학습 한영 사전

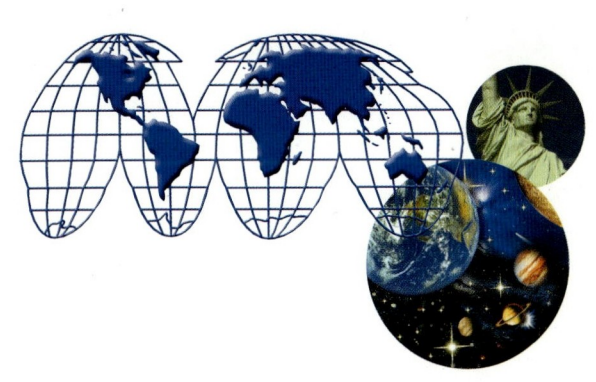

금성출판사

1.4.1 「-하다/-히」류

주표제어가 명사이고 그 명사에 「-하다/-히」가 붙어 용언 또는 부사가 파생되었을 때, 그 파생어는 명사의 풀이와 용례 끝에 별행을 잡지 않고 잇대어 제시하였다.「-당하다/-받다/-시키다/-되다」등의 파생어는 별도로 다루지 않고,「-하다」예문 끝에 ➔ 기호를 보인 뒤 예문의 형태로 다루었다. 다만,「-되다」의 경우에는「-하다」가 성립하지 않는 경우에 한해서 부표제어로 올리기도 하였다.

> **정확**(正確) correctness; ... **정확하다** correct; ... **정확히** correctly; ...
> **기습**(奇襲) a surprise (attack); ... **기습하다** raid; ... ➔¶기습당하다 be taken by surprise / ...
> **복종**(服從) obedience; ... **복종하다** obey; ... ➔¶복종시키다 subordinate ...
> **충혈**(充血) congestion (of the brain); ... **충혈되다** be congested; ...

1.4.2 복합어 명사류

주표제어가 2음절 이상의 명사일 때, 그것과 결합하여 이뤄진 복합 명사나 구는 주표제어의 풀이 및 용례를 보인 뒤 제시하되, 최초의 것은 ●표시와 함께 별행으로 제시하고 나머지의 것은 행을 바꾸지 않고 잇대어 제시하였다. 단, '주표제어+명사(또는 접미사)'의 경우에만 부표제어로 오를 뿐, '명사(또는 접두사)+주표제어'의 경우에는 예문으로 처리된다.

> **실내**(室內) indoors; ...
> ●**실내경기** indoor sports. **실내악** chamber music.
> **다이아몬드** 1 a diamond. ¶모조 ~ a rhinestone ...

1.4.3 속담/관용구

속담과 관용구는 그 어구의 최초 단어가 무엇인가를 따져서 그 단어 항목의 부표제어로 처리하였다.

1.5 전문 영역의 구분

전문어에 속하는 표제어는 그 전문 영역을 약어로 나타냈다. (4.2.3 참조)

2. 풀 이

2.1 뜻갈래 번호

어떤 단어가 두 가지 이상의 의미를 가지고 있을 때에는 **1**, **2**, **3**, ...으로 구별하여 뜻풀이를 제시하였다. 그리고 한 표제어에 대한 풀이가 15행 이상이거나, 또는 갈래 번호가 **5** 이상인 경우에는 각각의 번호를 별행으로 잡아 주었다.

> **바닥** 1 [평면을 이룬 부분] the broad; the flat. ... 2 [물체의 밑부분] the bottom; the sole; the bed. ... 3 [피륙의 짜임새] texture; weave; fabric. ... 4 [지역] an area; ...

2.2 우리말 핵심 정의

어떤 표제어가 여러 갈래의 의미를 가질 때, 역어 정보를 주기 전에 우리말 핵심 정의를 〔 〕 속에 짧게 제시하였다. 단일 의미를 가진 경우에도 그 단어가 지나치게 어렵다고 판단되면 같은 방식으로 핵심 정의를 제시하였다.

> **먹히다** 1 [먹음을 당하다] be eaten (up); ... 2 [먹게 되다] can be eaten[drunk]. ... 3 [재료·노력 등이 들다] take; require; cost. ...

2.3 역어 정보(譯語情報)

2.3.1 역어의 순서

역어가 2개 이상일 때에는 표제어의 의미에 좀 더 합치되는 것을 우선적으로 보였고, 그것

일러두기

이 비슷할 때에는 사용 빈도가 높은 것을 먼저 보였다. 한편, 역어와 역어는 세미콜론(;)으로 구분하였다.

2.3.2 역어의 호응어

어떤 역어에 수반하는 전치사, to 부정사, 동명사, that 절 등을 ( ) 속에 표시하여 역어의 활용도를 높일 수 있게 하였다. 또, 역어에 호응하는 목적어나 형용사, 동사 등을 ( ) 속에 표시하여 영작에 도움이 되도록 하였다.

> **권리**(權利) **1** [정당한 요구] a right (to / to do / of doing); ...
> **확신**(確信) ... **확신하다** ... be[feel] confident (of / that); ...
> **빼앗다 1** [억지로 제것으로 만들다] take (a thing) by force; snatch (something) from (a person); ...

2.3.3 역어의 보충 설명

역어를 의미적으로 한정하거나 부연 설명 하고자 할 때, 그 내용을 ( ) 속에 싸서 보였다. 또, 여러 역어의 의미상의 차이나 문법적인 주의 사항, 약어에 대한 원말의 완전한 철자를 보여 주거나 할 때 그 내용을 ( ) 속에 싸되, 내용 첫머리에 ▶ 표시를 보였다.

> **핸들**(*handle) (자동차의) a (steering) wheel; (자전거·오토바이의) handlebars.(▶. "handle"은 손잡이를 가리킬 뿐 자동차 조종 장치를 가리키지 않음)
> **라이온스 클럽** Lions Club(▶ Lions는 liberty, intelligence, our nation's safety의 약어).

2.3.4 가산 명사 / 불가산 명사

역어가 가산 명사일 경우에는 부정 관사 a나 an을 앞에 붙였고, 불가산 명사일 경우에는 부정 관사를 보이지 않았으며, 가산·불가산 양쪽으로 다 쓰이는 경우에는 (a)나 (an)을 보였다. 한편, 가산·불가산 여부에 상관없이 정관사 the가 늘 붙는 것은 the를 앞에 붙였다.

> **다짐** a definite promise; a promise; a pledge; an oath; an assurance; ...
> **모순**(矛盾) (a) contradiction; contradictoriness; (an) inconsistency; ...
> **내내년**(來來年) the year after next. ...

2.3.5 명사의 복수형

역어가 불규칙한 복수형을 가진 명사일 경우에, 단수형을 먼저 제시하고 복수형은 ( ) 속에 밝혀 주었다.

> **주사위** a die (*pl.* dice).
> **이**² [동] a louse (*pl.* lice).

2.3.6 미국 영어 / 영국 영어

미국과 영국이 어떤 개념에 대해 서로 다른 단어나 어구나 철자를 사용하는 경우, 해당 역어 앞에 (미), (영)을 표시함으로써 구별을 지었다.

> **캔디** (미) (a piece of) candy; (영) sweets.
> **화물**(貨物) (미) freight; (영) goods; ...

2.3.7 용법의 제시

어떤 역어가 용법상의 특징이 있을 때, 그 용법의 내용을 ( ) 속에 싸서 제시하였다. 가령, 우리말 형용사에 대해 역어를 제시할 때 일반적으로 역어 역시 형용사로 제시되나 때로 서술 동사를 필요로 할 경우가 있는데, 이 경우에는 (서술적)이라는 표시를 주었다. 또, 명사 역어를 제시할 때 그것이 집합 명사의 성질을 띨 때에는 (집합적)이라는 표시를 주었다.

> **창피**(猖披) ... **창피하다** ... (서술적) be embarrassed[abashed]; ...
> **새끼**² **1** [동물의 어린것] (집합적) the young; ...

2.3.8 동식물명

동식물명은 우리말에 해당하는 영어가 있으면 이를 밝혔으나, 그렇지 않을 경우에는 그 학명을 보였다.

참새 a sparrow.
버들치 [동] Moroco oxycephalus(학명).

2.3.9 한국 고유의 사물 이름

우리나라 고유의 사물이나 개념을 나타내는 명사를 역어로 제시할 때에는 우리 음을 로마자로 전사한 것을 우선적으로 보였으며, 영어권에서 통용되는 또 다른 표기나 표현이 있을 경우 이를 병렬하기도 했다. 이때, 전자의 표기는 현행 로마자 표기법(2000. 7. 7. 고시)을 따랐으며 이탤릭체로 나타냈다.

김치 *gimchi*; kimchi; ...
바둑 *baduk*; go. ...

2.3.10 관형어적 명사

우리말 명사 가운데 격조사가 붙지 않고, 다른 명사 앞에서 관형어적으로만 쓰이는 것은, [관형어적]이라는 정보를 주되 영어 역어는 명사가 아닌 형용사로 제시하였다.

국제(國際) [관형어적] international.
 ●**국제 가격** an international price. ... **국제 경기** an international game[match]. ...
대외(對外) [관형어적] foreign; external; oversea(s); ...
 ●**대외 관계** foreign[international] relations; ... **대외 무역** foreign[overseas /external] trade. ...

2.3.11 구어 / 문어, 속어 / 비어 / 완곡어, 기타

어떤 역어가 구어·문어이면 《구어》, 《문어》의 표시를, 속어·비어·완곡어이면 《속어》, 《비어》, 《완곡》의 표시를 역어 앞에 보였다. 이 외에도 《시어》, 《낡》, 《고》, 《농조》, 《격식》 등이 있는데, 이는 각각 '시어(詩語)', '현재 잘 안 쓰이는 낡은 투의 말', '고어(古語)', '농담조의 말', '격식체의 말' 등을 나타낸다. 한편, 〈속〉, 〈비〉, 〈소아〉 등은 표제어가 각각 속어·비어·소아어임을 나타낸다.

2.3.12 영어 속의 외래어

영어에도 프랑스 어, 독일어, 라틴 어, 이탈리아 어 등의 외국어에서 받아들인 외래어가 있다. 이러한 말에는 앞에 《프》, 《독》, 《라》, 《이》와 같은 표시를 주었다.

바캉스 ... 《프》 vacances.
라디오존데 [기상] 《독》 Radiosonde.
미사 [가] 《라》 Missa; ...
마카로니 《이》 macaroni.

2.3.13 역어를 달리하기 어려운 유사 계열어

동의어, 큰말 / 작은말, 여린말 / 센말 / 거센말, 높임말 / 낮춤말, 준말 / 본딧말 등과 같이, 개념의 동질성 때문에 역어를 서로 다르게 제시하기 어려운 말들에 대해서는, 어느 한쪽(A항목)에서만 완전한 풀이를 주되 다른 쪽(B항목)은 기본 풀이만 보였다. 그 대신 B항목 끝에 A항목으로 가 보라는 표시(⇨)를 보이되, 화살표 우측에 = < > ' " ↑ ↓ ← → 등의 기호를 첨부함으로써, 그 관계가 각각 동의어·큰말·작은말·여린말·센말·거센말·높임말·낮춤말·준말·본딧말임을 알게 하였다. 한편, 표제어가 어떤 말의 구용어 또는 구칭어거나 비표준어일 때에는, 역어 없이 ➡ 또는 → 표시와 함께 현 용어 또는 현 명칭이나 표준어를 제시함으로써 그 항목으로 풀이를 유도하였다.

가극(歌劇) an opera. ⇨="오페라
떵그렁 with a clang(or) ⇨'땡그랑
빤들빤들 smoothly; shrewdly; ... ⇨'반들반들
애² a child; a kid. ⇨아이

일러두기

> 국민학교 ➡초등학교(㊀초등)
> 자켓 →재킷

2.4 용례 정보

표제어의 역어가 우리말과 영어의 일대일 대응 관계를 보이는 평면적 정보라면, 용례는 문장이나 구 속에서 해당 단어가 어떻게 녹아 쓰이는지, 또는 문맥에 따라 어떻게 전혀 다른 표현으로 변용되는지를 보이는 입체적 정보라 할 수 있다. ¶ 기호는 용례의 시작을 나타내며, ~ 기호는 용례 속에서 표제어를 대신 나타낸다. 또, 용례 속의 어떤 단어나 일부 성분을 다른 말로 대체하여 보이고자 할 때 그 다른 말을 [ ] 속에 싸서 보였다.

2.4.1 용례의 구분

한 개의 우리말 예문에 대하여 그에 대응하는 영어 예문이 두 개 이상 있을 때 / 기호로 구분 지었다. 또, 우리말 예문과 영어 예문으로 이뤄지는 하나의 용례가 끝나고 다른 용례가 시작될 때 // 기호로 구별하였다.

> 말¹ [동] a horse; ... ¶경마용 ~ a race horse / a racer // ~을 타다 ride a horse / mount [get on] a horse ...

2.4.2 용례의 배열

예문의 배열은 복합어 → 구 → 문장의 순으로 하였다.

> 도시락 ... ¶소풍용 ~ a picnic lunch // ~을 담다 fill a lunch box (with boiled rice) // ... 난 오늘 ~을 싸 왔다 I brought lunch from home today. ...

2.4.3 구어 / 문어, 미국어 / 영국어 등의 구별

한 가지 주제에 대해 다양한 표현을 가급적 많이 제시하고자 했으며, 이때 그 용례가 구어나 문어, 미국 영어나 영국 영어, 속어나 비어 등의 특징을 띠고 있을 때에는 그 예 앞에 (구어), (문어), (미), (영), (속어), (비어) 등을 표시하였다.

3. 우리말 어문 규범

우리말 어문 규범은 '한글 맞춤법'(1988), '표준어 규정'(1988), '외래어 표기법'(1986)에 준거하되, 개개의 단어에 대해서는 '표준국어대사전'(국립국어연구원, 1999)을 따랐다.

4. 기호 및 약어

4.1 기호

( ) 표제어에서, 어원을 밝혀 한자 또는 로마자를 보일 때(1.3.1 참조)
    풀이에서, 역어의 의미를 한정하거나 약어·기호를 나타내거나 보충 설명을 할 때(2.3.3 참조)
    용례에서, 어떤 단어의 한자를 밝힐 때
    표제어·풀이·용례에서, 그 부분을 생략해도 의미적으로 거의 차이가 없음을 나타낼 때
( ) 어떤 역어에 호응하는 전치사, to 부정사, 동명사, that 절 등이나 목적어·형용사·동사 등을 속에 싸서 보일 때(2.3.2 참조)
    풀이에서, 명사의 복수형을 밝힐 때(2.3.5 참조)
    풀이에서, 용법을 제시할 때(2.3.7 참조)
〔 〕 풀이에서, 우리말로 그 뜻을 짧게 정의할 때(2.2 참조)
    풀이에서, 관형어적 명사를 제시할 때(2.3.10 참조)
[ ] 부표제어·풀이·용례에서, 어떤 단어나 일부 성분을 다른 말로 대체할 수 있음을 보일 때(2.4 참조)
- 표제어가 어미·접미사일 때 앞에, 접두사일 때 뒤에 붙이는 표시(1.3 참조)
- 영어 표기에서, 복합어 내부의 단어 사이에 경계를 보일 때, 어떤 단어가 행의 끝에 올

일러두기

　　　때 다음 행 첫머리의 철자와 이어짐을 나타낼 때
− 　표제어의 어원을 밝힐 때, 그 표제어의 구성이 고유어＋외래어, 또는 고유어＋한자어일 경우에 고유어 부분을 나타내는 표시
　　　복합어 형태의 부표제어 어원 표시에서, 주표제어 부분을 나타낼 때
~ 　용례에서, 표제어와 같은 말임을 나타낼 때(2.4 참조)
; 　풀이에서, 역어와 역어 사이의 구분을 나타낼 때(2.3.1 참조)
¶ 　용례의 시작을 나타낼 때(2.4 참조)
/ 　같은 뜻을 가진 복수의 부표제어를 제시할 때(1.4 참조)
　　　한 개의 우리말 예문에 대하여 영어 예문이 두 개 이상 있을 때, 그 영어 예문을 구분 짓는 표시(2.4.1 참조)
　　　역어의 호응어에서, 그 위치에 올 수 있는 성분을 병렬하여 제시할 때(2.3.2 참조)
// 　용례가 둘 이상 있을 때, 그 용례를 구분 짓는 표시(2.4.1 참조)
● 　복합어 명사류의 부표제어가 맨 처음 시작될 때(1.4.2 참조)
▶ 　어의·용례 등에서 그 앞의 어구에 대한 의미상의 차이, 약어에 대한 원말의 완전한 철자를 보여 줄 때, 문법적인 주의 사항 등을 보충 설명할 때(2.3.3 참조)
⇨< 　완전한 풀이를 큰말에서 하고자 할 때(2.3.13 참조)
⇨> 　완전한 풀이를 작은말에서 하고자 할 때(2.3.13 참조)
⇨＝ 　완전한 풀이를 동의어 또는 유사어에서 하고자 할 때(2.3.13 참조)
⇨′ 　완전한 풀이를 여린말에서 하고자 할 때(2.3.13 참조)
⇨″ 　완전한 풀이를 센말에서 하고자 할 때(2.3.13 참조)
⇨‴ 　완전한 풀이를 거센말에서 하고자 할 때(2.3.13 참조)
⇨↑ 　완전한 풀이를 높임말에서 하고자 할 때(2.3.13 참조)
⇨↓ 　완전한 풀이를 낮춤말에서 하고자 할 때(2.3.13 참조)
⇨￣ 　완전한 풀이를 본딧말에서 하고자 할 때(2.3.13 참조)
⇨⌐ 　완전한 풀이를 준말에서 하고자 할 때(2.3.13 참조)
⇨ 　기타 밀접한 관계가 있는 표제어를 보일 때
⇦ 　완전한 풀이가 있는 쪽으로 보내는 경우, 그 항목이 부표제어일 때 주표제어를 밝히는 표시
➡ 　표제어가 구용어 또는 구칭일 경우, 현재 통용되는 말로 보낼 때(2.3.13 참조)
→ 　표제어가 비표준어일 경우, 표준어로 보낼 때(2.3.13 참조)
➔ 　부표제어로 처리되는「-하다」류의 용언의 경우,「-하다」대신에「-당하다 / -받다 / -시키다 / -되다」등이 결합하는 예문을 보일 때(1.4.1 참조)
× 　영어권에서 쓰이지 않는 한국식 영어를 나타낼 때(1.3.1 참조)

4.2 약어

4.2.1 외래어의 국적

[표제어에서](1.3.1 참조)　　　　　　　　[역어에서](2.3.12 참조)

　㊅　네덜란드 어　　　　　　　　　　　(네)　네덜란드 어
　㊆　독일어　　　　　　　　　　　　　　(독)　독일어
　㊊　라틴 어　　　　　　　　　　　　　　(라)　라틴 어
　㊋　러시아 어　　　　　　　　　　　　　(러)　러시아 어
　㊌　범어　　　　　　　　　　　　　　　(범)　범어
　㊐　에스파냐 어　　　　　　　　　　　　(에)　에스파냐 어
　㊍　이탈리아 어　　　　　　　　　　　　(이)　이탈리아 어
　㊎　중국어　　　　　　　　　　　　　　(포)　포르투갈 어
　㊏　포르투갈 어　　　　　　　　　　　　(프)　프랑스 어
　㊑　프랑스 어

4.2.2 제약성의 표지

〈소아〉　표제어가 소아어일 때　　　　　〈비〉　　표제어가 비어일 때
〈속〉　　표제어가 속어일 때　　　　　　〈음역〉　표제어가 한자 음역어일 때

일러두기

(미)	역어가 미국 영어일 때	(고)	역어가 고어일 때
(영)	역어가 영국 영어일 때	(완곡)	역어가 완곡어일 때
(구어)	역어가 구어일 때	(농조)	역어가 농담조의 말일 때
(문어)	역어가 문어일 때	(격식)	역어가 격식체의 말일 때
(소아어)	역어가 소아어일 때	(시어)	역어가 시어(詩語)일 때
(속어)	역어가 속어일 때	(낡)	역어가 낡은 표현의 말일 때
(비어)	역어가 비어일 때	(드물게)	역어가 드물게 쓰이는 말일 때

4.2.3 전문어의 표지

[가]	가톨릭	[식]	식물학·식물명
[건]	건축·토목	[신]	신학
[경]	경제학	[심]	심리학
[고고]	고고학	[약]	약학·약품명
[공]	공업·공학	[언]	언어학
[광]	광물학·광물명	[역]	역사·고제도
[교]	교육학	[연]	연극
[군]	군사	[영]	영화
[기]	개신교	[예]	예술 일반
[기상]	기상학	[윤]	윤리학
[논]	논리학	[음]	음악
[농]	농업	[의]	의학
[동]	동물학·동물명	[인]	인쇄
[문]	문학	[전]	전기
[물]	물리학	[정]	정치
[미]	미술·공예	[종]	종교 일반
[민]	민속	[지]	지리학·지학·지명
[방송]	방송	[천]	천문학
[법]	법률·법학	[철]	철학
[불]	불교	[체]	체육
[사]	사회학	[컴]	컴퓨터
[사진]	사진	[통]	통신
[생]	생물학·생리학	[한]	한의학
[성]	크리스트교 성서	[항]	항공
[수]	수학	[해]	해양
[수산]	수산업	[화]	화학

ㄱ

ㄱ the first letter of the Korean alphabet. ¶~자자 an L square // ~자집 an L-shaped house // ~ㄴ순으로 (arrange names) in Korean alphabetical order // 그는 낫 놓고 ㄱ자도 모른다 He does not know A from B. / He is utterly illiterate.

가¹(音) [음계의 제6음] la; A. ¶~ 음A // ~ 조(調) the tone A // 내림~ A flat(기호 A♭) // 올림~ A sharp(기호 A♯) // ~장조[단조] (a piano concerto) A major [minor].

가² 1 [가장자리] an edge; a border; a margin; (절벽 등의) a brink; [경계·주변] a verge. ¶길~ the roadside / the wayside // 강~ a riverside / a riverbank // 바닷~ a beach / the seaside / the seashore // 호숫~에서 on the shore of a lake // 연못~에 서다 stand on the edge of a pond // 난롯~에 둘러앉다 sit around the stove [fire] // 우물~에 감나무가 한 그루 서 있다 There is a persimmon tree by the well. // 그 소녀는 연못~까지 걸어갔다 The girl walked to the edge of the pond. // 우리는 호숫~에 있는 호텔에 묵었다 We put up at a lakeside hotel [a hotel on the shore of a lake]. 2 [그릇 아가리의 언저리] a brim. ¶독~로 넘치는 물 water run [flow] over the brim of the pot.

가(可) 1 [학업 성적의] D. ¶~를 매기다 rate (an exam paper) as D // 그는 물리에서 ~를 받았다 He got a D in physics. 2 [찬성] approval; yes; yea; aye; OK. ¶~ 10, 부(否) 5 ayes 10 and noes 5. 3 [옳음] fairly [tolerably] good.

가-(假) 1 [임시의] temporary; [잠정적인] provisional; interim; [임시 변통의] expedient; makeshift; [시험적인] tentative. ¶~건물 a temporary [makeshift] building // ~계정 a suspense [temporary / nominal] account // ~면허 (미) a temporary licence / (영) a provisional license // ~배당 an interim dividend // ~수요 imaginary [fictitious] demand // ~제본 sample binding // ~처분 a provisional disposition // ~호적 a temporary census [family] register. 2 [가짜의] assumed; false; (미) bogus. ¶~명 an assumed name / an alias.

-가(家) 1 [전문인] a man; a specialist; a professional; a person noted for. ¶공상~ a daydreamer // 독지~ a charitable person // 수완~ a man of ability // 혁명~ a revolutionist / a revolutionary. 2 [가문] a family. ¶록펠러~ the Rockefeller family / the Rockefellers.

-가(哥) [성] the family name; the surname. ¶최~네 3형제 the three brothers of the Choes // 내 성은 남~요 My family name is Nam. // 이~는 한국의 두 번째로 흔한 성이다 Lee is the second largest family in Korea. // 한국에는 김~가 많다 There are many Kims in Korea.

-가(街) 1 [거리] a street; an avenue; a boulevard; a drive. ¶월~ the Wall Street. 2 [구역] a district; a center; a quarter; an area. ¶대학~ a university quarter // 번화~ a downtown / a shopping quarter // 유흥~ an amusement center / the gay quarters // 주택~ a residential quarter [district] / an uptown.

-가(歌) [노래] a song. ¶농부~ a farmer's song // 애국~ the national anthem // 유행~ a pop(ular) song // 응원~ a rooter's song // 자장~ a lullaby / a nursery rhyme.

-가(價) 1 [값] price. ¶공정~ an official price // 도매[소매]~ a wholesale [retail] price // 할부~ an installment price // 최저~ the rock-bottom [lowest] price. 2 [화] atomic value; valence. ¶2~ 알코올 dihydric [diatomic] alcohol.

가가대소(呵呵大笑) a loud laughter; a guffaw. **가가대소하다** laugh loudly; roar with laughter; guffaw; burst into an explosive laughter.

가가호호(家家戶戶) [각각의 집] every door [house]; house by house; [집집마다] from door to door; at every house [door]. ¶~를 방문하다 make a door-to-door [house-to-house] visit / ring every doorbell // 광복절을 맞아 ~에 국기가 게양되었다 Every house raised the national flag in celebration of the Liberation Day. // 그는 이웃을 ~ 찾아다니며 주문을 받았다 He canvassed the neighborhood from house to house for order.

가감(加減) 1 [더하고 뺌] addition and subtraction. **가감하다** add and [or] subtract. 2 [증감] increase and decrease; addition and reduction; [조절] adjustment; regulation. **가감하다** increase and decrease; regulate; adjust. ¶그의 말은 무엇이나 가감해서 들어야 한다 All he says must be taken with reserve [with a grain of salt]. / We must discount his story.

● **가감법** [수] the method of addition and subtraction. **가감승제**(-乘除) [수] the four fundamental processes of arithmetic; addition, subtraction, multiplication and division.

가건물(假建物) a temporary building. ¶~을 짓다 build a temporary house.

가게 a store; a shop(▶ (미)에서는 일반적으로 store를 쓰나, 작은 가게나 한 종류의 상품만을 다루는 가게는 shop이라고 함. (영)에서는 대규모의 상점은 store이나, 기타는 shop); (노점 등의) a stall; a stand; a booth. ¶구멍~ a penny candy store / a small store / a dime [ten-cent] store // 반찬 ~ a grocery store // 생선 ~ a fish shop // 큰 ~ a large establishment // 새로 낸 ~ a new [newly-opened] store [shop] // ~ 보는 사람 (영) a shopkeeper / a store keeper / a shop assistant / (미) a (sales) clerk // 잘되는 ~ a popular [prosperous] store // ~에서 일하다 serve in a store // ~를 내다[벌이다] open [start] a shop / set up shop [business] / ~를 비우다 leave one's store // ~를 닫다 [하루의 장사를 끝내다] close the store [door] / [장사를 그만두다] close [go out of] business / wind [give] up

가격

business / break up one's business // ~를 열다 open a store (usually for the day) / open business // ~를 보다 keep a shop[store] / tend[mind] the store // ~는 벌써 닫혀 있었다 I found the doors of the store closed. // 5시에 ~를 닫습니다 We shut up business at five. // 저 ~는 비싸게[싸게] 판다 Things are expensive[cheap] at that store. // 그는 종로에 ~를 두 채나 가지고 있다 He runs two stores in the Jongno. // 그 제품은 벌써 ~에 나돌고 있다 That product is already available in (the) stores[shops]. // 저 ~에는 상품이 많다 That store keeps a large stock of goods.
- **가겟방** a shop room; a store. **가겟집** a store; a house used as a store.

가격(價格) (파는 사람이 요구하는) (a) price; (대가·원가로서의) (a) cost; [가치] (a) value. ¶견적 ~ estimated value // 경쟁 ~ a competitive price // 공장도 ~ an exfactory price // 공정(公定)[협정/통제/신고] ~ an official [a stipulated / a controlled / a reported] price // 국내[국제] ~ a home[foreign] market price // 도매[소매] ~ a wholesale [retail] price // 독점 ~ the monopoly price // 매입[매출] ~ a purchase[sale] price // 생산자[소비자] ~ the producer[consumer] price // 수출[수입] ~ an export[import] price // 시장 ~ the market price // 시판 ~ a selling price // 정찰 ~ a net price // 최고 ~ the maximum price / price ceiling // 최저 ~ the minimum price / the floor (price) // 최저 ~ a check price system // 할인 ~ a bargain [reduce] price // 현행 ~ the present[current / ruling] price // 터무니없는 ~ a fancy price / an exorbitant price // 살 마음을 내키게 하는 ~ a tempting price // ~이 대중적인 상품 popular-priced[medium-priced] articles // 싼 [비싼] ~으로 at a low[high] price // 흥정한 ~으로 at an agreed price // 정가에서 20% 할인한 ~으로 at a discount of 20% off the regular price // ~을 매기다 mark the price on (an article) / fix a price tag on (an article) / ~을 올리다 raise[put up] the price // ~을 내리다 reduce[lower] the price // ~이 오르다 rise[advance / go up] in price // 내달 1일부터 ~을 10% 인상합니다 The price will be raised 10% from the 1st of next month. // ~은 5백 원에서 천 원까지 여러 가지입니다 The prices range from 500 won (up) to 1,000. // 그 ~이면 싸다 It is cheap at the price. // ~이 비싸다고 해서 반드시 좋은 물건이라고는 할 수 없다 A high price is not necessarily an assurance of good quality. // ~은 십만 원으로 어림되고 있다 The value is estimated at a hundred thousand won.
- **가격 경쟁** price competition. **가격 동결** price freeze. **가격 변동** fluctuation of price. **가격 분석** price analysis. **가격 인상** a price advance. **가격 조작**[조정] price manipulation[adjustment]. **가격 통제** price control. **가격표**(一表) a price list. **가격표**(一票) a price tag.

가결(可決) approval; passage; adoption; (미국속어) an O.K. **가결하다** pass[adopt] (a bill); carry (a motion); approve of (a bill). ¶원안대로 ~ pass (a bill) as drafted // 거수로 ~ decide (on a bill) by a show of hands. ➔ 가결되다 be passed[carried / approved] // 동의는 가결되었다 The motion was carried. // 예산안은 95대 80으로 가결되었다 The budget was passed by 95 to 80. // 그 불신임 결의안은 만장일치로 가결되었다 The non-confidence resolution was passed[adopted] unanimously. // 예산안은 30표의 차로 가결되었다 The budget bill passed[was carried / was adopted] by a majority of 30. // 그 의안은 가결되었습니까, 부결되었습니까 Was the vote for or against the resolution?

가결의(假決議) a temporary decision; a provisional resolution. **가결의하다** resolve temporarily; pass[adopt] a provisional resolution.

가경(佳境) [고비] the most interesting[exciting] part (of a story); the climax. ¶이야기는 ~에 접어들었다 We finally reached the most interesting part of the story. / The story reached its climax.

가계(家系) a family(▶ 집합적으로 씀); lineage. (▶ 일반적으로 가계에는 family를 써서 나타내는 일이 많음. 특히 어떤 한 조상으로부터의 혈통의 흐름을 나타내는 경우는 lineage라고 함) ¶훌륭한 ~ (의 사람) (a person from) a good family // 그 장군의 ~는 1920년에 끊겼다 The line of the general ended in 1920. // 그의 ~는 세종 대왕까지 거슬러 올라간다 He traces his genealogy back to King Sejong.
- **가계도** a family tree; a genealogical chart; a pedigree (chart).

가계(家計) [집안 경제] household economy; (금전상의) family finance(s); [생계비] house-keeping expenses; [가정의 예산] family budget; [생계] living; livelihood. ¶~에 보태기 위하여 to help family finances // ~가 넉넉하다[어렵다] be well[badly] off / be comfortably[poorly] off // ~를 돕다 help support a family // ~를 줄이다 use economy in the household // 그녀는 ~를 규모 있게 꾸려 나간다 She manages the family budget well. // 우리는 적은 수입으로 ~를 이럭저럭 꾸려 나가고 있다 We are scraping [getting / (영) rubbing] along on a small income. // 물가의 급등이 ~에 큰 영향을 미쳤다 Soaring prices strained the family budget. // 그녀가 일을 해도 ~에는 충분한 보탬이 되지 못했다 Her salary was not enough to make up for the deficit in their living expenses. // 우리 집에서는 아내가 ~를 맡고 있다 My wife minds the household accounts.
- **가계부** a household account book; a housekeeping log. ¶~를 적다 keep a record of household expenses / keep a household account book. **가계비** household expenses.

가계약(假契約) an interim[a provisional] contract. ¶~을 맺다 make a provisional contract (with).

가곡(歌曲) [노래] a song (in the classical style); [음] [리트] a lied (pl. lieder). ¶예술 ~ an art song // 소~ an arietta.
- **가곡집** a collection of songs. ¶슈베르트 ~ the collected lieder of Schubert.

가공(加工) (특히 식품·농산물 등의) processing; (기계에 의한 대량의) manufacturing; [법] specification; (보석 등의) cutting. ¶식품 ~ food processing // 치즈 process[processed] cheese. **가공하다** process; manufacture; (손으로) work. ¶과일을 ~ process fruit // 우유를 살균 ~ sterilize[pasteurize] milk // ~을 맺다 pasteurize는 저온 살균) // 이 금속은 (손으로) 가공하기 쉽다 This metal works easily[is easily worked].

●가공 공장 a processing plant. 가공 무역 processing trade; improvement trade. 가공식품 processed foodstuffs. 가공업 processing industries. 가공품 processed [wrought] goods.

가공(架空) **1** [공중에 가설함]. ¶~의 overhead / aerial / (미) trolley. **2** [터무니없음]. ¶~의 fanciful / visionary / imaginary / airbuilt / dreamy / fictitious // ~의 인물 a fictitious [an imaginary] character // 이것은 ~적인 이야기다 This is fiction. / This is a fictitious story. // 이 연극에 나오는 인명은 모두 ~의 것이다 All the names of the persons [characters] in this drama are fictitious. // 용은 ~의 동물이다 A dragon is an imaginary animal.

●가공 삭도(-索道) an aerial cableway [ropeway]. 가공선(전선·전화의) an overhead line [wire]; (전차의) a trolley line. 가공 전선 an overhead electric power line. 가공 철도 an aerial railway. 가공 케이블 an aerial [overhead] cable.

가공하다(可恐-) fearful; fearsome; terrible; dreadful; awesome; shocking; formidable. ¶핵무기의 가공한 파괴력 the annihilating power of nuclear weapons // 가공할 만한 적 a terrible foe // 각성제 오염의 가공할 실태 the terrifying realities of drug addiction // 거대 운석의 가공할 에너지 the awe-inspiring [enormous / tremendous] energy in gigantic meteorites.

가과(假果) [헛열매] [식] a pseudocarp; an accessory fruit.

가관(可觀) **1** [볼만함]. ¶~이다 be well worth seeing / be something to see // 경치가 ~이다 have a beautiful scenery / command a fine view // 설악산 정상에서 바라본 해돋이는 실로 ~이었다 The sunrise seen from the top of Seoraksan(Mt. Seorak) was a glorious spectacle. **2** [꼴사나움]. ¶~이다 be a sight / be unbecoming [unsightly] // 그 옷을 입고 있는 그녀는 정말 ~이었다 She was quite a sight in that dress. // 그것 참 ~이다 It really is something to see. // 네 꼴이 ~이군! What a sight you are! / You do look a sight!

가교(架橋) bridge-building; bridge-construction; bridging. 가교하다 build [construct] a bridge (over a river); span (a river) with a bridge; bridge (a river).

가교(假橋) a temporary [makeshift / flying] bridge.

가구(家口) (집합적) a household (기숙인을 포함한 집안 사람); (식구) a family. ¶열 ~가 사는 동네 a village of ten families // 그 마을에서는 대부분의 ~마다 남자 한 사람은 군대에 가 있다 Almost every family in the village has a man in the army. // 이 도시의 ~당 평균 인원수는 2.5명이다 The average number of people per household in this town is 2.5 [two and a half].

●가구 수 the number of household [families]. 가구주(-主) the head of a family [household].

가구(家具) (household) furniture [furnishings]; household stuff [(구어) things]. (▶ furniture는 어떤 방·건물 내의 모든 가구(융단 등을 포함)를 가리키는 불가산 명사. 양을 나타낼 때는 little, much 등을 쓰고, 가구 하나하나를 말할 때는 a piece of furniture, two pieces of furniture를 씀) ¶서양식 ~ Western-style furniture // 응접실용 ~ drawing room furniture // 외제 ~ foreign furniture // ~ 한 점 a piece [an article] of furniture // ~ 딸린 셋집 a furnished house for rent [(미) to let] // ~가 많다 [적다] have much [little] furniture // 방에 ~를 들여놓다 furnish a room / fit up a room // 실내의 ~는 모두 낡은 것이었다 All the furniture in the room was worn out.

●가구상(상점) a furniture store [shop]; (상인) a furniture dealer; an upholsterer. 가구장이 a furniture maker. 가구점 a furniture [furnishing goods] store [shop].

가극(歌劇) an opera. ⇨오페라 ¶경~ an operetta / a light opera // 대~ a grand opera // 희~ a comic opera / a musical comedy.

●가극단 an opera company [troupe]. 가극장 an opera house [theater].

가금(家禽) domestic fowls; (집합적) poultry. ¶~을 치다 keep chickens [poultry] // 우리는 정원 뒤쪽에서 ~을 치고 있다 Our poultry are kept [being fed] at the rear of the garden.

●가금 사육장 a poultry farm.

가급적(可及的) as ... as possible; as much [far] as possible; as ... as one can [may]; [가능한 한] to the best of one's ability. ¶~이면 if possible / if circumstances allow [admit] / if one can help it // ~ 속히 as soon [quickly] as possible [one can] / at one's earliest convenience / at the earliest possible opportunity // ~ 많이 as much [many] as possible / ~ 조속한 회답을 바랍니다 Please reply at your earliest convenience. / Please let me have your answer as soon as possible. // ~ 오도록 하겠습니다 I'll try (my best) to come. // ~ 늦지 않도록 해라 Don't be longer than you can help. // ~ 빨리 와라 Come as early as you can.

가까스로 with difficulty; just; barely; narrowly; laboriously. ¶~ ...하다 barely manage to do // ~ 연명해 가다 eke out a living / make a bare living // ~ 죽음을 모면하다 be snatched from the jaws of death // ~ 시험에 합격하다 just pass an examination / scrape through an examination / (구어) just managed to squeak by on the test // ~ 막차를 탔다 I just managed to catch the last train. / I barely made the last train. // 그는 ~ 당선되었다 He was elected by a narrow [bare] majority. // 우리는 ~ 제시간에 그곳에 당도했다 We managed to get there in time. // ~ 싸움을 말렸다 I had a hard time stopping the fight.

가까워지다 1 (거리가) get near to (a place); come up to; approach. ¶배가 육지에 ~ approach land / draw toward the shore. **2** (시간이) be near [close] at hand; draw near; be coming on. ¶끝에 ~ draw to a close // 점점 ~ get nearer to (a conclusion) // 겨울이 가까워지면 with the approach of winter // 봄이 가까워지고 있다 Spring is coming. // 마감이 가까워졌다 The deadline is nigh. // 일몰이 가까워지자 쌀쌀해졌다 It grew colder with the approach of sunset. **3** (친해지다) (남녀가) fall in love with; come to love (each other); (구어) take up with; (친구로서) make friends with; become intimate with; make a person's acquaintance; come into close association. ¶서로 곧 ~ soon become intimate with each other // 그녀는 나와 가까워지기를 꺼린다 She avoids my

가까이하다

company. ¶그들은 사이가 가까워지기 시작했다 A warm friendship sprang up between them. // 우리 사이는 더욱 가까워졌다 Our relations have grown[gained] in intimacy.

가까이하다 1 [사귀다] associate with; make friends with; make one's acquaintance with; keep company with; have connections[relations] with. ¶가까이하기 어려운[쉬운] 사람 a person who is difficult[easy] to approach / an unapproachable(or inaccessible)[accessible] person // 그는 보기에는 가까이하기 어려워 보이지만 아주 친절한 사람이다 He looks unapproachable[forbidding] but is really a very kind person. // 그녀는 딴 속셈이 있어서 그를 가까이하려고 했다 She has some secret motive for wanting to get to know him. // 그런 패들을 가까이하지 마라 Keep away from such company. // 그는 그녀를 가까이한 지 오래다 It is a long time since he had his affair [liaison] with her. // 그녀는 가난한 친척을 가까이하지 않았다 She spurned a poor relation from her door. // 그는 어딘지 모르게 가까이하기 어려운 데가 있다 There is something about him that discourages friendly advances.

2 [좋아하다]. ¶책을 ~ enjoy reading books / spend a lot of time reading books // 흙을 ~ get close to the earth / (원예·농경 등을) be fond of gardening[farming] // 담배를 가까이하지 마시오 You'd better refrain[abstain] from smoking. // 학생들은 文學을 더욱 가까이 해야한 한다 Students ought to acquire a closer acquaintance with good literature.

가깝다 1 (거리가) near; close[klous] (▶ close가 near보다 접근 정도가 강함); close[near] by; not far away; nearby. ¶가까운 집 a nearby house / a house close by // 서울에서 가까운 곳에 near Seoul / within easy reach of Seoul // 가장 가까운 길을 택하다 take the nearest route // 우리 집은 여기서 ~ My house is not far away from here. // 우리 집에서 가장 가까운 역은 신촌이다 Sinchon is the nearest [closest] station to our house. // 학교는 이 길로 가는 것이 더 ~ This is the shorter way [shortcut] to the school. // 해답은 가까운 곳에 있다 The solution is not far to seek. / You don't have to look very far for an answer. **가까이** near (to / by); close at hand; in the neighborhood. ¶~ 가다 go[come] near / approach // 위험! ~ 오지 마시오! (게시) Danger! Keep away!

2 (시간이) near; immediate; short. ¶가까운 장래에 in the near[immediate] future / at an early date // 거의 자정이 ~ It's almost [nearly] midnight. // 봄이 아주 ~ Spring is only a little while away. / Spring is just around the corner. / It will be soon springtime. // 벌써 크리스마스가 ~ Christmas is already near[close] at hand. **가까이** shortly; before long; close at hand. ¶그는 간밤에 11시 ~ 되어서야 돌아왔다 He came home shortly before eleven last night.

3 (사이·관계가) close (to); near; intimate (with); friendly (with). ¶가까운 친구 an intimate[a close] friend / a bosom buddy // 가까운 친척 a near relation[relative] // 그들은 가까운 친척이다 They are closely related to each other. // 그들은 그녀와 가깝게 지낸다 They are on the intimate terms with her. // 그들은 사이가 가깝게 지낸다 They are on the intimate terms with her.

4 [비슷하다] near; almost; close to; border on; approach (to). ¶무모에 가까운 용기 courage verging on foolhardiness // 나이 육십에 ~ be close to sixty years old / be pushing sixty // 완전에 ~ be almost perfect / approach perfection // 원숭이는 인간에 ~ The ape is closely allied to man. // 연민의 정은 사랑에 ~ Pity is near[akin] to love. // 그의 사상은 허무주의에 ~ His thought verges on nihilism. // 해마다 100만 원 가까운 돈이 학비로 들어간다 We spend nearly a million won a year on school fees. **가까이** nearly; almost(▶ almost가 nearly에 비해 근접 정도가 더 강함); (대략) about; around; approximately. ¶천 명 ~ nearly a thousand people // 이것은 5천 원 ~ 들었다 This cost me almost 5,000 won.

5 [비근하다] familiar; well-known. ¶가까운 예를 들다 take a familiar example / give a familiar example / cite a familiar instance.

가꾸다 1 (식물을) cultivate; raise; grow; rear ¶취미로 하는 난초 가꾸기 orchid growing [culture] as a pleasure[hobby] // 정원에 장미를 ~ cultivate roses in the garden // 뒤뜰에 채소를 ~ grow[raise] vegetables in a backyard. 2 [치장하다] dress (oneself) up; (장식물로) decorate; adorn; ornament; (얼굴을) make oneself up. ¶보석으로 옷차림을 ~ adorn oneself[deck oneself out] with jewels // 꽃을 심어 정원을 아름답게 ~ embellish a garden with flowers // 사람이 보는 데서 얼굴을 가꾸어서는 안 된다 You shouldn't make yourself up in public.

가꾸로 bottom up; the wrong way; headlong; instead. ⇨거꾸로

가끔 [때때로] sometimes; (every) now and then[again]; occasionally; [이따금] once in a while; [사이를 두고] at intervals. ¶그는 ~ 학교에 지각한다 He is sometimes late for school. // 그는 ~ 골프를 친다 He plays golf once in a while. // 나는 ~ 시골에 간다 Sometimes I go to the country. // 그는 ~ 찾아온다 Occasionally[Every now and then] he drops in on me. // 그에게서는 ~ 편지가 온다 I hear from him once in a while [at intervals]. // 그는 ~ 본 적이 있는 사람이다 I have caught glimpses of him occasionally. // 그는 ~ 오지 자주는 오지 않는다 He comes here once in a while but not often. // 작년에는 ~ 만났지만 올해는 통 만나지 못했군 Last year we saw each other now and then, but this year we haven't, have we?

가나다순 (-順) the order of the Korean alphabet. ¶~의 좌석 배열 the seating arrangement in Korean alphabetical order // ~으로 배열하다 arrange (names) in Korean alphabetical order / alphabetize (a list of words).

가나오나 [어디에서나] wherever one may go; everywhere one turns; [언제나] all the time; always; constantly. ¶그는 ~ 말썽이다 He is a constant troublemaker. / He makes trouble wherever he may be. // ~ 고생이다 I am never free from hardships.

가난 poverty; want; destitution; indigence; penury. ¶~에 쪼들리다 suffer extreme poverty // ~에서 벗어나다 emerge from poverty // ~ 속에 죽다 die poor / die in want [poverty] // 그는 ~을 면할 날이 없다 His poverty is chronic. **가난하다** poor; needy; poverty-stricken; destitute; impecunious; indigent. ¶가난한 집 a poor[needy] family / 가난한 사람 a poor person / (집합적) the poor // 가난하게 살다 live in poverty[need / want] / be in needy[straitened] circumstances / be badly off / eke out a scanty living // 찢어지게 ~ be extremely poor / be poverty-stricken / as poor as a church-mouse // 가난한 집에 태어나다 be born poor / be born in[of] a poor family // 가난해지다 become poor / be reduced to poverty // 그는 가난하게 자랐다 He was raised in poverty. // 사람은 가난해지면 거지 근성이 나타난다 When a man is reduced to want, the beggar in him crops out. // 그는 가난해서 학교에 다니지 못했다 Want kept him from school. // 우리나라에는 아직 가난한 사람이 많이 있다 There are still many needy people in our country.

가난 구제는 나라도 못한다(속담) There is no remedy for poverty.
가난한 집 제사 돌아오듯(속담) come as often as the bill collectors.
가난(이) 들다 1 [가난해지다] become poor; be reduced to poverty. 2 [부족하다] lack; want; be lacking[wanting] (in); run out [short] of; be scarce; run low. ¶인재에 ~ suffer from a dearth of talent.
● **가난뱅이** a poor man; a pauper; (집합적) the poor; the indigent; the needy; the have-nots.

가내(家內) (동거인도 포함한) a household; [가족] a family; one's people[folks]; members of one's family. ¶~의 domestic / family / household // ~가 평안하신지요 Are your family all well? / How are your people? / How is your family? // 그녀는 ~ 부업으로 재봉을 한다 She takes in sewing.
● **가내 공업** a home[household / domestic] industry; a cottage industry. **가내 공장** a domestic factory.

가냘프다 1 [목소리가] [힘이 없다] feeble; [희미하다] faint. ¶그 아이는 가냘픈 목소리로 울고 있었다 The baby was crying feebly. 2 [몸이] [호리호리하다] slim; slender; slight; [약하다] weak; feeble; frail. ¶가냘픈 팔 a thin and weak arm // 몸매가 가냘픈 여자 a woman with a slender figure // 가냘픈 소녀 a girl of slender build // 그녀는 여자의 가냘픈 손으로 가족을 먹여 살리고 있다 With the weak hands of a woman, she supports her family. // 그녀는 몸이 ~ She is of slender built.

가누다 control; keep under control; keep steady. ¶몸을 가누지 못하는 늙은이 a decrepit old man // 몸을 ~ keep one's balance / keep the balance of one's body / recover[regain] one's footing // 정신을 ~ collect one's senses / take[pick up] heart / collect oneself // 몸을 가누지 못하는 lose one's bodily control / lose control of one's body // 몸을 가누지 못하고 쓰러지다 be (thrown) off one's balance // 그는 몹시 취해서 몸을 가누지 못한다 He is so drunk (that) he can't keep himself steady. // 그는 비틀거렸으나 곧 몸을 가누어 회복했다 He staggered but soon recovered himself.

가느다랗다 very thin[fine / slender]; very slim; lean and long. ¶가느다란 팔 a slender arm // 가느다란 목소리 a thin voice // 가느다란 털실 extrafine[superfine] woolen[(영) woollen] yarn // 가느다란 펜 an extrafine [superfine] point(ed) pen // 목이 ~ have a slender neck.

가느스름하다 rather slender [thin / fine]; somewhat thin[slender]. ¶눈을 가느스름하게 뜨다 narrow one's eyes / (눈이 부셔서) squint one's eyes (at the glaring light).

가는귀먹다 be hard of hearing; be a little deaf; lose some of one's hearing; be slightly deaf. ¶그는 가는귀먹었다 He is hard of hearing. / His hearing is poor.

가늘다 1 [둘레가 작다] small; thin; fine; slender; slim. ¶가는 철사[끈] a small wire [string] // 가는 팔[허리] a slender arm [waist] // 가는 실 a small[fine] thread // 가는 나뭇가지 a twig // 가는 붓 a slender writing brush // 손발이 ~ have slender limbs // 가늘게 하다 thin / make thin / make slender.
2 [너비가 좁다] narrow. ¶눈을 가늘게 뜨다 narrow one's eyes // 눈을 가늘게 뜨고 보다 look (at a thing) with half-closed [narrowed] eyes // 그녀는 천을 가늘게 찢었다 She tore the cloth to shreds. // 그는 대를 가늘게 쪼갰다 He whittled a piece of bamboo into a thin stick.
3 [울림이 약하다] small; weak; feeble; faint. ¶가는 목소리로 in a feeble voice // 뒤뜰에서 아기의 가는 울음소리가 들려왔다 I heard the faint cry of a baby from the backyard.
4 [낟알이 작다] fine; small. ¶가는 모래 fine sand // 지금은 가는 비가 오고 있다 A fine rain is falling now. / It is drizzling now. // 그 바닷가는 모래가 ~ The beach has fine sand.
5 [아주 약하다] slight. ¶그녀의 손이 가늘게 떨리고 있었다 Her hands was trembling slightly.
6 [촘촘하다] fine; close. ¶가는 모시 fine ramie fabric // 올이 가는 직물 a fabric of close texture.

가늠 1 [겨냥] aim; sight. **가늠하다** take aim (at); aim (at); sight (a target); level[point] a gun (at). ¶총을 잘 가늠해서 쏘다 take a good aim and fire the gun // 잘못 ~ aim badly // 표적을 신중히 ~ take careful aim at the target.
2 [판단·어림] judgement; discernment; estimation; sense of proportion; a guess; a conjecture. ¶내 ~으로는 in my estimation [calculation] // ~을 잡을 수가 없다 have no idea (of) / be unable to figure (it) out / be utterly in the dark. **가늠하다** make a guess [conjecture]; use one's sense of proportion (on); watch; study; weigh (one plan against another). ¶정세를 ~ watch the development of a situation / see how the wind lies [is blowing] / see how things develop // 눈으로 ~ measure[estimate] (the distance) by the eye // 그 일이 언제 끝날지 아직 가늠할 수 없다 The end of the task is not yet in sight.
가늠(을) 보다 1 [목표를] aim (at); sight (a target). 2 [시세·기미를] estimate; make an estimate (of); guess.
● **가늠구멍** the notch of the backsight. **가늠쇠** the bead; the foresight; the front sight. **가늠자** the sight(s); a gunsight; the backsight.

가능성(可能性) (a) possibility; (잠재적인) (a) potentialities; (능력의) (a) capacity; (기회의)

가능하다

a chance; (객관적으로 본 바) likelihood. ¶~이 있는 젊은이 a promising youth // ~**이 있다** be possible (to do) / be feasible (to do) // ~**이 없다** be not possible (to do) / be impossible (to do) // ~이 충분히 있다 be quite within the realms of possibility // ~이 전혀 없다 be out of the bounds of possibility / be absolutely impossible // 그가 그 일을 맡은 ~은 희박하다 There is not much possibility [likelihood] of him taking the job. // 그런 방법으로 경영하는 회사는 도산할 ~이 크다 A company operated that way is very likely to go bankrupt. // 일이 잘될 ~은 충분히 있다 There is a good [fair] chance[possibility] of success. // 중국은 커다란 ~을 지닌 국가이다 China is a country with great potentialities [potential].

가능하다 (可能-)

possible; (실현이) practicable; feasible. ¶가능한 범위 내에서 as much [far] as possible / within the limits of the possible [possibility] // 가능한 빨리 as soon as possible // 가능하다면 if (it is [be/were]) possible / if (you) can // 가능하게 하다 make (a matter) possible // 불가능을 가능케 하다 turn an impossibility into a possibility / make the impossible possible // 그렇게 하는 것은 ~ It is possible for us to do so. / We can do so. // 그것은 얼마든지 가능한 일이다 That's quite possible. // 나는 그 일이 가능하다고 믿는다 I believe that it is possible. // 너의 소망은 실현이 ~ It is possible to realize your desire. // 가능한 일은 다해 보았다 We exhausted every possibility [possible means]. // 그가 그 일을 내일까지 끝내는 것은 ~[가능하지 않다] It is within [beyond] his power to finish it by tomorrow. / It is possible [impossible] for him to finish it by tomorrow. // 항생 물질의 사용으로 질병을 빨리 고치는 일이 가능해졌다 The use of antibiotics has made possible speedy recovery from many kinds of diseases. // 가능한 한 해 보지 I will do my best. / I will try to the best of my ability.

가다¹

1 [목적지를 향해 움직이다] go (to); [상대방 쪽으로 가다] come; [어떤 장소에 가서 잠시 머물다] be (at, in); (탈것을 타고) take; [출발하다] leave (for); [방문하다] visit. (참고) 어떤 장소를 기점으로 하여, 외부를 향해 나아가는 것은 go, 이에 대하여 어떤 도달점을 향해서 외부로부터 접근해 가는 것이 come이다. go는 흔히 우리말의 「가다」에, come은 「오다」에 해당되지만, come도 「가다」에 해당되는 경우가 있다. 그것은 2인칭에 대해 자기의 동작을 말하는 경우인데, 예를 들면 "내일 오후에 너의 집에 가겠다."는 "I'll come to your home tomorrow afternoon."이 된다. 이것은 말하는 상대방을 중심에 두고 자기의 동작을 생각하는 데서 온 것이다. 단, "나도 함께 가면 안 될까요?" "May I go with you?"와 같은 경우는 go도 사용된다. 이것은 상대방도 어디로 가는 도중이기는 하나 상대방이 도달점이라고 생각되지 않기 때문이다. 그러나 이 경우에도 상대방을 따라간다는 기분이 있으면 "May I come with you?"처럼 come도 사용된다. 다음의 우리말의 「가다」에 해당되는 말로서 종종 be가 사용된다. 어떤 장소에 가서, 거기서 얼마 동안 머무른다는 기분이 따르기 때문이다. (예) "지금 곧 갑니다." "I'll be there right away." 탈것을 이용해서 「…에 가다」라고 할 때는 take가 쓰인다. 「…으로[을 타고] 가다」는 go by taxi(택시로 가다)처럼 go by로 쓰지만, take a taxi to ... 쪽이 보다 구어적이다. 어떤 장소를 떠나서 다른 장소로 가는 것을 나타낼 때는 leave for ..., 어떤 장소를 방문한다는 뜻이 있을 때는 visit도 「가다」라는 우리말에 해당될 때가 있다. ¶서울 가는 기차 a train (bound) for Seoul // 부산에서 인천으로 가는 배 a ship bound from Busan to Incheon // 걸어서 ~ walk / go on foot(▶ foot, bus, ship 등 수단을 나타내는 것에는 관사를 붙이지 않는다) // 부산에 ~ go to Busan // 학교에 ~ go to school / attend school(▶ 「공부한다」는 본래의 목적을 위해 학교에 가는 경우는 school에 관사를 붙이지 않는다) // 부산까지 1등석을 타고 ~ travel[go] to Busan first-class // 시골에 ~ go down to the country // 동대문까지 ~ go as far as Dongdaemun // 똑바로 ~ go straight on[ahead] // 나는 매일 아침 8시에 학교에 간다 I go to school [leave for school] at eight every morning. // 나는 걸어서 학교에 간다 I go to school on foot. // 그는 내달에 미국에 간다 He will go to[leave for] America next month. // 나는 내주에 비행기로 런던에 갑니다 I'm flying to London next week. // 내일 댁에 가도 되겠습니까 May I come and see [call on] you tomorrow? // "어디 갔다 왔니?" "슈퍼에 쇼핑하러 갔다 왔어." "Where have you been?" "I've been to the supermarket to do some shopping." // 뉴욕에 가 본 적이 있니 Have you ever been to New York? // 그는 뉴욕으로 가 버렸다 He has gone to New York. (▶ have been은 갔다가 돌아와 있는 경우, have gone은 가서 지금은 여기에 없는 경우에 씀) // "이 버스는 신촌으로 갑니까?" "예, 갑니다." "Does this bus go to Sinchon?" "Yes, it does." // 그 역에서 공원으로 가는 버스가 있습니다 There is a bus that runs to the park from the station. // 은행으로 가는 길을 가르쳐 주십시오 Would you mind telling me the way to the bank? // 종로로 가려면 어느 길로 가면 됩니까 Which road shall I take to Jongno? // 이 길로 가면 종로가 나옵니다 This street leads to Jongno. // 역은 걸어서[차를 타고] 10분이면 갈 수 있다 You can get to the station in ten minutes on foot[by car]. // 그 역은 걸어서도 갈 수 있다 The station is within a walking distance. // 나는 인파를 헤치고 문 쪽으로 갔다 I made [headed] for the door, elbowing aside the crowd. / I elbowed my way toward the door. // (남이 불렀을 때) 곧 갑니다 I'm coming. // 이제 가 봐야겠습니다 I must be going[running] now. / I guess I'll leave now. / I'm afraid I have to go now. // 가는 말이 고와야 오는 말이 곱다고 마침내 싸움이 벌어졌다 Harsh words for harsh words led to a quarrel.

2 [떠나다] start; leave; go out. ¶여행을 ~ start on a journey / leave on a trip // 유학을 ~ go abroad for study // 시집을 ~ marry / be [get] married (to a person) // 사냥을 ~ go hunting // 낚시를 ~ go fishing / (강으로) fishing in the river // 그들은 산책을 갔다 They went out for a walk. // 나는 내년에 유학갈 예정이다 I'm planning to go abroad for study next year.

3 [도달하다] get to; arrive; reach. ¶그곳에 가면 편지를 주십시오 Please write me a letter [drop a line] when you arrive there. // 그 장소에는 10분이면 갈 수 있다 The place can be reached in ten minutes.

4 [들어가다] enter; join; go into. ¶군대에 ~ enlist in the army / join the colors[army] / enter the service // 수녀원으로 ~ enter a nunnery / become a nun / take the veil.

5 [걷다] walk. ¶시골길을 ~ walk along a country lane // 자갈길을 ~ walk along[up / down] a gravel road.

6 [전달되다] get to; come to hand; be received. ¶통지가 ~ have[receive] notice (of / that) / be informed (of / that) // 연락이 ~ get in touch (with) / have connection (with) // 그에게 기별이 갈 때까지 until one hears further from (a person) // 너한테도 소식이 갔니 Have you heard the news? // 다시 연락이 갈 때까지 기다려라 Wait till further notice.

7 [경과하다] pass (by); go by; (빨리) fly. ¶세월이 감에 따라 as time passes by [goes on] / with lapse[passage] of time // 세월은 간다 Time passes. // 세월은 빨리도 간다 How time flies! // 이야기에 열중하다 보니 시간 가는 줄도 모르고 있었다 We were so absorbed in talking that we almost forget the passing of time. // 겨울이 가고 봄이 왔다 Winter is over and spring has come. // 이달도 다 갔다 This month is up. // 세월이 감에 따라 아픔도 사라졌다 The pain died away as time went by. // 그의 작품은 세월이 가면서 잊혀졌다 His works were forgotten with the passage of time. / His work were forgotten as the years went by[passed].

8 [지속되다] hold out; last; (의복 등이) wear (well); (음식이) keep; (목숨이) live (out); pull through; (기계 등이) stand long use. ¶이런 좋은 날씨는 2, 3일 갈 것이다 This fine weather will last[hold / keep] for a few days. // 이 카세트테이프는 2시간이나 간다 This cassette tape lasts as long as two hours. // 이 건물은 앞으로 백 년은 더 갈 것이다 The building will stand another century. // 그 환자는 앞으로 사흘을 가지 못할 것이다 The patient will not outlive three days.

9 [음식이 변하다] go bad; turn sour[stale]; spoil. ¶맛이 간 맥주 stale[flat] beer // 이 두부는 맛이 좀 갔다 This bean curd has turned a bit sour. // 이 나물은 맛이 갔다 This vegetable dish lost its flavor. // 날씨가 더워지면 생선은 금방 간다 Fish will go bad quickly in hot weather. // 간 음식은 버려라 Throw away stale food[spoiled food, food which has gone bad].

10 [마음이 어떠한 상태로 되다]. ¶마음이 ~ become fond of / take a fancy to[for] / have a liking for[to] // 호감이 ~ be favorably disposed[inclined] toward (a person) // 이해가 ~ can understand[make out] // 납득이 ~ be convinced (of / that) // 이해가 가는 처사 an understandable[a comprehensible] measure // 그는 호감이 가는 인물이다 He has a pleasing[pleasant] personality. // 그때는 그의 의도가 이해가 가지 않았다 I could not make out his intentions at that time. // 나는 그에게 납득이 가도록 설명해 주었다 I explained it to him to his satisfaction. // 이 설명으로 납득이 갑니까 Is this explanation enough for you? // 당신 시계를 누가 훔쳤는지 짐작이 갑니까 Have you any idea who stole your watch?

11 [소요되다] take; require. ¶손이 많이 간 가구 furniture of elaborate workmanship // 손이 많이 ~ cost[require] much labor // 이 계획은 손이 많이 간 것이다 This is a carefully worked-out plan. // 이것을 만들려면 많은 손이 간다 It takes[requires] a lot of time and labor to make this.

12 [생기다] be caused; come about; form; make; take shape. ¶주름이 ~ get creased [wrinkled] // 금이 ~ be cracked / have a crack // 손해가 ~ lose / suffer a loss // 이 찻잔에는 금이 갔다 There is a crack in this teacup. // 눈 주위에 주름이 가기 시작했다 I have begun to develop wrinkles round my eyes. // 노령과 고생으로 그의 이마에는 깊은 주름살이 갔다 Age and care have made deep lines on his forehead. // 우리 팀의 단결에 금이 갔다 Cracks appeared in the unity of our team.

13 [죽다] die; pass away; depart (from) this life; be gone. ¶나이 육십에 홀연히 ~ pass away[die] suddenly at the age of sixty // 하늘나라로 ~ go to one's last home (in peace) // 그는 가고 없다 He is dead and gone. / He is no more.

14 [전깃불이] be out; go out; blow out. ¶전깃불이 갔다 The electric lights are out[have gone out]. / Electric lights has failed. // 어젯밤에는 폭풍우로 전깃불이 갔다 Our electric light was cut-off by a storm last night.

15 [값이] cost; be worth. ¶시가로 백만 원 가는 골동품 a curio worth of a million won in today's money // 이런 종류의 시계는 10만 원은 갈 겁니다 A watch of this kind will easily cost a hundred thousand won. // 쌀 한 가마에 십만 원 간다 The market price of rice is 100,000 won a bag. // 그것을 한국에서 사면 십만 원 이상 갈 겁니다 It would be worth more than 100,000 won in Korea.

16 [등급] rank; come (in an order, at a level). ¶첫째~ rank first // 그는 언제나 자기 반에서 으뜸갔다 He was always at the top [head] of his class. // 부산은 한국에서 둘째가는 대도시이다 Busan is the second largest city in Korea. // 이 공장은 그 규모에 있어서 첫째간다 This factory ranks first in size.

17 [한창때가 지나다] be out (of season). ¶한물간 과일 fruits out of season // 굴은 이제 한물갔다 Oysters are now out of season.

18 [어느 시기에 이르다]. ¶연말에 가서 toward the end[close] of the year // 결국에 가서는 in the long run / in the end / at last / after all // 얼마 안 가서 in a short time / before long.

19 [없어지다] come off[out]; be removed; be taken out. ¶아무리 씻어도 얼룩이 가지 않는다 The stain will not come out, however hard I may to try to wash them off. // 옷깃에 묻은 때가 여간해서 가지 않는다 The grime on the collar won't come out.

가다² [동작·상태가 계속되다]. ¶썩어 가고 있는 과일 a half-rotten fruit // 병이 나아 ~ be getting better // 해가 점점 짧아져 간다 The days are shortening[getting shorter]. // 그는 20세가 되어 간다 He is going on for twenty.

가다가 at times; occasionally; (구어) once in a while. ¶~ 실수를 하다 sometimes make a mistake / make an occasional slip // ~는 일찍 일어날 때도 있다 Sometimes[At times] I get up early. // ~는 아들과 테니스를 칠 때도 있다 I have an occasional game of tennis with my son.

가다듬다 1 [정신을 차리다] brace. ¶마음을 ~ brace oneself (up) / pull oneself together / brace (up) one's spirits / collect one's scattered mind // 마음을 가다듬고 시험을 치르겠다 I'll pull myself together and take the examination. // 마음을 가다듬고 더 힘차게 일을 시작하자 Let's brace ourselves up and start working harder. // 그의 결심을 알고 우리는 모두 마음을 가다듬었다 His determination made us pull ourselves together [made us buckle down].
2 [조절하다] put (things) in order; set in good order; tidy up; adjust. ¶의복을 ~ adjust oneself [one's dress] / straighten one's dress [clothes] // 목소리 [목청]를 ~ clear one's throat.

가닥 1 [줄] a strand; a strip; a ply; (머리의) braid a cut(ting). ¶~수 the number of strands // 실 한 ~ a piece of string // 두 ~으로 꼰 실 two-ply thread // 세 ~으로 꼰 밧줄 a rope of three strands // 두 ~으로 갈라진 꼬리 a furcated tail. **2** [줄기] a streak; a stripe; (빛의) a ray; a beam. ¶한 ~의 빛 a beam [ray] of light // 한 ~의 연기 a streak of smoke // 한 ~의 희망이 보였다 A ray of hope appeared.

가단성(可鍛性) malleability.

가담(加擔) [참여] participation; [공모] conspiracy. **가담하다** [편들다] take sides with; side with; stand by (a person's) side; [참여하다] participate [take part] in; be involved in; be a party to; join company with; [공모하다] conspire. ¶서방 측에 가담하고 있다 be aligned with the West // 어느 편에도 가담하지 않다 maintain neutrality // 그는 그 음모에 가담했다 He was a party to the plot. // 반역에 가담한 자는 처형되었다 Those who took part in the rebellion were executed. // 그 음모에 가담해서는 안 된다 Don't be a party to the conspiracy.
● **가담자** (從犯者) an accomplice; [공모자] a conspirator.

가당분유(加糖粉乳) sugared powder [pulverized] milk.

가당찮다(可當-) [부당하다] unreasonable; unjust; improper; undue; unsuitable; [터무니없다] wild; absurd; preposterous; [지나치다] excessive; outrageous. ¶가당찮은 생각 a preposterous idea // 가당찮은 값 an outrageous price / a ridiculously high price // 가당찮은 요구 an excessive [unreasonable] demand // 가당찮은 소리 마라 Don't talk nonsense. // 늙은 사람이 젊은 여자와 결혼하는 것은 ~ It is improper for an old man to marry a young woman.

가당하다(可當-) [합당하다] adequate; right; proper; appropriate; just; equitable; right and proper. ¶가당한 말이다 You are right in what you say. / You are right when you say. / You speak the truth.

가도(家道) [가계] family livelihood; [가풍] family customs [traditions].

가도(街道) **1** [주요 도로] a main road; a highway (▶ (영))에서는 주로 공적인 경우에 쓰임); a thoroughfare; (영) a trunk road. ¶경인 ~ the Gyeongin [Seoul-Incheon] Highway. **2** [진로] ¶출세 ~를 달리다 succeed in life / get ahead [on] in the world.

가돌리늄 [화] gadolinium (기호 Gd).

가동(可動) ¶~의 movable / mobile.

● **가동교**(-橋) a movable bridge. **가동 댐** a movable dam.

가동(稼動) operation; work. ¶완전 ~ full [full-scale] operation // ~ 중이다 be in (full) operation / be at work / be operated. **가동하다** operate; work; run; put into operation. ¶승강기를 ~ operate an elevator // 발전소는 주야로 가동한다 Power plants operate night and day [round-the-clock].
● **가동률** the rate of operation; the working ration. **가동 중지** a shutdown (of a factory).

가두(街頭) a street. ¶~에서 in [on] the street // ~에서 선전하다 propagandize in [on] the street // 선거 입후보자가 ~에서 연설을 하고 있었다 A candidate for the election was making a campaign speech on the street.
● **가두 검문** the on-the-street searching of a suspicious person (by a policeman). **가두녹음** a street-corner transcription; a man-in-the-street interview. **가두데모** a street demonstration. **가두모금** street fundraising. ¶~ 운동을 벌이다 launch [start] an on-the-street campaign for raising funds (for). **가두연설** street oratory; a wayside speech; a soapbox oratory. **가두판매** street peddling.

가두다 1 (사람을) shut in [up]; coop up; lock up (자물쇠를 채워서); confine; (가축을) impound; shut up in a pen; pen; (뱅쓰를) cage in. ¶남을 방 안에 ~ confine a person to [in] a room / shut a person up in a room // 죄수를 감옥에 ~ confine [keep] a convict in prison / imprison a convict // 수탉을 우리에 ~ coop up hens in a pen // 유괴범은 아이를 방에 가두었다 The kidnapper shut the child up in [confine the child to] a room. **2** (물을) store; impound. ¶저수지에 물을 ~ impound [store] water in a reservoir.

가두리 (손수건의) a hem; (직물의) the selvage; selvedge; (앞치마 등의) a border. ¶손수건에 ~를 대다 hem a handkerchief.

가드 (권투) one's guard. ¶~를 벌리고 at open guard // 그는 ~가 단단하다 [허술하다] It's hard [easy] to get inside [through] his guard. / His guard is good [bad].

가드레일 a guardrail; (영) a crash barrier.

가득 1 full; to the full; to capacity. ¶장내에 찬 청중 a full audience / a capacity crowd // 사람을 ~ 태운 버스 a jam-packed bus // 돈이 ~ 든 지갑 a purse full of money // 포도주를 ~ 부은 컵 a cup of brimful of wine // ~를 채우다 fill (up) / make full // 한 잔 ~ 따르다 fill a glass full [to the brim] // 여름철이면 해운대는 해수욕객으로 ~ 찬다 During the summer Haeundae is crowded with bathers. // 그는 언제나 불평으로 ~ 차 있다 He is always full of complaints. // 홀에는 사람들이 ~ 차 있었다 The hall was packed [crammed] with people. // 그녀의 눈에는 눈물이 ~ 괴어 있었다 Her eyes were filled [swimming / suffused] with tears. // 그 양동이에 물을 ~ 채워 주십시오 Please fill the bucket (to the brim) with water. // 장내를 ~ 메운 청중은 열광적으로 박수를 쳤다 The capacity audience applauded enthusiastically. // 이 방에 ~ 채우면 300명은 들어갈 수 있다 We could pack 300 men in this hall.

가득하다 full (of); chock-full; brimful; filled (to the brim); packed [crammed / crowded] (with people). ¶가득해지다 become full / be filled up / fill (up) / be packed (with)//방 안에는 술 냄새가 가득했다 The room reeked of liquor.//자루는 금과 은이 가득했다 The bag was bursting with gold and silver.//선반에는 책이 가득했다 The shelves groaned under the weight of [were loaded with] books.//그녀의 마음에는 근심이 가득했다 Many anxiety occupied her mind.//역에는 사람들이 가득했다 The station was crowded with people.//그녀의 마음은 자식들의 행복을 비는 생각으로 가득했다 All her thoughts were occupied with the happiness of her children.//그의 머릿속에는 멋진 아이디어가 ~ His head teems with bright ideas. **가득히** full; to the full; to capacity.

가등기(假登記) temporary [provisional] registration (at the recorder's office).

가뜩이나 to make matters worse; (and) what is worse; on top of that; besides; moreover. ¶그는 ~ 빚을 많이 지고 있는데 실직까지 했다 He was deeply in debt, and on top of that he lost his job.//그녀는 ~ 못생긴 데다가 다리까지 전다 She is plain-looking and cripples into the bargain.

가뜬하다 light; agile; feel good. ⇨<거든하다

가라사대 say. ¶예수 ~ as Jesus says ... //공자 ~ 왈 인(仁)이 멀리 있느냐 Confucius says, "Is virtue a thing remote?"

가라앉다 1 [내려앉다] sink; go down (to the bottom); go under; (문어) be submerged; (찌꺼기 등이) settle. ¶가라앉은 배의 보물 the treasure of a sunken ship//깊이 ~ sink deep//(사람이) 배와 함께 ~ go down with the ship//그 배는 선미부터 가라앉았다 The ship settled down by the stern.//그 보트는 순식간에 가라앉았다 The boat sank in a instant.//그 배는 태풍을 만나 가라앉았다 The ship was sunk in a typhoon.//찌꺼기가 가라앉아 포도주는 맑아졌다 The dregs is settled and the wine is clear.//비가 한바탕 오면 먼지가 가라앉을 텐데 A rain fall will settle the dust.//병 속에 뭔가가 가라앉아 있다 Something is settled [deposited] at the bottom of the bottle.
2 [진정되다] cool off; cool down; settle down. ¶마음이 ~ become composed / recover one's composure//그의 노여움은 가라앉기 시작했다 His anger began to subside.//그의 조용한 목소리에 사람들의 흥분도 가라앉았다 His quiet voice cooled their excitement.//그 그림을 보면 마음이 가라앉는다 The picture has a calming effect upon my soul.
3 [기세가 약해지다] calm [die] down; fall [drop] off; subside; abate. ¶저녁때가 되자 바람이 가라앉았다 The breeze went [died / calmed] down in the evening.//폭풍우가 가라앉자 배는 곧 출발했다 The ship set sail as soon as the storm abated.//이 소요도 불원간 가라앉겠지 This disturbance will blow over in time.//사태가 가라앉을 때까지 기다려 보자 Let's wait until things cool off.
4 (부기·통증 등이) abate; subside; soothe. ¶이 약을 먹으면 통증이 가라앉을 겁니다 This medicine will soothe [abate] the pain. / This medicine will remove [kill] the pain.//옆구리에 통증을 느꼈으나 곧 가라앉았다 I felt a pain in my side, but it has gone [stopped].//손가락의 부기가 가라앉았다 The swelling on my finger has gone away [down].//얼음으로 식혔더니 부기가 가라앉았다 The ice pack reduced the swelling. / The ice pack took [brought] the swelling down.
5 [조용해지다] become calm [quiet / still]. ¶연사가 일어서자 떠들썩했던 분위기가 가라앉았다 A dead silence fell over the room when the orator rose to speak.

가라앉히다 1 (물속으로) sink (a vessel); send (a ship) to the bottoms(전투 등에서); submerge(물속에 잠기게 하다); (찌꺼기 등을) settle; lay. ¶배에 구멍을 뚫어 ~ scuttle a ship//찌꺼기를 ~ make dregs settle//물을 뿌려 먼지를 ~ settle [lay] the dust by sprinkling of water//우리는 적함을 3척 가라앉혔다 We sunk three enemy's ships.
2 (감정을) calm; quiet; compose; [달래다] soothe; appease. ¶마음을 ~ calm one's mind / compose oneself//그는 마침내 마음을 가라앉히고 이야기를 시작했다 At last he got his feelings under control and began to speak.//아무도 그의 노여움을 가라앉히지 못했다 Nobody could soothe [ease] his anger.
3 (부기·통증 등을) relieve; soothe; allay; alleviate. ¶기침을 ~ relieve a cough//진통을 ~ allay [relieve] labor pains//치통을 가라앉히는 데는 이 약이 좋다 This medicine relieves toothache.
4 [진압하다] put down; suppress; quell. ¶학원 소요를 ~ put down [quell] a school disturbance.

가라오케 a karaoke. ¶~ 반주에 맞추어 노래를 부르다 sing a song with karaoke accompaniment.

가락¹ 1 [실 감는 꼬챙이] a distaff; a spindle. 2 [가늘고 긴 물건] a long, slender thing; a stick. **젓~** chopsticks//엿 한 ~ a stick of candy.

가락국수 noodles; wheat vermicelli.

가락² 1 [선율] a melody; a tune; an air. ¶거문고의 ~ a tune of a *Geomungo*//구성진 ~ a sweet tune / sweet music//~에 맞추어 춤을 추다 dance to the music. 2 [솜씨] skill; dexterity; [능률] efficiency.

가락(이) 나다 (일에) get into the swing of one's work; hit [get into] one's stride. ¶이제야 제 가락이 난다 I've got going at last.

가락(이) 맞다 1 (선율이) get [be] in tune. ¶그의 노래는 언제나 가락이 맞지 않는다 He always sings out of tune. / [음치이다] He is tune-deaf. 2 [비유]. ¶저 두 사람은 가락이 잘 맞는다 They get along [on] well with each other. (▶ get along은 (미), get on은 (영)의 표현)

가락지 a set of two rings; twin rings. ¶~를 끼다 [끼고 있다] put [wear] twin rings on one's finger // ~를 빼다 take [slip] twin rings off one's finger.

가람(伽藍) a Buddhist temple [monastery]; a cathedral.

가랑눈 powdery [fine] snow. ¶갑자기 ~이 내리다 (미) have a flurry (of snow) // ~이 온다 A light powdery snow falls.

가랑니 a nit; a baby louse.

가랑머리 hair braided in two plaits [pigtails] (hanging down the back). ¶~의 소녀 a girl with two plaits of hair hanging down the back//소녀는 ~를 하고 있었다 The girl wore [had] her hair in two plaits. / The girl had two pigtails.

가랑무 a forked radish.

가랑비 (a) drizzle; (a) mizzle; a fine [drizzling]

rain. ¶~가 온다 It is drizzling.// 오후 내내 ~가 왔다 It drizzled all afternoon.
가랑비에 옷 젖는 줄 모른다(속담) A small leak will sink a great ship.
가랑이 the crotch; the crutch; the fork. ¶바짓~ the crotch of (a pair of) trousers// ~가 찢어지다 as poor as a church mouse// ~를 벌리다 stretch[spread] one's legs apart// ~를 벌리고 서다 stand with one's legs [feet] apart//나무~에 걸터앉다 sit in the crotch of a tree// ~지다 branch off[away] / fork / bifurcate(두 갈래로) / ramify.
가랑잎 [낙엽] fallen[dead] leaves.
가랑잎에 불붙듯(속담) be short[quick] tempered; be impatient.
가랑잎이 솔잎더러 바스락거린다고 한다(속담) The pot calls the kettle black.
가래¹ [농기구] a spade. ¶~로 파다 spade (a trench) / dig with a spade.
● **가래질** [농] spading; spadework. **가랫날** the blade of a spade.
가래² [긴 토막] a stick; a rod; a long and slender piece (of). ¶엿[떡] 한 ~ a long piece of taffy[rice-cake].
● **가래떡** *garaetteok*; a long and slender rice-cake; rice-cake in form of rounded stick.
가래³ [담] phlegm[flem]. ¶피가 섞인 ~ bloody phlegm// ~ 삭이는 약 an expectorant (medicine)// ~ 덩어리 a clot of phlegm// ~가 많이 나오다 expectorate much / cough up much phlegm//목에 ~가 끓다 have a hard, obstructive phlegm in one's throat// ~를 뱉다 spit out phlegm / cough out[bring up] phlegm / expectorate phlegm //목에 ~가 걸렸다 The phlegm has stuck in my throat.
● **가래침** sputum (*pl.* -ta); phlegm and saliva.
가래톳 a bubo (*pl.* -es). ¶~이 서다 have a bubo.
가량(假量) 1 [어림짐작] a guess; a conjecture. 2 [쯤] about; around; some; almost; more or less; approximately. ¶1주일~ about a week (or so)//10마일~ about[some] ten miles / ten miles or so / round[(미) around] about ten miles//50살~의 남자 a man about 50 years of age//1만 원~ [(somewhere) around] 10,000 won//한 시간 ~ 지나면 돌아오겠습니다 I'll back in about an hour[an hour or so]./"비용은 얼마~ 들었습니까?" "3만 원~입니다." "How much did it cost?" "It cost me about 30,000 won."
가량없다(假量-) 1 [어림할 수 없다] immeasurable; inestimable. ¶가량없는 사막 an immeasurable expanse of sand//그 탑의 높이는 가량없었다 The tower was an immeasurable height. **가량없이** immeasurably; inestimably. 2 [어림도 없다] absurd; preposterous; outrageous. ¶가량없는 값 an outrageous[exorbitant] price. **가량없이** absurdly; preposterously.
가려내다 [분류하다] sort out; assort; classify; [골라내다] pick out; single out; [따로따로 하다] separate; winnow; sift. ¶쌀에서 뉘를 ~ winnow[separate] chaff from rice // 헌책을 ~ sort out old books//카드를 색깔별로 ~ sort cards according to their colors//좋은 사과를 나쁜 것에서 ~ sort out[separate] the good apples from the bad//여럿 중에서 ~ choose from among many//그들은 우수한 선수를 가려냈다 They picked[singled] out best players. / They selected[chose] best players.

가련하다(可憐-) [불쌍하다] poor; pitiable; pitiful; [애처롭다] pathetic; touching; sad; [비참하다] miserable; wretched. ¶꽃 파는 가련한 소녀 a poor flower girl//가련한 인생 a miserable man[life]//가련한 이야기 a sad [pathetic] story/(미) a sob story//가련한 처지 a miserable condition / a sad plight//가련하게도 그 아이는 3살에 부모를 잃었다 Poor child, he was orphaned at the age of three. **가련히** poorly; pitiably; sadly. ¶…을 ~ 여기다 take[have] pity[compassion] on (a person) / feel pity for (a person) / pity (a person).
가렴주구(苛斂誅求) extortion[exaction] of taxes; laying[imposing] crushing taxes. (on).
가렵다 itchy; itching. ¶등이 ~ My back itches. / My back feels itchy.//그는 가려운 곳을 북북 긁었다 He scratched the itchy place[spot] hard.//그녀는 얼굴에 난 발진을 가려워했다 She is bothered by the itchy rash on her face.
가려운 데를 긁어 주다 be very careful [scrupulous]; leave nothing to be desired. ¶그는 가려운 데를 긁어 주듯 나를 돌봐 주었다 He looked after me with scrupulous care.// 그의 설명은 가려운 데를 긁어 주는 듯했다 His explanation left nothing[little] to be desired.
가령(假令) 1 [예를 들어] for example; for instance; e.g.; let us say; […과 같이] such as; as; say. ¶~ 런던에서는 in London, for instance// 말일세, 누군가가 그런 짓을 했다면 if anyone, let me say you, had done so// 한 권에 백 원이라 치고 one hundred won per book, for example.
2 [가정하여] if; suppose (that); supposing [admitting / granting] that; even if [though]. ¶~ 그가 오지 않는다면 어떻게 하겠나 Supposing he doesn't come, then what are you going to do?// ~ 네가 나의 입장이라면 어떻게 하겠나 Suppose you were in my position, what would you do?// ~ 저 집이 오래 되었다 하더라도 그래도 사고 싶다 Granted [Granting] that the house is old, I still want to buy it.
가례(嘉禮) a celebration; a happy event; (왕실의) an auspicious ceremony at court. ¶혼인의 ~ a wedding ceremony.
가로 1 [폭] width; (문어) breadth; length(▶영어에서는 가로, 세로의 구별 없이 긴 쪽에 length를 쓴다). ¶(크로스워드퍼즐의) ~ 1번 number one across//그 그림은 가로 2미터이다 The picture is two meters wide[in width].// 표준적인 편지지의 크기는 ~ 18cm, 세로 23cm이다 The standard letter sheet is 18 centimeters wide by 23 centimeters long[18 by 23 centimeters]./나는 ~ 50cm, 세로 30cm의 판자를 찾고 있다 I am looking for a board fifty by thirty centimeters [50cm long and 30cm wide].
2 [옆으로 된 방향] across; crossways; crosswise; horizontally. ¶종이를 ~ 자르다 cut a piece of paper from side to side[from one side to the other]/글씨를 ~ 쓰다 write from left to right / write across the page//10cm의 선을 ~ 그어라 Draw a horizontal line of 10 centimeters. / Draw a 10 centimeter line

horizontally. ¶다음 숫자를 처음에는 세로, 다음에는 ~ 읽어라 Read the following digits first down and then across. ¶그는 머리를 ~ 저었다 He shook his head. / (안 된다고 말했다) He said no.
- **가로줄** a horizontal line. **가로축** [수] the horizontal axis; the x-axis.

가로(街路) a street; [큰 거리] an avenue. (▶ 미국의 대도시에서는 남북으로 달리는 도로를 avenue, 동서로 뻗은 것을 street라고 부르는 곳이 많음)
- **가로등** a streetlight; a streetlamp. **가로변** a roadside; a wayside. **가로수** a roadside tree. ¶~가 있는 보도 an arbored walk.

가로놓다 place [put / lay] across. ¶거리에 장애물을 ~ erect a barrier across a street // 우리는 개울에 널빤지를 가로놓았다 We laid a plank across the brook.

가로놓이다 1 [가로질러 놓이다] lie across. ¶그 강에 가로놓인 다리 a bridge across [over] the river // 길에 큰 나무가 쓰러져서 가로놓여 있었다 There was a big tree lying fallen across the road. // 긴 장대가 한길에 가로놓여 있다 A pole lies across the street. 2 [앞에 버티고 있다] stand in one's [the] way. ¶그의 앞날에는 큰 난관이 가로놓여 있었다 A great difficulty was lying in wait for him [was lying ahead of him].

가로누이다 lay (a thing) on its side. ¶몸을 ~ lay oneself down (on the grass) / lie down (on the bed) // 우리는 찬장을 문에서 가로누여 운반하였다 We carried the cupboard sideways through the door.

가로눕다 1 [옆으로 눕다] lie on one's side. ¶나는 피로하면 흔히 가로누워 잔다 I often sleep on my side when I'm tired. 2 [길게 눕다] lie (down); lay oneself down; stretch oneself out. ¶그는 마루에 큰대자로 가로누웠다 He lay at full length on the floor.

가로닫이 a sliding door [window]. ¶~창과 내리닫이창 a sliding window and a sash window.

가로되 say. ¶공자 ~ Confucius says ….

가로막다 1 [가로질러 막다] stop; stem; check. ¶강물을 ~ stop [stem] a stream / check a current // 강을 가로막고 댐을 만들다 build [construct] a dam across a river. 2 [앞쪽이 보이지 않게 하다] obstruct; shut out; (빛을) intercept. ¶시야를 ~ obstruct the view / 빛을 ~ block (off) [intercept] the light // 앞에 있는 큰 건물이 이 창문에서 보이는 경치를 가로막고 있다 A tall building in front obstructs [shuts out] the view from this window. 3 [방해하다] cut off; block; bar; hinder; (사람의 언행을) head off; interrupt. ¶적군이 아군의 퇴각로를 가로막았다 Our retreat was cut off [blocked] by enemy troops. // 트럭이 진창에 빠져 우리의 갈 길을 가로막고 있다 A truck has stalled in the mud, blocking [barring / standing in] our way. // 그는 군중이 잘못된 출구로 나가려는 것을 가로막았다 He headed the crowd off from the wrong exit.

가로막히다 be obstructed; be blocked (up); be intercepted; be screened. ¶산의 정상은 구름에 가로막혀 보이지 않았다 The summit of the mountain was screened by the clouds. // 언덕에 가로막혀 다리가 보이지 않는다 The bridge is shut out from view by the hill. / The hill blocked the view of the bridge.

가로맡다 1 [떠맡다] take over (another's task); take upon oneself; assume (another's responsibility); undertake. ¶남의 빚을 ~ shoulder another's debt // 남의 책임을 ~ undertake [assume] another's responsibility // 그는 남의 싸움을 가로맡아서 했다 He made the fight his own. 2 [나서다] meddle [interfere] (in); poke [put / thrust] one's nose (into). ¶남의 일이 이러니 저러니 가로맡고 나서지 마라 Don't stick your nose into other people's affairs.

가로새다 sneak [shirk] away (from company); slip [steal] away [off]. ¶수업 도중에 ~ (미국 속어) cut a lesson and beat it // 함께 가다가 도중에 ~ sneak away from company on the way // 손님은 한 사람 한 사람 슬그머니 가로새기 시작했다 The guests began to slip away, one by one, unnoticed.

가로세로 [가로와 세로] length and breadth. ¶~ 8피트의 양단자 an 8×8-foot carpet. 2 [사방으로] in all direction; in every direction; to all points. ¶철도가 전국을 ~ 누비고 있다 A network of railways covers the country.

가로쓰기 horizontal writing. ¶답안은 ~로 할 것 Write your answers from left to right. / Write across the page. **가로쓰기하다** write laterally [in lateral lines]; write from left to right.

가로지르다 1 [빗장을] put (a bar) across. ¶빗장을 가로질러 대문을 잠그다 bar [bolt] a gate. 2 [가로질러 지나다] cross; go [cut] across; traverse (똑바로 또는 비스듬히); intersect (교차하다); (바다·하늘을) sail [fly] across. ¶한반도의 허리를 가로지른 휴전선 a cease-fire line across the middle of the Korea Peninsula // 길을 ~ cross [go across] a street // 행렬을 ~ break through a procession // 산과 들을 ~ traverse hills and fields // 소로가 숲을 가로질러 나 있다 A path runs through the woods. // 그들은 강을 가로질러 정글로 들어갔다 They crossed [went across] the river and went into the jungle.

가로채다 1 [낚아채다] snap (away) (from / off); wrest (from); take by force; tear (off / away) (a thing) (from (a person)). ¶오토바이를 탄 젊은 남자가 그녀의 손에서 돈뭉치를 가로채어 도망갔다 A young man on a motorcycle snatched [grabbed] a roll of bills from her hand and ran off with it. 2 [자기 것을 만들다] seize (a thing) by force; steal; snatch; (횡령하다) embezzle; misappropriate; (권리·지위를) usurp. ¶땅을 가로채려는 음모 a vicious scheme to grab land // 공금을 ~ embezzle the public money // 왕위를 ~ usurp the throne // 남의 아내를 ~ steal a woman from her husband / win away another's wife // 남의 단골을 ~ intrigue with another's customer // 그 출납계원은 은행 돈 200만 원을 가로챘다 The teller embezzled two million won from the bank. 3 (남의 말을) cut (a person) short; interrupt (a person). ¶남의 말을 ~ interrupt a person's speech / interrupt a person in his speech // 그는 내 이야기를 가로채고 자기 이야기를 시작했다 Interrupting my speech [me], he started talking.

가로채이다 [낚아채이다] get seized (on the way); be snatched; (권리·지위를) be

가로퍼지다

usurped. ¶나는 그에게 재산을 가로채였다 He robbed me of my property. // 나는 가장 친한 친구에게 애인을 가로채였다 My best friend made off with my girl[boy] friend. / My best friend stole my girl[boy] friend.

가로퍼지다 1 [옆으로 커지다] spread (out); widen (out); broaden. ¶가로퍼진 가지 spreading branches. 2 [뚱뚱해지다] get stout[fat]; gain weight. ¶가로퍼진 남자 a stocky[stockily built] man / a chunky fellow.

가뢰 [동] a meloid; an oil beetle; a Spanish fly; a blister beetle; a cantharis.

가료 (加療) (medical) treatment; remedy. ¶~중이다 be under medical treatment // 1개월의 ~를 요하다 require a month's treatment.

가루 (일반적으로) powder; (금·석탄 등의) dust; [주로 체로 친 밀가루] flour; [곡식의 굵은 가루, 맷돌로 탄 것] meal. ¶~의[같은] powdered / powdery // 옥수수의 굵은 ~ corn meal // ~를 내다 powder / reduce to powder [dust] / (부수거나 갈아서) pulverize / (절구 등으로 빻아서) grind (corn) into meal[flour] // ~를 체로 치다 sift flour / put flour through a sieve.
- **가루분**(-粉) cosmetic[face] powder. **가루비누** soap powder. **가루약** powdered medicine; a (medical) powder.

가르다 1 [쪼개다] cut (into); divide (into). ¶생선의 배를 ~ cut[slash / open] the abdomen of a fish // [요리 준비를 하다] dress a fish // 사과를 넷으로 ~ cut an apple into four pieces / divide an apple into quarters / quarter an apple // 그녀는 케이크를 세 쪽으로 갈랐다 She divided the cake into three pieces.
2 [분할하다] divide (into); part (into); split (into); separate; sort out; classify. ¶머리를 ~ part one's hair (in[on] the middle / on the left) // 편을 ~ divide[split] (a group) into (two) rival teams // 코치는 선수들을 두 팀으로 갈랐다 The coach divided the players into two teams. // 나쁜 책과 좋은 책을 ~ sort out the good books from the bad // 그녀는 쌀과 겨를 갈랐다 She separated the rice from the chaff. // 선생님은 아이들을 키에 따라 갈랐다 The teacher classified the children by height.
3 [분배하다] share (with); distribute [divide] (among); allot. ¶그는 재산을 세[두] 아들에게 갈라 주었다 He divided his property among his three sons[between his two sons]. // 우리는 마지막 남은 빵 한 조각을 둘이서 갈라 먹었다 The two of us shared the last piece of bread.
4 [관계를 떼어 놓다] cut off; sever; separate; (문어) estrange. ¶사랑하는 두 사람 사이를 갈라놓다 separate a pair of lovers / tear a pair of lovers apart // 부부 사이를 갈라놓다 sever husband and wife / cut a husband from his wife // 아들과 며느리 사이를 억지로 갈라놓다 separate one's son and his wife against their will // 이 사건은 그와 그의 친구들 사이를 갈라놓았다 This incident estranged him from his friends.

가르랑거리다 wheeze; be wheezy. ⇨그르렁거리다 ¶그 노인은 천식으로 목을 가르랑거린다 The old man wheezes with asthma.

가르마 a part; (영) a parting. ¶~를 한가운데에[왼쪽으로/옆으로] 타다 part one's hair in the middle [on the left / at the side].

가르치다 1 [교육하다] (지식·기술 등을) teach; (음악·미술 등을 개인적으로) give lessons (in); [지도하다] instruct (in); train; educate; school. ¶아이에게 영어를 ~ teach a child English / teach English to a child // 그는 고등학교에서 수학을 가르치고 있다 He teaches[is a teacher of] mathematics in a high school. // 나는 그 학생들에게 역사를 가르치고 있다 I instruct the students in history. // 나는 그에게 개인적으로 영어를 가르치고 있다 I teach him English privately. / I give him private lessons in English. // 이 학교에서는 프랑스 어를 가르치지 않습니다 French is not taught at this school. // 젊은 세대를 가르치는 것은 매우 의의 있는 일이다 It is a task of great significance to educate young people. // 그는 개에게 재주를 가르쳤다 He trained his dog to do tricks. // 그들은 무엇보다도 먼저 소년 소녀 들에게 애국심을 가르쳤다 They inculcated love of their country above everything else into the young boys and girls.
2 [알려 주다] tell; direct; (실제로) show. ¶길을 가르쳐 주다 tell (a person) how to get to a place / direct (a person) [show (a person) the way] to a place // 죄송합니다만 역으로 가는 길을 가르쳐 주십시오 Excuse me, but will you tell me the way to the station? // 이 쿠키 만드는 법을 가르쳐 주세요 Please give me the recipe for these cookies / (함께 만들면서) Please show me how to make these cookies. // 이 연장의 사용법을 가르쳐 주지 I will tell [show] you instructions for using this tool. // 선생님 성함을 가르쳐 주십시오 May I have your name, please? // 안전벨트의 착용법을 가르쳐 주십시오 Please tell me how to fasten my seat belt.

가르침 1 [가르치는 일] teaching; instruction; lesson; [훈련] discipline; train. ¶~을 받다 be taught (a subject by a person) / study (a subject) under (a person) // ~을 **청하다** ask for a person's instruction // 나는 그에게서 직접 ~을 받기 위해 상경했다 I went (up) to Seoul to ask for his personal instruction [seek personal instruction from him]. (▶ 한정된 분야에서 가르침을 받는 경우는 일반적인 teaching보다 instruction을 쓰는 것이 좋음) // 그들은 부모를 공경하라는 ~을 받았다 They were trained[schooled / brought up] to respect their parents.
2 [교훈] a lesson; teachings; [행동의 규범] a precept; [교리] a doctrine. ¶부처의 ~ the teachings of Buddha / Buddhism // 나는 아버지의 ~에 따랐다 I followed my father's precepts. / I followed the lessons I learned from my father. // 이 책에는 공자의 ~이 쓰여 있다 This book contains the teachings of Confucius.

가름 [분할] dividing; splitting; [분리] separation; [분배] distribution; sharing; [분류] classification; grouping. **가름하다** cut (into); divide (into); share (with); cut off. ⇨가르다

가리¹ [고기 잡는 기구] a (fish) weir; a fish trap. ¶~를 **놓다** set[lay] a weir[fish trap].

가리² [더미] a pile; a stack; a cock. ¶볏 ~ a stack [shock] of rice straw / a rick // 건초 ~ a haystack / a hayrick // 노적 ~ an open-air stack of rice straw.

가리가리 to [in] pieces; into [in / to] shreds. ¶~ 찢다 tear [rend] to pieces [ribbons / shreds] // 그는 그녀의 편지를 ~ 찢었다 He tore her letter to pieces. // 내 옷이 ~ 찢어졌다 My dress was torn to [into] shreds.

가리개 [두 폭 병풍] a two-paneled [two-leaved] (folding) screen.

가리다[1] [덮다] cover; veil; shield; screen. ¶베일로 얼굴을 ~ cover one's face with a veil / veil one's face // 두 손으로 얼굴을 ~ cover one's face with one's hands / (슬퍼서) bury one's face with one's hands // 그녀는 손수건으로 입을 가렸다 She covered her mouth with her handkerchief. // 그 호수는 안개에 가려 보이지 않았다 The (view of the) lake was hidden by the fog. // 그는 신문 기자들에게 얼굴을 보이지 않으려고 모자로 가렸다 He shielded his face from several newspapermen with his hat. // 산의 정상은 구름에 가려 있다 The top of the mountain is covered with [hidden by] the clouds. // 나무가 해를 가리고 있다 A tree keeps the sun off. // 눈물이 앞을 가렸다 My eyes were dim [blurred] with tears.

가리다[2] 1 [고르다] choose; select; pick out; sort out. ¶그의 작품에서 최고의 것을 ~ select [choose] the best of his works // 친구를 가려서 사귀어라 Choose your companions well.
2 [싫어하다] be shy [bashful]. ¶낯을 ~ be shy of [with] strangers / 낯을 가리지 않다 take familiar to strangers // 그 아기는 엄마를 닮은 여자에게 낯을 가리지 않는다 The baby takes familiar to woman who resembles its mother. // 이 아이는 아직도 낯을 가립니다 This child is still bashful in front of strangers.
3 [따져 밝히다] look into; inquire; investigate. ¶시비를 ~ argue about whether it is right or wrong // 진위(眞僞)를 ~ inquire into the truth of the matter // 셈을 ~ adjust an account // 빚을 ~ pay (up) (the remainder of) one's debt // 정부는 그 수회 사건의 진상을 가리겠다고 약속했다 The government promised to inquire [look] into the bribery case.
4 [머리를 대강 빗다]. ¶헝클어진 머리를 ~ (빗으로) comb one's disordered hair roughly / (손으로) arrange one's disordered hair.
5 [식별하다] distinguish [discriminate] (A from B); tell (A from B). ¶그는 공과 사를 가릴 줄 모른다 He mixes [confuses] public affairs with private ones. / He fails to make a distinction between public and private matter. // 그 두 바이올리니스트는 우열을 가리기가 어려웠다 It was hard to tell which of two violin players was better. // 나는 그 당시 선악을 가릴 줄 모르는 어린애였다 I was then too young to know [tell] right from wrong.
6 (음식을) be fastidious [particular] (about food). ¶그는 가리는 음식이 너무 많다 He has too many likes and dislikes in what he eats. // 나는 음식을 가리지 않는다 I am not particular [choos(e)y] about food [what I eat].
7 (대소변을). ¶대소변을 ~ be grown up enough to go to stool by oneself.

가리다[3] [쌓다] pile up; stack; rick. ¶볏단을 ~ stack the bundles of rice straw / pile up rice straw in ricks. // 건초를 산더미처럼 ~ stack hay high.

가리마 → 가르마
가리비 [동] a scallop; a scollop.
가리새 [갈피] the drift [thread / direction] of an affair. ¶어찌된 일인지 ~를 모르겠다 I can't make out what it's all about.

가리키다 1 (손가락 등으로) point to [at] (▶ 는 대상물이 있는 방향을, at은 대상물 자체를 가리키는 경우); indicate; show; (눈금을) say; read; register (▶ register는 시계에는 쓰지 않음). ¶그는 누이동생을 손가락으로 가리켰다 He pointed his finger at his sister. / He pointed at his sister with his finger. // 그는 자기 집 쪽을 가리켰다 He pointed toward [in the direction of] his house. // 풍향계는 북쪽을 가리켰다 The weather vane pointed to the north. // 그는 달력에 동그라미를 친 날짜를 가리켰다 He indicated [pointed out] a circled date on the calendar. // 그는 지도의 한 점을 가리켰다 He pointed at [to] a spot on the map. // 시계는 12시를 가리키고 있다 The clock shows twelve. // 시곗바늘은 10시 5분을 가리키고 있었다 The hands of the clock stood at [indicated] 10:05. // 온도계는 영하 2도를 가리켰다 The thermometer said [registered / indicated] two degrees below zero.
2 [지칭하다] mean; refer (to). ¶'그것'은 3행 앞에 나온 「이상한 사건」을 가리킨다 "It" refers to "the extraordinary incident" mentioned three lines above. // 저런 사람을 가리켜 괴짜라고 한다 We call a man like him an eccentric. // 누구를 가리켜 말하는 것입니까 Who do you mean?

가마[1] 1 a cauldron; a kettle. ⇨→가마솥(⇨→가마) 2 [숯·벽돌을 굽는 시설] a gama; a kiln. ¶숯~ a charcoal kiln // 도자기 ~ a pottery [porcelain] kiln // 벽돌 ~ a brick kiln. // 벽돌을 굽기 위하여 ~에서 bake bricks in a kiln.
가마 밑이 노구솥 밑을 검다 한다 (속담) The pot calls the kettle black.
● **가마솥** a gamasot; a cauldron; a kettle; an iron pot.
가마[2] (머리의) the whirl [whorl] of hair (on the back of the head); a hair whirl [whorl].
가마[3] [탈것] (두 사람이 어깨에 메는) a palanquin; a palankeen; (두 사람이 허리 높이로 드는) a sedan chair. ¶~를 타고 가다 go by palanquin [sedan chair] // ~를 메다 carry a palanquin on the shoulder / carry a sedan chair.
가마[4] a straw bag; a bag; a bale. ⇨→가마니
가마니 1 [용기] a gamani; a straw bag. ¶쌀~ a straw rice bag [sack] / (쌀이 들어 있는) a bag of rice // ~에 넣다 put in a straw bag. 2 [단위] a bag; a bale; a sack. ¶쌀 두 ~ two bags of rice // 소금 한 ~ a bale of salt.
-가마리 a butt. ¶놀림~ a butt of ridicule // 욕 ~ a butt of good scolding // 웃음~ a laughingstock.
가마우지 [동] a cormorant.
가마조개 [동] a corbicula. ⇨→가무락조개
가만 ⇨→가만히6 ¶그가 무엇을 하든 ~ 내버려 두어라 Leave him alone to do anything. 2 (감탄사) Wait!; Hold on! ¶~, 그리 서두를 것 없네! Wait! You don't have to hurry. // 내 말도 좀 들어 보게 All right. But listen to me.
가만가만 calmly; softly; stealthily. ⇨→가만히2,3,4 ¶~ 이야기하다 talk [speak] in whispers.
가만두다 leave (a person) alone; do not disturb (a person); leave (a thing) as it is

가만있다

[stands]; leave (a thing) intact. ¶내 책상 위에 있는 것들을 치우지 말고 가만두시오 Leave the things on my desk as they were. // 당분간은 나를 가만두어 주시오 Please leave me alone for a while. // 건방지게 굴면 가만두지 않겠다 You'll pay dearly for your impertinence. / I won't let you get away with being impertinent. // 그를 가만두지 않겠다 I'll teach him a lesson.

가만있다 1 [움직이지 않다] be [remain] motionless [still]; be at a standstill; (구어) stay put. ¶온종일 방 안에 ~ keep (in) one's room all day long // 집 안에 가만있지 말고 밖에나 나가 봐라 You shouldn't shut yourself up in the house—go outdoors. // 내가 올 때까지 여기 가만있어라 Stick here till I get back. 2 [관계하지 않다]. ¶그가 훔친 것을 알면서 가만있을 작정이오 Are you going to let him off [go scot-free] when you know he stole it? // 아무것도 모르면 가만있어 That's none of your business. / Mind your own business.

가만있자 let me see; well. ¶~, 내가 그것을 어디에 두었더라 Let me see, where did I put it? // ~, 너의 질문이 무엇이었더라 Well, what was your question?

가만히 1 [움직이지 않고] motionlessly; quietly; still. ¶~ 앉아 있다 sit still [motionless] // ~ 누워 있다 lie motionless // ~ 바라보다 stare (fixedly) (at a person) // 그 아이는 잠시도 ~ 있지 않았다 The child was restless all the time. // 그는 활동가여서 잠시도 ~ 있지 못한다 He is too active to sit idle. / He is always on the go [the move]. // (사진을 찍을 때) 그대로 ~ 계세요 Hold on, please!
2 [조용히] calmly; silently; quietly; still. ¶~ 이야기하다 speak in a quiet tone [gentle voice / calm tone] // 떠들지 말고 ~ 있어라 Be quiet! / Shut up!
3 [살그머니] softly; gently; tenderly; lightly. ¶문을 ~ 두드리다 knock at [on] the door gently // 그는 환자가 깨지 않도록 ~ 걸었다 He walked softly [quietly] so as not to awaken the sick man. // 그녀는 방에서 ~ 나갔다 She left the room quietly. // 그녀는 ~ 내 손을 잡았다 She took my hand softly. // 깨뜨리지 않도록 ~ 놓으시오 Put it down gently so that it doesn't break.
4 [몰래] stealthily; secretly; in secret. ¶그는 아버지의 책상 서랍을 ~ 열었다 He stealthily opened the drawer in his father's desk. // 그는 ~ 내 방에 들어왔다 He stole [slipped] into my room. // 그녀는 ~ 비밀을 가르쳐 주었다 She whispered the secret to me [in my ear].
5 [곰곰이] deliberately; carefully; seriously. ¶~ 생각해 보다 think well / consider seriously // 선생님이 하신 말씀을 ~ 생각해 보아라 Think over what the teacher said.
6 [손을 쓰지 않고]. ¶이렇게 많은 사람이 곤란을 당하고 있는데 ~ 보고만 있을 수 없다 I cannot remain indifferent when so many people are suffering.

가망(可望) [장래성] hope; promise; [전망] prospect; [가능성] probability; possibility; (a) likelihood; (a) chance. ¶~이 있는 [없는] (사물이) hopeful [hopeless] / (사람이) promising [unpromising] // ~이 있다 be promising [hopeful] / have a bright prospect [future] / bid fair (to success) // ~이 없다 be hopeless / be unpromising // 그가 성공할 ~은 전혀 [거의] 없다 There is no [little] hope of his success. // 성공할 ~은 반반입니다 There is an even chance of success. // 이길 ~이 없다 The chances [odds] are against me. // 그들이 살아 있을 ~은 거의 [별로] 있다 There is little likelihood [not much hope] of their being alive. // 그는 완쾌될 ~이 없다 There is no hope [chance] of his recovery. / He is past [beyond] hope of recovery. // 현 상태로는 정식 협상이 이루어질 ~은 없다 Formal negotiations are not in the cards under present conditions. // 그 의안이 통과될 ~은 없었다 There was no possibility that the bill would be passed. / There was no likelihood of the bill being passed. // 핵 실험 금지가 실현될 ~은 보이지 않는다 There is no hopeful sign that the nuclear test ban will come into effect.

● **가망성** hope; prospect. ⇨가망 ¶~이 있는 학생 a hopeful [promising] student / ~이 있는 기업 a hopeless enterprise / ~이 있는 장사 a business which has bright prospect.

가매장(假埋葬) temporary burial [(문어) interment]. **가매장하다** bury temporarily. ¶그의 시체는 들판에 가매장되었다 His body was buried temporarily in a field.

가맹(加盟) joining; affiliation. **가맹하다** join (in); associate oneself with; be affiliated with; become a member. ¶단체에 ~ be affiliated with an organization / become a member of an association // 유엔에 ~ join the United Nations.

● **가맹국** a member nation (of the United Nations). **가맹자** a member; a participant. **가맹점** a member (store) (of a chain store association).

가면(假面) 1 [탈] a mask. ¶~을 쓴 댄서 a masked dancer // ~을 쓰다 [벗다] put on [take off] a mask // ~을 쓰고 있다 wear a mask.
2 [위선] a mask; disguise; a pretence. ¶자선이라는 ~을 쓰고 under the mask [pretence] of charity / behind a mask of charity // ~을 쓰다 mask one's real character // ~을 벗다 throw off a mask / reveal oneself // ~을 벗기다 unmask [take off the mask of] (a hypocrite) / debunk // 그녀의 애교는 야심을 가리기 위한 ~이었다 Her amiability was a mask for her ambition. // 저 신사인 체하는 녀석의 ~을 벗겠다 I will unmask that bogus "gentleman". // 그들은 우정의 ~을 쓰고 그에게 접근했다 They approached him under [in] the guise of friendship.

● **가면극** a masque; a mask (drama). **가면무도회** a mask(ed) ball.

가면허(假免許) a temporary license [(영) licence]; (단체 설립 허가 등의) a provisional charter.

가명(家名) [집안의 명예] the family name [honor]; the good name of a family. ¶~을 더럽히다 disgrace [blacken] the family name / bring disgrace on one's family // 그는 크게 ~을 날렸다 He enhanced the reputation of the family greatly.

가명(假名) [가짜 이름] a fictitious [made-up] name; [거짓 이름] an assumed [a false] name; (범죄자 등의) an alias; a pseudonym. ¶~을 사용하다 assume a fictitious name / use a false name // 편지를 ~으로 쓰다 write a letter under a fictitious [false] name // 그는

최민수라는 ~으로 행세하고 있다 He goes by the pseudonym[assumed name] of Choe Minsu.// 그 시체는 신원 불명인 채 홍길동이라는 ~으로 매장되었다 The unidentified corpse was buried under the name of Hong Gildong.

가무(歌舞) singing and dancing; all musical and other entertainments. ¶~를 즐기다 enjoy music and dancing// 정부는 ~음곡을 일체 금지했다 The government ordered a suspension of all public performances in music and dancing.

가무락조개 [동] a corbicula.
가무스름하다 dark; dusky; swarthy. ⇨<거무스름하다
가무잡잡하다 dark; swarthy; (햇볕에 타서) tanned; browned. ¶얼굴이 가무잡잡한 사나이 a dark-complexioned man// 피부가 ~ be dark[dark-skinned] / be tanned.
가문(家門) one's family[clan]. ¶최씨 ~ the Choe family / the Choes and their clan// ~의 영예 a credit[an honor] to one's family// ~을 빛내다 bring honor to one's family// 좋은 ~에 태어나다 come of (a) good stock[a good family] / be well-born// ~을 자랑하다 be proud of one's good birth// 그는 ~이 좋다 He has a good family background.// 그는 ~덕택에 출세했다 His rise in the world is due to the standing of his family.// 그의 ~은 어떤가 From[Of] what family is he sprung?
가문비나무 [식] a spruce.
가문서(假文書) a forged[counterfeit] document.
가물 a drought. ⇨가뭄
  가물에 콩 나듯(속담) be very scarce[rare]; be few and far between.
가물가물 (불빛이) flickeringly; shimmeringly; blinkingly. **가물가물하다** flicker. ⇨ˇ가물거리다 ¶촛불이 바람에 가물가물하다 꺼졌다 The candle flickered in the wind and went out. / The candle flickered out in the wind. **2** (먼 데 있는 것이) vaguely; dimly; hazily. **가물가물하다** haze. ⇨ˇ가물거리다 **3** (정신이) faintly; dizzily. **가물가물하다** have a dim consciousness. ⇨ˇ가물거리다 ¶정신이 가물가물해질 정도로 높은 곳에서 at a giddy [dizzy(ing)] height (from the ground).
가물거리다 1 (불빛이) flicker; glimmer; shimmer. ¶가물거리는 불빛 a flickering light // 먼 데서 불빛이 가물거렸다 I saw a flickering light in the distance.
  2 (먼 데의 물체가) haze; become misty [hazy]; (눈이) have dim sight; be purblind; be misty; grow dim; be blurred. ¶멀리서 가물거리는 섬 an island dim in the distance// 안개로 수평선이 가물거렸다 Mist blurred the horizon.// 눈이 가물거려 잘 보이지 않았다 I was dazzled and could not see very well.
  3 (정신이) have a dim consciousness [memory]; get fuzzy. ¶가물거리는 기억을 더듬다 trace back a vague memory// 배가 고파서 정신이 가물거린다 I am faint with hunger.
가물다 be in (a spell of) drought; be droughty [rainless]. ¶날씨가 7월 말부터 가물고 있다 We have had dry weather since the end of July.// 오랫동안 가물어서 우물물이 많이 줄었다 Owing to a long spell of dry weather, the well has considerably sunk.// 날씨가 가물어서 농작물이 죽어 가고 있다 The crops are suffering from lack of rain.
가물치 [동] a snakehead; a snakehead mullet [fish].
가뭄 a drought; dry weather; a dry spell. ¶오랜 ~ a long drought / a (long) spell of dry weather// 오랜 ~으로 인한 벼의 피해 damage to the rice crop caused by a prolonged drought// ~에 단비 (a) welcome rain during the dry season// ~으로 곤란을 겪고 있다 be suffering from want of rain// 오랜 ~으로 농사를 망쳤다 Owing to the long drought, the crops have failed. / Due to the long drought, the farmers have had poor crops.// 지난 한 달 동안 ~이 들었다 We haven't had a single drop of rain for the past month.// 이 벼의 새 품종은 ~을 탄다 This new variety of rice is easily damaged by droughts.
가뭇가뭇하다 black-spotted; speckled with black. ¶주근깨가 가뭇가뭇한 얼굴 a face sprinkled[peppered] with freckles / a freckled face// 가뭇가뭇한 수염이 자라 있다 have a stubble of black beard.
가뭇하다 blackish; darkish.
가미하다(加味~) **1** season; flavor; tinge; lace. ¶여러 가지 양념으로 가미한 고기 요리 a meat dish seasoned with many kinds of spices// 레몬을 가미한 아이스크림 ice-cream flavored with lemon// 그는 커피에 브랜디를 가미했다 He took his coffee laced with brandy. **2** [보태어 넣다] add. ¶유머를 가미한 연설 a speech seasoned with humor// 법에 인정을 ~ temper justice with mercy// 이 보고서는 시민의 의견도 가미한 것이다 This report takes into account the views of the citizens.
가발(假髮) (전체 가발) a wig; (부분 가발) a hairpiece(▶ wig보다 hairpiece가 머리숱이 없는 사람을 배려한 완곡어); (대머리에 쓰이는 남성용, 또는 옛날의 장식용) a toupee. ¶~을 쓰다 wear a wig.
가방 a bag; a portfolio(둘로 접게 된 것); a briefcase(서류용); a suitcase(소형); a trunk(대형). ¶(학생의) 책 ~ a satchel(흔히 멜빵이 있음)// 여행용 ~ a traveling bag / a valise / a portmanteau(양쪽으로 벌릴 수 있는 것)// ~을 들다 carry a bag// ~에 옷을 챙겨 넣다 pack clothes in a suitcase.
가법(加法) ➡덧셈
가법(家法) [가정의 법도] a family code of conduct; a family rules[regulations]; [예절] household etiquette[formality].
가변(可變) ¶~의 [바꿀 수 있는] variable / changeable / [조절할 수 있는] adjustable. ●**가변 비용** [경] variable cost. **가변성** variability; changeability. **가변 자본** [경] variable capital. **가변 저항기** [전] a variable resistor. **가변 축전기** [전] a variable condenser.
가볍다 1 (무게가) light; not heavy. ¶가벼운 짐 light baggage// 무게가 ~ weigh light / be light (in weight)// 가볍게 lightly// 짐을 가볍게 하다 lighten a load// 뱃짐을 가볍게 하다 lighten a ship's cargo// 이 천은 무게를 느낄 수 없을 만큼 매우 ~ This cloth is as light as air[a feather].// 그는 신장에 비해 체중이 다소 ~ For his height he's rather light[a bit on the light side].// 이 짐은 가벼워서 나도 들 수 있다 This baggage is light enough for me to carry.
  2 (가치·정도가) light; slight. ¶가벼운 범죄 a

minor [petty] offense // 가벼운 처벌 a light [mild] punishment // 가벼운 읽을거리 [농담] light reading [jokes] // 나는 그때 가벼운 실망을 맛보았다 I felt mild disappointment then. // 가벼운 이야깃거리로 화제를 돌립시다 Let's talk about a lighter topic. // 나는 때로 가벼운 읽을거리를 읽는다 I sometimes read light books. 가벼이 lightly; slightly. ¶목숨을 ~ 여기다 make light [little] of one's life.

3 [경솔하다] rash; thoughtless; careless; frivolous. ¶하는 짓이 ~ behave frivolously [flippantly] / act rashly // 그는 입이 ~ He cannot be trusted with a secret. / He doesn't know how to keep his mouth shut. // 그녀는 궁둥이가 ~ She never sits still for long. / She is restless [flighty]. // 그는 의장으로서는 아무래도 가벼워서 안 되겠다 He is no good as chairman—he lacks in seriousness. 가벼이 thoughtlessly; carelessly. ¶입을 ~ 놀리지 마라 Be careful what you say.

4 [책임·부담이). ¶세금을 가볍게 하다 lighten the taxes / reduce the tax // 형량을 가볍게 하다 reduce a sentence // 작업량을 가볍게 하다 lighten the work load // 그의 책임은 ~ His responsibility is not heavy.

5 [경쾌하다] light; nimble. ¶몸놀림이 가벼운 사람 an agile [a nimble] person // 가벼운 걸음걸이로 걷다 walk with light steps / step lightly // 가벼운 마음으로 with a light heart / without taking it (too) seriously // 그 일을 가벼운 마음으로 떠맡은 것이 잘못이었다 I shouldn't have undertaken the job so casually.

6 [심하지 않다] slight; not serious. ¶가벼운 병 a slight illness // 너의 상처는 ~ You are only slightly injured. // 그는 가벼운 홍역에 걸렸다 He had a light case of measles. // 나는 지난주에 가벼운 감기에 걸렸었다 I had a slight cold last week.

7 (음식이) light; not heavy. ¶가벼운 식사 a light meal // 여름에는 가벼운 음식이 좋다 I prefer light food in summer.

8 [수월하다] easy; light.

가보 (家寶) a family treasure; an heirloom. ¶~인 보석 family jewels // 그 병풍은 우리 집안의 ~로서 대대로 전해 내려오는 것이다 The folding screen has been handed down for generations [from generation to generation] as an heirloom in our family.

가보 (家譜) a genealogy; (a) lineage; [도표] a family tree; a genealogical chart.

가봉 (假縫) basting; tacking; (a) fitting. ¶~이 다 되었습니다 Your suit is ready for trying on. / We are ready to fit you. 가봉하다 baste; tack; try [fit] (a coat) on. ¶그는 양복점에 가봉하러 갔다 He went to the tailor's to be fitted.

가부 (可否) **1** [옳고 그름의 여부] right and [or] wrong; [적부 (適否)] propriety; advisability; [허락 여부] yes or no. ¶~를 가리다 distinguish between right and wrong / tell right from wrong // 모금 운동의 ~를 논하다 argue about the advisability of a fund-raising campaign // 그 설의 ~는 간단히 결정할 수 없다 We cannot decide readily whether the theory is right or wrong. // ~를 곧 알려 주십시오 Please let me know soon whether it is yes or no. // 나는 ~를 알려고 왔습니다 I've come for yes or no.

2 [찬성과 반대] ayes and nays; pros and cons; for and against. ¶투표로 ~를 묻다 decide (a matter) by vote / put (a matter) to vote / take a vote (on) // 투표로 ~를 결정합시다 We will vote to decide.

가부간 (可否間) [옳건 그르건] whether right or wrong; [찬성하거나 반대하거나] whether yes or no; [여하튼] at any rate; anyway; anyhow. ¶~ 오늘은 그 일을 매듭짓겠습니다 At any rate I'll settle the matter today. // ~ 최선을 다해 보겠습니다 Anyway (,) I will do what I can.

가부장 (家父長) a head of a family; a patriarch; [법] a paterfamilias. ¶~ 중심의 patricentric.
● **가부장제** (—制) patriarchy; patriarchal system.

가분수 (假分數) [수] an improper fraction.

가불 (假拂) **1** (봉급 등의) an advance; advance payment. 가불하다 advance; pay in advance. ¶월급의 절반을 가불해 드립니다 I'll advance you half your salary. // 월급에서 공제하기로 하고 20만 원까지 가불해 드립니다 You may borrow up to two hundred thousand won against your salary. →¶가불받다 borrow (50,000 won) in advance on one's pay [salary] / have (50,000 won) advanced on one's pay [salary] / have (50,000 won) paid in advance // 봉급의 절반을 가불받다 receive half month's salary in advance // 월급에서 20만 원만 가불받았으면 합니다 I would like an advance of two hundred thousand won on my salary.

2 [잠정 지불] a temporary payment. 가불하다 pay temporarily.
● **가불금** an advance; a temporary [suspense] payment.

가뿐가뿐 lightly; nimbly. **가뿐가뿐하다** [가볍다] light; [경쾌하다] nimble; airy; buoyant.

가뿐하다 1 (물건이) rather light; not heavy. ¶책가방이 ~ My satchel is not heavy. 가뿐히 lightly; easily; without (any) effort [difficulty]. ¶그는 거대한 돌을 ~ 들어 올렸다 He lifted the big stone without difficulty.

2 (몸·행동이) light; nimble; airy; lightsome; buoyant. ¶가뿐한 걸음걸이 (walk with) light steps // 몸이 ~ be [feel] well / be in good condition. 가뿐히 lightly; nimbly; buoyantly.

3 (마음이) light; carefree; without anxiety [worry]. ¶그 일을 해결하고 나니 마음이 ~ As the matter is settled, I am relieved of my worries [burden / anxiety]. // 그 소식을 듣고 그의 마음은 가뿐해졌다 The news lightened his gloom. / He was relieved in heart at the news. 가뿐히 lightly.

가쁘다 1 [숨이 몹시 차다] short-winded [-breathed]; gasping [panting] (for breath); (구어) puffy. ¶가쁜 숨을 몰아쉬며 out of breath / gaspingly // 달려왔더니 숨이 ~ I've come running and am out of breath. // 그는 심장이 나빠서 항상 가쁜 숨을 내쉰다 He is always short of breath because of his bad heart. // 나는 긴 계단을 오르면 숨이 ~ I run [get] out of breath when I go up a long staircase. // 숨이 가빠서 더 이상 달리지 못하겠다 I am out of breath and can't run any farther. **2** [힘에 겹다] burdensome; hard; trying. ¶이 일은 내게 ~ This task is beyond my ability [power].

가사 (家事) **1** [살림을 꾸려 나가는 일] (세탁·청소 등, 가정의 일상적인 일) housework; (집 안의 잡일) household [domestic] chores(▶ 복수형으로, chores는 「시시한 일」이라는 뉘앙스를 풍김); (살림살이) housekeeping. ¶~를 돌보다 do housework [household tasks] / keep house // ~에 쫓기다 be busy with housework [household chores] / be busy keeping house // 그녀는 ~를 잘 처리한다 She is a good housekeeper. / She runs her household well. // 나는 지금 ~를 돕고 있습니다 I help my mother with her housekeeping now. 2 [집안의 사사로운 일] family affairs; household matters.
● 가사 사건 [법] a legal case involving a family; [가정 분쟁] a family dispute.

가사 (假死) [의] suspended animation; apparent death; syncope; asphyxia(질식에 의한). ¶~ 상태에 빠지다 fall into a state of suspended animation / be in a syncopic state.

가사 (袈裟) [불] a surplice. ¶~를 입은 승려 a surpliced priest.

가사 (歌詞) (노래의) the words; the text; (오페라의) the libretto. ¶~를 짓다 write the words of a song // 홍길동 작의 ~ words by Hong Gildong // 이 노래의 곡은 ~와 잘 어울리지 않는다 The tune of this song does not quite fit the words.

가산 (加算) addition. **가산하다** [더하다] add; [산입하다] include. ¶원금에 이자를 ~ add interest to principal. ➔¶이 300만 원에는 이 자가 가산되어 있지 않다 Interest is not included in this three million won. // 특별 요금이 가산됩니다 An extra charge [A surcharge] will be added. // 요금에는 10%의 서비스료와 10%의 세금이 가산됩니다 // (게시) A 10% service charge and a 10% government tax will be added to the total price.
● 가산금 additional charges; (세금 체납 시의) a (tax defaulter's) penalty; a fine for default. 가산세 an additional tax; a deficit tax.

가산 (家産) family property [estate]; one's fortune. ¶~을 탕진하다 squander [dissipate] one's fortune / go [run] through one's fortune // 그의 ~은 기울었다 His fortune began to fall [ebb]. / He sank in fortune.

가산 명사 (可算名詞) [언] countable nouns.

가상 (假想) imagination; supposition. ¶~의 [적인] imaginary // ~의 적과 싸우다 fight [tilt at] windmills. **가상하다** imagine; suppose. ¶ 그를 적으로 ~ imagine him to be an enemy.
● 가상현실 virtual reality.

가상 (假像) (텔레비전·레이더 등의) a ghost (image); (결정(結晶)의) pseudomorph.

가상하다 (嘉尙-) admirable; laudable; commendable; praiseworthy; appreciate(높이 평가하다). ¶용돈을 쪼개어 빈민 구제에 기부를 하다니 어린 나이에 참으로 가상하군 It is highly praiseworthy for a child to contribute something out of its pocket money to the poor relief fund. **가상히** admirably; laudably; commendably; appreciatingly. ¶선행을 ~ 여기다 appreciate (a person) highly for his good deed // 사장은 그의 공적을 ~ 여겨 금일봉을 내렸다 The president granted [gave] him some money in appreciation of his remarkable achievement.

가새지르다 cross; lay [place] crosswise [crisscross]. ¶깃대를 ~ set up two flagpoles across each other // 국기를 ~ cross [entwine / intertwine] national flags.

가새표 (-標) a cross; an x. ¶~를 하다 mark with a cross / x (a ballot) // 잘못된 곳을 ~로 지우다 cross [x] out a mistake // 그녀는 자기가 쓴 것을 ~로 지웠다 She x-ed [crossed] out what she has written.

가석방 (假釋放) parole; release on parole; conditional [provisional] release. **가석방하다** parole (a prisoner); release [put] (a person) on parole. ➔¶가석방되다 be paroled / be released on parole / (영) be released on a ticket of leave.

가선 (架線) [선을 매는 일] (aerial) wiring; [매어 놓은 선] an aerial line; (an overhead) wire.
● 가선공 (-工) a lineman; (영) a linesman. 가선 공사 wiring work.

가설 (架設) (다리 등의) construction; building; (전화 등의) installation. **가설하다** construct; build; install(전화 등을). ¶강에 교량을 ~ construct [build] a bridge over a river // 전화를 ~ install a telephone / have a telephone installed // 그들은 전선을 가설하고 있다 (지하에) They are laying electric cables. / (지상의) They are putting up electric wires. // 전화를 가설하고 싶은데요 I would like to install a telephone in my house.
● 가설 공사 building [construction] work. 가설비 the building cost; (전화의) the installation cost.

가설 (假設) 1 [임시 설치] temporary establishment [construction]. ¶~의 temporary / provisional // ~ 매표소 a temporary ticket office. **가설하다** construct [put up] temporarily; build [install] for the time being. ➔ ¶그곳에 극장이 가설되었다 A temporary theater was built there. 2 [가정] assumption; [상정] supposition. **가설하다** assume; suppose; presume; postulate.
● 가설극장 a temporary theater. 가설무대 a makeshift stage.

가설 (假說) a hypothesis (pl. -ses). ¶~이라는 ~에 입각하여 on the hypothesis that ... // ~ 을 세우다 hypothesize / frame [formulate] a hypothesis / make [build] a hypothesis // ~ 은 증명되었다 The hypothesis was proved [verified].

가성 (苛性) ¶~의 caustic.
● 가성 소다 caustic soda; sodium hydroxide (수산화나트륨). 가성 알칼리 caustic alkali. 가성 알코올 caustic alcohol. 가성 칼리 caustic potash; potassium hydroxide(수산화칼륨).

가성 (假性) ¶~의 [의] false / pseudo-.
● 가성 근시 false nearsightedness; pseudomyopia. 가성 콜레라 pseudocholera.

가성 (假聲) 1 [음] (a) falsetto. ¶그는 ~으로 노래했다 He sang (in) falsetto. // 그는 대사를 ~으로 말했다 He spoke the lines in a falsetto tone. 2 [거짓 목소리] a feigned [disguised] voice. ¶~으로 말하다 talk in a feigned [disguised] voice // ~을 내다 disguise one's voice.

가성대 (假聲帶) [생] a false [superior] vocal cord.

가세 (家勢) economic [financial] conditions of a family; family circumstances. ¶~가 넉넉하다 be well [comfortably] off / be in easy circumstances // ~가 넉넉지 못하다 be badly [poorly] off / be in needy [narrow] circumstances // 그의 ~는 기울어 가고 있었다 His fortunes were on the wane [on the decline].

가세하다

가세하다 (加勢-) [편들다] side with; take sides with; be on a person's; [지지하다] support; back up; stand by (a person). ¶약한 편에 ~ side with the underdog / take side with [stand by] the weaker // 최 군이 우리 편에 가세해 주어서 정말 잘되었다 Mr. Choe was a welcome addition to our side. // 여론은 그에게 가세했다 Public opinion was in his favor [on his side]. // 너의 새 작업에 가세하겠다 I'll join [share / aid / assist] you in your new work.

가소롭다 (可笑-) ridiculous; laughable; absurd. ¶이야기 짝이 없다 be highly ridiculous / be quite absurd // 네가 나를 가르치겠다니 ~ It is ridiculous to imagine you teaching me anything. // 그가 남에게 검약을 설법하다니 ~ I am amused by the idea of his preaching thrift others.

가소성 (可塑性) plasticity. ¶~의 plastic // 열~의 thermoplastic.

가소제 (可塑劑) a plasticizer; (영) a plasticiser.

가속 (加速) acceleration; speed-up. **가속하다** accelerate; speed up; (미국 구어) soup up. ¶그 차는 급속히 가속했다 The car picked up speed rapidly.
● **가속기 / 가속 장치** an accelerator. **가속 차선** an acceleration line. **가속 페달** an accelerator (pedal).

가속도 (加速度) [물] acceleration. ¶등~ 운동 uniformly accelerated motion // 순간~ instantaneous acceleration // 중력 ~ acceleration of gravity // ~적인 accelerative // ~으로 at an increasing tempo / with increasing speed // ~가 붙어서 멈추지 못하고 문에 부딪혔다 I was going too fast to stop and ran into the door. // 사태는 ~적으로 악화하고 있다 The situation is deteriorating with increasing speed [at an ever increasing speed].
● **가속도 운동** an accelerated motion. **가속도 원리** [경] an acceleration principle.

가솔 (家率) one's family // [미] folks.

가솔린 (미) gasoline; (영) petrol; (미국 구어) gas. ¶차의 ~이 떨어졌다 We have run out of gas [petrol]. // 탱크에 ~을 가득 채워 주시오 Fill up the tank with gas [petrol].
● **가솔린 기관 / 가솔린 엔진** a gasoline engine. **가솔린차** a gasoline car.

가수 (假數) [수] a mantissa.

가수 (歌手) a singer; [여자 (유행) 가수] a songstress; [특히 밴드 연주로 노래하는 가수] a vocalist. **상송** [재즈] ~ a chanson [jazz] singer // **오페라** ~ an operatic [opera] singer // **유행가** ~ a popular (song) singer / a pop singer.

가수금 (假受金) a suspense receipt. ¶계약에 의한 ~ advance received on contract / key money.

가수 분해 (加水分解) [화] hydrolysis. ¶~의 hydrolytic.

가수요 (假需要) imaginary [fictitious / disguised] demand; [투기적] speculative demand. ¶~의 급증 a rapid [sudden] increase of imaginary demand.

가스 [기체] gas; [연료용의] (coal) gas. ¶천연 [도시] ~ natural [city] gas // 프로판 ~ natural gas // 독~ poison gas // 액화 천연 ~ liquefied natural gas // 액화 석유 ~ liquefied petroleum gas // 연탄 ~ coal gas // ~로 취사하다 cook by gas // ~를 켜다 [끄다] turn on [off] the gas / turn the gas on [off] // ~ 불을 약하게 [세게] 하다 turn the gas down [high] // ~가 나오는 것을 반으로 줄이다 reduce the gas to half // ~의 본관을 잠그다 turn off the gas at the main cock // 우리 집에는 ~가 들어와 있다 Our house has gas. / Our house is hooked up to the gas mains. / (영) We have gas laid on in our house. / ~가 나온다 [안 나온다] The gas is on [off]. // ~가 샌다 The gas is leaking. / The gas escapes. // 여기는 아직 ~가 들어오지 않았다 No gas is laid on here yet. // 그녀는 ~를 틀어 놓고 자살했다 She committed suicide by inhaling gas. / She killed herself with gas. / She gassed herself.
2 [배 속의] gas; wind (방귀). ¶배 속에 ~가 차다 have gas [wind] in the bowels // 배 속에 ~가 약간 차 있는 것은 염려할 것 없다 A bit of gas in the digestive tract [A slightly gassy stomach] is nothing to worry about.
● **가스관** a gas pipe (금속제); a gas hose (고무제); a gas main (본관). **가스등** (-燈) a gas lamp; a gaslight. **가스라이터** a gas (cigarette) lighter. **가스레인지** (미) a stove; a gas stove; a gas range; (영) a cooker. **가스마스크** [방독면] a gas mask; [군] a gas helmet. **가스버너** a gas burner. **가스 중독** gas poisoning. **가스총** (최루탄용) a tear gas gun. **가스 폭발** a gas explosion.

가슴 1 [가슴패] the breast; [흉곽] the chest; (여자의) the bust; [품] the bosom. (▶ 목과 배 사이의 부분은 남녀 불문하고 chest, 주로 여자의 유방은 breast, 신체 사이즈로서의 여자 가슴둘레는 bust) ¶~을 드러낸 bare-bosomed // ~이 풍만한 여자 a bosomy [full-bosomed / busty] woman // ~이 풍만하다 have a full bosom // (여자가) ~이 납작하다 be sag- [flat-] chested // ~이 아프다 have a pain in the chest // ~이 답답하다 feel oppressed in the chest // ~을 펴다 throw out one's chest / straighten [draw] oneself up // ~을 쓸다 [문지르다] pass one's hand over the breast // ~을 치다 [치며 울다] beat one's breast // ~을 펴고 걷다 walk with one's head held high // ~을 부풀리다 heave one's chest [bosom / breast] // ~에 손을 얹다 lay one's hand on one's heart // 그는 내 ~을 쳤다 He struck me a blow on the chest. // ~을 펴고 기운을 내라 Keep your chin up and be cheerful. // (의사가 환자에게) ~ 좀 볼까요 Let me have a look at your chest.

2 [심장] the heart. ¶~을 두근거리며 with one's heart throbbing // ~이 두근거렸다 My heart throbbed [beat fast]. // 내 ~이 뛰었다 I felt my heart pounding against my chest.

3 [마음] one's heart; one's mind; feelings; soul; bosom. ¶~ 깊이 deep in one's heart // ~ 깊이 간직한 생각 an idea cherished deep in one's heart // ~에 와 닿는 진실 a home truth // ~이 미어지는 듯한 슬픔 heartbreaking [heartrending] grief // ~이 뭉클해지다 feel a lump in one's throat // ~이 답답하다 be (all) choked up / have a pent-up [an oppressed] feeling / feel frustrated / feel hemmed in // ~이 후련하다 feel relieved [eased] / have a feeling of ease / breathe easy / feel free [unencumbered] / feel carefree // ~이 메다 [터지다] have one's heart break / be heartbroken [brokenhearted] / be heartbreaking [heartrending] / be enough to make one's heart break// ~이 터질 것만 같다 feel as if one's heart would break [rend] // ~을 태우다 be worried / be anxious / (사람이) pine [sign] (for) / burn with passion / (사물이) burn (a person's) heart / eat one's heart out //~에 와 닿다 (사물이) go to one's heart / come home to one [one's bosom] / come in (up)on one / cut one to the quick / appeal to one / impress one / ring the bell (속어) / (사람이) quickly understand (what a person is driving at)// 애인이 보고 싶어서 ~을 태우다 be dying [yearning] to see one's love // ~에 절이다 cut to the heart [to the quick] // ~ 깊이 묻어 두다 bury (a secret) within one's heart / keep (a confidence) within one's heart / hug (a secret) to one's bosom // ~이 후련해지도록 울다 weep oneself out / weep one's fill // ~이 찢어지는 아픔을 느끼다 feel heartbroken // 벅차서 말이 안 나왔다 My heart was too full for words. // 하고 싶은 말을 다 하고 나니 ~이 후련했다 After I had said my say, I felt as if a burden had been lifted off my mind. //그 마지막 한 마디가 내 ~을 절였다 The last word came home to me. // 나는 ~이 뿌듯했다 It was a proud moment for me. // 내 ~은 기대감으로 설렜다 My heart leaped (up) [bounded] with expectations. // 전화벨이 울리자 나는 ~이 섬뜩했다 When the telephone bell rang, my heart went into my boots [my heart was in my mouth]. / The telephone bell brought my heart into my mouth [boots].

가슴(이) 아프다 heart-stricken; heartbroken; heartrending; broken-hearted; lamentable; regrettable; (서술적) one's heart aches (at). ¶외아들을 잃는다는 것은 가슴 아픈 일이다 To lose one's only son is a heartrending experience. // 이제는 어머니가 안 계시거니 생각하면 나는 ~ It grieves me to think that my mother is no more. // 그것을 보고 그녀는 가슴이 아팠다 It hurt her in her breast to see it.

가슴이 내려앉다 be greatly surprised; be startled.

가슴이 부풀다 be buoyant (with).

● **가슴둘레** the girth; the bust (여자(옷)의); the circumference of one's chest. ¶넓은[좁은] ~ a broad [narrow] chest. **가슴속** one's heart; one's in(ner)most heart; the bottom of one's heart. ¶~ 깊이 간직한 생각 an idea cherished deep in one's heart // ~을 털어놓다 unbosom oneself (to) / speak one's mind (to) // ~에서 오가다 come and go [recur to] one's mind // 그것은 ~에서 우러나오는 말 같았다 The words seemed wrung out of his heart. **가슴앓이** heartburn; water brash; a sour stomach; [의] pyrosis; cardialgia; (a) chest trouble; chest disorder [ailment]; a pain in the chest. ¶~를 앓다 have heartburn. **가슴지느러미** [동] a pectoral (fin).

가습기 (加濕器) a humidifier.

가시 1 (장미 등의) a thorn; (풀잎 등의) a prickle; (선인장의) a spine; (밤송이 등의) a bur; [식] an acantha; an aculeus; an acicula. ¶~가 나는 [돋는] spinescent // ~가 있는 thorny / prickly / spined // 잎에 ~가 나는 prickly-leafed // 손을 ~에 찔리다 get a hand pricked by a thorn // 손을 ~에 긁히다 scratch one's hand on a thorn // 장미에도 ~가 있다 Roses have thorns. // ~ 없는 장미는 없다 There is no rose without a thorn. / No rose without a thorn.
2 (생선의) a fishbone; (지느러미의) a spine; (동물의) a (piece of) bone. ¶~가 많은 생선 a fish full of fine bones // 목에 ~가 걸리다 have[get] a bone stuck in the throat / have a bone in the throat.
3 [살에 박힌 나무 등의 거스러미] a splinter; (나무의) a sliver. ¶손가락에 ~가 박히다 get a splinter[thorn] in one's finger // ~를 빼다 pull [draw / pick] out a splinter // ~가 살에 깊이 박혔다 A splinter has been driven deep into the flesh.
4 [비유]. ¶눈엣 ~ an eyesore / a hateful [detestable] person / an encumbrance / ~돋친 말을 하다 speak daggers (to a person) / have a harsh tongue / say a biting thing / give the edge of one's tongue (to a person) / 그의 말에는 ~가 돋쳐 있었다 His words had a sting in them. // 그는 나를 눈엣~로 여긴다 He always looks on me as a thorn in his flesh.

● **가시덤불** a thorny thicket [shrub]; a bramble; a thorn; (찔레의) briars and brambles. **가시밭** brambles; a thornbush; a thorn(y) thicket. **가시밭길** a thorny path; a brambly way. ¶인생의 ~ the thorny path of life. **가시(鐵)** a barb; a prickle. **가시철사** barbed wire; barbwire; (구어) bob wire.

가시 (可視) ¶~의 visible.

● **가시거리** visibility range. **가시광선** a visible ray. **가시도** visibility.

가시나무 **1** [가시가 있는 나무] a thorny plant; a bramble; a brier. ¶~ 울타리 a thorn fence / a hedge of thorns. **2** [식] [가시목(木)] a beech.

가시나무에 가시가 난다 (속담) Like breeds like.

가시다 1 [씻다] wash (off / out); (입을) rinse (off / out). ¶그릇을 ~ wash dishes // 입을 ~ rinse out one's mouth. **2** [없어지다] disappear; be gone; fade away; leave (off); pass off; go away. ¶상처가 ~ the scar dies away [disappears] // 애타가 ~ grow up / outgrow one's children habits // 고통이 가셨다 The pain is gone [has left me]. / The pain is eased. // 이 약을 먹으면 아픔이 곧 가신다 This medicine will give instant relief from pain. // 피로가 아직 가시지 않았다 I have not quite recovered from the fatigue. // 그녀의 얼굴에서 핏기가 가셨다 The color fled [ebbed] from her face. / Her face drained of color.

가식 (假飾) affectation; dissemblance; dissimulation; ostentation; pretense; hypocrisy. ¶~적인 hypocritical / affected / false // ~이 없는 unaffected / plain / natural / unpretentious / [솔직한] artless / frank / candid / ingenuous / [~이 없는 말] words without trimmings // ~이 많은 사람 a showy [an ostentatious] person // 그는 ~ 없이 솔직하게 말하는 사람이다 He is a very frank and straightforward person. // 그는 ~적으로 말하지는 않는다 He does not mince matters [his words]. // 나는 ~ 없는 아름다움에 마음이 끌렸다 I was fascinated by her simple [uncontrived] beauty. // 나는 그 작가의 ~ 없는 문장을 좋아한다 I like the unadorned [plain] style of that writer. **가식하다** make outward show; put a good face on (a matter); put a varnish on (a matter); pretend; dissemble; dissimulate; do hypocrisy; play the hypocrite.

가신 (家神) a family god; a guardian [tutelar(y)]; deity [god / spirit] of one's family.

가심 [가시는 일] rinsing; washing. **가심하다** wash out; rinse; give (a thing) a rinse.

가십 gossip (about). ¶정계의 ~ gossip in political circles // ~을 좋아하는 사람 a gossip / a gossipmonger.
- **가십난** a gossip column.

가압 (加壓) pressurization. **가압하다** pressurize; apply [give] pressure (to). ¶가압하여 가열하다 heat (a solution) under pressure.
- **가압 장치** a pressure device.

가압류 (假押留) [법] provisional seizure [attachment]. **가압류하다** put under provisional attachment; attach [seize] (another's) property provisionally.

가야금 (伽倻琴) a *gayageum*; the *Gaya* harp; a Korean musical instrument with 12 strings. ¶~을 뜯다[퉁기다] play the *gayageum*.

가약 (佳約) a promise of marriage [to marry]; a marriage vow [promise]; a (marriage) contract; an engagement. ¶백년~ a pledge of eternal love [fidelity] / a conjugal [matrimonial] tie // ~을 맺다 tie the nuptial knot / pledge [plight] one's troth / get married / become man and woman.

가언적 (假言的) hypothetical; conditional. ¶~ 명제 a hypothetical proposition // ~ 삼단 논법 a hypothetical syllogism // ~ 판단 hypothetical judgment.

가업 (家業) 1 [직업] a family occupation; one's trade [business / calling / profession]. ¶~을 게을리 하다 neglect one's business // ~에 힘쓰다 pursue one's trade with diligence / be engrossed in one's business / attend closely to one's trade / be diligent in one's trade // ~은 목수다 be a carpenter by trade // 그는 ~이 무엇인가 What trade is he in? / What is his trade? / What is he by trade?
2 [세업 (世業)] one's father's occupation. ¶~을 잇다 succeed to [take over] one's father's business [occupation] // 차남이 ~을 이어받았다 I was succeeded in the business by my second son. // 나는 아버지의 ~을 이어갈 작정입니다 I will succeed to my father's business. / I am going to succeed my father in his business.

가없다 boundless; unlimited; endless. ¶가없는 바다 a boundless (expanse of the) ocean // 가없는 우주 limitless space. **가없이** boundlessly; unlimitedly; endlessly. ¶사하라는 ~ 펼쳐진 사막이다 The Sahara is an endless [a boundless] desert.

가역 (可逆) [물] [화] ¶~성의 reversible.
- **가역 반응** a reversible reaction. **가역 전지** a reversible cell.

가연성 (可燃性) combustibility; inflammability.

가열 (加熱) heating. ¶~ 살균하다 sterilize by heating / heat-treat (milk). **가열하다** heat (up); apply heat (to). ¶가열된 heated // 물을 ~ apply heat to water / heat water / 가열하여 압착하다 hot-press (a thing) // 이 굴은 가열하여 드시오 Please cook these oysters before eating them. // 그 철봉이 새빨개질 때까지 가열하시오 Heat the iron bar until it becomes red-hot.
- **가열기** a heater; a heating apparatus; a heating device. **가열 시험** a heating [heat] test.

가엾다 [불쌍하다] poor; pitiable; pitiful; [애틋하다] pathetic; sad; sorry. ¶가엾게도 sorry [sad] to say // 가엾은 고아 a poor orphan // 가엾은 신세 a miserable state / a sad plight // 가엾게 여기다 feel pity [sorry] for / take pity on / pity (a person) / sympathize with // 가엾어서 [가엾게 여겨] 용서해 주다 spare (a person) out of mercy [pity] // 가엾기도 하다 What a pity! / Poor thing! / Poor fellow! // 가엾어 볼 수 없었다 It was too pitiful to watch. // 가엾으니 살려 주어라 For pity's sake save the poor fellow. // 부모 없는 아이라 생각하니 더욱 가엾은 생각이 든다 I pity the child all the more because it [he / she] is an orphan. // 그들은 가엾은 처지에 있었다 They were in a pitiable situation. // 가엾게도 그 아이는 아버지의 죽음을 모르고 있었다 The poor child didn't know about his [her] father's death.

가오리 [동] a stingray; (미) a stingaree; a ray.

가옥 (家屋) [집] a house; [건물] a building; [건조물] a structure; [법] a messuage. ¶낡은 ~을 헐다 tear [pull] down an old house.
- **가옥대장** a house register [ledger]. **가옥 매매** dealing in real estate. **가옥세** a house tax.

가외 (加外) an extra; [여분] an excess; [잉여] a surplus. ¶~의 extra / spare / excessive / ~에 in addition to / besides / over and above // ~ 란 an extra member [person] / ~의 일을 하다 do extra work // ~로 천 원을 더 내다 pay 1,000 won extra // ~로 얼마 더 내면 됩니까 How much must I pay extra for it?
- **가외 비용** extra expense. **가외 수입** extra income. **가외 시간** time to spare. **가욋돈** extra money. ¶~을 가지다 carry some extra money / have some money to spare. **가욋일** extra work.

가요 (歌謠) [가곡] a song; [전승적인 전설 시] a ballad; (집합적) songs and ballads. ¶대중 ~ a popular song // 한국 ~사 a history of Korean songs and ballads.
- **가요곡** [민요] a folksong; [대중가요] a popular song. **가요제** a song fete [festival]. ¶국제 ~ the international song fete.

가용 (可溶) [관형어적] soluble.
- **가용물** a soluble body. **가용성** solubility.

가용 (可鎔) [관형어적] fusible.
- **가용 합금** a fusible alloy.

가용 (家用) 1 [비용] living expenses; housekeeping [family] expenses; the cost [price] of living. 2 [집안의 소용] home consumption; domestic [home] use; private use. ¶~의 for home [domestic] use // ~으로 남겨 두다 keep [spare] for use at home / put [set] aside for domestic [home] use.

가우스 [전] a gauss (약어 G.).

가운 a gown; [실내복] a dressing gown; [잠옷] a nightgown. ¶(졸업식에 참석한) 모자와 ~을 착용한 학생들 students in caps and gowns // 박사 ~을 입다 wear doctor's gown.

가운 (家運) the fortunes of a family. ¶그의 ~이 기울고 있다 His fortunes are on the wane [decline]. / His fortunes are at a low ebb. / His family is going downhill[beginning to ebb].

가운데 1 [중앙] the middle; the center. ¶~의 middle / central // 형 the middle brother // ~에(서) in the middle[center] of (the room) // ~에서 머리를 타다 part one's hair in the middle // ~를 잡다 hold (a thing) in the middle / hold the middle of (a thing) // ~를 취하다 take the mean / split the difference // 길 ~로 걸어가다 walk in[keep to] the middle of the road // ~를 싹둑 자르다 cut in two in the middle.
2 [중에·속에] in; in the midst of; in the heart[center] of; between; among; through; into; of; out of. ¶두 사람 ~ between the two // 너희들 ~ among you / some of you // 열 (사)람) ~ 아홉(사람)까지 nine out of ten (persons) // 이 ~에서 from among[out of] these // 한 반 ~ 가장 우수한 학생 the best student in the class // 둘 ~ 하나를 택하라 choose between the two / choose one of the two // 많은 ~서 하나를 가지다 take one of many // 군중 ~ 있다 be in the midst of a crowd // 이 ~서 어떤 것이든 셋을 취하라 Take any three of these. // 이것은 많은 예 ~ 하나에 불과하다 This is only one instance out of many. // 그들 ~에는 주디도 끼어 있었다 Among them was Judy. // 영국 근대 작가 ~ 하디를 제일 좋아한다 I like Hardy best of all the modern novelists of England.
3 […하는 중(에)] while[in the process of] doing; during(동안에); amid(ст); in(한창 …하는); with (a person) in attendance; in the presence of (a person). ¶박수갈채가 울려퍼지는 ~ amid(st) the applause of the audience // 그럭저럭하는 ~ (in the) meantime [meanwhile] // 책을 읽는 ~ while (I was) reading // 가난한 ~ 성장하다 grow up in poverty // 비가 [눈이] 오는 ~ 나가다 go out in the rain[snow] // 바쁘신 ~ 와 주셔서 고맙습니다 It's very kind of you to call on me in spite of your being pressed with work. // 어려움이 많은 ~서도 그는 임무를 다했다 He carried out his duties in spite of many difficulties.
● **가운데귀** [생] the middle ear; (라) auris media; the tympanum (pl. ~s, -na); the eardrum; the drum. **가운뎃손가락** the middle[second] finger.

-가웃 (and) a half. ¶석 자 ~ three feet and a half / three and a half feet // 네 말 ~ four mal and a half // 두 도 ~ two doe and a half.

가위 scissors; shears(큰); clippers(털 등을 깎는); snips(양철 등을 자르는); a punch(차표 등을 찍는). ¶~ 한 자루 a pair of scissors // ~로 자르다 cut (a thing) with scissors [shears] / scissor / shear // ~로 다듬다 [깎다] nip / snip / clip (the wool of a sheep) / prune[trim] (a tree) // ~로 표를 찍다 punch [clip] a ticket // ~를 갈다 sharpen scissors [shears] // ~를 대다 put scissors to (a tape).
● **가위질** scissoring; shearing; (정원수의) trimming; pruning. **가위춤** (엿장수 등의) a scissors rattling; (헛가위질) idling a pair of scissors. ¶~을 추다 rattle[clatter] one's scissors / fiddle[twiddle] with one's scissors.

가위눌리다 have a nightmare[an incubus]; be afflicted by[with] nightmare; suffer from a nightmare; be troubled[oppressed / tortured] by[with] a nightmare. ¶가위눌려서 소리를 지르다 cry out in one's sleep // 자주 ~ have the nightmare habits.

가위바위보 a gawibawibo game; the game of rock-paper-scissors. ¶~로 정하다 divide [decide] by gawibawibo / toss for (something) // ~에서 이기다[지다] win[lose] the toss // ~로 정하자 Let's toss (up) for it.

가윗날 Harvest Moon Day. ⇨ ☞추석

가으내 throughout the autumn[(미) fall]; all through the autumn[fall].

가을 [계절] autumn; (미) fall; (미) falltime. ¶늦~ late autumn / the latter part of autumn / (미) late fall // 초~ early autumn [(미) / (미) / the beginning of autumn // ~날 an autumn(al) day // 맑은 ~ 날씨 fine autumn weather / clear[fine] weather peculiar to autumn / a clear autumn(al) day // 독서의 계절인 ~ autumn, the best season for reading // ~에 피는 꽃 an autumn[a fall-blooming] flower // ~별 autumn sunshine / the autumn sun // 낙엽 한 잎이 ~을 알린다 A single leaf falling is a sign of autumn coming.
● **가을갈이** [추경] autumn plowing. **가을걷이** autumn[fall] harvesting[reaping]. **가을바람** an autumn wind[breeze]. **가을보리** autumn barley. **가을비** an autumn(al) rain; a drizzling autumn rain. **가을철** autumn (season).

가이거·뮐러 계수기 (-計數器) [물] a Geiger-Müller counter.

가이던스 [교] guidance; an orientation lecture(유학생에 대한). ¶신입생을 위한 ~ guidance for new students // ~를 하다 give guidance (to a person on).

가이드 [안내] guiding; [안내자] a (tour) guide; [안내서] a guidebook. ¶버스 ~ a bus tour guide.

가인 (佳人) a beautiful woman; a beauty. ¶재자(才子) ~ the wits and beauties // 절세 ~ a woman of unsurpassed beauty.
● **가인박명** (-薄命) Beauties die young.; Whom the gods love die young.; Beauty and fortune are often bad friends.; A beautiful woman is destined to be unlucky.

가일 (佳日) an auspicious[a lucky] day. ¶그들은 ~을 택하여 결혼식을 올렸다 They chose an auspicious day for their wedding.

가일층 (加一層) more (and more); still[much] more; all[only] the more. ¶~ 노력하다 make greater efforts / redouble one's efforts.

가입 (加入) (회·클럽 등의) joining; entrance; entry; admission; affiliation; (전화 등의) subscription; (조약의) signing; signature; (정당 등에 대한) adherence; accession. ¶공동 ~선(線) (전화의) a party line. **가입하다** enter (for); join (an association); become a member (of); affiliate oneself with (a society); send in[up] one's name (to); subscribe (for); sign (a treaty). ¶조합에 ~ become a member of a union // 팀에 ~ join a team // 이 나라는 10년 전에 국제 연합에 ~ 입했다 This country joined[was admitted to] the United Nations ten years ago. // 나는 어떤 정당에도 ~할 생각이 없다 I have no intention of joining any political party. ➔¶그는 1천만 원의 생명 보험에 가입되어 있다 He

가자미

is insured for ten million won.
● **가입금** an entrance [admission / initiation] fee. **가입 신청** an application for admission; subscription(전화 등의). **가입자** a member; a participant (in a game); a subscriber (to a magazine).

가자미 [동] a flatfish; a plaice; a turbot; a dab.

가작(佳作) 1 [우수 작품] a fine [a good / an excellent] (piece of) work; a work of merits. 2 [당선 외의] the next best work to the prizewinners (in a contest); an unawarded good work.

가장 [제일·최고로] most; extremely; exceedingly; to the extreme; supremely. ¶ ~ 안쪽의 innermost // ~ 바깥쪽의 outermost // ~ 중요한 일 the most important thing / a matter of the greatest [first] importance / a matter of prime importance // ~ 좋은 [나쁜] best [worst] // ~ 먼저 first and foremost / first of all // ~ 돈이 덜 드는 방법 the least expensive way [method] // ~ 사랑하는 아내 one's dear(est) wife // ~ 친한 친구 one's best [closest / dearest] friend // ~ 인상적이었던 것 the most impressive thing // 세계에서 ~ 높은 산 the highest mountain in the world // ~ 용감히 싸우다 fight most bravely // 나는 이것을 ~ 좋아한다 I like this best (of all). / I like this better than the others. // 그는 바쁠 때가 ~ 즐겁다 He is never happier than when he is busy. // 영어는 그가 우리 반에서 ~ 잘한다 He leads the class in English. // 이 강은 여기가 ~ 넓다 This river is widest at this point. // 지금까지 보신 영화 가운데 ~ 좋았던 것은 어느 것입니까 Of all the movies you have seen which did you like (the) best? // 그는 내가 ~ 싫어하는 타입의 사람이다 He is the type I like least. // 그가 ~ 먼저 [맨 나중에] 왔다 He came [arrived] first [last]. // 그가 ~ 나중 [last]에 도착하다 to arrive. // 이 삼촌이 누구보다도 ~ 잘 나를 이해해 주신다 Nobody understands me better than this uncle of mine. // 그의 친절한 말은 다른 무엇보다도 ~ 크게 나를 감동시켰다 His kind words moved me more than anything else. // 내가 ~ 애석하게 여기는 것은 자필 사인이 든 그의 사진을 잃어버린 일이다 The thing I regret most is that I lost the photograph with his autograph. / I regret the loss of his autographed photograph most of all. / 한국의 ~ 남쪽에 있는 항구는 어디입니까 Which [What] is the southernmost port in Korea? // 여기서 종로까지 어떻게 가는 것이 ~ 빠른 길일까요 What is the quickest [fastest] way to get to Jongno from here? // 신경통에는 온천이 ~ 좋다 Nothing is as good as (a bath in) a hot spring for neuralgia. // 따뜻하게 하고 집에 있는 것이 ~ 좋은 일이다 The best thing is to keep warm and stay indoors. // 따뜻한 것으로 말하자면 깃털 이불이 ~ 좋다 For warmth, nothing can beat [you can't beat] an eiderdown (quilt).

가장(家長) 1 [가구주] the head of a family [household]; a patriarch(남자); a matriarch(여자); a paterfamilias (*pl.* patresfamilias). 2 [남편] one's husband.
● **가장권** the rights of a patriarch; patriarchal rights. **가장 제도** patriarchal system; patriarchy; patriarchism.

가장(假裝) 1 [변장] disguise; guise; masquerade; a fancy dress. **가장하다** disguise oneself (as); be disguised (as); wear a disguise; dissemble; dress up. ¶ **가장하여** in disguise / in fancy dress // 여자로 ~ dress up [be disguised] as a woman // 그는 해적으로 가장했다 He disguised himself [was disguised] as a pirate. / 그는 선원으로 가장하여 밀항했다 He stowed away in [under] the disguise of a sailor.
2 [거짓 태도를 취함] pretense; (영) pretence; semblance; simulation; camouflage; feint; affectation. **가장하다** feign; pretend; affect; simulate; assume; make believe; put on a semblance of. ¶ ~을 가장하여 under pretense [cover / the guise / the cloak] of // 양민 [대학생]을 ~ counterfeit [pretend to be] a good citizen [a university student] // 출타 중으로 ~ pretend to be out // 최 선생이 오면 내가 출타 중인 것으로 가장해라 I am not at home to Mr. Choe. / If Mr. Choe should call, say I'm not at home.
● **가장무도회** a masked [costume] ball; a fancy dress ball. **가장행렬** a costume parade; a fancy dress parade.

가장귀 [나뭇가지의 아귀] a fork [crotch] (of a tree); [나뭇가지] a forked [furcate] branch. ¶ ~ **창** a forked spear // ~**지다** be forked / be furcate.

가장자리 the edge; the verge; the brink; the margin; the hem; the border; the fringe; the brim. ¶ **책상** ~ the edge of a desk // 벼랑의 ~ the edge of a precipice.

가장집물(家藏什物) household furnishings.

가재 [동] [미] a crawfish; (영) a crayfish.
가재는 게 편이라(속담) Like attracts like.; Birds of a feather flock together.
● **가재걸음** [뒷걸음] walking [crawling] backward; [지지부진] a snail's pace. ¶ ~**을 치다** walk [crawl] backward / crawfish / progress at a snail's pace.

가재(家財) 1 [가구] household effects [goods / belongings / stuffs]; furnishings; furniture and effects. ¶ ~를 꾸려 이사가다 move [remove] (to a town) with all one's belongings / pack up one's belongings and move (to a new home). 2 [가산] the family property [estate]; one's fortune.

가전제품(家電製品) electric home appliances; household electric(al) appliances.

가절(佳節) 1 [명절] an auspicious [a happy / a festive] occasion; a fete day; a jubilee. ¶ **중추**~ the midautumn festival. 2 [좋은 철] a beautiful season. ¶ **양춘**~ a pleasant springtime.

가정(家政) household [home] management; housekeeping; housewifery; homemaking. ¶ ~**을 맡아보다** run one's home / manage one's home / keep house.
● **가정 경제** domestic [household / home] economy. **가정과** a department of domestic science; a course in domestic science. **가정부**(-婦) a housekeeper; a housemaid(식모). **가정학** domestic science; home economics.

가정(家庭) (a) home; a family; a household; the home circle. ¶ ~**의** home / domestic / household / family // ~**에서** at [in] the home // **즐거운** [**단란한**] ~ a sweet [happy] home // **원만한** ~ a harmonious household // ~**의 행복** domestic happiness // **엄한** ~**에서 자라다** be brought up in a strict family // ~**을 꾸미다**

[가지다] make [start / build / establish] a home / get married and settle down / set up [keep] house / make one's home (at)∥팀은 앤은 3년 전에 ~을 꾸몄다 Tim and Anne got married and set up house (keeping) three years ago.∥에이미 아주머니가 이 ~의 살림을 맡아 하고 있다 Aunt Amy runs the household.∥그는 유복한 ~에서 태어났다 He was born into a well-to-do family. / He was born with a silver spoon in his mouth.∥청소년 범죄는 주로 ~에 그 책임이 있다 The home is mostly responsible for juvenile delinquency.∥그는 ~을 버리고 불문(佛門)에 들어갔다 He deserted his family to become a Buddhist priest.
● **가정교사** a private teacher; a tutor; a governess(여자). ¶~ 자리를 찾다 look out for a tutor's position / ~을 하다 teach (a boy) at his house / (act as a) tutor. **가정교육** home training [education / discipline]. **가정란** the home-life section [page]; a homemaker's column. **가정 방문** a home visit; making a round of calls (at homes); paying visits (to homes). **가정 법원** the Court of Family Affairs; the Family Court. **가정불화** (가족 간의) family [domestic] trouble [discord]; (부부 간의) a quarrel [friction] between husband and wife. **가정 사정** family affairs [matters]; family circumstances. **가정 상비약** a household medicine; a domestic remedy (for diarrhea). **가정생활** home [domestic / family] life. **가정용** ¶~ 전기 기구 household electric appliances. **가정의례** family rite [ritual]. ¶~ 준칙 the Simplified Family Rite [Ritual] Standards. **가정주부 / 가정부인** a housewife. **가정 학습** home work. **가정환경** a home background [environment]. ¶좋은 ~에서 자라다 be raised [brought up] in a perfect home environment.

가정(苛政) tyrannical government; despotic rule; tyranny; despotism. ¶~에 신음하다 groan under tyrannical government.

가정(假定) (a) supposition; (an) assumption; (a) postulation; [가설] a hypothesis (*pl.* -ses). ¶~적(인) hypothetic(al) / assumptive / presumptive∥그것은 어디까지나 ~에 지나지 않는다 It is a mere hypothesis. / That is just an assumption. **가정하다** suppose; assume; presume; take it for granted that; take (this fact) for granted; postulate; presuppose. ¶…이라고 가정하고 on the assumption that ... / supposing [assuming] that ...∥그것이 사실이라고 가정해 보자 Let us suppose that it is true.∥지금 당장 대지진이 일어난다고 가정할 때 맨 먼저 어떻게 하겠습니까 Suppose a great earthquake occurred right now. What would you do first?∥A와 B가 같다고 가정하자 Let A equal B. / Suppose A equals B.∥그것이 사실이라 가정하더라도 네가 잘못이다 Granting that it is so, you are still (in the) wrong.∥그가 했다고 가정해도 증거는 하나도 없다 Even if we assume that he did it, there is not a speck of evidence.
● **가정법** [언] the subjunctive mood.

가정적(家庭的) homely (air / atmosphere); domesticated [family-minded] (husband). ¶그녀는 사교적이기보다 오히려 ~이다 She is at her best in the home, not in social situations.∥그 레스토랑의 ~인 분위기가 좋다 I like the homelike [homey] atmosphere of that restaurant.

가제(假題) a tentative title.

가제본(假製本) [제책] [견본쇄] a dummy; a sample binding; 〔임시 제본〕 temporary binding. ¶~ 된 책 a book in a temporary binding.

가져가다 [몸에 지니고 가다] take (a thing) along [with one]; carry; [가지고 가 버리다] take [carry] away; take off; make off [away] (with). ¶도로 ~ take back∥도시락을 가져가거라 Take your lunch with you.∥누가 내 책을 가져갔느냐 Who has taken my book?∥누가 내 연필을 가져갔다 Somebody has taken (away) my pencil.∥밥상의 접시를 가져가거라 Take the dishes off the table.∥누군가가 그 돈을 가져가 버렸다 Someone made off with the money.

가져오다 1 〔지참하다〕 bring (over); fetch; get; bring [carry / take] (a thing) with (one); take (a thing) along. ¶가져오게 하다 get (someone) to bring send (to a shop) for (something)∥내 모자를 가져오너라 Fetch my hat.∥그는 내게 책을 세 권 가져왔다 He brought me three books.∥물 한 컵 가져오너라 Get me a glass of water.∥그것을 가져왔습니다 I have brought it [have it] with me.∥교무실에 가서 출석부를 가져오너라 I want you to go to the teacher's room for the roll book [(미) register].
2 〔초래하다〕 bring about [on / forth]; cause; induce; give rise [birth] to (confusion); result [end] in. ¶실패를 ~ cause a failure / result in failure∥파멸을 ~ bring down ruin (on a person)∥좋은 결과를 ~ produce (good) results∥집안에 불행을 ~ bring misfortune on one's family∥미국에 오늘날의 번영을 가져온 것은 무엇인가 What has brought America to her present prosperity?

가조약(假條約) a provisional treaty. ¶~을 맺다 conclude [make up / enter into] a provisional treaty (with).

가조인(假調印) an initial signature; initial signing. **가조인하다** initial (a treaty).

가족(家族) a family; a household; members of a family; one's people [folks]; 〔친족〕 kinsfolk. ¶대(大)~ a large family∥부양 ~ a dependent∥소(小)~ a small family∥핵(核)~ a nuclear family∥4인 ~ a family of four / a four headed family∥~의 일원 a member [one] of the family∥~이 많다 [적다] have a large [small] family∥~을 부양하다 support one's family∥우리 집은 5인 ~이다 We are a family of five in all. / There are five people in my family.∥그의 ~은 모두 개를 좋아한다 Everyone in his family likes dogs. / Members of his family like dogs.∥그는 ~을 데리고 유원지에 갔다 He took his family to an amusement park.∥공원은 근처의 ~들로 붐볐다 The park was crowded with neighborhood families.
● **가족계획** family planning [regulation]. **가족묘** a family burial ground. **가족법** [법] family law. **가족 수당** a family [dependency] allowance. **가족 제도** the family system. **가족회**의 a family council.

가죽 [피부] the skin; (a) hide(주로 쇠가죽); (무두질한) leather; [모피] (a) fur; [날가죽] a pelt [raw skin / rawhide]. ¶여우 ~ a fox fur∥호랑이 ~ a tiger skin∥~제(製)의 leather

가중

(belt) / leather-made ∥ ~을 벗기다 skin (a tiger) / flay (a rabbit) ∥ ~을 무두질하다 tan [taw / dress / bark] hide ∥ 그는 뼈와 ~만 남았다 He's all skin and bones. / He is reduced to a (mere) skeleton [bag of bones]. ●가죽 가방 a leather bag; a briefcase. 가죽 구두 / 가죽신 leather shoes. 가죽 띠 / 가죽 혁대 a leather belt. 가죽숫돌 a (razor) strap; a strop. 가죽 옷 leather garments. 가죽 장갑 leather gloves. 가죽 장정 leather binding. 가죽 점퍼 a leather jumper. 가죽 제품 a leather; leather products [goods]. 가죽 표지 a leather cover.

가중 (加重) (무게의) weighting; adding an extra weight; (형량의) [법] aggravation. 가중하다 increase; weight; [법] aggravate. ¶형을 ~ raise [aggravate] the penalty / stiffen [increase] the penalty. →¶정부의 증세(增稅) 정책은 국민의 부담을 가중시켰다 The Government's tax increase policy increased the burden laid on the people.
●가중치 (-値) [수] weight.

가증스럽다 (可憎-) hateful; abominable; detestable; cursed; damned; damnable; spiteful. ¶가증스러운 처사 spiteful conduct ∥ 가증스러운 놈 a detestable fellow ∥ 약탈자들의 가증스러운 잔학 행위 the detestable atrocities of the plunderers ∥ 가증스럽기 짝이 없는 죄 a most abominable crime.

가지[1] [식] an eggplant; (열매) an egg [a mad] apple; a garden egg.

가지[2] (나무의) a branch; [줄기에서 나온 큰 가지] a bough; a limb; [잔가지] a twig; [꽃·잎이 붙은 채 자른 잔가지] a spray (of cherry blossoms); a sprig (of jasmine) (spray 쪽이 꽃이 달린 이미지가 강함). ¶~가 잘 뻗은 소나무 a pine with graceful [shapely] branches / a shapely [gracefully shaped] pine tree ∥ ~를 내다 shoot out branches / ramify ∥ ~를 뻗다 put out branches / spread branches / branch out ∥ 죽은 ~를 잘라 내다 cut off dead branches ∥ ~를 꺾다 break (off) a branch ∥ ~를 치다 (가지가 뻗다) spread [put out] branches / branch out / (자르다) lop off [down] branches / lop [prune] a tree / take branches (off a tree) ∥ ~를 다듬다 prune [trim] a tree / prune [trim] the branches off.
가지 많은 나무에 바람 잘 날이 없다 (속담) A mother with a large brood never has a peaceful day.
●가지치기 trimming; pruning. ¶~를 하다 trim [prune] the branches (of a tree).

가지[3] (종류) a kind; a sort; a variety. ¶한 ~ a kind [sort] (of) / (동일 종류) 같은 kind [sort] ∥ 여러 ~ 물건 things of various kinds / varieties [different kinds] of things ∥ 거기에 가는 데는 두 ~ 방법이 있다 There are two ways of getting [to get] there. ∥ 신발에는 여러 ~ 종류가 있다 There are many kinds of footgear. ∥ 이 문장은 두 ~로 해석할 수 있다 This sentence can be interpreted in two ways. / (문어) It admits of a double interpretation. ∥ 이 꽃에는 두 ~가 있다 This flower comes in two varieties. ∥ 그의 잘못은 한두 ~가 아니다 He has a good many [more than one or two] faults. ∥ 한 ~ 청이 있습니다 I have a favor to ask of you. ∥ 여러 모로 감사합니다 Thanks for everything. ∥ 여러 ~로 괴로움을 끼쳤습니다 I caused you much trouble.

가지가지 various kinds (of); a variety (of); all sorts (of); of every kind [sort]. ¶~ 경험 a varied experience ∥ ~ 물건 articles of every sort and kind / a great variety of things / sundry articles / all sorts of things ∥ ~ 이유로 for various [many] reasons ∥ 담배도 ~다 There are many kinds of cigarettes.

가지각색 (-各色) every kind and description. ¶~의 various / varied / diverse / manifold / sundry / varicolored / of all kinds [sorts] ∥ ~의 사람들 all sorts (and conditions) of men / a motley of people ∥ ~의 인생 경험 various [a variety of] (human) experiences ∥ ~으로 바뀌는 무대의 조명 the varied lighting used on the stage ∥ 사람의 마음은 ~ So many men, so many minds. / Every man has his humor. ∥ 그 가게에선 ~의 물건을 팔고 있다 They sell all sorts of things in that store. ∥ 그들의 고민거리는 ~이다 They have worries of every kind. / They have all sorts of worries. ∥ 뉴욕의 주민은 ~의 인종으로 구성되어 있다 The New Yorkers comprise a medley of races. ∥ 그 책에 대한 비평은 ~이다 Opinion is divided about the book.

가지다 1 (손에) have; take; hold; (몸에) carry (with one); have (a thing) with one [about one]. ¶지금 돈 가진 것 있나 Do you have any money with you [on hand]? ∥ 지금 제가 갖고 있는 편지지를 사용해도 괜찮겠습니까 Will the letter pad I have on hand do? ∥ 성냥을 가지고 있나 Have you got any matches? / Do you have a light? ∥ 나는 지금 돈을 가지고 있지 않다 I have no money with [on] me now. ∥ 나는 단장을 가지고 다니지 않는다 I never carry a cane. ∥ 강도는 식칼을 가지고 있었다 The burglar was armed with a kitchen knife. ∥ 전 세계의 보화를 가지고도 그를 행복하게 할 수는 없다 All the treasure in the world cannot make him happy. ∥ 네 자신의 기준을 가지고 남을 가늠하지 마라 Don't measure others by your own standard. / Don't judge of others by yourself.
2 [소유하다] have; own; possess; be possessed of; be endowed with (타고나다). ¶가진 나라와 못 가진 나라 the haves and (the) have-nots ∥ 가게를 가지고 있다 keep [own] a shop ∥ 외서를 많이 가지고 있다 have many foreign books ∥ 이 그림엽서를 한 장 가져도 됩니까 May [can] I have one of these picture postcards? ∥ 그 나라 여성은 투표권을 가지고 있지 않다 In that country women do not have the rights to vote. ∥ 그 물건은 지금 내가 가지고 있다 The article is now in my possession. ∥ 그녀는 여러 가지 미덕을 가지고 있다 She possesses many virtues. ∥ 사람은 이성을 가지고 있다 Man is endowed with reason.
3 [마음에 지니다] have (an idea); hold (an opinion); harbor (hatred); cherish (hopes); bear (a grudge against). ¶호감 [악감정]을 ~ have [bear] a good [a bad] feeling (toward / against) ∥ …에게 의심을 ~ harbor suspicion against (a person) ∥ 큰 뜻을 가지고 있다 have [cherish] a great ambition ∥ 그는 불처럼 격하기 쉬운 기질 [성미]을 가지고 있다 He has a fiery temper. ∥ 그 사람은 익살맞은 면을 가지고 있다 There is [He has] something comical about him.
4 [아이를 배다] conceive; be pregnant. ¶아이를 ~ be (big) with child / be pregnant / be in the family way / be in a delicate condition

// (동물이) 새끼를 ~ be (big) with young / be in pup(개가) / be in[with] calf(소가).

가지런하다 arranged neatly; equal; even; uniform; regular (teeth); (서술적) be in order. ¶높이가 가지런한 of the same [uniform] height // 책을 가지런하게 세우다 put books in order // 신을 가지런하게 놓다 arrange shoes (in order) // 높이가 가지런하지 않다 be of unequal height // 각자의 발길음이 가지런하면 행진[행렬]이 아름답게 보인다 A march[parade] looks nice when everyone is in (perfect) step. **가지런히** evenly; uniformly; regularly; trimly; in order. ¶신발을 ~ 놓다 place one's shoes squarely (on the doorstep) / ~ 하다 make even [uniform] // 공구[연장]는 언제든지 쓸 수 있도록 ~ 놓아 두어라 Arrange[Put] the tools in order so they will be ready for use.

가집행(假執行) [법] provisional execution; a temporary injunction. **가집행하다** execute provisionally.

가짜(假-) [모조품] an imitation; a sham; a spurious[false] article; a fake; a make-believe (위조품) a counterfeit; a forgery; (미국 속어) a duffer; (사람) a charlatan; a pretender; an imposter; a fraud. ¶아주 정교하여 진짜 같은 ~ an exquisite imitation // ~의 sham / bogus / artificial / imitative / fake(d) / spurious / forged / false / mock // (미국 속어) phon(e)y // 그 5천 원권은 ~였다 The 5,000 won note was a forgery. // 이 증서는 ~ 다 This bond is a forgery. / This bond is counterfeit. // 이 진주는 ~다 This pearl is an imitation. // 이 목걸이는 ~다 This necklace is a fake. // ~에 조심하시오 Beware of imitation. // 나는 ~를 속아 샀다 I was cheated into buying a fake. // 추사(秋史)의 글씨에는 ~가 많다 There are many imitations in the works with Chusa's signature. / Many of the writings bearing the signature of Chusa are spurious imitations.

● **가짜 다이아몬드** a fake[false / sham] diamond. **가짜 증서** a counterfeit bond.

가차 없다(假借-) merciless; relentless; unrelenting; ruthless; scathing (remark); inexorable (creditor); unsparing; show no mercy (toward(s)). ¶가차 없는 법관 an unsparing [a merciless] judge // 가차 없는 철퇴를 내리다 mete out stringent punishment / take rigorous disciplinary action / crack down rigorously. **가차 없이** scathingly; severely; rigidly; ruthlessly; unrelentingly; rigorously; strictly; soundly; mercilessly; without mercy. ¶~ 처벌하다 punish (a person) without mercy / punish severely // 범법자에게 ~ 벌을 주다 punish the offender without the least consideration for the circumstances (involved) / allow[show] no mercy towards the offender // 그를 ~ 처벌해야 한다 You need not show him any mercy / You should punish him relentlessly. // 우리는 상대 팀을 ~ 완패시켰다 We gave our opponents a merciless thrashing. / We gave no quarter in beating our opponents.

가창(歌唱) singing; a song.
● **가창력** singing ability.

가책(呵責) scolding; chiding; blame; censure; imputation. ¶양심의 ~ compunction / the qualms[sting(s) / twinges / pangs / pricks / remorse / attack] of conscience / a pricking conscience / moral goadings // 양심의 ~을 받다 be conscience-stricken / feel the qualms of conscience / be tormented by a guilty conscience[with the stings of conscience] / be stung[convicted] by conscience / have [suffer] the qualms of conscience // 그는 양심의 ~을 견딜 수 없어 죄를 자백했다 He was so conscience-stricken that he confessed to his crime. // 나는 그것을 그에게 숨겨 온 것에 대해 양심의 ~을 받았다 I felt guilty for[felt qualms about] having kept it from him. // 그는 그 일 때문에 양심의 ~을 받고 있는 것 같다 He seems to have a bad conscience about it. **가책하다** scold; chide; rebuke; blame; censure.

가처분(假處分) [법] provisional disposition. ¶~ 신청을 하다 apply for an [a provisional] injunction. **가처분하다** make provisional disposition (of); arrange temporary disposition of; dispose of (something) for the time being.

● **가처분 소득** [경] a disposable income.

가청(可聽) audible; audio.
● **가청 거리** (within) earshot. **가청 범위** the range of hearing; the audible range. **가청음** audible sounds. **가청 주파수** [전] audio frequency(약어 A.F.).

가축(家畜) a domestic animal; (집합적) cattle; stock; livestock. ¶~의 떼 a herd of cattle (미) / [줄지어 가는 소] a drove of cattle // ~을 치다 keep[raise / breed] livestock // ~ 20마리 twenty head of cattle // ~은 목장에서 풀을 뜯고 있었다 Cattle were grazing in the pasture.

● **가축병원** a veterinary hospital; (애완동물의) a pets' hospital. **가축 사료** stock feed.

가출(家出) disappearance from home; abscondence(도망); an elopement(여자의). **가출하다** run[go / drift] away from home; leave home[one's house]; disappear[fly] from home; abscond; elope(특히 여성이 애인과). ¶가출하고 없다 be missing from home // 가출한 소녀들을 보호하다 shelter runaway girls // 요즘은 어린 소년 소녀가 이유 없이 가출한다 Recently many young boys and girls run away from home for no reason.

● **가출 소녀** [소년] a runaway girl[boy]. **가출인** a runaway; an absconder.

가출옥(假出獄) → 가석방(假釋放)

가치(價値) value; worth; merit. (▶ be worth 뒤에는 명사·대명사·동명사 또는 명사구, deserve 뒤에는 명사·명사구·대명사 또는 to 부정사가 옴. 금전으로 환산할 수 있는 가치로서는 value나 worth 모두 쓸 수 있지만 value는 주로 유용성·중요성 등에 관한 가치, worth는 정신적·도덕적 등 본질적인 가치에 대해서 말하는 일이 많음. merit는 칭찬할 만한 점을 나타냄) ¶건강의 ~ the value of good health // 경제적 ~ commercial[economic] value // 교환 ~ value in exchange / exchange [exchangeable] value // 본질적 ~ intrinsic value (of a coin) // 부가 ~ value added // 사용 ~ value in use // 실질적 ~ practical [actual] value // 이용 [실용] ~ utility value // 인간의 ~ a man's worth // 화폐 ~ money value / the value of money // 희소 ~ scarcity value // ~ 있는 valuable / worthy / of value // 매우 ~가 있는 invaluable / priceless / of great value / of considerable merit // 다소 ~가 있는 of some value // 사물의 ~를 판단하지

가치 못하는 사람 a poor judge of value.// 읽을 ~가 있는 책 a book worth reading / rewarding book// 우리가 진지하게 생각해 볼 만한 ~가 있는 일 a matter that merits our sober reflection// 거의[전혀] ~가 없는 것 a thing of little[no] worth// 시간을 들일 ~가 있다 be worth one's while / ~도 없다 be of no value / be entirely useless / be no good / be not worth a song[a button / a damn / a rush] / 한 푼의 ~도 없다 be not worth a whoop[a doit / a brass farthing]// 너는 시간의 ~를 모른다 You don't know the value of time.// 이 문제는 더 이상 논의할 ~가 없다 This question deserves no fuller[further] discussion.// 그의 우정은 무엇과도 바꿀 수 없는 ~가 있다 I value his friendship more than anything else. / His friendship is worth more than anything else in the world.// 꽃병은 100만 원의 ~가 있다 This vase is worth a million won.// 저 연극은 볼 만한 ~가 있다 That play is worth seeing.// 그의 근면함은 칭찬할 만한 ~가 있다 His diligence is worthy of praise[praiseworthy].// 이 그림은 내게 아무런 ~도 없다 This painting is worthless[of no value] to me.
● **가치관** one's sense of values. **가치 판단** judgement[estimation] of value; valuation; estimate.

가친(家親) my father.

가칭(假稱) 1 (잠정적인) a tentative [provisional] name; a tentative designation. ¶그 공원은 「어린이 공원」이라 부르고 있다 The park is tentatively called "Children's Park". **가칭하다** call[name] (a thing) ... tentatively [for the time being]. 2 (사칭) misrepresentation; a false representation; an assumed name[title]; a false name[title]. **가칭하다** assume another's[a false] name; represent oneself as (an official); designate tentatively. ¶그는 T라 가칭하고 살았다 He lived under the assumed name of T.

가택(家宅) a house; premises; a residence; domicile.
● **가택 방문** a house call; a visit to a house. **가택 수색** a house search; (법) a domiciliary visit[search]. ¶~ 영장 a search warrant// ~을 당하다 be subjected to a domiciliary search / have one's house searched.

가톨릭 Catholicism; the (Roman) Catholic Church. ¶~의 (Roman) Catholic// ~을 믿다 believe in Catholicism.
● **가톨릭교도** a Roman Catholic. **가톨릭교회** a Roman Catholic church.

가트 [관세와 무역에 관한 일반 협정] GATT (the General Agreement on Tariffs and Trade의 약어).

가파르다 steep (slope); sharp (climb); precipitous (cliff). ¶가파른 낭떠러지 a steep [sheer] cliff / a precipice// 가파른 산길 a steep mountain path// 가파른 비탈길 a steep slope[ascent] / a short but rough slope// 가파른 길 a steep path / a sharply rising road// 이 언덕은 동쪽보다 서쪽이 ~ The hill rises more steeply from the west than from the east.

가표(可票) an affirmative vote. ¶~를 던지다 cast an aye vote for (a bill) / vote for [in favor of] / ballot for// 투표 결과 ~가 20, 부표가 15였다 There were[The vote stood at] twenty ayes and fifteen noes.

가풍(家風) a family custom[tradition]; the ways of family. ¶~에 맞지 않다 be out of harmony[keeping] with the ways of a family// 그녀는 시대의 ~에 어울리지 못했다 She does not fit in with her husband's family traditions[customs].

가필(加筆) correction; retouch; revision. ¶회의록은 군데군데 ~이 있었다 There were some corrections in the minutes of the meeting. **가필하다** [정정하다] correct; [퇴고하여 바로잡다] improve; [수정하다] revise. ¶초고에 ~ add some touches to one's manuscript// 송 선생이 내 원고에 가필해 주셨다 Mr. Song touched up[corrected] my manuscript.// 선생님은 내 시를 가필하여 주셨다 My teacher improved my poem.

가하다(可−) (옳다) right; good; well; all right; (좋다) fairly good; passable. ¶…이라 해도 ~ we may rightly say that ... / it may safely be said that ...// 어느 쪽이든 ~ Either (of them) will do[be satisfactory].// 그것으로 ~ All right. / O.K. / That will do.// 그를 합격시켜도 ~ You may pass him.

가하다(加−) 1 [가산하다] add; add up; sum up. ¶3에 6을 ~ add six to three / add three and six// 5에 6을 ~ add 6 to 5// 2에 3을 가하면 5이다 Two and three make[are] five.
2 [부가하다] add (to); supplement with; include. ¶원금에 이자를 ~ add interest to the principal// 여비를 가해서 3천 원이 된다 It amounts to 3,000 won including travelling expenses.
3 [증가하다] increase. ¶박차를 ~ spur one's horse / (비유) spur[urge] (a person) [on to / on to] / 열차가 속도를 가했다 The train gathered[gained] speed.
4 [주다] inflict; give. ¶압력을 ~ pressure [put pressure upon] (a person) / apply pressure (to)// 열을 ~ apply heat / heat// 비판을 ~ criticize / pass judgment (upon)// 제재를 ~ punish / inflict punishment upon (a person) / discipline// 상해를 ~ inflict an injury (on person)// 그는 그 남자에게 강한 일격을 가했다 He dealt the man a hard blow.// 나는 그의 코에 일격을 가했다 I dealt him a blow on the nose.

가학(加虐) cruel treatment; maltreatment; cruelty. **가학하다** treat (a person) with cruelty; be cruel to (a person); maltreat.
● **가학성 성욕 이상** sadism.

가해(加害) doing harm; inflicting injury; violence; an offense; wrong (doing). **가해하다** do harm (to); commit a violence (on); [살인하다] murder.
● **가해자** an assaulter; an assailant; a wrongdoer; a murderer(살해자).

가호(加護) divine protection; providence; guardianship; blessing; grace. ¶신의 ~로 by the protection of Heaven// 신의 ~를 받다 call upon [pray to] God for help / invoke divine aid// 하나님의 ~가 있으시기를 May the grace of God be[go] with you.// 신의 ~로 그 참사에서 벗어났다 A special providence preserved me from the tragic accident. / I escaped the tragic accident through divine grace.

가혹하다(苛酷−) severe; hard; harsh; rigid; cruel; brutal. ¶가혹한 사람 a severe[cruel] person// 가혹한 비평 harsh[scathing] criticism// 가혹한 취급 cruel[merciless] treatment // 가혹한 규칙 severe[harsh] rules // (벌의) 가혹함 the severity of the punishment // 그 조건은 ~ Those terms are too enacting [harsh]. // 그는 가혹한 운명을 겪기에 이르렀다 He was to suffer a cruel fate. // 가혹한 요구를 해 왔다 They made enacting demands. // 세상은 ~ The world is stern[not easy to live in]. // 지금 곧 빚을 갚으라는 것은 좀 ~ It's a bit cruel to demand (of him) immediate payment of his debts. // 그렇게 어린 아이에게 매질을 하다니 ~ It's cruel of you to lash such a little child. 가혹히 severely; cruelly; harshly. ¶그녀는 나를 ~ 대한다 / She treats me harshly. / She is hard on me. // 그는 ~ 다루어졌다 He was used roughly [treated harshly].

가훈(家訓) family precepts; the family code of conduct.

가히(可-) (may) well; fairly well; (might) well; (can) rightly[suitably]. ¶~ 당대의 석학이라 할 만한 사람 a man who might well be called the greatest scholar of the age // ~ 그렇다 할 수 있다 You may well say so. // 그녀의 슬픔은 ~ 짐작할 만하다 We may well imagine how grieved she is. // 그가 얼마나 놀랐는지 ~ 짐작할 만하다 His surprise may well be imagined. // 그의 심정은 ~ 짐작할 만하다 I can easily figure out how he feels. // 이로 보아 그가 얼마나 부지런한지 ~ 알 수 있다 From this you can well imagine how diligent he is.

각(角) 1 [각도] an angle. ¶45도의 ~을 이루다 form[make] an angle of 45°(with).
2 [사각] a square.
3 [모퉁이] a corner.
4 [뿔] a horn; an antler(사슴의); a feeler(곤충 등의 촉각). ¶~도장 a horn seal.
5 [음] the middle note of the Korean pentatonic scale.

각(各) each; every; all. ¶~ 곳 every place / all the places // ~ 가정 each family // ~ 학교는 8시 반에 시작된다 Every school starts [begins] at 8:30. // A지, B지, C지를 ~ 1부씩 보내 주시오 Please send me a copy[one copy each] of The A, The B and The C.

각가지(各-) all sorts[kinds]; every sort [kind]; various kinds. ¶~의 various / varied / various kinds of / all sorts[kinds] of / of every sort (and kind) // ~ 물건 all sorts [kinds] of things / things of every sort.

각각(各各) each; all; every; respectively; individually; severally; separately. ¶~의 each / respective / individual / several // ~ 살다 live separately (from) / 물건을 ~ 따로 두다 keep things apart // 사람은 ~ 자기 할 일이 있다 Every man has his own duty to perform. // ~ 자기 할 일을 해라 Go to your respective jobs. // ~ 입장권을 지참할 것 Each (is expected) to bring his (own) ticket. // 우리는 ~ 자기 방이 있다 Each one of us has a room to himself. // 갈 때는 같이 갔으나 돌아올 때는 ~ 따로 왔다 We all went together but returned our separate ways. // 1등과 2등의 상품이 톰과 프랭크에게 ~ 수여되었다 This first and second prizes were awarded to Tom and Frank respectively.

각개(各個) each; each one; every one; one by one. ¶~의 each / individual / respective // 그 것은 ~의 문제이다 It is a problem that each of you[each person] must solve individually.
●**각개 격파** defeating one by one[one after another]. **각개 훈련** individual training.

각계(各界) every field[sphere] of life; every walk of life; various circles. ¶~의 명사 eminent people from various fields[walks of life] / notables representing various departments of society // ~의 의견을 듣다 listen to men of every social standing / collect opinions and comments from various walks of life.
●**각계각층** all social standings; all levels of society.

각고(刻苦) hard work; arduous labor; close application. ¶~의 작품 a painstaking work / a lucubration / a fruit of much labor // 그는 다년간의 ~ 끝에 드디어 이 발명을 완성해 냈다 He consummated this invention by years of hard application. // ~ 5년 그녀는 마침내 초지를 관철하였다 She accomplished his purpose after five years of hard work. **각고하다** work hard[diligently]; apply oneself closely to (one's studies).

각골난망(刻骨難忘) remembering forever; cherishing the memory of. **각골난망하다** (사람이) be deeply impressed (with / by); grave (the words) in the heart; (사물이) be brought home to (one); be deeply impressed on[engraved in] one's mind. ¶베풀어 주신 은혜는 실로 각골난망하옵니다 I shall never forget what[all the favors] you have done for me.

각광(脚光) (극장의) footlights; floats.
각광(을) 받다 (무대에서) appear before the footlights; (세상에서) be highlighted [spotlighted]; be in[move into / step into] the limelight; get into the spotlight. ¶그는 세계 외교 무대에서 각광을 받았다 He stood in the spotlight of world diplomacy. // 그는 매스컴의 각광을 받고 있다 He is in the spotlight [limelight] of mass communication. // 정치가들은 각광 받기를 무척 좋아한다 Politicians are very fond of the limelight. // 그는 마침내 제1급의 정치가로서 각광을 받기에 이르렀다 Now he is in the limelight[Now attention is being focused on him] as a politician of the first rank.

각국(各國) [각 나라] every[each] country [nation]; (여러 나라) various countries [states]; [만국] the world; all countries. ¶세계 ~ world nations // ~의 외교 사절 the foreign diplomatic representatives // ~에서 대표 한 사람씩 a representative from each country // 아시아 ~의 대표자 the representatives of the Asian countries // 유럽 ~을 시찰하다 make a tour of inspection in various European countries // ~의 무역 사정을 시찰하러 가다 go to various countries to observe commercial affairs.

각기(各其) [저마다의 사람이나 사물] each (one); every one; [각각 저마다] each; individually; respectively; severally; in one's own way. ¶사람은 ~ 장점과 단점이 있다 Each man has his merits and his faults. // 스튜어디스들은 ~ 모두 미인이었다 Each and every one of the stewardesses was beautiful.

각기둥(角-) [수] a prism.
각기병(脚氣病) beriberi. ¶~에 걸리다 have an attack of beriberi.

각다귀 1 [동] a gnat; a midge; a striped mosquito (*pl.* ~(e)s). 2 [착취자] a vampire; a sponge; an extortioner; a bloodsucker.

각도(角度) 1 [수] [각의 크기] an angle; the degree of an angle. ¶45도의 ~ at an angle of 45°// 선과 선이 엇갈렸을 때 생기는 ~ the angles formed where two lines cross each other // ~를 재다 take [measure] the angle (of) // 길은 30도 ~로 굽어 있다 The road curves at an angle of thirty degrees. 2 [관점] a point of view; a viewpoint; a standpoint; an angle (of vision). ¶이러한 ~에서 본다면 (looked at) from this point of view / viewed from this angle // 모든 ~에서 검토하다 survey [study] (a problem) from every angle [all angles / all viewpoints] // 다른 ~에서 보다 view (life) from a different angle.
● **각도계** an angle meter; a goniometer. **각도기** a protractor; a graduator.

각론(各論) (전문적인) a specialized study; [각 항에 걸친 논의] an item-by-item discussion; [각항 상설] detailed exposition. ¶해부학 ~ special anatomy / a detailed treatise on a special branch of anatomy // ~에 들어가다 go into details [particulars] // 총론에서 ~으로 들어가다 descend from generals to particulars // 이 의학 전서는 총론과 ~으로 이루어져 있다 This series of medical books contains both general discussion and detailed explanations [general and detailed discussion].

각료(閣僚) (집합적) the Cabinet [Ministerial] colleagues; a Cabinet member [minister / officer]. ¶~ 급의 (state minister) of cabinet level // 경제 ~ Cabinet minister in charge of economic affairs / economic minister // 전(前) ~ an ex-Minister / a former Minister // 한일 ~ 회담 the Korea-Japan Ministerial Meeting.
● **각료 회의** a Cabinet meeting.

각막(角膜) [생] the horny coat (of the eye); the cornea.
● **각막염** inflammation of the cornea; corneitis; keratitis. **각막 이식** corneal transplant(ation) [grafting]; keratoplasty.

각목(角木) a square bar; a scantling; a balk; a baulk.

각박하다(刻薄-) severe; harsh; hardhearted; stingy; heartless; unfeeling; merciless; pitiless; exigent; hard to live; miserly; niggardly. ¶각박한 인심 heartlessness / coldness / lack of consideration for others // 각박한 세상 the hard [tough] world / hard [stern] life // 그는 각박한 사람이다 He has a heart of stone. // 요즘 물가가 올라 인심이 각박해지고 있다 People are getting hardhearted in these days of high prices. // 각박한 세상이다 This is a rough world we are living in. / These are hard times.

각반(脚絆) (a pair of) gaiters; leggings; spats [짧은 것]; puttees. ¶~을 치고 있는 gaitered legs // ~을 **치다** put on gaiters / do up a puttee // ~을 치고 있다 be in [be wearing] gaiters.

각방(各方) everywhere; every direction; all directions. ¶~으로 in every direction [quarter] / in all quarters [directions] // ~으로 찾다 look for (a person) everywhere // ~으로 사람을 보내다 send messengers in all directions.

각방(各房) each [every] room; all rooms. ¶~에 거처하다 have each a room to himself // 그들은 ~을 쓴다 They live in separate rooms. / Each one of them has a room to himself. / They each have their own room.

각별하다(各別-) 1 [유다르다] particular; [특별하다] especial; special; extraordinary; unusual; [파격적이다] exceptional; [현저하다] marked; noticeable; remarkable. ¶각별한 호의 special favor // 각별한 일도 없이 uneventfully // 오늘 아침 추위는 ~ It is especially [exceptionally] cold this morning. // 각별한 볼일은 없읍니다 I have nothing in particular to do. **각별히** particularly; especially; exceptionally; remarkably. ¶~ 조심하다 take every precaution / be extremely cautious [prudent] / take the best possible care / be most careful (about) // 건강에 ~ 유의하시기 바랍니다 I hope you will take special care of yourself.
2 [깍듯하다] courteous; decorous; polite; civil. ¶각별한 대접을 받다 be received with much courtesy. **각별히** politely; courteously; with due courtesy. ¶~ 대접하다 treat with (much) courtesy / give a warm reception.

각본(脚本) [극본] a play; a drama; a playbook; (가극의) a libretto (*pl.* ~s, libretti); (영화의) a script; a scenario (*pl.* ~s, scenario). ¶~으로 만들다 dramatize / adapt for the stage [movies] / make a stage version of / make a screen version of // ~을 쓰다 write a play // ~을 상연하다 stage a play / put a drama on (the stage).
● **각본가** [작가] a dramatist; a playwright; (영화의) a scenario [script] writer; a scenarist.

각부(各部) [각 부분] each [every] part; all parts; [여러 가지 부분] various parts. ¶인체 ~의 구조 the structure of the parts of a body // 이 기계의 ~의 구조가 도해되어 있다 The structure of each part of this machine is illustrated.

각뿔(角-) [수] a pyramid. ¶정~ a regular pyramid. // 직~ a right pyramid.
● **각뿔대**(-臺) a truncated pyramid; a frustum of a pyramid.

각살림(各-) living separately; living apart. **각살림하다** live separately; live apart; maintain separate residences; set up one's own home. ¶그들 형제는 각살림하고 있다 The brothers live each by himself.

각색(各色) 1 [빛깔] every [each] color; all colors; various colors. 2 [각종] every kind; all sorts [kinds]; various kinds. ¶~ 인종 all races / people of various races // ~의 물건 all sorts of things / things of every sort and variety // 각양 ~ every kind and description // 각인 ~ Every man has his own humor / So many men, so many minds.

각색(脚色) 1 [각본으로 씀] dramatization; (an) arrangement. ¶~ 송수민 adapted by Song Sumin. **각색하다** dramatize (a novel); adapt [arrange] (a novel) for a movie [play]; (영화로) filmize; cinematize; scenarize; make a screen version of (a story). ¶외국 무대용으로 각색한 희곡 a drama arranged [adapted] for the foreign stage // 이야기를 텔레비전용으로 ~ arrange a story for TV // 이것은 어떤 외국 소설을 각색한 것이다 This was adapted from a foreign novel. 2 [분식(粉飾)]. ¶그의 이야기는 ~이 심하다 He tends to embellish

[embroider] stories.
● **각색가** a dramatizer; an adapter; a script writer(영화의).

각서(覺書) a memorandum (*pl.* ~s, -da) (on); a memorial; a note; (프) a mémoire; a protocol(의정서). ¶~의 교환 an exchange of notes[memoranda] // 이 문제에 관한 미국 정부의 ~ the American note on this subject.

각선미(脚線美) the beauty of leg lines; a nice leg line; "a well-turned ankle". ¶~가 멋진 여자 a woman with beautiful legs / a girl with shapely legs // ~를 강조한 사진 (미국 속어) a cheesecake.

각설이(却說-) [민] a singing beggar (begging for money at the marketplace).

각설탕(角雪糖) a lump sugar; cube[cubic] sugar. ¶~ 한 개 a cube of sugar.

각설하고(却說-) (말머리를 돌릴 때) now to resume our story; to return to the topic; now let us proceed. ¶~, 그 무렵에 큰비가 왔다 To resume our story, there was a heavy rainfall at that time.

각섬석(角閃石) [광] amphibole; hornblende.

각성(覺醒) awakening; disillusion; disenchantment. ¶영적(靈的) ~ spiritual awakening. **각성하다** (무지에서) awake (from / to); wake up (to); come to one's senses; (잘못에서) be disillusioned. ¶그 국민은 아직 각성하지 못하고 있다 The nation is not yet awakened. ➔**각성시키다** awaken; open (a person's) eyes / bring (a person) to (his) senses / disillusion / arouse // 패전은 국민을 크게 각성시켰다 The defeat was a great eye opener for the people.
● **각성제** an antihypnotic[a stimulant] (drug); (구어) a pep pill; (구어) an upper. ¶~ 중독 addiction to stimulant drugs.

각속도(角速度) [물] angular velocity.

각시 **1** [인형] a doll bride; a maiden doll. **2** [새색시] a bride; a newly married.
● **각시놀음** playing with dolls.

각양각색(各樣各色) every kind and description. ¶~의 various / varied / of all kinds [sorts] / varieties of // ~의 스타일의 자동차 cars of various styles // ~의 형태를 이루다 take various forms // 그들은 ~의 모자를 판매한다 They sell all kinds of hats. // 정부가 당면한 문제는 ~이다 The problems facing the government are manifold.

각오(覺悟) **1** [마음의 준비] readiness; preparedness; [결심] resolution; determination. ¶그 일을 완수할 ~가 있느냐 Do you have the firm determination to accomplish the job? // 우리는 ~를 새로이 하고 이 사태에 대처해야 한다 We must make up our minds to the situation. // 자넨 최악의 사태에 대한 ~가 되어 있는가 Are you prepared for the worst[for whatever may happen]? **각오하다** be ready[prepared] for; make up one's mind; form[make] a resolution; be determined. ¶죽음을 ~ be prepared for death // 노여움 살 것을 각오하고 말하다 dare a person's anger and say // 거절당할 것을 각오하고 부탁해 볼 생각이다 I intend to ask him anyway, though I don't expect he will consent to it.
2 [불] enlightenment; (a) spiritual awakening. **각오하다** be spiritually awakened.

각운(脚韻) a rhyme; [문] an end rime.

각운동(角運動) [물] angular motion.
● **각운동량** angular momentum.

각위(各位) [여러분] gentlemen; every one; (편지에서) Sirs; Gentlemen; Messrs.(Mr.의 복수형); messieurs(Mr.의 프랑스 어 monsieur의 복수형). ¶회원 ~에게 to the members // 관계자 ~에게 (편지에서) To whom it may concern // ~께서는 you all // ~의 건강을 위하여 축배를 올립니다 I drink to the health of all the guests present.

각의(閣議) a Cabinet meeting[council]. ¶정례[임시] ~ a regular[an extraordinary] Cabinet meeting // ~를 열다[소집하다] hold [call / summon] a Cabinet meeting // 문제를 ~에 회부하다 submit a problem to a Cabinet meeting.

각인(各人) each person; everyone; everybody.
● **각인각색** Every man has his own humor; So many men, so many minds. ¶~의 의견 various opinions // ~으로 취미가 다르다 Everyone has his own preference[likes and dislikes].

각인(刻印) a carved seal; a (carved) stamp. **각인하다** carve a seal; engrave a seal.

각자(各自) [각각의 자기 자신] each; each [every] one; [저마다 따로따로] each; individually; respectively; severally. ¶~의 each / respective / individual / one's own // ~의 의무를 다하라 Each of you fulfill your own duty. // ~ 집으로 돌아갔다 They returned to their several homes. // ~ 표를 사기 바람 Everyone is expected to buy his own ticket. // ~ 자유행동을 취하라 Each one for himself! // 우리는 ~ 자기의 일로 바쁘다 We are all busy at our several tasks. // 이것은 ~의 자유다 Each person may do as he likes about it.

각재(角材) squared timber[(미) lumber]; (작은) a scantling. ¶12센티미터의 ~ a twelve-centimeter square piece of lumber.

각종(各種) each[every] kind; all sorts [kinds]; various kinds; varieties. ¶~의 every kind / of all sorts / varieties of / of many species // ~의 자전거 bicycles of every description // ~의 나비 every species of butterflies // ~의 우표 수집 a collection of a large variety of stamps // ~의 것을 섞은 비스킷 mixed[assorted] biscuits // ~의 실험을 해 보았으나 그의 이론을 증명할 수는 없었다 Various experiments have failed to prove his theory.
● **각종 학교** one of miscellaneous schools.

각주(角柱) **1** [네모진 기둥] a square pillar. **2** ➔**각기둥**

각주(脚註) a footnote. ¶내용이 풍부한 ~ a copious footnotes // ~를 단 footnoted // ~를 달다 put in[add / append] a footnote / give footnotes (to a book) // ~로 인용문의 출전을 나타내다 give the sources of quotations in footnotes.

각지(各地) every[each] place[district / area]; [여러 지방] various places; various parts of the country; [전 지방] all parts of the country. ¶~에 everywhere / in several places // 세계 ~로부터 from all over [from every part of] the world // ~의 사정에 따라 according to the conditions in each place // 독감이 ~에 퍼졌다 The influenza spread everywhere. // 저기압은 한국 ~에 큰비를 내리게 했다 A low pressure system caused

각질(角質) (뿔·발톱 등의) keratin; (절지동물의) chitin; horny substance. ¶~의 horny / corneous / keratoid.
● **각질층** a horny layer; a stratum corneum (*pl.* strata cornea).

각처(各處) each[every] place; all places; various places[districts / quarters]. ¶~의[에] in every[each] place / everywhere / [여기저기에] here and there // 전국 ~에서 from every corner of the country // ~에 사람을 보내다 send a messenger to each place // ~에 경찰이 배치되어 있었다 Policemen were posted everywhere[all over the place].

각추(角錐) → 각뿔

각축(角逐) competition; rivalry; struggle (for mastery). ¶~을 벌이다 be at odds[variance] (with). **각축하다** compete; vie (with); struggle (for mastery); contend (against).
● **각축장** the arena of competition. **각축전** a hot[sharp] contest; keen competition. ¶선거에서 딴 후보자와 ~을 벌이다 compete with other candidates at an election.

각층(各層) (사회의) each class (of society); each stratum[segment] of society; (건물의) each[every] floor[story]. ¶~의 on[of] every floor // 각계 ~의 of all social standings / all levels of society // ~에 서는 승강기 an elevator that stops at every floor.

각파(各派) [정당] each party; all political parties[groups]; [파벌] each faction; [예술계 등의] all schools; [종파] all sects[denominations].

각판(刻版) a (printing) block; a woodcut; an engraving block.
● **각판본** a book printed from a block[plate].

각피(角皮) [생] cuticle.

각하(却下) rejection; turning down; [법] dismissal. **각하하다** reject; dismiss; turn down. ¶청원을 ~ reject a petition / turn down an application // ~ 상소를 ~ reject[dismiss] an appeal. → ¶그의 제안은 실행 불가능으로 각하되었다 His proposal was rejected[turned down] on the grounds that it was not practicable. // 그의 소송은 각하될지도 모른다 His suit may be dismissed. // 이의 신청이 각하되었다 His objection was overruled.

각하(閣下) (대사·총독 등을 지칭하여, 2인칭) Your Excellency; (3인칭) His[Her] Excellency (*pl.* Their Excellencies); (특히 영국의 재판관·공작 이외의 귀족 등을 지칭하여) Your[His / Her] Lordship; (미국의 판사·시장 등을 지칭하여) Your[His / Her] Honor. ¶시장 ~ Your[His] Honor the Mayor. // 요크 공 ~ His Grace the Duke of Yoke. // ~ 및 신사 숙녀 여러분 Your Excellencies, ladies and gentlemen.

각항(各項) each[every] item[paragraph / clause / provision].

각혈(咯血) [의] hemoptysis; emptysis; expectoration of blood. **각혈하다** expectorate blood; spit[cough] out blood; have a hemorrhage of the lungs and[or] trachea.

간 [염분의 정도] saltiness; a salty taste; [미] seasoning with salt; salting; [간장] soy (sauce). ¶~을 보다 taste (a dish) to see how it is seasoned with salt // ~이 짜다[싱겁다] be well seasoned with salt // ~이 짜다[싱겁다] be too salty[be not salty enough] // 생선에 ~을 하다 salt fish // 이 국은 ~이 좀 싱겁다 This soup wants a touch of salt. **간하다** season with salt; apply salt for seasoning.

간(肝) the liver.
간에 붙였다 쓸개에 붙였다 한다(속담) be two-faced; be not constant; be fickle.
간에 기별도 안 가다 be hardly enough to be worth eating; barely begin to satisfy one's stomach.
간을 녹이다 charm; fascinate; bewitch.
간이 작다 timid; faint-hearted; chicken-hearted.
간이 콩알만 해지다 be frightened out one's wits; be scared stiff.
간(을) 졸이다 worry oneself.
간(이) 크다 be plucky.
간(이) 타다 be anxious (for); pine.
● **간 경화** [의] cirrhosis of the liver. ⇨ 간경변증 **간기능 부전** hepatic insufficiency.

간¹(間) →칸

간²(間) 1 [두 곳 사이] between. ¶서울 인천 ~의 철도 the railway line between Seoul and Incheon / the Seoul-Incheon line[section]. **2** [⋯에 관계없이] regardless of; irrespective of; whether ... or ... ¶남자건 여자건 ~에 (no matter) whether it is man or woman // 비가 오든 안 오든 ~에 rain or shine / in all weather // 국적이야 어디든 ~에 irrespective of (a person's) nationality // 결과야 어떻든 ~에 나는 착수해야 할 것 같다 I feel I must begin it, no matter what the consequences may be.

-간(間) 1 [관계] relation; relationship. ¶형제 ~ brotherly[fraternal] relation // 그는 나와 사촌 ~이다 He is a cousin of mine. // 그들은 부자 ~이다 Their relation is that of father and son. / They are father and son.
2 [사이] between; among. ¶형제 ~의 싸움 a quarrel between brothers // 친구 ~에 among one's friends.
3 [간격] an interval; [기간] a period; for; during; in. ¶1개월 ~ for a month // 5일 ~ 계속되는 고교 대항 야구 시합 the five-days series of interschool baseball games // 10년 ~ 사귀어 온 친구 a friend of ten years' standing // 3일 ~에 그것을 완성할 수는 없다 It is impossible to finish it in three days. // 전람회는 4일부터 10일 ~ 개최된다 The exhibition will be open for ten days beginning on the 4th.

간간이(間間-) **1** [이따금] occasionally; now and then; at time; once in a while; at intervals; from time to time. ¶~ 오는 손님 a casual visitor // ~ 있는 사례 a rare instance // ~ 찾아오다 show up in a long while // 그는 ~ 우리를 만나러 온다 He comes to see us from time to time. **2** [듬성듬성] at intervals; here and there. ¶(일정한 간격으로) ~ 심다 plant them at regular intervals.

간간하다 (맛이) pleasantly salty; nicely salted; have a briny flavor; saltish. ¶이 음식은 좀 ~ This dish is a bit salty.

간격(間隔) 1 [공간·거리·시간] a space; spacing; an interval; a gap; a distance. ¶(열차의) 운전 ~ a headway // 넓은 ~ a wide interval // 15분 ~으로 at 15-minute intervals // 일정한 ~을 두고 at regular intervals // ~을 두다 leave spaces // ~을 좁히다 narrow the distance between / move closer together // 5분 ~으로 운행합니다 This is five minute service. // 앞차와의 ~을 충분히 두지 않고 운

전하는 것은 위험하다 It is dangerous to drive too close to the vehicle ahead.
2 [소원함] estrangement; coolness. ¶두 사람 사이에 ~이 생겼다 They have become estranged (from each other). / They have lost their former intimacy.
3 [틈·사이] a crevice; a chink; a gap; an opening. ¶울타리 판자의 ~ chinks between the boards of a fence.

간결하다(簡潔-) concise; terse; brief; compact (style); succinct; pithy. ¶간결하게 concisely / briefly / tersely / compactly // 간결한 편지 a briefly worded note // 간결하게 답하다 answer briefly // 말을 할 때에는 간결하고 요점이 분명해야 한다 In speaking one should be short [brief] and to the point. // 말이란 간결한 것이 좋다 Brevity is the soul of speech [wit]. // 그는 그 문제를 간결하게 설명했다 He explained the issue briefly and to the point.

간경변증(肝硬變症) [의] cirrhosis of the liver; hepatocirrhosis.

간계(奸計) a trick; a plot; an evil [a crafty] design; wiles; an intrigue. ¶~를 꾸미다 make crafty designs / resort to (ruses and) wiles // 적의 ~에 빠지다 fall a prey to the enemy's vile plot.

간곡하다(懇曲-) serious; earnest; sincere; cordial; hearty; warm; hospitable. ¶간곡한 청탁 an earnest request. **간곡히** seriously; repeatedly; sincerely; earnestly; kindly; cordially; hospitably. ¶~ 타이르다 admonish repeatedly / give (a person) a good talking-to // 그가 나빴다고 그를 ~ 타일렀다 I tried earnestly to make him see that he was to blame. / I talked to him over and over again to convince him that he was wrong. // 그녀는 담배가 해롭다는 것을 ~ 설명하였다 She explained earnestly how bad it was to smoke.

간과(干戈) [무기] shields and spears; arms; weapons; [전쟁] warfare.

간과(看過) **1** [못 보고 빠뜨림] passing over; failure to notice. **간과하다** fail to notice; overlook; miss; pass over [by / up]; lose sight of (an important fact). ¶간과해서는 안 될 요점 the point to see // 그의 눈은 무엇 하나 간과하지 않았다 Nothing escaped him[his attention]. / His eyes took in everything. // 나는 틀린 것을 간과했다 I overlooked [failed to notice] the mistake. // 우리는 그 문제의 본질을 간과했다 We missed the true nature of the problem.
2 [묵인] connivance; overlooking; condonation. **간과하다** look over; condone; connive at [in]; pass over (a matter) in silence; let (it) pass[go]; (구어) give (a person) the go-by. ¶과실을 ~ overlook a fault / 가볍게 ~ pass (a thing) over lightly / let (a thing) unchallenged. // 그 일은 그냥 간과할 수가 없다 I cannot let the matter pass (by) without making a protest.

간교하다(奸巧-) crafty; cunning; sly; wily; tricky; (속어) slick. ¶그 소년은 그가 원하는 것을 얻는 데에 상당히 간교했다 The boy showed a great deal of cunning in getting what he wanted.

간구(懇求) an earnest desire[request]; soliciting; begging; an eager wish[hope]. **간구하다** beg; ask; request earnestly; solicit; hope;

desire; wish. ¶간구하옵건대… we earnestly desire that … / it is my earnest hope[wish] that … // 그것은 본인이 간구하는 바이다 That is what I desire most. // 귀하의 조력으로 성공할 수 있기를 간구합니다 It is my earnest hope that I may succeed with your support.

간국 1 [잔물] salty liquids; a salt solution; brine. ¶~에 절이다 soak[steep] in brine. **2** [기름때] sweaty grime.

간균(杆菌) [생] a bacillus (*pl*. bacilli). ¶~의 bacillary.

간극(間隙) [틈] a gap; an opening; an aperture; a chink; [비유] an estrangement; a difference; discord; a cleavage. ¶~을 메우다 stop[fill up / bridge] a gap // ~이 생기다 fall out with (each other).

간난(艱難) hardships; difficulties; privations; afflictions; adversity. ¶~을 겪다 undergo[go through] hardships / have rough time [hard life / rugged life] // ~을 극복하다 overcome difficulties // ~을 참고 견디다 endure[bear] hardships[adversity]. **간난하다** hard; difficult; troublesome.

간뇌(間腦) [생] the diencephalon; the interbrain.

간단명료하다(簡單明瞭-) short and clear; simple and plain; terse; concise; laconic (style, expression, etc.). ¶간단명료하게 tersely / briefly / concisely and plainly // 간단명료한 문체 laconic style // 간단명료하게 말하다 speak in plain words / make one's explanation short and clear.

간단없다(間斷-) continuous; ceaseless; incessant. ⇨끊임없다

간단하다(簡單-) simple; brief; short; plain; easy. ¶간단한 문제 a simple problem [question] // 간단한 식사 a light meal / a snack // 간단한 일 a simple [light] matter / easy work // 간단한 절차로 through a simple procedure // "네"라는 간단한 대답이었다 "Yes" was the laconic response. // 그것은 설명이 너무 ~ That's far too facile an explanation. **간단히** [간결하게] simply; (speak) briefly; in brief; [손쉽게] easily; readily; with ease; [가볍게] lightly. ¶~ 말하면 in short[brief] / in a word // ~ 해치우다 lightly dismiss // ~ 승낙하다 readily comply with / give a ready consent // ~ 식사하다 take a light meal / have a snack / eat a cheap dinner // 그것에 대해 ~ 설명하시오 Give a brief account of it. // 그 문제는 ~ 풀 수 있다 The problem can be solved easily.

간담(肝膽) [간과 쓸개] liver and gall; [속마음] one's inmost feelings; one's innermost heart. ¶~을 서늘하게 하는 광경 an appalling[a gruesome] sight // ~을 서늘하게 하다 freeze (a person's) heart with terror / make (a person) shiver // 그의 날카로운 언변은 각료의 ~을 서늘하게 했다 His sharp tongue struck terror into the cabinet minister's hearts.

간담이 서늘하다 one's blood runs cold. ¶사자 소리에 간담이 서늘했다 My blood ran cold [chill] as I heard the roar of a lion. // 그 광경을 보고 그들은 간담이 서늘해졌다 The sight curdled their blood. / They were frozen with horror at the sight.

간담(懇談) a chat; a familiar[friendly] talk; a confabulation[confab]. ¶~식으로 이야기하다 have an informal talk (with) / talk in a

간댕거리다

friendly way [without restraint]. **간담하다** talk (with); chat (with); have a familiar talk (with). ¶털어놓고 ~ have a heart-to-heart talk (with)//교사들은 학부형과 간담했다 The teachers had a friendly [an informal] talk with their students' parents.//그는 학장[총장]과 마주 대하여 간담했다 He had a tête-à-tête with the president of the university. / He had a private conversation with the president of the university.
● **간담회**(-會) a social gathering [meeting]; a bull session; (미국 구어) a talkfest.

간댕거리다 [매달려 흔들거리다] dangle; tremble; (물건이) run short; get low; be almost out (of); (목숨 등이) be on the point of (doing). ¶마른 나뭇잎이 바람에 간댕거린다 A withered leaf trembles in the wind.

간독하다(懇篤-) kind; cordial; warm; hearty; genial. ¶간독한 감사의 편지 a cordial letter of thanks. **간독히** kindly; cordially; heartily; warmly; considerately.

간드랑거리다 swing gently; dangle; sway (to and fro); waver. ¶초롱이 바람에 간드랑거렸다 A lantern dangled in the breeze. ¶풍경이 바람에 간드랑거린다 The wind-bell is swinging in the wind.

간드러지다 coy; coquettish; willowy; charming; bewitching; fascinating; haunting. ¶간드러진 걸음걸이 a bewitching gait//간드러지게 웃다 laugh coquettishly [fascinatingly]//노래를 간드러지게 부르다 sing a song with a charming lilt.

간들거리다 1 (바람이) blow gently [softly]. 2 (물체가) shake; sway; dangle; waver; tremble. ¶바람에 간들거리는 나뭇잎 trembling leaves in the air. 3 (태도가) act coquettishly; play the flirt; put on coquettish air.

간디스토마(肝-) [동] a flukeworm; a liver fluke.

간략하다(簡略-) simple; concise; terse; brief; informal. ¶간략한 기사 a short account//간략하게 하다 make simple / simplify / abbreviate// 요점만 간략하게 말하다 touch (briefly) upon the principle points / outline the main points//결혼식은 가능한 한 간략하게 합시다 Let's make our wedding as simple as possible. **간략히** simply; concisely; tersely; briefly; informally; in short.

간만(干滿) ebb and flow; flux and reflux; rise and fall; tide. ¶~의 차 the difference between the rise and fall of the tide / the range of tide//(조수가) ~이 없는 tideless//조수에는 ~이 있다 The tide rises and falls. / The tide ebbs and flows.

간망(懇望) an earnest request [entreaty]; solicitation. ¶~에 못 이겨 being unable to refuse (a person's) earnest request//~을 받아들이다 listen to (a person's) entreaty / comply with (a person's) earnest request. **간망하다** earnestly request; entreat; implore; solicit (a person for).

간물 [소금물] salty water; [간국] brine.

간밤 last night; yesterday evening. ¶~의 불 last night's fire//그녀는 ~에 영국에 갔다 She went to England last night.//~부터 내린 비가 아직 그치지 않고 있다 It has been raining since last night.

간병(看病) nursing; tending (a sick person). ¶극진한 ~ careful nursing//그는 극진한 ~의 보람도 없이 어쩔재 죽었습니다 He died last night, all the care taken of him proving of no avail. **간병하다** nurse; tend; care for; attend on. ¶자지 않고 ~ sit up with a sick person.

간부(姦夫) an adulterer; a paramour. ¶~를 두다 cuckold [deceive] one's husband.

간부(姦婦) an adulteress; a paramour. ¶~의 남편 a cuckold.

간부(幹部) the executive members; the management; the leading [principal] members; the managing staff; the leaders; the governing body. ¶최고 ~ the top brass//회사의 ~ the executives of a company / (경영진) the management//~급에 있는 사람 a person in an executive position [on the executive] / an executive//~가 되다 become a leader.
● **간부 직원** officials in responsible posts. **간부 회의** an executive session [council]; a meeting of the managing staff. **간부 후보생** (육군의) a military cadet.

간사(幹事) 1 [일처리] administering affairs; management. 2 [일을 맡아서 처리하는 직무자] a manager; an executive secretary; (공공 기관의) a governor. ¶동창회의 ~ the secretary of an alumni association//그는 망년회의 ~로 일했다 He was in charge of arrangements for the year-end party.

간사하다(奸詐-) cunning; sly; foxy; craft; wily; deceitful; fawning. ¶간사한 놈 a foxy fellow. **간사히** cunningly; slyly; deceitfully; craftily.

간살 [아첨] flattery; adulation; sycophancy; toadyism; [교태] coquetry. ¶~ 떠는 adulatory / flattering//~부리다 [아첨하다] flatter / adulate / butter (a person) up / (구어) softsoap//그녀가 온갖 ~을 다 부려 호리도 그는 말러지 않았다 In spite of all her arts [wiles], he was not attracted to her.
● **간살쟁이** a flatterer; a sycophant; a toad-eater.

간살(間-) → 칸살

간상(奸商) a dishonest merchant; a crooked dealer; an illicit trader; a profiteer.
● **간상배** (a group of) racketeers.

간색(看色) [본보기를 봄] sampling; [눈비음으로 내놓는 물건] a sample. **간색하다** sample; test [judge] by a sample; assess by examining a small portion (of).

간색(間色) a compound [secondary] color; half tone; an intermediate [in-between] shade.

간석지(干潟地) a tideland; a dry beach; a beach at ebb tide; a tidal flat. ¶~를 개간하다 reclaim tidal land.

간선(間選) indirect election. ⇨ 간접 선거(⇨ 간접)

간선(幹線) (미) a trunk (line); (영) a main line; an artery of railroad traffic. ¶이 가도는 양국 간의 교통의 ~이다 This highway is an artery of communication between the two countries.
● **간선 도로** a principal [trunk] road; (영) an arterial road; (미) a boulevard.

간섭(干涉) 1 (참견함) interference; meddling; (타국의 내정 등의) intervention. ¶주제넘은 ~ an officious interference//외부의 ~ outside intervention//공동 ~ collective [joint] intervention//무력 ~ armed [military] intervention//3국 ~ the Triple [three-Power] Intervention//~을 받다 be

interfered (with) // ~을 받지 않다 be free from intervention. **간섭하다** interfere (in a matter / a person with); meddle (in); intervene (in); intrude oneself (into an affair); (구아) put [thrust] in one's oar; cut in. ¶남의 일에 ~ interfere in another's business // 내정을 ~ interfere in the internal [domestic] affairs (of another country) // 사생활을 ~ step into one's private life // 일일이 ~ meddle in everything // 쓸데없이 ~ make uncalled-for meddling // 내 일에 간섭하지 마라 Leave me alone. / Hands off my business. // 아이들에게는 너무 간섭하지 않는 것이 좋다 Children ought to be left alone [to themselves] sometimes. // 남의 일에 간섭하지 마라 Don't put [poke] your nose into other people's affairs.
2 [광파·음파 등의 겹침] interference.
● **간섭계** (-計) [물] an interferometer. **간섭색** [물] interference colors. **간섭자** an intervener. **간섭주의** interventionism; an interference policy.

간성 (干城) a bulwark; a stronghold; a defender; a safeguard; a tower of strength; [군인] a soldier; [집합적] soldiery. ¶국가의 ~ the bulwark of security to the state.

간소하다 (簡素-) simple; plain (and simple). ¶간소한 생활 a [the] simple life / plain living // 간소한 식사 a frugal meal // 간소한 옷차림을 하고 있다 be plainly dressed // 그의 집은 간소한 구조였다 His house was simply built. // 그들은 간소한 장례식을 치렀다 They held a simple funeral. **간소히** plainly; simply; with simplicity; (약식으로) informally; in an informal way. ¶~ 하다 simplify (a ceremony) / streamline (사무 등을).

간소화 (簡素化) simplification. ¶생활양식의 ~ simplification of one's way of life. **간소화하다** simplify (office procedure). ¶행정 기구를 ~ simplify the administration structure [setup] // 배달 과정을 ~ simplify a delivering process.

간수 keeping; safekeeping; custody; charge; storage. **간수하다** keep; save; store; take custody [charge] (of); put aside for future use. ¶소중히 ~ treasure (up) / lock away // 장 속에 간수해 두다 store (things) in a godown // 그것을 잘 간수해 둬라 Keep it in a safety place. // 그 서류는 한 씨가 간수하고 있다 The papers are in the custody of Mr. Han. // 이 책을 간수해 주시겠습니까 Will you please keep these books for me?

간수 (-水) bittern; brine.
간수 (看守) ➔ 교도관
간식 (間食) eating between meals; meals refreshments; a snack. ¶~으로 고구마를 먹다 eat sweet potatoes between meals / eat sweet potatoes for one's snack // 살찌고 싶지 않으면 ~을 삼가라 If you want to lose weight you'll have to stop eating between meals. **간식하다** eat (a snack) between meals; have a snack.

간신 (奸臣) a villainous retainer; a treacherous subject.
간신히 (艱辛-) [겨우] barely; narrowly; hardly; by the skin of one's teeth; by a (near) shave; [힘겹게] laboriously; with difficulty; [애써서] with an [much] effort; [근근이] just; only. ¶~ 도망치다 escape narrowly [by a·hairbreadth / by the skin of one's teeth] / have a narrow escape // ~ 이기다 win (a game) by a shave [narrow margin] // ~ 먹고 살아가다 make [earn] a bare living / eke out a scanty livelihood / rub along // ~ 기차를 잡았다 I barely managed to catch the train. // 그는 ~ 물에 빠지지 않고 살았다 He narrowly [barely] escaped drowning. / He had a narrow [hairbreadth] escape from drowning. // 그는 ~ 위기를 넘겼다 He got through the crisis with difficulty. // 그녀는 삯바느질로 ~ 생계를 유지하고 있었다 She eked out a living [made a bare living] by taking in sewing. // 그는 ~ 선거에 당선되었다 He was elected by a narrow majority. // 나는 발끝으로 서면 ~ 창에 닿는다 I can just reach the window on tiptoe. // ~ 목숨만은 구했다 I barely escaped death.

간악하다 (奸惡-) wicked; treacherous; villainous; knavish. ¶간악한 무리 a gang of scoundrels / rogues / rascals // 간악한 사람 a wicked person / a treacherous person / a traitor // 간악한 짓을 하다 do (a person) wrong / do a dishonest act / act dishonestly / commit injustice. **간악히** wickedly; treacherously.

간암 (肝癌) cancer of liver; liver cancer.
간언 (間言) mischief-making remarks; malicious gossip; estranging [alienating] words; sowing discord; mischievous gossip.

간언 (諫言) remonstrance; expostulation; admonition; [충고] advice; counsel. ¶~을 듣다 listen [yield] to (a person's) remonstrance // ~을 듣지 않다 give no ear to (a person's) expostulation // ~에 따르다 [따르지 않다] follow [reject] (a person's) advice // 나의 노(老)스승의 ~은 내 가슴에 와 닿았다 My old teacher's admonition came home to me [struck home]. // ~은 귀에 거슬리는 법이다 Good advice is [sounds] harsh to the ear. **간언하다** remonstrate [expostulate] (with); admonish (a person for his faults).

간염 (肝炎) [의] inflammation of the liver; hepatitis. ¶전염성 ~ infectious hepatitis // 혈청 ~ serum hepatitis [jaundice].
간엽 (肝葉) [생] the lobe of the liver.
간원 (懇願) (an) entreaty; solicitation; supplication; an earnest appeal; a petition (탄원). ¶그는 그들의 ~을 들어주었다 He granted [listened to] their entreaties. **간원하다** entreat [beseech / implore] (a person to do); beg earnestly; make an earnest appeal (to a person for something); solicit (for); supplicate (a person for). ¶그녀는 그에게 함께 가달라고 간원했다 She implored [entreated] him to go with her. / She begged him earnestly to accompany her. // 그들은 왕실의 기부를 간원했다 They solicited royal contributions.

간유 (肝油) (cod-)liver oil.
간음 (姦淫) adultery; illicit intercourse; (sexual) misconduct; fornication (미혼자의); [법] criminal conversation. **간음하다** commit adultery; have illicit intercourse (with); misconduct oneself; commit fornication (with); fornicate (with). ¶폭행 또는 협박으로 부녀를 간음한 자 [법] a person who, by violence or threat, has obtained carnal knowledge of a woman // 여자를 보고 음욕을 품는 자마다 마음에 이미 간음하였느니라 [성] Every one who looks at a woman lustfully has already

간이

committed adultery with her in his heart.
●**간음범** an adulterer(남자); an adulteress(여자). **간음죄** adultery.
간이(簡易) 〔관용어적〕 simple; easy; facile; handy.
●**간이 숙박소** (날품팔이 노동자용) day-laborers' lodgings[quarters]; (식사가 딸리지 않는) a rooming house[(영) a common lodging house]; (싸구려 여인숙) (미국 속어) a flop house. **간이식당** a quick-lunch room; a lunchroom; a chophouse; (셀프서비스식의) (영) a cafeteria[(미) a snack bar]; (즉석요리가 나오는) a fast-food restaurant; (카운터식의) a lunch counter; (열차 내의) a buffet. **간이식사** a light meal; a snack. **간이 재판소** a summary court. **간이 주택** a simple frame house; (조립식의) a prefabricated house; (미국 속어) a prefab; a Quonset hut.
간작(間作) 〔사이짓기〕 catch cropping; intercropping; (작물) a catch crop; 〔간접 소작〕 sharecropping. **간작하다** intercrop; grow (some vegetables) between the rows of another crop.
간장(-醬) ganjang; soy (sauce); (영) soya.
간장(肝臟) bowels and intestines; heart.
간장을 녹이다 charm; bewitch; captivate; fascinate; enslave. ¶그녀의 미소는 뭇 남성의 간장을 녹인다 Her smile captivates every man.
간장을 태우다 give (a person) trouble; cause anxiety to (a person); worry (a person). ¶그는 노상 부모의 간장을 태운다 He keeps his parents worried sick all the time.
간장이 타다 be deeply anxious [solicitous] (about); (사랑하여) burn (up) with love (for); be dying (for a woman).
간장(肝臟) 〔생〕 the liver. ¶~의[에 잘 듣는] hepatic / ~이 **나쁘다** I have liver trouble.
●**간장병** a liver disorder[complaint]; liver trouble; hepatitis; hepatopathia. ¶~의 liverish.
간절하다(懇切-) earnest; eager; fervent; ardent; sincere. ¶간절한 권고 earnest advice / 간절한 부탁 an earnest request / 간절한 마음 an ardent passion[love] / 간절한 소원 an earnest desire / one's fervent desire / one's ardent hope / 간절한 호소 an ardent [emotional] appeal // …하고 싶은 생각이 ~ be eager[impatient / anxious / dying] to (do) // 나도 가고 싶은 생각이 ~ I should very much like to go with you. / 한잔 생각이 ~ I'm thirsty for a drink. **간절히** eagerly; ardently; earnestly; heartily; sincerely. ¶~ 바라다 sincerely hope / desire earnestly / wish eagerly / ~ 권하다 urge (a person) strongly / strongly advise (a person to do) / ~ 부탁하다 entreat (a person to do) // ~ 호소하다 appeal to (the public) with great emphasis.
간접(間接) indirectness.
●**간접광**(-光) borrowed light. **간접 목적어** an indirect object. **간접 무역** indirect commerce[trade]. **간접비** (an) indirect cost; overhead costs; (생산의) indirect expenses. **간접 선거** indirect election; (미) (대통령 선출의) voting for the presidential electors. **간접세** an indirect tax; (물품세) an excise tax. **간접 조명** indirect illumination[lighting]. **간접 화법** the indirect speech[narration].
간접적(間接的) indirect; mediate; second-

hand; [말을 에둘러 하는] round-about; backhanded; oblique. ¶그는 ~으로 네 얘기를 했을 뿐이다 He made an indirect reference to you. / 그 일은 ~으로 들었다 I've heard about it indirectly. / I've got the information secondhand[at second hand]. // 그것은 우리나라의 경제에 ~으로 영향을 미칠 것이다 It will have an indirect influence on our economy. // 그를 ~으로 알고 있다 I know of him. / (친구 등을 통하여) I have heard of him.
간조(干潮) (an) ebb tide; low water [tide]. ¶~시에 at low tide [water] // 지금은 ~이다 The tide is out [down]. // 오후 8시에 ~가 된다 The tide will be on the ebb at 8 p.m.
●**간조선** a low-water level [line].
간주곡(間奏曲) 〔음〕 an interlude; an intermezzo (pl. ~s, -zi).
간주하다(看做-) regard (as); consider; think of (as); deem; reckon; count (as / for); look on [upon] (as); take (for). ¶법적으로 정당하다고 ~ give legal sanction (to) / legalize // 침묵을 승낙으로 ~ regard silence as consent // 요주의[위험] 인물로 ~ regard (a person) a dangerous [questionable] character / 다 해결된 것으로 ~ look upon (a matter) all squared up // 텔레비전 시청을 시간 낭비라고 ~ think of watching T.V. as a waste of time.
→ ¶최고 유력자의 한 사람으로 간주되다 be rated among the most influential members [men] // 그는 그 운동의 지도자로 간주된다 He is looked upon as a leader of the movement. // 불참자는 불합격으로 간주된다 Those who absent themselves will be considered to have failed in the examination. // 그 증거는 불충분한 것으로 간주되었다 The evidence was deemed inconclusive. // 그는 천재로 간주되고 있다 He is thought (to be) a genius.
간증(干證) 〔신앙 고백〕 a confession of faith; the profession of christianity; [범죄의 증인] an eyewitness. **간증하다** make profession of one's faith; confess; witness.
간지(干支) the sexagenary cycle; the zodiac signs.
간지럼 ticklish [tickling] sensation [feeling]; tickling; titillation. ¶~을 잘 타는 사람 a ticklish person.
간지럽다 1 (몸이) feel ticklish; feel a tickle. ¶간지러워하다 feel ticklish / [간지럼을 타다] be ticklish / be sensitive to tickling / 간지러워 못 견디다 be tickled to death // 온몸이 ~ I tickle all over. // 등 [귀 / 코 / 손바닥 / 발]이 ~ My back [ear / nose / palm / foot] tickles. // 그만둬, 간지러워 Stop! Don't tickle me!
2 [부끄럽다] be [feel] abashed; be shy; feel a touch of shame. ¶간지러운 수작 an obvious flattery / 낯간지러운 줄 모르다 lose one's shyness / be lost to the sense of shame // 낯이 ~ My face blushes with shame [uneasiness]. // 그처럼 칭찬을 받으니 낯이 ~ So much praise embarrasses me [makes me feel awkward]. // 이와 같은 작품으로 내가 상을 받다니 약간 낯이 ~ I feel a bit embarrassed to get a prize for a work like this.
간직하다 1 (물건을) keep; save; store; put aside; lay up; treasure (up); store [stow] away; tuck away (in a box); hide away (in a drawer). ¶소중히 ~ treasure (up) / lock away // 벽장 속에 ~ store (a thing) in a wall

closet // 훗날 쓰게 잘 간직해 두어라 Store it away for future use. // 네 병이 나을 때까지 이 자전거는 내가 간직하고 있겠다 I'll keep this bicycle until you get well. // 당신의 훌륭한 선물을 길이 간직하겠습니다 I shall long treasure your nice present.
2 [마음에 품다] harbor; entertain; cherish; keep; hold; hoard. ¶가슴속에 간직한 추억 memories enshrined in one's heart // 가슴속에 ~ keep (a thing) to oneself / bear in [within] mind // (가슴속에) 비밀을 ~ cherish a secret // 그 소녀는 그 일을 홀로 가슴속에 간직하고 있었다 The girl kept it all to herself. // 그는 그것을 추억 속에 고이 간직하였다 He treasured it in his memory.

간질(癎疾) [의] epilepsy; an epileptic fit(발작). ¶~을 일으키다 have an epileptic fit.
간질간질하다 feel creepy. ⇨근질근질하다
간질거리다 itch; feel ticklish. ⇨근질거리다
간질이다 tickle; titillate. ¶겨드랑이를 ~ tickle (a person) under his arm[at his armpit] / 발바닥을 ~ tickle the soles of (a person's) feet // 간질여서 웃기다 tickle a laugh out of (a person) // 남을 못 견디게 ~ tickle a person to death.

간책(奸策) a shrewd[dirty] trick; wiles; a sinister scheme[design]; a sly artifice. ¶~을 부리다 indulge in trickery / play a shrewd trick (on) / use wiles / scheme // ~에 말려[걸려] 들다 fall into (another's) snare / fall victim to a scheme // 그들은 ~을 부려 그를 함정에 빠뜨리려 했다 They schemed to trap him.

간척(干拓) land reclamation by drainage; inning. ¶아산만(牙山灣)의 ~ reclamation of the Asan Bay. **간척하다** reclaim (land) by drainage; drain off (a marsh). ¶호수를 ~ reclaim land from a lake.
● **간척 계획**[사업] a (land) reclamation program[project]. **간척 공사** reclamation work. **간척지** reclaimed land; innings.

간첩(間諜) a spy; an (espionage) agent; a secret agent; an emissary; espionage(행위). ¶경제 ~ an economic spy(사람) / economic espionage(일) // 고정 ~ a resident espionage agent // 군사 ~ a military spy // 무장 ~ an armed espionage // 대 ~ 대책 본부 the Counter-Espionage Operations // ~ 임무를 띠고 on a spy mission // ~을 보내다 send out a spy // ~을 색출하다 seek[hunt] out spies / dig up spies // ~ 혐의로 잡히다 be arrested under suspicion of being a spy.
● **간첩망** a network of spies; an espionage chain. **간첩선** a (North Korean) spy boat. **간첩죄** (the crime of) espionage.

간청(懇請) entreaty; solicitation; an earnest request; importunity; supplication; adjuration. ¶~에 의하여 at (a person's) earnest request / at (one's) solicitation // ~을 들어주다 listen to (a person's) entreaty / comply with (a person's) earnest request. **간청하다** entreat (a person to do); solicit (a person for); implore; supplicate; request earnestly; beg (earnestly). ¶허가를 ~ solicit (the authorities) for permission / request permission // 구명을 ~ supplicate (a person) to spare one's life // 원조를 ~ implore (a person) to give help / implore aid (from a person) // 우리 시(市)는 자매 도시에 대해 협력을 간청했다 Our city entreated[made an earnest request] to its sister city for cooper-ation.

간추리다 sum up; summarize; digest; epitomize; condense. ¶간추린 summarized / abridged / epitomized / 주장을 ~ epitomize an argument // 그것은 한마디로 간추려진다 It is summed up in a single word.

간취하다(看取-) [인지하다] perceive; notice; detect; find; see; grasp; [간파(看破)하다] see through (a trick).

간통(姦通) adultery; illicit intercourse [intimacy]; liaison; misconduct; [법] criminal conversation[(영) connection](약어 crim. con.). ¶기혼자와 독신자 간의 ~ single adultery // 기혼자끼리의 ~ double adultery. **간통하다** commit adultery[misconduct] (with); have illicit intercourse (with); have a liaison with.
● **간통자** an adulterer(남자); an adulteress (여자). **간통죄** criminal conversation; adultery.

간특하다(奸慝-) cunning; sly (as a fox); wily; artful; crafty; tricky; [속어] slick. ¶간특한 인간 a crafty[tricky] person / an old fox / a sly dog. **간특히** cunningly; craftily; artfully.

간파하다(看破-) penetrate (another's motive); see through (a fraud); read (another's thought); detect. ¶타인의 속셈을 ~ divine a person's thoughts // 사기꾼임을 ~ spot a shark[an impostor] // 한눈에 그가 위선자라는 것을 나는 간파했다 I saw at a glance that he was a hypocrite. // 우리는 한눈에 그의 속임수를 간파했다 We saw through his deceit at a glance. // 우리는 그의 변장을 간파했다 We penetrated his disguise. // 나는 그의 본심을 간파하기가 어렵다 It is difficult for me to read his true intentions.

간판(看板) **1** (상점의) a signboard; a sign; [광고판] (미) a billboard[(영) a hoarding]. ¶상점[이발소]의 ~ a store[hairdresser's] sign // 청과물상의 ~ a greengrocer's sign (board) // ~를 세워 놓은 a standing signboard // ~을 내걸다 put up[set up / hang out] a sign(board) / hang out a shingle(의사・변호사 등이) // ~에는 「한라 호텔」이라고 적혀 있었다 The sign read "Halla Hotel."
2 [겉으로 내세우는 방편] false front; a front (man); a figurehead; a dummy. ¶자선이라는 ~ 아래 under the cloak[in the disguise] of charity // ~ 노릇을 하다 serve as a front man[figurehead] // 우리 사장은 ~에 불과하다 Ours is just a president in name only. // 그 회사는 금융업을 ~으로 내걸고 있지만 실은 폭력단이다 That company has a moneylender's sign in front, but in actual fact they're gangsters.
3 [학벌] a school career; an academic career [background]. ¶~이 좋다 have a good[brilliant] academic career[background] // 그는 ~이 좋아서 출세했다 He has risen in the world with his brilliant academic background.
4 [인기 인물] a drawing card; an attraction; (미) a draw girl; a beauty lure; (극단 등의) the leading actor; the prima donna(여자). ¶저 예쁜 아이는 그 꽃집의 ~이다 That pretty girl is the florist's drawing card.
● **간판장이** a sign maker[painter].

간편하다(簡便-) convenient; simple; easy; handy; portable(휴대가 손쉬운). ¶간편한 방

간하다 법 an easy method / a simple and easy way // 간편한 옷 casual wear [clothes / attire] // 간편한 안내서 a handy guidebook // 간편한 테이프리코더 a conveniently-sized tape recorder // 간편한 생활을 하다 live a simple life // 가입 절차가 간편해졌다 The procedure for joining has been simplified. **간편히** simply; easily; conveniently. ¶짐을 ~ 꾸리다 pack things conveniently / pack things so that they will be handy.

간하다 season with salt [soy]; apply salt (to). ¶간장으로 살짝 간한 음식 food seasoned lightly with soy sauce.

간하다(諫-) remonstrate [expostulate] (with a king on his folly); admonish (one's superior against doing something); give (a king) candid [frank] advice. ¶…하지 않도록 remonstrate [reason] (with a person against …) // 간하는 말을 듣지 않다 give no ear to one's expostulation / turn a deaf ear to one's remonstration // 간하여 중지시키다 dissuade (a person from doing something).

간행(刊行) publication. **간행하다** publish; issue; bring out. ¶새 신문 [잡지]을 ~ start a new journal. ➔ ¶간행되다 be published / come out / appear // 영화에 관한 책이 영어로 간행되었다 A book on (the) movie has been published [has been brought out] in English. // 회보(會報)는 연 2회 간행된다 The bulletin is issued twice a year.
● **간행물** a publication. ¶정기 ~ a periodical. **간행본** a published book.

간헐(間歇) intermittence. ¶~적인 intermittent // ~적으로 내리는 비 an intermittent rain.
● **간헐열**(-熱) intermittent fever; ague; chill and fever. **간헐 유전** intermittent heredity; atavism. **간헐천 / 간헐 온천** a geyser; an intermittent fountain [spring].

간호(看護) nursing; care (of the sick); tending (a sick person). ¶극진한 ~ careful nursing // 그녀의 극진한 ~ 덕분으로 그는 완쾌했다 Thanks to her tender care [careful nursing], he recovered completely. // 그녀는 병원에서 극진한 ~를 받았다 She was well attended [looked after] in the hospital. **간호하다** nurse; tend (the sick and wounded); attend on (a sick person); care for. ¶자지 않고 ~ sit up with the sick / watch all night beside a sickbed / attend on a sick person all through the night // 그는 극진한 간호한 보람도 없이 어젯밤에 죽었다 He died last night, all the care taken of him proving of no avail. // 그녀는 남편을 간호하다 지쳐 쓰러지고 말았다 She broke down from the fatigue caused by nursing her husband (for such a long time).
● **간호병** a nurse; a hospital orderly; a medical corpsman; (미 해군) a corpsman. **간호사** (여자) a (hospital) nurse; a sick nurse; a sister; (남자) a male nurse [attendant]. ¶수(首)~ a chief [head / supervising] nurse // 수습 ~ (미) a practical nurse / (영) an unqualified nurse / a student nurse. **간호조무사** a nurse's aide. **간호학** the science of nursing; nursing science. **간호학교** a nurses' school [college]; a nursing school.

간혹(間或) [이따금] occasionally; at times; between times [whiles]; now and then; once in a while [way]; once in a long [great] while; at long [rare] intervals; on rare occasions. ¶~ 오는 손님 a casual [an occasional] visitor // ~ 있는 일 a rare occurrence / a thing of infrequent occurrence // 그는 ~ 들르다 drop in once in a while // 그는 ~ 술을 마신다 He takes a liquor occasionally. // 그도 ~ 농담할 때가 있다 He jokes between whiles. // ~ 도시는 견딜 수 없는 곳이 된다 At times the city becomes intolerable.

갇히다 be confined [shut up]; be kept indoors; be locked in; be imprisoned; be behind bars. ¶방 안에 ~ be confined in a room / be locked (up) in a room // 감옥에 ~ be put [landed] in prison / be sent to jail / (미) wear the stripes // 비에 ~ be kept [cooped up] within doors [indoors] by rain / be detained [kept in / shut up] by rain // 눈에 ~ be snowed in [up] / snowbound (기차 등이) // 비 때문에 온종일 집 안에 갇혀 있었다 The rain kept me indoors all day. // 감기로 지난 주일 꼬박 집에 갇혀 있었다 I have been confined in the house [kept in] with a cold for the past week.

갈가리 to [in] pieces. ➪가리가리

갈개 a small ditch; a drain; a gutter.

갈개꾼 [닥나무 껍질을 벗기는 사람] a person who skins paper mulberries; (훼방꾼) an interferer; a meddler; an obstructor.

갈개발 1 [연 귀퉁이의 종잇조각] two wedge-shaped tails of a kite. **2** [권세가에 붙어 세도 부리는 사람] a small man acting arrogantly through borrowed authority; an ass in a lion's skin; an hanger-on.

갈겨먹다 snatch (away) (from / off); seize; extort; wrest (from); take by force; tear (off / away) (a thing) from (a person).

갈겨쓰다 write hurriedly [carelessly]; scribble; scrawl; dash off. ¶편지를 ~ dash off a letter (to) // 몇 줄 ~ scrawl [scribble] a few lines (on a sheet of paper).

갈고리쇠 1 [갈고리 모양의 쇠] an iron hook. **2** [꼬부장한 성격의 사람] a perverse person [fellow]; a cross-grained person; (구어) a screwball; a crank; a crooked stick.

갈고랑이 a hook; a crook; a gaff. ¶~ 모양의 hooked / hook-shaped // ~로 상자를 걸다 hook a box.

갈고리 a hook. ➪갈고랑이

갈고쟁이 a hook made by forked branch.

갈구(渴求) a craving (for); a longing (for); an eager [earnest] desire (for); an ardent wish (for); thirst (for knowledge). **갈구하다** crave [yearn / thirst] for; long for [after] (fame); be thirsty after [for / of] (knowledge); hunger for [after] (affection); desire eagerly [earnestly].

갈근(葛根) the root of a kudzu [an arrow-root].

갈급증(渴急症) impatience; irritation; fretfulness. ¶~이 나다 be impatient / be irritable / be in suspense / be in a fret // 빨리 가르쳐 줘, ~이 나 죽겠어 Don't keep me in suspense, but let me know it at once.

갈기 a mane. ¶~가 있는 짐승 a maned beast.

갈기갈기 to pieces; into shreds. ¶~ 찢다 tear [rend] to pieces [ribbons / shreds / threads] / tear into strips / rip (the flag) into tatters // ~ 찢긴 torn in [to] pieces // ~ 찢기다 be torn to [be in] pieces [tatters / shreds].

갈기다 1 [때리다] beat; strike; knock; hit;

cuff; thrash; wallop; give[deal / deliver] (a person) a blow; punch; (구어) lick. ¶몽둥이로 ~ drub / club / cudgel∥채찍으로 ~ flog / lash / whip∥따귀를 ~ box[slap] (a person) on the ear / give (a person) a lick on the ear∥상판대기를 ~ strike (a person) across the face / punch (a person) in the nose∥호되게 ~ give (a person) a sound thrashing[good licking / hit (a person) hard∥녹초가 되게 ~ beat (a person) to a jelly[mummy] / beat (a person) up.
2 [쳐서 베다] cut; slash; strike a blow (with a sharp instrument). ¶낫으로 ~ cut with a sickle.
3 [글씨를 마구 쓰다] write hastily; scribble; scrawl; dash off. ¶두어 줄 ~ scrawl [scribble] a few lines (on a sheet of paper).
4 [총 등을 냅다 쏘다] fire (guns) by volleys; let fly[go] (with a rifle); loose off (a pistol).
5 relieve oneself[nature] indiscriminately. ⇨"깔기다
갈까마귀 [동] a jackdaw.
갈다¹ [바꾸다] renew; change (for a new one); replace (A by[with] B); substitute (B for A); attach[fix] anew. ¶이름을 ~ change one's name∥사람을 ~ replace (a person) by[with] (another)∥수건을 ~ get out a new towel / put a new towel into use∥탱크의 물을 ~ renew water in a tank∥더러운 셔츠를 깨끗한 것으로 갈아입다 change a dirty shirt for a clean one∥차를 갈아타다 change cars[carriages] / transfer (to another car)∥낡은 기계를 새것으로 갈 필요가 있다 The old machines need to be replaced by[with] new ones. / We need to replace the old machines with new ones.
갈다² **1** [칼 등을] whet; sharpen (a knife / a sword); grind (an axe); hone (a razor); strop (a razor). ¶칼(날)을 ~ sharpen a blade∥면도칼을 혁지에 ~ strap[strop] a razor / sharpen a razor on a strop∥숫돌에 칼을 ~ whet a knife on the whetstone.
2 [문지르다] polish; rub; file(줄로); grind (a lens); dress (stone); lap (a jewel). ¶먹을 ~ rub (down) an ink stick∥줄로 손톱을 ~ file one's fingernails∥보석을 ~ polish[cut] a gem.
3 (가루가 되게) grind[mill] (wheat) into[to] (flour); grind down; rub fine[into powder]; bray; pulverize; triturate. ¶곱게 ~ grind (wheat) to fine powder.
4 [이를] gnash; grate; grind; grit. ¶이를 ~ gnash[grind / grate] one's teeth.
갈다³ **1** [땅을 파 뒤집다] till; get (the soil) turned over; (미) plow; (영) plough; cultivate. ¶밭을 ~ till the field∥땅을 ~ till [cultivate] the land[soil]. **2** [곡물을 심다] plant; lay down. ¶밭에 밀을 ~ plant the field with[(미) to] wheat / lay down a field in wheat.
갈대 [식] a reed; a ditch reed. ¶여자의 마음은 ~와 같다 Woman is as fickle as a reed.∥사람은 ~에 지나지 않는다. 그러나 생각하는 ~다 Man is but a reed, but he is a thinking reed.
● **갈대꽃** reed flowers; the ears of a reed. **갈대발** a hanging screen made of reeds. **갈대밭** a field of reeds.
갈등(葛藤) trouble(s); discord; dissension; a complication; tangle; difficulties; [반목] a feud. ¶사랑[감정]의 ~ a love[an emotional] entanglement (between)∥~을 일으키다 cause[give rise to] complications (between) / breed discord[feud] (between)∥~을 해결 [해소]하다 disentangle / unravel (a complicated matter) / settle (a question)∥부모 자식 간의 정과 정의감의 ~에 시달리다 be caught[be torn] between family ties and one's sense of justice∥두 사람 사이에 ~이 생겼다 Trouble has arisen between them.∥그들의 혼인은 집안에 ~을 일으켰다 Their marriage caused difficulties[trouble / discord] between the two families.
갈라내다 1 [분할하다] divide; part; separate. ¶셋(세 부분)으로 ~ divide (something) into three (parts). **2** [이간시키다] estrange (people); alienate (a person) from (another); put a barrier (between). ¶부부 사이를 ~ separate husband and wife.
갈라붙이다 divide and assign[allocate].
갈라서다 1 [이혼·절연하다] divorce oneself (from); be divorced (from); break (with a person); break off relations (with a person); sever[cut] one's connection (with). ¶나는 그 친구와 갈라섰다 I have done[finished] with him. / (미) I'm through with him.∥그들은 결혼한 지 불과 2년 만에 갈라서고 말았다 They broke up only after two years of married life. **2** [따로 서다] stand apart; line up separately. ¶세 줄로 ~ line up into three separate group / stand apart in three rows / form three lines.
갈라지다 1 [째지다] split; cleave; fissure; [금이 가다] crack (a part); (땅 등이 크게) gape. ¶오랜 가뭄으로 갈라진 논 a rice paddy cracked from a long drought∥번개가 쳐서 나무가 둘로 갈라졌다 The tree was split in half by lightning.∥지진으로 땅이 갈라졌다 The ground was cracked by the earthquake.
2 [분할되다] be divided (into three parts); [분열되다] break up; split; rend (into two); part; [분리되다] branch off[out] (from); diverge (from); [분기(分岐)하다] fork (out). ¶세 부분으로 ~ be divided into three parts∥그 문제에 관해서 우리의 의견은 갈라졌다 We were divided in opinion on the subject.∥길은 여기서 세 갈래로 갈라진다 Here the road breaks[forks / divides / branches] into three. / 그 당은 여러 파로 갈라졌다 The party split into factions. / The party was rent into several factions.∥군중은 좌우로 갈라져서 일행을 통과시켜 주었다 The crowd parted right and left to make way for the party.
3 [사이가 틀어지다] be[become] estranged [alienated] (from); [헤어지다] part (from / with); part company with; be parted (from); be separated. ¶갈라져서 살다 live apart (from) / live separately∥그는 아내와 갈라졌다 He has left his wife. / He has separated from his wife.
갈락토오스 [화] galactose.
갈래 [분기(分岐)] a fork (of a road); [분파] a branch; an offshoot; a sect(종파); (당내의) a faction; a fraction; [구분] a division; a section. ¶두 ~ 길 a cross-road(s) / 세 ~ 진 trifurcate(d) / three-forked∥~가 지다 be forked / bifurcate / be divided into two branches∥여러 ~로 나뉘다 be divided into several parts[sections].

갈륨

● **갈래꽃** [식] a schizopetalous flower.
갈륨 [화] gallium.
갈리다¹ [분리되다] be divided (into); (be) split (into); be parted; separate; [분기(分岐)하다] branch off (from); be forked; fork (into). ¶남과 북으로 ~ be divided into north and south // 학생들은 작은 그룹으로 갈렸다 The students were divided into small groups. // 그 문제에 대해서는 구구하게 의견이 갈렸다 Opinions were divided on the issue. // 그 당은 세 파로 갈렸다 The party (was) split into three factions. // 여기서 샛길이 간선 도로에서 갈린다 Here a bypath branches off from the main road. // 경찰대는 두 갈래로 갈려 범인을 추적했다 The policemen separated into two groups to chase the criminal.
갈리다² 1 [(사람·물건이) 바뀌다] be changed (for); be replaced. ¶우리 담임선생님이 갈렸다 A new teacher has taken over our class. // 국무장관이 갈렸다 The Secretary of State has been replaced. 2 [(다른 것으로) 갈게 하다] get (a person) to change; have (a person) renew; have [get] (something) replaced. ¶구두창을 ~ have one's shoes resoled // 의자의 천을 ~ have a chair upholstered.
갈리다³ 1 [갈려지다] (칼 등이) be whetted; be ground; be sharpened; (옥돌 등이) be polished; be rubbed; be filed; (곡식 등이) be ground. ¶이 밀은 잘 [곱게] 갈린다 This wheat grinds [is ground] well [fine]. // 그것은 숫돌에 갈면 잘 갈린다 If it is whetted on a whetstone it will become sharp. 2 [갈게 하다] make (a person) whet [grind / hone]; get [have] (a knife / a sword) sharpened; (옥돌 등을) make (a person) polish; have (a person) rub; get (a person) to file.
갈리다⁴ 1 [(땅이) 갈려지다] be plowed [(영) ploughed]; get cultivated; be tilled; be under cultivation. 2 [(땅을) 갈게 하다] make (a person) plow [(영) plough]; have (a person) cultivate; get (a person) to till. ¶머슴에게 밭을 ~ have one's servant plow the field.
갈림길 1 [갈린 길] a branch road; a side road; a forked road; the fork of a road. ¶~에 이르다 come to the fork of a road // ~에서 오른쪽으로 접어들다 take the right-hand fork. 2 [기로(岐路)] turning point; a crossroad(s). ¶생사의 ~에서 헤매다 hover between life and death // 여기가 승패의 ~이다 This is the dividing line between victory and defeat. / Whether we win or not hangs [depends / hinges] on this point.
갈마들다 take turns; alternate; come on by turns; take by spell. ¶슬픔과 기쁨이 ~ have a mingled feeling of joy and sorrow // 만조와 간조는 갈마든다 The flood and ebb tides alternate with each other.
갈망 [수습] control; [처리] dealing; management; conduct; [뒤처리] setting (matters) right; settlement. **갈망하다** [수습하다] control; deal [cope] with; handle; [처리하다] manage (a matter); conduct (business); [뒤처리하다] settle; set (matters) right; wind up; deal with the aftermath.
갈망 [渴望] an earnest [eager] desire (for); an ardent wish (for); a craving [longing / thirst] (for). ¶명성에 대한 그의 ~을 풀어 줄 수 있는 것은 아무것도 없었다 Nothing could appease his thirst [craving] for fame. **갈망하다** crave (fame); long for [after]; crave [yearn / thirst] for; be thirsty after [for / of]; be eager [anxious] for; desire eagerly [earnestly]. ¶그들은 자유를 열렬히 갈망하고 있다 They have intense aspirations toward liberty. // 그들은 도서관이 생기기를 갈망하고 있다 They badly want [are eager for] a library. // 그는 부를 갈망하고 있다 He thirsts for [craves (for)] wealth. // 우리들은 평화를 갈망하고 있다 We are longing for peace.
갈매¹ [짙은 초록색] deep green (colo(u)r).
갈매² [열매] fruit of the (Dahurian) buckthorn.
● **갈매나무** [식] the Dahurian buckthorn.
갈매기 [동] a sea mew; a mew gull; a common gull; a sea gull; [군인 사병의 계급장] a chevron; a stripe.
갈무리 [정돈·간수] putting (a thing) away in good order; [마무리] finishing touches [strokes]. **갈무리하다** [정돈·간수하다] put [lay] (a thing) away [up] in good order; [마무리하다] finish (off / up); get (a thing) finished [done].
갈바람 a west wind.
갈밭 a field of reeds. ⇨ **갈대밭**(⇨갈대)
갈보 a prostitute; a harlot; a whore. ¶~ 노릇을 하다 go [live] on the street / walk the streets / prostitute oneself / practice prostitution / sell oneself for money.
갈비 1 a rib; (집합적) the ribs; [의] a costa (*pl.* -tae). ¶~의 costal. 2 (요리용) a *galbi*; a rib. ¶돼지 ~ ribs of pork // 쇠~ ribs of beef // ~를 굽다 roast [broil / grill] a rib. 3 [말라깽이] a skinny [lean / weedy / scrawny] person; a (living) skeleton; a mere [walking] skeleton; a bag of bones. ¶이봐, ~씨 Hey, skinny!
● **갈비뼈** a rib. ⇨ 늑골 **갈비찜** galbijjim; beef rib stew; steamed short-ribs. **갈비탕** galbitang; beef-rib soup. **갈빗대** a rib. ¶~를 부러뜨리다 break a rib / fracture a rib.
갈색(褐色) brown. ¶짙은 ~ dark brown / olive brown / umber / dun // 연한 ~ a light brown (color) // ~이 도는 brownish // ~ 눈 a brown eye // ~ 피부 brown skin / (햇볕에 탄) tanned skin // ~으로 되다 [하다] brown.
● **갈색 반점** chloasma. **갈색 인종** the brown races.
갈수기 (渴水期) the dry [low water] season; a period of water shortage [famine].
갈수록 as time goes on [by]; with the lapse [passage] of time; in the process of time; [할수록] the more [-er] ... the more [-er] ...; the more ... the less. ¶날이 ~ as days go by / as the days roll on // 해가 ~ with the year / as the years go on // ~ 해가 짧아진다 The days are getting shorter. // ~ 더위가 심해진다 It is growing warmer and warmer. / It is growing warmer every day. // 그가 더욱 그리워진다 As time goes on I miss him more and more.
갈수록 태산 (속담) Things go from bad to worse.; Things are worse than ever.; Things get worse and worse.; Out of the frying pan into the fire.
갈아대다 replace (an old one with a new one); put in a new one (as a replacement); repaper (a screen); recover; reupholster (a chair); renew (a plaster). ¶방의 공기를 ~

let fresh air into a room // 구두창을 ~ resole shoes // 그 의자는 천을 갈아대야 한다 The chair wants a new seating. // 그는 제2장을 새로 써 원고와 갈아댔다 He put in a newly written chapter in place of chapter two.

갈아들다 take the place of; take (another's) place; renew; replace; supplant. ¶새 식모가 갈아들었다 A new housemaid has replaced the old one. // A 씨 대신 B 씨가 새 국장으로 갈아들었다 Mr. A has been succeeded by Mr. B as (the) director (of the bureau).

갈아들이다 replace (a person) with (another); change (a person); substitute (a person). ¶가정부를 ~ take on [hire] a new housemaid // 그들은 해마다 가정교사를 갈아들인다 They change a tutor for their child every year.

갈아붙이다 attach [fix] anew; renew; change (for a new one). ¶책 표지를 ~ recover a book / renew the cover of a book // 이 의자는 바닥을 갈아붙여야겠다 This chair wants reseating.

갈아입다 change (one's clothes). ¶갈아입을 옷 a change of clothes / spare clothes // 갈아입을 옷 한 벌 없이 without a change of clothes // 옷을 갈아입고 in different clothes // 나들이옷으로 ~ change into one's best clothes [Sunday best] // 옷을 ~ change one's clothes // (군인이) 사복으로 ~ get back into civilian clothes // 옷을 갈아입으러 가다 go for a change (of clothes) // 급히 ~ make a quick change // 새 옷으로 갈아입히다 put a new dress (on) // 더러운 스커트를 깨끗한 것으로 ~ change a soiled skirt for a clean one // 그녀는 목욕하고 옷을 갈아입은 다음 외출하였다 Having bathed and changed, she went out. // 갈아입을 옷을 가지고 왔느냐 Did you bring a change (of clothes)? // 우리는 계절의 변화에 따라 옷을 갈아입는다 We change to a different set of clothing at the turn of the seasons. / When the seasons change, we change out wardrobe.

갈아주다 [물건을 사다] buy; purchase; get; take. ¶한 가게의 물건만 ~ patronize [trade only at] a store.

갈아타다 change (cars [trains / planes] at); transfer (to another car); (배를) tranship; change (for another train / to another line). ¶갈아타는 역 a station for changing cars / a junction (station) / a transfer point [stop] // 다른 배로 ~ transfer oneself to another ship // 다른 버스로 ~ switch to another bus // 기차를 세 번 ~ have three changes of train // 대전에서 기차를 ~ make railway connection at Daejeon // 용산에서 원주행 [경원선]을 ~ change at Yongsan for Wonju [to the Gyeongwon Line] // 목포에서 배를 갈아타는 것이 좋습니다 You may transship [take another boat] at Mokpo. // 여러분 갈아타 주십시오 All change. // (미) All out [off]! // 수원행 손님은 갈아타십시오 You must change (cars here) for Suwon. / (게시) Change here for Suwon.

갈음 substituting; replacing; switching; changing. **갈음하다** substitute; replace; change; renew.

갈이[1] [새것으로 바꿈] changing; replacement; remodeling. ¶구두창 ~ resoling shoes // 구두굽 ~ reheeling shoes.

갈이[2] **1** [논밭을 갈기] plowing; (영) ploughing; tilling; cultivating. ¶밭~ plowing of a field. **2** [넓이] the acreage that can be plowed by one person in (a given number of days). ¶사흘~ the acreage that can be plowed by one person in three days.

갈잎 1 fallen [dead] leaves. ⇨가랑잎 **2** leaves of an oak (tree). ⇨떡갈잎

갈조류(褐藻類) [식] brown algae.

갈증(渴症) **1** [목마름] thirst. ¶~을 나게 하는 음식 thirsty food // ~이 나다 feel thirsty // ~이 나게 하다 cause [produce] thirst // ~이 몹시 나다 be parched with thirst / be very thirsty // ~을 풀다 quench [appease / slake / relieve] one's thirst (with). **2** impatience; irritation. ⇨갈증

갈지자걸음(-之字-) a tottering step [gait / walk]; staggering [reeling] gait; a tipsy lurch. ¶~을 걷다 totter / reel (along) drunkenly / walk zigzag [in zigzags] / walk with unsteady gait / stagger (along) / walk with a staggering gait // 그들은 ~으로 거리를 걸어갔다 They went reeling down the street. // 그는 술에 취하여 ~을 걸었다 He walked zigzag under the influence of drink. // 술 취한 사람이 ~으로 길을 건너갔다 The drunken man lurched across the street.

갈지자형(-之字形) zigzag; a Z shape. ¶~의 지그재그 ~으로 나아가다 zigzag / go zigzag / ~으로 행진[데모]을 하다 snake-dance / stage a snake-dance.

갈참나무 [식] a white oak.

갈채(喝采) [환영의 목소리와 박수] applause; [환성] cheers; [환영·칭찬의 환호성] acclamation(s); [열렬한 찬사] plaudits; (자연적으로 터지는) an ovation. ¶~ 속에 amid cheers / (elect [carry a motion]) by acclamation // 터져 나오는 ~ a burst of applause / 열광적인 ~ enthusiastic applause / 그칠 줄 모르는 ~ round after round of cheers / prolonged applause // ~에 답하다 acknowledge applause [cheers] // ~를 받다 win [catch / draw / elicit] applause / receive [be accorded] an ovation / (미) get a (good) hand (박수갈채) / 기립 ~를 받다 win [receive] a standing ovation (from) // ~로 맞이하다 greet [receive] (a person) with (loud) applause / receive (a person) with acclamations // 그의 연기는 만장의 ~를 받았다 His performance won the applause of the whole house. // 그는 떠나갈 듯한[우레와 같은] ~를 받으며 단상에 올랐다 He stepped onto the platform amid a storm of cheers [applause]. // 그는 ~에 답하여 소품을 연주하였다 He acknowledged the cheers of the audience by playing a short piece. // 청중은 대통령의 연설에 ~를 보냈다 The audience applauded the President's address. // 장내가 떠나갈 듯한 ~였다 The hall echoed with applause. **갈채하다** applaud; cheer; give cheers; acclaim; shout applause; give an ovation. ¶총기립하여 ~ give (a person) a standing ovation / 장내가 떠나갈 듯이 ~ cheer (a person) to the rafters.

갈철석(褐鐵石) [광] limonite.

갈취(喝取) blackmail(ing); extortion by threats; exaction by threats; (미국 속어) a shake-down; (미국 속어) racketeering. **갈취하다** extort (money from a person) (by intimidation [threats]); practice extortions; blackmail; levy blackmail on (a person);

pinch; squeeze out; (미국 속어) racketeer. ¶금품을 ~ blackmail (a person) of his money and valuables / blackjack money and other valuables out of (a person) // 범죄자는 남자의 아내에게 그 사진을 주겠다고 으름장을 놓아 불쌍한 그에게서 금품을 갈취할 수 있었다 By threatening to give his wife the photograph, the criminal was able to screw money and other valuables out of the poor man. ➔ ¶돈을 갈취당하다 be blackmailed.
● **갈취자** blackmailer; racketeer.
갈치 [동] a hairtail; a cutlassfish; a scabbard fish.
갈퀴 a (bamboo) rake. ¶~로 낙엽을 긁어모으다 rake together dead [fallen] leaves.
갈탄 (褐炭) lignite; brown coal; wood coal.
갈파 (喝破) 1 [남의 이론 등을 뒤엎음]. **갈파하다** overthrow [overturn / explode / disprove] (a theory); knock the bottom out of (a theory). 2 [진리를 밝혀 말함] proclamation; pronouncement (of truth). **갈파하다** declare; affirm; proclaim; expound; pronounce. ¶지구는 둥글다고 갈파한 이는 누구인가 Who was it that proclaimed the earth was round?
갈팡질팡하다 1 [헤매다] move about in confusion; fool [knock] about [(미) around]; hang [wander / linger] about.
2 [당황하다] be flurried; be confused; be bewildered; be at a loss; be in a hurry-scurry. ¶갈팡질팡하여 confusedly / in confusion / in a flurry // 우리는 어느 길로 가야 할지 몰라 갈팡질팡하였다 We were at a loss which way to go. // 우리가 갈팡질팡하던 중에 이 일이 벌어졌다 This happened in the midst of all our confusion and bewilderment.
3 [주저하다] hesitate; vacillate; waver; hover. ¶두 의견 사이에서 ~ vacillate between two opinions // 꼭 필요한 때에 결단을 못 내리고 ~ hover on the brink of a decision // 우리는 집을 살지 임차할지 여러 해 동안 갈팡질팡하다가 결국 토지를 소유하는 편이 더 낫다는 결정을 내렸다 After years of hovering between buying and renting a house, we decided at last that it was better to own property.
갈포 (葛布) ko-hemp cloth; cloth woven of kudzu fiber.
● **갈포벽지** ko-hemp wallpaper.
갈피 1 [책장 등의 사이] a space between layers [folds / leaves]. ¶~에 돈을 넣어 두다 put money between the leaves of a book // 책장을 넘기다가 ~에서 그 사진을 발견하였다 I found that picture while I was turning over the leaves of a book. 2 [일의 어름] an interval (of / in / between); an interstice; [요점] the point; the sense; the thread (of meaning). ¶~를 못 잡다 cannot make head or tail (of a thing) / cannot catch [grasp] the point (of a subject) // 너의 이야기는 무슨 말인지 ~를 못 잡겠다 I can't catch [see] your point at all. / I can make neither head nor tail of what you say.
갈피갈피 (between) leaf after leaf; in every leaf; fold after fold; layer after layer; page after page. ¶옷을 ~ 뒤져 보다 search through the clothes one by one // 책을 ~ 넘기다 turn over [go through] the pages [leaves].
갉다 1 [(이·손톱·날카로운 도구 등으로) 깔짝깔

짝 문지르다] gnaw (at / on / through); nibble (at) (쥐 등이); scratch. ¶각설탕을 ~ nibble at a cube of sugar // 쥐가 벽 [상자]을 갉아 구멍을 내었다 The rats have gnawed a hole through a wall [in the box]. 2 [(갈퀴 등으로) 긁어모으다] rake up [together]; scrap together [up]; gather up. ¶낙엽을 갈퀴로 ~ rake together fallen leaves. 3 [남의 재물을 훑어 들이다] extort; squeeze; exploit. 4 [헐뜯다] find fault (with); cavil [carp at (another's) faults; pick holes in (a person's) coat; (미국 구어) pick on (a person / a thing).
갉아먹다 [빼앗아 가지다] extort; squeeze; exploit; (미국 속어) swear (one's employees). ¶돈을 ~ extort [squeeze] money from (a person) / screw money out of (a person).
갉작거리다 scratch repeatedly. ⇨ 긁적거리다
감¹ [과실의 하나] a persimmon. ¶곶~ a dried persimmon // 단~ a sweet persimmon // 떫은 ~ an astringent persimmon // 익은 ~ a ripe persimmon // 씨 a persimmon stone.
감² 1 [본바탕이 되는 재료] (a) material; matter; stuff; [천] texture; weave; fabric. ¶양복~ suit materials / suiting // 옷~ dress material / dress [clothing] fabrics // 좋은 ~으로 옷을 짓다 tailor with good materials. 2 [적격자] a suitable person; a man fit for the post. ¶훌륭한 사윗~ the most suitable man for one's son-in-law / a man who would make a good son-in-law / a likely son-in-law // 사장~ a man fit for presidency. 3 [옷감의 단위] a pattern. ¶모직 양복 한 ~ a pattern of woolen cloth.
감 (感) 1 [느낌] feeling; sense; sensation (feeling 쪽이 더 주관적); [인상] an impression. ¶만족 [적막 / 행복] ~ a feeling of satisfaction [loneliness / happiness] // 정의 [죄악] ~ a sense of justice [guilt] // …로[-ㄴ] ~이 있다 [들다] it gives the feeling that … / it feels [seems] like // …로[-ㄴ] ~을 주다 feel / be moved [impressed] / it feels like / strike (impress] (a person) as … / give (a person) an impression of … // 그는 책임~이 강하다 He has a strong sense of responsibility. // 완전히 겨울이 된 ~이 든다 I feel the touch of the cold season everywhere. // 그의 어조에는 얕잡아 보는 ~이 있었다 There was a touch [smack] of condescension in his tone. // 이 설명은 너무 자세한 ~이 있다 This explanation is rather too detailed. // 이 산들을 보니 한국에 돌아간 ~이 든다 Seeing these mountains I feel as if I were back in Korea. // 그것은 내게 이상한 ~을 주었다 [그것을 보고 이상한 ~이 들었다] It struck me as strange. / I was struck by the strangeness of the thing. // 이미 때늦은 ~이 있다 It gives the feeling you came a day (too late) after the fair.
2 [통신 기기의 감도] reception. ¶산지에서는 라디오의 ~이 좋지 않다 Radio reception is not good in mountainous districts.
감가 (減價) [할인] reduction of [in] price; (a) price reduction; depreciation; a discount; [할인한 값] a reduced price; a discounted price. **감가하다** reduce the price (of); depreciate; discount.
● **감가상각** (一償却) [경] depreciation. ¶~비 depreciation cost.
감각 (感覺) 1 [감각 기관을 통한 느낌] sense;

sensation; feeling; sensibility. ¶평형 the sense of balance[equilibrium]. // 시간[거리] ~ one's sense of time[distance] // 그는 그녀의 손을 잡았을 때의 따뜻한 ~이 아직도 느껴졌다 He still remembered the sensation of warmth he felt when he touched her hand. // 너무 추위 손발에 전혀 ~이 없어졌다 It was so cold that I lost all feeling in my hands and feet. / It was so cold that my hands and feet were numb. // 그의 다리는 ~이 없다 He has no feeling in the legs.
2 [사물을 느끼는 마음의 작용] sense. ¶예술적[음악적] ~ one's artistic[musical] sense // 미적(美的) ~ one's sense of beauty / one's (a) esthetic sense // ~이 둔하다 have dull senses / be insensitive (to) // ~이 예민하다 have keen[fine] senses / be (highly) sensitive (to) / be easily affected by (things) // 그에게는 도덕적 ~이 결여되어 있다 He lacks a moral sense [a sense of morality]. // 그녀는 음악[색채]에 대한 ~이 있다 She has an ear for music[an eye for color]. // 그는 젊은이다운 신선한 ~으로 현대 사회를 분석한다 He analyzes modern society with a fresh perceptivity[perceptiveness] typical of youth.
● **감각 기관** [생] a sense[sensory] organ; a sensory; receptor. **감각론** sensationalism; sensualism; aesthetics. **감각 상실** an(a)esthesia. **감각 세포** a sensory cell. **감각 신경** [생] a sensory nerve.

감각적(感覺的) [감각의] sensible; [감각에 호소하는] sensuous; [육체적 감각의] sensual.

감감(무)소식(−無消息) no news for a long time; having heard nothing for a long time. ¶그는 한번 다녀간 뒤로 ~이다 Nothing has been heard from him (for a long time) since he dropped in on me some time ago.

감감하다 1 [거리가] faraway; far off[away]; remote; [시간·차이 등이] far above[beyond]; long before. ¶감감한 옛날 a long time ago / remote antiquity // 감감한 수평선 the far horizon // 밀린 일을 다 끝내려면 아직 ~ It will be long before I can clear up belated business. // 그의 지식을 따라가려면 아직 ~ He is so far above us in his knowledge. // 바다 위에 감감하게 흰 돛이 보인다 A white sail is seen far out on the sea.
2 [기억·지식 등이] entirely forgotten; ignorant (of). ¶그 사람에 대해서는 ~ I don't know him at all[from Adam]. // 나는 그 일을 감감하게 잊고 있었다 It has entirely slipped from my mind[slipped my memory]. / I clean forgotten it.
3 [소식이] hear nothing from (a person); have no news from (a person); receive no word from (a person). ¶한번 간 뒤로 그 사람한테서 소식이 ~ Nothing has been heard from him since he left.

감개무량하다(感慨無量−) be filled with deep emotion; A thousand emotions crowd on one's mind; One's heart is full. ¶옛 스승을 10년 만에 뵙게 되어 감개무량하였다 My heart was full[I was filled with deep emotion. / I was deeply moved] when I saw my old teacher for the first time in ten years. // 지난날을 회상하니 ~ When I look back upon the past, a thousand emotions crowd on[well in] my mind.

감격(感激) **1** [격동] deep emotion; strong impression[feeling]. ¶~의 눈물을 흘리다 be moved to tears // 당신이 결정되는 순간의 ~이 새롭게 그의 가슴에 되살아났다 He recalled with renewed emotion the moment he had learned of his victory in the election. **감격하다** be deeply moved[touched] (by); be deeply impressed (with / by); be inspired (with); be carried away with emotion. ¶나는 그들의 친절에 감격하였다 I was deeply moved[touched] by their kindness. // 그는 처음 본 연극에 감격하여 배우가 되기로 결심하였다 Inspired by the first play he had ever seen, he decided to become an actor. →¶감격시키다 impress / move[touch / affect] (another's) heart deeply // 세계 평화를 호소하는 그의 연설은 청중을 감격시켰다 His speech advocating world peace moved the hearts of [deeply impressed] the audience.
2 [감사] a strong sense of gratitude; deep gratitude; heartfelt thanks. **감격하다** be very grateful; show gratitude.

감격적(感激的) moving; touching; impressive; dramatic. ¶~인 장면 a dramatic[moving / touching / soul-stirring] scene.

감관(感官) a sense[sensory] organ; a sensory.

감광(感光) exposure to light; sensitization. **감광하다** be exposed to light(감광되다). →¶감광시키다 expose (to light) // 필름이 감광되었다 The film has been exposed to light.
● **감광계** a sensitometer(사진의); an actinometer(화학선의). **감광도** (photo)sensitivity (of a film). ¶~가 높은 필름 highly sensitive film. **감광약** [화][사진] a (photo)sensitizer. **감광제 / 감광 유제**(乳劑) a sensitive emulsion. **감광지**(−紙) (photo)sensitive [sensitized] paper. **감광판** a sensitive plate. **감광 필름** a sensitive film.

감국(甘菊) [식] a mother chrysanthemum.

감군(減軍) the reduction of armed forces; a cut in the armed forces; a military manpower reduction; an arms cut[reduction]; a cutback in military strength. **감군하다** cut [reduce] armed forces[military manpower].

감귤(柑橘) [식] a tangerine; a mandarin.
● **감귤류** citrus fruits; oranges.

감극(減極) [수] the inferior limit; [전] depolarization.
● **감극제**(−劑) a depolarizer.

감금(監禁) confinement; imprisonment; detention in custody. ¶독방 ~ solitary confinement // 불법 ~ illegal[unlawful] detention / false imprisonment. **감금하다** imprison; confine; detain (a person) in custody; place (a person) in confinement; lock up. ¶그들은 아이를 방에 감금하였다 They confined the child in the room. →¶그는 독방에 감금되어 있었다 He was kept in solitary confinement. / He was placed under solitary confinement.

감기(感氣) a cold; (유행성) influenza; (구어) the flu. ¶기침 ~ a cold on the chest[lungs] // 코 ~ a cold in the head[nose] / a head cold // 가벼운 ~ a slight cold // 지독한 ~ a bad[severe] cold // ~가 들다[에 걸리다] catch[take / get] (a) cold // ~ 기운이 있다 have a slight[a touch of] cold // ~ 든 목소리 a husky[hoarse / nasal] voice[caused by a cold](nasal은 코 먹은 소리) // ~가 떨어지지 않다 can't get rid of[shake off / throw off] one's cold // ~에 걸려 열이 있다 get a fever

감기다

with a cold / be feverish with a cold // 그는 심한 ~에 걸려 있다 He has a bad cold. // 그는 ~로 누워 있다 He is in bed with a cold. / He is laid up[is down] with a cold. // ~가 유행하고 있다 There's a lot of flu about. // 나는 ~가 다시 든 것 같다 I seem to have caught a second[fresh] cold. / I am getting a cold again[twice]. // 친구에게서 ~가 옮았다 My friend has given me his cold. / I've caught a cold from my friend. // ~가 들려고 할 때는 무리한 일을 하지 않도록 해라 You should not overwork when you are coming down with a cold. // ~는 만병의 근원이다 A cold may develop into all kinds of illness(es).
감기 고뿔도 남을 안 준다(속담) be stingy; be niggardly; be closefisted; screw; pinch and scrape.
● **감기약** a medicine for cold; a cold remedy; (정제) cold tablets.

감기다[1] 1 (눈이) (one's eyes) be shut[closed] of their own accord (of themselves). ¶졸려서 눈이 ~ be so sleepy (that) one's eyes are falling shut / feel one's eyes heavy. 2 (눈을) make (a person's) eyes fall shut; shut [close] (a person's) eyes. ¶죽은 사람의 눈을 ~ close the eyes of a dead person.

감기다[2] 1 (감아지다) (실·끈 등이) be wound [rolled] (up); be coiled (around); (덩굴 등이) twine together; get twisted[wound] round; twist about. ¶실이 실패에 감긴다 Thread is wound on a reel. 2 (실·끈 등을 감게 하다) make[let] (a person) wind[roll / coil] (something) around. ¶그에게 시계태엽을 ~ have him wind the clock. 3 (옷이 몸에 달라붙다) be[get] caught in (a roller, a wringer, a wipe, etc.); cling[stick] to; hang on to. ¶젖은 옷이 몸에 ~ wet clothes cling to one's body // 그녀의 긴 옷자락이 다리에 감겼다 Her feet got caught in the train of her dress.

감기다[3] (머리·몸을) wash[bath(e)] (a person); make (a person) wash[bath]. ¶어린애의 머리를 ~ wash a baby's hair.

감나무 a persimmon tree.
감나무 밑에 누워도 삿갓 미사리를 대어라(속담) No pains, no gains.; No mill, no meal.
감나무 밑에 누워서 홍시 떨어지기를 기다린다(속담) One expects larks to fall ready roasted into his mouth.

감내하다(堪耐-) endure; persevere; stand (up to). ¶감내할 수 없는 unendurable / beyond endurance[one's perseverance] // 못 시련을 ~ stand[go through] many trials // 그들은 굶주림을 감내하고 계속 행진했다 They endured their hunger and marched on.

감다[1] (눈을) shut[close] (one's eyes). ¶눈을 감고 기도하다 give[say] one's prayers, with one's eyes shut.

감다[2] (씻다) wash; bath(e). ¶미역을 ~ bathe (in a river, in the sea, etc.) / have a dip / have a swim // 머리를 ~ wash one's hair.

감다[3] (실·끈 등을) wind[coil / twine / bind / tie] (something) round (another thing); reel. ¶실을 실패에 ~ wind thread on[to] a reel / wind a reel with thread / roll thread round a reel / reel (thread) // 털실을 공처럼 ~ wind wool into a ball / 연줄을 감다 reel in the string of a kite // 뼌 다리에 붕대를 ~ swathe a broken limb in bandage // 감은 것을 풀다 unroll / uncoil // 그는 재빨리 낚시

줄을 감았다 He rapidly reeled in the line. 2 (옷을 입다) put on; wear; be clothed[clad / dressed] (in); be wrapped[enveloped] (in). ¶몸은 누더기를 감고 있을지언정 마음은 깨끗하다 He is (clad) in rags, but is pure in heart.
3 (뱀 등이 서리서리 사리다) wrap coils around (a prey); loop (a victim) in several coils; throw turns of (its) body around (a prey). ¶그 방울뱀은 먹이를 몸으로 칭칭 감았다 The rattlesnake wound itself round a victim.

감당하다(堪當-) be equal to; be capable of carrying out[discharging / performing]; be up to (doing); be fit for (a job); be competent (to do); be able to fulfill the duties (of). ¶감당하지 못하다 be unfit for / be unequal to / be beyond one's capacity[power] / be too much for (one) / be beyond one's control // 그 친구라면 무슨 일이든 감당할 수 있을 것이다 He can fill any official. / He is equal to any task. // 이 일은 내가 감당할 수 없다 This task is beyond my power[depth]. // 그는 그 직책을 감당하기에는 너무 늙있다 He is too old for the post. // 그자는 기운이 너무 세어 나로서는 감당할 수 없다 He is so strong that he is more than a match for me. // 그는 부하들을 거칠게 몰아대어, 그자 밑에서의 일은 아무도 감당해 낼 수가 없다 As he drives his men hard, nobody can stand working under him. // 자네가 그런 서투른 글을 쓰면서 어떻게 일을 감당해 내는지 나는 알 수 없다 I don't understand how you can get away with writing so poorly.

감도(感度) sensitiveness; sensitivity (of an earthquake); sensibility (of a balance); reception (라디오·TV의). ¶~가 아주 좋다 be highly sensitive / be of high sensitivity / be hypersensitive // ~가 뛰어난[낮은] 필름 a fast[low] film / 라디오의 ~ the sensitivity [reception] of a radio[wireless] // 산이 많은 곳에서는 라디오의 ~가 좋지 않다 Radio reception is not good in mountainous districts.
● **감도 시험** a sensitivity test. **감도 측정** calibration; sensitivity measurement.

감독(監督) 1 [단속] superintendence; supervision; direction; control; [감시] surveillance. ¶~을 한층 강화하다[엄중히 하다] supervise more strictly / exercise a closer supervision (over) / enforce a more strict control (over) // ~ 소홀로 견책당하다 be reprimanded for lack of supervision[oversight] (of his subordinates). **감독하다** superintend; supervise; control; manage; exercise supervision over; oversee; direct; coach(경기를); look after; take charge of. ¶학생을 ~ look after one's pupils / take charge of one's class[pupils] // 시험을 ~ preside over an examination // 하에 두다 place (a thing) under (a person's) charge / put (a thing) under control[supervision] // 공원(工員)을 ~ oversee workman.
2 [단속자·감시자] a superintendent; a supervisor; an overseer; a director; an inspector; (인부·공원의) a foreman; (영) gaffer; (영화의) director; (교회의) a bishop; (경기 팀의) a manager; (무대의) an impresario (pl. ~s, -sari). ¶공사 ~ a taskmaster // **공장** ~ a factory inspector // **대리** ~ [아

구] an acting manager // 시험 ~ the supervisor of an examination.
● 감독관 an inspector; a superintendent. 감독관청 the supervisory office; the competent [proper] authorities.
감돌다 1 [주위를 돌다] go[turn] round; circle round; turn about.
2 [길·물굽이가] wind; meander; curve; follow (a bend); make a curve (around). ¶굽이굽이 감도는 winding (path) / meandering (stream) / serpentine (course of river) / sinuous (mountain path) // 강이 들판을 감돌며 흐르고 있다 The river meanders through the fields. / The river winds its way through the fields.
3 [어떤 분위기가 가득하다] linger; hang (in the air). ¶입가에 감도는 미소 a smile on one's lips / a smile playing about one's lips // 그들 사이에 무거운 침묵이 감돌았다 An oppressive silence hung between them. // 전운(戰雲)이 ~ War(-threatening) clouds hang[hover] over. // 그의 집에는 불안한 공기가 감돌고 있다 There is an air of uneasiness about his house.
감동(感動) impression; (deep) emotion; excitement; a sensation (among the audience). ¶그의 노래는 ~ 없이 들을 수가 없다 I cannot hear his song without emotion. // 그것은 그에게 아무런 ~도 주지 못하였다 It called forth no response in his heart [breast]. / It left him cold. // 그의 이야기에 그녀는 ~의 눈물을 흘렸다 She was moved to tears by what he said. **감동하다** be impressed (with); be moved [touched / inspired / affected / electrified] (by); feel emotion (at); be struck (by / with). ¶그의 용감한 행동에 주민들은 감동하였다 The villagers were impressed by his courageous deed. // 시민들은 그 소년의 용기에 감동하여 폭군 타도에 일어섰다 Inspired by the boy's courage, the citizens rose up against the tyrant. ➔¶그녀의 친절한 말이 그를 감동시켰다 Her gentle words touched[moved] him. // 그녀는 그의 열정에 감동되어 그와의 결혼을 승낙했다 Overcome[Moved / Touched] by his fervor, she consented to marry him. // 그는 아주 감동하여 말이 나오지 않았다 His heart was too full for words.
감동적(感動的) impressive; touching; moving. ¶~인 연설 a touching[moving] speech // 그것은 ~인 광경이었다 It was a very touching [moving] sight to see.
감득하다(感得-) [깨닫다] realize; perceive; become aware of; get conscious of; [눈치 채다] sense; get wind[scent] of; take hint of; (영감으로) take in; be inspired. ¶심상치 않은 형세를 ~ take in the extraordinary situation.
감등(減等) degradation; downgrading; (미) demotion. **감등하다** degrade; downgrade; reduce (a person) to a lower position [rank]; (미) demote.
감람나무(橄欖-) [식] a kanari; a canari; a Java almond.
감람석(橄欖石) [광] olivine; peridot.
감량(減量) 1 a loss in quantity[weight]; (운동선수의) reduction of one's weight. **감량하다** decrease[reduce] the quantity (of); (체중을) reduce (one's weight). ¶그 권투 선수는 감량하느라 고생하였다 The boxer have had a hard time reducing his weight. 2 (상품 운반 중의) outage; ullage. ¶2%의 ~을 어림잡다 estimate two percent for ullage.
감로(甘露) 1 [이슬] sweet dew; refreshing dew. 2 [달콤한 액즙] nectar; honeydew; [불] amrita.
● 감로수 sweet water; sugared water; syrup; nectar. 감로주 sweet liquor.
감리(監理) administration; management; supervision; superintendence. **감리하다** administer; manage; supervise; superintend.
감리교(監理教) [기] Methodism.
감리 교회(監理教會) a Methodist church.
감마선(-線) [물] γ-rays; gamma rays.
감마제(減磨劑) a lubricant.
감면(減免) (세금의) reduction (of) and exemption (from taxes); (형벌의) mitigation and remission; commutation. **감면하다** (세금을) reduce and exempt; (형벌을) mitigate and remit.
감명(感銘) a (deep) impression. ¶~적인 impressive // ~을 주다 make an impression on one's mind // 당신의 능란한 교수법에 깊은 ~을 받았습니다 I am deeply impressed by your skillful teaching. / I cannot but admire your teaching skill. // 그의 열변도 청중들에게 아무런 ~을 주지 못했다 The audience did not respond to his impassioned speech. / His impassioned speech fell flat. / The audience was immune to his impassioned speech. **감명하다** be impressed (with / by); be moved[deeply touched] (by); be engraved upon one's heart.
감미(甘味) sweetness; a sweet taste[flavor]; a sugary taste. ¶~를 내다 give a sweet flavor (to)[sweeten] // ~가 돌다[있다] taste sweet / be sweetened.
● 감미료 a sweetening agent; sweetening materials; a sweetener; sweetenings.
감미롭다(甘味-) sweet; mellow; dulcet; [음] dolce. ¶감미로운 목소리 a sweet[honey-sweet] voice / a voice of gold // 감미로운 선율 a sweet melody / an enchanting melody // 감미로운 음악 sweet music.
감발 [발감개] a cotton bandages for wrapping the feet (in place of socks); foot-bandages. **감발하다** wrap one's feet with bandages; bandage one's feet. ¶짚신을 감발하고 길을 떠나다 set out one's journey with footbandages and straw sandals on.
감방(監房) (a prison) cell; a ward. ¶~에 처널다 throw[cast] 《a person》 into a cell / land [run] 《a person》 in a ward.
감법(減法) ➔ 뺄셈
감별(鑑別) [구별] discrimination; [감정] judgment; discernment; differentiation. ¶병아리 ~사 a chicken sexer // 그는 병아리 -이 빠르다 He is quick at distinguishing the sex of chicks. **감별하다** distinguish; distinguish (between A and B); [감정하다] judge. ¶가짜와 진짜를 ~ distinguish between an imitation and the original[an imitation from the original].
감복(感服) admiration; wonder. **감복하다** admire; be impressed (with / by); be struck with admiration (at / for); wonder (at). ¶감복할 만한 행위 an admirable[a praiseworthy] deed // 용기에 ~ admire 《a person》 for his courage // 우리는 그의 깊은 통찰력에 감복

했다 We admired [were impressed by] the depth of his insight. →¶감복시키다 excite [demand] (a person's) admiration / strike (a person) with admiration / impress.

감봉(減俸) a salary [wage] reduction; a pay cut; a reduction in salary [pay]; a punitive wage cut; dockage. **감봉하다** reduce salaries [wages]; cut a person's pay; dock. →¶감봉당하다 have one's salary reduced [deducted] (by 100,000 won) / have one's pay cut down // 100만 원에서 80만 원으로 감봉되다 be reduced in pay from 1,000,000 won to 800,000 won // 그는 일의 실패로 1할 감봉되었다 His pay was cut [reduced] 10 percent because of his mistake.

감사(感謝) thanks; gratitude; gratefulness; appreciation; acknowledgment; (신에 대한) thanksgiving. ¶~의 말 words [a speech] of thanks [gratitude] // ~의 눈물을 흘리다 shed tears of gratitude / weep for gratitude // ~의 표시로 in token [as a token] of one's gratitude / as a proof of gratitude // ~ 기도를 올리다 say grace // 이것은 내 ~의 표시입니다 This is a small token of my gratitude. // 친절을 베풀어 주셔서 진심으로 ~를 드립니다 I thank you from the bottom of my heart [I am deeply grateful to you] for your kindness. // 호의에 대하여 깊이 ~드립니다 I am deeply grateful to you for your kindness [good will]. / I offer you my heartfelt thanks for your favor. **감사하다** 〔동사〕 thank (a person for his help); express [give / tender] one's thanks; express one's gratitude [appreciation]; appreciate; 〔형용사〕 thankful; grateful. ¶신에게 ~ thank God / give thanks to God / bless God (for) // 충심으로 ~ thank from the bottom of one's heart / express one's heartfelt thanks // 감사하게 받다 accept (a present) thankfully [with thanks] // 감사하여 reply [thanks] / in gratitude // (대단히) 감사합니다 Thank you (very much). / Thanks (a lot) (무간한 사이에서). / Many thanks. // 뭐라고 감사해야 할지 모르겠습니다 I can never [can't] thank you enough. / I don't know how to thank you. / I have no words to express my gratitude. // 이런 일을 한다고 감사하게 여길 사람은 없을 것 같다 This is likely to be a thankless job. / Small [A lot of] thanks I'm likely to get for doing this!! // 와 주셔서 대단히 감사합니다 Thank you very much for coming.
●**감사장** a letter [note] of thanks [appreciation]; a testimonial; a citation. **감사절** a harvest thank offering; (미) Thanksgiving (Day). **감사패** a plaque of thanks; an appreciation plaque.

감사(監事) **1**〔회원의〕 an auditor; an inspector; a supervisor. **2**〔불〕 a monk in charge of the property of a Buddhist temple.

감사(監司) a governor; the ruler of a province. ¶평안 ~도 제가 싫다면 그만이다 You may lead a horse to the water, but you cannot make him drink.

감사(監査)〔검사〕 inspection; superintendence; 〔회계〕 audit; auditing. ¶국정 ~ (국회의) parliamentary inspection of the administration / 자체 ~ a self-inspection / 엄중한 ~ a strict inspection / a strict [full] audit (회계의). **감사하다** inspect; superintend; (회계를) audit. ¶회계를 ~ audit accounts // 공장을 ~ inspect a plant [a factory].
●**감사과** the inspection department. **감사원** (~院) the Board of Audit and Inspection. **감사원장** the Chairman of the Board of Audit and Inspection.

감산(減産)〔자연적인〕 a decrease in production [output]; decreased production; 〔인위적인〕 reduction [curtailment] of output [production]. **감산하다** reduce [curtail] production. ¶2할 ~ curtail production by 20 percent.

감산(減算)〔수〕 subtraction. **감산하다** subtract.

감상(感想)〔생각〕 one's thoughts; 〔인상〕 one's impression(s); sentiments; 〔느낌〕 feelings. ¶~을 말하다 give [state] one's impressions (of) // ~을 묻다 ask for (a person's) opinion (about) / sound (a person) on a subject // 한국에 오신 ~은 어떻습니까 How does Korea strike you? / How do you find Korea? // 그는 선거 결과에 관한 ~을 말했다 He gave [stated] his impressions [thoughts] on the results of the election. // "~이 어떻습니까?" "별로 없습니다." "What did you think of it?" "I have no particular comments (to make)."
●**감상문** a description of one's impressions.

감상(感傷) sentiment; sentimentality. ¶저물어 가는 가을을 보고 ~에 젖다 sentimentalize over [about] the deepening of autumn // 그따위 ~은 질색이다 Please spare me such sentimentality [sentimentalism].
●**감상주의** sentimentalism.

감상(鑑賞) appreciation. ¶영화 ~회 a special show of films // 음악 ~ listening to music / the appreciation of music // 취미는 음악 ~입니다 My hobby is listening to music. **감상하다** appreciate; enjoy.
●**감상력** an appreciative power; an eye (for).

감상적(感傷的) sentimental; emotional; melodramatic; rosewater. ¶~인 소설 a sentimental story / (미) a sob story / a melodrama // ~이 되다 become [get / grow] sentimental / sentimentalize (over [about] the past).

감색(紺色) dark [navy / deep] blue. ¶~ 신사복 a navy blue suit.

감성(感性)〔감각력〕 sensitivity; (문어) sensibility; sensitiveness; the sense; 〔감수성〕 susceptibility. ¶~이 예민한 사람 a sensitive person.
●**감성 지수** an emotional quotient; an EQ. ¶그는 ~가 높다 He has a high EQ.

감성돔〔동〕 a black porgy.

감세(減稅) a tax reduction [cut]. **감세하다** reduce [cut / lower] taxes. →¶이 물품은 2퍼센트 감세되었다 The tax on these articles was reduced by 2 percent.
●**감세안** a tax reduction bill.

감소(減少)〔수량의〕 decrease; 〔모양이나 정도의〕 diminution; decline; drop; reduction. ¶가치의 ~ a shrinkage in values // 전년보다 50만 원의 ~ a decrease of 500,000 won compared with the previous year // 다소의 [끊임없는] ~를 보이다 show a slight [steady] decrease [decline] // 이것은 작년의 2할 ~다 This is a decrease of 20 percent compared with last year. / This is 20 percent less than last year. 감소하다 diminish; decrease; dwindle; fall off; shrink; lessen; drop; bring down; go down. ¶3분의 1로 ~ be reduced to one-third /수요가 감소하고 있다 be on the decrease / be on the ebb /수요가 감소했다 The demand fell off. // 금년의 식량 생산이 5퍼센트 감소했다 The food production of this year has decreased by 5 percent.

감속(減速) [물] speed reduction; deceleration. ¶눈비 올 때 ~ 운행 (개시) Low gear when wet. 감속하다 reduce the speed; slow down; decelerate. ¶차를 시속 20마일로 ~ reduce [decrease] the speed of a car to 20 miles an hour / bring[slow] a car down to 20 miles an hour.
●**감속 장치 / 감속 기어** a reduction gear; a speed reducer.

감손(減損) [감소] decrease; diminution; [손실] loss; waste; [마손] wear; [누손] leakage; draft. 감손하다 diminish; decrease; lessen; wear out.

감쇄(減殺) diminution; reduction; attenuation; detraction. 감쇄하다 lessen; diminish; reduce; [약화하다] attenuate; deaden (force); impair (the beauty); detract (from one's merits). ¶활동력을 ~ diminish the (vigor of) activity // 효과를 ~ lessen [weaken] the effect.

감쇠(減衰) decrement; decrease; attenuation; damping. 감쇠하다 damp; be attenuated. ¶감쇠하지 않은 undamped.

감수(甘受) submission; resignation. 감수하다 submit (tamely) to; put up with; be resigned to; be ready to suffer. ¶굴욕을 ~ swallow an insult // 고통을 ~ endure[put up with] hardship // 이런 가혹한 조건은 감수할 수 없다 I cannot submit to such severe terms. // 한국 팀은 4등을 감수해야 했다 The Korean team had to settle for[was beaten into] (the) fourth place. // 나는 운명을 감수하겠다 I'll accept my fate with resignation.

감수(減水) the fall of water; low water; the receding[subsiding] of water. 감수하다 fall; subside; recede; go down; sink. ¶홍수로 넘치던 물이 감수하기 시작했다 The floodwaters have begun to recede. →¶강물이 3피트 감수되었다 The water in the river has fallen (by) three feet. // 강이 [저수지가] 현저하게 감수되었다 The level of the river[reservoir] has fallen considerably.

감수(減收) a decrease in income[production]. ¶개인 소득세의 ~ a drop in the collections of individual income taxes. 감수하다 decrease; drop; fall off. →¶금년의 쌀 수확이 약 백만 톤이 감수됐다 The rice crop this year shows a decrease of about one million tons.
●**감수율** a rate of income decrease.

감수(減數) [수] a subtrahend; the number to be subtracted.
●**감수 분열** [생] reduction[reducing] division; meiosis.

감수(減壽) shortening one's life. 감수하다 one's life is shortened; shorten one's life. ¶십년~ feel as if one's life were shortened by ten years / be scared to death // 술을 한 잔씩 마실 때마다 그만치 감수하고 있는 셈이야 Every glass of spirits you take is a nail in your coffin.

감수(感受) reception; impression. 감수하다 be susceptible (of / to); receive (an impression); be impressed (with); (무전을) pick up.
●**감수성** sensitivity; sensibility; susceptibility. (▶ sensitivity는 외부의 자극에 대한 민감성, sensibility는 미적·정서적인 자극에 대한 과민한 반응력을 뜻하며 다소 에스러운 말. susceptibility는 감정적 자극을 받기 쉬운 성질) ¶~이 풍부한 시인 a sensitive poet // 그녀는 자연에 대한 ~이 예민하다 She is sensitive[susceptible] to nature. / She responds sensitively to nature.

감수(監修) (editorial) supervision. ¶민 박사 ~ edited by[compiled under the supervision of] Dr. Min // 이 사전은 스미스 씨의 ~에 따랐다 This dictionary was compiled under the supervision of Mr. Smith. 감수하다 supervise (the compilation of); be chief editor of the compilation (of). ¶교과서의 편집을 ~ supervise the compilation of a textbook.
●**감수자** a supervisor; a chief editor.

감숭감숭 darkly here and there; dotted sparsely. ¶털이 ~ 나다 sprout a fuzz. 감숭감숭하다 sparse and dark[darkish] (hair); thinly haired. ¶감숭감숭한 턱수염 fuzz on the chin.

감시(監視) 1 [지켜봄] watch; guard; lookout; vigil; observation; [감독] supervision. ¶~를 받다 be subject to[be under] (a person's superintendence) // ~를 게을리 하다 neglect [fail] to watch // ~를 두다 set a watch (on) // ~를 늦추다 slacken[loosen] the tight rope of surveillance. 감시하다 watch; keep watch on[over]; keep an[one's] eye on; observe; (죄수 등을) guard; (경찰이 장소 등을) (구어) stake out. ¶용의자의 행동을 ~ keep an eye on the movements of a suspect // 경찰은 그 용의자를 엄중히 감시했다 The police kept a close watch over[a close eye on] the suspect. // 경비원이 들치기들을 감시하고 있다 The guards are looking out[on the alert / on the lookout] for shoplifters. // 두 남자가 문 앞에서 감시하고 있었다 Two men were standing guard[(문어) sentinel] at the gate. // 경찰이 용의자의 집을 감시하고 있다 The police have staked out the suspect's house. // 저 소년은 감시할 필요가 있다 The boy needs watching[to be watched]. // 저 창문을 잘 감시해 주게 Keep watch[an eye] on that window.
2 (형법상의) surveillance; police supervision. ¶~하에 under police surveillance // ~의 눈을 피하다 elude the vigilance (of the police). 감시하다 conduct surveillance (of); exercise surveillance (over). →¶죄수들은 항상 감시당하고 있었다 The prisoners were under constant surveillance(▶ surveillance는 특히 죄수·용의자 등의 감시).
●**감시병** a guard; a lookout man. **감시소 / 감시 초소** a guard box; a watchhouse; (미) a lookout; [군] an observation post[point]. **감시원 / 감시인 / 감시자** a watchman; a guard; a guardian; a custodian; a keeper; a caretaker; a supervisor; an observer.

감식(減食) reduction of diet[food]; reduced [short] rations. 감식하다 reduce one's diet; cut down one's meals; underfeed (oneself); diet.
●**감식 요법** cure by reduction of diet; reduced diet cure.

감식(鑑識) 〔물건을 분별하기〕 discernment; 〔범죄의 감정〕 criminal investigation. ¶범죄~ 자료 materials of criminal identification∥지문 ~ fingerprint identification∥미술품의 ~에 능하다 be a good judge of[have an eye for] objects of art / be a good connoisseur of work of art / ~ 결과 피해자의 혈액형은 A형으로 밝혀졌다 The laboratory investigation made it clear[showed] that the victim's blood type was A. **감식하다** judge; be a judge of; discern; discriminate; appreciate.
● **감식가** a judge; a discerner; (미술품의) a connoisseur; 〔평가인〕 an appraiser. **감식과**(경찰의) the crime laboratory (investigation section); 〔구어〕 the lab; the Section of (Criminal) Identification. **감식안**(一眼) a discerning[critical] eye; discernment.

감실거리다 flicker at a dim distance; glimmer; gleam faintly. ¶감실거리는 불빛 a glimmer of light∥배가 먼 바다 위에 감실거린다 A ship is faintly discerned far out at sea.

감싸다 1 〔싸다〕 wrap (in); tuck up (in). ¶그녀는 온몸을 담요로 감싸고 있었다 She was covered from head to foot with a blanket. / 그 산꼭대기는 (짙은) 안개로 감싸였다 The summit was shrouded in fog. / The summit was veiled[enveloped] in mist. / 회장(會場)은 열기로 감싸였다 The hall was filled with enthusiasm.
2 〔비호하다〕 protect (the weak); cover (a guilty person); shield[screen / shelter] (a person from); take (a person) under one's wings; 〔변호하다〕 plead[speak up] for (a person). ¶그는 항상 그를 감싸 주고 있다 He is always under Mr. Hong's patronage. / 그녀를 감싸 줄 사람은 아무도 없었다 No one stood up[pleaded / spoke up] for her. / 경찰은 그녀가 아들을 감싸려고 범행을 자백한 것으로 생각하고 있다 The police believe she confessed to the crime, only to cover up for her son.

감안(勘案) 〔생각〕 consideration; 〔참작〕 allowance(s). **감안하다** take (a matter) into account[consideration]; give consideration (to); allow for; make allowance(s) for. ¶감안해야 할 여러 점 points to be duly considered∥계획을 실행하기 전에 실정을 ~ take the circumstances into consideration before one puts a plan into action.

감압(減壓) decompression. **감압하다** reduce pressure; decompress.
● **감압 밸브** a reducing valve.

감액(減額) a reduction; a curtailment; a cut; a cutback; diminution. **감액하다** reduce; curtail; diminish; abate; make a reduction; cut down. → 손해 배상액은 80만 원만큼[으로] 감액되었다 The amount of compensation for damages was reduced[cut down] by[to] eight hundred thousand won.

감언(甘言) flattery; honeyed words; coaxing; cajolery; wheedling. ¶~으로 속이다 deceive with honeyed words / coax∥그는 남의 ~에 잘 속는다 He is easily taken in by flattery. / 많은 여자가 그의 ~에 속아 넘어갔다 Many women were deceived by his honeyed words [smooth talk]. ∥그의 ~에 넘어가지 않도록 조심하라 Be careful not to be taken in by his glib talk[honeyed words].
● **감언이설** soft and seductive language; words of flattery; cajolery; blarney. ¶~에 속

다 be imposed upon by honeyed words.

감연하다(敢然−) daring; bold; brave; fearless; resolute; defiant; dauntless. **감연히** daringly; boldly; bravely; fearlessly; resolutely; defiantly. ¶~ 일어서다 bravely stand up (against the enemy) / arise to the occasion resolutely∥~ 난국에 대처하다 face a difficult situation resolutely∥그는 공무원의 독직(瀆職) 추방에 나섰다 He determinedly set himself to wipe out corruption among public officials.

감염(感染) (공기나 물에 의한) infection; (접촉에 의한) contagion; contamination. ¶공기 ~ aerial[airborne] infection∥재 ~ reinfection∥콜레라의 2차 ~ secondary infection of cholera. **감염하다** (병이 사람에) infect; (사람이 병에) catch; contract. ¶병에 감염된 사람 an infected person∥(면역이 되어) 감염되지 않다 be immune (from)∥사회악에 감염되다 catch social evils∥그는 적리(赤痢)에 감염됐다 He contracted dysentery.∥유행성 감기는 아주 감염되기 쉽다 Influenza is catching [highly contagious].∥이 병은 접촉에 의해 감염된다 This disease is contagious [spread by contagion].∥아이들은 한층 더 감염되기 쉽다 Children are more liable to infection.
● **감염 경로** an infection way; the route [a channel] of infection. **감염원**(−源) the source of infection.

감옥(監獄) a prison; a jail; (영) gaol(▶ (미)에서는 「유치장」의 뜻, (영)에서도 prison을 흔히 씀). ¶~에 넣다 put (a person) in prison / imprison[clap] (a person)∥~에서 나오다 come out of prison / be released from prison.
● **감옥살이** penal servitude; a prison life; living in the prison. ¶~ 하다 do penal servitude / serve a prison term∥그는 5년 동안 ~를 했다 He served a five-year sentence [five years] in prison.

감원(減員) reduction of the staff; cutting down of the personnel; a personnel cut [reduction]; (일시적인) a layoff. ¶1할의 ~ a ten percent cut in personnel. **감원하다** reduce[cut] the staff[personnel]; lay off. ¶대폭 ~ make a drastic cut in the staff.

감음정(減音程) 〔음〕 a diminished interval.

감읍하다(感泣−) be moved to tears (by / with); shed tears of gratitude (for). ¶온정이 넘치는 법관의 말에 그녀는 감읍했다 She was moved to tears by the judge's kind words.

감응(感應) 1 〔마음이 신에 통함〕 response; answer; 〔영감〕 inspiration; 〔공감〕 sympathy; effect. **감응하다** (종교적으로) respond to; be responsive to; 〔공감하다〕 sympathize with; be inspired[affected / moved] (by). ¶그의 기원에는 신명도 감응할 것이다 The god will answer[respond to / hear] his prayers.
2 〔전〕〔물〕 induction; influence; action. **감응하다** induce; be effective; act upon.
● **감응도** sensitivity. **감응 유전** 〔생〕 telegony.

감자 a potato; (미) a white potato; an Irish potato. ¶씨 ~ a seed potato∥햇 ~ a new potato∥~ 껍질을 벗기다 peel[pare] potatoes.
● **감자튀김** a fried potato; a potato chip(얇게 썬).

감자(減資) reduction[curtailment] of capital; a capital decrease. **감자하다** reduce[curtail] capital.

감장 self-help; doing by oneself; getting along without depending on others. **감장하다** help oneself; do by oneself; manage one's own concerns[affairs].

감적(監的) [군] marking.
● **감적수**(-手) a marker. **감적호**(-壕) a marking trench.

감전(感電) (receiving) an electric shock. **감전하다** receive an electric shock; be struck [affected] by electricity. ➔¶감전되어 죽다 be killed by an electric shock/전선을 만지지 마라, 감전된다 Don't touch the wire or you'll get a shock.
● **감전사**(-死) electrocution; a death from electric shock.

감점(減點) a demerit mark. ¶~을 당하다 receive a cut in marks. **감점하다** give (a person) a demerit mark; make a cut in marks.

감정(感情) feeling(s); [정서] emotion; sentiment; [열정] passion; [충동] impulse. ¶~이 메마른 사람 a prosaic person//이성과 ~ reason and emotion//~을 얼굴에 나타내다 show one's feelings/let one's feeling [emotions] show//그녀는 ~에 치우치기 쉽다 She tends to become emotional.//그렇게 말하면 남의 ~을 해치게 된다 That would create hard feelings./That would give offense.//그는 친구의 ~을 상하게 하는 말을 곧잘 한다 He often hurts his friends with his remarks.//그는 좀처럼 ~을 드러내지 않는다 He seldom betrays[shows] his feelings [emotions].//인간은 ~의 동물이다 Man is a creature of impulse.//그는 자연에 대한 ~을 시로 표현했다 He expressed his sentiments [feelings] about nature in a poem.//~이 격해졌을 때는 그는 방 안을 서성거리곤 했다 When he was excited he would walk up and down the room.//이 그림에는 작가의 자연에 대한 깊은 ~이 넘쳐흐르고 있었다 This painting was overflowing with the painter's deep feeling for nature.
● **감정 도착**(-倒錯) perversion of feelings. **감정 이입**(-移入) [심] empathy.

감정(憾情) [악감] an unpleasant[ill] feeling; ill[bad] blood; [유감] resentment. ¶~이 있다 be ill [unfavorably] disposed (toward)/have something on one's mind/~을 품다 bear[have] a grudge against (a person)/have something on one's mind/~을 사다 earn (a person's) grudge/incur (a person's) grudge[ill will]//나는 그에게 아무런 ~도 없다 I bear[own] him no grudge.

감정(鑑定) [판단] judgment; [전문가의] an expert opinion; [소송의] legal consultation [advice]; [평가] appraisal; estimation. ¶~을 받다 have (a thing) judged[appreciated] (by)/seek an expert opinion//…을 잘 하다[못하다] be a good judge[no judge] of ...//허위 ~을 하다 give false evidence (to)//문화재청은 보물급 골동품의 ~을 박물관에 의뢰했다 The Cultural Properties Administration referred to the museum the appraisal of the treasure level antiques. **감정하다** judge; give an (expert) opinion (on); identify (handwriting); (가치를) appraise (the value); estimate. ¶필적을 ~ give an expert[a professional] opinion on handwriting.
● **감정가/감정인** a judge; an identifier; (미술품의) a connoisseur; (골동품의) a virtuoso (pl. ~s, -si); [법] an expert witness; [평가자] an appraiser. **감정 가격** appraised[estimated] value; an appraisement. **감정서** (미술품의) a written statement of an expert opinion; (상품의) a surveyor's report; [법] an expert opinion in writing.

감정적(感情的) emotional; sentimental; impulsive. ¶~인 토론 an emotional discussion//~으로 말하다 speak with an emotioned bias/speak ill-disposedly//그녀는 매우 ~이다 She is very emotional.

감주(甘酒) a sweet drink prepared with rice and malt. ⇨단술

감지(感知) perception; sensing; becoming aware. **감지하다** perceive; sense; become aware (of); suspect; scent (a plot).
● **감지 장치** a sensor.

감지덕지(感之德之) very thankfully; with deep gratitude; with many[grateful/hearty/heartfelt] thanks. ¶내가 준 얼마 안 되는 돈을 그는 ~ 고마워했다 He was very grateful to me for the little money I offered him. **감지덕지하다** be[feel] very thankful[grateful] (for). ¶나는 그의 제의를 감지덕지하여 받아들였다 I accepted his offer with thanks.

감질나다(疳疾-) feel insatiable; never feel satisfied; feel eager to eat[have] more; feel tantalized; feel[be] dying for more. ¶감질나게 하다 make (a person) feel insatiable/tantalize//그는 늘 감질나 있다 He is hungry all the time.//그 보급으로는 감질날 따름이다 The supply did not give us entire satisfaction./The supply merely tantalized us.//아기는 감질나서 젖을 더 달라고 울었다 The unsatisfied child cried for more milk.//한 잔 더 하세, 감질나는군 Let's have another drink, I am all the more thirsty.

감쪽같다 (고친 물건이) as good as before; just as it was; restored to the former state; (거짓 등이) complete; perfect; successful; fair; artful. ¶그 의자는 수선을 하니 감쪽같았다 When repaired, the chair was as good as before.//세탁을 하니 감쪽같았다 When washed, it was as good as before. **감쪽같이** successfully; completely; perfectly; nicely; artfully. ¶~ 속다 be nicely[fairly/badly] taken in/~ 속이다 take in[deceive/cheat/fool] nicely[fairly]//~ 사라지다 vanish completely//약을 먹었더니 치통이 ~ 나았다 The toothache has clean gone by virtue of the remedy.

감찰(鑑札) a license (plate); (영) a licence; a permit; a certificate. ¶수렵 ~ shooting license//영업 ~ a business[trade] license/개의 등록 ~ a dog license//무~이 unlicensed/~이 있는 licensed/registered//~이 없는[없이] without a license/unlicensed//~을 교부하다 grant a license//~을 갱신하다 renew a license//~을 받다 get[obtain/take (out)] a license (for shooting)/~을 취소[몰수]하다 revoke a license//그는 노점상의 ~을 갖고 있다 He has a license for vending in the street.
● **감찰료** a license fee.

감찰(監察) [감사] inspection; [감독] supervision. **감찰하다** inspect; supervise.
● **감찰관** an inspector.

감채(減債) partial payment of a debt; reducing one's debt; amortization. **감채하다** pay a debt partially.

감청(紺青) Prussian blue; ultramarine; deep [navy] blue.
감초(甘草) a licorice (root).
감촉(感觸) (the sense of) touch; a feel. ¶~이 부드러운 smooth to the touch∥~이 딱딱하다[부드럽다] feel hard[soft] / be hard[soft] to the touch∥~이 좋다 be agreeable to the touch∥~이 꺼칠꺼칠하다 feel rough∥~으로 명주라는 것을 알 수 있습니다 You can tell it's silk by the touch[feel]. **감촉하다** touch; feel; sense; perceive through the senses.
감추다 (몸·물건 등을) hide (one's face); conceal (one's money); secrete (stolen goods); (덮어서) cover (a face); veil (one's displeasure); disguise (one's nationality); conceal (one's identity); [비밀로 하다] keep (a matter) secret[back] (from); [숨겨 주다] harbor (fugitives); shelter (a criminal). ¶감추지 않고 without concealing / frankly / openly / candidly∥몸을 ~ hide (oneself) (behind / under / in) / be in hiding∥마음의 동요를 ~ cover one's confusion∥자취를 ~ disappear / vanish (into thin air) / cover one's traces[tracks]∥서랍 속에 ~ put away (something) in a cabinet drawer∥나이를 ~ conceal one's age / make a secret of one's age∥나는 그 열쇠를 그들에게 보이지 않는 곳에 감추었다 I put the key out of their sight.∥사자는 흥분하지 않았을 때는 발톱을 감춘다 A lion retracts its claws when not excited.∥그는 얼굴에 기쁨을 감추지 못했다 He could not conceal his joy.∥그녀는 도둑질의 동기를 감췄다 She disguised her motive for stealing.

감축(減縮) reduction; diminution; retrenchment; curtailment. ¶주한 미군의 ~ the reduction of the US Forces in Korea. **감축하다** reduce; diminish; retrench; curtail; cut down. ¶경비를 ~ cut (down)[curtail] the expense / curtail[retrench] expenditures.
감치다 1 [꿰매다] hem; put a hem (in); sew up. ¶옷 가장자리를 ~ hem the edge of a garment. 2 [마음에 감돌다] linger[haunt] in one's mind.
감칠맛 1 (음식의) flavor; taste; savor; savory taste; relish. ¶~ 나는 요리 a tasty dish∥~이 있다 be flavory[tasty / savory / palatable / toothsome] / be nice to the palate∥~이 없다 be flat[tasteless / vapid / insipid]. 2 [매력] attraction; magnetism. ¶~ 있는 attractive / magnetic / engaging / appealing / sapid (sentence)∥~ 없는 글 a bald sentence.
감침질 hemming; darning; putting in hems. **감침질하다** hem; darn; sew up.
감탄(感歎) admiration (for / of); wonder; marvel; exclamation. **감탄하다** admire; be struck with wonder[admiration]; marvel (at); wonder (at); exclaim (over). ¶감탄할 만한 admirable (performance) / wonderful / marvelous / worthy of admiration∥감탄할 만씨 an admirable performance∥감탄할 만큼 끈기 있게 with admirable patience∥감탄해 마지않다 be greatly struck with admiration / be full of[filled with] admiration / be lost in admiration / express great admiration∥그들은 그 아름다운 경치에 감탄하여 소리를 질렀다 They exclaimed at the beautiful view.∥나는 너의 근면함에 감탄했다 I am deeply impressed with your diligence.∥나는 그의 기억력이 좋은 데에 감탄했다 I admired [marveled at] his good memory. ➔¶수많은 자연 애호가를 감탄시키다 inspire the admiration of many a lover of nature∥그는 이 어려운 일을 해냄으로써 모든 사람을 감탄시켰다 He accomplished this difficult task to the wonder and admiration of all.
●**감탄문** [언] an exclamatory sentence. **감탄부호** [언] an exclamation mark[point]. **감탄사** [언] an interjection; an exclamation.
감탕 1 [끈끈이] birdlime; lime. 2 [곤죽이 된 진흙] mud; a muddy place[spot] (in a road); mire; quagmire. ¶눈이 녹아 ~이 된 길 a muddy road caused by the melting of snow / a slushy road∥~에 빠지다 fall in the mire.
감퇴(減退) decline; ebb; failing; loss; decrease; recession. ¶…의 ~를 보이다 show a decline of …∥시력[기억력] ~ failing of eyesight[memory]∥나는 수년 전부터 시력의 ~를 느껴 왔다 I have been aware for several years that my eyesight is weakening [failing]. **감퇴하다** decline; ebb; recede; fall off. ¶식욕이 ~ lose one's appetite∥정력이 ~ decline in energy∥요즈음 그의 시력은 많이 감퇴하였다 His sight has failed sadly of late.∥나이를 먹으면 기억력이 감퇴한다 Our memory weakens[declines] as we grow older.∥그의 체력은 거의 감퇴하지 않고 있다 His physical powers are hardly dimmed.
감투 1 [모자] a horsehair cap formerly worn by gentry[officials]. 2 [관직] a government [an official] post[position]; [좋은 자리] a distinguished[responsible] post[office]. ¶~를 쓰다 become a government official / assume office / be appointed an high government official∥~를 벗다 leave one's post / resign a government[prominent] post.
●**감투싸움** a struggle for an influential post.
감투(敢鬪) fighting courageously[bravely]. **감투하다** fight courageously[bravely / gamely]; fight gallantly. ¶그들은 강적을 상대로 감투했다 They fought gallantly[bravely] against strong odds. / They put up a gallant[brave] fight against heavy odds.
●**감투상** a fighting-spirit prize[award]. **감투정신** a fighting spirit.
감표(減標) ➔ 뺄셈표(⇨뺄셈)
감하다(減-) 1 [빼다] subtract; deduct (from); take off. ¶30에서 20을 ~ subtract 20 from 30∥10에서 6을 감하면 4가 남는다 Six from ten leaves four. / Ten less[minus] six leaves four. 2 [줄이다] decrease; lessen; diminish; abate; reduce; [삭감하다] cut down. ¶3분의 1로 ~ reduce (something) to one-third∥3분의 1을 ~ reduce one-third∥1할 감해 드리겠다 We will discount[cut off] ten percent.∥현금이면 감해 드립니다 We allow a discount for cash. 3 [줄다] lessen; decrease; go down; fall off; be reduced; dwindle(차차). ¶수가 ~ decrease in number ∥3분의 1로 ~ be reduced to one-third.
감행(敢行) decisive[resolute / daring] action; [수행] carrying out; execution. **감행하다** take decisive[resolute] action; dare to do; venture (an attempt); carry out resolutely. ¶노동조합은 스트라이크를 감행했다 The labor union went ahead with the strike.∥그들은 억수로 쏟아지는 빗속에서 자동차 경주를 감행했다 They went through with the auto

race in spite of the pouring rain.

감형(減刑) reduction[mitigation / abatement] of penalty[a sentence]; commutation; remission. **감형하다** mitigate[commute] a sentence; remit; lower a penalty. ➔¶그는 사형에서 무기 징역으로 감형되었다 His death sentence was commuted[reduced] to life imprisonment[imprisonment for life].

감호(監護) [법] care and custody; superintendence. ¶~ 조치를 취하다 take a measure for care and custody. **감호하다** [감독하다] superintended; supervise; [보호하다] take care of; look after.

감홍(甘汞) [화] calomel; mercurous chloride.

감화(感化) influence; conversion; [교정] (moral) reform. ¶~ 사업 reformatory work∥도덕적 ~ a moral influence∥부모의 parental influence∥…의 ~를 받고 under the influence of …∥슈바이처의 ~를 받아 그는 의사가 되려고 결심했다 Under the influence of[Inspired by] Schweitzer, he made up his mind to be a doctor.∥그는 젊은이들에게 상당한 ~를 주었다 He had a good influence over[on] the young people. **감화하다** influence; (문어) exert an influence (on); inspire; infect; [바로잡다] reform; correct; [개심시키다] convert. ➔¶감화되다 be influenced[affected] (by) / [매혹되다] be under a person's spell.
● **감화력**(-力) influence; power to influence. **감화원**(-院) a (juvenile) reformatory; a correction[reformatory] school; (미) a reform school; a house of correction; a workhouse.

감회(感懷) [회포] sentiments; feelings; [회상] memories; reminiscences; retrospection. ¶~가 깊다 be deeply moved (by) ∥ ~에 젖다 give oneself up to deep emotion[recollection] ∥ 내 가슴은 ~로 벅차 있었다 My heart was filled[My breast heaved] with emotion.

감흥(感興) interest; fun; inspiration(영감). ¶~이 일다 be inspired (by) / become interested (in) / feel a sensation of pleasure ∥ ~을 깨뜨리다 spoil fun[interest] / break the spell∥그 그림을 보고 나는 큰 ~을 느꼈다 The picture excited[aroused] strong interest in me.∥그의 연설을 들어도 아무런 ~을 느끼지 못했다 His speech did not appeal to me. ∥그는 ~이 움직이는 대로 (계속) 써 내려갔다 He wrote (on and on) as inspiration[his fancy] directed.∥그런 것으로는 아무런 ~도 일지 않았다 That left me cold[cool].

감히(敢-) boldly; fearlessly; daringly; without hesitation; [주제넘게] affectedly; impudently; ¶~하다 (dare[venture / presume] (to do) / make bold (to do) / lend oneself to (a deed) ∥ ~ …이라고 말하다 venture to say …∥~ 죽음을 무릅쓰다 dare to risk one's life / challenge[brave] death∥~ 네가 그런 말을 내게 하다니 How dare you say such a thing to me? / (반어적) You're a fine one to talk to me like that!∥그들은 ~ 오지 못했다 They did not dare to come.∥어디서 ~ 그런 말이 나오느냐 How could you have the face to say so?∥그들은 ~ 공격을 하지 못했다 They did not dare to attack.∥네가 ~ 나를 속여먹다니 How did you dare to cheat me?∥아무도 ~ 그 유령이 나오는 집에 들어가지 않았다 No one dared to venture into the haunted house.

갑(甲) 1 [차례의 첫째] the first; No. 1; A. 2 [등급의 첫째] the first[top] (grade); A one; [최고 성적] grade A; class "A"; [여럿 중의 하나] A; the former; the one. ¶~과 을 A and B / the former and the latter / the one and the other∥~, … 쌍방 간에 between the two parties. 3 [등딱지] a shell; a tortoise shell(거북의); a carapace(갑각강의).

갑(匣) a case; a casket; a case; a box; a pack(담배 등의). ¶담뱃~ a cigarette case / a tobacco box∥담배 한 ~ a packet[(미) pack] of cigarettes∥하루에 담배를 몇 ~이나 피느냐 How many packs of cigarettes do you smoke every day?

갑(岬) a cape; a promontory; a headland; a spit.

갑각(甲殻) [동] a shell; a carapace; a crust. ¶~이 있는 loricate / testacean / testaceous / covered with the hard, protective shell.
● **갑각강**(-綱) [동] Crustacea(학명).

갑갑증(-症) ennui; irksomeness; boredom; tedium; tediousness.

갑갑하다 1 [답답하다] stifling; suffocating; stuffy; close; [좁다] confined (space); (uncomfortably) narrow; (구어) poky (little room).¶갑갑한 느낌이 들다 feel choky [suffocating]∥방이 갑갑해 못 견디겠다, 문좀 열어라 Please open the window, I feel stifled in this room.
2 [지겹다] boring; tedious; dull; tiresome; feel bored. ¶갑갑한 일 a boring[an irksome] job∥갑갑한 문체 a stodgy style∥지겹도록 ~ be bored to death / be bored stiff / be oppressed with tedium∥지루해서 갑갑하시겠습니다 I am afraid you find it a bore.∥생각만 해도 ~ The bare idea makes[turns] me sick.∥진도가 더뎌서 ~ I am sick of my slow progress.
3 (가슴이나 배가) (feel) heavy (in the chest [stomach]). ¶가슴이 ~ feel heavy in the chest.

갑골 문자(甲骨文字) [언] inscriptions on bones and tortoise carapaces.

갑근세(甲勤税) the income tax of Grade A; the Grade A income tax. ⇨갑종 근로 소득세 (⇨갑종)

갑년(甲年) [회갑의 해] the sixty-first anniversary of one's birth; one's 61st year.

갑론을박(甲論乙駁) arguments pro and con; the pros and cons. ¶회의는 ~으로 결론이 나지 않았다 The meeting was a seesaw battle of arguments for and against with no conclusion being reached. **갑론을박하다** argue back and forth; argue[discuss] the pros and cons (of a matter).

갑문(閘門) [물문] a floodgate; a penstock; a sluice (gate); (운하의) a lock gate.

갑부(甲富) the richest[wealthiest] person (in a community); a millionaire; a billionaire; a multimillionaire; (미) a plute.

갑사(甲紗) [품질이 좋은 사] fine (silk) gauze [gossamer].

갑상선(甲狀腺) [생] the thyroid gland[body].
● **갑상선 기능 항진** hyperthyroidism. **갑상선염** thyroiditis. **갑상선종**(-腫) [의] a goiter; a struma (pl. -mae). **갑상선 호르몬** (분비액) thyroid hormone; thyroxin(e).

갑옷(甲-) armor; (한 벌의) a suit[piece] of armor; a coat of mail. ¶~과 투구 armor and

갑자기

helmet // ~을 입은 무사 an armored warrior / a warrior in armor // 그들은 ~을 입고 싸움터에 나갔다 They put on their armor and came forth to battle.

갑자기 [별안간] suddenly; on a sudden; all of a sudden; all at once; abruptly; [뜻밖에] unexpectedly; without warning[notice]. (▶ suddenly는 불시에 신속하게 일어남을 강조. abruptly는 예고·암시가 없고 결과가 불쾌한 경우가 많음) ¶~ 나타나다 burst on the scene // ~ 돌아오다 return unexpectedly // 돌아서다 turn back abruptly // ~ 해고하다 dismiss (a servant) without notice // ~ 시험을 치르다 give an examination without notice // 그녀는 ~ 울음을 터뜨렸다 She burst into tears. / She burst out crying. // ~일이 생겨서 저는 참석할 수 없습니다 I cannot attend owing to an unexpected business. // 나는 ~ 제정신으로 돌아왔다 All of a sudden I came to my senses. // 그 사건 이후 그는 ~ 늙었다 He suddenly aged after that incident. // 한랭 전선이 다가옴에 따라 기온이 ~ 떨어졌다 The temperature dropped quickly [plummeted] with the arrival of a cold front. // 부친의 병세가 ~ 나빠졌다 My father's illness took a sudden turn for a worse. // ~ 물어서 죄송합니다만… Excuse my abrupt question, but ….

갑작스럽다 sudden; abrupt; unexpected; unlooked-for; unannounced. ¶갑작스러운 초대 a surprise invitation // 갑작스러운 일 an unexpected thing[happening] // 갑작스러운 변화 a sudden[an unexpected] change (in the weather) // 나는 갑작스러운 질문으로 말문이 막혔다 I was at a loss for a reply to his abrupt[unexpected] question. // 그의 구혼이 너무나 갑작스러워서 나는 당황했다 His proposal of marriage came so suddenly that I was caught off balance. // 그녀는 갑작스러운 손님으로 당황했다 The unexpected caller put her in a flurry. // 갑작스러운 정차였다 It was an abrupt stop.

갑절 1 [어떤 수량을 두 번 합치는 것] two times; twice; double; twofold; (셀 때) times; as much. ¶~ 반 half again as much // ~의 double / twice // ~의 폭 double width // 돈을 원금의 ~로 갚다 repay double the size [length] (of) // 그의 나이는 내 나이의 ~이다 He is twice my age. // 나의 수입은 이전의 ~이나 늘었다 My income is double what it was. // 이것은 그것보다 ~이나 좋다 This is twice as good as that. 2 [두 번 합친 만큼]. ¶~ 비싸다 cost twice as much // 남보다 ~ 일하다 work twice as hard as others.

갑종(甲種) grade A; first[top] grade; A1; A one.
● 갑종 근로 소득세 the income tax of Grade A; the Grade A income tax.

갑주(甲胄) helmet and armor; a panoply.

갑충(甲蟲) [동] a beetle; a coleopteron (pl. -ra). ¶~류의 coleopterous.

갑판(甲板) a deck. ¶뒤[후부 / 선미]~ the quarterdeck / the afterdeck // 앞~ the forward deck / the foredeck // 정[상 / 중 / 하] ~ the main[upper / middle / lower] deck // ~으로 가다 go on deck // ~에 나가 있다 be on deck // ~에 실을 것 (게시) on deck // 전원 ~으로 All hands on deck!
● 갑판 사관 a deck officer. 갑판실 a deckhouse. 갑판 여객 a deck passenger. 갑판장 a boatswain.

갑피(甲皮) the uppers of leather shoes; shoes without soles.

값 1 [가치] value; worth; merit(장점).
2 [가격] price; cost; charge. (▶ price는 특히 파는 값. charge는 노동 봉사에 대해서 구하는 대가. cost는 물건 노동 기타의 획득에 대해 지불하는 값) ¶~이 싼 low-priced / low in price / inexpensive / cheap // ~이 비싸다 be expensive[dear costly] / be high in price / be high-priced // ~이 오르다[내리다] go up [down] in price / rise[fall] in price / the price goes up[down] // ~을 올리다 raise the price / (정가를) mark up prices / (미국 속어) jack up // ~을 깎다 beat down the price / haggle over (the price) // ~을 묻다 inquire [ask] the price / (증권에) ~이 올랐을 때 팔아 치우다 sell out on the rise // ~을 정하다 fix the price // 그것은 (품질에 비해) ~이 싸다 That's a good bargain [buy]. // 이 ~이 드릴 최하의 것입니다 This is the lowest (possible) price I can offer you. // 그 ~으로는 본전도 안 됩니다 Your figure is below the cost. // ~이 얼마입니까 What is the price? / How much is it? // ~이 맞으면 팔겠다 I will sell it if you name a moderate price. // ~이 얼마면 쓰시겠습니까 About what price would you like, Sir?

3 [수] value. ¶x의 ~을 구하라 Find the value of x.

값(을) 놓다[부르다] (the buyer) name a price; bid; make a bid; (the seller) demand [ask] a price.

값(을) 보다 [값을 어림하여 보다] value; appraise; estimate; [값을 놓다] bid; offer a price. ¶이 물건 값을 좀 보아 주오 Please appraise this article. / Tell me what this is worth, please. // 내가 상당한 값을 봤는데도 그 사람은 팔려고 하지 않았다 I made a good offer, but he wouldn't sell it.

값나가다 valuable; expensive; costly; of value. ¶값나가는 물건 a valuable article / an expensive article / a golden-egg hen (속어) // 값나가는 보석 valuable jewels.

값비싸다 expensive; high in price; high-priced; dear costly.

값싸다 cheap; low-priced; low in price; inexpensive. ¶값싼 물건 a cheap[low-priced] article / a (good) bargain(헐값인 물건) / an inferior article(품질이 나쁜 물건).

값어치 value; worth. 1 [값에 알맞는 가치]. ¶~가 있는 그림 a valuable picture // 대단한 ~가 있는[그다지 ~가 없는] 반지 a ring of great [little] value // 그 토지는 현재 1억 원의 ~가 있다 The land is now worth a hundred million won. // 다이아몬드의 ~가 올랐다[떨어졌다] Diamonds rose[fell] in value. // 그것은 한 푼의 ~도 없다 It is not worth a farthing [hair straw]. // 그것은 백 원의 ~도 못 된다 It isn't worth 100won. // 그것은 얼마만 한 ~가 있는가 How much is it worth? // 보기보다 ~가 없다 It is showy but worthless. / It is not so good as it looks.

2 [사람·사물의 가치]. ¶그런 말을 하면 네 ~가 떨어진다 It is beneath your dignity to say such a thing. // 사람의 ~는 얼굴 생김새로 평가될 수가 없다 The worth of a man cannot be judged by his looks. // 그는 그런 상을 받을 만한 ~가 없다 He is not deserve (to be given) such a prize. / He does not worthy of

such a prize.// 이 사전은 추천할 ~가 있다 This dictionary is worth recommending.// 그것은 한 번 읽어 볼 ~가 있다 It is worth reading. / It is worthy of a perusal.// 그의 작품은 굉장한 ~가 있다 His works are worth their weight in gold.

값없다 [무가치하다] valueless; worthless; unworthy; not of merit; [귀하여 값을 따질 수 없다] priceless; invaluable.

값있다 worth; valuable; worthy; be of value.

값지다 [값나가다] valuable; of value; worthy; [비싸다] expensive; costly. ¶값진 물건 a precious object / [진귀한 물건] a rarity // 값진 선물 an (costly) gift[present] // 이 책은 내게는 아주 값진 것이다 This book is very valuable [is of great value] to me.

값하다 be worth; be worthy (of); deserve; merit. ¶밥 먹은 ~ render a service for what one has eaten / sing for one's supper / earn one's bread[board].

갓[1] [머리에 쓰는] a *gat*; a Korean hat made of bamboo[horsehair]. **2** [남포등 등의] a (lamp) shade; (버섯류의) a cap, a top. ¶전등 ~ a lampshade // 버섯의 ~ the cap of a mushroom / a pileus.

갓[2] [식] a leaf mustard; an Indian mustard. ¶~김치 leaf-mustard *gimchi*(kimchi).

갓[3] **1** [방금] fresh[green] from; just now; newly; recently. ¶~ 지은 집 a newly built house // 시골에서 ~ 올라온 처녀 a maiden fresh[green] from the country // ~ 만든 물건 a thing newly made // ~ 결혼한 부부 a couple who have just married / [미국 구어] the newlyweds // 대학을 ~ 나온 청년 a young man fresh from[just out of] college / a new[fresh] graduate // ~ 구운 빵 bread fresh[hot] from the oven / ~ 낳은 달걀 a new-laid egg / a fresh egg. **2** (나이 앞에서) just; exactly; neither more nor less than. ¶~ 마흔이다 be just forty years old // 저 처녀는 나이가 ~ 스물이다 The girl is just twenty years old.

갓길 a shoulder. ¶차를 ~로 몰아서 세우세요 You should pull off onto the shoulder.

갓난아이 a newborn baby; a baby; a babe; an infant. ¶~ 같은 babyish / babylike / infantile // ~ 취급을 하다 treat (a person) like a baby / baby (a person).

갓돌 a copestone; a cope; a tablet.

강- [호된] severe; harsh; intense; [억지의] forced; trying; [거짓의] pretended; [지나친] excessive; inordinate; [까닭 없는] unreasonable; unjustifiable; [순전한] pure; straight; dry. ¶~더위 a spell of intense heat with no rain at all // ~샘 intense [burning] jealousy // ~추위 dry cold weather.

강(江) a river; [강물] a stream; [시내] a brook. ¶~ 건너[에서] across[beyond] the river / on the other[opposite] side of the river / ~을 건너다 cross[go across] a river / (걸어서) wade (across)[ford] a stream / ~을 거슬러 올라가다 [내려가다] go up [down] a river / go upstream[downstream] / 이 범람했다 The river has overflowed its banks. / 이 ~은 황해로 흐른다 The river finds its way to the Yellow Sea.

강 건너 불구경 remain a mere [an idle] spectator [onlooker] stand by idly (and watch).

강(綱) [동] a class(▶ …강의 이름에는 어미에 -acea가 붙는다. (예) 갑각강 Crustacea).

강가(江-) a riverside; a riverbank; an edge of a river. ¶~의 풍경 the scenery along the river / ~의 산책길 a riverside promenade // ~에 살다 live on the banks of a river / ~를 거닐다 walk [stroll] along the river.

강간(强姦) rape; violation; outrage; assault. ¶~의 누명을 쓰다 be falsely [wrongly] accused of rape. **강간하다** rape; assault; violate; outrage; ravish. ¶열세 살 난 소녀를 ~ violate a 13-year-old girl. ➔¶강간당하다 be violated / be outraged / be attacked.

●**강간 미수** an attempted criminal assault [rape]. **강간범** a rapist; a violater[violator]. **강간죄** rape; criminal assault.

강강술래 [민] [춤] a *ganggangsullae*; a Korean circle [round] dance; [노래] the song that goes with the dance.

강건하다(剛健-) strong and sturdy; virile; vigorous; manly. ¶강건한 정신 a virile spirit // 강건한 기상을 기르다 cultivate the spirit of fortitude and manliness. **강건히** sturdily; manly; vigorously.

강건하다(强健-) strong; robust; hardy; healthy. ¶강건한 청년 a robust youngster // 강건한 신체 a strong[stout] body / a robust constitution // 그는 강건해 보인다 He looks sturdy[strong]. **강건히** strongly; robustly; healthily. ¶신체를 ~ 하다 build a strong body / strengthen one's body.

강경(强勁) [관형어적]. **강경하다** strong; firm; [단호한] resolute; unbending; unyielding; uncompromising. ¶강경한 결의문 a strongly-worded resolution // 강경한 태도를 취하다 take a firm [(구어) tough / stiff / hard-line] attitude[stand] / stand firm (against) // 강경한 수단을 쓰다 take [resort to] a drastic [strong] measure / take forceful action / have recourse to force // 강경한 반공 노선을 취하다 take a strong anti-Communist stand. **강경히** strongly; firmly; stoutly; resolutely. ¶~ 요구하다 strongly demand (an apology from …) // ~ 항의하다 protest vigorously (against) / file a vigorous protest (against) // ~ 주장하다 strenuously insist (on) / be very insistent (upon) // 그는 정부의 입장을 ~ 변호했다 He delivered a staunch defense of the government.// 그는 내 의견에 ~ 반대했다 He was firmly opposed to my view / He was dead against my opinion.

●**강경 노선** a hard line. **강경책** a hardline policy. **강경파** [주장을 고집하는 사람] hardliners; [매파] hawks.

강관(鋼管) a steel tube[pipe]; (집합적) steel tubing.

강괴(鋼塊) a steel ingot.

강구(講究) study; consideration; deliberation. **강구하다** study; consider; deliberate; devise; take. ¶적당한 수단을 ~ adopt[devise] a proper measure[means] (to) / take a proper step // 모든 수단을 강구했지만 허사였다 I tried every possible means, but nothing worked.// 그녀는 아직 아무런 수단도 강구하지 않았다 She has taken no action yet. // 그 사태에 대해 적절한 대책을 강구한 것은 스미스 씨였다 It was Mr. Smith who took the right steps [devised appropriate measures] to deal with the situation.

강국(强國) a great power; a strong nation [country]; a powerful state. ¶세계의 ~ the powers of the world / world powers // 5대 ~

강군 the Big Five / the five big[great] powers of the world.

강군(強軍) [강한 군대] a strong[powerful] army; a persistent force; [강팀] a strong team.

강권(強勸) recommending against (a person's) will; a persistent[an insistent] recommendation; urging; pressing. **강권하다** recommend against (a person's) will; urge; press. ¶술을 ~ press a drink on[upon] (a person)/환자에게 음식을 강권해서는 안 된다 Food should not be forced on the patient.

강권(強權) power; (the power of) authority; (법적인) legal authority. ¶~을 발동하다 invoke the power of the law (against) / bring the legal authority of the nation to bear on (a person)/그 건물은 ~에 의해 정발되었다 The buildings were requisitioned by the state.
● **강권 정치** power[a high-handed] politics. **강권주의** authoritarianism.

강기슭(江-) the banks[shores] of a river; a riverside. ¶~을 따라 상류 쪽으로 걸어가다 walk up the riverbank//~에 풀이 무성하게 자라나 있었다 The riverbank was overgrown with grass.

강남(江南) [강의 남쪽] the south of a river; [한강 이남] the south of the Hangang[Han River]; [양쯔 강 이남] the south of the Yangtze. ~의 **지역** the district south of the Hangang.

강낭콩 [식] a kidney bean; a haricot bean; a French bean.

강다짐 1 [맨밥을 먹음] forgoing the soup or other liquid one usually drinks while eating rice. **강다짐하다** eat (rice) without a beverage. 2 [보수 없이 부림] forcing (a person) to work without pay. **강다짐하다** force (a person) to work without pay. 3 [무턱대고 꾸짖음] scolding (a person) without listening to his side of the story. **강다짐하다** scold [reprove] (a person) without reason[listening to his side of the story].

강단(剛斷) 1 [결단력] decisiveness; determination; resolution. 2 [끈덕짐] latent[potential] energy; persevering strength; tenacity; perseverance. ¶~이 있는 strong / powerful / tenacious / sticky.

강단(講壇) a rostrum (pl. ~s, -tra); [학술의] a (lecture) platform; [설교의] a pulpit. ¶~에 서다 stand on a platform / take[occupy] the platform[rostrum] / preach a sermon.

강당(講堂) a lecture hall; (계단식) a lecture theater; a hall; (학교의) (미) an auditorium (pl. ~s, -ria); (영) an assembly hall. ¶졸업식은 ~에서 거행되었다 The graduation ceremony was held in the hall.

강대국(強大國) a powerful country; a big power.

강대하다(強大-) mighty; powerful; strong. ¶강대한 해군 a powerful navy.

강도(剛度) [물] (relative) stiffness.

강도(強度) intensity; powerfulness; degree of strength; [경도] solidity. ¶지진의 ~ seismic intensity.

강도(強盜) (사람) a robber; a burglar; a housebreaker; (행위) burglary; robbery. ¶권총 ~ (사람) a holdup man / a gunman / (행위) a holdup/노상 ~ (사람) a highwayman / a gentleman[knight / squire] of the road / (행위) highway robbery//살인 ~ (죄) burglary and murder//삼인조 ~ a trio of burglars//은행 ~ a bank burglar (사람) / bank robbery (행위)//흉기를 가진 [복면] ~ an armed[a masked] robber//노상 ~에게 털리다 be robbed by a highwayman//집에 ~가 들다 have one's house broken into / be robbed by a housebreaker//우리 집에 ~가 들었다 A burglar broke into my house.//요즘은 종종 ~ 사건이 있다 There have been several robberies lately.
● **강도질** robbery; burglary. ¶~을 하다 commit robbery[burglary].

강독(講讀) reading; translation. ¶원서 ~ textual exposition / reading original texts in class. **강독하다** read. ¶대학에서 셰익스피어를 ~ read Shakespeare(for[with] one's class) at the university.

강둑(江-) a river embankment[bank].

강등(降等) demotion; degradation. **강등하다** demote; degrade; lower the status[position] (of). ➔그는 과장에서 평사원으로 강등되었다 He was demoted from being a section head to the status of ordinary employee.

강력(強力) [관형어적]. ¶~ **비타민제** a high-potency vitamin preparation//초(超) ~ 수소 폭탄 a superpowerful hydrogen bomb[H-bomb]. **강력하다** strong; powerful; mighty. ¶강력한 내각 a strong[virile] Cabinet//강력한 후원자 a powerful[an influential] supporter//강력한 반대를 받다 meet with a stout[stubborn] opposition. **강력히** strongly; powerfully; [강경히] firmly; resolutely; with a high [strong] hand. ¶~ 항의하다 make a strong protest (against)//~ 요구하다 make a pressing demand//~ 거부하다 refuse (a person) flatly / give (a person) a flat refusal.
● **강력계** (사람) an officer[official] in charge of crimes of violence; (부서) a section in charge of crime of violence. **강력범** [범] (행위) a crime of violence; a major crime; a felony; (범인) a felonious[major] criminal; a criminal of violence.

강렬하다(強烈-) strong; intense; severe. ¶강렬한 색 loud colors//강렬한 자극 a strong stimulus. **강렬히** strongly; intensely; severely.

강령(綱領) 1 [으뜸 줄거리] a general plan; main[general] principles; [요점] an outline. ¶10대 ~ a 10-point program/철학 ~ an outline of philosophy. 2 [정당 등의 정책 요강] a platform. ¶당 대회에서 새로운 ~이 채택되었다 A new platform was adopted at the party convention.//그 정당은 어제 ~을 발표했다 The party set out its manifesto yesterday.

강론(講論) [토론] exposition; discussion; [설교] preaching; a sermon. **강론하다** expound; discuss; preach; teach.

강림(降臨) advent; descent; epiphany; Advent(그리스도의). ¶성령(聖靈) ~ the advent[descent] of the Holy Ghost. **강림하다** descend (upon); come down.

강매(強賣) coercive selling; high-pressure salesmanship; (구어) the hard sell. ¶모두들 ~에 화를 냈다 Everyone was angry at the hard sell.//~ 사절 (게시) Nothing Bought at the Door. / No Peddlers or Salesmen. / (영) No Hawkers or Salesmen. **강매하다** force a sale (on); force[press] (a person) to buy; force (a thing) on[upon] (a person). ¶학생들에게 참고서를 ~ press students to buy reference books// 외판원은 여자만 사는 가정인 줄 알고 강매하려고 했다 The salesman finding there were only woman in the house tried the hard sell.

강막(綱幕) ➡내림차

강모(剛毛) a bristle; a seta (*pl.* -tae); a striga (*pl.* -gae). ¶~이 있는[많은] bristled / setose // ~ 모양의 bristly / setaceous.

강목(綱目) an outline and details; divisions and subdivisions. ¶계획을 ~으로 나누어 검토하다 break a plan down and analyze it both generally and in detail.

강물(江-) river water; the river. ¶~이 넘친다 The river overflows[is flooded]. // ~이 준다 The river sinks. // ~이 불었다 The river is swollen[risen]. // 폭우로 ~이 범람했다 A heavy rain flooded the river. / The river was flooded by a heavy rain.

강바닥(江-) the river bed; the river bottom.

강바람 [건조하고 세찬 바람] a strong wind bringing no rain.

강바람(江-) a breeze from the river.

강박(强迫) compulsion; coercion; duress; constraint. **강박하다** compel; coerce; force; constrain.
● **강박 관념** an imperative idea[conception]; an obsession. ¶~에 사로잡히다 suffer from an obsession.

강밥 [강다짐으로 먹는 밥] boiled rice eaten without soup or water poured on it.

강변(江邊) a riverside. ⇨=강가
● **강변도로** a riverside road[drive].

강변(强辯) a quibble; (a) sophism; (a) sophistry. ¶그런 ~은 통하지 않는다 Such a far-fetched argument won't work. **강변하다** quibble; sophisticate; give a strained meaning. ¶네가 아무리 강변하더라도 그 사실을 은폐할 수는 없다 You can argue as much as you like but you can't hide the facts. // 그 시계가 자기 책상 위에 있었으니 그것이 자기 것이라고 그는 강변했다 He insisted (obstinately) that the watch was his because it was on his desk.

강병(强兵) a powerful army; a strong soldier; [병력의 강화] military buildup.

강보(襁褓) swaddling clothes; a swaddle; a baby's quilt. ¶아이를 ~로 싸다 wrap an infant in swaddling clothes / swaddle an infant.

강보합(强保合) ¶~의 [증권] firm [steady] with an upward tendency.

강복(降福) [가] benediction; blessing. **강복하다** bless.

강북(江北) [강의 북쪽] the north of a river; [한강 이북] the north of the Hangang[Han River]; [양쯔 강 이북] the north of the Yangtze. ¶~ 지역 the district north of the Hangang.

강사(講士) [연사] a speaker; a lecturer.

강사(講師) 1 [연사] a lecturer. 2 [대학의] (미) an instructor; (영) a lecturer. ¶대학 ~ a lecturer (on[in] English literature) / ~ 로 [in] a university / a college lecturer // 시간 ~ a part-time lecturer / (중·고교의) a part-time teacher // 전임 ~ an (a full-time) instructor // 철학 ~ a lecturer on[in] philosophy // ~로 임명되다 be appointed a lecturer [to lectureship].

강삭(鋼索) a wire rope; a cable; a steel rope; a hawser.
● **강삭 철도** a cable railway; a rope railway.

강산(江山) [강과 산] rivers and mountains; [경치] landscape; scenery; [강토] a country; a territory; a realm; a domain. ¶금수~ a beautiful[scenic] land / a country noted for the beauty in the landscape.

강상(江上) [강물 위] the surface of the river [water].

강샘 unreasonable[burning / intense] jealousy. **강샘하다** be[feel] burning jealousy (of / over); become intensely jealous; burn with jealousy; be green with envy.

강생(降生) incarnation. ¶신의 그리스도로의 ~ the Incarnation of God in Christ. **강생하다** become incarnate.

강선(鋼線) a steel wire.

강설(降雪) snowing; a snowfall. ¶어젯밤에는 20센티의 ~이 있었다 There was a snowfall of 20 centimeters [Twenty centimeters of snow fell] last night. // 대만에서는 ~을 볼 수 없다 Formosa is free from snow. // 대관령 일대에 큰 ~이 있었다 A heavy snowfall was experienced at Daegwallyeong and neighborhood.
● **강설량** (the amount of) snowfall. ¶이번 겨울에는 ~이 적었다 We have had little snow during the winter.

강설(講說) a lecture (on). ⇨=강의

강성하다(强盛-) [몸이] vigorous; energetic; [번성하다] powerful; thriving; prosperous. ¶강성해지다 become powerful and prosperous.

강세(强勢) 1 [언] stress; emphasis; accent. ¶~가 있는 음절 a stressed syllable // ~를 두다 put emphasis (on) // 이 말은 제2음절에 ~를 두고 발음한다 In pronouncing this word we stress[lay stress on / put the stress on] the second syllable. 2 [시장·주식 시세의 오름세] a strong feeling[market]; a firm [high] tone; a bull; a bullish tendency. ¶~의 strong / firm / bullish // ~로 나오다 be aggressive // 시장은 ~를 보이고 있다 The tone of the market is strong. // 하강세의 주식 시세가 ~로 돌아섰다 The declining stock market has firmed up[turned bullish].
● **강세 시장** (a) bull[strong] market. **강세주** bull shares.

강속구(强速球) [야구의] a fast[speed] ball; a fireball.

강수(降水) rainfall; precipitation.
● **강수량** (the amount of) rainfall [precipitation].

강술 a drink without any food; just liquor; alcoholic beverages without snacks. ¶~을 마시다 have a drink without eatables.

강술(講述) lecturing; expounding; a discourse. **강술하다** [강의하다] lecture (on); give a lecture (on); [설명하다] explain; give an explanation (of); expound.

강습(强襲) a storm; an assault; [야구에서] a vehement attack. ¶~대(隊) a storming party / a storm troop // 2루 ~ 땅볼[vicious] grounder to second baseman // ~ 점령하다 take (a fort) by storm // 그 타자는 투수쪽 ~의 내야 안타로 1루에서 살았다 The batter made it safely to first base on a smash too hot for the pitcher to handle. **강습하다** storm; assault. ¶3루를 강습하는 히트를 때리

다 send a hard-hit ball to third for a single // 우리는 적진을 강습했다 We made a fierce attack on the enemy's position.

강습(講習) a short training course[class]; studying; learning. ¶~을 받다 take short-term course (of English) / attend a class / take lessons (in English) // 수영 ~을 받다 take lessons in swimming // 요리 ~을 받다 take classes in cookery. **강습하다** give[offer] a course (in).
● **강습생** a student; a trainee. **강습소** a training school. ¶요리 ~ a cooking school. **강습회** an institute; a short course (of study); a (lecture) class.

강시(僵屍) a frozen corpse.

강신술(降神術) spiritualism; mediumism; typology. ¶~의 spiritistic / spiritualistic / mediumistic.

강심(江心) the "heart"[very middle] of a river.

강심제(強心劑) heart medicine; a cardiotonic drug; a cardiac; a cordial; a heart stimulant.

강아지 a puppy; a little dog; a doggie; a pup. ¶~ 때부터 기르다 raise (a dog) from a puppy // ~가 깽깽거렸다 The puppy whined.

강아지풀 [식] a foxtail.

강압(強壓) pressure; oppression; coercion; repression; compulsion; high-handedness. **강압하다** coerce; oppress; repress; put pressure (upon). ¶강압하여 복종시키다 coerce (a person) into submission.
● **강압 정책** a high-handed policy; (미) a big-stick policy. **강압 통풍** forced draft [draught].

강압적(強壓的) oppressive; overbearing; high-handed; [강제적인] coercive. ¶~인 수단으로 유권자를 누르다 coerce voters with a high-hand // 그의 태도는 매우 ~이다 His attitude is very heavy-handed[coercive].

강약(強弱) 1 [힘의 강함과 약함] strength and weakness; [강자와 약자] the strong and the weak. ¶~을 다투다 contend for the top position // 이 시합에서 ~이 판가름 난다 This game will make to clear which side is (the) stronger. 2 [음의] stress; (a) rhythm; [악센트] accentuation; [음악에서의 강약법] dynamics. ¶그 음절에서는 ~을 분명히 하라 Emphasize the dynamics in those passages.
● **강약 기호 / 강약 부호** [음] dynamic marks. ⇨ 셈여림표

강어귀(江-) the mouth of a river; [조수의 간만이 있는 넓은 강구] an estuary. ¶이 ~의 넓이는 2킬로이다 This river is two kilometers wide at the mouth.

강연(講演) a lecture; an address; a speech; a discourse. ¶공개 ~ public lecture // 시국 ~ a lecture on the current topics // 역사 ~ a lecture upon history // **연속** ~ serial [a series of] lecture (on) // 학회에서의 ~ a lecture to a learned society // 그 ~에는 상당한 청중이 있었다 There was a good[large] attendance at the lecture. **강연하다** (give a) lecture (on); address (a meeting); make an address (on); make a speech. ¶그 문제에 대해 ~ give a lecture[talk] on the subject // 라디오를 통해 ~ make a lecture over the radio[on the air] // 강연해 주기를 부탁하다 ask[invite] (a person) to give a lecture / ask (a person) to address[speak to] (students) // 브라운 박사는 오찬회에서 강연했다 Dr. Brown made a speech at the luncheon.

● **강연료** a lecture's fee. **강연자** a lecturer; a speaker. **강연회** a meeting to hear a speech; a lecture meeting.

강옥(鋼玉) corundum; ruby; sapphire.

강요(強要) a (forcible) demand; compulsion; enforcement; exaction; extortion. **강요하다** (상대방 의사를 거스르고) force[compel] (a person to do); (세금·벌금·의무·의견 등을) impose (a thing on a person); (권위를 갖고) demand forcibly; (지불·복종 등을) exact; (위협·압력으로) coerce; (구어) high-pressure (a person into doing). ¶복종을 ~ exact obedience from (a person) // 노동을 ~ force labor (upon a person) // 자백을 ~ extort a confession from (a person) // 당신은 내게 복종을 강요하려고 하는가 Are you trying to force me to obey? // 그는 자기 생각을 아들들에게 강요했다 He imposed his will on his sons. // 그는 내게 술을 마시도록 강요했다 He insisted on my drinking. // 그는 그녀에게 즉각 사직하도록 강요했다 He demanded that she (should) resign immediately. // 그들은 그에게 기부금을 강요했다 They coerced him into donating money. // 그는 빚을 갚으라고 강요했다 He put pressure on me to repay my debt at once. →¶**강요당하여** by[under / on] pressure (from) / under compulsion // 그는 꼼짝 못하고 그 일을 강요당했다 He was made [compelled / forced] to do it willy-nilly. // 나는 백과사전을 사도록 강요당했다 I was pressured to buy the encyclopedia. // 나는 자발적이기보다는 강요되어 기부금을 냈다 My donation was more forced than voluntary. // 그는 강요당하여 굴복했다 He was forced [compelled] to submit. // 그녀는 사직을 강요당하여 그만두었다 She has been forced out of office. / She was compulsorily relieved of his post.

강우(降雨) a rainfall; raining; [기상] precipitation. ¶심한 ~ a heavy rain / (미) a downpour // 많은 ~ a copious[an abundant] rain // ~가 계속되다 have a long spell of rainy [wet] weather // 작년에는 다량의 ~가 있었다 There was much rain last year. // ~로 인하여 강물이 불었다 The rain caused the rivers to rise. // ~ 부족으로 농작물이 자라지 않는다 The crops are suffering from little [deficient] rain. // 어제의 ~ 범위는 한반도 전역에 미쳤다 The rain area yesterday spread over most of the Korean Peninsula. **강우하다** it rains; rain falls.
● **강우계** a rain gauge. **강우기** the rainy season. **강우량** (the amount of) rainfall; a rainfall; (the record of) precipitation. ¶간밤의 ~은 50밀리를 넘었다 We had over fifty millimeters of rain last night. // 이 지방의 연간 ~은 500밀리를 넘는다 The annual precipitation[rainfall] in this district is over 500 mm. **강우림** a rain forest. **강우 전선** a rain front.

강의(講義) a lecture (on); a discourse; an exposition; (설명) an explanation. ¶공개 ~ an open class / (대학의) an extension lecture [course] // 과외 ~ an extracurriculum lecture // 문법 ~ a lecture on grammar // 집중 ~ an intensive course of lectures // 한국사의 ~ lectures on Korean history // ~을 시작하다 open one's course of lecture // ~에 나가다 (교수가) attend a lecture[one's classes] // ~를 노트하다 take notes on[of] a lecture

// ~를 빼먹다 cut a lecture / (미) play hooky / (영) play truant // 민 선생님 ~를 받고 있다 I am in Mr. Min's class. // 차 교수는 새 학기부터 햄릿의 연속 ~를 한다 Professor Cha will deliver a series of lectures on Hamlet beginning the new term. 강의하다 lecture (on a subject); give a lecture (on); give a course (in); teach. ¶영어로 ~ give a lecture in English // 그는 대학에서 철학을 강의한다 He lectures[gives lectures] on philosophy at the university.
● 강의록 a transcript of lectures; a correspondence course. 강의법 the manner of lecturing. 강의실 a lecture room.
강인성(強靭性) tenacity; toughness; solidarity.
강인하다(強靭─) strong; tough; persevering; tenacious; stiff. ¶무두질한 가죽처럼 강인한 as tough as tanned leather // 강인한 의지 a strong will / tenacity of purpose // 강인한 정신 a mind of steel // 강인한 신경의 소유자 a man of steely[iron] nerves.
강자(強者) a strong man; the strong; the powerful. ¶~와 약자 the strong and the weak // 싸움은 ~가 이기기 마련이다 The battle is to the strong.
강자성(強磁性) [물] ferromagnetism.
● 강자성체 [물] a ferromagnetic body [substance].
강장(強壯) robustness; healthiness. 강장하다 robust; sturdy; stout.
● 강장 음료 a tonic drink. 강장제 a tonic (medicine); a cordial; an invigorant; a restorative; (미국 속어) a pep pill.
강장강장 at a trot; with short steps. 강장강장하다 trot. ⇨강장거리다
강장거리다 trot; walk with short[mincing] steps.
강장동물(腔腸動物) a coelenterate.
강재(鋼材) steel (materials); (기계·건축용) structural steel. ¶압연 ~ rolled steel // 재생 ~ rerolled steel // 반제품 ~ semifinished steel products.
강적(強敵) a powerful enemy[adversary]; a formidable foe[rival]; (시합의) a powerful rival[opponent]. ¶~과 싸우다 fight against a powerful enemy[great odds] / contend against heavy odds // 일치단결하여 ~에 대항하다 unite themselves[present a united front] against a powerful enemy // ~이 나타났다 A powerful rival has come to the front. // 그는 ~이었다 I found a formidable rival in him. // 그녀는 사업상의 ~이다 She is a formidable[powerful] rival of mine in business.
강점(強占) occupation[possession] by force. ¶토지의 ~ [법] deforcement / detention. 강점하다 occupy[possess] (a person's house) by force.
강점(強點) one's strength[power]; a strong point; an element of strength. ¶~과 약점 one's strong and weak points // …의 ~이 있다 have the advantage of … // (상대에 대하여) ~을 갖고 있다 have an advantage over[an edge on] (a person) // 그의 ~은 수학을 잘한다는 데에 있다 His strength[strong point] lies in his mathematical ability. // 그의 글의 ~은 독창적인 의견이라기보다 명쾌한 설명에 있다 The strength of his writings lies in lucid exposition rather than in original ideas. // 그것이 그의 최대의 ~이다 That is

where he is at his strongest. // 정직만이 그의 ~이다 His only strength is honesty / He is nothing, if not honest.
강정 [찹쌀 과자] *gangjeong*; a fried glutinous rice cake; [물엿에 알곡을 버무린 것] a kind of cake made from rice[sesame / bean] mixed with glutinous rice-jelly.
강정제(強精劑) a tonic; the pills of extra strength and super potency; aphrodisiac.
강제(強制) compulsion; (문어) coercion; constraint; forcing; duress. ¶~적인 compulsory / coercive / forced // ~적으로 forcibly / by force / compulsorily / by compulsion / coercively // ~로 수용하다 take (a person) into custody. 강제하다 force; compel; coerce. ¶노동을 ~ force (a person) to work (against one's will). // 강제당하여 on [under] compulsion / under duress // 죄수들은 줄무늬의 제복을 입도록 강제되었다 The prisoners were forced to wear striped uniforms.
● 강제 가격 a forced price. 강제 결혼 a forced marriage; a marriage by force. 강제 공채 forced loan. 강제력 compelling power [force]; (법률상의) legal force. 강제 보험 compulsory insurance. 강제 송환 enforced [forced] repatriation. 강제 수용 detention by legal force. 강제 수용소 a concentration camp. 강제 집행 [법] (compulsory / forcible) execution; [압류] distraint. 강제 처분 legal disposition; compulsory execution. 강제 철거 forced demolition. 강제 통화 forced currency; legal tender.
강조(強調) stress; emphasis; accentuation. ¶방화[방범] ~ 주간 Fire[Crime] Prevention Week. 강조하다 emphasize; stress; accentuate; lay[place / put] stress[emphasis] (on); highlight; underline. ¶크게 ~ lay[place / put] great emphasis (on / upon) // 지나치게 ~ overemphasize / lay excessive[too much] emphasis (on) // 국방의 필요성을 ~ stress the need[necessity] of national defense // 안전 보장 문제를 ~ accentuate the idea of national safety and security // 이 점을 특히 강조하여 말씀드리고 싶습니다 I want to say this with special emphasis[to emphasize this in particular]. // 이 무늬는 특히 대각선을 강조하였습니다 I have accentuated the diagonal lines in this pattern. // 그것은 특히 강조할 가치가 있다 It deserves special emphasis. // 그는 문제의 중대성을 크게 강조했다 He was very emphatic on the importance of the matter. ➔별로 강조되지 않다 be[get] deemphasized.
강좌(講座) (대학의) a chair; a lectureship; professorship; (강습의) a course; a lecture. ¶음악 ~ lectures on music // 공개 ~ an [a university] extension course / an open lecture / (영) an extramural course // 라디오 영어 ~ English language lessons by radio / a radio English course / a radio lecture [course] in English // 성인 ~ an adult institute / ~ 특별 ~ a special course // 근대 미술 ~ a series of lectures on modern art // 자유 ~ a free chair // 공무원 수험 ~ a correspondence course for those preparing for the civil service examinations // ~를 개설하다 create [establish / found] a chair (of) // 그는 이 대학에서 역사[민법] ~를 맡고 있다 He holds[occupies] the chair of history[civil law] at this university.

강주정(-酒酊) feigned intoxication; an affected drunkenness. **강주정하다** pretend to be drunk.

강줄기(江-) the course of a river. ¶~를 따라 along a river∥~는 여기서 서쪽으로 꺾이고 Here the river turns to the west[westward]. ∥~가 평야를 가로지르고 있다 A river winds through a plain.

강즙(薑汁) ginger juice.

강직(強直) [의] rigidity; stiffness. ¶관절 ~ ankylosis / anchylosis.
● **강직성 경련** tetanus; tonic cramp.

강직하다(剛直-) incorruptible; upright; staunch; (서술적) have a moral courage. ¶ 강직한 사람 a man of integrity / an upright man∥그는 강직하기로 유명했다 He was famous for his integrity.

강진(強震) a severe[violent] earthquake; a severe tremor[shock]; a very strong earthquake. ¶근년에 없던 ~ the severest earthquake in recent years / one of the most terrific earthquake shocks ever felt in years[for years past] ∥ 간밤 이곳에 ~이 있었다 A severe shock[earthquake] was felt here last night.
● **강진계** a strong-motion seismograph.

강짜 unreasonable jealousy; burning [intense] jealousy. ¶~를 부리다 show burning jealousy.

강철(鋼鐵) steel. ¶~ 같은 의지[육체] an iron will[physique] / ~ 같은 마음 a heart of steel / ~제의 (made) of steel / steel / ~ 전부로 된 all-steel (car)∥잘 단련된 ~ steel of the finest temper.
● **강철관** a steel pipe[tube]. **강철판** steel plate[plank].

강청(強請) [강요] an importunate[a persistent] demand; exaction; (공갈로) blackmail; extortion. **강청하다** demand persistently; force (a person to do); importune (a person to do); exact (payment); blackmail; extort. ¶기부금을 ~ solicit (a person) importunately for contributions∥그 지도자는 부하들에게 충성을 강청했다 The leader extorted loyalty from his followers.

강촌(江村) a riverside village.

강추위 a spell of cold dry weather; intense [bitter] cold.

강치 [동] a sea lion; a hair seal.

강타(強打) 1 [강한 타격] a heavy[hard / hefty] blow; (구어) a wallop; (미국 구어) a slug; (권투에서) a Sunday punch. ¶~를 퍼붓다 rain hard blows (on). **강타하다** deal (a person) a heavy hit; hard; slog; (미국 구어) slug; (구어) swat[wallop] (a ball). ¶어깨를 ~ deal[strike] (a person) a hard [heavy] blow on the shoulder (with)∥계속해서 ~ rain hard blows (on). ➡¶가슴을 강타당하다 be hit hard[receive a hard blow] on one's chest∥옆구리를 강타당하여 숨이 막혔다 I was hit so hard in the ribs that I gasped.
2 [야구] a terrific[hard / heavy] drive[hit]; [골프·테니스] a powerful drive. ¶~를 터뜨리다 unleash a terrific drive.

강타자(強打者) a hard[heavy] hitter; (구어) a slugger; a (powerful) swatter; a slogger; a power[long-ball] hitter.

강탄(降誕) birth; nativity; [강림] advent; incarnation. ¶예수의 ~ the Nativity / the Advent / the birth of Jesus Christ∥그리스도~절 Christmas tide∥석존 ~제 the celebration of the nativity of Buddha. **강탄하다** be born; see the light; become incarnate.

강탈(強奪) extortion; [강도] (a) robbery; (선박·토지 등의) (a) seizure; plunder; [침입자 등에 의한 약탈] depredation; (미) hijacking; a stickup; [노상강도 행위] holdup. **강탈하다** extort; rob[despoil / plunder / loot] (a person) of (a thing); snatch (a thing) from (a person); seize; (미국 구어) hijack; stick up (a person / a bank). ¶그 도둑은 내게서 돈을 강탈하고 도망쳤다 The thief robbed me of my money and run away. ➡¶강탈당하다 be robbed of (a thing) / have (something) taken[snatched] away / have (something) stolen∥온 마을이 침략자들에게 강탈당했다 The whole village was plundered by the invaders.
● **강탈물** plunder; spoil; loot; booty. **강탈자** a robber; a plunderer; (미) a hijacker.

강태공(姜太公) an angler; a roadster; a Waltonian.

강토(疆土) a territory; a realm; a domain.

강판(鋼板) a steel sheet; sheet steel; a steel plate. ¶아연 도금 ~ a galvanized steel sheet.

강판(薑板) a grater. ¶~에 갈다 grate (an apple).

강평(講評) comment; criticism; review. **강평하다** criticize; comment on; review; make [offer] comment on.

강풍(江風) a breeze from the river. ⇨ 강바람

강풍(罡風) a strong[high] wind; a gale; [기상] a moderate gale. ¶~에 견디다 stand a strong wind∥~이 불고 있다 It is blowing a gale.∥태풍이 접근하여 부산 지방에는 이미 ~권에 들어 있다 Strong advance winds of the oncoming typhoon are already lashing the Busan area.
● **강풍 주의보** a strong-wind warning.

강하(降下) falling; dropping; a drop; descent; (기압의) depression. ¶급~ nose diving / a nose dive∥기온의 ~ a drop in (the) temperature. **강하하다** fall; drop; descend; glide down; [착륙하다] land. ¶고도 1천 피트까지 ~ descend[glide down] to a height of 1,000 feet∥이 지방에서 기온이 갑자기 강하했다 The temperature has shown a sharp fall in this part of the country. / There was a cold snap in this section of the country.
● **강하 지대** (낙하산 부대의) a drop zone.

강하다(強-) 1 [강력하다] strong; powerful; mighty. ¶강한 나라 a strong nation / a great power∥강한 자 a strong man∥강한 어조 an emphatic tone∥세력이 강해지다 increase in power / redouble the force∥강한 자가 이긴다 The battle is to the strong.∥저 학교는 스포츠가 ~ That school is strong on sports.
2 [강건하다] robust; stout. ¶심장이 ~ have a strong heart.
3 [강렬하다] severe; intense; hard; heavy. ¶강한 바람 a strong[severe / sharp] wind∥강한 소독약의 냄새 the sharp[strong] smell of a disinfectant∥강한 감정 an intense feeling∥강한 햇빛 bright[dazzling] sunshine∥광선이 너무 ~ The light is too strong.∥그 강연자[연사]는 교육자의 의무에 대해 강한 어조로 말했다 The speaker spoke forcefully about the duty of educators.∥연설을 듣고 그가 큰

인물이라는 인상이 더욱 강해졌다 His speech deepened[strengthened / 〈문어〉 enhanced] my impression that he was a great man.∥그는 내게 강한 인상을 심어 주었다 His image is deeply impressed on my mind.
4 〔굳세다〕 stout; strong; firm. ¶강한 의지 a strong will / an iron will∥도덕심이 강한 사람 a person of strict morals∥의지가 ~ be firm of purpose∥그는 책임감이 ~ He has a strong[keen] sense of responsibility.∥남자는 강하면서도 다정한 일면이 있어야 한다 Tender affection should go with strong manliness. / Strong manliness should be tempered with tender affection.
5 〔저항력이〕 resistant; tolerant. ¶추위에 강한 식물 a hardy plant∥병에 ~ be resistant to diseases∥이 식물은 추위에~ This plant is resistant to cold.∥이 나무들은 공해에 ~ These trees are tolerant of pollution.
강행(強行) enforcement; forcing. ¶~ 공사 rush[lightning / speedy construction] work∥무리한 계획의 ~ the enforcement of an impractical plan∥그들은 그 법안을 국회에서 ~ 가결시켰다 They rammed[〈구어〉 railroaded] the bill through the National Assembly. **강행하다** enforce; force. ¶증세(增稅)[고물가 정책 / 저물가 정책]를 ~ enforce a tax increase[high-price policy / low-price policy]∥호우 속에서 시합을 ~ keep playing a game in the downpour∥그는 무모한 계획을 강행하다가 목숨을 잃었다 He met his death trying to push ahead with his wild scheme.
강행군(強行軍) a forced march (of several days). ¶미국을 1주일 동안에 순회하는 ~ an exhausting tour around the U.S. in a week. **강행군하다** make[go on] a forced march. ¶우리는 이 작업을 강행군하여 끝내라는 명령을 받았다 We were ordered to rush this work.
강호(強豪) a veteran(player); a powerful man. ¶~끼리의 대전 competition between very strong teams∥전국에서 뽑힌 ~ 팀 powerful teams selected all over the country∥우리 팀은 첫날부터 ~ 와 맞부딪치게 되었다 Our team was paired against a powerhouse on the first day.
강호(江湖) 〔강과 호수〕 rivers and lakes; 〔자연〕 nature; 〔은둔처〕 a place[country] of seclusion; a retreat; 〔세상〕 the (general) public; the world.
● **강호 제현** the general public; people at large.
강화(強化) strengthening; solidification; consolidating; reinforcement; firming up; fortification. ¶전력의 ~ buildup of war potential∥그는 당내에서의 발언권 ~를 위해 애쓰고 있다 He is trying to strengthen his voice within the party. **강화하다** strengthen; intensify; solidify; firm up; reinforce. ¶입구의 경비를 ~ strengthen the guard at the entrance∥팀을 ~ strengthen a team / build up the strength of a team∥극좌 분자의 탄압을 ~ intensify the suppression of leftist extremists∥국방을 ~ strengthen[increase] the national defenses∥지위를 ~ consolidate one's footing[position] (in)∥통제를 ~ clamp[tighten] control (of / over)∥비타민을 넣어 식품을 ~ enrich[fortify] food with vitamins∥정부는 언론 자유 통제를 강화하려는 속셈이다 The government intends to tighten controls on freedom of speech.
● **강화미**(-米) enriched rice. **강화식품** (vitamin-)enriched foods. **강화 유리** tempered glass. **강화제** 〔화〕 a reinforcing agent. **강화 훈련** intensified training. ¶대표 선수들에게 합숙 ~을 실시하다 provide intensified camp training for the members of a (soccer) delegation.
강화(講和) an amicable settlement; peace; reconciliation. ¶다면 ~ a multiple peace / 다수 ~ a majority peace∥단독 ~ a separate peace∥전면 ~ an overall peace (settlement)∥굴욕적인 ~ a humiliating peace / an ignoble peace∥~의 제의 peace proposals / ~의 교섭 negotiations for peace / a peace talk∥양국 간에 ~가 성립되었다 The two countries made peace.∥정부는 ~를 밝혔다 The government made overtures of peace. **강화하다** make[conclude] peace (with); lay down one's arms; sheathe the sword; bury the hatchet (with).
● **강화 사절** a peace envoy[delegate]. **강화 조약** a peace treaty[pact]; a treaty of peace. **강화 회의** a peace conference.
강회(-膾) a small roll of boiled celery or scallion (eaten with drinks).
갖가지 various kinds (of); all sorts (of). ⇨가지가지
갖다 1 have; hold; conceive. ⇨가지다 ¶아이들이 성냥을 갖고 있지 못하게 하시오 Don't let children get hold of matches.∥그는 상업상의 지식을 충분히 갖고 있다 He has enough knowledge of business. **2** 〔가져다가〕. ¶물을 한 컵 ~ 다오 Get me a glass of water.∥사장님이 그 서류를 ~ 달라고 하십니다 The president is calling for the document.
갖바치 a maker of leather shoes; a shoemaker.
갖신 leather shoes.
갖옷 clothes lined with fur; fur-lined clothes.
갖은 〔모든〕 all; all sorts[manner] of; every; every possible; 〔빠짐없는〕 complete; perfect; well-made; 〔갖가지의〕 various; a variety of; 〔골고루 갖춘〕 assorted; well-assorted. ¶~ 것 all sorts of things / everything∥~ 고생 all kinds of hardships[troubles]∥~ 양념 all sorts of spices∥~ 고생을 하다 go through all kinds of hardships[troubles]∥~ 수단을 다 쓰다 try every means conceivable / try every possible means∥~ 욕을 다 보다 suffer all sorts of humiliation∥~ 죄를 범하다 have long list of criminal acts.
갖추 〔고루〕 exhaustively; (all-)inclusively; completely; fully; with no omissions; thoroughly. ¶가게에 물건을 ~ 벌여 놓다 put out all kinds of goods in a store∥음식을 ~ 차리다 prepare a full-course dinner.
갖추다 1 〔고루 준비하다〕 be[get] ready; be prepared; have. ¶준비는 갖추어졌다 Our preparations are complete. / We are ready.∥그들은 여장(旅裝)을 갖추었다 They prepared [got ready] for a journey.∥나는 파티 준비를 모두 갖추었다 I got everything ready for the party.∥이 도서관에는 생물 관계의 책이 갖추어져 있다 This library has a good collection of books on biology.∥저 가게에는 어린이용 상품이 모두 갖추어져 있다 They carry[stock] everything for children at that store.
2 〔제대로 완비되다〕 equip; furnish; com-

갖춘꽃

plete; assort. ¶이것으로 만찬 식기 세트가 갖추어진다 This completes the dinner set.∥이 사무실에는 소화기가 갖추어져 있지 않다 This office is not equipped with fire extinguishers.∥이 호텔은 방마다 냉장고가 갖추어져 있다 Each room in this hotel is provided [furnished] with a refrigerator.∥이 사무실에는 책상과 의자가 갖추어져 있다 This office is furnished with desks and chairs.∥적은 중무장을 갖추고 있었다 The enemy was heavily armed.

3 (재능·성질·능력 등을 지니다) possess; be blessed (with); be endowed (with talent). ¶그녀는 아름다움과 지성, 그리고 건강이라는 장점을 모두 갖춘 (이상적인) 여성이다 She is an all-round [ideal] woman — beautiful, intelligent and healthy.∥우리에게는 손님의 수효만큼의 유리컵이 갖추어져 있지 않다 We do not have enough glasses for all the guests.∥이 백과사전은 몇 권이 빠져, 제대로 갖추어져 있지 않다 Some volumes of this encyclopedia are missing.∥그녀는 법률 지식을 충분히 갖추고 있다 She has a thorough knowledge of law.∥그는 한국인의 전형적인 장점과 단점을 모두 갖추고 있다 He possesses both the typical strong and weak points of the Korean.∥그는 교사로서 충분한 자격을 갖추고 있다 He is well qualified as a teacher.∥그는 성악에 대한 천부의 재능을 갖추고 있다 He is endowed with vocal talent.∥그녀에게는 천부의 품위가 갖추어져 있다 She is endowed by nature with grace. / She possesses grace by nature. / She is naturally blessed with grace.

갖춘꽃 [식] a perfect[complete] flower.
갖춘마디 [음] a complete bar.
갖춘잎 [식] a complete leaf.
갚풀 glue (made from oxhide); gelatin(e).
같다 1 (동일하다) the same; identical (with); the self same. ¶거의 ~ be much[about / almost] the same (as)∥옛날과 같은 그 거리 the same old street∥양복과 같은 재료의 모자 a cap of the same material as a dress∥해마다 같은 날에 on the same day every year∥같은 소리를 몇 번이나 되풀이하다 say the same thing again and again / repeat oneself / harp on the same string (구어) rub (it) in∥우리는 서로 같은 인간이다 We are fellow human being.∥네 것과 같은 사전을 나도 갖고 있다 I have the same dictionary as yours.∥마크 트웨인과 새뮤얼 클레멘스는 같은 사람이었다 Mark Twain and Samuel Clemens were one and the same person.∥나도 당신과 꼭 같은 생각입니다 Your thoughts echo mine.∥두 사람은 꼭 같은 장점과 단점을 지니고 있다 The two have the same merits and the same faults.∥쾌락의 기대는 욕망과 같은 것이다 Expectation of pleasure is the same thing with desire.∥이 부근의 도로는 그 폭이 모두 ~ In this neighborhood the roads are all the same width.∥나는 같은 천으로 스커트를 기웠다[고쳤다] I mended a skirt with cloth of the same material.∥이와 꼭 같은 것을 어제 보았다 I saw just such another yesterday.

2 (동등하다) equal (to); uniform; equivalent (to). ¶같은 양의 물 an equal amount of water∥같은 액수 a like sum∥같은 입장에서 on an equal[the same] footing∥질이 같은 재료 materials of comparable quality∥같은 조건으로 교섭하다 negotiate on equal terms∥그와 나는 키가 거의 ~ He is about as tall as I.∥너의 넥타이는 내 것과 꼭 ~ Your tie is just like mine.∥기둥이 같은 간격으로 서 있다 The poles stand at equal intervals.

3 (비유) (…의 성격이 있다) like; alike; as. ¶악마 같은 사나이 a devil of a man∥천사 같은 소녀 an angel of a girl∥산더미 같은 파도 a mountain of a wave∥어머니 같은 애정 motherly love / affection like a mother's∥온 시가지가 하나의 커다란 공원 ~ The whole city strikes us as one big park.

4 (유사하다) similar (to); as. ¶죽은 거나 ~ be practically [virtually / as good as] dead∥새것 ~ be as good as new∥그는 꼭 갓난애와 ~ He is no better than a baby.∥이것은 내게 있어서 사형 선고를 받은 것과 ~ This is as much as [tantamount to] a death sentence to me.

5 (… 종류이다) a sort of; like; of the same kind; similar in kind; such ... as. ¶그와 같은 사람 a man like him / the like of him∥장난감 같은 것 toys or the like∥그는 네가 생각하고 있는 그런 같은 대학자가 아니야 He is not such a great scholar as you think.∥나는 그와 같은 말을 할 인간이 아니다 I am not the man to say such a thing.∥네가 학교 선생 같은 사람이 될 수 있겠느냐 Can you be a teacher or anything like that?∥이 같은 것은 어떻습니까 How about something like this?∥그는 일요일 같은 날에는 자주 찾아오곤 했다 He would call on us of a Sunday.

6 (…으로 추측되다) seem; appear; look; likely (to do). ¶눈이 내릴 것 ~ It looks like snow [as if it might snow].∥비가 올[오는 / 오던 / 왔던] 것 ~ It looks as though it were going to rain [were raining / has rained / has been raining / had been raining].∥그 남자는 장사꾼 같았다 The man was apparently a merchant.∥재미있을 것 ~ It sounds like fun.∥그는 이 사실을 알지 못하는 것 ~ He seems to be ignorant of this fact. / It seems that he is unaware of this fact.∥내가 뭐 같으냐 What do you take me for?∥그는 피곤한[기뻐하는] 것 ~ He looks tired [pleased].∥그는 정직한 사람 ~ He seems to be an honest man. / I suppose he is an honest man.∥그 대답이 실망시킬 만한 것이었던 것 ~ It would seem that the reply was a disappointing one.∥나도 할 수 있을 것 ~ I feel I can do it.

7 (…으로 가정하다) if it were; in case. ¶나 같으면 if it were me / if I were you∥옛날 같으면 if these were the old days∥나 같으면 그런 짓은 안 한다 (If I were you,) I would not do such a thing.∥이런 경우 너 같으면 어떻게 하겠니 What would you do in such a case?

8 (…답다) like; worthy of; becoming. ¶길 같은 길 a road worthy of the name [that can be called a road]∥사람 같은 사람 a real man∥집 같은 집이 없다 There is no house to speak of [worth mentioning].

9 (공통적이다) common. ¶기원이 ~ have a common origin (with)∥나 같은 일을 하고 있는 사람 a fellow worker∥삶을 사랑하고 죽음을 두려워하기는 사람이나 동물이나 ~ Love of life and fear of death are common to man and beasts.∥이 사람들은 국적은 다르지만 이해 관계는 ~ These men differ in nationality, but their interests are identical[common].

같은 값이면 다홍치마(속담) Other things [Prices] being equal, choose the better one.; Quality is preferable to size[quantity].

같은 값이면 preferably; other things being equal; if it is all the same (to). ¶~ 큰 것이 좋다 I will take the larger one, if I must take either.// ~ 잘하다 treat (men) if you do it at all, do it well.// ~ 나는 이것을 고르겠다 I should choose this in preference to any other.

같이 1〔같게〕 as; like; in the same way [manner]; similarly; in a similar way; alike; likewise. ¶어느 때와 ~ as usual// 위에서 말한 바와 ~ as (stated) above// 그가 하는 것을 보고 꼭 ~ 해라 Watch him and do likewise[as he does].// 그 두 형제는 똑~ 생겼다 The two brothers are much alike[have a lot in common]. 2〔동등하게〕 equally; impartially; alike; indiscriminately. ¶~ 분배하다 divide equally// ~ 취급하다 treat (men) without discrimination / treat (all men) alike // (혼동해서) mix up / confound[confuse] (A) with (B)// 사회학과 사회주의를 ~ 생각한다 confound sociology with socialism// 나를 저런 치들과 ~ 취급하면 곤란하다 I don't like to be classed[lumped / bracketed] with such fellows. 3〔처럼〕 as if[though]; like; as; as ... as. ¶눈~ 흰 as white as snow// 대낮~ 밝다 be as bright as day// 친딸~ 키우다 bring her up as if she were his own daughter// 그는 모든 것을 아는 것~ 떠벌린다 He talks as if he knew everything.// 그는 어린애니까 어린애~ 다루어야 한다 He is a child, and must be treated as such. 4〔함께〕 together; with; together with; along with; in company with. ¶다 ~ all together// ~ 살다 live together / live in the same house with (a person) // ~ 기뻐[슬퍼]하다 share joys[sorrows] with (a person)// 편지와 ~ 보내다 send (a thing) together with one's letter// ~ 책임지다 share a common responsibility// 자 다 ~ 사진을 찍읍시다 Let's have photo taken all in a group.// 어머니도 ~ 기뻐하고 계십니다 My mother joins me in congratulating you. 5〔동시에〕 at the same time; together. ¶둘이 ~ 도착했다 The two have arrived at the same time.// 두 가지 일을 ~ 해서는 안 된다 You must not do two things at a time. 6〔때를 강조하여〕. ¶매일~ almost every day / day after day// 새벽~ 떠나다 leave at dawn[daybreak / peep of day]// 그는 매일~ 바쁜 사람이다 His days are full.// 새벽~ 손님들이 찾아와다 I had early visitors this morning.

같이하다 share (something) with; take part[participate] in; partake of; have the same .... ¶때를 같이하여 at the same time [hour] / in the same instant / simultaneously (with) // 식사를 ~ eat at the same table // 고락을 ~ share joys and sorrows [one's fortunes] with // 일생을 ~ share one's life / be one's life companion[partner] // 운명을 ~ cast in one's lot (with) / share each other's fortune / face the same fate / be in the same boat // 이해를 ~ have common interests (in a matter with a person) // 마음을 ~ be of one mind[of the same mind] // 두 사람은 의견을 같이하고 있다 They agree with each other. / The two of them have[share] the same view[opinion]. / (문어) Their opinions concur.// 우리는 그와 그 일을 같이했다 We shared with him in that job.

같잖다〔눈꼴사납다〕 foolish; silly; absurd; nonsensical; unseemly; improper; bothersome; saucy; impertinent; 〔시시하다〕 trifle; trivial; small; slight; insignificant; of no account. ¶같잖은 물건 a no-good thing / a worthless object / wretched stuff / rubbish / trash / a white elephant// 같잖은 녀석 an impertinent fellow / a worthless[mean / good-for-nothing] fellow// 같잖은 수작을 하다 talk nonsense / say silly[absurd] things / say unseemly things// 같잖은 일로 화를 내다 get angry at trifles// 같잖은 소리를 하다 talk impudently (to) / give (a person) cheek [some lip] / (속어) get a mouth// 같잖은 짓 마라 Don't get fresh! / You needn't act smart.

갚다 1〔돈을〕 pay back (a loan); repay (a loan); clear; return; give back; refund; settle one's account. ¶빚을 ~ pay[repay] one's debts // 깨끗이 빚을 ~ clear off one's debts // (금전이 아닌) 물품으로 ~ pay (a person) back in kind// 품으로 빚을 ~ work out a debt// 자, 500원 갚겠네 Here's your five hundred won back.// 빌린 돈을 훗달에 갚겠습니다 I will pay back the money next month.// 빌려 간 돈을 갚아 주십시오 Please repay me the money you borrowed. 2〔보답하다〕 reward (a person) for; repay (another's kindness); requite (favors); 〔보상하다〕 recompense (a person) for; compensate for; 〔보복하다〕 retaliate (against a person) with; return; requite; 〔원수를〕 revenge; avenge. ¶선을 악으로 ~ return [render] evil for good[good with evil] // 똑같은 방법으로 ~ return[requite] like for like// 받은 것 만큼 ~ give as good as one gets // 여섯 배로 쳐서 ~ repay (a person) sixfold / 손해 본 것을 갚아 주다 compensate[indemnify] (a person) for the loss / repair the loss // 주먹을 주먹으로 ~ give measure for measure / give blow for blow / meet force with force// 언젠가 이 은혜는 꼭 갚겠습니다 Some day I will repay your kindness[repay you your kindness].// 그는 은혜를 원수로 갚았다 He returned evil for good. / He returned good with evil.

개[1]〔포구〕 the tidal reaches (of a river); the mouth of a river; an inlet; an estuary; a cove; an embayment; a small arm of the sea.

개[2]〔동〕 a dog; 〔암캐〕 a bitch[a she-dog]; a canine. ¶사냥 ~ a hound / a hunting [sporting] dog// 잡종 ~ a mongrel (dog) / a cur / (속어) a mutt // ~ 같은 doggish / doglike // ~의 canine // ~ 자식 a son-of-a-bitch / a dog / a bitch// 재주를 부리는 ~ a performing dog// ~를 기르다 keep[(미) have] a dog // ~에게 재주를 가르치다 teach a dog tricks// ~를 매다 chain up a dog // ~를 풀어 주다 let a dog loose / 가죽 끈을 달고 ~를 운동시키다 walk a dog on a leash// ~가 짖고 있다 A dog is barking.// 들~가 소리를 길게 뽑으며 짖고 있었다 A homeless [stray] dog was howling.// 그는 ~만도 못한 놈이다 He is worse than a beast.// 그는 나를 ~ 취

개

급하듯 했다 He used[treated] me like a dog. // 그런 것은 ~도 안 먹는다 Even a dog will turn up its nose at it. // ~ 조심 (게시) Beware of the Dog! / Beware — Fierce [Vicious] Dog. / Savage Dog — Look Out.
개 꼬리 삼 년 묵어도 황모 되지 않는다(속담) You can't make a silk purse out of a sow's ear.
개 발에 편자(속담) Caviar(e) to the general; to cast pearls before swine; be like the fox's skin sewed to the lion's.
개 보름 쇠듯(속담) miss[cannot afford] the good food appropriate to a feast day.
개(個·簡·介) a piece; a unit; an item. ¶도넛 한 ~ a doughnut // 사과 세 ~ three apples // 비누 두 ~ two cakes[pieces] of soap // 각설탕 두 ~ two lumps of sugar // 초콜릿 두 ~ two pieces of chocolate // 의자 다섯 ~ five chairs // ~당 가격 a unit price // ~당 5원 50 won each // 10~ 한 세트의 유리컵 a set of ten glasses // 이 달걀은 한 ~ 100원이다 These eggs cost a hundred won apiece.
개가(改嫁) remarriage[a second marriage / deuterogamy / digamy] (of a woman). ¶~를 권하다 advise (a woman) to remarry. 개가하다 marry again[second time]; remarry.
개가(凱歌) a triumphal song; a p(a)ean; a victory song. ¶현대 과학의 ~ a triumph of modern science // 민주주의의 ~ a triumph for democracy // ~를 부르다 sing in triumph / sing a song of triumph.
개가를 올리다 raise[give] a shout of victory [triumph]; cry[shout] triumphantly. ¶적에 대해 ~ triumph over one's enemies.
개가(開架) open[free] access; access to shelves; open shelves; an open stack. ¶~식 도서관 an open access[open-stack / open-shelf] library // ~식 열람실 an open-shelf [open-stack] reading room.
개각(介殼) a shell; shells.
개각(改閣) a cabinet reshuffle; a cabinet shake-up. ¶일부 ~ a partial cabinet reshuffle // 전면 ~ a sweeping cabinet reshuffle // ~을 단행하다 effect a cabinet reshuffle / reshuffle the cabinet portfolios. 개각하다 reshuffle the cabinet.
개간(改刊) reprinting; a reprint; a revised printing. 개간하다 reprint; print a revised edition.
개간(開墾) land clearing; reclamation; bringing (wasteland) under cultivation. ¶산림 ~ forest clearing. 개간하다 bring (land) under cultivation; reclaim (wasteland); clear (land). ¶호수[바다] 를 매립하여 개간한 토지 the land reclaimed from the lake[sea] // 토지를 개간하여 밭을 만들다 clear the land for a farm.
●개간지 developed land; a cultivated area. ¶미~ virgin soil / wild[waste] land.
개강(開講) beginning a series of one's lectures; the opening of a course (of study). 개강하다 give one's first lecture; begin a series of lectures; (대학에서) open a course; begin school. ¶9월 1일 ~ (게시) Lectures (will) begin on Sept. 1. // 월요일부터 ~ 개강하다 Lectures[Classes] will begin on Monday.
개개(個個·箇箇) (낱낱·각각) being individual; each one; an item; [모두] all; every one; everyone. ¶~의 individual / separate / several // ~의 문제 a separate problem // ~의

특질 individual characteristics // ~를 시험해 보다 try every one of (the light bulbs) // 그는 일반론에서부터 ~의 문제에 이르기까지 논급했다 He reasoned from the general to the particular.
●개개인 individuals; each and every person; each single person.
개개비 [鳥] the reed warbler.
개고기 [개의 고기] dogmeat; dog flesh; [막된 사람] a pest; a plague; a bad child; a wicked [a cruel / an ill-tempered] person; a devil; a nuisance.
개골 unreasonable[unprovoked] anger; a nasty temper; another's temper; anger; hot temper; rage. ¶~내다 get angry (with a person) / get into rage.
개골개골 ¶개구리가 ~ 울고 있다 A frog is croaking[chirping / singing].
개골창 a drain; a gutter; a sewer; a ditch. ¶~물 sewage / sewerage // ~을 치다 clear a ditch[sewer].
개과천선하다(改過遷善-) reform (oneself); correct a fault; repent (of); be repentant [penitent]; renounce (one's former sins); correct one's way; turn over a new leaf. ¶개과천선한 죄인 a reformed criminal // 개과천선하면 죄는 용서받는다 Repentance wipes out sin.
개관(開館) the opening (of a hall). ¶극장의 ~ the (formal) opening of a new theater [(영) theatre] // ~ 첫날의 입장자 수 the number of people who entered the hall on the day of its opening // 10시 ~ (게시) Open At 10 a.m. // 그 새 극장은 햄릿으로 ~ 공연을 했다 The new theater was opened with a performance of Hamlet. 개관하다 open (a hall).
●개관 시간 the opening hour. 개관식 the opening ceremony.
개관(槪觀) a general view; a survey; an outline; a conspectus; a general outlook. ¶근대사의 ~ a birds-eye view of modern history // 역사적 ~ a historical survey. 개관하다 survey; take a general[bird's-eye] view (of); make a general survey (of); give a conspectus (of). ¶정세를 개관하건대 시기가 아직 무르익지 않은 것같이 생각된다 A general survey of the situation leads me to believe that the time is not yet ripe.
개괄(槪括) a summary; a summing-up; [논] generalization. ¶~적인 general / generalized / sweeping // ~적으로 in general / generally. 개괄하다 summarize; sum up; generalize. ¶개괄하여 말하다 speak in broad generalities // 개괄해서 말하면 generally speaking / on the whole / to sum up / in short / in general terms / by and large / in a word.
개교(開校) the opening of a school. 개교하다 open[inaugurate] a school; found a school.
●개교기념일 the anniversary of the founding of a school.
개구리 a frog; (식용의) a bullfrog. ¶~ 같은 froggy / froglike // 청~ a tree frog // 참~ a leopard frog // 식용 ~ an edible[a table] frog // ~가 울고 있었다 Frogs were croaking [chirping / singing].
개구리 올챙이 적 생각 못한다(속담) Danger past, God forgotten[the Saint is mocked].; An upstart will often forget his old pinching times.
●개구리헤엄 the breaststroke. ¶~을 치다

개구리매 [동] a marsh harrier [hawk].
개구리밥 [식] a (great) duckweed.
개구리참외 [식] a spotted cantaloup(e).
개구멍 a doghole (in the wall [gate]).
● **개구멍받이** a baby abandoned [deserted] by the doghole; a foundling.
개구쟁이 a naughty boy; a mischievous boy; a brat; an urchin; an imp. ¶~의 [놀기 좋아하는] playful / [장난꾸러기의] mischievous // ~ 성질 [장난기] playfulness / impishness // ~ 짓 naughtiness / brattiness // (남에게) ~ 짓을 하다 play pranks (on a person) // 우리 집 ~ my dear little devil [monkey] // ~ 놈아 You [What a] little devil!

개국(開國) 1 [외국과의 국교 개시] the opening of a country. **개국하다** open a country [territory] to foreign trade and diplomatic relations. 2 [건국] the founding of a country [state]. **개국하다** found a country.
● **개국 공신** a meritorious retainer at the founding of a dynasty. **개국주의** the principle of opening the country to foreign intercourse; the open-door policy.
개국하다(開局-) open [set up / establish] a (new) post office [broadcasting station]; [국(局)이 업무를 개시하다] start (its) service.

개그 a gag. ¶그는 곧잘 ~를 내뱉는다 He often tells [tosses off] gags.
● **개그맨** a comedian; a gagman; a gagster. (▶ gagman은 실제로 잘 안 쓰는 말이며, 보다 일반적으로 쓰이는 말은 comedian임)

개근(皆勤) perfect attendance; non-absence (throughout a year); regular attendance (without a day's absence). **개근하다** attend regularly (without missing a single day); be not absent a single day.
● **개근상** [賞狀] a reward [certificate] for perfect attendance. **개근자** a person who has not missed a day.

개기(皆旣) [천] a total eclipse (of the sun).
● **개기식**(-蝕) a total eclipse; totality. **개기월식** a total eclipse of the moon; a total lunar eclipse. **개기 일식** a total eclipse of the sun; a total solar eclipse.

개기름 (natural) grease on one's face; skin oiliness. ¶~이 도는 그의 얼굴 his oily [greasy] face [complexion] // ~이 번질번질하고 살찐 40대 남자 an oilyfaced fleshy man in his forties.

개꼴 dishonor; disgrace; shame; wretched [miserable] condition. ¶~이 되다 be put to shame / bring disgrace upon oneself / lose face / disgrace oneself / humiliate oneself / be clothed with shame.

개꽃 [식] a scentless false-c(h)amomile.
개꿈 an empty dream; a silly [wild] dream.
개나리 [식] 1 a forsythia; a golden bell. ¶~는 봄의 상징이다 The forsythia is the symbol of the spring. // 새봄의 전조로 ~가 벌써 활짝 피었다 Forsythias are already in full bloom to herald the coming spring. 2 [들나리] a wild lily.
● **개나리꽃** (the blossom of) a golden bell.

개념(槪念) a notion; a general idea; [철] a concept; a conception; an idea. ¶기본 ~ fundamental notions // 동일 ~ an identical conception // ~적인 [의] notional / conceptional / general // 미(美)의 ~ notions of beauty // 우주라는 ~ the concept of the universe // ~화된 지식 a generalized knowledge // …에 대한 ~을 얻다 get [have] a general idea (of).
● **개념론** [철] conceptualism. **개념시**(-詩) a conceptional poem.

개다¹ [맑게 되다] (날씨가) clear up; become clear; (눈·비가) hold up; stop (raining / snowing); cease to (rain / snow); (안개가) lift; clear away [off]; break away. ¶어느 맑게 갠 아침 one fine morning // 활짝 갠 푸른 하늘 a cloudless [clear / serene] blue sky // 날씨가 갰다 The sky has cleared up [become clear]. / The sky is bright and clear. // 비가 갰다 The rain is over. // 날씨가 갤 것 같다 The weather shows signs of clearing. / It's likely to clear up. // 안개가 갰다 The fog lifted. / The mist cleared (away) [broke up]. (▶ clear away는 사라지다, break up은 갈라져 흘러가다, lift는 위로 올라가듯 사라지다) // 아침에는 비가 내렸지만 뒤에 갰다 It rained in the morning but the sun came out [it cleared up] later.

개다² [섞이게 이기다] soften with water; knead; mix up; temper; pug; work (clay / mortar). ¶가루 반죽을 ~ knead dough // 풀을 ~ temper paste (with water) // 진흙을 ~ temper [pug] clay // 모르타르를 ~ work mortar.

개다³ [접어 포개다] fold (up) (bedding); turn down. ¶다시 ~ refold // 이부자리를 ~ fold up [turn down] the beddings [bedclothes] / put [stow] away beddings // 옷을 ~ fold one's clothes / put the clothes away // 천막을 ~ fold up a tent / strike a tent.

개도국(開途國) a developing country. ⇨개발도상국(⇨개발)

개떡 a pie-shaped cake made of coarse barley flour; a bran cake. ¶~ 같은 trifling / trivial / worthless / rubbishy // ~ 같은 수작 nonsense / rubbish // ~ 같은 너석 a worthless fellow / (미) a punk // ~같이 여기다 make nothing of // ~ 같은 소리를 하다 talk nonsense [rot / rubbish] / talk idly / say useless things / tattle.

개똥 1 [개의 똥] dog dung [droppings]; a dog turd. 2 [천한 것] a rubbish [trash]; a garbage. ¶~ 같다 be rubbishy / be not worth a damn / be trash // ~같이 여기다 make nothing of / don't care a bit [fig / straw / pin] (about).
개똥도 약에 쓰려면 없다(속담) Sometimes it is difficult to get something very common for emergency use.
● **개똥참외** a wild melon. **개똥철학** a mockery of philosophy.

개똥밭 1 [땅이 건 밭] a rich [fertile / fruitful] field. 2 [더러운 곳] a dirty [squalid] place. ¶~에 인물 나다 rise from obscurity [the ranks] / spring from a humble origin / begin from the bottom.
개똥밭에 이슬 내릴 때가 있다(속담) Every dog has his day.

개똥벌레 [동] a firefly; a glowfly; (미) a lightning bug; [유충] a glowworm.

개똥지빠귀 [동] a thrush; a dusky thrush [ouzel].

개략(槪略) an outline; a summary; a compendium; a skeleton; the gist; [문학 작품의 줄거리] the epitome; (논문 등의) a résumé.

개량

¶~적인[의] rough / approximate // ~을 말하자면 roughly speaking / [간략하게] in brief // ~을 보고하다 make a summarized report (of) // 어림잡은 여비은 다음과 같다 The travel expenses are roughly as follows. // 나는 건설 회사로부터 ~적인 견적을 받아 놓았다 I got a rough estimate [an approximate figure] from the construction company. **개략하다** give an outline (of); outline; summarize; epitomize. ¶이상이 그 사건을 개략한 것이다 Such are the facts of the case in broad outline.

개량(改良) (an) improvement; betterment; (사회·정치상의) (a) reform. ¶사회 ~ social reform // 토지 ~ soil enrichment // 철자 운동 the spelling reform movement. **개량하다** improve; reform(사회를); make (a thing) better; better. ¶동물의 품종을 ~ improve the breed of an animal // 개량할 여지가 있다 [많다] There is some [much] room for further improvement. / 개량할 여지가 없다 There is no room for further improvement. / It can hardly be improved on. →¶이 기계는 내가 처음 사용하였을 때 이후로 많이 개량되어 있다 There have been a number of improvements in these machines since I started using them.
● **개량복** a reformed dress. **개량종** a select breed; an improved strain[variety]. **개량형** an improved model.

개런티 (*guarantee*) a performance [an appearance] fee.

개론(槪論) an outline (on); general remarks [consideration]; (입문) an introduction (to). ¶영문학 ~ an introduction to English literature // 인도 철학 ~ an introduction to Indian philosophy // ~에서 각론으로 들어가다 descend from generalities to particulars. **개론하다** outline; survey; give a survey [an outline / a summary account] (of).

개리 [동] the Chinese goose [swan].

개막(開幕) 1 [막을 엶] the raising of the curtain; the commencement of performance. ¶~ 중엔 자리에서 일어나지 마십시오 Please don't leave your seat during the performance. **개막하다** raise [draw up] a curtain; begin [commence] the performance. ¶오후 5시 반에 개막한다 The curtain rises at 5:30 p.m. 2 [일의 개시] the opening. **개막하다** open; commence. →¶내일 전국 대회가 개막된다 The national meet opens tomorrow. / 올림픽 대회가 개막되었다 The Olympic Games began [started].
● **개막극** a curtain raiser [lifter]. **개막식** the opening ceremony [pageant]. **개막전** an opening game; an [a season] opener.

개망나니 (구어) a tough; a rowdy; (미국 구어) a roughneck.

개망신(-亡身) a deep disgrace; a sore indignity; a burning [crying] shame. **개망신하다** disgrace oneself in public; bring burning shame on oneself.

개머루 [식] a wild grape [vine]; an ampelopsis.

개머리판(-板) a butt plate.

개명(改名) changing one's name; rechristening. ¶나는 ~ 신고를 했다 I registered my change of name. **개명하다** change one's name (from A to B); be renamed. ¶그는 태식을 태호로 개명했다 He changed his name from Taesik to Taeho.

개명(開明) (a) flowering of culture; civilization; enlightenment. **개명하다** open up new knowledge; be [become] civilized; be enlightened. ¶개명한 나라 a civilized country.

개문(開門) the opening of the gate. **개문하다** open the gate [door].

개미¹ [동] an ant; a pismire. ¶~의 formic // 여왕 ~ a queen (ant) // 일 ~ a worker ant // 사람들은 당밀에 꾀는 ~ 떼처럼 그 영화 스타 주위에 들끓었다 People swarmed [crowded] around [round] the movie star like ants round treacle. // 성은 포위되어 ~ 새끼 하나도 기어 나올 틈이 없었다 They lay close siege to the castle. / The castle was closely besieged (by the enemy).

개미 금탑 모으듯(속담) save up little by little.

개미 쳇바퀴 돌듯(속담) go [turn] round and round.

개미 새끼 하나 볼 수 없다 There is not a soul in sight.; There is not a thing to be seen.
● **개미구멍** an ant hole. **개미굴** an ant tunnel. **개미집** an ant's nest. **개미허리** a wasp [slender] waist. **개밋둑** an ant hill; an ant heap; a formicary.

개미² (연줄에 먹이는) powdered glass [porcelain] mixed with glue.

개미(를) 먹이다 coat (kite strings) with powdered glass [porcelain].

개미산(-酸) [화] formic acid.

개미취 [식] an aster; Michaelmas daisy.

개미핥기 [동] an anteater.

개발(開發) [개척] development; (자원의) exploitation; (식민지의) colonization; (우주 등의) exploration; [계발] enlightenment; development. ¶경제 ~ economic development [exploitation] // 경제 ~ 5개년 계획 a 5-year economic development plan // 국토 ~ land development // 전원(電源) ~ development of power resources // 저~국 an underdeveloped [a less developed] nation // 미~의 원시림 an undeveloped primeval forest // ~을 촉진하다 facilitate development. **개발하다** develop. ¶자원을 ~ develop resources // 신제품을 ~ develop new products // 천연자원을 ~ develop [exploit] natural resources // 황무지를 ~ bring a wasteland under cultivation / reclaim wasteland // 새로 개발한 기술 a newly-developed technique // 지능을 ~ develop the intellectual faculties.
● **개발 계획** a development project [program / plan]. // 우주 ~ a space development program // 유엔 ~ the United Nations Development Plan(약어 UNDP). **개발도상국** a developing country. **개발비** development expense [costs]. **개발 제한 구역** limited development district.

개발코 a snub [pug] nose.

개밥 dog's food [feed].

개밥에 도토리(속담) an outcast; an ostracized [a left-out] person.

개밥바라기 the evening star; [천] Venus; Hesper(us).

개방(開放) [열어 놓음] opening; throwing open; [허용] lifting the ban. ¶문호 ~ 정책 the open-door policy // (성질이) ~적인 frank and open [candid / openhearted] (person).

개방하다 open; throw open (a door); leave

(the door) open. ¶나라를 ~ open a country to foreign intercourse // 정원을 ~ throw open a garden to the public // …에 대하여 문호를 ~ open doors to …. ¶우리 대학의 운동장은 일반에게 개방되어 있읍니다 Our university's athletic field is open to the public.
● **개방 경제** an open economy. **개방 대학** an open college. **개방성** openness; [의] patency; persistence. **개방 요법** open-air treatment.

개백정(-白丁) a dog killer; a dog catcher; [막된놈] a blackguard; a thug.

개버딘 [직물] gabardine; gaberdine.

개벽(開闢) 1 [천지의 창조] the Creation; the beginning of the world. ¶~ 이래 since the beginning of the world / since the dawn of history / from time immemorial // 천지~ 이래의 사건 an unprecedented event. **개벽하다** (the world) be created. 2 [천지가 뒤집힘] a convulsion of the nature. ¶천지~이 되어도 though the heavens fall. **개벽하다** (the nature) be convulsed.

개변(改變) (a) change; (an) alteration; (a) renovation; innovation; reformation. **개변하다** change; alter; renovate; innovate. ¶제도를 ~ change[alter] a system.

개별(個別) an individual[a particular] case; individualization.
● **개별 개념** [논] a distributive concept. **개별 지도** individual guidance. **개별화** individualization.

개별적(個別的) individual. ¶~으로 individually / [따로따로] separately / [하나하나] one by one / severally / singly // 수상은 각 야당의 당수와 ~으로 회견했다 The prime minister met individually with the leader of each of the opposition party. / The prime minister met with the leaders of the opposition party one by one. // 그것들은 ~으로 다루어져야 할 문제다 They are problems that must be treated separately[one by one]. / 그들은 각자 ~인 방법으로 그것을 했다 They did it in their several ways. / Each of them did it (in) his own way. // 소년들에게는 ~으로 방이 배정되었다 A separate room was allotted to each of the boys. // 그것은 우리의 ~인 문제다 That's a matter for each of us to handle individually. // 그러니 너희들은 ~으로 결정해야 한다 So each of you has to decide independently[for yourself].

개병(皆兵) universal conscription. ¶국민 ~ 제도 a universal conscription system.

개복 수술(開腹手術) an abdominal operation; celiotomy; laparotomy. ¶~을 받다 undergo an abdominal operation[a laparotomy].

개복하다(開腹-) cut the abdomen open; [의] perform a laparotomy.

개봉(開封) 1 [봉한 것을 엶] opening; unsealing. **개봉하다** break[take off] the seal; open (a letter); tear (a letter) open; unseal (a letter). ¶편지를 개봉하지 않고 반송하다 send back a letter unopened // 편지를 개봉하여 부치다 mail an unsealed letter. 2 [영화의 첫 상영] a release; a first run; a premiere. **개봉하다** release[premiere] (a film). → ¶개봉되다 be released / have (its) premiere // 개봉되고 있다 be in release // 아주 최근에 개봉된 미국 영화 A very recently released American film.
● **개봉관** a first-run movie house[theater]; a first-runner; (영) a cinema that shows newly-released films. **개봉 영화** a first-run film[movie]; a newly-released film; a release.

개비 a piece of split wood[timber]. ¶성냥~ a matchstick // 장작 두 ~ two pieces of split firewood.

개비(改備) (a) renewal; replacing. **개비하다** renew; replace (one thing by[with] another); refurnish; refixture. ¶양복장을 ~ refurnish (a room) with a new wardrobe // 커튼을 ~ replace the curtains with new ones.

개산(槪算) a rough estimate[calculation]; approximate figures. ¶~으로 at a rough estimate / roughly / approximately / in round figures[numbers]. **개산하다** estimate [calculate] roughly; make a rough estimate [calculation] (of); approximate. ¶그 나라의 인구는 개산하여 8천만에 달한다 As roughly estimated, the country has a population of eighty million.

개살구 [식] a wild apricot.

개새끼 (욕) a son of a bitch[gun]; an s.o.b; a bitch; a dog. ¶이 ~야 You son of a bitch! / You dog! // 가면 ~다 I'll be dogged if I go.

개서(改書) [다시 쓰기] rewriting; [다시 쓴 것] a rewrite. **개서하다** rewrite; write over (again); [정서하다] copy clearly; write out fair. ¶원고를 세 차례 ~ work over manuscripts three times.
● **개서 어음** a renewed bill.

개선(改善) (an) improvement; (a) betterment; amelioration; reform(ation). ¶노동 조건의 ~ betterment[amelioration] of working conditions // 시설의 ~ improvement in accommodation // 체질의 ~ improvement of habitude / constitutional improvement // 두드러진 [미미한] ~ a marked[minor] improvement // 설비에 여러 가지 ~을 가하다 make various improvements in the facilities // 우리는 ~안을 작성하여 지체없이 실행해야만 한다 We should draft a reform[an improvement] plan and carry it out without delay. **개선하다** improve; better; ameliorate; make (a thing) better. ¶세제를 ~ improve the taxation system // 생활을 ~ better one's standard of living / improve one's way of life // 사태를 ~ remedy the state of things // 이 기술은 크게 개선할 여지가 있다 This technique leaves much room for improvement. → ¶개선되다 be improved / undergo improvements // 개선되는 중이다 It is being improved. / It is on the mend. // 낡은 제도가 많이 개선되었다 The old system was improved considerably.
● **개선책** a remedy; a reform measure.

개선(改選) reelection; [개편] reshuffle. ¶임원 ~ the reshuffle of the members of the board of directors. **개선하다** reelect (members). → ¶이번에는 의원의 반수가 개선된다 This time half the members are up for reelection.

개선(疥癬) the itch; scabies; [의] ascariasis; psora; (속어) scotch fiddle; mange (말·개의).

개선(凱旋) a triumphal return[entry]. **개선하다** return in triumph[with glory / from a victorious campaign]. ¶개선한 군인[용사] a returned soldier[hero] // 파리로 ~ return in triumph to Paris // 장군은 유럽에서 개선했다 The general returned from his victories in Europe.
● **개선가** a triumphal song; a paean. **개선군** victorious returning troops. **개선문** a tri-

개설 umphal arch; (파리의) the Arc de Triomphe. **개선장군** a triumphant general.

개설(開設) establishment; (공식적인) inauguration; opening; installation (of a telephone). ¶이 지역에 병원 ~이 요망된다 The establishment of a hospital is needed in this area. / It's necessary to set up[establish] a hospital in this area. **개설하다** establish; set up; inaugurate; open. ¶전화를 ~ have a telephone installed (in one's house)//학교[병원]를 ~ establish a school[hospital]//새로운 정부 기관을 ~ establish[inaugurate] a new Government agency//지점을 ~ open a branch (office)//신용장을 ~ open[establish / issue] a letter of credit[an L/C] (with a bank)//서울 뉴욕 간에 새 항로를 ~ open a new airline between Seoul and New York//이 빌딩에 사무실을 개설할 계획으로 I am planning to set up an office in this building.

개설(概說) a general[rough] statement; an outline; an introduction; a summary. **개설하다** give an outline[a summary account] (of); make a summary (of); treat (a subject) in outline; make an introduction (to).

개성(個性) individuality; personality; idiosyncrasy; individual character; characteristic traits. ¶~이 뚜렷한 사람 a man of marked individuality // ~이 없는 사람 a man with little personality // ~을 존중[무시]하다 respect[disregard / ignore] (a person's) individuality // ~을 발전시키다 develop[cultivate] one's personality[individuality] // ~을 발휘하여 show[display] one's originality / work out one's originality // ~을 억제하다 stifle a person's individuality // 그의 저술에는 그의 ~이 뚜렷이 나타나 있다 His writings are marked by his strong individuality. / All his writings are characterized by his personal taste. / 옷은 그 사람의 ~을 나타낸다 Dress expresses the wearer's individuality. // 그녀는 매우 ~적으로 자기를 표현한다 She has a way of expressing herself that is all her own.

● **개성 교육** individual upbringing[education].

개소(個所) a point; a place; a spot. ⇨군데

개소리 silly[foolish / pointless] talk; nonsense; rubbish. ¶~ 마라 Nonsense! / Don't talk nonsense[rubbish / rot]! / Bullshit! / Baloney! / 무슨 ~야 What arrant nonsense!

개수(改修) repair; mending; improvement; conservancy (하천의). ¶도로의 ~ road repairing // 건물은 ~ 중이다 The building is under repair. // 이 도로는 ~ 중이므로 통행 금지임 This road is closed for repairs. **개수하다** repair; mend; improve (a road). ¶대대적으로 ~ carry out large repairs / make extensive repairs // 그들은 그 제방을 개수했다 They repaired the banks.

● **개수 공사** repair works. ¶하천 ~ river conservancy / river improvement / riparian works.

개수(個數·箇數) the number (of articles). ¶~를 확인하다 ascertain[check] the number / count // ~가 얼마나 됩니까 How many (pieces / items) are there?

개수작(-酬酌) silly words; nonsense; rot; rubbish; a foolish remark. ¶~ 마라 Nonsense! / Stuff and nonsense! / Stuff! / Humbug!

개수통(-桶) a dishwater bucket; a dishpan.

개술하다(概述-) summarize; give an outline; sketch (its) outlines.

개숫물 dishwater; dishwash; slops. ¶~을 버리다 empty a dishpan.

개시(開市) 1 [시장을 엶]. **개시하다** open a fair; open up a market. 2 [마수걸이] the first sale of the day; an opening sale. ¶오늘 아침에는 아직 ~도 못했다 We haven't made a sale yet this morning. / We've sold nothing so far this morning. **개시하다** make the first sale of the day.

● **개시 손님** the first customer[buyer] of the day.

개시(開始) start; opening; inauguration; commencement; beginning. ¶~부터 from the outset // 시합 ~의 사이렌이 울렸다 A siren sounded to announce the beginning of the game. **개시하다** begin; commence; open (a game); enter upon[into] (negotiations); start (business); inaugurate (bus service); launch (an attack); make a beginning (with). ¶시판을 ~ begin to sell[market] / put[place] goods on the market // 이 지점은 4월 10일부터 업무를 개시한다 This branch (office) will open for[start] business on April 10(th). // 위원회는 그 건의 조사를 개시했다 The committee opened[launched] an investigation of the matter. // 그들은 핵 실험을 개시했다 They started nuclear bomb tests. // 자, 행동을 개시할 때다 Now we must go into action. // 한국과 미국은 내일 교섭을 개시한다 Korea and the U.S. open[enter into] negotiations tomorrow. ➔ ¶어제 두 도시 간의 버스 운행이 개시되었다 Bus service between the two cities was inaugurated yesterday.

개식(開式) the opening of a ceremony. **개식하다** open a ceremony.

● **개식사**(-辭) an opening address (of a ceremony).

개신(改新) (a) renovation; (an) innovation; (a) renewal; (a) reformation. **개신하다** renovate; innovate; renew; reform.

개심(改心) reform; amendment; (특히 종교적인) repentance; contrition. **개심하다** amend[correct] one's conduct; mend one's ways; reform (oneself); turn over a new leaf. ¶개심한 reformed (criminal) / repentant (sinner) // 그는 개심할 가망이 없다 He is incorrigible. / He is past[beyond] redemption. // 그는 개심하고 새출발할 것을 맹세했다 He swore to turn over a new leaf. // 그는 이제 완전히 개심했다 He is quite penitent[is another man] now. ➔ ¶비행 소년을 개심시키다 reform[reclaim] a juvenile delinquent.

● **개심자** a reformed man; a penitent.

개악(改惡) a change for the worse; deterioration. ¶노동법의 ~ the retrogressive revision of the Labor Law. **개악하다** change (a thing) for the worse; make a change for the worse; make (things) worse for the change; deteriorate. ¶헌법을 ~ change[revise] the constitution for the worse.

개안(開眼) 1 [눈을 뜸]. **개안하다** open one's eyes; [눈이 보이게 되다] gain eyesight. 2 [불][불공의 의식] a Buddhist ceremony on consecrating a newly made image; [진리를 깨달음-] spiritual (re)awakening; enlightenment. ¶대불(大佛) ~ the consecration of a huge image of Buddha. **개안하다** be awakened (to

a fact); be (spiritually) enlightened; open one's eyes to (the beauty of ...).
● **개안 수술** an eyesight recovery operation.

개암 [개암나무의 열매] a hazel; a hazelnut; a filbert.
● **개암나무** [식] a hazel (tree).

개업(開業) opening[commencement] of (a) business[a trade]; establishment in business. ¶~ 30주년 기념 대매출 a thirtieth anniversary sale. **개업하다** start (a) business; set oneself up[establish oneself] in business; enter (up)on business; (의사·변호사가) start practice; practice(medicine / law). ¶점포를 ~ open a shop to business / 생선 가게를 ~ start a fish shop / establish oneself as a fishmonger // 그 가게는 오늘부터 개업한다 The shop is open to business today. // 그는 내과의를 개업하고 있다 He is in practice as a physician.
● **개업식** the opening ceremony. **개업의**(—醫) a medical practitioner; a practicing doctor[physician].

개역(改譯) retranslation. ¶충실한 ~ a faithful retranslation. **개역하다** retranslate.
● **개역자** a retranslator. **개역판** a revised version.

개연(蓋然) probability; likelihood. ¶~적(인) probable / likely (to be).
● **개연론** [철] probabilism. **개연성** [철] probability.

개와(蓋瓦) →기와
● **개와장** a tiler. ⇨기와장이(⇨기와)

개요(概要) an epitome; a summary; an outline; a synopsis; an abstract; a résumé. ¶세계사 ~ the outline of World History / …의 ~를 들다[적다] outline (a fact) / give an epitome[an outline / a rundown] of / make a résumé of / give a brief account of.

개운하다 1 [상쾌하다] (feel) refreshed; feel well[fine / all right]. ¶푹 자고 나니 머리가 ~ My mind is refreshed with[after] a good sleep. // 이제 몸이 ~ I feel quite well now. / Now I feel refreshed. 2 [후련하다] (feel) relieved; feel free and easy; feel at ease. ¶할 말을 다 하고 나니 개운했다 I felt relieved[easier] after I had said[had had] my say. 3 [맛이 산뜻하다] plain; simple; refreshing.

개울 a brook; a brooklet; a streamlet; a rivulet.

개원(改元) the change of (the name of) an era; the change of a dynasty. ¶고려에서 조선으로 ~ the change from the Goryeo to the Joseon. **개원하다** change (the name of) an era; change a dynasty.

개원(開院) 1 (국회의) the opening of the National Assembly[a National Assembly session]. **개원하다** open the National Assembly. 2 (병원 등의) the opening[inauguration] (of a hospital). **개원하다** open[inaugurate] (a hospital). ¶병원은 오전 9시에 개원한다 The hospital opens at nine a.m.

개월(個月) month. ¶지난 몇 ~ 동안 for months past.

개의하다(介意—) mind; care about; be concerned about; trouble[concern] oneself about; worry[bother] about. ¶비용을 개의치 않고 regardless of expense / 남의 생각은 개의치 않고 no matter what other people (may) think // (조금도) 개의치 않다 do not care[mind] (a bit) / be (quite) indifferent (to) // 그는 그런 일에는 개의치 않는다 He doesn't mind[care about] such things. // 나에 대해 남이 뭐라든 나는 개의치 않는다 I don't mind[care] what people say of me. / People can say anything of me for all I care. // 그는 옷차림에 개의치 않는다 He is careless about his appearance. // 그들의 놀람에도 나는 개의치 않았다 Their ridicule didn't bother me. // 그는 남의 이익 따위는 개의치 않는다 He has no regard for others' interests. // 그런 일에 너무 개의하지 마십시오 Don't trouble yourself[never mind] about that. // 일의 성공 여부에 개의치 말고 최선을 다해라 Do your best without thinking about success or failure. / Do your best without worrying about the results. // 나는 칭찬이나 비난 따위에 개의치 않는다 I am indifferent to praise or blame. // 그들의 방해는 개의할 것도 없다 Their interference is not worth our consideration[is beneath our notice / isn't worth worrying about].

개인(個人) an individual; 〔사인(私人)〕 a private person[individual / citizen]; a person in his private capacity. ¶~ 또는 법인 [법] a natural or juridical person / 사장의 ~ 운전사 the company president's personal chauffeur[driver] / / ~으로서(는) as an individual / individually / personally / for oneself / in private / 나 ~으로서는 as for me [myself] / for my own part // ~ 자격으로 in one's private capacity / in the capacity of a private person // ~용의 for individual use // ~의 권리 the rights of the individual // ~의 존엄성 [자유] personal[individual] dignity [freedom] / 나 ~의 의견으로는 in my personal opinion[view] / individually (speaking) // 그것은 각 개인의 관점에 따라 다르다 That depends on one's individual[personal] viewpoint. // 그녀는 ~ 사정으로 사직했다 She resigned from her post for personal reasons. // 그것은 ~의 문제이다 That is a private affair. / That's a personal matter.
● **개인감정** personal feeling. **개인 경기** an individual sport[event]. **개인 교수** private lessons[instruction]; individual instruction [tuition]; tutoring. ¶피아노 ~ (게시) Piano lessons given. **개인기**(—技) individual skill. **개인 기업** a private enterprise. **개인 소득** an individual[a personal] income. **개인숭배** the cult of personality. **개인 어음** a personal check[bill]. **개인용 컴퓨터** a personal computer. **개인전**(—展) a private exhibition; a one-man show[exhibition]. ¶~을 열다 give [hold] a one-man show (at). **개인전**(—戰) a game between individuals; a tournament series in singles. **개인주의** individualism. **개인차**(—差) differences[variations] among individuals; individual variations; personal deviation. **개인택시** an owner-operator[a privately owned] taxi. **개인플레이** a personal action. ¶~를 하다 act personally / demonstrate one's personal skill(단체 경기에서). **개인 회사** a private firm[company].

개인적(個人的) [개인의] individual; [사적인] private; [일신의] personal; [이기적인] self-centered[-centred]. ¶~으로 individually / privately / personally / in person // ~ 감정에 지배되다 be affected by personal prejudice // ~으로 면담하다 talk personally (with) / have a personal interview (with) // 그는 ~으

론 좋은 사람이다 He is, personally, a nice fellow.//~으로는 그녀와 아무 관계 없다 I have no personal relations with her.//그것은 ~ 취미의 문제이다 It's a matter of individual taste.

개입(介入) intervention; meddling; interference. [군사] military [armed] intervention **개입하다** intervene [interfere] (in a dispute); meddle (in a matter). ¶분쟁에 ~ intervene in a dispute//타국에 군사 ~ intervene militarily in a foreign country / use military force to intervene in another country//외환 시장에 ~ intervene on the foreign exchange markets/the money market//~ take an active hand (in a dispute)//나는 너희들의 싸움에 개입하지 않겠다 I will not intervene between you in your quarrel.

개자리 [식] a bur clover; a snail clover; a medic; alfalfa.

개자식(-子息) a son of a bitch. ⇨개새끼

개작(改作) (an) adaptation (from / for); recasting. **개작하다** adapt (from / for); recast; rewrite. ¶한국에 맞게 개작한 극 a play adapted for the Korean stage//셰익스피어 극을 어린이에게 맞게 개작한 것 an adaptation from one of Shakespeare's plays for children//소설을 방송용으로 ~ adapt a novel for broadcasting//소설을 연극으로 ~ dramatize a novel / adapt a novel for a play //디킨스의「크리스마스 캐럴」을 개작함 Adapted from Dickens' Christmas carol.//이것은 뒤마의 작품을 개작한 것이다 This is an adaptation from one of Dumas's works.

● **개작자** an adapter.

개잠 [몸을 오그리고 자는 잠]. ¶~자다 sleep curled up / curl (oneself) up (in a ball).

개잠(改-) [다시 드는 잠] a sleep after waking up once in the morning. ¶~자다 fall [sink] into a sleep again (after waking up once).

개장(改裝) remodeling; refurbishing; conversion; modernization(현대식으로). ¶내부으로 임시 휴업 (게시) Closed Temporarily For Remodeling [Redecoration]. **개장하다** remodel; [장식을 고치다] redecorate; refit; reequip; refurbish; convert. ¶방을 현대식으로 ~ modernize a room / smarten up a room//군함을 ~ remodel a war vessel//개장한 백화점은 내일 개점한다 The refurbished department store opens tomorrow. ➔¶초라한 과자 가게가 다방으로 개장되었다 The shabby candy store was remodeled [converted] into a smart coffee shop.

개장(開場) opening; [증권] the opening session; a session; a call. ¶~ 중이다 be open//~과 동시에 사람들이 몰려들었다 People surged into the hall as soon as the doors were opened.//시세는 ~에 100달러였다 The market opened at $100. **개장하다** open; open the door; (증권 시장을) hold [open] a session [market]. ¶개장하자마자 사다[팔다] buy [sell] at the opening session//스타디움은 오전 10시에 개장한다 The stadium opens at 10 a.m.

● **개장 시간** the opening hour; market hours(시장의).

개장국(-醬-) *gaejangguk*; dog-meat broth [stock / soup].

개재(介在) interposition; intervention. ¶제3국의 ~를 불허한 permit no third power intervention. **개재하다** lie [stand] between; interpose (between); intervene (between).

개전(改悛) [뉘우침] (a) repentance; penitence; [개심] reform; amendment. ¶~의 정이 뚜렷하다 show clear signs of repentance [reformation]//그는 ~의 정이 조금도 보이지 않았다 There was not an ounce [a trace] of repentance in him.//그는 ~의 정이 뚜렷하다 It is clear that he is truly contrite. **개전하다** repent (of one's sins); be penitent (of); mend one's way; reform (oneself).

개전(開戰) the opening [commencement] of hostilities; the outbreak [beginning] of war. ¶~을 선포하다 declare war (against / on / upon). **개전하다** open [commence] war [hostilities] (against); make war (on); wage war (against).

개점(開店) **1** [개업] the opening of a shop [store]; opening of business. ¶~을 축하하여 in celebration of the opening of a shop//~휴업 상태입니다 Our store is open, but no customers come in.//금일 ~ (게시) Opened today. **개점하다** open [start] a shop [store]; open shop; establish a shop [store]. ¶이것은 최근 개점한 슈퍼마켓이다 This is quite a new [a newly opened] supermarket. **2** [그날의 시작]. **개점하다** open the store. ¶우리 가게는 아침 6시에 개점합니다 We open our business at 6 a.m.

● **개점 시간** the opening hour of a store.

개정(改正) [수정] (a) revision; (an) amendment; (a) reform; [변경] (an) alteration; (a) change. ¶조약 ~ treaty revision//헌법 ~ the amendment of the National Constitution / constitution revision. **개정하다** revise; amend; alter; change; remodel (the rules). ¶개정할 수 있는 amendable / correctable / rectifiable//교통 법규를 ~ revise traffic regulations.//상법을 일부 ~ make a partial amendment of the Commercial Code. ➔¶개정된 시행령의 발효 the effectuation of the revised enforcement regulations//다음과 같이 개정되도 be amended as follows / the following amendment is made (to).

● **개정안** a revised bill [plan]; an amendment.

개정(改定) a reform; (a) revision; fixing a new. ¶규칙의 ~ a revision of rules//운임 ~ a revision of fares. **개정하다** reform; revise; fix (a date) anew.

개정(改訂) revision. ¶전면 ~ total revision// ~ 증보 revision and enlargement// ~ 증보한 revised and enlarged//약간 ~ 증보하여 with some slight alterations and additions. **개정하다** revise; edit (a textbook) anew. ¶교과서를 ~ revise a textbook//사전을 전면 ~ revise a dictionary completely.

● **개정 증보판** a revised and enlarged edition. **개정판** a revised edition [version]; a revision. ¶전면 ~ a completely revised version [edition].

개정(開廷) [공판] a hearing; a trial. ¶~ 중이다 The court is now sitting. **개정하다** open the court; hold court [a trial]; give a hearing; sit. ¶7시에 개정한다 The court opens at 7.

개제(改題) a change of the title; retitling; a changed title. **개제하다** retitle; change the title of (a book). ¶영화 제목을 ~ change the title of a movie//그 음반은「사랑」으로 개

개조(改造) remodeling; reconstruction; reorganization; rebuilding. **개조하다** remodel; reorganize; reconstruct; rebuild. ¶다락방을 작업실로 ~ remodel[convert] an attic into a workroom // 부엌을 ~ have a kitchen made over // 사회를 ~ reorganize[reconstruct] society // 내각을 ~ reorganize[reshuffle] the Cabinet / (미) revamp the Cabinet // 이 상의는 약간 개조해야 한다 This jacket needs to be altered a little.

개조(改組) reorganization; reshuffle. ¶내각의 일부 ~ a partial cabinet reshuffle. **개조하다** reorganize (a company); reshuffle (a cabinet).

개조(開祖) 1 [불] the founder of a Buddhist sect. ⇨개종조(⇨개종(開宗)) 2 the founder of a Buddhist temple. 3 [시조] an originator; a father; a founder. ¶요가의 ~ the originator [initiator] of the Yoga.

개조(個條·箇條) [항목] an item; [법률·조약 등의 조항] an article; a clause. ¶신앙 ~ articles of faith // 요지를 5~로 나누다 divide the main point into five items // 조약은 20~로 되어 있다 The treaty consists of twenty articles. // 우리는 계약에 1~를 추가할 필요가 있다 We have to add a clause to the contract.

개종(改宗) (a) conversion (to); proselytism. **개종하다** change one's religion; be converted [proselyted] (to); proselyte. ¶기독교로 ~ be converted to Christianity / turn Christian. →¶개종시키다 convert (a person to Christianity) / make a convert of (a person) / proselytize.
● **개종자** a convert (to Buddhism); a proselyte.

개종(開宗) [불] founding a Buddhist sect. **개종하다** found a Buddhist sect.
● **개종조**(一祖) [불] the founder of a Buddhist sect.

개주(改鑄) (화폐의) recoinage; (종·대포 등의) recasting. **개주하다** recoin; mint again; remint; recast.

개죽음 throwing away one's life; an ignominious death; a stupid sacrifice of life; a useless death. **개죽음하다** die to no purpose [in vain]; throw away one's life. ¶그는 개죽음한 것은 아니다 He did not die for nothing.

개중(個中) [여럿 가운데]. ¶~에는 among them [the rest / others] / some of them / of the number // 너도 ~의 한 사람이다 You are (one) of the number. // 20명이 합격했는데 나도 ~의 한 사람이다 Twenty passed the examination, myself among them. // 재미있는 책이 있는가 하면 ~에는 지루한 책도 있다 Some books are interesting; others are boring.

개지랄 an improper and disgusting behavior; a mean and nasty act. ¶~ 마라 Don't be such a pig! / None of your fooleries.

개진(開陳) statement. **개진하다** state; make a statement (of); lay (one's views) before (a person); set forth (one's views); express (one's opinion). ¶그는 자기의 의견을 당당히 개진했다 He stated his views openly.

개집 a kennel; a doghouse.

개차반 a vulgar [mean] fellow; a churl; a hangdog. ¶행실이 ~이다 be mean in one's conduct / behave badly.

개착(開鑿) excavation; cutting; digging; sinking(우물 등의). ¶운하의 ~ excavation [building] of a canal. **개착하다** excavate (a tunnel); cut (a road); (운하 등을) build; construct; (우물 등을) sink.

개찰(改札) the examination of tickets. ⇨=개표(改票)

개척(開拓) (토지의) reclamation; opening-up of a land; bringing under cultivation; (삼림지대의) disafforestation; clearing; (자원의) exploitation; development; (식민지의) colonization. **개척하다** reclaim [clear] (wasteland); bring (wasteland) under cultivation; develop [exploit] (resources); open up (a new field in science); colonize. ¶새 시장을 ~ open up [find] a new market // 신천지[새 분야]를 ~ break fresh[new] ground // 운명을 ~ improve one's lot / hew out one's fortune / carve out a fortune // 황무지를 ~ reclaim waste land // 자원을 ~ exploit [develop] natural resources // 이 분야의 연구는 아직 개척할 여지가 있다 Research in this field still has many untouched possibilities [opportunities] to explore.
● **개척 사업** reclamation[exploitation] work.
개척자 [이주자] a colonist; a settler; (새로운 분야의) a pioneer; a trail blazer; a pathfinder; an early settler. **개척지** reclaimed land; a settlement area; (삼림의) a clearing.

개천(一川) a creek; a rivulet; a small stream; a streamlet; an open sewer [ditch]; a brook; a brooklet.

개천에서 용 난다(속담) It is a case of a black hen laying white eggs.; A great person may be born of perfectly ordinary parents.

개천절(開天節) the National Foundation Day (of Korea); Anniversary of the Dangun's Accession.

개체(個體) 1 [철] an individual; the individual; an independent [individual] existence; a separate entity. 2 [생] an individual; an individual [independent] organism; an organism existing independently.
● **개체 개념** [논] an individual concept. **개체군**(一群) [동] population. **개체 발생** [생] ontogeny; ontogenesis. **개체 변이** individual variation.

개초(蓋草) [이엉] thatch; [이엉으로 이기] thatching; roofing with thatch. **개초하다** thatch (a house / a roof); roof (a house) with thatch.

개최(開催) holding (a meeting). ¶~ 중인 회의 a council in session. **개최하다** hold (a meeting); open (an exhibition); have (a farewell [welcome] meeting); give (a garden party). →¶전국 체육 대회는 10월 3일에 개최된다 The National Athletic Meet will be held [open] on the third of October. // 미술 전람회는 10월 10일부터 11월 20일까지 개최된다 The art exhibition will be held from October 10 through November 20. // 대회는 내주 토요일부터 개최된다 The convention opens next saturday. // 평화 회담이 개최되고 있다 The peace conference is now meeting.
● **개최국** the host country (for a meeting). **개최지** the site (of an exposition / of an athletic meet); the locale (of a conference); a venue (of an exposition / for a conference).

개축(改築) reconstruction; rebuilding; remodeling; alteration (to a building). ¶~이

끝난 극장 a remodeled theater // ~ 중이다 be under reconstruction / be in course of reconstruction[rebuilding]. **개축하다** rebuild; remodel; reconstruct; alter. ¶빌딩을 ~ reconstruct a building // 점포를 사무실로 ~ remodel[convert] a store into an office
● **개축 공사** rebuilding[reconstruction] works.

개칠(改漆) 1 (칠의) repainting; recoating. **개칠하다** repaint; recoat; paint[plaster] afresh; give a new coat of (paint) to (the door). 2 (글씨의) correction; retouch. **개칠하다** correct[retouch] (a written letter); improve.

개칭(改稱) renaming; the changing of a name [title]. **개칭하다** (이름을) change the name (of); (칭호를) change the title[designation] (of). ➔¶그 지역은 마포에서 신촌으로 개칭되었다 The area changed its name[The name of the area was changed] from Mapo to Sinchon.

개키다 fold(up) carefully[elaborately] (clothes / bedding). ¶옷을 ~ fold one's clothes / fold the clothes up (neatly) // 이부자리를 ~ fold up beddings / put away beddings(치우다).

개탄(慨歎) deploring; lamentation; regret. ¶~을 금할 수 없는 일 a most deplorable. **개탄하다** deplore; lament; regret; grieve. ¶개탄할 행위 deplorable[lamentable] conduct // 그는 도덕 수준의 저하를 개탄했다 He deplored the decline in moral standards. // 도덕의 퇴폐는 실로 개탄하지 않을 수 없다 The corruption of public morals is simply deplorable. // 우수한 졸업생이 대학원에 진학하지 않는 것은 개탄할 일이다 It is regrettable[a matter for regret] that our brightest graduates do not go on to graduate school.

개탕(開鐋) [건] a groove; a fillister; a quirk. ¶~ 치다 groove / cut a groove.
● **개탕대패** a groover; a grooving plane; a fillister (plane).

개통(開通) opening to traffic. ¶새로운 철도의 전 구간 ~을 축하하는 식전이 열렸다 A ceremony was held in celebration of the opening of the entire length of the new railroad. **개통하다** (새로) be opened to[for] traffic; go into operation; open up; (막혔다가) be reopened for service; (교량을) open a bridge formally. ➔¶전 구간이[일부가] 개통되다 be fully [partially] opened to[for] traffic // 두 도시 사이에 철도[전화]가 개통되었다 Railroad[Telephone] service between the two cities has been started[(문이) inaugurated]. // 불통 구간은 오후 9시에 개통되었다 The closed section was reopened to[for] traffic at 9 p.m.
● **개통 구간** a section open to[for] traffic[in operation]. **개통식** the formal opening (of a railway); the opening ceremony (of a new bridge).

개판 utter confusion or disorder; a mess; a jumble; a topsy-turvy. ¶~이 되다 fall into utter confusion.

개판(改版) republishing; revision; [개판본] a revised edition. **개판하다** revise (the old edition); issue a revised[new] edition; reset(조판을).

개펄 a tideland; slime along the bank of an inlet; silt at an estuary; a tidal[mud] flat; a muddy riverside.

개편(改編) reorganization; (a) reshuffle; reform; modification. ¶내각의 ~ a Cabinet reshuffle // 정부 기구의 ~ reorganization of government setups // 당직 ~ reorganization of a party's hierarchy. **개편하다** reorganize; reshuffle; remodel. ¶교과서를 ~ re-edit a textbook // 기업을 ~ reorganize a firm // 진용을 ~ rearrange the disposition of troops.

개평 the winner's tip; a free handout; a (free) share of the winnings; a cut. ¶~ 주다 give away a share of one's winnings / give a cut. **개평(을) 떼다** take away the winner's tip.

개평(概評) a general comment[review / criticism]; an overall criticism. **개평하다** give a general comment (on); give an overall criticism (of).

개평근(開平根) ➡제곱근(⇨제곱)
개평(방)(開平方) ➡제곱근풀이(⇨제곱)

개폐(改廢) alteration and abolition; reorganization; a change. ¶사내 조직의 ~를 단행하다 reorganize a company / undertake organizational changes within the company. **개폐하다** reorganize; carry out a reorganization.

개폐(開閉) opening and[or] shutting; [전] make and break. **개폐하다** open and shut [close]; make and break (circuit). ¶문을 ~ open and shut a door. ➔¶문은 자동적으로 개폐된다 The door opens and shuts automatically.
● **개폐교** a drawbridge; a balance[swing] bridge. **개폐기** (전기의) a (break and make) switch; (사진기의) a shutter. ¶자동 ~ an automatic switch. **개폐 신호기** a switch signal. **개폐 장치** switchgear.

개표(開票) the official counting of votes; ballot counting; (미) official canvass of the votes. ¶선거 ~ 공표 official election returns // ~ 속보 a quick[flash] report of election results // ~는 내일 오전 6시에 시작된다 Vote counting will start at 6 a.m. tomorrow. **개표하다** count the votes[ballots]; (미) make a canvass (of the votes); open the ballot boxes. ¶즉일 ~ count the votes[ballots] on the same day as the election // 참관인 입회하에 ~ count the votes with witness attending // 개표한 결과 윤 씨가 당선되었다 On opening the ballot, it was found that Mr. Yun was returned.
● **개표소** a ballot-counting office[place]. **개표율** the percentage of (the) votes already counted. **개표 입회인** / **개표 참관인** a ballot-counting witness.

개표(改票) the examination of tickets; (철도에서) punching. **개표하다** examine tickets; [가위로 찍다] punch[clip] (a ticket). ¶개표하지 않고 승차하 board (a train) with one's ticket unpunched.
● **개표구** a (platform) wicket; a ticket barrier[gate]; a gate. **개표원** a ticket examiner [clipper / puncher].

개피떡 a rice-cake stuffed with bean jam.

개학(開學) beginning of school; (학년·학기 초의) opening of a school year[term]. **개학하다** open[begin] school; school begins.
● **개학식** the opening ceremony of the school year[term].

개항(開港) [항구의 개방] the opening of a port; [개방된 항구] an open port. **개항하다** [항구·공항을 개설하다] open a port[an air-

port]; [외국선의 출입을 허용하다] open a port (to foreign ships / for trade).
●**개항장** an open [a treaty] port.
개헌(改憲) (a) revision of the constitution; a constitutional revision; an amendment of the constitution. ¶~을 **제의하다** initiate a constitutional amendment // ~을 **발의하다** propose a constitutional amendment. **개헌하다** amend [revise / reform] the constitution.
●**개헌안** a bill for amending the constitution.
개헤엄 the dog paddle. ¶~을 **치다** do a dog paddle / dog-paddle / swim with the dog paddle.
개혁(改革) [혁신] (a) reform; reformation; renovation; innovation; [개선] improvement (of / on). ¶종교 ~ religious reformation / [역] the Reformation // 일대 ~ a large reform / (미) a shakeup // 근본적인 ~을 단행하다 make a radical [drastic] reform / reform from top to bottom // 정부는 세제의 일대 ~을 실시했다 The Government made [carried out] drastic reforms in the taxation system. // 즉시 ~을 요하는 것은 이 점이다 It is here that immediate reform is needed. **개혁하다** reform; make [carry out] reforms; renovate; innovate; improve(개선하다).
●**개혁안** a reform bill. **개혁자** a reformer; [역] a Reformer.
개화(開化) civilization; enlightenment. **개화하다** be [become] civilized; be enlightened; be illuminated. ¶개화한 나라 a civilized country. → ¶개화된 국민 civilized people // 개화되어 있지 않다 be backward in civilization // 그 나라는 이제 많이 개화되었다 It is now quite a civilized country.
개화(開花) blooming; bursting into bloom; efflorescence. ¶문명의 ~ the flowering [(문어) efflorescence] of civilization. **개화하다** flower; bloom; come into flower [bloom]; (특히 과수가) blossom; effloresce. ¶벚나무는 4월 초순에 개화할 것입니다 The cherry blossoms will come out early in April. / The cherry trees will [come into] blossom early in April. // 그의 재능은 개화할 기회가 없었다 His genius had no chance to flower [bloom].
●**개화기** the flowering time.
개황(概況) general condition; the general situation; an outlook. ¶일기 ~ the general weather outlook // ~을 **파악하다** get the bearings of the general situation / know how matters stand.
개회(開會) (회의의) the opening of a meeting; (의회·법정의) the opening of a session. ¶~를 **선언하다** (미) call (a meeting) to order / declare [announce] (the meeting) open // ~ 중이다 be open / (회의가) be in session // 국회는 지금 ~ 중이다 The National Assembly is now in session. **개회하다** (집회를) open; [집회가 열리다] meet; (의회·법정 등이) sit. ¶위원회는 주 1회 개회한다 The committee meets [A committee meeting is held] once a week. // 국회는 내일부터 개회한다 The National Assembly opens tomorrow.
●**개회사** an opening address [speech]. **개회식** an opening ceremony [(미) exercise]; an inauguration.
개회로(開回路) [전] an open [a broken] circuit.
개흙 mud [slime] on the bank of an inlet; silt at an estuary.
−**객**(客) a certain person. ¶불청~ an uninvited guest // 일등~ a first-class passenger / a cabin passenger.
객관(客觀) [철] the object; the material world(물질계).
●**객관 묘사** (an) objective description. **객관성** objectivity. **객관식 시험** an objective test. **객관주의** objectivism. **객관화** objectification.
객관적(客觀的) objective. ¶비~인 nonobjective (painting) // ~ 묘사 an objective description // ~ 정세 the true state of affairs // ~으로 objectively // ~으로 보다 take an objective view (of the situation) // ~으로 자신을 보기는 어렵다 It is not easy for us to see ourselves as others see us. // ~으로 보아 그의 주장이 옳은 것 같다 Viewed objectively, his claim seems more reasonable.
객기(客氣) ill-advised bravery; rashness; blind daring; youthful ardor; uncalled-for show of spirit. ¶~를 **부리다** be carried away by a rash impulse // 저렇게 큰소리치는 것도 술 마신 ~ 때문이다 All his big talk is just Dutch courage.
객담(客談) an idle talk; futile [empty] talk; bosh; an uncalled-for remark. **객담하다** talk nonsense; say silly things; waste words.
객담(喀痰) [담을 뱉음] expectoration; spitting. **객담하다** expectorate phlegm; cough up phlegm; spit (out).
●**객담 검사** an examination of one's sputum.
객사(客舍) a hotel; an inn.
객사하다(客死−) die away from home; die in a strange land; die abroad. ¶그는 멕시코에서 객사했다 He died (during his stay) in Mexico. // 바이런은 그리스에서 객사했다 Byron died (while) in Greece.
객석(客席) a seat (for a guest); (관객·승객용의) the seats (for the audience / for passengers); [관객·청중] the audience. ¶이 극장에는 5백 명이 앉을 ~이 있다 This theatre seats [has seats for] 500 people. // ~은 조용해졌다 A hush fell over the audience.
객선(客船) a passenger boat [ship].
객설(客說) an idle talk; prattle; tattle; useless talk; bosh; an uncalled-for [a superfluous] remark. **객설하다** talk idly [nonsense]; say useless things; tattle. ¶객설하지 마라 Quit your idle talk! / Don't talk nonsense!
객소리(客−) an idle talk; prattle. ⇨ᵇ**객설**
객수(客愁) loneliness on a journey; sadness felt while on a journey; nostalgia; homesickness. ¶~를 **느끼다** feel melancholy on a journey / be visited with thoughts of home while on a journey.
객스럽다(客−) unnecessary; needless; uncalled-for. ¶객스러운 짓 a useless [needless] act / an uncalled-for behavior.
객승(客僧) a traveling priest.
객식구(客食口) a hanger-on (pl. hangers-on); a dependant; a temporary addition to a family.
객실(客室) [여관 등의 방] a guest room; [선실] a passenger cabin; [특등실] a stateroom; (가정의) a drawing room [(미) a parlor].
●**객실 담당자** (호텔의) a room clerk.
객원(客員) an honorary [a guest] member; a non-regular member.

●**객원 교수** a guest [visiting] professor. **객원 지휘자** a guest conductor.
객주(客主) [거간꾼] a broker; a commission merchant [agent]; [객줏집 주인] the keeper of an inn for merchants.
●**객줏집** a peddlers' inn; an inn for merchants.
객지(客地) a strange land (where one is staying on a trip); one's staying place on a journey; foreign land. ¶~에 있는 stranger / an out-lander // ~에서 away from home / in a strange land // 나는 10년 동안 ~ 생활을 했다 I was absent from home for ten years. // 그는 ~에서 병으로 쓰러졌다 He fell ill while on a journey [far from home].
객쩍다(客-) unnecessary; needless; uncalled-for; [실없다] idle; silly. ¶객쩍은 소리 마라 Don't talk nonsense. / Tell that to the horse marines.
객차(客車) (미) a passenger car; a coach; (영) a (passenger) carriage. ¶일등 ~ a first-class car [carriage] // 특별 ~ a family saloon / a parlor car // ~ 편(에 / 으로) (by) means of a passenger train / (by) a passenger train.
객체(客體) 1 [법][철] the object. ¶범죄의 ~ the object of a crime // ~화하다 objectify / objectivize / objectize / objectivate // 영토와 국민은 국가의 ~다 The territory and people are the objects of the state. 2 [객지에 있는 몸] a person who is away on a journey [(far) away from home].
객토(客土) soil brought from an other place (to improve the soil). ¶~를 넣다 add fertile soil.
객혈(喀血) [의] hemoptysis. ⇨ 각혈
갤러리 a gallery.
갤런 a gallon. ¶1~으로 10마일 달리다 do ten miles to the gallon.
갭 a gap. ¶두 사람의 생각에는 큰 ~이 있다 There is a wide gap between the thinking of the two. // 세대 간의 ~을 메우기란 어렵다 It is difficult to bridge the generation gap.
갯가 the shore of an estuary; [물가] the waterside.
갯가재 [동] a squilla (pl. ~s, -lae); a mantis crab [shrimp / prawn].
갯값 dirt-cheap [dog-cheap] price; ridiculously [absurdly] cheap price. ¶~으로 for a mere [an old] song / at a large sacrifice // ~으로 팔다 sell (a thing) cheap as dirt / sell (an article) for a mere song // 그런 것은 팔아 봐야 ~이다 That would fetch only a small price.
갯바람 a sea breeze; briny [salt] air.
갯버들 [식] a pussy willow.
갯벌 beach.
갯지렁이 [동] a lugworm; a lobworm; a clam worm; a nereid.
갱 [강도] (한 사람) a gangster; a mobster; (한 무리) a gang (of robbers).
●**갱 영화** a gangster film.
갱(坑) 1 [광물 채취용 굴] a mine. 2 [갱도] a gallery; a drift. 3 [사금광의 도랑] a drain.
갱구(坑口) a pithead; a minehead; a pit mouth; a bank.
갱내(坑內) ¶~에서 inside a pit [mine shaft] // ~로 들어가다 go down pits.
●**갱내 노동자** a pit [an underground] worker; a miner; a mine worker. **갱내 작업** inside [pit] labor; underground work.
갱년기(更年期) the turn [change] of life; the critical age; (여성의) the menopause; [의] the climacterium. ¶~의 변화 climacteric changes.
●**갱년기 장애** a menopausal disorder.
갱도(坑道) [횡갱] a level; a head(ing); a gallery; a tunnel; [수갱] a shaft; a pit. ¶갱맥을 가로질러 만든 ~ a crosscut // ~를 파다 mine / drive (into rock) // ~가 무너져서 3명의 갱부가 갇혔다 Three miners were trapped by the collapse of the tunnel roof.
갱목(坑木) mine timber; a mine pillar [support]; a mine prop.
갱부(坑夫) a miner; a mineworker; a digger; a pitman (탄광의). ¶~로 일하다 work in a mine.
갱생(更生) rebirth; regeneration; rejuvenation; revival; resuscitation. ¶범죄자의 ~ the rehabilitation of an offender // 자력 ~ self-rehabilitation. **갱생하다** be born again; come to life again; be regenerated; revive; resuscitate; (범죄자가) be rehabilitated. ¶그녀는 나쁜 길에 들어섰다가 갱생했다 She has turned over a new leaf [given up her evil ways]. →¶ **갱생시키다** rehabilitate (an offender) / give (ex-convicts) a fresh start in life // 비행 소년을 갱생시키다 rehabilitate a juvenile delinquent.
●**갱생 시설** rehabilitation facilities; (중독 환자 등의) a halfway house; (학대받는 아내의) a hostel for battered wives; (가출한 아이 등의) a home for runaways. **갱생원** a rehabilitation center; a juvenile guidance center.
갱신(更新) renewal; renovation; innovation. ¶운전면허의 ~ renewal of a driver's license // 면허증의 ~ 시기가 되었다 It's time to renew my license. / My license has come up for renewal. **갱신하다** renew (a contract); renovate; innovate. ¶대차 계약을 ~ renew a lease // 공판 절차를 ~ recommence [renew] the proceedings of a public trial // 면허증은 3년마다 갱신해야 한다 The license must be renewed every three years. // 그는 세계 기록을 갱신했다 He broke the world record. / He established a new world record.
갱지(更紙) pulp paper; rough (printing) paper; newsprint (신문 인쇄용).
갸륵하다 praiseworthy; admirable; laudable; commendable; exemplary. ¶갸륵한 마음씨 a commendable purpose // 갸륵한 젊은이 an admirable young man // 갸륵한 일을 하다 do something good // 용돈을 절약해서 빈민 구제를 위해 기부한다는 일은 어린이로서 갸륵하기 그지없다 It is highly praiseworthy for [in] a child to contribute something out of its pocket money to the poor relief fund. **갸륵히** laudably; commendably; praiseworthily. ¶그의 효성을 ~ 여겨 in reward for [in consideration of] his filial heart.
갸름하다 somewhat long; slender; oval; pleasantly oval. ¶갸름한 얼굴 an oval face // 갸름한 손 a slender hand // 갸름한 예쁜 얼굴의 소녀 a girl with a sweet oval face // 얼굴이 ~ have an oval face.
갸웃거리다 peep (into); crane (one's neck). ⇨ ˇ기웃거리다
갸웃하다 1 [조금 기울이다] incline (one's head on one side); tilt (one's head); lean. 2 [조금 기울다] somewhat slanted [inclined].

갹출(醵出) donation; a contribution; sharing the expenses; chipping in; offering a share of money. **갹출하다** contribute (money to a fund); contribute each his own share; make contributions; (미국 구어) chip in; donate. ¶신체장애자를 위해 돈을 ~ donate money for physically handicapped people // 고아를 위해 장학금을 ~ contribute a scholarship fund for orphans // 구제 자금을 ~ make a donation to a relief fund.

거 [그것] Well!; Why!; There! ¶~ 참 잘되었다 That's good. // ~ 우습지 않은가 Why, isn't that funny! // ~ 참 아름답다 Why, that's beautiful! // ~ 누구냐 Uh, who is there?

거가대족(巨家大族) a distinguished and powerful[influential] family; a mighty clan.

거간(居間) 1 [중개업] brokerage. 2 a broker. ⇨ "거간꾼(⇨↗다) **거간하다** act as a broker; do brokerage; broker.
● **거간꾼** a broker; a middleman; [위탁 판매인] a commission agent.

거개(擧皆) [거의 모두가] most (of); the greater[best] part (of); (a) great part (of); a great[large / major] portion (of); [거의 모두] mostly; for the most part; largely; in large part; mainly; in the main. ¶이 학교 졸업생의 ~는 실업계로 진출한다 Most graduates of this school go into business. // 참석자는 ~가 대학생이었다 Those present were, for the most part, university students.

거구(巨軀) a huge [massive] figure; a big [gigantic] body [frame / physique]. ¶~의 사나이 a giant (of a man) // 280파운드의 ~ a massive figure of 280 pounds in weight // 그는 ~를 주체하지 못하는 듯했다 He looked as if he were in trouble, not knowing how to carry his big body.

거국일치(擧國一致) national unity; a united front; the whole nation in a body. ¶~로 국난에 대처했다 The whole nation faced the national crisis as one soled body.

거국적(擧國的) nationwide (movement). ¶~으로 on a nationwide scale / throughout[all over] the country // ~으로 정부의 정책을 지지했다 The whole nation supported[The people gave solid support to] the Government policy. // 그들은 ~으로 대통령을 환영했다 The whole nation welcomed the president.

거금(巨金) a large [big] sum (of money); a pile of money. ¶~ 백만 원 as much as [no less than] one million won / (구어) a cool million // ~을 투입하다 go to great expense / pay a big sum / (투자) invest a large sum (in) // ~을 요하다 cost a great deal of money.

거금(距今) ago; back from today. ¶~ 5백 년 전에 five hundred years ago // ~ 50년 전의 일이다 It dates back fifty years.

거기 1 [그곳(에)] that place; there; to that place; thither. ¶여기서 ~까지 from here to that place[there] // ~서 기다려라 Wait there. // ~ 누구요 Who's there ? // 최 선생 ~ 계십니까 Is Mr. Choe there? // 내가 ~로 가지요 I will come over (to your place). // ~서부터 울창한 숲입니다 There is a dense forest beyond there. // 길은 ~서부터 가파르게 된다 The road gets steep from that point[after that]. // 우리는 부산까지 함께 가고 ~서 헤어졌다 We went together as far as Busan, and

71   거꾸로

there[where] we parted. // ~는 벌써 눈이 왔겠지요 I suppose you've already had snow in your part of the country. // ~ 형편은 어떠하십니까 How are things going on in your place? // (전화에서) ~가 윤 박사님 사무실입니까? Is this Dr. Yun's office?
2 [그것(에)] that; so far; that far; to that extent. ¶~에 비하면 on the other hand / ~에다가 besides / moreover / [설상가상으로] what is worse / to make matters worse // ~까지는 좋았는데 so good, but ... // ~까지는 생각 못했는걸 I never thought of that. // ~까지는 나는 찬성이다 I agree with you so far [up to that point]. // 길을 잃었는데 ~에다 비마저 오기 시작했다 I lost my way and, what was worse, it began to rain. // 절약도 ~에 이르면 구두쇠가 된다 Economy carried to that extent is stinginess.

거꾸러뜨리다 1 [엎어뜨리다] make fall flat [headfirst / headlong / headforemost]; throw [bring] down; knock down (때려서); trip up(발을 걸어서); fell(나무를 찍어서); topple (a person in power); throw (a person) to the ground; get (a person) down; floor (a person). ¶씨름으로 ~ overmatch (a person) in wrestling // 폭도들이 그 기념비를 거꾸러뜨렸다 The mob razed the monument.
2 [멸망시키다] ruin; overthrow; subvert; unseat; undermine; [패배시키다] beat; defeat; vanquish; bring (a person) to (his) knees. ¶정부를 ~ overthrow [unseat / topple] the government // (미국 속어) give the government the bum's rush // 챔피언을 ~ beat [topple] a champion.
3 [죽이다] kill; make [do] away with; dispose of; (미국 속어) rub [blow] out; bump [knock] off; liquidate.

거꾸러지다 1 [엎어지다] fall head first [foremost]; fall flat [headlong]; fall (down); tumble down; go [roll] over; be off one's feet. ¶땅에 ~ fall to the ground / fall down on the ground // 술에 취하여 ~ collapse [fall down] dead-drunk // 앞으로 ~ fall forward // 지쳐서 ~ break down from exhaustion / break down from [through] over work // 그는 돌에 채어서 거꾸러졌다 He stumbled over a stone and fell.
2 [무너지다] go to ruin; collapse; fall; be overthrown; [패배하다] be defeated [beaten]; lose. ¶얼마 안 가서 그 왕조는 거꾸러졌다 It was not long before the dynasty was overthrown.
3 [죽다] die; succumb to (the wound); (속어) kick the bucket. ¶콜레라로 ~ be carried off [cut down] by cholera // 거꾸러져라 Go to hell [the devil]! / Curse upon you ! / Drop dead!

거꾸로 1 (아래위로) bottom up; upside down; wrong side up; (안팎을) inside out. ¶~ 하다 invert / turn (a thing) upside down / turn inside out // ~ 되다 be inverted / be turned upside down // ~ 매달다 hang (a person) upside down / hang (a person) by (his) heels // ~ 붙다 put a stamp the wrong side up // 철봉을 ~ 쥐다 grip a horizontal bar underhand // 꽃병이 ~ 놓여 있었다 The vase was placed upside down [bottom up] // 안팎[위아래]을 ~ 하면 어떨까 How about turning it inside out [upside down]?

2 [역으로] the wrong way; the other way (about[round]); in reverse order; reversely; topsy-turvy. ¶~ 말하면 conversely speaking / 일을 ~ 하다 put[set] the cart before the horse // 나이를 ~ 먹다 age reversely // ABC를 ~ 말하다 say the alphabet backward // 걷다 walk backward(s) // 카드의 순서가 ~ 되어 있다 The cards are in reverse order. / The order of the cards is reversed. // 수를 ~ 셀 수 있나요 Can you count backward? // 너는 내 말뜻을 ~ 받아들이고 있다 You put a wrong interpretation on what I say.

3 [곤두박혀] headlong; headforemost; headfirst; head over heels. ¶~ 떨어지다 fall headlong [headfirst / head over heels / upside down] // 그는 비계에서 ~ 떨어졌다 He fell headfirst[headlong] from the scaffold.

4 [오히려] instead; on the contrary. ¶칭찬은 커녕 ~ 책망해야겠다 Far from praising him, I must positively blame him.

-거나 [열거] and; or; [양보] (even) though [if]; no matter how[what / when / where / who]; whatever, etc; [상관] whether ... or .... ¶손뼉을 치~ 큰 소리로 웃~ 하지 마시오 Don't slap your hands or laugh loudly. // 날씨야 춥~ 말~ 예정 시간에 떠나자 Whatever the weather may turn out, let's leave on scheduled time. // 어떤 일이 일어나~ 그의 얼굴에서 온화한 미소가 떠나는 일은 없었다 No matter what happened, the gentle smile was still on his face. // 그것은 있~ 없~ 마찬가지다 It doesn't matter[It makes no difference] whether I have it or not. / I am just as well without it as with it.

거나하다 tipsy; mellow; (속어) happy; partly drunk[intoxicated]. ¶거나하게 feeling high[mellow] / 거나하게 취하다 get mellow[tipsy] with drink / get pleasantly drunk / get merry over one's cup // 그는 약간 거나하여 집에 돌아왔다 He came home a bit happy. // 그는 오늘 밤 거나하게 취했다 He is pretty high tonight. // 그는 거나하여 노래를 흥얼거리고 있었다 Feeling a bit tipsy[high after his drink], he was humming a tune.

거년 (去年) last year.

거느리다 [이끌다] lead; head (a party); be at the head (of); [지휘하다] command (an army); be in command (of an army); [부양하다] have; take care of. ¶K 장군이 거느리는 군대 the army under the command of General K // 일군을 거느리고 at the head of an army // 많은 가족을 ~ have [take care of] a large family / keep a large establishment / 처자를 ~ support one's wife and children / have one's family [dearest ones] // 십만 대병을 거느리고 처들어가다 invade (a country) leading an army a hundred thousand strong // 나는 많은 가족을 거느리고 있다 I have a large family to support[so many mouths to feed]. // 그는 숭배자들을 거느리고 회장으로 향했다 He set out for the hall, followed by his admirers.

거느림채 [건] a detached house[building]; an outbuilding[outhouse]; an annex(e) (to a house); (미) an extension.

-거늘 1 [원인] now that; since; as. ¶부자가 되었으~ 자선에 힘쓰시오 Since you are rich enough, render aid to the poor in charity. **2** [불구하고] though; although; in spite of; despite; with all ...; [한편] when; while. ¶자네는 부자 ~ 왜 만족을 모르느냐 Why not contented with all your riches? // 모두들 일하~ 나만 누워 있겠는가 How can I be confined to my bed while all my comrades are at work?

-거니 [...한테] since; as; so; but. ¶나는 젊었으~ 돌인들 무거우랴 Since I am young, can any stone be heavy (for me)!

2 [생각·추측·기대] with the thought that ... probably [surely]; with confidence [assurance] that. ¶그가 죽었다는 소식은 들었으나 지금도 살아 있겠~ 싶다 I was informed of his death, but I still presume him to be alive. // 자네가 오겠~ 생각했다 I thought you would come. // 내일이면 그를 만날 수 있겠~ 생각하면 몹시 기쁘다 Assured of seeing him tomorrow, I am very happy.

3 [교대 교대로] what with doing one thing and another (in alternation); now ... now ...; sometimes ... sometimes ...; by turns. ¶선물[인사말]을 주~ 받~ 하다 exchange gifts[greetings] with // 주~ 받~ 하나 exchange blows // 그들은 잔을 주~ 받~ 하며 실컷 마셨다 They drank their fill, now offering, now accepting cups. // 주~ 받~ 이야기는 끝이 없었다 What with my telling him and his telling me, there was no end to our talking.

-거니와 as well as; besides; admitting that; but (even so); not only ... but also ...; both ... and; futhermore; moreover; in addition. ¶돈도 없~ 틈도 없다 have neither money nor time to spare // 얼굴도 곱~ 마음씨도 곱다 have not only a pretty face but also a lovely disposition // 그건 그렇~ be that as it may ... // 그 학생은 공부도 잘하~ 운동도 잘한다 The student is a good athlete as well as a fine scholar. // 그것은 건강에도 좋~ 또한 경제적이다 It is not only good for health but also economical.

거닐다 walk[stroll] (aimlessly); saunter (leisurely); wander about; loiter; ramble. ¶거리를 ~ ramble[stroll] about the streets // 해변을 ~ take a stroll on the beach // 정원을 ~ take a turn in a garden // 거리를 거니는 것은 즐겁다 I enjoy strolling[sauntering] (in) the street. / It is enjoyable to walk [stroll] around the town. // 나는 정처 없이 산야를 거닐었다 I rambled[roamed] aimlessly through the hills and valleys[over hill and dale]. // 명동을 거니는 사람들이 많다 You can see a good number of strollers[promenaders / saunterers] on the Myeongdong (street).

거담 (祛痰) the discharge of phlegm. **거담하다** loosen[discharge] phlegm.
● **거담제** an expectorant.

거대 (巨大) hugeness; giganticness; enormousness. **거대하다** huge; gigantic; giant; enormous; mammoth; colossal. ¶거대한 건물 a massive [colossal] building / a stupendous structure // 거대한 재산을 모으다 build up a colossal fortune / (미) make a big pile.
● **거대과학** Big Science. **거대 도시** a megacity; a megalopolis. **거대 세포** a giant cell.

거덜 나다 collapse; crumble; break down; go to pieces; [결딴나다] be ruined; fail; burst (속어); [파산하다] go bankrupt [into bankruptcy]; go broke (속어). ¶거덜 난 살림 an eliminated livelihood // 거덜 난 사업가 a bankrupt[busted] businessman // 그 회사는

거딜 났다 The firm went down. / The company has passed out of existence [gone out]. // 그 은행은 거딜 났다 The bank broke [failed]. // 불경기로 저 가게는 거딜 나 버렸다 Owing to the business depression that store has folded up.

거동 (擧動) 〔처신〕 conduct; behavior; manner; carriage; demeanor; deportment; 〔행동〕 action; movements; doings. ¶~이 수상하다 act [behave] suspiciously // ~이 수상한 사람 a man who behaves suspiciously / a man of suspicious behavior // ~을 주시하다 watch (a person's) movements // ~이 점잖다 behave (oneself) gently / be gentle in one's movement [manners] // 그의 ~이 침착하지 않다 His movements lack composure. // 그의 ~은 매우 예측하기 어렵다 His actions [doings] are quite unpredictable [hard to predict]. // ~이 수상하다고 경찰이 나를 조사했다 The policeman demanded that I account for my strange [suspicious] behavior [conduct]. 거동하다 behave [conduct / bear] oneself; act (like).

거두 (巨頭) a prominent leader; a magnate; a prominent figure; a big shot [bug / whale / name] (미국 속어); a V.I.P. ¶재계의 ~ a leading financier // 정계의 ~ a political leader // 실업계의 ~들 big businessmen / the plutes (미).
● **거두 회담** a top-level [summit] conference [talk].

거두다 1 〔모아들이다〕 collect; gather; get [bring] together; take in. ¶기부금을 ~ get in donations / collect contributions // 빨래를 ~ take in washings // 세금을 ~ collect taxes / levy taxes (부과) // 회비를 ~ collect dues [membership fees] // 그는 소작료를 가혹하게 거두었다 He squeezed the rent out of his tenant.
2 〔수확하다·얻다〕 harvest; reap (fields); gather (in); gain; obtain. ¶곡식을 ~ gather [get] in crops / harvest crops // 만족할 만한 결과를 ~ obtain satisfactory result // 승리를 ~ gain [win] a victory // 투수의 교대가 효과를 거두었다 The change of pitchers was effective.
3 〔보살피다〕 look after; take care [charge] of; care for; attend on; see to; mind; tend. ¶아이를 ~ look after [take care of] a child // 거두어 먹이다 feed with care // 나는 그녀를 딸처럼 거두고 있다 I take quite a fatherly interest in her. / I take fatherly care of her. // 애처롭게도 그 아이는 거두는 사람이 없다 The poor child has no one to depend on.
4 〔정돈하다〕 right (a room); tidy [straighten] up (a room); put [set] (a room) straight [to rights]; clean up. ¶객실을 ~ put the parlor in order / tidy [fix] up the parlor.
5 〔그치다〕 stop; cease; end; quit; 〔철회하다〕 withdraw; recall. ¶숨을 ~ breathe one's last (breath) / gasp one's life away / give up one's breath // 눈물을 ~ stop crying [weeping] / dry one's tears // 명령을 ~ withdraw a command [an order] // 무기를 ~ lay down arms.

거두절미하다 (去頭截尾-) cut off the head and tail of (it); leave out the introduction and the conclusion of; make a short story of (it). ¶거두절미하면 to make [cut] a long story short.

거드럭거리다 show off; swagger; behave in a cocky way; hold one's head high; give oneself airs; put on airs. ¶거드럭거리면서 말하다 speak with an air of importance [in a lordly manner] // 거드럭거리면서 걷다 strut about / walk with a dignified air / swagger / stalk about // 거드럭거리지 마라 Don't be so puffed up! / None of your cheek [lip / sauce]!

거드름 a haughty attitude [air / demeanor]. ¶그가 ~을 피우는 것을 본 적이 없다 We never saw him behave haughtily [in an overbearing manner]. // 저 친구는 여기 주임이 되더니 되게 ~을 부리는군 How important he acts since he has been in charge here!
● **거드름쟁이** a high hat; a high-hatter; a swaggerer.

-**거든** 1 〔가정·조건〕 provided that; if; when. ¶바쁘지 않~ 놀러 오시오 Come and see me if you are free [not busy]. // 다 보았~ 그 책을 돌려주게 Return me the book when you have done with it. // 자라고 하~ 자 Go on to bed when I tell you to.
2 〔비교〕 still more; how much more. ¶개도 주인의 공을 알~ 하물며 사람에 있어서랴 If a dog is so faithful to its master, how much more should we human beings be! // 내 아니 잊었~ 너는 설마 잊었겠느냐 Since I haven't forgotten it, how could you?
3 〔까닭〕 as; so; since; owing to; due to; for. ¶그 사람이 있~ 방이 조용할 리가 있겠나 As far as he is staying in the room, how can it be quiet? // 내 눈으로 똑똑히 보았~ 다를 리가 있겠소 As I ascertain it with my own eyes, it cannot be otherwise.

거들 a girdle.

거들다 1 〔도와주다〕 help; assist; aid; lend [give] a (helping) hand; stand by. ¶남의 일을 잘 거드는 사람 a person who likes to do things for others / an obliging [accommodating] person // 거들어 주는 사람 a helper / an assistant // 일을 ~ help (a person) in [with] his work // 부모를 ~ help one's parents / be a help to one's parents // 옷 입는 [벗는] 것을 ~ help (a person) on [off] with his clothes // 당신을 위해 한몫 거들죠 I will make an effort for you. // 좀 거들어 주지 않겠나 Won't you lend me a hand?
2 〔참견하다〕 meddle [interfere] in; put one's nose into; 〔관여하다〕 participate (in); be concerned (in). ¶그는 항상 내 일에 거들려 한다 He is always trying to meddle in my affairs.

거들떠보다 lift one's eyes and look at (a person); glance up (at); notice; take notice (of); pay attention (to). ¶거들떠보지도 않다 do not even [so much as] cast a look at / do not so much as give the slightest attention to / barely glance up / do not care for / take no notice of / ignore completely // 내가 찾아갔으나 그는 거들떠보지도 않았다 I went to see him but he didn't even glance up at me. // 그녀는 너 따위는 거들떠보지도 않을 거다 She will not even look [glance up] at you. // 그녀는 자기 또래의 남자 아이는 거들떠보지도 않았다 She took no notice of [ignored] boys of her own age.

거들먹거리다 act rashly; behave imprudently; be elated (by success); let oneself go. ¶거들먹거리는 haughty / domineering / overbearing / pompous / important / lordly // 거들

거듭

먹거리면서 말하다 talk without reserve [restraint] // 거들먹거리면서 걷다 strut / swagger / walk swaggeringly [with a swagger].

거듭 [되풀이하여] over and over again; again; once again [more]; repeatedly. ¶~ 묻다 ask once more / ask the same question again / ask another question // ~ 부탁하다 ask repeatedly // 남에게 ~ 경고하다 warn a person again and again [repeatedly] // 감사드립니다 I am very grateful to you. / (구어) Many [A thousand] thanks to you. // ~ 사과 드립니다 I am terribly sorry. / I offer my sincere apologies. // ~ 묻고자 합니다 I want to [I'll] ask you this question again. / (다른 질문을) I have another question to ask you. // ~ 설명할 필요가 없다 There's no need to repeat the explanation. // ~ 말하지만 나는 그 일에 대해서 아무것도 모른다 I must repeat that I know nothing about that. **거듭하다** repeat; do again. ¶잔을 ~ drink cup after cup of wine // 실패를 ~ repeat a mistake // 우리 팀은 득점을 거듭했다 Our team piled up points. // 그 책은 5판을 거듭했다 The book went through [ran into] five editions. // 그는 고생에 고생을 거듭하여 재산을 모았다 He built up a fortune by struggling through one hardship after another. // 그 회사는 발전을 거듭했다 The firm was growing more and more prosperous. / The firm steadily expanded its business.

거듭나다 be born again; be reborn; come [return] to life again; resuscitate.

거듭제곱 [수] (raising (a term) to a higher) power; involution. **거듭제곱하다** raise to a higher power; involve.
● **거듭제곱근** [수] a radical root.

거뜬하다 light; nimble; agile; feel light; feel good(몸이). ¶거뜬한 짐 a light load / light baggage // 거뜬한 마음으로 with a light heart // 몸이 다시 ~ be well [all right] again / be restored to health / regain one's health. **거뜬히** lightly; (손쉽게) readily; easily; without difficulty [effort]. ¶~ 차려입다 be lightly dressed [clothed] / wear a light suit // ~ 들어올리다 lift (heavy baggage) light // ~ 이기다 win easily / win [gain] an easy victory (over) / win hands down / (구어) have a walkover // 그것쯤 ~ 할 수 있다 It will be no effort to do it. / Nothing can be easier. / (속어) It's a cinch. // 그는 100미터를 ~ 헤엄쳤다 He swam one hundred meters with ease.

거래 (去來) transaction; dealings; business; trade; (속어) a deal; (돈거래) lending and borrowing / (공정) ~ fair trade [transactions] / straight dealing / a square deal / (금전) ~ lending and borrowing money / (매수) bribery / payola / a payoff scandal / (이권에 관련된) graft / **무역** [무역 외] ~ visible [invisible] trade / **부정** [불법] ~ illegal [unlawful] transactions / black market(eer)ing / **현금** ~ business [dealings] for money [cash] / cash transactions / **국내** [지방 / 외국] ~ home [local / foreign] trade / **보통** ~ regular way contracts / **신규** ~ new business / **신용** ~ credit transactions / **부정한** ~ shady transactions / **실속이 있는** [없는] ~ a good [poor] bargain / ~의 범위 an extent of business / 은행과 ~ 가 있다 have a bank account // ~를 개시하다 [트다] enter into business (with) / (주로 은행 간의) open correspondent relation(ships) (with) / ~를 끊다 break off one's business connection (with) / close the account (with) / ~를 계속하다 keep an account (with) / maintain business relation(ships) (with) // 그 회사와의 ~는 중지되었다 Our business connections with the company were broken off. // 저 회사하고는 아버지 대부터 ~가 중단되지 않고 계속되어 왔다 Our transactions with that firm have continued unbroken since my father's generation. // 이번 ~에서 큰 손해 [이익]를 보았다 We lost [made] a great deal of money on this deal. // 저희는 쌀 ~는 하지 않습니다 We don't deal in rice. // 오늘의 주식 ~가(價)는 얼마입니까 What are today's quotations of shares? **거래하다** deal with (a person in a thing); transact [do] business (with); have an account (with); be connected in business dealings (with). ¶거래하지 않다 have no dealings with / 유리하게 ~ transact good business / 대규모로 ~ do a large (volume of) business / 월간 ···원으로 ~ turn over ... a month / 그 상사와 거래하고 있다 We have dealings with that firm.
● **거래량** the volume [amount] of business; (a) turnover. **거래소** an exchange; (주식) a stock exchange [market]. **거래 조건** terms and conditions of business. **거래처** [고객] a customer; a client; (거래 관계자) a business acquaintance; (전체) a (business) connection; (지방에 있는) a correspondent.

거론하다 (擧論─) make (it) a subject of discussion; make (it) an object of criticism. ¶거론할 여지가 없다 be out of the question // 이 책의 제1장은 노동 문제를 거론하고 있다 The first chapter of this book treats of [deals with] the labor problem.

거룩하다 divine; sacred; holy; sublime; solemn; venerable; great; grand; glorious. ¶(하느님의) 거룩하신 은혜 divine grace // 거룩하신 가르침 holy teachings // 거룩한 정신 lofty [noble] spirit // 거룩한 자기희생 sublime self-sacrifice // 높고 거룩하신 분 the high and lofty one / the God // 그 늙은 수녀의 얼굴은 거룩할 정도로 엄숙하였다 The old nun were a divinely solemn look.

거룻배 a lighter; a sampan; a barge.

거류 (居留) residence; residing. **거류하다** reside; dwell; live. ¶6개월 이상 거류한 외국인 a foreigner of more than six months residence.
● **거류민** residents. **거류민단** a settlement corporation. **거류지** a settlement; a concession. ¶외국인 ~ a foreign settlement [concession].

거르다[1] [여과하다] filter; strain (out); percolate; leach(물 등을); [가려내다] select; choose; pick out; sort out; single out. ¶물 거르는 기구 a (water) filter / a strainer // 불순물을 ~ filter out impurities // 국물을 ~ strain the stock // 물은 걸러서 마시도록 하시오 Drink filtered water only.

거르다[2] [건너뛰다] skip (over); omit; go without; dispense with. ¶한 집 걸러 이웃집 (the) next door but one // 아침을 ~ do [go] without [skip / omit / dispense with] breakfast / 하루 [이틀] 걸러 every other [every third] day // 한 줄씩 걸러 쓰다 write on every other line // 나는 바빠서 점심을 거르는 일이

자주 있었다 I was so busy that I often did [went] without lunch.
거름 [비료] manure; [인분] night soil; [소·말의 똥] dung; [화학 비료] (a) fertilizer. ¶~을 주다 spread manure (on) / apply fertilizer (to vegetables) // ~을 푸다 dip out night soil.
거름하다 manure; fertilizer; dress. ¶밭에 ~ cover a field with compost[manure].
● **거름통** a night-soil bucket[pail]; (미국 속어) a honey bucket; a manure tub.
거름종이 [불순물을 거르는 종이] a filter paper.
거리[1] [재료] material; matter; stuff; makings; [대상] the cause; the source; the subject; a butt. ¶걱정~ a source[cause] of anxiety [worry] // 이야깃[신문 기삿]~ a topic [subject] of conversation[a news story] // 웃음~ a laughingstock / a butt of ridicule / a subject of laughter // 말할 ~가 없다 I can't find any excuse[pretext] to approach him. / I don't have any subject to talk on. // 그는 우리의 조소~였다 He was the butt of our ridicule.
거리[2] [길거리] a road; a street. ¶번화한[쓸쓸한] ~ a busy[deserted / lonely] street // 큰 ~ a main street / a thoroughfare // 뒷~ a back street[lane] // 그 불량배 거리 roughs[hooligans] // ~를 지나가는 인파 the crowd passing along the street // ~의 여인 a woman of the streets / a street walker // ~를 걸어가다 walk on the street // 우리 집은 번화한 ~에 면해 있다 We live on a busy street. // ~를 깨끗이 합시다 (게시) Keep the town tidy.
거리 (距離) distance; [사정거리] range; [간격] an interval; a gap; a gulf; [차이] a difference. ¶일정한 ~에 at a certain distance // 상당한 ~ a pretty long distance // 한 시간의 ~ an hour's distance (from / between) // 5미터의 ~에서 발포하다 fire at 5-meter range // ~를 재다 measure the distance (between) // ~가 멀다 (공간이) be distant / be far / (상당한 차이가 있다) be very different (from) / be a far cry (from A to B) // 그 (지)점에서 같은 ~에 at equal distances from the point // 엎어지면 코 닿는 ~에 at a stone's throw // 짧은[2킬로미터의] ~를 두고 at a short distance[at a distance of two kilometers] (from) // 10미터의 ~를 두고 at intervals of 10 meters (from each other) // ~를 두다 keep one's distance // 안전한 ~를 유지하다 keep a safe distance (from) // ~를 떼어 놓다 [이기다] get a good lead (over one's opponent(s)) / open up a (big) lead (over) // ~가 벌어지다 [지다] lag behind (one's opponent(s)) // …까지의 사격 ~를 측정하다 find[get] the range of … // ~에 따라 다르다 (도금 둥이) vary with the distance // 서울에서 인천까지는 ~가 얼마나 됩니까 How far is it from Seoul to Incheon? / What is the distance between Seoul and Incheon? // 그는 그 ~를 2시간에 갔다 He covered[did / made] the distance in two hours. // 그곳은 우리 집에서 걸어서 갈 수 있는 ~에 있다 It is within walking distance of my house. // 걸어서 15분의 ~에 있다 It is a 15-minute walk from here. // 그 마을까지는 두 시간의 ~였다 It was a two hour journey [trip] to the village. // 그녀는 1위 선수와의 ~를 점점 좁혔다 She gradually closed the gap [shortened the distance] between herself and the front-runner. / She gradually caught up with the front-runner. // 그는 2위 주자와의 ~를 더욱 넓혀 가고 있다 He is putting more and more distance between himself and [is widening his lead over] the next runner. // 우리들의 의견에는 상당한 ~가 있다 We are very different in our opinion. / Our views are poles asunder. // 그것은 이상과는 ~가 먼 것이다 It is far removed from the ideal. / Nothing is farther from the ideal.
● **거리감** a sense of distance. **거리계** a range finder; a telemeter. **거리표** (철도의) a distance post; [이정표] a milestone; a mile marker.
거리끼다 [꺼림칙하다] be afraid of; be shy of; [주저하다] hesitate (to do); [가책을 받다] feel uneasy; have scruples about (doing); [방해가 되다] be restrained[hindered / prevented] (by). ¶그 일이 마음에 거리낀다 That matter weighs heavy on my mind. // 아무리 마음에 거리낀다 It haunts me. // 거리낄 게 뭐야 Why should I fear? // 나는 아무것도 거리낄 것이 없다 I can look the world in the face.
거리낌 [주저] hesitation; [양심의 가책] compunction; scruple; [사양] reserve. ¶~ 없는 비평 an unsparing criticism // 마음에 ~이 없다 do not weigh on one's mind // 그들은 아무런 ~도 없었다 They were free from care [worry]. / They had nothing to worry about. // ~ 없이 말하다 speak frankly[without reserve] / speak out / do not mince words // 남의 물건을 ~ 없이 쓰다 make free with another's possession // 그와는 아무 ~ 없이 그 문제를 논의할 수 있다 I can discuss the matter with him candidly and without reserve. // 자 ~ 없이 무엇이든지 물어보세요 Please feel free to ask us. / You are welcome to ask us. // 그가 나가 있는 동안 우리는 그의 방을 아무 ~ 없이 사용할 수 있었다 We made ourselves completely at home in his room while he was away.
거마 (車馬) horses and vehicles; traffic; transportation.
● **거마비** traffic expenses; carfare; carriage.
거 만 (巨萬) millions; a huge[colossal] fortune; vast[Croesus'] fortune. ¶~의 부를 쌓다 amass[pile up] vast[immense] wealth / make a vast fortune / make a big pile / become a millionaire // ~의 돈을 투입하다 spend millions (on a project).
거만하다 (倨慢—) proud; haughty; [건방지다] arrogant(▶ arrogant는 자기의 힘을 과신해서 우쭐댐, haughty는 자기의 지위를 자랑하며 남을 업신여김); pompous; puffed up; stuck up; toplofty; have one's nose in the air. ¶거만한 태도로 말하다 speak in a lofty manner // 거만한 태도를 취하다 assume an attitude of arrogant superiority (toward) / hold one's head (very) high // 그는 태도가 ~ He is haughty. / He has a grand[supercilious] manner. // 그는 누구에게나 ~ He is arrogant [haughty] toward(s) everyone. // 그는 거만한 태도로 남에게 명령한다 He orders people about arrogantly[high-handedly]. **거만히** haughtily; arrogantly; loftily. ¶~ 같보다 look down upon a person arrogantly // ~ 굴다 behave haughtily / be insolent (to) / assume an air of importance[superiority / hauteur] / stand over (a person) // 그가 ~ 구는 꼴이 마음에 안 든다 I don't like the way

거머리 he acts important.

거머리 [동] a leech; [달라붙어 괴롭히는 사람] a bur; a nuisance; a pest. ¶~처럼 달라붙다 stick like a leech // ~로 피를 빼다 bleed (a person) by the use of leeches // (치료하려고) ~를 붙이다 apply a leech (to) / 그들은 ~처럼 그의 재산을 송두리째 빨아먹었다 They leeched him until his entire fortune was exhausted.

거머잡다 grab[clutch / take hold of]. ¶멱살을 ~ grab (a person) by the collar // 실권을 ~ take[hold] the reins of (government).

거머쥐다 grab. ⇨ 거머잡다

거멀못 a clamp; a cramp; a rivet; a clincher.

거멀쇠 an iron clamp.

거목 (巨木) 1 [나무] a great[large / big] tree; a gigantic[towering] tree. ¶소나무 ~ a giant pine. 2 [인물] a great man.

거무데데하다 darkish; dusky; murky; swarthy; dark sallow(얼굴빛 등이).

거무스름하다 dark; darkish; dusky; swarthy; dark-colored; dark-complexioned. ¶피부색이 거무스름한 여자 a brunette // 얼굴이 ~ have a dark complexion / be dark-skinned / be dark-complexioned.

거무죽죽하다 blackish; dark; fuscous; somber. ¶거무죽죽한 벽지 dingy wallpaper // 눈 가장자리가 ~ have dark rings around one's eyes / (멍이 들어) have a black eye / (속이) have a mouse[shiner] // 온몸이 ~ be black and blue all over.

거문고 a geomungo; a Korean lute; a Korean harp (with six strings).

거물 (巨物) [영향력 있는 사람] a great man; a big[an important] figure; (구어) a bigwig; (구어) a VIP; [큰 사물] a big thing; a whopper. ¶당내의 ~ a big wheel in the party // 당대의 ~ the lion of the day // 정계의 ~ a leading figure[(구어) big wheel] in politics / a conspicuous figure in the political world // 산업계[재계]의 ~ an industrial [a financial] magnate // 문단의 ~ a great figure [lion] of the literary world / a literary star.

거뭇거뭇하다 black-spotted. ⇨ 가뭇가뭇하다

거미 a spider. ¶~가 집을 짓다 A spider weaves[spins] its web. 거미도 줄을 쳐야 벌레를 잡는다(속담) No gains without pains.

● **거미발** (보석의) a jewel chain shaped like a spider's legs. **거미줄** a spider's thread; cobweb. ¶~을 친 cobwebbed // 나비가 ~에 걸렸다 A butterfly was caught in a spider's web. // 방은 ~ 투성이다 The room is full of cobwebs.

거반 (居半) the (great) majority; mostly. ⇨ 거지반

거병하다 (擧兵-) raise[muster] an army; rise in arms; take up arms. ¶반란군은 북부에서 거병하였다 A rebel army was raised in the north.

거보 (巨步) a giant step; a mammoth stride; [훌륭한 공적] a brilliant achievement. ¶~를 내디디다 take a giant step (toward) / make a mammoth[giant] stride (forward) (in).

거봐라 I told you so!; Did I not tell you so?; Look!; See! You see! ¶~, 내 말이 맞지 I told you so, didn't I?

거부 (巨富) a man of (great) wealth; a millionaire; a multimillionaire; a billionaire; a person as rich as Croesus; a Croesus.

거부 (拒否) refusal; rejection; disapproval; [부정·부인] denial; veto disallowance; [법] traverse. **거부하다** refuse; deny; veto; reject; turn down; disapprove of. ¶요구를 ~ reject [turn down] a request // 의안을 ~ veto a legislative bill // 시인하기를 ~ decline to admit / deny any knowledge (of) // 회사 측은 조합의 임금 인상 요구를 전면 거부하였다 The management turned down[flatly rejected] the union's demand for a wage hike.

● **거부권** a veto; the veto right. ¶~을 행사하다 exercise one's veto (power) / put[place] a veto (on). **거부 반응** rejection (symptoms). ¶~이 나타나기 시작했다 Rejection set in.

거북 [동] a tortoise; a terrapin; a (sea) turtle. (▶ (미)에서는 거북은 모두 turtle이라 부르지만 육지에 사는 것은 tortoise라고도 함. (영)에서는 turtle은 주로 바다에 사는 것을 말하고 육지·민물에 사는 것은 보통 tortoise라 함)

● **거북선** a geobukseon; the "Turtle Boat"; an ironclad warship shaped like a tortoise.

거북하다 1 (마음이) awkward; embarrassing; ill at ease; uncomfortable. ¶듣기 거북한 disagreeable to hear // 입장이 ~ feel awkward / find oneself in an awkward position // 그 사람 앞에 가면 어쩐지 ~ I feel rather awkward in his presence. // 낯선 집에 가면 거북한 법이다 One feels ill at ease in a stranger's house. // 어쩐지 여기 있기가 ~ I feel out of my element here. // 나는 그가 마침 그곳에 있어 매우 거북했다 I felt quite embarrassed because he happened to be there. // 그 녀석이 거북해할까 봐 그런 말을 했지 I said so just to keep him in countenance. 2 (몸이) unwell; out of condition[order]. ¶배 속이 ~ have something wrong with one's inside // 오늘은 몸이 거북해서 그를 만날 수 없다 I do not feel equal to receiving him today. // 너무 먹었나 봐, 배 속이 거북해 It seems I ate too much, I feel quite unwell [I got my stomach out of order].

거뿐하다 (rather) light; carefree. ⇨ 가뿐하다

거사 (擧事) taking[initiating] an action; a revolt; an uprising; insurrection; insurgency. **거사하다** launch an undertaking; take an action; undertake (a riot); set (a plan / a movement) on foot; rise[revolt] (against). ¶혁명을 거사한 사람들 those who started a revolution.

거상 (巨商) a wealthy merchant; a merchant prince; a business magnate; (미국 속어) a baron.

거상 (巨像) a huge statue; a colossus (pl. -si, -es); a gigantic[mammoth] image.

거상 (居喪) [상중] being in mourning; [상복] a mourning attire. **거상하다** be in mourning.

거석 (巨石) a huge stone; [고고] a megalith.

● **거석문화** megalithic culture.

거성 (巨星) a giant star; [큰 인물] a great man; a luminary; a leading light; (구어) a big shot; a bigwig. ¶초~ a supergiant (star) // 화단의 ~ a great painter // 문단의 ~ a great writer / a literary genius / a leading figure of literary world // 그녀는 음악계의 ~이다 She is a musical superstar. // ~이 땅에 떨어졌다 A great star has fallen. / A great man is lost [has died].

거세 (去勢) 1 (동물의) castration; emasculation; gelding. **거세하다** castrate; emasculate; geld. ➡ ¶거세된 사나이 a castrated fellow / a

eunuch // 그는 기르는 개를 거세시켰다 He had his dog neutered.
2 (세력의) [약화] weakening; exclusion; [근절] eradication; [베제] a purge; a cleanup. **거세하다** purge (disloyal elements) from; destroy [undermine] (a person's) influence; weaken the power (of the opposing party). ➔¶지도자가 죽은 후, 그 운동은 거세되어 버렸다 After the death of the leader, the movement lost its former vigor. / (문어) The leader's death emasculated the movement. // 새 헌법에 의하여 그 나라의 반민주 세력은 거세되었다 The anti-democratic forces in this country were eradicated according to the new Constitution.

거세다 rough; wild; violent; fierce; strong; furious; tough; coarse; rude; aspirated. ¶거센 파도 wild [heavy] sea [waves / waters] // 거센 바람 a strong wind / a stiff breeze // 거센 여자 an unruly woman / a woman of spirit // 거센 성격 wild nature / uncontrollable temper / savage disposition // 거센 입심 unbridled tongue / violent language // 거센 말 aspirated intensives // 거센 세파에 시달리다 be tossed about in the storms of life.

거센소리 [언] aspirated sounds; an aspirate.

거소 (居所) one's residence; one's address; a dwelling place; one's whereabouts; [법] (a place of) abode. ¶확정된 ~ one's permanent address // ~를 정하다 [잡다] make one's home (at / in) / take up one's residence [quarters] (at / in) / settle down (in / at) // ~ 불명이다 one's whereabouts is unknown / be missing.

거수 (擧手) raising one's hand; a show of hands. ¶~로 표결하다 take (a) show of hands / decide (on a bill) by (a) show of hands // ~로 결정합시다 Let's decide by (a) show of hand(s). // 그 법안은 ~ 표결에서 부결되었다 The bill was defeated [negatived] by (a) show of hands. **거수하다** raise [show] one's hand. ¶질문이 있으면 거수하여 주십시오 If you any questions, please raise your hand.
● **거수경례** a hand salute; a military salute; cap-touching. ¶~를 하다 make [give] a military salute / raise one's hand in salute. **거수기** (一機) a rubber stamp; a yesman. ¶~ 노릇을 하다 rubber-stamp. **거수투표** voting by (a) show of hands.

거스러미 (손톱의) an agnail; a hangnail; (나무의) a splinter; a sticker. ¶~가 생긴 손가락 끝 a (torn) hangnail // 손~가 생기다 have a hangnail // 손가락에 ~가 박혔다 I've run a splinter into my finger. // 나무젓가락 끝에 ~가 생기기 시작했다 The tip of the chopstick began to splinter [split].

거스르다 **1** (성질이) become [grow] unmanageable [unruly / refractory / intractable]; get beyond control; get out of hand; grow stubborn. **2** (잔털이) bristle up; stand on end; get ruffled. ¶털이 거스러진 참새 a sparrow all ruffled up.

거스르다 **1** [반대 방향을 취하다] go [act] against; act contrary to; run counter to; oppose; disobey; defy; cross (another's will); offend (a person). ¶…을 거슬러 against / contrary to / in defiance of / in the face of // 바람을 거슬러서 나아가다 go in the teeth of the wind // 물결을 거슬러 헤엄치다 swim against the current [stream] // 부모의 말을 ~ defy [disobey / contradict] one's parents // 운명을 ~ strive [fight] against fate // 하늘의 뜻을 ~ fly in the face of Providence / give offense to the will of God // 중론을 ~ stem the tide of public opinion // 시대의 조류를 ~ swim against the current of the times / go against the stream of the times // 그는 남의 비위를 거스르지 않으려고 노력했다 He tried not to cause offense. // 그는 부모의 뜻을 거슬러 대학에 진학했다 He went to college against his parent's wishes.
2 [거스름돈을 주고받다] give change; make change. ¶…을 받고 10원을 거슬러 주다 give ten won (in return) for … // 거슬러 받다 get the change // 천 원짜리를 내시면 거슬러 받게 됩니다 You can get it at less than one thousand won. / You will get change if you give a thousand won note.

거슬러 올라가다 **1** (흐름을) go [row / sail] upstream. ¶강을 ~ sail upstream / go against the stream. **2** (과거로) go back (to the past); [소급하다] retroact (to); retrospect (to). ¶당시로 거슬러 올라가 생각하면 when I look back on that time // 과거로 거슬러 올라가서 적용시키다 apply (a law) retrospectively (to) // 이야기는 1790년대로 거슬러 올라간다 The story goes way back to the seventeen nineties.

거스름돈 change. ¶천 원짜리를 내고 받은 ~ the change from a thousand won note // ~을 주다 [받다] give [get] the change // ~을 주지 않다 refuse change // ~을 잘못 주다 count the wrong change // 여기 있습니다 Here's your change. // ~은 10원이 됩니다 That makes ten won change. // ~은 가지시오 You may keep [Keep / Never mind] the change. // ~은 동전으로 주시오 Give me my change in pennies. // 만 원짜리인데 ~이 있습니까 Have you change [Can you give me change] for a ten thousand won note? // ~은 없습니다 (잔돈을 준비하시오) (게시) No change given. // ~이 필요 없도록 잔돈을 준비하십시오 Please have the exact amount ready. // 그는 ~을 내게 잘못 주었다 [적게 주었다] He gave me the wrong change [short changed me]. // 나는 500원짜리로 지불하고 ~을 50원 받았다 I paid with five hundred won bill [(영) note] and got fifty won in change. // 만 원짜리를 드리면 ~을 주시겠습니까 Can you give me change if I pay with ten thousand won bill [(영) note]? // ~ 480원입니다 And here's 480 won (in) change.

거슬거슬하다 [거칠다] (성질이) rough; wild; stubborn; unruly; intractable; (살결이) rough; bristly; sharp; coarse. ¶거슬거슬한 피부 rough [coarse] skin // 손이 ~ have rough [chappy] hands // 그녀의 손은 일을 심하게 하여 거슬거슬했다 Her hands were rough with hard work.

거슬리다 [언짢은 느낌이 들다] offend; be offensive; give offense; be against the grain [one's taste]; be unpleasant; rub (a person) the wrong way. ¶귀에 거슬리는 소리 a harsh grating noise // 눈에 거슬리는 것 an eyesore // 비위에 ~ get on a person's nerves // 눈에 ~ be an eyesore / be unpleasant to the eye / be out of (a person's) favor // 귀에 ~ be [sound] offensive [harsh] to the ear // 거슬리는 말을 하다 make offensive remarks // 저 남

거슴츠레하다 아 빠진 빌딩은 눈에 거슬린다 That run-down building is an eyesore [offends the eye].// 그는 눈에 거슬리는 녀석이다 He's an offensive guy.// 그것은 내 성미에 거슬린다 It goes against the grain with me.// 이 아이의 하는 말, 하는 짓이 모두 비위에 거슬린다 Everything this child does or says rubs me the wrong way.// 저 드릴 소리가 귀에 거슬린다 That drilling noise grates on [offends] my ear.// 그가 하는 말은 모두 귀에 거슬린다 Everything he says irritates me.

거슴츠레하다 sleepy; dull; drowsy. ⇨ =게슴츠레하다

거시 경제학(巨視經濟學**)** macroeconomics.

거시기 1 [대명사] what-do-you-call-it; whatchama-call-it; what-you-may-call-it; whats-it; do-floppy; do-funny; what-not; thing-daddy; thingumbob. ¶내 ~ 어디 있지 Where is my whatchama-call-it?// 그 ~ 좀 집어 주게 Pass the doings to me. 2 [감탄사] what was it [he] called that ...; what. ¶~ 그게 뭐더라 That — what was it called? — that thingamajig ....

거시적(巨視的**)** macroscopic; (관점이) all-inclusive; comprehensive. ¶~ 세계 a macroscopic world / ~ 견해 a broad point of view / ~으로 보다 take a broad view (of) / see (something) in broad perspective.

거식하다 1 [동사] do something or other (with); fiddle around (with). ¶네 친구로 거식한 사람이 있지 않았니… 저… 언젠가 돈을 잃어버린 사람 말이야 Didn't you have a friend who ... uh ... did something or other with some money ... oh, yes, that man who once lost some money, you know. 2 [형용사] some sort of; somehow — I don't know —; hard to describe; [거북하다] reluctant (to say); uncertain whether one should (say). ¶그는 말하기 거식해서 말하지 않았다 He was in some doubt whether he should bring it up, so he said nothing.

거실(居室**)** (개인의) one's room; one's own [private] room; (가족의) a sitting room; (미) a living room; (영) a parlor. ¶(집 안의)~과 식당이 있는 곳 the dining-living area// ~ 겸 침실 (室) a bed-sitting-room.

거액(巨額**)** a huge [an enormous] amount of money; a colossal [stupendous] sum; a lot [a great deal] of money. ¶~의 돈 a large [an enormous] amount of money// ~에 달하다 amount to a huge sum// ~의 기부를 하다 make a big donation// ~의 공금을 착복하다 embezzle a large amount of public money // ~의 세금을 포탈하다 defraud a large amount of tax money // ~을 벌다 realize a large profit / make a lot of money // ~을 요하다 cost a great deal of money [a fortune] // 백만 달러는 ~이다 A million dollars is a mint of money.

거역(拒逆**)** disobedience; insubordination; opposition; objection. **거역하다** disobey; protest (against); object (to); oppose; go [act] against (a person's will). ¶상관의 명령을 거역하는 사병 an insubordinate soldier // 부모에게 ~ disobey [contradict] one's parents // 상관의 명을 ~ object to [protest against] the order of one's superior // 거역하기 어렵다 be unable to disobey // 그는 상사의 명령을 거역하고 가지 않았다 In defiance of [Disregarding] his boss's order he did not go.

거울 1 a mirror; a looking glass; a speculum. ¶~ 같은 glassy (surface) / smooth as glass // 손 ~ a hand mirror // 편면 ~ a one-way glass [mirror] // 화장 ~ a toilet mirror // ~ 같이 맑은 물 crystal-clear water // ~을 보다 look (at oneself) in a mirror // ~에 비치다 be reflected in a mirror // ~ 앞에서 치장을 하다 preen at one's mirror / tidy oneself at the glass // 신문은 시대를 반영하는 훌륭한 ~이다 The newspapers are a good mirror of the times. // 눈은 마음의 ~이다 The eye is the mirror of the soul. // 그는 ~에 자신을 비추어 보았다 He looked at himself in a mirror. 2 [귀감] a pattern; a model; an example; a paragon; a mirror. ¶덕행의 ~ a paragon of virtue // 부덕(婦德)의 ~ a mirror of womanhood // 정절의 ~ a model of chastity // …의 ~이 되다 exemplify oneself / set an example to the world // 그의 선행은 세상 사람들의 ~이 되었다 His good conduct set an example for the world. // 그는 군인의 ~이다 He is a model of what a soldier ought to be.

거울삼다 1 [본받다] pattern [model] after (a person); make an example; follow the example of (a person); take pattern by (a person); take (a person) for a model. ¶거울삼을 만한 exemplary / model // 거울삼을 만한 소녀 a model girl // 선인의 덕행을 ~ take the virtuous conduct of old sages for one's model // 부모를 ~ follow the pattern of one's parents.
2 [경계하다] take warning [example] (by); take a lesson (from). ¶남의 실패를 ~ take warning by another's failure // 과거의 실패를 거울삼아 in (the) light of the past failure // 남의 실패를 거울삼아라 Learn wisdom from the follies of others. / Take a lesson from another's failure.

거웃 [생식기에 난 털] pubic hair; pubes.

거위[1] a (domestic) goose (*pl.* geese); (소아어) a goosey. ¶수~ a gander.

거위[2] [회충] a roundworm; an intestinal worm; an ascarid. ¶~가 생기다 get (intestinal) worms.
● **거위배** stomach trouble caused by worms.

거의 [대체로] almost; nearly; practically; all but; as good as; no more than; next to; well-nigh; [대부분] for the most part; mostly; [약] about; some; (부정적) few; little; hardly; scarcely. ¶~ 전부 almost [nearly] all / mostly // ~ 불가능하다 be next to impossible // ~ 죽게 되다 be dying / be all but dead // ~ 한 시간 걸리다 take almost [just a little less than] an hour // ~ 1킬로 걷다 walk nearly a kilometer // ~ 모든 사람이 그것을 믿었다 Almost all the people [Most of the people] believed it. // 상태는 작년과 변함이 없다 Conditions are little better than last year. // 그는 한 마디의 말도 하지 않았다 He hardly uttered a word. / He said almost nothing. // 그것을 믿는 사람은 ~ 없다 Scarcely anybody believes that. // 희망은 ~ 없다 There is little hope. // 그 고양이는 ~ 죽어 있었다 The cat was almost dead. // 그는 ~ 60을 바라보고 있었다 He was almost sixty. // 그가 떠난 지 ~ 1년이 된다 It has been nearly [almost] a year since he left. // 나는 ~ 무일푼이다 I am little short of [as good as] broke. // 그는 ~ 거지나 다름없다 He is no more than a beggar.∥협상은 ~ 마지막 단계에 이르렀다 The negotiations have been brought well-nigh to a conclusion.∥그의 성공은 ~ 기적에 가까운 일이다 His success is little short of a miracle.∥그의 힘에 당할 사람은 ~ 없다 Very few can equal him.∥그 공사는 ~ 완성되었다 The construction (work) is almost [nearly] completed.∥이곳의 1에이커의 땅값은 그곳의 10에이커의 땅값과 ~ 먹는다 An acre of this land is approximately equivalent in price to ten acres of that land. ∥그 당시 아버지의 연세는 지금의 내 나이와 ~ 비슷했다 At that time my father was about the same age as I am now.∥학생들의 리포트는 ~ 비슷비슷하다 The students' papers are all more or less similar.

거인(巨人) a colossus; a Titan; [위인] a great man. ¶재계의 ~ a leading figure in financial circles / a financial magnate.
● **거인국** a land of giants; (걸리버 여행기의) Brobdingnag.

거장(巨匠) a (great) master; a great artist. ¶저명한 ~들 illustrious masters∥악단의 ~ a great [master] musician∥그림의 ~ a great [master] artist∥문단의 ~ an eminent writer / a great man of letters / a master writer.

거저 **1** [일을 안 하고] without doing anything (in particular); idly; lazily; slothfully. ¶~ 세월만 보내다 idle away one's time [days] / (미국 구어) fool around [about].
2 [빈손으로] without bringing anything; with nothing (in hand); with empty hands. ¶남을 ~ 방문하다 pay a visit to a person empty-handed [without some present for him].
3 [헐값으로] for a song; dog-cheap; dirt-cheap. ¶~나 다름없다 be quite a bargain / be fairly cheap∥~나 다름없는 값 a nominal price∥이것은 ~나 다름없습니다 It is an exceptional bargain.
4 [무료로] free; free of charge [expense / cost]; for nothing; as a gift; without cost; gratuitously. ¶~라도 at a gift / even for nothing∥~ 얻을 수 있다 can be had for the asking / can be got for nothing∥너에게 ~ 주겠다 You shall have it for nothing.∥그 일은 ~ 해 드리겠습니다 I will make no charge for the work.∥천 원이니 ~죠 It is one thousand won and a present at that.∥~ 줘도 않다 I would not have [take] it at a gift.

거저먹기 an easy job [task / thing] to do; soft job; a snap; (속어) a piece of cake. ¶그것은 ~다 That's nothing. / Nothing is easier. / That's a soft job. / That's as easy as pie. / That's cinch.

거적 a straw mat; a matting. ¶~을 깔다 spread a mat∥~을 덮다 cover (a thing) with matting∥~을 짜다 plait [make] a straw mat∥~에 싸다 wrap (a thing) in straw matting.
● **거적때기** a piece [fragment] of a straw mat. **거적문** a door made of matting.

거적눈 eyes with drooping eyelids. ¶피로하여 ~이 되다 one's eyelids droop with tiredness.

거절(拒絶) refusal; rejection; rebuff; disapproval; [법] repudiation; (미국 속어) brush-off. ¶~의 편지 a letter of refusal. **거절하다** refuse; reject; decline; rebuff; turn down; deny. ¶딱 ~ give a flat refusal / give (a person) a brush-off∥입장을 ~ deny (a person) admission [entrance]∥지불을 ~ refuse payment / decline to pay∥면회를 ~ refuse to see (a person) / deny oneself to (a caller)∥요구 [신청]를 ~ turn down [reject] (a person's) request [application]∥약속을 ~ pass up the engagement∥…하기를 끝내 ~ persist in one's refusal to (do)∥나는 아무래도 거절할 수가 없었다 I couldn't very well refuse it. / I couldn't but accept it.∥그는 우리의 제안을 딱 거절했다 He rejected our proposal point-blank.∥나는 재치 있게 [정중하게] 거절했다 I declined tactfully [politely].∥그녀는 나의 결혼 신청을 거절했다 She rejected [turned down] my offer of marriage.∥그는 충분히 이유도 없이 나의 제안을 거절했다 He refused [turned down / rejected] my offer without any good reason. ∥그는 완강하게 면회를 거절했다 He obstinately refused to see anyone.∥그는 그 계획에 나를 참가시키려 했으나 나는 거절했다 He wanted me to join him in the scheme, but I turned him down.∥그런 어리석은 제안은 거절한다 I refuse to accept such an absurd proposal.∥제발 거절하지 말아 주십시오 Please don't turn me down. ➔¶거절당하다 be rejected / meet with a refusal∥나의 제안은 거절당했다 My proposal was turned down.∥그들은 입장을 거절당했다 They were denied [refused] admission.∥근로자들은 임금 인상 요구를 거절당하자 파업에 들어갔다 The workers went on strike, their demands for higher wages being rejected.

거점(據點) a foothold; a base; a position; a pint; a stronghold. ¶공격 ~ a strongpoint for one's attacks (on the enemy)∥군사 ~ a military [naval] base / a strategic point [position]∥성장 ~ 도시 nucleus cities (in provincial areas)∥중요 ~ a key point [position]∥극렬분자들의 ~ radical strongholds∥~을 구축 [확보] 하다 establish [secure] a strongpoint∥작전상의 ~을 획득하다 obtain [secure] a strategic foothold∥이 서재가 나의 ~이다 This library is my stronghold.∥그는 출판계에 확고한 ~을 마련해 놓았다 He has got a strong foothold in the publishing business.

거족(巨族) a distinguished [powerful / influential] family; a mighty clan; a family of high social standing.

거족적(擧族的) nationwide; national. ¶~인 축제일 a day of national celebration∥~으로 on a national scale / throughout the nation ∥~인 관심을 끌다 attract a nationwide attention∥대통령은 자기의 정책에 대한 ~인 지지를 호소했다 The President appealed to the nation to support his policy.

거주(居住) residence; (문어) dwelling; abode; habitation. ¶~를 확인하다 ascertain (a person's) whereabouts / make certain of (a person's) address∥그는 ~가 일정치 않다 He is homeless. / He has no fixed residence.

거주하다 reside; live; (문어) dwell; inhabit; make one's home; take (up) residence. ¶6개월 이상 거주한 외국인 a foreigner of more than six months' residence (in / at).

거주 이전의 자유 the freedom of residence and change of residence.
● **거주권** the right of residence. **거주민** an inhabitant; a resident; a dweller; [시민] a

거죽 citizen; [토착민] a native; an indigenous inhabitant. **거주자** a resident; an inhabitant; a dweller; an occupant. ¶불법 ~ (공유지의) a squatter. **거주지** a place of residence.

거죽 [표면] the surface; the face; the right side; [외면부] the outside; the exterior; the external appearance. ¶융단의 ~ the right side of a carpet // 사물의 ~만 보다 look only at the surface of things // ~만 봐서는 모른다 Appearances are deceptive.

거중 조정(居中調停) mediation; intermediation; intervention; intercession; arbitration; good offices(주선). ¶~에 나서다 undertake mediation / ~을 제의[의뢰]하다 offer [ask] mediation // ~을 떠맡다 assume a mediation role.

거즈 (cotton, antiseptic) gauze; (거친 무명으로 된) thin cloth. ¶소독 ~ sterilized gauze.

거증(擧證) giving evidence; the establishment of a fact (by evidence). **거증하다** establish a fact (by evidence); present[produce] evidence[proof].
● **거증 책임** the burden of proof; the onus probandi.

거지 a beggar; a beggar woman(여자); a mendicant; a tramp; (미국 구어) a panhandler; (경멸) a wretch; a miserable being; a goodfor-nothing. ¶~ 같은 놈 a good-for-nothing (fellow) // ~같이 가난한 wretchedly poor // ~ 신세가 되다 be reduced to beggary / be brought to begging // ~ 취급을 하다 treat (a person) as a beggar // 배 속에 ~가 들다 have a wolf in the stomach.
● **거지 근성** a mean spirit; the beggar. **거지 꼴** shabby look; beggarly[miserable] appearance.

거지반(居之半) [반수 이상] the (great) majority; the bulk; [태반] the greater[best / most] part; [대개] mostly; for the most part; nearly all; very nearly; generally. ¶교사의 ~ the greater part of the school building // 전 시가의 ~이 파괴되었다 The bulk of the whole city was wiped out. // 나는 물에 빠져 ~ 죽을 뻔했다 I was nearly drowned. // 이달도 이제 ~ 다 갔다 This month is almost over now. // 그는 일생을 ~ 서울에서 살았다 He lived in Seoul for the most part of his life.

거짓 [속이기 위한 거짓말] a lie; untruth; [진실이 아님] falsehood; hypocrisy; a fabrication; [지어낸 말] misrepresentation; deceit. ¶~의 false / untruth / [속이는] deceitful (actions) / ~ 없는 truthful / [솔직한] frank // ~ 웃음을 forced[feigned] smile [laugh] // ~이 있다 be false[untrue / dishonest / deceitful] // ~임을 드러내다 prove (something) to be false // 그의 말에는 ~이 없다 All he says is true. / He always says the truth.

거짓말 (속이기 위한) a lie; [진실이 아님] a falsehood; an untruth; a fabrication; a fake; (사소한) a fib. ¶악의에 찬 ~ a black lie / 빤히 들여다보이는 ~ a transparent[hollow] falsehood [lie] / 그럴듯한 ~ a plausible [specious] lie / 계획적인 ~ a deliberate lie / 선의의[악의 없는] ~ a white lie / a fib / 새빨간 ~ a downright lie / an outright [outand-out] lie / a perfect fake // ~ 같은 이야기 an incredible story // ~투성이 a pack [tissue] of lies // ~을 퍼뜨리다 circulate a lie // 터무니 없는 ~을 하다 lie like a gas meter // 새빨간 ~을 하다 lie in a person's teeth // 그가 아프다는 것은 새빨간 ~이었다 His illness was a perfect fake. // 카메라는 ~을 하지 않는다 The camera never lies. // 어린애 같은 ~을 곧이듣지 마라 Don't take the childish fib so seriously. // 너는 ~을 하고 있다 You are not telling the truth. (▶ lie는 강한 표현이기 때문에 직접적으로는 말하지 않는 경우가 많음) / 그는 ~을 잘해서 곤란하다 The trouble with him is that he lies so easily [smoothly]. / 나는 절대로 ~을 안 합니다 I'm telling (you) the absolute truth. // 선의의 ~이라도 ~은 ~이다 A white lie is still a lie. // 그는 ~을 할 줄 모른다 He is incapable of telling a lie. // 그건 아무래도 ~ 같다 That sounds incredible. / He doesn't seem to mean it. // ~에도 한도 가 있다 There are limits in lying. // 때로는 ~도 하고 볼 일이다 A lie is sometimes expedient. / It is a case of pious fraud. // 그는 ~이 탄로 나도 태연하다 He shows little emotion when he is caught out in a lie. // ~이라고 할 지 모르겠지만 난 그 여자보다 열 살이나 아랩니다 Believe me [it] or not, man, I'm ten years younger than she. **거짓말하다** tell a lie; tell an untruth [a falsehood]; fib. ¶천연스럽게 ~ lie as though telling the truth / lie with a straight face // 거짓말하지 마라 Don't tell lies! / Don't lie to me! (▶ 전자는 일반적으로 거짓말을 하지 말라는 경고의 말이며 후자는 방금 한 말이 거짓말이 아니냐는 뜻)
● **거짓말쟁이** a liar; a fibber; a fibster; an Ananias; (완곡) a storyteller. (▶ liar는 의미가 강함. 우리말의 가벼운 뜻의 거짓말쟁이에 가까운 것은 fibber임) ¶그와 만나지 않았다는 것 ~ 같으니 You say you didn't see him? Ah, come on! (Do you expect me to believe that?) **거짓말 탐지기** a lie detector; a polygraph.

거찰(巨刹) a grand Buddhist temple; a cathedral.

거참 Indeed!; O my!; O dear!; (O) Dear me!; Bless me! (구어) By crikey! ¶~ 야단났다 O dear! What shall I do? // ~ 되게 어질러 놓았군 Oh, no! What a mess! // ~ 안됐군 Indeed, that was too bad! // ~ 큰 실수였군 Really, it was a miserable failure.

거창하다(巨創-) huge; enormous; gigantic; immense; monstrous. ¶거창한 건물 a huge building // 거창한 계획 a mammoth enterprise // 거창한 직함 a high-sounding [an ostentatious] title // 거창하게 on a large [grand] scale // 사업을 거창하게 하다 carry on a business in a large way // 그는 언제나 말은 거창하게 한다 He always talks grandiloquently [in high-sounding term].

거처(居處) dwelling (in); a dwelling place [house]; a residence; an abode. ¶일시적인 ~ a temporary abode // ~를 정하다 make one's home (at / in) / settle down / fix [take up] one's abode // ~를 옮기다 move [remove] (to / into) / change one's address (to) // 그는 자기의 ~를 밝히지 않았다 He didn't give me his address. / He didn't tell me where he lives. // 적어도 ~는 알려 주셔야지요 Let me know at least where you are. **거처하다** live [dwell / reside] (in / at); inhabit (a place).

거처(去處) one's whereabouts. ¶그의 ~를 알 수가 없다 His whereabouts are [is] unknown. // 마침내 그의 ~를 찾아냈다 At last I found out where he was.

거추장스럽다 burdensome; cumbersome; troublesome; cumbrous; bulky; unwieldy; ponderous. ¶거추장스러운 짐 a bulky load / 거추장스러운 것[존재] a burden / a drag (on) / a clog / a nuisance / a hindrance / an encumbrance // 거추장스러워지다 (사물이) become a drag (on a person) / (사물·사람 때문에) be encumbered (with) // 우산 등을 가지고 다니면 ~ I don't like carrying an umbrella. / It is burdensome to carry an umbrella. // 그런 것은 가지고 있어 봐야 거추장스럽기만 하다 It is a white elephant to me. // 그녀는 자식을 거추장스럽게 여기고 있다 She regards [looks upon] her children as so many encumbrances. // 이마에 내려온 머리카락이 거추장스러워 보인다 The hair hanging on your forehead looks as thought it bothers you.

거취(去就) [행동] one's course of action; [태도] one's attitude; manner; behavior. ¶~를 **결정하다** decide (on) one's course of action / decide one's attitude // ~를 분명히 하다 define[clarify] one's attitude // 의회의 대세는 무소속 의원들의 ~ 여하에 달려 있다 The situation in the House hinges upon the attitude of the Independents. // ~를 결정하기 전에 신중히 생각하는 게 좋겠다 You had better consider it carefully before you decide on your course of action. // 모두가 그의 ~에 주목하고 있다 Everybody is interested in whether he is going to leave or stay. // 그는 ~를 결정 못 하고 망설이고 있다 He does not know which course to take. // 지금이 당신의 ~를 결정할 때다 Now is the time to decide [clarify] your attitude. // 나의 ~ 문제는 오로지 이번 일의 성과에 달려 있다 Whether I must resign or I can continue in my office all depends on the result of this attempt.

거치(据置) (대출 등의) leaving (a loan) unredeemed; (지불 등의) deferment. ¶~의 undeemed / unredeemable / deferred // 5년 ~의 대출 a loan unredeemable for five years // 2년 ~ 10년 상환 조건의 차관 a loan payable in ten years following 2-year grace period // 5년 ~이다 be uncallable for five years. **거치하다** leave (a loan) unredeemed; defer [put off] (the payment of a loan). ¶예금을 5년 ~ leave a deposit untouched for five years.

● **거치 기간** (지불금의) the term unredeemed; the term of a loan; (지불의) a period of deferment.

거치다 pass by[through]; go by way (of); drop in on one's way; stop [call / touch] at on one's way; go via. ¶세관을 ~ pass a customhouse // 시험을 거쳐 [거치지 않고] on [without] examination // 많은 사람의 손을 거쳐 through many hands // 절차를 거쳐서 after going through the necessary formalities // 직업소개소를 거쳐서 through the employment agency // 모든 서류는 과장을 거쳐 이사에게 간다 All documents pass through the hands of the section chiefs before they reach the director. // 허가를 받기까지는 복잡한 절차를 거쳐야 한다 You have to go through complicated formalities before you (can) get a permit. // 모스크바를 거쳐 파리로 갔다 I went to Paris via[by way of] Moscow.

거치적거리다 be [stand / get] in (a person's) way; keep getting in the way; be a drag to [on] (a person); obstruct; hamper; (옷 등이) cling (to). ¶거치적거리는 cumbersome // 소용없는 상자들이 거치적거리는 통로 a passage encumbered with useless boxes // 그것을 거치적거리지 않는 곳에 치워라 Put it away where it is not in the way. // 치맛자락이 거치적거려 걷기 힘들다 I have trouble in walking with my skirt clinging to my legs.

거칠다 1 (가루·결 등이) coarse (texture); rough (skin). ¶거친 종이 coarse[poor-quality] paper // 거친 천 coarse material // 결이 거친 나무 timber of coarse grain // (피부가) 거칠어지다 roughen / become rough / get chappy // 부엌일로 손이 거칠어지다 get dishpan hands.

2 (일솜씨) rough; slovenly; slipshod; loose. ¶거친 솜씨 rough workmanship // 거친 번역 loose translation // 그의 예술이 거칠어졌다 His art has gone to seed.

3 (성질 또는 언행이) rude (behavior); wild (nature); harsh (tone); violent (language). ¶언행이 거친 사람 a rude fellow / a wild man // 거칠게 호흡하다 pant / breath hard / 거친 말투를 쓰다 employ rough language / 거칠어지다 grow wild / become rough // 거칠게 행동하다 behave rudely / play it rough // 거칠게 다루다 handle (a tool / a thing / goods) roughly // 저 집은 화목해서 거친 말 한 마디 들리지 않는다 Not a single angry voice is ever heard in that harmonious family. // 그는 성질이 ~ He has a violent temper. / (구어) He is a rough customer. // 그는 말씨가 ~ He uses harsh[violent / coarse] language. / He is rough in speech. // 그는 아랫사람을 거칠게 다룬다 He works his men hard. / He is a slave driver. // 그는 말투가 거칠어졌다 He spoke more roughly.

4 (물결·바람이) rough; wild; raging; violent; furious. ¶거친 바다[물결] a high [heavy] sea / wild waves / raging waters // 거친 세파에 시달리다 be buffeted about in the world / be tossed about in the storms of life / 거칠어지다 (바람·물결이) run high / become rough / (날씨가) become stormy / (바다가) grow violent / rage // 태풍이 접근하여 바다가 거칠어졌다 Because of the approach of the typhoon, the sea were rough. // 날씨가 거칠어져 등산은 불가능하다 Climbing the mountain is impossible on account of [because of] the threatening weather.

5 (길 등이) rough; rugged (surface); (논밭이) waste; wild; desolate. ¶거친 길 a rough road / 잡초가 우거진 거친 뜰 a garden wild with weeds // 거친 땅 desert land.

거칠하다 look emaciated [thin / skinny]; look wornout [tired / washed-out]; rough; coarse. ¶거칠한 얼굴 a haggard[worn] face // 그녀는 병으로 거칠해졌다 The disease has made her lose flesh. / She has become worn-out from illness. // 어머니는 걱정으로 얼굴이 거칠하시다 My mother looks haggard[worn out] because of anxiety.

거침새 an impediment; a hitch; a hindrance. ¶~가 많다 be full of snags.

거침없다 1 [막힘이 없다] unhindered; unobstructed; smooth. ¶거침없는 대답 a ready answer. **거침없이** without a hitch; without any trouble; without mishap; smoothly; swimmingly. ¶~ 진행하다 go on without a hitch [trouble] / keep going in good shape /

거포

run smoothly // 어려운 문제를 ~ 풀다 solve a hard problem easily[without (any) effort]. **2** [거리낌 없다] unreserved; unconstrained; unsparing; straightforward; free (from obstruction); without hesitation [reserve / being ashamed]. ¶거침없는 비평 an unsparing[honest] criticism // 그는 전혀 거침없는 태도였다 His manner was altogether free from constraint. **거침없이** without reserve [hesitation]; unreservedly; unhesitatingly; without restraint. ¶~ 말하다 say without reserve / speak out / do not mince one's words // 의견을 ~ 말하다 tell[give] one's opinion frankly[without reserve] // 그는 사람들 앞에서 ~ 거짓말을 하였다 He did not hesitate to tell a lie in public. / He told lies without compunction[shame] in public. // 그는 ~ 대답하였다 He answered without a moments hesitation.

거포(巨砲) a big[huge / mammoth] gun [cannon]; [야구의 강타자] a slugger.

거푸 again and again; over (and over) again; repeatedly. ¶~ 술잔을 기울이다 drink one cup[a glass of wine] after another / drink several cups of wine in rapid succession.

거푸집 1 [주형] a mo(u)ld; a cast; [활자 등의] a matrix; a die. **2** [붙인 종이·천 등의 뜬 곳] a blister[an air bubble] (caused by incomplete pasting). **3** [몸의 겉모양] one's figure [shape / constitution]; the outer appearance of one's body. **4** (콘크리트 공사의) a concrete form; a molding flask.

거품 a bubble; foam; froth; (발효의) barm; [표면에 뜨는 찌꺼기] scum; suds; (유리 속 등의) an air bell[bubble]; a seed; a blister; (곤충의) spit; spittle. ¶비누 ~ lather [soap suds / soap bubbles] / 물 ~ a water bubble [foam on water] // 맥주 ~ the froth of[on] beer / the barm of beer / beer suds / the head on a glass of beer // ~이 일다 bubble / foam / froth / rise in bubble / lather // 일게 하는 기구 a whisk / an eggbeater // ~이 이는 foamy [frothy / bubbly] / 입에서 ~을 내다 foam[froth] at the mouth / 달걀을 ~ 일게 하다 beat[whip] an egg / 크림을 ~ 일게 하다 whip cream // ~이 꺼진다 a bubble breaks[bursts] // **처럼 사라지다** come to nothing[naught] / end in smoke[a failure] // ~을 걷어 내다 scum // 이 비누는 ~이 잘 인다 This soap lathers properly[well]. // 그는 입에 ~을 물고 떠들어 대었다 He gabbled on foaming[frothing] at the mouth. // 인생은 물 ~ How brief is the span of life! / Life is but an empty dream. // 강물은 세제 때문에 흰 ~이 일고 있었다 The water of the river was foamy on account of detergents. // 맥주는 ~이 더 있는 게 좋다 I like more head on my beer.

거한(巨漢) a man of gigantic stature; a giant (of a man); a very big man.

거함(巨艦) a big[gigantic] warship; a mighty man-of-war; a superdreadnought.

거행(擧行) **1** [의식을 치름] celebration; performance; solemnization. **거행하다** perform [conduct / carry out] (a ceremony); observe [keep] (an anniversary); (특히 식전을) celebrate; hold[give]. ¶결혼식을 ~ celebrate a wedding[marriage] // 장례식을 ~ hold a funeral / perform a funeral service. ➔거행되다 be held[take place / come off] // 그들의 결혼식은 성 메리 교회에서 거행되었다 Their wedding ceremony was performed at St. Mary Church. // 졸업식이 내일 거행된다 The graduation ceremony [commencement exercises] will be held tomorrow.

2 [명령대로 행함] execution of an order. **거행하다** do as one is told; act according to orders[commands]. ¶분부대로 ~ act upon (a person's) order.

걱정 1 [근심] anxiety; concern; apprehension; worry; care; trouble. ¶돈 ~ money troubles / financial worries / worries about money // 집안 ~ family[domestic] cares / ~이 없다 be carefree / be free from worry / have nothing to worry about // ~이 되다 be anxious (about) / worry[be worried] (about) / (일의) ~이 (을) weigh[press] on one's mind / cause (a person) anxiety // 쓸데없는 ~을 하다 borrow trouble[sorrow] / be overanxious / ~ 없이 살다 live without worries / 그는 ~으로 병석에 누워 있다 He has taken to his bed with worry. // ~이 되어 견딜 수가 없어[죽을 것만 같아] Worry is killing me. / I am worried stiff[to death]. / I'm quite uneasy about it. // 그는 ~이 끊이지 않는군 He is never free from care[worry]. / He always has something to worry about. // 그는 아들 때문에 ~이 떠날 날이 없다 Her son is a constant source of worry to her. // ~ 없어 There is nothing to fear[worry about]. / Never mind! / Take it easy! // ~도 팔자군 [쓸데없는 걱정] You always overworry yourself. / You are worrying about little things [nothing]. / [남의 일에 참견함] Mind your own business. / It is none of your business. // 많은 ~을 끼쳐 드려 미안합니다 I am sorry to have troubled you so much. // 내 ~은 하지 마십시오 Don't trouble yourself about me I'm O.K. / There's no need to worry about me. // 이런 일로 당신에게 ~을 끼쳐 죄송합니다 I am sorry this has caused such anxiety to you. **걱정하다** feel anxiety; be anxious (about); take (a matter) to heart; be concerned (about / for / by); feel concern (about / for); take (it) seriously; be apprehensive (of); feel uneasy (about); worry (oneself) (about); feel worried (about). ¶아이들의 장래를 ~ worry about one's children's future // 걱정하여 병에 걸리다 worry oneself ill[sick] // 그녀는 소문을 걱정하고 있다 She is distressed[disturbed] by the rumors. / She takes the rumors to heart. // 그는 키가 작은 것을 걱정하고 있었다 He was sensitive about being so short. // 그녀는 몸이 약한 남편을 걱정하고 있다 She is worried [concerned] about her sick husband. // 나는 다음 날 비가 오지 않을까 걱정했다 I was afraid it would rain the next day. // 나는 그의 용태를 무척 걱정하고 있다 I am very anxious about his condition. / His condition causes me great anxiety. // 걱정하기 시작하면 끝이 없어 There is no limit to worries. // 가난쯤은 조금도 걱정하지 않는다 I don't mind poverty [being poor] at all. // 그녀는 무슨 일이든 걱정하지 않는다 She takes things in her stride. / She doesn't let things get her down. // 그런 일은 걱정해도 소용없는 일이야 It's useless to worry[fret] about such a thing. // 지레 걱정하지 마라 Do not worry yourself about the future needlessly. / Don't cross the bridge

till you get to it.// 형의 공부에 방해가 될까 걱정하여 우리는 집 안에서 발끝으로 다녔다 We tiptoed about the house for fear we might disturb our brother's study. ➔/시험 결과가 걱정된다 I'm anxious about the results of the examination.// 그의 안부가 갑자기 걱정되었다 I suddenly felt uneasy about him.
2 [나무라는 일] a scolding; reproof; reproach; lecture. ¶성적 때문에 선생님께 ~을 들었다 I was reproved for my poor grades by my teacher. / My teacher scolded me for my poor grades. **걱정하다** scold; chide; reprove; reproach; lecture.
걱정도 팔자(다) (속담) Mind your own business.; It's none of your business.
● **걱정거리** a source of anxiety; a matter of anxiety; a cause of anxiety. ¶그는 아들의 병이 ~였다 His son's illness was a worry to him. **걱정꾸러기** [늘 걱정거리가 많은 사람] a worrywart; a person given to worries; a (natural) worrier; [늘 남에게 걱정을 끼치는 사람] a (source of) constant trouble; a black sheep; a troublemaker; a troublesome [worrisome] child.
걱정스럽다 anxious; uneasy; troubled; concerned; apprehensive. ¶걱정스러운 일 cares / troubles / 걱정스러운 얼굴 a worried [an anxious] look// 그는 걱정스러운 얼굴을 하고 있었다 He had a care-worn [concerned] look. He looked worried [concerned].// 그녀는 걱정스러운 얼굴로 환자를 지켜보고 있었다 She was watching the patient with a concerned [an apprehensive / an anxious] look.
건 (巾) **1** [쓰개의 총칭] a head-cover made of cloth. **2** a mourner's hempen hood. ⇨**두건**
건 (件) a matter; an affair; a subject; a case. ¶긴급한 ~으로 on urgent business/나는 그 ~에 대해 아무것도 모른다 I know nothing about the matter.// 지난달 살인 사건이 두 있었다 There were two murders [murder cases] last month.// 그 ~은 어떻게 되었습니까 What has become of that matter?
건 (腱) [생] a tendon. ¶아킬레스~ Achilles' tendon.
건 (鍵) a key (of a piano / a typewriter). ¶88 ~의 피아노 a piano with 88 keys// 흑[백] ~ a black[white] key / a chromatic (natural) key/피아노 ~을 두드리다 play (on) the piano.
건각 (健脚) **1** [튼튼한 다리] strong [powerful] legs; iron legs. **2** [잘 걷는 사람] a good walker.
건강 (健康) health. ¶~에 좋다 be good for (the [one's]) health / be beneficial [conducive] to health / do (a person) good / ~에 해롭다 be bad for (the [one's]) health / be injurious to (the [one's]) health// ~을 해치다 injure [ruin / destroy] one's health / one's health breaks down// ~을 회복하다 regain [recover] one's health / be restored to (one's usual) health / become all right again // ~을 유지하다 keep [maintain / preserve] one's health / keep fit// ~에 유의하다 take (good) care of oneself [one's health] / be careful of oneself// 당신의 ~을 위하여 건배 To [Here's to] your health!// 나는 과로로 ~이 나빠졌다 My health has been failing as a result of overwork.// 과음하면 ~을 해치신다 You will ruin your health if you drink too much.// 요즘 그의 ~은 좋습니까 Is he well these days?// ~이 가장 중요합니다 Health is everything.// 먼저 ~을 증진시켜야 한다 First of all you must improve your health [get yourself fit].// ~이 아주 좋으시다니 반갑습니다 I congratulate you on your excellent health. **건강하다** healthy; sound; well; wholesome; (노인 등에) hale and hearty; fit; be in good health. ¶아주 ~ be in excellent [good] health// 그녀는 요즘 건강하지 못하다 She has not been very well recently.// 부모님은 건강하십니다 My parents are well. / 건강하시기를 빕니다 I wish you good health. **건강히** healthily; soundly.
● **건강관리** management of one's health; health care. ¶환절기의 ~ control of one's health [health care] at the change of season. **건강미** the glow of health; healthy beauty. ¶그녀는 ~가 넘친다 She is in the lovely bloom of health. **건강 상태** the condition [state] of one's health; a hygienic [health] condition. **건강식품** health [wholesome] food. **건강 진단** a medical [physical / health] examination; a medical inspection; (미) a physical [medical] checkup. ¶~을 받다 undergo a medical examination / get a physical (examination) / (구어) go in for a checkup. **건강체** a healthy body [condition].
건건하다 nicely salted. ⇨**간간하다**
건곤 (乾坤) heaven and earth; the universe.
건곤일척 (乾坤一擲) ¶~으로 sink or swim / kill or cure// ~의 승부를 하다 stake all (on) / play for all or nothing// 병원(病原)을 밝혀내는 것은 그에게 있어 ~의 일이었다 He staked his all on finding the cause of the disease. / He put everything he had into finding the cause of the disease.
건과 (乾果) dry [dried] fruits.
건국 (建國) the founding [establishment] of a country [nation]. **건국하다** found [establish] a country.
● **건국 기념일** National Foundation [Founding] Day. **건국 훈장** the Order of Merit for National Foundation.
건군 (建軍) ¶그는 그 나라 ~의 아버지이다 He is the founding father of his country's army [military forces]. **건군하다** build an army; form the military.
건너 the opposite side (of); the other side (of). ¶길 ~에 over the road / across the street// 그 마을은 강 ~에 있다 The village lies across the river.
건너가다 go across; cross over; cross; walk [run / ride / drive / sail] across. ¶길을 ~ cross [go across] a road [street] / 배로 강을 ~ cross a river by boat/횡단보도를 ~ cross at a pedestrian crossing// 영국으로 ~ go over to England.
건너다 **1** [넘다·가로지르다] go [pass] over; go [walk / run] across; cross; ferry (나룻배로). ¶다리를 ~ cross a bridge / 헤엄쳐서 강을 ~ swim across a river / 강을 ~ go [get] across a river / cross a river / (걸어서) wade a river. **2** [옮겨지다] be carried; be conveyed. ¶이 사람 저 사람을 건너 퍼진 소문 a rumor whispered [past] from mouth to mouth. **3** [지나다]. ¶한 해 건너 한 번씩 찾아가다 visit at one year apart [at one-year intervals]// 세 집 건너로 하나꼴로 술집이 있다 About every-third building is a bar [pub].
건너다보다 **1** (건너편에 있는 것을) look out

건너뛰다

across; look across; look out over. **2** (남의 것을) covet; hanker for[after]; cast a jealous eye (on). ¶남의 재산을 ~ covet another's property.

건너뛰다 1 [건너편으로 뛰다] leap[jump / spring] over; hop[jump / leap] from (one thing) to (another). ¶도랑을 ~ leap[jump / vault] over a ditch.//기선에서 보트로 ~ jump from a steamer into a boat. **2** [거르다] skip; miss out; omit; leave out. ¶한 페이지를 ~ skip a page//2학년을 건너뛰어 3학년이 되다 skip the second grade and enter the third //어려운 부분은 건너뛰어도 된다 You may skip the difficult parts.

건너오다 come across (to this side); come over (the sea). ¶태평양을 ~ come over the pacific.

건너지르다 put[place / lay] across. ¶도랑을 널빤지를 ~ lay a plank across a ditch.

건너짚다 1 [팔을 내밀어] reach across a thing to touch another; put[place] one's hands across[over]. **2** [넘겨짚다] guess; anticipate. ¶남의 뜻을 건너짚어 생각하다 guess what a person is thinking / read a person's mind.

건너편(一便) the opposite[other] side. ¶길 ~ 집 the house opposite[over the road / across the street]//그는 우리 집 ~에 살고 있다 He lives opposite our house[across the street from us].//길 ~에 우체통이 있다 There is a mailbox on the other side of the street.

건넌방(一房) a room opposite[on the opposite side of] the main living room.

건널목 1 [철도의] a (railway) crossing; (미) a grade crossing; (영) a level crossing. ¶무인 ~(에서) (at) an unattended crossing//~을 건너다 cross the railway tracks at a crossing// ~ 개폐기 없음 (게시) Level crossing without gates. / crossing—No gates.//~ 조심 (게시) Railroad crossing. / Stop, look, listen. **2** [횡단보도] a pedestrian crossing.
● **건널목지기** a gatekeeper; a gateman; a watchman (at a crossing); a flagman. **건널목차단기** a crossing gate[barrier].

건넛집 the house opposite[over the way / across the street].

건네다 1 [말을 붙이다] speak[talk] to (a person); address (oneself to) (a person). ¶지나가는 사람에게 말을 ~ talk to[address] a passerby. **2** [넘겨 주다] hand (over) (to); turn over; deliver. ¶돈을 ~ hand over the money. **3** [건너게 하다] pass (a person) over[across]; carry across; (배로) take[row] over; ferry (a person) over.

건달(乾達) an idler; a lazybones; a loafer; a good-for-nothing (fellow); a scamp.
● **건달패** a group of sluggards[scamps].

건답(乾畓) an easily drying rice paddy; a dry rice field.

-건대 on the ground of; according to; in accordance with. ¶듣~ I hear[we learn] (that) / according to the rumor / as the rumor goes//이러한 사실로 보~ in the light of these facts//내 경험으로 보~ judging from my experience//~ 일상생활을 뒤돌아보~ when I consider[think of] my every day life//바라~ I hope[pray] (that).

건더기 1 (국의) ingredients; a piece of meat and vegetables in soup. ¶국 ~ solid stuff [ingredients] in soup. **2** [내용] substance; [근거] a ground; a foundation. ¶변명할 ~가 없다 have little excuse (for).

건드리다 1 [움직이게 하다] touch; jog; give (a thing) a jog; move slightly; stir. ¶건드리지 마시오 (게시) Hands off! / Don't touch this article. **2** [노하게 하다] irritate; fret; provoke; nettle; vex. ¶남의 비위를 ~ get [jar] on a person's nerves / hurt a person's feelings / offend a person//그녀의 아픈 곳을 건드리지 마라 Don't touch (on) her sore spot.//그녀는 언제나 내 아픈 곳을 건드린다 She always touches me on a raw nerve. **3** [여자와 관계하다] make sport[fun] of; play [sport] with. **4** [일에 손을 대다] meddle (with); have a finger[a hand / an oar] in.

건들거리다 1 [흔들리다] dangle; swing; sway; totter; shake; be shaky; be unstable. ¶건들거리는 의자 a shaky[rocky / rickety / crazy] chair//건들거리는 loose tooth//수양버들이 바람에 건들거린다 A weeping willow sways to the wind. / A weeping willow rustles in the breeze. **2** (바람이) blow gently [softly]. **3** [빈둥거리다] idle[loiter / dawdle / fiddle / lounge] one's time away; fiddle about doing nothing.

건들건들 1 [흔들흔들] in a tottering[shaking] manner; unstably; danglingly. **2** (바람이) gently; softly. **3** [빈둥빈둥] idly; lazily; slothfully.

건듯건듯 [빠르게] in a hurry; in haste; hastily; hurriedly; [대강] roughly; loosely; in a rough-and-ready manner. ¶일을 ~ 해치우다 do a rough-and-ready job / make a quick job of it//나는 신문을 ~ 훑어보았다 I skimmed through[ran my eyes over] the newspaper.

건락(乾酪) cheese. ⇨치즈
● **건락소**(一素) [화] casein. ⇨카세인

건류(乾溜) dry[destructive] distillation; (석탄의) carbonization. **건류하다** dry (up) by distillation. ¶석탄을 ~ carbonize coal.

건립(建立) **1** (탑·동상 등의) erection; building; construction. **건립하다** erect; build; construct. ¶동상을 ~ erect a bronze statue//탑을 ~ construct a tower. **2** (기관·조직체 등의) establishment; foundation; organization. **건립하다** establish; found; organize; set up. ¶경제 연구소를 ~ constitute a research institute for economics.

-건마는 (even) though; although; while; still; however; in spite of; despite; for[after] all; notwithstanding; nevertheless. ¶최선을 다했 ~ 그는 실패했다 For all his efforts[Though he did his utmost] he failed.//물건은 좋~ 값이 비싸다 I admit its fine quality still it is too dear.//그는 돈은 많~ 행복하진 못하다 He is rich but not happy.//말썽을 그렇게 부리~ 그가 여전히 좋다 He gives us a lot of trouble, but I like him all the same.

건망증(健忘症) [의] amnesia; forgetfulness; failure[slip / loss] of memory. ¶~이 심하다[있다] be forgetful / have a short [poor / bad] memory / be apt to forget//나는 ~이 심하다 I have a bad memory. / I am so forgetful. / I forget soon what I have heard [been told]. / My memory is at fault [very short]./나는 요즘 ~이 심해졌다 My memory often fails me these days.//그는 ~이 심하니 중요한 일은 부탁하지 말아야 해 You had better not ask him to do anything important because he is very forgetful.

건목 [대강 만드는 일] a cursory[rough] job; [대강 만든 물건] a rough thing; a rough-wrought article.
건목(을) 치다 make a hasty job; do a cursory[rough / slapdash] job (of).
건목(乾木) dried lumber; seasoned timber.
건몸 달다 get all heated up to no avail; be mad[crazy] about (someone) in vain; run madly about to no purpose; struggle in vain. ¶그는 그 여자에게 건몸 달아 있다 He loves her in vain. / He is mad about her in vain. // 그는 돈을 마련코자 건몸 달아 다닌다 He runs about trying to raise money with no success.
건물(建物) a building; a structure; an edifice. ¶르네상스식 ~ a building in Renaissance style // 동양 최대의 ~ the largest structure of the kind in the East // 유지비 building maintenance expenses // 가~ a temporary building // 고층~ a high-rise (building) // 목조 ~ a wooden building. // 부속 ~ an attached building // 석조 ~ a stone building // 철근 콘크리트 ~ a ferroconcrete[concrete steel] building / a reinforced[armored] concrete building // 새 교사는 매우 단단한 ~이다 The new school building is a very solid construction. // 이 미술관은 조선 시대의 대표적인 ~의 하나이다 This museum is a good example of the architecture of the Joseon dynasty.
건물(乾物) dried[jerked] fish[meat]; (소금에 절이지 않은) stockfish.
건반(鍵盤) a keyboard; a clavier; a fingerboard; a manual.
● **건반 악기** a keyboard instrument.
건밤 새우다 sit[stay] up all night; keep[stay / remain] awake all night.
건방지다 (self-)conceited; pretentious; presumptuous; forward; impudent; impertinent; saucy; pert; (구어) cocky; (구어) cheeky; (구어) stuck-up. ¶건방진 대답 a pert answer / a saucy reply // 건방진 태도 a haughty bearing / a saucy manner // 건방진 인사 a supercilious[an insolent] greeting // 건방진 소리를 하다 say impudent[cheeky] things / talk impudently (to) // 그는 건방지게 말한다 He speaks pretentiously. / He talks as if he knew everything. // 그는 아주 ~ He's got plenty of cheek[(구어) nerve / (구어) gall]. // 그의 건방진 태도를 참을 수 없다 I can't stand his impudence[cocky attitude]. // 건방진 소리 하지 마라 None of your cheek! // 그는 건방지게도 나에게 명령을 했다 He had the insolence[He was impudent enough] to give me directions.
건배(乾杯) a toast. ¶(당신의 건강을 위해) ~! Cheers! / Toast! / Bottoms up! / Prosit! // 만찬회에서 대통령이 ~를 제의했다 At the banquet the President proposed a toast. **건배하다** toast; drink[give / make] a toast (to); drink the toast (of); drink to (a person's health). ¶건배하자고 제의하다 propose a toast (to) // 샴페인으로 ~ have [raise] a champagne toast / toast (a person) in champagne. // 그의 성공[건강]을 위하여 건배합시다 Let's drink (to) his success[health]. / Let's drink success [health] to him.
건빵(乾-) (미) a cracker; (영) a hard[dry] biscuit. (선원·병사용의) hardtack.

건사하다 1 [잘 돌보아 거두다] take care of; care for; attend to; look after. ¶내 딸은 아직 어려서 자기 몸도 건사할 줄 모른다 My daughter is too young to take care of herself. 2 [잘 간수하다] keep (carefully); put [lay] (a thing) away[up / by]. ¶귀중품을 자물쇠를 채워서 건사해 두다 keep valuables under lock and key. 3 [일을 수습하다] manage; deal[cope] with; supervise; direct.
건삼(乾蔘) (a) dried ginseng.
건선(乾癬) [한] psoriasis. ⇨마른버짐
건선거(乾船渠) a dry dock.
건설(建設) construction; erection; building; [설립] establishment. ¶~적인 의견 [비평] constructive opinion[criticism] // 최근에 ~이 된 다리 a bridge of recent construction // ~ 중이다 be under[in course of] construction / be going up // ~적인 의견을 내다 present a constructive idea // ~에 착수한 지 4년째이다 It has been four years in construction. // 새 도로는 아직 ~ 중이다 The new road is still under[in (the) course of] construction. **건설하다** construct; erect; build (up); [설립하다] establish; found. ¶댐[철도 / 교량]을 ~ construct a dam[a railway / a bridge] // 복지 국가를 ~ build up[establish] a welfare state.
● **건설 공사** construction[building] work. **건설 교통부** the Ministry of Construction & Transportation. ¶~ 장관 the Minister of Construction & Transportation. **건설비** construction cost[expenses]. **건설업** the construction industry. **건설업체 / 건설 회사** a building[construction] company. **건설 용지** a building lot[plot / site]. **건설자** (건물 등의) a constructor; a builder.
건성 half-heartedness; inattention; lack of attention; abstraction; absent-mindedness. ¶~으로 abstractedly / carelessly / mechanically / aimlessly / without purpose / for nothing / absent-mindedly / vacantly / inattentively / half-heartedly // ~으로 읽다 read (something) inattentively // ~으로 듣다 listen to (a person) in an absent sort of way / let (something) go in one ear and out the other // ~으로 대답하다 answer inattentively [in a halfhearted way] // ~으로 덤벼들다 try to do a thing without knowing anything about it // ~으로 인사하다 give a curt [perfunctory] greeting / greet a person unceremoniously // 그의 마음은 ~이다 His mind is faraway. // ~으로 듣고 있으니까 모르지 You cannot understand it, because you do not pay due attention (to it). // 그는 언제나 내 말을 ~으로 듣는다 He always listens to me absent-mindedly.
건성(乾性) dryness. ¶~의 dry.
● **건성유** drying oil.
건성건성 in a casual[superficial / desultory] way; halfway; in a half measure. ¶일을 ~ 해치우다 get one's work done in a casual [hit-or-miss] way / scamp[fudge / slur over] one's work / do a slapdash job // ~ 가르치다 teach in a perfunctory manner.
건수(件數) the number of cases[items]. ¶(경찰의) 단속 ~ the number of cases of crack down[clampdown] // 올들어 교통사고 ~가 줄었다 Traffic accidents have decreased in number this year. / The number of traffic accidents has decreased this year.
건습(乾濕) dryness and moisture; (degree of)

humidity.
- **건습구 습도계** a wet and dry bulb hygrometer; a psychrometer; a hygroscope.

건승(健勝) ¶~을 빕니다 I wish you good health. 건승하다 (서술적) be in [enjoy] good health. ¶건승하시다니 기쁩니다 I am glad to hear that you are in good health.

건시(乾柿) a dried persimmon. ⇨ 곶감

건식(乾式) the dry process.
- **건식세탁** dry cleaning.

건실하다(健實-) steady; steadfast; sound; solid; reliable. ¶건실한 직업 an honest occupation // 건실한 사람 a steady [trustworthy] person // 건실해지다 settle down to a proper way of living. 건실히 steadily; soundly; reliably. ¶사업을 ~ 하다 do [conduct] business on a sound basis // 그는 ~ 일을 하고 있다 He is steady at his work. / He works steadily.

건아(健兒) a vigorous youth; a stalwart youth. ¶대한의 ~ a virile son of Korea.

건어물(乾魚物) a dried [kippered] fish; a stockfish.

건울음 a sham cry; shedding unfelt [perfunctory] tears. ~ 울다 shed feigned [crocodile / sham / perfunctory] tears / feign [sham] weeping.

건위제(健胃劑) a peptic; a stomachic; a stomachal; digestive medicine.

건육(乾肉) dried meat; jerk.

건으로(乾-) (공연히) without reason [purpose / cause]; blindly; (터무니없이) absurdly; unreasonably; incredibly.

건의(建議) (제의) a proposal; a recommendation; a suggestion; (진언) a representation; a memorial. 건의하다 (제의하다) propose; recommend; suggest; (진백하다) make a representation (to); submit a petition (to). ¶정부에 ~ memorialize the Government / make a recommendation to the Government.
- **건의서** a petition; a memorial; a recommendation. **건의안** a proposition; a motion. ¶대정부 ~ a recommendation to the government. **건의함** a suggestion box.

건장하다(健壯-) healthy; robust; strong; sturdy; stout. ¶건장한 사람 a man of strong physique // 그는 건장한 체격이다 He has a robust build [constitution]. // 그는 60세까지는 건장했었다 He enjoyed robust health until the age of sixty.

건재(乾材) dried medicinal herbs.
- **건재 약국** a wholesale medicinal-herb store; a herbalist's.

건재(建材) building [construction] materials.
- **건재상** (상인) a building materials dealer [trader].

건재하다(健在-) be well; be in excellent health [condition]; be in good shape; be up and doing; be going strong; be as prosperous as usual (사업 등에). ¶부모님은 건재하십니까 Are your parents well? / How are your parents getting along [on]? // 우리 형제들은 모두 ~ All my brothers are alive and well [are in good health]. // 그 회사는 아직 ~ The company is still thriving.

건전지(乾電池) a dry cell [battery]; (미) a flashlight battery.

건전하다(健全-) healthy; sound; wholesome. ¶건전한 문학 healthy literature // 건전한 독서 [휴양] wholesome reading [recreation] // 건전한 재정 [투자 / 판단] sound finance [investment / judgment] // 심신이 건전한 사람 a man of sound body and mind // 건전하지 못한 생각 unwholesome [unhealthy] ideas // 건전한 정신을 갖고 있다 be sound minded // 그는 몸과 마음이 다 ~ He is sound both in mind and in body 건전히 healthily; soundly. ¶그 아이는 ~ 자라고 있다 The child is growing up soundly.

건전한 정신은 건전한 신체에 깃든다 (속담) A sound mind in a sound body.; Sound in body, sound in mind.

건조(建造) construction; building. ¶~ 중이다 be under [in course of] construction // 그 배는 지금 ~ 중이다 The ship is on the stocks [being built]. 건조하다 build; construct; lay down (a warship). ¶선박을 ~ build [construct] a ship. → ¶견고하게 건조된 선박 a strongly built ship.
- **건조물** a building; a structure.

건조(乾燥) dryness; aridity; (말리기) drying; seasoning(목재의). ¶이상 ~ abnormally dry weather // 급속 ~ 잉크 quick-drying ink // 급속-성의 quick-drying / quick to dry. 건조하다 [형용사] dry; arid; seasoned(목재가); [동사] become [get] dry [arid]; dry; season(목재를). ¶건조한 손 a dry hand // 건조한 목재 seasoned wood // 땅이 보송보송 건조해 있다 The ground is parched [dried up]. // 공기가 매우 ~ The air is exceedingly dry. // 건조시킨 감자 dehydrated potatoes // 이 목재는 잘 건조되었다 This timber is well seasoned.
- **건조기**(-期) the dry season. **건조기**(-器) a drier [dryer]; a drying machine; (밀크 등의) a desiccator. **건조 기후** an arid climate. **건조실** a drying room; a hothouse(도자기의). **건조제**(-劑) a drier [dryer]; a drying agent. **건조 주의보** a dry weather warning [alert]. **건조증** (의) xerosis.

건주정(乾酒酊) shammed [feigned] drunkenness. 건주정하다 sham [feign] drunkenness; pretend to be drunk; give a show of intoxication.

건지다 1 (물에서) take [bring] out of water; pull [draw] up; refloat(배를); pick up (a shipwrecked person). ¶물에 빠진 사람을 ~ save [rescue] a person from drowning / save a drowning man // 익사체를 ~ bring a drowned [dead] body to land.
2 (위험·죽음에서) help (a person) out of; rescue (a person) from; relieve (a person) from; release (a person) from. ¶사람을 파멸에서 ~ retrieve a person from ruin // 버스가 전복되었으나 전원이 목숨을 건졌다 The bus overturned, but the lives of all the passengers were saved. // 그는 간신히 목숨을 건졌다 He was saved from the brink of death. / He had a narrow escape from death.
3 (손해 등을) take [get] back; regain; save; retrieve; recover. ¶손해 본 것을 ~ recover [cover up] a loss // 손해를 좀 건졌느냐 Have you retrieved some of your loss? // 하나도 못 건지고 몽땅 불에 타 버렸다 All was lost in the fire. / Nothing was saved from the fire.

건초(乾草) hay; dry grass; dried herb. ¶~를 만들다 make hay // ~를 쌓아 올리다 cock hay.
- **건초 더미** a haycock; a haystack; a hayrick. **건초열** (의) hay fever.

건축(建築) [건조] construction; building; erection; [건축물] a building; a structure; (집합적) architecture. ¶목조[콘크리트] ~ a wooden[concrete] building∥~상의 architectural∥~ 중이다 be under[in course of] construction∥근대식 ~ modern architecture∥르네상스 양식의 ~ architecture [a building] in the Renaissance style∥그 아파트는 지금 ~ 중이다 The apartment house is now being built. **건축하다** build; construct; erect; set up; put up. ¶자기 집을 ~ build oneself a house(자신이) / have one's house built(타인이)∥이 교사는 근년에 건축한 것이다 The schoolhouse is of recent construction. →건축되다 get built.
● **건축가** an architect. **건축 공사** construction work. **건축 공학** architectural engineering. **건축물** a building; a structure; (집합적) architecture. **건축비** the cost of construction; construction expenditure. **건축사** an authorized architect and builder; a registered architect. **건축 설계** architectural design. **건축 양식** a style of building[architecture]. **건축업** the building trade. **건축업자** a builder; a constructor. **건축학** the science [art] of construction; architectonics; the science [art] of construction. **건축 허가** a building permit. **건축 회사** a building company; an architectural [a construction] firm.

건투(健鬪) a good fight; [노력] strenuous efforts. ¶~를 빕니다 Good luck to you! / I expect you to do your best. **건투하다** fight bravely; put up a good fight; [노력하다] make strenuous [vigorous] efforts. ¶건투의 보람 없이 after all one's hard work / in spite of one's strenuous efforts∥지방 팀은 건투하였으나 패배하였다 The local team fought hard but was defeated.

건판(乾板) [사진] a dry (photographic) plate; a plate; [인] a gelatin dry plate. ¶~을 현상하다 develop a dry plate.

건평(建坪) a building area; a floor space; floorage. ¶~ 25평의 아파트 an apartment with a floor space of 25 *pyeong*∥이 집은 ~이 100평방미터이다 This house has a floor space of 100 square meters (in all).

건폐율(建蔽率) coverage (ratio); building-to-land ratio. ¶~ 60퍼센트의 대지 a building site with a 60 percent coverage (ratio).

건포(乾脯) dried meat[fish].

건포도(乾葡萄) raisins; currants(작고 씨가 없는); dry grapes. ¶~가 든 케이크 a plum [raisin] cake.

건포마찰(乾布摩擦) [마른 수건으로 문지름]. ¶~을 하다 have a rubdown with a dry towel.

건필(健筆) a ready[facile] pen; vigorous writing. ¶~을 휘두르다 wield a facile [powerful] pen.
● **건필가** a prolific[productive] writer.

걷다[1] (안개 등이) clear away[off]; lift; break away.

걷다[2] walk; go on foot; tramp; step; hike. ¶걸어가면서 as one goes / on the way∥길을 ~ walk down[up / along] the road∥(어린아이가) 아장아장 ~ toddle[waddle] along∥사뿐사뿐 ~ walk lightly / walk with light steps∥살금살금 ~ walk with stealthy steps / walk on tiptoe∥뚜벅뚜벅 ~ tramp / tread heavily∥성큼성큼 ~ stride (along) / walk with long steps [strides]∥터벅터벅 ~ trudge along / plod on∥비틀비틀 ~ walk unsteadily / totter / stagger∥절뚝절뚝 ~ walk lame / limp along∥가만가만 ~ walk softly∥한가로이 ~ stroll / saunter∥마음이 내키는 대로 ~ go wherever one's humor dictates∥지치도록 걷게 하다 walk (a person) off his legs∥하루에 20마일을 ~ do 20 miles a day on foot∥지쳐 쓰러질 때까지 ~ walk till one is fit to drop∥걸어서 가다 walk (to) / go on foot / (속어) foot it∥학교에 걸어서 가다 go to school on foot / walk to school∥걸어서 집에 가다 walk home∥(환자·어린아이가) 걸을 수 있게 되다 find[feel / get on] one's legs∥직장까지 걸어서 20분 걸린다 It takes twenty minutes to walk to my office.∥역에서 걸어서 갈 수 있는 곳이다 It is within walking distance of the station.∥선생님은 수업 중에 교실 안을 걸어 다니신다 Our teacher paces up and down the classroom during class.∥자네는 잘도 걷는군 You are a good walker [pedestrian].∥어지간히 걸었군 We have done much walking.

걷기도 전에 뛰려고 한다(속담) do a thing out of proper order without going through proper channels.

걷다[3] **1** [말아 올리다] roll[turn / pull] up (one's sleeves); tuck up (one's skirt); bare [strip] (one's arm); gather up (curtain); fold up. ¶바지를 무릎까지 걷고 with one's trousers pulled up to the knees∥소매를 걷고 with bare arms / with one's sleeves turned over one's elbows∥셔츠 소매를 ~ roll up one's shirt sleeves∥커튼을 ~ gather up a curtain / draw aside a curtain (and fasten it)∥걷은 것을 도로 내리다 undo[let out] the tuck∥그녀는 스커트를 걷어 올렸다 She tucked up her skirt.∥그녀는 치맛자락을 걷어 올리고 바닷가를 거닐었다 She tucked up her long skirt and strolled along the shore.
2 [치우다] remove; take away; take off; [내리다] take down; strike; lower; pull down. ¶기를 ~ take[pull] down a flag / strike a flag∥돛을 ~ take in sails∥그물을 ~ haul [draw] in a net∥천막을 ~ strike [pull down] a tent∥그는 천막 자락을 걷고 안을 들여다보았다 He raised the flap of the tent and looked in.
3 [돈 등을 거두다] collect; gather; get. ¶걷은 돈 the collected money / the money collected∥기부금을 ~ get in subscriptions∥새로운 사업에 쓸 돈을 ~ raise money for a new undertaking∥빨래를 ~ gather up the laundry / take[bring] in the clothes∥빨래 걷는 것을 잊었다 I forgot to take[bring] in my laundry.
4 [일을 끝내거나 멈추다] settle (a matter); bring (a matter) to a conclusion. ¶일을 ~ settle one's affairs.

걷어붙이다 tuck[roll] up (one's sleeves). ¶바지를 무릎까지 걷어붙였다 I turned up my trousers to the knees.∥그는 소매를 걷어붙였다 He rolled his sleeves up above his elbows.∥그는 바지를 걷어붙이고 강으로 걸어 들어갔다 He waded into the stream with his trousers rolled up.

걷어차다 kick hard; give (a person) a hard kick. ¶정강이를 ~ give (a person) a hard kick on the shin∥말이 사람의 머리를 걷어찼다 A horse kicked a person hard on the head.

걷어채다 get a hard kick; be kicked hard. ¶옆구리를 ~ get a hard kick [get kicked hard] on the side // 그는 말한테 걷어챘다 He was kicked by a horse.

걷어치우다 1 [거두어 치우다] gather up and remove; clear away; put [take] away. ¶잡동사니를 ~ shift rubbish out of the way // 흩어진 물건을 ~ clear away scattered things. 2 [그만두다] leave off; stop; quit; give up. ¶일을 ~ throw [give] up one's job / abandon [leave off] one's work // 가게를 ~ close down a shop / go out of business // 그는 시골 살림을 걷어치우고 상경했다 He closed up his house in the country and came up to Seoul. // 그는 변호사를 걷어 치우고 실업계로 들어갔다 He retired from the bar and went into business.

걷잡다 [붙들다] hold; keep; stay; [참다] stop; keep back (one's tears); [막다] check (the enemy's advance); keep (a danger) at bay; control. ¶걷잡을 새 없이 swiftly / quickly // 걷잡을 수 없는 혼란에 빠지다 get into uncontrollable confusion // 저 은행은 걷잡을 수 없게 되었다 The bank cannot hold out any longer. // 흐르는 눈물을 걷잡을 수가 없었다 Try as I might, I could not keep back my tears.

걷히다 1 (구름·안개 등이) be lifted; be dispelled; be cleared away [off]; vanish; be broken up. ¶안개가 걷혔다 The mist cleared (off). / The fog lifted [disappeared / broke away]. // 구름이 걷혔다 The clouds lifted. // 연기가 걷히자 빨간 불꽃이 보였다 When the smoke cleared (away), we saw red flames. 2 (곡식·돈 등이) be gathered; be collected. ¶나락이 걷혔다 Crops were gathered. // 세금이 잘 걷힌다 The tax has a good yield. // 기부금이 잘 걷히지 않았다 The collection of the subscriptions was unsuccessful [far from satisfactory].

걸걸 hungrily; voraciously; greedily. **걸걸하다** be greedy; be gluttonous.

걸걸하다 (목소리가) guttural; husky. ¶걸걸한 목소리 a husky, resonant voice.

걸걸하다 (傑傑) open-hearted; free-hearted and cheerful. ¶그는 성미가 ~ He is nonchalant [cheerful / free-hearted] fellow.

걸귀 (乞鬼) (새끼를 낳은 암퇘지) a mother hog; a sow that has littered; [탐내는 사람] a glutton; a go(u)rmand; a gormandizer. ¶~들린 voracious / greedy / ravenous // ~들리다 have a wolf in one's stomach // ~같이 먹다 eat greedily [ravenously] / eat like a hog // ~처럼 굴지 마라 Don't be such a pig.

걸근거리다 1 [욕심내다] covet; be greedy (of / for); be covetous [gluttonous] (of). ¶돈에 ~ be greedy for money // 걸근거리며 돈을 모으다 love to make money. 2 [목구멍이 기침 등으로 근지러운 느낌을 주다] be tickled with phlegm. ¶목이 ~ have a scratchy throat.

걸다¹ 1 [매달다] hang (a thing on a peg); hook (걸쇠에); suspend; put up; set up. ¶간판을 ~ hang [put] up a signboard // 모자를 못에 ~ hang a hat on a peg // 달력을 ~ hang a calendar on the wall // 그림이 하나 벽에 걸려 있다 A picture is hanging on the wall.
2 [장치하다] fix; install. ¶솥을 ~ install a kettle.
3 [잠그다] (자물쇠·문고리 등을) lock; fasten; turn a key; (빗장을) bar [bolt] (the gate). ¶문의 자물쇠를 ~ lock a door // 창문에 자물쇠를 ~ latch [lock] a window / fasten a window.
4 (내기로 금품을) bet; stake; wager; (보증금 등을) deposit; pay (earnest money); (현상을) offer (a prize for). ¶돈을 걸고 마작을 하다 play mah-jongg for money // 대담하게 ~ make a risky wager // 계약금 3만 원을 ~ make a deposit of ₩30,000 // 차에 보험을 ~ insure a car / take out insurance on a car // 범인의 목에 현상금을 ~ set [put] a price on an offender's head // 이기는 자에게 상금을 ~ offer a prize for whomever wins // 그는 미지수의 말에 걸었다 He bet on a dark horse. / 그는 그 말에 꽤 많은 돈을 건 듯하다 He seems to have staked [bet / wagered] a considerable sum on that horse.
5 (목숨 등을) stake; risk. ¶목숨을 ~ risk [venture] one's life / stake one's life (on something) // 목숨 [지위]을 걸고 at the risk of one's life [position] // 운명을 ~ put the fate to a risk // 명예를 걸고 진실을 밀할 것을 맹세한다 I swear upon my honor to tell the truth. // 그녀는 목숨을 걸고 아이를 지키려고 했다 She tried to protect her child at the risk of her life.
6 (말 등을). ¶남에게 말을 ~ speak [talk] to a person / address (oneself) to a person // 영어로 말을 ~ talk to [address] (a person) in English // 농을 ~ play a joke on (a person) // 역에서 어떤 낯선 사람이 내게 말을 걸어왔다 A stranger spoke [called] to me at the station. (▶ called는 큰 소리로 말할 때)
7 (시비를) pick [seek] (a quarrel) with (a person); start a fight (with); provoke (a person to a quarrel). ¶남에게 시비를 ~ pick a quarrel with a person / provoke a person to a quarrel.
8 (재판을) put (a case) on trial; take (a matter) into court.
9 [희망 등을 가지다]. ¶희망을 ~ set [lay] hang] one's hopes on (a person) / have high hopes for (a person's future) // …에 기대를 ~ place one's hope on … / pin one's hope to … // 그는 아들에 희망을 걸고 있었다 He expected a great deal of his son. // 다음 경주에 그는 온 희망을 걸었다 He put all his hopes on the next race.
10 [통화하다] telephone; phone; make a telephone call (to); call (a person) up. ¶친구에게 전화를 ~ call a friend (on the telephone) / phone [telephone] a friend / (영) ring a friend up // 그에게 전화를 걸었다 I called him. / I rang him up. // 내일 아침에 전화 걸겠다 I'll call you [give you a call] tomorrow morning.
11 [작동시키다]. ¶발동을 ~ start an engine / set an engine going // 브레이크를 ~ put on [apply] the brakes // 재료를 기계에 ~ put the material in the machine.
12 (술책 등을) exert; exercise; practice; play; apply; lay (on); set (to). ¶최면술을 ~ mesmerize (a person) / hypnotize (a person) / practice hypnotism // 마법을 ~ cast [put / lay] a spell (upon a person) // 남의 다리를 ~ trip (a person) (up) // 남을 걸고 넘어지다 involve [entangle] in (a crime).
13 (기(旗) 등을) put up; hang out.

걸다² 1 [비옥하다] rich (soil); fertile (land). ¶

메마른 땅을 걸게 하다 make barren soil fertile // 이곳은 땅이 ~ The soil here is fertile.
2 [음식이 푸짐하다] heavy; rich; sumptuous (feast). ¶잔치가 ~ It is a sumptuous [rich] feast. // 음식이 ~ The table is well loaded with good things.
3 [식성이 좋다] gluttonous; omnivorous. ¶그는 식성이 ~ He is not particular [fastidious] about food. / He is not a fastidious eater. // 그는 입이 걸어서 무엇이든 잘 먹는다 He is an omnivorous glutton.
4 (액체가) thick; heavy; rich. ¶건 죽 thick gruel.
5 (입이) foul-mouthed; abusive; slanderous. ¶입이 건 사람 a foul-mouthed fellow // 그는 입이 ~ He is foul-mouthed [foul-tongued].
6 (손이) handy; dexterous (in / at). ¶손이 ~ be a good hand (at) / have a good hand (with) // 그는 손이 걸어 도박해서 잃은 일이 없다 With his luck [lucky hand], he never loses a gamble.

걸러뛰다 skip; pass over; bypass; leave out; omit. ¶제5페이지를 ~ omit [skip] page 5 / 5 페이지를 ~ skip over five pages // 2, 3행 걸러뛰고 읽다 skip a few lines in reading // 그는 재미없는 부분은 걸러뛰고 읽었다 He skipped the bad parts.

걸레 1 a floorcloth; a dustcloth; a duster; (자루가 달린) a mop; (갑판용) a swab. ¶마른~ a dry duster // 물~ a wet [damp] duster // ~로 훔치다 wipe (a pane) with a duster / swab [mop] up (water) // 마루를 ~로 닦다 wipe the floor with a damp cloth / mop the floor.
2 [너절한 물건] rubbish; trash; worthless stuff; [너절한 사람] a good-for-nothing; the social scum. ¶~ 같은 worthless / good-for-nothing.
●**걸레질** wiping with a damp cloth [duster]; mopping; scrubbing; swabbing. ¶마른 ~ wiping with a dry cloth.

걸리다[1] **1** [매달리다] hang (on / from); be suspended (on / from). ¶못에 걸려 있는 모자 a hat hanging on a peg // 벽에 그림이 걸려 있다 A picture is hanging on the wall. // 중천에 무지개가 걸려 있다 A rainbow is hanging in midair. // 달이 하늘에 걸려 있다 The moon is (hanging) in the sky.
2 [얽히다] catch; be caught (in / by); hitch (on a nail). ¶바지가 철조망에 ~ get one's pants snagged on the barbed wires // 못에 걸려 찢기다 have (one's coat) torn off at the nail // 밧줄에 걸려 넘어지다 trip over the rope // (먹은 것이) 가슴에 ~ lie heavy on the stomach // 연이 나무에 걸렸다 The kite lodged [got caught] in a tree. // 스커트가 못에 걸려 찢어졌다 I caught my skirt on a nail and tore it. // 가시가 목에 걸렸다 A bone stuck [got caught] in my throat.
3 [잡히다] be caught [entangled]; be hooked (낚시에). ¶거미줄에 ~ be entangled [get caught] in a cobweb // 큰 고기가 그물에 걸렸다 A big fish was caught in a net. // 물고기가 낚싯바늘에 걸렸다 A fish caught [took] the hook. // 비가 온 뒤에는 물고기가 잘 걸린다 Fish always take best after rain.
4 [관계되다] be concerned in; concern oneself in; have to do with. ¶사활이 걸린 문제 a vital question // 우승이 걸린 시합 the championship game // 나라의 운명이 그들의 양어깨에 걸려 있다 The destiny of the nation rest [falls] on their shoulders.
5 [말려들다] get entangled (with); be implicated (in); be involved (in). ¶부정 사건에 ~ be implicated [involved] in a scandal // 나쁜 여자에게 ~ get entangled with a bad woman // 장관이 의혹 사건에 걸렸다 The minister was involved in the scandal.
6 (덫 등에) be trapped; be entrapped; [속다] be cheated; be tricked. ¶덫에 ~ be caught in a trap [snare] / fall into a snare [trap] // 나는 그가 파 놓은 함정에 걸렸다 I fell right into the trap that he had set for me. // 그는 그들의 계략에 걸려들었다 He fell an easy prey to their plot.
7 [대항하다] play against; oppose; be up against; fight against. ¶그에게 걸리면 못 당한다 You are no match for him. // 너희들은 그에게 걸리면 어린아 다름없다 You are babies in his hands.
8 [위반되다] be against (a law); trespass (a law); be contrary [contradictory] to; [붙잡히다] be caught [taken]; (속어) be pinched. ¶법망에 ~ fall into the meshes of the law / be picked up by the law // 검열에 ~ fail to pass a censorship // 그는 경찰 검문에 걸렸다 He was caught in a police check. // 그는 교통순경에게 걸렸다 He was pinched by a traffic cop.
9 [병이 나다] become ill; get sick; fall ill; be taken ill; be attacked [affected] by (a disease); (특정한 병에) have [suffer from]. ¶홍역에 ~ catch the [have an attack of] measles // 감기에 ~ take [catch / get] (a) cold // 나는 전에 그 병에 걸린 적이 있기 때문에 이제는 걸리지 않는다 As I have had the disease, I am immune for it now. // 어린이는 병에 걸리기 쉽다 Children are susceptible to disease. / Children get sick easily. // 그는 뇌병 [폐병]에 걸려 있다 He has [is suffering from / (문어) is afflicted with] brain [lung] trouble. // His brain has [lungs have] been affected. // 그는 학질에 걸렸다 He contracted malaria.
10 [시간 등이 소요되다] take; need; require; cost. ¶이 책을 쓰는 데 10년 걸렸다 It took me as long as ten years to write this book. // 이것을 끝내는 데 1주일 걸릴 것이다 It will take (me) a week to finish this. // 그 일을 마치는 데 나흘이나 걸렸다 It took me no less than four days to finish the work. // 사고의 원인을 알아내는 데는 시간이 걸린다 To find out the cause of the accident will take [cost] much time.
11 [잠기다] be locked [fastened]; be barred (빗장이); catch; work. ¶빗장이 잘 걸리지 않는다 The bolt does not catch properly.
12 [작동하다] work; run; go; operate. ¶시동이 걸렸다 The engine has started. // 제동이 안 걸린다 The brake won't work.
13 [(전화가) 통하다] put through (a call); get connected (with). ¶그에게서 전화가 걸려 왔다 I had a call from him. // 전화가 안 걸려요 I could not get my call through [completed]. // 잘못 걸렸습니다 You've got the wrong number. / The wrong number.
14 [마음에 거리끼다] (사물이) weigh on one's mind; lie at one's heart; (사람이) feel uneasy about; be anxious about. ¶그의 말이 몹시 마음에 걸린다 His words weigh heavily with

걸리다

me[upon my mind]. ¶그 일이 몹시 마음에 걸린다 The matter weighs heavy on my mind. / It haunts me. // 아버지의 용태가 마음에 걸린다 I am anxious about my father's condition.
15 (상금 등이) hang (on). ¶이 경주에는 100만 원의 상금이 걸려 있다 There is a prize [purse] of a million won riding[hanging] on this race.

걸리다² [걷게 하다] make (a person) walk; walk (a person); force (a person) to walk(억지로). ¶남을 녹초가 되도록 ~ walk a person to exhaustion.

걸맞다 [정도가 비슷하다] well-balanced; well-matched; nicely-paired; [어울리다] suitable; be coming; fitting; befitting. ¶걸맞은 부부 a well-matched [-mated] couple / a well-assorted pair // 걸맞은 상대 a good match (for one) // 지출에 걸맞은 수입 an income which offsets expenditures // 능력에 걸맞은 월급 a salary proportionate to one's ability / 걸맞지 않은 ill-matched / unsuited / disproportionate / improper // 걸맞지 않은 부부 an unsuitable match / an ill-matched pair / an ill-assorted couple // 수입에 걸맞은 생활을 하다 live up to one's income // 신분에 걸맞지 않은 생활을 하다 live above one's means [social standing] // 일에 걸맞은 급료를 주겠다 We will pay according to the work you do [what your work deserves] // 그 옷은 추도식 행사에 걸맞지 않다 Your clothing is improper for[out of place at] a memorial service. // 그들은 걸맞은[걸맞지 않은] 부부이다 They are a well-matched[an ill-matched] couple.

걸머잡다 grasp; catch hold of; clutch at; seize. ¶머리채를 ~ seize (a woman) by the hair // 떡살을 ~ seize (a person) by the collar.

걸머지다 **1** (짐·책임 등을) carry (a burden) on one's back; shoulder (a burden); bear; be burdened (with). ¶짐을 멜빵으로 ~ strap a bundle on one's back // 책임을 ~ take the responsibility on one's own shoulders / shoulder[bear] responsibilities / assume responsibilities // 그는 대학 총장으로서 모든 책임을 걸머져야만 했다 As the president of the university he had to assume full responsibility. **2** (빚을) run into debt; contract a debt; be in debt. ¶그는 아버지의 빚을 걸머졌다 He shouldered[took responsibility for] his father's debts.

걸물 (傑物) a great[distinguished] person; an extraordinary character; a master man [spirit]. ¶법조계의 ~들 giants in legal circles.

걸상 (-床) a seat; a bench; a form(긴 것); a chair(의자).

걸쇠 (문을 잠그는) a latch(빗장); a hasp(갈고리); a clasp(물림쇠). ¶~를 걸다 latch / fasten with a hasp[latch] / fasten the clasp (of a handbag) // ~를 벗기다 unhasp / unlatch // 목걸이의 ~를 끄르다 unclasp [unfasten the clasp of] a necklace // 드레스 등 쪽의 ~를 채워 주시겠습니까 Would you hook my dress at the back?

걸식 (乞食) begging; mendicancy. ¶문전 ~ door-to-door begging / begging from door to door. **걸식하다** go (about) begging; beg food; live as a beggar.

걸신 (乞神) [빌어먹는 귀신] a hungry demon; [음식에 대한 욕심] a hunger; a greed; voracity; ravenousness.

걸신들리다 (乞神—) get greedy for food; have a wolf in one's stomach. ¶걸신들린 사람 a voracious[greedy] person / a man greedy for food // 걸신들린 듯이 먹다 eat greedily [ravenously] / eat like a hog.

걸어가다 go on foot; walk; pace one's way (to). ¶시골 길을 ~ walk along a country lane // 걸어갑시다 Let's walk it. // 걸어가십니까 Are you going on foot?

걸어오다 come on foot. ¶우리가 걸어온 길 the path we have followed.

걸어총 (-銃) [구령] Stack[Pile] arms!

걸음 walking; stepping; a step; [보조] pace. ¶첫 ~ the first step // 종종 ~ short and quick steps / mincing steps // 한 ~ 한 ~ step by step / by degrees // 황소~으로 at a snail's pace // 빠른 ~으로 at a rapid[quick / brisk] pace / with a rapid step / briskly // ~이 빠르다 [느리다] be quick[slow] of foot / be a good [bad] walker // 두 ~ 나서다[물러서다] take two steps forward[backward] // 한 ~ 앞서다 [뒤지다] be a step ahead[behind] // 갑자기 ~을 멈추다 come to a sudden stop // 나는 ~이 느리다 I have a weak leg. / I am a poor walker. // 그는 ~아 나 살려라 하고 달아났다 He ran away as fast as his legs could carry him. / He ran for his[dear] life.
●**걸음걸이** one's manner of walking; gait; walk; a step. ¶지친 듯한 ~ a weary walk // 무거운 ~로 with a heavy[leaden] step // 그는 취해서 비틀거리는 ~로 걷고 있었다 He was drunk and was walking unsteadily[with an unsteady gait].

걸음마 toddling. ¶~를 하다 toddle / find its feet // (아기에게) ~! Let's walk now! / Step firm. / Steady! Steady! // 아기는 ~를 하기 시작했다 The baby has begun to toddle. // ~ 잘 한다 Look! You are walking! Good boy[girl]!

걸인 (乞人) a beggar. ⇨거지

걸작 (傑作) **1** [뛰어난 작품] a masterpiece; a great work; a fine piece of work. ¶문학사상 최고의 ~ a masterpiece in the history of literature // 아동 문학의 ~ a masterpiece of juvenile literature // 이 그림은 르누아르의 ~이다 This is Renoir at his best. // 이것은 그의 일생일대의 ~이다 This is the crown of his life's work. **2** [웃기는 말·행동] a droll [funny] talk[behavior]; [그런 사람] a funny fellow; a droll. ¶그것 참 ~이다 That's hilarious[very funny]. // 그 친구 정말 ~이야 He is a jolly good fellow. / He is great[good] fun.

걸쭉하다 (액체가) thick; rich; heavy; mushy. ¶국물을 걸쭉하게 되도록 끓이다 let the broth simmer down to a rich stock // 딸기를 걸쭉해지도록 끓였다 We cooked the strawberries until they were reduced to a pulp.

걸출하다 (傑出—) excel (at / in); stand out (from); prominent; pre-eminent; distinguished; outstanding. ¶걸출한 작품 an outstanding work // 걸출한 정치가 a prominent [distinguished] politician // 그는 스키에서[학자로서] ~ He excels at skiing[as a scholar]. // 동료 가운데서는 그가 ~ He towers above [outshines] his colleagues. // 그는 변호사로서 ~ He cuts an outstanding figure as a lawyer. // 현대 화단에서는 그가 ~ He stands out among contemporary painters[in contemporary painting circles].

걸치다[1] 1 [얹어 걸다·놓다] put (a thing) on [over]; [건너질러 걸다] lay [place] over [across]. ¶도랑에 널빤지를 ~ lay a plank across a ditch // 두 다리를 도랑에 ~ straddle a ditch // 강 위에 다리를 ~ span a river with a bridge / build a bridge across a river // 책상에 다리를 ~ rest one's feet on a table top.
2 [옷을 되는대로 입다] throw [slip] on; huddle on. ¶급히 외투를 ~ huddle on one's overcoat / slip on one's overcoat hurriedly // 몸에 실오라기 하나 걸치지 않다 be stark-naked // 그는 상의를 걸치고 나갔다 He threw [slipped] on his coat [He threw his coat over his shoulder] and went out.
3 [술 마시다]. ¶한잔 ~ have a drink // 맥주를 한잔 ~ take a pull at one's beer.

걸치다[2] (시간·공간적인 범위에) range (from A to B); extend; spread (over); cover; last(계속되다). ¶그의 대방면에 걸친 지식 his multifarious learning // 5년에 걸쳐서 over a period of five years // 월요일부터 금요일에 걸쳐 extending from Monday through Friday / (미) (from) Monday through Friday // 10킬로미터 [10년]에 ~ extend [stretch] over ten kilometers [years] // 여러 번에 걸쳐서 강연하다 give [deliver] a series of lectures // 그는 다방면에 걸쳐서 활약하고 있다 He is actively engaged in various fields. // 이것은 내년도까지 걸쳐 있는 사업이다 This program extends into next year. // 그의 논문의 내용은 넓은 범위에 걸쳐 있다 His essay ranges over a wide field.

걸터앉다 (의자 등에) sit (on a chair); perch (on a stool); (다리를 벌리고) sit astride. ¶의자의 팔걸이에 ~ perch on the arm of a chair // 말 위에 ~ straddle a horse / ride on horseback / sit astride a horse.

걸터타다 (말 등에) sit [ride] astride [astraddle] (a horse); straddle [mount] (a horse); (모로) ride (a horse) sideways.

걸프렌드 a girlfriend (▶ 우리말 「걸프렌드」가 주로 10대 소년의 여자 친구를 가리키는 데 반해, 영어 "girlfriend"는 그 뜻 외에 성 관계를 맺고 있는, 성인 남자의 여자 애인을 가리키기도 함).

걸핏하면 too often; readily; easily; at the slightest provocation. ¶~ …하다 be apt [liable / prone] to (do) // ~ 화를 내다 be quick [ready] to take offense / be easily offended // ~ 사람을 치다 be ready to punch a person / punch a person at the slightest provocation // 그녀는 ~ 운다 She is apt to shed tears blindly. / She weeps just too often. // 그들은 ~ 상사의 욕을 한다 They are apt to criticize their superiors.

검(劍) [도검] a sword; [군도] a saber; [총검] a bayonet; [단검] a dagger.

검객(劍客) a swordsman; a master of fence; a fencer.

검거(檢擧) an arrest; [일제 검거] (구어) a roundup. ¶피~자 a person in custody / a person under arrest // 경찰의 용의자 일제 ~ a police roundup of suspects. **검거하다** arrest; take up; (구어) round up(일제히). ¶일제 ~ 하다 make a wholesale [mass] arrest (of) / round up // 폭력단을 대량 ~ 하다 make a sweeping [general] roundup of a gang of racketeers. ➔ 그는 선거법 위반으로 검거되었다 He was arrested for [on charge of] violating the election law. // 마침내 범인이 검거되었다 The criminal was arrested at last. / (용의자를) The police have picked up a suspect. // 살인범은 아직 검거되지 않았다 The murderer is still at large.

검뇨(檢尿) [의] an examination of urine; a urine test; uroscopy. **검뇨하다** examine (a person's) urine; [검사해 받다] have one's urine examined.
● **검뇨기**(─器) a urinometer.

검누렇다 blackish yellow; dark yellow.

검다 1 (빛깔이) black; dark; swarthy(살갗 등이). ¶검은 머리 black hair // 검은 옷 (a suit of) black clothes / a black costume // 얼굴이 ~ have a dark complexion / be dark-complexioned // 검게 타다 (볕에) be [get] tanned [sunburnt] // 검게 물들이다 [칠하다] dye [paint] (something) black // 검게 하다 blacken / black / make (something) black // 토스트가 검게 탔다 The toast was burned. // 그녀는 전신을 검은 옷으로 감싸고 있었다 She was dressed in black from head to toe.
2 [마음이 엉큼하다] black-hearted; wicked; evil-hearted. ¶속이 검은 사람 a black-hearted person / a schemer.

검댕 soot. ¶~투성이의 sooty / sooted / soot-covered // ~투성이의 얼굴 a sooty face / a face smudged with soot // ~이 끼다 [앉다] become sooty [sooted] / have soot (on it) // ~이 묻다 be smeared [stained] with soot // ~투성이가 되다 be covered with soot // 굴뚝에 ~이 끼었다 Soot has collected in the chimney.

검도(劍道) [검술] (the art of) fencing; swordsmanship. ¶~를 하다 practice fencing // 그는 ~ 5단의 실력이다 He has a fifth grade in fencing. / He is a fifth grade swordsman.

검둥개 a black dog.

검둥이 1 [흑인] a Negro (pl. ~es); a Negress(여자); a black (man / woman); a colored man [woman]; (구어) a darky; a blackie; (구어·경멸) a nigger. 2 [피부가 검은 사람] a dark-skinned person. 3 [검둥개] a black dog; (부를 때) Blackie.

검량(檢量) measuring; weighing; (공공 기관에 의한 화물의) metage. **검량하다** (양을) measure; take measure of; (무게를) weigh.
● **검량기** a gauging rod; a gauger.

검류계(檢流計) [전] a galvanometer; a galvanoscope.

검류의(檢流儀) (조류의) a current indicator.

검무(劍舞) a sword dance. ⇨ 칼춤

검문(檢問) (an) inspection; (a) check. ¶불심 ~ questioning (of a suspicious person by a patrolman) // ~을 통과하다 pass an inspection // 용의자의 차가 ~에 걸렸다 The suspect was caught at a traffic checkpoint [in a traffic check]. **검문하다** inspect; examine; check. ➔ 경찰관에게 검문당하다 be questioned by a policeman // 검문당하지 않고 나가다 go out unquestioned [unchallenged].
● **검문소** a check point; a control point.

검박하다(儉朴─) frugal; thrifty; plain; simple. ¶검박한 생활 plain living.

검버섯 black [dark] spots on an old man's skin. ¶얼굴에 ~이 돋다 have blotches on one's face.

검법(劍法) (the art of) fencing.

검부러기 remnants [bits] of dry grass or leaves. ¶짚 ~ bits of straw.
검불 dry grass or leaves.
검붉다 dark-red; of dark-red color; blackish red. ¶그는 햇볕에 검붉게 탔다 He was burnt dark-red from the sun. / He had a dark-red sunburn.
검사(檢事) a public prosecutor; (영) a counsel for the Crown; (집합적) the prosecution. ¶고검 ~ a public prosecutor of a high public prosecutor's office // 부장 ~ a chief public prosecutor // 지방 ~ a district public prosecutor / (미) a district attorney(약어 D.A.) // ~의 항소 a public prosecutor's appeal (to).
검사(檢査) (an) inspection; (an) examination; a test; an overhaul(기계·선박 등의); (an) audit(회계의). ¶~필 (게시) Examined. / Inspected. // ~를 받다 undergo[go through] an examination / be examined[inspected] // ~에 통과[합격]하다 pass the examination / stand the test // ~에 불합격하다 fail to pass the examination / be rejected // 그 기구는 ~에 합격하지 못했다 The instrument has not passed inspection. **검사하다** inspect; examine; audit (accounts); overhaul (a machine). ¶성병을 ~ examine (a person) for venereal disease // 당뇨병을 ~ test[give a test] for diabetes // 우물의 수질을 ~ examine[test] the water of a well // 공무원이 식당의 위생 상태를 검사하러 왔다 An official visited the restaurant to inspect sanitary conditions there. → ¶우리는 소지품을 검사받았다 We had our belongings examined.
● **검사관** an inspector; an examiner; (세관의) an examining officer; (미) a surveyor; (회계의) an auditor. **검사소** an inspection office [station].
검산(檢算) verification of accounts; checking accounts; proving a calculation. **검산하다** verify[check] accounts; (수) prove; check one's figures.
검색(檢索) 1 [찾아봄] reference; (컴퓨터의) retrieval. ¶~에 편리하다 be easy of[handy for] reference // 컴퓨터는 정보 ~에 편리하다 The computer makes it easy to get information. **검색하다** refer to (a dictionary); look up (a word) in (a dictionary). 2 [수색] a quest; a search; rummage(세관원의). ¶경찰의 ~에 걸리다 be caught in a police raid. **검색하다** search (for); make[prosecute] a search; rummage (a house for a thing). ¶배 안을 ~ search a ship (for contraband goods).
● **검색 엔진** a search engine.
검소하다(儉素－) [간소하다] simple; plain; [검약하다] frugal; thrifty; economical. ¶검소한 식사[생활] a frugal meal[way of life] // 매사에 ~ be economical in every way // 그 여인은 검소한 옷차림을 하고 있었다 The woman was plainly dressed. **검소히** simply; frugally. ¶~ 살다 live simply[plainly] / live in a small way.
검속(檢束) [구속] (a) restriction; (a) restraint; [구금] (an) arrest; custody; confinement; detention. ¶보호 ~ a protective arrest // 용의자에 대한 경찰의 일제 ~ a police roundup of suspects. **검속하다** [구속하다] restrict; restrain; [구금하다] arrest (for detention); take (a person) into custody.

검술(劍術) (the art of) fencing; swordsmanship. ¶~의 대가 a master swordsman [fencer] // 남과 ~를 겨루다 cross swords with a person // ~에 있어서는 그를 당할 자가 없다 No one is a match for him as a swordsman [in swordsmanship].
● **검술가** a swordsman; a fencer. **검술 사범** a fencing coach [master].
검시(檢屍) an autopsy; an [a coroner's] inquest; a post-mortem examination. ¶~ 결과 타살의 혐의가 엿보였다 The post-mortem examination raised a suspicion of foul play. **검시하다** examine a corpse to determine the cause of death; hold an inquest over (a corpse); make an autopsy.
● **검시관** a coroner; a medical examiner.
검안(檢案) [법] examination. **검안하다** examine. ¶시체를 ~ carry out[conduct] a post-mortem examination / make an autopsy.
검안(檢眼) an eye examination; optometry. ¶~을 받다 have one's eyes examined. **검안하다** examine (a person's) eyes.
● **검안경(一鏡)** an ophthalmoscope; an eye speculum.
검압기(檢壓器) a pressure gauge; a manometer.
검약(儉約) economy; thrift; frugality. **검약하다** be frugal; be thrifty; economize; exercise [practice / use] economy; save (money / expenses). ¶검약하는 thrifty / frugal / economical // 검약하기 위해 for economy's sake // 검약하며 생활했지만 돈을 모으지는 못했다 I have not saved much money in spite of my frugal living.
검역(檢疫) quarantine; quarantine [medical] inspection. ¶~필 (게시) Passed Medical Inspection. // ~을 받다 be quarantined // ~을 위해서 입항[상륙]이 금지되다 be held [detained] in quarantine // ~ 중이다 be in quarantine. **검역하다** quarantine; inspect.
● **검역관** a quarantine officer [doctor]; a healthguard. **검역선** a quarantine ship. **검역소** a quarantine station; a lazaretto (pl. ~s). **검역항** a quarantine port.
검열(檢閱) 1 [점검] inspection; examination. ¶~필 (게시) Passed Inspection. **검열하다** inspect; examine.
2 (간행물 등의) censorship. ¶사전[사후] ~ pre- [post-] censorship // 신문[영화] ~ press [film] censorship // ~필 censored / released by censorship // ~을 통과하다 pass censorship // ~에 걸리다 fail to pass censorship // ~을 받다 be censored // ~을 폐지[완화 / 강화]하다 remove [ease / tighten] the censorship // 서적과 정기 간행물은 ~을 받아야 한다 Books and periodicals shall have to be submitted for censorship. **검열하다** censor. ¶외국 우편물을 ~ censor foreign mail.
3 (군대의) inspection (of troops); a review. **검열하다** inspect; review. ¶사령관은 부대를 검열했다 The commander inspected the troops. → ¶검열받다 be inspected / be reviewed.
● **검열관** a censor; an inspector(군대의).
검은담비 [동] a sable.
검은자(위) (눈의) the (dark) colored part of the eye; the iris (pl. ~es, irides). ¶~가 많은 눈 eyes with large irises [pupils] / large dark

eyes.

검인(檢印) (검사필의) a seal[stamp] of approval; an "Examined" seal; (저자의) the seal of the author. ¶~을 찍다 seal / stamp / affix a seal[stamp] (of approval) (to) // ~이 찍혀 있다 be under seal // 이 책에는 저자의 ~이 없다 This book bears no seal of the author. // 여권에는 영사의 ~이 있어야 한다 The passport must be duly visaed by the consul.
● **검인증** an approval certificate.

검인정(檢認定) [검정과 인정] official approval[certification] and sanction; authorization.
● **검인정 교과서** an authorized textbook.

검전기(檢電器) [전] a galvanoscope; an electroscope; a rheoscope; a (voltage) detector(누전의).

검정 black; black color. ¶~ 물감 black dye // ~ 머리 black hair // ~ 옷을 입고 있다 be (dressed) in black.

검정(檢定) [면허] official approval[sanction / certification]; authorization; [시험·검사] (an) examination. ¶교과서 ~ 제도 the textbook authorization system / the textbook screening system. **검정하다** give official approval[sanction] to; approve; authorize; [시험하다] examine. ¶자격을 ~ test the qualification.
● **검정고시** a licensing[certification] examination; qualification examination. **검정 교과서** an authorized textbook.

검증(檢證) [법] a verification; identification(시체의); probate(유언의); [조사] (an) inspection. ¶현장 ~ an inspection of the scene (of a murder) / an on-the-spot inspection[investigation] / an on-site verification // 현장 ~ 조서 a protocol of on-the-spot inspection. **검증하다** verify; inspect; probate(유언을). ¶가설을 ~ verify a hypothesis // 유언을 ~ probate a will // 충돌 사고 현장을 ~ inspect the scene of a collision.

검지(-指) an index finger; a forefinger; the first finger.

검진(檢診) (a) medical examination[checkup]. ¶성병 ~ a V.D. check // 종합 ~ a comprehensive medical testing // 집단 ~ a group (tuberculosis) examination // ~을 받다 have a medical examination // 암의 정기 ~을 받다 have a periodic checkup for cancer. **검진하다** examine; give a medical examination; check up (a person's health).

검질기다 tenacious; persevering; pertinacious; persistent. ¶검질긴 사나이 a man of great tenacity[stamina] / (미) a tough guy // 검질기게 물고 늘어지다 give[offer] stubborn resistance (to) / stubbornly refuse to give up.

검찰(檢察) prosecution; investigation and prosecution. ¶~ 측 증인 a witness for the prosecution. // ~측과 변호인 측 the prosecution and the defense. **검찰하다** investigate and prosecute.
● **검찰관** a public prosecutor; a prosecutory official; (미) a United States attorney. **검찰청** the Public Prosecutions Administration. ¶고등 ~ the High Prosecutions Administration // 대 ~ the Supreme Public Prosecutions Administration // 지방 ~ a district public prosecutions administration. **검찰 총장** the Public Prosecutor General; (영) the Director of Public Prosecutions.

검출(檢出) [화] detection; (chemical) search. **검출하다** detect [find] (poison / strontium 90) (by chemical analysis); analyze out. ➔ ¶분석한 결과 독극물이 검출되었다 A poisonous substance was detected[found] by chemical analysis.
● **검출기** a detector.

검측측하다 (빛깔이) dark; dull and black; (마음이) black-hearted; wicked.

검침(檢針) the inspection[reading] of a meter; a gauge examination. **검침하다** check [read] a (gas) meter. ¶전기 미터를 ~ read an electric meter.
● **검침원** a (gas / water) meterman.

검토(檢討) (an) examination; (an) investigation; scrutiny; study. ¶재 ~ reexamination / restudying // ~ 중 under investigation [examination] // ~ 중인 법안 the bill under consideration // 예산안의 ~가 나에게 맡겨졌다 The examination of the draft budget was left to me. // 그 문제는 회의에 부칠 것인가를 ~ 중이다 We are considering whether to present the problem at the meeting. **검토하다** examine (a theory); investigate; inquire into; study. ¶세밀히 ~ (일을) examine thoroughly / inquire into (a matter) closely / (사람을) subject (a person) to a close examination // 더 검토할 필요가 있다 require further examination // 여러모로 ~ study[consider] the matter from all angles // 더 검토해서 보고 하겠습니다 We will make a report after conducting a further examination [investigation]. ➔ ¶철저히 검토되다 get a thorough going over.

검파(檢波) [전] detection; demodulation. **검파하다** detect; demodulate.
● **검파기**(-器) a (wave) detector; a cymoscope; a radio conductor.

검표(檢票) examination of tickets. **검표하다** examine[clip] tickets; (미) check up tickets.
● **검표원** a ticket inspector; a ticket examiner.

검푸르다 dark blue; blue-black. ¶검푸른 바다 a dark blue sea // 검푸른 색 a dark blue.

겁(怯) [공포] fear; fright; (a) terror; (a) dread; [소심] timidity; cowardice. ¶~이 많다 timid / cowardly / be a coward / chickenlivered // ~이 없다 fearless / bold / daring / ~ 없는 아이 a fearless child.

겁(劫) [불] (범) a kalpa; an (a)eon; an eternity; long ages.

겁나다(怯-) be frightened[scared]; be overcome with fright; be seized with fear[panic]; get in[to] a funk. ¶겁나서 소리 지르다 cry out for fear // 말할 수 없이 겁났다 I was scared to death. // 선생님에게 들킬까 봐 겁났다 I was afraid lest I should be found by the teacher. // 그녀는 꾸중 들을까 겁나서 잠자코 있었다 She did not say a word for fear of being scolded. // 죽기가 겁난다 I am afraid of dying. // 개가 짖어 대어 겁났다 I was frightened[scared] when a dog barked at me. // 낯선 곳에 혼자 남게 되자 겁났다 I was seized with fear[I got scared], when I found myself left alone in a strange place.

겁내다(怯-) fear; dread; be afraid (of); be in fear[terror]; have a horror of; show one's

겁먹다

cowardice. ¶겁내지 않다 be undaunted / be unawed / be fearless (of) // 겁내지 않고 without timidity // 그는 죽음을 겁내지 않았다 He did not fear[was not afraid of] death. // 그들은 불량배를 겁내어 모두 달아났다 They ran away in fear of the hooligan. // 실패를 겁내지 말고 하라 Don't be afraid of failing. Just do it. // 너는 아무것도 겁낼 것이 없다 You have nothing to fear.

겁먹다(怯-) be frightened (by / at). ¶그녀는 겁먹은 얼굴을 하고 있었다 She had a scared look on her face. // 어린이는 그 광경을 보고 겁먹었다 The child was frightened at the sight. // 그는 잔뜩 겁먹고 있었다 He was stiff with fright. // 그는 시험에 잔뜩 겁먹고 있으니 잘 치를 것 같지 않다 He is so frightened [scared] by examination that he is not likely to do well. // 일당의 가장 나이 어린 자가 잔뜩 겁먹었다 The youngest member of the gang lost his nerve [구어] got cold feet]. // 그는 시합 직전에 겁먹고 달아났다 Just before the match he panicked[lost his nerve] and ran away.

겁쟁이(怯-) a coward; a poltroon; a funk; a faint-heart; (미국 속어) a chicken; a mouse. ¶그는 진짜 ∼다 He is an absolute coward.

겁주다(怯-) threaten; scare; terrify; give a scare; (미) throw a scare into (a person). ¶남을 경찰에 알리겠다고 ∼ threaten to report a person to the police.

겁탈(劫奪) [약탈] pillage; plunder; [강간] violation; rape. **겁탈하다** [약탈하다] plunder; pillage; [강간하다] violate; rape. ¶여자를 ∼ violate[outrage / rape] a woman / commit a rape on a woman.
● **겁탈자** [약탈자] a plunderer; a looter; [강간자] a violator; a rapist.

것 1 [유형물] a thing; an object; [물품] an article; (대명사적) a one; the one; [사물] things; a matter. ¶∼ this / this one / 싼 ∼ a cheap one // 이 웃옷은 너무 작으니 큰 ∼으로 보여 주시오 This jacket is too small for me. Show me a larger one. // 시커먼 ∼이 물에 떠 있다 Something black is floating on the water.
2 [소유물] a possession. ¶내 ∼ mine // 네 ∼ yours // 남의 ∼ other people's possession / other's // 자기 ∼으로 만들다 secure / take possession of // 그 모자는 나의 ∼이다 That hat is mine. // 그 집은 그의 ∼이 되었다 The house passed[fell] into his hands[possession]. // 나는 어떤 일이 있어도 그 여자를 내 ∼으로 만들겠다 I will get the woman[make the woman mine] no matter what I have to do.
3 [사람·동물] a man; a person; (대명사적) a one; the one. ¶어린 ∼ a young one // 너 같은 ∼ such a man as you // 그런 대학자에 비하면 나 같은 ∼은 아무것도 아니다 When I compare myself with such a great scholar, I simply don't exist.
4 [사실] a fact; [일] a thing; what. ¶그가 언제 돌아올 ∼인지 잘 모르겠다 I don't know exactly when he will be back. // 그가 정직하다는 ∼은 사실이다 It is true that he is honest. // 내 말대로 하는 ∼이 좋을 거다 You'd better do just as I told you.
5 [필요] need; necessity. ¶그럴 ∼까지는 없다 It is unnecessary to do it. / You don't have to do it. // 서두를 ∼은 없다 There is no need for haste. / You need not hurry.
6 [확인·추측]. ¶∼일 ∼이다[이라 생각하다] I think / I suppose / [좋은 일을 예상하여) I hope / (언짢은 일을 예상하여) I fear / I am afraid / [아마 …이겠지] I dare say / I should say / perhaps // …인 ∼ 같다 [⋯처럼 보이다] look (like) / appear / seem / [⋯이라 생각되다] seem / it seems (to one) that / [⋯인 듯하다] be likely (to) / probably // 그는 내일 올 ∼이다 He will probably come tomorrow. // 그녀는 30세 미만일 ∼이다 She is under thirty, I should think.
7 [금지·의무]. ¶학생은 오전 8시에 등교할 ∼ The students are requested to school at 8 a.m. // 잔디밭에 들어가지 말 ∼ Keep off the grass.

-것-**1** [다짐] don't you(부가 의문); I suppose. ¶네가 가기는 가~ You are going there, aren't you? // 너 이 동네에 살~ You live in this town, don't you? // 나를 알 ∼ You must know me. **2** [조건이 충분함] given this and that. ¶돈 많∼, 권력 있∼, 그런데 무슨 걱정이오 You've got both money and power, and what's the matter with you? **3** [협박] surely[certainly] be[do]; you will do it (understand?) ¶내가 그리했~ You certainly did[have done] so. // 너 말 다했~ How dare you say such a thing to me?

겅중거리다 stride; walk with big (and bouncing) strides.

겉 1 [표면] the surface; the face; the right side(웃의); the obverse(메달 등의). ¶(가죽의) ∼쪽 the grain side // 양탄자의 ∼ the right side of a carpet // …의 ∼에 on the surface [face] of … // 어느 쪽이 ∼입니까 Which side is the front? / (옷감·종이 등에서) Which is the right side?
2 [외부] the exterior; the outside; [외관] the (outward) appearance. ¶∼으로 externally / outwardly / apparently // ∼을 꾸미다 make outward show // ∼만 보고 판단하다 judge (a person) by (his) outward appearance // 사물의 ∼만 보다 take a superficial view of things // ∼으로 태연한 체하다 remain[keep] calm outwardly // 그는 ∼과 속이 다르다 He looks one thing and means another. // 그녀는 ∼으로는 명랑해 보이나 사실은 비관적이다 She has a sunny manner[She looks cheerful], but actually she's rather pessimistic.

겉가량(-假量) a rough estimate; [눈대중] eye measure. ¶∼으로 at a rough estimate / by eye measure // 방문객은 ∼으로 만 명 정도다 The number of visitors is roughly estimated at 10,000. **겉가량하다** make a rough estimate; estimate roughly.

겉겨 chaff; bran; outer husks[hulls] of grain.

겉곡식(-穀食) unhulled grain.

겉귀 [생] the external ear; the concha (pl. -chae).

겉껍질 an outer cover; (과실·옥수수 등의) a husk; a shuck; (곡물의) a hull; (싹 등의) an envelope; (동식물체의) an investment; (피부의) the out(most) layer of the skin; the cuticle.

겉꾸리다 keep up appearances; put on a good face on (a matter); make outward show; put up a good front[a brave show].

겉날리다 scamp (one's work); do (one's work) in a careless manner; do a slapdash job. ¶그는 일을 겉날린다 He does his work halfheartedly[sloppily]. // 잠간 눈을 떼면 그 들은 일을 겉날리려고 한다 If you take your eyes off them for a moment, they try to cut corners in their work.

겉놀다 (못·나사 등이) slip; do not fit; [겉돌다] skid; race; do not get along well; be out of keeping with.

겉눈썹 an eyebrow.

겉늙다 look old for one's age; get old before one's time; be prematurely gray. ¶머리 모양을 그렇게 하니 겉늙어 보인다 That hair-do makes you look older than your age.

겉대 (푸성귀의) an outer stalk[leaf]; (대나무의) the outer part of bamboo.

겉대중 a rough estimate. ⇨ 겉가량

겉더께 (surface) scum; fur; scale.

겉돌다 1 [헛돌다] spin free(바퀴가); (톱니바퀴가) do not gear[engage] (with); be out of gear[mesh]. ¶기계가 겉돌았다 The machine failed to engage[catch]. // 두 톱니바퀴가 겉돈다 The two cogwheels don't engage each other. 2 [사람이 어울리지 못하다] do not get along well; be out of keeping (with); do not mix[mingle] (with). 3 [액체 등이 잘 섞이지 않다] do not mix (together). ¶기름과 물은 서로 겉돈다 Oil and water don't mix. / Oil doesn't mix with water.

겉똑똑이 a superficially bright[clever] person.

겉말 mere words; lip service; shallow compliments. ¶~로만 좋게 이야기하다 just talk fair words / be a little too ready with compliments.

겉맞추다 show a surface friendliness (to); flatter; gloss over; temporize.

겉모양 (-模樣) outward appearance; outward show; look; front; outlook. ¶~으로 사람을 판단하다 judge (of) a person by his appearance // ~에 속지 마라 Never be deceived by outward appearance. // 사물은 반드시 ~과 같지는 않다 Appearances are deceptive.

겉물 a liquid floating on another liquid and not mixing with it; supernatant fluid [liquid]. ¶~이 돌다 float on the surface without mixing.

겉보기 (outward) appearance; show; look. ¶~의 surface / outward / seeming // ~로 outwardly / on the surface / in appearance / apparently // ~로 판단하다 judge people by appearances // ~보다 무겁다 be heavier than (it) looks // 그는 ~에는 무뚝뚝하다 He is seemingly blunt. // 그는 ~와는 달리 겁쟁이가 아니다 He is not such a coward as he would appear to be. // 그는 ~에는 평온한 생활을 하고 있었다 To all outward appearances, he was living a peaceful life. // 그는 ~에는 정직해 보인다 He looks honest in appearance [to all appearances]. // 그것은 ~에는 신품이었다 It looked entirely new. // 그녀는 ~에는 온순하나 실로는 성질이 격하나 She looks mild mannered, but actually she has a passionate temperament. // 그는 ~와는 딴판이다 He looks totally different from what he really is.

겉보리 unhulled barley.

겉봉 (-封) an envelope; an outer envelope [wrapper]. ¶~을 뜯다 open[break (open)] an envelope / cut (a letter) open // ~을 쓰다 address an envelope.

겉씨식물 (-植物) [식] gymnosperm; a gymnospermous plant. ¶~의 gymnospermous.

겉약다 clever in a superficial way; superficially smart[sharp]; smart[sharp] merely in show.

겉옷 an outer garment.

겉잎 the outer leaves.

겉잠 [잠자는 체하기] sham[feigned] sleep; [선잠] a nap; a doze; a catnap; (구어) a snooze. ¶~ 자다 pretend to be asleep // ~들다 doze / catnap / snooze / take a nap.

겉잡다 make a rough estimate; estimate roughly. ¶손해는 걷잡아서 3천만 원이다 The (amount of) damage is roughly estimated at thirty million won. // 겉잡아 이틀이면 충분하다 In my estimation two days will be enough.

겉장 (-張) [표지] the cover (of a book); [일면] the front[first] page (of a newspaper).

겉절이 vegetables pickled right before eating.

겉짐작 (-斟酌) a rough guess[estimate] (based on appearances); a random guess. ¶그것은 ~에 지나지 않습니다 It's mere guesswork. 겉짐작하다 guess; make a rough estimate; make a random guess.

겉치레 ostensible decoration[display]; ostentation; outward show; keeping up appearances. ¶이 새 건물이 ~만 번지르한 데 놀랐다 I was appalled by the shoddy construction of the new building. 겉치레하다 dress up; keep up appearance; show off; cut a dash; put on a fair show.

겉치장하다 (-治粧-) dress up[decorate] the outside; make outward show; keep up appearances; put a good face on (a matter); gloss[smooth] over (a fault).

게¹ [동] a crab. ¶~의 집게발 a crab's claws [pincers] // ~한테 물렸다 I was nipped by a crab.

게 눈 감추듯 eat up in less than no time.

게² (것이). ¶네까짓 ~ such a guy[fellow] as you / 그까짓 ~ that sort of thing / a man like him / 제까짓 ~ 무슨 정치가냐 How could a fellow like him be a statesman? / 네까짓 ~ 할 수 있겠나 You never could do it.

게³ [거기] there. ¶~ 누구 있느냐 Is anybody there? / ~ 섰거라 Stop there! / Stop, you there! / ~ 좀 앉아라 Sit down there.

게⁴ [에게] for; to. ¶내~ 온 편지 a letter for me // 내~ 돈이 있다면 … If I had money, … / I wish I had money ….

-게¹ [친근한 명령] do. ¶들어오~ Come in. // 어서 앉~ Sit down. / You sit down. // 많이 먹~ Eat your fill. // 그 일은 자네가 맡~ You take care of the matter.
2 [가정] then won't (it) turn out that …?!; may[might]; will[would]. ¶그랬다간 매 맞~ If I do so, I will get whipped, won't I? / 숙제를 안 하면 큰일 나~ If I didn't do my homework, it would turn serious. // 그런 돈이 있으면 자동차를 사~ If I had so much money, I would buy a car.
3 [의문]. ¶이렇게 작은 책상이 무슨 도움이 되~ What good would such a tiny desk do to you? / 그런 돈을 가지고 무얼 사~ What can you afford to buy with such an amount of money?
4 [내용·정도의 제한]. ¶아름답~ 보이다 look beautiful // 똑똑하~ 생기다 look clever [smart] // 재미있~ 지내다 have a good time // 취하지 않~ 조심해라 See that you do not get drunk. // 감기 들지 않~ 조심해라 Be

게거품

5 [상태의 조성]. ¶행복하~ 하다 make (a person) happy // 흥미진진하~ 하다 make (something) very interesting // 방 안을 깨끗하~ 해 두어라 Keep the room clean.

6 [사역] make (a person) do; cause (a person) to do. ¶물을 마시~ 하다 make (a horse) drink water // 불을 타오르~ 하다 make the fire burn // 아들이 숙제를 하~ 하다 make one's son do his homework.

7 [···하게 되다] come to (do); get to (do); grow into. ¶좋아하~ 되다 begin[get / come] to like (a thing) / develop a fondness for (a girl) // 싫어하~ 되다 conceive a dislike for (a person) // 담배를 피우~ 되다 come to start smoking.

게거품 (게의) foam at the mouth of a crab; (사람·동물의) froth; foam. ¶말의 아가리는 ~투성이었다 The horse was foam-flecked. // 그는 말할 때 입에서 ~을 낸다 He foams[froths] at the mouth when talking.

게걸거리다 grumble; mutter; murmur; growl; complain; (미국 구어) grouch.

게걸들리다 become greedy for food; get an insatiable appetite; have a wolf in one's stomach.

게걸스럽다 greedy (for food); voracious; ravenous; gluttonous; have an insatiable appetite; have a wolf in one's stomach. ¶게걸스럽게 먹다 eat greedily / gobble / eat like a pig // 아이들은 식탁 위의 케이크를 게걸스럽게 먹었다 The children devoured[wolfed down] the cake on the table.

게걸음 a sidewise crawl[movement] of a crab.

게걸음(을) 치다 walk[crawl] sideways; sidle; move sidewise.

게꽁지만 하다 shallow; superficial; short. ¶게꽁지만 한 지식 a superficial knowledge // 게꽁지만 한 학문 가지고 무얼 안다고 그래 What do you know, with you two-bits' worth of education?

-게끔 [-게 5·6·7의 강조]. ¶그녀가 알아듣~ 똑똑히 이야기해라 Speak clearly. So that she understands you. // 그는 늦지 않~ 서둘렀다 He hurried up so as not to[so that he wouldn't] be late. // 뒤탈이 없~ 잘 처리하시오 Manage the matter carefully so that there will be no trouble in the future.

게놈 [생] a genom(e). ¶인간 ~ the human genome.

게다가 1 [그곳에] there; over there; in that place. ¶~ 쓰레기를 버리지 마시오 Don't dump refuse (over) there. // 책을 ~ 놓아라 Put the books there.

2 [거기에 더하여] in addition to (it); on top of (it); what is more; [그리고 또한] moreover; besides; [설상가상으로] to make matters worse. ¶~ 요리도 맛있었다 In addition to that, the food was delicious. // 여관 안주인은 매우 친절했고 ~ 미인이었다 The landlady was very kind, and what's more, she was a beauty. // ~ 그는 덜렁이다 Besides[More over / On top of that] he is a hasty fellow. // ~ 큰비가 쏟아지기 시작했다 To make matters worse, it began to rain heavily. // ~ 나는 50만 원의 상금까지 받았다 In addition I received a prize of five hundred thousand won. // 그는 낭비가 심하다. ~ 제멋대로다 On top of being extravagant, he's selfish as well. // ~ 이까지 쑤시기 시작했다 Moreover[Besides], my tooth began to ache.

게딱지만 하다 be small as a crab shell; be tiny. ¶게딱지만 한 집에 살다 live in a tiny house[a matchbox of a house].

게라 [인] a (printing) galley.
- **게라쇄**(-刷) a galley proof.

게르마늄 [화] germanium (기호 Ge).

게르만 the German (people). ¶~의 Germanic.
- **게르만 민족** the Germanic race. **게르만 어파** the German languages.

게리맨더링 gerrymandering.

게릴라 (전법) guer(r)illa; (사람) a guer(r)illa. ¶~ 도시 guer(r)illa fighting in city street.
- **게릴라 부대** a guer(r)illa band; a partisan unit. **게릴라전** guerrilla warfare. ¶대~ counter guer(r)illa warfare.

게슈타포 Gestapo.

게스트 a guest.
- **게스트 싱어** a guest singer.

게슴츠레하다 sleepy; dull; heavy; drowsy. ¶게슴츠레한 눈으로 bleary-eyed / with bleary eyes // 눈이 게슴츠레해지다 become[get] bleary // 잠이 와서 눈이 게슴츠레하군 Your eyes look heavy. / You are heavy-eyed. / You have heavy eyes.

게시(揭示) a notice; a notification; a placard; a bulletin. ¶입장 사절의 ~ a "No Admission" sign // ~를 벽에 붙이다 tack a notice to the wall(압정으로) / pin up a notice on the wall(편으로) / stick [fasten / fix] a sign on the wall(풀로). **게시하다** post [put up] a notice; notify; placard (a board with a bill). →¶다음 달 예정이 게시되었다 The schedule for next month has been posted. // 성적이 벽에 게시되었다 The results (of the examination) were posted on the wall.
- **게시판** a notice[bulletin] board; (미) a billboard.

게재비 [동] a water stick.

게양하다(揭揚-) put up; hoist; fly; raise; display. ¶국기를 ~ hoist[raise / put up] a national flag // 광복절을 축하하여 국기를 ~ display the national flag in honor of the Independence Day of Korea.

게염나다 become covetous.

게염스럽다 greedy; (서술적) be covetous. ¶너 정말 게염스럽구나 How covetous you are!

게우다 1 (먹은 것을) vomit; throw up; bring up. ¶먹은 것을 다 게웠다 I threw up [vomited] all I had eaten. // 게울 것 같다 I feel nauseated[sick]. / I feel like vomiting. **2** (부정 이익을) disgorge; repay [refund / give up] ill-gotten money. ¶그는 횡령한 돈을 게워 냈다 He repaid what he had seized unlawfully. // 도둑은 훔친 것을 게워 냈다 The thief disgorged his ill-gotten gains.

게으르다 lazy; idle; indolent; slothful; sluggish. ¶게으른 임원들 lazy executives // 그들은 자기 임무를 수행하는 데 ~ They are lax [remiss] in carrying out their duties. // 그는 손가락 하나 까딱 안 할 정도로 ~ He is a perfect[regular] lazybones. / He is laziness itself. // 그는 게으르게도 심부름꾼을 대신 보냈다 Out of laziness he sent[He lazily sent] a messenger instead of going himself.

게으름 laziness; idleness; indolence; sluggishness; sloth; [태만] neglect. ¶~ 피우다[부리다] be idle[lazy] / loaf / slacken one's efforts / idle one's time away.

● 게으름뱅이 an idler; a lazybones; a do-nothing; a sluggard; a dawdler.

게을러빠지다 very lazy[idle]; quite indolent [slothful]. ¶너는 게을러빠져서 못 쓰겠다 You are a good-for-nothing lazybones.

게을리 lazily; idly; indolently.; sluggishly; negligently. ¶~ 하다 [등한히 하다] neglect (one's duties); be negligent[neglectful] (of duty) / slight (one's work) // 학업을[근무를] ~ 하다 neglect one's studies[duties] // 일을 ~ 하다 slight one's work // 문단속을 ~ 하다 neglect[forget] to lock the door // 일[숙제]을 ~ 해서는 안 된다 Don't neglect your work [homework]. / 경계를 ~ 하지 마라 Don't be caught off guard. / Keep your eyes open.

게이 [남성 동성애자] a gay.

게이머 a gamer. ¶그는 훌륭한 ~이다 He is a good gamer.

게이지 [인] ga(u)ge; [측정 계기] a gage. ¶표준 ~ the standard gauge.

게임 a game. ¶실내 ~ an indoor game / a parlor game // 낮 ~ a day game // 콜드[드론 / 퍼펙트] ~ a called[drawn / perfect] game // 시범[비공식] ~ an exhibition game // ~ 을 하다 play a game // 그는 ~ 운영이 훌륭하다 He's very good at strategy.

● 게임차 [야구] games behind (the leading team)(▶ 신문 등에서는 G.B.라 생각함). ¶타이거즈는 자이언츠에 3~로 앞서고 있다 The Tigers are three games ahead of the Giants. 게임 포인트 game point.

게자리 [천] the Crab; the Cancer.

게장(-醬) 1 [게젓 간장] soy sauce in which crabs are preserved; crab preserved in soy sauce. 2 pickled[salted] crabs. ⇨ 게젓

게재(揭載) publication; insertion; printing. ¶잡지에 ~ 중인 연재물 a serial running in a magazine. 게재하다 (신문·잡지 등이) carry; run; (광고 등을) insert. ¶다음 호(號)에 게재할 예정 to appear in the next issue // 신문에 광고를 ~ insert[run] an ad(vertisement) in a newspaper // 신문은 일부러 그 사건의 기사를 게재하지 않았다 The paper deliberately left the affair unreported.➔¶회의의 진행 상황이 신문에 게재되었다 The progress of the conference was reported in the newspaper. / The newspaper ran a report of the progress of the conference. // 이 칼럼은 매주 목요일에 게재된다 This column appears every Thursday. // 짧막한 공식 통고가 그 신문에 게재되어 있었다 The newspaper carried a short official announcement about it.

● 게재 금지 a press ban; a ban on publication; prohibition of publication.

게젓 pickled[salted] crabs.

게정내다 grumble; complain; be querulous.

게트림 an arrogant belch; belching in a haughty manner. 게트림하다 belch arrogantly; belch in a haughty manner.

겔 [화] gel.

겟투 (*"get two") [야구] a twin killing; a double play. ¶~를 하다 get two runners out at once / make a double play // 그는 ~를 당했다 He hit into a double play.

겨 chaff; hulls[husks] of grain; bran. ¶겉~ (outer) husks / hulls / chaff // 쌀~ rice bran.

겨냥 1 [겨누기] aim; aiming. ¶~이 틀리다[빗나가다] aim wrong(ly) (at) / take one's mark amiss / miss one's aim[the mark] / go wild of the mark[target] // ~ 대다 bring into aim.

겨냥하다 aim[take aim] (at); set one's sights (on). ¶그는 총을 겨냥하여 발사하였다 He took aim with his gun and fired. // 그는 정확히 겨냥하여 과녁의 중심에 명중시켰다 He fired and hit the bull's eye with an unerring aim. 2 [치수] measure; size; dimension ¶발~ foot size // 신 ~ shoe size // ~ 내다 take the measure[dimension] (of). 겨냥하다 take dimension; measure off the size. ¶자로 ~ take measure with a rule.

● 겨냥대 a measuring rod; a yardstick. 겨냥도(-圖) a (rough) sketch; a sketch map [drawing].

겨누다 1 [겨냥하다] aim[take aim] (at); sight (a target); set one's sights (on); draw[get / take] a bead (on); level (a gun at); point (a gun at). ¶정확히 ~ take accurate aim (at) // 겨누지 않고 쏘다 shoot at random // 겨누어[군] Present! // 총으로 사냥감을 ~ aim at a game with one's gun / level one's gun at a game // 사나이가 총을 겨누고 다가왔다 A man approached with a gun leveled[aimed] at us. // 그는 새를 겨누어 총을 발사했다 He aimed[took aim with] his gun at the bird and fired. // 나는 그의 명치를 겨누어 공격했다 I struck at the pit of his stomach. 2 [대보다] measure; take measure[the dimensions] of; measure off the size.

겨드랑이 1 (신체의) the armpit; the axilla (pl. -lae, ~s). ¶~의 underarm / axillary / alar // ~에 땀이 나다 sweat under the arm // ~를 간질이다 tickle (a person) under the arm // ~를 긁다 scratch under[in] the armpit // 우산을 ~에 끼고 걷다 walk with an umbrella under one's arm. 2 (옷의) the armhole. ¶~가 타져 있다 There is a rip at the armhole.

겨레 [한 자손] offspring of the same forefather; [동포] brothers; brethren; fellow countrymen; one's countrymen; compatriots; [민족] a race; a people; a nation. ¶한~ one and the same people.

● 겨레붙이 members of a people[nation].

겨루다 pit (one's skill against); rival; compete [vie] (with); struggle (with). ¶힘을 ~ measure one's strength (with / against) / measure oneself against another in strength // 기량을 ~ match one's skill (against) // 힘 겨루기를 하다 compete (with a person) in physical strength // 솜씨를 ~ compete (with a person) in some art // 권력을 ~ struggle with one another for power // 너하고는 겨룰 재간이 없다 I am no match for you. // 그는 겨루어 볼 만한 상대다 He is one of my matching rivals. // 수수께끼로 지혜를 겨루자 Let's test each other's wits with riddles. // 우리나라는 문화 활동에서 다른 나라들과 겨루고 있다 Our country is competing with other countries for excellence in cultural activities. // 그들은 우승을 겨루고 있다 They are competing [vying] (with each other) for the championship. // 우리는 연인을 두고 겨룬 사이다 We were rivals in love. // 지금까지 그와 세 번 겨룬 적이 있다 I have been pitted[matched] against him three times.

겨룸 contest; competition; rivalry; contention; measuring[pitting] one's strength[talent] (with / against). ¶힘~ a contest of physical strength / a strength contest.

겨를 leisure; leisure time[hours]; free[spare] time; time to spare. ¶~이 없다 have no

거리 leisure / have no time to spare // 눈코 뜰 ~이 없다 be so busily engaged (in a matter) // 좀처럼 ~이 없다 I am seldom at leisure. // 아무리 바빠도 부모님에게 편지 쓸 ~은 있었을 거야 However busy you were, you might have had odd moments to write to your parents. // 불시에 일어난 일이라 숙고할 ~이 없었다 The accident was too sudden to allow time for calm deliberation. // 너무 바빠서 앉아 있을 ~이 없다 I'm busy every moment. / I don't have any time to sit down and vest. / (구어) I'm (so busy I have to be) on the go all the time. // 청소년 폭력의 사례는 열거할 ~이 없을 정도다 Instances of juvenile violences are too numerous to mention one by one.

거리 a plow drawn by a yoke of (two) oxen.

겨우 [간신히] barely; hardly; narrowly; [애써서] with much difficulty [effort]; [고작] only; merely; but; no more than. ¶~ 3일 동안 for only three days // ~ 입에 풀칠한다 live barely / keep body and soul together // 저녁이 되어서야 ~ 그 일을 마쳤다 I was not till evening that I finished the work. // 그는 ~ 기차 시간에 댔다 He barely managed to catch the train. // 우리는 시합에 ~ 이겼다 We won a game by a narrow [small] margin. // 그는 ~ 시험에 합격했다 He passed the examination with (great) difficulty. / (구어) He just squeezed through the exam. // 그는 적은 임금으로 ~ 살아간다 He makes out on a small wage. // 나는 ~ 그를 설득시켰다 I succeeded in persuading him with great difficulty. / It took a great deal of effort to persuade him.

겨우내 throughout the winter; all through the winter; all winter long. ¶~ 눈이 온다 It snows all winter through. // 작년에는 ~ 시골에 가 있었다 I stayed in the country all winter.

겨우살이¹ [겨울 용품] winter goods; (월동) passing the winter. ¶~ 준비 preparations for the winter // 나는 ~ 준비로 바쁘다 I am busy preparing for winter.

겨우살이² [식] a mistletoe; a parasite; a parasitic plant.

겨울 winter; the winter season. ¶~의 winter / wintry // 한~에 in midwinter / in the depth of winter // ~ 준비를 하다 prepare for the (coming) winter // ~을 지내다 pass the winter (in / at) // 날씨가 ~다워졌다 It is beginning to feel like winter. / It has grown wintry. // 산에서는 11월이면 ~이다 In the mountains winter comes in November. // (지난 ~은) 따뜻한[추운] ~이었다 We had a mild [severe] winter. // 그는 ~ 스포츠를 즐긴다 He enjoys winter sports. // ~이 오면 봄은 멀지 않으리 If winter comes, can spring be far behind? ●**겨울날** winter days; the winter weather. **겨울 방학** a winter vacation; winter holidays. **겨울잠** winter sleep; hibernation. **겨울철** the winter season; the winter (time)

겨워하다 feel something to be too much for one; feel something is more than one can manage; feel something is out of hand. ¶일을 (힘을) ~ feel the job is too much for one / be loath to take on a job // 그 젊은 과부는 혼자서 세 자녀를 기르는 것을 힘에 겨워하고 있다 The young widow feels it beyond her ability to take care of her three children by herself.

겨자 (양념) mustard; (풀) a mustard (plant). ¶~를 친 음식 food dressed with mustard. ●**겨자씨** (a) mustard seed.

격(格) 1 [지위·등급] (a) standing; (a) status; (a) rank; (a) class; (a) grade; (an) order. ¶우두머리 ~의 사람 the boss // 그 사람이 사회적으로는 나보다 ~이 위다 He is above me in social status. / He ranks above me socially. // 그는 우리와는 ~이 다르다 He is on a different level from us. / (구어) He's not in the same league as we are. // 그는 형과는 인물의 ~이 다르다 He stands no comparison with his brother. 2 [자격] capacity; character. ¶~에 맞지 않는 짓을 하다 go out of one's character / play an unbecoming part. 3 [언] (a) case. ¶주[소유/목적] ~ the nominative [possessive / objective] case. 4 [논] (삼단 논법의) a figure; a schema (*pl. -mata*). 5 (셈). ¶소 잃고 외양간 고치는 ~이다 That is (an instance of) shutting the stable door after the horse is stolen. // 그것은 공중에 누각을 짓는 ~이다 That is, as it were, building a castle in the air.

격감(激減) a sharp decrease; a marked decline. **격감하다** decrease [decline / fall off] sharply [remarkably]. ¶출석자 수가 격감했다 The attendance has fallen off markedly. // 수입이 격감했다 There is a big drop [a marked falling off] in imports. // 전쟁으로 인구가 격감했다 The population decreased sharply as a result of the war.

격납고(格納庫) a hangar; an airplane [aviation] shed; an airshed. ¶이동~ a portable hangar.

격년(隔年) every other [second] year; alternate years. ¶~ 간행의 biennial // 총회는 ~으로 개최된다 The general meeting is held every other [second] year. **격년하다** have not seen each other for more than a year.

격노(激怒) rage; fury; violent anger; wrath; exasperation. **격노하다** be enraged (by / at); be infuriated (by / at); fly into a rage. ¶격노하여 in a rage / in the fury of one's passion // 격노케 하다 infuriate / enrage.

격돌(激突) a clash. **격돌하다** clash. ¶그 문제로 나는 그와 격돌했다 I clashed with him about the matter.

격동(激動) excitement; agitation; (사회의) turbulence; convulsions. **격동하다** be greatly excited. ¶격동하는 사회 정세 turbulent social conditions // 전국적으로 민심이 격동하고 있다 Excitement prevails throughout [across] the country.

격랑(激浪) raging [angry] waves; a heavy [high] sea. ¶~에 휩쓸리다 be swept away [gulped down] by the angry waves // ~이 태산 같았다 Angry seas and frantic waves were mountain high. // ~이 하늘을 찌를 듯했다 Raging billows beat against the sky.

격려(激勵) encouragement; urging; incitement. ¶~의 encouraging // ~의 편지[말] a letter [words] of encouragement // 당신이 병문안 가면 환자에게 ~가 될 것이다 I think a visit from you would cheer the patient up. // 이 편지는 그에게 ~가 될 것이다 This letter will be a great encouragement to him. / This

letter will encourage him. **격려하다** encourage (a person to do); cheer (up). ¶선수를 ~ cheer a player on // 더욱 노력하도록 ~ inspire (a person) to further efforts // 그는 부하들을 격려했다 He encouraged his men. // 연구를 계속하도록 그를 격려하였다 I encouraged him to continue his research.
● **격려사** words of encouragement; stirring remarks; (미국 구어) a chin-up sermon.

격렬하다 (激烈-) violent; severe; intense. ¶격렬한 지진 a violent earthquake / 격렬한 말 violent language // 격렬한 폭풍우[공격] a violent storm[attack] // 격렬한 성질 a violent [fiery] temper // 격렬한 아픔 acute[intense / severe] pain // 격렬한 반대 vigorous opposition // 경쟁은 격렬했다 The competition was fierce. // 선거전이 더욱 더 격렬해졌다 The election campaign grew more and more heated. **격렬히** violently; severely; intensely. ¶~ 비난하다 criticize a person severely / make a scathing criticism.

격론 (激論) a heated[hot] discussion[argument]; a warm[a violent] controversy. ¶국회에서 ~이 벌어졌었다 A very vehement debate took place in the Assembly. / There was a hot passage of arms in the Assembly. **격론하다** argue[debate] hotly; have a heated discussion[a bitter controversy]. ¶나는 그 문제로 아버지와 격론했다[~을 벌였다] I had a heated argument with my father over the matter.

격류 (激流) a torrent; a swift current; rapids. ¶보트는 ~에 휩쓸리고 말았다 The boat was swallowed up in the torrent.

격리 (隔離) [고립] isolation; (전염병 환자의) quarantine; (흑인에 대한) (미) segregation. ¶그는 ~ 기간이 끝났다 He is out of quarantine. **격리하다** isolate; quarantine; segregate. ¶환자를 ~ isolate a patient / keep a patient in isolation. ➔격리된 집 a house in quarantine / 외부로부터 격리되어 있다 be hedged off from the outer world // 그는 콜레라로 격리되었다 He was quarantined[put in quarantine] with cholera.
● **격리 병실** [병동] an isolation[a segregation] room[ward]. **격리 환자** a patient segregated from the others; an isolated patient.

격막 (膈膜) [의] the diaphragm; [생] the septum (pl. -ta, -tums); a dissepiment.

격멸 (擊滅) destruction; extermination; annihilation. **격멸하다** destroy; exterminate; annihilate; wipe out; rout.

격무 (激務) hard[strenuous] work; a busy office; an exhausting post; a severe duty; an arduous task; [일의 분망] pressure of business. ¶~를 떠맡다 undertake [(구어) tackle] a demanding job // ~로 쓰러지다 break down under the strain of the hard work required // 매일 ~에 쫓기고 있다 I am extremely busy with pressing duties every day.

격문 (檄文) a written appeal; a manifesto (pl. ~(e)s); a declaration; [고급문(告急文)] a dispatch. ¶~을 띄우다 issue a written appeal / send a manifesto[declaration] (to) / [호소하다] appeal (to) / 전국에 ~을 띄우다 make a nationwide appeal in writing

격발 (激發) (병의) a sudden fit; a spasm; (감정 등의) an outburst; a fit; a flush. ¶감정의 ~ an outburst of emotion / (속어) a flare-up.

격발하다 burst forth; break out; explode; [야기시키다] provoke (a person) to (anger). ¶계급의식을 ~ awake (a person) suddenly to class consciousness. ➔정부의 조치는 반대 운동을 격발시켰다 The government's actions provoked[touched off] a protest movement.
격발 (擊發) percussion.
● **격발 장치** percussion lock.

격벽 (隔壁) a partition (wall); [해][광] a bulkhead; [동] a septum (pl. -ta, ~s); [식] a dissepiment; [화] a diaphragm. ¶방화용 ~ a fire wall // 방수[구면 / 선수(船首)] ~ watertight[spherical / collision] bulkhead.

격변 (激變) a sudden[violent] change; (사회의) an upheaval; (감정의) revulsion; [지] a cataclysm. ¶환경[기후]의 ~ rapid changes in the environment[weather] // 그 전쟁은 사회적 ~의 원인이 되었다 The war caused social upheavals[a rapid change of society]. **격변하다** undergo a sudden[violent] change; change suddenly[violently].

격 변화 (格變化) [언] (a) declension.

격분 (激忿) [격노] rage; fury; violent anger; wrath. **격분하다** be enraged (by / at); be infuriated (by / at); fly into a rage. ¶격분하여 in a rage[fury] // 격분한 군중이 그를 두들겨 팼다 The enraged crowd beat him up. ➔ ¶국무총리의 실언이 국민을 격분시켰다 The Prime Minister's careless remark enraged [infuriated] the people.

격분 (激奮) [몹시 분개함] vehement indignation[resentment]; great[high] dudgeon. **격분하다** become vehemently angry; burn with indignation; flare[blow] up. ¶격분하여 in great[high / deep] dudgeon / in hot[warm] blood // 그는 격분했다 He was stung to fury. // 그는 무시당하여 격분하고 있었다 He was boiling over with rage at finding himself ignored.

격상 (格上) elevation in rank. **격상하다** raise [promote] (a person to a higher rank); upgrade. ➔그 과는 독립 기관으로 격상되었다 The section was upgraded to (the rank of) an independent agency.

격세 (隔世) 1 [먼 세대] a distant[different] age; another age. 2 [세대를 거름] every second generation.
● **격세 유전** [생] (a) reversion; (a) throwback; (an) atavism. **격세지감** ¶텔레비전이 없었던 시절을 생각하면 ~이 있다 The days when there was no television seem to belong to a different age.

격식 (格式) [형식의 준수] formality; [사회의 관습] social rules; a (fixed) rule; an established form. ¶~을 차려 in a formal manner // ~을 차리다 be formal / be ceremonious / stand on ceremony / be stiff // ~을 차리지 않고 without formality / without ceremony // ~을 따지다 be particular about formalities / ~을 차린 말을 쓰다 use [speak in] formal[stiff] language // 그녀는 매사에 ~을 좋아한다 She likes to be ceremonious about everything. // 그는 ~에 까다로운 사람이다 He is a stickler for form. // ~은 생략하기로 합시다 Let's dispense with formalities [ceremony]. // 그는 언제나 너무 ~만 차리고 있다 He always stands on ceremony. // 그렇게 ~ 차리지 마세요. Please don't be so formal. / Please talk freely. // 그는 ~을 차

격심하다 러 인사를 했다 He greeted us in a stiff [ceremonious / formal] manner.// 이 집에서는 ~ 따위는 필요 없소 There is no need for ceremony in this house. / You needn't stand on formality in this house.

격심하다(激甚-) [세차다] violent; strong; vehement; fierce; furious; [심하다] intense; acute; severe; keen. ¶격심한 불황 acute business depression // 격심한 더위[추위] intense [extreme / severe] heat [cold] // 격심한 경쟁 keen competition // 격심한 폭풍우 a violent [heavy] storm // 격심한 타격을 입다 receive a terrible blow // 그는 격심한 경쟁을 이겨 왔다 He came through successfully in very tough competition. // 취직난이 격심해졌다 The difficulty of finding employment has become acute [aggravated].

격앙(激昂) [흥분] excitement; [분격] resentment; indignation. **격앙하다** be excited (about); flare up; lose one's temper [head]; be indignant (about / at); (구어) get (all) worked up. ¶격앙한 군중 an enraged crowd // 격앙하기 쉬운 excitable / choleric / hotheaded // 격앙하여 in a rage [fury]

격언(格言) [금언] a proverb; [속담] a (common) saying; [처세훈] a maxim. ¶~에 이르기를 「세월은 사람을 기다리지 않는다」고 했다 According to a maxim [As the proverb has it / As the proverb says / There is a saying that], "Time and tide wait for no man."

격월(隔月) every other [second] month; alternate months; a month's interval. ¶~의 bimonthly // 이 잡지는 ~로 나온다 This magazine is published every other month.

격의(隔意) reserve; [소원] estrangement; alienation. ¶~ 있는 reserved / distant / cold // ~ 없는 unreserved / confidential // ~ 없는 말투 an open [a frank] way of speaking // ~ 없는 회담 a frank [confidential] talk // 그와 ~ 없이 이야기를 나누었다 I talked with him frankly [without reserve]. / I had a heart-to-heart talk with him. // 우리는 서로 ~ 없는 의견을 교환한 후 더욱 친해졌다 After exchanging our frank opinions we became friendlier.

격일(隔日) every other [second] day; a day's interval. ¶~ 근무로 on a two-day shift // ~로 일하다 shift once in two days // 그는 ~로 백모를 방문한다 He calls on his aunt every other [second] day. **격일하다** have a day's interval.

격자(格子) 1 (창문 등의) a lattice; (쇠 등의) a grid; a grating; (문 등에 장식된) a grille; (천장들의) a coffer. ¶쇠 ~가 끼워진 창 an iron-barred window // ~로 된 of lattice / latticed / coffered (ceiling). 2 (대나무로 된 갓끈의) decorative beads threaded [put] on the string of a Korean top hat.

●**격자무늬** a checked pattern; cross stripes.
격자 세공 latticework; latticing. **격자창** a lattice(d) window.

격전(激戰) (전투의) a fierce [hot] battle; a severe fight [engagement]; (선거 등의) a hot contest. ¶~이 한창 벌어지고 있다 in the thick of a severe battle // ~이 벌어지고 있다 A fierce battle [violent fighting] is raging [going on] // 옛날 여기서 ~이 있었다 A fierce battle once have fought here. // 이번 선거는 ~이어서 전직 장관이 여러 사람 낙선했다 The last election was such a hot contest that several ex-ministers lost. **격전하다** fight fiercely [hotly]; (선거 등에서) contest (an election) hotly.

●**격전지** a hard-fought field; (선거의) a closely contested constituency; (미) a close district.

격정(激情) passion; a violent emotion; [분노] wild anger; fury. ¶~의 발작 a fit of passion [temper] // ~에 못 이겨 in a fit of passion [anger] / out of temper // ~을 억누르다 hold the passion in check

격조(格調) (문예 작품의) tone; style; rhythm; swing; (사람의) character; personality. ¶~ 높은 작품 a work of high tone // ~ 높은 연설 a speech with style.

격조하다(隔阻-) (소식을) be silent; be remiss in writing; neglect to write; (방문을) be remiss in calling; neglect to call. ¶격조하였습니다 (편지에서) I haven't written to you for a long time. / (만나서) I haven't been to see you for a long time. / 격조하였음을 용서하십시오 (편지에서) Excuse me for not writing for such a long time. / (만나서) It's been ages [a long time] since I saw you last.

격주(隔週) every other [second] week; a weekly interval. ¶~ 간행물 a fortnightly / a biweekly // ~의 잡지 a biweekly magazine / a fortnightly // ~(간행) fortnightly / biweekly // ~ 화요일에 every second [other] Tuesday / on alternate Tuesdays // 그는 ~로 상경한다 He comes to Seoul every two weeks [every other week]. **격주하다** have a weekly interval.

격증(激增) a sudden [rapid / marked] increase [rise]; (물의) a heavy swell. ¶주문의 ~ a rush of orders // 우리는 범죄의 ~으로 애를 먹고 있다 We are having trouble in dealing with the marked [sharp] increase in the crime rate. **격증하다** increase suddenly [rapidly / sharply]; show a sudden increase; (물의) rise [swell] rapidly. ¶백만으로 ~ jump [leap] to 1,000,000 (people / packages) // 이 도시는 인구가 격증했다 This town has grown rapidly in population.

격지다(隔-) be [become] estranged [alienated] (from); be on bad terms (with); be at odds (with).

격진(激震) a severe earthquake; a severe [violent] shock (of earthquake). ¶어젯밤 샌프란시스코에 ~이 있었다 A severe shock was felt in San Francisco last night. // 이 지방은 ~에 휩쓸렸다 This district was hit by a severe earthquake.

격차(隔差) [차이] a difference; [간격] a gap. ¶기술의 ~ a technological gap // 대기업과 중소기업 간의 노동 조건의 ~ disparity of working conditions between large-scale enterprises and smaller ones // 소득 ~을 없애다 abolish earnings differentials // 부유한 나라와 빈곤한 나라 간의 ~를 좁히다 narrow the gap between the rich and the poor nations // 그 물건은 값에 따라 품질에 ~가 있다 The goods differ in quality according to their price.

격찬(激讚) high praise; a high tribute. ¶~을 받다 win high praise // 그 소년은 착한 행동으로 ~을 받았다 The boy was highly praised for his good conduct. **격찬하다** praise highly; speak highly of; admire extravagantly. ¶용기를 ~ praise (a person) highly for (his)

courage // 두 음악 평론가가 이 젊은 지휘자를 격찬했다 Two music critics spoke very highly of[(문어) extolled] this young conductor.

격추하다(擊墜-) shoot down; bring down; down (a plane). ¶적기 가운데 두 대를 ~ shoot[bring] down two of the enemy planes. →¶폭격기는 격추되어 불꽃에 휩싸였다 The bomber was hit and went down in flames.

격침(擊沈) sinking; destruction. **격침하다** (attack and) sink (a ship); send (a ship) to the bottom. ¶어뢰로 ~ torpedo (and sink) (a ship). →¶잠수함에 격침당하다 be torpedoed and sunk by a submarine // 배는 미사일에 의해 격침되었다 The ship was hit and sunk by a missile.

격통(激痛) an acute[a sharp / a severe] pain. ¶위에 ~을 느끼다 feel an acute pain[a stab of pain] in one's stomach.

격퇴(擊退) a repulse; dislodgement. **격퇴하다** repulse; drive[beat] back[off]. ¶모든 공격을 ~ beat off[repulse / repel] all assaults // 그들은 적을 격퇴하는 데 성공했다 They succeeded in repelling the enemy. ¶격퇴당하다 be driven back / meet with a repulse.

격투(格鬪) a grapple; a fight; (구어) a tussle; fisticuffs; a hand-to-hand fight; (난투) a scuffle. **격투하다** fight (with); grapple (with); come to fisticuffs[blows]; fight hand to hand (with). ¶그는 격투하여 적병을 죽였다 He killed the enemy soldier in hand-to-hand combat.

격투(激鬪) a fierce[severe / furious] fight; hot [harsh / heavy] fighting. **격투하다** fight fiercely[severely / furiously / desperately].

격파(擊破) defeating; beating out; destruction. **격파하다** (적을) defeat (the enemy); beat; (put to) rout; crush; (때려 부수다) destroy (an enemy warship); [논파하다] refute (one's opponent). ¶적의 기갑 부대를 ~ smash the enemy's armored unit // 아군은 적을 격파하고 전진했다 Our troops smashed through the enemy lines and advanced.

격하(格下) demotion; degradation; downgrading. **격하하다** demote; lower the status [position] (of); lower (a person) in rank; demean (oneself); downgrade. →¶그는 과장에서 평사원으로 격하되었다 He was demoted from being a section head to the status of ordinary employee.

격하다(隔-) (거리를) separate; set apart; leave a space (between); [막다] screen; shield; [사이에 두다] interpose; (시간을) leave an interval (between). ¶길을 하나 격하여 across a street / over a road // 2주일을 격하여 after an interval of two weeks / after a two-weeks[two-weeks'] interval // 나는 그와 테이블을 격하고 앉아 있었다 I sat across the table from him.

격하다(激-) [흥분하다] (get) excited; [격노하다] (be) enraged; (말 등이) become violent. ¶격하여 excitedly / [격노하여] furiously // 격한 말 violent language // 격하기 쉬운 [흥분하기 쉬운] excitable / hot-tempered / [노하기 쉬운] irritable / touchy // 격한 어조로 말하다 speak in a harsh tone // 말이 점점 격해졌다 Words ran high.

격화(激化) intensification; [악화] aggravation; worsening. ¶당쟁의 ~ the intensification of the party strife. **격화하다** intensify; be intensified; be aggravated; worsen. ¶게릴라 전은 계속 격화하였다 The guerrilla war continued to intensify[get worse]. →¶내 말이 그의 감정을 격화시켰다 He grew excited at my words.

겪다 1 [경험하다] undergo; suffer; endure; experience; go through. ¶어려움을 ~ experience hardships / have a hard time (of it) // 수많은 고난을 ~ go through hardships and privations // 실제로 ~ have a personal experience of // 이런 추위는 처음 겪어 본다 This is the coldest weather I have ever experienced. // 그녀는 세상 고생을 겪어 보지 못했다 She has not experienced the troubles of this world. // 많은 곤란을 겪고 나서 마침내 그는 성공했다 After experiencing[going though] many difficulties, he finally succeeded. // 겪어 보니 그는 좋은 사람이었다 On further acquaintance I found him a jolly fellow.

2 [대접하다] entertain; have a guest. ¶손님을 ~ entertain a guest.

견(絹) silk.

견갑(肩胛) [생] the shoulder.
● **견갑골**(-骨) [생] a shoulder blade; a bladebone; a scapula (pl. -lae, ~s); an omoplate. **견갑 관절** the shoulder joint.

견강부회(牽强附會) a far-fetched[distorted / strained] reasoning[interpretation]. ¶~의 설명 a self-styled explanation. **견강부회하다** stretch a point; twist an argument.

견고하다(堅固-) strong; solid; [확고하다] steady; steadfast; firm. ¶견고한 요새 a strong fortress // 견고한 건물 a solid building / 견고한 창고 a strongly-built warehouse / 견고한 가구 solid furniture / a solid piece of furniture // 그의 견고한 결심 his firm resolve // 견고한 의지 a strong will / 방비(防備)는 be strongly fortified // 견 고 하 게 하 다 strengthen / make firm[solid] / solidify // 적의 방비는 예상외로 견고했다 The defense of the enemy was much stronger than expected.

견과(堅果) [식] a nut.

견디다 1 [참다] endure; bear; stand; put up with; tolerate; suffer. ¶견디다 어려운 unbearable / intolerable // 견디다 못해 unable to bear[endure] any longer // 꾹 참고 ~ bear (the pain) stoically[manfully / patiently / with patience] // 끝까지 ~ hold fast to the end // 여름 더위를 ~ bear[stand] the heat of summer // 견디기 어려운 더위다 The heat is unbearable. / It is intolerably hot. // 그의 가혹한 처사는 견디기 어려웠다 I could not endure his cruelty. / His cruelty was too much for me. // 그는 온갖 어려움을 견디어 냈다 He held up through all sorts of hardships. // 나는 그것을 더는 견딜 수 없다 I cannot endure[stand] it any longer. // 후덥지근해서 못 견디겠다 This hot humid weather is too much for me. // 방이 더워서 견딜 수가 없었다 I could not stand the heat in the room. // 저 냄새는 정말 견딜 수 없다 I can't stand[bear] that smell. / That smell is simply unbearable. // 시끄러워서 견딜 수 없다 The noise is beyond endurance. // 월급이 조금도 오르지 않으니 견딜 수 없다 The intolerable thing[what's so intolerable] is that my salary is never raised. // 나는 머리가 빠개지듯 아파 못 견디겠다 I can't bear the splitting headache. // 더 이상 견딜 수 없다 This

견문

is more than I can bear.// 참으로 견딜 수 없는 사람들이다 They are insufferable [obnoxious].

2 [지탱하다] support; stand; bear; hold (out); [오래가다] wear; last long. ¶열 stand [bear up against] heat// 그 다리는 홍수에 견디었다 The bridge held out against the flood.// 이 건물은 아직 백 년은 더 견딜 것이다 This building will stand another century.// 이 빌딩은 심한 지진에도 견딜 수 있게 지어져 있다 This building was constructed to stand even severe earthquakes.

3 [살아가다] make a living; subsist support oneself. ¶얼마 안 되는 월급으로 견디어 나가다 live on a small salary// 그럭저럭 견디어 나가다 manage to live / rub along.

견문(見聞) [지식] information; knowledge; [경험] experience; [관찰] observation. ¶~을 넓히다 add to [enlarge] one's experience / widen [increase] one's knowledge / see more of the world// 그 사람은 ~이 넓다 He is well-informed. / He has seen much of the world. **견문하다** observe; experience; see and hear.

● **견문록** a record of personal experiences.

견물생심(見物生心) Seeing is wanting.; The object gives rise to the desire.; Opportunity makes the thief.

견방(絹紡) silk-reeling. ⇨견사 방적(⇨견사(絹絲))

견본(見本) (상품의) a sample; [표본] a specimen; (무늬 등의) a pattern; (서적의) a sample copy. ¶상품 ~ a trade sample// 선적 ~ a shipment [shipping] sample// 수출 ~ an export sample// 표준 ~ a standard sample// 품질 ~ a quality sample// 만 못하다 be below the sample// ~과 같다 be [come] up to [correspond with] the sample// ~과 다르다 differ from sample// ~대로 according to [as per] sample / same as sample// 이것은 ~과 같지 않다 This does not correspond with the sample.// 보내온 물건은 ~과 같았다 [같지 않았다] The article sent to us was up to [did not come up to] the sample.// 자세한 내용을 알려 주십시오. ~을 보내 주시면 더욱 고맙겠습니다 We would like to be given further details. Samples would be specially welcome.

● **견본 검사** sampling inspection. **견본 매매** sales by sample. **견본 시장** a sample fair. ¶국제 ~ an international trade fair.

견본(絹本) silk cloth for painting on; silk canvas.

견사(絹紗) silk and (silk) gauze.

견사(絹絲) a silk-thread. ¶인조 ~ rayon.

● **견사 방적** silk-reeling; silk-spinning.

견습(見習) (일) probation; apprenticeship; (사람) a probationer; an apprentice. ¶~으로 일하다 serve as an apprentice / serve on trial [probation]// 그는 인쇄 공장에 ~으로 가 있다 He is apprenticed to a printer. **견습하다** receive training (in); practice oneself (in a trade); learn (by observation). ¶사무를 ~ learn the business routine of an office / learn how to conduct business// 그는 3년간 대장간에서 견습했다 He served a three years' apprenticeship under a blacksmith.

● **견습공** an apprentice. **견습 기자** a cub reporter; a junior reporter. **견습생** an apprentice; a student; a trainee; a probationer; (미국 구어) a cub.

견식(見識) [지식] knowledge; information; [뛰어난 판단력] judgment; [통찰력] discernment; insight; [견해] views; an opinion. ¶~이 있는 사람 a man of insight [good judgment / principle / penetration] / a discerning man / a well-informed person// ~이 있다 [자기 의견을 가지고 있다] have an opinion of one's own / [안식(眼識)이 있다] have a broad vision / be farsighted / have an insight / [견문·학식이 있다] be well-informed.

견실하다(堅實-) solid; steady; steadfast; sound; [믿음직하다] trustworthy; reliable. ¶견실한 청년 a steady [trustworthy / reliable] young man// 견실한 사람 a sterling fellow// 견실한 사상 [판단] sound thought [judgment / ideas]// 견실한 사업 a sound line of business// 견실한 은행원 a trustworthy [reliable] bank clerk// 견실한 투자 a safe [solid / sound] investment// 경영 방침이 ~ have a sound management method// 그런 종류의 사업이라면 ~ That kind of business is stable [safe]. **견실히** steadily; soundly; reliably; fairly; step by step; straight; in an honest way. ¶~ 해 나가다 go straight / draw a straight furrow / pursue an honest career / follow the beaten track / proceed slowly but steadily// ~ 사업을 하다 do [conduct] business on a sound basis// 그는 사업가로서 기반을 닦았다 He steadily went about establishing a foothold as a businessman.// 그는 ~ 일을 하고 있다 He is steady at his work. / He works steadily.

견우성(牽牛星) [천] Altair.

견원지간(犬猿之間) mutual dislike [hatred / enmity]. ¶~이다 be on (extremely) bad terms (with) / hate each other like poison / be at enmity (with) / be at loggerheads (with) / there is bitter enmity between (them) / lead a cat-and-dog life(특히 부부 사이가) / (구어) be at [on the] outs (with) / (구어) hate each other's guts.

견유주의(犬儒主義) [철] Cynicism.

견유학파(犬儒學派) [철] the Cynics.

견인(堅忍) (dogged) perseverance; fortitude; stoicism. **견인하다** persevere; bear patiently; endure undauntedly.

● **견인불발** (indomitable) perseverance; (invincible / unshakable / adamantine / steadfast) fortitude. ¶~의 정신 an indefatigable spirit / an indomitable mind / a heart of oak / an iron [adamant] will.

견인(牽引) traction; hauling. **견인하다** pull; draw; haul; tow. ¶내 차를 다른 차로 견인하였다 I had my car towed by another car.

● **견인력** the force of traction; tractive force; pulling capacity; traction (power). **견인차** a tow truck; a wrecker. ¶~ 역할을 하다 play the role of locomotive.

견장(肩章) a shoulder strap [mark / ensign / knot]; (정장의) an epaulet(te).

견적(見積) an estimate; an estimation; assessment; valuation; computation; calculation. ¶가(假)~ a preliminary estimate / 개산(槪算)~ an approximate [rough / rude] estimate / 건물의 ~ an estimate for a building// 과대 [과소] ~ overestimation [underestimation]// 세부 ~ a detailed estimate// 정밀 ~ a close estimate// 지출의 대략적인 [줄잡은]

~ a rough[conservative] estimate of the expenses. 견적하다 estimate (at); make [form] an estimate (of); calculate (at); value (at); rate (at); [경] quote (a commodity at ...); quote a price (for); give a quotation (for). ¶싸게[비싸게] ~ estimate (the cost) low[high] / rate (a thing) low[high] / underestimate[overestimate]∥줄잡아 ~ make a conservative[moderate / mean / low] estimate∥아무리 싸게 견적해도 at the lowest[most sparing] estimate∥아무리 많이 견적해도 at the highest estimate[at most / at the outside]∥그들은 집수리의 비용을 견적했다 They estimated for the repair of a house.∥그 물품에 대한 손해액을 견적하기에는 아직 시기상조이다 It is too early to form an estimate of the damage incurred on the article.∥나는 나무 울타리 페인트칠에 대하여 견적해 주도록 그에게 요청했다 I asked him to quote a price for[to give me an estimate of the cost of] painting the board fence.∥하기 물품에 대한 귀사의 최저 가격을 견적해 주십시오 Please quote us your lowest[rock-bottom] prices for the following goods. ¶기부금의 총액은 줄잡아 견적해도 100만 원은 된다 The total sum of the contributions is conservatively estimated at a million won. → ¶비용은 2만 원으로 견적된다 The expense is estimated at 20,000 won.∥견적된 비용은 얼마가량입니까 What is the estimated expense?
●**견적 가격** an estimated[assessed] value; a valuation. **견적서** an estimate; a written estimate; an estimate[estimation] sheet.

견제(牽制) **1** [자유를 방해함] a check; a restraint; curbing. ¶~와 균형 check and balance. **견제하다** check; keep[hold] in check; restrain. ¶서로 ~ hold each other in check∥그가 입을 열 때마다 그의 형이 견제하여 말을 못하게 했다 Whenever he opened his mouth to speak, his brother checked [stopped] him.∥미국은 그 나라를 견제할 정책을 취했다 The United States adopted a containment policy toward(s) that country. **2** [야구] a pick-off. **견제하다** peg (a runner on the base). ¶주자를 견제하여 아웃시키다 pick a runner off base∥그 투수는 1루 주자를 견제했다 The pitcher held the runner on [kept the runner close to] first base.
3 [군] [양동] a diversion; containment. **견제하다** contain; make a feint; make a diversion; divert.
●**견제구** a pick-off throw; a feint ball. ¶~를 던지다 throw a ball to peg a runner on the base. **견제력** a restraining influence.

견주다 [비교하다] compare (one thing) with (another); weigh[measure] (one thing) against (another); take (something) for comparison; [겨루다] rival; compete (with). ¶…과 견주어 보면 as compared with / as weighed against∥견주어 보아 판단하다 judge[decide] by comparison∥힘[기술]을 ~ measure one's strength[skill] with[against] (a person's)∥수학에서 그와 견줄 만한 사람은 없다 He has no equal[No one equals him] in mathematics.∥문장의 아름다움에서 그와 견줄 소설가는 없다 No novelist can compare with him for beauty of style.∥그것에 견줄 만한 것이 없다 Nothing can compare with it. / Nothing can stand comparison with it. / It stands unrivaled [unequaled / without a peer].∥그는 고흐와 견줄 수 있는 화가다 He is an artist who ranks with Van Gogh.∥그의 극은 셰익스피어의 극과는 견줄 바가 못 된다 His plays cannot compare with Shakespeare's.

견지 a bamboo fishing troll[reel / spool]. ¶~질하다 fish with a roll / troll (for) fish.

견지(見地) [입장] a standpoint; [관점] a viewpoint; a point of view; an angle. ¶내 ~에서 보면 from my point of view[standpoint / viewpoint] / viewed in my[this] light / viewed from my[this] angle∥새로운 ~에서 from a new angle of view∥예술적 ~에서 말하면 from an artistic point of view∥문제를 다른 ~에서 보다 view a problem from another angle[a different standpoint] / look at a problem in another light∥넓은 ~에서 보다 take a long[broad] view / take a higher and broader view / view[judge] things from a broader point of view∥모든 ~에서 검토하다 examine[study] (it) from all angles [points].

견지하다(堅持-) adhere (to); stick (to); hold fast (to); firmly maintain; hold on (to). ¶자기주장을 ~ hold fast to one's opinion / stick to one's principle∥군비 축소 노선을 ~ stick to a policy of disarmament∥낙관적 견해를 ~ maintain[hold fast to] an optimistic view∥현 정책을 ~ adhere closely to the present policy / play up a policy∥당신이 뭐라고 주장하더라도 난 내 결정을 견지할 것이다 Whatever your argument, I shall hold to my decision.

견직물(絹織物) silk fabrics; silk goods[stuff]; silk(s).
●**견직물 공장** a silk mill. **견직물상** a silk merchant.

견진 성사(堅振聖事) [가] (the sacrament of) confirmation. ¶~를 받은 사람 a confirmed man∥~를 행하다 confirm.

견책(譴責) a reprimand; (a) rebuke; (a) reproof; (a) censure. **견책하다** reprimand; rebuke; give[administer] a rebuke; reprove; censure. →¶견책당하다[받다] receive a reprimand[rebuke] / be reprimanded (for) / be subjected to reprimand∥나는 직무 태만으로 견책받았다 I was reprimanded for neglect [dereliction] of duty.

견치(犬齒) [생] a cuspid; a canine tooth. ⇨ 송곳니

견학(見學) study by inspection[observation]. ¶현장 ~ on the spot study / a field trip∥새 공장을 ~ a tour of[through] a new factory. **견학하다** inspect; observe; visit (a factory) for study[information]; (체육 시간 등에) look on; sit out (a game) and watch. ¶과학관을 ~ visit a science museum for information[study]∥6학년 학생들은 신문사를 견학하였다 The sixth-grades visited a newspaper office as part of their study.∥오늘 체육 시간은 견학하게 해 주십시오 Let me sit out the action and just watch today.

견해(見解) an opinion; a view; an outlook (on); (구어) a slant. ¶~의 차이 a difference of view / conflict of views / divergence of opinion / discrepancy in opinions∥그릇된 ~를 가지다 take a wrong view of (a matter) ∥중간적인 ~를 취하다 take a middle point of view∥그것은 ~ 차이야 [~상의 문제다]

결다

That's a mere difference of opinion. // 국무총리는 그 문제에 대한 정부의 ~를 발표했다 The Prime Minister announced the government view[position] on the matter. // 그들은 ~가 다르다 They see things from different points of view.

결다¹ 1 [기름이 배다] become oily[greasy]; be oiled; be saturated with oil. ¶기름에 결은 종이 oiled paper[oilpaper] // 맷국에 결은 옷 a garment greasy with grime // 종이가 잘 결었다 The paper has been well oiled. 2 [손에 익다] become experienced (in); get skillful; be quite at home (in); become skilled. 3 [기름에 배게 하다] oil (paper); saturate[soak / infiltrate / treat] (a thing) with oil. // 장판지를 기름에 ~ oil floor-paper.

결다² 1 [엮어 짜다] weave; plait; braid. ¶돗자리를 ~ weave a rush mat // 골풀로 결은 망태기 a bag woven from rushes. 2 [어긋매끼다] stack; pile up crisscross. ¶총을 ~ stack[pile] arms // 국기를 ~ cross[entwine / intertwine] national flags.

겯지르다 cross; place crosswise; intercross.

겯질리다 1 [엇걸리다] be crossed[intercrossed / intersected]; be placed crosswise. 2 [일이 엇갈리다] get entangled with each other; become complicated; become intricate. 3 [기진맥진하게 되다] be exhausted; be wrung out.

결¹ [나무·돌의] grain; [직물의] texture; [피부의] grain; (skin) texture. ¶비단 ~ a silky[velvety] texture // ~이 촘촘한 피륙 closely-woven cloth // ~이 고운[거친] 목재 fine-grained[coarse-grained] wood // ~이 곱다[촘촘하다] be fine / be fine-grained / have a fine grain / be of fine grain / be of fine texture // ~이 거칠다 be rough / be coarse-grained / be coarse / have a coarse grain / be rough-grained / be of loose texture.

결² 1 [성질] disposition; temper; temperament; spirit. ¶~이 고약한 사람 a man of ill nature[evil mind] / malicious[vicious] man / a person of nasty[rough] disposition. 2 [결기] a quick[hot / short / bad / hasty / violent] temper.

결이 바르다 be straight[straightforward / upright].

결³ [때] the time; the moment; [사이] a while. ¶아침 ~에 before the morning is out / in the morning // 잠 ~에 in one's sleep / while asleep // 꿈 ~에 듣다 listen half asleep // 어느 ~에 일 주일이 지나갔다 A week has passed in a flash[before we knows it].

결가부좌(結跏趺坐) [불] sitting cross-legged[with legs crossed] (as in Buddhist statues).

결강하다(缺講-) (교수가) do not give one's lecture; cancel a lecture[class]; (학생이) cut a class[lecture].

결격(缺格) disqualification; rejection; [법] incapacity.
● **결격 사유** reasons for disqualification[rejection]; reasons for being disqualified.
결격자 a disqualified[an unqualified] person; (구어) a reject.

결과(結果) a result; an effect; an outcome(▶effect는 원인 작용에서부터 생기는 직접적 결과, result, outcome은 최종적인 결과); [자연스런 과정] a consequence; (문어) the issue. ¶원인과 ~ cause and effect // 좋은[좋지 않은] ~ a good[a poor / an unfavorable] result // 최종[최후] ~ a final[an end] result / the end product // 최종 ~ 집계표 the final tabulation // 문의해 본 ~ an inquiry proves that ... // 지금까지의 ~로 미루어 보아 in view of the results so far achieved // …의 ~로(서) as the[a] result of ... / in consequence of ... / as a sequel to [of] // ~가 좋지 않은 [성공하지 못한] unsuccessful / abortive / [헛된] ineffectual // ~에 책임을 지다 take[answer for] the consequences // 좋지 않은 ~로 끝나다 end in failure / end up failing[a failure] / prove fruitless // ~가 …으로 되다 result[end / issue] in ... / come in effect to ... / turn out (fine / well) // 좋은 ~를 얻다 [맺다] obtain[produce] a good[bad] result / bear[produce] good[bad] fruit / come to good[bad] // 이렇다 할 확실한 ~가 나타나지 않다 produce no tangible[appreciable] result // 바라던 ~를 얻다 attain a looked-for[desired] effect / yield[produce] desirable results // 시합의 ~는 어떠했습니까 What was the result of the game? // 그들은 협상의 ~를 근심하고 있다 They are worrying about the outcome of the negotiations. // 시험 ~가 발표되었다 The results of the examination were announced[declared / published]. // 그것은 그의 노력[노고]의 ~이다 It is a result of his hard work. / It is the fruits of his labor[efforts]. // 그 ~는 손해를 볼 것이 뻔하다 It's bound to result[end] in a loss. // 협상의 ~ 타협이 이루어졌다 The negotiations resulted in a compromise. // 서로 양보한 ~ 사건은 곧 원만히 해결되었다 We made mutual concessions with the result that the matter was settled at once. / Our mutual concession resulted in a speedy settlement of the affair. // 해 보기는 하겠지만 ~는 약속할 수 없다 I will try but I cannot promise what the outcome will be. // 그 ~가 어찌될 것인지 나도 알 수가 없다 I don't know what result it would lead to[how it would end]. // 그런 ~가 되리라고 생각했다 I thought it would end up that way[like that]. // 의외의 [뜻밖의] ~가 나왔다 It came to[reached / attained] an unexpected result[ending]. // 그것이 반대의 ~를 가져왔다 It brought (about) a reverse effect[an opposite result]. // 그것은 생각했던 바와는 반대의 ~를 가져왔다 It produced an effect opposite to what was designed[intended]. // 세관에 문의해 본 ~ 전적으로 그의 잘못임이 판명되었다 An inquiry at the customs house proved that it was all because of his mistakes. // 네가 시험에 불합격한 것은 나태다 ~다 Your idleness is responsible for your failure in the examination. / Your failure in the examination comes of your idleness. // 그 ~ 어떻게 되든 나는 가겠다 Whatever results follow, I will go. // 그 ~ 그는 해고당했다 As a result[In consequence], he was dismissed. / The outcome[consequence] was that they fired him[he lost his position]. // 일이 이런 ~가 되어 유감으로 생각합니다 I regret that things have come to this pass.
● **결과론** criticism (on past events) based on the result.

결구(結構) [구조] structure; construction; framework; [구성] a build-up (of a story); a plot (of a novel); [건] a truss. **결구하다** frame; construct; map[plan / work] out (a

결국(結局) 1 [끝장] an end; a close; a finish; a termination; [결말] conclusion. 2 [마침내] after all(긍정·부정 양쪽에 쓰임); finally; in the end; in conclusion; in the long run; in the result; in the last resort; in the last [final / ultimate] analysis; ultimately. ¶~ …이 될 것이다 It will come [boil] down to …. / It will result [end] in …. / The question will go down to …. // 그래서 ~ 그는 나타나지 않았군요 So he didn't show up after all. // ~ 그들 두 사람은 화해했다 They were reconciled in the end. // ~ 그는 파산을 면할 수 없었다 After all he could not escape bankruptcy. // ~ 그 모든 비용을 내가 떠맡았다 [내 자신이 부담했다] In the end I bore all the expenses [paid for it myself]. // ~ 공부라는 것은 남의 강요로 되는 성질의 것이 아니다 After all, studying is not the kind of thing that you force a person to do. // 그 문제는 ~ 아무도 풀지 못했다 The problem remained unsolved after all. // 난 ~ 지고 말았다 I was finally defeated. // 여러모로 노력해 보았지만 ~ 실패였다 All my efforts resulted in failure. // ~ 돈이 문제다 It is after all [at root] a question of money. // ~에 가서는 실력이 이긴다 Real ability will win out in the end. // ~에 가서는 손해보다 득이 많을 것으로 생각한다 I think the gains will surpass the losses in the long run. // ~은 더 비싸게 치일 것이다 It will prove rather expensive. // 소문은 ~ 근거 없는 것이었다 The rumor turned out to be false. // ~ 모두 경찰서에 연행되었다 In consequence, all were taken to the police station.

결근(缺勤) absence (from); nonattendance (at). ¶무단 ~ an absence without notice [leave] / 장기 ~ a long (-term) absence. **결근하다** be absent (from duty [office / one's work]); be away from work; stay home (from the office). ¶그는 오늘 아파서 결근했습니다 He is out sick today. // 어제는 병이 나서 결근하였습니다 Yesterday I stayed home from work because of illness. // 내일은 새집으로 이사하는 관계로 결근해야겠습니다 I must take a day off tomorrow to move into our new house. // 나는 하루도 결근한 날이 없습니다 I have never missed a day at the office. ● **결근계** a report [notice] of absence. **결근자** an absentee; a non-attendant.

결기(-氣) impetuousness; vehemence; a quick [hot / short / hasty] temper. ¶~가 있는 quick- [hot-] tempered / irascible / passionate / impetuous / hasty / impatient // ~가 나서 in a fit of ill temper / out of temper. **결나다** get angry; be enraged; flare [flame] up ¶결나서 (남을) 때리다 beat (a person) up in a fit of anger. **결내다** lose one's temper; fall [fly / get] into a passion [rage / temper]; flare up. ¶툭하면 ~ be liable to lose one's temper / be easily roused to temper.

결단(決斷) (a) definite decision; determination; (a) resolution. ¶~이 빠르다 [느리다] be quick [slow] in decision / 망설이기만 하고 ~을 내리지 못하는 사람 a waverer // ~을 내리다 make a decision / reach [come to / arrive at] a definite decision / make a final decision / give one's decision // ~을 못 내리다 [~이 서지 않다] cannot decide (on / to do) / cannot [be unable to] make up one's mind / vacillate / hang fire // 그는 ~을 강요받았다 He was urged [pressed] to make a definite decision. // 아직 아무런 ~도 내리지 않았다 No decision is reached yet. // ~이 내려지지 않는다 I am undecided [vacillating / wavering]. // 그는 진학을 해야 할지 어떨지 ~ 내리지 못하고 있다 He is still uncertain whether to go on to college or not. // 그는 ~을 내려 결혼했다 He made up his mind and got married. / He went ahead [take the plunge] and got married. // 노조는 파업하기로 ~을 내렸다 The union determined to strike. **결단하다** decide; determine; resolve. ● **결단력** the strength of one's mind; resolution; determination. ¶~이 있다 be quick in decision / be firm of purpose // ~이 없다 be irresolute / lack (in) decision / be infirm [weak] of purpose / be vacillating. **결단성** firmness of character; decidedness; decision.

결단식(結團式) an inaugural meeting [rally]; a ceremony celebrating the establishment of an organization.

결단코(決斷-) decisively; certainly; surely; by all (manner of) means; at any cost; never; (not) ever; not … at all [in the least]; on no account; by any means; by no means; for all the world. ¶어떤 일이 있더라도 ~ 나는 그 일을 해내고야 말겠다 I will carry it out at any cost [(구어) no matter what]. // 그는 ~ 사실대로 고백하지 않을 것이다 He will never for the life of him confess the truth.

결단하다(結團-) form [establish] an organization; set up [organize] a group. → ¶전 한국 축구 대표 팀이 결단되었다 They put together an all-Korean soccer team.

결당(結黨) the founding [formation] of a party. **결당하다** found [form / organize] a party. ● **결당식** an inauguration ceremony of a party.

결딴나다 1 [망가지다] be broken (down); be destroyed [smashed / demolished / razed]; be spoilt [ruined]; go to wreck [ruin]; collapse; go to pieces. ¶그 지진으로 많은 집이 결딴났다 A number of houses were destroyed by the earthquake. // 그는 건강이 결딴났다 His health has been much broken [ruined]. / His health has gone to pieces. 2 [망하다] fall; fall in one's circumstances; go to ruin; go under; be ruined; be wrecked; go to the bad; become [go] bankrupt. ¶그 집안이 결딴나 버렸다 The family has been ruined. // 단 한번의 실패로 그의 인생은 결딴나 버렸다 Just a single failure ruined his life.

결딴내다 1 [망가뜨리다] spoil; ruin; destroy; break; wreck. ¶그는 술로 몸을 결딴내 버렸다 He wrecked himself with wine. / He ruined his health with wine. 2 [망하게 하다] ruin; bring [reduce] to ruin. ¶그의 상습적인 도박은 그의 일생을 결딴내 버렸다 His habitual gambling has reduced him to ruin for life. / His habitual gambling has made a wreck of his life. / His habitual gambling has blasted his career.

결렬(決裂) a rupture; a breakdown. **결렬하다** come to a rupture; break off [down]; end in a rupture. → ¶협상은 결렬되었다 The negotiations were broken off.∥그들의 회담은 결렬되고 말았다 They failed to come to an agreement at the meeting. / The meeting ended in a stalemate.∥그들 두 사람은 세 시간 동안 협상했지만 견해가 일치되지 않아 결렬되었다 They talked for three hours but parted with their views still unreconciled.

결례(缺禮) lack of courtesy; negligence of etiquette; failure[omission] to pay one's compliments; want of respect. **결례하다** omit [fail] to pay one's compliments[to offer one's greetings].

결론(結論) a conclusion; a concluding remark. ¶~에 도달하다 come to[reach / arrive at] a conclusion / 서둘러 ~을 내리다 jump to a conclusion / form a hasty conclusion /~을 짓다[내리다] draw[form] a conclusion / ~적으로 나는 스미스 씨의 의견에 찬성합니다 In conclusion I agree with Mr. Smith. / 이렇게 저렇게 그들이 논의했으나 결국 도달한 ~은 이것이었다 This was the conclusion they've come to after discussing it this way and that.

결리다 1 (몸이) feel a stitch (in); have a crick (in). ¶옆구리가 ~ feel[have] a stitch in one's side∥목이 결린다 I have a crick in the neck. 2 (기를 펴지 못하다) be cowed; feel constrained[oppressed]; be overpowered; flinch (from); shrink (from); quail (at).

결막(結膜) [생] the conjunctiva (pl. ~s, -vae).
●**결막염** [의] conjunctivitis. ¶유행성 ~ epidemic[contagious] conjunctivitis / pinkeye.

결말(結末) [끝장] an end; a close; a conclusion; a termination; [결과] a result; an outcome; [낙착] settlement; fixing up; [대단원] the denouement; the catastrophe(비극의). ¶그것이 타당한 ~이다 That is a proper conclusion.

결말 나 다(結末-) be settled; come[be brought] to a conclusion[an end]. ¶우리는 내일 출발하기로 의논이 결말났다 It has been agreed that we will start tomorrow.∥협상이 결말났다 An agreement has been reached in the negotiations.∥그 분쟁이 마침내 결말났다 The dispute was finally settled.∥그 문제는 아직 결말나지 않았다 The matter has not been settled yet. / The matter still remains unsettled. / The matter is yet to be settled.∥그 문제는 어떻게 결말날까 What will be the final outcome (of the matter)? / How will the matter end[result / come out]?∥그 일은 머지않아 결말나겠지 That affair will soon be concluded.

결말내다(結末-) settle. ⇨결말짓다

결말짓다(結末-) settle; bring (a matter) to a settlement[conclusion / an end]; put an end to; fix up; (미) wind up. ¶협상에 결말을 짓다 bring the negotiations to a conclusion∥일[논쟁]을 ~ settle a matter[dispute] / 서로의 의견이 갈라져 그들은 결말지을 수 없었다 They were divided in opinion and could reach no conclusion.∥그는 모든 일에 신속한 결말을 지었다 He brought everything to a speedy conclusion.∥그들이 질질 끌던 분쟁을 마침내 결말지었다 They settled[put an end to] a prolonged difficulty at last. / 곧 그와 결말짓지 않으면 안 되겠다 I will have to fix things with him soon.

결맹하다(結盟-) conclude[make up / enter into] a treaty; form a league[federation / union]; conclude[form / enter into] an alliance.

결미(結尾) the end; the close; the conclusion; the finis.

결박(結縛) binding; tying; pinioning. **결박하다** bind; tie (up); pinion; [수갑을 채우다] shackle (a person's) hands; put (a person) in irons. ¶단단히 ~ tie fast[hard]. →¶결박당하다 be bound[tied up]∥양손을 뒤로 결박당하여 with one's hand tie behind.

결백(潔白) [깨끗함] purity; [무죄] innocence; [청렴] integrity. ¶일신의 ~을 입증하다 prove one's innocence / vindicate one's character / 나는 그의 ~을 믿는다 I believe he is innocent (of the charge).∥그의 ~이 입증되었다 His innocence was established. / He was cleared (of suspicion). **결백하다** [깨끗하다] pure; stainless; immaculate; [죄가 없다] innocent; guiltless; [청렴 하다] upright; cleanhanded. ¶결백한 사람 a man of integrity[an innocent man / a man with a clean record]∥그 일에 있어서 나는 ~ I am innocent[not guilty / have clean hands] in that matter.∥그가 결백한지 그렇지 않은지 아직 우리는 모른다 We don't know yet whether he is guilty or not.

결번(缺番) a missing[wanting] number. ¶5번은 ~이다 The number five is blank on the roll. / No. 5 is missing.

결벽(潔癖) [유달리 깨끗함을 좋아함] love of cleanliness; [기호가 까다로움] fastidiousness; finicality; daintiness.

결별(訣別) 1 [작별] parting; separation; [고별] leave-taking; farewell; good-bye. **결별하다** part with; take leave of; say[bid] good-by (to); bid farewell (to). ¶그는 가족과 결별하고 전선으로 떠났다 He parted from his family and left for the front. 2 [관계·교제를 끊음] a breach (of friendship); a rupture. **결별하다** break with[off] (a person); part with[from] (a person); cut[drop / sever] one's acquaintance[connection] (with). ¶그는 낡은 유파와 결별했다 He broke with the old school.

결본(缺本) a wanting[missing / lacking] volume. ¶제3권이 ~이다 The third volume is missing.

결부(結付) relation; connection; a junction. **결부하다** join[link] together; connect with. →¶결부되다 link oneself (to) / be linked (up) (with) / be related (with) / 공산당과 직접 결부되어 있는 여러 단체 organizations with direct ties to the Communist Party∥A를 B와 결부시켜 생각하다 consider A in relation to B / consider A in connection with B.

결빙(結氷) freezing; frost; ice formation. **결빙하다** freeze; be frozen over; become[be] ice-bound[ice-locked]; (항구 등이) be closed by ice. →¶항구는 현재 결빙되어 있다 The harbor is icebound.∥호수는 완전히 결빙되어 있다 The lake has completely frozen over.
●**결빙기** the freezing season. **결빙점** the freezing point.

결사(結社) an association; a society. ¶비밀 ~ a secret society / an underground organization. **결사하다** form an association[a society / a fraternity].
결사의 자유 freedom of association.

결사(決死) a do-or-die[death or glory] spirit; determination to die; preparedness for

death. ¶~의 전투 desperate battle // 그는 ~의 각오로 적지에 잠입하였다 He smuggled himself into enemy territory, ready to die if necessary.
● 결사대 a forlorn hope; a death-defying [do-or-die] corps; a suicide corps [squad].

결사적 (決死的) desperate; death-defying; last-ditch. ¶~으로 desperately / in desperation / at the risk of one's life [death] / setting death at naught // ~으로 싸우다 fight desperately / fight for one's life [to the death].

결산 (決算) settlement of accounts; balancing [closing] accounts. ¶반기(半期) ~ a semi-annual [half-yearly] settlement // ~은 3월과 9월입니다 We settle accounts in March and September. **결산하다** settle [balance / square] accounts; balance the books; close the books. ¶우리는 월말마다 장부를 결산한다 We settle accounts at the end of every month.
● **결산기** an accounting period; a settlement term. **결산 보고** a statement of accounts. **결산일** a settling [settlement] day; a closing date.

결석 (缺席) absence; nonattendance; (구어) a cut; [법] default; nonappearance. ¶무~ regular attendance / non-absence // 무단~ absence without leave // 병고 ~ absence on account of illness // 장기 ~ a long absence. **결석하다** be absent (from); absent oneself (from); stay away (from); fail to attend; miss [cut] (one's class); [법] default; make default. ¶병으로 학교에 ~ be absent from [miss] school because of illness // 오늘 많은 [37명 중 4명의] 학생이 결석했다 Many [Four out of the thirty-seven] pupils are absent [not have] today. // 나는 어제 회의에 결석했다 I did not attend the meeting yesterday. // 피고는 재판에 결석했다 The accused failed to appear in court. // 그는 위원회에 곧잘 결석한다 He is irregular in his attendance at committee meeting. // 오늘은 결석한 사람이 하나도 없습니다 No one is absent today.
● **결석계** a notice of absence; a report of nonattendance. **결석자** an absentee; (재판의) a defaulter. **결석 재판** (형사 사건의) trial in absentia; (민사 소송의) judgment by default.

결석 (結石) [의] a calculus (pl. -li); a stone. ¶신장 ~ a renal calculus.

결선 (決選) 1 (투표의) a final election; a runoff. **결선하다** elect by final vote. 2 [경기] the final contest; the finals. ¶~에 진출하다 go into [advance to / move into] the finals. **결선하다** play [run] in the finals.
● **결선 투표** a final [decisive] vote [ballot]; a showdown vote; a runoff election [ballot].

결성 (結成) organization; formation. **결성하다** organize; form. ¶정당을 ~ form [organize] a political party.
● **결성식** an inaugural [organizational] meeting.

결속 (結束) 1 (한 덩이로 묶음) binding together; banding [sticking] together; pulling together. **결속하다** bind together. 2 [단결] union; unity; solidarity. ¶~을 굳히다 [강화하다 / 다지다] strengthen [solidify] the solidarity [unity] / tighten the union (of) / cement unity // 당내의 ~을 다지다 solidify [strengthen] the party's unity // 종업원의 ~은 단단하다 The workers are closely united. **결속하다** band [stick] together; unite; hang together; get [be] united; pull [hold] together; present a united front (toward). ¶결속하여 in a body / united (together) / in unity // 결속하여 일어서다 stand up in a body / rise in unity.

결손 (缺損) (특히 금전상의) a deficit; deficiency; a loss. ¶~을 메우다 cover the loss [deficit] / make up the deficit [a loss] / make good the losses // ~의 연속이다 suffer loss upon loss / run at a series of losses // 크게 ~을 내다 run a large [heavy] deficit / suffer [incur] a heavy [great] loss // ~이 200만 원이 되었다 The deficiency came to two million won. // 그 회사는 금년 영업에서 10만 달러의 ~이 났다 The company had a deficit of $100,000 in this business. // 이 일로 100만 원의 ~이 났다 This cause a deficit of one million won. // 우리는 연속적인 ~을 보았다 We have suffered a series of losses.
● **결손금** the deficit; the amount of loss. **결손 처리 / 결손 처분** deficits disposal.

결승 (決勝) 1 the decision (of a contest). ¶동점 ~ a play-off // 준 ~ a semifinal / 준준~ a quarterfinal // ~까지 올라간 주자는 5명이었다 Five runners reached the finals. **결승하다** decide victories; fight to the finish [last]; fight it out; play off (무승부 시합에서). 2 the final round. ⇨결승전(⇨)결승)
● **결승선** the goal line; the finishing line. **결승전** the final round [game / match / contest]; the finals; a run-off; (비긴 경기 등의) a play-off. **결승점** the goal (line); the home; the finish line.

결식 (缺食) going without a meal. ¶~ 아동 a schoolchild without lunch. **결식하다** go without [skip] a meal.

결실 (結實) 1 [열매 맺기] ripening; fruition; bearing (of fruit); fructification. ¶~의 계절 the fruiting season // ~이 늦다 ripen late // 가을은 ~의 계절이다 Autumn is a harvest season [time]. // 올해는 벼의 ~이 좋았다 [좋지 않았다] We had a good [poor] rice crop this year. **결실하다** bear fruit; fructify; fruit; go to seed; develop into fruit. ¶결실하지 않는 나무 a sterile plant // 결실하지 않다 be sterile [bear no fruit / be fruitless].
2 [좋은 결과] realization; a result. ¶~을 보는 연구를 하다 do productive research // ~을 못 보다 [결실하지 못하다] come to naught [nothing] / bear no fruit // 오랜 노력 끝에 그 ~의 이상이 ~을 보았다 His ideal was realized after many years of endeavor. // 이 기사는 취재자의 노고의 ~이다 This article is the fruit [result] of the reporter's hard work. // 당신에게 ~이 있는 한 해가 되기를 빕니다 Best wishes for a fruitful year. **결실하다** be successful; achieve [attain] success.
● **결실기** the fruiting season.

결심 (決心) determination; resolution. ¶굳은 ~ a firm [a determined / an unshakable / an inflexible] resolution // ~이 서지 않은 irresolute [hesitating / vacillating] // ~이 서 있다 know one's own mind // ~이 약해지다 be [get] weakened in one's resolution // ~을 굳히다 make a firm resolution / stiffen one's resolution // 어느 길을 택할 것인가 ~이 서지 않습니다 I can not decide which way to take. // 나는 마지막 순간에 ~이 흔들렸다 My resolution wavered at the last moment. / My resolution was shaken [staggered] at the last

결심 moment. **결심하다** determine; be determined; make up one's mind; resolve; be resolved; decide. ¶나는 담배를 끊기로 결심하였다 I am determined to give up smoking.// 올해에는 일기를 쓰기로 나는 결심했다 I resolved [made up my mind / made a resolution] to keep a diary this year.// 그는 아직 결심하지 못하고 있었다 He still remained undecided. / He was still wavering. / He was still unable to decide. / He still couldn't make up his mind.// 나는 사장에게 승급을 부탁하려고 결심했다 I made up my mind to ask my boss for a pay raise.// 먹고살기 위해서는 어떤 힘든 일이라도 하려고 나는 결심했다 I was determined to do any job, no matter how hard, to earn my living.// 자네가 단단히 결심하고 시작하면 잘될 거야 If you steel yourself for it, it will go well.// 그는 일단 결심하면 전력투구한다 Once he makes up his mind, he goes full tilt.

결심 (結審) the conclusion of a hearing [trial]. **결심하다** close (a hearing); decide (a case).
● **결심 공판** the final trial.

결여 (缺如) (a) want; (a) lack; absence (of a proof); deficiency; privation. ¶상식의 ~ a want [a lack / an absence] of common sense. **결여하다** want; lack; be lacking [wanting / deficient] (in). →¶그는 공덕심이 결여되어 있다 He is lacking [wanting] in public spirit. / He lacks public spirit. / He has no public spirit.// 필요한 자료가 결여되어 있다 We don't have the data we need.

결연 (結緣) 1 [인연을 맺음] forming a connection [relationship]. ¶자매~ establishment of sisterhood relationship [ties] // 자매~을 맺은 학교들 sister schools. **결연하다** form [establish / enter into] a connection (with); establish relations (with). 2 [불문에 드는 인연을 맺음]. **결연하다** become a (devout) believer in Buddhism; embrace the Buddhist faith; be converted to Buddhism.

결연하다 (決然—) resolute; decisive; determined. **결연히** decisively; resolutely; in a decisive [determined / resolute / firm] manner. ¶그는 자신이 하겠다고 ~ 선언했다 He declared resolutely that he would do it.

결원 (缺員) a vacancy; a vacant position [post]; an opening. ¶~이 생기다 a vacancy occurs / (일이) cause a vacancy / vacate a post // ~을 보충하다 fill (up) a vacancy // ~을 그대로 두다 leave a position unfilled [vacant] // ~이 생기면 당신을 채용하겠습니다 I shall employ you if there is a vacancy.

결의 (決意) resolution; determination. ¶단호한 ~ inflexible determination / firm resolution // ~를 새로이 하다 make a fresh determination // ~를 다지다 strengthen [firm up] one's will [determination / resolve] (to do) // ~를 표명하다 declare one's will // 중대한 ~를 하다 take a decisive step / cross [pass] the Rubicon // 자넨 ~가 대단하군 You are very determined, aren't you?// 그는 ~를 가다듬고 일에 착수했다 He tightened his resolve and set to work. / He set to work with determination. **결의하다** determine; resolve; make up one's mind; decide on (a course of action).

결의 (決議) a resolution; a decision; a vote. ¶부대 (附帶) ~ (pass) an additional resolution // 감사의 ~ a resolution of thanks // 국회의 ~ a resolution of the National Assembly / (미) a Congressional decision / (영) Parliamentary decision // 총괄적인 ~ an omnibus [a catchall] resolution // 국회의 ~에 의거하여 in accordance with a decision of the National Assembly // 그들은 그 계획안에 찬성[반대] ~를 했다 They decided [voted] for [against] the plan. **결의하다** resolve; pass [adopt] a resolution; decide; vote. ¶안건을 ~ vote for a scheme / vote on a bill // 불신임을 ~ pass a vote of nonconfidence (in the cabinet) // 다음과 같이 결의함 Be it resolved [Resolved] that .... // 공장 유치를 시의회에서 결의했다 It was resolved [decided] in the municipal assembly to try to attract factories.

● **결의권** the right of voting; the voting right. **결의 기관** a voting [resolutionary] organ. **결의문** a resolution. **결의안** a (draft) resolution. ¶불신임 ~ a nonconfidence resolution.

결의하다 (結義—) swear to be (brothers); take an oath of brotherhood. ¶부자(父子)가 되기로 ~ contract the relations of father and son / swear to enter into the father-and-son relationship.

결의형제 (結義兄弟) sworn [pledged] brothers.

결자 (缺字) an omitted word; an omission; a missing character; [인] a blank type. ¶이 교정쇄는 ~투성이다 Those proof sheets are full of blanks.

결장 (結腸) [생] the colon. ¶~의 colonic.
● **결장염** colonitis.

결재 (決裁) sanction; approval; decision. ¶~를 얻다 obtain an approval // ~를 올리다 submit a matter for a person's approval // ~가 나다 be approved / go from 'In' tray to 'Out' tray // 이 안은 장관의 ~가 남아 있다 This plan remains to be sanctioned by the Minister. / This plan is awaiting the Minister's approval. **결재하다** sanction; approve; decide (upon).
● **결재권** the right of decision; decisive power. **결재투표** a deciding [casting] vote.

결전 (決戰) (fight) a decisive battle (with); a tug-of-war; a showdown; (경기의) a deciding match [race]; (무승부 후의) a run-off; a play-off. ¶대(大)~ an Armageddon / a most decisive battle // ~의 시기 the decisive stage (of a war) / the zero hour // ~ 단계에 돌입하다 reach [enter into] a decisive stage // 드디어 ~이다 Now we have reached zero hour. / We have reached the decisive stage at last. / This is it. **결전하다** fight a decisive battle; fight it out; (동점이 되어) run [play] off.

결절 (結節) [뼈나 식물의 뿌리의, 또는 결핵의] a tubercle; [피부에 생긴 응기] a node; [마디] a knot; [~ 모양] tubercular / nodular.

결점 (缺點) [불완전한 점] a fault; a defect; a demerit; a flaw; a blemish; an imperfection; [약점] a weak point; a weakness; a shortcoming; a failing; one's blind side; [난점] a drawback; a disadvantage. ¶~이 있는 faulty / defective / flawed // ~이 없는 faultless / flawless / perfect // ~을 고치다 correct [remedy / cure] (a person's) defect // 남의 ~을 찾다 find fault with a person / pick [point] out another's defects // ~투성이다 have many faults [shortcomings] // ~을 드러내다 expose one's faults [defects] // ~을 감추다 conceal one's defects // 소심한 [접 많은] 것

이 그의 ~이다 Timidity is his weakness [defect].∥그의 태도에는 ~이 없다 I cannot find fault with his manner. / His manner is flawless [perfect].∥이 집의 ~은 부엌이 좁은 데에 있다 The weak point [drawback] of this house is that the kitchen is too small.∥~ 없는 사람은 없다 No man is free from faults. / There is no man but has some faults.∥이 설비의 ~은 그 크기이다 The problem with [The drawback of] this equipment is its size.∥그는 잔꾀를 부리다가 오히려 ~을 드러냈다 His petty tricks served to betray him [(구어) give game away].∥~이 드러나기 전에 그만두자 Let's quit before we're found out.∥이렇게 하면 내 ~이 가려질 것이다 This will cover up my defects [weaknesses].∥그 학설의 ~은 문화의 차이를 무시하고 있는 데에 있다 The weak point in that theory is that it ignores cultural differences.

결정(決定) (a) decision; 〔결의〕 (a) determination; 〔결론〕 (a) conclusion; 〔해결〕 (a) settlement. ¶~에 관해 ~을 내리다 make a decision over [about] ∥ ~을 연기하다 put off [postpone] one's decision∥~을 서두르다 hurry in reaching a decision∥위원회의 ~에 따르다 abide by a committee's decision∥어떻게든 ~을 내리셨습니까 Have you arrived at any conclusion? **결정하다** decide (on/to do); determine; set; fix (upon) (▶ decide는 불확실했던 것을 결정함. determine은 decide 보다도 강한 결단의 뜻을 가짐. fix와 set는 보통 일시·장소 등을 정할 때 씀); 〔결론을 내리다〕 conclude; 〔결심하다〕 resolve; determine; 〔판정하다〕 rule. ¶날짜를 ~ fix [set] the date (for)∥학교 [직업]을 ~ decide on one's school [profession] ∥방침을 ~ decide on one's policy [a course of action] / 태도를 ~ determine one's attitude∥나는 가기로 결정했습니다 I have decided to go.∥그것은 세계의 장래를 결정하는 전투였다 It was a battle that decides the future of the world.∥그들은 소풍 날짜를 10월 6일로 결정했다 They decided on [set fixed on] the sixth of October as the date of the excursion. ➔¶아직 어느 쪽으로도 결정되지 않은 상태로 hang [be] in the scale [balance] ∥내 후임자가 결정되었다 My successor was chosen [decided on].∥그분의 한마디로 내 진로가 결정되었다 That remark of his determined my course in life.∥선거 유세 일정이 결정되었다 The campaign schedule was set up [was fixed].

●**결정권** decision-making authority; the right of decision; decisive power. ¶나에게는 ~이 없다 I have no power [authority] to decide the matter. / (구어) I don't have the (final) say. **결정론** 〔철〕 determinism. **결정타** (야구에서) a game-winning hit; the winning hit; (권투에서) a decisive [finishing] blow; (이야기 등의) (구어) a clincher. ¶타자가 ~를 치는 바람에 투수는 물러났다 The pitcher was knocked out when even his best pitch was hit. **결정투표** the deciding [casting] vote. **결정판** a definitive [an authorized] edition; (번역본의) the most authentic version ever published.

결정(結晶) 1 〔물질의〕 crystallization; 〔결정체〕 a crystal. ¶~의 crystalline. **결정하다** crystallize. 2 〔노력 등의 소산〕 a fruit. ¶그 아이는 그들의 사랑의 ~이었다 The child was the fruit of their love.

●**결정계**(~系) a system of crystallization. **결정 구조 / 결정 조직** crystal structure. **결정수**(~水) water of crystallization; combined water. **결정체** a crystal; a crystalloid. **결정학** crystallography. **결정형** a crystal form.

결정적(決定的) definite (reply); final (judgment); decisive (factor); definitive (answer); conclusive (evidence); determinate (reply); clinching (proof). ¶(수험생들의) ~ 순간 a decisive moment (for the examinees)∥~ 승리 a decisive victory / (사건 등의) ~ 요인 a decisive [conclusive] factor / (구어) a clincher∥그것은 양측의 ~ 전투였다 That was a crucial battle for the two parties.∥그 카메라맨은 미사일 발사의 ~ 순간을 포착했다 The cameraman took a picture of the missile at the decisive moment when it was launched.∥변호사는 그의 무죄의 ~ 증거를 제출했다 His lawyer produced [introduced] decisive proof [conclusive evidence] of his innocence. ∥(야구에서) 자이언츠가 ~인 추가점을 얻었다 The Giants added an insurance run.∥(미식축구에서) 제츠는 제4쿼터에서 ~인 터치다운 2점을 덤으로 추가했다 For good measure, the Gets added two more touchdowns in the fourth quarter.

결제(決濟) settlement; liquidation (빚의). ¶미~ 계정 an account outstanding∥국제 ~ 은행 the Bank of International Settlements∥대차 ~ settlement of accounts / closure (of accounts)∥부분 [전액] ~ partial [full] settlement∥삼각 ~ the triple settlement. **결제하다** settle an account; square accounts; make up accounts; liquidate [square up] (one's liabilities.

●**결제일** a settlement [(영) settling] day.

결집(結集) concentration; regimentation. **결집하다** 〔모이다〕 gather together; 〔하나로 묶다〕 collect in a mass; 〔집중하다〕 concentrate. ¶총력을 ~ concentrate [concert] all one's effort∥동지를 ~ call together our comrades∥무장한 시민이 광장에 결집했다 Armed citizens massed [gathered / rallied] in the public square.

결착(決着·結着) settlement; conclusion; decision; end. **결착하다** be settled; be closed; come to a close [an end / a conclusion]; reach an ending. ➔¶결착시키다 settle / bring (a matter) to a conclusion [close].

결초보은하다(結草報恩−) requite [return / reciprocate / repay] another's kindness even after one's death; carry one's gratitude beyond the grave. ¶결초보은하겠습니다 I shall never forget your kindness (as long as I live).

결코(決−) 〔절대로 … 않다〕 never; by no means; assuredly [positively] ... not; 〔어떤 경우에도 … 않다〕 under no circumstances; 〔어떤 이유로도〕 on no account [occasion]; 〔조금도 … 않다〕 not (bad) at all; not in the least. ¶나는 ~ 거짓말을 하지 않겠다 I simply do [will] not lie. / (속어) I'll be damned if I('ll) lie.∥나는 그것을 ~ 허용하지 않겠다 I positively [absolutely] forbid it.∥나는 ~ 뒤로 물러서지 않겠다 I will never [on no account (whatsoever)] retreat.∥그는 ~ 자기가 한 말을 뒤엎지는 않을 것이다 He would be the last man to retract his words. ∥나는 이 경험을 ~ 잊지 않을 것이다 I shall never forget this experience.∥그 값은 ~ 비

싸지 않다 The price is none too high. // 결과는 ~ 만족할 만한 것이 아니었다 The result was far from satisfactory. // 이것은 ~ 나쁘지 않다 This is not bad in the least. // 나는 그를 용서할 수 없다 I cannot forgive him on any account. // ~ 그렇지 않다 No, never, it isn't so. / I am positive that it is not so. / (구어) Not on your life. // 사태는 ~ 위급하지 않다 The situation is in no way serious. // 그의 병세는 ~ 중태는 아니다 His condition is in no way serious. // 그는 ~ 바보가 아니다 He is by no means a fool. / He is no fool. // 그녀는 ~ 미인은 아니다 I think she is far from [none too] pretty. // 남에게 의혹을 살 만한 행동을 ~ 해서는 안 된다 You mustn't act in such a way as to cause even the slightest suspicion.

결탁(結託) [함께 꾸미기] conspiracy; (문어) [사전 비밀 협약] collusion. **결탁하다** conspire (with); be in collusion [league] (with). ¶친구와 결탁하여 in conspiracy [collusion] with one's comrades / in league with one's pals // 그는 그 악당과 결탁하여 온갖 나쁜 짓을 다 했다 He did all manner of evil things in league with that villain. // 그들은 결탁하여 가공의 출장비를 빼냈다 They conspired to get allowances for imaginary business trips. // 모두가 결탁하여 그걸 내게 숨기려 하고 있는 것 같다 Everyone seems to be conspiring to keep it from me.

결투(決鬪) a duel; an affair of honor; [되받아침] (구어) a shootout; a gunfight. ¶~를 신청하다 challenge (a person) to a duel / throw down the gauntlet [glove] // ~에 응하다 accept a person's challenge to a duel / take up the gauntlet. **결투하다** duel (with); fight a duel (with).
● **결투자** a duelist; a dueler. **결투장**(-狀) a challenge (to a duel); a cartel.

결판(決判) [판가름] a judg(e)ment; [결말] settlement; fixing (up). ¶~이 나다 be settled [fixed] / be finished / come [be brought] to an end [a conclusion] // 그건 이제 ~이 났다 It's over and done with. // 이제 ~을 지어도 될 때다 It's about time we are through with it. // 사건이 원만히 ~났다 The case was settled amicably. / The case was brought to an amicable settlement.

결핍(缺乏) [없음] (a) want; (a) lack; (a) dearth; (a) famine, poverty; absence; [부족] shortage; deficiency; scarcity; scantiness. ¶비타민의 ~ (a) vitamin deficiency // 연료의 ~ a fuel shortage // 노동자의 ~ a labor famine // 비료의 ~으로 수확이 줄었다 We had a poor crop for want of fertilizer. **결핍하다** [필요한데 없다] want; lack; be wanting [lacking] (in); [부족하다] run short (of); run low [out of]. → ¶너는 비타민 C가 결핍되어 있다 You need vitamin C.
● **결핍증**(비타민 등의) (a) deficiency disease.

결하다(決-) determine; decide (on / to do); settle; [판정하다] judge. ¶승부를 ~ decide a contest / try conclusions (with) / (무승부일 때) run off / play off (against) // 자웅을 ~ fight a decisive battle (with a person) for hegemony / try conclusions (with).

결하다(缺-) (be) wanting; lacking; short; deficient; missing.

결함(缺陷) (중대한) a defect; (완전함에서 약간 모자라는) a flaw; a fault; a shortcoming; (미국 비어) bugs; a deformity (of one's nature); [부족] deficiency; shortage; a gap. ¶~이 있는 defective / faulty / flawed / deficient / ~이 없는 faultless / flawless / perfect / complete // 성격상의 ~ a defect [deformity] in one's character // 제도의 ~ a defect [flaw] in the system // 경영상의 ~ a defect in management // 정신적 [육체적]으로 ~이 있다 be mentally [physically] deficient // ~이 많다 be badly flawed // ~을 드러내다 (사람이) betray one's weakness // ~을 보완하다 [메우다] make good [make up for] a defect // 그는 성격상 몇 가지 ~이 있다 He has some defect [Something is lacking] in his character. // 그의 시력(視力)에 ~이 있다 His vision is imperfect. // 그의 논리는 ~투성이이다 There are many flaws [holes] in his reasoning. // 그의 논법에서 나는 ~을 조금도 찾아볼 수 없다 I can't find anything wrong with his logic. // 만일 이 물품에 품질상의 ~이 발견되면 경비를 본사에서 부담하는 조건으로 반품하셔도 좋습니다 If you should find any defects in the quality of these goods, you are quite free to return them at our charge.

결합(結合) union; combination; cohesion; conjunction (of discoveries and inventions); [전/물] coupling; linkage; bond; (원자핵의) fusion; (우주선의) docking. **결합하다** combine; unite; (두 개의 것이) couple; weld (into one body); consolidate; be [get] tied up (with); be brought together; be united; bring (the two) together; join [band] together; conjoin; wed (to); (미국 구어) connect up. ¶두 개의 물건을 ~ couple [unite] two things // …과 결합하여 in combination with ... / conjointly with ... // 여러 파(派)가 결합하여 당을 만들었다 Several factions combined [united] to form a party. // 그 부부는 다시 결합했다 The couple got back together again. / The couple resumed their former relationship. // 이것은 두 개의 원소가 결합한 것이다 This is a combination of two elements. → 그들은 양국 관계를 보다 가까이 결합시키는 데에 많은 고생을 했다 They had a hard time bringing the two countries closer to each other. // 이해 관계에 의해 결합되다 be linked together by interest // 그 큰 두 재벌은 혼인으로 결합되었다 The two great business groups were brought together [were united] by that marriage. // 서로가 바흐의 음악을 좋아한 것 때문에 그 두 사람은 결합되었다 A common love of Bach's music brought the couple together.
● **결합력** unifying force; cohesiveness; [화] bonding strength; coherence. **결합 법칙** [수] associative law. **결합체** a corporation; a corporate body. **결합 효과** [물][화] a packing effect.

결항(缺航) (배·항공기의) a flight cancellation; a canceled flight; suspension of (ferry) service. **결항하다** (배가) do not sail (as scheduled); (비행기가) do not fly (as scheduled). → ¶결항시키다 cancel a ship [a flight] // 이번 김포발 편은 결항되었다 The next flight from Gimpo has been canceled. // 103편(便)은 결항되었습니다 Flight 103 has been canceled. // 연락선은 (폭풍우로) 결항되었다 The sailing of the ferryboat was canceled (because of the storm).

결핵(結核) [의] [결핵균에 의한 작은 멍울] a tubercle; [병] tuberculosis(약어 T.B., t.b.); consumption; [지] concretion. ¶장(腸)~ intestinal tuberculosis // 폐(肺)~ [성] phthisis / pulmonary tuberculosis // ~성의 tubercular / tuberculous / [지] concretionary // ~에 걸리기 쉬운 소질 a predisposition to tuberculosis // 폐~을 앓다 suffer from tuberculosis of the lungs // ~에 걸리다 contract tuberculosis // ~을 박멸하다 eradicate [uproot] tuberculosis.
● 결핵균 a tubercle bacillus (*pl.* -li); tuberculosis germs. 결핵 예방 prevention of tuberculosis. 결핵 요양소 a sanitarium[(영) sanatorium] for tuberculosis; a T.B. sanatorium. 결핵 환자 a tuberculosis patient.

결행(決行) decisive action; a resolute step. **결행하다** carry out (resolutely); take decisive action (on); take a resolute step. ¶일행은 내일 아침에 등정(登頂)을 결행하기로 했다 The party has decided to carry out the climb tomorrow morning. // 조합은 파업을 결행했다 The union staged[carried out] the strike [walkout] as scheduled. / The union went on strike. →¶경기는 우천임에도 불구하고 결행되었다 The game was held[They went ahead with the game] in spite of the rain.

결혼(結婚) (a) marriage; a union; (문어) matrimony. ¶강제 ~ (a) forced[coercive] marriage[match] // 국제~ (an) international marriage // 근친~ a near-kin[consanguineous] marriage // 맞선 ~ (an) interview[arranged] marriage // 매매 ~ (a) purchase marriage // 사진 ~ a picture[photo] marriage // 시험 ~ a trial marriage // 약탈 ~ (a) marriage by capture // 연애 ~ a love match [marriage] // 이민족 (간) ~ an intermarriage / a mixed marriage // 이중 ~ (commit) bigamy // 정략 ~ (a) marriage of convenience / (an) expedient marriage / a marriage forced by political expediency // 정식 ~ a legal marriage // 중매 ~ a marriage arranged [made up] by go-between // 집단 ~ (a) group marriage // 합의 ~ (a) consensual marriage // ~의 matrimonial / marriage / marital / conjugal // 행복한 ~ a happy union // ~ 전의 관계[여자 친구] one's premarital relations[girl friend] // (여자로부터) ~의 승낙을 받다 gain[win] (her) hand // ~에 성공[실패]하다 succeed[make a blunder] in marrying (a man, a woman, etc.) // ~을 신청하다 propose to a person / make a proposal (of marriage) to a person // ~을 해소하다 dissolve[break off] one's marriage (with a person) / annul a marriage // [이혼하다] get a divorce // ~을 승낙하다[거절하다] accept [reject] a marriage proposal // ~을 약속하다 engage to marry / engage oneself (to) // ~을 축하하다 [축사를 하다] congratulate a man on his marriage / wish a woman great happiness in her marriage(▶ 보통 남성에 대해서는 congratulate, 여성에 대해서는 wish ... happiness라고 함) / [식·축연을 하다] celebrate a person's marriage // 모두 알고 있는 바와 같이 ~은 연애의 무덤이다 As everyone knows, marriage is death to a love affair. **결혼하다** marry; be[get] married (to); be united; wed; join (hands)[unite] in marriage; enter into matrimony; (미국 속어) hitch (up); (구어) tie the knot. ¶결혼한 남자[여자] a married man[woman] // 갓 결혼한 부부 newlyweds / a just-married couple // 재산을 목적으로 결혼하는 사람 a fortune hunter // 장차의 신부 [장차의 신부] a prospective bride // 그는 그 처녀와 결혼했다 He married that girl. // 그녀는 농부[은행원]와 결혼했다 She married[got married to] a farmer[bank employee]. // 그들은 10대에 결혼했다 They got married (while they were still) in their teens. // 우리는 결혼한 지 3년이 되었습니다 We have been married for three years. // 그는 평생 동안 결혼하지 않았다 He remained single all his life. // 나는 결혼할 나이의 딸이 하나 있다 I have a daughter of marriageable age. // 딸이 결혼하는 것을 보기 전에는 내가 안심하고 눈을 감을 수 없다 I cannot die in peace before I see my daughter married. →¶결혼시키다 (딸을) marry (one's daughter to a person) / get (a daughter) married / (남녀를) marry (the two of) them / make one / unite (a couple) in marriage / couple.
● 결혼기념일 a wedding anniversary. 결혼반지 a marriage[wedding] ring. 결혼상담소 a matrimonial agency[center]. 결혼 생활 a married[wedded / conjugal / marital] life; wedlock; conjugality. ¶~에 들어가다 embark in[on] matrimony / enter into the bonds of matrimony // ~을 하다 live a married life / live in double harness. 결혼식 a marriage [(문어) nuptial] ceremony; a wedding (ceremony). ¶~을 올리다 hold a wedding ceremony / solemnize a marriage. 결혼식장 a wedding hall. 결혼 적령기 a marriageable [nubile] age; the age for marriage. 결혼 피로연 a wedding reception. 결혼 행진곡 the wedding march.

겸(兼) and; in addition; combining; concurrently; at the same time. ¶국무총리 ~ 외무부 장관 the Prime Minister and (concurrently) Minister of Foreign Affairs / the portfolio of Foreign Minister together with the Premiership // 서재 ~ 응접실 a room used both for study and for receiving visitors / a study-cum-drawing room // 편집인 ~ 발행인 the editor and publisher (of a magazine) // 여기가 거실 ~ 침실입니다 This room doubles as a living room and a bedroom. // 나는 그의 운전기사 ~ 비서를 하고 있다 I am his chauffeur besides acting as his secretary. // 나는 관광 ~ 상용으로 경주에 갔다 I went to Gyeongju partly on business and partly for sightseeing.

겸무(兼務) an additional post; another post [office]; plural offices; an extra post. **겸무하다** hold an additional[a concurrent] post (of); hold also the post (of); serve concurrently (as); hold another office concurrently [simultaneously / in addition]. ¶두 학교에 ~ teach in both schools // 그는 이사와 판매부장을 겸무하고 있다 He holds the posts of director and head of the sales department concurrently.

겸비하다(兼備-) combine (one thing) with (another); have both; have[possess] (A and B / two things) at the same time; join. ¶재색(才色)을 ~ combine wit with beauty / be as wise as fair // 재색을 겸비한 여성 a woman with beauty and intelligence / a beautiful and intelligent woman // 그는 세 가

겸사

지 특징을 겸비하고 있다 He combines all the three characteristics.∥그는 문무를 겸비하고 있다 He combines both learning [He excels at both scholarship] and the martial arts.∥그는 지용(智勇)을 겸비하고 있다 He has both courage and wisdom.

겸사(謙辭)〔겸손〕modesty; humility;〔겸손한 말〕humble speech;〔사양함〕declining humbly; humble refusal [denial / declination]. **겸사하다** be modest; be humble; humble oneself and give way to another; decline humbly.

겸사겸사(兼事兼事) at the same time; simultaneously; for a double purpose; for two reasons; combined with; partly ... and partly .... ¶상용 유흥 ~로 partly on business and partly for pleasure∥만나도 보고 이야기도 하려고 ~ 왔다 I have come with a double purpose of seeing you and of having a talk with you.

겸상(兼床) (상) a table for two; (식사) a tête-à-tête dinner. ¶~을 차리다 prepare [lay / set] the table for two∥~을 받다 sit down to a tête-à-tête dinner. **겸상하다** take a tête-à-tête dinner; sit at the same dinner table; eat a meal face to face at the table.

겸손(謙遜) modesty; humility; diffidence; self-effacement. ¶~이 지나치면 비굴이 된다 Excessive modesty lapses into servility. **겸손하다** modest; diffident; humble; unassuming; humble [efface] oneself; (아랫사람에게) condescending;〔삼가다〕reserved. ¶겸손한 태도[사람] modest attitude [a modest person / a self-effacing person]∥겸손해하다〔사양하는 듯한 태도를 취하다〕be modest [self-effacing / unassuming] / take a modest approach [attitude] /〔겸양하다〕be humble∥지나치게 ~ think too meanly of oneself∥그는 말씨[태도]가 ~ He is modest in his speech [behavior].∥그녀의 태도는 항상 ~ She always takes a self-deprecating attitude. / (구어) She's always putting herself down.∥그녀는 겸손한 말씨를 쓴다 She speaks humbly [in a humble tone].∥저 녀석은 겸손한 데가 조금도 없다 He hasn't the slightest touch of modesty.∥그는 너무 겸손하여 아무 말도 하지 못했다 He was too modest to speak up.∥그는 겸손하여 잠자코 있다 Modesty keeps him from speaking. **겸손히** with modesty; in a modest way; modestly; humbly. ¶~ 말하다 talk in a modest manner / talk with modesty.

겸양(謙讓) humbleness; modesty; humility; diffidence. ¶~의 미덕 the virtue of modesty∥~의 미덕을 발휘하다 behave modestly [with modesty] / hide one's light under a bushel∥지나친 ~은 오만 Too much humility is pride. **겸양하다** be modest; humiliate oneself; humble oneself; condescend. ¶겸양하는 compliant / self-effacing.

겸업(兼業) a side job [business / line]; a subsidiary business; a by-business; (미) bywork; a job [business] on the side. ¶~의 금지 prohibition of side job. **겸업하다** take up a side job; pursue [follow] (another trade) as a side business [in addition to a trade]; have two jobs at the same time. ¶그의 가족은 다방과 꽃집을 겸업하고 있다 His family is running a coffee shop and a flower shop simultaneously.∥그 집은 음식점과 여관을 겸업하고 있다 That house combines restaurant and hotel business.

겸연쩍다(慊然-) abashed; embarrassed; disconcerted. ¶겸연쩍게 shamefully / shame facedly∥겸연쩍어하다 be [feel] abashed / be [feel] embarrassed / be put out of countenance / feel awkward∥겸연쩍게 만들다 make (a person) self-conscious / put (a person) out of countenance∥겸연쩍은 듯이 쓴웃음을 웃으며 grinning sheepishly∥겸연쩍은 얼굴을 하다 be shamefaced / (꾸중을 듣고) have a hangdog look∥겸연쩍어 나는 그에게 부탁을 하지 못하겠다 I cannot with any grace make the request to him.∥너무 추어올리지 마라. 내가 ~ You praise me too much. Spare my blushes.

겸용(兼用) a combined [double / multiple] use; combination. ¶청우(晴雨) ~ 우산 a combination parasol and umbrella / a sunshade umbrella / (프) an en-tout-cas (pl. -cases)∥서재 ~ 응접실 a library and parlor in one / a library which also serves as a parlor / a combination library and parlor / parlor-cum-study∥이 부엌은 식당 ~입니다 This kitchen also serves as a dining room. **겸용하다** use in two or more ways; use (both) as (A) and (B); make (a thing) serve a double purpose. ¶서재를 응접실로 ~ use a study as a reception room∥이것은 소파와 침대로 겸용할 수 있다 This can be used both as a sofa and a bed. / This sofa does double duty as a bed.

겸임(兼任) a concurrent office. ⇨겸직 **겸임하다** hold an additional [also] post [office] (of); hold two or more positions concurrently; have part-time business in two or more places. ¶3개교에서 겸임해 가르치다 teach (at) three different schools∥그는 회사의 상무이사와 판매 부장을 겸임하고 있다 He holds the posts of director and head of the sales department concurrently.

겸자(鉗子)〔의〕a forceps (pl. ~, -cipes); an extractor; (외과용의) clamps.

겸직(兼職) a concurrent office [position]; an additional job [post / office]. ¶~으로 일하다 work in two or more places∥공무원의 ~에는 규정에 따른 제한이 있다 There are restrictions on civil servants holding other jobs. **겸직하다** hold (a position) concurrently with the principal; hold an additional position; hold concurrent posts. ¶그는 두 병원에서의 일을 겸직하고 있다 He works at two different hospitals.∥그는 대학의 교수와 도서관장을 겸직하고 있다 He is serving concurrently as professor of a university and director of the library.

겸하다(兼-) 1〔아울러 가지다〕combine [unite] (one thing with another); possess both (A and B);〔겸용되다〕serve both as (A and B); double as; [A이기도 하고 B이기도 하다] be both (A and B). ¶일과 놀이를 ~ combine business with pleasure∥공부를 겸하여 외유하다 go abroad partly for pleasure [sightseeing] and partly to learn about the world∥산책을 나갔던 길에 겸하여 도서관에 들렀다 While I was out for a walk, I dropped in at the library.∥이 상자는 책상과 의자를 겸하고 있다 This box serves both as a desk and a seat.∥그가 작곡과 작사를 겸하여 했다 He both composed the music and wrote the words.

2 [겸직하다] hold (a post) as an additional office [in addition to one's regular office]; combine the office of (A) with that of (B); hold (two offices) simultaneously [concurrently]; double as (cook). ¶내가 입원 중이므로 나는 그녀의 일을 겸하여 하지 않으면 안 된다 I have to do my wife's work too, now that she's in the hospital. // 그는 혼자서 교장, 교사, 경리, 수위를 모두 겸하고 있다 He is principal, teacher, treasurer, and janitor, all in one. // 총리는 국방 장관을 겸하고 있다 The Premier is also (serving as) the Minister of Defense at the same time.

겸행(兼行) [아울러 함] doing more than one job at the same time; [밤에도 일함] double duty; working overtime. ¶주야 ~으로 일하다 work day and night [round the clock] // 주야 ~으로 가동시키다 set (a machine) on the 24 hour job // 불도저를 주야 ~으로 운전하다 operate a bulldozer around the clock [twenty-four hours a day]. **겸행하다** do (more than one job) at the same time; work a double shift; work overtime at.

겸허하다(謙虛-) humble; modest; retiring. ¶겸허하게 in a humble way / with modesty / modestly // 겸허한 태도 a modest attitude // 겸허한 태도로 부탁하다 make a modest request // 겸허하게 여론에 귀를 기울이다 listen humbly to the voice of public opinion // 그 가족은 겸허하게 살아가고 있다 The family lives unpretentiously. // 나의 잘못을 겸허한 마음으로 사과합니다 I apologize most humbly for my mistake. // 나는 인생을 사랑하며 죽음 앞에서는 ~ Life I love, and before death I am humble.

겹 1 [포개어 거듭됨] a fold; [거듭된 켜] a fold; a layer; [쌓아 올린 켜] a pile; [맞줄 등의 가닥] a ply; [두 배] double; twofold. ¶두 ~ twofold // 여러 ~ many folds / over and over again / repeatedly // 담요를 두 ~으로 접다 double a blanket // 종이를 여러 ~으로 접다 fold a piece of paper over and over again. **2** [이중] double; twofold; twin; duplication; doubleness; duplexity. ¶~문 double doors [windows] // 병사들이 5~, 6~으로 서서 문을 지키고 있었다 Soldiers stood five and six deep guarding the gate.

겹겹이 in many folds; manifoldly; one upon another; fold on fold; layer upon layer; ply on ply; row on row; range on range; heap on heap(s); in piles. ¶~ 쌓아 올리다 lay one upon another / lay in piles [layers] // 종이로 ~ 싸다 wrap (a thing) in several sheets of paper // 적을 ~ 둘러싸다 surround the enemy thick and fast // 산으로 ~ 둘러싸이다 be surrounded by range of range of mountains // 그의 집을 경찰관이 ~ 둘러쌌다 His house was besieged tightly by the police. // 내가 도착하자마자 신문 기자들이 ~ 내게 몰려들었다 On arriving, I was besieged by the reporters.

겹꽃 [식] a double flower [blossom].

겹눈 [동] compound eyes; an ommateum (*pl.* -tea). ¶~의 ommateal.

겹다 1 [참기 어렵다] uncontrollable; unrestrainable; irrepressible; irresistible; beyond restraint; be difficult to stand (against); be unable to bear up. ¶흥에 겨워 in the excess of mirth / driven by one's enthusiasm // 설움에 겨워 in (the fullness of) one's sorrow [grief] / in a passion of grief // 눈물겨운 광경 a tearful [pathetic] scene // 그는 슬픔에 겨워 소리 내어 울었다 He wept loudly in a passion of grief.

2 [힘에 부치다] beyond [above] one's capacity; too much for (one). ¶이 일은 내 힘에 ~ I am not equal to the task. / This work is too much for me. // 이 일은 힘에 겨워 못 해내겠다 I find it difficult to deal successfully with this business. // 그 일은 젊고 연약한 여자에게는 힘에 겨운 것 같다 The task seems too much for a young and fragile woman.

겹말 tautology; redundant words; a pleonasm.

겹문자 (-文字) a redundant [pleonastic] passage.

겹사돈 (-査頓) a relative doubly related by marriage.

겹세로줄 [음] double bar.

겹옷 lined clothes; clothes with a lining.

겹질리다 be sprained; (a joint) be wrenched; have a strain in (one's leg). ¶다리를 ~ have a strain [sprain] in one's leg.

겹창 (-窓) a double window; a storm window.

겹치다 overlap each other [one another]; be piled up. ¶불행이 ~ have misfortune after misfortune / have a series of misfortunes // 손해가 ~ sustain loss upon loss.

겹치다 1 [포개다] pile up; heap up; put [place] one upon [over] another; lay one on top of another [the other]. ¶겹친 판자(기와처럼) overlapping boards // 슬레이트를 ~ lap a piece of slate over another // 벽돌을 5개 ~ pile [stack] up five bricks // 종이를 3장 ~ lay three sheets of paper one on top of another // 스웨터를 겹쳐 입다 wear one sweater over another // 두 사람은 겹쳐 쓰러졌다 [쓰러져 있었다] The two of them fell down on top of each other [were lying sprawled on top of each other]. // 더러운 접시를 겹쳐 놓지 말아 주십시오 Please don't stack the dirty dishes.

2 [포개어지다] be piled up; overlap each other [one another]. ¶상자가 많이 겹쳐져 있다 There are a lot of boxes piled up. / There is a big pile of boxes.

3 [추가되다·맞물리다] overlap; fall on. ¶겹친 행운 a happy combination of good lucks // 불운은 겹치게 마련이다 Misfortunes come in succession [one after another]. // 나는 일이 겹쳐 정신을 못 차리고 있다 I am swamped with work. // 그는 수면 부족이 겹쳐 앓아 눕게 되었다 He became ill from chronic [cumulative] lack of sleep. // 이 두 분야는 서로 겹치는 부분이 있다 These two fields overlap each other in some places. // 빈곤과 무지(無知)가 겹쳐 그가 그런 범죄를 저지르게 되었다 Poverty and ignorance combined to lead him to such a crime. // 이 두 권의 책의 내용에는 겹친 데가 있다 The contents of the two books overlap. // 이 두 사람의 목소리가 겹쳐 나는 그들이 무슨 말을 하는지 알아듣지 못했다 The two spoke at the same time, and I could not understand what they were saying. // 올해는 추분 날과 일요일이 겹친다 *Chubun* falls on Sunday this year. // 우연히 두 사고가 겹쳐 일어났다 The two accidents happened to occur at (almost) the same time.

겹치마 a lined skirt.
겻섬 a sack of rice hulls.
경(更) a night watch; [시각] one of the five watches of the night. ¶삼~ midnight / (in) the dead[depth] of night.
경(京) [수] ten-million billion.
경(卿) 1 [그대] You my liege(임금이 신하에게). ¶~들은 you all. 2 [호칭] Lord; Sir. ¶넬슨 ~ Lord Nelson // 처칠 ~ Sir Winston / Sir Winston Churchill(Lord는 성에 붙이고, Sir는 이름 또는 성명에 붙일 때 쓴다).
경(經) 1 [경서] Chinese classics of Confucianism.
2 [불경] the sutras; the Buddhist scriptures. ¶~을 읽다 chant[recite / intone] a sutra / read a service.
3 [기도문·주문] spells [incantations] of sorcerers. ¶~을 외다 chant a spell / make an incantation.
4 [직물의 날] the warp.
5 [경도] longitude.
경-(輕) light; light-weight; simple; easy. ¶~ 기관총 a light machine gun.
-경(頃) about; (미) around; toward(s); circa. ¶3시~ about[around] three o'clock // 15세기 말~ toward the end of the 15th century // 작년 봄 4월~의 일이다 It was in the last spring, sometime in April. // 그것은 1940년~에 일어났다 It took place in 1940 or thereabouts.
경가극(輕歌劇) an operetta; a light opera.
경각(頃刻) a moment; an instant; a second; a minute. ¶~간에 in a moment[an instant] / within a moment / in a split second / in the twinkling of an eye // ~을 다투다 fight the clock // ~도 지체할 수가 없다 Not a moment is to be lost. / There is no time[not a moment] to lose.
경각(傾角) 1 [수] amplitude. ⇨ˆ편각(偏角) 2 [물] a dip of the compass). ⇨ˆ복각(伏角).
경각(警覺) warning; awakening; remonstration; caution; precaution. **경각하다** warn; awaken; remonstrate; give a warning; caution; admonish.
●**경각심** (self-)consciousness; (self-)awakening. ¶~을 불러일으키다 arouse[provoke] (a person's) attention / bring (a person) to (his) senses.
경감(輕減) reduction; mitigation; abatement; (고통 등의) alleviation; (형의) commutation. ¶국민들은 세금의 ~을 바라고 있다 The people want to have their taxes reduced [lightened]. **경감하다** (형을) reduce; (부담·세금 등을) lighten; (벌을) mitigate; (고통을) alleviate[allay / soothe]; relieve; (벌을) commute; (세금을) abate. // (형(刑)을) ~ reduce[lighten] a penalty[sentence] / commute the punishment (from death to life imprisonment)(▶ commute는 보통 사형의 감형에 쓰임) // 고통을 ~ alleviate[relieve / ease] the pain. ➔¶우리의 부담은 훨씬 경감되었다 Our burdens have become much lighter.
경감(警監) a police inspector; a police captain(약어 pol. capt.).
경거망동(輕擧妄動) rash[hasty] attempt and blind behavior. ¶~을 삼가다 behave [proceed] prudently / refrain from rash acts. **경거망동하다** do[act] rashly; commit a rash act.

경건하다(敬虔−) pious; devotional; devout; godly; God-fearing. ¶경건하지 않은 impious / profane // 경건한 기독교 신자 a devout [pious] Christian // 경건한 기도를 드리다 offer a most reverential prayer / pray devoutly (to God) // 경건한 느낌을 갖다 feel reverence (for) // 교황이 나타나자 경건한 침묵이 흘렀다 There was a reverential silence when the Pope appeared. **경건히** reverently; respectfully; humbly.
경계(境界) a boundary; a border; a frontier; [법] metes and bounds. ¶시(市)의 ~ the city limits // 주(州)의 ~ the state border // 토지의 ~ the boundary of the estate // 중국의 ~ the border with China // 연민과 동정의 ~ the borderline between pity and sympathy // 생사의 (cross) the Great Divide // 밤과 낮의 (on) the confines of night and day // 생사의 ~를 헤매다 hang[hover] between life and death // ~를 접하다 border (on) / abut (on) // ~를 접하고 있지 않다 share no common boundary (with) // ~를 정하다 demarcate / delimit / fix [define] the boundary (between) // ~를 봉쇄하다 close the borders // ~를 이루다 adjoin (a place) / border on (a place) // 만주는 시베리아와 ~를 접하고 있다 Manchuria borders on Siberia. // 핀란드는 서쪽으로 스웨덴과 ~를 접하고 있다 Finland is bounded on the west by Sweden. / Finland borders Sweden on the west. // 산등성이가 두 도(道)의 ~로 되어 있다 The mountain ridge forms the boundary between the two prefectures.
●**경계선** (토지의) a boundary line; (미) a border (line); a line of demarcation; (시대 구분의) a dividing line (between). ¶~을 긋다 draw a line of demarcation (between). **경계인** [사] a marginal man. **경계표**(−標) a landmark; a mete; a boundary stone[mark]; a demarcation post.
경계(警戒) 1 [경고] caution; warning; admonition; [주의] precaution. ¶경찰의 엄중한 ~ stringent police precautions // ~를 엄중히 하다 make strict precautions // 폭풍의 우려가 있으므로 연안 지방은 ~를 요한다 Since there is fear of a storm, precautions ought to be taken along the coasts. **경계하다** warn; give warning of; exercise[take] precaution; caution (a person) against; admonish. ¶너는 그녀를 경계해야 해 You must be on your guard against her. // 너는 특히 음주를 경계해야 한다 You must on your guard especially against drink.
2 [감시·경비] watch; vigilance; lookout; guard. ¶삼엄한 ~ strict watch // 전면 ~ 태세에 돌입하다 be on a full alert // 물샐틈없는 ~를 하다 be on strict watch[guard] // ~를 게을리 하지 않다 keep a sharp lookout (for) // ~를 늦추다 lower one's guard // 그는 적군에 대한 특별 ~ 태세를 취할 것을 군에 명령했다 He ordered the armed forces to be put on special alertness against the enemy. // 교사들은 교내 폭력에 대하여 ~를 강화하고 있다 The teachers are growing increasingly wary of[are redoubling their precautions against] school violence. **경계하다** watch; look out for; keep an eye on; be on the watch; be watchful; [순찰하다] patrol. ¶소매치기를 경계하라 Look out for pickpockets. // 수상 관저를 엄중히 ~ keep strict guard

[watch] over the Prime Minister's official residence // 그를 경계해야 한다 You must be on your guard against him. / Beware of him. // 경찰은 폭동에 대비하여 엄중히 경계하고 있다 The police are on the strict alert for a riot.
● **경계경보** (공습의) air-raid warning; a preliminary alert. **경계관제** warning control of lights; an alert; (등화관제의) dim-out. **경계망** a cordon of police; a police cordon[net]. ¶~을 치다[빠져나가다] lay[slip through] a police cordon. **경계색** protective coloring (of animals); warning[semantic] coloration. **경계선** a police line[cordon]. ¶~을 돌파하다 (범인이) slip through a police cordon / (군중이) break through[across] a police line. **경계수위**(-水位) the danger level (of a river). **경계심** wariness. **경계표지** a warning sign.

경고(警告) warning; admonition; (영) caution; advice; notice. ¶사전 ~ an advance warning // 엄중한 ~ a sharp[serious] warning // ~를 발하다 send out[issue / announce] a warning // ~를 받다 take warning (from) / be warned (against) // 그는 아무런 ~도 없이 발포했다 He fired (his gun) without warning. // 친구들의 ~도 듣지 않고 그녀는 강에서 헤엄치기 시작했다 She began to swim in the river against the advice of her friends. **경고하다** warn; caution (a person) against; give warning; admonish. ¶강경히 ~ thunder words of warning in (a person's) ears // 국민에게 ~ sound a warning to the nation // 술을 과음하지 않도록 나는 그에게 경고했다 I advised him not to drink too much. // 정부는 국민에게 인플레의 위험을 경고했다 The government alerted the nation to the dangers of inflation. // 내가 경고해 두지만 그런 일이 있으면 너는 파면이다 I'm warning you[This is a warning]. You'll be fired [dismissed from the service] if you do it again.
● **경고 사격** (fire) a warning shot.

경골(脛骨) [생] the shinbone; the tibia (pl. -ae, ~s). ¶~의 tibial.
경골(硬骨) 1 (뼈의) (a) hard bone. 2 [강직] a firm character; firmness (of character); inflexibility; stubbornness. ¶~의 firm / staunch / uncompromising / inflexible.
● **경골한**(-漢) a man of firm character; a man of principle [sturdy heart].
경골(頸骨) the neck bone. ⇨*목뼈
경공업(輕工業) light industry.
● **경공업 제품** light industry articles.
경과(經過) (시간의) passage; lapse; flight; (기한의) expiration; [사건·상태의 귀추] progress; development; the course (of events); a tendency. ¶재판의 ~ the progress of a case // 사건의 ~ the course [run / development] of events // 수술 후의 ~ the postoperation course // 회의의 ~ the progress of a conference [negotiations] // 일에 대한 ~를 말하다 tell how things turned out // ~를 일일이 보고하다 regularly report (to one's senior) how things are going // ~를 살피다 watch the development of the affair // 그는 수술이 성공하여 ~가 좋다 He is progressing favorably after successful operation and is doing well. // 지금까지의 교섭의 ~를 말씀드리겠습니다 I will tell you how the negotiations are progressing. // 사건의 ~를 알고 계십니까 Do you know how the affair has developed? // 사태의 ~를 그대로 내버려 두자 Let things take their course [take care of themselves]. // 지금까지의 ~로 보아 그가 의장으로 틀림없이 선출될 것 같다 Judging from the course of things so far, he is sure to be elected chairman. **경과하다** pass; elapse; go by; expire. ¶10년이 경과하여 after (the lapse of) ten years // 유효 기간이 ~ the term[period] of validity expires // 그로부터 5년이 경과했다 Five years have passed since then. // 시간이 경과함에 따라 그의 마음의 상처도 아물었다 As time passed, he recovered from his emotional wounds. // 그는 4세기가 절반쯤 경과할 무렵에 태어났다 He was born halfway through the fourth century A.D. // 그의 사후 5시간이 경과했다 He has been dead these five hours. // 시간이 경과하면서 그 영웅적 행위는 잊혀졌다 With the passage of time, that heroic act was forgotten. // 세월이 경과했다 The years rolled on[by].
● **경과보고** a progress report; (회의의) a report on the proceedings; (사건의) a report on the development of an affair.
경관(景觀) a view; a vista; a scene; a spectacle; a sight; scenery. ¶장대한 ~ a grand view / a panorama // 남알프스의 웅장한 ~ the magnificent panorama of the Southern Alps // ~을 해치다 destroy[spoil] the scenic beauty
경관(警官) a policeman; a police officer. ⇨*경찰관(⇨*경찰)
경교(景敎) Nestorianism. ¶~의 Nestorian.
● **경교도**(-徒) a Nestorian.
경구(硬球) a hard ball; a regulation ball.
경구(警句) an epigram; an aphorism; a witticism; a witty remark; a good thing; a laconicism; (속어) a crack. ¶~를 말하다 make witty remarks // ~가 많은 문체 an epigrammatic style.
경구 감염(經口感染) oral infection.
경구개(硬口蓋) [생] the hard palate; the roof of the mouth.
경구 피임약(經口避妊藥) an oral contraceptive pill; a birth control pill; the pill.
경국(經國) running a country; administration; statesmanship.
● **경국지재**(-之才) the caliber of a statesman; administrative talent[abilities].
경국(傾國) decline of a nation; ruining a country.
● **경국지색**(-之色) a woman beautiful enough to cause the downfall of a country; a Helen of Troy; a siren.
경극(京劇) [중국의 가극] (a) Beijing (classical Chinese) opera.
경금속(輕金屬) light metals.
경기(景氣) business conditions; transactions; (the tone of) the market. ¶가짜 ~ a false show of activity / false prosperity / a fake boom // 벼락 ~ a boom (in the market) // 불 ~ a depression / a slump / a recession / bad business / a dull market // 전쟁[전후 / 전시] ~ a war[postwar / wartime] boom // 호 ~ prosperity / activity / a boom // 조작된 ~ borrowed[false / artificial] prosperity[boom] // ~의 내리막 a business[an economic] slowdown / an economic downturn // ~의 냉각 cooling down of the economy // ~가 좋다 [나쁘다] Business is brisk[dull]. // ~가 호황

이다 Business is flourishing.// ~가 상승[하강]하고 있다 Business is improving[falling off].//그의 회사는 ~가 좋다 His company is doing a good business.//~가 회복되었다 Business has rallied. / (시장의) The market picked[looked] up.//국내 ~는 명백한 회복의 조짐을 보이고 있다 The domestic business shows clear signs of recovery.// 장사의 ~는 어떻습니까 How is your business doing?/ How's business?// 금년의 ~ 전망도 역시 어둡다 The economic prospects for this year are dark again.//이 장사만은 ~를 타지 않는다 This trade is above business fluctuation.//아파트 건설의 과열 ~는 고비를 넘겼다 The boom in apartment house construction has passed its peak.
●**경기 관측 / 경기 예측** the business forecast. **경기 변동 / 경기 순환** a business[(영) trade] cycle. **경기 부양책** steps to stimulate the economy; reflation measures[policy]; expansionary[expansionist] policy. **경기 상승** a business upturn. **경기 예고 지표** the business warning index(약어 WI). **경기 지수**(一指數) a business barometer[index]. **경기 침체** stagnancy of business activities; economic slump. **경기 회복** a business[an economic] recovery; return to prosperity; a perk-up; boom after depression. **경기 후퇴** a business[an economic] recession; a business setback.

경기(競技) [시합] a game; a match; a contest; a competition; a meet; a tournament; [경기의 종목] an event; a sporting event. ¶근대 5종 ~ the modern pentathlon //3회전 ~ a three-game match// 수상(水上) ~ the water[aquatic] sports[events] // 수영 ~ a swimming competition / a swim race// 실내[야외] ~ indoor[field] games// 10종 ~ ten events / decathlon// 연습 ~ a practice game / a workout game// 육상 ~ track and field events//주요 ~ a main event//7종 ~ the heptathlon// 학교 대항 ~ an interschool match / (대학의) an intervarsity[a collegiate] match//~에 참가하다 take part in a contest / enter for an event / take the field//~에 이기다[지다] win[lose] a match[the game]//~에 도전하다 challenge (a person) to a match / enter for an event//~를 포기하다 throw up a game //~의 승패가 났다 The game is over[finished]. / The contest has been decided.// 무승부로 ~가 끝났다 The game ended in a draw.// 마지막 한 ~가 남았을 뿐이다 There is only one game[bout] left.//이 복싱 ~만은 안 보고 넘길 수 없다 I'm determined not to miss this boxing match. **경기하다** have a match[contest / game] (with); play a game[match] (with).
●**경기 대회** (운동의) an athletic meet(ing); a sports meeting; (기술 등의) a contest; a competition. **경기자**(一者) a contestant; a competitor; an athlete; a player; a racer; a swimmer. **경기장** [경기 진행의 장소] a (sports) ground[field]; (관람석을 포함하여) a (sports) stadium (pl. ~s, -dia); (주위에 관람석이 있는 원형 시합장) an arena.

경기(驚氣) [의] convulsions.
경기관총(輕機關銃) a light machine gun. ¶소형 ~ a submachine gun.
경기구(輕氣球) a dirigible balloon; a hot-air balloon. ¶계류 ~ a captive balloon.

경기병(輕騎兵) (부대) light cavalry; (병사) a light cavalryman[horseman].
경내(境內) the precincts[grounds / compound]; the precincts of a temple[shrine]. ¶~ 건물 precinct buildings//~의 수목 tree in the precincts (of a shrine)//사당의 ~에[에서] in the precincts (compound) of a shrine / within the pale of a shrine.
경노동(輕勞動) light labor[work]. ¶~에 고용되다 be employed on light work.
●**경노동자** a light worker; (사무직) a business worker.
경단(瓊團) a rice cake dumpling covered with bean paste[jam]; a dumpling.
경대(鏡臺) a dressing[mirror] stand; a dresser; a toilet[dressing] table; (미) a vanity.
경도(硬度) hardness; solidity. ¶다이아몬드의 ~는 10이다 The hardness of diamond is 10.
●**경도계** a durometer; [물] a hardness meter; [광] sclerometer; a sclerascope.
경도(經度) 1 [지] longitude. ¶~는 동경 10도 15분이다 It is situated at 10 degrees 15 minutes[10° 15′] of east longitude. 2 [월경] the menses; menstruation; monthlies; menstrual discharge; monthly sickness.
경도(傾度) inclination; [건] batter; [물] gradient.
경도(傾倒) [넘어짐] falling down; toppling (over); [기울어 쏟음] tilting; tipping; (마음을) devoting oneself; concentration. **경도하다** fall down; topple; tilt; tip; devote oneself to; concentrate (one's mind, one's energy, etc.) on; be wholly devoted to; be given to. ¶전력을 ~ concentrate all one's energies [powers] on (a subject)// 온 정신을 ~ bring all one's mind (to bear) upon (a matter)//나는 10년 동안 미국 문학 연구에 경도해 왔다 I have concentrated on the study of American literature for the past ten years. ◆그는 입센에 경도되어 있다 He is an ardent admirer of Ibsen.
경도(輕度) ¶~의 slight / trifling / not serious //~의 부상[화상 / 손해] a slight injury[burn / damage].
경동맥(頸動脈) [생] the carotid (artery).
경락(競落) auctioning.
●**경락물**(一物) objects knocked down. **경락인** [경매인] an auctioneer; [낙찰자] a successful bidder.
경량(輕量) light weight.
●**경량 골재** lightweight aggregate. **경량급** a lightweight (boxer). **경량품** light goods.
경력(經歷) one's (past) career[record]; one's life[personal] history; a career record; personal experiences; antecedents. ¶무대 ~ one's stage career// 연구 ~ one's academic history// 회사 ~서 the historical record of a company //~이 다양한 사람 a man with a varied career / a man of varied experiences //~이 수상한 사람 a man with a dubious past //~이 수상쩍은 여자 a woman with a past //~이 다년간 ~는 선교사 a missionary of many years' standing //~이 좋다[나쁘다] have a good[bad] record //~을 조사하다 check up[trace] (a person's) career[record] //그는 어떤 ~을 가진 사람이냐 What is his past career?// 그들은 그 여자의 ~에 대해 초보적인 조사도 하지 않고 채용했다 They employed the woman without first investi-

gating [looking into] her past life [background]. // 그는 ~이 좋으므로 어디든지 일자리를 구할 수 있을 것이다 He is sure to find situation anywhere, as he is a man of commendable antecedent. // 그녀의 ~은 소설이나 다름없다 Her story is a romance in real life.
- **경력 소개** a biographical introduction. **경력자** an experienced man.

경련(痙攣) convulsions; a spasm; a spasmodic; contraction; (근육의) crick; cramp; a jerk; (안면의) a tic; a twitch. ¶**강직성** ~ a tonic spasm // **손가락** ~ (문필가의) writer's cramp [palsy / spasm] / (전신 기사의) telegrapher's cramp // **안검** ~ a nictitating spasm // **안면** [얼굴] ~ a (facial) tic // ~성의 spasmodic / spastic / convulsive // ~이 **일어나다** be convulsed / have a convulsive fit / fall into a fit of convulsions / have a spasm [cramp] // 격심한 ~을 일으키다 fall into a fit of violent convulsions // 다리에 ~이 일어나다 get cramps in one's leg // 나는 목에 ~이 일어났다 I've got [I had] a crick in my neck. // 그는 헤엄치다가 ~이 일어났다 He was seized with a cramp while swimming. // 그의 눈꺼풀이 ~하고 있다 His eyelids are twitching. / He has a twitch in his eyelids.

경례(敬禮) salutation; a salute; an obeisance; a courtesy; a bow; (구령) Salute! ¶**거수** ~ a hand [military] salute // 거수~를 하다 raise one's hand in salute // 그들은 ~의 자세를 취했다 They stood at salute. // 사령관은 ~를 받았다 The commander took the salute. // 장교는 사병의 ~에 답했다 The officer returned the private's salute. **경례하다** salute; make a salutation; bow (to). ¶**차려 하고** ~ salute at attention // 정중히 ~ make a profound reverence // 국기에 대하여 ~ salute the colors // 모자를 벗어 올리며 ~ raise one's hat to (a person) // 그 병사는 손을 번쩍 올려 경례하였다 The soldier's hand snapped up a salute.

경로(經路) [지나는 길] a course; a channel; a route; [단계] a stage; [과정] a step; a process. ¶**외교** ~ a diplomatic channel // **전염** ~ the trace of an epidemic // 어떤 ~로 through what channel / how // 발달의 ~ the process of growth // 진화의 ~ the evolutionary process // **버스** ~ [노선] a bus service route // 같은 ~를 밟다 follow the same course (of) // 발달의 ~를 더듬다 trace the growth (of) // 이 지경에 이른 ~를 말하다 describe how it has come to this pass // 어떤 ~로 네가 그 정보를 입수했느냐 Through what channel did you get the information? // 그들은 전염 ~를 조사 중이다 They are investigating the path by which the epidemic spread. // 성공한 사람들은 모두 이런 ~를 밟아 온 것이다 This is the path trodden by all successful men of the world. // 다른 ~로 그것을 보내 드리겠습니다 I will send it by [via] another route.

경로(敬老) respect for the old [aged]. **경로하다** respect the aged; tend the aged; be kind to old folks.
- **경로잔치** a feast [party] in honor of the aged. **경로회** a respect-for-age meeting [association].

경륜(經綸) government; administration; (국가의) statecraft; statesmanship. **경륜하다** govern; administer; rule.

- **경륜지사**(-之士) a man of great administrative ability.

경륜(競輪) cycling race; (미) a bike race; a bicycle [cycle] race. ¶~에 내기를 걸다 play [bet on] cycle races // ~에서 돈을 벌다 [잃다] make [lose] money on cycle races
- **경륜 선수** a (professional) bicyclist; a cycle racer. **경륜장** a bicycle race track; a cyclodrome; a velodrome.

경리(經理) [처리] management; administration; [회계] accounting; [사무] accountant's business. ¶**회사의** ~ 관리 the control of corporate accounts [finances] // 그는 그 회사의 ~를 맡고 있다 He is in charge of accounting for the company. / He is an accountant for the company. **경리하다** manage; administer.
- **경리과 [부]** the accountants' section [department]. **경리 사원** an accounting clerk.

경마 a rein to lead a mounted horse with; a halter; a bridle.
경마(를) 잡다 serve as a groom; hold [lead] a horse by the bridle.
경마(를) 잡히다 have a groom lead a horse.

경마(競馬) horse racing; the races; a horse race. ¶**지방** ~ a local horse race // ~ **순번표** [출마표] a race card // ~의 승리자 racing tips // ~에 이긴 말 a winning racer // ~로 한몫 잡다 carry off a big race // ~에 돈을 걸다 bet on horse races / play the races // ~에서 돈을 잃다 [따다] lose [make] money on the turf [race] // ~에 맞히다 hit a dark horse // ~로 재산을 날리다 race one's fortune [property] away. **경마하다** hold [have] a horse race.
- **경마광**(-狂) a turf fan; a racing man. **경마 말** a race horse; a racer. **경마장** a racecourse; a race track; the turf.

경망하다(輕妄-) rash; imprudent; hasty; indiscreet; careless; flippant; light; frivolous. ¶**경망한 짓** a rash act // **경망한 여자** a frivolous woman // **경망한 사람** a reckless man // 경망한 언동 frivolities // 경망한 짓을 하다 act hastily [imprudently] / commit a rash act // 그녀는 경망한 데가 있다 She is apt to become indiscreet [frivolous]. // 그들은 경망한 데가 전혀 없다 There is nothing unstable [frivolous] about them. // 그 장관은 너무 경망하다는 비난을 받았다 The Minister was criticized for being too frivolous. **경망히** rashly; hastily; lightly; imprudently. ¶~ 입을 놀리다 talk flippantly / use flippant language // 그는 매사를 ~ 처리하지 않는다 He does not treat anything lightly.

경매(競賣) auction; a public [an open] sale; a sale at [(영) by] auction. ¶**강제** [**강제**] ~ a forced [compulsory] sale by auction // **부정** [**사기**] ~ a mock [fake] auction // 격렬한 ~ spirited bidding // 깎아 내리는 ~ Dutch auction // ~에서 값을 매기다 bid a price at auction // 집을 ~에 부치다 put up a house for auction // 피아노를 ~에 내놓다 put a piano up for auction // ~**에 부쳐지다** come under the (auctioneer's) hammer / be sold at auction // 나는 이 그림을 ~에서 샀다 I got this painting at an auction. // 그 가구는 ~에서 30만 원에 팔렸다 The furniture was sold at auction [auctioned off] for 300,000 won. // 가재도구는 모두 ~에 부치기로 되어 있다 All

경멸

the household goods are to be auctioned off (to the highest bidder) [come under the hammer]. 경매하다 sell at[(영) by] auction; auction off; bring[send] (a thing) to the hammer; put up (an article) to[at] auction.
● 경매 가격 a bid; a price offered by a successful [the highest] bidder. 경매물 an article for sale at auction. 경매 시장 an auction market. 경매 업자 an auction dealer. 경매인 an auctioneer; the promoter of an auction; [입찰자] a bidder. 경매장 an auction room [house / hall / site / a sale room]. 경매 처분 disposition by public sale [auction]; a tax sale; selling up.

경멸(輕蔑) contempt; scorn; disdain. (▶ contempt는 열등·무가치하다고 생각되는 것에 대한 비웃음의 기분, scorn은 목소리나 태도에 나타난 노엽고 조소적인 멸시, disdain은 경멸의 감정 이외에 자기를 높이 보고 자기는 단연 그런 짓을 하지 않는다는 기분》 ¶~의 눈초리로 보다 eye (a person) with contempt / look at (a person) contemptuously // ~을 당하다 be held in contempt[irreverence] // 그는 그들에 대한 경멸을 공공연히 드러냈다 He openly showed his contempt for them. 경멸하다 despise; hold (a person) in contempt; look down on[upon]; scorn; slight; think meanly of. ¶경멸하는 투로 말하다 talk[speak] disrespectfully (of) / speak in contempt // 그런 너석은 경멸할 가치도 없다 Such a fellow is beneath contempt. // 나는 그의 천한 근성을 경멸한다 I despise him for his mean nature. // 가난하다고 해서 남을 경멸해서는 안 된다 You should not despise a man because he is poor.

경모(敬慕) a admiration; adoration; love and respect; esteem. ¶~에게 ~의 정을 품다 conceive an adoration for (one's teacher). 경모하다 admire; adore; have a high regard for; hold in esteem; love and respect. ¶내가 경모하는 인물 중의 한 사람 one of my heroes // 학생들은 자기 담임선생님을 경모하고 있다 The children adore their homeroom[(영) class] teacher. // 시민들은 아직 그를 경모하고 있다 The townspeople have a great reverence and affection for him.

경묘하다(輕妙—) light and pleasant[easy]; smart; free; ready; clever. ¶경묘한 익살 a witty joke // 경묘한 문체 a light and witty style // 그는 곤란한 처지를 경묘한 답변으로 벗어났다 He got out of the difficult situation with a smart answer. 경묘히 lightly; wittily.

경무(警務) police affairs[duties / administration].
● 경무관 a police commissioner[director]; an inspector general.

경문(經文) [불] the text of a sutra; the Buddhist scriptures; a sutra; sutras; sacred books; [도교 서적] the Taoist scriptures [classics]; [가] ➡기도문(➪)기도(祈禱) ¶~을 읽다 read a sutra.

경미하다(輕微—) slight; little; not serious; trifling; negligible; insignificant. ¶경미한 문제 a trifling[trivial] matter // 경미한 범죄 a minor offense // 그는 경미한 부상을 입었다 He was slightly wounded[injured]. // 작물의 피해는 경미했다 The crop suffered slight damage.

경박하다(輕薄—) [불성실하다] insincere; [부박하다] light; frivolous; flippant; flighty; [변덕스럽다] fickle; volatile. (▶ flippant는 주로 일시적인 태도나 언동에 대해서, frivolous는 그 사람이 갖고 있는 성질·생활 태도 등에 대해서 쓰임》 ¶경박한 말씨 flippant way of talking / 경박한 사람 a frivolous person // 경박한 행동 frivolous behavior / a flippant act // 경박한 생각 a foolish[shallow] idea // 그가 하는 말은 언제나 ~ His remarks are always frivolous [flippant / shallow]. // 저런 사람이 하는 일에 편승하다니 너도 참 경박하군 How imprudent of you to follow such a man blindly! // 그는 영리하지만 경박한 데가 있다 He is clever, but rather frivolous. 경박히 frivolously; flippantly; insincerely.

경배(敬拜) bowing respectfully; a respectful bow. 경배하다 bow respectfully.

경범죄(輕犯罪) a minor offense; a misdemeanor. ¶그는 ~로 체포되었다 He was arrested for a misdemeanor.
● 경범죄 처벌법 Minor Offense Law.

경변증(硬變症) [의] cirrhosis (of the liver).

경보(競步) (competitive) walking; a walking race; a walking marathon; (미·캐나다) a walkathon. ¶1만 미터의 ~ the 10,000-meter walk (on the track).
● 경보 선수 a walker.

경보(警報) an alarm; a warning; a signal. ¶공습 ~ an air-raid alarm // 비상 ~ an alarm (signal) // 원거리 조기 ~망 the (distant) early warning // 조기 ~기(機) an early-warning plane / a radar picket plane // 폭풍 ~ a storm warning // ~를 내리다[전하다] warn / give [raise / sound] an alarm / give warning / (소리를 질러) shout an alarm / (징을 쳐) beat an alarm (on a gong) // ~를 해제하다 give[sound] an all clear // ~가 나자 사람들은 곧 집합하였다. // 그 지방 일대에는 지금 홍수 ~가 내려 있다 A general flood warning is now in operation all over the district.
● 경보기(—器) an alarm (signal). ¶도난 ~ a burglar alarm // 화재 ~ a fire alarm / a heat sensor.

경부 고속도로(京釜高速道路) the Gyeongbu [Seoul-Busan] expressway[superhighway / (미) speedway].

경부선(京釜線) the Gyeongbu [Seoul-Busan] Line.

경비(經費) [비용] expense(s); cost(s); upkeep; [지출] expenditure; (an) outlay. ¶일반 ~ general expenses // 제(諸) ~ overhead expenses[charges] // 여행에 필요한 ~ traveling expenses // 의복을 위한 ~ an outlay on [for] clothing // ~ 관계로 for financial reasons // 많은 ~를 들여서 at a great cost // ~에 관계없이 without regard to [for] expense[cost] // ~가 많이 들다 require [involve] great expense // ~를 절감하다 reduce [cut down] the expenses / curtail // 얼마의 ~가 들건 나는 금년 여름에 유럽에 갈 작정이다 Regardless of the cost, I'm going to Europe this summer. // ~는 모두 12만 원이었다 In all, the expenses amounted to 120,000 won. // 모든 ~를 빼고 순익 7만 4천 원이다 The net profit after the deduction of all expenses, is 74,000 won. // 이 집을 유지하는 데는 무척 많은 ~가 든다 It costs a lot to maintain [keep up] this house. // 거기에는 많은 ~가 소요될 것이다 It will involve a

swim a race (with); have a swim race (with).
●**경영 대회** a swim(ming) meet. **경영자 / 경영 선수** a (competitive) swimmer; (미) a merman(남자); a mermaid(여자).

경옥(硬玉) [광] jadeite. ¶~의 jaditic.

경외(敬畏) awe; dread. **경외하다** dread; stand in awe (of); have a dread (of); be awestruck.

경우(境遇) [때] an occasion; a time; a moment; [형편] circumstances; conditions; a situation; [사례] a case; an instance. ¶지금 같은 ~에(는) at this time[occasion] / as things stand [the case stands] (now) // 화재의 ~에(는) in case of fire / in the event of fire // 그런 ~가 생기면 if[when] such occasion arises // 내 ~에는 in my case // ~에 따라서 according to circumstances / as circumstances require / when occasion demands / if necessary[need be] // 위험한 ~에 in time of danger / at a critical moment // 최악의 ~에(는) in the worst case / when (the) worst comes to (the) worst // 대개의 ~에(는) in most cases / generally / in general // 그런[이런] ~에(는) in such a case / in [under] such[these] circumstances // 어떤 ~에(는) in certain[some] cases / sometimes / under certain circumstances / on a certain occasion // 어떤 ~에도 on[at] all occasions / under all circumstances / in all cases / no matter what the circumstances / always / (부정) under no circumstances / in no case / on no account // …의 ~에(는) in case of … / in the case of … // 그[이] ~에(는) in that[this] case // 필요한 ~에(는) in case of need / if circumstances require / when [where / if] (it is) necessary // 한 ~를 제외하고(는) except in the case[event] of (a fire, a person's death, etc.) / except where … / except in cases where [in which] (he fails) // 만약 그렇게 되는 ~에(는) should things come to such a pass // 비가 내릴 ~ 체육 대회는 중지된다 In case of rain[If it rains], the athletic meet will be called off. // 이 옷은 어떤 ~에도 입을 수 있다 This dress can be worn on all occasions. // 이 규칙은 당신의 ~에 적용되지 않는다 This rule does not apply to your case. // ~에 따라서는 거짓말을 해도 좋을 때가 있다 Falsehood is excusable in certain circumstances. // Circumstantial lies may be justified. // 만일의 ~를 위해 신분증을 갖고 가시오 Take your identification card with you, just in case. // 그렇게 하지 않으면 안 되는 ~가 흔히 있다 There are frequent occasions when it is imperative to do so. // 현재와 같은 ~에는 부득이하다[하는 수 없다] It cannot be helped under the present circumstances[conditions]. // ~에 따라서는 허용될 수 있다 That may be permitted depending on the situation. // 그 ~에 우리는 무엇이든 하겠소 We will do whatever the occasion demands. // 이런 ~, 많은 이야기를 해서는 안 될 것이라고 나는 생각했다 I thought I should not talk much on such an occasion as this. // 정직한 사람이 손해 보는 ~도 있다 There are instances where honesty does not pay. // 그것은 ~ 나름이다 That depends on circumstances. // 그것과 이것은 ~가 다르다 We must discriminate between the two cases. // 너의 ~는 예외로 한다 We make an exception in your case. // ~가 ~인 만큼 너그럽게 보아주자 We'll let it pass under these[the present] circumstances. / The circumstances being what they are[The situation being what it is], we'll overlook it. // 온갖 ~가 이 조항 속에 포함되어 있다 All possible circumstances are covered by this clause.

경운기(耕耘機) (drive / run) a cultivator; a tiller. ¶동력 ~ a power cultivator.

경원하다(敬遠-) keep (a person) at a (respectful) distance; give (a person) a wide berth; sidestep (an issue); [야구] give (a batter) a walk intentionally. ¶투수는 다음 타자를 경원했다 The pitcher gave the next batter an intentional walk. / The pitcher walked the next batter intentionally. // 학생들은 교장을 경원했다 The students kept away from the principal. // 그녀는 그를 경원하고 있다 She gives him a wide berth. ➔¶아무래도 나는 부하들로부터 경원당하고 있는 것 같다 My men seem to be keeping me at a distance[at arm's length].

경위(涇渭) [옳고 그름] right and[or] wrong; good and[or] bad[evil]; vice and virtue; [판단·식별력] judgment; discernment; good sense. ¶~야 어떻든 whether it is right or wrong / for good or bad[evil] // ~에 벗어난 짓 unreasonable doings / an improper act // ~에 어긋나다 be out of reason // ~를 알다 [~가 밝다] know[can tell] right from wrong // ~를 모르다 do not know what is right and what is wrong / be unreasonable / lack propriety // ~를 따지다 distinguish between right and wrongs (of) / distinguish between right and wrong / tell right from wrong // 그는 ~에 밝은 사람이다 He is a man of fair judgment. / He is a man of good sense.

경위(經緯) 1 [경도와 위도] longitude and latitude.
2 [직물의 날과 씨] warp and woof[weft].
3 [전말] details; particulars; circumstances. ¶사건의 ~ the whole story of an affair / the procession of an event / the circumstance [pictures] of an affair // 사건의 ~를 이야기하다 tell (a person) the circumstances of the case / tell the whole story of the affair / talk all about the affair // 그것이 시작된 ~를 말씀해 주십시오 Tell me how it started. // 일이 이렇게 된 ~는 나는 모른다 I don't know how things got this way[how it came about]. // 그가 이혼하게 된 ~를 들려주게 Give me the details of his divorce. // 그 ~로 보아 우리 쪽이 그 손해를 부담할 수밖에 없습니다 Under the circumstances we have no alternative but to bear the loss on our part.
●**경위도** longitude and latitude. **경위선** lines of longitude and latitude.

경위(警衛) 1 [호위] guard; patrol; escort. **경위하다** guard; patrol; escort. 2 [경찰관의 계급] a police lieutenant; (국회의) an Assembly guard.

경유(經由) ¶… ~로[의] via / by way of … / through … / 홍콩 ~ 전보 a cable via [sent by] the Hong Kong route // 대전 ~ 대구행 열차 a train for Daegu via[by way of] Daejeon // 앵커리지 ~ 파리에 가다 go to Paris via [by way of] Anchorage // 파나마 운하 ~의 배로 뉴욕에 가다 sail to New York by way of[via] the Panama Canal. **경유하다** go via[by way

경유(輕油) of]; pass[go] through.
경유(輕油) light oil; diesel oil[fuel]; kerosene. ● 경유 기관 a diesel engine.
경유(鯨油) whale[train] oil; whale fat; blubber.
경음(硬音) [언] a fortis (*pl.* fortes). ⇨된소리
경음악(輕音樂) light music.
경의(敬意) respect; regard; homage; esteem; deference; honor; reverence. ¶…에 대한 ~의 표시로서 as a token of respect to / as a mark [token] of respect for / in honor of / in deference to∥심심한 ~를 표하여 with all due respect / with full honor∥~를 표하다 pay one's respects (to) / show one's respect (to) / regard[treat] (a person) with respect (to / honor (to) / do[pay] homage (to) / take off one's hat[take one's hat off] (to a person) / ~를 표하여 남[집]을 방문하다 honor a person[house] with a visit∥그의 용기에는 ~를 표하여야 한다 We should show respect for his courage.∥먼저 내 전임자에게 ~를 표하고 싶습니다 First of all, I'd like to pay tribute to my predecessor.∥그을 사람들은 그 위대한 음악가에게 ~를 표하여 조상(彫像)을 세웠다 The townspeople built a statue in honor of the great musician. / The townspeople paid homage to the great musician by erecting a statue.

경이(驚異) (a) wonder; a miracle; a marvel. ¶자연계의 ~ prodigies of nature / nature's wonder / ~을 느끼다 excite wonder / inspire wonder (into a person)∥~의 눈으로 바라보다 stare in wonder (at) / open one's eyes in astonishment (at). **경이하다** wonder (at); amaze (at); marvel (at). ¶그것이 깨지지 않았다는 것은 경이할 만한 일이다 It is a wonder[You may well wonder] that it did not break.∥학생들이 모두 영어 회화에 매우 능란한 것에 대해 나는 경이하였다 I marveled at the fact that all the students were so good at speaking English.

경이적(驚異的) wonderful; marvelous; amazing; miraculous; (미) eye-opening. ¶~(인) 사건 an eye-opening event / an eye-opener∥~인 진보를 이룩하다 make wonderful[remarkable] progress (in).

경인(京仁) Seoul and Incheon; the Gyeongin district. ● 경인 고속도로 the Gyeongin[Seoul-Incheon] Expressway. **경인선** the Gyeongin [Seoul-Incheon] Line.

경작(耕作) cultivation; farming; tillage. ¶~에 적합하다 be arable / be tillable. **경작하다** cultivate; farm; till (a field); plow (land). →¶경작되어 있다 be under cultivation / be cultivated / be under[in] crop. ● 경작권 the right of cultivation. **경작물** farm [agricultural] produce[products]; farm crops; the products of a farm. **경작자** a tiller (of the soil); a plowman; a peasant; a farmer. **경작지** arable land; cultivated [plowed] land; land under cultivation.

경쟁(競爭) (a) competition; a contest; rivalry; emulation; a race. ¶가격 ~ competitive pricing / 가격 인하 ~ a price cutting race / underselling competition / 치열한 ~ keen [cutthroat] competition / a tight (election) race / 공개 ~ open competition / 과당 ~ excessive competition / 국내[대외] ~ domestic[foreign] competition / 군비 확장 ~ an arms[armament] race / 생존 ~ a struggle for existence[survival] / 자유 ~ free competition / 두 학교 사이의 ~ rivalry between two schools / 선의(善意)의 ~ competition in good faith / ~이 없는 선거구 an unopposed constituency / an uncontested division / ~에 참가하다 participate [take part] in a competition[contest] / become an entrant (for) / ~에 이기다[지다] defeat [be defeated by] one's competitor / win out over [lose out to] one's competitor(s) / win [lose] a race / be victorious [defeated / beaten] in a competition / ~을 벌이다 enter into competition [rivalry] (with) / ~을 유발하다 provoke competition [rivalry] / 부당한 ~을 규제[방지]하다 control [prevent] an unfair competition / ~권 안에[밖에] 있다 be in [out of] the running (for the championship) / 격렬한 ~이 그들 사이에 계속되고 있다 A close contest [race] is being fought out between them.∥신진 작가들의 ~ 작품이 방송될 예정이다 They will televise plays by new writers in a competition.∥그 산업에서의 ~이 치열하다 There's cut throat [keen] competition in that industry.∥도지사에 대한 ~이 격렬하다 There was a hot race [contest] for governor. / The governorship was hotly contested.∥그 와는 ~이 되지 않는다 (그가 너무 약해) He is no match for me. / (그가 너무 강해) I'm no match for him.∥그는 ~ 없이 의장으로 선출되었다 He was elected chairman uncontested [unopposed].∥~이 없으면 침체되기 쉽다 A lack of competition [rivalry] often leads to stagnation.∥우리는 옆집 가게와 ~에 들어갔다 We entered into competition with the shop next door.∥한국의 수출업계는 유럽 시장에서 치열한 ~에 부딪치고 있다 Korean exporters have been meeting with cutthroat competition in European market. **경쟁하다** compete [contend] (with [against] a person for something); rival (another in something); vie [cope] with (another in); contest (an election); emulate each other [one another]. ¶우승배를 차지하기 위해 서로 ~ compete with each other for the cup / 신제품의 개발을 놓고 ~ compete in the development of new products / 그는 다른 3명의 남자들과 상을 놓고 경쟁했다 He competed with three other men for the prize.∥한국은 자동차 산업에서 다른 나라들과 경쟁하고 있다 Korea is competing against [with] other countries in automobile production. / Korea's automobile industry is in competition with those of other countries.∥그들은 국회의 의석 하나를 두고 경쟁했다 They contended for a seat in the National Assembly.∥같은 주제를 갖고 5명의 화가가 그리기 경쟁했다 Five artists vied with one another in painting on the same subject.∥가격과 품질에 있어서 폐사의 상품과 경쟁할 수 있는 것은 없다고 확신합니다 It is our firm belief that no other goods can compete with ours in both price and quality. →¶경쟁시키다 bring [put] (persons) into competition (with).

● 경쟁 가격 a competitive price. **경쟁력** (develop) competitive power; competitiveness; competitive edge. ¶국제 ~ international competitiveness / ~이 있는 상품 competitive goods / …의 ~을 강화하다 strengthen [sharpen] the competitiveness of. **경쟁률**

the competitive rate; the ratio of successful (applicants) to total applicants. ¶~이 높다 [그다지 높지 않다] be highly [not very] competitive. 경쟁시험 a competitive [screening] examination. 경쟁심 a competitive spirit; spirit of emulation [competition]. 경쟁의식 (a sense of) rivalry; a competitive sense. 경쟁 입찰 a competitive bid; a public tender. 경쟁자 a rival; a competitor; a contestant; a contender; (집합적) the competition.

경적(警笛) an alarm whistle; (경관의) a police whistle; (자동차의) a (warning) horn; a honker; a foghorn(농무 때에). ¶~을 울리다 whistle a warning / give an alarm whistle / (자동차의) sound [blow] a horn [honker] / honk (a car horn) / hoot // ~ 금지 (게시) No horn [honking]!

경전(經典) scriptures; sacred books; (불교의) Buddhist scriptures; the Sutras; (크리스트교의) the Scriptures; the (Holy) Bible; (회교의) the Koran; the scripture of Islam.

경정(警正) [경찰의 계급] a police superintendent.

경정(更正) correction; revision; rectification. ¶추가 ~ 예산 a supplementary (additional) budget. 경정하다 correct; rectify; revise.

경정맥(頸靜脈) [생] the jugular (vein).

경제(經濟) [경] economy; [경제 상태] economics; [재정] finance; [절약] thrift; frugality; saving; economy. ¶계획 ~ planned economy // 국가 [국민 / 가정 / 농촌 / 사회] ~ state [national / domestic / rural / social] economy // 복합 ~ plural economy // 자립 ~ self-supporting economy // 자유 [통제] ~ free [controlled] economy // 자유 [자본] 주의 ~ liberal [capitalistic] economy // 정치 ~ political economy // 국내 ~의 회복 추세 the recovery trend of the domestic economy // 그것은 불 ~ 다 It is uneconomical [poor economy]. // 그것은 내 ~ 사정이 허락지 않는다 I can't [am not rich enough to] afford it. / It is beyond my means. // 싸구려를 사는 것이 실제로는 불 ~ 이다 There is no real economy in buying cheap things.
● 경제 개발 economic development. 경제 개발 5개년 계획 a five-year plan [program] for economic development. 경제계 the economic world; economic [financial] circles. 경제 계획 economic plan. 경제 공황 a financial panic. 경제 구조 an economic structure [setup / buildup]. 경제권(-圈) an economic bloc. 경제 대국 a great [major] economic power. 경제란 [신문] the financial section [column(s)]. 경제력 economic [financial] power [strength]. 경제면 [신문] the financial page. 경제 백서 a white paper on economics. 경제 봉쇄 an economic blockade. 경제 사범 an economic offense(죄); an offender of economic laws(사람). 경제 사회 이사회 (UN의) the Economic and Social Council(약어 ECOSOC). 경제성 [경] economical efficiency. 경제 성장 growth of economy; economic growth. 경제 성장률 the rate of (Korea's) economic growth; the economic growth rate. 경제속도 an economical speed. 경제인 an economic man. 경제 정책 an economic policy. 경제주의 economism. 경제 지리(학) economic geography. 경제 지표 economic indicators. 경제학 economics; political economy; economic science. 경제 협력 economic cooperation. 경제 협력 개발 기구 the Organization for Economic Cooperation and Development(약어 OECD).

경제적(經濟的) economic; financial. ¶~으로 economically / financially / ~ 견지 an economic point of view // ~인 여행법 an economical way of traveling // 천연자원을 ~으로 사용하다 be economical in our use of natural resources / use natural resources sparingly // ~으로 궁핍하다 be financially embarrassed // 나는 늘 ~으로 생활해 왔다 I have always been thrifty [frugal]. // 그렇게 하는 것이 시간과 돈의 ~ 소비가 될 것이다 It would be economy of time and money to do so. / That will save time and money. // 가스는 숯보다 ~이다 Gas is more economical than charcoal.

경조(敬弔) condolence. ¶~의 뜻을 표하다 express [offer] one's condolence (to a person on something).

경조(慶弔) congratulations and condolences.
● 경조비 expenses for congratulations and condolences. 경조사 matters of congratulations and condolences.

경조(競漕) a boat [rowing] race; a regatta. ¶~용 보트 a race [racing] boat. 경조하다 row a race (with); have a boat race (with).

경종(警鐘) an alarm bell; a fire bell [alarm] (화재의); [경고] warning. ¶~을 울리다 ring [sound] an alarm (bell) / [경고하다] warn / give warning // 화재 ~이 울리고 있다 There goes the fire bell! // 이 사건은 시 당국에 대한 ~이 되었다 This incident served as a warning to the city authorities.

경죄(輕罪) (commit) a misdemeanor; a minor [slight] offense.

경주(傾注) devotion; concentration. 경주하다 devote oneself (to); concentrate (on). ¶전력을 ~ devote oneself entirely [one's whole mind] (to) / concentrate one's energies (on) // 연구에 전력을 ~ concentrate one's energies on [throw energy into / bend one's energies to] one's research.

경주(競走) a (foot) race; a run; a running match; (단거리의) a dash; a sprint. ¶100미터 ~ the 100-meter dash [race] // 10,000미터 ~ the 10,000-meter run // 도보 ~ a foot-race / a walking race(경보) // 마라톤 ~ a marathon race // 모터사이클 ~ a motorcycle race // 이인삼각 ~ a three-legged race // 자동차 ~ a motor (an auto mobile) race // 자전거 ~ a bicycle [bike] race / cycle racing // 장애물 ~ a hurdle race / the hurdles(단수 취급) / an obstacle race / 장(중)거리 ~ a long-distance [middle-distance] race // 평지 ~ a flat race // ~용 자전거 a racing bicycle // ~에 나가다 run [compete] in a race / enter [take part in] a race // ~에 내보내다 enter (a car) in a race / race (a horse) // ~에 이기다 [지다] win [lose] a race. 경주하다 run [have / do / engage in] a race (with); race (another). ¶나는 친구와 학교까지 경주했다 I raced to school with a friend.
● 경주로 a course; a (race) track. 경주마(-馬) a racehorse. 경주용 자동차 a racer; a race [racing] car. 경주자 a runner; a racer; (단거리의) a sprinter.

경중(輕重) (relative) importance; relative weight(물체의). ¶병의 ~ the (relative) seriousness of an illness // 일의 ~ the gravity of the affairs // 형(刑)의 ~ [법] the relative gravity of penalties[punishments] // ~을 재다 weigh the importance[gravity] of (a matter) // 사물의 ~을 올바르게 인식하다 see things in their true proportions // 그는 사물의 ~을 모른다 He doesn't know what is important and what is not.

경증(輕症) a slight illness[attack]; a minor ailment; a mild case[form] (of measles). ¶ ~의 콜레라 a mild form of cholera // ~에 걸려 있다 have a slight attack[touch] of dysentery // 다행히 그의 병은 ~이었다 Fortunately his illness was not serious.

● **경증 환자** a mild[light] case (of cholera [typhus]).

경지(耕地) (경작에 적합한) arable[tillable] land[soil]; (경작한) a cultivated field[area]; plowed[cultivated] land; plowland; a plantation; land under cultivation; farmland.

● **경지 면적** acreage under cultivation; cultivated acreage. **경지 정리** the redevelopment [readjustment] of arable land.

경지(境地) **1** [상태] a state; a condition; a stage; [심경] a mental state. ¶…의 ~에 도달하다 reach[attain / come to] the stage of … // 무아의 ~에 이르다 attain a state of perfect self-effacement // 그는 그러한 마음의 ~에 도달해 있었다 He had attained that state of mind. **2** [분야·영역] a field; a sphere; a ground; a territory; a province. ¶ 그는 문학에서 마침내 독자적인 ~를 개척했다 He finally broke[struck out / opened up] new ground[a new path] in literature. **3** [경계지] a boundary; a borderland; a frontier.

경직(硬直) stiffness; stiffening; rigidity. ¶사후(死後) ~ cadaveric rigidity / rigor mortis. **경직하다** stiffen; get stiff; become stiff[rigid].

경질(更迭) a change; a switch; a reshuffle; a shake-up. ¶대 ~ a big[wholesale / radical] change / a shake-up // 간부의 ~ a shake-up in the higher echelons (of an organization) // 내각의 ~ a Ministerial[Cabinet] change / a change of government / reshuffle of the Cabinet // 내각의 ~을 단행하다 reshuffle the Cabinet. **경질하다** change (the members); make a change (in the staff); switch (the commanders). ➜ 내달에는 국장이 경질될 것이다 The bureau chief will be replaced next month. // 사원들이 대대적으로 경질되었다 Sweeping changes have been made among the staff.

경질(硬質) ¶~의 hard / rigid / scleroid(동물의 피부 등이).

● **경질 고무** hard rubber. **경질 섬유** hard fiber. **경질 유리** hard glass.

경찰(警察) the police; the police force; [경찰서] a police station; [경찰관] a policeman. ¶ 서울특별시 ~국 Seoul Metropolitan Police Bureau[Headquarters] // 서울특별시 ~국장 the Chief of Seoul Metropolitan Police // 비밀 ~ the secret police // 사법[경제] ~ the judicial[economic] police // 수상(水上) ~ the water[harbor] police // 이동 ~ the mobile police // ~의 급습 a police raid (on a gambling house) // ~을 부르다 (전화로) call [phone] the police // ~에 신고하다[알리다] report to[inform] the police (of a matter) // ~에 고발하다 complain to the police // ~에 넘기다[인도하다] deliver[hand over] (a person) to the police // ~과 말썽을 빚다 get into trouble with the police // ~의 수배를 받고 있다 be wanted by the police // ~에 출두하다 report (oneself) to the police // ~에 도난 신고를 하다 notify the police of the theft // ~에 자수하다 give oneself up to the police // (기자가) ~에 출입하다 work on the police beat (for a newspaper) // ~이 그를 뒤쫓고 있다 The police are on his track. // 그것은 ~에 고발해야 할 사건이다 It is a case for the police. // 나는 아직 ~에 끌려간 적이 없다 I have no police record. // 그는 ~에 유치되었다 He was taken into police custody. / He was detained at the police station. // 그는 ~의 감시를 받고 있다 The police are keeping an eye on him. // 이 일을 ~ 문제로 끌고 가고 싶지 않다 I don't want to have this reported to the police. // 그는 마침내 ~에 입건되었다 At last the law caught up with him.

● **경찰견** a police dog; (영) a bloodhound. **경찰관** a police officer; a policeman; (영) a constable; (집합적) the police; (속어) a cop. ¶빨리 ~을 불러 주시오 Call a policeman right away. **경찰국가** a police state. **경찰권** police authority[power]. ¶~을 발동[하]다 exercise[abuse] the police authority [power]. **경찰력** police force. **경찰 법규** the police laws. **경찰 병원** a police hospital. **경찰봉** a policeman's billy[club]; a truncheon; a baton. **경찰서** a police station; (미) a station house. ¶~로 연행되다 be taken[marched off / escorted] to a police station. **경찰서장** the chief of a police station; (미) a police chief; (미) a city marshal. **경찰청** the National Police Agency. **경찰학교** a police school [institute].

경천동지(驚天動地) ¶~의 world-shaking / earthshaking / startling / astounding / marvelous // ~의 대사건 an astounding[earthshaking / extraordinary] event / a world-shaking[most sensational] event. **경천동지하다** startle[astound] the whole world; create[cause / make] a sensation in the world; set the world on fire.

경첩 a hinge. ¶~이 달린 문 a hinged door // ~을 달다[메다] hinge[unhinge] // 그 문은 ~이 빠졌다 The door is off its hinges. // 그 문은 ~으로 여닫힌다 The door opens[turns] on its hinges.

경첩하다(輕捷−) light; agile; deft; nimble; swift.

경청(傾聽) listening closely[intently / attentively]. **경청하다** listen (intently / attentively) to (what is said); have a listen (to); give ear (to); be all attention[ears]. ¶경청할 만하다 be worth listening to // 그는 한마디도 놓칠세라 열심히 경청하였다 He listened devouring every word. ➜ ¶그의 연설은 아주 흥미 있게 경청되었다 His speech was listened to with great interest.

경축(慶祝) congratulation; felicitation; celebration. ¶~의 노래 a song of congratulation [celebration] // ~의 뜻을 나타내다 convey one's congratulations. **경축하다** congratulate; felicitate; celebrate (an event). ¶…을 경축하여 in celebration[honor] of … / congratulating … / …식을 거행하여 그날을 ~ celebrate the day with appropriate ceremonies // 온 국민이 그 일을 크게 경축했다 The whole nation made a great celebration over the event.

●**경축일** a flag[red-letter / festival] day; a national holiday; a gala[fête] day. **경축 행사** festivities; a celebration program(me); a celebration.

경치(景致) [어느 고장 전체의 경관] scenery; [개개의 경관] a view; [한정된 풍경] a scene; [육지의 경관] a landscape; [바다의 경관] a seascape. ¶~가 좋은 scenic / 한국의 ~ Korean scenery // 아름다운 ~ fine[beautiful] scenery / a fine view // 아늑한 봄 ~ a peaceful spring scene // 눈 ~ a snow scene // ~가 좋은 곳 a place of scenic beauty / a beauty[scenic] spot // 도시의 확 트인 ~를 내려다보다 command an extensive[get a wide] view of the city // ~의 아름다움에 넋을 잃다 be overpowered with the beauty of the scene // 그곳은 ~ 좋기로 유명하다 The place is noted for its scenic beauty. // 창에서 바라본 ~는 더없이 좋았다 The view from the window was very fine. // 속리산은 저녁 ~가 특히 아름답다 Songnisan[Mt. Songni] looks especially beautiful in the evening. // ~가 좋은 방을 주시오 I want a room with[commanding] a good view.

경치다(黥-) [벌을 받다] suffer torture; suffer severe punishment; be severely[heavily] punished; [야단맞다] have a good scolding; [혼나다] have a hard[rough / bad] time of it (with a person); have[get] the worst of it; pay dearly (for); bitter experience; go through an ordeal; catch it; go through hell. ¶너 그런 짓 하면 경친다 If you do (that), you will catch it. / You will have to pay for that. // 경치 이 경칠 놈아 God damn you! // 경칠 것 What's the hell! / Damn it! // 그는 게으름을 피우다가 선생님한테 경쳤다 He was sharply reproved by his teacher for idleness.

경칩(驚蟄) [24절기의 하나] *gyeongchip*; the day on which insects appear from their holes in the earth.

경칭(敬稱) an honorific title; a title of honor[courtesy]; a term of respect. ¶~을 생략하다 omit titles from names / dispense with the titles / cut out[leave out] prefixes from the names // ~을 붙여 부르다 call a person by the proper (courtesy) titles // ~을 생략하고 부르다 call (a person's) name without title.

경쾌하다(輕快-) [날렵하다] light; nimble (movement); airy (manner); [쾌활하다] light hearted; cheerful (tone); buoyant. ¶경쾌한 발걸음으로 with light steps // 경쾌한 동작 nimble[swift] movements // 경쾌한 가락 a cheerful tone // 경쾌한 음악 rhythmical[lilting] music // 그녀는 경쾌한 복장을 하고 있다 She is in casual clothes. **경쾌히** lightly; nimbly; airily; cheerfully; [음] leggiero.

경탄(驚歎) admiration; wonder. **경탄하다** admire (the skill); wonder[marvel] at (the beauty); be struck with admiration[wonder]; have a great regard[respect] (for). ¶경탄해야 할 admirable / estimable / 묘기에 ~ marvel at (a person's) skillful performance / 경탄할 만하다 deserve the admiration (of) // 자연의 아름다움에 ~ wonder at the beauty of nature // 나는 그의 의견에 나는 경탄하고 있다 I have great respect for his opinions. / I hold his opinions in high esteem. // 나는 그의 고결한 정신에 경탄했다 I was deeply impressed by his noble spirit. // 그 용맹한 행위는 경탄할 만하다 That brave act is worthy of admiration. // 그는 경탄할 만한 속도로 그것을 완성했다 He accomplished it with marvelous[amazing / impressive] speed. // 그 정세[사태]에 대한 그의 깊고 넓은 해석에 우리는 경탄할 뿐이었다 His profound reading of the situation filled us with admiration[wonder].

경토(耕土) arable soil; mold; rich[fertile / fine] soil.

경포(輕砲) a light gun.

경폭격기(輕爆擊機) a light bomber.

경품(景品) a premium; a free gift; a present; (구어) a giveaway. ¶~부 대매출 a grand sale with gifts[presents] / a gift enterprise // ~ 증정 (광고) Customers offered premiums. // ~을 제공하다 offer premiums[(미) giveaways].

●**경품권** (미) a gift certificate; (영) a gift voucher[token]; a gift coupon.

경풍(輕風) [기상] a light air[breeze]; a soft wind.

경풍(驚風) [어린아이의 신경성 질환] nervousness; sensitiveness; [경련] convulsion. ¶~을 일으키다 fall into a fit of convulsion / have a convulsive fit.

경하(慶賀) congratulation; felicitation; celebration. **경하하다** congratulate[felicitate] (a person on his success); celebrate; offer one's congratulations (to a person on the occasion of). ¶경하할 만한 일이다 It is a matter for congratulations (that ...). / Let me offer you my hearty congratulation (on your success). // 이번의 성과를 경하하여 마지 않습니다 I heartily congratulate you on your brilliant achievement. // 우리 회사가 80주년 기념일을 맞이한 것은 충심으로 경하할 일입니다 It is truly a matter for congratulation that our company is celebrating its eightieth anniversary.

경하다(輕-) (무게가) light; not heavy; lack weight; (사태 등이) slight; trivial; trifling; not serious; do not carry weight; (중요도가) light; insignificant; unimportant; (언행이) rash; imprudent; careless; flippant; frivolous; precipitate. ¶책임이 ~ be not in a very responsible position // 그는 입을 경하게 놀리지 않는다 He weighs[picks] his words.

경학(經學) (the study of) Chinese classics; the study of Confucian classics[Confucianism].

경합(競合) [경쟁] (friendly) rivalry; conflict; competition; contest; [연합 작용] concurrence. **경합하다** concur; conflict; compete[contend] (with a person for a thing); vie with each other (for); contest (an election); bid against each other. ¶2개 회사가 토지 개발의 권리를 둘러싸고 경합하고 있다 The two companies are vying[competing] for the right to develop the land. // 이 범행에는 3가지 범죄가 경합하고 있다 This offense is a combination of three violations. / This offense contravenes three laws.

●**경합범** concurrent offenses.

경합금(輕合金) a light alloy.

경향(京鄕) the capital and the country. ¶~ 각지에서 모여든다 come from every corner of the country // ~ 각지를 여행하다 travel around the country far and wide.

경향

경향(傾向) **1** [사물이 쏠리는 방향] a tendency (to / toward / to do); [정세] a trend. (▶ tendency는 일정한 방향으로, trend는 불규칙한 움직임 속에서 볼 수 있는 방향성이나 어떤 시기에 나타나는 특유의 경향을 가리킴) ¶영문학의 최근의 ~ a recent trend [recent trends] in English literature // 앙등의 ~ a rising [an upward] tendency // 물가는 상승 ~ 을 나타내고 있다 Prices are showing a tendency to rise. // 여론의 ~은 전쟁 [전쟁 반대] 쪽으로 기울고 있다 The drift of public opinion is toward [against] war. // 나는 살이 찌는 ~이 있다 I tend to gain weight.
2 [성질이 향하는 방향] a tendency (to / toward / to do); (문어) a propensity (to / toward / for / to do); an inclination (to / to do). (▶ inclination은 특히 자기가 좋아하는 방향으로 나가는 성질, propensity는 종종 바람직하지 않은 방향으로 나가는 성질에 쓰임) ¶외동아들은 경쟁심이 부족한 ~이 있다 An only son is apt to lack competitive spirit. // 그는 윗사람에게 아첨하는 ~이 있다 He tends to flatter his superiors. // 그에게는 남의 말을 곡해하기 잘하는 ~이 있다 He has a tendency to twist another person's words. // 그 여자는 과장하여 말하는 ~이 있다 She has a tendency to exaggerate things. // 그들에게는 보수적인 ~이 있다 They tend towards [lean towards / are inclined to] conservatism. // 그는 일을 게을리 하는 ~이 있다 He is apt to neglect his work. // 그녀는 자기 자신을 비하하는 ~이 있다 She tends [has a tendency] to run herself down.
● **경향극** a tendency play. **경향 소설** a tendency novel.

경험(經驗) (an) experience (of / in). ¶간접 ~ indirect [vicarious] experience // 내 [외] ~ inner [outer] experience // 사회 ~ practical [worldly] experience // 직접 ~ direct [firsthand] experience // 잊혀지지 않는 [즐거운 / 새로운 / 고통스러운] ~ an unforgettable [a pleasant / a new / a bitter] experience // ~이 풍부한 사람 a person with wide experience / a widely experienced person // ~을 살리다 make use of one's experience // 조수 구함, 불문(不問) [광고] Help wanted, Experience not necessary. // 호된 ~을 하다 have a terrible experience // ~으로 알다 learn by experience // 나는 여러 가지 고통스러운 ~을 겪어 왔다 I have undergone [gone through / experienced] many hardships. // 자넨 아직 ~이 없군 You are still inexperienced. / You have little experience. // 그는 강연자로서 많은 ~을 쌓은 사람이다 He is a veteran lecturer. // 나는 이 일에 ~이 없다 I am new to [at] this job. // 그는 이 방면의 사업에 ~이 없다 He is inexperienced in this line of business. // 우리 모두가 캠핑에 ~이 없었다 Camping was a new experience for every one of us. // 그는 ~을 쌓은 [~이 없는] 외교관 [판매원]이다 He is an experienced [inexperienced] diplomat [salesman]. // 그는 인생 ~이 풍부하다 [하지 못하다] He has seen much [little] of life. // 그녀는 환자를 다룬 ~이 많다 [별로 없다] She has had a great deal of [lacks] experience handling patients. // 이런 ~은 난생처음이다 This is quite new [quite a new experience] to me. // 사회에 나가 ~을 넓히고 싶다 I want to broaden experience by becoming a working member of society. / I want to see more of the world by working. // 해외에서의 ~을 살려 취직을 하고 싶다 I want to get a job in which I can put my experience abroad to good use. // 그것을 고통스러운 ~으로 배웠다 I learned it the hard way. // 이것은 내 직접 ~을 통해 말하는 것이다 I say this from personal [firsthand] experience. // 내 ~으로는 그렇게 하는 편이 낫다 Judging from my experience, it would be better to do so. // 옛날에 익힌 ~으로 아직도 젊은 사람에게 지지 않을 자신이 있다 Using my experience from the past, I can still keep up with young people. // 내게도 그런 쓰라린 ~이 있다 I had a bitter experience like that, too. // 그 실패가 좋은 ~이 되었다 The failure was a good experience [lesson] to me. **경험하다** experience; (특히 괴로운 등을) go through; undergo. ¶내가 경험한 바로는 … I know from my experience that … // 이미 경험한 바이다 be proved by experience to be true // 이런 추위는 지금까지 경험한 일이 없다 This is the coldest weather I have ever experienced.
● **경험 과학** empirical science. **경험담** a story of one's (personal) experiences. **경험론** empiricism; experientialism. **경험론자** an empiricist; an experientialist. **경험자** an experienced person; a man of experience. **경험 철학** empirical [experiential] philosophy.
경험적(經驗的) experiential; empirical. ¶~ 사실 an empirical fact // ~ 지식 experimental [empirical] knowledge.

경혈(經穴) [한] spots on the body suitable for acupuncture.

경호(警護) guard; escort; convoy; patrol. ¶무장 ~ an armed guard // ~ 아래 under guard [escort / convoy] // ~를 맡다 act as escort / be on guard / stand [keep] guard (over) // 대사관은 경찰의 엄중한 ~를 받고 있었다 The embassy was placed under heavy police guard. **경호하다** guard; (호위하다) escort; (군함이 수송선을, 무장 차량이 병사를) convoy.
● **경호원** a bodyguard; a (security) guard; (미국 속어) a muscleman; (술집·나이트클럽·호텔 등의) a bouncer. ¶대통령 ~ a presidential guard / (미) a secret service man.

경화(硬化) (물건의) hardening; vulcanization (of rubber); setting; induration; (의견·태도의) stiffening. ¶동맥 ~ sclerosis of the arteries. **경화하다** stiffen; harden; become stiff [hard]; metalize (rubber). ¶쇠를 ~ harden steel // …에 대한 태도를 ~ stiffen one's attitude towards // 노령이 되면 동맥이 경화한다 The arteries harden with age. →¶경화된 firm and determined (attitude) // 여야의 태도가 경화되었다 The attitudes of ruling and opposition parties have stiffened [become firm].
● **경화 고무** ebonite; vulcanite (hard rubber). **경화유** hardened [hydrogenated] oil. **경화증** sclerosis.

경화(硬貨) hard money [cash]; metallic currency; effective money; (집합적) coinage.

경화기(輕火器) [군] light firearms [weapons].

경황(景況) (여유) time to spare; (급한 상황) an urgent state of affairs. ¶~**이 없다** be busy [preoccupied] for / have no time (to spare) / one's mind is too much occupied (to think about other things) // 노는 데 정신이 팔려 공부할 ~이 없다 be too much absorbed in play to think of one's study // 일에 ~이 없어서 문안 편지도 드리지 못했습니다 I have been so busy that I have failed to write to you. // 그녀는 어머니가 돌아가신 뒤로는 공부할 ~이 없어 보였다 She didn't show any inclination to study in the wake of her mother's death.

곁 [옆] a side; [부근] neighborhood; vicinity. ¶~의 near by / neighboring // ~에 by (the side of) / at one's side / beside / near // ~에 close [near] by / close at hand // 길 ~에 by the roadside // ~에 가다 come [go] near / draw near // ~에 앉다 sit by (a person) / sit by (a person's) side // ~에 살다 live in the neighborhood // ~에 서다 stand by the side of // ~에 놓다 put [leave] (a thing) at one's side // ~에 두다 keep (a thing) (close) at hand [at one's elbow] // ~을 지나다 pass by (a thing / a person) // ~으로 다가가다 draw [come / go] near (to a person) // 부모 ~을 떠나다 leave the parental roof [one's parents] // ~에서 시중들다 wait [attend] on // ~에서 참견하다 butt in // 남이 그것을 하는 것을 ~에서 보면 틀림없이 쉽게 보인다 It no doubt looks easy when you watch someone else do it. // 그것은 ~에 있는 사람에게 보이는 것처럼 그렇게 재미있는 것은 아니다 It is not so interesting as it looks to others [bystanders]. // 그는 상관 않겠지만 ~의 다른 사람들이 곤란을 겪게 될 것이다 He may not mind, but others will be inconvenienced. // (나처럼) 제3자라도 ~에서 보기에 그가 참 안되었다[가엾다] Even an outsider (like me) cannot help feeling sorry for him. // 그는 ~으로 피하여 차를 지나가게 했다 He stepped aside to let the car pass. // 너 따위는 그의 ~에도 못 간다 You are no match for him. / You are not to be put beside him. // 그는 자기 딸을 ~에 두고 싶었다 He wanted to keep his daughter by his side. // 나는 영원히 당신 ~에서 살고 싶습니다 I wish to live with you forever. // 위험이 닥쳐오고 있는 동안 그는 총을 ~에 두고 있었다 He kept his gun handy as long as danger was near. // 애야, 내 ~에서 떨어지지 마라 Keep close to me, my dear. // 내 ~을 떠나지 마라 Don't leave my side. // 제발 내 ~에 있어 다오 Stick with me please.

곁가지 a side branch; a lateral branch.
곁길 a side path [road]; an alley; a bystreet.
곁눈 a side(long) glance [look]. ¶~으로 보다 look askance (at) / look with a sidelong glance (at) / glance sidewise (at) / give (a person) a sidelong look / cast a side glance / eye (a person) askance // 그는 그 아름다운 처녀를 ~으로 보았다 He looked sideways [cast a side glance] at the beautiful girl. // 그는 ~으로 아내를 뚫어지게 바라보았다 He gazed at his wife intently out of the corner of his eye.
곁눈(을) 주다 give a suggestion with a look; give a wink; wink at; cast sheep's eyes [an amorous glance] at; make (sheep's) eyes at; roll one's eyes at.
곁눈(을) 팔다 take one's eyes off; look at something else; look away [off].
곁눈질 a side glance; a slant; [추파] an amorous [a coquettish] glance; sheep's eyes.

곁눈질하다 look askance [sideways] (at a person); cast a side(long) glance [look] (at); take a slant (at); squint [leer] (at); leer one's eye (at); [추파를 던지다] wink (at); ogle (at). ¶그들은 의자에 기대앉아 지나가는 여자들에게 곁눈질하고 있었다 They leaned back in their chairs, leering at the girls as they passed.
곁달이 [딸린 것] a secondary thing; an appendage; [딸린 사람] a participator as an outsider. ¶~를 끼다 participate as an outsider / join in a party as a special member / ~를 들다 say [remark] from the sidelines / put [poke / thrust] one's nose into.
곁두리 snacks for farmhand.
곁들다 lend [give] a (helping) hand to; lend one's help to; aid; assist; take the part of; side with. ¶일을 곁들어 주다 help out with the work // 곁들어 싸우다 take (a person's) part in a fight // 이 가방이 무거우니 좀 곁들어 주십시오 Please help me up [down] with this heavy trunk.
곁들이다 1 (음식을) garnish (a dish with some vegetable); add (some vegetable) as a relish; put all on one plate; dress. ¶케이크에 버찌를 ~ garnish a cake with cherries // 생선 요리에 야채를 ~ garnish fish with a green vegetable. 2 (일을) do (things) at a time; do all at once; do along with; accompany. ¶말에 몸짓을 ~ accompany one's speech with gestures // 소나무 밑에 바위를 곁들여 돋보이게 하다 place a rock at the foot of a pine tree to set it off.
곁땀 sweat from the armpit; underarm sweat. ¶~이 나다 sweat under the arm.
곁말 [변말·은어] an argot; a cant; a jargon; a lingo; a slang; [빗댄 말] an allusive [a periphrastic] remark (with a bantering simile or metaphor).
곁방 (-房) 1 (협실) a small room attached to the main one; a side chamber; a closet. 2 [셋방] a rented room.
●**곁방살이** living in a rented room.
곁붙이 [먼 친척] a distant relative [relation].
곁뿌리 [식] a lateral root; a rootlet.
곁상 (-床) a small dining table set at the side of the main one; a side table; a tray with extra dishes.
곁쇠 (대용의) a passkey; a skeleton key; a false key; (같게 만든) a duplicate key; a fellow key.
곁순 (-筍) sprouts [buds] from the side; lateral buds; extra sprouts [buds]. ¶~치기 [농] nipping off extra sprouts / picking the (superfluous) buds.
곁쐐기 a side wedge; an accessory [additional] wedge.
곁자리 a side seat; seats on either side.
곁줄기 [식] a side [lateral] stalk (of a vine).
곁집 a neighbo(u)ring house; the house next door; an adjoining house. ¶~에 살다 live nextdoor.
곁채 an annex (of a house); a shed; an attached house.
계 (戒·誡) [훈계] admonition; remonstrance; (불교 등의) a (Buddhist) commandment; discipline. ¶~를 지키다 [어기다] observe [break] the Buddhist commandments // 모세의 십 ~ the Ten Commandments.
계 (計) 1 [계략] a plot; a stratagem; a trick. 2 [합계] the total; the sum total; (합계하여) in total; in all; all told. ¶~ 3만 원이 되다 be

계 30,000 won in total[in all / all told] / total 30,000 won // ~를 내다 add up / find the total of.

계(係) [담당] charge; duty; business; [부서] a (sub)section (in charge of); [a front / an information] desk; [담당자] a person in charge; a clerk (in charge). ¶접수~ a reception clerk / a receptionist // 출납~ [부서] the cashier's section / (사람) (영) a cashier / (미) a teller.

계(契) a gye; a fraternity; a fraternal order [society]; a friendly society; a benefit club [society / association]; a mutual aid association; a mutual financing[loan] association; a mutual savings club. ¶~를 조직하다 organize a fraternity // ~를 타다 get one's share [dividend] from a savings club // 낙찰 ~에서 당첨되다 secure credit from a mutual financing association by lottery.

-계(系) 1 [계통] a system. ¶태양~ the solar system // 혈관~의 병 a vascular disease // 제3~ [지] the Tertiary system. 2 [혈통] a family line; lineage; descent; extraction; origin. ¶남[여]~ the male[female] line // 프랑스~ 미국인 an American of French ancestry[descent] // 라틴~ 국민 people of Latin origin[extraction] // 그는 한국~의 사람이다 He is of Korean extraction. 3 [정치·사상의 경향] a faction; a clique. ¶혁신[보수]~ 후보 a progressive[conservative] candidate // 우[좌]익~의 단체 a rightist (or right-wing)[leftist / left-wing] organization.

-계(界) [… 사회] a community; a world; a circle; [생] a kingdom; [지] a group. ¶동물[식물 / 광물]~ the animal[vegetable / mineral] kingdom // 문학[실업]~ the literary [business] world // 미술~ the artistic community // 자연~ nature / the natural environment // 사교~ social circles / society // 모스크바의 서방 외교~에서는 그 협상에 희망을 걸지 않고 있다 Western diplomatic circles in Moscow is not hopeful[optimistic] about (the outcome of) the negotiations.

-계(屆) [신고 서면] a notice; a report; a notification. ¶결석~ a report[notice] of absence note.

-계(計) [재는 기구·계기] a meter; a gauge. ¶온도~ a thermometer // 우량~ a rain gauge.

계가(計家) [바둑] taking count of crosses [each territory].

계간(季刊) (a) quarterly publication. ¶~의 quarterly.

● **계간지(―誌)** a quarterly (magazine).

계고(戒告) 1 [경고] a warning; (a) caution. ¶지각하지 않도록 ~를 하다 warn a person not to be late for work. **계고하다** give a warning; warn[caution] (a person against something). ¶상사는 그의 경솔한 행동에 대해 계고했다 His superior warned[cautioned] him against careless behavior. 2 [징계 처분] a reprimand. ¶그는 직무 태만으로 ~ 처분을 받았다 He was reprimanded for neglecting his duty.

● **계고장(―狀)** a monition; (경고장) a written warning; a reminder.

계곡(溪谷) a valley; a gorge; a glen; a ravine; a dale; a canyon.

계관(鷄冠) 1 [닭의 볏] a cockscomb; a (cock's) crest. 2 [식] a cockscomb. ⇨맨드라미

● **계관초(―草)** a cockscomb. ⇨맨드라미

계관 시인(桂冠詩人) a poet laureate.

계교(計巧) a scheme; a trick; a design; a plot; an artifice. ¶~을 꾸미다 devise a scheme / plot / scheme // ~를 부리다 play a trick (on).

계급(階級) 1 [계층] (a) class; estate; caste(봉건적인). ¶지식 ~ the intellectual class(es) / the intelligentsia // 지배[노동] ~ the ruling [working] class(es) // 유산 ~ the propertied class(es) // 자본가 ~ the bourgeoisie // 무산 ~ the proletariat // 상[중 / 하]층 ~ the upper [middle / lower] class(es) // ~을 타파하다 level[equalize] classes / demolish [break down] the distinction of classes // 그는 사회의 훨씬 상층 ~에 있다 He is higher up the social scale.

2 [위계] (a) rank; a grade; (크리스트교 성직자의) (an) order. ¶~이 오르다 be promoted / be raised in rank // ~이 강등되다 be degraded / be reduced to a lower grade [rank] / (미) be demoted // 그는 나보다 ~이 위[아래]이다 He is higher[lower] in rank than I am. / He ranks above[below] me.

● **계급값(―수)** class value. **계급 문학** proletarian literature. **계급 사회** a hierarchical society. **계급의식** class consciousness; a sense of class distinction. **계급장** an insignia [a badge] of rank; an ensign. **계급 제도** the class[caste] system. **계급투쟁** a struggle of classes; a class strife[struggle].

계기(計器) (길이·양 등을 재는) a gauge; (사용량을 재는) a meter; a scale; an instrument. ¶가정용 ~ a house-service meter // 공업용 [항해용] ~ industrial [nautical] instruments // 항공 ~ an aircraft instrument.

● **계기등(―燈)** (가스·불 등의) a gauge lamp. **계기반** an instrument board [panel]; (자동차 등의) a dashboard; a fascia board. **계기 비행** instrumental navigation; instrument [blind] flight. **계기 착륙 (장치)** instrument [blind] landing (system).

계기(契機) [근거·기회] a moment; an impetus; a chance; an opportunity; an occasion. ¶이를 ~로 해서 마음을 고치시오 Take this opportunity to reform. // 새 교사 신축을 ~로 클럽 활동이 활발해졌다 With the construction of the new school building, the students became more involved in club activities. // 그는 병에 걸린 것을 ~로 술과 담배를 끊었다 On falling ill, he gave up both drinking and smoking. // 수상을 ~로 그녀는 직업적인 작가가 되었다 She became a full-time writer upon winning the award. // 그 음악가의 망명을 ~로 많은 지식인들이 외국으로 망명하였다 That musician's defection led to a stream of intellectuals seeking refuge in other countries. / Stimulated by that musician's defection, many intellectuals sought refuge in other countries.

계단(階段) 1 [층계] stairs; (통로로서의) a stairway; the stairs; [한 계단] a step; [난간 등을 포함한 전체] a staircase. ¶나선 ~ a spiral [corkscrew] staircase / a winding stair // 뒷 ~ a back stair // 만곡 ~ a geometrical staircase // 비상 ~ an escape stairway / (화재용의) a fire escape // 가파른 ~ steep stairs // (층계참과 층계참 사이의) 일련의 ~ a flight of stairs // 정면의 대~ (극장 등의) the grand staircase // 30층계의 나선 ~ a spiral staircase of thirty steps // ~의 최상[하] 단에서 on

the top[bottom] step∥~의 디딤판 a tread∥ ~을 오르다 go up[climb] the stairs∥~을 뛰어오르다 run up the stairs∥~을 몇 층계 오르다 go up a few steps∥~에서 떨어지다 fall down the stairs∥그는 ~을 두 단씩 뛰어 올라갔다 He flew up the steps, two at a time. **2** [단계] a stage; phase. ¶그는 출세의 ~을 쌓아 올라갔다 He climbed (the ladder of success) all the way to the top.
- **계단 농업** solid farming. **계단식 농장** a terraced farm; terraced fields.

계도(系圖) [계보] (a) genealogy; (a) lineage; [도형] a family tree; a genealogical table. ¶~의 genealogy∥그는 16세기까지 거슬러 올라가면서 자신의 ~를 추적했다 He traced his genealogy[roots] back to the sixteenth century.

계도(啓導) guidance; leading; instruction; teaching; enlightenment. **계도하다** guide; lead; instruct; teach; enlighten.

계란(鷄卵) an egg. ⇨달걀
- **계란지**(一紙) [사진] albumenized paper.

계략(計略) [책략] a stratagem; an artifice; a design; a trick; a ruse; [함정] a trap; a snare; [계획] a plan; a scheme; [음모] a plot; [공동 모의] a conspiracy. ¶깊은 ~ dark designs∥~이 뛰어난 사람 a resourceful[crafty] person(crafty는 나쁜 계략이 많음) ∥그가 생각해 낸 ~ a stratagem[scheme] he thought up∥~에 빠뜨리다 entrap / ensnare∥~에 걸려들다 [빠지다] be entrapped / fall a prey to (another's) plot / fall into (another's) snare / step into a trap laid by (a person)∥~을 꾸미다 devise[prepare] a stratagem / work[think] out a scheme / make a plan∥그가 무엇인가 비열한 ~을 꾸미고 있는 것 같다 I suspect he has some sort of dirty trick up his sleeve. / I suspect him of hatching some sort of plot.∥너의 그런 ~에 내가 넘어가지 않는다 None of your tricks. / I won't fall for that trick.∥그들의 의표를 찌를 ~은 잘되어 갔다 The scheme to outwit them worked well.∥그는 그들의 ~에 빠지고 말았다 He fell into their trap[snare]. ∥그는 장사꾼의 온갖 ~을 알고 있다 He knows all the tricks of the trade.∥이 ~으로 그가 알리바이를 조작했다 This is how he faked[the trick he used to fake] his alibi.

계량(計量) (무게의) weighing; (길이·부피의) measuring. **계량하다** (길이·양을) measure; gauge; (무게를) weigh. ¶권투 선수들을 ~weigh a boxer. →¶그 레슬링 선수는 80킬로그램으로 계량되었다 The wrestler weighed in at 80kilograms.
- **계량 경제학** econometrics. **계량기** a weighing machine; a meter; a gauge; a gauger; a scale. **~가스** a gasometer∥**~수도** a water gauge[meter]. **계량컵** a measuring cup.

계루(繫累·係累) **1** [딸린 식구] dependents; (family) ties; encumbrances; relatives and in-laws. **2** [연루] involvement; implication; complicity. **계루하다** involve; implicate; encumber; tie (a person) down [to a job).

계류(溪流) a mountain torrent[stream].

계류(繫留) **1** [붙잡아 매 놓음] mooring. ¶배는 ~중이다 The ship is at its moorings[is berthed]. **계류하다** moor (at/to); take up moorings (at a buoy). ¶애드벌룬을 옥상에 ~ moor an advertising balloon to the top of a building∥보트를 선창에 ~ moor a boat at [to] the pier. **2** [미해결]. ¶~중인 pending / outstanding / unsolved / unresolved / unsettled∥~중인 문제 a pending[outstanding] problem / a question at issue∥~중이다 remain unsettled∥그 사건은 아직도 법원에 ~중이다 The case is still pending in court.
- **계류기구**(一氣球) a captive balloon; a kite balloon. **계류부표** a mooring buoy. **계류선**(一船) (서로 붙잡아 맨) boats moored [tied up] to each other; (기슭·잔교·말뚝에 매어 놓은) a boat moored to the shore [a jetty]; a moored [laid-up] vessel; a vessel on the berth. **계류장** moorings; a moorage; a berthage. **계류탑** (비행선·기구의) a mooring mast[tower].

계리사(計理士) →공인 회계사(⇨공인(公認))

계면(界面) the interface.
- **계면 장력**(一張力) [물] interfacial[surface / phase / boundary] tension.

계명(戒名) [불] (사후의) a posthumous Buddhist name[honorific appellation]; (생전의) a Buddhist name.

계명(階名) [음] the name of each note in the sol-fa system (of the musical scale). ⇨계이름

계명(誡命) [종] religious precepts; commandments; discipline. ¶십 ~ (모세의) the Ten Commandments / the Decalog(ue).

계명성(啓明星) [천] Venus; the morning star; (문어) Lucifer.

계모(繼母) a stepmother.

계몽(啓蒙) enlightenment; education; instruction (of the ignorant); illumination. ¶~적 enlightening / (교육적) educative / (초보의) elementary∥~적인 책 an enlightening book / (초보자용의) an elementary [introductory] book. **계몽하다** enlighten; illuminate; educate; edify; develop the intellect of (backward people). ¶민중을 ~ enlighten [educate] the public. →¶그의 연설을 듣고 크게 계몽되었다[깨우쳤다] I learned a great deal from his speech.
- **계몽기** the period of enlightenment. **계몽문학** the literature of enlightenment. **계몽운동** a campaign for enlightenment; an enlightenment [edification / educational] movement[campaign]; (18세기 유럽의) the Enlightenment. ¶농촌 ~을 벌이다 launch a rural enlightenment drive. **계몽주의** illuminism. **계몽 철학** philosophy of enlightenment.

계발(啓發) enlightenment; illumination; edification; education; development. ¶~적인 enlightening / edifying. **계발하다** develop; enlighten (the ignorant); illuminate; irradiate (the mind); edify; educate. ¶지능을 ~ develop the intellectual faculties.
- **계발자** a developer.

계보(系譜) (a) genealogy; (a) pedigree; lineage; a genealogical record [table]; a family tree. ¶한국 문학의 ~ genealogy of Korean literature∥~를 조사하다 look into (a person's) genealogy[pedigree] / genealogize.
- **계보학** genealogy. **계보학자** a genealogist.

계부(季父) the youngest brother of one's father.

계부(繼父) a stepfather.

계분(鷄糞) chicken droppings.

계사(繫辭) [논] a copula (pl. ~s, -lae); a copulative (verb).

계사(鷄舍) a henhouse; a chicken house.

계산(計算) 1 〔숫자셈〕 calculation; reckoning; computation; counting; accounts; figure work; an estimation; balancing. ¶~이 아무래도 맞지 않는다 The figures simply won't [don't] add up. / The calculation doesn't come out right.∥~상의 이익은 실지와는 다르다 A profit on paper does not always mean a profit in the bank. / What is correct in theory is not always right in practice.∥~은 나한테 달아 주시오 Charge it to my account. / Put it on my bill.∥"(음식점 등에서) ~이 얼마 나왔어요?" "8,000원 나왔습니다." "How much is my bill?" "Bill [(미) Check], please." "Your bill comes to 8,000 won."∥~이 맞다[맞지 않다] The figures add up (don't add up).∥~은 내가 할게 It's on me. / I'll pick up the tab[check]. **계산하다** calculate; compute; figure (out); reckon(calculate는 복잡한 계산에, compute는 그보다 약간 간단한 계산에 쓰이는 경향이 있음. figure, reckon은 간단히 계산하기); 〔합계하다〕 add [sum] up; total. ¶이 상자의 부피를 계산하시오 Compute [Calculate] the volume of this box.∥비용이 얼마나 들지 계산해 주게 Calculate [Figure out] how much it will cost.∥그는 거스름돈을 잘못 계산했다 He miscalculated the change.∥그는 하루의 매상을 약 10만 원으로 계산했다 He reckoned that a day's proceeds would be about 100,000 won.∥그는 손가락을 꼽으면서 날수를 계산했다 He counted the number of days on his fingers.∥계산해서 얼마나 됩니까 How much does it come to?∥내가 잘못 계산한 것 같다 I must[seem to] have miscalculated[made a mistake in calculation].

2 〔고려〕 consideration; account. ¶그들에 대한 계산은 ~에 넣지 않아도 돼 You need not take them into account.∥내가 이렇게 하면 그가 당황하게 되는 것이라는 ~이 나왔다 My behavior had been calculated to upset him.∥그것은 ~에 넣지 마라 Leave it out of consideration. **계산하다** reckon; calculate; count on; take into account. ¶그는 그런 사건에 말려들리라고는 계산하지 않았다 He had not reckoned on being involved in such an affair.∥자네는 한테서 돈을 빌릴 수 있을 것으로 계산하고[믿고] 있었나 Did you count on me to lend[count on my lending] you some money?∥그들이 온다는 것은 계산하지 않았다 We did not take their coming into account[consideration]. ➔¶그가 하는 짓은 모두 계산되어 있다 Everything he does is studied.

● **계산기** a calculating[a counting / an adding] machine; a calculator; a computer; an adder. ¶**디지털** ~ a digital computer / **전자** ~ an electronic computer[brain]∥~처럼 정확히 분석하다 analyze (the facts) with computerlike precision. **계산대** 〔카운터〕 a counter; (호텔의) the front [reception] desk; (슈퍼마켓의) a checkout counter. **계산법** a system of measuring[calculation]. **계산서** a statement of accounts; an account (of charges); 〔청구서〕 a check; a bill; (미) a tally card[sheet]. ¶~를 갖고 오시오 Fetch [Get] me the bill. / Check [Bill], please. **계산자 / 계산척** a slide rule; (미국 속어) a slipstick. **계산 착오** miscalculation; an error[a mistake] in calculation.

계상하다(計上-) 〔셈하다〕 sum [add] up; 〔할당하다〕 appropriate (a sum for some purpose). ¶예산으로 ~ appropriate (ten million won) in the budget (for). ➔내년도 예산에 계상되어 있다 be earmarked for the next fiscal year budget∥새 도서관을 위해 10억 원이 계상되었다 One billion [(영) One thousand million) won has been appropriated [been earmarked] (in the budget) for the new library.

계선(繫船) mooring; (출항 불능 때문인) laying up; 〔배를 매어 둠〕 a moored boat; an idle [a laid-up] ship. **계선하다** moor (at / to); tie [lay] up (vessels); berth.

● **계선거**(-渠) a wet dock. **계선료** quayage; mooring charges. **계선소** moorings; a berthage; a moorage; a quay side. **계선주**(-柱) a mooring post.

계속(繼續) continuation; continuance; succession. ¶이야기의 ~ the sequel [continuation] of a story / ~적(인) continuous / continual / uninterrupted∥~(적)으로 〔끊임없이〕 continuously / 〔짧은 간격을 두고 연속적으로〕 continually / uninterruptedly / 〔연이어·잇달아〕 one after another∥이것은 7페이지의 ~이다 This is continued from page 7. **계속하다** 〔이어지다〕 continue; last; run on; follow; 〔계속 하다〕 continue; maintain; keep up (with); go on (with one's work); 〔갱신하다〕 renew. ¶며칠이나 계속하여 for days on end∥세 번 계속하여 three times running [in succession / in a row]∥계속하여 10시간 동안 for ten hours at a stretch∥이야기를 ~ go on talking / keep up a conversation∥수업을 ~ continue at school∥노력을 ~ follow up on one's effort(s) (to do)∥계속하여 서 있다 keep standing / stay on one's feet∥계속하여 빠른 걸음으로 걷다 keep walking at a rapid pace∥그저께부터 계속하여 비가 내리고 있다 It has been raining (incessantly / without letup / continuously) since the day before yesterday.∥레이건은 두 임기 동안 계속하여 대통령 직을 차지하고 있었다 Reagan occupied the presidency for two terms running[in succession].∥그는 협상을 계속했다 He proceeded[went ahead] with the negotiations.∥나는 3일 동안 계속하여 울었다 I cried for three straight days.∥그는 계속하여 3년간 개근했다 He never missed a day in three years.∥비가 계속해서 내린다 It keeps on raining.∥나는 번역 일을 계속하였다 I continued at the work of translation.∥그 계약은 계속하기로 되어 있다 The contract is to run.∥나는 숲 속을 계속하여 걸어갔다 I walked on and on [kept walking] in the forest.∥그들은 하나하나 계속하여 나를 추월해 갔다 They passed me one after another. / They passed me in rapid succession.∥지진이 일어나고 있는 동안에도 그는 강의를 계속했다 He continued to lecture even during the earthquake. / He proceeded [continued] with his lecture even during the earthquake.∥우리는 밤늦게까지 이야기를 계속했다 We went on talking until late at night.∥내게 신경 쓰지 말고 일을 계속하시오 Please don't let me interrupt your work.∥가수를 계속하는 한, 당연히 상을 타 보고 싶다 As long as I remain a singer, of course I'll hope to win a prize.∥휴식 뒤에 그들은 다시 회의를 계속했다 They resumed the meeting after a recess.

// 토지 가격이 계속하여 올랐다 The price of land continued to rise [kept rising / kept going up]. // 눈이 10일 동안이나 계속하여 내렸다 It snowed for ten consecutive days. // 그는 쉬지 않고 일을 계속했다 He went [kept] on working without taking a rest. ➔¶계속되는 불황 a continuous [lasting] recession // 계속되는 가뭄[한발] a long spell of dry weather / a long drought // 계속되는 맑은 날씨[우천 / 가뭄 / 추위] a fine [wet / dry / cold] spell / a spell of fine [wet / dry / cold] weather // 9월까지 계속되다 last until [into] September // 다음 페이지로 계속됨 Continued on the following page. // 좋은 날씨가 계속될 것 같다 The fair weather looks lasting. / The weather seems to stay fine. // 내 두통이 계속되었다 My head kept aching. // 그 회의는 세 시간 내내 계속되었다 The meeting was held for three hours running. // 노래 소리가 한밤중까지 계속되었다 The singing went on continuously until the middle of the night. // 그 전시회는 이달 말까지 계속된다 The exhibition will remain open [will continue] till the end of this month. // 치열한 전투는 며칠을 두고 계속되었다 The fierce battle continued for days. // 계속되는 장마로 각지에 홍수가 일어났다 A long spell of rain caused floods in various parts of the country. // 비참한 사건이 계속되었다 Disastrous events occurred one after another [in quick succession]. // 바겐세일이 오늘부터 3일간 계속된다 The bargain sale will run for three days, beginning today. // 우리 집안에 최근 불행한 일이 계속되었다 Recently we have had a run of bad luck in our family. // 나는 하루 종일 우울한 기분이 계속되었다 I have been depressed all day. // 전쟁은 언제까지 계속될까요 How long will the war continue [last]?
●**계속범** a continuing crime. **계속비**(-費) a continuing expenditure.
계속(繫屬) [법] pendency.
계수(季嫂) a younger brother's wife. ⇨제수(弟嫂)
계수(係數) [수] a coefficient; [물] a modulus; a factor. ¶미분 ~ a differential coefficient // 숫자 ~ a numeral coefficient // 엥겔 ~ Engel's coefficient // 문자 ~ literal coefficient // 노동 ~ a labor coefficient // 증발 ~ the evaporation factor // 탄성(彈性) ~ the modulus of elasticity // 팽창[수축] ~ a coefficient of expansion [contraction] // x의 ~ the coefficient of x.
계수(計數) calculation; counting; computation; figures. ¶~에 능한 사람 a person with a skill with figures // ~에 밝다 be good at figures. **계수하다** count; calculate; compute; figure.
●**계수관**(-管) (방사능의) a counter. **계수기**(-器) a calculating [counting] machine; a comptometer; an arithmometer.
계수나무(桂樹-) [식] a cinnamon [cassia] tree; (달 속의) the great laurel tree in the moon.
계승(繼承) succession; accession; inheritance. ¶왕위 ~ succession to the throne. **계승하다** succeed (to); accede (to); inherit; take over. ¶(조상으로부터) 계승한 [생] inherited // 왕위를 ~ succeed [accede] to the throne // 위대한 전통을 ~ uphold [cherish] the great traditions (of the early pioneers) // 우리는 여러 가지 문화적 유산을 계승하고 있다 We have inherited various cultural legacies. // 그는 아버지의 작위를 계승했다 He succeeded to his father's title. // 홍 씨의 뒤를 계승하여 그가 사장이 될 것이다 He will succeed Mr. Hong as president.
●**계승자** a successor (to the throne); an heir (of liberty).
계시(啓示) revelation. ¶신의 ~ a revelation of God // 신의 ~로 쓴 책 writings inspired by God // ~를 받다 receive a divine revelation [message]. **계시하다** reveal.
●**계시록** [성] The Book of Revelations [Apocalypse] of St. John. ⇨요한 계시록 **계시 문학** apocalyptic literature; apocalypses. **계시 종교** a revealed religion.
계시(計時) a time check. **계시하다** clock; keep time; check time. ¶소요 시간을 정확하게 ~ clock the time required accurately.
●**계시기** a timer. **계시원** a timekeeper; a timer.
계시다 (someone esteemed) be; stay; be located. ¶아버지 계시냐 Is your father in [at home]? // 잠깐만 계십시오 Please wait a minute [moment]. // 좀 더 계십시오 Stay a little longer. // 런던에 얼마나 계셨습니까 How long have you been in London?
계씨(季氏) (a person's) younger brother.
계약(契約) a contract; a compact; a covenant; an agreement(협정); [매매 계약] a bargain. ¶가~ a provisional contract // 구두 ~ a verbal [an oral] contract // 무효[유효] ~ a void [valid] contract // 불법[적법] ~ an illegal [a legal] contract // 성문 ~ a written contract // 수의 ~ a private contract // 쌍무[편무] ~ a bilateral [an unilateral] contract // 약식 ~ a simple contract // 정식 ~ a formal contract / a contract under seal // ~의 만기[만료] expiration [termination] of a contract // ~ (기간)의 연장 extension of a contract // ~의 이행 performance [fulfillment] of a contract // ~의 파기 annulment of a contract // ~대로 according to the contract / as per contract / as contracted // 3년 ~으로 on a three-year contract // …와 구두 ~을 하다 make a verbal contract with ... // ~을 취소하다 cancel [break off] a contract // ~을 이행하다 carry out [fulfill / fill up / perform] a contract // ~을 위반하다[파기하다] break [violate] a contract [an agreement] // 회사와의 ~에 서명하다 sign a contract with a firm // ~ 중이다 be under contract (to build a ship) // 이 ~은 유효하다[무효이다] This contract holds good [will not stand]. // 아직 아무런 ~도 성립되지 않았다 No contract has yet been concluded. // 머지않아 ~(의 기한)이 끝난다 The contract expires soon. // 그는 레코드 회사와 ~을 맺고 있다 He is under contract to the record company. // 한국 건설 회사가 이 공사의 ~을 땄다 The Korea Construction Company has received [won] the contract for this (construction) work. **계약하다** contract; make [enter into] a contract [an agreement] (with); promise; sign a contract [an agreement]. ¶나는 외야수로 저 구단과 계약하고 싶다 I want to sign (on) with that team as an outfielder. // 그 건축업자는 그의 집을 6개월 이내에 짓기로 그와 계약했다 The builder contracted [entered into a contract] with him to build his house

계엄

within six months.// 우리는 이 일을 20억 원으로 정 건설 회사와 계약했다 We contracted this work out to Jeong (and Company) for two billion won. / We awarded Jeong (and Company) a two billion won contract for this job.
● **계약 갱신** renewal of a contract. **계약금** (a) down payment; a contract deposit; earnest money. **계약서** a (written) contract; a contract document; an agreement; a bond; an indenture. ¶~를 작성하다 draw up a contract[an agreement]. **계약설** the theory of social contract. ⇨사회 계약설(⇨사회(社會)) **계약 위반** (a) breach [violation] of a contract. **계약 조건** a contract basis. **계약 조항** contract clauses. **계약 해제** cancellation of a contract.

계엄 (戒嚴) guarding against the threat of danger; exercising vigilance.
● **계엄령** (the) martial law. ¶~을 선포하다 proclaim martial law. //~을 해제하다 lift [withdraw] martial law. **계엄 사령관** the chief martial law administrator. **계엄 사령부** the Martial Law Enforcement Headquarters.

계열 (系列) [생] a system; an order of descent; succession; [물] a series(스펙트럼의); (산업의) interrelationship (among industries); (대학의) department. ¶같은 ~의 점포 stores belonging to the same chain// 기업의 ~화(化) the systematization of enterprises// 대학의 ~별 모집 admission of students to a university by department.
● **계열 기업** [산업] interrelated enterprises [industries]. **계열사 / 계열 회사** the affiliates; the allied enterprises; an affiliated company; a collateral firm.

계영 (繼泳) relay swimming.

계원 (係員) a clerk in charge; an attendant. ¶접수 ~ an information clerk / a receptionist.

계원 (契員) a member of a loan club [mutual financing association].

계율 (戒律) religious precepts; commandments; discipline. ¶~을 지키다 observe the commandments / practice [act up to] the precepts // ~을 어기다 violate the commandments [precepts].

계이름 (階一) [음] the name of each note in the sol-fa system (of the musical scale).
● **계이름부르기** [음] solmization.

계인 (契印) a tally (impression); a joint seal; (the impression of) a seal over the joint of two papers. ¶~을 찍다 affix a seal over two edges / impress a seal over the joint of two sheets of paper.

계장 (係長) a chief clerk; a chief; the head [clerk] (of a section).

계쟁 (係爭) dispute; contention; controversy; [소송] a law suit. ¶~ 중인 문제 a question at issue / an issue in dispute // ~ 중이다 be in dispute / be at issue / (법정의) be pending in court. **계쟁하다** dispute; have a dispute; engage in a controversy.
● **계쟁물** property under dispute. **계쟁점** the point at issue; a disputed point.

계전기 (繼電器) [전] a relay.

계절 (季節) a season; the time of the year. ¶사 ~ the four seasons // 더운 ~에 in the hot season / in summer // ~의 꽃 flowers of the season // ~이 바뀔 때에 at the change of seasons // ~에 어울리지 않는 폭풍우 an unseasonable storm // 이 ~에 어울리는 추위 the degree of cold one can expect at this time of year // 버섯의 ~ the mushroom season / the season for mushrooms // ~에 관계없이 in all seasons / all the year (round) // 지금은 장사가 안되는 ~이다 We're now in a dull season in trade. // 벚꽃이 피기에는 ~이 좀 이르다 It is a little too early for cherry blossoms. // 올해는 벚꽃이 ~에 앞서서[늦게] 피었다 The cherry blossoms came out ahead of time[late] this year. // 이 스포츠는 ~에 관계없이 인기가 있다 This sport is popular in all seasons [all the year round].
● **계절감** a sense of the season(s). **계절상품** seasonal goods. **계절풍** a periodic wind; a seasonal wind; a monsoon(인도양의).

계절적 (季節的) seasonal; for the season; in season. ¶기후의 ~ 변화 seasonal changes of climate.
● **계절적 실업** seasonal unemployment.

계정 (計定) accounts; (구어) tab. ¶당좌 ~ current account // 대체 ~ postal transfer account // 미지급 ~ outstanding account // 잡 ~ sundry account // 지급 ~ account payable // …의 ~에 넣다 charge [put] (a sum) to (a person's) account.
● **계정 과목** a title of account.

계제 (階梯) [단계] a step; a phase; a stage; a gradation; the course [process] (of things); [기회] an opportunity; an occasion; a chance. ¶~가 나쁜 untimely / ill-timed // 문제 해결을 위한 좋은 ~를 놓치다 miss a perfect chance to settle the matter // 지금은 행동을 취할 ~가 아니다 This is not a good time to go into action. // 그는 ~를 살피다가 그 문제를 끄집어낼 생각이었다 He was watching for a chance to broach the subject. // 문제를 해결하기에는 지금이 좋은 ~다 Now is the perfect time to settle the matter. // ~가 되면 들러 주십시오 Please call on me if you happen to come this way. // ~가 있으면 카탈로그를 보내 주십시오 Please send us a catalog when you have an opportunity. // 이 ~에 또 한 가지 예를 들겠습니다 While I'm on the subject [(구어) While I'm at it], let me give one more example. // 이 ~에 다음 회의 의제를 말씀드립니다 I'd like to take this opportunity to announce the agenda for our next meeting. // 이 ~에 말씀드리고 싶은 것이 있습니다 Incidentally, there's something I'd like to tell you about. // 물러나기에는 ~가 좋지 않다 This is not a proper time to withdraw.

계좌 (計座) an account. ¶대체 ~ a postal transfer account // 별도 ~ a separate account // 은행 비밀 ~ secret bank accounts // (은행에) ~를 트다 [개설하다] open an account (with a bank) // 예금 ~의 수 the number of one's bank accounts.
● **계좌 번호** an account number.

계주 (契主) the organizer of a mutual finance association [credit union].

계주 경기 (繼走競技) a relay (race). ¶400미터의 ~ a 400 meter relay.

계집 a woman; a female; the fair sex; [아내] one's wife; [정부] a mistress; a concubine. ¶~이라면 사족을 못 쓰는 사내 a man who has a weakness for woman // ~을 좋아하는 fond of women / amorous / lustful // ~의 말

계집 을 잘 듣는 남편 a fond husband // ~을 얻다 take (to oneself) a wife / get married to a woman // ~을 보다[두다] get a mistress / keep a mistress [concubine] / ~을 버리다 discard [desert / leave] one's wife.
● **계집아이** a girl; a lass. ¶깜찍한 ~ precocious girl. **계집자식** [처자] one's wife and children; one's family; [딸] one's daughter. **계집종** a servant [slave] girl. **계집질** womanizing; whoring; [난봉] debauchery; woman hunting.

계책 (計策) a stratagem; an artifice; a design; a trick; a plan; a scheme. ¶좋은 ~ a good [clever] scheme // ~을 쓰다 adopt [use] a stratagem // ~이 풍부하다 be resourceful; be full of resources // ~을 생각해 내다 devise [think out / work out] a plan / invent a scheme / draw up a plan // 그들은 세력을 만회하려고 갖은 ~을 다 쓰고 있다 They are resorting to every stratagem to retrieve their power.

계측 (計測) measuring; measurement. **계측하다** measure; [토지 등을] survey.
● **계측 공학** instrumentation engineering. **계측기** a measuring instrument [machine].

계층 (階層) (사회의) a level; a stratum (*pl.* strata, ~s)(사회적·경제적 지위); (언어의) a hierarchy. ¶모든 ~의 사람들 people from all levels [strata] of society // 사회의 각 ~에 in all strata of society [social strata] // ~이 다르다 belong to a different class // 그는 모든 ~의 사람들에게 인기가 있다 He is popular with all sections and classes.

계통 (系統) 1 [조직·체계] a system. ¶신경[근육 / 소화] ~ the nervous [muscular / digestive] system // 지휘 [명령] ~ a channel [chain] of command // ~이 선 [서지 않은] 설명 a systematic [confused] explanation // ~을 세우다 systematize // ~을 세워 대화를 진행하다 proceed with a talk systematically [methodically] // 그의 연구는 ~이 서 있지 않다 He lacks [has no] system in his study.
2 [계보] genealogy; [유파] a school; [당파] a party. ¶같은 ~의 빛깔 a color of a similar shade // 아리스토텔레스의 ~을 이어받은 학파 the Aristotelian school // 이들 부족은 모두 같은 ~이다 All these tribes are of the same descent [stock]. / All these tribes are related to one another. // 이 말은 인도·아리아 어 ~의 말이다 This language belongs to the Indo-Aryan language family. / This is an Indo-Aryan language. // 밤색 ~에는 여러 가지 색깔이 있다 There are many shades of brown.
● **계통도** a distribution diagram; a genealogy. **계통 발생** [생] phylogeny.

계통 (繼統) succession to the throne. **계통하다** succeed to the throne.

계통적 (系統的) systematic; methodical. ¶표본을 ~으로 분류하다 classify the specimens systematically // 근대 과학을 ~으로 연구하다 make a systematic study of modern science.

계피 (桂皮) cinnamon (bark); cassia bark.
● **계피유** cinnamon oil. **계핏가루** cinnamon powder.

계획 (計劃) a plan (for / of); a project; a scheme; a design. (▶ plan이 가장 일반적으로 말. project, scheme은 plan보다 계획이 구체적인 느낌. scheme은 때로 나쁜 음모. design은 딱딱한 느낌과 동시에 때로 엉뚱한 일을 꾀

함을 암시. project는 상상력이 풍부한 계획을 나타냄.) ¶단기[장기] ~ a short- [long-] range plan // 도시 ~ town [(영) city] planning // 사업 ~ a business program [project] // 5개년 ~ a five-year plan [program] // 탁상 ~ a desk plan // 막연한 [불투명한] ~ an indefinite plan // 실행 불가능한 ~ an impracticable plan // ~대로 according to plan / as planned [scheduled] / as previously arranged // ~대로 하다 follow a fixed plan [a plan as laid out] (in reading) // ~을 세우다 make [form] a plan / form a scheme / make [plan / work out / map out] a program / lay [map] out a schedule (for the coming vacation) // ~을 정하다 work out a plan // 하이킹 ~을 세우다 [실행하다] make [carry out] a plan for hiking // 그 일은 ~이 소홀했다 The affair was carelessly arranged. // 도서관 신축 ~이 유산되었다 The scheme of [for] building a library fell through. // 우리는 학급 파티의 ~을 확정지었다 We made [laid] definite plans for our class party. // 먼저 세밀한 ~을 결정짓자 First, let's decide on a precise plan. // 우리는 축하회 준비의 ~에 대한 ~을 세웠다 We made arrangements for the celebration (party). // 내가 그를 내리누르고 조지가 그의 돈을 빼앗는다는 것이 그 ~의 진행 순서다 Here's how it goes — I'll hold him down and then George will take his money. // 시초의 우리 ~이 완전히 빗나갔다 [실패했다] Our original project [plan] failed [fell through] completely. // 만사가 ~대로 진행됐다 Everything went according to plan [worked out exactly as scheduled]. // 나는 제주도행 ~을 세웠다 I have mapped out a plan for my trip to Jeju-do. // 그들은 5개년 ~으로 사전을 편찬하기로 했다 They decided to compile a dictionary on a five-year plan. // 사업은 ~대로 진행되었다 The undertaking was carried out as planned [scheduled]. // 그들의 공중 납치 ~은 실패했다 [성공했다] Their scheme to hijack the plane failed [succeeded]. // 시(市)의 하수도 건설은 아직 ~ 단계에 있다 A sewage system for the city is still in the planning stage. // 체육관 건설이 ~ 중에 있다 Construction of a gymnasium is under consideration [is being planned]. // 한 해의 ~은 설날에 세워야 한다 New Year's Day is the day to make your year's plan. / You should make plans for the year on New Year's Day. // 하루의 ~은 이른 아침에 세워야 한다 The day's plan should be made out early in the morning. **계획하다** plan (to do); make a plan; project; scheme; design. ¶이곳 도(道) 당국은 이 지역의 개발을 계획하고 있다 The prefectural authorities are planning the development of [to develop] this region. // 그들은 도서관 건축을 계획하고 있다 They are planning to construct a library [the construction of a library]. // 그가 무엇을 계획하고 있는지 나는 전혀 추측할 수가 없다 I have no idea what he is after. // 그는 무엇인가 나쁜 짓을 계획하고 있는 것 같다 He seems to be scheming [up] to some mischief.
● **계획 경제** a planned economy. **계획성** (lack) planning. ¶그는 매사에 ~이 있다 [없다] He always [never] plans ahead. **계획안** a schedule; a plan; a blueprint. **계획표** a plan.

계획적 (計劃的) (계획된) planned (crime); studied (insult); systematic (study /

겟돈

research); (일부러 꾸민) intentional; deliberate(d) (fraud); calculated (crime); premeditated (crime). ¶~인 범죄 a premeditated crime//~인 탈세 deliberate tax evasion//이번의 사건은 대규모의 ~인 범죄로 판명되었다 The case turned out to be a systematic crime carried out on a large scale.//그는 ~으로 연구를 계속해 왔다 He has been studying according to a schedule [systematically]. (▶ according to a schedule는 「계획에 따라서」, systematically는 「체계적으로」의 뜻)

겟돈(契-) money for [from / owned by] the mutual assistance society [the credit union]; lodge money.

고¹ [고리] a loop (of string / in a rope); a bight.

고² that; the same; (the man) in question; the very. ⇨<그² ¶~놈 that (little) man / ~모양이다 be just the same as before / that is (just) the way it is.

고³ [인용]. ¶머리가 아프다~ 말하다 complain of a headache//사실이 아니라~ 말하다 deny it to be true//방문하겠다~ 약속하다 promise to visit//그는 나에게 돈을 꿔 주겠다~ 말했다 He offered to lend me money.

-고 1 [대등 연결] and (also); as well as; and then; both; as well. ¶정직하고 ~ 근면한 (both) honest and industrious//바쁘~ 피곤하다 be busy and tired//그는 지식도 있~ 경험도 있다 He has experience as well as knowledge.
2 [욕망] to do. ¶집에 가~ 싶다 I want to go home.
3 [진행·완료] be doing; have done. ¶나는 책을 읽~ 있다 I am reading a book now.//나는 저녁밥을 먹~ 났다 I have just finished my dinner.//그녀는 아들을 보내~ 몹시 울었다 Having seen her son off, she cried bitterly.
4 [동작의 선행·이유] (do) and (then); because. ¶문을 열~ 집 안으로 들어가다 open the door and go into the house.

고(故) the late ...; the (late) lamented ...; the deceased ...; ... of blessed [happy] memory. ¶~ 브라운 씨 the late Mr. Brown / Mr. Brown of blessed [glorious] memory.

고-(高) high. ¶~혈압 high blood pressure.

-고(高) 1 [높이] ~ . ¶물가~ high prices of commodities / the increased cost of living. 2 [수] a number; [양] a quantity; an amount; a volume; [금액] a sum; an amount of money. ¶매상~ the amount sold / the sales / the returns / the turnover//생산~ an output / a yield / an outturn//수확~ the yield / the crop//어획~ a haul [catch] (of fish) / a fish catch//매상~ the amount sold.

고가(古家) an old house; [폐가] a deserted [dilapidated] house.

고가(高架) [관형어적] overhead; high-level; elevated.
●**고가교** an elevated bridge; a viaduct. **고가도로** (미) an overpass; (영) a flyover.

고가(高價) a high [good] price; costliness; expensiveness. ¶엄청난 ~ a fancy [fabulous] price / an exorbitant [a prohibitive] price//~의 expensive [costly / high-priced / dear//~로 팔다 sell (something) at a high price//고본 ~ 매입 (게시) Best prices offered for used books.
●**고가주**(-株) high-priced stocks. **고가품** a costly [high-priced] article; a valuable.

고갈(枯渴) (물의) drying up; (자원 등의) exhaustion; drain. ¶인재의 ~ a dearth [lack] of talent. **고갈하다** be dried up; run dry; be parched; (자원 등이) become exhausted; be drained. ➔¶그 전쟁은 국가의 재원을 고갈시켰다 The war has drained the country of its financial resources.//오랜 가뭄으로 우물이 고갈됐다 A long drought dried up the well. / The well ran dry after a long spell of dry weather.//그는 모든 아이디어[상상]가 고갈되었다 He has run [gone] dry of all ideas. / The fountain [source] of his imagination has been exhausted. / (소설가의 소재가) He has written himself out.

고개¹ [머리] the head; [목뒤] the back [scruff] of the neck; [목] the neck. ¶~를 갸우뚱하다 lean over his head to one side / tilt one's head//~를 꾸벅이다 (인사로) bow [nod] one's head / nod (to [at] a person in the street) / (졸려서) nod / sit nodding / ~를 끄덕이다 (찬성하여) nod one's approval [assent / agreement / 'yes'] (to) / nod in assent//~를 밖으로 내밀다 put [stick] one's head out of (the window)//~를 돌리다 turn one's head / (…쪽을 보다) look toward / look back / (외면하다) look away / avert one's eyes//그는 마침내 ~를 끄덕였다 At long last, he nodded his assent.//그녀는 그 제의에 대해 ~를 옆으로 저었다 She shook her head at the proposal. / She refused the offer.//그는 낯선 사람을 보고 ~를 갸웃거렸다 He tilted [inclined] his head slightly [a bit] to one side as he looked at the stranger.//그는 내 말이 못마땅하다는 듯이 ~를 획 쳐들었다 He tossed his head to show his dissent at my words.//그녀는 그게 정말이냐는 듯 ~를 갸웃거렸다 She bent her head as if questioning its truth.//해바라기가 태양을 향해 ~를 들었다 The sunflower lifted its head to the sun.//우리는 ~를 숙여 고인의 명복을 빌었다 We bowed our heads praying for the repose of the soul of the dead.
●**고개(를) 들다** (물가 등의 상승세) go up; rise; soar. ¶고개를 든 민중의 불만 the rising tide of public discontent//물가가 고개를 들었다 Prices are rising.//질투의 싹이 고개를 들었다 Jealousy began to rear its (ugly) head. **고개를 흔들다** shake one's head; shake one's head no [in denial]. **고개를 숙이다** (굴복하다) bend the neck; surrender; give in; (물가 등이) go [come] down; fall; drop; give in; decline. ¶물가가 고개를 숙이고 있다 Prices are declining [falling].//마침내 더위가 고개를 숙이기 시작했다 The heat is losing at last. / At last the hottest season is over.
●**고갯짓** (거부의) a shake of the head; (찬성의) a nod.

고개² 1 [산길] a ridge; a (mountain) pass. ¶심플론 ~ Simplon Pass//~를 오르다 [내려가다] go uphill [downhill]//~를 넘다 cross (over) a mountain pass [ridge / peak] / pass over the peak [crest]. 2 [고비] a critical moment [turn]; a crisis; a turning point; [절정] the crest; the summit; the height; the climax. ¶인생의 ~ the vicissitudes of life//50 ~를 넘다 be [have] turned fifty / be over [on the wrong side of] fifty//pass one's fifty-year milestone//50 ~를 갓 넘은 사람 a person just turning fifty//그녀는 50의 ~를

넘지 않았다 She is on this side[(구어) on the sunny side] of fifty.
* **고개턱** the head of a pass[slope]. **고갯길** an uphill pass; an ascent.
고객(顧客) a customer; a patron; (변호사 등의) a client; (집합적) patronage; custom. ¶오랜[단골] ~ an old[a regular] customer∥~을 끌다 draw[attract / win] custom[customers] (to a store, shop, house, etc.)∥~을 잃지 않으려고 노력하다 try to retain[keep] one's customers∥이 상점은 ~이 많다[적다] This store has a lot of[few] customers.∥그들은 상점을 개장(改裝)하여 ~을 끌어 모으려 했다 They refurnished their store in order to draw more customers[custom] to it.∥이 상점에는 주부 ~이 많다 This shop is well patronized by housewives.∥요즈음 그들에게 ~이 늘었다[줄었다] They have gained[lost] customers recently.∥이 가게의 ~은 고급이다 This store is patronized by top people[the upper echelons of society].∥이 가게의 ~은 하층이다 This store draws its customers from the lower income groups.
고갱이 (식물의) the pith; the medulla (pl. ~s, -lae); the heart of a plant; (핵심) the core; the kernel; the essence. ¶양배추의 ~ the heart of a cabbage.
고검(高檢) a high public prosecutor's office. ⇨고등 검찰청(⇨고등)
고견(高見) 1 [뛰어난 의견] a valuable[an excellent] opinion. 2 [상대방의 의견] your opinion[views / ideas]. ¶이 문제에 대해 기탄 없는 ~을 듣고자 합니다 Please feel free to express your views on[to say what you think of] this matter.
고결하다(高潔-) lofty; noble; pure; high-minded [-souled]. ¶고결한 사람 a man of noble character / a high-souled [noble-minded] person∥고결한 인격 lofty[noble / high] character∥고결한 마음 a noble[pure] heart∥고결함을 잃지 않다 retain one's noble character∥그의 고결한 정신에 모두 경의를 표했다 Everybody respected him for the nobility of his mind.
고고 the go-go[gogo] dance; go-go; gogo. ¶~를 추다 dance go-go.
고고(呱呱) a baby's cry at its birth.
고고하다(孤高-) proud in loneliness[isolation / solitude]; aloof from others. ¶고고한 생활 a life of proud loneliness[splendid isolation]∥고고한 태도를 지키다 remain apart[aloof] from others.
고고학(考古學) arch(a)eology. ¶~적 자료 archeological evidence[specimens / relics] / ~상 arch(a)eologically / from the arch(a)eological point of view.
* **고고학자** an arch(a)eologist.
고공(高空) (a) high altitude; the high sky. ¶그 비행기는 1만 미터의 ~을 비행하고 있었다 The airplane was flying at an altitude of ten thousand meters.
* **고공병**(-病) altitude sickness. **고공비행** high-altitude flight[flying].
고과(考課) consideration of service[efficiency]; evaluation of merits. ¶인사 ~ merit[efficiency] rating.
* **고과표** efficiency report; (공무원의) a service record; a personnel record(인사 기록).

고관(高官) [높은 직위의 관리] a high (government) official; a dignitary; [높은 직위] a high office.
* **고관대작**(-大爵) [높은 직위의] a high and prominent office; [지위가 높은 사람] a high official; a man of high office; a dignitary.
고교(高校) a (senior) high school. ⇨고등학교(⇨고등)
고구마 a sweet potato (pl. ~es). ¶군 ~ a roast[baked] sweet potato∥찐 ~ a steamed sweet potato∥~ 밭 a sweet-potato field[patch].
고국(故國) one's native[home] country[land]; one's homeland; one's old home. ¶~에 돌아오다 return to one's native country / return home∥~을 생각하다[그리다] pine[long] for one's home∥~을 떠나다 leave one's homeland[native land] / be away from the homeland / go into exile(망명하다).
고군분투하다(孤軍奮鬪-) fight alone (with / against); fight unsupported; struggle single-handed. ¶우리는 고군분투하여 포위망을 뚫고 돌아왔다 My forlorn band has cut its way through the besieging enemy.
고궁(古宮) an ancient[old] palace; a time-honored palace.
고귀하다(高貴-) (지위·인품이) noble; exalted; highborn; (값이) expensive; valuable; rare. ¶고귀한 사람 a high[noble] personage / a person of high rank / a person of royal blood(왕족)∥고귀한 태생이다 be of high[noble] birth / (제왕·귀족 등) be born in the purple∥그 부인은 고귀한 집안에서 태어났다 The lady was born into[of] a noble family. / The lady is of noble birth.
고금(古今) ancient and modern times; time past and present; all ages; any age. ¶~의 ancient and modern / in [of] all ages∥동서~의 작가 writers of all ages and countries∥동서~에 걸쳐 (be true) for all ages and in all places / (be applicable) to all times and places / East and West, past and present∥동서~의 민요 ballads of all ages and countries∥~을 통하여 in history / through all ages∥이 작품은 예술적 가치에 있어서 ~ 미증유(未曾有)이다 In its artistic value this work is unparalleled[unequaled] in history.∥이것은 ~ 미증유의 대발견이다 This is the greatest discovery on record[in history]. / This is the greatest discovery that has ever been made.
고금리(高金利) high interest; a high rate of interest; usury. ¶~로 돈을 빌려 주다 lend money at high interest[at a usurious rate of interest].
고급(高級) [높은 계급] high rank; seniority; [훌륭한 품질] high class[grade]. ¶~인 [질이 좋은] high-quality[-class / -grade] / [사치스러운] luxury (food).
* **고급 공무원** a high[senior] official; higher [high-ranking] officials; high functionaries. **고급 승용차** a deluxe car; an expensive automobile. **고급 장교** a high-ranking officer; a senior officer. **고급품** high-quality articles; luxury items[goods]; goods of higher grade; an article of quality; quality[high-grade] articles[goods]. **고급 호텔** a deluxe[a first-class] hotel; an exclusive[an international (-class)] hotel; a five-star hotel(제1급의).
고기[1] 1 (동물의) meat (fish와 poultry를 제외한

고기

식용육); game(사냥한 들새·짐승의); flesh (of a beast)(들짐승의 살). ¶날~ raw meat/닭~ chicken//돼지~ pork//말~ horsemeat/horseflesh//불~ roast meat/쇠~ beef/송아지~ veal/양~ mutton//요리 a meat dish/~ 한 점[파운드] a piece [pound] of meat/(두껍게 썬 토막) a chop (of meat)//~ 여러 토막 small bits [pieces] of meat//저민 ~ minced [hashed] meat//연한[질긴] tender [tough] meat//~ 저미는 기계 a mincing machine / a meat chopper [grinder] //~ 단자 a meat ball//~를 썰다 cut [carve / chop] meat//~는 잘 구워진[중간 정도의 / 설구워진] 것을 나는 좋아한다 I like my meat well-done [medium / rare].
2 a fish. ⇨ 물고기

● **고기만두** a meat bun; a rissole. **고기밥** (먹이) fish food; food given to fish; (미끼) a fish bait. ¶~이 되다 become food for fishes / be drowned. **고기잡이** fishing; [어업] fishery; [낚시질] angling. ¶~ 가다 go fishing. **고깃간** (一間) a butcher's (shop). ⇨ 푸줏간 **고깃국** (meat) juice(s); (고기 수프) broth; (육즙에 가루를 혼합하여 군고기에 끼얹어 먹는) gravy. **고깃것** plants used as fish-lures. **고깃덩어리** (짐승의) a lump [piece / hunk / hunch] of meat [fish]; [육체] the flesh; the body; the fleshy envelope; the outer man. ¶그는 이제 영혼이 없는 단순한 ~에 지나지 않는다 He is now a mere body without a soul. / He is just a husk of a man. **고깃배** a fishing boat. ⇨ 어선

고기² that place; there; that. ⇨ 거기

고기압 (高氣壓) high atmospheric pressure; anticyclone; the barometric maximum. ¶대륙성 ~ the continental high pressure//~이 발달하다 a high pressure develops itself (over)//한반도 남부 지방은 ~으로 덮여 있다 The southern part of Korean peninsula are covered by [enveloped in] a high pressure system [area]. / High atmospheric pressure overlies the southern part of Korean peninsula.

고까짓 such; so trifling; so small; so trivial. ¶~ 일로 화내지 마라 Don't be offended at such a trifle.//~ 것쯤은 알고 있다 I know as [that] much.//~ 일로 소란을 피우지 마라 Don't make a fuss about such a trifle.//~ 빚 갖고 걱정 말게 Don't worry about that nominal debt. / Such a trifling [small] debt is not worth worrying about.//~ 상처로 크게 떠들어 대다니 Why should you make a fuss over such a slight injury?

고깔 a peaked hat worn by Buddhist monks and nuns.

고깝다 regrettable; reproachful; spiteful; hateful. ¶~게 여기다 have a grudge (against) / feel bitter (against a person) / be reproachful [rueful] / think ill of (a person) / feel bad (about a person's lack of kindness) / take (it) ill [amiss] //악의로 그런 것이 아니니, 고깝게 여기지 말아 주시오 Please, don't think ill [hard] of me. I meant no harm.//고깝게 생각지 않겠다고 나에게 약속해 줘 I want you to promise you won't feel bad.

고꾸라뜨리다 let (a person) fall forward.

고꾸라지다 fall [tumble] forward; fall on one's face; topple down. ¶술에 취해 ~ fall down dead-drunk.

고난 (苦難) distress(es); suffering(s); affliction(s); (박해 등에 의한) tribulation; hardship(s). ¶인생의 ~ the trials [ills] of life//~의 길을 걷다 muddle through the bitters of life//온갖 ~을 견디다 stand [bear / endure] any kind of trials / possess oneself under all trials//모든 ~을 극복하다 conquer [overcome / get over] all trials [afflictions / hardships]//그녀는 ~을 견뎠다 She bore her hardships.//그에게는 끊임없는 ~의 일생이었다 His was a life of constant suffering.//그는 ~의 길을 걸어 갈 각오가 되어 있었다 He was prepared to take a thorny path [(문어) a path beset with difficulties].

고녀 (鼓女) a woman with undergrown sexual [genital] organs; a sexually deficient woman.

고뇌 (苦惱) gnawing; suffering(s); distress; (an) affliction; anguish; agony; pain. ¶~에 찬 마음 a heart full of trouble / an anguished conscience//~의 생활 a life of suffering / a hell of life//~의 빛이 그의 얼굴에 나타났다 A look of distress came over his face.//그는 ~의 일생을 보냈다 He lived life of agony [suffering].//그의 얼굴에는 짙은 ~의 빛이 드러났다 His face revealed the depth of his affliction [distress].//그의 창백한 얼굴은 깊은 ~에 싸 있었다 His ghastly face was full of intense pain.//그는 심한 ~를 맛보았다 The iron entered into his soul. **고뇌하다** suffer; be agonized; anguish.

고니 (동) a swan; a whistling swan. ¶큰~ a whooper swan//혹~ a black swan.

고다 1 [푹 삶아서 흐무러지게 하다] boil (something) (until it is reduced) to pulp; [푹 끓여서 달이다] boil down; boil dry; (끓지 않도록 오래도록) stew. ¶너무 ~ overdo / overboil//고기를 흐무러지게 ~ boil meat to pulp//엿을 ~ boil down grains into taffy / make boiled sweet [hard candy]//닭을 ~ stew a chicken (for a long time)//고아서 과당을 만들다 boil down (fruit juice) into syrup. **2** [양조하다] brew; distill. ¶소주를 ~ distill spirits.

고다지 (not) very; so. ⇨ 그다지

고단자 (高段者) a person holding a high rank (in Judo).

고단하다 tired; fatigued; exhausted; weary; worn out. ¶고단한 일 exhausting [tiring / fatiguing] work//고단하여 잠자리에 들다 go to bed fatigued//몸이 ~ have a weary body / feel worn out [done in]//몹시 ~ be ready to drop (with fatigue) / be worn [tired / fagged] out / be tired to death / (~에 의해) be done up [in]//그는 여행 끝이라서 고단해 보였다 He looked tired after his journey.//몹시 고단해 보이는군요 You look done up [all in / run down / beat / fagged].

고달 [괴통] a metal cap [ring]; a ferrule; [슴베] a tang; a tongue; a prong.

고달이 a handle; a hanger; an attached finger loop (on a package).

고달프다 1 [심신이] tired [fagged / worn] out; quite [dead / dog] tired; done [used / knocked] up; (totally) exhausted; (구어) all [done] in. ¶몸이 ~ have a tired body / be all worn out//마음이 ~ be worried / be fatigued in mind / be mentally fatigued. **2** (일·시간이) tiring; fatiguing; wearing; weary; wearisome; tiresome; hard. ¶고달픈 일

tiring[wearing / fatiguing / hard] work∥고달픈 인생 **a weary[hard] life**∥고달픈 나날 **wearisome days**.

고담(古談) an old tale[story]; a legend; folklore.

고답적(高踏的) transcendent; (구어) highbrow; high-toned ¶~인 문학 **highbrow literature** / (작품) **a highbrow literary work**∥그는 평생을 통하여 ~인 생활 방식을 지켰다 **He kept aloof from the world throughout his life**.

고답주의(高踏主義) transcendentalism.

고답파(高踏派) (일반적으로) the highbrows; [선험론자] the transcendentalists; the Parnassian.

고당(高堂) [높은 집] a lofty[tall] house; a mansion; [남의 집] your[his] house[residence / mansion]; [남의 양친] your[his] parents; your[his] father and mother.

고대 [지금 막] just[right] now; a moment ago; [즉시] this instant; this very minute; at once; immediately. ¶~ 돌아왔습니다 **I have just come home. / I came back just now.**∥그는 ~ 다녀갔다 **He has just been here.**∥~ 들었다 **I have just now heard it.**

고대(古代) ancient[old] times; remote ages; antiquity. ¶~의 ancient / antique / of antiquity / ~의 유물 **antiquities / relics of ancient times** / ~로부터 **from ancient times** / **from time immemorial**.

● **고대 문학 ancient literature. 고대사** ancient history. **고대 소설 a story of ancient times. 고대인** the ancients; ancient people; (집합적) antiquity.

고대광실(高臺廣室) a grand residence; a palatial mansion.

고대하다(苦待-) wait impatiently[eagerly] (for); feel[be] impatient (for); long for; eagerly look forward to (an event). ¶고대하던 소식 **the long-awaited news**∥남이 오기를 ~ **long for a person to come**∥나는 그와 만날 날을 고대하고 있다 **I can hardly wait to see[meet] him.**∥젊은 사람들은 그 가수가 나타나기를 고대하고 있었다 **The young people were impatient[waiting impatiently] for the singer to appear.**∥그 노인은 아들이 돌아오기를 고대하며 나날을 지내고 있다 **The old man is living in expectation of[is living for] his son's return home. / The old man is looking forward patiently to his son's return.**∥학생들은 여름 방학을 고대하고 있다 **The pupils are impatient[can scarcely wait] for the summer holidays to come.**∥조속한 회신을 고대합니다 **I am looking forward to your earliest reply.**

고도(古都) [옛 도시] an ancient city; [옛 수도] an ancient capital.

고도(孤島) a solitary[an isolated / a lonely] island; a desert island. ¶절해의 ~ **a solitary island in the distant ocean[far out on the sea]** / **an islet in[on] the ocean[on the high seas]**.

고도(高度) **1** [높이] (an) altitude; (a) height. ¶비행 ~ **flight[flying] altitude**∥3천 미터의 ~를 날다 **fly at an altitude[a height] of 3,000 meters**∥(비행기의) ~를 낮추다 **lower (its) altitude / fly lower**∥5천 미터의 ~를 유지하다 **keep[maintain] the altitude[height] of 5,000 meters**∥~를 측정하다 **measure the altitude**∥그 비행기의 ~는 어느 정도였는가 **What altitude did the plane reach?** **2** [정도가 높음] a high degree; a high power. ¶~의 **intense / high-power / high-degree[-grade] / high** / (발전한) **advanced / highly developed**∥~의 문명 **a high level[standard] of civilization**∥~의 경제 성장 **high growth of (Korean) economy / high level of (Korea's) economic growth**∥~로 **to a high degree**∥~로 기계화[물질화]한 문명 **highly mechanized[materialized] civilization**∥거기에는 ~의 기술과 최~의 정밀 작업이 필요하다 **It requires advanced[a high degree of] technical skill and precision work of highest order[caliber]**.

● **고도계** an altimeter; an altometer; a height indicator. **고도 기록** an altitude record. **고도성장** high[speedy / rapid] growth. **고도 제어** (장치) [항] altitude control (system). **고도 측량** [천] altimetry.

고독(孤獨) [혼자임] solitude; [혼자 있어 외로움] loneliness (solitude는 자기 뜻에 의해서 혼자 있는 것이며, 반드시 외로움이 포함되는 것은 아님). ¶~을 느끼다 **feel lonely[alone]**∥~을 사랑하다 **love[be fond of] solitude[one's own company]** / ~을 참다 **bear solitude**∥나는 깊은 ~감을 느끼고 있다 **I feel a deep sense of isolation. / I feel very lonely.**∥때때로 ~도 또한 즐거운 것이다 **I enjoy my own company, too, at times. 고독하다 solitary; friendless; lonely; lonesome.** ¶고독한 사람 **a solitary person**∥그는 평생을 고독하게 보냈다 **He lead a lonely[solitary] life.**

● **고독단신** a solitary[lonely] person; a solitary.

고동 **1** [기계 장치] a starter (of a machine / of an apparatus); a switch; a cock; a handle. ¶~을 틀다 **turn on (the water)** / ~을 잠그다 **turn off (the gas). 2** [기적] (steam) whistle; a siren. ¶~을 울리다 **sound [blow / give] a whistle / blow a siren / whistle**∥~이 울렸다 **The whistle blew. 3** (물레의) two flywheel type rings on a spinning wheel spindle.

고동(鼓動) (심장의) a beat; beating; pulsation; palpitation; throbbing. ¶심장의 ~ **heartbeats / the beating of the heart**∥심장의 ~이 들리다 **hear (a person's) heart throbbing**∥이 기계는 심장의 ~을 기록한다 **This machine records the heartbeat[the beating of the heart].**∥심장의 ~이 빠르다[불규칙하다] **My heart is beating fast[irregularly].**∥심장의 ~이 빨라졌다[격렬해졌다] **My heart began to beat fast[violently].**∥나는 내 심장의 ~ 소리가 그에게 들릴지도 모른다는 생각이 들었다 **I thought he might be able to hear the pounding[thumping] of my heart.**∥그의 심장은 ~을 멈추었다 **His heart stopped beating. 고동하다 beat; pulsate; palpitate; throb.**

고동색(古銅色) brown; reddish brown.

고동치다(鼓動-) beat; pulsate. ⇨**고동하다** (⇨**고동**(鼓動)) ¶희망으로 고동치는 가슴 **a heart throbbing with hope**∥내 심장이 새차게 고동쳤다[고동치는 것을 느꼈다] **My heart beat fast. / I felt my heart beating fast.**

고되다 tired; fatigued; (일 등이) trying; hard (to bear); painful; tough; difficult; laborious; arduous. ¶고된 일 **hard[heavy] work / a toilsome [painful] task / an awful [a horrible] sweat**∥고된 노동 **hard[intense]**

고두밥

labor // 고된 경험 a trying experience // 고된 생활[세상] a hard life[world] // 고되게 일하다 work like a dog / toil and moil // 이 일은 몹시 ~ This work is very tiring[fatiguing]. / This work wears me out[takes it out of me].

고두밥 hard-boiled[-steamed] rice.

고둥 [동] a snail; a spiral shellfish; (열대산 대형의) conch (pl. ~s, ~es); spirals.

고드름 an icicle. ¶처마 끝에 주렁주렁 매달린 ~ a fringe of ice on the eaves // ~이 매달려 있다 an icicle hangs (from the eaves) // ~이 생기다 an icicle forms.

고들개 1 [안장의 가슴걸이에 다는 방울] a horsebell; a cowbell. 2 (채찍의) a knobbed (whip) lash; a loaded lash. 3 (굴레의) a throatlatch. 4 (처녑의) the manyplies; an omasum (pl. -sa).

고들고들하다 dry and hard. ⇨ 꼬들꼬들하다

고들빼기 [식] a Korean lettuce.

고등(高等) high grade; high class. ¶~의 high / [상급의] higher / advanced / supreme / [고급의] high-grade / high-class / first-class. ●**고등 검찰청** a high public prosecutor's office. **고등 교육** (receive) (a) higher[liberal] education. ¶~을 받은 사람 a highly educated person / a college[university] graduate / (집합적) the highly educated / the intellectuals. **고등 동물** a higher animal. **고등 법원** a High Court (of Justice); [상고 법원] an appellate court. **고등 수학** higher mathematics; (구어) higher math. **고등 식물** higher plant life. **고등 정책** higher politics. **고등학교** (미) a (senior) high school(▶ 9-12, 또는 10-12학년의 학생이 다니는 학교를 가리킴. 한편, (영)에서는 중고등학교를 통칭하는 secondary school이라는 말이 있음). ¶인문 [여자 / 공업 / 농업 / 상업] ~ an academic[a girls' / a technical / an agricultural / a commercial] high school. **고등학생** a (senior) high school student.

고등어 [동] a mackerel (pl. ~(s)); a scombroid.

고딕 Gothic. ●**고딕 건축** Gothic architecture; (건축물) a Gothic building. **고딕식** Gothic; Gothic style. **고딕체** Gothic type; a black letter.

고락 [낙지의 배] the abdomen of an octopus; [낙지 먹물] ink of an octopus; [먹물집] the ink bag of an octopus.

고락(苦樂) joys and sorrows. ¶인생의 ~ the sweets and bitters of life // ~을 같이하다 share one's joys and sorrows [one's fortunes] (with) // 세상의 ~을 다 겪다 have tasted sweets and bitters of life // 우리는 ~을 같이해 온 사이다 We have come through good and bad times together. / We have been great friends both in joy and in sorrow. // 그는 ~을 함께해 온 아내를 잃었다 He lost the wife who had shared all his joys and sorrows with him.

고랑¹ [두둑의 사이] a furrow; a trough. ¶~을 짓다 make furrows / furrow. ●**고랑창** a narrow deep trough; a ditch.

고랑² handcuffs. ⇨ 쇠고랑

고래¹ [동] a whale. ¶혹등~ a humpback whale / 큰~ a black right whale / 긴수염~ a finback / a fin whale / a razorback / 향유~ a sperm whale / a cachalot / ~ 목(目)의 cetacean // 수[암]~ a bull[cow] whale // 새끼~ a whale calf / ~ 같다 be as big as a whale / be huge // ~가 물을 내뿜고 있다 A whale is blowing[is spouting water]. **고래 싸움에 새우 등 터진다**(속담) An innocent bystander gets badly hurt[gets a heavy by-blow] in a Titanic struggle. **고래 등 같다** grand; magnificent; palatial; imposing. ¶고래 등 같은 집 a stately[grand] mansion / a palatial house. ●**고래 고기** whale meat. **고래 기름** whale oil; blubber. **고래수염** baleen; whalebone; [경] a whalefin. **고래자리** [천] the whale; Cetus. **고래작살** a harpoon; a gaff. **고래잡이** whale fishing; whaling.

고래² [방고래] flues in a hypocaust[a floor heater].

고래(古來) ¶~의 old / ancient / time-honored // ~로 유례가 없다 have no parallel[equal] in history[in any age].

고래고래 shoutingly; in a voice of thunder. ¶~ 소리 지르다 shout (at) / yell / roar / bawl / thunder / cry in a loud voice // 화가 나서 ~ 소리를 지르다 raise one's voice in a huff [rage] // 우리는 ~ 소리 지르며 반대하여 (그것을) 저지했다 We stopped it by raising a roar of opposition. / (구어) We stopped it by screaming bloody murder.

고량(高粱) [수수] kaoliang; koaliang; kowliang; sorghum. ●**고량주** kaoliang wine[spirits].

고량진미(膏粱珍味) rich fare; a dainty; a food of delicate flavor; luxurious viands; good[fat] things; all sorts of delicacies. ¶~로 손을 대접하다 entertain (a person) with all sorts of delicacies.

고려(考慮) consideration; deliberation; reflection; thinking; careful thought. ¶~에 넣다 take (a person / a thing) into account [consideration] / make allowance for (a person's youth) // …을 충분히 ~에 넣어 with due regard to … / in due consideration of … // ~에 넣지 않다 leave (a matter) out of consideration[account] / discount // ~를 요하다 be worth due consideration / demand deliberation // ~ 중이다 (사람이) have (a matter) under consideration[contemplation] / (사물이) be under consideration [contemplation] / be in view. **고려하다** consider; think[ponder] over; give consideration[thought] to; take (a matter) into consideration[account]; deliberate on; reflect upon; bear (it) in mind. ¶고려해야 할 점들 points to be duly considered // 충분히 고려한 후에 after due consideration[deliberation] // 상대방의 사정도 충분히 ~ pay due regard to their convenience // 고려하지 않다 take no thought (of) / have no regard [consideration] (for) / pay no regard (to) // 고려해 볼 만하다[고려할 가치가 없다] be [be not] worth deliberation[consideration] / deserve much [little] consideration // 고려의 여지가 있다 There is no room for consideration. // 그것은 아직 고려의 여지가 있다 It leaves some room for consideration. // 이것들은 특히 고려해야 할 점이다 These are the points to be specially considered. // 그는 내 나이를 고려해 주지 않았다 He did not take my age into consideration[account]. // 여러 가지를 고려해 볼 때 그것은 비싸게 산 것이 아니다 All things considered, it is not a bad bargain. // 젊음을 고

고려(顧慮) [잘 생각함] consideration; thinking over; [걱정] concern; solicitude. **고려하다** consider; think over; take (a matter) into consideration; be concerned about. ¶…을 고려하지 않고 without respect to ... / regardless of ... / with little[no] thought of ... //고려하지 않다 be indifferent (to) / take no notice (of) / pay no attention (to) / have no regard (for)//그는 남의 이해 관계는 전혀 고려하지 않는다 He has no regard[respect] for other's interests.

고려인삼(高麗人蔘) *Goryeo insam*; Korean ginseng.

고려자기(高麗瓷器) Goryeo (ceramic) ware [porcelain / pottery].

고려장(高麗葬) an ancient burial practice whereby an [a dying] old person is left to die in an open tomb.

고령(高齡) an advanced [a great / a venerable / a ripe] age. ¶~의 aged / old / advanced in years // ~에도 불구하고 in spite of (his) great age // ~에 달하다 attain an advanced age // ~으로 죽다 die very old / die in advanced life [at an advanced age] // 80세의 ~으로 죽다 die at the great [advanced / ripe / old] age of eighty // 그는 ~이다 He is advanced in age. / He is very old. // 그는 88세의 ~까지 살았다 He lived to the ripe age of eighty-eight.

● **고령자** (집합적) the aged [old]; [나이가 많은 개인] a very old [an aged] person; a person of advanced age. ¶최~ the oldest / the most aged.

고령토(高嶺土) [도자기 원료] Kaolin; kaolinite; china [porcelain] clay.

고례(古例) an old practice; an established custom; tradition.

고로(故-) therefore; accordingly; hence; consequently; so (that) ...; and so; for the reason that.

고료(稿料) [원고료] copy money; fee for a manuscript [an article]. ¶~ 생활자 a commercial writer // ~가 많다[적다] (사람이) be paid well[poorly] for one's writing / (원고가) be paid for high[low] // ~를 한 페이지[장]에 얼마로 지불하다 pay so much per page [sheet].

고루(均一) [균일하게] evenly; equally; uniformly; [공평하게] fairly; impartially; [차별없이] indiscriminately. ¶~ 나누어 주다 distribute evenly[all round] // ~ 가르다 divide (a thing) equally / go share and share alike // 여러 방면의 서적을 ~ 섭렵하다 read through books covering all sorts of field// 케이크에 ~ 크림을 바르다 cover a cake with whipped cream / spread whipped cream all over a cake // 음식을 ~ 먹도록 하라 Try to eat well-balanced meals. // 그는 모든 학과를 ~ 잘한다 He does very well in every subject. // 그는 그 문제를 빠짐없이 ~[모든 각도에서] 조사했다 He investigated the matter thoroughly [from all angles].

고루거각(高樓巨閣) a lofty and stately building.

고루하다(固陋-) bigoted; narrow-minded; stubborn; obstinate; extremely conservative. ¶고루한 늙은이 an old fog(e)y.

고르다¹ [선택하다] choose; select; make choice of; pick[single / sort] out(선발하다); fix upon(선정하다). ¶자기가 고른 책 a book of one's own choice // 둘 중에서 ~ choose [make one's choice] between the two // 잘못 ~ make the wrong selection / make a bad choice // 고르고 ~ pick and choose // 며느리를 ~ choose a future daughter-in-law // 가장 좋은 것을 ~ select the best one // 좋은 날을 ~ choose[fix upon] an auspicious day // 쌀에서 돌을 ~ pick sand out of the rice [grain] // 골라 잡아 1,000원 All one thousand won apiece. / Take your choice [Choose whichever you like] for 1,000 won. // 골라 잡아 이 스카프 두 장에 만 원이오 You can have your choice of two scarfs for ten thousand won. // 내 옷은 어머니가 골라 주신다 My mother chooses the right kind of clothes for me. // 아버지는 그녀를 나의 아내로 고르셨다 My father fixed upon her for my wife. // 그것은 제가 고른 것입니다 It is my choice. / I chose it myself. // 이것이 내가 고른 그림이다 This is the picture I chose. // 내가 고른다면 노랑이로 하겠다 I would take yellow, for choice. // 그녀는 우리 아이에게 적합한 장난감을 골라 주었다 She selected[chose] a suitable toy for my child. // 이 무늬를 참 잘 고르셨습니다 You were wise in selecting this pattern. / This pattern is a very good choice. // 나는 내 옷을 고르는 일을 그녀에게 맡겼다 I left the choice of clothes to her. / I let her choose my clothes. // 그는 좋은 것을 골랐다 He made a good[the right] choice. // 어느 책이든 원하는 것을 고르시오 Select [Choose] any book you want. // 이 둘 중에서 어느 하나를 고르시오 Choose between these two. / Choose one of the two. // 그들은 그의 작품 가운데서 최고의 것을 골랐다 They selected [chose] the best of his works.

고르다² [평평하게 하다] level (the ground); smooth; make even; roll(롤러로); bulldoze(불도저로). ¶표면을 ~ bring a surface to a level // 뜰을 갈퀴로 ~ smooth the uneven spots in a garden with a rake // 집을 짓기 전에 땅을 ~ level ground[make the ground level] before building / bulldoze a building site // 우리는 땅을 골라 운동장을 만들었다 We rolled [leveled] the land and made a playground.

고르다³ 1 [한결같다] even; uniform; equal; regular. ¶고르지 않은 uneven / not uniform / unequal / irregular / rugged(울퉁불퉁한) // 고르게 evenly / equally / uniformly / regularly // 고르게 따뜻한 방 a room heated evenly // 대소 규격이 고르지 않은 irregular in size // 기량이 고르지 못한 선수 an erratic player // 고르지 못한 길 a rough[bumpy] road // 이가 ~ [고르지 않다] have regular [irregular / uneven] teeth // 복장이 ~ be dressed all alike / be uniformed // 고르게 칠하다 paint evenly // 땅이 ~ The ground is even. // 이 학생은 시험 성적이 고르지 못하다 This student performs unevenly on tests. // 각 조합의 의견이 고르지 않다 The unions are in disagreement. // 어린이들의 학교 성적이 고르지 못했다 The children's school records were not uniform. // 이 사과는 지금 막 거두어들여 분류가 안 되었기 때문에 고르지 못하다 These apples have just been picked and are unsorted. // 우리 대학은 학생들의 능력이 고르다는 점을 자랑으로 삼고 있다 Our university is proud of the uniform level of the students'

고르 ability.// 그는 모든 것을 고르게 잘한다 He is equally good at everything.// 그는 나무들의 키를 고르게 했다 He made the trees the same[a uniform] height.// 그들은 건물 내부 전체의 온도를 고르게 했다 They equalized the temperature in all parts of the building. **2**〔공평하다〕equal; fair; impartial. ¶고르지 못한 unfair / unjust / partial / unequal // 고르게 equally / fairly / justly / impartially // 고르게 나누다 divide《money》equally[into equal part] / go share and share alike // 몫이 고르지 못하다 The share is not equal. **3**〔날씨가 순조롭다〕seasonable; favorable. ¶고른 날씨 seasonable[favorable] weather // 고르지 못한 unseasonable / unsettled / changeable / unfavorable / irregular(불규칙한) // 가을 날씨는 고르지 못하다 Autumn weather is changeable.

고름¹ 〔농즙〕pus; matter; purulent matter; discharge. ¶〔눌리〕부스럼에서 ~을 짜내다 press out pus from a boil / pop a pimple // 부스럼을 따서 ~을 짜내다 lance a boil / 부스럼에서 ~이 나왔다 Pus came out of the boil. /〔여드름 등의〕The pimple popped. // 상처에 ~이 생겼다 The wound contains[has formed / has produced] pus. / Pus has gathered in the wound.
● **고름집** a pustule.

고름² 〔옷고름〕a breast-tie; a coat string. ¶~을 매다 tie with a bow.

고리¹ 〔끼우는 물건〕a ring; a link(사슬의); 〔실·끈 등의〕a loop. ¶귀~ an earring / 문~ a door-ring // 손잡이 ~〔서랍의〕a drawer handle // ~를 만들다 loop(실 등으로) / form a ring.

고리² 〔쪼갠 고리버들 가지〕split osiers[willow] branches; wicker; 〔고리짝〕a wicker portmanteau[suitcase]; a wicker trunk(큰 것).
● **고리장이** a wick worker; a maker of wicker (articles). **고리짝** 〔고리로 엮은 상자〕a wicker portmanteau[suitcase / trunk];〔짐〕(미) baggage; (영) luggage.

고리(高利) high interest; a high rate of interest; usury. ¶~로 돈을 빌려 주다[빌려 오다] lend[borrow] money at high interest[at a usurious rate of interest].
● **고리대금**〔이자가 비싼 돈〕a loan at high interest;〔이자가 비싼 돈놀이〕usury; loan-sharking. **고리대금업자** a usurer; a usury man; (미국 속어) a loan shark; a Shylock. **고리채** a usurious loan.

고리다 ill-smelling; suspicious. ⇨<구리다

고리못 a ring-shaped nail[hook].

고리버들 〔식〕an osier; a basket osier.

고리타분하다 1〔냄새가〕ill-[foul-] smelling; stinking; malodorous; rancid; offensive; fetid; rank; rotten(썩어서). ¶고리타분한 냄새가 나다 smell offensive[foul / rancid] / give out a bad smell / stink // 고리타분한 냄새가 코를 찔렀다 A rancid smell greeted my nose. / It stank to (high) heaven. **2**〔성질·행동이〕low; mean; petty; shallow; narrow-minded; stale; trite; commonplace; banal; meticulous. ¶고리타분한 생각[사상] a stereotyped [hackneyed] idea / moth-eaten[outdated / old-fashioned] ideas / 고리타분한 학설 a worn-out[threadbare] theory.

고린내 a foul[nasty] smell; a stench; a stink. ¶~를 풍기다 give[send] out an offensive smell / emit a foul[bad] odor // ~가 나다 have a bad smell / smell bad / stink // 그들의 발~가 확 내 코를 찔렀다 The stink from their feet greeted my nose.

고릴라 〔동〕a gorilla.

고립(孤立) isolation; helplessness. ¶국제적 ~(avoid) international isolation // ~무원으로 싸우다 fight alone (and unaided). **고립하다** be isolated; stand alone[isolated]; be in isolation; be helpless[friendless];〔정치·경제적으로〕be quarantined. ¶외계로부터 완전히 ~ be entirely cut off from the outside world [from the rest of the world]. ➔ **고립된** solitary / isolated / lone / friendless / helpless // **고립시키다** isolate (a person) (from) // 침략국을 고립시키다 quarantine an aggressor nation // 고립된 생활을 하다 live in isolation (from others) / play the Robinson Crusoe // 그는 동업자 사이에서 고립되어 있다 He has no friends among those in the same line of business.
● **고립어** an isolated language. **고립 정책** an isolation policy. **고립주의** isolationism. **고립화** isolation; encirclement.

고마움 〔감사〕gratitude; thankfulness;〔가치〕value[virtue]《of money》;〔은혜〕(a) favor; 〔혜택〕blessing《of health》. ¶~을 알다 know[appreciate] the value《of a thing》/ know how much one owes (to a person) / know how good it is to ... // 돈의 ~을 알다 know[appreciate] the value[worth] of money // 병이 나야 비로소 건강의 ~을 안다 No one can appreciate the bliss of health till he loses it. // 나는 이제야 부모님의 ~을 알았다 Now I acknowledge[understand] how much I owe (to) my parents. // 그는 돈의 ~을 모른다 He is a stranger to the value of money. // 우리는 진심에서 우러나온 ~을 표하려고 선생님들을 저녁 식사에 초대했다 We invited our teachers to dinner as an expression of our heartful gratitude. // 그는 건강의 ~을 모르고 있다 He doesn't know what a blessing it is to be healthy. // 우리는 흔히 부모님의 ~을 잊어버린다 We often forget how much we owe (to) our parents.

고마워하다 〔고맙게 여기다〕be thankful (for); feel grateful (for); show one's gratitude; appreciate; be appreciative (of); be obliged[indebted] (for). ¶그는 나의 사소한 친절을 몹시 고마워했다 He was very grateful to me for the little kindness I had shown him. // 그는 조그만 일에도 고마워한다 It takes so little to make him thankful. // 그녀는 아주 고마워하며 그것을 받았다 She accepted it with great thanks.

고막〔동〕→꼬막

고막(鼓膜) the eardrum; the drumhead; the drum membrane; the drum of one's ear;〔생〕the tympanum (pl. ~s, -na); the tympanic membrane. ¶~이 tympanic / tympanal // ~이 찢어질 것 같은 earsplitting / ear-blasting // ~이 터지다 have one's eardrum split [ruptured] // ~이 찢어질 듯한 소리를 내며 제트기가 이륙했다 The jet took off with an earsplitting[a deafening] roar.
● **고막염** myringitis; tympanitis.

고만¹ (a) little (amount of). ⇨<그만¹

고만² that much and no more; as soon as; carelessly. ⇨<그만³

고만고만하다 be about the same. ⇨그만그만

하다

고만두다 stop (doing); abolish; stop (drinking); resign (one's post). ⇨ 〈그만두다

고만하다 tolerable; much the same. ⇨ 〈그만하다

-고말고 certainly; (as a matter) of course; indeed; to be sure; enough; rather; needless to say; no doubt; it goes without saying that ...; why not? ¶그렇~ It's just as you say. / You are certainly right. / Oh, yes, to be sure / Yes, indeed! / Of course, it is. // 그것으로 좋~ Certainly, that will do. // "이것 좋아하나?" "좋아하~." "Do you like this?" "Rather." // "음악 좋아하나?" "그렇~." "Do you like music?" "I'll say." // "나를 기억하십니까?" "기억하~요." "Do you remember me?" "Of course (I remember)." // "바쁩니까?" "바쁘~요." "Are you busy?" "Sure, I am." // 그가 위인이~ 여부가 있나 He is, without a doubt, a great man. // 그는 정직한 사람 같은데." "그렇~." "He seems to be an honest man." "So he is." // "아무렴, 그런 일은 허용할 수 없~." "I'm not going to permit such a thing. Never!"

고맘때 that time of day. ⇨ 〈그맘때

고맙다 1 (사물이) grateful; welcome; blessed; appreciated; gracious; benevolent. ¶고마운 비 a welcome rain // 고마운 선물 a much appreciated present // 고마운 말씀 kind [gracious] words // 고마운 주인 a benevolent [kind] master // 고마지 않은 unwelcome (guest) / thankless (task) / undesirable // 전등이란 참으로 고마운 것이다 What a blessed device [a happy invention] the electric lamp is!
2 [감사하다] thankful; appreciative; gratefully acknowledged; obliged; (미) obligated; indebted. ¶고맙게도 fortunately / luckily / mercifully / thankfully / by good luck / I am glad (to say) that ... / I am thankful that ... // 고맙게 여기다 [생각하다] be thankful [grateful] (to a person for something) / appreciate (a person's kindness) / gratefully acknowledge (a favor) / be obliged (to) / (미) be obligated // 고맙게도 그는 내게 돈을 꾸어 주었다 He was kind enough to lend me some money. / He has kindly lent me money. // 깨어나 보니 고맙게도 날씨는 갰다 A welcome change in the weather awoke me. // 대단히 고맙습니다 Thank you very much. / Thank you for your trouble. / How kind of you! / (강조) I don't know how to thank you! / Many thanks. / (구어) Thanks a lot. / I'm much obliged to you. // 그렇게 말씀해 주시니 고맙습니다 It is very kind [nice] of you to say so. // 당신의 친절에 대해 매우 고맙게 생각합니다 I deeply appreciate your kindness. / Thank you very much for your kindness. // 생일 축하연에 초대해 주셔서 고맙습니다 Thank you for inviting me [It's kind of you to invite me] to your birthday party. // 그는 아내의 배려를 무척 고맙게 여겼다 He was very thankful [grateful] to his wife for her consideration. / He greatly appreciated his wife's consideration. // 조속히 회답해 주셔서 고맙습니다 I am much obliged to you for your prompt reply. // 그를 도와주시면 정말 고맙겠습니다 I should be very much obliged to you if you would help him. // 친구들이 보내 준 생일 선물을 받고 나는 퍽 고맙게 생각했다 I deeply appreciated the birthday presents sent by my friends. // 원조를 해 주시어 고맙게 여기고 있습니다 I am grateful for the help you have given me. // 항상 저의 곤경을 보살펴 주셔서 고맙습니다 Thank you for your constant attention to my needs. // 네가 와 주어 고맙다 I appreciate your [Thanks for] coming. // 나는 항상 그녀의 친절 [조언] 을 고맙게 여기고 있다 I am always thankful [grateful] for her kindness [advice]. / I always appreciate her kindness [advice]. // 나는 부모님의 사랑이 그렇게 고마울 수가 없었다 I have never felt so grateful [thankful] to my parents for their loving concern.

고매하다 (高邁－) noble; lofty; high-minded. ¶고매한 이상 a lofty ideal // 고매한 기품 a noble spirit // 아무리 ~ have exalted ideas / 그런 고매한 이상을 편다고 해도 너는 아무런 성과를 얻을 수 없을 것이다 Such lofty (-minded) ideals will get you nowhere.

고명 (요리의) a garnish; (미) fixings; garnishings; (속어) trimmings; a condiment; a relish; decorative [colo(u)rful] seasonings; an ornamental accompaniment; (a) garniture. ¶파슬리를 ~으로 얹은 생선회 raw fish garnished with parsley.

고명 (高名) 1 [유명함] fame; high reputation; repute; renown; a famous name. **고명하다** famous; renowned; celebrated; famed; noted. ¶소설가로서 ~ with fame as a novelist / be well known as a novelist // 그는 세계적으로 고명한 사람이다 He is world-famous. / He is a man of world-wide fame. 2 [남의 이름을 높여 일컫는 말] your name. ¶~은 이미 들어 알고 있습니다 I have heard much of [about] you. / I have often heard of you. / Your name is quite familiar to me.

고명딸 one's [the] only daughter among many sons.

고명하다 (高明－) 〔겸하고 현명하다〕 noble and wise; perspicacious; 〔식견이 높다〕 high-minded.

고모 (姑母) an aunt; one's dad's [father's] sister; (문어) a paternal aunt. (▶ 영미에서는 우리나라와 달리 「고모 / 이모 / 숙모 / 외숙모」 등을 aunt로 총칭해서 쓰는 것이 일반적이며, 그것을 굳이 구별하고자 할 때, 「고모」의 경우 "dad's sister / paternal aunt" 등을 씀)
● **고모부** an uncle; the husband of one's father's [dad's] sister.

고목 (古木) an old [aged] tree. ¶떡갈나무 ~ an old oak (tree).

고목 (枯木) 〔말라 죽은 나무〕 a dead [decayed / withered] tree; dead [rotten] wood. ¶~이 쓰러지듯 죽다 die as a decayed old tree falls.

고무 1 (가공품으로서의) rubber; 〔탄성 고무〕 India rubber; (재료로서의) gum. ¶생 ~ raw [crude] rubber // ~를 입힌 rubber(-coated) / gummed / rubberized // ~바닥[창]의 rubber-soled // ~를 입힌 천 rubberized cloth // ~를 입힌 방수 외투 (영) a mackintosh [mac]. 2 an eraser. ⇨ 〈고무지우개(⇨)고무〉
● **고무공** a rubber ball; a bouncing ball. **고무관** a rubber tube. **고무나무** a rubber tree [plant]; a gum tree. **고무밴드** a rubber band (포장용). **고무신** rubber shoes. **고무 제품** rubber goods. **고무줄** 고무 끈 an elastic cord [string]; a rubber band. **고무지우개** an eraser [a rubber]; an India [india] rubber; a rubber. **고무창** a rubber sole. **고무풀** gum

고무래 (arabic); mucilage; (사무용) glue. **고무풍선** a (toy) balloon; a rubber balloon.

고무래 a solid wooden rake (used to spread grain, to rake ashes, or to level soil).

고무적 (鼓舞的) encouraging; inspiring; stimulative. ¶당신의 ~인 말씀에 용기를 얻었습니다 I was cheered by your encouraging remark.∥섬유 공업의 전망은 매우 ~이다 The future [prospect] of the fiber industry is very bright [encouraging].

고무하다 (鼓舞-) encourage; inspire (a person with patriotism); inspirit (a person to an action); incite; stimulate; stir up (one's mind); arouse (a person to activity); cheer up. ¶사기를 ~ arouse [stir up] the morale (of the troops)∥남을 고무하여 더욱 노력하게 하다 stimulate a person to (make) greater efforts∥그 책은 소년들에게 모험심을 고무했다 The book inspired the boys with an adventurous spirit.

고문 (古文) ancient writing(s); archaic texts; (집합적) classics.

고문 (拷問) torture; the rake; (미) the third degree. ¶~을 당하다 be tortured / be put to torture∥~을 당해 자백하다 [죽다] confess [die] under torture∥나는 어떤 ~에도 입을 열지 않겠다 No torture would make me speak. **고문하다** torture; use torture on (a person); give (a person) the third degree; put (a person) to torture [the rack]; put (a person) on the rack. ¶물로 ~ [물고문을 하다] torture a person by water / put a person to water torture∥그들이 아무리 고문해도 그는 입을 열지 않았다 They couldn't torture him into talking.

● **고문치사** (-致死) torture resulting in death.

고문 (顧問) an advisor [an adviser] (to); a counselor [(영) a counsellor] (adviser는 지식이나 경험에 입각한 실제적인 조언을 해 주는 사람, counselor는 신중히 숙고한 뒤에 조언을 해 주는 사람); a brain truster; (컨설턴트) a consultant. ¶기술 ~ a technical adviser∥대통령 ~ an aide-de-camp to the President∥법률 ~ a juridical counselor∥편집 ~ an advisory editor∥~으로 있다 act in an advisory capacity / act as consultant∥~으로 삼다 engage (a person) as an adviser∥외국인 전문가를 ~으로 초빙하다 employ a foreign expert as adviser.

● **고문관** a counselor. **고문 기관** an advisory [a consultative] council. **고문단** an advisory group [body / committee / council]; a brain trust; (미) brain trusters. **고문 변호사** a legal advisor; (회사의) a corporation lawyer [attorney]; (가정의) a family lawyer.

고문서 (古文書) ancient [antique] documents; a paleograph; diplomas.

고물[1] [떡에 묻히는 가루] powdered bean [sesame / pea] (used for covering or coating rice cake). ¶콩~을 묻힌 떡 a rice cake dressed with bean flour∥떡에 깨~을 묻히다 cover rice cakes with powdered sesame.

고물[2] [배의 뒤쪽] the stern; the poop. ¶이물에서 ~까지 from bow to stern / fore and aft∥~ 쪽에 [으로] aft / astern / abaft∥~ 쪽부터 가라앉다 sink by the stern.

고물 (古物) **1** [골동품] antiquities; antiques; curios; (집합적) bric-a-brac. **2** [낡은 것] a used item; used things; a worn-out [secondhand] article; used [old] furniture (가구). ¶이 소파는 이제 ~이다 This sofa is on its last legs.∥저 친구 이젠 ~이 다 되어 쓸모가 없다 He is worn-out [a back number] and good for nothing.

● **고물상** (商人) a dealer in secondhand articles; secondhand dealer; a used article dealer; (상점) a secondhand store [(영) shop]. **고물 시장** the flea market.

고미 [건] a kind of plaster panel ceiling. ¶~를 누르다 lay [put in] a plaster panel ceiling.

● **고미다락** an attic. **고미혀** rafters between supporting beams and boards.

고미 (苦味) [쓴맛] bitterness; a bitter taste.

고민 (苦悶) agony; anguish (agony는 심신의, anguish는 주로 마음의 괴로움); worry; trouble; affliction. ¶~거리 the source of trouble∥청춘의 ~ nameless longings of youth / torments of awakened love∥마음의 ~ anguish of heart / mental affliction / a weight on one's mind∥그의 ~은 거의 견딜 수 없는 것이었다 His distress was almost unbearable.∥그는 ~으로 밤새껏 잠을 이루지 못했다 His mental anguish kept him awake all night. **고민하다** be in agony [anguish / distress]; suffer mental anguish; agonize (over one's failure); be worried (about); be troubled (with); worry (oneself) (about / over). ¶사랑에 ~ languish for love / be lovesick / be lovelorn (실연하여)∥너는 그렇게 고민할 필요가 없었다 You need not have worried (yourself) so much.∥나는 장래의 진로에 대해 여러 가지로 고민했다 I just didn't know what to do about my future.

고발 (告發) [법] prosecution; indictment; accusation; charging; a complaint; a formal charge [accusation] (against). ¶~에 따라 on complaint (of a person). **고발하다** (검찰청이) prosecute [indict] (a person for a crime); file a complaint (against) (경찰, 수사관에 영장을 받기 위해 법원에 제출하는 것); (민간인이) lodge [lay] a complaint [an information] (against a person); inform (the authorities against a person). → 그는 절도 혐의로 고발되었다 He was charged with stealing.∥질서를 문란케 하는 자는 고발된다 Prosecution will follow any violation of order.

● **고발인** an accuser; [법] a plaintiff. **고발장** a bill of indictment.

고방 (庫房) a storeroom; a lumber room [closet]; a go-down; (영) a boxroom.

고배 (苦杯) a bitter cup; (승부에서) a sad defeat; hardships. ¶~를 마시다 [들다] drink a bitter cup / drink the cup of agony [humiliation] / go through an ordeal [a trial] / drain the cup of sorrow / have a bitter experience / experience [taste] the bitterness of life / (승부에서) (문어) taste the bitterness of defeat / suffer a defeat∥우리는 작년에 저 팀과의 시합에서 ~를 마셨다 We were humiliated [miserably defeated] by that team last year.

고백 (告白) confession; acknowledgment (자인); profession (공표). ¶사랑의 ~ a declaration of love∥신앙 ~ a confession [an avowal] of faith. **고백하다** confess (of). ¶나는 모든 것을 고백했다 I confessed everything. / I made a clean breast of the whole affair.∥그는 자기의 죄를 신부에게 고백했다 He confessed his sins to the priest.∥그녀는

지하 조직의 일원임을 고백했다 She confessed herself to be a member of the underground organization.// 그는 그녀에게 사랑을 고백했다 He declared his love for her.
●**고백 성사** [가] the sacrament of penance; penance.
고법(高法) a High Court (of Justice). ⇨"고등 법원 〈고등〉
고변하다(告變−) inform (the authority) of a rebellion [mutiny]; report [bring news of] treason.
고별(告別) leave-taking; farewell; valediction; parting; good-bye. **고별하다** take leave (of); bid farewell [adieu] (to); pay last respects (to).
●**고별사**(−辭) 〔인사〕 a farewell speech [address]; parting words; 〔졸업생의〕 a valediction; valedictory address; 〔조사(弔辭)〕 a funeral oration. **고별식** 〔송별식〕 a farewell ceremony; 〔영결식〕 a funeral service.
고본(古本) **1** 〔옛 판〕 an old [a former] edition. **2** 〔헌책〕 a used [secondhand] book. ¶나는 이 책을 ~으로 샀다 I have bought this book secondhand.// **고가 매입** (게시) High prices offered for used books.
고봉(高峯) a high [lofty] peak; a high mountain; an alp; a cloudkissing mountain peak.
●**고봉준령** high mountains and steep peaks.
고봉(高捧) a heap [mountain] (of); a full measure (되 등); (음식의) a generous [large] helping [serving]. ¶~의 brimful / heaping full / full to overflowing// ~으로 3인분 three large servings// ~으로 되다 give a heaping measure (of).
고부(告訃) an obituary (notice) 〔신문의〕; the announcement of (a person's) death. **고부하다** announce [report] (a person's) death.
고부(姑婦) mother-in-law and daughter-in-law. ¶그의 ~간의 사이가 별로 좋지 않다 His mother and wife don't get along so well.
고부라뜨리다 bend (one's back); curve (a wire); crook (one's arm). ¶철사를 ~ bend a wire.
고부라지다 bend; curve; swerve; be bent; be crooked; (길이) turn (to the right). ¶고부라진 길 a winding path// 고부라진 소나무 a crooked pine (tree)// 늙어 허리가 ~ be bent (in the back) with age / stoop from age// 혀가 ~ be tonguetied / have an impediment in one's speech// 길이 왼쪽으로 고부라졌다 A road turns [strikes] to the left (hand).// 열차는 산모퉁이에서 고부라져 갔다 The train curved around the hill.
고부리다 (몸을) stoop (over); blow; (물건을) bend; crook; curve; inflect. ¶철사를 ~ bend a wire / bend oneself [one's back] / 허리를 ~ / double up one's body / 안쪽으로 ~ bend [turn] in / inflect.
고부장하다 slightly bent. ⇨"고부장하다
고부조(高浮彫) high relief; alto-relievo.
고분(古墳) an old burial mound; an ancient [old] tomb; a tumulus (pl. ~es, -li). ¶~을 발굴하다 unearth [dig up] an old tomb.
고분고분 obediently; submissively; gently; meekly; docilely; tamely; like a lamb. ¶부모님의 말씀을 ~ 잘 듣다 be obedient to one's parents. **고분고분하다** submissive; obedient; docile; gentle; meek; tame; pliable. ¶고분고분한 성질 a meek [pliant] disposition / a

gentle nature// 성격이 ~ be amenably disposed.
고분자(高分子) a macromolecule; a high molecule [polymer]. ~적 macromolecular.
●**고분자 물질** a high molecular substance. **고분자 화학** high polymer chemistry; chemistry of high polymers. **고분자 화합물** a high molecular compound; a highly polymerized compound.
고불거리다 wind. ⇨"꼬불거리다
고불고불 meanderingly. ⇨"꼬불꼬불
고불탕하다 winding. ⇨"꼬불탕하다
고비¹ 〔절정〕 the climax; the crest; the height; the peak; the summit; 〔위기〕 the crisis (pl. crises); brink; the crucial [trying] moment; the critical situation [stage]; the turning point (of an illness). ¶중대한 ~ a crucial moment// 이판사판의 ~ a now-or-never [do-or-die] situation// 마지막 아슬아슬한 ~에서 at the last moment / at the eleventh hour// ~를 넘(기)다 pass the crisis / turn the corner(병세가) / pass the peak [crest] of(물가가)// 우리는 이 일의 가장 어려운 ~를 넘겼다 We have finished the most difficult part of this job. / The hardest part of this work is over. / (구어) We are over the hump on this job.// 더위는 지금 ~이다 We are now in the height of summer./ The summer is now at its hottest.// 환자는 오늘이 ~다 The invalid is passing the crisis today. / Special care must be taken of the patient today. / Today will tell the tale.(의사의 말)// 이제 우리는 결정적인 ~를 맞게 된다 Now we are coming to the crucial point [the moment of truth].// 지금부터의 1년이 우리로서는 ~다 Whether we make it or not [survive or not] will depend on this coming year.// 이 사업도 이제 전환해야 할 ~에 다다랐다 This business has reached [come to] a turning point [a crisis].// 그의 병은 ~를 넘겼다 He has passed the crisis. / He is out of danger now.// 더위도 ~를 넘었다 [지금이 ~다] The heat has passed [reached] its peak.// 우리 회사는 지금 존망(存亡)의 ~에 서 있다 Our company's fate is now hanging in the balance.// 지금이 승패의 ~이다 Now we are treading the narrow line between victory and defeat.
고비² 〔식〕 a flowering fern; an osmund; a royal fern.
고뿔 a cold; influenza. ⇨"감기
고삐 a bridle; reins; ribbons; a halter. ¶~를 당기다 draw rein / draw in the reins / rein in (a horse) / check (a horse) with reins// 이 말은 ~로 다루기가 쉽다 [어렵다] This horse has a good [hard / bad] mouth.
고삐 놓은 말 a runaway horse; a riderless horse.
고삐를 늦추다 〔감시·통제를 누그러뜨리다〕 relax one's supervision. ¶조금이라도 고삐를 늦추면 그는 게으름을 피운다 The moment you relax your supervision, he becomes lazy.
고사(古事) an ancient event [happening]; an event of former days.
고사(故事) **1** an ancient event. ⇨"고사(古事) **2** a historical fact [allusion]; 〔전설〕 tradition; folklore; 〔내력〕 a source; an origin. ¶중국의 ~ historical events in China// ~를 인용하다 allude to a historical event// 이 말에는 ~가

있다 This word has its origin in a historical fact.

고사(古史) ancient history.

고사(考査) 〔고찰〕 consideration; 〔시험〕 examination; a test; (미) a quiz. ¶고입 선발 ~ the qualifying examination for high school entrance∥인물 ~ a character test∥지능 ~ an intelligence test∥학력 ~ an achievement test∥~를 치르다 be tested / sit for a test[quiz]. **고사하다** consider; inquire; test; examine; quiz; put (a person) through a test.

고사(告祀) offering a sacrifice to spirits. **고사하다** offer a sacrifice to spirits.
● **고사떡** rice-cake offered to spirits.

고사(固辭) a positive refusal. **고사하다** decline[refuse] positively. ¶고사하다 받지 않다 positively decline to accept (an offer)∥그는 장관 직을 고사했다 He categorically [flatly] refused to take office as a minister.

고사(枯死) withering to death. **고사하다** wither and die; wilt; (병으로) be blighted. → ¶고사시키다 kill down∥오랫동안의 한발로 모든 초목이 고사되어 있었다 All the plants were withered and dead after the long drought.

고사 기관총(高射機關銃) an anti-aircraft machine gun; an A.A.-machine gun.

고사리 〔식〕 a bracken; a fernbrake; a brake. **고사리 같은 손** the cute little hands of a baby.

고사포(高射砲) an antiaircraft[antiair] gun; an A.A. gun; (속어) an ack-ack (gun); (속어) an Archie.
● **고사포 대**(一隊) antiaircraft[A.A.] artillery [battery]. **고사포 진지** an A.A. battery position; an anti-aircraft emplacement. **고사포탄** an anti-aircraft shell.

고사하고(姑捨-) 〔별도로 하고〕 setting aside; apart from; 〔…은 커녕〕 anything but; far from; not at all; let alone; 〔말할 것도 없이〕 not to mention; not to speak of; to say nothing of. ¶농담은 ~ joking aside∥비용은 ~ apart from the expense / let alone the expense / to say nothing of the expense∥미인은 ~ 도깨비 같다 She is far from beautiful — she is a fright.∥그는 사치는 ~ 먹고살기도 힘들다 He has nothing to live on, to say nothing of luxuries.∥그는 택시는 ~ 버스도 안 탄다 He does not take a bus, let alone a taxi.∥나는 불어는 ~ 영어도 모른다 I don't know English, not to speak of French.∥친구들은 ~ 형제들도 오지 않았다 Even his brothers did not come, to say nothing of his friends.

고산(高山) a high[lofty] mountain; an alp. ¶~의 alpine.
● **고산대**(一帶) 〔식〕 an alpine belt[zone]. **고산병** mountain[altitude] sickness. ¶~에 걸리다 develop[suffer from] altitude sickness. **고산 식물** an alpine plant; an alpine; an alpine flora (pl. ~s, -rae)(식물상). **고산 지대** an alpine region; the high reaches (of Tibet).

고상하다(高尙-) noble; lofty; high; (품위가) refined; elegant; high-minded; high-toned; elevated. ¶고상한 독자 a highbrow reader / 고상한 목적 a lofty aim∥고상한 사상 a lofty [noble] idea∥고상한 잡지 a high-toned [highbrow] magazine∥고상한 부인 a noble lady / an elegant[graceful] lady∥고상한 취미 an elegant[a well-cultivated] taste / refined[cultured] taste∥고상한 옷 a decent suit of clothes∥고상한 학문 advanced learning∥그녀는 몸가짐이 ~ She has graceful manners.∥그녀는 너무 고상한 체해서 나는 싫다 She is too much of a fine lady for me.∥고상한 취미가 사치스러운 생활을 의미하는 것은 아니다 Elevated taste does not mean high living.∥그의 고상한 태도에 나는 매우 감명을 받았다 I was greatly impressed by his noble[refined / graceful] bearing. **고상히** nobly; elegantly. ¶방을 ~ 꾸미다 furnish a room elegantly.

고색(古色) an antique[a hoary] look[appearance]; (청동기 등의) patina. ¶~을 띠다 have a note of antiquity / give evidence of antiquity / wear a look of age.

고색창연하다(古色蒼然-) (서술적) be hoary with antiquity; look hoary; look very old; be venerable; be quite black with age. ¶이 절은 ~ This temple has an ancient look about it. / This temple looks very old. / This temple looks hoary[time-honored] in everything.

고생(苦生) **1** 〔어려운 생활〕 a hard[tough] life; privation. **고생하다** be badly off; be in needy[straitened] circumstances. ¶고생할 때 (the hour of) need / when one is hard up∥그때만 해도 나는 돈 때문에 고생하고 있었다 In those days I was pressed for money. **2** 〔고난〕 trouble(s); hardship(s); suffering(s); difficulty; distress; adversity. ¶~을 견디다 endure hardships∥온갖 ~을 겪다 undergo[go through] all sorts of hardships [troubles] / experience[taste] the bitters of life[hardships] / have a hard[(구어) tough] time∥~를 함께 하다 share (with a person) in his hardships[distress]∥그는 ~이 많은 일생을 보냈다 He led a life full of cares.∥그는 아무런 ~도 모르고 자랐다 He was brought up free from[of] all care.∥그는 온갖 ~ 끝에 그 소설을 완성했다 He sweated blood to finish writing the novel.∥나는 부모에게 많은 ~을 시켰다 I have given[caused] my parents much trouble[anxiety].∥너는 아직 ~이라는 것을 잘 모른다 You have not seen enough of life[the world].∥~을 해 봐야 사람이 된다 Adversity makes a man wise. **고생하다** be distressed[troubled] (by / with); have trouble[difficulty]; undergo [suffer / go through] hardships; have a hard[thin] time; be (hard) put to it. ¶이가 아파 ~ have trouble with one's teeth / suffer from (a) toothache∥가족을 부양하느라 ~ be hard put to it to support one's family.∥그 미망인은 숱하게 고생하면서 아이들을 길렀다 The widow went through many hardships to raise her children.∥자네가 젊을 때 고생해 보는 것도 좋을 것이다 It will be good for you to go through hardships while you are young.∥길이 미끄러워 나는 고생하여 앞으로 나아갔다 I advanced with much difficulty, because the path was slippery. **3** 〔수고〕 toil; labor; pains. ¶헛~ vain efforts / lost labor∥그는 그녀를 기쁘게 하기 위해서라면 ~도 마다하지 않을 것이다 He would have spared no pains to please her.∥이러한 ~ 끝에 나는 그 기술을 배웠다 Thus I learned the technique the hard way. **고생하다** labor; toil; take pains. ¶고생하여 번 돈

hard-earned money // 나는 고생한 보람이 있었다 All my effort has been rewarded. / I have not suffered in vain. // 그들은 고생하면서 대설(大雪) 속을 헤치고 나아갔다 They labored [struggled] through the heavy snow.
고생 끝에 낙이 온다(속담) No gain without pain.; No cross, no crown.; No pain, no gain.; After a storm comes a calm.; Every cloud has a silver lining.
● **고생길** a thorny way; a hard row to hoe.
고생문 the threshold of a future filled with hardships. ¶~이 훤하다 be heading for hard times. **고생살이** a hard life; a life of hardship. **고생주머니** a person who is never free from troubles; a person with hard luck.
고생대(古生代) [지] the Pal(a)eozoic (era). ¶~의 Pal(a)eozoic.
● **고생대충** Pal(a)eozoic strata.
고생물(古生物) extinct animals and plants (that existed in ancient times); [화석물] fossils.
● **고생물학** pal(a)eontology.
고생스럽다(苦生-) trying; hard (to bear); painful; painstaking; bitter; tough; afflicting; laborious; toilsome; troublesome; distressful. ¶고생스러운 일 a trying [bitter] thing / a hard [tough] job / a trial // 살아가기 ~ It is hard to get along. // 나는 고생스럽게 자랐다 I was brought up the hard way.
고서(古書) an old [ancient] book; the classics; [희귀서] a rare book; [헌책] a secondhand book; [옛 글씨] an old [ancient] handwriting.
고성(古城) an old [ancient] castle.
고성(孤城) **1** [외딴 성] an isolated [forlorn / lone / solitary] castle. **2** [포위·고립된 성] a besieged castle; helpless castle.
고성(高聲) a loud [stentorian] voice; loud talking. ¶~으로 loudly / aloud // ~방가하다 sing with a loud voice / sing boisterously.
고성능(高性能) high effectiveness [efficiency]. ¶~의 highly efficient / high-performance (machine) / high-powered (gasoline) / high-yield (hydrogen bomb).
● **고성능 수신기** a highfidelity receiver; hi-fi.
고성능 폭약 a high explosive; TNT.
고소(告訴) an accusation; a charge; a (law) suit; a complaint; legal proceedings [steps]; a legal action. ¶~를 수리 [기각] 하다 accept [reject] a complaint // ~를 취하하다 withdraw [drop] a complaint / retract a charge // ~는 각하되었다 The complaint was rejected. // 그들이 당사자 간 해결책으로 50만 원의 화해금을 내겠다고 하여 우리는 ~를 취하했다 They offered to settle out of court for 500,000 won, so we withdrew our complaint [dropped our suit]. **고소하다** complain (to the magistrate of a crime); make [lay] a complaint (against); proceed against (a person); take legal steps (against); file a suit (in the court); bring (institute) a suit (against); charge (a person with a crime); accuse (a person of theft); bring a charge against (a person); sue (a person for damages); lodge a complaint (against a person). (▶ accuse는 당국 또는 개인이 제소하는 일로, 형사·민사 양쪽에 모두 쓰. charge는 당국이 주로 형사 사건에 대하여 기소하는 일. sue는 당국, 개인의 양쪽에 쓰이지만 민사적인 사건에 대하여 제소하는 일. complain은 개인이

고속(도)

한 민사상의 제소임) ¶나는 송 씨를 채무 불이행으로 고소했다 I sued Mr. song [filed a suit against Mr. song] for default of his obligation. // 당신을 고소하겠소 I'm gonna sue. / I'm gonna take you court. / You'll be hearing from my lawyer. // 피해자가 경찰에 고소함으로써 그 문제가 공개되었다 The matter came to light because the victim reported it to the police. ➔ ¶사기로 고소당하다 be accused of fraud // 그는 불법 침입죄로 고소했다 He was accused of trespassing. / They brought a complaint against him for trespassing. // 그는 폭행죄로 고소당했다 He was charged with [was accused of] assault and battery.
● **고소인** an accuser; a complainant; [원고] plaintiff. **고소장** a (letter [bill] of) complaint; a written accusation.
고소(苦笑) a forced [wry / bitter / ghastly / grim / sour / vinegary / sardonic] smile; a strained laugh. ¶나는 아무것도 모르므로 나는 ~를 금할 수 없었다 I could not suppress a wry [bitter] smile at his ignorance. **고소하다** smile a bitter [wry / grim] smile; smile wryly [grimly]; force a smile; give a strained laugh.
고소(高所) [높은 곳] a high place [ground]; an eminence; (산 등의) heights; altitudes; an elevation.
● **고소 공포증** fear of heights; [의] acrophobia.
고소득(高所得) a large [big] income.
● **고소득자** a large income earner; people in the high-income brackets. **고소득층** the high-income bracket.
고소하다 1 (맛·냄새가) taste of sesame oil; tasty; sweet; savory; nice; fragrant; (서술적) have a flavor of nut. ¶콩을 볶는 고소한 냄새 the aroma of beans being roasted // 고소한 냄새를 풍기다 diffuse a savory aroma.
2 (남의 일이) (서술적) be pleased to see a disliked person makes a mistake. ¶고소한 듯이 gloatingly // 고소해하다 gloat (over a hateful person) / take an unholy pleasure (in seeing a disliked person make a mistake) // 남의 실패를 보고 고소해하다 gloat over another's failure // 아이 고소해라 Serves you [him / her] right! / Serve [It will serve] / That will serve] you [him / her] right! (앞의 것은 이미 일어난 일에 대해 쓰고, 뒤의 것은 그렇게 되면 고소하겠다고 하는 뜻) // 그는 자못 고소하는 표정이었다 He looked on as if [though] to say "Serves you right!" // 그녀가 그 남자의 불행을 고소하게 여기는 것은 당연하다 She has good reason to rejoice over the misfortune of that man.
고속(도)(高速度) high [full] speed; (교통) rapid transit. ¶~의 high-speed // ~(으)로 at high speed / at a high rate of speed / at high velocity // 최~(으)로 달리다 run at (the) maximum speed / run at full [top] speed // 그 자동차는 ~(으)로 달렸다 The car traveled at high speed.
● **고속도강**(-鋼) high-speed steel. **고속도로** a superhighway; an expressway; an express highway; a speedway; a freeway; (영) a motorway. ¶경부 ~ the Gyeongbu [Seoul-Busan] expressway // ~의 진입로 a ramp // ~의 통행료 a toll. **고속버스** a highway bus; an express bus. **고속 영화** a fast motion picture. **고속 철도** a rapid transit railway. **고**

고수 속 촬영 high-speed photography.

고수(固守) persistence; adherence (to); adhesion; tenacity. **고수하다** [고집하다] adhere[cling] to (the principle); keep[stick] to (old customs); hold fast to (one's ideal); persevere[persist] in (a course); stand pat (on one's views); stand by one's guns; [막다] hold out; defend stubbornly. ¶옛 습관을 고수하는 사람들 people who cling to old customs / adherents to old customs // 자기의 주장을 ~ adhere to one's opinion // 주의를 ~ hold fast[stick] to one's principle // 진지를 ~ hold out[cling to] a position / defend a position stubbornly // 그들은 요새를 고수했다 They tenaciously[stubbornly] defended the fortress. // 그는 끝까지 전통을 고수하려고 했다 He was set on keeping[following] the tradition. // 그는 자신의 견해를 고수한다 He holds[sticks] fast to his views.

고수(高手) [수가 높음] superiority (in ability); excellent skill; mastery; [수가 높은 사람] a good[great / capital] hand; a superior (to another in something); [고단자] a high-grade player; a master. ¶바둑[장기]의 ~ a high-ranking *baduk*[chess] player.

고수(鼓手) a drummer; a tambour.

고수레하다 [민] scatter food (on the ground) as an offering to hungry devils; (술을) make a libation to thirsty demons.

고수머리 [곱슬곱슬한 머리털] curly[frizzled / fuzzy] hair; (흑인의) kinky hair; [머리털이 곱슬곱슬한 사람] a person with curly hair; a curly-haired[-headed] person; a curlyhead; a curly-pate; a kinky-top; ringleted person.

고수부지(高水敷地) the terrace land on the river.

고수위(高水位) [건] high-water level; flood stage.

고스란히 [그대로] just as it was; with nothing touched; with no change; [손상 없이] without a damage; with nothing damaged; safely; [모두] completely; entirely; wholly; all. ¶~ 그대로 있다 remain intact / be left untouched / be just as it was // (이익이) ~ 남다 get a clear gain[profit] (of) // ~ 다 가져가다 leave nothing behind / take away everything // 임자가 나서지 않아 그 돈은 ~ 그의 것이 되었다 As no one claimed the money, it was all given to him.

고슬고슬하다 properly cooked; (서술적) be cooked just right; be nice to eat; be neither too hard nor too soft.

고슴도치 [동] a hedgehog; porcupine. ¶~ 같은 hedgehoggy.

고슴도치도 제 새끼가 함함하다면 좋아한다 (속담) No one is immune to flattery.

고승(高僧) (덕이 높은) a learned and virtuous priest; a priest of (high) virtue; (지위 높은) a high priest; a prelate; a religious dignitary.

고시(古詩) 1 [옛 시] ancient poems. 2 free verse (in ancient China). ⇨고체시⇨고체(古體)

고시(考試) an examination; a test; [법] the civil service examination. ¶검정~ a certificate examination // 국가~ a state examination // ~를 치르다 sit[enter] (for) an examination / take an examination. **고시하다** examine; give an examination[a test] (to).

고시(告示) a notification; a notice; a bulletin; an (official) announcement; a proclamation. ¶이 규약에 관한 ~가 신문에 나와 있다 There is a notice of the regulations in the paper. **고시하다** notify (the public of something); give notice (of); issue a notification; proclaim; promulgate; announce. ➡¶···이라고 고시되었다 It has been officially announced that .... // 도서관은 내주 중에 폐관한다고 고시되었다 It has been announced that the library will be closed next week.
● **고시 가격** an official price; an officially fixed price.

고시(高試) the Higher Civil Service Examination.

고시랑거리다 1 [중얼거리다] mumble; murmur. ¶혼자 ~ mumble to oneself. 2 [잔소리를 늘어놓다] grumble. ¶그 노인은 아내에게 뭔가를 고시랑거렸다 The old man grumbled at his wife, muttering something. // 그는 언제나 이러쿵저러쿵 고시랑거리기만 한다 He is always grumbling about one thing or another. // 마누라가 항상 고시랑거려 나는 진절머리가 난다 I'm sick and tired of always having my wife griping at me.

고식적(姑息的) [임시변통으로 하는] makeshift; patch-up; timeserving; (문어) temporizing. ¶~인 해결 halfway solution // ~으로 for a shift / by way of a makeshift / to temporize // ~인 치료 a temporizing treatment // ~ 인 수단을 쓰다 take half measures / employ a stopgap policy temporize / take temporizing[stopgap] measures / resort to makeshifts.

고심(苦心) pains; labor; efforts; trouble; hard work; close application. ¶~의 작품 a fruit of much labor / a lucubration // ~을 알아주다 appreciate (a person's) efforts // 모든 나의 ~이 수포로 돌아갔다 All my pains have gone for nothing. // 그것은 대단한 ~작이다 It is the result of an immense amount of labor. **고심하다** work hard; take pains; labor; apply oneself to; make every possible effort; [머리를 짜라] rack[cudgel] one's brains. ¶고심하여 by hard work / with a great deal of trouble // 고심하여 문제를 풀다 work out a problem // 이 작품에는 저자가 상당히 고심한 흔적이 보인다 The author seems to have taken great pains over this work. // 이 일을 잘해 보려고 나는 고심하고 있다 I'm at great pains to do this work well. // 고심한 만큼의 보람은 있었다 It was worth the effort.
● **고심담** an account of one's hard experiences.

고아(孤兒) an orphan (child). ¶전쟁~ a war orphan // ~ 신세 orphanhood // ~로 만들다 orphanize // 그 소녀는 다섯 살 때 ~가 되었다 The girl was left an orphan[was orphaned] at the age of five. // 그는 ~나 다름 없다 He is no better than an orphan.
● **고아원** an orphanage; an orphan asylum [home]; a home for orphans. ¶~을 세우다 build[establish / found] an orphanage.

고아하다(高雅-) elegant; refined; graceful. ¶고아한 필치 a elegant stroke (with a writing brush).

고안(考案) a design; a device; a plan; a conception; an idea; a project; (문어) a contrivance. ¶착상이 좋은 ~ an ingenious contrivance // 쓸모 있는 ~ a helpful device // ~ 중이다 (사람이) be working on a plan / (일이)

be under contemplation [consideration]. **고안하다** devise; contrive; conceive; design; plan; originate. ¶고안해 내다 think out / work out / invent // 그는 자동차의 새 디자인을 고안했다 He devised a new design for a car. // 그는 새 어학 교수법을 고안했다 He schemed out a new method of language teaching. // 이것은 내가 고안한 것이다 This is my own invention. / I thought this up myself.
● **고안자** a designer; a deviser; an originator.

고압 (高壓) [전] high tension; high voltage; (증기의) high pressure.
● **고압계** (-計) a piezometer. **고압선** a high-tension wire [line]; a highly charged line; (미) a high-voltage cable; a power cable. **고압수단** a high-handed measure [action]. **고압 전기** high-tension electricity. **고압 전류** a high-tension current; a high-voltage current. **고압 정책** a high-handed policy.

고압적 (高壓的) highhanded; coercive; overbearing. ¶~으로 with the strong hand / highhandedly // ~으로 나오다 act [speak] highhandedly // ~으로 억누르다 hold (a person) down with a high hand // ~으로 남을 복종시키다 coerce a person into obedience // ~인 수단을 취하다 take high-handed measures (against) // ~인 태도로 그는 그들에게 나가라고 호령했다 In an overbearing manner he ordered them to go away. / (문어) He peremptorily ordered them away. // 그의 말씨는 ~이다 He has an overbearing manner of speech.

고액 (高額) a large amount [sum] (of money). ¶~의 소득이 있다 have a large income.
● **고액권** a large denomination bill [(영) bank note]. **고액 납세자** a high [an upper-bracket] taxpayer. **고액 소득자** a large-income earner.

-고야 1 [조건]. ¶알~ 내가 그런 짓을 했겠느냐 If I had known, I wouldn't have done it. // 네 행동이 그러해~ 어찌 성공하기를 바랄 수가 있나 With the way you act, how can you expect to succeed? // 이래 가지~ 어찌 내가 외국 가기를 바랄 수 있겠나 With the way things stand at the moment, I can't hope to go abroad.
2 [각오]. ¶나는 기어이 그것을 하~ 말겠다 I will do it come what may. // 일단 약속을 하면 그는 반드시 그것을 지키~ 만다 If he makes an appointment, he keeps it without fail.
3 [결과]. ¶마침내 그는 암으로 죽~ 말았다 He died of cancer at last. // 그것이 결국 큰 문제를 일으키~ 말았다 It caused eventually a great trouble.

고약 (膏藥) [상처에 붙이는 약] a plaster; a patch; (상처에 바르는 약) (an) ointment; (a) salve; an unguent. ¶~을 바르다 salve / dress (the wound) with an ointment // ~을 붙이다 apply [stick] a plaster (to) / plaster // ~을 떼다 take off [remove / peel off] a plaster // 그는 다리에 ~을 붙였다 He put a plaster on his leg.

고약스럽다 ugly; bad; nasty. ⇨**고약하다**

고약하다 1 (보기에) ugly; bad-looking; unsightly; (마음이) bad; nasty; ill-natured; evil; wicked; crooked; malicious; foul; troublesome. ¶고약한 성미 an ill [bad] nature [disposition] // 고약한 사람 a wicked man // 고약하게 생긴 사람 an ill-looking person // 고약한 녀석 What a man [nasty guy]! / (비꼬아) What a nice [fine] fellow! // 읽기가 ~ be hard to read / be a mess to read // 고약한 말을 쓰다 use vulgarisms / speak in vicious words
2 (냄새·맛이) bad; foul; nasty; disgusting; repulsive; offensive; (날씨가) nasty; vile; bad; foul. ¶고약한 날씨 nasty [wretched / beastly] weather // 고약한 냄새가 나다 smell offensive [foul] / give out a bad smell / stink // 이 냄새가 아주 ~ This smell disgusts me. // 그것은 맛이 ~ It is disgusting to the taste. // 고약한 날씨로군 What a nasty day! / Rotten day, isn't it?
3 (정도 등이). ¶고약한 감기 a bad [nasty] cold / malignant influenza // 고약한 병 a virulent disease // 일이 고약해진다 Things are getting tough. // 그녀는 고약한 감기에 걸렸다 She came down with a nasty cold.

고양 (高揚) exaltation; elevation; uplift. ¶정신의 ~ spiritual elevation [uplift]. **고양하다** exalt; enhance; raise; promote. ➔¶이 실험의 성공으로 관계자의 사기가 고양되었다 The success of this experiment raised the morale of those concerned.

고양이 a cat; a puss (특히 부르는 말); a feline (고양잇과의 동물); a pussy (cat) (애칭·유아어). ¶도둑~ a stray [an ownerless] cat // 새끼~ a kitten / (소아어) a kitty // 수~ a tomcat / a he-cat / a male cat // 암~ a tabby cat / a she-cat / a female cat // 얼룩~ a mottled cat // 페르시아 (샴)~ a Persian [Siamese] cat // ~의 catlike / feline // **고양잇과 felid** // ~ 목에 방울을 달다 bell the cat // ~가 야옹하고 울었다 A cat mewed [meowed / miaowed]. // 교미기의 [암내 낸] ~가 울고 있다 A cat in mating season is caterwauling. // ~가 갈그랑거리고 있다 The cat is purring. // ~가 얼굴을 닦고 [핥고] 있다 The cat is washing [licking] its face.

고양이보고 반찬 가게 지켜 달란다 (속담) That's like setting the wolf to guard the sheep.; It is like trusting a cat with milk.

고어 (古語) an archaic [obsolete] word. ⇨**옛말1**

고언 (古諺) an old proverb [saying]; an ancient saw [adage].

고언 (苦言) bitter counsel; candid [outspoken] advice; exhortation. ¶~을 하다 [드리다] give candid advice (to a person) / offer bitter counsel // ~을 받아들이다 swallow the bitter pill // 그는 친구에게 ~을 서슴지 않았다 He gave his friend frank advice. // 나는 ~을 감수했다 I swallowed the bitter pill.

고언 (古言) an archaic [obsolete] word. ⇨**옛말1**

고역 (苦役) hard work [toil]; a tough job; drudgery; toil; fag. ¶~을 치르다 have a hard time of it / sweat // 나는 그 ~을 견딜 수 없었다 I couldn't stand the burden of it. // 사는 것이 ~이다 Life hangs heavy upon me. // 나는 그 땅을 개간하는 데 여러 해의 ~을 치렀다 I spent years of hard work opening up the land.

고열 (高熱) 1 (높은 열) a super-heat; intense [high] heat. ¶~을 발산하다 emit [give off] high heat. 2 (신열). ¶~과 싸우다 fight [struggle] with a feverish disease // ~에 시달리다 suffer from a high fever // 그는 몸에 ~이 났다 He had [ran] a high fever [temperature]. // 그녀는 ~로 정신이 혼미 상태였다 [헛소리를 했다] She was delirious with fever. / She uttered meaningless words [talked in delirium] while sick with a high fever.

고엽 (枯葉) a dead [withered / dry] leaf.
- **고엽제** (-劑) a defoliant.

고옥 (古屋) an old house; an ancient building.

고온 (高溫) a high temperature. ¶이 지방은 여름에 대개 ~이다 The temperature is generally high [It is generally very hot] in summer in this region. // 물은 ~으로 가열하여 살균해야 한다 The water must be sterilized by boiling at a high temperature.
- **고온계** a pyrometer. **고온 다습** high temperature and humidity.

고요 silence; stillness; calm(ness); tranquility; quietude; serenity; peace. ¶밤의 ~ the stillness [silence] of night // 죽음 같은 ~ a dead [deathlike] silence / silence like the grave // 폭풍 전의 ~ the silence [calm] before a storm / the hush before the tempest // 밤의 ~를 깨고 사이렌 소리가 울려 퍼졌다 A siren sounded, breaking the silence of the night. **고요하다** [조용하다] still; quiet; hushed; silent; [평온하다] calm; serene; tranquil; peaceful; pacific. ¶고요한 마음 a tranquil mind // 고요한 바다 a calm [placid] sea // 고요한 밤 a silent night // 고요한 산간 a quiet mountainside // 고요한 아침의 나라 Korea, the Land of the Morning Calm // 집 안은 아주 고요했다 It was very quiet in the house. / Silence reigned in the house. // 주위는 쥐 죽은 듯이 고요했다 All was deathly still. / All was so quiet there (that) a pin might have been heard to drop. **고요히** quietly; still; calmly; peacefully; placidly.

고음 a lotus persimmon.

고음 일흔이 감 하나만 못하다 (속담) Quantity is no substitute for quality.; Number is no substitute for size.

고용 (雇用) employment; hiring. **고용하다** employ; hire. ¶재~ 중대 call back to work // 운전사로 ~ take (a person) on as one's chauffeur // 그는 많은 노동자를 고용하고 있다 He has a lot of workers in his employ. →**고용되다** be employed [engaged] / enter (a person's) service [employment] // 그녀는 가정교사로 고용되기를 원하고 있다 She wishes to go out as governess.
- **고용주** an employer.

고용 (雇傭) employment; an engagement; being employed. ¶국내 ~ 증대 domestic employment enlargement // 과잉 ~ overemployment / surplus employment // 불완전 ~ underemployment // 완전 ~ full employment // 장기 ~ long-term employment // 종신 ~ lifetime employment // ~의 최저 연령 the minimum age of employment // 초과 [필요 이상]의 ~을 요구하다 featherbed // 이 회사에서 여성의 ~이 늘고 있다 The number of women employed by this company is on the increase. **고용하다** be engaged; be employed; be hired.
- **고용 계약** a contract of employment; an employment agreement; a hiring [service] contract. **고용률** hiring rate. **고용살이** service as an employe(e); apprenticeship. **고용인** [종업원] an employe(e), an employé; (농장 등의) a hired hand; [하인] a servant. ¶~을

해고하다 dismiss [fire] a servant / discharge [discard] an employe. **고용 조건** employment terms [conditions].

고우 (故友) an old friend; a long-time friend; a friend of long standing; (구어) an old pal [crony].

고원 (高原) a plateau (pl. ~s, -eaux); a highland; a tableland; [고지] heights. ¶개마~ the Gaema highlands.

고원 지대 highlands.

고원하다 (高遠-) lofty; noble; high; elevated; exalted. ¶고원한 이상을 품다 have a lofty ideal.

고위 (高位) high rank; honors; distinction. ¶~에 있다 be highly placed.
- **고위 관리** a high official [officer]; a high-ranking officer. **고위 인사** ranking personalities [officials]; dignitaries. **고위층** high-ranking officials; persons holding positions.

고위도 (高緯度) a high latitude.
- **고위도 지방** high latitudes; a district in a high latitude; [한랭 지방] cold latitudes.

고유 (固有) [특유] characteristics; peculiarity; [천성] inherence; [본질] essence; nativeness. ¶그들 ~의 언어 a language of their own // 한국 ~의 예술 an art native to Korea // 동양 ~의 풍습 a custom peculiar to the Orient // 이 지방 ~의 방언이 있다 The people of this district speak [have] their own dialect. // 코알라는 오스트레일리아 ~의 동물이다 Koalas are indigenous to Australia. // 투쟁 본능은 동물 ~의 것이다 A fighting instinct is innate in animals. **고유하다** peculiar (to); proper (to); characteristic (of); (of) one's own; essential; inherent (in); native; inborn; indigenous.
- **고유 명사** [언] a proper noun. **고유색** [미] a local color. **고유성** a characteristic; a peculiarity.

고육지계 (苦肉之計) a desperate plan; one's last resort. ¶~를 쓰다 have recourse to the last resort / take a desperate measure under the pressure of necessity / torture oneself to deceive the enemy.

고육책 (苦肉策) a desperate plan. ⇨**고육지계**

고율 (高率) high rate; a high(er) interest rate. ¶~의 이자 a high (rate of) interest // 90퍼센트의 ~로 at the high rate of ninety percent.
- **고율 관세** a high tariff. **고율 배당** high-rate dividend. **고율 임금** a high rate of wages; high wages.

고을 a district (of a province); a county.

고음 (高音) a high-pitched tone [sound]; a high key; a loud sound; soprano. ¶~의 loud / high-pitched / stentorian.
- **고음부** soprano; treble. **고음부 기호** [음] the treble clef. ⇨**높은음자리표**

고의 men's short trousers (for summer wear). ¶~춤에 손을 넣다 thrust one's hands into the waistband of summer shorts.

고의 (故意) 1 [의도적임] intention; deliberation; design; purpose; willfulness; bad faith. ¶~의 [의도적인] intentional / deliberate / designed / studied / willful / contrived // ~의 [고의로] purposely / on purpose / intentionally / with design / deliberately // ~가 아닌 unintentional / accidental // ~거나 우연이거나 intentionally or accidentally / whether by design or accident // ~적인 방해 intentional interference // ~의 과실 [탈세] willful negligence

[evasion of taxes] // ~로 의무를 태만히 하다 willfully neglect one's duty // 그때 그의 행동이 우연인지 ~인지 판단하기 어렵다 It is difficult to decide whether his action at the time was accidental or deliberate. // 이 통계에는 ~로 꾸며 낸 흔적이 보인다 There is something contrived about these statistics. // ~로 한 것이 아니니 용서해 주게 Pardon me, for I meant no harm (to you). // ~가 아니었지만 그녀의 감정을 상하게 했다 I unknowingly hurt her feelings.
2 [법] feasance; commission.
● **고의범** [죄] a crime of commission; a deliberate [an intentional] offense; [고의로 범행한 사람] a deliberate offender.

고이 [곱게] beautifully; finely; nicely; lovely; well; [소중하게] tenderly; gently; carefully; with care; [편히] peacefully; in peace; at rest; [온전히] soundly; perfectly. ¶ ~ 다루다 handle carefully // ~ 키우다 bring up (a child) with tenderest care // ~ 잠들다 fall gently to sleep / pass away peacefully // ~ 간직하다 treasure (up) / lock away // ~ 돌아오다 come back safe // ~ 차려입다 dress oneself beautifully // 빌려 온 책을 ~ 돌려주다 return (a person) a borrowed book in good condition // ~ 잠드소서 Rest in peace!

고인 (古人) the ancients; ancient people; men of old. ¶ ~의 말씀에 의하면 as the ancients used to say / as they used to say in the old days / according to an old saying / as an old saying has it / an old saying goes (that).

고인 (故人) the deceased; the departed; the late lamented; (미) [법] the decedent; the dead. ¶ ~의 유족 the family of the deceased [the dead man] / the bereaved family // ~이 되다 be numbered among the dead / pass away / join the majority // ~이 된 최 씨 the late Mr. Choe // 윤 선생은 이미 ~이시다 Mr. Yun is dead [is no longer with us]. / Mr. Yun has died [has passed away].

고인돌 [고고] a dolmen.

-고자 (욕망) wanting to; wishing to; ready [prepared] to; intending to; going to; willing to; (목적) (in order) to; so as to; with the intention of; (so) that ... may; for (the purpose of). ¶그가 내가 말한~ 했던 거였 That is what I was going to say. // 충분한 수면을 취하~ 그는 일찍 잔다 He goes to bed early so as to get plenty of sleep. // 그가 사~ 하는 차는 없었다 There was no car he was interested in having. // 당신을 만나~ 왔소 I have come to see you.

고자 (鼓子) a man with underdeveloped genital organs; an impotent man; [거세된 남자] a eunuch; a spado.

고자세 (高姿勢) an aggressive [an overbearing / a highhanded] attitude. ¶ ~로 highhandedly / overbearingly / domineeringly // ~를 취하다 assume a high posture / act highhandedly [overbearingly] // 그는 ~로 나왔다 He took a highhanded attitude.

고자질 (告者-) taletelling; tattling; squealing; a tale. **고자질하다** tell [squeal / tattle] on (a person); tell tales (about a person); inform (a person against another); (구어) let on. ¶그는 나의 일을 선생님에게 고자질했다 He told on me to the teacher. / (구어) He ratted on me to the teacher. // 엄마한테 고자질하지 마라 Don't tell mother on me. // 학교에서 친구들을 고자질한 일은 없다 I have never snitched on a fellow student in school. // 그녀는 동료들의 일을 남에게 고자질할 사람이 아니다 She's not the sort of person who would tell tales about her colleagues.

고작 at (the) most; at (the) best; at the highest [greatest / largest]; at the outside; as much as one can (do); no more than; merely; only; but. ¶ ~ 3년 가다 last[wear] for three years at most [at the outside] // 하루에 만 원밖에 벌지 못하다 earn at most 10,000 won a day / get no more than 10,000 won a day // 매일 먹는 것이 ~ 그 양밖에 되지 않습니까 Is that all you eat every day? // 참석자가 ~ 그 정도밖에 안 되다니 나는 놀랐다 I was surprised that the attendance was so poor [so few people were present]. // ~ 그만한 일로 우는 게 아니야 Don't cry over such a little thing. // ~ 2천 원 정도의 손해겠지 The loss will not be more than two thousand won. // ~ 이 정도입니다 This is the utmost I can do. / This is about as far as I can go. / This is the limit. // 길게 걸려야 ~ 15일간이다 I should think it will take fifteen days at (the) longest. // ~ 그는 20세밖에 안 된다 He is twenty at the most. // 큰소리를 쳐 보았자 그는 ~ 평사원이 아닌가 He talks big, but after all he's only [just] a run-of-the-mill office worker. // 애들을 먹여 살리는 것이 ~ 이다 It is all [as much as] I can do to feed my children. // ~ 그 정도의 사람이다 He is worth no more than [the way] he looks. // 에게 새 외투 한 벌 사 줄 수 있는 것이 ~일 것이다 It may be only enough to buy him a new overcoat. // 나 혼자 겨우 살아가는 것이 ~ 이다 It is all I can do to support myself. // 나중에 그는 발을 동동 구르는 것이 ~일 것이다 At most, all he'll be able to do is stamp in vexation later. // 하루 종일 내가 강가에 앉아 있을지라도 내가 낚을 수 있는 물고기는 ~ 한두 마리밖에 되지 않을 것이다 Even if I sit on the riverbank all day, one or two fish is about all I can hope for [about the best I can do].

고장 [지방] a locality; a district; a region; [산지] the place of production; [서식지] the home; the habitat; [고향] one's home; one's native place. ¶담배의 ~ a tobacco-growing district // 자기가 사는 ~ the place [town] where one lives // 그 ~ 사람 a native of a place // 그 ~의 산물 the local products // 나는 이 ~을 잘 모른다 I am a stranger here [in this locality / in this region]. // 그는 이 ~에 밝다 [익숙하다] He is familiar with this area. // 나는 그 ~에서 자랐다 I was raised there. // 제주도는 귤의 ~으로 유명하다 Jeju-do is famous for its production of oranges [tangerines / mandarins].

고장 (故障) trouble; a breakdown; [결함] defect; something wrong. ¶기계[엔진 / 전화]의 ~ mechanical [engine / telephone] trouble / 전기의 ~ an electricity failure // ~ 없이 without trouble / smoothly / well / all right // 기관 ~으로 due to engine trouble // ~이 나지 않는[없는] trouble-free (machine) // ~이 나게 하다 put [throw] out of order // ~이 나다 get out of order / break (down) / (something) go wrong (with) // ~이 없다 be in (good) order / work well // ~ 난 곳을 찾다

trace a fault (in) 어디가 ~ 났습니까 What is the trouble? / What's wrong? // 기관 ~으로 열차가 연착했다 The train was delayed owing to some trouble in the engine. // 엔진이 ~ 났다 The engine is out of order. / Something has gone wrong with the engine. // 배가 기관 고장을 일으켰다 The ship developed engine trouble. // 브레이크 ~이 있다 Something is wrong[the matter] with the brake. // 이 녹음기가 ~이 났다 Something is wrong with this tape recorder. / This tape recorder is out of order. // 이 시계는 ~이 나지 않는다 This watch keeps good time.

고장애물 경주(高障礙物競走) [체] the high hurdles; a high hurdle race.

고쟁이 a kind of loose underpants worn by women; drawers; bloomers.

고저(高低) [기복] rise and fall; undulation; (시세) fluctuation; (음성의) pitch; (목소리의) modulation. ¶~가 있는 undulating / uneven / fluctuating // ~가 없는 even / level // 기온의 ~ the fluctuation of temperature // 토지의 ~가 심한 지방 undulating[rolling] country // 물가의 ~ fluctuation in prices / the ups and downs of prices // 목소리의 [높이] pitch / [억양] modulation // 임금의 ~에 따라 according to the wages.
● **고저각**(~角) angle of elevation.

고적(古跡) relics; a historic place[spot]; historic remains; ruins; a place of historical interest; an ancient landmark. ¶~을 탐승하다 visit places of historical interest // 이곳은 이순신 장군으로 ~지다 This is a historic spot associated with Admiral Yi Sunshin. // 경주 일대에는 ~이 많다 There are many spots of historical interest in Gyeongju and its vicinity.

고적대(鼓笛隊) a drum and fife band[corps]; a drum and bugle corps.
● **고적대장** a drum major[majorette(여자)].

고적운(高積雲) [기상] an altocumulus (pl. -li).

고적하다(孤寂-) solitary; lonely; lone; lonesome. ¶고적한 생활을 보내다 lead a solitary [lonely] life / live in solitude // 고적하게 살다 live in retirement.

고전(古典) [옛날의 뛰어난 예술 작품] classics; classical literature; [고서] an old book; (희랍·로마의) the classics. ¶고금의 ~을 읽다 read ancient and modern classics // 그의 작품은 이미 ~이 되었다 His work has already become a classic. // 로빈슨 크루소는 영문학의 ~이다 Robinson Crusoe is a classic of English literature.
● **고전 건축** classical architecture. **고전 경제학** classical economics. **고전극** classical [ancient] drama. **고전 문학** classical literature; the classics; humane learning. **고전미** classical beauty. **고전 음악** classical music. **고전주의** classicism; classicalism. ¶~ 의 classical / 신~ neoclassicism. **고전파** a classical school. **고전학** the classics.

고전(古錢) an ancient[old] coin.

고전(苦戰) a hard fighting; a hard[severe] fight; a desperate battle; a bitter battle; (경기·경쟁의) a hard-fought game; a close contest; a tight game[match / race]; hard [tough] going. ¶~ 끝에 이기다 win a bitter fight[hard-fought game] (from) // 경기는 상당한 ~이었다 It was[We had] a very tight [close] game. / The game was close and tough. // 그는 선거에서 ~ 끝에 주지사로 선출되었다 He was elected governor after a close election contest. **고전하다** fight hard; struggle desperately; fight against heavy odds; have a tough[close] game. ¶이번 선거에서 그는 상당히 고전했다 He had a tough game in the recent election. // 당 총재는 고전하고 있는 송 씨의 지원 유세에 나섰다 The party leader went on the stump to bolster Mr. Song who was in a hard race.

고전적(古典的) classic; classical; Attic. ¶~ 용모를 지니다 look classic / have clear-cut features.

고정(固定) fixation; fixing; (자금의) lockup; tie-up. **고정하다** fix; be fixed; fasten; settle; put (a thing) in place[position]; (자본의) be locked[tied] up; [진정하다] calm oneself; calm down (one's excitement[temper]). ¶텐트를 ~ anchor a tent. → ¶고정된 fixed / stationary / permanent / immovable // 고정된 장 a built-in bookcase // 핀으로 고정시키다 fasten (a thing) with a pin // 가격을 고정시키다 fix prices // 전체 자본을 고정시키다 tie up all capital // 게시판에 게시문을 핀으로 고정시키다 pin a notice to a bulletin board // 자금이 고정되어 있다 Capital is tied[locked] up. // 그 작가는 고정된 독자를 가지고 있다 The writer has a fixed circle of readers. // 이 주식은 2천 원에서 고정되어 있다 This stock is pegged at 2,000 won. // 이 핀으로는 그것이 고정되지 않는다 These pins will not hold it. // 이 책상은 마룻바닥에 고정되어 있다 This desk is fixed to[nailed to] the floor. // 그는 땅에 버팀기둥을 고정시켰다 He fixed the post in the ground. // 그는 그림에 시선을 고정시킨 채 움직이지 않았다 He stood still with his eyes fastened on the picture.
● **고정 가격** a fixed[firm] price. **고정간첩** a spy[an agent] recruited from among the residents of the land; a resident spy. **고정관념** [심] a fixed idea; (프) idée fixe. **고정급** a (basic) regular pay; a fixed pay[salary]. **고정 독자** a regular reader; (잡지·신문 등의) a regular subscriber (to the Korea Times). **고정비** fixed charges[costs]. **고정 자본** fixed capital; locked-up capital. **고정 자산** fixed assets[property]; permanent assets. **고정표**(~票) a fixed vote; loyal votes. **고정화** fixation; freezing. **고정 환율**(제) the fixed exchange rate (system).

고정하다 [흥분 등을 가라앉히다] calm oneself; calm down. ¶고정하시오 Calm down. / Take it easy. / Don't be upset.

고제(古制) an old law; an ancient statute.

고조(高調) 1 [높은 가락] a high tone[pitch]; a high-toned melody. 2 (감정의) a rise; a swell; an elevation. ¶감정의 ~ an uprush of emotion // 긴장의 ~ an increase[a buildup] of tension. **고조되다** rise; be raised; (구어) up; increase. ¶기분이 ~ get into high spirits // 양국 간의 긴장이 고조되었다 Tension has built up between the two countries.

고조(高潮) 1 (조수의) high tide[water]; floodtide. ¶~에 달하다 rise to its flood mark. 2 [절정] the climax; the culmination; the acme; the high point. ¶최~에 이르다 come to[reach] the climax / culminate // 야구 열은 ~에 이르고 있다 Baseball fever is at its

high pitch.
●**고조선**(-線) the high-water line.
고조모(高祖母) one's great-great-grandmother.
고조부(高祖父) one's great-great-grandfather.
고종 (**사촌**)(姑從四寸) a child of[cousin by] one's father's sister.
고주망태 dead drunkenness. ¶~가 되다 get[be] dead[beastly] drunk / be under the table / (구어) get boozy // ~가 되어 쓰러져 자다 go to bed in one's boots.
고주파(高周波) 〔물〕 a high frequency(약어 H.F., HF., h.f.); high-frequency (radio) waves.
●**고주파 발전기** a high-frequency generator. **고주파 전류** a high-frequency current.
고중합체(高重合體) 〔물〕〔화〕 a high polymer.
고증(考證) (a) historical investigation [research / inquiry / study]. ¶시대 ~ historical research // 그가 이 연극 의상의 시대 ~을 했다 He was in charge of researching authentic period costumes for the play. // 이 그림 속의 인물의 복장은 ~상 잘못이 있다 The dress[costume] of the figure in this picture is wrong from the historical point of view. **고증하다** study[ascertain] historical evidence; investigate; inquire into; refer to the original.
●**고증학** the study of old documents; a bibliographical study of Chinese classics; the methodology of historical research.
고지 (호박 등의) chopped and dried pumpkins [eggplant].
고지(告知) a notice; a notification; an announcement; a representation; a bulletin. ¶~ 의무 duty of declaration. **고지하다** notify (a person of / that); announce.
●**고지서** a (written) notice; a bulletin.
고지(高地) high ground[land]; highlands; the uplands; a heights; 〔고원〕 a plateau (pl. -x, -s); tableland. ¶2백 ~ the 200-meter Hill // ~에 살다 inhabit highland // ~를 점령하다 capture (an enemy's fortress on) a hill / 〔유리해지다〕 get[gain] an advantage of [over].
고지대(高地帶) a hilly section[area] (of a city); an eminence; the high elevated areas; a hill. ¶그의 집은 ~여서 전망이 좋다 His house stands on an eminence, commanding a fine view.
●**고지대 식수난** water shortage in the hilly sections[areas]. **고지대 주민** hillside residents.
고지식하다 simple and honest; guileless; simple-minded; rigid; naive; formalistic; tactless; too serious[grave]; serious to a fault. ¶고지식하게 too seriously / in dead earnest // 고지식한 사람 a man of strict morals // 그는 너무 ~ He is stupidly honest. // 그는 고지식한 구식 사람이다 He is a simple and honest fellow of the old form. // 그는 고지식해서 남의 말을 잘 믿는다 He is naive and gullible. // 고지식하면 손해 보는 세상이다 We live in a world where simple honesty does not pay.
고진감래하다(苦盡甘來-) Sweet after bitter.; Pleasure follows pain.; Pain is gone, and pleasure is come.; No gains without pains.
고질(痼疾) an inveterate[a chronic] disease; a deep-seated disease[trouble]. ¶대학의 ~적인 재정난 the chronic financial predicament of colleges and universities // 인플레이션과 국제 수지 역조가 그 나라 경제의 ~이었다 Inflation and adverse balance of trade have been the chronic disease of the country's economy. // 나는 ~인 신경통에 시달리고 있다 I am a chronic sufferer from neuralgia. / I suffer chronically from neuralgia. / I suffer from chronic neuralgia. // 그의 ~인 천식이 재발했다 He had a return of his old complaint of asthma.
고집(固執) 〔완고〕 obstinacy; stubbornness; obduracy; 〔집착〕 adherence (to); persistence. ¶~이 센 obstinate / stubborn / obdurate / headstrong // ~이 센 영감 an obstinate old man / an old man of an obstinate nature // ~을 부리다 have one's own way // 사소한 일에 ~을 부리다 be stubborn about[over] little things // ~을 부려 반대하다 disagree for the sake of disagreement / object out of contentiousness // 그녀는 무엇이든지 제 ~대로만 하려고 한다 She will have everything her own way. // 그렇게 너무 ~을 부리지 마라 Don't be so stubborn [obstinate]. // 아버지는 마침내 ~을 꺾고 우리의 결혼에 동의하셨다 My father finally gave in[yielded] and consented to our marriage. // 그는 전혀 ~이라는 것이 없다 He has no backbone. // 내가 시작한 일이니까 ~으로라도 해내 보이겠다 Since I started it I will see it through to the end, if only to show I'm no quitter. // 그는 ~이 센 사람이라 싫은 소리를 들으면 꼭 말대꾸를 한다 He's so stubborn [strong-willed] that if he's criticized, he's bound to answer back. // 그 소년은 묘하게 ~센 데가 있다 That boy has a contrary streak in him. // 그는 내심으로 그 제안에 찬성하면서도 단순한 ~으로 반대 의견을 말했다 He was really for the proposal, but spoke against it out of sheer orneriness. **고집하다** stick to; adhere to; hold fast to; stand firmly by; persist in; insist upon. ¶즉시 반환을 강력히 ~ strenuously insist upon the immediate return (of) // 내가 고집할 생각은 없지만 … I won't insist, but …. // 그는 자기 의견을 끝까지 고집했다 He obstinately [stubbornly] stuck to his own opinion. // 그는 학교를 그만두기를 고집하고 있다 He insists on leaving school. // 그녀는 자기 생각을 고집하고 있다 She insists on her own way. / She won't give in to others.
●**고집불통** extreme stubbornness[obstinacy / persistence / bigotry / perversity]. ¶그는 천하의 ~이다 He is obstinacy itself. / He is obstinate as an ass. **고집쟁이** / **고집통이** an obstinate[a stubborn / a headstrong] person; a hardheaded fellow; a self-opinionated person.
고차 방정식(高次方程式) 〔수〕 an equation of higher degree.
고차적(高次的) high-level; high-grade; high-degree. ¶사라진 그 문명은 ~인 것이었다 The lost civilization was of a high order[highly advanced].
고착(固着) adherence; sticking; fastening; fixing. **고착하다** adhere[stick / cohere] (to).
●**고착 관념** 〔심〕 a fixed idea. ⇨**고정관념**(⊖고정) **고착제** a binder.
고찰(古刹) an old[an ancient / a historic old] temple.

고찰(考察) consideration; an examination (of); (a) study; (an) investigation (of); (an) inquiry (into). ¶청소년 범죄에 대한 ~ a study of juvenile delinquency // 사회 문제에 관한 ~ a study of the social problem. **고찰하다** consider; examine; study; contemplate; (문의) inquire into; investigate. ¶문제를 신중히 ~ give careful consideration to a question // 주택 문제를 ~ investigate the housing problem / 이 문제를 다른 각도에서 고찰해 보라 Consider this problem from another angle [point of view]. // 그것은 여러모로[여러 각도에서] 고찰해 볼 필요가 있다 It requires [involves] consideration from various angles [in all its aspects].

고참(古參) seniority; (사람) a senior; an old-timer; a long-time member. ¶최~자 the father / the doyen // 최~의 직원 the senior member of the staff / (구어) the staff member who has been around the longest / 클럽의 ~(자)들 the old [senior] members of the club / club members of long standing // 그는 나보다 훨씬 ~이다 He is many years my senior (in service). // 그는 이 회사에서 ~에 속합니다 He is one of the oldest members of this company. / He is one of the senior members [old-timers] in this company.
● **고참병** a long service soldier; a veteran; a veteran soldier; a senior comrade.

고창하다(高唱―) [노래하다] sing loudly; [주창하다] advocate; urge; [강조하다] emphasize; stress.

고철(古鐵) scrap iron; iron scraps; pieces of old metal. ¶~로 팔다 sell (an old car) for junk.
● **고철상** (상인) a junkman; a junk dealer; (상점) a junk shop.

고체(古體) an archaic style [form]; archaism.
● **고체시**(―詩) (한시(漢詩)에서) free verse (in ancient China).

고체(固體) a solid (body); solid matter. ¶~의 solid // ~화하다 solidify (liquid).
● **고체 연료** solid fuel.

고초(苦楚) hardships; difficulties; trouble; trials; privation; distress. ¶~를 겪다[당하다] suffer [go through] hardships / have a bitter experience / be hard put to it / have a hard time of it / be in dire distress / have one's trials.

고추 a Guinea pepper; a cayenne (pepper); (구어) a red [bird] pepper; a hot pepper; a capsicum.
고추는 작아도 맵다(속담) The smaller, the shrewder.; Though small in body one is fierce or strong.; He may be little, but when he gets mad, watch out!
● **고추바람** a cutting [biting / piercing] wind. **고추잠자리** a red dragonfly. **고추장** *gochujang*; thick soypaste mixed with red peppers. **고춧가루** powdered red pepper.

고충(苦衷) distress; a predication; a dilemma; mental suffering [anxiety / conflicts]. ¶~을 헤아리다 [이해하다 / 알아주다] appreciate a person's painful situation [position] / sympathize with a person in a predicament // 우리는 그의 ~에 동정하지 않을 수 없다 We cannot help sympathizing with him in his dilemma [predicament].

고취(鼓吹) inspiration; instillation; inculcation; advocacy; propagandism. **고취하다** inspire; instil; inculcate; advocate; propagandize; stir up; arouse. ¶예술 취미를 ~ stir up interest in art // 그는 자연주의를 고취했다 He advocated naturalism enthusiastically. / He was a passionate advocate of naturalism. // 그는 청소년들에게 애국심을 고취했다 He inspired [inculcated] patriotism in the young [the young people with patriotism].

고층(高層) 1 (건물의) higher stories; upper floors. ¶~의 multistory / multistoried / high-rise / lofty. 2 (대기의) a high layer.
● **고층 건축 / 고층 건물** a multistory [multistoried] building; a high [tall / lofty] building; a high-rise building; (미) a skyscraper. **고층 기류** an upper air current. **고층 기상학** aerology. **고층 아파트** a high-rise apartment building. **고층운** [기상] an altostratus (*pl.* -ti); an altostratus cloud.

고치 a cocoon. ¶~에서 실을 뽑다 reel silk off cocoons // 누에는 ~를 짓는다 The silkworm spins a cocoon.

고치다 1 [바로잡다] correct; reform (an evil practice); redress (abuses); remedy (an evil); amend (one's conduct); mend (one's ways); rectify (a mistake); cure; revise; set [put] right. ¶잘못을 ~ correct an error // 오자(誤字)[잘못된 철자]를 ~ correct a wrong character [misspelled word] // 악폐를 ~ reform abuses / redress evils // 결점을 ~ correct one's shortcomings / remedy one's defects / gloss [smooth] over one's faults // 나쁜 버릇을 ~ (자신의) get rid of [get over / overcome] a bad habit / break [cure / divest] oneself of a bad habit / (남의) break [cure] (a person) of a bad habit / wean (a person) from a bad habit // 날짜의 「3월」을 「4월」로 고치다 (정오표 등에서) Read "April" for "March" in the date. // 다음 문장에서 틀린 곳이 있으면 고치시오 Correct mistakes, if any, in the following sentences. // 너는 그 버릇을 고쳐야 한다 You must get over [break] that habit. // 그는 그의 행동을 고쳤다 He has reformed. / He has mended his ways. // 내가 자네 넥타이를 똑바로 고쳐 주겠다 Let me straighten your tie. // 그녀는 화장을 고치러 갔다 She has gone to repair [fix] her makeup. // 그는 실수로 말을 잘못해서 즉시 고쳐 말했다 Having made a slip of the tongue, he corrected himself immediately.
2 [병을 낫게 하다] heal; cure. ¶고칠 수 없는 병 an incurable [uncurable] disease // 병을 ~ cure a disease // 상처를 ~ heal a wound // 부디 내 병을[상처를] 고쳐 주십시오 Please cure me of my illness [heal my wound]. / 당신은 그 감기를 고치지 않으면 외출을 할 수 없습니다 You cannot go out until you get over [get rid of] your cold. // 어떤 명의도 그 환자를 고칠 방법을 알지 못했다 No doctor, no matter how good, knew how to cure that patient. / (문어) The most excellent physician knew of no remedy for that patient.
3 [수선하다] repair; mend; patch up; set [put] right; put in order; (미국 구어) fix (up). (repair는 고장 난 것으로서 비교적 큰 것을 고치다 mend는 비교적 작은 것을 수선하다 fix는 양쪽에 쓰임) ¶기계를 ~ repair a machine / put a machine in order [to right] / get [put] a machine in (working) order // 구두를 ~ mend shoes / have one's shoes mended // 나는 시계[자동차]를 고치게 했다

고향

[고쳐 달랬다] I had my watch[car] repaired [(미) fixed].∥지금 지붕을 고치고 있는 중이다 They are repairing the roof now. / The roof is under repair.
4〔변경하다·새롭게 하다〕change; alter; modify; remodel; renew; make renew[again / afresh]; renovate; improve; 〔번역하다〕translate[render / put] (into). ¶고쳐 표하다 express (one's idea) differently / restate ∥ 쳐 쓰다 rewrite / write over (again) / 〔정서하다〕copy cleary∥(집을) 고쳐 짓다 rebuild / reconstruct / re-erect / build again [anew]∥낡은 여관을 호텔로 ∼ remodel an old inn into a hotel∥계약을 ∼ renew a contract∥시간표를 ∼ alter the schedule∥이름을 ∼ change one's name (to) / assume the new name (of)∥마음을 고쳐먹다 change one's mind∥우리말을 영어로 ∼ translate[render / put] Korean into English∥그는 그의 태도를 고쳤다 He changed his attitude.∥그는 처음부터 그 수필의 원고를 고쳤다 He rewrote the essay from the very beginning.∥12월 말까지 그 규칙이 고쳐지기로 되어 있다 The regulations will[are to] be changed[revised] by the end of December.

고칭(古稱) an old name[designation]; an archaic term[title].

고탑(古塔) an old tower; an ancient tower.

고통(苦痛) pain; agony; 〔심한 괴로움〕great pain; anguish; 〔일시적 격통〕pang; suffering; affliction. ¶마음의 심한 ∼ anguish of heart∥해산(解産)의 ∼ pains (of childbirth) / labor pains∥죽음의 ∼ mortal agony / the agonies of death∥남에게 ∼을 주다[가하다] inflict pain on a person / cause pain to a person∥∼을 느끼다 feel a pain / feel painful / suffer pains∥∼을 호소하다 complain of pain∥이 약은 그 ∼을 덜어 줄 것이다 This medicine will relieve[ease / allay / soothe] the pain.∥나는 무릎의 ∼으로 빨리 달릴 수가 없다 I have trouble with my knee[I have knee trouble] and cannot run fast.∥단말마[죽음]의 ∼ 속에서 그는 아들의 이름을 불렀다 He called his son's name in his death agony.

고통스럽다(苦痛−) painful; afflicting; tormenting; distressing; harassing. ¶고통스러운 듯한 걸음걸이로 with painful steps∥그는 고통스러워 몸을 비틀었다 He writhed in pain.∥그는 고통스러운 나머지 신음 소리를 내고 있다 He is giving a moan of pain. / He is moaning[groaning] in pain[agony].∥(be in agony가 보통이지만 be in agonies 라고 복수형을 쓰는 경우도 있음)∥계단을 뛰어 올라갔더니 숨 쉬기가 고통스러웠다 As I had run up the stairs, I was out of breath.∥그는 고통스러운 표정으로 이야기했다 He spoke with a look of anguish.

고투(苦鬪) a bitter[an uphill] struggle; a hard fight; a tussle. **고투하다** have[fight] a hard fight.

고판(古版) **1**〔옛 목판〕an old printing [engraving] block. **2** an old edition. ⇨고판본(⇨고판).
● **고판본**〔옛 목판본〕an old block book; old books in block print; 〔신판 이전의 책〕an old edition.

고패 a pulley; a small-sized block.

고평(高評) your[his] esteemed opinion. ¶∼을 바랍니다 (저서 증정의 문구) With the author's compliments.

고풍(古風) **1**〔풍속〕old manners and customs. ¶∼을 지키다 stick[adhere / keep] to old customs / follow the old ways / keep [maintain] the traditions. **2**〔모습·방식의 예스러움〕being antique[archaic / old-fashioned / antiquated / out-of-date / outmoded].

고풍스럽다(古風−) antique; archaic; old-fashioned; antiquated; out-of-date; outmoded. (▶ old-fashioned는 옛것의 장점을 인정할 때나 경멸할 때나 공통적으로 쓰임. antique는 오래되고 정취 있는, archaic은 말이나 표현이 낡았다는 뜻.) ¶고풍스러운 가구 antique furniture∥고풍스러운 건물 an old-fashioned [antique] building∥고풍스러운 사고방식 antiquated views∥고풍스러운 문체 archaic style.

고프다 hungry; famished. ¶배가 ∼ be hungry / feel[get] hungry.

고하(高下) (사회적 지위의) rank; grade; (품위의) quality; (가격의) rise and fall; fluctuations. ¶신분의 ∼를 막론하다 be irrespective of rank∥값의 ∼를 막론하고 내가 사겠다 I will buy it irrespective[regardless] of its price.

고하다(告−) tell; inform; 〔알리다〕announce. ¶사실대로 ∼ tell[reveal] the truth∥작별을 ∼ say[bid / wish] (a person) good-by(e) / take (one's) leave[farewell] of (a person) / bid (a person) farewell / bid farewell to (a person)∥일반에게 널리 ∼ announce to the public∥그 소년이 선생님에게 너의 일을 고해바쳤다 The boy told the teacher on you.

고학(苦學) paying[working] one's own way through school. **고학하다** support oneself through school; earn one's own school expenses. ¶그는 고학하여 대학을 졸업했다 He worked his way through college[(영) university].
● **고학생** a working[self-supporting] student; a student who is paying his own way.

고함(高喊) a shout; a yell; a roar; a howl; a scream; a shriek; an outcry. ¶객석에서 ∼ 소리가 들렸다 A shout was heard from the audience.

고함지르다(高喊−) shout; shriek; set up a shout; (떠들썩하게) clamor; bawl (out); cry [call out] loudly; (응원 등에서) yell; give a yell (to a player). ¶그는 화가 나서 고함질렀다 He roared with anger[in rage].∥그는 나에게 나가라고 고함질렀다 He shouted to me to get out.∥그는 목청껏 고함질렀다 He shouted at the top of his voice.∥경찰관이 내게 고함질러 꾸짖었다 I was yelled at by a policeman.

고함치다(高喊−) shout; shriek. ⇨고함지르다

고해(苦海) 〔불〕this (weary) world.

고해 성사(告解聖事) ➡고백 성사(⇨고백)

고행(苦行) (속죄의) penance; (수도자로서의) asceticism; an ascetic practice[penance]; religious austerities; self-mortification; a religious penance. ¶∼을 견디다 endure religious austerities. **고행하다** do penance; practice asceticism.
● **고행자** an ascetic.

고향(故鄕) one's home; (미) one's hometown; one's native place; one's birthplace; one's home country[village]; one's native town [village]. ¶제2의 ∼ one's second home /

고현학(考現學) the study of modern social phenomena.

고혈(膏血) hard-earned money; sweat and blood. ¶백성의 ~을 짜다 exploit[sweat / squeeze] people[the poor] / grind down the poor / exact from the poor the fruits of their labor[toil] / put the poor under the screw / suck all the juice from the poor / suck the life's blood of the poor / grind the faces of the poor.

고혈압(高血壓) [표준 이상의 혈압] high blood pressure; hypertension. ¶나는 ~이다 I suffer from[I have] high blood pressure. / I am suffering hypertension.
● **고혈압증** [의] hyperpiesia. **고혈압 환자** a hypertensive.

고형(固形) a solid body; solidity. ¶~의 solid // ~ 수프 a soup cube.
● **고형물** a solid (body). **고형 알코올** solid alcohol; solidified alcohol. **고형 연료** solid fuel.

고 혹(蠱惑) fascination; enchantment; bewitchment; glamo(u)r. ¶~적인 captivating / bewitching / enchanting / fascinating / attractive / alluring. **고혹하다** fascinate; enchant; bewitch; enamor; allure; seduce; captivate.

고혼(孤魂) a lonely spirit[soul] of the deceased; a spirit for whom there is no one to offer sacrifices. ¶~이 되다 die with no one in attendance / die in solitude / 수중~이 되다 die at sea[in water] / go to a watery grave / be gone to Davy Jones's locker.

고화(古畫) an ancient[old] picture[painting].

고환(睾丸) [생] the testicles; the testes (sing. -tis); the stones; (속어) the balls; (속어) the family jewels. ¶~의 testicular.
● **고환염**(-炎) orchitis; testitis.

고희(古稀) three score and ten; seventy years of age; one's 70th birthday. ¶~를 넘다 go well beyond the allotted (span of) three score years and ten / be on the wrong side of seventy / be in one's 70's // 그들은 부친의 ~를 축하드렸다 They celebrated their father's seventieth birthday.
● **고희연**(-宴) the celebration of one's 70th birthday.

곡(曲) (a piece of) music; [곡조] a tune; a melody; an air. ¶그리그의 피아노~집 Grieg's piano pieces // 바이올린~ music for the violin // 그는 그 시에 ~을 붙였다 He set the poem to music. / He wrote the music for a song. // 그는 독주회에서 바흐의 ~을 연주하였다 He played a Bach composition[piece] at his recital. // 자 한 ~ 들려주십시오 Please let me hear you play a piece. // 그녀는 조용한 ~을 연주했다 She played a quiet tune.

곡(哭) wailing; a moan; lament(ation). **곡하다** bewail; lament; wail; moan.

곡가(穀價) the price of grain; grain price. ¶이중~제 a double-tiered grain price system / a dual-price system designed to protect both farmers and consumers.
● **곡가 정책** a grain price policy.

곡괭이 a pick; a pickax; (영) pickaxe; a hack. ¶~로 땅을 파다 dig in the ground with a pickax(e).

곡구(曲球) [야구] a curve (ball); [당구] a fancy shot.

곡기(穀氣) food. ¶~를 끊다 abstain from food.

곡류(曲流) [지] meandering; a winding watercourse; a bent flow. **곡류하다** meander; wind its way (through).

곡류(穀類) cereals; (미) grain(s); (영) corn.

곡률(曲率) [수] curvature.
● **곡률 반지름** the radius of curvature.

곡마(曲馬) circus[stunt] riding; a riding stunt; a feat of horsemanship; an equestrian feat.
● **곡마단** a (traveling) circus troupe[company]. **곡마사** a circus[stunt / trick] rider.

곡면(曲面) a curved surface.

곡명(曲名) the title of a musical composition.

곡목(曲目) [연주곡의 목록] a program; (영) a programme; the selection (for the concert); one's repertoire; (한 곡) a (musical) number; a (musical) selection. ¶다음 ~은 무엇입니까 What's the next number (on the program)? / What will he sing[play] next? // 너의 ~ 선택은 좋았다 You selected the music well. // ~은 전부 바흐의 것이었다 The whole program consisted of works by Bach.

곡물(穀物) cereals; (미) grain; (영) corn.
● **곡물상**(-商) (미) a grain dealer; (영) a corn dealer; a dealer in grain.

곡사(曲射) high-angle fire. **곡사하다** fire at a high angle.
● **곡사포** a howitzer; a high-angle gun.

곡선(曲線) a curved line; a curve. ¶상승[하강] ~ a rising[falling] curve // ~으로 된 curvilinear[curvilineal] // ~을 그리다 draw [describe] a curve / curve // ~상승 ~그리며 curve up // 그 공은 큰 ~을 그리며 날아갔다 The ball flew through the air in a tremendous arc.
● **곡선 도표** a curve graph. **곡선미** (그림·건축 등의) linear beauty; (여성의) the beauty of one's curves; curvaciousness; curvaceousness; curvesomeness. ¶~가 있는 여자 a curvaceous[curvacious / curvesome] woman / a woman with a voluptuous[sexy] figure. **곡선 운동** a curvilinear motion.

곡성(哭聲) a wail; a wailing cry; a moan.

곡식(穀食) cereals. ⇨곡물

곡예(曲藝) acrobatics; a trick; an acrobatic

feat; a stunt; fancy performances. ¶자전거 ~ trick cycling / a bicycle stunt[trick] // 기마 ~ trick riding / equestrian acrobatics [feats] / car(r)ousels // 다이빙 fancy [somersault] diving / a fancy dive // ~ 스케이팅 fancy skating // ~를 하다 do[perform] acrobatics // 공 ~ 를 하다 do stunts while balancing (oneself) on a ball / 그는 좌측 끝에서 우측 끝으로 옮겨 가는 ~를 해냈다 He pulled off the acrobatic feat of switching from ultra left to ultra right. // 그는 오토바이로 ~를 했다 He did stunt riding on a motorcycle.
●곡예비행 stunt flying; a flying feat; an acrobatic[aerobatic] flight; aerobatics; aerial acrobatics; a loop-the-loop flight. 곡예사 an acrobat; a tumbler; a stunt performer; a trick cyclist(자전거의).

곡절(曲折) 1 [까닭] reason; the whys and hows; ground(s). ¶여러 가지 ~이 있어서 for many reasons combined // 거기에는 필시 무슨 ~이 있을 것이다 There must be some reason for it. / There must be something in it.
2 [복잡한 사정] intricacies; complications; [변화] vicissitudes; ups and downs. ¶~이 많은 일생 a checkered[vicissitudinary / vicissitudinous] career / a colorful life // ~이 많다 be very complicated / be full of turns and twists // 그는 인생의 우여~을 경험하였다 He experienced the ups and downs[vicissitudes] of life. // 이 소설은 줄거리의 ~이 많다 This novel has an intricate[a complicated] plot. // 여러 가지 ~는 있었지만, 마침내 쌍방간에 합의가 이루어졌다 There were a lot of difficulties, but the two sides finally came to an agreement. / After many turns and twists the agreement between two sides came to a fruitful end.

곡조(曲調) a melody; a tune; strains. ¶한 ~ 부르다 sing a tune // 가사에 ~를 붙이다 set a song to music / put tunes to a song / write the music to a song // 그 노래의 ~는 이렇다 This is how the song goes.

곡직(曲直) right and wrong. ¶불문 ~ 하고 without inquiring into the right or wrong / without any preambles or explanations // ~을 가리다 distinguish right from wrong / inquire into the rights (of a case).

곡창(穀倉) 1 [곡식 창고] (미) a grain elevator; a granary; a cornloft. 2 [곡식 양산지(量産地)] (미) a breadbasket; a rich grain district; a rice bowl; a granary. ¶호남평야는 한국의 ~이다 Honam plain is the granary[rice bowl] of Korea.
●곡창 지대 a grain belt; a grain-growing district; a grain-producing region; a breadbasket; a granary.

곡척(曲尺) a square. ⇨곱자

곡해(曲解) misinterpretation; misunderstanding; distortion; a strained[forced] interpretation. 곡해하다 willfully put a false [wrong] construction (on); interpret wrongly; misconstrue; misunderstand; strain[distort / contort / pervert] (the sense of a passage); twist (a person's words) around[round] (the meaning / twist a person's words. ➔친절한 마음에서 한 나의 일이 훼방[간섭]으로 곡해받았다 My kindness was misinterpreted as interference.

곤경(困境) distressed[adverse / straitened] circumstances; straits; a fix; a predicament; an awkward[a hard / a difficult] position [situation]. ¶~에 처하다 be[find oneself] in difficulty / (구어) be in a fix[hot water] / be in trouble[distress] // 재정적으로 ~에 처해 있다 be in a financial predicament // ~에서 헤어나오다 struggle out of a morass // ~에 빠지다 get into trouble / be driven to the wall / be thrown into a fix / be placed in a painful position // ~을 넘기다 [극복하다] get over [overcome] a difficulty // 아내의 재빠른 재치가 나를 ~에서 구해 주었다 My wife's quick wit helped me out of a difficult spot.

곤궁(困窮) poverty; need; want; destitution; straightened[needy / narrow] circumstances. ¶~에 허덕이다 [빠지다] suffer[get into] destitution // ~을 견디다 bear[endure] hardship and privation // 유족들은 ~에 처해 있다 The bereaved family are in great [extreme] distress. / The bereaved family are in dire want[sink into the depths of misery]. / The bereaved family are having great financial difficulties. / The bereaved family are poverty-stricken. // 우리는 엄청난 ~을 겪었다 We underwent great hardship [went through many hardships]. 곤궁하다 poor; needy; destitute (of); distressed; (서술적) be in want[need / distress]; be hard pressed; be hard up. 곤궁히 needily; distressfully.

곤돌라 a gondola. ¶~ 사공 a gondolier // ~를 젓다 row[pole] a gondola.

곤두박질 falling headlong[head-over-heels]. **곤두박질하다** fall headlong; fall head foremost[head-over-heels]; topple; nosedive; fall (upside) down. ¶물속으로 곤두박질하듯 뛰어들다 plunge[dive] head over heels into the water // 그는 계단에서 곤두박질하여 떨어졌다 He fell headlong down a flight of stairs.

곤두서다 feel[be] on edge; stand on end; (머리털이) bristle up. ¶머리털이 ~ one's hair bristles up // 그 광경에 내 머리털이 곤두섰다 The sight made my hair stand on end. // 모두의 신경이 곤두서 있었다 Everyone's nerves were on edge.

곤두세우다 set on end; bristle up; erect. ¶머리털을 곤두세우고 with one's hair erect[on end] // 신경을 ~ pay one's attention to / be all ears have one's nerves on edge // 작은 실수에 그리 신경을 곤두세우지 마라 Don't get so upset over small errors.

곤드라지다 fall asleep dog-tired[dead-drunk]; drop off to sleep; sink into a slumber. ¶술에 만취하여 ~ drink oneself to sleep / go off into a vinous sleep // 지친 나머지 그녀는 방에 들어서자마자 이내 곤드라졌다 Being overcome with fatigue, she sank into a slumber like a dog as soon as she got into the room.

곤드레만드레 dead-drunk; staggering. ¶그는 ~ 취했다 He is dead[helplessly] drunk. / He is (as) drunk as a fish[lord] // 나는 ~가 될 때까지 마셨다 I got myself blind drunk. / I drank myself under the table[into oblivion] // 마침내 그는 ~가 되어 잠들어 버렸다 He finally drank himself to sleep. **곤드레만드레하다** stagger; lose one's sense of balance.

곤란 (困難) difficulty; a hurdle; a trouble; suffering(s); hardship(s); distress; embarrassment; perplexity. ¶재정 ~ financial [pecuniary] embarrassment [difficulty] // 우리는 문제의 해결에 ~을 겪고 있다 We are having difficulty (in) finding a solution to the problem. // 그들은 계속되는 가뭄으로 ~을 겪고 있었다 They were in trouble because of the long dry spell. / They were suffering from a long drought. // 우리는 심한 비를 만나 ~을 겪었다 We were caught in a heavy rain and had a hard time of it. // 우리는 해결책이 전혀 없어 크게 ~에 처해 있다 Having found no solution, we are in great difficulty. **곤란하다** (困-) difficult; hard; tough; troublesome; embarrassing; perplexing; awkward; (서술적) be in trouble; be in a fix; have a hard time. ¶곤란한 사건 a troublesome [serious / difficult] affair // 곤란한 문제 a difficult problem [a troublesome question] // 말하기가 ~ be hard up / be in needy circumstances / live in poverty / live from hand to mouth // 곤란하게 하다 annoy [trouble / worry] / 숨 쉬기가 ~ breathe with difficulty / have difficulty in breathing // 사태가 곤란하게 되었다 The situation grew complicated [serious]. // 그는 어려운 질문을 하여 남을 곤란하게 하는 것을 재미로 여긴다 He takes pleasure in annoying people with difficult questions [making people feel uncomfortable by asking difficult questions]. // 남을 곤란하게 하는 질문은 하지 마라 Don't ask embarrassing questions. // 그녀는 새 옷을 사 달라고 졸라 대어 남편을 언제나 곤란하게 하고 있다 She is always worrying her husband to buy her new clothes. // 우리는 곤란하게 되었습니다 We are in an awkward [embarrassing] position. / (빈정대어) Things have come to a pretty pass. / This is a nice business, indeed! / (미국 구어) This is a fine how-do-you-do. / (미국 구어) 더욱 곤란하게도 거기 오지 않았다 To make matters worse [what was even worse], he didn't come. // 그는 곤란한 아이 [녀석]이다 He is a problem child [a nasty fellow]. // 그것을 지금 쓰는 것은 ~ It is not proper [good] to write about it now. // 그렇게 하면 당신 입장이 곤란해진다 That would place you in an awkward [a compromising / a difficult / delicate] position [situation].

곤봉 (棍棒) a club; a cudgel (짧고 굵은 것); (체조용의) an Indian club; (경찰용의) a (policeman's) club [truncheon]; (미국 구어) a billy.
● **곤봉 체조** Indian club exercise.

곤색 (-色) →감색 (▶「곤색」의 「곤」은 일본어 こん(紺)에서 온 말임)

곤약 (菎蒻) [식] a devil's-tongue; (식품) a paste made from the starch of the devil's-tongue.

곤욕 (困辱) bitter insult; contempt; indignity. ¶~을 치르다 be insulted [disgraced] / suffer a bitter insult.

곤장 (棍杖) a cudgel; a stick; a club (for beating criminals). ¶~을 안기다 flog (a person) / beat (a person) with a cudgel // ~을 열 대 맞다 receive ten cudgels [strokes of the cudgel].

곤죽 (-粥) **1** [진창] sludge; mire; a quagmire; muddiness. ¶눈이 녹아 ~이 된 길 a slushy [slush-filled] road. **2** [뒤범벅] a mess; a jumble; utter confusion. ¶일을 ~으로 만들 다 make a mess of an affair // 만사가 ~이 되어 있었다 I found everything at sixes and sevens.

곤지 the red spot on a bride's brow. ¶~ 찍다 put a rouge spot on one's forehead / wear a rouge spot on one's brow.

곤충 (昆蟲) an insect; (미국 구어) a bug.
● **곤충류** [동] Insecta; insects. **곤충망** an insect net. **곤충 채집** insect collecting; (구어) bugging; bughunting. ¶~ 하러 가다 go hunting for insects / (구어) go bugging. **곤충학** entomology; insectology. **곤충학자** an entomologist.

곤하다 (困-) weary; tired; fatigued; exhausted. ¶몹시 ~ be dead [dog] tired / be tired out / feel exhausted // 곤해 죽겠다 I'm tired with a fatigue that goes to the bone. / (미국 구어) I'm completely frazzled out. **곤히** tiredly; in a weary manner. ¶~ 자다 sleep like a log // ~ 잠들다 fall fast asleep.

곤혹 (困惑) embarrassment; perplexity; puzzlement; discomfiture. **곤혹하다** be at a loss (what to do); be at one's wit's end. ¶교감의 갑작스런 사직은 교장을 곤혹케 했다 The sudden resignation of the vice-principal upset the principal. / The principal was at a loss what to do when the vice-principal suddenly resigned.

곤혹스럽다 (困惑-) embarrassed; perplexed; (서술적) be at one's wit's end.

곧 1 [금방] immediately; instantly; directly; soon enough; at once; quick(ly); straight off; [즉석에서] on the spot; [오래잖아] soon; shortly; presently; before long. ¶(약이) ~ 효력이 나타나다 [듣다] be quick [prompt] in effect // 저 아이는 책상에 앉자마자 ~ 졸기 시작한다 That boy begins to nod as soon as he sits at his desk. // 나는 ~ 부산으로 이사하니다 I am going to move to Busan before long. // ~ 크리스마스가 된다 Christmas is just around the corner. // 그는 ~ 마흔 살이 된다 He is nearly [close upon] forty. // ~ 배달해 드리겠습니다 We will deliver it at once. // 지금 ~ 갑니다 I'm coming right now. // 열차는 ~ 도착합니다 The train will arrive in a minute. // 그의 열은 ~ 내릴 것입니다 His fever will soon go down. // 우리는 ~ 결혼합니다 We are going to get married soon [before long]. // 나는 ~ 미국으로 떠납니다 I am leaving shortly for the United States. // ~ 세 시가 된다 It will soon be three o'clock. / It's almost three o'clock. // 어머니께서 ~ 오실 것이다 My mother will come before long. / My mother will soon be here. // 그는 ~ 돌아올 것이다 He will be back in a moment [in a short while]. // 비는 ~ 갤 것이다 The rain will stop pretty soon. // ~ 날씨가 갤 것이다 It will clear up soon [presently / shortly / before long]. // ~ 알게 될 것이다 Wait and you'll see. / You'll understand in time. // 그는 ~ 후회하게 될 것이다 He will regret it before long [by and by]. // 이 비행기는 ~ 마닐라에 착륙합니다 This plane will land at Manila shortly [before long]. // ~ 실행하지 않으면 된다 No time must be lost in doing it [putting it into practice]. // 약효가 ~ 나타났다 The medicine took immediate effect [took effect immediately]. // 전쟁은 ~ 끝날 것이다 It will not be long before the war ends. // 집에 돌아가면 ~ 그에게 답장을 써야겠다 I'll write

him an answer as soon as I get home.∥그에게 전화해요 You'd better call him right away.
2 [다시 말하자면] namely; that is to say; that is; no other than; in other words. ¶고향을 사랑하는 마음은 ~ 나라를 사랑하는 마음이다 To love one's hometown is to love one's country.∥그것이 ~ 뇌물이다 It is nothing but a bribe.∥그의 발명은 우리나라에 대한 공헌이며 그것은 ~ 전 세계에 대한 공헌이기도 하다 His invention will be a great contribution to our country, which means that it will also be a boom to the whole world.

곧다 1 (물건이) straight; upright; erect; direct. ¶곧은길 a straight road∥곧은 기둥 an upright post∥길은 수 마일이나 곧게 뻗어 있었다 The road ran straight for several miles. **2** (마음이) honest; straightforward; upright; righteous. ¶곧은 사람 an honest [(문어) righteous] person / a man of integrity∥곧게 honestly / straightforwardly∥세상을 곧게 살아가다 lead an honest life / pursue an honest career∥그는 마음이 곧은 사람이다 He is upright at heart.

곧바로 [똑바로 곧게] straight; direct(ly); [즉시] at once; immediately; directly. ¶~ 집으로 가다 go home straight∥서울로 돌아오자 나는 ~ 그의 집으로 달려갔다 Directly after my returning[On returning] to Seoul I hastened (to go) to see him.∥나는 호텔에 도착하자마자 ~ 그에게 전화를 걸었다 I telephoned him as soon as I arrived at the hotel.

곧은창자 [생] the rectum (pl. -ta). ⇨"직장(直腸)

곧이곧대로 [사실 그대로] plainly; straightforwardly; honestly; frankly; just as it is. ¶~ 말하다 speak plainly[frankly] / speak without reserve / speak out∥그녀의 말은 ~ 들어서는 안 된다 We had better take what she says with a grain of salt. / We had better not swallow everything what she says whole.∥나는 그의 말을 ~ 받아들였다 I took him at his words.

곧이듣다 take (a thing) for truth; accept (a remark) (as true / as truth); believe (a statement) (to be true); take (it) seriously; believe one's ears. ¶쉽게 ~ swallow something whole∥남의 말을 ~ take a person at his word(s)∥농담을 ~ take a joke seriously∥나는 그의 말을 곧이들었다 I believed him [took him seriously / took him at his words].∥그런 소문을 곧이들었느냐 Did you believe such a rumor? / Did you take [accept] such a rumor as truth?∥그런 말을 누가 곧이들어 Who would believe it? / Tell that to (the horse) marines.∥그녀는 그의 말이라면 무엇이든지 곧이듣는다 She swallows any story he tells.

곧잘 [제법 잘] pretty [fairly] well; well enough; [쉽사리] (all) readily; quite readily; easily; [자주] often; frequently. ¶젊은이들이 ~ 저지르는 잘못 a blunder (that) young men are apt to make∥~ 화를 내다 be quick to take offense / be easily offended∥~ …하곤 했다 used to (do) / would (do)∥그는 ~ 화를 낸다 He is easily offended. / He gets angry easily.∥그녀는 피아노를 ~ 친다 She plays the piano fairly well.∥내가 어렸을 때 어머니는 ~ 책을 읽어 주셨다 When I was a child, my mother used to read me books.∥그는 ~ 남의 말을 믿는다 He is (all) ready to believe others.∥약이 ~ 듣는다 A drug is fairly effective.∥~ 그런 사고가 일어난다 That sort of accident occurs too often.∥그 녀석이 ~ 쓰는 수법이다 That's his usual tricks.∥그녀는 탁구도 ~ 한다 She is not half bad at table tennis.

곧장 [똑바로 곧게] straight; direct(ly); [즉시] right (away); straight [right] off; without delay. ¶~ 가다 go[keep] straight on / make straight (toward / for)∥~ 집으로 돌아가다 go straight home∥그 길로 ~ 떠나다 leave without delay∥나는 역으로 ~ 갔다 I went directly[straight] to the station.∥모퉁이에서 돌지 말고 ~ 가시오 Go straight without turning at that corner.∥역이 보일 때까지 ~ 가십시오 Keep straight on till you see the station.∥그는 사무실에서 나와 ~ 병원으로 갔다 After leaving the office he went direct(ly) to the hospital.

곧추 [일직선으로] straight; in a straight line; [수직으로] perpendicularly; vertically; upright.

곧추서다 stand upright[erect] / erect oneself.
곧추세우다 erect. ¶몸을 ~ hold oneself erect / straighten one's body∥그 새는 꽁지를 멋지게 곧추세우고 있었다 The bird thrust its tail rakishly in the air.

곧추안다 hold (a baby) out straight.
곧추앉다 sit up straight[erect].

골¹ (the) (bone) marrow. ⇨"골수¹ **2** (속) a brain; a cerebrum. ⇨뇌 **3** a brain. ¶~이 아픈 문제 a difficult question / a hard problem to solve.

골(이) 비다 have no one's sense[discretion].
골² [성] anger; dander; temper. ¶~을 잘 내다 be apt to get angry.
골³ [틀] a block; a mold; a cast. ¶구두에 ~을 넣다 tree a shoe.
골⁴ [구멍] a cave; a hollow; [골짜기] a gully; a valley; a dale; (기암) a trough.
골로 가다 die; lose one's life.
골⁵ [금] the crease made when a sheet of cloth, paper or cardboard is folded into two equal parts.
골⁶ a goal. ¶~을 넣다 [득점하다] make [score] a goal∥~에 들어오다 reach[make] the finish line.
골간(骨幹) **1** [뼈대] physique; framework. **2** [골자] gist; substance; essentials.
골격(骨格) **1** [고등 동물의 뼈의 조직] a framework; a skeletal structure; a skeleton; [체격] a frame; build; physique. ¶~이 좋은 말 a horse with plenty of bone∥그는 강건 [섬약]한 ~을 하고 있다 He has a solid [delicate] build [frame].∥그는 ~이 튼튼하다 He has a sturdy build[physique]. **2** [기계·건물 등의 구조] a structure; a frame(work). ¶학교 건물의 ~ the framework of the schoolhouse.
●**골격근** skeletal muscle.
골고루 equally; fairly; indiscriminately. ⇨"고루
골골하다 suffer from a chronic disease; suffer constantly from weak health; be sick all the time. ¶골골하는 사람 a chronic invalid / a sickly person∥골골하는 사람이 도리어 오래 산다 Creaking doors hang the longest.
골나다 be angry. ¶골나서 in a fit of passion /

골내다 in anger / in heat // 골나게 하다 make (a person) angry [(구어) mad] / anger / provoke (a person) to anger // 그녀는 골나서 가 버렸다 She left angrily [in a huff]. // 그는 쓸데없는 말을 해서 그녀를 골나게 했다 His careless remark offended her [made her angry].

골내다 get angry (about a thing / with [at] a person); (구어) get mad (at a person / about a thing); get one's dander up.

골다 (코를) snore. ¶코를 (요란하게) 고는 사람 a (heavy) snorer // 코를 드렁드렁 ~ snore loudly / (구어) snore like a grampus // 코를 (요란하게) 골며 자다 sleep with (loud) snores // 코를 골기 시작하다 fall to snoring // 자기의 코 고는 소리에 잠을 깨다 snore oneself awake.

골동품 (骨董品) 1 a curio (pl. ~s); objects [articles] of virtu; bric-a-brac; an antique (object). ¶가짜 ~ a faked antique // 그 꽃병은 ~적 가치가 있다 This vase is valued among connoisseurs (of antiques). // 그는 ~에 대한 안목이 있다 He has an eye for curio. 2 [시대에 뒤진 사람·물건] (경멸) a museum piece.
● **골동품상** (상점) a curio store; an antique shop; (상인) a curio [an antique] dealer. **골동품 애호가** an antiquarian; an antiquary.

골든 골 [연장전에서의 결승 골] a golden goal.
골든 디스크 a golden disk [disc].
골든아워 (*golden hour) (TV·라디오의) prime [peak] time. (▶ golden hours는 「가장 행복한 시간」을 뜻함)

골똘하다 absorbed [engrossed / lost] (in); intent [keen] (on); concentrated (on); given (to); completely taken up (with). 골똘히 absorbedly; intently; with an absorbed attention. ¶~ 생각하다 think intently / meditate [ponder] deeply // ~ 바라보다 give an intent look (to) / stare (at something) with all one's eyes.

골라내다 [선발하다] pick [single] out; choose (from); select (out of many); sort out (the best); [선별하다] assort; sort; sift; pick and choose. ¶좋은 사과를 ~ sort out [separate] the good apples from the bad // 많은 작품 중에서 볼 만한 것을 ~ pick out [select] the good ones from among a lot of works // 그는 검사용 샘플을 골라냈다 He selected [picked out] random samples for inspection.

골라인 a goal line.
골라잡다 choose; select; take [have] one's choice. ¶골라잡아 천 원 1,000 won a piece at your choice. / Take your choice for 1,000 won. // 둘 중에 하나를 골라잡으시오 Choose between these two. / Choose one of the two. // 구색을 다 갖추고 있으니 마음대로 골라잡으세요 We have a rich variety of goods in stock from among which you can make any choice.

골리다 (약자를) bully; tease; annoy; torment; be hard on (a person); be cruel to (a dog); (신입생 등을) (미) haze. ¶약자를 ~ bully the weaker / tyrannize over the weak // 그가 오면 골려 줘야겠다 I will take it out of him when he comes. // 학생들은 어려운 질문을 해서 선생님을 골려 주었다 The students vexed their teacher with difficult questions.

골막 (骨膜) [생] the periosteum (pl. ~s, -tea).
● **골막염** (-炎) periostitis.

골머리 a brain.
골머리(를) 앓다 be annoyed [troubled].

골목 a side street; an alley; a byway; a bystreet; a narrow street; (미) an alleyway. ¶뒷 ~ a back street // 어귀 an alley entrance // 막다른 ~ a blind alley // 그 집은 이 ~의 막다른 곳에 있다 The house is at the end of the lane. // 그 ~을 들어서서 두 번째 집이 그의 집이다 The second house down that alley is his. // 그의 집은 변두리의 ~에 있다 His house faces an alley in the outskirts.
● **골목대장** a bully; the cock of the walk; the boss of youngsters of the neighborhood.

골몰 (汨沒) absorption; immersion; engrossment. **골몰하다** be immersed [absorbed / engrossed] in; devote oneself to (a task); give oneself up to; bury oneself in; be hung up ¶연구에 ~ be absorbed in the research // 그는 골프에 골몰하여 왔다 He has thrown himself completely into golf. // 그는 그 문제의 해결에 골몰하고 있다 He is intent on [absorbed in] solving the problem. // 그녀는 그림 그리기에 골몰하고 있었다 She was completely absorbed in drawing the picture.

골무 a thimble; a thumbstall. ¶~를 끼다 wear [put on] a thimble [thumbstall].

골반 (骨盤) [생] the pelvis (pl. -ves); the basin.

골방 (-房) a small end-room; a back room; a closet.

골병 (-病) a deep-rooted illness [injury]; a disease [an injury] in the inmost part.

골병들다 (-病-) fall into deep-rooted sickness; be hurt [injured] internally; have one's vital parts affected.

골분 (骨粉) powdered bones.
● **골분 비료** bone manure.

골상 (骨相) [뼈대] physique; [인상(人相)] physiognomy; one's features; one's head; the shape [conformation] of the skull. ¶~을 보다 look into one's future [character] phrenologically / make a phrenological study (of) / examine one's physiognomy.
● **골상학** phrenology; physiognomy. **골상학자** a phrenologist; a physiognomist.

골생원 (骨生員) [옹졸한 사람] a narrowminded [an illiberal] man; [골골하는 사람] a weak [sickly] man; a man in delicate health.

골 세리모니 (*goal ceremony) goal celebration.

골수 (骨髓) 1 [생] (the) (bone) marrow; the marrow (of a bone); the medulla (pl. -lae). 2 [요점] the pith. ¶~ 공산주의자 a Communist to the core // ~ 보수주의 bone-deep conservatism. 3 [마음속] heart. ¶~에 사무치다 cut [go] deep into one's heart / sting [cut / hurt] (one) to the quick / pierce one's heart / pierce into [penetrate to] the marrow // 그에 대한 원한이 ~에 사무쳐 있다 I bear him a deep grudge. / I have a deep grudge against him.
● **골수분자** a hard core. **골수염** osteomyelitis; myelitis.

골육 (骨肉) [육친(肉親)] one's own flesh and blood; a blood relative; kindred. ¶~의 정 love for one's own flesh and blood.
● **골육상쟁 / 골육상잔** family discord [trouble].

골인 (*goal in) scoring a goal; a finish; breasting of the tape. 골인하다 (구기에서) make [score] a goal; (농구에서) score a basket; (육상 등에서) reach the goal (line); reach the finish line; breast the tape; [성공하다] succeed. ¶결혼으로 ~ be happily married.

골자(骨子) the essential part; the main point(s); the gist; the essence; the substance. ¶그의 연설의 ~ the gist of his speech // 계획의 ~를 말하다 outline the essential features of a plan // ~는 이렇다 The point is this.

골재(骨材) aggregate.

골절(骨折) a bone fracture; [부러진 뼈] a broken bone.

골절(骨節) a joint.

골조(骨組) 1 [골격] the (bony) frame; a skeleton; physique; build. 2 [구조] framework; a frame; framing; structure; a skeleton; the carcass(선체 등의).

골질(骨質) [생] bony[osseous] tissue; [골상물질] bony substance.

골짜기 a valley; a vale; [협곡] a canyon; a ravine; a dale; a gorge. ¶산~ a gorge / a ravine / a glen / 한없이 깊은 ~ an abysmal gorge // 산~를 흐르는 물 a mountain stream // 산을 넘고 ~를 건너 up hill and down dale // ~에서 ~로 넘어가다 go over from valley to valley.

골초(-草) [질 낮은 담배] tobacco of low quality; cheap tobacco; (영국 속어) a gasper; [심하게 담배를 피우는 사람] a heavy smoker; a chain smoker.

골치 a brain.

골치(를) 앓다 worry about (a matter); be troubled.

골칫거리 a headache; a (source of) trouble; a nuisance; a bother; a pain in the neck. ¶사회의 ~ a burden to the community / a public nuisance // 두 번째 문제가 ~였다 The second question was a floorer. / The second question baffled me. // 그는 가족에게 큰 ~다 He is a great distress to the family. / He is the black sheep of the family. // 너는 정말 ~구나 You really are hopeless. / I really don't know what to do about you. // 그는 회사로 봐서는 ~다 As far as the company is concerned, he's just an excess baggage. // 자식이 게을러서 ~다 I don't know what to do about my lazy son. / (구어) My lazy son is a headache.

골칫덩어리 a problem child; a nuisance; a black sheep. ¶개는 정말 ~야 He is a nuisance[black sheep]. / He is a bull in a china shop.

골키퍼 a goalkeeper.

골킥 a goal kick.

골탕 a great loss[injury]; heavy [serious] damage.

골탕(을) 먹다 suffer a big loss; [애먹다] have bitter experiences; have a hard time (of it) (with a person). ¶그 친구를 믿었다가 골탕 먹었다 I was taken in, trusting that guy. // 그녀는 고스란히 골탕 먹었다 She was easily taken in. She fell neatly for the trick.

골통 〈속〉 the head. ⇨머리1 (구어) the noddle; (미국 구어) the noggin; (속어) the pate. ¶~이 터지다 have one's head hurt // ~을 가 버리겠다 I'll blow your brains out. / I'll brain (the life out of) you.

골판지(-板紙) corrugated cardboard.

골패(骨牌) a domino.
골퍼 a golfer; a golf player.
골포스트 a goalpost.
골풀 [식] a (candle) rush.
골프 golf. ¶~ 치는 사람 a golfer / a golf player // ~를 치다 play (at) golf / golf. ●골프공 a golf ball. 골프 연습장 a golf practice ranger; a driving range. 골프장 a golf links; a golf course; a green. 골프채 a golf club; an iron (club)(철제의); a driver; a wood(en club)(목재의).

골필(骨筆) a stencil pen; a steel pen; a stylus; an iron pen.

골함석 a corrugated iron sheet.

골회(骨灰) (animal) bone ashes.

곪다 (상처가) gather; fester; form pus; (일이) (an affair) come to a head; ripen. ¶상처가 곪았다 The wound festered. / The wound formed [(문어) generated] pus. / Pus has gathered in the wound. // 여드름이 곪았다 The pimple has come to [formed] a head.

곬 1 (길) a fixed direction; a set way; a direct road. ¶세상사를 외~으로만 생각하다 see things from only one point of view [from the same viewpoint]. 2 [물길] a waterway; a watercourse; a (water) channel.

곯다1 1 (배를) go hungry; be (always) hungry; be famished; starve. ¶곯은 배를 채우다 satisfy[gratify] one's hunger // 그 아이는 배를 곯고 있었다 The child was very hungry. // 배를 곯아서는 아무 일도 할 수 없다 You can't do anything on an empty stomach. // 애들을 배곯게 할 수는 없다 My children must not be left hungry. // 어떻게 식구들의 배를 곯게 할 수 있단 말인가 How can I let my family go hungry? 2 [그릇에 덜 차다] unfilled; (서술적) be (still) not full; be a little short of full.

곯다2 1 (상하다) rot; go bad; spoil; be spoilt; become stale; addle(달걀 등이). ¶곯은 rotten / bad / spoilt / addle / 곯은 달걀 addle[bad] eggs // 곯기 쉽다 be easy to spoil[go bad] / be perishable // 참외가 ~ a melon spoils // 달걀은 곯기 쉽다 Eggs are apt to addle. 2 [해를 입다] suffer (secret) damage; suffer [sustain] a loss; (미국 구어) be left holding the bag; [골병들다] suffer (an) internal injury. ¶그 사람들 농간에 나는 되게 곯았다 I suffered heavily from their tricks. / Their wiles made me sustain great damage. // 그는 폭음을 해서 몸이 곯았다 Excessive drinking did him bodily harm.

곯리다1 (배를) underfeed; leave (a person) to starve. ¶간신히 식구들을 안 곯릴 정도다 I barely support my family.

곯리다2 1 (상하게 하다) rot; spoil; addle; putrefy; make (a thing) stale. ¶달걀을 (오래 두어) ~ spoil an egg. 2 (골병들게 하다) inflict damage upon (a person); do harm to; cause damage to.

곯아떨어지다 (잠에) fall fast asleep; be dead asleep; sleep like a top; (술에) be overcome with liquor; be dead drunk; be helplessly drunk; (구어) pass out. ¶그는 맥주 한 잔에 곯아떨어졌다 He got quite drunk after only a glass of beer. // 그들은 잠에 곯아떨어져 있었다 They were sprawled out sound asleep. // 그녀는 피로해서 곯아떨어졌다 She fell into a deep sleep from exhaustion.

곰1 [고기를 삶은 국] a thick broth made of

곰 thoroughly cooked meat.

곰² 1 [동물] a bear. ¶흰~ a white[polar] bear // ~ 새끼 a bear's cub // ~의 쓸개[웅담] dried bear's gall bladder (used as medicine) // ~ 사냥 bear hunting. 2 [미련한 사람] a slowpoke; a slow-witted person. ¶그는 ~ 같은 사람이다 He is a regular bear.
● 곰 가죽 (a) bearskin.

곰곰(이) deliberately; thoroughly; deeply; profoundly; seriously; mulling[thinking] over; musing. ¶~ 생각하다 think it over / mull (the matter) over / deliberate / consider carefully / muse / reflect upon / ponder (over / on) // ~ 생각해 보아라 Put that in your pipe and smoke it. / You should take time to consider it. // 결론을 확정하기 전에 ~ 생각해 보아라 Think it over and over again before you come to a definite conclusion. // 모든 가능성은 시간을 두고 ~ 생각해 보시오 Take your time and think over all the possibilities.

곰국 *gomguk*; a thick beef soup.

곰방대 a (tobacco) pipe; a short (smoking) pipe.

곰배팔 a disabled[deformed] arm.
● 곰배팔이 a person with a deformed arm.

곰보 a pockmarked person; a person with a pitted face.

곰삭다 1 (옷이) wear thin; be worn out; be outworn; (old and untouched clothes) reach the point where it will fall apart at a touch. 2 (젓이) (pickled stuff) get well[thoroughly] pickled.

곰살갑다 [다정스럽다] tenderhearted; kind; cordial; gentle; delicate; [너그럽다] generous; broad-minded; magnanimous.

곰살궂다 gentle; kind; warm (-hearted); cordial. ¶곰살궂게 kindly / gently / tenderly / cordially // 그녀는 곰살궂게 나를 보살펴 주었다 She took kind care of me.

곰실거리다 wriggle; writhe; squirm; wiggle; twist.

곰탕(—湯) a thick beef soup. ⇨ ˚곰국

곰팡 mold; mould. ⇨ ˚곰팡이(⇨ ˚곰팡)
● 곰팡내 [곰팡이 냄새] a musty[stale] smell; mustiness; fustiness; [진부함] commonplaceness; triteness. ¶~ 나는 방 a musty room // ~ 나는 사상 moth-eaten [outdated] ideas. **곰팡이** (미) mold; (영)mould; mildew; must. ¶푸른 ~ blue[green] mold // ~가 슨 빵 moldy bread // ~투성이다 be covered with mold / get mildewed all over // ~를 없애다 remove the mold // ~ 피는 것을 막다 keep (something) from getting moldy // 치즈에 ~가 피었다 The cheese got moldy. / Mold gathered on the cheese. // 책에 ~가 슬었다 The books got mildewed.

곱¹ mucous discharge; a crust of mucus; a film of pus. ¶상처에 낀 ~ a crust of mucus formed on a wound // 헌데에 ~이 끼었다 A mucous discharge formed on a wound.

곱² 1 double; times. ⇨ ˚곱절 2 [수] the product.

곱다¹ 1 (손발이) numb (with cold); benumbed (with cold); stiff. ¶추워서 손발이 곱았다 My hands and legs are numb with cold. // 나는 손가락이 곱아 펜을 잡을 수가 없다 My fingers are so stiff with cold that I cannot hold my pen. 2 (이가) (one's teeth) be set [put] on edge.

곱다² 1 [아름답다] beautiful; lovely; fine; nice; handsome. ¶고운 소녀 a nice-looking [pretty / lovely] girl // 고운 얼굴 pretty features / a fair face [countenance] // 고운 꽃 a pretty [beautiful] flower // 곱게 차려입다 dress oneself beautifully / be finely dressed // 곱게 피어 있다 be in beautiful bloom.
2 [마음이] sweet; gentle; pure-minded; noble-minded. ¶마음씨 고운 소녀 a kindhearted [a tenderhearted / an affectionate] girl // 마음씨가 ~ be kindhearted / be pure in mind [heart].
3 [말·소리가 맑고 부드럽다] sweet; charming; soft. ¶고운 목소리 a sweet[soft] voice // 고운 말 refined language [words] // 고운 말로 노래 부르다 sing in a charming voice.
4 (살결·가루 등이) fine; fair. ¶고운 살결 a fine [fair / delicate] skin // 고운 모래 [가루] fine sand [flour].

곱다랗다 1 [아름답다] quite pretty; beautiful; lovely; handsome; nice. 2 [깎축없다] whole; intact; safe; undamaged.

곱돌 [광] agalmatolite.

곱들다 [갑절 들다] cost twice as much (as); take twice as much (as). ¶시간이 ~ take double [twice] the time / take twice as much (as) // 힘이 ~ be twice as hard [difficult] (as).

곱들이다 spend [put out] twice as much (as); consume twice as much (as).

곱똥 (white) diarrhoetic stools; mucous stools.

곱빼기 1 (음식의) double measure; a double-measure of wine; a double (-size) glass; a double-the-ordinary dish. 2 [거듭함] double; twice.

곱사등 a humpback; a hunchback.
● 곱사등이 a humpback; a hunchback; a hunchbacked person.

곱살스럽다 (용모가) comely; pretty; fair; good-looking; (마음씨가) nice; tender; gentle. ¶얼굴이 곱살스러운 소녀 a charming [pretty] girl // 곱살스럽게 굴다 be gentle.

곱새기다 1 [오해하다] misunderstand; misconstrue; [곡해하다] twist (a person's words). 2 [거듭 생각하다] think over (and over) again.

곱셈 (a) multiplication. **곱셈하다** multiply; do multiplication.
● 곱셈표 the sign for multiplication; the multiplication sign(기호 ×).

곱슬곱슬하다 curly; curled; frizzled; frizzly; wavy. ¶곱슬곱슬한 머리 curly [frizzled] hair.

곱씹다 [말 등을 되풀이하다] rechew; repeat (a word); (다짐받듯) harp (up)on (a question); emphasize.

곱자 a square.

곱장다리 bowlegs.

곱절 [두 배] double; [배] times. ¶~이 되다 double / be doubled (in value) // 세 ~의 treble // A의 ~이나 크다 be twice [two times] as large as A // 몇 ~이나 many times over // 몇 ~의 노력을 하다 redouble one's efforts // 값의 ~을 지불하다 pay double [twice] the price // 1,000은 100의 몇 ~이나 How many times a hundred is a thousand? // 2의 세 ~은 6이다 Three times two is (equals to) 6. // 값이 다섯 ~이나 뛰었다 The price went up fivefold.

곱창 the small intestines of cattle.
곱치다 [반으로 접다] fold; [곱절하다] double. ¶값을 ~ double a price∥담요를 ~ fold [double] a blanket∥신문을 ~ fold up a newspaper.
곱하기 multiplication.
곱하다 [수] multiply. ¶두 수를 ~ multiply two numbers together∥2에 2를 ~ multiply 2 by 2∥2에 2를 곱하면 4가 된다 Two times two is[are] four. (2×2=4는 "Two times [multiplied by] two is four. / Two twos [Two 2's] are four."라고 읽음)∥3곱하기 2는 6 Two times three makes[is] six.
곳 a place; (좁은) a spot; (현장) a scene; (지방) locality. ¶사고가 일어난 ~ the spot of the accident∥안전한 ~ a place of safety∥귤이 많이 나는 ~ an orange-producing district∥~에 따라 다르다 be different in different localities∥그~ 형편은 어떻습니까 How are things going on in your place?∥여기는 젊은이가 오는 ~이 아니다 This is no place for young people.∥나는 조용히 있을 ~을 원한다 I want a place where I can be quiet.∥나는 갈 ~이 없다 I have nowhere to go.∥그는 안주할 ~을 찾아 헤맸다 He wandered about looking for a place where he could live in peace.∥참 마음에 드는 ~이다 What a pleasant place it is!∥사고가 난 ~이 여깁니까 Was this the scene of the accident?∥오늘은 ~에 따라 비가 오겠습니다 Some areas are likely to have rain [There will be scattered rainfall] today.∥소풍하기에 알맞은 ~을 발견했다 We found a good spot for a picnic.∥사는 ~이 어디요 Where is your home? / What is your address?∥비키니 차림의 아가씨들에게 둘러싸여 그는 눈 둘 ~을 몰랐다 Surrounded by girls in bikinis he was at a loss where to look[turn his eyes].
곳간(庫間) a storeroom; a repository; a shed; a warehouse.
곳곳 several places; everywhere. ¶시내 ~에서 in several[various] parts of the city∥그 회사는 거의 전국 ~에 지점이 있다 That company has its branches in almost all parts of the country.∥같은 사건이 ~에서 일어났다 Similar cases occurred in many[various] places.
공¹ [볼] a ball; a handball; [원구] a circle; a sphere; a globe. ¶고무~ a rubber ball∥~을 던지다[받다 / 치다] throw[catch / hit] a ball∥~을 차다[튀기다] kick[bounce] a ball∥~을 줍다 pick up a ball∥~을 몰다 drive a ball∥치기 좋은 ~을 놓치지 않다 be sure to hit a good pitch∥투수가 오늘은 ~이 빠르다 The pitcher's fast today. / The pitcher's got a lot of speed today.
공² a gong. ¶~이 울렸다 (권투에서) There is the bell.
공(公) **1** [공무(公務)] public matters; public affairs. ¶~과 사를 구별하다 draw the line between public and private matters∥~과 사를 혼동하다 mix up[confuse] public and private affairs[matters]. **2** (영) a prince; (영) a duke. ⇨*공작*(公爵) ¶웰링턴 ~ the Duke of Wellington. **3** [2인칭] you (sir); sir; [3인칭] he; the gentleman.
공(功) **1** meritorious deeds. ⇨*공로*(功勞) ¶특히 ~이 있는 사람 a person of exceptional merit / ~을 치하하여 for[in recognition of] a person's services∥~을 세우다 render meritorious[distinguished] services / perform a meritorious deed∥~을 다투다 claim credit (for an invention)∥그는 나라를 위해 큰 ~을 세웠다 He rendered distinguished [meritorious] service to the state.∥전투에서 그는 큰 ~을 세웠다 He distinguished himself in this battle.∥그들은 일을 완성한 ~을 그에게 돌렸다 They let him take the credit for the completion of the work. **2** [수고] exertion; efforts; labors. ¶~을 들인 계획[장식] elaborate plans[ornaments].
공(空) **1** [영] (a) zero; (a) cipher; [무] (a) naught; nothing(허사). ¶나의 모든 노력은 ~으로 돌아갔다 All my efforts have come to naught. **2** [동그라미] a circle; an 'O'. ¶~을 치다 draw a circle / write an 'O' / mark down a zero∥~을 하나 붙이다 put a zero to.
-공(工) [일꾼] an artisan; a worker; a mechanic. ¶금속~ a metal worker∥선로~ (미) a trackman / (영) a plate layer.
-공(公) (존칭) a lord.
공간(空間) **1** (우주의) space. ~의 spacial∥시간과 ~ time and space∥무한의 ~ the infinite∥시간과 ~을 초월하다 neglect[take no notice of] time and space∥~을 날다 travel through space. **2** [장소] room; [틈] a space; a gap; [문어] discontinuity. ¶위상-[수] topological space∥~을 만들다 make room∥책상 두 개가 더 들어갈 ~이 있습니까 Is there room for two more desks?∥페이지 아래쪽에 10센티의 ~이 있었다 There was a space of ten centimeters at the bottom of the page.
● **공간 개념** [철] the concept[notion] of space. **공간 예술** spatial[plastic] art. **공간 지각** [심] space perception.
공갈(恐喝) a threat; intimidation; a menace; blackmail. ¶~ 혐의로 (체포되다) (be arrested) on a charge of blackmailing. **공갈하다** threaten; intimidate; make a threat; blackmail; bluff; threaten (a person) with bluff. ¶공갈하여 돈을 빼앗다 blackmail (a person) of his money / blackjack money out of (a person)∥그는 나를 공갈하여 뇌물을 받아 갔다 He extorted a bribe from me.∥그는 나를 죽인다고 공갈했다 He threatened to kill me. / He threatened me with death.∥그들은 그를 공갈하여 거짓말을 시켰다 They intimidated[(미국 속어) bulldoged] him into lying about it.∥그는 그녀를 공갈하여 돈을 빼앗았다 He extorted money from her by threats. / He blackmailed money out of her. / He intimidated her into giving him money.
● **공갈죄** (the crime of) blackmail; the crime of intimidation; extortion.
공감(共感) sympathy; response. ¶~을 불러일으키다 evoke[excite / rouse] (a person's) sympathy / call forth a response in (a person's) heart∥~을 얻다 win[gain] the sympathy (of)∥호소했지만 아무런 ~도 못 얻었다 No response came to the appeal on our side.∥그의 연설은 많은 청중의 ~을 불러 일으켰다 His speech aroused sympathy from [gained the sympathy of] a large audience.
공감하다 sympathize with (a person); respond to (an appeal). ¶남의 의견에 ~ sympathize with a person in his point of view / sympathize with a person's point of view.

공개(公開) ¶~의[적인] open (to the public) / public // ~ 석상에서 in public / in a meeting open to the public // ~가 금지되다 be closed to the public // 그는 ~ 석상에 나가기를 좋아하지 않는다 He does not like to attend public functions. **공개하다** open (a thing) to the public; throw (a thing) open to the public; [전시하다] place (a thing) on exhibition; exhibit; (기업을) go public. ¶회의를 ~ make public the proceedings (of a committee) // 주식을 ~ offer shares of stock for public subscription // 신문 기자에게 ~ open to the press // 이런 일은 공개하여 말할 수 없다 This is no the kind of thing I can say in front of everybody. / We cannot talk about this openly[freely]. ➔ ¶이 탑의 내부는 일반에게 공개되고[공개되지 않고] 있다 The interior of this tower is open[closed] to the public.

● **공개 강좌** (대학의) an extension lecture. **공개 방송** open broadcasting. **공개 법인** a corporation which is opened to public subscription. **공개수사** an open criminal investigation. **공개 시장** an open market. **공개 입찰** a public tender; an open bid. **공개 재판** a (public) trial. **공개 토론회** a[an open] forum (pl. ~s, fora).

공것(空-) something free; what can be had for nothing; a thing got for nothing; an article obtained without cost; a gift; a windfall. ¶~으로 얻다 get[gain] (a thing) as a gift[without efforts] // ~보다 비싼 것은 없다 You never get something for nothing.

공격(攻擊) 1 [침] an attack; [강공] an assault; [맹공] an onslaught; [급습] a raid; [공세] an offensive movement; an offense. ¶기습 ~ a surprise attack // 배면 ~ a rear attack // 정면 [측면] ~ a frontal[flank] attack // ~적인 offensive / aggressive // ~을 개시하다 open[launch] an attack (on / against) // ~을 가하다 deliver[launch] an attack against / attack // ~을 막다 defend oneself against an attack // 적의 ~을 저지하다 check the advance of the enemy // 기회를 잡아 ~으로 전환하다 seize a chance to take the offensive // ~은 최선의 방어다 A good offense is the best defense. / The best defense is attack. // 적은 총~을 개시했다 The enemy launched an all out attack. // 적의 ~은 아군의 허를 찔렀다 The enemy attack took us by surprise. // 저 씨름꾼의 ~은 맹렬하다 That *ssireum* wrestler has a powerful charge. **공격하다** attack; assail; assault; charge; storm; make an attack [assault] (on); make[carry out] a raid (on). ¶적의 배후를 ~ take[attack] the enemy in the rear // 세차게 공격하여 요새를 점령하다 take[win] a fortress by assault // 우리는 전력을 다하여 적을 공격했다 We went at the enemy with all our might.

2 [비난] an attack; a charge; (a) censure; denunciation; criticism. ¶~적인 말 offensive[highly critical] language / (구어) fighting talk. **공격하다** attack; charge; criticize; denounce; censure. ¶신문에서 사람을 ~ attack[pound] a person in the newspaper // 상사는 그의 직무 태만을 공격했다 His superior reprimanded him for neglecting his duties.

3 [야구] batting (side). **공격하다** go[come] to bat.

● **공격 개시 시간** [군] H-hour; zero (hour). **공격력** striking power. **공격 목표** an attack objective. **공격 정신** an offensive spirit.

공경(恭敬) respect; reverence; veneration; deference. **공경하다** respect; esteem; honor; revere. ¶공경할 만한 respectable / venerable / esteemable // 어른을 ~ be respectful to one's elders // 스승을 ~ honor[respect / revere] one's teacher. **공경히** respectfully; deferentially; reverently; venerably; in a reverent manner.

공고(公告) a public[an official] announcement[notice]; a (public) notification. ¶경매 ~ an auction announcement // 특허 ~ a patent announcement. **공고하다** notify publicly; announce; give a public notice (of). ➔ ¶시험 날짜가 어제 공고되었다 The date of the examination was publicly announced yesterday. / The public announcement of the date of the examination was made yesterday.

공고하다(鞏固-) firm; stable; solid; sound; strong. ¶~공고한 의지 a strong[an iron] will // 공고한 지반 firm[solid] ground // 공고한 기반을 구축하다 firmly establish one's sphere of influence // 공고한 기초 위에 서 있다 It is based on a sound[solid] foundation. **공고히** firmly; strongly; solidly. ¶~ 하다 make solid / solidify / strengthen / consolidate // 자기 지위를 ~ 하다 make one's position secure.

공공(公共) the public society; the community. ¶~의 public / common / communal // ~의 이익을 도모하다 promote public interests / work in the interests of the public // ~을 위하여 봉사하다 render public services to the public / work for the public benefit // 그는 ~의 이익을 위해 일했다 He worked for the common good. // 그는 ~의 이익을 위해 크게 기여했다 He rendered great service to the community.

● **공공 기관** a public institution. **공공 기업체** (영) a government corporation; (미) a public corporation. **공공 단체** a public organization. **공공사업** a public enterprise; public works; (public) utilities. **공공 생활** community[communal] life. **공공시설** public facilities. **공공심** public spirit; sense of public duty. **공공요금** charges for public service; public utility charges. **공공 재산** public property. **공공 투자** public investment; government investment.

공공연하다(公公然-) open; public; open and public; avowed (enemy); overt (hostility). ¶공공연한 사실 a fact as clear as day / a fact known to everybody // 공공연한 비밀 an open secret // 전무와 비서의 정사가 공공연한 사실이 되었다 The managing director's affair with his secretary has become public knowledge. **공공연히** openly; publicly; in public. ¶~ 반대하다 oppose[assail] openly // 나는 ~ 말할 수 없는 일이 있다 There is something that I can't say out in the open[openly]. // 십대 소년들이 ~ 담배를 피우고 있었다 Teenage boys were smoking in public.

공과(工科) the department of engineering.

● **공과 대학** a college of engineering; a college specializing in engineering; an institute of technology.

공과(功過) merits and demerits. ¶이 개발 계획은 ~가 반반이다 The pluses and minuses [advantages and disadvantages / strengths and weaknesses] of this development project are evenly balanced.

공과금(公課金) public imposts[charges]; taxes.

공관(公館) 〔저택〕 an official residence; 〔공사관〕 a legation; 〔공공의 집〕 a public hall. ¶재외 ~ diplomatic missions[establishments] abroad / (영사관 포함) diplomatic and consular offices in foreign countries // 대법원장[도지사] ~ The official residence of the Chief Justice[the governor].

공교롭다(工巧-) 〔뜻밖이다〕 coincidental; wholly unexpected; quite accidental; opportune[inopportune]; timely[untimely]; lucky [unlucky]. ¶공교로운 일치 a coincidence // 공교로운 때 an opportune [inopportune] time[occasion / moment] / a likely[unlikely] time // 공교로운 실수 an unfortunate mistake. **공교로이** unexpectedly; accidentally; opportunely[inopportunely]; at a likely [unlikely] time; luckily[unluckily]; fortunately[unfortunately]; by a lucky [an unlucky] coincidence; as luck would have it; happen[chance] to. ¶~ 가진 돈이 없다 Unfortunately[It so happens that] I have no money with me. // ~ 그날 비가 내렸다 The day happened to be rainy. // ~ 때마침 전화벨이 울렸다 The telephone rang at a most inconvenient[unwelcome] moment. // ~ 집에 아무도 없을 때 그녀가 찾아왔다 Unfortunately[As luck would have it], she called on us when no one was at home.

공교하다(工巧-) **1** (솜씨가) skillful at complicated[fine] things. ¶공교한 솜씨 dexterity / deftness / cleverness with one's fingers. **2** coincidental. ⇨ 공교롭다

공구(工具) a tool; an implement; an instrument. ¶~ 한 벌 a set of tools // 기계 ~ a machine tool // 정밀 ~ a precision tool.

공구(工區) 〔건〕 a section of works; a building construction area.

공국(公國) a dukedom; a duchy; a principality. ¶리히텐슈타인 ~ the Principality of Liechtenstein.

공군(空軍) an air force; the air service; a flying corps. ¶한국 ~ the Republic of Korea Air Force(약어 ROK A.F.) / 영국 ~ the Royal Air Force(약어 R.A.F. RAF) / 미국 ~ the United States Air Force(약어 U.S.A.F. USAF).

●**공군기** an air-force plane. **공군 기지** an air base. **공군력** air power. **공군 본부** the Air Force Headquarters. **공군 사관학교** an air-force academy.

공권(公權) civil rights; citizenship.

●**공권력** governmental authority[power]. **공권 박탈** deprivation of civil rights; disfranchisement.

공권(空拳) a bare hand; a naked fist. ⇨ 맨주먹 ¶(적수)~으로 with one's naked[bare] hands.

공그르다 blindstitch; whip (a seam).

공극(空隙) an opening; a gap; a crevice; an aperture.

공글리다 1 〔다지다〕 harden; make hard; consolidate; solidify; firm up; strengthen; stabilize. **2** 〔알뜰히 끝맺다〕 finish up; settle [fix up] (a matter) neatly.

공금(公金) public money; government funds. ¶~을 횡령하다 embezzle public funds // ~을 낭비하다 be extravagant with the public purse // ~으로 해외여행을 하다니 너무 심하다 That's terrible-taking a trip abroad at public expense!

●**공금 횡령** embezzlement of public money; peculation.

공급(供給) supply; provision; (전기·수도 등의) service. ¶수요와 ~ (의 법칙) (a law of) demand and supply // 수요와 ~의 균형 a balance between supply and demand // ~을 끊다 cut off the supply (of) // ~을 받다 be supplied (with) / get a supply (of) // 전력 ~을 끊다 cut off the supply of electric power / cut off a person's electricity // ~이 수요를 따라잡지 못한다 The supply cannot meet the demand. **공급하다** supply [provide] (a person with something / something for a person); furnish (with); serve (a town). ¶원료를 ~ supply (a factory) with material / 인력을 ~ supply with manpower / man up // 그들은 우리에게 식량을 공급했다 They supplied [provided / furnished] us with food. / They provided food for us. / They supplied [furnished] food to us.

●**공급 가격** a supply price. **공급로** a channel of supply; a supply route. **공급 부족** a short supply; an undersupply. **공급원** a source of supply. **공급자** a supplier; a provider.

공기 〔아이들의 놀이용 돌〕 a jackstone; a pebble; (그 놀이) jackstones; marbles. ¶~ 놀다 play [shoot] marbles [jackstones] (with).

공기 놀리듯 하다 〔농락하다〕 turn [twist] (a person) round[around] one's (little) finger; make sport [a toy] of (a person).

공기(公器) a public institution; a public organ [instrument]. ¶~를 남용하다 abuse public instruments // 신문은 여론을 전달하는 ~이다 Newspapers are organs of public opinion.

공기(空氣) **1** 〔기체〕 air. ¶신선한 ~ fresh air // 더러운[탁한] ~ impure[foul] air // 실내의 ~ the air in the room // 바깥 ~ the air outside // ~의 흐름 the air current // ~의 유통 circulation of air // ~가 통하지 않는 airtight / airproof // ~의 유통이 좋다[나쁘다] be well [ill] ventilated // ~를 넣다 ventilate (a room) / let (fresh) air in / (타이어 등에) fill with air / pump up (a tire) / inflate // ~를 빼다 deflate (a tire) // ~를 갈다 air out (a room) // 신선한 ~를 마시다 breathe (in) fresh air // 창문을 열고 신선한 ~를 쐬었다 I opened the window for a breath of fresh air. // 이 방은 ~가 나쁘다 This room is stuffy. // 이 방은 ~ 유통이 잘된다[잘 안 된다] This room is well [poorly] ventilated. // 그는 타이어의 ~를 뺐다 He let the air out of [deflate] the tire.

2 〔분위기〕 atmosphere. ¶긴장된 ~ a tense atmosphere // 사내(社內)의 ~가 매우 험악하다 A tense atmosphere reigns at the office. / There is something tense in the air at the office. // 불온한 ~가 느껴졌다 We felt a disturbing [threatening] atmosphere. // 좌중에 불쾌한 ~가 가득했다 An uncomfortable atmosphere spread over the whole gathering.

●**공기뿌리** 〔식〕 an aerial root; a cram-

공기 po(o)n. 공기 압축기 an air compressor. 공기 오염 air[atmospheric] pollution. 공기 저항 air resistance. 공기 전염 (병균의) infection by air; aerial[airborne] infection. 공기 정화기 an air cleaner. 공기 제동기 / 공기 브레이크 an air[a pneumatic] brake. 공기주머니 an air sac. ⇨기낭1 공기총 an air gun [rifle]. 공기 펌프 an air pump.

공기(空器) [빈 그릇] an empty vessel[dish]; (식사용의) bowl. ¶밥 한 ~ a bowl of rice // ~에 담아 주다 serve in a bowl.

공기업(公企業) a public[government / state] enterprise.

공납금(公納金) (학교의) regular school payments; (관공서의 부과금) taxes; public imposts[charges].

공단(工團) an industrial complex. ⇨공업 단지(공업)

공단(公團) a public corporation.

공단(貢緞) silk satin (without patterns).

공대(工大) a college of engineering. ⇨공과대학(⇨공과(工科))

공대(恭待) 1 [공손한 대접] respectful[hospitable] treatment. 공대하다 treat respectfully; treat (a person) with courtesy. ¶그녀는 언제나 시어머니를 공대하였다 She always paid due respect to her mother-in-law. 2 [공대말을 씀]. 공대하다 address with respect; use polite language.

공대공(空對空) air-to-air.
● 공대공 미사일 an air-to-air (guided) missile.

공대지(空對地) air-to-surface[-ground].
● 공대지 미사일 an air-to-surface (guided) missile.

공덕(功德) charity; piety; a pious act; a charitable[virtuous] deed; an act of merit; virtue. ¶~을 베풀다 [자선하다] perform an act of charity / [선행하다] do good[virtuous] deeds // ~을 쌓다 build up one's credit in Heaven // ~이 불쌍한 사람들을 돕는 일은 ~이 됩니다 Helping these unfortunate people will help you earn salvation.

공덕심(公德心) public spirit; public sense; a sense of public duty. ¶~이 없다 be wanting in public spirit.

공도(公道) 1 a highway. ⇨공로(公路) 2 [정의] justice; equity. ¶~를 걷다[~에서 벗어나다] keep to[stray from] the right path.

공돈(空-) an unearned[a windfall] income; easy money; (부정한) filthy lucre; (미국 속어) gravy. ¶~은 오래 못 간다 Lightly come, lightly go. / Easy come, easy go.

공동(共同) cooperation; collaboration; union; association; partnership. ¶~의 common / communal / joint / concerted / united / public(공공의) // ~의 적 a common enemy // ~의 이익을 위하여 for the common benefit [interests] (of) // ~으로 in conjunction [cooperation / collaboration / concert / association / participation] (with) / jointly // ~으로 보조를 취하다 take joint steps // ~으로 가게를 경영하다 run a store in partnership with // ~으로 부담하다 share (the losses) with (another) / bear (the expenses) jointly with (another) // ~으로 차를 사용하다 share the use of a car // 나는 그와 ~으로 그것을 만들었다 I collaborated with him[I was his partner] in making it. // 우리는 ~으로 책임을 져야 한다 We are jointly responsible for it. / We must take joint responsibility for it. // 그들은 세 사람이 ~으로 차 한 대를 샀다 They bought a car between the three of them. 공동하다 cooperate (with); collaborate (in); work together; act in concert (with).
● 공동 가입 [전화] joint subscription. 공동 가입선 a party wire[line]. 공동 가입자 a joint subscriber. 공동 가입 전화 a telephone on a party line; a party-line telephone; (시설) two-party telephone service. 공동 경영 joint management. 공동 관리 joint control; [국제법] condominium. 공동묘지 a (public) cemetery; a common burial ground. 공동 사업 a joint enterprise [undertaking]. 공동 사회 a communal society; a commune. 공동 상속 joint inheritance; (토지의) (co)parcenary. 공동생활 community[communal] life; communal living; living together; (남녀의) cohabitation. 공동 성명 a joint statement[communique]. 공동 소유 joint ownership; coproprietorship. 공동 시설 public facilities; facilities for common[communal] use. 공동 연구 joint research(es). 공동 작업 group work; teamwork; cooperation. 공동 작전 concerted [united / combined] operations. 공동 재산 joint property. 공동 전선 a common[united] front. ¶~을 펴다 form[make] a common front (against) / present[put up] a united front (against) / join forces (with) / make common cause (with / against). 공동 제작 joint production; coproduction. 공동 주최 joint auspices. 공동 책임 (위원회·내각 등의) corporate responsibility; [부채 등의 연대 책임] joint liability. 공동 출자 joint investment; pooling of funds. 공동 협찬 joint auspices. ¶(라디오·텔레비전의) ~ 프로 a program with more than one sponsor / a cosponsored program.

공동(空洞) a hollow; [텅 빈 동굴] a cave, a cavern; a cavity; (폐의) a vomica (pl. -cae).

공들다(功-) require much labor[trouble]; cost strenuous efforts[exertion / labors]. ¶공드는 일 laborious[toilsome] work.
● 공든 탑이 무너지랴 (속담) Hard work is never wasted.; A man's labors will be crowned with success.

공들이다(功-) make a strenuous effort; labor assiduously; spend[expend] one's labor; put great care (in one's work); take pains. ¶공들여 with great effort[labor / care] / elaborately / carefully // 공들인 작품 an elaborate (piece of) work // 공들인 문장 an elaborate sentence // 공들여 화장하다 make one's toilet carefully // 이것은 꽤 공들인 작품이다 This is a nice little job. / This is an elaborate piece of work. // 공들인 보람이 없었다 All my labor were wasted[lost / in vain].

공떡(空-) a godsend; a windfall; a thing won for nothing. ¶이게 웬 ~이냐 What a welcome windfall!

공란(空欄) a blank[an empty / a vacant] column; a blank (space); empty space; margin. ¶~에 기입하다 fill in the blanks // ~에 알맞은 말을 넣으시오 Insert the appropriate words in the blank spaces.

공랭(空冷) air cooling. ¶~(식)의 air-cooled (cylinder).

공략(攻略) capture; conquest; reduction; occupation; [침략] (an) invasion; taking by

storm. 공략하다 carry; capture; conquer; reduce; take (a fortress) by storm; [침략하다] invade (a country). ¶공략하기 어려운 impregnable (fortress) // 적의 진지를 ~ capture an enemy position.

공력(功力) (노력) effort; labor; elaboration; [불] the merit of one's austerities[penance]. ¶그의 ~도 마침내 허사였다 All his efforts ended in vain.

공로(公路) a highway; a public road[way]; (미) a highroad.

공로(功勞) meritorious deeds[services]; merits; an exploit. ¶~가 있는 meritorious / of merit // ~에 의하여 in recognition of a person's distinguished services // ~를 세우다 distinguish oneself in (war) / render distinguished service to (the state) / perform a meritorious deed / do much for (social welfare) // ~를 세워 훈장을 받다 be decorated for one's distinguished services // 그것은 전적으로 그의 ~다 The credit for it goes to him. // 그것은 나의 ~가 아니다 The credit for that is not mine. // 그는 국민 복지에 ~가 많았다 He rendered distinguished service to [He contributed a great deal to / He did much for] the welfare of the people.

● **공로자** a person of merit; a person who has rendered distinguished service (to the state). **공로주** [경] a bonus stock.

공로(空路) an air route; an airway. ¶~로 by air[air plane / plane] // ~로 돌아오다 fly back (home / to Seoul) // ~로 수송하다 transport by airplane / fly (goods to New York) / ship by aircraft // ~로 …으로 fly for (France) // 그는 ~로 부산으로 향했다 He left for Busan by air[airplane]. // 책은 ~로 서울로 보내졌다 The books were flown to Seoul. // 그는 내일 ~로 귀가할 예정이다 He is to fly[flying] home tomorrow.

공론(公論) 1 [여론] public opinion; the consensus. ¶만사를 ~으로 결정하다 decide all affairs by public opinion // 국사를 ~으로 결정하다 refer all state affairs to public opinion. 2 [공평한 의논] an impartial opinion[view]; fair criticism; an unbiased [a disinterested] view.

공론(空論) an impractical theory; (무익한) a futile discussion; (근거 없는) an unfounded [a groundless] argument; (비현실적인) a desk[a paper] argument[theory]. ¶탁상~ a useless theory which looks good only on paper / an impractical argument / a desk theory. **공론하다** talk a desk theory.

● **공론가** an armchair philosopher [theorist]; a doctrinaire; a doctrinarian.

공룡(恐龍) [동] a dinosaur; a dinosaurian; a titanosaur.

공리(公利) public good[interest(s) / welfare]; the common[general] weal. ¶~를 도모하다 promote the public interest / serve for the common good.

공리(公理) 1 [수] an axiom; a maxim; a postulate. 2 [도리] a self-evident truth(자명한 이치).

공리(空理) an empty[impractical] theory; doctrinairism.

● **공리공론** an empty, impractical theory; doctrinarianism; academicism. ¶그는 ~에 치우치는 경향이 있다 He tends towards doctrinairism[abstract theories].

공리적(功利的) utilitarian. ¶~으로 in a utilitarian[practical] way // ~인 사람 a matter-of-fact fellow / a businesslike man // 사물을 ~으로 생각하다 take a utilitarian view of things / view things in a most practical way.

공리주의(功利主義) utilitarianism.

공립(公立) a public institution. ¶~의 public / communal / (지방자치제의) provincial / municipal.

● **공립 도서관** a public library. **공립학교** a public school; (시립의) a municipal school; (도립의) a provincial school.

공막(鞏膜) [생] the sclera (pl. ~s, -rae); the sclerotica.

공매(公賣) (a) public sale; (a) public auction; (미) (a) vendue. ¶~에 붙이다 put up (a thing) for[to] public sale / put up (a thing) to [(미) at] auction / sell by [(미) at] auction // 그 집은 ~에 붙여졌다 The house was put to public sale. **공매하다** sell in public; sell by [(미) at] auction.

● **공매 처분** (disposition by) public sale; (a) public sale of confiscated property; (a) tax sale; selling sale.

공매(도)(空賣渡) [증권] short sale; short selling. **공매(도)하다** sell short.

공명(功名) a great exploit[feat]; a glorious deed; distinguished services; [명예] credit; distinction; fame; renown; honor. ¶~을 세우다 perform a glorious deed / achieve a great exploit / distinguish oneself // 그는 그 전투에서 ~을 세웠다 He distinguished himself[He performed great feats] in the battle.

● **공명심** ambition; aspiration; love of fame. ¶~에 불타다 be ambitious / be eager [thirsty] for fame.

공명(共鳴) 1 [공감] sympathy; unison; [반향] a response; an echo. **공명하다** sympathize (with); echo (a person's sentiment); respond (to). ¶~에 공명하고 있다[공명하고 있지 않다] be in[out of] sympathy with … // 그는 나의 사상에 공명하였다 He responded to my thoughts. / He sympathized with my thoughts. // 급진주의에 공명하는 젊은이가 많다 Many young people are in sympathy with radicalism. / Many young people have radical sympathies. // 그는 나의 의견에 공명하지 않았다 He had no sympathy for my view. / He did not accept[go along with] my opinion.

2 [물] sympathy; sympathetic vibration; resonance; consonance; [음] resonance. ¶핵자기 ~ nuclear magnetic resonance // ~을 일으키다 cause[produce / set up] resonance. **공명하다** be resonant (with); resonate. ¶현들이 공명했다 The strings resonated with each other.

● **공명기** a resonator. **공명 상자** a resonance box[chamber]; a sound box. **공명자** a sympathizer. **공명판** (악기의) (sounding) board; a resonator. **공명 현상** (양자 역학적) mesomerism. **공명 효과** a resonance [mesomeric] effect.

공명선거(公明選擧) a clean[fair] election.

공명정대하다(公明正大─) fair (and square); just and upright; aboveboard; open (as the day); open[fair] and aboveboard; just and fair. ¶공명정대하게 fairly / justly / aboveboard / on the square // 공명정대한 태도 an

공명하다 impartial attitude // 공명한 조치를 취하다 adopt impartial measures // 공명정대하게 싸우다 play fair // 공명정대하게 행동하다 act fair and square // 그는 무슨 일에나 ～ He is always fair and upright in his dealings. / He is aboveboard in everything.

공명하다(公明-) fair; just; open; (open and) aboveboard; (fair and) square; straight. **공명히** fairly; justifiably.

공모(公募) (an appeal for) public subscription[contribution]; (주식 등의) public offering. **공모하다** invite public participation; (사람을) advertise for (a secretary); (기부금 등을) solicit (a contribution). ¶현상 소설을 ～ open a prize list of novels / invite the public to join in a prize contest for best stories // 그 대학에서는 수학 교수를 공모하고 있다 The university is accepting applications for the post of professor of mathematics. // 출연 희망자를 공모했다 We have advertised for people who want to take part. / We have invited applications from those who would like to perform. // 당사에서는 지금 주를 공모하고 있다 This firm is now offering stocks for public subscription[has placed its stock on the market].

공모(共謀) (a) conspiracy; collusion. **공모하다** conspire[plot] (with a person); conspire [plot] together; collude (with). ¶…와 공모하여 in conspiracy[collusion] with … // 그들은 공모하여 내 재산을 횡령했다 They conspired together to usurp my property. // 그는 동생과 공모하여 부친의 토지를 승낙을 받지도 않고 팔아 버렸다 He conspired with his brother and sold their father's land without his consent.

●**공모자** a conspirator; an accomplice (in a crime).

공목(空木) [인] (행간용) a reglet; a blind [filling] material; a lead; (자간용) a spacer.

공무(工務) engineering works.

●**공무국** the engineering works department; (신문사·출판사의) the printing bureau.

공무(公務) [공공 사무] public service; government affairs; official [public] business; [공무원 직무] official [public] duties. ¶～로 인한 부상 [질병] an injury [a disease] incurred in line of (public) duty // 다망하여 owing to the pressure of official business // ～를 집행하다 execute [exercise / perform / carry out] one's official duties // 그는 ～로 출장 중이다 He is away on official business. // ～와 사무를 구별해야 한다 You must discriminate between public and personal affairs. // ～ 외 출입 금지 (게시) Official business only.

●**공무원**(-집행직) the civil service; public service personnel; government employees; (개인) a public employee; an official; a civil servant; a servant of the state; a public service worker; a government official; (미) an officeholder. ¶국가 ～ a national civil servants // 기술 [기능]직 ～ a public official in technical [skill] post // 고급 ～ high-ranking public officials // 하급 ～ a petty official. **공무 집행** execution [performance] of one's official duties; exercise of one's office.

공문(公文) an official document. ⇨**공문서**(☞ 공문)

●**공문서** an official document [paper / note]; a state document; archives (보존된); a communiqué (외교의). **공문서식** formalities for official documents.

공문(孔門) the Confucian school. ¶～의 십철(十哲) the ten leading disciples of Confucius.

공문(空文) a dead letter; a (mere) scrap of paper. ¶～에 become [end as] a mere scrap of paper / prove a dead letter.

공물(供物) a Buddhist offering [oblation]. ¶～을 바치다 make an offering to Buddha.

공물(貢物) a tribute; a tributary payment. ¶～을 바치다 pay [offer] a tribute (to).

공미리 [동] a halfbeak.

공민(公民) a citizen; a burgess; a denizen; a freeman.

●**공민 교육** civic [citizenship] education. **공민권** citizenship; civil rights; franchise. **공민학교** a civil education school.

공박(攻駁) refutation; confutation; an attack; a charge; denunciation. **공박하다** refute; confute; argue against; attack (by argument); charge; denounce; denunciate. ¶남의 주장을 ～ refute a person's argument.

공밥(空-) food [a meal] one has not paid [worked] for; (놀고먹는) idle bread. ¶～을 먹다 [놀고먹다] eat idle bread / [식객이 되다] eat (a person's) salt / [공으로 얻다] take one's reward without working for it.

공방(攻防) offense and defense.

●**공방전** an offensive and defensive battle. ¶치열한 ～을 전개하다 launch a desperate offensive and defensive warfare.

공방(空房) 1 [빈방] a vacant room; an unoccupied room [chamber]. 2 [공규(空閨)] the bedchamber of a widow [a neglected wife].

공배수(公倍數) [수] a common multiple. ¶최소 ～ the least [lowest] common multiple (약 이 L.C.M., l.c.m.).

공백(空白) [책 등의 여백] a blank; blank [empty] space; [비움] a vacuum (pl. ～s, vacua); a void; a gap. ¶정치 [힘]의 ～ a political [power] vacuum // ～을 메우다 fill a gap (in) / fill up [in] a blank // ～이 생기다 leave [produce] a vacuum / make a blank (in one's life) // 부상한 5번 타자의 ～을 보결 선수로 메우다 fill in [plug] the gap left by the injury to the number five batter with a substitute player // 신청서의 ～에 써넣다 fill in the blanks on an application form // 7월 1일 이후 그의 일기는 ～인 채였다 After July 1, his diary remained blank. // 그는 전시 중의 ～을 독서로 메웠다 He read books to fill in [up] the blank [void] left by the war. // 그것에 관한 모든 일이 기억 속에서 ～으로 되어 있다 Everything concerning that has faded from my memory. // 수상의 갑작스런 죽음이 정국에 일시적 ～을 초래했다 The Premier's sudden death created [caused] a temporary vacuum in the political world.

공범(共犯) [공모하여 죄를 범함] complicity (with a person in a crime); conspiracy (공모). ¶～으로 체포되었다 He was caught as a party to the crime. // 그는 살인 ～의 혐의를 받고 있다 He is suspected of complicity in the murder.

●**공범자** an accomplice (with [of] a person in a crime); a confederate (in a crime); a partner (in a crime). ¶～로 기소하다 prosecute (a person) for a party to a crime. **공범죄** complicity (in a crime).

공법(工法) a method of construction. ¶예로부터의 ~으로 using a time-tested method of construction.
공법(公法) public law. ¶국제 ~ international law.
● **공법학** the study of public law.
공법인(公法人) a public judicial person; a public corporation.
공변되다 fair; just; square.
공변세포(孔邊細胞) 〔식〕 a guard cell.
공병(工兵) a military engineer; (영국 군인 속어) a sapper.
● **공병대** an engineer[engineering] corps [battalion]; (미) a construction battalion(약어 CB).
공보(公報) 〔정부·관청의 보고〕 an official report[communication]; an official bulletin [notice]; an official gazette(관보); a communiqué(외교상의); 〔홍보〕 (public) information. ¶선거 ~ an election bulletin // ~에 의하면 according to an official report / It is officially reported (that) // ~로 발표하다 publish in a gazette.
공복(空腹) 〔배 속이 빔〕 an empty stomach; 〔배고픔〕 hunger; being hungry. ¶~이다 [~을 느끼다] be[feel / go] hungry / (구어) be starving // ~에 술을 마시다 drink on an empty stomach // ~을 채우다 satisfy one's appetite (with some food) / gratify one's hunger (on) / 그는 물을 마셔서 간신히 ~을 면했다 He staved off his hunger with[by drinking] water.
공부(工夫) study; learning; work (on one's studies); scholarly activity. ¶시험을 ~ study for an examination / cramming for an examination // ~를 잘하다 be good at one's studies / learn nicely // ~를 잘 못하다 be poor at one's studies / be a poor student // ~를 게을리 하다 neglect one's studies // 너는 ~가 좀 부족하다 You don't study hard enough. // 그는 학생 시절에 별로 ~ 하지 않았다 He did not study hard when he was a student. // 그는 시험에 대비해서 벼락치기 ~를 하고 있다 He is cramming[(영국 구어) swotting] for the examination. // 나는 스미스 씨에게 ~를 배우기 시작했다 I began my studies with Mr. Smith. // 그는 학교에서 ~를 잘한다[못한다] He does well[poorly] at school. **공부하다** study; work at[on] (one's studies). ¶법률을 ~ study[(영) read] law // 시험에 대비하여 ~ study for an exam / 열심히 ~ study hard / work hard at one's studies / grind (away) (at examination subjects) / 밤늦도록 ~ study till late at night / stay[sit] up late over one's books // 지나치게 ~ overstudy / overwork oneself / study too hard // 공부하고 있다 be at one's studies [books] // 화가가 되려고 ~ study for a painter. ➔ **공부시키다** get (a boy) to study.
● **공부방** a study (room). **공붓벌레** a greasy grind; a grinder; (미국 속어) a dig; a swot.
공분(公憤) 〔민중의 분노〕 indignation[rage / resentment] of the general public; 〔의분〕 public indignation [rage / resentment]; righteous[moral] indignation. ¶~을 느끼다 be morally indignant (at / about it / with him) // ~을 일으키다 raise public indignation (over) // 세제 불공평에 ~을 느끼다 feel righteous indignation at[over / about] the unfair taxation system.

공분모(公分母) 〔수〕 a common denominator. ⇨ ═공통분모(⇦)공통)
공비(工費) the cost of construction; construction expenses. ⇨ ═공사비(⇦)공사(工事))
공비(公費) public expenditure; public expenses. ¶~로 at public expense // ~를 절감하다 reduce[cut down / curtail] public expenditure // ~를 낭비하다 waste[throw away] public money.
공비(公比) 〔수〕 a common ratio.
공비(共匪) 〔공산군〕 a Red [Communist] army; 〔공산 유격대〕 Red [Communist] guerrillas. ¶잔존 ~를 소탕하다 mop up [clean up / clear out] the remnants of Communist guerrillas.
공사(工事) construction; construction work; work of construction; engineering work. ¶건설 ~ construction works // 날림 ~ jelly building / flimsy [slipshod / shoddy] construction (work) // 도로 ~ road work [building / construction] // 철도 ~ railway [(미)] railroad] construction // 보수 ~ repair work // 토목 ~ engineering [public] works // ~중이다 be under [in course of] construction / be under way // 건설 ~를 시작하다 start construction work // ~를 감독하다 supervise work direct construction // ~는 이미 시작되었다 Ground has already been broken. // 교사는 지금 ~중이다 The schoolhouse is under construction. / The construction of[work on] the school building is now in progress. // ~ 중 (게시) Under construction [repair]. / Men working [at work]. / Road Work(s) Ahead. **공사하다** construct; do [execute] construction work (on); work (at); build.
● **공사비** the cost of construction; construction expenses [cost]. **공사 입찰** a bid for construction work.
공사(公私) 〔공적인 일과 사적인 일〕 public and private matters; official and personal affairs; 〔사회와 개인〕 society and individual; 〔관청과 민간〕 government and people. ¶~ 모두 both in public and private / both officially and privately // ~를 혼동하다 mix up public and private matters / fail to draw a line between official and personal matters [affairs] // ~를 구별하다 draw the [a] line between public life and private one // 나는 ~ 간에 바쁜 나날을 보내고 있습니다 I have been busy both officially and privately.
공사(公事) public service; official duties. ⇨ ═공무(公務)
공사(公使) a (diplomatic) minister. ¶각국 ~ diplomatic representatives / the heads of foreign missions // 대리 ~ (프) a chargé d'affaires (ad interim) (pl. chargés d'affaires) // 전권 ~ an envoy extraordinary (and minister plenipotentiary).
● **공사관** a legation. **공사관원** 〔집합적〕 the staff [personnel] of a legation; a legation staff; (한 사람) a legation attaché; a member of a legation staff.
공사(公社) a public corporation. ¶한국 전력 ~ the Korea Electric Power Corporation // 대한 주택 ~ the Korea Housing Corporation.
공사채(公社債) 〔공채와 사채〕 bonds; public and corporate bonds; 〔공사의 채권〕 public corporation bonds.

공산

●공사채 투자 신탁 a bond investment trust.

공산(公算) probability; likelihood; a (good) chance. ¶…할 ~이 크다 There is a strong [high] probability that … // 성공할 ~이 크다 stand a fair[good] chance of success / bid fair to succeed // 성공할 ~이 적다 have a poor[slim] chance of success // 내일은 폭풍우가 불 ~이 크다 There is a good chance that there will be a storm tomorrow. // 자이언츠가 우승할 ~이 크다 The chance are that the Giants will win the pennant. // 보수당이 분열할 ~이 커졌다 The likelihood[probability] of a split in the conservative party has increased. / A split in the conservative party seems increasingly likely.

공산(共產) common property; community of property; [공산주의] communism.
●공산 국가 a Communist country. 공산군 the Communist army[force]; the Red Army. 공산권 the Communist bloc[orbit]. 공산당 the Communist Party(약어 CP); the Communists. 공산당원 a Communist; a member of the Communist Party; a commie. 공산주의 communism. ¶~의[적인] communist(ic) // ~에 물든 사람 a pink. 공산주의자 a communist. 공산 진영 the Communist camp. 공산화 communization. ¶~를 막다 defend[safeguard] (a country) against Communists.

공산명월(空山明月) 1 [산에 외로이 비치는 밝은 달] the bright moon shining on a lone mountain. 2 [대머리] a bald head.

공산품(工產品) industrial products.

공상 (an) imagination; a daydream; a fantasy; fancy. ¶~적인 imaginary / fanciful / visionary // 엉뚱한 ~ a wild fancy // ~적인 이야기 a fanciful tale // ~에 잠기다 indulge in[be lost in] (a) reverie / be given to daydreaming // 그는 ~에 잠겨 있다 He is daydreaming. 공상하다 imagine; dream; daydream. ¶마음껏 ~ give full play to one's fancy // 나는 미래의 나 자신을 공상해 보았다 I drew an imaginary picture of what I would [(영) should] be[I imagined myself] in the future. // 그녀는 자기가 영화 스타라고 공상해 보았다 She fancied[imagined] herself as a movie star.
●공상가 a visionary; a dreamer; a daydreamer; a Utopian. 공상 과학 소설 a science fiction novel; a SF novel. 공상 과학 영화 a science fiction film.

공생(共生) [생] symbiosis; commensalism. [광] paragenesis. 공생하다 live together[in symbiosis]; symbiose.
●공생체 / 공생 생물 a symbiont; a commensal.

공서 양속(公序良俗) public order and standards of decency.

공석(公席) [공적인 모임] (the presence of) the public; the meeting; [공무 보는 자리] a place where public affairs are attended to. ¶~에서 in public[company] / before[in the presence of] others.

공석(空席) [빈 좌석] a vacant[an unoccupied] seat; (지위 등의) a vacancy; a vacant post. ¶~을 메우다 fill (up) a vacancy // 그가 사임하여 부지점장 자리가 ~이 되었다 As he resigned, the post of assistant manager fell vacant. // 그 자리는 ~인 채로 있다 The post remains[is still] vacant.

공선(公選) [공중 선거] public election; election by popular vote; official selection; [공명 선거] a fair election. 공선하다 elect by popular vote; select officially. ¶위원은 모든 관계자가 공선한다 The committee members are elected by a vote of all concerned.

공설(公設) ¶~의 public / municipal / communal.
●공설 기관 a public institution. 공설 시장 a public[municipal] market. 공설 운동장 a public stadium.

공성(攻城) a siege. 공성하다 siege; besiege.

공세(攻勢) an offensive (movement); the offensive; the aggressive; aggression. ¶평화[외교] ~ a peace[diplomatic] offensive // 노동 ~ a labor offensive // 테러 ~ a wave of terror[terrorism] / 선전 ~ a propaganda offensive // ~의[적인] offensive / aggressive / ~로 전환하다 change over to the offensive // ~를 취하다 take[assume] the offensive / launch[open] an offensive (movement) (against) // 질문 ~를 하다 torment (a person) with inquiries / assail (a person) with questions // ~로 나왔다 The army took the offensive. / The army launched an offensive (operation). // 그의 팀은 후반전에 들어서 ~를 취했다 His team rallied and took offensive in the second half. // 그는 처음부터 끝까지 ~로 나왔다 He was on the offensive[kept his opponent on the defensive] from beginning to end.

공소(公訴) [법] arraignment; prosecution; accusation; public action; a criminal action. ¶~를 제기하다 institute a public action / prosecute a case // ~를 기각[철회]하다 dismiss[withdraw] a public action. 공소하다 arraign; prosecute; accuse; impeach.
●공소권 authority[power] of prosecution; authority to indict. 공소 사실 a count; a charge. 공소 유지 institution and support of a public action; maintenance of a public action. 공소장 a written arraignment.

공손하다(恭遜-) polite; civil; courteous. ¶공손한 태도로 in a polite attitude / with a respectful attitude / in a reverential manner // 공손한 말을 쓰다 use decent words[polite language] // 그는 누구에게나 ~ He is polite[courteous] to everybody. 공손히 politely; courteously; nicely; civilly. ¶~ 대하다 treat (a person) with courtesy[respect / civility] // ~ 말하다[절하다] speak[bow / salute] politely / make a low[deep / polite] bow // 그 학생은 교장 선생님께 ~ 절을 했다 The student made a respectful[deep] bow to the principal.

공수(攻守) offense and defense; (야구의) batting and fielding. ¶그 팀은 ~가 다 강하다 The team is powerful enough both in batting and fielding[offensively and defensively].
●공수 동맹 an offensive and defensive alliance.

공수(空輸) [항공 수송] air transport[transportation]; transportation by air; airlift; air service. ¶대규모 ~ an airlift on a large scale / a massive airlift // ~ 가능의 air-transportable. 공수하다 transport[carry] by air; fly (goods); airlift (a corps). ¶우편물을 ~ carry[send] mail by air // 신선한 식품을 ~ transport[carry] perishables by air // 화물을

뉴욕으로 ~ fly goods to New York // 정예 부대를 전방으로 공수했다 The crack troops were airlifted to the front.
● 공수 부대 an airborne troops; an airlift troop; (수송의) an air transport corps(약어 A.T.C.). 공수 작전 an airborne [airlift] operation. 공수 화물 air freight; (미) airlift (goods); air cargo.

공수래공수거(空手來空手去) "come empty, return empty"; the vanity of life.

공수병(恐水病) [의] hydrophobia.

공수표(空手票) (상업에서) a bad check [(영) cheque]; a kite; a fictitious bill; an accommodation bill of exchange; [빈말] an empty promise. ¶~를 발행하다 [떼다] fly a kite / [비유] give [make] an empty promise // ~로 끝나다 end in an empty pledge / prove to be an empty promise // 그의 약속은 ~가 되었다 His promise proved to be worthless [empty].

공순하다(恭順-) submissive; gentle; meek; docile. **공순히** submissively; meekly; gently; docilely.

공술(空-) free liquor; a gratis drink.
공술(供述) a statement; a deposition. ⇨진술
● 공술서 a (written) statement. ⇨진술서(⇨진술)

공술인(供述人) (공청회 등의) a speaker [witness] at a public hearing.

공습(空襲) an air raid [attack]; an aerial strike. ¶~으로 다 타서 없어지た be burnt out in an air raid / be bombed out // ~을 받다 undergo [suffer] an air raid // 그 도시에 대한 ~으로 5만 명이 소사하였다 Fifty thousand people were burned out in the air raid on that city. // 미군 폭격기는 일본에 대해 새벽 ~을 감행하였다 American bombers made a dawn strike on Japan. **공습하다** make an air raid (on); attack (a city) from the air.
● 공습경보 an air-raid alarm [warning / alert]. ¶~를 발하다 give an air-raid warning / sound an air-raid alarm [alert] // ~를 해제하다 sound the "all clear" [a white alert].

공시(公示) a public announcement [notice]; an official notice. ¶국회의원 선거 ~의 proclamation of a general election for the National Assembly // 왕의 국장은 6월 1일 거행한다는 ~가 있었다 It has been publicly [officially] announced that the state funeral for the king will be held on the first of June. **공시하다** make public; publish; announce publicly; make known to the public. ¶운임과 요금을 ~ publish the rates and charges.
● 공시가 the declared value. 공시 송달(-送達) [법] conveyance by public announcement. 공시 최고 a public summons.

공식(公式) 1 [수] a formula (*pl.* ~s, -lae). ¶~으로 나타내다 express in a formula / formulate. 2 [의식·정식] formality; an official ceremony. ¶~의 state / formal / official // ~으로 formally / officially // ~으로 환영을 받다 be officially feted (by) // 아직 ~ 통고를 받은 바 없다 I have not received any official notice yet.
● 공식 경기 / 공식 시합 (야구의) a regulation match; (권투의) a title match. 공식 발표 an official announcement. ¶그의 은퇴는 아직 ~가 되지 않았다 His retirement has not been officially announced yet. 공식 방문 a formal [an official] visit; (국가 원수의) a state visit. 공식 성명 an official statement (on); (신문발표의) a handout. 공식주의 formalism. 공식화 formulation.

공식적(公式的) public; open; official. ¶~으로나 비~으로나 both openly and secretly / both in public and private // ~인 조치를 취하다 take open measures // ~으로는 그렇게 발표되었다 It is officially so announced. / It is known that way ostensibly.

공신력(公信力) public trust (in banking institutions). ¶~을 잃다 lose public confidence.

공신(功臣) a worthy [meritorious] retainer; a vassal of merit; a retainer who has rendered distinguished services. ¶~을 포상하다 reward deserving retainers.

공안(公安) public peace (and order); public safety [security]. ¶~을 유지하다 maintain peace and order // ~을 해치다 disturb the public peace.
● 공안 경찰 a public peace police; a security police. 공안 사범 a public safety [security] offender.

공액(共軛) ➡켤레

공약(公約) a pledge; a public promise [commitment]; (선거의) an election [a campaign] promise. ¶정당의 ~ the public commitment of a party // ~을 실행하다 implement [follow through on / make good (on)] one's campaign promises // ~을 재확인하다 reaffirm (the U.S.) commitment to (Korea).
공약하다 pledge [commit] oneself (to). ¶정책을 ~ commit oneself to a policy // 그는 감세를 공약했다 He pledged to reduce taxes. / He pledged himself to a tax reduction.

공약수(公約數) [수] a common measure [divisor]. ¶최대 ~ the greatest common measure(약어 G.C.M).

공양(供養) 1 (어른에 대한) providing (one's elders) with food. **공양하다** provide (one's elders) with food. 2 [불공] a service for the dead; a memorial service (for / in honor of); a mass (for). **공양하다** hold [say] a mass (for); have a mass read for the repose of (a person's) soul. 3 [승려가 음식을 먹음] eating food. **공양하다** eat food.
● 공양미 consecrated rice (offered to the Buddha). 공양주 a person who gives alms to Buddhist temple.

공양드리다(供養-) offer food to the Buddha.

공언(公言) declaration; profession; avowal. **공언하다** declare openly; profess; proclaim; tell the world. ¶그는 애국자라고 공언했다 He avowed himself (to be) a patriot. // 당신은 그래도 휴머니스트라고 공언할 수 있는가 Can you still claim to be a humanist? / Can you still avow [profess] yourself (to be) a humanist? // 나는 그 사건과는 아무런 관계가 없음을 공언할 수 있다 I can publicly declare that I have no connection whatever with that affair. // 그는 양심의 가책을 받을 만한 일이 없다고 공언하였다 He declared openly that he had a clear conscience.

공업(工業) (an) industry; manufacturing industry; (집합적) the industries. ¶주요 ~ key industries // 중 [경] ~ heavy [light] industry // 가내 ~ the household industry / 기계 ~ machine industry // ~의 industrial / technical / technological // ~용으로 industrial use // ~을 진흥시키다 promote the industries // ~의 발전을 촉진하다 promote the development of industry.
● 공업가 an industrialist; a manufacturer.

공업계 industrial circles; the industrial world. 공업 고등학교 a technical high school. 공업국 an industrial nation. 공업 규격 industrial standard. 공업 단지 an industrial complex. ¶울산 ~ the Ulsan industrial complex∥임해 ~ a coastal industrial complex. 공업 도시 an industrial [a manufacturing] city; a factory town. 공업 약품 industrial chemicals. 공업용수 industrial water. 공업 제품 industrial goods [products]. 공업 지대 an industrial area [district]. 공업 폐수 industrial effluent [waste water]. 공업화 industrialization.

공여(供與) giving; a grant. 공여하다 give; grant; make a grant (of). ¶차관을 ~ extend credit (to). →¶이 나라는 모 대국으로부터 무기를 공여받고 있다 This country is supplied with weapons by a certain big power.

공역(公役) public service. ¶~에 복무하다 do [undergo] public service.

공역(共譯) joint translation. 공역하다 translate (a book) jointly [in collaboration] (with). ¶A와 B가 공역한 translated by A and B∥이 책은 한 교수와 서 교수가 공역하였다 This book was translated (jointly) [is a joint translation] by professors Han and Seo.

공연(公演) a public performance. ¶낮 ~ a matinee / an afternoon performance∥자선 ~ a charity performance [show]∥지방 ~ a road [traveling] show∥첫 ~ the first public performance∥추모 ~ a memorial performance∥장기 ~ a long run∥하룻밤만의 ~ (미) a one-night stand∥~ 중인「햄릿」 "Hamlet" on the stage∥지금까지의 최장 브로드웨이 ~ 기록 the longest Broadway run record in show history∥두 번째의 ~ a second series of presentation. 공연하다 perform; play; stage; present. ¶하루에 2번 공연한다 There are two performances a day. / They give two shows a day.∥일행은 하루 3회 공연했다 The troupe performed [put on the show] three times a day. →그 연극은 국립 극장에서 공연된다 The play will be presented [is on] at the National Theater.

공연(共演) coacting; co-starring. ¶A 양과 B 씨 ~의 영화 a film co-starred by Miss A and Mr. B∥폴 뉴만과 로버트 레드퍼드 ~의 영화 a film co-starring [jointly featuring] Paul Newman and Robert Redford. 공연하다 costar (in a film); play together (in a film); do a play with (another); coact.

● 공연자 a coactor; a co-star; fellow members of the cast.

공연하다(空然-) useless; futile; unavailing; needless; unnecessary; fruitless; ineffectual; empty. ¶공연한 노력 a fruitless effort∥공연한 걱정 an idle fear∥공연한 걸음을 하다 go on a bootless errand / make a visit (on a person) in vain [to no purpose]∥그에게 친절을 베풀어 봤자 공연한 짓이다 All kindness is wasted [lost / thrown away] upon him. 공연히 to no purpose; needlessly; uselessly; without reason; fruitlessly; in vain. ¶~ 우쭐대다 be vainly pretentious∥~ 소란을 피우다 make a great fuss about nothing / (구어) make waves (over) / make much ado about nothing∥~ 서두르다 make needless haste ∥~ 애만 썼다 We've labored in vain.∥우리는 ~ 기적이 일어나기를 기다렸던 것이다 We were waiting in vain for a miracle to take place.

공염불(空念佛) a fair but an empty phrase; cant. ¶~로 끝나기 쉬운 선거 공약 an empty election promise∥~로 그치다 end in an empty talk∥~을 외다 chant empty prayers.

공영(公營) public management. ¶~의 public (-managed) / (시영의) municipal. 공영하다 place [bring] (an undertaking) under public [municipal] management.

● 공영 주택 a public-financed house; a house built under a public housing project.

공영(共榮) mutual prosperity; co-prosperity. ¶공존 ~ coexistence and co-prosperity.

공영(共營) joint management [operation].

● 공영화 collectivization.

공예(工藝) industrial arts; technology. ¶~의 industrial / technological∥미술 ~ arts and crafts.

● 공예가 a craftsman; an industrial artist. 공예 미술 applied fine arts. 공예품 an industrial art object; a handicraft objects of craftwork [applied arts]; a craftwork. 공예 학교 a polytechnic (school); a technological school.

공용(公用) [공무] official [public / government] business [duty]; [공공의 비용] public expense; [공공용] (for) public use; public service. ¶~으로 on official business [duty] ∥ ~의 public / official∥그는 ~으로 해외 출장 중이다 He is overseas now on official [government] business. 공용하다 use publicly.

● 공용물 objects for public use. 공용어 [관청용어] official language [terminology]; (국제회의 등의) an official language (of an international conference). 공용지 land for public use.

공용(共用) common [joint] use. ¶~의 부엌 a kitchen for common use∥이 쓰레기 소각장은 이웃 사람들의 ~이다 This incinerator is for neighborhood use. 공용하다 use (something) in common; share (a thing) with (another). ¶나는 누이동생과 아파트를 공용하고 있다 I share an apartment with my younger sister.

● 공용물 public property.

공원(工員) a factory worker [hand]; machine operator; an industrial worker. ¶~ 모집: 경험 유무 불문 Wanted; machine operators, both experienced and inexperienced.

공원(公園) a park; a public garden; [작은 공원] (영) a square. ¶국립 ~ a national park ∥서울 대 ~ Seoul Grand Park∥옥상 ~ a roof garden∥자연 ~ a wilderness park / a natural park∥~을 만들다 lay out a park / provide a park (for a city)∥언덕을 허물고 작은 이 만들어졌다 The hill was laid out for [as] a small park.

공유(公有) public ownership [property]. ¶~의 public / public (ly)-owned∥~의 건물 buildings forming public property / buildings for common use.

● 공유 재산 public assets [property]. 공유지 public [common] land; land for common use; public domain; (영국사) folkland.

공유(共有) joint [common] ownership; co-ownership; community. ¶~의 common / jointly owned∥재산의 ~ community of property. 공유하다 have [possess] a thing jointly; hold (something) in common. ¶재산

을 ~ communize property // 나는 이 집을 아내와 공유하고 있다 I own this house jointly [in common] with my wife. // 이 밭은 양가가 공유하고 있다 This field belongs to the two families.
● **공유 결합** [화] a covalent bond. **공유물** common property. **공유 재산** common property; property in co-ownership. **공유지** a common (land).

공으로(空-) free (of charge); for nothing. ¶~얻다[일하다] get[work] for nothing.

공의(公醫) a community doctor[physician].

공이 a pestle; a pounder; (총의) a firing pin. ¶~로 치다 pound (rice) with a pestle / crush (grains) with a pounder.

공이치기 the hammer (of a rifle); a gunlock; a cock. ¶총의 ~를 당기다 cock a gun / draw back the hammer of one's gun.

공익(公益) public[common] benefit; common weal. ¶~을 위하여 in the interest[cause] of the public / for the public good // ~을 도모하다 promote the public interest / work for the public good // ~을 해치다 be prejudicial [detrimental] to the public interest // ~을 위해 힘쓰다 work for the benefit[good] of the public // 개인의 이익보다 ~을 앞세우다 give priority to the public interest over individual interests.
● **공익 단체** a public corporation. **공익 법인** a nonprofit foundation; a juridical person for the public good[benefit / welfare] ; a public service corporation. **공익사업** public utilities[works]; an enterprise for the public good. **공익 우선** public interest first. **공익 재단** a public utility foundation.

공익(共益) public good; common benefit [interest]. ¶~을 위하여 for the public good / in the interest of the public.

공인(公人) [사회를 위하여 일하는 사람] a public person[character / figure]; [공직에 있는 사람] a governmental official; (미) an officeholder. ¶~으로서의 생활 one's public life // 신문 기자는 ~이다 Newsmen are public, not private, writers.

공인(公認) official recognition[approval]; authorization. ¶~의 officially recognized / authorized / official / officially-adopted // 비 ~의 unofficial / unauthorized / unrecognized // ~을 받다 gain official approval // 그는 자유당에서 후보자로서 ~을 받고 있다 As a candidate he has the endorsement of the Liberal Party. // 이 기록은 미~이다 We are awaiting certification of this record. **공인하다** recognize[approve] officially; give (a person) official recognition; authorize; (법률로) legalize. ¶후보자를 ~ officially adopt a candidate / nominate a candidate. →¶이것은 세계 기록으로서 아직 공인되어 있지 않다 This has not yet been officially recognized as the world record. // 그는 노동당의 후보로서 공인되어 있다 He [His candidacy] has the endorsement of the Labor Party. / He has been nominated as the candidate of the Labor Party.
● **공인 기록** official record. **공인 중개사** a licensed real estate agent. **공인 회계사** (미) a certified public accountant (약어 CPA); (영) a chartered accountant (약어 C.A.).

공일(空-) [거저하는 일] free service; work for nothing; a job in vain; [헛수고] lost labor. ¶이것은 ~이나 마찬가지다 This will bring you practically nothing (for your service).

공일(空日) [노는 날] a holiday; a red-letter day; [비번일] a day off; [일요일] Sunday.

공임(工賃) a wage; wages; pay; the charge for one's work. ¶~을 내리다[줄이다] cut down [reduce] the wages // ~을 올리다 raise [increase] the wages // 싼 ~으로 일하다 work at low wages // ~이 비싸서 수지가 맞지 않는다 As labor is very expensive, the work will not pay.

공자(公子) a young nobleman; a young[little] prince.

공작(工作) 1 [기계·기물의 제작] construction; building; engineering work; [수공] handicraft; handiwork. **공작하다** construct; build; make. 2 [일을 꾸밈] maneuvering; a move; activities; operations. ¶이면 ~ maneuvering [(구어) pulling the wires] behind the scenes // 정치 ~ political maneuvering // 지하 ~ underground activities // 선전 ~ propaganda maneuvers // 그들의 화평 ~이 주효했다 Their work for peace proved effective. **공작하다** maneuver; scheme. ¶배후에서 ~ maneuver behind the scenes // 평화 ~ make a peace move.
● **공작금** operational funds. **공작 기계** a machine tool. **공작대**(-隊) a group of underground activists. **공작대**(-臺) a work-table. **공작실** a workshop. **공작원** an espionage operator; an agent.

공작(孔雀) [동] a peacock (수컷); a peahen (암컷); a peafowl; a pea-chick (새끼 공작). ¶~같은 peackokish // 꽁지를 편 ~ a peacock in his pride / a peacock with his tail spread [expanded] // ~이 날개를 펴고 있다 The peacock is displaying his tail [spreading his tail feathers].
● **공작석** [광] malachite.

공작(公爵) a prince; (영) a duke. ¶웰링턴 ~ the Duke of Wellington // ~의 ducal // ~을 제수받다 be created prince.
● **공작 부인** a princess; (영) a duchess.

공장(工匠) a craftsman; an artisan.

공장(工場) a factory; a plant; a mill; a works; a manufactory. ¶기계 ~ a machine shop // 조립 ~ an assembly plant // 철 ~ an iron-works // 하청 ~ an affiliated work shop / a supplier // 자동차 ~ a car factory / an auto(mobile) plant // 방적 ~ a spinning mill / a cotton mill // ~에서 일하다 work at a factory // ~을 폐쇄하다 close down a factory / lock out (파업으로) // ~에 다니다 work in a factory / be a factory worker.
● **공장 감독** a factory superintendent; (현장의) a foreman of machine operators; a labor foreman; a supervisor. **공장 관리** factory management[control]. **공장도 가격** an ex-factory price. **공장 부지** a plant site. **공장장** a plant manager. **공장주** the owner of a factory; a mill owner; a factory proprietor and operator. **공장 지대** an industrial zone [area]. **공장 폐쇄** closure of a factory; a lockout. **공장 폐수** industrial sewage [waste water]; trade waste. ¶~ 처리 장치 a waste water disposal plant // (강 등이) ~로 오염되다 be polluted with industrial sewage // 그들은 ~를 강에 흘려보냈다 They discharged liquid wastes from the factory into the river.

공저 (共著) a joint work; collaboration; coauthorship. ¶~로 in collaboration with / under joint authorship with∥매켄지 씨와의 ~ a book written jointly [in collaboration] with Mr. Mackenzie.
● 공저자 a coauthor; a joint author.

공적 (公的) public; official; formal. ¶~으로 publicly / officially∥~ 성격을 띠고 있다 be of [have] public character∥~으로 책임을 지다 publicly answer (for) / be publicly answerable (for)∥그것은 아직 ~으로 발표된 것이 아니다 It is not officially announced yet.∥그는 ~ 입장에서 그 파티에 참석했다 He attended the party in an official capacity.∥그는 ~ 사업에 종사하고 있다 He is working on a public project.∥그런 ~인 장소에서 칭찬을 받으리라고는 전혀 생각을 못했다 I had never thought I would be praised on such a formal occasion.

공적 (公敵) a public [common] enemy.

공적 (功績) a meritorious deed; achievement(s); service(s); merit(s); an exploit. ¶과학상의 ~ scientific achievements∥~ 있는 사람 a man of merit∥~을 기념하여 in commemoration of a person's services∥~을 세우다 perform great services (in society) / render distinguished services (in war / to the country)∥자기의 ~이라고 주장하다 claim credit∥그는 세계 평화를 위하여 큰 ~을 세웠다 He rendered remarkable services to the cause of world peace.∥회사는 그의 ~을 인정하여 승진시켰다 The company promoted him in recognition of his achievements [services].∥그것은 그의 ~이다 The credit rests with him.∥그것은 내 ~이 아니다 The credit for that is not mine.

공전 (工錢) a wage; wages; pay.

공전 (公轉) [천] revolution (of the earth around the sun). ¶지구의 ~과 자전 the earth's revolution and rotation∥지구의 ~은 1년 걸린다 The revolution of the earth around the sun takes a year.∥지구는 자전과 ~을 한다 The earth revolves on its own axis and around [( )] round] the sun. **공전하다** revolve (round the sun); move around the sun.
● 공전 운동 orbital motion. 공전 주기 the cycle of revolution round the sun.

공전 (空前) unprecedentedness. ¶~의 unprecedented / unexampled / unheard-of / unparalleled / record-breaking / epoch-making∥~의 기록 an all-time record∥~의 대성공 a phenomenal success∥전람회는 ~의 성황이었다 The exhibition was an unprecedented [unparalleled] success.∥벼농사는 ~의 풍작이었다 We had a record [record-breaking] rice crop.∥물가는 ~의 오름세를 보였다 The prices have hit an all-time high.

공전 (空電) atmospheric electricity. ⇨ 공중 전기 (⇨공중 (空中))

공전 (空轉) 1 (자동차의) skidding; (엔진의) racing. **공전하다** skid; (기계 등이) race; run idle. → ¶공전시키다 race (an engine)∥그는 차의 엔진을 공전시켰다 He raced the engine of his car. 2 (사업 등의) ineffective business activity; fruitless effort. ¶토론은 ~을 거듭할 뿐 아무런 진전을 보지 못했다 The argument went round and round in circles and did not get anywhere. **공전하다** prove [turn out] ineffective; make a poor show (in business); (토론이) run round in circles. ¶국회는 1주일 동안 공전하였다 The National Assembly remained idle for a whole week.

공정 (工程) [진척 정도] the progress of the work; construction progress; [과정] a manufacturing process; [공률] [물] power. ¶생산 ~ a manufacturing process∥~을 2분의 1 단축하다 reduce [shorten] the length of the process by (one) half∥~의 반이 끝났다 We are halfway through the work.∥~은 순조롭다 The work is progressing [going] satisfactorily [smoothly].∥~은 약 80%가 끝났다 The work is about 80 percent finished.∥완성까지 아직 4개의 ~이 남아 있다 It has to go through four more processes before it is finished.
● 공정 관리 process [production] control. 공정표 progress schedule; time schedule of work.

공정 (公正) justice; impartiality; fairness; equity. ¶~을 기하기 위해서 in order to do justice (to) / to ensure fairness (in)∥남에게 완전히 ~을 결여하고 있다 be far from their part on a person∥~을 기하기 위해 기명 투표를 했다 We had an open vote in order to ensure fairness. **공정하다** just; fair; equitable; righteous; impartial. ¶공정한 조치 a fair measure∥공정한 처사 a fair [square] deal∥공정한 평가로 사들이다 purchase at a fair valuation∥나는 공정한 취급을 받지 못하고 있다 I am not getting justice.∥재판은 공정했다 The trial was fair.∥그녀는 공정한 의견을 가지고 있다 She is impartial [unbiased] in her opinions.∥그의 판단은 공정하지 못하다 He does not judge fairly. / He makes partial judgement. **공정히** justly; fairly; on the square. ¶모든 사람에게 ~ 대하다 treat all men justly [with justice]∥그들이 ~ 행동한다고 믿어도 될까 Can we trust them to act on the square?
● 공정 가격 a fair price. 공정 거래 위원회 the Korea Fair Trade Commission. 공정 증서 a notarial [an authentic] deed; an attested [authentic] document.

공정 (公定) [관형어적] official; officially fixed. **공정하다** decide publicly; fix (a price) officially. ¶물가를 ~ fix prices officially.
● 공정 가격 an official price [rate]; an officially fixed price; (최고의) a ceiling (price). ¶~에 팔다 [사다] sell [buy] (articles) at official [legal] prices [rates]. 공정 시세 an official quotation; (최고의) a ceiling quotation; a (price) ceiling. 공정 이율 the official discount rate; the bank rate. 공정 환율 an official exchange rate.

공제 (共濟) mutual aid [benefit]. **공제하다** aid [help] each other.
● 공제 사업 a mutual-aid project. 공제 조합 a cooperative; (미) a benefit [mutual aid] society [association]; 《영》 a friendly society.

공제 (控除) subtraction; deduction. ¶소득세 ~ an income tax deduction∥근로소득 ~ an earned income credit [allowance]∥기초 ~ a basic deduction∥특별 ~ a special deduction. **공제하다** subtract; deduct; take away [off]; cut off. ¶공제할 수 있는 deductible (expenses)∥세금·경비를 공제한 순수입 a net income / take-home pay∥수입

에서 지출을 공제한 것이 이익이다 The profit is determined by deducting[subtracting] expenses from revenues.// 그중에서 영업비를 공제하면 잔금 25,000원이 된다 The sum less [minus] the operating expenses stands at 25,000 won.// 교제비를 경비로 공제했다 He deducted entertainment expenses as a necessary expenditure. →¶집세는 내 봉급에서 공제된다 The rent is deducted from my salary[pay].// 화재 보험료는 과세 소득에서 공제된다 The fire insurance premium is deducted from taxed income.// 우리는 매월 봉급에서 소득세가 공제되고 있다 Our income tax is deducted from our salary every month.
● **공제액** an amount deducted; a deduction (from); an abatement. ¶소득 ~ the amount deducted from one's income.

공조(共助) mutual assistance; cooperation. **공조하다** mutually assist; cooperate; help [aid] one another.

공존(共存) coexistence. ¶소극적 ~ negative coexistence// 평화 ~ peaceful coexistence. **공존하다** coexist; live together; live and let live. ¶두 종파가 공존하기는 어려웠다 It was difficult for the two sects to coexist[live together].
● **공존공영** prosperous coexistence; coexistence and co-prosperity; mutual prosperity in papers notarized.

공주(公主) a (royal) princess.
공준(公準) [수][논] a postulate.
공중(公衆) the public. ¶~의 public / common// ~ 앞에서 in public / in the public eye// ~을 위하여 for the general good// ~의 이익 the public interest// ~에게 개방되다 be opened to the public// ~의 방해가 되다 be a common nuisance// ~ 앞에서 연설하다 speak in public// ~의 편익을 도모하다 work for the public benefit// 그는 ~을 위해 헌신했다 He devoted himself to the good[He served the cause] of the public.
● **공중도덕** public morality[morals]. ¶~을 지키다 take care not to trouble others / act the gentleman in public / be a gentleman in public. **공중목욕탕** a public bath house. **공중변소** a public lavatory[toilet]; a public [street] latrine; a public convenience; (미) a (public) comfort station; a comfort room. **공중위생** public health; public hygiene; public sanitation. **공중전화** a public telephone; a pay phone; a pay telephone. (▶ 미국의 공중전화는 우리나라의 것과는 달리 고유의 전화번호가 있어 걸려 오는 전화를 받을 수도 있음) ¶~ 《게시》 Public Telephone. / 《영》 Call Box.

공중(空中) the air; the sky; midair; space. ¶~의 aerial / in the air// ~에(서) in the air [sky] / in midair / in space// ~을 날다 fly in the air// ~으로 사라지다 disappear into space[thin air]// ~ 높이 떠오르다 soar up to the sky / soar skyward// ~에 매달리다 hang[be suspended] in midair / dangle in space// ~으로 던져 올리다 toss up in the air// 그 성은 조명을 받아 ~에 떠 있는 것처럼 보였다 Floodlit, the castle looked as if it were floating in midair.// 꽃불이 ~으로 날아 올라갔다 Fireworks shot (up) into the air.// 연이 ~에 높이 떠 있었다 A kite was flying high in the sky.// 마치 ~를 걸어가는 기분이었다 I felt as though I were walking in the air.// 그 계획은 ~에 떠 있다 The plan is up in the air[pending].
● **공중 곡예** (서커스의) an aerialist act; an aerial stunt performance; [곡예 비행] aerobatics; aerial acrobatics; stunt flying. **공중 급유** air-to-air refueling; inflight [aerial] refueling. **공중 납치** a skyjack; hijacking of an airplane; skyjacking. ¶~범 a skyjacker / a hijacker. **공중누각** a castle in the air; an air[a cloud] castle; a dream. ¶~을 그리다 [짓다] build castles in the air / build air castles. **공중 보급** air-to-air refueling; [항공기에 의한 물품 보급] an airlift. **공중분해** disintegration in midair; a midair disintegration. ¶비행기가 ~ 했다 The airplane fell [broke] apart in midair. **공중선**(−線) an antenna. ⇨°안테나 **공중 수송** air transportation. ⇨°항공 수송(⇨항공) **공중 어뢰** an aerial torpedo (*pl.* ~es). **공중 전기** atmospheric electricity. **공중 정찰** air[aerial] reconnaissance[scout / patrol]. **공중제비** a somersault; a somerset; a tumble. ¶~을 하다 turn[make] a somersault. **공중 질소** atmospheric nitrogen. **공중 투하** airdrop. **공중활주** gliding (in the air); volplane.

공증(公證) a notarial act; authentication; official endorsement. **공증하다** notarize; authenticate; attest; exemplify. ¶서류를 ~ have papers notarized.
● **공증료** notarial fees[charges]. **공증인** a notary public(약어 N.P.); a notary.

공지(公知) common[universal] knowledge. ¶~ known to all[everybody] / universally [widely / well] known //···은 ~의 사실이다 It is (a matter of) common knowledge that ....
● **공지 사항** the (items of) official announcement.

공지(空地) vacant land; (구획한) an empty [(미)] unoccupied] lot; a vacant lot.

공직(公職) a public office; an official position. ¶~에 있다 hold[be in] a public office / be in government service // ~에 있는 사람 a public official[servant] / a public office holder // ~에서 추방하다 purge (a person) from public office // ~을 그만두다 resign [give up] one's public office // ~에서 물러나다 resign from public life // 모든 ~에서 물러나다 stay away all public positions // ~에 복귀하다 be restored to one's public office // 그는 ~에 있다 He is a public official[servant]. // 조부는 ~에서 추방되었다 My grandfather was removed from public office. // 그는 ~에 취임했다 He entered government service.
● **공직 생활** a public career[life]; government service. **공직자** a public official; a government official; a public post holder.

공진(共振) [전] resonance; [공명(共鳴)] [물] sympathetic vibrations; resonance; consonance; sympathy. **공진하다** resonate.

공진회(共進會) a competitive exhibition; an exposition; an expo. ¶농업 ~ an agricultural show // 가축 ~ a cattle show.

공집합(空集合) [수] an empty set.

공짜(空−) [무료] free[no] charge; [거저 얻은 물건] a thing got for nothing; a present; a gift. ¶~의 free / gratuitous / gratis // ~ 관람객 [승객] a free spectator[passenger] // ~표 a free ticket // ~로 free / without[free of] charge / gratis / for nothing // ~나 마찬가지

공차

로 사다[팔다] buy[sell] for almost nothing // ~로 타다 get a free ride / steal a ride / cheat a railway // ~라도 싫다 I would not have [take] it at a gift[even as a gift]. // ~보다 싼 것은 없다 Nothing freer than a gift. // ~보다 비싼 것은 없다 Nothing costs so much as what is given us.

공차(公差) [수] a common difference; (도량형의) allowance.

공차(空車) 1 [빈 차] an empty carriage[car / vehicle]; [철도] an idler; [게시] Vacant. 2 [무료로 타는 차] a free ride; a stolen ride. ¶~를 타다 steal a free ride / get a free ride / (미국 속어) snag a pick-up.

공창(公娼) [허가를 받은 창녀] a licensed[a registered] prostitute.
● **공창 폐지** abolition of licensed prostitution.

공채(公債) 1 [공적인 채무] a public loan [debt]. 2 a government securities. ⇨공채증권(⇨공채) ¶교부 ~ government compensation bonds // 군사 ~ a war loan[bond] // 등록 ~ registered bonds // 무이자 ~ passive bonds // 장기[단기] ~ a long-term[short-term] loan[bond] // ~를 공모하다 offer bonds for subscription // 5푼 이자 ~를 발행하다 issue five percent bonds // ~를 모집하다 raise[float] a loan // ~를 개서[상환]하다 convert[redeem] a loan[a bond] // ~를 청약하다 subscribe for a public loan // ~의 상환을 청구하다 (미) call a bond // 10억 원의 ~를 모집하다 float[raise] a loan of a thousand million won.
● **공채 시장** the bond market. **공채증권** a government securities; public loan bond.

공책(空册) a notebook.

공처가(恐妻家) a hen-pecked husband; a man afraid of his wife; (속어) a wifephobe. ¶그는 대단한 ~다 He is terribly afraid of his wife.

공천(公薦) [합의에 의한 천거] public nomination[recommendation]; [의원 선거 출마자에 대한 정당의 추천] party nomination of parliamentary candidates. ¶~의 nominated / accepted // ~을 받은 사람 a nominee // 공화당 ~으로 입후보하다 stand (for the Assembly) on the Republican ticket. **공천하다** recommend publicly; nominate (a candidate). ¶후보자를 ~ officially adopt a candidate / nominate a candidate.
● **공천 후보자** a recognized[an official / an authorized] candidate.

공청회(公聽會) a public hearing. ¶~를 열다 hold a public hearing (on).

공출(供出) offering; delivery (of rice to the government). ¶초과 ~ above-the-quota delivery // 할당 ~ quota delivery // 쌀의 ~ compulsory delivery of rice to the government. **공출하다** deliver; give[deliver] the allocated toll of (harvest). ¶쌀을 ~ deliver rice (to the government) // 물자 대신에 노동을 공출해야 했다 We were ordered to supply labor instead of goods.
● **공출 가격** a delivery price.

공치다(空-) [허탕 치다] be unsuccessful; be fruitless[vain / in vain]; be futile.

공치사(功致辭) self-praise of one's good conduct; admiration of one's merit; self-congratulation. **공치사하다** praise[congratulate] oneself; value one's own deed; admire[talk

about] one's merit; sing one's own praises.

공칭(公稱) [공식 명칭] the official name. ¶~의 nominal / official.
● **공칭 자본** nominal[authorized] capital.

공탁(供託) deposition; deposit; trust; lodgement. ¶법원에의 공금[재산] ~ payment into [deposit in] court. **공탁하다** deposit (in, with); place (money) on deposit (in); lodge (with); post (with). ¶은행에 [남에게] 돈을 ~ deposit money in a bank[with a person] // 보증금으로 2천만 원을 지정 은행에 ~ deposit twenty million won as a guarantee in a designated bank // 나는 집세를 변호사에게 공탁했다 I placed my rent on deposit[deposited my rent] with a lawyer.
● **공탁금** money on deposit; deposit money; a (security) deposit. **공탁물** a deposit; a deposited article. **공탁서** a document that goes with a deposit. **공탁소** a deposit office; a depository. **공탁자** a depositor.

공터(空-) vacant land. ⇨공지(空地)

공통(共通) commonness. ¶~의 common // ~의 이해 a common[shared] interest / an interest held in common // ~의 이익을 위하여 for the public good // …과 ~으로 in common with ... // 전체에 ~적인 성질 a characteristic common to all // 그는 우리의 ~의 친구이다 He is a common friend of ours. // 이혼의 급증은 세계 ~의 현상이다 The rapid increase in divorce is phenomenon common throughout the world. // 두 사람이 같은 잘못을 ~으로 저질렀다 Both of them made the same mistakes. **공통하다** be common (to). ¶만인에게 ~ be common to us all.
● **공통분모** [수] a common denominator. **공통성**(-性) community; commonness. **공통어** a common language. **공통 인수** [수] a common factor. **공통점** a common point; a point of sameness. ¶~이 있다[없다] have something[nothing] in common (with).

공판(公判) a trial; a (public) hearing. ¶사건의 ~ the trial of a case // 현재 ~ 중인 사건 a case no being tried (in court) // ~ 중이다 be on (one's) trial / be under public trial // ~을 열다 hold (a) court // ~에 붙이다 commit (a case) for trial / put (a case) on trial / try (a case) / bring (a case) to trial // 절도 혐의로 ~에 붙여졌다 He stood[went on] trial for theft. / He was tried for theft. // 사건의 ~은 월요일에 열린다 The case will come to trial [will be tried] on Monday.
● **공판 기일** a court day; a fixed day for public trial; a date for hearing. **공판 절차** procedure in a public trial. **공판정** the court; a public trial court; a court in session; a court room.

공판장(共販場) a joint market. ¶농협 [수산물] ~ an agricultural cooperative's[a fishery] joint market.

공편(共編) coeditorship; joint compilation. ¶A 씨와 B 씨의 ~ 사전 a dictionary (jointly) edited by Mr. A and Mr. B.
● **공편자** a coeditor.

공평(公平) impartiality; fairness; fair play; equity; equitability. ¶~을 유지하다 maintain impartiality / hold the scale even // ~하지 않다[잃다] be unfair (to) / be partial[unjust] (to) // ~을 기하다 try to be fair / endeavor to see justice done. **공평하다** [정실이 없다]

impartial; unbias(s)ed; [공정하다] **fair; equitable;** [공평무사하다] **disinterested;** (구어) **fair and square.** ¶공평한 대우 equitable treatment // 공평한 의견 an impartial opinion / an unprejudiced view // 공평한 판단을 내리다 hand down [render] an impartial judgment. **공평히** impartially; without partiality; fairly; justly; (미) squarely. ¶~ 말하자면 to do (a person) justice / to be fair // ~ 다루다 treat (a person) fairly [squarely] // ~ 분배하다 distribute fairly [evenly] // ~ 말하면 이것은 그의 허물이 아니다 To do him justice, he is not to blame for this.

공평무사하다 (公平無私-) fair and disinterested.

공포 (公布) [법] promulgation; proclamation; (official) announcement. **공포하다** promulgate; proclaim; make public; announce officially. ¶법률을 ~ promulgate a law // 이 규칙은 공포한 날로부터 이를 시행한다 The present regulations shall come into force on and after [as from] the day of promulgation.

공포 (空砲) (fire) a blank shot [cartridge]. ⇨ 헛총 ¶연습에서는 ~를 사용했다 Blanks were used for the maneuvers.

공포 (空胞) [생] a vacuole. ⇨액포(液胞)

공포 (恐怖) fear; dread; terror; fright; horror; panic(공황). ¶이유 없는 ~ a groundless [baseless] fear // ~에 떨다 shiver [tremble] with fear // ~에 떨리다 terrify // ~에 사로잡히다 be seized [overcome] with fear [terror] // ~를 느끼다 be terrified / be frightened // ~로 기절하다 faint in terror // 그녀는 서 있을 수 없을 만큼 ~에 질려 있었다 She was in such fear that she could hardly stand. // 그는 ~에 질려 안색이 창백해졌다 He became pale with fear.

●**공포감** (a sensation of) fear. **공포심** fear; horror. **공포 정치** terrorism; a reign of terror. **공포증** morbid fear; a phobia; [의] psychasthenia. ¶고소 ~ acrophobia // 대인 ~ anthropophobia.

공표 (公表) publication; (an) official announcement; proclamation. ¶그들은 일정의 ~를 보류했다 They withheld the publication of the schedule. // 그들은 그녀 이름의 ~를 머뭇거렸다 They hesitated to announce her name officially. **공표하다** announce (publicly); make public; release; publish; give publicity (to an affair); (미) publicize. ¶왜 그 사람의 이름을 공표하지 않는가 Why are you keeping that person's name secret? ➔¶다음 날 그의 사인이 공표되었다 The next day the cause of his death was made (known to the) public. // 그 일은 그의 사후에 공표되었다 It was made known [public] after his death.

공학 (工學) engineering; technology. ¶기계 [전기 / 토목] ~ mechanical [electrical / civil] engineering.
●**공학 박사** (사람) a doctor of engineering; (학위) Doctor of Engineering(약어 D. Eng.). **공학사** (사람) a bachelor of engineering; (학위) Bachelor of Engineering(약어 B. Eng.).

공학 (共學) (미) coeducation; (영) mixed education. ¶남녀 ~반 a mixed class // 흑인과 백인의 ~을 실시하다 carry out school integration // 저 대학은 남녀 ~이다 That college is coeducational. **공학하다** have coeducation; be coeducational [coeducated].

공한지 (空閑地) unused [idle / vacant] land; land lying idle; land in fallow.

공항 (空港) an airport; an aerial port; airdrome; an aviation field; (영) an aerodrome. ¶김포 ~ Gimpo Airport // 인천 국제 ~ Incheon International Airport // ~에 착륙하다 land at an airport.
●**공항 출입국 관리소** the airport immigration office.

공해 (公海) the high seas; international waters; the open ocean; mare liberum. ¶~의 자유 freedom of the seas // ~에서 어업하다 fish in open waters [on the high seas] // 우리는 ~ 상을 항행하고 있었다 We were sailing in international waters.

공해 (公害) (environmental) pollution(환경오염); environmental disruption(환경 파괴); a public nuisance; (a) menace [a threat] to public health; public hazard. ¶산업 ~ industrial pollution // 소음 ~ noise pollution // 열 ~ thermal pollution // 원자 ~ atomic pollution // 무~ 차 a nonpolluting car // 무~ 채소 chemical free vegetables // ~ 없는 환경 pollution-free environment // ~를 일으키다 cause harm to the public // ~를 없애다 get rid of [wipe out] pollution // 소음 ~에 시달리다 be bothered by [suffer from] noise pollution.
●**공해 대책** an antipollution measure. **공해 문제** the pollution problem; the pollution issue. **공해 방지법** [법] the Environmental Pollution Prevention Act; a pollution-control [an antipollution] law. **공해병** a public hazard disease. **공해 추방 운동** an antipollution campaign [drive].

공허감 (空虛感) a sense of emptiness.

공허하다 (空虛-) empty; (문어) void; vacant; hollow. ¶공허한 표정 an empty [vacant] look // 공허한 마음으로 with an emptiness [empty feeling] in one's heart / (문어) with a void in one's heart // 공허한 느낌이 들다 feel hollow // 노인은 공허한 미소를 띠었다 The old man gave a hollow smile. // 그의 이야기의 내용은 공허하였다 There was nothing useful [memorable] in what he said. // 그의 말소리는 공허하게 울렸다 His voice sounded hollow. / He sounded insincere.

공헌 (貢獻) a contribution; services. **공헌하다** contribute (to); make a contribution (to); do much (for / towards); render services (to). ¶대외 무역에 크게 ~ render great services to foreign trade // 평화에 크게 ~ make a great contribution towards peace / do much for peace // 그는 의학계에 크게 공헌했다 He rendered great service [made a great contribution / contributed much] to the medical profession. // 그는 이 마을의 복지 증진에 나름대로 공헌했다 He has contributed his share to [done his part in] the promotion of welfare in this village.

공화 (共和) [관형어적] republican.
●**공화국** a republic; a commonwealth. **공화당** (미국의) the Republican Party; the Republicans; (구어) the Gop(▶ the Grand old Party의 약어). **공화 정치** (a) republican government. **공화 제도** republican government; republicanism.

공황 (恐慌) a panic; a scare; consternation; [경] a financial panic [crisis]. ¶주식 ~ a stock market [exchange] panic // 금융 ~ a

공회 financial panic // ~을 초래하다 (사람이) be thrown into a panic / be panic-stricken / (사건이) cause [bring on] a panic // ~ 상태에 있다 be in a state of panic / be panic-stricken.

공회(公會) a public meeting [assembly].
● **공회당** a public hall; a town hall (미); a community center; a civic auditorium (*pl.* ~s, -ria).

공훈(功勳) an exploit; a great deed [feat]; a credit; a merit; a meritorious deed; a distinguished service. ¶빛나는 ~ brilliant exploits // ~이 있는 meritorious // ~을 세우다 distinguish oneself / perform great deeds / render distinguished services // ~을 세워 훈장을 타다 be decorated for one's distinguished services.

공휴일(公休日) [법정 휴일] a legal holiday; (영) a bank holiday; [정기적 휴일] a regular holiday; a day-off.

곶(串) a cape; a promontory; a headland; a point (of land); a spit. ¶장산~ Jangsan Point / the headland of Jangsan.

곶감 a dried [cured] persimmon.
곶감 꼬치에서 곶감 빼 먹듯(속담) eat away [up] one's savings; spend up one's savings bit by bit.

과 1 [그리고] and. ¶말~ 소 ox and horse // 술~ 담배를 샀다 I bought liquor and tobacco. 2 [함께] with; along [together] with. ¶어머니~ 여행하다 travel with one's mother // 수학~씨름하다 struggle with mathematics // 중국~손을 잡다 go hand in hand with China // 은행~ 거래하다 have dealings [do business] with a bank // 그 사람~는 완전히 손을 끊었다 I have done with him. / I'm through with him.
3 [비교] with. ¶저 사람~는 달리 in contrast with him // 전~ 마찬가지로 대답하다 answer the same as before // 내 그림은 네 것~는 비교가 안 된다 My painting cannot be compared with yours. // 그 모자는 이것~ 꼭 같다 That hat is just like this one.

과(科) 1 [학과] a department; a faculty; (병원의) a department; [병과] an arm (of the military service). ¶수학~의 학생 a student majoring in mathematics // 문~ the liberal arts department // 보병~ the infantry arm // (병원의) 신경 정신~ the department of neuropsychiatry. 2 [교과]. ¶사회~ social studies. 3 [생] a family. ¶고양잇~ 동물 animals belonging to [of / in] the cat family.

과(課) [학과] a lesson; [업무 분담의 한 구분] a section; a department; an office. ¶인사~ the personnel (affairs) section // 후생~ the welfare section // 제10~ Lesson 10 [ten] // 국은 여러 느 나누어져 있다 The bureau is divided into a number of sections.

과감하다(果敢-) [단호하다] resolute; determined; [용감하다] bold; daring; [두려움을 모르다] dauntless. ¶과감한 공격 a daring [bold] attack // 과감한 수단을 취하다 take a decisive [resolute] step / go drastic. **과감히** resolutely; boldly; daringly; in a decisive manner. ¶~ 맞서다 fight resolutely [boldly] against // ~ 말하다 express oneself daringly.

과객(過客) a passer-by (*pl.* passers-by); a foot passenger; [나그네] a wayfarer; a transient.

과거(科擧) [역] the civil service examination.

과거(過去) 1 [지나간 때] the past. ¶~를 회상하다 recall [think of] the past // ~ 5년 동안 for the past [last] five years // 그것은 먼 ~의 일이다 It happened in the distant past. / That happened long ago. // 그녀는 ~의 사람이다 [인기가 없어졌다] She is through [(구어) a has been]. / [죽었다] She is no more. / She is dead. // ~는 돌이킬 수 없다 What is done cannot be undone.
2 [남의 경력] one's past. ¶~가 있는 사람 a person with a past [something to hide] // 저 사람의 ~는 알 수 없다 I do not know the past history [former career] of that man. // 그는 ~가 있는 사람이라고 한다 He is rumored to have shady past.
3 [언] the past (tense); the preterit(e) (tense).
● **과거 분사** [언] a past participle (약어 p.p.). **과거사** past affairs; bygones. ¶~는 잊어버리자 Let bygones be bygones. **과거 완료** [언] the past perfect; the pluperfect.

과격분자(過激分子) radical [extremist] elements.

과격파(過激派) the extremists; the radicals.

과격하다(過激-) extreme; excessive; radical; drastic; ultra; violent; rabid (terrorists). ¶과격한 수단 a drastic [an extreme / a radical] measure // 과격한 사상 radical ideas / revolutionary thought // 그들은 과격한 행동으로 치닫기 쉽다 They are apt to go to extremes [go too far]. // 과격한 운동은 삼가라고 의사가 말했다 The doctor told him to avoid strenuous exercise. // 그는 곧잘 과격한 말을 쓴다 He often uses violent language. // 너의 생각은 ~ Your idea is too drastic.

과공(過恭) ¶~은 비례라 It is impolite to be too modest. **과공하다** overmodest.

과꽃 [식] a China aster.

과납(過納) payment in excess. **과납하다** pay in excess.
● **과납액** an amount paid in excess.

과냉각(過冷却) supercooling. **과냉각하다** supercool; superfuse.

과녁 a mark; a target. ¶~의 복판 the bull's-eye // ~의 복판을 맞히다 [빗나가다] hit [miss] the bull's-eye // ~을 넘다 overshoot the mark.
● **과녁판** a target board.

과녁빼기 the right opposite side [direction]; the place one faces right ahead; the place directly opposite.

과년(瓜年) 1 [결혼에 적당한 여자의 나이] marriageable [nubile] age; pubescence. ¶~ 찬 딸을 출가시키다 marry one's marriageable daughter. 2 [임기가 다한 해] the last year of one's term of service.

과년하다(過年-) overage for the marriage; past the marriageable age. ¶과년한 처녀 an old maid / a spinster // 과년한 딸 a daughter delayed in marriage.

과다(過多) excess; superabundance; overplus; surplus. ¶공급 ~ oversupply / an excessive supply / excess of supply // 인구 ~ overpopulation // 지방 ~ excessive fat **과다하다** excessive; superabundant; too many [much].

과단성(果斷性) firmness of character; promptness in decision; decisiveness. ¶~있는 사람 a decisive person.

과당(果糖) fruit sugar; fructose; levulose.

과당 경쟁(過當競爭) an excessive competitions (in sales); overheated vying (for). ¶~을 삼가다 refrain from excessive competitions (among themselves).

과당하다(過當-) excessive; undue; [과분하다] undeserved; [터무니없다] exorbitant; extravagant. ¶과당한 요구 an exorbitant [unreasonable] demand∥과당한 보수를 지불하다 pay a person more than he deserves ∥과당한 요금을 강요당했다 I was forced to pay an excessive charge.

과대(誇大) [관형어적] exaggerated; bombastic; magnified; extravagant; stretched; inflated. **과대하다** exaggerate; magnify; overstate; stretch; inflate. ¶과대한 exaggerated [bombastic / magnified / extravagant / stretched / inflated]∥사실을 과대하게 말하다 exaggerate matters / stretch the truth / [신문이] play up∥그는 과대하게 말하는 버릇이 있다 He has a tendency to exaggerate things.
● **과대광고** an exaggerated [a bombastic] advertisement; (구어) a puff. **과대망상** delusion of grandeur; expansive delusion. ¶~에 빠지다 fall into expansive delusion. **과대망상증** megalomania.

과대평가(過大評價) overestimation; overrating; overvaluation. **과대평가하다** overestimate; overrate; overvalue; think too highly of. ¶작품을 ~ overrate [overestimate] a work∥그의 인격을 과대평가하였다 I overestimated his character.∥저를 너무 과대평가하시는군요. 순전히 운이 좋아 성공한 것뿐입니다 You're giving me too much credit. My success was entirely due to good luck. ➔¶저는 너무 과대평가받고 있는 것 같습니다 I'm afraid I am much overrated.

과대하다(過大-) excessive; exorbitant; unreasonable; undue; too big [great]; inordinate; too big [great]. ¶과대한 요구 an unreasonable [exorbitant] demand∥노조는 과대한 임금 인상을 요구했다 The union demanded an excessive wage increase.∥과대한 기대는 하지 마라 Don't expect too much of me. **과대히** excessively; unduly; too much; extravagantly.

과도(果刀) a fruit knife.

과도(過渡) [관형어적] transitional.
● **과도기** a transitional period; a period of transition; an age of transition. ¶~의 문화 culture in a transitional period∥~적 현상 a transient phenomenon. **과도 정부** an interim government.

과도하다(過度-) excessive; immoderate; too much; inordinate. ¶과도한 노동 excessive [too much] work / overwork∥과도한 요구 an unreasonable demand. **과도히** excessively; immoderately; to excess; unduly; to an undue extent. ¶~ 머리를 쓰다 overtax one's brains / use one's head to excess.

과두 정치(寡頭政治) oligarchy; oligarchic government. ¶~의 oligarchic(al).

과람하다(過濫-) undeserved; unmerited; undue; more than one deserves.

과량(過量) an excess (of quantity); overmeasure. **과량하다** excessive; too much.

과로(過勞) overwork; overexertion; strain. ¶그는 ~로 병이 났다 He became ill [broke down] through overwork. / He fell ill from [got ill by] overwork [overworking himself]. **과로하다** work too hard (oneself); overwork; exert oneself too much. ¶자네는 병후 요양

중이니까 과로해서는 안 되네 You've just gotten better, so you'd better not overdo things.

과료(過料) ➔과태료

과립(顆粒) a granule. ¶~ 모양의 granular / granulated.

과명(科名) [생] a family name.

과목(科目) 1 [분류 조목] items. ¶계정 ~ items of an account∥~별로 on each item∥~별로 구분하다 itemize / classify / break down into details [particulars]∥청구서를 ~별로 하다 itemize a bill∥자료를 ~별로 나누다 classify the data. 2 [학과] a subject; a course; a[the] curriculum(전과목). ¶교양 ~ the academic liberal arts subject∥선택 ~ an optional subject / an elective (course)∥필수 ~ a compulsory [required] subject∥사회학을 두 ~ 이수하다 complete two courses [classes] in social studies.

과묵하다(寡默-) taciturn; reticent. ¶과묵한 사람 a taciturn [reticent] person / a man of few words / an oyster of a man∥그는 과묵한 사람이다 He is reserved [reticent].

과문하다(寡聞-) have little knowledge (of); ill-informed; limited in knowledge. ¶과문한 탓으로 그 일은 아직 모르고 있습니다 I'm afraid I haven't heard anything about it yet. / I've heard nothing about it, I'm sorry to say.

과물(果物) fruit. ➪"과실(果實)1
● **과물전**(-廛) a fruit store [shop / parlor]

과민(過敏) oversensitiveness; nervousness; hypersensitivity. **신경~** neurosis / morbid sensitiveness. **과민하다** (over)sensitive; hyperacute; hypersensitive; morbidly sensitive; [신경질적이다] jumpy; edgy. ¶그는 항생 물질에 ~ He is sensitive to antibiotics.∥그녀는 남편의 건강에 대해 ~ She worries too much about [over] her husband's health. ➔¶오토바이 소음으로 모든 사람의 신경이 과민 되어 있다 The noise of motorcycles was grating on everyone's nerves [was setting everyone's nerves on edge].
● **과민증** [의] erethism; hyperesthesia; anaphylaxis; hypersensitiveness.

과밀(過密) overcrowding; congestion. ¶인구 ~ overpopulation. **과밀하다** overcrowded; congested; crammed.
● **과밀 도시** an overpopulated city.

과반수(過半數) the majority; the greater part [number] (of). ¶국회에서 ~를 차지하다 [차지하지 못하다] hold [lack] a majority in the National Assembly∥~를 얻다 win [gain / obtain] a majority∥의결은 ~로 한다 The decision will be made by majority.∥그 법안은 ~의 득표로 통과되었다 The bill was passed by a majority of vote.

과보호(過保護) overprotectiveness. ➪"과잉보호(㊤)과잉)

과부(寡婦) a widow; a woman bereft of her husband. ¶그녀는 스물 다섯에 ~가 되었다 She lost her husband [She became a widow] at the age of twenty-five.∥그 후로 죽 그녀는 ~로 있다 She has remained a widow [lived in widowhood] ever since.∥전쟁으로 많은 ~가 생겼다 The war produced many widows. / The war widowed many wives. / A great many women were widowed by the war.

과부는 은이 서 말이고 홀아비는 이가 서 말이다(속담) Widows are thrifty and can be

과부족

counted on to save money, but widowers are apt to remain poor. **과부 사정은 과부가 안다**(속담) It takes a widow to know a widow's difficulties.

과부족(過不足) overs and shorts; excess and deficiency. ¶~ 없는 neither more nor less / neither too much not too little / just enough / in exact[proper] quantities∥세 가지 재료를 ~ 없이 섞다 mix the right amounts of three ingredients∥그는 재산을 자녀들에게 ~ 없이 분배하였다 He divided his property equally among his children.

과분하다(過分−) unmerited; undeserved; unworthy (of). ¶과분한 사례를 주셔서 황송합니다 It's very kind of you to give me such generous remuneration.∥과분한 그의 찬사에 나는 어쩔 줄 몰랐다 I felt embarrassed by his lavish compliments.∥이런 선물은 제게 과분합니다 I don't deserve such a gift. / Such a gift is too good for me.∥그녀는 네게는 과분한 마누라다 She is too good a wife for you. / She's wasted on a husband like you. /이것은 내게는 과분한 명예다 This is a great honor I hardly deserve. / This is an undeserved honor.∥저에게는 과분한 칭찬의 말씀입니다 Your praise is more than I deserve. / I don't deserve such words of praise.∥그녀는 미인으로 그의 아내라기에는 ~ She is too beautiful to be his wife. **과분히** unmeritedly; undeservedly; above one's deserts.

과산화나트륨(過酸化−) natrium peroxide.
과산화망간(過酸化−) manganese peroxide.
과산화물(過酸化物) peroxides.

과세(過歲) celebration [observation] of the New Year. **과세하다** celebrate [observe] the New Year.

과세(課稅) taxation; imposition of taxes; assessment. ¶누진 ~ progressive taxation /분리 ~ separate taxation /배당 ~ levying tax on stock dividends /비~ 소득 non-taxable income∥인정 ~ optional taxation /자본 ~ a capital levy /종합 ~ general [consolidated] taxation /중~ heavy taxation∥~가 면제되다 be exempt(ed) [immune] from taxation. **과세하다** tax; lay [put / impose] a tax (on); levy duties (on). ¶개인 소득에 ~ tax the income of an individual
● **과세 가격** the taxable amount; the assessed value. **과세 물건** / **과세 대상** [경] an object of taxation; a taxation article. ¶~이 되다 be liable for taxation / be taxable / be assessable / be dutiable(관세의)∥그 물건은 ~이 됩니다 That article is taxable. **과세율** [법] tax rates. **과세 표준** [법] a standard of assessment; tax basis. **과세품** a taxable article; articles subject to taxation; (세관에서의) a dutiable [(미) customable] article.

과소비(過消費) overconsumption. **과소비하다** overconsume.

과소평가(過小評價) underestimation; underrating. **과소평가하다** underestimate; underrate; belittle; set too low a value on (a person).

과소하다(過少−) too little; too few; too small (in quantity).

과소하다(寡少−) very little [few]; scanty.

과속(過速) overspeed. ¶~으로 달리다 overspeed /~ 위험, 안전 제일 (게시) Speeding is dangerous, safety first.
● **과속 차량** an overspeeding vehicle.

과수(果樹) a fruit tree.
● **과수원** an orchard; a fruit garden; (미) a fruit farm. **과수 재배** fruit-growing; pomiculture.

과시(誇示) ostentation; display; showing off; parade. ¶힘의 ~ an ostentation [a display] of one's power. **과시하다** show off (proudly); display ostentatiously; make a display [show / parade] of; parade. ¶재능을 ~ show off one's talents∥지식을 ~ make a show [display / parade] of one's knowledge / parade one's knowledge∥무력으로 국력을 ~ flaunt [proudly show off] the nations power by the use of arms∥그는 학식을 과시한다 He shows off [parades / makes a display of] his knowledge.

과식(過食) overeating; excessive eating; surfeit. **과식하다** eat too much; eat to excess; overeat (oneself). ¶과식하여 탈 나다 overeat oneself sick /과식하여 토하다 vomit from repletion /과식하여 위를 해치다 injure one's stomach by overeating /그는 과식해서 배탈이 났다 He upset his stomach by eating too much [overeating].∥위가 아픈 것은 과식했기 때문이다 Your stomachache comes from overeating.

과신(過信) overconfidence. **과신하다** put [place / have] too much confidence (in); be credulous; be overconfident. ¶자신을 과신하지 마라 Don't be too confident of yourself.∥나는 그의 능력을 과신하였다 I overestimated [overrated] his ability. / I had too much confidence in his ability.∥그들은 서전에서의 승리를 과신하여 다음의 대비를 하지 않았다 Overconfident from their victory in the first encounter, they failed to prepare themselves for the next one.

과실(果實) 1 (집합적) fruit(age); (낱낱의) a fruit; (딸기류) a berry. ¶작은 ~ a fruitlet /~을 맺다 (나무가) bear [produce] fruit / (꽃이) develop into fruit / fructify / fruit /~을 재배하다 grow fruit. 2 [수익] profits; returns; [법] fruit. ¶법정 [천연] ~ legal [natural] fruit /~이 생기다 yield a profit.
● **과실주** fruit wine; ratafia.

과실(過失) 1 [잘못] a mistake; an error; [실책] a blunder; a fault. ¶~을 인정하다 admit one's error / admit that one is in error / acknowledge one's mistake∥~을 사과하다 apologize for an error [a mistake] /그는 큰 ~을 저질렀다 He committed an awful blunder. / He made a terrible mistake. /모두가 나의 ~이다 It's all my fault. / I am to blame for it all. / The fault lies entirely with me.∥그는 자신의 ~임을 인정하였다 He admitted that it was his fault [that he was to blame].∥그의 ~이지 내 ~이 아니다 The fault lies with him, not me.∥사람에게는 누구나 ~이 있다 To err is human.

2 [법] [사고] an accident; [태만] negligence; [부주의] carelessness; oversight. ¶그건 ~이 아니라 고의로 한 짓이다 It was not done by accident, but by design. /살인이 ~인지 고의인지 결정할 길이 없다 There is no way of telling whether the killing was accidental or intentional. /그는 업무상 ~ 치사 혐의로 체포되었다 He was arrested on suspicion of professional negligence resulting in death.

● **과실범** criminal negligence; an offense committed through negligence. **과실 치사죄** accidental homicide; unpremeditated homicide; involuntary manslaughter.

과언(過言) saying too much; going too far (in one's talk); exaggeration. ¶그는 당대 제일의 화가라 해도 ~이 아니다 It is no exaggeration [not going too far / not too much] to say that he is the greatest artist of the day. / It may safely be said that he is the greatest artist of the day.

과업(課業) 1 [임무] a task; a duty. ¶~을 맡기다 assign[set] (a person) to a task[job] / place[impose] a duty[task] upon (a person). 2 [학과] a lesson. ¶~에 힘쓰다 work at one's lessons[studies].

과연(果然) as expected; sure enough; just as one thought; indeed; really. ¶~ 그것은 사실일까 Is it really true? / ~ 그렇군 So it is, to be sure! / ~ 사실이었다 It proved to be true. / It was really the case. // ~ 그는 위대하다 He is indeed[truly] a great man. // ~ 일은 잘되었다 As (had been) expected, things went well. // ~ 그녀는 독신이었다 She was single just as I had thought. / (구어) Sure enough, she was single. // 그런 질문을 하다니 ~ 자네답군 It's just like you to ask that (question). // ~ 그는 의사의 아들이다 He is, after all, a doctor's son. // ~ 그는 우승했다 I should[might] have known that he'd win.

과열(過熱) 1 [너무 뜨거워짐] overheating; superheating. **과열하다** overheat; superheat. →¶모터가 과열되어 있다 The motor is overheated. 2 [지나치게 활기를 띰]. ¶~ 경제 an overheated economy // ~ 입시 경쟁 excessive[hot] competition for entrance tests // 반정부 운동은 ~ 상태에 이르렀다 The antigovernment movement got out of hand [went too far].

● **과열 경기** an excessive (economic) boom. **과열 경보** a temperature alarm.

과염소산(過鹽素酸) [화] perchloric acid.

● **과염소산염** a perchlorate.

과오(過誤) a mistake; a fault. ⇨**과실**(過失)1 ¶~를 범하다 commit a fault / make a mistake[an error] // ~를 뉘우치다 repent one's fault // ~를 고치다[바로잡다] correct[remedy / amend] a fault / mend oneself / mend one's ways.

과외(課外) 1 extracurricular work. 2 an extracurricular lesson. ⇨**과외 수업**(⇨**과외**) ¶~ 강의 an extracurricular lecture.

● **과외 공부** out-of-school studies. **과외 수업** an extracurricular lesson; off-campus tutoring. **과외 활동** extracurricular activities.

과욕(過慾) avarice; greed; greediness; covetousness. **과욕하다** avaricious; greedy; covetous.

과욕하다(寡慾-) unselfish; disinterested; wantless.

과용하다(過用-) spend too much[in excess / excessively]; be extravagant[prodigal] (with); (약을) take an overdose of medicine [a drug]. ¶수면제를 과용하여 죽다 die of an overdose of sleeping pills // 그녀는 의복에 돈을 과용한다 She spends too much money on [for] clothes.

과원(課員) (개인) a member of the section staff; (집합적) the staff of a section.

과유불급(過猶不及) Too much is as bad as too little.; Too much water drowns the miller.

과육(果肉) [식] flesh (of fruit); sarcocarp.

과음(過飮) excessive drinking; overdrinking; intemperance in drinking. ¶~ 과식은 몸을 해친다 Immoderate eating and drinking will ruin your health. **과음하다** drink too much [to excess]; overdrink. ¶과음하여 병나다 drink oneself ill / drink too much and fall ill // 과음하셨군요 You had too many drinks. / You had one too many.

과인산(過燐酸) [화] perphosphoric acid.

● **과인산 석회** calcium superphosphate; superphosphate of lime.

과일 (집합적) fruit; (낱낱의) a fruit. ¶바구니 가득한 ~ a basketful of fruit // ~을 많이 먹다 eat a lot of fruit // 망고나 파파야 같은 ~ fruits such as mangoes and papayas.

● **과일 가게** a fruit shop[store / parlor]. **과일 장수** a fruit dealer[seller / man]; (영) a fruiterer. **과일칼** a fruit knife.

과잉(過剩) [잉여] an excess; a surplus; overabundance; superabundance; superfluity. ¶공급 ~ an oversupply // 정력 ~ a plethora of energy // ~의 surplus / superabundant // 그는 자의식이 ~이다 He is too self-conscious. // 이 지역의 농산물은 생산 ~이다 This district has a surplus of agricultural products. // 그녀는 친절 ~이다 She is overly kind. **과잉하다** superfluous; surplus; excessive; more than enough; overmuch; plethoric; (서술적) have[show] a surplus; become overabundant[excessive].

● **과잉보호** overprotectiveness. **과잉 생산** [경] overproduction. **과잉 인구** surplus[overflowing] population; overspill. **과잉 투자** [경] overcapitalization.

과자(菓子) (집합적) confectionery; sweet stuff; (케이크) a cake; (당과) (미) candy; (영) sweets; (파이 등) pastry. ¶~ 그릇 a cake tray[dish / bowl].

● **과자 상자** a box of cake; a package of cake; a carton of biscuits[candy]. **과자 장수** a confectioner. **과자점** (영) a sweet shop; (미) a candy store; a confectionery.

과장(課長) (대학의) the head[director] of a department; (병원의) the head[chief] doctor [physician / surgeon]. ¶소아과 ~ the head [chief] of the pediatric department.

과장(課長) the chief[head] of a section; a section chief.

● **과장 대리** an acting head of a section.

과장(誇張) exaggeration; overstatement; grandiloquence; magniloquence; magnification. ¶…라고 해도 ~이 아니다 It is not too much to say that …. **과장하다** exaggerate; overstate; magnify; overdraw; overshoot oneself; stretch; go too far; overpitch; blow up; paint (a thing) in high colors; make a mountain out of a molehill. ¶그녀는 언제나 과장해서 말한다 She always exaggerates[makes too much of] things. // 그는 과장하는 버릇이 있다 He is given to exaggeration. / He is in the habit of piling it on. →¶과장된 exaggerated / bombastic / high-flown / grandiloquent // 과장된 이야기 a story full of exaggeration(s) // 과장된 말 an exaggeration / tall talk / bombastic[high-flown] language // 과장된 문장 a high-flown sentence // 과장된 몸짓으로

with exaggerated gestures.∥그의 말은 늘 과장되어 있다 His stories are always exaggerated.
● **과장법** [문] hyperbole.
과점(寡占) [경] oligopoly.
과정(過程) (a) process; a course; a stage. ¶생산[제조] ~ a process of production[manufacture]∥ ~을 **밟다** undergo[follow] a process / pass[go through] a process[stage]∥양모는 어떤 ~을 거쳐서 옷감이 됩니까 By what process is wool made into cloth?∥포장 ~에서 약간 착오가 있었음이 분명하다 There must have been some mistake during the packing process.∥여기에 이르기까지의 ~을 더듬어 보자 Let's look back upon how it has developed.
과정(課程) a course; a curriculum. ¶대학 ~ a university[college] course / one's course in a university[college]∥3년 ~ a course of three years / a three-year course∥그는 고등학교 ~을 마쳤다 He finished[completed] the (whole) course of high school. / He finished high school.∥그는 석사 ~을 마치고 박사 ~에 들어갔다 He completed the master's course and went on for a doctorate.∥위 사람은 본교 소정의 ~을 수료하였음을 증명함 This is to certify the above-mentioned has completed the prescribed course of this school.
과제(課題) 1 [문제] a question; a problem. ¶해결해야 할 ~ a problem awaiting solution [to be solved]∥이것이 우리가 당면한 ~이다 This is the problem which confronts us. 2 [숙제] homework; a home task; (미) an assignment; exercises(연습 문제). ¶여름 방학 ~ a summer assignment / summer homework∥ ~를 **주다** set a task (to) / give an assignment (to)∥오늘은 문법에 대한 ~을 많이 내겠다 I will give you a lot of grammar exercises (to do).
과중하다(過重-) too heavy; burdensome. ¶과중한 노동 excessively heavy work / overwork∥과중한 부담 too great burden / a heavy burden∥과중한 부담을 지우다 overburden; burden too heavily∥나에게는 이 새 일이 ~ This new job is too much[heavy] for me.
과즙(果汁) fruit juice.
과찬(過讚) overpraise; an undeserved praise; excessive compliment. ¶ ~의 말씀이십니다 You flatter me (immensely). / I am (so) flatted. / This is very flattering. **과찬하다** overpraise; praise[compliment] excessively.
과태료(過怠料) [법] a fine for default; a negligence fine; penalty; a penalty fee; a civil fine. ¶5만 원의 ~를 부과하다 impose a 50,000 won correctional fine.
과표(課標) [법] a standard of assessment. ⇨과세 표준(⇨과세(課稅))
● **과표액** the taxable amount; (영) the ratal; (영) the rateable value.
과피(果皮) the rind (of a fruit); the seedcase; the pericarp.
과하다(科-) (형벌을) inflict (a punishment on a person); impose (a penalty on a person).
과하다(課-) 1 (세금·벌금 등을) levy[lay / put] (a tax upon a person); impose (a fine on a person). ¶수입품에 높은 관세를 ~ charge[impose / levy] high duties on imports∥정부는 국민에게 중세를 과하였다 The government imposed[levied] heavy taxes on the people. / The government taxed the people heavily. / The government burdened the people with heavy taxes.∥그에게 주차 위반으로 벌금이 과해졌다 He was fined for a parking violation.∥그에게 경범죄로 5,000원의 벌금이 과해졌다 He was fined five thousand won for a minor offense. 2 (업무 등을) assign (a task to a person); impose (a task on a person); task (a person). ¶학생에게 숙제를 ~ give a student some homework.
과하다(過-) too much[good / heavy / severe]; excessive; overly; beyond (all) bounds [limits]; undue; undeserved; unreasonable. ¶술을 과하게 마시다 overdrink oneself / drink too much / drink to excess∥농담이 ~ carry a joke too far∥그에게는 과한 부인이다 She is too good for him. / She is worthy of a better husband than him.∥그 집은 내게 ~ The house is too good[too big / too fine] for me. **과히** [지나치게] too (much); excessively; (미) overly; [그다지] (not) very; (not) quite; (not) much. ¶이것은 ~ 좋지 않다 This is not very good.∥ ~ 심한 병은 아니다 It is not a very serious illness.∥나는 그것을 ~ 좋아하지 않는다 I do not like it so much.
과학(科學) science. ¶사회 ~ social science∥순수 ~ pure[abstract] science∥응용 ~ applied science∥인문 ~ cultural science∥자연 ~ natural[physical] science∥정신 ~ mental science∥ ~의 진보 development [advance] of science∥ ~을 응용하다 apply science.
● **과학관** a science museum. **과학 교육** science education. **과학 기술** science and technology; scientific technique. **과학 기술부** the Ministry of Science and Technology. **과학자** a scientist; a man of science.
과학적(科學的) scientific. ¶ ~으로 scientifically∥ ~으로 사고하다 think scientifically.
곽 → 갑(匣)
관(官) the government; the authorities; the government office. ¶ ~에 **있다** hold a government post[office] / be in government service.
관(冠) 1 [역] (머리에 쓰던 쓰개) a crown; a coronet(소형의). ¶ ~을 **쓰다** put on[wear] a crown. 2 (족보에서) a married man.
관(貫) 1 one's ancestral home. ⇨ 본관(本貫) 2 [무게 단위] a gwan (=8.267 lbs., 3.75 kg).
관(棺) a coffin; (미) a casket. ¶ ~ 메는 사람 a pallbearer / a coffin bearer∥ ~에 **넣다** lay in a coffin / put[place] in a coffin[casket].
관(管) 1 [둥글고 긴 속이 빈 물건] a pipe; a tube; [도관(導管)] a duct. ¶유리 ~ a glass tube∥수도 ~[가스 ~]를 설치하다 install a water[gas] pipe. 2 [관악기] a wind instrument.
관(款) [조항] an article; a subsection; a part; a title.
-**관**(觀) an outlook; a view. ¶인생 ~ one's view of life / an outlook on life∥세계 ~ an outlook on the world / a view of the world.
관가(官家) an official building; a local [provincial] government; a district office (of the government)
관개(灌漑) irrigation; watering. **관개하다** irrigate; water.
● **관개 공사** irrigation works. **관개용수** water

for irrigation; irrigation water.
관객(觀客) a spectator; an audience; an attendance. ¶많은[적은] ~ a large[small] audience // 많은 영화 a box-office film // 가장 싼 관람석의 ~ (the spectators in) the gallery // **이 적다** have a small audience / draw a poor house / have a thin house // 영화의 ~은 대부분이 십 대의 소년 소녀 들이다 The audience for this film is mostly teenagers. // 정초의 흥행엔 ~이 많이 몰린다 The New Year performance draws a large audience[house].
● **관객석** a seat (in the audience).
관건(關鍵) 1 [문빗장] a bolt; a (locking) bar. 2 [가장 중요한 부분] a key[pivotal] point; an important point[post]. ¶문제 해결의 ~을 쥐고 있다 hold[have] the key to the solution of the question.
관견(管見) [좁은 소견] a narrow view; [사견·견해] one's point of view; one's personal view.
관계(官界) the official world; officialdom; official circles. ¶~에 있는 사람 a man in official life / a man in the government service // ~에 진출하다 enter government service.
● **관계 쇄신** a renovation of officialdom.
관계(關係) 1 [관련] relation; relationship; reference; bearing; respect; [이해관계] an interest; a concern; [연고] connection; [교제] relations. ¶거래 ~ trade connections // 국제[외교] ~ international[diplomatic] relations // 인간 ~ human relations // 수요와 공급의 ~ relation(ship) between supply and demand // 적대 ~ hostile relations // (문장의) 전후 ~ the context // 의료 ~의 일 work connected with medicine // 사회학과 다른 학문과의 ~ the correlation of sociology with other studies // 양국 간의 ~가 개선되었다 The relations between the two countries have been improved. // 그 클럽과는 오래전에 ~를 끊었다 I severed[cut / broke off] my connection with the club long ago. // 이 두 사건은 서로 밀접한 ~가 있다 These two events are closely related[connected]. // 이것과 그것은 아무 ~가 없다 There is no connection[relation] between this and that. // 음식과 건강은 밀접한 ~가 있다 Food is closely related to[connected with] health. // 그는 이 사업에 어느 정도 이해~가 있다 He has some interest in this undertaking. // 나는 그것과 다소 ~가 있다[~가 전혀 없다] I have something[nothing] to do with it. // 연령에 ~없이 콘테스트에 참가할 수 있다 You can take part in the contest regardless[irrespective] of age. // 네가 하는 말은 이 문제와는 ~가 없다 Your remarks are irrelevant to this matter. // 이것은 지금 논의되고 있는 문제와는 아무 ~가 없다 That is irrelevant to the topic under discussion. // 이것은 주변의 생활 향상과는 아무런 ~도 없다 This has no bearing whatever on the betterment of the living conditions of the inhabitants. // 그것은 한미 간의 여러 문제에 중요한 ~를 갖고 있다 It has an important bearing on the relations of Korea to the United States. // 나는 그의 죽음과 아무 ~가 없다 I have nothing to do with his death. // 저 사람과는 어떤 ~입니까 (친척 관계) How are you related to him? / (교제 관계) How are you connected[related] with him? // 나는 그와 친척 ~이다 I am related to

him by blood. / He is a relative of mine. // 우리는 그 회사와는 아무 ~가 없다 We have no connection[have nothing to do] with that company. **관계하다** relate[be related] (to); have relation (to); concern; be connected (with).
2 [관여] participation; concern; [연좌] involvement. ¶~을 **끊다** wash[wipe] one's hands of (an affair) // 너와는 ~없는 일이다 That's no concern of yours. / That's none of your business. **관계하다** participate (in); take part (in); concern oneself (in); be concerned (in); be involved (in); have[take] a hand (in). ¶음모에 ~ be involved in a plot / be a party to a plot // 그러한 일에 관계해서는 안 된다 You must not concern yourself in such an affair. / Keep[Stay] out of such an affair. // 그는 정치에 관계하고 있다 He is involved[(문어) engaged] in politics. // 그도 그 음모에 관계했습니까 Did he participate [take part] in the plot, too? // 나는 어느 정당과도 관계하고 있지 않다 I am independent of any political party. ➔ ¶그는 이 사건에 관계되었을까 Is he involved in this affair? // 그는 그 수뢰 사건에 관계되어 있다 He is involved in that bribery case.
3 [영향] influence; an effect; [이유·까닭] reason. ¶그것은 나에게는 별 ~가 없다 It matters little to me. // 기압 ~로 머리가 아프다 I have a headache caused by atmospheric pressure. **관계하다** affect; have influence (on / upon); matter. ➔ ¶그것은 생사에 관계되는 일이다 It is a matter of life and death. // 내 명예에 관계되는 일은 아무것도 하지 않았다 I have not done anything to affect [which reflects on] my honor. // 그는 자신의 출세에 관계되는 일밖에는 생각하지 않는다 He thinks of nothing but what affects his getting ahead. // 나의 체면에 관계되는 일이다 My honor is at stake.
4 [성 관계] (sexual) relations[intercourse]; connection. ¶그녀와 ~가 있는 남자들 the men who are intimate with her[who have connection with her] // 유부녀와 ~를 갖다 have relations with a married woman // 두 사람은 사랑하는 ~이다 The two are in love with[on intimate terms with] each other. **관계하다** have connection[relations] (with); misconduct oneself (with). ¶한 씨는 저 여자와 관계하고 있는 것 같다 Mr. Han seems to have relations with that girl.
● **관계 기관** the organs[agencies] concerned. **관계 당국** the authorities concerned; the competent[relevant] authorities. **관계 대명사**[**부사**] [언] a relative pronoun[adverb]. **관계 법규** the related laws and regulations. **관계 서류** the relevant[related] documents [papers]; documents related (to the matter). **관계자** the persons[parties] concerned; (이해의) an interested party; (계약의) the contracting parties; a participant; a participator. ¶~ 이외 출입 금지 (게시) No Entry[(미) Off Limits] To Unauthorized Persons.
관공서(官公署) a government office; a public office.
관광(觀光) sightseeing; tourism. ¶시내 ~ city-sightseeing. **관광하다** go sightseeing; go on a (sightseeing) tour; see[do] the sights (of). ¶제주도를 ~ see[do] the sights of

Jejudo.
● **관광객** a tourist; a sightseer; a visitor; (미국 속어) a rubberneck(특히 단체 여행의); (집합적) tourism. ¶~ 유치 inducement of tourists[sightseers]. **관광단** a sightseeing [tourist] party[group]. **관광버스** a tourist [(미국 속어) rubberneck] bus. **관광 사업** the tourist industry[business / trade]; tourism. **관광 시설** tourist[sightseeing] facilities. **관광 여행** a (sightseeing) tour. **관광 열차** a sightseeing train. **관광 자원** tourist attractions. **관광지** a tourist resort; a sightseeing resort [place]; vacationland; a tourist attraction. **관광 코스** a tourist route. **관광호텔** a tourist hotel.

관구(管區) a (territory [district] under someone's) jurisdiction; a district (under jurisdiction); [가] a province.

관군(官軍) the government army; government forces.

관권(官權) governmental[official] authority; government power. ¶~을 남용하다 abuse government authority / make an improper use of government power.

관급(官給) government supply; (미) government issue(약어 GI, G.I.).
● **관급품** articles supplied by the government.

관기(官紀) official discipline. ¶~ 문란 laxity in official discipline / corruption of officialdom // 요즘 ~가 눈에 띄게 해이해졌다 These days official discipline has been remarkably slack[lax].

관내(管內) ¶~에 within[throughout] the jurisdiction[province] / ~를 순시하다 make a tour of inspection through one's (area of) jurisdiction / make one's rounds / walk one's beat // 이 경찰서 ~에서 절도가 두 건 발생하였다 There were two cases of theft in [within] the jurisdiction of this police station.

관념(觀念) 1 [개념·생각] an idea; a concept(ion); a notion. ¶고정~ a fixed idea // 도덕 ~ a moral idea / ~적(인) ideological (viewpoint) / ideal (happiness) // ~적으로 ideally / in idea // 잘못된 ~을 가지고 있다 have a wrong idea[mistaken notion] (of success) // 그녀는 미국인에 대해 고정~을 가지고 있었다 She had a fixed idea of Americans. // 전쟁의 비참함을 ~적으로만 알고 있을 뿐이다 I know the tragedy of war only conceptually.
2 [··· 정신] a sense; a spirit. ¶의무[책임 / 정의] ~ a sense of duty[responsibility / justice] // 시간~이 없다 take no thought of time / have no sense of time // 책임 ~이 없다 have no sense of responsibility // 그는 책임 ~이 강하다 He has a strong sense of responsibility.
● **관념론** [철] idealism; [공론] an empty theory; an academic argument. **관념주의** idealism.

관능(官能) 1 [육체 기능] organic [physical / bodily] functions. ¶~의 functional. 2 [육체적 감각] (fleshly) sense; [육욕] carnal desires[lust]. ¶~을 자극하는 묘사 a sexually stimulating description // ~을 만족시키다 satisfy one's carnal desire.
● **관능미** voluptuous beauty[charm / attraction]. **관능주의** sensualism.

관능적(官能的) [감각적] sensuous; [육욕적] sensual. ¶~인 여자 a glamor(ous) girl / (속어) a sexpot // ~인 그림 a sensual painting // 그녀의 ~인 지체 her voluptuous[sexy] figure.

관다발(管−) [식] vascular bundle; fibrovascular bundle.

관대하다(寬大−) broad-minded; generous; liberal; magnanimous; tolerant; indulgent; lenient. ¶관대한 태도 a generous attitude // 반대파에 대하여 ~ be liberal to one's opponents // 관대한 처벌 a mild [lenient] punishment // 관대한 처분을 탄원하다 plead for leniency // 그는 누구에게나 관대했다 He was generous to everybody. // 그는 종파를 달리하는 사람들에게도 관대했다 He was tolerant to those who belonged to other sects. // 당신은 학생들에게 지나치게 ~ You are too lenient [easy] with the students. / You are not strict enough with the students. **관대히** generously; liberally; magnanimously; tolerantly; leniently; indulgently. ¶그는 포로들을 ~ 다뤘다 He dealt leniently with the prisoners. // 경찰은 그가 장관의 아들이라고 해서 ~ 대한 것 같다 The police seem to have been easy on him[have dealt with him leniently] because he is a minister's son.

-관데 so ... that; such ... that. ¶무슨 일이 있었기~ 그가 그리 슬퍼하느냐 What makes him so sad? / Why is it that he is so unhappy? // 요즈음 무엇이 그리 바쁘~ 한 번도 오지 않느냐 What in the world makes you so busy that you never come to see me these days? // 네가 무엇이~ 그런 짓을 하느냐 What on earth are you doing such a thing?

관등(官等) an official rank; civil service grade. ¶~이 높은 사람 a high-ranking official / an official of high rank // ~이 오르다 be elevated to a higher rank / be promoted in rank / ~이 떨어지다 be reduced in rank[to a lower grade] / (미) be demoted.
● **관등 성명** one's official rank and name.

관등(觀燈) the Lantern Festival; the Festival of Lantern. **관등하다** have the Festival of Lanterns; celebrate Buddha's birthday.
● **관등놀이** merrymaking at the Lantern Festival. **관등절** the Lantern Festival.

관람(觀覽) inspection; viewing. ¶일반의 ~을 허가하다[불허하다] be open[closed] to the public. **관람하다** see; view; inspect. ¶축구 시합을 ~ see a soccer game.
● **관람객 / 관람자** a spectator; a visitor; (집합적) an audience; the gallery. **관람권** an admission ticket. **관람료** an admission fee; admission. **관람석** a seat; (극장의) an auditorium; a front; a box; the (spectators') gallery; (야구장 등의) a stand; a grandstand(정면의); a bleacher(s)(지붕이 없는).

관련(關聯) connection; reference; relation; correlation; association. ¶이것은 그것과 아무 ~이 없다 This has no connection with it. / This has nothing to do with it. // (청소년) 비행 문제는 가정환경과 ~이 있다고 생각해야 한다 We should consider that the problem of delinquency is related to the home environment. **관련하다** be connected (with); be related (to); relate (to); be correlated (to); bear (on); have a bearing (on); refer (to); connect (up) (with). ¶··· 과 관련하여 in con-

nection with / in relation to // 방금 말씀하신 것과 관련하여 생각나는 것이 있습니다 I am reminded of something related to [in connection with] what you said just now. // 관련 시키다 correlate (one thing with another) / relate (facts to events) // 관련되다 be connected (with) / be related (to) // 그 사건에 관련된 문제 matters connected with [related to] the incident // 식물의 성장은 날씨와 깊이 관련되어 있다 The growth of plants is closely connected with [related to] the weather. // 이 두 사건이 어떤 식으로 관련된 것은 틀림없다 There is no doubt that the two incidents are connected [linked / related] in some way. // 그도 그 음모에 관련된 것 같다 He seems to be involved in [to have something to do with] the plot, too. // 이 사건에 관련된 사람이 한 사람 더 있다 There is one more person who is connected with [involved in] the case. // 이것은 당신도 관련되어 있다 This is related to you too. // 그는 그 사건에 관련되어 기소되었다 He was indicted for [charged with] complicity in that affair. // 이 사건들은 서로 미묘하게 관련되어 있었다 These events were all subtly linked together.
● 관련 기사 a related article [story]. 관련 산업 allied industries. 관련성 relation; relevance; relevancy. 관련 업계 related business circles. 관련자 the persons concerned; those who have something to do (with).

관례(冠禮) [성년식] a rite to mark one's attainment of manhood; the celebration of one's coming of age; a coming-of-age ceremony; [혼례] a wedding ceremony. ¶~을 치르다 celebrate one's coming of age / celebrate one's attainment of manhood.

관례(慣例) (a) custom; a usage; a usual practice; a precedent(전례); a convention(관습). ¶사회의 ~ a social custom // ~의 customary / usual / conventional // ~상 conventionally / traditionally / habitually // ~에 따라 in accordance with the custom / according to custom [usage] // ~에 따르다 follow [observe / conform to] custom // ~에 어긋나다 offend against the custom / act contrary to custom // ~를 깨뜨리다 violate [break with] custom // 그렇게 하는 것이 우리의 ~이다 It is the custom [practice] with us (in this country) to do so. // 그것은 기성의 ~에 어긋나는 생각이다 The idea goes against accepted practice. // ~에 따라 지난달에 총회가 소집되었다 According to regular practice a general meeting was convened last month. // ~에 따라 6월에 종업원에게 보너스가 지급되었다 In accordance with custom [As is the custom], the employees received bonuses in June. // 이 같은 잘못을 간과한다면 좋지 않은 ~가 될 염려가 있다 I am afraid we will set a bad precedent if we overlook this mistake. // 이 조치는 ~에 어긋나는 것이다 This move is a deviation from custom.

관록(官祿) a stipend; an official salary. ¶~을 먹다 receive a stipend [an official salary].

관록(貫祿) weight of character; presence; dignity; importance. ¶~이 있는 사람 a man of dignity [presence] // ~이 붙다 gain in dignity / [노련해지다] be experienced in (business) // 선수권 보유자의 ~을 보이다 uphold the dignity of a champion // 그는 베테랑 선수의 ~을 보여 주었다 He showed what a seasoned player can do [is made of]. // 그녀는 최근에 ~이 붙었다 She has gained an air of confidence lately. // 그는 장관으로서의 ~이 충분하다 He is fully qualified for the portfolio.

관료(官僚) [관리] a bureaucrat; a government official; (집합적) the bureaucracy; officialdom; government officials. ¶고급 ~ a high-ranking official // ~적인 bureaucratic // ~ 출신의 정치가 a politician from officialdom / a bureaucrat-turned politician // ~화하다 bureaucratize / become bureaucratized // 이것은 전형적인 ~적 처리 방식이다 This is a typically bureaucratic way of working. / This is a typical example of red tape for you.
● 관료 정치 bureaucratic government; bureaucracy. 관료주의 bureaucratism; bureaucracy; officialism.

관류하다(貫流-) flow [run] through (a city).

관리(官吏) a government official; a public official [servant]; (영) a civil servant; a public functionary; (집합적) bureaucracy; officialdom. ¶고급 ~ a high-ranking government official // 하급 ~ a petty [minor] official // 유능한 ~ an able official // ~가 되다 enter government service / become a public official // 그의 아버지는 ~다 His father is in government service. // 그는 어느 관청의 말단 ~인 듯하다 He seems to hold a humble [minor] post in some ministry.
● 관리 근성 bumbledom; officialism; bureaucratism.

관리(管理) **1** [지배·감독] administration; management; control; supervision; superintendence. ¶국가 ~ state [government] control // 법정 ~ legal management // 생산 ~ production management // 공장 ~ the management [supervision] of a factory // 업무 ~ business administration // 인사 [노무] ~ personnel [labor] management // 품질 ~ quality control // ~상의 managerial / administrative // 정부 [국제] ~하에 두다 place (a matter) under government [international] control // ~의 ~를 명령받다 be put [placed] in charge of .... 관리하다 administer; manage; control; superintend; supervise. ¶학교를 ~ manage [administrate] a school // 회사의 사무를 ~ manage the business affairs of a company // 그는 산림을 관리하고 있다 He is in charge of the forest.
2 [돌봄] charge; care. ¶유산 ~ [법] administration // 재산의 ~를 위임하다 entrust one's property to (a person's) care / put one's property in (a person's) charge // 나는 그의 재산 ~를 맡았다 I was entrusted with the care of his property. // 공원은 ~가 잘되어 있다 The park is well kept [taken care of]. 관리하다 take [have] charge of; care for. ¶남의 재산을 ~ take charge of another's property // 모든 가사는 어머니가 관리하신다 The entire house is run by my mother. // 선장은 배와 승무원을 관리한다 A captain commands his ships and crew.
● 관리권 the right of management; (hold) a supervisory authority (over). 관리법 (방법) the method of administration [management]; (법률) the Administration Law. 관리부 an executive department. 관리비 management expenses. 관리 사무소 a superintendent's office; a control office. 관리인 a

manager; an administrator; a supervisor; a superintendent; an executor(유산·유저 등의); a caretaker; a trustee; a custodian; a keeper; (아파트 등의) a concierge; (미) a superintendent. **관리직** (직위) an administrative [a managerial] post; (사람) an administrator; a person holding an administrative [a managerial] position; a member of the management; a managerial officer; (집합적) (the) management; the management staff.

관립(官立) ¶~ 학교 a government school.

관망(觀望) observation; watching; fence-sitting. **관망하다** observe; watch; (wait and) see; look on(방관하다). ¶형세를 ~ 하다 observe [watch] developments / follow the turn of events / watch to see how a matter will turn out // 관망하는 태도를 취하다 assume a wait-and-see attitude // 사태를 좀 더 관망해 보자 Let's wait a little longer and see.

관명(官名) an official title. ¶~을 사칭하다 assume an official title spuriously / lie about one's official position / assume a false title.

관명(官命) official [government] orders; [관용(管用)] an official mission [business]. ¶~에 의하여 by government [official] order // ~을 띠고 under official orders / on official business [mission] // 그들은 ~에 따라 해외 시찰을 나갔다 They were sent abroad on an official [government] inspection tour. / They went on a foreign inspection tour under official [government] orders.

관모(冠毛) (새의) a crest; (식물의) a pappus (pl. -pi); plume.

관목(灌木) a shrub; a bush.
● **관목림** bushes; shrubbery. **관목 지대** a shrubbery zone.

관문(關門) 1 [요새·국경의 문] a barrier (station); a barrier-gate; a gateway (to); a boundary gate(지계(地界)의); [검문소] a checking station; a checkpoint. ¶동양의 ~ a gateway to the Orient // ~을 통과하다 pass a barrier / pass through a checkpoint. 2 [난관] a difficult situation; [장벽] a barrier; a hurdle; an obstacle. ¶사법 시험의 ~을 돌파하다 successfully pass the state law examination // 그는 입시의 ~을 무사히 통과했다 He has safely got over the hurdle of the entrance examination. // 그는 그녀와 결혼하기까지 몇 가지 ~을 통과해야만 했다 He had to surmount various obstacles before he was able to marry her.

관민(官民) officials and people; [정부와 민간] the government and the people. ¶~이 협력하여 by the joint [united] efforts of government and people // ~이 일체가 되어 부정을 뿌리 뽑아야 한다 The officials [government] and the people must unite and root out corruption.

관변(官邊) government [official] circles; official quarters. ¶~에서 나온 소식 news coming from an official source // ~에 의하면 according to official quarters / government circles say (that) // 그 소식은 소식통에서 나온 것 같다 The news seems to have come from an official source.

관보(官報) 1 (정부 발행의) an official daily gazette; a daily government newsletter. ¶~로 발표하다 gazette / publish [announce] by [in] the official gazette // ~에 실리다 [나다] be reported in the official gazette // 그의 사임은 ~로 발표되었다 His resignation was announced in the gazette. 2 [공용 전보] an official telegram.

관복(官服) an official uniform [outfit / garb / attire].

관불(회)(灌佛會) [불] the rite of perfuming the image of Buddha on an anniversary of Buddha's birth.

관비(官費) government expenditure. ¶그는 ~로 미국에 유학 갔다 He was sent to America for study at government expense.

관사(官舍) an official residence. ¶~를 제공하다 be provided with an official residence.

관사(冠詞) [언] an article. ¶정 ~ a definite article // 부정 ~ an indefinite article.

관상(冠狀) ¶~의 coronary / coronal / coronate.
● **관상 동맥** [정맥] the coronary arteries [veins].

관상(管狀) ¶~의 tubular / tubal / tubiform / tubulous.
● **관상 기관** [동] a fistula (pl. -lae). **관상화**[식] a tubular [tubulous] flower.

관상(觀相) physiognomy; physiognomic judgment of character; phrenological interpretation. ¶~을 보아 주다 read (a person's) physiognomy / tell (a person's) fortune by physiognomy // ~을 보다 get (a person) to tell one's fortune by physiognomy.
● **관상가** / **관상쟁이** a physiognomist; one who reads character [people's fortune] from facial features. **관상술** / **관상학** physiognomy; phrenology.

관상(觀賞) admiration; enjoyment. **관상하다** admire; enjoy. ¶나는 일찍 일어나 나팔꽃을 관상한다 I get up early to enjoy the morning glories.
● **관상식물** a decorative plant; an ornamental (plant). **관상어** an aquarium fish.

관서(官署) a government [public] office. ¶중앙 ~ the offices of the central government // 지방 ~ local government offices.

관선(官選) [관형어적] chosen by the authorities; official.
● **관선 변호인** ➡ 국선 변호인(⇨국선) **관선 이사** (학교 재단 등의) a government-appointed trustee.

관설(官設) a government establishment [installation / facility]. ¶~의 established by the government [state].

관성(慣性) [물] inertia.
● **관성 모멘트** the moment of inertia. **관성의 법칙** the law of inertia.

관세(關稅) customs (duties); a custom duty; a (custom) tariff. ¶보복 ~ retaliatory tariffs [duties] / 보호 ~ a protective tariff / 수입 [수출] ~ import [export] duties / 종량 ~ specific duties // 특혜 [호혜] ~ a preferential [reciprocal] tariff // ~의 인상 [인하] the raising [the lowering] of customs duties // ~ 일괄 인하 overall [across-the-board] tariff cut / tariff reduction in package // 다국 간 ~ 인하 교섭 the multilateral tariff negotiations (약어 MTN) // ~가 붙는 dutiable (goods) / (미) customable // ~가 붙지 않는 undutiable / duty-free // ~를 부과하다 levy [impose] a custom duty (on) // ~를 징수하다 collect customs (on imported goods) // ~를 치르고 화물을 인수하다 clear goods // 보석

류에는 아주 높은 ~가 붙는다 There is[They levy] a very high tariff on jewelry.
● **관세법** [법] the Customs Law[ACT]. **관세 수입** customs revenue. **관세율** a customs tariff; a tariff rate. **관세 장벽** a customs[tariff] barrier[wall]; a trade barrier. **관세 정책** a tariff policy. **관세청** the Office of Customs Administration.

관세음보살 (觀世音菩薩) [불] the Goddess of Mercy; the Merciful Goddess.

관솔 a (resinous) pine knot; a resinous part of a pine wood.
● **관솔불** a fire set to pine knots; a pine torch.

관습 (慣習) custom; usage; (a) usual[common] practice; convention; tradition. ¶상거래 the custom of trade / a commercial practice[usage] // 일반화된 ~ accepted [established] usage // 사회의 ~ the custom of society / a social custom / (social) mores // 오래된 ~ a custom of long standing // ~적인 customary / usual / ~상 customarily / usually // ~에 따라 according to custom / 옛 ~을 지키다 keep on old usage alive // 1년에 두 번 선물하는 것이 이곳의 ~이다 It is the custom here to give presents twice a year. // 이것은 이 지방의 오랜 ~이다 This is a custom[common practice] of long standing in this district. // 그는 ~에 얽매이는 사람이 아니다 He is unconventional. / He's an unfettered man.
● **관습법** (the) common law; (the) custom.

관심 (關心) interest (in); concern (about / over). ¶…에 ~을 갖다 be concerned about / take[have] (an) interest in / be interested in / …에 ~이 없다 be indifferent to / be unconcerned with / care nothing for / ~을 끌다 arouse[awake] one's interest (in) // ~을 기울이다 give thought (to) / take[have] (an) interest (in) // 그는 그것에 ~을 나타냈다 He showed an interest in it. // 그녀는 그런 일에는 아무 ~도 없다 She has no concern for[have no interest in] that sort of thing. / 나는 정치에는 별로 ~이 없다 I have little interest in politics. // 그녀는 남의 일에 ~을 갖고 있다 She is interested in other people's affairs. // 그들은 이 계획에 별로 ~이 없는 것 같다 They don't seem very enthusiastic about this project. / They seem to be little interested in this plan. // 그 소년의 박식은 반에서 ~의 대상이 되었다 The boy's wide knowledge became the center of interest [attention] in his class. // 그는 그 일에 전혀 ~이 없는 것처럼 행동했다 He acted quite unconcerned about it. // 그는 음식에는 ~이 없는 것처럼 보인다 He seems indifferent to food. // 그는 명성에는 전혀 ~을 두지 않았다 He cared nothing for[was unconcerned about] fame. // 그녀는 옷차림에는 전혀 ~이 없다 She pays no attention [is indifferent] to her appearance. // 본사는 귀사 제품에 큰 ~을 가지고 있사오니 견본을 보내 주시기 바랍니다 We take much interest in your products and would like to have samples of them.
● **관심사** a matter of concern and interest; a (matter of) concern. **최대** ~ a matter of primary concern / one's greatest concern.

관아 (官衙) a government office.

관악 (管樂) [음] the wind (instrument) music; pipe music.
● **관악기** a wind instrument. **관악대** a brass band.

관여 (關與) participation (in). **관여하다** participate[take part] in; have[play] a part (in); be concerned in[with]; have something to do with. ¶계획에 ~하고 있는 사람 a participant in a plan / 국정에 ~ participate in the national government // 사건에 ~ be involved in a case / take part[participate] in an affair // 정치에 ~ participate[mix / have a part] in politics // 경영에 ~ engage in management // 그것은 네가 관여할 일이 아니다 It is no affair[concern] of yours. / It is none of your business. // 그는 여러 가지 사업에 관여하고 있다 He is involved[has a finger] in all sort of businesses. // 나는 그 일에는 관여하고 있지 않다 I have nothing to do with[I'm not concerned with] that matter.

관엽 식물 (觀葉植物) a (potted) plant with beautiful leaves; an ornamental (plant).

관영 (官營) government management[control / operation]. ¶~의 government-controlled [-managed / -run / -operated] // ~으로 **하다** nationalize / put under government management.
● **관영사업** a government enterprise[undertaking].

관용 (官用) [관청의 용도] official[public] use; [관청의 용무] government[official] business; an official mission. ¶~으로서 for official use // ~으로 on official business[duty].
● **관용어** official language.

관용 (慣用) usage; common use. ¶~의 common / customary / (어구의) idiomatic(al) // ~상 by usage // **이 되다** get into common [popular] use // 그것은 ~상 허용되고 있다 It is accepted as established usage. // 이것은 ~적 표현이니까 그대로 욀 수밖에 없다 Since this expression is idiomatic you just have to memorize it as it is. // ~에 따르면 of는 for가 되어야 한다 According to usage, this "of" should be "for". // 그런 표현은 ~적이 아니다 Such an expression is unidiomatic.
● **관용구** an idiom; an idiomatic phrase; a set phrase; a phrase of common use. **관용어** an idiom; a idiomatic phrase; a word of established use.

관용 (寬容) tolerance; magnanimity; generosity; liberality; leniency; forgiveness; forbearance. ¶~의 tolerant (of) / lenient (to / toward / with) / magnanimous / generous (to / toward) // ~을 바랍니다 Please be patient with us. **관용하다** tolerate; be tolerant of; bear[put up] with; be generous (to / toward); forbear; forgive. ¶그는 나의 무례를 관용해 주었다 He had the magnanimity to forgive my rudeness. // 그들은 아직 어린애들이니까 장난을 치더라도 좀 더 관용해야 할 것 같다 I think you ought to be a little more lenient[understanding] towards children when they are naughty.

관원 (官員) a government official[clerk]; a public official[servant]; (영) a civil servant; a public functionary.

관위 (官位) [관직과 위계] office and rank; [관등] an official rank. ¶~을 박탈하다 divest (a person) of his official rank.

관음보살 (觀音菩薩) [불] the Goddess of Mercy. ⇨ 관세음보살

관음증(觀淫症) voyeurism; scop(t)ophilia.
관인(官印) an official [government] seal. ¶~을 **적다** affix an official [a government] seal.
관자놀이(貫子-) [생] the temple.
관작(官爵) an office and titles; official rank.
관장(管掌) charge; management; control. ¶업무를 **관장하는 사무원** the business in one's charge / one's duty. **관장하다** take charge of; have (a matter) in charge; manage. ¶경리를 관장하는 사무원 a clerk in charge of accounting / an accounts clerk / a bookkeeper // 사무를 ~ take charge of [supervise] business affairs // 그 문제를 ~ deal with the question // 이 과 경리 사무를 관장한다 This section takes [is in] charge of accounting. // 그는 하느님이 인간의 운명을 관장하고 있다고 믿는다 He believes that God controls [presides over] human destiny.
관장(館長) a director; a superintendent; (도서관의) a chief [head] librarian; (박물관의) a curator. ¶미술관 ~ the director [curator] of an art museum.
관장(灌腸) [의] an enema (*pl*. ~s, ~ta); rectal injection; intestinal irrigations; a clyster. **관장하다** administer [give] an enema to (a person); apply a clyster (to). ¶환자에게 ~ give an enema to a patient.
관재(管財) administration of an estate; custodianship; receivership(파산 시의). **관재하다** administer; put property under one's custody [custodianship].
● **관재인** (공물의) a trustee; [법] a committee; [영국 법률] a manager; (유산의) an administrator(남자); an administratrix(여자); (청산 시의) a receiver; (정부·점령군의) a property custodian.
관저(官邸) an official residence (of the Prime Minister). ¶대통령 ~ the Presidential residence.
관전기(觀戰記) a witness's account (of a chess match).
관전하다(觀戰-) witness a battle; observe military [naval] operations; (경기를) watch a game [contest / match]. ¶텔레비전으로 럭비 경기 관전하기를 좋아한다 I like watching rugby games on TV.
관절(關節) [생] a joint; an articulation. ¶가동 ~ diarthrosis // 팔꿈치 ~ an elbow joint // ~이 있는 articular // ~을 **빼다** have a joint dislocated / put (the knee) out of joint // 발[팔]의 ~을 빼다 put one's leg [arm] out of joint // 무릎[팔꿈치] ~을 뺐다 I sprained my knee [elbow]. / 무릎 ~이 아프다 My knee hurts [pains me]. // 모든 ~이 쑤셨다 Every joint ached. // 오른팔의 ~이 뼜다 I had my right arm out of joint.
● **관절 류머티즘** articular [joint] rheumatism. **관절염** arthritis; inflammation of a joint. **관절 탈구** dislocation of a joint; disarticulation.
관점(觀點) a point of view; a viewpoint; a standpoint; an angle (of vision). ¶문제를 보는 새로운 ~ a new angle on the problem / 이 ~에서 본다면 (judging) from this point of view // 모든 ~에서 검토하다 examine (it) from all angles // 다른 ~에서 보다 view (a matter) from a different standpoint [angle] // 당신과 나는 ~이 다르다 You and I have different points of view. // 이 ~에서 생각하면 그의 말이 옳다 Viewed in this light, what he says is right. // 그가 그런 ~을 취하는 것은 당연하다 It is natural that he should take such a stand. // ~을 바꾸어서 보면 어때 How about looking at things from a different angle?
관제(官制) a system [an organization] of government; government organization; official regulations. ¶~를 **정하다** establish a government organization.
● **관제 개혁** reform of government organization; reorganization of the government offices.
관제(官製) government manufacture. ¶~의 government-manufactured / of government manufacture [make] / made [manufactured] by the government.
● **관제엽서** a government [an official] postcard; (미) a postal card.
관제(管制) control; controlling. ¶지상 ~ (진입) ground control (approach)(약어 GCA) // 당시에는 전국적으로 보도 ~가 내려져 있었다 In those days there was news censorship all over the country. **관제하다** control. ¶등화를 ~ black [dim] out.
● **관제소** (우주선의) a (satellite) tracking station. **관제탑** (비행장의) a control tower.
관조(觀照) contemplation; meditation; (미) intuition. **관조하다** contemplate; meditate. ¶자연[인생]을 ~ contemplate nature [life].
관족(管足) [동] a tube [an ambulacral] foot.
관존민비(官尊民卑) making much of officialdom and little of the people; putting government above people. ¶~의 폐풍 the corrupt [evil] custom of putting government above people.
관중(觀衆) spectators; viewers; onlookers; (집합적) an audience. ¶축구 시합의 ~ spectators at a football match // ~이 **많다**[적다] have a large [small] audience // ~을 끌다 draw an audience // 이 스타디움은 5만 명의 ~을 수용할 수 있다 This stadium can seat 50,000 spectators. // 그녀는 ~의 우레와 같은 박수를 받으며 등장했다 She appeared on the stage amid a thunderous handclapping of the audience. // 이 영화의 ~은 대부분이 십대 소년 소녀 들이다 The audience for this film is mostly teenagers.
관직(官職) a government [an official] post [position]; the government service. ¶~에 있다 be in government service // ~을 **떠나다** leave [resign from] government service // 아버지는 ~에 몸담고 계시다 My father is a government official. / My father is in government service. // 그는 중요한 ~에 임명되었다 He was appointed to an important government post [office].
관찰(觀察) observation; view. ¶물체의 ~ 방법 a way of looking at [observing] things // 정확[면밀]한 ~ an accurate [a minute / a close] observation // 개미의 습성에 관한 ~ observations on the habits of ants // ~이 **예리하다** be sharp in observation / have a keen power of observation // 내 ~에 잘못이 없다면 unless my observation deceives [my eyes deceive] me // ~을 **그르치다** make an incorrect observation // 남의 옷차림에 대한 그녀의 ~은 날카롭다 She has a sharp eye for the way other people dress. **관찰하다** observe; make observation (of); watch. ¶내가 관찰한 바로는 according to my observation / as I

look at it // 천체의 움직임[물고기의 생태]을 ~ observe the movements of the heavenly bodies[the ecology of fish] // 나는 이야기를 주고받으면서 그녀를 관찰했다 While talking with her, I watched her closely.
● **관찰력** (one's) power of observation. ¶~이 예리한 사람 a man of keen observation // ~을 기르다 foster one's power of observation. **관찰사** a (provincial) governor. **관찰안** an (observing) eye (for). **관찰자** an observer. **관찰점** a point of view; a viewpoint; an object of observation.

관철(貫徹) accomplishment; attainment; realization; fulfillment. **관철하다** carry (a thing) through; hold out to the last; accomplish (one's purpose); achieve (one's end); realize (one's intention). ¶초지를 ~ carry out one's original goal [intention] // 목적을 ~ accomplish[achieve] one's purpose[end] / attain one's object[goal] // 신념을 ~ stick to one's belief to the last // 그는 자기의 주장을 관철하였다 He stuck to his opinion. // 그것을 관철하려는 당신의 결의에 나는 감명을 받았다 I am impressed by your determination to carry it through. // 무슨 일이 있어도 이것을 관철할 결심이다 Nothing shall prevent me from accomplishing this. / I am determined to go through with the undertaking. // 끝까지 요구를 관철하자 Let us push on our demand to the last.

관청(官廳) a government office; [당국] the authorities. ¶행정 ~ an administrative office // 당해 ~ the authorities concerned // 주무 ~ the competent authorities // 감독 ~ the authorities supervising the affairs (of) // ~에 근무하다 serve in an office.

관측(觀測) **1** [관찰] observation; survey. ¶기상 ~ weather observation // 남극 ~대 the Antarctic expedition (party). **관측하다** observe; make[take] an observation; survey. ¶별을 ~ observe the stars / make astronomical observation // 태양[일식]을 ~ make observations of the sun[a solar eclipse] // 기상[기압 / 천체]을 ~ make meteorological[barometric / astronomical] observations.
2 [생각·의견] thinking; an opinion. ¶내 ~으로는 사태는 더 이상 악화되지 않을 것 같다 In my opinion the situation will not get any worse. // 이것은 나의 희망적 ~에 지나지 않습니다 This is merely my wishful thinking.
● **관측기구** an observation balloon; (기상 관측의) a sounding balloon. **관측소** an observatory; an observation station. **관측자** an observer.

관통(貫通) piercing; penetration; perforation. **관통하다** pierce; bore (through / into); pass through; penetrate; perforate; (탄환이) shoot [go] through. ¶탄환이 그의 다리를 관통했다 The bullet went through his legs. // 터널이 산을 관통하여 만들어졌다 A tunnel was bored through the mountain. // 철도는 대평원을 관통하고 있다 The railroad goes all the way across the great plain.
● **관통상** a piercing bullet wound. ¶그는 가슴에 ~을 입었다 He was shot through the chest. / He had his chest shot through.

관포지교(管鮑之交) a Damon and Pythias [David and Jonathan] friendship. ¶그들은 ~의 사이였다 They were inseparable friends.

관하다(關─) **1** [대하다] be connected[concerned] with; be related to; concern; be about; refer to. ¶종교[과학]에 관한 책 a book on religion[science] // 정치에 관한 강연 a lecture on politics // 방위에 관한 논쟁 a dispute over[concerning] defense // 이 건에 관한 일체의 서류 all the documents referring to this matter // 이 일에 관하여 in this connection[respect] / about this matter // 그에 관한 한 문제는 없다 As far as he is concerned, there is no problem. // 그 일에 관해서는 아무것도 모른다 I know nothing about the matter. // 이 건에 관하여 들은 이야기가 있다 There's something that I have heard in connection with this affair.
2 [영향을 미치다] affect (one's honor); concern (one's welfare); involve (one's prestige). ¶명예에 관한 문제 a question affecting one's honor // 생사에 관한 문제 a matter of life and death // 그의 생명에 관한 일이 될지도 모른다 It may affect his life. // 그것은 국가의 위신에 관한 문제다 It is a problem in which national honor and prestige are involved.

관학(官學) a national[government] university.

관할(管轄) jurisdiction; control; competence. ¶…의 ~하에 있다 fall under the jurisdiction of ... / ~ 내[밖]의 within[outside] the jurisdiction // 이 지역은 서대문 경찰서 ~이다 This district is under the jurisdiction of the Seodaemun Police Station. // 그 지역은 당 경찰서의 ~ 내[밖]에 있다 The area is within [outside / beyond] the jurisdiction of this police station. **관할하다** exercise jurisdiction [control] (over a district); have competence (over a matter); control. ¶그 관청은 북부 지방을 관할한다 The office has jurisdiction over the northern district. // 이 과(課)는 회사의 문화 시설을 관할하고 있다 This department has control over the cultural facilities of the company.
● **관할 관청** the competent[relevant] authorities station. **관할 구역** (법원의) the district boundaries of a court; (경찰서의) a police district[(미) precinct]. **관할권** jurisdiction.

관행(慣行) (a) traditional practice; (a) custom; routine. ¶~의 habitual / customary / practical // ~을 지키다 follow a custom [traditional practice] // ~에 따라 지사가 시구를 했다 In accordance with tradition, the governor threw out the first ball.

관향(貫鄕) a place of origin. ⇨본관

관허(官許) government permission; (government) license. ¶~를 얻은 licensed / authorized // ~를 얻다 obtain an official permit[a license]. **관허하다** give official permission [recognition]; license.
● **관허요금** (government-)licensed charge.

관헌(官憲) **1** a government office. ⇨관청 **2** a government official. ⇨관리(官吏)

관현악(管絃樂) orchestral music; an orchestra.
● **관현악단** an orchestra (band).

관형사(冠形詞) an unconjugation adjective.

관혼상제(冠婚喪祭) the ceremonies of coming of age, marriage, funeral and ancestral worship; ceremonial occasions.

괄괄하다 **1** (성질이) virile; spirited; hot-tem-

괄다 pered; impetuous; rash. ¶성미가 괄괄한 남자 a man of violent[impetuous] temper // 성미가 괄괄한 여자 a spirited[manly] woman / a woman of masculine temper. **2** (풀기가) sticky; stiff with starch.

괄다 1 [불길이 세다] too high[strong]. ¶불이 너무 괄아 밥이 탔다 The rice was scorched because the fire was too intense. **2** virile; spirited. ⇨ 괄괄하다₁

괄목하다 (刮目-) watch eagerly[closely]; watch with keen interest. ¶괄목할 만한 진보 eye-opening[startling] progress // 괄목할 만하다 be worthy of close attention // 그의 새로운 연구는 괄목할 만하다 His new research deserves close attention.

괄시 (恝視) negligence; slight; [냉대] a cold reception. **괄시하다** neglect; slight; treat (a person) coldly. ¶너무 괄시하지 마라 Don't hold me so cheap.

괄약근 (括約筋) [생] a sphincter (muscle); a constrictor; a sphincteral muscle. ¶항문 ~ the anal sphincter / the sphincter ani.

괄태충 (括胎蟲) [동] a slug.

괄호 (括弧) (미) parentheses (*sing.* -sis) [(영)] (round) brackets; [대괄호] brackets; square brackets; [중괄호] braces (▶ 모두가 복수형으로 쓰임). ¶이중 ~ double parentheses // ~ 안에 넣은 어구 parenthesized[bracketed] phrase / a phrase in parentheses[brackets] // ~ 를 없애다 remove the parentheses[brackets] // ~ 로 묶다 put (a word) in parentheses[brackets] / parenthesize.

광 a store-room; a storehouse; a cellar(땅광); a granary(곡식 광); a barn.

광 (光) **1** [물] [빛] (a) light; [광선] rays (of light); a ray. ¶태양~ the light[rays] of the sun. **2** [유기] gloss; luster; glaze; brightness. ¶진주의 ~ the luster of a pearl // ~이 나는 lustrous / glossy / bright / sheeny // ~이 안 나는 dim / dull / dry / lusterless // ~이 안 나는 가죽 dull leather // ~을 내다 gloss / glaze / bring out the luster / polish up // 보석을 닦아 ~을 내다 polish a jewel to bring out the shine[its luster] / 천[종이]에 ~을 내다 calender cloth[paper] // ~을 죽이다 take off the gloss[luster / shine].

광 (廣) [넓이] (an) area; (an) extent; [나비] width; breadth.

광 (鑛) [갱(坑)] a pit; a mine; [덩어리] a (mineral) ore.

-광 (狂) a fan; a fanatic; (미국 구어) a buff. ¶경마~ a turfman / a race maniac / a horse racing enthusiast[(구어) nut] / 낚시~ a fishing addict // 살인~ a homicidal maniac // 야구~ a baseball fan // 재즈~ a jazz freak // 영화~ a film[movie] enthusiast // 그는 연극~이다 He is a theatre buff. / He is crazy about the stage. // 그는 경마~이다 He is mad about horse racing.

광각 (光角) [물] an optic angle.
광각 (光覺) the light sense[sensation].
광각 (廣角) a wide angle.
●**광각 렌즈** a wide-angle lens; a pantoscope.

광견병 (狂犬病) [의] (the) rabies; hydrophobia; lyssa; canine madness. ¶~에 걸리다 be affected with rabies // ~ 예방 주사를 맞다 get an antirabies injection.

광경 (光景) [벌어진 일의 상태] a spectacle; a sight; a scene; a view; an aspect. ¶즐거운 [무서운 / 슬픈] ~ a pleasant[horrid / sad] sight // 손에 땀을 쥐게 하는 ~ a thrilling [dramatic] scene[spectacle] // …의 도착 ~을 방송하다 broadcast a description of the arrival of … // 그것은 보기 흉한 ~이었다 It was an unseemly sight. // 그 순간 이상한 ~이 벌어졌다 A curious spectacle was witnessed.

광고 (廣告) an advertisement; (구어) ad; (영국 구어) an advert; [알림] a notice; an announcement; [선전] advertising; publicity. ¶구인 ~ a help-wanted advertisement / a want ad // 삼행 ~ classified ads // 사망 ~ an obituary / a death notice // 미아 [잃은 것]를 내다 advertise for the recovery of a missing child[a lost article] // 방송[텔레비전] ~에 ~를 넣다 insert a commercial (message) in a radio[TV] program // 건설 회사에서 신축 아파트의 세입자 모집 ~를 내고 있다 The construction company is advertising for tenants for its new apartment house. // 그들은 최신형 자동차의 ~를 신문, 잡지에 냈다 They placed[put / ran] advertisement for the latest model cars in newspapers and magazines. / They advertised the latest model cars in the press. // 그는 신문에 구직 ~를 냈다 He was advertising for employment[a job] in the newspaper. **광고하다** advertise (for a book); announce; give publicity (to); make (something) widely known. ¶신문에 ~ advertise in a newspaper / put an ad in the papers // 대대적으로 ~ advertise extensively.

●**광고란** an advertising column[section]; [신문의 3행 광고] the classified ad; a want column. **광고료** advertisement rate[charge]; advertising rates[charge]. **광고문** (게재된) an advertising description; a written advertisement; [초안·원문] an advertisement draft; an original copy of advertisement. **광고 방송** [라디오·TV] a commercial (broadcast); [문구] a commercial (message); (미국 속어) a plug. **광고업** advertising business. **광고 전단** (뿌리는) a handbill; [붙이는] a poster; a placard. **광고탑** (거리의) a poster column; (옥상 등의) an ad pillar; an advertising tower. **광고판** a billboard; a signboard.

광공업 (鑛工業) the mining and manufacturing industries.

광구 (光球) [천] a photosphere.
광구 (鑛區) a mining area; diggings; a mine lot; a mining claim.

광궤 (廣軌) a broad gauge; (구미(歐美)의) the standard gauge. ¶~의 broad-gauge.
●**광궤 철도** (미) a broad-gauge railroad [(영) railway].

광기 (狂氣) insanity; madness; craziness; lunacy. ¶~의 insane / mad // 그의 행동은 ~에 가깝다 His conduct borders upon madness.

광나다 (光-) gloss; glaze; shine; have a gloss [shine / luster / glaze]. ¶광나지 않다 be dull [dim / lackluster] / (a table) won't polish // 구두가 광난다 The shoes are shiny.

광내다 (光-) shine (shoes); polish; make (a thing) shine[bright]. ¶광내는 가루약 polishing powder // 구두를 ~ shine shoes // 쇠조각을 ~ burnish a piece of metal // 때 빼고 ~ [몸단장하다] smarten oneself up.

광년 (光年) [천] a light-year.

광대 (가면극의) a masque performer; (인형극의) a puppeteer; [곡예사] an acrobatic performer; a tumbler; [어릿광대] a clown; a buffoon; a jester; (창극의) a feat singer. ¶~가 되다 go on the stage // ~ 노릇을 하다 play the jester[fool].

광대뼈 the cheekbone; zygomatic bone. ¶~가 나온 사람 a person with high cheekbone.

광대하다(廣大-) vast (plains); extensive; immense. ¶광대한 사막 a vast expanse of desert // 광대한 평원 a vast[extensive] plain // 미국은 모든 것이 규모가 ~ Everything is on a grand scale in America.

광도(光度) luminous[light] intensity; intensity of lightness; [행성의 밝기] brightness (of a star). ¶~의 차이 the different degree of brightness // 별의 ~ the brightness[magnitude] of a star.
●광도계 a photometer. 광도 계급 luminosity classification. 광도 측정 photometry.

광독(鑛毒) mining[mineral] pollution; [독물] pollutants produced in the (copper) mining process.

광란(狂亂) madness; craziness; fury; frenzy; raving. ¶반~ 상태의 half-mad[-crazed] // 너는 화가 나서 ~ 상태가 되어 있다 She is frenzied[in a frenzy / beside herself] with anger. 광란하다 go mad; be[become] frantic; get wild; be beside oneself; rage; rave.

광량(光量) the intensity of radiation.
●광량계 an actinometer.

광력(光力) (전등 등의) light; [물] illuminating power.

광림(光臨) your visit[call / presence]. 광림하다 condescend to come[be present]. ¶광림하여 주시면 영광이겠습니다 We request the honor of your company (at dinner).

광막하다(廣漠-) vast; extensive; wide; boundless. ¶광막한 황야 a vast wilderness // 광막한 사막 a vast[boundless] expanse of desert // 광막한 초원 a vast expanse of grass / (미) the vast plains[prairies].

광맥(鑛脈) a vein of ore; a lode; a deposit. ¶매장량이 많은 ~ a rich vein (of coal) // ~을 찾아내다 strike a vein of ore / strike a lode.

광명(光明) [빛] light; [희망] hope; a bright future[prospect]. ¶한 줄기의 ~ a ray [gleam] of hope / a beam of hope (on the horizon) // 생활에 ~을 주다 brighten (a person's) life // 그의 앞날에는 ~이 있다 His future prospects are bright. ¶ He has a bright future before him. // 그는 맹인에게 ~을 찾아 주었다 He restored sight to the blind.

광목(廣木) cotten (broad) cloth.

광물(鑛物) a mineral. ¶금속 ~ a metallic mineral // ~(성)의 mineral // 풍부한 ~ 자원 rich mineral resources.
●광물계 the mineral kingdom. 광물성 mineral. 광물질 mineral matter. 광물학 mineralogy.

광범위(廣範圍) a wide area[range]; a wide scope. ¶~에 걸치다 cover a wide area. 광범위하다 extensive; wide; widespread; wide-ranging (studies); comprehensive (plan); far-reaching (program). ¶광범위하게 extensively / widely / largely // 광범위한 개혁 a far-reaching reform // 광범위한 영향을 주다 exercise a far-reaching influence (upon / over) // 광범위한 권한이 주어지고 be given wide power // 광범위하게 논하다 discuss (a subject) at large / deal with generalities // 그녀의 독서 폭은 ~ Her reading is of very wide range[covers a wide range]. // 그의 지식은 ~ He is widely informed. // 이 식물은 광범위하게 분포되어 있다 This plant grows[is distributed] over a wide area. // 그의 영향은 광범위하게 미쳤다 His influence extended [reached] far and wide.

광복(光復) glorious restoration; [주권 회복] the restoration of independence (to a country). 광복하다 regain (a country's) independence.
●광복군 the Independence[Liberation] Army. 광복절 Independence Day of Korea.

광부(鑛夫) a miner; a mine worker; a pitman; a digger. ¶석탄 ~ a coal miner.

광분하다(狂奔-) 1 [미쳐 날뛰다] rush about; run madly about; run wild[amuck]. 2 [바삐 돌아다니다] make desperate efforts; be very busy (in) (doing). ¶구직에 ~ be busily hunting for a job / keep oneself busy in search of work // 돈 벌이에 ~ be busy making money / be absorbed in moneymaking // 그는 선거 운동에 광분하고 있다 He is busily engaged in an election campaign. // 그는 막후 공작에 광분하였다 He rushed about madly working[He made desperate efforts] behind the scenes.

광산(鑛山) a mine; a mine field. ¶~을 개발하다 develop[open up] a mine // ~을 채굴하다 work[exploit] a mine // ~을 경영하다 run [operate] a mine // ~에 투자하다 invest in a mine // ~을 폐쇄하다 shut down a mine // 폭발 사고 이후 그 ~은 폐쇄되었다 The mine was closed after the explosion.
●광산 기사 a mining engineer. 광산 채굴권 mining rights[concessions]. 광산촌 a miners' town; (미) a camp. 광산학 mining (science); (the study of) mining.

광산(鑛産) [광업 생산] mining production; [광산물] mineral products.
●광산업 mining; the mining industry; the mines. 광산지 a region[an area] rich in mineral deposits.

광상(鑛床) a (mineral) deposit.

광상곡(狂想曲) [음] a capriccio.

광석(鑛石) an ore; a mineral; a crystal(라디오의).
●광석 검파기 a crystal[mineral] detector.

광선(光線) a ray[beam] of light; light. ¶태양 ~ sunbeams / the rays of the sun // 반사[굴절] ~ reflected[refracted] light // 살인 ~ death rays // 직접 ~ a direct ray of light // 간접 ~ an indirect ray of light // ~이 잘 드는 [안 드는] 방 a well-[an ill-]lighted room // ~을 방사하다 send out light / ~을 차단하다 cut off light / (갓을 씌워서) shade from the direct rays (of the sun) // 태양 ~이 창문으로 들어와 카펫을 비추었다 The sun shone in through the window onto the carpet. // 이 필름은 ~이 들어갔다 This film is affected.
●광선 요법 phototherapy; action therapy.

광섬유(光纖維) optical fiber.

광속(光束) a pencil of light[rays]; [전] luminous flux.

광속(도)(光速度) [물] the speed[velocity] of light.

광수(鑛水) mineral water.

광시곡(狂詩曲) [음] a rhapsody. ¶헝가리 ~

광신 Hungarian Rhapsodies.

광신(狂信) (religious) fanaticism. ¶~적인 fanatic(al) // ~적 공산주의자 a fanatical [rabid] Communist. **광신하다** fanatically believe (in); be devoted blindly (to).
● **광신자** a fanatic; a fanatic believer (in).

광심(光心) [물] an optical center.

광야(曠野·廣野) a wilderness; (미) a prairie; a wide field [plain]; open country.

광양자(光量子) [물] a photon; light quantum.

광어(廣魚) [넙치] a flatfish; a dried flatfish(말린 것).

광언(狂言) unreasonable [crazy] talk; nonsense.

광업(鑛業) the mining industry.
● **광업가** (미) a mine operator; a mine owner. **광업권** a mining right [concession]. **광업소** a mining station [office].

광역(廣域) a wide area. ¶살인범의 ~ 조사가 행해졌다 A search for the murderer was conducted over a wide area.
● **광역 수사** a search (for a suspected criminal) conducted over very wide area. **광역시** a metropolitan city.

광열비(光熱費) expenses for lighting and fuel; electricity and heating expenses.

광염(光焰) a flame.

광우리 →광주리

광우병(狂牛病) mad cow disease; (공식명) bovine spongiform encephalopathy(약어 BSE).

광원(光源) [물] a light source; the source of light.

광음(光陰) time (and tide). ¶일촌~ a minute.

광의(廣義) a wide [broad] sense. ¶~로 해석하다 interpret [understand / take] (it) in a broad sense // 이 표현은 ~로 해석할 수 있다 This expression can be interpreted broadly [in wider sense]. / (문어) This expression admits of wide interpretation.

광인(狂人) a madman; a lunatic; an insane [a crazy] person.

광자(光子) [물] a photon; a light quantum.

광장(廣場) an open space; (도시의) a public square; (대광장) a plaza. ¶역전 ~ a square [plaza] in front of a station.

광재(鑛滓) slag; dross.

광적(狂的) lunatic; insane; frantic; fanatic(al); mad. ¶~인 신앙 fanatic belief // ~인 행위 an insane act // ~인 열의 wild enthusiasm // 신흥 종교의 ~인 신자 a fanatic believer in a new religion.

광전관(光電管) [컴] a phototube; a photoelectric tube.

광전기(光電氣) [전] photoelectricity.

광전자(光電子) [물] a photoelectron.

광전지(光電池) a photocell; a photoelectric cell.

광점(光點) a luminous point; [천] a radiant; a facula(태양의).

광주(鑛主) the owner [proprietor] of a mine.

광 주 리 a (bamboo [wicker]) basket; a hamper(뚜껑 있는).

광증(狂症) insanity; madness; lunacy; frenzy. ¶~을 일으키다 go mad / become insane.

광차(鑛車) a mine car; a coal tub(석탄차).

광채(光彩) brilliance; luster; splendor; effulgence. ¶~ 나는 진주 lustrous pearls // ~가 나다 be brilliant / be in all (its) splendor // ~를 발하다 shed luster / shine // 그 소년의 눈은 흥분으로 ~가 났다 The boy's eyes shone with excitement. // 그녀의 눈은 ~를 잃었다 Her eyes lost their luster. // 그녀의 다이아몬드 반지가 ~를 발했다 Her diamond ring sparkled brightly. // 그녀의 연기는 특히 ~를 발했다 Her performance outshone all the others.

광천(鑛泉) a mineral spring; mineral water(광수(鑛水)); a spa(온천).

광체(光體) a luminous body. ⇨ 발광체(發光)

광축(光軸) [물] an optical axis.

광층(鑛層) an ore bed.

광태(狂態) disgraceful behavior [[영] behaviour]; shameful conduct. ¶~를 부리다 behave scandalously [disgracefully] / (취하다) get wild in drink [on the drink] / (실수하다) get into a mess.

광택(光澤) gloss; sheen; luster; polish; brilliance; a shine. ¶~ 있는 lustrous / glossy / brilliant / ~ 없는 dull / lusterless // 은은한 ~ quiet [subdued] gloss [sheen] // ~을 내다 polish / burnish / glaze / give luster [brilliance] // ~을 잃다 lose luster [brilliance] // 니스를 칠한 가구에서 ~이 잘 난다 That varnished furniture has a nice gloss.
● **광택지** glossy [slick / coated] paper.

광파(光波) [물] light wave.

광포하다(狂暴-) furious; frenzied; outrageous; wild. ¶광포해지다 go berserk / fly into a frantic rage.

광폭(廣幅) double [extra] width; an (extra) wide width (of cloth).

광풍(狂風) a raging wind; a violent gale.

광학(光學) optics; optical science.
● **광학 기계** an optical instrument. **광학 병기** optical weapons.

광합성(光合成) photosynthesis.

광행차(光行差) [천] an aberration. ¶연주(年週) ~ annual aberration.

광화학(光化學) [화] photochemistry.
● **광화학 반응** [화] (a) photochemical reaction.

광활하다(廣闊-) spacious; vast; extensive. ¶광활한 사막 a vast expanse [extent] of desert // 광활한 평야 a vast (fertile) plain / a vast open field // 광활한 땅 a vast expanse [spread / extent] of land // 전망이 ~ command an extensive view. **광활히** spaciously; extensively.

광휘(光輝) brilliance; brightness; splendor; glory; glow. ¶~를 발하다 shine brilliantly / emit dazzling rays // 그의 명성은 이미 ~를 잃었다 His fame has lost its brilliance.

광휘롭다(光輝-) glorious [brilliant / splendid] (victory).

광희(狂喜) wild joy; rapture(s); extreme delight; exultation; ecstasy. **광희하다** be mad [wild] with joy; be beside oneself with joy; go [fall] into raptures (over).

괘(卦) (주역의) a trigram from the Book of Changes; a divination sign.

괘념(掛念) care; concern; worry. **괘념하다** mind; care; be concerned (over); take (a matter) to heart; worry (about). ¶조금도 괘념하지 않다 do not care a bit [straw] (about) // 나는 세상 사람들이 뭐라고 하든 괘념하지 않는다 I don't care at all [a bit] what people say of me.

괘도(掛圖) [지도] a wall map; [도표] a wall

괘선(罫線) a ruled line; a rule; [인] a rule mark. ¶～이 있는[없는] 종이 ruled[unruled/plain] paper.

괘씸하다 [무례하다] rude; impertinent; insolent; [밉살스럽다] hateful; detestable; disgusting; [은혜를 모르다] ungrateful; [발칙하다] outrageous; [믿을 수 없다] unfaithful; untrustworthy. 괘씸한 놈 a disgusting[an intolerable] fellow∥괘씸한 짓 an improper act / an offensive deed∥나를 이렇게 기다리게 하다니 참으로 ～ It is perfectly monstrous to keep me waiting like this.∥그는 어른한테 인사도 할 줄 모르는 괘씸한 놈이다 He is an insolent fellow who doesn't know how to greet his elders properly.∥선생님에게 말대꾸하다니 괘씸한 것이다 It is unpardonable to have talked back to the teacher.∥내 편지에 답장도 보내지 않다니 괘씸한 놈이다 It is inexcusable[unpardonable] of him not to answer my letter. **괘씸히** rudely; impertinently. ¶～ 생각하다 hold (a person) culpable.

괘종(掛鐘) a wall clock.
괘지(罫紙) ruled[lined] paper.
괜찮다 1 [쓸 만하다] nice; good; not so bad; passable; fair; fine. ¶괜찮은 값[수입] a good [fair] price[income]∥괜찮은 사람 a good [fine] man∥괜찮은 여자 a fairly pretty woman∥맛이 ～ taste good (enough)∥그것 ～ That's good[OK].∥이건 좀 괜찮은 포도주다 This wine is not (half) bad.
2 [무방하다] (사람이) may; can; (서술적) be allowed to (do); be justified in (doing); (사물이) justifiable; warrantable; all right; O.K.; (서술적) will do. ¶괜찮으시다면 if you don't mind (it) / if it is convenient to you∥문을 열어도 ～ You may open the door.∥비가 와도 ～ I don't care if it rains.∥담배를 피워도 괜찮습니까 Do you mind if I smoke?∥어느 쪽이든 ～ Either will do.∥휴일은 아무리 많아도 ～ There is no such thing as too many holidays. / Holidays cannot be too many.∥괜찮습니다 (사과에 대하여) Never mind. / That's all right.∥고맙습니다. 이젠 괜찮습니다 Thank you. I'm all right now.∥11월에는 겨울 코트는 안 입어도 ～ You can do without a heavy[winter] coat in November.∥네 노트를 빌리지 않아도 괜찮을 것 같다 I believe I can manage without borrowing your notes.
3 [안심이다] safe; secure; free from danger; all right; (미) O.K. ¶…라고 말해도 ～ It is safe to say that ….∥(위험을 벗어나) 이젠 ～ Now we are out of danger[the woods]. / We are in the clear now.∥이 건물은 지진이 일어나도 ～ This building is proof against earthquakes.∥"도둑맞지 않을까?" "아니, 괜찮아." "Will it not be stolen?" "No, there is no fear of that."

괜하다 useless. ⇨공연(空然)하다
괜히 to no purpose; needlessly. ⇨공연히(⇨공연하다)
괭이¹ a hoe; a pick; (뿌리 캐는) a mattock. ¶～로 **파다** hoe up the soil / dig with a hoe∥밭을 ～로 갈다 hoe a field / till a field with a hoe∥～로 풀을 뽑다 hoe up[out] weeds.
괭이² a cat.
괴경(塊莖) [식] a tuber; a seed. ⇨덩이줄기(⇨덩이)
괴괴망측하다(怪怪罔測－) [야릇하다] very strange; grotesque; most weird[uncanny/mysterious]; [흉측하다] outrageous; monstrous; scandalous. ¶괴괴망측한 소문 a wildest[most scandalous] rumor∥괴괴망측한 일 a strange thing / an odd thing / a mystery.

괴괴하다 [조용하다] quiet; still; silent; deserted. ¶괴괴한 거리 a quiet[deserted] street∥괴괴한 밤 a very silent[still] night.
괴기(怪奇) (a) mystery; (a) wonder. **괴기하다** weird; grotesque; bizarre; mysterious. ¶복잡괴기한 사건 a complicated and inscrutable affair.
● **괴기 소설** a mystery[spook] story; a thriller.
괴나리봇짐(－褓－) a traveler's knapsack; a back bundle. ¶～을 등에 메고 길을 떠나다 take the road, carrying a bundle on one's back.
괴다¹ [모이다] gather; collect; [정체하다] stagnate; be stagnant. ¶괸 물 stagnant [standing] water∥오목한 땅에 괸 빗물 rainwater collected[gathered] in depressions∥그의 눈에 눈물이 괴었다 Tears gathered in his eyes.∥시궁창 물은 괴어 있었다 The water lay stagnant[stood] in the gutter.∥비가 그친 후 길의 여기저기에 물이 조금씩 괴어 있었다 After the rain there were many small puddles in the road.
괴다² [발효하다] ferment; undergo fermentation.
괴다³ 1 [받치다] prop; support; sustain. ¶두 손으로 턱을 ～ cup one's chin in one's hands / support one's chin on one's hands∥쓰러져 가는 담장을 받침으로 ～ prop [support] a leaning fence with a post∥그녀는 턱을 괴고 창밖을 바라보고 있었다 She was looking out of the window with her chin resting[propped up] on the hand(s). 2 [쌓다] arrange[pile up] (food). ¶음식을 접시에 ～ arrange food on a dish.
괴담(怪談) [무서운 이야기] a ghost story; (미) a spooky story; [이상한 이야기] a strange story.
괴란(壞亂) (풍의) corruption; demoralization. **괴란하다** corrupt; subvert; destroy.
괴력(怪力) marvelous (physical) strength; Herculean[prodigious/superhuman] strength; Amazonian strength(여자의). ¶～을 **발휘하다** put forth[out] Herculean[a giant's] strength.
괴로움 [곤란·고난] distress; troubles; hardships; sufferings; [근심] worries; [수고] trouble; annoyance; [고뇌] agony; anguish; affliction; [고통·병고] pain; pangs; [문어] throes; [시련] trials; ordeals. ¶～의 원인 the source of trouble∥삶의 ～ the worries [troubles] of life∥죽음의 ～ death agony∥마음의 ～ anguish of heart / a weight on one's mind∥가난의 ～ the gripe of poverty∥인생의 ～ the bitters of life / life's trials∥～이 많다 have a lot of trouble / be full of woe / have many difficulties∥～을 **주다** inflict pain on a person∥～을 **견디다** bear one's sufferings∥～을 **덜다** alleviate one's sufferings∥～을 **당하다** suffer troubles / undergo hardships∥그는 여러 가지 ～을 겪어 왔다 He has gone through various hardships.∥아이 기르는 일은 ～이기도 하지만 즐거움이기도 하다 The upbringing of children is a source

괴로워하다

of pleasure as well as of anxiety. // 아내의 참견이 그에게는 큰 ~이었다 His wife's meddlesomeness was an agony [quite painful] to him.

괴로워하다 1 [고통을 느끼다] suffer (from); feel [be in] pain; be afflicted (with). ¶갈증으로 ~ suffer from thirst // 그는 치통으로 괴로워하고 있다 He is suffering from toothache [(미) a toothache].
2 [고민하다] be distressed; be worried (by); worry oneself (about / over); torment with the thought (of). ¶돈 문제로 ~ be pinched [pressed / hard up] for money // 그는 양심의 가책에 괴로워하고 있다 He is tormented by a guilty conscience. // 그는 사업의 실패로 몹시 괴로워하고 있다 He is terribly distressed by the failure of his business. // 그는 갈 것인가 말 것인가로 괴로워하고 있다 He is worrying whether he should go or not. // 그는 아들의 비행으로 괴로워하고 있다 His son's misconduct caused him great distress [pain]. // 그녀는 자신의 장래 문제로 괴로워하고 있다 She is worried about her future. // 그는 실패한 것을 아직도 괴로워하고 있다 He is still troubled by his failure. / He can't get over his failure.

괴롭다 [고통스럽다] painful; afflicting; distressing; agonizing; [곤란하다] troublesome; hard; difficult; [난처하다] awkward; embarrassing; [곤궁하다] straitened; needy; reduced; (서술적) be indisposed of. ¶괴로운 나머지 driven by pain [distress / despair] / out of desperation // 괴로운 임무 a painful duty // 괴로운 일 a hard [difficult / (구어) tough] job // 괴로운 세상 a hard world // 괴로운 마음 an aching [a troubled] heart // 괴로운 입장 an awkward situation // 과식을 해서 속이 ~ I have eaten so much that my stomach feels heavy. // 그 일은 생각만 해도 ~ It pains me even to think of it. // 외아들을 잃은 것은 그의 생애에 가장 괴로운 경험이었다 The loss of his only son was the bitterest experience of his life. // 그의 일생은 괴로운 일뿐이었다 His life was full of hardships. // 여러 해 동안 살아 정든 집을 파는 것은 괴로운 일이었다 It was hard for me to sell the house I had lived in for so many years. // 아무리 괴로운 때에도 그녀는 결코 불평을 하지 않았다 No matter how trying the circumstances, she never complained. // 환자는 괴로운 듯이 숨을 쉬고 있었다 The patient was breathing with difficulty. // 괴로운 1년이었다 I had a trying year. // 어린 자식을 두고 집을 나간다는 것이 그녀에게는 괴로운 일이었다 It was distressing [agonizing] for her to go, leaving her small child behind at home. // 모기에 뜯기는 괴로운 한밤을 보냈다 I had a bad night as I was pestered by mosquitos.

괴롭히다 [괴로움을 주다] afflict; torment; harass; agonize; torture; [고통을 주다] cause (a person) pain; distress; excruciate; [난처하게 하다] trouble; worry; annoy; bother; embarrass; [못살게 굴다] persecute; tease; be hard on; [억압하다] oppress. ¶강아지를 ~ torment a small dog / be cruel to a puppy // 어린이들은 흔히 약자를 괴롭힌다 Children tend to bully [pick on] the weak. // 그녀는 며느리를 괴롭힌다 She is hard on her daughter-in-law. // 신혼부부를 너무 괴롭히지 말게 Don't tease the newlyweds too much. // 동생의 비행이 나를 괴롭힌다 My brother's misconduct weighs on my mind. / It hurts me to see my brother acting improperly. // 류머티즘이 오랫동안 그를 괴롭혔다 He has been suffering from [troubled with] rheumatism for a long time. // 밤새도록 모기가 우리를 괴롭혔다 We were annoyed by mosquitoes all night long. // 송 선생님은 어려운 문제를 내어 학생들을 괴롭히기를 좋아하신다 Mr. Song likes tormenting his students with difficult questions. // 주정뱅이 남편이 저를 폐나 괴롭혔죠 My drunk of a husband caused me great distress [so much trouble]. // 그는 나를 괴롭히려고 줄곧 문을 시끄럽게 여닫았다 He kept opening and shutting the door noisily just to annoy me.

괴뢰(傀儡) [꼭두각시] a puppet; a marionette; a dummy; [앞잡이] a tool; a cat's paw; [허수아비] a robot. ¶~ 노릇을 하다 act as another's tool / be made a cat's-paw (of).
● **괴뢰 정부** a puppet [dummy / robot] government.

괴리(乖離) estrangement; alienation; [분리] detachment; separation; dissociation. **괴리하다** be estranged [alienated] (from).

괴멸(壞滅) [파괴] destruction; [전멸] annihilation; ruin. **괴멸하다** be destroyed [demolished / ruined]; moulder away; be annihilated. ¶반대 세력을 괴멸시키다 annihilate an opposition force // 집중 폭격으로 그 도시는 괴멸되었다 The town was utterly destroyed by the intensive bombing.

괴문서(怪文書) (출처를 알 수 없는) a mysterious [dubious] document; an anonymous document; a document from an unidentified source; (중상적인) a libelous [(영) libellous / defamatory] publication [document]. ¶후보자를 비방한 ~가 나돌고 있다 A document containing defamatory statements about the candidate is being circulated.

괴물(怪物) [도깨비] a monster; [정체를 알 수 없는 인물] a mysterious figure; a mystery man. ¶바다의 ~ wonders of the deep / a sea goblin // ~의 정체를 밝히다 unmask the apparition.

괴벽스럽다(乖僻—) eccentric; fastidious. ⇨ 괴벽하다 ¶그런 추녀와 결혼하다니 ~ How whimsical of him to marry such a fright!

괴벽하다(乖僻—) eccentric; fastidious; queer; unusual; odd; peculiar. ¶괴벽한 사람 a queer man / an eccentric man / an oddity // 괴벽한 노인 an eccentric [a queer / an unusual] old man // 괴벽한 취미 fastidious taste(s) // 그 화가는 괴벽하기로 유명했다 The painter was pretty well known for his eccentricity.

괴변(怪變) a strange accident; an odd mishap.

괴병(怪病) a mysterious disease; an unidentified disease. ¶~이 퍼졌다 An unidentified disease has spread over.

괴사(壞死) [생체 내의 조직·세포의 사멸] necrosis. **괴사하다** become necrotic.

괴상야릇하다(怪常—) quite odd [strange]; most peculiar [grotesque]. ¶괴상야릇한 얼굴 a face that would stop a clock.

괴상하다(怪常—) [묘하다] strange; queer; curious; [이상하다] odd; fantastic; grotesque. ¶괴상한 물건 a strange thing / an oddity // 괴상한 모자 an absurd [a funny-looking] hat // 괴상한 옷차림을 하고 있다 be fantastically dressed // 그 괴상한 옷을 입고 나가려 하느냐 Are you going out in those weird clothes [that peculiar dress]? 괴상히 strangely; queerly; curiously.

괴석 (怪石) an oddly shaped stone.
괴수 (怪獸) a monster; a monstrous beast.
괴수 (魁首) the ringleader; the leader. ¶도둑의 ~ the head [boss] of robbers // 폭도의 ~ the ringleader of a mob.
괴이다 1 [받쳐지다] get propped; be supported; be sustained; [쌓아 올려지다] be arranged; be piled up. 2 [사랑받다] win (a person's) favor; be a favorite with (one's master); be in (a person's) favor.
괴이하다 (怪異 ‑) [이상야릇하다] mysterious; strange; grotesque; odd; weird; uncanny; (구어) funny. ¶괴이한 사람 a queer person // 괴이한 죽음 mysterious death / death from an unknown cause // 괴이한 소문 a strange [wild] rumor // 괴이한 행동 a strange behavior / a funny way to behave // 괴이한 현상 a strange [mysterious] phenomenon // 초자연의 괴이함 a strange happening belonging to the realm of the supernatural. 괴이히 mysteriously; strangely; grotesquely; oddly; weirdly.
괴인 (怪人) a monster man; a mystery man. ¶복면의 ~ a masked mystery man.
괴저 (壞疽) [의] gangrene; necrosis.
괴질 (怪疾) 1 a mysterious disease. ⇨ ¨괴병¨ ¶그 지방에는 ~이 번지고 있다 An unidentified epidemic is prevalent in the district. 2 〈속〉 cholera. ⇨ 콜레라.
괴짜 (怪‑) an eccentric (person); an odd [a peculiar] fellow; a queer fish [fellow]; (미국속어) a screwball; (구어) a character; (구어) an oddball. ¶저 사람은 ~ 야 He is an odd fish. / He is quite a character. // 그런 짓을 하다니 너도 ~ 다 It is rather eccentric of you to do such a thing. // 그는 ~ 다 He is a very strange person. / He is really eccentric [odd]. // 당신도 ~ 구먼 You are a funny one, aren't you?
괴철 (塊鐵) an iron ingot; bloom (iron).
괴춤 (the area) between abdomen and belt.
괴팍하다 (乖愎‑) [별나다] eccentric; cranky; [까다롭다] fastidious; finical; fussy; finicky; [완고하다] obstinate; bigoted. ¶괴팍한 사람 an eccentric person / a fastidious [finical] person // 그는 괴팍한 버릇이 있다 He has eccentric ways. // 그런 일을 하다니 자네도 꽤 나 괴팍하군 It is rather eccentric of you to do such a thing.
괴퍅하다 →괴팍하다
괴한 (怪漢) a suspicious(-looking) fellow; a suspicious guy; a strange-looking character. ¶~이 집 주위를 어슬렁거리고 있다 A suspicious fellow is loitering around the house.
괴현상 (怪現象) a strange phenomenon; an extraordinary phenomenon. ¶~이 일어났다 A strange phenomenon presented itself.
괴혈병 (壞血病) [의] scorbutus; scurvy. ¶~[~에 걸린] scorbutic.
● **괴혈병 환자** a scorbutic.
굄돌 a stone prop [support].
굉음 (轟音) a roar; a roaring sound; a thundering sound; a deafening roar; earsplitting sound; a peal; a rumble; a boom; booming; a booming sound. ¶대포의 ~ the roar [boom] of a gun // ~을 내며 with a roaring [booming] sound // ~을 내다 make [produce] a thundering noise // ~을 내며 치솟다 roar up // 몇 대의 오토바이가 ~을 내며 지나갔다 Several motorcycles thundered by.

굉장하다 (宏壯‑) [크다] grand; magnificent; imposing; [대단하다] splendid; glorious; grand; excellent; superb; [엄청나다] awful; terrible; tremendous. ¶굉장한 부자 an awfully rich man // 굉장한 미인 a dazzling [stunning] beauty // 굉장한 저택 a palatial residence // 굉장한 성공 a phenomenal [dazzling] success // 우리는 거기서 굉장한 환영을 받았다 We met with a wonderful [royal] reception there. // 그 가수의 인기는 ~ The singer is tremendously popular. // 그것은 굉장한 소리를 내며 폭발했다 It exploded with a terrific noise. // 그의 노래는 굉장한 히트였다 His song was a smash hit. // 야 굉장하구나! 어떻게 그녀와 데이트를 하게 되었지 That's really something [Wow]! How did you get a date with her? // 백악관에 초대받다니 굉장하군 How wonderful to be invited to the White House! // 그것 참 굉장한데 That's great. // 오늘 더위는 굉장하군 The heat today is really terrific. / (구어) This heat is really something else. // 그의 새 차는 굉장한 속력을 낸다 His new car can go at a terrific speed. / His new car can get up an awesome speed. **굉장히** [대단히] very; very much; exceedingly; greatly; immensely; [놀랄 만큼] strikingly; wonderfully; [엄청나게] awfully; terribly. ¶~ 덥다 be terribly [unbearably] hot // 머리가 ~ 아프다 I get a most beastly headache. // 배가 ~ 고프다 I'm good [rare] and hungry. // 그는 힘이 ~ 세다 He is super strong. // 오늘 밤은 ~ 춥다 It's bitterly [terribly] cold tonight. // 이 책은 ~ 재미있다 This book is extremely entertaining [amusing]. // 그 영화는 ~ 재미있다 The movie is really [(구어) super] interesting. / That's a great movie. // 그는 테니스를 ~ 잘한다 He is a terrific tennis player. / He's an awfully good tennis player. // 오늘은 ~ 좋은 날씨였다 We had wonderful weather today. / The weather was marvelous today. // 그의 연주는 ~ 좋았다 His performance was really superb. / He gave a stunning [terrific] performance.

-교 (橋) a bridge. ¶인도~ a footbridge.
교가 (校歌) a school [college] song; an alma mater song. ¶~를 합창하다 sing in chorus a school [college] song.
교각 (交角) [수] an angle of intersection; a crossing angle.
교각 (橋脚) [건] pier; a bent.
교각살우 (矯角殺牛) a deadly effect of a good intention.
교감 (交感) rapport; mutual response; [생] consensus; (mutual) sympathy. **교감하다** sympathize (with each other); respond [be responsive] to each other; share each other's feeling.
● **교감 신경** the sympathetic nerve.
교감 (校監) a head teacher; an assistant principal; a vice-schoolmaster; a principal [director] in charge.
교갑 (膠匣) (약의) a capsule; (프) a cachet.
교과 (教科) a lesson; a subject; a course of study; the curriculum.

●**교과 과정** a curriculum. ⇨ ˝교육 과정(⊙)교육) **교과목** a subject; a course (of study). **교과서** a textbook; a schoolbook; (구어) a text. ¶**검인정 ~** an authorized textbook ∥ **국정 ~** a national textbook / a government-[state-] designated textbook ∥ **수학 ~** a textbook on mathematics.

교관(敎官) an instructor; a teacher; (교련의) a drill instructor.

교교하다(皎皎-) bright; brilliant. ¶**달빛이 ~** The moon shines bright(ly). **교교히** bright(ly); brilliantly.

교구(敎具) teaching tools[items]; instruments of education.

교구(敎區) a parish; an ecclesiastical district. ¶**~의 목사** a parish priest.

교권(敎權) (교육상의) educational authority; (종교상의) ecclesiastical authority; ecclesiasticism. ¶**~을 확립하다** establish teacher's authority.

교기(校旗) a school banner[flag].

교기(驕氣) a haughty[proud] attitude[air]. ¶**~를 부리다** act proudly / assume a haughty attitude / hold one's head high / ride the high horse.

교내(校內) school grounds; (미) a campus(대학의). ¶**~의** intramural (game / team) ∥ **~에(서)** in the school building / within school bounds / on the school grounds / (대학의) in the university / (미) on the campus.

교단(敎團) an order; a religious society [association]; a religious brotherhood; a religious sisterhood(여자의). ¶**프란체스코 ~** the Franciscan order.

교단(敎壇) (학교의) the (teacher's) platform; [교육계] the educational world. ¶**~에 서다** be a teacher / teach (at a) school / teach a class ∥ **~에서 물러나다** give up teaching / (정년으로) retire from teaching.

● **교단생활** a teacher's life; a teaching career.

교대(交代) [교체] (an) alternation; (a) change; (직무의) relief; (근무 시간의) a shift. ¶**위병 ~** change of guards ∥ **심야 ~** a midnight shift ∥ **주야 ~** a day and night shift / **~로** in turn / by turns / alternately ∥ **~로 말하다** speak one after the other [another] / speak in turn / by turns / alternately ∥ **~로 감시하다** keep watch by turns ∥ **자매가 ~로 어머니를 도왔다** The sisters took turns helping their mother. ∥ **우리들은 ~로 보트를 저었다** We rowed the boat in turn[by turns]. ∥ **그 공장은 3~제다** The factory operates on three shifts. ∥ **누이동생과 내가 ~로 방을 소제한다** My sister and I take turns cleaning our room. **교대하다** [교대로 하다] take turns; take one's turn (in doing something); [교체하다] relieve (a person); alternate (with another); rotate; [대신하다] take another's place; (보초가) change[relieve] (guard); (상호 간에) interchange. ¶**나는 그와 교대했다** I took his place. / I relieved him. / I took over from him. ∥ **당직은 4시간마다 교대한다** The watches are alternated[changed] every four hours.

● **교대 시간** changing time; relief time(보초 근무의); a shift. ¶**~은 몇 시입니까** When will you be relieved? / When is your shift over? **교대자** a shift; a relief.

교도(敎徒) a believer (in); an adherent (to); a follower (of). ¶**불교 ~** a Buddhist ∥ **기독교 ~** a Christian.

교도(敎導) instruction; teaching; training; guidance. **교도하다** instruct; teach; train; coach; guide. ¶**비행 소년을 ~ reform a juvenile delinquent.

교도관(矯導官) a prison officer; a (prison) guard; a warder; a jailor; (영) a gaoler; a turnkey.

교도소(矯導所) a prison; a jail(jail은 특히 (미)에서는 미결수, 경범죄자용을 가리킴. (영)에서는 공용어로 gaol이 쓰임); (미) (주·연방의) a penitentiary; (속어) a pen. ¶**~에 수감하다** put (a person) in prison / send (a person) to prison / **~에 수감되다[들어가다]** be sent to prison [jail] / be imprisoned ∥ **그는 어제 ~에서 나왔다** He left[was released from] prison yesterday. ∥ **그는 언젠가는 ~에 가게 될 것이다** He will land[wind up / end up] in prison someday. ∥ **그는 살인죄로 ~에 수감되어 있다** He is held on a murder charge at a jail.

교두보(橋頭堡) a bridgehead; a beachhead(해안의). ¶**~을 확보하다** establish [secure] a bridgehead [beachhead] ∥ **그들은 노조를 ~로 하여 임금 투쟁을 시작하였다** Spearheaded by the labor union [With the labor union in the forefront], they began their drive for higher wages.

교란(攪亂) a disturbance; a commotion; derangement; turbulence. **교란하다** disturb; derange; upset; stir up; throw into confusion; agitate. ¶**평화를 ~** disturb peace ∥ **후방을 ~** harass the rear (guard) ∥ **마음을 ~** upset [perturb] a person.

교량(橋梁) a bridge. ⇨**다리¹**

교련(敎鍊) (military) drill; training; drilling. ¶**대대 ~** battalion drill ∥ **사격 ~** target practice ∥ **~을 받다** be drilled / drill / practice drilling. **교련하다** drill (soldiers); train; exercise.

● **교련 교관** a drill instructor.

교료(校了) [교정 완료] finishing proofreading; [부호] O.K.; proofed. ∥ **책임 ~** O.K. with corrections. **교료하다** O.K. (the proofs); finish proofreading; finish correcting the proofs.

교류(交流) 1 [전] an alternating current(약어 AC, A.C., a-c, a.c.). 2 [교환] interchange; exchange. ¶**한미간의 문화 ~** cultural exchange [interchange] between Korea and America ∥ **지방 자치 단체 간의 인적 ~** an interchange of personnel between local governments ∥ **두 나라 사이에 문화 ~가 활발해졌다** Cultural exchanges between the two nations have become very active. **교류하다** interchange; exchange.

● **교류 발전기** an AC [alternating current] generator; an alternator.

교리(敎理) a doctrine; a creed; a dogma (pl. ~s, -mata); a tenet. ¶**기독교의 ~를 설교하다** teach Christian doctrines.

● **교리 문답** catechism.

교린(交隣) friendship among[between] neighboring countries; relations of neighboring countries; [선린] good-neighbor relations.

● **교린 정책** a good-neighbor policy.

교만(驕慢) arrogance; haughtiness; pride; conceit. **교만하다** arrogant; haughty; proud;

교만하다 conceited; puffed-up. ¶그녀는 아주 교만한 여자다 She is a very conceited woman. / She is as proud as a peacock. // 그는 교만한 얼굴을 하고 있다 He looks high and mighty. // 나의 교만한 코를 꺾어 놓겠다 I'll teach him to act so arrogantly! **교만히** arrogantly; haughtily; conceitedly; proudly. ¶~ 굴다 bear oneself haughtily / act in a lordly manner.

교모(校帽) a school cap.

교목(校牧) a (school) chaplain.

교목(喬木) a tall [high] tree; a forest tree; an arbor.

교묘하다(巧妙―) skillful; ingenious; clever; dexterous; shrewd; adroit; deft; adept. ¶교묘한 대답 a tactful [subtle] reply // 교묘한 세공 ingenious [clever / skillful] handiwork / elaborate workmanship // 교묘한 솜씨 a deft performance // 교묘한 수법 a shrewd [crafty] trick // 그는 교묘한 변명을 한다 He makes smart [clever] excuses. // 장관은 교묘한 답변으로 난처한 질문을 피했던 The minister evaded the embarrassing question with an adroit reply. // 나는 교묘한 속임수를 간파하지 못했다 I was unable to see through the clever trick. **교묘히** skillfully; dexterously; ingeniously; cleverly; shrewdly; adroitly; with skill [dexterity]; tactfully. ¶너는 ~ 속은 것이다 You were nicely [neatly] taken in. // 도둑은 ~ 도망친 듯하다 The thief seems to have made good his escape. // 그는 ~ 그 자리를 얼버무렸다 He adroitly glossed things over [patched things up] for the moment. // 그것은 놀랄 정도로 ~ 만들어져 있었다 It was made very cleverly [with wonderful skill]. // 그것은 ~ 짜여진 함정이었다 It was an ingeniously set trap.

교무(教務) (학교의) school affairs; academic affairs [administration]; (교회 등의) the business affairs of a sect, temple, etc. ¶(학교의) ~를 맡아보다 be in charge of school affairs // ~를 관장하다 manage [handle] school affairs.

● **교무과** the educational affairs department; the instruction section; (미국 대학의) the registrar's office. **교무실** a teacher's room; (영) a staff room. **교무 주임** a curriculum coordinator; the director of the instruction section. **교무처** the office of academic affairs.

교문(校門) the gate of a school; a school gate. ¶~을 나서다 leave the school gates / leave school / graduate from school.

교미(交尾) copulation; mating; coition; leap. ¶~ 중인 잠자리 dragonflies in connection // ~의 copulative / copulatory. **교미하다** copulate; mate; couple; (새 등이) tread (a hen); pair; (짐승이) cover.

● **교미기** (발정기) (암컷의) heat; estrus [(영) oestrus]; (교접 시기) the breeding [mating / pairing] season.

교민(僑民) Korean residents abroad; overseas Korean.

교배(交配) crossbreeding; crossing; (식물의) cross-fertilization; hybridization; interbreeding. ¶과실의 ~ the cross-fertilization of fruit. **교배하다** cross; crossbreed; hybridize; interbreed; mate; cross-fertilize. ¶불도그와 진돗개를 ~ cross a bulldog and a *Jindotgae* // 2종을 교배하여 신종 식물이 만들어졌다 A new plant was made by crossing [crossfertilizing] two others.

● **교배종** a cross (between a peach and a grapefruit); a crossbred; a hybrid (from a donkey and a horse).

교법(教法) a religious doctrine; a religion; a creed; (부처의 가르침) the teachings of Buddha.

교복(校服) a school uniform. ¶~의 자율화 the liberalization of the dress code (for secondary school students).

교본(教本) a textbook (on / in); a manual (of); (음) a school. ¶피아노 ~ a book of études [drills] for the piano // 운전 ~ a manual for driving.

교부(交付) delivery; transfer; handing over; grant; issue. ¶영장의 ~ a delivery of writ. **교부하다** deliver (a deed); grant; issue; hand over; pass along; transfer; serve (a person) with. ¶통지서를 ~ serve a notice on (a person) / transfer a slip to (another) // …에게 여권을 ~ issue a passport to [for] (a person).

● **교부금** a grant; a bounty (공공 사업 원조를 위한) a grant-in-aid (*pl.* grants-in-aid); (보조금) a subsidy.

교부(教父) a Church Father; (대부) a godfather.

교분(交分) friendship; intimacy; friendly relations. ¶~이 두텁다 be good friends with / enjoy a close intimacy with // ~을 새롭게 하다 renew one's companionship (with) / get in closer contact (with) // 그들은 날로 ~이 두터워지고 있다 They are growing daily in intimacy.

교사(校舍) a schoolhouse; a school building. ¶~를 증축하다 extend [add to] the school building.

교사(教師) a teacher; an instructor; (주로 초등학교의) a schoolteacher; a master; (미국 속어) a schoolman; (초등학교의) a schoolmaster; a schoolmistress(여교사); a tutor(가정교사); a governess(여자 가정교사). ¶역사 ~ a history teacher / a teacher of history // 무용 ~ a dancing master // 어느 학교의 ~ a teacher in a school // 그가 다니는 school masterish (attitude) // 당신은 왜 ~가 되었습니까 Why did you go into teaching? // 아버지는 고교 ~이시다 My father is a high school teacher [teacher at a high school]. // 그는 화학 ~이다 He teaches chemistry. / He is a teacher of chemistry [chemistry teacher]. // 그는 ~로서 빈틈이 없다 He is all there as a teacher.

● **교사 자격증** teacher's license; a teaching certificate.

교사(教唆) instigation; incitement; abetment. ¶…의 ~로 at (a person's) instigation [incitement] // 이 폭동은 어떤 정치인의 ~로 일어났다 The riot broke out at the instigation of a certain politician. **교사하다** instigate; abet; incite; set [egg] on. ¶범죄를 ~ incite [instigate] (a person) to (commit) a crime / abet (a person) in a crime // 폭동을 ~ instigate a rebellion // 정부 전복의 음모를 ~ instigate a plot to overthrow the government // 틀림없이 그 녀석이 교사했을 것이다 That fellow must have egged him on to do it.

● **교사 방조죄** (the crime of) aiding and abetting.

교살(絞殺) strangulation; strangling; hanging. ¶~의 흔적 marks of strangulation. **교살**

교상

하다 strangle (a person) to death; hang; string up. ¶밧줄로 죄인을 ~ hang a criminal by a rope. ➔교살당하다 be strangled (to death) / [교수형을 받다] be hanged (to death).

교상(咬傷) a bite; an injury by biting. ¶뱀의 ~ (die from) a snake bite. **교상하다** be bitten; be injured by a bite.

교생(教生) a student teacher; a practice teacher. ¶~으로 가다 do practice teaching.

교서(教書) a message; [가] a (papal) bull. ¶대통령의 ~ a presidential message to Congress // 연두 ~ (미국의) the State of the Union Message // 대통령이 의회에 예산 ~를 보내다 deliver the Budget Message to Congress.

교섭(交涉) [담판] negotiation; bargaining; a parley; an overture; [논의] discussion; conversation; [관계] connection; relation; dealing. ¶단체 ~ collective bargaining // 예비 ~ preliminary negotiations // 직접 ~ direct negotiation // 비공개 ~ a closed door negotiation // ~의 결렬 rupture of negotiations // ~ 중이다 be in [under] negotiation / be negotiating // ~ 단계에 있다 be in the negotiation stage // ~을 계속하다 carry on negotiations // ~을 중단하다 discontinue [interrupt] negotiations // 이 문제는 ~의 여지가 있다 [없다] This matter is negotiable [nonnegotiable]. // ~이 성립되었다 The negotiations have been concluded. / We have come to terms. // ~은 교착 상태에 빠져 실패로 끝났다 The negotiations got stalled [become deadlocked] and ended in failure. // 한국은 중동 제국과 석유 무역 협정을 ~ 중이다 Korea is negotiating an oil agreement with Middle East nations. // ~은 아직 거기까지는 이르지 않고 있다 The negotiations are not yet so far advanced. **교섭하다** negotiate; bargain; confer; parley; make an overture (to); approach (a person with a proposal); communicate (with). ¶직접 ~ negotiate directly with (a person) / enter [go] into direct negotiations with (the boss) // 그 건으로 그가 나에게 교섭해 왔다 He approached me about the matter.

●**교섭 단체** a bargaining body; (국회의) a negotiation body.

교성(嬌聲) a woman's lovely [charming] voice; seductive tones. ¶~을 지르다 utter a coquettish voice.

교세(教勢) religious influence; [신도 수효] the total number of believers.

교수(教授) [가르침] teaching; instruction; tuition; [대학의 강의자] a professor; [집합적] faculty. ¶개인 ~ private lessons // 명예 ~ an emeritus [honorary] professor // 지도 ~ an adviser // (영) a supervisor // 조 ~ an assistant professor // 부 ~ an associate professor // 정 ~ a (full) professor // 부산 대학교 언어학 ~ a professor of [in] linguistics at Busan University // ~의 직 [지위] professorship / the chair (of physics) // ~진을 강화하다 form a strong professorial staff / strengthen the teaching staff (of an university) // A 선생의 ~를 받다 study under (the tutorship of) Mr. A // 그와 같은 저작은 그의 ~로서의 명성을 손상시키게 될 것이다 Writing a book like that would hurt his professorial standing. // 이 대학교에 경제학 ~ 자리가 새로 만들어졌다 A chair of economics was created at this university. // 그는 최 선생의 ~를 받고 있다 He is studying under professor Choe. // 송 선생으로부터 피아노 개인 ~를 받고 있다 I am taking private lessons in piano from Miss Song. **교수하다** teach; instruct (in); give instruction (in); give lessons to (a person) in. ¶한국어를 ~ teach (a person) Korean // 사용법을 ~ show (a person) how to use it // 나는 20년간 수학을 교수한 경험이 있다 I have twenty years' experience of teaching mathematics.

●**교수법** teaching methods; pedagogics. ¶구두 ~ an oral method of teaching (foreign languages). **교수회** [교수의 자치적 조직] a faculty; [교수의 집회] a faculty meeting.

교수(絞首) strangulation; hanging; strangling. ¶~용 밧줄 a halter / a hempen collar [cravat]. **교수하다** strangle; strangulate; hang (a criminal).

●**교수대** the gallows; a gibbet; a scaffold; [영국 역사] the Tyburn tree. ¶~에 오르다 mount [go to] the gallows [scaffold]. **교수형** (death by) hanging; punishment by hanging. ¶~에 처해지다 be hanged / be executed by hanging.

교습(教習) training; teaching instruction. ¶음악 ~을 받다 take lessons [a course] in music / have [learn] music lessons // 한국어 ~ (게시) Korean instruction [lessons] given. **교습하다** give lessons (in); train; drill; teach; instruct.

●**교습소** a training school [institute] (for). ¶댄스 ~ a dancing school.

교시(教示) instruction; teaching. **교시하다** teach; instruct; enlighten. ¶…을 ~ enlighten (a person) as to [upon] ….

교신(交信) communication(s); contact; correspondence. ¶~을 시작하다 start communication (with) / open correspondence (with) // 그와의 ~이 끊어졌다 The communication with him was cut off [interrupted]. // 관측소와의 ~이 갑자기 끊어졌다 Suddenly, we lost contact with the observation post. **교신하다** contact; make (radio) contact (with); communicate (with). ¶신호로 배와 ~ communicate with a ship by signals.

교실(教室) a classroom; a schoolroom; a lecture room; (미) a recitation room; (대학의) a department. ¶계단 ~ an amphitheater // 화학 ~ a chemistry room // 합반 ~ a combined classroom // 콩나물 ~ an overcrowded classroom // 어머니 ~ a class for mothers // 외국어는 ~에서만 배울 수는 없다 Foreign languages cannot be learned in class alone.

교안(教案) a teaching plan; lesson plans. ¶~을 짜다 make a teaching plan / form a lesson schedule.

교양(教養) culture; refinement; education; cultivation. ¶~이 있는 cultured / cultivated / educated // ~ 없는 uneducated / uncultured / ill-cultivated // ~이 있는 사람들 men of culture / well-educated classes / cultured circles // ~을 쌓다 acquire culture // ~을 높이다 cultivate oneself / heighten the level of one's culture // 나는 ~을 위해 프랑스 작품을 읽는다 I read French novels because I think I can learn from them something conducive to my general education. // 그는 꽤 ~이 있어

보인다 He seems to have some cultural background.
● **교양 과목** cultural studies[subjects]; liberal arts; the arts. **교양 프로** an educational program. **교양 학부** a college[school/faculty] of general education; the liberal arts school.

교언(巧言) flattery; fair[fine / honeyed] words; blarney; soft soap. ¶그의 ~에 속았다 I was taken in by his honeyed[sweet] words. **교언하다** flatter; use sweet[smooth] words; coax; cajole; say nice things.
● **교언영색**(-令色) fine words and insinuating countenance.

교역(交易) trade; commerce; barter; interchange. **교역하다** trade (with); carry on commerce; barter; exchange. ¶외국과 ~ trade with foreign nations.
● **교역 조건** terms of trade.

교역(教役) [종] religious work.
● **교역자** a religious worker.

교열(校閱) revision; revisal; recension. ¶스미스 박사 ~ Revised by Dr. Smith ¶원고는 지금 ~ 중이다 The manuscript is under revision now. **교열하다** look over and correct (a manuscript); revise.
● **교열자** a person who checks the accuracy (of a manuscript); a reviser.

교외(郊外) the suburbs; the outskirts; the environs; suburbia. ¶~의 suburban ¶ ~를 산책하다 go for[take] a walk in the suburbs ¶그는 서울 ~에 살고 있다 He lives in the suburbs[on the outskirts] of Seoul.
● **교외 생활** suburban life; life in the suburbs.

교외(校外) ¶~의[에서] outside (the)[out of] school / off campus.
● **교외 활동** extramural activities.

교우(交友) [벗을 사귐] making friends (with); [친구] a friend; a companion; an acquaintance; an associate. ¶넓은 ~ 범위 a large circle of friends ¶그는 ~ 범위가 넓다 He has a lot of friends[acquaintances]. / He knows a lot of people. **교우하다** make friends (with); keep company (with); associate (with).
● **교우 관계** one's company; one's associates. ¶~가 나쁘다[좋다] keep bad[good] company.

교우(校友) a school friend; a schoolfellow; a schoolmate; (동창생) graduates of the same school; an alumnus (*pl.* -ni) (남자); an alumna (*pl.* -nae) (여자); (영) an old boy.

교우(教友) a fellow believer; a brother (*pl.* brethren); a fellow Christian[Buddhist].

교원(教員) a teacher; an instructor; (초중고의) a schoolteacher; [한 학교 전체의 교사] the (teaching) staff; the faculty(대학의). ¶ ~자격을 따다 obtain a teacher's license ¶고교 ~이다 be a high school teacher.
● **교원 자격증** a teachers' license[certificate].

교유(交遊) social intercourse; association; friendship; companionship. ¶그의 ~ 관계를 조사했다 We investigated his associates. / We checked to see who he associated with. **교유하다** associate with; keep company with; (구어) run around with.

교육(教育) education; [학교 교육] schooling; [교수] instruction; teaching; [훈련] training; [훈육] discipline; [교양] culture; (양육) upbringing; breeding. ¶의무 ~ compulsory education ∥ 초등[중등 / 고등] ~ elementary (or primary) [secondary / higher] education ∥ 대학 ~ a university [college] education ∥ 보통[직업] ~ general [vocational] education ∥ 기술 ~ technical education ∥ 음악 ~ musical training ∥ 전문 ~ professional training[education] ∥ 가정 ~ home training [education] ∥ 성인 [평생] ~ adult[lifelong] education ∥ 군대 ~ military training ∥ ~을 많이 받은 사람 a highly educated person ∥ 학교 밖의 ~ out-of-school education ∥ ~에 극성스러운 어머니 a mother oversolicitous over her children's education ∥ ~의 educational / educative / cultural ∥ ~상(으로) viewed from an educational viewpoint / educationally ∥ 폭넓은 ~ education with latitude ∥ ~을 받은 educated / cultured ∥ ~을 받지 못한 uneducated / (문맹의) illiterate / undereducated ∥ ~을 받다 receive [get / have] an education / be educated [trained] (by) ∥ ~에 종사하다 engage [be engaged] in education / be a teacher ∥ ~의 기회를 균등하게 하다 equalize educational opportunities ∥ 가정교사에게 아이들의 ~을 맡기다 entrust a tutor [governess] ∥ ~을 마치다 complete [finish] one's schooling [school education] ∥ ~상 어린이에게 좋지 않다 be not good for children from the educational standpoint ∥ 그는 정규 ~은 받지 않았다 He has had no formal education [schooling]. ∥ 어머니는 ~을 받지는 않았지만 교양이 없지는 않았다 My mother had no formal education but she was not uneducated. ∥ 저는 ~을 좀 받았습니다 I have had some education. ∥ 그는 처음에는 프랑스에서 ~을 받았다 His early education was received in France. **교육하다** educate; give (a person) an education; instruct; teach; discipline; bring up; train; school. ¶아이에게 순종하도록 ~ educate a child to obey ∥ 남을 의사가 되도록 ~ educate a person for medicine.
● **교육가 / 교육자** an educator; a teacher. **교육감** the superintendent of education (in Seoul). **교육계** the educational world; educational circles. **교육 공무원** the educational public service (employee); an educational personnel and staff. **교육 공학** education technology. **교육 과정** a course of study; a curriculum. **교육 기관** an educational institution. **교육 대학** a teachers' college; a college of education. **교육 방송** educational broadcasting. **교육법** a teaching method. **교육 보험** educational endowment insurance. **교육비** educational [school] expenses; the cost of school education (per person). ¶요즈음은 아이들의 ~도 무시 못 한다 Children's education costs us no small money nowadays. **교육세** education taxes. **교육 시설** educational facilities. **교육 심리학** educational psychology. **교육 영화** an educational film [picture]. **교육 인적 자원부** the Ministry of Education and Human Resources Development. **교육장** a superintendent of education. **교육 제도** an educational system. **교육학** pedagogy; pedagogics. **교육 행정** educational administration.

교육적(教育的) educational; educative; instructive. ¶~인 영화 an educational film

교의 [picture].
교의(校醫) a school physician [doctor].
교의(教義) a religious doctrine; a dogma; a tenet.
교인(教人) [종교를 믿는 사람] a believer; an adherent; a devotee; a follower; [교회원] a member of a church. ¶(기독교의) ~이 되다 become a Christian / embrace Christianity.
교자상(交子床) a large [dining] table.
교잡(交雜) 1 [뒤섞임] being interlaced and intertwining (as tangled growths); disorder; confusion. 교잡하다 interlace and intertwine; be tangled [confused]; be in disorder; be mixed [jumbled] up. 2 [식] crossing; [동] hybridization. 교잡하다 cross; hybridize.
교장(校長) (초중고의) a principal; (영) a schoolmaster; a headmaster; (여자) a schoolmistress; a headmistress.
교장(教場) a (military) drill ground; a drill [training] field.
교재(教材) teaching material(s); teaching aids. ¶영자 신문을 ~로 쓰다 use an English paper for teaching [in class].
교전(交戰) [전쟁] war; warfare; [전투] a battle; [전쟁 상태] belligerency; hostilities. ¶~을 중지하다 break off the engagement // 우리는 그 나라와 ~ 중이다 We are at war with the country. // 그들은 곧 ~을 중지했다 They soon ceased fire [firing]. // 그는 ~ 중에 부상했다 He was wounded in action. 교전하다 [전쟁] engage in a battle; wage war; join battle (with). ¶적과 ~ engage [fight with] the enemy (troops).
● 교전 상태 a state of war; belligerency. 교전지 a battlefield; a field of battle; the theater [seat] of war.
교전(教典) a canon; (교육상의) the canon of education.
교점(交點) a point of intersection; an intersection point; [천] a node.
교접(交接) [접촉] contact; [성교] sexual intercourse [union]; coition; copulation. 교접하다 [접촉하다] contact; make contact (with); [성교하다] have sexual intercourse (with); copulate (with).
교정(校正) proofreading; correction of the press; correcting the press. ¶최종 ~ the press [final] revise // ~상 실수 a proofreading [proof-reader's] error // ~에서 오식을 놓치다 overlook errors in proof // ~ 중에 정정하다 make corrections in [on the] proof // 이 책은 ~을 잘못 보아 오자가 많다 This book has many misprints owing to careless proofreading. // ~는 몇 번 보았느냐 How many times was the proof read? // 두 번 ~ 보았다 (초교와 재교) I read two proofs. / I proofread it twice. 교정하다 proofread; read proofs; correct the press. ¶원고를 ~ correct a manuscript // 세밀히 ~ read proofs with religious care // 세 번 ~ read the proofs three times / make corrections in three proofs // 소홀하게 ~ read a proof carelessly // 녹음을 ~ proof-listen.
● 교정 기호 proof-correction marks; proof-reader's marks. 교정쇄 a (galley) proof; a proof sheet. 교정원 a proofreader; a corrector; a press reader. 교정지 a proof sheet; a (galley) proof. 교정필(-畢) a correct proof; Corrected; O.K. ¶~의 corrected.
교정(校庭) the school grounds; (초등학교의) a playground; (특히 대학의) the campus.
교정(矯正) reform; correction; rectification; remedy; redress. ¶치열 ~ straightening teeth / [의] orthodontia. 교정하다 reform; correct; rectify; remedy; set right. ¶교정하기 어려운 incorrigible / incurable / irreclaimable // 말더듬이를 ~ cure a person of stammering // 발음 [언어 장애]을 ~ correct bad pronunciation [a speech impediment] // 나쁜 풍습을 ~ rectify [remedy] an abuse.
● 교정시력 corrected eyesight.
교제(交際) association; (문어) social intercourse; intercourse; society; company; friendship; acquaintance; fellowship. ¶남녀 간의 ~ dating // ~상 as a matter of social courtesy / for company's sake / to be sociable / for the sake of friendship // ~가 넓다 have a large acquaintance / be widely acquainted // ~가 서투르다 (미국 구어) be a bad mixer // ~를 좋아하다 be fond of society [company] // ~를 끊다 cut (a person) / break off one's friendship (with) // ~를 맺다 form a friendship (with) / get acquainted (with) / make (a person's) acquaintance // ~가 깊다 be on intimate terms (with) / be closely associated (with) // 그녀는 ~를 싫어한다 She doesn't like social gatherings. / She shuns society. // 그는 ~가 넓다 He has a large circle of friends [acquaintances]. // 그는 그녀와의 ~를 끊었다 He broke off his friendship with her. // 그와의 ~는 즐겁다 I enjoy his company. // 정치가와의 ~는 없다 I have no association with politicians. // 아버지께서는 그와의 ~를 끊으라고 충고하셨다 My father advised me not to associate with him. / (특히 딸에게) My father warned me not to see him any more. // 그 사건 때문에 그들의 친밀한 ~에 금이 갔다 The incident caused a crack in their close relationship. // 이런 일은 ~상 거절할 수 없다 I shall be very rude if I decline an offer like this. // 이건 낭비가 아니라 ~상 필요했던 거야 This was not a matter of wasting money, but rather of filling social obligations. // 단지 ~상 그와 바에 갔었다 I went to a bar with him just to be nice. 교제하다 associate (with); (구어) mix with; have intercourse (with); keep company (with); cultivate one's acquaintance. ¶좋은 [나쁜] 사람과 ~ keep good [bad] company // 교제하기 어려운 be hard to get along with // 그와 친하게 교제하고 있다 He is a very good friend of mine. // 나는 그와 형제처럼 교제하고 있다 He is like [as close as] a brother to me. // 우리는 오랫동안 교제하고 있다 We have been friends for a long time. / We are old acquaintances. // 그 사람과는 교제하고 싶지 않다 I don't like his society. / I wouldn't seek his acquaintance. // 그는 많은 영국 사람과 교제하고 있다 He has a lot of acquaintances among Englishmen.
● 교제가 a sociable person; a society man [lady]; (미국 구어) a good mixer; a club man [woman]. 교제 범위 a circle of acquaintance(s). ¶~가 넓다 [좁다] have a large [small] circle of acquaintance(s). 교제비 social expenses; table money; [접대비] entertainment costs; (회사의) an expense account. 교제술 social tactics; the art of social intercourse.
교조(教祖) the founder of a religion; the head

교조(敎條) a tenet (of faith); a doctrine; a dogma.
● **교조주의** doctrinairism; dogmatism.
교주(校主) the proprietor [founder] of a school.
교주(敎主) the founder of a religious sect; the highest priest of a religious body.
교지(校誌) a school magazine.
교지(敎旨) 〔옛날의 사령장〕 a writ of appointment; 〔교리〕 doctrines [precepts] of a religion; 〔교육의 취지〕 principles of education. ¶기독교의 ~ the doctrine of Christianity.
교직(交織) a mixed [-weave] fabric; a blended fabric; a mixture; a blend.
● **교직물** union cloth.
교직(敎職) the teaching profession; (대학의) professorship; (종교의) the ministry; (religious) orders; the priesthood. ¶~에 있다 follow the teaching profession / be a teacher / (미) teach school // ~에 몸을 담다 enter the teaching profession / become a teacher / [목사가 되다] enter the ministry // 30년간 ~에 있다 have a 30 years' teaching experience // ~을 지망하다 want to enter the teaching profession / apply for a teaching post // 그는 ~에 있다 He is a teacher.
● **교직원** the teaching staff; the faculty; 〔교원과 직원〕 the (teaching and clerical) staff (of a school). **교직자** a school teacher; those in the teaching profession.
교질(膠質) a colloid. ¶~의 colloidal / gluey / glutinous / gelatinous.
교차(交叉) intersection; crossing; 〔통신〕 transposition; 〔식〕〔동〕 crossing over. ¶평면 ~ (미) a grade crossing / (영) a level crossing // 입체 ~ an overhead crossing / a two-level crossing. **교차하다** intersect; cross; (전선을) transpose. ¶교차하는 intersecting / crossing // 직각으로 ~ intersect at right angles // 두 도로가 거기서 교차한다 The two highways cross each other [intersect] there. ➔ 총을 교차시키다 stack arms // 두 개의 막대기를 교차시키다 cross the two sticks.
● **교차로** a crossing; an intersection; a crossroads; a cross street; a crossway. **교차 승인** the cross-recognition. **교차점** 〔두 선의 교점〕 a crossing; the point of intersection; an intersecting point; 〔네거리〕 a cross; a crossover; crossroads; an intersection; (선로의) a crossing.
교착(交錯) 〔뒤섞임〕 mixing; a mixture; blending; 〔복잡하게 엇갈림〕 complication; intricacy; complexity. ¶꿈과 현실의 ~ a mixture of dream and reality. **교착하다** get [be] complicated [involved]; cross [mingle with] each other; mix. ¶희비가 교착하여 with mingled joy and sorrow.
교착(膠着) adhesion; agglutination; stalemate. ¶~ 상태 a deadlock / a standstill / a stalemate // ~ 상태에 빠지다 come to a standstill [deadlock] / be brought to a stalemate // 교섭은 ~ 상태에 빠졌다 The talks [negotiations] have reached a deadlock [an impasse]. / The negotiations got bogged down. // 전선은 ~ 상태에 빠졌다 The war has come to a deadlock [standstill]. // 그들의 계획은 ~ 상태에 빠졌다 Their plans got bogged down. **교착하다** adhere (to) agglutinate; conglutinate; stick (to); glue (to); ce-

ment; (사태가) come to a standstill.
교체(交替) replacement; a change; a switch(투수의).
교칙(校則) school regulations; the statutes. ¶~에 의하면 [의하여] under the school regulations // ~을 지키다 [어기다] observe [violate] the school regulations.
교칙(敎則) rules for teaching.
교탁(敎卓) the teacher's desk (in a classroom); a teaching desk.
교태(嬌態) coquetry; flirtatiousness; coquettish behavior [attitude / ways]. ¶~를 부리다 flirt / play the coquette / put on coquettish airs / behave coquettishly // 그녀는 ~를 부리며 내게 기대었다 She leaned against me flirtatiously [amorously / coquettishly]. // 그녀는 아무 남자에게나 ~를 부렸다 She made up to [flirted with] every man she saw.
교통(交通) 〔왕래〕 traffic; 〔수송 (방법)〕 transportation [(미) transport]; 〔연락〕 communication; 〔교제〕 (영) intercourse. ¶혼잡한 ~ traffic congestion / (영) a traffic jam // 중심가의 혼잡한 ~ the dense [heavy] traffic of a main street // ~이 편리한 [불편한] 곳 a place easy [difficult] of access / a place conveniently [inconveniently] situated // ~ 혼잡을 덜다 relieve the congestion of traffic // ~을 정리하다 regulate [control] traffic // ~을 일시 차단하다 suspend traffic // ~이 두절되다 traffic is interrupted [tied up] // 그의 고장은 ~ 편이 좋다 His town is easy to reach. // 그 호텔은 ~이 편리하다 The hotel is easy to get to. // 이 거리는 ~이 혼잡하다 There is heavy traffic on this street. // 지진 때문에 곳곳에 ~이 마비되어 있다 Traffic has been paralyzed in places by the earthquake.
● **교통경찰** traffic police. **교통 규칙** traffic regulations [rules]; the rule of the road. **교통 기관** (a means) of transportation; transport [traffic] facilities; means [a mode] of conveyance; a public conveyance. **교통난** a traffic congestion [jam]. **교통도덕** traffic morality [morals]. ¶~을 지키다 follow traffic morals. **교통량** the volume of (wheeled) traffic; traffic volume [density]; traffic. ¶~이 많은 도로 a road where there is much traffic. **교통로** a traffic route; a line of communication. **교통마비** the traffic paralysis; a traffic jam. **교통망** a network of roads; a transportation network. **교통 방해** a traffic obstruction. **교통비** transportation [traveling / (영) travelling] expenses; carfare. **교통사고** a traffic accident; a smash-up. ¶~를 일으키다 cause [bring about] a traffic accident. **교통수단** a means of transportation. **교통순경** (미) a traffic policeman; (영) a traffic warden. **교통 신호** a traffic light [signal]; blinkers; (영국 구어) a stop-go sign. ¶~를 지키다 [무시하다] observe [neglect] traffic signal. **교통안전** traffic [road] safety; the security of smooth traffic. **교통 위반** violation of traffic regulations; a traffic offense. ¶~은 철저히 단속해야 한다 We must exercise strict control over any violation of traffic regulations. **교통 위반자** a traffic offender [violator]; (추월 등의) a road hog; 〔속도위반자〕 a speeder; 〔보행 위반자〕 (구어) a jaywalker. **교통정리** traffic control [regulation]. ¶~를 하고 있는 순경 a policeman directing traffic [on traffic duty]. **교통지옥** a traffic

chaos; horrible traffic congestion; hazardous conditions of traffic. **교통질서** a traffic order. **교통 체증** traffic congestion; a traffic tie-up [jam]. ¶도심 지역의 ~을 덜다 ease traffic jams[congestion] in the downtown area. **교통 표지** a traffic sign.

교파(敎派) a (religious) sect; a denomination. ¶새로운 ~를 형성하다 form a new denominations.

교편(敎鞭) [강의용 막대기] a teacher's pointer[ruler]; a birch (rod); [학생을 가르침] teaching. ¶그는 고등학교에서 ~을 잡고 있다 He teaches at a high school. / He is a teacher at a high school.

교포(僑胞) a Korean resident [national] abroad; a Korean residing abroad; (집합적) overseas Koreans. ¶재미[재일] ~ a Korean resident in America [Japan] / a Korean [Koreans] (residing) in America [Japan] ∥ 해외 ~ overseas Koreans.

교풍(校風) school tradition [spirit / morals]; the esprit de corps of a school. ¶~을 수립하다 establish[form] the traditions of a school.

교향곡(交響曲) a symphony. ¶베토벤의 제9번 Beethoven's ninth symphony ¶슈베르트의 미완성 ~ Schubert's Unfinished Symphony.

교향시(交響詩) [음] a symphonic poem.

교향악(交響樂) a symphony; symphony music.
● **교향악단** a symphony orchestra. ¶국립[시립] ~ the National [Municipal] Symphony Orchestra.

교화(敎化) enlightenment; culture; edification; education; civilization; illumination; (야만인에 대한) reclamation; domestication; taming; (복음에 의한) evangelization. **교화하다** enlighten; civilize; culture; educate; illuminate; (야만인 등을) reclaim; domesticate; tame; [전도하다] evangelize. ¶토인을 ~ civilize the wild tribes ∥ 비행 소년을 ~ guide a delinquent boy aright.

교환(交換) exchange; interchange; reciprocation; reciprocity; give-and-take; (물물 교환) barter; (속어) swap; trade; substitution; (어음 교환) clearing. ¶의견의 ~ an exchange [interchange] of views ∥ 문화의 ~ cultural exchange ∥ ~이 가능한 exchangeable / transferable (currency) ∥ …과 ~으로 in return [exchange] for … ∥ 한미간에 교수 ~이 있다 There is an exchange of professors between Korea and the United States. **교환하다** exchange (one thing for another); make an exchange; trade; barter; interchange; give and take; counterchange; reciprocate; change (one thing for another); (속어) swap; (어음을) clear (a check). ¶의견을 ~ exchange views (on) / compare notes (as to) ∥ 친서를 ~ exchange personal letters ∥ 어음을 ~ clear a draft [bill / note] ∥ 영수증과 교환하여 물품을 드립니다 We deliver (the) goods in exchange for a receipt. ∥ 그녀는 그와 자리를 교환하였다 She changed [switched] places [seats] with him. ∥ 그는 낡은 타이어를 새것으로 교환하였다 They replaced the old tire with a new one. ∥ 그들은 소금을 생사와 교환하였다 They bartered salt for silk. ∥ 이 기계의 부품은 서로 교환할 수 있다 The parts of these machines are interchangeable.

● **교환 가격** the exchange price. **교환 가치** an exchange(able) value; value in exchange. **교환 교수** [문화 교류를 목적으로 파견된 교수] an exchange [interchange] professor; [그 교수의 수업] exchange lessons (어학 등의). **교환국** (전화의) a central telephone office; a telephone exchange. **교환기** (전화의) a switchboard. **교환대** (전화의) a switchboard. **교환소** (어음의) a clearing house. **교환원** a telephone operator. ⇨ 전화 교환원 ⓢ 전화(電話) **교환 조건** a bargaining point. **교환품** an exchange; a thing bartered; a barter; (미) a trade-in.

교환 경기(交歡競技) a good-will match; a courtesy [friendly] game. ¶양국 실업 팀이 공식적인 탁구 ~를 재개하다 resume official binational business teams' table tennis exchanges.

교활하다(狡猾−) cunning; sly; crafty; wily; sneaky; foxy; tricky. ¶교활한 사람 a crafty [tricky] person / (속어) an old fox / (속어) a sly dog ¶교활한 꾀 a sly[an underhand / a sneaky] trick ¶교활한 상행위 underhand business practice ¶그는 교활한 짓을 한다 He behaves dishonestly. / (경기에서) He plays foul [dirty]. ∥ 그는 ~ He is a wily person. / He is full of guile [cunning]. **교활히** cunningly; slyly; with a trick.

교황(敎皇) a pope; (로마의) the Pope; the Sovereign [Supreme] Pontiff; the Vicar; the Holy Father; His Holiness the Pope (경칭). ¶~의 papal.
● **교황권**(−權) the popedom; the papacy; the tiara. **교황 사절** a pope's envoy; an apostolic delegate. **교황청** the Vatican; the Papal court; the (Roman) Curia; the Holy [Papal / Apostolic] See.

교회(敎會) 1 [기독교의 단체·종파] (the) Church; an ecclesia. ¶가톨릭 ~ the (Roman) Catholic Church ∥ 장로 [감리 / 침례 / 감독] ~ the Presbyterian [Methodist / Baptist / Episcopal] Church ∥ ~에 다니는 사람 a churchgoer ∥ ~에 다니다 attend [go to] church ∥ ~에서 예배하다 attend church services. 2 [그 건물] a church; a chapel. ¶~에서 결혼하다 be married in church.
● **교회당** a church; a chapel; a place of worship.

교회사(敎誨師) a prison chaplain.

교훈(校訓) school precepts [motto(e)s].

교훈(敎訓) a lesson; (우화 등의) a moral; instruction; edification; teachings; a precept; an injunction. ¶~적인 instructive / moral / edifying / (설교풍의) didactic ¶산 ~ a living lesson ¶~을 주다 give a lesson (to a person) ∥ ~을 얻다 learn a lesson (from) / draw a moral (from) ∥ 이 아이들은 부모의 ~을 잘 지키고 있다 These children follow their parents' instruction faithfully. ∥ 이 실패는 나에게 좋은 ~이 되었다 This failure taught me a good lesson. / I learned a valuable lesson from that failure. ∥ 이것은 그에게 좋은 ~이 될 것이다 This will be a good lesson for him [teach him a lesson].

구(九) nine; (로마 숫자) IX. ¶제 ~ the ninth ∥ ~ 분의 1 a ninth.

구(句) a phrase; an expression; a passage.

구(區) 1 (도시의) a gu; a ward; (뉴욕의) a borough. 2 [구역] a district; a section. ¶선거 ~ an electoral district / a constituency ∥ 우편 ~

구(球) [구체] a globe; a sphere; (야구 등의) a ball; (전구·온도계 등의) a bulb; (라디오 등의) a tube. ¶5~ 수신기 a five-tube radio set [receiver] // ~의 부피 the volume of a sphere // 1~, 2~ 모두 볼이었다 The first and second pitches were both balls.

구-(舊) former; one-time; ex-; old; outgoing (퇴임한). ¶~세대 the old generation // ~제도 the old system.

-구(口) an opening; a mouth; a window; a hole; a wicket. ¶개찰~ a (platform) wicket // 출입~ an entrance and exit // 접수~ an usher's desk [desk] / an inquiry [information] office / a reception counter // 출납~ (은행의) a teller's window [cage].

구가(謳歌) glorification; eulogy; applause; a panegyric. **구가하다** glorify; admire; extol; eulogize; applaud; praise; sing the praises of. ¶인생을 ~ sing the joys of life // 평화[자유]를 ~ eulogize the blessings of peace [liberty] // 청춘을 ~ sing the praises of youth // 그는 사업에 성공하여 인생의 봄을 구가하고 있다 Because the enterprise succeeded he thinks the world is his oyster.

구각(舊殼) [낡은 껍질] old skin; [오랜 인습] old customs; tradition. ¶~을 탈피하다 cast off the old skin / discard the tradition / break with the tradition / shake off the fetters of old customs and matters.

구간(舊刊) (서적의) an old edition [printing]; an old publication; (잡지의) a back number (of a magazine).

구간(區間) the section (between A and B); a block (of railroad track); a service area; [수] an interval. ¶승차 ~ the section of a (railway) line one travels // 불통 ~ a damaged [disrupted] section // 전 ~ 운임 a through (freight) rate // 전 ~ 차표 a through ticket (to Pohang) // 제1 ~ 공사 work on the first section // 수원-오산 ~ 이 불통이다 The Suwon-Osan section is blocked.

구강(口腔) the mouth; the oral cavity. ¶~의 oral / of the mouth.
●**구강외과** oral [dental] surgery. **구강 위생** oral hygiene; the hygiene of the mouth.

구개(口蓋) [생] the palate; the roof of the mouth. ¶경(硬)~ the hard palate // 연(軟)~ the soft palate / the velum.
●**구개음** [언] a palatal (sound); a gutturo-al (연구개음). **구개음화** [언] palatalization.

구걸(求乞) begging; asking alms; mendicancy. **구걸하다** beg (one's bread); go begging; live by begging; ask alms [charity]. ¶구걸하며 다니다 go about begging // 집집마다 다니며 ~ beg from door to door // 그 사람은 행인에게 돈을 구걸했다 The man begged money of [from] passers-by.

구겨지다 be crumpled; be wrinkled; become creased; crumple. ¶구겨진 신문지 a crumpled piece of newspaper // 옷이 구겨졌다 My dress got wrinkled [rumpled].

구경 1 [관광] sight-seeing; a visit. **구경하다** see (a play); visit (a museum); see [do] the sights of; watch (a game). ¶연극을 ~ see a play // 경기를 ~ watch a game // 서울 ~ go sightseeing in Seoul // 서울 시내를 ~ [do] the sights of Seoul // 우리는 이틀 동안에 파리를 구경했다 We did the sights of Paris in two days. // 경주에는 구경할 만한 곳이 많다 There are many sights to see in Gyeongju. **2** [방관]. **구경하다** watch (with interest); look on (at). ¶군중은 그들의 싸움을 구경하고 있었다 The crowd looked on at their fight.
●**구경가마리** a laughingstock; a byword; an object of ridicule. **구경거리** [구경감] a sight; a spectacle; an object of interest; an attraction; a feature; [흥행] a show; a circus. ¶~로 삼다 put something on show / make a show of. **구경꾼** [관객] a sightseer; a visitor; a tourist; [관객] a spectator; the audience; onlookers; [구경만 하는 사람] loafers; window-shoppers; [방관자] a looker-on; a bystander; an on-looker; an inquisitive (crowd) (군중); (영) a rubberneck.

구경(口徑) [지름] a diameter; (총포의) a caliber; bore; (렌즈의) aperture. ¶대 [중 / 소] ~ 대포 a large- [medium- / small-] caliber gun // 38~ 권총 a 38-caliber revolver // ~ 20 인치의 포 a 20-inch gun // 대 ~ 렌즈 a lens of large diameter [aperture].

구경(球莖) [식] a corm.

구경나다 a spectacle takes place [occurs].

구관(舊官) the former governor.

구관이 명관이다(속담) Better the devil you know than the devil you don't know.

구관(舊館) the old [older] building.

구관조(九官鳥) [동] a (hill) myna(h); a mina; a myna (bird).

구교(舊交) an old friendship; [친구] an old friend. ¶~를 새로이 하다 renew one's (old) friendship (with) / brush up one's acquaintance (with).

구교(舊教) Roman Catholicism; the Roman Catholic Church.
●**구교도** a (Roman) Catholic.

구구 [닭 부르는 소리] chuck-chuck; [비둘기 우는 소리] coo-coo.

구구(九九) 1 [수] the rules of multiplication. ⇨**구구법**(⇨~구구) **2** [구구표로 계산함] calculating by the multiplication table. **구구하다** calculate by the multiplication table.
●**구구법** [수] the rules of multiplication. **구구표** the multiplication table.

구구하다(區區-) 1 [변변찮다] trifling; trivial; petty; small; insignificant; of little importance; of no account. ¶구구한 소리 마라 (속어) Don't talk nonsense [rod]. / Don't say silly things. **구구히** trivially; pettily.
2 [각각 다르다] various; diverse; different; divergent; divided; varied; conflicting. ¶구구한 보도 conflicting reports // 풍문이 ~ Rumors are conflicting. / Conflicting rumors are in the air [afloat]. // 그것의 기원에 관한 전문가의 설은 ~ Expert opinion is divided as to its origin. // 그의 이혼 이유에 대해서 구구한 소문이 떠돌고 있다 There are all sorts of rumors about the reason for his divorce. // 그 문제에 대해서 그들은 의견이 구구했다 They were divided in opinion [They all had different opinions] on the matter. **구구히** severally; variously; diversely.
3 [용렬하다] mean; base; sordid; squalid; low. ¶구구한 변명 a lame [sorry / poor] excuse // 소액을 가지고 다투는 것은 구구한 짓이다 It is unworthy of us to wrangle over a little money. **구구히** squalidly; sordidly; basely.

구국(救國) national salvation; salvation

[rescue] of one's country. ¶~ 병사의 기념상 a monument to the soldiers who saved their country. 구국하다 save[rescue] one's country.

구균 (球菌) [생] a micrococcus (*pl.* -cocci); a coccus (*pl.* -ci). ¶포도상 ~ a staphylococcus (*pl.* -cocci).

구근 (球根) [식] a bulb. ⇨⁼알뿌리
● **구근 식물** a bulbous[bulbaceous] plant; (속어) a bulb.

구금 (拘禁) [판결 전의 유치] detention; [감금] custody; confinement; imprisonment. **구금하다** detain (a person); hold (a person) in custody; confine; put (a person) in detention; imprison; lock up; intern. ➡¶자택에 구금당하다 be detained in one's home / be confined to one's own home // 그는 피의자로서 (심문을 위해) 경찰에 구금되었다 He was detained as a suspect (for questioning) by the police. // 그는 곧 구금될 것이다 They will take him into custody at once. / He will be placed under arrest immediately.

구급 (救急) [관형어적] first-aid. ¶~ 처치를 하다 administer first aid (to). **구급하다** relieve; rescue.
● **구급법** (knowledge of) first aid. **구급붕대** (an) emergency dressing. **구급상자** a first-aid kit. **구급약** emergency remedies; first-aid medicine. **구급차** an ambulance (car). **구급치료** a first-aid treatment. **구급 환자** an emergency case.

구기 a small ladle[dipper / scoop]. ¶~로 뜨다 scoop (up) with a ladle[dipper].

구기 (球技) a game of ball; a ball game.

구기다 1 [옷 등이[을] 금이 생기(게 하)다] crumple; wrinkle; rumple; crease; crush; muss. ¶구겨진[구긴] 종잇조각 a crumpled sheet of paper // 구겨지다 be crumpled [wrinkled] / be rumpled / get mussed / get rucked up / become crease // 구겨진[구긴] 바지를 펴다 take creases out of the trousers // 신문지를 구겨 부드럽게 하다 crumple a piece of newspaper until it's soft // 이 천은 잘 구겨진다[구긴다] This material creases very easily. // 그녀의 옷이 많이 구겨졌다 Her dress was crushed. 2 [형편이 어렵게 되다] take a turn for the worst; grow bad[unfavo(u)rable / difficult].

구기자 (枸杞子) the (dried) fruit of the Chinese matrimony vine.

구기적거리다 crumple[rumple / wrinkle / crease] up (a sheet of paper).

구김살 1 [주름] wrinkles; creases; rumples; folds; cockles. ¶~이 간 wrinkled / crumpled // ~이 지다 be crumpled / be wrinkled / become creased // ~을 펴다 smooth (down) / iron out wrinkles // 바지에 보기 흉한 ~이 생겼다 Ugly creases were left in my trousers. 2 [비유]. ~ 없는 미소 an angelic smile // 진 살림 poor[needy] circumstances // ~ 없는 미소를 짓다 laugh an innocent laugh.

구깃구깃하다 crumpled; wrinkled; full of wrinkles; creasy. ¶구깃구깃한 지폐 a crumpled bank note // 구깃구깃한 저고리 a coat full of wrinkles.

-구나 [감탄] how; what; indeed. ¶참 불쌍하~ What a pity! / Poor thing! / Poor fellow! // 참 아름답~ How beautiful it is! // 향기가 참 좋~ How lovely it smells!

구난 (救難) rescue; salvage(난파선의).

● **구난선** a salvage vessel. **구난 작업** rescue work; salvage work[operation].

구내 (構內) [시설·부지의 안] premises; precincts; [담벽이 있는 소유지] a compound; [학교 등의] ground; an enclosure; [건물에 인접한] a yard; a close(사원·학교의). ¶역~에(서) in the station yard // 국회 도서관 ~에서 on the premises of the National Assembly Library // 학교 ~에서 on the school grounds / (고교·대학의) (미) on the campus // ~ 금연 No smoking in the area. // ~ 무단출입 금지 (게시) No admittance except on business. / No trespassing.
● **구내식당** a refectory(학교 등의); a refreshment room(역·열차 내의). **구내전화** an interphone; an (internal) office telephone. **구내전화 번호** an extension number.

구내염 (口內炎) [의] stomatitis.

구단 (球團) a corporation which owns a professional baseball[soccer] team.

구대륙 (舊大陸) the old World(유라시아); the European Continent(유럽).

구더기 a maggot; (영) a gentle(낚싯밥). ¶썩은 고기에 ~가 끓고 있다 The rotten meat is full of maggots.

구덩이 [팬 땅] a (ground) depression; a hollow (place); a cavity; a pit. ¶땅에 판 ~ a hole dug in the ground // 비가 와서 ~에 물이 괴었다 The rain water has collected in a depression. / The rain has formed a pool in a sunken place.

구도 (求道) seeking after truth. **구도하다** seek after truth.

구도 (構圖) [미] composition (of a painting); planning. ¶~를 잡다 compose (a picture) / draw a rough sketch (of) / design (a picture / a sculpture) // 이 그림은 ~가 좋다[나쁘다] This picture is well[poorly] composed.

구도 (舊道) an old road; a former road; an old highway[highroad].

구도 (舊都) an old capital[metropolis]; a former capital.

구독 (購讀) subscription. ¶~을 신청하다 send a subscription (to a magazine). **구독하다** subscribe for[to] (a newspaper / a magazine); (미) take; (영) take in. ¶그는 수종의 잡지를 구독하고 있다 He subscribes to[has a subscription to / takes] several magazines.
● **구독료** a subscription (fee). **구독자** a subscriber; a reader; [집합적] the constituency (정기 간행물의); the audience(책의).

구두 [단화] (a pair of) shoes; [장화] (미) high shoes; (영) boots; [집합적] footwear; footgear. ¶새 ~ 한 켤레 a new pair of shoes // 예장용(禮裝用) ~ dress shoes // 굽이 높은 (낮은) ~ high-heeled[low-heeled] shoes // 고무창 ~ rubber-soled shoes // ~의 발등 부분 [굽] the instep[heel] of a shoe // ~를 신다 [벗다] put on [take off] one's shoes // ~를 닦다 polish [clean] shoes // (미) shine shoes / (남을 시켜서) have one's shoes cleaned [polished / (미) shined] // ~를 (한 켤레) 맞추다 have a pair of shoes made // 그녀의 ~는 너무 꼭 죄었다 Those shoes pinched [were too tight for] her feet. // 이 ~는 오래 신습니다 These shoes wear long[well]. / You can wear these shoes long. // ~를 닦으세요 Give your shoes a shine, sir? / Shine, Sir?
● **구두끈** a shoelace; a shoestring; (영)

bootlaces. ¶~를 매다[풀다] tie[untie] one's shoestrings / lace[unlace] one's boots [shoes]. **구두닦이** a shoeblack; a bootblack; (미) shoeshine boy[man]; (호텔의) a boots. **구두약**(-藥) shoe polish; (shoe) blacking(검은). ¶~을 바르다[으로 닦다] black[polish] one's shoes / (미) shine one's shoes. **구두장이** a shoemaker; a cobbler. **구두창** the sole of a shoe; a boot sole. **구둣발** feet with shoes on; shoed feet. ¶~로 차다 kick (a person) with boots on. **구둣방** a shoe store [(영) shop]. **구둣솔** a shoe[boot] brush. **구둣주걱** a shoehorn; a shoeing-horn; a shoe lift.
구두(口頭) word of mouth. ¶~로 verbally / orally / by word of mouth // ~ 또는 문서로 either by word of mouth or writing / in word [speech] or writing // ~로 전하다 convey [communicate] verbally // ~로 보고하다 make an oral report // ~로 신청하다 make an application by word of mouth / apply verbally (for a position) // 메시지는 ~로 전달되었다 The message was conveyed verbally[by word of mouth].
●**구두 계약** a verbal[parol] contract [agreement]. **구두 변론** [법] oral proceedings [pleas]; oral argument[pleadings]; hearing. **구두선**(-禪) a fair word; a mere talk; an empty slogan. ¶~에 그치다 become mere talk[empty slogan]. **구두시험** an oral examination[test]; [면접] an interview. **구두 심리** a verbal[an oral] trial; hearing.
구두법(句讀法) punctuation; pointing. ¶~이 틀리다 be wrongly punctuated.
구두쇠 a miser; a niggard; a stingy [close fisted / tightfisted] fellow; a skinflint; a screw; (구어) a penny pincher; (구어) a tightwad. ¶~ 영감 an old screw // ~로 유명하다 be notorious for parsimony // 그는 ~다 He is a tightfist type[(구어) a tightwad].
구두점(句讀點) a punctuation mark[point]; a full stop; (미) a period. ¶~을 찍다 punctuate / mark with punctuation marks / put [use] punctuation marks (between / after / before) // ~ 없이 쓰다 write (a poem) without punctuation.
구들 a Korean underfloor heating system; a hypocaust; a Korean floor heater. ¶~을 놓다[고치다] install[repair] a Korean hypocaust.
●**구들방** a room with a Korean hypocaust system. **구들장** a piece of flat stone used for hypocaust flooring.
구라파(歐羅巴) 〈음역〉 Europe. ⇨유럽
구락부(俱樂部) 〈음역〉 a club. ⇨클럽1
구랍(舊臘) last December; the end of last year.
구래(舊來) from old times; from times past. ¶~의 old / old-time / time-honored // ~의 습관을 지키다 keep to old customs.
구럭 1 [새끼로 그물처럼 엮은 것] a straw network; anything made of straw netting. 2 →망태기
구렁 1 [팬 곳] a hollow (place); a depression; a pit; a cavity. ¶깊은 ~ a bottomless pit // ~에 빠지다 fall into a pit[hole]. 2 [심연] the depths; a gulf; an abyss; an abysmal chasm; nadir. ¶죄악의 ~ an abyss[a pit] of sin / the Slough of Despond // 불행의 ~ 속에 빠져 있다 be at the bottom of fortune's wheel / be (sunk) in the depths of despair //

사업에 실패하여 그는 절망의 ~에 빠졌다 When he failed in business, he sank into the depths[(문어) an abyss] of despair.
구렁이 1 [동] a yellowish brown serpent. 2 [음흉한 사람] a snake; a serpent; a deep one. **구렁이 담 넘어가듯**(속담) play tricks cautiously without arousing suspicion.
구렁텅이 1 [깊은 구렁] a deep hollow[hole]; a bottomless pit. 2 the depths. ⇨ =구렁2
구레나룻 sideburns; (남) whiskers(▶ 오늘날 whiskers는 사람의 「구레나룻」을 가리키기보다는 고양이·쥐 등의 수염을 가리킴). ¶~이 난 사람 a whiskered man.
-**구려** 1 [감탄] ¶참 아름답~ How beautiful it is! / What a (beautiful) sight! 2 [허용] may. ¶들어오~ You may enter. // 좋도록 하~ Do as you please. // 갈 테면 가~ You may go if you want to. 3 [권유] I advise you (to do / that); you had better (do). ¶조심하~ Be careful.
구력(舊曆) the lunar calendar. ⇨＝태음력(⇨)태음)
구령(口令) a (word of) command; a (verbal) order[command]. ¶~에 따라 at the word of command // ~을 내리다 give an order [a command] // ~이 떨어지자 차려자세를 취하다 stand at attention at the word of command // 발사 ~을 내리다 give the order to fire // 선생님의 ~에 따라 학생들은 행진하기 시작했다 The pupils began to march at the teacher's command. **구령하다** command; order; give an order; dictate.
구령(救靈) salvation; redemption.
구례(舊例) an old custom; a precedent; a usage.
구루병(佝僂病) rickets; rachitis.
구류(拘留) custody; detention; commitment. ¶재(再)~ (a) remand // ~ 중이다 be in [under] detention / be kept in custody // 10일간의 ~에 처하다 be sentenced to ten days' detention // 그는 ~에서 풀려났다 He was released from custody. **구류하다** detain; lock up; (미) hold. ¶재구류되다 be remanded to custody // 경찰에 구류되어 취조를 받고 있다 be detained[(미) held] for questioning by the police // 그는 절도 혐의로 구류되었다 He was taken into custody on a theft charge.
구르다[1] 1 (데굴데굴) roll (over). ¶굴러 떨어지다(공 등이) roll down (a slope) / [쓰러져 떨어지다] tumble[fell] down (the stairs) // 공이 뜰로 굴러들었다 A ball rolled into the garden. // 공이 길 건너편으로 굴러 갔다 The ball rolled across the road. // 나에게 행운이 굴러 들어왔다 Suddenly fortune smiled on me. / I had an unexpected piece[turn] of good luck. // 큰돈이 그에게 굴러 들어왔다 A big sum of money suddenly fell[plopped] into his hands. // 그에게 큰 재산이 굴러 들어왔다 He came[stepped] into a big fortune. / A big fortune came[fell] into his hands. // 이것은 귀중한 물건이라서 아무 데나 굴러다니는 것이 아니다 This is a valuable article and does not grow on trees. / This is a valuable article. You'll have a hard time finding anything like it. // 그런 것은 아무 데나 굴러다닌다 You can find that kind of thing (lying around) anywhere. // 그는 침대에서 굴러 떨어졌다 He fell out of bed. // 언덕길에 세워 둔 차가 굴러 내리기 시작했다 The car parked on

구르다
the slope began to roll down the hill. **2** [반동으로 되튀다] recoil; rebound; kick. ¶대포는 뒤로 구른다 A gun recoils.
굴러 온 호박(속담) a (unexpected) windfall.
구르다² (발을) stamp (one's feet); tread noisily; beat one's shoes (on the floor). ¶초조하게 발을 ~ tap one's foot impatiently / 발을 구르며 울다 cry stamping one's feet // 발을 동동 구르며 분해하다 stamp with vexation [mortification / chagrin] / be hopping mad.
구름 a cloud; (집합적) the clouds. (▶ 구름의 종류. 권운 cirrus / 권적운 cirrocumulus / 권층운 cirrostratus / 고층운 altostratus / 고적운 altocumulus / 적란운 cumulonimbus / 난층운 nimbostratus / 적운 cumulus / 층적운 stratocumulus / 층운 stratus) ¶솜 같은 ~ fleecy clouds // 얇은[두꺼운] ~ thin[thick / heavy] clouds // ~이 많은[없는] 날 a cloudy [cloudless] day // ~ 사이 a break in the clouds // ~ 뒤에 숨다 go behind a cloud // 검은 ~이 드리워져 있었다 Dark clouds were hanging low. // ~이 끼었다 Clouds have gathered. // ~이 걷혔다[개었다] The clouds have broken[lifted]. // 하늘에는 한 점의 ~도 없었다 There was not a speck of cloud in the sky. / Not a cloud was to be seen in the sky. // 하늘이 온통 ~에 덮여 있다 The sky is overcast. // ~의 움직임으로 보아 당분간 좋은 날씨가 계속될 것 같다 From the look of the sky[clouds] I'd say the good weather will hold for some time. // 산꼭대기가 ~ 사이로 나타났다 The mountain peak appeared from behind the clouds. // 달이 ~ 사이로 숨었다 The moon disappeared[hid itself] behind the clouds. // 해가 갑자기 ~ 속으로 숨어 버렸다 Suddenly the sun went behind the clouds.
● **구름장** a mass[sheet] of cloud.
구름다리 a viaduct; an overpass; a railway bridge; a land bridge; a girder bridge.
구릉(丘陵) a hill; a hillock. ¶중첩된 ~ hills piled on hills.
● **구릉 지대** hill areas; hilly country[areas]; downland.
구리 copper. ¶~를 입힌 coppered // ~를 함유한 coppery.
구리다 1 (냄새가) ill-[foul-]smelling; fetid; stinking. **2** (행동이) suspicious; dubious; shady. ¶밑 밑에 ~ have something on one's conscience.
구린내 a bad[foul / nasty] smell; an offensive odor; a stink. ¶~를 풍기다 have[give out] a bad smell / emit an offensive smell / smell bad / stink // ~가 코를 찌른다 An offensive smell greets my nose.
구린내가 나다 [수상한 점이 있다] smell fishy.
구릿빛 copper color; brown. ¶~의 brown / copper(-colored) / (햇볕에 타서) bronzed / (sun)tanned / sunburnt.
구매(購買) purchase. ⇨ =구입
● **구매력** purchasing[buying] power; (화폐의) the buying value. ¶~이 증대하고 있다 Buying power is growing. **구매욕** customers' interest. **구매자** a buyer; a purchaser. **구매조합** a cooperative (society); a consumers' association; a purchasing association; (미국구어) a co-op.
-구먼 [감탄] ¶아 그렇~ Oh is that it! / Indeed, that's right. / I see what you mean. / So it is. / Well I'll be! / 비가 왔~ Why it's rained! / 비가 오겠~ I see it's going to rain! / 똑같~ Why it looks just like it! / 그 동네는 외국촌 같겠~ That part of town must be a kind of foreign colony! / 화려한 빛깔이 좋겠 ~ I guess a fancy color would be nice! / 그럼 문제는 간단하~ Then the question is simple. / 그래? 그럼 수재들이었~ Really? Then they were a talented lot! / 그럼 그 많은 돈은 그 남편이 다 가졌겠~ Then the husband must have got all her money! / 참고된 일이었~ It was hard work, I tell you. // 내가 잘못 했~ I acknowledge[admit] that I was wrong. // 거기 있었겠~ Sure enough there it was. // 벌써 정오~ Well, well, it's noon already.

구멍 1 a hole; [틈] an aperture; an opening; a perforation(뚫은); a slit(가늘고 긴); an orifice(관(管) 등의). ¶바늘 ~ [바늘귀] the eye of a needle / [바늘로 뚫은 구멍] a hole made by a needle / 창에 난 ~ a chink in a paper window / 깊이 2미터의 ~ a hole two meters deep / 우편물을 투입하는 ~ a slit for mail // 호스의 ~ the nozzle of a hose // 빠져나갈 ~ a loophole / a way out / a way[means] of escape // 빠져나갈 ~이 많은 법률 a law full of loopholes // ~을 뚫다 make[start] a hole (in) // 널빤지에 ~을 뚫다 drill[bore] a hole in a board / 카드에 ~을 내다 punch a hole in a card // 땅에 ~을 파다 dig a hole[a pit] in the ground // ~을 넓히다 broach / 벽에 ~을 내다 make a hole [an opening] in the wall // ~을 막다 (up) a hole / fill[stop] a gap (with rags) // ~을 메우다 fill[stop] (up) a hole // 탈세할 ~을 막다 plug a tax loophole // 네 양말에 ~이 뚫렸다 There is a hole in your socks. // 옷에 좀이 먹어 ~이 났다 Moths have eaten [made] a hole in my jacket. // 동전을 ~에 넣으면 표가 나온다 Drop a coin into the slot, and you get a ticket. // 배 바닥에 ~이 났다 The boat sprang a leak in the bottom.
2 [결함] a defect; a blind point(맹점). ¶국경은 ~투성이여서 얼마든지 다닐 수 있다 The border is porous. // 그 계획은 ~투성이다 There are a number of holes in the scheme.
3 [결손] a loss(손실); a deficit(부족금). ¶장부상의 ~ shortages in one's accounts // ~을 내다 make a hole (in one's capital) // ~을 메우다 make up (a deficit) / make up for (a loss) // 그는 회사 경리에 큰 ~을 냈다 He caused the firm a great loss. / He made a great hole in the firm's finances.
구멍가게 a mom-and-pop store; a small store[shop]. ¶~를 내고 있다 keep a small store / engage in small trade [retail business].
구면(球面) [수] a spherical surface. ¶~의 spherical.
● **구면경** [물] a spherical mirror. **구면 기하학** spherical geometry. **구면 삼각법** spherical trigonometry[geometry]; spherics. **구면 삼각형** [수] a spherical triangle. **구면 수차**(-收差) [물] spherical aberration. **구면 투영법** a spherical projection.
구면(舊面) an old acquaintance; a familiar face. ¶그와 나는 ~이다 I have known him for a long time. / Our acquaintance is of long standing.
구명(究明) study; (an) investigation; (an)

inquiry. **구명하다** study; investigate (into) (a matter); look [inquire] into (a matter); bring (a matter) to light. ¶원인을 ~ clear up [look deep into] the cause (of) // 문제를 ~ bring light on a subject / bring a subject to light // 원인은 철저히 구명해야 한다 The cause should be thoroughly investigated. // 과학자들은 암의 원인을 구명하고 있다 Scientists are trying to discover the cause of cancer.

구명(救命) lifesaving; sparing a person's life; clemency(죄수의). ¶~을 빌다 beg for mercy [for a person's life] / appeal for mercy [clemency] // 그들은 헛일임을 알고 있었기 때문에 ~을 탄원하지 않았다 They asked for no quarter as they knew that none would be given. **구명하다** save a person's life; save a person from death; spare a person's life; (항복자를) give quarter (to a person). ➜그는 구명되었다 His life was saved.
●**구명구**(-具) a life preserver; lifesaving equipment [apparatus]; (집합적) survival equipment. **구명대**(-帶) a life belt; a safety belt; (영) an air-jacket. **구명정**(-艇) a lifeboat; a rescue boat.

구명(舊名) an old name [designation / appellation].

구무럭거리다 move slowly. ⇨꾸무럭거리다

구문(口文) (a) commission; a percentage; brokerage; (구어) a cut. ¶1할의 ~ commission (on the sale) // ~을 받다 take [receive] a commission (on the sale) // 매상고의 20프로를 ~으로 주겠다 I will give you a commission of 20 percent on sales [a 20 percent sales commission]. // 그는 ~을 받고 그 기계를 팔았다 He sold the machine on commission. / He took a commission on the sale of the machine.

구문(構文) construction (of sentences); sentence structure [building]. ¶문법상의 ~ grammatical construction // 불완전한 ~ defective construction // 분사 ~ a participial construction.
●**구문론** syntax.

구문(舊聞) old news; an old story. ¶그것은 ~에 속한다 It's an old story. / It took place a long time ago.

구문서(舊文書) an ex-proprietor's bill of sale; a sales note of the prior owner.

구물거리다 wriggle; move slowly. ⇨꾸물거리다

구미(口味) [입맛] (one's) taste; (one's) palate; appetite. ¶~를 돋우는 tempting / inviting / appetizing // ~에 맞다 suit one's taste / be nice to the palate // ~를 돋우다 stimulate [tempt] one's appetite / make one's mouth water // 그 음식은 내 ~에 맞는다 The food is pleasant to my taste. // 포도주는 내 ~에 맞지 않는다 Wine doesn't agree with me. // 그것은 ~가 당기는 제안이다 It is a very attractive [tempting] proposal.

구미(歐美) Europe and America; the West; the Occident. ¶~ 각국 Western countries // ~의 European and American / Western / Occidental // ~에서는 in Western countries / in the West // ~식 사고방식 the Western way of thinking.

구미호(九尾狐) an old fox; (교활한 사람) a sly dog; a tricky [cunning] person.

구민(區民) the inhabitants of a ward.

구박(驅迫) ill-treatment; maltreatment; cruel treatment; mistreatment; abuse. ¶~을 참아 내다 endure [bear] the severity of the treatment. **구박하다** persecute; ill-treat; maltreat; abuse; treat (a person) harshly [roughly / cruelly]; be cruel to (a maidservant). ¶아내를 ~ treat one's wife cruelly / abuse one's wife // 며느리를 ~ pick [be hard] on one's daughter-in-law // 그는 나를 구박했다 He gave me a hard time. / He treated me harshly. ➜**구박받다** be ill-treated / be maltreated / be handed roughly.

구배(勾配) a slope; (an) inclination. ⇨"물매³

구법(舊法) [옛 법] an old [ancient] law; [낡은 방법] an old method.

구변(口辯) oratorical talent [skill]. ⇨"언변

구별(區別) **1** [차이] a difference; (a) distinction; [차별] discrimination. ¶~ 없이 without discrimination / indiscriminately // 인종·연령·성의 ~ 없이 irrespective of race, age, or sex // 남녀의 ~ 없이 without distinction of sex // ~을 못 하다 cannot distinguish [discriminate] (A from B / between A and B) // 당시는 계층의 ~이 매우 뚜렷했다 In those days class distinctions were very clear. // 그는 공사간의 ~을 분명히 하는 사람이다 He draws a sharp [clear] line between official and private matters. // 모든 사람은 인종이나 신조의 ~ 없이 평등하게 취급되어야 한다 Everybody ought to be treated alike without (making any) distinction as to [of] race or creed. // 여관과 호텔은 어떤 ~이 있습니까 What is the difference between a yeogwan and a hotel? **구별하다** tell [know] (A from B); distinguish (between A and B); make a distinction (between); discriminate (between the two things). (▶ difference는 일반적인 말, distinction은 미묘한 차이, discrimination은 가치의 인식이 따름) ¶새를 우는 소리를 듣고 ~ differentiate one bird from another by their calls / tell what kind of bird it is by its song // 좋은 일과 나쁜 일을 ~ make a distinction [discriminate / distinguish] between right and wrong // 옳고 그름을 ~ distinguish right from wrong [between right and wrong] // 이 새는 색깔과 모양만으로는 암수를 구별할 수가 없다 In the case of this bird, we cannot distinguish [tell] the male from the female by color or shape. // 그녀는 자기 자식과 의붓자식을 구별하지 않고 사랑했다 She loved her own child and her stepchild equally. // 너는 이제 옳고 그름을 구별하지 못할 나이가 아니다 You are old enough to know right from wrong. // 사실과 소문을 구별하기는 어렵다 It is difficult to tell the difference between fact and rumor. // 나는 물개와 해마를 구별하지 못한다 I cannot tell [distinguish] a seal from a walrus.
2 [차이에 따라 나눔] (a) classification. **구별하다** classify.

구보(驅步) a run; (군대의) double-quick; double time; (말의) a canter; a gallop. ¶~로 at double-quick / at a canter(말이) / at the running pace // ~로 가다 go at a run [on the double] / (말이) (go at a) gallop // ~로 행진하다 march at [on] the double // 그는 ~로 왔다 He came running. // ~ [구령] Double march! // 그는 ~가 빠르다 He runs fast. / He is a fast runner. **구보하다** run; (군) double; (말이) canter.

구복(口腹) mouth and stomach; 〔생계〕 living; subsistence. ¶~지게 a means of living∥~을 채우다 satisfy one's appetite / eat one's fill.

구부러뜨리다 bend (one's back); curve (a wire); crook (one's arm). ¶철사를 ~ bend a wire.

구부러지다 bend; bow; curve; stoop; turn. ¶구부러진 곳 a curve / a bend / 길이 구부러진 곳 a curve[turn] in the road / 구부러진 나무 crooked[gnarled] tree / 허리가 구부러진 노인 an old man stooped[bent] with age∥활등처럼 구부러진 철도 a railway line curved like a bow∥그 모퉁이를 원편으로 구부러지면 우체국이 있다 If you turn left at that corner, you'll find a post office.∥노인은 허리가 구부러져 있다 The old man is bent with age.∥거기서 길이 왼쪽으로 구부러져 있다 There the road curves to the left.

구부리다 (몸을) stoop (over); bow; (물건을) bend; crook; curve; inflect. ¶철사를 ~ bend a wire∥허리를 ~ bend oneself[one's back] / double up one's body∥안쪽으로 ~ bend [turn] in / inflect.

구부정하다 rather[slightly] bent[curved / arched]; somewhat crescent shaped. ¶그는 몸이 수척하고 ~ He is slender and slightly bent.

구분(區分) 〔분할〕 a division; 〔구획〕 a section; 〔분류〕 classification; 〔한계〕 demarcation. ¶종(種)은 속(屬)의 하위 ~이다 Species is a subdivision of genus. **구분하다** 〔나누다〕 divide; 〔분류하다〕 sort (out). ¶땅을 작게 구분하여 팔다 divide land into small lots and sell it / subdivide and sell land∥우편물을 ~ sort mail∥그 거리는 도시를 남과 북으로 구분하고 있다 That street divides the city into north and south.∥이 표에서는 직원을 직능에 따라 명확히 구분하지 않았다 This table did not classify the staff members clearly according to function.∥그는 공부할 시간과 놀 시간을 아주 잘 구분한다 He knows very well when to study and when to enjoy himself. →¶구분된 짐 luggage[baggage] which has been sorted / sorted luggage.

구붓하다 slightly bent[curved / warped]. ¶구붓한 등 a bent[rounded] back / a stoop.

구비(口碑) (an) oral tradition; 〔전설〕 a legend; 〔민간전승〕 folklore. ¶~로 전하여지다 be handed down by tradition[orally / by word of mouth].

구비하다(具備—) possess; have; be possessed of. ¶모든 조건을 ~ fulfill all the conditions / satisfy all the requisites∥그는 교사의 자격을 충분히 구비하고 있다 He is well qualified as a teacher.∥그는 한국인의 장점과 단점을 구비하고 있다 He possesses both the typical strong and weak points of the Korean.

구빈(救貧) relief of the poor; poor relief.
●**구빈사업** settlement work.

구사(驅使) 1 〔부림〕 driving. **구사하다** have (one's men) at one's beck and call; turn (a person) round one's little finger; order (a person) about; command the service of (one's subordinates). 2 〔자유자재로 씀〕 free use. **구사하다** use freely; command; have a command of. ¶영어를 자유로이 ~ have a good[perfect / excellent] command of English / be a master of English∥그는 5개 국어를 구사한다 He has a good command of five different languages. / He can speak five languages.

구사상(舊思想) old-fashioned[antiquated / moss-grown] ideas.

구사일생(九死一生) a narrow[hairbreadth] escape from (the jaw of) death. ¶그는 죽음을 모면했으나 그야말로 ~이었다 He fortunately escaped death, but it was a very near thing. **구사일생하다** have[make] a narrow escape from death; narrowly escape death; escape death by a hair's breadth; have a hair's breadth escape from death. ¶그는 곰을 만났다가 구사일생했다 He had a hairbreadth escape from a bear.

구상(求償) claim for compensation[indemnity / damages].
●**구상권** a right to indemnity; a right of demanding[claiming] compensation; a claim for damages. **구상 무역** compensation trade.

구상(具象) concreteness; embodiment. ¶~의 [적인] concrete / figurative∥~화하다 exteriorize.
●**구상 개념** a concrete concept. **구상 예술** the plastic arts.

구상(球狀) a globular[spherical] shape; globularity; globosity. ¶~의 spherical / spheroidal / globular / globe-shaped.

구상(鉤狀) ¶~의 hooklike / hook-shaped.

구상(構想) 〔계획〕 a plan; 〔면밀한 계획〕 a design; 〔착상〕 (a) conception; an idea; 〔문예 작품의〕 a plot. ¶소설의 ~ the plot of a novel∥논문에 대한 ~을 다듬다 work out a detailed plan for one's thesis∥~이 떠오르다 conceive an idea[a plan]∥~을 가다듬다 beat[tax / rack] one's brains (about / over) / elaborate a plan∥그 소설의 ~은 참으로 웅대하다 The novel is truly grand in conception.∥나는 논문의 ~을 바꾸어 다시 썼다 I changed the basic idea[conception] of my paper and rewrote it.∥교장 선생님은 우수 학생을 위한 특별 커리큘럼의 ~을 가지고 있다 The principal[(영) head master] has a design of[has designed] a special curriculum for the advanced students. **구상하다** map out (a scheme); crystallize[shape] one's idea (of); visualize a plan (of); formulate a plan[plot] (of).

구상유취(口尙乳臭) 〔유치〕 being babyish [boyish / puerile]; 〔미숙〕 being green [unfledged / callow].

구새 먹다 become[get] hollow; be eaten hollow.

구색(具色) assortment. ¶~이 맞는 assorted / matched / suited∥~을 갖추다 assort a stock of goods / keep[have] a rich[large] assortment of goods (in stock) / have a well-assorted stock. **구색하다** assort.

구석 1 〔모퉁이의 안쪽〕 a corner; a nook. ¶~자리 a corner seat∥아늑한 ~ a cosy[snug] corner∥방 한~에 앉다 sit[take a seat] in the corner of a room∥종일 방 ~에 박혀 있다 keep (in) one's room all day long∥모든 ~을 다 뒤지다 search every nook and corner (for) / comb (a room)∥나는 이 사진의 왼쪽 아래 ~에 있다 You can see me in the lower left-hand corner of the picture.
2 〔치우친 곳〕 a recess; a nook; 〔외딴 곳〕 a remote[a secluded / a retired / a sequestered / an out-of-the-way] place[corner].

¶시골~ a remote country place / an out-of-the-way corner in the country / (미) the backcountry // 마음 한~에 somewhere in the back(ground) of one's mind / somewhere at the bottom[back] of one's heart / somewhere in the inner(most) recesses of one's heart // 그는 시골~에 살고 있다 He lives in a remote country place. / (미) He lives way back in the country.

3 [점·면] a point; a respect; an aspect; a side; an angle; a way; a manner. ¶약한 ~ a weak point / one's weakness // 모르는 ~이 없다 know every inch of (the neighborhood) / know (a thing) down to the last detail // 그의 이야기에는 다소 미심쩍은 ~이 있다 There are some points in his statement which do not sound quite convincing to me.

구석구석 every corner; every nook and corner; all the corners (of); everywhere. ¶나라 안 ~까지 all the country over / throughout[all over] the country // 세계의 ~까지 to the four corners of the World [earth] // ~ 다 뒤지다[찾아보다] search[look in] every nook and corner (of) / search everywhere / leave no corner unsearched // 그는 이 근방은 ~ 훤히 알고 있다 He knows every inch of the neighborhood. // 경찰은 그 건물을 ~ 뒤졌다 The police searched every nook and corner [cranny] of the building. // 그 방은 ~ 꽃으로 장식되어 있었다 There were floral arrangements in every corner of the room. // ~ 다 찾아보았느냐 Have you looked everywhere [searched every nook and cranny]? // 환한 달빛이 사방을 ~ 비췄다 The whole area was flooded with bright moonlight. / The moon cast its bright light all over the ground. // 우리는 그것을 ~ 찾아보았으나 발견하지 못했다 We searched every nook and corner for it, but in vain. // 그 식탁보는 ~까지 수가 놓여 있었다 The table cloth was embroidered all over.

구석기(舊石器) a pal(a)eolith; a pal(a)eolithic stone implement.
●**구석기 시대** [고고] the Old Stone Age; the Pal(a)eolithic period[era].

구석지다 recessed; retired; sequestered; secluded; covert; out-of-the-way. ¶구석진 곳 a recess / a (covert) nook / an out-of-the-way place[corner] / (미) the backcountry.

구설(口舌) adverse criticism; malicious gossip. ¶~을 듣다 be on the stinging tongues of (people) / be talked about maliciously by (others) / (자기의 실언으로) suffer from a[an unfortunate] slip of the tongue.
●**구설수** the bad luck to hear abusive language[to be verbally abused].

구성(構成) [각 요소를 하나의 통일체로 만들기] composition; constitution; organization; formation; construction; make-up; [화] configuration(분자의); (문어) plot. ¶인원 ~ personnel organization / line-up // 소설의 ~을 마치다 construct[lay out] the plot of a novel // 문장의 ~을 분석하다 analyze the structure of a sentence / parse a sentence // 그는 문장(의) ~에 고심했다 He took pains with the structure of his sentences. // 문장의 ~이 어색하다 The sentence structure is awkward. **구성하다** make; compose; constitute; organize; form; comprise; construct. ¶사회를 ~ form a community / constitute a society // 이론을 ~ frame a theory. →¶물질은 원자로 구성되어 있다 Matter is composed of atoms. // 극단은 30명의 단원으로 구성되어 있다 The troupe has [consists of] thirty members. // 우리 클럽은 30인의 학생으로 구성되어 있다 Our club is composed [consists] of thirty students.
●**구성 분자** a component; constituent elements; part (of). **구성비** the component [distribution] ratio. **구성원** a constituent (member); members; (한 사람) a member (of a community); (계약의) a signatory (member).

구성지다 [매력적이다] attractive; charming; tasteful; [어울리다] becoming. ¶구성진 음악 enchanting[melodious / tuneful] music // 구성진 목소리로 in a soft[beautiful] voice.

구세계(舊世界) the old World; the old continent.

구세군(救世軍) the Salvation Army.

구세대(舊世代) the old generation.

구세주(救世主) the savior of the world; [예수] the Savior[(영) the Saviour]; the Redeemer; the Messiah; the Messias. ¶~ 예수 그리스도 Jesus Christ, our savior / the Savior // ~의 [같은] Messianic (ardor).

구속(拘束) (a) restriction; (a) restraint; constraint; binding; [감금] confinement; detention (in custody); [체포] (an) arrest. ¶~이 없는 free / unrestrained // ~을 풀다 remove restrictions / set a person free. **구속하다** [제한하다] restrict; place restrictions (on); [규제하다] restrain (a person from doing); [속박하다] bind; curb; be binding (upon / on); place (a person) under restraint; detain (a person) in custody; arrest. →¶구속받다 [되다] be bound / be placed under restraint [control] / suffer restriction. // 그는 일 주일 동안 구속되었다 He was kept in custody for a week. // 나는 그런 무리한 약속에 구속받고 싶지 않다 I refuse to be bound by such unreasonable restrictions.
●**구속력** binding power[force]; [법] vigor; validity. ¶~을 잃다 lose (its) binding power // 법적 ~이 있다[없다] carry[carry no] legal binding force. **구속 영장** a warrant of arrest; an arrest warrant. **구속자** a person under restraint; (집합적) the restrained.

구수(口授) [입으로 가르침] oral instruction [teaching]. **구수하다** instruct[teach] orally; dictate.

구수하다 **1** (맛이) tasty; pleasant-tasting; savory; (냄새가) nice-[sweet-]smelling; sweet. ¶구수한 맛 a delicate flavor[savor / taste] // 구수한 냄새 a sweet[a savory] smell // 고기 굽는 구수한 냄새 the savory smell of meat being barbecued // 커피콩 볶는 구수한 냄새 the pleasant aroma of coffee beans being roasted // 맛이 ~ taste good / be good [pleasant] to the taste[palate] // 냄새가 ~ smell good[sweet].
2 (인품·이야기 등이) engaging; appealing; attractive; entertaining; interesting. ¶구수한 이야기 an entertaining[amusing / interesting] talk / a humorous[witty] story // 구수한 사람 an attractive[affable] person / a man of delicate charm.

구수회의(鳩首會議) a (closed-door) conference. **구수회의하다** consult (on a matter); put[lay] (their) heads together (about);

hold [have] a secret [closed-door] conference (with); go into a huddle.

구순하다 friendly; harmonious. ¶둘 사이가 ~ They are on good terms. **구순히** harmoniously; on good terms; in harmony.

구술(口述) an oral statement; dictation. ¶~의 oral / verbal. **구술하다** state orally; dictate (a letter to one's typist). ¶그는 연설을 비서에게 구술하였다 He dictated his speech to his secretary.
● **구술서** a verbal note; an oral statement. **구술시험** an oral examination [test].

구슬 〔유리알〕 a glass bead; 〔진주〕 a pearl; 〔보석〕 a precious stone; a gem; a jewel; a bijou. ¶~ 같은 like a gem / gemlike / pearly / perfect // ~이 구르는 것 같은 목소리 a silvery voice.
구슬이 서 말이라도 꿰어야 보배(라) (속담) Nothing is complete unless you put in final shape.
● **구슬 백** a beaded bag.

구슬땀 beads of sweat [perspiration]; sweat in beads. ¶~을 흘리며 일하다 work with sweat running down in beads.

구슬리다 1 〔그럴듯한 말로〕 cajole; coax; wheedle; talk (a person into [out of] doing); win (a person) over. ¶슬슬 구슬려서 만 원을 내도록 하다 wheedle [coax] (a person) out of 10,000 won // 아이를 구슬려 학교에 보내다 〔약을 먹이다〕 coax a child to school [to take a medicine] // 여자가 남자를 마음대로 have a way with a man / have a man in (her) pocket / twist [turn] a man round (her) (little) finger // 그녀는 남편을 구슬려서 조건을 수락하게 했다 She sweet-talked her husband into accepting the condition. // 나는 아이들에게 후에 무엇을 사 주겠다고 구슬려서 마당 청소를 시켰다 I talked [coaxed] the children into cleaning up the yard with promises of buying them something later.
2 〔이리저리 생각하다〕 consider; deliberate; meditate (on); reflect (on); ponder (over).

구슬프다 sad; sorrowful; plaintive; pathetic; touching; doleful; melancholy; mournful. ¶구슬픈 목소리 a plaintive [sorrowful] voice / 구슬픈 이야기 a sad [pathetic / sob] story / a sorrowful tale // 구슬픈 노래 a doleful [plaintive] song // 구슬픈 곡 a mournful [plaintive] tune // 구슬퍼지다 feel sad. **구슬피** sadly; sorrowfully; plaintively; dolefully; mournfully. ¶~ 울다 weep sorrowfully.

구습(舊習) an old custom; an old-fashioned [out-of-date] practice; a time-honored [time worn] usage; conventionalities. ¶~을 고수하다 stick to old customs // ~을 타파하다 break through [do away with] conventionalities.

구시렁거리다 〔잔소리를〕 give (a person) a long lecture; nag; 〔군소리를〕 keep grumbling (at / over / about).

구식(舊式) an old type [style / fashion / school]. ¶~의 old-fashioned / out-of-date / out of fashion / of the old type / (미) out-moded // ~ 생각 an old-fashioned idea // ~ 무기 outdated [obsolete] weapons // 그런 모자는 이제는 ~이다 That kind of hat is out of style [fashion]. // 그 옷은 ~이다 The clothes are out of date. // 그는 ~ 집안에서 자랐다 He was brought up in an old-fashioned [a conventional] family.

구실 〔직무·역할〕 (a) duty; an office; a function; a job; a mission; a role; a part; 〔책무〕 (a) duty; (an) obligation. ¶자식 ~ a son's [daughter's] duties / one's filial duties // 제~을 (다)하다 do [perform / fulfill] one's (share of) duty / discharge [fulfill] one's function // 제~을 다하지 못하다 fail in [fall short of] one's duty // 제~을 하다 discharge one's full duty as man / behave like a human being // 이 소파는 침대 ~도 한다 This sofa serves as a bed, too. / This sofa doubles as a bed. // 이 명사는 이 구절에서 형용사 ~을 한다 The noun functions as an adjective in this phrase. // 우산일지라도 만약의 경우에는 무기 ~을 할 수 있다 Even an umbrella will serve as a weapon in time of need. // 그는 제~을 훌륭히 다했다 He performed his part with great success.

구실(口實) 〔핑계〕 an excuse (for); a pretext; a pretense; a plea; make-believe. ¶그럴듯한 ~ a plausible excuse / a specious pretense // 빤한 ~ a flimsy [transparent] pretext // …을 ~로 on the pretext [pretense / plea] of / under (the) pretext [pretense] of / under the cloak [mask / veil] of / making (it) an excuse to … // ~을 대다 make [find / invent / trump up] an excuse [a pretext] (of) / (미) concoct [cook up] an excuse (for delay) // 그들은 물가 상승을 ~로 택시 요금을 인상했다 They raised taxi fares, using the excuse that prices had gone up. // 그는 언제나 이러쿵저러쿵 ~을 대어 할 일을 아니하려 한다 He always tries to shirk his duty on one pretext or another. // 그것은 ~에 불과하다 That's a mere excuse. // 나는 어머니의 병환을 ~로 학교를 결석했다 I used my mother's illness as an excuse for not going to school. / I stayed away from school, giving my mother's illness as an excuse.

구심(求心) 1 〔중심으로 쏠림〕. ¶~적인 centripetal // ~적으로 centripetally. 2 〔참선〕 religious meditation [contemplation].
● **구심력** 〔물〕 centripetal force.

구심(球審) 〔야구〕 the umpire-in-chief; the plate umpire; the chief umpire.

구십(九十) ninety; (로마 숫자) XC. ¶~ 노인 an old man of ninety.

구악(舊惡) (개인의) one's past misdeed; one's old crime; (사회 등의) the old [deep-rooted] evils. ¶~을 들추어내다 expose (a person's) past misdeeds / rake up (a person's) secret past // ~을 일소하다 make a clean sweep of [sweep out / root out] the old evils // 그의 ~이 드러났다 His past crime came to light.

구애(求愛) courting; courtship. ¶동물의 ~ 행동 courtship behavior among animals. **구애하다** court; (문어) woo; make advances. ¶그는 그녀에게 열심히 구애하고 있다 He's doing everything he can to win her love. / He has been making impassioned advances to her. / (구어) He is chasing her like mad.

구애(拘礙) adherence (to); prejudice (against); scruples. **구애하다** adhere (to); stick (to); be particular [fussy] (about). ¶~애하지 않고 freely / irrespective of // 형식에 ~ be particular about [stick to] formality.
→ ¶비용에 구애받지 않고 without regard to cost / regardless of expense // 인습에 구애되다 be tied to [bound by] tradition // 세속적인 일에 구애받지 않다 be free from worldly

cares / be indifferent to vulgar affairs // 사소한 일에 너무 구애되지 마라 Don't be such a stickler for detail. / Don't be so scrupulous [particular] about little things.// 그는 작은 일에 구애받지 않았다 He wasn't particular about the details.// 그는 세속적인 일에 구애되지 않는 사람이다 He is never concerned about worldly matters.// 참된 예의는 형식에 구애되어서는 안 된다 Real etiquette should be free from formalities [should not be a prisoner of form].// 그는 사소한 일에 구애되어 중요한 점을 보지 못하고 있다 He is fussy about minor matters and misses the important points. / He can not see the wood for the trees.// 법의 자구(字句)에 구애되어 그 정신을 몰각해서는 안 된다 You must observe the spirit, not the letter of the law.

구약(舊約) **1** 〔옛 약속〕 an old promise [commitment]. **2** 〔가〕〔기〕〔하느님의 약속〕 the old Covenant.
● **구약 성서** the Old Testament. **구약 시대** the Old Testament era; Old Testament days.

구어(口語) (the) spoken [colloquial] language; (a) colloquialism; a colloquial word. ¶~을 spoken / colloquial / conversational // ~로 쓰다 write in (a) colloquial [conversational] style.
● **구어문** a colloquial sentence. **구어체** (a) colloquial [conversational] style.

구역(區域) 〔지역〕 an area; a district; a zone; a quarter; 〔한계〕 the limits; the boundary. ¶담당 ~ a district assigned [allotted] to one / a district in one's charge / one's rounds / (경찰관의) one's beat / one's territory (판매원의) ~ 순찰 a beat / a round / **안전** 〔위험〕 ~ a safety [danger] zone // **상업** ~ a business zone [district / quarter / section] // **경찰**〔군대〕 관할 ~ a police [military] district // **우편** ~ a postal zone / **배달 구역** a delivery zone // ~을 정하다 set the limits / fix the boundary // 두 순경은 담당 ~을 순찰 중이다 Both policemen are on their rounds [beats].

구역질(嘔逆-) nauseation; vomiting. ¶~이 나다 feel sick [nauseated] / want to throw up [vomit] / (사람에) be disgusted (at / with / by) / (사물이) be disgusting / be sickening / ~ 나는 냄새[맛] a nauseating [nauseous / sickening] smell [taste] // ~을 참다 stifle [repress] a feeling of nausea / 그의 얼굴만 보아도 ~ 난다 The mere sight of him is quite disgusting [makes me sick].// 그의 뽐내는 말투를 듣고 있으면 ~이 난다 His affected manner of speech is disgusting.// 저 광고 방송을 보고 있으면 ~이 난다 That commercial makes me sick.// 그의 태도는 ~ 난다 His attitude is nauseating. / I am disgusted by [with] his attitude. **구역질하다** vomit.

구연(口演) an oral narration. **구연하다** narrate (orally); recite.
● **구연동화** an orally narrated fairy tale.

구연(舊緣) old ties; (an) old relationship.
구연산(枸櫞酸) 〔화〕 citric acid. ⇨시트르산

구옥(舊屋) 〔고옥〕 an old house; 〔전에 살던 집〕 one's former house.

구우(舊友) an old friend; 〔구어〕 an old pal [crony].

구우일모(九牛一毛) a drop in the bucket [ocean].

구워삶다 twist [wrap] (a person) around one's little finger. ¶그 여자는 할아버지를 용케 구워삶아 왔다 She has managed to wrap grandpa around her little finger.

구원(久遠) eternity; permanence; perpetuity. ¶~의 여성 the eternal feminine // ~의 평화 lasting [permanent] peace. **구원하다** eternal; permanent; perpetual; everlasting.

구원(救援) 〔구조〕 relief; rescue; succor; deliverance; [7] salvation; redemption. ¶~의 손길을 뻗치다 extend a helping hand (to) // ~을 요청하다 ask for [seek] help [relief] / call upon (others) for help // 그는 파산 직전에 친구에게 ~을 청했다 On the verge of bankruptcy he begged his friend(s) for assistance.// 읍 사람들은 홍수로 집을 잃은 사람들에게 재빨리 ~의 손길을 뻗쳤다 The townspeople were quick to lend a helping hand to those left homeless by the flood. **구원하다** relieve; rescue; deliver (a person out of trouble); succor (a person in distress). ¶...을 구원하러 가다 go to the rescue of ... // 그를 구원해 줄 생각은 없다 I have no intention of lending him a helping hand [(문어) extending a helping hand to him].
● **구원군** / **구원병** reinforcements; (군대) a relief [rescue] column. **구원 투수** 〔야구〕 a relief pitcher; a reliever; 〔구어〕 a fireman.

구월(九月) September (약어 Sept.).
구유 a manger; a trough.
구이 meat [fish] roasted [broiled / grilled] with seasonings; grill (불고기). ¶갈비~ roasted ribs / 닭~ fried [roast] chicken // 돼지고기 ~ roast pork.

구인(求人) the offer of a job; a job offer. ¶~ (게시) Help Wanted. // ~의 구직을 웃도다 The number of (job) vacancies exceeds that of job hunters. **구인하다** offer a job; seek help.
● **구인 광고** an advertisement for help; a help-wanted advertisement; (미국 구어) a want ad; (영) a situation-vacant advertisement. **구인난**(-難) a labor shortage; a shortage of labor. **구인란**(-欄) an appointments column; a help-wanted column; a section of the jobs vacant (in a classified advertisement).

구인(拘引) (an) arrest; custody (구류). **구인하다** arrest; seize; place (a person) under arrest; take (a person) into custody. ➔구인되어 있다 be held [taken] in custody / be detained / be under arrest // 절도 혐의로 구인되다 be taken to a police station on suspicion of theft.
● **구인장** a warrant of arrest; a summons (pl. ~es).

구입(購入) purchase; buying. **구입하다** purchase; buy. ¶대량 ~ make [effect] a heavy purchase (of) // 우리는 최신형 구두를 다량 구해 놓았다 We have a large stock of [We are well stocked with] the latest styles in shoes. // 우리는 등유를 다량 구입해 놓았다 We've laid in a large stock of kerosene.
● **구입 가격** the purchase price.

구작(舊作) an [one's] old work.
구잠정(驅潛艇) a submarine chaser; a sub-chaser.
구장(球場) a ball ground [park]; a stadium; 〔야구〕 a baseball stadium [ground]; a diamond; (미) a ball park.

구저분하다 filthy; squalid; sordid; dirty; shabby. ¶구저분한 빈민굴 a sordid slum.

구적(求積) [수] the finding [computation] of areas [volumes] (of).

구전(口傳) transmitting [conveying] by word of mouth; (oral) tradition. **구전하다** transmit by word of mouth; hand down (by word of mouth); (소문을) spread; circulate. ¶마을 사람들은 두 사람의 비련의 이야기를 오늘에 이르기까지 구전하고 있다 The villagers have handed down to the present day the tragic story of the two lovers. ➜¶구전된 비법 a secret method transmitted [handed down] orally [by word of mouth] // 추문이 입에서 입으로 구전되었다 The scandal was spread by word of mouth. // 괴 정보가 비밀리에 구전되고 있다 Strange news is being circulated clandestinely.

구전(口錢) (a) commission. ➪"구문(口文)

구절(句節) [구와 절] phrases and clauses; [글 도막] a phrase; a passage; a paragraph.

구절양장(九折羊腸) a meanders; a winding path. ¶∼ 같은 소로 a winding [zigzag] path // 길이 ∼을 이루며 오르막이 되다 The path climbs zigzag // 그 길은 ∼이다 The path is full of turns and twists.

구접스럽다 (사물이) dirty; shabby; messy; (행동이) mean; base; nasty; filthy; foul; (미) dirty. ¶구접스러운 방 a dirty room // 구접스러운 짓 a mean action / a shameful conduct.

구정(舊正) ➜설

구정(舊情) old friendship. ➪"옛정

구정물 1 [더러워진 물] dirty [filthy / foul] water; waste water; washings; used wash water(빨래한 물); dishwater(설거지한 물); (kitchen) slop(s). **2** (종기의) serous fluid (oozing [seeping]) out of a boil [tumor] after all the pus has been discharged.

구제(救濟) relief; help; aid; (문어) succor; deliverance; redemption; salvation(영혼의). ¶실업자 ∼ 계획 an unemployment relief project // ∼를 받다 get [receive] relief // ∼를 중단하다 cut off relief aid // 그녀는 빈민 ∼에 일생을 바쳤다 She devoted her life to the relief of the poor. **구제하다** relieve; give relief [aid] to; help; succor; save; deliver; redeem. ¶구제할 수가 없는 beyond remedy / past salvation [redemption] / irredeemable (criminal) // 빈민 [이재민]을 ∼ relieve the poor [sufferers] / give relief [extend a helping hand] to the poor [sufferers] // 이렇게 재정 사정이 악화되면 회사를 구제할 길이 없다 There is no remedy for [no way to save] a firm in such a bad financial state.

●**구제 기금 / 구제 자금** a relief fund. **구제 사업** relief work. **구제 조치** relief steps. **구제책** (문어) redress; a relief [remedial] measure; a remedy. ¶정부의 실업 ∼ the Government measures for the relief of the unemployed.

구제(驅除) extermination; destruction; stamping out. ¶이 약은 회충 ∼에 효과가 있다 This medicine is effective in getting rid of round worms. **구제하다** exterminate; destroy; stamp out; get rid of. ¶해충을 ∼ exterminate harmful insects // 쥐를 ∼ get rid of rats.

구제도(舊制度) the old [former] system. ¶∼를 폐지하다 abolish [do away with] the old order (of things).

구제역(口蹄疫) foot-and-mouth disease.

구조(救助) rescue; relief; (문어) succor; deliverance; aid; help; assistance. ¶인명 saving a life // 해난 ∼ sea rescue / salvage // ∼를 청하다 ask [call] for help [aid] / cry for help(큰 소리로) // …의 ∼에 나서다 go to the rescue of … / go to (a person's) rescue // ∼를 청하는 난민이 해상에 표류하고 있다 Refugees seeking relief are adrift on the sea.

구조하다 rescue; relieve; save; aid; help; assist; salvage; succor; pick up(난파선의 사람을). ¶인명을 ∼ save a life // 남을 익사로부터 ∼ save [rescue] (a person) from drowning // 인명을 구조하여 표창받다 receive an award for saving a person's life // 강 한가운데에서 오도 가도 못하게 된 사람들을 구조하기 위해 헬리콥터가 출동했다 A helicopter was sent to rescue the people who were stranded in the middle of the river. ➜¶조난자는 구조되었다 The disaster victim was saved [rescued]. // 난파선의 선원들은 지나가던 기선에 의해 구조됐다 The shipwrecked crew were picked up by a passing steamer.

●**구조대**(一袋) (고층 건물의 화재 등에 쓰이는) an escape chute. **구조대**(一隊) a relief squad; a rescue team [party / unit]; a wrecking crew(구난대). ¶∼의 도착이 늦어 그 아이는 익사했다 The child drowned, help [the rescue team] having arrived too late. **구조선** a lifeboat; [구난선] a rescue ship. **구조 신호** an SOS call. **구조 작업** rescue [relief] work; rescue operations; (난파선의) salvage work [operations].

구조(構造) structure; (a) construction; (a) make; makeup; fabric; fabrication; set up; [조직] constitution; organization. ¶산업 ∼ industrial structure // 상부 [하부] ∼ the superstructure [the substructure] // 이중 [사회] ∼ (a) dual [social] structure // 파이프 오르간의 ∼ the structure of a pipe organ // 기계의 ∼ the mechanism of a machine // ∼상의 structural // 인체의 ∼ the structure of the human body // 문장의 ∼ the construction of a sentence / sentence structure // 사회의 ∼ the organization of society // 우리 사회의 ∼적인 모순 a structural contradiction in our society // ∼상의 결함 a structural defect // ∼는 간단 [복잡] 하다 It is simple [complicated] in construction. // 한국식 ∼이다 It is Korean in structure [style]. // 이들 단체들은 ∼상으로는 서로 별로 다른 것이 없다 These organizations are not very different from one another in makeup.

●**구조 개혁** structural reform. **구조 공학** structural engineering. **구조물** a fabric; a structure. **구조식** [화] a structural formula (pl. ∼s, -lae). **구조 언어학** [언] structural linguistics. **구조주의** structuralism.

구좌(口座) ➜계좌(計座)

구주(救主) the Savior; the Redeemer. ➪"구세주

구주(歐洲) Europe. ➪"유럽

구주(舊株) [경] an old stock [(영) share].

구중중하다 (물이나 축축한 곳이) filthy; dirty; foul.

구지레하다 dirty and untidy; filthy; squalid; sordid. ¶구지레한 집 a squalid [sordid] house // 구지레한 꼴을 하고 있다 be dressed untidily / be shabbily [slovenly] dressed.

구직(求職) job hunting; a hunt for a job. ¶∼을 신청하다 apply for a position // 그는 ∼ 중

이다 He is looking for a job. **구직하다** seek (for) a job [employment]; look [hunt] for a job.
● **구직 광고** a classified ad for a job; a situation-wanted advertisement [ad]; a want ad. ¶~를 **내다** advertise [put an advertisement] (in a newspaper) for a (vacant) situation.
구직자 a job hunter [seeker]; an applicant (for a position).
구질구질 1 (상태가) dirtily; untidily; squalidly; slovenly. **구질구질하다** dirty; untidy; squalid; slovenly; filthy; foul. ¶구질구질한 날씨 nasty [foul] weather. 2 (하는 짓이) meanly; basely; despicably; indecently. **구질구질하다** mean; base; sordid; despicable; indecent. ¶구질구질한 수를 쓰다 use a mean [dirty / slimy] trick // 그는 돈에 대해서는 폐 ~ He is very mean [greedy] about money.
구차하다 (苟且-) 1 (변변하지 못하다) clumsy; awkward; strained; ignoble; humiliating; unworthy; insignificant; worthless. ¶구차한 목숨 an ignoble existence / a humiliating life // 구차한 변명을 대다 make a clumsy [lame / forced / poor] excuse // 남에게 구차한 소리를 하다 beg [plead] for a person's mercy [sympathy]. 2 (가난하다) very poor; poverty-stricken; needy; hard-up; badly off; wretched. ¶구차한 살림 형편 narrow [needy / straitened] circumstances // 구차하게 살다 live a wretched life / live poorly [in poverty] / be in poverty [in need / in want] / be badly off.
구척장신 (九尺長身) [매우 큰 키] extraordinary stature; towering height; [매우 키가 큰 사람] a person of towering height; a person of extraordinary stature.
구천 (九天) 1 [하늘] the sky; the highest heavens. 2 [불] the nine celestial bodies.
구천 (九泉) [저승] Hades; the other [under / lower / nether] world; the region [land] of the dead.
구청 (區廳) a ward [district] office; (미) a borough office. ¶마포 ~ the Mapo Ward Office.
● **구청장** the head [chief] of a ward; the ward head [chief]. **구청 직원** a ward official.
구체 (球體) a sphere; a global body. ¶~의 spherical / global.
구체안 (具體案) a definite [concrete] plan; a definite proposal. ¶~을 세우다 set up [make] a concrete plan / ~을 제시하시오 Show me a concrete plan (of it).
구체적 (具體的) concrete; definite. ¶~으로 concretely / in the concrete / in a concrete way [form] // ~으로 말하면 be concrete / to put it concretely / in concrete terms // ~ 예를 들다 give a concrete example // ~인 내 생각을 ~으로 말해 보라 Put your idea into concrete language. // ~인 것은 아직 아무것도 듣지 못했다 I have not yet heard anything definite [specific].
구체제 (舊體制) the old order [system].
구체화 (具體化) [형체 부여] embodiment; concretization; [실현] materialization; actualization. **구체화하다** embody; concretize; give shape [body] to; take (concrete) shape; materialize; actualize. ¶계획을 ~ give shape to a plan. ➔¶나의 오랜 꿈이 구체화되었다 My long-cherished dream has materialized.
구축 (構築) construction; building. ¶제방 (堤防) ~ levee construction. **구축하다** construct; build. ¶기반을 ~ establish [build up] the foundation (of) // 공병대가 토루를 구축하였다 The engineers constructed the bulwarks.
구축 (驅逐) expulsion; ousting; driving away. **구축하다** expel; drive (from / away / out); oust. ¶그들은 적군을 그들의 영토에서 구축했다 They expelled [drove] the enemy from their territory [land]. // 악화가 양화를 구축한다 Bad money drives out good.
● **구축함** [군] a destroyer. ¶어뢰 ~ a torpedo-boat destroyer.
구출 (救出) rescue; deliverance; saving. **구출하다** rescue; save (a person from danger); relieve; deliver. ¶물에 빠진 사람을 ~ rescue [save] (a person) from drowning // 위험에서 ~ rescue [extricate] (a person) out of danger // 침몰하는 배에서 승객을 ~ rescue the passengers from a sinking ship // 그 여자는 말을 구출하려다가 희생되었다 She sacrificed herself in an attempt to save her daughter. // 용감한 소방수가 두 어린아이를 불타고 있는 집에서 구출했다 A brave fireman rescued two small children from the burning house. ➔¶그의 기지로 나는 궁지에서 구출되었다 I was helped out of difficulty by his quick wit.
구충제 (驅蟲劑) [의] 1 (기생충의) a vermicide; a vermifuge; an anthelmintic. 2 an insecticide. ⇨ ⁼살충제
구취 (口臭) foul [bad] breath; [의] halitosis. ¶그는 ~가 난다 He has bad [foul] breath.
구치 (臼齒) a molar (tooth). ⇨ ⁼어금니
구치 (拘置) detention; confinement. **구치하다** detain; confine; keep [hold] (a person) in custody.
● **구치소** a house of detention; a detention house [cell]; a jail; (영) a gaol; a prison (for confinement); (미국에서) a tank.
구칭 (舊稱) the old name; the former title. ¶한양은 서울의 ~이다 Hanyang is the old [former] name for Seoul.
구타 (毆打) a blow; (a) beating; [법] assault and battery. **구타하다** give [deal] (a person) a blow; beat; assault; drub; make an assault on (a person); assail with blows. ¶머리를 ~ strike a person on the head // 구타하여 기절시키다 stun (a person) by a blow.
구태여 [일부러] intentionally; on purpose; [특별히] especially; particularly. ¶그 모임에 ~ 출석할 필요는 없다 You need not bother to attend the meeting. / You don't have to take the trouble to attend the meeting. // ~ 반대하지는 않겠다 I have no particularly objection to it. / I will not object to it particularly. // ~ 그녀에게 방문안하러 가지 않아도 된다 You need not take the trouble to inquire after her health. / Don't trouble (yourself) to inquire after her health.
구태의연하다 (舊態依然-) (서술적) remain as it was [as before]; remain unchanged. ¶구태의연한 사고방식 obsolete way of thinking // 그의 주장은 ~ His is the same old claim. / His claim remains unchanged [the same].
구토 (嘔吐) vomiting; [의] emesis (pl. -ses). **구토하다** vomit; throw up; be sick (at one's stomach).
● **구토 설사** emesis [vomiting] and diarrhea. **구토제 / 구토약** an emetic.

구투(舊套) a conventional usage[practice]; conventionalism; an old fashion[custom]. ¶~를 벗다 shake off the bounds of convention / get out of conventionalities.

구파(舊派) 1 [구래의 양식을 좇는 파] conservative people; the conservatives. 2 [이전에 이루어진 파] the old school.

구판(舊版) an old[a former] edition. ¶~을 개정하다 revise an old[a former] edition.

구폐(舊弊) [구식의 생각] an old-fashioned notions[idea]; [오래된 폐단] an old evil; an abuse of long standing. ¶~를 일소하다 sweep away old abuses / eradicate old evils.

구포(臼砲) [군] a mortar.

구하다(求-) 1 [찾다] look for; seek (for / after); search for; pursue; want; need. ¶셋방을 ~ look for a room to let / 일자리를 ~ hunt[seek] for a job / 점원을 ~ want[need] a clerk // 점원[가정부]을 구함 [광고] Help [Domestic help] wanted. // 판매원 구함 Salesman Wanted. / Wanted: A Salesman. // 타이피스트 1명 구함 Wanted a typist. // 그는 일자리를 구하고 있다 He is hunting for a job. // 좋은 의사를 구해 주시오 Please help me find a good doctor. / Could you introduce me to a good doctor? // 그는 친절하게도 좋은 일자리를 구해 주었다 He kindly found a good job[position] for me. // x의 값을 구하라 (문제에서) Find the value of x.
2 [청하다] ask for; call for; solicit (for); look [turn] to (a person for something). ¶자비를 ~ ask mercy of (a person) // 남의 도움을 ~ ask for a person's help // 남에게 원조를 ~ look[turn] to a person for assistance // 주지사[군수]는 이 문제에 관한 전문가의 의견을 구했다 The governor invited[gathered] the opinions of specialists on this matter.
3 [얻다] get; have; obtain; [찾아내다] find (out); [사다] buy; purchase. ¶서울에서 구한 물건 a thing bought in Seoul // 그 사전을 구해 주마 I'll get you the dictionary. // 그에게 좋은 아내를 구해 주지 I'll find him a good wife.

구하다(救-) (위험·죽음에서) rescue (a person) from (danger); save (a person) from (death); (고통·가난·나쁜 환경 등에서) relieve (a person) from (suffering); release (a person) from (pain / distress); help (a person) out of (a difficulty); deliver[extricate] (a person) from (a difficulty); (죄에서) redeem; reclaim. ¶인명을 ~ save a person's life / rescue (a person) from death // 물에 빠진 사람을 ~ rescue[save] (a person) from drowning // 사람을 불 속에서 구해 내다 save a person from a fire // 빈민을 ~ relieve the poor / give relief to the poor // 구할 길이 없다 be helpless[hopeless / incurable] / be beyond remedy / be past[beyond] redemption[salvation] // 수색대가 눈보라로 오두막집에 갇힌 등산객들을 구해 냈다 The search party rescued the stranded climbers from the mountain hut. // 그를 죽음에서 구한 것은 아내의 극진한 간호의 손길이었다 It was his wife's careful nursing that saved his life. // 이 개는 조난 등산객을 구하기 위해 훈련되었다 This dog is trained to rescue climbers who have met with accidents. // 내가 어려움에 처할 때마다 형이 나를 구해 주었다 Whenever I had some difficulty, my brother used to help me out of it. // 우리는 가난한 사람들을 구하기 위해 모금을 한다 We raise funds for the relief of the poor. // 하느님이시여, 우리를 악에서 구하옵소서 (May) God deliver us from evil.

구현(具現) incarnation; embodiment; materialization; realization. ¶그들의 이상의 ~ the embodiment of their ideals. **구현하다** embody; materialize; realize; give concrete form (to). ➔그작가 자신의 철학이 주인공 속에 구현되어 있다 The writer's own philosophy is embodied in the hero.

구형(求刑) [법] the prosecutor's demands; the prosecutor's recommendation for punishment. **구형하다** demand a penalty; suggest[propose] a punishment for the accused. ¶사형을 ~ demand a sentence of death / demand the death penalty // 검사는 피고에 대하여 무기 징역을 구형했다 The prosecutor demanded life imprisonment for the accused.

구형(球形) a globular shape; globularity. ¶~의 globular / spherical / globe-shaped.

구형(舊型) an old model[style / type]. ¶~ 자동차 an old-fashioned[a vintage / a classic] car / an old-model car // ~ 모델 an out-of-date model.

구호(口號) 1 [주장을 나타내는 간결한 말] a slogan; a motto (pl. ~(e)s); a catchword; a catchphrase; a rallying word. ¶…의 ~를 내걸고 under the slogan of … // 선거 [선전] ~ an election[propaganda] slogan // 단순한 ~에 그치고 말다 end in mere gesture. 2 a (military) password. ⇨구호(軍號).

구호(救護) 1 (재난·어려움에 처한 사람의) relief; aid. ¶따뜻한 ~의 손길을 뻗치다 extend a warm helping hand (to). **구호하다** aid; give aid to; give relief[help] to; relieve; help and protect. 2 (병자·부상자의) nursing; tending; (medical) care[treatment]; cure. **구호하다** nurse; tend [attend on]; care for; treat; give (a person) a medical treatment; cure. ¶부상자를 ~ give aid to the injured [the wounded].
●**구호물자** relief; relief goods[supplies]. ¶수재민에게 ~를 보내다 send a relief to the victims of the flood. **구호미**(-米) relief rice.
구호반 a relief squad[party]; [군] an ambulance corps.

구혼(求婚) a proposal[an offer] of marriage; courtship; wooing. ¶~을 승낙 [거절] 하다 accept[decline] (a person's) suit[hand]. **구혼하다** propose (marriage) (to); court; pay court (to); seek (a lady's) hand in marriage; woo. ¶그는 수에게 구혼했다 He proposed to Sue. / He asked Sue to marry him.
●**구혼 광고** an advertisement for a spouse. **구혼자** a suitor; a wooer. ¶돈이 목적인 ~ a fortune hunter / (미국 속어) a gold digger (여자).

구황(救荒) relief from famine; relief of famine victims; relief of the famished. **구황하다** relieve (the sufferers from) famine; give relief[aid] to the famine-stricken people.
●**구황 작물** hardy crops[plants] (that can be relied on for food in famine years).

구획(區劃) [구분] division; demarcation; [한 구획] a section; a division; a compartment; (시가 등의) a block; (토지의) a lot[plot] (of land); [경계] a boundary. ¶행정 ~상 이 집의 반은 이웃 구에 들어가 있다 In terms of administrative division half of this house is in the neighboring ward. **구획하다** draw a line of demarcation; mark off (one lot from another); divide; partition; demarcate; compartment; mark out (land). ¶토지의 한쪽을 구획하여 채소밭을 만들다 mark off a piece of ground for a vegetable garden. →그 땅은 놀이터로 구획되어 있다 The lot is marked off as a playground.

● **구획 정리** land readjustment; (도시의) replanning of streets; readjustment of town lots. ¶농지 ~ the adjustment of partitions of agricultural land.

구휼(救恤) relief (of the poor). **구휼하다** relieve; give relief (to). ¶재해자를 ~ aid (disaster) victims / give aid to the victims.

● **구휼금** relief fund [money].

국 1 [탕] soup; broth. ¶~ 건더기 solid stuff [ingredients] in soup // ~에 말다 put (rice) into soup. 2 [국물] the liquid part of a dish; (fish / meat) stock.

국에 덴 놈 냉수 보고도 분다(속담) A scalded cat [dog] fears cold water.; The burnt child dreads the fire.; One bit [bitten], twice shy.

국(局) 1 (관청·회사 등의) a bureau; a department. ¶사무 ~ a secretariat // 편집 ~ the editorial department // 업무 ~ the business department // 1 ~ 4과로 나누다 divide (an office) into one department and four sections. 2 [바둑·장기의 승부] a game (of go [chess]). **대** ~ (playing) a game of go [chess] (with).

-국(國) a state; a country; a nation. ¶선진~ an advanced [a developed] nation // 강대 ~ a superpower.

국가(國家) a nation; a state; a country. (▶ nation은 하나의 독립 정부하에 통일된 것, state는 주권이 있는 국가, country는 사람이 국민으로서 귀속되는 곳) ¶독립 ~ an independent nation [country] // 자본주의 ~ a capitalist country [nation] / a capitalistic state // 복지 ~ a welfare state // ~의 national / state // ~의 정책 state policy // ~의 흥망에 관한 문제 an issue that concerns the fate of the nation // ~의 주권을 침해하다 infringe on a nation's sovereignty // ~의 보조를 받다 be granted national assistance.

● **국가 경제** the national economy. **국가고시** a state [national] examination. **국가 공무원** a government official; a government worker; a national public servant; (집합적) national civil service personnel. **국가 권력** national power; the power of the state. **국가 기관** the administrative machinery of a state; state organ. **국가 대표 선수** a state amateur; a national athlete; a member of the national team. **국가 보훈처** the Ministry of Patriots and Veterans Affairs. **국가 정보원** the National Intelligence Service. **국가주의** nationalism.

국가(國歌) a national anthem.

국가적(國家的) national. ¶~ 사업 an enterprise of national importance / a national undertaking [project] // ~ 견지에서 보면 from a national point of view // 아름다운 자연은 ~ 재산이다 The beauties of nature are a national heritage.

국거리 materials for soup.

국경(國境) a border; a frontier; the (national) boundary [border]; the boundaries of a country. ¶~의 요새 a fortress on the frontier // ~의 수비 border defense / fortifications on a frontier [along a border] // ~을 넘어서 over the border // 두 나라 사이의 ~ the border between two countries // ~을 **침범하다** violate the border // 그는 ~을 넘어서 프랑스에 들어갔다 He crossed the border into France. // 캐나다는 남으로 미국과 ~을 접하고 있다 Canada is bordered on the south by the United States. // 에스파냐는 동쪽으로 프랑스와 ~을 접하고 있다 España is bordered on France on the east. // 사랑에는 ~이 없다 Love has no frontier.

● **국경 경비대** border [frontier] guards [army]; border posts [patrols]; border garrison. **국경 도시** a border town; a town on a frontier. **국경 분쟁** a border [boundary] dispute. **국경선** a border (line); a boundary line.

국경일(國慶日) a national holiday.

국고(國庫) the (National) Treasury; (영) the Exchequer; the coffers of the State; the public purse; the fisc. ¶~ 부담이 되다 be borne by the National Treasury / be provided [paid] from the National Treasury // 의무 교육비는 전액 ~ 부담으로 해야 한다 The National Treasury should provide all expenses for the compulsory education. // 전매 수입은 ~에 들어간다 Monopoly proceeds are placed into the state coffer. // 그것은 ~에서 부담해야 한다 That should be paid out of the National treasury. // ~는 텅텅 비어 있다 The coffers of the state are empty. / The nation is bankrupt.

● **국고금** national funds; government money. **국고 보조** a state [government] subsidy. **국고 수입** national revenues; National Treasury receipts. ¶~이 되다 go to the national treasury. **국고 지출** defrayment out of [appropriation from] the National Treasury. **국고 차입금** a national loan.

국교(國交) diplomatic relations; national friendship; intercourse between nations. ¶~를 **맺다** enter into diplomatic relations (with) // ~를 **단절하다** break off [sever] diplomatic relations (with) // 네팔과 ~를 맺다 establish [enter into] diplomatic relations with Nepal // ~를 **회복하다** restore [reestablish] diplomatic relations (with).

● **국교 단절** a severance [rupture / cessation] of diplomatic relations; a diplomatic break; a break of diplomatic relations. **국교 정상화** normalization of diplomatic relations. ¶중국과 ~를 도모하다 make an effort to normalize diplomatic relations with the People's Republic of China. **국교 회복** a restoration of diplomatic relations.

국교(國敎) a state religion [church]; the established church. ¶영국 ~회 the Church of England / the Anglican Church // ~로 정하다 establish (church).

국군(國軍) 1 [한 나라의 군대] a nation's armed [military] forces; government troops. 2 [자기 나라의 군대] our troops; our armed forces; [한국군] the Korean Army, Navy and Air Force; the Korean armed forces; the armed forces of the Republic of Korea.

● **국군의 날** Armed Forces Day.

국권(國權) [국가 권력] the power of the state; [통치권] national sovereignty. ¶~을

국그릇

신장하다 expand [extend] national power [strength] / enhance national prestige // ~을 발동하다 exercise the right of the state // ~을 침해[주장]하다 violate [claim] national sovereignty.

국그릇 a soup bowl; a bowl for containing soup [broth].

국기(國技) the national sport [game]. ¶씨름은 우리나라의 ~이다 Ssireum(Wrestling) is one of our national sports.

국기(國旗) the national flag [emblem / colors]; [해] an ensign. ¶미국 ~ the American flag / The Stars and Stripes / the star-spangled banner // 영국 ~ the British flag / the Union Jack // 프랑스 ~ the French flag / the Tricolor // ~를 게양하다 hoist [raise / put up] the national's [country's] flag // ~를 제정하다 decide on the national flag // ~에 대하여 경례하다 salute the national flag // 배는 한국 ~를 달고 항해했다 The ship sailed under the Korean flag.
● **국기 게양식** a flag hoisting ceremony.

국기(國基) the foundation of a nation.

국난(國難) a national crisis (pl. -ses); a national danger [peril]; a national disaster [calamity]. ¶~을 면하다 be delivered from a national danger // 그 장군은 ~에서 나라를 구했다 The general saved the nation in a (national) crisis. / The general led his country out of its difficulties.

국내(國內) the interior. ¶~의 internal / domestic / home (▶ 영)에서는 home을, (미)에서는 domestic을 쓰는 일이 많음) // ~산 사과 (미) domestic [(영) home-grown] apples // ~ 뉴스 domestic news // 올해의 쌀 생산량은 ~ 수요를 겨우 충족시키는 정도다 The rice crop this year hardly meets the domestic need [demands]. // 이 문제를 놓고 국외뿐만 아니라 ~에서도 열띤 논쟁이 있었다 This question has been heatedly discussed at home as well as abroad.
● **국내 경제** domestic [home] economy. **국내 관세** internal customs; domestic tariff. **국내법** [법] municipal [civil] law. **국내선**(-線) domestic lines; domestic [internal] air service (항공의). **국내 소비** home [domestic] consumption.

국내외(國內外) the inside and outside of the country. ¶~의 internal and external / home [domestic / native] and foreign // ~ 사정 home [domestic] and foreign affairs // 그 사건은 ~의 신문에 보도되었다 The incident was reported in domestic and foreign papers. // ~에서 실업자 수가 늘고 있다 The number of the unemployed is increasing both at home and abroad.

국도(國道) a national [state] road; a national highway [road / route].

국란(國亂) a national [public] disturbance; an uprising; a rebellion; a civil war.

국력(國力) the strength [power] of a nation; (자원) the resources of a nation. ¶~ 신장 continued buildup of national strength // 수년간의 전쟁으로 ~이 피폐하였다 The nation's resources were exhausted by years of warfare.

국록(國祿) a government salary. ¶~을 먹다 be on the government payroll / be in government service.

국론(國論) public opinion [sentiment / view].

¶~의 통일 national consensus // ~에 귀를 기울이다 give ear [lend an ear / pay attention] to the public opinion / have [keep] one's ear to the ground // ~의 분열을 막다 prevent splits in national opinion // ~을 들 끓게 하다 excite public opinions / lead to heated public discussions // ~을 양분하다 split [divide] public opinion in two.

국립(國立) ¶~의 national / government-established.
● **국립공원** a national park. **국립 극장** a national theater. **국립대학** a national [government] university. **국립 도서관** a national library. **국립묘지** the National Cemetery.

국면(局面) 1 (어떤 일의 형세) the state of affairs; the situation. ¶새로운 ~에 접어들다 take a new turn / enter (up) on a new phase / take on a new aspect // ~을 타개하다 break a deadlock / bring the deadlock to an end // 중대한 ~에 이르다 reach a crucial phase // ~을 일변시키다 change the whole aspect of things [situation] // ~이 일변했다 The situation has completely changed. / The situation has been completely reversed. // ~은 아직 호전되지 않고 있다 The state of affairs is still unimproved [is yet to be improved]. // 이 계획은 여러 가지 ~에서 생각해야 된다 We must consider this plan in its various aspects.
2 (바둑·장기의) a stage [phase] of a game; the situation on the chessboard. ¶~을 재현하다 reconstruct the position on the board.

국명(國名) the name of a country.

국명(國命) a government order.

국모(國母) the mother of the state; the Empress; the Queen.

국무(國務) the affairs of state; state affairs. ¶~를 관장하다 administer state affairs // ~를 처리하다 transact [conduct] state affairs.
● **국무부** (미) the Department of State; the State Department. **국무 위원** a minister of state; a state minister. **국무 장관** (미) the Secretary of State; the State Secretary; (영) a State Minister. **국무 차관** an Undersecretary of State. **국무총리** the Prime Minister; the Premier. **국무 회의** a Cabinet council [conference / meeting].

국문(國文) [문자] the national script; [한글] the Korean alphabet; [국어] the Korean language; the national language; [문학] the national literature; Korean literature; [국문으로 쓴 것] writings in Korean. ¶~의 Korean / vernacular // ~ 영역 Korean-English translation // ~ 타자기 a typewriter with Korean keyboards.
● **국문법** Korean grammar; grammar of the national language. **국문학** [한국 문학] Korean literature; [학문] the study of Korean literature.

국물 1 (국 등의) soup; broth; gravy; (fish / meat) stock. ¶김치 ~ gimchi(kimchi) [pickle] juice // 멸치 ~ stock made by stewing anchovies / anchovy sauce // 고기 ~ gravy // 맑건 ~ clear soup // ~을 우려내다 prepare stock // ~ 맛이 좋다 The soup tastes good [is richly flavored]. 2 [부수입] an additional gain [profit]; a perquisite; an emolument; a privilege attached to one's position. ¶~이 없으면 그런 일은 하지 않겠다

I won't do anything of that sort unless I can get something for myself out of it.
국민(國民) 〔집합적〕 a nation; 〔인민〕 a people; 〔개개인〕 a national; a member of a nation; (미) a citizen; (영) a subject. ¶한국 ~ the Korean people[nation] ∥ ~의 national / 1인당 소득 the per capita income of a nation ∥ ~의 축제일 a national holiday ∥ ~의 의무 a national obligation ∥ ~의 심판 people's judgment ∥ ~의 후원 a national backing[support] ∥ ~의 화합과 단결 national harmony and unity ∥ ~을 계몽하다 enlighten one's fellow countrymen ∥ ~에게 호소하다 appeal to the country ∥ 주권은 ~에게 있다 Sovereign power resides in[with] the people. ∥ 한국인은 근면한 ~이다 The Koreans are a hardworking people[nation]. ∥ ~ 전체가 그 안에 반대했다 All the [The whole] country opposed the plan.
●**국민감정** national sentiment. ¶~을 자극하다 provoke the national sentiment ∥ 한국에 대한 그들의 ~은 좋다 They have no enmity against Korea. **국민 건강 보험** national health insurance. **국민 경제** national[state] economy; (strengthen) the nation's economy. **국민 생활** the national life; the life of the people. ¶~을 안정시키다 stabilize national life. **국민성** the national character; national traits; the character[characteristics] of a nation; nationality. **국민 소득** the national income; the annual income of the whole nation. ¶1인당 ~ the national income per head / national per capital income. **국민 연금** a state pension. **국민운동** a popular [national] movement[campaign]. **국민정신** the national spirit. **국민 주권** the sovereignty of the people. **국민 총생산** the gross national product (약о GNP). **국민 투표** a plebiscite; a referendum; a popular [national] vote. **국민학교** ➡초등학교(⇨초등)
국민학생 ➡초등학생(⇨초등)
국밥 gukbap; boiled rice served in soup.
국방(國防) national defense [(영) defence]; the defense of a country. ¶~상 for defensive reasons ∥ 자주 ~ independent national defense (capability) ∥ 전면적 ~ 태세 the overall defense posture (of the United States) ∥ ~의 완비 the completion of national defense preparations / (미) preparedness ∥ ~의 제1선 the first line of defense ∥ ~을 강화하다 strengthen [(구어) beef up] the national defense.
●**국방 계획** a national defense plan; a national security plan. **국방부** the Ministry of National Defense; the Defense Ministry; (미) the Department of Defense; the Pentagon; (영) the Ministry of Defence. **국방비** national defense expenditures. **국방색** khaki color. **국방 예산** a defense budget.
국번(호) (局番號) a telephone exchange number. ¶시외 ~ an out-of-town telephone exchange number.
국법(國法) national law; the law of the land; (미) federal law. ¶~을 지키다 obey [abide by] the law (of a country) ∥ ~을 어기다 violate [break] a national law ∥ ~으로 금지하다 prohibit by (national) law ∥ 그것은 ~에 저촉되는 행위이다 That is against national law.
국보(國寶) a national treasure; a treasure of the country; an asset to the nation. ¶~로 지정 [보존]되다 be designated [preserved] as a national treasure ∥ 그는 ~적 인물이다 He is a national asset.
국부(局部) 1 〔일부〕 a part; a section. ¶~화하다 localize (a disease, etc.) / arrest the spread (of a disease). 2 〔음부〕 the private parts; the privates.
●**국부 마취** local an(a)esthesia.
국부(國父) the father of the[one's] country; a founding father (of a country).
국부(國富) national wealth; the wealth of a nation. ¶~의 증진을 꾀하다 seek to increase the nation's wealth.
●**국부론** (아담 스미스의 저서명) The Wealth of Nations.
국부적(局部的) local; sectional; partial. ¶~으로 locally / sectionally / partially ∥ 전염[동란]을 ~으로 저지하다 localize infection [a disturbance] ∥ 그의 영향은 ~인 것에 지나지 않았다 His influence was limited to one particular locality.
국비(國費) national expenditure (expenses / outlay]; 〔나라의 자금〕 public funds; public money. ¶~의 낭비 a waste of public funds ∥ ~로 유학하다 study abroad at government expense ∥ ~를 절감하다 cut[slash] governmental spending.
●**국비 유학생** a student sent abroad at state expense. **국비 장학생** a state scholarship student; a student receiving state scholarship.
국빈(國賓) a guest of the state; a state guest; a national guest. ¶~ 대우를 하다 accord (a person) the treatment of a national guest ∥ 그는 ~으로 영접받았다 He was received as a state guest [a guest of the state].
국사(國史) the history of a nation; a national history; 〔한국사〕 the history of Korea; Korean history.
국사(國事) the matters [affairs] of state; national affairs. ¶~를 논하다 discuss the affairs of a nation ∥ ~에 다망하다 exert oneself in the interests of one's country ∥ ~에 참여하다 take part in the affairs of state.
●**국사범** 〔국가 권력을 침해하는 범죄〕 a political crime; (a) political crime; high treason; 〔정치범〕 a political offender; a state prisoner.
국산(國産) home[domestic] production; 〔한국산〕 Korean production. ¶~의 domestic / homemade / domestically produced / home-produced / made in Korea ∥ ~ 자동차 a domestic car / a home-manufactured car / a Korean car / a car made[manufactured] in Korea.
●**국산품** (자기 나라의) a domestic product; domestic goods; home products; homemade articles; home-produced [-manufactured] articles; (한국의) Korean (-made) products; articles made in Korea. ¶~을 애용하다 use [buy] homemade articles (in preference to foreign-made ones). **국산화** (-化) localization. ¶~하다 begin home production (of) / localize.
국상(國喪) a state [national] funeral; national mourning.
국새(國璽) guksae; the Seal of State; the Great Seal.
국서(國書) 〔외교 문서〕 credential(신임장); a

sovereign's message (to a foreign state); 〖일국의 문헌〗 national literature. ¶~를 봉정하다 present one's credentials (to a sovereign).

국선(國選) 〖관형어적〗 chosen [appointed] by the government.
- **국선 변호인** a court-appointed lawyer [attorney]; a public defender.

국세(局勢) 〖형세〗 an aspect [a phase] of an affair; 〖바둑의〗 the position; the situation. ¶뚜렷하지 않은 ~ a situation whose outcome is uncertain // ~가 일변하다 take a new turn / enter upon a new phase // ~는 우리에게 불리하다 The aspect of affairs is black for us. // 승패를 가릴 수 없는 ~이다 The game is anybody's guess.

국세(國稅) a national [state] tax. ¶직접 [간접] ~ a direct [an indirect] national tax // ~를 징수하다 collect national taxes.
- **국세청** the Office of National Tax Administration. **국세 체납** nonpayment [arrears] of national taxes.

국세(國勢) the state of the nation; the strength of the nation. ¶~가 진작되지 못하고 있다 The state of the nation is at a low ebb. // 한국의 ~는 크게 신장되고 있다 Korea's star is in the ascendant.
- **국세 조사** a national census.

국소(局所) 〖국부〗 a (limited) part; a section; the affected part [region]; 〖관절〗 joints (of the body). ¶~에 통증을 느끼다 feel localized pain / feel pain in just one place.
- **국소 마취** local an(a)esthesia.

국수 guksu; noodles; vermicelli; spaghetti.
- **국수물** noodle broth. **국수틀** a noodlemaker; a vermicelli-press.

국수(國手) 〖바둑·장기의〗 a national champion (of baduk); a master player of the game of baduk(go); 〖명의〗 a great doctor; an excellent [a noted] physician.

국수주의(國粹主義) ultranationalism; extreme patriotism.
- **국수주의자** an ultranationalist.

국시(國是) national policy. ¶~를 정하다 fix [formulate] the national [state] policy / orientate a government policy // 그 나라는 반공을 ~로 하고 있다 The country is thoroughly anticommunist. / The country takes an anticommunist line.

국악(國樂) Korean classical music; Korean folk music. ¶~ 무대 the stage of Korean classical music // 국립 ~원 the National (Classical) Music Institute.

국어(國語) 〖한 나라의 말〗 the national language; one's native language; one's mother tongue; the vernacular; 〖한국말〗 the Korean language; Korean. ¶2개 ~의 bilingual / 여러 개 ~를 말하는 사람 a multilingual person / a polyglot // ~로 된 사전 a bilingual dictionary // 제2의 ~ one's second language // 그는 여러 개 ~를 할 줄 안다 He can speak several languages.
- **국어 국문학과** the department of Korean language and literature. **국어사전** a Korean language dictionary. **국어학** the study of the national language.

국영(國營) government [state] management; management by state. ¶~의 state-operated [-run] / under government management. **국영하다** nationalize (railways); place under government [state] management.
- **국영 기업** a national [state] enterprise; a government enterprise [undertaking]. ¶~체 a state policy corporation [company] / a government-run [state-run] firm. **국영 방송국** government-run broadcasting station. **국영화** nationalization.

국왕(國王) 〖왕〗 a king; 〖세습 군주〗 a monarch; 〖주권자〗 a sovereign; 〖통치자〗 a ruler. ¶~의 monarchic // 프랑스 ~ 루이 14세 Louis XIV, King of France.

국외(國外) ¶~로[에] outside the country / abroad / overseas / beyond seas // 국내에서도 ~에서도 both at home and abroad // ~에서 범한 죄 an offense committed while outside the territory of a country // ~로 도망치다 fly the country / ~로 추방하다 deport (a person) from the country / expatriate / exile / put (a person) out of the country // ~로 추방되다 be expelled from the country // ~로부터의 통신에 따르면 The news from overseas says that .... // 그는 지금 ~에 있다 He is abroad now. // 그는 국내나 ~에서도 잘 알려져 있다 He is well known both at home and abroad.

국외(局外) the outside; an independent position. ¶~의 outside / external // ~에서 관찰하다 observe from the outside.
- **국외자** an outsider; an outlier; a third party; an onlooker. **국외중립** neutrality. ¶~을 선언하다 declare one's neutrality // ~의 태도를 취하다 take neutral stand. **국외중립국** a neutral country.

국운(國運) the fate of a country; the national destiny. ¶~의 성쇠 the prosperity and decline of a country / the rise and fall of a nation // ~이 기울다 Fortune deserted the country. // 잇따른 실정으로 ~이 기울었다 The country's fortunes declined because of continuing misgovernment.

국위(國威) national prestige [glory / dignity / honor / power]. ¶~에 관한 문제 a point of national honor / a matter of national prestige // 해외에서 ~를 선양하다 enhance (the) national prestige abroad // ~를 손상시키다 tarnish [〖문어〗 sully] (the) national prestige [dignity].

국유(國有) state [government] ownership. ¶~의 state / state- [government-] owned / national // ~ 하다 make (something) a national possession.
- **국유림** a national [state] forest. **국유 재산** national property [assets]; government property. **국유지** national land; state-owned land; a state demesne. ¶~를 불하하다 sell (at auction) a lot in national land. **국유 철도** national railways; a government [state] railway. **국유화**(-化) nationalization. ¶기간 산업의 ~ the nationalization of key industries.

국은(國恩) one's debt to one's country; favors benefited by one's country. ¶~에 보답하다 pay one's debt to one's country.

국익(國益) national interests. ¶~을 우선하다 give priority to national interests.

국자 a dipper; a ladle; a scoop. ¶~ 모양의 dipper-shaped / spatulate // ~ 한 ~ a scoop (of broth) // ~로 국을 푸다 ladle [dip up] soup (into a bowl).

국장(局長) 〖관청의〗 the director [chief] of a

bureau; (우체국 등의) the head of a post [telephone / telegraph] office. ¶우체국 ~ a postmaster.

국장(國章) a national emblem.

국장(國葬) a state [national] funeral. ¶~으로 하다 give [(문어) accord] (a person) a state funeral / hold a state funeral for (a person).

국적(國賊) a traitor (to the country); a rebel; an insurgent; an insurrectionist. ¶~의 낙인이 찍히다 be branded as a public enemy // ~이라고 비난하다 call (a person) a traitor / (미) call (a person) down as a traitor.

국적(國籍) nationality; (미) citizenship. ¶~불명의 비행기 a plane of unknown nationality // 이중 ~자 a person with [of] dual [double] nationality [citizenship] // 무~자 a stateless person // ~이탈 renunciation of nationality // 한국 ~의 배 a ship of Korean registry // ~을 상실[회복]하다 lose [regain / recover] one's nationality // ~을 박탈당하다 be deprived [stripped] of one's nationality // 그는 한국 ~을 취득했다 He was naturalized in Korea. // 그는 일본 ~을 버렸다 He divested himself of [renounced] his Japanese nationality. // 당신의 ~은 어디입니까 What is your nationality? / What nationality are you? // 그녀는 ~은 미국이지만 이탈리아계이다 She is an American of Italian origin [an Italian American].

● **국적 상실** loss of nationality; denationalization. **국적 포기** renunciation of nationality [citizenship]. **국적 회복** reinstatement of citizenship.

국전(國展) an art exhibition sponsored by the nation [state]; the National Art Exhibition.

국정(國定) government authorization. ¶~의 statutory / authorized by the state.

● **국정 교과서** a government designated textbooks; a state [an authorized] textbook.

국정(國政) (national) administration; government; [국무] affairs of state; state affairs. ¶~에 참여하다 participate in administration // 그는 국회의원으로서 ~에 참여하고 있다 He participates in the government as a member of the National Assembly.

● **국정 감사** (parliamentary) inspection of the administration [of government offices]. **국정 조사권** a parliamentary right to investigate. **국정 홍보처** the Government Information Agency.

국정(國情) the conditions of a country; the state of affairs in a nation. ¶~을 시찰하다 inspect the actual condition of a country // 한국 ~에 어둡다[밝다] be ignorant of [well informed of] Korean affairs // 그것은 한국 ~에 맞지 않는다 It is against the customs of Korea. / It does not harmonize with the actual condition of Korea. // 그는 한국의 ~에 밝다 He knows a great deal about the state of affairs in Korea

국제(國際) [관형어적] international.

● **국제 가격** an international price. **국제 결제 은행** the Bank for International settlement(약어 BIS). **국제결혼** an international marriage; an intermarriage. **국제 경기** an international game [match]. **국제 경쟁력** international competitive power. **국제공항** an international airport. **국제 관계** international relations. **국제 교류** international (culture) exchange. **국제도시** a cosmopolitan city. **국제무대** the international stage. **국제 박람회** a world's fair; an international exposition [exhibition]. **국제 방송** international broadcasting. **국제법** the (public) international law. **국제 사회** international society [community]; the community [family] of nations. **국제 수지** [경] the international balance of payments; international payments; balance of international payments [accounts]. **국제 시장** an international market. **국제어**(一語) an international [universal] language. **국제 연맹** the League of Nations. **국제 연합** the United Nations (약어 U.N., UN). **국제 올림픽 위원회** the International Olympic Committee(약어 IOC). **국제 의회 연맹** the Inter-Parliamentary Union(약어 IPU). **국제 전화** an international telephone call. **국제 정세** the international situation. **국제주의** internationalism. **국제 통화 기금** the International Monetary Fund(약어 IMF). **국제화** internationalization.

국제적(國際的) international. ¶~으로 internationally / universally // ~ 견지에서 from the international point of view // ~ 명성을 얻다 win an international reputation // 그는 ~으로 알려져 있다 He is internationally known. // 그는 피아노 연주자로서 ~ 명성을 얻었다 He won worldwide fame as a pianist. / He became internationally famous as a pianist.

국지(局地) a locality; a definite place; a limited region [area]. ¶~화하다 localize (a war).

● **국지전 / 국지 전쟁** a local war limited warfare; a brush-fire war.

국지적(局地的) local. ¶~ 해결 settlement on the spot / regional settlement // 농작물은 ~으로 태풍의 피해를 받았다 The crops in some regions were damaged by the typhoon. // 정부는 분쟁을 ~으로 해결하려 하고 있다 The Government intends to settle the disputes locally.

국채(國債) [부채] a national debt [loan]; [공채] a public loan; [증권] national bonds; (미) government bonds; (영) government securities. ¶내(외)~ a domestic [foreign] loan // ~를 발행[구입]하다 issue [buy] national bonds // ~를 상환하다 redeem [sink] a national loan // ~를 모집하다 float [raise] a national loan // 거액의 ~를 지고 있다 be saddled [burdened] with heavy national indebtedness [debts].

● **국채 발행고** the amount of government bond issue. **국채 상환 기금** an amortization [a consolidation] fund; a sinking fund.

국책(國策) (a) national policy. ¶~에 따라 in line with the national policy / along the line of national policy // ~ 수행의 도구로서 as an instrument of national policy // ~을 수립[수행]하다 fix [carry out] a national policy // 어떤 나라에서는 산아 제한이 ~으로서 장려되고 있다 In some countries, birth control is being encouraged as a matter of national policy.

● **국책 은행** a government-run bank. **국책 회사** a national policy concern; a state policy corporation [company].

국체(國體) the national polity; national structure; the form of the state. ¶~를 유지하다 retain the fundamental character of the

국치 state.

국치(國恥) national humiliation[disgrace / dishonor]; a disgrace to the nation. ¶~이다 be a disgrace to the national prestige / ~를 초래하다 bring disgrace upon one's country // 그것은 한국의 ~이다 It is a matter of national humiliation for Korea. / It is a disgrace to Korea.
● **국치일** National Humiliation Day.

국태민안(國泰民安) the prosperity and welfare of a nation.

국토(國土) a country; a territory; a realm; a domain. ¶인구가 많고 좁은 ~ a small, overpopulated country // ~를 개발하다 reform [cultivate] the land // ~를 방위하다 defend one's country // ~가 협소함을 느끼다 feel confined within narrow frontiers // 그 사건은 독일 ~에서 일어났다 The incident occurred in German territory. // 우리나라의 ~는 경지 면적의 비율이 비교적 적다 The percentage of arable land in our country is comparatively small.
● **국토 개발** (national) land development. **국토 계획** national land planning; a land development program(me). **국토방위** the defense of the country; national defense.

국판(菊判) a small octavo (▶ 22×15cm); (미) a medium octavo [8 vo]. ¶~ 250페이지의 책 a 250-page octavo book.

국풍(國風) national customs (and manners).

국학(國學) study of Korean classical literature; the national classics.
● **국학자** a scholar of Korean literature.

국한(局限) localization; limitation. ¶~적인 local. **국한하다** localize; confine; limit; set limits to. ¶문제의 범위를 …에 ~ narrow one's subject down to ... // 오늘의 의제는 이 문제로 국한합시다 Let's confine [limit] today's discussion to this matter. ➔ ¶빈곤은 반드시 한 지역에 국한되어 있는 것은 아니다 Poverty is not necessarily is confined to only one area. // 그러한 체험을 가진 사람은 전 인구 중 일부에 국한되어 있다 Only a few in the whole population have had such experiences.

국한문(國漢文) Korean and Chinese characters. ¶~을 혼용하다 use Korean and Chinese characters in combination // ~에 능통하다 be versed in Korean and Chinese literature.

국헌(國憲) the national constitution; the laws of the land. ¶~을 준수하다 respect the national constitution.

국호(國號) the name of a country. ¶그때 ~를 고쳐 고려라고 칭했다 At that time the country was renamed Goryeo.

국화(菊花) a chrysanthemum; (미국 속어) a mum. ¶~과 식물 a composite (plant).

국화(國花) a national flower. ¶무궁화는 한국의 ~이다 Mugunghwa is regarded as the national flower of Korea.

국회(國會) (한국・프랑스의) the National Assembly; (미국의) Congress; (영국의) Parliament; (일본・스웨덴의) the (National) Diet. ¶제10차 임시[특별] ~ an extraordinary [special] session of the National Assembly // ~ 모의 ~ a mock parliamentary meeting / a sham Assembly session // 제10차 정기 ~ the 10th regular session of the National Assembly // ~ 회기 중 during the session of the National Assembly / while the House of Representatives is in session // ~를 소집하다 convene [call / summon] the National Assembly // ~를 해산하다 dissolve the National Assembly // 내일 ~가 열린다 The House meets tomorrow. // ~가 개회 중이다 The National Assembly is in session now. // ~는 국권의 최고 기관이며 나라의 유일한 입법 기관이다 The Assembly is the highest organ of state power and the sole lawmaking organ of the state.
● **국회 도서관** the National Assembly Library; (미국의) the Library of Congress. **국회법** [법] the National Assembly Law. **국회 사무처** the Secretariat of the National Assembly. **국회 상임 위원회** the National Assembly standing Committee. **국회 의사당** the National Assembly building; (미국의) the Capitol; (영국의) the House of Parliament; (일본의) the Diet Building; the House of the National Diet. **국회의원** a member of the National Assembly; an [a National] Assemblyman; (미국의) a member of Congress; a Congressman; a Congresswoman(여자); (영국의) a member of Parliament; an M.P. (pl. M.P.s, M.P.'s). **국회 의장** the Speaker; the President.

군- extra; needless; unnecessary; uncalled-for. ¶~식구 a hanger-on (pl. hangers-on) / a dependent / a sponge / a boarder // ~걱정을 하다 worry (oneself) unnecessarily // ~소리를 하다 say unnecessary things / make an uncalled-for remark // ~짓을 하다 do unwanted things / gild refined gold.

군(君) 1 [경칭] Mister [Mr.] (▶ 동료・친구・손아래 남자를 부를 경우, 영어에서는 이름에 경칭을 붙이지 않음). ¶손 ~ (Mr.) Son. 2 [자네] you. ¶~들 you fellows [people / chaps] / 그것은 ~의 잘못이다 You are to blame for that. 3 [역] Lord; Sir. ¶광해 ~ Lord Gwanghae.

군(軍) [군대] an [the] army; a force; (armed) forces; troops; [단위] an army; [군부] military authorities. ¶~의 military // ~의 본연의 임무 the military's proper duty // 육해공 ~ the armed forces // 상비 ~ a standing army [navy / air force] // 제 8 ~ the Eighth United States Army // 삼 ~ the whole army / three armed services // 청 [백] ~ a blue [white] team // ~ 당국 military authorities // ~에 입대하다 enter [go into / join] the army // ~에 복무하다 serve in the army // ~에서 제대 [퇴역]하다 leave [retire from] the army.

군(郡) a gun; a county; a district; (미국의) a township. (▶ county는 (미)에서는 대다수의 주(state)에서 가장 큰 행정 구획을, township은 county 내의 행정 구분, (영)에서는 군에 해당하는 것이 district이며, county는 주(州)에 상당함) ¶양주~ Yangju-gun.

군(群) [무리] a group; [군중] a crowd; a throng.

군가(軍歌) a war song [chant]; a martial song; an army song; a marching song. ¶~를 부르다 sing a war song.

군거(群居) gregarious [social] life; aggregation. ¶~성의 gregarious. **군거하다** live gregariously [together / in flocks]. ¶이 지대에는 까마귀가 군거하고 있다 Crows live in flocks in this area.

군것 a superfluous [useless] thing; a super-

군것질하다 eat between meals; (미국 방언) piece; spend one's pocket money on candy [sweets].

군견(軍犬) a war [military] dog. ⇨군용견(숙용).

군경(軍警) the military and the police.

군계일학(群鷄一鶴) the only figure among ciphers; the sun among inferior lights; a Triton among[of] minnows. ¶우리 사이에서 그 청년은 ~ 같은 존재였다 Among us, the youth looked like a jewel in a heap of trash.

군고구마 a roast[baked] sweet potato.

군관구(軍管區) a military district. ¶6~ 사령부 the 6th Military District Command.

군국(軍國) 〔군사(軍事)를 중시하는 나라〕 a militant nation; 〔전쟁 중인 나라〕 a nation at war.
- **군국주의** militarism.

군기(軍紀) military discipline; troop morals. ¶~의 해이 relaxation of military discipline // ~를 유지하다 maintain[enforce] military discipline // ~를 문란케 하다 offend against [violate] military discipline / commit a breach of military discipline // ~가 문란해 있다 Military discipline is lax.

군기(軍旗) the (regimental) colors[(영) colours]; a standard; a battle flag; an ensign.

군기(軍機) a military secret; (서류 등의) a classified military document. ¶~상 for reasons of military secrecy // ~를 누설하다 divulge[disclose] a military secret.
- **군기 누설** disclosure[betrayal / leakage] of military secrets.

군기침 a dry cough.

군납(軍納) the purveyance of supplies or services for an army. **군납하다** provide (supplies or services) for an army; purvey for an army.
- **군납업자** a purveyor for an army; a military goods supplier; service contractors for the military. **군납품** supplies provided by a purveyor. **군납 회사** a military purveyance firm; a military supply contract firm.

군내 an unwanted[extra] smell; an unpleasant smell; a stale smell.

군단(軍團) an army corps; a corps. ¶제1~ the First Corps.
- **군단 사령부** the corps headquarters. **군단장** the commander[commanding general] of an army corps.

군대(軍隊) the troops; armed forces; the forces; an army; a corps; the military. ¶3만의 ~ an army thirty thousand strong // ~에 들어가다 enlist in[join] the army / join up / enlist // ~ 에 복무 중이다 be [serve] in the army // ~ 를 보내다 send troops // 나폴레옹은 러시아에서 그의 ~를 철수시켰다 Napoleon withdrew his troops from Russia.
- **군대 생활** (a) military life.

군더더기 〔쓸데없이 덧붙은 물건〕 an excrescence; a superfluity; 〔공연히 따라다니는 사람〕 an unwanted follower; a hanger-on. ¶~를 붙이다 add something superfluous.

군데 a place; a spot; a point; a part. ¶한두 ~의 잘못 one or two mistakes // 한 ~ 오래 머물다 stay long in the same place // 여러 ~ 상처를 입다 receive several wounds // 이 등산로에는 위험한 곳이 세 ~ 있다 There are three dangerous spots[places] on this climbing trail.

군데군데 here and there; sporadically(산재하여); at[in] places; (in) various places; sparsely. ¶~ 눈이 쌓이다 be covered with snow here and there // (페인트 등이) ~ 벗겨져 있다 be off in places // ~ 나무를 심다 plant trees here and there // 들판에 ~ 집이 서 있다 Houses stand scattered in the field. // 전방에 초소가 ~ 서 있다 Guard posts are placed sporadically along the front line.

군도(軍刀) a military sword; a saber; (영) a sabre.

군도(群島) a group of islands; an archipelago (pl. ~s, ~es).

군도(群盜) a group[gang] of robbers.

군돈 money spent unnecessarily; unnecessary expenses.

군락(群落) 〔많은 촌락〕 a group of hamlets; 〔식물이 떼 지어 자람〕 a community. ¶설악산에는 앉은부채가 ~을 이루며 자라고 있다 Skunk cabbages grow in groups[colonies] in Seoraksan[Mt. Seorak].

군란(軍亂) an insurrection of troops; an army rebellion; a coup (d'etat).

군략(軍略) strategy; a stratagem; tactics. ¶~상 strategically // ~상의 strategic // ~을 사용하다 resort to a stratagem // 그들은 ~에 걸려들었다 They fell into the trap laid by the enemy.
- **군략가** a strategist; a tactician.

군량(軍糧) (military) provisions; (food) supplies; ration. ¶~이 떨어지다 be short of provisions // 군대는 ~이 떨어졌다 The army ran out of provisions. / The provisions for the army were exhausted[ran out].

군령(軍令) a military command[order].

군림(君臨) reigning. **군림하다** reign (over a kingdom / people); rule (over millions); lord it over. ¶인민 위에 ~ reign over the people // 그는 미술계에 군림하고 있다 He is a leading figure in the artistic world. / He dominates the artistic world. // 영국 왕은 군림하나 통치하지 않는다 The English sovereign reigns, but does not rule.

군마(軍馬) 〔군사와 말〕 soldiers and horses; 〔군대용 말〕 a military horse; a charger(장교용); a (war) steed; a war horse.

군말 an unnecessary[uncalled-for] remark; an expletive; (문장 등의) redundant[superfluous] words. ¶건강의 중요성에 대해서는 ~이 필요 없다 We do not need to dwell on [emphasize] the importance of health. **군말하다** say unnecessary things; make an uncalled-for remark.

군매점(軍賣店) (미) a post exchange; a PX (pl. PXs); a canteen.

군명(君命) the orders[commands] of one's lord. ¶~을 받들어 in obedience to one's lord's[king's] command / by order of one's lord[king] // ~이라면 어쩔 수 없다 Our lord's[king's] word must be obeyed.

군모(軍帽) a military cap; (육군의) an army cap; (해군의) a navy cap.

군목(軍牧) a chaplain.

군무(群舞) group[formation] dancing. ¶~를 추다 dance in groups.

군무(軍務) military[naval] affairs; military service. ¶~를 수행하다 perform military duties / serve in the army[navy / air force].

군문

●**군무원** a civilian attached to the military; an army [a naval] civilian employee. **군무 이탈** desertion from military service.
군문(軍門) [군영 입구] a camp gate; [군영 내] a camp; [군대] an army. ¶~에 들어가다 enlist in the army / enter the service.
군민(軍民) the military and the people; the fighting services and the civilians.
군민(郡民) inhabitants of a county; county people.
군밤 a roast(ed) chestnut.
군번(軍番) (a soldier's) serial number (약어 SN); service number; [인식표] an identification [a dog] tag.
군벌(軍閥) a military [an army] clique; a militarist party; the (powerful) militarists.
●**군벌 정치** military dictatorship; militaristic government; warlordism.
군법(軍法) martial [military] law.
●**군법 회의** ➡ 군사 법원(➪군사(軍事))
군복(軍服) a military uniform; (육군의) a army uniform; (해군의) a navy [naval] uniform; (공군의) an air-force uniform. ¶~을 입고 있다 be in military uniform // ~을 입은 병사 a soldier in uniform / a uniformed soldier.
군부(軍部) military authorities; army circles; the militarists; [집합적] the military.
군불 a fire for heating an *ondol*. ¶~을 때다 heat an *ondol* (with firewood) / burn (firewood) to heat an *ondol*.
군비(軍備) [준비] military [warlike] preparations; (미) preparedness (for war); [설비] armaments; arms. ¶~를 확장하다 increase [expand] armaments // ~를 축소하다 reduce armaments // ~가 갖추어져 있다 be militarily prepared / be ready for war // ~를 철폐하다 disarm.
●**군비 경쟁** an arms race. ¶치열한 ~ a fierce armament [arms] race. **군비 제한** the limitation of armaments; arms control. **군비 축소** the reduction of [a cut in] armaments; an armament reduction; an arms cut.
군비(軍費) military expenses; war [army] expenditure; [군자금] the sinews of war.
군사(軍士) a (common) soldier; a private (soldier); [집합적] (enlisted) men; the rank and file.
군사(軍事) military affairs. ¶비~적인 nonmilitary (means) // ~상의 목적으로 for military [strategic] purposes.
●**군사 고문** a military adviser. ¶~단 the military advisory group. **군사 기지** a military [an army / a navy / an air] base. **군사 동맹** a military alliance. **군사력** military strength [might / capacity]. **군사 법원** a court-martial (*pl.* courts-martial); a military tribunal. ¶~에 회부하다 try (a soldier) by court-martial / court-martial (a soldier). **군사 분계선** the Military Demarcation Line. **군사비** war expenditure [funds]. **군사 우편** military mail. **군사 원조** military aid [assistance]. **군사 재판** a military trial. **군사 정권** a military regime; (잠정적인) a junta. **군사 행동** military operations; hostilities. **군사 훈련** military drill.
군사령관(軍司令官) an army commander.
군사령부(軍司令部) military headquarters.
군살 1 [군더더기살] (구어) flab; superfluous [waste] flesh. ¶~을 빼다 get rid of extra flesh / wear [work] off surplus fat // 배에 ~이 찌다 put on excess weight around waist / (구어) develop a spare tire // 나는 중년의 ~이 찌고 있다 I'm developing middle-age flab [spread]. // 여름휴가 전에 ~을 다 뺄 작정이다 I'm determined to get rid of this flab before the summer vacation. **2** proud flesh. ➪"굿은살
군상(群像) a large group of people; (조각의) a sculptured group.
군색하다(窘塞-) destitute; poor; needy; hard-up. ¶군색한 변명 a poor [sorry / lame] excuse // 군색한 집안에 태어나다 be born in a poor family / be born poor [to poverty] // 군색하게 살다 lead a life of want / make a poor [scanty] living / earn [pick up] a scanty livelihood.
군생(群生) [모든 생물] animate things; living creatures; [생] a community; gregariousness. **군생하다** grow in banks [colonies]; (송이를 이루어) grow in clusters.
군서(群棲) [생] gregariousness. **군서하다** live gregariously; (소·말·돼지·고래 등이) live in herds; (양·염소·새가) live in flocks; (곤충·새가) live in swarms. ¶이 섬에는 바다코끼리가 군서하고 있다 Walruses live in colonies on this island.
군세(軍勢) [군사력] military strength [power]; [군의 형세] the military situation (of a country); [병사 수] the number of soldiers; [군대] an army; a force; troops.
군소(群小) the small; the vulgar; (a large number of) small fry. ¶~의 minor / petty.
●**군소국** the lesser nations. **군소 정당** minor [petty] political parties.
군소리 [헛소리] talking in one's sleep [delirium]; [쓸데없는 말] an uncalled-for remark. **군소리하다** make an unnecessary remark; talk in one's sleep [delirium]; utter meaningless words.
군속(軍屬) ➡ 군무원(➪군무(軍務))
군수(軍需) munitions.
●**군수 공업** / **군수 산업** the munitions [war] industry. **군수 공장** a munitions [an armament] factory [works / plant]. **군수품** / **군수물자** munitions (of war); war supplies [materials / stores]; ordnance.
군수(郡守) a county headman [governor]; the magistrate of a county.
군식구(-食口) a hanger-on (*pl.* hangers-on); a dependent; a parasite; a sponger.
군신(君臣) sovereign and subject; ruler and ruled; lord and vassal.
군신(軍神) [전쟁의 신] the god of war; [로마 신화] Mars; [그리스 신화] Ares; [군인] a war hero.
군신(群臣) a crowd of retainers [subjects]; a large group [number] of (one's) retainers.
군실거리다 feel itchy [creepy / crawly].
군악(軍樂) military [martial] music. ¶~을 연주하다 play military music.
●**군악대** a military band; (해군의) a naval band. **군악대원** a bandsman.
군영(軍營) a military camp; an encampment. ¶~을 치다 camp / encamp.
군왕(君王) a monarch; a king.
군용(軍用) military use [purpose]. ¶~의 military / for military use / [전쟁용의] war.
●**군용견** a war [military] dog. **군용기** a war plane; a service airplane; a military [naval

plane. 군용 도로 a military road. 군용 열차 a troop train. 군용품 military equipment [supplies].

군웅(群雄) rival leaders [barons].
● **군웅할거**(-割據) rivalry of local barons. 군웅할거 시대 the age of rival chiefs [war lords].

군율(軍律) [군의 규율] military discipline; [군대의 형법] martial law; the articles of war. ¶~을 지키다 observe military discipline // ~이 엄하다 Military discipline is quite severe.

군음식(-飮食) a between-meals snack; a snack (between meals); extra food.

군의(관)(軍醫官) (육군의) an army surgeon [doctor]; (해군의) a naval surgeon; (공군의) a flight surgeon.

군인(軍人) a serviceman; a servicewoman(여성); a soldier(병사); an officer(장교); (해군의) a sailor; (공군의) an airman; (육군의) a soldier. ¶작업 [장교] a career officer // 그에게는 ~ 기질이 많다 He has much of the soldier in him.
● **군인 정신** the military spirit.

군일 unnecessary [needless] work; extra work. 군일하다 do unnecessary [extra] work.

군자(君子) a man of virtue [honor / (영) honour]; a (true) gentleman. ¶~인 체하다 assume a virtuous air / pose as a man of culture.
● **군자표변**(-豹變) Wise men are quick to adapt themselves to circumstances.

군자금(軍資金) [군사 자금] war funds; a war chest; [선거 등의 자금] campaign funds. ¶~을 공급하다 supply the sinews of war / subsidize // 선거전의 ~이 부족하다 be short of election campaigning funds.

군자란(君子蘭) [식] a scarlet kaffir lily.

군장(軍裝) (a) military uniform; (전투의) a combat uniform; [군대 장비] a soldier's kit. ¶~을 하다 wear uniform // 완전 ~으로 in full uniform / (전투복으로) in full gear [(영) kit].

군정(軍政) (a) military government [administration]. ¶~을 펼치다 establish military administration / impose military rule (on the people) // ~하에 있다 be under military administration.

군제(軍制) a military system; (a) military organization.

군졸(軍卒) a soldier; the rank and file.

군주(君主) (왕국·제국의) a monarch; [최고의 지배자] a sovereign; [통치자] a ruler. ¶전제 ~ an autocrat / an absolute monarch.
● **군주국** a monarchy. **군주 독재** absolute monarchy; autocracy. **군주 정체** monarchism; monarchy. **군주 정치** monarchy. **군주제** a monarchial system; monarchism.

군중(群衆) a crowd (of people) (▶ 집합체를 가리킬 때는 단수, 군집 속의 하나하나를 지칭할 때는 복수 취급); a multitude; a throng. ¶~으로 붐비다 be crowded [thronged] with people // ~을 헤치고 나아가다 force [push / elbow] one's way through the crowed // ~을 제지하다 keep back a crowd // ~이 모였다 [밀어닥쳤다] A crowd gathered [surged forward]. / ~이 흩어졌다 [줄어들었다] The crowd scattered [ebbed / thinned]. // 많은 ~이 그것을 보러 모였다 Soon a large crowd of people gathered to look at it.
● **군중대회** a (mass) rally. **군중 심리** mob [mass / crowd] psychology; the group [crowd] mind. ¶그것이 ~라는 것이다 That is the mentality of the masses.

군집(群集) a large group of people. 군집하다 crowd; throng; congregate; gather in crowds.

군청(群靑) ultramarine; sea blue. ¶~색의 바다 [하늘] a deep blue sea [sky].

군청(郡廳) a gun [county / district] office. ¶~ 소재지 the seat of a county office.

군체(群體) [동] a colony (of corals).

군축(軍縮) the reduction of armaments. ⇨ 군비 축소(⇨군비(軍備)).

군침 excessive saliva; slaver; slobber; drool. ¶~을 흘리다 drivel / slaver / salivate / run [dribble] at the mouth / [부러워하다] be envious (of).

군침(이) 돌다 feel an appetite. ¶군침이 도는 appetizing / tempting (offer) / attractive (woman) // 그는 불고기 냄새를 맡고 군침이 돌았다 His mouth watered when he smelled the roast meat. // 나는 좋아하는 뱀장어구이 냄새에 군침이 돌았다 My mouth watered at the aroma of grilled eels, my favorite food. // 보기만 해도 군침이 도는 물건이다 Only a momentary sight of the article will make you crave for it. // 저런 다이아몬드를 보면 군침이 돈다 The sight of such a diamond is tempting [a temptation] to me. // 냄새만 맡아도 군침이 돌았다 The mere smell of it made my mouth water [made me drool]. // 이건 수집가들이 보면 군침이 돌 물건이다 This is an item that would make collectors' mouths water [that collectors would drool over].

군턱 a double [an extra] chin.

군표(軍票) military scrip [currency]; an army [a war] note. ¶미 ~ an American MPC [military payment certificate].

군함(軍艦) a warship; a man-of-war; a battleship. ¶~을 건조하다 construct a warship.
● **군함기**(-旗) a naval ensign; (영국의) the white ensign.

군항(軍港) a naval base [station / port]; (영) a naval dockyard.

군호(軍號) a (military) password; a watchword; a countersign.

군화(軍靴) military shoes; combat boots; (미) G.I. shoes.

굳건하다 strong and steady; solid; reliable; firm; strong-minded; stout-hearted. ¶굳건한 정신 a stout heart / a firm spirit // 굳건한 의지 an iron [indomitable / adamant] will // 굳건한 사람 a firm character / 정신적인 굳건함 strength of character / strong-mindedness // 토대가 ~ The foundation is solid [secure].

굳건히 strongly; firmly; solidly; tightly.

굳다¹ [굳어지다] become hard [hardened]; harden; become solid; [뻣뻣해지다] become stiffened; stiffen; [응결하다] set; congeal(엉기다); clot(피가); curdle(우유가). ¶알맞게 굳은 빵 bread of just the right consistency // 습관이 ~ be confined in one's habit // 계란을 굳게 삶다 hard-boil an egg // 추워서 온몸이 굳었다 I was stiff all over from cold. // 풀이 딱 딱하게 굳었다 The paste dried up completely. // 석고는 빨리 굳는다 Plaster of Paris sets quickly. // 젤리는 식으면 굳는다 Jelly sets as it cools.

굳다² 1 [딱딱하다] hard; solid; adamant(ine); unyielding. ¶굳은 땅 hard[stiff/tough] soil // 굳은 표정으로 with a stern look // 고양이는 죽어서 몸이 굳었다 The cat lay stiff in death. 2 [확고·견고하다] strong; firm; fast; tight; secure; steady; steadfast; stable; solid; sound. ¶굳은 결심 a firm resolve[resolution] // 굳은 신념 a firm[strong] belief // 의지가 굳은 사람 a man with a strong[an iron] will // 굳게 약속하다 promise definitely // 그의 결백함을 굳게 믿고 있다 I firmly believe that he is innocent. / I am confident of his innocence. // 그들은 굳게 단결하고 있다 They are closely[firmly] united. // 그들은 서로 굳게 손을 잡았다 They grasped each other's hands firmly. // 문은 굳게 닫혀 있었다 The door was shut tight. // 그의 결의가 굳은지 시험해 보겠다 I will test the firmness of his resolution.

굳세다 (몸이) strong; firm; stout; (마음이) strong-minded; stout-hearted (woman). ¶굳세게 undauntedly / bravely / stout // 굳센 의지 an iron[a bulldog] will // 굳센 신념 a firm conviction // 굳센 마음 strong mind // 굳센 마음으로 살아가다 with the avowed intent (to do) // 험한 세상을 굳세게 살아가다 face the reality of life with firm determination / meet bravely the grim reality of life // 그녀는 눈물 한 방울 보이지 않는 마음이 굳센 여자다 She is really strong[tough] and not shed a single tear.

굳어지다 become stiff; stiffen; (표정 등이) freeze. ¶굳어진 손 stiff hands // 그는 선생님을 본 순간 얼굴이 굳어졌다 He stiffened[froze] when he saw his teacher.

굳은살 hardened skin; (손의) a callus; (발의) a corn. ¶발가락에 ~이 박이다 get a corn on a toe // 손가락에 ~이 박였다 A callus has formed on my finger.

굳이 strongly; firmly; decisively; strictly; obstinately(고집스럽게). ~ 묻다 inquire importunately // ~ 원하신다면 if you particularly wish it / if you insist (upon it) // ~ 사양하다 decline once for all // 네가 ~ 혼자 가겠다면 할 수 없지 If you insist on going alone, please do so. // ~ 사시겠다면 (그것을) 내놓더라도 (저는) 상관없습니다 If you really want to buy it, I don't mind parting with it. // 이미 결정된 것이라면 ~ 바꾸라고는 하지 않겠다 If it has already been decided on, I won't insist that you change it[insist on a change]. // ~ 비교하자면 영수가 작문은 좀 낫다 If forced to compare them, I'd say that Yeongsu is a little better at composition. // 그 모임에는 ~ 참석할 필요가 없다 It's not absolutely necessary for you to be present at the meeting.

굳히다 1 [굳게 하다] harden; make hard; (응결시키다) congeal; condense; curdle; freeze. ¶자갈을 시멘트로 ~ bind gravel with cement // 말려서 ~ harden by drying / dry up // 우리는 눈을 밟아 굳혔다 We trod [tramped] down the snow. 2 [강화하다] strengthen; [견고히 하다] solidify; consolidate; make secure. ¶기초를 ~ strengthen the basis // 지반을 ~ strengthen[solidify / consolidate] the foundation[one's footing] / make one's position secure // 신념[결심]을 ~ strengthen one's belief[resolution] // 지위를 ~ solidify [strengthen] one's position // 터전을 ~ improve one's footing // 결속을 ~ tighten the bond of union.

굴 [동] an oyster. ¶생 ~ a raw oyster // ~을 양식하다 cultivate oysters.
● 굴 껍데기 oyster shells. 굴 양식 oyster farming[culture]; ostreiculture. 굴 양식장 an oyster bed; an oyster farm.

굴(窟) 1 [터널] a tunnel. ¶~을 파다 dig a tunnel / build [bore / drive / cut / excavate / pierce] a tunnel (through) / tunnel (through) / excavate (the side of a hill). 2 [동굴] a cave; a cavern; a grotto (pl. ~s); an excavation (in a rock). ¶~의 어귀[입구] a cave mouth // ~투성이의 cave-pocked [-riddled] (beach). 3 [짐승이 사는 구멍] a lair; a den; a holt; an earth(여우 등의); a burrow[barrow] (토끼 등의). ¶늑대 ~ a wolve's den[lair] // ~ 파는 동물 a fossorial animal / a burrower / an earth excavator // ~을 파다 dig a burrow / burrow. 4 a den. ⇨소굴

굴곡(屈曲) a bend; a curve; (관절의) flexion; (해안선 등의) indentation; (광선의) refraction. ¶~이 진 crooked / winding / indented // 한국의 남해안은 ~이 심하다 The southern coast of Korea frequently runs in and out[is very rugged].

굴광성(屈光性) [생] phototropism. ¶~의 phototropic.

굴다 behave (toward); conduct[bear] oneself; act; treat; (고) demean oneself (like a man). ¶심하게 ~ act harshly (toward a person) // 못살게 ~ treat (a person) harshly / be hard on (a person) // 신사답게 ~ behave as a gentleman / do like a gentleman // 비열하게 ~ play foul[false] // 버릇없이 ~ (구어) carry on // 스스럼없이 ~ conduct oneself without reserve // 바보처럼 ~ make an ass[a fool] of oneself // 거만하게 ~ have an imperious[arrogant] bearing (toward one's underlings) / be insolently[impetuously] proud // 그녀는 손님에게 친절하게 군다 She receives her visitors kindly. / She is a good hostess.

굴다리(窟-) an overpass; (영) a flyover; a viaduct; a land bridge.

굴대 [차축] an axle; (기계의) a shaft; an arbor; a mandrel; (팽이의) a stem; a roller.

굴뚝 (집의) a chimney; (여러 개 한 묶음의) a (chimney) stack; (기관·기선의) a funnel; (난로의) a stovepipe. ¶~ 청소 chimney sweeping // ~ 청소부 a chimney sweep(er) [cleaner] // ~이 둘인 기선 a two-funneled steamer // ~을 청소하다 sweep a chimney // ~이 막혔다 The chimney is blocked[clogged up].

굴뚝같다 be quite anxious[eager] (to do); have a strong urge (to do); feel an irresistible impulse (to do). ¶나도 가고 싶은 마음은 굴뚝같지만 다른 데 방문할 약속이 있다 I would very much like[I am dying] to go, but I have another appointment to visit.

굴뚝새 [동] a wren; a jenny wren(암컷).

굴렁쇠 a hoop. ¶~를 굴리다 drive[trundle / roll] along a hoop.

굴레 1 (마소의) a bridle; a halter; a headgear. ¶~ 벗은 말 an unbridled horse // ~를 씌우다 put a bridle (on a horse) / bridle / halter up // ~를 벗기다 take off a bridle[headgear] / unbridle / unhalter. 2 [얽매임] restraint; a yoke; fetters; ties; bonds. ¶~를 쓰다 be bridled [restrained / curbed / bound] // ~를 벗다 free oneself from restraints / shake [throw / break] off the yoke [fetters] / get released // 아이가 부부간을 묶어 두는 ~가 되는 경우가 많다 A child is often a tie binding its parents together.

굴리다 1 [구르게 하다] roll (a barrel / a wheel); trundle (a cask); tumble over (a barrel). ¶구슬을 굴리는 듯한 목소리 a sweet silvery voice // 묵주를 가락으로 ~ tell [finger] one's beads / 굴려 떨어뜨리다 roll (a stone) down (a slope) // 혀를 굴리며 말하다 speak with a trill / trill [roll] one's r's / 소년은 눈을 굴렸다 The boy rolled [goggled] his eyes.
2 [방치하다] neglect; lay aside. ¶책을 함부로 ~ toss a book to one side // 함부로 굴리면 못 쓰게 된다 If you leave it unattended, it will not last.
3 [모나지 않게 깎다] round off (the corners [angles]); pare off [away]; smooth the surface (of woodwork).
4 [돈놀이하다] lend out. ¶돈을 ~ lend one's money out at interest / practice usury // 돈을 잘 ~ invest one's money profitably.
5 [운행하다] run. ¶그는 버스를 5대 굴린다 He has five buses running for business purposes.

굴복(屈服) submission; surrender. **굴복하다** submit [surrender / yield / succumb / give in] (to); bow one's head (to); lick [kiss] the dust. ¶적에게 ~ succumb [yield / surrender] to the enemy // 적에게 굴복하느니 죽는 편이 낫다 I'd rather die than surrender to the enemy. // 그들은 그의 명령에 굴복했다 They submitted to his orders. // 마침내 그의 집요함에 굴복하고 말았다 At last his persistence wore me down and I gave in. / At last I gave in [yielded] to his pertinacity. // 아무도 그의 금력에 굴복하는 사람이 없었다 No one bowed [yielded] to his money. // 그는 마침내 굴복하여 우리들의 제안에 동의했다 He gave away [gave in] at last and agreed to our proposal. // ¶굴복시키다 make (a person) give in / bring (a person) to (fall on) his knees / put down / floor.

굴비 a dried croaker [yellow corbina].

굴속(窟~) 1 [굴의 안] the inside of a cave [den / tunnel]. ¶~에 살다 [숨다] live [hide itself] in a burrow (여우가) / ~으로 달아나다 run to earth. 2 [어두운 곳] a dark place; the dark. ¶~ 같다 be as dark as the inside of a cave / be very dark / be inscrutable.

굴수성(屈水性) [식] hydrotropism.

굴신(屈伸) bending and stretching; extension and contraction. ¶~이 자유로운 elastic / flexible / pliable. **굴신하다** bend and stretch; extend and contract; be elastic.

굴욕(屈辱) humiliation; indignity; disgrace; dishonor; shame; an insult. ¶~을 받다 be subjected to humiliation / 남에게 ~을 주다 humiliate a person / subject a person to humiliation // 나는 지난 2년 동안 ~을 참아왔다 I have been enduring humiliation [eating humble pie] these two years. // 나는 말이없이 ~을 참았다 I swallowed [put up with] the insult in silence.
●**굴욕감** a sense of humiliation.

굴욕적(屈辱的) humiliating; disgraceful; shameful. ¶~인 외교 humiliating diplomacy / crow-eating diplomacy // ~인 강화 조약을 맺다 conclude a humiliating [an ignoble] peace treaty (with).

굴절(屈折) 1 [꺾임] bending; a turn. ¶~이 많은 해안선 an uneven coastline. **굴절하다** bend; turn; make a turn. →¶그는 그녀에게 굴절된 감정이 있다 His feelings toward her are warped. 2 [물] refraction. ¶~성의 [굴절시키는] refractive / [굴절하는] refrangible. **굴절하다** be refracted. 3 (어형(語形) 등의) inflection; (영) inflexion. **굴절하다** inflect; be inflected.
●**굴절각** (광선의) an angle of refraction; (프리즘 등의) a refracting angle. **굴절 광선** a refracted ray of light. **굴절률** a refractive index; index of refraction. **굴절 망원경** a refracting telescope; a refractor. **굴절어** an inflected language. **굴절파** a refracted ray of wave.

굴젓 pickled oysters.

굴종(屈從) submission; subservience. **굴종하다** submit (tamely / meekly) (to); yield (to); succumb (to); bend [bow] the knee (to / before). ¶적에게 ~ succumb [yield / surrender] to the enemy // 그는 순순히 굴종할 사람이 아니다 He is not the sort of man to submit tamely. // ¶굴종시키다 bring (a person) to his knees / keep (a person) down // 나는 어떻게든 그를 굴종시키지 않으면 안 된다 I must bring him to his knees [bring him into submission] by some means (or other).

굴지(屈指) [손가락을 꼽음] counting on one's fingers; [뛰어남] eminence; prominence. ¶~의 leading / prominent / preeminent / outstanding / distinguished / foremost // 한국 ~의 상업 도시 the leading commercial cities in Korea // 그는 당대 ~의 화가였다 He was one of the foremost painters of his day [time]. // 그는 세계 ~의 명지휘자다 He is one of the leading [prominent] conductors in the world.

굴지성(屈地性) [식] geotropism.

굴진하다(掘進~) dig through [into / under].

굴착(掘鑿) [굴을 파서 뚫음] digging; boring; [토사를 파내기] excavation. **굴착하다** dig out [through]; excavate; hollow (out). ¶터널을 ~ dig [bore] a tunnel (through a mountain) // 운하를 ~ build a canal.
●**굴착기** an excavator; (증기식의) a steam shovel.

굴참나무 [식] an oriental species of oak.

굴하다(屈~) yield [submit / succumb / give in / bow / knuckle under] (to). ¶굴하지 않고 undauntedly / unflinchingly / nothing daunted (by failure) / in defiance of / in spite of / 유혹에 ~ yield under pressure // 그는 마침내 유혹에 굴하고 말았다 He at last yielded [gave in] to temptation. // 그는 부당한 처사에 굴하지 않았다 He did not submit [bow] to the unfair treatment he received. // 그들은 당국의 탄압에도 굴하지 않고 반정부 운동을 계속했다 They continued their antigovernment movement in defiance [spite] of suppression by the authorities.

굵다 (몸피가) big; thick; burly; (목소리가) deep; thick; (선이) heavy; (활자 등이) fat; (피륙의 바탕이) coarse; large. ¶굵게 thickly / deeply // 굵은 팔 a big arm // 굵은 실 (a) heavy thread // 굵은 가지 a thick bough // 굵

굵다랗다 very thick; very big; (목소리가) very deep.

은 목 a thick neck // 굵은 선 a bold[heavy / thick] line // 굵은 목소리 a deep voice // 굵게 쓰여지는 만년필 a broad-pointed fountain pen // 굵은 글씨로 쓰다 write in bold strokes // 인생을 굵고 짧게 살다 lead a short life and a merry one.

굵다랗다 very thick; very big; (목소리가) very deep.

굵직굵직하다 all thick[big / burly / deep]. ¶ 굵직굵직하게 썰다 cut into big[thick] pieces.

굵직하다 somewhat thick[big / burly / deep / fat]; thickish.

굶기다 let (a person) go hungry[foodless]; starve; make (a person) starve. ¶굶겨 죽이다 starve (a person) to death // 처자식을 굶길 수는 없잖나 How can I let my family go hungry?

굶다 go foodless[hungry]; skip[miss / lose] a meal; starve; famish; fast. ¶굶어 죽다 die of [from] hunger / be starved[famished] to death // 종일 굶었다 I haven't eaten all day. / I have not touched food all day. // 그해에는 많은 사람들이 굶어 죽었다 Many died of hunger[starved to death] that year. // 굶어 죽을 지경이다 (구어) I'm (almost) starved. / (구어) I'm (simply) starving. / (구어) I'm famished. // 그들은 여러 날 굶었다 They went hungry for days. // 굶어 죽기 전에 일자리를 찾아야 한다 I have to find a job before I starve.

굶주리다 1 [먹을 것이 없어 주리다] starve; be famished; be hungry. (▶ starve는 식량 부족으로 쇠약 또는 아사하다, be hungry는 배가 고프다, be famished는 be hungry를 과장한 표현) ¶가뭄 때문에 많은 사람이 굶주렸다 Many people starved during the drought. // 굶주린 늑대의 무리가 소를 습격했다 A pack of famished wolves attacked the cattle.
2 [욕구가 충족되지 않다] hunger[hanker / thirst] for[after]. ¶그는 지식에 굶주리고 있었다 He was hungry for knowledge. // (문어) He hungered after knowledge. // 그녀는 사랑에 굶주리고 있었다 She was starved for[(영) of] love. / She yearned for love. // 굶주린 짐승처럼 그는 사람을 죽였다 He killed people like a beast thirsting after blood.

굶주림 [배를 곯음] hunger; [기아] starvation. ¶~을 면하다 starve[keep] off hunger // ~ 때문에 많은 사람이 죽었다 A great many people died of hunger[starved to death]. // 그는 한 조각의 치즈로 ~을 달랬다 He starved off his hunger with a piece of cheese. // 이렇게 적은 음식물로는 내 ~을 채울 수가 없다 Such a small amount of food cannot satisfy my hunger.

굼뜨다 slow; tardy; sluggish; slow-moving; slowgoing. ¶굼뜬 동작 sluggish behavior // 굼뜬 사람 a dawdler / a laggard // 일에 ~ be slow at the job // 그의 굼뜬 동작에 짜증이 났다 His slowness made me impatient. // 그녀는 굼뜨지 않다 She does things[acts] quickly. / She gets down to work[moving] right away.

굼벵이 [유충] a (white) grub; a maggot; [동작이 굼뜬 사람] a sluggard; a laggard; a slow (-moving) person. ¶~ 같은 slow(-moving) / snail-slow / sluggish // ~ 걸음으로 나아가다 go at a snail's pace.

굼벵이도 구르는 재주가 있다 (속담) Every man for his own trade.

굼실거리다 [느릿느릿 움직이다] writhe; wriggle; squirm; creep about (over one's body); crawl over (one).

굽 1 (마소의) a hoof (pl. ~s, hooves). ¶갈라진 ~ cloven hoofs // ~이 있는 동물 a hoofed animal. 2 (신발의) a heel; (그릇의) a foot; a base; a stem (of a glass). ¶~이 높은[낮은] 구두 high-heeled[low-heeled] shoes // 구두의 ~이 완전히 닳아 버렸다 The heels of my shoes are completely worn down. // 그는 ~이 닳아 빠진 구두를 신고 있었다 He was down at heel (▶ 초라한 옷차림의 뜻으로도 씀).

굽다¹ [만곡하다] bend; curve; be crooked [stooped]; warp. ¶굽은 길 a winding path // 굽은 계단 a dogleg(ged) staircase // 굽은 나무 줄기 a crooked tree trunk // (나이가 들어) 허리가 ~ be bent with age / stoop from age.

굽다² 1 roast (고기), broil (고기·생선을); bake (빵을); toast (빵 조각이나 김을). (▶ roast 는 육류·감자 등을 직접 불에 익히거나 오븐 속에 넣고 가열하는 것이고, broil은 고기나 생선을 직접 불에 접촉시켜 가열하는 것이며, bake는 빵·과자·감자 등을 오븐에 넣고 가열하는 것임) ¶잘 구워진 well done / well baked // 덜 구워진 medium(중간) / rare(덜 구워진) // 지나치게 ~ overdo / overcook / overroast / overbroil // 빵을 ~ bake bread / (토스트로) toast (a slice of bread) / 김을 살짝 ~ pass laver lightly over a flame // 빵이 갈색으로 멋지게 구워졌다 The bread was baked to a perfect brown. // 생선이 구워졌다 The fish is roasted. // 고기가 구워질 때까지 기다려라 Wait till the meat is roasted. // 고기가 잘 구워졌다 The meat is well done. // 고기가 덜 구워졌다 This meat is underdone[rare]. // 이건 너무 구워졌다 It is overdone. // 스테이크를 잘 [덜 / 중간 정도로] 구워 주시오 I like my steak well done[rare / medium]. // 이 고기를 한 번 더 구워 주세요 Please do this meat again thoroughly. // 이 돼지고기는 덜 구워졌다 This pork is undone[not completely cooked].
2 (도자기 등을) bake; fire; make (china); burn (bricks / lime); (숯을) produce; burn (charcoal). ¶도자기[벽돌]를 ~ bake[fire] pottery[bricks] // 숯을 ~ make charcoal / char wood / burn wood into charcoal // 단지가 훌륭하게 구워졌다 The pot was fired [baked] beautifully.
3 (윷에서) start another marker on the first position of a yut board (while the first marker is still there).

굽도리 [벽의 아랫도리] the skirting (of a wall); the lower walls of a room.

굽실 bowing[kowtowing] obsequiously [fawningly]. ¶소년은 ~ 절을 하였다 The boy dropped[dipped] his head in a bow. **굽실하다** bow one's head; bow low; kowtow; fawn (upon). ¶머리를 ~ bow one's head // 몸을 ~ make an obeisance.

굽실거리다 [복종하다] bow (and scrape); truckle[yield] (to); [아첨하다] kowtow (to); cringe (to); crouch. ¶그는 사장 앞에서 늘 굽실거린다 He always kowtows[humbles] himself before the president.

굽어보다 1 [내려다보다] look down (at); overlook; command[take] a bird's-eye view of. ¶들판을 굽어보는 산 a mountain dominating the plain // 골짜기를 ~ look down into a valley. 2 take a kindly interest in. ⇨

굽어살피다 take a kindly interest in; pay attention to. ¶민정을 ~ look into the condition of the people∥하느님이시여 굽어살피소서 Heaven be my witness.

굽이 a turn (of a river); a bend [turning] (of a road); the curve (of a street). ¶물~ the bend of a river / a turn in a stream / an arm of the sea∥~마다 at every turn∥배는 강의 ~를 돌았다 The boat turned a bend in the river.

굽이굽이 1 [굽이마다] at every turn[bend]. 2 [물이 굽이쳐 흐르는 모양] windingly; meanderingly; serpentinely; zigzag; in zigzag; back and forth; round and round. ¶~ 흐르는 강 a winding [meandering / serpentine] river∥냇물이 계곡을 ~ 흐르고 있었다 The stream meandered along the valley.

굽이돌다 wind [curve] around; (강이) meander; make a curve (around). ¶굽이도는 길 a winding path∥굽이돌며 흐르는 시내 a meandering stream.

굽이지다 make a bend [turn / curve]. ¶강이 산모퉁이에서 굽이진다 The river makes a bend at the corner of a mountain.

굽이치다 run [flow] back and forth [round and round (a series of curves)]; wind; meander; undulate; swell (파도가). ¶냇물이 굽이쳐 흐른다 The stream meanders back and forth.∥먼 바다에서는 파도가 크게 굽이친다 Surges run high in the open sea.∥동진강은 호남평야의 여러 고을을 굽이쳐 흐른다 Dongjingang(Dongjin River) meanders through the various towns on the Honam plain.

굽죄이다 have qualms [misgivings]; have an uneasy conscience; have a sense of having done wrong; feel compunction; be apprehensive; feel small [intimidated / overawed / frightened]; be ashamed [embarrassed]. ¶그는 부인한테 굽죄어 지낸다 He is henpecked.

굽히다 1 [구부리다] bend (one's knees); stoop (oneself); hook (one's finger); crook (one's arm); bow (one's head). ¶허리를 ~ bend one's back / bend forward / bend over / bow∥그녀는 몸을 굽혀서 마루의 종잇조각을 주우려 했다 She stooped [bent] down to pick up the scraps of paper on the floor.∥그녀는 몸을 굽혀 아이에게 무엇인가 말했다 She bent down and said something to the child.∥그녀는 허리를 조금 굽혀 나에게 절했다 She greeted me by making a slight bow [by bowing slightly].∥그 노인은 허리를 조금 굽히고 걸었다 The old man walked with his back slightly bent.
2 [굴하다] yield; submit; give in; bend (to / before). ¶주장을 ~ concede a point∥의지를 ~ bend one's will / act against one's will∥주장을 굽히지 않다 hold fast to one's own views / stick to one's guns∥필요한 때는 자기를 굽혀야 한다 We must bow to necessity.∥결국 그는 뜻을 굽히고 말았다 After all he gave up his ambition.∥그는 한사코 자기의 의견을 굽히려 하지 않았다 He won't change his opinion for anything.

굿¹ [벅적거리는 구경거리] a spectacle; an object of interest; a show (연극 등의); a sight.

굿² (무당의) *gut*; an exorcism; practices of an exorciser. ¶~ 들은 무당 a person who is only too happy to be of service.

굿 뒤에 날장구 친다 (속담) flog[mount on] a dead horse.

굿거리장단 a tune performed during exorcism.

궁(宮) 1 a (royal) palace. ⇨궁전 ¶덕~ the Changdeokgung. 2 [천] a sign; [점성] a (mundane) house. ¶황도(黃道) 12~ the (twelve) signs of the zodiac∥백양(白羊)~ Aries / the Ram. 3 [장기] the king or the queen; the *janggi*(chess) position of the king or queen.

궁궐(宮闕) the royal palace. ¶~ 같은 집 a palatial residence / a palace.

궁극(窮極) finality; extremity; eventuality. ¶~의 ultimate / final / extreme∥~의 승리 a final victory∥~의 목적 one's ultimate purpose [object]∥~적으로 in the final [last] analysis / ultimately / in the long run / in the end∥~적으로는 같은 결과가 된다 Ultimately [In the long run / In the end] the result will be the same.

궁글다 [속이 비다] hollow; empty; (소리가) deep; hollow; 《서술적》 be left empty. ¶속이 궁근 나무 a hollow tree.

궁금증(-症) [호기심] curiosity; [염려] anxiety. ¶~을 풀다 gratify [satisfy] one's curiosity.

궁금하다 anxious [worried / concerned / nervous] (about); 《서술적》 feel wonder [curious / curiosity]; wonder (about / if / whether / how / when / who). ¶소식이 ~ be anxious to hear from (a person)∥시험 결과가 ~ be worried about the result of the examination∥무슨 일이 일어났는지 ~ I wonder what happened.∥그들의 안부가 ~ I am anxious to know how they are.

궁기(窮氣) [궁한 기색] a meager appearance; a wretched look; wretchedness. ¶~가 낀 poor-looking.

궁내(宮內) the royal palace [court].

궁녀(宮女) a court lady; a lady-in-waiting (*pl.* ladies-in-waiting); a maid of honor.

궁노루 [동] a musk (deer).

궁도(弓道) archery; bowmanship.

궁둥이 the buttocks; the hips; the backsides; the seat (of one's pants); (구어) the bottom; (마소의) the rump. ¶~가 질기다 stay too long / overstay [outstay] one's welcome∥여자의 ~를 쫓아다니다 dangle after [about] a girl / philander∥내 바지 ~가 거의 닳았다 The seat of my trousers [(미) pants] is almost worn through. / My trousers are almost worn out in the seat.

궁둥이가 가볍다 [민첩하다] be ready [willing] to work; be quick to act. ¶궁둥이가 가벼운 여자 a wanton girl / a woman of loose [easy] morals [virtue]∥그녀는 ~ She is restless [flighty]. / She never sits still for long. / She can't sit still [stay put] for long.

궁둥이가 무겁다 be unwilling to work; be slow in starting work. ¶그는 ~ He is lazy [indolent]. / He is slow to get moving [act].

궁리(窮理) [연구] study [research] of the laws of nature; [생각함] deliberation; consideration; thinking [pondering] over. ¶~ 끝에 after much thinking∥밤새 ~ 끝에 집을 팔기로 했다 After thinking long and hard about it overnight, he decided to sell his house. **궁리하다** [연구하다] study the laws of nature; [생각하다] ponder [think / mull

궁박하다 over; cast about (in one's mind) (for a good plan). ¶그들은 사전을 사용하기 쉽도록 만들기 위해 여러 가지로 궁리했다 They came up with various ideas to make the dictionary easy to use. /어떻게든 궁리해 보죠 I'll see if I can't come up with something.

궁박하다(窮迫-) very poor; destitute; penurious; impecunious; poverty-stricken; distressed in a fix; in needy circumstances.

궁벽하다(窮僻-) secluded; remote; unfrequented; out-of-the-way. ¶궁벽한 곳 an out-of-the-way place / a secluded [remote] place / (미) the backcountry.

궁사(弓師) a bowyer, a bow maker.

궁상(窮狀) a sad [sorry] plight; a distressed state [condition]; straitened circumstances. ¶농촌의 ~은 실로 형언할 수 없다 The miserable life of farmers is really hard to describe.

궁상(窮相) a meager face; a poor [distressed] outlook.

궁상떨다(窮狀-) reveal one's straitened circumstances; complain of [grumble at] one's sad plight.

궁상맞다(窮狀-) miserable-looking; (서술적) have a look of poverty.

궁상스럽다(窮狀-) poor-looking. ¶궁상스러운 사람 a poor-looking man // 궁상스러운 옷차림을 하고 있다 be poorly [shabbily / seedily] dressed.

궁색하다(窮塞-) poor; destitute (of); distressed. ¶살림이 ~ be in needy [straitened] circumstances / be badly off.

궁성(宮城) a royal palace.

궁수(弓手) an archer; a bowman.

궁술(弓術) archery; bowmanship. ¶~ 사범 a master of archery.

궁여지책(窮餘之策) the last resort [expedient]; a desperate measure. ¶~으로서 as the last resort [expedient] / as a desperate measure [shift] // ~을 강구하다 resort to a last-ditch measure / fall back on [try] one's last resort // 나는 ~을 생각해 냈다 I have thought out a plan as the last resort.

궁인(宮人) a court lady.

궁전(宮殿) a (royal) palace. ¶~의 palatial // ~ 같은 집 a palace of a house / a palatial mansion // ~같이 호화로운 집 a house of palatial splendor / a house as gorgeous as a palace.

궁정(宮廷) the Court; Court circles. ¶~에서 at Court.
● **궁정 시인** a cavalier poet.

궁중(宮中) the Royal Court. ¶~에서 within the palace.
● **궁중 문학** court(ly) literature.

궁지(窮地) a difficult situation; a predicament; a sad [sorry] plight; a dilemma; extremity; a fix; (속어) a hot-seat. ¶~에 몰리다 [몰려 있다] stand [be] at bay / be pushed to the wall / be driven into a corner / (구어) be placed in a fix // ~에 몰아넣다 [빠뜨리다] drive [push] (a person) into a (tight) corner / put (a person) in a hole [fix] / (미국 속어) have (a person) over a barrel // 그는 ~에 빠졌다 He was caught in a dilemma. // 그는 ~에서 겨우 빠져나왔다 He managed to escape from his predicament. // 그는 친구를 ~에 빠뜨렸다 He drove his friend into a corner. // 나는 파산하여 ~에 빠져 있다 I've gone bankrupt and am in a terribly difficult situation.

궁지에 빠진 쥐가 고양이를 문다(속담) Despair makes [turns] cowards courageous.; A stag at bay is a dangerous foe.

궁체(宮體) the court style of Hangeul calligraphy.

궁핍하다(窮乏-) destitute; poor; penurious; needy; (서술적) be in poverty [need]; be reduced to poverty; be in needy [straitened] circumstances. ¶궁핍한 생활 a needy life / a life of distress [want] / (영) a life of austerity // 궁핍한 생활을 하다 live in destitution / 자금이 ~ We are in need of funds. // 시가 재정적으로 ~ The city is in financial difficulties.

궁하다(窮-) **1** (경제적으로) destitute; needy; hard up; indigent; penurious. ¶돈이 ~ be in need of money // 생활이 ~ be unable to make a living // 나는 지금 돈이 ~ I'm hard up (for money) now. // 그는 돈이 궁해서 집을 팔았다 Hard up [pressed] for money, the man sold his house. **2** [일이 난처하다] be at a loss; be at one's wit's [wits] end. ¶대답이 ~ be at a loss for an answer. **3** [궁지에 몰리다] cornered; (서술적) be driven to the wall; be in a dilemma [fix]; get into a scrape. ¶궁한 새가 품에 날아들면 포수도 쏘지 않는다 Even the hunter will refrain from killing the bird that has flown to him for shelter. / We help those who appeal to us in distress.

궁하면 통한다(속담) A person in dire enough need will find a way.; There is always a way out.; Want makes wit.

궁합(宮合) marital harmony as predicted by a fortuneteller. ¶~을 보다 compare the horoscopes of a young couple // 그 두 사람은 ~이 맞는다 The horoscopes of a young couple agree [assure married bliss].

궁형(弓形) **1** [활처럼 굽은 꼴] an arc; a bow; a crescent form. ¶~의 bow-shaped / arched / bowed / (건축의) arcuate. **2** ➡ 활꼴

궂다 1 [언짢다] bad; ill; undesirable; irksome; [불길하다] ominous; (성질이) cross; bad. ¶궂다 말이 없다 say neither good nor bad. **2** [날씨가] bad; foul; nasty; inclement; rainy; snowy; wet; soggy. ¶궂은 날씨 nasty weather.

궂은비 a long and nasty rain.

궂은살 proud flesh; granulation; an excrescence.

궂은일 1 [언짢은 일] an ugly job; an untoward event. ¶좋은 일이 있으면 ~도 있다 Good and evil are interwoven. / Every cloud has a silver lining. **2** [흉사] unlucky affairs; death.

권(卷) **1** (책의) a volume; a book; a copy. (▶서점 등에서 특정한 책을 「한 권, 두 권 …」하고 셀 때에는 book 대신 copy를 쓰는 경우가 많음) ¶제1~ the first volume / volume one / book one / 전(全) 3~의 책 a three-volume book / 전 6~의 저서 a work in six volumes // 책을 한 ~ 사다 buy a copy (of the Bible) // 이 책은 상하 두 ~으로 나누어져 있다 This book [work] is divided into two volumes. // 「천문학 입문」을 다섯 ~ 보내 주세요 Please send me five copies of An Introduction to

Astronomy.∥그는 한 ~의 저서도 없다 He has not published a single book.
2 [한지(韓紙)의 단위] twenty sheets of Korean paper; a Korean quire. ¶한지 두 ~ forty sheets of Korean paper.
3 [영화 필름 길이의 단위] a reel; a part. ¶전 5~의 영화 a five-reel picture[film] / a five-reeler.

권(勸) [추천] recommendation; [권고] advice; suggestion; [장려] encouragement. ¶…의 으로 on[at] the recommendation of ... / by [at] the advice of ... ∥ 의사의 ~에 따르다 follow one's doctor's advice.

-권(券) a bond; a ticket; a card; a (bank) note. ¶백 원 ~ a 100-won note[(미) bill] / 우대 ~ a complimentary ticket∥상품~ a merchandise bond[coupon].

-권(圈) a sphere; a circle; a range; a radius. ¶북극 ~ the Arctic Circle∥태풍 ~ 내에 in the typhoon area.

-권(權) [권력] authority; power; [권리] a right; a claim; [이권] a concession. ¶입법 ~ legislative power∥재산 ~ the right of property∥채굴 ~ a mineral power / a mining concession∥통치 ~ sovereignty.

권고(勸告) (a piece of) advice; counsel; recommendation; expostulation(충고). ¶간절한 ~ an earnest exhortation∥ ~ 사직을 당하다 resign (one's post) on an official suggestion∥친구의 ~로 by[at] the advice of a friend / at the instance [urging] of a friend∥ ~에 따르다 follow a person's advice∥의사의 ~로 조깅을 시작했다 I started jogging on my doctor's advice.∥의사의 ~에도 불구하고 그는 술을 끊지 않았다 He did not give up drinking in spite of the doctor's advice.∥조합은 중재 재판소의 ~를 따르지 않았다 The union did not comply with the recommendation of the court of arbitration. **권고하다** advise (a person to do / that); (문어) counsel a person (to do). ➔¶그는 사직을 권고받았다 He was urged to resign.
● **권고안** a recommendation.

권내(圈內) ¶~에 within the range[sphere] (of).

권농(勸農) encouragement of agriculture. **권농하다** encourage [promote] agriculture.
● **권농책** a farm encouragement policy.

권능(權能) competency; power; authority. ¶~을 부여하다 empower (a person) / authorize / vest (a person) with power.

권두(卷頭) the first[opening] page (of a book); the beginning[commencement] of a book.

권력(權力) power (over / with); authority (over / with); [세력] influence (over / with). ¶~과 금력 power and money / political and financial powers∥절대적 ~ absolute power∥…의 ~하에 under the authority of ...∥ ~의 행사 the exercise of power∥~이 있는 powerful / influential∥~이 없는 powerless / without authority[power]∥ ~을 얻다[잃다] gain[lose] power∥~을 휘두르다 exercise [use / wield] one's power[authority] (over)∥~을 쥐다 seize [take / assume] power / come to[into] power∥~을 쥐고 있다 be in the saddle / retain (absolute) power.
● **권력가** a man of power [influence]; a person in power; a power holder. **권력욕** (a) desire[lust] for power. **권력 투쟁** a struggle for power; a power struggle.

권리(權利) **1** [정당한 요구] a right (to / to do / of doing); a claim (to) (청구권); a privilege(특권); a title(소유권). ¶법률상의 ~ a legal right∥인간 고유의 ~ inalienable rights∥정당한 ~ a just right[claim]∥당연한 ~ a natural [due] right∥평등한 ~ an equal right∥법률[종교]상의 ~ a legal[religious] right∥ ~의 양도 the transfer of rights∥ ~와 의무 rights and duties∥평등한 ~로 on terms of equality∥ ~가 있다 have a right (to the title) / be entitled (to better treatment / to do)∥ ~가 없다 have no right (to (do) something / of doing) / be not entitled (to) ∥ ~를 부여하다 invest (a person) with rights / empower (a person to do)∥ ~를 취득[상실]하다 acquire [lose / forfeit] a right∥ ~를 포기하다 give up [waive / relinquish] one's rights∥ ~를 침해하다 infringe (up)on (a person's) right∥ ~를 빼앗다 deprive a person of a right / (부당하게) usurp a right∥ ~를 주장하다 assert one's right (to do) / insist[stand] (up)on one's rights∥ ~를 요구하다 claim [demand] one's rights∥ ~를 행사[남용]하다 exercise [abuse] one's rights∥ ~를 다투다 claim a right / contest a claim(법정에서) ∥시민은 생명, 자유, 행복을 누릴 ~를 갖는다 A citizen has the right to life, liberty and happiness.∥나는 그 편지를 읽을 ~가 있다[없다] I have the [no] right to read that letter.∥우리는 아무도 그 땅에 대한 ~가 없다 None of us can lay claim to the estate.
2 [영업권] goodwill. ¶~가게의 ~를 넘기다 transfer the goodwill of one's store.
● **권리금** (토지·영업 등의) a premium; (셋방·셋집 등의) key money. ¶비싼 ~이 붙은 임대 점포 a rented store[shop] with a high premium. **권리 능력** capacity of enjoyment of rights. **권리 행위** a rightful act.

권말(卷末) the end of a book[volume]. ¶~에 색인이 있다 There is an index at the back of the book.

권면(券面) the face of a bill; a denomination.

권모술수(權謀術數) scheming; trickery; wiles; machinations; Machiavellism. ¶~에 능한 사람 an expert[master] schemer∥~을 쓰다[부리다] resort to trickery / employ Machiavellian tactics∥그는 ~를 부려 정권을 잡았다 He seized power after some clever scheming.

권문세가(權門勢家) [권세가 있는 집안] an influential [a powerful] family; [권세가 있는 사람] a powerful [an influential] person; the great and powerful. ¶~에 아첨하다 curry favor with the powerful / be servile to those with influence / lick the boots of people in power.

권선(捲線) [전] a coil. ⇨ⁿ코일
● **권선기**(~機) a (coil) winding machine.

권선징악(勸善懲惡) promotion of virtue and reproval of vice; encouraging good and punishing evil.

권세(權勢) power; influence; authority. ¶아버지의 ~로 through the influence of one's father∥ ~를 쥐다 seize power / hold the reins of power∥ ~를 부리다 wield [exercise] power[authority]∥그는 시 의회에서 ~를 휘둘렀다 He exercised influence in the city council. / He wielded power [He was a

권속(眷屬) 1 [친족] one's (whole) family; [집안 사람·가신(家臣)] one's household; one's dependents. ¶일가~ a whole family / one's kith and kin // 그는 일가~을 거느리고 남미로 이주했다 He emigrated to South America with his whole family. 2 [아내] my wife.

권수(卷數) the number of volumes.

권신(權臣) an influential vassal; a powerful courtier.

권외(圈外) ¶~에 out of the range[sphere] (of) / outside the circle[range / radius] (of) // 그는 의장 입후보 선발에서 ~로 밀려났다 He has been dropped from the list of candidates for chairman.

권운(卷雲) [기상] a cirrus (*pl.* -ri).

권위(權威) 1 authority; power; [위엄] dignity; majesty; prestige. ¶국회의 ~ 향상 promotion of the authority of the Assembly // ~ 있는 authoritative (opinion) / (a historian [figure]) of authority / magisterial (words / opinion) / ~ 있는 책 an authoritative book // ~ 있는 소식통으로부터의 정보 a report from an authority / information received from an authority[authoritative source] // 경제학의 최고 ~ the greatest authority on economics // 그는 가정에서는 전혀 ~가 서지 않는다 He has no control at all over his family. / He has no authority in his home. // 교장은 학생들에게 ~가 있었다 The principal had great authority[power] over the boys and girls.
2 an authority. ⇨˚권위자(⇨권위)

● **권위자** an authority; [전문가] an expert; a specialist; [대가] a master. ¶현대[사계(斯界), 이 방면]의 최고 ~ the highest[foremost] authority of the day[in that line / on the subject]. **권위주의** authoritarianism.

권유(勸誘) an invitation (to); [운동] canvassing; solicitation; [장려] persuasion; encouragement. ¶만찬회의 ~ an invitation to a banquet. **권유하다** ask; invite (to do); induce; persuade (a person to do / into doing); canvass (for contributions). ¶보험을 [기부를] ~ canvass for insurance[subscription] // 가입을 ~ invite (a person) to join (a club) / 어떤 사람이 신문 구독을 권유하러 왔었다 A man came to solicit (me for) my subscription to a newspaper. // 그는 그녀에게 보험을 권유하였다 He tried to persuade her to buy insurance. ➔나는 최 군에게 권유받아 테니스부에 들어갔다 I have been persuaded by Mr. Choe to join the tennis club. // 나는 권유받아 그들의 극단에 가입했다 I was talked into joining their theatrical troupe. // 나는 그들의 계획에 참여하도록 권유받았다 I was invited to join[participate] in their plan. / They asked me to come in on their scheme.

권익(權益) (rights and) interests. ¶국가의 ~ national interests // ~을 옹호하다 protect [defend] one's interests.

권장(勸獎) encouragement; recommendation; promotion. ¶영어 선생님의 ~으로 이 테이프를 샀다 I bought this tape on the recommendation of my English teacher. **권장하다** encourage; recommend; promote. ¶운동 경기를 ~ encourage athletic sports // 국민에게 저축을 ~ encourage the people to save money // 임산부에 …할 것을 ~ give advice to the expectant and nursing mothers to (do).

권적운(卷積雲) [기상] a cirrocumulus. (*pl.* -li) (▶ 보통 복수형); a small, white, fleecy cloud.

권좌(權座) the seat of power; a position of authority[power]. ¶~를 떠나다 resign one's power // ~에서 쫓겨나다 be forced[removed] from power // ~에 있다 hold the seat of power / be in the saddle // ~에 앉다 come to [into] power.

권척(卷尺) a tape (measure); a tapeline. ⇨˚줄자

권총(拳銃) a pistol; a revolver(연발총); (미) a handgun; (미국 구어) a gun; a rod. **자동[연발] ~** an automatic[a six-chambered] revolver // 구경 38밀리의 ~ a 38 revolver // ~을 겨누다 point [level] a gun (at) // ~을 발사하다 fire[discharge] pistol[revolver] // ~으로 협박하다 threaten (a person) with a revolver // 그는 ~에 탄환을 장전했다 He loaded a gun. // 그는 나에게 ~를 들이댔다[발사하였다] He pointed [fired] a pistol at me. // 그는 ~으로 위협을 받아 돈 있는 곳을 알려 주었다 He was forced at gunpoint to tell where the money was.

● **권총 강도** an armed robber; a robber armed with a gun; a pistol burglar. **권총 자살** killing [shooting] oneself with a pistol [revolver].

권층운(卷層雲) a cirrostratus (*pl.* ~, -ti).

권태(倦怠) weariness; fatigue; languor; tedium; ennui. ¶~를 느끼다 feel tired [languid] / become weary [tired / fatigued] / feel languor / be [get] bored / have a tired feeling.

● **권태기** the stage of ennui in married life; a period of lassitude. ¶(부부의) ~에 들다 become weary of one's married life.

권토중래하다(捲土重來一) rally; make redoubled efforts; come back with renewed strength; [정] roll back.

권투(拳鬪) boxing; pugilism; a prize-fight(흥행). **권투하다** box (with); (구어) put on the gloves.

● **권투 선수** a boxer; a pugilist; (프로의) a professional [prize] fighter. **권투 시합** a boxing match; a (glove) fight; a prize fight(프로의). **권투 장갑** boxing gloves.

권하다(勸一) 1 [권고하다] ask; exhort; advise; suggest; encourage; persuade. ¶담배를 끊으라고 ~ advise (a person) to give up[quit] smoking / advise against smoking // 나는 담임선생님이 권해서 이 대학에 진학했다 I entered this university on my homeroom teacher's advice. // 그 교수는 나에게 외국 유학을 권했다 The professor encouraged [advised] me to study abroad. // 그에게 생명보험에 가입하라고 권해도 아무 소용없다 It is no use trying to persuade him to take out a life insurance policy. // 점원은 나에게 코트를 입어 보라고 권했다 The salesgirl suggested that I [urged me to] try the coat on.
2 [추천하다] recommend. ¶책을 ~ recommend a book (to a person) // 형이 이 사전을 나에게 권했다 My brother recommended this dictionary to me.
3 [음식·물건을] offer (a person something); present (a person with something). ¶담배 [차]를 ~ offer a cigarette[a cup of tea] // 술을 ~ offer (a person) (a glass of) wine

[liquor] / ask 《a person》 to have some liquor // 손님에게 억지로 음식을 권하지 마라 You must no press food on your guest. // 스튜어디스는 손님들에게 사탕을 권했다 The stewardess offered candy to the passengers. // 그는 나에게 술을 억지로 권했다 He pressed wine on me[me to drink the wine].

권한(權限) right; authority; power; [관할권] jurisdiction; [법] (관청·법원 등의) competence; competency; (권능의 한도) the authorized limit of rights[powers]. ¶관청의 ~ the competence of a government office // ~의 위임 delegation of power // ~ 다툼 conflict of attribution // ~ 내에[밖에] within[outside] one's rights[power] // ~ 밖의 unauthorized / outside one's authority // ~을 부여하다 empower 《a person》 / authorize // ~이 있다 have the right[authority / power] to 《do》 // ~을 벗어나다 exceed one's authority // …에게 ~을 위임하다 delegate authority[power] to // 당신은 명령할 ~이 없다 You have no authority[right] to give orders. // 무슨 ~으로 나를 심문하는가 On what authority are you questioning me? // 위원회는 그 문제를 조사할 ~이 부여되었다 The committee was authorized to investigate the matter. // 그것은 법관의 ~을 초월하는 행위다 That exceeds the competence[authority] of a judge.
● **권한 대행** ¶**대통령** ~ the acting President.

권화(權化) incarnation; personification; avatar.

궐기 대회(蹶起大會) an indignation meeting; a rally.

궐기하다(蹶起-) rise and go into action; rise; rouse 《oneself》 to action; spring up; stand up 《against》. ¶지금이야말로 궐기할 때이다 Now is the time for action. // 학생들은 그 법안 반대를 위해 궐기했다 The students rose in protest against the bill. ➔¶궐기시키다 rouse 《a person》 to action / stir up.

궐련 a cigarette. ¶~ 한 갑 a pack(et) of cigarettes // ~을 피우다 smoke a cigarette // ~을 입에 물고 with a cigarette between one's lips [in the corner of one's mouth].
● **궐련갑** a cigarette case.

궐석 재판(闕席裁判) judgment by default.

궐위(闕位) a vacancy; a vacant post[position]. ¶~가 생겼을 때 on the occurrence of a vacancy. **궐위하다** become vacant.

궤 a chest; a coffer; a box; a case.

궤간(軌間) a gauge; the gauge of a track. ¶표준 ~ the standard gauge.

궤도(軌道) 1 (천체의) an orbit; a circle. ¶~의 orbital // 극 ~ a polar orbit // 정지 ~ a geostationary orbit // 대기 ~ a parking orbit // 달 ~ the lunar[moon] orbit // 원 ~ a circular orbit // 주기 ~ a synchronous orbit // 지구 ~ the earth's orbit // 타원 ~ the elliptic orbit // 위성을 ~에 올려놓다 put a satellite into orbit / orbit a satellite // ~를 벗어나다 go out of orbit // 위성의 ~를 수정하다 adjust the orbit of a satellite // 인공위성이 ~에 올랐다 The satellite has gone into orbit.
2 (철도의) (미) a (railroad) track; (영) a railway track; a line; (전차의) a streetcar line; (영) a tramline. ¶단선[복선] ~ a single[double] (railroad) track // 전기 ~ an electric tramway // ~를 부설하다 lay tracks[a line].
3 [어떤 일의 과정] (a) track. ¶~에 오르다 (일이) be started along the right lines / get going / get on track // ~에 올라 있다 be well under way / be on the (right) track // ~에 올리다 set 《a business corporation》 on to way // 계획은 ~에 오르기 시작했다 The program is just getting under way.
● **궤도 비행** an orbital flight; orbiting.

궤멸(潰滅) [파괴] destruction; [전멸] annihilation. **궤멸하다** be destroyed; be annihilated. ➔¶반대 세력을 궤멸시키다 annihilate an opposition force.

궤범(軌範) an example; a model; a pattern; a standard.

궤변(詭辯) (a) sophism; (a) sophistry; quibbling; a false[vicious] syllogism; a paradox(역설). ¶~적(인) sophistic(al) / quibbling / paradoxical // ~을 부리다 quibble / use sophistry / sophisticate / chop logic [words] 《with a person》 // 그는 ~을 부리고 책임을 모면했다 He used some clever talk to get out of his responsibility. // 그는 ~을 늘어놓는 버릇이 있다 He has a way of using sophistry. // ~만 늘어놓지 말고 한번 실천해 보면 어떠하냐 Why don't you put it into practice instead of quibbling? // 하찮은 일에 ~을 늘어놓지 마라 Don't quibble over trivial matters. // ~으로 나를 속여 넘길 수는 없지 You can't fool me with that absurd[ridiculous / farfetched] argument.
● **궤변가** a sophist; a quibbler.

궤양(潰瘍) [의] an ulcer. ¶~의 ulcerous.

궤적(軌跡) 1 [바퀴 자국] a rut; a (wheel) track; the print of a wheel; a furrow. 2 [수] ➔자취2

궤주(潰走) a rout; a flight; (동물군의) a stampede. **궤주하다** be routed; be put to flight [rout]. ¶그의 연대는 궤주했다 His regiment retreated in disorder. ➔¶적을 궤주시키다 put the enemy to rout[flight] / have the enemy on the run.

궤짝(櫃-) a box; a case. ¶사과 한 ~ a box of apples // ~에 담다 put 《a thing》 in a box.

귀 1 [듣는 기관] an ear; [청각] hearing. ¶손으로 ~를 가리다 cover one's ears with one's hands / put one's hands over one's ears // ~에 펜을 꽂다 have a pen (stuck) behind one's ear // ~를 우비다 pick one's ears // 한쪽 ~로 듣고 한쪽 ~로 흘리다 go in (at) one ear and go out (at) the other // 그녀는 내 ~에 대고 속삭였다 She spoke in my ear. // 그는 병으로 ~가 들리지 않게 되었다 He lost his hearing because of an illness. // 그 개는 이상한 소리에 ~를 쫑긋 세웠다 The dog pricked up its ears at the strange sound. // 낮에 들은 여자의 비명 소리가 아직도 ~에 쟁쟁하다 The screams of the woman (that) I heard during the day are still ringing in my ears. // 그 말이 아직도 ~에 생생하다 His words still ring in my ears[linger in my heart / haunt my memory]. // 이 규칙은 ~에 걸면 귀걸이 코에 걸면 코걸이식이다 This rule admits of several interpretations. / This rule reads several ways. // ~ 좀 빌립시다 May I have a word in your ear? / Could I have a word with you?
2 [귓바퀴] a concha (pl. -chae); an auricle. ¶그녀는 ~가 작다 She has small ears.
3 a spout. ➪귀때
4 [모서리] a corner; (문어) a nook. ¶책장의

~ the corner of a page (in a book) // 책장의 ~를 접다 make a dog-ear / dog-ear // 손수건을 ~를 맞추어 접다 fold a handkerchief neatly.
5 [바늘구멍] the eye of a needle; an eye.
6 [돈머리에 붙은 우수리] an additional [odd] amount; an odd sum [fraction]. ¶값은 만 원에다가 ~가 달린다 The price is ten thousand won and a little in addition.
귀가 번쩍 뜨이다 have one's attention drawn (to); have (it) brought to one's ears. ¶그 일에 ~ have the matter come to one's attention.
귀가 솔깃하다 ¶귀가 솔깃해지는 이야기 welcome [encouraging / good] news // 귀가 솔깃해지는 조건 a tempting offer / inviting terms // 그에게는 귀가 솔깃해지는 이야기였다 That was welcome news to him. / He was very glad [happy] to hear that.
귀가 절벽이다 1 [아주 들리지 않다] be as deaf as a adder [door post]. **2** know but little [have but little knowledge] of (the ways of) the world; be out of touch with the world. ¶그들은 회사의 속사정에 대해서는 ~ They were ill-informed about the inside affairs of the company.
귀(를) 기울이다 listen to (music); strain one's ears (to). ¶그는 내 탄원에 귀를 기울이지 않았다 He turned a deaf ear [would not hear] to my pleas.
귀(가) 따갑다 ¶그 이야기는 귀가 따갑도록 들었다 I am sick (and tired) of hearing the story. / I have heard enough of the story.
귀가 뜨다 begin [start] to hear for the first time (after the birth); begin to perceive a voice [sound] by the ear.
귀를 의심하다 ¶나는 그의 말을 들었을 때 내 귀를 의심했다 When I heard what he said, I couldn't believe my ears.
귀에 거슬리다 ¶귀에 거슬리는 충고 a piece of advice that is hard to take // 귀에 거슬리는 소리 a harsh grating noise / a jarring noise.
귀에 못이 박히다 ¶그것은 귀에 못이 박히도록 들었소 I'm sick and tired of hearing it. / I'm fed up with it.
귀(가) 울다 ¶내 귀가 운다 I have a buzzing in my ears. / My ears are ringing.
귀(에) 익다 get used to hearing; be familiar to one's ears. ¶귀에 익은 목소리 a familiar voice // 수화기에서 귀에 익은 그녀의 목소리가 들려왔다 I heard her familiar voice over the phone.
귀(貴) [당신의] your; your esteemed. ¶~ 상점 your store [shop] / (지점 등) your branch / your office // ~ 정부 your government.
귀-(貴) [귀한] valuable; noble; precious. ¶~ 금속 the precious [noble] metals.
귀가(歸家) return(ing) home; home-coming. ¶~ 도중에 on one's way home // ~ 후 after one's return home // ~가 늦다 be late in returning home. **귀가하다** [돌아오다] come home; return home; [돌아가다] go home. ¶그는 늘 밤늦게 귀가하곤 했다 He used to return home late at night. / ¶이제 슬슬 귀가할 시간이다 It's about time to go home.
귀감(龜鑑) a model; a paragon; a pattern; a good [shining] example; a mirror; an exemplar. ¶군인의 ~ a model soldier / a pattern [paragon] of soldiery // 남의 ~이 되다 exemplify oneself / set an example to the world.

귀갑(龜甲) (a) tortoise shell; the carapace of a tortoise.
귀걸이 1 [귀걸이안경] spectacles with strings for bows; [귀에 거는 방한용 물건] earmuffs. **2** an earring. ⇨▷귀고리
귀결(歸結) [결말] a conclusion; [결과] a consequence; a result. ¶~을 짓다 bring (a matter) to a conclusion [an end] / draw [form] a conclusion // 입학시험에 실패한 것은 당연한 ~이다 It was a foregone conclusion that he would fail his entrance examinations. / His failure to get into the school was only to be expected. **귀결하다** end; be concluded; come to an end; [결과가 되다] result. ➔그 소송은 원고의 패소로 귀결될 것이다 The plaintiff will lose the case in the end.
귀경(歸京) one's return to Seoul [the capital]. **귀경하다** return to Seoul [the capital].
귀고리 an earring; a pendant.
귀골(貴骨) [귀한 집안의 사람] a person of noble birth; high personage; [귀인의 골격] noble feature.
귀공자(貴公子) a young nobleman; (문어) a scion of a noble family. ¶~다운 princely (young man) / noble-looking / aristocratic (air / appearance).
귀국(貴國) your (esteemed) country.
귀국(歸國) returning home from abroad; homecoming; return to one's country. ¶~ 명령을 받다 be ordered home [back to Korea] // ~ 길에 오르다 leave for home / start [set out] on one's journey home // ~ 길에 있다 be on one's way home / be homeway bound // ~ 도중에 on one's journey [way] home / on one's homeward voyage [trip]. **귀국하다** go [come / return] home; return [go back] to one's country. ¶그는 미국에 귀국했다 He is back home in the United States. // 우리는 전쟁 후 중국에서 귀국했다 We returned [were repatriated] from China soon after the war.
귀금속(貴金屬) [쉽게 화학 변화를 일으키지 않는 금속] a noble metal; [값비싼 희귀 금속] a precious metal.
● **귀금속상** (상인) a dealer in precious metals; (미) a jeweler; (상점) a jewelry store.
귀납(歸納) [논] induction; generalization. **귀납하다** induce; generalize; make an induction (from). ¶경험에서 일반적 원리를 ~ induce general principles from one's experience.
● **귀납법** the inductive method; induction.
귀납적(歸納的) inductive. ¶~ 논리 inductive logic [philosophy] // ~ 추리 inductive reasoning [inference] // ~으로 추론하다 reason inductively [a posteriori].
귀넘어듣다 take no notice of; pay no attention to; let (an advice) go by; [무시하다] neglect; ignore. ¶그는 내 충고를 귀넘어들었다 He paid no attention to [took no attention of / neglected] my advice.
귀농하다(歸農-) return to [go back to] farming; (원래 농민이 아닌 사람이) become a farmer [rancher]; take up farming [ranching].
귀담아듣다 listen willingly [attentively]; listen carefully; stuff one's ears with (a person's words). ¶그는 내 충고를 귀담아듣지 않았다 He turned a deaf ear to my advice.

귀대하다(歸隊-) return to one's unit [company / regiment]; (장교가) rejoin one's command.

귀댁(貴宅) your home.

귀동냥 hearsay; second-hand knowledge. ¶~으로 배우다 pick something up from others [others conversation] / learn about something by listening to what people say // 그는 ~으로 많은 것을 알고 있다 He has a smattering knowledge of many things. // ~도 쓸모가 있다 Picked-up knowledge is useful, too. **귀동냥하다** learn (a thing) by ear; pick up (information).

귀동자(貴童子) a precious [beloved] son.

귀두(龜頭) [생] the glans (*pl*. glandes).
● **귀두염** [의] balanitis.

귀둥이(貴-) a pet [beloved] child.

귀매 [주전자의 부리 같은 물 따르는 구멍] a spout. ¶항아리의 ~ the spout of a pot.

귀뚜라미 [동] a cricket. ¶~가 운다 A cricket chirps.

귀띔 a suggestion; a hint; a tip; an intimation. ¶~을 받다 receive secret [confidential] information / get the tip (on / about). **귀띔하다** give a hint [tip]; suggest; tip off; intimate; give [make] suggestion. ¶남에게 사실을 귀띔해 주다 tip a person off to the fact // 너에게 귀띔해 줄 일이 있다 I have something for your private ear. // 그가 사실을 귀띔해 주었다 He told me about the fact under the rose. // 먼저 가라고 귀띔했다 He suggested that I go first.

귀로(歸路) one's way home; one's homeward way. ¶~에 on one's way home [back] // ~에 오르다 make one's way home / start on one's way home // ~를 서두르다 hurry home / quickly make one's way home // ~에 …에 들르다 stop over [off] at … on one's way home // 유럽 여행의 ~에 on one's return trip from Europe // 7시에 ~에 올랐다 I left for home at seven. // ~에 그의 집에 들렀다 I dropped in on him on my way home. // 비가 올 것 같아 ~를 서둘렀다 As it looked like rain, I hurried home. // ~에는 비행기를 탔다 I returned [came back] by plane.

귀리 [식] oats (▶ 보통 복수형).

귀머거리 a deaf person; (집합적) the deaf. ¶~이다 be deaf / be hard of hearing // ~가 되다 become deaf.

귀먹다 lose one's hearing; be deaf. ¶그는 병으로 해서 귀먹었다 He lose his hearing because of an illness.

귀물(貴物) [진품] a rare articles; a curio; [귀중품] an article of value; a treasure; (집합적) valuables.

귀밑머리 hair braided behind the ears.

귀부(龜趺) the turtle base of a stone monument.

귀부인(貴婦人) a lady; a titled lady; a noblewoman; a society dame(사교계의). ¶~다운 ladylike.

귀빈(貴賓) an honored [a distinguished] guest; an important guest.
● **귀빈석** seats reserved for honored guests; the royal box. **귀빈실** room reserved for special guests; a room for VIPs [Very Important Persons].

귀뿌리 the root of the ear. ¶~까지 빨개지다 blush to the roots of one's ears.

귀사(貴社) your company [firm].

귀성(歸省) homecoming; coming home; visiting one's parents at home. ¶~ 중에 during one's return visit. **귀성하다** go [come / return] home; visit one's parents at home. ¶귀성하는 학생 a student going home for the holidays / a homecoming student.
● **귀성객** homecoming people. **귀성열차** a (special) train for homecoming people.

귀소 본능(歸巢本能) the homing instinct.

귀속(歸屬) reversion; return; [소속] possession. ¶남극 대륙의 ~ 문제 the question of title to Antarctica. **귀속하다** (재산 등이 복귀되다) revert (to); (소속되다) belong (to); return to; be returned to. ¶국고에 ~ revert to the State (Treasury). → 그녀의 재산은 국가에 귀속될 것 같다 Her property will probably revert to the state. // 그 섬들은 한국에 귀속된다 Those islands belong to Korea.
● **귀속 재산** government-vested property; properties reverted to the government.

귀순(歸順) defection; submission; return to allegiance; defection(변절); surrender(항복). ¶반란군은 항복하고 정부군에 ~을 서약했다 The rebels surrendered and swore allegiance to the government forces. **귀순하다** submit; defect; surrender; return to allegiance.
● **귀순병** a soldier returned to allegiance; a submitted soldier. **귀순자** a defector.

귀신(鬼神) 1 [혼령] a departed soul; a spirits; [유령] a ghost; [요괴] apparition. ¶~이 나오는 집 a haunted house // 피살된 여자의 ~ the apparition [ghost] of a murdered woman // ~을 내쫓다 drive away [exorcise] evil spirits (from [out of] a person [place]) / exorcise (a person) of evil spirit // 저 방에는 ~이 나온다고 한다 That room said to be haunted. // 그날은 ~이 나올 듯한 밤이었다 It was a ghostly night. // 그는 ~의 존재를 믿지 않았다 He didn't believe in spirits.
2 [뛰어난 사람] a master; an expert; a proficient (in); a demon (at golf). ¶그는 돈을 버는 데는 ~이다 He is an expert at money-making. // 그는 남의 마음을 읽는 데는 ~이다 He has an amazing ability to read other people's minds.

귀신도 모르다 ¶그는 귀신도 모르게 그것을 했다 He did it without attracting anybody's attention. // 그것은 귀신도 모른다 No one knows it.

귀신(이) 들리다 be possessed (by / with). ⇨귀신(이) 씌우다(⇨귀신)

귀신(이) 씌우다 be possessed (by / with). ¶그 여자는 귀신이 씌어 있었다 The woman was possessed [in a religious frenzy].

귀신이 곡할 노릇이다 be strange [mysterious / unaccountable]. ¶그 서류가 감쪽같이 없어지다니 귀신이 곡할 노릇이다 How the documents have disappeared is a mystery. / I wonder how the papers could have disappeared.

귀신같다(鬼神-) (재주가) be a master [an expert / a demon]; be proficient. ¶그것은 정말 귀신같은 솜씨였다 I couldn't imagine that such a feat was humanly possible. / It was beyond human power. // 그는 귀신같은 재주를 보여 주었다 He gave [put on] an inspired performance.

귀싸대기 ¶~를 올리다 slap (a person) on the face / box (a person's) ear // ~를 맞다 be slapped on the face.

귀얄 a paste[paint] brush.
귀양 banishment; exile; deportation; transportation. ¶그들은 그를 절해의 고도에 ~을 보냈다 They banished[exiled] him to a solitary faraway island.
  귀양(을) 가다 be exiled to a remote place; be banished to a distant[remote] place; go into exile. ¶그는 먼 섬으로 귀양을 갔다 He was sent in exile on a remote island.
  ● **귀양살이** living in exile.
귀엣말 a whisper. ⇨⁼귓속말
귀여겨듣다 listen[bend an ear] (to); listen carefully[with attention]; be all attention [ears]. ¶내 말을 귀여겨듣고 명심해라 Listen to what I say and bear it in your mind.
귀여워하다 love; be affectionate to; treat with affection; pet; make a pet of; be attached to; treat tenderly[kindly]; [애무하다] caress; fondle. ¶귀여워하는 아이 one's pet[beloved] child / one's darling (child) /개를 ~ make a pet of a dog /어머니들은 종종 아이들을 너무 귀여워한다 Mothers often spoil their children. /아이는 인형을 귀여워했다 The child fondled her doll. //그 부인은 나를 친자식처럼 귀여워합니다 She holds me as dear as her own child.
귀염 love; affection; attachment. ¶~을 받다 be loved (by) / be beloved (by / of) / be favored (by) / be liked[petted] (by) / be a favorite (with a person) / win (another's) love[heart] //그는 모든 사람에게 ~ 받고 있다 He is beloved of[by] all. / He is liked by everybody. //그 아이는 이웃 사람들에게 ~ 받고 있다 The boy is a favorite with his neighbors.
  ● **귀염둥이** a beloved[favorite] child; a darling (child); a pet (child). **귀염성** the charm of childhood; attractiveness; amiability; lovableness; sweetness. ¶~ 있는 얼굴 a lovely[sweet] face.
귀엽다 lovely; charming; cute; attractive; winning; dear; darling; [예쁘다] sweet; nice; pretty; (미국 구어) cute (girl / hat). ¶귀여운 애 a lovable[sweet / charming] child //귀여운 자식 one's dear[precious] child //귀여운 인형 a lovely doll //귀여운 태도 a charming manner / fetching ways //귀여운 목소리로 in a sweet voice //그녀는 얼굴이 ~ She has a lovely face. //그녀에겐 제법 귀여운 데가 있다 There's something pretty[charming / appealing] about her. //손녀가 귀여워 죽겠다 I have a real soft spot (in heart) for my granddaughter.
귀영하다(歸營─) return to barracks.
귀울음 ear noises. ⇨⁼이명(耳鳴)
귀의(歸依) [믿음] faith; devotion. **귀의하다** come to believe [have faith] (in Yahweh); become a (devout) believer (in Buddhism); (문어) embrace (Christianity). ¶불교에 귀의하여 생애를 보내다 lead a devoted[devout] Buddhist life.
  ● **귀의자** a devotee.
귀이개 an earpick.
귀인(貴人) a man of distinction; a noble man.
귀일하다(歸──) be united into one; be reduced to one; be unified.
귀임(歸任) return to one's post ¶~ 중이다 be on the way back to one's post. **귀임하다** return[go back / come back] to one's post [duty]; resume one's official duties. ¶서울로 ~ return to one's post in Seoul.

귀재(鬼才) [뛰어난 재능의 소유자] an unusual genius; a prodigy; a man of remarkable talent; a man of no common ability; (구어) a wizard; [뛰어난 재능] unusual [remarkable] talent. ¶금세기 제일의 바이올린의 ~ the greatest violinist of this century.
귀족(貴族) [집합적] the nobility; nobles; the peerage; the aristocracy; blue blood; [훌륭한 가문의 개인] a noble; a nobleman; a noblewoman; a peer; an aristocrat. ¶~의 noble / aristocratic / titled / noble-[blue-]blooded // ~적인 취미 aristocratic taste // ~ 출신의 blue-blooded //그는 ~ 출신이다 He is of noble birth.
  ● **귀족 계급** the aristocratic class. **귀족 정치** aristocracy.
귀중(貴中) Messrs(▶ Messieurs의 약어). ¶스미스 상회 ~ Messrs. Smith & Co. //서울 대학교 ~ (To) Seoul National University.
귀중품(貴重品) an article of value; [집합적] valuables. ¶~을 금고에 보관하다 keep valuables in a safe.
귀중하다(貴重─) precious; valuable. ¶귀중한 보물 precious treasures //귀중한 시간 precious time //귀중한 충고 priceless [valuable] advice //귀중한 생명과 재산 valuable life and property //건강은 귀중한 재산이다 Health is a precious possession. //참으로 귀중한 경험이었다 It was very valuable experience. //귀중한 것은 부근에 놓아 두지 마시오 Don't leave valuables lying around. **귀중히** preciously; valuably. ¶~ 여기다 prize / value / treasure.
귀지 earwax; wax; cerumen. ¶~를 파내다 clean the wax out of one's ears.
귀지(貴紙) your paper; your honored [valued] paper; your (esteemed) columns. ¶~를 통하여 through the medium of your columns // 4월 20일자 ~ 보도대로 as stated in your paper dated April 20.
귀지(貴誌) your magazine.
귀착(歸着) 1 [돌아옴] return; coming back. **귀착하다** return; come [get] back; be back (home). ¶무사히 ~ reach home in safety / arrive back (in Korea) safely //그는 서울에 귀착했다 He arrived back in Seoul. //전투기는 기지에 귀착했다 The fighter planes returned to base.
2 [귀결] conclusion. ¶논의의 ~점 the logical conclusion of an argument. **귀착하다** arrive at (a result / a conclusion); result [end] in; resolve itself into[to]; add up to; boil down to. ¶결국은 돈 문제로 귀착한다 After all it is a question of money. / The question resolves itself into a question of money. / Ultimately it comes[boils] down to a question of money. //이 문제들은 결국 세 점에 귀착한다 These problems will resolve into three points.
귀찮다 troublesome; annoying; bothering; harassing; bothersome; tiresome; (미국 구어) pesky; irksome (work). ¶귀찮은 일 troublesome [bothersome] task / a bother / 귀찮은 소리 annoying remarks / nonsense // 귀찮은 듯이 with an annoyed look [air] // 귀찮게 annoyingly / tiresomely / irksomely / 귀찮게 굴다 behave in an annoying way / annoy [bother / trouble] a person / make a nuisance of oneself //귀찮게 조르다 ask

importunately for (money) / importune (a person) for (money) / importune (a person) to give one (money) // 귀찮게 질문하다 trouble [pester / plague] (a person) with questions // 귀찮게 따라다니다 pay (a person) cumbrous attentions / dance attendance on (a person) / tag [dangle] after (a person) // 귀찮아하다 feel annoyed (at / by) / regard (a matter) as a nuisance / find [consider] (a matter) troublesome [annoying] // 귀찮게 하지 마라 Don't bother me. / Leave me alone. // 세상이 ~ I am sick (and tired) of the world. // 긴 머리는 ~ Long hair is troublesome [gets in the way]. // 파리가 ~ Flies are a nuisance. // 그는 내 질문을 조금도 귀찮아하지 않고 친절히 대답해 주었다 He answered my questions kindly without regarding them as a nuisance. // 그는 급우들의 귀찮은 존재였다 He was a nuisance to his classmates. // 이렇게 바쁜 때에 그것은 참으로 귀찮은 이야기다 It is really a bother [annoying] when I am so busy. // 그가 귀찮은 일을 가지고 왔다 He brought in a troublesome task. // 귀찮아하지 말고 매일 조깅을 하시오 Go jogging everyday without telling yourself it's too much trouble. // 나는 그것들을 그들에게 개별적으로 되돌려 주는 일이 귀찮았다 I am tired of sending them back to each person individually. // 더 이상 귀찮게 하지 않겠다 I won't put you to [cause you / give you] any further trouble. // 귀찮게 해서 미안하지만 복사기 쓰는 법 좀 가르쳐 주시오 I am sorry to trouble [bother] you, but will you show me how to use the copying machine? // 그는 이발소에 가는 것을 매우 귀찮아했다 He thought it too much trouble to go to the barber's. // 그녀는 귀찮아하지 않고 시어머니 시중을 든다 She does not spare herself in taking care of her mother-in-law. // 그녀는 아이들이 따라다녀도 조금도 귀찮아 하지 않는다 She does not look at all annoyed [doesn't seem to mind at all] when children tag along after her.

귀천 (貴賤) the noble and the base; patrician and plebeian; high and low; dear and cheap. ¶~을 가리지 않고 [의 구별 없이] regardless [irrespective] of rank / without distinction of rank (or position) / high and low alike / from palace to hovel // 빈부 ~의 구별 없이 민주주의를 위해 모두가 힘을 합쳤다 Rich and poor, high and low united in the cause of democracy. // 직업에는 ~이 없다 All occupations [honest trades] are equally honorable. / Every honest occupation deserves esteem.

귀청 the eardrum. ⇨ ☞고막(鼓膜)

귀추 (歸趨) a tendency; a trend; a drift; [낙착점] the issue; the outcome; the consequence. ¶마땅한 [당연한] ~로서 as a natural course of events / as a natural consequence // ~를 지켜보다 watch the development [course] of events / wait for the turn of events / wait and see how things will turn out // 문제의 ~를 지켜보다 ascertain how the issue will develop // 당연한 ~로서 우리 당은 두 파로 분열되었다 As a natural consequence [In the natural course of events] our party broke up into two factions.

귀퉁이 1 [귀의 언저리] parts around the ear. 2 [모퉁이] a corner; an edge. ¶탁자 ~ the corner of a table.

귀티 (貴-) [고귀한 태도] a noble [an elegant / a graceful] figure [manner / attitude]; [귀여운 태도] a charming [a lovely / an attractive] manner [attitude / air]. ¶~가 나다 be [look] noble [elegant / graceful] / be charming [lovely / attractive].

귀하 (貴下) 1 [당신] you. 2 [께] (남자에게) Mr. (pl. Messrs.); (영) Esq.; (여자에게) Ms [Ms.] (pl. Mses, Ms's); (기혼녀에게) Mrs [Mrs.] (pl. Mrs., Mmes.); (미혼녀에게) Miss (pl. ~es). ¶아담 스미스 ~ Mr. Adam Smith / Adam Smith, Esq.

귀하다 (貴-) 1 [고귀하다] noble; (문어) august; high; exalted; honorable; venerable. ¶귀한 가문 a noble family // 귀한 분 a high personage / a person of noble birth / a person of high rank // 어떤 귀하신 분 a certain nobleman [(문어) an august personage].
2 [드물다] rare; scarce; few; [진귀하다] uncommon; unusual; curious; [소중하다] precious; valuable; highly prized. ¶귀한 물건 a precious [valuable] thing / a rare article // 귀한 자식 one's beloved child // 귀한 손님 a welcome visitor // 귀한 경험 a unique [valuable] experience // 요즈음은 좋은 쌀이 ~ Nowadays good rice is rather rare [hard to get]. // 생명보다 귀한 것은 없다 Nothing is so precious as life.

귀함 (貴函) your (esteemed) letter.

귀함하다 (歸艦-) return to one's warship; rejoin one's ship.

귀항 (歸航) a homeward [return] voyage [trip]; an inward voyage; a return passage. ¶~ 길에 오르다 start on the return [homeward] voyage [trip] // ~ 중이다 be homeward-bound / be on a return [homeward] trip. 귀항하다 make a homeward voyage [trip]; make a return passage; sail for home; resail; sail back.

귀항하다 (歸港-) return to port; put [sail] back to port.

귀향 (歸鄕) a homecoming; going home; return to one's native place [birthplace]. 귀향하다 go [come] (back) home; return (to one's old) home; return to one's home town [birthplace]. ¶휴가로 귀향해 있다 be home for the holidays / (미) be vacationing at one's home (town) / be back home for the vacation.

귀화 (歸化) [국적 이전] naturalization. ¶~ 캐나다 시민 a Canadian citizen by naturalization // ~를 허가하다 (미) confer citizenship (upon). 귀화하다 be [become] naturalized (in America / as an American citizen). ¶그는 한국에 귀화하였다 He became a naturalized Korean citizen. / He was naturalized as a Korean citizen. // 그는 귀화하여 미국 사람이 되었다 He is American by naturalization.
● **귀화인** a naturalized citizen; (영) [법] a denizen.

귀환 (歸還) one's return (home); repatriation (본국으로의). 귀환하다 return; return [come] home; be repatriated. ¶기지로 무사히 ~ return safely to the base / make it back to the base // 지구에 무사히 ~ return to earth safely // 그는 일선에서 무사히 귀환했다 He came back from the front in safety.
● **귀환병** a returned [repatriated] soldier

[serviceman]. **귀환자** a returnee; [본국 송환자] a repatriate.

귀휴(歸休) [군] temporary release (of a soldier) before the expiration of his term of service. ¶~ 중이다 be on leave from the service. **귀휴하다** be released (before the expiration of one's term of service).
● **귀휴병** a soldier (sent) home on leave; a soldier released temporarily before his time.

귓가 the rim of the ear.

귓결 hearing by chance. ¶~에 unexpectedly / accidentally / casually / by chance / by accident // ~에 듣다 happen to hear / hear by chance // ~에 여인의 울음소리가 들려왔다 By chance a woman's sobbing came into my ears.

귓구멍 the earhole; the (external) auditory canal[meatus]; the opening of the ear. ¶~을 후비다 pick[clean] one's ears / ~이 막히다 one's ears are clogged up[blocked off].

귓등 the back of the ear. ¶~으로 듣다 do not listen carefully / take no notice (of) / pay no attention (to) / be deaf to (a person's remonstrances) // 그는 내 충고를 ~으로 들었다 He paid no attention to[(문어) took no heed of] my advice. / (구어) He didn't give two hoots about my advice.

귓문(-門) the auditory opening; the outer part of the earhole.

귓바퀴 [생] a concha (*pl.* -chae); an auricle; a pinna (*pl.* ~s, -nae).

귓밥 [귓불의 두께] the thickness of an earlobe.

귓병(-病) an ear disease[ailment / trouble]; an earache; [의] otalgia. ¶~을 앓다 have an earache / have a pain in the ear.

귓불 an earlobe; an earlap; the lobe of the ear. ¶~이 크다 [두툼하다] have thick lobes to one's ears // ~을 잡아당기다 pull (a person) by his lobe / pull the lobe of (a person's) ear // ~만 만지다 be at a loss / do not know (what to do) / be fogged / be in a quandary // 그녀는 ~까지 빨개졌다 She blushed to the roots of her hair.

귓속말 a whisper; whispering. ¶~로 in a whisper // ~을 주고받다 whisper to each other / talk in whispers. **귓속말하다** whisper (to a person); speak[tell] in a person's ear.

귓전 the ear rims. ¶~에서 about[close to] one's ears / ~에 대고 소리치다 yell into (a person's) ear // ~으로 듣다 hear casually / happen to hear.

규격(規格) a standard; a norm; a gauge. ¶KS ~ Korean (Industrial) Standards // ~ 외 품 a nonstandardized article / an article that does not meet (government) standards / (규격 미달의) a substandard article // ~에 맞다 meet standard requirements / ~에 맞추다 make a thing meet (come up to) standards // ~을 통일하다 standardize.
● **규격품** standardized goods[articles]. **규격화** standardization; normalization.

규명(糾明) a close examination; a searching [grilling / minute] examination. **규명하다** examine (a matter) closely; look[inquire] into (a matter) minutely. ¶죄상을 ~ grill a suspect to establish his guilt / 사건의 진상을 ~ find out the real truth of the matter / get to the bottom of the case // 사고의 원인을 ~ investigate the cause of an accident // 진위를 규명해야 한다 We must find out whether it is true or not. // 이 독직 사건은 철저히 규명하자 We will carry out a thorough investigation of[into] this corruption case.

규모(規模) 1 [규범] a rule; a pattern; [짜임새] a scale; [범위] (a) scope; [설계] (a) plan; [구조] structure. ¶~가 큰 large-scale (warfare) / large in scale // ~가 작은 small-scale (plan) / small in scale // 대[소]~로 on a large[small] scale / in a large[small] way // 국제적[전국적]인 ~로 on an international [a nationwide] scale / ~를 확대[축소]하다 enlarge[reduce] the plan (of) / upscale [downscale] // 그들은 핵 실험 반대 운동을 전국적 ~로 벌였다 They started a movement against nuclear test on a nationwide scale. // 저 공장은 매우 ~가 크다 That factory is run on a very extensive scale.
2 [씀씀이의 한도] a budget limit. ¶~ 있게 돈을 쓰다 make effective use of one's money.

규방(閨房) women's quarters; a boudoir; a lady's (living) room.
● **규방 문학** literature depicting women's life in feudal society.

규범(規範) [본보기] a model; an example; a pattern; [법칙·원리] a law; a (fundamental) rule; a regulation; a principle; [표준] a standard; a norm; a criterion (*pl.* -ria, ~s). ¶~적인 normative // 건전한 사회 ~ a sound social ethos / 도덕적 ~ a moral precepts / ~에 따르다 follow an example / 행동의 ~이 되다 be a model of (good) behavior.
● **규범 법칙** a normative law.

규산(硅酸) [화] silicic acid.
● **규산염** a silicate.

규석(硅石) [광] silicon dioxide; silica.

규소(硅素) [화] silicon(기호 Si).

규수(閨秀) 1 [처녀] a maiden; a virgin; a maid. ¶민 씨 댁 ~ Mr. Min's daughter. 2 [학식 있는 여자] an accomplished lady [woman]. ¶~ 시인 a poetess / a female poet // ~ 작가 a woman[female / lady] writer / an authoress.

규약(規約) [협약] an agreement; a covenant; a pact; a compact; [규정] rules; a bylaw(내규); [정관] the articles[statutes] (of an association). ¶협회의 ~ the articles of an association / ~을 정하다 make[lay down] rules / ~을 맺다 make[fix up] an agreement (between / with) / enter into an agreement [a covenant] (with) // ~을 어기다 break the terms of an agreement.

규율(規律) 1 [질서] order; discipline; observance(수도회의); [조직] system. ¶엄격한 rigid discipline // ~이 엄격한 사람 a disciplinarian / a methodist // ~ 있는 orderly / systematical / (well-)disciplined / regular // ~ 없는 disorderly / irregular / undisciplined / tumultuary (troops) // ~ 있게 [바르게] in good order / in an orderly manner / systematically // ~을 유지하다 maintain discipline // ~ 있는 생활을 하다 lead an ordered[disciplined] life // 군대는 ~이 엄격하다 Discipline is strictly enforced in the army. // 그 학교 학생들은 ~이 썩 잘 잡혀 있다 The students of the school are under perfect discipline.
2 [준칙] rules; regulations; law. ¶~에 어긋나다 be against the rules[regulations] / ~을 지키다[어기다] observe[break] the rules.

규정(規定) [규칙] rules; regulations; [정한

것] stipulations; prescriptions; [조항] provisions. ¶직무 ~ the regulations defining the duties of the staff // 통행 ~ the rules of the road / the traffic regulations // …에 관한 ~ the regulations affecting … // 도서 대출 ~ library regulations for lending books // ~대로 [에 따라] according to [in conformity with] the rules / as laid down // ~의 서식으로 in due form // 현행 ~으로는 under the existing provisions [standing rules] // 제1조의 ~에 따라 in accordance with the provisions of Article I / under the requirements of Rule I // ~에 어긋나다 be against the rules // ~에 따르다 obey [follow] the rules // ~을 어기다 go against [infringe / violate] the rules // ~을 만들다 make provisions (against gambling) / make [lay down / prescribe] rules // 12시까지는 돌아와야 한다는 것이 기숙사의 ~으로 되어 있다 The dormitory regulations require that we return by 12 o'clock. **규정하다** prescribe; ordain; (법률 등으로) provide (for); (계약 조건으로서) stipulate (for). ¶우리 시의 건축법은 이 지역에 4층 이상의 건물을 짓지 못하도록 규정하고 있다 The building law of our city provides [stipulates] that no building higher than four-stories may be built in this area. ➔¶규정된 prescribed (method) / ordained (process) / regular (course) / stipulated (quality) // …이라고 법률에 규정되어 있다 be expressly provided (for) in the statute / the statute provides that … / it is stipulated [laid down] in the statute that … // 규정된 절차를 밟다 go through the necessary formalities // 그것은 법률에 의해 규정되어 있다 It is prescribed by law. / It is provided in the law.

● **규정액** [화] a normal solution.
규제 (規制) [규칙] regulation; [제한] restriction; [통제] control. ¶교통 ~ traffic control // 소비 ~ regulation [restriction] of consumption. **규제하다** regulate; control; restrict. ¶교통을 ~ regulate traffic // 보도를 ~ control the news / suppress the news // 소비성 품목의 수입을 ~ restrict imports of consumer items // 수출을 자율 ~ control [curb] exports voluntarily. ➔¶파업은 법으로 규제되어 있다 Strikes are regulated by law.
규조토 (硅藻土) diatomite; diatomaceous earth; silicious marl.
규준 (規準) a canon; a criterion (*pl.* -ria, ~s); a standard; [교] a norm.
규중 (閨中) a woman's living room; (프) a boudoir.
● **규중처녀** of an innocent girl (brought up in the bosom) of a good family; a naive girl who knows nothing of the world; a hidden flower; (프) an ingénue.
규칙 (規則) a rule; regulations. ¶~에 따라 [~대로] according to the rules / in conformity [conformance] with the rules // ~에 맞다 conform to the rule / ~에 위배되다 be against [contrary to] the rules [regulations] // ~에서 벗어나다 deviate from an established rule / ~에 따르다 go by rule // ~을 지키다 observe [stick by] the rules / act upon a rule / keep [conform] to a rule / follow [obey] a rule // ~을 마련하다 [정하다] lay down [make] a rule / establish regulations / ~을 시행하다 put the rules into effect / enforce the rules // ~을 무시하다 disregard the established rules // ~을 어기다 break [violate / go against / (문어) infringe on] the rules // ~을 폐지하다 abolish a rule // 예외 없는 ~은 없다 Every rule [There is no rule but] has its exceptions. // 이 학교는 ~이 엄격하다 This school has strict rules. / Strict discipline is enforced at this school. // 그것은 ~ 위반이다 It is against the rule. // 이곳에의 주차는 ~ 위반입니다 It is against [It is a violation of] the rules to park a car here. // ~ 대로만 해야 한다면 조직 운영이 원활해지지 않는다 We can't run the organization smoothly if we have to do everything exactly according to the book. // 그는 매사를 ~대로 한다 He always sticks to the rules [goes by the book]. / He is a stickler for rules and regulations.

● **규칙 동사** [언] a regular verb.
규칙적 (規則的) regular; systematic; methodical; orderly. ¶~으로 regularly / methodically / systematically / on [with] system // ~인 생활을 하다 have regular habits / keep regular hours / live [lead] a well-regulated life / lead an orderly life.
규탄 (糾彈) impeachment (▶ 특히 (미)에서는 공무원에 대한 탄핵의 뜻이 있음); censure; denunciation; arraignment. **규탄하다** impeach; censure; denounce; arraign (a person for something); take [call / bring] (a person) to task (for something). ¶정부의 실정을 ~ impeach [censure / denounce] the government for maladministration // 그들은 정 씨의 수회를 규탄했다 They denounced [impeached] Mr. Jeong for taking bribes. // 야당은 정부의 태만을 규탄했다 The opposition parties censured the government for being negligent.
규토 (硅土) [화] silica; silex.
규폐(증) (硅肺症) [의] silicosis; (구어) the dust disease. ¶~ 환자 a silicotic.
규합 (糾合) rally; muster. **규합하다** rally; muster; gather [call] together. ¶동지를 ~ rally [call together] men of like mind // 동지를 규합해서 정당을 조직하다 form a political party with men of the same mind.
규화 (硅化) [광] silicification. **규화하다** silicify; become silicified.
● **규화물** a silicide.
균 (菌) 1 fungi (*sing.* -gus). ➪⁼**균류** 2 a bacilus (*pl.* bacilli). ➪⁼**세균** ¶결핵 ~ tuberculosis bacilli // 콜레라 ~ a cholera bacillus // ~ 배양 bacterial culture / bacteria cultivation / germiculture // 이질 ~ a dysentery. 3 a disease germ. ➪⁼**병균** ¶~이 묻은 옷 infectious clothing.
균등 (均等) equality; uniformity; evenness; (a) parity (세력·처우 등의). ¶기회 ~ equality in opportunity. **균등하다** equal; even; uniform. ¶균등한 대우를 받다 obtain parity (of treatment) (with) // 우리는 균등한 대우를 요구했다 We demanded equal treatment. **균등히** equally; evenly; uniformly. ¶~ 하다 equalize / even / make equal [alike] / render uniform // ~ 배분하다 distribute (the money) equally // 비용을 ~ 부담하다 share the expenses equally // 납세의 부담을 ~ 하다 equalize the burdens of taxation // 그들은 건물 내의 온도를 ~ 했다 They equalized the temperature in all parts of the building.
균류 (菌類) fungi (*sing.* -gus).

●**균류학** fungology; mycology.

균배(均配) division into equal parts. **균배하다** divide into equal parts; divide equally.

균분(均分) equal division. **균분하다** divide [share] equally; equalize. ➔¶유산은 형제들에게 균분되었다 The inheritance was equally distributed between[among] the brothers.

균열(龜裂) 1 (물체의) a crevice; a chap; a crack; a fissure; a cleft; a crevasse (빙하 등의). ¶지면의 ～ a crack [fissure] in the ground//지진에 의한 도로의 ～ the cracks in the road made by the earthquake//땅에 ～이 생겼다 The ground opened in fissures. //지진으로 길에 군데군데 ～이 생겼다 The roads were cracked [fissured] in places owing to the earthquake. **균열하다** crack; be cracked; fissure; cleave.
2 (관계의) a break; a rupture; a crack. ¶그것 때문에 두 사람의 우정에 ～이 생겼다 That has impaired [caused a crack in] their friendship.//노동조합의 단합에 ～이 생겼다 Cracks appeared in the labor coalition. **균열하다** break (with); fall out (with); split (with); be at odds (with).

균일(均一) uniformity; equality. ¶천 원 ～ a uniform rate of 1,000 won//수수료를 ～화하다 standardize handling charges [fees]//개당 모두 천 원 ～이다 They are all 1,000 won a piece. **균일하다** uniform (price); equal; even. ¶균일한 품질 uniform quality//균일하게 하다 make (things) uniform / uniformalize / equalize (tax burdens)//균일하게 배분하다 distribute uniformly [equally]//같은 균일합니다 They are all one-priced. / They are of a uniform price.

●**균일 가격** a uniform [flat] price.

균점(均霑) equal allotment of profits. **균점하다** share (in); participate (in); have equal shares (in); have equal portions (of).

균제하다(均齊—) symmetrical; well-proportioned (form); well-balanced (development).

균질(均質) homogeneity. ¶～의 homogeneous.

●**균질 우유** homogenized milk. **균질체** a homogeneous substance.

균할(均割) equal division [allotment]. **균할하다** divide [allot] equally.

균형(均衡) balance; (an) equilibrium; equipoise. ¶세력의 ～ the balance of power //소비 ～ consumer equilibrium//힘의 ～ the equilibrium of forces//수급의 ～ the balance of demand and supply//무역의 ～ equilibrium of trade/～이 잡힌 식사 a balanced diet//～이 잡히지 않은 예산 an unbalanced budget//～이 잡혀 있다 be (well-)balanced / be in balance [equilibrium / equipoise]//～을 유지하다 keep [hold] the balance (between) / maintain (the) equilibrium//세력 ～을 유지하다 [깨다] maintain [upset] the balance of power//한 발로 몸의 ～을 잡다 balance oneself on one leg/～을 잡다 balance / balance [poise] oneself (자체의) / equilibrate / keep in equilibrium [harmony] (with) / poise / make proportionate to /～을 잃다 lose (the) balance//～을 회복하다 redress the balance//생산과 소비의 ～을 맞추다 balance production with consumption//그는 몸의 ～을 잃고 넘어졌다 He lost his balance and fell.//수요와 공급의 ～을 잘 이루고 있다 Supply and demand are balanced well [are in good balance].//이번 예산은 수지 ～이 잡혔다 The current budget is balanced.//수출입 ～이 잘 잡혀 있다 There is a good balance between exports and imports. / Imports and exports are well balanced.//그는 마음의 ～을 잃었다 His mental equilibrium was upset.//그는 ～을 잃고 말에서 떨어졌다 He lost his balance and fell from the horse.//양측의 힘의 ～이 무너졌다 The balance of power between the two opposing sides has been lost.//그는 육체와 정신의 성장의 ～이 잡혀 있지 않다 His mental development hasn't kept pace with his physical growth.

●**균형 가격** an equilibrium price. **균형 예산** a balanced budget.

귤(橘) an orange; (중국 원산의) a mandarin; (북아메리카·남아프리카 원산의) a tangerine.

귤껍질(橘—) orange peel; the peel of an orange.

귤나무(橘—) [식] an orange [a citrus] tree; a mandarin orange.

귤밭(橘—) an orange orchard [plantation].

그¹ 1 [3인칭 단수 대명사] [그 사람] (주격) he; (소유격) his; (목적격) him; (소유 대명사) his; (재귀 대명사) himself; that man.(▶ 드물게「그」가 여자를 나타낼 때도 있으나 대개 남자를 가리킴) ¶그는 [가] he/그의 ～의 것 his/～에게 [를] him/～는 위대한 사람이다 He is a great man.//～도 사람이요 나도 사람이다 He is no more a man than I.//～에 대한 얘기는 더 이상 듣고 싶지 않다 I don't want to hear any [anything] more about him. 2 [3인칭 지시 대명사] [그것] (주격) it; (소유격) its; (목적격) it; (소유 대명사) itself; that. ¶～로 인하여 on that account [score] / therefore / consequently.

그² that; those; the; [앞에서 말한] the same; [불확실한] (the man) in question; (강조하여) the very; [그것의] its. ¶～ 사람 he/she / that person / that [the] man [woman]/～ 근처에 about there //～ 무렵에 in those days //～ 같은 like that / such/～ 같은 사람 a man like that [him] / the like of him / his like//～처럼 like that / (in) that way/～ 때문에 for that reason / on that account / so / therefore / consequently//～ 책들 말입니까? 가지십시오 You mean those books? You may have them.//～ 이야기는 그만둡시다 Let's drop that subject.//누구나 ～ 나름의 생각이 있기 마련이다 Each man has his own ideas.//그래, ～거야 That's it!/(미국 구어) Attaboy [Attagirl]!(▶ Atta는 That's the의 단축형)//～ 학생들은 벌써 퇴학당했다 The boys in question have already been expelled (from school).

그간(—間) the while. ⇨ᆞ그사이

그것 1 that one; that; it. ¶～은 그렇지만 it may be so, but .../～은 그렇다 치고 setting [putting] it aside / apart from the question / be that as it may/～이 중요한 점이다 That's the point.//～이 바로 네가 나를 도와 주어야 할 일이다 That's just where I need your help.//～이 이것보다 크다 That one is larger than this (one).//～은 무엇이냐 What's that?/～은 10년 전의 일이다 That was ten years ago.//～은 지금도 분명히 기억하고 있다 I still remember clearly.//거기 있는 ～ 좀 이리 주게 Hand me that thing over there.//～ 좀 보여 주시오 Please show me

that one. / Please show it to me.∥ ~은 어느 갠 날의 일이었다 It was[happened] on a fine day.∥사과 편지 한 통이면 ~으로 족하다 All you have to do is to write a letter of apology.∥ ~ 말고 나머지는 모두 만족스럽다 Apart from that[that aside] everything is satisfactory.∥ ~은 그렇고 당신의 대답은 언제 들을 수 있습니까 Well then, when can we have your answer?∥ ~은 좋은데 지금 돈이 없다 That's fine, but I don't have the money now.∥ ~도 내 탓이라고 하는 겁니까 Do you blame me for that, too?∥ ~은 그의 노력의 대가이다 That is the fruit of his efforts.∥ ~ 만은 줄 수 없다 I will give you anything but that.∥ ~으로 그의 정치가로서의 생명은 끝났다 That means the end of his career as a statesman. **2** [그 사람] that fellow; (미) that guy; he; she. ¶~이 그 사실을 모를 리가 없다 He can't help knowing about the matter.∥ ~들에게 저녁을 주시오 Give the little ones their dinner.

그곳 that place; there. ¶~에(서) in that place / there∥ ~까지 가다 go that[so] far∥그도 ~ 출신이다 He comes from the place too.∥ ~ 형편은 어떻습니까 How are things going on in your place?∥ ~은 별고 없으신지요 Are you all getting along well?∥나는 우연히 ~에 있었다 I happened to be in the scene[be there].

그글피 three days after tomorrow; four days hence[from now].

그까짓 [그 정도의] so trivial; so trifling; [그와 같은] like that. ¶~ 일 such a trivial matter / so trifling a matter / such trifles / a trifle like that∥ ~ 것 Oh! It is nothing.∥ ~ 일로 울다니 You must not weep over a trifle like that.∥ ~ 것은 누구라도 할 수 있겠다 Everyone can do such a thing.∥ ~ 빚으로 속태우지 말게 Don't worry about that nominal debt.∥ ~ 일로 내 결심은 변하지 않는다 I would not change my mind for so little.

그끄러께 three years ago; last year but two; two years before last; the year before last.

그끄저께 three days ago; two days before yesterday. ¶~ 밤 the night before the night before last / last night but two / three nights ago.

그나마 and that; at that; and yet; still; even so; nevertheless. ¶불과 몇 마디, ~ 작은 소리로 이야기했을 뿐이다 They spoke little and that in whispers.∥그 커피는 2천 원이나 했는데 ~ 질이 좋은 편이 아니었다 The coffee cost 2,000 won and not a very good one at that.

그날 (on) that day; (강조하여) (on) the very [same] day. ¶~의 일 the day's work∥따라 on that particular day / on that day of all days (in the year)∥ ~ 중으로 before the day is over[out] / within the day∥내가 돌아온 ~ 그는 떠났다 He left on the very day I came back.∥ ~ 이다 Each day is just like every other day. / Nothing is ever changed.∥그 부친은 그가 태어나던 바로 ~에 돌아가셨다 His father died on the very day that he was born.

그날그날 everyday; daily; day after[by] day; from day to day. ¶~ 겨우 살아가다 eke out a bare existence from day to day / scrape a living day by day.

그냥 1 [그대로] as it is; as it stands; intact; in the same way as before; still. ¶~ 두다 leave (something) intact[as it is] / let (a matter) rest there / let (a person) alone∥ ~ 그대로 있다 remain as it was / remain intact / be left untouched∥집이 쓰러진 채 ~ 있다 The house remains as it fell.∥그 문제를 ~ 내버려 둘 수는 없다 We cannot afford to leave[let] the matter alone. / The matter cannot be allowed to stand as it is. **2** [줄곧] all the time[way]; (all) through; throughout; continuously. ¶~ 울고만 있다 do nothing but cry∥ ~ 서 있다 keep standing / stay on one's feet∥밥 먹지 않고 ~ 학교에 가다 go to school without breakfast∥ (지금까지) ~ 기다리고 있었다 I have been waiting all this while.

그네 a swing; (미) a trapeze. ¶앉아서 타는 ~ a seat swing∥ ~ 타는 곡예사 a[an aerial] trapeze performer[artist]∥ ~ 뛰다 get on a swing / sit in a swing / swing in a swing∥ ~ 를 타고 있다 be on a swing / sit in a swing / ~를 구르다 propel a swing / rock back and forth a swing / ~를 매다 put up a swing.
●그넷줄 a swing rope.

그네(들) those people; they; them.

그녀(-女) [3인칭 단수 대명사] (주격) she; (소유격) her; (목적격) her; (소유 대명사) hers; (재귀 대명사) herself. ¶~는 수줍음이 많은 소녀였다 She was a shy girl.

그놈 that fellow[chap / rogue]; (미) that guy; (영) that blighter; (속어) that bastard. ¶~이 ~이다 They're all bastards!(다 시원찮다) / There is little to choose between them(엇비슷하다).∥ ~은 사기꾼일지도 모른다 The fellow might be an imposter.

그늘 1 [응달] shade. ¶큰 나무 ~에서 in the shade of a big tree∥나무 ~에서 잠간 쉬다 rest for a while in the shade of a tree∥그것은 ~에서 말리시오 Dry it in the shade[out of the sun].∥그 나무는 좋은 ~을 만들어 준다 The trees give[afford / provide] a pleasant shade.∥우리 집은 새로 들어선 아파트의 ~에 가려져 있다 My house is in the shadow of a newly-built apartment house.∥정원의 반이 ~에 져 있었다 Half of the garden was in shadow.
2 [남의 보호] protection; care. ¶부모님 ~에서 자라다 grow up under the protection [good care] of one's parents / grow up under one's parents wings[one's parental roof].
3 [드러나지 않는 처지] obscurity. ¶~에서 사는 사람 a social outcast / a person with a shady past / an ex-convict / a fugitive from justice.

그늘지다 1 [응달이 지다] be shaded; be shady. ¶그늘진 a shady lane / 가로수로 그늘진 거리 a street shaded with trees. **2** [드러나지 않다] be in obscurity[the shade / the shadow]. ¶그늘진 곳에서 외로이 살다 live in the shade[the shadow / obscurity] / keep shady. **3** [표정·마음이] gloom; cloud; feel gloomy; look dismal. ¶그늘진 얼굴 gloomy face∥그녀의 얼굴은 근심으로 그늘져 있었다 Her face was clouded with anxiety.∥그는 어딘지 그늘진 데가 있다 There is something gloomy about him.

그다지 1 [별로·그리] (not) very[much/greatly]; rarely; seldom; little. ¶~ 춥지 않다 It is not very cold. / I do not feel very cold. // 오늘은 몸이 ~ 좋지 않다 I am not too[so] well today. // 이름 따위는 ~ 중요하지 않다 Names matter little. // 이 책은 ~ 재미가 없다 This book is not very interesting. // 그의 집은 ~ 훌륭하지 않다 His house is not particularly impressive. / His house is nothing special. // 그는 ~ 유식하지 않다 He is not much of a scholar. // 나는 그런 일에 ~ 마음 쓰지 않는다 I do not mind it very much. // 나는 그 사람을 ~ 좋아하지 않는다 I do not like him too well.
2 [그러한 정도로까지] so; so much; to that extent; that much; to such an extent. ¶~ 먼 길인 줄은 몰랐다 I never thought it would be such a long way.

그대 [예스러운 2인칭 대명사] (주격) thou; (소유격) thy; (목적격) thee; (소유 대명사) thine. ¶~ 간음하지 말지니라 Thou shalt not commit adultery.

그대로 as it is[stands]; in the same way as before; like that; that way; intact; untouched. ¶있는 ~ 의 사실 a plain[an unvarnished / a straight / an undisguised] fact / 있는 ~ 말하다 give an accurate account / (구어) tell it like it is // ~ 두다 leave (a thing) as it is[stands] / leave (a thing) intact[alone / untouched] / let (a person) alone // 있다 remain intact[as it was] / be left untouched[alone] // ~ 본 ~ 이야기하다 tell as one saw it // 금고는 ~ 있었다 The safe was left intact[untouched]. // 외투는 ~ 입고 계십시오 Keep your coat on, please. // 그 문제를 ~ 둘 수는 없다 We cannot afford to leave[let] the matter alone. / The matter cannot be allowed to stand as it is. // 그 건은 ~ 있다 The matter has been left as it is. / The matter has not been settled yet. // 그 서류는 ~ 두시오 Please leave the papers untouched[alone]. // 그들이 ~ 갔더라면 지금쯤 목적지에 도착해 있을 텐데 If they had kept on going at that rate, they would have reached their destination by now. // 그가 한 말을 ~ 믿었단 말인가 Did you believe[(구어) swallow] everything he said? // 그의 말을 ~ 받아들여서는 안 된다 You should not take him at his word[take his word] for it. // 부모님은 죽은 형의 방을 여러 해 동안 ~ 두고 계신다 My parents have left my dead brother's room untouched [exactly as it was] for all these years. // 그 문장은 ~ 좋다 That sentence is all right as it stands[just as it is]. // 그는 곤란한 상황을 있는 ~ 이야기했다 He gave a straightforward account of the difficult situation.

그동안 (in the) meantime. ⇨ 그사이
그득 to the full. ⇨ 가득
그득하다 full (of). ⇨ 가득하다
그들 [3인칭 복수 대명사] [그 사람들] (주격) they; (소유격) their; (목적격) them; (소유 대명사) theirs; (재귀 대명사) themselves. ¶~은 6시까지 오지 않았다 They're not coming until 6:00.
그들먹하다 almost[nearly] full.
그따위 a thing[person] of that sort[kind]; such a one; that sort[kind] (of). ¶~ 일로 화내지 말게 Don't be offended at such a trifle. // 여기에는 ~ 인간은 필요 없다 We don't want his kind in here.

그때 then; (at) that time[moment]; (on) that occasion. ¶마침 ~ just at that moment / just then // ~는 then / in that case[event] // ~부터 since then / ever since / from that time onward // ~까지 (과거·미래) until then / (과거) up to that time // ~의 대통령 the then President // ~에는 긴치마를 입었다 We wore long skirts in those days. // 그는 ~까지는 착한 아이였다 He had been a good boy till then. // ~ 이후로 그들은 사이가 좋지 않다 They have been on bad terms since then. // ~까지 그것을 마쳐라 Finish it by then. // 그들은 ~까지 참을성 있게 기다렸다 They had waited patiently until then. // ~까지는 일이 잘되어 갔었다 All had gone well so far. / All went well to that point. // 파티는 7시부터니까 ~까지는 와 주십시오 The party begins at 7 o'clock, so we expect you by that time.

그라비어 photogravure; gravure. ¶~ 인쇄로 하다 photogravure.
그라운드 a ground; an athletic field. ¶홈~ a team's home ground.
그랑프리 (프) a grand prix; a grand[principal / main] prize. ¶이 영화는 ~를 차지했다 This film won the grand prize.

그래¹ 1 [대답이] yes; so. ¶"너 오겠니?" "~ 갈게." "Will you come?" "Yes, I will." // ~ 그게 유일한 방법이야 Yes, that's the only possible way. // ~ 알았다 I see. / I've got it. // ~ ~ 생각났어 Oh yes, now I remember. // ~ ~ 그런 약속이었지 Yes, yes, that was our agreement, wasn't it?
2 [다짐아 물음·강조] so. ¶~ 정말인가 So? / Is that so? // ~ 너 진담이야 What! Do you really mean it? // ~ 정말이야 Oh, Really? // ~ 그럴 수가 있을까 Really! Is that possible? // ~ 너는 뭐라고 말했나 And (then) what did you say? // ~ 이제는 내 말을 알아듣겠지 Now you know what I mean.
3 [감탄·놀람] indeed. ¶과연 ~ You are quite [too] right. / So it is. // ~ 잘했어 Well done! // ~ 정말 멋지군 Oh, how wonderful!

그래² and; (and) so. ⇨ 그래서
그래도 but (still); and yet; nevertheless; though; still; however; all the same; for all that; at any rate. ¶이상하게 들릴지 모르지만 ~ 사실이다 It may sound strange, but it is true for all that. // ~ 이것이 나은 편이다 This is less unsatisfactory than that. // 그녀는 상냥하고 친절하지만 나는 그녀가 싫다 She is gentle and kind to me, but I still don't like her[but all the same I don't like her / but for all that I don't like her]. // 아무도 그 그림을 칭찬하지 않지만 ~ 나는 그 그림이 훌륭하다고 생각한다 Nobody praises that picture, still I think it's very good. // 결점이 있긴 하지만 ~ 그는 본바탕은 좋은 녀석이야 He's basically a good man for all his faults. // 그는 ~ 아직 정신을 못 차린 모양이야 Even this doesn't seem to have taught him anything[to have gotten through to him]. // ~ 불만이라면 마음대로 하시오 If you are still dissatisfied, do as you like.
그래미상(-賞) a Grammy (award).
그래서 and; (and) so; (and) then; thereupon; hereupon; accordingly; for that [this] reason; on that account. ¶~ 나는 인천으로 이사 가기로 했다 So I decided to move to Incheon. // ~ 건축을 1년 연기했다 Therefore

[As a result] we postponed the construction.// ~ 결국했단 말이지 Was that why you were absent?// 어제는 비가 왔다. ~ 하루 종일 집에 있었다 It rained yesterday and so I stayed home all day.// ~ 나는 가기가 싫었다 That was why I did not want to go.// ~ 우리는 당신에게 도움을 청하기로 했다 That was why we decided to ask you to help us.//우리는 개업 자금이 부족합니다. ~ 천만 원 정도의 빚을 내고 싶습니다 We do not have enough capital to set up in business. Therefore [(문어) In this connection] we would like to request a loan of ten million won.// ~ 어쨌단 말이냐 So what?// ~ 그만두고 싶다는 건가 And so you wish to resign?

그래야 only so; unless so; only if one does [says] that. ¶~ 내 아들이지 That's what I expect of my son. / That's the boy! / (미국 속어) Attaboy!// 서둘러라, ~ 시간 안에 갈 수 있어 Hurry, and you will be in time.

그래프 a graph. ¶선 ~ a line graph // 막대 ~ a bar graph // ~로 만들다 make a graph (of) // ~를 그리다 draw a graph (of).
● **그래프용지** graph [section] paper.

그래픽 graphic.
● **그래픽 디자이너** a graphic designer.

그랜드 슬램 [야구·테니스·골프] grand slam.

그랜드 오페라 the grand opera.

그랜드 피아노 a grand piano.

그램 a gram(me) (기호 g., g).

그러구러 somehow or other; in one way or another; bit by bit; little by little; gradually; in the meantime; meanwhile. ¶~ 일을 끝냈다 Somehow, I got the job done.// ~ 고향을 떠난 지도 10년이 지났다 It is ten years [Ten years have passed] since I left my hometown.

그러그러하다 so-so; be about the same; be neither good nor bad; be neither better nor worse. ¶그 영화는 그저 그러그러했다 The movie was so-so [tolerable].

그러나 but; however; though; and yet. ¶나는 가고 싶었다. ~ 갈 수 없었다 I wanted to go, but I couldn't.// 나는 멋있는 차를 발견했다. ~ 값이 너무 비쌌다 I found an ideal car. It was however, [However, it was] too expensive for me.// 오늘 밤에 찾아뵙겠어요. ~ 잠시 동안밖에 머물 수 없겠습니다 I'll come and see you this evening — I can only stay a few minutes, though.

그러나저러나 anyway; anyhow; at any rate; in any case. ¶~ 준비는 해 놓겠다 In any case, I will make preparations for it.// ~ 그것을 말할 수 없다 I cannot say it anyway.

그러내다 rake out; take out; scrape out. ¶난로의 재를 ~ rake [scrape] out the ashes from a stove.

그러넣다 rake in; shovel (food) into (one's mouth). ¶삼태기에 자갈을 ~ rake gravels into a straw basket.

그러니까 so; for that [this] reason; therefore. ¶~ 그는 친구가 많다 That is why he has so many friends.// ~ 그는 가난한 거야 That explains [accounts for] his poverty.

그러니저러니 this or that; one thing or another. ¶~ 할 것 없이 without saying this or that / setting aside all objections // ~ 말이 많아서 그 계획은 결국 그만두게 되었다 As they made objections to the scheme, it was dropped at last.

그러담다 rake [scrape / gather] up (something) (and put it) into. ¶낙엽을 가마니에 ~ rake up dead leaves into a straw bag.

그러당기다 pull. ¶머리채를 ~ pull (a person's) tuft of hair.

그러들이다 rake in; gather in; collect. ¶판돈을 ~ rake in the money on the gambling table // 빚 준 돈을 ~ collect debts.

그러면 1 [그렇게 하면] and. ¶구하라. ~ 너희에게 주실 것이다 Ask and it shall be given you.// 사진을 다시 한번 보자. ~ 생각이 날지도 모른다 Let's look at the photo again. Then we may remember.// 바로 떠나시오. ~ 다섯 시까지는 집에 도착할 것이오 Leave at once, and you will reach home by five.
2 [그러하다면] if (it is) so; if that is the case; in that case; then; well; well then. ¶~ 내일 오죠 Well then, I shall come tomorrow. ~ 나는 어떻게 해야 하지 In that case, what shall I do?// ~ 담배를 끊는 것이 좋겠다 Then you may as well give up smoking. ~ 내가 거짓말을 하고 있다는 말입니까 Then do you mean I am lying?

그러면 그렇지 Well, all right!; Well, it's about time!; That's the way!; That-a-boy!; Attaboy!; That's what I mean!; Now you [they] have got it!; I told you so!; I thought so!; See what I mean!; as (was / had been) expected; it should be so. ¶~ 그녀가 불평 안 할 리가 있나 No wonder that she makes complaints. ¶~ 집에서 오늘 편지가 없을 리가 있나 Well it's about time! There just had to be a letter from home today.// ~ 그가 가난할 리가 없지 Quite so. He can not be poor.

그러모으다 gather up; scrape up [together]; rake up [together]; round up; collect. ¶그러모은 것 a medley // 낙엽을 ~ scrape up fallen leaves // 그는 휴가 자금을 그러모았다 He scraped up [together] enough money to take a holiday.// 상자 속에는 그러모은 잡동사니들이 들어 있었다 In the box there was a jumble of odds and ends.

그러므로 so; therefore; hence; for that reason; accordingly; on that ground; on that account; consequently. ¶~ 나는 나의 의도를 단념했다 I accordingly gave up my intention. ~ 그를 최우수 선수로 인정한다 Therefore [And so / (문어) Hence] we declare him the outstanding player.

그러안다 embrace; hug; hold [take / clasp] in one's arms; fold in one's arms; press to one's bosom; hug [clasp] to one's breast. ¶아이를 ~ embrace a child / hug a child to his breast // 그는 딸을 포근히 그러안았다 He held his daughter to him in a warm embrace. / He gave his daughter a warm hug. // 그녀는 어린애를 그러안고 볼을 비볐다 She hugged the chick to her cheek.

그러자 and then; just then; then; and (▶ 앞 뒤 관계로 우연히 뜻이 되는 일이 있음. ¶~ 그 일이 벌어졌다 And then it happens. // ~ 거기에 경찰관이 지나갔다 Just then, a policeman happened to come along. // 연기가 피어올랐다. ~ 마법사가 사라져 버렸다 There was a puff of smoke and the witch had gone. // 그는 문간에 섰다. ~ 문이 저절로 열렸다 He stood at the doorstep. Then the door opened of itself.

그러잖아도 even if it were not so; all the more; in addition (to); on top of (it); more-

그러잡다 over; what is more; to make matters worse; to add to the surplus. ¶~ 한번 만났으면 하던 참이었소 I was going to visit you even if you were not to come to see me. / I intended to see you one of these days. / You are welcome. I myself was going to see you.∥~ 피곤한데 그가 한 시간 일을 더 하란다 I am already tired, and still he asks me to work one hour longer.∥~ 벌이가 시원찮아 살아가기가 어려운데 식구가 하나 더 늘면 어떡합니까 We hardly earn enough to live on now. What are we going to do with another mouth to feed?∥그에게 쓸데없는 말을 하지 말아 줘. ~ 는 불만이 많다 Don't go putting any more ideas into his head. He is dissatisfied as it is.

그러잡다 grasp; grip; clasp; clutch; grab; take [get] hold of. ¶손을 ~ clasp[grasp] (a person's) hand∥머리털을 ~ grasp[clasp] (a person's) hair / seize (a person) by hair.

그러저러하다 so and so; such and such. ¶그러저러해서 for such and such reasons∥그러저러한 날에 on such and such a day∥그는 어저께 그러저러한 사람과 만났다고 하였다 He said he had met such and such a person the day before.

그러쥐다 seize; catch; grasp; grip; grab; take [catch / grab] hold of; hold. ¶손잡이를 ~ hold[clutch] a handle∥머리털을 그러쥐고 질질 끌다 drag (a person) by the hair∥너무 많이 그러쥐려다가는 다 잃어버린다 A person who grasps at too much may lose everything.

그러하다 [그와 같다] so; such; like that; that sort [kind] of. ¶사정이 그러하여 당신과 함께 갈 수가 없다 Such being the case[under the circumstances], I cannot go with you.

그럭저럭 somehow (or other); (in) one way or another; by some means (or other); by hook or by crook; barely. ¶~ 살아간다 I manage to get along, one way or another.∥하는 것 없이 ~ 하루가 지나갔다 The day has been wasted on this and that (getting nothing accomplished). ∥~ 6시다 It's nearly [almost] six o'clock.∥여기 온 지도 ~ 5년이 된다 It is five years since I came here.∥나는 여행에 필요한 돈을 ~ 마련하였다 I scraped up expenses for trip.∥그 문제는 ~ 해결이 되었다 The matter has been settled somehow or other.∥우리는 ~ 위기를 모면하였다 We somehow managed to ride out[get through] the crisis.

그런 [그러한] such; like that. ¶~ 사람 such a man (as that) / a man like that / that sort of man / the like of him / his like∥~ 식으로 so / (in) that way / in that manner / like that∥~ 경우에는 in that case / in such a case / in case like that∥세상이란 ~ 거야 Such is the way of the world. / The world is just the way it is.∥~ 것은 본 적이 없다 I never saw anything of the sort before.∥~ 소동을 벌이지 않아도 된다 You needn't make such a fuss.∥~ 더러운 것은 버려라 Throw that dirty thing away!∥~ 이유로 그녀는 해고되었다 That is why she was fired.∥~ 식으로 말한다면 반대할 수 없다 If you put it that way. I can't object.∥그가 ~ 짓을 했을 리 없다 He can't have done such a thing.∥~ 넓은 집에서 살고 싶다 I wish I could live in such a large house.∥~ 영화는 싫다 I don't like films like that[films of that sort].∥~ 부류의 남자는 참 다루기 힘들다 That type of man is hard for me to deal with. / I have trouble dealing with men like that.∥~ 종류의 모자는 다 떨어졌소 We are out of stock in that sort of hats.∥~ 식으로 말해서는 안 된다 You must not speak like that[(in) that way].∥~ 사람하고는 협상할 수 없다 You can't negotiate with that kind of person [such a person].∥~ 소설에는 흥미가 없다 I'm not interested in that type of novel.∥~ 이유로 내가 먼저 돌아왔다 That's why I came home before the others.∥~ 사정이라면 회의는 연기하자 If that is the case[that's the way it is / If so], we will postpone our meeting.

그런대로 rather; tolerably; enough; I should say ...; (구어) (fair-to-)middling. ¶~ 쓸 만한 사람 a good enough man in his way∥그 영화는 ~ 볼 만했다 The movie was so-so [mildly enjoyable].∥~ 쓸모가 있다 He is not altogether worthless. / (물건이) It may answer[serve] some purpose.∥"경기는 어떻습니까?" "~ 괜찮습니다." "How's business?" "Oh, not too bad." / "Just so-so." / "Well I can't complain."

그런데 but; however; and yet; by the way; by the bye; now. ¶~ 그 일은 어떻게 되었습니까 By the way, how does the matter stand? / Now, what has become of the matter you spoke of?∥~ 어디서 식사를 하지요 Well, where shall we eat?∥~ 당신의 계획은 어떻게 되었습니까 By the way, what happened about your plans?∥~ 그 문제는 결말이 났습니까 By the way has the matter already been settled?∥~ 다음 모임은 언제입니까 Well, then, when shall we have our next meeting?∥그녀는 인물은 좋아, ~ 키가 좀 작구나 She is nice-looking, but she is rather short in statue.

그런데도 and yet; still; in spite of that; for all that; nevertheless; notwithstanding; all the same; none the less. ¶그녀는 소심하다. ~ 그 위험한 묘기에 도전하려 할 것이다 Although she is timid, she will try the stunt nevertheless.∥그는 꽤 열심이긴 한데, ~ 학교 성적이 신통치 않다 With all his diligence, he doesn't cut a very brilliant figure in school.

그런즉 therefore; accordingly; thereupon; hence; consequently; such being the case; then.

그럴듯하다 1 [있을 법하다] likely; [수긍할 만하다] plausible. ¶그럴듯한 이야기 a likely story∥그럴듯한 변명 a plausible excuse∥그럴듯한 구실을 대다 give a plausible [(문어) specious] excuse∥그럴듯한 거짓말을 하다 tell a plausible lie∥그녀는 그 이야기를 아주 그럴듯하게 했다 She told the whole story quite as if it were true.∥그는 그럴듯한 거짓말을 잘한다 He is good as telling lies which found like the truth.∥그럴듯한 제의에 너무 덤비지 마라 Don't get excited about offers that sound too good to be true.∥그의 말은 그럴듯하게 들린다 His words ring[sound] true[like truth].

2 [제법 훌륭하다] fair; passable; considerable; respectable; decent. ¶그럴듯한 연설 a speech worth hearing[listening to]∥그럴듯하게 살다 live respectably[decently] / make a decent living / be comfortably off.

그럼¹ and; if (it is) so. ⇨그러면
그럼² [긍정] yes; (미국 속어) yah; yeah; indeed; right; quite so; certainly; of course. ¶"뜰에 들어가도 됩니까?" "~." "May I go into the garden?" "Yes, certainly." "~요, 내 우산을 빌려 가도 좋아요 Certainly, you may borrow my umbrella.∥"~요, 좀 도와주겠니?" "~요." "Can you help me?" "Surely[certainly]!"
그렁그렁 1 (액체가) almost full (to the brim); all watered up; (눈물이) tearfully; suffused with tears. **그렁그렁하다** almost full (to the brim); brimful; all watered up; tearful; suffused with tears. ¶눈물이 그렁그렁한 눈 tearful[watery] eyes / eyes filled[suffused / brimming] with tears∥눈물이 그렁그렁하여 with tears in one's eyes∥그녀의 눈에는 눈물이 그렁그렁했다 Her eyes were watery [brimming / swimming] with tears. / Tears stood[gathered] in her eyes.
2 [국물이 많음]. **3** [배 속이 그득 찬 느낌]. **그렁그렁하다** feel bloated [charged / loaded] with water; be full from drinking too much water. ¶물을 너무 많이 마셔서 배 속이 ~ I have a feeling of fullness after drinking too much water. / My stomach feels too full of water.
그렇게 [그러한 정도까지] so; so much; like that. ¶~까지 to such an extent / so[thus] far / that much∥~ 화내지 말게 Don't be so angry.∥~ 춥진 않아 I don't feel very[so] cold.∥~까지 말할 필요는 없었는데 You need not have said all that. / You didn't have to carry it that far.∥그가 ~까지 냉정한 사람인 줄은 몰랐다 I had never thought that he was so coldhearted.∥~ 총명한 사람은 보기 드물다 Such a clever person is rarely found.∥~까지 무서워할 것은 없다 You don't have to be so afraid.∥사람들은 그녀를 굉장한 미인이라고 하는데 내가 보기에는 ~까지 말할 정도는 아니다 People say she is a great beauty, but I don't think she is all that beautiful.∥나는 그가 (당신이 생각하는 것처럼) ~ 나쁜 사람은 아니라고 생각한다 I don't think he is such a bad person (as you seem to think).∥이 책은 ~ 재미있지는 않다 This book is not very interesting.∥내가 ~까지 부탁했는데 그는 거절했다 He refused in spite of all my entreaties.∥~ 대담한 사람은 처음 보았다 I have never seen such a daring man. / He is the most daring man I have ever seen.∥그가 ~까지 고집하는 데는 틀림없이 이유가 있을 것이다 Since he insists so strongly, there must be some reason.
2 [그러하게] in that manner; (in) that way; like that; so. ¶사정이 ~ 되었다 Such is the case.∥그가 ~ 말했을 리 없다 He can't have said so.∥일을 ~ 처리해서는 안 된다 You should not deal with it that way[like that]. ∥~ 해 보시오 Try it like that[that way].∥~ 해서 그는 부자가 되었다 In that way[(문어)] Thus] he became rich.∥그때 ~ 했더라면 좋았을 것을 I should have done so then. ∥~ 하면 나는 틀림없이 성공한다 If I do it that way, I'm sure to succeed.∥그는 ~ 해서 다섯 사람을 속였다 He deceived five people with that trick[that way].
그렇다 [그러하다] so; such; like that; that way; (대답) Yes; No; That's right. ¶바로 ~ be just[quite / exactly / precisely] so / be just that way∥그렇다고 대답하다 answer [say] yes / answer in the affirmative / affirm ∥그렇다고는 하나 nevertheless / but / however / be that as it may∥그렇습니까 Yes? / Is that so? / Really? / You don't say so?∥그렇습니다 You are right. / That's right [so]. / That's what it is! / So it is.∥그렇지 않아도 서투른 글씨가 서둘러 써서 더 알아보기 힘들다 Haste made my normally poor handwriting even harder to read.∥그렇지 않아도 성미가 급한데 그는 요즘 더위 때문에 형편없이 화를 낸다 Always short-tempered, he is now hopelessly irritable because of the heat. ∥나는 확실히 그렇다고 생각해 I feel certain about it.
그렇고말고 Indeed!; Of course!; Certainly!; So it is.; Quite so.; Indeed it is.; That's it.; (미국 구어) Sure!; You can say that again.; I'll say.; You're telling me.; You said it.
그렇다고 해서 yet; for all that; nevertheless; be that as it may; one may well say so, but .... ¶~ 그의 도움을 청할 수도 없다 For all that, I can't ask for his help now.∥~ 달리 좋은 방안이 있는 것도 아니다 But still, that doesn't mean there's a better plan. / That doesn't mean there's a better plan, though.∥~ 그만둘 수도 없다 Even so [(문어) For all that] I cannot give up.
그렇지 않으면 otherwise; else; or (else); if not so; were it not so. ¶자유를 달라, ~ 죽음을 달라 Give me liberty, or give me death!∥자 이제 출발해요.. ~ 비행기를 놓칠 거예요 You'd better leave now or else you'll miss your plane.∥제가 전화를 걸까요. ~ 전화를 해 주시겠습니까 Shall I call you, or will you call me?
그렇지 1 (긍정하여) yes; yes, it is; you are right; just[quite / exactly] so. **2** (상대방의 동의를 구하여) isn't it?; doesn't it?; don't you?; I dare say. ¶매우 피곤할 거야, ~ You must be very tired, I dare say.∥걱정하지는 않았겠지, ~ You weren't worried, were you?
그렇지마는 but; however. ⇨그렇지만
그렇지만 but; however; still; nevertheless; though; although; and yet; be that as it may; for all that. ¶~ 값이 비쌌어요 It was expensive, though.∥~ 그는 틀림없이 위인이야 For all that, he is certainly a great man. ∥~ 그것은 별로 쓸모가 없을 것이다 It won't be of much use though.∥~ 이제 너무 늦다 But it's too late.∥그는 책임감이 없다. ~ 양친을 만년에 잘 돌봐 드렸다 He has no sense of responsibility. Never the less he did take good care of his parents in their old age.∥~ 그 문제는 이대로 내버려 둘 수는 없다 All the same I can hardly leave the problem like this.
그레셤의 법칙 (一法則) [경] Gresham's law.
그레코로만형 (一型) [레슬링] the Greco-Roman style.
그려 (옹낙·감탄). ¶갑시다~ Let's go.∥앉게~ Sit down.∥한잔합시다~ Let's have a drink, shall we?∥자네 말 잘하네~ You are very eloquent fellow.
그로기 groggy. ¶잇단 펀치를 맞아 그는 완전히 ~ 상태이다 He is dazed after all the blows he's taken. / He is absolutely groggy after that rain of blows.
그로테스크하다 grotesque; bizarre.
그루 1 (나무의) a stump; a stock; (곡식의) stubbles (of rice plants). **2** [식물을 세는 단

위) a plant; a tree. ¶감나무 세 ~ three persimmon trees / 한 ~의 느티나무 a zelkova (tree). 3 (농사짓는 횟수) a crop. ¶두 ~ 심는 농사 two crops a year / a semiannual crop.
●그루갈이 [농] double cropping. ⇨"이모작
그루밭 a stubble (field); an aftercrop field; a field used again after a barley crop. **그루벼** rice plants raised after harvesting the barley. **그루콩** an aftercrop of beans. **그루터기** (나무의) a stump; a stub; a stock; (벼 등의) stubbles. **그루팥** a aftercrop of redbeans.
그룹 a group. ¶독서 ~ a reading circle // 연구 ~ a study circle // ~을 지어 in groups // ~을 만들다 form a group // ~으로 나누다 divide (students) into groups.
그룹사운드 (*group sound) a musical band.
그르다 1 (옳지 않다) wrong; erroneous; false; incorrect; mistaken; (서술적) be in error; be in the wrong; be at fault. ¶옳고 그름을 가리다 tell [know] right from wrong / discriminate between right and wrong // 그는 그른 판단을 하지 않는다 He is infallible [unerring] in his judgement. // 자네가 ~ You are wrong. / You are in the wrong. / It's your fault.
2 (잘될 가망이 없다) hopeless; (서술적) be done for; be all over; (구어) be all fouled up. ¶그 환자는 이제 글렀다 The patient has little chance to pull through. / The patient is hopeless. // 난 글렀어 I am done for. / It's all up [over] with me. / I'm gone. / (구어) I'm a goner. // 그 애 사람되기는 글러 먹었다 The boy is far from promising. / The child will never be a good man [become a man of character]. // 우리 팀이 우승하긴 글렀다 There is no chance [hope] that our team will win. / Our team has no chance to win. / Our team doesn't have a dog's chance of gaining a victory. / The chances are ten to one that our team will lose the day.
3 (상태·조건 등이 좋지 않다) bad; foul; nasty; ill. ¶맛이 글렀다 It tastes bad [flat]. / It is unsavory [unpalatable]. // 오늘은 날씨가 글렀다 It's foul [bad / nasty / rainy] weather today.
그르렁거리다 wheeze; be wheezy. ¶그 노인은 천식으로 목을 그르렁거린다 The old man wheezes with asthma.
그르치다 spoil; ruin; destroy; botch; mar; corrupt; mislead; make a mess [hash / muddle / (구어) mush / (영국 구어) mull] (of); muff; mess up. ¶대사를 ~ muff one's lines / (영국 속어) fluff // 신세를 ~ ruin one's fortune / ruin oneself / be ruined // 일생을 ~ make a failure [both] of one's life / be ruined for life / blast one's career / make a wreck of one's life / be fouled up for the rest of one's life.
그릇¹ 1 [용기] a receptacle; a container; a bowl; [액체를 담는 용기] a vessel. ¶밥 ~ a rice bowl // 놋 ~ a brazen vessel // 질 ~ an earthen vessel / an earthen ware.
2 [능력·도량] caliber; ((영) calibre); capacity; capability; ability. ¶~이 큰 [작은] 사람 a man of high [poor] caliber // 그 사람은 그 일을 할 만한 ~이 못 돼 He is not equal to it. / He is by no means qualified for it. // He has not got what it takes. // 그는 대통령이 될 ~이 아니다 He is not of the stature of a president. / He is not presidential material. / He doesn't have what it takes [isn't cut out] to be president. / He is not of presidential caliber [stature].
그릇² [그르게] wrongly; misguidedly; falsely; erroneously; mistakenly. ¶~ 생각하다 misunderstand / mistake // ~ 판단하다 judge wrong / misjudge / miscalculate / err in one's judgement // 사람을 ~ 보다 judge a person wrongly / misjudge a person / make a wrong estimation of a person / make a mistake in one's estimate of a person / be deceived in a person.
그릇되다 be mistaken; go amiss [wrong]; be apt to pot; end in a failure; fail; be spoiled [ruined]; come to naught [nought]. ¶그릇된 생각 mistaken / wrong / false / incorrect / erroneous / errant / improper // 그릇된 생각 a mistaken [an erroneous] idea / a wrong opinion // 그릇된 길을 밟다 err [stray / deviate] from the path of righteousness / take the wrong way [an evil course]
그리 1 so; in that manner. ⇨"그렇게 ¶~ 생각합니까 Do you think so? // 그의 작품은 ~ 인기가 없다 His works are not so [overly] popular. 2 [그쪽으로] in that direction; that way; to that place; there; (고) thither. ¶~ 가겠습니다 I am going there. // ~ 가지 말게 Don't go there. / You must not go in that direction.
그리고 and; (and) then; and also; as well as. ¶방을 먼저 치우고 ~ 공부를 시작했다 First I tidied up my room, and then I began studying. // 그는 나에게 음식과 ~ 옷을 주었다 He gave me clothes as well as food. // 설탕과 소금 ~ 식초가 조금 필요하다 We need sugar, salt, and some vinegar. // ~ 다음은 내 차례였다 Then it was my turn. // ~ 우리는 목적을 달성했다 And so we ended up achieving our purpose. / And that was how we came to achieve our purpose.
그리니치시 (-時) Greenwich (Mean) Time (약어 G.M.T.).
그리니치 천문대 (-天文臺) the Greenwich Astronomical Observatory.
그리다¹ long [sigh / languish / pine] for; yearn after [for]; be sick for; miss; be attached to. ¶고국을 ~ pine for homeland / be homesick / be filled with a longing to see one's home again // 옛 시절을 ~ view the past with nostalgia / be nostalgic of the good old days / look back to the past with nostalgia // 돌아가신 어머니를 ~ sorely miss one's dead mother // 애타게 자유를 ~ have a great yearning [longing] for liberty.
그리다² 1 (그림 등을) draw; picture; paint (채색하여); sketch (약도로); (도형을) construct; describe. ¶유화를 ~ paint in oil // 산수를 ~ paint [draw] a landscape // 지도를 ~ draw a map [draw] // 원 [삼각형]을 ~ describe a circle [triangle] // 눈썹을 ~ use an eyebrow pencil / pencil one's eyebrow // 입술을 ~ rouge one's lips // 초상화를 그리게 하다 have one's portrait drawn [painted] / sit for one's portrait // 병풍에 모란꽃이 그려져 있었다 Peonies were painted on the (folding) screen. / The (folding) screen had a picture of peonies on it. // 독수리가 원을 그리며 날고 있다 The condor is flying in a circle. // 능선이 완만한 호를 그리고 있었다 The ridge of the moun-

tain formed [described] a gentle arc.
2 [묘사하다] depict; describe; delineate; portray. ¶그 작품은 현실 생활을 그린 것이다 The work is a picture of real life.//발자크는 그 당시 사회의 다양한 현상을 생생하게 그렸다 Balzac vividly described [(문어) depicted] the various social phenomena of his time.
3 [상상 [회상] 하다] imagine; picture [figure] (a thing) (to oneself); image a picture (to oneself); conjure up an image (of). ¶아름다운 풍경을 마음에 ~ picture [imagine] beautiful scenery to oneself//그는 자기의 결혼을 그려 보았다 He pictured his wedding to himself.//미래의 내 모습을 그려 본다 I picture to myself my future self./I imagine my future self.

그리마 [동] a house centipede; a galley worm.
그리스 grease. ¶차축(車軸)에 ~를 치다 grease an axle.
그리스도 Christ; Jesus Christ; the Nazarene; the Messiah; the Savior; the Lord. ¶예수 ~ Jesus Christ.
그리스도교(-敎) Christianity. ⇨ ˝크리스트교
그리스 문자(-文字) The Greek alphabet; a Greek letter.
그리스 신화(-神話) Greek mythology.
그리스 어(-語) Greek; the Greek language.
그리스 인(-人) a Greek; (집합적) the Greeks.
그리스 정교회(-正敎會) the Greek Orthodox Church.
그리움 yearning; longing; attachment; affection; nostalgia. ¶~을 못 이기다 feel an irresistible yearning for [after] //당시를 회상하니 ~으로 가슴이 메인다 Looking back to that time, I am filled with nostalgic sweetness.
그리워하다 long [yearn / pine] for. ¶고향을 ~ have a longing for home; be homesick / pine for home//어머니의 모습을 ~ think of [remember] my (dead) mother//옛 친구를 ~ yearn for one's old friend//조국을 ~ long for one's home-land//돌아가신 할머니를 ~ miss one's dead grandmother very much//그녀는 고향을 그리워하고 있다 She is yearning [longing] for her home.//그녀는 역사 선생님을 그리워하고 있다 She misses her history teacher. / She remembers her history teacher.
그리저리 [되어 가는 대로] at random; at [by] haphazard; in a hit-or-miss manner; by trial and error; in a desultory way. **그리저리하다** try this way and that; do (a thing) at random [haphazard]; do (a thing) by trial and error.
그린 [골프장 구멍 주위의 퍼팅 구역] a putting green.
그린벨트 a greenbelt. ¶~ 지역 a greenbelt zone.
그림 (일반적으로) a picture; [연필·펜·크레용화] a drawing(무채색의); [수채화·유화] a painting; [사생화] a sketch; [삽화] an illustration(▶ 페이지 내의 일부에 넣는 삽화는 a cut, 전면적인 삽화는 a plate 라고 함); [도형] a figure; [설명도] a diagram. ¶고흐의 ~ 같은 picturesque a picture by Van Gogh//~ 같은 picturesque //~이 있는 illustrated / pictorial//~이 있는 신문 [잡지] an illustrated paper [magazine] / a pictorial//~이 들어 있는 책 an illustrated book//~처럼 아름다운 곳 a picturesque place//~을 그리다 paint [draw] (a picture) / make a picture [drawing / painting]//말을 ~을 그리다 paint a picture of a horse / draw a picture of a horse//~이 많이 들어 있다 be illustrated with many cuts [pictures] / be replete with many illustrations//그는 (풍경의) ~을 잘 그린다 He is good at painting [drawing] (landscapes). / He paints [draws] (landscapes) well. / He is a good landscape painter.//그는 서재에 르누아르의 ~을 걸어 놓고 있다 He has a Renoir in his study.//그녀는 ~처럼 아름답다 She is as lovely [pretty] as a picture.
그림의 떡 a prize beyond one's reach; (미국 속어) pie in the sky.
●**그림물감** paints; colors; (영) colours; (주로 분말) (a) pigment; (유화용) oil colors; oils; (수채화용) water colors. **그림엽서** a picture postcard; a picture card. **그림책** a picture book; [삽화가 든 책] an illustrated book; [그림 이야기책] an illustrated story book.

그림자 1 [음영] a shadow; a silhouette. ¶검은 ~ a dark shadow//죽음의 ~ the shadow of death//~놀이 a shadowgraph//~ 같은 shadowy / ghostly//어두운 ~가 드리우다 an ominous shadow looms (across)//~처럼 쫓아다니다 follow (a person) like a shadow//그의 부인은 ~처럼 언제나 그의 곁에 있다 His wife sticks to him as if she were his shadow.//사람의 ~가 창호지에 비쳤다 The shadow of a man fell on the paper window.//그 건물의 ~가 보도 위에 깔려 있었다 The shadow of the building lay across the pavement.//그 집안은 온통 어두운 ~에 싸여 있다 The whole house is wrapped in gloom. / A dark shadow is hanging over the whole family.//그 불행은 집안에 어두운 ~를 던졌다 The misfortune cast a blight over [came like a blight to] the family.//그의 얼굴에 죽음의 ~가 비쳤다 The shadow of death was on his face.
2 [영상] a reflection; an image; a figure; a shadow. ¶거울에 비친 ~ the picture in a mirror//호수에 비친 산의 ~ the mountain reflected [mirrored] in the lake//물속에 비친 자신의 ~를 보다 look at one's own shadow in the water//아치 다리의 ~가 연못에 비치고 있었다 The arched bridge was reflected in the pond. / The pond reflected the image of the arched bridge.
3 [자취] a shadow; a sign; a trace; a clue. ¶~도 보이지 않다 be completely [entirely] out of sight / there is no sign of (a person) there//거리에는 사람의 ~도 보이지 않는다 Not a soul was to be seen on [in] the street.//적의 ~도 보이지 않았다 Not a shadow of the enemy was seen. / There was no sign of the enemy anywhere.//어찌된 셈인지 그는 요즘 ~도 비치지 않는다 I don't know why but he never comes to see me these days.

그립다 dear; sweet; beloved; longed-for; (서술적) yearn after [for] (a person); miss (a friend). ¶그리운 사람 my beloved / my dearest//그리운 내 고향 my dear old home//그리운 추억 [sweet] memories / memories dear to one//20년 전의 그리운 옛날 the nostalgic past of twenty years ago//옛날이 ~ I long for the days past.//그 사람이 ~ I miss him.//고국이 ~ I am homesick for my native country.//고향이 ~ I am sick for home. / I am homesick. / I long for my old home.//친구가 ~ I pine for [miss] my friend.//그 노래를 들으니 옛날이 ~ That song conjures up memories of the good old days.//나는 그것을 그리운 마음으로 회상하니 다 I look back on it with nostalgia.

그만[1] [그만한] (a) little (amount of); so little [small] as; such (a trifle); as [that] much; to that (small) extent; no more than; only. ¶~ 일로 화내지 말게 Don't let so slight a thing put you out [ruffle your temper].//~ 빚으로 무슨 걱정이냐 Don't worry about such a nominal debt.//~ 돈이 없다니 웬일이냐 How comes it that you don't have that little amount of money?//~ 일에 낙심 마라 Don't be disappointed about such a trifle.//~ 일은 어린애라도 할 수 있다 Even a child can do that.//~ 일은 바보라도 안다 Even a fool knows as [that] much.

그만[2] **1** [그 정도로] that much and no more; to that extent only; no more than that; (명령형) Stop (doing). ¶~ 지껄여라 Stop talking! / Don't talk any more!//~ 울어라 Do not cry any more.//이제 ~ 자는 게 좋겠다 You'd better go to bed now.//술은 이제 ~ I have had quite enough wine. / I've drunk enough. / I want no more of drink.//자랑 좀 ~ 해라 No more of your bragging.//~ 해 두는 것이 좋겠다 You had better not go farther.
2 [곧] as soon as; no sooner than; immediately; directly. ¶그는 화를 버럭 내면서 ~ 가버렸다 He went off immediately in a fit of sudden temper [anger].//그녀는 남편의 사망 소식을 듣자 ~ 기절했다 She fainted instantly at the news of her husband's death.//자리에 들자 그는 ~ 잠이 들었다 As soon as he went to bed, he fell asleep.//그는 나를 보자 ~ 달아났다 He ran off at the moment he saw me.
3 [부주의로] carelessly; by mistake [accident]; [본의 아니까] involuntarily; unintentionally. ¶~ …하다 do by mistake / be careless enough to do//그릇이 ~ 방바닥에 떨어져 산산조각이 났다 The dish just fell on the floor and broke to pieces, that's all.//오늘 외출한다고 말하는 것을 ~ 잊었다 I forgot to say that I should go out today.//나는 ~ 입을 잘못 놀리고 말았다 I let slip the truth.//곧 답장을 쓰겠다고 생각하면서도 바빠서 ~ 실례했습니다 I meant to answer your letter promptly, but I was so busy I never got around to it.//나는 꾸지람을 들을 것이 두려워 ~ 고백할 기회를 놓쳤다 I missed my chance to confess because I was afraid of being scolded.//가난 때문에 ~ 죄를 저질렀습니다 I was tempted by poverty to commit a crime.//일을 ~ 잡치고 말았다 Things were finally broken off in spite of my desire.

그만그만하다 [어슷비슷하다] (서술적) be nearly [about] the same; be much the same; be much of a muchness; (구어) be of a hair; be six of one and half-a-dozen of others. ¶나이가 ~ be about the same age//모두 ~ All of them are about the same. / All of them are so-so.//영어 실력이 다 ~ All the students have about the same amount of English.//손익이 ~ The gains and losses are about on a par.//참석자들은 나이나 실력이 ~ All participants were of a sort of both age and competence.//두 사람은 ~ They are both of a hair. / There is little difference between two persons (in their circumstances).//내 병은 그 후로도 여전히 ~ I have been more or less ailing ever since.

그만두다 1 [중지하다] stop (doing / a fight); discontinue (doing); cut out; [포기하다] give up; abandon; renounce; [취소하다] call off (a meeting). ¶계획을 ~ abandon [give up / lay aside / drop] a plan / give up a project [an idea / a scheme]//갑자기 ~ cut [stop] short [suddenly] / break off//공부를 ~ give up one's studies / stop studying//이야기를 ~ cease talking//거래를 ~ close an account (with a person)//사업을 ~ give up one's business//그녀는 2학년 때 대학을 그만두었다 She left [quit / gave up / dropped out of] college in her second year [(미) sophomore].//그만두었더라면 좋았을 것을 I wish I had not done it.//나는 연습을 그만둔 지 오래다 I have long been out of practice.//(구어) 그만둬라 Enough [None] of that! / Drop it! //농담은 그만둬라 None [Enough] of your jokes!//그 사건 이후로 그는 저술 [글쓰기]을 그만두었다 He has quit [given up] writing since that incident.//그는 어떤 이야기를 끄집어내다가 그만두었다 He started to say something but checked himself.//나는 그에게 고함치려고 생각했다가 그만두었다 I felt inclined to shout at him, but I held myself back [checked myself].//나는 당분간 영어 공부를 그만두었다 I have discontinued [left off] studying English for some time.//그가 들어오자 그들은 이야기를 그만두었다 They stopped [ceased] talking when he came in.//잘 안 되거든 그만두시오 If you do not succeed, please do not trouble further.
2 [폐지하다] abolish; do away with; discontinue. ¶허례를 ~ dispense [do away with] formalities//형식적인 것은 그만두자 Let us do away with all ceremony.
3 (술·습관 등을) stop (drinking); give up (smoking); break oneself of (a habit); [삼가다] refrain [abstain] from (drinking). ¶술을 ~ give up drinking / (미) go on the wagon //그의 술 마시는 [담배 피우는] 습관을 내가 그만두게 해 주리라 I will cure [break] him of the habit of drinking [smoking].
4 [사임하다] resign (one's post); leave [quit / throw up] (one's job); retire (from office). ¶회사를 ~ leave (the service of) the company//공무원 직을 ~ leave [retire from] government service//그는 직장 [직업]을 그만두었다 [사직하다] He quit [left] his job. / [무직이다] He is out of a job. / [해고되다] He was dismissed [fired] from the company [his job]. / [은퇴하다] He retired from office.//그는 국회의원을 그만두었다 He resigned his seat in the House.//그는 의장을 그만두었다 He resigned as chairman. / He resigned from the chairmanship.//그녀는 몇 년 전에 교사 직을 그만두었다 She gave up his job as a schoolteacher several years ago.

그만이다 1 [그뿐이다] be the end (of it); be no more than that; [상관없다] do not mind [care / matter]. ¶그것만 있으면 ~ That is all I want.//헤어지면 ~ That's the end of all if they take apart.//늦어도 ~ It doesn't matter if you are late.//해 보고 안 되면 ~ If I try and fail, that's the end of it.//자네가 가서도 그를 만나지 못하면 ~ If you go and

still can't meet him, that's that[all there is to it, the end of it].
2 〔더 할 나위 없〕 the best; the finest; superb; matchless; 〔이상적이다〕 ideal; best fit (for); most suitable (for); 〔충분하다・만족스럽다〕 satisfactory; enough; sufficient. ¶낚시에 그만인 곳 a capital spot for fishing∥날씨가 ~ This is ideal weather.∥그녀의 요리 솜씨는 ~ She is a perfect cook.∥따끈한 커피 한 잔이면 ~ Just a cup of coffee will suffice me.∥그 일에는 그가 ~ He is the best man for the job.∥여름 휴양지로는 호숫가가 ~ No other place than the lakeside would be better for a summer recreation site.∥천 원만 있으면 ~ A thousand won will do[is enough].∥이 맛은 정말 ~ This taste is just out of this world.

그만저만 to about that extent[degree]; about so far[much]; half way; reasonably; tolerably; ever so much. ¶날도 저물었는데 ~ 끝냅시다 Darkness has got around and let's quit today up. **그만저만하다** so[as many [much]; that[thus] much; about the same; so-so; be not too good and not too bad. ¶일을 그만저만해 두다 do one's work halfway (병이) ~ be more or less ailing (ever since) ∥내 건강은 ~ I am in tolerable health.

그만큼 〔그 분량〕 as much as that; as[that] much; 〔그 정도〕 to that extent; in that degree. ¶~ 더 as much[many] again [more] ... ~ 말했는데도 after all I have said / after all advice I gave∥~이나 돈이 있으면서도 for all one's riches / for all one's wealth∥~ 있으면 되겠다 That[So] much will do.∥~은 내가 알고 있다 I know as much.∥~으로는 충분하지 않다 That much is not enough.∥~ 노력했는데도 그는 실패하였다 For[In spite of] all his effort, he failed.∥~ 피아노를 잘 친다면 그가 콩쿠르에 입상할 것이다 If he plays that well, he will probably place in the piano contest.∥겨우 ~ 밖에 안 되는 돈으로는 우리가 아무것도 할 수 없다 We can't do anything with such a small sum of money.∥그것은 그가 ~ 애썼다는 것을 나타내는 것이다 It shows how much he went through.∥지금 떠나면 ~ 빨리 돌아올 수 있다 If you start now, you will be back the sooner.∥이 아이가 몸이 약하니까 ~ 더 측은하다 I love this boy all the more because he is weak physically.∥내 딸이 불평을 하지 않으므로 ~ 더 불쌍한 느낌이 듭니다 I feel all the sorrier for my daughter because she doesn't complain.∥~은 나도 할 수 있을 것 같다 I'm flattering myself that I can do that much.∥~의 노력은 나도 했다 I too have done that much effort.∥~ 충고를 해도 그는 듣지 않았다 All my advice was lost upon him.∥~이라도 그에게는 폐 위안이 되었지 Such as it was, it was a great comfort to him.∥~ 성공했으면 만족해야지 You ought to be content with that measure of success.∥이 구두는 비싸지만 ~ 발이 편하다 These shoes are as comfortable as they are expensive.∥내 장서는 이것이 전부가 아니고 2층에 ~ 또 있다 These are not all the books I have, I have as many more upstairs.∥노력하면 ~ 보답이 있을 것이다 Every effort you make will be rewarded.∥일을 더 많이 하면 ~ 자네가 돈을 더 받는다 If you do more work, you are paid that much more.

그만하다 1 〔웬만하다〕 tolerable; so-so. ¶그의 학교 성적은 ~ His school record it tolerable.∥"장사는 잘됩니까?" "~ 그만합니다." "How's business?" "Oh, not too bad." / "Well, I can't complain."∥환자의 병세는 ~ The patient is getting neither better nor worse.∥사고가 그만하기 다행이다 It was fortunate for you that the accident wasn't so bad.
2 〔정도가 그것만 하다〕 much the same; alike; similar; so many[much]; as many [much]; that much; so trifling; so small. ¶내 모자의 크기도 ~ My hat is of the same size with it.∥나도 그만한 것쯤은 알고 있다 I know as much.∥그만하면 충분하겠다 So [That] much will be enough.∥그만한 일로 내가 놀랄 줄 아느냐 You can't surprise me with anything so trivial as that. / It takes more than that to surprise me.∥그녀에 대한 그의 태도는 항상 ~ He has been always the same to her.∥그만한 노력도 안 하고 어찌 성공하기를 바라느냐 Don't complain about such a trifle.∥그만한 빚을 가지고 근심할 것 없네 Such a trifling[small] debt is not worth worrying about.

그맘때 about that time; that time of day [night / year]. ¶사과는 ~가 제일 맛난다 That is the time when apples taste most delicious.∥~의 천 원은 내게 큰돈이었다 For me in those days a thousand won was a big amount (of money).∥~가 사내로서 한창 기운이 왕성한 때다 Men are most vigorous at that time of life.∥~까지는 일이 끝날 것입니다 My work will be finished by that time.∥나도 ~는 무척 장난이 심했다 I was quite naughty when I was that age.

그물 1 〔구멍이 나게 얽은 물건〕 a net; (집합적) netting; network; mesh. ¶새 ~ a fowling net∥물고기 잡는 ~ a fishing net∥~에 걸린 물고기 a netted fish∥~ 모양의 netlike / reticular∥~에 걸리다 be caught in a net / be netted / be enmeshed∥~로 물고기(새)를 잡다 net fish[birds]∥~을 뜨다[짜다] make a net / net∥강에 ~을 던지다 cast[throw] a net into the river∥~을 끌어 올리다 haul in [draw up / pull in] a net∥~을 치다 pitch [lay / stretch] a net∥물고기를 잡기 위해 강에 ~을 장치하다 net a river to catch fish∥새를 막기 위해 과수에 ~이 처져 있었다 The fruit tree were netted against birds.
2 〔남을 꾀는 수단 방법〕 a net; a web; meshes; 〔수사망〕 a dragnet. ¶그는 음모의 ~에 걸렸다 He was caught in a web of intrigue.∥경찰은 범인을 검거하기 위해 ~을 쳤다 The police put out a dragnet for the criminal.
● **그물채** a netted ladle; a skimmer. **그물코** a mesh of a net.

그믐 the end of the month. ⇨**그믐날**(⇨)**그믐**
● **그믐날** the end[last day] of the month. ¶섣달 ~ (on) New Year's Eve / the last day of the year. **그믐달** the old moon. **그믐밤** the last night of a lunar month. **그믐사리** a yellow corvina caught around the end of the month.

그사이 the while; (in the) meantime; the interval. ¶~에 우리는 저녁을 먹을 수 있다 We can take our supper in that time.∥~에 그 소년은 달아났다 The boy ran away in the meantime.∥~ 안녕하십니까 How have you been all this while?∥~ 오래도록 그를 만나

그슬리다 지 못했다 I have not seen him for a long [good] while.

그슬리다 [약간 태우다] scorch; sear; roast; broil; [불에 약간 타다] get smoked [fumigated]; get scorched. ¶까맣게 ~ char / burn to a cinder // 새털을 ~ scorch the hair of a fowl / roast a fowl (unpicked) // 고기를 ~ sear the meat [steak] / broil a fish (over a fire).

그악스럽다 [장난이 심하다] naughty; mischievous; [부지런하다] diligent; industrious; [너무하다] excessive. ¶그악스러운 소년 a naughty boy // 그악스러운 사람 a fierce person // 그악스럽게 돈을 벌다 be engrossed in money-making / be all eagerness to make money // 그악스럽게 굴다 conduct outrageously [roughly] // 그악스럽게 일하다 work too hard // 남을 그악스럽게 부리다 drive a person hard / sweat a person // 그 애는 너무나 그악스러워서 다룰 수가 없다 The boy is too naughty to be controlled [persuaded].

그악하다 naughty; diligent; excessive. ⇨ 그악스럽다

그야 it; that. ¶~ 그렇지만 It may be so, but …. // ~ 물론이지 It is a matter of course (that). // ~ 그렇지 Oh, that is true. / That's right. // ~ 그럴 수도 있지 That is quite possible. // ~ 누가 모르나 Who wouldn't know that?

그야말로 [참으로] really; indeed; certainly; [그것이야말로] that is … certainly [indeed]; that is the very thing (that). ¶~ 아름답다 It is really beautiful. // ~ 구사일생이었구나 You really had a narrow escape. // 그렇다면 ~ 내가 매우 기쁘겠다 If so, I shall be very happy. // ~ 네가 잘못이다 Certainly you are wrong. / You are really to blame. // ~ 힘든 일이다 That is indeed a difficult job. // ~ 그것은 내가 원하고 있던 그대로의 것이었다 That was the very [just the] thing I had been wishing for. // 만일 건초에 불이 붙는다면 ~ 큰일이다 If the hay caught fire, it would be a real disaster. // 자넨 ~ 재산이라도 잃은 것 같은 표정을 짓고 있구나 You look (just) as if you had lost a fortune.

그예 [기어이] at last; at length; at long last; finally; ultimately; in the long run; in the last [final] analysis; after all. ¶그는 술 때문에 ~ 죽고 말았다 Drink ended [was the end of] him. // 그는 그 일을 근심하던 끝에 ~ 미치고 말았다 He took the matter too much to heart, until (at last) he went mad.

그윽하다 1 [장소가] secluded; secret; retired; sequestered; hidden; out-of-the-way; solitary lonely; peaceful. ¶그윽한 곳 a secluded spot // 그윽한 골짜기 quiet and secluded valley. **그윽이** in secret [private]; quietly. ¶먼 절의 종소리가 ~ 들려왔다 The muffled sound of a distant temple bell came to my ear.
2 (생각·뜻 등이) deep; private; secret; deep-down; profound; recondite; abstruse. ¶그윽한 생각 a secret [private] idea // 그윽한 애정 profound affection. **그윽이** profoundly; deep.
3 (정취가) refined; tasteful; (향기가) sweet. ¶그윽한 향기 a sweet scent // 뜰에는 꽃향기가 ~ The garden is fragrant with the smell of flowers. // 공중에 그윽한 백합꽃 향기가 풍겼다 The air was laden with the scent of lilies. **그윽이** sweetly; tastefully.

그을 1 (햇볕에) become suntanned; get sunburnt [browned]; be tanned with the sun; get a tan. ¶새까맣게 그은 deep- [heavily-] tanned // 햇볕에 그은 얼굴 a sunburnt [sunbrowned] face // 바닷바람에 구릿빛으로 그은 어부 a fisherman tanned leathery in the salt air // 그의 피부가 햇빛에 새까맣게 그을었다 His skin is bronzed by the sun.
2 (연기에) smoke; fume; smolder; get sooty; fumigate; get covered [black] with soot. ¶그은 sooty / smoke-stained // 연기에 그은 천장 a smoke-stained ceiling // 그은 유리 a glass stained [covered / coated] with soot // 그을 정도로 생선을 굽다 grill (a) fish until it begins to brown.

그을리다 (훈제 가공을 위해) smoke; (소독·살충을 위해) fumigate; (산화를 위해) oxidize; (연기에) cover [stain] with soot; make (all) sooty; (햇볕에) sunburn. ¶그을린 smoked / fumed // 쉽게 그을리는 피부 a skin that burns easily // 검게 그을린 오크 목재 fumed oak / 램프가 천장을 그을린다 The lamp smokes the ceiling.

그을음 soot; black dirt. ¶~이 끼다 become sooty / have soot on it / be soot-covered // ~을 쓸어 [닦아] 내다 sweep away [wipe off] the soot.

그이 that person; he; she.

그저 1 [줄곧] yet; still; without ceasing [stopping]; so far. ¶비가 ~ 계속해 내리고 있다 It keeps on raining. // 그녀는 ~ 책만 읽고 있다 She is still reading. // 그는 아침부터 ~ 텔레비전만 보고 있다 He has been watching television all through the morning. // 그는 ~ 가족에게 걱정만 끼치고 있다 He is a constant source of anxiety to his family.
2 [생각 없이] recklessly; wildly; immoderately; aimlessly; heedlessly; at random; [이유 없이] without any reason; [어쨌든] anyhow; anyway; [하는 일 없이] without doing anything (in particular). ¶~ 자꾸 두드리다 hit wildly / beat (a person) blind // ~ 빚을 마구 지다 go into debt recklessly // 그녀는 ~ 웃기만 하였다 She said nothing but smiled. // 그녀는 ~ 앉아 있다 She is sitting down doing nothing. // 그는 아무 말도 하지 않고 ~ 가 버렸다 He went away without a word.
3 [신통하지 않다] so-so; all right (but not terribly good). ¶~ 쓸 만하다 be just passable // "영화가 재미있었느냐?" "~ 그렇더라." "Was the movie interesting?" "It was so-so."
4 [단지] merely; slightly; just; only. ¶~ 약간 just a little [bit] // 지나는 길에 ~ 들렸네 As I happened to come this way, I have just dropped in at your house. // ~ 농으로 한 말일세 I said it merely [only] as a joke [just for fun]. / I did not mean what I said. // 그는 ~ 이름만의 총재이다 He is a president only in name. // ~ 제가 해야 할 일을 했을 뿐입니다 I only have done what I ought to (do).
5 [제발] please; I beg of you. ¶~ 네가 참아라 Won't you be patient, please? // ~ 살려만 주십시오 Please save me. / Spare me for mercy's sake.

그저께 the day before yesterday. ¶~ 아침 [밤 / 저녁] the morning [night / evening] before last.

그전 (-前) former days [times]; the other day; the past. ¶~에 in the past / formerly / before / in old days / previously // ~ 주소

former address // ~같이 as before / as usual // 우리는 ~부터 아는 사이다 We've known each other for a long time. // 모든 것이 ~과는 다르다 Things are not what they used to be. // ~에 빌려 갔던 책을 그녀가 가져왔다 She has returned the book she borrowed sometime ago.

그제야 only then; not until; at that ... for the first time; only when; only after; at last; for the first time. ¶며칠이 지나서 ~ 나는 그 사실을 알았다 It was not until a few days later that I learned the truth. // 사람들은 건강을 잃고 나서 ~ 그 고마움을 안다 People do not know the blessing of health till they lose it. // 나는 ~ 화재의 무서움을 깨달았다 Then I realized for the first time how horrible a fire was. // 내 말을 듣고 ~ 그는 자기가 잘못된 것을 깨달았다 I had to explain it to him before he realized he had made a mistake. // 선생님이 떠나신 후 ~ 우리는 그 고마움을 알게 되었다 We understood the teacher's worth only when he left.

그중 (-中) [가장] the most; the best. ¶이것을 나는 ~ 좋아한다 I like this better than the others. // 나는 수학이 ~ 싫다 I like mathematics least.

그즈음 about[at] that time; then; in those days. ¶~ 아버지는 공무원이었다 In those days my father was a government official. // ~의 여성은 기본적 인권을 거의 가지고 있지 않았다 Women in those days had few fundamental human rights. // ~은 여자는 20살 이전에 결혼하는 관습이 있었다 It was then[at that time] customary for girl to get married before the age of twenty.

그지없다 [끝없다] limitless; boundless; endless; [더할 나위 없다] extreme; exceeding; [표현할 수 없다] beyond expression [description]. ¶유감스럽기 ~ be extremely sorry《for》 // 가엾기 ~ be too pitiful for words // 고맙기 그지없습니다 I offer my heartiest thanks. // 사람의 욕심은 ~ There are no bounds[limits] to man's greed. // 그 경치는 아름답기 ~ I can't fully describe the beauty of the view. / The beauty of the view is beyond description. **그지없이** limitlessly; boundlessly; endlessly; extremely; exceedingly. ¶~ 넓은 바다 a boundless expanse of the ocean // 저는 ~ 기쁩니다 I couldn't be happier. / Nothing could make me happier. // 효도에 바친 당신의 노력은 ~ 훌륭합니다 I greatly admire your efforts to do your duty to your parents.

그쯤 1 (정도) so[as] many[much]; that much; to that extent. ¶글쎄 ~ 되겠지 That is about right. // ~은 나도 안다 I know as [that] much. 2 (장소) about[near] there. ¶~에서 좀 쉬어 가자 Let's take a rest about there.

그치다 1 [멈추다] stop; [끝나다] lift; end; come to stop[an end]; [문이] cease; (소리가) die out[fade away]; (바람 등이) die down; (비·눈이) hold up. ¶그칠 새 없이 ceaselessly / continuously / without cease / with no break / 그칠 새 없는 걱정 constant worry / ceaseless anxiety // 비가 그쳤다 The rain has stopped[lifted]. / 폭풍이 그친 것 같다 The storm seems to have stopped. // 비가 잠시도 그치지 않고 내리고 있다 It went on raining without a break. // 비가 잠시 그친 사이에 나는 쇼핑을 하러 나갔다 I went out shopping during a lull in the rain. // 통증이 그칠 때까지 나는 일어나지 못했다 I could not get up till the pain subsided[left me]. // 치통이 그쳤습니까 Is your toothache gone? // 그녀는 울음을[눈물을] 그치지 않았다 She went on crying. / Tears flowed down her cheeks ceaselessly.
2 [⋯을 그만두다] stop; cease; [끝내다·제한하다] put an end[a stop] to. ¶울음을 ~ stop crying // 나는 그가 비행(非行)을 그치기 바란다 I hope he will stop misbehaving. // 그녀가 그 방에 들어가자 그들은 애기를 뚝 그쳤다 On her entering the room they suddenly ceased talking. // 그 이름만 들어도 우는 아이가 울음을 그칠 정도였다 The name alone was enough to stop a crying child. // 단지 나는 내 희망을 말하는 것에 그쳤다 I simply expressed my desire. // 그의 야심은 그칠 줄을 모른다 His ambition knows no limits. // 눈이 그쳤다 The snow has stopped falling.

그토록 so (much); such an extent. ¶자네가 ~ 심하게 말할 것까지는 없다 You don't have to use such harsh words. // ~ 소중히 그들은 그 아이를 키웠다 They had gone to all that trouble to bring up the child. // ~ 잘해 주시니 고맙습니다 Thank you so much. // ~ 돈이 많아도 그는 불만인 것 같다 He seems discontented for all his wealth. // ~ 내가 충고해도 그는 듣지 않았다 All my advice was lost upon him. // ~ 만나고 싶다면 만나게 해 주지 You shall see him if you are so anxious to. // ~ 완고한 사람은 내가 본 적이 없다 He is the most obstinate fellow I have ever seen.

극 (劇) a drama; a play. ¶사회 ~ a social-life drama // 역사[현대] ~을 상연하다 stage a historical[modern] play // 이 ~은 대단한 호평이었다 The play had a tremendous hit. / The play was very popular.

극 (極) 1 (지구의) the terrestrial poles; (전기의) the electric poles; (자석의) the magnetic poles. 2 [절정] the height; the zenith; the climax; the acme; the extreme; extremity. ¶~에 달하다 go to extremes / run to an extreme / reach its climax // 절망의 ~에 달해 자살하다 kill oneself in despair // 피로의 ~에 달하다 be exhausted to the extreme / be dead tired // 빈곤의 ~에 달하다 be reduced to extreme poverty // 도덕의 퇴폐는 그 ~에 달해 있다 They are extremely corrupt in morals.

극과 극은 서로 통한다 (속담) Extremes meet.
극값 (極-) [수] extreme value; extremum (pl. -ma).
극거리 (極距離) [천] polar distance.
극광 (極光) the aurora; the polar lights.
● **극광대** an auroral zone.
극구 (極口) ¶~ 변명하다 go to extremes in excusing oneself / make every sort of excuses / spare no pains to defend oneself // ~ 칭찬하다 speak highly of / speak in high terms of / praise[laud] 《a person》 to the skies // 그녀는 신부의 장점을 ~ 칭찬했다 She praised the bride's virtues to the skies. / She spoke with the highest praise of the bride's virtues.
극권 (極圈) the polar circles.
극기 (克己) [금욕] self-denial; [자제] self-restraint; self-control; self-abnegation; stoicism; self-command. ¶~적인 self-denying

극난하다

∥~력이 있는 사람 a self-denying[stoic] person / a man of self-restraint.*∥그는 ~력이 있다[없다]* He was[has no] self-control. **극기하다** deny oneself; exercise self-denial. *¶체중을 줄이려면 식사 때에 극기를 필요가 있다* To reduce, one has to practice self-denial at the dinner table.
● **극기심** a self-denying spirit; the spirit of self-restraint.

극난하다(極難-) most (extremely) difficult; very hard.

극단(極端) an extreme; extremity; a pole. *¶인간성의 양~* the extremes of human nature *∥~으로 흐르다* go to extremes[excess] / run to an extreme / go too far *∥양~은 상통한다* Extremes meet. *∥젊은 사람들은 ~으로 흐르기 쉽다* Young people are apt to go to extremes. *∥그의 견해는 ~에서 ~으로 흐르는 경향이 있다* His views have a tendency to swing from one extreme to the other.
● **극단론** an extreme view. **극단론자** an extremist; a radical; an ultraist. **극단주의** extremism; radicalism; ultraism.

극단(劇團) a dramatic[theatrical] company; a theatrical troupe; a theater group; a troupe[company]. *¶국립 ~* the National Drama Company *∥지방 순회 ~* a provincial touring company / a troupe on the road / a traveling troupe.

극단(劇壇) the stage; the theatrical world; the theater. *¶~에 서다* come[go] on the stage / appear before the footlights *∥~을 떠나다* leave[go off] the stage *∥저 여배우는 ~ 출신이다* That actress comes from the legitimate stage.

극단적(極端的) extreme; excessive. *¶~으로* extremely / to the extreme degree / too far *∥~인 예* an extreme case *∥~인 좌파* the ultra-left *∥그것은 ~이다* That's going too far. *∥~인 표현을 한다면 그는 인간 쓰레기라고 할 수 있다* To put it in an extreme way, he is the scum of mankind. *∥그렇게 생각하는 것은 너무 ~이다* Thinking that way is going too far. *∥그가 그렇게 ~인 짓을 하리라고는 생각지 못했다* Little did I think that he should go to that length.

극대(極大) the greatest; the largest; [수] the maximum. *¶~의 maximal / ~의 이익[이윤]을 추구하다* seek the maximum profit.
● **극댓값** the relative maximum; the maximum value.

극도(極度) the extreme; [최대한] the maximum; [정상] the zenith. *¶~의* extreme / utmost *∥~로* extremely / in the extreme / to the highest degree / to an extreme / to the utmost *∥~로 흥분하다* be extremely excited / be excited in the extreme / be highly wrought up *∥~에 달하다* reach an extreme *∥~의 신경 쇠약에 걸리다* suffer from neurasthenia[nervous debility] of the worst kind *∥~의 근시이다* be extremely short-sighted *∥그는 ~의 위험에 처했다[놓였다]* He was in[was expose to] the utmost danger. *∥그 아이는 ~로 자기 선생을 두려워하고 있었다* The child was in extreme[great] fear of his teacher. *∥그는 ~로 감수성이 예민하다* He is extremely sensitive. / (문어) He is sensitive in the extreme. *∥그의 피로는 ~에 달했다* His fatigue reached the utmost limit of his endurance. *∥요즘 도덕의 퇴폐는 ~에 이르렀다* In these days, the depravity of morals is at its worst. *∥그는 ~의 불면증[신경증]에 시달리고 있다* He is suffering from acute[severe / serious] insomnia[nervous ailment].

극동(極東) the Far East. *¶~의* Far Eastern.
● **극동 문제** Far Eastern problems.

극락(極樂) paradise; heaven; the abode of the blessed; Elysium; [희열] supreme happiness; perfect bliss. *¶지상의 ~* an earthly paradise / an Eden *∥저 다락방과 비교하면 여기는 아주 ~이다* Compared with that attic, it is simply heaven here[this is a real paradise]. *∥아, ~에 온 것 같구나* Oh, what bliss[how pleasant]!
● **극락세계** the abode[world / land] of perfect bliss; paradise. **극락왕생** euthanasia; a gentle and easy death; an easy passage into eternity. **극락정토** the Land of Happiness[Perfect Bliss]; the Elysian fields. **극락조** [동] a bird of paradise; a king bird; a bee martine.

극량(極量) [약의 최대 투여량] the maximum dosage; (1회분의) a fatal dose.

극력(極力) [있는 힘을 다함] one's utmost exertion; the utmost; [힘껏] with all one's might; to the best of one's ability; to the utmost. *¶~ 반대하다* oppose stubbornly[to the last] *∥~ 응원[성원]하다* cheer with all one's might / [원조하다] help as much as one can *∥회사의 영업 성적을 올리기 위해 ~ 힘쓰다* do one's utmost[try as hard as possible] to improve the company's business performance *∥힘썼으나 그것이 실패로 돌아갔다* It ended in (a) failure in spite of my best efforts. *∥나는 ~ 그를 달랬다* I tried to soothe him in every way. **극력하다** exert oneself to the utmost; make an all-out effort.

극렬분자(極烈分子) a radical; an extremist.
극렬하다(極烈-) violent; severe; vehement; acute; keen. *¶극렬한 경쟁* keen competition / a sharp contest. **극렬히** violently; severely; intensely; keenly; acutely.

극론(極論) an extreme argument; sophistry. **극론하다** make[advance] an extreme argument.

극명하다(克明-) scrupulous; [정성 들이다] painstaking; [자세하다] minute. *¶극명한 묘사* a minute description. **극명히** scrupulously; painstakingly; minutely. *¶문제를 ~ 설명하다* explain a matter in detail.

극 문학(劇文學) dramatic literature.

극미하다(極微-) infinitesimal; microscopical; ultramicroscopic; atomic. *¶극미한 세계* a microscopic[an infinitesimal] world.

극복(克服) conquest; subjugation. **극복하다** overcome; conquer; surmount; subjugate; cope with; deal successfully with. *¶반대를 ~* break down[overcome] opposition *∥인플레이션을 ~* deal successfully with inflation *∥온갖 난관을 ~* conquer[overcome / surmount] all[various] difficulties *∥약점을 ~* overcome one's weaknesses *∥시국을 ~* cope with the situation *∥위기를 ~* weather a crisis *∥그는 난관을 극복하고 훌륭한 소설을 많이 썼다* He overcame his handicap and wrote many fine novels. *∥그들은 재정상의 곤란을 잘 극복했다* They successfully tided over their financial difficulties. *∥그는 불굴의*

정신으로 장애를 극복했다 His indefatigable spirit carried him over the obstacles.∥극복해야 할 여러 가지 어려움이 있었다 There were a number of difficulties to be overcome.

극본(劇本) a play; a drama. ⇨각본

극북(極北) [가장 북쪽] the extreme north.

극비(極祕) strict[absolute] secrecy; (미) top secret. ¶~의 closely guarded / in strict secrecy∥~리에 with utmost secrecy / in the greatest secrecy∥~에 부치다 keep (a matter) a strict secret / guard (a matter) with great secrecy∥나는 그에게 ~의 서한을 보냈다 I have sent him a top-secret letter.∥그것은 ~로 되어 있다 It is kept a close secret.∥의사(議事)는 ~리에 진행되었다 The proceedings were conducted in profound secrecy.∥그 제조 방법은 ~다 The process of manufacture is a jealously guarded secret.∥이 일이 ~임을 양해해 주시오 You will understand this is absolutely[strictly] confidential.
● **극비 서류** confidential documents.

극빈자(極貧者) a needy[destitute] person; a pauper; (집합적) the destitute[indigent].

극빈하다(極貧-) extremely poor; destitute; indigent; as poor as a church mouse. ¶그들은 극빈한 생활을 하고 있다 They are in utter destitution. / They live in extreme poverty.

극상(極上) the first; the best; the highest quality. ¶~의 the best / the first-rate / extrafine / excellent∥~의 장소 a tiptop place.
● **극상품** the finest[choicest] stuff; an article of the finest[best] quality; an A1 article.

극성(極性) [전] polarity. ¶~의 polar.

극성(極盛) (세력이) highly flourishing [thriving]; being very prosperous; being rampant; (성질이) extremity. ¶~을 떨다[부리다] grow impatient / run to extreme. **극성하다** impatient; impetuous; mad; frantic; furious.

극성스럽다(極盛-) impatient; impetuous; mad; frantic; furious. ¶극성스러운 사람 an impatient[impetuous] person∥극성스러운 언동 intemperate[intemperate] conduct∥자녀 교육에 극성스러운 어머니 a mother oversolicitous for her children's education∥그는 직공들이 쓰러질 때까지 극성스럽게 일을 시켰다 He drove the workers unmercifully until they collapsed.

극소(極小) the smallest; the minimum. ¶~의 생물 a microscopic form of a life. **극소하다** infinitesimal; minimal. ¶양자 간의 차이는 극소했다 The difference between the two was infinitesimal.
● **극솟값** [수] the local[relative] minimum; the minimum value.

극소량(極少量) the minimum (pl. ~s, -ma).

극소수(極少數) the minimum number; a small minority.

극시(劇詩) a verse drama; a drama in verse; dramatic poetry.

극심하다(極甚-) extreme; excessive; intense; severe; heavy; enormous; tremendous; terrible; keen. ¶극심한 더위 an intense heat∥극심한 추위 a severe cold∥농작물은 극심한 피해를 입었다 The crops suffered extremely heavy damage.∥재계의 불황은 요새처럼 극심한 때는 없었다 Never before has the financial world experienced such a heavy depression.∥후진국들은 극심한 인재난을 겪고 있다 Underdeveloped countries are faced with serious shortages of talented people.

극악하다(極惡-) extremely wicked; heinous; atrocious; devilish; brutal. ¶극악한 사람 an accomplished villain / a devil / a fiend∥극악한 행위 infernal deed∥극악한 대죄 a heinous[flagrant] crime / a crime of deepest dye.

극약(劇藥) [위험한 약품] a powerful[drastic] medicine[drug]; [독약] a poison; a violent [deadly] poison.

극언(極言) unreserved criticism; unsparing words. **극언하다** go so far as to say[declare]; be bold enough to say; speak in unsparing words; utter an extreme view; give unreserved criticism. ¶극언하자면 perhaps I am going too far in saying this, but ... / strictly speaking ...∥반역자라고까지 ~ go so far as to brand (a person) as a traitor.

극영화(劇映畫) a film drama (play); a play film.

극예술(劇藝術) the dramatic art.

극우(極右) the extreme right; the ultraright. ¶~의 extreme-rightist / ultranationalist / ultraconservative∥~의 테러리스트 extreme right wing terrorists∥그는 ~로 치우쳤다 He turned ultraconservative.
● **극우파** extremists of the right; ultranationalists.

극작(劇作) playwriting. **극작하다** write a play [drama].
● **극작가** a dramatist; a playwright. **극작법** dramaturgy.

극장(劇場) a theater; a playhouse. ¶개봉 ~ a first-run theater∥국립 ~ the National Theater∥오페라 ~ an opera house∥영화 ~ a movie theater[house] / (영) a cinema∥원형 ~ an amphitheater.
● **극장가** a theater district[quarter]; (미) a rialto.

극적(劇的) dramatic. ¶~으로 dramatically∥~인 장면[정경] a dramatic scene[sight]∥~인 사건 a dramatic event∥~인 효과 a dramatic effect∥그녀는 ~인 생애를 보냈다 She had an eventful life.

극점(極點) 1 [남위·북위 90도의 지점] a pole. ¶남~ the South Pole. 2 [극한] a limit; [절정] a climax; the extreme[highest] point; [맨 밑] the bottom; the nadir. ¶긴장의 도가 ~에 달했다 The tension rose to a climax.

극좌(極左) the extreme left. ¶~의 extreme left-wing / ultra-leftist.
● **극좌파** extremists of the left; extreme leftists.

극중(劇中) ¶~의 사건 an incident in the play / the plot(대략의 줄거리)∥~에서 불린 노래 the songs that were sung during the performance∥~에 등장하는 인물 the characters in the play.

극지(極地) 1 [남극·북극 지방] the polar region; the pole. ¶~를 횡단하다 cross the polar region. 2 [땅 끝] the ends of the earth.

극진하다(極盡-) very kind; cordial; hearty; hospitable; devoted. ¶극진한 대접 heartwarming hospitality∥나는 극진한 간호를 받았다 I was nursed with great care. / I was given the best of nursing care. **극진히** very

극찬 kindly; cordially; heartily; hospitably; warmly; with all one's heart. ¶~ 사랑하다 love deeply [devotedly] // 우리는 ~ 대접받았다 We were warmly [hospitably] received.

극찬(極讚) high praise. ¶~을 **받다** win high praise // 소년은 선행을 하여 ~을 받았다 The boy was highly praised for his good conduct.

극찬하다 praise (a person) sky-high; speak very highly of (a person). ¶두 사람의 음악 평론가가 이 젊은 지휘자를 극찬했다 Two music critics spoke very highly of [(문어) extolled] this young conductor.

극초단파(極超短波) microwave; [물] ultrahigh frequency(약어 UHF).

극치(極致) the culmination; the acme; the height. ¶완벽한 ~ the acme of perfection // 아름다움의 ~ ideal beauty // ~에 달하다 attain the highest perfection / achieve [reach] the ultimate (in) // 그의 예술은 원숙의 ~에 도달했다 His art has attained the acme of maturity.

극피동물(棘皮動物) [동] an echinoderm (*pl.* -mata).

극하다(極─) [끝까지 가다] go to the end (of), attain [reach] the summit (of); [극도에 달하다] carry (a thing) to extremity; go to extremes; run to an extreme. ¶사치를 ~을 most luxurious // 참상을 ~ present a most miserable sight.

극한(極限) the utmost limits; the bounds; (문어) an extremity (of pain); [수] limit. ¶~에 달하다 reach the limit (of patience) // ~을 넘다 [넘지 않다] go beyond [keep within] the bounds [limits] (of) // 인내의 ~에 도달하다 reach the limit of one's endurance.

●**극한값** a limiting value. **극한 상황** (독) a grenzsituation; an extreme situation. **극한투쟁** struggle to the extremes; fight to the end; resort to the extremism.

극한(極寒) severe [intense / arctic] cold.

극형(極刑) [사형] a capital punishment; the death penalty. ¶~에 처하다 condemn [put] (a person) to death.

극화(劇化) dramatization. **극화하다** dramatize. ¶소설을 ~ dramatize a novel / make a novel into a drama.

극화(劇畫) [만화] comics with a realistic narrative; [그림 연극] a picture story show.

극히(極─) very; exceedingly; excessively; extremely; remarkably; greatly; immensely. ¶~ 미묘한 most delicate // ~ 드물게 very rarely / once in a blue moon // ~ 정확하게 with religious exactitude // ~ 중요한 문제 a very important matter / a problem of paramount importance // ~ 만족해하다 be altogether satisfied (at) // ~ 유감이다 be most regret table // 나는 ~ 운이 좋았다 I had capital luck.

근(斤) a *geun* (단수·복수 동형) (=약 600 g, 1.323 lbs); a catty.

근(根) 1 (부스럼의) the core (of a boil). 2 [수] a root. ¶세제곱 ~ a cubic root // 제곱 ~ a square root. 3 [물] bases of sensation (=eye, ear, nose, tongue, body and mind).

근(筋) a muscle; [힘줄] a sinew; a tendon.

근(近) about; almost; near(ly). ¶~ 30리 nearly thirty *ri* // ~ 한 달 동안 for about a month.

근간(近刊) 1 [곧 나올 출판] forthcoming publication. ¶~의 in preparation / forthcoming // ~ 예정인 책 books to be published / forthcoming books. 2 [최근의 출판] a recent publication. ¶~의 잡지 recently published magazines.

●**근간 도서** (최근 나온) a recent publication; (곧 나올) a forthcoming book.

근간(近間) recently; lately. ⇨"요사이

근간(根幹) 1 [뿌리와 줄기] the root and the trunk. 2 the foundation; the basis. ⇨"근본

근거(根據) 1 [이유] ground(s); [기반] a basis (*pl.* -ses); [전거] authority. ¶~를 두다 (사람에) base (one's argument) on ... / find one's reasons in ... / (사물에) afford [provide] a basis for ... // ~가 있는 well-grounded [-founded] // ~가 없는 unfounded / groundless / without foundation // ~ 있는 [없는] 정보 information from a reliable [an unreliable] source // 의혹의 ~가 몇 가지 있다 There are several reasons [There is ample ground] for suspicion. // 그의 추론은 언제나 사실에 ~를 두고 있다 He always bases his inferences upon actual fact. / His inferences are always grounded in (actual) fact. // 이 소설은 사실에 ~를 두고 쓰인 것이다 This novel is based on fact. // 무엇을 ~로 당신이 나를 의심하는가 On what ground do you suspect me? // 당신이 그렇게 말하는 ~는 무엇인가 What is your authority for saying that? // 그의 의혹은 이 점에 ~를 두고 있는 것 같다 His doubts seem to have arisen from this point. 2 a base (of operations). ⇨"근거지(⇨근거)

●**근거지** a base (of operations); headquarters; a stronghold.

근거리(近距離) a short distance; a close range. ¶~에서 at close range [quarters] // ~에 있다 be located a short way off / be within a stone's throw (of) // ~에서 쏘다 shoot (at a thing) at short range // 시청은 이곳에서 ~에 있습니다 The city hall is only a short distance from here.

●**근거리 경주** a short-distance race. **근거리 전화** a short-distance (telephone) call.

근검(勤儉) thrift and diligence [industry]; diligence and economy. ¶~과 저축을 장려하다 promote thrift and saving. **근검하다** thrifty (and diligent); frugal. ¶근검한 가정주부 a frugal housekeeper.

근경(近景) a near [close-range] view (of).

근경(根莖) [식] a rootstock; a rhizome. ⇨"뿌리줄기(⇨뿌리).

근경(近境) [부근] neighboring districts; [비슷한 경우] a similar condition [case].

근계(謹啓) (친척에게) Dear [My dear] Father [Aunt Clara / Kate] (▶ my를 붙인 편이 미국에서는 보다 형식적, 영국에서는 보다 친애적, 수신자가 여자일 경우는 dear대신에 dearest를 쓸 때도 있음); (친구에게) Dear [My dear] Mary (▶ 그다지 친하지 않거나 손윗사람의 경우는 Dear Mr. [Mrs. Miss. Dr.] Smith처럼 칭호를 붙임. 여자의 경우 미혼·기혼의 구별을 싫어하는 상대에게는 Ms.를 붙이는 경우가 있음; (형식적으로) Dear Sir [Madam]; Sir [Madam]; (회사·단체 앞으로) (미) Gentlemen, (영) Dear Sirs, (여성 단체) Ladies; (수신자가 분명치 않을 때) To whom It May Concern.(▶ 사신(私信)에서는 이들 인사말 뒤에 콤마를 찍고, 상용 편지에서는 콜론을 찍음)

근고(近古) the early modern age.

●**근고사** a history of the early modern age.

근골(筋骨) **1** [근육과 뼈대] sinews and bones; (체격) build; physique; setup. ¶~이 실팍한 muscular / sinewy 《arms》 / stringy 《young man》 / powerfully-built. **2** physical strength; stamina. ⇨ 체력

근교(近郊) the suburbs; the outskirts; the neighboring[《영》neighbouring] districts. ¶~의 suburban / neighboring // 서울과 그 ~ Seoul and the neighboring districts // ~에 있는 주택 suburban residence // 부산 ~에 in the suburbs of Busan / on the outskirts of Busan // 나는 서울 ~에 살고 있다 I live in the suburbs of Seoul.
● **근교 농업** agriculture in suburban areas.

근근이(僅僅-) [간신히] barely; narrowly; hardly; with difficulty; [겨우] just; only. ¶~살아가다 make a bare living / eke out a bare existence / rub along.

근년(近年) recent years; late years. ¶~에 of late years / in recent years // ~에 없었던 추위 the coldest weather we have had in recent years // ~의 걸작(傑作) one of the best literary works in recent years.

근대 [식] (Swiss) chard.

근대(近代) recent[modern] times[ages]. ¶~의 modern / recent // ~적인 modernistic / modern // 전~적인 premodern // 초~적인 ultramodern.
● **근대 국가** a modern nation[state]. **근대 문학** modern literature. **근대사** modern history. **근대 사상** modern ideas. **근대성** modernity. **근대화** modernization; 《영》modernisation.

근동(近東) the Near East. ¶~의 Near East(ern).

근들거리다 swing; rock; sway; play loosely [to and fro]. ¶바람에 ~ be swayed by the wind / sway (about) to the wind.

근래(近來) recent days; these days ¶~의 사건 recent events // ~의 late / recent.

근량(斤量) weight. ¶~을 속이다 give short weight.

근력(筋力) muscular strength[power]; physical strength; brawn. ¶우리 할아버지는 아직도 ~이 좋으시다 My grandfather enjoyed robust health yet.

근로(勤勞) work; labor[《영》labour] (▶ work 는 일반적인 말, labor는 육체 노동 또는 일반적으로 힘이 드는 일); service; industry. ¶~에 대한 보수 compensation [remuneration] for one's service. **근로하다** labor; work; toil; serve.
● **근로 기준법** [법] the Labor Standard Act. **근로 봉사** service provided through physical labor. **근로 소득** an earned income. ¶~세 earned income tax. **근로자** a worker; a laborer; a wage earner. **근로자의 날** May Day; (미국·캐나다의) Labor Day(9월의 첫째 월요일). **근로 조건** working[labor] conditions.

근류(根瘤) [식] a (root) tubercle. ⇨ 뿌리혹(⇨ 뿌리)

근린(近隣) the neighborhood; the vicinity.

근면(勤勉) diligence; (문어) industry; hard work; (close) application; assiduity. ¶~은 성공의 어머니 Diligence is the mother of success. // 그의 성공은 ~ 덕택이다 His success was due to industry. **근면하다** diligent; hardworking; industrious. (▶ diligent는 세

부까지 정성 들여 열심인, 그 결과 일이 훌륭히 마무리됨을 의미함. industrious는 바쁘게 일함을 강조함) ¶근면한 백성 a hardworking[an industrious] people. **근면히** industriously; diligently. ¶~ 일하다 work hard [diligently / like a bee].

근멸(根滅) eradication; extirpation; extermination. **근멸하다** eradicate; extirpate; exterminate; root out; eliminate (something) root and branch.

근모(根毛) [식] a root hair. ⇨ 뿌리털(⇨ 뿌리)

근무(勤務) service; duty; work; business. ¶시간 외 ~ overtime (work) // 야간 ~ night duty / a night shift // 육상 [해상] ~ shore [sea] service // 주간 ~ day duty / a day shift // 나는 금주에 주간 ~다 I am on the day shift this week. // 초과 ~ 수당 allowance for overtime work // 특별 ~ 수당 specific duty allowance // 8시간 ~제 the eight-hour day system / the portal-to-portal 8-hour system // 해외 ~ 수당 a foreign service [an overseas] allowance // ~ 중(에) while on duty / when being in charge (of) // ~를 게을리 하다 neglect[slight] one's duties // ~를 충실히 하다 serve faithfully / be faithful to one's duty / attend faithfully to one's work // ~ 중에 술을 마시면 안 된다 You must not drink alcohol (while) on duty. // 지금 그는 6시간 ~에 종사하고 있다 He is on a 6-hour shift at present. **근무하다** do duty; be on duty; work; serve. ¶하루 8시간 ~ work 8 hours a day / work an 8-hour day // 그녀는 병원에서 간호사로 근무하고 있다 She works in [for] a hospital as a nurse. // 그는 무역 회사에 ~근무하고 있다 He works at[for] a trading company. // 그는 45년간 병원에서 근무한 후 퇴직했다 He retired after forty-five years' service at a hospital [after he had worked at a hospital for forty-five years].
● **근무 성적** one's performance record; one's record in the performance of one's duties. ¶그는 ~이 양호하다 He has a record of good service. **근무 시간** office [business / working] hours; on-duty hours. ¶지금은 ~이 아니다 [이다] I am off[on] duty now. **근무 연한** the length of one's service. **근무자** men in service; men on duty; workers. **근무 조건** conditions [terms] of employment. **근무처** one's place of employment; one's place of business [work]; one's office.

근묵자흑(近墨者黑) Who keeps company with the wolf will learn to howl.; He who touches pitch shall be defiled there with.

근방(近方) [근처] the neighborhood; the vicinity; [주변] the surrounding; the environs (of a city). ¶~에 있는 nearby / close by / in the neighborhood (of) // 서울 ~에 in and around Seoul / in the vicinity of Seoul // 나는 그 ~에 대한 것을 잘 모른다 I am a stranger around there. // 그의 집이 그 ~에서는 가장 크다 His house is the largest one thereabouts [in the neighborhood]. // 그 ~에 사는 사람에게 물으면 그의 집을 찾을 수 있을 것이오 You can find his house if you ask someone who lives in the neighborhood. // 이 ~에 우체국이 있습니까 Is there a post office in this neighborhood [(구어) around here]? // 이 ~을 모조리 뒤져서 없으면 나는 단념하겠다 If I cannot find it after searching this whole area [(구어) all over the place], I will

근배(謹拜) (편지의 끝말) Yours truly [faithfully / respectfully / sincerely].

근본(根本) 〔기초〕 the foundation, the basis (*pl.* -ses); 〔근원〕 the root; the origin; 〔본질〕 the essence. ¶모든 일은 그 ~을 바로잡아야 한다 Everything must be put right from the root.∥나는 한국의 역사를 ~부터 다시 연구했다 I studied the history of Korea all over again from the very beginning [from its origins].∥그는 선(禪)의 ~을 터득했다 He attained the essence of Zen.∥문제의 ~은 그녀가 좀 더 자립하고 싶다는 데에 있었다 The root of the trouble lay in her desire for more independence.∥그는 그들의 정책의 ~을 규명하고 싶었다 He wanted to study the basis [root] of their policy. / He wanted to discover what their policy was based on.
● **근본 문제** a fundamental problem; a key question. **근본 원리** the fundamental [basic / guiding / underlying] principle; the bedrock absolutes. **근본 원인** the basic [root] cause. ¶도산의 ~은 그의 무모한 경영에 있었다 The basic cause of the bankruptcy was his reckless management.

근본적(根本的) 〔기본적인〕 fundamental; basic; 〔철저한〕 radical, drastic; 〔각 세부에 걸친〕 thorough. ¶~인 의견의 차이 a basic disagreement∥사건을 ~으로 조사하다 examine a matter to the last detail / make a thorough investigation of an affair [a matter] ∥~인 개편이 필요하다 A thorough [radical] reorganization is needed.∥그 생각은 ~으로 틀렸다 The idea is fundamentally [basically] wrong.

근사하다(近似-) **1** 〔비슷하다〕 approximate; close; 《서술적》 closely resemble; be closely akin to. ¶인간에 가장 근사한 동물 animals most nearly allied to man [human beings]. **2** 〔멋지다〕 chic; fine; smart; excellent; splendid; wonderful; nice; OK. ¶근사한 생각 a happy [good / splendid / capital] idea∥입구가 근사하게 생긴 레스토랑 a restaurant with an impressive entrance∥근사한 소리를 하다 say nice [smart / pretty / clever] things.

근삿값(近似-) an approximate value; an approximation.

근성(根性) **1** 〔좋지 못한 성질〕 an evil nature; an unpleasant disposition. ¶관리 ~ a bureaucratic nature∥노예 ~ a servile spirit ∥상인 ~ a mercenary spirit∥섬나라 ~ an insular spirit [prejudice]∥속물 ~ snobbery / philistinism∥그는 비뚤어진 ~을 갖고 있다 He is jaundiced. / He was born with a chip on his shoulder. **2** 〔끈질긴 성질〕 willpower; 《구어》 guts. ¶~이 있는 사람 a man who has guts [plenty of grit]∥~이 없다 have no guts / be weak-willed.

근세(近世) modern time [ages]; recent times / latter days. ¶~의 modern / recent∥~의 한국 작가 Korean writers of modern times.
● **근세 국가** a modern nation. **근세사** a modern history.

근소하다(僅少-) few(수); little(양); 〔사소하다〕 trifling (cost); small; scanty; insignificant; meager. ¶근소한 차로 (win / lose) by a narrow margin∥근소한 차로 2등이 되다 be a close second∥그는 근소한 차로 선거에 이겼다 He was elected by a small majority.∥우리의 피해는 근소했다 We suffered very little damage. / We suffered only slight damage.

근속(勤續) continuous [long] service; continuance in office. ¶장기 ~ 공무원 a public official on long-term service∥아버지는 장기 ~으로 표창받았다 My father was honored in recognition of his long service. **근속하다** serve for long years; be in continuous service; continue in the service. ¶그는 그 회사에서 30년 근속했다 He served [worked] in the firm for thirty years.
● **근속 수당** a long-service allowance. **근속 연한** the length of (one's) service. **근속자** a person in long service; a long-service man.

근수(斤數) the weight (expressed) in *geun* [catties]; 〔무게〕 the weight. ¶~를 달다 weigh 《a commodity》 on a scale / check weight∥~는 근수다 give short weight∥~가 모자라다 be short of weight / be underweight ∥~를 후하게 주다 give good weight.

근시(近視) near[short]-sightedness; near vision; 〔의〕 myopia. ¶~의 near[short]-sighted / myopic∥~인 사람 a short-sighted person / a myope∥그는 ~이다 He is short-sighted [near-sighted].
● **근시안** near-sightedness; a myopia. ¶~적 사고방식 a short-sighted [narrow-minded] way of thinking.

근신(謹愼) **1** 〔언동을 삼가함〕 good behavior [conduct]; prudence; discretion; 〔자제〕 self-control; self-restraint; 〔개전〕 penitence. ¶~을 명하다 order a person to put a rein on his own behavior∥~의 뜻을 표하다 show one's penitence [repentance]. **근신하다** behave oneself; be on one's good behavior; be prudent (in speech and action); be penitent. ¶금후 근신하겠습니다 I'll behave myself better after this.∥그는 근신하고 있다 He is behaving himself. / He is behaving in a restrained way.
2 〔처벌〕 disciplinary confinement. **근신하다** be confined to one's home. ¶그 학생은 흡연하다 발각되어 1주일간의 자택 근신하라는 명령을 받았다 The student was caught smoking and ordered not to leave his house for a week.

근실하다(勤實-) diligent; assiduous; hard-working; sincere; honest. ¶근실한 학생 an assiduous student∥근실한 생활을 하다 live straight / live honestly. **근실히** diligently; assiduously; painstakingly; sincerely; honestly. ¶~ 일하다 work diligently / serve faithfully / be assiduous in one's work.

근심 anxiety; concern; solicitude; uneasiness; apprehension; fear; care; worry; trouble. ¶~이 있다 be careworn / be worried 《about》 / have worries [anxieties] / have something to worry about∥~이 없다 be free from care [worry] / be carefree / be expansive∥~을 끼치다 cause 《a person》 anxiety / give 《a person》 trouble∥그녀의 얼굴에는 ~의 빛이 보였다 There was a look of distress [a deeply troubled look] on her face. **근심하다** feel anxious 《about》; worry 《about / over》; be troubled [worried / concerned] 《about》; feel concern 《for》; be afraid of[for]; be uneasy about; be alarmed; care for. ¶근심한 나머지 in an excess of anxiety∥쓸데없이 ~ over-worry oneself∥그는 그 소문을 듣고 대단히 근심했다 He was deeply concerned at the news.∥뭘 그리 근심하고 있는가? What are

you worrying[nervous] about? / What's the trouble[worry]? / What's on your mind? // 근심하느라 나는 식욕을 잃었다 I am so worried that I have lost my appetite.
● **근심거리** a cause of anxiety; a source of a worry.

근심스럽다 anxious; worried; concerned. ¶근심스럽게 anxiously / with a worried air // 근심스러운 얼굴을 하다 wear a worried [troubled] look / have a careworn look on one's face.

근엄하다(謹嚴—) [진지하다] serious; [엄숙하다] solemn; grave; austere. ¶근엄하고 솔직한 사람 a sober, honest person // 근엄한 태도 a dignified mien // 그는 매우 ~ He is as grave as a judge[an owl]. // 우리 선생님은 근엄한 분이시다 Our teacher is an austere man.

근염(筋炎) [의] myositis; inflammation of a muscle.

근엽(根葉) [뿌리와 잎] roots and leaves.

근영(近影) a recent photograph[(구어) photo]; one's latest photo.

근원(根源) the root; the origin; the source; the basis (*pl.* bases); the fountainhead; the beginning; [원인] the cause; [정수] the essence. ¶모든 사회악의 ~ the root of all social evils // ~을 캐다 trace (something) to its origin[source] / get at[go to] the root of (something) // ~을 이루다 lie at[be] the root of (a thing) // 그 사건의 ~을 추적하다 trace the incident to its origin / look into the background of the case // 입은 재난의 ~이다 The less said, the better. / Your tongue will get you into trouble. // 증대하는 실업(失業)이 이 사회 불만의 ~이다 This social unrest has its origin in[can be traced to] increasing unemployment. // 우리는 모든 악의 ~을 규명하여 이를 박멸해야 할 것이다 We should get to[at] the root[source] of every evil and stamp it out. // 돈에 대한 집착이 모든 악의 ~이다 The love of money is the root of all evil.

근위대(近衛隊) the Royal Guards; court guards.

근위병(近衛兵) a Life Guardsman.

근육(筋肉) muscle(▶ 신체 각부의 근육을 구체적으로 가리킬 때는 a muscle); brawn(팔·다리 등의 불거진 근육). ¶~의 muscular // ~내의 intramuscular // ~이 발달한 powerfully-muscled / well-muscled / muscular / sinewy // ~이 억센 어깨 muscular[brawny] shoulders // 단단한 ~ solid[hard] muscle(s) // 어깨의 ~ a shoulder muscle.
● **근육 주사** an intramuscular injection. **근육질** muscularity. ¶~의 muscular. **근육통** muscular pain; [의] myalgia; myodynia.

근인(近因) an immediate[a proximate] cause.

근인(根因) the basic[root] cause.

근일(近日) 1 recently; lately. ⇨ 요사이 2 [가까운 미래]. ¶~ 중에 in a few days / one of these days / in a couple of days / before long // 그것은 ~ 중에 발매된다 It will be put on sale in a few days[soon / shortly]. // ~ 중에 뵙고 싶습니다 I'd like to see you one of these days. // 그것은 ~ 중에 도착할 겁니다 It will be sent to you before long. // **개점** Opening Soon!

근일점(近日點) [천] the perihelion (*pl.* -lia). ¶~의 anomalistic.

근자(近者) these[recent] days. ¶~에 these days / recently / lately / of late // ~의 recent / late / latter-day.

근작(近作) one's recent work; one's latest product.

근저(近著) one's recent (literary) work.

근저(根底) [근본] the root; [기초] the foundation; the basis (*pl.* -ses). ¶~의 fundamental / basic // ~로부터 radically / fundamentally / thoroughly / from the ground [bottom] up // 문제의 ~에 있는 것은 인종적 편견이다 The root of the problem lies in racial prejudice. / Racial prejudice is at the root[heart] of the problem. // 개인의 자유가 민주주의의 ~를 이루고 있다 Individual freedom forms the basis of democracy.

근저당(根抵當) fixed collateral; a collateral security. **근저당하다** give (a thing) in fixed collateral[as a collateral security].

근전도(筋電圖) an electromyogram.

근절(根絶) eradication(특히 범죄·병 등의); extermination; annihilation; extirpation; stamping[wiping] out. **근절하다** exterminate; stamp out; eradicate; uproot; kill off [out]; destroy completely; annihilate. ¶근절할 수 없는 악폐 ineradicable evils // 교통사고를 ~ put an end to[eradicate] traffic accidents // 독직을 ~ root[stamp] out bribery // 악의 씨를 ~ nip evil in the bud. ➜ ¶이들 다년간의 폐습은 근절시키기 힘들다 These evil practices of long standing are very hard to uproot[eradicate].

근점(近點) 1 [가까운 점] a near point. 2 [천] the perigee (point). ⇨ 근지점 3 [천] the perihelion (*pl.* -lia). ⇨ 근일점

근접(近接) approach; nearing; close contact; approximation; [천] appulse; [심] contiguity. **근접하다** draw near; come[go] close (to); approach. ¶근접한 neighboring[(영) neighbouring / nearby] (cities) / [인접한] contiguous[adjacent] (territories) // …에 근접하여 in close vicinity to … // 근접해 있다 be [stand] near[close (to)] // 그의 땅은 사찰의 경내와 근접해 있다 His land lies adjacent to the temple compound.

근정(謹呈) [삼가 드림] presentation; (책에) with the author's compliments. **근정하다** present (a person) with (a thing); make (a person) a present of (a thing).

근조(謹弔) (I respectfully express my) condolence. ¶~ 고(故) 신근호 In memorium: Sin Geunho.

근종(筋腫) [의] a myoma (*pl.* ~ta, ~s). ¶자궁 ~ (a) myoma of the uterus.

근지럽다 itchy; scratchy. ¶등이 ~ My back itches. / I feel itchy in my back. // 근지러워 죽겠다 The itching is quite unbearable [unendurable].

근지점(近地點) [천] the perigee (point); (달의) the lower apsis. ¶~의 perigeal / perigean // ~에 있다 be at perigee.

근질거리다 itch; feel ticklish; feel a tickle.

근질근질하다 (사람이) feel creepy[crawly]; feel itchy; (가려운 데가) be itchy; (마음이) be impatient (of); be anxious[eager] (for / to do); be spoiling (for); ache[itch] (to do). ¶한 대 먹이고 싶어 손이 ~ feel one's back itchy[creepy] // 사실을 말하고 싶어서 속이 ~ burn to tell the truth // 그를 한 대 먹이고 싶어 내 손이 ~ My hands itch to deal him a blow.

근착(近着) recent arrival; (게시) just arrived. ¶~의 recently received / just arrived // ~의 학술지 a newly arrived learned journal.

근채류(根菜類) edible [esculent] roots; rootcrops.

근처(近處) 〔이웃〕 the neighborhood; the vicinity; 〔주위〕 the surroundings; the environs. ¶~의 neighboring / nearby / adjacent / close by // 이 ~ around [about] here // ~에서 첫째가는 미녀 the most beautiful woman in this neighborhood // 시합이 끝나면 ~의 역들이 혼잡해진다 When the game is over, nearby stations are crowded with people. // 이 ~는 너무 번잡하다 This is a very busy area [quarter]. // 명동 ~를 안내하겠소 I will show you around the Myeong-dong. // 이 ~에는 우체국이 없다 There is no post office in this neighborhood [near here]. // 그의 집이 이 ~의 어딘가에 있다고 생각한다 I think his house is somewhere around [about] here. // 이 ~에서 쉬자 Let's rest somewhere around here. // 이 ~는 밤에 위험하다 This neighborhood is unsafe at night. // 간밤에 이 ~에서 화재가 있었다 Last night there was a fire near here.

근청(謹聽) (listening with) attention. **근청하다** listen to (a person) with attention; hear attentively. ¶학생들은 노교수의 강의를 근청하고 있었다 The students were all attention [ears] when the old professor gave his lecture.

근치(根治) radical [complete / permanent] cure. **근치하다** 〔고치다〕 cure radically [completely]; effect a radical [permanent] cure. ¶근치하기 어렵다 be hard of radical cure / be hard to cure completely. →¶근치되다 be completely [radically] cured.

근친(近親) a near [an immediate] relation; a near [close] relative; (kith and) kin; (관계) near relationship. ¶그들은 ~ 간이다 They are near related [near each other in blood]. // 그의 ~ 가운데는 유명한 작가가 있다 One of his near relative [relations] is a famous writer.
● **근친결혼** (a) consanguineous marriage. **근친상간** incest.

근친(覲親) a bride's visit to her parents; a bride's (first) call on her parents. **근친하다** pay [make / give] a visit to one's parents after one's marriage; call on [upon] one's parents.

근하신년(謹賀新年) (I wish you) a Happy New Year; Allow me to offer you my hearty congratulations on the arrival of the New Year.; I hope you may have a happy New Year and that all things may prosper with you.

근해(近海) the adjoining [near] seas; the neighboring [home] waters. ¶~의 coastal / inshore / offshore // 한국 ~에서 in Korean waters // 제주도 ~에서 off the Jejudo // 인천 ~에서 in the sea near Incheon // 그 배는 한국 ~를 순항하고 있다 The ship is cruising in Korean waters.
● **근해어** a shorefish. **근해 어업** inshore fishery [fishing]. **근해 항로** a coasting line [route].

근호(根號) 〔수〕 a radical sign.

근황(近況) the recent [present] condition [situation]. ¶우리나라 대외 무역의 ~ the recent state of our foreign trade // ~이 어떻습니까 How goes the world with you? / How is the world using you? / (편지에서) Please let me know how you are getting along.

글 1 〔문장〕 writings; a composition; (문법상의) a sentence; 〔본문〕 the text; 〔문체〕 style. ¶세련된 ~ a polished sentence [style] // 알기 쉬운 ~ an easy [a simple] style // 생각을 ~로 나타내다 express one's thoughts in writing [written words] // ~을 짓다 build [make] up a composition [sentence] / form a sentence // ~을 쓰다 write (something) / do (some) writing / make [write] a composition // ~을 다듬다 polish [elaborate] one's style // 나는 「봄」이라는 제목으로 ~을 썼다 I wrote an essay [a composition] entitled "Spring". // 그는 훌륭한 [명쾌한] ~을 쓴다 He writes in an excellent [a clear] style. // ~이 바로 그 사람이다 The style is the man. // ~ 속에 애매한 점이 있다 There are some obscure points in the text. // 나는 ~쓰기를 직업으로 삼기로 결심했다 I decided to live by my pen [be a professional writer]. // 그는 교묘한 ~ 솜씨로 독자를 끌어당겼다 He attracted readers with his exquisite skill in writing.
2 〔글자〕 a letter; a character; an ideograph (한자 등). ¶~을 모르다 be unlettered [illiterate].
3 〔학식·학문〕 learning; studies; scholarship; scholarly attainments; knowledge. ¶~이 없는 사람 a person without learning / an unlettered [uneducated] person // ~이 있는 사람 a learned man / a man of learning / a scholar // ~깨나 배웠다고 뽐내다 be proud of one's learning [scholarship] // ~을 배우다 study / learn / pursue learning / follow one's studies.

글겅이 a currycomb.

글겅이질 〔빗질〕 currying; currycombing; 〔착취〕 exploitation; exploiting; sweating; squeezing. **글겅이질하다** curry (a horse); clean [brush] (a horse) with a currycomb; exploit [squeeze] (a person).

글귀(-句) 〔어구〕 words; terms; 〔구절〕 a phrase; a clause; a sentence; a passage; an expression; 〔시가〕 a line(1행); a verse(1절); a stanza(1연); a poem. ¶흔히 쓰는 ~ stock phrase // ~가 어색하다 be poorly worded // ~를 외다 memorize a passage // 초대장은 보통 이런 식의 ~로 쓰여 있다 In invitations the text is usually worded in this manner. // 이런 ~로 쓰기 시작하면 어떤가 How about beginning (your essay) with these words? // 그 1절의 (정확한) ~는 생각나지 않지만 그것은 매우 감동적이었다 I don't remember the (exact) wording of the passage, but it was very moving.

글꼴 a fo(u)nt. ¶그는 기사를 보다 수월하게 읽기 위해 ~을 바꿨다 He changed the font to make the report easier to read.

글동무 a schoolmate; a schoolfellow; a fellow student; a classmate.

글라디올러스 〔식〕 a gladiolus (pl. ~, -li, -es).

글라스 〔유리잔〕 a glass. ¶~를 비우다 empty one's glass.

글라이더 〔항〕 a glider. ¶~를 조종하다 maneuver [control] a glider.

글래머 a glamor girl; a glamorous-[voluptuous-]looking girl.

글러브 〔운동용 가죽 장갑〕 〔야구〕 a (leather)

글로불린 [생] globulin.
글로빈 [생] globin.
글루타민 [화] glutamine.
글루탐산 (-酸) glutamic acid; glutamate.
글리세린 [화] glycerin(e).
글리코겐 [화] glycogen.
글발 1 [적어 놓은 글] jotting; notes. **2** [글씨의 모양] the appearance of one's letters; [필적] handwriting; penmanship. ¶~이 고르다 the letters are even. **3** [문맥] the context (of a passage); coherence(일관성). ¶~이 서다 be coherent.
글방 (-房) a private[home] school (for the study of Chinese classics); a village school.
글벗 a comrade in letters.
글썽글썽 with tearful eyes. **글썽글썽하다** (서술적) be filled[brimming / swimming] with tears. ¶눈물이 글썽글썽한 눈 eyes suffused [filled] with tears. / 그녀의 눈에는 눈물이 글썽글썽했다 Her eyes swarm[were filled] with tears. / Tears stood[gathered] in her eyes. / Her eyes were wet[moist] with tears. // 그녀는 눈물이 글썽글썽한 눈으로 편지를 다시 읽어 보았다 She read the letter again with tearful eyes[with eyes brimming with tears].
글썽하다 be filled with tears. ⇨ **글썽글썽하다** (⇨ 글썽글썽)
글쎄 1 [강조·고집] just; please. ¶~ 내 말을 들어 All right. But listen to me. // ~ 해 보라고 Just try it. // ~ 조용히 하라니까 Please be quiet! // 그 아이디어라면, ~ 홍 씨한테서 나왔을거야 That idea may have come from, say, Mr. Hong. **2** [주저] well; say; I think; let me see; (생각할 때) ah; uh; er—. ¶~ 아무래도 모르겠는데 Well, I am sure I don't know. // ~ 어디다 두었더라 Let me see — Where have I put it? // ~ 네 잘못인지도 모를 일이지 Well, you may be wrong. // ~ 내주까지 기다릴까 Well, shall we wait until next week? // ~ 그럼 돈이 얼마 더 필요하니 Well, then, how much more money will you need?
글쎄요 Well, let me see. ¶"몇 사람이나 됩니까?" "~, 한 300명쯤 되겠죠." "How many people are there?" "Well, I should say about three hundred." // ~ 그럼 내가 직접 가지요 Well, let me see. I'll go myself, then.
글씨 1 [글자] a character; a letter(a, b, c등); an ideograph(한자 등). ¶굵은[가는] ~ a heavy[slender] character // ~를 휘갈겨 쓰다 write hastily / scribble / scrawl // 이 ~는 빨간색으로 써야 했다 This character should have been written in red.
2 [글자를 쓰는 일] writing; [글자를 쓰는 법] how to write; penmanship; calligraphy. ¶~를 가르치다 teach how to write // ~ 연습을 하다 practice penmanship[handwriting] / learn calligraphy.
3 [필적] handwriting; a hand; penmanship. ¶알아보기 힘든 ~ a handwriting hard to read // ~를 잘[못] 쓰다 write a good[poor] hand / be a good[poor] penman // 이것은 스미스 씨의 ~이다 This is Mr. Smith's handwriting. // 이 편지는 여자 ~로 되어 있다 This letter is in a feminine[female] hand [woman's handwriting.].
● **글씨체** a style of penmanship[handwriting]; a calligraphic style.
글월 1 [글] a writing; a letter(글자); a sentence(문장). **2** [편지] a letter; a note; an epistle.
글자 (-字) a letter; a character; an ideograph(한자 등). ¶큰 ~ [대문자] a capital letter / a cap // 작은 ~ [소문자] a small letter // ~ 그대로 as it might be understood without explanation / literally / to the letter // ~를 모르다 be unlettered / illiterate / be an ignoramus // 아이에게 ~를 가르치다 teach a child his letters.
글재주 literary talent[ability]. ¶~가 있다 have a talent for writing // ~가 있는 사람 a person of[gifted with] literary ability.
글제 (-題) the subject[theme / title] of a composition[an article / a poem]. ¶~를 내다 give[set] a subject[theme] (for a composition) // "민주주의"라는 ~로 글을 짓다 write a composition on the theme, "Democracy."
글줄 a line[row] of writing.
글짓기 composition; writing. **글짓기하다** write [make] a composition; (미) write a theme.
글피 two days after tomorrow; three days from today[now]. ¶~까지 in three days.
긁다 1 (손톱·연장 등으로) scratch; scrape (off / away / out / down). ¶머리를 ~ scratch one's head // 가려운 데를 ~ scratch an itchy spot[place] / scratch where one itches // 벌레 물린 데를 ~ scratch an insect bite // 구두의 흙을 ~ scrape one's shoes / scrape the mud off one's shoes // 긁어 부스럼을 만들지 마라 Let sleeping dogs lie. / Let[Leave] well enough alone.
2 (네발짐승이 앞발로 땅·바닥·문을) paw. ¶말이 앞발로 땅을 긁고 있다 A horse is pawing (at) the ground.
3 [그러모으다] scrape[rake] up[together]; gather up. ¶낙엽을 긁어모아 수북이 쌓다 rake up[together] fallen leaves in a heap // 난로에서 석탄재를 긁어내다 rake (out) the coal ashes from a stove // 냄비의 누룽지를 긁어내다 scrape (away) the burned bits of food from[off] a pan // 문의 페인트를 긁어내다 scrape the paint off the door // 돈을 긁어모으다 rack one's money together / collect all the money one has // 우리는 그럭저럭 사람을 긁어모아 야구팀을 만들었다 We scraped together a baseball team.
4 [남의 마음·감정·기분을 자극하다] offend; provoke; irritate; stimulate; nag (at); gripe (at); [헐뜯다] find fault with; carp[cavil] at. ¶남을 ~ irritate[offend] a person / find fault with a person / nag[pick] at a person // 바가지를 긁어 남편을 못살게 굴다 nag one's husband to death.
5 [착취하다] extort; squeeze; exploit; (속어) soak; (미국 속어) sweat. ¶돈을 긁어내다 extort[squeeze] money from (a person) / fleece (a person) of his money / bleed[soak / milk] (a person).
긁어먹다 extort; squeeze; exploit; (속어) soak; (미국 속어) sweat (one's employees). ¶그는 가난한 사람들에게서 돈을 긁어먹고 산다 He lives on the money squeezed out of poor people. / He lives off the poor.
긁적거리다 scratch[scrape] repeatedly [successively]. ¶머리[등]를 ~ scratch one's head[back] again and again.
긁적긁적 scratching and scratching; scraping and scraping. **긁적긁적하다** scratch repeatedly. ⇨ **긁적거리다**

긁히다 1 (손톱·연장 등으로) be scratched; clawed; be scraped. ¶긁힌 자국 a scratch // 얼굴을 ~ be scratched on the face / 가시에 손을 긁혔다 I've scratched my hand with the thorns. / I got my hand scratched with the thorns. **2** [그러모이다] be raked; rake. ¶낙엽이 잘 긁힌다 The leaves rake up easily. / 이 갈퀴는 잘 긁힌다 This rake rakes well. **3** (기분·감정 등이) be offended [provoked]; be nagged [griped]; be irritated; [헐뜯기다] be found fault with; be carped [cavilled]. **4** (착취당하다) be extorted [exploited / squeezed]; be fleeced (of one's money); be bled [soaked / sweated].

금[1] (값) a price; a cost; value; worth. ¶적당한 ~ a moderate [reasonable] price / ~이 오르다 the price goes up [rises / advances] / (물건이) rise [advance] in price / ~이 내리다 the price falls [goes down] / (물건이) come down [fell / decline] in price // ~이 맞으면 if the price is satisfactory [moderate / reasonable] // ~이 나가다 cost much / be high in price / be dear [expensive].

금[2] **1** [균열] a crack; a crevice; a cleft; a chink; a fissure. ¶벽의 ~ a crack in the wall // 우정의 ~ a crack [rift] in a friendship // ~이 가다 crack / be cracked / ~이 간 꽃병 [사발] a cracked vase [bowl] / ~이 간 갔다 The cup has cracked. / There is a crack in the cup. / 이 종은 ~이 간 소리가 난다 This bell sounds cracked. / 그것 때문에 두 사람의 우정에 ~이 갔다 That has impaired [caused a crack in] their friendship. **2** [선] a line; [접은 자국] a fold; a crease; [주름] a wrinkle. ¶~을 긋다 draw a line.

금(金) **1** [황금] gold. ¶~시계[반지 / 메달] a gold watch [ring / medal] / ~의 gold / golden // ~을 입힌 gold-plated / gilded / ~빛의 golden-colored / golden // ~을 입히다 plate (a thing) with gold // 이에 ~을 씌우다 crown a tooth with gold. **2** Friday. ⇨ 금요일

금가락지(金-) a pair of gold ring.
금가루(金-) gold dust; powdered gold.
금강산(金剛山) the Geumgangsan (Mt. Geumgang).
금강산도 식후경(속담) The spectacles of the Geumgangsan cannot interest the hungered.; Bread is better than the song of the birds.
금강석(金剛石) [광] a diamond. ⇨ 다이아몬드. ¶~을 갈다 cut [polish] a diamond.
금고(金庫) **1** [화재·도난 방지용 철제 궤] a safe; a strong box; a moneybox; a cashbox; (미국 속어) a coffin; a vault (금고실). ¶내화 ~ a fireproof safe // 휴대용 ~ a portable safe [cashbox] // ~용 경보기 a safe alarm // ~에 넣다 put [keep] (a thing) in a safe // ~을 억지로 열다 break [force] open a safe // ~을 잠그다 lock a safe / 나는 보석을 은행의 대여 ~에 맡겨 놓았다 My jewels are in a safe(ty) - deposit box at the bank. **2** [국가·공공 단체의 현금 출납 기관] a cash office; a depository.
금고(禁錮) [법] imprisonment; incarceration; confinement. ¶20일간의 ~ imprisonment for twenty days // ~중(重)[경]~ major [minor] imprisonment // ~형에 처하다 imprison / confine / incarcerate // 그는 5년의 ~형을 받았다 He was sentenced to five year's imprisonment.
금과옥조(金科玉條) golden rule. ¶~로 삼다 adhere strictly (to) / stick fast (to) / recognize no other authority (than) // 나는 아버지의 가르침을 ~로 삼고 있다 I follow my father's teachings faithfully. / I treat each of my father's teachings as a golden rule.
금관(金冠) **1** [왕관] a gold crown [coronet]. **2** (치과의) a (gold) crown. ¶~을 씌우다 crown (a tooth) with gold.
금관 악기(金管樂器) the brass.
금광(金鑛) **1** [금을 캐내는 광산] a gold mine. **2** [금을 함유한 광석] (a) gold ore.
금괴(金塊) a lump [nugget] of gold; (무역·주조용의) gold bullion; (봉상(棒狀)의) a gold bar; [주괴] a gold ingot. ¶~ 밀수 smuggling of gold.
금권(金權) the power of money; financial [monetary] influence.
금궤(金櫃) a cash [money] box; (매상금을 넣는) a till; [금고] a strong box.
금기(禁忌) (a) taboo; tabooing; [의] contraindication. ¶배합 ~ 약품 incompatible drugs. **금기하다** taboo; (음식물을) abstain voluntarily from (certain food).
금남(禁男) off-limits to men; forbidden to men; "Women Only". ¶~의 집 a home without a man.
금납(金納) cash payment; payment in money. **금납하다** pay in money.
금낭화(錦囊花) [식] a bleeding heart.
금년(今年) this year. ⇨ 올해
금니(金-) a gold(-capped) tooth; the gold casing of one's tooth. ¶~를 하다 have a gold tooth put in / have a tooth capped with gold / stop [fill / plug] a tooth with gold.
금단(禁斷) prohibition; (마약의) withdrawal. ¶~의 열매 the forbidden fruit / 여기는 살생 ~의 장소이다 Catching fish or hunting birds is prohibited here. **금단하다** prohibit (a person from doing); forbid (a person to do).
금덩이(金-) a nugget of gold.
금도금(金鍍金) gilding; water-gilding; gold plating. ¶~의 [~을 한] overlaid with gold / gilt / gilded / gold-plated / ~을 한 시계 a gold-plated watch. **금도금하다** plate (a thing) with gold; gild. ¶촛대를 ~ gild a candlestick / plate a candlestick with gold.
금띠(金-) golden belt [band / sash / girdle].
금란지계(金蘭之契) close [fast] friendship.
금력(金力) the power of money [wealth]; the influence of money. ¶~으로 by employing [using] one's financial power / under [through] the influence of money / by force of money // 무력과 ~ sword and purse // ~에 좌우되다 be influenced by money.
금렵(禁獵) prohibition of shooting [hunting]. **금렵하다** prohibit the hunting [shooting] (of).
● **금렵구** a (game / hunting) preserve; a (wildlife / bird) sanctuary. **금렵기** (미) the closed season; (영) the close time [season].
금령(禁令) a prohibitory [an interdictory] decree; a prohibition; a ban; an embargo (pl. ~es); an interdict. ¶~을 내리다 issue a ban [an embargo] (on something) / publish a decree prohibiting (the use of the Book of Common Prayer) / interdict // ~을 어기다 violate the prohibition [ban] // ~을 해제하다 lift [remove] the ban [embargo] (on something).

금리(金利) interest (on money); money rates; [이율] a rate of interest. ¶대출 ~ loan rate // 예금 ~ deposit rate // 은행 ~ a bank rate // 표면 ~ coupon rate // 연 6%의 ~로 at an annual interest rate of 6 percent // ~를 인상[인하]하다 raise[lower] the rate of interest // 하루 5백 원의 ~로 돈을 빌려 주다 lend money at an interest rate of 500 won a day // 꾼 돈에 8%의 ~를 지불하다 pay 8 percent interest on a loan // ~가 비싸다[싸다] Money is dear[cheap] // ~가 올랐다[내렸다] Money rates have been stiffened[eased] in the Seoul Olympics. ●금리 수준 the level of interest rates; the interest rate level. 금리 자유화 the liberalization of interest rates. 금리 정책 a bank-rate policy.

금맥(金脈) **1** [금이 나는 광맥] a vein of gold. **2** [돈줄] a patron; a source of money.

금메달(金-) a gold medal. ¶그는 서울 올림픽에서 ~을 땄다 He won a gold medal at[in] the Seoul Olympics.

금명간(今明間) today or tomorrow; sometime today or tomorrow; in a day or two; in a couple of days; within forty-eight hours. ¶편지는 ~ 당신에게 도착할 것입니다 The letter will reach you in a day or two. / The letter will be delivered sometime today or tomorrow.

금모래(金-) [사금] gold dust; [금빛 모래] golden sand(s).

금몰(金-) a gold braid; (미) gold lace. ¶~이 달린 gold-braided / gold-laced.

금물(禁物) [금한 것] a tabooed thing; a taboo; a prohibited[forbidden] thing; a thing to be (carefully) avoided; a thing to be abstained from; an anathema; [해로운 것] an injurious thing; a poison. ¶~의 forbidden / taboo(ed) // 여기에서의 흡연은 ~이다 Smoking is strictly forbidden here. // 기름기 있는 음식은 그 환자에게 ~이다 All fatty food is bad for the patient. // 밤늦게까지 안 자는 것은 ~이다 Late hours are taboo. // 점잖은 사람들과의 교제에서는 그런 화제가 ~이다 Such topics are taboo in decent society.

금박(金箔) [얇은] (a) gold leaf; [두꺼운] gold foil; beaten gold. ¶~을 입히다 plate (a thing) with gold / gild // ~이 벗겨졌다 The gilt came[was rubbed] off.

금반지(金半指) a gold ring.

금발(金髮) golden[fair] hair; hair of gold. ¶~의 golden- [fair-] haired / blond (man) / blonde (woman) // ~ 벽안의 with golden hair and blue eyes // ~의 미소녀 a beautiful [lovely], fair-haired girl / a beautiful blonde.

금방(今方) [지금 막] just[right] now; just; now; [바로 전에] (just) a moment ago; [곧] at once; in a moment; immediately; [금시라도] every[at any] moment. ¶나는 ~ 도착했다[돌아왔다] I arrived[came back] just now. // 나는 ~ 죽는 줄 알았다 I expected every moment to be killed. // ~ 비가 올 것 같다 It threatens to rain. // 하늘 모양이 ~ 비를 뿌릴 것 같다 The sky looks as if it's going to rain any minute now. / It's threatening to rain any moment now. // 그녀는 ~ 울음을 터뜨릴 기색이었다 She was about to cry. / She was on the verge of tears.

금배(金杯) a gold cup[goblet].

금번(今番) (부사적) lately; recently. ¶~의 학생 분규 the school trouble we have had lately // ~ 도미하게 되어 on this occasion of my departure for America // ~ 우리 회사는 기구 개편이 있었다 Our company was reorganized recently.

금법(禁法) a prohibitory decree. ⇨금령

금 본위(金本位) the gold standard. ●금 본위국 a country on the gold standard. 금 본위 제도 the gold standard system.

금부처(金-) a gold[gilded] image[statue] of Buddha.

금분(金粉) gold dust; powdered gold.

금불(金佛) a gold image of Buddha. ⇨금부처

금붕어(金-) a goldfish. ¶~를 기르다 keep goldfish.

금붙이(金-) things made of gold; (집합적) gold; goldwork.

금비(金肥) (a) chemical[commercial] fertilizer.

금비녀(金-) a gold(en) hairpin.

금빛(金-) (a) gold[golden] color; gold. ¶~으로 빛나다 give off a golden gleam // 찬란하다 glitter in[with] golden color // 지는 해가 하늘을 ~으로 물들였다 Sunset gilds the sky. / The sky is tinted with a golden color as the sun is sinking.

금사(金沙) [금가루] gold dust; [금빛 모래] golden sand(s).

금산(禁山) a forest reserve; a reserved forest.

금상(金賞) a gold prize.

금상(金像) a gold statue; a gilded[gilt] statue.

금상첨화(錦上添花) ¶이것은 ~다 This is an additional attraction.

금새 [물건 값] price.

금색(金色) (a) gold color. ⇨금빛

금서(禁書) prohibited[banned] books.

금석(金石) **1** [쇠붙이와 돌] metals and rocks. **2** [견고한 것] an adamant. ¶~지교 a firm friendship // ~지약 a firm promise. **3** an epigraph. ⇨금석 문자(⇨금석) **4** [금을 함유한 돌] a gold-bearing rock. ●금석 문자 / 금석문 an inscription on a stone monument; an epigraph. 금석학 studies in ancient monumental inscriptions; epigraphy.

금석지감(今昔之感) ¶~을 금할 수 없다 be stuck with the change of times.

금성(金星) [천] Venus; Hesperus; the evening star.

금성철벽(金城鐵壁) an impregnable fortress; a citadel; a stronghold.

금세 [곧·바로] in a moment; at once; immediately; without delay. ¶~ 돌아오다 come back immediately // ~ 가겠다 I'll go at once.

금세공(金細工) gold-work; goldsmithing; goldsmithery.

금세기(今世紀) this century. ¶이것은 ~ 최대의 행사이다 This is the greatest event of the century. / There has been no greater event than this since the beginning of the century.

금속(金屬) (a) metal. ¶귀[비(卑)] ~ precious [base] metal // 중[경] ~ heavy[light] metals // ~의 metallic // ~제의 made of metal / metal (tube) // ~성 a metallic sound // 이 ~은 열에 녹는다 This metal melts with heat. // 철은 유용한 ~이다 Iron is a useful metal.
●금속 가공 the processing of metal; metalworking. 금속 공업 the metalworking industry. 금속 공학 metal engineering. 금속 세공

금수(-輸) an embargo on the export [import] (of). ¶자동차의 ~를 해제하다 lift the embargo on the export [import] of cars // 그 나라에서 농산물은 ~로 되어 있다 In that country agricultural products are under an embargo.
● **금수품** contraband (goods); articles under an embargo.

금수(禽獸) birds and animals [beast]; a brute; a beast. ¶~ 같은 bestial / beastly / ~와 같은 행위 a beastly conduct // ~만도 못한 놈 a fellow little better than a brute / a person worse than a brute.

금수강산(錦繡江山) (a land of) picturesque rivers and mountains; a country noted for the beauty in the landscape. ¶삼천리~ the beautiful land of Korea.

금슬(琴瑟) 1 [거문고와 비파] a Korean harp and a lute. **2** → 금실(琴瑟).

금시(今時) this [the present] time [moment]; now; nowadays. ¶~에 in a moment / at once / without delay // ~에 마음이 변하다 change one's mind in a flash.

금시계(金時計) a gold watch.

금시초문(今時初聞) ¶그것은 ~이다 I have never heard of that. / This is the first time for me to hear about that. / I didn't know that. / (It) beats me. // 그가 죽었다니 ~이다 His death is news to me.

금식(禁食) a fast; fasting. **금식하다** fast; observe a fast; go without food; abstain from food.

금실(金-) gold thread; spun gold. ¶~로 수놓다 embroider with gold threads.

금실(琴瑟) [부부의 화목] conjugal harmony; connubial bliss. ¶~지락 a happily married life / the happiness of conjugal harmony / ~이 좋다 live in conjugal harmony / lead a happily married life.

금싸라기(金-) a thing of great value.
● **금싸라기 땅** an exceedingly high-priced plot of land. ¶이곳은 ~이다 The land here is worth its weigh in gold.

금액(金額) an amount [a sum] of money. ¶큰 [작은] ~ a large [small] amount of money // 상당한 ~ a considerable [sizable / good] sum of money // 막대한 ~ an infinite [enormous] sum of money // 손해 ~은 500만 원에 달한다 The damage amounts to five millions won. // 전부 합하면 상당한 ~이 된다 The whole comes to an enormous sum.

금어(禁漁) prohibition of fishing [fishery].
● **금어구 / 금어장** an area closed to fishing; no-fishing area [zone]; a marine preserve. **금어기** (미) the closed season (for fishery); (영) the close time [season].

금언(金言) a wise [golden] saying [saw]; a proverb; a maxim; an adage.
● **금언집** a collection of maxims and proverbs.

금연(禁煙) prohibition of smoking; no smoking. ¶차내 ~ (게시) No Smoking in This Car [Carriage] / Smoking Prohibited in This Car. // 교내에서는 ~입니다 Smoking is prohibited within the school compound. **금연하다** give up [quit] smoking. ¶그는 설날부터 금연하고 있다 He gave up smoking on New Year's Day. / He has not smoked since New Year's Day. // 의사는 내게 금연하라고 말했다 My doctor advised me to give up [quit] smoking.
● **금연석** a non-smoking seat. **금연 운동** an antismoking [anti-tobacco] campaign. **금연자** a nonsmoker.

금요일(金曜日) Friday (약어 Fri.). ¶성(聖) ~ [기] Good Friday // 13일의 ~에 on Friday the 13th [▶ 서양에서는 불길한 날] // 다음 주 ~에 만납시다 See you again next Friday.

금욕(禁慾) abstinence; ascetic practice; (성욕의) continence; sexual abstinence. ¶~ 생활을 하다 lead an ascetic [continent] life. **금욕하다** control one's passions and desires; be ascetic [continent]; practice asceticism [continence].

금월(今月) this month; the present [current] month; instant (약어 inst.). ¶~ 10일 (on) the 10th inst // ~ 중에 in the course of this month / before the end of this month.

금융(金融) [자금의 대차] finance; financing; monetary circulation. ¶수출 [수입] ~ export [import] financing // ~의 money / monetary / financial / banking // ~이 긴축되어 있다 Money is tight.
● **금융 감독 위원회** the Financial Supervisory Commission. **금융계** [금융업자들의 사회] the financial world; the financial [banking] circles. **금융 공황** a financial crisis; a banking [financial] panic. **금융 기관** a financial institution; a banking agency. **금융 긴축** monetary stringency; tight credit. **금융 긴축 정책** a tight-money policy. **금융 시장** (좁은 뜻의) the money market; (넓은 뜻의) the financial market. **금융업** financial [banking] business; money lending business. **금융 자본** financial capital. **금융 회사** a financial company [firm].

금은(金銀) gold and silver.
● **금은방** a jeweler's (shop). **금은보배 / 금은보화** money and valuables; treasures; worldly goods. ¶건강은 ~보다 귀한 것이다 Health is better than wealth.

금의환향하다(錦衣還鄕-) go home loaded with honors; return to one's old home in glory.

금일(今日) today; this day. ¶~의 신문 today's newspaper / ~ 오후 this afternoon / ~ 휴업 (게시) Closed (For) Today. / 이 표는 ~에 한해서 유효합니다 This ticket is good [valid] only today. // 전람회는 ~로 끝납니다 The exhibition ends today. / This is the last [closing] day of the exhibition.

금일봉(金一封) an enclosure [a gift] of money. ¶~을 주다 [하사하다] grant [give] (a person) money (in appreciation of his services) // 나는 회사로부터 장기 근속으로 ~을 받았다 I was given a sum of money as a special gift [bonus] for my long (years of) service at the office.

금자탑(金字塔) a pyramid; [비유] a monumental achievement. ¶출판계의 ~ a monument of the publishing business / a monumental publication // ~을 세우다 accomplish a monumental work (in) // 그는 그 작품으로 현대 미술계에 ~을 세웠다 With that work he erected a monumental landmark in modern art.

금잔(金盞) a gold cup; a golden goblet.
금잔디(金-) [식] Korean lawn grass. ¶골프장에 ~를 깔다 lay the golf course with Korean lawn grass.
금잔화(金盞花) [식] the pot marigold.
금장(襟章) a collar badge [mark / ensign / bar].
금장도(金粧刀) a gilded pocketknife(도금한).
금장식(金粧飾) gold(en) decoration. **금장식하다** decorate with gold.
금전(金錢) money; [현금] cash. ¶~의 노예 a slave to money [(문어) of mammon] // ~상의 monetary / (문어) pecuniary // ~상의 원조 pecuniary [monetary] aid / financial help [support] // ~상의 문제 a matter [question] of money // ~상의 이익 financial profit // ~을 취급하다 handle money // 무엇이든 ~의 면에서 보다 see everything in terms of money // 그와는 ~상 관계가 없다 I have no money relations with him. // 이 문제가 ~으로 해결되지는 않는다 Money will not solve this problem. // 그것은 ~의 문제가 아니다 It is not a question of money. // 그들은 ~상의 문제로 크게 다투었다 They had a big quarrel over the money.
● **금전 등록기** a cash register. **금전 출납계** a cashier(창구에서 현찰을 다루는 사람); a treasurer(단체·관공서 등의 출납 계원); a teller(은행의). **금전 출납장**(부) a cashbook; an account book.
금제(金製) ¶~의 (made of) gold / golden.
금제(禁制) prohibition; a ban; taboo. ¶~를 풀다 lift a ban / remove a prohibition. **금제하다** forbid; prohibit; ban. ➔¶금제되어 있다 be under a ban.
금족(禁足) confinement; detention. ¶~을 명하다 confine / keep (a person) indoors // 군대의 규칙을 어긴 탓으로 1주일간의 ~을 명령받았다 I was ordered to stay in for a week [I was placed under a week's confinement] for breaking army regulations.
● **금족령** a standstill order.
금종이(金-) golden paper; gilt paper.
금주(今週) this week. ¶~나 내주 this week or next // ~ 중에 during this week / before the end of this week // ~ 월요일에 on Monday of this week / this Monday / this (past) Monday // 그가 ~ 중에 방문할 것이다 He will call on you sometime this week [before the end of the week]. // ~ 내내 바빴다 I've been busy all (this) week.
금주(禁酒) abstinence (from alcohol drinks); temperance(▶ temperance는 절주를 말하나 완전히 술을 끊는 경우에도 쓰임). ¶~를 맹세하다 swear off drinking // ~를 명하다 prohibit drinking / (의사가) order (a person) to abstain from drinking. **금주하다** abstain from alcohol [drinking]; give up [stop / quit] drinking; (속어) go on the wagon; be temperate; (미) go dry. ¶의사는 1년 동안 금주하라고 내게 말했다 The doctor advised me not to drink for a year. // 그는 금주하기로 맹세했다 He took an oath [a vow] of temperance.
● **금주가** an [a total] abstainer; a teetotaler; a nondrinker. **금주법** the prohibition law; (미) the Volstead Act; the Dry Law (1933년 폐지); Prohibition. **금주 운동** a temperance movement; a dry campaign; (미) a pussyfoot campaign.
금준비(金準備) the gold reserves.

금줄(金-) [금으로 된 줄] a gold chain (on a watch); (계급장 등의) gold stripes (on the sleeves); [금실] gold thread.
금줄(禁-) an exorcistical rope (stretch across the door, etc.). ¶~을 치다 stretch an exorcistical rope (between / across).
금지(禁止) prohibition; inhibition; a ban; an embargo; taboo; interdiction; (발행의) suppression. ¶문[도어] 개방 ~ (게시) Don't Leave The Door Open. // 벽보 ~ (게시) (미) No Posters Allowed. / (영) Post [Stick] No Bills. // 주차 ~ (게시) No Parking. / Parking prohibited. // 상연 ~ a stage ban // 수출입 ~ 품목 items on the contraband list // 흡연 ~ (게시) No Smoking. / Smoking is forbidden. // (게시) No Smoking. // U턴 ~ (게시) No U-turns. // 판매 ~ a ban on sales / prohibition of sale // 금 수출 ~ an embargo on the export of gold / a gold embargo // 통행 ~ (게시) No Thoroughfare. // ~를 풀다 withdraw the prohibition (on / against) / lift the ban (on) // ~를 어기다 violate a prohibition // 그 절의 오랜 동안에 걸친 여자 출입 ~는 마침내 풀렸다 At last women were admitted to the temple after long years of exclusion. **금지하다** prohibit; forbid; (법에 의해) ban(▶ forbid는 주로 개인적인 금지, prohibit는 법률이나 국가에 의한 금지, ban은 법적·사회적인 금지); place a ban (on); put an embargo (on). ➔¶금지된 사랑 a forbidden love // 남자 출입이 금지된 학원 an academy closed to boys // 판매 금지시키다 place [put] a thing under a ban / prohibit [ban] the sale (of a thing) / (출판물을) suppress // 그녀는 밤의 외출을 금지당했다 She was forbidden to go out at night. // 마약 거래 [그런 종류의 양귀비 재배]는 법으로 금지되어 있다 Dealing in narcotics [The culture of that species of poppy] is banned [under a ban / prohibited] by law. // 법에 의해 이 상품의 매매는 금지되어 있다 The purchase and sale of this article is prohibited by law. // 이 상품의 판매는 금지되어 있다 The sale of those goods is prohibited. // 그는 그녀의 집 출입이 금지되었다 He wasn't allowed to visit her home. / He was forbidden entrance to her home. // 그 기사는 검열에 의해 발표가 금지되었다 The article was banned by the censor. // 우리 집에서는 대머리에 관한 이야기는 금지되어 있다 Any mention of bald heads is banned at our house. / Talk about baldness is a no-no at our house. // 이 전화의 사용은 금지되어 있다 We are forbidden to use this telephone.
● **금지 구역** a restricted area. ¶통행 ~ a restricted area. **금지령** a prohibition order; a prohibitory [an interdictory] decree; a negative order [command]; an interdict; a law forbidding. ¶~을 내리다 [풀다] issue [lift / remove] the ban [embargo] (on something). **금지법** prohibitional law. **금지 조항** a forbidden clause. **금지 처분** prohibitive measure; prohibition.
금지옥엽(金枝玉葉) [임금의 집안·자손] a person of royal birth; [귀한 자손] precious sons and daughters. ¶~으로 자라다 be brought up like a prince.
금치산(禁治産) [법] incompetency. ¶정신병에 의한 ~ 선고 interdiction of lunacy // ~의 선고를 받다 be declared incompetent.
● **금치산자** [법] a person adjudged incompe-

금테(金-) gilt edges; (액자의) a gilded [gilt] frame; (안경의) gold rims. ¶~의 gilt-framed / gold-rimmed.
● **금테 안경** gold-rimmed [gilt-edged] spectacles.
금패(金牌) a gold medal [plaque].
금품(金品) money and goods. ¶~을 요구하다 demand a person of (his) money and valuables // 그것은 ~으로 보상될 수 없는 손실이었다 That was a loss that could never be made good in money or in kind.
금하다(禁-) 1 [금지하다] forbid (a person wine / a song to be sung); prohibit; proscribe; ban; taboo; bar (the use of poison gas); interdict (foreign trade); inhibit (a person from doing); (미) enjoin (an action / a person from doing); (금제품으로서) place (something) under a ban; lay an embargo on (something); place ban (on). ¶도박을 ~ prohibit [illegalize] gambling / prohibit (a person) from gambling // 흡연을 ~ prohibit [prescribe] smoking // 사담을 금합니다 Don't whisper among yourselves. // 회의 중의 흡연을 금합니다 No smoking during the meeting. // 이곳에서의 사진 촬영을 금합니다 Photographing is forbidden here. / You are not allowed to take photographs here. // 학교에서는 극장 출입을 금하고 있다 The school forbids us to go to the theater. / The students are debarred by the school from going to the movie. // 미성년자의 흡연은 법률이 금하고 있다 Minors are prohibited by law from smoking. // 의사는 내게 1주일간의 외출을 금했다 The doctor kept me in for a week. // 이 방의 출입을 금합니다 I forbid you this room. 2 [억누르다] suppress; repress; restrain; check; keep under [back]. ¶기쁨을 금할 수 없다 cannot contain oneself for joy // 눈물을 금할 수 없다 cannot keep [hold] back one's tears / cannot repress one's tears // 웃음[실소]을 금할 수 없다 cannot help laughing (at the sight).
금혼식(金婚式) a golden wedding (anniversary). ¶~을 올리다 celebrate one's golden wedding (anniversary).
금화(金貨) a gold coin [piece]; (집합적) gold currency [coin / coinage]. ¶~로 (have the money) in gold / ~로 지불하다 pay in gold.
금환식(金環蝕) an annular eclipse.
금후(今後) [이제부터] after this; [장래] in (the) future (▶ (영)에서는 the를 붙이지 않음); hence(forth); hereafter; for the future; from this time on. ¶~의 future / coming / ~의 논제 a topic for further discussion // 수일[주 / 개월 / 년]간 for a few days [weeks / months / years] ahead [from now] // ~의 발전을 지켜보다 watch future developments // ~ 더욱 조심하겠습니다 I will be more careful after this. // 나는 퇴원은 했으나 몇 주일 동안은 조용히 집에 있지 않으면 안 된다 I have been discharged from the hospital but I have to stay home quietly for a few weeks. // 나는 탐이 ~ 어떻게 될지 모른다 I cannot tell what will become of Tom (after this). (▶ 영어에서는 시간에 관한 부사구를 그대로 번역하지 않으며, 시제에 따라 그 의미를 나타내는 경우가 흔히 있음. "지금까지 몇 페이지 읽었느냐?"는 "How many pages have you read?"이고, 「지금까지」는 번역할 필요가 없음)

급(級) a class; a grade; a rate. ¶대사~ 회담 a conference on the level of ambassadors [at the ambassadorial level] / an ambassador level conference // 메가톤~ 핵폭발 a nuclear explosion in the megaton range // 전문가~의 기술 skill on a level with professionals // ~을 올리다 promote (a person) [move (a person) up] to a higher grade [rank] // ~을 내리다 demote [reduce] (a person) to a lower grade // 주산에서 나는 한 ~이 올라갔다 I have been moved up to the next rank in the use of the abacus. // 그는 제1~의 변호사다 He is a first-rate lawyer. // 그 배는 1,500톤~이다 The ship is in the 1,500 ton class. // 그는 중량~의 권투 선수다 He is a heavyweight boxer.
급감(急減) a rapid decrease (in population). **급감하다** decrease [diminish] rapidly; be sharply reduced. ¶택지 개발로 이 지역의 녹지가 급감하고 있다 Housing developments are rapidly reducing the green areas of land in this district.
급강하(急降下) 1 (온도의) a sudden drop. **급강하하다** drop suddenly. ¶기온이 급강하했다 The temperature dropped suddenly [plummeted]. 2 (비행기의) a swoop; a (nose) dive. **급강하하다** do a nose dive; nose-dive.
● **급강하 폭격** dive bombing. ¶~을 하다 dive-bomb.
급거(急遽) hurriedly; hastily; in haste; in a hurry. ¶~ 상경하다 hurry up to Seoul / rush [fly] to Seoul / ~ 귀국하다 speed homeward from abroad // 그는 ~ 상경했다 He hurried to Seoul. // 의료진이 ~ 재해지로 파견되었다 A group of doctors were dispatched in haste to the stricken area.
급격하다(急激-) [돌연하다] sudden; [빠르다] rapid; [심하다] sharp. ¶급격한 정책의 변화 a sudden [rapid] change in policy. **급격히** suddenly; rapidly. ¶자동차에 의한 사망자의 수가 ~ 증가했다 The number of deaths from car accidents has increased rapidly. / There has been a sharp increase in the number of deaths from automobile accidents. // 오후부터 기온이 ~ 상승했다 The temperature went up suddenly in the afternoon. // 그의 병세가 ~ 악화되었다 His illness took a sudden turn for the worse.
급경사(急傾斜) a steep slope [incline]; [치받이] steep ascent [acclivity]; [내리받이] steep descent [declivity]; (배의) a heavy list. ¶~의 steep / high-pitched (roof) // ~의 계단 a steep flight of stairs // 감속! ~ 커브 (게시) Slow! Sharp curve steep hill.
급고(急告) an urgent notice [notification]. **급고하다** give an urgent notice; make an urgent notification (of); make an immediate announcement; notify urgently. ¶~ — 긴급 위원회가 오늘 오후 3시에 개최됨 Urgent — An emergency committee meeting has been called for 3 p.m. today. // ~ — 금일 제2교시 종료 후 전교생 교정에 집합할 것 (게시) Urgent — All students are to line up in the schoolyard after the second period.
급급하다(汲汲-) intent [bent] on; engrossed [absorbed] in; busy oneself about; too eager [very anxious] (to do); think only of. ¶명리에 급급하고 있다 be striving hard after fame and gain / be hungry for fame / be thirsty for reputation // 그는 돈벌이에 급급하고 있다

He is bent on making money.

급기야(及其也) at (long) last; finally; in the end; in the long run; in time; ultimately; after all. ¶돈을 물 쓰듯 하더니 ~ 그는 빈털터리가 되었다 He went on squandering his money until (at last) he became penniless. ∥ ~ 타협하고 말았다 The upshot of the matter was that they came to a compromise. ∥ ~ 그는 파면되고 말았다 To crown all, he lost his place. ∥질투는 ~ 비극을 초래했다 The final outcome[result] of jealousy was a tragedy.

급등(急騰) a jump; a sudden rise; (물가 등의) skyrocket. ¶식료품 가격의 ~ a sudden rise [jump] in the price of food ∥물가의 ~ a sudden rise in prices. **급등하다** jump; rise [shoot up] suddenly; rocket. ¶급등하는 인기 rapidly increasing popularity / rocketing popularity ∥급등하는 주식 stocks[(영) shares] whose value has suddenly risen ∥물가는 나날이 급등하고 있다 Prices are skyrocketing every day. ∥ 금년에 건축비가 급등했다 Building costs have leaped this year.

급락(急落) (시세의) a sudden[sharp] drop [decline / fall]; a sharp break; a steep decline; a slump. ¶시세의 ~ a sudden drop [a slump] in the market. **급락하다** drop[fall] suddenly; slump; drop sharply; plunge. ¶오늘 달러 시세가 700원으로 급락했다 The dollar plunged[plummeted] to 700 won today.

급랭(急冷) rapid[quick] cooling; [화] quenching. **급랭하다** cool rapidly[quickly]; [화] quench.

급료(給料) a salary; wages; pay. (▶ wages는 일급·주급 등. salary는 매달 나누어 지불하는 연봉을 뜻하며, pay는 일반적으로 보수로 지불되는 것) ¶높은 ~ a high[large] salary ∥낮은 ~ a low[small] salary ∥미불의 ~ unpaid wages / (미) back salary[pay] ∥실지 수령의 ~ take home pay ∥월 50만 원의 ~ a salary of 500,000 won ∥ 생활이 가능한 ~ a living wage ∥ ~를 받다 receive one's salary / have one's wages paid ∥ ~를 올리다 raise (a person's) pay[salary / wages] ∥ ~를 내리다 lower[reduce] (a person's) wages / cut [slash] (a person's) pay ∥ ~로 생활하다 live on one's salary ∥ ~ 인상을 요구하다 demand an increase[a raise / (영) a rise] in salary ∥ 그는 그 회사에서 ~를 받고 있다 He draws a salary from the company. / He is in the pay [on the payroll] of the company. ∥그 회사는 ~가 좋다 That company pays good salaries. ∥당신 ~는 얼마입니까 How much do you make[earn]?
● **급료일**(-日) (미) (a) payday; (영) a wage day.

급류(急流) a fast flowing[rushing] stream; a rapid[swift / fast] stream; a swift[strong] current; [격류] a torrent; rapids. ¶ ~에 휩쓸리다 be swept away by a strong current ∥ ~를 내려가다 shoot down the rapids / shoot a rapid (in a canoe).

급모(急募) an urgent[a pressing] invitation (to subscribe to a fund); [신병·새 회원 등의] hurried recruiting (of personnel). ¶종업원 ~ (게시) Employees urgently needed [wanted]. **급모하다** recruit[enlist] hurriedly [in great haste]; issue[send] (a person) an urgent invitation (to subscribe to a relief fund).

급무(急務) urgent business; an urgent [immediate] necessity; a pressing[crying] need; a matter requiring immediate attention. ¶초미의 ~ the pressing need of the hour ∥ 현하의 ~에 부응하다 meet the exigencies of the times ∥목하의 ~는 폭동을 진압하는 일이다 The first thing we must do [Our most urgent task] is to quell the riot. ∥외화 자금의 유출을 방지하는 일이 우리나라가 당면한 ~이다 It is of urgent necessity for our country to check the drain on our foreign exchange reserve.

급박하다(急迫-) pressing; urgent; imminent; exigent. ¶급박한 문제 a pressing[burning] question / an urgent problem ∥매우 급박한 문제 a problem of great urgency ∥중동의 급박한 정세 an acute situation in the Middle East ∥식량 문제가 급박해졌다 The food question has become acute. ∥사태가 급박해졌다 The situation has become tense [critical / acute]. / The situation has come to a head.

급변(急變) 1 [갑작스런 변화] a sudden change[turn]. **급변하다** change suddenly; undergo a sudden change; (병이) take a sudden turn for the worse. ¶급변하는 주위 환경[세계 정세] the rapidly changing circumstances[world situation] ∥아버지의 병세가 급변했다 My father's condition took a sudden turn for the worse. ∥날씨가 급변했다 There was a sudden change in the weather. / The weather suddenly changed. ∥그의 태도가 급변했다 His attitude changed suddenly.
2 [예기치 못한 변고] an emergency; an (unforeseen) accident. ¶ ~이 일어나지 않는 한 unless some unforeseen accident occurs ∥ ~에 대비하다 provide[be prepared] for emergencies ∥ ~에 대비하여 항공모함이 파견되었다 An aircraft carrier was dispatched in readiness for an emergency[contingencies].

급보(急報) an urgent message[report]; [경보] an alarm. ¶ ~에 접하다 receive the urgent news (of) ∥ ~를 받고 다수의 경찰관이 현장으로 급히 달려갔다 At the report a large number of policemen rushed to the scene. **급보하다** report promptly; send an urgent message (to); (화재 등의) give the alarm (for a fire); (구원·요구 등을) send an emergency call (for).

급부(給付) presentation; bestowal; delivery; (보험 등의) payment; (a) benefit. ¶반대~ a consideration / counter-presentation / a benefit in return (for) / [비유] a compensation (for) ∥부가 ~ [경] fringe benefits ∥의료 ~ medical[sickness] benefits. **급부하다** confer; provide; make a presentation (of); deliver; grant; bestow; pay (a benefit). ¶물품을 ~ furnish[provide] (a person) with goods ∥노인에게 연금을 ~ pay pensions to the elderly ∥사원에게 제복을 ~ provide [furnish] employees with uniforms.

급비생(給費生) a scholarship student[holder]; a student on scholarship; (영) a scholar. ¶ ~이다 be on scholarship / be a scholarship student.

급사(急死) a sudden[an untimely] death. **급사하다** die suddenly; meet with an untimely death; (구어) pop off. ¶그는 심장 마비로 급사하였다 He died suddenly of heart failure.

급사(給仕) an attendant. ⇨ⁿ사환(使喚)
급사(急使) an express messenger; a running [quick] messenger; a dispatch rider; a fast courier. ¶~를 보내다 dispatch [send] an express messenger (to) / dispatch an envoy (to).
급사면(急斜面) a steep slope [incline].
급살(急煞) the most unlucky [sinister] star; [비유] the worst fate.
급살(을) 맞다 die suddenly [a sudden death]; drop dead; (속어) pop off (the hooks). ¶급살 맞을 놈아 Drop dead! / Go to hell [the devil]! / Curse upon you! / A plague on you!
급상승(急上昇) a sudden rise; skyrocketing; [항] zooming; a zoom; a chandelle. **급상승하다** rise suddenly; skyrocket; [항] zoom; chandelle.
급서(急逝) a sudden death. ⇨ 급사(急死)
급선무(急先務) the most urgent business [necessity]; the most important matter requiring immediate attention; an exigency. ¶우리의 ~는 우선 그의 소재를 알아내는 일이다 It is of the most urgent necessity for us to find out where he is.
급선봉(急先鋒) a vanguard; a forerunner; an active leader. ¶…의 ~이다 be an active leader of ... / be in the van of ... / be at the forefront of ... // 그는 이 운동의 ~이다 He is in the van of this movement. // 그는 개혁파의 ~으로 활약했다 He played an active role as a reform leader.
급성(急性) ¶~의 acute (disease) // ~이 되다 run an acute course.
● **급성 류머티즘** [폐렴] acute rheumatism [pneumonia]. **급성 신장**[간 / 맹장]염 acute nephritis [hepatitis / appendicitis].
급소(急所) **1** [몸의] a vital part [point]; [집합적] the vitals. ~의 일격 a fatal [mortal] blow // ~에 一撃 be hit in the vitals // (탄환 등이) ~를 빗나가다 miss a vital point // ~를 찌르다 stun (a person) (by a strike at a vital point) / attack [strike with the fist at] a vital point // 공이 그의 ~에 맞은 것 같다 The ball seems to have hit him where it hurts.
2 [가장 중요한 곳] the main [vital / key] point. ¶문제의 ~ the key [essential] point of a question // ~를 찌른 질문 a question that touches [goes to] the heart of the matter / a question which touches on a vital [key] point / a home question / a question to the point // ~를 벗어난 질문 a question out of the point [beside the mark] // ~를 찌르다 strike [hit] home // 그의 비평은 ~를 찔렀다 His remarks hit home.
3 [약점] a venerable spot; one's Achilles' heel. ¶~를 찌르다 hit (a person) in a venerable spot.
급속하다(急速-) rapid; swift; quick; fast; speedy; expeditious; prompt. ¶급속한 성장 rapid growth (of a plant) // 급속한 해결 a prompt settlement (of a matter) // 급속한 진보를 하다 make rapid progress // 그 나라는 급속한 산업 발전을 이룩했다 The country underwent rapid industrialization. / The country developed its industry rapidly. **급속히** rapidly; swiftly; in haste; fast; promptly; quickly; expeditiously. ¶그들은 그 문제를 ~ 해결했다 They settled the matter quickly [in quick order]. // 한국 내 거주 외국인의 수가 ~ 증가하고 있다 The number of foreigners living in Korea is growing rapidly.
급송하다(急送-) send (a thing) in haste [by express]; dispatch; (미) ship (goods) by express; (미) express; (미) rush (a message). ¶소화물을 ~ send [ship] a package (to a person) by express / express a package (to) / (항공 편으로) fly a package (over).
급수(級數) [수] a series; (a) progression (수 그 자체를 문제 삼을 때는 "a series"를 씀). ¶기하[등비] ~ geometric series [progression] // 무한 ~ an infinite series [progression] // 산술 [등차] ~ an arithmetic series [progression] // 순환 ~ a recurring series // 유한 ~ a finite series // 산술[기하] ~적으로 증가하다 increase [grow (in number)] in arithmetic [geometric] progression.
급수(給水) [물의 공급] water supply [service]; water feeding; [공급된 물] service water; feed water. ¶시간 ~ a water supply restricted to certain hours // ~ 부족으로 고통을 받다 suffer from a water famine [short water supply] // ~를 제한하다 restrict the water supply. **급수하다** supply (a town) with water; feed water (to the boiler); feed (a boiler) with water. ¶불모지에 급수하기 위해 운하를 만들다 build a canal to supply water to waste land.
● **급수관** a water [service] pipe; a feed (-water) pipe (on a boiler). **급수난** a water shortage [famine]. **급수차** a water-supply wagon; a water wagon.
급습(急襲) a surprise [sudden] attack; a raid; (경찰의) a (police) raid (on gamblers); a round-up (일제 단속). ¶경찰의 ~을 받다 be raided by the police // 어젯밤 그 도박장에 (경찰의) ~이 있었다 A raid was made on the gambling house last night. **급습하다** make a surprise [sudden] attack (on); suddenly descend (upon); take (the enemy) by surprise; raid; storm. ¶공중에서 ~ make an air raid (on) / air-raid / blitz (a city) // 현금 수송차를 ~ make a surprise attack on a cash delivery car.
급식(給食) (provision of) meals; feeding (동물 등의). ¶학교 ~ 제도 a school lunch program. **급식하다** provide (free) lunch for (school-children); supply [provide] (the poor) with meals; provide meals for (employees); feed (a bird).
● **급식 시설** feeding facilities; equipment for cooking.
급신(急信) an urgent message; a dispatch. ¶~을 보내다 send an urgent message.
급여(給與) (an) allowance; a grant; (a) supplies; [봉급] pay; salary; wages. ¶임시 ~ an extra allowance [pay] // 현물 [현품] ~ an allowance in kind // 특별 ~ fringe benefits (주택·건강·보험·질병·휴가 등의) // 음식 [피복]의 ~ an allowance of food [clothing] // ~가 좋다 [나쁘다] be well [ill / poorly] paid. **급여하다** allow; grant; supply [furnish / provide] (a person with something); pay (a monthly salary of 450,000 won). ⇨ ¶여비로서 약간의 수당을 급여받다 be allowed a certain sum of money to cover the traveling expenses.
● **급여금** an allowance; a grant; a dole (실업

의). **급여 소득** an (annual) income (of a white-collar worker). ¶~**자** a wage earner / an employment income earner / a salaried employee.

급우(級友) a classmate. ¶최 군은 나의 고등학교 ~ 중의 한 사람이었다 Choe was one of my high school classmates.

급유(給油) oil supply; supply of oil; (기계의) oiling; lubrication; (연료의) refueling; (미) fill-up. **급유하다** feed [supply] (a machine) with oil; oil [lubricate] (wheels); refuel (an airplane); put gas in (a car); [자동차·모터사이클 등에 가득 채우다] fill up; gas up; top off(top offs는 이미 상당한 양의 연료가 들어 있는 경우).
● **급유기**(-機) a tanker plane. **급유선** a tanker; an oiler. **급유함** a naval tanker [fuel ship].

급작스럽다 sudden; abrupt. ⇨갑작스럽다

급장(級長) the president [headboy] of a (homeroom) class; a (homeroom) class president.

급전(急電) an urgent telegram [message]. ¶~을 치다 wire an urgent message (to) / send an urgent telegram (to) // ~을 받다 have [receive] an urgent telegram.

급전(急錢) urgently needed money; money for immediate use; money for emergencies.

급전(急轉) a sudden change [turn]. ¶~직(로) suddenly / all of a sudden / all at once / precipitately // 형세가 ~ a sudden turn [change] of events // 사건은 ~직하로 해결되었다 The matter has come to an abrupt settlement. / The situation was suddenly resolved. **급전하다** change suddenly; take a sudden turn. ¶형세는 급전하였다 The situation took a sudden turn.

급정거(急停車) a sudden stop. **급정거하다** stop suddenly [short]; come [be brought] to a sudden stop. ¶버스가 급정거했다 The bus made [came to] a sudden stop. → **급정거시키다** bring (a car) to a sudden stop / apply [put on] the emergency brake // 운전기사는 차를 급정거시켰다 The driver brought his car to a sudden stop.

급제하다(及第-) pass [be successful in] an examination; make the grade; pass muster(기준에 달하다); be promoted(진급하다). ¶간신히 ~ scrape through an examination / pass an examination with difficulty.

급조(急造) hurried construction; (an) improvisation(즉흥). ¶조립식의 ~ 가옥 a prefabricated house / (구어) a prefab. **급조하다** build in haste; construct hurriedly; throw [run] up; (임시변통으로) produce [prepare / make up] (something) in a hurry. ¶급조한 hurriedly [hastily] constructed [built] / improvised / jerry-built // 급조한 판잣집 a temporary shack // 급조한 무대 an improvised [a hurriedly built] stage.

급증(急增) a sudden [rapid] increase (in numbers); a (populational) jump. ¶인구 ~ 에 대한 대책이 시급하다 The populational jump calls for an immediate countermove. **급증하다** increase rapidly [suddenly]; jump (to). ¶급증하는 교통량 rapidly increasing traffic // 인구가 급증하고 있다 The population goes on rapid growing [multiplying] // 요즈음 은행 강도가 급증하고 있다 Recently bank robberies have rapidly increased in number.

급진(急進) 1 [빨리 나아감] rapid progress [advance]. **급진하다** advance rapidly; make rapid progress; speed up; push forward; rush. 2 [과격] going to extremes; radicalism. ¶~적인 radical / extreme.
● **급 진 사상** radical ideas [thought / thinking]. **급진주의** radicalism. **급진주의자** a radical(ist); an extremist. **급진파** the radicals; a radical faction; the extremists.

급커브(急-) a sharp curve [turn]. ¶도로의 U 자형 ~ a hairpin curve [bend] / a hairpin ~ **를 틀다** make a sharp turn (at the corner) / turn (a corner) sharply // 여기서 길은 ~가 된다 The road makes a sharp curve here. / There is a sharp bend in the road here. // 그는 그 아이를 피하려고 ~를 틀었다 He turned the steering wheel sharply in an effort to miss the child. // 버스는 ~를 틀지 못하고 골짜기로 굴러 떨어졌다 The bus couldn't make the sharp curve and plunged into the valley. // 전방에 ~ 있음 (게시) Warning: Sharp Curve Ahead.

급템포(急-) quick [fast] tempo. ¶~의 rapid / speedy / fast-moving [-paced] // ~로 in quick tempo / double-quick / speedily / rapidly // (일이) ~로 **진척되다** progress very rapidly // 이 악장은 ~로 연주된다 This movement is played at a quick tempo.

급파(急派) dispatching. **급파하다** dispatch; despatch; rush; expedite. ¶경찰을 현장에 ~ rush [dispatch] a police squad to the scene (of disaster) // 현장에 구조대를 ~ dispatch [rush] a rescue party to the scene. → ¶그 비행기 추락 사고의 원인 조사를 위해 전문가들이 급파되었다 A group of specialists were dispatched to investigate the causes of the plane crash.

급하다(急-) 1 [다급하다] urgent; pressing; hurried; impending; imminent; [갑작스럽다] sudden; abrupt. ¶급한 주문 a rush order // 급한 문제 a pressing question // 급한 식사 a hurried [hasty] meal // 급한 볼일로 on urgent business // 급할 때에는 when time is short / [긴급 시에는] in case of emergency // 나는 돈이 ~ I am in dire [urgent] need of money. // 급한 일이 좀 생겼다 Some pressing business has turned up. // 이 일은 급합니다 I want (to get) the work done quickly. // 이건 급하지 않아 This can wait. // 양국 간의 형세가 매우 급해졌다 The situation between the two states are dangerously strained. // 일은 급하게 하면 못 쓴다 It's no good rushing things. // 아버지는 급한 볼일로 시내에 나가셨습니다 My father has gone to town on urgent [pressing] business. **급히** [서둘러] in a hurry; in haste; hastily; hurriedly; [빨리] speedily; quickly; quick; (미국 속어) on the double; at a brisk pace(빠른 걸음으로); [즉시] without delay; promptly; immediately; at once. ¶~ **나가다** hurry out of (a room) // ~ **걷다** walk hurriedly [briskly] / go with (all) speed / make the best of one's way // ~ 떠나다 hurry off [away] / hustle off // ~ 몰다 drive in haste // ~ 멈추다 stop short // ~ 쓰다 write in haste // ~ 타다 [내리다] hurry on [off] // ~ 집으로 돌아가다 hurry [hasten] home // ~ 밥을 먹다 take a hasty [hurried] meal / rush through one's meal / snatch a hurried meal // ~ 돈이 필요하다 be in urgent [immediate] need of money.

급행

2 [성급하다] impatient; impetuous; hasty; quick-[short-]tempered. ¶급한 성미 a quick [short / hot] temper / impatience / impetuosity∥성미가 급한 사람 a person of an impetuous disposition / a hothead∥그는 성미가 급하다 He is hot-tempered.

3 [위중하다] critical; serious; dangerous; bad. ¶급한 병 a serious[severe] illness∥급한 환자 a serious case [중환자] / [긴급 환자] an emergency[urgent] case∥그는 병세가 매우 ~ He is seriously ill. / He is in a critical condition.

4 [가파르다] steep; precipitous; [날카롭다] sharp. ¶급한 비탈 a steep slope[gradient] / 급한 언덕 a steep hill / 급한 굽이[커브] a sharp turn[curve].

5 [빠르다] swift; rapid; speedy. ¶급한 흐름 a swift current / a rapid stream∥급한 발전 rapid growth (of a town).

급할수록 돌아가라(속담) Make haste slowly.; (The) more haste, (the) less speed.

급행(急行) **1** [급히 감]. ~의 express / fast / (미) hot-shot (freight train). **급행하다** hasten[hurry / rush] (to); go in a hurry; go posthaste (to). ¶현장으로 ~ rush[shoot off] to the scene∥경찰관은 사건 현장으로 급행했다 The policeman hurried[rushed] to the scene of the accident. **2** an express train. ⇨ **급행열차**(⇨**급행**) ¶7시 30분 부산행 ~ the 7:30 express for Busan∥~으로 가다 travel (to a place) by express / take an express (to)∥나는 10시 30분 ~으로 대전에 갔다 I went to Daejeon by the 10:30 express.

●**급행권** an express ticket. **급행 버스** an express bus. **급행열차** an express train; a fast train; (미) a highball. **급행요금** an express charge.

급환(急患) [급병에 걸린 환자] an emergency case; [급병] a sudden illness[disease]. ¶의사 선생님은 ~이 있어 왕진 중이십니다 The doctor is out on an emergency call.

굿다[1] **1** [선 등을 그리다] draw. ¶금을 ~ draw a line / 경계선을 ~ draw a line of demarcation (between) / demarcate / 획을 ~ draw a stroke (of a character)∥잘못된 낱말에 금을 그어 지우다 cross out a wrong word. **2** [성냥을 문지르다] strike[scratch] (a match). ¶벽에 (황린의) 성냥을 ~ scratch a match against a wall. **3** [외상값을 적다] charge (expense) to one's account[to the account (of)]. ¶굿고 먹다 eat on credit[tick]∥요금을 내 앞으로 그어 놓으시오 Charge this against me[to my account].∥저 가게에서는 그을 수 있다 I have a charge account at the store.

굿다[2] [비가 그치다] stop; hold up; [비를 피하다] take shelter[refuge] from (rain); shelter oneself from (rain); get out of the rain. ¶처마 밑에서 비를 ~ stand under the eaves (of a house) to get out of the rain.

긍정(肯定) affirmation; approbation(시인). **긍정하다** affirm; answer in the affirmative; answer "yes"; acknowledge. ¶그들은 긍정하지도 부정하지도 않았다 They refused to deny or confirm. / They declined either to affirm or deny. / They said nothing[made no comment] either way.∥나는 마르크시즘 이론을 전면적으로 긍정하지는 않는다 I do not entirely[completely] agree to the Marxism theory.∥나는 그 비판[보고]을 긍정했다 I acknowledged[affirmed] the criticism [report].∥증인은 사실을 긍정했다 The witness affirmed the fact.

●**긍정 명제** [논] an affirmative (proposition). **긍정문** [언] an affirmative sentence. **긍정 판단** [논] an affirmation.

긍정적(肯定的) affirmative. ¶~ 개념 [논] an affirmative concept / ~으로 대답하다 answer in the affirmative / give an affirmative answer∥그는 전적으로 ~이라고는 할 수 없었다 He didn't agree with us wholeheartedly.

긍지(矜持) pride; dignity. ¶~를 느끼다 feel proud∥~를 지키다 maintain one's dignity / save one's honor[face] / 한국 국민으로서의 ~를 가지다 have one's (national) pride as a Korean.

긍휼(矜恤) pity; compassion; commiseration; sympathy. **긍휼하다** pity; take[have] pity (on); sympathize (with). **긍휼히** with pity [sympathy / compassion]. ¶~ 여기다 feel compassion for[toward] / feel pity for / take pity[compassion] on.

기(忌) [상(喪)] (a period of) mourning; [연기(年忌)] an anniversary of (a person's) death. ¶선친의 6주~ the sixth anniversary of one's father's death.

기(紀) [지질] a period. ¶석탄~ the Carboniferous period.

기(氣) **1** [기력·원기] vigor; energy; vitality; strength; force; spirits; stamina; (미) pep. ¶~가 나다 cheer up / take heart / feel triumphant / swell up / be puffed (at) ∥~가 나서[등등하여] exultantly / in triumph / triumphantly∥~가 찬[왕성한] 사람 an energetic person / a man full of (push and) go / ~가 부족하다 be lacking[deficient] in energy / be in low[poor] spirits∥~가 왕성하다 be full of energy[vigor / vitality] / be in high spirits / be full of life∥~가 질리다 lose one's courage[heart] / have one's spirit broken.

2 [숨] breath; wind.

3 [정신력·용기] spirit(s); heart. ¶~가 죽다 feel small[(미국 구어) mean] / have a feeling of inferiority / feel depressed[dispirited]∥~를 꺾다 depress (a person's) spirit / dishearten / discourage / damp the ardor∥청중을 앞에 두고 나는 ~가 죽었다 In front of the audience I lost my nerve[got nervous / got stage fright].∥그것을 보고 나는 ~가 죽었다 My heart sank at the sight.

4 [정기(精氣)] ether; essence; spirit; [철] natural passion; the life force; (프) élan vital.

기(를) 쓰다 be hot[bent] (on); be very eager [going all out] (to); be mad[frantic] (for); do with great zeal; vehemently[heatedly / excitedly] do (something); make desperate [strenuous] efforts; do one's best; exert oneself to the utmost; strain; struggle. ¶기를 써서 일하다 work with all one's might / work to the best of one's ability / 기를 쓰고 달아나다 run (away) for one's life / take to one's heels / 저 회사는 새 시장을 개척하려고 기를 쓰고 있다 That firm is very eager [is going all out] to open new markets.∥그는 기를 쓰고 공부했다 He worked hard with great zeal[in real earnest].∥그는 기를 써서 돈을 벌려고 했다 He made desperate efforts[He struggled hard] to make money. / He was all for making money. / He was intent on moneymaking.// 꼭 이기겠다고 그는 기를 쓰고 있다 He has got himself all worked up to win.

기(를) 펴다 make oneself comfortable [at home]; put oneself at ease; cheer up; heighten one's spirit; relax. ¶기를 펴지 못하다 feel constrained [oppressed] / feel ill at ease / cower // 그 소식을 듣고 나는 기를 폈다 The news gave me relief. / I felt relieved to hear that. / I was relieved at the news.

기(基) [화] a radical; a radicle; a group; [수] radix (*pl.* ~es, radices).

기(期) [시대] a period; an age; [기일] a date; a time; [기간] a period; a term; [계절] a season; [병의] a stage. ¶제1~의 폐병 tuberculosis [consumption] in the first stage // 이번 ~의 의회 the present session of the National Assembly.

기(旗) a flag; a banner(주로 문어·비유에 쓰임); a standard(군기); an ensign(함선기); the colors(연대기); [긴 삼각기], a pennant; a pennon(삼각기); [집합적] bunting; [국기(國 旗)] a national flag. ¶~를 앞세우고 with banners flying / with flying colors // ~를 흔들다 wave a flag // ~를 흔들어 (열차를) 세우다 flag down (a train) / flag (a bus) // ~를 올리다 hoist [display / raise / lift / fly out / set up] a flag // ~를 내걸다 hang out a flag // ~를 내리다 take down a flag / [항복하다] throw up one's hands // ~를 접다 furl a flag // ~를 펴다 unfurl a flag // ~가 바람에 펄럭이고 있다 The flag is streaming [floating / waving / fluttering] in the wind. // 읍내에는 경축을 위한 ~가 걸렸다 The town was beflagged [gay with flags] in honor of the occasion. // 집집마다 현관에 ~가 걸려 있었다 There was a flag hung out at the front door of every house.

-기(氣) a feeling (of ...); a flavor; a touch; a shade; a tinge. ¶바람~가 있는 남자 a man with a roving eye // 바람 ~가 있는 여자 a fickle woman / 기름 ~가 많은 음식 greasy [rich] food // 시장 ~를 느끼다 feel hungry // 익살~가 있다 have a touch of humor / be tinged with humor // 그는 감기~가 있어 누워 있다 He is laid up with a touch of cold [with a slight cold].

-기(機) a machine. ¶비행~ an airplane // 세탁~ a washing machine.

-기(記) [기록] a record; [기술] an account; a description; [역사] a chronicle; a history; [연대기] annals. ¶체험~ memoirs.

기각(棄却) [각하] turning down; rejection; [법] dismissal; [포기] abandonment; renunciation. **기각하다** turn down; reject; dismiss; throw (a suit) out of court. ¶신청을 ~ reject [turn down] an application.

기간(基幹) a mainstay; a nucleus (*pl.* -clei).
● **기간산업** basic [key] industries.

기간(既刊) ¶~의 previously published [issued].

기간(期間) [한정된 시기] a period (of time); a term. ¶상환 ~ a period of redemption // 유효 ~ a term of validity // 일정한 ~ 내에 within a fixed [certain / set] period of time // ~을 연장하다 extend the time [period] // 그가 의장으로 일할 ~이 1년으로 되어 있다 He is to serve as chairman for a term of one year. // 대매출 ~ 중에 출혈 서비스를 할 예정이다 There will be special bargains during the big sale. // 이 표의 유효 ~은 벌써 지났다 The validity of this ticket has long since expired.

기갈(飢渴) hunger and thirst; starvation. ¶~이 들다 suffer from [be pressed by] hunger and thirst / experience the pangs of hunger // ~을 면하다 keep [drive] the wolf from the door.

기갑 부대(機甲部隊) an armored [a mechanized] unit; armored forces [(영) armoured troops].

기강(紀綱) [관기(官紀)] official [government] discipline; [질서] public order; law and order. ¶~ 문란 a (gross) breach [the degradation] of (official) discipline // ~을 바로잡다 improve the moral fiber (of) / tighten discipline (among) // ~을 어지럽히다 lower discipline.

기개(氣槪) (unyielding) spirit; (문어) mettle; (구어) grit; [기골] backbone; pride; self-respect. ¶~가 있는 spirited / mettlesome / mettled / plucky / proud // ~가 있는 사람 a man with backbone / a man of mettle [pluck / noble spirit] // ~를 보이다 show one's mettle // ~가 없다 have no spirit / be backboneless // 나는 그 연로한 성직자[지도자]의 ~에 감동되었다 I was moved by the firmness of the old priest's will [resolution].

기거(起居) [일상생활] one's daily life; daily living. ¶~를 함께 하다 live together / live under the same roof / live with a person // 그는 10년 동안 ~를 같이하면서 일해 왔다 He and I have lived and worked together for ten years. **기거하다** live; get on [along]; lead [live] a life. ¶그녀와는 한집에 기거하고 있다 She and I live in the same house [under the same roof].

기겁하다(氣怯-) be astonished [shocked / thunderstruck]; be frightened out of one's wits; [소리 지르다] cry out in astonishment [surprise]. ¶기겁하여 in a fright / in alarm / with yells of horror // 개가 짖는 바람에 도둑은 기겁하여 달아났다 The burglar was frightened away by the barking of the dog.

기결(既決) ¶~의 decided / settled / [법] convicted. **기결하다** have already decided [settled].
● **기결수**(-囚) a convict; a convicted prisoner. **기결안** a settled matter.

기계(奇計) a clever plan; a cunning scheme. ¶~를 쓰다 resort to a bit of ingenuity // ~로 적을 제압하다 use an ingenious plan to get the better of the enemy.

기계(器械) an instrument; an apparatus (*pl.* ~, -tuses); an appliance. ¶공작 ~ a machine tool // 광학 ~ an optical instrument // 의료 ~ medical appliances [instruments].
● **기계 체조** heavy gymnastics; gymnastics [(구어) gym] with apparatus.

기계(機械) a machine; a gin; (집합적) machinery; gear; [기계 장치] a mechanism; machinery; setup; works(시계 등의). ¶복잡한 ~ an intricate piece of machinery / complex mechanism // 정교한 ~ delicate mechanism // 상자 만드는 ~ a machine for making boxes // ~와 같은 machinelike // ~처럼 정확히 like clockwork // ~를 설치하다 install a machine / set up machinery // ~를 조립하다 assemble a machine / put a machine up [together] // ~를 분해하다 take a machine to pieces // ~를 검사하다 overhaul a machine //

기계적

~를 다루다 manage [handle / control / operate / work] a machine // ~가 섰다 The machine has come to a standstill. // 자동 장치를 한 ~는 저절로 움직인다 An automatic machine goes by itself. // 틀림없이 ~에 잘못된 데가 있다 Something must be wrong with the works. // 새 공장에는 ~를 10대 설치했다 Ten sets of machinery were installed in the new plant. // ~에 손대지 마시오 《게시》 Hand off the machinery. // 그는 ~에 불과하다 He is a mere machine.

● **기계공** a mechanic; a mechanician; machine hand [operator]; a machinist; 《미》 a machiner. **기계 공업** the machine industry. **기계 공장** a machine [mechanics] shop; an engineering works. **기계 공학** mechanical engineering. **기계류** machinery. **기계 부품** a machine part. **기계실** a machine [machinery] room; an engine room. **기계어** [컴] a machine language. **기계유** machine [lubricating] oil. **기계학** mechanics. **기계화** mechanization. ¶농촌 ~ farm mechanization.

기계적 (機械的) mechanical; machine. ¶~인 일 mechanical work // ~으로 mechanically / automatically / (do) by rote / routinely // ~으로 외다 have [get / learn] by rote / learn by repetition.

기고 (寄稿) (a) contribution (to); a piece written (for). ¶잡지의 ~를 의뢰받다 be asked to write an article for a magazine / be asked to contribute an article to a magazine. **기고하다** contribute 《to a newspaper》; write (for a magazine). ¶신문에 ~ write in [for] the paper [press].

기고만장하다 (氣高萬丈-) 1 [몹시 성이 나다] exasperated; enraged; infuriated; 《서술적》 get wild like a madman; fly into a violent anger [a passion]. ¶기고만장하여 in the fury of one's passion / in a rage / with anger [rage].
2 [기세가 대단하다] elated; 《서술적》 be in high [roaring / towering] spirits; be puffed up; be big with pride; wear a high hat. ¶기고만장하여 in high spirits [feather] / in triumph / triumphantly / with colors flying (and band playing) // 성공을 거두어 ~ be elated [flushed / intoxicated / puffed up] with success / pride oneself on one's success // 그들은 기고만장했다 Their spirits were sky-high [rose to the skies].

기골 (氣骨) [기개] spirit; soul; mettle; (moral) backbone; 《구어》 pluck; 《구어》 grit; [골격] (the body) frame; build; physique. ¶~이 있는 spirited / plucky // ~이 없는 spineless.

기공 (技工) [기술] craftsmanship; workmanship; [솜씨] skill; [기술자] an artisan; a craftsman; a technical hand. ¶치과 ~ a dental technician.

기공 (起工) the start of (construction) work; [토목 공사의] breaking ground; [배] keel laid. **기공하다** begin [start] work [construction]; set to work; [토목의] break ground (for); [건축의] lay the cornerstone (of). ¶하수도 공사를 ~ begin work on a sewer system.

● **기공식** (-式) a ground-breaking ceremony; (빌딩의) the laying of a cornerstone; a cornerstone-laying ceremony; (배의) a keel laying; a keel-laying ceremony.

기공 (氣孔) 1 a pore; (식물의) a stoma 《pl. ~ta》; (곤충·거미류 등의) a stigma 《pl. ~s, ~ta》. 2 (바위나 광물 속의) a vesicle; a gas cavity.

기관 (汽管) [공] a steam pipe.
기관 (汽罐) a boiler; a steam generator.
● **기관실** a boiler room; (배의) a stokehold; a fireroom.

기관 (氣管) [동] the trachea 《pl. ~s, -cheae》; the windpipe. ¶~의 tracheal / ~ 절개(술) tracheotomy / bronchotomy.
● **기관지** [생] the bronchus 《pl. -chi》; a bronchial tube.

기관 (器官) [동] [식] an organ. ¶감각 ~ a sense organ // 발성 ~ a vocal organ // 소화기 ~ the digestive organs [apparatus] // 운동 ~ a locomotive organ // 청각 ~ a hearing organ // 호흡 ~ the respiratory organs // 신체의 중요 ~ vital organs of the body // 신체의 여러 ~ the (individual) organs of the body.

기관 (機關) 1 an engine. ⇨엔진. ¶가솔린 ~ a gasoline engine // 가역(可逆) ~ a reversible engine // 공랭 [수랭] 식 ~ an air-cooled [water-cooled] engine // 내연 ~ an internal combustion engine // 디젤 [터빈식] ~ a Diesel [turbine] engine // 보조 ~ an auxiliary engine // 선박용 ~ a marine engine // 수압 ~ a hydraulic engine // 왕복 ~ a reciprocating engine.
2 [수단] an organ; a means; a vehicle; a medium; an instrument; an agency; a system; [시설] facilities; service; accommodations; an institution; [기구] an organization; machinery. ¶관리 ~ the governing body // 교육 ~ an educational institution // 교통 ~ transportation facilities // 국제 ~ an international agency // 금융 ~ banking facilities // 대행 ~ an agency // 심의 ~ a deliberative body // 언론 ~ organs of public opinion / mass media // 입법 ~ a law-making organ // 정부 ~ the apparatus of government / government agencies // 집행 ~ an executive organization // 통신 ~ a means of communication // 행정 ~ administrative machinery [agencies] // 국가의 최고 ~ the highest state body // ~을 설치하다 set up an agency // 텔레비전은 현재 중요한 보도 ~이다 Television is now an important information medium.

● **기관 단총** a submachine gun; (미국 군인 속어) a burp gun. **기관사** (기선의) an engineer; (기차의) an engineman; an engine driver; (미) an [a locomotive] engineer; (영) a locomotiveman; (비행기의) a flight engineer. **기관실** an engine room; a machinery room. **기관원** (기관실의) a fireman; a stoker; (정보기관의) a secret service man. **기관장** a chief engineer. **기관지** an organ; a bulletin. **기관차** an engine; a locomotive (engine); a loco. ¶증기 ~ a steam locomotive (engine). **기관총** a machine gun; a maxim gun. ¶~으로 마구 쏘아 대다 rattle away 《at the enemy》 with a machine gun. **기관포** a (heavy) machine gun.

기괴망측하다 (奇怪罔測-) quite strange [mysterious / weird / monstrous]; outrageous. ¶그가 내게 그런 말을 했다니 정말 기괴망측한 일이다 It's outrageous that he should have said such a thing to you.

기괴하다 (奇怪-) [괴이하다] strange; mysterious; weird; uncouth; uncanny; [망측하다]

outrageous; extraordinary; monstrous; scandalous. ¶기괴한 풍설 a bizarre rumor // 기괴한 행동 strange behavior // 그의 기괴한 실종은 아직도 이야깃거리가 되고 있다 People still talk about his mysterious disappearance.

기교(技巧) art; craftsmanship; workmanship; technical skill; technique; technics; mechanism(예술의); [계책] an artifice; a trick; finesse. ¶광고 ~ advertising technics / the knack of advertisement // ~에 치우친 문체 a sophisticated style // ~에 치우친 작품 an excessively elaborate work // 그의 새 작품은 ~적으로 뛰어났다 His latest work is technically outstanding. // 저 도예가는 ~가 뛰어났다 That potter is a fine craftsman [technically accomplished]. // 저 배우의 연기는 너무 ~적이다 His acting is artificial [too studied].

기구(氣球) a balloon. ¶계류(繫留)~ a captive balloon // 관측~ an observation balloon // 광고 ~ an ad balloon // 기류 관측~ an observation balloon // 무인 관측~ a pilotless balloon // 유동(遊動)~ a dirigible balloon // 헬륨 ~ a helium-filled balloon // ~를 띄우다 send up [fly] a balloon(fly는 특히 놀이에서) // ~에 타다 ride in a balloon // ~를 타고 올라가다 ascend in a balloon.

기구(器具) [도구] a tool; a utensil; [간단한 기계(器械)] an appliance; an apparatus; an instrument. ¶가스 ~ a gas appliance // 난방 ~ a heating apparatus // 소독 ~ a sterilizer // 의료 ~ a medical appliance / a remedial apparatus // 전기 ~ an electrical appliance // 조명 ~ an illuminator // 주방 ~ kitchen utensils // 측정용 [정밀] ~ a measuring [precision] instrument // ~를 장치하다 mount an apparatus // 그 부엌에는 최신식 전기 ~가 있었다 The kitchen was furnished with the latest model electric appliances.

기구(機構) 1 [조직] a system; (an) organization; (a) structure; machinery. ¶국제~ an international organization // 북대서양 조약 ~ the North Atlantic Treaty Organization(약칭 NATO) // 유통 ~ a distribution system // 행정 ~ a governmental [an administrative] organization / governmental machinery // 유엔의 ~ the organization [machinery] of the United Nations // ~를 개편하다 reorganize the system.
2 [내부의 구조] the structure; the (internal) works. ¶기계의 ~ a mechanism / the mechanical structure // 인체의 ~를 조사하다 investigate the structure of the human body // 이 시계의 ~는 아주 간단하다 The mechanism of this clock is very simple.
● **기구 개편** reorganization; structural reform; the reorganization of a system.

기구하다(崎嶇-) [세상살이가 험하다] checkered; vicissitudinous; adverse; hapless; unlucky; strange; unfortunate; ill-fated. ¶기구한 생애 a checkered [an eventful / a stormy] career / a life marked by vicissitudes / a life full of ups and downs // 기구한 운명 a checkered lot [fortune] / a hapless [an evil] fate // 기구한 운명을 밟다 be the puppet [sport] of fortune / lead a checkered life / pass through strange vicissitudes of fortune // 기구한 운명을 타고나다 be born under an unlucky star // 기구한 신세를 한탄하다 grieve over one's ill [tough] luck // 그녀의 생애는 아주 기구했다 Hers was an extremely unlucky [unhappy] life. / She led a very miserable existence. // 그의 기구한 경력은 바로 한 편의 소설이다 The ups and downs of his life [career] are just like something out of a novel. // 그녀만큼 기구한 운명에 시달려온 사람을 나는 알지 못한다 I know of no one who was been made so much sport of by Fortune as she. / (구어) I don't know of anyone who was been kicked around by Fortune so much as she has.

기권(氣圈) (지구의) the atmosphere.

기권(棄權) abstention (from voting); renunciation [waiver] (of one's rights); (경기의) absence; cancellation (of the [one's] entry). ¶찬성 53, 반대 20, ~ 13 (투표에서) 53 in favor, 20 opposed, 13 abstentions. **기권하다** abstain (from voting); (권리를) renounce [waive] (one's right); (경기에서) give up (the race halfway). ¶그는 시장 선거 투표를 기권했다 He did not vote in the mayoral election. // 그는 레이스 직전에 기권했다 He withdrew from the race at the last minute. // 그는 경기를 기권했다 He dropped out of the tournament. / He defaulted.
● **기권율** an abstention rate. **기권자** an absentee (from voting); a nonvoter; an abstentionist; [법] a releasor. **기권표** a blank ballot.

기근(氣根) [식] an aerial root. ⇨ㄱ공기뿌리(⇨공기(空氣))

기근(饑饉) (a) famine; failure of crops; [부족] a dearth; (a) shortage. ¶대(大)~ a great [big / severe / huge / grievous] famine // 물 ~ shortage of water supply / a water famine [dearth] / water shortage // 석탄 ~ a coal famine / a famine of coal // ~이 든 해 a lean year // ~이 들었을 때 when a famine visits us [them] / in time of dearth // ~으로 고생하다 suffer from a famine // ~으로 죽다 perish with [by] famine / die of famine // 이 나라는 현재 ~에 시달리고 있다 This country is suffering from (a) famine now.

기금(基金) a fund; a foundation; an endowment. ¶감채(減債) ~ a sinking fund // 구제 ~ a relief fund // 국제 통화 ~ the International Monetary Fund(약어 IMF) // 전도 ~ a mission fund // ~을 설정하다 create [establish] a fund // 병원에 ~을 기부하다 donate a fund to a hospital / endow a hospital // 사회사업의 ~을 조달하다 raise a fund for social work.
● **기금 모집** collection of a fund; raising fund.

기기(機器) [비품] equipment; [특수한 기능을 가진 기구 일습] (an) apparatus(▶ 복수는 드묾); [기계(器械)] an instrument. ¶전자 ~ electronic equipment // 정밀 [천문] ~ precision [astronomical] instruments // 시청각 [난방] ~ audiovisual [heating] apparatus.

기기묘묘하다(奇奇妙妙-) [기이하다] very strange [curious / queer / odd / funny]; singular; weird; (구어) curiouser and curiouser; [기묘하다] wonderful; wondrous; marvelous; miraculous; magical.

기꺼워하다 be pleased with; be happy with. ⇨ㄱ기뻐하다

기껍다 [기쁘다] joyful; joyous; glad; delightful; happy; [유쾌하다] pleasant. ¶기꺼운 대답 a pleasing [favorable] answer // 기꺼운 소

기껏

식 glad[happy / joyful] news[tidings] // 기꺼운 얼굴을 하고 있다 look happy / have a happy face. **기꺼이** [기쁘게] joyfully; gladly; with pleasure[delight]; (쾌히) willingly; heartily; (선뜻) readily; with readiness; with a good grace. ¶~ …하다 would fain[gladly] (do) / be willing[pleased] to (do) // ~ 승낙하다 readily[willingly] consent (to it) / give a ready consent (to) // 내가 그것을 ~ 맡겠소 I will undertake it gladly[willingly / readily]. // 그는 나의 사과를 ~ 받아들였다 He accepted my apology with good grace. // 무슨 일이든지 ~ 해 드리겠습니다 I am quite willing [prepared] to do you any service.

기껏 1 [힘껏] as far[much] as one can; with all one's might; with might and main; to the utmost (of one's power). ¶~ 모은 돈을 다 써 버리다니 바보 같은 짓을 했다 I was foolish enough to spend the money I had saved at no small pains. 2 [고작] only; merely; at (the) most; at the utmost; at (the) best. ¶~ 한다는 소리가 그거냐 You say, at best, such a stupid[trifle] thing! / What a nonsense you are talking!

기껏해야 at (the) most; at the very most; at the utmost; at (the) best; only; merely; after all. ¶그건 ~ 4시간 정도 걸릴 것이다 I think it'll take about four hours at most. // 나는 80점밖에 못 따겠지 I may get on eighty[(영) get eighty], at best. // ~ 5,000원 정도 들 것이다 It will cost five thousand won at the (most. / It won't cost more than five thousand won. // ~ 5명 정도가 성공할 것이다 Only about[No more than] five of them will succeed.

기낭 (氣囊) 1 (새 등의) an air sac. 2 (비행선·기구 등의) a gasbag; an envelope.

기내 (機內) [항공기의 안] the inside of a plane; the cabin. ¶~용의 in-flight // ~에서[에] on the plane / during the flight // ~에서 식사를 하다 have a meal on the plane // ~의 온도를 일정하게 유지하다 maintain a constant temperature in the plane.

● **기내식** a meal on the plane; an in-flight meal; airline food.

기네스북 the Guinness Book of Records.

기념 (記念·紀念) commemoration; (추억) a memory; remembrance. ¶~의 commemorative / memorial // ~으로 in memory [commemoration] (of) / to the memory (of) / in remembrance[honor] (of) / as a souvenir (of) // 이거, ~으로 받아 두겠소 I will take this as a memento[souvenir]. // 그녀는 자기 사진을 ~으로 내게 주었다 She gave me her picture as a remembrance[token]. **기념하다** commemorate; (축하하다) celebrate. ¶우리는 학교의 창립을 기념하여 나무를 심었다 We planted some trees in commemoration of [to commemorate] the founding of our school. // 그들은 창립자를 기념하여 동상을 세웠다 They erected a bronze statue in memory[remembrance] of the founder. // 오늘은 나로서는 기념할 만한 날이다 This is a special[memorable] day for me. // 그들은 은사의 회갑을 기념하여 논문집을 출판했다 They published a collection of essays in celebration of[to celebrate] their teacher's 60th birthday.

● **기념관** a memorial hall. **기념물** a souvenir; a keepsake; a token; a memory. **기념비** a monument; a memorial; a cenotaph. **기념사진** a commemorative[souvenir] photograph[picture]. **기념식** a commemorative ceremony; commemoration exercises. **기념식수** (—植樹) a memorial tree. **기념우표** [주화] a commemorative stamp[coin]. **기념일** a memorial day; (해마다의) an anniversary. ¶독립 ~ (미국의) Independence Day / the Fourth of July // 창립 ~ foundation day // 오늘은 우리의 10회째 결혼 ~이다 This is our tenth wedding anniversary. **기념장** (—章) a commemoration[commemorative] medal [badge]. **기념제** a commemoration; an anniversary; a memorial festival. **기념품** a remembrance; a memento; a souvenir. (▶ remembrance는 상당히 추상적이고, 특정한 것에 대해서는 memento를 쓰는 일이 많음. souvenir는 이를테면 여행지에서 사는 것 등) **기념행사** a memorial event.

기능 (技能) skill; ability; capacity. ¶특수한 ~ special[expert] skill // ~이 있는 skilled // ~이 뛰어나다 be highly skilled (in) // ~이 뛰어난 사람 a person of masterly skill (in) / a person skilled in the technique[art] (of) // ~을 연마하다 polish[improve] one's skills.

● **기능 검사** skill measurement. **기능 교육** technical education. **기능 올림픽** Olympics in Technology; (공식명) the International Vocational Training Competition. **기능직** technical service. ¶~ 공무원 a technical official.

기능 (機能) a function. ¶~적인 functional // 생식[생활] ~ generative[vital] function // 소화 ~ the digestive function // ~적으로 functionally // ~을 하다 function / work / operate // ~을 발휘하다 fulfil(l) (one's / its) function / function // 심장의 ~ the function of the heart // 뇌의 ~ the function(ing) of the brain / be functionally disordered // 모든 ~이 정지되었다 All its functions were suspended. // 이 책상은 상당히 ~적이다 This desk is quite functional.

● **기능어** [언] a function word. **기능 장애** a functional disorder. ¶~를 일으키다 be functionally disordered.

기다 1 (몸을 엎드려) crawl; creep(▶ 보통 crawl은 발이 없어도 짧은 생물, 엎드려 기는 사람 등에 대하여 씀. creep는 네 손발로 기는 사람이나 네발짐승이 천천히 살금살금 나아가는 모양; grovel(배를 붙이고). ¶기어 나오다 craw[creep] out / worm oneself[one's way] out // 한 어린아이가 토관(土管)에서 기어 나왔다 A child crawled out of the earthen pipe. 2 [남에게 꼼짝 못하다] cringe; crouch; be servile; grovel. ¶권위 앞에 설설 ~ grovel before[to] authority // 상사 앞에서 설설 ~ cringe to one's superiors / humble[abase] oneself before one's superiors.

기는 놈 위에 나는 놈이 있다 (속담) You cannot always outdo others.; Greatness is comparative.; Everyone has his master.; There is always someone who do it[who knows it] a little bit better.

기어 다니다 creep[crawl] about[around]. ¶아기는 잔디 위를 기어 다녔다 The baby crawled around[about] on the grass. // 네 등에서 벌레가 기어 다니고 있다 A worm is crawling on your back.

기다랗다 rather long; lengthy; long and boring[tedious]; long-winded-long-spun. ¶

기다란 막대 a long pole // 기다란 이야기 a long(-spun) story / a shaggy dog story // 기다랗게 이야기를 늘어놓다 have a long talk [chat] (with) / dwell for a long time [at length] on (a subject) / spin out a story.

기다리다 1 [대기하다] wait (for); await; watch for; be in wait for; be on the lookout (for). ¶기회를 ~ wait [watch] for an opportunity // 때를 ~ bide [watch] one's time // 끝까지 ~ wait out (the long hours) // 차례를 ~ wait one's turn // 남아서 ~ wait behind // 안에서 ~ wait inside // 자지 않고 [외출하지 않고] ~ wait up [in] for (a person) // 한 달을 꼬박 ~ wait out a whole month // 밤새워 ~ wait the whole night (for) / pass the night in waiting // 기다리다가 지치다 grow [get] tired [weary] of waiting (for) // 애타게 ~ wait impatiently [eagerly / anxiously] (for) // 몹시 ~ wait for on tiptoe // 오래 기다리게 해서 미안합니다 I'm sorry to have kept [left] you waiting for a long time. // 장마가 계속되니 햇빛이 몹시 기다려진다 This long spell of rain makes me yearn [long] for the sunshine. // 당신과 만날 날을 손꼽아 기다리고 있어요 I am counting the hours till I can be with you. // 나는 이야기를 하려고 그를 기다리고 있다 I'm waiting to talk to him. // 나는 그에게서 전화가 오기를 하루 종일 기다렸다 I wanted all day for a call from him. // 지난 10년 동안 그녀는 아들이 돌아오기를 기다리며 살아왔다 She has spent the last ten years waiting for her son's return. // 나는 초조하게 기다리던 편지를 받았다 I received the letter that I had been waiting for impatiently. // 그를 기다리다가 지쳐 나는 집으로 돌아왔다 I got quite tired of waiting for him and went home. // 좀 늦어질 테니 나를 기다리지 말고 회의를 시작하시오 Don't wait for me to start the meeting. I'll be late. // 나는 자지 않고 남편이 돌아오기를 기다렸다 I stayed up waiting for my husband to return. // 아무리 기다려도 그로부터는 아무런 소식이 없었다 We waited and waited, but we heard nothing from him. // 기다리는 사람의 처지도 좀 생각해 보시오 Just think how tedious waiting is. // 그가 어떻게 나오는가 기다려 보자 Let's wait and see what line he takes. // 기회란 참을성 있게 기다릴 수밖에 없다 Opportunities must be patiently waited for. // 잠깐만 기다려 주십시오 Wait a moment [minute / little / bit], please. / (지금 갑니다) Just a moment, please. / (전화) Please hold the line [hold on] a minute [moment]. // 이 근처에서 기다려, 곧 돌아올 테니 Wait [Stick] around, will you? I'll soon be back with you.

2 [기대하다] expect; look for; anticipate; await; look forward to. ¶이제나저제나 하고 ~ expect (a person) every moment / be on (the) tiptoe of expectation // 기다리고 기다리던 사람이 왔다 The expected man has come. // 기다리고 기다리던 날 [여름 방학] 이 왔다 The long-awaited day [summer vacation] has come. // 일요일에 만나 뵙기를 기다리겠습니다 I look forward to seeing you on Sunday. (to 뒤에는 명사나 동명사가 옴) // 만나 뵙게 될 날을 기다리겠습니다 I shall expect you when I see you. // 뜻하지 않은 행운이 우리를 기다리고 있었다 Unlooked-for good fortune awaited us. // 우리는 좋은 소식이 오기를 기다리고 있다 We are looking forward to receiving good news.

기단(氣團) [기상] an air mass. ¶한랭 [온난] ~ a cold [warm] air mass // 시베리아 ~ the siberian air mass.

기담(奇談·奇譚) a strange and interesting tale [story].

기대(期待·企待) expectation; expectancy; anticipation; hope. ¶그것은 내 ~에 미치지 못했다 It fell short of my expectations. / It did not live up to my expectations. // 그는 사랑하는 제자에게 ~를 걸었다 He counted [placed his hopes] on his favorite pupil. // 그는 아버지의 ~에 부응할 게다 He will live [come] up to his father's expectations. // 그는 아버지의 ~에 미치지 못했다 [어긋났다] He fell short of his father's expectations. / He did not come up to his father's expectations. // ~와 달리 그는 낙선했다 Contrary to our expectations, he failed in the election. // 그 부모는 아들의 장래에 큰 ~를 걸었다 The parents cherished [entertained] great expectations [hopes] for the future of their son. // 우리에게 ~를 갖게 [품게] 하는 그런 말투는 삼가 주시오 Please do not talk so as to raise our hopes like that. // 내 ~는 어그러졌다 I was disappointed of [was deceived in] my hope. / My hopes were disappointed. **기대하다** expect; anticipate; hope for; look forward to; look for; count on [upon]; reckon on; look to (a person) for. ¶…을 기대하고 in expectation [anticipation] (of) // 나는 그가 쉽게 나를 용서해 주리라고 기대하고 있다 I expect that he will forgive me readily. // 그 사업은 그가 기대했던 대로 성공했다 The undertaking went successfully, just as he had expected. // 나는 그의 도움을 기대했었지만 빗나갔다 I counted on his help, but was disappointed [(구어) was let down]. // 우리는 그의 성공을 기대하고 있다 We expect him to [that he will] succeed. // 그는 승진을 기대하고 열심히 일했다 He worked hard in expectation of promotion. // 그에게는 너무 기대하지 마라. Don't expect too much of [from] him. // 우리는 새로운 요법의 결과로 그의 용태가 뚜렷이 호전되기를 기대하고 있다 With the new treatment, we are hoping for a marked improvement in his condition. // 우리는 봉급 인상을 기대하지 않는다 We have little hope of a raise in salary. // 그 테니스 선수는 내가 기대했던 것 이상으로 잘 싸웠다 The tennis player put up more of a fight than I had expected. // 나는 그의 도움을 기대하고 있었다 I was counting on his help. / I was hoping that he would help me.

● **기대주** [장래성 있는 사람] a coming man; a promising person. ¶저 선수는 올해의 ~다 He is the most promising player this year.

기댓값 [수] expected value; expectation.

기대다 1 (몸을) lean against [on / over]; stand against; recline on [against]; rest on [against]. ¶지팡이 [남의 팔]에 ~ lean on a stick [a person's arm] // 의자의 등에 ~ lean back in a chair // 책상에 ~ lean on a desk / 난간에 ~ lean over the railing // 몸을 벽에 ~ rest [lean] one's body against a wall // 사다리를 벽에 기대어 세우다 rest [prop] a ladder against a wall // 그는 힘없이 나의 어깨에 기댔다 He leaned weakly against [on] my shoulder. // 그녀는 그의 가슴에 기댔다 She snuggled against his chest.

기도

2 [의지하다] rely on[upon]; lean on; depend on[upon]; count on[upon]. ¶남의 호의에 ~ depend on other's kindness // 아버지에게 기대어 살다 be dependent on one's father / depend on one's father for support / lean on one's father // 나는 너밖에 기댈 사람이 없다 I have nobody but you to turn to[rely on] for help. // 남에게 기대지 않겠다는 것이 그의 주장이다 Self-help [-reliance] is his motto.

기도(企圖) [시도] an attempt; a try; an essay; [기획] an enterprise; an undertaking; a project; a design. ¶살해 ~ an attempt upon (a person's) life. **기도하다** attempt; try; undertake; plan; design; project; scheme; plot; intend; contemplate; have (something) in mind. ¶자살을 ~ attempt suicide / attempt one's own life // make an attempt at suicide // 살해를 ~ make an attempt on (a person's) life / plot the murder (of) / attempt the life (of).

기도(祈禱) a prayer; (식전·식후의) (a) grace; (one's) devotions (▶ 언제나 복수로). ¶아침의 ~ morning prayer / matins // 저녁의 ~ (an) evening prayer / vespers. **기도하다** pray; offer[say] a prayer; (식전·식후에) say (a) grace. ¶무릎을 꿇고 ~ kneel in prayer // 그녀는 기도하고 있었다 She was praying [saying her prayers]. / She was at her prayers [devotions]. // 아버지의 병이 낫기를 나는 하느님께 기도했다 I prayed to God that my father would recover from his illness. // 하느님의 가호가 있기를 기도합니다 I pray that you may be protected by Providence. // 그녀는 남편이 무사히 귀국하기를 기도하고 있다 She praying for her husband's safe return home.

● **기도문** a prayer; the Lord's Prayer. **기도서** a prayer [service] book; [가] a breviary; (영국 성공회의) the Book of Common Prayer. **기도원** a prayer house [retreat]. **기도회** a prayer meeting; a devotional service.

기도(氣道) [생] the respiratory tract.

기독교(基督敎) **1** Christianity. ⇨ 크리스트교 **2** [기] Protestantism.

● **기독교도** / **기독교 신자** a Christian; (집합적) Christendom. **기독교 여자 청년회** the Young Women's Christian Association(약어 Y.W.C.A.). **기독교 청년회** the Young Men's Christian Association(약어 Y.M.C.A.).

기동(起動) **1** [움직임] one's movement. ¶~이 자유롭지 못하다 [어렵다] have difficulty in moving[getting] about. **기동하다** move; stir; get about; (병후에) be up[out] and about. ¶노인은 기력이 없어 기동하지 못했다 The old man's debility prevented him from getting out of bed. **2** starting. ⇨ 시동(始動)

기동(機動) maneuver; [군] movement. ¶~적인 mobile.

● **기동력** mobile power[strength]; mobility. ¶~을 발휘하다 demonstrate one's mobility. **기동 부대** mobile troops; a mechanized unit; (특수 임무를 띤) a task force. **기동성** (군대 등의) mobility. **기동 연습** / **기동 훈련** maneuvers; (영) manoeuvres; (야외의) a field maneuver. **기동 작전** mobile operations. **기동 타격대** a special strike [task] force (ready to act).

기둥 1 (건축물의) a pillar; a column (두리기둥); a post; a pole. ¶불~ a pillar of fire // 물~ a column of water // ~을 세우다 erect[set up] a pillar. **2** [의지가 될 만한 사람] a support; a prop; a stay; a mainstay; a pillar. ¶집안의 ~ the prop[breadwinner] of a family / the support[prop and stay] of a family // 나라의 ~ a pillar of the state // 그는 우리 회사의 ~ 이다 He is one of the pillars[mainstays] of our firm.

● **기둥머리** a capital; a chapiter; a cap piece. **기둥목**(-木) logs for pillars and columns. **기둥뿌리** the base of a column.

기둥서방(-書房) a fancy man (of a whore); a guardian lover (of a bargirl); a gigolo (pl. ~s); (포주) a pander; a pimp.

기득(旣得). ¶~의 already acquired [obtained] / vested. **기득하다** be already acquired [obtained].

● **기득권** vested rights; vested interests(권익). ¶~을 지키다 infringe upon [protect] (a person's[one's]) vested rights.

기둥차다 〈속〉 grand and special; awesome; cool; (서술적) be out of this world.

기라성(綺羅星) glittering [bright] stars. ¶~ 같은 고관들 a galaxy [fine array] of dignitaries // 집회장에는 재계의 쟁쟁하신 양반들이 ~같이 늘어서 있었다 In the hall there was a splendid array of leading financiers.

기략(機略) resources; shifts; expedients; tact; wit. ¶~이 뛰어난 사람 a man of resources [ideas] / a resourceful person // ~이 뛰어난 full of resources [ideas] / full of shifts and devices / resourceful.

기량(技倆) skill; ability. ⇨ 기능(技能)

기량(器量) ability; talent; capacity; caliber. ¶~이 있는 able / talented // 그는 큰 인물이 될 ~이 없다 He lacks the stuff of greatness. // 그는 지도자가 될 ~이 있다 He has the caliber of leadership. / He has what it takes to be a leader of people.

기러기 [동] a (wild) goose (pl. geese).

기러기발 (현악기의) a bridge (on a string instrument).

기력(氣力) **1** [기운] energy; vigor; (영) vigour; force; spirit; vitality; virility; (미국 속어) pep; will power. ¶~이 왕성한 energetic / vigorous / full of vitality // ~이 없다 be in low spirits / be spiritless / be listless [languid / weak-kneed] // ~을 되찾다 regain one's vigor / recover one's spirits / recuperate one's (used-up) strength // 대단한 ~인걸 What energy! // 그는 옛날의 ~을 잃었다 He has lost his old vigor. // 그는 나이를 먹어 ~을 상실했다 He has lost most of his drive with age. // 그 환자는 오직 ~만으로 살고 있었다 He stayed alive by sheer force of will. / He was living solely upon his own spirit. // 나는 심하게 병을 앓고 났더니 ~이 완전히 없어졌다 Since my serious illness I have completely lost my vigor [(미국 구어) I just don't have any pep].

2 [물] air pressure.

-기로 1 [까닭·조건] as; because; since; on account of; owing to. ¶네가 떠난다~ 전송을 나왔다 Hearing that you are leaving, I have come to see you off. **2** [아무리 …이다 하더라도] however; whatever; even if [though]. ¶아무리 돈 [재산]이 많~ however rich a man may be / no matter how rich a man may be / be a man ever so rich // 아무리 달이 밝~ 어찌 햇빛에 견줄 수 있으랴 No matter how bright the moonlight may be, how can it

possibly rival the sun?
기로(岐路) turning point. ⇨﹦갈림길2
-기로서(니) however. ⇨﹦-기로2
-기로선(니) however. ⇨﹦-기로2
기록(記錄) 1 [적음] recording; [기록한 것] a record; [문서] a document; documentary literature; [공문서] archives; [의사록] the minutes, proceedings; [연대기] annals; a chronicle. ¶~에 남기다 leave (an event) on record / keep a record (of an event) // ~에 빠지다 [남아 있지 않다] fall to be recorded / be offrecord // ~에서 삭제하다 strike (off) (a word) from the record. **기록하다** record; register; write [note] down; put on (something) record. ¶그는 전쟁의 참상을 기록하여 자손에게 전하려고 했다 He tried to record the misery of war for posterity. ➔¶기록되다 be (put) on record / be recorded // 그 전쟁의 사망자 수는 기록되어 있지 않다 It is not recorded how many people died in the war.
2 [경기 등의 성적] a record. ¶100미터 자유형의 ~ the record for the 100-meter freestyle // 우승 ~ the winning record [time] // ~을 깨다 break [beat / smash / shatter] the record // (세계 신)~을 세우다 set [establish / make] a (new world) record [mark] // ~을 경신하다 better [renew] one's record.
● **기록계원** a recorder; a record keeper; an archivist; (경기의) a scorer; a timekeeper; (영화 촬영의) a director's assistant. **기록 보유자** a record holder. **기록 영화** a documentary (film [movie]); a record film.
기뢰(機雷) an underwater mine. ¶부유(浮遊) ~ a drifting mine // 수압 ~ a pressure mine // 음향 [자기(磁氣)] ~ an acoustic [a magnetic] mine // ~를 부설하다 place [lay] mines (in the sea) / mine (a harbor) // ~에 걸리다 [~를 건드리다] hit [strike] a mine // ~ 방지 장치를 하다 provide (a ship) with an anti mine device // 우리는 항구의 입구에 ~을 부설했다 We mined [laid mines at] the entrance to the harbor.
기류(氣流) an air [atmosphere] current; an atmospheric [aerial] current; a current of air. ¶난(亂)~ (air) turbulence / turbulent air // 상승 [하강] ~ an ascending [a descending] air current // 상층 [하층] ~ the upper [lower] air current // 악~에 휩쓸리다 be caught [trapped] in a treacherous air current // 행글라이더는 ~을 타고 천천히 내려왔다 The hang glider came down slowly on the air current.
기류(寄留) temporary residence [domicile]. **기류하다** live [stay] temporarily (at a person's house / with a person); reside temporarily (at); temporarily domiciled (at); sojourn. ¶그는 대학 재학 중 서울의 삼촌 댁에 기류했다 He stayed [lived] with his uncle in Seoul while attending college.
● **기류지** the place of one's temporary residence [domicile]; [법] one's domicile of choice.
기르다 1 [키우다] raise (애완동물 등에는 쓰지 않음); keep; breed; rear; feed (먹이다); grow; cultivate; bring up; foster; nurse. ¶새끼 때부터 기른 곰 a bear raised (by a man) since it was a cub / a bear kept from young // 주인집에서 길러 온 점원 a clerk brought up in his master's house // 닭[양]을 ~ raise chickens [sheep] // 앵무새를 ~ keep a poll parrot (새장에서) // 가축을 ~ raise livestock / breed domestic animals // 난초를 ~ cultivate [grow / raise] the orchids // 아기를 우유로 ~ nourish an infant with milk / feed [raise] a child on the bottle // 어릴 때부터 ~ raise [rear] from an early age // 아이를 훌륭하게 [잘] ~ nurture a child the way a child should be brought up // 나는 부모가 안 계셔서 형이 나를 길러 주었다 I have no parents and was brought up [reared / raised] by my brother. // 그는 소를 기르며 생계를 잇고 있다 He makes his living by raising cattle. // 그는 개를 2마리 기르고 있다 He keeps two dogs. // 사랑으로 길러져 자란 아이는 참으로 행복하다 A child brought up with love is indeed lucky.
2 [가르치다] educate; train; cultivate. ¶인재를 ~ cultivate men of talent [ability] / foster men to be great // 그 대학은 교사를 길러 낸다 That college trains teachers.
3 [단련·배양하다] train; build (up); develop; cultivate; culture. ¶어릴 때부터 길러 온 운동선수 an athlete trained (by a coach) since he was young // 비판력 [심미안]을 ~ develop [cultivate] one's critical powers [sense of beauty] // 음악에 대한 감각 [음감]을 ~ train one's sense of music [ear] // 도덕심을 ~ cultivate a sense of morality // 우리가 젊었을 때 상상력을 기르자 Let's cultivate [foster] our imaginative powers while (we are) young. // 여름 방학이야말로 아이들이 체력을 기를 때다 Summer vacation is the time when children develop [build up] their physical strength.
4 [버릇·기술 등을 익히다] form; develop; cultivate; acquire; gain. ¶어학 실력을 ~ acquire linguistic skill / gain ability in a language // 그들은 어렸을 때 좋은 습관을 길렀다 They formed [cultivated] good habits in their childhood.
5 [머리털·수염 등을 자라게 하다] grow; cultivate. ¶머리를 ~ let one's hair grow (long) // 턱수염을 ~ grow [cultivate] a beard // 턱수염을 기르고 있다 have [wear] a beard.
기름 [식물유·동물유·광물유] oil; (기계용) grease; [동물의 지방] fat; (정제한 돼지 기름) lard; (소·양의) suet; (고래의) blubber. ¶샐러드 ~ salad oil / ~의 [~을 함유한] oily / greasy // ~이 많은 고기 fatty meat // ~에 튀긴 생선 fried fish // ~이 배다 [묻다] become oily [greasy] / be stained with oil [grease] // ~에 데다 be burned by oil // ~으로 지지다 fry (a fish) with oil // ~에 튀기다 fry (a fish) in oil / deep-fry (a fish) // ~과 물은 섞이지 않는다 Oil and water do not mix. // 이 기계는 ~이 다 되었다 This machine needs oiling. // 자동차에 ~이 떨어졌다 The car ran out of gas. // 그 두 사람 사이는 마치 물과 ~ 같다 The two can't [don't] mix like oil and water. / They simply don't [can't] get along well together.
기름(을) 먹이다 oil. ¶기름을 먹인 종이 oiled paper / oilpaper // 장판에 ~ oil the floor paper.
기름을 치다 [뇌물을 쓰다] grease [oil] a person's palm. ¶그의 여비서에게 기름을 치면 그의 사무실 열쇠를 그녀가 줄지도 모른다 If you grease his secretary's palm, she might give you a key to his office.
기름(을) 짜다 [착취하다] extort; squeeze; sweat. ¶가난한 자들의 ~ squeeze the poor.

기름지다

- **기름걸레** oilcloth. **기름기** [기름 덩이가 섞인 고기] the fat (of meat); fat meat; [기름기운] oiliness; greasiness. ¶~ 많은 greasy / oily // ~ 있는 음식 rich[greasy] food // ~ 도는 얼굴 an oily face. **기름때** oil dirt[stain]; a grease spot[stain]. **기름병** an oil bottle. **기름옷** greasy[grimy] clothes. **기름종이** oiled paper; oilpaper. **기름콩** a sprouting bean. **기름틀** an oil press.

기름지다 1 (음식물 등이) greasy; fat; fatty. ¶기름진 음식 greasy food / rich food / fat diet / nourishing[nutritious] food(영양분이 많은) // 기름진 식사를 하다 take a greasy meal. 2 (사람·동물) fat; fleshy. ¶기름진 말과 여윈 말 a fleshy horse and a worn-out horse. 3 (땅이) fertile; rich; fat; fruitful; productive. ¶기름진 땅 rich[fat / mellow] soil / fertile land // 그들은 밭에 거름을 주어 기름지게 하였다 They fertilized the field with manure.

기름하다 longish; somewhat long. ¶기름한 얼굴 a moderately[rather] long face / a longish face // 얼굴이 기름한 사람 a long-faced person / a person with an oval face [egg-shaped face].

기리다 applaud; praise; admire; extol; give high praise to; speak highly of. ¶…의 유덕을 기리어 비석을 세우다 erect a monument to the illustrious memory of … // 본교의 창설자의 유덕을 기리기 위하여 이 동상을 건립합니다 We erect this statue to pay (a) tribute to the memory of the founder of this school.

기린 (麒麟) 1 [동] a giraffe. 2 [상상의 동물] a unicorn; a fabulous and auspicious beast.
- **기린아** (-兒) a genius; a (young) prodigy [wonder]. **기린자리** [천] the Camelopard; the Giraffe; Camelopardalis.

기립 (起立) rising; standing up. ¶~ [구령] Stand up! / Rise! // 일동 ~ Everybody up! **기립하다** stand up; rise; get[rise] to one's feet. ¶우리는 기립하라는 요청을 받았다 We were asked to rise[get to our feet].
- **기립 박수** a standing ovation. ¶~를 받다 receive a standing ovation. **기립 투표** standing[rising] vote.

기마 (騎馬) 1 [말타기] horse riding. **기마하다** ride a horse; mount [get on] a horse; ride horseback. ¶기마하고 가다 go on horseback. 2 [타는 말] a riding[saddle] horse.
- **기마경찰** (집합적) the mounted police. **기마 민족** a horse-riding people; an equestrian people; mounted nomads. **기마병** a cavalry [mounted] soldier; a cavalryman; (집합적) cavalry. **기마전** (play) a mock cavalry battle. **기마행렬** a cavalcade.

기막히다 (氣-) 1 [놀랍다·어이없다] amazed; appalled; dum(b)founded; astonished; stunned; taken aback. ¶기막히는 일 a horrible thing / an absurdity // 기막힌 사정 a reason[matter] hard to tell / [무참한 상태] a wretched[miserable] condition // 기막혀 말이 안 나오다 be (struck) dumb with amazement / feel[be] utterly scandalized (at) // 어린애가 그런 소리를 하다니 기막히군 I am (struck) dumb with amazement to hear a child say such a thing. // 우리는 모두 기막혀서 얼굴만 바라보았다 We all gazed at each other in blank dismay. // 너의 바보 같은 짓에는 기막힌다 Your stupidity really beats [shocks] me. 2 [정도가 높다] breathtaking; striking; wonderful; astounding; great. ¶기막힌 풍경 a breathtaking view // 기막힌 연주 a marvelous [superb / (미) standout] performance // 기막히게 구성된 정원 garden of exquisite composition // 그가 파리에서 샹송을 배우더니 저렇게 기막히게 잘 부른다 He learned to sing chanson in paris, which is why he sings them so superbly[he is so very good].

기만 (欺瞞) [남을 속임] deception; deceit; imposition; imposture; cheat. **기만하다** deceive; cheat; delude; impose (on a person); play (a person) a trick; pull[draw / put] the wool over (a person's) eyes. ¶세상을 ~ deceive[blear the eyes of] the world / impose upon public.
- **기만성** deceitfulness. **기만행위** a fraudulent act.

기말 (期末) the end of a term; a term end.
- **기말 결산** a term-end account. **기말 시험** a semester test; a term exam(ination); (학년말의) a final[term-end] exam(ination).

기맥상통하다 (氣脈相通-) be congenial (to / with); be like-minded; find in (a person) a kindred soul; get along (with).

기명 (記名) a signature; register; inscription. **기명하다** sign (one's name); register; inscribe; put down one's name (for). ¶서류에 기명하고 날인하다 sign and seal a document.
- **기명 투표** an open vote[ballot]. ¶무~ an unopen vote.

기명 (器皿) vessels and dishes.

기묘하다 (奇妙-) strange; curious; queer; odd; singular. ¶기묘한 일치 a curious coincidence // 기묘한 모양을 한 상(像) an oddly-shaped statue // 기묘한 사람 an odd person // 기묘한 이야기 a queer story / a strange sort of story / a mystery story // 기묘한 짓을 하다 act oddly // 기묘한 복장을 하고 있다 be dressed in singular fashion[in an odd style]. **기묘히** strangely; oddly; curiously; peculiarly.

기문 (奇聞) a strange news[report].

기문 (氣門) [동] a stoma (pl. ~ta); a stigma (pl. ~s, ~ta).

기물 (器物) [용기] a receptacle; a container; [특히 액체를 담는 것] a vessel; [기구] a utensil; an implement; [가구] (a piece of) furniture.

기미 freckles; liver spots. ¶~ 낀 얼굴 a freckled face // ~가 끼다 freckle // 그녀는 ~가 잘 낀다 She freckles easily.

기미 (幾微·機微) a touch; a dash; a shade; a smack; a tinge; a suspicion; a tendency; signs; indication. ¶히스테리 ~가 있는 사람 a person who tends to be hysteria / a person predisposed to hysteria // ~가 있다 There is a smack of. // 금리는 내려갈 ~를 보이고 있다 The bank rate is showing a downward tendency. / The bank rate is showing a tendency to slip a little. // 이 집에는 남자가 살고 있다는 ~가 없다 This house hold lacks a masculine touch.

기민하다 (機敏-) quick; prompt; astute; shrewd; smart; alert; (구어) cute. ¶기민한 동작 quick movements // 기민한 사람 an alert person / (구어) a person who's always on the ball // 기민하게 행동하다 move quickly / make an adroit move // 기민하지 못하다 be slow(-going) / be tardy / be unbusinesslike // 그는 어떤 일이든지 기민하게 해치운다 He is smart in all things [quick at everything].

기밀(機密) secrecy; secret information; a secret. ¶국가 ~ a state secret // ~의 secret / confidential / classified // 군사 ~ military secret // ~에 관한 일 confidential duties // ~로 해 두다 keep (a matter) secret / keep (a matter) under wraps // ~을 누설하다 let out [leak out / divulge / disclose] a secret // ~을 지키다 keep a secret / observe secrecy.
● **기밀 누설** a leak of secret information; an intelligence leak. ¶~죄 divulgence of a (state) secret. **기밀문서** confidential [secret] papers.

기박하다(奇薄-) unlucky; ill-starred; ill-fated; hapless; unfortunate. ¶기박한 팔자를 타고나다 be born under an unlucky star // 팔자가 기박한 것을 한탄하다 grieve over one's ill [tough] luck // 그녀는 한평생 팔자가 기박했다 She led an ill-fated life. / She was hapless throughout her life.

기반(羈絆) restraint; a yoke; fetters; ties; bonds; shackles.

기반(基盤) a foundation; a base; a basis; [지위] footing; foothold; [세력 범위] a sphere of influence; (선거의) a constituency; constituents; (지질의) bedrock. ¶…을 ~으로 하다 be based [founded] on … // …의 ~을 이루다 form the basis [foundation] of … // ~을 굳히다 solidify [establish] one's footing // 확고한 ~을 잡다 gain a firm foothold // 농촌을 ~으로 하여 입후보하다 run for (the National Assembly) with agricultural districts for the constituency // ~을 쌓다 establish a constituency.

기발하다(奇拔-) uncommon; extraordinary; peculiar; novel; original; unconventional; fanciful (drawing / pattern). ¶기발한 도안 a fantastic design // 기발한 광고 방법 an original way of advertising // 기발한 말을 하다 say a clever [smart] thing // 기발한 생각으로 사람을 놀라게 하다 set people agape by some original idea.

기백(氣魄) spirit; soul; vim; vigor. ¶~ 있는 사람 a man of spirit // 호매한 ~ an intrepid spirit // ~이 있다[없다] be full of [be lacking in] spirit // ~을 떨치다 prove [show] one's mettle // 말씨가 부드러운 그 남자에게서 나는 강한 ~이 깃들어 있음을 느꼈다 I felt a strong drive in that soft-spoken man. // 그의 연설은 ~에 차 있었다 He made a powerful speech.

기백(幾百) hundreds. ¶~만 millions // ~만 명 millions of people.

기법(技法) techniques. ¶영화의 ~ cinematic technique // ~을 터득하다 acquire [master] the technique (of) // 목각의 ~을 배우다 learn the craft of a wood-carver.

기벽(奇癖) an eccentric [a queer] habit; an eccentricity; a peculiarity; a singularity. ¶그는 취하면 남의 귀를 잡아당기는 ~이 있다 When he's drunk he has the odd habit of pulling people's ears.

기별(奇別) a notice; information; news; word; tidings; a letter; report; a message. ¶미리 아무 ~도 없이 without previous notice // ~을 듣다 hear of / have [receive] news of / get word from // 아무런 ~도 없다 hear nothing from (a person) // 며칠이 지나도 ~이 없다 Days passed without a line from him. // 그에게서 무슨 ~이 있었나 Have you heard anything from him? **기별하다** let (a person) know; tell; inform (a person) of [that]; advise (a person) of; give (a person) notice; report; write to (a person). ¶일 주일 전에 ~ 해 (give a person) a week's notice // 그에게 내가 기별하기까지는 올 필요가 없다고 일러 주게 Tell him he need not come till I send him word. // 무사히 도착하거든 기별해 주게 Please send me word of your safe arrival.

기병(騎兵) a cavalry [mounted] soldier; a cavalryman; a trooper; (집합적) cavalry. ¶~ 3천 three thousand horse [cavalrymen] // 경[중]~대 light [heavy] cavalry.
● **기병 장교** a cavalry officer; a cavalry.

기병(起兵) raising an army; rising in arms; an uprising. **기병하다** raise an army; rise in arms (against).

기보(既報) a previous report; prior information. **기보하다** have already reported. ¶기보한 바와 같이 as already [previously] reported [announced] / as stated in a previous issue // 기보한 대로 방화 훈련이 실시된다 As previously announced, there will be a fire drill.

기보(棋譜·碁譜) the record of a game of go.

기보법(記譜法) [음] musical notation.

기복(起伏) ups and downs; undulations; [지] accident; relief. ¶~이 있는 undulating / rolling // ~이 많은 생애 a checkered [a colorful / an eventful] career / a life full of ups and downs // ~이 완만한 in easy undulations // ~이 많은 사업 a peak and valley enterprise // 그의 작품은 질의 ~이 심하다 His works are of uneven [are not uniform in] quality. // 그는 감정의 ~이 심하다 He goes through a lot of emotional ups and downs. / He is very moody. // 생산고는 곳에 따라 ~이 있다 The output fluctuates depending on the location. **기복하다** rise and fall; roll; undulate; wave.

기본(基本) [기초] a foundation; a basis; basics; [기준] a standard. ¶댄스의 ~ 동작 the basic movements of a dance // ~을 이루다 be fundamental (to) / form the groundwork (of) // ~에서 시작하다 begin with the ABC (of) // 농업은 국가의 ~이다 Agriculture forms the basis of [is basic to] a nation. // 그는 수학의 ~을 아버지로부터 배웠다 He learned the elements [basics / fundamentals] of mathematics from his father. // 이것이 구두 및 필기 연습의 ~이 된다 This is made the basis of frequent oral and written drill. // 아마추어 운동선수의 ~ 요건은 무엇인가 What is most important (of all) for an amateur athlete?
● **기본 계획** general planning; a master plan. **기본급** a basic [base] salary; basic [base] wages; basic [regular] pay. **기본 단위** a basic [standard] unit. **기본 방침** a basic policy. **기본법** an organic law. **기본 설계** a basic design. **기본요금** a basic rate [charge]; (택시의) minimum fare. **기본형** a fundamental form.

기본적(基本的) fundamental; basic. ¶~으로 fundamentally / basically // ~ 소비재 vital consumption goods // ~ 인권 the basic [fundamental] human right.

기부(寄附) (a) donation; (a) contribution; (a)

기부

subscription. ¶물품에 의한 ~ contributions in kind∥개인의 ~로 설립된 대학[도서관] a privately endowed university[library]∥운동회 비용으로 ~를 청합니다 Please give something toward the sports fund.∥~는 액수의 다과를 불문하고 고맙게 받겠습니다 The smallest contribution is thankfully received. **기부하다** contribute (to/toward); donate; subscribe; make a donation[contribution] (to). ¶강제로 기부하다 force (people) to make contributions∥나는 바자에 의류를 기부했다 I contributed some clothes to be sold at the bazaar.∥여기에 백만 원을 기부합니다 Here is a million won toward it.∥음악회의 수입은 적십자 기금에 기부한다 The proceeds of the concert will go to the Red Cross Funds.∥지방의 몇몇 기업체가 1,000달러씩 기부하겠다고 신청했다 Several local businesses have offered to chip in with 1,000 dollars a piece. ● **기부금** a contribution; a donation; an endowment; a gift of money. ¶~을 모으다 collect[raise] donation[contribution] (from) / make a purse (for). **기부자** a contributor; a subscriber; a donator; a donor.

기부(基部) the base; the foundation; the basal part (of). ¶이 기둥의 ~는 썩었다 The bottom of this pillar is rotten.

기분(氣分) feeling; sensation; a frame of mind; mood; atmosphere. ¶**정초** ~ the New Year feeling[atmosphere]∥유쾌[불쾌/우울]한 ~으로 in a pleasant[sulky/gloomy] mood∥일시적인 ~으로 on the spur of the moment∥감상적 ~ a melting mood∥차분한 ~ a quiet mood∥그때 ~에 따라서 in [according to] the mood of the moment/as one's humor[whim] dictates∥~에 따라 움직이다 be swayed[influenced] by sentiment∥~이 좋다 feel well[good] / be in good humor[mood] / be comfortable∥~이 나쁘다 be in a bad mood / get up on the wrong side of the bed / feel unwell[ill/bad/poorly/low] / be out of sorts / be unpleasant∥~이 울적하다 be[feel] down / be depressed∥~을 내다 get in the spirit of things / (분위기를) create an atmosphere (of)∥(남의) ~을 상하다 hurt (a person's) feelings / offend∥그것은 그의 ~ 나름이다 It depends on how he feels about it.∥시골 길을 걸으면 ~이 좋다 It's pleasant walking along a country road.∥감미로운 향기 덕분에 나는 ~이 좋다 The sweet fragrance makes me feel good.∥남에게 뒷손가락질을 받는다면 ~이 나쁘겠지요 You would be hurt if you were laughed at behind your back.∥카드놀이를 할 ~이 아니다 I'm in no mood for playing card.∥춤출 ~이 나지 않는다 I'm not in a mood for dancing.∥그것은 다분히 ~의 문제이다 The problem is largely a matter of feeling.∥오늘 ~이 좀 어떻습니까 (환자에게) How are you feeling today?∥도시는 온통 축제 ~이었다 The town was full of a festive spirit.∥어머님의 ~이 제대로 풀리기 전에는 난 집으로 돌아갈 수 없다 I can't go home until my mother recovers her temper.∥여행을 하면 ~이 풀리겠지요 Going on a trip will give you some diversion[will cheer you up].∥~ 나쁘게 생각하지 말고 내 말을 들어 다오 Please listen to what I have to say without taking offense.∥오늘은 고기가 많이 잡힐 것 같은 ~이 든다 I've got a feeling that we're going to catch a lot today.∥우리가 시합에 이겼기 때문에 나는 ~이 좋았다 We had won the game, so I was in a good mood.∥그는 일시적인 ~으로 직장을 바꾼다 He is always changing jobs on a whim.∥내 차를 타고 달리면 ~ 만점이다 It feels great to be in my car and punch[get on] it.∥나는 지루한 강의를 들을 ~이 나지 않는다 I don't feel like attending a dull lecture.∥그때 나는 절망적인 ~이었다 I was in despair then.∥희미한 오르간 소리가 내 귀에 ~ 좋게 들렸다 The faint organ music was pleasing[sweet] to my ear.∥그는 ~ 나쁠 정도로 침착하다 He is disgustingly calm about it.

● **기분 전환** (a) diversion; a pastime; (a) recreation; (a) relaxation. ¶~을 위해 여행을 떠나다 go away from home to get a change. **기분파** a man of moods; a moody person. ¶그는 ~다 He is apt to indulge in moods.

기뻐하다 be pleased[delighted] with[at]; be happy with; be glad for; rejoice over[at]; congratulate oneself on; [즐겁게 여기다] enjoy; consider (something) to be pleasant [enjoyable/delightful]. ¶몹시 기뻐하여 in high glee (at) / highly delighted / with great joy / much pleased∥성공을 ~ be pleased with one's success∥고향 소식을 듣고 ~ be delighted at the news from home∥뛸 듯이 ~ dance[jump] with[for] joy∥아이들은 눈이 오면 기뻐한다 Children have a glad time when snow falls.∥이 선물을 받으면 누구나 기뻐할 것이다 This gift would be acceptable to anyone.∥나는 꿈이 아닌가 하고 기뻐했다 My rapture was so intense that I could scarcely believe my sense.∥나는 행운을 기뻐하고 있었다 I was felicitating myself on my good luck.∥그 계획을 기뻐하지 않는 사람들도 있다 Some people are none too pleased with the project.

기쁘다 joyful; delightful; happy; pleasant; glad; gratifying; [기쁘게 생각하다] delighted; pleased; gratified. ¶기쁘게 하다 please / satisfy∥기쁜 소식 a glad[delightful/pleasant/joyful/welcome] news[tidings]∥기쁜 날 a joyous occasion∥기쁜 일 a happy event / (행사) a happy[(문어) felicitous] occasion / a glad[delightful] thing / cream and sugar∥기뻐서 for[in/with] joy∥기쁘게도 to one's joy∥얼굴로 with a delightful look∥기쁘기도 하고 슬프기도 하다 have mixed feelings of joy and sorrow∥기쁠 때나 슬플 때나 in joy and in sorrow∥기쁨 나머지 울다 cry for[with] joy / shed tears of joy∥만나 뵙게 되어 기쁩니다 I'm happy to see you.∥모시고 함께 갈 수 있다면 기쁘겠습니다 I would be very happy[(구어) love] to go with you.∥나는 눈물이 나오려고 할 정도로 기뻤다 I nearly wept for joy.∥그의 생존이 확인되어 나는 말할 수 없이 기뻤다 I was overjoyed to hear that he was alive.∥자네가 양쪽 시험에 합격했다니 얼마나 기쁜 일이냐 How wonderful that you passed both exams!∥그가 돌아왔다고 하는 기쁜 소식을 우리는 받았다 We received the joyful news of his return.∥전원 합격했다는 것이 나는 매우 ~ I am very happy[pleased] that everyone passed the examination.∥당신에게 기쁜 소식이 있습니다 Here's some delightful news for you.∥아들의 말은 그 아버지를 기쁘게 했다 The son's words pleased[delighted] his father.∥그는 언제나 남을 기쁘게 하는 말을 한다 He always has something pleasing to say.∥기쁜 빛이 그의 얼굴에 넘치고 있다 His face beams with joy[delight].∥그는 기뻐서 어쩔 줄을 몰랐다 He was beside himself[transported] with joy.∥당신의 편지를 기쁘게 읽었 습니다 I have read your letter with great pleasure.∥건강하시다니 기쁩니다 I'm glad to find you in good health.∥오랜만에 고향 산들을 바라보고 정말 기뻤다 It was really a sweet pleasure to gaze upon the mountains of my hometown again after such a long time.∥이보다 더 기쁜 일이 없습니다 Nothing would make me happier than this.

기쁨 〔희열〕 joy; delight; glee; gladness; rejoicing; pleasure; 〔환희〕 rapture; exultation; ecstasy; 〔축의〕 congratulation; felicitation; 〔만족〕 gratification. ¶삶의 ~ joy of life∥여러 가지 ~과 슬픔 joys and sorrows∥~이 없는 devoid of joy / joyless∥~으로 가슴이 뛰놀다 one's heart pounds with delight∥~을 참지 못하다 be unable to contain one's joy∥아름다운 것은 영원한 ~이다 A thing of beauty is a joy for ever.∥그녀의 가슴은 ~으로 두근거렸다 Her heart beat high with delight.∥그 비보에 그녀의 ~도 쓰디쓴 것이 되었다 Her joy was soured by the sad news.∥그녀는 ~의 눈물을 흘렸다 She shed tears of joy.

기사 (技師) an engineer; (전문 분야의) a technical expert.(▶ 미국에서는 engineer란 말이 아주 넓은 뜻으로 쓰임, 예를 들면 미화원을 sanitation engineer, 창문 수리공을 casement window engineer라고 하는 경우가 많음) ¶건축 ~ a building engineer / an architect∥토목 [기계 / 전기] ~ a civil[a mechanical / an electrical] engineer.

기사 (記事) 1 〔사실을 적음〕 describing; (a) description; an account; a statement. ¶∼체의 descriptive (story)∥(일기에서) 오늘 ~ 없음 Nothing happened worth jotting down today.
2 (신문의) news; a news item[story]; a report; 〔논설〕 an article; an account. ¶사망 ~ an obituary (notice) / a necrology∥사회 ~ social news[items]∥삼단 ~ a three-column article∥신문 ~ a newspaper account / press news / a news item∥지방 ~ local news∥특종 ~ exclusive news / a scoop / a new beat∥짧은 ~ news in brief∥(신문의) ~로 쓰기 위한 회견 a story interview∥특종 ~를 싣다 publish an exclusive (on)∥수해 ~를 싣다 carry an item about flood damage∥~를 삭제하다 erase a news item / (일부를) blue-pencil∥~의 정확[확실]성 accuracy[reliability] of news∥~ 게재를 금지하다 prohibit printing the news∥오늘 신문에는 최근의 선거에 관한 ~가 실려 있다 Today's paper carries an article on the recent election.∥신문 ~를 전면적으로 믿을 수는 없다 We cannot believe all that the newspaper says[reports].∥신문은 일제히 그 재판 ~를 다루었다 All the papers featured [played up] the trial.∥그것은 아름다운 이야기입니다. ~화하겠습니다 It is a charming story. I will use it in print.
● **기사문** a description; a descriptive composition.

기사 (棋士) a baduk(go) player; (장기의) a janggi player. ¶프로 ~ (바둑의) a professional baduk player.

기사 (騎士) 〔승마자〕 a rider; a horseman; (유럽 중세의) a knight. ¶~의 갑옷 knightly armor.
● **기사도** knighthood; chivalry.

기사회생 (起死回生) resuscitation; revival. ¶~의 묘약 a medicine of the virtue of reviving the dead / (미) a miracle[wonder] drug∥그 융자는 파산 직전의 회사에 있어서 ~의 기회였다 The loan gave the nearly-bankrupt company a chance to recover. **기사회생하다** restore from death; revive; resuscitate.

기산 (起算) reckoning[counting / computing] from a certain date. **기산하다** reckon [compute] from; measure from. ¶이자는 예금한 다음 날부터 기산하여 지불한다 Interest is paid from the day following that of deposit. ➔¶네 승급(昇給)은 3개월 전으로 거슬러 올라가 기산된다 The increase in your salary is to be reckoned from three months back.
● **기산일** the initial date in reckoning; the day from which a reckoning is made. **기산점** a starting point for reckoning; the point where one starts counting.

기상 (起牀) rising (in the morning). **기상하다** rise; get up; turn out; (미국 속어) roll out.
● **기상나팔** 〔군〕 the reveille; the morning bugle. ¶~을 불다 sound[blow] the reveille. **기상 시간** the hour of rising; the turnout.

기상 (氣象) weather (conditions). ¶이상 ~ abnormal weather∥~을 관측하다 make meteorological observations.
● **기상 관측** (a) meteorological[weather] observation. **기상대** a meteorological observatory. **기상도** a weather chart[map]. **기상청** the Meteorological Administration. **기상통보** weather news; a weather report[bulletin]. **기상학** meteorology; aerology.

기상 (機上) ¶~에 오르다 get on[board] an airplane∥~에서 내려다보다 look down from an airplane (over a city).

기상 (氣像) spirit; temperament; nature; temper; disposition; appearance; bearing. ¶쾌활한 ~의 사람 a man of cheerful disposition∥~씩씩한 ~ a manly[valiant] spirit∥진취적 ~ an enterprising spirit.

기상천외 (奇想天外) ¶~의 most fantastic∥그것은 ~의 생각이다 It is a most unexpected idea.

기색 (氣色) 〔표정〕 looks; countenance; appearance; 〔감정〕 mood; humor; feeling; 〔표시〕 a sign; an indication. ¶조금도 두려워하는 ~ 없이 without showing the slightest sign of fear∥~이 좋지 않다 look bad / be out of sorts∥~이 변하다 change color [countenance]∥~을 살피다 read (a person's) face / study the pleasure of (a person)∥~가 좋은 ~을 보이다 look uneasy [anxious]∥그녀는 내게 감사하고 있다는 ~을 전혀 보이지 않았다 She showed no sign whatsoever of being grateful to me.∥기뻐하는 ~이 그녀의 얼굴에 나타났다 A look of pleasure came to her face.∥그의 ~은 별로 변하지 않았다 His face did not show any emotion.∥~으로 보아 그가 성난 것을 알았다 I read anger in his countenance.∥비가 올 ~이 없다 There is no sign of the rain.∥실망의 ~이 그의 얼굴을 스치고 지나갔다 A look

기생 of disappointment passed over his face. // 그는 그러한 ~을 조금도 보이지 않았다 There was nothing in his look or manner to show that.

기생(妓生) a gisaeng. ¶~집 a gisaeng house // ~을 불러 놀다 have a gisaeng spree [party].

기생(寄生) parasitism. ¶공(共)~ 〔생〕 symparasitism // ~의 parasitic(al). **기생하다** be parasitic (on); be a parasite (on / to); live (upon / in); be a hanger-on. ¶조충은 동물에 기생한다 Tapeworms are parasites on animals.

● **기생 동물** a parasitic animal. **기생물 / 기생체** a parasite. **기생 미생물** a microparasite. **기생 식물** a parasitic plant. **기생충** a parasite; a parasitic insect[worm].

기선(汽船) a steamship; a steamboat; a steamer; a liner. ¶정기 ~ a regular liner / a steam packet // ~를 타다 take a steamer / ~으로 가다 go by steamer / go (to Honolulu) on[in] a steamer.

기선(機先) forestalling; getting ahead of (a person); taking the initiative. ¶~을 꺾다 damp (a person's) ardor // 적의 ~을 제압하다 anticipate the enemy's movements / forestall the enemy.

기설(既設) being already constructed. ¶~의 established / existing // ~ 설비를 이용하다 utilize the existing facilities.

기성(棋聖·碁聖) a great master of go[chess]; an accomplished go[chess] player.

기성(旣成) ¶~ 완료 completed / accomplished / established / (현존의) existing / (만들어져 있는) manufactured / ready-made // ~의 학설 an accepted theory / ~의 체제[권력 조직]에 반대하는 학생들 students opposing the establishment.

● **기성 개념** a preconceived idea. **기성관념** ready-made ideas. ¶~을 버리다 get rid of one's stereotypes. **기성도덕** the established moral principles. **기성복** ready-made[ready-to-wear] clothes; store clothes; (미) hand-me-downs; slops(싸구려). **기성세대** the older generation. **기성 작가** a writer of established fame; an established[a well-known] writer [author]; a writer of standing. **기성 정당** the existing political parties; established parties. **기성품** manufactured goods; ready-made articles.

기성(奇聲) a peculiar[queer / weird] voice. ¶~을 지르다 raise a queer voice / squeak.

기세(氣勢) vigor; ardor; 〔형세〕 a position; a situation. ¶맹렬한 ~로 (구어) like a hundred[thousand / ton] of bricks / like forty / with an irresistible [overwhelming] force // ~가 오르다 [떨어지다] be in high[in low / out of] spirits // ~를 꺾다 dispirit / discourage / throw a wet blanket on // ~를 올리다 arouse one's enthusiasm / show one's nerve / drum up opposition (to) // 정부에 대한 공격의 ~가 더 한층 격렬해졌다 The attacks on government were growing more and more severe. // 그는 무서운 ~로 내게 대들었다 He turned on me with an angry look. // 그의 질책으로 우리의 ~가 꺾였다 His reproof discouraged us [dampened our spirits]. // 그가 합류함으로써 우리 팀 전체의 ~가 올라갔다 Since he joined us, team morale has risen. / Since he joined the team, our spirits have risen. // 폭풍의 ~는 조금도 꺾이지 않았다 The storm has not let up a bit. // ~다 ~다 That's the spirit!

기소(起訴) 〔형사상의〕 prosecution; indictment; legal proceedings. ¶불~ 처분 a disposition not to institute a public action. **기소하다** prosecute[indict] (a person for a crime); charge (a person with a crime); bring in an indictment (against); (민사에서) institute an action; bring an action[a suit] (against); go to law (with); proceed (against). ¶살인죄로 ~ indict (a person) for murder // 법률 위반으로 ~ prosecute (a person) for the violation of the laws // 검찰국은 폭력단을 기소하지 않기로 결정했다 The public prosecutor decided not to press charges against the gang. → ¶적국을 위해 간첩 활동을 한 행위로 기소된 피고에게 사형을 선고하다 sentence the accused indicted for having conducted espionage activities for the enemy, to death // 그 사건은 기소되지 않았다 The case was dropped. // 그는 수회로 기소되었다 He was prosecuted [indicted / charged] for taking bribes.

● **기소 각하 / 기소 기각** dismissal of indictment. **기소 유예** 〔법〕 suspension of indictment; stay of prosecution. **기소장** an indictment; a written indictment; an information.

기수(奇數) an odd[uneven] number. ⇨홀수

기수(基數) 〔수〕 a simple [cardinal] number; a fundamental number.

기수(旗手) a standard-[color-]bearer; an ensign; a flagman. ¶연대 ~ a bearer of the regimental colors // 평화와 협력의 새로운 ~ a new standard-bearer for peace and cooperation (in the world) // 신문학(新文學)의 ~ the standard-bearer of a new literary movement.

기수(機首) the nose (of an airplane). ¶~를 내리다 nose down // ~를 서쪽으로 돌렸다 The plane took a westerly course. / The plane headed[turned to the] west. // 파일럿은 ~를 올렸다[내렸다] The pilot lifted[lowered] the nose of the plane.

기수(騎手) a rider; a horseman; (경마의) a jockey.

기수(既遂) consummation; completion. ¶~의 consummated.

● **기수범** a consummated crime.

기수법(記數法) 〔수〕 notation; numeration system. ¶십진 ~ decimal notation / the common scale of notation.

기숙(寄宿) lodging; boarding; board and lodging. **기숙하다** lodge[board / room] (at a person's house / with a person); take up one's lodgings (in). ¶그는 아저씨 집에 기숙하고 있다 He is boarding[lodging] at his uncle's[with his uncle].

● **기숙사** a boarding house; (미) a dormitory; (영) a hostel; (구어) a dorm; (영국 대학의) a hall of residence; a residence hall ((영)에서 dormitory는 침대가 많이 놓인 기숙사의 넓은 방). ¶~에 들어가다 board in the school // ~ 생활을 하다 live in a dormitory. **기숙생** a boarding[resident] student; a boarder.

기술(技術) art; technique; 〔기량〕 ability; skill; (과학·공업의) (a) technology; (미) (technical) know-how; (학과목) manual training. ¶공업 ~ (engineering) technology

기압

//생산 ~ manufacturing technic//**첨단[최신] ~** up-to-date technology//**~상의 technical**//~적으로 technically//**~상의 곤란[어려움]** a technical difficulty//**새로운 ~의 개발** development of new technology//**~을 배우다[가르치다]** learn[train a person in] a trade//익힌 ~이 있으면 너는 일자리를 쉽게 얻을 수 있을 것이다 You will find a job easily if you are trained in a skill.//그것은 ~상 곤란하다 That is technically difficult.//가르친다는 것은 하나의 ~이다 Teaching is an art.//이 공장은 프랑스에서 ~을 도입하여 건설되었다 This factory was built with the help of technological know-how from France.//그것은 전문적인 ~을 필요로 한다 It requires technical skill.//그 나라에는 아직 항공기 제작 ~이 발달되어 있지 않다 The technical side of aircraft manufacture is still backward in that country.//~이 입신의 경지에 이르렀다 His skill approached the level of the superhuman.

● **기술 개발** technical development. **기술 도입** the introduction of technology. **기술 원조** technical[technological] assistance [aids]. **기술 이전** the transfer of technical know-how. **기술 인력** (secure) skilled technical hands; (highly) skilled technical manpower. **기술자** a technician; a technical expert; [기사] an engineer. **기술 제휴** a technical tie-up; technical cooperation. ¶~를 하다 join in a technical tie-up / provide technical assistance//…과 ~를 하고 있다 be technically tied up with (another company)//우리 회사는 미국의 제약 회사와 ~를 했다 We secured the technical cooperation of[entered into a technical tie-up with] a pharmaceutical company in the U.S. **기술 집약 산업** a technology-intensive industry. **기술 축적** the accumulation of technology[industrial knowhow]. **기술 혁신** technical[technological] innovation[revolution].

기술 (記述) (a) description; an account; writing. ¶~적 과학 the descriptive science//~식 문제 an essay question. **기술하다** describe; give an account of; write up. ¶기술하기 어렵다 be beyond description//토론의 내용을 ~ take notes of what was said during the debate//그는 소년 시절의 추억을 영어로 기술했다 He wrote down his boyhood memories in English.

기슭 (강의) the bank(s); (호수·바다의) the shore; the coast; the border; (산의) the foot. ¶강~ the edge[brink] of a river//산~ the foot of a mountain//언덕의 ~에 자리 잡은 마을 a village nestling under a hill//강~을 위로 걸어 올라가다 walk up the riverbank//파도가 ~을 때리고 있다 Waves are beating [dashing] against the shore.//여기서는 온 산이 ~까지 잘 보인다 From here we can see the whole mountain right down to the base.

기습 (奇習) a strange custom[practice]. ¶인디언의 ~ a queer Indian practice.

기습 (奇襲) a surprise (attack); a sudden [sneak] attack. ¶~적인 시험 a surprise examination / a pop[snap] quiz[test]//~으로 요새를 탈취하다 take a fortress by surprise. **기습하다** raid; make a surprise attack (on); attempt a surprise; take unawares; take (a person) off his guard. ¶나무 뒤에서 ~ snipe at (a person) from behind a tree// 요새를 기습하여 함락시키다 take a fortress by surprise//우리는 적을 기습했다 We surprised the enemy.//경찰대는 폭력단을 기습하여 검거했다 The police arrested the gang in a surprise raid. ➔¶기습당하다 be taken by surprise / be attacked unawares//기습당하지 않도록 조심하라 Be careful not to be caught off guard.

● **기습 작전** shock action.

기승 (氣勝) an unyielding spirit; strong-mindedness; spiritedness. **기승하다** unyielding; unbending; strong-minded; spirited.

기승떨다 (氣勝−) do not give in; be obstinate. ⇨¶기승부리다

기승부리다 (氣勝−) do not give in; be obstinate; be stubborn; refuse to yield; rage; be rampant; grow more violent. ¶그 지방에는 아직도 콜레라가 기승부리고 있다 Cholera is still raging in that district.//금년에는 늦더위가 유달리 기승부린다 The heat of late summer is severer this year.

기승전결 (起承轉結) (한시(漢詩)의) the four steps in composition; the introduction, the development of the theme, conversion, and summing up. ¶~에 유의하여 문장을 구성하다 write a passage being careful to construct it with an introduction, adequate development and a conclusion.

기식 (寄食) parasitism; dependence; sponging on. **기식하다** board and lodge; live with; sponge[live] on (one's relative); be a parasite (on / to).

● **기식자** a dependent; a sponger; a hanger-on; a parasite.

기신호 (旗信號) flag-wagging; flag signal(l)ing.

기실 (其實) [실제의 사정] the truth; the reality; [실제로] really; in reality; to tell the truth; as a matter of fact. ¶그는 자기 자랑을 늘상 하지만 ~ 아무 일에도 성공한 적이 없다 He is always bragging about himself, but in reality[in actual fact] he has never succeeded in anything.

기아 (棄兒) an abandoned[a deserted] child (pl. children); (문어) a foundling.

기아 (飢餓·饑餓) hunger; starvation. ¶~로 고통을 받다 suffer from hunger//~ 직전에 있다 be on the brink of starvation / be faced with starvation//우리는 ~에 직면했다 Famine stared us in the face.//많은 사람이 ~에 처해 있다 Many peoples are starving.

● **기아 수출** hunger export.

기악 (器樂) [음] instrumental music.

● **기악곡** an instrumental piece. **기악 연주** an instrumental performance. **기악 편성법** instrumentation.

기안 (起案) drafting. **기안하다** draft; prepare [make out] a draft (of); draw up a plan. ¶법률을 ~ draft[draw up] a bill.

● **기안자** a drafter.

기암 (奇巖) strangely shaped rocks.

● **기암괴석** (−怪石) strange rocks and bizarre stones; oddly formed stones and weirdly shaped rocks.

기압 (氣壓) atmospheric[air / barometric] pressure. ¶고[저] ~ high[low] atmospheric pressure / barometric maximum[minimum] //절대 ~ absolute atmosphere//~ 관계로 owing to the atmospheric condition.

● **기압계** a barometer; a manometer; a baroscope; an air gauge. **기압골** a trough of low

기약

atmospheric pressure; a low pressure trough. **기압 배치** the distribution of atmospheric pressure.

기약(期約) promise; pledge; engagement; appointment. **기약하다** pledge; promise. ¶필승을 기약하고 resolved to win∥우리는 재회를 기약하고 헤어졌다 We parted, expecting to meet again. / We parted with a promise to meet again.

기약 분수(既約分數) [수] an irreducible [a simple] fraction.

기어 a gear; gears. ¶감속(減速) ~ a reduction gear∥후진 ~ reverse (gear)∥~를 넣다 put the car in gear∥~를 바꾸다 shift gear∥자동차의 ~를 톱[로]에 넣다 put a car in high [low] gear[(영) top[bottom] gear].

기어가다 go on all fours. ¶쐐기벌레가 가지를 타고 기어가고 있다 A caterpillar is crawling along the branch.∥우리는 네발로 기어갔다 We crawled along on all fours[on our hands and knees].∥고양이가 새를 보고 살금살금 기어갔다 The cat crept silently toward the birds.∥공사는 굼벵이가 기어가듯 진행되고 있다 The work is proceeding at a snail's pace.

기어들다 crawl [creep] in [into]; worm oneself into. ¶이불 속으로 ~ get [slip] into bed∥쌓아 올린 건초 밑으로 그가 기어들었다 He crawled [crept] under a pile of hay.

기어오르다 1 (벌레 등이) crawl [creep] up; (사람이) climb [shin] (up) (a tree); (미국 구어) shinny up; clamber (over / up); scramble (up); claw one's way up (a cliff). ¶가파른 경사면을 ~ clamber up the steeps slope / work one's way up the steep slope∥그는 밧줄을 사용하여 바위 산을 기어올랐다 With the aid of a rope he scrambled [climbed] up the rocky mountain.∥그는 덩굴을 붙잡고 벼랑의 꼭대기까지 기어올랐다 He hauled himself up by the vines to the top of the cliff.∥담쟁이가 벽을 기어올랐다 The ivy crept up the wall.∥뱀이 나무를 기어오르고 있다 The snake is slithering up a tree.
2 (버릇없이 굴다) presume on; take liberties (with); be overfamiliar (with). ¶친절히 대해 주면 기어오른다 have one's kindness taken advantage of∥가만 놔두면 기어오른다 presume upon (a person's) patience.

기어이(期於-) **1** [꼭] by all (manner of) means; by hook or by crook; without fail; at any cost [price / risk]. ¶나는 ~ 이기고야 말겠다 I intend to win no matter what.∥나는 ~ 가려고 말겠다 I will do it, or I am a Dutchman.∥그들은 만나면 ~ 싸우고야 만다 They never meet without quarrelling.∥이번에는 ~ 성공해 보이겠다 I give you my word what I shall make it a success this time. **2** [마침내] at last; in the end; finally; after all. ¶그는 그 일에 너무 몰두하다가 ~ 미치고 말았다 He took the matter too much to heart, until (at last) he went mad.

기억(記憶) memory; mind; memorization; remembrance; [추억] recollection. ¶어린 시절 이후로 만난 적도 없는 ~ 속의 어머니 the mother one has not seen since childhood∥확실[불확실]한 ~ an unfailing [a treacherous] memory∥~을 잘한다[못한다] have a good [poor] memory∥~에 남다 remain [be retained] in one's memory / be impressed on one's memory∥~을 되살리다 bring back one's memory∥~을 더듬다 trace back in memory / retrace [search] one's memory (to)∥아버님은 내 ~ 속에 살아 계신다 My father lives in my memory.∥그런 말을 한 ~이 없다 I don't remember having ever said anything like that.∥그는 노령 때문에 ~이 흐려졌다 Old age has dimmed [clouded] his memory. / His memory has faded because of old age.∥내 ~이 틀림없다면 그가 그녀의 남편이다 If I remember correctly [right / rightly], he is her husband.∥어릴 적 일은 어렴풋한 ~밖에 없다 I have only a dim [vague] memory [recollection] of my childhood.∥그 광경은 아직도 ~에 새롭다 The scene is fresh in my memory.∥결국 그 사건은 사람들의 ~에서 사라져 갔다 Eventually the event vanished [slipped] from memory. / Eventually the event was forgotten.∥그 문제에 대해서는 통 ~이 나지 않는다 My memory is perfectly blank on the subject. **기억하다** [기억하고 있다] remember; remain [live] in one's memory; (잊지 않도록) bear [keep] (something) in mind [remembrance / memory]; commit (something) to memory; memorize; [외다] learn [get] (something) by heart. ¶단단히 ~ fix [bear] (something) firmly [indelibly] in one's memory [mind]∥똑똑히 [어렴풋이] 기억하고 있다 have a clear [dim] recollection of / remember clearly [vaguely]∥내가 기억하기로는 그가 결혼한 적은 없다 As far as I can remember [To the best of my recollection], he has never married.∥이것만은 기억해 두십시오 Never forget this. / Be sure to keep this in mind.∥나는 아버지에 대해서 아무것도 기억하고 있지 않다 I don't remember my father at all. / I have no recollection of my father.∥자네 말은 기억해 두겠다 I will keep what you say in mind. / I shall never forget your words.∥그는 그 편지의 내용을 기억해 두었다 He committed the content of the letter to memory. / He memorized the content of the letter.

●**기억력** (one's power of) memory; the retentive faculty. ¶그는 ~이 좋다 [나쁘다] He has a good [bad / poor] memory. **기억 상실증** [의] amnesia. **기억 장치** [컴] a memory; a storage. ¶전자 ~ an electronic memory machine / a ticketer∥주~ a main storage unit / a main memory unit.

기엄기엄 crawling (along); creeping (up / down / about); on all fours; on hands and knees. ¶~ 가다 go [crawl] on all fours [on (one's) hands and knees]∥산꼭대기에 ~ 기어오르다 climb up to the top of a mountain on hands and knees.

기업(企業) an enterprise; a business. ¶공영 ~ a public corporation / a state-owned company / a government enterprise∥대(大) ~ a large business [corporation / company]∥독점 ~ a monopolistic enterprise∥민간 [개인] ~ a private enterprise∥부실 ~ (체) an insolvent [an improperly-run] enterprise∥영세 ~ a small business∥외국 자본 ~ a foreign capital firm∥중소 ~ smaller business / small and medium-sized enterprises∥~을 일으키다 set up a business / go into business∥~을 합리화하다 rationalize an enterprise / streamline a company.

●**기업가** an enterpriser; a man of enterprise; an enterprising man; an industrialist; a captain of industry. **기업 공개** a corporation's public offering[sale] of stocks [shares]; going public. **기업농** market farming. **기업 연합** a cartel; (공동 판매를 위한) a syndicate. **기업 진단** management consulting. **기업체** a business entity. ¶**복합**~ a conglomerate corporation[company]. **기업 합동** a trust; [법] a merger. **기업 합병** amalgamation; an industrial merger.

-기에 [때문에] as; because; since; on account of; owing to. ¶**덥**~ 나는 저고리를 벗었다 As it was warm, I took off my coat. // **책이 싸**~ 한 권 샀다 As the book was cheap, I bought a copy. // 경영자가 나가고 없~ 비서에게 말을 전하고 왔다 The manager was out, so I left a message with his secretary.

-기에 망정이지 fortunately ... otherwise; or (else); only owing to[because of]; if not so. ¶돈이 있었~ 창피당할 뻔했다 It was fortunate that I had some money with me, otherwise I would have to lose my face. // 열심히 공부했~ 그는 시험에 떨어질 뻔했다 He had worked hard, otherwise he would have failed in the examination.

기여 (寄與) contribution; service. **기여하다** contribute (to); render services (to); add (much) to; do much toward. ¶그는 한국의 경제 발전에 크게 기여했다 He contributed greatly to the economic development of Korea. // 그의 보고가 금후의 연구에 크게 기여할 것이다 His report will be a great contribution to future research. // 그는 평화를 위해 크게 기여했다 He made great contributions [rendered great services] to the cause of peace.

기연 (奇緣) a strange fate[chance]; a curious coincidence; an uncanny[a karmic] relationship[connection].

기염 (氣焰) [기세] high spirits; enthusiasm; [큰 소리] tall[big] talk; bombast. ¶~**을 올리다**[**토하다**] argue heatedly[enthusiastically] // 모교를 위하여 ~을 토하다 do a good job[put up a good show] for the sake of one's alma mater // 그는 학회에서 크게 ~을 토하고 있다 He is very active in the academic society. // 팀 멤버 중에서 오직 그만이 ~을 토했다 He alone of all the team members played very well[made a good showing].

기예 (技藝) [예술] arts; [수예] (handi)crafts; [예능] (artistic) accomplishments.
● **기예가** an artist.

기예하다 (氣銳-) spirited; energetic; active; impetuous.

기온 (氣溫) (atmospheric) temperature. ¶**평균**~ average temperature // ~의 변화 a change of temperature // ~의 급상승[급강하] a sudden rise[fall] in temperature // ~**이 오른다**[**내린다**] The temperature rises[falls]. // 금년 봄은 대체로 ~이 낮았다 Temperature were on the whole low this spring.
● **기온 조절** (-調節) air conditioning.

기와 a (roofing) tile; 《집합적》 tiling. ¶**평** (平) ~ a plain[flat] tile // 얹은 담 a tile-capped wall // ~**를 이다** lay tiles on a roof / roof (a house) with tiles / tile a roof // 집의 지붕을 ~로 덮다 roof a house with tiles / tile the roof of a house.
● **기와장이** a tiler; a tile layer. **기와지붕** a tiled roof. **기와집** a *giwajip*; a tile-roofed house. **기왓장** a tile.

기왕 (既往) [지금보다 이전] the past; bygones; the bygone days; [이미] already; since. ¶~**의** past / bygone // ~**이면** if it is done / if it has already happened / (선택) if I must take[choose] // ~**이면 큰 쪽을 갖겠다** I will take the larger one, if I must take either.

기왕지사 (既往之事) bygones. ¶~는 깨끗이 잊어버리자 Let bygones be bygones. // ~는 묻지 않는다 I do not call on you to account for what has been done.

기용 (起用) appointment; employment. **기용하다** [발탁하다] promote; [임명하다] appoint. ¶국방부 장관에는 홍길동 씨를 기용하기로 정해졌다 It was decided to appoint Mr. Hong Gildong[that Mr. Hong Gildong be appointed] to the post of the Ministry of National Defense. ➔ 그는 과장으로 기용되었다 He was promoted to chief of his section. // 그는 우리 대학 팀의 투수로 기용되었다 He was chosen to be the pitcher for our college team.

기우 (杞憂) unfounded[groundless / imaginary] fears[apprehensions]; baseless anxiety. ¶~로 끝났으면 좋으련만 I hope my fears will prove groundless. // 그 일에 대해서 그녀는 ~를 갖고 있었다 She had groundless fears[《문어》 apprehensions] about the matter. / She worried needlessly about the matter.

기우 (祈雨) praying for rain. **기우하다** pray for rain.
● **기우제** (-祭) a ritual (praying) for rain; a shamanist service to pray for rain.

기우듬하다 somewhat slanting[aslant / oblique]; slant; inclined a little; (서술적) be on the tilt. ¶**오른쪽으로** ~ have a tilt to the right // (집이) 한쪽으로 ~ be leaning to one side / be out of the perpendicular // 피사의 탑은 한쪽으로 ~ The tower of Pisa is leaning to one side. **기우듬히** in a somewhat slanted way; slightly askew; at a bit of an angle; (so that it is) a bit out of line; at a tilt; on a slant.

기우뚱거리다 1 [흔들리다] rock; totter; wobble; sway[move] from side to side. ¶기우뚱거리는 의자 a shaky[rocky / rickety] chair // 기우뚱거리며 일어서다 reel[stagger] to one's feet // 배가 기우뚱거린다 A boat is rolling[rocking]. / 차가 몹시 기우뚱거렸다 The car received a tremendous jolting. 2 [흔들다] move (a thing) from side to side; rock; sway; tilt[incline] (one's head). ¶몸을 ~ sway one's body.

기우뚱기우뚱 swayingly; rolling; shakily; totteringly. **기우뚱기우뚱하다** rock; sway. ⇨ ＝기우뚱거리다

기운 1 [힘] (physical) strength; force; power; might. ¶~**이 센** strong / powerful / energetic // ~**이 없는** weak / feeble / of little strength // ~**을 다해서** with all one's might [strength] / with might and main // ~**만으로** by sheer strength alone // ~**이 나다** gain in strength // ~**을 내다** put forth[out] one's strength // ~**이 빠지다** one's strength ebbs / (사람이) be exhausted[spent up] // ~**을 회복하다** regain strength / (환자가) recover one's strength // 나는 스테이크를 먹고 나서 ~이 났다 I felt more energetic[livelier] after

기운

(eating) a steak. // 그는 ~이 빠진 기색도 없이 다음 기획에 착수했다 Nothing daunted [Not at all daunted], he started on his next enterprise.
2 [원기·생기] vigo(u)r; energy; life; spirits; vitality; get-up-and-go; (속어) pep; gumption; go. ¶~을 **잃다** lose heart / be discouraged // [노초가 되다] be exhausted // ~**이 나다** cheer up / become heightened in spirits / get encouraged // ~**을 내다** take courage [heart] / pluck [muster] up courage / buck up // ~**이 없다** be low spirits / be off colo(u)r / be disheartened // ~**이 왕성하다** be in high spirits // ~**이 넘치다** brim over with good spirits / be full of vigor [pep] // ~**을 돋우다** buck a person up / put fight into a person // ~**을 회복하다** [차리다] recover [restore] one's spirits / be refreshed // 경기에 임하여 ~을 차리다 (미) get [fire] oneself up for a match / (구어) psyche oneself up for a match // ~**을 내라** Pull yourself together! / Don't let yourself get depressed [discouraged]. / Cheer up! / (미국 구어) Pep up! / (스포츠에서) Show your nerve! / (일 등에서) Make it snappy! // 너무 곤해서 말할 ~도 없었다 I was too tired to speak. // 자넨 ~이 아주 다 빠진 모양이군 You look down in the mouth.
3 [독한 기운 등] vapo(u)r; fume; gas; breath; [기미] an air (of); a look (of); an indication; a sign; a symptom; a mark; a trace; (약·술 등의) efficacy. ¶**불** ~ a spark [flash] of fire // **약** ~ the virtue(s) of a medicine // 독한 ~ poisonous character / virulence // **술** ~이 있다 be under the influence of liquor / have the odor of liquor on one's breath / be (a little) tipsy // 감기 ~이 있다 have a slight [a touch of] cold // 붉은 ~이 돌다 be tinged with red.
4 (천지만물의) anima; the universal spirit thought to underlie living things and to be manifest in negative ["dark"] and positive ["bright"] aspects.

기운 (氣運) a tendency; a trend; the tide; a movement. ¶한국 문단에 있어서의 새로운 ~ the new trend in the Korean literary world // …의 ~이 고조되다 show a strong tendency to (do) // 사람들 사이에 전쟁을 기피하려는 ~이 대두되었다 (특정한 전쟁에 대하여) A desire to stay out of the war grew among the people. / (일반적으로 전쟁 그 자체에 대하여) Antiwar feeling built up among the people.

기운 (機運) **1** [기회] an opportunity; the time. ¶양사 합병의 ~이 무르익었다 The time is ripe for the merger of the two companies. **2** [운] fortune; luck.

기운차다 full of vitality [vigor]; high-spirited; cheerful; (노인이) hale and hearty. ¶기운차게 in high spirits / cheerfully // 더 기운차게 노래해라 Sing with more life.

기울다 1 [한쪽으로 쏠리다] tilt; (특히 서 있는 것이) lean; (배 등이) list. ¶기운 지붕 a slanted [sloping] roof // 그 로켓의 방향이 서쪽으로 약간 기울었다 The direction of the rocket leaned slightly westward. // 나침반이 동쪽으로 5도 기울었다 The compass has moved east [edged eastward] by 5 degrees. // 비행기가 한쪽으로 기울면서 떨어졌다 The plane tilted to one side and crashed. // 태풍으로 배가 좌[우]로 기울었다 The storm caused the ship to list to port [starboard]. // 그의 몸이 별안간에 오른쪽으로 기울었다 His body suddenly lurched to the right. // 그 땅은 완만하게 기울어 있었다 The land sloped gently. // 제도판이 기울어 있었다 The drawing board was slanted. (incline, slope, slant는 주로 기운 상태에 대해 쓰임)
2 [해 저물다] decline (toward); go down; sink; set. ¶해가 기울고 있다 The sun is sinking [going down]. // 해가 기울자 추워지기 시작했다 When the sun went down, it became chilly.
3 [쇠퇴하다] decline; fall (away); wane; be reduced; ebb. ¶그의 운이 기울기 시작했다 His fortunes are on the wane [on the decline].
4 [어떤 경향을 띠다] be inclined (to); lean (to / toward(s)). ¶그들은 좌경으로 기울어 있다 They lean [are inclined] toward the left. // 그는 찬성 쪽으로 기울고 있다 He is in favor of it.

기울어뜨리다 tip; tilt; lean; incline; list; slant. ¶병을 ~ tip a bottle.

기울어지다 incline; slant. ¶기울어진 널빤지 an inclined [a slanting] board // 그들은 쾌락주의에 기울어지고 있다 They lean [are inclined] toward(s) hedonism. // 이 나무는 10도쯤 기울어졌다 This tree leans about ten degrees. // 달력이 기울어져 있다 The calendar is crooked [aslant]. // 이 건물은 심하게 기울어져 있다 This building leans badly. // 꽃병이 기울어져 넘어졌다 The vase tipped over. // 낡은 헛간이 한쪽으로 기울어져 있었다 The old shed leaned [tilted] to one side.

기울이다 1 [한쪽으로 쏠리게 하다] tilt; (서 있는 물건을) lean; incline. ¶고개를 ~ lean one's head to one side / tilt one's head // 책상을 ~ tilt a desk // 그는 몸을 앞으로 45도 기울였다 He bent [leaned / leant] his body forward 45 degrees. // 우리는 수없이 많은 잔을 기울였다 We emptied a great many cups of liquor.
2 [집중하다] concentrate (one's energy, powers, etc.); devote oneself (to); [향하게 하다] direct one's attention (to); bend (one's mind) to. ¶귀를 ~ strain one's ears / listen clearly [carefully] // 그는 자기 일에 전력을 기울였다 He devoted [bend] himself to his work. / He concentrated on his work. // 자, 귀를 기울이고 들으세요 Now listen to me carefully. // 그것에는 특별한 주의를 기울여야 한다 You should pay special attention to that.

기웃거리다 [엿보다] peep (through / into); snoop (around); get a peep (at); look in on (a person / a thing); (고개를) crane (one's neck); incline [tilt] (one's head). ¶기웃거리는 사람 a snooper / a peeping Tom / a voyeur // 기웃거리고 다니다 pry about // 이 방 저 방 ~ peek [snoop] around this room and that // 모두 신부를 보려고 고개를 기웃거리고 있다 Everybody is craning to see the bride.

기웃기웃 peeping; snooping. **기웃기웃하다** peep (through / into); crane (one's neck). ⇨**기웃거리다**

기웃하다 1 somewhat slanting. ⇨**기우듬하다**
2 [조금 기울이다] incline [tilt / tip / slant] (something) a little; put (a thing) a bit askew; place (a thing) a little out of line [off center]. ¶몸을 오른쪽으로 ~ lean one's body to the right. **기웃이** peeping; snooping. ¶빈 틈으로 ~ 들여다보다 peep through a

기원(祈願) prayer; supplication; petition. ¶필승의 ~ a prayer for victory. **기원하다** pray; supplicate; petition; wish. ¶영원한 평화를 ~ pray for everlasting peace // 하느님에게 열심히 ~ pray fervently to the god // 입시 합격을 ~ pray to pass the entrance examination // 그를 살려 달라고 기원했다 I prayed that he might be saved.

기원(紀元) an era; an epoch. ¶단군~ 4310년 the 4310th year after the accession of Dangun // 서력~ 1990년 A.D. 1990 / 1990 A.D. / the year 1990 by the Western calendar // (비)碑 등에 쓸 때) in the one thousand nine hundred and ninety ninth year of our Lord // ~전 50년 50 B.C. / fifty years before (the birth of) Christ // 신~을 그은 발견 a discovery that marked the beginning of a new era / an epoch-making discovery.

기원(起源·起原) the origin(s); the beginning(s); the rise; the genesis. ¶생명의 ~ the beginnings [origin] of life // 종의 ~ The Origin of Species(저서명) // ~을 찾다 trace (a thing) to its origin [source] // ~...으로 하다 originate in ... / (문어) derive from ... / have its origin(s) in ... / [어떤 연대에서부터 시작되다] date back to ... / ~을 더듬어 찾다 trace a thing back to its origins [roots] // 이 행사의 ~은 그리스이다 This event originated in Greece. // 이 풍습의 ~은 15세기로 거슬러 올라간다 This custom dates back to the fifteenth century. **기원하다** originate (in); have (its) origin [genesis / rise] (in); be stemmed from; derive (its) origin (from).

기원(棋院) a baduk(go) club(house).

기율(紀律) order; discipline; [규율] rule. ¶~을 지키다 [어기다] observe [break] the rules.

기음(氣音) [언] aspirated sounds; an aspirate. ⇨거센소리

기이하다(奇異-) strange; queer; odd; singular; curious; eccentric; extraordinary. ¶기이한 광경 a curious sight // 기이한 풍설 a strange rumor // 기이한 행동 an unaccountable action / eccentric conduct // 남에게 기이한 느낌을 주다 It strikes (a person) as strange (that ...). // 사실은 소설보다 ~ Truth is stranger than fiction. **기이히** strangely; oddly; curiously.

기인(奇人) an eccentric; (구어) a crank; (미국 구어) an oddball; (구어) an odd fish; a queer fellow; an oddity; (속어) nut.

기인(起因) the cause; the root. **기인하다** be caused by; originate in; come [arise / spring] from; result from; be due [owing] to. ¶불경기에 기인하는 범죄 a crime that is caused by [has its roots in] bad economic conditions // 이 비극은 질투에 기인하였다 Jealousy was the cause of this tragedy. / This tragedy arose from jealousy. // 그것은 그의 오해에 기인한다 That comes [arises] from a misunderstanding on his part. / That is the result of a misunderstanding on his part. // 그것은 단순히 뜬소문에 기인한 것이었다 It originated in a mere rumor. // 그의 실패는 그의 소심함에 기인하는 것으로 우리는 생각한다 We attribute his failure to his timidity. / We think his failure was caused by [due to] his timidity. // 이 병은 과로에 기인한다 This disease is caused by overwork.

기일(忌日) the anniversary of (a person's) death; the deathday. ¶어머니의 3회 ~ the third anniversary of one's mother's death.

기일(期日) a (fixed) date; an appointed day; [기한] a time limit; a deadline; a due date. ¶납일 ~ (제품의) the delivery date / (세금 등의) the deadline for payment // ~ 안에 within the time limit / (문어) by the appointed day // ~을 정하다 fix the date / set a time limit // ~을 단축 [연장]하다 shorten [extend] the date [term] // ~까지 지불하다 pay (the bill) when due // ~을 앞당기다 advance [move up] the date // ~이 되다 (오다) mature [fall due / expire] // ~을 하루 연기하다 extend the date one day // 서류 제출 ~을 지키다 comply with the deadline for submitting papers // ~까지 일을 마쳐야만 한다 I must finish the work by the deadline [fixed date]. / I must finish the work on time.

기입(記入) entry; filling up(용지에); recording. ¶난외의 ~ marginal notes // ~필 Entered. **기입하다** make an entry; enter; fill up; (미) register; write in. ¶인명록에 이름을 ~ enter a name in a directory // 필요 사항을 서류에 ~ fill out [(영) in] a form // 신청서에 이름을 ~ write [fill in] one's name on an application form // 호텔에서 숙박자 명부에 이름을 ~ register at a hotel // 등록부에 주소와 성명을 기입해 주십시오 Please, write your name and address in the registration book. ➔¶여백에 많은 것이 기입되어 있다 There are many notes written in the margins.

● **기입 누락** an omission. **기입장** an entry book.

기자(記者) 〔탐방 기자〕 a reporter; 〔신문 기자〕 a newswriter; a newspaperman; 〔통신원〕 a correspondent; 〔저널리스트〕 a journalist. ¶가십 ~ a gossip writer / (속어) a keyhole reporter // 수습 [올챙이] ~ a junior reporter / (미국 속어) a cub reporter // 여~ a woman reporter / a newswoman / (속어) a newshen // 종군 ~ a war correspondent // 취재 ~ a (news) reporter / a legman (pl. -men) / a legger // 탐방 ~ a (newspaper) reporter / an interviewer // 타일지의 해외 통신 ~ a foreign correspondent for The Times // ~를 하고 있다 be (engaged) on the staff of a newspaper / hold a reporter's job on a (local) paper // 그는 주간지 ~로 일하고 있다 He is on the staff of [a reporter for] a weekly magazine.

● **기자단** a press corps. **기자석** (흥행장의) press box; (의회의) a press [reporters] gallery; (경기장의) a press stand. **기자증** a press card. **기자 클럽** a press club; a journalist club. **기자 회견** a press interview; a news [press] conference(기자단과의). ¶~을 하다 meet the press.

기장¹ 〔식〕 (chinese) millet.

기장² 〔옷의 길이〕 the length of a suit; the dress length. ¶이 옷의 ~은 너무 짧다 This dress is too short for me. // 나는 소매의 ~을 줄였다 I shortened the sleeves.

기장(記章·紀章) a commemoration medal. ¶종군 ~ a war [service] medal // 옷깃에 학교의 ~을 달다 wear a school badge on one's collar.

기장(記帳) register; entry. ¶복식 ~ double entry // 판매의 ~을 마치다 finish the sales accounts. **기장하다** register; enter [post up]

기장

accounts; make an entry; book. ¶그날의 지출을 ~ enter the day's expenditures (in the account book).

기장(機長) a (plane) captain; a crew chief.

기재(奇才) [뛰어난 재능] exceptional talent; [뛰어난 재주를 지닌 사람] a genius. ¶화단의 ~ a genius in the world of art.

기재(記載) (장부의) entry; (신문의) publication. ¶허위 ~ a false entry. **기재하다** state; mention; record; (신문·잡지에) print; report; carry; (장부에) enter. ¶별항에 기재한 바와 같이 as stated[reported] else. ➔¶위에 기재된 바와 같이 as stated[mentioned] above // 그의 이름은 선거인 명부에 기재되었다 His name was entered[registered] in the poll book. // 그 사항은 장부에 기재되었다 They made an entry of the item in the notebook.

● **기재 사항** the items mentioned.

기재(器材) [기구의 재료] materials for making tools; [기구와 재료] tools and materials. ¶실험용 ~ apparatus and materials for an experiment // 통신 ~ signal equipment.

기재(機材) 1 [기계를 만들기 위한 재료] materials needed for the manufacture of machinery. 2 [생산에 필요한 기계와 재료] machinery and materials (needed to manufacture a product).

기저(基底) a base; a basis; a foundation. ¶~의 basal // 이것이 사회 보장 제도의 ~를 이루고 있다 This forms the foundation[base] of the social security system.

기저귀 (미) a diaper; (영) a napkin; (영국 구어) a nappy. ¶종이 ~ a paper diaper[nappy] // ~를 채우다 diaper (a baby) / put a diaper on (a baby) // ~를 갈다 change the diaper (of an infant) // 이 아이는 아직도 ~를 차고 있다 The child is still in diapers[nappies].

● **기저귀 커버** a diaper cover.

기적(汽笛) a (steam) whistle; a siren. ¶~을 울리다 blow[sound / give] a whistle / whistle // ~ 소리가 울린다 A whistle is sounded. / A whistle blows. // 기차는 ~을 울리며 떠났다 A train pulled out with a whistle. // 발차를 알리는 열차의 ~ 소리가 들렸다 I could hear the whistle signaling the train to start.

기적(奇蹟) a miracle; a marvel; a wonder; a mystery. ¶~을 행하다 work[accomplish / perform] miracles / work wonders // ~이 일어났다 A miracle was wrought. / A miracle occurred[came up] // 그가 회복된 것은 ~이다 His recovery was a miracle. // 그의 성공은 참으로 ~이다 That he has succeeded is a complete miracle.

기적적(奇蹟的) miraculous. ¶~으로 miraculously / (escape death) by[to] a miracle // 우리는 ~으로 살았다 God saved us. // 나는 ~으로 구조되었다 I was saved by a miracle. / I was saved miraculously.

기전(起電) [전] electric generation; generation of electricity.

● **기전기** an electric motor; an electromotor. **기전력** electromotive force(약어 E.M.F., e.m.f.).

기절(氣絶) fainting; a swoon; a fainting fit [spell]. **기절하다** faint (away); lose consciousness[one's senses]. ¶기절할 듯이 놀라다 be frightened out of one's senses[wits] // 기절하여 쓰러지다 fall senseless[unconscious] / fall [drop] in a faint // 그는 맞아서 기절했다 He was knocked unconscious. / He was knocked out. // 그렇게 많은 피의 광경을 보고 그녀는 기절했다 At the sight of so much blood she fell into a swoon. ➔ **기절시키다** deprive (a person) of his senses / make (a person) insensible / stun(때리어) // 목 조르기로 상대를 기절시키다 cause one's opponent to pass out[make one's opponent faint] in a strangle hold.

기절초풍하다(氣絶-風-) ¶그는 소식을 듣고 기절초풍했다 He was frightened (to death) at the news. // 우리는 그 광경을 보고 기절초풍했다 We were dumbfounded at the sight. // 그것은 기절초풍할 계획이었다 It was a mind-boggling [stupendous] project.

기점(起點) the starting point; the origin; (도로의) the top; the head; (배의) the home port; (철도의) the terminus (pl. -ni, ~es). ¶~을 ~으로 하다 start (from) // 이 건물을 ~으로 하여 거리를 측정하다 measure the distance with this building as its starting point.

기정(旣定) ¶~의 established / fixed / prearranged / predetermined // ~ 방침에 따라 according to a prearranged[fixed] plan.

● **기정사실** an established [accomplished] fact; a settled matter.

기제(忌祭) a memorial service held on an anniversary of (a person's) death.

기조(基調) 1 [기본적인 흐름] the basic tone; a basic theme. ¶경제 ~ the basic economic condition // 인상주의가 이 음악의 ~를 이루고 있다 Impressionism forms the basis of this music. / Impressionism is the underlying theme upon which this music is based. 2 [음] the keynote.

● **기조연설** a keynote address. **기조연설자** a keynoter.

기존(旣存) ¶~의 existing / established // ~의 시설 the existing facilities // ~의 사회 조직 the existing social structure.

기종(機種) (비행기의) kinds[types] of airplanes[(영) aeroplanes]; (기계의) kinds [types] of machines. ¶제조를 중지한 ~ a model which is no longer being made [produced] // ~ 신~을 발매하다 release a new model of a machine.

기주(寄主) the host. ⇨ "숙주(宿主)

기죽다(氣-) 그렇게 높은 연단 위에서 연설을 하려니까 기죽어 말도 잘 나오지 않는다 It makes me feel self-conscious to speak from such a high platform.

기준(基準) [표준] a standard; (판단·결정 등의) a criterion (pl. -ria, ~s); [기초] a basis. ¶근로 ~법 the Labor Standards Act // 도덕의 ~ moral standards / an ethical standard // 새 ~을 정하다 set a new standard (for) // ~에 맞추다 standardize // …을 ~으로 해서 정하다 set[fix] (wages / price) on the basis of … // 선약을 판단할 ~이 없다 There is no yardstick for judging right and wrong. // 네 신념의 ~은 무엇이지 What is the basis of your beliefs? // 승진 결정의 ~이 무엇이오 What criteria do you use in deciding whether a person should be promoted?

● **기준 가격** a standard price. **기준량** a norm; standard amount. **기준면** a datum plane[level]; a base level. **기준선** a datum

[base] line. **기준 시세** (외국환의) the central rate. **기준 연도** the basic period [year].

기중(忌中) the period of mourning. ⇨상중

기중(其中) [그 가운데] among the rest [others / other things]. ¶~ 가장 나은 소년 the best boy among them.

기중기(起重機) a crane; a derrick; a hoist; a jack. ¶**고정식** ~ a stationary crane // **삼각** ~ a gin // **수동식** ~ a hand operated crane // **운반식** ~ a portable crane // **이동식** ~ a travelling crane // ~**로 들어 올리다** crane / lift (a thing) with a crane.

기증(寄贈) presentation; contribution; donation. **기증하다** present; contribute; donate.
● **기증본** a complimentary [presentation / free] copy; a gift book. **기증자** a contributor; a donor; a giver; a donator. ¶**혈액** ~ a blood donor. **기증품** a gift; a donation; a present.

기지(既知) ¶~**의** (already) known / familiar / well-known / established // ~**의 사실** a well-known fact / an established fact.
● **기지 사항** a datum (pl. data).

기지(機智) wit; quick wits; a flash of wit; ready wits; resources. ¶~ **있는** witty / tactful / resourceful / smart // ~**에 넘치는 말솜씨** a witty way of talking // ~**의 번득임** a flash of wit // ~**가 풍부하다** be witty / be resourceful / be full of resources // ~**와 유머를 겸비하다** be possessed of both wit and humor.

기지(基地) [군] a base; [터전] a site; a home(탐험대의). ¶**공군** ~ an air(-force) base // **군사** ~ a military base // **미사일** ~ a missile base // **작전** ~ a base of operations / an operating base // **전진** ~ an advance base // **전초** ~ a garrison base // **중계** ~ a relay base // **해군** ~ a naval base // **남극의 관측** ~ an antarctic observation base // **항공기 야간 훈련** ~ a base for the nighttime training of pilots // **무사히** ~**로 돌아오다** return safely to the base // **인도네시아가 일식 관측** ~**로 되었다** They based their observation of the solar eclipse in Indonesia.
● **기지국** a base station. **기지촌** a military campsidetown.

기지개 straightening one's back; stretching oneself. ¶~**를 켜다** stretch (oneself) / stretch one's body with raised hands // ~**를 켜며 하품하다** yawn with a stretch // **잘 자고 일어나서** ~**를 한 번 켜다** stretch oneself after a sound sleeping.

기직 a rough mat; a straw-and-rush mat.

기진(氣盡) exhaustion; (overwhelming) fatigue. **기진하다** be exhausted; be tired out; be worn out.

기진맥진하다(氣盡脈盡-) be worn [tired] out; be wearied [tired] to death; be utterly [totally] exhausted. ¶**나는 기진맥진하였다** I am completely exhausted [(구어) beat / drained of energy]. // **긴 행군으로 군대는 기진맥진했다** The long march has quite exhausted the troops.

기질(氣質) (a) disposition; (a) temper; (a) temperament(▶ disposition은 타인과의 관계 등에 있어 나타나는 천성적인 기질, temper는 자기 억제 등과 관계가 있는 기분·성향, temperament는 정서와 관련된 기질); (a) nature; a cast [frame] of mind; make-up. ¶~**이 대쪽 같은 사람** a person with an open disposition // **온순한** ~ a mild disposition // **발끈하는 쉬운** ~ a hot temper // **예술가적** ~**의 사나이** a man with an artistic temperament // **학자** ~**인 사람** a man'of a scholarly turn of mind // **그의** ~ **속에는 목적을 향해 돌진하는 경향이 있다** It is his nature to rush headlong towards a goal. // **나는 저런** ~**의 사람과는 뜻이 맞지 않는다** I find it difficult to get along with that type of man. // **네가 타고난** ~**이니 어쩔 수 없다** You cannot help your nature.

기질(基質) [생] a stroma (pl. ~ta); [화] a substrate.

기차(汽車) 1 [증기 기관차] a steam locomotive. 2 a train; a railroad. ⇨**열차** ¶**서울발** [행]**의** ~ a train from [for] Seoul // **9시**[**9시 20분**] ~ the nine o'clock [nine-twenty] train // ~**로 가다** go by train / (미) go on a train ride // ~**를 타다** ride in a train / take (a) train / (미) board a train // ~**에서 내리다** get off a train // ~ **시간에 대다**[**놓치다**] be in time[be too late] for a train / catch [miss] a train // ~**가 10분 늦었다** The train is ten minutes behind schedule. // ~**는 제시간에 도착했다**[**떠났다**] The train arrived [departed] on schedule [time]. // **나는 황급히** ~**에 올랐다** I quickly got on [(영) in] the train.
● **기차 여행** railroad traveling; (미) a train journey [trip]. **기차표** (a railroad) ticket. ¶**왕복** ~ a return ticket / a round-trip ticket // **편도** ~ a single ticket / (미) a one-way ticket // ~**를 끊다** buy a ticket / [**개찰하다**] punch [clip] a ticket. **기찻길** (미) a railroad track; (영) a railway (line).

기차다(氣-) 〈속〉 breathtaking; wonderful. ⇨**기막히다**2 // **기차게** awfully / terribly / extremely / wonderfully / (구어) so // **기찬 솜씨** remarkable [exceptional] ability / great skill // **기찬 미인** a stunning beauty // **기차게 맛있다** be exceedingly palatable / be so delicious / be very palatable [tasty].

기착(寄着) a stopover; (a) stop-off. **기착하다** stop over [off]; make a (brief) stop.

기채(起債) an issue of bonds; a bond issue; flotation[(영) floatation] of a loan. **기채하다** float [raise] a loan; issue bonds.

기척 [기색] a sign; [기미] a touch; an indication; traces; a hint. ¶**인**~**이 있다** There is a sign of somebody present. // **아무도 다녀간** ~**이 없다** There is no sign of anyone having been here. // **그러한** ~**은 전혀 없다** There are no such indications. / No such indications are to be sensed [observed].

기체(氣體) [가스] (a) gas; [증기] (a) vapor [(영) (a) vapour]. ¶~**의** gaseous / aerial / pneumatic / gasiform.
● **기체 연료** gaseous fuel. **기체화** vaporization; gasification; aerification.

기체(機體) a body; a machine; [비행기 동체] a fuselage; an airframe. ¶~**가 박살 났다** The plane broke up (in the crash). // ~**에 고장이 났다** Something went wrong with the machine. // **그 비행기는** ~**의 파손이 막심했다** The airplane was badly damaged.

기초(起草) drafting. ¶~ **중이다** It is being drafted. **기초하다** draft (a bill); draw up (a constitution); make a draft (of). ¶**헌법**[**법안**]**을** ~ draw up [draft] a constitution [bill] // **조약을** ~ make out the draft of the treaty.
● **기초 위원**(**회**) (a meeting of the) drafting committee. **기초자** a drafter; a draftsman.

기초

기초(基礎) **1** [건축물의 토대] the foundation. ¶건물의 ~를 쌓다 lay the foundation [groundwork] of a building // 이 건물의 ~는 튼튼하다 This building has a solid foundation.
2 [밑바탕이 되는 것] a basis (*pl*. bases); a foundation; the groundwork. ¶문법의 ~ 지식 elementary knowledge of grammar // ~ 없는 groundless / baseless // …에 ~를 두다 be based[founded / established] of / base [establish] (a thing) on // ~를 만들다 lay the foundation(s) (for / of) // 나는 영어를 기초부터 다시 공부할 생각이다 I am going to begin studying English again from the beginning. // 그는 수학의 ~가 착실히 되어 있다 He has mastered the fundamentals of mathematics. // 질문표를 ~로 하여 우리는 새로운 계획을 세웠다 We developed our new plan on the basis of the questionnaire. // 그 이론은 실험의 결과를 ~로 하고 있다 The theory is based on the results of experiments. // 그는 음악가로서의 ~를 유럽 유학 중에 쌓았다 He laid the groundwork [foundation] for his career as a musician during his stay in Europe. // 이들 작품의 ~를 이루고 있는 것은 작가의 인간애이다 What underlies these works is the author's love of humanity. // 그의 업적이 후세 과학자들의 거점이 되는 ~를 만들었다 His work laid the groundwork [foundations] for later scientists to build on. // 그는 현대 언어학의 ~를 닦았다 They laid[established] the foundation for modern linguistics. // 그의 논문은 다년간의 공들인 실험에 ~를 두고 작성된 것이다 His thesis is based on years of laboratory tests.
● **기초 공사** foundation work; ground-making. **기초 공제** basal deduction. **기초 대사**(-代謝) basal metabolism. **기초 산업** a basic[key] industry. **기초 지식** a (good) grounding (in); an elementary[basic / fundamental] knowledge (of). **기초 학과** the fundamental studies [courses]; primary subject (of study); a basic subject.

기초적(基礎的) fundamental; elementary; basic. ¶~ 요소 the elements (of) // ~인 지식 a basic [fundamental / elementary] knowledge (of).

기총(機銃) a machine gun. ⇨기관총(⇨기관(機關))
● **기총 소사** machine-gunning; strafing (raids) (비행기에서의).

기축(機軸) [중추] an axis (*pl*. -es); an axle; [방안] a plan; a device; a contrivance; [기계의 축] a shaft; [활동의 중추] the center[(영) centre] of activity. ¶신~ a new departure / a novel contrivance / a new device.

기축(基軸) a criterion; a standard.

기치(旗幟) **1** [깃발] a flag; a banner; an ensign; a pennant; an emblem; a standard; colors(군기). ¶…의 ~ 아래 (fight) under the flag[banner] of … // 자유의 ~ 아래 싸우자 Let's fight under the flag[banner] of freedom [for the cause of freedom]. // 그들은 평화의 ~ 아래 협력할 것을 맹세했다 They pledged to cooperate with one another under the banner of peace. // 이 당은 「정계의 정화」를 ~로 내걸고 결성되었다 This party was organized under the slogan "Clean Up Politics!"
2 [태도] one's attitude; one's position; one's stand; [정강(政綱)] the platform; the plank. ¶~를 선명히 하다 make one's attitude [position] clear / assume a definite attitude / show one's hand.

기침 a cough; coughing; [의] a tussis. ¶마른 ~ a dry cough / a hacking cough(잇달아 나오는) // 잔 ~ a slight cough // 이 나다 have a cough // ~으로 고생하다 suffer from[be troubled with] a cough // 감기가 다 나았는데도 아직도 가벼운 ~이 난다 I still have a slight cough even though I have got(ton) over my cold. **기침하다** cough; have a cough. ¶심하게 ~ cough violently / cough one's lungs out / be taken with a fit of coughing // 기침하여 가래를 뱉어 내다 cough up phlegm.
● **기침약** a cough medicine; a remedy for cough.

기타(-憚). ¶클래식 ~ a classical guitar // ~를 치다 play (on) the guitar // ~를 뜯다[퉁기다] strum[twang] a guitar.

기타(其他) the others; the rest; and others; and so forth; and the like; etc. ¶피복과 서적 ~ 품목 clothes, books, and so forth // ~ 여러 가지 and many other things.

기탁(寄託) deposition; [법] bailment. **기탁하다** deposit (a thing with a person); entrust (a person with a thing).
● **기탁금** trust money; money consigned. **기탁자** a depositor; a truster; a bailor. **기탁 증서** a deposit certificate.

기탄없다(忌憚-) frank; outspoken; unreserved; candid. ¶기탄없는 비평 candid criticism. **기탄없이** without reserve; unreservedly; frankly; candidly. ¶~ 말하자면 to be frank (with you) / plainly speaking // 말하다 speak freely / do not mince matters // 그는 그것에 대해 ~ 비평을 했다 He was outspoken [uninhibited] in criticizing it.

기통(氣筒) a (steam) cylinder. ¶4[6] ~ 엔진 a 4-[6-] cylinder engine.

기특하다(奇特-) commendable; admirable; praiseworthy; laudable. ¶기특한 마음씨 a good intention / a commendable purpose // 기특한 행동 a commendable deed // 그녀는 기특하게도 동생들의 뒤를 보살피고 있다 It is quite a praiseworthy [an admirable] thing that she is looking after her younger brothers. // 그는 부모를 기쁘게 하려는 기특한 마음에서 열심히 공부했다 He studied hard out of a commendable desire to please his parents. // 그녀의 기특한 마음가짐은 언젠가 보상될 것이다 Some day her good intentions will be rewarded. // 그는 기특하게도 그 어려운 일을 혼자 할 결심을 했다 He commendably determined to do that arduous work by himself. // 그 기특한 소녀는 앓고 계시는 어머니 대신에 일하러 나섰다 The commendable [admirable] little girl went to work in place of her sick mother. // 내가 기특하게 생각하는 점은 그의 성실성이다 What I admire [(문어) What is commendable] about him is his sincerity.

기틀 the key[pivotal] point; the crux (of a matter); [계기] a (most appropriate) moment; a chance; an occasion; [토대·기반] a base; a basis (*pl*. bases); a foundation. ¶~을 잡다 seize an opportunity (to do / of doing) / take the tide (as it offers) // 성공의 ~이 되다 serve as a stepping-stone [a springboard] for (future) success // 성공의 ~

을 쌓다 pave the way [lay the groundwork] for one's success // ~이 잡히다 be settled (down [in]) / get a firm stand.

기포(氣泡) an air bubble; a blowhole(주물의); a bubble(유리의). ¶물이 괸 웅덩이에서 ~가 일고 있었다 Gas bubbles were rising from the stagnant pond water.
● **기포제**(~劑) a foaming agent.

기포(氣胞) 1 (물고기의) a fish sound; a swimming bladder. 2 [생] an alveolus. ⇨폐포

기폭(起爆) ignition; detonation. **기폭하다** explode.
● **기폭 장치** a triggering device; detonator. **기폭제** an initial explosive; priming (powder). ¶그의 연설이 ~가 되어 의사당 회의장은 소란이 일어났다 His speech triggered [set off] an uproar on the floor of the House.

기표(記票) balloting. **기표하다** fill in [out] a ballot (paper); fill out a voting card.
● **기표소** a polling booth.

기품(氣品) [위엄] dignity; nobility; grace; [세련] refinement. ¶~이 있는 dignified / refined // ~이 가득한 몸가짐 graceful [refined] movements // 그는 ~이 있는 풍모를 하고 있다 He has a refined look. // 그녀에게는 어딘지 모르게 ~이 있다 There is something noble about her.

기풍(氣風) (개인의) character; disposition; temper; (단체의) morale; tone; [사] ethos; [정신] spirits; [특성] traits; characteristics. ¶국민의 ~ the traits [characteristics / tone] of a nation // 옛 ~의 노인 an old-fashioned old man // 학교의 ~ the spirits [morale] of a school // 진취의 ~ an enterprising spirit // ~을 진작하다 arouse[enhance] the (national) spirit // 신입 사원이 회사의 ~을 몸에 익혔다 The new employees have acquired [are imbued with] the company spirit.

기풍(棋風·碁風) one's way of playing baduk(go) [chess]. ¶그의 바둑은 자유롭고 느긋한 ~이다 He has a free and easy style at baduk.

기피(忌避) 1 [꺼리어 피함] evasion; avoidance. ¶징병 ~ draft evasion / avoidance [evasion] of military service. **기피하다** avoid (doing); evade; shirk. ¶자기의 책임을 ~ shirk [evade] one's responsibility. 2 (법률상 법관 등에 대한) a recusation; a challenge. (▶ recusation은 주로 법관에 대하여, challenge 는 법관에도 쓰이지만 주로 배심원에 대하여) ¶재판관 ~ challenge to judges. **기피하다** recuse; challenge. ¶판사를 ~ challenge a judge.
● **기피 인물** [외교] an unwelcome [unacceptable] person. **기피자** an evader (of service); a shirk (of military service); a shirker; [법] a challenger.

기필코(期必─) [꼭] certainly; surely; assuredly; [틀림없이] without fail; [어떤 일이 있어도] by all (manner of) means; at any cost; at all costs; whatever may happen. ¶~해야 할 일 a thing that has to be done // ~ 나는 그것을 성취하고야 말겠다 I will have it done one way or the other. // ~ 너를 실망시키지는 않겠다 I'll never let you down.

기하(幾何) 1 [얼마] how many; how much. 2 geometry. ⇨기하학 ⇨기하
● **기하급수** [수] a geometric series. ⇨~등비급수(⇨등비) ¶인구는 ~적으로 불어난다 Population increases by [in] geometric(al) progression. **기하 평균** geometric average [mean]. **기하학** geometry. ¶~적(인) geometric(al) (figure).

기하다(期─) 1 [날짜·기한 등을 정하다] fix [decide upon] the date; set [fix] a term [time limit / deadline] (for); [약속하다] promise; pledge. ¶가까운 장래를 기하여 in the near future // 두 사람은 재회를 기하고 헤어졌다 The two parted, pledging [promising] to meet again. // 3월 1일을 기하여 그들은 공사를 착수한다 They have chosen march 1 to begin [start] the work. / They will begin the work on march 1.
2 [목표로 삼다] aim (at something / to do); have (something) in one's mind [in view]; [기대하다] expect; anticipate; hope for; look forward to; look to; [결심하다] determine; resolve; decide. ¶만전을 ~ aim at perfection // 필승을 ~ resolve to secure [win / gain] a victory (at any cost) // 우리는 안전을 기하기 위해 위험에 대한 만전의 예방 조치를 취했다 To ensure safety we took every possible precaution against danger.

기한(期限) a time limit; a term; a period; a deadline; time; [법] limitation(법률의 효력 등의). ¶예정 ~ the target date // 유효 ~ the term of validity // ~부로 [로] with a time limit (fixed) / (미) with a (six-month) deadline // ~ 전에 before the time set / before the date fixed // ~ 내에 within the period (fixed by law) // 지불 ~ the term for payment // 엄격한 ~부의 일 a job with a strict time limit // ~이 지난 정기 승차권 a commuter's pass which is no longer valid // 일정 ~ 안에 within a certain [set] period // 신청 ~을 선정하다 set a deadline for applications [an application deadline] // 이 표는 유효 ~이 지났다 This ticket is no longer valid. / The validity of this ticket has expired. // 지불 ~이 끝났다 The deadline for payment has passed. / Payment is overdue. // 계약 ~이 내일로 끝난다 The term of the contract expires [runs out] tomorrow. // 1주일이면 어음의 ~이 된다 The bill falls due in a week. / 어음의 ~이 지났다 The bill is overdue. // 다음 달에 꾼 돈의 지불 ~이 다가온다 The payment of our loan falls due next month. // 이 일에는 ~이 없다 There's no time limit for this work. // ~을 정하는 것이 좋겠소 You had better fix a deadline.
● **기한 만료** the termination [expiration] of a term.

기한(飢寒) hunger and cold. ¶~에 떨다 suffer from hunger and cold.

기함(旗艦) a flagship.

기합(氣合) 1 [정신 집중] concentration of spirit; [집중을 위하여 지르는 소리] a yell; a shout. ¶~을 넣다 [소리치다] shout [yell] at (at person) / give (a person) a yell / [독려하다] urge (a person) to get a move [start] on (his) work // 그는 상대의 ~에 압도되어 패배했다 He lost because he was cowed [overawed] by his opponent's show of determination. // 그는 좀 더 ~을 넣어 줄 필요가 있다 He needs to have it hammered [drilled] into him. / He needs to have it beaten into him. 2 [군] disciplinary punishment (upon a group); ¶단체 ~ disciplinary punishment upon a group // ~을 주다 chastise / punish.

기항술 the art of mesmerizing by one's will power.

기항(寄港) a call[stop] at a port. **기항하다** call[stop/touch] (at); put in (at); make a call (at). ¶부산에 ~ touch at Busan//그 배는 항해 도중 많은 곳에 기항했다 The vessel called at many ports on her route.

기행(紀行) an account of travels; a traveler's journal; a book of travels; a travelog. ¶(영화의) ~물 a travelog//경주 ~ (제목) A Trip to Gyeongju//그는 이탈리아 ~을 출판했다 He published a book on[a record of / an account of] his travels in Italy.
● **기행문** an account of trip; one's travel sketches.

기행(奇行) a strange[an eccentric] conduct; an eccentricity. ¶~으로 알려져 있다 be notorious[well-known] for one's eccentricities//그는 ~이 많은 사람이었다 He was full of eccentricities.

기형(畸形) deformation; (a) malformation; (a) deformity; (a) monstrosity; abnormality(형태상의). ¶~의 deformed / malformed / abnormal//선천성 ~ congenital malformation.
● **기형물** a monster; a monstrosity. **기형아**(-兒) a deformed[malformed] child; a freak of nature.

기호(記號) a sign; a symbol; a mark(▶ 보통 문자·숫자 이외의 기호); emblem; an ideogram[ideograph] (1, 2, +, - 등); [음] a clef; a signature(조(調)·박자의). ¶+[-]의 ~ a plus[minus] sign//삭제 ~ a deletion mark[sign]//수학 ~ a mathematical symbol//음악 ~ a musical sign//음성 ~ a phonetic symbol//화학 ~ a chemical symbol//~를 붙이다 mark (with a symbol)//OX의 ~를 붙이다 put a circle or a cross (before)//이것은 무엇을 나타내는 ~입니까 What does this symbol stand for? / What does this mark mean?//$는 달러를 나타내는 ~이다 $ is a dollar sign.//언어는 사상의 ~이다 Words are the sign of ideas.

기호(嗜好) (a) taste(s); (a) liking; fancy; gusto; one's likes; (a) preference. ¶~에 따라 according to one's liking[preference]//~에 맞다 be to one's taste / suit one's taste//~가 까다롭다 have a fastidious taste / be fastidious[nice / finical] in one's taste / have a delicate palate//대중의 ~에 맞다 capture [strike / hit / catch] the public fancy//재즈는 모든 사람의 ~에 맞는 것은 아니다 Jazz is not to[does not suit] everyone's taste.//그 와인은 그의 ~에 맞았다 That wine suited[was to] his taste. **기호하다** have a taste[fondness / fancy] for ...; have a liking for ....
● **기호품** [개인적으로 좋아하는 식품] one's favorite [(영) favourite] food; (차·술 등) table luxuries.

기혼(既婚) ¶~의 married.
● **기혼자** a married person; the married.

기화(奇貨) [진기한 물건] a curiosity; a rarity; [호기] a rare[good] opportunity. ¶…을 ~로 (삼아) taking advantage of / 비열하게도 (남의) 무지를 ~로 삼다 take (a) mean advantage of (a person's) ignorance//남의 약점을 ~로 삼다 practice upon another's weakness//그녀는 자신의 미모를 ~로 삼고 있다 She trades on her beauty. / She has made her (good) looks her selling point.

기화(氣化) evaporation; vaporization; gasification. **기화하다** evaporate; vaporize; gasify.
● **기화기** a vaporizer; an evaporator; a carburet(t)or. **기화성** vaporability.

기회(機會) an opportunity; a chance; an occasion. ¶좋은 ~ a good chance[opportunity]//절호의 ~ a golden[rare] opportunity/(천재일우의) 천에 하나의 ~ an opportunity in a thousand//~ 있을 때마다 at every opportunity / whenever the opportunity arises//~ 있는 대로 at the first opportunity / as opportunity permits//다음 ~에 some other time / on another occasion / [나중에] later//절호의 ~를 놓치다 miss a perfect chance[a golden opportunity] / let a wonderful opportunity get away//~를 잡다 grasp[seize] an opportunity to do//~를 얻다 get[gain] an opportunity to do//~를 타다 take advantage of an opportunity//~를 기다리다[놓치다] wait for [miss] a chance//~를 보아 물러나다 seize [grasp] an opportunity to withdraw[leave] (▶ leave는 그만두다)//다음 ~에 전화드리겠습니다 I will telephone you[call you up] later[some other time].//그것에 대해서는 다음 ~에 말씀드리겠습니다 I will speak about it on another occasion.//~가 닿는 대로 알려주시기 바랍니다 Please let me know at your earliest convenience[at the first opportunity].//내가 그를 사귈 수 있는 ~를 네가 만들어 주겠니 Will you give me an opportunity to get acquainted with him?//~가 있으면 또 만납시다 Let's meet again if we have a chance.//이상하게도 우연한 ~에 그와 왕복 모두 같은 비행기를 탔다 By a strange chance, he and I happened to take the same plane both ways.//우연한 ~에 우리는 공동 사업을 시작했다 A chance happening led us to start a joint business venture.//나는 어머니가 돌아오신 것을 ~로 아내와의 말다툼을 그만두었다 On my mother's return, I left off the argument with my wife.//그는 ~가 있을 때마다 그 일을 화제로 삼는다 He brings up the subject at every opportunity[whenever possible].//그는 ~를 보다가 우세한 쪽에 붙는다 He jumps whichever way the wind is blowing.//나는 ~를 보아 돈 대출에 대한 이야기를 꺼냈다 I waited for a suitable time and then broached[raised] the matter of a loan.//이쪽에 오실 ~가 있으면 들러 주십시오 If you have a chance to come this way [When you are in the area], please drop by.//이 건은 다음 ~로 돌리겠다 We will take this matter up at the next opportunity.//나는 모든 ~를 이용해서 자기선전을 했다 I used every opportunity to sell myself.//그는 고대하던 ~가 왔다는 듯 자기선전을 시작했다 He leaped at the opportunity to sell himself. / He started to sell himself as if this were the very chance he had been waiting for.//사과할 ~는 얼마든지 있었다 There was ample opportunity to apologize. / You had plenty of chances to apologize.//이 ~에 새 차를 사자 Let's take advantage of this opportunity and buy a new car.//이런 ~는 평생에 다시 없을 것이다 A chance like this comes but once in a lifetime. / There will never be another opportunity like this. / It's now or never.//이건 일생에 한 번 있을까 말까 한 ~야 This is a once-in-a-life-time chance.//그는 ~를 포착하는 데 민첩한 사람

이다 He is quick to grasp[seize] an opportunity. / He never missed a chance.∥매사에는 ~라는 것이 있다 There is a time[tide] for everything.∥누구에게나 ~는 온다 Every dog has his day.∥그는 적당한 ~를 기다렸으나 그녀에게 말을 걸었다 He waited for a good chance[picked his time / chose the proper time] and spoke to her.∥이 ~에 여러분에게 감사의 뜻을 표합니다 Let me take this opportunity of thanking you all.
● 기회균등 equality of opportunity; equal opportunity. ¶교육의 ~ equal educational opportunities. 기회균등주의 the principle of equal opportunity; the open-door principle. 기회주의 opportunism; timeserving; wait-and-see policy. 기회주의자 an opportunist; a timeserver; (미) a fence-sitter; a fence straddler.

기획(企劃) [계획함] planning; [계획] a plan; a project. ¶새로운 ~ a new program ∥ ~을 세우다[짜다] make[draw up] a plan / (구어) come up with a plan. **기획하다** plan; make [form / set up] a plan; work out a scheme [program].
● 기획 관리 planning and management. 기획부[실] planning department[office]. 기획 예산처 the Ministry of Planning and Budget. 기획자 a planner; a plan maker. 기획 조정실 the Office of Planning & Coordination.

기후(氣候) (a) climate; [날씨] the weather(▶ weather는 나날이 변하는 것, climate는 어떤 지방의 풍토를 가리키며 오랜 동안에 걸쳐 그 의 변화하지 않는 것을 지칭함); [절후] a season. ¶해양성 ~ a marine[an oceanic] climate∥온화한 ~ a mild climate∥대륙성 ~ a continental climate∥좋은 ~ a fine climate∥불순한 ~ unseasonable weather / 변하기 쉬운 ~ a variable climate / changeable[unsettled] weather∥~가 불순한 때이 므로 in this unseasonable weather∥~가 바뀔 때에 when the seasons change / at the change of seasons∥그곳은 ~의 변화가 심하 다 The place is subject to extreme[violent] climatic changes.

긴급(緊急) urgency; [긴급 사태] (an) emergency; (an) exigency; (서류 등에 쓸 때) (미) "Rush"; (영) "Urgent". ¶매우 ~을 요하는 문제 a problem of great urgency∥치료는 ~을 요한다 Immediate treatment is necessary. **긴급하다** urgent (demand); pressing (problem); emergent (state); burning (problem); exigent (problem); crying (want). ¶긴급한 용무로 on urgent business∥긴급한 경우에 in an emergency∥내 부친은 긴급한 용무로 상경하셨다 My father went to Seoul on urgent business. **긴급히** urgently; exigently. ¶이 문제에 ~ 대처하지 않으면 안 된다 We must take emergency steps[act at once] to deal with this problem.
● 긴급 대책 an urgent countermeasure. 긴급 동의 an urgent motion. 긴급 명령 an emergency order; (미) a rush order. 긴급 사태 a state of emergency; an emergency; an exigency; a crisis (pl. crises). 긴급 조치 an emergency measure. 긴급회의 an urgent conference[meeting]. ¶~가 소집되었다 An emergency meeting was called.

긴말 a long[lengthy] talk[speech]; a long and boring[tedious] talk; a long-winded [-drawn] talk; a yarn; a screed. ¶~을 늘어 놓다 spin a yarn / tell a long boring story. **긴 말하다** speak long-windedly[lengthily]; dwell on (a subject) at (great) length; give a tedious talk (to); spin a yarn; talk round. ¶긴말하지 않겠습니다 I'll not bother you with a long talk. / I shall not enlarge[expatiate] upon the subject. / I'll cut it short.

긴밀하다(緊密-) strict; rigid; tight; tightly knit (alliance). ¶긴밀한 접촉 close touch [contact]∥긴밀한 연락을 취하다 keep in close contact (with) / 이것은 그것과 긴밀한 관계에 있다 This is closely connected with it. / This has a close connection with it.∥귀 사와의 긴밀한 제휴가 필요합니다 We need close ties with your company. **긴밀히** strictly; closely; rigidly; tightly. ¶~ 협력하여 in close cooperation (with).

긴박하다(緊迫-) tense; acute; strained. ¶긴 박한 국제 정세 a tense[strained] international situation∥긴박해지다 grow strained / become acute∥두 나라 관계는 점점 긴박해지 고 있다 The relation between the two countries are growing more and more strained [tense].∥긴박한 국제 정세를 어떻게 완화시 킬 것인지가 문제이다 The problem is how to ease the tense international situation.

긴병(-病) a long[protracted] illness; a lingering disease; a siege of illness. ¶~을 앓다 suffer from a long illness / be ill[(미) sick] in bed for a long time∥그는 ~에서 막 회복 되었다 He has just recovered from a long illness.

긴병에 효자 없다(속담) A protracted illness wears out filial devotion.; A long visit[stay] wears out one's welcome.; Never overstay [outstay] one's welcome.; Enthusiasm is short-lived.

긴요하다(緊要-) important; of vital importance; vital; momentous; of moment; weighty; [필요하다] necessary (to); [없어서 는 안 되다] essential; [주요하다] main; indispensable (to); requisite (to). ¶긴요한 문제 a problem of vital importance∥성공을 위해 긴요한 조건 conditions vital[crucial / most important] to our success / 건강을 유 지하기 위해서는 적당한 운동이 ~ Moderate exercise is essential for the preservation of health. **긴요히** importantly; vitally; momentously.

긴장(緊張) strain; tension. ¶~이 계속되고 있 다 The tension[(미국 속어) heat] is on.∥곧 시험이 닥쳐오니까 이제 와서 ~을 풀 수는 없 다 As the examination is approaching, I cannot relax my efforts[let up] now.∥안심하 는 순간 나는 ~이 풀렸다 My tension melted away the moment I stopped worrying.∥아직 은 ~을 풀 때가 아니다 I cannot breathe easy yet. **긴장하다** be strained; become tense; be on the strain[stretch]; be keyed up; gird[string] oneself up (to do); prepare. ¶ 긴장하여 tensely / in strain∥긴장한 표정 a tense look / a strained countenance∥지나치 게 ~ overstrain oneself / be strained to the limit∥긴장할 것 없다 Relax! / Take it easy. ∥사장 앞이라 긴장하여 변변히 의견을 말하지 못했다 I was so nervous in front of the president that I had difficulty expressing my opinion.∥요즘 나는 쭉 긴장하여 일하고 있다 I have been working under a strain lately.
➔¶긴장된 공기 a tense[highly-charged]

긴지름

atmosphere // 긴장된 생활 high-tension living / an intense life // 신경을 극도로 긴장시키다 stretch one's nerves keyed up // 나는 신경이 극도로 긴장되어 있었다 My nerves were taut. / I was tense [very nervous]. // 회장에는 긴장된 공기가 감돌고 있었다 The atmosphere in the hall was tense.
● **긴장 상태** a state of tension. **긴장 완화** (국제간의) the relaxation [relief] of international tensions; a détente; a thaw. ¶동서의 ~ easing [relaxation] of East-West tensions // 한반도의 ~ the easing of tensions of the Korean Peninsula.

긴지름 [수] the major axis.

긴축(緊縮) [절약] (strict) economy; (문어) retrenchment; curtailment; (통화의) deflation; (생활 태도의) austerity; belt tightening.

긴축하다 [절약하다] economize; tighten; [삭감하다] retrench; curtail; cut down (expenses); (통화를) deflate. ¶재정을 ~ cut down on spending [expenditure] / (문어) retrench (the nation's) finances // 금융을 ~ tighten the money market // 시장을 ~ firm up the market // (은행의) 신용 대출을 ~ tighten up on credit.
● **긴축 생활** an austere life. **긴축 예산** an austerity budget. **긴축 재정** a reduced budget; a curtailed budget. **긴축 정책** a policy of retrenchment [restraint / austerity]; a belt-tightening [tight-financing] policy.

긴팔원숭이 [동] a long-armed ape; a gibbon.

긴하다(緊—) [긴요하다] important; of vital importance; vital; momentous; weighty; [필요하다] necessary (to); indispensable (to); essential (to); requisite (to); [유용하다] useful; of use; [급하다] urgent; pressing. ¶긴한 일 urgent [pressing] business / business demanding immediate attention / pressing need / an urgent [a vital] matter / 긴한 사람 an indispensable person / 긴한 물건 a necessary [an indispensable] article / a useful object (to have around) // 긴한 ині, in time [hour] of need // 긴한 부탁을 드리러 왔습니다 I have come with an important [urgent] favor to ask of you. // 곧 해결해야 할 긴한 문제들이 있다 There are urgent problems which require immediate settlement. // 긴할 때의 친구가 참다운 친구다 A friend in need is a friend indeed. **긴히** importantly; vitally; momentously. ¶~ 드릴 말씀이 있는데요 May I speak to you in private?

긷다 (물을) draw; ladle(바가지 등으로); pump(펌프로). ¶우물의 물을 ~ draw water from a well // 두레박으로 물을 ~ draw water (from a well) with a (well) bucket // 길어 올리다 draw up / pump up // 단수에 대비하여 물을 길어 놓다 set aside some drinking water in case the water is shut off.

길[1] **1** [도로] a road; a way; [거리] a street; a thoroughfare; [가도] a highway; a highroad; [코스] a route; [작은 길] a path; a lane; a walk(정원 등의); a pass; a trail(산·숲 속의); a track(밟아 다진); an alley(골목길); [통로] a passage; an approach (road) (to) [입구로 가는]. ((미) 뉴욕 시 등에서 avenue는 남북으로 통하는 대로, street는 동서로 통하는 것) ¶가로수 ~ an avenue / a boulevard / a tree-bordered road / an arbored walk // 지름~ a

288

shorter way / a shortcut // ~ 가는 사람 a passerby (pl. passersby) / a wayfarer // ~에서 on [in] the road [street] // ~을 걷다 [가다] walk down [up / along] the road // ~을 막다 stand in (a person's) way / bar the way / block the passage // ~을 내다 [트다] make [cut through] a road (to) / cut a path (to) / ~을 열다 open up a road / pioneer // ~을 묻다 ask one's [the] way (to a place) / ask direction(s) (to a place) // ~을 잘못 들다 take the wrong way / mistake the road / go wrong // ~을 가르쳐 주다 tell (a person) the way (to) / (안내하여) show (a person) the way (to) // ~을 비켜 주다 make way [room] (for) / yield the right of way // ~을 잃다 lose [miss] one's way / lose one's bearings / get lost // ~을 고르다 level a road // ~을 치우다 clear the way (for) // ~이 막혀 있다 A road is blocked [comes to a dead end]. // ~이 나 있다 A road [way] is open. // ~을 물어 그곳까지 갔다 I got there inquiring along the way. // ~이 틀린다 You are going the wrong way. / It's the wrong way. // 은행으로 가는 ~을 가르쳐 주시겠습니까 Would you please tell me how to get to the bank? / Could you show me the way to the bank? // 어느 ~로 가야 가장 빠릅니까 Which route [course / way] is the quickest? // 큰 트럭이 ~을 막고 있었다 A huge truck was in [blocking] our way. // 우리는 눈을 치워서 ~을 텄다 We cleared a path through the snow. // 소방차 오니까 ~을 비키시오 Make way for the fire engine. / A fire engine is coming — get out of the way! // 나는 지나가는 사람에게 도서관으로 가는 ~을 물었다 I asked a passerby the way to the library. // 돌아갈 때 나는 다른 ~로 갔다 I took a different route [went another way] on my return. // 이 ~을 따라가면 정거장 [역]에 이르게 됩니다 Follow [Keep on / Stay on / Go along] this road, you will come to the station. / This road leads to the station.
2 [행정(行程)] a way; journey; [거리] distance. ¶인생 ~ the journey of life / life's journey // 하룻 ~ a day's distance // 상경 ~ 오르다 start for Seoul // ~을 떠나다 start [set out] on a journey // ~을 서두르다 make the best of one's way / hurry along [on] // 문제 해결의 ~은 아직도 멀다 There is still a long way to go toward solution of this problem. // 먼 ~을 가야 할 것을 생각하니 걱정스럽다 I feel uneasy about the long way we have to go. // 그는 세계 일주의 ~을 떠났다 He started [(문어) embarked] on a trip around the world [a world tour].
3 [도중] the midst of a way [course]; incidental to a course of action. ¶대전으로 가는 ~에 on my way to Daejeon // 우체국으로 가는 ~에 시장이 있다 There is a market on the way to the post office. // 학교 가는 ~에 한 가지 심부름 좀 해 주겠니 Will you run an errand for me on your way to school? // 나는 학교로 가는 [에서 돌아가는] ~에서 그를 만났다 I met him on my way to [back from] school.
4 [진로] a course; a way; [경로] a route; a channel; [방법·수단] a way; a means; [취할 길] a course; a step. ¶성공하는 ~ the road [way] to success // 취할 ~ the course to take [to be taken] / the course of action (to follow [to be followed]) // 안전한 ~ a safe

course // 살아가는 ~ a means of livelihood // 성공과 번영에 이르는 ~ an avenue to success and prosperity // …으로의 ~을 트다 pave the way for[to] / ~의 승진에 ~을 열어 놓다 keep the door open to promotion / give an opportunity[clear the way] for promotion // 자신의 ~을 가다 go one's way // 후진을 위해 ~을 열어 주다 make way for one's juniors / give the younger people a chance // 살아갈 ~이 막연하다 I don't know how to make a living. // 빠져나갈 ~이 없다 There is no way out[through]. // 이 밖에 달리 ~이 없다 This is the only way[course] open to me. / I have no choice[nothing] but to (do) this. // 그의 안부를 알 ~이 없다 There is no way of knowing if he is all right.
5 [지켜야 할 일] a duty; [도의] morality; [가르침] teachings; [진리] truth; [도리] reason. ¶세속의 ~ the way(s) of the world // 자식으로서의 ~ filial duty // 사람의 ~ one's path of duty // 공맹의 ~ the teachings[doctrines] of Confucius and Mencius // 올바른 ~에서 벗어나다 err[stray / deviate] from the path of righteousness.
6 [분야·방면] a line; [직] a career; [기술·기예] an art. ¶그 ~의 대가 a (past) master of the art[profession] / an expert in this field[in the line] // 그들은 각기 그 ~의 전문가다 They are specialists in their respective fields.

길² **1** [동물의 부리기 좋게 된 버릇] domestication; tameness. **2** [익숙해진 솜씨] skill; dexterity. **3** [윤기] polish; gloss; luster; shine.

길³ [품질의 등급] a class; a grade. ¶윗~의 first-class / first-rate / of superior grade[quality] / superior / choice // 윗~의 털실 a fine quality of yarn // 아랫~의 inferior / of lower grade[quality] // 좀 더 윗~의 것을 보여 주시오 Show me a better one. // 이보다 윗~의 것은 없습니다 This is the best we have.

길⁴ a wrapper; a set of books. ⇨질(帙)

길⁵ **1** [사람 키의 길이] the height of a man; [깊이] a fathom. ¶천[만] ~ 골짜기 an unfathomable[a bottomless] ravine / an abysmal valley / an abyss // 한 ~이나 되는 담장 a manhigh[-tall] fence // 깊이가 열 ~이다 be ten fathoms deep. **2** [길이의 단위] a measure of length; either 10 or 8 *ja*(=11′9″ or 9′5″).

길가 the roadside; the wayside. ¶~의 roadside / wayside // ~에 by the roadside[wayside] // ~ 꽃 wayside flowers // ~의 찻집 a teahouse by [along] the roadside.

길거리 a street; a road; an avenue; a thoroughfare. ¶~에 나앉다 be turned adrift / be turned in[on] the streets // ~를 쏘다니다 roam about the streets // ~를 헤매다 wander about the town[the streets].

길길이 **1** [높이] high; to a great height; tall; aloft; [수북이] in a heap[pile]; in heaps. ¶~ 쌓다 pile up high[in a heap] / pile (goods) mountain-high // ~ 자라다 grow tall / grow high up in the sky // 불길이 ~ 치솟다 go high up in flames / burst into flames. **2** [몹시] extremely; to the highest[last] degree; to the utmost. ¶화가 나서 ~ 뛰다 get hopping[be raging] mad / get mad with anger / be wild with anger / (구어) hit the ceiling[roof].

길나다 **1** become used (to). ⇨길들다 **2** **2** (연장 등이) be well used; be broken in. ¶길난 만년필 a well-used[broken-in] fountain pen // 도구는 모두 길나 있었다 All the tools were well used[broken in].

길년 (吉年) [결혼에 좋은 나이] the marriageable[nubile] age; [연운年運] an auspicious year for marriage.

길눈 [방향 감각] a sense of direction. ¶~이 밝다 have a good sense of direction // ~이 어둡다 have no sense of direction.

길다 **1** (물체가) long; lengthy. ¶긴 소매 a long sleeve // 긴 치마 a trailing skirt // 길어야 at the longest // 길게 하다 make longer / lengthen / draw long // 길어지다 be lengthened / become [grow] longer // 길게 눕다 lie down / lie at full length // 이 끈은 그것보다 5센티 더 ~ This string is five centimeters longer than that one. / This string is longer than that one by five centimeters.
2 (시간·공간적으로) long; prolonged(오래 끈); lengthy. ¶긴 세월 a long time / a long stretch of time / many years // 긴 장마 a long rainy season // 길어야 3일 three days at (the) longest // 긴 눈으로 보면 in the long run // 긴 안목으로 보다 take a long(-range) view (of) // 길어지다 be prolonged / be extended // 긴 세월이 걸린다 It takes a long time[many years] (to do). // 그는 앞날이 길지 못하다 He will not last long. / His days are numbered. // 낮이 점점 길어지고 있다 The days are getting[growing] longer. // 신청 기간이 길어졌다 The deadline for applications has been extended. // 의학의 발전 덕분에 사람의 수명이 길어졌다 Progress in medical science has prolonged[lengthened] our life span. // 사람은 길게 두고 봐야 안다 It takes a long time to understand a person. // 이야기는 길어졌다 Our talk took time.

길고 짧은 것은 대어 보아야 안다(속담) A real test will prove who[which] is better[greater, stronger, etc.].; It ain't over till it's over.

길동무 a fellow traveler[(영) traveller / passenger]; a traveling companion. ¶~와 ~가 되다 (happen to) travel together (with) / fall in[into company] with … // 여행에는 ~가 있어야 즐겁다 Traveling is more enjoyable with companions[company] (than alone). // 당신 같은 ~라면 좋습니다 I shall be very glad of your company. **길동무하다** travel[go] with (a person) as a companion; travel together (with); keep (a person) company.

길드 a guild.
● **길드 사회주의** guild socialism.

길들다 **1** [동물이 잘 따르게 되다] become [grow] tame; become[get] domesticated; get housebroken[trained]; ¶길든 고양이 a tame [housebroken] cat // 길들지 않은 undomesticated / untamed / unbroken / wild // 길들지 않은 새 a wild bird // 이 개는 잘 길들어 있다 The puppy is quite tame with me.
2 [익숙해지다] become[get] used[accustomed] (to); get familiar with; get inured (to); grow experienced in; become skil(l)ful [good] at. ¶길든 practiced / experienced / familiar // 길들지 않은 unexperienced // 사치에 ~ be lapped in luxury // 곧 길들게 될 것이다 You will soon get used to it.
3 [윤나다] take[get / admit] a polish; get [show] a gloss[shine / luster]; get glossy. ¶

길들이다 길들어 반들반들한 glossy / lustrous / bright / sheeny // 노상 닦았더니 양복장이 길들었다 The wardrobe has got a polish from constant rubbing. // 이 목재는 길들지 않는다 This wood wouldn't polish.

길들이다 **1** (동물을) tame (an animal); domesticate; break in (a horse); make [reclaim] (a hawk); charm (a snake); (구어) gentle (a wild pony); (훈련시키다) train (a dog); practice (dogs in guiding the blind). ¶고릴라를 ~ tame a gorilla // 돌고래를 재주를 부리도록 ~ train[teach] a dolphin to do tricks // 말을 ~ break in a horse // 개에게 신문을 갖고 오도록 ~ train the dog to fetch the newspaper // 잘 길들여져 있다 be kept well under / be quite tame // 그들은 코끼리를 길들여 무거운 물건을 운반하게 한다 They tame elephants and use them to carry heavy things. **2** [익숙해지게 하다] inure; habituate; accustom; make (a person) used [accustomed / inured] to (something); train [improve] (a person) in (something); (능란하게 하다) make (oneself / a person) skillful [skilled / proficient / expert] (in / at). ¶길들인 연장[도구] a wellused tool // 아내에게 길들여진 남편 a tame [well-trained / meek] husband // 직장에 완전히 길들여진 회사원들 office workers who have been completely broken in [have lost their independent spirit] // 몸을 추위에 ~ inure oneself to cold // 프라이팬은 오래 쓸수록 잘 길들여진다 The longer you use a frying pan, the better it becomes for cooking. **3** [윤나게 하다] gloss; glaze; bring out the luster; give a gloss [polish / luster / shine] to; put a gloss [polish] on; polish up; make (it) glossy. ¶가구를 닦아 ~ give a polish to furniture [polish furniture] by rubbing it.

길잡이 a guide. ⇨ ⇒길잡이2
길례(吉禮) [경사스러운 예식] a happy [an auspicious] ceremony; a ceremony for congratulation.
길마 a packsaddle. ¶~를 지우다 put a packsaddle on / fix a packsaddle / saddle up.
길모퉁이 the corner (of a street); (at / on) a street corner; a turn; a turning. ¶~의 파출소 a police box on a street corner // ~에서 나는 그를 만났다 I met [ran into] him on the street corner. // 나는 세 번째 ~를 왼편으로 돌았다 I turned left at the third corner. / I took the third turning [road] to the left.
길목 **1** [길모퉁이] a street corner; a turning of a road; (at) a turn in a road; (at) a bend of a road; a road bend. ¶~에 있는 가게 a corner store // ~을 돌다 turn [go round] the corner (of a street) / round a bend // 둘째 ~을 오른편으로 돌다 take the second turning to the right / turn right at the second corner // ~에 가게를 내다 open a shop on a street corner // ~을 잘못 든 것 같다 It seems I made a mistake and took the wrong turn. **2** [중요한 어귀] an important position [place]; an important center [focus]; (군사상의) a point of strategic importance; a strategic point. ¶~마다 at important points [positions] / at every strategic point // ~을 지키다 fortify the points of strategic importance / station troops at strategic points.
길몽(吉夢) a lucky [an auspicious] dream; a dream of good [lucky] omen.
길바닥 [길의 표면] the surface of a road; a roadbed; [길 가운데] the middle of road.
길벗 a fellow traveler. ⇨ ⇒길동무
길보(吉報) (a piece of) good news. ¶~를 가져오다 bring good news.
길사(吉事) [경사] a happy event; (문어) an auspicious event.
길섶 (at / by / on) the roadside; (by / on) the wayside; the shoulder of a road.
길손 a traveler; a tourist; a wayfarer; a stranger.
길쌈 weaving (by hand); handweaving; handloom-weaving. **길쌈하다** weave by hand; handweave; make cloth.
길운(吉運) good fortune; (good) luck; (미) a lucky [good] break.
길이¹ [긴 정도] length; (문어) stature. ¶드레스[옷의] ~ the length of a dress [coat] // 무릎 ~의 (overcoat) of knee length // ~가 얼마냐 How long is it? / What is its length? // 그것은 ~가 3미터이다 It is three meters long [in length]. // 이 막대는 네 것보다 2배의 ~이다 This stick is twice as long as yours. // 이 리본을 같은 ~로 5조각으로 잘라라 Cut the ribbon into five pieces of equal length. // 이 판자는 ~가 5센티 모자란다 This board is five centimeters too short. // 내 재킷의 ~를 줄일 필요가 있다 My jacket needs to be shortened [taken up].
길이² [오래도록] (for) long; for a long time; [영원히] forever; everlastingly; eternally; for many and many years to come. ¶~~ forever (and ever) / eternally / everlastingly / to [through all] eternity / forever // ~ 보존하다 preserve [cherish] (a thing) for good // 이름을 ~ 남기다 immortalize one's fame [name] // 그의 이름은 청사에 ~ 빛날 것이다 His name will be long noted in history. / He will remain long [be recorded / live] in history.
길일(吉日) a lucky day; (문어) an auspicious day. ¶~을 택하다 choose a lucky day.
길잡이 **1** [지침] a guiding principle; a guideline; [안내서] a guide (to); a handbook; a manual. ¶작문의 ~ hints on composition // 문제 해결의 ~ an index to the solution of a problem // 이 책이 초심자의 ~가 되기를 바란다 I hope this book will provide guidance for [serve as a guide to] the beginners. **2** [길을 인도하는 사람] a guide. ¶~가 되다 act as (a) guide / show (a person) the way (to) / direct [guide] (a person to a place).
길조(吉兆) a good [a lucky / an auspicious] omen; a lucky [propitious / favorable] sign; a happy [good] augury. ¶~의 auspicious // ~를 보이다 be of good omen / augur [bode] well (for our scheme).
길짐승 a creeping animal; creeping things; creepers.
길쭉길쭉하다 (all) longish; somewhat long. ¶길쭉길쭉한 막대기 longish [long] sticks // 대를 길쭉길쭉하게 자르다 cut a piece of bamboo in long sections.
길쭉하다 longish; moderately [somewhat] long. ¶다리가 길쭉한 의자 a chair with spindly legs // 길쭉한 나뭇조각 a sliver // 길쭉한 호리병박 [호박] a long-necked gourd [pumpkin] // 얼굴이 ~ have a longish face.
길쭉이 somewhat long. ¶좀 ~ 자르다 cut (something) a little longer.

길하다 (吉-) good; fortunate; lucky; (문어) auspicious. ¶점괘가 길하다고 나왔다 Good fortune was foretold for me.

길항 (拮抗) rivalry; contention; competition; antagonism; a struggle for supremacy. **길항하다** [항쟁하다] rival; contend [cope / vie / compete] with; stand [put oneself] against; struggle with (a person) for supremacy; [비견하다] compare with.
- **길항 작용** [생] antagonism.

길흉 (吉凶) one's fortune; one's (good or bad) luck. ¶카드로 ~을 점치기 fortune-telling with playing cards.

김[1] [해태] laver; sloke; sloak; dried seaweed. ¶맛~ seasoned laver // 구운 ~ toasted laver // 한 장의 ~ a large sheet of laver // ~을 재다 [굽다] season [toast] laver.
- **김 양식** laver farming.

김[2] **1** [수증기] (white) steam; vapor. ¶온천에서 솟아오르는 ~ steam rising from a hot spring // ~이 무럭무럭 나는 스튜 요리 steaming hot stew // ~이 나다 [을 내다] steam / reek / emit [give off / send up] steam // ~을 쐬다 fume / fumigate // 주전자에서 ~이 나고 있다 The kettle is steaming. // 수프에서 ~이 오르고 있다 Steam is rising from the soup. **2** (입·코의) breath. ¶입~ breath // 콧~ breath through the nose. **3** (향기) flavor; savor(풍미); smell; fume; [맛] taste.

김[3] [기회] an occasion; an opportunity; a chance. ¶(하는) ~에 while / when / as / by the way / by the by(e) / incidentally / on the occasion / at the same time / apropos / while one is at [about] it / in passion // 나가는 ~에 just as one is going out // 술에 취한 ~에 그는 상사에게 불평을 늘어놓았다 Emboldened by drink [Under the influence of alcohol], he complained to his superior. // 산책하는 ~에 그의 집에 들렀다 I dropped in on him while taking a walk. // 존의 이야기가 나온 ~에 하는 말인데, 그의 어머니는 어떻게 지내고 계십니까 Speaking of John, I wonder how his mother is doing? // 나는 그곳에 간 ~에 그에게 전화를 했다 I telephoned him while I was there.

김[4] [논·밭의 잡초] weed. ¶~을 매다 weed / pick weeds out of / root out [remove] weeds.

김밥 *gimbap*; rice rolled in dried laver.

김빠지다 1 (맥주 등이) run vapid; become flat [insipid]; flatten; (차·커피 등이) lose its flavor; become flavorless. ¶김빠진 맥주 flat [stale / vapid] beer // ~이 위스키는 김빠졌다 This whisky tastes flat.
2 (일이) flag; fall off in interest; become dull; lose (its) relish. ¶김빠진 대화 a dull lecture // 김빠진 농담 a flat joke // 김빠진 대답을 하다 answer absently [in a half-hearted manner] / give a cold [dry] answer // 너의 익살은 제삼자가 들으면 김빠진 것이 된다 Your joke falls flat on outsiders. // 부정행위에 대한 정부의 조사는 겨우 2주일로 김빠진 상태가 되어 버린 것 같다 The government's investigation of corrupt practices seems to have run out of steam after only two weeks.

김새다 lose interest [enthusiasm] (in); one's enthusiasm dies down. ¶김새게 하다 dampen [chill / cool down] (a person's) enthusiasm [zeal / ardor] (for) // 김샜다 The fervor of my passion died. / My enthusiasm wore off. // 그의 태도를 보고 우리는 완전히 김샜다 His attitude was enough to cool down our ardor (for it).

김장 [겨우내 먹을 김치를 담그기] *gimjang*; *gimchi*(kimchi)-making [preparing *gimchi* / pickling vegetables] for the winter; [담근 김치] *gimchi* prepared for the winter. **김장하다** prepare [make] *gimchi* for (use during) the winter; pickle vegetables for winter use.
- **김장독** a *gimjangdok*; a *gimchi*[pickle] jar [pot]; a pickle tub; a steeper. **김장철** *gimjangcheol*; the *gimchi*-making season; the time for preparing *gimchi* for the winter.

김치 *gimchi*; kimchi; kimchee; pickled vegetables. ¶무[배추/오이] ~ radish[cabbage / cucumber] *gimchi*[pickles] // 익은[덜 익은/신] ~ mellow[rare / sour] *gimchi* // ~를 담그다 prepare [make] *gimchi* / pickle [salt] vegetables.
- **김치찌개** *gimchijjigae*; *gimchi* soup; pork stew with *gimchi*.

김칫국 *gimchi*(kimchi) juice.

김칫국부터 마시다 (속담) count (one's) chickens before they are hatched; sell the skin before one has killed the bear; run before one's horse to market; jump the gun.

깁다 sew; stitch; mend; patch up(헝겊을 대고); darn(양말을). ¶기운 옷 patched clothes // 여기저기 흉하게 기운 상의 a coat patched [renewed] badly in places // 더덕더덕 기운 full of patches / patchy // 더덕더덕 기운 양말 socks darned over and over again // 옷을 ~ patch up clothes // 양말을 ~ darn socks // 신을 ~ mend one's shoes // 찢어진 데를 ~ darn [knit up / stitch up] a rent // 상의를 깁게 하다 get [have] one's coat patched up // 코트의 터진 곳을 ~ mend a rip in a coat // 나는 바지의 무릎을 헝겊을 대어 기웠다 I sewed patches on the knees of my trousers.

깁스 (⑤Gips) [석고] gypsum; plaster (of Paris); [석고 붕대] a (plaster) cast. ¶~를 하고 있다 wear a (plaster) cast / be put in plaster // 그는 다리에 ~를 하고 있다 His leg is in a (plaster) cast.

깃[1] [외양간 등에 까는 짚·풀] litter. ¶~을 깔다 litter down (a horse / a stable) / spread litter [straw bedding] // 마구간에는 새로운 ~이 듬뿍 깔려 있었다 The stable was well littered down with fresh straw.

깃[2] **1** [깃털] a feather; a plume; plumage. ¶아직 ~이 나지 않은 unfledged // ~이 나다 fledge / ~이 빠지다 shed feathers / feathers come off // ~을 갈다 molt // ~을 뽑다 pluck feathers (from a fowl) // ~을 다듬다 (a bird) preen its feathers / (a bird) plume itself. **2** (화살의) a feather; a wing. ¶화살에 ~을 달다 fean arrow.

깃[3] **1** a collar; a neckband. ⇨옷깃 ¶접는[세우는] ~ a turn-down[stand-up] collar // ~이 달린 블라우스 a blouse with a collar // ~이 없는 코트 a collarless coat / a coat without a collar // 양복 ~ 에 다는 배지 a lapel badge // 코트의 ~을 세우다 turn[pull] up the collar of one's overcoat // ~을 달다 sew a collar on a coat. **2** [이불깃] the upper strip on the outside of a quilt.

깃[4] tinder; touchwood. ⇨부싯깃.

깃대 (旗-) a flagpole; a flagstaff. ¶~에 기를 달다 run a flag up the flagpole.

깃들다 (정신이) dwell (in); (생각이) lodge (in).

깃들이다 (새가) build a nest; nest; put up a

깃발

nest; roost; [비유] lodge; dwell. ¶새는 나무에 깃들인다 Birds roost in[on] trees.

깃발 (旗―) a flag; banner; a standard(군기); a pennant [pennon] (긴 삼각형의); (집합적) bunting; [기치] one's attitude[stand] (태도); the platform[plank] (정강); [구호] a slogan; a motto (pl. ~(e)s). ¶자유의 ~ 아래[자유의 ~을 내걸고] under the slogan [watchword] of freedom / with "Freedom" as the slogan // ~을 휘날리며 with banners flying / with flying colors // …의 ~ 아래 모이다 flock to (a person's) standard // ~을 올리다 hoist [display / raise / lift / fly out] a flag // ~을 흔들다 wave a flag // ~을 내리다 take down a flag / strike[lower] a flag // ~이 바람에 펄럭이고 있다 The flag is streaming[floating / waving / fluttering] in the wind.

깃이불 a feather[down] quilt; a down coverlet; a feather bed; an eiderdown (quilt).

깃털 a feather; (장식용) a plume; (집합적) plumage; (얇은 털) down. ¶~이 다 난 새 a full-fledged[fully fledged] bird // ~이 뜯긴 새 a plucked bird // 그 새는 ~이 빠졌다[새 털로 갈았다] The bird shed its feathers [molted]. // 이것은 ~처럼 가볍다 This is as light as a feather. // 공작은 ~이 아름답다 Peacocks have beautiful plumage. // 그녀는 ~ 달린 모자를 쓰고 있었다 She wore a hat with a plume on it.

깊다 1 [바닥·속까지의 거리가 멀다] deep; [외지다] secluded; remote. ¶깊은 곳 a depth / a deep place / the deeps // 깊은 동굴 a deep cave // 깊은 산골짝 a deep valley // 깊은 협곡 a deep gorge // 깊은 산속에 deep in the mountains / far up (in) the mountain // 바닥을 알 수 없을 정도로 깊은 bottomless / fathomless // 늪지대의 깊은 곳에 빠지다 get stuck in[fall into] the depths of a swamp // 깊은 곳에 가지 마라 Keep within your depth. // 그 어린아이는 깊은 물속에 가라앉았다 The child sank into deep water. // 물은 그다지 깊지 않았다 The water was not very deep. / There was no great depth of water.

2 [심원하다] deep; profound; in(ner)most; [강렬하다] intense; strong. ¶깊은 애정 deep affections // 깊은 잠 (fall into) (a) deep [profound / sound / heavy] sleep [(문어) slumber] // 깊은 뜻 a deep[profound] meaning // 깊은 슬픔[사랑] deep sorrow [love] // 깊은 인상 a strong[deep / profound / an indelible] impression // 깊은 증오 intense[deep-seated / deep-rooted] hatred // 깊은 학식 profound learning[knowledge] // 우정을 깊게 하다 cement a friendship // 지식 [슬픔]을 깊게 하다 deepen one's knowledge [sorrow] // 이번 여행에서 그 나라에 대한 이해를 깊게 했다 My recent trip deepened my understanding of the country [made me understand the country better]. // 깊은 흥미를 갖고 있다 be deeply [profoundly] interested (in) // 그들의 애정은 날이 갈수록 깊어졌다 Their love deepened day by day. // 나는 그것에 대한 흥미가 더욱 더 깊어졌다 I became more and more interested in it. // 이야기에는 무엇인가 내게 깊은 감명을 주는 바가 있었다 There was something in the story that impressed me deeply. // 그 둘 사이의 대립은 아주 뿌리가 ~ The rivalry [bad feeling] between the two is deep-rooted.

3 [친밀하다] close; fast; intimate; (속어) thick. ¶깊은 관계 close connections / intimate relations / intimacy // 깊은 사이다 be an intimate terms[relations] (with) / be strongly bound by love (with) // …과 깊은 사이가 되다 become intimate with … // 그는 그녀와 깊은 사이다 He is thick [deeply in love] with her. // 그는 그녀와 깊은 관계에 있다 He has a serious relation-ship with her. // 그 두 남녀 사이는 깊은 관계다 They're deeply involved with each other. / They're not mere friends.

4 [시간이 늦다] late. ¶깊은 밤 the dead of night / midnight // 깊은 가을 late autumn / the latter part of autumn / (미) late fall // 밤이 깊어 감에 따라 as the evening wears on // 가을[밤]이 깊어 가고 있다 Autumn[The night] is getting far advanced. // 가을이 깊어졌다 It is late autumn. / We are well into autumn.

5 (상처가) serious; deep. ¶깊은 상처 a severe [bad] wound / a serious [mortal] wound / a gash // 깊은 상처를 입다 sustain[receive] a deep[severe] wound / be mortally [seriously] wounded.

깊숙하다 [깊다] deep; [으슥하다] sequestered; secluded; retired; covert; inmost. ¶깊숙한 골짜기 a deep valley // 깊숙한 방 a secluded [sequestered] room / an inner room / (미) a back room // 깊숙한 곳에 recess / a nook // 깊숙한 벽촌 a secluded villages // 안이 깊숙한 집 a house extending for back. **깊숙이** deep (down); deeply; far. ¶장롱에 ~ 넣다 put deep into a chest // 모자를 ~ 눌러쓰다 pull [draw down / slouch] one's hat (well) over one's eyes / wear one's hat low over one's eyes // 그녀는 안락의자에 ~ 앉았다 She sat deep in the armchair. // 탐험대는 그 나라 ~ 들어갔다 The expedition advanced deep in the country. // 정원 ~ 나무로 지은 오두막이 있었다 There was a wooden shed at the bottom of the garden.

깊이¹ depth; deepness; profundity. ¶~를 알 수 없는 bottomless / fathomless / unfathomable / abysmal // 매우 ~가 있는 사람 a man of great depth // 그녀의 지식의 ~ the profundity of her knowledge // 생각의 ~ profundity of thought // 애정의 ~ the depth of affection // 연못의 ~ the depth of a pond // ~가 있는 deep / profound // ~가 없는 lacking depth / shallow / superficial // ~는 5미터이다 be five meters deep[in depth] // ~를 재다 measure the depth (of a lake) / sound (the sea) / sound [plumb] the depth (of) / take depth measurements (of) // 그의 소설에는 ~가 없다 His novels lack depth[profundity]. // 그의 지식은 넓기는 하나 ~가 없다 His knowledge is wide [extensive] but not deep [profound]. / He knows something of everything but not everything of something. / He has put all his goods [has everything] in the shopwindow. // 이 작품은 인생의 ~를 느끼게 한다 This work makes one feel the profundity of life.

깊이² deep(ly); dead (asleep); profoundly; [충분히] up to one's lips; [진심으로] heartily; sincerely; [강력히] intensely; strongly; very much. ¶~ 뿌리박은 deep-rooted[-seated] / ingrain(ed) // ~ 파다 dig deep(ly) // ~ 숨을 쉬다 breathe (in) deep(ly) / take [draw] a deep breath // ~ 연구하다[배우다] study throughly / make a profound study (of) / make an exhaustive study of//~ 사랑하다 love (a person) deeply [dearly]//~ 잠들다 sleep soundly / sleep like a log[top]//잠 들어 있다 be sound[fast] asleep//생각에 ~ 잠겨 있다 be deep in thought//~ 머리를 숙이다 make a deep courtesy[bow]//너무 ~ 말려들다 go too far into an affair//나는 나의 그 행위를 ~ 뉘우치고 있다 I deeply regret (having done) it. / I'm very sorry I did it.//그는 그녀를 ~ 사랑하고 있다 He is deeply in love with her.//그는 그 사건에 너무 ~ 관련된 것 같다 He seems to have gotten[(영) got] too deeply involved in the matter.

까까머리 (a person with) a shaven(-bald) head; a close cropped head; (삭발한) a tonsure. ¶~**가 되다** have one's head shaved / have one's hair clipped//~로 깎았다 I had my hair close-cropped[cut close].

까까중 a person with a head shaved bald; (중) a bonze; a Buddhist priest[monk]. ¶~이 되다 have one's hair cut close.

까뀌 an adz(e). ¶~질하다 hew (a timber) with an adz(e) / adz(e) (a timber).

까끄라기 [식] (보리 등의) an awn; an arista (*pl.* -tae); a beard. ¶~가 있는 bearded / awned / aristate.

까놓다 (털어놓다) open one's heart (to); speak (out) one's mind; unbosom oneself (to); confide in (a person); confide (a secret) to (a person); lay bare one's mind. ¶까놓고 말하면 to be frank with you / frankly speaking / to speak honestly / in plain terms//까놓고 말하다 speak without reserve / exchange confidences with (each other) / be outspoken / talk frankly//까놓고 의견을 교환하다 have a frank and candid exchange of views (with)//까놓고 말하라 Speak your mind.//자네에게 까놓고 이야기하고 싶네 I want to confide in you.//너의 계획을 까놓고 말해 봐라 Come[Give] out with your plan.//그는 그 일의 전말을 까놓았다 He opened the whole affair.//까놓고 말하지 will be open[frank] with you. / I'll conceal nothing from you.

까다[1] **1** [제하다] take (away / out) (from); deduct (from); subtract (from). ¶세금을 까고 월 40만 원의 수입 a monthly income of 400,000 won after taxes//봉급에서 월부금을 ~ deduct a monthly installment from one's salary//본전에서 이자를 ~ take off[deduct] interest from the principal. **2** [가산을 축내다] reduce (one's fortune); lessen (one's fortune). **3** (줄다) become thin[thinner]; slim down.

까다[2] **1** (껍질을) peel; husk; crack; shell. ¶귤을 ~ peel a tangerine//밤을 ~ crack a chestnut//콩을 ~ hull beans//삶은 달걀을 ~ shell a boiled egg.
2 (살갗을) graze; abrade; skin. ¶무릎을 ~ have one's knee skinned//팔꿈치를 ~ scrape[skin] one's elbow//그 소년은 넘어져서 무릎을 깠다 The child fell and skinned his knees[scraped the skin off his knees].
3 [부화하다] hatch (out); incubate. ¶갓 깐 새 새끼 a nestling / a hatching//알을 ~ hatch an egg//암탉이 병아리를 깐다 A hen hatches out chickens.
4 [안의 것을 밖으로 내다] turn out; turn up.

¶불알을 ~ castrate / emasculate / geld / (미) alter//화투짝을 ~ turn up a card.
5 [치다] strike; hit; [차다] kick; give a kick. ¶이마를 돌로 ~ strike (a person) on the forehead with a stone//정강이를 ~ give (a person) a kick on the shin / kick (a person) in the (right) shin / [럭비] (미) hack.
6 [나쁘게 말하다] speak ill of; (구어) run down; [비판하다] criticize; (글로 써서) write down. ¶그는 선거 연설에서 상대 당을 호되게 깠다 In his campaign speech he really blasted the other party.//그는 정부의 시책을 호되게 깠다 He severely criticized the policy of the government.

까다[3] [입만 놀리다] talk glibly; quibble; sophisticate; have a clever tongue; be fair-spoken. ¶그는 입만 까고 실천이 없는 사람이다 He is all talk and no action. / He does not mean what he says.

까다롭다 1 (성미·취향이) fastidious (about); overnice; particular (about); hard to please. ¶성미가 까다로운 사람 a fastidious person / a person hard to please//식성이 ~ be fastidious[particular] about one's food / have too many likes and dislikes in what one eats//의복에 ~ be fastidious about one's dresses / have a fastidious taste in dress//그는 날 때부터 식성이 ~ He was born with a dainty tooth.//그는 넥타이를 고르는 데 ~ He's particular in his choice of[about his] ties.//그녀는 까다로운 시어머니를 잘 모셨다 She served her faultfinding mother-in-law faithfully.//그렇게 까다롭게 굴지 마 Don't be so fastidious.
2 [복잡하다] complicated; complex; intricate; [어렵다] difficult; hard; [성가시다] troublesome; vexing; delicate. ¶까다로운 문제 a knotty[complicated] problem / a hard nut to crack//까다로운 법률 용어 cramp law terms//까다로운 절차를 밟아 비자를 얻다 go through a complicated procedure[rigmarole] to get a visa//이 문제는 좀 ~ This problem is a little too hard to solve.//그런 짓을 하면 일은 더욱 까다로워진다 It will make the situation more delicate.
3 [엄격하다] strict; stringent; exacting; punctilious. ¶까다로운 규칙 a strict[stringent] rule / hard and fast rules//예절에 까다로운 사람 a stickler for etiquette//세관에서 까다롭게 굴 것 같다 The customs will make difficulties.//그렇게 까다롭게 굴지 말고 용서해 주어라 Don't be so exacting, and let him go.

까닭 1 [이유] a reason; [원인] a cause; [근거] ground; [동기] a motive; account. ¶무슨 ~으로 why / for what reason / on what ground//어쩌된 ~인지 for this[that] reason//…할 ~이 없다 there is no reason for ... / it cannot be ...//그렇게 생각한 ~이 있다 I have every reason to think so.//그것으로 ~을 알았다 That accounts for it.//거기에는 무슨 ~이 있음에 틀림없다 There must be some reason for it.//네가 저 선생을 미워하는 ~은 무엇인가 What is your reason for hating that teacher? / What makes you hate that teacher? / Why do you hate that teacher?(▶ 첫째와 둘째 예문은 부드러운 질문, 셋째는 단도직입적이나 좀 힐문조로 들리는 일이 많음)//그가 그렇게 바쁠 ~이 없다 He

까딱 can't be so[that] busy.//무슨 ~으로 사직했나요 What is your reason for resigning? / How come you left your company?//내가 빌어야 할 ~이 없다 Why should I apologize? / 그가 알 ~이 없다 How can he know it!//그는 ~이 있어 삼촌의 양자가 되었다 He was adopted by his uncle for a certain reason [for some reason] (▶ for a certain reason은 말하는 사람이 이유를 알고 있을 때, for some reason은 말하는 사람이 이유를 모를 때).
2 [연유] the history. ¶~이 붙은 with a history[past / story] / 그것에는 ~이 있다 There is a story about it. / 저 얼굴에는 무슨 ~이 있음에 틀림없다 That face must have a story.//집세가 굉장히 싸다고 생각했더니 역시 ~이 붙은 집이었다 I thought the rent was awfully low, and, sure enough, later I found out that the house had a strange history.

까딱 1 (고개를). **까딱하다** bob; nod. ¶알았다고 고개를 ~ nod in assent // 고개를 까딱하고 인사하다 bob one's head (in a bow) (to) / 그녀는 내게 머리를 가볍게 까딱했다 She nodded slightly to me. / She gave me a slight nod. **2** [조금 움직이는 모양]. **까딱하다** move slightly; budge. ¶저 게으름쟁이는 손가락 하나 까딱하지 않는다 That lazy fellow would not stir a finger [do a stitch of work]. **3** [자칫]. ¶여기서 ~ 잘못하면 큰일 난다 A false step at this point would lead to disaster.

까딱도 하지 않다 1 (물체가) do not move a muscle[turn a hair]; do not budge an inch. ¶그 문은 아무리 밀어도 까딱도 하지 않았다 No matter how I shoved, the door wouldn't budge an inch. **2** (사람이) keep cool and calm; remain unmoved; stand firm (against). ¶그는 아무리 욕을 퍼부어도 까딱도 하지 않았다 He remained calm [unmoved] in spite of the shower of abuse heaped on him.

까딱거리다 bob (one's head) up and down; nod (one's head) again and again. ¶알았다고 고개를 ~ nod in assent / show one's approval with a nod // 고개를 까딱거리며 졸다 nod in a doze / nid-nod.

까딱까딱하다 nod; bob; bubble. ¶고개를 서너번 ~ nod one's head several times.

까딱없다 1 (사물이) undamaged; uninjured; unspoiled; unimpaired; unaffected. ¶이 건물은 지진이 일어나도 ~ This building can withstand any earthquake. / This building is earthquake-proof.//그 회사는 불황에도 까딱없었다 The firm was quite unaffected by the economic panic.//그 불에도 금고는 까딱없었다 The safe remained intact in spite of the raging flames. **까딱없이** intactly; unaffectedly.
2 (마음이) unmoved; unruffled; unperturbed; cool; calm. ¶어르고 달래도 그는 까딱없었다 Neither threats nor coaxing could make him moved.//그는 그 소식을 듣고도 까딱없었다 He remained cool as a cucumber when he heard the news. **까딱없이** unmovedly; unperturbedly.

까라지다 (몸이) become feeble[droopy]; languish. ¶배가 고파 몸이 ~ languish from hunger.

까르르 ¶아이들의 ~ 웃는 소리가 밖에까지 들려왔다 Shrieks[Peals] of children's laughter was heard outside.

까르륵 ¶젖먹이가 ~ 울고 있었다 The baby was crying frantically.

까마귀 [동] a crow; a raven(갈까마귀); a bird of ill omen(별명). ¶~ 떼 a flock of crows // ~의 울음소리 cawing of a crow.

까마귀 고기를 먹었나(속담) Why are you so forgetful?

까마귀 날자 배 떨어진다(속담) It is just a coincidence that the two events has happened at the same time.

까마득하다 1 (거리가) far; faraway; remote; (구어) a long way (off). ¶그의 집은 저 언덕 너머 까마득한 곳에 있다 His home is far (away) beyond that hill.//비행기가 까마득한 하늘을 날아가는 것이 보였다 I saw an airplane flying in the distance.//부산까지 갈 길이 아직 ~ It is a long way yet to Busan. **까마득히** far away[out]; in the distance. ¶바다 위에 ~ 배가 보이기 시작했다 A ship came in sight far out at sea.
2 (시간이) distant; remote. ¶내가 런던에 갔던 것은 까마득한 옛날이다 I was a long time ago that I went to London.//그 전설은 까마득한 옛날부터 전해 내려오고 있다 The legend has been handed down from ancient times[the remote past]. **까마득히** far back; a long time ago. ¶그 이야기는 ~ 먼 옛날로 거슬러 올라간다 The story goes far back into the past.

까마아득하다 far; distant. ⇨까마득하다
까마중 [식] a (black) nightshade; a morel; a wonderberry.
까막눈 the eyes of an ignoramus.
● **까막눈이** an illiterate (person); an unlettered person.

까맣다 1 (빛깔이) deep-black; jet-[coal-] black; inky(-black). ¶까만 머리 raven (-black) hair / (윤기가 나는) jet-black hair / 그녀는 해변에 갔다가 까맣게 타서 돌아왔다 She returned home from the beach tanned all over. **2** [아득하다] far; far-off[-away]; in the distance; long way off. **3** [모르고 잊고 있다]. ¶나는 그것을 까맣게 잊고 있었다 I've forgotten all about it. / It has entirely slipped from my mind[slipped my memory]. // 나는 그 일을 까맣게 모르고 있었다 I know absolutely nothing about the matter.

까매지다 become[turn] black; blacken. ¶햇볕에 타서 ~ be[get] thoroughly tanned / be tanned almost black // 그의 얼굴은 햇볕에 타서 까매졌다 The sun bronzed his face.

까먹다 1 [까서 먹다] peel[rind / shuck / shell / crack] and eat. ¶귤을 ~ peel[rind] an orange and eat it // 호도를 ~ crack a nut and eat it.
2 [없애다] use up; spend all; squander; run through. ¶밑천을 다 ~ live on one's capital // 재산을 다 ~ lose [run through] one's fortune // 나는 병이 나서 저축한 돈을 다 까먹었다 My savings were eaten up by illness.//그는 아버지의 유산을 다 까먹었다 He used up[squandered] all the money he had inherited from his father.
3 [잊다] forget; be forgetful[oblivious] (of); lose. ¶가사[대사]를 ~ go blank // 나는 그녀의 이름을 까먹었다 Her name escapes me. / Her name has escaped[has slipped from / has eaten up] my memory.
4 [군것질하다] spend one's pocket money on candy[sweets].

까무러치다 faint[away]; lose consciousness

까무러치다 [one's senses]; swoon; black out(특히 비행 중에); (구어) pass out. ¶까무러쳐 쓰러지다 fall senseless[unconscious] / fall[drop] in a faint /까무러칠 듯이 놀라다 be frightened out of one's senses[wits] // 그 권투 선수는 얼굴에 일격을 맞고서 까무러쳤다 A blow to his face stunned the boxer. /그는 얻어맞고 까무러쳤다 He was knocked unconscious. / He was knocked out.

까무스름하다 a dark(-colored); darkish; sallow; dusky; swarthy. ¶피부가 까무스름한 사나이 a dark-complexion[-skinned] man.

까무잡잡하다 darkish; dusky; murky; dark; blackish. ¶까무잡잡한 피부 dark red skin.

까뭉개다 level (off). ¶아파트를 짓기 위해 야산을 ~ level the hill before building an apartment house // 철도를 건설하기 위해 산을 ~ cut through a mountain to construct a railway.

까바치다 tell tales (about); tell on (a person). ¶그 소년은 빌의 일을 선생님에게 까바쳤다 The boy told the teacher on Bill. //그는 동료의 일을 까바칠 그런 사람이 아니다 He's not the sort of person who would tell tales about his colleagues.

까발리다 1 (속에 든 것을) peel[shuck / sell] (something) out. 2 (비밀 등을) expose; disclose; reveal; uncover; bring to light. ¶남의 스캔들을 ~ bring a person's scandal to light // 남의 정체를 ~ unmask a person / disclose a person's identity.

까부라지다 1 (부피가 줄다) become smaller; diminish[dwindle] (in size). 2 (나른해지다) feel languid[weary / tired]; become heavy [dull]. ¶더워서 몸이 까부라진다 The heat makes me feel languid.

까부르다 1 (키로) winnow; fan. ¶곡식을 ~ winnow grain (from the chaff, dirt, etc.) / drive[blow] (chaff, dirt, etc.). 2 (위아래로 흔들다) dandle; dance. ¶까불러서 우는 아이를 달래다 pacify a baby by dandling[dancing] it.

까불거리다 1 (위아래로 흔들리다) move up and down lightly; flicker; flare; (배가) pitch; (차가) jolt. ¶촛불이 산들바람에 까불거렸다 The candle[candlelight] fluttered [quivered] in the breeze. //그 배는 폭풍우 속에서 상하 좌우로 까불거렸다 The ship was pitching and rolling in the storm. // 차는 울퉁불퉁한 길에서 몹시 까불거렸다 The car jolted badly over the rough road. 2 act like a clown. ⇨ ☞까불다2

까불까불 (등불이) flickeringly; flaringly; (경망하게) frivolously; flippantly. **까불까불하다** move up and down lightly; act like a clown. ⇨ ☞까불거리다

까불다 1 move up and down lightly. ⇨☞까불거리다1 ¶촛불이 간들간들 까불다가 꺼져 버렸다 The candle flickered out. 2 (우스꽝스러운 짓을 하다) act like a clown; clown; droll; be facetious; be merry; (어린이가) frisk; frolic; make merry. ¶(어린이에게) 까불지 말고 얌전히 있어라 Where're your manner? / Behave yourself. / Be a good boy. //까불지 마 (건방지게 굴지 마라) None of your cheek[sauce]!

까불다¹ [재물을 날리다] dissipate; squander; run through (one's fortune).

까불리다² [까부름을 당하다] be[get] winnowed; (까부르게 하다) make let (a person) winnow.

까불이 [까부는 사람] a droll[facetious] person; a droll; a merry-andrew; a buffoon; a joker; [까부는 아이] a jocose[sportive] boy.

까슬까슬하다 1 (성질이) hard-grained (character); intractable; rough; not docile. 2 (촉감이) rough (skin); rugged (surface); sandy. ¶까슬까슬한 촉감 a rough[sandy] feel // 까슬한 옷감 cloth of (a) rough texture // 이 종이는 ~ This paper feels rough. // 표면이 ~ The surface touches rough.

까옥 [까마귀 소리] cawing; a caw. ¶까마귀가 ~ ~ [깍깍] 울면서 날아갔다 The crow flew off cawing.

까지 1 [시간 또는 공간의 종결점] till; until; to; up[down] to(▶ until과 till은 그 뜻의 차이는 없으나 until 쪽이 다소 격식을 차린 감이 있음); [기한] by; by the time; not later than; before. ¶지금~ till[until by] now / by this time / up to now[the present] / hitherto // 오늘날~ up to this day / up to date // 최후~ to the last // 밤늦게~ till late at night // 아침부터 밤~ from morning till night // 봄부터 여름~ from spring to summer / all through spring and summer // 두 시부터 네 시~ from 2 to 4 o'clock // 이달 20일~ not[no] later than the 20th of this month / before the 21st of this month // 죽을 때~ 싸우다 fight till death // 백살~ 살다 live to (be) a hundred // 막판~ 버티다 hang on to the very end / stick around until the very end // 주말~ 비가 내릴 것이다 It will rain over the weekend. // 나는 여기서 절~ 자주 산책을 하곤 했었다 I often used to take a walk from here to that temple. // 회의가 정오~는 끝날 것이다 The meeting will be over by noon. // 그가 올 때~ 기다리시오 Wait until he comes. // 그는 12살 때~ 큰아버지 댁에서 자랐다 He was raised at his uncle's up to the age of twelve. // 전쟁이 언제~ 계속될지 아무도 알 수가 없다 No one could tell how long the war would continue. // 5시~는 돌아오마 I will be back by 5. // 찌는 듯한 더위가 9월~ 계속되었다 The heat of the summer lasted into September. // 그가 올 때~는 완성됩니다 It will be ready by the time he comes here. // 지금~는 좋다 So far, so good.

2 [장소] to; as far as; [정도·범위] to the extent of; even; [한도] up to; to the limit; so much. ¶부산~의 차표 a ticket to Busan // 부산~ 가는 열차 a train for Busan // 10피트의 깊이~ 가라앉다 sink to a depth of ten feet // 10페이지~ 읽다 read to [as far as] page 10 // 마지막 한 방울~ 마시다 drink (the wine) to the very last drop // 어디~ 가십니까 Where are you going? / How far do you go? // 열차로 두 시간~ 걸리지는 않는다 It won't take even two hours by train. // 옷~ 다 타 버렸다 Even my clothes were burnt. // 그렇게~ 할 필요는 없다 There is no need of going so far[to go that far]. // 회사에서 50만 원~ 빌릴 수 있다 I can get a loan of money to the extent of ₩500,000 from my company. // 이 홀은 2,000명~ 수용할 수 있다 This hall can hold[accomodate] up to two thousand people.

3 [게다가] moreover; besides; what is more; in addition to (that); to make matters worse; what is worse. ¶길이 바쁜데 차~ 고장 났다 I was in a hurry[pressed for time] and, to

까지다 make matters worse, even the car broke down.// 그는 책뿐만 아니라 많은 그림~ 내게 주었다 He gave me books and many pictures besides.// 노인들~ 춤추고 있다 Even old people are dancing.// 엎드리기~는 하지 않더라도 사과의 말 한 마디쯤 하는 것이 어떤가 Even if you don't go so far as to grovel, how about a simple apology. / Nobody is asking you to prostrate yourself, but you could say you're sorry!

까지다 1 (피부 등이) be grazed [abraded / chafed]; (껍질이) peel (off). ¶무릎이 ~ have one's knee skinned. **2** [줄이다] (재산 등이) decrease; diminish; run low.

-까짓 […만한 정도의] such as [like]; any [some] such; [하찮은] so trifling; so little. ¶네~ such as you / (a person) like you// 제~ such as him [her / them].

까치 [동] a Korean magpie.
● **까치걸음** a bouncy walk [gait].

까치발 [건] a bracket; tripod; a brace; a cross-arm; a strut; (집합적) bracketing.

까칠하다 haggard; exhausted; emaciated; gaunt; thin; careworn; look worn out. ¶까칠한 얼굴 a haggard [worn] face// 까칠해지다 get [become] thin [haggard / emaciated] / be worn out / waste [pine / fall] away.

까탈 [방해] a hindrance; a hitch; an obstacle; an obstruction; an impediment; a stumbling block. ¶~ 없이 without a hitch / without let or hindrance / smoothly// ~ 없이 진행되다 proceed unhindered [without hindrance] / 일이 끝날 때까지는 여러 가지 ~이 있을지도 모른다 You may run into all sorts of obstacles before you finish the job. // 그는 이러니저러니 ~을 부려서 그 혼담을 깨려고 했다 He tried to break off the engagement on some pretext or other.

까탈스럽다 →까다롭다
까투리 [암꿩] a hen pheasant.
까풀 the outer layer of the skin; the film; scum; skim. ¶~이 지다 get a skin on it / be coated.

깍깍 (까마귀가 우는 소리) caw; crow. ¶까마귀가 ~ 울고 있었다 A crow was cawing [croaking].

깍두기 kkakdugi; sliced [cubed] radish gimchi (kimchi).

깍둑거리다 cut [chop] in uneven bits.

깍듯하다 well-mannered; mannerly; polite; civil; courteous. ¶예의범절이 깍듯한 사람 a well-mannered person// 그는 예의범절이 ~ He has good manners. / He is well-mannered. **깍듯이** politely; courteously; with much courtesy; civilly; in a civil way; respectfully. ¶남에게 ~ 대하다 be polite [civil] to others// ~ 인사하다 greet [salute] politely [deeply] // ~ make a low [deep / polite] bow.

깍쟁이 1 [약빠른 사람] a shrewd person; a sharp customer; a cunning fellow; a sly dog. ¶서울 ~ a shrewd Seoulite// 저 서울 ~들을 조심하세요 Watch out for those Seoul slickers. // 그렇게 ~ 노릇 하지 말아요 Don't be such a stinker. **2** [인색한 사람] a stingy person; (미국 구어) a tightwad; a niggard; a miser. ¶~ 짓을 하다 be stingy with one's money.

깍지¹ [꼬투리] a pod; a hull; a shell; a shuck; (완두의) a peas(e)cod. ¶~ 속에 든 콩 beans in the pods // ~를 까다 shell [pod] (peas).

깍지² (활 쓸 때의) a horn ring for the thumb (in archery).
깍지(를) 끼다 put the archer's thimble on the thumb.
깍지(를) 떼다 shoot [discharge / let off] an arrow.

깎다 1 (머리를) cut; clip; crop; dress; (단발로) bob; (미국 속어) shingle. ¶머리를 짧게 깎고 with one's hair cropped short [close] // 갓 깎은 머리 newly cropped (head) / just clipped [dressed] (head) // 머리를 짧게 ~ cut one's hair short / have one's hair cut short // 머리를 깎고 중이 되다 take the tonsure (to be a monk) // 머리 좀 깎아 주시오 I want to have my hair cut. / I want a hair-cut. // 네 머리를 깎아야겠구나 Your hair wants cutting [dressing].

2 (잔디·손톱·나무 등을) trim; prune; dress; mow. ¶잔디 깎는 기계 a lawn mower // 손톱을 ~ trim [cut] one's nails // 철쭉을 깎아 다듬다 trim an azalea // 오늘 잔디를 깎아야겠소 I need my lawn yard be mowed today.

3 (수염·양털 등을) shave; shear; fleece. ¶수염을 갓 깎은 freshly shaven // 수염을 ~ shave oneself / (남을 시켜서) get oneself shaved (by) // 전기면도기로 수염을 ~ shave with an electric razor // 양털을 ~ shear wool from a sheep // 천의 보풀을 ~ shear cloth // 그는 닷새 동안 수염을 깎지 않아 텁수룩하다 He has five day's stubble on his face. / He wears a five-day beard.

4 (연필·목재 등을) shave (wood); plane (a plank); sharpen (a pencil); whittle; chip. ¶판자를 ~ plane a piece of board // 그는 나뭇조각을 깎고 있었다 He was whittling at a piece of wood. // 그는 나무를 깎아서 대체적인 모양을 만들었다 He whittled the wood into a rough figure.

5 [껍질을 벗기다] pare; peel. ¶배 [사과]를 ~ peel a pear [an apple].

6 [예산 등을 삭감하다] cut down; curtail; reduce; retrench; slash; whittle down [away / off]. ¶비용을 ~ curtail [cut down / reduce] the expenses // 월급을 만 원 ~ cut down (a person's) salary by 10,000 won // 예산을 ~ reduce the budget // 정부의 지출을 ~ slash government expenses // 그는 그 계획의 비용을 깎았다 He whittled down the cost of the project.

7 [체면 등을 손상시키다] bring disgrace upon; dishonor; disgrace; stain; make (a person) lose face [countenance]; run down; put to shame. ¶집안의 체면을 ~ throw [reflect] discredit upon one's family // 아들이 못되어서 아버지 낯을 깎는다 The son disgraces his father by his misbehavior.

8 (값을) cut; reduce; come down; beat [knock / whittle] down the price; lower; take off; abate; make (it) cheaper; slash; bargain down. ¶값을 천 원으로 ~ beat (the dealer) down to 1,000 won // 값을 몹시 깎아 내리다 drive a hard bargain // 1할 깎아 주다 take off ten percent // 좀 더 깎아 주시오 Come down a little more. // 깎아 주시지 않겠습니까 Can't you make it cheaper? / Can't you take something off of that? // 백 원 깎아 드리죠 I'll take a hundred won off the price. // 값은 깎지 마십시오 We do not bargain; our prices are fixed. // 최대로 깎아서 천 원에 드리겠습니다 Slashing the price to the lowest, I will let it

go at a thousand won.
9 [주었던 지위를 빼앗다] dismiss from (an office); fire. ¶벼슬을 ~ dismiss (a person) from his office.
10 [절삭하다] cut; turn. ¶금속을 ~ turn metal∥(녹로로) 책상 다리를 ~ turn the legs of tables.
11 (공을) cut.

깎아내리다 speak ill [evil] of; speak slightingly of; condemn; abuse; slander.

깎아지르다 be precipitous; be very [extremely] steep. ¶깎아지른 듯한 암벽 a precipitous wall of rock.

깎이다 1 [깎게 하다] make [have] (a person) cut [trim]; get (a person) to cut [mow / peel / pare]. ¶머리를 ~ have one's hair cut [trimmed]∥손톱을 ~ have one's fingernail pared [cut / trimmed].
2 [깎음을 당하다] be shaved [trimmed / sharpened / cut / pared / mowed]. ¶풀이 깎였다 The grass was cut. / The lawn was mowed.∥저 연필은 잘 깎인다 That pencil sharpens nicely.
3 (값·예산·봉급 등이) be reduced; be slashed; be bargained [beat] down; be cut down. ¶값이 3할 깎였다 The price was reduced thirty percent.∥영업 부진으로 그의 봉급이 대폭 깎였다 His salary was slashed as business became dull.
4 [삭제되다] be rubbed out; be deleted; be erased; (신문 검열에서) be blue-penciled. ¶법안이 한 항목 깎였다 A section in a bill is deleted [stricken out].
5 (명예·체면이) be disgraced; be put to shame; be blemished. ¶낯이 ~ lose one's honor [face] / disgrace oneself∥그런 짓을 하면 네 체면이 깎인다 Such conduct will disgrace you.
6 (직책·계급이) be taken away; be fired (from); be dismissed (from). ¶그는 부주의 탓으로 깎였다 He was dismissed from the service for carelessness.
7 [침식되다] be wave-beaten; be weather-beaten. ¶물에 깎인 바위 water-worn rocks∥오랜 세월에 깎여서 보이지 않게 된 묘비명 an epitaph worn away by the years.

깐 →**따**²

깐깐하다 [끈질기다] sticky; [완고하다] pertinacious; tenacious; [세심하다] meticulous; inquisitive; careful; [까다롭다] fastidious; particular; hard-grained (character). ¶성미가 깐깐한 사람 a man of hard-grained character / a particular person∥깐깐한 기질 a fastidious mind∥그렇게 깐깐하게 굴지 마라 Don't be so tenacious. **깐깐히** carefully; strictly; scrupulously; meticulously; exactly. ¶~ 조사하다 examine carefully∥~ 캐어묻다 grill (a person) / inquire (a person) in great details∥일을 ~ 하다 put great care into one's work / work conscientiously.

깔개 an underlay (물건 밑에 까는); a carpet; a rug (융단); matting (돗자리 등); a cushion (방석); a footcloth; a floorcloth (마루의). ¶마루에 ~를 깔다 lay [put down] a carpet on the floor.

깔기다 (오줌·똥을) relieve oneself [nature] indiscriminately; discharge (excrements) irrespective of [regardless of] places; (알을) lay eggs all over. ¶길가에다 오줌을 ~ make [pass] water by the side of the road∥똥을 아무 데나 ~ use a fresh-air toilet.

깔깔 ¶~ 웃으면서 with a high laugh∥~ 웃다 laugh aloud [loudly] / roar with laughter / laugh uproariously [heartily]∥소녀는 ~ 웃었다 The little girl laughed merrily.

깔깔거리다 laugh loudly [aloud]; scream [roar] with laughter; guffaw; burst out laughing; burst into laughter; cachinnate; cackle. ¶그는 깔깔거렸다 He gave a loud, cheerful laugh.

깔깔하다 1 (감촉이) rough (surface / texture); coarse (grain); sandy. ¶깔깔한 촉감 a rough [sandy] feel∥깔깔한 피부 rough skin∥이 종이는 ~ This paper feels rough.∥혓바닥이 ~ My tongue is rough. / I have a rough tongue. **2** (성미가) particular; fastidious; moody; touchy; fussy; unrefined. ¶성미가 깔깔한 사람 a touchy person.

깔그럽다 1 [거칠다] rough (surface); coarse. ¶깔그러운 나무껍질 rugged bark∥먹으면 혀가 ~ feel rough to the tongue. **2** [따끔거리다] prickly; prickling. ¶깔그러운 털내복 itchy woolen underwear∥이 내복은 ~ This undershirt scratches.

깔끔거리다 prick; prickle; tingle; be irritated.

깔끔하다 (외양이) sleek and clean; smart; neat and tidy [trim]; (성질이) sharp; harsh; fastidious. ¶깔끔하지 못한 slovenly / untidy∥깔끔한 사람 a person fond of cleanliness / a stickler for cleanness∥깔끔한 성질 a sharp temper∥차림새가 ~ be neatly dressed / be neat in appearance∥그는 깔끔한 사람이다 He has neat habits. / He is habitually clean and tidy.∥그녀는 언제나 차림새가 ~ She always dresses neatly. / She is always neat and clean.∥그녀는 옷차림 [행동]이 깔끔하지 못하다 She is slovenly [untidy] in appearance [her conduct].∥그의 일은 깔끔하지 못하다 He works in a slipshod way. / He does his work any which way [(영) any old how].

깔다 1 (깔개 등을) spread; lay [put down] (a carpet on the floor). ¶마루에 돗자리를 ~ lay mats on the floor∥상자 바닥에 종이를 ~ cover the bottom of a box with paper∥이부자리를 ~ make a bed.
2 (자갈 등을) pave; pitch. ¶도로에 아스팔트를 ~ pave (streets) with asphalt.
3 (방석 등을) sit on [seat oneself] (a cushion). ¶이 방석을 깔고 앉으십시오 Please take your seat on this cushion. / Please take [use] a (floor) cushion.
4 (돈·상품 등을) lend out (money / grain) widely; invest (in). ¶빚을 몇 군데 ~ lend money to several persons∥여러 가지 사업에 돈을 깔아 놓다 invest [put] money in various business.
5 [억누르다]. ¶남편을 깔고 앉다 dominate one's husband / keep one's husband under one's thumb.

깔딱 [삼키는 소리] with [at] a gulp; [숨이 넘어가는 모양] with gasps; [뒤집히는 소리] cracking; crackling; popping; snapping. ¶~ 삼키다 gulp down / drink at a gulp∥숨이 ~ 넘어가다 breathe one's last (breath) / gasp one's life away / give up one's breath / die.

깔딱하다 gulp; gasp for breath; crack; crackle; pop; snap.

깔딱거리다 1 (목이) gulp; drink with a gulp. **2** (숨이) pant; gasp. ¶숨을 ~ breathe with dif-

깔딱깔딱 with a gulp.
깔때기 a funnel. ¶~ 모양의 funnel-shaped.
깔리다 1 [널리 흩어져 있다] be (over)spread; be covered; be scattered; be dispersed. ¶자갈이 깔린 길 a road covered with gravel / a graveled road // 낙엽이 땅에 깔려 있다 The fallen leaves lie scattered on the ground. / The ground is scattered with fallen leaves. // 시내에 온통 경찰이 깔려 있었다 The policeman covered the whole city. // 구름이 낮게 깔려 있다 Clouds are hanging low. **2** [밑에 눌리다] be buried [pressed / pinned / held / caught]; be knocked down (by); be sat on (by). ¶자동차에 ~ be run over by a car // 그는 떨어진 바위에 깔려 죽었다 He was crushed to death under the loosened rocks.
깔보다 look down on; think [make] little [nothing] of; despise; disparage; depreciate; belittle. ¶남의 능력을 ~ undervalue a person's ability // 사람을 깔보는 버릇이 있다 have a habit of looking down on people // 그것은 나를 깔보고 하는 말이다 You slight me by saying that. // 너의 처사는 나를 깔보고 하는 짓이다 I take your treatment as an insult to me. // 그는 항상 나를 깔보고 있다 He always looks down on [makes light of] me. // 가진 것이 없다고 깔보지 마라 Do not hold me so cheap [in contempt] only because I have nothing [I am penniless].
깔아뭉개다 1 [깔고 뭉개다] press down; compress; squeeze; [앉아서 뭉개다] sit on (a thing) and mash it.
2 (일을) pigeonhole; put [lay / cast] on the shelf; (미) lay on the table; (미) side track; (미) table; (사실 등을) keep [conceal / hide] (a matter from a person); [secrets] [cover up / stifle up / smother up] (a fact). ¶제안을 ~ shelve [smother up] a proposal // 법안을 ~ shelve [pigeonhole / strangle / burke / kill] a bill.
3 [억누르다] press [put / hold / keep] down; hold in check; keep back; suppress. ¶남편을 ~ dominate one's husband / keep one's husband under one's thumb / have one's husband in one's pocket // 자존심을 ~ put one's pride in one's pocket / pocket one's pride.
깔짝거리다 [따짝거리다] eat a bit of everything; gnaw (at). ¶쥐들이 그 목공품을 깔짝거리고 있었다 Rats were eating away the woodwork.
깔쭉거리다 feel rough; be sandy [gritty]; be rough to feel [touch].
깔쭉깔쭉하다 rough; coarse; sandy; granular; gritty; notched; jagged; (화폐가) milled. ¶깔쭉깔쭉한 상어의 이빨 the jagged teeth of a shark // 깔쭉깔쭉하게 하다 notch / jag / make notches / mill (동전의 가장자리를) // 그 100원짜리 동전은 가장자리가 ~ The 100 won coin has a milled edge.
깜깜하다 1 [어둡다] very dark; pitch-dark; (as) dark as pitch; (as) dark [black] as midnight. ¶깜깜한 밤 a jet black [pitch-dark] night // 깜깜한 속에서 in utter [dead / thick] darkness // 깜깜해지다 become [get] dark / darken // 방 안은 아주 깜깜하였다 It was pitch-dark within the room. // (어지러워서) 눈앞이 깜깜해진다 Everything is going black. **2** [모르다] ignorant; blank; unlearned. ¶나는 과학에는 ~ I am unlearned in science. // 그런 일이라면 아주 ~ I know nothing about matters of that kind.
깜둥이 1 [흑인] a Negro (pl. ~es); a colored man; (구어) a nigger; a darky; a blackie; a black(e)y. **2** [얼굴이 검은 사람] a dark-faced person.
깜박 1 (등불·별빛 등이) with a flash; with a twinkle. **깜박하다** flicker; twinkle; blink. ¶촛불이 바람에 깜박하다가 꺼졌다 The candle flickered out in the wind. // 별이 ~ a star twinkles.
2 (눈을) with a blink [blinking]; with a wink. **깜박하다** blink; wink. ¶눈을 ~ blink one's eyes // 그녀는 알았다는 듯이 눈을 깜박했다 She winked knowingly at me.
3 (정신이) 순간적으로 흐려지는 모양). ¶~ 속다 be nicely [fairly] taken in / be taken in unawares / be swindled before (a person) knows it // ~ 졸다 have a snatch of sleep // 나는 약속을 ~ 잊어 먹었다 The appointment slipped my mind. / I carelessly forgot my appointment. **깜박하다** forget for the moment; (일이) escape one's memory; slip from [out of] one's memory. ¶나는 가끔 깜박한다 My memory often fails me. // 정신이 깜박한다 My mind dims [gives away] for a moment.
깜박거리다 1 (별이) twinkle; (불이) flicker; waver; shimmer. ¶깜박거리는 등불 a blink of light / a flickering light // 깜박거리는 별들 twinkling stars. **2** (눈을) blink (one's eyes); wink; nictitate. ¶그녀는 눈물을 감추려고 눈을 깜박거렸다 She blinked to stop the tears.
3 (정신이) be vague [indistinct / hazy / misty / dim]. ¶정신이 깜박거린다 My mind keeps giving way [dimming / blacking out].
깜박깜박 flickeringly; waveringly; faintly; dimly; with repeated blinking [flickering / wavering]. ¶~ 졸다 doze off / nod [rock] in a doze // 멀리서 등불이 ~ 비치고 있었다 I saw a flickering light in the distance. **깜박깜박하다** twinkle; flicker; blink (one's eyes); be vague. ⇨깜박이숯⇨깜부기) 눈이 부셔 ~ blink in the strong light.
깜부기 1 [깜부깃병으로 까맣게 된 이삭] a smut ball; a smutted ear (of barley); a blighted ear of grain. **2** [얼굴이 까만 사람] a dark-complexioned [-faced] person. **3** cinders. ⇨깜부기숯⇨깜부기)
● **깜부기숯** cinders; charred firewood. **깜부깃병** (一病) smut; dustbrand; bunt.
깜빡 with a flash; with a blink. ⇨깜박
깜빡깜빡 flickeringly; waveringly. ⇨깜박깜박
깜짝 with a wink. ⇨깜짝¹
깜짝거리다 keep winking. ⇨깜짝거리다1
깜짝이다 wink (one's eyes). ⇨깜짝이다
깜장 [검은 빛깔] black.
깜짝¹ [눈을 떴다 감는 모양] with a wink; with a blink [blinking]. **깜짝하다** wink [blink] (one's eyes); (미) bat one's eyes [eyelids]. ¶눈 하나 깜짝하지 않다 do not flicker an eyelash / [태연자약하다] be perfectly calm and collected.
깜짝² [놀라는 모양] with surprise; with a start. ¶~ 놀라다 be startled out of one's wits / be struck all of a heap / be thunderstruck / one's heart leaps into one's mouth / bat an eyelid / eyebrows go up / be rocked on one's heel // ~ 놀라게 하다 startle /

astonish / take (a person) by surprise / take (a person's) breath away / knock the breath out of (a person) / strike (a person) dumb // 세상을 ~ 놀라게 하다 startle the world / cause the public to gasp with surprise // ~ 놀라 기절하다 faint from fright // 놀라 눈을 뜨다 awake with a start // 나는 ~ 놀랐다 I was very surprised. // 이제 봐, 자네들을 ~ 놀라게 하겠다 Watch this, because it's going to amaze you. // 그는 그 기발한 학설로 세상을 ~ 놀라게 했다 He astonished the public [caused a sensation] with his novel theory. // 그는 감쪽같은 요술로 모두를 ~ 놀라게 했다 His trick was so exquisite that it took people's breath away. // 자네를 ~ 놀래 줄 일이 있다 I have a surprise (in store) for you. // 그 소리에 ~ 놀라 사슴은 귀를 쫑긋 세웠다 Startled at [by] the noise, the deer pricked up its ears. // 검은 그림자를 보고 나는 ~ 놀랐다 I started at the sight of a dark figure. // 무서움에 ~ 놀라 나는 그 자리에서 꼼짝 않고 섰다 Struck with terror, I stopped dead in my tracks.

깜짝거리다 1 (눈을) keep winking. 2 (놀라다) repeatedly start up with surprise; jump with a start again and again.

깜짝깜짝 1 (눈을 깜박거리는 모양) with repeated winking [blinking]. **깜짝깜짝하다** blink repeatedly; wink (one's eyes). 2 (놀라는 모양) with repeated starts. ¶자면서 ~ 놀라다 startle repeatedly in one's sleep.

깜짝이다 wink [blink] (one's eyes); (미) bat one's eyes [eyelids]; (의미 있는 눈짓으로) give (a person) a significant wink; wink (at). ¶알았다는 듯이 눈을 ~ give (a person) a knowing wink.

깜짝이야 Oh, shocks!; Oh my!; My eye; What a surprise!; Goodness gracious!; What a start you gave me!

깜찍하다 1 (영악하다) too clever for one's age; precocious; too sharp; overly shrewd; cunning; crafty; sly; selfish. ¶깜찍한 놈 a foxy fellow // 그 계집애 참 ~ The girl is quite precocious. / What a clever girl!! / 어린것이 참 깜찍한 소리를 한다 Though a mere child, he says quite a sensible [smart] thing. 2 (작고 귀엽다) surprisingly [cleverly] small; saucy; cute. ¶깜찍한 모자 a saucy little hat // 그 개 깜찍하게도 작다 What a tiny dog it is!

깜죽거리다 behave frivolously; put on airs. ⇨껍죽거리다

깡 〈속〉 a competitive spirit. ⇨깡다구

깡그리 all; wholly; entirely; utterly; without (an) exception. ¶빚을 ~ 갚다 pay [repay] all one's debts // ~ 자백하다 make a clean breast of / make a complete confession // 나는 그 일을 ~ 잊고 있었다 I've clean [utterly] forgotten the matter. // 그것을 ~ 먹어 치워라 Eat it all up.

깡그리다 complete [finish]; bring (a matter) to finish; round out [off].

깡깡 (악기) a two-stringed fiddle.

깡다구 〈속〉 a competitive spirit. ⇨오기(傲氣)

깡똥하다 (옷이) unbecomingly short; very [too] short. ¶깡똥한 옷 a garment too short for (a person) // 깡똥한 옷을 입고 있다 be in [wear] a very short garment.

깡마르다 1 (바싹 마르다) dry and hard; dry as a brick; parched. ¶깡마른 논 a parched [suncracked] paddy. 2 (야위다) thin; skinny; haggard; lean; gaunt; rawboned. ¶깡마른 사람 a lean and scrawny person / a slender person.

깡충깡충 1 ~ 뛰다 hop / skip / jump up and down / (뛰어다니다) romp / frisk [gambol] about // ~ 뛰면서 좋아하다 skip about for joy / leap [jump] for [with] joy // ~ 뛰듯이 (미국 구어) hippety-hop(pety).

깡통 (-筒) (미) a can; (영) a tin; an empty (tin) can; (머리가 텅 빈 사람) an empty-headed fellow; a rattlebrain. ¶빈 ~ an empty can // ~ 맥주 canned beer // ~을 따다 open a tin [can].

깡통(을) 차다 be reduced to begging; go [become] bankrupt; fail; (구어) go bust; go to pot.

● **깡통 따개** a can [(영) a tin] opener. ¶~가 붙어 있는 뚜껑 a cutter lid // ~가 필요없는 깡통 a pop-top can.

깡패 (-牌) hoodlums; a rough; a good-for-nothing; a gangster; a ruffian; a racketeer; a blackguard; (속어) a heavy; a hood; a tough. ¶정치 ~ a political adventurer // ~ 사회의 규율 the code of the underground.

깨 (식) (참깨) sesame; a gingili (plant); (들깨) wild sesame; green perilla; (씨) sesame seed; perilla seed. ¶검은 ~ black sesame // ~를 빻다 grind sesame seeds // 그 신혼부부는 ~가 쏟아진다 The newly-married couple live very happily together.

깨갱깨갱 (강아지의 소리) whining; yelp; yip; yap. ¶강아지가 ~ 을었다 The puppy cried, "Yap, yap, yap." **깨갱깨갱하다** whine; yap; yelp; yip.

깨끗하다 1 (청결하다) stainless; unsoiled; clean; (단정하다) neat (and clean); tidy; trim; smart. ¶깨끗한 방 a neat [clean] room // 그녀의 차림은 깨끗하고 단정하였다 Her appearance was tidy and neat. // 그녀는 목욕하고 깨끗한 옷으로 갈아입었다 She bathed and put on a clean dress. // 모든 것이 깨끗하고 잘 정돈되어 있었다 Everything was clean and in perfect order. // 이 행주는 깨끗합니까 Is this dishcloth clean? **깨끗이** (청결히) clean(ly); cleanlily; (단정히) neatly; tidily. ¶~ 하다 clean / cleanse / make clean / purify / (치우다) put in order / tidy (up) / make tidy [neat] // 방을 ~ 쓸다 sweep a room clean / tidy up a room // 손을 ~ 씻어라 Wash your hands. // 그 아이는 언제나 ~ 차려입고 있었다 The child was always neatly dressed. // 방은 ~ 치워져 있었다 The room was clean and tidy. // 거리를 ~ 합시다 (게시) Keep the town tidy.

2 (맑다) clear; limpid; clean; (순수하다) pure. ¶깨끗한 물 clear [clean] water / (오염되지 않다) unpolluted [pure] water // 깨끗한 공기 clean [fresh] air (of the morning) / unpolluted air // 하늘은 맑고 ~ The sky was bright and clear. // 호수는 바닥이 보이도록 ~ The lake is clear to the bottom.

3 (완전하다) clean; complete; entire; all; whole. ¶깨끗한 청산 clean liquidation // 그의 태만은 드디어 깨끗한 실패를 가져왔다 At last his idleness gave rise to a complete failure. // 병이 완치되어 그는 깨끗한 몸이 되었다 He recovered from illness and felt well in his mind and body. **깨끗이** clean; completely; wholly; thoroughly; entirely; once (and) for

all. ¶셈을 ~ 치르다 settle the accounts in full[completely]//빚을 ~ 갚다 pay[clear] off one's debts//(병이) ~ 낫다 recover completely (from one's illness) / be quite well again.
4 [결백하다] pure; clean; immaculate. ¶깨끗한 사랑 platonic[pure] love//깨끗한 마음 a pure heart[soul]//깨끗한 일생 a career with a clean record//마음이 깨끗한 사람은 행복하도다 Blessed are the pure in heart.//그는 마음이 ~ He is fair[honest] at heart.//그의 경력이야 깨끗하지요 There is no stain in his personal history.//그는 금전에 관해서는 ~ He has clean hands as regards money. **깨끗이** clearly; purely; cleanly. ¶~ 교제하다 have a real friendship (with) / (남녀간에) be in platonic love (with)// ~ 살다 live cleanly / live an honest[a clean / a pure] life / lead an immaculate life// 그는 ~ 죽었다 He died a noble death. / He died honorably.
5 [공정하다] fair; clean; (fair and) square; just. ¶깨끗한 태도 a fair[impartial] attitude//깨끗한 승부 fair play//깨끗한 선거 a clean election//깨끗한 한 표 an honest[a clean] vote//깨끗한 한 표를 던지다 cast a vote for (a person) from one's free will//이번 선거에서는 깨끗한 투표를 합시다 In the forthcoming election let's vote conscientiously.//이기든 지든 깨끗한 승부를 하라 Play fair to win or to lose. **깨끗이** fairly (and squarely); openly; clean. ¶~ 싸우다 play fair / fight openly and squarely// ~ 처리하다 deal fairly with (a matter)// ~ 사과하다 have the grace to apologize//그는 자신의 잘못을 ~ 인정했다 He frankly admitted his fault.//그 사람은 질 때는 ~ 진다 He is good loser.//그는 ~ 질 줄 모른다 He is a bad loser.// ~ 겨루자 Let's play fair.

깨끼(옷) kkaekki clothes; an early summer outfit for ladies which has silk gauze lining, hemmed with elaborate seams.

깨나다 **1** [의식을 찾게 되다] regain[recover] consciousness; return[come back] to life; come to life (again); come round (to oneself); come to oneself; be brought (back) to life; be restored from apparent death; rise from the dead[grave] (죽었던 사람이). ¶기절했다가 ~ regain one's consciousness after a fainting spell / come out of a faint//마취에서 ~ come out from under the anesthesia//남을 깨나게 하다 bring a person back to life / restore a person to consciousness / revive a (drowned) person (by artificial respiration).
2 (미몽에서) be awakened from an illusion[a delusion]; be disillusioned[undeceived]; come to one's senses. ¶그는 아직도 환상에서 깨나지 못했다 He is not yet awakened from the illusion.
3 (술에서) become sober; sober up[off]. ¶술에서 깨나 보니 내가 도랑에 자고 있었다 When I came to, I found myself lying in the ditch.
4 [생기를 되찾다] be brightened up; be freshened; be refreshed; be brought out; be invigorated.

깨나른하다 languid; weary; dull; wearisome; listless. ¶더워서 몸이 ~ The heat makes me feel languid.//깨나른해서 일하기가 싫다 I feel too lazy to work.

깨다[1] **1** (잠·꿈에서) wake (up); awake from sleep[a dream]. ¶잠이 ~ awake[be roused] from one's sleep / have one's sleep interrupted//자주 잠이 ~ be a light sleeper / have a broken sleep / awake often from one's sleep//잠이 덜 ~ be half awake [asleep] / be sleep-drunk//나는 심한 폭풍우 때문에 잠이 깼다 I was awakened[(문어) aroused] from my sleep by a heavy storm.//나는 여섯 시에 잠에서 깼다 I woke (up) at six.//잠이 깨어 정신이 맑아지도록 나는 커피를 마셨다 I drank coffee to wake myself up.//어느 날 아침 깨어 보니 나는 일약 유명해진 것을 알았다 I awoke one morning to find myself famous.
2 (미혹·환상에서) awake (from); be aroused; become sensible; come to one's senses; be disillusioned; have one's eyes opened. ¶환상에서 ~ wake from one's reverie[the illusion]//악몽에서 ~ (a person) awake from[come out of] a bad[an evil] dream//그는 악에서 깨어났다 He came to his senses and abandoned his evil ways.//이로써 그의 생각이 깰 것이다 This would bring him to his senses.
3 (술이) become[get] sober; sober off[up]; take off the effects of drink; recover from one's intoxication; [술기운이 가시다] wear off. ¶술이 깰 때까지 자라 Sleep yourself sober. / Sleep and get sober.//밤바람을 쐬었더니 술이 깼다 The night wind sobered me up.//그는 서서히 술이 깼다 He sobered up slowly. / The drunk inside him wore off gradually.
4 [개화하다] be[become] civilized[enlightened / awakened]; know the (way of the) world; open one's eyes. ¶깨지 못한 사람 a person not used to the world's way / an unsociable person//그는 깬 사람이다 He talks senses. / He is quite a man of the world. / He is a civilized man.//그 여자는 깬 사람이다 She is modern. / She is a sensible woman.//신교육을 받아 많은 사람들이 깼다 The people have been enlightened by new education.

깨다[2] **1** [부수다] break (into pieces); crack (an egg / a nut); crush; smash. ¶접시를 ~ break[smash] a dish//얼음을 ~ break [crack] ice//머리를 ~ crack one's head//산산이 ~ break (a thing) to pieces[bits] / crash (a thing) to atoms / smash (a thing) into fine pieces[into atoms].
2 [좌절시키다] frustrate (a person's plan); [파괴하다] break; destroy. ¶평화를 ~ destroy the peace//침묵을 ~ break one's [the] silence//기록을 ~ break[beat] the (world / Olympic) record//쓸데없는 잡담이 그들의 우정을 깨고 말았다 The gossip ruined their friendship.
3 [취소하다] cancel; dissolve; [어기다] break (off); violate. ¶혼담을 ~ break up a proposed marriage//계획을 ~ frustrate a plan//그들은 화해 교섭을 깼다 They wrecked the peace negotiations.
4 [감퇴시키다] diminish; reduce; [망치다] spoil; mar. ¶남의 흥을 ~ spoil[dampen / wet-blanket] a person's fun[pleasure / sport] / kill joy / cast a chill over//그의 발언이 대화를 깼다 His remark spoiled the conversation.//그의 말이 회의에 대한 우리의 흥미를 깼다 His remarks dampened our

enthusiasm for[interest in] the conference. //그는 항상 남의 감흥을 깨기만 하는 사람이다 He is a wet blanket.

깨다³ 〔부화하다〕 be hatched; hatch; 〔부화시키다〕 make hatch; cause (a chicken) to hatch (eggs). ¶갓 깬 새 nestling birds / a hatch / 병아리가 깼다 The brood are out [hatched]. / Some chicks are hatched.

깨닫다 1 〔인식하다·깨치다〕 understand; comprehend; realize; 〔알아채다〕 see; perceive; discern; be aware of; get wind of; sense. ¶위험을 ~ perceive[sense] danger / 자기 잘못을 ~ see[(문어) awake to] one's error / find out[be convinced of] one's mistake / 의무를 ~ be conscious[aware] of one's duty // 사실을 깨닫게 하다 convince (a person) of a truth / awake (a person) to the truth (to) // 그는 자기가 잘못되었다는 것을 깨달아야 한다 He must (be made to) realize that he is mistaken. // 세상은 그저 그런 것이라고 나는 깨달았다 I have learned to take the world as it is. // 그는 자기가 그녀의 감정을 해치고 있다는 것을 깨닫지 못했다 It didn't occur to him[He didn't realize] that he was hurting her. // 나는 깨달은 바 있어 담배를 끊었다 Realizing the harmfulness of the practice, I have given up smoking. 2 〔진리를 터득하다〕 be spiritually awakened; attain (spiritual) enlightenment[higher perception]; find true philosophy. ¶그는 마치 심원한 진리를 깨달은가 한 것처럼 말한다 He talks like a philosopher. // 석가모니는 그 나무 아래 앉아서 도를 깨달았다 Gautama sat under that tree and experienced spiritual awakening. // 나는 인생의 무상함을 깨달았다 I realized the transience of life.

깨뜨리다 break (into pieces); frustrate (a person's plan); cancel; diminish. ⇨깨다²

깨물다 bite; gnaw; crunch. ¶(분해서) 입술을 꼭 ~ bite[gnaw] one's lip (in rage) // 어금니로 땅콩을 ~ chew peanuts with one's molars[back teeth] // 전병을 바삭바삭 ~ crunch a rice cracker into bits // 얼음을 오도독 ~ crush an ice cube with one's teeth // 혀를 ~ bite one's tongue.

깨소금 parched[powdered] sesame seeds mixed with salt; salt with parched sesame.

깨소금 맛이다 be tasty[delicious]; taste good[nice]; (조롱조로) serve one right. ¶고녀석 경치는 것을 보니 ~ It serves him right to get punished. / The punishment served him right.

깨알 a grain of sesame; sesame seed. ¶~ 같은 글씨 very minute handwriting // ~ 같다 be tiny as a grain of sesame // ~만 해서 보이지 않다 be so tiny that one can't see it / be too small to be seen // 그는 동정심이라곤 ~만큼도 없다 He has not a grain[an ounce] of sympathy.

깨어나다 regain consciousness; be awakened from an illusion; become sober; be brightened up. ⇨깨나다

깨어지다 break; get a wound; fall through; be broken; be defeated. ⇨깨지다

깨우다 (잠에서) wake up (a person); awake [arouse / rouse] (a person) from[out of] (his) sleep; call (up) (a person). ¶문을 두드려 ~ tap[knock] up (a person) // 흔들어 ~ shake (a person) out of (his) sleep // 잊지 말고 6시에 깨워 주시오 Don't forget to call me at six o'clock. // 몇 시에 깨워 드릴까요 What time shall I wake you? // 7시에 깨워 주시오 Please wake me up at 7:00. / (호텔의 교환수에게) Please give me a morning call at 7:00. // 빗소리가 나를 깨웠다 The sound of rain woke me up. / I woke to the sound of rain. // 급한 환자 때문에 한밤중에 의사를 깨웠다 I woke the doctor up[roused the doctor] in the middle of the night for an emergency case.

깨우치다 awake[awaken] (a person) to (the realities[facts] of life); wake (a person) up to; make (a person) realize[understand]; call (a person's) attention to. ¶도리를 ~ bring (a person) to reason. // 잘못을 ~ reason with (a person) on (his) mistake // 사실을 ~ convince (a person) of a truth / awake (a person) to the truth (of) // 그 사건은 국민에게 위험을 깨우쳐 주었다 The event woke up the nation to the realization of danger.

깨죽 (—粥) porridge made of ground sesame and rice.

깨죽거리다 complain; eat without appetite. ⇨께죽거리다

깨지다 1 〔조각이 나다〕 break; be broken [smashed / crushed; come [go] to pieces(산산조각으로); go smash. ¶깨진 접시 a broken dish[plate] // 깨지기 쉬운 breakable (porcelain) / brittle (ice) / fragile (glass) / frail / easily cracked[split] // 깨지지 않도록 하다 keep[prevent / protect] (something) from breaking // 산산조각으로 ~ be crushed to pieces / be smashed into atoms[fragments] // 깨지기 쉬운 물건 — 취급 주의 (게시) Fragile — Handle with care. // 창유리 깨지는 소리가 들렸다 I heard the smash[crash] of a window(pane). // 유리는 깨지기 쉽다 Glass breaks easily[is easily broken]. // 사발이 떨어져서 깨졌다 The bowl tumbled down and broke[cracked]. 2 〔상처가 나다〕 get[receive] a wound; get hurt; be broken. ¶날아온 돌에 머리가 ~ get hurt in the head by a thrown stone. 3 〔성사되지 않다〕 fall through; be broken off; come to[end in] a rupture; be frustrated [ruptured]; fail. ¶흥정은 깨졌다 The bargain failed. // 평화 회담이 깨지고 말았다 The peace talks were broken off. // 약혼〔혼담〕은 부모의 반대로 깨졌다 The engagement [match] was broken off because of their parents' opposition. // 양국 간의 힘의 균형이 깨졌다 The balance of power between the two countries was upset. // 정상 회담은 핵 실험 금지 문제로 깨지고 말았다 The summit conference blew up over the nuclear test ban. 4 〔기록 등이 돌파되다〕 be broken[beaten / smashed]; (흥이) be dampened; be spoiled. ¶흥이 ~ one's fun is spoiled (by) / one's enthusiasm is dampened (by) // 올림픽 기록이 깨졌다 The Olympic record was broken. // 싸움 때문에 흥이 깨졌다 The quarrel cast a chill over the merrymaking. 5 〔패배하다〕 be defeated; suffer a defeat; lose a game[battle]. ¶그녀는 경쟁 상대에게 한판도 깨지지 않았다 She did not lose a single match to her rival.

깨지락거리다 do (something) with reluctance. ⇨께지럭거리다

깨치다 [깨닫다] see; perceive; understand; [배우다] learn; master; [이해하다] understand; comprehend; apprehend. ¶한글을 ~ learn from (a person) how to read and write *Hangeul*//문장의 뜻을 ~ understand the meaning of a sentence//진리를 ~ perceive a truth//그것으로 그는 깨친 바가 있었다 His eyes were opened by it. / It taught him a lesson.

깩 shrieking; shouting. ⇨ ˂ 끽

깻묵 sesame dregs[pulp]; oil cake; seedcake of sesame. ¶콩 ~ bean cake.

깻잎 a sesame leaf; a perilla leaf(들깻잎).

깽 with a moan[whimper]. ¶강아지는 꼬리를 밟혀 ~ 하고 비명을 질렀다 The puppy let out a yelp when someone stepped on its tail.

깽깽 yap, yap, yap. ¶강아지가 ~거렸다 The puppy cried, "Yap, yap, yap."//강아지가 빗속에서 ~거리고 있었다 A puppy was whining in the rain.

꺼내다 1 [밖으로 내다] take[bring] out; draw [pull] out; pick out. ¶호주머니에서 지갑을 ~ take one's purse out of one's pocket//지갑에서 돈을 ~ take out some money from a purse / take some money out of a purse//가구를 ~ carry furniture out (of a room)//그는 호주머니에 손을 넣어 담배를 꺼냈다 He reached into his pocket and came up with a cigarette.//나는 서류함에서 서류철을 꺼냈다 I drew out my file from the cabinet.//그는 지갑에서 천 원짜리 한 장을 꺼냈다 He took out a thousand-won bill from his wallet.//강도가 호주머니에서 식칼을 꺼냈다 The robber whipped out a kitchen knife from his pocket.
2 [이야기를 시작하다] bring out (a question); bring (a matter) up (for discussion); broach (a matter); open (the case); start (one's discourse). ¶이야기를 ~ broach a matter / introduce a topic[subject]//난문제를 ~ bring up a difficult problem / put a hard question to[before] (a person)//그 말을 꺼내기가 난처했다 I felt embarrassed as to how to break the ice about it.//그 문제를 어떻게 꺼내야 할지 몰라 망설이고 있다 I'm hesitating to broach the subject.//나쁜 소식을 꺼내기가 매우 힘들었다 I found it very hard to break the bad news.//그녀는 무슨 말을 꺼내다 말고 그만두었다 She started to say something, but did not finish it.//자네가 먼저 꺼냈으니 자네부터 하게 You're the one who brought it up[You suggested it (first)], so you did it first.//그는 알맞은 때를 기다렸다가 이야기를 꺼냈다 He waited for the right moment and then brought up the subject.

꺼두르다 grab[grasp] and pull[drag / lug] about; shake (by the collar). ¶머리채를 휘어 잡고 ~ drag (a woman about the floor) by the hair.

꺼둘리다 get grabbed and pulled about; get dragged.

꺼뜨리다 put out a fire[light] by mistake; let the fire[light] die[go] out. ¶불을 꺼뜨리지 않다 keep the fire alive[from going out]//불씨를 꺼뜨려 버렸다 Now there is no live coal to start the fire.//불을 꺼뜨리지 말아 주게 Don't let the fire die[go] out. / See that the fire is kept alive.

꺼리다 1 [싫어하다] dislike; have a dislike to [for]; have a distaste for; be reluctant (to do); [피하다] shun; avoid; alienate. ¶세상의 이목을 ~ avert people's eye/세상에 나가기를 ~ shun society / dislike to see[keep] company//사진 찍기를 ~ be shy of camera / be camera-shy//승낙하기를 ~ seem[act] unwilling to give one's consent//돈 내기를 ~ be unwilling[reluctant] to pay / begrudge money//그녀는 수줍어서 낯선 사람을 만나기를 꺼린다 Being shy, she shrinks from meeting strangers.//그는 거기 가기를 꺼리고 있다 He is reluctant to go there.//남의눈을 꺼릴 것 없다 You need not fear[be afraid of] what others may say.
2 [주저하다] hesitate (to do); scruple. ¶속이는 것을 ~ scruple deceiving[deceit].

꺼림칙하다 (서술적) feel uneasy; feel uncomfortable (about); (something) weigh on one's mind. ¶꺼림칙한 예감[꿈] an ominous premonition[dream]//꺼림칙한 데가 없다 have an easy[a clear / a clean] conscience / feel no prick of conscience / have no feeling of shame//그녀를 전송하러 공항에 가지 못해 ~ I feel sorry that I failed to see her off at the airport.

꺼멓다 jet-black. ⇨까맣다 1

꺼벙하다 big but shaky.

꺼지다¹ [불 등이 사라져 없어지다] go [die] out; blow out; be put out; be extinguished. ¶꺼진 불[숯] a dead fire[coal]//꺼져 가는 등불 a failing light//꺼지려고 하다 be about to go[die] out//불이 꺼지지 않도록 하다 mend the fire / keep the fire alive[going]//전등이 ~ electric light fails//바람에 촛불이 꺼졌다 The candle was blown out by the wind.//불은 곧바로 꺼졌다 The fire was soon put out.//담뱃불이 반쯤 타다가 꺼졌다 The cigarette went out half-smoked.//숯불이 타다 말고 꺼졌다 The charcoal died out halfburned.
2 [분이 풀리다] be appeased[softened].
3 [사라지다] go[get] away. ¶꺼져 버려 Go away! / Be off! / Beat it!
4 [거품이 가라앉다] break; burst.

꺼지다² [움푹 들어가다] become hollow [depressed]; [땅이 내려앉다] sink (into the ground); fall[cave] in; subside; [얼음이 깨지다] give; crack; (배가) get hungry. ¶눈이 꺼진 사람 a person with sunken eyes//볼이 꺼진 사람 a man with sunken[hollow] cheeks //그는 피로하면 눈이 꺼진다 He gets hollows under his eyes whenever he gets tired.//지진으로 도로가 꺼졌다 The road sank[caved in] because of the earthquake.

꺼풀 the outer layer of the skin; scum. ⇨까풀

꺽다리 a tall lank person; (영국 구어) a daddy longlegs; (미) a gangling fellow.

꺽둑꺽둑 chopping unevenly. ¶무를 ~ 썰다 cut radish in uneven bits.

꺾꽂이 cuttage; planting a cutting. **꺾꽂이하다** plant a cutting. ¶이 나무는 간단히 꺾꽂이할 수 있다 This tree can be grown easily from a cutting.

꺾다 1 [부러뜨리다] break (off); snap. ¶꽃을 ~ break off a spray of flowers / (꽃을) pluck[pick / pull off] a flower//꽃나무 가지를 ~ break off a twig of a flower tree//그는 꽃을 꺾었다 He plucked the flower. / He pulled the flower off.//그는 신경질적으로 연필을 둘로 딱 꺾어 버렸다 Nervously, he snapped the pencil in two.//나무를 꺾지 마

시오 Please do not damage the trees.
2 [방향을 돌리다] turn; make a turn; shift; veer (round); change direction. ¶왼쪽으로 ~ turn to the left / 핸들을 오른쪽으로 ~ wheel right // 핸들을 꺾을 때에 주의하라 Be careful when you turn the steering wheel. // 그는 핸들을 딱 꺾어 충돌을 피했다 He cut the wheel sharply (in the other direction) and avoided a collision. // 두 번째 모퉁이에서 오른쪽으로 꺾으시오 Turn to the right at the second corner. / Take the second turn to the right.
3 [기세를] crush; break; squelch; daunt; shake; unnerve; damp(en); discourage; [고집을] yield (to); concede (to); give in (to). ¶용기를 ~ discourage [dispirit / dishearten / unnerve] // 사기를 ~ depress [sap] the morale (of the troops) // demoralize (an enemy) // 약자를 돕고 강자를 ~ help [side with] the weak and crush the strong // 고집을 ~ concede [yield] a point (in argument) / bend [yield] to another's will // 그 녀석의 콧대를 꺾어 놓고 싶다 I'd like to deflate that guy's ego. / (구어) I'd like to take him down a peg or two. // 우리는 그들의 계략을 꺾어 버렸다 We frustrated their scheme [conspiracy].
4 [접다] fold; double (up); turn (down). ¶둘로 ~ fold in two / fold on itself // 칼라를 ~ turn down the collar // 표를 하기 위해 페이지를 ~ double over a leaf to mark the page / turn down a leaf to mark the page.

꺾쇠 an iron clamp; a cramp (iron); a staple; a clam. ~를 치다 fix a cramp iron // ~로 단단히 고정시키다 make (things) fast with cramps / fasten [hold] (things) with cramps.

꺾어지다 **1** [부러지다] break; be broken; snap; give way; come off. ¶세 동강으로 ~ be broken in three / 잘 꺾어지지 않는 지팡이 a tough stick / 태풍에 많은 소나무가 꺾어졌다 Many pine trees were snapped [broken] off by the typhoon. **2** [접히다] be folded; be doubled. ¶둘로 ~ be doubled // 셋으로 ~ be folded in three.

꺾은선 (-線) [수] a polygonal [broken] line.
● **꺾은선 그래프** [수] a graph of broken line.

꺾이다 **1** [부러지다] break; be broken; snap; give way. ¶참나무는 휘기는 하지만 잘 꺾이지는 않는다 Oak may bend, but will not break. **2** [방향·길이] turn; make a turn; be bent; be crooked. ¶크게 꺾인 커브 a sharply breaking curve / a curve which breaks well // 공이 오른쪽으로 꺾였다 The ball broke [curved] to the right. // 길은 여기에서 갑자기 꺾인다 There is a sharp turn in the road here. / The road makes an abrupt turn here.
3 [기세·용기가] be discouraged; be disheartened; lose heart [courage]; be dispirited; (의지가) bend [bow] (to); submit [yield] (to). ¶그는 실패로 용기가 꺾였다 He was discouraged by this failure. / He lost heart through this failure. // 나의 열의는 꺾이고 말았다 My enthusiasm was dampened [weakened]. / My ardor was cooled [chilled]. // 이 재난에도 그는 조금도 기가 꺾이지 않았다 He was not in the least daunted by this disaster. // 그는 시작이 시원찮아서 기가 꺾인 것 같다 His poor start seems to have discouraged him. // 소년은 온갖 고생에도 기가 꺾이지 않고 훌륭한 청년으로 성장했다 Not beaten [discouraged] by hardships, the boy grew into a fine young man.

껄껄 껄깔.
껄껄거리다 laugh loudly. ⇨깔깔거리다
껄껄하다 rough (surface / texture); particular. ⇨깔깔하다
껄끄럽다 rough (surface); prickly. ⇨깔끄럽다

껄떡 with a gulp; with gasps; cracking. ⇨깔딱
껄떡거리다 gulp; pant; crackle. ⇨깔딱거리다
껄떡껄떡 with a gulp. ⇨깔딱깔딱
껄렁껄렁하다 worthless; trashy; good-for-nothing; (서술적) be no good. ¶껄렁껄렁한 사람 a good-for-nothing fellow / a worthless scamp // 나는 그런 껄렁껄렁한 짓은 안 한다 I am worthy of better course. / I know much better.

껄렁이 a wretched [good-for-nothing] fellow; a silly [stupid] fellow.

껌 chewing gum; a stick of gum(막대기 모양의); a tablet of gum(정제 모양). ¶풍선~ bubble gum // ~을 씹다 chew gum / have a chew of gum.

껌껌하다 **1** very dark. ⇨깜깜하다1 ¶껌껌해서 아무것도 보이지 않았다 Nothing was to be seen in the utter darkness. // 굴속은 껌껌했다 It was pitch-dark [as dark as pitch] in the tunnel. // 우리는 껌껌해지기를 기다렸다 We waited for full darkness. **2** [마음씨가] black-hearted; evil hearted. ¶속이 껌껌한 사람 a black-hearted [treacherous] person / a schemer.

껍데기 **1** (조개·달걀 등의) a shell; a valve. ¶굴 ~ an oyster shell // 달걀 ~ an egg-shell // ~를 벗기다 take the shell off // 굴 ~을 벗기다 shell oysters. **2** [외피(外皮)] a castoff skin; a slough. **3** (화투 등의) a blank; a cipher.

껍죽거리다 [까불거리다] behave frivolously; (잘난 체하다) put on [give oneself] airs; hold one's head high.

껍질 (나무의) bark; (과일 등의) skin(엷은 껍질); rind(단단한 껍질); a peel(주로 벗겨진 껍질). ¶사과 [복숭아] ~ the skin [peel] of an apple [a peach] // 수박 ~ the rind of a watermelon // 바나나 ~ a banana peel // 옥수수 ~ the husk(s) of an ear of a corn // 땅콩 ~ the skin of a peanut // 나무의 ~을 벗기다 strip the bark off a tree / bark a tree // ~을 벗기다 (손가락 또는 칼로) peel / (칼로 일부를 깎아 내며) pare // 귤 [바나나 / 사과] ~을 벗기다 peel a tangerine [a banana / an apple] // 옥수수의 ~을 벗기다 husk corn // 감자를 ~째 삶다 boil potatoes in their jackets / boil a potato unpeeled // 토마토를 ~째 먹다 eat a tomato skin and all.

-껏 **1** [있는 대로 모두] as far [much] as possible; to the extent (of); to the utmost (of). ¶힘~ 일하다 work as hard as one can // 양~ 먹다 eat one's fill // 마음~ 먹다 eat to one's heart's content / make [have] a hearty meal of // (손님을) 정성~ 대접하다 entertain (a person) cordially // 마음~ 울다 have a good (long) cry / weep to one's heart's content. **2** [까지] (right) up to (now). ¶여태~ all this while // 저렇게 훌륭한 사람은 여태~ 본 적이 없다 I have never seen such a great man in my life. // 여태~ 어디에 있었니 Where have you been all this while? // 그는 여태~ 오지

않았다 He has not come as yet.
껑충 with a jump [leap]. ¶담을 ~ 뛰어넘다 jump [leap] over a fence.// 물가가 ~ 뛰어올랐다 Prices have jumped (up).// 그는 시내를 ~ 뛰어넘었다 He cleared a brook in one vault.
껑충거리다 walk in a leaping manner; stride along bouncing [leaping].
껑충하다 tall and long-legged; lank; lanky; (구어) gangling. ¶키가 껑충한 사람 a lanky [gangling] man / a man tall as a church steeple // 두루미는 다리가 ~ A crane has long, slender legs.
께 [에게] to [by / for] (a person). ¶하느님~ 맹세하다 swear by God // 아버지~ 온 편지 a letter for my father // 이 편지를 어머니~ 갖다드려라 Give this letter to your mother.// 최선생~ 올림 To [Presented to] Mr. Choe with best wishes from ….
-께 1 [때] about; (미) around; toward (a time). ¶그믐~ about the end of the month. **2** [장소] around; in the vicinity [neighborhood] of; near (a place). ¶이 근처 어디~ somewhere around [about / near] here // 시장 ~ near the market / in the vicinity of the market.
께끄름하다 (사람이) be anxious [nervous] (about); feel uneasy (about); have misgivings (about); feel a bit unpleasant; (사물이) weigh on one's mind; get on (one's) nerves. ¶뒷맛이 께끄름한 꿈 a dream remembered with discomfort // 답장을 내지 않고 보니 마음이 ~ I feel guilty about not answering his letter.
께서 from (a person). ¶아버지~ 주신 선물 the present that my father gave me // 춘부장~는 무고하신가 Is your father well? / How is your father? // 선생님~는 올여름 방학에 어디로 가시겠습니까 Could I ask where you are going for the summer vacation?
께적거리다 do (something) with reluctance. ⇨께지럭거리다
께죽거리다 [투덜대다] grumble; growl; complain; (음식을) eat without appetite; pick at one's food; chew dryly at (one's food).
께지럭거리다 do (something) with reluctance [with half a heart]; go at (something) reluctantly [half-heartedly]; (음식을) pick at one's food. ¶께지럭거리지 말고 먹어 치워라 Stop picking at your food — eat it up!
께지럭께지럭 reluctantly; half-heartedly; begrudgingly; (음식을) picking (at one's food).
껴들다 (두 팔로) lift [take] (a thing) in one's arms; (두 물건을) hold both at once.
껴안다 embrace; hug; hold (a person) to one's breast [in one's arms]; take into one's arms; (떠맡다) undertake (many responsibilities). ¶서로 ~ embrace [hug] each other / be in [go into] each other's arms // 꼭 ~ give (a person) a tight hug // 애인을 ~ embrace [hug] one's beloved // 그들은 서로 껴안고 울었다 They wept in each other's arms. // 소녀는 아버지의 목을 껴안았다 The girl flung [threw] her arms around her father's neck. // 어머니와 딸은 서로 꼭 껴안았다 The mother and daughter embraced [hugged] each other tightly. // 두 사람은 서로 껴안고 절벽에서 몸을 던졌다 They threw themselves from the cliff with their arms around each other. // 아이는 장난감을 꼭 껴안고 있었다 The child was hugging the toy tightly.
껴입다 wear (a shirt) underneath one's clothes; wear extra (layers of) clothing. ¶셔츠를 석 장 ~ wear three undershirts one over another // 겨울에는 사람들이 옷을 잔뜩 껴입어서 차내 혼잡의 한 요인이 된다 One reason the trains are so crowded in winter is that people are wearing extra layers of clothes.
꼬기다 crumple; wrinkle; rumple; crease.
꼬기작거리다 crumple (up); wrinkle; rumple; crease.
꼬깃꼬깃 ¶그녀는 그 편지를 ~ 구겼다 She crumpled (up) the letter (into a ball). **꼬깃꼬깃하다** crumpled; wrinkled; creasy. ¶꼬깃꼬깃하게 하다 crumple (up) (paper).
꼬꼬 <소아> a chicken.
꼬꼬댁 cackle. ¶암탉이 알을 낳고 ~ 울었다 The hen cackled on laying an egg.
꼬꾸라뜨리다 let (a person) fall forward. ⇨' 고꾸라뜨리다
꼬꾸라지다 fall [tumble] forward. ⇨고꾸라지다
꼬끼오 cock-a-doodle(-doo). **꼬끼오하다** (roosters) cry cock-a-doodle; crow. ¶수탉이 꼬끼오하고 울고 있다 The cock is crowing [is going cock-a-doodle-doo / is cock-a-doodle-dooing].
꼬느다 1 [치켜들다] lift up with a stretched arm. **2** [잔뜩 가다듬다] be on standby; make ready (to do); be ready [prepared / posed] (for); (정신적으로) nurse [toy with] (an idea). ¶만년필을 꼬느고 발표를 기다리다 wait for an announcement with a pen couched in hand.
꼬다 1 (새끼 등을) twist; entwist; twine; throw. ¶금실 은실을 합쳐 꼬아 만든 끈 a string made of gold and silver threads twisted together // 노끈을 ~ twist threads into a string / braid a cord // 밧줄을 ~ make [twist / strand] a rope // 생사를 ~ throw silk into threads // 철사를 ~ twist wires together // 갖가지 색실을 한데 ~ twist threads of various colors together (into a string) // 아마의 섬유와 나일론사를 꼬아 실을 만들다 intertwine flax and nylon into a thread // 우리는 짚으로 새끼를 꼬았다 We twisted pieces of straw into a rope. // 이 로프는 50가닥의 실을 꼰 것이다 This rope is twisted from fifty threads.
2 (몸을) twist; writhe. ¶다리를 꼬고 앉다 sit with one's legs crossed // 그는 고통스러워 몸을 비비 꼬았다 He writhed [twisted] in pain [agony].// 그녀는 온몸을 비비 꼬며 누구에게나 아양을 떤다 She makes herself delightful [pleasant] to every person with her whole body motion.
3 make sarcastic remarks (on). ⇨'비꼬다2
꼬드기다 1 [꾀다] tempt; allure; seduce; entice; (선동하다) incite; abet; instigate; egg on; stir up. ¶꼬드겨 …하게 하다 entice [allure / tempt] (a person) to (do) / egg [set] (a person) in a crime / put (a person) up to (commit) a crime // 누군가 꼬드기고 있음에 틀림없다 Someone must be at the bottom of the affair. **2** (연줄을) tug at the string of a kite (to make the kite go up higher).
꼬들꼬들하다 dry and hard. ¶꼬들꼬들한 밥 hard boiled rice.

꼬락서니 shape; appearance. ➪`꼴¹
꼬랑지 〈속〉 a tail (of a bird). ➪꽁지
꼬르륵 rumbling; cackling; gurgling. ➪`꾸르륵
꼬리 **1** 〔전반적 동물의〕 a tail. ¶굵은 다람쥐[여우]의 ~ a squirrel's[fox's] tail[brush] // 〔짧은〕 사슴[토끼]의 ~ a deer's[rabbit's] tail[scut] / 공작의 ~ a peacock's tail[train] // ~ 끝 a tail end / the end[tip] of a tail // 뭉툭한 ~ a stumpy tail // ~가 없는[없는] tailed [tailless] / 개가 ~를 흔들었다 The dog wagged its tail. // 말이 휙 ~를 쳤다 The horse swished its tail. // 개는 ~를 늘어뜨리고 주인을 따라갔다 The dog followed its master with its tail hanging[drooping].
2 〔밑동〕 a tail; 〔끝〕 the end. ¶무 ~ the end of a radish / 연~ the tail of a kite / 혜성의 ~ the tail[train / trail] of a comet / 제트기가 길게 ~를 끌었다 The jet left a long tail behind it.
3 〔비유〕 the rear(뒤쪽); one's true self[colors / character] (정체); a clue(단서).
꼬리가 길면 밟힌다(속담) The pitcher goes (once too) often to the well but is broken at last.; An evil deed will be discovered.
꼬리(를) 감추다 hide[conceal] oneself; cover one's trace.
꼬리(를) 물고 one after another[the other]; in rapid succession.
꼬리(를) 밟히다 give a clue to (the police); furnish a clue to the discovery; be traced by.
꼬리(를) 잡다 find another's faults; catch (a person) tripping. ¶오래지 않아 그도 꼬리를 잡힐 것이다 He will give away one of these days. // 그 협박범은 언젠가 결국 꼬리를 잡혀 경찰에 체포될 것이다 The extortionists will slip up eventually, and then the police will get them.
꼬리(를) 치다 〔유혹하다〕 seduce; entice; (al)lure; 〔아첨하다〕 flatter; butter (a person) up. ¶그는 자기 사장에게 꼬리를 치고 있다 He is fawning on his boss.
● **꼬리뼈** 〔생〕 the coccyx (pl. -cyes, -cyges).
꼬리지느러미 〔동〕 a caudal[tail] fin.
꼬리표(-票) a label; a tag; a docket. ¶~를 달다 fasten[attach / (미)fix] a label[tag] to (a trunk) / tag[label] (one's baggage).
꼬마 **1** 〔어린아이〕 a kid; a child; a tot. **2** 〔작은 사람〕 a dwarf; a pygmy; a pigmy; a squirt; a shrimp; a midget. **3** 〔소형〕 miniature (tube); midget (airplane); pocket (battleship).
● **꼬마 자동차** a baby[midget / mini-sized] car; a minicar. **꼬마전구** a miniature (electric) bulb; a midget [fairy] lamp.
꼬막 〔동〕 an ark shell.
꼬맹이 a kid; a dwarf.
꼬무락거리다 move slowly. ➪꾸무럭거리다
꼬물거리다 wriggle; dawdle. ➪`꾸물거리다
꼬박¹ 〔계속〕 straight through; without any break; 〔밤새껏〕 without sleeping a wink; 〔완전히〕 fully; completely; whole. ¶~ 사흘 동안 (for) a full[whole] three days / (for) three whole[clear] days // ~ 밤을 새우다 do not sleep a wink / pass a sleepless night / sit up for the whole night without sleeping a wink // 하루 종일 ~ 기다리다 wait for (a person) to come all day long / 그 일은 ~ 하루가 소요되는 작업이다 It is a good day's work. / It will take a whole day to finish that job. // 그는 ~ 12시간 잤다 He slept for a good [full] twelve hours.
꼬박² 〔졸기〕 nodding; 〔절하기〕 bowing; 〔조아리기〕 ko(w)towing. **꼬박하다** 〔졸다〕 doze; nod; fall into a doze; snooze; 〔절하다〕 bow; make a bow; ko(w)tow. ¶책을 읽다가 꼬박하며 졸다 nod [doze] over a book // 절을 ~ bow / ko(w)tow.
꼬박꼬박 〔머리를 계속 숙였다가 들어〕 niddle-noddle; bowing repeatedly; 〔어김없이〕 humbly obeying; faithfully; obediently; without fail; 〔고대하여〕 waiting intently [anxiously]. ¶~ 졸다 doze off / nod[rock] in a doze / nid-nod // 어른의 말을 ~ 잘 듣다 readily obey one's elders // 대출금을 매월 갚아 나가다 make the monthly payment on one's loan regularly[right on time] // 일기를 ~ 적다 make regular entries in one's diary // 그는 그들에게 ~ 인사말을 했다 〔문어〕 He thanked them punctiliously. // 그는 관습을 ~ 지키는 사람이다 He is very careful [(문어) punctilious] about conventions.
꼬박이 straight through; fully. ➪`꼬박¹
꼬부라뜨리다 bend. ➪`고부라뜨리다
꼬부라지다¹ bend. ➪`고부라지다
꼬부라지다² 〔마음이 비틀어져 있다〕 crooked; perverse. ¶성격이 꼬부라진 사람 a perverse [cross-grained] person / a person of vicious nature.
꼬부랑글자(-字) 〔졸필〕 a poor hand; "hen tracks[scratches]"; 〔서양 글자〕 alphabetic letters; Roman or Cyrillic script.
꼬부랑길 a winding[tortuous] path.
꼬부랑꼬부랑 ¶시냇물은 논밭 사이를 ~ 흐르고 있다 A brook meanders[winds its way] through the fields. // 좁은 길이 산을 ~ 누비고 있다 A narrow path led on through the hills with twists and turns. **꼬부랑꼬부랑하다** bent here and there; winding; meandering; crooked; sinuous; serpentine. ¶꼬부랑부랑한 길 a winding[crooked] road / meandering path / a road that winds every now and then // 그 꼬부랑꼬부랑한 길이 산마루까지 이어져 있다 The winding road leads to the top of the hill.
꼬부랑 늙은이 a bent[stooping] old person.
꼬부랑하다 (등이) bent; (나무 등이) crooked; (길이) twisty; winding; (개천 등이) meandering; (진로 등이) zigzag. ¶꼬부랑한 나뭇가지 a crooked bough // 늙어 허리가 ~ be bowed with years / be bent with age / stoop from age // 나는 꼬부랑한 숲 속의 길을 더듬어 갔다 I followed a path meandering through the woods.
꼬부랑 할머니 a bent old woman; an old woman bent with age.
꼬부리다 stoop (over); bend. ➪`고부리다
꼬부스름하다 somewhat bent; slightly curved; crooked a little.
꼬부장하다 slightly bent[curved]; (자세가) slightly slouchy[stooping]. ¶허리가 ~ be slightly bent (in the back).
꼬불거리다 wind; meander; zigzag. ¶시내는 여기서부터 꼬불거리기 시작한다 The brook begins to zigzag from here.
꼬불꼬불 meanderingly; windingly; zigzag. ¶~ 흐르는 시내 a meandering stream. **꼬불꼬불하다** crooked; meandering; winding; zigzag; tortuous (curve); (나무가) snarled. ¶꼬불꼬불한 산길 a meandering[a zigzag / a

꼬불탕하다 winding] mountain path // 길이 아주 ~ The road turns and twists a good deal.
꼬불탕하다 winding; meandering; zigzag. ¶꼬불탕한 길 a winding road // 꼬불탕한 개천 a meandering stream.
꼬빡[1] straight through; fully. ➪ '꼬박'[1]
꼬빡[2] nodding; bowing. ➪ '꼬박'[2]
꼬이다[1] 1 (실 등이) get snarled[twisted]; be entangled; (일 등이) go wrong[amiss]; get fouled up; suffer[meet with] a setback. ¶꼬인 것을 풀다 untwist / disentangle / straighten out // 사업이 꼬여서 고생하다 suffer from the unsatisfactory state of one's business // 만사가 꼬였다 Everything went against me. / Nothing came up to my expectations. // 실이 꼬였다 Strings were twisted. // 너의 허리띠[혁대]가 꼬였다 Your belt is twisted. // 그 철사는 너무 가늘어 꼬이기 쉽다[잘 꼬인다] The wire develops kinks easily because it is so fine.
2 (마음이) become crooked[distorted / peevish / perverse]; get cross[sour]; get cranky. ¶배알이 ~ get cranky / grow peevish // 일이 뜻대로 안 돼 비위가 ~ get perverse as (something) does not turn out the way one expected.
꼬이다[2] swarm; flock. ➪ '꾀다'[1]
꼬이다[3] tempt; lure. ➪ '꾀다'[2]
꼬장꼬장하다 (물건이) straight and strong; (노인이) hale and hearty; vigorous; (성미가) stern; unbending; upright. ¶그는 성미가 ~ He has a stern character. // 칠십 노인이지만 아직도 ~ Though a septuagenarian, he is still vigorous and erect in figure.
꼬집다 1 (살을) pinch; give a pinch; nip. ¶세게 ~ give (someone) a sharp pinch (on the arm) // 꼬집어 멍 들게 하다 pinch (a person) black and blue // 꿈이 아닌가 하고 꼬집어 보다 pinch oneself to see if it is real // 그는 내 무릎을 세게 꼬집었다 He pinched my knee sharply. 2 (비꼬다) make cynical[cutting / sarcastic] remarks about (something); say spiteful things; criticize. ¶아픈 데를 ~ criticize (a person) on a sore spot // 남의 잘못을 ~ catch (a person) tripping / trip (a person) up // 결점을 꼬집어 내다 pick[point] out (another's) defects.
꼬집어 말하다 tell frankly[pointedly]; make cynical[cutting / sarcastic / ironical] remarks; say spiteful things.
꼬챙이 (굽는 데 쓰는) a skewer; (통째로 굽는 데 쓰는 대형의) a spit; [불고기용 쇠꼬챙이] a broach; (농업용의) a dibble. ¶생선[고기]을 ~에 꿰다 skewer[spit] a fish [a piece of meat] / thread a fish on a skewer[a spit] / skewer a fish // 생선을 ~에 꿰어서 굽다 skewer a fish and grill it / roast[grill] fish on skewer[broach].
꼬치 1 [꼬챙이로 꿴 음식] food on a skewer; skewered food. ¶~구이한 수퇘지 a spit-roasted[barbecued] boar // 고기를 ~구이 하다 roast a meat on a skewer // 경단 ~를 빼먹다 gobble dumplings off a stick. 2 & skewer. ➪ '꼬챙이'
꼬치꼬치 1 (몸이 마른 모양). ¶~ 마르다 be nothing but skin and bones / be worn [wasted / reduced] to a shadow[skeleton] / be as thin as a lath[wafer].
2 (따지고 캐묻는 모양) inquisitively. ¶~ 따지고 들다 examine (a matter) to a bottom / search into the root of (a matter) / (미국 구어) give (a person) a (severe) going-over // 그는 내게 내 계획에 대해 ~ 따져 물었다 He questioned me even to the minutest details about my plan. / He subjected me to searching inquiry on my plan. / He catechized me to searching inquiry on my plan. / He catechized me (to the last detail) about my plan. / He was inquisitive about my plan. / He questioned me about my plan closely [inquisitively].
꼬투리 1 [식] (깍지) a (pea) pod; a hull; a peascod(완두의); a shell; a shuck. ¶~는 까다 shell[pod] (peas / beans). 2 [담배꼬투리] the unusable refuse of tobacco leaves. 3 [일의 실마리] cause; reason; a lead; a beginning; a start; origin. ¶~를 잡다 invent[make up] a pretext (for a fight[quarrel]) / trail one's coattails // 싸움의 ~가 뭐냐 Where does the quarrel start?
꼭 1 [단단히] firmly; tightly; fast; close(ly). ¶끈을 ~ 묶다 tie[fasten] the strings tight(ly) // 수건을 ~ 짜다 wring a towel tightly [hard] (tightly는 짠 결과가 단단한 것이고 hard는 힘을 주어 짜는 일을 말함) // 병마개를 ~ 닫다 cork a bottle tightly // ~ 쥐다 grasp firmly / hold (a thing) tightly [fast] / take fast hold // ~ 누르다 press hard // 문을 ~ 닫다 shut the door close[tight] // 눈을 ~ 감다 squeeze the lids over the eyeballs // 문은 ~ 닫혀[잠겨] 있었다 The door was tightly closed [locked]. // 그는 손잡이를 ~ 잡았다 He grasped the handle tightly. // 어머니는 내 손을 ~ 쥐셨다 My mother pressed my hand hard. / My mother squeezed my hand. // 그 어머니는 자기 아이를 ~ 껴안았다 The mother hugged[embraced] her child tightly [with all her might].
2 (빈 틈이 없는 모양) exactly; to a tittle; to a nicety; perfectly. ¶~ 알맞은 사람 a suitable person / the right man // ~ 맞는 뚜껑 a close lid // ~ 끼는 모자 a tight cap // ~ 끼는 구두[장갑] tight shoes[gloves] // 그의 옷이 내게 ~ 맞았다 His clothes fitted me to perfection[(구어) to a T]. / His clothes were tightly fitting. // 내겐 이 옷이 ~ 낀다 I can just barely get into this dress. / This dress is too tight for me.
3 [수량·시간 등이 맞는 모양] exactly; precisely; punctually; sharp; just; to the minute. ¶시간에 ~ 맞게 punctual to the moment // ~ 3마일 exactly three miles [three miles to an inch] // ~ 9시 just at nine (o'clock) [at nine sharp / precisely at nine] // 강연은 ~ 1시간이 걸렸다 The lecture lasted for just [exactly] an hour. / The lecture lasted for one hour to the minute. // 계산이 ~ 맞았다 The calculations came out exactly. / The figures tallied up exactly. // 그 답이 ~ 맞다 The answer is perfectly correct.
4 [틀림없이] certainly; surely; undoubtedly; at any cost; on all accounts; in any case; by all means; by hook or by crook; without fail; always. ¶~ 들러 주십시오 Please drop in by all means. / Do come and see me. // 이것은 내가 ~ 읽고 싶었던 책이다 This is the book I wanted so badly [so much] to read. // 오시기 전에 ~ 전화를 걸어 주십시오 Please be sure to telephone us before you come. // ~ 보라고 그녀가 말했기 때문에 나는 그 영화를

보러 갔다 I went to see the film because she had insisted that I go.∥이 구두는 내게 ~ 맞는다 These shoes fit me perfectly[just right].∥~ 오십시오 Be sure to come. / Please come without fail.∥~ 그렇다고 생각합니다 I am sure of it.∥그녀는 아들이 ~ 돌아오리라고 믿었다 She believed that her son would surely come back some day.∥그가 한 말은 ~ 실현될 것이다 What he said will undoubtedly[certainly] be realized.∥1주일에 한 번씩은 ~ 부모님께 편지를 드려라 Be sure to write to your parents once a week.∥무슨 일이 있어도 그것은 ~ 해내겠습니다 I will carry it out at any cost[(구어) no matter what].∥그는 ~ 앞자리에 앉았다 He always took a seat in the front row.∥그는 외국으로 나갈 때는 딸을 ~ 데리고 갔다 He took his daughter with him whenever he went abroad.∥그녀는 외출하면 ~ 과자를 사 온다 She never goes out without buying sweets.∥나는 아침마다 ~ 조깅을 하기로 하고 있다 I make it a rule to go jogging every morning. / I go jogging every morning without fail.∥무슨 말에도 그는 ~ 말대꾸를 한다 If you say anything to him, he always talks back.∥그는 약속은 ~ 지킨다 He keeps his promise scrupulously. / He never fails to keep his promise.
5 [참는 모양] patiently. ¶웃음을 ~ 참다 hold back one's laughter∥모욕을 ~ 참다 bear an insult patiently∥그는 아픔을 ~ 참았다 He endured the pain stoically.
꼭대기 1 [맨 위] the top; the summit(산의); the apex; (머리·모자의) the crown; (뾰족한 것의) the spire. ¶산~에 at the mountaintop / at the top[summit / peak] of a mountain∥언덕 ~에 on the hilltop∥머리 ~ the crown∥투구의 ~ the crest of a helmet∥지붕 ~ a rooftop[the top of a roof]∥나무 ~ a treetop[a head of a tree]∥나무 ~에 올라가다 climb to the top of a tree.
2 [단체 등의 윗자리] the highest rank; the top place; (윗자리의 사람) a boss; the chief; the head; the leader; a top man. ¶~를 차지하다 hold (the) top place / rank first∥사람들의 ~에 서다 be a leader of men / stand above others / stand at the head of others / lead others.
꼭두각시 (철사나 손으로 놀리는) a puppet; (실을 달아 놀리는) a marionette; (비유) a tool; a cat's paw; a robot. ¶~놀음 a puppet show [play] / a marionette show[play]∥남의 ~ 노릇을 하다 act as another's tool[instrument] / cat's paw∥그는 정부의 ~가 되었다 He was made a puppet of the government.∥그는 그들의 ~에 지나지 않다 He's nothing but their puppet.
꼭두새벽 the peep of day[dawn]. ¶~에 quite early in the morning / before dawn [daybreak] / at the crack of dawn.
꼭두서니 1 [식] a madder; the madder plant. **2** [꼭두서니로 만든 붉은 물감의 빛깔] madder (red).
꼭지 1 [식] a stem; a stalk; a peduncle. ¶~가 떨어진다 Fruit is ripe. / Fruit falls[drops].
2 [뚜껑의 손잡이] a knob; a handle. ¶주전자 ~ the handle of a kettle.
3 (연의) a decorative strip pasted near the top of a kite.
4 (도리깨의) the pivot of a flail.
5 [우두머리] the boss (of a band of beggars).
6 [묶음] a bunch; a bundle. ¶미역 네 ~ four bunches[bundles] of seaweed.
꼭지각(-角) [수] a vertical angle.
꼭짓점(-點) [수] an apex; a vertex; the angular point.
꼴[1] [모양] shape; form; [외양] appearance; [복장] clothes; [상태] a state; plight; [광경] a sight; a spectacle. ¶~이 말이 아니다 be out of shape / look miserable∥네 ~이 그게 뭐냐 Look at you! / What a sight! / How dreadful (of you)!∥이게 무슨 ~이람 (맞대놓고) For shame! / Shame on you! / (제3자를 말할 때) What a plight he is in! / What a sorry figure he cuts!∥그 ~이 뭐냐 How did you ever get into mess? / Shame on you!∥그 놈은 ~도 보기 싫다 I hate the very sight of him.∥이런 ~로는 남 앞에 나갈 수 없다 I am not fit to be seen.∥그는 경고를 무시해서 저 ~이 된 거야 Look what happened to him after he ignored the warning.
꼴[2] (마소의) pasture; forage; fodder; provender; hay. ¶~을 베다 cut fodder (for animals) ∥말에게 ~을 먹이다 give a horse fodder / feed a horse (with fodder).
-꼴 [비율] rate; proportion; ratio. ¶한 다발에 3,000원~로 at the rate of 3,000 won a bundle∥천 명에 한 사람~로 in the ratio of one to a thousand persons∥쇠고기가 한 근에 10,000원~로 판매되고 있다 Beef is sold at the rate of 10,000 won a *geun*.∥세 집에 한 집~로 술집이 있다 About every third building is a bar[pub].
꼴깍 at a gulp; as if by swallowing. ⇨꿀꺽
꼴딱 at a gulp. ⇨꿀떡
꼴뚜기 [동] a small kind of octopus.
꼴리다 1 (성기가) stand erect; become stiff [rigid]. **2** (배알이) be roused to anger; flare up (in anger); anger burns in one.
꼴불견(-不見) unsightliness; unpresentableness; shabbiness; indecency. ¶~이다 be unsightly[ugly / indecent] / cannot bear to see / be unable to stand the sight (of)∥옷차림이 ~이다 [어울리지 않는다] be unbecomingly dressed / [초라하다] be shabbily dressed∥나이 들어 가지고 ~이다 Shame on you! You are old enough to know better.∥~이니 그런 짓은 그만두어라 Stop it! You're making a laughing stock of yourself.∥와이셔츠 차림으로 만찬회에 가는 것은 ~이다 It's most unsuitable to go to a dinner in your shirt sleeves.∥늙은이가 그런 식으로 여자를 쫓아다니는 것은 ~이다 It is obscene for an old man to chase around after women that way.
꼴사납다 [보기 흉하다] ugly; unsightly; shabby; [창피스럽다] indecent; unbecoming; disgraceful. ¶꼴사나운 놈 a disgusting [despicable] fellow / "a nasty customer"∥꼴사나운 짓 unbecoming behavior / a shameful act∥꼴사납게 굴다 behave disgracefully [indecently] / make a sight of oneself∥옷을 꼴사납게 입다 be shabbily dressed∥꼴사나운 짓 하지 마라 Don't disgrace yourself.∥그런 짓을 하다니 You are mean to act like that.∥그는 꼴사나운 옷차림을 하고 왔다 He came in unpresentable attire[not properly dressed].∥그는 꼴사납게 땅바닥에 쓰러졌다 He tumbled to the ground in an ungainly

꼴좋다 sprawl. / He fell in an unsightly heap on the ground.

꼴좋다 It serves you right!; What a fine mess (you've gotten yourself into)!

꼴깍 1 [소리] squelching; squashing; squishing (sound). **꼴깍하다** squelch; squash. 2 [우는 모양] sniffling. **꼴깍하다** sniffle.

꼴깍거리다 squelch and squelch; squash and squash; sniffle and sniffle(울다).

꼴깍꼴깍 squashing and squashing; sniffling and sniffling.

꼴찌 the last; the bottom; the tail (end); the tailender(최하위자). ¶맨 ~에서 둘째[셋째] the last but one[two] // 그는 ~로 졸업했다 He graduated last on the list. // 그는 반에서 ~다 He is at the (very) bottom of his class. // 그는 달리기에서 ~를 했다 He finished last. / He was the tailender. // 나는 달리기에서는 ~었다 I brought up the rear[came in last] in every race. // 그는 백 미터 경주에서 ~에서 두 번째를 했다 He was second to last [(영) the last but one] in the hundred meter dash.

꼼꼼하다 very careful; meticulous; scrupulous; precise; deliberate; elaborate. ¶꼼꼼한 편집자 a scrupulous editor // 꼼꼼한 성격 a meticulous nature // 저 배우는 ~ That actor is meticulous about details. **꼼꼼히** carefully; meticulously; scrupulously; in detail; elaborately. ¶~ 일을 하다 do (one's) work carefully // 의사는 그녀의 병의 원인을 ~ 조사했다 The doctor investigated the cause of her illness with scrupulous care. // 그 형사는 뭔가 작은 물건을 주워 ~ 살펴 보았다 The detective picked up something small and examined it carefully [with careful attention / with scrupulous care].

꼼지락거리다 move sluggishly; stir leisurely; get about lazily.

꼼짝 budging; stirring; moving. ¶그는 그 자리에서 ~도 못 했다 He was rooted to the spot. // 내 차는 눈 속에서 ~도 못 했다 My car got stuck[got stalled] in the snow. // 교통 혼잡으로 ~ 못 했다 We were help up in a traffic jam. // 일이 쌓여 ~ 못 한다 I am swamped with work. // ~ 마, 경찰이다 Police! freeze! **꼼짝하다** budge; stir; move (slightly); make a move. ¶꼼짝하지 않다 remain motionless / do not stir[budge] an inch / stand[stock-]still // 꼼짝할 수 없다 cannot move at all / can not stir[budge] an inch // 꼼짝하지 말고 거기 있어라 Stay put there! / Don't move from that spot! // 그는 꼼짝하지도 않고 그 자리에 서 있었다 He stood there motionless [stock-still]. // 꼼짝하면 죽는다 One move and you are a dead man. / If you dare budge, I will kill you. // 바위가 꼼짝하지 않는다 The rock won't budge an inch. // 그는 손가락 하나 꼼짝하지 않는다 He does not stir a finger. // 그는 꼼짝하지 않고 집에 틀어박혀 있다 He is holed up at home and never stirs (outside).

꼼짝 못하다 be in a fix; be quite helpless; be at a loss; stick in the mud. ¶적을 꼼짝 못하게 하다 hold the enemy in check // 그는 빚을 많이 져서 꼼짝 못한다 He is up to his ears in debt. // 우리는 지배인에게 꼼짝 못한다 The manager always keeps us under his thumb. // 그는 주인 앞에서는 꼼짝 못한다 He is always cowed in the presence of his master. // 그는 마누라한테 꼼짝 못한다 He is henpecked by his wife. // 우리는 꼼짝 못하고 졌다 We were beaten all hollow. // 그는 나를 말로 꼼짝 못하게 한다 He talks me down.

꼼짝달싹 ¶~ 못 하다 be in a fix[hole] / be in a tight corner / be at a pinch / find oneself in a dilemma[predicament] // 그는 빚으로 ~ 못 하고 있다 He is involved deeply in debt.

꼼짝없다 helpless; unavoidable; inevitable. **꼼짝없이** helplessly; without any means; with no way out; inevitably; unavoidably. ¶~ 내쫓기다 be helplessly forced out / be obliged to get driven out // ~ 붙잡히다 be held [arrested] with no way out // ~ 죽게 되다 face the inevitable death // 정전으로 많은 열차가 ~ 서게 되었다 A number of trains were brought to a standstill due to a power failure.

꼽다 count (on one's fingers); number; reckon; take a count (of). ¶날짜를 ~ count the days on one's fingers // 우리 동네 부자로는 그를 꼽는다 He is one of the richest people in our town.

꼽추 a humpback. ⇨`곱사등이`

꼿꼿하다 strong; firm; upright. ⇨`꿋꿋하다`

꽁꽁¹ groaning. ⇨`끙끙`

꽁꽁² 1 [언 모양]. ¶~ 얼다 be thickly frozen (over) / be frozen stiff[hard / solid] // 물이 ~ 얼었다 The water has frozen hard. // 스케이트를 할 수 있을 만큼 얼음이 ~ 얼었다 The ice is strong enough to skate upon. // 나는 몸이 ~ 얼었다 I feel as cold as ice. / I am chilled to the bone. 2 [묶는 모양]. ¶~ 묶다 tie up (a parcel) / ~ 뭉이다 be tied up in a ball // 도둑을 ~ 묶었다 We bound the thief firmly hand and foot.

꽁무니 [척수 끝] the lower end of the backbone; the rear end; [궁둥이] the buttocks; the rear; [끝] the tail (end). ¶~가 빠지게 달아나다 take to one's heels / turn tail and run away // 줄의 ~에 서다 be last in [at the tail end of the] line // 여자 ~를 따라다니다 dangle after[hang about] a girl / chase [run after] a woman // 여자 ~를 따라다니는 것은 좋은 행실이 못된다 Dangling about[Hanging about] a girl is not a good behavior.

꽁무니(를) 빼다 flinch (from); shrink (back) (at / from); hold[hang] back (from); [달아나다] run away; run off; turn tail (and run away); beat a retreat. ¶약속해 놓고 나오면 꽁무니를 뺀다 He dodges whenever I talk of the matter. // 꽁무니 빼지 말고 해 봐라 Don't hang back. Give it a try. // 그는 언제나 막판에 가서 꽁무니를 뺀다 He always hangs back at the last moment.

꽁보리밥 boiled barley (for a meal).

꽁지 a tail (of a bird); a train(공작 등의).

꽁초(-草) a cigarette butt[end / stub]; [엽궐련의] a cigar end; [미국 속어] a snipe. ¶~ 줍는 사람 a cigarette butt picker / a stub collector // ~를 버리다 throw away a cigarette end // 복도에 ~를 버리지 마시오 Don't throw away a cigarette butt on the floor.

꽁치 [동] a Pacific saury; a saury.

꽁하다 introvert and narrow-minded; reserved and unsociable; moody; reticent and unadaptable; be a cold fish. ¶꽁한 성질 introvert nature // 꽁하게 생각하다 bear in mind / feel badly [sore (about) / have[harbor] a grudge against (a person).

꽂다 1 [박아 세우다] stick (in / into); put (into / through); fix (in / into); [찌르다] drive (into); stab; pierce; thrust; [끼워 넣다] insert (in); inset; [핀으로] pin (up / down); impale. ¶감자에 포크를 ~ stick a fork into a potato // 국기를 ~ fix the national flag at (the gate) // 책을 ~ put[set] a book (on a shelf) // 꽃을 ~ put[set / arrange] flowers (in a vase) / stick a flower (in one's hair) / 머리에 장식 핀을 ~ place an ornamental hairpin in one's hair / adorn one's hair with an ornamental hairpin // 스위치를 ~ plug in / insert a plug (in) // 호주머니에 손을 ~ put [stick] one's hand in(to) one's pocket // 서류를 핀으로 꽂아 철하다 pin papers together // 헝겊에 바늘을 ~ stick a needle into cloth // 나는 눈 속에 장대를 꽂아 단단히 세웠다 I planted[set] the pole firmly in the snow. 2 [가로지르다] put (a bar) across. ¶문에 빗장을 ~ bar[bolt] the gate // 상투를 ~ wear a topknot.

꽂을대 (탄약을 다져 넣는 꼬챙이) a rammer; a ramrod; (총포 청소용) a gunstick; a cleaning rod; a sponge(대포의).

꽂히다 [찔리다] be stuck[pinned / impaled]; be stabbed[pierced]; [맞히다] hit; [끼이다] be inserted; [박히다] be embedded; [걸리다] be bolted. ¶타이어에 못이 꽂혀 있었다 I found a nail sticking in the tire. // 화살이 과녁에 꽂혔다 The arrow hit the target right in the center. // 창은 호랑이의 심장에 꽂혔다 The spear pierced into the tiger's breast.

꽃 1 (초목의) a flower(특히, 관상용의); (과수의) a blossom; [헌화] a floral tribute. (▶ flower 는 가장 널리 쓰이는 말, blossom은 결실을 기대하는 뜻이 포함됨) // 일찍[늦게] 피는 ~ an early[late] flower // ~ 파는 소녀 a flower girl // ~이 편 들 a field of flowers // ~이 피는 초목 a flowering plant // ~의 floral // ~ 같은 flowery / flowerlike // ~ 피는 시절 the flower season // ~이 만발한 in full blossom[bloom] // ~를 가꾸다 cultivate[grow] flowers // ~을 (병에) 꽂다 arrange flowers (in a vase) // ~을 따다 pluck[pick] flowers // ~을 꺾다 break off a spray of flowers // ~이 핀다 Flowers open. / Trees blossom[bloom]. / Buds come into flower[bloom]. // ~이 시든다 The flowers wither[shrivel / fade]. // 이 ~들은 이른 봄에 핀다 These flowers bloom[blossom] early in spring. // 과일나무는 대개 봄에 ~이 핀다 Most fruit trees flower in spring. // 벚~이 피었다 The cherry blossoms are out. // ~이 졌다 The flowers are gone. / The blossoms have finished.
2 [정수] essence; flower; spirit; the pride; pearl; the pick; the élite; [청춘] youth; [시절] best days; [미인] a fair woman. ¶임자 있는 ~ a married beauty // 사교계의 ~ the flower[the belle] of society // ~을 꺾다 deflower(처녀의 순결을) // ~필 날이 있었지 Let us hope for the best. // 청춘은 인생의 ~ 이다 Youth is the flower of life. / Youth is a treasure.

● **꽃 가게** a flower[florist's] shop; a flower stall(노점). **꽃 소식** news of (cherry) blossoms[the blossoming of (cherry) trees]; (문어) tidings of the approach of the (cherry) blossom season.

꽃가루 [식] pollen; anther-dust. ⇨화분(花粉).
꽃가지 a spray[sprig] (of flowers).
꽃게 [동] a blue crab.
꽃구경 flower[blossom] viewing. ¶~을 가다 go (out) flower viewing.
꽃꽂이 flower arrangement[arranging / composition]. ¶~를 배우다 take lessons in flower arrangement. **꽃꽂이하다** arrange [set] flowers; put flowers in a vase.
꽃놀이 flower viewing; a picnic for viewing flowers. ¶~ 가다 go on an outing to see the flowers / go flower-viewing // 비 때문에 ~를 완전히 잡쳤다 The rain has entirely spoilt the flower viewing picnic. **꽃놀이하다** enjoy an outing among the flowers.
꽃다발 a bunch of flowers; (프) a bouquet; a nosegay; a posy; a corsage.
꽃다지 1 [식] a whitlow grass. 2 [첫 열매] the first fruit (of cucumber, eggplant, etc.).
꽃답다 lovely[pretty / beautiful] (as a flower); flowerlike. ¶꽃다운 청춘 the bloom[flower / charm / glow] of youth / the springtime [prime] of life // 꽃다운 처녀 a girl (as) pretty as a flower / a girl (as) fair as a May rose / a flower of a girl // 꽃다운 나이이다 be in the flower of maidenhood / be sweet sixteen // 그녀는 꽃다운 청춘에 죽었다 She was cut off in the flower of her youth.
꽃대 [식] a flower stalk; a floral axis; a rachis (pl. ~es, -chides); a peduncle.
꽃덮이 [식] the perianth; the floral envelope; the perigonium (pl. -nia).
꽃동산 a flower garden; a flowery hill.
꽃말 flower[floral] language; the language of flowers.
꽃망울 a flower bud[button]. ¶~이 서다 have [bear] buds / put forth[shoot out] buds / be in bud / bud.
꽃무늬 floral design; flower[flowery] patterns; flowerings; [인] a printer's flower. ¶장미 ~ a rosette // ~의 floral-patterned // ~가 있는 카펫[양탄자] a carpet with a floral pattern [design].
꽃 바구니 a flower basket; a basket of flowers(꽃 한 바구니).
꽃받침 [식] a calyx (pl. ~es, -lyces); a (flower) cup; a receptacle; a torus (pl. -ri); a thalamus (pl. -mi).
꽃밥 an anther.
꽃밭 [화원] a flower garden; [화단] a flower-bed; (고산의) a field of alpine flowers.
꽃병 (一瓶) a flower vase. ¶~에 꽃을 꽂다 arrange flowers in a vase.
꽃봉오리 a (flower) bud; a button; a budding flower; [청춘] the youth. ¶~ 같은 소녀 a budding beauty / a young maiden / a girl of sweet seventeen // ~가 맺히다 bear [have] buds / put forth[put out] buds // ~가 피다 a bud develops into a flower[bursts into blossom] // ~를 꺾다 pluck a flower in the bud / [비유] pluck the bud of maidenhood / deflower a girl // ~가 커져서 막 피어나려 하고 있었다 The buds were swollen to bursting.
꽃부리 [식] the corolla of a flower.
꽃불 1 (이글이글 타는) a blazing fire. 2 [폭죽] fireworks; a fireworks display. ¶~을 올리다 let[set] off fireworks // 오늘 밤 ~ 놀이가 있다 There will be a fireworks exhibition this evening. / Fireworks will be let off this

꽃샘 a cold[windy] weather in the blooming.
꽃샘하다 suddenly get cold in the flowering season.
꽃송이 an open flower; a blossom.
꽃술 [식] a stamen(수술); a pistil(암술).
꽃시계(-時計) a floral[flower] clock.
꽃잎 [식] a (flower) petal. ¶여섯 ~의 꽃 six-petal(l)ed flower∥많은[한] ~의 many-[single-] petal(l)ed.
꽃자루 [식] a flower stalk; a footstalk; a peduncle.
꽃집 a flower[florist's] shop; a flower stall(노점).
꽃차례(-次例) [식] an inflorescence; anthotaxy.
꽈리 [식] a bladder cherry; a Chinese lantern plant; a ground[winter] cherry; a husk tomato; (입으로 부는) a mouth clacker. ¶~를 불다 blow on a ground cherry. **2** (피부의) a blister.
꽉 1 [힘을 주는 모양] tight(ly); fast; firmly. ~ 쥐다 grasp firmly / grip with force / take a firm grip of / squeeze / 주먹을 ~ 쥐다 tighten[clench / double] one's fists / 허리띠를 ~ 죄다 wear a belt tight / tighten[buckle / notch] one's belt / 기둥을 ~ 붙들다 hold on tight to a pole / 입을 ~ 다물다 close one's lips tightly∥그녀는 입을 ~ 다물고 있었다 She sealed her lips tightly. ∥나는 라켓을 ~ 쥐었다 I gripped the racket firmly.∥그는 내 손을 ~ 쥐었다 He squeezed my hand. / He pressed my hand hard.∥그녀는 입을 ~ 다물고 나를 노려보았다 She stared at me with her mouth tightly shut. / She stared at me shutting her mouth tight.
2 [가득 찬 모양] close(ly); tight(ly); fully; compactly; to the full; chock-full. ¶트렁크에 ~ 채워 넣다 pack a trunk tight(ly)[close] / ~ 차 있다 be packed to the full / be chock-full of / be crammed with∥상자에는 옷이 ~ 들어차 있었다 The box was packed tightly with clothing.∥이 근처에는 집들이 ~ 들어차 있다 In this neighborhood, the houses are closely packed[crowded close] together.∥그녀는 헌 옷을 상자에 ~ 채웠다 She stuffed the old clothes into a box. / She stuffed the box with old clothing.∥그는 스케줄이 아침부터 밤까지 ~ 차 있다 His schedule is jam-packed from morning to night.∥홀에는 사람들이 ~ 들어차 있었다 The hall was filled[packed / crammed] to capacity with people.
3 [참고 견디는 모양] patiently; firmly. ¶~ 참다 bear up (under) / suffer patiently / bear firmly∥그는 괴로움을 ~ 참았다 He bore his affliction patiently[bravely].∥그녀는 울고 싶은 충동을 ~ 참았다 She resisted an impulse to cry out.
꽉꽉 1 [여러 번 힘을 주는 모양] firmly; tightly; fast. ¶~ 눌러 담다 squeeze into / 밥을 ~ 눌러 담다 stuff (a bowl) full of rice / 백에 이것저것 ~ 쑤셔 넣다 cram one's bag full of things∥그는 옷을 옷가방에 ~ 쑤셔 넣었다 He stuffed[crammed] his clothes into the suitcase. **2** [가득 찬 모양] compactly; fully; close(ly). ¶방마다 모두 사람들로 ~ 찼다 All the rooms were packed[crammed] with people.
꽝 1 with a bang[boom]; with a thump [thud]. ¶대포를 ~ 쏘다 bang off a gun / boom a gun / 문을 ~ 닫다 shut the door with a bang / bang the door shut∥의자가 ~ 하고 넘어쳤다 The chair fell over with a crash.∥그는 서류에 도장을 ~ 쩍었다 He affixed his seal to the papers with a thump.∥그는 훅을 한 대 ~ 얻어맞고 나가떨어졌다 He took a hook and went down.∥그는 차를 전봇대에 ~ 부딪혔다 He ran his car smack into a telephone pole.∥차가 ~ 하고 기둥을 들이받았다 The car crashed[banged] into the pole.
2 [당첨 안 된 제비] a blank. ¶~ 없는 제비뽑기 a lottery without any blanks.
꽝꽝 bang-bang; boom-boom. ¶대포를 ~ 쏘다 boom a cannon continuously∥문을 ~ 두들기다 thunder at[thump on] a door. **꽝꽝하다** go bang bang.
꽝꽝거리다 [꽝 소리를 내다] go[keep] bang-bang[boom-boom]; bang-bang; [큰소리치다] talk big[tall]; talk boastfully.
꽤 [제법] quite; pretty; rather; fairly(바람직한 일에 쓰임); considerably; [비교적] comparatively; relatively; [생각보다 더] beyond one's expectation. ¶~ 먼 거리 a good distance / ~ 많은 금액 a considerable[sizable] sum of money / ~ 많은 수입 a handsome income∥이 파이는 ~ 맛이 있다 This pie tastes pretty[rather] good.∥그는 영어를 ~ 잘한다 He speaks English fairly well.∥우리는 ~ 오랫동안 기다렸다 We waited for quite a long time.∥그들은 ~ 좋은 집에 살고 있다 They live in a fine house.∥그 아이는 ~ 즐거운 모양이었다 The child seemed to be quite happy.∥그것 ~ 좋소 It's pretty good.∥그는 술을 ~ 마신다 He can drink quite a bit.∥그는 나이보다 ~ 젊어 보인다 He looks quite a bit younger than his age.∥그는 ~ 곤란을 겪고 있는 것 같다 He seems to be greatly troubled.∥~ 많은 돈이 들었다 It cost us a great deal[a considerable sum] of money.∥오늘은 ~ 덥다 It's rather hot today.∥그는 그것을 ~ 잘 설명했다 He explained it pretty[fairly] well.∥그것은 ~ 많은 이익을 가져올 것이다 It will bring in no small[a great deal of] profit.∥우리가 회답을 받기까지는 ~ 오래 걸릴 것이다 We won't get an answer for some time yet.∥세상에는 그런 사람이 ~ 많다 There are plenty of people like that (in the world).
꽥 with a shout[scream / shriek / yell]. ¶~ 하고 소리치다 utter[give] a shriek[shout / yell]∥~ 하며 쓰러지다 fall down with a shriek∥그는 놀라서 ~ 하고 소리쳤다 He was frightened and yelled.
꽥꽥 quacking; shouting and shouting. ¶그렇게 ~ 소리를 질러서는 안 돼 Don't scream [squeal / screech] like that! **꽥꽥하다** cry; quack; gaggle. ⇨꽥꽥거리다
꽥꽥거리다 1 [소리치다] cry; shout; yell; roar; give an angry word. ¶화가 나서 ~ roar with anger∥사소한 일로 ~ roar at[about] trifles. **2** (오리가) quack; (거위가) gaggle; (갈매기가) squawk.
꽹과리 a kkwaenggwari; a (small) gong. ¶~를 치다 beat[hit / sound] a kkwaenggwari.
꾀 [슬기] wise counsel; wit; resources. ¶~ 많은 사람 a man of resources / a resourceful person∥우리 모두 ~를 모아 보자 Let's combine our wits. / Let's put our heads

together.//우리는 없는 ~를 짜냈다 We cudgeled[racked] our empty brains. 2 [계략·계책] a trick; a ruse; an artifice; a stratagem(군략 등의); a device; a design; a scheme. ¶얕은~ a shallow cunning // ~가 있다 be resourceful / be tricky / be clever / be wily // ~가 없다 be brainless / be harebrained / be tactless // ~가 늘다 grow clever [intelligent] // ~가 모자라다 be wanting in sense / be on the dull side // 일에 ~가 나다 get tired[weary] of a work // ~를 짜내다 cudgel[rack / beat] one's brains / strain one's wits // ~를 써서 이기다 outwit (a person) // ~를 피우다 be idle / get lazy / neglect // 그녀는 아프지 않다, ~를 부리고 있을 뿐이다 She's not sick, she's just being lazy. // 나는 그의 ~에 넘어갔다 I was entrapped by him. // 제 ~에 제가 넘어간다 Schemers are caught in their own schemes. / He is deceived by his own trick. // 그는 제 ~에 넘어갔다 He was done in his own cleverness.

꾀까다롭다 fastidious; particular; finical; hard to please; hard to handle; fretful (baby); overnice (about); hard-grained (character); dainty (feeling / taste). ¶꾀까다로운 상사 a superior hard to be contented // 꾀까다로운 취미 dainty[finicky] taste(s) // 꾀까다로운 고객 a difficult customer // 그는 꾀까다로운 사람이다 He is hard to please. // 그는 음식에 ~ He is particular about his food. // 그녀는 옷에 대해 ~ She is particular[choosy] about her clothes. / She is hard to please when it comes to clothes. // 그는 꾀까다로운 주인이다 He is a difficult master to please. // 그녀는 매사에 ~ She is picky about everything.

꾀꼬리 [동] (한국의) an oriole; (유럽의) a golden oriole; (열대 아메리카의) a cacique. ¶~ 같은 목소리 a beautiful voice.

꾀꼴꾀꼴 warbling and warbling; singing away (of an oriole). ¶~ 울다 (an oriole) warbles away / trill / sing.

꾀다¹ (벌레 등이) swarm; gather; crowd; flock; collect; fester; be infested with. ¶파리가 꾀지 않도록 하다 keep flies away from (the food) // 이 건어물에 구더기가 꾀어 있다 Maggots have bred in this dried fish. // 썩은 고기에 파리가 꾀어 있었다 Flies were swarming over the rotten meat. // 케이크에 개미가 꾀어 있었다 Ants were crawling all over the cake. // 꽃에 진딧물이 꾄다 The flower is infested with aphides.

꾀다² [유혹하다] tempt; lure; entice; seduce; decoy. ¶그는 미망인을 꾀어 돈을 빼앗았다 He coaxed[cajoled] money out of the widow. // 그는 부자의 딸을 꾀어 결혼했다 He tricked the daughter of a rich man into marrying him. // 그는 그녀를 꾀어 기밀 서류를 훔치도록 했다 He (sweet-)talked her into stealing classified documents from her office. // 그는 그녀를 꾀어 불량 주식을 사게 했다 He talked her into buying a bad stock. // 그는 그녀를 꾀어 돈을 훔치게 했다 He enticed her to steal money. // 나쁜 친구들이 담배를 피우도록 그를 꾀었다 Bad friends tempted him to smoke [into smoking].

꾀다³ get snarled; become crooked. ⇨꼬이다¹

꾀바르다 crafty; clever; shrewd; cunning; sly (to get off hard work); (미) smart (boy). ¶꾀바르게 굴다 act smartly[sly].

꾀병(-病) feigned[pretended] illness; counterfeit illness[sickness]; (미) fake sickness; (군) malingering. ¶~을 앓다 feign illness / pretend to be sick / malinger // 그의 병은 단지 ~이었다 His illness was only a sham [fake]. / He was not really ill but only shamming. **꾀병하다** malinger; feign[sham] illness.

꾀보 a man of resources. ⇨꾀쟁이

꾀부리다 1 [몸을 아끼다] spare oneself; spare oneself the trouble of (doing); be stingy of effort; grudge working. ¶꾀부리지 않고 일하다 labor without stint / work without sparing oneself. 2 [게으름 피우다] be sluggish; be indolent; be idle; be lazy. ¶꾀부리는 사람 a sluggard (man) / a lazy fellow / (구어) a lazybones // 공부에 ~ shun real study. 3 [책임을 피하다] shirk (one's duty); be sly; neglect. ¶어려운 일에는 ~ be sly on the difficult[important] problem.

꾀쓰다 use a trick; play a trick (on); resort to wiles[a ruse]. ¶목적 달성을 위해 ~ use tricks to achieve one's object // 꾀써서 달아나다 escape by trickery.

꾀어내다 lure (a person) away; decoy[entice] out. ¶위험한 곳으로 ~ lure (a person) into a dangerous position // 그 냄새가 사자를 굴에서 꾀어냈다 The smell lured the lion away from[out of] the den.

꾀이다 be lured; be enticed[tempted]; be seduced. ¶친구에게 ~ be enticed by a friend // 그녀는 감언에 꾀여 가출하였다 She ran away from home, allured by honeyed words. // 그는 나쁜 친구들에게 꾀여 나쁜 길로 빠졌다 Tempted by bad companions, he fell into evil ways.

꾀잠 sham[feigned / pretended] sleep; make-believe sleep; a simulation of sleep. ¶~을 자다 sham[feign / simulate] sleep / pretend to be asleep.

꾀쟁이 a man of resources[ideas]; a tricky [wily] person; a person full of wiles [schemers]. ¶그는 대단한 ~이다 He has more wit in his little finger than in your whole body.

꾀죄죄하다 shabby; dirty; filthy; squalid; sordid; seedy; dowdy. ¶옷차림이 ~ be shabbily dressed[clothed] / be dressed with dirty [soiled] clothes // 그가 왜 저렇게 꾀죄죄해졌는지 모르겠다 I hardly understand what has made him so shabby.

꾀피우다 spare oneself; be sluggish; shirk (one's duty). ⇨꾀부리다

꾀하다 [계획·획책하다] scheme; plan; devise; contrive; design; project; [서두르다] attempt; (나쁜 짓을) plot; conspire; hatch (a plot); machinate; (미) frame up; [추구하다] seek; intend (to do); aim at; (노력하다) strive[labor] (for); exert oneself (for). ¶실각을 ~ plot[design] a person's downfall // 공익을 ~ work for the good of the public / serve the public interest // 독립을 ~ strive for national independence // 사건의 조기 해결을 ~ aim at[strive for] an early settlement of the matter // 그는 재기를 꾀하였다 He tried to recover his lost standing. // 그녀는 자살을 꾀하였다 She attempted suicide. // 그는 무엇인가를 꾀하고 있는 모양이었다 He seemed to be nursing a scheme. // 그들은 정부의 전복을

꾀하고 있다 They are plotting to overthrow the government.// 그가 그런 일을 꾀하고 있을 줄은 꿈에도 생각지 못했다 I never dreamed that he was harboring such artful schemes.

꾐 〔유혹〕 temptation; allurement; enticement; seduction. ¶~에 빠지다 fall into [yield to] temptation / fall a victim to (a person's) temptation// 그는 나쁜 친구의 ~에 빠져 나쁜 길로 들어섰다 Bad companions tempted him into wrong ways.// ~에 빠지지 마라 Beware of sweet words.

꾸기다 crumple; take a turn for the worst. ⇨'구기다

꾸기적거리다 crumple up. ⇨ 구기적거리다

꾸깃꾸깃하다 crumpled. ⇨ 구깃구깃하다

꾸다[1] 〔꿈을〕 dream. ¶꿈을 ~ dream[have] a dream / 〔꿈에 보다〕 dream (a thing) / dream of / see in a dream// 좋은 [나쁜] 꿈을 ~ dream a good [bad] dream// 마치 꿈을 꾸는 기분이었다 I felt as if I were in a dream.

꾸다[2] 〔빌려 쓰다〕 borrow (a thing from a person); have (money) on loan; have a loan (of). ¶꾼 돈 만 원 the owing 10,000 won// 토지를 저당 잡혀 돈을 ~ raise [borrow] money on one's estate// 여기저기서 돈을 꾸어 들이다 borrow (money) from many people // 꾼 돈은 갚아야 한다 One must pay what one owes.// 돈 좀 꾸어 주시겠습니까 May I trouble you for some money?// 그녀는 첫날엔 꾸어다 놓은 보릿자루처럼 얌전했다 The first day, she was very quiet [diffident]. / The first day, she was as meek as lamb(▶ 영어에서는 lamb을 관용적으로 쓴다). **꾸어다 놓은 보릿자루**(속담) being like a cat in a strange garret.

꾸들꾸들하다 dry and hard. ⇨ 꼬들꼬들하다

-꾸러기 an overindulger; a person who overdoes (something). ¶말썽~ a burden / a bother / a handful / a nuisance / an imp / a bully// 심술~ a cross-grained [an ill-natured] fellow / a dog in the manger / a cynic / a crosspatch// 잠~ a late riser / a sleepy head / a slugabed / a heavy sleeper// 장난~ a mischievous boy / an urchin / a little monkey / a limb of the devil [Satan] / slyboots.

꾸러미 1 〔싼 물건〕 a bundle (in a wrapper); a package; (작은) a packet; a parcel; (큰) a bale. ¶bundle은 운송이나 저장에 편리하도록 한 묶음으로 만들어 놓은 것. parcel은 수송이나 판매의 목적으로 비교적 조그맣게 꾸려 놓은 것이며, package는 보통 상자나 용기 안에 담은 것을 말함) 〔옷〕 a bundle of clothes// 책 ~ a package of books// ~를 만들다 make a bundle [parcel / package / packet] / bundle (clothes) / pack (goods) // ~를 풀다 unpack / undo a package [bundle] // 그것을 모두 한 ~로 해서 운반해 주시오 Please carry them all in one bundle. **2** 〔짚으로 만든 물건〕 a straw wrapper. ¶달걀 한 ~ ten eggs in a straw wrapper.

꾸르륵 1 〔배 속이〕 rumbling; growling; gurgling. **꾸르륵하다** 1 give a growl; make a rumble; gurgle. ¶배에서 꾸르륵하는 소리가 난다 (곧, 배가 고프다) I am so empty. / I can hear my stomach. **2** 〔닭이〕 cackling. **꾸르륵하다** cackle; let out a cackle. **3** 〔물이〕 gurgling. ¶~ 솟아오르다 gurgle up / well up with gurgles. **꾸르륵하다** gurgle; make a gurgle [gurgling sound].

꾸리 a ball. ¶실~ a ball of thread// 털실 두 ~ two balls of yarn.

꾸리다 1 〔짐을〕 pack (up); tie up; do up; wrap up; bundle. ¶짐을 ~ make a bundle [package] // 소지품을 ~ pack up one's belongings// 그는 자기 짐을 꾸리고 떠나 버렸다 He packed his things and left. **2** 〔일을〕 manage; deal with; have control of. ¶살림을 ~ manage household affairs// 회사를 꾸려 가는 수완이 있다 have the ability to control one's firm// 나라의 재정을 꾸려 나가다 finance a government// 이 돈으로 살림을 꾸려 나가기는 무리다 It is impossible to cover [pay] all the expenses with this amount of money.// 나는 적은 예산으로 꾸려 나가야 했다 I had to manage on [make shift with] a small budget.// 그는 다달이 받는 송금으로 꾸려 나가고 있었다 He was making do on his monthly allowance.// 20만 원으로 꾸려 나갈 수 있을 것 같다 I will be able to manage [get along] on two hundred thousand won. **3** 〔정돈하다〕 put (things) in order; put [set] (things) to rights; tidy [do] up (a room). ¶여장을 ~ equip [outfit] oneself for a journey // 매무새를 ~ adjust oneself [one's dress].

꾸무럭거리다 move slowly [lazily / leisurely / idly]; linger; idle about; dillydally; dawdle (over). ¶꾸무럭거리지 말고 without delay / right [straight] away// 이불 속에서 ~ dally [potter] away one's time// 뭘 꾸무럭거리고 있는 거야 What's the delay? / Why on earth have you been so long?// 꾸무럭거리고 있을 때가 아니다 There is no time to lose. / It admits of no delay.// 꾸무럭거리지 말고 대답하라 Answer me and be quick about it.

꾸물거리다 1 〔꿈틀거리다〕 wriggle; writhe; wiggle; squirm. ¶꾸물거리며 나아가다 wriggle along// 구더기가 ~ Worms wriggle. **2** 〔굼뜨다〕 move slowly; dawdle. ¶그는 무슨 일에나 꾸물거린다 He is slow [inefficient] about everything.// 뭘 꾸물거리고 있나 Be quick about it! / What's taking you so long? // 꾸물거리고 있을 시간이 없다 I have no time to lose.// 꾸물거리다가 자리를 못 잡았다 We were too slow to get seats.// 꾸물거리지 말고 해라 Don't be long about it.

꾸미다 1 〔장식하다〕 ornament; decorate (a room with flowers); adorn; bedeck; dress (a window); 〔화장하다〕 make up (one's face); put on makeup. ¶꽃으로 꾸민 방 a room decorated [blazoned] with flowers// 호화롭게 꾸민 응접실 a gorgeously furnished drawing room// 무덤을 꽃으로 ~ decorate a grave with flowers// 보석으로 화려하게 ~ bedizen oneself with jewels// 연단을 꽃으로 화려하게 ~ decorate a stage lavishly with flowers// 오랜만에 가 보았더니 그 가게는 새로 꾸며져 있었다 I found the store had been redecorated when I visited it again after a long time. **2** 〔수식하다〕 embellish; garnish. ¶문장을 ~ use a flowery style / embellish one's style// 말을 ~ use fancy [decorative] words. **3** 〔가장하다〕 affect; be affected; feign; pretend; assume; disguise; put on [assume] a semblance of (honesty). ¶꾸민 태도로 in an affected manner// 겉을 ~ make outward show / put a good face on (a matter) // 그는

걸을 꾸미는 사람이다 He is a showy person.
4 [조작하다] fabricate; forge; invent; make [cook] up (a story); coin; (음모 등을) plan; scheme; plot. ¶꾸며 낸 기사 a cooked-up report∥음모를 ~ lay a plot (against) / form [lay] a conspiracy against (a person's life)∥정부의 전복을 ~ plot [scheme] the downfall of the government∥그는 그 일에 대해서 터무니없는 이야기를 꾸며 냈다 He invented some farfetched [(구어)] made up a cock-and-bull] story about it.∥그녀는 그럴듯한 구실을 꾸며 냈다 She cooked up [concocted] a clever excuse.∥그들은 정부에 대해 반역 음모를 꾸몄다 They plotted treason against the government.∥그것은 교묘하게 꾸며진 사기였다 It was a cleverly engineered fraud.∥돈을 도둑맞았다는 것은 그녀가 꾸며 낸 거짓말이었다 That story about having her money stolen was just a put-up job.∥당신은 도대체 무슨 일을 꾸미고 있는가 Whatever are you up to?
5 [조직하다] make; compose; organize; form; establish; (가정 등을) keep (house); set up (a house). ¶가정을 ~ (get married and) make a new home (at/in) / make one's home (at).
6 [작성하다] draw up; write out; prepare (a deed). ¶서류를 ~ draw up [write out] a document∥소설을 연극으로 ~ dramatize a story / arrange a novel for the stage∥(계약서를) 두 통 ~ make out (a contract) in duplicate.

꾸밈새 [장식] decoration; [장식법] the way one decorates [fixes up]; [모양새] a shape; a form; appearance. ¶~가 좋은 shapely (figured) / well-formed [-shaped]∥~가 좋은 방 a decently furnished room∥~가 흉한 ill-shaped / ill-formed / shapeless / unseemly∥이 공원의 ~는 영국식이다 The park is laid out in the English style.∥그 소나무를 심어서 정원의 ~가 좋아졌다 The garden has improved in appearance with the newly planted pine.

꾸밈없다 an simple; plain; [솔직한] candid; frank; artless; straightforward. ¶꾸밈없는 simple / plain / [솔직한] candid / frank / artless / straightforward∥꾸밈없는 말 words without trimmings∥그의 문체는 ~ He writes in an unaffected style. **꾸밈없이** simply; plainly; [솔직히] candidly; in a straightforward way; frankly. ¶~ 말하다 speak in a straightforward way / say frankly.

꾸밈음 (-音) [음] an ornament; a grace; (프) agréments.

꾸벅 nodding; bowing. ⇨²꼬박²

꾸벅거리다 nod (in a doze); make repeated bows. ¶책을 읽으면서 ~ nod [doze] over a book∥그는 고개를 꾸벅거리는 버릇이 있다 He has a way of jerking his neck up and down.

꾸벅꾸벅 niddle-noddle. ⇨²꼬박꼬박

꾸부러뜨리다 bend (one's back); curve (a wire). ⇨'구부러뜨리다

꾸부러지다 bend; bow. ⇨'구부러지다

꾸부렁꾸부렁 ⇨²꼬부랑꼬부랑

꾸부렁하다 bent; crooked. ⇨²꼬부랑하다

꾸부리다 stoop (over); bend. ⇨²구부리다

꾸부스름하다 somewhat bent. ⇨²꼬부스름하다

꾸부정하다 rather bent. ⇨'구부정하다

꾸불꾸불 meanderingly; windingly. ⇨²꼬불꼬불

꾸불텅하다 winding; meandering. ⇨²꼬불탕하다

꾸역꾸역 in a stream; in succession; one after another; in droves. ¶많은 사람이 다방으로 ~ 들어왔다 People streamed [filed] into the coffee house in droves.∥사람들이 홀에서 ~ 나왔다 The people came out of the hall in a stream.

꾸준하다 [한결같다] steady; constant; [부지런하다] assiduous; strenuous; [끈기 있다] untiring; unflagging; persistent. ¶꾸준한 성격 a steady [stable / solid] character∥꾸준한 우정 constant [steadfast] friendship∥꾸준한 노력으로만 성공할 수 있는 것이다 You will succeed only with unceasing [untiring / persistent] effort. **꾸준히** steadily; constantly; ceaselessly; assiduously; strenuously; untiringly; unflaggingly; persistently; undefatigable. ¶~ 발전하다 make steady progress∥~ 노력하다 make steady and persistent effort∥그는 훌륭한 정치가가 되려고 ~ 노력했다 He made a constant effort [(문어) exerted himself assiduously] to become an outstanding statesman.∥그는 ~ 실험을 되풀이 하였다 He repeated the experiment indefatigably [untiringly].∥강물은 ~ 불기만 한다 The (water level of the) river is steadily [just goes on] rising.∥저 가게에는 손님이 ~ 드나든다 That store has a steady flow of customers. /(영) That shop enjoys brisk custom.

꾸중 a scolding; a rebuke. ⇨='꾸지람

꾸지람 a scolding; a rebuke; a reproof; a reproach; a reprimand (공무상의). ¶~을 듣다 be scolded [reproved / rebuked] / catch [have / get] a scolding / (구어) catch it (hot) / get it∥나는 아버지에게 ~을 들었다 My father gave me a lecture.∥선생님한테 ~을 들었다 I was scolded by my teacher. / The teacher gave me a scolding.∥지각하여 ~을 들었다 I was scolded for being late. **꾸지람하다** scold; chide. ⇨=²꾸짖다

꾸짖다 scold; chide; rebuke; (문어) upbraid; (문어) reprove; reproach; reprimand; give (a person) a scolding [lecture / lesson]. ¶호되게 ~ scold severely / give (a person) a good scolding [sound rating] / give (a person) a sharp [severe / good] scolding / chew (a person) out∥지각했다고 학생을 ~ scold a student for being late∥그 녀석을 붙잡으면 호되게 꾸짖어 주겠다 When I get my hands on that brat, I'm going to give him a piece of my mind.∥선생님은 학생들이 제시간에 교실에 들어오지 않아 호되게 꾸짖었다 The teacher reprimanded the students for not coming to class on time.∥그는 그 일을 알게 되자 아들을 호되게 꾸짖었다 When he found about it, he gave his son a good scolding.

꾹 firmly; tightly; patiently. ⇨²꼭1·5

꾹꾹 [꽉·잔뜩] with no room [not an inch] to spare; to the full; tight. ¶~ 눌러 담다 pack in tightly / fill chock-full.

-꾼 a person notorious [noted] for; a man occupied with …. ¶씨름~ a wrestler.

꿀 honey; nectar (꽃의); molasses; honeydew. ¶~처럼 달콤한 honey-sweet (love) / mellifluous (music)∥~을 따다 collect honey∥

꿀꺽

~을 빨다 suck nectar [honey] (from a flower) // ~같이 달다 be sweet as honey // 꿀벌이 꽃에서 꽃으로 ~을 빨다 다닌다 The bees are sucking nectar from flower to flower. // ~ 먹은 벙어리라도 되었니 (Has) the cat got your tongue? / Did you lose your tongue?

꿀 먹은 벙어리 (속담) a person who could not open one's heart to another.

꿀꺽 1 [삼킴] at a gulp; holus-bolus. ¶~ 마시다 [삼키다] gulp (down) / drink [swallow] at a gulp / gulp (it) down holus-bolus // 침을 ~ 삼키다 swallow one's saliva // 남자는 컵의 위스키를 ~ 들이켰다 The man gulped down the cup of whisky with relish. // 맥주를 ~ 마셨다 I gulped my beer (down). **꿀꺽하다** gulp; make a gulping sound. 2 [참는 모양] (keep back) as if by swallowing; (swallow down) with effort; patiently. ¶분을 ~ 참다 swallow [gulp down] one's resentment.

꿀꺽꿀꺽 gulping(ly). ¶~ 마시다 gulp (down) / drink (water) in big swallows / take a long noisy drink / swill / take a swig (at). **꿀꺽꿀꺽하다** gulp and gulp; gulp away; swig; swill.

꿀꿀 [돼지 소리] grunting(ly); [물소리] bubbling; gurgling. ¶돼지가 ~거리고 있다 The pigs are oinking. **꿀꿀하다** (돼지가) grunt; (물이) bubble; gurgle.

꿀떡 (음식물 등을) at a gulp.

꿀렁 1 (물이) splashing about inside. **꿀렁하다** splash about inside. 2 [부푼 모양] baggily; puffily. **꿀렁꿀렁하다** baggy; puffy.

꿀리다 1 [구겨지다] be creasy [wrinkled / crumpled]; cave [fall] in; wrinkle; become creased; cockle.
2 [형편이 옹색하게 되다] be impoverished; be hard up (for money); be in needy [straitened] circumstances. ¶살림이 ~ be in needy [narrow] circumstances / find it hard to make a living / be badly off / (미) be poorly fixed / be ill off // 집안 형편이 ~ be in straitened circumstances.
3 [켕기다] have something on one's conscience. ¶양심이 ~ have scruples about (doing).
4 [기세·형세가 눌리다] feel small [overshadowed]; be [feel] inferior (to); compare unfavo(u)rably (with); [굴하다] give in; give up; succumb; be overwhelmed; get cornered. ¶조금도 꿀리지 않고 dauntlessly / without flinching // 누구에게도 꿀리지 않다 yield [be second] to none / prove oneself equal to anyone // 위엄에 ~ feel small in the presence of an awe-inspiring person / be overawed // 말에 ~ be cornered in an argument // 부자 친구를 만나면 어쩐지 꿀린다 I feel somehow small in the presence of a rich friend.

꿀물 honey-water; honeyed water.

꿀벌 [동] a honeybee. ¶~ 집 a honeycomb / [벌통] a beehive.

꿀샘 [식] a nectary; a honey gland.

꿀쩍 squelching; sniffling. ⇨>꼴짝

꿀쩍거리다 squelch and squelch. ⇨>꼴짝거리다

꿀쩍꿀쩍 squashing and squashing. ⇨>꼴짝꼴짝

꿀풀 [식] a self-heal.

꿇다 bend one's knees; kneel (down); fall [drop / go down / throw oneself] on one's knees. ¶무릎을 꿇고 on one's knees // 무릎을 꿇고 용서를 빌다 beg a person's forgiveness on one's knees // 무릎을 꿇고 기도를 드리다 kneel in prayer // 나는 비틀거리다가 나도 모르게 무릎을 꿇었다 I staggered and fell to my knees in spite of myself. // 골라인에 뛰어든 순간 주자는 무릎을 꿇고 쓰러졌다 Just as the runner crossed the finish line, his knees buckled [gave out] and he collapsed.

꿇리다 1 (무릎을) make (a person) kneel (down). 2 [억지로 복종하게 하다] bring (a person) to his knees; force to yield; keep (a person) down.

꿇어앉다 sit on one's knees [legs].

꿈 a dream; [환상] a vision; an illusion; [망상] a delusion; a chimera; [백일몽] a day-dream. ¶~이 없는 dreamless // 참[개] ~ a true [false] dream // 불길한 ~ an evil [ill-boding] dream // 무서운 ~ a terrifying dream / a nightmare // 청춘의 ~ the dream of youth // 헛된 ~ an empty dream / a crushed hope // 많은 소녀 ~ a girl full of romance / a starry-eyed girl // ~에도 생각지 않은 undreamed-of [undreamt-of] (success) / (a thing) never dreamed of // ~ 해몽 the interpretation of a dream // ~을 꾸다 dream a dream [have] a dream // …의 ~을 꾸다 dream of [about] (bears) // ~에서 깨다 awake from sleep [a dream] // (허황된 것에서) wake from one's reverie / come [be brought] to one's senses // ~이 아닌가 하고 의심하다 wonder if it is only a dream // ~에도 생시에도 잊지 못하다 can never forget [get (it) off] one's mind] asleep or awake / remember day and night // ~을 해몽하다 interpret a dream // 오랜 ~을 실현하다 realize [give shape to] one's long cherished dream [vision] // 인도에 가게 될 줄은 ~에도 생각지 못했다 I never even dreamed that I would be able to go to India. // 어머니가 ~에 나타났다 My mother appeared in my dream. / My mother appeared to me in sleep. // 그는 인생 설계의 큰 ~을 꾸었다 He had a great dream for his life. // 나는 즐거운 ~을 꾸었다 I had a pleasant dream. // 나는 긴 ~에서 깨어났다 I awoke from a long dream. // 나는 어머니 ~을 꾸었다 I dreamed [dreamt] of my mother. // 아버지를 만난 ~을 꾸었다 I dreamed that I met my father. / I met my father in my dream. // 파리에 가게 되다니 ~만 같다 It's like a dream to be able to go to Paris. // ~을 꾸는 것 같은 기분이었다 I felt as if I were in a dream. // 인생은 ~에 불과하다 Life is but a dream. // 그는 대정치가가 될 ~을 가졌다 He had dreams of being [becoming] a great politician. / It was his dream to be a great politician. // 그의 ~은 산산이 깨졌다 His dream has been shattered. / His hopes are gone. // 그들은 ~이 없다 They have no lofty ambitions [dreams]. // 그는 아버지의 죽음으로 ~에서 깨어났다 His father's death brought him to his senses. / He came to his senses when his father died. // 그녀는 우주비행사가 될 ~을 꾸고 있다 She dreams of becoming an astronaut. // ~은 맞았다 [맞지 않았다] The dream came true [turned out false]. // 지난 10년의 ~이 이루어져 우리는 집을 장만했다 Our dreams of the past ten years have been fulfilled, and now we have a home

꿈같다 dreamy; dreamlike; visionary; illusory; chimerical. ¶꿈같은 dreamy / dreamlike / illusory∥꿈같은 이야기 a fantastic story / nonsense / a wild tale / a story too good to be true∥꿈같은 세상 an illusory[a chimerical] world∥꿈같은 이야기를 하다 speak of a remotest possibility∥꿈같은 여행이었다 It was a dream of a trip. **꿈같이** as in a dream.

꿈결 (the midst of) a dream; a passing dream; a dream state; [꿈꾸는 상태] a dreamy[an ecstatic] state of mind; [덧없이 빠른 사이] emptiness; uncertainty. ¶~ 같은 세상 a chimerical[fleeting] world∥~ 같다 be like a dream / be dreamy[illusory] ∥ ~같이 지내다 live[go about] in a dream / dream away∥~에 듣다 listen (to a noise) dreamily[half asleep]∥그 후 한 달간은 ~처럼 지나갔다 After that we spent a month in a trance.

꿈꾸다 [바라다] dream (of); fancy (oneself); desire; wish; have an ambition (to ...). ¶그러한 날이 오기를 ~ dream forward to such a day∥그는 앞날의 행복한 생활을 꿈꾸었다 He drew a fine picture of his future happiness.∥그는 아들의 성공을 꿈꾸었다 He dreamed of his son's success.∥나는 장차 정치가가 되기를 꿈꾸었다 I used to dream of becoming a statesman.∥영화를 보면서 그녀는 주연 여우가 된 자기 자신을 꿈꾸었다 Watching the movie, she fancied[imagined] herself as the leading actress.

꿈나라 [꿈속의 세계] a dreamland; [환상 세계] a fairyland; a never-never land; a utopia; [잠] sleep. ¶~로 가다 [의식을 잃다] go to never-never land / [잠들다] fall asleep.

꿈속 a dream. ¶~에 나타나다 appear[come] in one's dream / come to one in a dream.

꿈자리 a dream; the happenings in a dream. ¶~가 좋았다[사나웠다] I had a good[bad] dream.∥그래서 그런지 어젯밤 ~가 사나웠다 I now see that the dream I had last night boded ill.

꿈지럭거리다 move sluggishly. ⇨꿈지락거리다

꿈쩍 stirring. ⇨꿈짝

꿈쩍없다 (서술적) remain unmoved.

꿈틀 with a wriggle[squirm]. **꿈틀하다** give a wiggle; wiggle; wriggle; writhe; twist; make a short writhing motion. ¶몸을 ~ (a worm) twist its body.

꿈틀거리다 wriggle (about); squirm; wriggle oneself. ¶꿈틀거리며 나아가다 wriggle along ∥뱀이 꿈틀거린다 A snake twists[wiggles] to and fro.∥아래에 있는 사람들이 꿈틀거리는 벌레처럼 보였다 The people below looked like so many squirming[wriggling] worms.∥지렁이가 꿈틀거리고 있다 An earthworm is wriggling about.

꿉꿉하다 dampish; (빨래가) damp-dry.

꿋꿋하다 [견고하다] strong; firm; solid; tough; hard; [언행이] upright; firm; inflexible; unyielding. ¶꿋꿋한 의지 a strong[an iron] will∥꿋꿋한 기상 an upright[unyielding] spirit∥꿋꿋한 마음 a firm[determined] mind / an unyielding mind∥꿋꿋한 자세 a straight posture. **꿋꿋이** strongly; firm(ly); unyieldingly. ¶~ 서다 stand firm∥~ 버티다 take a firm stand / show a firm[an unyielding] front∥~ 저항하다 make[offer] a stubborn resistance / put up a stiff resistance∥자기주장을 ~ 관철시키다 hold fast to one's views / stick to one's guns.

꿍꿍¹ [앓는 소리] groaning; moaning (with pain). ¶~ 앓다(병으로) moan with one's ailment / [걱정하다] worry (oneself) (about / over) / brood[grieve] (over) / repine (at) / mope (oneself) / indulge in vain regrets. **꿍꿍하다** groan (with pain). ⇨꿍꿍거리다

꿍꿍² with thumps; bang. ⇨쿵쿵

꿍꿍거리다 groan (with pain); moan. ¶아파서 꿍꿍거리고 있다 be groaning with pain.

꿍꿍이속 an underhand scheme; an underlying motive; a secret design. ¶~이 있다 have a plot in mind / have a secret design / have an ax to grind∥그는 무슨 ~이 있어 원조를 제의한 것 같다 He seems to have offered his aid for some hidden reason[from some ulterior motive].∥그는 돈을 빌릴 ~으로 술을 한 병 들고 찾아왔다 He brought along a bottle of wine for me as part of a scheme to get me to loan him money.

꿩 [동] a pheasant; a ring-necked[Chinese] pheasant(한국산). ¶**수**[암]~ a cock[hen] pheasant∥~ **사냥** pheasant hunting∥한 쌍의 ~ a brace of pheasants.

꿩의비름 [식] an orpine.

꿰다 1 [관통시키다] pass[run] through; thread; string. ¶바늘에 실을 ~ thread a needle / run[pass] a thread through a needle∥구슬을 ~ string[thread] beads. **2** [찔러 꽂다] pierce; thrust; put through. ¶꼬챙이에 ~ skewer / transfix∥꼬챙이에 생선을 꿰어 굽다 roast fish on skewers∥고기를 꼬챙이에 ~ skewer the meat. **3** [입다·신다] put on; wear. ¶신을 ~ put on one's shoes∥옷을 ~ wear one's clothes.

꿰뚫다 1 [관통하다] pierce; pass[run] through; shoot through(총알이); perforate(구멍을 뚫다). ¶정글을 꿰뚫은 도로 a road that pierces the jungle∥창으로 옆구리를 ~ pierce (a person's) side with a spear∥칼을 찔러 남의 심장을 ~ thrust a sword through a person's heart∥못이 벽을 꿰뚫었다 The nail pierced the wall.∥화살은 과녁을 꿰뚫었다 The arrow pierced[went through] the target.∥총알이 그의 왼쪽 허벅다리를 꿰뚫었다 A bullet went through his left thigh. **2** [통찰하다] discern / penetrate[see] into. ¶꿰뚫어 보다 discern / penetrate[see] into / see through / have an insight into (a person's character)∥그의 말은 문제의 실상을 꿰뚫은 것이었다 What he said went[got] to the root of the matter.∥그는 사람의 성격을 꿰뚫어 보는 힘이 있다 He is a shrewd judge of character.

꿰매다 [깁다] work in needle and thread; sew; stitch; (조각을 대고) sew (in) a patch; patch (up); put[add] a patch on (a coat); [수선하다] mend. ¶손으로 ~ sew by hand∥재봉틀로 ~ sew (something) on[with] a (sewing) machine∥옷을 ~ sew a garment∥해진 곳을 ~ sew up a torn seam∥저고리의 해진 데를 ~ sew up a rip in a jacket∥타진 솔기를 ~ sew up an open seam∥양말을 ~ darn socks∥듬성듬성 ~ sew with large stitches∥촘촘히 ~ sew a fine seam∥스커트의 찢긴 곳을 ~ mend a tear in a skirt∥웃옷 팔꿈치에 천 조각을 대고 ~ put patches on the elbows of a jacket∥의사는 상처를 다섯 바늘 꿰맸다 The doctor sewed up the cut

꿰미 with five stitches.

꿰미 a string (for coins / fish / persimmons / mushrooms); [꿴 것] things on a string. ¶생선 한 ~ a string of fish // 돈 ~ a string of coins.

꿰지다 [미어지다] rip; be torn; tear; [터지다] rend; burst; be broken; [해지다] wear out; [드러나다] be exposed; lay bare; be disclosed[revealed]; [일이 틀어지다] go wrong [amiss / ill]. ¶쉬 ~ tear easily // 일이 꿰지기 전에 손을 쓰다 take a counter-measure before something goes wrong with it // 자루가 ~ a bag bursts.

꿰찌르다 thrust through; run through; pierce. ¶단도로 가슴을 ~ plunge a dagger into (a person's) breast.

꿰차다 [제 것으로 만들다] make (a thing) for one's own possession; (속어) latch onto.

꿱 with a shout. ⇨꽥

꿱꿱 quacking; shouting and shouting. ⇨꽥꽥

꿱꿱거리다 cry; quack; gaggle. ⇨꽥꽥거리다

뀌다 break; release (flatulence). ¶방귀를 ~ break[make] wind / pass gas / (속어) fart.

끄나풀 1 [끈] (a piece of) string[cord]. ¶~로 묶다 tie with a string // ~을 풀다 untie [undo] the strings. 2 [앞잡이] a tool; an implement; a cat's-paw; a pawn; (경찰 등의) an agent; (소매치기의) an assistant. ¶경찰의 ~ a police agent[spy] // ~ 노릇을 하다 work as (another's) instrument / act as an agent (for).

끄다 1 (타는 불을) put out; (문어) extinguish; blow out(입으로 불어서); snuff (a candle); put (a fire) under; bring[get] (a fire) under control. ¶밟아서 ~ trample[tread out / stamp out] a fire // 촛불을 불어 ~ blow out a candle // 물을 끼얹어 ~ put out [quench] a fire with water // 담요로 덮어 불을 ~ smother a fire with a blanket // 두들겨서 ~ beat out (the flame) // 소방수가 불을 껐다 The firemen put the fire out. // 그는 담뱃불을 발로 밟아서 껐다 He stamped out the cigarette with his foot. // 우리는 풀밭의 불을 두들겨서 껐다 We beat out the grass fire. 2 (전기 등을) switch off (an electric light); turn off[out] (the television / the gas / the radio); put off[out] (the light). ¶시동을 ~ stop[kill] an engine // 텔레비전을 ~ turn off the TV [television set]. 3 (덩어리로 된 물건을) break; crush; crack; smash. ¶흙덩이를 ~ break a clod (of earth) / crush a lump of earth. 4 (빚 등을) pay[repay] (one's debts). ¶다달이 빚을 꺼 나가다 pay one's debts by the month.

끄덕 (머리를) with a nod. **끄덕하다** nod; give a nod. ¶찬성의 뜻으로 ~ nod one's agreement [in agreement] / nod one's approval [in approval / approvingly] / nod one's head in agreement[with approval] / nod in the affirmative // 그는 지나가면서 나에게 머리를 끄덕하였다 [머리를 끄덕여 인사했다] He nodded to me as he passed.

끄덕이다 nod. ¶재빨리 [가볍게] 고개를 ~ nod a quick nod / nod lightly / give a slight nod // 그는 대답 대신 그렇다고 고개를 끄덕였다 He nodded yes making no answer. // 아버지는 승낙의 뜻으로 고개를 끄덕였다 My father nodded his consent. // 그녀는 그에게 고개를 끄덕였다 She nodded him yes. / She nodded yes to him.

끄덩이 1 [머리털·실 등의 뭉친 끝] the ends of a bunch of hair [thread]. ¶머리를 잡고 seize[grab] (a person's) hair / seize (a person) by the hair. 2 (일의 실마리) a beginning; a clue; a lead.

끄떡 with a nod. ⇨끄덕

끄떡(도) 않다 do not budge an inch; do not turn a hair; do not move a muscle; remain unmoved[unflinching]; maintain[preserve] one's composure. // 문은 아무리 세게 밀어도 끄떡도 하지 않았다 No matter how hard I pushed, the door would not move an inch. // 그는 아무리 욕을 퍼부어도 끄떡도 하지 않다 He remained calm[unmoved] in spite of the shower of abuse heaped on him.

끄떡없다 [탈없이 온전하다] safe (and sound); all right; (물·불 등에) proof (against); [태연하다] unmoved; unflinching; withstand. ¶이 구두는 함부로 신어도 ~ These shoes will withstand much hard wear. // 이 건물은 화재에도 ~ This building is proof against damage from fire. // 어떤 일이 있어도 우리의 결속은 ~ We will stick together no matter what happens. // 불황이 닥쳐도 우리 회사는 ~ A recession will not affect[will have no effect on] our company. // 그녀는 두 시간 계속해서 수영해도 ~ Swimming two hours at a stretch is nothing to her [(미국 구어) doesn't faze her a bit]. // 그는 위스키 한 병을 다 마셔도 ~ He can drink a bottle of whisky without feeling the effects[with impunity].

끄르다 [맨 것을 풀다] undo; untie; unfasten; unpack; (잠근 것을) unlock; take off. ¶구두 끈을 ~ unlace one's boots // 매듭을 ~ untie a knot // 꾸러미를 ~ open[undo] a parcel / open[untie] a package // 상의의 단추를 ~ unbutton[undo the buttons of] one's coat.

끄르륵 with a belch[burp]. **끄르륵하다** belch; burp; eruct.

끄르륵거리다 keep burping; belch continually.

끄무레하다 cloudy; overcast; dull. ¶끄무레한 날씨 dim and cloudy weather / a cloudy day // 하늘이 ~ The sky has clouded up.

끄물거리다 get clear and cloudy at intervals; get cloudy off and on[from time to time]; remain unsettled. ¶끄물거리는 날씨 unsettled weather // 요 며칠 동안 날씨가 좀 끄물거리고 있다 The weather has been somewhat unsettled for the last few days.

끄집다 take[pick] up; hold and pull; draw; drag. ¶여럿 중에서 하나를 ~ take one among many // 의자를 끄집어 불 가로 가져오시오 Draw your chair up to the fire.

끄집어 내리다 take[bring / carry] down. ¶사람을 의자에서 ~ drag (a person) out of a chair // 책을 2층에서 ~ bring down books from upstairs.

끄집어 올리다 take[bring / carry] up; pull [draw / drag] up. ¶높은 지위로 ~ promote (a person) to a high position // 침몰선을 ~ salve a sunken vessel.

끄집어내다 1 (물건을) take[bring / carry] out; draw[pull] out; drag out. ¶호주머니에서 편지를 ~ take a letter out of one's pocket // 그는 호주머니에 손을 넣어 담배를 끄집어냈다 He reached into his pocket and came up

with a cigarette.
2 (말을) bring up 〔a new subject〕; bring 〈something〉 into conversation. ¶슬슬 금전 문제를 ~ lead up to the question of money // 이야기를 ~ broach a matter / introduce a topic[subject] // 대화 중에 장사 이야기를 ~ bring[〈구어〉] lug] business matters into conversation // 그는 회의 석상에서 자기의 개인적인 이야기를 끄집어냈다 He brought up his own personal affairs at the meeting. / He dragged his own personal affairs into the discussion at the meeting. // 모두가 바쁜 것 같아 나는 그 이야기를 끄집어낼 기회를 찾지 못했다 As everyone appeared to be busy, I couldn't find an opportunity to broach[bring up] the subject. // 그런 제안을 끄집어낸다고 하더라도 그는 들어주지도 않을 것이다 He will not listen to such a proposal. // 나는 그 말을 끄집어내기가 힘들었다 I found it difficult to broach the matter.

끄집어들이다 pull[take / carry / bring] in; gain; win[bring] over; enlist; interest 〈a person〉 in. ¶짐을 ~ carry luggage in // 사람을 자기 편으로 ~ win〈a person〉 over to one's side // 집 없는 거지들을 ~ take in homeless beggars // 사업에 자본가를 ~ interest capitalist in an enterprise // 사람을 방으로 ~ draw〈a person〉 into a room.

끄트러기 〔자질구레한 부스러기〕 chips; scobs; scraps; 〔나머지〕 odd pieces; odds and ends. ¶나무 ~ odd pieces of wood // 종이 ~ a scrap of paper // 천 ~ remnants[odds and ends] of cloth // ~의 scrap / odd.

끄트머리 1 〔맨 끝〕 the end; the tip; the edge; the last; the bottom; the extremity; the tail end. ¶~에서 ~까지 from end to end / from one end〈of ...〉 to the other // ~에 서다 stand at the tail end // ~로 졸업하다 graduate last on the list / come out bottom man in the class // ~를 뾰족하게 하다 cut to a point / point an end // 그는 행렬의 ~에 있었다 He was at the very end[tail end] of the procession. / He brought up the rear of the procession. **2**〔실마리〕 a clue; the beginning 〈of〉.

끈 1 a string; a cord (▶ cord는 string보다 굵고 rope보다 가늘); a ribbon; a lace; 〔꼰 끈〕 a braid; a line; a plait; a band. ¶가죽 ~ a strap / a thong // 구두 ~ a shoestring / shoelaces // ~을 매다[풀다] tie[untie / undo] / a string[the strings] // ~이 풀렸다 The strings came untied[loose]. **2**〔연줄〕 influence; ties; connection; 〈속어〉 a pull.

끈기(-氣) **1**〔끈끈한 기운〕 viscosity; stickiness; glutinousity; adhesiveness. ¶~ 있는 sticky / adhesive / glutinous // ~ 있는 쌀 glutinous rice.
2〔참을성〕 patience; perseverance; persistence; endurance; energy; stamina; staying power; tenacity; 〈미국 속어〉 stick-to-itiveness; ability to hang on; grit. ¶~ 있는[있게] persevering(ly) / patient(ly) / (싫증 내지 않고) untiring(ly) // ~ 있게 기회를 기다리다 patiently await an opportunity // ~ 있게 공부하다 concentrate all one's efforts on studying / put all one's efforts into one's studies / persevere in one's studies // 〈구어〉 stick to one's studies // 그에게는 ~가 없다 He lacks tenacity[〈미국 구어〉 stick-to-itiveness]. // 나이를 먹어 나는 ~가 없어졌다 With old age I have lost my perseverance. //

그녀는 ~ 있게 미싱 일을 했다 She worked untiringly at the sewing machine. // 그녀는 시어머니의 꾸지람을 가만히 듣고 있을 ~가 없었다 She did not have the patience to listen quietly to her mother-in-law's criticism. // 스웨터를 짜려면 ~가 필요하다 You need perseverance to knit a sweater. // 그는 ~ 있게 노력하지 않으니까 성공하지 못한다 He doesn't succeed because he does not persevere in his efforts.

끈끈이 lime; birdlime(새 잡는); something sticky; slime(더럽거나 고약한 냄새가 나는 것). ¶파리 잡는 ~ 종이〔a piece of〕 flypaper // ~로 새를 잡다 catch a bird with lime[a limed pole].

끈끈이주걱 〔식〕 a sundew; a drosera.

끈끈하다 1〔끈적끈적하다〕 sticky; adhesive; viscous; gluey. ¶끈끈한 액체 a sticky liquid // 끈끈한 풀 sticky[gluey] paste // 셔츠가 땀으로 ~ one's shirt is sticky with sweat // 이 풀은 끈끈하지 않다 This paste doesn't stick very well. **2**〔검질기다〕 tenacious; persistent; glutinous; sticky. ¶성질이 끈끈한 사람 a stickler / a man of great tenacity / (미) a tough guy. **끈끈히** stickily; viscously; persistently. ¶~ 캐묻다 ask questions persistently[inquisitively].

끈덕거리다 be loose[shaky / rickety / unsteady / unstable]. ¶끈덕거리는 이 a loose tooth // 끈덕거리는 책상 a swaying[wobbly] table // 책상다리가 끈덕거린다 The legs of the table are groggy.

끈덕지다 sticky; persistent; tenacious; pertinacious; patient; persevering; 〈문어〉 importunate. ¶끈덕지게 tenaciously / persistently / with persistence[tenacity] // 끈덕지게 질문하다 pester[plague]〈a person〉with questions // 그는 끈덕지게 설명을 요구했다 He persisted in demanding an explanation. // 그는 끈덕지게 말을 하는 사람이다 He speaks slowly and tenaciously[doggedly]. // 그렇게 끈덕지게 캐물으려고 하지 마라 Don't be so inquisitive. // 세일즈맨이 끈덕져서 나는 혼이 났다 The salesman was so insistent[persistent] that I didn't know what to do. // 정말 끈덕진 아이군 What a pest you are! // 그렇게 끈덕지게 조르지 마라 Don't keep after me like that! // 그의 끈덕짐에는 질려 버렸다 I am fed up with[I've had enough of] his doggedness. // 〈그의〉 빚 갚으라는 요구는 ~ He is hounding me for repayment of my debt. / 〈속어〉 He keeps bugging me to pay him back.

끈목 〔a〕 braid; 〔a〕 braided[plaited] cord; 〔장식용의〕 a gimp.

끈적거리다 1〔끈끈하여 자꾸 들러붙다〕 be sticky; be gluey; 〈미국 속어〉 be gooey; adhere〈to〉. ¶풀이 묻어 손이 끈적거린다 My hands are sticky with paste. // 땀으로 내 속셔츠가 끈적거렸다 My undershirt was sticky with perspiration. // 땀이 끈적끈적 clung to my sweaty body. // 나는 무엇인가 끈적거리는 것을 밟았다 I stepped on something gooey[sticky]. **2**〔검질기다〕 stick〈to〉; (be) tenacious; persistent; persist〈in〉; get on〈a person's〉 nerves; irritate by being persistent. ¶끈적거리는 사람 a person of tenacity.

끈적끈적 1〔끈끈하게 들러붙는 모양〕. ¶알사탕이 ~ 손에 들러붙었다 Some[The] candy stuck to my hands. / My hands were sticky [〈구어〉 gooey] with candy. // 땀으로 셔츠가

끈질기다

~ 몸에 들러붙고 있다 My shirt is clinging [sticking] to my body with perspiration. **끈적끈적하다** be sticky. ⇨"끈적거리다1 ¶손이 기름으로 끈적끈적하다 My hands are greasy. //인쇄용 잉크는 매우 끈적끈적하다 Printer's ink is a very viscous substance. 2 [검질기게] tenaciously; persistently. **끈적끈적하다** stick (to). ⇨"끈적거리다2

끈질기다 strong and sticky; strongly adhesive; [집요하다] steadfast; persistent; tenacious; obstinate; unyielding; (서술적) have tenacity of purpose; stick to (a task); persist in (doing). ¶끈질긴 노력 a steadfast endeavor / (a) persistent effort//끈질기게 협상하다 negotiate indefatigably [tenaciously] //그는 끈질기게 자기 의견을 고집한다 He clings tenaciously to his own opinion.//그는 참으로 끈질긴 녀석이다 What nerve he's got! //그는 전혀 아는 바 없다고 끈질기게 버텼다 He persistently denied all knowledge of the matter. / He persisted in denying all knowledge of it.//그는 끈질긴 노력으로 오늘의 지위에 올랐다 He has risen to his present position by sheer effort.//그는 네스호(湖)의 괴물[피수]의 존재를 끈질기게 믿고 있었다 He held a persistent belief in the existence of the Loch Ness monster.

끊기다 be cut; break off; come to an end; expire; terminate. ⇨"끊어지다

끊다 1 [절단하다] sever; cut (off); chop off; break. ¶둘로 ~ cut in two//사지를 ~ cut off the limbs / dismember a body//밧줄을 cut[break] a rope//직각으로 ~ cut at right angles//불에 녹여 ~ burn off//금속 토막을 전기로 녹여 ~ cut off a piece of metal with electricity//도둑이 금고의 문을 가스 버너로 녹여 끊어 버렸다 The burglar burned off the safe door with a blowtorch.

2 [단절하다] sever (one's connections with); break off (relations with a person); break with; cut (connection); cut off (communication); [중단·차단하다] cut off; stop; shut off; intercept; interrupt; (꼭지·스위치 등을 조작하여) turn off (the gas / water). ¶끊을래야 끊을 수 없는 인연 an indissoluble tie / a fatal connection//적의 정보망을 ~ cut[sever / break up] an enemy's intelligence network //끊으려야 끊을 수 없는 관계에 있다 be inseparable bound up (with)//교제를 ~ sever [cut / drop] acquaintance with (a person) / break off friendship with / break with (a person) / have done with / (미) be through with//연락을 ~ sever[cut off] the connection [communication] (between the two) / [행방불명되다] disappear//발을 ~ stop visiting / keep oneself away from / cease to visit//외교 관계를 ~ break off [sever] all diplomatic relations//전기[가스]를 ~ cut off electricity[gas]//전류를 ~ switch off the electric current//회로를 ~ kill a circuit//보급로를 ~ block the supply route//적의 퇴로를 ~ cut off the enemy's retreat//나는 그녀와의 관계를 끊기로 했다 I decided to break off[sever] my relationship with her.//나는 폭력단과의 관계를 끊었다 I have broken off (my connection) with the racketeers.//나는 그와의 교제를 끊었다 I've broken with him.

3 [계속하던 행위를] 그치다] pause; stop; break off; (전화를) cut off; switch off; disconnect; (미) hang up (the receiver); (영) ring off. ¶그는 갑자기 말을 끊었다 He suddenly stopped talking. / He broke off abruptly.//그는 전화를 끊었다 He hung up.//전화를 끊지 말아 주시오 Hold it [Hold on] just a minute, please. / Hold the line, please. / Please do not cut off (the phone).

4 [말·문장을 마디 지어 자르다] punctuate; mark[set] off (a clause) by a comma. ¶이야기를 ~ punctuate a story//한 구(句)씩 끊어서 읽다 read (a text) with pauses between phrases.

5 [그만두다] abstain from (fish and flesh); give up (drinking / smoking); for(e)go; deny oneself; abjure; abnegate(좋아하는 것 등을). ¶술을 ~ abstain from wine / quit[stop / give up / leave off] drinking / forswear [(속어) swear off] drinking(맹세를 하고) / (미국 속어) be on the water wagon//담배를 ~ give up [quit] smoking//나는 2개월 전부터 술[담배]을 끊었다 I quit[gave up] drinking[smoking] two months ago.

6 (목숨을) kill; take (a person's) life. ¶스스로 목숨을 ~ kill oneself / suicide//그는 스스로 목숨을 끊었다 He killed himself. / He committed suicide.

7 [사다] buy. ¶옷감을 ~ buy a piece of cloth//차표를 ~ buy a ticket / [개찰하다] clip a ticket.

8 [발행하다] issue; write out; draw. ¶전표를 ~ sign [give / write out] a chit / issue a voucher [a payment slip]//수표를 ~ issue [write out / make out / draw] a check.

끊어지다 1 [절단되다] be cut; break; snap(실 등이). ¶열에 녹아 ~ burn out//전열기[전기 스토브]의 니크롬선이 열에 녹아 끊어졌다 The nichrome wire in the heater has burned out. //실이 끊어졌다 The thread snapped.//전선이 끊어졌다 An electric wire is down.//퓨즈가 끊어졌다 The fuse is gone [blown]. / The fuse blew.//전구가 끊어졌다 The electric bulb has burned [(영) burnt] out.

2 [두절·차단·중단되다] break off; be [get / become] broken; be cut off; be interrupted [suspended / blocked]; cease; discontinue; pause; intermit; be switched off; be disconnected. ¶이야기가 끊어졌을 때 in pauses of the conversation / between talks//교통이 ~ traffic [transportation] is stopped [interrupted]//소식이 ~ communication is cut off [interrupted]//연락이 ~ a connection is cut off / lose contact (with)//전화가 끊어졌다 A telephone call was cut off [interrupted]. //통화 중에 전화가 끊어졌다 We were cut off in the middle of our telephone conversation. //그 후 그는 소식이 끊어졌다 He was never heard of again. / That was the last letter we had from him.//그와의 연락이 끊어졌다 We have lost contact with him.//모든 통신이 끊어졌다 All correspondence ceased [was cut off].

3 [관계가 멀어지다] come to an end; be cut [severed]; break (off) with; have done with; be off with (her former husband); be through [over / done / finished] with. ¶관계가 ~ break off with (a person) / be through with (a person) / relations [connections] are severed//인연이 ~ be separated / be divorced(부부의) / be finished with each other.

4 [죽게 되다] expire; end; die. ¶숨이 ~ breathe one's last (breath) / expire / die // 그는 숨이 끊어지기 전에 이와 같이 말했다 This is what he said (just) before he breathed his last [passed away]. // 그는 병원으로 운반하는 도중에 숨이 끊어졌다 He died on the way to (the) hospital. // (내가 갔을 때) 그는 숨이 끊어지려 하고 있었다 I found him breathing feebly. / I found him at his last gasp.

5 [거래·기한이 끊기다] expire; terminate; become [fall] due; run out; be up; (공급 등이) run out; be out; be exhausted; be used up; fail; be sold out of stock. ¶상품이 끊어졌다 Merchandize was out of stock. // 1년이 지나면 계약 기간이 끊어진다 The contract holds good for a year. // 그와는 거래가 끊어졌다 The business with him has been terminated. // 태풍으로 전기와 수도가 끊어졌다 Because of the typhoon both the electric current and the water supply failed [were cut off]. // 계속되는 가뭄으로 급수가 끊어졌다 The supply of water ran out [We were cut off from the water supply] on account of a continued drought.

끊음표(―標) [음] staccato. ⇨ =스타카토

끊이다 cease; discontinue; come to an end. ¶걱정이 끊이지 않다 be never free from care(s) // 저 집안에는 말썽이 끊이지 않는다 There is no end of troubles in that family. / There are constant troubles in that family.

끊임없다 continued; continual; continuous; ceaseless; unceasing; incessant; uninterrupted; endless; perpetual; constant; successive. ¶끊임없는 비행기의 소음 the incessant noise of airplanes // 끊임없는 주의 constant attention // 끊임없는 걱정 endless worries // 끊임없는 발전 continuous development // 끊임없는 손님 a constant stream of visitors // 외국어를 유창하게 구사하기 위해서는 끊임없는 노력이 필요하다 Constant [Unremitting] effort is necessary to achieve fluency in a foreign language. // 나는 그녀의 끊임없는 잔소리에 넌더리가 난다 I am sick of her incessant [constant] nagging. // 오늘은 하루 종일 내객이 끊임없었다 Today we had one visitor after another. **끊임없이** constantly; continually; continuously; incessantly; ceaselessly; unceasingly; in succession; successively; without cease [ceasing / cessation / interruption / intermission / letup]; without a break; [영원히] perpetually; everlastingly; [항상] always; ever. ¶~ 지껄이다 talk without a pause [all the time] / have no end of talk / chatter ceaselessly // ~ 노력하다 make a constant effort / continue one's unremitting exertions // ~ 감시하다 keep a constant watch (over) / be always on the watch (over) // ~ 전화가 걸려 오다 have telephone calls almost without a break // 젖먹이가 ~ 울었다 The baby never stopped crying. / The baby cried constantly. // 화산은 ~ 불을 뿜고 있었다 The volcano erupted without cease [intermission]. // 물이 ~ 솟아 나오고 있다 Water is gushing out (ceaselessly). // 그는 ~ 담배를 피우고 있다 He is smoking all the time [endless cigarettes]. // 이 거리에는 차가 ~ 다닌다 There is a continuous stream of traffic on this street. // 피난민의 행렬이 ~ 이어졌다 The line of refugees went on unbroken. // 눈물이 ~ 그녀의 뺨을 흘러내렸다 Tears streamed incessantly down her cheeks. // 그는 ~ 영어를 공부하고 있다 He continually studies English. // 시계는 ~ 똑딱 소리를 내고 있다 The clock ticks constantly [all the time]. / The clock makes a constant ticking sound.

끌 a chisel. ¶둥근 ~ a gouge / (조각용) a scauper // ~로 파다 chisel / cut with a chisel.

끌끌 1 [혀 차는 소리] tut(-tut); tsk(tsk). ¶혀를 ~ 차다 click [clack] one's tongue / tut / go tut-tut [tsktsk]. **2** [트림하는 소리] belching; burping.

끌다 1 [잡아당기다] pull; draw; give a pull; jerk(갑자기); drag [tug / lug / haul] (at) (세게); tow(밧줄로). ¶양쪽에서 ~ tug from both sides // 남을 사방으로 끌고 다니다 drag a person around (a city) // 남의 소매를 ~ pull (a person) by the sleeve / tug at a (person's) sleeve // 달구지를 ~ draw [pull] a cart // 배를 밧줄로 ~ tour a boat with a rope // 땅 위로 통나무를 ~ drag [pull] a log along the ground // 우리는 적의 깃발을 끌어 내렸다 We hauled [dragged] down the enemy flag. // 그들은 침몰선을 끌어 올렸다 They salvaged [raised] a sunken ship.

2 [질질 끌다] drag; draggle. ¶발을 질질 ~ drag one's feet // 그는 발을 질질 끌며 걷는다 He walks with dragging feet. / He scuffs. / He drags his feet as he walks. / He drags himself along. / He shuffles (his feet) along. // 그녀는 치맛자락을 끌며 걷는다 She walks with a trailing skirt.

3 [이끌다] lead; guide. ¶말을 ~ lead a horse (by the bridle) // 아이의 손을 ~ lead a child by the hand.

4 [연행하다] pull along by force; take (a person) to (a place); walk (a person) off to (a place). ¶경찰서로 끌고 가다 drag [take] (a person) off to the police station.

5 [늦추거나 미루다] prolong; protract; delay; draw [drag] out; drag on. ¶오래 끄는 병 a long disease / a lingering [protracted] disease // 오래 끌어 온 협상 [교섭] long-pending [-drawn-out] negotiations // 지불을 ~ put off [delay] payment // 회답을 ~ delay one's reply [in answering] // 약속을 ~ put off [delay on] a promise // 차일피일 ~ put off from day to day // 마지막까지 ~ put (a matter) off to the last moment // 그는 연설 [이야기]을 질질 끌었다 He dragged out his speech. // 전쟁은 끝없이 질질 끌었다 The war dragged on endlessly. // 그의 병은 오래 끌었다 He was long in recovering from his illness. // 반드시 감기가 오래 끌지 않도록 하시오 Be sure not to let your cold hang on for a long time. // 재판 [협상]은 질질 끌었다 The trial [negotiations] dragged on [along]. // 그들은 협상을 1주일 동안이나 끌어 왔다 They have dragged the negotiation for a whole week. // 질문이 계속 잇달아 인터뷰는 시간을 끌었다 The interview was prolonged by a long succession of questions. // 토론은 한밤중까지 질질 끌었다 The discussion dragged on until the middle of the night. // 중재는 질질 끌어 한 달간이나 걸렸다 The arbitration was spun out for a month. // 올해는 장마가 오래 끌어 쌀의 작황이 나쁠 것이다 The rice crop this year will be poor on account of the lingering rainy season.

끌러지다

6 [마음을 쏠리게 하다] attract; draw; catch; arrest; win; [매혹하다] charm; bewitch; fascinate; captivate. ¶남을 끄는 힘 attraction / magnetism∥세인의 주목을 ~ attract[draw] popular attention∥눈길을 ~ draw[attract / engage] one's attention / attract (one's) notice / catch the eye∥여자 마음을 ~ win the heart[love] of a woman∥인기를 ~ catch[win / gain] popularity∥주의를 ~ attract[draw / call] (a person's) attention (to)∥손님을 ~ draw custom[customers] / (호객꾼이) tout / entice / (try to) call in customers / (매춘 등을 위해) solicit∥그녀의 일하는 방식이 내 눈길을 끌었다 The way she worked attracted my attention.∥그에게는 어딘가 사람을 끄는 데가 있다 He has something about him that fascinates others. / There is something engaging[attractive] about him.∥그 연극은 관객을 많이 끌고 있다 The play is a great draw.∥그가 만드는 광고문은 여성의 마음을 끈다 The advertising copy he writes attracts women[appeals to women's imaginations].∥저 슈퍼마켓에서는 손님을 끌기 위해 온갖 수단을 다 쓰고 있다 That supermarket is trying every means to draw[attract] customers.∥이 고장으로 사람들을 끄는 것은 뭐니뭐니해도 온천이다 What attracts people to this place is, above anything else, the hot springs.

7 [시설하다] lay on (gas / water); install (a telephone). ¶파이프로 물을 ~ pipe water (to a place)∥강물을 ~ draw water off a river (into)∥전화를 ~ have a telephone installed∥집에 수도며, 가스, 전등을 끌어 놓았다 Water, gas and electricity has been laid on in my house.

8 [인용하다] cite; quote; refer to. ¶예를 끌어 오다 cite[give] an example.

끌러지다 come[get] loose; be loosened; come [get] untied[undone]; (one's shoestring(s)) become unlaced. ¶구두끈이 끌러졌다 My shoestring came untied.∥네 허리띠가 끌러졌어 Your belt has come loose.

끌리다 **1** [당겨지다] be pulled; be drawn (by); be tugged; be lugged; be hauled; (질질) be dragged; be draggled; be trailed; drag; draggle; trail. ¶신발이 ~ one's shoes drag (on the ground)∥친구에 끌려 그는 경마에 손을 대기 시작했다 Under the influence of bad company, he began to gamble on horse races.∥그런 타입의 사람은 나쁜 길에 끌려 들어가기 쉽다 A man of that type is easily led[tempted / enticed] into evil ways.∥그는 남이 시키는 대로 질질 끌려 다니기만 한다 He is being led (around) by the nose.∥나는 그들의 운동에 끌려 들어갔다 I was dragged into[got involved in] their movement.∥그녀가 걸어갈 때 흰 웨딩드레스[긴 스커트]가 바닥에 끌렸다 Her white wedding dress[long skirt] trailed along the floor as she walked.

2 [연행·소환되다] be taken to (a place); be walked off to (a place). ¶경찰서에 끌려가다 be taken[walked off] to a police station∥나는 공청회에 끌려 나오게 되었다 I was summoned to the public hearing.

3 [늦추어지다·미루어지다] be prolonged; be protracted; be delayed; be retarded; drag on [pulled off]. ¶지불이 질질 끌리어졌다 The payment was delayed.

4 (마음이) be attracted; be drawn; [매혹되다] be charmed; be fascinated; [감동되다] be moved; be touched (with emotion); (뭠에) be touted[enticed / solicited]. ¶광고에 끌려 attracted[enticed] by the advertisement∥인정에 ~ be overcome by one's affection∥인정에 ~ be touched with humanity∥부모 자식 간의 사랑에 ~ be drawn by the ties of parent and child∥나는 그 음모에 끌려 들어 갔다 I was enticed into the plot.∥무의식중에 그의 이야기에 끌려 들어갔다 I was carried away by his speech. / I was caught up in his speech[story].∥그녀는 그에게 마음이 끌리는 것을 억제할 수 없었다 She found her affections drawn irresistibly toward him.∥그는 그녀의 매력에 끌렸다 He was attracted [fascinated / drawn to her] by her charm.

끌어내다 take[get / pull / draw] out; drag out [forth] (질질); carry (a thing) out of (a house). ¶침대[집]에서 ~ rout (a person) out of bed[the house]∥나는 그 개를 개집에서 끌어냈다 I dragged the dog out from the kennel.∥그는 마구간에서 말을 끌어냈다 He led a horse out of the stable.∥그들은 그 남자를 방에서 억지로 끌어냈다 They dragged the man out of the room against his will.∥그녀는 침대 밑에서 여행 가방을 끌어냈다 She dragged[pulled] out a suitcase from under the bed.∥그들은 나를 설득하여 파티에 끌어냈다 They talked me into attending the party.

끌어내리다 (지위를) demote; degrade; lower in rank. ¶낮은 자리로 ~ reduce (an officer) to lower grade / lower (a person) in rank / demote[degrade] (a person).

끌어넣다 draw[drag] in[into]; pull in[into]; take[bring] (a person) into (a room); lead in; (가입시키다) enlist; (유인하다) win[gain / bring] over (to); (유혹하다) tempt[entice] in[into]. ¶음모에 ~ tempt (a person) into an intrigue∥자기 편에 ~ win (a person) over to one's side / bring (a person) over to one's camp∥미국을 극동의 분쟁에 ~ lead the United States into entanglements in the Far East∥우리는 그를 우리의 싸움[분쟁]에 끌어넣었다 We involved him in our quarrel [dispute].

끌어당기다 draw (a thing) near[toward / up to] (one); pull nearer; drag in; (마음 등을) attract; draw. ¶밧줄을 ~ pull[haul] in a rope hand over hand∥(남의) 소매를 ~ pull (a person) by the sleeve / tug at (a person's) sleeve∥재떨이를 가까이 ~ draw an ashtray near∥난롯가로 의자를 ~ draw a chair up to the fire∥자석은 철분을 끌어당긴다 A magnet attracts iron.∥그는 어딘지 사람을 끌어당기는 데가 있다 There is something engaging[attractive] about him.∥나는 전기스탠드를 내 가까이에 끌어당겼다 I drew the lamp near[up to / close to] me.

끌어대다 **1** (돈을) borrow[collect] money (necessary) for (a business); raise money [funds / a loan]. ¶돈을 여기저기서 ~ scrape together a sum of money∥집을 사려고 돈을 ~ raise money to buy a house∥토지를 저당 잡히고 돈을 ~ raise money on one's land / 자금을 ~ finance an enterprise∥천만 원가량 ~ scrape together 10,000,000 won. **2** [맞추어 대다] bring together; join together; introduce.

끌어들이다 ¶손님을 ~ solicit[draw] a customer // 남의 팔을 잡고 ~ drag[pull] a person in by the arms // 남을 클럽에 ~ cajole[persuade] a person to join a club // 수상한 여자를 방 안에 ~ take a questionable woman into one's private room // 음모에 ~ entangle (a person) in a plot // 범죄에 ~ induce (a person) to evil doing // 자기 편에 ~ win[gain] (a person) over to one's side / bring (a person) over to one's camp // 자본가를 사업에 ~ interest capitalists in an enterprise // 그는 나를 방으로 끌어들였다 He dragged[pulled] me into the room. // 한 남자가 통행인들을 유인하여 바 안으로 끌어들이려 하고 있다 A man is trying to lure passersby into the bar. // 그런 일에 사사로운 감정을 끌어들여서는 안 된다 You should not bring personal feelings into it. // 최근 야구 시합이 많은 관중을 끌어들이고 있다 Recently baseball games have been drawing[attracting] large crowds (of spectators). // 이 조약은 한국을 전쟁에 끌어들일지도 모른다 This treaty may drag Korea into a war. // 그 두 극장은 아주 비슷한 영화로 서로 더 많은 관중을 끌어들이려고 한다 The two theaters are trying to out draw each other with very similar films.

끌어안다 draw (a person) closer to one's breast; hold[clasp / carry] (a person) in one's arms; give (a person) a hug; embrace; hug. ¶어린애를 ~ hug a child // 서로 ~ embrace[hug] each other / be in[go into] each other's arms // 어머니는 아기를 꼭 끌어안았다 The mother clasped her baby to her breast. // 그는 소녀를 꼭 끌어안았다 He held the girl tightly in his arms. // 그는 힘차게 그녀를 끌어안았다 He gave her a squeeze. // 두 사람은 서로 끌어안고 울었다 The two threw themselves into each other's arms and wept.

끌어올리다 drag[pull / draw / lug]; (성적·수준을) grade[level] up. ¶네 이야기의 수준을 학급 수준으로 끌어올려라 Level up your speech to the class.

끌채 a thill; a shaft; a pole; a tongue. ¶~에 맨 말 a thiller.

끌탕 affliction; anguish; agony; worry. **끌탕하다** be troubled (with); be worried (about); worry (oneself) (about / over); be afflicted (with).

끓는점 (-點) [물][화] the boiling point. ¶~이 낮은 가솔린 high-test gasoline.

끓다 1 (비등하다) boil; seethe; be on the boil. ¶끓는 물 boiling[scalding] water // 끓어 넘치다 boil up // 끓기 시작하다 come to the boil / begin to boil // 물이 끓는다 Water boils. / Water bubbles up. // 밥이 끓는다 The rice is boiling over. // 냄비가 끓어 넘친다 The pot is boiling over.

2 (뜨거워지다) become very hot; become boiling hot. ¶방이 설설 끓는다 A (heated) room is boiling hot.

3 (들끓어 오르다) ferment; stir; burn; glow; be aflame; fret; fume. ¶노여움으로 속이 부글부글 ~ fret and fume / seethe[boil] with anger / be convulsed with anger // 그는 애국의 피가 끓고 있었다 He was a boil with patriotism. // 젊은 피가 끓는다 One's youthful blood tingles.

4 (배가) rumble. ¶배 속이 끓었다 The bowels rumbled.

5 (가래가) make a rattling[guggling] sound; rattle in the throat; ruckle. ¶목에 가래가 끓는다 Phlegm obstructs[sticks in] the throat.

6 [우글거리다] (벌레 등이) swarm; gather; flock; collect; (사람이) crowd; gather. ¶파리가 ~ be infested with flies // 설탕에 개미가 끓고 있다 Ants are swarming upon the sugar. // 광장에는 사람들이 끓고 있다 The public square was crowded with people.

끓어오르다 boil[seethe] up. ¶물은 이내 끓어올랐다 Water soon boiled up. // 나는 분노로 피가 끓어올랐다 My blood boiled with indignation[rage / anger]. // 그의 말에 배알이 끓어올랐다 His words made my blood boil. // 그는 증오감이 끓어오르고 있다 He is seething with hatred.

끓이다 1 [끓게 하다] boil; heat; make hot. ¶펄펄 ~ boil up / bring (water) to the boil // 국을 ~ make soup // 물을 ~ boil water // 차를 ~ draw[brew] tea / make[prepare] tea // 뭉근한 불에 서서히 ~ simmer / boil gently // 목욕물을 ~ prepare[heat] the bathe // 물은 반드시 끓여 먹어라 Do not fail to boil water once before you drink it. **2** [속태우다] worry; bother; trouble; vex; annoy. ¶그 일로 나는 속을 끓였다 This weighed[pressed] heavy on my mind. // 속을 끓일 만한 일이 아니다 That is nothing serious. / It is nothing to worry about.

끔벅 1 (등불·별빛 등이) with a flash; with a twinkle. **끔벅하다** flicker; twinkle; blink. **2** (눈을) with a blink[blinking]; with a wink. **끔벅하다** blink; wink.

끔벅거리다 1 (별이) twinkle; (불이) flicker; waver; shimmer. **2** (눈을) blink (one's eyes); wink; nictitate.

끔찍하다 1 [참혹하다] cruel; atrocious; horrible; heartless; [으스스하다] ghastly; grim; gruesome; appalling. ¶끔찍한 살인 a cruel [cold-blooded] murder // 끔찍한 광경 a cruel [horrible] sight // 끔찍한 죽음 a horrible death // 생각만 해도 ~ The mere thought of it makes me shudder. // 끔찍한 짓을 다하는군 It is cruel of you to do such a thing.

2 [지독하다] terrible; awful; horrible; tremendous. ¶끔찍한 인파 an awful turnout of people / a mammoth crowd // 끔찍한 속도로 at a terrific[devil-defying] speed // 끔찍하게도 크다 be awfully big[large]. **끔찍이** terribly; horribly; awfully; tremendously.

3 [극진하다] terribly kind; awfully thoughtful[considerate]; very courteous[cordial]; devoted; warmhearted. ¶끔찍한 대접 cordial [hearty] hospitality // 끔찍한 사랑 fond [ardent] love. **끔찍이** kindly; courteously; cordially; heartily; devotedly. ¶~ 사랑하다 love very much / dote[doat] on (one's child).

끗수 (-數) points; a score; (낱장의) spots; pips. ¶~가 높은 패를 잡다 get a higher number of pips // 내 ~는 넷이다 My point is 4.

끙끙 (아파서) with groans[moans]; (불평으로) grumbling; (힘이 들어) laboriously. ¶~ 앓다 (아파서) groan[moan] with[in] pain. [비유] worry (oneself) (about / over) / fret (about) / brood[grieve] (over) / repine (at) / indulge in vain regrets(돌이킬 수 없는 일을). // 그렇게 ~ 않지 마라 Don't worry! / No dark brooding! / Cheer up! / Take it easy! / 무슨 일로 ~ 앓느냐 What's your worry [trouble]? / What are you worried about? /

끙끙거리다

What has made you so unhappy?/그 일로 나는 ~ 앓고 있었다 I was worrying myself sick about it.//~ 앓아 보아야 별 도리가 없다 It is no use worrying[fretting] about [over] it. **끙끙하다** groan; moan. ⇨*끙끙거리다*

끙끙거리다 groan; moan; grumble; labor. ¶끙끙거리며 물건을 나르다 drag[carry] a thing with great effort//끙끙거리며 가파른 언덕을 오르다 toil[make one's way] up a steep hill//몸의 열이 높아 그 아이가 끙끙거리고 있었다 The child had a high temperature and was moaning and groaning. / The child was moaning with fever. /나는 끙끙거리며 힘껏 밀어 보았지만 아무리 해도 문이 열리지 않았다 I shoved on the door[gave the door a couple of good strong pushes], but it just wouldn't open.

끝 1 [최종] an end; a close; a finish; a termination; [종말] the end; the extremity; [결말] (a) conclusion; [기한의 만료] expiration. ¶여로의 ~ the journey's end / the end of a journey//세계의 ~ the world's end / the end of the world//집회의 ~ the close of a meeting//~으로[에 가서] lastly / finally / at (long) last / at length / in conclusion / in the end / in the long run(결국)//~을 잘 맺다 end well / come to a good end / come to a happy ending[termination] / make a happy ending (of) / (맺게 하다) bring to a successful issue//~으로 한 말씀 드리겠는데… In concluding my speech, I would like to say….//~에 가서 그 아이는 울기 시작했다 In the end the child began to weep. /행렬의 맨 ~에 간호사들이 왔다 Last in the procession came the nurses.//(설명 등을 한 뒤에) 이것으로 ~입니다 That's all there is to tell. /이만 ~. That's that. / That's it. / (교실에서) So [This] much for today.//이 길의 ~에 절이 하나 있다 There is a temple at the end of this road.//무엇이든지 그 ~이 있다 All things have an end.//~이 어떻게 될지 아무도 모른다 There is no knowing how it will end.//정치가로서의 그의 생애도 이제 ~이다 His political career is now at an end.//내 이름은 명단의 ~ 쪽에 있다 My name stands near the bottom of the list.//그는 맨 ~에 왔다 He was the last to come.//우리의 우정? 그건 그것으로 ~이야 Our friendship? That was the end of it.//우리는 ~까지 싸울 각오가 되어 있다 We are prepared to fight to the last man.//그 사건은 ~이 났다 The case came[was brought] to an end.//이 이야기는 뜻밖의 결말로 ~을 맺는다 This story has an unexpected[a surprise] ending.

2 [첨단] the point (of a pencil); the (pointed) head (of a spear); the tip (of a finger); the nib (of a pen); the end[top] (of a pole); the nozzle (of a hose); an end; a tip; the tail end; the extremity; [맨 마지막 부분] the edge; the verge; the brink; the border. ¶붓 ~ the tip of a writing brush//창 ~ a spear head//칼 ~ the point of a sword//혀 ~ the tip of a tongue//코 ~ the end[tip] of a nose//처마 ~ the edge of the eaves//편 ~ a pinpoint//갑(岬)의 ~ the tip[horn] of a promontory//이삭의 ~ the tip of an ear (of grain)//부지의 북쪽 ~에 at the northern end of the lot//이 ~에서 저 ~까지 from this end to the other end//머리에서 발 ~까지 from head to toe//~이 가는 tapering//~이 가는 손가락 tapering fingers//~이 굵은 claviform / club-shaped//의자 ~에 걸터앉다 sit on the edge of the chair//~이 점점 가늘어지다 taper (to a point)//**~이 뾰족하다** be pointed[sharp] at the end//**~이 둥그렇다** be rounded at the end//**~을 자르다** cut at the end / cut off the end / trim the end//실의 ~에 매듭을 지어라[만들라] Knot the end of a thread. / Put a knot in the end of a thread.//이 연필은 ~이 뾰족하다 This pencil has a sharp point.//그 반도는 ~이 점점 가늘어진다 The peninsula tapes off to a narrow point of land.//이 막대기의 ~은 가늘다 The end of this stick is tapered.//손가락 ~을 바늘에 찔렸다 I hurt the tip of my finger with a needle.

3 [한도] a limit; limits; bounds; an end. ¶**~이 없다** be endless[limitless / boundless] / know no end//(사람의) 욕심에는 ~이 없다 There is no limit to one's desire. / Avarice knows no bounds.//토론하기 시작하면 ~이 없다 There is no end to argument.//그녀의 야망에는 ~이 없다 Her ambition knows no bounds. / There is no end[limit] to her ambition.//그녀가 수다를 떨기 시작하면 ~이 없었다 There was no end to her chatter.//그는 내버려 두면 ~도 없이 지껄일 것이다 He will go on talking forever, if he is allowed to.

4 [결과] (in the) end; (as the[a]) result; (in) consequence. ¶충분히 생각한 ~에 after due consideration//심사숙고 ~에 after much thinking//다년간의 노력 ~에 after many years' efforts//그는 온갖 죄를 다 지은 ~에 살인까지 하였다 He went to the extent of committing murder to top off the varieties of crimes he had perpetrated.//그것은 그가 신중히 생각한 ~에 취한 행동이었다 He did it after careful thought.//말다툼 ~에 그들은 주먹다짐을 하게 되었다 They proceeded from words to blows.//수술 ~이 좋지 않았다 The surgical operation resulted in failure.

끝갈망 [뒷수습] setting (matters) right; settlement; after adjustment; clearance work; winding up; liquidation. ¶싸움의 ~을 하다 settle a quarrel / deal with the aftermath of a quarrel//파산 은행의 ~을 하다 liquidate [clear up the affairs of] an insolvent bank//**~을 잘하다** bring something to a successful issue. **끝갈망하다** settle; set (matters) right; take remedial measures; wind up (one's affairs); deal with the aftermath.

끝끝내 [최후까지] to the last; to the (bitter) end; to the finish; throughout; [완강히] persistently; doggedly; stubbornly; tenaciously. ¶~ 싸우다 fight desperately (to the last man) / fight to the death[to a finish / to the last] / fight it out//~ 반대하다 persist in one's opposition / stick out against / oppose stoutly[stubbornly / stiffly]//~ 버티다 persist to the bitter end / hold on to it through thick and thin / make a stubborn resistance//그는 그 제안에 ~ 반대했다 (구어) He was dead against the proposal.//그녀는 ~ 시치미를 떼려고 했다 She tried to brazen it out.//그는 ~ 돈을 갚지 않았다 He didn't pay the money to the last.//그는 ~ 그것을 부인했다 He persistently refused to admit it. / He denied it to the end[last].//그는 ~ 모른다고 버티었다 He persisted in asserting his innocence. / He persisted to the last, denying his knowledge (of it). // 나는 ~ 참아 낼 수가 없었다 I couldn't stand it [stick it out]. // 모른다고 ~ 우길 작정이냐 You mean to go on insisting that you don't know. // 그녀는 ~ 독신으로 늙을 모양이다 She seems to remain an old maid through life.

끝나다 [마치다] end; come[be brought] to an end [a close / a conclusion / a termination]; close; be concluded; be over (with); be done; terminate; [완료되다] be finished; be completed; (기한이) expire; [결과를 가져오다] result [end] in; [산회하다] break up; rise; adjourn. ¶끝날 무렵에 toward the end [close] (of) // 이 주일이 끝나기 전에 before the week is out[up] // 방문이 끝난 뒤에 upon completion of a visit // 학교가 끝난 뒤에 after school (is over) // 근무가 ~ be off duty // (결국) …으로 ~ end [result / terminate / culminate] in ... / lead to ... // 실패로 ~ result [end up] in failure // 지불 기한이 ~ be overdue // 장마철이 끝났다 The rainy season is over [has ended]. // 방학이 끝났다 The vacation came to a close. / The vacation is over. // 전쟁이 끝났다 The war has come to an end. / The war ended. // 협상이 끝났다 The negotiations have been terminated. / (타결되었을 경우) The negotiations have been concluded [wound up]. // 만사가 끝났다 The game is up. / All is over[up]. // 시험은 곧 끝난다 The examinations will soon be over. // 언제 일이 다 끝나십니까 When will you be through with your work? // 나는 벌금으로 끝났다 I got off with a fine. // 사과문을 써서 끝난다고 생각하면 큰 오산이다 If you think you can get off just by writing a letter of apology, you are greatly mistaken. // (일·식사가) 끝났다 I am through. / I have[am] finished. // 파티는 10시에 끝났다 The party broke up at ten. // 연극은 9시에 끝났다 The curtain was dropped at 9 p.m. // 오늘 일도 끝났다 The day's work is done. / I'm finished for today. / (미) I'm through for today. // 우리 집의 개축은 아직 끝나지 않았다 The rebuilding of our house has not been completed yet. // 내 임기는 끝났습니다 My term of office has expired. // 그는 내 산기슭에서 끝나고 거기서부터는 울창한 숲이 있었다 The path came to an end at the foot of the mountain, where a dense forest began. / The path was lost in the thick forest at the foot of the hill. // 그것은 완전히 실패로 끝났다 It proved [ended in] a complete failure. // 오늘로 3일간의 연습이 끝난다 Today is the last day of our three-day practice session. // 수술은 무사히 끝났다 The operation was completed successfully. // 회의는 아무 성과 없이 끝났다 The conference broke up resultless. // 모든 일이 무사히 끝났다 Everything went off all right [without a hitch]. // 그는 내 말이 채 끝나기도 전에 나가 버렸다 He went out without waiting for me to finish what I was saying.

끝내 **1** to the last; persistently. ⇨ˮ끝끝내 **2** [결국] in the end; finally; ultimately; on top of all this; as the last consequence; as the final outcome; after all. ¶그는 ~ 철창 신세가 되었다 He ended [wound] up behind bars. // 그는 ~ 술로 인해서 죽었다 Drink ended[was the end of] him. // 4시간이나 기다렸으나 그는 ~ 오지 않았다 I waited for him four hours, but he did not come after all.

끝내기 (바둑의) the last [concluding / clinching] moves; the end game; an ending. ¶~를 그르치다 commit an error in the ending / fail to beat the opponent by an eleventh-hour error.

끝내다 [마치다] end; finish (off) (with); complete; terminate; get [be] through (with); [마감하다] close; stop; conclude; wind up (one's trip); put an end [a period] (to); bring (a thing) to a close [finish]; make an end of. ¶하루의 일을 끝내고 after a day's work // 일을 ~ finish [leave off] one's work / get [be] through with one's task / get one's work done // 이야기를 ~ wind up a talk // 용무를 ~ make an end of one's business / finish one's business // 토의를 ~ shelve an argument // 여행을 ~ complete one's itinerary / accomplish one's journey // 곧 일을 끝내겠다 I will soon be [get] through with the work. // 그는 지금 막 목욕을 끝냈다 He has just finished bathing [gotten out of the bath]. // 되도록 돈이 덜 드는 방향으로 끝내 주게 Do it as cheaply as possible. // 파티 비용은 1인당 5,000원 이내로 끝내 주기 바란다 We don't want the cost of the party to go over 5,000 won per person. // 그녀는 척척 일을 끝냈다 She finished off her work efficiently. // 나는 이 일을 금주 안에 끝내지 않으면 안 된다 I must finish[get through with] this work before[by] the end of the week. // 이 단편 소설을 끝내는 데 하루가 더 필요하다 I need one more day to finish off this short story. // 오늘은 이쯤에서 공부[일]를 끝내기로 한다 We will [Let's] stop [leave off] our work here for today. / Class is dismissed. // 이쯤에서 끝낼까 Shall we finish off? / Shall we wind up [call it quits] here? // 그는 자기 이야기를 서둘러 끝냈다 He concluded his speech promptly. / He quickly wound up his talk. // 그들은 1개월 만에 지방 공연을 끝냈다 They finished the local performances in a month. // 네 일을 빨리 끝내라 Finish (off) [Get done with] your work quickly. // 나는 어젯밤 이 책 읽기를 끝냈다 I finished reading this book last night. // 그들은 회의를 6시에 끝냈다 They closed the meeting [brought the meeting to a close] at six. // 나는 그와의 회견을 간단히 끝냈다 I made short work of his interview. // 그는 무엇이든지 "됐지?"라는 말 한마디로 끝낸다 He just finishes off everything with "OK?"

끝닿다 reach [get to] the end [bottom / top]; come up to the end; touch bottom; hit (the) bottom.

끝동 a cuff. ¶~을 달다 sew a cuff on a sleeve.

끝마감 conclusion; an end; closing. ⇨ˮ마감

끝마무리 finishing; the finish. ⇨ˮ마무리

끝마치다 end; finish (off) (with). ⇨ˮ끝내다

끝맺다 end; finish (off) (with). ⇨ˮ끝내다

끝머리 [끄트머리] the end; a tip; the tail end; the extremity; [말미] the close; finish (서적의). ¶~에서 at the end [close] (of) // 내 이름은 명부의 ~ 쪽에 있다 My name stands near the bottom of the list. // 이 책은 ~에 갈수록 재미가 없어진다 The interest flags towards the end of the book. / The book drags toward the end.

끝물 the last product of the season. ¶~의

끝손질 finishing; the finish. ⇨마무리

끝수 (-數) a leftover amount; an odd amount; [수] a fraction. ¶~를 버리다 calculate to the nearest whole number / round off fractions.

끝없다 endless; boundless(넓이가); unfathomable(깊이가); [영원하다] eternal; everlasting; [무한하다] unlimited; limitless; interminable; infinite; [다함이 없다] inexhaustible; never-ending; [긋없이] ceaseless; incessant; [걷잡을 수 없다] uncontrollable. ¶끝없는 대양 a boundless ocean // 끝없는 사막 an endless desert // 끝없는 욕망 insatiable [unbounded] desires (for) // 끝없는 걱정 endless worries // 조국에 대한 끝없는 사랑 undying love for one's homeland // 끝없는 망망대해 a boundless (expanse of the) ocean // 끝없는 인생 행로 the endless journey of (human) life // 나는 그의 끝없는 푸념에 질렸다 I was exasperated by his endless grumbling. // 부모의 끝없는 슬픔을 생각지도 않고 그는 집을 떠났다 He left home, disregarding the immeasurable sorrow he was causing his parents. **끝없이** boundlessly; endlessly; without end; interminably; eternally; infinitely; to an unlimited extent. ¶~ 깊은 바다 a bottomless abyss // ~ 지껄이다 have an interminable [no end of] talk // 그들의 논쟁은 ~ 계속되었다 Their dispute went on without end. // 그녀는 ~ 수다를 떨었다 She chattered on endlessly. // 물가는 ~ 뛰고 있다 Prices are soaring forever. // 수요는 ~ 늘어날 것이다 The demand will increase to an unlimited extent. / An open-end increase of demand is expected. // 밀밭이 ~ 이어져 있었다 The wheat field extended endlessly.

끝일 [맨 나중 일] the final job[affair]; the last work; [뒷정리] after adjustment; clearance work; windup; liquidation.

끝장 [결말] (an) end; (a) close; (a) conclusion; (a) termination; [낙착] (a) settlement; fixing (up); [결과] a result; an outcome. ¶싸움의 ~ the end [outcome] of a quarrel // 비극의 ~ the catastrophe [(프) dénouement] of a tragedy // ~을 보고야 마는 사람 a thoroughgoing person / a perfectionist // 파업도 ~이 보인다 The end of the strike is now in sight. // 여기서 만났으니 너는 이제 ~이다 Now I've seen you here, you're doomed [done for / finished]. // 이 신제품이 팔리지 않으면 우리 회사는 ~이다 If we can't sell this new product, our company will be finished [it'll be curtains for the company]. // 나는 이제 ~이다 I'm cornered. / I've got my backs to the wall. / This is the end. / There's no way out. / It is all up [over] with me. / All is over (with me). // 이것을 못 풀면 나는 ~이다 If I can't solve this, it will be all up with me [I'm finished.]. // 우리가 실패하면 만사 ~이다 If we fail, that's the end of everything.

끝장나다 [끝나다] end; close; come [be brought] to a conclusion [an end]; be over; [낙착되다] come to a settlement; be settled; (미) be fixed. ¶비극으로 ~ end in a sad failure / come to a sad end // 원만하게 ~ be brought to a happy end [termination] // 마침내 그 일은 끝장났다 It finally came to a settlement [an end]. // 이 전쟁은 어떻게 끝장날까 How will the war end [result]? / What will be the consequence of this war? // 그 사건[문제]은 아직 끝장나지 않았다 The matter [problem] has not been settled [solved] yet. / The matter still remains unsettled [is yet to be settled].

끝장내다 [종결짓다] end; finish; conclude; terminate; bring (a matter) to a conclusion [a close / an end]; put an end [a period] to; wind up; [해결하다] bring to a settlement; settle; (미) fix (up). ¶싸움을 ~ put an end to a strife [quarrel] // 그 문제는 속히 끝장내는 것이 좋겠소 You had better settle that question promptly. // 그는 만사에 끝장낼 줄 모른다 He never finishes what he undertakes [sets out to do].

끝판 1 [끝 단계] the last stage (of); the end; the close; the conclusion; the finish; the windup; the finale. ¶~에 이르다 come [be brought] to an end [a close / a conclusion] // 토론 ~에 가서 싸움이 났다 A quarrel was started at the end of the discussion. // 전쟁도 ~에 가까워졌다 The war is drawing to a close. 2 [승부의 결판] the last round (of a game); the end (of a game of *baduk*). ¶~에 지다 lose a game in the last round.

끼[1] 1 [바람기]. ¶그 여자는 ~가 있다 She is a flirt [vamp]. 2 [연예인 기질]. ¶그는 연예인이 될 만한 ~가 있다 He has what it takes to be an entertainer.

끼[2] [끼니·식사] a meal; a diet. ¶한 ~ 거르다 skip a meal // 하루에 세 ~ 먹다 take three meals a day / eat three times a day // 세 ~ 먹고 방 값이 2만 원이다 charge 20,000 won for full board.

끼니 a meal; daily meals. ¶세 ~ three meals // ~때 a mealtime // ~를 거르다 miss [skip / do not have] a meal // 겨우 ~를 이어 가다 manage to live / live by hook or by crook // ~를 잇지 못하다 fail to keep the pot boiling // ~를 잇기가 어렵다 find it hard to earn one's daily bread / be badly pressed for living // ~를 걱정하다 worry (about) where meals is coming from // ~ 걱정은 없다 have enough to live on / be well [comfortably] off / be assured of livelihood // 여기의 하숙비는 세 ~가 딸려 얼마입니까 How much do you charge for this room with board [three meals]?

끼다[1] 1 get between; lie between; be tight; take one's place among. ⇨끼이다 2 insert (in); fix into. ⇨끼우다

끼다[2] 1 (안개·연기 등이) gather; hang over; envelop; shroud; screen. ¶아침 안개가 끼어 있는 마을들 villages wrapped [veiled / enveloped] in a morning mist // 구름이 ~ become covered with clouds / become cloudy [overcast] // 안개가 ~ / cloud up // 안개가 ~ become foggy / be enveloped [wrapped / folded] in a fog / be shrouded by fog // 들에는 안개가 끼어 있었다 The mist was hanging over the field. // 저녁때가 되자 안개가 끼기 시작했다 In the evening a mist began to foam. / In the evening, it began to get foggy [misty].
2 (때·먼지 등이) become dirty; be soiled; be stained (with); (이끼 등이) be mossed. ¶이끼 낀 돌 stones covered with lichens / a stone fleeced with moss // 기름기가 낀 바지 greasy trousers / trousers stained with grease // 얼굴에 기미가 ~ have a freckled face // 눈곱이 ~ matter forms in the eyes / one's eyes are

gummy[mattery] // 먼지가 공중에 뽀얗게 끼어 있다 The air is thick with dust. // 옷에 온통 기름때가 끼어 있었다 The clothes were smeared all over with greasy dirt.

끼다[3] **1** [끌어안다] embrace; hug; fold (a person) into one's arms; hold (a person) in one's arms; (팔 을)fold [link] (one's arms); (몸의 벌어진 사이로) hold (a thing) (under / between / behind). ¶연필을 귀에 끼고 있다 [holding] a pencil behind one's ear // 손가락에 연필을 ~ hold a pencil between one's fingers // 겨드랑에 손가방을 ~ hold a portfolio under one's arms // 서로 팔을 끼고 걷다 walk arm in arm // 팔짱을 (남과) link arms / link one's arms in another's / (자기의) fold one's arms // 노파는 그 아이를 가슴에 꼭 끼었다 The old woman pressed [clasped / hugged] the child to her breast. // 그는 팔짱을 낀 채 출입구에 서 있었다 He stood in the doorway with his arms folded. // 노동자들이 팔짱을 끼고 시가를 행진했다 Arm in arm, the workers marched through the streets.
2 [착용하다] put on; pull on; wear; slip on. ¶장갑을 ~ pull[put] on one's gloves // 손가락에 반지를 끼고 있다 have[wear] a ring on one's finger // 골무를 ~ wear a thimble [thumbstall] // 단추를 ~ fasten buttons / button (up) (one's coat).
3 […을 따르다] skirt; run along. ¶…을 끼고 along / by / parallel to [with] // (길 등이) 강을 끼고 뻗다 parallel a stream / run [lie] parallel with [to] a river // 해안을 끼고 초가집들이 있었다 There were thatch-roofed houses along the shore. // 우리는 깎아지른 벼랑을 끼고 나아갔다 We advanced around the sheer cliff.
4 [사이에 두다] put[hold] between. ¶우리는 책상을 끼고 마주 앉았다 We sat facing each other across the table [with a table between].
5 [덧붙이거나 겹치다] combine; link. ¶그 법안은 다른 법안에 끼어 상원을 통과했다 That bill passed the Upper House in linkage with another one. / The Upper House passed that bill in combination [by linking it] with another.
6 [배경이 있다] be backed (up) by ...; have (a person) at one's back. ¶권력을 ~ have an influential person at one's back // 관의 권력을 끼고 횡포를 일삼다 carry matters with high hand under the backing[pull] of the high ranking boss's power.

끼루룩 honking. **끼루룩하다** honk; make a honk.

끼룩거리다 1 (기러기가) honk. **2** [목을 빼다] make a long neck; crane [stretch out] one's neck; (미국 속어) rubberneck.

-끼리 ¶가족~의 모임 a family party [gathering] // 우리~의 이야기지만 사태가 아주 좋지 않은 것 같다 Just between you and me, the situation looks very bad. // 우리는 마음 맞는 사람들~ 그룹을 만들었다 We organized a group of congenial people. // 승객~ 싸우기 시작했다 The passengers began to quarrel among themselves. // 너무 깜깜해서 뜻하지 않게 아군~ 싸움이 벌어졌다 It was so dark that they (accidently) began to attack on their own side. // 우리~ 갑시다 Let's go by ourselves.

끼리끼리 in groups; group by group; in separate groups. ¶~ 해 먹다 each group looks to its own interests [feathers its nest] // 사람은 ~ 모이는 법이다 Birds of feather flock together. / Like attracts like.

끼어들다 intrude into[upon]; wedge (oneself) in(to); thrust oneself into; (이야기 등에) break [cut / shove] in (on). ¶줄지어 선 틈바구니에 ~ break into the queue / cut in / (영국 속어) jump the queue // 남의 이야기에 끼어들면 못 쓴다 Don't break[chip] into other people's conversation.

끼얹다 pour[splash] (on); shower [sprinkle] (on / over); dash (water) (on a person). ¶몸에 물을 ~ pour[splash] water over[on] oneself / douse oneself with water // 잔등에 물을 ~ dash water on one's back // 머리에 모래를 ~ sprinkle sand over (one's head) // 그는 매일 아침 냉수를 몸에 끼얹는 습관이 있다 He makes it a rule to dash (cold) water over himself every morning.

끼우다 [사이에 넣다] put [get / let] in; insert (in); hold between; (빠지지 않게) fix[fit] into; set (in); inlay; [참가시키다] take (a person) into one's circle; let (a person) join (in). ¶유리를 끼운 fitted with glass // 책에 서표(書標)를 ~ insert a marker between the pages of a book // 빵에 햄을 ~ sandwich [put] ham between slices of bread // 종이를 클립으로 ~ fasten sheets of paper together with a paperclip // 열쇠를 열쇠 구멍에 [플러그를 콘센트에] 끼워 넣다 insert a key in a lock [a plug in an outlet] // 광고지를 신문에 끼워 넣다 insert an advertisement in a newspaper // 그 교수는 강의 중에 농담을 끼워 넣기를 좋아한다 The professor likes to insert some jokes into his lecture. // 그 일에 나도 한몫 끼워 주지 않을래 Let me in on [have a share in] that job, won't you.

끼이다 1 (물건 사이에) get between; be caught in; get jammed [hemmed] in; be sandwiched between; (틈에 박히다) fit (in(to)); be fit for. ¶음식물이 잇새에 끼었다 A particle of food got caught between my teeth. // 한복의 소맷자락이 닫히는 문에 끼었다 The sleeve of her Korean clothes was caught in a door as it closed.
2 (양자 사이에) lie [get] between. ¶어머니와 아내 사이에 끼여 난처한 처지에 있다 Caught between my mother and my wife, I am in an awkward position. // 나는 아름다운 두 여성 사이에 끼었다 I was sandwiched between two beautiful woman.
3 (구두 등이) be tight [close]. ¶이 옷은 내게 너무 끼인다 This jacket is too tight [small] for me. // 바지의 허리가 끼인다 The trousers pinch me around the waist. // 네가 그렇게 바짝 붙어 앉으니 내가 빽빽하게 끼인 기분이다 It makes me feel cramped if you sit so close to me.
4 [참여하다] take one's place among; rank with [among]. ¶이 수지 맞는 돈벌이 일에 한몫 끼이지 않겠니 Don't you want to be in on this profitable scheme?

끼인각(-角) [수] an included [a contained] angle.

끼적거리다 scribble; scrawl; scratch; dash [write] off. ¶종이에 몇 자 끼적거려 놓다 scribble something on a piece of paper / write a hasty line / dash off a letter.

끼치다[1] (소름이) get (the) gooseflesh; become

끼치다

(all) goose pimples; feel a chill creep over one; shudder; shiver; thrill (with horror); feel a thrill; be gooseflesh all over; (사물이) make one's blood run cold; curdle one's blood; send a thrill[chill]; make one's flesh creep. ¶무서워서 소름이 ~ shudder in horror / feel one's hair stand on end with terror∥추워서 소름이 ~ shiver with cold.

끼치다² 1 (폐·영향 등을) cause (harm); exert [exercise] (influence upon); give; render. ¶폐[괴로움]를 ~ trouble (a person) / give [cause] (a person) trouble / get (a person) into trouble[mischief] / 걱정을 ~ give [cause] (a person) occasion to feel anxiety / cause anxiety to (a person)∥그는 자기 회사에 큰 손실을 끼쳤다 He caused a great loss to his company.∥폐 많이 끼쳤습니다 I am afraid I have put you to much trouble.∥남에게 폐를 끼치니 그만둬라 Stop, or you may cause trouble[be a nuisance] to other people.∥나는 부모님께 많은 걱정을 끼쳤다 I caused my parents a great deal of anxiety [a lot of trouble].
2 (후세에) hand down; leave (behind); bequeath. ¶오명을 ~ leave a bad reputation [name].

끽 shrieking; shouting; yelling; in a choking voice; with a scream[screech].

끽소리 a yell of; a squawk of complaint. ¶~ 못하다 be (utterly) silenced / be in blank dismay[surprise] / be completely nonplused ∥ ~ 못하게 하다 put[reduce] (a person) to silence / beat (a person) all hollow∥그는 ~도 못했다 He was left without a word to say. / He couldn't utter a word in reply.∥이 말에 그는 ~ 못했다 He couldn't utter a syllable in reply.∥나는 그를 ~도 못하게 했다 I beat him hollow.

끽연 (喫煙) smoking (tobacco). ⇨흡연

끽해야 at (the) most; at the utmost; at (the) best; at the outside. ¶그는 ~ 스무 살쯤이다 He is twenty at the most[outside].∥~ 보름쯤 걸리겠죠 I should think it will take fifteen days at the longest.∥~ 그녀가 빚 없이 사는 정도겠지 It may be all[as much as] she can do to keep out of debt.

낄낄 ¶~ 웃다 giggle / titter / chuckle(▶ titter 나 giggle은 주로 여자가 웃음을 참으면서 웃는 경우에 씀. chuckle은 조용히 소리를 내지 않고 웃다) / snicker / (영) snigger∥그는 책을 읽으면서 ~ 웃었다 He chuckled to himself while reading. 낄낄하다 giggle; titter. ⇨낄낄거리다

낄낄거리다 giggle; titter; chuckle; snicker; (영) snigger. ¶숨어서 ~ laugh in one's sleeve∥노는 아이들은 낄낄거리며 웃고 있었다 The playing children were squealing with laughter.∥계집애들이 즐겁게 낄낄거리고 있다 The girls are laughing merrily.

낌새 [되어 가는 형편] the course (of events); the development (of an affair); the turn (of events); [기미] niceties; secrets; secret devices; inner workings; delicate signs; the delicate turn (of a situation); [조짐] a sign; an indication. ¶옆방에 누가 있는 ~를 느꼈다 I felt[sensed] someone in the next room.∥그 일에 대하여 그들이 상의한 ~는 없었다 There were no signs of their having discussed the matter.∥물가가 오를 것 같은 ~가 짙다 There is every indication that prices will go up.∥정국이 달라질 ~는 보이지 않는다 We can't see any sign that there will be a change in the political situation.∥재정 상태는 회복의 ~를 보이고 있다 There are signs [indications] that our financial conditions are about to rally.∥그에게서 양보할 것 같은 ~를 볼 수 없다 He shows no sign(s) [indication] of relenting. / There are no indications that he will relent.

낌새채다 sense[get at] the secrets of (an affair, a plan, etc.); sense[get at] (a person's) intimate thoughts[the delicate turn of a situation]; scent; get wind of; smell out. ¶상대방의 계략을 ~ get wind of one's opponent's plans / (구어) get wise to one's opponent's tricks.

낑낑 groaning (and grunting); moaning. **낑낑하다** groan (and groan). ⇨낑낑거리다

낑낑거리다 groan (and groan); groan away; moan. ¶무거운 짐을 지고 ~ groan under a heavy load on one's back∥낑낑거리는 소리가 들리다 hear a person's moans / hear someone groaning∥아파서 낑낑거리고 있다 be groaning with pain.

ㄴ

- **ㄴ가** 1 [의문]. is it?; isn't it?; aren't you[they]?; isn't he[she]?; if[whether] it is .... ¶이게 뭔가 What is it?//저건 누군가 Who is he?//아니, 자네 최·군 아닌가 Oh, you are Mr. Choe, aren't you?//자네 기쁜가 Are you happy?//그는 믿을 만한가 Is he reliable?//그것이 사실인가 아닌가 확인해 보자 Let's see if it is true or not.
2 [막연한 사람·시간·장소] someone; sometime[day]; somewhere. ¶누군가 했더니 삼촌이었다 It was no other[no less a person] than my uncle.//그는 이 근처 어딘가에 살고 있다 He lives somewhere about here[in this neighborhood].//언젠가 만난 적이 있지요 I remember I've met you before.//그는 아마 바쁜가 보다 He seems to be busy.//그의 얘기는 정말인가 보다 His story has the appearance of truth.
- **ㄴ다고** [인용]. ¶그의 아버지가 다음 달에 서울에 온다고 합니다 His father is coming to Seoul next month, I hear. 2 [원인·근거] because; as.
- **ㄴ다니** 1 [의문]. ¶그는 언제 돌아온다니 When is he supposed to come back? / When do you think he will come back?//그녀가 왜 온다니 Do you know what she comes for? 2 [ㄴ다고 하니]. ¶공부를 잘한다니 기쁘다 I am delighted to hear that you are a good student.//내가 그래 주기를 바란다니 그 친구 참 어지간하군 He is rather[pretty] calm of him to expect me to do so.
- **ㄴ다면** [가정적 조건] if; unless; when; whenever. ¶원한다면 and; if you like/둘이서 함께 이야기한다면 오해가 풀릴 것이다 If you talk it over together, the misunderstanding will clear up.
- **ㄴ다손 치더라도** (even) though; (even) if; granted[granting] that; no matter how[who/what/when/which]. ¶누가 그렇게 말한다손 치더라도 믿지 않겠다 Whoever may say so[No matter who say so], I won't believe it.//실패한다손 치더라도 해 볼 가치가 있다 It is worth attempting though we fail.
- **ㄴ대서** [ㄴ다고 해서]. ¶증기선은 증기로 간다서 그렇게 부른다 A steamer is so called because it is run by steam.
- **ㄴ대서야** [ㄴ다고 해서야]. ¶금방 여기 있던 것을 네가 모른대서야 말이 되냐 You can't help knowing about a thing that was here a minute ago, can you?
- **ㄴ대야** even so; even if. ¶지금 떠난대야 만나기는 글러서 Even if you start now, you will not be able to see him.//이런 아이들은 자란대야 별수 없을 것이다 Such naughty children will come to no good after all.
- **ㄴ데** 1 [그리고] and; [그러나] but. ¶난데, 왜 문을 안 여니 It's me. Why don't you open the door?//그는 겉보기는 온순한데 심지는 굳다 He is gentle in appearance, but strong at heart.
2 [한편] when; while. ¶시험이 내일모렌데 그는 놀고만 있다 He keeps on idling when the examination is in sight.//무일푼인데 내가 집을 어떻게 삽니까 How can I buy the house when I have no money?//이것은 내 책인데 보고 주게 This is my book, return it to me when you are through with it.
3 [상대의 의견을 들으려는 스스로의 감탄]. ¶날씨가 매우 찬데 It is very cold, isn't it?//훌륭한 사진기인데 What a nice camera!//좋은 곳인데 Why, it's a very nice place!//과연 가을인데 It's certainly autumn, isn't it?
- **ㄴ들** [···하다 할지라도 어찌] granted that; though; even though[if]. ¶난들 못할쏘냐 I can do it too. / I also can do it.//자넨들 나을 게 뭐냐 You are no better than I.//힘이 약하다 한들 너보다 약하랴 I may be weak, but I am sure I'm no weaker than you.//간다 한들 아주 가랴 Though I leave, I'm not going away for good.//남들이 뭐라 한들 대수랴 I don't care what people say of me.
- **ㄴ바** [···하고 보니까]. ¶그의 말을 들어 본바 사실과 틀림없었다 According to what he says, it is true to the fact.//그곳에 가 본바 과연 절경이었다 I visited the place, which I found really picturesque.
- **ㄴ즉** as; now that; so far as (it is) concerned; speaking of. ¶그런즉 어떻게 하면 좋겠느냐 Well then, what would you like me to do? / Such being the conditions[circumstances], what shall we do?//알아본즉 그의 말은 거짓말이었다 On inquiry, what he had said proved false.//경치인즉 금강산이 한국에서 제일이다 As far as scenic beauty goes, the Geumgangsan(Mt. Geumgang) are the best in Korea.//일이 벌어진 시초인즉 이렇다 This is how it happened.//시골에 가 본즉 풍년이 있다 I went to the country, where I realized we had a bumper year.//그의 말을 듣고 본즉 그럴듯하다 As I heard him say so, it seems quite plausible.
- **ㄴ지** [막연한 의문·감탄] if; or; either ... or; I wonder .... ¶무엇인지 하얀 것 something that looks white//정가인지 하는 사람 a (certain) Mr. Jeong / a man named Jeong or something//어떻게 하는 것인지 가르쳐 주시오 Tell me how to do it.//그가 하는 소리는 뭐가 뭔지 통 모르겠다 I cannot make head or tail of what he says.//그는 어딘지 외국인 냄새가 난다 He has something outlandish about him.//그가 어떻게 된 것인지 모르겠다 I wonder what has become of him. / How is he getting along, I wonder?

나[1] 1 [1인칭 단수 대명사] (주격: 나는) I; (소유격: 나의) my; (목적격: 나를, 나에게) me; (소유 대명사) mine; (재귀 대명사: 나 자신) myself. ¶~라면[~로서는] as for me / for my part/~ 자신 myself / my own self/~도 모르게 in spite of myself / unconsciously / involuntarily//너 ~ 하는 사이가 되다 achieve a first name friendship (with)//이것은 ~의 사진입니다 This is my picture.//(남들은 어떠하건) ~는 상관없다 As for me[For my part], I do not care.//"누구세요?" "~예

요." "Who is it?" "It's me." // ~라면 그런 짓은 하지 않겠다 If I were in your[his] place, I would not do such a thing. // 잘못한 것은 ~ 다 It is who am guilty. // ~도 처음에는 그렇게 생각했다 I thought so myself at first. // ~로서는 그를 믿었다 As for me, I trust him. // ~야말로 천하제일의 수재라고 생각하고 있었다 I was conceited enough to think myself an intellectual wonder.
2 [자아] self; ego. ¶이전의 ~ my former [present] self / 제2의 ~ my second self / (라) alter ego.

나² [음] si; B. ¶~장조[단조] B major[minor].

나³ 1 [선택] ... or ...; ... and ...; either (A) or (B); neither (A) nor (B) (부정). ¶나무 ~ 돌 trees and[or] stones // 너 ~ 나 ~ 누구 한 사람이 가야 한다 Either you or I must go. // 이 가운데 어느 거 ~ 갖고 싶은 걸 가져라 Take which ever you like of these.
2 [어느 것을 막론하고] and; as well as; (두 가지 물건일 때) both ... and. ¶그는 독일어 ~ 프랑스 어 ~ 다 말할 줄 안다 He can speak both German and French. / He can speak not only German but also French. // 그 ~ 나 ~ 영리하지 못하다 Neither he nor I am clever. // 누구 ~ 그의 승리를 믿고 있었다 Everybody believed he would win. // 그 고장은 어느 곳이 ~ 눈으로 덮여 있었다 The town was covered with snow everywhere. / The whole town was covered with snow.
3 [양보]. ¶영화 ~ 보러 갈까요 What do you say to seeing the movies, for instance? // 일요일에 ~ 그녀를 만나러 가겠다 I'll go to see her, say, on Sunday.
4 [정도] as many[much] as; no less[fewer] than; as long[far] as. ¶남편은 때로는 말 한 필에 5파운드 ~ 걸었다 My husband sometimes put as much as five pounds on a horse.

-나 1 [앞뒤의 상반] but; though. ¶가난하 ~ 거짓말을 할 사람은 아니다 Though (he is) poor, he is above telling a lie. // 그녀는 얼굴은 미우 ~ 마음씨는 곱다 She is plain but sweet-tempered.
2 [동작·상태를 가리지 않음] (whether ...) or; or the like; or what not. ¶크 ~ 작으나 가리지 않고 regardless of whether it is big or small // 보 ~ 마 ~ 마찬가지다 There is no difference whether I see it or not.
3 [형용사를 강조하기 위해 붙이는 연결 어미] quite; very; ever so (much). ¶머 ~ 먼 길 a long long road [distance].
4 [의문]. ¶점심 먹었 ~ Did you eat lunch? // 안 가겠 ~ Won't you go? // 내 말 알아듣겠 ~ Do you understand what I mean?

나가다 1 [밖으로] go[get / head / stir / turn] out; step out (잠깐 나가다). ¶방에서 ~ go [get] out of a room // 뜰로 ~ go out into the garden // 산책 ~ go out for a walk // 점심 먹으러 [장 보러] ~ go out for lunch[shopping] // 밖에 나가지 않다 keep to one's house // 그는 지금 나가고 있다 He has gone out. // 그는 물건 사러 나갔다 He is out shopping. / He has gone shopping. // 그는 점심 먹으러 [볼일 보러] 나가고 없습니다 He is out for lunch [on business]. // 막 나가려는 참에 그에게서 전화가 왔다 I had a call from him just as I was going[was about to go] out.
2 [출근·출석하다] be present at (a ceremony); attend (a meeting); [출두하다] appear; report (at). ¶회사에 ~ go to office / go to work // 모임[강의]에 ~ attend[be present at] a meeting[lecture] // 회의에 ~ attend[be present at] a conference / join[take part in] a conference // 법정에 ~ appear in court.
3 [근무하다] work (in); serve (in); be in the service (of); be employed (in); hold an office (in) (관청에). ¶회사에 ~ serve a company / be employed in a company / be in the service of a company // 시청에 ~ serve in the Municipal office // 신문사에 ~ be connected with[be working in] a newspaper office // 학교에 ~ teach in a school.
4 [진출하다] go[sally] forth into (the world); go upon (the world's stage); launch into; enter upon. ¶정계에 ~ enter upon a political career / make one's debut on the political stage // 실업계에 ~ go into business // 사회에 ~ launch[go out] into the world.
5 [참가·출전하다] join; participate in; take part in; enter for; go out for; [출마하다] stand (for); (미) run (for). ¶올림픽에 ~ take part in the Olympic games // 미인 선발 대회에 ~ enter[go in for] a beauty contest // 백 미터 경주에 ~ run in[enter (for)] a 100-meter race // 대통령 후보로 ~ run for the Presidency // 나는 경기[웅변대회]에 나갔다 I took part in a game [a speech contest].
6 [태도를 취하다] assume (an attitude); take (a move). ¶고압적으로 ~ act high-handedly // 그에게는 세게 나가는 것이 좋다 We had better take a firm attitude toward him.
7 [퇴거하다·떠나다] leave; take one's leave; move out; quit; [물러나다] withdraw; go away; (조수가) ebb; go out; flow back; be on the ebb. ¶집을 ~ leave home[the house] / get[cut / (소에) shove] out of the house // 나가라 Go away! / Get out! / Be off with you! // 이달 말에 그들은 이 집에서 나간다 They will move out of this house at the end of this month.
8 [정신이 없어지다] go out of one's mind; go off one's head; take leave of one's wits [sense]; go mad; become insane; [멍청해지다] grow absentminded; become absent in one's mind. ¶정신 나간 짓 a crazy act.
9 [팔리다] sell. ¶잘 나가는 물건 a good [quick] sell[seller] // 가장 잘 나가는 책 the top[best] seller // 잘 ~ sell well / be in good [great] demand / (책이) have[enjoy] a large circulation // 잘 안 ~ be unsalable / find no purchase / be in poor demand // 이 소설은 잘 나간다 This novel is a good seller. // 이 잡지가 국내에서는 제일 잘 나간다 This magazine has the largest circulation in our country. // 금년에는 가스스토브가 잘 나갔다 Gas stoves were in great demand this year.
10 [닳다] wear [be worn] out [off]; wear threadbare. ¶소매 끝이 ~ be frayed in the edges of sleeves // 내 바지는 무릎이 나갔다 My trousers are worn out at the knees. // 그의 구두는 뒤축이 나갔다 The heels of his shoes wore down. / His shoes wore down at the heels.
11 (비용이) be spent; be paid out; (수중의 물건이) be out. ¶지난달에는 생각보다 비용이 훨씬 많이 나갔다 The expenses last month were much more than I had expected. // 어린이 교육에 많은 돈이 나간다 Children's edu-

cation costs us a great deal.// 들어오는 것은 없고 나가는 것뿐이다 All outgo and no income.
12 (가치가) cost; be worth; (무게가) weigh. ¶그는 10만 원이나 나가는 시계를 나에게 주었다 He gave me a watch worth one hundred thousand won.// 뱀장어 큰 것은 무게가 3파운드나 나간다 A large eel will weigh (as much as) three pounds.
13 [나아가다] advance; go forward; make one's way. ¶한 걸음 더 나가서 going[making / taking] one more step forward// 앞으로 한국이 나갈 길 the course Korea should take in the future.// (교실에서) 지난번에는 어디까지 나갔어요 How far did we get?[where did we get to] (in the textbook) in our last lesson? // 18페이지의 12행까지 나갔습니다, 선생님 We got up to page 18, line 12, sir.
14 [못 쓰게 되다] be broken; go wrong; get out of order; (전기 등이) go out; fail; be cut off. ¶(전기의) 퓨즈가 나갔다 The fuse was gone[blown].// 폭풍우로 전기가 나갔다 The electric light went out by a storm.

나가동그라지다 tumble down[over]. ⇨ 나동그라지다

나가떨어지다 1 [넘어지다] fall flat on one's back; (맞아서) be knocked down; (멀리) be thrown off; be hurled away (from). ¶큰대 자로 ~ fall full length (on the floor)// 한 방에 ~ be knocked down at[by] a (single) blow.
2 [실패하·지다] fail; lose (one); fall to the ground; meet with defeat. ¶경쟁에서 ~ lose in a contest// 싸움 [소송 / 경기] 에서 ~ lose a battle[lawsuit / game]// 노름에 지고 ~ run through all one's money through gambling / drop all one's money at cards.
3 [녹초가 되다] be ready to drop (with fatigue); be worn[tired / fagged] out; (술에) be done up; be all in; (술에 취하여) drink oneself down; be[get] dead[blind] drunk; (구어) pass out. ¶술 석 잔에 ~ be under the table with three glasses of wine// 그는 완전히 나가떨어졌다 He is absolutely done up.

나가자빠지다 1 fall flat on one's back. ⇨ 나가떨어지다1 **2** [이행하지 않다] fail (to); fall down on; cease to do with (it); withdraw oneself (from); back out. ¶계약을 해 놓고 ~ back out of a contract / draw back[cry off] from a contract // 빚을 지고 ~ fail to pay [(구어) run out on] one's debts / (속어) be a dead beat / 약속을 했으니 네가 이제 나가자빠질 수 없다 After all your promise you can't withdraw now.

나귀 an ass; a donkey. ⇨ 당나귀
나그네 [길손] a traveler; a tourist; a wayfarer; [타관 사람] a stranger; [방랑객] a wanderer; a vagabond; [손님] a visitor; a guest.
● **나그넷길** a journey.

나굿나굿하다 1 [촉감이] soft; tender; [매끈하다] smooth; velvety. ¶나굿나굿한 살결 the soft fair velvety skin// 살결이 ~ have soft skin. **2** [태도가] mild; amiable; affable; smooth. ¶나굿나굿한 성미 a mild[an amiable] disposition.

-나기 → 내기
나날이 everyday; daily. ⇨ 날마다
나누기 [수] divide. ¶6 ~ 2는 3이다 6 divided by 2 is[gives / equals] 3. **나누기하다** divide.
나누다 1 [분할하다] divide; part; sever; split (up); (속어) whack (up). ¶나눌 수 없는 indivisible / inseparable // 둘로 ~ divide [split] (a thing) into two // 다섯(부분)으로 ~ divide (something) into five parts // 사과를 반으로 ~ divide an apple into halves // 땅을 세 필지로 나누어 팔다 sell land in three lots // 세 사람은 노획품을 똑같이 나누었다 The three men divided (up) the booty equally. // 그들은 그 돈을 똑같이 나누었다 They split the sum equally. // 이 과자를 셋으로 나누어 하나씩 먹자 Let's divide this cake into three and each take one piece. // 이익은 둘이서 반으로 나누자 Let's go half-and-half[halves / fifty-fifty] with each other on the profit. // 이익을 모두가 똑같이 나누어 가진다면 각자의 몫은 거의 없다 If we have to split[share / go shares] with everyone, the profit will be next to nothing. // 8을 2로 나누면 4가 된다[8 나누기 2는 4이다] Eight divided by two gives four. / Divide eight by two and you get four. / Two into eight goes four times. // 20은 5로 나누어떨어진다 Twenty can be divided by five without a remainder. / Twenty is (exactly) divisible by five.
2 [분배하다] distribute[divide (up)] (among); share; allot; portion out; (트럼프의 카드 등을) deal (out). ¶돈을 둘[셋]이서 ~ divide the money between the two[among the three] // 아이들에게 과자를 나누어 주다 divide[distribute] the cakes among the children // 자식들에게 재산을 나누어 주다 settle property on one's children // 이익을 종업원에게 나누어 주다 distribute the profits among one's employees.
3 [구분하다] draw a line between; [분류하다] classify; sort (B); assort. ¶책을 항목별로 ~ classify books by subjects // 카드를 색깔별로 ~ sort cards according to their colors // 그것은 다시 여러 항목으로 나눌 수 있다 It is to be classified into many items.
4 [함께하다] share (something) with (a person); partake of. ¶점심을 ~ have lunch together // 슬픔 [기쁨] 을 ~ share one's sorrow[joy] with (a person) // 고락을 ~ share joys and sorrows with // 술을 ~ keep company in drinking / help each other to drink / drink together // 술을 나누면서 이야기하다 talk[have a chat] with (a person) over a bottle.
5 [주고받다] exchange (words / greetings). ¶이야기를 ~ talk (with) // 인사를 ~ greet each other / exchange greetings // 그들은 상대방의 연주에 대해 서로 의견을 나누었다 They exchanged opinions about each other's performances.

나누이다 be divided; be separated. ⇨ 나뉘다
나눗셈 [수] division. **나눗셈하다** divide.
나뉘다 be[get] divided; be separated; be split up; be classified. ¶두 패로 ~ be divided into two groups // 그 교회는 여러 파로 나뉘어 있다 The church is split by parties and factions. // 그 마을은 강 때문에 둘로 나뉘어 있다 That village is divided[split] into two parts by the river.

나다[1] **1** [태어나다] be born; come into the world; come into being[existence]. ¶날 때부터 from (the day of) birth / 내가 난 고장 my birthplace // 나서 여태까지 ever since my birth[I was born] / (내) all my born days // 미국에서 ~ be born in America.
2 [자라다] grow; [돋아나다] come out; bud

나다

(out); spring up; sprout. ¶비 온 뒤에 난 죽순 bamboo shoots[sprouts] after a rain // 깃털이 다 난 새[아직 깃털이 다 나지 않은 새] a full-fledged [an unfledged] bird // 풀이 ~ grass grows[sprouts] // 이가 ~ cut a tooth / erupt // 싹이 ~ bud (out) / sprout / spring up // 턱에 수염이 ~ one's chin sprouts a beard // 깃털이 난다 A bird grows wings [feathers its wings]. // 뜰에 모를 풀이 나고 있다 Some unknown plant is coming up in the garden. // 이 식물은 고산 지대에 난다 This plant grows in alpine regions. // 이 아이는 첫 이가 났다 This child has cut his first tooth. // 이 아이는 이가 막 나려 하고 있다 The baby is teething. // 이 약을 쓰면 머리털이 납니다 This medicine will grow hair on your head. // 소년은 턱수염이 나기 시작했다 The boy has begun to develop a beard. // 사슴의 뿔은 봄에 떨어지고 또 새 뿔이 난다 Deer shed their antlers in the spring and then grow new ones.

3 〔흘러나오다〕 flow[run / gush] out; spring (from). ¶샘이 ~ a fountain flows // 눈물이 ~ tears flow / tears come into one's eyes // 콧물이 ~ have a running nose / one's nose runs [drips] // 땀이 ~ sweat / perspire.

4 〔발생하다〕 happen; come to pass [happen]; come about; occur; take place; turn up; break out; rise; arise; spring [come] up. ¶연기가 ~ have smoke / be smoky / smoke rise[goes up] // 사건이[사고가] ~ have an incident / an incident happens[occurs / takes place] // 홍수가 ~ have a flood / a flood rises // 고장이 ~ break (down) / have [there is] a breakdown / get out of order / (something) go[be] wrong (with) // 야단이 ~ have trouble[a fuss] / difficulties arise [break out] // 탈이 ~ run into a hitch [hindrance / trouble] / get[become] ill (병이 나다) // 전쟁이 났다 A war broke out. // 옆집에서 불이 났다 The fire broke out in the house next door. // 그 도시에 홍수가 났다 The town was flooded. // 그에게 사고가 났음이 틀림없다 An accident must have happened to him.

5 〔길·구멍이 생기다〕 be built; be constructed; be made; be open(ed). ¶새 길이 났다 A new road is built[opened]. // 구멍이 났다 A hole is made[opened]. // 골짜기로 내려가는 길이 나 있다 A road leads down the valley. // 작년에 이 읍으로 철도가 났다 A railway was built to this town last year.

6 〔감정·생각 등이 들다〕 occur; feel. ¶성이 ~ get[become / grow] angry // 심술이 ~ get cross[cranky] / become perverse // 생각이 ~ (something) come into one's mind / occur to one / remember / recollect // 흥이 ~ get merry[excited] (over a thing) // 재미가 ~ become interesting / be interested (in) // 싫증이 ~ become sick[tired / weary] (of) / lose interest (in) / (음식에) be fed up (with) // …할 마음이 ~ be[feel] inclined (to do) / feel like (doing) // 막판에 와서 용기가 나지 않았다 My courage failed me at the last moment.

7 〔약효·능률 등이 생기다〕 get; take; produce. ¶약효가 ~ tell[act / work] (on) / talk effect // 열성이 ~ get enthusiastic / become assiduous // 능률이 ~ become efficient / produce efficiency.

8 〔생산되다〕 be produced; be yielded; be raised; be grown; be found. ¶대구에서 사과가 난다 Apples are grown in Daegu. // 이 지방은 쌀이 많이 난다 This part of the country yields much rice. // 이 밭에서는 밀이 난다 This field yields wheat. // 이 지방에서는 감자가 많이 난다 A lot of potatoes are produced in this area. // 이 광산에서 금이 난다 Gold is found in this mine.

9 〔냄새가〕 smell; (맛이) taste. ¶좋은[나쁜] 냄새가 ~ smell sweet[nasty] // 맛이 ~ be tasty / taste good[nice] / be delicious // 매운 맛이 ~ have a hot[biting] taste / be hot to the taste // 신맛이 ~ taste sour / be sour to the taste // 장미꽃 향기가 ~ have scents [a scent] of a rose.

10 〔소리가〕 sound; come out[forth]; make a sound[noise]. ¶높은[날카로운] 소리가 ~ sound loud[shrill] // 박수 소리가 난다 There is a handclap. // 문 두드리는 소리가 난다 There is a knock at the door.

11 〔티가〕 have an air[a look]; look like; look; show. ¶장사꾼 티가 나는 사람 a man looking like a shopkeeper / a man apparently a merchant // 시골티가 ~ wear a rustic [countrified] air / have a bit of the country about one / look rustic // 학자 티가 ~ have the air of a scholar / have a smack of the pedant / be scholarlike [scholarly]

12 〔병 등이〕 get; become; have. ¶병이 (미) get sick / (영) fall[be taken] ill // 기침이 ~ have a cough / cough // 상처가 ~ be [get] wounded [hurt / injured] // 열이 ~ become feverish / run[develop] a fever / come to have fever // 구역질이 ~ feel like vomiting / suffer from nausea / feel sick(ish) // 그는 감기로 몸에 열이 났다 He ran a fever because of his cold. // 그것을 보고 구역질이 났다 The sight made me sick. // 그녀는 어젯밤부터 고열이 나고 있다 She has had a high fever since last night.

13 〔흔적·흠·결말 등이〕 leave; turn out (to be); come out as a result; result[end] in. ¶자국이 ~ leave a trace (behind) // 흠집이 ~ flaw / crack / have a flaw[crack] / leave a scar // 결말이 ~ be settled / come [be brought] to a conclusion // 끝장이 ~ come [be brought] to an end / be finished // 가루가 ~ turn to powder / get crushed / get ground // 동이 ~ become scarce / run short (of).

14 〔더해지다〕 gain (in); gather. ¶속력이 ~ gain in velocity / gather speed // 힘이 ~ gain strength / (기운이) cheer up / take heart.

15 〔인품이 뛰어나다〕 be outstanding [eminent / distinguished]; 〔잘생기다〕 be good-looking [handsome]; be well-favored. ¶난 사람 an outstanding person / an extraordinary character / (속어) a bigwig // 난 체하다 look big / give[put] oneself airs.

16 〔나타나다〕 appear; make one's appearance; turn[show] up. ¶시장에 사과가 났다 Apples appeared in[on] the market. // 그 시대에는 많은 충신이 났다 The age was productive of many loyal subjects.

17 〔명성·소문 등이〕 acquire; circulate. ¶명성이 ~ acquire [win / gain] fame / win one's renown / win [gain / earn / acquire / achieve] a reputation // 소문이 ~ a rumor circulates [gets abroad] / a rumor is abroad [current / in circulation] about … // 그는 여색에 빠져 있다고 평판이 나 있다 He has the

reputation of being a womanizer.
18 [실리다] be recorded[mentioned / registered / listed]; be put on (a book); be given (in a program). ¶신문에 ~ appear[be printed / be reported] in a newspaper / be carried[published] in a daily// 그 사건은 신문에 났다 The affair appeared[was reported] in the papers. / The newspapers carried an account of the affair.
19 [틈이 생기다] be vacated; become vacant[empty]; empty; open up. ¶시간이 ~ be free / have leisure[spare time]// 자리가 났다 A place[job / seat] opened up[became available]. / 방이 났다 A room was available[vacant]. // 빈집이 났다 A house was vacant (for rent).
20 (계절을) pass (a season); tide over; go[get] through. ¶겨울을 ~ pass the winter / see winter through / winter// 외투 없이 겨울을 ~ go through the winter without an overcoat.
21 (나이가). ¶여덟 살 난 아이 a child of eight // 열두 살 난 여학생 a twelve-year-old schoolgirl.

나다[2] [완료되다] have (just) finished (doing). ¶한잠 자고 나니 정신이 새롭다 I have had a nap and now I feel much refreshed. // 할 말을 하고 나니 속이 후련했다 After I had said my say I felt my mind unburdened[as if a burden had been lifted off my mind]. // 숙제를 끝내고 나니 마음이 놓인다 I feel much relieved to have finished my homework.

나다니다 [외출하다] go out; gad[wander] about; go about. ¶늘 나다니는 사람 a regular gadabout// 밤에 나다니는 여자 a girl gadding about at night// 늘 ~ be always on the gad / be a gadabout / live in the street// 그녀는 나다니기를 대단히 좋아한다 She is a great gadabout. / She doesn't like to stay at home. // 밤에 혼자 나다니는 것은 위험하다 It is dangerous to go out alone at night.

나돌다 **1** go out; gad about. ⇨나다니다 ¶쓸데없이 ~ wander about to no purpose. **2** (말·소문이) get abroad; be rumored; (상품이) arrive[appear] on the market; hit[come on to] the market; be moving. ¶딸기가 시장에 나돌기 시작했다 Strawberries are beginning to appear on the market. // 지금 사과가 한창 나돌고 있다 Apples are now in season.

나동그라지다 tumble down[over]; topple over[down]; fall on one's back; have oneself tripped off. ¶파도에 쓸리어 ~ be carried off one's feet by the waves.

나뒹굴다 roll about; be spread all over. ⇨뒹굴다1·3

나들다 come in and go out. ⇨드나들다1

나들이 going out; an outing; a short visit. ¶결혼 후 처음으로 친정집에 ~를 가다 pay the first postmarriage visit to (her) native home. **나들이하다** go out; pay a short visit (to); go on a (short) visit (to). ¶이웃집에 ~ pay a visit to the neighbors.

● **나들이옷** one's best (clothes); one's Sunday best[best]; a gala[holiday] dress; a go-to-meeting dress; a visiting wear.

나라 **1** [국토] a country; a land; [영토] a territory. ¶머나먼 ~ a far-off land / a distant country.
2 [국가] a state; a nation; a country; an empire(제국); a kingdom(왕국); [국적] one's nationality; [고국] one's (native) country; one's home[mother] country; one's homeland[fatherland / motherland]. ¶~의 중대사 a matter of national importance// ~를 위하여 for the sake of one's country// ~ 없는 사람들 stateless people// ~가 위급한 때에 at[on the occasion of] a national crisis// ~를 생각하는 마음 the love of one's (home) country / patriotism// ~를 **다스리다** govern a nation[state / country] // ~를 **세우다** found[establish / build up] a country[state] // ~를 **재건하다** reconstruct[rebuild / rehabilitate] one's country// ~를 **팔다** sell[betray] one's country// 온 ~가 그의 죽음을 애도했다 The whole nation mourned his death. // (외국인에게) 어느 ~ 사람입니까 What is your nationality? / What country are you from?
3 […세계] a world; a realm. ¶꿈~ the dream-world / the dreamland / the realm[a land] of dreams / the cloudland// 달~ the lunar world / the moon// 별~ the starry world// 공상의 ~ the realm of fancy.

● **나라님** the king; the monarch; the sovereign; the ruler. **나랏일** the affairs[matters] of state; the state[national] affairs.

나락(奈落·那落) [지옥] Hell; Hades; the infernal regions; (범) Naraka. ¶~으로 떨어지다 fall into the bottomless pit.

나란하다 even; equal; uniform; regular; (be) lined up; (be) in a regular line[row / file]; [평행하다] (be) parallel (to / with). ¶대열이 ~ be in regular ranks / be in perfect order.

나란히 [줄지어] in a (regular) line[row / file]; side by side; abreast; [가지런히] evenly; uniformly; regularly; in (good / neat / trim) order. ¶철로와 ~ 뻗은 길 a road running parallel with the railway// ~ 움직이는 자동차들 cars moving side by side[abreast] // ~ 하다 arrange in a row// 높이를 ~ 하다 make (them) all of the uniform[same] height// 어깨를 ~ 하다 (곧, 대등하다) rank[vie] (with) / bear[stand] comparison (with) / be equal (to) / equal[rival] (another) / ~ 서다 stand shoulder to shoulder / (한 줄로) stand in a row[line] / line up// 옆으로 ~ 서다 stand side by side / stand abreast (of) // 우로[좌로] ~ 서다 dress to[by] the right[left] // 어깨를 맞대고 ~ 가다 go shoulder to shoulder[side by side] / walk abreast (with)// 우로[앞으로] ~ [구령] Right[Forward] dress!// 그들은 교실에서 ~ 앉았다 They sat side by side in class. // 거리에는 상점이 ~ 줄지어 있다 The street is lined with shops.

나루 **1** [배가 건너다니는 일정한 곳] a ferry. **2** →나룻배(⇨나루)

● **나루터** a ferry (crossing). **나루(터)지기** a ferryman; a ferry guard. **나룻가** the vicinity of a ferry. **나룻배** a ferryboat; a ferry.

나르다 [운반하다] carry; [문어] convey; [수송하다] transport(▶ convey는 주로 탈것으로 나르는 경우에 씀. transport는 장거리를 나르는 경우. convey와 transport는 날라서 상대방에게 건네줄 때까지를 말하고 carry는 단순히 나른다는 뜻뿐임); (바람·물 등이) waft. ¶짐을 ~ carry luggage// 날라 가다 carry away// 손으로[수레로] ~ carry (a thing) by hand[cart] // 비행기[기차 / 트럭]로 ~ transport (goods) by air[train / truck] // 위층으로 ~ get (tables) upstairs// 탁자를 방에서 밖으로

나르시시즘

~ carry a table out of the room.// 다음 역까지 승객을 ~ carry[convey] passengers to the next station.// 비행기[배]로 그 기계를 날랐다 The machine was transported by air [sea].// 탁자를 여기로 날라다 주게 Bring the table over here.// 우리는 인부들을 시켜 짐을 날랐다 We engaged men to carry our baggage.

나르시시즘 [심] narcissism.

나른하다 [고단하다] languid; weary; listless; log(g)y; tired; dull; heavy; [맥이 풀려 있다] slack. ¶나른한 봄날 a lazy spring day.// 나른한 날씨 slack[sweltering] weather.// 나른한 오후 a slack afternoon.// 나른한 목소리 in a listless voice.// 날씨가 더워서 몸이 나른했다 The hot weather made me feel sluggish [listless/languid].// 몸이 나른해서 일할 생각이 없다 I feel too lazy to work.// 오늘은 어쩐지 ~ Somehow I feel languid[listless] today.// 몸과 마음이 모두 ~ I am weary in body and mind. **나른히** languidly; wearily; languorously; lazily; listlessly.

나름 ¶… ~이다 depend on / hang[turn] on / be conditional[dependent] on / rest[lie] with / 자기[그] ~대로 in one's[its] own way / after one's[its] kind / 능력 ~으로 according to one's ability / 자기 ~대로 하다 do a thing in one's own way / 값은 품질 ~이다 Prices vary with the quality.// 그것은 사람 ~이다 That depends on the person.// 만사는 그들의 움직임 ~이다 Everything depends on what move they make.// 그것은 모두 네가 말하기 ~이다 It all depends on how you put [say] it.// 무슨 요리든 나는 내 ~대로 만든다 I have my own recipes for the dishes I cook.// 그 영화는 그 ~대로 재미있다 That film is interesting in its own way.// 이것은 그 ~대로 좋은 점이 있다 This has a merit of its own.// 이 책은 그 ~대로 읽을 만한 가치가 있다 This book has a certain worth of its own.

나리¹ [식] **1** a lily. ⇨ "백합(百合) **2** a tiger lily. ⇨ 참나리

나리² [존칭] your honor; sir; [왕사님] Your Highness. ¶시장 ~ Your[His](간접적으로)] Honor the Mayor.

나마 […라도] though; however; but anyway; if only; […마저] even. ¶그만한 비 ~ 와 주니 크게 다행이다 Even that much of rain is of great help.// 주소 ~ 알았어도 편지는 내었을 텐데 If only I had known your address, I would have written to you.// 늙은 마누라 ~ 나에게는 소중하다 Though old, she is my good wife.

-나마 though; however; even if; even. ¶맛은 좋지 못하~ 좀 들어 보세요 These are not very tasty, but just have some anyway.// 그 집은 크지 못하~ 아늑하다 Though small, the house is cozy.// 그녀는 가난하~ 거짓말은 안 한다 Though (she is) poor[Poor as she is], she is above telling a lie.

나막신 a *namaksin*; (wooden) clogs; wooden shoes (with high supports); sabots; patterns. ¶~을 신다 put on *namaksin* / wear *namaksin*.

나머지 1 [잔여] the remainder; the remnant; the rest; the remaining(s); the balance[잔고]; [잉여] the surplus; the residue; [남긴 것] leavings; remnants; things left over; left-overs. ¶~의 remaining / remnant / residuary / residual (quantity) / outstanding (debt) / surplus(과잉의) ~ (잡동사니) 물건 odds and ends / oddments / ~ 재산 what is left of one's property / the residue of one's property.// ~ 빚 the remainder [what is left] of one's debt (to).// ~ 일 the remaining work / the rest of the work.// ~ 반 the other half.// ~ 없이 wholly / entirely / all / 먼저 ~ 일을 끝내다 finish the rest of the work first.// ~는 네가 혼자 해라 You do the rest by yourself.// ~ 일은 내일 하겠다 I will do the remaining work tomorrow.// 연필 세 자루는 내가 갖고 ~를 네게 주겠다 I will take three pencils and give you the rest.// 식탁에 올리고 난 ~ 음식은 버릴까요 Shall I throw away the leftovers from dinner?// 분배하고 난 ~ 도시락이 5개 있었다 There were five lunches left(over).// 15에서 8을 빼면 ~는 얼마입니까 What does 8 from 15 leave? / What is the remainder if you subtract 8 from 15.// 15에서 8을 빼면 ~는 7이다 8 from 15 leaves 7.// ~는 내달에 지불해 주십시오 Please pay the rest[remainder] next month.// 나는 휴가의 ~를 집에서 보냈다 I spent much remained[was left] of my vacation at home. / I stayed at home during the rest of my vacation.// ~ 다섯 개는 어떻게 할까 What shall we do with the odd five?// 책을 샀다지? ~ 돈은 어떻게 했어 Bought a book, have you? And what have you done with the balance?// ~ 돈이 얼마나 있느냐 How much money have you left?// ~ 돈으로 무엇을 살까 What shall I buy with the leftover money?// ~ 사람은 어디 있는가 Where are the rest of people?// 스커트를 만들고 난 ~ 천으로 전화 커버를 만들었다 I used the remnants of cloth left over from making my skirt to make a cover for the telephone.// 그것으로 됐다, ~는 알겠다 That's enough, I can guess the rest. / ~는 내게 맡겨 주시오 I'll take care of the rest. / Leave the rest to me.

2 [(…한) 끝(에)] (in) the excess (of); (as) a result (of). ¶기쁜 ~ in the excess[fullness] of one's joy / through excess of joy / in one's joy / for joy.// 슬픈 ~ in one's grief / in a passion of grief.// 괴로운 ~ driven by pain [despair].// 당황한 ~ all in a fluster.// 분한 ~ in a fit of anger[passion].// 질투한 ~ driven by jealousy.// 미워한 ~ out of hatred.// 사랑한 ~ in an excess of love.// 바쁜 ~ 소식을 전하지 못했습니다 I have been too busy to write[call on] you.// 심한 언쟁을 한 ~ 싸움이 되었다 Their severe quarrel resulted in fighting. / As a result of much quarreling they began to fight[came to blows].

3 [수] the residue.

나무 [수목] a tree; a shrub(관목); [초목] a plant; [목재] wood; timber; (미) lumber; [맨나무] firewood. ¶~가 우거진 산 a wooded(woody) hill / ~가 없는 산 a hill bare of trees / a bald hill.// ~ 책상 a wooden desk.// 산에서 ~를 베어 내다 bring down timber[lumber] from a mountain.// ~를 베다 fell[(미)] fall / cut] a tree.// ~에 물을 주다 water a plant.// ~를 치다 trim a tree.// ~에 올라가다 climb (up) a tree.// ~를 때다 burn wood.// ~가 우거지다 be thickly wooded.// ~를 보고 숲을 못 보다 cannot[be unable to] see the wood for the trees.// ~에서 사과를 한

개 따 먹었다 I picked an apple from a tree and ate it. **나무하다** gather firewood; cut wood for fuel. ¶나무하러 가다 go to gather [cut] firewood.
● **나무 그늘** the shade of a tree; a leafy recess[shade]; a bower. **나무껍질** the bark of a tree. ¶~을 벗기다 bark (a tree) / strip a tree of its bark / strip the bark from a tree. **나무꾼** a firewood gatherer; a woodman; a woodcutter; (미) a lumberjack. **나무못** a wooden peg[nail]; a treenail. **나무 상자** a wooden box. **나무장수** a firewood seller; a fuel dealer. **나무줄기** the trunk of a tree. **나무토막** a piece[chip / splinter] of wood; a block(큰 것). **나무가지** the branches of a tree; a bough(큰 가지); a spring(잔 것). **나뭇결** the grain (of wood). ¶~이 곱다[거칠다] be fine-grained[coarse-grained]. **나뭇단** a fag(g)ot; a bundle of firewood. **나뭇등걸** the stump of a tree. **나뭇잎** leaves (of trees); (집합적) foliage; leafage. ¶~이 다 떨어졌다 The leaves are all gone off the trees. / The trees are bare of leaves. **나뭇조각** a splinter; a piece[chip / block] of wood; a chunk (of wood)(큰 것).

나무라다 [꾸짖다] rebuke (a person for something); scold; blame; reprove; reproach; [비난하다] censure; accuse; [문책하다] call (bring) (a person) to account; take[call / bring] (a person) to task. ¶나무랄 데 없이 impeccably / perfectly /조용히[호되게] ~ scold mildly[severely] / give (a person) a mild[sharp / severe] scolding // 잘못을 ~ censure[blame] (a person) for his error[fault] // 배은망덕을 ~ rebuke (a person's) ingratitude // 남을 맞대 놓고 ~ run a person down to his face / 나무랄 데 없다 have no fault to find with / be faultless [flawless] / be impeccable[perfect] / be free from blemishes // 조심성이 없다고 아내를 나무랐다 He reproached[reproved] his wife for her carelessness. // 그는 부하의 직무 태만을 나무랐다 He took his subordinate to task for his neglect[dereliction] of duty. // 선생님은 그의 태만을 나무라셨다 The teacher reproached[censured / (문어) rebuked] him for being lazy. // 결과는 나무랄 데 없이 좋다 The outcome is very satisfactory[leaves nothing to be desired]. / His character is without blemish.

나무람 (a) rebuke; a reproach; a reproof; a blame; a censure. ¶~을 듣다 receive a rebuke (from) // 그는 불려 가서 ~을 들었다 He was summoned to receive a proof. // 그런 짓을 하면 ~을 듣는 정도로 그치지 않을 것이다 If you do a thing like that, you can't get away with a mere scolding.

나무아미타불 (南無阿彌陀佛) I sincerely believe in Amitābha; (위험을 만났을 때) Save us, merciful Buddha!; (명복을 빌 때) May he [his soul] rest in peace.

나물 1 (생것) potherbs; (edible) herbs; wild greens[vegetables]; salad makings. ¶콩~ bean sprouts // 나물을 캐다 pick herbs / gather greens. 2 (무친 것) cooked potherbs[greens / vegetables]; herb salad. ¶~을 무치다 cook greens.
● **나물국** vegetable soup; soup with greens in it.

나박김치 *nabakgimchi*; watery *gimchi*(kimchi) made of radish sliced flat.

나발 a *nabal*; a trumpet; a bugle. ¶규칙이고 ~이고 있느냐 Regulations be hanged! // 이 판에 예절이고 ~이고 어디 있느냐 Decorum is an idle word in this case.

나발(을) 불다 1 (술 등을) drink (beer) from [out of] a bottle; drink out of an upended (beer) bottle. 2 (어린아이가) cry; shout; yell. 3 [떠벌리다] trumpet; talk big. 4 [자백하다] confess (to).

나방 [동] a moth.

나변 (那邊) [어디] where. ¶그 이유가 ~에 있는가 Where is the reason? / What on earth is the reason? // 그의 진의가 ~에 있는지 알 수가 없다 I cannot understand what he really means.

나병 (癩病) [의] leprosy; lepra; Hansen's disease. ¶~에 걸려 있다 be leprous.
● **나병원** [요양소] a leper house; a leprosarium (*pl*. ~s, -ria). **나병 환자** a leper; a leprous patient.

나부 (裸婦) a woman in the nude; a nude woman.

나부끼다 flutter; wave; stream; flap; float. ¶바람에 ~ flutter[wave / flap] in the wind // 바람에 나부끼는 기 a flag fluttering[waving / streaming] in the wind // 초목이 바람에 나부끼고 있다 The grass is bending before [in] the wind. // 버들가지가 바람에 나부끼고 있다 The willows are flowing in the wind.

나부대다 (입을) gabble; talk glib and flippant; (몸을) keep budging nervously; move restlessly; fidget (about).

나부랭이 1 [조각] a piece; a bit; a scrap; a fag end; remnant; odds and ends. ¶종이 ~ a scrap[slip] of paper / 헝겊 ~ pieces [scraps / strips] of cloth. 2 [시시한 것·사람] a fag end. ¶관리 ~ a petty official / 순경 ~ a petty policeman / (속어) a flatfoot.

나부시 (내려오는 모양) (going down) smoothly; lightly; softly; gently; (다소곳이) politely. ¶~ 절하다 bow with a gentle sweep / make a polite bow.

나부죽이 flatly; pronely. ⇨¹너부죽이

나부죽하다 somewhat broad and flat. ⇨너부죽하다

나부거리다 1 [나부끼다] flutter[flap / stream] away. ¶선풍기에 매단 리본이 나부거리고 있다 The ribbons tied to the electric fan in motion are whipping[fluttering]. 2 (입을) chatter; prattle; (구어) rattle; wag one's tongue; flap about. ¶잘도 나부거리는군 How your tongue runs!

나불나불 [나부끼는 모양] fluttering[flapping / streaming] away; [지껄이는 모양] chattering; wagging one's tongue; flapping about.

나붓거리다 keep fluttering[flapping / waving / flowing].

나붙다 be posted up[stuck] (on a wall). ¶무용자 출입 금지」라는 경고가 나붙어 있었다 There was a notice up, saying, "No admission except on business." // 벽보판에 갖가지 포스터가 나붙어 있었다 Various posters appeared on the wall-newspaper board.

나비¹ [피륙 등의 폭] width (of cloth).

나비² [동] a butterfly. ¶~ 모양의 butterfly / butterfly-shaped // ~처럼 날다 fly like a butterfly // ~가 꽃을 찾아 날고 있다 Butterflies are fluttering from flower to flower. // ~가 꽃을 찾듯 꽃이 ~를 찾는가 Men court women,

나비

●**나비넥타이** a bow (tie). **나비매듭** a bow-knot; a bow. **나비춤** a butterfly dance; (in a Buddhist dance) dancing in the manner of a flying butterfly.

나비³ [고양이] puss; tabby; kitty.

나빠지다 grow[get] worse; go wrong; go [turn] bad; (점점 되) go from bad to worse; (품질 등이) spoil; become deteriorated; deteriorate. ¶(환자가) 또 ~ suffer a setback [relapse] / 더 나빠지기만 하다 grow worse and worse / 보다 더 나빠지다 be worse than ever // 사태는 더한 층 나빠졌다 Things went from bad to worse. / 그의 병세는 더욱 나빠졌다 He has taken a turn for the worse. // 그는 과로 때문에 건강이 서서히 나빠졌다 His health was undermined by overwork. // 날씨가 나빠지고 있다 The weather is getting worse.

나쁘다 1 [옳지 않다] bad; evil; ill; wrong; immoral; sinful. ¶나쁜 짓[악행] a wrong / an evil [a wrong] deed / a misdeed / [악덕] a vice / [죄악] a crime / a sin // 나쁜 짓을 하다 do wrong / commit a sin[crime] // 생물을 괴롭히는 것은 ~ It is wrong to torment any creature. // 나는 나쁜 짓을 한 적이 없다 I have a clear[nothing on my] conscience.

2 [사악하다] bad; evil; wicked; ill-natured; malicious. ¶나쁜 마음 an evil [a wicked] heart // 나쁜 마음을 먹다 let evil thoughts arise / be tempted to do evil // 나쁜 인간 a wicked man / a rascally fellow / a rascal // 나쁜 친구들 bad companions // 너는 참 나쁜 아이로구나 What a bad [naughty] boy you are! / 그녀는 듣던 것보다는 나쁜 사람이 아니다 She is not so black as she is painted.

3 [잘못이다] wrong; be in the wrong; be to blame; be in fault. ¶내가 나빴어 It's my fault. / The fault lies with me. / I am to blame (for it). / I take the blame on myself. // 그는 자기가 나빴다고 말했다 He acknowledged[owned] himself in the wrong. // 둘 다 ~ Both are to blame. // 그런 말을 한 것은 네가 ~ You are to blame [It's your fault] for having said such a thing.

4 [해롭다] bad; harmful; injurious; [악성이다] malignant (influenza); virulent (disease); nasty. ¶눈에는 ~ be bad [injurious to] the eyes // 과음은 몸에 ~ Over-drinking is bad for your health. / Excessive drinking is not good for you. // 이 날씨는 농작물에 ~ The weather is bad for the crops. // 이런 책을 아이들한테 읽히는 것은 ~ Such books should not be placed in children's hands.

5 [건강이 좋지 않다] ill[sick]; indisposed. ¶병세가 아주 ~ dangerously[critically] ill // 심장이 ~ have [suffer from] a heart disease [trouble] / be troubled with a weak heart // 위가 ~ have a complaint in one's stomach / have a weak stomach // 안색이 ~ look pale / have a bad complexion // 눈이 ~ have a bad eye / have defective eyesight // 장(腸)이 ~ suffer from a bowel complaint // 몸이 어디 나쁜가요 What is wrong with your health? / Is anything the matter[wrong] with you? / What is the matter with you? / What ails you?

6 [정도·품질이 좋지 않다] bad; inferior; of low grade; of inferior make; coarse(날림의). ¶나쁜 물건 inferior goods / a bad [defective] article // 품질이 ~ be of inferior [poor] quality.

7 [머리·기억력이] poor; weak; feeble. ¶머리가 ~ be weak-headed / be muddleheaded / be slow of understanding / be slow at learning // 기억력이 ~ have a poor[bad] memory.

8 [날씨가] bad; foul; nasty; inclement. ¶나쁜 날씨 foul[bad / nasty] weather.

9 [도로가] muddy; bad; rough; execrable. ¶길이 몹시 ~ The road is very rough.

10 [불길·불행하다] ill; unlucky; bad; ominous. ¶나쁜 징조 a bad [an ill] omen // 나쁜 소식 sad[ill / unwelcome] news // 오늘은 일진이 나쁜가 보다 It seems this is an evil [bad / a black] day.

11 [불쾌하다] bad; unpleasant; disagreeable; displeased; ill-humored. ¶기분이 ~ feel uncomfortable / feel hurt / be displeased (with / at / by) / take offense (at) / be out of sorts.

12 [불편·불비·고장 등이 있다, 부적당하다] bad; wrong; ill; out of order(고장 난); ill-timed(시기가). ¶엔진의 어딘가가 ~ Something is wrong[the matter] with the engine. // 이 시계의 어디가 나쁜지 좀 봐 주십시오 I want you to see what this watch wants doing to it.

13 [모자라다] insufficient; unsatisfactory; deficient; inadequate; (서술적) be not enough. ¶저녁이 내겐 좀 나빴다 The supper wasn't enough for me [didn't fill me up]. // 그렇게 먹고도 아직 나쁘냐 You really ate much. And are you not filled[satisfied] yet? // 밥은 좀 나쁜 듯하게 먹어야 탈이 없다 Feed by measure and defy the physician. / Temperance is the best physic[medicine]. / Moderation is everything to the health.

나뻐 [나쁘게] bad; ill. ¶(남을) ~ 말하다 speak ill of (a person) / talk against (a person) // 악의로 한 말이 아니니 그렇게 ~ 여기지 마십시오 Don't take my words so ill [amiss] since I didn't make them out of spite.

나사 [미국 국립 항공 우주국] NASA(▶ the National Aeronautics and Space Administration의 약어).

나사(羅紗) woolen cloth; (thick close-woven) wool cloth. ¶능직 ~ twilled cloth / twills. // ~상(인) a dealer in woolen cloth / (영) a woolen draper[dealer].
●**나사점**(-店) a woolen draper's[dealer's] shop.

나사(못)(螺絲-) a screw nail; a wood screw(나무로 된); a screw eye(대가리가 고리 모양인). ¶수~ a male[a positive / an external] screw / a bolt // 암~ a female [a negative / an internal] screw / a nut // 박다 [죄다·돌리다] drive[put on / turn] a screw / screw // ~로 죄다 [고정시키다] screw (hinges to the door) / screw (a board) // ~를 단단하게 죄다 drive home a screw // ~를 빼다 take off (a board) / unscrew // ~를 풀다 loosen a screw // ~를 죄다 tighten a screw // 뚜껑을 ~로 고정시키다 screw down the lid // 경첩의 ~를 풀다 loosen a screw from a hinge / unscrew a hinge // ~가 풀어졌다 The screw is loose. // ~를 한 번 더 돌리시오 Give another turn to the screw. // [비유] 그 친구 머리의 ~가 좀 빠졌군 There is something loose about his brainwork. / He

나아지다

has lost some of the mental power[strength of character] that he used to have. / (속이) He has a screw loose. / He wants[needs] screwing up.
● **나사돌리개** a (screw) driver.

나상(裸像) [미] a nude statue[figure]. ⇨나체상(⇨나체)

나서다 1 [나와 서다] come[step] forward; appear; come out[forward / forth / up / along]; turn up; make one's appearance; present oneself. ¶줄에서 ~ get[step] out of line // 무대에 ~ appear on the stage / be on the stage // 표면에 ~ appear in the limelight.
2 [나타나다] (구하던 것이) turn up; be found; (구하던 사람이) apply (for); make application (for); go in for. ¶일자리가 ~ find a job[position / situation] / find employment / get a place // 학비를 대겠다고 ~ offer to provide (someone) with (his) school expenses // 나서는 희망자가 없다 No one applied for it. // 아들에게 좋은 혼처가 나섰다 An offer of marriage has come up for my son.
3 [시작하다] go into; enter upon; launch into; embark upon; get started; (정계나 각 분야의 제일선에) make one's debut; appear; [출마하다] run[stand] for. ¶실업계[사교계 / 정계]에 ~ go into business[society / politics] // 국회의원 후보로 ~ run for the National Assembly // 지사 선거에 ~ be a candidate[(미) run / (영) stand] for governor // 경찰이 조사에 나섰다 The police started an investigation. // 그는 다음 선거에서 정계에 나설 작정이다 He is going to make his political debut in the next election.
4 [가로맡거나 간섭하다] intrude; interfere; obtrude; intermeddle; push[put / thrust] oneself forward; thrust[poke] one's nose into. ¶쓸데없는 일에 ~ intrude where one is not wanted // 주제넘게 나서는 사람 a forward [pert] man // 주제넘게 나서서 죄송합니다 Excuse me for being too forward. // 주제넘게 나서는 것 같습니다만… Excuse me for being [sounding] impertinent, but …. // 넌 이 일에 나서지 마라 You keep out of this. // (이것은) 네가 나설 일이 아니야 This is none of your business. / Mind your own business. / You have nothing to do with this matter. // 지금이야말로 내가 나설 때다 It is time for me to take[go into] action. // 그는 언제나 남의눈에 띄게 나서려고 한다 He is always thrusting [forcing] himself upon[on] the notice of others. // 그 신출내기는 건방지게 나서서 별것 아닌 지식을 과시하려고 하였다 That green boy was forward enough[had the impudence / (구어) had the cheek] to try to show off his smattering of knowledge. // 여기서는 내가 나서서 할 일이 없다 I have no part to play here. // 뒤늦게 내가 나설 자리가 아니다 At this late date, it is not my place to say [do] anything.
5 [떠나다·출발하다] leave; set out; start; get out (of). ¶집을 ~ leave home[one's house] // 여행에 ~ start[leave / set out] on a journey // 몇 시에 집을 나설까요 When shall we leave home?

나선(裸線) a naked electric wire; a bare wire.
나선(螺旋) a spiral; a helix; a screw(나사). ¶~의 spiral / helical // 독수리는 크게 ~을 그리며 상공으로 날아올랐다 The vulture climbed by vast spirals into the upper air. // 연기는 ~ 모양으로 올라갔다 The smoke spiraled up[rose in a spiral.]
● **나선 계단** a spiral[corkscrew] staircase; a spiral stairway; a circular[winding / spiral / screw] stair. **나선균** a spirillum (pl. -rilla). **나선상 / 나선형** screw shape; spirality. ¶~의 screw-shaped / spiral. **나선 운동** screw motion.

나스닥 NASDAQ: (공식명) National Association of securities Dealers Automated Quotations.

나신(裸身) a naked body. ⇨알몸1

나아가다 1 [전진하다] advance; go forward; move on[forward]; progress; march; make way. ¶한 걸음 나아가서 going[taking] a step forward / [게다가·그 위에] moreover / besides / further(more) // 한 걸음 앞으로 ~ go[make / take] a step forward // 거친 바다로 ~ sail[go] out on the rough sea // 해변으로 ~ advance towards the coast // 바람 불어오는 쪽으로 ~ make headway against the wind / (배가) work[beat] to windward / tack [beat] against the wind // 시속 50마일 속도로 ~ make 50 miles an hour // 하루에 50킬로 ~ make fifty kilometers in a day // 한 걸음 더 나아가서 생각해 보시오 Go a step further in your thinking. // 그 사람뿐만 아니라 나아가서는 공무원 전체의 명예가 걸려 있다 Not only his honor but that of all public officials is at stake. // 나는 목적지로 나아갔다 I went [stepped] ahead toward my destination. // 그들은 목표를 향하여 꾸준히 나아가고 있다 They are making steady progress toward their goal. // 배는 파도를 헤치며 나아갔다 The ship plowed[buffeted] her way through the waves. // 눈이 많이 쌓여서 더 나아갈 수가 없었다 Further progress was hindered by deep snow. // 행렬은 천천히 절을 향해 나아갔다 The procession advanced slowly toward(s) the Buddhist temple. // 그는 나침반을 길잡이로 삼아 북쪽으로 나아갔다 With a compass as his guide, he headed north. // 우리는 숲 속을 몇 킬로 더 나아갔다 We went [moved] ahead[forward] a few kilometers through the wood. // 그들은 군중을 헤치고 나아갔다 They elbowed[pushed] their way through the crowd. // 구조선은 난파선을 향해 나아갔다 The rescue boat made its way toward(s) the wrecked ship. // 우리는 하루에 몇 마일밖에 나아가지 못했다 We were unable to cover more than a few miles a day. // 빛은 1초에 몇 미터 나아가느냐 How many meters a second does light travel? // 그는 호명을 받자 한 걸음 앞으로 나아갔다 When his name was called, he stepped[took a step] forward.
2 [진척·진보하다] make progress; progress; advance; improve; come[get] better; change for the better. ¶이대로 나아가면 at the present rate of progress // 이라크의 경제는 급속히 나아가고 있다 The economy of Iraq is making rapid progress.

나아지다 become[get] better; improve[be improved]; change for the better; take a favorable turn. ¶성적이 ~ show a better school record // 살기가 ~ get better off / be in easier-circumstances // 조금도 나아진 게 없다 It's none the better for the change. // 새 각료의 진용에는 조금도 나아진 게 없다 The

나약하다

new cabinet lineup is no improvement over [is not much different from] the last one.∥식량 사정이 나아졌다 The food situation has improved.∥환자의 병세가 나아지고 있다 The patient is not doing well. / There has been not improvement in the patient's condition.∥그 환자는 (병이) 나아지고 있다 The patient is taking a turn for the better. / The patient is getting better.

나약하다(懦弱·儒弱-) effeminate; emasculate; feeble-minded; spiritless. ¶나약한 남자 an effeminate man∥나약한 국민 a soft and spiritless people∥나약해지다 lapse into effeminacy / become effeminate∥그 정도 일로 울다니 참 나약하구나 What a weakling to cry over such a thing!

나열(羅列) marshaling; an array. **나열하다** arrange (in a row); marshal; enumerate. ¶미사여구를 나열한 문장 a composition full of flourishes∥통계 숫자를 ~ marshal statistical figures / give a wealth of statistics∥단편적으로 정보를 ~ enumerate bits of information∥그는 자신의 장점을 나열하였다 He listed his own virtues [merits].

나오다 1 [안에서 밖·앞을 향하여 오다] go [come / get / head] out of; take one's way out; step out. ¶집에서 ~ get out of the house / leave home∥탕[욕조]에서 ~ step out of the tub [bath]∥풀장에서 ~ get [climb] out of the pool∥정원으로 ~ come out into the garden∥앞으로 한 발 나오시오 Step forward.∥방에서 나와 Come [Get] out of your room!∥나는 간신히 차에서 나왔다 I struggled out of the car with great difficulty.∥나는 한 달 동안 방에서 나오지 않았다 I kept [was confined in] my room for a month.
2 […에 모습이 나타나다] appear; show oneself; emerge (from / out of / on); make one's appearance; come forward; turn [show] up; (출몰하다) haunt; infest; (드러나다) show itself; be revealed [exposed]; assert [reveal / betray] itself; peep out; (시장에) arrive [appear] (on the market); hit [come out to] the market. ¶별이 ~ the stars appear in the sky∥나쁜 버릇이 ~ one's bad habit peeps [crops] out∥습관적인 [평소의] 고집이 ~ one's usual stubbornness asserts itself / one shows his customary obstinacy∥그는 텔레비전 [무대]에 자주 나온다 He often appears on television [the stage].∥남 앞에 나오면 쑥스럽다 I feel shy in the presence of others.∥구름 사이로 해가 나왔다 The sun emerged from behind the clouds.∥밭에서 많은 옛 금화가 나왔다 A lot of ancient gold coins have been dug up from the field.∥이 집에는 귀신이 나온다 A ghost haunts [walks] this house.∥부엌에 쥐가 많이 나온다 The kitchen is infested with [by] rats.∥화가 나자 그의 본성이 나왔다 Anger has made him betray himself.∥수박이 시장에 나왔다 Watermelons have appeared on the market. / Watermelons are out on the market.
3 (싹이) shoot; sprout; bud. ¶크로커스의 싹이 나왔다 The crocus buds have come out.∥나무에 싹이 나오기 시작했다 The trees have begun to bud [to shoot forth buds].
4 [참석·출석·출근하다] be present at; attend; [출두하다] appear; report (at). ¶(사람이) 모두 ~ appear all together / be all present /

be all out∥법정에 ~ appear in [before] court∥그는 회의에 안 나왔다 He is not present at the meeting.∥그가 파티에 나오다니 뜻밖이다 His attendance at the party was unexpected.∥교실에 와 보니 전원이 나와 있었다 I came to my class and found full attendance.∥오늘 모임에 있는데 좀 나와 주지 않겠습니까 We have a meeting today; won't you come along [join us]?
5 [진출하다] launch into; enter upon; (참가하다) join; participate in; take part in; enter for. ¶사회에 ~ launch [go out] into the world∥정계에 ~ enter upon a political career / make one's debut on the political stage∥시합에 ~ take part [participate] in a game∥그녀는 15살 때 서울로 나왔다 She came (영) up) to Seoul at the age of fifteen.∥영국도 올림픽에 나온다 England is also taking part in the Olympic games.
6 [없어진 것이] be found; turn up; be restored (to); get (a thing) back. ¶도둑맞은 반지가 곧 나왔다 The stolen ring was soon found.∥없어진 당신의 펜이 나왔습니까 Has your missing pen turned up?∥잃어버린 줄 알았던 시계가 서랍에서 나왔다 The watch I thought I had lost turned up in the drawer.
7 [내밀다] project; protrude; jut [stick] out. ¶이마가 ~ have a prominent forehead∥못 대가리가 나와 있다 The head of a nail is sticking out.∥그는 배가 나와 있다 His belly is protruding. / His stomach sticks out.∥당신 슬립이 나와 있어요 Your slip is showing.∥그는 배가 나오게 되었다 He became potbellied [developed a paunch].∥그녀는 (임신하여) 배가 나오고 있다 Her pregnancy has begun to show.
8 [흘러나오다] flow out; run out; issue (forth); spring forth [out]. ¶코피가 ~ bleed at the nose∥재채기가 ~ have a fit of sneezing∥그의 눈에서 눈물이 나왔다 Tears fell [flowed] from his eyes.∥아이의 콧물이 나오고 있다 The child's nose is running.∥그의 팔에서 피가 나오고 있다 His arm is bleeding.∥나는 입에서 침이 나왔다 My mouth watered.∥이 골짜기에는 온천이 나온다 There is a hot spring in this valley.∥이 펜은 잉크가 잘 나오지 않는다 This pen doesn't write smoothly.∥이 만년필은 잉크가 잘 나온다 This fountain pen has a good flow of ink.∥그의 상처에서 피가 나오고 있다 Blood is running from his wound.
9 (길이) lead to; [도달하다] come to [upon]; hit upon; find oneself (at / in). ¶이 길을 따라가면 바다가 나온다 This path leads [goes] to the sea.∥곧 어느 마을이 나왔다 Soon we came to a village.∥20분 더 갔더니 간선 도로가 나왔다 We reached [struck] the highway after twenty minutes. / Another twenty minutes saw us on the highway.
10 [출판되다] be published; be issued; be brought out; be given to the world. ¶최근에 나온 책 a newly published book / a new publication∥내 책이 곧 나온다 My book will come [be] out soon.∥특별호는 언제 나옵니까 When will the special number be issued [come out]?∥창간호는 15일에 나온다 The first number will come out [appear / make its appearance] on the 15th.
11 [게재되다] appear [come out / be reported] (in); go into (a newspaper). ¶그 뉴

스는 내일 신문에 나옵니다 The news will appear[be] in tomorrow's papers.// 그 사건은 주간지에 자세히 나와 있다 The incident is reported in detail in a weekly magazine.// 그의 사진이 신문에 나왔다 His picture appears in the paper.// 이것은 그의 소설에서 자주 나오는 여성형이다 This is the type of woman that often appears in his novels.

12 [주어지다] be brought; be served; be given; (급료 등이) be paid. ¶여권[연금] 이 ~ be granted a passport [a pension] // 나는 일주일의 휴가가 나왔다 I was given a week off. // 그 일을 하면 5만 원의 보수가 나온다 Fifty thousand won will be paid for the work. // 식사가 나왔다 Dinner was served. // 진수성찬이 나왔다 We were served[treated to] a sumptuous dinner. // 생선 다음에 베이컨이 나왔다 Fish was removed by bacon. // 마침내 비자가 나왔다 My visa has been issued at last. // 경찰의 허가가 좀처럼 나오지 않았다 We had difficulty getting police permission. // 나는 65세에 연금이 나왔다 I was entitled to a pension at sixty-five.

13 [제출·제시되다] be given; be brought up. ¶시험에 열 문제가 나왔다 Ten questions were given in the examination. // 시험에 어떤 문제가 나왔나 What kind of questions were on the examination? // 회의에서 그 문제가 나왔다 The problem was brought up at the meeting.

14 [산출·배출되다] be produced; be raised [grown]; be found; be turned out. ¶이 근방에서 석유가 나온다 Oil is found around here. // 이 도시에서 많은 위인이 나왔다 This town has produced many great men. // 이 학교에서는 유명한 학자가 많이 나왔다 This school has turned out a number of eminent scholars.

15 [유래하다] spring[issue / come] (from); originate (in / from); be derived (from); be traced (to). ¶이 말은 그리스 어에서 나온 것이다 This word is derived[comes] from Greek[of Greek origin]. // 그 이야기는 그에게서 나왔다 He first told the story. // 그것은 최 군에게서 나온 소문이다 Mr. Choe started [originated] the rumor. // 그의 집안은 권씨 가문으로부터 나왔다 His family is descended from the Gwon clan. // 비용은 그에게서 나온 것이라고 들었다 I heard he paid the expenses[(구어) footed the bill]. // 그의 그 행동은 호기심에서 나온 것이었다 He did it from[out of] curiosity. // 그의 여비는 어디서 나온 것입니까 Where has he got his traveling expenses? // 그 보도는 믿을 만한 소식통에서 나온 것이다 The report comes from a reliable source.

16 [(결과로서) 생기다] come out (as a result); work out. ¶마침내 결론이 나왔다 At last we came to[arrived at] a conclusion. // 여간해서 좋은 생각이 나오지 않는군 I'm having a hard time coming up with a good idea. // 12를 2로 나누면 6이 나온다 Twelve divided by two gives six.

17 [(소속·단체에서) 물러나다] resign (one's office); quit; leave. ¶직장에서 ~ leave a job.

18 [졸업하다] graduate from; leave; finish. ¶그는 어느 대학을 나왔습니까 What university did he graduate from? // 그는 건축과를 나왔다 He graduated (from a university) in architecture. // 그는 초등학교도 나오지 않았다 He didn't even finish elementary school.

19 [풀려나오다] be released. ¶교도소에서 ~ be released from prison / leave prison / be let out of prison // 그 남자는 교도소에서 나온 지 겨우 한 달 됐다 The man was released from prison only last month.

20 [태도를 취하다] assume (an attitude); take[make] (a move). ¶모든 것은 그들이 어떻게 나오느냐에 달렸다 Everything depends on what tack[line] they take[what move they make]. / Nothing can be done until their attitude is known. // 그녀가 어떻게 나오는지 두고 보자 Let's wait and see what moves she will take.

21 [(후보로) 나서다] stand (for); (미) run (for). ¶선거에 ~ run for an election // 국회의원 후보로 ~ stand for Parliament[(미) run for Congress] // 서울 종로구에서 ~ run from the Jongno constituency of Seoul.

22 [찍히다] come out; show; be taken. ¶이 사진은 잘 나왔다 This photo has come out well[is taken well]. // 이 사진에서 네가 잘 나왔구나 You came out well in this photo. / You look fine in this picture. // 이 사진은 실물보다 잘 나왔다 This picture flatters you. // 이 사진은 잘 안 나왔다 This photo is badly [not well] taken.

23 (전화에). ¶나왔습니다(교환수의 말) You are connected[in connection]. / Your party is on.

나왕(羅王) [식] a lauan; [목재] lauan.
나위 [여지] room; a margin; [필요] necessity. ¶말할 ~도 없다 be needless to say / be not worth mentioning / faultless / complete / most satisfactory / matchless / superb / left nothing to be desired // 그 비행기의 시설은 더할 ~ 없이 훌륭하다 The accommodation at that airplane is perfect[leaves nothing to be desired]. // 그는 남편으로서 더할 ~ 없다 He is a perfect husband. / He is everything a husband should be. / He is all that can be desired as a husband. // 좀 더 부지런하기만 하면 그녀는 더할 ~ 없는 사람인데 If she were only a little more diligent, there would be nothing to be said against her. // 그녀는 더할 ~ 없이 행복하다 She is as happy as happy can be. // 그 증거는 의심할 ~가 없다 The evidence admits of no [leaves no room for] doubt. // 날씨가 더할 ~ 없이 좋다 This is ideal weather. / The weather is all that could be wished for.

나이 age; years. ¶~별로 by age group // ~순으로 according to age[years / seniority] // ~가 40쯤 되는 여자 a woman of about forty // ~에 상관없이 with no age limit // 네 ~ 때는 when I was (of) your age // ~**가 지긋하다**[패 들다] be well up[advanced] in (one's) years // 제 ~로 보이다 look as old as one is / look one's age // 학교 갈 ~다 be old enough to go to school / be of school age // 아직 결혼할 ~가 아니다 be too young to marry // ~가 40에 가깝다 I'm pushing[nearing] 40. // 그는 ~가 마흔 몇 살이다 He is forty-something. // 그는 ~가 마흔쯤 되었다 He is fortyish. // 저는 ~가 열두 살인데 곧 열세 살이 됩니다 I'm 12, going on 13. // 당신과 같은 ~입니다 I am just your age. // 형은 나보다 ~가 훨씬 많다 My brother is much older than I am. // 그도 이젠 벌이를 할 만한 ~이다 He is old enough to be earning his own living. // 그 여자의 ~를

나이 샷

모르겠군 I can't tell her age. / 계단을 올라가는 데 숨이 차니 ~는 못 속이겠군 I ran out of breath going up the stairs. "Age will tell." as they say.

나이(를) 먹다[나이(가) 들다] put[take] on years; advance in age[years]; grow older; grow[get / become] old; get on in years. ¶또 한 살 ~ grow older by one year / grow a year older // 나이가 들었어도 in spite of one's advanced age // 나이는 먹었어도 마음은 젊은 old in years but young in vigor // 사무실에서는 모두가 내가 10년이나 더 나이가 들어 보인다고 하는군 They all put on[aged] ten years — that's what they say at the office! // 그는 나이를 먹어 감에 따라 원숙해졌다 He mellowed with age[years]. / He has not put on years[gotten old] in vain[for nothing]. / 나이가 들면 지혜가 생긴다 Wisdom comes with age. / Years bring wisdom. / The older, the wiser. // 그는 경험도 있고 나이도 충분히 들었다 He has enough experience and he is old enough for it.

나이(가) 아깝다 (a person) should know better at his age; (a person) seem to have gotten old in vain. ¶그는 젊은 여자의 꽁무니를 따라다니니 그 ~ He runs after young girls as though he had forgotten his age. / 손자와 다투다니 자네 나이가 아깝군 How unbecoming for a man of your age to quarrel with your grandchild!

나이에 비해서[나이치고는 / 나이보다] for one's age[years]; beyond (one's) years; than one's years. ¶나이보다 많이 늙어 버리다 have aged beyond one's years // 그는 나이에 비해서 영리하다[순진하다] He is clever [naive] for[beyond] his years. // 그는 나이치고는 배짱이 좋다 He has a lot of courage [구어] guts] for his age. // 그는 60세인데 나이보다 적어도 10년은 젊어 보인다 He looks at least a decade younger than his 60 years.

나이(가) 차다 be[become] of marriageable age; arrive at the age of marriage; be ripe for marriage; reach a marriageable age. ¶그녀도 이젠 나이가 찼다 She is now of marriageable age.

●**나이배기** a person older than he looks. **나잇값** one's sayings and doings appropriate to[befitting] one's age. ¶~도 못하다 be thoughtless[disgraceful] for one's age / be unworthy of one's years / ought to know better at one's age // ~ 좀 해라 Act[Be] your age! / A man of your age ought to know better. / You're gotten old for nothing[in vain]. **나잇살** a mature[an advanced] age. ¶~이나 먹은 사람 a man stricken in years / a man well advanced in years // ~이나 먹어 가지고 in spite of one's mature[advanced] age / being old enough to know better.

나이스 샷 (*nice shot) [골프] fine [good] shot.

나이테 [식] an annual ring.

나이트 [기사] a knight. ¶그는 ~ 작위를 수여받았다 He was dubbed a knight.

나이트가운 [여성의 잠옷] a nightgown; (영) a night robe.

나이트 게임 a night game. ¶~ 설비가 되어 있는 구장 a baseball stadium with facilities for night games.

나이트캡 a nightcap.

나이트클럽 a night club; a nightclub; (구어) a nightspot.

나이팅게일 [동] a nightingale.

나이프 a knife (*pl.* knives); (식탁용) a table knife; (접람) a jackknife; a claspknife; (소형의) a pocketknife; (식탁용 큰 고기 써는 칼) a carving knife. ¶잘 드는[들지 않는] ~ a sharp[dull] knife // ~와 포크로 식사하다 eat with a knife and fork.

나인 [역] a lady attendant in the palace; an attendant court lady; a court lady; a maid of honour.

나일론 [화] nylon.

나자식물(裸子植物) [식] gymnosperm. ⇨겉씨식물

나전칠기(螺鈿漆器) *najeonchilgi*; lacquerwork [lacquer(ed) ware] inlaid with mother-of-pearl.

나절 ¶한~ half a day / a half day // 점심~ (in) the afternoon // 아침~ (in) the forenoon / (in) the morning / morning hours.

나졸(邏卒) a patrol (man).

나중 the last; the latter part; the future; the end; the consequences; the next. ¶~의 latter / the next / the following / the succeeding / later / future / coming // ~에 after / afterwards / later (on) / subsequently / some time later / by and by // ~ 뵙겠습니다 I'll come later (on). // ~에 또 봅시다 See[I'll see] you later. // ~에 그에게 편지를 쓰겠습니다 I'll write to him by and by. // 이 문제는 ~ 부분에서 논급되어 있다 This issue is discussed in a later section. // 그녀가 맨 ~에 왔다 She was the last to come. // 그것은 ~으로 미룹시다 Let's put it off till some other time. // 이 문제는 ~에 처리하자 Let's deal with this problem later. // 당신은 ~의 편에 속해 있지 않았든가요 Didn't you belong to the later group? // 더 자세한 것은 ~에 말씀드리겠습니다 I will tell you further details later on. // 너는 ~에 후회할 거야 You will repent for it later[in future]. // 그는 ~ 일은 생각할 줄 모른다 He is not a man to think about the future. // ~에 전화할게요 I'll call[phone / (영) ring] you later on. // 누가 맨 ~에 사무실을 나왔지 Who was the last to leave the office? // ~ 일은 알 게 뭐냐 I don't care what happens afterwards. / The consequences are not my concern.

나중 난 뿔이 우뚝하다(속담) The younger generation is better prepared.

나지막하다 rather low; lowish. ¶나지막한 집 a low-built house // 나지막한 소리로 in an undertone / in a low voice / in whispers [a whisper] / under one's breath. **나지막이** low; humbly; softly. ¶~ 말하다 say in a low voice.

나직하다 rather low; lowish. **나직이** low; humbly; softly.

나체(裸體) a naked[nude] body. ¶반~ semi-nudity // 전 ~ a stark-naked body / complete nudity / stark-nakedness // ~의 naked / nude // 완전 ~의 stark-naked // ~의 여자 a naked woman // 반~의 남자 a half-naked body man // ~로 in the nude // 완전 ~가 되다 undress completely // ~가 되다 strip oneself naked / strip oneself of one's clothes / become naked // ~로 만들다 strip (a person) naked / denude // ~로 걷다 walk in the nude // ~로 질주하다 streak.

●**나체상**(~像) a nude statue[figure]. **나체**

주의자 a nudist. **나체화** [미] a nude (picture).
나치(스) 〔나치스 당원·신봉자〕 a Nazi; 〔당〕 the Nazis.
● **나치즘** Nazism.
나침반(羅針盤) a compass. ¶삼각 ~ a triangular compass // 선박용〔항해용〕 ~ a mariner's compass // 항공 ~ an aero compass // 회전 ~ a gyrocompass // ~ 바늘 the needle of a compass // ~에 표시된 방위 the points of the compass // ~ 없이 항해하다 navigate without compass.
● **나침반자리** 〔천〕 Pyxis.
나침의(羅針儀) a compass. ⇨⁼나침반
나타나다 1 〔모습이 보이다〕 appear; come out [forth / forward]; come into view; emerge; take form; come in sight; become visible. ¶연극 장면에 ~ appear in a scene of a play // 산 너머로 보름달이 나타났다 The full moon came out[appeared] from behind the mountain. // 우리가 차를 몰고 계속 가니, 교회의 첨탑이 전방에 나타났다 As we drove on, a church spire come into view in front of us. // 안개 속에서 여자의 형체가 나타났다 The figure of a woman emerged from out of[took form in] the mist. // 그 집에는 귀신이 나타난다 The house is haunted. / A ghost haunts the house. // 이 혜성은 75년마다 나타난다 This comet is visible once in every seventy-five years. // 이윽고 섬이 하나 나타났다 It was not long before an island came in sight.
2 〔그곳에 오다〕 arrive; show up; turn up; make one's appearance; appear; put in an appearance; show[present] oneself. ¶그가 나타났을 때는 식사가 이미 끝난 뒤였다 The meal was over when he finally arrived[(구어) showed up / (구어) turned up]. // 때마침 경관이 그 자리에 나타났다 A policeman made a timely appearance upon the scene.
3 〔(없었던 것이) 출현하다·생기다〕 come into existence; appear; make one's appearance; (문제 등이) crop up; arise. ¶몇 년 전에 여성 회원 전용의 클럽이 나타났다 A few years ago there came into existence[was born] a club whose members were exclusively women. // 그는 19세기에 나타난 위인이었다 He was one of the great men to appear in the nineteenth century. // 내가 하는 일에는 언제나 예기치 않은 문제가 나타난다 Problems are always cropping up in my work.
4 〔드러나다〕 show[display / manifest] itself; be expressed; be described; be revealed; assert[envisage / reveal / express] itself; appear (on); come (over); pass (over); (효과 등이) take[produce] effect; have an effect (on). ¶고뇌의 빛이 그의 얼굴에 나타났다 A look of anguish crossed[passed over / appeared on] his face. / His face registered mental anguish. // 실망의 빛이 어머니의 얼굴에 역력히 나타났다 My mother looked clearly disappointed. / My mother's disappointment showed clearly on her face. // 갑자기 의혹의 빛이 그의 얼굴에 나타났다 A sudden doubt came over him. // 이 작품에는 그가 노력한 흔적이 나타나 있다 This work bears[shows] traces of his effort. // 놀란 기색이 그의 얼굴에 나타났다 His surprise showed on his face. / He looked astonished. // 영상이 인화지에 나타났다 An image appeared on the photographic paper. // 나는 포도주의 술기운이 즉시 얼굴에 나타난다 The effect of wine appears immediately on my face. // 토마토에 붉은 빛깔이 나타나기 시작했다 The tomatoes have begun to turned red. // 그 아이에게 어느 정도 지능의 싹이 나타나기 시작했다 The child is beginning to show some signs of intelligence. // 그 약의 효력이 나타났다 The medicine took effect[showed its effect].
5 〔발견되다〕 be found (out); be discovered; (사실 등이) be exposed; be disclosed; be laid bare; come to light; be brought to light; be revealed; come out. ¶진실은 나타나기 마련이다 Truth always comes out[comes to light]. / Truth will out. // 잃어버렸던 시계가 서랍에서 나타났다 My lost watch turned up in the drawer. // 용의자가 나타난 모양이다 A suspect seems to have appeared[emerged]. / They seem to have come up with a suspect. // 이 사실에서 그가 믿을 만한 사람이라는 것이 나타난다 This fact shows him to be a reliable person. // 불탄 자리에서 그녀의 시체가 나타났다 Her dead body was found[discovered / recovered] in the debris of the fire. // 「정」이라는 남자가 용의자로 나타났다 A man named Jeong loomed up[emerged] as a possible suspect. // 좋은 결과가 나타났다 It produced fine results. // 새로운 사실이 나타났다 A new fact came to light.
6 〔기록 등에 실려 있다〕 be mentioned; be given. ¶미국 문헌에 나타난 한국 Korea mentioned in American literature // 그것은 문헌에 나타나 있다 It finds mention in literature.
나타내다 1 〔모습을〕 appear; show oneself; turn[show] up; make one's appearance. ¶우리가 모퉁이를 돌자 높은 건물이 모습을 나타냈다 As we turned the corner a tall building appeared before our eyes[came into view]. // 그는 불쑥 모습을 나타냈다 His figure burst on our sight. // 그는 무대 위에 모습을 나타냈다 He showed himself on stage.
2 〔표시하다〕 show; indicate; be indicative of; manifest; 〔발휘하다〕 display; exhibit; 〔증명하다〕 prove; speak for; bespeak; 〔드러내다〕 expose; disclose; reveal; bare; betray; lay bare. ¶감정을 얼굴에 ~ show one's feelings // 죄수에게 연민과 친절을 ~ show pity and kindness to the prisoners // 수완을 ~ display[show] one's ability // 결백함을 ~ prove[indicate] one's innocence // 자기의 무지를 ~ expose one's ignorance // 정체〔본색〕를 ~ betray oneself / show oneself in one's true light / show one's true colors // 그녀의 태도는 불만을 나타내고 있다 Her attitude shows[betrays] her dissatisfaction. // 책의 제목이 반드시 내용을 나타내는 것은 아니다 The title of a book doesn't always reflect its contents. // 그의 기침은 분명히 천식의 증상을 나타내고 있다 His cough is a clear symptom of asthma. // 그 약은 1시간 만에 효능을 나타낼 것이다 The effects of the medicine will be felt in one hour. / The medicine will take effect in an hour. // 그는 고갯짓으로 찬성의 뜻을 나타냈다 He indicated his approval with a nod. // 오도미터는 주행 거리를 나타낸다 An odometer indicates the distance traveled.
3 〔표현하다〕 express; give expression (to); convey. ¶말로 나타낼 수 없는 inexpressible // 생각을 말로 ~ put one's thoughts into words // 필설로 다 나타낼 수 없다 be beyond expression[description] / have no word for

나태

/ do not know how to put it // 이 깊은 감사를 말로 나타낼 수가 없군요 I cannot express the depth of my gratitude in words. / My gratitude is beyond[too deep for] words. // 그 장대한 전망은 붓으로는 나타낼 수 없다 The grandeur[magnificence] of the view is beyond description[is indescribable].
4 〔의미하다〕 signify; 〔기호로서 나타내다〕 represent; 〔상징하다〕 symbolize; stand for. ¶이 경우 빨간색은 위험을 나타낸다 Red in this case signifies[stands for] danger. // MP는 Military Police를 나타낸다 The initials "MP" represent[stand for] "Military Police". // 그 메달의 월계수 잎은 승리를 나타낸다 The laurel leaves on the medal symbolize victory. // 이 기호는 무엇을 나타냅니까 What does this sign represent[stand for]?
5 〔두드러지게 하다〕 distinguish. ¶두각을 ~ distinguish oneself / cut a figure / stand out // 이름을 (세상에) ~ make a name for oneself (in the world) / become famous [known] // 그가 단연 두각을 나타내고 있다 He is head and shoulders above his fellows.

나태(懶怠) laziness; idleness; indolence; sloth; sluggishness. **나태하다** idle; lazy; indolent; slothful; sluggish. ¶나태한 마음 sloth / a lazy mind / a disinclination to work // 나태한 생활 a lazy[an idle] life // 나태한 사람 an idler / a lazybones / a drone / a sluggard / a lazy[an idle] man.

나토 the NATO(▶ the North Atlantic Treaty Organization의 약어).

나트륨(⑤Natrium) 〔화〕 sodium(기호 Na).

나팔(喇叭) (악단의) a trumpet; (군대의) a bugle. ¶소집 ~ 신호 a trumpet[bugle] call // ~ 모양의 trumpet-shaped // 진군[돌격 / 후퇴] ~ 을 불다 sound the advance[charge / retreat] // 행진 ~ 이 울렸다 The trumpets sounded the march.

나팔(을) 불다 drink (beer) from a bottle; cry; trumpet; confess (to). ⇨¹나발(을) 불다 (☞나발)

● **나팔관** 〔생〕 the trumpet; the oviduct; the Fallopian tubes. **나팔꽃** 〔식〕 a morning glory. **나팔바지** bell-bottom(ed) trousers; bell-bottoms. **나팔 소리** a bugle note; a trumpet[bugle] call. ¶~ 가 울려 퍼졌다 A bugle call rang out. / A bugle was sounded. **나팔수** a bugler; a trumpeter; a trumpet player.

나포(拿捕) capture; seizure. ¶불법 ~ illegal seizure. **나포하다** capture; seize.
● **나포선** a captured ship; a prize.

나풀거리다 flutter[flap] away. ⇨¹나불거리다₁

나프타 1 〔화〕 naphtha. **2** 〔북대서양 자유 무역 지역〕 NAFTA(▶ North Atlantic Free Trade Area의 약어).

나프탈렌 1 〔화〕 naphthalene; naphthaline. **2** (의류용의) mothballs. ¶옷에 ~ 을 넣어 두다 put mothballs among the clothes.

나한(羅漢) an arhat; an arahat; a Buddhist monk who attained nirvana.

나한에도 모래 먹는 나한이 있다(속담) High position is no guarantee against hardship.

나흗날 the fourth day of the month.

나흘 1 〔4일간〕 four days. **2** the 4th day of a month. ⇨초나흗날

낙(樂) 〔즐거움〕 pleasure; enjoyment; delight; happiness, 〔오락〕 amusement, 〔기분 전환〕 a diversion, 〔취미〕 taste; hobby, 〔위안〕 comfort. ¶인생의 ~ the pleasure[joy / enjoyment] of life // 이 없는 joyless / unhappy / mirthless // ~ 이 없는 사람 a man of few pleasures // 낚시질을 ~ 으로 삼다 take pleasure[delight] in angling / delight in angling // 자녀 교육을 유일한 ~ 으로 삼다 find one's sole comfort in the education of the children // 그의 주된 ~ 이라면 독서였다 His chief amusement was reading. / He found his chief amusement in reading. // 나는 이 일을 돈 때문에 하고 있는 게 아니라, ~ 으로 하고 있는 겁니다 I'm not doing this for money. It's my pleasure. // 나무 그늘에서 독서하는 것이 요즈음의 내 ~ 이다 It's now my daily delight to read under the trees. // 그 여자는 대체 무슨 ~ 으로 살까 What does she live for I wonder? // 그녀에게는 어린애를 자라는 것을 보는 것이 유일한 ~ 이다 Her sole pleasure is to see her children growing up.

낙관(落款) (a painter's) sign and seal; (a writer's) signature. ¶~ 이 없는 unsigned / 〔작자의〕 ~ 이 있다 bear the writer's[painter's] signature // 이 그림에는 ~ 이 없다 This picture bears neither the artist's signature nor his seal. **낙관하다** sign (and seal).

낙관(樂觀) optimism; an optimistic[a rosy / a hopeful] view; sanguine[optimistic / high] hopes. ¶~ 을 불허하다 be far from reassuring / do not warrant any optimism // 사태는 ~ 을 불허한다 The situation is very unpromising. / The situation does not allow much room for optimism. **낙관하다** be optimistic (about); be sanguine (of). ¶전도를 ~ be optimistic about the future / take an optimistic view regarding the future // 그는 승리를 낙관하고 있다 He is sanguine of victory. // 너무 낙관하지 마라 Don't be too sure of success.

● **낙관론** an optimistic[a rosy] view. **낙관론자** an optimist. **낙관주의** optimism.

낙관적(樂觀的) optimistic; rosy; hopeful; sanguine; upbeat. ¶~ 인 생각 an optimistic[a rosy] view[idea] // 매사를 ~ 으로 보다 take a rose-colored view of things / view[see] things in an optimistic light / take things easy // 지나치게 ~ 이다 be too optimistic / paint too rosy a picture of thing / look too much on the bright side of things // 그것은 지나치게 ~ 인 생각이다 That's taking too optimistic a view of it. / That's expecting too much. // 그는 매사에 ~ 이다 He takes an optimistic view[look on the bright side] of everything. / He is optimistic about everything.

낙낙하다 enough; big enough; sufficient; adequate. ¶낙낙한 웃옷 a loose jacket.

낙농(酪農) dairy (farming). ¶그는 ~ 에 종사하고 있다 He runs a dairy farm. / 《문어》 He is engaged in dairy farming.

● **낙농가** a dairy farmer; a dairyman. **낙농업** dairy farming; the dairy business (industry). **낙농장** a dairy (farm); 《미》 a milk ranch. **낙농품** dairy products.

낙담(落膽) discouragement; despondency; disappointment; dejection; dismay. **낙담하다** be[get] discouraged; be disheartened [dispirited]; be dejected; be disappointed; be cast down; lose heart. ¶그렇게 낙담하지 말게 Don't be so cast down. / Never say die! / Cheer up! // 그 혹평에 그는 낙담해서 소설

쓰기를 그만두었다 That severe criticism discouraged him from continuing to write novels.//그는 시험에 떨어져서 낙담하고 있다 He is discouraged by his failure in the examination.//그는 기대가 빗나가서 낙담하고 있다 He is let down because things didn't work out as he expected.//그는 하나뿐인 자식이 죽어서 낙담하고 있다 He is heart broken over the death of his only child. ➔¶낙담시키다 discourage / dishearten / disappoint.

낙도(落島) an outisland; a remote [distant] island; a deserted island.
● 낙도 주민 outislanders.

낙락장송(落落長松) a tall and exuberant pine tree.

낙뢰(落雷) the falling of a thunderbolt. ¶~로 큰 소나무가 쪼개졌다 The lightning splintered a big pine tree.//그는 ~로 인하여 죽었다 He was killed by lightning. **낙뢰하다** (장소가) be struck by (a bolt of) lightning.

낙마(落馬) a fall [tumble / (구어) spill] from a horse. **낙마하다** fall from [be thrown off] one's horse; fall off one's horse. ¶기수가 낙마하였다 The rider [jockey] fell from his horse.

낙망(落望) disappointment; despair; dejection; discouragement; hopelessness. ¶~의 빛을 띠다 look disappointed//~의 빛을 보이지 않다 swallow one's disappointment. **낙망하다** be disappointed (at / in / of / with); despair (of); lose one's heart [hope]; be thrown into despair. ¶낙망하여 disappointedly / in despair of / in despair//낙망하지 마라 Keep your heart up!//그는 낙망한 나머지 자살하였다 Despair drove him to commit suicide. ➔¶낙망시키다 (원인이) disappoint / let down / dash [crush] a person's hope.

낙반(落磐) (a) cave-in; the fall of roof in a mine. ¶~이 되다 cave in//터널에 ~이 있었다 The roof of the tunnel caved in.
● 낙반 사고 a cave-in (disaster). ¶~가 있었다 The mine roof caved in.

낙방(落榜) failure in an examination; (미국 구어) flunk. **낙방하다** fail in an examination; (영국 속어) get plucked; (미국 구어) flunk (an exam). ¶내가 이 대학의 입학시험을 치른 것은 딴 데에서 낙방할 경우에 대비하기 위한 것이었다 I took the entrance exam for this university just in case I fail to be admitted elsewhere.

낙부(諾否) approval and [or] disapproval; yes and [or] no.

낙산(酪酸) [화] butyric acid. ⇨부티르산
● 낙산 발효(-醱酵) butyric fermentation.

낙상(落傷) an injury [a hurt / a bruise] from a fall. **낙상하다** get hurt from a fall; fall and hurt oneself.

낙서(落書) scribbling(s); a scrawl; (공중 변소의) graffiti(▶ 단수는 graffitio인데 보통 복수로 쓰임); (종이쪽지나 노트 등의) a doodle. ¶화장실 벽의 ~를 지우다 clean the graffiti off the wall of a lavatory. **낙서하다** scribble; scrabble; scrawl; doodle. ¶벽에 ~ scribble on the wall//담벼락에 낙서하지 마라 Don't put marks on fences.
● 낙서 금지 No Scribbling.; No graffiti.; Do not deface.; Scribbling forbidden.

낙석(落石) [떨어지는 암석] a falling rock; [돌이 떨어짐] a fall of rock; a rock-slide.
● 낙석 주의 Beware of [Watch out for / (영) Mind] falling rocks.

낙선(落選) (선거의) defeat [failure] (in an election); (출품의) rejection. **낙선하다** (선거에서) lose an election; be defeated [unsuccessful] in an election; (출품이) be rejected. ¶당의 간부들은 모두 낙선했다 All the officers of the party failed to get elected [failed of election / were defeated].//그는 불과 한 표 차이로 낙선했다 He failed to win [missed winning] the election by only one votes.//현상 소설에 응모했으나 낙선했다 I entered for the prize novel contest, but failed to win anything.//그는 총선거에서 낙선하였다 He was defeated [He lost] in the general election.//그의 그림은 국전에서 낙선하였다 His painting was rejected [not accepted] for the National Art Exhibition.
● 낙선자 an unsuccessful [a defeated] candidate; (미국 속어) an also-ran. 낙선작 a rejected [an unaccepted] work [article].

낙성(落成) completion (of a building). ¶도서관 ~ 축하회 a ceremony to celebrate the completion of a library. **낙성하다** complete; finish. ➔¶낙성되다 be completed / be finished//그 건물은 곧 낙성된다 The building is nearing completion.//호텔은 다음 달에 낙성된다 The hotel will be completed next month.
● 낙성식 an inauguration ceremony; a celebration of the completion (of a building). ¶~을 거행하다 inaugurate [dedicate] (a new building) / celebrate the (official) opening of (a building).

낙수(落水) raindrops (falling from the eaves). ⇨=낙숫물(⇨낙수)
● 낙수받이 (평행 홈통) an eave trough [spout]; (수직 홈통) (미) a downspout. 낙숫물 raindrops (falling from the eaves); eavesdrops. ¶~ 소리 the patter of raindrops//~이 떨어진다 Eavesdrops are falling.

낙수(落穗) 1 [이삭] gleanings; fallen ears (of grains). ¶~를 줍다 glean. 2 [뒷얘기] an episode.

낙승(樂勝) an easy victory; a walkaway; a walkover; a pushover. **낙승하다** gain an easy victory (over); ease out; walk over; have a walkover; win in a breeze; (구어) win (a game) hands down. ¶미국 팀은 일본 팀에게 낙승하였다 The U.S. team won an easy victory over the Japanese team.

낙심(落心) disappointment; discouragement; disheartenment. ¶그는 성적이 나빠 ~천만이다 He is terribly depressed [dejected] because of his poor grades. **낙심하다** be disheartened. ¶그렇게 낙심하지 마라 Don't take it so hard.//중요한 시합에 져서 나는 몹시 낙심했다 I was terribly let down [I lost heart] after losing the important match.//그 말을 듣고 나는 몹시 낙심했다 My heart sank when I heard it. ➔¶낙심시키다 dispirit / deject / dishearten / disappoint.

낙양(落陽) the setting sun. ⇨=석양

낙엽(落葉) [나뭇잎이 떨어지기] defoliation; [떨어진 잎] fallen [dead] leaves. ¶~성의 deciduous (trees)//~이 지다 (나무가) shed [cast] (its) leaves / (잎이) fall//~이 지기 시작했다 The leaves are falling. / The trees are shedding their leaves.//나무들은 완전히 ~이

낙오

졌다 The leaves are all (gone) off the trees. ●**낙엽송** a larch. **낙엽수** a deciduous tree.

낙오(落伍) (대열에서의) falling behind; straggling; (시대·사회에서의) being out of step with the times. **낙오하다** drop [fall] out of line [the ranks]; drop [fall] behind; drop out (to the rear); straggle. ¶행군 중에 ~ fall out while on the march // 시대의 진보에서 ~ fall [be left] behind in the march of progress / lose touch with the world // 경주에서 ~ [뒤떨어지다] drop out of a race / 대열에서 ~ fall behind in a race // 그는 너무 느긋하게 굴다가 일자리를 얻는 데 낙오하였다 He was so easy-going that he failed to find a job.
●**낙오자** a straggler; a dropout; a (social) failure; a man behind the times. ¶인생의 ~ a derelict / a (social) failure / a social outcast.

낙원(樂園) a paradise; Eden; Elysium. ¶지상의 ~ an earthly paradise / a paradise on earth // 자연의 ~ Nature's paradise / paradisiacal nature // 많은 이민자들에게 미국은 ~ 이었다 America has been a promised land for many immigrants.

낙인(烙印) 〔불에 달궈 찍는 도장〕 a brand; a brand(ing) iron; 〔그 자국〕 a brand; a stamp (pl. -mata, -s). ¶~이 찍힌 악당 a certified scoundrel // ~을 찍다 brand (a horse with a red-hot iron) / stigmatize / (비유) brand (a person as a Communist) // 가축에 ~을 찍다 brand one's cattle / put a brand on one's cattle // 그는 술고래라는 ~이 찍혀 있다 He has the reputation of being a vicious drinker. // 그는 사기꾼으로 ~이 찍혔다 He was branded a swindler.

낙일(落日) the setting sun; sunset; (미) sundown.

낙자(落字) an omitted word; an omission.

낙장(落張) missing pages; a missing leaf. ¶이 책은 ~이 5, 6페이지나 된다 Several pages are missing from this book. // 7페이지에서 12페이지까지가 ~이다 Pages seven to twelve are missing.
●**낙장본** a book with missing pages; a defective book.

낙제(落第) failure in an examination; (검사에서) rejection. ¶그는 교사로서는 ~다 He is a failure as a teacher. // 그 물건은 수출품으로서는 ~였다 The article was rejected [eliminated] from the list of exports. **낙제하다** fail (in [to pass]) an examination; (구어) flunk (an examination); (속어) get plucked; (유급하다) stay back in the class. ¶두 과목에 ~ fail in two subjects // 50점 미만은 낙제한다 Those who get [score] under 50 will not pass. // 그는 두 번이나 낙제했으니까 우리보다 두 살 위였다 He was two years older than the rest of us because he had flunked his exams twice. // 그는 장기 결석으로 낙제하지 않으면 안 되었다 He had to repeat the same grade [(영) repeat the year / stay down] because he had been absent for so long. // 나는 화학에서 낙제하였다 I failed [(구어) flunked] (in) chemistry. → **낙제시키다** fail [(구어) flunk / (영국 구어) plough] (a student) // 선생님은 수학에서 다섯 사람을 낙제시켰다 The teacher failed [(구어) flunked] five students in mathematics.
●**낙제생** (미) a repeater; a failure; a flop; (영국 구어) a plucked student; a holdover (유급생). **낙제점** a failing mark. ¶그는 세 과목에서 ~을 받았다 He failed (in) three subjects.

낙조(落照) the glow of the setting sun; a setting sun.

낙지 a small octopus.
●**낙지볶음** panbroiled octopus (seasoned with red pepper).

낙진(落塵) (atomic) fallout. ¶방사성 ~ radioactive [radiation] fallout / (속어) silent killer.

낙질(落帙) a lacking [missing] volume.

낙차(落差) 1 〔물〕 a head; a fall; a water level. ¶고 [저 / 중] 위 ~ a high [low / medium] head / 수압 ~ a pressure head / 유효 ~ an effective [a net] head / ~ 10미터의 폭포 a 10-meter waterfall // 물은 20미터의 ~로 골짜기에 떨어지고 있다 The water drops 20meters into the gorge below. 2 〔높낮이의 차〕 a gap. ¶이전의 일과 이번 일은 급료의 ~가 크다 There is a great difference in pay between this job and my former one.

낙착(落着) a settlement; an end; a conclusion; a termination. ¶사건의 ~ the settlement [winding-up] of an affair // ~을 보다 be settled / come to settlement [conclusion / close] / come [be brought] to an end // (사건이) 아직 ~을 못 보다 be still pending. **낙착하다** be settled; come to a settlement [conclusion / close]. → **낙착될 곳은 그것밖에 없다** It is the only conclusion we can come to. // 결국 우리가 가기로 낙착되었다 After all we decided to go. // 그 사건은 순조롭게 낙착되었다 The incident was brought to a happy end. / The case was settled satisfactorily.

낙찰(落札) a successful bid; awarding of a contract. **낙찰하다** bid successfully; make a successful bid; (물건이) be knocked down to (a person). → ¶나에게 낙찰되었다 My bid was successful [accepted]. / The contract was awarded to me. // 그 그림은 나에게 낙찰되었다 The picture was knocked down to me. // 저 조각은 이천만 원에 그에게 낙찰되었다 That sculpture was knocked down to him for twenty million won. // 교량 공사는 우리 회사에 낙찰되었다 The contract for building the bridge was given to our company.
●**낙찰 가격** a contract price; the highest bid price. **낙찰자** a successful bidder.

낙천(落薦) a failure in an application (for nomination). **낙천하다** fail in (one's) application (for nomination).
●**낙천자** an unsuccessful applicant [candidate].

낙천(樂天) optimism.
●**낙천가** an optimist; an easygoing person. **낙천주의** optimism. **낙천주의자** an optimist.

낙천적(樂天的) optimistic (about); hopeful; cheerful; sanguine; rosy; rose-colored; happy-go-lucky. ¶~인 인생관을 갖다 have an optimistic [cheerful] view of life // 그는 천성이 ~이다 He is optimistic [happy-go-lucky] by nature.

낙체(落體) 〔물〕 a falling body.

낙타(駱駝) 〔동〕 a camel. ¶~의 혹 a camel's hump / 단봉 ~ an Arabian camel / a dromedary // 쌍봉 ~ a Bactrian camel [two-humped] camel.

●**낙타털** camel's hair.
낙태(落胎) a (criminal) abortion; a miscarriage; aborticide. ¶**인공** ~ an induced [artificial] abortion. **낙태하다** abort; miscarry; commit feticide. ➔¶낙태시키다 procure abortion / commit feticide / cause [induce] abortion.
●**낙태 수술** a surgical operation to cause abortion. ¶~을 하다[받다] perform [undergo] a criminal operation (on). **낙태 약** an abortive (medicine / drug); an aborticide. **낙태죄** aborticide; feticide; illegal abortion.
낙토(樂土) paradise; Heaven; Elysium. ¶지상의 ~ an earthly paradise.
낙하(落下) falling; dropping; descent. ¶~의 법칙 [물] the law of falling. **낙하하다** fall; come down; drop; descend; come to the ground. ¶수직으로 ~ fall plumb down // 비행기의 파편이 건물에 낙하했다 Part of an airplane fell [dropped] on the building. // 거대한 바윗돌이 산허리에 낙하하였다 A huge rock rolled down the mountainside.
●**낙하지점** (미사일 등의) an impact point.
낙하산(落下傘) a parachute; (구어) a chute. ¶(소형의) 보조 ~ a drogue parachute // 회전 ~ a rotochute // ~을 펴다 release a parachute // ~으로 강하하다 parachute (down) / descend by parachute / (부대가) make an airborne landing // ~으로 비행기에서 탈출하다 bail out / hit the silk // 부대 [식료품]를 ~으로 섬에 투하하다 parachute troops [provisions] onto the island // 우리는 ~으로 추락기에서 탈출했다 We bailed [(영) baled] out of the falling plane.
●**낙하산병** a parachutist; a paratrooper. **낙하산 부대** a parachute troop [unit]; a paratroop; airborne infantry; paratroopers. ~의 강하 the landing of paratroopers (an airborne troop). **낙하산 인사** [남데없이 외부 인사를 임명하는 인사] high-handed personnel administration; appointment of a former official to an important post in a private company (through influence from above).
낙향(落鄕) rustication; exile from the capital [city]; a leaving for the countryside. **낙향하다** rusticate; move to [bury oneself in] the country; go back to the rural life. ¶그는 생활난으로 낙향했다 The difficulty of living drove him out of Seoul into the country.
낙화(落花) [꽃이 짐] falling of blossoms [flowers]; [진 꽃] fallen blossoms; [지는 꽃] falling blossoms [petals]. ¶분분한 ~ a shower of falling blossom petals // ~처럼 떨어지는 눈 snow whirling down like falling cherry blossom petals. **낙화하다** flowers [blossoms / petals] fall [scatter].
낙화(烙畫) poker work [picture]; a poker engraving; a pyrography; poker drawing. ¶~의 꽃무늬 a design of flowers in poker work // ~을 그리다 poker.
낙화생(落花生) [식] a peanut. ➪=땅콩
낙후(落後) falling behind; straggling. **낙후하다** lag [fall] behind (another in something); be behind [backward]; be in arrear (the times); drop [fall] out of line [the ranks]; be out of touch with. ➔¶낙후된 lagging behind / backward [underdeveloped] (country) // 그 나라는 문화가 낙후되어 있다 The country is backward in civilization.
낚다 1 (물고기를) angle for; fish (with rod and line); catch (a fish). ¶물고기를 ~ (낚싯바늘로) hook a fish / catch a fish on [with] a hook / (낚싯줄을 드리우고) angle for a fish // 잉어를 많이 ~ get a good catch of carp // 지렁이를 미끼로 고기를 ~ fish with the bait of an earthworm // 여기는 낚이지 않는다 This is not a good (fishing) spot. 2 [솔깃한 말로 꾀다] allure; decoy; entice; entrap; draw on; attract; take in; cheat; ensnare. ¶여자를 ~ pick up [entice] a woman // 돈에 낚여 그는 비밀을 누설했다 Enticed by the money, he let out the secret.

낚시 1 [낚싯바늘] a fish [fishing] hook. ¶~를 드리우다 drop a line // ~에 미끼를 달다 bait a hook / put [fix] a bait on a hook // (물고기가) ~에 걸리다 be hooked / be caught on the hook // (물고기가) ~를 물다 bite (the hook / at a bait) / have a (powerful) bite. 2 angling. ➪=낚시질(⇨낚시) ¶강 ~ river fishing // 바다 ~ sea fishing // 민물 ~ fresh-water fishing // 밤 ~ night fishing [angling] / fishing by night // ~를 하러 가자 Let's go fishing.
●**낚시꾼** a fisherman; a rodster; a Waltonian; an angler(▶ angler는 취미·스포츠로 낚는 사람). **낚시질** angling; fishing (with rod and line). ¶~을 하다 fish (with rod and line) / angle (for trout / in a brook). **낚시찌** a float; a cork; a quill; a bob. ¶~가 까딱거린다 A float is bobbing up and down. **낚시터** a fishing spot [hole]; a place for angling. **낚싯대** a fishing rod; an angling rod. **낚싯바늘** a fishhook. **낚싯밥** a bait. **낚싯배** an angler's [fisherman's] boat; a fishing boat. **낚싯봉** a sinker; a bullet; a lead; a plummet. **낚싯줄** a fishing line; a fishline. ¶~을 드리우다 drop a line.
낚아채다 1 (낚시로) strike (a fish). 2 [잡아채다] snatch (away) (from / off); wrest (from); take by force. ¶그는 내 손에서 그 편지를 낚아챘다 He snatched the letter (away) from me. // 나는 그녀의 지갑을 낚아챘다 I snatched her pocketbook.
난(卵) an egg.
난(亂) an uproar; a war; a revolt. ➪=난리
난(欄) (신문 등의) a column; a page; a section; (기입하는) a blank; a column; a space. ¶두 ~에 걸친 광고 an advertisement occupying two whole columns // 그 신문은 그 사건을 여러 ~에 걸쳐 특종 기사로 다뤘다 The paper featured the affair, running column after column in reporting it.
난(蘭) an orchid; an orchis. ➪=난초
난-(難) troublesome; difficult; hard; tough. ¶~문제 a difficult [stiff / tough] problem / a hard nut to crack.
-**난** [곤란] trouble; difficulty; hardship; [부족] shortage. ¶생활~ difficulty in making a living // 그들은 심각한 주택 [식량] ~을 겪고 있다 They are suffering from a serious housing [food] shortage.
난가(亂家) a family in turmoil; a disturbed family.
난각(卵殼) an eggshell.
난간(欄干·欄杆) a handrail; a railing; (계단 등의) a handrail; a guardrail(▶ 잡는 부분); a balustrade(▶ 잡는 부분과 그것을 떠받치는 기둥을 포함함); a parapet. ¶다리의 ~ the parapet of a bridge / a bridge-railing // ~에 기대다 lean over [upon] the balustrade // 육교에 ~을 설치하다 provide a footbridge with a

난감하다(難堪-) [힘겹다] beyond one's capacity[power]; be too much for (one); be not equal to (the task); [견디기 어렵다] unbearable; intolerable; insufferable; [할 바를 모르다] be at a loss; be at one's wit's [wits'] end. ¶나는 어떻게 해야 할지 몰라 난감했었다 I was completely at a loss (what to do). / I was at my wit's end, not knowing what to do.∥나는 어려운 문제로 난감했었다 I was terribly perplexed by the difficult problem.∥그는 난감한 얼굴로 들어왔다 He came in with a distressed[troubled] look. **난감히** unbearably; intolerably; hopelessly. ¶일이 ~ 됐어 We are in a hopeless situation. / We are in a sad fix. / (구어) What a pretty kettle of fish!

난거지든부자(-富者) a poor-looking rich man.

난경(難境) a predicament; a difficult situation. ¶~에 처하다 be in a fix / be in hot water / find oneself in a fix∥~을 벗어나다 get out of the predicament.

난공불락(難攻不落) impregnability; inexpugnability. ¶~의 impregnable / inexpugnable∥~의 요새 an impregnable fortress∥~이다 be hard of approach / defy attack∥그 성은 지금까지 ~이었다 The castle has so far resisted[defied / withstood] all attacks.∥그 여자는 ~이야 (구어) She is simply impossible to get anywhere with her.

난공사(難工事) a difficult construction [building] work.

난관(卵管) [생] an oviduct. ⇨나팔관(⇨나팔)
● **난관염** salpingitis; inflammation of an oviduct. **난관 임신** tubal pregnancy.

난관(難關) [장애] a barrier; an obstacle; [곤란] a difficulty; [난국] a difficult situation; [교착] a deadlock; the crux of the situation. ¶~을 타개하는 길 a way out of the difficulty∥~에 봉착하다 encounter a difficult situation / (교섭 등이) come to a deadlock / strike a snag∥~을 극복하다 tide over[overcome] a difficulty / get over a barrier∥~을 뚫고 나아가다 muddle through a difficulty∥이 ~을 넘기면 쉽다 Once over this barrier, the rest will be plain sailing.∥힘을 합쳐 우리 가정이 직면한 ~을 극복하자 Let's join hands in overcoming the difficulties [trouble] facing[confronting / (문어) besetting] our family.

난국(難局) a grave[difficult / delicate] situation; a crisis (*pl.* crises); a difficulty; [교착상태] a deadlock. ¶~에 처하다 be in a difficult position / be in a fix∥~을 바로잡다 straighten[iron] out a bad situation∥~을 수습하다 save[settle] a difficult situation∥~을 타개하다 break the deadlock / find one's way out of the difficulty∥그들은 큰 ~에 직면해 있었다 They were in a highly touch-and-go situation.∥그는 어떤 ~에도 대처할 수 있다 He is equal to any situation.∥우리는 국가의 존망이 걸려 있는 ~에 처해 있다 We are now facing[confronting] a national crisis.

난국(亂國) a disturbed[disrupted / troubled] country; a nation in turmoil.

난국(亂局) a tumultuous situation[time].

난군(亂軍) [문란한 군대] a lawless[disorderly] army; [반란군] a rebel army; insurgent troops.

난기류(亂氣流) [기상] (air) turbulence; turbulent air. ¶지금 비행기가 ~에 휘말려 있습니다 (기장이 승객에게) We are experiencing some air turbulence just now. / We have [The plain has] hit some turbulence.

난대(暖帶) the subtropical zones. ⇨아열대

난데없다 [뜻밖이다] unexpected; never dreamed of; sudden; abrupt; be out of the blue; unanticipated; [영동하다] wild; fantastic; eccentric; absurd. **난데없는 손님** an unexpected visitor. **난데없이** unexpectedly; abruptly; to one's surprise; without warning; out of the blue; outrageously. ¶~한 사나이가 나타났다 A man appeared from out of nowhere.

난도질(亂刀-) hacking; mangling; (고기 등의) mincing; chopping; hashing. **난도질하다** mangle; hack to pieces; (고기 등을) mince; chop; hash. ¶사람을 ~ slash (a person) again and again. ➔ 난도질당한 시체 a corpse covered with slash wounds.

난독(亂讀) desultory[unsystematic] reading; random reading. **난독하다** read at random [desultorily / without system]. ¶난독하지 마라 Don't read every book that you come across[comes your way].
● **난독가** an omnivorous[indiscriminate] reader.

난동(暖冬) a mild[warm / green] winter. ¶이상(異常)~ an abnormally warm winter∥올해는 이상 ~이다 We have an abnormally [unusually] warm weather this winter.∥이상 ~으로 야채 값이 싸다 Thanks to the abnormally warm winter, vegetables are cheap.

난동(亂動) a disturbance; a commotion; a strife; a riot. ¶~을 부리다 raise[make] a disturbance / stir[get] up a riot / kick up a row / commit excesses∥군중은 크게 ~을 부렸다 Pandemonium broke loose among the crowd.∥술집에서 술에 취한 자가 ~을 부렸다 A drunk ran amuck in the bar.∥~을 부린 군중은 경찰서에 난입했다 The riotous [unruly] crowd broke into the police station. **난동하다** [난폭하게 굴다] act violently; (흥분하여) rage; (미친 듯이) run amuck[amok]; (군중이) riot; (말 등이 날뛰다) become unruly; [발버둥 치다] struggle.

난딱 easily; with ease; without any trouble [difficulty / effort]; just like that; in an instant; (구어) in a jiffy. ¶큰 돌을 ~ 들어올리다 lift up a huge stone as if it were made of cotton.

난로(暖爐) a stove; a heater(▶ stove는 요리용 렌지도 뜻함); (벽난로) a fireplace. ¶가스~ a gas heater[stove]∥석유~ an oilstove / an oil heater∥석탄[장작] ~ a coal[wood] stove ∥전기 ~ an electric stove[heater]∥~를 둘러싸고 around the stove∥벌겋게 단 ~ a red glowing stove∥~을 쬐다 warm oneself at a stove∥~를 때다[피우다] light a stove [heater] / make a fire in the stove / turn on the electric stove∥~는 잘 타고 있다 The stove is well burning.
● **난롯가** the fireside.

난류(暖流) a warm current.

난리(亂離) [소동] an uproar; a disturbance; [전쟁] a war; [반란] a revolt; a rebellion; a riot; [혼란] confusion; commotion. ¶~가 나다 a war breaks out / have a war / have a disturbance[an uproar] // ~를 일으키다 start a war / cause a riot / raise a rebellion / lead to confusion // 풀~ a flood disaster // ~를 가라앉히다 quell a disturbance[riot] / put down a revolt ¶그렇게 되면 ~야 If things should come to that pass, we shall be in trouble.

난립하다 (亂立-) 1 [무질서하게 세워지다]. ¶빌딩이 난립해 있다 Many different sorts of buildings are jumbled up close together. 2 [후보들이 무턱대고 나서다] run[stand / bid] for (mayor) in great numbers; scramble for (an election). ¶그 선거구는 입후보자가 난립하고 있다 The constituency is flooded with candidates. / There are too many candidates running from the constituency.

난마 (亂麻) chaos; anarchy; imbroglio. ¶~ 같은 상태에 빠지다 be reduced to a chaotic state / be thrown into confusion[disorder] // ~같이 얽히다 be entangled / be in a chaotic state / be chaotic // 그 나라의 정국은 ~처럼 뒤얽혀 있다 The political situation of the country is chaotic.

난막 (卵膜) [동] an egg membrane; (어란의) a chorion.

난만하다 (爛漫-) 〈서술적〉 be in full bloom; be in all (their) glory; be at (their) best. ¶ 벚꽃이 ~ The cherry blossoms are in all their glory // 백화~ All the flowers are in full bloom[at their best]. **난만히** in full bloom; in all (their) glory; in dazzling brilliance; in luxuriance.

난망 (難忘) unforgettableness. ¶~의 never to be forgotten / unforgettable // 그 은혜 백골~이옵니다 I shall never forget your kindness [what you have done for me].

난맥 (亂脈) disorder; confusion; disarrangement; chaos; a mix-up. ¶~을 이룬 confused / chaotic / disturbed / turbulent // ~에 빠지다 be thrown into disorder[confusion] / fall into chaos // 당의 운영은 심한 ~ 상태에 빠져 있다 The leadership of the party is in utter disorder. // 당의 결속에 ~상을 보이고 있다 Party unity is in disarray. // 그 회사의 회계는 실로 ~ 상태였다 The finances of that company were chaotic[in a chaotic state / (구어) in shambles].

난무 (亂舞) [어지럽게 추는 춤] a boisterous dance; [날뜀] rampage. **난무하다** [춤추다] dance boisterously; [날뛰다] rampage; be rampant. ¶폭력배가 난무하는 거리 a gangster-ridden street // 괴상한 정보가 난무했다 All sorts of false rumors were flying around. // 대도시에는 온갖 악이 난무하고 있다 Wickedness of all kinds thrives in big cities. // 나비가 바람에 난무하고 있었다 The butterflies were dancing in the wind.

난문 (難文) a difficult sentence[passage]; a sentence[passage] hard to understand; a crabbed style.

난문제 (難問題) a difficult [stiff / tough / knotty / thorny / puzzling] problem[question]; a hard[tough] nut to crack; a puzzle; a crux (*pl.* ~es, cruces); a poser; conundrum; a vexed question. ¶~를 풀다 solve [work out] a hard problem / (비상수단으로) cut the Gordian knot // ~에 부닥치다[봉착하다] encounter a thorny problem / catch a Tartar / ~와 씨름하다 be at grips with a difficult question / tackle a hard problem // 그것은 내게는 ~이다 That is a hard nut for me to crack. // 그것이 그들에게 과해진 ~이다 It is the great question put to[before] him.

난민 (亂民) riotous[lawless] people; insurgents; rioters; a mob; rebels.

난민 (難民) [피난민] refugees; displaced persons(약어 D.P.); [빈민] the destitute; [이재민] sufferers; 《flood》 victims. ¶팔레스타인~ the displaced Palestinians // 전화(戰禍)에서 도망친 ~의 무리 a flood of refugees fleeing (from) the disasters of war.
● **난민 구제** refugee relief; the relief of the destitute[sufferers]. **난민 수용소** a refugee camp[reception center]. **난민촌** a shanty quarter; a ghetto.

난바다 the open sea (far from land); the far-off sea; the offing. ¶~에 떠 있는 배 a ship in the offing / a ship (far) out at sea.

난반사 (亂反射) [물] diffused reflection; scattered reflection.

난발 (亂發) 1 firing at random. ⇨**난사**(亂射) 2 an excessive issue. ⇨남발

난발 (亂髮) dishevelled[ruffled / unkempt / uncombed] hair.

난방 (暖房·煖房) [데움] heating; [덥게 한 방] a heated[warm] room. ¶중앙~법 central heating // 온수~ hot-water heating // 증기~ steam heating // 지역[방사(放射)] ~ district [panel] heating // ~이 되어 있다 be heated (by) // ~ 완비 (게시) Air-Conditioned. // ~이 들어온다 [들어오지 않는다] (방·건물 등의 한난(寒暖)) The house is well[poorly] heated. / (난방 장치의 기능) The heating is[isn't] on [working].
● **난방 장치 / 난방 시설** [난방 기구의 설치] heating; air conditioning; [난방 기구] a heating apparatus[arrangement / system]; a heater; a radiator(복사 난방기). ¶~가 된 heated / air-conditioned // ~가 없는 unheated // ~를 하다 install a heater (in a room) // 새 건물에는 중앙~가 되어 있다 The new building has central heating.

난백 (卵白) the white (of an egg); the albumen; glair.

난봉 dissipation; profligacy; prodigality; debauchery; vicious courses; a fast life. ¶~으로 패가망신하다 be ruined by dissipation. **난봉(을) 부리다 [피우다]** live fast; lead a fast [dissipated / dissolute / riotous] life. ¶그는 젊었을 때 난봉을 피웠다 He led a wild life [sowed wild oats] in his youth.
● **난봉꾼 / 난봉쟁이** a libertine; a fast liver; a debauchee; a Lothario; a rake; a playboy; a rip.

난봉나다 fall into vicious[ill] courses; take to fast living.

난부자든거지 (-富者-) a wealthy-looking poor man.

난사 (亂射) firing[shooting] at random; a random[wild] shot; unaimed fire. **난사하다** fire[shoot] at random; fire blindly; spray bullets. ¶적은 기관총을 난사하였다 The enemy fired machine guns blindly[indiscriminately].

난사 (難事) a difficult thing[matter]; a hard task[undertaking]; a trouble. ¶~ 중의 ~ the most difficult of all things / the hardest thing to do // ~를 처리하다 tackle [grapple with] a difficulty / 《미국 구어》 take the heat (for a person).

난사람 a distinguished [a prominent / an outstanding / an eminent] person; a person of extraordinary ability [large caliber]. ¶세계적으로 ~ a world figure // 그 고을에는 아직 이 별로 없다 There have been almost no outstanding people in that town.

난산(難産) hard labo(u)r; difficult delivery [birth]. ¶아내는 아들을 낳았는데 꽤 ~이었다 My wife gave birth to a baby boy, but it was an extremely difficult birth. // 이번 조각(組閣)은 꽤 ~이었다 The new Cabinet was formed with much difficulty. **난산하다** have a hard labo(u)r; have a difficult delivery.

난삽하다(難澁-) difficult to understand; hard to make out; knotty. ¶난삽한 글 a difficult passage / an article hard to understand / a crabbed style. **난삽히** with difficulty.

난색(暖色) [미] a warm color [(영) colour].

난색(難色) [곤란해하는 기색] disapproval; reluctance; unwillingness. ¶~을 보이다 show [express] disapproval (of) / be opposed (to a plan) / hesitate (to do) / be reluctant (to do) // 아버지는 그녀를 외국으로 보내는 데 대해 ~을 표했다 Her father was reluctant to let her go abroad. // 그 계획에 대해서는 일부 사람들이 ~을 표했다 Some people were opposed [There was some opposition] to the project. // 그는 그 계획에 ~을 보였다 He showed [expressed] disapproval of the plan.

난생(卵生) [생] oviparity; oviparousness. ¶~의 oviparous // 물고기는 ~이다 Fish are egg-layers. **난생하다** bear (offspring) by egg; be oviparous.

● **난생 동물** an oviparous [egg-laying] animal; (집합적) an ovipara.

난생처음(-生-) for the first time in one's life; in all one's born days. ¶~ 당하는 일 the first experience in one's lifetime // ~ 보는 사람 an utter stranger // 연단에 서기는 ~이다 This is the first time that I have ever stood on the platform.

난세(亂世) troublous [troubled] times; turbulent days. ¶이 ~ these troubled [chaotic / turbulent] times // ~의 영웅 a hero in a warlike [turbulent] age // 그는 ~에 태어났다 His country was in a state of anarchy when he was born.

난세포(卵細胞) an egg cell; an oocyte; an ovum (pl. ova).

난센스 nonsense. ¶그것은 완전한 ~다 It's sheer nonsense.

난소(卵巢) [생] the ovary; the ovarium (pl. -ria). ¶~의 ovarian.

● **난소 낭종** ovarian cyst. **난소염**(-炎) ovaritis; oophoritis. **난소 임신** ovarian pregnancy. **난소 호르몬** ovarian [follicular] hormones.

난수표(亂數表) a table of random numbers.

난숙(爛熟) 1 (과일의) overripeness; overmaturity. **난숙하다** overripe; overmature. ¶난숙한 멜론 an overripe melon. 2 [더할 수 없는 성숙] mellow ripeness; full [ripe] maturity [development]. ¶문화의 ~ the mellow ripeness of culture // 문명의 ~기에 at the apex [full glory] of civilization // 그의 서예는 ~의 경지에 도달했다 His calligraphy has reached full maturity. **난숙하다** attain full maturity; reach [come to] complete maturity; become fully mature. ¶난숙한 문장 a mellow style // 난숙한 문화 a decadent culture.

난시(亂視) astigmatism; distorted vision; astigmia. ¶~의 astigmatic // ~인 사람 an astigmatic.

● **난시안** astigmatism; astigmatic eyes.

난시(亂時) troublous times; a time of confusion [disorder / anarchy].

난신(亂臣) [나라를 어지럽히는 신하] a traitorous [treacherous] subject; rebellious minister; a traitor; a rebel; [난세의 충신] a loyal subject in turbulent days.

난외(欄外) the margin; a marginal column. ¶~의 여백 marginal space // ~에 in [on] the margin (of a page).

● **난외 기사** stop-press news. **난외주**(-註) marginal notes; notes on the margin.

난이(難易) hardness and easiness; (relative) difficulty. ¶일의 ~성에 따라 according to the relative difficulty // 보수는 일의 ~성에 달렸다 The remuneration depends on how hard the work is. // 나는 일의 ~를 묻는 것이 아닙니다 I don't care whether the work is difficult or not.

● **난이도** the degree of difficulty. ¶시험 문제의 ~에 따라 점수가 달리 배정되어 있다 The marking varies with the relative difficulty of the question.

난입(亂入) intrusion; trespass(ing); a raid; forced entry. **난입하다** break into; intrude; trespass; force one's way into; force an entrance into a house. ¶사무실에 ~ break into an office // 데모대가 국회 의사당에 난입했다 The demonstrators broke into the National Assembly Building. // 데모대는 앞을 다투어 회의장에 난입했다 Demonstrators struggled to rush into the hall.

● **난입자** an intruder; a trespasser.

난자(卵子) an egg cell; an ovum (pl. ova); (식물의) an ovule.

난자(亂刺) ruthless [wild] stabbing; (외과의) scarification. **난자하다** stab (a person) ruthlessly; [의] scarify. ¶단도로 ~ stab (a person) all over with a dagger / make stabs in (a person's chest).

난잡하다(亂雜-) be in disorder [in a mess]; disorderly; confused; unsystematic; untidy; jumbled up. ¶난잡한 옷차림 untidy dress // 난잡한 방 a disorderly room // 난잡한 학생 a student lacking discipline // 난잡해지다 fall into disorder / get out of order // 방이 ~ The room is untidy [at sixes and sevens]. // 그는 술을 마시면 난잡해진다 He loses control of himself when in cups. // 그는 난잡한 생활을 하고 있다 He's leading an unsettled [a disordered] life. // 간밤의 연회는 난잡했다 The party last night was a bit wild [got out of control]. // 난잡하기 짝이 없었다 Things were all in a jumble [in utter disorder]. // 그는 서류를 난잡한 채로 두었다 He left his papers in confusion. **난잡히** in disorder [confusion]; at sixes and sevens; in a mess. ¶책이 ~ 놓여 있다 The books are arranged in bad order. // 방바닥에 책이 ~ 흩어져 있었다 Books were scattered in a disorderly manner on the floor. / The floor was cluttered up with books.

난장(亂杖) random beating; reckless [wild] beating; indiscriminate flogging.

난장(을) 맞다 get beaten wildly; get a hard

flogging
난장(을) 치다 beat wildly[mercilessly].
난장판(亂場−) a scene of confusion and disorder; a chaotic scene; a tumult; a turmoil; a mess. ¶~을 이루다 go for a free-for-all / be in confusion / have a rough tumble with (a person)/불이 나서 그 부근은 ~이었다 The fire occasioned terrible confusion in that neighborhood.//주먹다짐이 시작되어 ~이 되었다 Blows were traded, and there was a great fight.//주인이 죽어서 집안이 온통 ~이 되었다 The master's death threw the whole house into utter confusion.//그 도시는 3일간 완전히 ~이었다 Perfect chaos reigned the city for three days.
난쟁이 a dwarf; a pigmy; a midget; a manikin; a shrimp; Tom Thumb. ¶~의 homuncular //서커스의 ~ a circus midget.
난적(亂賊) rebels; rioters; traitors; insurgents. ¶그는 ~이다 He's no everyday opponent [no common enemy].
난전(亂戰) a confused fight; a dogfight; a scuffle; a melee. ¶~을 벌이다 start a confused fight / engage in a scuffle / have a melee / fight in confusion.
난점(難點) a difficult[knotty] point; a crux of a matter; [결점] a fault; a flaw. ¶~을 모두 설명해 주다 explain away a difficulty / get rid of a difficulty by explanation//제일 ~은 …이다 The worst of it is (that) ….
난제(難題) [어려운 문제] a knotty subject; a difficult problem; a puzzling[baffling] question; a hard nut to crack; a crux; poser; a floorer; [무리한 제안] unreasonable terms; an unjust proposal. ¶한국 외교상의 ~ the greatest crux of Korean diplomacy//교육상의 ~의 하나 one of tantalizing problems in education//~를 안고 있다 have a difficult problem to solve.
난조(亂調) (음악의) discord; ragtime tune; [혼란] disorder; confusion; (맥박의) irregularity; [전] hunting. ¶~를 보이다 (투수가) lose control//~를 이루다 be out of tune//~에 빠지다 be thrown into disorder[confusion] / [현재 경제계는 ~를 이루고 있다 The economic situation is confused[in confusion].//맥박이 ~를 이루고 있다 The pulse has become irregular.
난중(亂中) the midst of turmoil[commotion]; time of war; a tumultuous[strife-ridden] period. ¶~에 during a war[revolt] / in wartime / in the midst of turmoil.
● **난중일기** (저서명) A War Diary.
난중지난(難中之難) the most difficult of all things; the hardest thing (to do); the toughest problems.
난처하다(難處−) embarrassing; awkward; annoying; be at a loss; be in a dilemma. ¶난처한 표정으로 with a perplexed[troubled] look//난처한 입장 awkward position / a difficult situation//더욱 난처한 것은 to make matters worse / what's worse//뭐라고 대답해야 할지 난처합니다 I am puzzled for an answer. / I don't know how to answer you.//그녀는 꼬치꼬치 캐묻는 삼촌을 난처한 눈으로 빤히 쳐다보았다 She stared at her uncle in perplexity[bafflement / bewilderment], for he had demand too much of her.//그녀가 바싹 다가서자 그는 난처해서 뒷걸음질을 쳤다 As she drew closer to him, he stepped back in embarrassment.//열차 안에서 주머니를 털려 나는 난처했다 Having had my pocket picked in the train, I was at a loss what to do.//그의 말은 난처한 나머지 하는 평계다 He just said that to get out of the pinch he was in.//당신이 지금 그만둔다면 난 참으로 난처하게 됩니다 I shall be put in an awkward position[(구어) be in a fix] if you quit now.//그는 난처할 때 입술을 깨무는 버릇이 있다 He has a habit of biting his lips when puzzled.//난처한 일이 또 하나 있다 Here is another difficulty.//가기도 무엇하고 안 가기도 무엇하여 아주 ~ I am in a dilemma none too eager to go but none too eager to stay either.
난청(難聽) hardness of hearing; [의] bradyacusia. ¶~의 hard of hearing.
● **난청 지역** (라디오의) a fringe area where reception is poor; a blanket area.
난초(蘭草) an orchid; an orchis.
● **난초 재배가** an orchidist.
난층운(亂層雲) [기상] nimbostratus(약어 Ns, Ns).
난치(難治) incurableness; incurability. ¶~의 intractable / hard to cure / incurable / fatal.
난치하다 be hard to cure; incurable; fatal; hopeless.
● **난치병** disease hard to cure; an incurable disease.
난타(亂打) beating at random; pommeling; repeated knocking[blows]; random blows.
난타하다 pommel; give (a person) a shower of blows; beat at random; strike[knock] violently; batter; [야구] make successive hits; (미국 구어) slog. ¶화재의 경종을 ~ strike the firebell violently[wildly]//문을 ~ knock the door violently / pound on the door//우리는 상대방 투수의 공을 좌우로 난타하기 시작하여 일거에 5점을 올렸다 We started hitting their pitcher right and left and got five quick runs.
● **난타전** (야구·권투의) a slugfest.
난투(亂鬪) a confused fight; a free fight; a free-for-all; a rough-and-tumble; a scuffle; a scrimmage; a scrum. ¶~를 벌이다 come to fisticuffs[scuffles / blows]//양편 사이에 ~가 벌어졌다 A free fight developed[ensued] between both sides.//그는 지난번의 ~로 머리를 다쳤다 He got hurt of the head in the recent free-for-all. **난투하다** have a confused [free] fight; scrimmage.
● **난투극 / 난투 장면** a scene of violence and confusion; (연극·영화의) a fight scene.
난파(暖波) warm wave; a current of warm air.
난파(難破) shipwreck; wreck. **난파하다** be wrecked; be shipwrecked. ¶그 배는 암초에 걸려 난파했다 The ship was wrecked on a sunken rock.//배는 당장이라도 난파할 듯했다 The ship was in momentary danger of shipwreck.//그 배는 아프리카 해안에서 난파했다 The ship was cast away on the coast of Africa.
● **난파선** a wrecked ship. **난파 신호** a signal of distress; an SOS. ¶배가 ~를 보냈다 The ship signaled its distress.
난폭(亂暴) violence; outrage; roughness; rudeness; wildness; rampage; recklessness. ¶~ 차량 신고함 (게시) Report box[booth] for careless or reckless driving. **난폭하다** violent; rude; wild; reckless; rough; outra-

난필 geous; rowdy. ¶**난폭한 짓**[행동] outrageous [riotous / rude] behavior / rough manners // 난폭한 사람 a wild [an unruly / a disorderly] fellow / a rough // 난폭한 운전 reckless driving // 난폭한 언사를 쓰다 use violent [abusive] language / utter wild words // 그는 기질이 ~ He has a violent temper. // 그는 난폭한 목소리로 고함쳤다 He roared in an angry voice. / He shouted in a harsh tone (of voice). // 그는 취하면 난폭해진다 He becomes violent when he drinks too much. // 폭도들은 난폭한 짓을 많이 했다 The rioters committed many outrages. **난폭히** violently; roughly; rudely. ¶노인을 ~ 다루어서는 안 된다 You must not treat the old people rudely [roughly]. // Please excuse me for my hasty writing. // 그는 ~ 행동하고 있다 He is acting violently. // 이 자전거는 소년이 ~ 다루었는데도 견더 냈다 This bicycle withstood rough handling by the boy.

난필(亂筆) a scribble; a scrawl; scratchy [bad] writing; a cursive writing. ¶~을 용서하십시오 Excuse my writing in haste. / Please excuse me for my hasty writing.

난하다(亂−) gaudy; garish; loud (color); flashy; showy. ¶난한 빛깔 a loud color // 난하게 화장을 한 얼굴 a thickly [flashly] painted face // 난한 영화 포스터를 응시하다 stare at a lurid cinema poster // 이 빨간 스카프는 그 나이의 여자에게는 너무 난한 것 같다 The red scarf looks too gay [young] for a woman of her age. // 그녀의 치마 무늬가 좀 ~ The pattern of her skirt is a bit too flashy. // 그녀는 난하게 차려입고 있다 She is showily [gaudily] dressed.

난할(卵割) [생] cleavage.

난항(難航) a stormy passage [voyage]; (항공기의) a hard flight; rough going; tough going. ¶조각(組閣)은 ~을 거듭하고 있다 Difficulties are being felt in the formation of the new Cabinet. // 연안에서의 항해는 ~이었다 Sailing was bad near the coast. // 수사는 ~에 부딪쳤다 The investigation ran into difficulties. // 협상은 ~이다 The negotiations are proceeding with difficulty [having a hard going]. // 그 세법안은 국회에서 ~ 중이다 The tax bill is facing rough going in the National Assembly. **난항하다** have a difficult sailing; (일이) meet with a difficulty; have rough going. ¶배는 격랑 속에서 난항했다 The ship sailed laboriously in a heavy sea.

난해하다(難解−) difficult to understand; hard to make out; knotty; unintelligible; abstruse. ¶난해한 글 a difficult passage (in a book) / an article hard to understand // 난해한 문제 a difficult problem [question] / a knotty problem // 본문 중의 난해한 곳 a textual crux // 난해한 작가 a recondite author // 그 논문에는 난해한 부분이 몇 군데 있다 There are several puzzling passages in that thesis. // 이것은 ~ This is a puzzle [riddle]. // 헨리 제임스의 소설은 ~ Henry James's novels are hard reading.

난행(亂行) debauchery; misconduct; violation; immoral conduct; profligacy. **난행하다** lead a dissipated [fast] life; [강간하다] assault; violate; rape.

난행(難行) 1 (불교의) asceticism; austerity; severity; penance; religious austerities. **난행하다** do penance; practice austerity or asceticism. ¶난행하는 성자 a self-mortifying saint. 2 [행하기 어려움] being hard to practice; being hard to put into effect. **난행하다** be hard to put into practice.

난형(卵形) an egg shape; ovalness; an ovoid figure. ¶~의 ovate (leaf) / egg-shaped / oviform / oval / ovoid.

난형난제(難兄難弟) being almost equal; hard to tell who is better. ¶~다 There is little to choose between the two. / They are six of one and half a dozen of the other. // 두 사람의 기량은 ~다 The two are nearly equal in their skill.

난혼(亂婚) promiscuous sexual relations; promiscuity.

난황(卵黃) the yolk; the yellow (of an egg); [생] the deutoplasm; a vitellus (pl. -li). ¶~의 vitelline.

낟가리 a stack of grain stalks; a rice stack; a rick. ¶~를 가리다 stack / rick.

낟알 a grain; a kernel.

날[1] 1 [하루] a day; [시일] time; [일진] the kind of day. ¶어느 ~ one day // 좋은 ~ a happy day / a red-letter day / a lucky [an auspicious] day // ~마다 day by [after] day / from day to day / every day // 이 감에 따라 as days go by / as the days roll on // 다음 ~ the next [following] day // ~이 밝기 전에 before dawn [day] // ~이 저물어서 after dark // ~을 정하다 fix [set] a date // 그의 슬픔은 ~ 이 갈수록 더해 갔다 His sorrow deepened as the days went by [passed]. // 시험 볼 ~이 며칠 안 남았다 We have but a few days left before the examination. // 하루라도 난 그것을 이용하지 않는 ~이 없다 There does not pass a day without my using it. // 오늘은 아무래도 ~[일진]이 좋지 않다 This just isn't my day.

2 the weather. ⇨ '날씨 ¶~이 좋건 나쁘건 in fair weather or foul / rain or shine // 좋은 (on) a fine [clear] day // 궂은 ~ foul [bad / nasty] day [weather] // ~이 좋으면 if weather permits / if the weather is favorable // ~이 좋아질 것 같다 The weather is likely to improve. // 이런 ~에는 나가지 않는 것이 좋다 It is better not to go out into such weather. // ~이 좋으면 내일 출발하겠다 I will start tomorrow if it is fine. // **~이 사납다** It is foul [bad] weather.

3 [시절·때] on the morrow of; a time when; in time [case / the event] of. ¶내가 성공하는 ~에는 when I have succeeded // 작품을 완성하는 ~에는 on the completion of the work // 전쟁이 일어나는 ~에는 in the event of a war (breaking out) // 그 일이 완성되는 ~에는 그가 유명해질 것이다 When the work is completed [On the completion of the work] he will become famous. // 당신을 만난 ~을 나는 기억하고 있다 I remember the day when I met you.

4 a date. ⇨ '날짜[1]

날(이) 들다 clear up; become clear [fine weather]. ¶날이 들기 시작한다 It is clearing up. // 날이 들 것 같다 Weather looks promising. / It is going to be fine.

날(을) 받다 [잡다] set the date; fix a date; fix upon the day [date]; name the day.

날 샐 녘 dawn; daybreak; daylight. ¶~에 at dawn [daybreak] / at the peep of day [dawn] // ~까지 일하다 work until daylight.

날² (칼 등의) an edge; a blade. ¶**칼~** the blade of a knife // **대팻~** the blade[bit] of a plane // **면도~** a razor blade // **무딘[예리한] ~** a dull[sharp] edge // **~이 상하다** be broken / be nicked // **그것을 칼로 자르면 ~이 상한다** If you try to cut it with the knife, the edge will be nicked.

날(이) 서다 be edged; take an edge; become sharp[keen]. ¶**날이 선 칼** a sharp[keen] knife // **날이 선 무기** an edged weapon // **그것은 숫돌에 갈면 날이 선다** If it is whetted on a whetstone, it will become sharp.

날(을) 세우다 put an edge on; give an edge to; edge; sharpen; whet.

날³ (직물의) the warp; the lengthwise threads. ¶**~실** warp threads // **베를 ~** the warp on a loom // **~과 씨** the warp and woof[weft].

날- [익히지 않은] raw; uncooked; [가공하지 않은] crude; unprocessed; [신선한] fresh; [익지 않은] unripe; green. ¶**~고기**[생선] raw meat[fish] // **~계란** a raw egg // **~가죽** raw hide / a pelt // **~감** green[unripe] persimmons.

날강도(一强盜) a robber; a racketeer.

날개 the wings; (곤충의) an ala (pl. alae); [항] an airfoil[aerofoil]. ¶**비행기 ~** the wings of an airplane // **~ 달린** winged // **~ 치는 소리** the flappings[clappings] of the wings // **~를 치다** flap[clap / beat] the wings / flutter // **~를 펴다** spread[unfurl] the wings // **그것들은 ~ 돋친 듯이 팔렸다** They sold like hot cakes. // **새가 ~를 폈다[접었다]** The bird spread [folded] its wings. // **그 새의 ~는 펴서 길이가 50센티다** The bird has a wingspread of 50 centimeters. // **그 새는 두세 번 ~를 치고 나서 날아갔다** The bird flapped[fluttered] its wings a couple of times and then flew away. ●**날개옷** a robe of feathers. **날갯죽지** the wing; the (shoulder-)joint of a wing. ¶**~가 늘어지다** have a drooping wing.

날것 uncooked; raw fish[meat] (생선·고기); unripe[green] fruits(과일); untreated articles. ¶**~으로 먹다** eat (fish) raw[fresh] // **이 고기는 아주 ~이다** This meat is quite raw[rare].

날김치 fresh gimchi(kimchi); freshly-prepared gimchi.

날다¹ 1 (공중을) fly; soar; take wing; take flight; rise in the air; (나비·곤충이) flutter [flit] about; (솔개·수리가) wheel; (바람에) blow. ¶**나는 새** a flying bird / **나는 새** a bird flying in the air / a bird on the wing // **날지 못하는 새** a flightless bird // **하늘을 ~** fly in the air[sky] // **높게[낮게] ~** fly high[low] in the air // **떼 지어 ~** take wing in a flock // **그 거리를 6시간에 ~** cover the distance in six hours // **갈매기가 날고 있다** Gulls are wheeling about. // **비행기는 북극 상공을 날았다** The airplane flew over the North Pole. // **내 모자가 날아 시궁창에 빠졌다** My hat blew into the gutter. // **내게로 공이 날아 왔다** A ball came flying at me. // **종달새가 지저귀며 하늘 높이 날아올랐다** The singing lark soared higher and higher in the sky. 2 [빨리 가다] fly; go very fast; run; rush. ¶**나는 듯이 달려가다** run with flying feet / run like the wind // **나는 기별을 듣고 나는 듯이 집으로 달려왔다** At the news I flew home like the wind. 3 [달아나다] fly; flee; run away. ¶**정부와 함께 ~** elope with a lover // **그는 빚쟁이에게 졸려서 날아 버렸다** He has given the creditors the slip. // **그 범인은 국외로 날아 버린 지 오래다** The criminal had long since fled the country.

나는 새도 깃을 쳐야 날아간다(속담) One can't attain one's object without preparing oneself for it.

난다 긴다 하다 be incomparably deft[adroit]; display versatility[flexibility]; have many strings to one's bow. ¶**난다 긴다 하는 사람** a man of unusual ability.

날려 보내다 1 [놓아주다] fly; let fly; make fly; set free; (바람이) blow off[away]; (바람이) have (a thing) blown away. ¶**새를 ~** let loose a bird / set a bird free // **바람이 그 집의 지붕을 날려 보냈다** The wind blew the roof from the house. // **바람에 모자를 날려 보냈다** I had my hat blown[snatched] off. 2 [탕진하다] dissipate[squander] (a fortune); lose; waste; throw away. ¶**주색으로 한 재산 ~** blow in a fortune on women and liquor // **도박으로 3만 원을 ~** lose 30,000 won in gambling.

날다² 1 [색이 바래다] fade; discolor; lose color. ¶**색이 난** faded / discolored // **빛깔이 날기 쉬운** quickly fading / fugitive // **빛깔이 날지 않는** fadeless / fast / standing // **이 빛은 빨아도 색깔이 날지 않는다** This color will stand wash. // **햇볕을 쬔 데는 색이 날았다** The part exposed to the sunlight has discolored. 2 [냄새가 없어지다] lose odor; go away; vanish; (알코올·수증기 등이) evaporate; volatilize. ¶**이 향수는 냄새가 날았다** This perfume lost its fragrance. // **휘발유는 날기 쉽다** Gasoline is volatile.

날다³ [실을 만들다] spin (a thread); [베틀에 날을 걸다] thread the warp of (a loom).

날다람쥐 a flying squirrel.

날도둑놈 a barefaced scoundrel; a shameless swindler[crook].

날도마뱀 a flying dragon[lizard].

날뛰다 jump (up); leap (up); bound (up); (사납게) rage; rave; raise a row; go[run] wild; get rowdy; become excited[furious]. ¶**날뛰는 폭도** a raging mob // **기뻐 ~** jump[leap] for joy / dance with joy / fly into raptures // **성이 나서 ~** rave with fury / fret and fume / raise a row // **미친 듯이 ~** run amuck / be[go] on a wild rampage // **술에 취해 ~** be drunk and disorderly // **그는 미친 듯이 날뛰어 어쩌할 수가 없었다** He was raving mad and was beyond our control. // **그들은 미친 듯이 날뛰며 몇몇 버스에 불을 질렀다** They went on a rampage and set fire to several buses.

날라리 [음] →태평소

날래다 quick; speedy; swift; fast; agile; nimble. ¶**날랜 말** a speedy horse // **날래게 quickly** / speedily / swiftly // **그는 걸음이 ~** He is swift of foot. / He has swift feet. // **범인은 날래게 자취를 감추었다** The culprit disappeared in a flash.

날렵하다 smart; sharp; cute; shrewd; quick; keen; prompt. ¶**아주 날렵한** as smart as steel-trap // **그는 모든 일에 있어서 ~** He is smart in all things[quick at everything]. **날렵히** smart(ly); quickly. ¶**~ 비켜서다** jump back[aside] nimbly.

날로¹ [날이 갈수록] day by day; from day to day; every day. ¶**~ 번창하다** enjoy increasing prosperity as time goes on // ~ 나아지다 get better day by day // ~ 더워지고 있다 It is getting hotter every day. // 그 아기는 ~ 귀여워진다 The baby is getting sweeter[nicer / cuter] every day.

날로² [날것으로] raw; uncooked. ¶~ 먹다 eat (fish) raw // 당근을 ~ 먹다 eat a carrot uncooked // 생선을 ~ 먹다 fish raw[raw fish].

날름 1 (혀를) darting in and out. ¶혀를 ~ 내밀다 put[stick / thrust] out one's tongue (at). 2 [잽싸게] quickly; like a flash; with a quick snatch. ¶책상 위의 책을 ~ 집어들다 snatch a book off the table // 핸드백을 ~ 채 가다 snatch a handbag from[out of] her hand // 그는 음식을 ~ 먹어 치웠다 He gobbled up every bit of food in no time.

날름거리다 1 (혀 등을) let (a tongue / an arm) dart in and out; (손을) take one's hand in and out quickly. ¶개구리를 보자 뱀이 혀를 날름거리기 시작했다 On seeing a frog, the snake began to dart its tongue in and out. 2 [탐내다] be greedy for; peep stretching one's neck; crane one's neck to see.

날름날름 darting[taking / thrusting] in and out repeatedly. **날름날름하다** let (a tongue / an arm) dart in and out; be greedy for. ⇨ 날름거리다

날름쇠 (무자위의) a valve; (종의) a tumbler; cock; [스프링] a metal spring; (자물쇠의) a tumbler; a tongue.

날리다¹ 1 (공중으로) fly; let fly; make fly. ¶연을 ~ 날리다 fly a kite // 비둘기를 ~ let loose a pigeon // 돌을 ~ let fly a stone // 신문을 접어 ~ sail a folded newspaper // 그 아이는 종이 비행기를 공중에 날렸다 The child flew [sailed] a paper airplane through the air. // 그는 2루타를 날렸다 He hit[banged out] a double.
2 (이름을) make famous; distinguish; be popular (with / among); be widely[well] known. ¶이름을 ~ win[rise to] fame / make one's name / distinguish oneself // 전 세계에 이름을 ~ be known all over the world // 그는 작가로서 한창 날리고 있다 He is just booming as a writer. // 그도 한때는 날렸다 He has seen better days. // 그는 당시 소설가로서 크게 날렸다 He enjoyed great popularity as a novelist at that time.
3 [일을 대충 하다] scamp[skimp] one's work; do slipshod; do hasty job. ¶이 집은 꽤 날려 지었다 There is a lot of slapdash(work) about this house. // 그 목수는 절대로 일을 날리지 않는다 The carpenter is very conscientious in his work. / The carpenter never scamps his work.
4 [없애다] lose (all); waste; throw away; bring to naught. ¶갑작스런 가격 하락으로 지금까지 번 것을 모두 날리고 말았다 The sudden fall in prices has blown away all the profits hitherto accumulated. // 그는 얼마 안 가서 재산을 노름에 날려 버렸다 He soon lost all his fortune in gambling.

날리다² (바람에) wave; flutter; flap. ¶국기가 바람에 날리고 있다 The national flag is flapping in the wind. // 재가 날린다 Ashes blow. // 바람이 불 때마다 먼지가 날렸다 Every gust of wind stirred (up) dust.

날림 slapdash; doing[making] carelessly [slapdash / negligently]. ¶~으로 지은 jerry-built / of jerry-building // 이 작문은 ~이다 This is a slipshod composition. // 도처에 ~ 건물들이 올라가고 있다 Slapdash buildings are going up everywhere.
●**날림 공사** a jerry-building; slapdash construction work.

날마다 every day; daily; day after day; day by day. ¶~ 하는 일 daily routine // 거의 ~ almost every day // 그는 ~ 아침이면 내게 들르곤 한다 He calls on me every morning. // 나는 ~ 당신 생각을 하고 있습니다 Not a day passes without my thinking of you. // 마찬가지였다 One day was quite like another. // 그런 일은 ~ 있는 일이 아니다 Such things do not happen every day.

날밑 a blade guard; a sword guard.
날바닥 the bare floor[ground].
날반죽 cold-water dough; kneading with cold water. **날반죽하다** knead with cold water.
날밤¹ [지새우는 밤] a night one stays up [keeps awake] all night.
날밤(을) 새우다 stay[sit] up all night; kill the night.
날밤² raw[unroasted] chestnuts.
날벌레 a winged insect.
날벼락 1 [꾸중] an unreasonable reproof [scolding]. ¶~이 떨어지다 get an unreasonable scolding[rebuke]. 2 [재앙] an unexpected disaster; a sudden calamity. ¶~을 맞다 meet a sudden calamity / meet an unexpected stroke of misfortune.
날불한당 (-不汗黨) a shameless rascal [scoundrel]; a barefaced villain[crook].
날붙이 an edged tool; a cutting-instrument; bladeware; cutlery.
날삯 daily pay[wages]; a day's wage.
날수 (-數) 1 [날의 수효] (the number of) days. ¶~가 많이 걸리다 take many days[a long time] // 끝내려면 꽤 ~가 필요하다 Days are required for finishing it. 2 [그날의 운수] the luck[fortune] of a particular day. ¶~가 좋다[나쁘다] have a lucky[an unlucky] day // ~를 보다 tell one's fortune for the day.
날숨 an outbreath; exhalation; expiration. ¶~을 쉬다 exhale / breathe out / expire.
날실 [세로로 놓인 실] warp threads; [삶지 않은 실] raw[untreated] thread.
날쌔다 quick; agile; nimble; alert; swift; prompt; fleet. ¶날쌘 청년 a nimble young man // 날쌘 짐승 a fleet animal // 날쌔게 quickly / speedily / swiftly / quick as a flash // 행동이 ~ be quick[prompt] in action / act quickly[promptly] // 그는 일을 날쌔게 해치웠다 He finished his work in quick order. // 그 달필가는 멋진 필적으로 날쌔게 써 내려갔다 The talented calligrapher wrote in a beautiful running hand. // 그는 날쌔게 검을 칼집에서 뽑았다 He drew the sword (from its sheath) in an instant. // 그 소년은 군중 속을 날쌔게 빠져나갔다 The boy made his way nimbly through the crowd.
날씨 the weather; atmospheric conditions; the elements. ¶화창한 ~ fine[fair / favorable / good] weather // 온화한 ~ calm[mild / genial / serene] weather // 나쁜[궂은] ~ foul [bad / nasty / rainy] weather // 변덕스러운 ~ fickle[broken / changeable / unsettled] weather // 음산한 ~ gloomy[oppressive]

weather // 더할 나위 없는 ~ perfect[ideal] weather // 어떤 ~에도 in all winds and weathers / in fair weather or foul / regardless of weather // ~의 급변 an abrupt[a sudden change in weather] // 지금 ~로는 judging from the look of the sky // ~가 좋아지는 대로 on the first fine day // ~를 보다 have a look at the weather / read the sky // ~를 예보하다 make a weather forecast / forecast the weather // ~를 잘 맞추다 be weather-wise // ~를 탓하다 put down (anything) to the weather // 그는 ~에 관계없이 매일 조깅을 한다 He jogs every day regardless of the weather. // ~가 고르지 않다 The weather is unsettled. // 이 ~가 얼마나 갈까 How long will this weather hold[last]? // ~가 좋으면 8시에 출발하자 If the weather permits, let's start at eight. // ~가 심상치 않다 The weather[sky] looks threatening. // ~를 봐서는 내일 비가 올 것이다 Judging from the look of the sky, it will rain tomorrow. // 오늘 ~는 어때 How is the weather today? // ~가 개기 시작했다 The weather began to clear. // ~가 차차 좋아진다 The weather is changing for the better. / The weather is improving. // 이와 같은 ~가 오래 계속되지 않을 것이다 The weather will not hold so long. // 추운 ~가 여러 날 계속되고 있다 The weather has been cold for several days. // ~ 탓인지 머리가 무겁다 I feel heavy in the head, probably because of[due to] the weather. // 오늘은 겨울 ~ 같군요 It is winter weather today, isn't it? // 비가 올 ~다 We'll have falling[bad] weather. // We shall have some rain. // 이맘때 치고는 ~가 꽤 춥다 It's a little too cold for this time of (the) year. // ~가 풀렸다 The weather became warmer. // ~가 좋군요 It's a nice[sunny / lovely / beautiful / fine] day, isn't it? // 오늘은 ~가 좋으니 산책하러 가자 Since it's a nice day, let's go for a walk. // 아마 ~ 때문인지 졸려서 못 견디겠다 I am very sleepy, perhaps because of the weather.

날씬하다 (몸매가) slender; delicate(-looking); thin; slim; svelte; lithe; (자태가) smart; spruce. ¶날씬한 여자 a slim woman / a woman with a slender figure // 날씬한 허리 a slender[supple] waist // 날씬한 다리 race-horse legs // 날씬해지다 become slender [slim] // 옷차림이 ~ be smartly[sprucely] dressed // 그녀는 몸매가 ~ She is trim and slender in figure. **날씬히** sprucely. ¶~ 차려 입다 spruce oneself up (for dinner) / dress oneself neat and tidy.

날아가다 1 (공중을) fly away; take wings; (바람에) be blown away[off]. ¶남쪽으로 날아가는 제비들 swallows winging southward // 태풍에 기와가 날아갔다 Our roof tiles were blown off[away] by the typhoon. 2 (없어지다) be gone[out]; be used up; go. ¶돈이 어느새 다 날아간다 My money is all gone already. // 1주일에 5만 원의 돈은 곧 날아가 버린다 The fifty thousand won a week will not go far[will go quickly].

날아다니다 fly[flit / flutter] about[around]. ¶이 꽃 저 꽃으로 ~ fly from flower to flower // 나방들이 등불 주위를 날아다녔다 Moths flew about[around] the light. // 개똥벌레가 이리저리 날아다니고 있었다 Fireflies were flitting about.

날아들다 fly in[into]; (소식 등이) come (in); have. ¶이상한 편지가 ~ (사람이) have[get] a strange letter // 잠자리 한 마리가 방 안으로 날아들었다 A dragonfly came flying into the room. // 불행[행운]이 날아들었다 We suffered misfortune[were blessed with good fortune]. // 이내 첩보(捷報)가 날아들었다 It was not long before word came that they won the battle. // 흥분한 관객석에서 방석이 링 쪽으로 마구 날아들었다 The excited spectators hurled their seat cushions at the ring from every corner.

날염 (捺染) (textile) printing. ¶양면 ~ duplex printing. **날염하다** print. ¶날염한 천 printed cotton / print / (미) calico.
● **날염기** a printing machine.

날인 (捺印) sealing; affixing a seal. ¶톱누꼴 절취선이 있는 ~ 증서 an indenture // 조건부 ~ 증서 [법] an escrow. **날인하다** seal; put [affix / set / stamp] one's seal to. ¶기명 ~ write one's name and verify it by affixing one's seal / sign and seal // 증서에 ~ seal a deed.
● **날인자** a sealer.

날일 daywork; day labor.

날조 (捏造) (a) fabrication; (an) invention; (a) concoction; (미) (a) frame-up. **날조하다** concoct[cook up / make up] (a story); manufacture (a false report); fabricate; invent; (특히 문서·수표 등을) forge. ¶그것은 전적으로 그가 날조한 이야기이다 The story is a pure invention on his part. // 그 기사는 주간지가 날조한 것으로 판명되었다 The report proved to be the invention[a fabrication] of a weekly magazine. // 그는 자기에게 유리하도록 이야기를 날조했다 He fabricated a story to his own advantage.
● **날조 기사 / 날조 이야기** a fabrication; a fabricated report; a cooked-up report; a made-up[getup / trumped-up] story. **날조자** a fabricator.

날짐승 winged animals; the feathered tribe; birds; fowls.

날짜¹ 1 [정해진 날] a date; dating. ¶~ 소인 a day mark[stamp] // 계약[약속] ~ the date of contract[an appointment] // 5월 10일 ~의 편지 the letter dated[of] May 10th // ~가 없는 undated / dateless // ~를 늦추다 put off the date // ~를 앞당기다 move up[advance] the date // ~를 정하다 fix a date / name the date // (실제 날짜보다) 앞선 ~로 하다 ante-date / foredate / predate / date backward // ~를 매기다 date (a letter) / put a date to (a document) // 우리가 출발할 ~를 정하자 Let's fix the date of our departure. // 그 편지는 8월 5일 ~로 되어 있었다 The letter bore the date of[was dated] August 5. // 두 사람의 결혼 ~는 정해져 있었다 The date has been set [decided / fixed / chosen] for their wedding. 2 [일수] (the number of) days; time. ¶~는 얼마나 걸립니까 How long[many days] will it take? // 완성하는 데 여러 ~가 걸린다 Days are required for finishing it. // 감기가 낫는 데 꽤 많은 ~가 걸렸다 It took me many days to get over my cold.
● **날짜 변경선** a date line; the International Date Line.

날짜² 1 uncooked food. ⇨날것 2 [익숙하지 못한 사람] an inexperienced person; a greenhorn; a rank amateur; a mere novice; a

날짝지근하다

crude fellow. ¶그 배우는 ~다 The actor lacks experience.//그런 ~는 처음 보았다 I have never seen such a greenhorn.

날짝지근하다 (feel) languid. ⇨늘쩍지근하다

날치[1] [새 사냥] catching [shooting] birds on the wing; [날쌤] promptness; quickness; nimbleness; agility.
● **날치꾼** a master shot; an excellent hunter (so skilled as to shoot a bird on the wing).

날치[2] [동] a flying fish.
● **날치자리** [천] Volans.

날치기 [재빨리 채뜨려 가는 행위] purse-snatching; (속어) swiping (things); [재빨리 채뜨려 가는 사람] a purse-snatcher; a (handbag) snatcher. ¶의안을 ~로 통과시키다 rush a bill through the Assembly by surprise. **날치기하다** snatch (away) (from). ¶남자는 그에게서 돈뭉치를 날치기하여 도망쳤다 The man snatched a bundle of notes from him and ran away. ➔¶날치기당하다 have (a thing) snatched¶날치기당하지 않도록 소지품에 주의하십시오 Keep an eye on your belongings so that no one will walk off with [snatch / swipe] them.¶노상에서 가방을 날치기당했다 I had my bag snatched away on the road.//정거장에서 나는 카메라를 날치기당했다 I had my camera ripped off at the station. / Someone swiped my camera at the station and ran off with it.

날카롭다 1 [예리하다] sharp; [끝이 뾰족하다] pointed. ¶날카로운 칼 a sharp knife//날카로운 커브 a sharp curve [turn]//날카로워지다 get [become] sharp.
2 [형세가 매섭다] sharp; (문어) poignant. ¶나는 왼쪽 다리에 날카로운 통증을 느꼈다 I felt a sharp [stabbing] pain in my left leg.//신문은 정부에 대해 날카로운 공격을 가했다 The papers attacked the government bitterly. / The press leveled cutting remarks at the government.//그의 에세이는 날카로운 풍자로 가득 차 있다 His essays are full of stinging [biting] sarcasm.
3 [두뇌·감각이 뛰어나다] keen; quick; [통찰력 등이 예민하다] acute. ¶날카로운 관찰 keen [acute] observation//날카로운 눈 keen [piercing / penetrating] eyes//청각 [후각] 이 ~ be keen of hearing [scent] //그의 판단력은 ~ He can make acute judgments.//이 작가는 관찰이 ~ This writer has a keen eye.//너는 신경이 ~ You are very sensitive [perceptive].//너의 관찰은 폐 ~ You have a keen observing eye.

날탕 a person with no means; a penniless [empty-handed] person.

날파람 1 [서슬에 나는 바람] a gust of wind raised by a swiftly passing object. **2** [날카로운 기세] roaring spirits; keenness; fierceness.

날품 day labor [work]. ¶~을 팔다 be hired [(미) hire out] by the day / work by the day//~으로 일하다 work by the day//~으로 고용되다 be hired by the day.
● **날품삯** daily wages. **날품팔이** [날품팔이꾼] a day laborer [(영) labourer / worker]; [날품을 파는 일] work done on a daily wage basis.

낡다 [오래되다] old; aged; antiquated; time-worn; grow old; used worn; worn-out; [시대에 뒤지다] old fashioned; outmoded; antique; [진부하다] stale; threadbare; hackneyed; commonplace; outdated; out of date; outworn. ¶낡은 관습 an obsolete custom / a worm-eaten custom//낡은 양복 an old-fashioned dress / an old clock//낡아서 누렇게 된 신문지 a newspaper yellow with age//낡아 빠진 바지 (a pair of) worn-out [ragged] trousers//낡은 생각 an old-fashioned idea//낡아 빠진 가구 worn out furnitures//좀 낡은 표현이지만 to use a somewhat trite expression//자네 신발은 몹시 낡았군 Your shoes are really worn out, aren't they?//그는 항상 낡은 옷을 입고 있었다 He was always in worn-out clothes.//이 타자기는 낡았다 This typewriter is worn out.//낡은 기름으로 튀겼는지 이 새우 프라이는 맛이 없다 These fried shrimps are not good. They must have been cooked in old oil.//그는 기사도의 낡은 생각을 버리지 못하고 있다 He still clings [hangs on] to out-dated [outmoded] ideas of chivalry.

남 1 [타인] another; other people; others. ¶~ 앞에서 in public / in the presence of others//~처럼 like others//~ 하는 대로 like common run / like others//~이야 어떻든 나는 so far as I am concerned / as for me//~의 손을 빌리지 않고 without assistance//~을 거들떠보지도 않다 be arrogant//~ 앞에 나서기를 꺼리다 shun company [the public]//~ 앞에서 의견을 말하다 give people one's view//~의눈을 피하다 avoid the eyes of others / shun the public eye//그녀는 ~의 이야기하기를 좋아한다 She likes to talk about others. / She is a gossip.//~은 ~이고 나는 나다 Let others mind their own business.//~의 마음도 모르고 어떻게 그런 말을 한담 How can you say such a thing? As if you didn't understand my good intentions!//그들은 ~ 보기에는 행복해 보인다 They look happy to others [other people].//그들은 ~이 보기에는 의좋은 부부다 Anybody can see that they are a happily-married couple.//그는 ~의 눈치를 보고 말을 한다 He waits to see others attitude [to see which way the wind is blowing] before he says anything.//그의 불행이 ~의 일 같지 않다 I feel as if his misfortune were my own.//나도 ~처럼 대학으로 진학했다 I entered a university like everyone else.//~ 걱정은 하지 마라 Don't worry about others.//넌 ~이니 잠자코 있어 줘 Being an outsider, you had better keep silent.//그는 생판 ~이오 He is an utter stranger to me.//그녀는 ~들 앞이어서 그 말을 꺼내지 않았다 She did not refer to it because other people were present.//이대로는 ~ 앞에 나갈 수 없다 I am not fit to be seen.//~의 말에 신경 쓸 것 없다 Let people talk and dogs bark!//~을 나쁘게 말하지 마라 Don't speak ill of others.//~도 아닌 네가 그런 말을 하다니 To think that you, of all persons, should say so!
2 [친척이 아닌 사람] an unrelated person. ¶촌수는 멀지만 그는 아주 ~은 아니다 Though distant, he is still my relative.
3 [국외자] an outsider; [관계를 끊은 사람] an estranged person; a stranger. ¶생면부지의 ~ a complete [utter] stranger//~이 참견할 일이 아니다 A third party should not thrust his nose into these matters.//그들은 이혼했으니 이젠 ~이다 Since they got divorced, they have nothing to do with each

others.// 이것은 ~의 이야기가 아니야 It is warning to you.
남을 물에 넣으려면 제가 먼저 물에 들어간다 (속담) To dig pit for another and fell into it oneself.
남의 밥에 든 콩이 굵어 보인다(속담) The apples on the other side of the wall are the sweetest.; The grass is always greener on the other side of the fence.
남의 손을 빌리다 [도움을 받다] get help [assistance] from another.
남(男) 1 [남자] a man; a male; [아들] a son. ¶그는 슬하에 3~2녀를 두고 있다 He is blessed with three sons and two daughters. 2 baronage. ⇨ 남작(男爵)
남(南) the south. ⇨ 남쪽
남-(男) masculine; male.
남가일몽(南柯一夢) vain [fleeting / passing] glory.
남계(男系) the male line; the spear side; the male issue. ¶~의 on the male line / on the father's [spear] side [line] // ~의 친족 관계 agnation // ~의 자손 the descendants in the male line // ~의 조상 (아버지 쪽의) the ancestors on the father's [paternal] side.
남구(라파)(南歐羅巴) Southern Europe.
남국(南國) a southern country [land]; the south countries.
남극(南極) (지구의) the South Pole; the Antarctic; (자석의) the south pole. ¶~자(磁)~ the South Magnetic Pole.
● **남극광**(-光) the aurora australis (*pl.* aurorae australes); southern lights. **남극구**(-區) (동물·지리학상의) the Antarctic Region. **남극권**[대] the Antarctic Circle [Zone]. **남극 대륙** the Antarctic Continent; Antarctica. **남극 탐험** an Antarctic expedition [exploration]; a south-pole exploration.
남극해 the Antarctic Ocean [Sea].
남근(男根) the penis (*pl.* penes, ~es). ⇨ 음경
● **남근 숭배** phallicism; phallic worship.
남기다 1 [사람·물건을] 뒤에 남게 하다] leave (behind); keep back [in]; [후세에 전하다] leave; hand down. ¶발자국을 ~ leave one's footprints // 나쁜 인상을 ~ leave a bad impression behind [on] // 북극에 자기 발자국을 ~ leave one's footprints at [set one's feet on] the North Pole // 역사에 자기 이름을 ~ leave one's name in history // 전쟁의 비참함을 말해 주는 기록을 후세에 ~ hand down records describing the misery of war to posterity // 그는 아내와 두 어린아이를 남기고 죽었다 He died leaving his wife and two small children (behind). // 그는 당신에게 주려고 이 꾸러미를 남겨 두고 갔습니다 He left this package for you. // 우리는 몇몇 해결해야 할 문제를 더 남겨 두고 있다 We have a few more problems to solve. / There are still two or three more problems. // 선생님은 벌로서 두 학생을 남겨 두었다 The teacher kept two pupils after school as a punishment. // 그녀는 아직도 어린 시절의 모습을 얼굴에 남기고 있다 She still retains something of her looks as a child. // 산림은 개발되어 이전의 모습을 아무것도 남기고 있지 않다 The forest has been developed and nothing remains to remind us of what it used to be. // 그의 추방은 여러 사람의 마음에 검은 오점을 남겼다 His expulsion left a dark spot in everyone's heart. // 나 하나만 남기고 다들 놀러 갔다 They went out to play, leaving me all alone. // 그는 위대한 음악가로서의 명성을 남겼다 He left behind a reputation as a great musician.
2 [하지 [쓰지] 않고 두다] leave over [undone]; [따로 떼어 두다·돈을 저축하다] save; spare; have in store; set aside. ¶일을 ~ leave one's work unfinished [half-done] / leave one's job over (till the next week) // 한 푼도 안 남기고 다 써 버리다 spend all the money one has / spend one's money to the last cent // 봉급에서 조금 남겨 두다 have a little money left over from one's wages // 나는 도넛을 아이들 먹으라고 남겨 놓았다 I left doughnuts for the children to eat. // 대회까지 이제 1주일을 남겨 두었을 뿐이다 We have only one week left before the general meeting. / Only one week remains before the general meeting. // 내일을 위해 작업의 일부를 남겨 두겠다 I will leave part of the work for tomorrow. // 이제 연말까지 며칠을 남겨 두었을 뿐이다 There are only a few days left before the end of the year. // 아직 푸른 사과는 따지 않고 남겨 두었다 I left the green [unripe] apples on the tree. // 아무것도 나는 남겨 둘 여유가 없다 I have nothing to spare. // 그는 자기 노후를 위해 돈을 남겨 두었다 He saved money for his old age. // 나는 종이를 한 장도 남기지 않고 써 버렸다 I used up all the paper down to the last sheet. // 그는 10만 원 가운데 3만 원을 남기고 나머지는 책을 샀다 He set aside 30,000 won out of the 100,000 won, and spent the remainder on books.
3 [이를 보다] gain profit; make [get / obtain] a profit. ¶만 원 ~ make a profit of 10,000 won // 1할 ~ clear [net] ten percent // 거래에서 많이 ~ make a large profit on a deal // 별로 못 ~ realize little [just a bare] profit.
남김없이 all (together); wholly; entirely; without exception [reserve]. ¶한 사람도 ~ to the last man / to a man // ~ 털어놓다 make a clean breast of (a matter) / make a complete [full] confession of (a fact) // 그는 언제나 지기가 번 돈을 ~ 써 버리곤 했다 He always spent all the money he earned [got]. / He always spent all his wages. // 그는 그때의 사정을 ~ 설명했다 He gave a complete [full] explanation of the situation [the circumstances] at that time. // 제가 알고 있는 것은 ~ 말씀드렸습니다 I have told you all I know. // 한 사람도 ~ 부적격이라는 것이 판명되었다 They proved to be disqualified to a man [to the last man / without exception]. / Everyone of them proved to be disqualified. // 달걀은 한 개도 ~ 부패되어 있었다 Every single egg was addled. // 그는 큰 비프스테이크를 ~ 먹어 치웠다 He ate up every bite [scrap] of the big steak.
남남동(南南東) the south-southeast (약어 SSE).
남남북녀(南男北女) The best men are found in the south and the best women in the north.
남남서(南南西) the south-southwest (약어 SSW).
남녀(男女) man and woman; male and female; persons of different sexes; both sexes. ¶~를 막론하고 regardless of sex // ~

남녀 양성의 of both sexes / bisexual ∥ ~간에 between male and female ∥ 젊은 ~ (속어) Jack and Gill[Jill] / crew-cuts and ponytails ∥ ~의 역할 male and female roles ∥ ~의 차별 discrimination based on sex / sex discrimination ∥ ~를 불문하고 지원할 수 있음 You can apply regardless of sex. ●**남녀 공학** coeducation. ¶~의 coeducational ∥ ~ 대학의 여학생 (미국 구어) a coed. **남녀 관계** sexual relations; the relation of the sexes. **남녀노소** people of all ages and both sexes; people, young and old, men and women. ¶~를 막론하고 without distinction of age or sex / people, young and old, men and women all alike. **남녀동등권주의** feminism. **남녀유별** distinction between the sexes. **남녀칠세부동석** A boy and a girl should not sit together after they have reached the age of seven (according to Confucian idea). **남녀평등** the equality of sexes.

남녘(南-) the south; the south side; the southern districts.

남다 1 [여분이 있다] remain (over); be left (over); [너무 많다] be too many[much]; be in excess[surplus]. ¶남은 돈 the money left over ∥ 남은 일 the remainder of work / the remaining work ∥ 20에서 8을 빼면 12가 남는다 Taking 8 from 20 leaves 12. ∥ 돈은 이제 얼마 남아 있지 않다 There is only a small sum of money left (over). ∥ 다시 해 볼 만큼의 시간은 우리에게 남아 있다 We still have time enough to do it over again. / 9를 2로 나누면 몫이 4이고 1이 남는다 When nine is divided by two, the answer is four with a remainder of one. / When you divide nine by two, you get four with one left over. ∥ 지난주에는 내 돈이 한 푼도 남지 않았다 Nothing was left of[I used up all] my pocket money last week. ∥ 밥이 많이 남았다 A lot of rice was left over. ∥ 카드놀이의 브리지를 하기에는 한 사람이 남았다 We had one person too many to play bridge. ∥ 내 지갑에는 돈이 얼마 남아 있지 않았다 There was little money left in my wallet. ∥ 시간이 남았기에 그는 영화관에 들어갔다 Since he had some free time, he entered a movie theater. ∥ 우리는 돈이 쓰고 남을 정도로 있다 We have more money than we can spend[than we know what to do with]. ∥ 남은 것을 내게 달라 Give me what is left over. ∥ 우리는 남는 돈은 은행에 맡긴다 We deposit our surplus money in the bank. ∥ 나에겐 남아도는 시간이란 없다 I have no time to spare. ∥ 남은 돈이 있니 Have you[Is there] any money left? ∥ 그의 장점은 단점을 보충하고도 남는다 His merits more than offset his demerits. ∥ 예산에서 얼마나 돈이 남았습니까 How much money was left over (from what we budgeted)? ∥ 사과는 2개밖에 남아 있지 않다 There are only two apples left. ∥ 출발까지 아직 3일이 남아 있다 We have still three days before our departure. 2 [잔존하다] remain; linger. ¶마음에 ~ remain[stay] in one's mind ∥ 역사에 ~ be written[recorded] in history ∥ 귀에 ~ linger[ring] in one's ears ∥ 집은 파괴되었지만 석조 대문은 남았다 The stone gate was left[remained] after the house was destroyed. ∥ 그들이 떠난 뒤에는 먼지 하나 남아 있지 않았다 There was not a speck of dust left after they departed. ∥ 그의 얼굴에는 흠터[상처 아문 자리]가 남아 있다 He still has a scar on his face. ∥ 그들 사이에 봉건적인 생각이 아직도 남아 있다 Feudalistic ideas still persist[linger] among them. ∥ 그의 마지막 말이 아직 내 귀에 남아 있다[쟁쟁하다] His last words still ring in my ears. ∥ 역한 냄새가 아직 방에 남아 있다 There is a bad smell lingering in[still hanging about] the room. ∥ 그 광경은 내 기억에 아직 생생하게 남아 있다 The sight is still fresh in my memory. ∥ 그 분쟁은 미해결인 채 그대로 남아 있다 The conflict remains unsettled.

3 [체류하다] remain (behind); stay; stop; linger. ¶최후까지 ~ remain[stay] to the last ∥ 나는 늦게까지 회사에 남아 있었다 I remained in office till late. ∥ 방과 후에 남아 우리는 노래 연습을 했다 We remained[stayed] after school to practice singing. ∥ 그녀는 들판에 혼자 남게 되었다 She was left all alone in the field. ∥ 두 팀이 결승까지 남았다 These two teams were left[remained] after the semifinals / These two teams survived to the finals.

4 [살아남다] survive; outlive. ¶뒤에 남은 처자 one's bereaved family ∥ 아내 뒤에 남아 생존하다 outlive one's wife.

5 [후세에 전해지다] be handed down. ¶이 지방에는 재미있는 전설이 남아 있다[전해 내려온다] An interesting legend has been handed down in this district. ∥ 그것에 관한 기록은 이제 남아 있지 않다 All the documents about it are gone[lost]. ∥ 그의 이름은 영원히 남을 것이다 His name will be immortal[will live forever]. ∥ 그의 악명은 그의 사후에도 남았다 His notoriety lived on after his death.

6 [이익을 보다] (사람이) make a profit; make; gain; earn; (사물이) be profitable; yield profits. ¶남는[남지 않는] 장사 a profitable[an unprofitable] business ∥ 꽤 ~ make a good profit ∥ 그것은 천 원 이하로 팔아서는 남는 것이 없다 It wouldn't pay to sell it for less than 1,000 won.

7 [웃돌다·우월하다] surpass; be beyond one's power. ¶그 계곡의 웅장한 경치는 상상하고도 남음이 있다 The spectacular view of the canyon surpasses[eclipses] the imagination.

남다르다 peculiar; (서술적) be different from others; be unlike other people; be out of the common[ordinary] (run). ¶남다른 노력 a great effort ∥ 남다른 취향 a new departure / a novel idea[plan] ∥ 그는 어딘지 남다른 데가 있다 He has something out of the common. ∥ 그는 어릴 때부터 남다른 재능을 나타냈다 He began to show outstanding ability in his childhood.

남단(南端) the southern extremity[end / tip / rim]. ¶제주의 ~ the southernmost tip of Jeju ∥ 공원은 시의 ~에 있다 The park is located at the southern end of the city.

남달리 in a different way than others; out of the common; uncommonly; unusually; extraordinarily; especially; exceptionally; more than others. ¶~ 노력하다 work harder than others ∥ ~ 알뜰하다 be thrifty to a fault ∥ ~ 추위를 타다 be unusually sensitive to the cold ∥ ~ 고집이 세다 be unique in one's stubbornness ∥ 그는 ~ 근면하다 He

남대문(南大門) Namdaemun; the South Gate (of Seoul).

남독(濫讀) [닥치는 대로 읽음] hit-or-miss [haphazard / desultory] reading.

남동(南東) (the) southeast(약어 SE). ¶남~ (the) south-southeast(약어 SSE) / ~의 southeast(ern) / ~에 [으로] southeast / southeastward // 도서관은 시의 ~부에 있다 The library is in the southeast part of the city.
● **남동풍** a southeasterly wind.

남루(襤褸) [누더기] rags; shreds; scraps; [헌옷] tatters; tattered clothes; (속어) duds. **남루하다** tattered; shabby; threadbare; ragged; (서술적) be in rags. ¶남루한 옷을 입은 사람 a person in rags [threadbare clothes] / a ragged [tattered] man // 남루한 옷을 입고 있다 be (clad) [go] in rags (and tatters).

남매(男妹) brother and sister. ¶4~ a brother-and-sister foursome // 그들은 ~간이다 They are brother and sister. // 그는 8~를 두었다 He has a son-and-daughter eight-some.

남모르다 unknown to others; unseen; hidden; secret; (내심의) inward. ¶남모르게 secretly / inwardly // 남모르는 고생 inward trouble / hardships unknown to others // 남모르는 슬픔 a hidden sorrow // 그녀에게는 남모르는 괴로움이 있다 She has a secret trouble. // 내게도 남모르는 고민이 있다 I have troubles of my own that are unknown to others. // 그녀는 남모르게 고아들의 학비를 도와주었다 She secretly helped orphans with their school expenses. **남몰래** secretly; in secret; inwardly. ¶그녀는 ~ 울었다 She cried in secret [in private].

남미(南美) South America. ¶~의 South American.
● **남미 대륙** South America; the South American Continent.

남반구(南半球) the Southern Hemisphere.

남발(濫發) an excessive [a reckless] issue; an overissue. ¶어음[지폐]의 ~ an overissue of bills [bank notes]. **남발하다** issue excessively [recklessly]; overissue.

남방(南方) the south; the southward; the direction of the south(방향). ¶~의 southern / southerly // ~으로 가다 go south.
● **남방셔츠** an aloha shirt.

남벌(濫伐) reckless deforestation; indiscriminate felling (of trees). **남벌하다** deforest [cut down trees] recklessly; fell trees indiscriminately.

남복(男服) men's clothes [wear]; male attire; clothes in which a woman disguises as a man. **남복하다** be dressed like a man; wear men's clothes.

남부(南部) the southern part [district / portion]; (미국의) the South. ¶~에 in the south of (Korea) / (live) down South // 한반도의 ~ the southern part of the Korean Peninsula / 호남의 ~ the southern part of Honam // ~의 군대 (미국의) the Southern Army / (남북 전쟁 시의) the Confederate Army.

남부끄럽다 ashamed; disgraceful; shameful; scandalous; disreputable. ¶남부끄럽지 않은 살림 a decent living // 어디 내세워도 남부끄럽지 않은 인물 a fine [worthy] person // 남부끄러운 짓 a disgraceful [shameful] act // 남부끄럽지 않다 have nothing to be ashamed (of) / be up to the mark / be worthy [decent / honorable] // 남부끄럽지 않게 차려입고 있다 be decently dressed // 남부끄러워 그런 말은 못 하겠다 I am ashamed to say such a thing. // 그런 짓을 하고도 남부끄럽지 않으냐 Aren't you ashamed of what you have done [having done such a thing]?

남부럽다 envious of others. ¶남부럽지 않게 살고 있다 be well off / have no need to envy others.

남부럽잖다 well-to-do; well-off; wealthy; rich. ¶남부럽잖게 살다 be well [comfortably] off / be well-to-do / live in plenty [abundance].

남부여대하다(男負女戴-) set out on a wandering [vagabond] life; become poor wanderers [refugees].

남북(南北) north and south(▶ 어순에 주의). ¶~으로 가로놓이다 [에 걸쳐 있다] lie from north to south / extend north and south // 강은 ~으로 흐르고 있다 The river flows from north to south. // 거리는 ~으로 통해 있다 The street runs north and south.
● **남북 교류** exchange between north and south Korea. **남북 대화** the North-South dialogue. **남북문제** (부국·빈국 간의) North-South problems; problems between the industrialized North and the impoverished South; (한국의) Korean problems. **남북 분단** the division of Korea into north and south. **남북 전쟁** [역] the Civil War. **남북통일** the reunification of North and South (Korea). **남북한** north and south Korea; the North and the South of Korea.

남비 →냄비

남빛(藍-) indigo; deep blue.

남사당(男-) a wayfaring male entertainer; a strolling actor; actors on the road.
● **남사당패** a troupe of players.

남산골샌님(南山-) a penniless scholar; a wretched scholar.

남상(男相) a woman's face having masculine features; an unwomanly face.
남상(을) 지르다 have a mannish face.

남상(濫觴) the origin; the source; the genesis; the rise; the beginning. ¶연극의 ~ the origin [beginning] of the drama.

남새 vegetables; greens.
● **남새밭** a vegetable garden [patch].

남색(男色) sodomy; buggery. ⇨*비역

남색(藍色) 1 indigo. ⇨남빛 ¶~ 물을 들이다 dye (a cloth) deep blue. 2 [남색짜리] a newlywed [married] woman around twenty.

남생이 [동] a Chinese pond turtle; a Korean terrapin; (미국산의) a spotted turtle [terrapin / tortoise].

남서(南西) the southwest. ¶~의 southwest / southwestern // ~로 가다 go southwest [southwestward] // 호수는 마을의 ~2킬로미터 지점에 있다 The lake is two kilometers (to the) southwest of the village.
● **남서풍** a southwestern wind.

남성(男性) 1 [남자] the male (sex); manhood; (a) man; the sterner [stronger] sex; a man; [남자 성질] masculinity; manliness. ¶~의 male / of the male sex / man (friend) // ~용 잠옷 men's pajamas / pajamas for men // ~만의 파티 a stag party // 여성이 ~보다 못하다는 근거는 없다 There is no proof that

남성

woman is inferior to man. 2 [언] the masculine gender.
● 남성미 masculine [manly] beauty. 남성 호르몬 male hormone; testosterone.

남성 (男聲) a male voice.
● 남성 사중창 a male quartet. 남성 합창 a male chorus.

남성적 (男性的) masculine; manly; virile. ¶~인 여자 a girl of masculine spirit // ~인 오락 a manly sport // ~인 태도 [의연함] a manly attitude // ~인 문체 a masculine style // 걸음걸이가 ~인 여자 a woman with a masculine walk // ~인 데가 없다 lack manliness [masculinity] // 자신의 잘못을 인정하는 데는 ~인 용기가 필요했다 It took a great deal of manly courage to admit that he had been wrong. // 그 방이나 세간이 ~인 느낌이었다 There was a masculine air about the room and its furnishings. // 그녀에게는 어딘지 모르게 ~인 데가 있다 She's a bit mannish [masculine] in some ways. / She's a little bit like a man in some ways.

남실거리다 covet; surge. ⇨ 넘실거리다

남실남실 stretching one's neck avidly (to see); wavily. ⇨ 넘실넘실

남십자자리 (南十字-) [천] the Southern Cross; the Cross; Crux.

남아 (男兒) [남자 아이] a boy; a son; [대장부] a man; a manly man. ¶~답게 like a man / in a manly manner // 그는 진짜 한국-이다 He is a true Korean (man) [son of Korean].
● 남아일언중천금 A man's word is as good as a bond.

남아돌다 (물건이) be in excess; be superabundant [superfluous]; (사람이) have too many [much]; have more than enough. ¶남아도는 surplus / excessive / superfluous / superabundant // 사람이 남아도는 회사 an overstaffed firm // 우리 집 소로부터 우리 5명 식구에게 남아돌 만큼의 젖이 나온다 Our cow gives more than enough milk for the five of us. // 그녀는 돈이 남아돌 만큼 많다 She has more money than she can spend [knows what to do with]. / She has money enough and to spare.

남아메리카 (南-) South America.
남아프리카 (南-) South Africa.
남안 (南岸) the southern coast; (영국의) the South Coast.
남양 (南洋) the South Seas.
남용 (濫用) abuse; misuse; misappropriation; an extravagant [improper] use (of). ¶권리 [권력]의 ~ an abuse of one's rights [power] // 직권 ~ misfeasance // 직권 ~ 죄 [법] oppression. **남용하다** misuse; abuse; use improperly [unlawfully]; use to excess; misappropriate. ¶권력을 ~ abuse [make an improper use of] one's power // 직권을 ~ abuse one's official authority // 시장이 되자마자 그는 직권을 남용하기 시작했다 As soon as he became mayor, he began to abuse his authority.

남우 (男優) [남자 배우] an actor.

남우세스럽다 [창피스럽다] indecent; disgraceful; scandalous; [꼴사납다] unsightly; unbecoming; disreputable; unpresentable. ¶남우세스럽지도 않으냐 Shame on you!

남위 (南緯) the south latitude [parallel]. ¶~ 15도 20분에 in lat. 15°20′S [latitude fifteen degrees twenty minutes south].

● 남위선 a line of south latitude.
남유럽 (南-) Southern Europe.
남의집살이 domestic service; (미) living out (as a maid); working as a domestic servant. **남의집살이하다** be in domestic service.

남자 (男子) [사내] a man (pl. men); (집합적) man (▶ 관사를 붙이지 않음); a gentleman. ¶~의 male // ~ 중의 ~ a man among men // ~ 옷 men's wear // ~용 men's / gentlemen's / for gentlemen's use // ~다운 manly / manful / virile // ~에 어울리는 무늬 patterns for gentleman // ~용 의류 men's wear // ~용 화장실 the men's room [toilet] / (게시) Gentlemen // 그는 ~답게 행동했다 He behaved in a manly way. // 저 회사에서는 아직 여자는 ~와 차별되고 있다 That company still discriminates between the sexes [against women]. // 이 클럽은 ~ 전용입니다 This club is for men only. / This is a stag club. // 그녀는 아직 ~를 모른다 She's never had [known] a man. / She's still a virgin. // 그녀는 ~를 써서 점포를 운영하고 있다 She runs the store with a male employee. // 그는 비열해서 자리를 같이 못할 ~다 He is a disgrace to (all) men. // ~답게 죽기 아니면 살기로 해 보라 Do or die if you are a man. // 너를 ~라고 믿고 부탁하는 거야 I ask this of you because I consider you a man. // 나도 자존심이 있는 ~다 I am a man of honor. // 그렇게 해 주면 ~로서의 체면이 선다 I can save face if you will do that for me. // 그런 짓을 하면 ~로서의 체면이 손상된다 If I did such a thing, it would reflect on my honor. // 너도 ~라면 그런 짓은 못 하겠지 You should be man enough not to do a thing like that.
● 남자 사무원 a male clerk. 남자 친구 a boyfriend; a man friend (pl. men friends). ¶나는 ~가 한 사람도 없다 I have no men friends.

남작 (男爵) (사람) a baron; (작위) baronage. ¶K ~ Baron K // 골드윈 ~ (영국에서) Baron Goldwin / (드물게) the Baron of Goldwin (▶ of를 쓰는 것은 지명인 경우).
● 남작 부인 a baroness.

남장 (男裝) male attire [disguise]. ¶~의 여인 a fair woman (dressed) in male attire / a beautiful girl masquerading as a man. **남장하다** disguise oneself as a man; be dressed like a man; wear [be in] men's clothes. ¶그녀는 남장하고 있다 She is dressed like a man. // 그녀는 남장하고 파티에 잠입했다 She sneaked into the party disguised as a man.

남정 (男丁) an adult man.
● 남정네 [사내들] the menfolk(s); [남의 남편들] the husbands.

남정석 (藍晶石) [광] cyanite.

남존여비 (男尊女卑) predominance of men over women; treatment of women as inferior to men; subjection of women. ¶~의 사회 a male-dominated society // 그 지방에서는 ~ 사상이 아직도 일반화되어 있다 In that district the idea that men are superior to women [women are inferior to men] is still prevalent.

남종 (男-) a servant. ⇨ 사내종 (⇨ 사내)
남중 (南中) (천체의) southing; culmination. **남중하다** south; cross the meridian.
남중일색 (男中一色) an uncommonly handsome man; an Adonis.

남진(南進) southward advance [movement / expansion]. **남진하다** go [advance] south.

남짓하다 (서술적) be a bit over [above / more than]; be upward of. ¶20명 ~ be more than twenty people / be twenty strong // 나이가 쉰 ~ be a little over fifty // 나는 만 원 남짓한 돈을 가지고 있다 I have a little more than 10,000 won. // 10마일 남짓한 거리다 It is a little over ten miles. // 여기 온 지 5년 ~ It is upward of five years [five years and more] since I came here. **남짓이** over; above; more than; upward of; odd. ¶5년 ~ over [more than] five years / five years and more // 3마일 ~ over [more than] three miles // 1세기 ~ (for) something over a century // 천 원 ~ 1,000 won odd / 1,000 odd won // 30명 ~ 출석했다 Upward(s) of [more than] thirty people came [were present]. / Over thirty [Thirty-some / Thirty-odd] people attended the meeting.

남쪽(南−) the south (약어 S). ¶~의 south / southern // ~으로 toward the south / southward // ~에 [떨어진 곳에] to the south (of) / [남부에] in the southern part (of China) / [경계를 접하여] on the south side (of the house) // 북쪽에서 ~으로 from north to south // 서울의 ~ 300마일 지점의 an island three hundred miles (to the) south of Seoul // ~으로 여행하다 travel (to the) south // 그 도시는 ~에 있다 The city is south of us. // 바람은 ~에서 불어 온다 The wind blows [is] southerly [from the south]. / The wind is in the south.

남창(男唱) [여자가 남자 소리로 부르는 노래] a song sung by a woman in male voice; [남자가 부르는 노래] a man's song; [남자 소리로 부르는 여자] a woman singing the man's part.

남창(男娼) a male prostitute; a professional catamite.

남창(南窓) a window facing the south.

남천(南天) [남쪽 하늘] the southern sky.

남청(藍靑) indigo blue.

남치마(藍−) a deep-blue skirt.

남침(南侵) a southward invasion; an invasion of the south. ¶북한의 ~ 야욕 a North Korean plot to invade the south / the North Korean scheme of war against the Republic of Korea. **남침하다** invade the south.

남탕(男湯) the men's section of a public bath.

남태평양(南太平洋) the South Pacific.

남파(南派) [남쪽으로의 파견] sending [dispatching] to the south. **남파하다** send [dispatch] (an armed agent) to the south.
● **남파 간첩** an espionage agent sent (by the north) to the south.

남편(男便) a husband; one's man; (구어) a hub(by); [법] a baron; one's worse half (익살로). ¶~다운 husband-like // ~의 권리 marital rights // ~ 있는 몸 [여자] a married woman / ~ 없는 single / unmarried // 사랑하는 ~ the lord of one's bosom / ~을 섬기다 be obedient [devoted / attentive / faithful] to one's husband / ~을 얻다 get a husband / get married // ~을 잃다 become a widow / be widowed / ~을 깔고 뭉기다 wear the breeches [pants] // 여자 팔자는 ~에게 달려 있다 A good [bad] husband makes a good [bad] wife. / A good Jack makes a good Jill.

남포[1] (화약) dynamite. ¶~질하다 dynamite /

shatter [destroy / blast / blow up] (a rock) with dynamite.

남포[2] [남포등] a lamp; an oil [a petroleum / a kerosene] lamp.
● **남포 심지** a lamp wick. **남폿불** lamplight; a lamp.

남풍(南風) the south [a southerly] wind; a wind from the south; the Auster.

남하(南下) southward advance; southward movement. **남하하다** go [come] south; advance southwards. ¶자유를 찾아 ~ come to the south seeking for freedom // 부대는 남하했다 The unit moved south.

남학생(男學生) a schoolboy; a boy student.

남한(南韓) South Korea; ROK(▶ Republic of Korea의 약어).

남해(南海) the southern sea; the straits of Korea(현해탄).

남행(南行) going south; southing. **남행하다** go (down to the) south.
● **남행 열차** a south-bound train.

남향(南向) a southern exposure; facing (the) south. ¶~의 방 a room facing (the) south. **남향하다** face the south; be exposed to the south.
● **남향집** a house facing [looking towards] (the) south; a house open to the south; a house with a southern exposure.

남회귀선(南回歸線) the Tropic of (the) Capricorn.

남획(濫獲) (물고기의) indiscriminate fishing; (새·짐승 등의) indiscriminate hunting; reckless [excessive] fishing [hunting]; overfishing; overhunting. ¶그 새는 ~으로 멸종의 위기에 처해 있다 That species of bird is endangered because of overhunting. **남획하다** fish [hunt] recklessly [indiscriminately]; overfish; overhunt. ¶고래를 ~ catch whales in excessive numbers.

납 lead (기호 Pb); [화] plumbum. ¶~의 leaden.

납(蠟) wax; beeswax; white [refined] wax. ¶~으로 형을 뜨다 make a wax impression (of).

납(鑞) solder. ⇨땜납

납골(納骨) laying (a person's) ashes to rest. **납골하다** lay a person's ashes in a tomb. ¶아버지의 유골을 납골했다 We laid our father's ashes in the tomb.
● **납골당** a charnel house; [교회·묘지의 지하 납골소] a crypt; a vault.

납기(納期) (금전의) the time [period] for payment; (물품의) the appointed date [time limit] of delivery. ¶세금의 ~일 the date of tax payment // 소득세의 ~ the deadline for paying one's income tax // 수업료는 ~ 내에 납입할 것 School fees should be paid by the due date.

납덩이 a lead ingot.

납덩이같다 [얼굴이 창백하다] be pale; be dull as lead; [몸이 무겁다] be [feel] as heavy as lead.

납득(納得) [승낙] assent; consent; compliance; [이해] understanding; conviction; satisfaction. ¶~이 가는 설명 a satisfactory explanation // ~이 가지 않는 대답 an unsatisfactory answer // 그들이 그처럼 화를 낸 것에 ~이 간다 They had good reason to be so angry. / It is natural that they were so angry. // 비로소 ~이 가는군 Now it makes sense. **납득하다** [승낙하다] assent (to);

납땜

consent (to); [묵인하다] acquiesce in (a proposal); [이해하다] understand; comprehend; [알아듣다] listen to reason; [깨닫다] be convinced (of / that …); satisfy [persuade] oneself (of / that …). ¶당신이 하는 말은 납득할 수 없다 I cannot understand what you're saying. / Your story [explanation] is incomprehensible [unconvincing]. (▶ incomprehensible은 이해할 수 없다. unconvincing은 납득시킬 수 없다는 뜻) I am not satisfied with your account.∥그 이야기에는 납득할 수 없는 점이 있다 Some aspects of the story fail to convince me.∥납득할 수 있도록 설명하겠습니다 I will explain to your satisfaction.∥그 보고가 사실이라는 것을 납득하셨습니까 Have you satisfied yourself of the truth of the report? / Are you satisfied [convinced] that the report is true? ∥그것은 서로가 잘 납득한 후에 한 일이다 We did it by mutual agreement [consent].∥그는 납득할 수 없다는 얼굴이었다 He looked dubious [doubtful].∥구체적인 예를 들어 설명해 주어도 그는 좀처럼 납득하지 않을 게다 Even an explanation with concrete examples will not go down easily with him.∥이 설명으로 충분히 납득할 수 있는지요 Is this explanation enough for you?

납땜(鑞-) soldering. **납땜하다** solder (a leaky pot).
● **납땜인두** a soldering iron.

납량(納涼) enjoying the cool air; cooling oneself. **납량하다** enjoy the cool air; cool oneself.
● **납량객** people who go out to enjoy the cool evening breeze; a cool-breeze hunter. **납량특집** a special summer evening program.

납본(納本) [책의 납품] delivery of books; (출판물의 점검 등을 위한) presentation of a specimen copy; [납품된 책] a specimen copy (for censorship). **납본하다** deliver books (to); present a specimen copy to the authorities.

납부(納付) (금전의) payment; (물품의) delivery (of goods). ¶분할 ~ divided payments / payment on an installment basis. **납부하다** pay (taxes); deliver (goods); supply (goods). ¶세금을 ~ pay one's taxes.
● **납부금** (지불된) money paid; (지불할) money due. **납부 기한** the deadline for payment. **납부서** a statement of payment [delivery]. **납부자** a payer.

납북(拉北) kidnap(p)ing to the north. **납북하다** kidnap [abduct] (a person) to the north; hijack (an airplane) to the north.
● **납북 어선** [어부 / 인사] a fishing boat [a fisherman / a person] kidnaped to North Korea.

납세(納稅) payment of taxes; tax payment. **납세하다** pay one's taxes.
● **납세 고지서** tax papers; a notification for tax payment; a tax notice. **납세 관리인** a tax payment administrator; a tax manager. **납세 미필** (게시) Tax [Duty(물품세)] unpaid [in arrear]. **납세 신고** income tax returns. **납세액** the amount of one's taxes. **납세 의무** a legal obligation to pay one's taxes; liability to taxation. ¶국민은 ~를 진다 The people shall be liable to taxation. **납세자** a taxpayer. ¶고액 ~ a large taxpayer. **납세 증지** a tax payment stamp. **납세필** (게시) Tax

[Duty(물품세)] paid. **납세필증** a certificate of tax [duty] payment.

납신거리다 [입을 경망스럽게 놀려 말하다] chatter; patter; rattle; talk glib and flippant. ¶입을 ~ wag one's tongue / run off at the mouth.

납입(納入) payment. ⇨=납부
● **납입금** money paid; money due. ⇨=납부금 (⇨납부)

납작¹ [몸을 바닥에 대고 냉큼 엎드리는 모양] flat; low. ¶~ 엎드리다 lie down flat (on the ground, on one's belly, etc.) / fall prostrate ∥~ 절하다 bow with one's hands laid flat on the floor / bow low. **2** [입을 재빨리 벌렸다 닫는 모양] with one's mouth wide open. ¶~ 받아 먹다 seize upon [snatch up / gobble up] with one's mouth wide open.

납작납작¹ [입을] with one's mouth open. [서슴없이] without hesitation.

납작납작² [납작하게] flatwise; flatly; all flat. ¶떡을 ~ 썰다 cut a rice cake into flat pieces.

납작보리 pressed barley; rolled barley.

납작얼굴 a person with a flat face. ⇨=넓적이

납작코 [납작한 코] a flat [squat / button / button-shaped] nose; [코가 납작한 사람] a flat-nosed person.

납작하다 flat; low; thin. ¶납작하게 flatly / level∥납작한 얼굴의 flat-faced∥납작한 가슴 a flat chest∥납작하게 만들다 (형태를) make flat [low / thin] / [굴복시키다] snub / put down / beat (a person) hollow / bring (a person) to (his) knees∥모자를 납작하게 짜부라뜨리다 crush a hat∥납작해지다 (형태가) be flattened / become flat / be crushed flat / [끽소리 못하다] be shut up / be nonplus(s)ed / be dum(b)founded / be snubbed ∥코를 납작하게 하다 (구어) knock (a person) into a cocked hat∥그 녀석 코를 납작하게 해 줄 필요가 있다 I had him there.∥그는 좀 납작하게 해 줄 필요가 있다 He wants sitting on. ∥개구리가 차에 납작하게 깔려 죽었다 The frog was squashed as flat as pancake by a car.

납 중독(-中毒) lead poisoning.

납지(蠟紙) wax paper.

납지(鑞紙) silver paper. ⇨=은종이

납채(納采) wedding presents sent from the bridegroom's house to the bride's house. **납채하다** send wedding presents to the bride's house.

납치(拉致) (사람의) kidnaping; abduction; (물건의) seizure by force; hijacking. **납치하다** kidnap; carry away; take (a person) away [captive]; hijack. ¶여자를 ~ abduct a woman. ➔¶이북으로 납치되다 be kidnaped to north Korea∥카이로행 항공기가 납치되었다 A plane (bound) for Cairo was hijacked [skyjacked]. (▶ 비행기 이외의 경우에는 skyjacked는 쓸 수 없음)∥그의 아들은 납치당했다 His son was kidnapped. / Someone made off with his son.∥그는 반대파에 의해 납치되었다 He was abducted by an opposing group.
● **납치범** a kidnaper(유괴범); a hijacker(탈취범).

납폐(納幣) sending blue and red silks to the bride's house(행사); blue and red silks sent to the bride's house(예물). **납폐하다** send blue and red silks to the bride's house.

납품(納品) 〔물품을 바침〕 delivery of goods; 〔바친 물품〕 delivered goods. ¶그 책은 ~을 완료했습니다 We have completed the delivery of the books. / We have already delivered the books. **납품하다** deliver (goods); supply (the government with goods). ¶우리는 저 병원에 기기를 납품하고 있다 We supply the hospital with equipment. // 부품은 수요일까지 납품해 주시오 Please supply us with the parts[deliver the parts to us] by Wednesday.
● **납품서** a statement of delivery. **납품업자** a supplier.

납회(納會) the last[final] meeting of the year; (증권 거래소의) the last[closing] session of the month.

낫 (자루가 짧은 것) a sickle; (자루가 긴 것) a scythe. ¶~으로 벼를 베다 cut rice with a sickle // ~으로 풀을 베다 mow grass with a sickle / sickle down weeds / scythe grass.

 낫 놓고 기역 자도 모른다(속담) be so ignorant as not to know his ABC; can hardly read or write; do not know A from B; be utterly illiterate.

낫다¹ 〔병이〕 recover (from illness); get well; be cured; (상처 등이) heal. ¶낫지 않는 incurable // 저절로 ~ get well of itself / heal by itself / clear up // 낫게 하다 〔고치다〕 heal / cure(▶ heal은 주로 외부 상처에, cure는 질병에 쓰임) // 그 나이 많은 의사는 그들의 상처를 낫게 했다 The old doctor healed their wounds. // 당신의 슬픔은 세월이 낫게 해 줄 것이다 Time will heal your grief. // 내 기침은 이 약으로 나았다 I got rid of my cough with this medicine. // 감기는 나았소 Have you got over your cold? // 저 병은 현대 의학으로도 낫지 않습니다 Even modern medical science has no cure for that disease. // 상처가 완전히 나을 때까지 움직여서는 안 됩니다 You must lie still until the wound has healed completely. // 환자는 자기의 병이 낫지 않는 병이라는 것을 알고 있었다 The patient knew his disease was incurable[past remedy]. // 병이 나아 갈 때 조심해야 합니다 You must take good care of yourself when you are convalescing [starting to get better].

낫다² prefer (than); superior (to); preferable (to); best (another); surpass; excel; exceed; outdo; have an advantage (over). ¶보다 나은 지혜로 by superior wisdom[cunning] // …보다 조금 나은 정도의 better by a hair's breadth[just a little better] than … // 나아지다 become better / be improved // 누구보다도 ~ surpass[be superior to] all // …보다 나은 것이 없다 nothing can be better than … / the best way is to do … // 아버지보다 ~ outdo[surpass] one's father // 아이를 보다 나은 학교에 보내다 send one's children to a better school // 영어에서는 그가 다른 학생들보다 ~ He excels the other boys in English. / 건강은 재산보다 ~ Health is above wealth. // 셰익스피어는 그 재능이 다른 모든 인간보다 훨씬 ~ The genius of Shakespeare transcends that of all other human beings. // 모국보다 나은 곳은 없다 There is no better place than our mother country. // 피로할 때는 목욕보다 나은 것이 없다 There is nothing to touch[beat] a hot bath when you are tired. // 이것은 그것보다 나으면 나았지 못하지는 않다 This is in no way[not at all] inferior to that. // 그가 자네보다 나을 것이 하나도 없네 He has no advantage over you. / (미국 구어) He has nothing on you. // 내 집보다 나은 곳은 없다 There's no place like home. // 이 점에서는 그보다 나은 사람이 없다 He is second to none in this respect. / In this respect he is unrivaled. // 나로서는 배반하기보다는 가난이 ~ I prefer poverty to treachery. // 조금뿐이라도 없는 것보다는 ~ Something is better than nothing. / Half a loaf is better than no bread. / 늦더라도 전혀 안하는 것보다는 ~ Better late than never. // 그렇게 살 바에야 차라리 죽는 게 ~ I would rather[sooner] die than lead such a life. / I prefer death to such a life. // 그런 일에 돈을 쓰려면 차라리 버리는 편이 ~ You might as well throw money away as spend it on such a thing. // 맨션이라고 해 봤자 연립 주택보다 좀 나을 정도다 Though called a "mansion" it is not much better than a tenement house).

낫살 a mature age. ⇨ 나잇살(⇨나이)

낫질하다 scythe; use[wield] a scythe[sickle].

낭군(郎君) (my) dear husband[hubby].

낭독(朗讀) (a) reading (aloud); (a) recitation(암송); (연설투의) (a) declamation. ¶햄릿의 ~ a recital of Hamlet // 각본 ~ dramatic reading // 자작시의 ~회를 열다 give a recital[public reading] of one's own poems. **낭독하다** read aloud (to a person); recite; declaim; give[deliver] a reading (of). ¶셰익스피어의 작품을 ~ give a reading of Shakespeare // 영시를 ~ recite an English poem // 연설문을 ~ read a speech (from notes) / read an address.
● **낭독법** elocution. **낭독자** a reader; a reciter.

낭떠러지 a cliff; (바다에 면한) a bluff; (깎아지른) a precipice. ¶~의 소나무 a pine tree hanging over a cliff // ~의 가장자리 the edge of a precipice // ~에서 떨어지다[내려다보다] fall[look] over a precipice // ~를 기어오르다 climb (up) a cliff // 거기에는 ~가 깎아지른 듯 내리닫고 있다 The bluff falls away sharply there.

낭랑하다(朗朗-) (목소리가) clear and ringing; sonorous; full; clarion; silvery (voice); (달빛 등이) bright and clear. ¶낭랑한 목소리로 in a rich, resonant voice.

낭만(浪漫) being romantic.
● **낭만주의** romanticism. **낭만주의자** a romanticist. **낭만파** 〔낭만주의를 신봉하는 유파〕 the romantic school; 〔낭만주의 신봉자〕 the romanticists.

낭만적(浪漫的) romantic. ¶~인 생각에 잠기다 indulge in romantics.

낭보(朗報) good[happy / glad / cheering] news; glad tidings.

낭비(浪費) waste; extravagance; squandering; wasteful spending; dissipation; prodigality. ¶국가 자원의 ~ the squandering of the nation's resources // 전기의 ~를 막다 prevent waste of electricity // 공무원의 공금 ~를 단속하다 caution government officials against being extravagant with public funds // 묘안이 없을 때는 아무리 생각해 봐야 시간 ~다 It is a waste of time to think a matter over when one has no good ideas. // 우리는 그런 ~는 할 수 없어요 We cannot afford to be that extravagant. **낭비하다** waste; use [spend] wastefully; use to no purpose; dis-

sipate; throw away; squander; be prodigal of. ¶낭비하는 wasteful // 보잘것없는 일에 시간을 ~ waste time doing unimportant things // 그는 재산을 낭비했다 He wasted[squandered] his fortune. // 요즘 아이들은 물건을 낭비한다 Today's children waste things. // 시간을 낭비하지 마라 Save your time.
● **낭비벽** spendthrift habits. ¶~이 있다 have [be in] the habit of wasting money (on luxury). **낭비자** a waster; (금전의) a spendthrift.

낭설(浪說) a wild[false] rumor; an unfounded[a groundless] report. ¶~을 퍼뜨리다 set a false rumor afloat // ~을 믿다 take rumor as it is // ~이 퍼지다 a rumor is abroad [current / circulated] // …이라는 ~이 떠돌고 있다 There is a rumor afloat (that) …. / Rumor has it (that) …. / It is noised abroad (that) …. // 그것은 전혀 ~이다 That is a pure fabrication.

낭송(朗誦) recitation; reading. ¶각본 ~ reading a play / (배우의) rehearsal. **낭송하다** recite; give a recitation; read aloud; narrate. ¶시를 ~ recite a poem.
● **낭송자** a reciter.

낭음(朗吟) recitation; a recital. **낭음하다** recite (a poem); sing.

낭자 (딴머리) a chignon; a toupee.
낭자(娘子) a virgin; a maiden; a maid.
● **낭자군** Amazons; Amazonian troops.

낭자하다(狼藉—) 1 [산재하여 어지럽다] be in wild disorder; be in great confusion; be scattered all over. ¶유혈이 ~ be covered with blood. 2 [시끌벅적하다] (서술적) be widely rumored[spread]; be gossiped about; be in everybody's mouth.

낭종(囊腫) [의] a cystoma (pl. ~s, ~ta); a cystic tumor. ¶난소 ~ anovarian cystoma.

낭중(囊中) one's pocket; one's purse. ¶~ 무일푼이다 be penniless / be stonebroke / have not a penny in one's purse // ~ 무일푼이 되다 become[go] penniless / (미국 속어) go broke.
● **낭중물**(一物) what is in one's pocket; things one has with him.

낭창낭창하다 pliant; pliable; flexible; limber; supple. ¶낭창낭창한 대나무 pliant bamboo // 낭창낭창한 나뭇가지 a flexible[pliable] twig / a switch.

낭패(狼狽) [실패] failure; frustration; defeat; miscarriage; a blunder; a fiasco; (곤경) (a) trouble; straits; a fix. ¶영어를 잘 몰라 ~다 The trouble is that I don't know English very well. // 이것이 ~로구나 Good heavens! / We are in for it. / What a most awkward case [way] this is! **낭패하다** fail (in); fall down (on / at); make a failure; meet with failure; be frustrated; fall through; miss fire; be in a fix[dilemma].

낭하(廊下) 1 a passage (way). ⇨ ᵇ복도 2 the servants' quarters (on both sides of the gate). ⇨ ᵃ행랑

낮 [해가 떠 있는 동안] day; the daytime; [한낮] noon; noonday; noontime; midday; high noon. ¶~에 by day / in the daytime / during the day(time) // 달이 ~같이 밝다 The moon is as bright as day. // ~에 보니 그것은 낡은 옷이었다 Seen in the daylight, the dress looked worn-out. // 그는 ~에는 농사를 짓고 밤에는 책을 읽고 있다 He works on a farm by day and reads books by night.

낮 말은 새가 듣고 밤 말은 쥐가 듣는다(속담) Walls[Pitchers] have ears.

낮거리 sexual intercourse performed in the (broad) daytime. **낮거리하다** have sexual intercourse in the daytime.

낮결 early afternoon; the first half of the afternoon. ¶비는 그날 ~부터 오기 시작했다 It began raining early that afternoon.

낮다 1 (높이·정도가) low; (숫자가) low; small. ¶낮은 언덕 a low hill // 낮은 임금 low wages // 낮아지다 become low / lower / go down // 생활수준이 ~ have a low standard of living // 이 방은 천장이 ~ This room has a low ceiling. // 나는 코가 ~ I have a flat nose. // 물은 낮은 곳으로 흐른다 Water tries to find its level.
2 (신분이) low; humble; mean. ¶신분이 ~ (태생이) be of low social position // 지위가 ~ be low in position / be placed low (in a company) // 그는 나보다 신분이 ~ He is beneath me in rank(▶ beneath는 단순히 쓰면 상대를 얕보는 뜻이 들어 있음. 단순히 상하 관계를 나타낼 때는 below를 씀).
3 (목소리가) low. ¶낮은 음 a low-pitched sound // 낮은 목소리 a low voice / (속삭임) a whisper // 낮은 소리로 말하다 speak in a low voice / speak under one's breath / whisper // 그들은 갑자기 목소리가 낮아졌다 They suddenly lowered their voices[began to speak in whispers]. // 그는 그것에 이제 싫증이 나고 물렸다고 낮은 목소리로 말했다 He said in an undertone that he was sick and tired of it.

낮도깨비 [낮에 나타난 도깨비] a goblin [ghost] haunting in broad daylight; (체면 없이 마구 행동하는 사람) a shameless bastard; a woman in a heavy makeup.

낮도둑 [낮에 훔치는 도둑] a sneak thief; a noonday thief; (비어) a gutter prowler; [몰염치한 욕심쟁이] a shark; a shameless hog; a greedy[grasping] person.

낮은말(賤한 말) a vulgar word; a vulgarism.
낮은음자리표(—音—標) [음] the bass clef; the F clef.

낮일 day work.

낮잠 a (midday) nap; a noon's nap; a siesta; forty winks; (속어) a snooze. ¶~을 자다 take[have] a nap[siesta] // 드러누워 ~ 자다 lie down for a nap.

낮잡다 estimate[rate / appraise / evaluate] low; underestimate; underrate. ¶낮잡은 액수 [숫자] a conservative amount[figure] // 낮잡아서 at a conservative[moderate] estimate // 아무리 낮잡아도 at the most sparing[the lowest] estimate / at (the very) least // 건물 값을 ~ rate the price of a building low // 낮잡아 평가하다 underrate / make a conservative[moderate / low] estimate // 기부금의 총액은 낮잡아도 백만 원은 될 것이다 The total sum of the contributions is conservatively estimated at a million won. // 그는 아무리 낮잡아도 초등학교 선생쯤은 되어 보인다 He must be a primary[(미) grade] school teacher at the very least.

낮참 1 [점심 전후에 먹는 간식] a snack taken before or after lunch. 2 [점심 전후의 휴식 시간] a recess before or after lunch.

낮추다 1 [낮게 하다] lower; make low; drop; bring [let] down; (음성을) subdue; drop; lower; sink; turn down(라디오를). ¶목소리를 ~ lower one's voice // 허리를 ~ bend over /

stoop // 고도를 ~ reduce one's altitude // 스테레오[텔레비전]의 소리를 ~ turn down the volume of a stereo [television] // 나는 이야기의 수준을 낮추어 다 알기 쉽게 했다 I simplified [lowered the level of] my speech to make it understandable. // 그 기장[조종사]은 기수를 낮추었다 The pilot lowered the nose of the plane. // 그는 정도를 좀 낮추어 강의했다 He simplified the content of his lecture [gave an easier lecture] when he spoke to us. // 좀 자세를 낮추어 주시겠습니까 Could you bend your knees a bit [lower your head a little]? // 그는 목소리를 낮추어 말했다 He spoke in a restrained tone [in an undertone].
2 [강등시키다] reduce (a soldier) to a lower rank; (미) demote (to); [(품질을) 저하시키다] degrade; debase (the quality). ¶(공무원이) 1호봉 낮추어지다 be demoted by a step in payroll.
3 [하대하다] speak in familiar [plain] terms. ¶말씀 낮추십시오 Please drop honorifics. / Your words sound too polite to me.

낮추보다 look down on [upon]; have a low opinion (of); hold (a person) cheap [in contempt]; [낮잡아] undervalue; make a low estimate of. ¶가난하다고 해서 그를 낮추보지는 마라 You should not despise [look down upon] him because he is poor.

낮춤말 [언] [하대 말] intimate [friendly] speech [terms]; [겸손어] humble [modest] words.

낯 1 [얼굴] a face; a visage; features (이목구비); (속어) a phiz; (미국 속어) a pan; [얼굴 표정] a look; looks; a countenance. ¶두 손으로 ~을 가리고 with one's face buried in one's hands // 웃는 ~으로 사람을 대하다 welcome (a person) with a smile // ~을 가리다 cover [hide] one's face // ~을 대하다 face each other / look at each other // 부끄러워서 ~을 들지 못하다 be ashamed to face (a person) // ~을 씻다 wash oneself [one's face] / have a wash / wash up // ~을 찡그리다 make a wry face / frown / contort [pucker up] one's face // 좋은 [좋지 않은] ~을 하다 look pleased [displeased] / look satisfied [dissatisfied] / 싫은 ~을 하다 make a bad face / look hurt [displeased] // wear a frown // 그녀는 비웃는 ~으로 나를 보았다 She threw a look of contempt at me.
2 [면목·체면] face; honor; dignity; prestige. ¶…의 ~을 보아 taking (a person's) face [reputation / honor] into consideration / for (a person's) sake // ~에 똥칠을 하다 disgrace / discredit / dishonor / scandalize / sully [stain] (a person's) good name / be a disgrace (to) / bring a disgrace [dishonor] (on) // ~이 깎이다 be put out of countenance / lose (one's) face [countenance / reputation / honor / dignity] / disgrace [humiliate] oneself // 볼 ~이 없다 have no face [countenance] / be ashamed of (oneself) // ~이 팔려 있다 be widely known / be popular // ~을 못 들다 be ashamed of oneself (toward a person) / cannot face (a person) // ~을 세우다 save (a person's) honor [face] / relieve (a person) from disgrace / keep (a person) in countenance // 너를 볼 ~이 없다 I'm ashamed to see you. // 그에게 부탁할 ~이 없다 I cannot with any grace make the request to him. // 무슨 ~을 들고 다시 너를 보겠니 I am too ashamed of myself (ever) to see you again. // 세상 사람들을 대할 ~이 없다 I dare not show myself [my face] in public. // How can I face people? // 내 ~을 보아 그 애를 용서해 주시오 Please forgive the boy for my sake [just to save my face]. // 내가 어제 저지른 실수로, 오늘은 남 보기가 ~ 뜨겁고 매우 곤혹스럽다 Because of the blunder I committed yesterday, I'm too embarrassed [abashed] today to look anyone in the face.

낯(이) 두껍다 thick-skinned; shameless; unabashed; unblushing; brazen-faced; impudent; saucy; audacious; cheeky. ¶낯 두껍게도 …하다 have the nerve [heart / face / impudence / audacity] to (do) … / be shameless [impudent] enough to (do) … / make bold to (ask a favor) // 그는 낯 두껍게도 돈을 꾸러 왔었다 He had the crust to ask for a loan.

낯을 붉히다 become [turn] red in the face; (부끄러워) blush (with [for] shame); color up; (흥분하여) flush (up) (with excitement); (성나서) redden [flush / turn purple] (with anger); get angry; be enraged. ¶낯을 붉히고 with a blush / blushingly / angrily (성나서) // 그는 여간해서 낯을 붉히지 않는다 He is slow to get angry. // 그녀는 부끄러워 낯을 붉혔다 Shame flushed her cheeks. / Her face flamed with shame.

낯가리다 1 (어린애가) be afraid [shy] of strangers; be bashful. ¶낯가리어 울다 cry at the sight of strangers // 이 애는 아직도 낯가린다 This child is still bashful in front of strangers. // 그 아기는 엄마를 닮은 여자라면 낯가리지 않는다 The baby takes to women who resemble his mother. **2** [차별 대우 하다] treat with discrimination; discriminate against (a person). **3** [체면을 세우다] save one's face [honor]; relieve (a person) from disgrace; keep up [maintain] appearances.

낯가죽 the skin of the face.

낯가죽(이) 두껍다 have lots of nerve (in one); have plenty of cheek; be brazen-faced; be thick-skinned. ¶낯가죽이 두꺼운 brazenfaced / thick-skinned / cheeky / impudent / shameless // 참 낯가죽도 두꺼운 녀석이다 What a brazen-faced fellow he is! / What an affront! / What nerve he's got!

낯간지럽다 ashamed; blushed; conscience-stricken. ¶그토록 칭찬해 주니 ~ So much praise embarrasses me [makes me feel awkward]. // 이 작품으로 상을 타다니 약간 ~ I feel a bit embarrassed to get a prize for a work like this. // 나는 낯간지러워 그런 말은 할 수 없다 I am ashamed to say such a thing.

낯나다 [생색이 나다] gain [win] honor; get credit; reflect honor [credit] on (a person); feel oneself honored; (something) do (a person) credit.

낯내다 [생색을 내다] take credit to oneself (for); do oneself proud [credit]; act so as to gain the respect of others. ¶낯내기 위하여 기부하다 make a donation just to reflect credit on oneself // 자네 이 하찮은 선물로 낯내려 드네그려 You are doing yourself proud by giving me this small present, aren't you. // 그런 일로 낯내지는 못한다 We could not get credit for that. / That is nothing to be proud

낯바닥 〈속〉 a face; a visage. ⇨낯1
낯부끄럽다 ashamed; shameful; disgraceful. ¶낯부끄러운 행위 a shameful[disgraceful] behavior[conduct].
낯빛 complexion; colo(u)r. ⇨얼굴빛⟨얼굴⟩
낯설다 〔알지 못하다〕 unknown; 〔친숙하지 않다〕 strange; unfamiliar. ¶낯선 세계 an unknown world / the unknown // 낯선 사람 a stranger // 회의의 자리에는 낯선 얼굴들이 보였다 There was a row of unfamiliar faces at the meeting table. // 이것은 낯선 광경이다 This is an unfamiliar[a new] scene to me. // 나는 술 취한 사람들을 어렸을 때부터 보아 와서 낯설지 않다 I have been used to seeing drunken people since my childhood. // 나는 낯선 사람 앞에서는 언제나 조심스러워진다 I am always shy with strangers. // 자네 어쩐지 전연 낯선 사람[아주 남]으로는 느껴지지 않는다 For some reason you don't seem at all like a stranger to me.
낯없다 (have) not face to; (구어) not in a position to; ashamed of (oneself); (be put) out of countenance. ¶정말 낯없습니다 I am really ashamed of myself. / I have no excuse to offer.
낯익다 (사람이) (get / become) used to seeing (a thing); (사물이) familiar (to); well known (to). ¶낯익은 얼굴 a familiar face // 서로 낯익은 사이다 be on nodding terms with each other[one another] / be a nodding acquaintance // 낯익은 얼굴이지만 이름은 모르겠다 I recognize him but don't know his name. // 그 사람 낯익은 얼굴인데 I fancy I have seen him somewhere before. / I remember seeing him once. / His face seems familiar to me.
낯익히다 get (a person) familiar with oneself; cultivate the familiarity of. ¶나는 이곳을 아직 낯익히지 못했다 I am as yet rather new to this place.
낯짝 〈속〉 a face; a visage. ⇨낯1 ¶무슨 ~으로 부탁을 하러 왔느냐 How cheeky you are to come to ask me a favor!
낱 a piece; an item; a unit; each piece.
낱개 (-個) a piece; each piece; one item in a set. ¶~에 (얼마) a piece / each // ~ 100원 a hundred won a piece[each] // ~로 파는 loose (flowers / pencils) // ~로 팔기 selling piecemeal / selling things loose // ~로 팔다 sell piece by piece / sell by the piece // 이 가게에서는 세탁 비누를 ~로 판다 They sell washsoap by the cake[stick / bar] in this store. // 이 포크는 ~로는 팔지 않습니다. 세트로 팝니다 You can't buy these forks separately[just a fork by itself], they are only sold in place settings. // 그 디너 세트는 ~로는 팔지 않습니다 We do not sell single pieces[items] of the dinner set.
낱권 (-卷) a volume (in a set); a single volume(단권); an odd volume(짝이 안 맞는).
낱낱이 〔하나하나〕 one by one; piece by piece; singly; individually; severally; separately; 〔모조리〕 in everything; all; entirely; without omission[exception]; each and every one; in every case; 〔자세히〕 in detail; in full; fully. ¶이름을 ~ 들다 mention[single out] each by name // 물건을 ~ 세다 〔조사하다〕 count[examine] articles one by one // 집을 ~ 방문하다 make a door-to-door visit // ~ 간섭하다 meddle in everything // 그는 내가 하는 일에 ~ 트집을 잡는다 He finds faults with everything I do. // ~ 보고[질문]하다 report[ask questions] in detail // ~ 말하다 particularize / give full particulars // ~ 설명하다 give full explanation.
낱돈 small change; loose money[cash]; a small coin; money of small denominations. ¶~으로 바꾸다 change[break] (a 1,000 won bill) into small change.
낱말 a word; a vocabulary. ⇨단어
낱알 a grain (of rice). ¶~이 굵다[잘다] be large-[fine-] grained / be oversized[undersized].
낱장 (-張) a sheet[piece] (of paper); a copy (of photograph); a leaf.
낳다¹ 1 〔출산하다〕 bear; give birth to; be delivered of; bring forth; breed(동물이); (알을) lay (eggs); spawn(물고기가). ¶자기가 낳은 자식 one's own child // 소가 송아지를 ~ a cow calves a calf // 말이 망아지를 ~ a horse foals a colt[filly] // 개가 새끼를 ~ a dog drops[has] a pup // 그녀는 언제 아기를 낳을까 When will she have a[the] baby? (▶ 임신 중의 여자에 대해서 말할 때는 the baby, 그렇지 않으면 a baby) // 그녀는 사내아이를 낳았다 She had[gave birth to] a (baby) boy. / She became the mother of a baby boy. // 우리 집 고양이가 새끼를 낳았다 Our cat had kittens. // 이 닭은 이제 알을 낳지 못하게 되었다 This hen has stopped laying (eggs). // 돼지는 1년에 몇 번 새끼를 낳는가 How many times a year does a sow have a litter? // 물고기는 일반적으로 많은 알을 낳는다 Generally fish spawn many eggs. // 그녀는 그와의 사이에서 자식을 일곱 낳았다 She has borne him seven children.
2 〔생기게 하다·배출하다〕 bring forth; produce; yield; bear; give rise to. ¶좋은 결과를 ~ produce[get] good results // 그는 한국이 낳은 최대의 건축가다 He is the greatest architect Korea has ever produced. // 그 뉴스는 여러 가지 소문을 낳았다 The news gave rise to a variety of rumors. // 그의 행동은 의혹을 낳기 쉽다 His conduct is likely to arouse[excite] suspicion. // 이 투자는 9퍼센트의 이자를 낳을 가망이 있다 This investment is expected to bear[yield] 9 percent interest. // 돈이 돈을 낳는다 Money begets money.
낳다² (실을) spin; make yarn; (피륙을) weave. ¶무명실을 ~ spin thread[yarn] out of cotton / spin cotton into yarn // 명주를 ~ weave silk.
내¹ 〔연기〕 smoke; fume.
내² (a) smell; (an) odor. ⇨냄새1 ¶무엇이 타는 ~가 나지 않습니까 Can't you smell something burning?
내³ 〔시내〕 a stream; a streamlet; a brook; a brooklet; a rivulet; a rill; (미) a creek. ¶~를 건너다 cross[go across] a river / (걸어서) ford a stream / wade (across) a stream // ~를 거슬러 올라가다 go up the river / go up stream // ~를 끼고 가다 go along a stream // 이 ~는 흐름이 완만하다 This brook flows lazily[gently].
내⁴ 1 〔나〕 (주격: 내가) I. ¶~가 했다 I (myself) did it. // ~가 생각해도 나 자신에 정나미가 떨어진다 I am disgusted with myself. // ~가 나쁘오 I (myself) am to blame. / It was my (own) fault.

2 [나의] (소유격) my. ¶~ 것 mine.∥~ 집 my home[house]∥~ 것 네 것 mine and thine∥~ 것 네 것을 혼동하다 get confused as to what is (his) and what isn't / confound meum and tuum∥~ 것 네 것을 가리지 않다 make no distinction between meum and tuum / draw no line between what is one's own and what isn't∥그는 ~ 친구다 He is a friend of mine. / He is my friend.∥무슨 일이 있어도 저 그림을 ~ 것으로 하고 싶다 I want to make that picture mine no matter what the cost.

-내 [내내] through; throughout; all through; in the course of (the day). ¶겨우~ throughout[all through] the winter∥금주~ all this week∥일 년~ all the year round / the year around∥그해 봄~ all during the spring of that year∥이 나무는 일 년~ 푸르다 This tree is green all the year round. / This tree is evergreen.∥그 섬은 일 년~ 덥다 Summer never dies in that island.

내(內) within; within the scope of. ¶기한 ~에 within the period (of)∥권한 ~에 within the scope of authority∥선박 ~에서 on board [aboard] the ship.

내가다 take[bring] out; carry out[away]; out with (something); remove. ¶몰래 [슬쩍] ~ smuggle (something) out of (the house)∥나는 정원에 의자를 내갔다 I brought a chair into the garden.

내각(內角) [수] an interior angle; [야구] the inside (corner). ¶~을 찌르다 pitch a ball inside∥삼각형의 ~의 합은 2직각과 같다 The three (interior) angles of a triangle add up to[are equal to] two right angles.

내각(內閣) a cabinet; [영] a ministry; [정부] the government; (미) the administration. ¶거국일치 ~ an all-nation Cabinet∥약체 ~ an effete[a frail] Cabinet∥연립 ~ a coalition cabinet / a fusion administration∥재야(在野)~ a shadow cabinet∥정당 ~ a party Cabinet∥초당파 ~ a nonparty Cabinet∥현 ~ the present Ministry[Cabinet]∥~의 분열 a split in the Cabinet∥~의 경질 a Cabinet [Ministerial] change / a change in the Ministry / a change of Ministry∥~의 위기 a Cabinet[Ministerial] crisis∥2대의 ~에 걸친 각료 a member of two administrations∥솔즈베리 ~ 시대에 during the Salisbury regime [ministry]∥~에 끼다 [입각하다] hold [occupy] a seat in the Cabinet / hold a portfolio / become a Cabinet Minister / go into the Cabinet∥~을 조직하다 form[organize] a Cabinet[Government / Ministry]∥~을 개편하다 reorganize[reshuffle] the Cabinet∥~을 쓰러뜨리다 overthrow[unseat] the Cabinet∥~이 흔들리고 있다 The Cabinet is tottering.∥Y~ 타도 Down with Prime Minister Y and his Cabinet.∥새 ~의 면면은 다음과 같다 The new Cabinet has been constructed [formed] as follow: ….

●**내각 각료** Cabinet members. **내각 불신임 투표** a vote of nonconfidence in the Cabinet. **내각 총사퇴** a general resignation of the Cabinet; a resignation of the Cabinet en bloc[in a body].

내갈기다 **1** [후려치다] thrash; slap; strike; hit. ¶몽둥이로 ~ club / cudgel∥채찍으로 ~ lash / whip∥뺨을 ~ slap (a person's) cheek[face] / slap (a person) on the cheek.

2 [글씨를 마구 쓰다] scribble; scrawl; dash. ¶편지를 ~ dash off a letter / scribble a few lines.

내객(來客) a caller; a visitor; a guest; (집합적) company. ¶오늘은 ~이 많았다 We have had a good many visitors[much company] today.

내걸다 1 [게양하다] put up; hang out (a sign / a lantern); hoist; display (a flag). ¶간판을 ~ put up[set up / hang out] a sign[signboard]∥기를 ~ put up[hang out] a flag∥시내 가가호호마다 8·15를 기념하여 국기를 내걸었다 Every house in the city put up the national flag in commemoration of the Liberation Day.

2 [목숨 등을 내놓다] risk (one's (own) life / one's head); stake; hazard. ¶목숨을 내걸고 at the risk[hazard / peril] of one's life.

3 [내세우다] stand for; advocate; maintain; (문제 등을) take up (a problem). ¶슬로건을 내걸고 under the slogan (of)∥조건을 ~ impose conditions∥이상을 ~ hold up an ideal∥방침을 ~ declare[state] one's policy.

내경(內徑) **1** the inside diameter. **2** [총·포 등의 구경] the gauge; the caliber; the bore.

내계(內界) the inner world[sphere]; the internal world.

내공(內攻) [의] retrocedence; retrocession. **내공하다** strike in[inward]; retrocede.

내공(耐空) endurance in flying[flight]. **내공하다** stay in the air; make an endurance flight.

내과(內科) (병원의) the internal department; [대과학] internal medicine. ¶~의 권위자 an authority on internal diseases∥~의 치료를 받다 be internally treated.

●**내과 병동** a medical ward. **내과 병원 / 내과 의원** a hospital (for internal diseases); a medical establishment. **내과의**(-醫) a physician; an internist; a medical practitioner(개업의). **내과 질환** an internal disease. **내과 치료** internal treatment.

내과피(內果皮) [식] the endocarp.

내관(內官) a eunuch. ⇨환관

내관(內觀) [불] inward contemplation[looking]; [심] introspection. **내관하다** introspect; turn over's thoughts inward.

내관(來觀) a visit (for inspection). **내관하다** visit; view; inspect.

내교섭(內交涉) preliminary[informal] negotiations. **내교섭하다** carry on preliminary negotiations (with).

내구(耐久) [지속] endurance; persistence; [지구] permanence; durability.

●**내구 경쟁** an endurance contest. **내구력 / 내구성** durability; persistence; lasting quality; staying power; [지구력] stamina. ¶~이 있다 be durable / be lasting / last[hold out] long / be of lasting quality / wear long [well] (옷·신발 등이). **내구 소비재** consumer(s') durables; durable consumer goods. **내구재** durable[hard] goods; durables.

내국(內國) home; the home country. ¶~산의 domestic / native / home-grown / home-produced / homebred (horses)∥~제의 of home [domestic] manufacture[make] / home-made∥~의 home / domestic / internal / native.

●**내국 공채** an internal[a domestic] loan

내규 [debt]. **내국 무역** home [inland / domestic] trade. **내국세** an inland [internal] duty [tax]. **내국인** a native. **내국환** domestic [inland] exchange. **내국환 어음** an inland bill.

내규(內規) private rules [regulations]; customary rules; bylaws. ¶회사의 ~ the bylaw of a business company // ~에 위반되다 [위반하다] violate [infringe] the bylaw / offend against the tradition // 그것은 협회 [회사] 의 ~에 (…이라고) 규정되어 있다 That is provided [laid down] in the bylaws of the association [company] (that …).

내근(內勤) indoor [inside] service; desk [inside / room] duty; an office [desk] work. ¶~으로 전직되다 be transferred to desk duty [indoor service] // 그는 ~이다 He works in the office. // 그는 올해 ~으로 전직되었다 This year he has been transferred to a desk job. **내근하다** work inside [indoors]; be on room duty.
● **내근 경찰관** a policeman on inside duty; a desk policeman.

내기 (금품을 거는) a bet; a wager; betting; staking; gambling. ¶돈 ~ a money bet / betting money // 과자 ~ a bet of cakes // 큰 [작은] ~ a heavy [paltry / petty] bet / high [low] stakes // ~에 이기다 [지다] win [lose] a wager [bet] // ~ 마작 [바둑] 을 하다 [두다] play mah-jongg [baduk] for money [stakes] // ~에 응하다 take [accept] a wager [bet] // ~ 로 돈을 잃다 lose money in [on] a bet / lose one's bet / gamble away (one's fortune). **내기하다** wager (on); bet (on); lay [have] a wager (on); make a bet (on); lay down a stake; see who will win (in a contest). ¶트럼프로 ~ gamble at cards // …과 ~ bet against [with] (a person) / lay (a person) a bet // 백원 ~ make a bet of 100 won // 그는 나에게 오천 원 내기하자고 했다 He offered to bet me five thousand won (that it won't rain tomorrow). // 내기하자 I will lay you a bet. / I will bet with you. // 축구 경기에 대해서 그와 5불 내기했다 I made a bet [wager] of [I bet / I wagered] five dollars with him on a football game. // 어느 편이 이기는지 내기하자 Let's make [have] a bet as to which side will win. // 그가 한 것이 틀림없어, 내기해도 좋아 I'm sure he did it, I'd even bet on it. // 물속에서 누가 오래 있나 내기하자 Let us see who can remain under water longest.
● **내기 돈** stakes; a bet; a wager.

-내기 1 […태생] a person from …; a person born in [at] …. ¶서울~ a person from [born in] Seoul / a Seoulite // 시골~ a person from the country / a country born person. 2 […한 사람]. ¶풋~ a greenhorn / an inexperienced person.

내깔기다 discharge forcefully [at random]. ¶똥을 ~ defecate // 오줌을 ~ urinate.

내남없이 without any exceptions to us all; irrespective of persons; indiscriminately; anyone; anybody; everybody; everyone. ¶~ 다 같은 처지에 있다 We are all in the same boat. // 그것은 ~ 다 아는 사실이다 It is a fact known to everybody.

내 내 all the time [way]; (all) through; throughout; all along (the line); all during (the vacation). ¶1년 ~ throughout the year / all the year round / the year around / from year's end to year's end / [줄곧] always // 아침 ~ all through the morning // ~ 선두를 달리다 lead the race from start to finish // 우리는 아침 8시부터 밤 9시까지 ~ 일했다 We were made to work without a break from 8 in the morning till 9 at night. // 우리는 하룻밤 ~ 술을 마셨다 We drank all through the night. // 그녀는 3시간 ~ 피아노를 쳤다 She played the piano for three hours running [on end / straight]. // 그 후 ~ 나는 여기서 살고 있다 I've lived here ever since. // 나는 지난봄 ~ 부산에 있었다 I stayed at Busan all last spring. // 대전서부터 ~ 서서 와야만 했다 (차중에서) I was kept standing all the way from Daejeon. // 그 일은 다음 주 ~ 걸릴 것이다 The work will take all (of) next week. // 그녀는 4년 동안 ~ 수석이었다 She has been at the top of the class for the whole four-year period. // 그는 (1년) ~ 쪼들리고 있다 He is always in needy [straitened / narrow] circumstances. / He is badly off all the year round. / He remains always poor. // ~ 내가 주의하라고 말하지 않았느냐 Haven't I been warning you all this time? // ~ 안녕히 계십시오 Good-bye! / Farewell! / Good luck (to you)! / Peace be with you!

내내년(來來年) the year after next. ¶내년이나 ~ next year or the year after.

내내월(來來月) the month after next. ¶내월이나 ~ next month or the month after.

내년(來年) next year; the coming year. ¶~ 겨울 next winter // ~ 3월 next March / (in) March next (year) // ~ 초에 early next year // ~ 이맘때 about this time next year // ~의 오늘 this day next year // ~의 예정표 a schedule for next year [the coming year] // ~도 예산안 the budget for next year [next fiscal year] // 그는 ~ 5월에 [~ 이맘때] 귀국한다 He will return home next May [about this time next year]. // ~에 무슨 일이 일어나지는 아무도 모른다 There is no telling what will happen next year.

내놓다 1 (밖으로) put out; take out; bring out; pull [draw] out. ¶책상을 밖으로 ~ take a desk out // 주머니에서 돈을 ~ take [pull] money out of one's pocket // 창밖으로 머리를 ~ stick one's head out of the window // 횡령했던 돈을 도로 ~ disgorge the embezzled money / cough up the money one has embezzled.

2 (가둔 것을) set [make] free; free; liberate; let go [loose]; put [let] out of; release. ¶소를 목장에 ~ turn cattle out to graze / put cattle to grass // 개를 내놓아 기르다 leave a dog at large / give a dog free run of (one's house) // 죄수를 감옥에서 ~ let a prisoner out of jail / set a prisoner free / let go a prisoner.

3 [드러내다] expose; bare; show. ¶종아리를 ~ bare [expose] one's leg // 가슴을 ~ show [expose] one's chest // 어깨죽지를 ~ bare [expose] one's shoulders.

4 (팔려고) have (articles) out for sale; put up [offer] (a thing) for sale; place (a thing) on sale; [진열하다] exhibit (an article) at a show; put (an article) on show. ¶내놓은 집 a house for sale // 집을 ~ put up one's house for sale // 물건을 쇼윈도에 ~ exhibit an article in the show window // 그 회사는 완공 주택을 내놓을 예정이다 The company is

planning to offer ready-built houses for sale.∥금년에 이 회사에서 소형 승용차 두 종류를 시장에 내놓을 예정이다 Two types of compact cars are to be put on the market by this company this year.
5 〔발간하다〕 publish; issue; bring[put] out. ¶책을 ~ publish a book.
6 〔돈을〕 pay; give; contribute(기부); invest(투자). ¶교회 짓는 데 돈을 ~ contribute money for building a church∥사업에 돈을 ~ invest money in an enterprise∥선뜻 천만원을 ~ generously give a donation of ten million won (to / towards).
7 〔음식 등을〕 offer; serve (up); set out (a meal). ¶차를 ~ serve tea / offer (a person) a cup of tea∥술을 ~ serve up wine[drinks]∥과자를 ~ set cake before (a person)∥방석을 ~ offer (a person) a cushion.
8 〔제출하다〕 present; send in; submit (one's view); tender; bring forward[up]. ¶의안(議案)을 ~ present a bill∥사표를 ~ tender [send in / hand in] one's resignation∥명함을 ~ send in one's card∥회의에 동의안을 ~ bring forward a motion at the meeting∥나는 내놓을 만한 증거가 없다 I have no evidence to produce.
9 〔제외하다〕 exclude; except; leave out; omit. ¶토요일을 내놓고는 매일 수학이 들어 있다 We have a mathematics lesson every day except Saturdays.∥나를 내놓고는 다 부자다 All are rich but[except] me.
10 〔포기하다〕 give up; abandon; desert; leave; part with; resign; sacrifice. ¶지위를 ~ throw up[resign from] one's office[position]∥재산을 ~ deliver up one's possession / 〔제공하다〕 offer[place] one's property at the disposal of another∥목숨을 ~ lay down [sacrifice] one's life / risk[hazard] one's life∥그는 어렵게 차지했던 자리를 내놓을 수밖에 없었다 He was forced to resign from[give up] his post he had worked so hard to obtain.∥나는 아버지가 나에게 남겨 주신 시계를 내놓을 수밖에 없었다 I had to part with the watch my father had left me.

내다¹ 〔연기가〕 smoke; smolder; become smoky. ¶불이 낸다 The fire is smoking.∥난로가 낸다 The stove is smoking[smokes].∥생나무가 내기만 하고 타지 않는다 The green wood smolders and will not burn.∥되게 내는군 Oh, how smoky!

내다² **1** 〔밖으로〕 put out; 〔꺼내다〕 take out; bring out; pull[draw] out; 〔제시하다〕 show. ¶책상을 밖으로 ~ take a desk out∥표를 ~ show one's ticket∥차표를 내 주십시오 Please show (me) your ticket.
2 〔발휘하다〕 put[call] forth; muster[pluck / rouse / stir / summon] up (one's courage); exert; display. ¶기운을 ~ cheer up / brace oneself up∥온 힘을 ~ put forth all one's strength∥실력을 ~ display one's ability∥용기를 내라 Pluck[Screw] up your courage. / Take your courage in both hands.∥힘을 내어 당겨라 Pull with all your might.∥나는 있는 힘을 다 내어 공을 던졌다 Exerting[Calling forth] all my strength I threw the ball.∥용기를 내어 나는 그에게 물었다 I plucked up (my) courage and asked him.∥그는 시험에서 실력을 충분히 내지 못했다 He did not do himself justice[do as well as he could have (done)] in[(미)on] the examination.

3 〔이름을〕 attain[gain / win] distinction; distinguish; raise; elevate. ¶이름을 ~ distinguish oneself / make one's name familiar [known] to the public / make[win] a name (for oneself) / make oneself famous.
4 〔발설하다〕 set forth; put forward; start (a rumor); 〔감정 등을〕 vent; give vent to; give expression to; express. ¶화를 ~ get angry (at a matter / with a person) / take offense (at) / lose one's temper (with a person for something)∥소문을 ~ set a rumor afloat / circulate[spread] a rumor∥말을 ~ start talk / broach[get on] a subject∥비밀을 입밖에 ~ let out[divulge / reveal] a secret.
5 〔얻다〕 take; get; have; receive; obtain. ¶허가를 ~ take out[get] a license∥여권을 ~ have a passport issued / obtain[get] a passport∥빚을 ~ get[take out] a loan / raise a loan of money / borrow money (from / of).
6 〔만들다·마련하다〕 set up; make; fix; arrange (for). ¶길을 ~ make way (for) / build[open / cut] a road∥방을 ~ put a room in / build a room∥앉을자리를 ~ make[arrange] a seat / make room for (a person) to sit∥구멍〔창문〕을 ~ put in [make] an opening[a window]∥시간을 ~ arrange the hours / make[find] time (for something / to attend the meeting)∥저를 위해 시간을 10분만 내 주시지 않겠습니까 Could you spare ten minutes for[to see] me?∥나는 시간을 내어 부모님께 편지를 썼다 I made time to write to my parents.∥바쁜 스케줄에 매어 있는데도 그는 시간을 내어 회의에 참석했다 He made time in his busy schedule for a meeting[to attend a meeting].
7 〔출품하다〕 exhibit (an article) at a show; put (an article) on show.
8 〔보내다〕 send (a messenger); forward (goods); post (a letter); (미) mail (a letter); send out (an invitation). ¶황 씨 앞으로 낸 편지 a letter addressed to Mr. Hwang∥편지를 ~ send a letter / post[(미)mail] a letter∥초대장을 ~ send out an invitation.
9 〔발행·발간하다〕 publish; issue; bring[put] out. ¶새 잡지를 ~ publish a new magazine∥나는 5년 동안 책을 한 권도 내지 않았다 I haven't had a book out in five years.∥이 출판사는 잡지를 다섯 종류 내고 있다 This firm publishes[issues] five kinds of magazines.
10 〔발표하다〕 publish (a story in a magazine); print (an affair in a paper); insert (an article in a paper). ¶신문에 광고를 ~ put an ad in the papers / advertise in a newspaper[through the press] / place [run] an advertisement in a newspaper∥소설을 잡지에 ~ publish a story in a magazine.
11 〔제출하다〕 present; send in (an application); hand in (a composition); give in (one's examination paper); tender (one's resignation); submit (one's view); produce; bring out (evidence). ¶지원서를 ~ submit [send in] an application∥의안을 ~ present a bill∥사표를 ~ tender one's resignation∥문제를 ~ present a problem / set[give] a question∥전시회에 작품을 ~ submit one's work for[enter one's work in] an exhibition∥그는 사표를 냈다 He has presented[(문어)tendered] his resignation∥나는 고등학교에

내다

입학 원서를 냈다 I sent in an application for admission to a high school.// 모두 답안지를 내시오 Hand in[Give me] your papers.// 그는 어려운 문제를 우리에게 냈다 He set us a poser.// 선생님은 학생들에게 숙제를 내셨다 The teacher gave his pupils homework.

12 [음식을 대접하다] serve (up) (wine); offer (tea); treat (a person to something). ¶점심을 ~ treat (a person) to lunch// 다과를 ~ serve tea and cake / serve (a person) with light refreshments// 우리는 손님에게 차와 과자를 냈다 We served our guests tea and cake.// 내가 맥주 한 병을 내지 I'll treat you to a bottle of beer.// 그가 한잔 냈다 He stood us drinks.// 이것은 내가 내는 거다 This is my treat. / This is on me.

13 [운행하다] run[operate] (a special train); put out (a boat).

14 [산출·배출하다] produce; yield; turn out. ¶많은 사상자를 ~ cause heavy casualties// 좋은 결과를 ~ produce[bring about] good results// 천 명의 졸업생을 ~ turn out 1,000 graduates// 많은 수재를 ~ produce[turn out] many brilliant men// 저 학교는 좋은 교사를 많이 냈다 That school has turned out a number of good teachers.

15 [돈을] pay; give; contribute (to / toward); invest; [공급하다] supply[furnish] (a person with money). ¶물건 값을 ~ pay for an article// 자금을 ~ furnish (a person) with funds / advance (the) capital / invest in (an enterprise)// 세금을 ~ pay one's taxes// 집세를 ~ pay one's rent// 수업료를 ~ pay a school fee// 학교 짓는 데 천만 원을 ~ contribute 10,000,000 won toward building a school house// 그는 책값으로 5천 원을 냈다 He paid five thousand won for the book.// (물건을 살 때) 만 원까지 내겠다 I will go as high as ten thousand won.// 숙부님이 내 대학 학비를 내 주셨다 My uncle paid my way through college.// 이 식사 대금은 내가 내겠다 Let me pay for this meal. / This meal is on me.// 당신의 출장비는 회사가 내 준다 The company will pay[bear] the expenses for your business trip.// 비용은 각자가 냈다 Each paid his share in the expenses.

16 [속력을] achieve[develop] (a speed of ...); gather[get up] (speed); speed up. ¶80마일 속도를 ~ make 80 miles// (기선이) 전속력을 ~ put on full steam// 차가 속도를 내기 시작했다 The car is gathering[gaining] speed.// 우리는 시속 100킬로를 냈다 We built up[(문어) put forth] a speed of 100 kilometers an hour.// 이 도로에서라면 속도를 낼 수 있다 We can speed up[drive fast] on this road.// 여기서는 100킬로까지 속도를 내도 된다 You can increase your speed here to 100 kilometers.// 그 차는 속력을 내어 도망쳤다 The car sped away.

17 [시장에] take[bring] (commodities to market); [팔다] market; sell. ¶쌀을 장에 ~ transport rice to the markets (from farms) / put rice on sale[on the market].

18 [모를] transplant (rice seedlings); plant (rice); set[bed] out (rice plants); (거름을) manure (a field).

19 [발산하다] issue forth[out]; emit; send [give] out. ¶빛을 ~ emit[give out] light / send out rays of light / radiate// 김을 ~ emit[give out / send up] steam// 열을 ~ generate heat// 먼지를 ~ raise[stir up] dust// 큰 소리를 ~ cry out / give a loud cry// 불을 ~ cause a fire// 이상한 소리를 ~ make a strange noise// 크게 소리 내어 울다 cry in a loud voice / cry aloud// 부자티를 ~ give oneself the air of a millionaire / act the lord// 그녀는 깔깔거리는 웃음소리를 냈다 She gave a loud peal of laughter.

20 [개시하다] open (a shop); start (a school); set up; run; keep; commence; inaugurate. ¶가게를 ~ open[start / set up] a store// 살림을 ~ set up one's own home// 그는 종로에 가게를 냈다 He opened a store on the [in] Jongno.

21 [선출하다] put forward; select; appoint; offer. ¶후보자를 ~ select a candidate// 대표자를 ~ offer[put forward] a representative.

22 [비우다] empty; clear; (집 등을) vacate; quit; surrender. ¶김칫독을 ~ empty a *gimchi*(kimchi) pot// 집을 ~ move out / clear out of house.

내다³ [제 힘으로 …을 끝내다]. ¶잘라 ~ cut out[away / off] / tear off(손으로)// 가지를 잘라 ~ cut off[prune] branch// 모든 고생을 견뎌 ~ endure all hardships (to the last)// 찾아 ~ find out / discover// 끝까지 절개를 지켜 ~ remain faithful[loyal] to the last.

내다보다 **1** [밖을 보다] look out (of / over / on); see from within. ¶창밖을 ~ look out of a window// 거리를 ~ look out on the street// 바다를 ~ look out over the sea// 창에서 내다보는 경치가 좋다 The window commands a fine view.

2 [예상하다] anticipate; expect; forecast; foresee; look ahead. ¶…을 내다보고 in expectation[anticipation] of ...// 앞날을 ~ foresee[forecast] the future / look ahead into the future / 장래 일을 ~ anticipate future events / have an insight into the future// 앞일을 내다보지 못하다 fail to foresee / be short-sighted / be lacking in foresight// 가격 양등을 내다보고 투기를 하다 speculate on a rise of the price// 값이 오를 것을 내다보고 주식을 내놓지 않다 hold one's stocks for a rise// 우리는 추운 겨울을 내다보고 등유를 여분으로 사 놓았다 We bought extra kerosene in expectation[anticipation] of a cold winter. / Anticipating a cold winter, we bought extra kerosene.// 그는 이율이 인상될 것을 내다보고 저축을 늘렸다 In anticipation[expectation] of a rise in interest rates, he increased his savings.

내다보이다 **1** (밖이) be[can be] seen from within; be seen out of; see through. ¶바다가 내다보이는 집 a house with an outlook over [a view of] the sea// 창으로 바다가 내다보인다 The sea can be seen through the window.// 창에서 거리가 내다보인다 The street is seen from the window.// 그 높은 창으로부터는 마을의 절반이 내다보인다 The high window overlooks half of the town.

2 [예상되다] be anticipated[expected / foreseen]. ¶장차 곤란이 있을 것이 ~ difficulties are anticipated// 네 장래가 빤히 내다보인다 It is easy to see what will become of you.// 그 일이 언제 끝날는지 아직 내다보이지 않는다 The end of the task is not yet in sight.

내다지 [건] a hole through a column[pillar].

내닫다 [뛰어나가다] run[rush] out; [뛰기 시작하다] start running; break into a run;

break into a gallop(말 등이). ¶**밖으로 ~** run [rush] outdoors / dash out into the street [the open] // **후다닥 ~** break suddenly into a clattering run.

내달(來-) (the) next month; the following [coming] month; proximo(약어 prox.). ¶**~ 초이튿날(에)** (on) the second of next month / (on) the 2nd prox // **~로 돌리다**[이월하다] carry (a thing) forward to the next month.

내담(來談) ¶**본인 ~ 요망** Apply in person. // **Personal application (is) requested.** // **내일을 바랍니다** Please come and see me [I beg you to call on me] tomorrow. **내담하다** come to talk (about something); come to see (one).

내당(內堂) woman's quarters. ⇨**내실**(內室)

내던지다 1 [냅다 던지다] throw[cast / hurl / fling] out[away]. ¶**창밖으로 ~** throw (a thing) out of the window // **의자를 ~** hurl a chair at (a person) // **그는 화가 나서 컵을 바닥에 내던졌다** He got angry and flung [threw] a glass against the floor. // **그 남자는 절벽 위에서 바다로 몸을 내던졌다** The man threw himself from the top of the cliff into the sea. // **그는 달리는 열차에서 밖으로 내던져졌다** He was flung[thrown] out of a moving train.
2 [포기하다] give[throw] up; abandon; [내버려 두다] neglect; lay aside; leave[let] (a thing) alone. ¶**일을 ~** throw[give] up one's job / abandon one's work // **지위를 ~** throw up[resign from] one's position[office] // **그는 왕위를 내던지고 그녀와 결혼했다** He gave up the throne to marry her. // **다른 모든 것을 내던지고 그는 그 작품을 완성했다** Throwing everything else aside, he completed the work.
3 [제공·희생하다] offer; deliver; lay down; sacrifice. ¶**목숨을 ~** lay down[sacrifice] one's life // **재산을 ~** deliver up one's possessions / offer[place] one's property at the disposal of another // **선뜻 5천만 원을 ~** generously give a donation of 50 million won (to / towards) // **그 사나이는 자기 목숨을 내던지고 다른 승객들을 구했다** The man saved other passengers at the cost [sacrifice] of his own life. / He laid down his life to rescue other passengers.

내도(來到) the advent; the arrival; incoming. **내도하다** arrive (at); come (to); (기회가) offer[present] itself; occur.

내돋다 rise to surface; come out; spring up; sprout; put forth(싹이); grow; appear. ¶**어드름이 내돋는다** Pimples come out on my face.

내돌리다 pass (a thing) round; pass (a thing) from hand to hand; hand round.

내동댕이치다 throw out; give up. ⇨**내던지다**·2

내두르다 1 [휘두르다] brandish; wave (about); flourish; swing (around); wield. ¶**지팡이를 ~** flourish one's cane[stick] // **칼을 ~** brandish[wield] a sword // **손을 ~** wave one's hand / give a wave of one's hand. 2 [남을 부리다] control; dominate; lead (a person) by the nose; have (a person) under one's thumb[control]. ¶**금융계를 마음대로 ~** have a firm grip on the banking business.

내둘리다 1 [남에게 쥐이다] be pushed around; be led by the nose; be at the mercy of (a person). ¶**남한테 ~** be at a person's back and call / be under a person's thumb.
2 [어지러워지다] get dizzy; be[feel] dizzy.

내디디다 [발족하다] step forward; advance; set foot (on); tread (up)on; [(사업계 등에) 나서다] enter upon; launch forth[out]. ¶**첫발을 ~** make the first step (toward) // **일보를 ~** take a step forward // **무대에 첫발을 ~** make one's first appearance on the stage // **해결을 향해 한걸음 ~** take a step towards solution // **정계에 발을 ~** enter into politics / enter upon a political career // **새로운 인생의 첫발을 ~** embark[set forth] on a new life // **인생의 첫발을 잘못 ~** make a wrong start in one's life // **방 안에 책이 흩어져 있어 발을 내디딜 곳이 없다** The room is littered with books, leaving no place to plant a foot on.

내딛다 step forward; enter upon. ⇨**내디디다**

내뚫다 bore; pierce; penetrate; go[pass / run] through; (구멍을) punch through; perforate. ¶**산에 굴을 ~** bore[cut / build] a tunnel through a mountain // **판자에 구멍을 ~** bore a hole through a board // **총알이 그의 오른쪽 허벅지를 내뚫었다** A bullet went through his right thigh.

내뜨리다 throw[hurl / cast / fling] away.

내란(內亂) [내전] a civil war[strife]; [폭동] an insurrection; [반란] a rebellion; [국내의 소요] internal disturbances[troubles]; a domestic conflict. ¶**~을 일으키다**[진압하다] raise[suppress / settle] a rebellion // **~을 선동하다** instigate[incite / agitate] a rebellion // **~이 일어났다** A civil war broke out. // **~은 마침내 진압되었다** The rebellion was suppressed at last. / [자연히 가라앉다] The rebellion died down at last.
● **내란죄** high treason; an offense against the safety of a state.

내레이션 narration.

내레이터 a narrator(남자); a narratress(여자).

내레이터모델(×narrator model) a pitch girl.

내려가다 1 (아래로) go[come] down; get down; step down; move down[to]; descend. ¶**내려가는 기차** a down train / an outbound train // **언덕을 ~** go[get / climb] down a hill / descend a hill // **산에서 ~** come[climb] down a mountain / go down[descend] a hill // **층계를 ~** descend[go down / climb down / come down] the stairs // **사다리를 ~** get down a ladder // **2층에서 ~** go down stairs // **지하실로 ~** descend into a cellar / go down to the basement // **시골로 ~** move[go] down to the country // **우리는 서둘러 산을 내려갔다** We hurried down the mountain. // **나는 경부선으로 부산까지 내려갔다** I went (down) to Busan on the Gyeongbu[Seoul-Busan] Line. // **내 바지가 헐거워 밑으로 내려간다** My trousers are falling down. // **이 양말은 내려가지 않는다** These socks stay up.
2 [소화되다] digest. ¶**빨리 ~** be quick of digestion // **점심 먹은 것이 잘 안 ~** get one's lunch ill digested // **먹은 것이 잘 안 내려간다** The food is slow of digestion.
3 [(도수가) 낮아지다] drop; fall; go down. ¶**온도가 5도 ~** fall[drop] by 5 degrees // **기온이 영하로 ~** fall (down) below zero // **온도[습도]가 내려갔다** The temperature[humidity] fell [dropped]. // **신열이 내려간다** The fever abates. // **오늘은 정오 무렵부터 기온이 내려갔다** The temperature started to fall around

내려놓다

noon today.
4 [하락하다] fall; drop; go down; decline; sag; depreciate. ¶기록적인 싼 값으로 ~ sag [fall] to a new low / 물가가 내려갔다 Prices have gone down.∥시세가 내려가기만 한다 The market (price) is on the decline [goes on declining].
5 [하위가 되다] come down; drop; sink down; [강등되다] be degraded (from); (미) be demoted (to). ¶아랫자리로 ~ sink down to a lower level∥석차가 ~ come down on the list∥일곱째로 ~ go down to [slip into] the seventh place∥시험에서 석차가 10등이나 ~ be ten places down in class after examination∥그는 지위가 내려갔다 He was demoted.

내려놓다 take down; set down; lower; bring down; put [pull] down; reach down(선반 등에서); let down [fall / off]. ¶책을 선반에서 ~ take down a book from a shelf∥냄비를 ~ take the pot off [from over] the fire∥배 [수레] 에서 짐을 ~ unload a ship [cart]∥수화기를 전화기에서 ~ leave the (telephone) receiver off (the hook)∥책상 위에 책을 내려놓아라 Put your book down on the table.

내려다보다 **1** [아래를] look down (at); overlook; take a bird's-eye view (of); see (a place) below one's eyes. ¶평야를 내려다보는 산 a mountain dominating the plain∥창문에서 거리를 ~ look down the street from the window∥고양이 한 마리가 지붕 위에서 나를 내려다보고 있었다 A cat was looking down at me from the roof.∥이 높은 건물에서는 전 시가지가 내려다보인다 This tall building overlooks [commands] the whole city.∥그 언덕에서는 아름다운 바다의 경치가 내려다보인다 The hill overlooks [commands] a fine view of the sea.
2 [얕보다] look down upon [on] (a person); hold (a person) in contempt; despise; belittle; slight; make light [little] of.

내려디디다 step upon; tread on.

내려뜨리다 drop; let (a thing) fall; throw down. ¶강에 낚싯줄을 ~ drop [lower] one's line into the river.

내려본각(-角) [수] a dip; an angle of depression [declination].

내려서다 come down on one's feet; go down and stand; land on one's feet; step down.

내려앉다 **1** [아랫자리로] come [get] down (and sit); take a lower seat. ¶의자에서 ~ get off a chair (and sit on the floor)∥윗목에서 아랫목으로 ~ take a seat in the lower part of a Korean room moving from the upper part∥그는 전무 직에서 감사로 내려앉았다 He was demoted to auditor from managing director.
2 [무너지다] come [fall] down; break down; collapse; give way; cave [fall] in; (지붕 등이) subside; sink; dip. ¶천장이 내려앉았다 The ceiling has sagged. / The roof fell [caved] in.∥나는 밟고 섰던 마루가 내려앉는 것을 느꼈다 I felt the floor give way [begin to cave in] under my feet.∥그 큰 지진으로 이 부근의 지반(地盤)이 내려앉았다 The ground around here sank as a result of the big earthquake.

내려오다 (높은 데서) come [go] down; get [step / climb] down; descend; (명령 등이) given; be issued. ¶산에서 ~ go down a hill / descend (from) a mountain∥나무에서 ~ come down from a tree∥하늘에서 ~ descend from heaven∥아래층으로 ~ come downstairs∥연단에서 ~ descend [step down] from the platform∥시골로 ~ come down (from town)∥독수리가 먹이를 채러 내려왔다 An eagle swooped down upon its prey.∥전진하라는 명령이 내려왔다 We were ordered to march.
2 (탈것에서) alight from; get [step] off [out of]. ¶버스에서 ~ get down from [get off / alight from] a bus∥비행기에서 ~ get off [alight from] an airplane∥말에서 ~ dismount [get off] a horse.
3 (전하여) be handed down; be transmitted; come down (from one's ancestors). ¶대대로 ~ be transmitted [handed down] from generation to generation∥가보로 전해 내려오는 칼 a sword handed down as an heirloom∥그 풍습은 태곳적부터 전해 내려왔다 The custom has come down to us from remote antiquity.

내려쫓다 (높은 곳에서) chase down; (시골로) drive [hound] from the capital.

내려찍다 cut (straight) down. ¶내려찍어 두 쪽을 내다 cleave [cut] (a thing) in two.

내려치다 strike (a person) a blow (on the head); bring (a stick) down (on a person's head); flick [swing] downwards. ¶책상을 주먹으로 ~ hit the table with one's fist∥그는 번개같이 상대방의 목에 칼을 내려쳤다 He brought down his sword with the speed of sunbeam on the other's neck.

내력(來歷) **1** [경력] a career; one's (personal) history; one's background; one's past life; [유래] an origin; a history. ¶절의 고사(故事) ~ the history and legends connected with a temple∥(일의) ~을 캐다 investigate the origin (of) / trace (a thing) to (its) origin∥행사의 ~을 캐다 trace an event to its origins∥그는 파란만장한 ~을 갖고 있다 He has had a checkered career.∥이것이 우리 학교의 설립 ~입니다 This is the story of the founding of our school.∥그 ~을 들려 다오 Tell me the story that hangs round it [lies behind it].∥이 관습의 ~을 아십니까 Do you know how this custom came about?∥그 일의 ~을 이야기해 줄게 I'll tell you how it all came about.
2 inheritance. ⇨=내림¹

내륙(内陸) inland.
● **내륙국** a landlocked country; a country without a seaport. **내륙 지방** inland areas; the interior (provinces) of a country.

내리 **1** [위에서 아래로] down; downward. ¶지붕에서 ~ 구르다 fall [roll] down from the roof.
2 [줄곧] all through; throughout; on end; consecutively; continuously; successively; in succession; ceaselessly; without stopping [a break]. ¶ 닷새 동안 for five consecutive days / for five days running [on end / at a stretch]∥~ 이기다 win through / win (three) straight victories / win one victory after another / keep on winning / (경기에서) make a clean score∥책만 ~ 읽다 read books constantly∥네 시간이나 ~ 연설하다 speak four hours continuously / make a continuous speech for four hours∥열두 시간 ~ 잠자다 sleep (a)round the clock∥나는 여섯 시간 ~ 일했다 I worked for six hours

내리갈기다 flog[beat / strike] (a person on the head); bring (a stick) down (on a person's head).

내리굿다 draw a vertical line.

내리깔기다 void (urine / feces) down. ¶2층에서 오줌을 ~ urinate down from upstairs.

내리깔다 (눈을) drop[cast down] one's eyes; look downward. ¶내리깐 눈 a downcast look / downcast eyes∥눈을 내리깔고 with downcast eyes∥그녀는 눈을 내리깐 채 대답했다 She answered with downcast eyes.

내리누르다 1 (위에서) press down; press upon (a thing); push down; force down. 2 〔압박하다〕oppress; suppress; 〔구어〕clamp down; 〔윽박지르다〕force; compel; urge. ¶언론을 ~ shackle speech and writing / place [put] a gag upon the freedom of speech / (일을) 떠맡도록 ~ urge[compel / constrain] (a person) to undertake (a task)∥억지로 내리누르는 바람에 하는 수 없이 그 일을 떠맡았다 I was coerced to undertake it.

내리다¹ 〔자동사〕. 1 (높은 데서) come[go] down; get[step] down; descend. ¶사다리에서 ~ get down a ladder∥연단에서 ~ descend from the platform∥막이 내렸다 The curtain dropped[fell]. ∥비행기가 내렸다 The airplane[(영) aeroplane] descended.
2 (탈것에서) alight from; get[step] off[out of]; leave. ¶기차에서 ~ get off a train∥버스에서 ~ get down from[get off] a bus∥배에서 ~ disembark∥비행기에서 ~ get off [alight from] an airplane / deplane∥택시에서 ~ get out of a taxi∥말에서 ~ dismount [get off] a horse∥종로에서 ~ get out[get off] at Jongno∥다음 정거장에서 내립니다 I'm going to get off at the next stop.∥차장, 세워 줘요, 내릴 테니 Stop, conductor, I want to get out.∥그는 버스의 문쪽으로 가서 "내려요." 하고 말했다 He stepped to the door of the bus and said, "Out!"∥승객이 다 내리는 타 주세요 Wait for all the passengers to get off (before you board / before you get on). / Let the passengers off the train first.∥잘못 내렸다[정류장이 틀렸다] We got off at the wrong stop.
3 alight; settle (on the ground); swoop; drop down(새가); 〔활주하다〕plane down; 〔착륙하다〕land. ¶공항에 ~ land on an airport∥꿩이 골짜기에 ~ Pheasants descend on the valley.
4 (비·눈·서리 등이) fall; come down; descend. ¶서리가 내렸다 Frost fell. / There was a frost. / The ground was frozen.∥비가 계속 내리고 있다 It is raining steadily.∥눈이 내리기 시작했다 It started snowing.∥이슬이 내렸다 Dew fell. / There was dew on the ground.
5 (온도 등이) drop; fall; go down. ¶(한란계가) 5도 ~ fall[drop] by 5 degrees∥(한란계가) 0°이하로 ~ fall down below zero∥기온이 내린다 The temperature falls[drops / goes down].∥몸의 열이 내린다 The fever abates.∥열이 아주 내렸다 The fever has entirely left me.∥열이 내리지 않는다 There is no abatement in his fever.
6 (물가가) fall; drop; go down; decline; sag; depreciate. ¶물가가 ~ prices go down[fall off / decline]∥버터 값이 10원 내렸다 Butter has gone down[dropped] ten won in price.∥종이 값이 갑자기 내렸다 There has been a sharp[sudden] drop in the price of paper.∥겨울 옷값이 대폭으로 내렸다 There were big reductions in the prices of winter clothes.∥풍어로 고등어 값이 2할가량 내렸다 As there was a big catch of mackerel, the price dropped[fell] (by) about twenty percent.
7 (뿌리가) take[strike / make] (root); live; root. ¶땅속에서 뿌리가 ~ take root in the ground∥뿌리가 깊게 ~ take[spread] deep root / root deep∥요새 나무를 옮겨 심어 봤자 뿌리가 내리지 않습니다 If the tree is transplanted at this time of year, it will not take root.
8 (살이) become[grow / get] lean[thin]; fall away (in flesh); lose flesh. ¶부기가 ~ the swelling goes down∥체중이 ~ lose weight∥전보다는 살이 많이 내렸군요 You have got much thinner than you were. / You appear to have lost flesh.
9 (먹은 것이) digest. ¶(음식이) 잘 내리는[안 내리는] digestible[indigestible] / (be) easy [hard] of digestion[to digest] / 빨리[더디] ~ be quick[slow] of digestion.
10 (신령이) be possessed (by). ¶신령이 무당에게 내렸다 A god entered into the holy woman[sorceress].
11 (명령 등이) be given; be issued. ¶전진 명령이 내렸다 We were ordered to march.
12 (상·허가 등이) be given; be bestowed [conferred]; be granted. ¶상이 ~ be given a reward / be rewarded∥허가가 ~ be granted permission.

내리다² 〔타동사〕. 1 (높은 데서) take down; lower; bring down; put[pull] down; reach down(선반 등에서); lift down; let down[fall]; drop. ¶돛을 ~ strike sail∥기를 ~ lower [pull down] a flag∥닻을 ~ cast[drop] (an) anchor∥선반에서 책을 ~ take down a book from a shelf∥냄비를 ~ take the pot off [from over] the fire∥트럭에서 짐을 ~ unload goods from a truck∥보트를 ~ lower [launch] a boat∥그 배는 짐을 내리고 있다 The ship is unloading.
2 (승객 등을) set (a passenger) down; drop; get (a person) off. ¶부축하여 내려 주다 help (a person) off (a car) / hand (a woman) down from[out of] (a cab)∥어디서 내려 드릴까요 Where would you like to be dropped off?∥역 앞에서 내려 주시오 Drop me (off) in front of the station.∥그는 노인을 부축하여 전차에서 내려 드렸다 He helped the old man down from the streetcar.
3 (셔터·커튼 등을) drop; let fall; let down. ¶셔터를 ~ pull[roll] down the shutter∥커튼을 ~ draw[drop / bring down] the curtain ∥차양을 ~ pull[draw] down the blinds / lower an awning.
4 (값 등을) cut; reduce / lower / drop / bring down] (the price / wages / fare / freight). ¶작년의 수준으로 값을 ~ reduce[cut down / lower] the prices to last year's level∥값을 2천 원으로 ~ cut[lower / reduce] the price to 2,000 won∥임금을 만 원 ~ cut wages by 10,000 won.
5 (지위를) degrade; demote; reduce (an offic-

내리닫다

er) to a lower rank[grade]; (정도를) lower; bring[let] down. ¶기준을 ~ lower the standards // 반음 ~ [음] flatten // 한 음(音) ~ lower the key (of a song).
6 [하사하다] deign to give; grant; give; bestow; award; honor (with); confer (upon). ¶상금을 ~ confer a prize [an award] // 허가를 ~ grant permission // 연금을 ~ grant (a person) a pension / grant an annuity to (a person) // 관직을 ~ confer a rank on (a person).
7 (명령 등을) issue (orders); order; give[lay on] (a command). ¶사격 명령을 ~ give the word to fire // 특사령을 ~ grant pardon // 최종적인 명령을 내리는 것은 사장이다 The president is the one who will give the final order.
8 (판결 등을) pass (judgment on a person); pronounce; hand down one's decision; render a decision. ¶결론을 ~ draw a conclusion // 단안을 ~ form[make] a conclusion // 사형 선고를 ~ pronounce a death sentence to (a person) / condemn [sentence] (a person) to death // 그는 그 문제에 대해 공평한 판결을 내렸다 He handed down a fair decision on the matter. // 나는 결론을 너무 빨리 내렸다 I have formed too hasty a conclusion. / I came to a conclusion too hastily. // 피고에게 징역 2년의 판결이 내려졌다 The defendant was sentenced to two years imprisonment.
9 (뿌리를) take[strike] root; root. ¶나무가 뿌리를 내렸다 The tree has taken root. // 꺾꽂이한 진달래가 뿌리를 내렸다 The azalea cutting has taken root.
내리닫다 run[dash] down; rush downward.
내리닫이[1] [어린이 옷] children's overalls with a convenience slit.
내리닫이[2] [건] a sash window; a push-up window.
내리뜨다 drop[cast down] (one's eyes); look downward. ¶내리뜬 눈길 a downward glance [look] // 그는 눈을 내리뜨고 말했다 He talked with downcast eyes. // 그녀는 눈을 내리뜨고 한두 번 나를 훔쳐보았다 She stole a glance or two at me while standing with lowered eyes. // 연사(演士)는 눈을 내리뜨고 원고를 보았다 The speaker cast a downward look [glance] at his manuscript.
내리막 1 (길의) a downward path[slope]; a downhill; a descent; a declivity; (철도의) a down grade. ¶~이 되다 (길이) slope [go] down / go [run] downhill // 거기서 길은 ~이 된다 There the road slopes down. / There the road goes [runs] down (the) hill. // 여기서부터 길은 ~이다 The road descends [slopes downward / goes down] from here.
2 (쇠퇴) (a) decline; an ebb; wane. ¶인생의 ~ the downhill of life / the afternoon of life // 그 권투 선수 는 ~ 에 있다 a boxer on the downgrade // ~이 되다 be down on one's luck / be on [in] the wane [downgrade] / be at the ebb / go downhill // 이제 더위도 ~이다 The heat is on the decline. // 그의 인기[운]도 이제는 ~이다 His popularity[fortune] is declining [waning]. / His popularity[fortune] is now on the wane. / His star is on the wane. // 그의 화가로서의 명성도 이제 ~이다 His reputation as a painter is declining [on the decline].

내리막길 1 (길의) a downhill road; a descending[downhill] path. ¶앞에 가파른 ~ 있음 (게시) Sharp drop in road level ahead. **2** [쇠퇴기] a downward course; adversity. ¶~에 들어선 여자 a woman (already) past her prime // 그 집안은 ~을 달리고 있다 That family is going fast downhill.
내리밀다 push down; force down.
내리받이 a downhill path. ⇨내리막1
내리비치다 shine[reflect] down.
내리사랑 parental love toward youngsters; love of the young by the elders.
내리지르다 1 (비·바람이) blow[pour / fall] down violently. **2** (주먹·발로) kick [knock / beat] down [on] (a person / a thing).
내리쬐다 beat[strike] down on; shine[glare / blaze] down upon. ¶따갑게 내리쬐는 햇볕 (under) a burning[scorching] sun // 볕이 ~ burn / beat down on // 머리 위에 햇볕이 ~ have the sun beating down[straight] upon one's head // 햇볕이 쨍쨍 내리쬐고 있다 The sun is pouring down its full strength from the sky. // 햇볕이 그녀의 얼굴에 온통 내리쬐고 있었다 The sun was beating fully into her face. // 해는 이 불쌍한 아이의 맨머리에 내리쬐고 있었다 The sun was beating down on the uncovered head of this poor little fellow.
내리치다 strike downward; strike (a person) a blow (on the head); bring (a stick) down (on a person's head). ¶이마를 ~ strike straight on the forehead // 그는 지팡이로 미친 개의 머리를 내리쳤다 He brought[swung] his stick down on the mad dog's head.
내리퍼붓다 (비가) rain incessantly; rain hard; (눈이) snow incessantly; fall thick and fast. ¶내리퍼붓는 눈 a thick snow // 비가 내리퍼붓고 있다 The rain is pouring down. / It is raining in torrents. / (구어) It rains cats and dogs.
내리훑다 thresh downward.
내릴톱 [세로 켜는 톱] a ripsaw.
내림[1] [혈통으로 유전되어 오는 특성] inheritance; heredity; patrimony. ¶~**이다** be transmitted [handed down] from generation to generation // 정신병은 그 집안의 ~이다 There is hereditary insanity in the family. / Insanity runs in the family. // 그의 용기는 집안의 ~이다 He has courage in his blood.
내림[2] [건] a frontage; a front; a façade; (폭) width; breadth.
내림굿 [민] an invocatory rite of a would-be (spiritualistic) medium.
내림세(-勢) (시세·물가의) a downward trend; a falling [declining] tendency; a drop in price trends; a weakness; sagging. ¶~**를 보이다** show a downward tendency / decline / go down / sag (증권이) // 시세가 ~다 (증권이) The market sags. / (물가가) Prices show a downtrend. / Prices are on the decline. // 물가 ~로 바뀌었다 Prices started going down.
내림차(-次) [수] a descending series; a descending powers.
내막(內幕) the inside (facts); concealed [undisclosed] circumstances; inner workings (of a business). ¶~ **이야기** an inside account [report / story] / a behind-the-scenes story / inside information // ~을 아는 사람 an insider // ~ 이야기를 하다 give (a person) the lowdown [inside information]

(on)∥~을 폭로하다 expose a secret (of)∥~을 알고 있다 have an inside knowledge (of) / have the lowdown (on) / be in the know∥회사의 ~을 탐색하다 find out about[dig into] the inside affairs of a company∥그의 사직에 대한 ~을 들려줄까 Do you want to hear the (real) story behind his resignation?∥사건의 ~을 자네에게 말해 줄 수도 있다 I can give you inside information[(구어) the lowdown] on the affair.∥대체 누가 ~을 폭로하였을까 Who could have exposed the inside facts[the real story]?∥나는 그 ~에 대해서 알고 있다 I have inside knowledge about it.

내맡기다 leave (a matter) (entirely) to[with] (a person); commit (a matter) to a person's care; entrust (a person) with the task (of). ¶아이를 식모에게 ~ commit one's child to the care of a maid∥자기의 몸을 ~ submit [resign] oneself to (another's) will / throw oneself on[upon] (a person) / give oneself to (a person)∥운(하늘)에 ~ resign [abandon] oneself to one's fate / trust to luck[chance] / leave (it) to chance∥결국 그에게 몸을 내맡겼다 At last she gave [yielded] herself to him.∥그에게 이 일을 내맡길 수는 없다 This work must not be entrusted to him. / He cannot be entrusted with this work.

내면(內面) the inside; the interior. ¶그는 표면으로는 경기가 좋은 것 같지만 ~으로는 어려운 것 같다 He seems to be straitened in real circumstances though he poses big outside.
● **내면 묘사** (an) inner description. **내면생활** one's inner life. **내면세계** the inner world. **내면화**(-化) internalization; interiorization.
내면적(內面的) internal; inside; inner. ¶~ 고찰 introspection∥~으로 internally.
내명(內命) private[secret / informal] orders [instructions]. ¶~을 내리다[받다] issue [receive] an unofficial order∥그는 사장의 ~을 받고 유럽에 갔다 He went to Europe under[on] secret orders from the president.
내명년(來明年) the year after next. ⇨ˀ후년
내몰다 drive out[away]; turn[force / send] out; bundle off[out]; (직위에서) oust[expel / dislodge] (a person from a position); (구어) hoof out. ¶소를 목장으로 ~ turn out cattle to graze∥방 밖으로 ~ drive[force] (a person) out of the room∥지위에서 ~ oust (a person) from a position∥(씨름에서) 상대방을 링 밖으로 ~ drive one's opponent out of the ring∥나는 고양이를 방 밖으로 내몰았다 I shut the cat out of my room.
내몰리다 be driven out[away]; be forced out; be expelled. ¶셋집에서 ~ be forced out of a rented house∥그는 일을 못하게 내몰렸다 He was shut out from work.∥근로자들은 직장에서 내몰려 있다 The workers have been locked out.∥그는 그 무리에서 내몰렸다 He was shut out of the group.
내무(內務) 1 [국내의 정무] domestic affairs of state. 2 [내부 사무] a desk job.
● **내무반** [군] (living) quarters; barracks. **내무 사열** an inspection of the soldiers' living quarters.
내밀다 1 [앞·밖으로 나가게 하다] push [thrust] out; stick out (of); force out. ¶손을 ~ hold[reach] out one's hand∥혀를 ~ stick[thrust] out one's tongue∥그는 창문에서 머리를 내밀었다 He stuck his head [leaned] out of the window.∥그는 배를 내밀고 걷는다 He walks with his stomach thrown forward[stuck out].∥난간 밖으로 몸을 너무 내밀지 마십시오 Don't lean too far out over the railing.∥그는 사인첩을 내 앞에 내밀었다 He held out an autograph album before my eyes.
2 [남에게 미루다] throw (on); shift (on); switch (over to). ¶책임을 남에게 ~ shift the blame[responsibility] on to another.
3 [쫓아내다] drive[force] out; expel. ¶사람을 방 밖으로 ~ push[shove / throw / thrust] (a person) out of the room.
내밀리다 be thrust[pushed / thrown] out; be pressed. ¶뜰 밖으로 ~ be thrust[pressed / pushed / thrown] out of the garden∥회사에서 ~ get shoved[pushed] out of one's job with the company∥하마터면 만원 버스에서 내밀릴 뻔했다 I was just in danger of being pushed out of a crowded[jampacked] bus.
내밀하다(內密-) private; secret; confidential; backdoor; under-the-table. ¶내밀한 이야기 a secret[confidential] talk∥이것은 내밀한 이야기인데, 돈을 크게 버는 수를 내가 알고 있어 Between you and me, I know of a way to make a lot of money. **내밀히** [남몰래] in secret; secretly; confidentially. ¶당신께는 그것을 ~ 털어놓겠소 I will confide in you about it.∥그들은 ~ 한 달에 한 번씩 만나고 있다 They meet secretly[in secret] once a month.∥그의 장례식은 ~ 치러졌다 His funeral was held privately[in private].
내방(來訪) a visit; a call. ¶~ 중인 미국 실업가 an American businessman now on a visit (to Korea). **내방하다** visit; call on (a person); call at (a house); pay (a person) a visit; make a visit to (a person). ¶여가가 있을 때 내방해 주십시오 Please come and see me when you are free[at leisure].
● **내방자** a visitor; a caller.
내배다 ooze out; exude; soak through; transude; saturate; percolate. ¶땀이 내밴 셔츠 a sweat-stained shirt∥붕대에 피가 내배어 있었다 The bandage was saturated with blood. / Blood oozed out of the bandage.
내배엽(內胚葉) [생] the endoderm; the endoblast; the hypoblast.
내뱉다 spit (out); spew; spue; expectorate. ¶내뱉듯이 말하다 spit it out / say disdainfully∥길에 침을 ~ spit on the road∥이 말을 내뱉고 그는 집을 나갔다 Flinging these words behind him, he left the house. / With this parting verbal shot, he left the house (without waiting for a reply).
내버리다 throw[cast / fling] away; dump (refuse). ¶현관에 내버린 아이 a baby left on the doorsteps∥담배를 ~ cast[chunk] one's cigarette∥쓰레기를 ~ throw away garbage / dump refuse∥그것은 돈을 내버리는 짓이다 It is a mere waste of money.
내버려 두다 [등한히 하다] neglect (one's work); lay aside; [방치하다] leave[let] (a thing / a person) alone[unattended / untended]; let (a thing) as it is[stands]. ¶일을 하지 않고 ~ leave one's work undone∥병을 ~ leave the disease untreated∥울게 ~ leave (a person) alone and let him cry∥어린아이를 제멋대로 ~ let a child have his own way∥제 마음대로 하게 ~ let (a per-

son) do what he wants / leave (a person) to his own devices // 그냥 내버려 둘 수는 없다 I can't leave it alone. / I can't pass it unnoticed. / I can't pass it over in silence. // 그가 하고 싶어 하는 대로 내버려 두어라 Let him do as he lives. // 그 일은 되어 가는 대로 내버려 두겠다 I'll let the matter take its own course.

내벽(內壁) an inside [inner / interior] wall.

내보내다 1 (안에서 밖으로) let go [get] out; let [send] out; forward; turn (a person) out-of-doors; show (a person) the door. ¶전파를 내보내는 천체 a celestial body which sends out [emits] radio waves // 자기 외아들을 미국으로 ~ send one's only son to the U.S.A. // 스파이를 ~ send out a spy // 사내아이들을 밖으로 ~ let the boys go outside // 그는 (장기의) 말을 내보냈다 He moved the pawn forward.
2 (직장·거주지에서) give (a person) the sack; send (a person) packing; put [send / drive / kick] out; (미) fire; evict (셋방 등에서). ¶세든 사람을 ~ evict [eject] a tenant from the house / put a tenant out // (그들은) 식모를 내보냈다 The maid was discharged [dismissed / let go / (구어) fired]. // 이 학교는 우수한 문예 비평가들을 다수 내보냈다 This school has produced many fine literary critics. // 그는 집세가 밀린 세든 사람을 내보냈다 He evicted his tenant [gave his tenant notice to move out] for not paying the rent. // 그 학교는 올해 50명의 졸업생을 사회에 내보냈다 The school sent fifty graduates out into society [graduated fifty students] this year.

내복(內服) 1 underwear; underclothes. ⇨속옷 ¶~을 갈아입다 change one's underwear. 2 [약을 먹음) internal use. ¶~용 "To be internally used." **내복하다** take [use] (a medi-cine) internally [orally]. ¶하루 3번 ~ take medicine three times a day.
● **내복약** a medicine (for internal use); an internal medicine.

내부(內部) the inside; the interior; the inner part. ¶신체 ~ the inner [internal] parts of the body / (내장) one's inwards / (미국 구어) one's internals // ~의 internal / inner / inside / interior / inward / intestine (체내의) / domestic (국내의·가내의) // 가장 ~의 inmost / the innermost // ~ 소리에 귀를 기울이다 listen to one's inner voice [what one's heart says] // 이것은 건물 ~에서 한 짓일 것이다 This must have been an inside job. // ~에 대립이 있다 There is internal strife among the staff. // 그들은 건물 ~에 폭약을 장치했다 They placed an explosive within [inside] the building.
● **내부 감각** inner sensation. **내부 분열** a split [rupture] among friends; internal discord. **내부 사정** the internal affairs; the inside story (내막). **내부 에너지** internal energy. **내부 저항** (물) internal resistance.

내분(內分) [수] interior division. **내분하다** divide internally.

내분(內紛) an internal trouble [strife]; domestic discord; a storm in a teacup. ¶정당의 ~ internal troubles in a political party / an intraparty conflict [strife] // ~을 일으키다 give rise to an internal trouble / raise a storm in a teacup // ~에 시달리다 suffer from internal troubles [dissention] // 저 당은 ~이 끊이지 않는다 There are constant troubles within the party.

내분비(內分泌) [생] internal secretion; incretion; endocrine.
● **내분비선**(-腺) endocrine glands; a ductless gland. **내분비액** an endocrine [internal] secretion; a hormone.

내불다 1 (입김을) breathe out [forth]; give out breath; breathe upon. ¶입김을 내불어 손을 녹이다 blow (on) one's fingers to warm them. 2 (바람이) blow away (from / toward). ¶바람이 바다 쪽으로 내분다 The wind blows away toward the shore.

내비치다 1 (빛·빛깔이 밖으로) be [grow] transparent. ¶내비치는 openwork (skirt) // 내비치는 옷감 transparent cloth // 내비치는 무늬가 있는 지폐 a watermarked bank note // 옷이 얇아서 팔이 내비쳐 보인다 Her arms are seen through her thin dress. 2 (짐짓 말을 꺼내어) hint (at / that); intimate; insinuate; suggest. ¶사직을 ~ hint at resignation // 그는 승낙할 뜻을 내비치고 있다 He gives us to understand that he will consent.

내빈 명단 a guest; a visitor. ¶다음에는 ~께서 축사를 해 주시겠습니다 Next our honored guest will give a congratulatory address.
● **내빈** 명단 a list of guest [visitors'] book; a visitors' register. **내빈석** the visitors' seats [gallery]; the seats for invited guests. **내빈실** a special room reserved for honored visitors; (게시) For guests; a guest room; a reception room.

내빼다 flee; run away; (속어) scram; make [take / run] off; make a getaway; (질정하여) scamper off [away]. ¶이런 때는 내빼는 것이 상책이다 The wisest thing to do in this case is to run away.

내뻗다 put forth [out]; spread [stretch] out; extend. ¶다리를 쭉 ~ stretch out one's legs // 등넝쿨이 ~ A wisteria puts out its vine.

내뻗치다 put forth; stretch; (물 등이) gush out; spout (out); spurt (out / up); jet.

내뿜다 (물·피 등) spout (out); spurt (out / up); gush out; (가스·증기·불 등) blow off [up]; emit; (연기 등) send out; (화산·증기) erupt; break out. ¶불을 내뿜는 괴수(怪獸) a monstrous beast breathing fire // 연기를 내뿜고 있는 굴뚝 a chimney sending forth [emitting] smoke // 코끼리는 우리에게 물을 내뿜었다 The elephant blew water over us. // 기관차가 연기를 내뿜고 있다 The engine is emitting [puffing out] smoke. // 물이 호스에서 내뿜었다 Water spouted [shot / spurted] from the hose. // 주전자에서 김이 내뿜기 시작했다 Steam began to shoot from the kettle. // 분화구에서 연기[마그마]를 내뿜었다 Smoke billowed [Magma erupted] from the crater.

내사(內査) secret examination [inspection / investigation]; a private inquiry. ¶지금 ~ 중이다 A secret investigation is proceeding. **내사하다** make private [secret] inquiries into (a matter); investigate [examine / inspect] secretly.

내사(來社) a visit to a company [an office]. **내사하다** visit a company [an office]. ¶10시에 내사하여 주십시오 Please come to our office [company] at ten o'clock.

내색(-色) one's facial expression [countenance]; expression of one's feeling; betrayal of one's emotion; a revealing look. ¶그녀는 기쁜 ~을 하고 있었다 A look of pleasure came to her face. **내색하다** betray one's emotion; show[display] (anxiety) on one's face; let one's face show one's thoughts. ¶내색하지 않다 pocket[suppress] one's feelings(감정) / master one's anger(화) / veil one's displeasure(불쾌) / disguise one's grief(슬픔)∥그는 증권에서 큰 손해를 보았지만 전혀 내색하지 않는다 He shows no sign of having lost a lot of money on stocks[(주) shares]. / From the way he acts you'd never guess that he had lost a lot of money on the stock market. ∥그는 마음에 느낀 것을 반드시 내색한다 There is nothing in his mind that does not show on his face. ∥그는 자기감정을 내색하지 않는다 He keeps his feelings to himself.

내생(來生) [불] the life to come; the future life; life after death. ¶~의 행복 happiness in next life[world] / one's welfare in another world[after death] ∥ ~을 위하여 기도하다 pray for salvation.

내선(內線) (전기의) indoor[interior] wiring; (전화의) an extension(약어 ext.); (작전상의) an inner line; (인터폰) an interphone; an intercom line; an inside line. ¶~ 253번 대 주세요 Extension[Give me extension] 253 [two five three], please. / May I have extension 253, please?

● **내선 전화** an extension (tele)phone; interphone.

내성(內省) [심] introspection; (intimate) reflection; inward-looking; self-communion; self-examination. **내성하다** introspect; introvert; reflect on oneself; turn one's thought inward; examine one's own heart. ¶깊이 ~ engage in intimate introspection / hold communion with oneself.

내성(耐性) [의][식] tolerance (to radioactivity). ¶~이 있다 tolerate∥그 약에 대해서는 몸에 ~이 생기지 않는다 The body develops [builds up] no tolerance to the drug.

● **내성균** resistant bacteria. ¶**페니실린**(에 대한) ~ penicillin-resistant bacteria.

내성적(內省的) introspective; introversive; introvertive; reflective; indrawn. ¶~인 사람 an introvert / a reflective person∥~인 기질 an introspective nature.

내세(來世) a better[the next / other] world; the future life[existence] after death; the world to come; the hereafter; Kingdom(기독교의); (속어) kingdom come. ¶현세와 ~ this world and the next∥~를 믿다 believe in the future existence / believe in the world beyond the grave∥~의 명복을 빌다 pray for one's welfare in the future life∥~로 떠나다 go on journey to the next world∥~에는 남자로 태어나고 싶다 I hope I would be reincarnated as a man in the next life.

내세우다 **1** [나와 서게 하다] make (a person) stand; stand; support. ¶대열 앞에 ~ make (a person) stand before ranks.

2 [나서게 하다] nominate; designate; put up; make[have] (a person) represent[stand for]. ¶후보로 ~ put up[nominate] (a person) as a candidate / have (a person) stand for (the Assembly)∥남을 회사 대표로 ~ have a person represent the company / present a person as the company's representative∥그들은 신 씨를 지도자로 내세워다 They made Mr. Sin their leader.∥우리는 그를 대변자로 내세우고 교섭에 임했다 We attended the negotiations with him as our chief spokesman.∥우리는 그를 사장으로 내세웠다 We supported him for president.

3 [어떤 문제·의견 등을 주장하다] stand on; insist; bring (a matter) up to one's advantage; speak highly of (one's own achievement); single out (for praise); recommend; display. ¶권리를 ~ stand on one's right∥~한 조건을 ~ take up the position that ...∥그에게는 내세울 만한 재주가 없다 He has no talent to speak of.∥소인은 자기를 내세우고 남을 헐뜯는 법이다 Mean fellows will advertise themselves at the expenses of others.∥그는 그것에 대하여 아는 바 없음을 내세우고 자기 잘못이 아니라고 주장했다 He insisted that it was not his fault on the plea that he had known nothing about it. / He used his ignorance of the matter to shield himself from blame[as an excuse].∥그들은 그 규칙을 내세워 우리의 요구를 거절했다 They used the regulation as an excuse for rejecting our demands.

내셔널리스트 a nationalist.

내셔널리즘 nationalism.

내소박(內疏薄) mistreating[despising / alienating] one's husband; jilting one's husband. **내소박하다** mistreat[jilt / despise / alienate / abuse] one's husband. ➔¶내소박당하다 be forced out by one's wife.

내솟다 spring up; spout out; spurt (out / up); gush out.

내수(內需) domestic[home] demand[requirements]; (소비) domestic consumption.

● **내수 산업** an industry for domestic demand; enterprises producing commodities for domestic markets. **내수용 원자재** raw materials for domestic demand[consumption].

내수면(內水面) inland waters.

● **내수면 어업** fish-water fishery.

내수성(耐水性) water-resistance; water-proofing. ¶~이 있는 목재 water-repellent[water-resistant] lumber.

내숭 treacherousness; trickiness; wickedness; sneakiness; underhandedness. **내숭하다** wicked; treacherous; sneaky; tricky; sly; wily. ¶내숭한 사람 a tricky[sneaky] fellow / a snake.

내숭스럽다 wicked; treacherous. ⇨내숭하다 (⑤내숭) ¶내숭스러운 웃음 an insidious smile.

내쉬다 (숨을) breathe out; exhale. ¶숨을 ~ breathe out one's breath∥숨을 크게 ~ exhale deeply∥한숨을 ~ give[heave] a sigh.

내습(來襲) [침입] an invasion; [습격] an attack; [소규모의 급습] a raid. ¶적의 ~에 대비하다 provide[guard] against the enemy's assault[attack]. **내습하다** attack; assault; invade; raid; make an attack[a raid] (on); (태풍이) hit. ¶내주엔 서울에 한파가 내습할 것이다 A cold wave will hit[is coming to] Seoul next week.∥우리 진지에 적기가 내습했다 Enemy planes attacked [raided / made a raid on] our camp.

내습성(耐濕性) ¶이 타일은 ~이 강하다 This tile is moistureproof[withstands dampness

very well].
내시(內侍) a eunuch; a gelding.
내시경(內視鏡) [의] an endoscope.
● **내시경 검사**(법) endoscopy.
내식성(耐蝕性) corrosion resistance. ¶~이 있는 쇠 anticorrosive [corrosionproof / rust-proof] iron.
내신(內申) an unofficial [a confidential] report. **내신하다** report unofficially [confidentially] (to a higher office).
● **내신 성적** (고교의) the academic reports (from high schools to colleges and universities); the high school records.
내실(內室) **1** [거실] a living room; [안방] women's quarters; the main room. **2** [남의 아내] your [his] wife.
내실(內實) substance; substantiality. ¶~을 기하다 insure substantiality.//~화하다 make (a matter) substantial [solid].
내심(內心) **1** [속마음] one's (inmost) heart; one's mind. ¶~으로는 at heart [bottom] / in one's heart / inwardly / secretly //~ 후회하다 repent at heart //~ …하고 싶어 하다 have a secret desire to (do)//그는 ~ 좋아했다 He was inwardly pleased. / He was pleased at heart.//그는 ~ 거절할 셈이었다 His real intention was to refuse.//그는 ~의 동요를 감출 수 없었다 He was not able to conceal his inward [inner] agitation.//그녀는 ~을 털어놓으려 하지 않았다 She would not unburden herself to me. **2** [수] the inner center.
내앉다 sit forward.
내앉히다 let [have] (a person) sit forward; let (a person) come out and occupy a seat.
내야(內野) [야구] the infield; the diamond.
● **내야석** an infield stand; an infield bleachers (▶ bleachers 는 지붕 없는 좌석). **내야수** an infielder; a baseman; (집합적) the infield. **내야 안타** an infield hit.
내약(內約) a private agreement [contract]; a secret [tacit] understanding(묵계); a secret treaty(밀약). **내약하다** make a private agreement [contract]; have a tacit understanding (with). ¶나는 네가 가입하겠다고 내약했으니까 승낙한 것이다 I consented on the understanding that you would join it.
내역(內譯) particulars (on / about). ⇨명세 ¶지출의 ~ a breakdown of expenditures [expenses] // 계정(비용)의 ~을 적으시오 Itemize the account (expenses).
내연(內緣) an informal [an unlegalized / an unregistered / a common-law] marriage; a marriage of consent; (미) a companionable marriage. ¶~의 처 a common-law wife / a wife not legally married //~의 남편 an unmarried husband //~ 관계를 맺다 contract [make] a de facto marriage (with) / (영) jump over the broomstick //~의 부부 생활을 하다 live together without being legally married / live as man and wife without being married / live out of wedlock (with).
내연(內燃) internal combustion.
● **내연 기관** an internal-combustion engine; a motor.
내연(來演) ¶우리 시에 보스턴 교향악단이 ~하였다 The Boston Symphony Orchestra came to our town to give a performance.
내열(耐熱) heatproof; heat-resistance. ¶~의 heatproof / heat-resisting / heat-resistant /

refractory // ~성의 [공] thermostable.
● **내열 시험** a heat(-resistance) test. **내열 유리** heat-resisting glass.
내오다 (안에서 밖으로) take [carry / bring] out; remove. ¶의자를 뜰로 ~ bring a chair out into the garden.
내왕(來往) [통행] come-and-go; comings and goings; (street) traffic; (편지의) communication; an exchange of letters; [교제] (friendly) intercourse; association. ¶차량의 ~ vehicular traffic //~이 많다[적다] Traffic is heavy [light]. **내왕하다** come and go; pass; intercommunicate; (사귀다) hold intercourse [exchange visits] (with). ¶그들은 서로 내왕하는 사이다 They are on visiting terms.//지금도 우리는 가끔 서로 내왕합니다 We often see each other even now.
내외¹(內外) **1** [안팎] the interior and exterior; within and without; the inside and outside. ¶~의 internal and external //~의 공격 an attack from inside and outside / an onslaught from within and out //학교 건물은 ~가 다 깨끗하다 The schoolhouse is kept clean inside and out.
2 [국내외] the inside and outside of the country; home and abroad; home [domestic / native] and foreign. ¶~가 다사다난하다 be eventful [busy] at home and abroad.
3 [부부] man [husband] and wife; a (married) couple. ¶그들은 잘 어울리는 ~다 They make a handsome couple.
4 [약간 넘거나 덜한] some; about; around; or so; thereabouts; a matter of. ¶1주일 ~ a week or there abouts // 5백 원 ~ 500 won or so / around 500 won.
● **내외간** relationship between man and wife. **내외분** you and your wife [husband]; he and his wife; she and her esteemed husband; the esteemed couple. **내외 사정**[정책] home [domestic] and foreign affairs [policy].
내외²(內外) [이성을 대하기를 피함] avoidance of the opposite sex; men and women keeping away from each other. ¶~ 술집 a simple pub with no hostesses. **내외하다** keep their distance (from each other); avoid society with the opposite sex.
내용(內容) **1** [속에 든 알맹이] contents (of a bag). ¶이 상자의 ~은 무엇입니까 What does the box contain? / What is in the box?
2 [표현된 것의 의미] content(구체적인 하나하나의 내용을 생각할 때에는 contents); import(취지); substance(실질). ¶형식과 ~ form and substance [content] // 교육의 ~ the quality of education // 연구의 ~ the substance of one's study // 직무의 ~ the substance of one's duties and responsibility // 조례의 ~ the subject matter of an act // 잡지[그의 강연]의 ~ the content of a magazine [his lecture] //~이 풍부한 토론 a discussion full of meat //~이 없는 연설 an address of little substance //~이 있는[없는] 사람 a person with a lot [nothing] to him // 중요한 것은 ~이다 It is a subject matter that counts.//그 책의 ~은 2페이지에 있다 The contents of the book are on the second page.//이 편지의 ~을 복사하시오 Copy the text of this letter.//전갈의 ~은 무엇입니까 What does the message say?//사건의 ~을 모르겠다 I don't know the details of the affair.

- **내용물** the contents. **내용 증명** certification of contents. ¶~ 우편 contents-certified mail[post].

내용 연수(耐用年數) [사용 가능 연한] the life (of a machine). ¶~가 긴 자산 long-lived assets∥이 기계는 ~가 5년이다 The life of this machine is five years.∥이 재봉틀은 이미 ~가 지났다 This sewing machine is no longer serviceable.

내우(內憂) domestic discord; internal troubles.
- **내우외환**(-外患) troubles both at home and abroad[from within and without]; internal and external troubles.

내원(來援) coming to help; coming to the aid (of)[to (a person's) aid]; assistance; aid; help; support. ¶~을 요청하다 ask (a person) to come and help one / ask (a person) to come to one's assistance. **내원하다** come to help[(a person's) aid].

내월(來月) (the) next month. ⇨ 내달

내응(內應) a secret communication[understanding]; collusion; treachery within; betrayal. **내응하다** collude[conspire] (with); be in collusion[secret communication] (with); join hands secretly (with); (구어) tip (the enemy) off (on a matter); (성내(城內) 군사를) assist the attackers. ¶적과 ~ communicate secretly with the enemy / betray (us) to the enemy.

내의(內衣) underwear; underclothes. ⇨ 속옷

내의(內意) [의중] one's mind; one's (secret) intention; [사견(私見)] one's private[personal / confidential] opinion. ¶~를 받고 by secret order (of) / under the private injunction[personal instructions] (of)∥~를 말하다[전하다] reveal[make known] one's intention[wishes] (to) / confide one's opinion (to).

내의(來意) the object of one's call[visit]; the purpose of one's visit. ¶~를 묻다 ask the object of (a person's) call∥~를 알리다 tell [state] the object of one's call∥~를 말씀해 주십시오 Kindly tell me what you have come for.

내이(內耳) the internal ear; the labyrinth. ⇨ 속귀
- **내이염**(-炎) [의] labyrinthitis; inflammation of the internal ear; otitis interna.

내인(內因) an internal cause; an intrinsic motivation.

내일(來日) **1** [명일] tomorrow. ¶~부터는 after today∥그는 ~ 아침에 이곳에 옵니다 He's coming here tomorrow morning.∥~의 예정은 어떻게 되어 있습니까 What is your schedule for tomorrow?∥일은 ~부터 시작된다 The work starts tomorrow.∥~부터 나는 6시에 일어나겠다 Beginning tomorrow, I'll get up at six.∥~ 어찌 될지 모를 인생이다 Life is precarious. / We don't know what may befall us tomorrow.∥오늘 남에게 일어난 일은 ~ 우리에게 일어날 수도 있다 What befalls others today might befall us tomorrow. / Tomorrow it might be me.∥~의 일을 걱정하지 마라 Take no thought for the morrow.(▶ 성경의 말씀)
2 [장래] the future. ¶한국의 ~을 짊어질 사람들 those who will be the support and driving force of future Korea / those who will bear the destiny of future Korea on one's shoulders∥~의 서울을 위한 계획 plans for the Seoul of tomorrow[the future]∥가족을 위해 ~에 대비하라 Provide for the future of one's family.

내입(內入) **1** [돈의] partial[part] payment; payment on account. **내입하다** pay in part; pay on account[as part payment / in part settlement]. ¶책값 5만 원 중에서 2만 원만 ~ pay 20,000 won as part payment for books totalling 50,000 won. **2** [궁중에 물건을 들임] delivery (of goods) to the Royal Court [Household]. **내입하다** deliver[supply] (goods) to the Royal Court.
- **내입금** [대금의 일부] money paid on account; [착수금] a deposit; [첫 지불금] a down payment. ¶차의 ~을 지불하다 pay [put down] money on a car / place a deposit down on a car / make a down payment on a car.

내자(內子) my wife.

내자(內資) [자금] local[domestic / home] capital[fund]; [물자] domestic[home] resources[materials]. ¶~를 동원하다 mobilize domestic capital.

내장(內粧) [실내 장식] interior design; interior decoration; [실내 구성] the interior; (자동차 등의) upholstery.
- **내장 공사** (신축 건물의) interior finishing; (기존 건물의) interior decorating; redecorating.

내장(內臟) the internal organs; the internals; [창자] the intestines; the bowels; the entrails; the guts; (가축의) innards; viscera; (구어) guts; (새의) giblets. ¶닭의 ~을 꺼내다 remove the insides from a chicken.
- **내장병** an internal disease. **내장 신경** the splanchnic nerve. **내장 질환** a trouble of an internal organ; internal disease[complaint]. **내장학** splanchnology.

내장안(內障眼) [흑내장] amaurosis; [백내장] cataract; [녹내장] glaucoma.

내장하다(內藏−) have (a thing) within; have (a thing) built-in. ¶현대 한국이 내장하고 있는 여러 문제 various problems inherent in modern Korea. ➔자동 셔터가 내장된 카메라 a camera with a built-in self-timer.

내재(內在) [철] immanence; indwelling; inherence. ¶신의 ~ [신] the divine immanence. **내재하다** (문어) be immanent (in); indwell (in); be inherent (in). ¶인간 사회에 내재하는 온갖 모순 all kinds of contradictions inherent in human society.

내재율(內在律) (시의) (inner) rhythm [cadence] (of free verse [prose]).

내재적(內在的) immanent; indwelling; inherent; intrinsic; internal. ¶사물의 ~ 가치 the intrinsic[inherent] value of a thing.

내적(內的) [내부의] inner; internal; (고유의) intrinsic; (마음의) mental; (유전의) inherited.
- **내적 경험** inner experience. **내적 생활** inner life.

내적(內積) [수] the inner product; the scalar product.

내전(內殿) **1** [궁전의 안채] the penetralia (of the Royal Palace). **2** [왕비] a queen; an empress.

내전(內戰) an internal[a civil] war.

내전(來電) [전보] an incoming telegram [dispatch]; an incoming cablegram(해외로부터의) [전화] an incoming telephone[phone] call. ¶뉴욕발 ~ (according to) a dispatch from New York / a New York dispatch [cable] // 런던에서의 ~에 의하면 a London telegram reports [says] that ... / according to a dispatch from London ...

내접(內接) [수] inscription. **내접하다** touch internally; be inscribed (in a circle). ¶내접한 inscribed.
● **내접원** an inscribed circle.

내젓다 (손·기를) wave; (팔을) swing; (신체·물병을) shake; (머리·꼬리·손가락을) wag; (배를) row out; pull [put] out (to sea). ¶팔을 내저으며 걷다 swing one's arms as one goes [walks].

내정(內定) private [informal / unofficial / tentative] decision; informal settlement. **내정하다** decide unofficially [informally / tentatively]. → ¶내정되다 be informally [provisionally / tentatively] arranged [decided] // …하기로 내정되었다 It has been unofficially decided to (do). // 그는 새 은행의 은행장으로 내정되어 있다 He has been informally designated as president of the new bank.
● **내정 가격** a reserve price.

내정(內政) 1 [나라 안의 정치] domestic [internal] administration; domestic policies; state [internal] affairs. ¶다른 나라의 ~에 간섭하다 intervene [interfere] in the domestic [internal] affairs of another country. 2 [가정의 살림살이] house management; housekeeping.
● **내정 간섭** intervention [interference] in the domestic [internal] affairs of another country.

내정(內庭) 1 [안뜰] an inner yard; a courtyard. 2 [아낙] women's quarters; one's wife's quarters.

내정(內情) [내부 사정] the internal [domestic] condition(s); the inside (of a company); [실정] the real state of affairs; the real circumstances. ¶~에 밝은 사람 (미국 구어) an insider // ~을 탐지하다 inquire into the real state // ~을 폭로하다 expose [reveal] an inside story // 그는 그 회사의 ~에 밝다 He is conversant with the internal conditions of the company. / (미국 속어) He has the lowdown on the company. // 이 절도 사건은 회사의 ~에 밝은 자의 소행인 것 같다 This theft at the company looks like an inside job. / This theft seems to be the work of someone familiar with the inner workings of the company.

내조(內助) the wife's help [assistance / aid]. ¶~의 공[덕]으로 through the assistance of one's wife // 그녀의 ~의 공이 컸다 She did much to help her husband along. // 그는 아내의 ~ 덕택으로 출세하였다 Thanks to his wife's help, he got ahead in life. **내조하다** help one's husband.

내종(사촌)(內從四寸) a cousin by a paternal aunt.

내주(來週) next week; the coming week. ¶~토요일 Saturday next week / next Saturday / (영) on Saturday next // ~의 오늘 와 주세요. Please come a week from today [(영) a week today].

내주다 1 (금품을) take [bring / put] (a thing) out; give; give out [away]. ¶돈을 지갑에서 ~ give money out of one's purse // 짐을 ~ deliver goods // 이 교환권을 가져오면 현품을 내줍니다 We will give [deliver] the article in exchange for this coupon. // 이것은 그에게 내줄 돈이다 This money is to him.
2 (자리·길 등을) give; offer; yield; surrender; (실권을) hand [turn / make] over; transfer; resign. ¶권리를 ~ devolve rights upon (a person) / transfer one's right to (another) // 왕위를 ~ turn the throne over (to) / abdicate the throne in favor (of) // 후진에게 자리를 ~ resign one's post in favor of a junior // 재산을 채권자에게 ~ make over one's estate to one's creditor // 마침내 그들은 요새를 적에게 내주었다 Finally they surrendered their fortress to the enemy. // 그는 회장 자리를 아무에게도 내주지 않으려 하고 있다 He is trying to hang on to the post of president.

내주장(內主張) petticoat government; gynecocracy. **내주장하다** exercise petticoat government; tie one's husband to one's apron strings; henpeck one's husband. ¶그녀는 내주장한다 She dominates [henpecks] her husband. / (미) She wears the pants (in that family). // 저 집은 내주장한다 The wife is the ruler in that house.

내지(內地) [안쪽 지방] the interior; inland; hinterland; back country. ¶~의 interior / inland / domestic / internal // ~에 들어가다 go into the interior // (해안에서) go [strike] inland // 일본 ~를 여행하다 travel in the interior of Japan.

내지(乃至) 1 [셈·정도의 얼마에서 얼마까지] from (ten) to (fifteen); between (ten) and (fifteen). ¶100원 ~ 200원 from 100 to 200 won / between 100 and 200 won // 제12조 ~ 제16조의 규정 the provisions of Articles 12 to 16 inclusive // 비용은 3000원 ~ 4000원 들 것이다 The cost will be between three thousand and four thousand won. // 아동의 나이는 7세 ~ 13세다 The ages of the pupils ranges from seven to thirteen.
2 [또는] or; and; and/or. ¶과학적 ~ 합리적 방법 a scientific or rational method // 5 ~ 그 이상[이하] five or more [under] // 이런 유의 가난한 사람들에 대한 원조는 정부 ~ 각 지방 관서에서 행한다 Assistance to the needy of this type is financed by the State and / or each local government.

내직(內職) [부업] a job done on the side; a side job; bywork; homework; a sideline; outside [extra] work; (가정에서의) piecework done at home. ¶~으로 as a side job [line] // ~으로 수입을 보충하다 supplement one's salary [income] by outside work // ~으로 저작을 하다 write books as a side line. **내직하다** do something else (on the side); do a side job; do [pick up] odd jobs.

내진(內診) an internal [gynecological] examination; endoscopy. **내진하다** make an internal examination (of).
● **내진경** an endoscope.

내진(耐震) ¶~의 earthquake-proof.
● **내진 건물** an earthquake-proof [-resistant] building.

내집단(內集團) an in-group.

내쫓기다 1 [추방되다] get driven [put / sent / turned] out; be forced out; be ousted (from a party); be kicked out. ¶집 밖으로 ~ be turned out of the house // 시집에서 ~ be compelled to leave one's husband's home // 그는 빈손으로 내쫓겼다 He was cut off without a cent.//우리는 무슨 일이 있어도 이 집에서 내쫓기지 않겠다 We are not going to be turned out[forced out] from this house.//그는 아파트에서 내쫓겼다 He was evicted from[was ejected from / was forced to move out of] the apartment. **2** [해고되다] be dismissed[discharged / fired]; get the sack. ¶회사에서 ~ be fired [sacked] by the company//그녀는 사직했으나 사실은 상사에게 내쫓긴 것이다 She quit because her boss made it too uncomfortable for her to stay.

내쫓다 1 [밖으로 몰아내다] expel; turn[get / put / send / drive] out; bundle off[out / away]; kick (a person) out (of the house [company / army]); (셋집 등에서) evict [eject] (a tenant from the house); put (a tenant) out. ¶집에 세들어 있는 사람을 ~ evict a tenant//학생을 학교에서 ~ expel a student from school/throw a student out of school//그들은 그를 위원장 자리에서 내쫓으려고 했다 They tried to remove him from the post of chairman.//그녀는 며느리를 내쫓았다 She tormented her daughter-in-law so mercilessly that she left home. / She was so hard on her daughter-in-law that she left home.//스스로 나가지 않으면 내쫓겠다 If you won't go yourself, I shall turn[rush] you out.//기동 경찰이 학생들을 강제로 건물에서 내쫓았다 The riot police forcibly evicted the students from the building.//그는 손님을 내쫓았다 He showed his visitor the door. **2** [해고하다] dismiss; discharge; (구어) fire; give (a person) the axe[sack]; send (a person) packing. ¶하인을 ~ send a servant packing//사전 예고도 없이 급료를 주어 ~ pay (a person) off without previous notice.

내차다 kick[boot] out; [냅다 차다] kick hard; give (a person) a hard kick (on the shin); (속어) give (a person) the boot.

내착(來着) arrival. **내착하다** reach; arrive (at / in); come; get to. ¶그는 근간 이곳에 내착할 예정이다 He is expected[due] here shortly.

내채(內債) an internal loan. ⇨내국 공채(⇨내국)

내처 1 [줄곧] throughout; all the time[way]; [잇달아] continuously; without intermission [a break]; at a stretch. ¶~ 손해만 보다 suffer a series of losses / suffer loss upon loss//3시간을 ~ 가르치다 teach for three hours at a stretch//그는 3마일이나 되는 길을 ~ 달렸다 He ran every inch of the three miles.//나는 어제저녁부터 ~ 잤다 I have kept on sleeping from yesterday evening. **2** [하는 김에 끝까지] straight; to the very end. ¶일을 시작한 김에 ~ 끝내 버리다 finish one's work straight out//올라가는 김에 ~ 꼭대기까지 가다 go on and climb straight up to the top of a hill.

내추럴리즘 [자연주의] naturalism.

내출혈(內出血) [의] internal hemorrhage [bleeding]; extravasation. ¶~을 일으키다 bleed[hemorrhage] internally//그는 가슴을 맞아 ~을 일으켰다 He suffered internal bleeding as a result to being hit in the chest.

내치(內治) **1** (병의) cure by internal treatment [medicine]. **내치하다** cure by internal medicine. **2** (내정) home administration[policy]; internal[domestic] affairs. **내치하다** administer the affairs of state.

내치다 [쫓다] drive away; send away; expel; [내던져 버리다] throw away; cast away; abandon; desert.

내치락들이치락 1 [변덕스럽게] capriciously; whimsically; frivolously; fickly; fitfully; blowing hot and cold; on-again-off-again. **내치락들이치락하다** be capricious[whimsical]; be full of whims; blow hot and cold. ¶내치락들이치락하는 사람 a man of moods / a capricious[whimsical] person. **2** (병세가). **내치락들이치락** change constantly; have (its) ups and downs. ¶그의 병세는 내치락들이치락한다 His illness hangs in the balance[gets better one day and worse the next].

내친걸음 having set about doing (a thing); having crossed the Rubicon. ¶~에 while one is at[about] it / on passing / at the same time//~에 들르다 look[drop] in on one's way//~이니 끝까지 해 볼 수밖에 We are in for it. / Over shoes, over boots, let's go through with it. / In for a penny, in for a pound.//이미 ~이라 물러설 도리가 없다 Now I've set about it, there is no turning back. / The die is cast.//~에 그에게 전화를 걸었다 I telephoned him while I was there.

내키다[1] [마음이] have a mind (to); be[feel] inclined (to do); feel like (doing); have an inclination; care to; be disposed (to do); be willing (to do / for doing). ¶마음 내키는 대로 as one's humor dictates / as the spirit prompts//마음이 내키지 않다 have no mind [inclination] (to do) / be unwilling[loath / reluctant] (to do)//편지 쓸 마음이 내키지 않는다 I don't feel like writing the letter.//어쩐지 일할 마음이 내키지 않는다 I am in no mood for work.//그는 마음이 내키면 몇 시간이든지 계속해서 공부를 한다 He studies for hours together when the whim is on him.//아무도 마음이 내키지 않는다면 이 계획을 포기한다 If no one is particularly interested, we'll give up the plan.//나는 마음이 내키지 않으면서도 그 일을 떠맡았다 I undertook the work though against my will.//마음이 내키면 가겠다 I'll go if I feel like it.//마음이 내키지 않는 날에는 능률도 오르지 않는다 I can't get much done on days when I don't feel interested.

내키다[2] [공간을 넓히려고 물리어 내다] make [leave] room for; remove farther; set farther ahead.

내탐(內探) a private inquiry; a secret investigation. **내탐하다** make private[secret] inquiries into (a matter); investigate secretly[in secret].

내통(內通) **1** [내응] secret communication; collusion. **내통하다** hold secret communication (with); communicate secretly (with the enemy); be in collusion with (an outsider); collude with (an undercover agent); [배반하다] betray (a person to the enemy). ¶이장은 산적과 내통하고 있다 The headman of the village is in league with the brigands. **2** [남녀가 몰래 정을 통함] illicit intercourse; misconduct; intimacy. **내통하다** commit adultery (with); have improper relations (with); misconduct oneself (with); become intimate (with).

●**내통자** a betrayer; [사통자] a fornicator;

내팽개치다

[간통자] an adulterer; an adulteress(여자).

내팽개치다 throw (a thing) out (forcefully); fling out; [일 등을] lay aside (one's work); abandon. ¶나는 자포자기가 되어 카드를 내팽개쳤다 I threw up my cards in despair. // 말을 안 들으면 밖으로 내팽개쳐 버리겠다 I will kick you out, if you don't obey me.

내포(內包) intention; comprehension; [논] connotation. **내포하다** contain; involve; [논] connote. ¶내포하는 여러 문제 the problems involved // 그의 말은 거부의 뜻을 내포하고 있었다 His words implied rejection.

내피(內皮) the inside skin; [동] the endothelium (*pl.* -lia).

내핍(耐乏) austerity; voluntary privation; putting up with poverty. **내핍하다** put up with poverty; practice austerities.

● **내핍 생활** a hard[an austere] life; a life of austerity; austerity; belt tightening. ¶~을 하다 bear a hard life / tighten one's belt.

내한(來韓) a visit to Korea; arrival in Korea. **내한하다** visit[come to] Korea; arrive in this country.

내한(耐寒) proof against the cold; cold-proof. ¶~성의 cold-proof / cold-resistant // 이 산막(山幕)의 ~ 설비는 불충분하다 This mountain hut is not adequately equipped for cold weather. **내한하다** endure the cold; be cold-proof.

● **내한 식물** a plant which can survive cold weather. **내한 훈련** training to build up resistance to cold weather.

내항(內港) the inner harbor.
내항(內項) [수] internal[inner] terms.
내항(內航) a coastwise service[line].

● **내항로** a coasting line[route]; a route in home waters. **내항선** a home-waters liner; a coastwise[coasting] vessel; a coaster.

내항(來航) a visit to these shores[this country]. ¶영국 함대의 ~ a visit of the British fleet to Korea. **내항하다** visit this [Korea's] shore (in a ship).

내항성(耐航性) seaworthiness; (항공기의) airworthiness. ¶~이 있는 seaworthy / airworthy / (우주선이) spaceworthy.

내해(內海) an inland sea; an arm of the sea; [큰 호수] a big lake.

내향성(內向性) [심] introversion. ¶~의 introvert(ed) / introversive / introvertive // ~의 사람 an introvert / an introverted person // 그는 ~이다 He is apt to turn inward(s).

내화(內貨) local currency; the coin of the realm.

내화(耐火) proof against fire; fireproof. **내화하다** resist fire; be fireproof.

● **내화 건물**[금고] a fireproof[fire-resistant] building[safe]. **내화 구조** fireproof[fire-resisting] construction. **내화 벽돌** a firebrick; a refractory brick. **내화성** resistance to fire; fire resistance. **내화재** fireproof material; refractory material; fireproofing.

내환(內患) [아내의 병] one's wife's illness; [나라 안의 걱정] domestic[internal] troubles. ¶외우~ troubles both at home and abroad / troubles from within and without.

내후년(來後年) the year after next; three years hence. ¶~까지는 in three years.

냄비 (바닥이 얕은) a pan; a saucepan; (바닥이 깊은) a pot; a cookpot. ¶스튜 ~ a stewpan / a stewpot / a saucepan // 큰 ~ a ca(u)ldron / 탁상용 ~ (풍로가 달린) a chafing dish // 프라이 ~ a frying pan // ~를 불에 올려놓다 put a pot over the fire // ~에 끓이다 boil (something) in a pan over the fire // 우리는 쇠고기 ~ 요리를 먹었다 We ate cooked beef from the pot.

● **냄비 뚜껑** the lid of a pot; a potlid. **냄비 받침** a pot stand. **냄비 손잡이** the bail of a pan.

냄새 1 (a) smell; (an) odor; (a) scent; [방향] perfume; aroma; fragrance; [악취] a stench; a stink; reek. ¶좋은 ~ a sweet[nice / pleasant] smell / an agreeable smell // 나쁜[역한] ~ a bad[disgusting / vile / foul / nasty] smell / an unpleasant[offensive] smell // ~에 민감한 사람 a person sensitive to odor / a person of sensitive nostrils // 기름 ~의 smell of oil // ~를 피우다 emit [give out / send forth] a smell / stink / reek // 그녀의 손수건에서 향수 ~가 났다 Her handkerchief smelled of perfume. // 그의 입에서 ~가 난다 He has bad breath. // 그의 셔츠에서 땀 ~가 난다 His shirt smells[reeks] of sweat. // 돼지우리의 ~가 코를 찔렀다 The pigsty stank. / The smell of the pigsty assailed my nose. // 지독한 ~군 What a smell[an odor]. // 썩은 양배추가 고약한 ~를 풍긴다 The rotten cabbage stinks [smells bad / gives off a bad smell]. // 치즈는 ~만 맡아도 싫다는 사람이 있다 Some people cannot stand the smell of cheese. // 감기가 들어서 ~를 모르겠다 I can't smell because I have a cold. // 그녀의 옷에는 신선한 풀 ~가 배어 있었다 Her dress was impregnated[soaked] with the odor of fresh grass. // 그가 지나가자 향기로운 엽궐련 ~가 풍겼다 I got a whiff of a good cigar as he passed. // ~를 맡아 보면 향수의 이름을 알 수 있다 I can tell the name of this perfume by its scent. // 그녀는 에테르 ~를 맡자 곧 의식을 잃었다 She went off at the first whiff of ether. // 개가 탈주자의 은신처를 ~를 맡아 찾아냈다 The dog smelled[sniffed] out the runaway's hide-out.

2 [느낌·티] a smack; a flavor; an odor. ¶관료 ~가 짙다 smack[savor] strongly of the bureaucrat // 그는 아직도 문학 청년의 ~가 빠지지 않았다 He still has something of the smell of a young literature buff about him.

냅다[1] (연기가) smoky. ¶아이 내워라 Oh, how smoky! // 연기 때문에 눈이 ~ The smoke irritates my eyes.

냅다[2] [몹시 빠르고 세차게] with force; hard; actively; with all one's strength; violently. ¶~ 후려치다 give a hard blow // ~ 걷어차다 kick hard // ~ 달아나다 run away for one's (dear) life / flee in all haste // 빰따귀를 ~ 갈기다 box (a person) on the ear / give (a person) a lick on the ear // 그는 문을 ~ 열고 안으로 들어갔다 He flung open the door and went in.

냅킨 a (table) napkin; a serviette. ¶무릎에 ~을 펴다 lay one's napkin across one's lap // ~을 개다 fold a napkin.

냇가 the bank of a river; a riverbank; a riverside. ¶~에서 at the side of a river / at the riverside // ~에 늘어선 포플러나무 a row of poplars on the bank(s) of a river.

냇물 [시내] a stream; (물) water of a stream. ¶~을 건너다 wade across a stream.

냇버들 [식] a purple willow; a purple osier.

냉(冷) **1** (배의) a chill stomach; a stomach

chill. 2 (몸의) a chill; a body chill. 3 leucorrh(o)ea. ⇨대하증

냉-(冷) iced; cold; chill(ed); cooled. ¶~커피 iced coffee // ~국 cold soup.

냉가슴(冷-) a hidden[secret] pain; inward pang; agony unknown to others. ¶그는 혼자서 ~을 앓았다 He had a secret trouble. / His heart pained inwardly.

냉각(冷却) cooling; refrigeration. ¶공기 ~ 발동기 an aircooled motor. **냉각하다** [차가게 하다] cool (down); refrigerate; [차가워지다] cool (off); get cool. ¶수증기를 냉각하면 물이 된다 When cooled, vapor is condensed into water. →물을 냉각시키다 cool[refrigerate] water // 고조된 베를린의 위기를 냉각시키다 take the heat out of the Berlin crisis // 그의 감정이 냉각될 때까지 기다리자 Let's wait till he cools off[calms down].

● **냉각기** a refrigerator; (미) a freezer; (음료 등의) a cooler; (자동차 엔진의) a radiator; (공기에 의한) an air condenser. **냉각기간** a cooling-off period; cooling time. ¶조금 참으면서 잠시 ~을 두는 게 좋을 것 같다 You had better be patient for a while and allow some time for things to cool off. **냉각수** cooling water; a coolant. **냉각 장치** a cooling device; a refrigerator.

냉국(冷-) cold soup; soup prepared cold.

냉기(冷氣) [찬 공기] cool air; a chilly draft [draught]; [찬 기운] cold; chill; [추위] a cold wave; cold weather. ¶아침 ~가 몸에 스미다 feel the chill of the morning air // (물의) ~를 가시게 한 다음에 마셔라 Drink the water after taking off the chill.

냉담하다(冷淡-) 1 [무관심하다] cool; half-hearted; indifferent; apathetic; phlegmatic. ¶냉담한 태도 an indifferent attitude // 정치에 대해 ~ be indifferent to[unconcerned with] politics // 그녀는 교육 문제에 대해서는 극히 ~ She is extremely indifferent about[takes little interest in] educational matters. // 그는 이기주의자로서 남의 일에는 아주 ~ He is selfish and indifferent to others. // 회사는 정년 연장 문제에 대해 ~ The company is indifferent to[about / as to] the question of postponing the fixed retirement age. **냉담히** cooly; indifferently; half-heartedly; luke-warmly; apathetically; phlegmatically.
2 [냉정하다] cold; cold-hearted; heartless; icy; frigid. ¶냉담한 성질 a cold temperament // 냉담한 인간 a cold-hearted man / an unfeeling person // 냉담한 대답 a cold reply // 그는 원래 냉담한 사람이다 He is coldhearted by nature. // 그들은 나에게 냉담했다 They were cold to me. / They gave me the cold shoulder. // 무엇 때문에 두 사람 사이가 냉담해졌을까 What caused the relationship between the two? **냉담히** coldly; icily; cold-heartedly; heartlessly. ¶이웃 사람들은 스미스 일가에게 ~ 대했다 The neighbors gave the Smiths the cold shoulder.

냉대(冷待) unkind treatment. ⇨푸대접

냉동(冷凍) freezing; refrigeration; cold storage. ¶급속 ~ quick[fast] freezing. **냉동하다** cool down; refrigerate; deep-freeze. ¶고기를 ~ refrigerate[freeze] meat // 빵은 냉동해 둘 수가 있다 Bread can be kept frozen.

● **냉동 건조** freeze-drying; lyophilization. **냉동기 / 냉동 장치** a refrigerator; a refrigerating machine; a freezer. **냉동선** a refrigerator ship; (미국 속어) a reefer. **냉동식품** frozen food. ¶급속 ~ quick-[fast-]frozen food. **냉동실** a freezer; a deep freeze. **냉동어** (a) frozen fish. **냉동육** frozen meat. **냉동차** a refrigerator car[van]; a chill car.

냉랭하다(冷冷-) 1 [차갑다] cold; chilly; frigid; icy; freezing. ¶방바닥이 얼음장같이 ~ The floor is as cold as ice. **냉랭히** coldly; frigidly; icily. 2 [태도가 쌀쌀하다] cold; cool; indifferent; half-hearted. ¶그들의 우정은 냉랭해졌다 Their friendship had cooled off [turned cold]. **냉랭히** coldly; coolly; indifferently; half-heartedly. ¶그들은 나를 ~ 대했다 They gave me the cold shoulder. // 그들은 ~ 대답했다 They gave a cold[curt] reply. / They replied curtly[coldly].

냉면(冷麵) naengmyeon; a cold noodle dish; iced vermicelli.

냉방(冷房) [찬방] a cold[an unheated] room; [온도를 낮춤] air conditioning; air cooling. ¶이 건물은 ~이 약하다 The air conditioning in this building is too weak. // 모든 사무실은 여름에는 ~, 겨울에는 난방이 되어 있다 All the offices are air-cooled in summer and heated in winter. // ~ 중 ― 문을 닫으시오 (게시) Space cooled[Air-conditioned]. ― Keep door closed.

● **냉방 완비** (게시) Air-conditioned. **냉방 장치** an air conditioner; air conditioning; an air-conditioning unit. ¶~가 된 건물 an air-cooled[-conditioned] building.

냉소(冷笑) a cold[sardonic / derisive / cynical] smile; [조소] a sneer; a jeer; a derision; a scornful laugh. ¶~를 띠고 with a sneer / with a cold smile // 그녀는 언제나 얼굴에 ~를 띠고 있다 She is always sneering [smiling coldly]. **냉소하다** smile mockingly; sneer (at); jeer (at); deride; mock at; laugh in scorn. ¶그는 나의 그림을 냉소하였다 He sneered at my picture.

냉소적(冷笑的) sardonic; cynical; mocking. ¶그의 말에는 ~인 데가 있다 There was something derisive in his words.

냉수(冷水) cold water. ¶~를 끼얹은 것처럼 소름이 끼쳤다 A cold shudder ran through me. // ~도 잠간 요기는 된다 A cup of tea may stay[stave off] hunger for a time. / Anything is better than nothing.

냉수 먹고 된똥 눈다(속담) Make something from nothing.

냉수 먹고 이 쑤시기(속담) pretending to have eaten one's fill; showing off; putting on a big act.

● **냉수마찰** a rubdown with a cold wet towel; cold-water rubbing. ¶~을 하다 rub oneself down with a cold wet towel. **냉수욕** cold-water bathing; a cold bath[douche / shower].

냉습(冷濕) [한] a disease caused by cold and dampness; rheumatism.

냉습하다(冷濕-) [차고 습하다] cold and humid[moist].

냉엄하다(冷嚴-) grim; stern; stark. ¶냉엄한 현실 a grim reality[fact] // 냉엄한 조치를 취하다 take stern measures // 시국의 냉엄한 현실을 국민에게 알리다 let the people know the hard facts of the situation.

냉육(冷肉) cold meat; (썰어 담은) cold cuts.

냉이 [식] a shepherd's purse; a pickpurse; a mother's-heart.

냉장(冷藏) cold storage; refrigeration. ¶요~(게시) Keep Refrigerated. // 이 궤짝은 ~용으로 쓰기에 좋다 This chest is good for cold-storage purpose. **냉장하다** keep (a thing) cold; keep (a thing) on ice; keep (things) in cold storage; refrigerate. ¶생선을 ~ keep fish in cold storage / 〔냉동하다〕 freeze fish.
● **냉장고** a refrigerator; a freezer; an ice chest; an icebox; (구어) a fridge. ¶전기~ an electric refrigerator. **냉장법** refrigeration. **냉장실** a cold-storage room; a cool chamber. **냉장차** a refrigerator car [van]; a cold-storage car; (미) a reefer.

냉전(冷戰) a cold war; (특히 미소간의) the Cold War. ¶~의 긴장을 완화하다 ease [alleviate] cold war tensions.

냉정(冷靜) calmness; coolness; composure; serenity; presence of mind. ¶~을 잃다 lose one's presence of mind / be perturbed / be upset // ~을 유지하다 keep calm [cool] / keep one's head (cool) / maintain one's composure / remain serene / be philosophical // ~을 회복하다 recover one's mental balance / regain one's self-possession // 그는 곧 ~을 회복하였다 Soon he regained his composure [self-possession]. / 그는 자주 ~을 잃는다 He is easily upset. / He often loses his head [his presence of mind / his composure]. // 그녀는 애써 ~을 가장하였다 She tried hard to look calm [composed / self-possessed]. / (문어) She tried hard to feign calmness. **냉정하다** calm; cool; composed; self-possessed; cool-headed; serene; dispassionate. ¶냉정한 판단 calm [cool] judgements // 냉정한 태도를 취하다 take a calm attitude (toward) / assume a dispassionate attitude // 그렇게 흥분하지 말고 좀 냉정해져요 Don't be so excited, calm yourself. // 그는 언제나 ~ He always keeps his presence of mind [maintains his composure / (구어) keeps his cool]. **냉정히** calmly; coolly; composedly; serenely; dispassionately. ¶~ 대처하다 take a calm attitude (toward) // ~ 검토하다 examine in cold blood // 사물을 ~ 생각하다 take a cool view of things // 그가 ~ 생각한다면 자기의 잘못을 깨달을 것이다 If he thinks about the matter calmly, he will find out his mistake. / Calm reflection will convince him of his error.

냉차(冷茶) iced tea.

냉채(冷菜) a cold (vegetable) dish dressed with various seasonings. ¶새우 ~ prawns and vegetables // 해파리 ~ jelly fish and vegetables.

냉천(冷泉) a cold mineral spring.

냉철하다(冷徹−) cool-headed; level-headed. ¶냉철한 사람 a level [cool-] headed person. **냉철히** cool-headedly; level-headedly.

냉큼 [곧·당장] at once; (미국 구어) straight [right] away; right now; (재빨리) quickly; promptly; swiftly; briskly; hastily; without delay. ¶~ 다녀오다 (go and) come back right away // ~ 대답하다 answer promptly [readily] // ~ 나가라 Get out at once [right now]! / Make yourself scarce! / (미국 속어) Scram! / Beat it! // ~ 해라 Hurry up! / We have no time to lose. // ~ 말해라 Tell me quick. / Spit it out!

냉하다(冷−) cold; chilly; icy; freezing.

냉한(冷汗) (a) cold sweat. ⇨=식은땀

냉해(冷害) cold-weather damage. ¶~를 입다 suffer damage due to [from] cold weather // ~ 대책을 강구하다 study how to protect cold weather damage // 농작물을 ~로부터 보호하다 protect crops from being damaged by cold weather.

냉혈(冷血) [동] cold-bloodedness. ¶~h(a)ematocryal / poikilothermal / cold-blooded.
● **냉혈 동물** a cold-blooded animal. ⇨=변온동물 **냉혈한**(−漢) a cold-hearted [heartless] fellow; a hellkite.

냉혹하다(冷酷−) cruel; heartless; callous; cold-hearted; inhuman; unfeeling; merciless. ¶냉혹한 사나이 a heartless man // 그는 아주 냉혹한 녀석이다 He is as cold as a stone. / 그녀는 냉혹한 여자다 She is as cold as ice. / She is a cold-hearted woman. // 그는 나에게 냉혹한 짓을 했다 He did something very cruel [cold-hearted] to me. / He treated me mercilessly.

-냐 [의문을 나타냄]. ¶몇 살이~ How old are you? // 지금 몇 시~ What time is it now? // 그게 뭐~ What is it?

냠냠 yum-yum. **냠냠하다** [먹고 싶어 하다] want [wish / desire] to eat; [갖고 싶어 하다] wish for; long [itch] for; be anxious for.

냠냠거리다 smack one's lips; go yum-yum; eat with much gusto [zest]; dine with a good appetite.

냥(兩) [화폐의 단위] a nyang; an old Korean monetary unit; a tael; [중량 단위] a nyang; an old Korean unit of weight equivalent to 37.5 gr. or 1⅓ oz; a tael. ¶엽전 열닷 ~ fifteen copper nyang // 한 ~종의 a nyang (weight) of (silver).

너[1] [2인칭 단수 대명사] (주격: 너는) you; (소유격: 너의) your; (목적격: 너를, 너에게) you; (소유 대명사: 너의 것) yours; (재귀 대명사: 너 자신) yourself; (고) (시어) thou (주격); thy (소유격); thee (목적격); thine (소유 대명사). ¶그것은 ~의 책임이다 That's your responsibility, you know.
너 자신을 알라 Know yourself [thyself].

너[2] [넷] four. ¶쌀 ~ 되 four doe of rice.

너구리 [동] a raccoon dog. ¶~ 모피 raccoon / coonskin.

너그럽다 broad-minded; generous; liberal; magnanimous; tolerant; lenient; indulgent. ¶너그러움 generosity / magnanimity // 너그러운 마음을 가진 사람 a person with a big heart // 너그러운 생각 a liberal mind // 지나치게 ~ be generous to a fault [to excess] // 너그러운 처분을 바라다 plead for leniency [clemency] // 반대파에 대하여 ~ be generous [liberal] to the political opponent // 여자에게 ~ be indulgent with women / have a weakness for women // 그녀의 너그러운 마음씨에는 감탄할 따름이다 I can't help admiring her broad-mindedness [generosity]. // 그는 참으로 너그러운 사람이다 He is a very generous [liberal] person. // 그는 마음이 너그러웠다 He was big-hearted [broad-minded / generous]. / He had a big heart. // 그는 나의 무례함을 너그럽게 용서해 주었다 He had the magnanimity to forgive my rudeness. // 아버지는 아이들에게 너그러우셨다 My father was lenient with us children. // 그는 종파를 달리하는 자들에게도 너그럽게 대했다 He was tolerant to those who belonged to other sects.

너그러이 generously; liberally; with leniency; with a broad mind; tolerantly; magnanimously; indulgently. ¶잘못을 ~ 대하다 deal leniently with another's errors[faults] // ~ 용서하다 generously forgive // 이번만은 너의 행동을 ~ 봐주겠다 I will overlook your behavior for this once. // 그는 그녀의 행동을 ~ 봐줄 수가 없었다 He was not able to view her conduct with a broad mind.

너글너글하다 broad-minded; generous. ⇨너그럽다

너나없이 without[making no] distinction of persons; all equally; all alike. ¶~ 모두 all [both] (of us) / everyone // ~ 컴퓨터를 쓸 줄 아는 시대가 올 것이다 The time is likely to come when (anybody and) everybody knows how to use a computer. // 우리는 ~ 그 계획에 반대다 We are (one and) all against the plan. // 우리는 ~ 같은 운명이다 We are all in the same boat. // ~ 미국의 유행을 따른다 Everybody goes after American fashion. // 그 소리를 듣고 우리는 ~ 비통했다 We all[All of us] were unhappy at the news. // ~ 정치가가 되고 싶어 한다 Everyman jack wants to be a politician.

너더댓 about four or five; several. ¶~새 about 4 or 5 days.

너더분하다 1 [지저분하다] untidy; disorderly; messy; (서술적) be in disorder[out of order]; be at sixes and sevens; be a mess. ¶너더분한 방 a room in a mess / an untidy room // 이 방은 너더분하구나 This room is in a terrible mess. **너더분히** confusedly; in disorder. ¶책을 ~ 쌓아 놓다 pile up books in a disorderly fashion. 2 [장황하다] long and boring; lengthy; long-winded; tedious; diffuse. ¶너더분한 이야기 an old wives' tale // 그의 문장은 ~ His style is rather wordy. / He writes a prolix. **너더분히** lengthily; tediously; diffusively. ¶그는 ~ 말을 한다 He talks tediously.

너덕너덕 patchily; in tatters[pieces / rags]; torn and tattered; in shreds[ribbons]. ¶~ 기운 patchy / full of patches // 옷을 ~ 집다 patch up one's clothes all over // 벽보가 ~ 붙어 있다 The wall is plastered all over with bills[posters].

너덜거리다 1 (가닥이) dangle[hang] in tatters; flutter; flap. ¶(옷이) 다 해어져 ~ in tatters[in rags and tatters] // 찢어진 옷소매가 팔을 움직일 때마다 너덜거린다 The torn sleeve of my coat is fluttering as I move my arm. 2 [함부로 지껄이다] chatter; prattle; gabble; behave fresh[forward].

너덜너덜 in tatters; in shreds; in rags and tatters. ¶그의 옷은 ~ 찢어졌다 His clothes were torn[worn] to rags. **너덜너덜하다** tattered; tagged; torn; worn-out; seedy; threadbare. ¶너덜너덜하게 낡은 가방 a worn-out bag // 노인은 너덜너덜한 옷을 입고 있었다 The old man was dressed in rags. // 이 사전은 너덜너덜하게 닳았다 This dictionary has been worn to tatters.

너덧 about four. ¶~ 사람 a four or five people.

너도나도 both you and I. ¶~ 불조심 Let's keep a vigilant guard over fire. / Let's take precautions against fire. // 아랍 어를 모르는 것은 ~ 마찬가지다 You can't speak Arabic and neither can I. // 세계 각국은 ~ 아랍의 석유를 공급받으려고 아귀다툼이다 Nations of the world are in a competitive scramble for Arab oil supplies.

너도밤나무 [식] a beech (tree).

너럭바위 a broad flat rock.

너르다 wide; spacious; open; extensive; roomy; commodious. ¶너른 마당 an open space / a plaza // 너른 벌판 an open field // 너른 수면 an expanse of water // 넓고 너른 바다 위에 on a wide, wide sea // 그는 이 너른 세상에 몸 붙일 곳도 없다 He is a forsaken man in this wide world.

너머 beyond; over; the other[opposite] side (of a mountain). ¶산 ~ across[beyond] a mountain // 재 ~ 마을 a village beyond [across] the hill // 강 ~에 across the river (from) // 안경 ~로 보다 look over (the rims of) one's spectacles // 담 ~로 말을 엿들은 것이 사실이냐 Is it true that you overheard [eavesdropped] what was said on the other side of the wall? // 서산 ~로 해가 졌다 The sun has set beyond the mountain. // 공이 지붕 ~로 날아갔다 The ball flew over the roof.

너무 too; too much; ever so much; excessively; to excess; to a fault; (미) overly. ¶~ 많은 too many[much] // ~ 크다 be entirely too big / be awfully big // ~ 빨리 끝나다 end all too soon // 그의 작가로서의 생애는 ~도 짧았다 His career as a writer was all too brief. // 내게 ~ 기대하지 말게 Don't expect too much of me. // 그놈은 세상을 몰라 How little he knows the world! // 그는 ~ 온순해서 탈이야 He is gentle to a fault. // 이 책은 ~ 어려워서 못 읽겠다 This book is too difficult for me to read. // ~ 서두르다 지갑을 두고 왔다 I have forgotten my purse in my hurry. // ~ 심한 말이군 What a thing to say! / You put it too strongly! // 그는 ~ 놀라서 말도 못했다 He was speechless with astonishment. // ~ 더워서 모두가 물만 마셔 대고 있었다 The heat was so intense[It was so hot] that everybody was drinking a lot of water. / In the intolerable[unbearable] heat, everybody kept drinking water. // 그녀는 ~ 기뻐서 춤을 추었다 She was so happy that she danced for joy. / Overjoyed, she began to dance (in spite of herself). // ~ 서두르는 바람에 자네가 실수를 저지른 것이야 You made a mess of it because you were in too much of a hurry.

너무나 [너무의 강조형]. ¶입장료가 3만 원이라고 하던데, 그건 ~ 비싸다고 생각한다 I'm told the admission fee is 30,000 won, I think it's too expensive[that's too much]. // 그녀는 ~ 화려한 차림을 하고 있어서 그녀의 딸로 오인되었다 She was wearing such bright clothes that she was mistaken for her daughter. // 그가 공처가라는 사실은 ~ 유명하다 It is too well known that he is a henpecked husband. // 그가 성공할 가능성은 ~ 적다 There is little hope of his success.

너무하다 unreasonable; (too) bad; too hard. ¶그건 ~ That's too much. / That's going too far. // 그런 짓[말]을 하다니 너도 ~ It is too bad [heartless / inconsiderate] of you to do [say] such a thing. // 이렇게 열심히 일하고서 도 욕을 먹으니 ~ It is too much to be blamed after all the work I have done.

너부데데하다 unpleasantly flattish[flat] (face). ¶너부데데한 얼굴 a flat ugly face.

너부시 (going down) smoothly. ⇨²나부시

너부죽이 flatly; pronely; levelly. ¶~ 엎드리다 lie flat[prone / prostrate] / lay oneself flat // 노예는 주인의 발 아래 ~ 엎드렸다 The slave lay prostrate at his master's feet.

너부죽하다 somewhat broad and flat.

너불거리다 flutter away; chatter. ⇨나불거리다

너비 width; (문어) breadth; range. ¶~가 넓다[좁다] be wide[narrow] in width // ~가 넉 자다 be four feet wide // ~을 넓히다 widen / increase the width // ~를 좁히다 narrow the width // ~가 5센티이다 be five centimeters broad[in breadth] // 그것은 길이 20미터 ~ 15미터이다 It is 20 meters long by 15 wide. // 강의 ~는 30피트이다 The river is thirty feet across[wide]. / ~가 5피트이다 It is five feet wide[in width / in breadth].

너비아니 slices of roast; seasoned beef in width.

너스래미 loose ends[strips]. ¶명석의 ~를 뜯다 pluck the short bits of straw from a straw mat.

너스레 1 [걸쳐 놓는 것] a frame of crosspieces[twig]. 2 [허튼소리] idle remarks; nonsense; [허풍] big[tall] talk. ¶~를 놓다 set up a frame-support // ~를 떨다 talk nonsense / make idle remarks / talk big[tall] / brag.

너울 a thin black hood worn by women for going out; a lady's veil.

너울거리다 (물결이) wave; surge; roll; swell; (나무나 풀이) flutter; undulate; waver; sway (to and fro). ¶바람에 너울거리는 벼 이삭 waving heads of rice plants // 너울거리는 불꽃 wavy flames // 머리카락이 바람에 너울거린다 The hairs swing[sway] around in the wind.

너울너울 wavily; undulatingly; waveringly; flutteringly. ¶~ 춤을 추다 dance with swaying arms // 나비가 ~ 춤추며 이 꽃 저 꽃으로 날아다닌다 A butterfly is fluttering from flower to flower. // 햇빛이 수면에 ~ 춤을 춘다 The sun is dancing on the water. **너울너울하다** wave; flutter. ⇨너울거리다

너울지다 (물결이) be rough in the distance; run high; surge; swell; billow.

너저분하다 (모양이) shabby; untidy; disorderly; messy; squalid; (행실이) slovenly; slatternly; untidy; sloppy. ¶너저분한 방 an untidy room / a room in a mess // 너저분한 집 a shabby house // 방이 ~ The room is awfully in a mess[jumble]. **너저분히** shabbily; untidily; squalidly; slovenly; in a jumble[mess]. ¶~ [너저분하게] 책을 늘어놓다 leave books in a mess[jumble].

너절하다 1 [허름하다] shabby; worn out; threadbare; unsightly; ugly; unpresentable; (구어) sloppy. ¶너절한 의복 shabby clothes / sloppy dress // 너절한 환경 shabby surroundings.
2 [시시하다] poor; shabby; worthless; paltry; petty; insignificant; trivial; unimportant; trifling; of no account. ¶너절한 변명 paltry excuse // 너절한 녀석 a good-for-nothing fellow / a person of no account // 너절한 작품 a trashy work[novel].
3 [품위가 없다] shabby; mean; vulgar(야비한); poor; despicable(치사한); contemptible(비열한); deteriorated(타락된); disgraceful(창피한). ¶너절한 취미 vulgar tastes // 너절한 거짓말쟁이 a despicable liar // 너절한 생각 mean thoughts.

너클 볼 [야구] a knuckle ball; a knuckler. ¶~을 던지다 hurl[pitch] a knuckle ball.

너털거리다 1 dangle in tatters; chatter. ⇨너털거리다 2 [너털웃음을 웃다] laugh loudly[boisterously / heartily]; roar with laughter; burst out laughing; (문어) cachinnate; guffaw.

너털웃음 a loud[hearty / boisterous] laugh; a guffaw; (문어) cachinnation; a roar of laughter. ¶~을 웃다 laugh aloud[boisterously].

너트 a nut. ¶볼트를 ~로 고정하다 fasten a bolt with a nut.

너펄거리다 flutter[flap / sway / wave] (in the wind). ¶깃발이 바람에 너펄거린다 The flag is flapping in the wind.

너풀거리다 flutter[flap / stream] away.

너풀너풀 fluttering[flapping] away.

너희(들) [2인칭 복수 대명사] (주격) you; (소유격) your; (목적격) you; (소유 대명사) yours; (재귀 대명사) yourselves. ¶오늘 밤 ~들 뭘 하고 싶니 What do you all want to do tonight?

넉 four; fourth(순서). ¶~ 달 four months // ~ 줄째의 in the fourth line (of the page).

넉가래 a wooden shovel; a snow shovel; a snowplow (미); a snowplough (영). ¶~질하다 shovel with a wooden shovel.

넉넉하다 1 [충분하다] enough; sufficient; adequate; plenty[plentiful]; ample; full. ¶넉넉한 돈 enough amount of money // 넉넉한 보급 sufficient supply // 넉넉한 치수 ample measure // 세 사람이면 넉넉할 거다 Three men will be enough for the job. // 시간은 ~ We have enough[ample] time. // 식량은 ~ We have enough[sufficient] provisions. // 2만원 정도이면 ~ Twenty thousand won or so will do[(문어) suffice]. // 이 주차장은 100대를 수용하기에 넉넉한 크기다 This parking lot is large enough to accommodate a hundred cars. / There is enough space for a hundred cars in this parking lot. **넉넉히** enough; sufficiently; fully; amply; plentifully. ¶옷을 짓다 cut clothes full / give a loose[ample] fit // 역까지 3마일은 ~ 된다 It is a good three miles to the station. // 걸어서 이틀은 걸린다 It is a full[good] two days journey on foot.
2 [풍족하다] rich; wealthy; well-to-do; well-off; comfortably off. ¶넉넉한 가정 a well-to-do family // 살림이 ~ live well / be well [comfortably] off // 그 임금으로 넉넉하게 살아갈 수 있다 I can well afford to live on the pay. **넉넉히** richly; wealthily. ¶~ 살다 live comfortably / be well off // 그는 돈은 ~ 있지만 머리가 모자란다 That fellow is short on brains, though long on cash.
3 [도량이 넓다] big-[broad-] minded; generous; lenient; liberal. ¶마음이 ~ have a lenient mind / have a broad[big] mind.

넉살 shamelessness; impudence; cheekiness; brazen-facedness; sauciness; sassiness. ¶~을 부리다 behave shamelessly[saucily] / act brazenly[audaciously] // ~ 좋은 친구로군 What nerve he has got! / What a shameless[cheeky] fellow he is!

넋 a soul; a spirit; a ghost; one's spirit(s)(기력). ¶~을 위로하다 pray for the repose of the departed soul // ~을 빼앗다 captivate /

charm / bewitch // **~을 빼앗기다** be captivated[enthralled] (by) // **…의 ~을 달래다** propitiate[appease] the souls[names] of // 그의 ~을 위로하여 기도하였다 I prayed that his soul might rest in peace.

넋(을) 놓다[잃다] get absentminded; forget oneself; [기절하다] swoon; faint. ¶그는 그녀의 아름다움에 넋을 잃었다 He was captivated[enthralled] by the girl's beauty. / He fell under the spell of her charms. // 그는 그 광경에 넋을 놓고 오랫동안 바라보고 있었다 He gazed enraptured at the scene for a long while. // 나는 넋을 잃고 그의 그림을 바라보았다 I looked at his picture with admiration[in fascination]. // 그녀의 아름다움에 그는 넋을 잃고 바라보고 있었다 He stared, dumbstruck by her beauty. // 아름다운 경치에 넋을 놓고 있다가 하차하는 것을 잊었다 Lost in admiration of[Fascinated by] the scenery, I missed my stop.

넋(이) 없다 be absentminded[halfhearted].

넋두리 **1** (무당의) utterances of a shaman given as those of a deceased spirit. **넋두리하다** (a shaman) transmit[convey] the words of the departed spirit to the bereaved family. **2** [불평·푸념] a grumble; a mutter; a murmur; a complaint. **넋두리하다** [불평하다] grumble (at / about / over); mutter [murmur] (at / against); complain (of / about).

넌더리 aversion; loathing; repulsion; disgust; revolt; repugnance; dislike. ¶공부에 ~가 나다 be sick and tired of studying // 틀에 박힌 일상생활에 ~가 난다 I am sick of[am fed up with] my daily routine. // 그녀의 불평에는 ~가 난다 I have had enough of her complaints.

넌더리(를) 대다 behave disgustfully[revoltingly / repugnantly]; weary (a person) with requests.

넌지시 secretly; indirectly; tacitly; allusively; implicitly; covertly; by hints; quietly. ¶~ 놀려 대는 말 words with a hint of teasing // ~ 말하다 hint (at) / drop a hint / allude // ~ 남을 비난하다 rebuke a person indirectly // ~ 돈을 요구하다 make an indirect demand for money // ~ 추파를 던지다 make eyes at (a person) secretly // ~ 사의를 표명하다 hint at one's resignation // 남을 ~ 떠보다 beat about the bush / sound a person (about) // 그는 ~ 나에게 손을 떼라고 말했다 He indicated vaguely that I should withdraw. // 그는 이혼할 뜻을 ~ 알렸다 He hinted at getting a divorce. // 그녀는 승낙할 뜻을 ~ 비치고 있다 She gives us to understand that she will consent. // 그는 ~ 제의를 거절했다 He indirectly declined the offer. / He intimated that he did not want to accept the offer.

넌출 [식] a bine; a vine(포도 등의); a tendril(넝굴손); a runner(고구마 등의).

넌출지다 (tendrils) hang[dangle] down.

널 **1** a board. ⇨ **널빤지** **2** a coffin; (미) a casket. ⇨ **관(棺)** **3** (널뛰기의) a seesaw board; a teeter(ing)-board.

널다 [펼쳐 놓다] spread out; stretch; [펴서 걸다] hang (something) out (to dry). ¶빨랫줄에 옷을 ~ hang out clothes on a clothesline // 옷을 널어 말리다 hang out clothes to air // 멍석에 곡식을 ~ spread grains out on a straw mat // 젖은 옷을 햇볕에 ~ spread wet clothes in the sun // 세탁물을 ~ hang out the washing.

널따랗다 wide; broad; roomy; spacious; extensive. ¶널따란 공지 wide open spaces // 널따란 밭 extensive fields // 널따란 홀[방 / 길] a spacious hall[room / street].

널뛰기 *neolttwigi*; seesaw; seesawing; teeter-totter(ing). **널뛰기하다** play at *neolttwigi*. ⇨ **널뛰다**

널뛰다 play at seesaw; seesaw; teetertotter.

널름 darting in and out; quickly. ⇨ **날름**

널리 [너르게] widely; broadly; extensively; far and wide; [보편적으로] universally; generally; at large; [도처에] everywhere; all over; throughout; at every turn. ¶~ 알려져 있다 be widely known // ~ 광고하다 advertise extensively // ~ 읽히고 있다 be widely read // 명성이 천하에 ~ 퍼지다 have a worldwide reputation // 이 교과서는 ~ 쓰이고 있다 This textbook is widely used. // 그것은 ~ 알려진 일이다 It is a matter of universal[common] knowledge. / The fact is known to the general public. // 그 사실은 나라 안에 ~ 알려졌다 The fact was known throughout[all over] the country. // 그 사실을 국민에게 ~ 알려야 할 것이다 The general public must [The people must all] be informed of the fact. // 그의 스캔들이 세상에 ~ 알려졌다 The scandal about him became generally [widely] known. // 그 사건은 국내에 ~ 알려졌다 The case received wide publicity in the country.

널리다 [흩어져 있다] be spread[scattered] (over / around); (빨래 등이) be hung out. ¶줄에 널린 빨래 the wash(ing) hung on a string // 공원에는 휴지가 널려 있었다 The park was littered with rubbish. // 낙엽이 뜰에 널려 있다 The fallen leaves are spread all over the garden. // 휴지 조각이 온 방 안에 널려 있다 Waste-paper is scattered all over the room.

널마루 a wooden floor.

널브러지다 spread (out); scatter (widely). ¶사방팔방으로 ~ scatter all directions.

널빈지 board[wooden] shutters.

널빤지 a board; a plank(두꺼운); [집합적] planking; boarding. ¶1인치 (두께)의 ~ an inch board // ~로 막다 board (over / up) / plank (over / up) / lay boards (on) // ~로 이은 집 a shingle-roofed house // ~로 지붕을 이다 shingle a roof // 큰 방의 바닥은 ~가 깔려 있다 The hall has a board[wooden] floor. // 부지는 ~로 둘러싸여 있다 The site is fenced in with (wooden) boards.

널어놓다 spread out; hang out (a thing to air or dry it); stretch out.

널조각 a piece of board[plank].

널찍널찍하다 all rather spacious[wide]. ¶널찍널찍하게 자리를 잡다 take[occupy] ample space.

널찍하다 large; roomy. ¶널찍한 집 a large [roomy] house // 선실은 생각보다는 널찍하였다 The cabin was unexpectedly roomy. **널찍이** rather widely[broadly / spaciously]. ¶구멍을 ~ 파다 dig a rather big hole [pit].

널판때기(-板-) a plank; a thick board; (집합적) planking.

널판장(-板牆) a board(ing) fence; a wooden wall.

넓다 **1** (폭이) wide; broad (road); (면적이)

넓어지다

large (territory); extensive; vast; spacious; expansive; commodious (room); roomy (house); open(널찍한). ¶넓은 길 a wide road // 넓은 방 a spacious [large] room // 넓은 집 a large [roomy] house // 넓은 사막 a vast [an extensive] desert // 넓은 풀밭 an extensive [a spacious] meadow // 넓게 펼쳐진 솔밭 a stretch of pine trees // 넓게 퍼진 가지 the spread of the branches // 폭이 넓은 강 a wide river // 어깨가 넓은 사람 a broad shouldered person // 언덕을 올라가니 넓은 경치가 눈앞에 펼쳐졌다 We got a wide [an open] view from the top of the hill. (▶ wide는 저쪽까지 거리가 있는 넓이, open은 눈앞이 활짝 트인 느낌)
2 (마음이) generous; broad-[large-]minded; magnanimous. ¶마음이 넓은 사람 a broad-minded [generous] person.
3 (범위가) large; wide; extensive; comprehensive. ¶넓은 지식 comprehensive knowledge // 넓은 범위에 걸친 독서 wide-ranging reading // 시야가 넓은 사람 a man of broad outlook // 교제가 ~ have large social connections // 넓은 의미로 in a broad sense // 넓은 시야가 요구되고 있다 One must have a broad outlook. // 그는 화제 범위가 ~ His topics cover a wide range. / He can talk about a wide range of subjects. // 그는 천문학에 관해서 넓은 지식을 갖고 있다 He has a broad [a wide / an extensive] knowledge of astronomy.

넓어지다 widen; broaden; become wider [broader]. ¶강어귀에서 ~ (the river) widen [broaden] at its mouth // 노폭은 거기서 갑자기 넓어진다 There the road widens suddenly.

넓이 [면적] (an) area; (an) extent; dimensions. ¶삼각형의 ~ the area of a triangle // 이 땅의 ~는 얼마나 되느냐 What is the area [extent] of this land? // 이 방의 ~는 20제곱미터다 The area of this room is twenty square meters.

넓이뛰기 ➡멀리뛰기

넓적넓적 flatwise; flatly. ⇨ ²납작납작²

넓적다리 a thigh; a ham(뒤쪽); a femur (pl. -mora). ¶~ 안쪽 the inside [inner side] of the thigh // 소의 ~ 고기 a round of beef // 돼지의 ~ 고기 ham // 총알이 ~를 관통했다 A bullet went through [penetrated] the thigh.
● **넓적다리뼈** the thighbone. ⇨ ²대퇴골(⇨대퇴)

넓적부리 [동] a spoonbill; a shovel(l)er; shovelbill.

넓적이 [얼굴이 넓적한 사람] a person with a flat face; a flat-faced person.

넓적하다 flat; low. ⇨ ²납작하다

넓히다 [넓게 하다] widen (a path); broaden (a road); [확대하다] extend; expand; enlarge; ream(구멍 등을). ¶세력을 ~ extend one's (sphere of) influence // 강폭을 ~ widen [broaden] a river // 운동장[영토]을 ~ enlarge [extend] the playground [one's territory] // 집을 ~ build an extension to [enlarge] a house // 사업을 ~ extend [expand] one's business / extend the scope of one's business // 경험을 ~ enlarge one's experience // 그는 활동 범위를 넓혔다 He extended his field of activity. // 해외여행으로 시야를 넓히고 싶다 I want to broaden [widen] my outlook on life by traveling abroad.

넘겨다보다 **1** [탐내다] covet; lust (for / after); have a desire [lust] for. ¶남의 재산을 [아내를] ~ covet another's property [wife]. **2** [look over] (a wall). ⇨ 넘어다보다

넘겨쓰다 be made the scapegoat (for); be falsely charged (with); have (something) wrongly imputed to one. ¶억울하게 남의 죄를 ~ find oneself in the sorry position of being charged with another's crimes // 친구의 잘못을 ~ take the blame for one's friend's fault.

넘겨씌우다 shift the blame (on to); put [lay / cast] the blame (on / upon); impute the fault (to) charge a crime (upon another). ¶책임을 남에게 ~ shift [shuffle off / slough off] one's responsibility onto another's shoulders // 자신이 저지른 실수의 책임을 동생에게 ~ shift the blame for one's own mistake on to one's brother.

넘겨잡다 guess; surmise; conjecture; [알아채다] anticipate; forecast; foresee; look ahead. ¶넘겨잡고 by guess / as a shot // 남의 생각을 ~ guess a person's intention // 잘못 [바로] ~ guess wrong [right] // 값이 오를 것을 넘겨잡고 투기를 하다 speculate on a rise of the price.

넘겨주다 **1** [인도하다] hand [turn] over; hand [pass] (a thing) to (a person); deliver; give. ¶돈을 ~ hand over money (to a person) // 시체를 유족에게 ~ hand over (a person's) remains to the family // 물건을 주인에게 ~ hand over a thing to the owner // 그에게 내가 하던 일을 넘겨주었다 I handed my work over to him.
2 [양도하다] transfer; make over; turn over (a business to); assign; alienate; convey; part with(내주다). ¶소유권을 ~ yield [transfer] ownership (of something to a person) // 정권을 ~ hand over the reins of government [power] // 재산을 채권자에게 ~ make over [assign] one's estate to one's creditor.

넘겨짚다 guess; conjecture; surmise; suppose; make [try] a shot (at). ¶남의 생각을 ~ guess a person's intention // 넘겨짚어 말하다 hazard a conjecture // 넘겨짚은 것이 맞다 make a good shot (at) / guess right.

넘고처지다 be either too long [big] or too short [small]; be good neither for one thing nor the other; [부적합하다] be unsuitable [unfit]. ¶취직 자리는 몇 군데 있으나 모두 그에게 넘고처진다 There are several positions [vacancies], but none of them is suitable for him. // 지원자는 여러 사람 있으나 모두가 ~ There are many applicants, but none of them is suitable for the position.

넘기다 **1** [넘어가게 하다] pass (a thing) over; make pass [go] over. ¶담 너머로 ~ pass (something) over a wall.
2 [쓰러뜨리다] fell; throw down; trip(다리를 걸어서). ¶나무를 베어 ~ fell [cut down] a tree // 다리를 걸어 ~ trip a person.
3 [젖히다] turn over; turn up; go over (one's notes). ¶페이지를 ~ turn over the leaves (of a book) / turn [leaf] the pages (of) / leaf through (a book) // 달력을 ~ turn over the pages of a calendar / [한 장씩 뜯어내다] tear off a sheet of a calendar // 사전을 (한 장씩) ~ leaf through a dictionary // 나는 5페

지까지 넘었다 I turned to page 5.// 그는 그 책의 책장을 넘겨 230페이지를 펼쳤다 He leafed[riffled] through the book to page 230.
4 [이월하다] carry[bring] over; [다음으로 이루다] carry forward; [연기하다] defer; postpone; put off. ¶이 문제 해결은 내년으로 넘기게 될 것 같다 This problem will probably be carried over to next year.// 그 결정은 다음 회의로 넘겨졌다 The decision was put off to the next meeting.// 결의는 다음 회기로 넘깁니다 The resolution will stand over until the next session.
5 [극복하다] keep[hold] over; get through [over]; pass[go] through; tide[bridge] over; pull through. ¶겨울을 ~ keep over the winter / (환자가) survive[live through] the winter// 하루하루를 간신히 ~ live from hand to mouth// 난관을 ~ surmount a difficulty // 재정 위기를 ~ weather a financial crisis // 우리는 그럭저럭 급한 고비를 넘길 수 있었다 Somehow we managed to tide over[ride out] the crisis.// 겨울을 넘길 만큼의 연료는 있다고 생각한다 I think we have enough fuel to see the winter out.// 이 겨울을 넘기면 환자는 회복할 것이다 The patient will survive if he can get through this winter. / The patient will recover if he can survive the winter.// 폭풍우가 고비를 넘긴 것 같다 The storm seems to have passed its peak. / The worst of the storm seems to be over.// 교섭이 고비를 넘겼다 The negotiations have passed the critical point.// 여기까지 왔으니 일의 고비는 넘긴 셈이다 We've gotten this far, so we're over the hump.// 이 환자는 오늘 밤을 넘기지 못할 것이다 The patient won't last till morning [through the night].
6 [시기를 지나가게 하다] pass; spend; (기한을) exceed. ¶겨울을 ~ pass the winter / winter// 해를 ~ pass[speed on] the old year / enter a new year// 신청 기한을 ~ pass [miss] the deadline for application.
7 [인도하다] hand[turn] over; deliver; give. ¶범인을 경찰에 ~ send an offender to the police / hand[turn] over a culprit to the police// 이 표를 가지고 오시면 현품을 넘겨 드립니다 We will give[deliver] the article in exchange for this coupon.// 그 소매치기는 경찰에 넘겨졌다 The pickpocket was turned [handed] over to the police.
8 transfer; make over. ⇨ "넘겨주다2
9 [돌리다] transmit; send round (a bill to). ¶사건을 다른 관청으로 ~ refer a matter to another office.
10 [음식을] swallow; gulp down; drink in. ¶음식을 너무 급히 ~ swallow one's food too quick.

넘나들다 frequent; visit here and there [many places]; go and come often. ¶문턱이 닳도록 ~ frequent a (person's) house.

넘다 1 [넘어가다] go over (a mountain); [get] beyond; get over (a fence); clear[take] (a hedge / a fence / a ditch); hurdle[take / clear] (an obstacle); [가로지르다] cross; go across (a mountain); [통과하다] pass. ¶산을 ~ cross[go over] a mountain// 담을 ~ go over a wall// 고개[국경]를 ~ cross a pass [the border]// 저 산을 넘으면 우리 행군은 끝이다 The march will end when we get over [across] the mountain.// 그는 대문을 타고 넘어 우리 뜰 안으로 들어왔다 He climbed over the gate into our garden.
2 [초과하다] top; exceed; go[pass] beyond (the limit); rise above; be more than; be over. ¶권한의 한계를 ~ overstep [exceed] one's authority// 50세가 ~ be more than fifty / be on the wrong[other / shady] side of fifty// 비용은 2만 원을 조금 넘었다 The expenses ran a little over 20,000 won.// 그는 키가 2미터를 넘는 거한이었다 He was a big man, topping two meters.// 그 노인은 나이가 70이 넘었다 The old man was more than seventy years old.// 이 화물은 20킬로가 넘는다 This baggage exceeds[is over / is above] twenty kilograms.// 우리의 지출은 예산을 넘었다 Our outlay has exceeded the budget.// 그녀는 30이 넘었음에 틀림없다 She must be over[more than] thirty.// 기온이 30도를 넘는다 The temperature is above 30°.
3 [때·시한이 지나다] be over[past]; fall due; run out. ¶1시가 넘었다 It is past one o'clock.// 계약 기한이 넘었다 The contract has run out[expired].// 그 일은 일 주일 넘게 걸린다 It will take over a week.
4 [들고 나아가다] tide over; pull[muddle] through. ¶넘을 수 없는 사랑의 장벽 an insuperable barrier to love// 죽을 고비를 ~ tide over a crisis.
5 [뛰어넘다] jump; hop; clear. ¶도랑을 ~ clear[take / jump] a ditch// 줄을 ~ jump [skip] rope.
6 [범람하다] overflow; run[flow] over. ¶강물이 둑을 넘었다 The river overflowed its banks.

넘버 [번호] a number. ¶~원 number one(약어 No. 1) / an ace// 병에 ~를 붙이다 number the bottles.
● **넘버링** numbering. **넘버링머신** a numbering machine. **넘버판 / 넘버 플레이트** (미) a license plate; (영) a license plate; (영) a number plate.

넘보다 1 [얕잡아 깔보다] look down on; underestimate; underrate; undervalue; hold (a person) cheap; think meanly of; disparage; belittle; make light of. ¶사람의 재간을 ~ underrate (a person's) talent// 그를 어린애라고 넘보아서는 안 된다 You should not make light of him as a mere boy. **2** covet. ⇨ "넘겨다보다1

넘실거리다 1 [탐을 내다] covet; be greedy for. ¶남의 것을 넘실거려서는 못쓴다 You should not covet anything that belongs to others. **2** (물·물결이) surge; roll; swell; be brimful. ¶물이 뱃전에 넘실거린다 The water is about to overflow the side of the boat.

넘실넘실 1 [탐을 내는 모양] stretching [craning] one's neck avidly (to see); rubbernecking. **2** wavily; undulatingly; waveringly; flutteringly.

넘어가다 1 go over; go beyond (a mountain). ⇨ "넘다1 공은 우익수의 머리 위를 넘어갔다 The ball sailed over the right fielder's head.
2 [쓰러지다] fall over[down]; go[roll] over; drop. ¶나는 뒤로 넘어갔다 I felt flat on my back.
3 [해·달이 지다] set; sink; go down. ¶해가 넘어가기 전에 before dark[dusk]// 해가 ~ the sun sets[sinks]// 해가 서산에 넘어갔다 The sun has sunk behind the western mountains.
4 [옮아가다] pass (into / to); come[fall]

넘어다보다

(to); drift; (권리 등이) pass[fall] into another's hand; be transferred. ¶화제가 판 대로 ~ drift from one subject to another // 그럼 다음 장(章)으로 넘어갑시다 Well, let's come to the next chapter. // 소유권은 A 씨에게 넘어갔다 The ownership was transferred to Mr. A.

5 [속다] be deceived[cheated]; be taken in; be imposed upon; be played upon. ¶계략에 ~ fall into a trap (set by a person) // 남에게 ~ be cheated[done in] by a person // 그런 수작에는 안 넘어간다 So that is your little game! // 그는 유혹에 넘어가기 쉽다 He is easily tempted. // 그는 내 말에 홀딱 넘어갔다 He fell completely for [He was completely taken in by] my words.

6 (음식물이) be swallowed; be taken[got] down; be drunk in. ¶버찌 씨가 목구멍에 넘어가지 않도록 주의해라 Take care not to swallow the cherry stone.

7 [젖혀지다] be turned over. ¶책장이 바람에 ~ a leaf of the book is turned over by the wind.

8 be over; fall due. ⇨넘다3

넘어다보다 look[peep] over (a wall). ¶담을 ~ look[peep] over a wall[fence].

넘어뜨리다 (서 있는 것을) let fall; bring [throw] down; (사람을) throw (a person) (to the ground); get (a person) down; knock down; trip up(발을 걸어서); (바람이) blow down; level; tip down (뒤집어엎다); pull down (무너뜨리다); push down (밀어서). ¶밀어 ~ push down // 의자를 ~ tip over a chair // 다리를 걸어 ~ trip (a person) // 남을 ~ throw[floor] a person to the ground // 나무를 베어 ~ fell a tree / cut a tree down // 집을 ~ demolish[destroy] a house(지진 등이) / pull [take] down a house // 폭풍이 벼를 넘어뜨렸다 The storm leveled[blew down] the rice plants.

2 [전복시키다] overthrow; undermine; ruin. ¶정부를 ~ overthrow[unseat] a government.

넘어서다 pass[get] over. ¶어려운 고비를 ~ get over the hump[the hard period].

넘어오다 1 (넘어서 이쪽으로) come over (a mountain); come beyond; come across. ¶국경을 ~ come over[across] the border (line) (to) // 산을 ~ come over a mountain // 물이 둑을 ~ the water overflows the bank.

2 (쓰러져) come down; fall[topple / collapse] (this way). ¶담이 뜰 쪽으로 ~ a wall topples over toward the garden.

3 [옮겨 오다] come into; transfer; be made [turned] over; be passed on; change hands. ¶내 손에 넘어온 재산 the property transferred to me (from my father) // 감독권이 A 씨로부터 B 씨에게 넘어왔다 The control [superintendence] was transferred from A to B.

4 [다음으로 이월되다] be carried forward (to). ¶잔고가 금년도로 넘어왔다 The balance has been carried over to the present year.

5 [토하다] vomit; throw[bring / fetch] up (food); spew; puke. ¶아침 먹은 것이 ~ vomit one's breakfast // 먹은 것이 넘어올 것 같다 fell nausea / feel sick / feel like vomiting // 그는 먹었던 것이 다 넘어왔다 He vomited[fetched up] all he had eaten.

6 [자기편에 붙다] come over (on our side); [투항하다] surrender. ¶(자기편에) 넘어오게 하다 get[win / gain] (a person) over / win (a person) to one's side // 자유 진영으로 ~ come over to[for] the free world.

넘어지다 1 (서 있는 것이) fall; come[go] down; topple; collapse. ¶넘어져 있다 be lying / (폭풍 등으로) be laid low // 바람에 나무가 넘어졌다 The wind brought[blew] down the trees. // 우유병이 넘어졌다 The milk bottle was over turned[knocked over]. // 차가 미끄러져서 넘어져 The car skidded and turned over[over-turned]. // 테이블 위의 병이 넘어졌다 The bottle on the table fell over.

2 (사람·동물이) tumble (down / over); fall (down / over / to the ground); go[roll] over. ¶벌렁 ~ fell on one's back // 곤두박이로 ~ fall head over heels / fall upside down // 돌부리에 채여 ~ fall[tumble] over a stone // 나는 돌부리에 걸려 넘어졌다 I stumbled over[on] a rock and fell. // 그는 한 방에 넘어졌다 One push sent him tumbling. / One push and he tumbled over[fell down]. // 그는 넘어져 무릎을 다쳤다 He fell down and hurt his knee. // 그는 얼음 위에서 미끄러져 한바탕 굴러 넘어졌다 He slipped on the ice and did a flip-flop. // 그는 세게 떠밀려 뒤로 벌렁 넘어졌다 He was pushed hard and fell on his back. // 어린이는 미끄러져 넘어졌다 The child slipped and fell (down). // 그는 돌에 걸려 앞으로 넘어졌다 He tripped over a stone and fell on his face. // 어린이들은 넘어질 듯이 달려갔다 The children ran away, half falling. // 그는 계단을 잘못 디뎌 넘어진 듯하다 He seems to have missed a step and tumbled down the stairs.

3 [패배하다] be defeated[beaten]; [망하다] be ruined; collapse; be overthrown. ¶그 정부는 곧 넘어질 것이다 The government will be overthrown before long.

넘치다 1 [흘러나오다] overflow (the bank); run[flow] over (the brim); brim over (with); be overflowing (with); [넘칠 만큼 많다] teem[swarm] (with); be superabundant [overabundant]. ¶넘치는 기쁨 an overflowing joy // 강물이 ~ a river overflows[floods] its bank // 애교가 철철 ~ be overflowing with charms // 투지가 ~ be full of fight // 그의 젊은 가슴에는 정의감이 넘쳐 있었다 His young heart was overflowing with a sense of justice. // 나는 기쁨이 넘쳐 울었다 I wept overwhelmed with joy. // 양동이에 물이 넘친다 The bucket is overflowing. // 그녀의 눈에는 눈물이 넘쳐흐르고 있었다 Her eyes were brimming with tears. // 나는 넘쳐흐르는 눈물을 참을 수가 없었다 I could not hold back the tears. // 강물이 넘쳐 마을이 침수되었다 The river flooded[inundated] the village. // 어제의 큰비로 논에 물이 넘쳐흘렀다 The paddy fields were flooded[inundated] by yesterday's heavy rainfall. // 욕조에 물이 넘쳐 The bathtub overflowed. // 물이 끓어 넘치고 있다 The water is boiling over. // 소파에 누워 있는 여자는 성적 매력이 넘쳐흘렀다 The woman lying on the sofa was overflowing [oozing] with sex appeal. // 이것은 행복이 넘치는 가족의 사진이다 This is a picture of the family, beaming with happiness. // 그들은 기운이 넘쳤다 They were full of spirit. // 이런 종류의 상품이 시장에 넘쳐흐르고 있다 The market is glutted[oversupplied] with article

of this sort.// 그는 희망에 넘쳐 있었다 He was full of[was brimful of / filled with] hope. // 아이들은 활력이 넘쳐 있었다 The children were bursting[brimming] with energy.// 그 젊은 부부는 행복에 넘쳐 있었다 The young couple were brimming over with[brimful of] happiness.
2 [지나치다] exceed; be above; be over; be more than; go too far[to excess]. ¶분에 넘치는 영광 an undeserved honor // 힘에 넘치는 일 work beyond one's power[capacity] // 분에 ~ be undue[undeserved] / be above one's means(생활 방식이)// 분수에 넘치게 살다 live beyond one's means // 그것은 넘치로 처친다 It is good neither for one thing nor for the other.

넙데데하다 unpleasantly flattish (face). ⇨>너부데데하다
넙적넙적 with one's mouth open; without hesitation. ⇨>납작납작¹
넙치 [동] a flatfish; a fluke; (북태평양산의) a halibut; (유럽산의) a turbot.
넝마 [해어진 옷] tattered clothes; rags; tatters; [해어진 천] rag; shred; scrap.
● **넝마장수** a ragman; a rag-and-bone man; a junkman; (미) a junk dealer. **넝마주이** [넝마 줍는 사람] a ragpicker; a ragman; (구어) a guttersnipe.
넝쿨 a bine; a vine. ⇨>덩굴
넣다 1 (속에) put [take / bring] in; let in; pack (something) in(to); [가하다] add (to); (액체를) pour (in(to)); fill; drop (into); [찔러 넣다] thrust; stick. ¶공에 바람을 ~ pump [blow] air into a ball // 상자에 물건을 ~ get a thing into a box // 차고에 자동차를 ~ run a car into a garage // 호주머니에 손을 ~ put one's hand in[into] one's pocket // 안약을 ~ drop a lotion into the eye // 머릿속에 넣어 두다 bear[keep] (something) in mind // 타이어에 바람을 ~ pump up the tires // 이 약 세 방울씩을 눈에 넣어라 Put three drops of this medicine into eyes. // 그 아이는 양동이에 손을 넣고 물을 휘저었다 The child plunged [stuck / thrust] his hands in the bucket and stirred the water.
2 [수용하다] accommodate; admit (into); take in (a patient); hold (so many people); [들어가게 하다] send [put] to. ¶(부모가) 아이를 학교에 ~ put[send] a child to school // 아이를 병원에 ~ send a child to (the) hospital // 회에 넣어 주지 않다 exclude (a person) from membership / deny admission to (an applicant) // 나는 두 자식을 대학에 넣었다 I've sent both my children to college. // 그 호텔은 1,000명까지 넣을 수 있다 The hotel can accommodate up to a thousand people.
3 [포함시키다] include; count among[in]. ¶이자를 넣어서[넣지 않고] inclusive [exclusive] of interest // 셈에 ~ reckon in one's calculation / count in // 계산에 넣지 않다 leave (a thing) out of count // 합격자는 나까지 넣어 10명이다 Ten applicants passed the examination, myself among the number. // 나는 그 속에 넣지 마시오 Count me out, please. // 이것도 계산에 넣어 주십시오 Add this to the bill, too. // 모든 어린이를 같은 틀에 넣으려고 하는 것은 잘못이다 It is wrong to try to fit [squeeze] all children into the same mold.
4 (중간에) put (a person) between (two parties); make (a person) a mediator. ¶통역을 넣어 이야기하다 speak through (the aid of) an interpreter // 사람을 넣어 교섭하다 negotiate (a matter) through an intermediary.
5 [예금하다] deposit. ¶나는 매월 5만 원씩 은행에 넣는다 Every month I deposit fifty thousand won in the bank.

네¹ 1 [너] (주격: 내가) you. ¶~가 틀렸어 You are wrong. // ~가 해 봐라 Try it. / Try it yourself. // ~ 이놈 You rascal! // ~가 잘못했다 You are to blame. // ~가 관여할 바 아니다 That's no business of yours. / It is none of your business. // ~**가 옳다** You are right. **2** [너의] (소유격) your. ¶~ 것 your thing // ~ 집 your (own) house // ~ 책 좀 빌려 다오 Lend me your book.
네² [넷] four. ¶~ 사람 four people // ~ 살 먹은 소녀 a girl of four (years old) // ~ 시에 일어나다 get up at four // ~ 식구 a family of four.
네³ yes; here. ⇨>예²
-네 [사람·집안의 한 무리]. ¶우리~ we all // 당신~ you all // 브라운~ Mr. Brown and his family / the Browns.
네거리 a crossroads; crossing streets; an intersection; an X-road. ¶종로 ~ the Jongno intersection [crossing] // ~마다 at every crossing // ~에서 오른쪽으로 돌아가시오 Turn to the right at the crossroads.
네거티브 negative.
● **네거티브 필름** (a) negative film.
네글리제 (@négligé) a negligee.
네까짓 the likes of you; (a person) like you. ¶~ 놈 such a fellow[creature] as you // ~ 것한테 지겠느냐 I shall never be beaten by a fellow like you. // ~ 놈이 할 수 있겠나 It cannot be done by a character like you.
네눈박이 a dog with black spots above the eyes.
네다섯 four or five.
네댓 about four or five. ¶~새 about four or five days.
네모 a square (shape); a quadrilateral.
● **네모꼴** a quadrilateral; a tetragon; a quadrangle; (영) a trapezium (pl. ~s, -zia). ¶~의 quadrilateral / tetragonal / quadrate.
네모나다 be square. ¶네모난 square / four-cornered // 네모난 종이 a square (piece) of paper / a paper square // 네모난 얼굴 a square face // 네모나게 자르다 cut square.
네발 four feet [legs]. ¶~의 [~ 달린] four-footed / quadruped // ~로 (go) on all fours / on (one's) hands and knees // ~로 가다 crawl [go] on all fours [on (one's) hands and knees] // 그는 ~로 기어 손자의 말이 되어 주었다 He became his grandson's horse, crawling along the floor on all fours [on his hands and knees].
네발(을) 타다 be allergic to (four-footed) meat.
● **네발짐승** a four-footed animal[beast]; a quadruped (animal); a beast.
네안데르탈인 (-人) [고고] a Neanderthal man; a Neanderthaler; (라) Homo (sapiens) neanderthalensis.
네오디뮴 [화] neodymium(기호 Nd).
네오로맨티시즘 neo-romanticism.
네온 [화] neon(기호 Ne).
● **네온사인** a neon sign[light]. ¶~이 깜박이는 거리 a street illuminated by neon lights.

네이팜 [화] napalm.
* **네이팜탄** a napalm bomb.

네커치프 a neckerchief (pl. ~s). ¶~를 목에 두르다 wear a neckerchief about one's neck.

네크라인 a neckline.

넷 1 [그물] a net. ¶~ 터치를 하다 touch the net / 공을 ~에 닿게 하다 net the ball / hit a ball into the net. **2** [골프] a net.
* **네트 플레이** net play; playing close to the net.

네트워크 [방송망] a network. ¶전국 30국 ~에서 방송되고 있는 텔레비전 프로 a TV program broadcast on thirty stations throughout the country.

네티즌 a netizen.

네티켓 netiquette.

넥타이 a necktie; a tie. ¶나비 ~ a bow (tie) // ~를 매지 않고 without a (neck)tie // ~를 매다 put on a tie.
* **넥타이핀** (*necktie pin) a tiepin; a tie clasp [clip]; (미) a stickpin. ¶~을 꽂다 wear a tiepin.

넵투늄 [화] neptunium.

넷 four. ¶~으로 자르다 cut (an apple) into quarters // 사과를 ~으로 잘라 모두에게 도르다 pass around the quarters of an apple.

넷째 the fourth; No. 4; the fourth place. ¶~로 fourthly // ~의 the fourth.

녀석 1 [놈] (구어) a fellow; (미) a guy; (친근 감을 가지고,) (영) a chap; a rogue; (속어) a bird; (영국 속어) a blighter; a male. ¶경칠 ~ a cursed fellow // 묘한 ~ [괴짜] a queer [an odd] fish / a funny customer // 불쌍한 ~ a poor thing [wretch] // 재수 좋은 ~ a lucky dog // 재미있는 ~ a jolly fellow // 콧대 센 ~ a plucky little devil // 저 ~ that fellow [swine / brute] // (미) that guy // 힘에 벅찬 ~ a tough customer / an ugly customer to deal with // 이 ~ You rascal! // 이 바보 ~ You fool! // 그자는 참 보기 싫은 ~이다 What a nasty fellow he is! // 그는 이상한 ~이다 He is an odd fish. // 그 ~은 대단한 사기꾼이다 He is a regular impostor [hypocrite]. / He is a complete phony.
2 [사내아이] a boy; a kid; an urchin; a chap; (구어) a young shaver. ¶장난꾸러기 [코흘리개] ~ a mischievous [sniveling] urchin // 귀여운 ~ a sweet little rascal of a boy // 요 ~ You young [little] rascal!

년 [여성의 멸시·하대의 표현] a wench; a hussy; a slut; a bitch; a whore. ¶망할 ~ a damned wench // 미친~ a crazy bitch // 이~ You wretched slut!

년 (年) a year. ¶1~에 한 번 [두 번] once [twice] a year; annually [biannually / semi-annually] // 5~ 5개월 five years and five months // 1~은 365일이다 Three hundred and sixty-five days make a year. / There are 365 day in a year. // 그 사건이 난 지 몇 ~이나 되었습니까 How many years have passed since that incident? // 그는 서울로 이사한 지 몇 ~ 되지 않았다 Not many years have passed since he moved to Seoul.

녘 1 [무렵] about; around; toward(s). ¶새벽~에 around dawn / toward(s) dawn [daybreak] // 아침~에 toward(s) morning / in the wee hours of the morning / in the early morning // 날 샐 ~에 around daybreak // 해질 ~에 about [around] sunset. **2** [방향] a direction; a way; in the direction of ...; toward(s) ...; to (the east). ¶동~의 east / eastern / easterly // 북~ the north / the northern way.

노 [노끈] a string; a cord; a small-gauge rope. ¶삼~ a hempen cord // 지(紙)~ a twisted paper string // ~를 꼬다 braid [make] a cord.

노 (櫓) an oar; a paddle (짧고 넓적한); a scull (혼자서 젓는 두 개의 노 중의 하나). ¶~ 젓는 사람 a rower / an oarsman (pl. -men) // ~를 젓다 put an oar / scull (a boat) / paddle // 박자를 맞추어 ~를 젓다 keep stroke in rowing // ~를 저어 배를 전진시키다 propel a boat with oars // 그는 15분 저었다 He worked at the oars for 15 minutes.

노 (爐) [화덕] a hearth; a fireplace; [용광로] a furnace; a kiln.

노- (老) old; aged. ¶~처녀 an old maid / a spinster / (영) a tabby // ~총각 an old bachelor.

노가다 → 막일꾼(⇨막일).

노각 (老-) an overripe cucumber.

노간주나무 [식] a juniper tree; a needle juniper.

노경 (老境) old [advanced] age; senescence; one's declining years. ¶~에 들어서서 in one's old [advanced] age / in the evening of life / when one is old // ~에 들다 be advanced in life [age] / become senescent / be well on in years / be in the decline of one's life / grow old.

노고 (勞苦) [애씀] labor; pains; toil; travails. ¶아무런 ~도 없이 without (any) effort // ~에 보답하다 remunerate (a person) for (his) labor // ~를 위로[치하]하다 reward (a person) for (his) labors // 이 저작은 신 박사 필생의 ~의 결정이다 This work embodies the lifelong labors of Dr. Sin. // 그는 그녀를 즐겁게 해 주기 위해서는 어떠한 ~도 아끼지 않았을 것이다 He would have spared no pains to please her.

노곤하다 (勞困-) languid; heavy; weary; tired; exhausted. **노곤히** languidly; heavily; tiredly.

노골적 (露骨的) **1** [숨기지 않는] naked; plain; open; undisguised; unreserved; broad; frank; candid; blunt; outspoken; plain-spoken; straightforward. ¶~인 사람 an outspoken person // ~인 비평 a bareknuckle(d) criticism // ~인 암시 a broad hint // ~으로 plainly / openly / unreservedly / broadly / frankly / outspokenly / candidly / straight out / straightforwardly / downright // ~으로 말하면 to be plain [frank] with you / to tell you the plain truth / in plain words [terms] / frankly speaking // 경멸의 표정을 ~으로 나타내어 with a look of open [undisguised] contempt // ~으로 말하다 speak plainly [openly] / speak in plain terms / call a spade a spade / talk straight / be brutally frank // 그는 ~으로 말하는 사람이다 He is outspoken [plain-spoken]. / He is not a man to mince his words. // 그는 불만을 ~으로 얼굴에 드러냈다 His look plainly expressed his dissatisfaction. // 나는 그의 ~인 비난에 움츠러들었다 I shrank back at his direct [straightforward] accusation. // 자넨 그렇게 ~인 말을 하는 것이 아니야 You shouldn't put it so crudely.
2 [표면화된] conspicuous; salient; striking;

acute. ¶양자 간의 알력은 ~인 것이 되었다 The friction between them has become more conspicuous [come to the fore].

3 [음란한] broad; lewd; [선정적인] suggestive. ¶~인 이야기 a broad story // ~인 그림 [책] an indecent picture [book] // 저 그림은 너무 ~이다 That picture is too suggestive. // 그의 농담은 점잖은 사람들에게는 지나치게 ~이다 His jokes are too broad for gentle folk.

노구(老軀) one's old bones; one's old and weak limbs; an advanced age. ¶80의 ~에도 불구하고 in spite of one's venerable [advanced] age of 80.

노그라지다 1 [지치다] be dead tired; be dog-tired; be tired [fagged] out; be washed-out; be exhausted; be worn out. ¶지쳐 ~ become as limp as a rag [doll]. 2 [마음이 쏠리다] give [abandon / surrender] oneself (to); be engrossed (in); be infatuated [taken] (by); be wholly given up (to); be addicted (to); lose one's heart (on); (구어) be crazy [mad] (about).

노글노글하다 1 [부드럽다] soft; tender; plastic; pliant; limp. ¶노글노글한 가죽 soft [limp] leather // 노글노글한 손가락 flexible [supple] fingers. 2 [유순하다] mild; meek; lamblike; obedient; submissive; docile.

노긋노긋하다 1 [아주 부드럽다] very soft [limp]; very soft and flexible; supple; elastic. 2 [유순하다] gentle; mild; docile; meek.

노기(怒氣) (a fit of) anger; an angry mood; fume; indignation; wrath; resentment; bile. ¶~를 띠고 with a trace of rising temper // ~가 등등하다 be in a black rage / be furious // ~가 충천하다 boil with rage // 그는 ~가 등등했다 Fury and anger filled his heart [head]. // 그는 눈에 ~를 띠고 일어섰다 He stood up with anger in his eye. // 그는 ~를 띠고 말했다 He said it in an angry tone.

노끈 a string; a cord; a small-gauge rope; (삼으로 된) a hempen cord. ¶종이로 꼰 ~ a twisted paper string / a twisted piece of paper // ~으로 묶다 tie with a string / cord (up) (a box) // ~을 꼬다 make a cord / 삼으로 ~을 꼬다 twist hemp into a string / make a hempen cord.

노년(老年) old [advanced] age; declining years; the winter [evening] of life. ¶~에 이르러 in one's old age [later years] / in the decline [evening] of one's life // ~에는 시골에서 살고 싶다 I want to live in the country in my old age [when I get old].

● **노년기** senescence; old age. ¶~로 접어들다 arrive at senescence / become senescent.

노농(勞農) laborers and farmers.

노느다 [분배하다] distribute [divide (up)] (among); share; allot; apportion; portion (out); (음식을) serve out (식탁에서); (트럼프의 카드 등을) deal (out). ¶돈을 둘 [셋] 이 ~ divide the money between the two [among the three] // (이익을) 반반씩 ~ split (the profit) half and half [fifty-fifty] // 음식을 노나 먹다 share food with others // 그는 재산을 세 [두] 아들에게 노나 주었다 He divided his property among his three sons [between his two sons].

노느매기 division; sharing; distribution; allotment; apportionment; a share. **노느매기하다** divide; share; distribute; apportion; portion; deal out; allot. ¶노획품을 ~ divide (their) booty.

노닐다 stroll [ramble] about; saunter [loiter / lounge] a long; wander about; hang [dawdle / hover / linger] about [around] (a place); putter about [(미)] around). ¶정원을 ~ take a turn in a garden.

노다지[1] 1 [광] a bonanza; a rich vein [mine]. ¶~를 만나다 [캐다] strike a bonanza / be in bonanza // 그는 ~를 발견했다 [광맥을 찾았다] He struck a vein. / 그는 ~를 캐냈다 He achieved a great success. 2 [큰 이익] a killing; a cleanup; a bonanza. ¶~를 만나다 [캐다] make a killing [cleanup] / strike a bonanza.

노다지[2] →언제나

노닥거리다 keep talking [chatting / chattering / joking] playfully; keep saying funny things; wag one's tongue humorously [jokingly].

노닥이다 talk [chat / chatter / joke] playfully; talk away one's time; say funny things; wag one's tongue humorously [jokingly].

노대(露臺) (건물의) a balcony; (공연·행사 때의) an open-air platform [stage / stand].

노대가(老大家) an old master; a veteran [venerable] authority (on). ¶문단의 ~들 leading figures in literary circles.

노도(怒濤) raging billows; angry [surging] waves; a high [boiling / tumultuous] sea; rough waters. ¶~처럼 밀려오는 군중 surging crowds // ~를 무릅쓰고 [헤치고] 나아가다 advance in the face of high seas // 적은 ~처럼 밀어닥쳤다 The enemy surged upon us.

노독(路毒) fatigue of travel. ¶~을 풀다 take a good rest [refresh oneself] after a journey.

노동(勞動) labo(u)r; manual labor; work; toil; industry. ¶강제 ~ compulsory [forced] labor // 경 [중] ~ light [heavy] labor // 계절 ~ seasonal [migrant] labor // 근육 ~ muscular labor // 두뇌 ~ brain work // 생산적 [비생산적] ~ productive [unproductive] labor // 시간외 ~ overtime work // 육체 ~ physical work [labor] // 1일 8시간 ~ (work) an eight-hour day // 저임금 ~ cheap labor // 정신 ~ mental work [labor] // 조직 ~ organized labor // ~의 신성 the sacredness [dignity] of labor // ~으로 생활하다 live by labor. **노동하다** labor; work; toil; engage in labor. ¶그는 노동해 본 적이 없다 He hasn't done any manual labor.

● **노동 가치설** the theory of labor value. **노동 계급** the working [laboring] class(es). **노동권** the right to labor [work]. **노동당** the Labour Party. **노동력** labor; manpower; work [working] force; labor power [force]; working power. ¶저렴하고 풍부한 ~ cheap and plentiful labor // ~의 부족 a shortage of manpower [labor]. **노동 문제** a labor question [problem]. **노동 법규** labor laws; industrial laws. **노동부** the Ministry of Labor. **노동 시간** working hours; the hours of labor; man-hours (연(延) 노동 시간수). ¶~을 단축 [연장]하다 shorten [lengthen] the working hours. **노동 시장** [사] the labor market. **노동 운동** a labor movement [campaign / drive]. **노동 인구** labor force; labor population; working population. **노동 임금** wages; pay. **노동자** a laborer; a worker; a workman; a workingman; a wage earner; (집합적) the laboring [working] population; work people; labor. ¶계절 ~ a seasonal laborer // 숙련 ~

a skilled laborer // ~의 권익을 보호하다 protect the interests of labor // ~를 착취하다 sweat[exploit] laborers // ~ 처우를 개선하다 better[ameliorate] labor conditions. **노동 쟁의** a labor dispute[trouble / strife / struggle]; 〔파업〕 a strike; a walkout; 〔영〕 a turnout. **노동절** May day. ⇨ 〝근로자의 날(⇔근로) **노동 조건** working[labor] conditions. **노동조합** 〔미〕 a labor union; 〔영〕 a trade(s) union. **노동조합원** a member of a labor union; a (trade) unionist; a union man.

노두(露頭) 〔광〕 an outcrop; a basset; a crop.

노둔하다(駑鈍−) imbecile; stupid; doltish; dull; dense; thickheaded.

-노라면 ¶그러 ~ meanwhile // 사 ~ 별일 다 당하는 법이다 You have to put up with a lot of things to stay alive.

노랑 〔노란빛〕 yellow; 〔노란 물감〕 yellow dyes. ¶~ 빛을 띤 yellowish / cream-colored / creamy / cream.
●**노랑나비** 〔동〕 a yellow (butterfly). **노랑머리** a yellow head; yellow hair.

노랑이 1 〔노란색의 물건〕 a yellow thing; yellow stuff; a yellow one; 〔노란 개〕 a yellow dog. 2 〔구두쇠〕 a miser; a niggard; a stingy [closefisted] fellow; a skinflint; a screw. ¶지독한 ~ 다 be as close as a vice // ~ 다 〔인색하다〕 He's a real skinflint. / 〔소심하다〕 He's a petty-minded little bastard.

노랗다 yellow. ¶노란 셔츠 a yellow shirt // 피부가 ~ be yellow-skinned // 노란 옷을 입고 있다 be dressed in yellow.

노래 〔가요〕 a song; a ballad; 〔장가〕 singing. ¶~를 부르다 sing a song // ~를 배우다 take lessons in singing / take vocal lessons // 너 ~ 잘하니 Do you sing well? // 그녀는 ~를 잘 부른다 She is a fine[good / beautiful] singer. // 우리 다 같이 ~ 부르자 Let's have a song. **노래하다** 〔노래를 부르다〕 〔가락을 붙여〕 sing; 〔작은 목소리로 감상적으로〕 croon; 〔표현하는〕 〔문어〕 sing (of); 〔새가 지저귀는〕 sing; 〔찍찍하고〕 chirp. ¶소리 높여 ~ sing (out) in a loud voice // 노래하여 갓난애를 잠재우다 sing a baby to sleep // 그녀는 「토스카」 중에서 아리아를 한 곡 노래했다 She sang an aria from Tosca. // 그는 기타 반주로 노래했다 He sang to the accompaniment of) the guitar. // 그녀는 갓난아기에게 자장가를 노래해 주고 있었다 She was crooning a lullaby to her baby. // 그는 사랑의 노래를 낭랑하게 노래했다 He sang the love song sonorously[in a sonorous voice]. // 그는 그녀의 아름다움을 시로 노래했다 He sang of her beauty in a poem. // 그는 이 작품에서 청춘의 애환을 노래하고 있다 In this work he expresses the joys and sorrows of youth.
●**노래방** a *noraebang*; a karaoke club. (▶ 엄밀한 의미의 「노래방」은 서양에 없음. 최근에 「가라오케 클럽」이 생기고 있으나 이 역시 무대 시설이 있다는 점에서 우리의 「노래방」과 차이가 있음) **노래자랑** 〔신인의〕 an amateur singing contest; 〔프로그램 이름〕 Amateur Singers on the Air. **노랫가락** 〔무당들의〕 a shaman's song; 〔속요〕 a popular[folk] song; a ballad. **노랫소리** singing; a singing voice; the voice of a singing person.

노래기 〔동〕 a milliped(e); a millepede; a myriapod; a wireworm.

노래지다 turn[become] yellow; yellow. ¶노래지는 나뭇잎 the yellowing leaves.

노략질(擄掠−) pillage; plunder; loot; spoilage; spoliation; despoliation; despoilment; depredation. **노략질하다** plunder; pillage; depredate; despoil; loot; sack; strip (a person of something); ravage (a land) // 남의 재물을 ~ despoil a person of his goods // 도시를 ~ plunder[sack] a town // 해적이 연안의 도시들을 노략질했다 Pirates pillaged the towns along the coast.

노려보다 glare (at); scowl (at); stare fiercely (at); look angrily[sharply / daggers] (at). ¶서로 ~ glare (defiance) at each other / stare fiercely[look daggers] at each other // 꼼짝 못하게 ~ scowl down (a person) / stare (a person) into silence // 기분 나쁘게 ~ stare (a person) down[out of countenance] // 그는 화가 난 눈으로 노려보았다 He was glaring angrily. // 궁수는 꼼짝 않고 과녁을 노려보았다 The archer stared fixedly at the target. // 그가 노려보자 그의 아내는 입을 다물고 말았다 He stared his wife into silence.

노력(努力) effort; 〔문어〕 endeavour; (an) exertion; labor; strain; industry. ¶피눈물 나는 ~ blood-and-tears endeavor // 헛된 ~ fruitless[futile] effort // …에 ~을 집중하다 concentrate[focus] one's effort on … // 최후의 ~을 하다 make last-ditch efforts // 그의 ~이 결실을 보았다[보답되었다] His efforts bore fruit[were rewarded]. // 나의 최대한의 ~도 허사였다 My utmost efforts[endeavours] were in vain. // ~ 없이는 아무것도 획득할 수 없다 Nothing can be got without effort[pains]. // 이 책은 그의 많은 ~이 결실한 것이다 This book of his is the fruit of much labor[a lot of hard work]. // 이번 성공은 주로 그의 ~에 힘입었다 We owe this success to his effort. // 온갖 ~에도 불구하고 그는 어찌할 수가 없었다 In spite of all his efforts it was beyond him. // 교섭이 순조롭게 진척되도록 그는 온갖 ~을 다하였다 He took great pains [made every effort] so that the negotiations would proceed smoothly. **노력하다** endeavor; do one's best; make an endeavor[effort]; strive (for); exert[bestir] oneself; make[put forth] efforts; work hard. ¶끊임없이 ~ persevere in one's efforts // 최대한으로 ~ exert all possible efforts / do one's best[utmost] / exert oneself to the utmost / make utmost efforts / make a supreme effort / take the utmost pains / put forth every ounce of one's energy // 노력하여 나아가다 work one's way (to) // …을 얻으려고 ~ strive[labor] for … // 조금도 노력하지 않다 do not lift a hand // 필사적으로 ~ make desperate efforts / strain every nerve // 사건의 조기 해결에 ~ aim at[strive for] an early settlement of the matter // 그는 있는 힘을 다해 노력했다 He exerted himself to the utmost. // 최대한 노력하겠다 I will make every effort[do my best]. // 나는 일몰까지 이 일을 마치려고 노력하였다 I exerted myself to finish the work by sundown. // 그는 사업을 성공시키려고 무척 노력하였다 He worked hard[endeavored] to make his business success. // 다시는 이런 잘못을 되풀이하지 않도록 노력하겠습니다 I will try not to repeat the same mistake again. // 그녀는 아내로서의 의무를 다하려고 노력했다 She endeavored to do her duty as a wife. // 우리는 이 난국을 극복하도록 노력하지 않으면 안 된다 We must strive to overcome this dif-

ficulty.// 그는 10년 동안이나 노력한 보람이 있어 성공했다 His ten long years of exertion were crowned with success.// 그는 밑바닥에서부터 꾸준히 노력해서 올라갔다 He has worked himself up steadily from the lowest rung of the social ladder.
● **노력가** a hard worker; a hard-working[an industrious] person. **노력상** a prize awarded in recognition of (a person's) efforts.

노력(努力) [노동] labor; [수고] effort; trouble; toil; labors. ¶~을 **제공하다** offer personal labor // ~을 **덜다** save one's trouble // ~이 많이 들다 require a great deal of labor.

노련하다(老鍊-) experienced; veteran; old; expert; skilled. ¶노련한 작가 a practiced[trained] writer // 노련한 노동자 a worker of experience / a skilled worker // 노련한 교사 an experienced[expert] teacher // 노련한 병사 a veteran soldier // 노련한 목수 a skilled carpenter // 그는 등산에 관해서는 ~ He is an old hand at mountaineering. // 그는 강연자로서 ~ He is a veteran lecturer.

노령(老齡) old[advanced] age; one's increasing age[advancing years]. ¶~에 **이르다** attain an advanced age / reach a great age / live to a ripe old age[a goodly age] / grow old // 그는 ~이라 그 직책을 감당 못한다 He is too old for the post. // 그는 ~임에도 불구하고 일에 착수했다 He undertook it in spite of his age.

노루 [동] a roe deer. ¶수~ a roebuck.
노루잠 a doze; a short and wakeful sleep; (미) a cat nap.
노르께하다 tinged[stained] with yellow.
노르딕 종목(-種目) [스키] the Nordic events.
노르마 (러) norma; a norm; a work[production] quota; one's assigned task. ¶생산 ~ a production norm // 종업원의 ~는 정해져 있습니까 Do you set quotas for your workers? // 오늘 ~를 아직 다하지 못했다 I haven't yet fulfilled my quota for today.
노르스름하다 yellowish; cream-colored; creamy; cream. ¶빵을 노르스름하게 굽다 toast a slice of bread to a beautiful brown.
노른자(위) [난황] the yolk of an egg; the yellow; the vitellus; [알짜] the pith; the cream; the best.
노름 gambling; gaming; a game of chance; gambling game. ¶~에 **미치다** be given to gambling / indulge in gambling // ~에서 돈을 많이 따다[잃다] gain[lose] much money in gambling // ~으로 패가망신하다 gamble away one's fortune // ~을 크게 하다 play for high stakes / play high // 쩨쩨한 ~을 하다 play for low stakes / play low. **노름하다** gamble; bet; wager; play for money; play (a game) for stakes.
● **노름꾼** a gambler; a gamester. ¶사기 ~ a card sharper / a rook. **노름빚** a gambling debt. **노름판** a gambling place[room / house / establishment / den]; a gambler's den; a casino (pl. -s); (미국 구어) a gambling joint.
노름패 a gang of gamblers[gamesters].
노릇 [일] a job; work; [기능] function; [직분] duty; an act; a place; [역할] a part; a role; [직업] an occupation. ¶**선생** ~ a teaching job / teaching // 중매쟁이 ~을 **하다** act as go-between // 주인 ~을 잘하다 play the host well // 그는 위원장 ~을 아주 훌륭히 해냈다 He performed his duties as chairman of the committee quite admirably.

노릇노릇하다 spotted[dappled] with yellow; yellow here and there; yellowish. ¶노릇노릇하게 잘 구워지다 be done to a beautiful brown / be beautifully browned.

노리개 1 [패물] a *norigae*; a pendent trinket worn by ladies; personal ornaments; (집합적) trinketry. 2 [장난감] a toy; [농락물] a sport; a trifle. ¶여자를 남자의 ~로 보다 regard women as the plaything of men // 여자를 ~로 삼다 make sport of a woman / sport with a woman / make a plaything[toy] of a woman / seduce a woman // (여자가) 남자의 ~가 되다 fall a prey to a man's lust / be seduced by a man / be made a plaything of a man / be trifled with by a man.

노리다¹ 1 [노려보다] glare[scowl] (at); stare fiercely (at). ¶무서운 눈으로 ~ look with glaring eyes / glare fiercely (at).
2 [목적하다] aim (at); have an eye (on); [기회를 엿보다] watch for; [추구하다] seek; be after. ¶…을 노리고 with the aim of ... / with the eye on ... // 그는 1등상을 노리고 있다 He is aiming at[trying for] (the) first prize. // 그가 노리는 것은 그 회사의 사장 자리다 What he is after is the presidency of the company. // 이 광고가 노리는 것은 10대 소녀들이다 This commercial is aimed at girls in their teens. // 그의 비평이 노렸던 것이 적중했다 His criticism struck[went] home. / His criticism hit the mark. // 그 권투 선수는 상대를 녹아웃시킬 틈새를 노리고 있었다 The boxer was looking for an opening so that he could knock out his opponent. // 사자가 얼룩말을 노렸다 The lion had its eye on a zebra. // 그는 도망칠 좋은 기회를 노리고 있었다 He was watching for a good chance to run away. // 그의 목숨을 노리고 있는 자가 있다 Someone is seeking[after] his life. // 그는 위원장[의장]의 자리를 노리고 있다 He is aiming at the chairmanship. // 카메라의 셔터를 누를 순간을 노리고 있었다 I watched for the right moment to press the shutter. / I was ready to press the shutter at any moment.

노리다² 1 (냄새가) stinking; fetid; rank; foul-smelling; smelled like burning hair(털이 타듯); smelled like a skunk(동물의). 2 [인색하다] stingy; niggardly; miserly; (미국 속어) pinchpenny.

노리쇠 (소총의) a breechblock.
노린내 a stink; a stinking[fetid / nasty] smell; the smell of burning hair[fat](털이 타는); the smell of a skunk(동물의).
노린재 [동] a stinkbug; a shield bug.
노망(老妄) dotage; senility; anility; second childhood. ¶~이 들었군요 You've gone gaga. // 우리 할아버지가 요즈음 ~기를 나타내기 시작했다 My grandfather has recently begun to show signs of senility. **노망하다** become senile; (구어) go dotty; (구어) go gaga; fall into one's dotage. ¶노망한 사람 a dotard / a senile (person).
노면(路面) a road surface. ¶~을 **개수하다** resurface the road.
● **노면 전차** a surface car; a streetcar; (영) a tram(car). **노면 포장** (re)surfacing the road; road-surfacing; pavement.

노모(老母) one's old[aged] mother.
노무(勞務) labor; work. ¶~를 제공하다 offer one's services.
● 노무과 the labor section. 노무 관리 personnel[labor] management. 노무자 a worker; a laborer; a workman.
노반(路盤) roadbed.
노발대발(怒發大發) wild rage; violent[raving] anger; wrath; fury. 노발대발하다 fly into a rage[passion]; burn with wrath; give one's wrath full swing; boil with rage[anger]; flare up; be in hot anger[a fume]; get into a rage; (미) get mad with anger; (구어) hit the ceiling[roof]; (속어) blow one's top. ¶그는 그 소식을 듣고 노발대발하고 있다 He is burning with anger at the news.
노방(路傍) the roadside. ⇨ 길가
노벨상(-賞) a Nobel prize[award].
● 노벨상 수상자 a Nobel prize winner; a Nobelist.
노변(路邊) the roadside. ⇨ 길가
노변(爐邊) the fireside. ⇨ 화롯가(⇨화로) ¶~에서 by the hearth / by the fireside[fire].
● 노변담화 a fireside chat[talk].
노병(老兵) an old soldier; a campaigner; a war veteran; (미국 속어) a vet. ¶~은 죽지 않고 다만 사라질 뿐이다 Old soldiers never die; they just fade away.
노병(老病) decrepitude; senile decay[infirmity]; infirmities of (old) age. ¶그는 ~으로 죽었다 He died of old age.
노복(奴僕) a servant. ⇨ 사내종(⇨사내)
노부모(老父母) one's aged[old] parents.
노브라 ¶그녀는 언제나 ~였다 She never wears a bra[brassiere] / She does without a bra.
노비(奴婢) male and female servants; slaves.
노사(勞使) labor and management; capital and labor.
● 노사 관계 the relations between labor and capital; labor-management relations; industrial relations. 노사 분규 / 노사 분쟁 a labor dispute; a labor-management dispute; a conflict between labor and capital. 노사 협의회 a joint labor-management conference. 노사 협조 union-management cooperation; harmonious labor relations; cooperation [collaboration / harmonization] of capital and labor; cooperation between labor and management; industrial conciliation[peace].
노상 always; all the time; at all times; usually; habitually; constantly; ever; every time; whenever. ¶~ 책만 읽다 always read books // 부모에게 ~ 걱정을 끼치다 be a constant source of anxiety to one's parents // 그녀는 ~ 거짓말만 한다 She is a habitual liar. // 그는 ~ 허풍을 떤다 He always talks big. // 나는 ~ 그렇게 생각하였다 I thought so all along. // 그들은 만나면 ~ 싸운다 They never meet without quarreling. // 그렇게 ~ 말만 듣고 있을 수는 없다 I can't accommodate your every whim. // 그는 ~ 호주머니에 손을 넣고 걸어 다닌다 He is in the habit of walking with his hands in his pockets.
노상(路上) (on) the road[street]. ¶~에서 in [on] the road[street] // ~에서 흔히 볼 수 있는 광경 a sight usually seen[met with] on the road // ~에서 놀다 play on the road.
● 노상강도 [행인의 재물을 강탈하는 짓] highway robbery; (a) holdup; [행인의 재물을 강탈하는 사람] a footpad; a highwayman(▶ 옛날에 말을 타고 대로에 출몰하였음); a bandit; 《미국 속어》 a holdup (man). ¶~를 만나다 fall in with footpads / be held up in the street.
노새 〔동〕 a mule.
노색(怒色) flush of anger; an angry face [look]; anger. ¶얼굴에 ~을 띠다 show anger / look black with anger.
노선(路線) 〔일정한 교통선〕 a route; 〔기본 방침〕 a line; a course. ¶민주주의 정치 ~ the democratic line // 강경 ~ a tough[hard] line / a hard-line policy // 버스 ~ a bus service route // 정책 ~ a policy line // 항공 ~ an airline // 사회당의 외교 ~ the Socialist party's foreign policy line // 공산주의의 ~을 따르다 take[follow] the communist line.
● 노선도(-圖) a route map.
노성(怒聲) an angry voice; an excited voice.
노소(老少) young and old; age and youth. ¶~를 막론하고 without distinction of age / both young and old // 죽음은 ~를 불문하고 찾아온다 Death comes to young and old alike. / Death is no respecter of age.
노송(老松) an old pine tree.
노쇠(老衰) infirmity of old age; senility; anility; senile decay[weakness]; decrepitude. ¶~ 현상을 보이는 show signs of decrepitude. 노쇠하다 senile; decrepit; old and infirm[feeble]. ¶노쇠하여 죽다 die of [from] old age.
● 노쇠기 senescence.
노숙(露宿) camping; camping-out; sleeping outdoors; bivouac(군대의). 노숙하다 sleep [pass the night] in the open (air); camp (out); bivouac.
● 노숙자 street people; the homeless.
노숙하다(老熟-) mature; mellow; experienced; practiced; veteran; seasoned. ¶노숙한 사상가 a mature thinker // 노숙해지다 be [become] matured / attain maturity [consummate skill] // 그는 아주 노숙한 사람이다 He is a very mature man.
노스탤지어 〔향수(鄕愁)〕 nostalgia.
노승(老僧) an old[aged] priest.
노심초사(勞心焦思) exertion of the mind; solicitude; anxiety; care; worry. 노심초사하다 exert oneself mentally; worry oneself; rack[tax] one's brains; be worried[anxious]. ¶노심초사한 끝에 after taking great pains / with a great deal of trouble // 노심초사하여 with a great deal of trouble // 나는 그 문제를 풀려고 노심초사하고 있다 I am racking my brains for a solution to[to solve] this problem.
노아 Noah. ¶~의 홍수 the Deluge / Noah's flood / the Noachian deluge / the Flood.
노 아웃 〔야구〕 no out. ¶~에 만루이다 The bases are loaded with no outs[nobody out].
노안(老眼) 〔의〕 presbyopia; the eyesight of the aged; long-sightedness. ¶~의 presbyopic // ~인 사람 a presbyope // ~이 되다 one's eyes get dim with age.
● 노안경 convex glasses for the aged. ⇨ 돋보기 1
노약자(老弱者) the old and the weak.
노약하다(老弱-) infirm with age[years].
노어(露語) Russian; the Russian language.
노여움 anger; indignation; rage; fury; wrath; displeasure; (은근한) quiet resentment. ¶

을 풀다 relent towards (a person) // ~을 라앉히다 quell [appease] one's anger // ~을 억누르다 [참다] restrain [hold in / contain] one's anger / suppress [repress / master] one's anger / restrain [bridle / keep down] one's wrath.

노여움(을) 사다 excite [arouse] (a person's) anger; incur [arouse / provoke] (a person's) wrath [displeasure]; give offense (to); offend (a person). ¶그는 상사의 노여움을 샀다 He incurred his superior's displeasure. / He fell into disfavor with his superior.

노여워하다 be displeased by [with / at]; take offense at; feel hurt; feel displeasure over; be indignant over [at]; be given offense. ¶노여워하여 in resentment [indignation] // 남의 행동 [말]에 ~ resent a person's actions [remarks] // 그는 매우 노여워했다 He was very much displeased. // 그녀 말에 너무 노여워하지 마시오 Please do not be offended by her remark. // 그녀는 푸대접을 받고 그에게 노여워하고 있다 She is indignant with him over the treatment she received.

노역(老役) the part [role] of an aged person. ¶~을 하다 play the part [role] of an aged person.

노역(勞役) labor; toil; drudgery; work. **노역하다** labor; toil; do hard work.
● **노역장**(一場) a workhouse; a labor house; (죄수의) a prison workshop.

노염 anger. ⇨노여움

노엽다 unpleasant; displeased; displeasing; offensive; indignant. ¶노여운 얼굴로 with a look of displeasure // 그를 노엽게 할 생각은 없었네 I did not mean to offend him.

노예(奴隸) 1 [자유 없는 사람] a slave; a bond(s)man; a bondslave. ¶반~ 상태 a condition of semislavery // ~ 같은 slavish // ~처럼 부리다 put (a person) to a practical slave labor / use (a person) like a slave // ~처럼 일하다 work like a slave / slave (away) / drudge // ~로 만들다 enslave / enthrall / make a slave // ~를 해방하다 set a slave free // 그들은 ~나 다름없다 They are no better than slaves. 2 [비유] a slave. ¶술의 ~ a slave of drink // 정욕의 ~가 되다 become a slave to passion // 사랑의 ~가 되다 be a slave to love // 금전의 ~가 되다 let oneself be a slave of mammonism.
● **노예근성** a servile spirit. **노예 매매** slave trade; flesh [human] traffic. **노예 신세** slavery; bondage; peonage; thral(l)dom; serfdom. **노예 제도** slavery. **노예 해방** emancipation of slaves.

노옹(老翁) an elderly gentleman; an old [aged] man.

노을 (하늘의) a glow in the sky; a red sky. ¶저녁~ an evening [the sunset] glow / an after-glow of the sunset / a red sunset // 아침~ a morning glow / a rosy morning // ~ 진 하늘 the sky aglow with the rising [setting] sun / the sky bright with the morning [evening] glow // 서쪽 하늘에 저녁~이 붉게 타오르고 있다 The western skies are lit up with the glow of the setting sun.

노이로제 (독) Neurose; a nervous breakdown; [의] (a) neurosis. (▶한국어로 노이로제라고 하는 경우는 nervous breakdown이 뜻에 가까움. neurosis는 병명으로서 신경증의 뜻) ¶~에 걸리다 become neurotic / suffer from neurosis / have a nervous breakdown // 그는 ~로 밤잠을 못 잔다 He is on the verge of a nervous breakdown.
● **노이로제 환자** a neurotic.

노익장(老益壯) a vigorous old age. ¶~을 자랑하다 enjoy a green old age / be hale and strong.

노인(老人) an old [aged] person; an elder; (미) an oldster; (집합적) the aged [old]; old people; old folks. ¶~ 같은 소리를 하다 talk as if one were quite old // ~을 공경하다 respect [revere] the old [aged] / make much of the old // ~을 돌보다 look after [take good care of] one's old folks / be kind to old people // 65세 이상 ~에게는 특별 할인 혜택이 있다 There is a special discount for people of sixty-five or over.
● **노인병** geriatric diseases; the infirmities of age. **노인병학 / 노인 의학** geriatrics; geriatric medicine. **노인학** gerontology.

노일 전쟁(露日戰爭) The Russo-Japanese War. ⇨러일 전쟁

노임(勞賃) wages; pay. ¶기본 ~ basic wages // 실질 [명목] ~ real [nominal] wages // 최저 [최고] ~ minimum [maximum] wages // ~을 인상 [인하] 하다 raise [reduce] the wages [cost of labor] // ~을 지급하다 pay (a person) // 싼 ~을 받고 일하다 work at low wages / work at poor pay // ~이 싸다 [비싸다] Labor is cheap [dear].
● **노임 인상** an increase [a raise] of wages; a wage hike. **노임 인하** reduction [curtailment] of wages. **노임 투쟁** wage struggle.

노자(勞資) capital and labor; labor and management.

노자(路資) travel expenses. ⇨여비(旅費)

노작(勞作) 1 [역작(力作)] a laborious work; a work to which considerable labor was devoted; a lucubration. ¶다년간의 ~ a laborious work taking years to finish / a work completed after many years' labor // 이 그림은 아버지의 다년간의 ~이다 My father spent years on this picture. 2 [힘써 일함] toil and moil; labor; elaboration.

노장(老將) [싸움에 경험이 많은 장수] a veteran general; [노련한 시합] a veteran; [노련한 선수] an experienced player. ¶테니스의 ~ an experienced [a veteran] tennis player / an old hand at tennis.

노적(露積) a stack [rick] of grain; stacked grain.
● **노적가리** stacks of grain.

노점(露店) a street stall; a roadside stand; an open-air stall; a booth. ¶~을 내다 [벌이다] open [keep] a stall on the street / engage in street stalling // 시장에는 많은 ~이 있었다 There were many booths at the fair. // ~이 일제히 철거되다 All the street stalls were pulled down simultaneously.
● **노점가**(一街) open-air stall quarters. **노점 상인** a stall [booth] keeper; a stallman; (미) a pitchman.

노점(露點) [물] the dew point. ⇨이슬점(⇨이슬)

노정(路程) [이수(里數)] mileage; (a) distance; [여행 경로] a route; an itinerary; a course. ¶10킬로의 ~ a distance of ten kilometers / a ten kilometers' journey // 기차로 1시간 정도의 ~ about an hour's ride by train [train ride / railway journey] // 자동차로 두 시간의

~이다 It is just two hours' ride in a motor-car.
●노정표 a table of itinerary.
노조(勞組) a labor union. ⇨노동조합(⇨노동)
노즐 a nozzle.
노지(露地) [지붕이 덮이지 않은 땅] the bare ground.
●노지 재배 raising outdoors.
노질(櫓-) rowing; sculling; paddling; pulling an oar. 노질하다 row (a boat); paddle; pull [ply] an oar; scull; work at (oars).
노처녀(老處女) an old maid; a spinster(▶ old miss는 한국식 영어임). ¶~ 같은 old-maidish / spinsterish // ~더러 시집가라 하다 make a superfluous remark.
노천(露天) the open air; the open. ¶~의 open-air / outdoor // ~에서 in the open (air) / out of doors / outdoors.
●노천 교실 an open-air schoolroom[class].
노천굴 opencut[(미) strip / (영) opencast] mining; open-air mining; openwork. 노천극장 an open-air theater. 노천 운동장 an open-air playground.
노총각(老總角) an old bachelor.
노출(露出) 1 [드러남·드러냄] exposure; disclosure; outcrop(광맥의). 노출하다 expose; disclose; lay bare; leave (a thing) to view; crop out(광맥이). ¶어깨를 ~ expose one's shoulders. →비바람에 노출된 벤치 a weather-beaten bench // 노출되다 be exposed [disclosed / bared] / crop out(광맥이) // 비바람에 노출시키다 expose a thing to wind and rain // 햇볕에 노출시켜 말리다 dry a thing in the sun // 위험에 몸을 노출시키다 expose oneself to danger // 창피스러운 일[수치]을 노출시키다 bring disgrace on oneself / disgrace oneself in public // 광상이 노출되었다 The deposit has cropped out[up].
2 [사진] exposure. ¶이 사진은 ~이 부족[과다]하다 This picture is underexposed[overexposed].
●노출계 an actinometer; an exposure [a light] meter; a photometer. 노출 부족[과다] underexposure[overexposure]. 노출증 exhibitionism. ¶국부 ~ a mania for indecent exposure.
노 카운트 no count. ¶~로 하다 do not count // ~가 되다 be called no count // 지금의 서브는 ~가 되었다 That serve didn't count.
노코멘트 no comment. ¶그는 그 문제에 대해서 ~였다 He refused to comment[He said he had no comment to make] on the matter.
노크 1 [문 등을 두들김] a knock. 노크하다 knock (at / on). ¶누군가가 문을 노크했다 Someone knocked at[on] the door. 2 [야구] a knock. 노크하다 hit fungoes for the outfielders; knock fungoes for infield practice.
노트¹ [배의 속도 단위] a knot. ¶25~의 배 a ship of 25 knots / a 25 knot ship // 이 배는 30~를 낼 수 있다 This ship can make [do] 30 knots.
노트² 1 [필기·각서·주석] a note. ¶~를 보고[없이] 연설하다 make a speech from[without] notes // 네 ~를 좀 보여 다오 Let me see your lecture notes, can't you? 노트하다 note [put / write / jot] down; take [make] notes of[(미) on] (a lecture). ¶강의를 ~ take notes of a lecture // 그는 선생님의 말을 한 마디도 빠뜨리지 않고 노트했다 He noted down every word the teacher said. 2 [필기장]

a notebook.
●노트북 컴퓨터 a notebook (computer); a laptop (computer). ¶~를 가지고 가다 take the laptop // ~를 이용하다 use a laptop.
노티(老-) signs of (old) age; looking old. ¶나이치고는 ~가 나다 look older than one's age [one really is] / look old for one's age.
노파(老婆) an old woman; (나쁜 뜻으로) a beldam; a hag.
노파심(老婆心) grandmotherly[old-womanish / excessive] solicitude; solicitude for another's welfare. ¶나는 ~으로 이러한 말을 하는 거야 I say this out of kindness [for your (own) good]. // 그는 그저 ~에서 그렇게 말했을 뿐이다 He only said so out of concern for you. // ~ 일는지 모르지만 그의 행동이 요즘 좀 이상하다 I may be worrying unnecessarily, but I think he has been acting strangely lately.
노폐물(老廢物) effete [waste] matter; waste material [product].
노폐하다(老廢-) superannuated; aged. ⇨노후하다
노폭(路幅) the width of a street[highway].
노하다(怒-) get [become / grow / be] angry (with a person / at something); be angered [offended / enraged / furious]; be stirred to anger; get [fly] into a rage; show temper; lose one's temper; fume; (미) get mad. ¶노하여 angrily / in one's anger / in a fit of anger // 불처럼 ~ be hot with anger [rage] / boil with rage // 그는 어떤 일에도 노하는 법이 없다 His temper is equal to any trial.
노하우 [기술적 지식] know-how. ¶그는 그 일의 ~을 익혔다 He has acquired the know-how to do the job.
노형(老兄) my respected aged friend.
노호(怒號) a roar (of anger); a howl; a bellow; an outcry. ¶폭풍우의 ~ the raging of the storm / the howling of the wind // 청중의 ~ the roar of the audience. 노호하다 roar (in anger); howl (with rage); bellow.
노화(老化) ag(e)ing. ¶외국어 공부는 두뇌의 ~를 방지한다 Learning a foreign language prevents our minds from growing old [helps keep our minds young]. 노화하다 age. ¶여자보다 남자가 더 빨리 노화한다 Men age more rapidly than women.
●노화 현상 the phenomena of ag(e)ing; (the symptom of) senility; the aging process.
노환(老患) the infirmities [diseases] of old age; senile infirmity. ¶~으로 죽다 die of old age.
노회하다(老獪-) crafty; astute; cunning; wily; foxy; insidious. ¶노회한 사람 an old [a cunning] fox / a sly old dog // 노회한 방법 a cunning way to do it / a crafty method // 저 정치가는 아주 ~ That politician is as cunning [crafty / wily] as a fox.
노획(鹵獲) capture; seizure; plunder; pillage. ¶군수 물자의 대량 ~ the seizure of a large quantity of military supplies. 노획하다 seize (the enemy's weapons); capture; plunder; grab; pillage (goods).
●노획물 a prize; a trophy; booty; loot; spoils; (집합적) plunder. ¶~을 똑같이 나누다 divide the spoils equally // 그 총포들은 적군으로부터의 ~이었다 Those guns were captured from the enemy.
노후(老後) one's old age; one's declining

years; the winter[evening] of life. ¶~의 낙(樂) consolation of one's old age // ~의 대비로 against one's old age // ~에 대비하다 provide for[against] one's old age // ~를 안락하게 지내다 live comfortably in one's old age / spend one's declining years in peace // 그는 그녀가 ~에 의지할 유일한 사람이다 He is the only prop of hers for her old age. / ~에는 편히 지내고 싶다 I want to spend my last days[remaining years] comfortably. / I want to live comfortably in my old age. // ~의 낙이 한 가지 더 늘었다 This added something else to look forward to in my old age.

노후하다 (老朽-) superannuated; aged; antiquated; senescent; time-worn; worn-out.

노히트 노런 (*no-hit no-run) ¶투수는 상대 팀을 ~으로 눌렀다 The pitcher pitched a no-hit, no-run game. / The pitcher shut the other team out on a no-hitter.

녹 (祿) a fief; a stipend; (a) salary; pay; a ration of rice; (an) allowance. ¶하는 일 없이 ~만 타 먹다 receive a stipend without rendering any service.

녹(을) 먹다 receive a stipend; eat the bread (of).

녹 (綠) 1 [금속 표면의 산화물] rust; tarnish. ¶~이 슬다 gather[form] rust / become rusty // ~을 문질러 없애다 rub off the rust // ~을 방지하다 proof (a thing) against rust / (미) rustproof (a thing) // 이 은그릇에는 ~ 방지가 되어 있다 A tarnish preventive has been applied to this silverware. / This silverware has been treated with a tarnish preventive. // 쇠는 ~이 잘 슨다 Iron is apt to rust. ⇨ Iron gathers rust easily. 2 green rust. ⇨ 동록

녹각 (鹿角) an antler; a deer horn.
녹나무 [식] a camphor (tree).
녹내장 (綠內障) [의] glaucoma.
녹는점 (-點) a melting[fusing] point; the point of fusion.

녹다 1 [열에 물러지다] melt (away); thaw; fuse. ¶불에 ~ melt in the fire / be fused by the fire // 녹아서 한 덩어리가 되다 fuse into one // 그 금속은 열에 녹는다 The metal melts with heat. // 눈이 녹았다 The snow melted away. // 보도의 얼음은 완전히 녹았다 The ice has melted off the sidewalks. // 서리가 하루종일 녹지 않았다 The frost did not give all day.
2 [용해되다] dissolve; liquefy; melt. ¶물[지방]에 잘 ~ be soluble in water[fat] // 소금이 물에 잘 녹는다 Salt is easily soluble in water. / Salt easily dissolves in water. // 이 세제는 물에 잘 녹지 않는다 This cleanser [detergent] doesn't dissolve easily in water.
3 [추워서 굳어진 몸이 풀리다] warm up; be warmed; get warm. ¶손이 ~ one's hands warm // 술을 마셔 몸이 ~ get heated with wine // 자리가 녹는다 My bed is warmed. // 몸이 차차 녹아 온다 I'm gradually thawing.
4 [반하다] be enraptured[captivated] (by); be stuck (on); be gone on (a girl); be crazy (about); be infatuated (with); be over head and ears in love. ¶그녀의 매력에 녹아 떨어졌다 I am stuck by her charms. // 그 노래에 아주 녹았다 That song really melts me.

녹다운 a knockdown. ¶~ 병의 knockdown / knocked-down // ~시키다 knock (a person) down / put (a person) on the canvas

/ (미) floor.
녹두 (綠豆) [식] mung beans; green gram.
●녹두묵 mung-bean jelly. 녹두죽 mung-bean gruel.

녹록하다 (碌碌-·錄錄-) poor (in); insignificant; worthless; good-for-nothing; trifling; of little value. ¶녹록잖은 적 a formidable enemy // 나는 그런 녹록한 짓은 안한다 I don't go for such worthless things. / I know much better.

녹림 (綠林) 1 [푸른 숲] a greenwood. 2 [도둑의 소굴] a bandits' den.
녹말 (綠末) starch; (영) farina; [화] dextrin(e).
녹말당 starch sugar. 녹말질 starchiness.
녹물 (綠-) [동록의 얼룩] rust stain; [동록의 빛깔] rust (color); reddish brown.
녹변 (綠便) green stool.
녹봉 (祿俸) a fief. ⇨ 녹(祿).
녹비 deerskin; buckskin.

녹비에 가로왈 (속담) be easily swayed by others.

녹비 (綠肥) green manure.
녹색 (綠色) a green color; green; verdure. ¶~의 green / verdant / emerald // 짙은 ~ dark [deep] green.
●녹색신고 a green return; a green-paper (on business income). 녹색 혁명 the green revolution.

녹슬다 (綠-) 1 [금속이] rust; get rusty; gather [form] rust. ¶녹슨[녹슬지 않는] 칼 a rusty [rustproof] knife // 수분은 철을 녹슬게 한다 Water rusts iron. // 뚜껑이 녹슬어 열리지 않는다 The lid is rusted shut and won't open. 2 [기능 등이 둔해지다] become dull[blunt]; weaken; be weakened. ¶게으름을 피우고 있으면 재능이 녹슨다 You'll just rust away in idleness. // 내 영어는 다소 녹슬어 버렸다 My English has gotten a bit rusty.

녹신녹신하다 very soft and flexible; quite pliant; very elastic; (녹초가 되어) limp.

녹십자 운동 (綠十字運動) a tree-planting movement symbolized by a green cross.

녹아나다 [망하다·혼나다] have bitter experiences; pay dearly (for); have a hard time of it; be ruined[exhausted]. ¶악말 고리대금업자한테 걸려서 녹아났다 I had a hell of time dealing with a bad usurer.

녹아웃 1 [권투] a knockout(약어 KO, K.O.); (미국 속어) a kayo. ¶~시키다 knock out / put (a person) down for the full count of ten / floor (a person) for a knockout / (미국 속어) K.O. / (미국 속어) kayo. 2 [야구] [투수가 계속 강타를 맞고 물러남]. ¶~시키다 (투수를) knock (a pitcher) out (of the box) / drive (a pitcher) from the mound // 우리 팀은 3회 말에 상대 팀의 투수를 ~시켰다 Our team knocked out the opposing pitcher in the bottom half of the third inning.

녹옥 (綠玉) 1 [녹색 구슬] a green bead[marble]. 2 [광] an emerald. ⇨에메랄드
녹용 (鹿茸) the young antlers of the deer; deer antlers.
녹음 (綠陰) the shade of trees; a shady nook; a leafy recess[shade]; bower. ¶~에서 쉬다 take a rest in the shade of trees / in a shady nook // ~이 우거진 거리를 산책하다 go for a walk down a well-shaded street.
●녹음방초 (-芳草) green shades and fragrant plants.

녹음(錄音) (sound) recording; phonographing; (electrical) transcription. ¶동시 ~ synchronous recording // 드라마를 ~으로 방송하다 broadcast a transcribed play. **녹음하다** record (a speech / music); (테이프에) tape; phonograph; transcribe (a program). ¶테이프에 녹음한 audio-taped (lecture) // 녹음한 음악 recorded music // 새소리를 성공적으로 녹음할 수 있었다 We were able to record the songs of birds successfully. // 그의 연설을 녹음하겠다 I will make a tape recording of his speech. // 나는 음악을 테이프에 녹음했다 I recorded the music on tape.
● **녹음기** a recorder; a tape recorder; a recording[transcribing] machine; a transcription machine. **녹음 기사** a recording engineer; a recordist. **녹음 방송** (a) transcription; a transcribed broadcast. **녹음실** a recording room. **녹음 재생기** a transcription machine. **녹음테이프** a (magnetic) tape; (카세트용의) a cassette tape. **녹음판** a record.

녹이다 1 (열에) melt (up / down); fuse; smelt; (얼음 등을) thaw. ¶버터[쇠]를 ~ melt butter[iron] // 광석을 ~ smelt ore // 얼음[초]을 ~ melt ice[wax] // 녹여서 ~을 만들다 melt down (one thing) into (another) // 그들은 눈을 녹여서 음료수로 사용했다 They melted snow to get drinking water.
2 [용해시키다] melt; dissolve; liquefy. ¶물에 ~ dissolve (a thing) in water // 그녀는 물에 설탕을 타서 녹였다 She dissolved sugar in the water. // 이 약품은 쇠를 잘 녹인다 This chemical liquefies iron easily.
3 (굳은 몸을) warm (oneself) up; take warmth; make oneself warm; thaw. ¶손을 비벼서 ~ warm one's hands by rubbing them together // 화로에 손을 ~ warm one's hands over a brazier // 그들은 불 옆에 앉아 몸을 녹였다 They sat by the fire and thawed out. // 불을 쬐어 몸을 녹여라 Warm yourself by the fire.
4 [반하게 하다] enchant; charm; bewitch; fascinate; captivate; steal the heart of; enslave; kill (a man). ¶살살 녹이는 눈짓 a killing wink // 남자의 간장을 ~ captivate [fascinate] a man // 그녀의 미소는 뭇 남자의 마음을 녹였다 Her smile captivated every man.

녹주석(綠柱石) [광] beryl.
녹지(綠地) a green tract of land; greens(초원). ¶~하다 afforest.
● **녹지 계획** a plan for afforestation. **녹지대** a greenbelt; a green zone; a tree lawn(가로와 보도 사이의).
녹진녹진하다 quite soft and sticky. ¶녹진녹진한 떡 soft and glutinous rice cake // 아교를 녹이면 녹진녹진해진다 Glue gets all soft and sticky when it is heated.
녹차(綠茶) green tea.
녹초 1 [기진맥진] utter exhaustion; dog-tiredness. ¶~가 되다 be exhausted [bushed] / be washed out / be worn [tired] out / be reduced to pulp / be dead tired / (구어) be dog-tired / (미국 속어) be pooped (out) / (영국 속어) be knackered // 피곤하여 ~가 되었다 I am dead tired. // 그는 ~가 되어 돌아왔다 He came back exhausted. // 그는 산에 오르는 도중에 ~가 되었다 He collapsed halfway up the mountain. // 3일 동안 밤낮의 협상으로 그들은 ~가 된 것 같다 After three days and nights of negotiations, they looked completely exhausted [(구어) done in]. // 겨우 300미터를 달렸을 뿐인데 벌써 ~가 되었느냐 Are you already fagged out[pooped] after running three hundred meters? // 힘든 일을 하여 그는 ~가 되었다 He was worn out[(구어) done in] by the hard work.
2 [못쓰게 됨] all tattered[out of shape].

녹초(綠草) green grass.
녹턴 [음] a nocturn(e).
녹화(綠化) tree-planting; afforestation. ¶산림 ~ 운동 an afforestation campaign / a campaign to make hills green. **녹화하다** plant trees (in an area); plant (an area) with trees.
● **녹화 장려** encouragement of afforestation.
녹화(錄畵) (a) video (tape) recording; (a) filming; telerecording. **녹화하다** record (a scene on video tape). ¶드라마를 비디오로 ~ record a drama on video tape / videotape a drama.
● **녹화 방송** a filmed TV broadcast.
녹황색(綠黃色) greenish yellow.
논 a rice paddy; a rice field; [무논] a paddy field. ¶비옥한[메마른] ~ a rice field of rich [poor] soil // ~에 물을 대다 irrigate[water] a rice field // ~에 모를 심다 plant rice / plant out rice-seedlings // ~을 갈다 till[plow] a rice field.
논갈이 plowing[(영) ploughing] a rice field. **논갈이하다** plow[till] a rice field.
논객(論客) a controversialist; a disputant; (신학의) a polemic.
논거(論據) the basis[grounds] of an argument; data. ¶…의 ~가 되다 supply argument for … // 그의 ~는 확실하다 His argument is well grounded. // ~가 아주 박약하다 Your ground is anything but convincing. // 나의 ~가 되는 사실이 몇 가지 있다 There are some facts in favor[support] of my argument.
논고(論考·論攷) a study (on[in] Korean literature).
논고(論告) the prosecutor's closing argument; the concluding[final] speech of the prosecutor; prosecution; the state's address. ¶~를 개시하다 open the arguments (on a case) // 2시에 검사의 ~가 있었다 The prosecutor addressed the court at two. **논고하다** prosecute; (the prosecutor) address the court.
논공행상(論功行賞) a granting of rewards [honors] according to each person's merits (after examining his services); the awarding [distribution] of rewards according to (each person's) merits; weighing (a person's) merit and making appropriate award; citation; the official recognition of distinguished services. ¶~이 공평하지 못했다 The conferment of honors was not fair. / The honors were not justly[fairly] distributed. // 종군자에 대한 ~이 어제 있었다 The grant of rewards to the participants in the war was made [announced] yesterday. **논공행상하다** award [distribute] rewards according to (each person's) merits; distribute[confer] honors; grant honors.
논구(論究) an exhaustive discussion. **논구하다** discuss thoroughly[exhaustively]; make a full discussion (of a matter); conduct an

exhaustive discussion.

논급(論及) reference; mention. **논급하다** mention; touch on[upon]; refer to; enter into. ¶그는 그 문제를 상세히 논급했다 He entered into a detailed discussion of the problem.

논길 a footpath between rice fields; a paddy path; a lane through rice fields.

논꼬 an irrigation gate[a sluice] for irrigating a paddy field.

논농사(-農事) rice-field farming. ¶~를 짓다 do rice-field farming / cultivate paddy fields.

논다 distribute (among); share. ⇨노느다

논다니 a prostitute; a harlot; a courtesan. ¶~ 노릇을 하다 practice prostitution.

논단(論壇) [토론 장소] a (public) platform; a forum; a rostrum; [언론계] the press; the world of journalists[criticism]; [평론계] the world of public criticism; the circle of critics [publicists]. ¶~의 거물 [문예 비평가] a great literary critic / [평론가] an eminent publicist / [언론계의 거물] a leading figure in the press circles // 그 문제는 ~을 떠들썩하게 했다 The question evoked much controversy among the publicists.

논도랑 a ditch[waterway] of a rice paddy.

논두렁 the levee of a rice paddy.
● **논두렁길** a footpath between rice paddies.

논란(論難) (adverse) criticism; denunciation; charge; (a) censure; disproof. **논란하다** criticize; denounce; take to task; attack (by argument); pass strictures (on). ¶현행 세제에 대해 ~ denounce the present taxation system.

논리(論理) logic. ¶~를 무시하고 regardless of logic // ~에 맞지 않다 be illogical / be contrary to logic / be not logically defensible // 그의 ~는 박약하다 His logic is not sound. // 당신의 ~에는 비약이 있다 There is a leap in your logic. // 그의 의론은 ~가 정연하다[성립되지 않는다] His argument is perfectly logical [is untenable].
● **논리성** logicality. **논리주의** [철] logicism. **논리학** logic. **논리학자** a logician.

논리적(論理的) logical; dialectic. ¶~ 추리 logical reasoning // ~ 필연성 logical necessity // 비~인 illogical / fallacious // ~으로 logically / dialectically // 그것은 ~으로 옳다 That is logically correct. // 그의 이론은 언제나 ~으로 짜여 있다 His theory is always founded on a logical basis. // 당신의 말은 비~이다 What you say is illogical.

논마지기 a small plot [a patch] of rice paddy. ¶그는 ~나 갖고 있다 He is something of a landowner.

논매기 the weeding of a rice paddy. **논매기하다** weed a rice paddy.

논매다 weed a rice paddy.

논문(論文) (일반적인) a treatise; an essay; (연구상의) a thesis (*pl.* theses); a dissertation; (학회 등의) a paper; (전문적인) a monograph; (신문 등의) an article. ¶박사 ~ a thesis for a doctorate [doctor's degree] / a doctor's thesis / [졸업] a graduation thesis // 미국 문학에 관한 ~ a treatise [theme / paper] on American literature // ~을 쓰다 write a paper [thesis / monograph] (on) // ~을 심사하다 examine (a person's) paper (on) // 대학에 학위 ~을 제출하다 submit a dissertation to a university // ~을 제출하여 박사 학위를 받다 obtain a doctorate by presenting a thesis [dissertation] // 그녀가 제출한 ~은 입상(入賞) 수준에 이르지 못했다 The paper submitted by her did not measure up to the standard deserving of a prize.
● **논문 심사** the examination of a thesis. **논문집** a collection of learned papers.

논문서(-文書) the title deed of a rice paddy.

논물 water in a rice paddy. ¶~을 대다 draw water for a rice paddy.

논박(論駁) refutation; confutation; attack. **논박하다** argue against; attack the weak points in one's opponent's[a person's] argument; confute; refute; contradict(반박하다).

논밭 rice paddies and dry fields; fields; a farm.

논법(論法) a line of argument; logic; reasoning. ¶삼단 ~ a syllogism // ~의 정확성 logical soundness / logicality // 같은 ~을 쓰다 use the same argument // ~을 바꾸다 change the line of argument / approach from another standpoint // 그것은 잘못된 ~이다 You are following [That's] a false [wrong] line of argument. // 그는 그 나름의 ~이 있다 He has a logic of all his own. / He has his own brand of logic. // 그는 ~에 맞지 않는 말을 한다 He is not governed by logic.

논변(論辯) discussion. ⇨변론(辯論)1

논보리 barley planted in a paddy field; a paddy-cultivated barley.

논봉(論鋒) [의론하는 기세] the force of an argument; [논법] logic. ¶날카로운 ~ an incisive [a keen] argument // ~을 …으로 돌리다 turn the force of one's argument against … // 그는 최 씨의 ~에 말문이 막혔다 He was silenced by Mr. Choe's argument. // 그의 ~은 아주 날카로웠다 His argument was very powerful.

논설(論說) [논문] a discourse; a dissertation; [사설] a leading article; a leader; (미) an editorial. ¶국제 정의에 관한 ~ an editorial [a leading article] on international justice // 사건을 ~로 다루다 devote a leader to the case / (미) editorialize on the case.
● **논설란** the editorial column. **논설위원** a leader writer; an editorial writer; an editorialist.

논술(論述) statement; enunciation. **논술하다** enunciate; state; set forth.

논어(論語) the Analects [Discourses] of Confucius.

논외(論外) ¶~의 [문제가 안 되는] out of the question / [논의의 범위를 벗어난] beside the question / irrelevant / impertinent // ~다 be not germane [pertinent / relevant] to the subject.

논의(論議) (서로 주장하는) (an) argument; [토의] (a) discussion; [논쟁] (a) dispute; [토론] a debate. ¶활발한 ~ a lively discussion [exchange of views] // 정치상의 ~ a political discussion // 승산이 없는 [의미가 없는] ~ a loosing [meaningless] argument // ~에서 이기다[지다] win [lose] an argument // (일이) ~중이다 be under discussion [debate] // 열띤 ~를 벌이다 develop heated discussions // 그의 ~는 논리 정연하다 His argument is quite logical [sound]. // 그의 발언은 활발한 ~를 불러 일으켰다 His statement aroused a great deal of controversy. // 그 점에 대해서 나는 그와 열띤 ~를 했다 I wrangled [had a hot dis-

논의 cussion] with him about that point. **논의하다** discuss (a matter); argue (about); debate (on / about). ¶문제를 ~ argue about[over] a matter // 충분히 ~ discuss (a subject) fully[at length] / have a full discussion // 그것은 논의할 만하다 That is debatable[is a disputable point]. // 저 사람하고는 논의해 보아야 소용없다 There is no arguing with that man. // 그 문제는 논의할 가치가 없다 The matter is not worth discussing. // 계획에 대해서는 충분히 논의하였다 We discussed the plan through and through. / We had a thorough discussion of the plan.

논의(論意) the point of an argument. ⇨ **논지**(論旨)

논자(論者) [논객] a debater; a disputant; [주창자] an advocate; an apostle (of); [논문의 집필자] the (present) writer. ¶~ 쌍방은 논의하고 있던 문제에 대해 알지 못했다 The disputants on both sides were ignorant of the matter they were disputing about.

논쟁(論爭) a dispute; a controversy; a contention; an argument; a polemic. ¶법률상의 ~ a dispute over a point of law // 열띤 ~ a heated controversy // ~ 중인 문제 the question at issue // ~의 여지가 없다 be indisputable[incontestable / incontrovertible / be beyond[past] dispute // ~에 끼어들다 enter into[join in] a dispute // ~을 벌이다 go into a dispute // 그 일은 ~의 여지가 있다 The matter is beyond[past] dispute. // 그는 교묘하게 ~을 피했다 He maneuvered himself out of the argument. // 그 건은 ~ 중이다 The matter is being disputed. // 그들 사이에서는 ~이 끊일 새 없다 There are constant disputes between them. // 그것은 ~의 여지가 있는 이론이다 It is a controversial theory. // 그 법안을 둘러싸고 국회에서 열띤 ~이 일고 있다 There is a hot controversy [dispute] in the National Assembly about the bill. // 그들은 개정안을 놓고 열띤 ~을 벌였다 They had a heated[hot] dispute over the amendment. // 그 문제를 둘러싸고 찬성파와 반대파가 격심한 ~을 벌였다 The supporters and the objecting members had a heated argument on the matter. **논쟁하다** argue; have an argument (with); dispute; contend; controvert; take issue (with). ¶어떤 문제에 관해 남과 ~ argue[(문어) dispute] with a person about[on / concerning] a subject.

● **논쟁자** a disputant; a controversialist; a debater.

논적(論敵) one's opponent[adversary] (in argument / debate).

논전(論戰) a dispute. ⇨ = **논쟁**

논점(論點) a (disputed / moot) point; an arguing point; the point at issue[in dispute / in question]. ¶의견이 분분한 ~ a very moot point // ~을 분명히 하다 make one's point clear // ~을 파악하다 get (a person's) point // 그 질문은 ~에서 벗어나 있는 것 같다 That question seems to be off[beside] the point. // 주된 ~은 그 돈의 사용처에 있었다 The main (point at) issue was what the money had been used for.

논제(論題) the subject[theme / text] of one's argument[article / lecture]; a topic for discussion. ¶~에서 벗어나다 digress from one's text[theme] // ~에서 벗어나지 않다 stick to one's text[theme].

논조(論調) the tone[tenor / drift] of argument. ¶이 문제에 관한 각 신문 사설의 ~는 한결같다 The editorial on this question are the same in tenor[tone]. // 그의 ~는 최근 부드러워진 것 같다 He seems to have softened tone of his argument recently. // 이 논평은 권력에 영합하는 ~로 쓰여 있다 This commentary caters to the wishes of the authorities.

논죄(論罪) ruling; finding. **논죄하다** rule; find.

논증(論證) (a) demonstration; proof. ¶직접[간접] ~ direct[indirect] demonstration // ~적(인) demonstrative // ~적으로 demonstratively. **논증하다** prove; demonstrate; bear (something) out by fact[proof]; adduce arguments.

논지(論旨) the point[gist / drift / tenor] of an argument. ¶~를 분명히 해 주시오 Please make your point clear. // 그의 논문의 ~를 이해할 수 없다 I cannot make out what he is aiming at in his paper[(문어) the purpose of his paper]. // 너의 ~는 분명치 않다 Your argument is not convincing[to the point].

논총(論叢) a collection of treatises.

논파하다(論破-) [반론하다] refute (an argument); confute (one's opponent); disprove; [꺽소리 못하게 하다] argue[talk] (a person) down; argue (a person) into silence; defeat (a person) in argument. ¶그녀는 냉정한 논리로 상대를 논파했다 Her cool logic beat [vanquished] her adversary.

논평(論評) (a) criticism; a comment; a review; commentary. ¶이 문제에 관한 신문의 ~ newspaper[press] comments on this subject // 남의 작품에 ~을 가하다 make a review of a person's work // ~을 피하다 eschew comment (on) // ~을 삼가다 withhold comment. **논평하다** criticize; review; comment (on current topics). ¶신문은 그 계획에 대해 신랄하게 논평했다 The newspapers commented harshly on the plan.

논풀다 make land into rice fields.

논픽션 nonfiction.

● **논픽션 작가** a nonfictioneer; a nonfiction writer; a writer of nonfiction.

논하다(論-) 1 [논의하다] discuss (a matter); argue (on / about); dispute (on / about); [평론하다] comment (on). ¶논할 것도 없이 needless to say // 정치[문학]를 ~ discuss politics[literature] // 시사 문제를 ~ comment on current topics // 논할 필요가 없다 be beyond question // 그는 그 문제에 관하여 막힘없이 논했다 He talked[argued] on the subject with flowing eloquence. 2 [(문제)를 다루다] treat of; deal with. ¶이 책은 자연주의에 대해 논하고 있다 This book deals with naturalism.

놀 a glow in the sky. ⇨ **노을**

놀[2] [파도] a big[heavy / giant] wave; a high sea; a billow; a swell; a big roller. ¶~이 잇달아 그 배의 갑판을 쓸었다 Heavy waves washed[broke] over the deck of the ship.

놀다[1] 1 [유희하다] play. ¶화투를 가지고 ~ play (at) cards // 장난감을 갖고 ~ play with a toy // 소꿉장난[숨바꼭질]을 ~ play house [hide-and-seek] // 놀고 있다 be at play // 노는 데 여념이 없다 be hard at play / be lost in play // 놀러 나가다 go out to play // 놀며 시간

놀라다

을 보내다 play away one's time // 아이가 개와 놀고 있다 A child is playing with a dog. // 나가서 놀아라, 싸우지는 말고 Go and play, and don't fight. // 놀러 나가도 돼요 Can I go out to play? // 놀고 있는 아이들의 목소리가 들렸다 We heard the voices of children at play. // 그 아이는 같이 놀 친구가 없다 The children has no one to play with. // 공부만 하고 놀지 않으면 애가 못쓰게 된다 All work and no play make Jack a dull boy. // 노는 시간에 교실에 남아 있으면 안 된다 You must not stay in the classroom during playtime.

2 [즐기다] amuse [divert] oneself; enjoy oneself. ¶놀기 좋아하는 fun-[amusement-]loving / pleasure-seeking // 그림책을 보며 ~ amuse oneself with picture books // 노래를 부르며 ~ divert oneself in [amuse oneself with] singing // 장기를 두며 ~ amuse oneself playing chess // 아이들과 함께 ~ have some fun with the kids // 우리는 아주 즐겁게 놀았다 We had a very good [nice] time. / We had a lot of fun. // 아이들은 들에서 아주 즐겁게 놀았다 The children had a lot of fun in the field. / The children had a merry [pleasant] time in the field. // 아이들이 신나게 놀고 있다 The children are having a merry time. // 그 소년은 비누 거품을 불어 만들며 놀았다 The boy enjoyed blowing soap bubbles. // 남들은 일하고 있는데 그는 놀고 있었다 He was enjoying himself [(구어) fooling around] while the others were at work. // 나는 지금 놀 기분이 아니다 I am not in the mood for fun. // 볼 일도 보고 놀기도 할 겸 왔습니다 I've come partly on business and partly for pleasure. // 거기는 놀러 간 게 아니라 일이 있어 간 겁니다 I went there on business, not for pleasure.

3 [소풍·방문하다] ¶놀러 가다 make [go on] an excursion (to) / make a (pleasure) trip (to) / go on a picnic (to) / visit // 시골에 놀러 가다 go into the country for pleasure // 다음 일요일에는 용인에 놀러 간다 We are going on an excursion to Yongin next Sunday. // 또 놀러 오게 Come and see me again.

4 [유흥하다] make merry; have a spree; take one's pleasure; [방탕하다] lead a fast [dissolute] life; frequent the gay quarters; visit the red-light district. ¶…과 마음껏 have an all-out fling with (a gisaeng) // 그는 젊은 시절에 많이 놀았다 He frequented the red light district in his youth. / He used to go out on the town in his younger days.

5 [일하지 않다] be idle; be doing nothing; be loafing and lolling; take one's ease. ¶노는 사람 an idle man / an idler // 노는 날 a holiday / an off day (비번 날) // 하루 (쉬며) ~ take a holiday / take a day off // 놀며 지내다 idle [loaf] one's time away / live in idleness / spend one's time (in) doing nothing // 놀고 먹다 eat the bread of idleness / live a life of ease // 놀고 월급 받다 be paid for no work / have an unearned income // 나는 퇴직 후에 놀고 있다 I'm taking life easy after my retirement. // 나는 자동차 사고 후 1년 동안 놀고 지냈다 After the car accident I spent a year doing nothing. // 계속 공부만 하지 말고 가끔 놀기도 해야 한다 You ought to take your ease once in a while instead of working continuously.

6 [사용되지 않고 있다] be not in use; lie [stand] idle. ¶놀고 있는 기계 an unused [idle] machine / a machine not in use [standing idle] // 놀고 있는 돈 idle money // 놀고 있는 자본 unemployed capital / idle [sleeping] funds // 놀고 있는 땅 land lying idle [fallow] // 컴퓨터가 놀고 있다 The computer is not used.

7 [실직하다] be out of work [employment / job]; be unemployed. ¶놀고 있는 사람 an unemployed person / a jobless man / a man out of work [employment] / the unemployed (집합적) // 그는 요즘 놀고 있다 He is out of work these days. // 나는 한 달 가량이나 (일자리를 얻지 못해) 놀고 있다 I have been out of work [been unemployed] for about a month.

8 [고정된 것이] totter; shake; give; be loose [unstable / unsteady / rickety / shaky / wobbly]; have play. ¶바퀴와 굴대가 잘 놀도록 하다 give a wheel more play on the axle // 나사가 논다 The screw is loose. // 이가 논다 I have a loose tooth. // 의자가 논다 The chair is rickety. // 바위가 논다 The rock shakes [gives].

9 [멋대로 행동하다] act rashly [flippantly] as one pleases; [주책없이 굴다] play [act] the fool [ass]. ¶멋대로 놀게 하다 allow (a person) to go [have] his (own) way / give (a person) a free hand // 허수아비냐, 남의 춤에 놀게 You must be a puppet to be rash [flippant] enough to follow in the wake of another [to move at another's beck and call]?

10 [이리저리 움직이다·꿈틀거리다] move; get about. ¶연못에서 물고기가 놀고 있다 Some fish are swimming in the pond. // 배 속에서 아이가 놀고 있다 The baby is quickening.

놀다² [던지다] throw; cast; shoot (dice); play. ¶윷을 ~ throw *yut* sticks / play (a game of) *yut* // 주사위를 ~ throw dice / play at dice / shoot craps.

놀라다 **1** [경악하다] be surprised; be astonished; be amazed; be astounded; start at; be startled; be taken aback (대경하다); (나쁜 일에) be shocked. ¶깜짝 놀랄 surprising / astonishing / striking / shocking // 깜짝 놀라서 in amazement // 놀랍게도 to one's surprise [astonishment] // 총소리에 ~ be startled at the sound of a gun // 자기의 그림자에 ~ startle at one's own shadow // …을 보고 [듣고] ~ be surprised at the sight [news] // 조금도 놀란 기색이 없다 exhibit no surprise (at) // 놀라서 말문이 막히다 be dumb struck [struck dumb] / be speechless with surprise // 놀라서 소리치다 cry out in surprise [astonishment / amazement] // 놀라서 눈이 휘둥그레지다 open one's eyes wide in surprise // 그는 깜짝 놀랐다 He was dumb(b)founded [flabbergasted]. // 그는 너무 놀란 나머지 오금도 못 썼다 He stood transfixed with astonishment. // 나는 놀라서 그의 얼굴을 쳐다보았다 I stared back at him in surprise [in astonishment]. // 그의 이야기는 깜짝 놀랄 만한 것이었다 His story was astonishing. // 그가 결혼했다는 말을 듣고 놀랐다 I was surprised [astonished] to hear that he had gotten married. // 그가 죽었다는 소식을 듣고 깜짝 놀랐다 I was shocked by the news of his death. // 우리는 범인이 어린아이라는 것을 알고 깜짝 놀랐다 We were shocked to find that the offender was a child. // 그가 아

놀라움

직 독신이라니 놀랐다 I was amazed to learn that he was still single[a bachelor]. / His still being single surprised me. // 그가 특상을 탔다는 말을 듣고 정말 놀랐다 His gaining the top prize astonished me[made me open my eyes]. // 그의 성공은 놀랄 만한 것이 못 된다 It is only natural that he should succeed. / There is nothing surprising about his success. // 그 뉴스에는 약간 놀랐다 The news took us rather by surprise. // 그 소리에 그녀는 깜짝 놀랐다 The noise brought her heart up into her mouth. // 아이쿠 놀랐다 What a surprise! // 남편이 체포되었다는 것을 알고 그녀는 얼마나 놀랐을까 How shocked she must have been to learn that her husband had been arrested!

2 [질리다] be frightened; be alarmed; be horror-struck[-stricken]; be terrified; have a fright; (미) scare. ¶놀라서 in one's fright / with alarm // 놀라서 병이 나다 be ill [from] fright // 도보 여행자들은 큰 곰을 보고 놀랐다 The hikers were frightened[horrified] to see a big bear. // 새들은 총소리에 놀라서 날아갔다 The gun frightened the birds away. // 그 일은 놀랄 만한 일이 못 된다 It need cause no alarm.

3 [경탄하다] wonder[marvel] at; be amazed at. ¶놀랄 만한 wonderful / marvelous / strange // 놀랄 만큼 wonderfully / wondrously / marvelously // 참으로 놀랄 만하다 be perfectly astounding // 놀라서 바라보다 stare in wonder / look with wonder (at) // 그의 박식에 놀랐다 I marveled at his profound scholarship. // 그녀의 끈기에 놀랐다 I wondered [marveled] at her perseverance. // 그런 것에는 놀라지 않는다 I shouldn't wonder at it. // 별로 놀랄 만한 일이 못 된다 Well, that's no wonder. / That's nothing wonderful. // 그녀의 학력은 조금도 놀랄 것이 못 된다 Her attainments are nothing out of the way. // 그는 놀랄 만큼 유창하게 에스페란토 어를 말했다 He spoke Esperanto with surprising[amazing] fluency.

놀라움 [경악] surprise; astonishment; [경탄] amazement; wonder; [질림] fright; horror; terror; scare. ¶~을 드러내 보이다 show one's surprise[wonder] // ~으로 눈을 크게 뜨다 stare in surprise[wonder] // 그것을 들었을 때 부모님의 ~은 어떠했을까 What was (not)[You can imagine] the surprise of the parents when they heard it! // 그 광경을 보았을 때의 나의 ~을 상상할 수 있을 것이다 You can imagine my surprise when I saw the sight.

놀랍다 wonderful; marvelous; surprising; startling; astonishing; astounding; amazing; alarming. ¶놀랍게도 to one's surprise [astonishment / shock] / to one's dismay // 놀라운 사건 a remarkable incident / (미) an eye-opener // 놀라운 사람 a wonderful man // 놀라운 재간 [솜씨] amazing talent[skill] // 놀라운 소식 surprising[astonishing] news // 놀라운 무기 a formidable weapon // 놀라운 기억력을 갖다 have a remarkable memory // 놀랍게도 그 회사가 도산했다 To my surprise, that company went bankrupt. // 놀랍게도 지갑이 없어졌다 To my dismay, my wallet was gone. // 이 약은 효험이 ~ This drug works wonders. / This medicine works[does] miracles. // 놀랍게도 그는 그 일을 불과 사흘 만에 해치웠다 The marvel is that he accomplished the task in only three days. // 그녀가 겨우 서른 살이라니 ~ It comes as a surprise to learn that she is only thirty years old. // (여기서 뵙게 되다니) 놀랍습니다. 어디로 가시는 길입니까 Well, well, What a surprise! Where are you off to? // 그녀가 배우가 되겠다니 놀라운 일이다 I wonder[marvel] that she should become an actress. / It's amazing that she's going to be an actress.

놀래다 **1** [놀라게 하다] surprise; astonish; amaze; astound; shock; startle; give (others) a start; alarm. ¶깜짝 ~ knock the breath out of (a person) / take (a person's) breath away / strike (a person) dumb // 새로운 설(說)을 내어 세상을 ~ startle the world with a novel theory // 너를 깜짝 놀래 줄 일이 있다 I have a great surprise in store for you. // 그들을 깜짝 놀래 주겠다 I'll make them sit up and take notice. / I'll give them a surprise[something to think about]. / (미국 구어) I'll bowl them over. // 놀래 드려 죄송합니다 I am sorry for alarming you.

2 [겁에 질리게 하다] frighten; terrify; terrorize; scare; throw (people) into a panic; freeze (a person's) blood. ¶세상 사람을 ~ strike terror into people's hearts.

놀리다 **1** [놀게 하다] let[have / make] (a boy) play; [쉬게 하다·쓰지 않다] have [leave] (a person / a thing) idle; leave (a thing) unused. ¶돈을 쓰지 않고 ~ have one's money lying idle[dormant] // 아이를 밖으로 데리고 나가 ~ take a child out for play // 땅을 ~ keep a land idle // 공장을 ~ leave a factory idle[unused] // 남을 한동안 ~ leave a person idle for a while / give a person some days off // 저 기계[방]를 쓰지 않고 놀려 두는 것은 낭비다 It's a waste to leave that machine idle[not to use that room]. // 돈을 놀려 두면 큰 손해입니다 It will mean a great loss if you leave your money lying idle. // 나는 너를 놀려 둘 처지가 못 된다 I cannot (afford to) have you idle. // 직공들을 놀릴 수는 없다 I would not do to keep the workmen idle.

2 [조롱하다] banter; chaff; tease; make fun [sport / game] of; poke fun at; play[come] a joke on; jest at (a person on his poverty); (구어) kid. ¶그를 놀리는 것은 재미가 있다 It is amusing to make fun of him. // 아이들은 그를 울보라고 놀려 댔다 The children jeered at him, calling him a cry. // 그는 나를 놀리면서 웃어 댔다 He laughed at my expense. // 놀리지 마라 Quit your kidding! / Stop your teasing! // 개를 놀리지 마라 Stop teasing the dog. // 그가 아둔하다고 놀려서는 안 된다 You must not make fun of him just because he moves slowly. // 그는 그들이 자기를 놀리고 있다는 것을 깨닫지 못했다 He was not aware that they were playing[having] a joke on him. // 나를 놀리는 거냐 Are you teasing me? / You're pulling my legs, aren't you? / Are you trying my patience with those wisecracks? // 사람을 놀리는 것도 분수가 있다 There is a limit in befooling one. // 그는 자네를 놀리고 있는 거야 He's fooling[making a fool of] you.

3 [조종하다] handle; manage; manipulate; play (a tool); (이면에서) pull (the) wires. ¶인형을 ~ manipulate[work] a puppet / put a

marionette through its paces[act] // 사람을 제 마음대로 ~ make a puppet of a person.
4 〔움직이다〕 move; set[put] in motion; operate. ¶손발을 ~ move[work] one's arms and legs // 입을 ~ move one's lips // 기계를 ~ operate a machine // 레코드를 ~ play a record // 입 좀 작작 놀려라 Shut up! / Hold your tongue! // 나는 무심결에 입을 잘못 놀렸다 I made a slip of the tongue.

놀림 banter; jeer; chaff; ridicule; fun; teasing; a joke; jest. ¶반 ~ 조로 half for[in] fun / partly for fun / banteringly / teasingly.
● **놀림감** an object[a butt] of ridicule; a subject of derision[for laughter]; a laughingstock. ¶~으로 삼다 make fun[sport] of / make a plaything of / treat (a person) as a plaything // ~이 되다 become a laughing-stock[an object of ridicule] / be played with.

놀부 심보(-心-) 〔심술궂은 마음씨〕 wickedness; ill-naturedness; cross-grainedness; perverseness.

놀아나다 1 〔방탕해지다〕 take to fast living; go [run] wild; become a playboy; begin to dissipate; begin to lead a fast life. ¶그녀는 놀아난 계집이다 She is a loose woman. / She sleeps around. / (속어) She's an easy lay. // 얌전하던 사람이 갑자기 놀아나기 시작했다 He used to be so nice, but now he has started on the life of a playboy. // 그녀의 남편은 젊었을 때 꽤 놀아났었다 Her husband has sown his wild oats. **2** 〔들뜨게 행동하다〕 act imprudently[thoughtlessly / rashly]. ¶남의 장단에 ~ dance[do] after a person's tune[pipe].

놀음(놀이) play; merrymaking; a spree; pleasure; fun; (good) sport; (an) amusement. **놀음(놀이)하다** play; make merry; go on a spree; have fun[a good time].

놀이 1 〔유희〕 play. ¶어린이들의 ~ children's play // ~ 친구 a playmate / a playfellow // 카우보이 ~를 하다 play at (being) cowboys (and Indians) / play cowboy // 술래잡기 ~를 하다 play tag // 학교 ~를 하다 play school // 병정 ~를 하다 play (at) soldiers. **놀이하다** play. ¶놀이하는 데 끼어들다 join (their) play.
2 〔경기〕 a game; a sport. ¶화투 ~ a game of (picture) cards // 알아맞히기 ~를 하다 make a game of guessing at …. **놀이하다** have[play] a game.
3 〔오락〕 a pastime; (a) recreation; (an) amusement; pleasure; fun. ¶반은 ~ 삼아 half[partly] for diversion[pleasure / fun] // 잡히기만 하면 낚시는 재미있는 ~다 Fishing is fine fun when there is a good take[catch]. // 옛날에 귀족의 ~는 사냥이었고 귀부인의 ~는 악기 연주였다 In old days the noblemen's pastime was hunting, while the ladies' diversion was playing on musical instruments.
4 〔행락〕 an excursion; a pleasure trip; an outing; holidaymaking. ¶꽃~ flower viewing // 뱃~ (a) boating / a river[sea] outing // 단풍~를 가다 go maple-viewing. **놀이하다** make an excursion (to); go on a pleasure trip (to).
● **놀이꾼** 〔떠들며 노는 사람〕 a merrymaker; a carouser; a junketer; 〔행락객〕 a person on [a member of] an outing; a picnicker; a holidayer; an excursionist. **놀이터** a playground; a play yard; a playing field; a playing space; a recreation ground; 〔행락지〕 an amusement place; a pleasure resort; a holiday haunt. ¶**어린이** ~ a playground for children. **놀잇배** a pleasure boat; an excursion barge.

놀치다 (big waves) rise roughly; run high; swell; billow; surge. ¶사납게 놀치는 바다 a furious sea / angry waves[waters] // 바다는 거칠게 놀치고 있었다 The waves tossed and raged.

놈 1 〔남자〕 a fellow; a chap; (속어) a bird; (미국 구어) a guy; (영국 속어) a blighter. ¶고약한 ~ an unsavory[immoral] character / a dreadful[an awful] person / a loathsome creature // 더러운 ~ a dirty bastard / a mean guy / a stinker / a rotter // 나쁜 ~ a bad egg // 괴상한 ~ a queer[an odd] fish / a funny customer // 미친~ a crazy guy / a screwball // 불쌍한 ~ a poor wretch // 재수 좋은 ~ a lucky dog // 이~ (친밀감을 담아) You little rascal! / (경멸·증오심을 담아) You rat! / Damn you! // 그놈은 참 좋은 ~이다 He's a truly fine fellow. // 그놈은 참 멍청한 ~이다 He's a real jerk, that one.
2 〔남자 아이〕 a boy; (구어) a kid; a youngster; (경멸하여) a brat. ¶재미있는 ~ a funny little chap // 고얀 ~ You little imp[monkey]!
3 〔동물·물건〕 thing; one. ¶이~의 옷 this wretched coat // 저~을 보여 주시오 Show me that one. // 그~의 개를 방에서 끌어내라 Get that damned dog out of the room!

놈팡이 1 〔사내〕 a fellow; a man; a guy; a chap; 〔빈둥거리는 남자〕 a bum; a loafer. **2** 〔여자의 상대〕 a girl's boyfriend.

놉 a casual laborer (paid by the day); a day laborer.

놋 brass. ⇨놋쇠.

놋그릇 brassware; brass tableware.

놋대야 a brass basin.

놋쇠 brass. ¶~로 만든 brazen.
● **놋쇠 세공**(-細工) brass-work.

농(弄) a joke; a jest. ⇨농담(弄談). ¶~으로 해보다 do a thing for a joke[in jest] // ~으로 받아들이다 take a thing as a joke // 남의 진담을 ~으로 돌리다 turn a person's earnest story into ridicule.

농(膿) pus; matter. ⇨고름¹.

농(籠) **1** 〔상자〕 a wicker trunk[basket]; a (wicker) portmanteau; a (wicker) suitcase. **2** 〔장롱〕 a chest (of drawers); a wardrobe.

농가(農家) 〔농사로 생계를 꾸리는 집〕 a farmhouse; 〔농사로 생계를 꾸리는 가정〕 the household of a farmer; a farm(ing) family; an agrarian home. ¶~의 마당 a farmyard // ~는 가을에 매우 바쁘다 Farmers are very busy in autumn. // 그녀는 ~에서 자랐다 She was brought up on a farm.

농간(弄奸) an artifice; a device; a trick; an intrigue; wiles; a wicked design; an evil scheme. ¶~에 빠지다 walk into[fall for] a trap set by (a person) / fall a victim to another's scheme // 여자의 ~에 빠지지 않도록 조심해라 Be careful not to be taken in by feminine wiles. // 그녀는 온갖 ~을 부려 그를 속이려고 했다 She used every trick in the book to try to deceive him. // 아무래도 무슨 ~이 있다 I suspect some trick. **농간하다** resort to artifices[wiles]; use artifice [tricks]; play[use] tricks on (another);

농게(籠-) [동] a sand crab.
농경(農耕) agriculture; farming; farm labor; tillage. ¶그들은 그곳에 정착하여 ~을 시작했다 They settled there and started farming.
● **농경민족** an agricultural people. **농경 시대**[역] the Agricultural Age. **농경지** farm land.
농공(農工) [농업과 공업] agriculture and industry; [농부와 직공] farmers and artisans.
농과(農科) [학부] the department of agriculture; [과정] an agricultural course; a course in agriculture.
● **농과 대학** an agricultural college.
농구(農具) a farm [an agricultural] implement [appliance]; a farming [farm] tool.
농구(籠球) basketball.
● **농구 선수** a basketball player; a cage star; a cager. **농구화** sneakers; basketball shoes.
농군(農軍) a farmer; a peasant; a farm laborer [hand]; a ploughman.
농기(農期) the farming season. ⇨ "농사철(⇨농사)
농기구(農器具) a farm implement. ⇨ "농구(農具)
농노(農奴) a (predial) serf.
● **농노 신분** serfdom; serfhood; serfage; villeinage. **농노 해방** emancipation of serfs.
농단(壟斷) [독점] monopoly; monopolization; assumption of an exclusive right [privilege]. **농단하다** monopolize; engross; make a monopoly of; take exclusive possession of; have (things) to oneself. ¶이익을 ~ monopolize the profit / have all the profit to oneself.
농담(弄談) a joke; a jest; fun; pleasantry; badinage; witticism. ¶가벼운 ~ a light jest // ~을 좋아하는 사람 a jesting [larky] man // 반~으로 half in joke [play] / half jokingly // 자~은 그만하고 joking [jesting] apart [aside] / to be serious / seriously speaking / now, seriously // ~으로 jestingly / playfully / jokingly / in joke [jest] / out of fun / in [for] fun // ~으로 …하다 do a thing for a joke [in jest] // ~으로 돌리다 treat (a matter) as a joke / take (something) as a joke / make sport of (a serious matter) // ~을 주고 받다 exchange pleasantries [badinage] (with) // ~을 건네다 make a joke (at) / poke fun (at) / pass a pleasantry (to) // ~을 곧이 듣다 take a joke seriously // 그건 ~이야 I don't mean what I say. // ~이 아냐 It's no joke. // 서투른 ~에는 손님들이 웃지 않는다 The audience won't laugh at bad jokes. // 그는 늘 ~을 잘한다 He is always cracking jokes. // ~으로 그랬을 뿐이야 I said it only in fun [as a joke]. // 그는 긴장을 풀려고 줄곧 ~을 했다 He kept telling jokes to ease the tension. // 아이들한테는 섣불리 ~도 할 수 없다 You have to be careful when joking with children. // 진담이 아니라 ~으로 그렇게 말했을 뿐이다 I said it just as a joke [in jest] and not in earnest. // ~으로라도 그런 말은 말게 Don't say such a thing even in jest. // ~이시 겠지 You're kidding. / You pulling my leg. / 그 사람한테는 ~도 못해 He can't take a joke. // ~이 진담 된다 What was said as a joke comes true. // ~ 속에 진실 있다 There's many a true word said in jest. **농담하다**

crack [break / make / cut] a joke; joke; make a crack; wisecrack; quip; jest; be merry.
농담(濃淡) shading; a shade; light and shade. ¶빛깔의 ~ a shade of color // 갈색으로 몇 가지의 ~을 나타낸 스커트 a skirt in several shades of brown // 그림에 ~을 나타내다 shade a picture [drawing] // 이 그림에는 ~이 잘 나타나 있다 This painting is successful in producing fine effects of light and shade.
농도(濃度) density; thickness; consistency; intensity; [화] concentration. ¶빛깔의 ~ the depth [strength] of color // 차 [커피] 의 ~ the strength of tea [coffee] // ~가 짙은 수프 thick soup // ~ 높은 우유 creamy milk (유지(乳脂)가 많은) // ~를 높인 설탕물 water containing a high concentration of sugar // ~가 높다 [낮다] be in high [low] concentration // 교차로 주변의 일산화탄소의 ~는 꽤 높았다 The air around the intersection contained a rather high density of carbon monoxide.
● **농도계** (물질을 재는) a densimeter; (빛을 재는) a densitometer.
농땡이 ¶~를 부리다 shirk one's duty [task] / loaf on the job / (속어) soldier on the job / (구어) lie down on the job.
● **농땡이꾼** an idler; a lazybones; a man of sloth; a sluggard.
농락(籠絡) cajolement; inveiglement. **농락하다** cajole (a person into doing); make a person one's puppet; inveigle; wheedle; take in; ensnare; entice; (특히 여자 등을) sport [toy / trifle / fool] (with); make sport [a plaything / a fool] (of). ¶여자를 ~ make sport of a woman / sport with a woman // 남자를 ~ flirt with a man / twist [turn] a man round one's (little) finger // 정조를 ~ trifle with a woman's virtue // 돈으로 ~ entice (a person) with money // 그는 나의 애정을 농락했다 He played with my affections. ➔남자에게 농락당하다 fall a prey to a man's lust / be seduced by a man // 그녀는 자기 고용주에게 농락당했다 She was a plaything by her employer. / Her employer made a plaything of her.
농로(農路) a farm road.
농림부(農林部) the Ministry of Agriculture and Forestry.
농무(農務) [농사일] agricultural affairs; farming; [농정(農政)] agricultural administration.
농무(濃霧) a dense [thick / heavy] fog. ¶~를 틈타서 under cover of a fog // ~가 끼기 시작했다 A thick fog came on. // 해상은 지독한 ~였다 It was very foggy on the sea. / There was a heavy fog on the sea. // 등산객들은 ~ 속에서 길을 잃었다 The climbers lost their way in a dense [thick] fog.
● **농무 경보** a dense fog warning.
농민(農民) [소작인] a peasant; [자작농] a farmer; [집합적] the farming population; [소작 농민 계급] the peasantry. ¶토지가 없는 가난한 ~ poor landless peasants.
● **농민 문학** peasant [agrarian] literature. **농민 운동** a peasant movement.
농번기(農繁期) a busy season for farmers; the (busy) farming season.
농본주의(農本主義) physiocracy; the 'agriculture-first' principle.
농부(農夫) [농장주] a farmer; [소작농] a

tenant farmer; a peasant; (닭) a plowman. (▶ farmer는 거대한 농장을 경영하는 부유한 사람을 가리키는 어감이 있으나, peasant는 소규모로 농사를 짓는 가난한 사람을 가리키는 어감이 있음)

농사(農事) agriculture; farming; farm work; agricultural affairs. ¶올해 벼는 평년 이하라고 한다 This year's rice crop is estimated to be below the average.
● **농사꾼** a farmer. **농사 시험장** an agricultural experiment station. **농사철** the farming season.

농사짓다(農事−) engage in farming; do farming (farm work); cultivate [till] the soil; farm.

농산물(農産物) agricultural [farm] products; farm produce. ¶~이 부족하다 be poor in farm products.
● **농산물 가격** farm prices.

농성(籠城) 1 [성을 지킴] holding a castle. **농성하다** be besieged; be sieged; hold a castle. ¶적에게 포위되어 한 달 동안 농성했다 The castle was besieged by the enemy for a month. 2 [스트라이크의 하나] a sit-in; a sit-down (strike); (영) a stay-in strike. **농성하다** go on a sit-down (strike); stage a sit-down demonstration.
● **농성 투쟁** a sit-down strike.

농수산물(農水産物) agricultural and marine products; agrofishery products; agro-marine items. ¶~의 가격 안정 the price stabilization of agricultural and fisheries products.

농아(聾啞) deaf and dumb; a deaf and dumb person; a deaf-mute.
● **농아 교육** education for the deaf and dumb. **농아 학교** a deaf-mute school; a school for the deaf and dumb; a deaf and dumb school.

농악(農樂) a *nongak*; instrumental music of peasants; farm music.
● **농악대** a farm [peasant] band; a farmer's folk band.

농액(濃液) a thick liquid; a concentrated solution.

농약(農藥) agricultural chemicals [medicines]. ¶~을 뿌리다 scatter agricultural chemicals // 인체에 위험이 없는 ~을 개발하다 develop agricultural chemicals that do not endanger the human body.
● **농약 중독** poisoning by agricultural chemicals; parathion poisoning (특히 파라티온에 의한).

농양(膿瘍) [의] an abscess.

농어 [동] a sea bass; a perch.

농어민(農漁民) farmers and fisherman. ¶~ 소득 증대 사업 a project to increase the income of farmers and fishermen.

농어촌(農漁村) farming and fishing villages [communities].

농업(農業) agriculture; farming; agricultural industry. ¶고도 기계화 ~ highly mechanized agriculture // 집약적 [조방적] ~ intensive [extensive] agriculture // ~에 종사하다 farm / (문어) engage in agriculture [farming] / follow the plow.
● **농업 경영** agricultural [farm] management. **농업 경제** agricultural economy. **농업 고등학교** an agricultural high school. **농업국** an agricultural country. **농업용수** agricultural water. ¶~ 개발 계획 an agricultural

water resources development project. **농업 인구** the farming population. **농업 협동조합** an agricultural cooperative (association).

농예(農藝) [농사 기술] agricultural technology; (the art of) growing plants; husbandry; [농업과 원예] agriculture and horticulture; farming and gardening.
● **농예 화학** agricultural chemistry.

농우(農牛) farming cattle; a plow ox; a draft ox.

농원(農園) a farm; a plantation. ¶자작 ~ a home farm.

농익다(濃−) get overripe; mature fully. ¶농익은 과일 overripe fruits.

농자(農者) agriculture. ⇨ 농업
● **농자천하지대본**(−天下之大本) Agriculture is the foundation of a nation [the basis of national existence].

농작(農作) farming; husbandry; cultivation of land; tillage of the soil; farming. **농작하다** till.
● **농작물** the crops; a harvest; farm produce [products]. ¶~이 잘되었다 The harvest turned out well.

농장(農場) a farm; (대규모의) a plantation; (토지·건물 포함) a farmstead; (목장) a ranch. ¶공동 [집단] ~ a collective farm / ~ a kolkhoz (Russ) / 국영 ~ a state farm // 실험 ~ an experimental farm // 그는 ~을 경영하고 있다 He runs a farm. / He is the owner of a farm. // 그녀는 ~에서 일하고 [살고] 있다 She works [lives] on a farm.
● **농장 경영** farm management. **농장 관리인** a farm bailiff. **농장주** a farmland proprietor; a farmer; (면화 등의) planter.

농정(農政) agricultural administration; farm policy.

농지(農地) agricultural land; farmland.
● **농지 개량** improvement of farmland. **농지 개혁** a farmland [an agrarian] reform. **농지세** farmland tax.

농지거리(弄−) joking; bantering; jesting; pleasantry; poking fun. **농지거리하다** joke; banter; jest; poke fun (at); pass pleasantries (with).

농촌(農村) a farm [farming] village; an agricultural village; a rural community. ¶~의 rural / agricultural / agrarian / ~의 공업화 industrialization of agricultural villages.
● **농촌 경제** rural economy. ¶한국 ~ 연구원 the Korean Rural Economics Institute (약어 KREI). **농촌 계몽** enlightenment of the farmers. **농촌 문제** a rural [an agrarian] problem; a farm problem. **농촌 봉사 활동** enlightenment service for rural communities. **농촌 진흥청** the Rural Development Administration.

농축(濃縮) concentration; enrichment. **농축하다** concentrate; enrich. ¶농축한 오렌지 주스 concentrated orange juice / orange juice concentrate. ➔ **농축된** concentrated / condensed.
● **농축기** a concentrator. **농축 우라늄** enriched [concentrated] uranium.

농탕(弄蕩) flirtation; dalliance.

농탕치다(弄蕩−) flirt [dally] with (a woman); be jolly with (a girl); bill and coo; (구어) spoon.

농토(農土) farmland. ⇨ 농지 ¶매마른 ~ barren [sterile] land // 전천후 ~ all-weather

농학 farmland.
● 농토 확장 expansion of farmland.

농학(農學) (the science of) agriculture. ¶~의 agricultural.
● 농학 박사 a doctor of agriculture(사람); Doctor of Agriculture(학위). 농학자 an agronomist; an agricultur(al)ist.

농한기(農閑期·農開期) the slack season on the farm; the agricultural off-season. ¶농민들은 ~ 되면 대부분 서울로 벌이를 하러 간다 When the peasants are free from farm work, most of them go to Seoul to work.

농협(農協) an agricultural cooperative (association). ⇨ 농업 협동조합(⇨농업)

농후하다(濃厚-) thick; dense; heavy; strong; rich. ¶농후한 색채 a heavy[rich] color // 농후해지다 deepen / become strong[pronounced] // 전쟁 기운이 농후해졌다 The war atmosphere grew tense. // 살인 혐의가 ~ There is a strong suspicion that he committed the murder. // 패색이 ~ The odds are against us. / Our defeat seems certain.

높낮이 1 [고저] high and low; pitch(소리의). 2 [울퉁불퉁함] unevenness; ruggedness; irregularity of surface; undulation(땅의). ¶~있는 uneven / unlevel / rugged (road) // ~가 없는 even / smooth / level // ~를 없애다 level (the ground).

높다 1 (높이가) high; tall; lofty; eminent; elevated; prominent(코가). ¶높은 산 a high[(문어) lofty] mountain // 높은 나무 a tall [high] tree // 높은 코 a long[prominent / big / high-bridged] nose // 아주 ~ be sky-high // 바람이 몹시 불어 파도가 높았다 The sea was choppy as a stiff wind was blowing. // 쏟아지는 눈을 보면서 얼마나 높은 곳에서 떨어지는 것일까 하고 생각했다 I stared at the snowflakes and wondered how high they were falling from.

2 (지위·신분·희망 등이) high; lofty; noble; exalted; superior. ¶높은 사람 a dignitary / a personage / (구어) a VIP(▶ very important person의 약어) / (구어) a big shot / (구어) a bigwig / (경멸적으로) a panjandrum // 지위가 높은 사람 a person of high position // 직위가 높은 관리 a high-ranking official // 정도가 높은 학교 a school of high academic standing // 인격이 아주 높은 사람 a person of the first quality // 눈이[희망이] 너무 ~ aim[set one's hopes] too high.

3 (값이) dear; high; expensive; costly. ¶높은 생활비 a high cost of living // 높은 급료 a high[large] salary // 값이 매우 ~ be very high in price // 물가가 너무 high. // 생활비는 작년의 배나 ~ Living costs are twice as high as they were last year.

4 (음성이) loud, stentorian; (음정이) high-pitched. ¶높은 소리 a high-pitched sounds // 높은 소리로 말하다 speak in a shrill voice // 그녀는 평소보다 높은 목소리로 말했다 She spoke in a voice that was several tones higher than usual.

5 (정도·비율이) high. ¶높은 율 a high rate // 도수 높은 안경 strong[powerful / thick] glasses // 정도가 높은 교과서 a high-level textbook // 높은 이자로 at a high interest // 체온이 ~ have a high temperature // 이 지방은 위도가 높은 곳에 있다 This region is in[at] a high latitude. // 환자가 열이 ~ The patient has a high fever. // 나는 혈압이 ~ I have high blood pressure. // 그는 격조 높은 문장을

쓴다 He writes in a refined style.

높다랗다 remarkably high; lofty.

높아지다 rise; be raised; (구어) up; swell; be elevated; increase; build (up) (위험 등이). ¶지위가 ~ rise in position / be raised to a higher position // 고도가 높아짐에 따라 기온은 내려간다 The higher you go, the colder it grows. // 반대하는 소리가 높아졌다 Opposition to it became more clamorous. // 아시아에서의 한국의 지위가 높아질 것이다 Korea's position in Asia will be enhanced. // 그는 명성이 높아짐에 따라 자만심이 생겼다 His growing reputation made him self-conceited. // 그의 연설로 그 계획에 대한 관심이 높아졌다 There was a surge[ground swell] of enthusiasm for the plan after his speech. // 석유주에 대한 투자가들의 관심이 점점 높아지고 있다 Investors are growing more and more interested in oil shares. // 온 나라에 민주화의 기운이 높아지고 있다 There is a growing tendency toward democratization throughout the country.

높은음자리표(-音-標) [음] the treble[violin] clef; the G clef.

높이[1] 1 [높은 정도] height; altitude; elevation. ¶~가 200피트다 be 200 feet high[in height] // 8천 피트의 ~를 날다 fly at a height of 8,000 feet // 어린애는 10미터 ~에서 떨어졌다 The child fell from a height of 10 meters. // 이 책장의 ~는 2미터이다 This bookcase is 2 meters high[in height]. // 저 건물의 ~는 얼마입니까 How high is that building? / What is the height of that building? // 나무는 5미터 ~로 자랐다 The tree has grown to a height of 5 meters. // 그 ~에서는 공기가 매우 희박하다 In those altitudes the air is extremely thin. // 키가 창문 ~에 미치지 못했다 My stature was lower than the height of the bottom of the window from the floor.

2 (소리의) pitch(음정); loudness(음량). ¶곡조의 ~ the pitch of a tone[tune] // 음성의 ~ the height[loudness] of a voice // 라디오 소리의 ~를 조절하다 modulate / adjust (the tune) // 그는 음성의 ~를 여러 가지로 바꾸면서 이야기했다 He varied the pitch of his voice as he spoke.

● 높이 제한 (육교 밑을 지나는 차에 대한) a height limit.

높이[2] 1 [높게] high; highly; aloft. ¶하늘 high up in the air // 손을 ~ 들다 hold one's hand up high // ~ 평가하다 highly appreciate / set a high value (on) / esteem // 머리 위 ~ 기가 펄럭이고 있다 A flag is fluttering high above our heads. // 나뭇잎이 하늘 ~ 날아 올라갔다 The leaves whirled around high up in the air. // 그녀는 유능한 교장으로서 ~ 평가되고 있다 She is valued highly as an efficient principal. // 나는 그의 학식을 ~ 사고 있다 I have great respect for his scholarship. 2 (소리를) loud; loudly; in a high pitch; in a loud voice. ¶소리 ~ 노래하다 sing in a loud[high] voice.

높이다 1 [높게 하다] raise; lift; (증진하다) promote; heighten (an effect); make higher; elevate (one's ideal); exalt (one's tone of voice); [좋게 하다·향상시키다] improve (one's condition); enhance (value); ennoble (one's character). ¶둑을 ~ build a bank higher / raise a bank // 담을 ~ make a wall higher // 품질을 ~ raise[improve / better] the quality of a product [manufactured goods] // 방 안의 온도를 ~ raise the temperature of a room // 생산을 5년 동안 2배로 ~ double the output in five years // 언성을 ~ raise one's voice (in anger) // 지위를 ~ promote (in rank) / raise (a person's) position // 사기를 ~ raise [boost] morale // 국민의 문화 수준을 ~ improve [raise] the cultural level [standard] of the nation // 여성의 지위를 높이는 데 기여한 사람들 those who contributed to the elevation of the status of women // 원색의 대담한 사용이 효과를 높이고 있다 The bold use of primary colors has heightened the effect. // 우리 아이의 성적을 높이려고 가정교사를 두었다 We employed a tutor for our child so that he would get better grades.

2 [받들다] respect; honor; reverence; do [show] honor (to). ¶남을 신으로 ~ deify a person // 말을 ~ use polite expressions / use honorifics.

높이뛰기 a high jump; a high leap; (말의) a capriole. ¶장대 ~ a pole vault [jump] // 제자리 ~ the standing high jump.

높임말 an honorific (expression / word); a term of respect.

높직하다 rather high; slightly elevated; rather loud (목소리가). **높직이** rather [slightly] high; rather [some what] loud.

놓다[1] [두다] put; lay; set (세워서) place. ¶손을 테이블 위에 ~ rest one's hands on a table // 펜을 놓으세요 Put [Lay] down your pen(s). / Stop writing. // 의자를 그리 ~ Put a chair there. // 다 쓴 후 제자리에 놓아라 Put it back where it was when you are through. // 우산은 어디다 놓고 왔느냐 Where did you leave your umbrella? // 그는 명함을 놓고 갔다 He left his card. // 그가 당신에게 편지를 놓고 갔소 He left a note for you. // 책은 책장의 제자리에 갖다 놓아라 Please put the book back on the shelf where you found it [it belongs].

2 [해방하다] set free; release; unloose; turn [let] loose; (손을) let go [off]; take off one's hand; let go one's hold (of); quit one's grasp. ¶그는 그녀의 손을 쥐고 있다가 ~ He held her hand and then let it go. // 권총을 놓아라 Take your hand(s) off the gun. // 그는 밧줄을 놓았다 He let go (his hold) of the rope.

3 (총포를) fire; discharge. ¶한 방 ~ have a shot // 총을 ~ fire a gun.

4 (불을) set (a fire). ¶집에 불을 ~ set fire to a house / set a house on fire.

5 [가설하다] build; construct; lay on (water); install (a telephone); lay down (a railway). ¶강에 다리를 ~ build [throw] a bridge over a river // 그들은 여우를 잡으려고 덫을 놓았다 They set [laid] a trap for foxes. // 그들은 아파트에 전화를 놓았다 They have had a telephone installed in the apartment house.

6 (주사를) inject; inoculate (a person with); apply; syringe; (침을) acupuncture. ¶주사를 ~ give [make] an injection // 침을 ~ needle / apply acupuncture (on).

7 (마음을) ease; set (one's mind) at ease [rest]; give (one's mind) relief; [방심하다] be in attentive; relax one's attention. ¶마음을 ~ feel easy (about) / make oneself at ease // 한시름 ~ feel [be] relieved / breathe freely again // 그 사람이라면 마음 놓고 일을 맡겨도 된다 You may trust him to do the work for you. // 잠깐 마음 놓은 사이에 가방을 잃었다 My suitcase was stolen in an unguarded moment.

8 (자수를) embroider; adorn with. ¶금실로 수를 ~ embroider figures on (velvet) in gold thread // 무늬를 ~ provide [decorate with] a pattern.

9 [셈하다] calculate; reckon; figure; compute; estimate. ¶수판을 ~ figure it out [reckon] on an abacus.

10 (값을) offer (a price); bid; name ¶5만 원의 값을 ~ offer [bid] 50,000 won // 그녀는 테이블에 6달러의 값을 놓았다 She bid six dollars for the table.

11 (돈을) lend [loan] (at interest); (세를) hire (out); let (out); let (a room) on hire; rent; (부동산을) lease. ¶돈을 4푼 이자로 ~ lend money at four percent interest // 집을 ~ rent [let] a house // 방을 ~ let a room on hire // 땅을 ~ put out land to lease.

12 [돈을 걸다] pay; bet (money on); wager. ¶천 원 놓고 점치다 consult a fortuneteller with a fee of one thousand won // 너는 얼마 놓겠느냐 Name your wager.

13 (속력을) accelerate; increase. ¶속력을 ~ accelerate [increase] speed / speed up.

14 (말을) lower one's style of speech; talk plainly; relax one's honorifics. ¶말씀 놓으시지요 Please don't hesitate to drop your honorifics in talking to me, sir.

15 [중간에 사람을 두다] put in (as an intermediary); send (a person). ¶사람을 놓아 교섭하다 negotiate through a third party // 사람을 놓아 수소문하다 get information through an agent / send a person for information.

16 (솜 등을 채우다) stuff [pad] with cotton. ¶방석에 솜을 ~ stuff a cushion with cotton.

17 [기타]. ¶목을 놓아 울다 cry unrestrainedly // 퇴짜 ~ refuse / reject / give the cold shoulder to (a person) // 엄포를 ~ make a threat // 석 점을 ~ (바둑에서) accept a three-stone handicap.

놓다[2] […해 두다] keep; have; leave. ¶문을 열어 ~ leave [keep] the door open // 방을 깨끗이 정돈해 ~ have one's room clean and tidy // 잠 못 자게 해 ~ keep (a person) awake // 표를 사 놓으세요 Buy the tickets in advance (now). // 논을 갈아 놓고 비를 기다린다 We have finished plowing the paddy field and are waiting for rain. // 그는 급료에서 언제나 3달러를 떼어 놓는다 He always keeps back three dollars from his wages. // 그가 좌석을 예약해 놓았다 He has reserved a seat for me. // 당신을 위해 방을 청소해 놓았습니다 I've cleaned the room for you.

놓아두다 [내버려 두다] leave; allow; let. ¶개를 그냥 놓아둬. 놀리면 물 테니까 You had better leave that dog alone, it will bite you if you tease it. // 홍차가 너무 묽으니 더 우러나게 놓아두시오 The tea is too weak, let it stand for a little while.

놓아먹이다 graze; pasture; put (cattle) to grass; leave (a dog) at large; keep (a pig) loose. ¶놓아먹이는 닭 yard fowls / fowls ranging freely // 개를 ~ let a dog run loose // 소를 놓아먹이고 있다 The cows are at pasture. // 그들은 여름에는 고지에서 소를 놓

놓아주다

아먹인다 In summer they take their cattle up to high ground and turn them out to pasture.

놓아주다 turn[let / cast] loose; let go[off]; release; unloose; free; set free; liberate. ¶새를 ~ set a bird free // 죄수를 ~ set a prisoner free / release a prisoner // 잡았던 물고기를 ~ put the fish back (into the water) // 이번만은 놓아준다 I will let you off this time once. // 나를 놓아주오 Let me go. / Let go of me.

놓이다 1 (물건이) be put[laid / placed / set]. ¶책상 위에 놓인 꽃병 a flower vase set on the table // 강에 놓인 다리 a bridge that spans the river // 여러 가지 장난감이 가게에 놓여 있다 Many toys are exhibited[on show] at the store. // 건너편 섬과의 사이에 다리가 놓였다 A bridge was built between here and the island. // 불단에 촛불이 놓였다 A lighted candle had been placed on the Buddhist altar. 2 (마음이) feel[be] relieved; feel at ease; be relaxed. ¶마음이 놓일 때가 없다 have no moment of ease // 그 소식을 듣고 한결 마음이 놓였다 I was greatly relieved at the news.

놓치다 1 (잡고 있던 것을) miss one's hold (of); drop (a bottle); (죄인 등을) let (a prisoner) escape; let[turn] (a captive) loose; lose; (모습 등을) lose sight of; (정보·사람 등을) lose track of. ¶그릇을 ~ drop a dish // 물고기를 ~ lose a fish // 나는 안개 속에서 그들을 놓쳐 버렸다 I lost sight of them in the fog. // 탐정은 수상한 그 사나이를 놓쳤다 The detective lost track of the suspicious man. // 유감스럽게도 소매치기를 놓치고 말았다 Unfortunately, I let the pickpocket get away [escape]. / Unfortunately, I failed to catch the pickpocket. // 그 어린이는 인파 속에서 부모를 놓쳤다 The child got separated from his parents in the crowd. // 나는 그들을 놓치지 않도록 바로 뒤를 따라갔다 I followed right behind them so as not to get lost. // 경찰은 유괴범을 놓쳤다 The police failed to catch the kidnapper. 2 (기회 등을) let (an opportunity) slip; throw away; miss; lose. ¶좋은 기회를 ~ miss[pass up] a good opportunity[chance] // 아깝게도 상을 ~ miss a prize by a slight mischance // 좋은 일자리를 ~ lose a good position // 어머니의 병환으로 유학의 기회를 놓쳤다 On account of my mother's illness I missed the chance to go abroad to study. // 나는 큰돈을 벌 기회를 뻔히 알면서도 놓쳤다 I missed the chance to make a lot of money knowing it all the while. // 그 영화를 놓치고 말았다 I missed that picture. // 그는 무엇 하나 놓치지 않고 주시하였다 Nothing escaped his notice. // 나는 목표를 놓치고 대신 나무를 쏘아 버렸다 I missed my mark and hit a tree instead. // 가장 중요한 점을 놓치고 못 들었다 I failed to hear[catch] the most important point. // 그는 그녀의 표정 변화를 하나도 놓치지 않으려고 했다 He was very sensitive to every change in the expression on her face [in her expression]. // 나는 그에게 사과할 기회를 놓쳤다 I missed the chance to apologize to him. // 그의 연설은 한 마디도 놓치지 않고 들었다 I did not miss a single word of his speech. 3 (차를) miss; lose; fail to catch. ¶기차를 놓쳤다 I missed my train. // 3분 늦어서 막차를 놓쳤다 I missed the last train by three minutes.

4 (구기에서). ¶공을 ~ fail to catch a ball / miss[fumble] a ball // (타자가) 좋은 공을 ~ let a good ball go by // 그는 공을 놓쳤다 He fumbled the ball.

놓친 고기가 더 크다[커 보인다] (속담) It is the fish you lose that are the biggest.

뇌(腦) a brain; a cerebrum; [생] an encephalon; [두뇌] brains. ¶~의 cerebral // ~의 활동 cerebral activity // ~를 쓰는 일 brain work // ~의 손상 brain damage // ~를 쓰다 [너무 쓰다] tax[overtax] one's brains // 과도한 공부로 ~를 상하게 하다 hurt one's brains with overstudy // 때로는 ~도 쉬게 해야 한다 You must give a rest to your brains at times.

● 뇌 수술 brain surgery; a surgical operation on brain. 뇌 장애 a brain injury; brain trouble. ¶~를 일으키다 suffer from brain trouble / suffer injuries in the brain.

뇌경색(腦硬塞) cerebral infarction.

뇌관(雷管) a percussion cap; a detonator; an exploder.

● 뇌관 장치 a percussion lock. 뇌관화약 percussion powder.

뇌까리다 repeat[reiterate] the same remark unpleasantly; harp on[upon]. ¶화려했던 옛날을 자꾸만 ~ harp upon the glories of one's former days // 임금이 적다고 ~ grumble repeatedly at a low pay.

뇌꼴스럽다 disgusting; detestable; loathful.

뇌다 1 (가루를) resift (through a sieve of finer mesh). 2 [되풀이하다] repeat; reiterate. ¶같은 말을 ~ repeat oneself / say over and over again.

뇌동맥 경화증(腦動脈硬化症) [의] cerebral arteriosclerosis.

뇌리(腦裏) the brain; one's mind; one's memory. ¶~에서 떠나지 않다 haunt one [one's memory] / be ever present in one's mind // ~에 새기다 make a deep impression on one's mind // 어떤 생각이 ~를 스쳤다 An idea occurred to me[crossed my mind]. // 그는 죽은 아내가 한시도 ~에서 지워지지 않았다 His dead wife always haunted him[his memory]. / He could never forget his dead wife even for a moment. // 나는 조용한 전원 풍경을 ~에 그렸다 I pictured the quiet pastoral scenery in my mind. / I imagined the quiet pastoral scene.

뇌막(腦膜) [의] (cerebral) meninges. ¶~의 meningeal.

● 뇌막염 meningitis; brain fever.

뇌명(雷鳴) thunder; a thunderclap; a roll [peal / clap / crack] of thunder; the rumbling of thunder.

뇌문(雷紋) a fret; a meander; a key pattern; a Greek fret.

● 뇌문 세공 fretwork; fretting.

뇌물(賂物) a bribe; (속어) palm oil[grease]; the golden[silver] key; (미국 속어) boodle; soup; a pie; [부정한 돈] money passed under table. ¶~을 받은 사람 a bribee / (미국 속어) a boodler / a sellouter // ~을 준 사람 a briber // ~이 통하는 corruptible / bribable // ~이 통하지 않다 be proof against corruption // ~을 먹다 be bribed / receive [accept / take] a bribe // ~로 매수하다 buy

off (a person) // 공무원에게 ~을 주다 give a bribe to [grease the palm of] a government official // 그는 ~ 따위를 받는 사람이 아니다 He is superior to bribery. // ~의 효과가 있었다 The bribe has worked. // 그 회사는 공무원에게 ~을 주고 입찰 가격을 알아냈다 The company bribed government officials into leaking the bidding price. / The company greased government officials palms in order to learn the bidding price. // 그들은 ~ 공세로 나왔다 They resorted to bribery.
● 뇌물 수수 bribery.

뇌병(腦病) a brain disease[affliction].

뇌병원(腦病院) a mental hospital. ⇨"정신 병원(⇨정신(精神))

뇌빈혈(腦貧血) [의] cerebral anemia; anemia of the brain. ¶~을 일으키다 have an attack of cerebral anemia.

뇌사(腦死) [의] brain death; cerebral death.

뇌성(雷聲) a peal of thunder. ⇨"천둥소리(⇨천둥)
● 뇌성벽력 thunder and lightning.

뇌성 소아마비(腦性小兒痲痺) [의] cerebral infantile paralysis.

뇌쇄(惱殺) ¶~적인 웃음 a smile that wins (a person's) heart away / a winning smile // ~적인 눈길을 보내다 cast a killing glance [eye] (at) // 그녀의 아름다움은 ~적이다 Her beauty is enchanting[irresistible]. **뇌쇄하다** fascinate; enchant; captivate; bewitch; (속어) kill (a man).

뇌수(腦髓) [생] the brain; the encephalon (pl. -la).

뇌신경(腦神經) [생] a cranial [cerebral] nerve.
● 뇌신경 세포 a brain cell. 뇌신경외과 neurosurgery; (병원의) the department of neurosurgery.

뇌염(腦炎) brain inflammation; encephalitis; cerebritis; phrenitis. ¶기면성 ~ [의] sleeping sickness // 유행성 ~ epidemic encephalitis // 일본 ~ Japanese encephalitis // ~의 발생 an outbreak of encephalitis // ~에 걸리다 be stricken with encephalitis.
● 뇌염 경보 a warning against the outbreak of (Japanese) encephalitis. 뇌염모기 a culex mosquito; an encephalitis-bearing mosquito. 뇌염 환자 an encephalitis patient. ¶~로 확인되다 be confirmed an encephalitis patient.

뇌우(雷雨) a thunderstorm; a thundershower. ¶심한 ~ a heavy [severe] thunderstorm // ~를 만나다 be overtaken by a thunderstorm.

뇌운(雷雲) a thundercloud.

뇌일혈(腦溢血) [의] cerebral hemorrhage. ⇨"뇌출혈

뇌전(雷電) thunder and lightning; thunderbolts.

뇌조(雷鳥) a snow grouse; a ptarmigan.

뇌졸중(腦卒中) (cerebral) apoplexy. ¶~에 걸리다 have a stroke [fit] of apoplexy.

뇌종양(腦腫瘍) [의] a brain tumor.

뇌진탕(腦震盪) concussion of the brain; cerebral concussion. ¶~을 일으키다 have a concussion of the brain.

뇌척수(腦脊髓) [생] the brain and spinal chord.
● 뇌척수막 [생] the brain and spinal chord. 뇌척수액 cerebrospinal fluid.

뇌출혈(腦出血) [의] cerebral hemorrhage; (a stroke of) apoplexy; effusion of blood on the brain. ¶~을 일으키다 have a fit of apoplexy / be stricken with a cerebral hemorrhage // ~로 죽다 die of apoplexy.

뇌충혈(腦充血) [의] congestion of the brain; cerebral hyperemia.

뇌파(腦波) [생] brain waves. ¶~를 기록하다 take electroencephalogram readings.
● 뇌파 검사 a brain wave test. 뇌파도 an electroencephalogram.

뇌하수체(腦下垂體) [생] a pituitary gland [body]; a pituitary; a hypophysis.
● 뇌하수체 호르몬 pituitary hormone.

뇌혈전증(腦血栓症) cerebral thrombosis.

뇌홍(雷汞) [화] fulminating mercury; mercury fulminate.

누(累) implication; involvement; trouble; an evil influence[effect]. ¶~가 되다 be annoying[harassing / troublesome] // 남에게 ~를 끼치다 give [cause] a person trouble [annoyance / worry / inconvenience] / implicate [involve] others in trouble // 그렇게 하면 자기뿐만 아니라 남에게도 ~를 끼치게 된다 That would bring trouble to others as well as yourself. // 남에게 ~를 끼치지 않도록 해라 You must not make yourself a nuisance to others.

누가(累加) acceleration; cumulative rise; progressive increase. **누가하다** accumulate; increase progressively; accelerate.

누가복음(-福音) [성] (The Gospel according to St.) Luke.

누각(樓閣) a tower; a castle. ¶사상(沙上)~을 짓다 build a house on sand // 공중~을 짓다 build castles in the air.

누계(累計) the total; the total amount [sum]; the aggregate. ¶~가 10만 원이다 total [amount to] 100,000 won // ~ 이천팔백 명 2,800 men in total [in all / all told]. **누계하다** total; sum[add] up. ¶누계하여 in the aggregate.

누관(淚管) [생] the tear duct. ⇨"눈물길(⇨눈물¹)

누구 1 [특정인인 경우] (주격) who; (소유격) whose; (목적격) whom. ¶아니, 이게 ~야 Well, look who's here! // ~가 그러더냐 Who told you? // 그는 (도대체) ~냐 Who (on earth) is he? // ~를 만났느냐 Who [Whom] did you see? // ~에게 줘야 할지 모르겠다 I don't know to whom to give it. // ~시라고 여쭐까요 What name shall I say? // ~십니까 (노크에 대한 응답) Who is it? / (전화에서) Who's speaking[calling], please? // ~ 였다 It was no other than my father. // ~를 데리고 가셨습니까 Whom [Who] did you take with you? // 그것은 어떤 친구한테 들었는데 ~ 라고 지적하지는 않겠다 I heard it from a certain friend of mine, who, however, shall be nameless. // 혼잡 속에서 누가 ~인지 잘 알 수 없었다 Identities were hardly distinguishable in the bustling crowd.

2 [일정치 않은 사람] (긍정문) somebody; someone(좀 형식적); some(누군가); (누구나 다) everybody; everyone; (의문문·조건문) anybody; anyone; any; (부정문) anybody; anyone; none. ¶~ 딴 사람 somebody else // ~에게도 뒤지지 않다 be second to none / have no equal // 누군가 찾아왔나 보다 Somebody is at the door. // 규칙을 어기는 자

는 ~를 막론하고 처벌을 받는다 Anyone who violates the rules will be punished.// 누군가 가 그 보물을 가져간 거다 Someone has made off with the treasure.// ~도 그쪽에 가지 않았다 Nobody went there.// 아직 ~에게도 말을 안 했다 I haven't told it to anybody.// ~든 그 책을 찾으면 돌려주시오 If anybody should find the book, please return it to me.// ~나 다 알고 있다 Everybody knows that.// ~ 딴 사람에게 물어라 Ask someone else.// ~ 이 책이 필요한 사람 있어요 Is there anybody who wants this book?// ~나 그 방법으로 그것을 할 수 있는 것은 아니다 Not everybody can do it that way.// 그런 문제는 ~나 풀 수 있다 Anyone could solve such a problem.// ~도 그 문제를 풀 수 없었다 Nobody was able to solve the problem.// ~보다도 너를 만나고 싶었다 I wanted to see you more than anyone else.

3 (양보절에서) whoever; whosever; whomever. ¶~라도 이 법률을 위반하는 자는 처벌받는다 Whoever breaks this law shell be punished.// ~든지 그 그림을 원한다면 가져도 좋아 Whoever wants the picture may have it.// 누가 뭐라 해도 그것은 거짓이다 Whoever said so, it is false.// 흠, 참 좋은 집이군. 집 임자야 ~든 말이야 Well, it's a very fine house, whoever it belongs to.

4 [비교하는 투] I; me; someone. ¶누가 할 말을 네가 하는구나 You blame me, but I should be blaming you. / You are saying what I should say.// 그러면 누가 무서워할 줄 아느냐 Do you think I will be afraid if you do that?// ~는 밤에 자다가 오줌 쌌대요 Someone I know wet his bed last night!// 누가 안대 How should I know?// ~를 놀리는 거냐 Are you kidding me?

누구누구 this or that person; just who and who; who all; [많은 사람] (many) people. ¶~ 할 것 없이 누구 everybody / each and all / every one (of them) / without distinction of person// ~ 왔나 Who all is here?// ~ 할 것 없이 이 나쁘다 You are all to blame, every last one of you.// 그곳에 ~ 있었는지 전혀 기억이 없다 I forgot who all were there.

누그뜨리다 soften (one's attitude); appease (one's anger). ¶말소리를 ~ soften one's voice// 그는 목소리를 누그러뜨렸다 He softened his voice. / He spoke gently [in a gentle voice].

누그러지다 1 (날씨가) get milder [warmer / better]; become less severe; ease up; (바람 등이) abate; subside; lull; go down; lose the sharpness. ¶추위가 누그러졌다 The cold has abated [moderated] . / The cold has decreased [relaxed] in severity.// 바람이 누그러졌다 The wind abated [went down].

2 (값이) get lower; decline; be on the decline. ¶물가가 ~ prices become lower / prices are on the decline.

3 (감정·태도 등이) soften; become conciliatory; grow calmer; be mollified; cool [calm] down. ¶그녀의 친절한 말에 그는 마음이 누그러졌다 He melted at her kindly words.// 그는 몹시 화가 나 있었으나 차차 누그러졌다 He was very angry, but he has cooled down gradually.// 그는 누그러져 얼굴에 웃음을 띠었다 His features relaxed into a smile.// 고통이 누그러졌다 The pain was relieved [eased].// 그의 태도가 누그러졌다 His attitude softened [become less aggressive].// 그는 부인의 설득에 고집스러운 태도가 누그러졌다 His obstinate attitude was softened by his wife's urging.

누글누글하다 soft; mild. ⇨노글노글하다
누긋누긋하다 very soft; gentle. ⇨노긋노긋하다
누긋하다 soft; tender; docile.
누기 (漏氣) moisture; humidity; damp(ness); wet(ness). ¶~가 찬 방 a damp [humid] room.
누기(가) 치다 become damp [moist / wet]; dampen; moisten. ¶방에 누기가 쳤다 The room has become damp.
누나 one's older [elder] sister; (구어) one's big sister (▶ 종종 아이가 말하는 경우). ▶ 우리말에서는 남자의 손위 동기 여자를 「누나」, 여자의 손위 동기 여자를 「언니」로 구별하여 말하고 있으나, 영어에서는 그런 구별이 없이 모두 older sister임). ¶큰~ the eldest [oldest] sister(▶ (구어)에서는 older, oldest를 쓰는 경향이 많음)// 이복~ one's [an] older half sister.
누년 (累年) successive years; many years; several years; a series of years.
누누이 (累累-) many times (over); several [a dozen / a good many / a thousand] times; time after time; time and (time) again; over and over again; again and again; over and over (again); repeatedly; frequently. ¶어머니는 아이에게 철도 근처로는 가지 말라고 ~ 말하였다 Mother has told her child time and (time) again not to go near the railway.// 나는 그런 짓을 하지 말라고 그에게 ~ 타일렀다 I have admonished him a thousand times not to do such a thing [against doing such a thing].// ~ 주의를 주었는데도 그는 듣지 않는다 He turns a deaf ear to my repeated warnings.

누다 evacuate; discharge; pass. ¶오줌을 ~ make [pass] water / pass urine / urinate / (비어) take [have / do] a leak / (속어) have [take] a piss / (속어) piss / (속어) have [take] a pee / (속어) have a pee// 똥을 ~ have a bowel movement / (문어) defecate / evacuate / evacuate [relieve] the bowels / have a stool / (비어·속어) shit / relieve [ease] nature.
누대 (累代) successive generations. ¶~에 걸쳐 from generation to generation.
누더기 tattered clothes; tatters; rags; (구어) duds. ¶~를 걸친 사람 a person (dressed) in rags / a ragged [tattered] man / a ragamuffin / a tatterdemalion// ~를 걸치고 돌아다니다 go about in rags// ~를 걸치다 be (clad) in tatters// 이 외투는 오래 입어서 ~가 되었다 This overcoat has been worn threadbare [to rags].// 노파는 ~ 옷을 입고 있었다 The old woman was in rags [tatters].
누덕누덕 in patches; full of patches; patched and repatched. ¶옷을 ~ 깁다 patch and repatch one's clothes.
누드 nude. ¶~의 nude / naked// ~의 그림 [상(像)] a nude// 그 모델은 ~로 포즈를 취했다 The model posed in the nude.
● **누드모델** a nude model. **누드 사진** a nude photo [photograph]. **누드쇼** a striptease; a nude show.
누락 (漏落) an omission; a lacuna (pl. -nae, ~s). **누락하다** omit; leave out; fail to enter. ¶몇 자 ~ miss out a few words. ➔¶누락되

다 be omitted[left out] / be missing // 이 게 산서에는 누락된 것이 있습니다 There are some items omitted in this bill. // 두세 사람의 이름이 명단에서 누락되어 있었다 A few names had been left off[omitted from] the list. // 이 페이지에서 한 절이 누락되어 있다 A paragraph is missing on this page.

누란(累卵) ¶~의 위기에 처해 있다 be in imminent peril[danger] / be in a most perilous situation / be threatened with ruin / be in a precarious position / sit on a volcano.

누렁 yellow; yellow dyes(물감).

누렁이 1 [누런 물건] a yellow thing; [누런 개] a yellow dog. **2** [황금] gold.

누렇다 quite[deep] yellow; golden yellow. ¶누렇게 변해 가는 스냅 사진 a yellowing snapshot // 보리가 누렇게 익었다 The barley is ripe and golden.

누룩 malted rice[wheat]; malt; (효모) yeast.
●**누룩곰팡이** [식] an aspergillus (*pl.* -gilli).

누룽지 *nurungji*; the crust of overcooked rice; the scorched part of boiled rice.

누르께하다 yellowish; yellowy. ¶누르께한 얼굴 a sallow face // 커튼이 때가 묻어 누르께해졌다 The curtain has been yellowed.

누르다¹ 1 [어느 부분에 힘을 가하다] press; push; hold[press / keep / pin] down; weigh on. ¶벨을 ~ push[press] the bell // 발로 step[tread / trample] on // 돌로 눌러 놓다 press (something) under a stone / place [put] a stone as a weight on (something) // 도장을 ~ stamp (a document) with a seal / set a seal (to) / fix[affix / stamp] a seal // 카메라의 셔터를 ~ press the shutter (of a camera) // 서진(書鎭)으로 종이를 ~ keep papers down by a paperweight // 무릎을 눌러 보면 아프다 My knee hurts when I press on it.
2 [억압하다·진압하다] suppress; put down; repress; subdue; control; oppress; [저지하다] check; [위압하다] overpower; overwhelm; dominate; overawe; domineer over. ¶반란을 ~ suppress a rising / put down a rebellion // 약자를 ~ oppress the weak // 모든 반대를 ~ bear down all opposition.
3 [심리 작용을 억제하다] restrain; control; repress; suppress; get[keep] under control; keep[hold] back; check. ¶누를 길 없는 분노 uncontrollable[irrepressible] anger // 감정을 ~ suppress[control] one's feelings // 화나는 것을 ~ control[contain / repress] one's anger / master[swallow] one's anger / keep [gulp] down one's anger // 격정을 ~ restrain one's passions / hold one's passions in check / keep a rein on one's passion // 기쁨을 누를 길 없었다 I could not contain myself for joy.
4 [국수를 뽑다] squeeze out. ¶국수를 ~ make noodles / squeeze out noodles (through a perforated press).
5 [제압하다] beat (a person, a team, etc.); defeat. ¶선거에서 경쟁자를 ~ beat one's rival in the election // 수영에서 그를 ~ defeat him at swimming // 적을 ~ hold the enemy in check // 상대방을 무득점으로 ~ shut out the opposing team / hold the opposing team scoreless.

누르다² yellow(ish); golden (yellow). ¶누른 빛깔이 되다 turn yellow.

누르스름하다 yellowish; somewhat yellow.

누르퉁퉁하다 dull yellow; unpleasant [unhealthy] yellow; sallow. ¶얼굴이 ~ look sallow / have a sallow face.

누름단추 a push[press] button; (초인종의) a bell push.

누릇누릇하다 spotted with yellow. ⇨노릇노릇하다

누리 〔세상〕 the world. ¶온 ~에 in all the world / all over the world.

누리다¹ enjoy; have; be blessed with. ¶행복을 ~ enjoy happiness / have felicity // 건강을 ~ enjoy good health // 장수를 ~ live a long life / enjoy longevity // 부귀영화를 ~ live in splendor[wealth and honor] // 이 나라는 천연자원의 혜택을 누리고 있다 The country is blessed with natural resources.

누리다² **1** (냄새가) rank; foul-smelling; fetid; stink. **2** (식은 국물처럼) be[smell / taste] rancid.

누린내 a stink. ⇨노린내

누명(陋名) a false[an unjust] charge[accusation / imputation]; groundless[unfounded] suspicion. ¶~을 벗다 clear oneself of false accusation // ~을 쓰다 be falsely[unjustly / wrongly] accused (of stealing) / be falsely charged (with murder) / be unjustly suspected of a guilt // ~을 씌우다 accuse (a person of theft) unjustly / make[bring] a false charge (of espionage) against (a person) / charge (a person) unjustly (with bribery).

누범(累犯) a repeated offense; the repetition of offenses; cumulative offense. **누범하다** repeat an offense.

누비 1 [피륙 사이에 솜을 넣어 홈질하는 바느질] quilting. **2** [누빈 물건] quilted work.
●**누비옷** quilted clothes. **누비이불** a quilt.

누비다 1 (피륙을) quilt. ¶이불을 ~ quilt / form into a quilt. **2** [요리조리 뚫고 나가다] thread; weave. ¶인파 속을 ~ thread[weave / wade / twist] one's way through the crowd / thread[snake] through the crowd // 그녀는 아이를 따라 잡으려고 행렬 사이를 누비고 다녔다 Threading her way through the procession, she ran to catch up with her child. // 그들은 장식 수레를 타고 읍내를 누비고 다녔다 They paraded floats[decorated vehicles] around the town. **3** twist up (one's face) into a scowl. ⇨찡그리다

누선(淚腺) [생] a lachrymal gland. ⇨눈물샘(⇨눈물¹)
●**누선염** [의] dacryadenitis.

누설(漏泄·漏洩) **1** (액체 등의) a leak; leakage. ¶가스 ~ a gas leak // ~을 막다 stop[plug] a leak. **누설하다** leak; let leak.
2 (비밀의) leakage; disclosure; divulgence. ¶군기 ~ a leakage of military secret. **누설하다** tell others; let (a secret) out; (문어) divulge (one's secret); reveal; disclose; betray; break; give away; leak (out). ¶기밀[비밀]을 ~ break[let out / give away / betray / tell / divulge / reveal] a secret / (구어) let the cat out of the bag(무심코) / blurt out a secret(무심코) / babble a secret out(무심코) // 적에게 내부 정보를 ~ leak inside information to the enemy // 그 소식을 기자에게 ~ leak the news (out) to the press // 그는 무심결에 비밀을 누설하고 말았다 He carelessly let the secret slip[babbled out the secret]. / He inadvertently let the cat out of

the bag.∥누설해서는 안 된다 Keep it secret. / Don't tell anybody. / Don't let[blurt] it out. / Keep it to yourself. / Don't breathe a syllable[word] about it to anyone.∥비밀은 아무한테도 누설해서는 안 된다 You must not let out[divulge] the secret to anybody. →¶시험 문제가 누설되어 큰 소동이 일어났다 The leakage of some examination papers led to a grave complication.
누수(漏水) a water leakage; a leakage of water; leaking water.
● 누수 검출기 a hydrostat.
누습(陋習) a bad habit; a corrupt[evil] custom; a vice; abuses. ¶~을 타파하다 do away with an evil custom.
누승(累乘) ➡거듭제곱
누심(壘審)〔야구〕a base umpire. ¶1~ the umpire at first base.
누에〔동〕a silkworm. ¶~에서 실을 뽑다 obtain silk from silkworms∥~를 치다 rear [raise / keep / breed] silkworms∥~가 고치를 치기 시작했다 The silkworms have begun spinning.
● 누에고치 cocoon. ⇨"고치 누에 농사 / 누에 치기 sericulture; silk-farming.
누옥(陋屋) 1〔누추한 집〕a squalid[wretched] hut; a humble cottage. 2〔자기 집을 낮춰 일컬음〕my (humble) dwelling[house].
누워먹다 eat idle bread; eat the bread of idleness; live[lead] an idle life; live in idleness.
누이 a boy's sister.
누이 좋고 매부 좋다(속담) Scratch my back and I'll scratch yours.
누이다[1] 1〔눕히다〕lay down; lay on the side. 2〔피륙을 잿물에 담갔다가 솥에 찌다〕gloss; give a gloss (to); (명주를 쪄서) soften. ¶누인[누이지 않은]명주 glossed[unglossed] silk.
누이다[2]〔대소변을〕make[let / have] (a child) urinate[defecate].
누이동생(-同生) one's (younger) sister(▶ younger을 생략하는 것이 보통임); one's little sister; (배다른 누이) one's half-sister. ¶~ 남편〔매제〕one's brother-in-law / one's (younger) sister's husband.
누적(累積) accumulation; cumulation. **누적하다** accumulate; cumulate; increase cumulatively. ¶~된 악폐 accumulated evils∥누적된 결과〔영향〕the cumulative effects (of)∥빚이 누적되어 총 백만 원이 되었다 The debts went on accumulating till the whole sum reached one million won.
● 누적 투표 cumulative voting.
누전(漏電)〔전〕an electric leakage; a leak(age) of electricity; a short circuit; a leak; a fault. ¶~에 의한 화재 a fire started by a short circuit / a fire caused by a leakage of electricity∥~을 일으키다 cause a short circuit / cause a leak (of electricity). **누전하다** short(-circuit); leak.
● 누전계(-計) a ground[a leakage / an earth] detector; a leakage indicator.
누정(漏精) spermatorrh(o)ea.
누증(累增) acceleration; cumulation; cumulative rise[increase]; progressive increase. **누증하다** accelerate; cumulate; accumulate; increase progressively[cumulatively].
누지다〔축축하다〕damp; dampish; humid; slightly wet.
누진(累進) successive[gradual] promotion. ¶~적으로 progressively / gradually / on a graduated scale. **누진하다** be promoted from one position to another; be gradually promoted; rise step by step.
● 누진 과세 progressive taxation. 누진세 a progressive[cumulative / graduated] tax.
누차(累次) successively; in succession; one after another; many times; over and over; time and again; time after time; repeatedly. ¶~ 말했듯이 as I have told you repeatedly.
누추하다(陋醜-) filthy; squalid; sordid; shabby; untidy. ¶누추한 살림살이 squalid [sordid] living conditions∥누추한 집 a messy house∥누추한 차림을 하다 be shabbily dressed∥누추한 곳을 찾아 주셔서 고맙습니다 How good of you to visit us!(▶ 우리말처럼 지나친 겸양어를 영어에서는 쓰지 않음)
누출(漏出) leakage; leak; escape. ¶가스 ~로 인한 폭발 사고 an explosion caused by a gas leak. **누출하다** leak (out); ooze out; escape(가스가). →¶가스관에서 가스가 누출되고 있었다 Gas was leaking[escaping] from the pipe.
눅눅하다 damp; (공기 등이) humid; moist; dampish. ¶눅눅한 날씨 soft[humid] weather / a damp[muggy / humid] day∥눅눅한 옷 wet[damp] clothes∥더위로 초콜릿이 눅눅해졌다 The chocolate has melted in the heat.
눅다 1 (반죽 등이) soft; tender. ¶눅은 반죽 soft dough.
2 (습기로) soft and damp; soft with wet; damp. ¶담배가 ~ The tobacco is damp.
3 (성질이) calm; quiet; placid. ¶성질이 눅은 사람 a person of placid temper / a person of a quiet disposition.
4 (춥던 날씨가) become mild(er); become agreeable; warm up. ¶날씨가 눅었다 The weather turns warm[has become milder].
5 (값이) cheap; inexpensive; low(-priced); of low price; moderate.
눅신눅신하다 very soft and flexible. ⇨"눅신눅신하다
눅이다 1 (굳은 것을) soften; make soft [tender]; (물에 적셔) macerate. ¶반죽을 ~ soften the dough. 2 (마음을) appease; pacify; calm; mollify. ¶마음을 ~ soften [appease] (a person's) heart∥노여움을 ~ appease[calm] (a person's) anger∥그의 친절한 말이 내 마음을 눅였다 His kind words melted my heart. 3 (목소리를) soften; tone down. ¶목소리를 눅여 말하다 modify one's tone. 4 [적시다] damp; moisten; make (a thing) damp[moist]; moisturize. ¶다리미질 하기 위해 옷을 ~ damp clothes prior to ironing.
눅진눅진하다 quite soft and sticky. ⇨"눅신눅진하다
눈[1] 1〔물체를 보는 기관〕an eye(▶ 보통 복수형);〔안구(眼球)〕an eyeball. ¶~의 optic / 〔문어〕ocular∥~을 감고 with one's eyes shut[closed]∥~을 크게 뜨고 with one's eyes open〔(속어) peeled〕∥~의 근육 an ocular muscle∥~의 신경 the optic nerve∥ 눈꼬리가 처진 ~ drooping eyes∥치켜 올라간 ~ slant[peaked] eyes∥멍청한 ~ dull [fishy] eyes∥파란[검은] ~ blue[dark] eyes ∥~ 깜짝할 사이에 in the twinkling of an eye / in an instant∥졸리는 듯한 ~ sleepy [heavy] eyes∥한쪽 ~으로 보다 look with one eye∥~을 감다 close one's eyes∥~이 아프다 have sore eyes∥~을 부비다 rub one's

eyes∥~이 핑핑 돌다 be[feel] dizzy∥~을 내리깔다 lower[drop / cast down] one's eyes∥~에 티가 들어가다 have a note in one's eye∥~에 설다 be unfamiliar / be strange∥~을 가늘게 뜨다 narrow one's eyes/(눈이 부시어) squint one's eyes∥~을 부릅뜨다 glare in one's eyes∥~이 휘둥그레지다 be popeyed∥그 경치가 ~이 설었다 The sight was strange to me.∥그것을 알아보지 못하다니, 도대체 ~이 어디다 두었어 You didn't notice it? Where are your eyes?∥내 ~으로 그것을 직접 보았다 I saw it with my own eyes.∥~에 보이는 것 모두가 신기했다 Everything I saw was new to me.

2 [시력·시각] sight; eyesight; vision; eyes. ¶~의 optical / visual∥~의 착각 an optical illusion∥~이 밝다[좋다] have good eyes [eyesight] / have a good sight[vision]∥~이 어둡다[나쁘다] have bad eyes[defective vision] / have a poor[bad] sight[vision]∥~이 멀다[안 보이게 되다] lose one's (eye)sight / become blind /(one's (eye)sight) be gone∥한쪽 ~이 멀다 be blind in one eye∥~을 버리다 impair one's vision[eyesight]∥내 ~이 점점 나빠지고 있다 My eyesight is failing.

3 [눈매] a look; a gaze; an eye. ¶다정스러운 ~으로 with a gentle[kindly] look∥성난 ~으로 with an angry look in the eye∥그는 날카로운 ~으로 나를 노려보았다 He gave me a sharp[keen] look. / He fixed me with a piercing look.

4 [눈처럼 생긴 것]. ¶태풍의 ~ the eye of a typhoon.

5 [주목·주시] (public) notice; attention; watch. ¶~을 딴 데로 돌리다 turn one's eyes away (from) / look away[aside]∥세상 사람들의 ~이 두렵다 I am afraid of the eye of the people[the public eye].∥~ 둘 곳을 몰라 정말 난처했다 To my embarrassment I didn't know where to turn my eyes[look].∥여기는 남의~이 너무 많은 곳이군 This place is too public.∥너는 남의~을 지나치게 걱정하고 있다 You worry too much about the public eye.∥그들은 남의~도 꺼리지 않고 서로 껴안았다 They hugged each other in public.∥나는 그 광경을 차마 보고 있을 수가 없어서 ~을 돌렸다 I could not stand watching the scene and looked away.

6 [안목·안식] an eye; judgment; insight; discernment. ¶사물을 보는 ~이 있다[없다] have[haven't] the seeing eye / have an eye[no eye] (for) / be a good[poor] judge (of) / be[be not] sharp-eyed∥그는 ~은 틀림이 없다 He is a good[fine] judge of people. / He has a discerning eye for character.∥그는 도자기를 보는 ~이 있다[없다] He has an eye [no eye] for chinaware. / He is a good[poor] judge of chinaware.∥그는 골동품을 보는 ~이 있다 He is a connoisseur of antiques.

7 [사물을 보는 태도] a point of view; a viewpoint. ¶의사의 ~으로 보면 from a doctor's point of view∥공평한 ~으로 보다 look upon (a person / a matter) with an impartial eye∥그의 ~에는 내가 그저 어린애로밖에 보이지 않는다 I am a mere baby in his eyes.∥남들은 나를 이상한 ~으로 보고 있다 People regard me with prejudice.∥그들의 쾌락의 관념은 외국 사람의 ~에는 좀 이상하게 보인다 Their ideas of enjoyment are rather strange in foreign eyes.

8 (이성의) judgment; reason. ¶그는 욕심에 ~이 멀었다 Greed blinded him. / He was blinded by greed.∥그는 탐욕에 ~이 멀어 판단력을 잃은 것 같다 Greed seems to have blinded his (good) judgment.∥나는 단지 돈에 ~이 멀어 그 짓을 한 건 아니다 I didn't do it merely for love of money.

눈 가리고 아웅(속담) try to deceive by a transparent guile; bury one's head ostrich-like in the sand.

눈 감으면 코 베어 먹을 세상(속담) a cut-throat competitive world.

눈에는 눈, 이에는 이 An eye for an eye, a tooth for a tooth(▶ 성경에서).

눈 깜짝할 사이에 in the twinkle[wink] of an eye; in a twinkling; in an instant; in a flash. ¶일 주일이 ~ 지나갔다 A week has passed in a flash.

눈(이) 꺼지다 one's eyes shrink[droop]; one's eyes become hollow. ¶배가 고파 ~ one's eyes are hollow with hungers.

눈(이) 높다 [정도 이상의 좋은 것만 찾다] aim high; be desirous of things beyond one's means; have ambitions[dreams] beyond one's station; [안목이 높다] have a good[a sharp / a keen / an expert] eye (for); be appreciative (of); be a connoisseur (of). ¶그 여자는 눈이 높아서 웬만한 남자는 거들떠보지도 않는다 She aims high and will not even look at ordinary men. / She has high standards and doesn't play attention to ordinary men.∥그는 골동품에 관한 한 꽤 ~ He is quite knowledgeable about antiques. / When it comes to antiques, he has a good[discerning] eye.∥그는 그림을 보는 ~ He has a good eye for paintings.∥그는 도자기를 보는 ~ He is quite a connoisseur of ceramics. / He has a sharp eye for ceramic art objects.

눈도 깜짝 안 하다 not[never] bat an eyelid [eye / eyelash]. ⇨"눈 하나 깜짝하지 않다(⇨ 눈¹)

눈(을) 돌리다 turn[direct] one's eyes[attention] (to); bend one's eye (on); bring one's gaze to bear (upon). ¶중동 문제로 ~ turn one's eyes[attention] to the problems of the Middle and Near East∥이번에는 인구 문제로 눈을 돌려 봅시다 Now let us turn our eyes to the population problem.

눈(이) 뒤집히다 be blinded; lose one's sober judgment; lose control of oneself; lose one's mind[wits]; run[go] wild[mad]. ¶눈이 뒤집힌 군중 a frenzied[wild] crowd.

눈 뜨고 볼 수 없다 be disgusting; be shocking; be repulsive; be hideous; be frightful; be too piteous to look at. ¶그 참상은 눈 뜨고 볼 수 없었다 I could hardly bear to look at the scene of the disaster.

눈(에) 띄다 [눈에 보이다] come in sight; come into view; greet[meet] the[one's] eye; be found; one's eyes fall[rest] upon (a thing); [두드러지다] attract[catch] one's attention[eye]; strike[catch] the eye (of); come[be brought] to[under one's] notice; be noticeable[remarkable / visible]. ¶눈에 띄게 noticeably / remarkably / perceptibly∥눈에 띄게 향상되다 make remarkable [visible] progress∥그는 눈에 띄게 건강이 회복되고 있다 He is recovering his health very quickly.∥책상에 놓인 꽃이 눈에 띄었다 The flowers on the table caught my eye [attention]. // 요즈음 그녀의 결점이 눈에 잘 띈다 Her faults are particularly noticeable these days. // 그의 근면이 사장 눈에 띄었다 His diligence caught the president's eye [the attention of the president]. // 이것이 내 눈에 띄었다 My eye fell on this.

눈(이) 맞다 fall in love (with); take a shine (to). ¶둘은 눈이 맞아 달아났다 They fell in love with each other and ran away together.

눈(을) 맞추다 [눈을 마주 보다] look eyes with each other; look at each other; exchange looks [glances] with each other.

눈 밖에 나다 be out of [lose] favor (with a person); be out of [lose] a person's favor; lose a person's confidence; get on a person's bad side; get on the bad side (of a person). ¶그는 주인의 눈 밖에 났다 He lost favor with his master. / He lost his master's confidence.

눈(을) 붙이다 sleep; fall asleep; go [get] to sleep; doze; take a nap; take [have] forty winks [a short nap] (특히 점심 식사 후의 낮잠). ¶깜빡 눈을 붙였나 했는데 벌써 아침이었다 I thought I'd just dozed off, but it's already morning.

눈(을) 속이다 do (a person) in the eye; throw dust in (a person's) eyes; cheat; deceive; trick; take in; impose upon; play a trick upon; hoodwink. ¶죄수는 눈을 속이고 도주했다 The prisoner outwitted his guards and escaped. / The prisoner deceived [tricked] his guards and got away successfully.

눈에 거슬리다 be unpardonable [intolerable]; offend [affront] the eye [sight]; be an offense to the eye [sight]; become an eyesore; obstruct [spoil] the view. ¶눈에 거슬리는 행동 unpardonable behavior // 그것은 눈에 몹시 거슬리는 장면이었다 It was a sight too offensive to look at. // 그들의 무례함은 눈에 거슬렸다 Their rudeness was beyond endurance.

눈에 넣어도 아프지 않다 be the apple of one's eye. ¶딸아이는 ~ My daughter is the apple of my eye.

눈에 밟히다 haunt (one / one's memory); be haunted (by the image of a person). ¶죽은 아들의 모습이 자꾸 눈에 밟힌다 I am haunted by the phantom of the departed son.

눈에 불을 켜다 ¶그는 눈에 불을 켜고 화를 냈다 He glared in anger. // 그는 입학시험이 한 달 뒤로 다가와서 눈에 불을 켜고 공부하고 있다 With only one month left to the entrance examination he is studying flat out [like mad].

눈에 불이 나다 ¶뺨을 맞아 눈에 불이 났다 I had a slap across my face that lighted flashes of light in the eyeballs.

눈에서 번개가 번쩍 나다 ¶그와 머리를 부딪쳐서 눈에서 번개가 번쩍 났다 When I bumped my head against his, I saw stars.

눈에 선하다 be clear [vivid] in one's memory [mind]. ¶그의 실망한 표정이 눈에 선했다 His hurt expression rose again in my mind.

눈에 익다 familiar; (서술적) (사물이) be familiar (to); (사람이) get [become] used to seeing (a thing); become familiar (with the sight of). ¶눈에 익은 광경 a familiar sight // 눈에 익지 않은 unfamiliar / strange // 눈에 익은 얼굴들 familiar faces // 눈에 익어 아무렇지도 않다 be hardened to the sight // 이것은 눈에 익은 광경이다 This is a familiar scene to me. // 이 애는 동물원에 자주 가기 때문에 호랑이는 눈에 익어 있어요 As the child often goes to the zoo, he is familiar with the tiger. / The tiger is familiar to the child because he often visits the zoo.

눈에 차다 be satisfactory.

눈에 흙이 들어가다 ¶내 눈에 흙이 들어가기 전에는 while [as long as] I live / so long as I am alive // 내 눈에 흙이 들어가기 전에는 그런 짓은 어림도 없다 I won't permit such a thing as long as I live. / You may do so only over my dead body. / Over my dead body!

눈을 끌다 catch [strike] one's eye; attract one's attention [notice]; be striking; be attractive. ¶전시품 가운데서 그의 대담한 작품이 사람들의 눈을 끌었다 Among the exhibits his bold work attracted the attention of the people.

눈을 의심하다 ¶야윈 노인이 달리기 시작했을 때 나는 내 눈을 의심했다 I watched in disbelief [I could hardly believe my eyes] as the emaciated old man began to run.

눈이 둥잔만 하다 ¶그들은 깜짝 놀라 눈이 둥잔만 해졌다 Their eyes were popping with amazement. // 앵무새가 노래하기 시작하자 아이들은 눈이 둥잔만 해졌다 When the parrot began to sing, the children stared at it in round-eyed wonder. // 노인은 스트리킹을 하는 남자들을 보고서 눈이 둥잔만 해졌다 The old man stared after the streakers, round-eyed with amazement.

눈(을) 주다 give (a person) the eye; wink (significantly) (at); make a sign with one's eye(s); eye (a person) meaningly.

눈(을) 피하다 avoid another's observation [eye]. ¶그들은 선생님들의 눈을 피해 학교 화장실에서 담배를 피웠다 They smoked in the school lavatory to avoid the eye of their teachers. // 그 아이는 부모의 눈을 피해 담배를 피우고 있었다 The boy was smoking, when his parents weren't looking.

눈 하나 깜짝하지 않다 not [never] bat an eyelid [eye / eyelash]. ¶그는 아내가 중병에 걸렸다는 말을 듣고도 눈 하나 깜짝하지 않았다 He didn't bat an eyelid when he was told his wife was very ill. // 그는 눈 하나 깜짝하지 않는 강심장이다 He has the nerve to face [brazen] it out.

눈[2] [식] a bud; a sprout; a shoot; a germ. ¶~이 트다 (the buds) come out / sprout / shoot (up / out) / bud (out) / come into bud.

눈[3] a division (on a scale). ⇨=눈금1 ¶저울~을 속이다 give short weight.

눈[4] [그물 등의 구멍] a mesh. ¶그물~ the meshes of a net // ~이 가는 체 a sieve of fine [close] mesh // ~이 성긴 [촘촘한] 그물 a wide-[fine-] mesh(ed) net.

눈[5] [설(雪)] snow; a snowfall (강설); snows (적설). ¶~의 snowy // ~ 오는 날 a snowy day // ~ 가루 powdery snow // 함박~ large [feathery] snowflakes // 적은 [약간의] ~ a light snowfall / a little snow / 큰 ~ a heavy (fall of) snow / a heavy snowfall // 진~ wet snow / sleet / snow mixed [mingled] with rain / 첫~ the first snow(fall) of the season // ~ 덩이 a ball of snow / a snowball // ~ 뭉

치 a snowball // ~ 덮인 벌판 a snowfield / a field [an expanse] of snow // 바람에 날리는 ~ snowflakes that come riding on the wind // 녹은 ~ melted snow // 바람에 날려 쌓인 ~ (더미) a snowdrift / a snow bank // 산봉우리의 ~ a snowcap // ~ 녹은 길 a slushy [slush-filled] road // ~ 덮인 꼭대기가 ~ virgin snow // 꼭대기가 ~ 에 덮인 북악산 snowcapped [영] snow-capped // Bugaksan (Mt. Bugak) // ~치기 snow shoveling [영] shovelling // ~이 덮인 snow-covered / snow-laden / snow-blanketed / snow-mantled // ~이 많이 오는 지역 a region of heavy snows [snowfall] // ~에 묻히다 be buried under [in] the snow / be snowed under // ~에 갇히다 be snowbound / be snowed up [in] / be snowstalled // ~에 덮이다 be covered with [mantled in] snow // ~을 치다 rake [shovel / sweep] away snow / clear away [off] snow / clear (a road) of snow / remove snow // ~을 털다 knock snow off (one's coat, the fence, etc) / stamp the snow from (one's boots) (발을 굴러) // ~을 맞다 get snowed on / be exposed to snow // ~을 헤치고 나아가다 plow (one's way) through the snow // ~이 내린다 [온다] It snows. / Snow falls [flies]. // ~이 (much / little) snow. // ~이 평평 [몹시] 내린다 It snows heavily [hard / thick and fast]. // ~이 펄펄 내린다 Snowflakes flutter in the air. // 비가 섞인 ~이 내리고 있다 It is snowing with (a mingling of) rain. // ~이 쌓인다 Snow lies [piles up / heaps] (on the ground). // ~이 올 것 같다 It threatens to snow. / It [The sky] looks like snow. / There are signs of snow. // ~이 그 대로 있다 The snow is staying [remaining]. // ~이 내려 1미터나 쌓여 있었다 Snow lay one meter deep on the ground. // ~이 1미터 내렸다 There was a one-meter snowfall [a snowfall of one meter]. // 산에 큰 ~이 내렸다 A heavy snow fell in the mountains. // 간밤에 ~이 약간 내렸다 We had a light snow(fall) last night. / There was a light snowfall last night. // ~이 10센티 쌓였다 The snow lies [is] ten centimeters deep. / We had a ten-centimeter snowfall [ten centimeters of snow]. // 어제는 20년 만에 가장 많은 ~이 내렸다 Yesterday we had the heaviest snowfall we have had for twenty years. // 올해는 ~이 많이 왔다 [조금밖에 오지 않았다] We've had a lot of [We haven't had much] snow this year. // 도로 옆에 ~이 수북이 쌓여 있었다 There was a mass of snow heaped [piled] up by along the roadside. // 그들은 ~에 갇혀 오두막에서 이틀을 보냈다 They were snowed in [up] and spent two days and nights in the hut. // ~이 녹았다 The snow has disappeared [melted / thawed]. // 나는 집 앞 보도의 ~을 치웠다 I shoveled the snow (away) from the pavement in front of our house.

눈가 the eye rims; parts around the eye.

눈가리개 a bandage; a blindfold; (말은) blinkers; (미) blinders. // ¶~를 하다 blindfold (a person) / put a bandage over (a person's) eyes / bandage (a person's) eyes / (말에) put blinkers on a horse.

눈가림 (a) sham; (a) pretense; camouflage. **눈가림하다** pull the wool over (a person's) eyes; hoodwink; camouflage; blind the eyes (of); blindfold; cover up; gloss over; make (A) look like (B); give (a thing) an air [appearance] of. ¶어물어물 눈가림하여 넘기다 shuffle [rub] along [through].

눈감다 1 [죽다] die; breathe one's last. ¶그는 어린 자식들을 두고 편히 눈감을 수가 없었다 He could hardly die in peace leaving behind such young children. 2 [못 본 체하다] shut [close] one's eyes (to); blink [wink] at; connive at; turn a blind eye (on / to); overlook.

눈감아 주다 shut [close] one's eyes (to); keep one's eyes closed (to); overlook; look over; pass over; let (it) pass [go]; let (a person) go unchallenged [unpunished]; connive (at); wink (an eye) (at); blink (at). ¶비행을 ~ connive at a person's wrongdoing // 남의 허물을 ~ blink at another's mistakes // 남의 부정행위를 ~ wink at a person's misconduct // 밀렵자를 ~ shut one's eyes to a poacher // 불쌍하니 이번만은 눈감아 주겠다 For pity's sake I will let the matter pass for this once. // 이번만은 눈감아 주시기 바랍니다 I hope you will overlook my mistake [forgive me] just this once. // 그는 내 실수를 눈감아 주었다 He was good enough to overlook my mistakes.

눈결 a glance; a glimpse. ¶~에 언뜻 보다 get [catch] a glimpse of.

눈곱 1 (눈에 끼는) discharge from the eyes; eye mucus [discharges]; gum [matter] (in the corner of the eye); (구어) sleep; (영국 구어) sleepy dust. ¶~이 낀 눈 a waxy [blear] eye // ~이 끼다 matter forms in the eyes / one's eyes matter (up) / one's eyes are gummy [mattery] // 네 왼쪽 눈에 ~이 꼈다 There's some sleep [sleepy-dust] in your left eye. // 그 노인은 ~으로 눈이 흐릿하다 The old man has bleary eyes because of mucus discharges. // 네 눈에 ~이 끼었구나 (속어) (어린아이에게) You've got some sleep [(영) sleepy-dust] in your eye.
2 [비유] a very small thing [amount]; a grain; a bit; a whit; a modicum. ¶~는 개의치 않았다 He did not care a fig [whit / bit] about it. // 그녀는 퇴직금을 ~만큼 받았다 She received only a pittance in retirement money [a miserably small amount as retirement money]. // 그녀는 ~만큼의 위자료를 받았을 뿐이다 She was given only a modicum of a solatium. / She received only a token solatium. // 그의 말에는 진실이라고는 ~만큼도 없다 There isn't a grain of truth in what he said.

눈구멍 an eyehole; the eye socket; an eyepit.
눈구석 the inner corner of the eye.
눈금 1 (자·저울·온도계 등의) a division (on a scale); a scale (on a beam balance); graduations (on a thermometer); [광] a graticule. ¶온도계의 ~ graduations [gradations] on a thermometer // ~을 매기다 graduate / divide / mark with degrees / calibrate // 글라스에 ~을 매기다 graduate a glass / mark a scale on a glass // 이 자는 ~이 밀리미터로 되어 있다 This ruler is graduated in millimeters. // 이 계량컵은 1cc 마다 ~이 그어져 있다 This measuring cup is graduated in cubic centimeters. 2 [눈짐작으로 긋는 금] a line which is drawn according to eye measure. ¶~을 긋다 draw [make] a line by (the) eye.

눈기이다 deceive; hoodwink; (미국 구어) draw [pull] the wool over (a person's) eyes.

눈길[1] one's eyes. ⇨ 시선(視線) ¶~이 닿는 [닿지 않는] 곳에 within [beyond / out of] eyeshot // ~을 피하다 avoid a person's eyes / escape another's gaze // ~을 주고받다 look at each other / exchange glances [looks] (with) // ~을 돌리다 turn [direct] one's eyes [attention] (to) / bend one's eyes (on) // 의미심장한 ~을 주고받다 exchange significant glances // ~을 끄는 포스터 an eye-catching poster / ~을 끄는 광고 an attention-getting advertisement // 그녀의 모자가 폐 ~을 끌었다 Her hat attracted a lot [a good deal] of attention.

눈길(을) 모으다 attract public gaze.

눈길을 거두다 take one's eyes off [from]; look aside [away].

눈길[2] [눈 덮인 길] a snow-covered [laden] road; a snowy road.

눈까풀 an eyelid. ⇨ 눈꺼풀

눈깔사탕(—沙糖) toffees; taffies; (영) a bull's eye. ¶~을 빨다 suck on a piece of taffy.

눈깜짝이 a blinkard.

눈꺼풀 an eyelid; the lid (of an eye); [생] a palpebra (*pl.* -rae). ¶쌍겹[한 겹] ~ an eyelid with a [no] fold // 윗 [아랫] ~ an upper [a lower] eyelid / 처진 ~ a drooped eyelid.

눈꼴사납다 1 [모양이 사납다] hard-featured; villainous-looking; unsightly; shabby; ugly. ¶눈꼴사나운 놈 a hard-feature fellow // 눈꼴사나운 광경 an ugly scene. 2 [아니꼬워 비위에 거슬리다] offensive to the eye; hateful to see; disgusting. ¶그의 하는 짓이 ~ His behavior is disgusting. // 그가 거드럭거리는 꼴이 눈꼴사나워 못 봐 주겠다 I hate to see [am sick of seeing] him swaggering.

눈꼴시다 (서술적) hate to see; be disgusting; be sick of. ¶그가 잘난 체하는 것이 ~ I hate to see him pretending he is somebody. // 그가 사장에게 아첨하는 꼴이 ~ I am sick of the way he fawns upon the boss. / I am sick of him licking at the boss's heels.

눈꼴틀리다 hate to see. ⇨ 눈꼴시다

눈대중 eye measurement [estimation]; measuring with one's eye. ¶~으로 by the [one's] eye / by eye measure / at a rough estimate / by the rule of thumb / at a [by] guess // ~으로 재다 estimate by (the) eye / 설탕을 ~으로 재다 measure sugar by (the) eye. **눈대중하다** measure [estimate] by the eye.

눈독(—毒) a covetous steady gaze; gazing at; having [keeping] an eye to.

눈독(이) 들다 become greedy [covetous] in one's look; (a thing) get eyed [gazed at]; (a thing) make (a person) drool. ¶아내는 그 모피 코트에 눈독이 들었다 The fur coat made my wife drool.

눈독(을) 들이다 have an eye on; fix one's eyes on; have [keep] an eye to; can't keep one's eyes off; mark for a victim; look over closely [avidly]. ¶도둑이 눈독 들인 집 a house a thief has his eyes on // 재산에 ~ have an eye to the property // 소매치기는 졸고 있는 여자의 핸드백에 눈독을 들였다 The pickpocket fixed his eyes on the dozing woman's handbag. // 도둑은 벌써부터 그 집에 눈독을 들이고 있었다 The robber had marked out the house for burglary.

눈동자(—瞳子) the pupil (of the eye); the apple of the eye. ¶검은 ~ (dark) brown eyes. (▶ black eye라고 하기 쉬우나 이는 눈 주위가 멍이 든 상태를 가리키는 말임)

눈두덩 the brow. ¶~이 붓다 have swollen eyes.

눈딱부리 [툭 불거진 큰 눈] protruding [protuberant / projecting / bulging] eyes; goggle [pop / lobster] eyes; [툭 불거진 큰 눈을 지닌 사람] a lobster-eyed person. ¶~의 goggle-eyed / bug-eyed / (미국 속어) popeyed.

눈뜨다 [잠을 깨다] wake (up); awake; [깨닫다·본능 등이 발동하다] awake [awaken / wake up] (to); be awakened (to); be awake (to). ¶미(美)에 ~ be awaken to beauty // 성(性)에 ~ experience a sexual awakening / be awakened to sex [sexually] / experience the awakening of erotic impulse // 현실에 ~ be awakened [have one's eyes opened] to the stern realities (of life).

눈뜬장님 [눈뜨고도 보지 못하는 사람] a person with unseeing eyes; [흑내장이 있는 사람] an amaurotic person; a bat-blind person; [문맹자] an unlettered person; an illiterate (person); an ignoramus; (집합적) the illiterate. ¶그는 ~이야 He can't read or write. / He is an illiterate. // 그것도 알아보지 못하다니 ~이로구나 You are a blind fool not to recognize it.

눈망울 an eyeball.

눈매 the shape of one's eyes; the eyes. ¶귀여운 ~ charming [lovely] eyes // ~가 사나운 사람 a fierce-looking man // ~가 또렷한 소녀 a girl with clear [bright] eyes // 온순한 [부드러운] ~의 여인 a woman with a tender [gentle] look // ~가 매섭다 have hard eyes // 자네는 ~가 어머니 닮았네 You and your mother have very similar eyes.

눈맵시 the eyes. ⇨ 눈매

눈멀다 lose one's sight; become [go] blind. ¶눈먼 사람 a blind person / (집합적) the blind / 눈먼 사랑 blind love / 돈에 ~ covet money / be lured [blinded] by gain // 사랑에 ~ be blind in the matter of love.

눈물[1] a tear; [동정심의 비유] sympathy. ¶거짓 ~ sham [false / fictive / crocodile] tears / forced tears / 뜨거운 ~ hot [burning / scalding] tears / 기쁨의 ~ tears of joy / happy tears / tears of pleasure / ~ 젖은 눈 eyes misted [dimmed / blurred] with tears / moist [tearful] eyes / ~ 젖은 얼굴 a tearful face / a crying face / weeping eyes / ~ 젖은 목소리로 with tears in one's voice / in a tearful voice / ~도 없는 사람 a tearless [an unfeeling / a cold-blooded] person / ~이 날 정도로 웃다 laugh till the tears come // 그의 이야기를 듣고 있자니 눈에 ~이 나는 것을 느꼈다 As I listened to his story, I felt tears come to my eyes. // 양파를 썰고 있으니 ~이 나기 시작했다 As I was chopping an onion, tears came into my eyes [my eyes began to water]. // ~ 어린 눈 liquid eyes // 그녀의 눈에 ~이 어렸다 Tears gathered [stood] in her eyes. // ~이 글썽하다 bring tears to one's eyes // ~이 비 오듯 하다 shed a shower of tears // ~을 흘리다 shed [drop] tears / give way to tears / weep // 억지로 ~을 짜다 squeeze out a tear // 감동으로 ~을 흘리다 be moved to tears // 회한의 ~을 흘리다 shed bitter tears of remorse // ~을 닦다 dry [wipe (away)] one's tears / wipe one's wet eyes / (급히)

dash away one's tears // ~을 참다 keep [choke / hold / fight] back one's tears / choke down one's tears / repress one's tears / keep tears from one's eyes // ~을 감추다 hide one's tears // 그들은 손을 맞잡고 기쁨의 ~을 흘렸다 Taking each other's hands, they shed tears of joy. // 내 눈에 ~이 솟아났다 Tears welled up in [sprang to] my eyes. // 나는 고마움에 ~을 흘릴 뿐이었다 I could only shed tears of gratitude. // 그녀는 절대로 남에게 ~을 보이지 않는다 She never cries in front of other people. / She never shows her tears to others. // 양친과 아이들은 ~로 이별하였다 The parents and the children parted in (a flood of) tears. // ~이 흘러 그녀의 베개를 적셨다 The tears trickled [rolled] down and wet(ted) her pillow. // 어머니는 ~이 많으시다 My mother is easily moved to tears. // 잠자는 아이의 뺨에 ~ 자국이 있었다 There were traces of tears on the sleeping child's cheeks. // ~이 그녀의 뺨을 흘러내렸다 A tear rolled down her cheek. // 그 영화는 상투적으로 짜게 하는 이야기이다 The movie is a stereotyped tearjerker [sob story]. // 고아가 된 그 아이를 보니 ~을 참을 수가 없었다 Looking at the bereaved infant, I could not hold back my tears. // 우리는 그 처참한 광경에 ~을 흘렸다 The pitiful sight moved us to tears. // 장례식 날은 우리의 ~이 빗물이 된 듯이 비가 내렸다 On the day of the funeral it was as wet as if our tears had changed into rain. // 임종의 여인은 딸에게 ~로 자신의 비밀을 털어놓았다 The dying woman confided her secret to her daughters in tears. // 그녀는 ~에 목이 메어 아무 말도 하지 못했다 She was choked with tears and was unable to say anything. // 그 소녀는 ~을 참으려고 애썼다 The girl tried hard to hold back her tears. // 참았던 ~이 마침내 터져 나왔다 My pent-up [long-stored] tears burst forth at last.

눈물(을) 거두다 stop weeping.
눈물(을) 삼키다 swallow [gulp down] one's tears; repress one's tears; choke down one's tears; hold [choke / keep back] one's tears. ¶진 팀은 눈물을 삼키며 경기장을 떠났다 The defeated team walked out of the stadium swallowing [holding back] their tears.
눈물을 자아내다 move (a person) to tears; draw [force] tears from (a person); call forth (a person's) tears; make (a person) weep. ¶눈물을 자아내는 이야기 a moving [touching] story.
● **눈물길** [生] the tear [lachrymal] duct. **눈물샘** [生] a lachrymal gland.
눈물² [눈 녹은 물] melted snow.
눈물겹다 touching; moving; tearful; pathetic; tear-provoking. ¶눈물겨운 장면 a moving [touching / pathetic] scene // 눈물겨운 이별 parting in tears / tearful parting // 눈물겨운 노력 pathetically sincere efforts // 눈물겨운 이야기 a pathetic [touching] story.
눈물지다 tears fall [flow].
눈물짓다 shed tears; (눈이) be filled with tears; one's eyes moisten [glisten] with tears; moisten at one's eyes. ¶그녀는 눈물짓으며 고개를 떨구었다 She hung her head with tears in her eyes.
눈바람 1 [눈과 바람] wind and snow. 2 [심한 고난] terrible afflictions; great sufferings.
눈발 snow flakes. ¶굵은 ~ big flakes of snow // ~이 선다 It threatens to snow. / It looks like snow. // ~이 날리기 시작한다 Snowflakes begin to flutter in the air.
눈방울 a glaring eyeball. ¶~을 굴리다 goggle (about).
눈밭 1 snow-covered ground. 2 a snowfield.
눈병 (-病) an eye disease [trouble / complaint]; sore eyes; ophthalmic ailment [case]. ¶~이 나다 suffer from an eye disease [trouble] / have an eye trouble / be afflicted with an eye disease.
눈보라 a snowstorm; a shower of snow; a snowdrift; a driving snow. ¶심한 ~ a severe snowstorm / a blizzard // ~가 치다 (snow) be driven by the wind / drift hard // 밤새도록 ~가 몰아쳤다 The snowstorm raged all through the night. // 우리는 ~를 무릅쓰고 행군하였다 We marched in the teeth of a blizzard.
눈부시다 1 (빛이) dazzling; glaring; blinding (flash). ¶매우 눈부신 태양 the hot glaring sun // 눈부신 햇빛 brilliant sunlight // 눈부신 전등불 a glaring light // 눈부시게 희다 be dazzlingly white // 눈부시게 빛나다 dazzle / glare / flare (전등 등이) // 햇빛이 눈부셨다 The sunlight dazzled my eyes. // 눈부시어 눈을 뜨고 있을 수 없다 The light is so bright that I cannot keep my eyes open. // 빛이 세어 눈부셨다 The strong light dazzled my eyes. / My eyes were dazed by the glare of the light. // 빛이 눈부시어 눈을 뜰 수가 없었다 My eyes were blinded by the glare. / The dazzling light blinded my eyes.
2 [현란하다] gorgeous; showy; gaudy; dazzling; brilliant; radiant. ¶눈부신 광경 a glittering scene // 눈부시게 차려입다 be gaudily dressed / be attired in gala dress.
3 [비유] striking (achievement); remarkable (development); conspicuous (part); signal (victory); splendid (exploit); brilliant (success); wonderful (deed). ¶눈부신 발전 remarkable [striking] development // 농기구의 눈부신 개량 a remarkable improvement in farming tools // 눈부신 활약을 하다 perform a brilliant exploit [distinguish oneself] (in a battle) / play a conspicuous part (in) // 눈부신 업적을 올리다 succeed in a splendid [wonderful / striking] achievement // 그는 사건 해결에 눈부신 역할을 했다 He played a conspicuous role [He distinguished himself] in settling the matter. // 최근 과학의 발달은 눈부신 바 있다 Modern science has made startling progress.
눈비 [눈과 비] snow and rain.
눈빛¹ 1 [눈의 빛깔] the color of one's eyes; [표정] the expression of one's eyes. ¶애원하는 듯한 ~ a look of appeal // ~이 달라지다 change color (at the news) // 성이 나서 ~이 달라지다 be furious with anger. 2 [안광] the glitter of one's eyes.
눈빛² [흰색] the color of snow; white.
눈사람 a snowman. ¶~을 만들다 make [build] a snowman.
눈사태 (-沙汰) a snowslide; an avalanche (of snow)(큰). ¶~로 많은 집들이 파괴되었다 [휩쓸려 갔다] Many houses were destroyed [carried away] by the avalanche [snowslide]. // ~가 났다 Avalanches rushed down the mountainside. // ~가 우리를 덮쳤다 An avalanche came [fell] down on us. // 산 중턱

에 ~가 났다 The snow slid down the mountainside. / There was an avalanche on the mountainside.

눈살 the furrow[wrinkles] between the eyebrows.

눈살(을) 찌푸리다 draw one's eyebrows together; knit one's brows; frown (at / on); make a penthouse of the eyebrows. ¶눈살을 찌푸리고 with a frown / with knitted eyebrows // 그는 난처하여 눈살을 찌푸렸다 He frowned in his distress. / He drew together his troubled brows. // 그는 눈살을 찌푸리며 이야기했다 He talked with his brows knitted. // 그는 눈살을 찌푸리며 날 보았다 He looked at me with a frown[with knitted eyebrows]. // 그녀의 머리 모양을 보고 모두들 눈살을 찌푸렸다 Everyone looked askance[frowned] at her hair style.

눈석임 a thaw; the thawing of snow. **눈석임하다** thaw.
● **눈석임물** snow water; meltwater.

눈속임 cheating; deceiving; hoodwinking; camouflage. **눈속임하다** deceive; cheat; trick; hoodwink. ¶노름에서 ~ cheat in gambling // 근수를 ~ give short weight.

눈송이 a flake (of snow); a snowflake.

눈시울 the edge of an eyelid; the eye rims. ¶~이 뜨거워지는 광경 a pathetic[moving] sight // ~이 뜨거워지다 be (almost) moved to tears / melt into tears / one's eyes moisten (with tears) / be touched (by) // 그 불쌍한 이야기를 듣고 ~이 뜨거워졌다 The pathetic story appealed to my tender emotion.

눈싸움[1] [눈겨룸] a game of staring each other; an staring game. **눈싸움하다**[1] have [play] an staring game; try to stare each other[one another]; try to stare another person down[(영) out].

눈싸움[2] [설전(雪戰)] a snowball fight[battle]; snowballing. **눈싸움하다**[2] have a snowball fight[battle]; snowball. ¶아이들이 눈싸움했다 The children snowballed each other. // 눈싸움 하자 Let's throw snowballs. / Let's have a snowball fight.

눈썰미 a quick eye for learning things. ¶~가 있다[없다] be quick[slow] in visual learning / have a quick[dull] eye for learning things.

눈썹 an eyebrow. ¶굵은 ~ strong eyebrows // 그린[가짜] ~ painted eyebrows // 찌푸린[팔자] ~ slanted eyebrows // 한 쌍의 ~ (a pair of) thick[heavy / bushy / shaggy] eyebrows // 반달 같은 ~ arched[crescent-shaped] eyebrows // ~을 치켜 올리다 arch[raise / lift] one's eyebrows // ~을 그리다 pencil one's eyebrows // ~이 짙다 have abundant[thick] eyebrows.

눈썹도 까딱하지 않다 remain unperturbed. ¶눈썹도 까딱하지 않고 with a poker face / without changing one's expression / without batting an eyelid[eye] // 그녀는 아주 침착하여 눈썹도 까딱하지 않았다 She was so cool that not a muscle of her face moved.
● **눈썹연필** an eyebrow pencil.

눈알 an eyeball. ¶~을 굴리다 roll[goggle] one's eyes // ~이 툭 불거지다 have protruding eyes / be goggle-eyed // (미국 속어) popeyed // ~이 뛰어나올 정도로 놀라다 be frightened out of one's wits // ~을 부라리다 goggle (one's eyes) / stare one's eyes out / glare (at / upon).

눈앞 1 [면전]. ¶~에서 before (a person's) eyes / under (a person's) (very) eyes[nose] / in (a person's) presence[sight] / (just) before one // 그것은 바로 네 ~에 있다 It is right in front of you. // 내 ~에서 문이 쾅 하고 닫혔다 The door was slammed in my face. // 네 ~의 상자를 열어라 Open the box that's just in front of you. // 애는 엄마의 ~에서 차에 치였다 The boy was run over by a car before his mother's eyes. // 그것은 바로 내 ~에서 도난 당했다 It was stolen right out from under my very nose! // 웅대한 경치가 ~에 펼쳐졌다 A splendid view opened out before us. // 나는 그의 ~에서 100불짜리 지폐를 흔들어 댔다 I waved a hundred bill before his eyes. // 바로 내 ~을 자동차가 획 지나갔다 A car whizzed by right in front of me. // 증거가 내 ~에 내밀어졌다 Evidence was shoved under my nose. // 그 광경이 ~에 보이듯이 묘사되어 있다 The scene is described so vividly that I feel as if I actually saw it. // 내 아이의 얼굴이 ~에 어른거린다 My child's face haunts me[my eyes]. // 새로운 세계가 우리의 ~에 펼쳐졌다 A new world has opened up[appeared] before our eyes.

2 [직전]. ¶~에 close[near] at hand / just ahead // ~에 닥치다 [다가오다] be near [close] at hand / be imminent / be directly [just] ahead // 시험이 ~에 다가왔다 The examination is close at hand[is just ahead]. // 그들의 결혼식 날짜가 ~에 다가와 있었다 Their wedding day was close at hand. // 그녀는 결혼식을 ~에 두고 병에 걸렸다 She became ill just before the wedding. // 완성을 ~에 두고 시간이 다 되어 버렸다 Just as I was within the sight of finishing, time ran out.

3 [현재]. ¶~의 immediate / at hand / direct // ~의 이익 an immediate profit // ~의 일만 생각하다 think only of the present[the immediate future] / take a short view of things / be short-sighted.

눈앞이 깜깜하다 ¶은사의 갑작스런 서거에 눈앞이 깜깜해졌다 On the sudden death of my teacher, I was thrown into despair[everything before me went black].

눈약(-藥) eyewash; eye drops. ⇨*안약

눈어림 eye measurement. ⇨*눈대중

눈언저리 parts around the eye. ⇨*눈가 ¶~에 멍이 들었다 The blow gave him a black eye.

눈엣가시 1 [눈에 거슬리는 사람] a very disgusting[disagreeable / hateful] person; an offense to the eye; a pain in the neck[ass] ; a thorn in one's flesh[side]; an eyesore. ¶~로 여기다 regard (a person) as an eyesore / regard (a person) with enmity / hate (a person) (to death) // ~가 되다 be an eyesore / be hated // 계모는 나를 ~처럼 여겼다 My stepmother regarded me as an eyesore[as if I always stood in her way]. // 저 과장은 ~ 같은 존재다 I cannot act freely because the section chief always stands in my way. 2 [남편의 첩] a concubine; a (kept) mistress.

눈여겨보다 observe carefully; watch intently; take a good[close] look (at). ¶눈여겨볼 만하다 be worth notice / be worthy of attention // 행동을 ~ observe (a person's) behavior carefully // 그녀는 그 옷을 눈여겨보았다 She had a good look at the dress.

눈요기(-療飢) a feast[joy] to the eye; visual pleasure. ¶~가 되다 be a feast[joy] to the eye / delight[please] the eye / give (a person) visual pleasure.∥회장을 가득 메운 한복을 차려입은 여성들이 내 ~가 되었다 The sight of the women in Korean costumes who filled the hall was a feast for my eyes.∥그 멋진 그림은 내게 ~가 되었다 The beautiful paintings (I saw) were a delight to the eye. **눈요기하다** feast one's eyes on (something).
눈웃음 a smile with[about / in] one's eyes.
눈웃음치다 [눈으로만 살짝 웃다] smile with one's eyes; wear a smile about[in] one's eyes; [추파를 던지다] cast[make] sheep's eyes (at). ¶그녀는 그 남자에게 눈웃음쳤다 She cast sheep's eyes at the man.
눈인사(-人事) a nod; nodding. ¶~를 **교환하다** exchange nods. **눈인사하다** nod (to); greet with a nod[one's eyes]; give (a person) a nod.
눈자위 the eyeball area.
눈접(-椄) [농] bud grafting; budding; inlay (graft). **눈접하다** graft a bud (in / upon); bud.
눈정기(-精氣) the vivacity[animation] of the eyes; the glitter of the eyes; the keenness of the eyes. ¶~가 있다 have lively[animated] eyes / have glittering eyes / be keen-eyed.
눈짐작(-斟酌) eye measurement. ⇨눈대중
눈짓 winking. ¶~으로 with talking eyes. **눈짓하다** wink (significantly) (at); give (a person) a wink; make a sign with one's eyes; eye (a person) meaningly. ¶서로 ~ exchange glances[significant looks]∥그들은 서로 눈짓했다 They exchanged significant looks.∥그녀가 눈짓하자 하인은 슬그머니 방을 나갔다 At a sign from her eyes the servant gliden out of the room.
눈초리 1 [눈꼬리] the outer corner of the eye; the tail of the eye. ¶~의 주름 the lines at the corners of the[one's] eyes / crow's-feet / crowfeet (wrinkles) / ~가 치켜 올라가[처져] 있다 have upward[downward] slanting eyes ∥그녀는 ~가 치켜 올라가 있다 Her eyes slant upwards.
2 [눈매] a look (in a person's eyes); an expression of the eyes. ¶매서운 ~ a dreadful[menacing] look∥~가 무서운 사람 a fierce-looking man∥성난 ~로 노려보다 look daggers[fiercely] (at) / glare furiously (at) ∥의심하는 ~로 보다 view (something) with suspicious eyes / eye[regard / look on] (something) with suspicion∥그는 묘한 ~로 사람을 본다 He has a strange way of looking at people.∥그는 의심스러운 듯한 ~로 나를 보았다 He gave me a suspicious look.
눈총 a glare; a sharp look; looking daggers (at); a scowl.
눈총(을) 맞다 be hated[detested] (by); make oneself hated (by); be in detestation. ¶뭇사람의 ~ be a common eyesore / be [become] a common object of hatred∥그렇게 하면 그분의 눈총을 맞을 거야 If you do that you will make yourself obnoxious to him.
눈총기(-聰氣) the mind's eye. ¶~가 있다[좋다] have a photographic memory.
눈치 1 [센스] tact; sense; quick[ready] wit. ¶~ 있게 …하다 have the good sense to (do) / be sensible[tactful] enough to (do)∥~가 빠르다 be quick-witted / be ready-witted / have quick wits / be tactful[sensible] ∥~가 없다 be slow-[dull-]witted / have slow wits / have no sense / be tactless[senseless] ∥그 사람은 ~가 빠르다 He has all his wits about him.∥그는 직업상 ~가 빠르다 From his business habits he has quick perception. ∥ 우리는 ~ 빠르게 그들 둘이서만 있게 해 주었다 We tactfully left them alone together.∥ "어떻게 알아냈습니까?" "~지요." "How did you make it out?" "It was a hunch[I knew it in my bones]."
2 [마음의 기미] one's frame of mind; one's mental attitude toward (a person); one's intention[design / wish]; [기색] looks; (facial) expression; a sign; a hint; an indication. ¶싫어하는 ~ 하나 안 보이고 without showing the least sign of reluctance∥~를 **살피다** study the pleasure of (a person) / read[study] (another's) face[countenance] ∥~를 **보이다** express (one's emotions) by outward signs / betray (one's mind) in one's look∥좋아하는[좋아하지 않는] ~를 보이다 give[show] signs of pleasure[displeasure]∥찬성하지 않는 ~를 보이다 hint one's disapproval∥그런 ~는 전혀 보이지 않는다 There are no such indications. / No such indications are to be observed.∥그녀는 슬쩍 남편의 ~를 살폈다 She secretly studied her husband's facial expression. / She cast a furtive glance at her husband.∥그런 ~를 몰랐다 It did not come under my notice.∥그는 ~가 좀 이상하다 He is somewhat strange in his manners.∥그녀는 내가 마음에 든 ~다 She seems pleased with me.
눈치(를) 보다 study the pleasure of (a person); read[study] (another's) face [countenance]; have a regard for (a person's) feelings; see how the wind blows. ¶성나지 않았나 ~ study (a person's) face to see if he is angry∥눈치 보아 가며 의견을 진술하다 venture an opinion studying (another's) face∥눈치 보아 가며 행동하자 Let's see which way the wind is blowing actions before we take.
눈치(를) 채다 become aware of[that]; be suspicious of; suspect; sense; scent; get wind[scent] of; smell; have an inkling of; take hint of. ¶위험을 ~ perceive[sense] danger∥그가 사기꾼이 아닌가 하고 어렴풋이 눈치 채고 있었다 I had a hunch[I vaguely suspected / I had a vague suspicion] that he was an imposter.∥주인은 마침내 두 사람 사이를 눈치 챘다 In the end the relation between the two came to the knowledge of their employer.∥그에게 숨겨진 면이 있다는 것을 전혀 눈치 채지 못했다 I did not have the faintest inkling of his secret side[that he had a secret side].∥식구들이 눈치 채지 않게 집을 빠져나올 수 있었다 I was able to get away without attracting my family's notice [unnoticed by my family].
● **눈치작전** a wait-and-see policy.
눈치레 mere show; outward show; showy appearance; vain ornamentation; putting on a good front[face]. ¶~로 for show / for the sake of appearance. **눈치레하다** make outward show; dress up to appeal to the eye; stress eye appeal; make a good showing; put on a good front.

눈칫밥 a meal offered unwillingly; perfunctory hospitality. ¶~을 먹다 eat another's salt / eat salt with (a person) / feed [live] on (a person).

눈코 [눈과 코] the eyes and the nose.

눈코 뜰 사이 없다 be (kept) very busy; have eggs on the spits. ¶눈코 뜰 사이 없이 바쁘다 be in a whirl of business / be pressed by business [work] / be so busy that one feels as if going to faint // 그녀는 아기를 돌보기에 눈코 뜰 사이 없이 바쁘다 She has her hands full [is busy enough just] taking care of her baby. // 오늘은 손님이 잇따라 찾아와서 눈코 뜰 사이가 없었다 I have had a hectic [busy] time today with visitors coming one after another. // 그는 지금 논문 교정에 ~ He is now fully occupied with the proofreading of his thesis. // 손님이 오시는 날은 어머니는 아침부터 눈코 뜰 사이 없이 바쁘시다 Whenever we have visitors my mother is busy [hard at work] from early in the morning.

눈트다 sprout; shoot; bud; germinate.

눋다 scorch; burn; singe; be [get] scorched [burned / charred]. ¶눋은 내 a burnt smell / 시커멓게 ~ be burnt [scorched] black / 뜨거운 다리미로 셔츠를 눋게 만들다 scorch a shirt with a hot iron / 무엇인가 눋는 내가 난다 I (can) smell something burning. / 밥이 눋었다 The rice has got scorched. / 밥에서 눋은 내가 난다 The rice has a smoky [burnt] smell. / 눋지 않도록 계속 저어라 Stir it constantly to prevent burning [scorching].

눌러듣다 [너그러이 듣다] take (a person's) remark] with kindly tolerance [with good grace]. ¶철없는 말이거니 하고 ~ forgive (a person) for his thoughtless remarks.

눌러보다 [너그러이 보다] overlook (a person's fault); deal [treat] leniently [tolerantly] with (a person); pass over; shut [close] one's eyes to; look through one's fingers at. ¶남의 잘못을 ~ overlook (a person's) faults / regard (a person's) errors with kindly tolerance / deal leniently with another's mistakes // 이번만큼은 네 행동을 눌러봐 주겠다 I will overlook your behavior for this once.

눌러앉다 continue to stay; stay on and on; [유임하다] remain in the same position; remain in power [office]; stay on. ¶그는 한번 눌러앉으면 일어설 줄 모른다 He never knows when to leave. / 그들은 내 집에 오기만 하면 몇 시간이고 눌러앉아 있다 When they come to see me they always stay planted for hours. / 그 가족이 이 고장에 눌러앉은 지 3년이 된다 Three years have passed since the family settled down in this town.

눌리다[1] [누름을 당하다] be pressed down; be kept [held] down. ¶납작하게 ~ be pressed flat // 눌려 죽다 be crushed to death. **2** [압도당하다] be suppressed; be put down; be repressed; be oppressed. ¶다수에 ~ be overwhelmed by numbers / 말에 ~ be overwhelmed [overpowered] by the eloquence [argument] / be talked down // 아내에게 ~ be henpecked / be wife-ridden / be tied to one's wife's apron strings / be (right) under one's wife's thumb // 작은 가게는 큰 상점에 눌러서 장사가 안된다 Little shops are jostled out of trade by big ones. // 그의 위엄에 눌려 나는 아무런 반대도 할 수가 없었다 I was so awed by his air of dignity that I wasn't able to make any objections.

눌리다[2] [눋게 하다] burn; scorch; singe. ¶다리미질하다가 셔츠를 ~ scorch a shirts while ironing it // 밥을 ~ overcook [burn / scorch] rice.

눌변(訥辯) slowness of speech. ¶~인 slow of speech / inarticulate / awkward [clumsy] in speech / ineloquent // ~인 사람 a poor [an awkward] speaker // 그는 ~이다 He does not have a glib tongue. / He is not a fluent speaker. / He's a poor talker. / He doesn't talk well.

눌어붙다 [타서 붙다] scorch and stick to. ¶솥 바닥에 ~ get scorched and stick to the bottom of a pot // 내가 요리하던 음식이 냄비에 눌어붙었다 The food I was cooking burned and stuck to the pan. **2** [한곳에 오래 머물며 떠나지 않다] remain in the same place [position]; settle down; stay on. ¶눌어붙어 일어날 줄 모르는 사람 a sticker // 눌어붙어 앉아서 남의 눈총을 받다 outstay [wear out] one's welcome // 집에 ~ stay indoors [at home] / keep (to) the [one's] house / 시골에 눌어붙어 살다 settle down in the country / live in rural retirement // 한자리에 눌어붙어 움직이지 않다 squat down in one place and don't move / stay on in the same place / remain in the same position.

눌은밥 burned [scorched] rice at the bottom of the pot.

눕다 lie down; lay oneself down; stretch oneself; prostrate oneself. ¶반듯이 ~ lie on one's back [facing upward] / 모로 ~ lie on one's side / 자리에 ~ lay oneself [repose] on the bed // 길게 ~ lie [stretch out] at full length (on) / 큰대 자로 ~ lie [be stretched] at full length / lie in the form of capital X / lie spread-eagled / stretch oneself // 그는 폐렴으로 병상에 누워 있다 He is laid up with pneumonia. // 나는 소파에 누웠다 I lay down [(문어) reclined] on the sofa. // 그는 감기로 자리에 누워 있었다 He was in bed with a cold. // 그는 작년부터 병상에 누워 있다 He has been bedridden [sick in bed] since last year. // 하루 종일 누워 있지 그래 Why not stay in bed all day? // 그는 잔디밭에 누워 책을 읽고 있었다 He was lying on the lawn [grass] reading a book. // 나는 자리에 눕자마자 잠들었다 I went to sleep as soon as my head touched the pillow. // 잔디밭에 (다리를 뻗고) 누워 나는 푸른 하늘을 우러러보았다 I lay [stretched out] on the lawn, and I looked up into the blue sky. // 당분간 누워 있어야 한다 You must keep in bed [ought to be in bed] for some time. // 그 노인은 중풍으로 7년간 누워 있다 The old man has been laid up with palsy for seven years.

누워서 떡 먹기(속담) (It's) a very [quite an] easy task [job]; (It's) a cinch [snap]; (구어) (It's) a piece of cake.

누워서 침 뱉기(속담) Curses, like chickens, come home to roost; wash one's dirty linen in public; piss in the wind.

눕히다 lay down. ⇨¹누이다₁

눙치다 soothe [calm / appease] with nice words. 눙쳐서 노여움이 풀리게 하다 pacify [allay] (a person's) wrath [rage] / soothe [calm down] an angry man.

뉘[1] (쌀의) an unhulled [a half-hulled] grain of

rice (found in polished rice).

뉘² 1 [누구] who. ¶당신은 ~시오 Who are you? 2 [누구의] whose. ¶이것은 ~ 펜이냐 Whose pen is this? / Whose is this pen?

뉘³ a boy's sister. ⇨ '누이'

뉘다¹ lay down; gloss. ⇨ '누이다¹'

뉘다² make (a child) urinate. ⇨ '누이다²'

뉘앙스 a nuance; a shade of difference (in meaning / feeling). ¶말의 ~ a shade of difference in meaning[expression] // 시적 표현의 미묘한 ~ a delicate [subtle] nuance in poetic expression.

뉘엿거리다 1 (해가) be going [ready] to set; be about to set [sink]. ¶지평선으로 뉘엿거리는 해 the sun (now) verging [sinking] toward the horizon // 해가 뉘엿거린다 The sun is sinking in the west. 2 (속이) ~ feel nausea; feel sick; nauseate. ¶속이 ~ feel nausea / have a sick stomach / be sick at the stomach // 보기만 해도 속이 뉘엿거린다 The mere sight of it makes me sick [turns my stomach]. / My stomach turns [rises] at the mere sight of it.

뉘엿뉘엿 1 (해가) ~ 지다 the sun is sinking in the west. **뉘엿뉘엿하다** be ready [about / going] to set [sink]. 2 (속이). **뉘엿뉘엿하다** feel nausea [sick]; nauseate.

뉘우치다 regret (▶ 후회, 또는 유감의 뜻); repent (▶ 변심, 자신의 결점, 잘못된 행위를 자각하고 자인하여 자신을 책함); be sorry (for); be penitent [repentant] (for); feel regret [remorse] (for). ¶뉘우친 사람 a penitent / a contrite sinner // 뉘우치는 빛도 없이 without any contrition [repentance] // 깊이 ~ be smitten with remorse // 자기가 한 일을 ~ regret one's act / be sorry for [repent of] what one has done // 죄를 ~ be penitent for one's sin // 뉘우치는 빛이 보이다 show repentance // 뉘우치지 않다 be impenitent // 뉘우칠 일이 없다 have no regrets / have nothing to repent of // 그녀는 뉘우치는 빛이 조금도 없다 She makes no sign of repentance. // 뉘우쳤을 때는 이미 늦었었다 I repented too late. / It was too late for me to be sorry. // 그는 자신의 어리석은 언동을 뉘우치고 있다 He is sorry for [repents] his foolish talk and behavior. // 나는 그때 거짓말을 한 것을 뉘우치고 있다 I regret that I lied then. / I regret having told a lie. // 당신의 충고를 따르지 않은 것을 뉘우치고 있습니다 I regret not having taken your advice. // 그런 짓을 하면 너는 나중에 뉘우치게 된다 If you do such a thing, you will regret it [be sorry] later. // 이제는 뉘우쳐도 소용없다 It is no good regretting it now. / What is done cannot be undone. / It is no good regretting it now. / It's too late to regret it. / It's no good crying over spilt milk.

뉴스 news (▶ 단수 취급이지만 부정 관사를 붙이지 않으며, 한 개의 뉴스의 경우는 a piece of news, a news item 등으로 함). ¶해외 [국내] ~ foreign [home] news // **전광** ~ an electric news tape // **스폿** ~ spot news // 짤막한 news in brief // 좋은 ~ good news // 중대한 ~ (a piece of) big news // …에 관한 최신 ~ the latest news on ... // 7시 ~에 의하면 according to the seven o'clock news // ~ (거리)가 되다 make news / get in the news // 중동에 관한 ~는 없습니까 Is there any news about the Middle East? // 대통령이 저격당했다는 ~가 들어왔다 [퍼졌다] A report came in [spread] that the president had been shot. // 이것은 ~거리가 되겠는걸 This will make news. // 그 기자는 ~의 출처를 밝히려 하지 않았다 The reporter refused to reveal the source of the news [the name of his source].

● **뉴스 방송** newscasting; a newscast; a news show. **뉴스 영화** a newsreel; a news picture [film]. **뉴스 캐스터** a newscaster. **뉴스 해설** (radio / TV) news commentary. **뉴스 해설자** a (TV / radio) (news) commentator; a news analyst.

뉴트론 [물] a neutron.

느글거리다 feel nausea; feel sick [queasy]; nauseate; keck; retch; heave; gag. ¶속이 ~ feel nausea / be sick at the stomach / have a sick stomach // 차를 타고 있는 동안에 속이 느글거리기 시작했다 I began to feel sick while riding in the car. // 그 냄새를 맡았더니 속이 느글거렸다 The smell made me sick.

느긋하다 [만족하다] quite satisfied [contented / gratified] (with); well pleased; [마음 편하다] comfortable; relaxed; carefree. ¶느긋한 사람 a happy-go-lucky person // 기분이 ~ feel (much) relieved [relaxed] / feel easy [at ease] // 저녁을 잘 먹고 나니 ~ After such a good dinner, I feel wonderful. // 그는 항상 느긋해 보인다 He always looks carefree. // 집에 돌아오면 마음이 느긋해진다 I feel relaxed when I come home. // 백부님과 함께 있으면 마음이 느긋해진다 Being with my uncle puts me at ease [makes me feel at home]. // 이 산장에 있으면 느긋한 기분이 된다 The life at this mountain cottage relaxes me. **느긋이** comfortably; at ease; in a leisurely manner; in a carefree [relaxed] mood. ¶그는 소파에 ~ 앉아 있었다 He was sitting comfortably [at ease] on a sofa. // 그녀는 하루 종일 ~ 그림을 그리고 있다 She has been painting a picture in a leisurely manner all day long. // 그는 ~ 만화책을 읽고 있었다 He was reading a comic book in a carefree [relaxed] mood. // 모든 근심을 잊고 ~ 있을 수만 있다면 좋겠는데 I wish I could forget my cares and relax.

느끼다 1 [감각·지각하다] feel; be conscious of; experience (inconvenience); be sensible of [to]; have a feeling (that ...). ¶배고픔을 ~ feel hungry [empty] // 아픔을 ~ feel a pain (in the chest) / suffer pain // 더위 [추위]를 ~ feel the heat [cold] // 기쁨을 ~ feel [experience / know] joy // 불편을 ~ feel inconvenienced / experience inconvenience / find it inconvenient (to do) // 어려움을 ~ feel [have] difficulty (in doing) // 친밀감을 ~ feel friendly (toward) // 애착을 ~ have an attachment (for / to) // 의분을 ~ have righteous indignation (about / against / with) // 필요를 절실히 ~ feel keenly the necessity (for) // 팔에 무엇이 닿는 것을 ~ feel a touch on one's arm // 가슴속 깊이 슬픔을 ~ realize true sorrow // 아픔을 느끼지 않다 be insensible of [to] pain // 어쩐지 쓸쓸하게 느껴진다 Somehow I feel lonesome. // 고도에 혼자 남겨진 것같이 느껴진다 I feel as if I had been left alone on a remote island. // 집이 흔들리는 것을 느꼈다 I felt the house shaking. // 나는 그것에 대해 웬지 모를 애착을 느꼈다 I felt an indescribable attachment to it. // 그가 나한테 뭔가 숨기고 있다고 느꼈다 I felt that he was keeping something from me. // 그는 생명의

느끼하다

위험을 느꼈다 He sensed that his life was in danger. // 시골에 살아도 프로판 가스가 있어서 불편을 느끼지 않는다 Thanks to propane gas, we feel [experience / find] no inconvenience in living in the country. // 내가 무식하다는 것을 이때만큼 뼈저리게 느낀 적은 없었다 Never had I realized my ignorance more keenly than at that time. // 그는 연민이라고는 조금도 느끼지 못하는 사람이다 He knows no pity. / He is dead to all feelings of pity. // 느낀 점이 있으면 무엇이든 말씀하십시오 Tell me any idea that may flash upon[occur to] your mind.
2 [감동하다] be impressed (by / with); be struck (by / with); be affected [moved / touched] (by). ¶친절을 고맙게 ~ appreciate[be moved by] (a person's) kindness // 깊이 느끼게 하다 touch (a person) to the heart / impress (a person) profoundly // 세상의 덧없음을 ~ realize the uncertainty of life // 그 소설을 읽고 느끼는 바가 많았다 I was deeply stirred by the novel. // 그때 처음으로 어머니의 사랑을 깊이 느꼈다 I had never felt my mother's love so strongly.
3 [흐느끼다] sob; be choked with [drowned in] tears. ¶그녀는 느껴 울면서 이야기했다 She told her story with tears in her voice. / Her voice was strangled with tears when she told her story.

느끼하다 1 (맛이) greasy; fatty; oily; thick; heavy. ¶느끼한 음식 greasy food // 이 요리는 너무 느끼해서 내 입에 맞지 않는다 This dish is too heavy[rich] for me. **2** [느글느글하다] (be) sick to the stomach; nauseated; queasy. ¶기름진 음식을 먹었더니 속이 ~ I feel sick[I have a sick stomach] after a greasy meal.

느낌 1 [감각] feeling; sense; sensation; [감촉] touch; feel. ¶뭐라고 말할 수 없는 ~ an indefinable[indescribable] sensation // 피곤한 [어지러운] ~ a sensation of weariness [dizziness] // ~이 들다 feel / have a (queer) feeling[sensation] / [예감이 있다] have a hunch.
2 [인상] an impression; [기분] sentiment; feeling; a mood; (예술품의) an effect (of a painting). ¶선생 같은 ~을 주는 사람 a person who reminds one of a teacher // 좋은 [나쁜] ~을 주다 make[produce] a favorable [an unfavorable] impression on (a person) / impress (a person) favorably [unfavorably] // ···한 ~을 주다 impress [strike] (a person) as / affect (a person) as / give an impression of // 그곳은 어딘지 모르게 동양의 도시 같은 ~을 준다 The place has the feeling[feel] of an Oriental town. // 그것을 보았을 때 이상한 ~이 들었다 When I saw it, it struck me as odd. // 전시회를 관람하신 ~이 어떻습니까 What was your impression of the exhibition? // 그는 어쩐지 서먹서먹한 ~이 든다 There is something distant [unfriendly] about him. // 누가 방에 숨어 있을 것 같은 ~이 들었다 I had a feeling that somebody lay concealed in the room. // 무슨 큰일이 생길 것 같은 ~이 들었다 I had a hunch that something serious would happen. // 그녀는 이전지 그에게 맞지 않는 것 같은 ~이 든다 It is my impression that the woman is not his type.
3 [기미] a tinge; a smack; a touch; a suspicion. ¶그의 문장은 매너리즘에 빠진 ~이 있다 His style has a touch of mannerism.

느낌표(-標) [언] an exclamation mark [point].

-느냐 ⇨-냐 ¶어디로 가~ Where are you going? // 어째서 매일 지각하~ Why are you late for school everyday? // 무슨 일로 왔~ What has brought you here? // 무슨 일이 있~ What is the matter (with you)? // 영어를 할 줄 아~ Can you speak English?

-느니 1 and; or; and the like; and so forth. ⇨-니4·5 ¶어쩌~ 저쩌~ 핑계를 대어 with suchlike excuses // 자식은 부모에게 순종해야 하~ Children should obey their parents. **2** [차라리] rather; as soon; sooner ... than. ¶항복하~ 차라리 죽는 편이 낫다 I would sooner[rather] die than give in. // 버스를 타~ 걷자 I would (just) as soon walk as ride in a bus.

느닷없다 sudden; abrupt; unexpected; unheralded. ¶느닷없는 말 an abrupt [unexpected] remark // 느닷없는 짓 unexpected [strange] behavior // 느닷없는 해고 unheralded discharge // 느닷없는 물음에 대답할 바를 몰랐다 I was at a loss for a reply to his abrupt question. // 그의 느닷없는 제의에 깜짝 놀랐다 I was surprised at his completely unexpected offer. **느닷없이** [돌연히] abruptly; suddenly; (all) of a sudden; unexpectedly; out of the blue; [예고 없이] without notice[warning]. ¶~ 남의 뺨을 때리다 slap a person on the cheek all of a sudden // ~ 덤벼들다 make a sudden spring at (a person) // ~ 나타나다 appear unexpectedly // ~ 사직하다[해고하다] resign (one's post) [dismiss (a person)] without (giving) notice // 그가 ~ 찾아왔다 He called on me without notice[unnoticed]. // ~ 그는 짐을 챙겨 떠나 버렸다 Quite abruptly he packed his things and left. // 그는 ~ 내일 미국으로 가겠다고 말했다 He said abruptly [All of a sudden he declared] that he was going to America the next day.

-느라고 [원인·이유] because (of); owing to; due to; as; since. ¶점심 먹~ 늦었다 Lunch made me late. // 자~ 무슨 일이 있었는지 몰랐다 I was sound asleep, so I did not know what happened.

느럭느럭 slowly; tardily; leisurely; lazily; sluggishly; idly. ¶~ 움직이다 move sluggishly // ~ 나아가다 go [proceed] at a slack pace // ~ 걷다 walk slowly / loiter along. **느럭느럭하다** tardy; slow; slow-going; sluggish; (서술적) linger; idle about. ¶···하는 것이 ~ be slow in (doing).

느른하다 languid; slack. ⇨나른하다
느릅나무 [식] an elm (tree).
느리광이 a laggard. ⇨느림보
느리다 1 [더디다] slow; tardy; slow-going; sluggish. ¶느린 기차 a slow train // 걸음이 느린 기부 a slow-going tortoise // 동작이 ~ be slow in action / be slow-moving // 걸음이 ~ go at a slow pace / be slow-footed / be slow of foot / be a slow walker // 행동을 취하는 것이 ~ be slow in taking action // 말이 ~ speak slowly / drawl // 이해가 ~ be slow to understand [grasp] things / be dull / (문어) be slow of understanding // 진보가 ~ be laggard / be lagging / make slow progress // 그의 맥박이 ~ His pulse is sluggish [slow]. // 그는 걸음이 ~ He is slow of foot. / He is a

slow walker.∥그는 일이 ~ He is slow in his work. / He is a slow[dilatory] worker.∥그는 계산이 ~ He is slow at[with] figures.∥그는 만사에 ~ He is slow in everything.∥저놈은 굼벵이처럼 ~ He is as slow as a snail.
2 [짜임새가 성글다] loose (in weave); slack. ¶올이 느린 천 loose cloth.

느림 [장식으로 늘어뜨린 것] a streamer; a tail; a tag; a tassel.

느림보 a laggard; a dawdler; (속어) a slow coach. ¶그 사람은 ~다 He is slow[a slow coach].

느릿느릿 1 (동작이) slowly; sluggishly; tardily; idly. ¶~ 전진하다 go[proceed / make progress] at a snail's[slack] pace / crawl ~ 걷다 walk slowly[at a snail's pace] / loiter along∥말하다 speak slowly / drawl∥그는 ~ 일어섰다 He rose slowly to his feet.∥그는 ~ 담뱃불을 끄고 나서 이야기를 시작했다 He took his time stubbing out his cigarette and then began to speak.∥짙은 안개 속을 열차는 ~ 기다시피 나아갔다 The train crawled through the thick fog.∥지쳐버린 나그네는 ~ 마을 밖으로 떠나갔다 The exhausted traveler trailed[dragged himself] out of the village. **느릿느릿하다** slow(-moving); snail-slow; sluggish. ¶느릿느릿한 동작 sluggish behavior∥그는 느릿느릿하게 말을 하는 버릇이 있다 He has a slow, lazy way of speaking.
2 [성기게] loose(ly); slack. ¶이 천은 ~ 짜였다 This cloth[textile / fabric] was woven loosely. **느릿느릿하다** loose; slack.

느물거리다 talk[behave] insidiously[snakily]; act craftily[trickily / treacherously].

느물느물 insidiously; craftily; snakily; trickily; treacherously. **느물느물하다** talk insidiously. ⇨⁼느물거리다

느슨하다 1 [헐겁다] loose; slack; lax. ¶느슨한 밧줄 a slack rope∥느슨해지다 loosen / slacken / become[get] loose / be loosened∥매듭이 ~[느슨해졌다] The knot is loose[has came loose].∥밧줄이 느슨해졌다 The rope has worked (itself) loose.∥벨트가 ~ The belt is loose.∥기계의 볼트가 느슨해졌다 A bolt has loosened on the machine. **느슨히** loosely; slackly; laxly. ¶~ 매다 string[tie] loosely.
2 (마음이) relaxed; slack. ¶느슨해지다 become[get] remiss / remit / relax / slack(en) / (경계가) be off one's guard / be unguarded∥학생의 규율이 느슨해진 것 같다 Discipline seems relaxed among the students.∥규제가 매우 느슨했다 The regulations were not at all strict.

느즈러지다 1 [느슨해지다] (조인 것이) loosen; slacken; become[get] loose; (팽팽한 것이) slacken; hang slack; be loosened. ¶느즈러진 밧줄 slack rope∥허리띠가 ~ one's waistband loosens[becomes loose]∥매듭이 ~ a knot comes[gets] loose. **2** (기한이) be postponed; be put off; be prolonged[delayed]. **3** (마음이) become[get] remiss; relax; slack(en); remit. ¶그는 정신이 느즈러졌다 His attention[mind] relaxed.

느지감치 a little late[later]; later (than usual); rather late. ¶아침 늦 일어나다 get up rather late in the morning∥저녁 ~ 집에 돌아오다 come home a little late in the evening∥~ 조반을 먹다 have a latish breakfast.

느지막하다 rather[quite] late. ¶이런 느지막한 시간에 어딜 가는 거요 Where are you going at this time of night? / Where are you going this late? **느지막이** rather[quite] late. ¶~ 자다 go to bed rather late at night∥일요일에는 ~ 일어난다 I get up late on Sundays.

느직하다 1 [늦다] somewhat[a little] late; latish. ¶느직한 아침 식사 a late[latish] breakfast. **느직이** somewhat[a little] late. ¶~ 아침을 먹다 take a latish breakfast. **2** [느슨하다] a little loose[slack]. **느직이** rather loose(ly)[slack]. ¶~ 매다 tie rather loose.

느치 [동] a cadelle.

느타리(버섯) [식] an agaric.

느티나무 [식] a zelkova (tree).

느헤미야(서) (-書) [성] (The Book of) Nehemiah(약어 Neh.).

늑간 (肋間) ¶~의 intercostal / between the ribs.
● **늑간근** the intercostal muscle. **늑간 신경** the intercostal nerve.

늑골 (肋骨) [생] a rib; a costa (*pl*. -tae); (집합적) the ribs. ¶~의 costal∥~ 아래의 subcostal.

늑대 a wolf (*pl*. wolves). ¶~의 / ~ 같은 wolfish / lupine∥~ 같은 인간 cruel and avaricious persons.

늑막 (肋膜) [생] the pleura (*pl*. -rae). ¶~의 pleural.
● **늑막염** pleurisy.

늑목 (肋木) Swedish[wall] bars; a stall bar.

늑연골 (肋軟骨) [생] costal cartilage.

늑장 부리다 dawdle (over); linger; loiter; loaf (on the job); dally away; tarry; slow up (work); be slow(-going); be tardy; idle about; dillydally. ¶늑장 부리지 않고 without delay[lingering] / promptly / straight off∥도중에서 ~ loiter on the way∥늑장 부리다가 기회를 놓치다 dally away one's opportunity∥늑장 부리며 직무를 다하지 않다 linger in discharging one's duties∥늑장 부리지 말고 곧 다녀오너라 Come back without delay. / Don't linger along the way.∥네가 늑장 부리는 바람에 버스를 놓쳤다 You were so slow that we missed the bus.∥파티가 끝난 뒤에도 우리는 얼마 동안 늑장 부리면서 남아 있었다 We lingered a while after the party. ¶늑장 부리지 마라 Look sharp! / Step on it! / Make it snappy!

는 ¶그~ 의사다 He is a doctor.∥나~ 가지 않는다 (As for me,) I won't go.∥그~ 술은 마시지만 담배는 피우지 않는다 He drinks but doesn't smoke.∥하기~ 했지만 실패했다 I (really) did do it, but it was a failure.∥내일까지~ 마칠 수가 없다 I can't finish it by tomorrow.

-는 -ing. ¶흐르~ 물 running[flowing] water / a running stream∥오르~ 물가 rising prices∥신문을 읽고 있~ 신사 a gentleman who is reading a paper.

-는가 is it? ⇨⁼-ㄴ가 ¶무엇하러 왔~ What have you come for?∥그녀는 언제 시집갔~ When did she get married?∥어디에 살고 있~ Where do you live?

-는구먼 ⇨⁼-구먼 ¶비가 오~ Well I see it's raining!

-는다고 because; as. ⇨⁼-ㄴ다고

-는다니 ⇨⁼-ㄴ다니

-는다면 if; unless. ⇨⁼-ㄴ다면

-는다손 치더라도 (even) though; (even) if. ⇨-ㄴ다손 치더라도

-는대서야 ⇨-ㄴ대서야 ¶이런 좋은 날씨에 집에 틀어박혀 있~ 말이 되나 It is absurd for you to stay at home on such a fine day.

-는데 and; but; when; while. ⇨-ㄴ데 ¶어제는 소풍을 갔었~ 대단히 즐거웠다 We went on a picnic yesterday, and (we) had a very good time.//그에게는 딸이 셋이 있~ 모두 시집갔다 He has three daughters, who are all married.//최 씨가 그러~ 당신 장사가 잘된다면서요 Mr. Choe said your business was prosperous.//정 선생에게 편지를 쓰~ 무슨 부탁할 말씀이 없으십니까 I'm writing to Mr. Jeong — Is there anything you want me to tell him?//저 책을 사야겠~ 지금은 돈이 없다 I have to buy that book, but I have no money with me now.//비가 오~ 어딜 가요 Where are you going in spite of the rain? 그가 일을 하고 있~ 내가 어떻게 놀러 갈 수 있겠니 How can I go and play when he is working?//잘하~ You're doing well!//야, 맛있는 냄새가 나~ How lovely it smells!//비가 점점 많이 오~ The rain is coming down harder than ever!//그 아이 잘생겼~ What a handsome child (he is)!//해외로 갈 수 있으면 좋겠~ I wish I could go abroad.//어머니가 곧 오시면 좋겠~ I hope mother will come soon.

는적거리다 be pulpy[flabby / squashy] from rot.

는적는적 pulpily; flabbily; squashily. **는적는적 하다** be pulpy from rot. ⇨는적거리다

-는지 if; or; either ...; or; I wonder .... ⇨-ㄴ지 ¶그가 집에 있~ 사무실에 있~ 모른다 I don't know whether he is at home or in[at] the office.//몇 사람이나 가~ 아시오 Do you know how many people are going?//내 묻는 말을 못 들었~ 그는 이야기를 계속하고 있다 Apparently he didn't catch my question — he went on with what he was saying.//목욕물이 데워졌~ 물어보십시오 Please ask if the bath is ready.//어느 것을 가장 좋아하~ 말해 보아라 Say which you would like best.//그는 지금 어떻게 지내고 있~ How is he getting along, I wonder?//도대체 언제쯤이라야 되~ It pains me to think when it will be ready.//그가 올~ 안 올~ 모르겠다 I don't know whether he will come or not.

는질거리다 feel squashy[pulpy / soft and mushy]; be flimsy[crumbly / crumby / decomposed].

는질는질 squashily; softly; pulpily; flimsily. **는질는질하다** feel squashy. ⇨는질거리다

는커녕 anything but; far from; not at all; in no wise. ¶그렇기~ far from it / on the contrary/¶실망하기~ far from being disappointed//그는 위스키~ 맥주도 못한다 He does not drink beer, to say nothing of whisky.

늘 [어느 때나·항상] always; all the time; usually; habitually; ceaselessly; continuously. ¶그녀는 ~ 웃는 얼굴로 사람을 응대했다 She always greeted people with a smile.//전화를 걸면 ~ 통화 중이다 Whenever [Every time] I call him, the line is busy.//그는 ~ 집에 없다 He is never at home.//그의 반대는 ~ 있는 일이다 There is nothing unusual about[out of the ordinary in] his opposing it. / He habitually opposes things.//~ 그 생각이 난다 I am reminded of it all the time [quite frequently].//그는 ~ 투덜대고 있다 He is always grumbling.//그녀는 아침이면 ~ 정원의 나무[화분]에 물을 주었다 She usually waters the garden[pot] plants every morning.//경관들이 ~ 수상 관저를 지키고 있다 Policemen are on the alert at the premier's residence at all times.//"그는 또 투덜대고 있군." "뭐, ~ 하는 짓이지." "He is complaining again." "It's the same old thing."

늘그막 old[advanced] age; senescence; one's declining years; the winter of one's life. ¶~에 이르러 in one's old age[later years] / in the decline[evening] of one's life//~에 의지할 곳이 없다 have no one to depend upon in one's later life//~에 호강하다 live in luxury in one's old age//~에 고생하다 have a hard time late in one's life//~에 아들을 얻다 have a son in one's old age.

늘다 1 (수·양이) increase (in number, in quantity, etc); multiply(배로); gain(힘·무게 등이); swell(팽창하다); augment; rise(강물이); accrue(증식되다). ¶100이 ~ increase by 100//체중이 ~ gain (in) weight//무게가 퍽 ~ put on a lot of weight//두 배로 ~ multiply two times//세력이 ~ become more powerful / gain in influence//늘지 않도록 하다 keep (the population) from increasing / check the (further) increase (of)//그는 아이가 또 하나 늘었다 He had another addition to his family.//수출이 작년보다 30% 늘었다 The export increased by 30 percent over last year.//비용이 생각했던 것보다 늘었다 The expenses amounted[ran up] to a larger sum than I had expected.//소년 범죄가 늘고 있다 Juvenile delinquency is on the increase [rise].//체중이 5킬로나 늘었다 I have gained five kilograms.//술이 느는 것 같군 You seem to be able to drink more than you used to. / Your capacity for alcohol seems to have increased.

2 [향상되다] improve; advance; make (good) progress. ¶재간이 ~ improve one's skill (at / in) / improve in ability//지혜가 ~ grow wiser[in one's wisdom]//영어 실력이 ~ improve oneself in English//최근에 그는 테니스 솜씨가 늘었다 His tennis has improved lately.

늘름 darting in and out; quickly. ⇨날름

늘름거리다 let (a tongue) dart in and out; be greedy for. ⇨날름거리다

늘리다 1 (수량을) increase; add (to); raise; multiply; augment. ¶인원을 ~ increase the personnel[number of men]//일손을 ~ add to the staff / increase hands(직공의)//재산을 ~ increase[add to] one's fortune//판매량을 ~ increase[boost] sales//약의 복용량을 ~ step up the dose//자격자의 수를 ~ increase the number of qualified persons. 2 [확대하다] extend; expand; enlarge. ¶운동장을 ~ enlarge the playground//장사를 ~ extend one's business//구두를 ~ stretch shoes / have one's shoes stretched//바지 허리를 ~ let out the waist of trousers//길을 ~ widen the road.

늘비하다 [늘어놓여 있다] spread out[over]; displayed; [늘어서 있다] arrayed; drawn up. ¶늘비하게 in a row[line]//진열장에는 여러 가지 장난감이 늘비했다 A great variety of toys were displayed in the show window.//

선반에는 병이 늘비했다 There was an array of bottles on the sideboard.//그 길 한쪽에는 가게가 ~ On one side of the street is an unbroken succession of shops.//교통사고로 길이 막혀 버스, 택시, 트럭이 늘비하게 섰다 The accident held up a long line of buses, cabs, and trucks.

늘썽하다 coarse (texture); large (meshes); rough; loose (fabric); porous (cloth); coarse [loose-]woven (cloth). ¶늘썽한 천 cloth with a loose weave [texture] / cloth of open texture //늘썽하게 짜다 knit with large stitches.

늘씬하다 1 slender; slim; smart. ⇨*날씬하다 2 [기운이 없어 늘어지다] (서술적) be exhausted; be fagged[worn] out; be reduced to pulp. ¶늘씬하게 때려 주다 beat (a person) soundly[to a pulp] / pommel (a person) to a jelly //늘씬하게 얻어맞다 be struck hard / be pommeled to a jelly.

늘어나다 extend; lengthen; stretch; grow longer; expand. ¶늘어나는 extensible / expansible / elastic//잘 늘어나는 나일론 elastic[stretchy] nylon//열을 받으면 금속은 대개 늘어난다 Heat expands most metals.// 고무줄이 늘어났다 A rubber band stretched [has gone slack].//햇볕에 엿이 늘어난다 A gluten candy expands[grows longer] under the sun's heat.//빚이 늘어나고 말았다 I have gotten deeply into debt.//그렇게 미식(美食)을 하면 식비가 늘어난다 If you go on eating so well, your food bill will go sky-high.//콘크리트로 지으면 비용이 50프로가 늘어난다 Building it with concrete will add fifty percent to the cost.

늘어놓다 1 [벌여 놓다] arrange (goods); range; [정돈하다] put[place] (things) in order; [진열하다] display (goods); show (samples); exhibit (paintings); (요리를) spread (dishes). ¶한 줄로 ~ place (things) in a row//크기의 순으로 ~ range[arrange] things by size//명패를 알파벳순으로 ~ put name plates in alphabetical order//식탁에 식기를 ~ set the table//요리를 식탁에 ~ put the food on the table.
2 [흩어 놓다] scatter (about); put in disorder; leave (one's clothes) lying about (in the room). ¶옷을 방 안에 ~ leave one's clothes lying about in the room//그는 마루에 장난감을 늘어놓고 놀고 있었다 He was playing with the toys scattered on the floor. //그 작은 방에는 책이 잔뜩 늘어놓여 있었다 Books were lying all over the little room.
3 (사업을) put one's hand to (various enterprises); attempt (tasks); extend one's business in all directions. ¶아버지는 여러 가지 사업을 늘어놓았다가 실패했다 My father took a hand in various enterprises only to fail.
4 (말을) enumerate; marshal (facts); multiply (instances); itemize (details). ¶결점을 ~ enumerate (a person's) faults//장광설을 ~ launch into a long harangue//허튼수작을 ~ talk a lot of nonsense//그가 길게 늘어놓는 아침의 말을 나는 참을 수 없다 I can't stand his profuse compliments.//그는 갖가지 불평을 늘어놓았다 He set forth a number of grievances. /(구어) He rattled off a lot of grievances.

늘어뜨리다 hang down; suspend; slouch(축); droop (the tail); drop; lower (one's head). ¶옷자락을 길게 늘어뜨린 야회복 an evening dress with a long train//축 ~ hang loose / dangle//치맛자락을 ~ let down one's skirt / trail one's skirt//(개가) 혀를 ~ loll out the tongue//다리를 늘어뜨리고 with one's legs dangling (in the air)//커튼을 ~ hang down a curtain//꼬리를 ~ droop the tail//시곗줄을 ~ dangle the chain of a watch//나무에서 밧줄을 ~ hang[suspend] a rope from a tree //앞머리를 ~ (미) have bangs /(영) have [wear] one's hair in a fringe//그 소녀는 그 머리를 뒤로 늘어뜨리고 있었다 The girl had let her long hair hang down her back.

늘어서다 in a row; stand in a row[line]; form in line[a line]; be drawn up; [열을 만들다] line up; rank; (차례를 기다리며) queue [line] up; line up in a queue. ¶옆으로 ~ stand side by side / stand abreast (of)//두 줄로 ~ form[stand in / be drawn up in] two rows//배급을 타려고 죽 ~ make a queue waiting for the ration//그 도로를 따라 집들이 늘어서 있었다 Houses stood in a row along the road.//새 우표를 사려고 사람들이 늘어서 있었다 People had lined up[(영) had queued] to buy the new stamp.//항구에는 낡은 창고들이 늘어서 있었다 Old warehouses stood in a row along the harbor.//여왕은 거리에 늘어선 군중에게 손을 흔들었다 The queen waved to the people lining[lined up along] the street.//흰 벽의 집들이 빽빽이 늘어서 있었다 White-walled houses were jammed close together.

늘어앉다 sit in a row; sit in line; sit around. ¶많은 사람이 방에 죽 늘어앉아 있다 Many people are sitting around in the room.//정장을 한 신사들이 죽 늘어앉아 있었다 There was a long row of gentlemen seated in full dress.

늘어지다 1 [아래로 처지다] hang down; dangle; droop; be pendent. ¶귀가 늘어진 개 a button-[drop- / flap- / flop- / lop-]eared dog//가슴까지 늘어진 흰 수염 a long white beard that comes down to one's chest//늘어진 근육 flabby muscle//늘어진 입 a slack [loose-lipped] mouth//천장이 늘어져 있다 The ceiling is sagging.//눈의 무게로 가지가 늘어져 있다 The branches are hanging down [drooping] under the weight of the snow.// 수양버들 가지가 땅에 닿도록 늘어져 있었다 The weeping willow branches hung [drooped] down close to the ground.// 중년에 살이 올라 허리가 늘어져 있다 He has developed middle-aged spread and is flabby around the waist[middle].//물을 주지 않았기 때문에 방 안의 화분이 모두 늘어졌었다 All the plants in my room were drooping because I hadn't watered them.
2 [길어지다] extend; lengthen; stretch; spread. ¶늘어지게 기지개를 켜다 stretch (oneself).
3 (몸이) droop; languish; get exhausted; grow languid. ¶몹시 지쳐 ~ be dog-tired / be dead tired / feel as limp as a rag//의식을 잃고 ~ fall senseless//나는 축 늘어지도록 얻어맞았다 The blow left me limp[groggy].// 그녀는 의자에 늘어진 채 앉아 있었다 She sat slouched in the chair.//그녀는 공포에 질려 그 자리에 축 늘어졌다 Struck with fear, she sank down (helplessly) on the spot.//요새 젊은이들은 걸핏하면 늘어져 버리기를 잘한다

늘이다

The young people of today get exhausted [worn out] easily.

늘이다 1 [길게 하다] lengthen; make (something) longer; stretch; extend; draw out. ¶고무줄을 ~ stretch a rubber band // 6미터 ~ lengthen (a rope) by six meters / make (a rope) six meters longer // 수명을 ~ prolong[lengthen] one's life / 금을 두들겨 늘여서 금박으로 만들다 beat gold into foil // 철사를 잡아 늘여 아주 가늘게 하다 draw out the wire until it is very thin // 끈을 이어 3미터로 ~ tie pieces together to make a string three meters long.

2 [아래로] hang down; droop; suspend. ¶발을 ~ hang a bamboo screen // 앞머리를 ~ (구어) have bangs / (영) have [wear] one's hair in a fringe // 목을 늘이어 칼을 받다 let one's neck droop under the sword // 소녀는 긴 머리를 등 뒤로 늘이고 있었다 The girl had left her long hair hang down her back.

늘임표 (-標) [음] a fermata; a length mark.

늘쩍지근하다 (feel) languid; (feel) weary; (feel) listless; (feel) logy; (feel) tired; (be) dull; (be) heavy. ¶온몸이 ~ feel languid all over // 잠을 설쳐서 ~ feel languid for want of sleep // 날씨가 더워 몸이 ~ The heat makes me feel languid.

늘쩡거리다 be tardy; be slow(-moving); be slow-going; be sluggish; idle about; dawdle (over); linger. ¶이불 속에서 ~ dally in bed // 일을 늘쩡거리며 하다 slight[scamp] one's work / slack at one's job / shirk[be neglectful of / let up on] one's duty.

늘컹거리다 be soft (pulpy / mushy / flabby / limp / squashy). ¶늘컹거리는 것을 밟다 step upon something squashy.

늘컹하다 soft; pulpy; flabby; limp; squashy.

늘컹거리다 be soft and droopy; be flabby [pulpy / mushy].

늘큰하다 soft and droopy; flabby.

늙다 grow [get] old; age; advance in years [age]. ¶걸 ~ look older than one's age / look old for one's age // 그는 요 몇 해 사이에 부쩍 늙었다 He has aged visibly for these years. // 자네 갑자기 늙었군그려 You've aged suddenly, haven't you? // 그는 나이에 비해 늙어 보인다 He looks old for his age. // 그는 늙었어도 정정하다 He is hale and hearty in his old age. // 그녀는 늙지 않는 것 같다 She doesn't seem to age[get any older]. // 그 머리 모양은 나이보다 더 늙게 보인다 That hairdo makes you look older than your age. // 고생을 하거나 병을 앓으면 늙는다 Worry and illness age a man. // 자네는 조금도 늙지 않았군 You haven't aged a bit.

늙어 빠지다 decrepit; senile; (서술적) grow senile; become awfully old; get weak [become feeble] with age; grow weak from age; sink under age. ¶늙어 빠진 노인 a decrepit old man // 노인의 늙어 빠진 육체 an old man's decrepit [enfeebled] body // 늙어 빠진 개 a feeble old dog.

늙다리 a dotard; a doddered; a silly old man; a superannuated person; (구어) an old crock. ¶~ 말 an old nag / a hack // ~ 할멈 a withered old woman / a hag / a geezer.

늙수그레하다 fairly [considerably] old; oldish.

늙은이 an old person; an aged person; an elder; (미) an oldster; (집합적) the aged [old]; old people; the elders. ¶나 젊은이나 both young and old [old and young] (alike) // ~ 같은 말을 하다 use an old man's speech / talk older for one's age.

늙정이 (속) an old person. ⇒늙은이

늙히다 make (a person) old; let (a person) get old. ¶처녀로 ~ let (a girl) pass her marriageable age.

늠름하다 (凜凜-) gallant; brave; imposing; manly; commanding; dignified; awe-inspiring. ¶늠름한 모습 a dignified figure // 늠름한 태도 a manly attitude // 기상이 ~ be full of spirit / be in high spirits // 늠름한 데가 있다 have a manly [commanding] mien.

능 (陵) a royal mausoleum (pl. -lea); a royal tomb.

능 (稜) ➡ 모서리2

능가하다 (凌駕-) surpass; exceed; excel; be superior to; outdistance; outdo; outrival; stand above; outstrip. ¶아버지를 능가하는 유능한 아들 a son superior in ability to his father // ~ ···에서 나머지를 ~ excel the rest in ... // 젊은이를 ~ outdo[surpass] the young // 훨씬 ~ far surpass / be far superior to (others) // 수에 있어서 적을 ~ outnumber the enemy / surpass in numerical strength // 그의 힘[능력]을 능가할 만한 것은 아무것도 없다 Nothing is beyond his power[ability]. // 토론에서 그를 능가할 사람이 없었다 No one could get the better of him in an argument. // 그는 기량에서 부친을 능가하였다 He surpassed his father in skill. // 그의 학식은 동료들을 훨씬 능가하고 있다 He towers high above his colleagues in scholarship.

능구렁이 1 [동] a yellow-spotted serpent. 2 [음흉한 사람] an insidious person; a deep one; a snake; a snaky person; an old fox.

능글능글하다 tricky; sly. ⇨=능글맞다

능글맞다 tricky; sly; snaky; cunning; insidious; wily; crafty; foxy; slick. ¶능글맞은 웃음 (make) an insidious smile.

능금 a crab apple.

● **능금나무** [식] a crab apple tree. **능금산** (-酸) [화] malic acid.

능동 (能動) activity; activeness.

● **능동태** [언] the active voice. ¶~의 문장 a sentence in the active voice / an active sentence.

능동적 (能動的) active; voluntary. ¶~으로 spontaneously / actively / voluntarily // 문제와 ~으로 씨름하다 grapple with a problem in an active manner [in a positive manner / actively].

능란하다 (能爛-) skillful; dexterous; accomplished; proficient; good (at); clever; adroit; expert; deft; ingenious; masterful; slick. ¶···에 ~ be skillful [skilled] in [at] / be master of / be expert in [at] / be good at // 그는 흥정에 ~ He is good at bargaining. // 그는 말솜씨가 ~ He is a glib speaker. / He has a glib [smooth] tongue. // 그는 춤이 [흉내가] 매우 ~ He is very good at dancing [mimicry]. / He is a very good dancer [mimic]. // 글씨를 능란하게 쓰다 write a good hand / be a good hand at penmanship. **능란히** skillfully; adroitly; dexterously; cleverly; neatly. ¶그는 3개 국어를 ~ 구사한다 He speaks three languages fluently.

능력 (能力) [일을 할 수 있는 힘] (an) ability; [특수한 지력] a faculty; [적성] competence;

[그 자체에 갖추어진 잠재적인 힘] capacity. ¶생산 ~ productive [production] capacity / productivity // 정신 ~ the mental capacity [faculty] // 지불 ~ solvency / the ability to pay (one's debts) // ~이 있는 남자 an able man / a man of ability // ~ 없는 남자 a good-for-nothing fellow // 남자로서의 ~을 보이다 show one's worth as a man // 그는 그 일을 할 ~이 없다 He is not competent for that job. / That work is beyond his ability. // 가난한 아버지에게는 배상 ~이 없었다 The poor father was unable to pay for the damage. // 나는 그 문제를 풀 ~이 없다 I don't have the ability [capacity] to solve the problem. // 그 홀은 2,000명의 수용 ~이 있다 The hall has a seating capacity of 2,000. / The hall seats 2,000 people. // 그에게 ~ 이상의 일을 기대해도 헛일이다 It is no good to expect more of him than he is capable of. // 그는 남을 지도할 ~이 없다 He has no ability to lead others. // 그는 시키는 일밖에는 할 ~이 없는 사람이었다 He could only do what he was told to do. // 그는 이렇다 할 ~도 갖고 있지 않다 He has nothing to recommend him. // 그는 프로의 뛰어난 ~을 똑똑히 보여 주었다 He showed clearly the superior ability of a professional.
● 능력급(-給) payment based on ability; efficiency wages. 능력자 a person of great capacity; a competent [capable] person.

능률(能率) **1** [일의 진척] efficiency. ¶노동 ~ efficiency of labor / labor efficiency // 작업 ~ efficiency of work // ~이 좋은[나쁜] efficient [inefficient] // ~을 올리다[낮추다] raise [lower] efficiency // ~을 몇 배나 올리다[낮추다] multiply efficiency severalfold // 최소의 노동력으로 최대의 ~을 올리다 secure the maximum of efficiency with the minimum of labor // 그런 식으로는 아무리 해도 ~이 오르지 않는다 Efficiency will never improve by that method. // 나는 무엇보다 ~을 중시한다 I value efficiency above all things. **2** (기계의) moment.
● 능률급(-給) efficiency wages. 능률 저하 lowering [decrease / diminution] of efficiency. 능률 증진 increase [improvement / enhancement] of efficiency; promoted [higher] efficiency. 능률화 the promotion of efficiency.

능률적(能率的) efficient. ¶~인 방법 an efficient method // ~으로 일을 처리하다 do one's work efficiently // 복잡한 절차를 ~으로 하다 streamline complicated procedures.

능멸(凌蔑) contempt; disdain; scorn; slight. **능멸하다** despise; scorn; slight; disdain; look down (up)on (a person); have contempt for (a person).

능변(能辯) eloquence; oratory; fluency of speech. ¶~의 eloquent / fluent // 타고난 ~ unstudied eloquence // 그는 ~이다 He is an eloquent [a fluent] speaker. / He has a fluent tongue. / He has the gift of eloquence.
● 능변가 an eloquent [a good] speaker; orator.

능사(能事) proper and suitable work (for a person); the right thing [job] (for a person); one's work [business]; one's line (of business); a competent task. ¶~을 ~로 삼다 consider (something) one's work / make it one's business to (do) // 먹고 마시는 것만이 인생의 ~는 아니다 There is something in life besides eating and drinking. // 돈을 버는 것만이 장사꾼의 ~는 아니다 Moneymaking is not the only business [concern] of merchants. // 돈을 모으는 것만이 ~가 아니다. 잘 쓰는 일도 중요하다 It is not everything to accumulate money; to spend to good purpose is also important.

능선(稜線) a ridge(line) a mountain ridge. ¶~에 포진하다 take up [occupy] a position on the ridge of the mountain // ~을 따라 내려오다 come down along the ridge.

능소능대하다(能小能大-) skillful in everything; dexterous [expert] at all things; versatile; (교제에) tactful in society; affable.

능소화나무(凌霄花-) [식] a trumpet creeper.

능수(能手) **1** [능란한 솜씨] skill; dexterity; cleverness; adroitness; proficiency. **2** [능란한 사람] a good [master] hand (at); a person of ability; an expert (in moneymaking); an adept (at); a proficient (in); a skillful man; (구어) a wizard (at); (영국 구어) a dab; (미국 구어) a crackerjack. ¶그는 그 장사에는 ~이다 He is no slouch at the business.

능수버들 [식] a weeping willow.

능숙하다(能熟-) skilled; skillful; expert (in / at); proficient (in); good (at); clever (at); dexterous; deft. ¶영어 회화에 능숙한 사람 a good [fluent] speaker of English // 검도에 ~ be proficient in fencing // ~ 수예에 ~ be skilled in handicrafts // 그녀는 요리에 ~ She is good at cooking. / She is an excellent cook. // 그녀는 피아노에 ~ She plays the piano well. // 그 소년은 암산[산수]에 능숙했다 The boy was good at mental calculation [arithmetic]. // 그는 중국어에 ~ He is proficient in [good at] Chinese. // He speaks Chinese fluently. // 그는 문장에 ~ He is a good writer. // 그는 글씨에 ~ He writes a good [an attractive] hand.

능욕(凌辱) **1** [모욕] insult; affront; indignity. ¶~을 참다 pocket [brook / swallow] an insult. **능욕하다** insult; affront; disgrace; treat (a person) with indignity; subject (a person) to indignities; put (a person) to shame. →¶능욕당하다 be insulted / be subjected to insult / be humiliated / be put to shame. **2** (여자를) outrage; violation; rape. **능욕하다** (문어) violate; outrage; rape; ravish; attack; assault; commit a rape [an outrage] on. ¶처녀를 ~ deflower // 폭력으로 ~ assault and rape (a woman). →¶능욕당하다 be violated / be outraged / be attacked.

능지처참하다(陵遲處斬-) put (a criminal) to death by dismemberment; behead and dismember (a criminal).

능직(綾織) (방법) twill (weave); (직물) diagonal cloth; figured cloth; lease; leash; twilled fabrics [weaves].

능철석(菱鐵石) [광] siderite; chalybite; sparry iron; spathic iron.

능청 dissimulation; dissemblance; feigning; false pretense; hypocrisy. ¶~을 떨다[부리다] dissimulate / dissemble / play the hypocrite / feign [assume an air of] innocence / play innocent / look as if butter would not melt in one's mouth (여자가).
● 능청이 a guileful [wily] person; a sly one.

능청맞다 dissembling; deceitful. ⇨ 능청스럽다

능청스럽다 dissembling; deceitful; cunning; tricky; wily; guileful; double-faced; double-hearted; hypocritical. ¶능청스러운 웃음 a hypocritical [deceitful] smile // 능청스러운 사람 a deceitful person / [교활한 사람] a sly dog / an old fox // 능청스러운 짓 a hypocritical act / a make-believe.

능통하다(能通-) skillful; skilled; accomplished; proficient; expert; versed. ¶사업에 능통한 사람 a man versed in business // …에 ~ be skillful [skilled] in[at] / be a master of / be expert in[at] / be good at / be well versed in / be proficient in / be at home in [on] // 어학에 ~ be a good linguist // 사무에 ~ proficient in office work // 영어에 ~ be versed[well up] in English / have a good command of English.

능필(能筆) [잘 쓴 글씨] a skillful [(영) skilful] hand; [사람] a good[skilled] penman [calligrapher]. ¶그녀는 ~이다 She writes a skillful [very good] hand.

능하다(能-) skillful; dexterous; adept; adroit; expert; competent; proficient; (서술적) be (well) versed in; be good at; be at home in. ¶문장에 ~ be a good[an excellent] writer // 영어에 ~ be good at English // 만사에 ~ be skillful in[good at] everything / be a master of all trades / be versatile // 그는 말을 다루는 데 아주 ~ He has a way with a horse. / He has an admirable[a happy] knack of managing a horse. // 그는 돈벌이에 ~ He is an expert at moneymaking. **능히** capably; competently; ably; [손쉽게] easily; with ease; without difficulty [trouble]. ¶(재주가 있어) 다른 일도 ~ 해낼 수 있는 사람 a man of versatile talent[adaptable ability / adaptability / solid worth] // 해낼 수 있다 be competent to do / be competent in[at] doing // 어떤 범죄라도 ~ 저지를 수 있다 be capable of (committing) any crime // 다른 일도 ~ 해내다 be good[useful] for some other work // 그는 ~ 살인을 할 사람이다 He is capable of murder.

늦- late; tardy; belated. ¶~곡식 late crop.

늦가을 late autumn; the latter part of autumn; (미) late fall. ¶~에 in late fall / late in autumn / toward the end of autumn.

늦겨울 late winter. ¶~에 in late winter / late in winter.

늦다[1] late. ¶늦은 봄 late spring // 늦게 late // 늦게까지 up to[till] a late hour // 어젯밤 늦게 late last night // 늦어도 at (the) latest // 너무 늦기 전에 before it's too late // 늦게까지 자지 않고 있다 sit up late at night / stay up till late // 늦게 돌아오다 come back (home) late / be late (in) coming back // 늦도록 (집에) 안 돌아오다 be long in returning // 이해가 ~ be slow to understand[grasp] things / be dull /(문어) be slow of understanding // 늦게 아들을 얻다 have a son late in one's life // 아침 늦게까지 자다 sleep late into the morning // 그는 늦게 자고 늦게 일어난다 He keeps late hours. // 이렇게 늦은 밤에 어디 가느냐 Where are you going this late [at this time of night]? // 지금 새삼스럽게 후회해도 이미 ~ It is too late to repent. / It's no good being sorry now. // 금년은 봄이 ~ Spring is late in coming this year. // 지금 출발하기는 너무 ~ It is too late to start now. // 너무 늦기 전에 그 일에서 손을 떼시오 Quit that job before it's too late. // 지금이라도 늦지 않다 It is not too late now. // 늦더라도 안 하느니보다는 낫다 Better late than never. // 정부의 공해 대책은 너무 늦었다 The government's antipollution measures were much too late [came too late].

늦다[2] [일정 시간 안에 못 미치다] be late; be delayed. ¶학교[열차 / 식사]에 ~ be late for school [for the train / for dinner] // 나는 출근 시간에 늦었다 I was late for work. / I was late getting to the office. // 나는 원서 제출이 늦었다 I sent in my application too late. // 회의는 예정보다 10분 늦게 시작되었다 The meeting started ten minutes late [behind schedule]. // 비행기는 2시간 늦었다 The plane was delayed two hours. // 이 학급은 작년의 학급보다 교과서 진도가 늦어 있다 This class hasn't gotten as far in the textbook [isn't covering the textbook as quickly] as last year's class. // 이 손목시계는 하루에 1분 늦는다 This watch loses one minute a day. / 저 괘종시계는 5분 늦는다 That clock is five minutes slow. // 이 시계는 시간이 늦어지는 일이 자주 있다 This watch tends to lose time.

늦더위 the lingering summer heat; the heat of late summer. ¶올해는 ~가 심하다 The heat of late summer is severer this year.

늦되다 [늦게 익다] grow [ripen / mature] late; be slow to mature; (지능이) be slow in mental development. ¶늦되는 late grown / [식] serotinous / late // 늦되는 과일 [농작물] late fruit[crop] // 늦된 아이 a retarded child // 금년에는 농작물이 늦된다 The crops are late this year.

늦둥이 1 [늦자식] a child born of an old couple. 2 [지진아] a retarded child; [얼뜬 사람] a slow-witted person; a coward.

늦바람 1 [저녁 바람] an evening wind [breeze]. ¶선선한 ~ a cool evening breeze. 2 [빠르지 않은 바람] a gentle [light] breeze; a soft wind; a breath of air. 3 [나이 들어 피우는 난봉] old-age passion; dissipation [prodigality] in one's later years; amorous pursuits in the decline of one's life. ¶~이 나다 take to fast living late in one's life / play the prodigal in one's later years / debauch oneself in one's old age.

늦벼 late-ripening rice; late rice; a slow-maturing variety of rice.

늦복(-福) good fortune in one's old age; happiness in one's later years.

늦봄 late spring; the latter part of spring.

늦부지런 1 [뒤늦은] a belated effort. 2 [노인의] diligence in one's old age.

늦서리 late frost; frost in the late spring.

늦여름 late summer; the last [latter] part of summer. ¶~에 toward the end of summer / late in summer.

늦잠 oversleeping; late rising. ¶~을 자서 회사에 지각했다 I overslept and was late getting to the office. // 오늘 아침에 두 시간이나 ~을 잤다 I woke up two hours late this morning. ● **늦잠꾸러기** / **늦잠쟁이** a late-rising person; a late riser [sleeper]; a sleepyhead; a lie-abed; a slugabed. ¶그는 ~다 He gets up late. / He is a late riser [a sleepyhead]. (▶ sleepyhead는 특히 아이들 잠꾸러기).

늦장마 a late rainy [wet] season; the rainy spell in late summer. ¶올해는 ~가 들었다 We have a late rainy spell this summer.

늦추다 1 (띠·고삐를) loosen; slacken; (마음을) relax; ease. ¶조금 ~ make (one's belt) a little looser // 고삐를 ~ slacken the reins / let the rein go // 허리띠를 ~ loosen the belt // 경계를 ~ relax one's guard [vigilance] / let down one's guard // 고삐[누른 손/낚싯줄]를 늦추지 않다 keep a tight rein [hand / line].
2 (속도를) slow down; reduce one's speed; ease (up) (the speed); slack; slacken. ¶걸음[속도]을 ~ slack(en) [relax / reduce / slow down] one's pace [speed] // 차의 속도를 ~ slow one's car down // 그는 속도를 늦추어 달리고 있다 He is running at a reduced speed.
3 (시간·날짜를) delay; defer; put off; postpone; extend; protract. ¶시계를 1시간 ~ put [set / turn] back a clock [watch] one hour // 기간을 ~ extend the term (from ... to ...) // 마감 날짜를 이틀 ~ put the deadline off two days // 1시간 늦추어 출발하다 [귀가하다] leave [come home] an hour late [behind] // 일요일까지 ~ put off [defer] till Sunday // 빚 청산을 한 달만 늦추어 주시오 Let the debt stand over for another month.

늦추위 the lingering cold (of early spring); the cold of late winter. ¶아직도 ~가 계속되고 있다 The cold of (late winter) still lingers.

늪 a marsh; a swamp; a bog.

-니 1 [원인·근거] since; because; as; for; seeing that; so ... that; now (that). ¶아무 말도 없는 걸 보~ 그는 그것을 모르는 것 같다 Since he said nothing, it seems that he doesn't know about it yet. // 여기서 너를 만나다~ 뜻밖이다 This is the last place where I expected to meet you. / I little dreamed [had no thought] of meeting you here.
2 and also.
3 [의문]. ¶너 어디 가~ Where are you going? // 저 사람이 네 누나~ Is that your sister?
4 [진리 등의 서술을 끝맺는 말]. ¶고생 끝에 낙이~ No cross, no crown. / No pains, no gains.
5 [여러 가지] and; or; and the like; and so forth. ¶세상에선 날더러 이러~저러~ 한다 People say one thing or another of me.

니그로 a black (man / woman); (집합적) the blacks (▶ a Negro, a Negress는 경멸적이므로 보통은 쓰이지 않음).

-니까 [이유·원인] now that; since; because; due to; and so; when (in the past) then; and [but] then. ¶네가 그렇게 말하~ now that you say so ... // 그는 개를 무서워하~ 검둥이를 보자 도망쳐 버렸다 Being afraid of dogs, he ran away at the sight of Blackie. // 식사 준비가 다 된 모양이~ 식당으로 가십시다 As the meal seems to be all ready, let's go along to the dining room. // 오늘은 토요일이~ 일찍 돌아오겠다 I'll be back home earlier than usual because it is Saturday today.

-니만큼 because (of); since; as; for. ¶그녀는 직업이 직업이~ 화려하게 옷을 입어야 한다 She must be gaily dressed, because of her profession. // 매우 신중한 사람이~ 그는 사고를 일으키지 않을 것이다 He is so careful that he will not cause an accident.

니스 [화] varnish. ⇨▷바니시 ¶~를 칠하다 varnish (over) (the surface) / apply varnish to (the surface).

니켈 [화] nickel (기호 Ni). ¶~의 nickel / nickelous / (도금의) nickel-plated // ~을 함유하는 nickeliferous

니코틴 nicotine. ¶~의 nicotinic // ~이 없는 담배 denicotinized [nicotineless] cigarettes // ~을 제거하다 denicotinize / denicotine (from).
● **니코틴 중독** nicotinism. ¶~에 걸리다 suffer from nicotinism.

니크롬선 (─線) Nichrome wire.

니트 ¶~의 knit (suit) / knitted (garment) // ~의 원피스 a knit dress.
● **니트웨어** knitwear.

니트로글리세린 nitroglycerine.

니트로벤젠 nitrobenzene.

니힐리스트 [허무주의자] a nihilist.

니힐리즘 [허무주의] nihilism.

닉네임 [별명·애칭] a nickname. ¶아이들은 그에게 「점보」라는 ~을 붙였다 The boys nicknamed him "Jumbo". // 그녀는 눈이 크기 때문에 「잠자리」라는 ~으로 통하고 있다 She goes by the nickname of "Dragonfly" on account of her big eyes.

님 [경칭]. ¶주시경 ~ Mr. Ju Sigyeong / (영) Ju Sigyeong, Esq.

-님 [경칭] (남자의) Mr. (Mister의 약어); Esq.(Esquire의 약어); (여자의) Mrs.(Mistress의 약어); Mme.(Madame의 약어); Miss(미혼 여성). ¶사장~ Mr. President / (여자) Madam President // 선생~ My respected teacher / Sir! // 신부~ reverend Father / Father! // 예수~ Lord Jesus // 임금 ~ (3인칭) His [Her] Majesty / (2인칭) Your Majesty // 주인~ my honorable master / (미) Mr. ... // 형~ my dear brother.

님프 a nymph.

닢 ¶가마니 두 ~ two straw bags // 동전 한 ~ a piece of copper // 엽전 열 ~ ten brass coins.

ㄷ

다[1] [음] do; C. ¶~장조[단조] C major[minor]// ~장조 소나타 a sonata in C major.

다[2] **1** [모두] all; wholly; altogether; all through; in all[full]; everything; everybody; everyone; both. ¶둘 ~ both of them / both together// ~ 함께 all together// ~ 해서 in all// 아이들이 ~ all the children// 빠짐없이 ~ without omission[exception]// 먹어 치우다 ~ eat up all// 조건을 ~ 들어주다 accept the conditions in full// ~ 가져가라 Take away the whole lot.// 두 사람이 ~ 그것을 알고[모르고] 있었다 Both[Neither] of us knew it.// 세 사람이 ~ 알고[모르고] 있었다 All [None] of the three knew it.// ~ 내 잘못이다 It's all my fault.// 영식도 나도 ~ 열다섯 살이다 Yeongsik and I are both fifteen years old.// 시험에 두 사람이 ~ 떨어졌다 Both of them failed in[Neither of them could pass] the examination.// 세 사람이 ~ 지치고 말았다 The three were all tired. / All three got tired.// 내 형제들은 ~ 독신이다 My brothers are bachelors without exception.// 나는 용돈을 ~ 써 버렸다 I have spent the last penny of my pocket money.// 우리가 ~ 간 것은 아니다 Not all of us went there.// 나는 이 책장에 있는 책을 ~ 읽었다 I have read every book on this bookcase.// ~ 합해서 삼천 원입니다 It comes to 3,000 won altogether.// 준비가 ~ 되었다 Arrangements have been thoroughly made.// 누구나 ~ 자기의 의무를 다하지 않으면 안 된다 Everybody must do his duty.// 반짝인다고 ~ 금은 아니다 All that glitters is not gold.

2 [완전히] completely; quite; all; utterly; perfectly; thoroughly; [거의] almost; nearly; all but. ¶~ 죽어 가는 목소리 a faint voice// ~ 죽어 가다 be dying / be almost to die / be at the point of death / be at death's door// 집이 ~ 되었다 The house is now completely built.// 그 책을 ~ 읽으신 뒤에 제가 빌려 가고 싶습니다 I would like to borrow the book when you are finished[through / done] with it.

3 [강조·조소]. ¶별일 ~ 봤다 Now I've seen everything.// 별말씀 ~ 하십니다 Don't mention it. / Not at all.// 별꼴 ~ 보겠네 What a shame! / Shame on you!// 비가 ~ 온다 And now it has to rain, on top of everything else.// 주제에 양복까지 ~ 입었네 What a sight he looks in that coat!

4 [최상의 것] at best; at (the) most; as much as one can. ¶말을 잘한다고 해서 그것만으로 ~는 아니다 It is not everything[the most important thing] to talk in fine language.// 내 월급으로 네 식구 먹여 살리는 게 ~다 My salary is scarcely enough to support a family of four.

-다[1] [상태·동작] be; do. ¶비싸~ expensive// 높~ high// 마시~ drink// 그는 환자~ He is a patient.// 그녀는 아름답~ She is beautiful. **2** while; as. ⇨-다가

다가 [장소] at; in; into; on; over. ¶판자에 구멍을 뚫다 bore a hole in a board// 그것을 어디~ 둘까요 Where shall I put it?

-다가 1 [다른 동작으로 넘어감] while; as; during; over; with. ¶그녀는 집에 오~ 그를 만났다 She met him on her way home.// 책을 읽~ 잠들었다 I fell asleep reading. **2** [동작이 번갈아 일어남]. ¶왔~ 갔~ 하다 go to and fro / walk back and forth// 섰~ 앉았~ 하다 be now standing and now sitting// 울~ 웃~ 하다 weep and laugh by turns. **3** [어떤 일의 근거가 됨]. ¶그는 감기를 그대로 놔두었~ 목숨을 잃었다 He died of a neglected cold.

다가가다 go[come / get] near; approach; step[come] up to; steal up. ¶다가가지 않다 keep [stay] away[aloof] from (a person) / do not go near// 배후로 몰래 ~ steal up behind a person// 우리는 산꼭대기에 바짝 다가갔다 We approached[got close to] the top of the mountain.// 그녀는 그 자동차로 다가갔다 She walked[stepped] up to the car.// 개는 주인에게 바짝 다가갔다 The dog nestled close[snuggled up] to its owner.// 표범은 먹이를 향해 살며시 다가갔다 The leopard stalked its prey.// 톰은 제3위에 바짝 다가가며 달리고 있었다 Tom was running a close third.

다가붙다 stick nearer (to); draw[sit / stand] close[near]; snuggle against[up to]. ¶바짝 다가붙어 close together// 바로 옆에 ~ in [under] the shadow of.

다가서다 get near(er); come[walk / step] up to; approach closer; come[go] nearer. ¶다가서서 보다 take a near[get a closer] view of / see (a picture) close at hand// 내게 바짝 다가서렴 Come closer to me.// 안으로 다가서 주세요 (버스에서) Move on, please.

다가앉다 sit close[closely]; sit up; move forward (on one's knees); slide oneself forward; take one's seat closer. ¶얘기 좀 하게 다가앉아라 Sit a little closer, so we can have a talk.// 좀 다가앉아 주십시오 Please sit [squeeze] up a little closer[sit closer together].// 거기는 추우니까 좀 더 난로에 다가앉아라 It's cold there. Sit closer to the fire.

다가오다 1 [접근하다] approach; near; step [come / go / walk] up to; get near (a place); move on toward. ¶(배가) 육지에 ~ approach land / close with the land / draw toward the shore// 점점 ~ get nearer to (a place)// 여자는 내게 바짝 다가왔다 The woman stealthily edged over to me[drew close to me / sidled up to me].// 낯선 사람이 다가왔다 A stranger walked up to me.

2 [임박하다]. ¶다가오는 coming / to come / next// 다가올 선거 the forthcoming election// 종말이 ~ draw to a close / near one's end// 여름이 다가오고 있었다 Summer was drawing near. / It was almost summer.// 회합의 종료가 다가왔다 The party drew to a close.// 추석이 다가온다 Chuseok is drawing near.// 연말이 다가왔다 It is almost the end of the year. / The end of the year is fast approaching[is almost upon us].∥시험이 가까이 다가왔다 The examination is close at hand[is drawing on].∥시험이 3일 후로 다가왔다 The examination is only three days away[off].∥경기가 다가오니 그들은 안절부절 못하고 있다 With the match near at hand, they are restless.∥파멸이 그의 목전에 다가왔다 Ruin stared him in the face.∥새해가 다가왔다 The New Year is coming on us.

다각(多角) ¶~의 many-sided / multilateral / diversified / multiple.
• **다각 경영** diversification; multiple[diversified] management[operation]. **다각 무역** multilateral trade. **다각형** [수] a polygon. ¶~의 polygonal∥정~ a regular polygon. **다각화** (기업 등의) diversification. ¶~하다 diversify.

다각적(多角的) many-sided; versatile; diversified; multilateral. ¶~인 투자 diversified investment∥~인 천재 a versatile genius∥문제를 ~으로 생각하다 consider a problem from different[many other] angles.

다갈색(茶褐色) (dark) brown; liver brown; yellowish brown. ¶~의 brown / liver-colored.

다감하다(多感−) [느끼기 쉽다] susceptible; [감동하기 쉽다] emotional; impressionable; sensitive. ¶다감한 소녀 a sentimental girl∥다감한 청년 a susceptible[sensitive] youth∥다감한 소녀기에 in one's impressionable girlhood∥성품이 ~ be of a sentimental[emotional] nature.

-고 because; as. ⇨-ㄴ다고 ¶그는 일이 느리~ 합니다 He is slow in his work, I hear.∥가난하~ 경멸해서는 안 된다 You should not despise a man because he is poor.

다공질(多孔質) porosity; porousness. ¶~의 porous / [통기성의] poromeric.

다과(多寡) [많고 적음] many or few; more or less; large or small; (양) a quantity; (수) a number; (액수) an amount. ¶~를 불문하고 regardless of (its) quantity[number / amount]∥손해의 ~에 따라 in proportion to the damage suffered∥팁의 ~에 따라 대우를 달리하다 treat (guests) differently according to the amount of tips∥모든 주문은 ~를 불문하고 신속히 조달해 드립니다 All orders, large and small, will be promptly executed.

다과(茶菓) (light) refreshments; tea and cake. ¶~를 대접받다 partake of light refreshments∥~ 있음 (게시) Refreshments provided.∥그들은 우리에게 ~를 대접했다 They served us light refreshments. / Tea and cakes were served.
• **다과회** a tea party; a tea. ¶~에 초대하다 ask (a person) to come in to tea.

다구(茶具) (여러 가지의) tea things; tea utensils; (한 벌로 된) a tea service[set]. ¶한 벌 a set of tea things.

다국적 기업(多國籍企業) a multinational corporation[enterprise]; a transnational (corporation).

다그다 1 [가까이 옮기다] bring near; draw near; put[bring] (a thing) close (to). ¶촛불을 가까이 ~ bring a candle closer to oneself∥그는 난롯가로 의자를 다가 놓았다 He drew[moved] his chair near the fire. 2 [앞당기다] (날짜 등을) advance; move[carry] up; (시간을) quicken. ¶…의 기일을 ~ advance[put forward] the date of …∥닷새 ~ shift five days ahead / advance[move up] (the date) by five days∥6교시의 국어 시간을 3교시로 ~ move up the Korean lesson from the sixth hour to the third.

다그치다 urge; prompt; impel; spur on; press. ¶다그쳐 묻다 press (a person) (hard) for an answer / ply (a person) with question∥다그쳐서 움직이게 하다 spur (a person) into action∥대답을 다그치는 바람에 대꾸할 말을 잊었다 Pressed for an answer, I did not know how to reply.∥그의 동료들은 그를 배은 망덕한 놈이라고 다그쳤다 His colleagues took him to task[gave him a hard time] for being an ingrate.

다극(多極) ¶~의 multipolar∥세계 정치의 ~화 시대 the age of multipolarized world politics.

다급하다(多急−) pressing; urgent; imminent; exigent; impending. ¶다급한 문제 a pressing question∥다급한 볼일로 on urgent business∥다급한 경우에는 in case of emergency∥시간이 ~ be pressed for time∥그런 것은 다급할 때 아무 도움이 되지 않는다 It won't do in an emergency. **다급히** urgently; exigently; imminently.

다기지다(多氣−) daring; gritty; bold; dauntless; intrepid; fearless; hardy; stout-hearted; courageous. ¶다기진 행동 a daring act[deed]∥그는 몸은 작아도 다기진 사람이다 Though small in stature, he is a man with plenty of guts.∥그는 다기지게도 혼자 적진에 들어갔다 He was bold enough to make an entry into the enemy's camp all alone.

다난하다(多難−) full of difficulties[troubles]; fraught with difficulties; eventful. ¶다난한 해 a tumultuous year∥그는 다난한 삶을 살았다 He led an eventful life.

다녀가다 drop in for a short visit; call at (a house); drop in (on a person)[come round to see (a person)] and then go on; look (a person) up; stop[come] by. ¶어제 형님이 다녀가셨다 My brother dropped by to see me yesterday.∥상경하거든 다녀가시오 Look me up when you are in Seoul.

다녀오다 drop in (on a person) and then come back; go round to see (a person) and then return; get[come] back (from visiting); return; be (back) home. ¶학교에 ~ get home from school∥곧 다녀와야 한다 You have to come back without delay.∥곧 다녀올게 I shan't[won't] be long.∥대전에 좀 다녀오겠다 I'm going to run down to Daejeon.∥저녁때까지 다녀오기는 어려울 게다 It will be difficult for us to be back before evening.∥"어디 갔다 왔습니까?" "부산에 다녀왔습니다." "Where have you been?" "I have been to Busan."∥다녀왔습니다 (인사말) Hullo, here I am!∥어머니, 다녀왔습니다 Hullo, mother! [Well mother,] I'm back[home].∥지금 막 전시회에 다녀오는 길입니다 I have just come back from a visit to the exhibition.

다년(多年) many years; a number of years.
• **다년간** a long time; many years; (부사적) (for) a long time; (for[over / through]) many years; for a number of years; through the years. ¶~의 long / of long standing / of many years∥~ 사귀어 온 친구 a friend of long standing / a longtime friend∥~의 경험 a long experience∥~의 연구 many years' study / long-continued study / years of

study / years' research // ~의 노력 years of labor[efforts] // ~의 교제 an intercourse of many years // ~의 실험으로 증명이 끝난 방법 a time-tested formula[method] // ~에 걸쳐서 for (many) years / for a number of years / over a period of years / through many years / over a long term of years // ~에 걸친 전쟁 a war of long duration // ~에 걸치다 extend over many years / cover a long period of years / last for many years // 그와는 ~ 만나지 못했다 I haven't seen him for years. // ~의 노고 끝에 드디어 그것을 완성했다 At last he accomplished it after many years' labor. // 그것은 그의 ~의 소망이었다 It was his long-cherished desire. // ~의 습관을 좀처럼 버릴 수 없다 We cannot readily give up customs of long standing.

다년생 (多年生) [식] perennation. ⇨ "여러해살이

● **다년생 식물** [식] a perennial herb. ⇨ "여러해살이풀(⇨여러해살이)

다뇨증 (多尿症) [의] polyuria. ¶~의 polyuric.

다능하다 (多能-) versatile; many-sided; accomplished; all-(a)round; multiple-skilled. ¶다능한 사람 a man of great versatility / a many sided person.

-다니 1 ⇨ "-ㄴ다니

2 [의외] how[why] should ...; I am sorry that ...; I regret ...; It is a pity that .... ¶여기서 너를 만나~ (생각도 못했다) This is the last place where I expected to meet you. // 이런 곳에서 그를 만나~ Fancy meeting him here (of all places)! // 그런 짓을 하~ 미쳤느냐 Are you mad that you should do such a thing? // 그가 저 훌륭한 저택에서 살고 있~ Just think of him living in that fine residence! // 사태가 이 지경이 되~ 유감천만이다 It is a great pity that things should have come to this pass. // 그가 80세로 한라산을 오르~ How marvelous that he should climb Hallasan(Mt. Halla) at eighty! // 그가 실패하~ 정말 안됐다 It is a great pity that he should have failed. // 내가 외롭~, 천만에 Why should I feel lonesome? // 그런 정직한 사람을 내쫓~ The idea of kicking out such an honest fellow!

다니다 1 [왕래하다] go to and from (a place); go to (a place) and back; make a trip to and from (a place); (전차 등이) run; (배가) ply (between / from ... to ...); (개통하다) be opened to traffic; be open for traffic. ¶부산과 제주를 다니는 배 a ship plying between Busan and Jeju // 왼쪽으로 ~ keep to the left // 답례하러 ~ make a round calls to return thanks // 이 길은 사람이[차가] 많이 다닌다 Many people[cars] pass on this road. // 사람이 다니지 않는 뒷길은 피하는 것이 좋다 You had better avoid deserted back streets. // 역과 절 사이에는 버스가 다니고 있다 Buses run between the station and the temple. // 한국에서는 차가 우측으로 다닌다 Cars keep to the right in Korea. // 나는 매일 병원에 다닌다 I go to hospital every day. // 이 강은 대형 기선이 다닐 수 있다 The river is navigable for large steamers.

2 [통근·통학하다] commute; attend (school); go to. ¶버스로 학교에 다니고 있다 I go[commute] to school by bus. // 그들은 매일 아침 걸어서 공장에 다닌다 They walk to the factory every morning. // 어느 학교에 다니느냐 What school do you attend? // 가정부는 1주일에 두 번 다니러 온다 A helper comes twice a week. // 어디 다니십니까 Where do you work?

3 [자주 가다] go frequently (to); frequent; hang around; hang out at. ¶자주 다니는 찻집 a familiar teahouse // 술집에 ~ hang around a saloon // 젊었을 때에는 그곳에 잘 다녔다 When young, I used to be a frequenter[frequent visitor] of the place. // 이 길은 늘 다니던 길이다 This is the road I usually take.

4 (직무·취미로). ¶구경[사냥]을 ~ go sightseeing[hunting] // 출장을 ~ go on a business trip (利事) // 그는 이사(理事)들의 개별적 결재를 얻기 위해 서류를 이리저리 들고 다녔다 He took the papers around to the directors individually for approval.

5 [들르다] stop at (a place); drop in for a short visit; call at.

다니엘서 (-書) [성] (the Book of) Daniel(약어 Dan).

다다르다 1 [장소에 닿다] come to; arrive (at); reach; get to (a place); gain; attain. ¶목적지에 ~ arrive at[come to] one's destination / come to the end of one's journey // 우리는 마침내 산꼭대기에 다다랐다 We arrived at the top of the mountain at last. / We finally made it to the top of the mountain.

2 [최종 상태에 이르다]. ¶그는 밑바닥에서 시작했지만 마침내 정상의 위치에 다다르는 데 성공했다 Though he started at the bottom, he managed to work his way to the top. // 그대로 계속된다면 다다를 곳은 파산뿐이다 If he continues that way he can only end up bankrupt. // 거기까지 했다면, 마지막 다다를 때까지 해 보는 거다 If you have done that much, you might as well go all the way[as far as you can].

다다이즘 Dadaism; Dada.

다다익선 (多多益善) The more, the better.

다닥다닥 in clusters. ⇨ <더덕더덕

다닥치다 come (round); arrive; draw near; impend; be imminent; be near at hand; be around the corner. ¶눈앞에 다닥친 위험 a pressing[an impending] danger // 죽음이 다닥치고 있다 one's time is drawing near / (사람이) be on the verge[brink] of death // 시험이 다닥쳤다 The examination is at hand. // 약속한 날이 다닥치고 있다 The appointed day is now close[near] at hand.

다단식 로켓 (多段式-) a multistage[multiple-stage] rocket.

다달이 every[each] month; from month to month; monthly; a[per] month. ¶~ 얼마씩으로 by the month // ~ 한 번씩 once a month // ~ 이자를 ~ 지불한 pay interest every month // 나는 회비를 ~ 꼬박꼬박 지불했다 I paid my monthly membership fee regularly.

다당류 (多糖類) [화] polysaccharide; polysaccharose.

다대하다 (多大-) great; much; considerable; heavy; serious. ¶대대한 희생자 a huge cost of life // 대대한 손해를 입다 suffer a heavy [great] loss / sustain a serious[severe] loss // 대대한 노력이 필요하다 require much labor // 대대한 영향을 받다 be seriously affected / be hard hit / be greatly influenced // 폭풍우로 작물은 대대한 피해를 입었다 The crops suffered serious[great] damage from the storm.//그는 자기의 과실로 인해 다대한 희생을 치렀다 He paid dearly for his mistake.//인간은 태양으로부터 다대한 은혜를 입고 있다 Man is under a great debt[greatly indebted] to the sun.//그는 국가에 대한 다대한 공적으로 표창을 받았다 He won commendation for his great services to the State.

다도(茶道) the tea ceremony[cult]; the art of ceremonial tea-making. ¶~를 가르치다[익히다] teach[practice / take lessons in] the tea ceremony

다도해(多島海) 〔에게 해〕 the Aegean Sea; the Archipelago; (보통 명사로서) an archipelago.

다독(多讀) wide[much / extensive] reading; a great deal of reading. **다독하다** read extensively[widely]; read many books.
● **다독주의** the principle of extensive reading.

다독거리다 (물건을) gather (things) up and press in order; arrange in good order; (아기를) caress; pat (a child on the head).

다듬다 1 [매만지다] trim[spruce] up; adorn; embellish; refine; polish; elaborate; file; make beautiful. ¶잘 다듬은 머리 well-groomed hair//머리끝을 ~ trim the ends of a person's hair (skillfully)//말을 ~ refine a language//문장을 ~ polish one's writing//구상을 ~ develop[work out] an idea.
2 (나무·잔디 등을) prune; trim. (▶ prune은 불필요한 가지를 자르기, trim은 잘라서 가지런히 손질하기)//장미나무를 ~ prune a rose bush//산울타리를 ~ trim a hedge//잔디를 ~ mow a lawn / cut the grass//애완견의 털을 ~ trim one's pet dog//양털을 ~ shear a sheep//죽은 잎을 다듬어 내다 nip off dead leaves//나무를 ~ shave a piece of wood smoothly / (널빤지를) plane a piece of board smoothly / (각재를) trim a square timber.
3 (깃털을) plume; preen. ¶독수리가 (부리로) 깃털을 다듬고 있었다 An eagle was pluming its feathers (itself).
4 (피륙을) smooth (starched cloth) by beating with round fulling sticks; full (cloth).
5 [마무리하다] give the final touches to; finish (up); do up.

다듬이 1 [다듬이질할 옷감] *dadeumi*; cloth to be fulled[smoothed by pounding]. 2 fulling (cloth). ⇨ 다듬이질(⇨다듬이)
● **다듬이질** *dadeumijil*; fulling (cloth). ¶~소리 the sound of fulling[beating] cloth. **다듬잇돌** a *dadeumitdol*; a fulling block; a block for beating cloth. **다듬잇방망이** (a pair of) round fulling sticks.

다듬질 1 [다듬기] the final polish; finish; the finishing touches. **다듬질하다** give the final touches to; finish (up); do up. 2 fulling (cloth). ⇨ 다듬이질(⇨다듬이)

다라지다 bold; daring; dauntless; fearless; hardy; plucky; spunky. ¶그는 몸집은 작지만 다라진 사람이다 He may be small but he sure has spunk.

다락 an upper stor(e)y; a loft over a kitchen.
● **다락방** a garret; an attic; a loft.

다락같다 very high (in price); expensive; very costly. ¶다락같은 물가 soaring prices / (미) boom prices // 다락같이 뛰다 rise suddenly / (미) boom / jump / soar // 물가(物價)가 다락같이 뛰었다 Prices took a jump.

다람쥐 〔동〕 a squirrel; a (Asiatic) chipmunk.
다람쥐 쳇바퀴 돌듯 (속담) go round and round; repeat the same thing forever; be in a vicious circle.

다랍다 1 dirty. ⇨ 더럽다 2 [인색하다] stingy; niggardly; miserly; mean; parsimonious; grasping; (속어) screwy; (미국 속어) pinch-penny. ¶다라운 녀석 a niggard / miser // 먹을 것에 다랍게 굴다 be mean about food // 그런 부자가 고것밖에 내지 않다니 ~ It is mean in a man of his wealth to give so little.

다랑어 a tuna. ⇨ 참다랑어 ¶~ 통조림 canned[(영) tinned] tuna.

다랑이 a small lot[strip] of terraced paddy field.

다래 〔다래나무 열매〕 the fruit of Actinidia arguta; [목화의 열매] a (cotton) boll.

다래끼 〔의〕 a sty(e); a hordeolum (*pl.* -la). ¶내 왼쪽 눈에 ~가 났다 I have a sty on my left eyelid.

다량(多量) a large quantity (of); a great deal (of); (구어) plenty (of); a lot (of). ¶~의 방사능 a high degree of radioactivity // 재해 지역에 ~의 의약품이 보내졌다 A great quantity[A lot] of medicine was sent to the stricken area.//소년은 ~ 출혈로 위독하다 Having lost a great deal of blood, the boy is in critical condition.//이 나라는 구리를 ~으로 수입한다 This country imports copper in great quantity[large quantities of copper].//이 사막에는 석유가 ~으로 매장되어 있는 것 같다 It is thought that there are abundant oil reserves lying under this desert.//이 지방은 사과의 ~ 생산지로 유명하다 This area is wellknown for its abundant production of apple.

다루다 1 [처리·취급하다] handle; manage; deal with; treat of (a subject); transact [carry on / handle / conduct] (business); deal in (goods). ¶다루기 쉬운 manageable / easy to handle[to deal with] // 다루기 편한 머리털 hair that is easy to manage // 말을 ~ handle[manage] one's horse // 다룰 수 없다 be out of control // 책을 조심해서 ~ handle books with care // 이 차는 거칠게 다루어졌다 This car has been used roughly.//그는 영어를 잘 다룬다 He has a good command of English. / He can speak English fluently.//그 문제를 다룬 책이 있다 There is a book that deals with the problem.//이런 문제는 다루지 않기로 작정하고 있다 I make it a rule not to deal with this sort of problem.//이런 일은 내가 전에 다룬 적이 있다[없다] I have (never) handled this type of job before.//신문은 그의 발견을 대대적으로[3단 기사로] 다루었다 The paper gave a big write up [devoted three columns] to his discovery.
2 [(사람을) 대하다] treat; deal with. ¶다루기 쉬운 사람 an easy person to handle // 다루기 힘든 아이 an unmanageable child // 아이들을 엄하게 ~ tighten the reigns on one's children // 그는 사원을 어떻게 줄 줄 모른다 He doesn't know how to treat[handle] his employees.//그는 부하를 거칠게 다룬다 He works his men too hard.//그녀는 환자를 잘 다룬다 She is an expert at humoring invalids.//막무가내인 판매원을 어떻게 다루어야 할지 모르겠다 I don't know how to deal with pushy salesman.//저 아이는 요즘 다루

다르다

기 어렵게 되었다 That child has recently gotten out of control[hand]. // 저런 손님은 다루기 쉽다 That sort of customer is easy to deal with. // 부하를 더 공정하게 다루시오 Treat your subordinates more fairly. // 새로 온 사람은 그가 다룬다 He takes care of the newcomers.

3 〔조작하다〕 handle; manipulate; work [operate] (a machine). ¶기계를 ~ handle [operate] a machine // 그는 고삐를 능숙하게 다루었다 He handled the reins. // 이 기계는 다루기가 쉽다[어렵다] This machine is easy [difficult] to handle [operate / run]. // 깨지는 물건은 조심해서 다루어라 Handle the fragile articles carefully.

4 〔가죽 등을〕 work (smooth); soften; make pliant. ¶다루지 않은 untanned [raw] (hide) // 가죽을 ~ dress [tan] a hide [skin].

다르다

1 〔일치하지 않다〕 be not in accordance (with); be contrary (to); be not in keeping with; disagree; 〔상이하다〕 differ (from); be different [from], vary (from). ¶아주 ~ be quite [entirely / utterly] different (from) // 가격은 품질에 따라 ~ Prices vary according to the quality. // 이 두 개의 드레스는 스타일이 ~ These two dresses are different in style. // 그의 사고방식은 나와 ~ His way of thinking differs [is different] from mine. // 그의 말은 진실과 ~ His statement is at variance with the truth. // 그 점에서 나는 당신과 의견이 다르오 I disagree with you in that respect [there / on that]. // 그렇다면 약속과는 다르지 않소 You're not keeping your promise. // 우리는 그와는 생각이 ~ We think differently from him. // 고장이 다르면 풍습도 ~ Different places, different customs. // 말하는 것 다르고 행동하는 것이 다른 그런 사람은 신용할 수 없다 The kind of person who says one thing and does another cannot be trusted. // 보는 것과 듣는 것과는 크게 ~ There is a great difference [a world of difference] between seeing and hearing. / Rumor and fact are miles apart. // 이 둘은 다를 바가 없다 There is little to choose between the two.

2 〔그 밖의·별개의〕 other; further; additional; else; distinct. ¶눕는 것과 자는 것은 ~ It is one thing to lie down, and another to sleep.

3 〔유별나다〕 extraordinary; peculiar; unusual; uncommon. ¶천재는 역시 ~ There is something extraordinary in a genius.

다름(이) 아니라

just; nothing but; no more [less] than; no other than. ¶그것은 ~ the fact is that ... // 그가 여기 온 것은 ~ 자네를 보러 온 것일세 He came here for nothing else but to see you. // 내가 말하려는 것은 ~ 당신이 과장으로 승진하게 되었다는 것이오 What I want to say to you [All I want to say] is that you are being promoted to section chief. // ~ 부탁할 것이 있어서 왔네 I have come for other reason than to make a request of you.

다름 아닌

¶그녀는 ~ 국무총리였다 She was no less personage than the Prime Minister. // 그 신사는 ~ 대통령이었다 The gentleman was none other than the President. // ~ 그녀의 부탁이니 최선을 다해 보겠네 Since the request comes from her and none other, I will try my best. // 석탄은 ~ 돌의 일종이다 Coal is nothing but a kind of stone.

다른

1 〔그 밖의·별개의〕 other; further; additional; else; distinct. ¶~ 것 something else / the other thing // ~ 책 another book / other books // ~ 사람을 이롭게 하다 benefit others // 누군가 ~ 사람에게 물어보자 Let's ask someone else. // ~ 이야기를 하자꾸나 Let's change the topic (of conversation). // 그에게 줄 선물은 ~ 데서 사자 Let's buy his present somewhere else [at some other store / else where]. // ~ 사람에게 말하면 안 된다 Don't tell anybody. / Keep it a secret. // ~ 펜을 보여 주시오 Show me another pen, please. // 어떤 ~ 호텔로 옮기는 편이 낫다 We had better move to some other hotel. // 그것에 관한 토론은 ~ 기회에 넘기겠다 I will leave the discussion of that for another [a different] occasion.

2 〔보통의·여느〕 usual; common; ordinary. ¶그녀는 확실히 ~ 사람과는 다르다 She is certainly out of the common run of men.

다름없다

〔같다〕 the same; not different (from); similar (to); alike; 〔변함없다〕 constant; never-changing; steady; unwavering. ¶전과 다름없는 우정 steady [constant] friendship // 선전 포고나 다름없는 중대하고도 심각한 도발 행위 a grave and serious provocation tantamount to a declaration of war (against) // 한가족이나 ~ be almost [be as good as] one of the family // 그는 거지나 다름 없는 꼴을 하고 있었다 He looked no better that a beggar. // 그녀는 청혼을 받아들인 거나 ~ She as good as accepted the offer. // 정세는 이전과 ~ The situation is unchanged. // 거의 없는 거나 ~ I have [There is] almost nothing. // 가난하기는 옛날과 ~ We are just as poor as we used to be. // 그가 한 짓은 사기나 ~ What he did amounts to fraud. // 그의 부탁은 협박이나 다름없었다 His request was equivalent to [the equivalent of] a threat. // 네가 하는 말은 모욕이나 ~ Your remark is no better than [amounts to] an insult. // 그의 재산은 없는 거나 ~ His fortune is practically gone. // 그가 완쾌된 것은 기적이나 ~ His recovery is little short of a miracle. // 네가 훔친 거나 ~ You virtually stole it. // 받은 거나 ~ I will take the will for the deed. / I thank you just the same. // 그것은 공짜나 ~ It is dirt cheap. / The price is so low the thing is as good as free. // 그 건물은 완공된 거나 ~ The building is nearly [almost] completed. // 그의 안중에는 부모의 위엄은 없는 거나 ~ In his eye the parents' authority counts for nothing. // 거저나 다름없는 헐값으로 샀다 I bought it for next to nothing. // 그런 놈에게 돈을 주는 것은 돈을 버리는 거나 ~ You might as well throw away your money as give it to such a fellow. // 너는 원숭이나 ~ You are for all the world like a monkey. // 그것에 대해서는 모르는 거나 ~ Very little is known about it. 다름없이 〔똑같이〕 similarly; equally; alike; in like manner; 〔변함없이〕 unvaryingly; unchangingly; without a change; 〔한결같이〕 uniformly. ¶전과 ~ as before / as usual / as always / (as ...) as ever / no better [worse] than before // 전과 ~ 영리하다 be as clever as before // 제 자식과 ~ 사랑하다 love (a child) like one's own // 그는 보통 때와 ~ 5시에 퇴근했다 He left the office as five as usual. // 전과 ~ 애호해 주십시오 Please give me favor as usual.// 그녀는 예나 ~ 가난하다 She remains as poor as ever.// 그는 괴짜나 ~ 여겨진다 People think him little better than an eccentric.

다리¹ **1** (사람·동물의) a leg; (구어) pins; a limb(동물의); an arm(낙지·문어·오징어 등의). ¶~ 운동 (체) leg exercises // ~ 벌려 앞으로 구르기(매트 운동에서) a forward roll with legs astride // 비쩍 마른 ~ a lean[thin] leg // 무~ thick legs // 굽은 ~ pudgy legs / piano legs // ~가 안으로 굽은 knock-kneed // ~가 밖으로 굽은 bowlegged / bandy-legged // ~가 긴 long-legged / leggy // ~가 짧은 short-legged // ~가 굵은 heavy-legged // **~가 있다 [없다]** have legs [be legless] // ~가 길다 have long legs / be leggy / be long-legged // ~가 짧다 have short legs / be short-legged // ~가 굵다 have thick legs // ~가 비틀거리다 be wobbly[dotty] on one's legs // ~가 튼튼해지다 get stronger on one's legs // (피곤하여) ~가 말을 듣지 않다 be worked off one's legs // ~를 다치다 get hurt in the leg / get one's leg hurt // ~를 굽히다 bend one's legs // ~를 뻗다 stretch out one's legs // ~를 벌리다 stretch[spread] one's legs apart // ~를 벌리고 서다 stand with one's legs[feet] apart // ~를 뻗고 자다 sleep stretching one's legs / sleep carefree // ~를 쉬다 rest one's feet // ~를 꼬다 cross one's legs // 책상~를 하고 앉다 sit with one's legs crossed / sit cross-legged // (꼰) ~를 풀다 unwind one's legs // ~를 편하게 하고 앉다 sit at ease // ~가 뻣뻣해지도록 걸었다 I walked until my feet were almost worn to stumps.// 그는 한쪽 ~를 전다 He is lame in one leg.// 오징어의 ~는 몇 개인가 How many arms does a cuttlefish have?// 그는 술 취한 사람처럼 ~가 휘청거렸다 His legs were as shaky[unsteady] as a drunken man's. / He staggered[reeled] like a drunk.// 그 소년은 거리낌 없이 두 ~를 뻗고 앉아 있었다 The boy sat with his legs too freely extended.

2 (책상 등의) a leg; a leg piece. ¶안경~ the bows of a pair of glasses[spectacles] // 책상 ~ the leg of a table // ~가 긴 탁자 a long-legged[tall] table // ~가 셋 달린 탁자 a three-legged table.

● **다리뼈** a leg bone. **다리통** the girth of the leg.

다리² **1** [교량] a bridge; [구름다리] a viaduct; [현수교] a suspension bridge. ¶홍예~ an arch bridge // 돌~ a stone bridge // 공사 the construction[repair] of a bridge // ~ 통행세 a bridge toll // ~의 난간 a bridge rail // ~ 밑을 지나가다 pass under a bridge // ~를 건너다 cross a bridge / go across a bridge // ~를 지나 강을 건너다 cross a river by a bridge // 강에 ~를 놓다 build[lay / throw] a bridge a cross[over] a river / span a river with a bridge // 그 강에는 ~가 둘 있다 There are two bridges across the river. / Two bridges span the river.// 그 ~는 1989년에 개통되었다 The bridge was opened in 1989.// 무거운 차 때문에 ~가 무너졌다 The bridge gave way under a heavy wagon.// 이 ~의 길이는 얼마나 됩니까 How long is (the span of) this bridge?// 바꿔 타실 분은 이 ~를 건너시오 (역의 게시) Passengers changing trains are requested to cross this bridge.

2 [중개] mediation; good offices.

다리(를) 놓다 mediate [intermediate] (between); act as an intermediary [a go-between]. ¶다리를 놓겠다고 나서다 offer one's services as a mediator // 누군가 양자 사이에 다리를 놓지 않으면 안 된다 Someone has to bring the two parties together. / Someone has to bridge the gap between the two parties.

● **다릿목** the foot of[the approach to] a bridge.

다리³ (여자의 머리에 덧넣는) a tress of false [artificial] hair; a hairpiece; a switch; (미국구어) a rat. ¶~를 넣다 put on a tress of false hair / wear a hairpiece // ~를 넣어 머리털을 부풀리다 use[add] a hairpiece to give one's hair more fullness.

● **다리꼭지** a bunch[clump] of false hair.

다리다 iron (out) (a shirt); press (the trousers); do the ironing. ¶바지를 ~ iron out trousers[pants] / crease one's trousers (주름 잡다) // 대충 ~ run over (the clothes) with an iron // 옷을 다려 드릴까요 Can't I press out a dress for you?

다리미 an iron; a flatiron; a goose ¶전기~ an electric iron // 증기 ~ a steam iron // ~로 주름을 펴다 smooth the wrinkles with an iron // ~를 켠 채 두다 leave an iron heated // ~로 식탁보를 다렸다 The table-cloth was smoothed out with an iron.

● **다리미질** ironing. ¶~을 하다 iron (out) / press / do the ironing. **다리미판** an ironing stand[board].

다림 (수직의) plumbing; (수평의) level(l)ing.

다림(을) 보다 (수직을) plumb; ascertain perpendicularity; (수평을) level; (이해 관계를) keep alert to one's own interest; reckon in advance one's interests and losses.

● **다림줄** a lead [plumb] line. **다림추** a plumb (bob); a plummet.

다림질 ironing. ⇨ 「다리미질(⇨다리미)」

다만 1 [오직 그뿐] only; merely; simply; just; but; alone. ¶~ …하기만 하면 되다 have [need] only to (do) / an one has to do is to (do) // ~ 울기만 하다 do nothing but cry // ~ 돈벌이만 생각하고 있다 be solely bent on moneymaking // ~ 물어보았을 뿐이오 I just wanted to know it (and nothing more). / I just asked.// 그녀의 장점은 ~ 정직하다는 것뿐이다 Honesty is her only merit.// 그것은 ~ 소문에 지나지 않는다 It is merely a rumor.// ~ 내 의무를 다했을 뿐이다 I have done nothing but my duty.// 그녀와는 ~ 편지를 주고받는 사이다 My relations with her are confined to the exchange of letters.// 이것은 ~ 나 자신뿐만 아니라 우리 가족 전체에 도움이 된다 It will benefit not only myself, but (also) all my family.// ~ 한 가지 말해 두고 싶은 일이 있다 There is only one thing which I wish to tell you.// 언어 숙달에는 ~ 연습이 있을 뿐이다 Practice is the only way of mastering a language.// 우리는 ~ 그의 명령을 따를 따름이다 We have no alternative [choice] but to obey his order.// ~ 시키는 대로만 하면 된다 You have only to do as you are told.

2 [그러나] but; however; only; provided (that); on condition that; excepting that. ¶그는 좋은 결심을 한다. ~ 지키지 못할 뿐이다 He makes good resolutions, only he never keeps them.// 피곤하지는 않다. ~ 배가 고플

뿐이다 I am not tired, but I am hungry. // 외출은 자유다. ~ 10시까지는 돌아와야 한다 You are free to go out, however, [but] you must be back by ten. // 그 친구 무척 좋은 너석이야. ~ 가끔 과음하지만 않는다면 말이야 He's a good guy, only he sometimes drinks too much. // 무엇을 해도 좋다. ~ 남에게 폐를 끼치지 마라 You may do anything you like, provided (that) you do not give trouble to others. // 기꺼이 떠맡겠소. ~ 건강이 허락하면 말이오 I will be glad to undertake it, provided that I am well enough.

다망하다(多忙-) busy; busily engaged; fully occupied; have much work; have many things[much] to do. ¶다망한 1주일 a busy [rush] week // 공무 다망하여 by[on account of] pressure of official business // 다망한 중에도 불구하고 though one is very busy / despite the claims of a busy life // 다망한 생활을 하다 lead a busy life // 다망하신 데 죄송합니다만… (I'm) sorry to trouble[intrude on] you when you are so busy, but … // 일 때문에 몹시 ~ I am very busy with my work. / I'm pressed with business. // 그는 공사다망하여 학급 회의에 불참했다 He was unable to attend the class reunion on account of the pressure of official and private business. // 그녀는 여러 가지 일로 ~ She is fully occupied with lots of work.

다매(多賣) a large sale [turnover].

-다면 if; unless; when. ⇨ㄴ다면 ¶가능하~ if possible // 불편하시~ 오지 않아도 됩니다 You don't have to come if it's inconvenient. // 필요하~ 내일 다시 전화하세요 Please call again tomorrow if necessary.

다면적(多面的) many-sided; versatile; multilateral; diversified. ¶문제의 ~인 연구 a many-faceted attack on the problem.

다면체(多面體) a polyhedron (pl. -dra, ~s). ¶정~ a regular polyhedron / ~의 polyhedral / polyhedric.

다모작(多毛作) multiple cropping.

다모증(多毛症) excessive growth of hair; [의] hypertrichosis; hirsutism; hirsuties.

다목적(多目的) multipurpose. ¶~의 multiple-purpose // ~의 가구 (a piece of) furniture with many uses.

● **다목적 댐** a multipurpose [a multiple-purpose] dam.

다문박식(多聞博識) wide[much] information and extensive[encyclopedic] knowledge. ¶~한 사람 a man of various information and wide knowledge / an erudite (person).

다물다 shut[close] (one's mouth). ¶굳게 다문 입 a compressed[a firm] mouth / tense lips // 입을 ~ be silent / hold one's tongue / be shut up // 잠시 입을 다물면 어떻겠니 How about holding your tongue for a minute? // 마을 사람들은 입을 다물고 말하지 않았다 The villagers kept their mouth shut. // 그는 굳게 입을 다물고 있었다 He shut up like a clam. / His lips were tightly sealed[closed]. // 그는 그 일에 관해서는 입을 꼭 다물었다 He kept quiet[silent / (구어) mum] about the matter. / He said nothing about the matter. // 그의 꼭 다문 입은 강인한 의지를 나타내고 있다 His firm-set lips bespeak an iron will.

다민족 국가(多民族國家) a multiracial nation [country].

다반사(茶飯事) [일상의 사건] an everyday occurrence[affair]; a daily event; [사소한 일] a trifling matter; a matter of no importance. ¶뭐, 그야 ~지 Well, it's just one of those things. // 요즈음은 살인 사건이 ~로 일어난다 Murders are daily events these days.

다발 a bundle; a bunch; a sheaf (pl. sheaves) (벼 등의); a faggot(장작 등의); a stack; a coil(새끼 등의). ¶꽃~ a bunch of flowers // 열쇠 ~ a bunch of keys // 건초[장작] ~ a bundle of hay[firewood] // 편지 ~ a batch of letters // 지폐 ~ a roll[(구어) wad] of // 한 ~에 700원 seven hundred won a bundle // ~로 하여 in a bundle[bunch] // ~로 하다 tie (goods) into a bundle / bundle (things) up together // ~로 팔다 sell (things) in a bundle[bunch] // 장작은 ~로 판다 Firewood is sold by the bundle.

다발식(多發式) ¶~의 multiengine (plane) / many-engined.

다발하다(多發-) (사고 등이) occur frequently (often); (질병 등이) occur in many places[localities]; (증상이) occur in many cases. ¶교통사고가 ~ 다발하는 지점 a spot where traffic[(영) road] accidents occur frequently / (영) a black spot // 각지에서 콜레라가 다발했다 Many cases of cholera occurred [Cholera broke out] in various places.

다방(茶房) a teahouse; a tearoom; a teashop; (미) a coffee shop[a coffee house]; (영) a coffee bar (● 미국과 영국에서는 모두 차뿐 아니라 경양식도 파는 식당). ¶~ 레지 a teahouse waitress / a tearoom hostess // ~ 마담 a tearoom manageress // ~ 음악 a coffee shop[a tearoom] where you can listen to music.

다방면(多方面) [여러 방면] many quarters; [여러 방향] many directions; [여러 취미] many-sidedness; [여러 재능] versatility. ¶~의 many-sided / various / varied / manifold / versatile // ~으로 in many directions [fields] // ~에 걸친 학식 wide-ranging erudition / multifarious learning // ~에 걸친 재능의 소유자 a man of many[(문어) manifold] talents // ~으로 친구가 있다 have a wide [varied] circle of acquaintances // 이야기가 ~에 걸치다 talk on many[various] topics // 그는 ~에 걸친 수집을 하고 있다 He has a great variety of collections. / His collections cover a number of areas. // 문제는 ~에 걸쳐 있다 The problem has so many facets. // 그의 ~에 걸친 화제에 놀랐다 We are surprised at the wide variety of topics he can converse on. // 문제는 ~에서 출제되었다 Questions were put on various[a wide range of] subjects. // 그는 ~에 취미를 가진 사람이다 He is a man of catholic taste. / He has many-sided interests.

다변(多辯) talkativeness; loquacity; garrulity; volubility; verbosity. ¶~한 talkative / loquacious / garrulous / voluble / long-tongued // ~은 웅변이 아니다 A wealth of words is not eloquence.

● **다변가**(-家) a great talker; a chatterbox; a prattler; a garrulous person.

다변적(多邊的) multilateral.

다변형(多邊形) ¶a polygon. ⇨다각형

다변화(多邊化) diversification. ¶수출 시장의 ~ diversification of export markets. **다변화하다** diversify; be diversified.

다병하다(多病-) weak; infirm; delicate;

fragile; sickly. ¶대병한 사람 a man in delicate health / a sickly person / a valetudinarian.

다복다복 in bunches[thickets / groves]; densely; luxuriantly; thickly. **다복다복하다** thicketed; dotted[covered] with thickets. ¶소나무가 다복다복한 언덕 a hill covered with thickets of pine trees / a hill thickly wooded with pine trees.

다복하다(多福-) lucky; blessed; happy; fortunate; be blessed with good luck. ¶다복한 생활을 하다 live a happy life / live comfortably[in comfort] // 그녀는 가정적으로 다복하지 못하다 Her home life is not a happy on.

다부지다 1 [과단성 있다] staunch; firm; determined; plucky; strong-minded; solid. ¶다부진 사람 a tough guy / a stout-hearted person / a person of staunch character // 다부지게 일하다 work hard[indefatigably] // 자네는 키는 작아도 사람이 ~ Though small in stature, you are a man of firm character. 2 [생김새가 옹골차다] strong and firm; sturdy. ¶다부지게 생긴 사람 a person with firm [well-defined / strong / compact] features / a solidly-built person // 그는 다부진 몸매다 He has good muscle tone. / He is in good shape[fit].

다분히(多分-) much; a good deal (of); mostly; greatly; quite a lot. ¶그녀는 시인의 소질이 ~ 있다 She has very much of the poet in her. // 그럴 염려가 ~ 있다 It is a matter much to be apprehended. / We fear it very much. // 자네는 ~ 자기 본위인 데가 있네 You have a very selfish disposition. // 전쟁이 발발할 가능성이 ~ 있다 There is a very strong possibility that war will break out.

다불다불 in tufts. **다불다불하다** tufty; fringy; fleecy. ¶다불다불한 머리 tufty[flowing] hair.

다붓다붓 close(ly); dense(ly); at short intervals. ¶~ 앉다 sit close together.

다붓하다 close; dense; thick; crowded. **다붓이** closely; densely.

다비(茶毘) [불] cremation; burning (the body) to ashes. **다비하다** cremate; burn (the body) to ashes.
●**다비소**(-所) a crematory; a crematorium (pl. ~s, -ria).

다사다난하다(多事多難-) eventful. ¶다사다난한 한 해 an eventful year // 그는 다사다난한 생활을 보냈다 He led an eventful life. // 다사다난한 해였다 I had one difficulty after another that year. // 작년에 내외로 다사다난한 한 해였다 Last year was a very eventful one both at home and abroad.

다사스럽다(多事-) meddlesome; officious. ¶다사스러운 사람 a meddler / a busybody / (속어) a Nosy Parker // 자네도 어지간히 다사스럽네 How meddlesome you are!

다사하다(多事-) [일이 많다] busy; eventful; (서술적) have much to do.

다산(多産) [자식·새끼를 많이 낳음] fecundity; bearing many young; [물품을 많이 생산함] productivity. ¶~의 fecund / multiparous / prolific / fruitful / productive // ~계(系)의 동물 a prolific[fertile] animal. **다산하다** bear many young; be fecund. ¶이 닭들은 다산한다 These hens are good layers. // 이 지방의 여자들은 다산한다 The women in this region have many children.
●**다산부**(-婦) a prolific woman.

다색(多色) many colors. ¶~의 multicolored / many-colored / varicolored / polychromic / polychrome / versicolor.
●**다색 인쇄** multicolor(ed) printing.

다색(茶色) light brown; drab. ¶~의 light brown / brownish.

다선 의원(多選議員) a Congressman[an Assemblyman] elected for many terms.

다섯 five. ¶~ 배(의) fivefold / quintuple // ~개 한 벌 a set of five / a quintet // (영) ~ 중주 quintette // 우리 ~이 같이 간다 Five of us will be going together. // 내 딸은 ~ 살이다 My daughter is five (years old).

다섯째 fifth. ¶~ 사람 the fifth person // 지난 시험에 ~가 되었다 On the last test I came out fifth.

다소(多少) 1 [많고 적음] many or[and] few; more or[and] less; number(수); quantity(수량); amount(양). ¶~에 따라서 according to the number[quantity / amount] of / ~를 불문하고 regardless of amount / large or[and] small // 참가자의 ~에 따라 예정이 바뀔지도 모른다 The schedule may vary with[according to] the number of participants. // ~를 불문하고 쓰레기는 스스로 처리하여 주십시오 Please dispose of the garbage yourself regardless of the amount. // ~를 불문하고 주문에 신속히 응하겠습니다 All orders, large and small, will be promptly executed. // ~를 불문하고 기부를 부탁드립니다 Contributions gratefully accepted. / We solicit you to contribute any amount you like. // 이러한 때에 금액의 ~는 문제가 아니다 Under these circumstances the cost doesn't matter. // 중량의 ~에 관계없이 무료로 배달해 드립니다 Any article, light or heavy, will be delivered without charge. / Any article will be delivered free regardless of its weight.

2 [어느 정도] a little; some; (의문·조건) any; somewhat; to some extent[degree]; in some [a] measure; (구어) kind of; sort of. ¶~ 이름이 알려진 사람 a man of some note // ~ 성공하다 win some[a] measure of success // ~ 춥다 be a bit cold // ~ 피로하다 be a little[be kind of] tired // 나도 그것에 대해서는 ~ 책임이 있다 I am also more or less responsible for the matter. // 그녀는 ~ 건방진 데가 있다 She is fresh in a way. // 이것은 네게 ~ 어려울지도 모른다 This may be rather[a little too] difficult for you. // 프랑스 어를 ~ 할 줄 압니다 I can speak a little French. // 거기엔 ~ 의심스러운 점이 있다 There is something doubtful about it. // 그는 ~ 의학 지식이 있다 He has some knowledge of medicine. // 그는 ~ 이름이 알려진 화가이다 He is an artist of some renown[acclaim]. / He is not totally unknown as an artist.

다소곳하다 [고개를 숙이다] modest and quiet with one's head lowered; [온순하게] modest; quiet; gentle; obedient. ¶다소곳한 태도 an obedient (and courteous) attitude.

다소곳이 [온순하게] obediently; quietly; submissively; gently; [머리를 숙이고] with one's head drooped[dropped / bowed]; with a drooping[hanging] head. ¶~ 남의 말을 듣다 listen to another's advice obediently[with one's head dropped] // 신부는 ~ 앉아 있었다 The shy bride sat mum with downcast eyes.

-다손 치더라도 (even) though; (even) if. ⇨ -ㄴ다손 치더라도 ¶그렇~ even if it were so /

다수

granting that it is so // 그렇게 말했~ even if [granted that] one did say so // 아무리 돈이 있~ however [no matter how] rich one may be // 무슨 일이 있~ whatever [no matter what] may happen / come what may // 그가 늙었~ though he is old.

다수(多數) **1** [많은 수] a large number; a multitude (of readers); numbers; a heap; a multiplicity (of errors); a plurality (of causes); a host; an army. ¶~의 (a great) many / numerous / a large number of / a lot of / innumerable / manifold // 국민의 ~ the large mass of the people // ~의 사람들 a great number of [a great many] people / numbers [scores] of people // ~의 적 the numerous enemy // ~를 위해 소수를 희생하다 sacrifice the few to the many // ~를 믿다 trust to numbers // 그들은 ~의 힘을 믿고 횡포를 부렸다 They acted highhandedly by [relying on] force of numbers. // 적은 우리보다 ~다 The enemy are superior in number. // 그 문제에 관해서는 ~의 책이 있다 Books written on this subject are legion. // 그런 실수를 한 사람은 ~였다 Quite a few people made the same mistake.
2 [과반수] (a) majority (of); a predominance (of); a greater part (of). ¶압도적인 [절대] ~ an overwhelming [an absolute / a clear] majority // ~의 횡포 the tyranny of the majority // ~의 의견을 따르다 agree to the views of the majority // 압도적 ~로 대통령에 선출되다 be elected president by a landslide // ~를 **차지하다** have [command] a majority / get [win] a majority // 양원 모두 지금 ~를 차지했다 The Republican Party has won plurality in both houses. / Both houses are now Republican-dominated. // 3분의 2 이상의 ~에 의한 의결이 필요하다 It must be decided by a majority of two-thirds or more. // 시의회에서는 혁신파가 ~를 차지하고 있다 The progressives hold a majority in the city council.
● **다수결** decision by majority. ¶~ 원칙 majority rule / majoritarian principle // ~에 의한 표결 majority voting // ~에 **따르다** abide by the decision of the majority // ~로 **결정하다** decide by (a) majority vote. **다수당** majority [dominant] party. **다수 대표제** a majority representation system. **다수 의견** a majority opinion. **다수표** majority vote. ¶~를 **획득하다** poll a majority.

다수확(多收穫) a high yield; a bumper crop. ¶~의 high-yield(ing) // 과수 지대의 ~은 기후 조건 덕택이다 A fruit belt owes its abundant yield to climatic conditions.
● **다수확 품종** a high-yield variety (of grain).

다스 a dozen(약어 doz., dz)(▶ two dozen cups, several dozen apples처럼 수사(數詞), several, a few 등을 붙여 단수형으로 형용사적으로 쓰는 것이 보통). ¶연필 1~ a dozen pencils // 2~들이 상자 a box containing two dozen // 10~ ten dozen / a small gross // 반 ~ half a dozen // 여러 ~의 (many) dozens of ... // 연필은 ~로 팔고 있다 Pencils are sold by the dozen.

다스리다 1 [통치하다] rule [reign] over; govern; administer; [관리하다] conduct; manage; direct; preside over. ¶나라를 ~ rule over [govern] a country / manage a state // 집안을 ~ manage [regulate / order] a household // 국정을 ~ direct [conduct] the affairs of state.
2 [바로잡다] put (things) in order [trim]; put [set] (things) to rights. ¶교내를 ~ keep the school in order.
3 [통제하다] control; keep control over; regulate; keep under control. ¶엄중히 ~ exercise strict control over / control strictly // 규칙을 마련하여 ~ control with regulations // 물을 ~ control floods / take flood-control [river conservancy] measures.
4 [평정하다] suppress; put down; quell; subdue; pacify. ¶난리를 ~ subdue [suppress] a rebellion // 싸움을 ~ make up a quarrel // 폭도를 ~ suppress [put down] the rioters.
5 [병 등을 고치다] cure; heal; remedy. ¶상처를 ~ salve [heal] a wound // 환자를 ~ cure a patient / heal the sick.
6 [죄에 대해 벌을 주다] punish; bring (a person) to justice. ¶죄를 ~ punish a crime.

다슬기 [동] a marsh snail; a black snail; a horn shell.

다습하다(多濕-) humid; damp. ¶다습한 날씨 damp [humid] weather // 올여름은 고온 다습했다 This summer has been very hot and humid.

다시 1 [되풀이하여 또] again; once more [again]; another time; a second time; repeatedly; twice. ¶몇 번이고 ~ many times over / over and over (again) // ~ 말할 것도 없이 needless to repeat // 언제 ~ some other time / another time // ~ 하다 do over again [once more] / try again / have another go [try] (at) // ~ 보다 look at (it) again [twice] / have another look (at) / give (it) a second look // ~ 한번 해 보다 make a second attempt // ~ 읽다 read (a book) (all over) again // ~ 세 번 쓰다 write thrice again // 일을 ~ 시작하다 begin one's work again / resume one's work // ~ 말하다 say again / repeat / say over again // ~ 말하(자)면 in other words / that is to say / namely // 근간 ~ 한번 찾아뵙겠습니다 I will call again one of these days. // ~ 뵙게 되기를 바랍니다 I hope I shall see more of you. // 그것은 ~ 해야 한다 It needs to be done [tried] again. // ~ 그 유명한 정원을 찾았다 I visited the famous garden again [for a second time]. // ~ 그에게 충고를 했으나 허사였다 I cautioned him second time, but in vain. // 우리는 ~ 한 번 사고의 원인을 조사했다 We investigated the cause of the accident once more. // 우리는 ~ 교섭을 시작했다 We resumed negotiations. // 그는 예전처럼 ~ 튼튼해졌다 He has become as strong as he used to be. / He has regained his health. // ~ 전화하겠습니다 [찾아오죠] I will call [come] again. // 이런 실수를 두 번 ~ 되풀이하지 않겠다 I swear that I shall never repeat the same error. // ~ 한두 해가 지나갔다 Another year or two passed. // 이제 ~는 돈을 요구하지 않겠습니다 This is the last time I will ever ask you for money.
2 [새로이] anew; afresh; (do) over again. ¶~ 시작하다 begin anew / start afresh / start all over again // 다리를 ~ 놓다 rebuild a bridge // 집을 ~ 꾸미다 remodel [redecorate] a house // 그의 가슴은 ~ 희망으로 부풀었다

Hope sprang afresh in his heart.// 기와를 ~ 이어야겠다 We must have our roof retiled.// 그는 헤어진 아내와 ~ 결혼했다 He remarried his divorced wife.// 그는 ~ 국장 자리에 복귀되었다 He was reinstated as bureau chief.

다시다 ¶입맛을 ~ (맛이 있어서) smack one's lips / (불쾌하여) click[clack] one's tongue// 입맛을 다시며 먹다 eat (a thing) with much gusto[keen relish].

다시마 [식] a (sea) tangle; a tangleweed; a devil's apron; (짐합적) tang; kelp.

다시없다 unique; matchless; unparalleled; unequaled; without a peer. ¶다시없는 협력자 a superb helper / the best possible collaborator// 다시없는 일품 a unique article / the only one of its kind/ 다시없는 친구 a once-in-a-lifetime friend// 이렇게 경치가 좋은 곳은 ~ The place is unequaled[has no equal] in its scenic beauty.// 다시없는 좋은 이야기를 들었다 I have never heard such a good story.// 이처럼 쓸모 있는 사전은 ~ This dictionary has no parallel in usefulness.// 이 반지는 다시없는 추억이 될 것입니다 This ring will be a reminder of this marvelous experience. / This ring will be a perfect memento. / 다시없는 기회 a golden opportunity / an opportunity one will never have again// 이건 다시없는 기회다 This is a unique chance.// 이런 기회는 ~ We shall never have such a good opportunity again. / Such an opportunity knocks but once at the door.

-다시피 [마찬가지로] as; like; similar to; sort of; in the same way (that); [같은 정도로] almost; nearly; practically; all but; as good as. ¶보~ as you (can) see// 알~ as you know / as you must realize// 무상으로 일하~하다 work for next to no wages// 그녀는 거의 죽~ 되었다 She was as good as dead.// 그 책을 외~ 읽었다 I've read the book to the point where I have it practically memorized.// 그들은 여기서 살~ 한다 They practically live here.// 함대는 거의 전멸하~ 했다 The fleet was all but annihilated.// 보시~ 나는 돈이 없습니다 As you can see, I have no money.// 누구나 알~ 런던은 영국의 수도다 London, as everyone knows, is the capital city of England.// 그는 술집에서 살~ 한다 He spends most of his time at the public house.

다식(多食) eating much; heavy eating; gluttony; voracity. **다식하다** eat much; overeat; eat to excess; gluttonize.
● **다식증** [의] polyphagia; bulimia.

다식(茶食) a kind of pattern-pressed candy made of sesame, chestnut, greenpea flour, honey, etc.

다식하다(多識-) well-informed; erudite.

다신교(多神教) polytheism.
● **다신교도** a polytheist.

다실(茶室) a teahouse. ⇨ 다방

다액(多額) a large sum[amount]. ¶~의 much / a large[huge] sum[amount] of / considerable// ~의 돈 a large sum[amount] of money// ~의 기부 a generous contribution// ~의 비용 a huge cost// ~의 자본[자금] large capital [funds].

다양성(多樣性) variety; diversity; multiformity.

다양하다(多樣-) various; diverse (▶ 서로 다름을 강조함); manifold. ¶다양한 직업을 가진 사람들 men of diverse occupations// 내용이 ~ contain a wide variety// 사물을 다양한 각도에서 보다 see things from various angles// 그는 취미가 ~ He has many-sided interests. / He is a man of catholic taste.// 이 말에는 다양한 의미가 있다 This word has various meanings.// 최근에는 다양한 잡지가 출판되고 있다 A great variety of magazines are published now.

다염기산(多鹽基酸) [화] polybasic acid.

다예(多藝) versatility.

다용도(多用途) many purposes.
● **다용도 건물** a multipurpose building. **다용도실** a multipurpose room.

다우(多雨) a great deal[a lot] of rain.
● **다우 지역** a high-rain area.

다우존스 산식(-算式) the Dow-Jones formula.

다우존스 주가 평균(-株價平均) the Dow-Jones average[index]; (구어) the Dow; the average price computed under the Dow-Jones formula.

다운 1 [권투] a knock-down. **다운되다** be knocked down. ¶다운되었다가 일어나다 climb off the canvas// 그는 제3라운드에서 다운되었다 He was downed in the third round. → 다운시키다 knock down / (미국 속어) floor. **2** [지처서 떨어짐]. **다운되다** ¶지난주에는 독감으로 다운되고 말았다 I was down with (the) flu last week. **3** [내림] down. **다운하다** fall; go down.

다운로드 [컴] [내려받기] a download.

다원(多元) pluralism. ¶~화 현상 polycentrism (in communist world).
● **다원론** pluralism. **다원 방송** a broadcast originating from multiple locations.

다원적(多元的) plural; pluralistic. ¶~ 국가론 pluralistic conception of the State.

다육(多肉) [식] fleshiness. ¶~질[성]의 fleshy / pulpy.

다음 the next; the second; the sequel (of a story); (형용사적) [바로 뒤의] (the) next; following; ensuing; [오는] coming; [둘째] second; the rest; [인접한] adjacent; adjoining. ¶이~ next time / [언젠가] another time// ~ 역 the next station// ~ 기사 the adjoined[following / subjoined] article// ~ 금요일 (현재에서 보아) next Friday / (과거 또는 미래의 어느 날에서 보아) the next [following] Friday// ~ 세대 the next[coming] generation// ~부터는 from now on// ~에 next / secondly / in the second place / then / after (that) / next [another] time [occasion] / in the following// ~ 방 the next[adjoining] room / (곁방·대기실) antechamber// ~과 같다 it is[runs] as follows / it is to this effect// ~ 문장을 번역하시오 Translate the following sentence.// ~의 주의서를 잘 읽어 주십시오 Please read the following instructions carefully.// 그녀의 편지에는 ~처럼 씌어 있었다 She writes as follows.// 이야기의 그~을 계속해 주십시오 Please go on with your story. / Let me hear the rest of the story.// 이 이야기 [소설] 줄거리의 ~은 어떻게 전개됩니까 I wonder how the story will develop after this.// 제 ~ 회장은 민 여사입니다 Mrs. Min succeeds me as president.// ~은 What (comes) next?// ~ 열차는 몇 시입니까 What is the next train?// ~은 누구 차례입니까 Whose

다음가다

turn comes next? / Who's next? // ~에는 송씨가 이야기할 차례입니다 The [Our] next speaker is Mr. Song. // 그는 ~ 토요일에 파리로 떠났다 He left for Paris the following Saturday. // ~에 또 봅시다 I'll see [catch] you later. // 명동에는 ~ 에 가자 Let's go to the Myeongdong some other time. // 이 ~부터는 꼭 조심하겠다 I will (promise to) be careful in (the) future. (▶ (영)에서는 the를 쓰지 않음) // 이 ~ 시험에는 합격하고 싶다 I hope to pass the next [coming] examination. // 이 ~ 일요일에 오너라 Come and see me next [this] Sunday. // ~에는 서울에서 만납시다 Let's meet in Seoul next time. // 중요한 점이 둘 있다. 먼저 누가 그것을 했나이고, ~에 왜 그것을 했나이다 There are two important points. First, who did it? Second [Secondly], why did he do it? // 내 바로 ~에 도착한 사람은 누구였습니까 Who arrived right after me? // 목욕은 너 ~에 하겠다 I'll take a bath after you. // 한라산 ~으로 높은 산은 무슨 산입니까 Next to [After] Hallasan (Mt. Halla), which is the highest mountain? // 출석자 중에는 ~과 같은 분들이 계셨다 Among those present were the following. // 그 ~은 말할 필요가 없다 You need not go any further. / We know the rest. // 이것이 제일 마음에 들고 그 ~은 저것이다 I like this best and that next. // ~으로 무엇이 필요하십니까 (가게에서) Anything else?
● **다음 날** [이튿날] the next [following] day. ¶도착한 ~ the day after [following] one's arrival // ~ 아침 일찍이 early the next morning // ~ 떠나다 leave the next day // ~ 은 맑게 개었다 It was fine the next [following] day. // 그들은 운동회 ~은 휴교했다 They had no school (on) the day after the sports meet. // 그는 귀국한 ~ 아침에 죽었다 He died the morning after he returned home. **다음 달** (the) next month; the following [coming] month; proximo(약어 prox.). ¶ ~의 오늘 this day next month // ~로 돌리다 [이월하다] carry (a thing) forward to the next month. **다음 해** the next [following] year; the ensuing year; the year ensuing. ¶ 가뭄이 있던 ~ the year after the drought // 그 문제를 ~로 넘기다 carry the matter over to next year // 계정을 ~로 이월하다 carry the account forward into next year's.

다음가다 [버금가다] be [come] next (to); rank next [second] to; be second [next] to; in the second place. ¶서울 다음가는 대도시 the largest city next [second only] to Seoul // 지위 [나이]가 그의 다음가는 사람 the person next (to) him in rank [age] // 그녀는 그에 다음가는 지위에 있다 She is [comes] next to him in rank. // 그는 주(州) 지사 다음가는 실력자다 He is the most influential man next to [after] the governor. // 밀턴은 셰익스피어 다음간다 Milton is placed after Shakespeare.

다음날 [훗날] someday; another [some other] day; some time later. ¶ ~ 다시 보자 I will see you someday again. // 그것은 ~로 미루기로 합시다 Let us leave that for another time.

다음다음 next but one; the one after the next; after next. ¶ ~ 날 the next day but one / the day after next / two days after [later] // ~ 해 two years later / the year after next // ~ 정거장 the station after next / the next but one station // ~ 월요일에 on the Monday after next // 그는 상경한 ~ 날 나를 찾아왔다 Two days after he came up to Seoul, he came to see me. // 결혼한 ~ 달에 일선으로 떠났다 I went to the front two months after I got married.

다음자(多音字) a polyphone.
다음절(多音節) a polysyllable. ¶ ~의 polysyllabic.
다의(多義) polysemy; ambiguity; many [various / diverse] meanings. ¶ ~의 (a word) of many meanings / multivocal / ambiguous / equivocal (▶ equivocal은 의도적인 다의성을 나타냄) / having a multiplicity of meaning.
● **다의어** an ambiguous [an equivocal / a multivocal] word; a word with [of] many [manifold] meanings.
다이내믹하다 dynamic. ¶다이내믹하게 dynamically // 다이내믹한 스피커 a dynamic speaker.
다이너마이트 (a stick of) dynamite. ¶ ~로 폭파하다 shatter [blow up] (a rock) with dynamite / dynamite (a rock) // 그들은 ~로 다리를 폭파했다 They blew up the bridge with dynamite. / They dynamited the bridge. // 그들은 회의장에 ~를 장치했다 They set a charge of dynamite in the conference hall.
다이빙 diving. ¶공중 회전 ~ somersault diving // 스프링보드 ~ springboard diving // 플랫폼 ~ platform diving // 저 아이는 ~을 잘한다 That child is a good diver. / That child is good at diving. **다이빙하다** dive.
● **다이빙대** a diving [spring] board.
다이아 [광] a diamond; the diamond. ⇨다이아몬드
다이아몬드 1 [광] a diamond. ¶모조 ~ a rhinestone // ~를 깎다 [다듬다] cut [polish] a diamond. 2 [야구] a diamond.
다이아진 [약] sulfadiazine. ⇨술파다이아진
다이어그램 a diagram.
다이어트 a diet. ¶그는 ~ 중이다 He is on a diet. / He is dieting.
● **다이어트 식품** diet food.
다이얼 a dial; a radio dial; a dial plate(문자반). ¶ ~을 돌리다 turn a dial / dial // 라디오 ~을 돌리다 turn a dial (of the radio) // ~을 돌려 112번 [경찰]을 부르다 dial 112 [the police] // 라디오 ~을 KBS에 맞추다 turn in to KBS / turn the radio dial to KBS.
다이얼로그 a dialog(ue).
다이오드 [전] [2극 진공관] diode. ¶크리스털 ~ a crystal diode.
다이제스트 a digest; [잡지] a magazine digest. ¶ 「종(種)의 기원」의 ~판 an abridged version of The Origin of Species.
다인 [물] a dyne(기호 dyn).
다작(多作) abundant production; prolificacy in writing. **다작하다** produce [write] abundantly; be prolific (in writing). ¶그는 다작하는 작가였다 He was a prolific writer. / He wrote many books.
다잡다 1 (사람을) excercise close supervision (over); tighten the control (of the students); keep a close check (on); keep a tight rein [hand]. ¶부하들을 다잡아 일을 속히 끝내다 urge one's men to push the work // 학생들을 ~ put the pupils under strict discipline. 2 (일을) concentrate on (a job); stick close to (one's work); manage (a job). 3 (마음을) reform (one's attitude); brace oneself (up); brace (up) one's spirits; gird (up) one's

loins. ¶마음을 다잡고 …하다 do (something) with a quiet purpose ∥ 마음을 다잡고 공부하다 settle [set] down to one's studies.

다재다능하다(多才多能-) versatile; talented; gifted; many-sided; (서술적) have many talents. ¶다재다능한 예술가 a versatile artist / an artist of many talents ∥ 다재다능한 사람 a versatile person / a person of varied accomplishments [attainments] / an all-(a)round person ∥ 그는 다재다능한 작가이다 He is a versatile writer.

다정다감하다(多情多感-) sentimental; passionate; emotional; ardent. ¶다정다감한 사람 a man of sentiment [feeling] ∥ 다정다감한 여학생 a sentimentalist ∥ 다정다감한 여학생 a sentimental schoolgirl.

다정다한하다(多情多恨-) emotional; sensitive; full of tears and regrets. ¶다정다한한 일생을 보내다 lead a life full of tears and regrets.

다정불심(多情佛心) tender-heartedness; warm-[kind-]heartedness; compassion.

다정하다(多情-) 1 [정이 많다] affectionate; tender; kind-[warm-/tender-]hearted; emotional; passionate. ¶다정하게 손을 잡다 affectionately press (a person's) hand ∥ 여자는 남자보다 ~ Women have warmer affection than men. ∥ 그는 다정한 사람이다 He is an emotional man.
2 [사귄 정이 두텁다] intimate; familiar; close; friendly; chummy; (속어) thick. ¶다정한 친구 an intimate friend / a good [close / great / fast] friend / a familiar / (구어) a chum ∥ 다정한 사이다 [다정하게 지내다] be on good [intimate / friendly] terms (with) / have a close [friendly] relation (with) / be intimate [friends] (with) / be thick with / …과 다정한 사이가 되다 become intimate [familiar] (with) / get in with / make friends with / get thick with / come into close association with ∥ 두 사람은 아주 다정한 사이다 They are hand and [in] glove with each other.

다족류(多足類) [동] millipeds. ⇨=다지류
다중(多重) [관형어적] multiplex; multiple.
●다중 방송 a multiplex broadcast; multiplex broadcasting.
다중(多衆) a crowd; a great [large] number of people; a host; hosts; a multitude.
다지다 1 [단단하게 하다] harden; make hard. ¶땅을 ~ harden the ground / tamp (down) / ram ∥ 흙[눈]을 밟아 ~ tread down so as to harden soil [snow] ∥ 밟아 다져서 길을 만들다 tread a path ∥ 우리는 눈을 밟아 다졌다 We trod [tramped] down the snow.
2 [강조하다] emphasize; underscore; [확인하다] make sure of [that …]; press (a person) for a definite answer [promise]; keep after (a person). ¶꼭 오라고 ~ call (a person) special attention to come ∥ 몇 번씩이나 ~ make assurance double [doubly] sure ∥ 마음을 다지고 그 난문제에 착수했다 I tackled the difficult problem with determination.
3 [강화하다] strengthen; confirm; [견고히 하다] solidify; consolidate. ¶지반을 ~ strengthen the basis ∥ 결의를 ~ confirm one's determination / be fully determined [resolved] (to do) ∥ 사회적 지위를 ~ consolidate one's position in society.
4 [고기·양념 등을 잘게 만들다] mince; hash; chop fine; chop (up); cut fine. ¶잘 다진 고기 well-minced meat ∥ 고기를 ~ mince meat ∥ 마늘을 ~ smash (up) garlic.
5 [눌러서 잠재우다] press (seasoned food) with a stone.
다지류(多肢類) [동] millipeds; myriapods.
다짐 [확약] a definite promise; a promise; a pledge; an oath; an assurance; vouching. ¶~을 받다 get an assurance from (a person) / make (a person) pledge [promise] ∥ 그렇다면 처음에 ~을 받은 것과는 다르다 If so, it doesn't agree with the original arrangement. ∥ 그들은 다시는 죄를 짓지 않겠다는 ~을 받고 그를 석방시켰다 They set him free on his oath that he would never commit a crime again. 다짐하다 assure; pledge; make sure; pledge oneself (to); give one's word. ¶확실히 다짐하기 위하여 to make (it) double sure / to make assurance doubly sure ∥ 그는 정말 가도 되느냐고 재차 다짐했다 He made doubly sure that it was all right for him to go. ∥ 다시는 거짓말하지 않겠다고 다짐할 수 있겠는가 Can you give me your definite answer that you will never tell a lie? ∥ 그에게 저녁 식사 때까지 돌아오도록 다시 다짐했다 I told him again that he had to be back by suppertime. ∥ 그에게 그 점에 대하여 신중을 기하도록 다짐했다 I called his special attention to that point. ∥ 나는 그에게 편지를 보내 달라고 다시 다짐했다 I reminded him [I told him again to be sure] to mail the letter for me.

다짜고짜(로) [예고 없이] without notice [warning]; [느닷없이] suddenly; abruptly; unexpectedly; without preamble; [이유 없이] with neither rhyme nor reason; peremptorily; arbitrarily. ¶~ 따귀를 때리다 slap (a person) on the cheek all of a sudden ∥ ~ 끌고 가다 walk (a person) off by force ∥ ~ 집을 비우라고 하다 order (a person) out of the house without notice ∥ ~ 해고당했다 I was discharged without notice.

다채롭다(多彩-) colo(u)rful; multicolo(u)red; varicolo(u)red; variegated. ¶다채로운 행사 variegated functions ∥ 다채로운 생애를 보내다 lead a colorful life ∥ 다채로운 여흥이 베풀어졌다 There was entertainment of all sorts. ∥ 다채로운 사람들이 모였다 People working in various fields [People from various walks of life / All kinds of people] gathered there.

다처(多妻) many wives. ¶일부~ polygyny / polygamy.

다치다 1 [부상을 입다] be [get] hurt [wounded / injured]; hurt oneself; (구어) come to grief. ¶다친 개 an injured dog ∥ 발을 ~ hurt [injure] one's foot ∥ 자동차에 ~ be injured in an auto accident ∥ 크게 [몹시] ~ be badly hurt [wounded] (on the head) / be seriously injured ∥ 다치게 하다 do (a person) an injury / inflict an injury on (a person) / injure / hurt ∥ 다행히도 그는 다치지 않았다 Luckily, he escaped unhurt. ∥ 어디 다치셨습니까 Have you got hurt? ∥ 그녀는 다친 팔에 삼각건을 하고 있다 She has her injured arm in a triangle (bandage). ∥ 그는 넘어져서 머리를 다쳤다 His head was hurt by his fall.
2 [손상하다] be damaged; sustain an injury. ¶다치기 쉬운 fragile / delicate ∥ 어두운 곳에서 책을 읽으면 시력을 다치게 된다 You will ruin your sight if you read books in

다큐멘터리

a dark place.
3 〔손으로 건드리다〕 touch; give a jog. ¶물건을 다치지 마라 Don't touch this article / Hands off!

다큐멘터리 documentary.
● **다큐멘터리 영화** a documentary (film).

다크호스 a dark horse. ¶알려지지 않은 ~가 의외로 승리하는 경우가 있다 Sometimes a dark horse [an unknown new] candidate comes out victorious. // 그는 이번 선거에서 ~로 지목되고 있다 He is regarded as a dark horse in the coming election.

다투다 **1** 〔말다툼하다〕 quarrel [have a quarrel] (with a person over a matter); have a cross word (with); squabble; wrangle; brawl. ¶사소한 일로 ~ quarrel about [over] trifles // 그는 늘 이 사람 저 사람과 다투고 있다 He is always quarrelling with this man or that.
2 〔논쟁하다〕 dispute; argue; have a dispute [an argument]; engage in a controversy. ¶다툴 여지가 없는 indisputable / incontrovertible / 다툴 수 없는 an indisputable [undeniable] fact // 새로운 교육 제도를 두고 ~ argue (for) a new educational system // 한 발짝도 양보하지 않고 ~ dispute every inch of ground // 더 이상 다툴 필요가 없다 It is beyond further dispute. // 그들은 그 문제에 대해 열심히 다투고 있었다 They engaged in a heated dispute over the question.
3 〔겨루다〕 compete [vie] (with a person for); contend (with others for a prize); struggle (for supremacy). ¶시간을 다투는 문제 an urgent problem // 의석(議席)을 ~ contest a seat // 앞을 다투어 …하다 strive to be first (for / in doing) / scramble (for / in doing) / vie with one another (for / in doing) // 앞을 다투어 들어가다 try to be the first to enter // 이것은 일각을 다투는 문제다 The problem must be solved without a moment's delay. // 우리 팀은 그들과 1위를 다투었다 Our team competed with them [theirs] for first place [prize]. / 한국은 자동차 수출에서 일본과 다투고 있다 Korea is competing [in competition] with Japan in the export of automobiles. // 사람들은 앞을 다투어 버스를 타려 Trying to push ahead [in front] of one another, the crowd got into the bus. // 각 백화점들은 앞을 다투어 연말 세일을 개시했다 (순번을 다투어) All the department stores have tried to get in first with their year-end sales. / (유리하도록) All the department stores are trying to gain an edge with their year-end sales. // 그들은 주도권을 다투었다 They struggled [vied with each other] for supremacy. // 그들은 스타디움에 들어가려고 앞을 다투어 달렸다 They raced to be the first to enter the stadium.

다툼 **1** 〔말다툼〕 a quarrel (with / between); a (verbal) dispute; a wrangle; a brawl; a squabble; 〔불화〕 discord (with)(▶ fall out은 의견 대립의 원인으로 다툼). ¶말~ an altercation / a quarrel / a wrangle. **2** 〔논쟁〕 a controversy; an argument; a debate; a dispute. ¶학문상의 ~ an academic controversy. **3** 〔경쟁〕 a contest; a struggle [fight] (for); (a) competition (for); a contention. ~자리 the competition for a position / 세력 〔정권〕 ~을 하다 vie [struggle] for influence [political power] // 그는 주도권 ~에 휘말렸다 He was dragged into the struggle for supremacy [leadership].

다하다¹ **1** 〔다 없어지다〕 be exhausted; run out; be used up [consumed / spent / gone]. ¶기름 [식량] 이 ~ run out of oil [food] / The oil [food] is all gone. // 힘이 다할 때까지 while [as far as] one's energy lasts // 이 세상 다하도록 for ever (and ever) / to the end of time // 시간이 다했다 Time is up. // 힘이 다했다 My strength is gone. **2** 〔죽다〕 die; pass away; meet one's end [fate]. ¶목숨이 다할 때까지 as long as one lives // 천수를 ~ die a natural death / die of old age. **3** 〔끝나다〕 (come to an) end; be over. ¶장마철이 다했다 The rainy season is over.

다하다² **1** 〔있는 대로 다 들이다〕 exhaust; use up; run out of; do everything possible. ¶최선을 다하여 to the best of one's ability // 온갖 수단을 ~ try [exhaust] every means (in one's power) / try everything // 있는 힘을 ~ exert all one's powers // 배방으로 힘을 ~ use every exertion // 갖은 고생을 ~ drain the cup of sorrow to the dregs // 있는 힘을 다해 보자 Let's go for broke. // 그는 있는 힘을 다하여 몸으로 부딪쳤다 He hurled himself at it with all his strength. // 있는 힘을 다하여 해 보겠습니다 I will do my best. / I will make every possible effort. // 온갖 말을 다하여 그녀를 위로했다 I used every work of consolation I could think of to comfort her. // 그들은 갖은 사치를 다한 생활을 한다 They live in the utmost luxury. // 그 참상은 필설로 다할 수 없었다 The horror of the scene was beyond description. // 그는 자기 회사를 위해 할 수 있는 모든 일을 다했다 He did all he could for his company. // 그들은 인류를 위한 모든 봉사를 다했다 They rendered great service to humanity.
2 〔이행하다〕 discharge; keep; perform; fulfill; 〔완수하다〕 accomplish. ¶의무 [임무] 를 ~ do [fulfill / discharge] one's duty / ~책임을 ~ fulfill [perform / discharge] one's responsibility (as a teacher) // 대임(大任)을 ~ fulfill [carry out] an important mission // 약속을 ~ keep one's promise.

다한증(多汗症) 〔의〕 excessive sweating; hyper(h)idrosis.

다항식(多項式) 〔수〕 a polynomial [multinomial] (expression).

다핵 세포(多核細胞) 〔생〕 a coenocyte.

다행(多幸) (good) luck; good fortune; happiness. ¶불행 중 ~ a happy feature of a misfortune // 목숨을 건진 것이 무엇보다도 ~이다 You may bless your stars that you have escaped with your life. // 여기서 너를 만나게 되어 ~이다 It's rare good luck that I could see you here. // 즉시 회답을 주시면 ~으로 생각하겠습니다 If we could hear from you soon, we would be much obliged. / We would appreciate an immediate reply to this letter. // 최근의 태풍 피해가 아주 적어서 ~으로 생각합니다 I am happy to assure you that we suffered very little damage from the recent typhoon. // 다과회에 참석해 주시면 천만~으로 생각하겠습니다 We should like very much to have the pleasure of your company at the tea party. / It we could give me great pleasure if you could attend [be at] the tea party. **다행하다** lucky; fortunate; happy. ¶내가 오늘 여기에 있었던 것은 정말 다행한 일이다 It is a lucky stroke for me that I happened to be here today. **다행히** fortunately; luckily; by good luck[fortune]. ¶~ 일이 잘 되면 with luck on one side / if fortune smiles upon on // ~ (도) …하다 be lucky enough to do / have the good fortune[luck] to do // ~ 난국을 타개하다 get successfully out of difficulty[trouble] / fall on one's legs [feet] // ~ 도중에서 그를 만났다 Luckily, I met him on the way. // ~ 빚을 모두 갚을 수 있었다 Luckily, I was able to repay my loan completely. // ~ 내일은 일요일이다 Fortunately, it is Sunday tomorrow. // ~ 비가 개었 다 Luckily, it stopped raining. // ~ 우리는 모 두 잘 있습니다 Happily we are all well. // ~ 그와 아는 처지였다 Fortunately I happened to know him. // ~ 나는 늘 건강하다 Fortunately I am always healthy. / I am always blessed with good health.

다혈질 (多血質) a sanguine temperament. ¶~ 의(중세의 생리학에서) sanguine // ~의 사람 a sanguine person / a full-blooded man / (격하 기 쉬운) a man of excitable temperament.

다홍 (―紅) deep red. ⇨ 다홍색(⇨ 다홍)
● **다홍색** deep red; crimson. **다홍치마** a crimson skirt.

닥나무 [식] a paper mulberry.

닥뜨리다 1 [직면하다] be faced with; meet with; come upon[across]; be confronted with[by]; hit upon; encounter. ¶곤란에 ~ be faced with difficulty / run[bump] against a wall / strike[hit / run] against a snag(불의 의 곤란) // 죽음에 ~ be confronted by death / face[confront] death. **2** [몰아치다] press hard. ¶돈을 빨리 갚으라고 ~ dun (a person) to repay the money.

닥치다 [다가오다] approach; draw[come] near; come round; be near at hand; be in the offing; [임박하다] impend; be impending; hang over; overhang; imminent. ¶눈앞에 닥친 위험 (an) impending[pressing] danger // 곧 닥처올 폭풍우 an impending storm // 죽 음이 눈앞에 ~ death stares (a person) in the face / (사람이) be on the verge[brink] of death // 시간이 닥처오다 time is pressing / (사람이) be pushed[pressed] for time // 커다 란 재난이 그에게 닥쳤다 A great misfortune [dire calamity] befell him. // 시험 날이 닥처온 다 The examination is near at hand[is drawing near]. // 중간고사가 눈앞에 닥처졌다 The midterm exam is just around the corner. // 어떠한 재난이 닥처와도 그는 흔들리 지 않을 것이다 No matter what happens to him[(문어) Whatever befalls him], he won't lose his composure. // 닥처오는 위험에 속수무 책이었다 I could not do anything about the danger staring me in the face[the impending danger].

닥치는 대로 at random; haphazardly; randomly; in a desultory way; desultorily. ¶~ 뭣이나 whatever[anything that] comes handy[along / one's way / to one's hand] / whatever one can lay hands on // 그는 ~ 아 무것이나 먹었다 He ate anything he could lay[get] his hands on. // 그는 ~ 책을 모두 읽었다 He read everything that came his way.

닦다 1 [윤내다] polish; give (a thing) polish; burnish (metal); brighten; shine(▶ 이 뜻으 로는 규칙 동사); grind (a lens); cleanse (a watch). ¶반들반들하게 닦은 작은 시렁 a well-polished display shelf // 잘 닦은 마루 a highly polished[well-scrubbed] floor // 이를 ~ brush[clean] one's teeth // 구두를 ~ shine[polish] one's shoes / (닦게 하다) have one's shoes shined // 은그릇을 ~ polish a silverware // 주전자를 번쩍번쩍하게 ~ put a good shine on kettle by polishing it // 마루는 거울같이 닦아 놓았다 The floor was so well polished that it shone like a mirror.

2 [물로 씻다] clean; wash; brush; [훔치다] wipe (off[from]); mop (up); dry(물기를); wipe clean. ¶창문을 ~ clean a window // 수 건으로 손을 ~ wipe one's hands on a towel // 얼굴의 땀을 ~ wipe the perspiration off [from] one's face // 손수건으로 눈물을 ~ wipe[dry] one's tears with a handkerchief // 행주로 접시를 닦다 dry dishes with a cloth // 엎질러진 물을 ~ sop up the spilt water (with a cloth) // 욕탕에서 몸을 ~ scrub oneself in the bath / give oneself a scrub in the bath // 그녀는 이마의 땀을 닦았다 She wiped the perspiration from her forehead. // 그는 욕탕에서 나와 수건으로 몸을 잘 닦았다 After his bath he dried himself thoroughly with a towel.

3 [길·터를 다지다] level; improve; make even; smooth. ¶길을 ~ improve a road // 터 를 ~ level[smooth] the ground // 운동장을 ~ level a playground.

4 [단련·힘쓰다] practice; cultivate; pursue; train; drill; improve; school. ¶갈고 닦은 문체 a refined style // 갈고 닦은 장인의 솜씨로 만 든 유리 꽃병 a glass vase made by a craftsman with consummate skill // 기술을 ~ improve one's skill // 덕을 ~ cultivate one's character / improve upon one's virtue // 학업 을 ~ pursue knowledge[one's studies] / complete one's education // 그런 환경 속에서 는 훌륭한 인격을 갖고 닦을 수 없다 You cannot develop a fine character in an environment like that.

5 [기반·토대를 마련하다] prepare the ground (for); pave the way (for); solidify one's footing. ¶선거 기반을 ~ nurse one's constituency / (미) mend one's (political) fences.

6 nag (an). ⇨ 홀닦다

닦달(질) [닦아세움] scolding; rebuking; taking[calling] to task; giving (a person) a piece of one's mind. **닦달(질)하다** scold (a person for). ⇨ 닦아세우다

닦아세우다 scold[rebuke / rate] (a person for); give (a person) a good talking-to[a scolding / a piece of one's mind]; dress down; speak roughly (to a person); blame; reproach. ¶호되게 ~ subject (a person) to a severe rebuke / (구어) give it hot // 잘못했 다고 ~ take (a person) to task for his mistake // 상대를 닦아세웠다 I silenced my opponent. // 그를 닦아세웠다 I shut him up.

닦이다 1 [닦음을 당하다] be polished[shined / burnished / brightened]; be wiped [mopped]; be cleaned[brushed / scrubbed / washed]. ¶이 마루는 잘 닦였다 This floor is well polished. **2** [홀닦이다] be rebuked; be scolded; be given a talking-to. ¶호되게 ~ have [be given] a good scolding.

단[1] [묶음] a bundle; a bunch; a sheaf (pl. sheves) (짚 등의); a load; a faggot(장작 등 의). ¶벼[보리] (한) ~ a sheaf of rice[wheat]

단

// 장작 (한) ~ a bundle [load] of firewood // 시금치 세 ~ three bunches of spinach // ~으로 묶다 tie [do] up in a bundle / make into a bundle // ~으로 팔다 sell by the bunch.

단² a hem. ⇨옷단 ¶~을 올리다 take the hem up // ~을 내리다 let the hem down // ~을 짧게 하 shorten [take up] (a dress / a skirt) // 그녀는 스커트 ~을 잡아 내려 무릎을 감추었다 She pulled the hem of her skirt over her knees. / She pulled down her skirt to hide her knees.

단(段) 1 [계단의 1단] a step; a stair(1단); a flight of steps [stairs] (계속된 단); a rung (사다리의). ¶20~의 계단 a staircase with twenty steps // 꼭대기 [밑바닥]의 ~ the top [bottom] steps // 위 [아래]로부터 두 번째 ~ the step next to the top [bottom] // 사다리의 ~ a rung of a ladder // 2~ 침대 a bunk bed // 3~ 로켓 a three-stage rocket // 층계의 ~을 오르[내리]다 go up [down] the steps [stairs] // 한 번에 2~씩 계단을 오르다 go up the stairs two at a time.
2 (인쇄물의) a column. ¶3~ 조판 the triple column setting // 4~(짜리) 표제 a four-column heading // 이 신문은 한 면이 16~이다 This paper consists of sixteen columns a page. // 이 수필은 5~으로 되어 있다 This essay is composed of five paragraphs.
3 [바둑 등의 등급] a grade; a rank; a class. ¶바둑 2~ (사람이) a second grader in baduk(go) / a baduk player of the second grade.
4 [넓이의 단위] a dan(=0.245 acre). ¶~당 수확량 production per dan // 밭 3~보 three dan of fields // 이 땅은 약 4~쯤 된다 This lot covers (an area of) about an acre.

단(單) [하나·홀] only (one); no more than; single; [겨우] mere(ly); sole. ¶~ 한 사람 only one man // ~ 한 번 only once // ~ 하나도 not a single one / only one // ~ 벌옷 the only suit of clothes one has // ~ 한 번도 … 않다 never once / not even once // ~ 한 번 여기 온 적이 있다 I've been here just one. / 지난 한 해 동안 ~ 하루도 결석한 일이 없다 I have never missed a day in the past year.

단(但) however; but; only; provided (that).

단(壇) [높게 가설한 자리] a platform; a podium(▶ 지휘자·강연자 등이 서는 자리); a stage; a dais; a raised floor; an altar(제단). ¶~ 위에 서다 take [stand on] the platform // ~ 위에서 말하다 [내려오다] speak [descend / step down] from a podium // 중앙에 ~을 마련하다 lay a platform in the center // 그녀는 우레와 같은 박수를 받으며 ~에 올랐다 She took the rostrum admits a thunderous clapping of hands.

-단(團) [모임] a group; a body; a corps; a team(경기의); a gang(악한의); [일행] a party; [극단] a company; a troupe. ¶관광~ a tourist party // 외교~ a diplomatic corps // 재일 동포 모국 방문~ a home-visiting group of Korean residents in Japan.

단가(短歌) [시조] a danga; a Korean Verse; a kind of short poem.

단가(單價) a unit cost [price]. ¶생산 ~ the unit cost of production // ~ 100원에 at 100 won a piece // ~를 절감하다 reduce the unit cost of (an item) // ~를 매기다 put a unit cost of (an item).

단가(團歌) the official song of an association [organization].

단거리 1 [단으로 묶은 땔나무] firewood in bundles [faggots]. **2** [단으로 파는 땔나무] firewood sold by the bundle [faggot].

단거리(短距離) a short distance; (사격의) a short [close] range. ¶~에서 (shoot) at short distance [close range].
● **단거리 경주** a short-distance race; a sprint (race); a dash. **단거리 선수** a sprinter; a sprint runner; a dash man.

단검(短劍) a short [small] sword; a stiletto (pl. -(e)s); a dirk; a dagger. ¶~으로 찌르다 stab with a poniard [dagger].

단것 sweet things; sweet-stuff; sweets(과자). ¶~을 좋아하다 be fond of sweets / have a sweet tooth // 여자는 대개 ~을 좋아한다 Most girls have a sweet tooth [go in for sweets].

단견(短見) 1 [좁은 견해] shortsightedness; a narrow [short-sighted] view [opinion]. ¶~적 shortsighted. **2** [자기 의견] my personal views; my humble opinion. ¶제 ~으로는 in my opinion / to my thinking.

단결(團結) unity; union; (공통의 목적·이해에서 생기는) solidarity; combination. ¶국민의 ~ national solidarity // 우방국 간의 ~ the solidarity of the friendly nations // 그 사건은 그들의 ~을 강화하는 데 도움이 되었다 The incident served to strengthen their solidarity. **단결하다** unite; stand [hand / hold] together; combine. ¶단결한 united / combined / leagued / solid // 단결하여 solidly / combinedly / in union / in a body / in combination / in one united body // 단결하여 일하다 work as one [a united body] // 단결하여 …에 저항하다 be united [banded together] against … // 단결하여 행동하다 act in a body // 그들은 공동의 적에 맞서서 단결했다 They united against their common enemy. // 단결하면 살고 흩어지면 망한다 United we stand, divided we fall. ➔ ¶굳게 단결되어 있다 be closely banded together / be strongly united.
● **단결권** [법] the right of organization. **단결력** the power of combination; the capacity for united action. **단결심** (프) esprit de corps; the spirit of unity; a cooperative spirit.

단결에 [기회가 지나가기 전에] while there is a chance; before the chance slips away; [열기가 식기 전에] while it is hot; [즉시] at once; on the spot; without delay.

단계(段階) 1 [등급] a level; a rank; a grade. ¶4~로 나누다 divide into four levels [ranks] // 이 물품에는 A에서 E까지의 ~가 있다 These articles are graded [ranked] from A to E. // 급여에는 여러 ~가 마련되어 있다 The pay is severally graded.
2 [순차적인 과정] a step; a stage; [국면] a phase. ¶지금의 ~에서는 at the present stage // 예비적 ~ preliminary stages // ~적으로 by [in] stages // 세 ~를 거치다 pass through three phases [stages] // ~를 밟아 설명하다 explain a thing step by step // 전쟁은 최후의 ~로 돌입했다 The war has reached its final stages. // 이 치료법은 아직 실험 ~에 머물러 있다 This method of treatment is still in the experimental [trial] stages. // 교섭은 새로운 ~에 접어들었다 The negotiations have now entered a new phase. // 인플레이션은 ~적으로 증대되고 있다 Inflation is escalating.

단곡(短曲) a short piece of music; (프) a morceau.
단골 〔늘 거래하는 손님〕 a (regular) customer; a patron; a client; a frequenter; 〔늘 거래하는 집〕 a customary[regular / familiar] establishment; (집합적) custom; connection; patronage. ¶~ 가게 a permanent store[ship] / a familiar shop / a shop one knows well // ~ 미장원[바] one's favorite beauty parlor[bar] // ~ 싸전 one's rice dealer // ~ 술집 one's favorite drinking house // ~ 의사 one's family[regular] doctor // ~ 정육점 one's (usual) meat shop / one's favorite meat store // ~ 오랜 ~ an old customer / a customer of long standing // ~의 favorite / accustomed // 연극의 ~ 관객 a (frequent) theater goer[play goer] // ~이 되다 become a regular customer (of) // ~이 많다 have a large custom[connection] / enjoy a large patronage // ~을 얻다[잃다] gain [lose] custom[a customer] / secure a customer's account // ~을 만들다 build customer[connection] / establish a connection // 그분은 우리 ~입니다 He patronize us[our store]. / He is a good customer of ours. // 이 가게는 예술가들 사이에 ~이 많다 This establishment enjoys the patronage of many artists. // 그는 자신이 근무했던 은행의 ~을 방문[순방]했다 He visited[went the rounds of] the customers[clients] of the bank he worked for.
단공(鍛工) a metalworker; a hammersmith.
단과(單果) a simple fruit. ⇨ 홑열매
단과 대학 a college.
단광(單光) 〔물〕 monochromatic rays.
단교(斷交) (a) rupture; a break of relations; 〔외교 단절〕 diplomatic cessation; severance of diplomatic relations. 단교하다 break off relations (with); sever the relation (with). ¶두 나라는 마침내 단교하고 말았다 The two countries finally broke off diplomatic relations.
단구(段丘) a bench; a terrace; a theater. ¶하안 ~ a river[stream] terrace // 해안 ~ a marine terrace.
단구(短句) a phrase; a short sentence.
단구(短軀) short[small] stature. ¶~의 of short stature / stocky.
단군(檀君) Dangun; the founding father of the Korean nation. ¶~의 자손 descendants of Dangun.
●단군 신화 Dangun mythology; the myth of Dangun's birth.
단궤(單軌) 〔단선 궤도〕 a monorail.
●단궤 철도 a monorail (railway).
단극(單極) 〔전〕 a single pole[electrode]. ¶~의 unipolar.
단근(單根) 1 〔화〕 a simple radical. 2 〔식〕 a simple root.
단근질 torturing with a red-hot iron. 단근질하다 torture (a criminal) with a red-hot iron.
단금지교(斷金之交) close[warmest] friendship; a Damon-and-Pythias friendship. ¶~를 맺다 swear eternal friendship.
단기(單記) (a) single entry.
●단기 투표 a single-entry ballot; single voting.
단기(單機) 〔한 대의 비행기〕 a single[lone] plane.
단기(短期) a short period (of time). ⇨ 단기간

¶~의 short / short-period / of short duration // ~의 계획 a short-run project // ~ 지불 payment within a short period // ~ 흥행 a short run // 분쟁의 ~ 해결 a short-term settlement of the conflict.
●단기 강습 a short(-term) course. ¶여름휴가 이용의 일어 ~ a special class of Japanese for the summer vacation. 단기 대출 a short-term loan. 단기 복무 a short service. 단기 자본 〔경〕 short-term capital. 단기 체류 a short stay.
단기(團旗) the flag of association; an association banner; the official flag of an association.
단기(檀紀) the Dangun Era. ¶서기 2002년은 ~ 4335년이다 The year 2002 in the Christian Era falls on 4335 in the Dangun Era.
단기간(短期間) a short period (of time); a short space[span] of time.
단김에 while there is a chance. ⇨ 단결에
단꿈 a sweet[good / happy] dream. ¶~을 꾸다 dream[have] a sweet dream.
단내 1 〔열에 달아서 나는 냄새〕 a scorched [burnt] smell. ¶~가 나다 smell burning / give a burning smell // 그 피자는 ~가 난다 The pizza tastes scorched. 2 〔열이 높을 때 코에서 나는 냄새〕 a stuffy smell from one's nostril due to physical fever.
단념(斷念) abandonment; despair; resignation; relinquishment. 단념하다 give up (an idea); (문어) abandon, forego; relinquish; despair (of); get resigned to (one's loss); 〔손 떼다〕 wash one's hands (of). ¶죽은 것으로 ~ give up (a person) for[as] lost [dead] // 그는 출세를 아주 단념했다 He gave up all hope of success in life. // 어떤 일이 있어도 단념할 수 없다 Nothing can make me give it up. // 그는 아직도 그녀를 단념하지 못하고 있다 He still retains a lingering love for the woman. // 나는 심사숙고 끝에 그와의 결혼을 단념하기로 했다 After considerable thought I gave up the idea of marrying him. // 자금 부족으로 기획을 단념했다 We abandoned the project for lack of funds. // 그는 발이 아팠기 때문에 출전을 단념케 했다 As he hurt his foot, I persuaded him to withdraw from [(문어) dissuaded him from taking part in] the race. // 그런 사업은 단념해 버리시오 Wash your hands of[Give up] that business. // 그들은 회사 재건을 단념하고 말았다 They have abandoned any hope of reconstructing the company.
단단하다 1 〔굳다〕 hard; solid; adamantine; 〔견고하다〕 firm; 〔오래 견디다〕 durable. ¶단단한 돌 a hard stone // 단단한 기초 a solid foundation / a firm basis // 단단한 가구 solidly-built[sturdy] furniture // 쇠같이 ~ as hard as iron // 단단해지다 harden / became hard // 이 집은 지반이 ~ This house stands on firm ground. // 이 감자는 아직 삶아지지 않았군, 아직도 단단하거든 This potatoes are not cooked yet, they are still hard. 단단히 hard; solidly; firmly. ¶땅을 ~ 다지다 stamp[tramp] the earth down hard // 기초를 ~ 닦다 make a solid foundation / establish a firm ground // 집을 ~ 짓다 build a house solidly.
2 〔속이 차서 야무지다〕 solid; hard. ¶단단한 재목 hard wood // 이 생선은 살이 ~ The

단당류

meat of this fish is firm. **단단히** solidly; hard.
3 [몸·뜻·생각이 강하다] strong; firm; solid; stable; steady. ¶단단한 결심 a firm resolution / a strong determination / a steady resolve // 단단한 체격의 (남자) (a man) of solid build // 요즘의 젊은이들은 아주 자유스러운데 그 만큼 마음도 단단해야 할 것이다 It requires more character to be as free as youth is today. **단단히** firmly; solidly; strongly; stably; steadily. ¶~ 결심하다 make a firm resolution / be firmly resolved [determined] // ~ 약속하다 make[give] a solemn[firm] promise // 마음을 ~ 먹다 keep up one's spirits / steel one's heart (against).
4 [느슨하지 않다] tight; compact; close. ¶단단한 매듭 a tight knot (of a rope) // 이 마개는 단단하여 뽑을 수 없다 This cork is too tight to draw[to come out]. // 선수들이 단단한 스크럼을 짰다 The players formed a tight scrum. **단단히** firmly; tightly; fast. ¶~ 매다 tie fast [firmly] / fasten tight // ~ 붙들다 cling to (a thing) / take a firm hold of / hold[hang] on fast (a thing) / 손발을 ~ 묶다 bind hand and foot tightly // 밧줄을 나무에 ~ 감다 coil a rope tightly round a tree // 남의 팔을 붕대로 ~ 감다 bind a person's arm tightly with a bandage // 문단속을 ~ 하다 fasten the doors / be very careful about locking up // 나사를 ~ 죄다 tighten (up) a screw // ~ 잡다 catch a thing firmly // 짐을 ~ 꾸리다 pack a bundle tight // 그녀는 밴드로 허리를 ~ 죄었다 She tied the band very tightly around her waist. // 나는 병에 공기가 들어가지 않도록 뚜껑을 ~ 했다 I fastened the lid tightly so that air couldn't get into the bottle.
5 [대단하다] great; extraordinary. ¶단단한 재산가 a very rich person. **단단히** greatly; severely. ¶~ 재미 보다 have great fun / have a very good time / (이득을) make a sizable profit // ~ 꾸지람을 듣다 be severely scolded.
6 [건실하다] sound; [믿을 만하다] reliable. ¶단단한 투자 a sound[solid] investment // 그는 단단한 인물이다 He is a reliable man. **단단히** reliably.
단단한 땅에 물이 괸다(속담) Only a frugal man can save money.

단당류(單糖類) [화] a monosaccharide.
단대목(單—) **1** [큰일을 앞둔] the high tide (of). **2** [중요한 고비] an important opportunity; a turning point. ¶~에 가서 포기하다 give up at a critical[crucial / decisive] moment.
단도(短刀) [짧은 칼] a short sword; [작은 칼] a knife; [단검] a dagger; a dirk; a poniard; a stiletto (pl. ~(e)s). ¶~를 품고 with a dagger in one's bosom // ~로 찌르다 stab (a person) with a dagger / give a thrust of cold steel // ~로 목을 찔러 자살하다 commit suicide by cutting one's throat with a dagger.
단도직입적(單刀直入的) point-blank; direct. ¶~인 질문 a point-blank[direct] question // ~으로 directly / point-blank / straightforwardly // ~으로 말해라 Go right to the point. / Don't beat around the bush. / Come to the point promptly.
단독(單獨) [관용어적] independent; [개개의] individual; separate; [하나만의] single; sole; single-handed; unassisted. ¶~으로 [독립적으로] independently / [개별적으로] individually / separately / [혼자서] singly / alone / by oneself / [독력으로] single-handed(ly) / ~으로 가다 go alone[by oneself] // ~으로 행동하다 act independently[by oneself / single-handed] // 각자가 ~으로 책임을 져야 한다 Each of them should individually take the responsibility.
● **단독범** a single-handed offense; a one-man crime. ¶경찰은 이 살인을 그의 ~으로 보고 있다 The police think he was acting on his own when he killed the man. **단독 비행**(—飛行) a solo flight. **단독 행동** an independent action. ¶~을 하다 act independently / take independent action. **단독 회견** an exclusive interview.

단돈 a small amount of money. ¶~ 십 원도 없다 haven't even got a ten won // 그는 ~ 만 원을 구하지 못해 쩔쩔매고 있다 He is at a loss how to raise a paltry sum of ten thousand won.
단두대(斷頭臺) a guillotine; a scaffold; a block. ¶~에 오르다 go to the guillotine / mount the scaffold.
단두대의 이슬로 사라지다 die on the scaffold [block]; be guillotined.
단둘 only two persons. ¶방엔 ~밖에 없다 There are only two persons in the room. // 그들은 ~이 남았다 The two were left alone.
단락(段落) **1** [일의 결말] settlement; conclusion; an end; a stop. ¶일에 ~을 짓다 put an end to a job // 이쯤 해 두고 ~을 짓자 Let's stop[leave off] our work here for the time being. // 이 문짝을 다 칠하고 나면 일을 ~ 짓자 When we've done[painted] this door, let's call it a day. **2** (문장의) the end of a paragraph; a full stop. ¶이 작문은 세 ~으로 되어 있다 This composition is made up of three paragraphs.
단락(短絡) (전기의) a short circuit; a short. ¶~ 시험 a short-circuit test. **단락하다** short-circuit; short; have a short circuit.
단란하다(團欒—) harmonious; happy; (서술적) sit in a happy circle; make a happy group. ¶단란한 가정의 즐거움 the pleasure of a happy home circle // 단란한 가정에서 in the bosom of one's family.
단량체(單量體) [화] a monomer. ⇨**단위체**(⇨ 단위)
단련(鍛鍊) **1** (금속을) temper; forging. **단련하다** temper; forge; anneal. ¶쇠를 ~ temper iron.
2 (심신의) training; discipline; drilling. ¶정신의 ~ the training of the mind // 유도는 심신 ~에 도움이 된다 Judo is helpful in training the body and spirit. **단련하다** train; drill; discipline. ¶심신[의지]을 ~ train[discipline / harden] one's mind and body[will] // 추위를 견디도록 몸을 ~ season[inure / harden] oneself to cold // …의 솜씨를 ~ train oneself in … / improve one's skill in … // 나는 정신을 단련하기 위해 철학 서적을 읽는다 I read books of philosophy in order to discipline my mind. ➔ **단련된** tempered / trained // 고난[전쟁]에 단련되다 be schooled by adversity[in war] // 우리 학교에서는 유도로 신입생을 단련시킨다 At our school the freshmen are disciplined through training in judo[the freshmen are given training in judo for dis-

단리(單利) simple interest. ¶~로 계산하다 calculate at simple interest.
● 단리법 the method of simple interest.
단막(單幕) one act.
● 단막극 a one-act play[drama].
단말기(端末機) [컴] a terminal.
단말마(斷末魔) one's last moments[gasp / breath]; the point[verge / hour] of death. ¶~의 고통 death agony / the agonies[throes] of death / dying struggles // ~의 고함 a death cry // ~에 이르다 be at death's door // ~의 고통으로 몸부림치다 writhe[squirm] in one's death agonies.
단맛 sweetness; a sweet flavor[(영) flavour]; a sweet taste; a sugary taste. ¶~을 내다 sweeten / make a thing sweet // ~이 나다 taste[be] sweet / have a sweet taste // ~이 들다 be sweetened // 인생의 ~ 쓴맛을 다 보다 tasted the sweets and bitters of life / go through hell and high water // 이 배는 ~이 있다 This pear is sweet // 이 과자는 ~이 강하다 This cake is very sweet.
단면(斷面) 1 [잘라 낸 면] the cut end; a section; (지층의) a profile. ¶수평 ~ a horizontal section // 종[횡] ~ a longitudinal[a cross] section. 2 [부분적인 측면]. ¶사회생활의 한 ~ a slice[phase] of social life // 한 ~을 나타내다 reveal a cross section (of).
● 단면도 a cross section; a cross-sectional view. ¶부분 ~ a cutaway view[picture] // 기계의 ~를 나타내다 show a machine in section.
단명(短命) [명이 짧음] a short life; a brief span of life; [일찍 죽음] an early death. ¶그의 ~은 과음 탓이었다 His early death was caused by heavy drinking. / He died young on account[as a consequence] of heavy drinking. // 그 내각은 ~으로 끝났다 The cabinet did not last long. 단명하다 short-lived; ephemeral. ¶단명한 잡지 a short-lived periodical // 단명한 집안 a short-lived family // 그 아이는 단명했다 The boy died young [are short-lived].
단모음(單母音) a single[simple] vowel; a monophthong. ¶~의 monophthongal // ~화 monophthongization.
단무지 pickled radish.
단문(單文) [언] a simple sentence.
단문(短文) a short sentence[composition / piece]. ¶열 단어로 된 ~ a composition of 10 words // 다음 어구들을 써서 ~을 지어라 Make[Compose] short sentences using each of the following phrases. // 그는 잡지에 가끔 ~을 발표한다 He often publishes short pieces in magazines.
단물 1 [민물] fresh water. 2 [실속 있는 부분] the cream; the best portion[part]; the lion's share. ¶~을 빨아 먹다 get all the profit (out of) / take the lion's share / skim the cream off // 결국 ~을 빤 것은 그였다 In the end, he was the one who pocket the rewards. 3 [맛이 단 물] sweet water [juice]. 4 [연수(軟水)] soft water.
단박에 at once; immediately; promptly; instantly; quickly; in a flash; in a jiffy; right off[away]; without delay. ¶일을 ~ 해치우다 finish a job at a sitting / finish up one's work in a jiffy // 그만한 일은 ~ 할 수 있다 I can do that in no time. // ~ 답장을 드릴 수 없습니다 I cannot give you an immediate answer.
단발(單發) 1 [한 발] a (single) shot; a round. ¶~에 at a shot. 2 [발동기의] a single engine.
● 단발기 a single-engined plane.
단발(斷髮) bobbed hair; a bob. ¶~머리 소녀 a bobbed-haired girl // ~ 미인 a beautiful woman with bobbed hair / a bobbed-haired belle. 단발하다 cut[bob] one's hair; have one's hair bobbed; wear bobbed hair. ¶그녀는 단발하고 있다 She wears her hair bobbed.
단방(單放) 1 (총포의) a single shot [charge]. ¶~에 맞히다 kill (a bird) at a shot [at the first fire] // 사냥감을 ~에 쓰러뜨리다 down one's quarry with a single shot. 2 just once. ⇨ ‟단번(單番)

단배 a strong[keen / sharp] appetite. ¶~를 곯리다[주리다] go hungry in spite of a good [strong] appetite / be underfed.
단백뇨(蛋白尿) albuminuria.
단백석(蛋白石) opal. ¶~의 opaline.
단백질(蛋白質) (화학의) protein; proteide; (동물·야채의) albumin. ¶~의 proteinic / albuminous / proteinaceous / proteidic // ~이 풍부한 음식물 protein-rich food / highly protein food // 동물성 [식물성] ~ animal [vegetable] protein // ~이 풍부하다 be rich in albuminous substances.
단번(單番) [단 한 번] just[only] once; once for all; [한 차례] a single stroke. ¶금번의 임금 인상은 ~의 교섭으로 결정되었다 This year's wage increase was decided in a single negotiation round[in the first round of bargaining].
단번에(單番-) at a stroke; at one coup; at one try; in a single effort; at once. ¶붓을 떼지 않고 ~ 그린 그림 a picture drawn without lifting the pen from the paper // 써내다[그리다] write[draw] in one stroke // ~ 시험에 합격하다 succeed in an examination at one's first attempt // ~ 결정하다 decide (a matter) by one effort.
단벌(單-) [유일한 것] a single one; the only one; [오직 단 한 벌] one's only suit. ¶~ 나들이옷 one's sole Sunday best // 일년 내내 ~로 지내다 keep wearing the same clothes all the year round // 그는 ~의 나들이옷을 입고 식에 참석했다 He attended the ceremony (dressed) in his sole Sunday best.
● 단벌 신사 a poor gentleman in his only suit.
단복(單複) 1 [단수와 복수] the singular and plural. ¶영어의 명사 「양」은 ~ 동형이다 The English noun sheep has the same form in both the singular and the plural. 2 [단식과 복식] singles and doubles.
단복(團服) a uniform (of an association).
단본위제(單本位制) monometallism; a single standard (system). ¶~를 채택하다 adopt a single standard.
단봇짐(單褓-) a handy bundle; a parcel in a wrapper. ¶~을 싸다 wrap up one's personal belongings in a kerchief // 그녀는 ~만 달랑 들고 서울로 올라왔다 She came up to Seoul with nothing but her personal belongings.
단봉낙타(單峯駱駝) [동] a dromedary; an Arabian[a single-hump] camel.
단분수(單分數) [수] a simple fraction.
단비 a welcome[timely / long-awaited / sea-

단비(單比) [수] simple ratio.

단비례(單比例) [수] simple proportion.

단사(丹砂) [광] cinnabar.

단산(斷産) natural cessation of childbearing. **단산하다** stop one's childbirth; pass the age of childbearing. ¶내 아내는 몸이 허약해서 40세에 단산했다 My wife has stopped her childbirth at the age of forty because she was weak.

단상(壇上) (on) the platform. ¶~에 서다[오르다] stand on[take] the platform // 의정(議政) ~에 서다 become a member of the National Assembly // 내빈은 ~에 앉아 있었다 The guests are seated on the dais [platform].

단상(斷想) fragmentary thoughts; random thoughts; stray thoughts.

단상 교류(單相交流) a single-phase current.

단색(單色) a single [solid] color [(영) hue / colour]; monochrome. ¶~의 unicolored / monochromatic // ~의 차 a monotone car / a car in a single color // ~의 흰 벽 a solid white wall / a wall painted all in white // ~으로 그리다 paint in one [a single] color.
● **단색광** monochromatic light. **단색화** a monochrome.

단서(但書) a proviso (pl. ~(e)s); a provision; a provisory [conditional / saving] clause. ¶~가 붙은 conditional // …이라는 ~를 붙여서 with [add] the proviso that … // 그의 말을 누설하지 않겠다는 ~를 붙이고 그와의 면담을 허락받았다 I was allowed to interview him with the proviso that he would not be quoted.

단서(端緒) [발단] the beginning; the start; [시초] the first step; [실마리] a clue (to); a key; a trace. ¶문제 해결의 ~ the first step toward the solution of the question / a clue for solving a problem // 범인 수사의 ~ a clue for tracking the culprit down // ~를 얻다[잡다] have [get / find / gain] a clue (to / for) / have a key (to) // ~를 놓치다 lose a (the) clue (to) // 아직 문제 해결의 ~가 발견되지 않았다 Not a clue has yet been found to solve the problem. // 그것이 ~가 되어 사건이 해결되었다 It served as the clue that led to the solution of the case. // 증거가 적어서 이 사건의 ~를 잡기 어렵다 With so little evidence, it is hard to know where to begin work on this case. // 경찰은 사건의 ~를 잡지 못하고 있다 The police don't have any clues [leads] to help them solve the case. // 지문이 범인 체포의 ~가 되었다 The fingerprints gave a clue that led to arrest of the culprit. // 저당 잡힌 시계가 경찰 수사의 ~가 되었다 The watch he had pawned put the police on the scent. // 그것이 문제 해결의 ~가 되었다 It provided a key to the solution of the problem.

단선(單線) 1 [외줄] a (single) line; (전선의) solid wire. 2 [단궤(單軌)] one [a single] track; monorail. ¶경춘선은 ~이다 The Gyeongchun [Seoul-Chuncheon] Line is single-tracked. // 사고로 인하여 그 구간은 1~으로 왕복 운행을 하고 있다 Because of an accident, the train is shuttling on single track in that section.

단선(斷線) the snapping [cutting / breaking] of a wire. ¶~으로 on account of broken wires. **단선하다** (선이) snap; be down. ➔ ¶바람으로 전화선이 단선되었다 The telephone wires are down [out] because of the wind. // 폭설로 각처에서 전선이 단선되었다 Owing to the snow wires were down in several places.

단성(單性) [생] one sex; unisexuality. ¶~의 unisexual.
● **단성 생식** [생] parthenogenesis. ⇨ **단위생식** **단성화**(-花) a diclinous flower.

단세포(單細胞) [하나의 세포] a single cell; one cell. ¶~의 unicellular.
● **단세포 동물** [식물] a unicellular animal [plant].

단세포적(單細胞的) [생각하는 것이 단순함] simple-minded. ¶~인 사고방식 one-[a single-] track way of thinking // ~인 인간 a person with a one-celled mind // 저 녀석이 생각하는 것은 ~이다 He can't see anything but what's right in front of him. / He's really simple-minded.

단소(短簫) a *danso*; a short bamboo flute. ¶~ 구멍 a stop [a finger hole] of a flute // ~를 불다 play on the flute.

단소하다(短小-) small and short; little; stunted.

단속(團束) [규제] control; regulation; a crackdown; [감독] supervision. ¶집중 ~ intensive control // ~ 기관 a regulatory agency // ~ 대상 a subject of control // 도박 [매춘] ~반 the vice squad // 마약 ~반 a narcotics squad // 보행 위반에 대한 집중 ~ an intensified police control of traffic violations by pedestrians // ~의 소홀로 책망받다 be reprimanded for lack of supervision // ~을 할 수 없게 되다 lose control over / be unable to maintain discipline among // 음주 운전에 대한 엄한 ~이 전국적으로 시작되었다 A nationwide crack down [clampdown] on drunk drivers has been launched. // 당국은 지나치게 엄중한 ~을 했다 The authorities enforced too rigid a control. // 학내 폭력에 대한 ~이 강화되었다 Regulations against violence in schools were strengthened. // 폭력단에 대한 ~을 더욱 강화해야 한다 There should be a crackdown on gangsters. **단속하다** control; regulate; manage; supervise; keep control over; keep (anything) in order. ¶엄중히 ~ exercise strict control over / control strictly // 학생을 ~ keep students under control // 풍기를 ~ watch over [control] public morals // 폭력 행위를 ~ keep control over terroristic activities // 경찰관은 여기서 교통을 단속하고 있다 Policemen are on duty here regulating the traffic.
● **단속자** a controller; a regulator; a supervisor.

단속기(斷續器) an interrupter; a rheotome.

단속적(斷續的) intermittent; snatchy; fitful; sporadic. ¶~으로 intermittently / fitfully / by snatches / at intervals / on and off [off and on] / in an off-and-on way // 토의는 아침부터 저녁까지 ~으로 계속되었다 The discussion continued from morning till night with breaks now and then. // 하루 종일 ~으로 비가 내렸다 It rained off and on all day long. // 군중들의 웅성거림이 ~으로 들려왔다 The racket made by the mob could be heard intermittently.

단손(單-) 1 [혼잣손] a lone hand; but one hand. ¶~으로 single-handed(ly) / for oneself / without help[a helping hand] // 그녀는 ~으로 집안 살림을 꾸려 갔다 Single-handed, she managed all her household chores. 2 [일격] a blow; a stroke; a hit; a poke. ¶~에 by a (single) blow / at a [one] blow // ~에 때려눕히다 knock (a person) down with a blow.

단수(段數) 1 (바둑·유도 등의) the grades; the class; the rank; the level. ¶~의 차이 difference in grade / ~가 틀리다 be not in a class (with) / stand on different levels. 2 [술수] resource; quick wit. ¶~가 센 사람 a man full of resource / a quick-witted person // ~를 부리다 exercise expedient / adopt[use] a stratagem.

단수(單數) 1 [언] the singular number. ¶~의 singular // ~와 복수 singular (number) and plural (number) // 3인칭 ~ the third person singular // 이 낱말은 ~이다 This word is in the singular. 2 [홀수] a unit.

단수(端數) ➔끝수

단수(斷水) (a) suspension of water supply. ¶시(市) 전역에 걸친 ~ the failure of water supply over the whole city. 단수하다 cut [shut] off the water supply; stop[suspend] the supply of water. ➔수도관 파열로 시 전체에 걸쳐 단수되었다 The water supply throughout the city was cut off because of a burst waterpipe.
● **단수 구역** a section from which to cut off water supply.

단순(單純) [관형어적]. 단순하다 simple; uncomplicated; plain; simple-minded [-hearted]; unsophisticated. ¶단순한 사람 a simple-minded person / 단순한 일 simple work / a simple task // 단순한 무늬 a simple pattern // 단순한 생활을 하다 lead a simple life // 그의 머리는 ~ He is simple-minded. 단순히 simply; easily. ¶그는 ~ 문인만은 아니다 He is not a mere [simple] writer. // 너는 사물을 너무 ~ 생각해 버린다 You oversimplify the matter. // 그는 외판원의 말을 ~ 믿고 말았다 He believed the salesman's story too easily.
● **단순 개념** a simple concept. **단순 재생산** simple reproduction. **단순화** simplification.

단순호치(丹脣皓齒) red lips and white teeth; [아름다운 용모] a beautiful face; [미인] a beauty.

단술 a sweet drink prepared with rice and malt.

단숨에(單-) [한 번에] at[in] a breath; in one breath; [계속하여] at[on] a stretch; in a single spell; at a heat; without a break; [한 모금에] at a draught[draft / gulp]. ¶책을 읽다 read a book at a [one] stretch[sitting] // ~ 마시다 swallow[empty the glass] at a gulp[draught] / gulp the whole thing / toss off // 술 한 병을 ~ 들이켜다 drink up a bottle of liquor at one gulp // ~ 일을 해치우다 finish one's work straight out / finish a job at a [one] sitting[(속어) ~ in one go] // ~ 언덕에 뛰어오르다 go up a hill with one rush // ~ 부산까지 비행하다 make a nonstop flight to Busan // ~ 곧장 straight to Busan // ~ 편지를 쓰다 dash off a letter // ~ 학교까지 달려가다 rush to school without stopping for breath // 그는 그 나무를 ~ 쓰러뜨렸다 He felled the tree with one bold stroke. // 그녀는 한 조끼의 맥주를 ~ 마셨다 She downed a mug of beer in one gulp.

단승식(單勝式) [경마] a winning system. ¶~으로 걸다 bet (one's money) on a horse to win.
● **단승식 마권** a beak; a win ticket.

단시(短詩) a short poem[verse]; a little verse; a verselet; a sonnet.

단시간(短時間) a short time. ¶~ 테스트 a short-time test // ~에 in a short time / in a short period[space] of time / soon // ~에 보고서를 다 쓰다 write up a report in a short time.

단시일(短時日) a short time; a short period [space] of time. ¶~에 in a short (period [space] of) time / in a day / 사회 개혁은 ~에 이루어지는 것은 아니다 Social reform will not be effected in a day.

단식(單式) 1 [단순한 방식] a simple system. 2 bookkeeping by single entry. ⇨단식 부기(⇨단식) 3 [테니스·탁구] singles. 4 a winning system. ⇨단식
● **단식 부기**(-簿記) bookkeeping by single entry; the single-entry system of bookkeeping. **단식 화산** a simple volcano.

단식(斷食) a fast; fasting; abstinence (from food). ¶7일간의 ~에 들어가다 go on a seven day fast[a fast of seven days] // ~을 중지하다 break one's fast. 단식하다 fast; observe a fast; abstain from food. ¶5일간 ~ fast (for) five days // 단식하여 수양하다 train oneself while fasting // 그는 그날 하루 단식했다 He went without food the whole of that day.
● **단식 요법** a starvation cure; a fasting treatment. **단식일** a fast day. **단식 투쟁** a hunger strike.

단신(單身) a single person. ¶~으로 (all) alone / by oneself / single-handed(ly) / without a companion / solitarily / apart from family // ~으로 상경하다 come up to Seoul all alone[unaccompanied] // ~으로 버티다 hold out single-handed // ~으로 적지에 잠입하다 penetrate single-handed into the enemy's territory // ~으로 돌격하다 make a solo assault (on) // 그는 ~으로 장사를 시작하기로 했다 He decided to start a business single-handed.

단신(短身) a short[small] stature.

단신(短信) a short letter; a (brief) note; a brief message; brief news; a short news item.

단심(丹心) a sincere heart; single-heartedness; sincerity; devotion. ¶애국 ~ sincere sentiment of patriotism.

단심제(單審制) [법] the single-trial system.

단아하다(端雅-) graceful; elegant; refined; decent. ¶용모가 단아한 사람 a man of regular features[good looks] // 옷차림이 ~ be dressed in good taste // 그녀는 머리 모양이 ~ Her hair is done elegantly.

단안(單眼) [동] a stemma. ⇨홑눈

단안(斷案) a conclusion; [결론] a conclusion; [결정] a decision. ¶~을 내리다 form[make] a conclusion / conclude that ... / 최후의 ~을 내리다 say the last word (on a subject) / give a final verdict[judgment] // ~을 내리지 않다 offer no conclusion.

단안경(單眼鏡) [한쪽 눈으로 보는 안경] a monocle; an eyeglass; an quizzing glass; [한

단애 쪽 눈으로 보는 망원경〕 a monocular telescope.

단애(斷崖) a precipice; a cliff; a bluff. ¶~ 위의 등대 a lighthouse on a bluff.

단야(短夜) 〔짧은 여름밤〕 the short nights of summer.

단어(單語) a word; a vocabulary(어휘). ¶기본 ~ basic words / a basic vocabulary // 중요 ~ most frequently used words // ~ 실력 테스트 a vocabulary test // 알고 있는 영어 ~ 수 one's English vocabulary // ~ 실력을 늘리다 build up one's word power / increase one's vocabulary // ~를 찾아보다 look up[look out] a word (in a dictionary) / ~를 많이 알고 있다 have a large[rich] vocabulary.

● **단어장** a vocabulary; a glossary. **단어집** a collection of words; a wordbook.

단언(斷言) affirmation; (positive) assertion; asseveration; a positive[definite] statement; declaration. **단언하다** affirm; assert; asseverate; declare; say[state] positively; avouch; give one's word. ¶그것이 사실임을 단언한다 I affirm[assert] it to be a fact. // 그것에 관해서는 단언할 수가 없다 I am not positive about it. // 당신은 그게 거짓말이라고 단언하겠소 Can you say for certain[sure] that it is a lie? / Can you declare positively that it is a lie?(▶ 한층 격식 차린 말투) / 그 일을 맡겠다고 단언할 필요는 없다 You need not commit yourself to the task. // 그는 그 사건과는 아무런 관계가 없다고 단언했다 He swore that he had nothing whatever to do with the case. // 그는 오늘은 날씨가 좋을 것이라고 단언했다 He assured us that it would be good weather today.

단역(端役) 〔대단치 않은 역할〕 a minor role[part]; a small part; a bit; a walk-on (part); 〔대단치 않은 역을 맡은 배우〕 an extra; a bit player; (속어) a super; a utility (man). ¶~ 여배우 an extra girl[lady] / a utility cinema[screen] actress // ~을 맡아 하다 play a small[a minor / a bit / an extra] part / walk-on // ~을 배정받다 get a walk-on.

단연(斷然―) 1 〔단호히〕 resolutely; decisively; firmly; without hesitation. ¶~ 거절하다 refuse flatly[positively] / give a flat[point-blank] // ~ 반대하다 oppose stoutly / be unalterably opposed (to) / ~답은 「노」다 The answer is a resounding "no". // ~ 금연키로 했다 I have firmly resolved to give up smoking.
2 〔확실히〕 decidedly; positively; absolutely; definitely; 〔훨씬〕 by far; far and away; by a long way; 〔부정〕 never; by no means; on no account. ¶~ 뛰어나다 show decided superiority / be a class in itself // ~ 일 등이다 be by far the best of all // ~ 아니다 Far from it! / Decidedly[Positively] no. // 나는 ~ 그에게 이긴다 I swear to beat him. // 나는 ~ 그 자리를 차지할 것이다 / I will do anything to get the position. / I will move heaven and earth to get the position. // 전체 중에서 이것이 ~ 크다 This is far and away the largest.

단열(斷熱) 〔열의 전도를 막음〕. ¶이것은 ~용이다 This is used for insulation.

● **단열 변화**〔압축 / 팽창〕 adiabatic change [compression / expansion]. **단열재** an insulating material; insulation; heat shield (material).

단엽(單葉) a simple leaf. ⇨홑잎1

● **단엽 비행기** a monoplane.

단오(端午) 〔민〕 *dano*; the festival on the fifth day of the fifth month of the year according to the lunar calendar.

단원(單元) 〔교〕 1 〔학습 단위〕 a unit. ¶교과(敎科)의 5~을 마치다 cover five units of a subject. 2 〔철〕 the monad.

단원(團員) a member (of an association[a party]); 〔집합적〕 the company. ¶청년단 ~ a member of a young men's association / ~ 일동을 대표해서 representing[on behalf of] all the members of our troupe.

단원제(單院制) the unicameral[the single chamber] system. ¶~ 의회 the unicameral legislature.

단위(單位) 1 〔기준 수치〕 a unit; (화폐의) a denomination; (유수(流水) 측정의) module. ¶기본 ~ a standard[fundamental] unit // 실용 ~ 〔물〕 a practical unit // 유도〔절대〕 ~ 〔물〕 a derived[an absolute] unit // 화폐 ~ a monetary unit // 계산[매매]의 ~ the unit of calculation[trading] // ~가 같다 be commensurable // ~는 천으로 하다 be expressed in (terms of) thousands // 너의 계산은 ~가 틀리다 You calculate on a wrong unit.
2 〔기준 수량〕 a unit. ¶가족을 사회의 (구성) ~로 보다 take the family as the unit of society // 그 회사의 주식 청약 ~는 10주다 The shares of the company are to be sold in blocks of ten. // 부부가 하나의 ~가 되어 사회 생활을 해 나간다 People lead their social lives with a husband and wife as a unit.
3 〔대학 등의 일정한 학습량〕 a unit; (미) a credit. ¶필수 ~ required credits // 영어에서 8~〔학점〕을 따다 take eight credits in English.

단위체(單位體) 〔화〕 a monomer. ¶~의 monomeric. **단위행렬**(―行列) 〔수〕 a unit matrix.

단위생식(單爲生殖) 〔생〕 parthenogenesis; unisexual reproduction; monogenesis; apomixis.

단음(短音) a short sound. ¶~ 기호 a breve / ~ short horn.

단음(單音) 1 〔최소 단위의 음〕 a single sound; a monosyllable. 2 〔음〕 monotony; a simple tone; a monotone. ¶~ 하모니카 a simple [non chromatic] harmonica.

단음(斷音) 〔언〕 a stop; 〔음〕 a staccato (pl. ~s, -ti).

단음계(短音階) 〔음〕 the minor (scale); the minor mode. ¶가락 ~ the melodic minor scale // 자연 ~ the natural minor scale // 화성 ~ the harmonic minor.

단음절어(單音節語) a monosyllable; a monosyllabic word.

단음정(短音程) 〔음〕 a minor interval.

단일(單一) singleness; unity; simplicity. ¶~ 행동 independent action // ~ 사례 a single instance // 이 물질은 ~ 성분이다 This substance consists of only one element. // 이 구(句)는 ~의 뜻을 갖고 있다 This phrase has only one meaning. **단일하다** single; singular; sole; simple; (개별적) individual; (일원적) unitary.

● **단일 국가** a unitary state. **단일 변동 환율제** the unitary fluctuation[floating] foreign exchange system. **단일화** simplification; unification; unitization. ¶정부는 여러 기구의 ~를 꾀하고 있다 The government is aiming at the unification of[wants to streamline]

단일신교(單一神教) henotheism.
단자(單子) (부조 등의) a list of gifts [presents]; (후보자 등의) a list of candidates.
단자(短資) a short-term [dated] loan; a call loan; a short loan.
● 단자 회사 a short-term financing company.
단자(端子) [전] a terminal.
단자엽(單子葉) [식] monocotyledon. ⇨ˮ외떡잎
단작(單作) [농] a single crop; single culture.
단작스럽다 mean; stingy. ⇨ˮ던적스럽다
단잠 a sweet [good / sound] sleep. ¶~이 들다 fall [drop] off into sound sleep // ~을 자다 sleep a sound sleep / have a good sleep // ~을 깨다 wake up from a sound [good] sleep.
단장(丹粧) 1 [화장] a make-up; a toilet; [옷차장] dressing. 단장하다 [화장하다] make up (one's) face; put on (one's) makeup; make one's toilet; (옷치장하다) dress [attire] oneself; dress up; pretty [smarten] up; doll oneself up. ¶잔뜩 단장한 마을 여자들 village women all decked out in their finery / (구어) village women dressed to the teeth // 곱게 단장하고 나서다 go out beautifully dressed up. 2 [장식] decoration; ornament; [채색] painting. 단장하다 [장식하다] decorate; ornament; adorn; deck (up / out); [채색하다] paint; [다시 꾸미다] refurnish; do over. ¶새로 단장한 건물 a newly finished building // (사무실을) 새로 ~ newly decorate / give a new look (to) / refurnish / remodel / furnish up // 상점가는 크리스마스를 앞두고 새로 단장했다 With Christmas just ahead, the shopping streets assumed a different appearance.
단장(短杖) (미) a cane; (영) a (walking) stick.
단장(團長) the head (of a group); the leader (of a party); a commandant; a boss; (극단의) the (proprietor and) leader of a troupe; the leading actor. ¶소년단 ~ a scout master / a chief scout // 관광단 ~ the head of a tourist party // 신 박사는 ~으로 하는 경제 사절단 an economic mission headed by Dr. Sin.
단장(斷腸) heartbreak; a lacerated heart. ¶~의 heartbreaking / heartrending // ~의 비애 heartbreaking grief // ~의 비애를 느끼다 feel one's heart rent [torn to pieces] / one's heart bleeds / feel as if one's heart were breaking // ~의 아픔을 무릅쓰고 그것을 단념했다 I gave it up through it broke my heart (to do so).
단적(端的) ¶~인 direct / straightforward / point-blank / frank / blunt // ~으로 directly / straightforwardly / point-blank / flatly / plainly / frankly // ~으로 말하면 frankly speaking / to be frank (with you) / to come to the point // ~으로 말하다 speak plainly [frankly] / talk straight // ~으로 묻다 ask (a person) point-blank // 내적 생활을 ~으로 나타내다 go full into the inner life (of) / be truly descriptive of the inner life (of).
단전(丹田) the abdomen; the hypogastric region. ¶~의 [에] under the navel // ~에 힘을 주다 strain the abdomen / put [concentrate] one's whole strength in the abdomen.
단전(斷電) [정전] power failure; [전력 공급의 중단] suspension of power supply. 단전하다 suspend power supply (to); shut [cut] off electricity.
단절(斷絕) 1 [소멸] extinction; [중단] (an) interruption; stoppage; discontinuation. 단절하다 become extinct; cease to exist; die out. ➔¶그 집안은 비참한 사건으로 단절되고 말았다 The family was wiped out in a tragic accident. // 그의 집안은 그 사람을 마지막으로 단절되겠지 He is the last of his family. / The family name will die (out) with him.
2 [관계를 끊음] severance; (a) rupture. ¶국교 ~ a severance [a rupture] of diplomatic relations / diplomatic break (with) // 세대 간의 ~ a generation gap. 단절하다 sever (the relations); cut [break] off. ¶이웃 나라와 국교를 ~ break off diplomatic relations with a neighboring country.
● 단절감 a sense of alienation; a credibility gap.
단절(斷折) cutting; severance; section; amputation. 단절하다 cut; cut off; chop; sever; amputate.
단점(短點) [결점] shortcoming; a fault; a defect; [약점] a weak point. ¶장점과 ~ merits and demerits // ~을 보완하다 [고치다] make up for [remedy] one's defects // 자기의 ~을 깨닫다 be aware [conscious] of one's own weak point // 남의 장점을 취해 자신의 ~을 고치다 correct one's own defects by following the good example of others // 소심한 게 그의 ~이다 Timidness is his weak point. // 그녀에겐 ~이 많다 She is full of shortcomings. // 그것엔 장점도 있지만 ~도 있다 It has both advantages and disadvantages [pluses and minuses].
단정(短艇) a cutter (군함의).
단정(斷定) [결론] conclusion; [결정] decision; [판단] judgment. ¶~적인 언사 a conclusive remark // ~를 내리다 form [draw] one's conclusion / make one's decision. 단정하다 conclude; decide; judge; come to a conclusion; make up one's mind (that ...). ¶성급하게 단정해서는 안 된다 We must not jump at conclusions. // 우리는 그것이 그의 소행이라고 단정할 수는 없다 We cannot conclude that it was his doing. // 그를 범인이라고 단정하기에는 아직 이르다 It is too early to conclude [jump to the conclusion] that he is the criminal. // 그녀가 안 온다고 누가 단정할 수 있나 Who can say that she will not come?
단정하다(端正-) correct; right; just; upright; decent; proper; (복장이) neat; tidy; (정조가) chaste; constant. ¶단정한 얼굴 a well-featured [well-made up] face // 품행이 단정한 사람 a man of good [irreproachable] conduct // 단정치 못한 slovenly / slatternly / loose / untidy / disorderly // 용모가 ~ have classical [neat] features // 옷차림이 ~ be properly dressed // 그녀는 몸가짐이 단정했다 She carried herself with grace and dignity. // 그는 항상 행실이 ~ He is always proper [correct] in his behavior. 단정히 upright; straight; properly; neatly; tidily; smartly. ¶~ 앉다 sit straight [upright / properly] / sit up square // ~ 하다 adjust (one's dress) / put (things) in order [trim] / set (things) in (good) order // 옷차림을 ~ 하다 adjust oneself [one's dress] / tidy oneself / (미) fix

단조 oneself.

단조(短調) [음] a minor (key). ¶~로 in a minor key // 마~의 소나타 a sonata in E minor // 다~의 교향곡 a symphony in C minor.

단조(鍛造) forging.

단조롭다(單調-) monotonous; dull; flat; humdrum; drab; (음악이) monotonic; (억양이) singsong; (일하는 방법이) simple; tactless. ¶단조로운 a dull[flat] style // 단조로운 경치 a scene lacking variety // 단조로운 설교 a monotonous sermon // 단조로운 생활을 하다 lead a monotonous[dull] life / live a humdrum[treadmill] existence // 단조로움을 깨뜨리다[덜다] break[relieve] the monotony // 그의 작품은 ~ His works lack diversity [follow one and the same pattern]. // 그는 단조롭게 이야기한다 He speaks in a monotone [in a boring manner]. // 이런 단조로운 생활에는 싫증이 났다 I'm tired of this drab life. // 그 사건은 전원생활의 단조로움을 깼다 The monotony of rural life was broken by that incident. **단조로이** monotonously; in a monotone; on[in] one key.

단종(斷種) [의] sterilization; [거세] castration.
●**단종 수술** a sterilization (operation).

단좌(單座) ¶~(식)의 single-seated (fighter).
●**단좌기** a single-seat(ed) plane; a single-seater.

단좌하다(端坐-) sit straight[upright / properly].

단죄(斷罪) [유죄의 판결] judgment of a crime; decision on a punishment; conviction; condemnation. **단죄하다** convict; condemn; punish. ¶재판관은 그를 살인범으로 단죄했다 The judge found him guilty of murder. →**단죄되다** be convicted (of a crime) / be condemned (to death) / be executed // 그는 절도죄로 단죄되었다 He was convicted[found guilty] of theft.

단주(端株) [증권] odd-lot[broken-lot] stocks; an odd lot; a fractional[broken] lot.

단주(斷酒) (total) abstinence from alcohol [wine / drink / drinking]; giving up from drinking. **단주하다** abstain from wine [liquor]; give up drinking; leave off alcohol; (미) go dry; (미국 속어) be on the wagon.

단지 a jar; a pot; a crock; an earthenware pot [jar]. ¶꿀 ~ a honey jar // ~의 아가리 the mouth of a jar // ~에 넣다 pot.

단지(團地) a (public) housing development; an apartment development[area]; a development; a housing[an apartment-house] complex; (영) a housing estate; a housing project(저소득층을 위한). ¶공무원 주택 ~ a government employees' housing area // 공업 ~ an industrial complex // 아파트 ~의 주민 dwellers in modern apartments // 아파트 ~에서의 생활 living in a development apartment house // 그들은 구릉에 택지용 ~를 조성했다 They terraced the hillside with housing lots.

단지(但只) only; merely; simply; solely; alone; just; no more than. ¶~ 1분만 있으면 in just a minute // 지금은 ~ 한 가지만을 설명하겠다 I will explain just one point now. // 이유는 ~ 그것만이 아니었다 That was not the only reason. // 그는 ~ 회화뿐만 아니라 조각에도 뛰어났다 He was distinguished not only in painting but (also) in sculpture. / He was distinguished in sculpture as well as in painting. // 그것은 ~ 소수파의 의견에 불과하다 It is merely[no more than / nothing but] the opinion of a small minority. // 그것은 ~ 여자의 허영에서 나온 것이다 It arose simply from feminine vanity. // 그는 들은 것을 ~ 반복할 뿐이었다 He only repeated[All he did was to repeat] what he had heard. // 그녀는 ~ 웃을 뿐이었다 She did nothing but laugh. // ~ 우리는 명령에 복종할 수밖에 없었다 There was nothing we could do but obey. // ~ 하라는 대로 네가 하면 된다 You have only to do as you are told.

단지증(短指症) [의] phocomelia; phokomelia. ¶~의 phocomelic.

단짝(單-) a bosom[an intimate] friend; a great[close] friend; (구어) a chum; one's pal[partner / mate / fellow]; a crony; (미국 속어) a sidekick. ¶~이 되다 become friendly (with) / make friends (with) / (구어) chum up (with) // 두 사람은 아주 ~이다 They are great[close] friends.

단창(短槍) a short spear; a javelin.

단채(單彩) ¶~의 monochromatic.
●**단채화** monochrome.

단철(鍛鐵) **1** [단련함] tempering iron. **2** (선철(銑鐵)에 대하여) malleable cast iron.

단청(丹靑) *dancheong*; a picture of many colors and designs; (a) painting. ¶~ 공사 a painting work[finish] // ~의 기술이 뛰어나다 be a good[great] painter / be good at painting. **단청하다** paint; finish with painting.

단체(單體) [화] a simple substance. ⇨"홑원소 물질

단체(團體) **1** [일단] a party; a company; a group; a body; a corps (*pl.* corps). ¶~를 구성하다[만들다] make up a party[body] // ~로 관람하다 go to (a theater) in a party[group] // ~로 신청하다 apply in a body / book (a room) for a (sightseeing) party // 30명 이상의 ~에는 운임을 할인해 준다 For a party of not less than thirty persons reduced fares are allowed. // 우리는 20명이 ~가 되어 경주 구경을 갔다 Twenty of us made up a party and went to Gyeongju for sightseeing.
2 [조직체] an organization; a corporation; a society; an association; a unit. ¶교섭[연구] ~ a negotiation[research] body // 자선[실업] ~ a charity[business] organization // ~를 조직[해산] 하다 form[dissolve] an organization // ~에 가입하다 join[become a member of] a society[an association] // ~에서 빠지다 leave[quit] a society // 그들은 정 씨를 후원하는 ~를 결성했다 They organized[formed] a society in support of Mr. Jeong.
●**단체 경기** a team sport[event / competition]. **단체 관람** a group viewing[inspection]. **단체 교섭** collective bargaining. ¶경영자 측과 ~을 하다 bargain collectively with the management. **단체 생활** a group [corporate] life. **단체 여행** traveling in a party; a group tour; [여행업자의 알선에 의한 패키지 여행] a package tour. **단체전** a team sport [event]; a team competition. **단체정신** a team spirit; esprit de corps. **단체 행동** a collective action.

단총(短銃) a short gun; [권총] a pistol; a revolver. ¶기관 ~ a submachine gun // 6연발 ~ a six-shooter / a six-chambered revolver.

단추 a button; a stud(장식의). ¶금~ (금으로 만든) a gold button / (놋쇠로 만든) a brass button // 배자[호박] ~ a vest[an amber] stud // 자개 ~ a shell button // 장식 ~ a fancy button // 커프스 ~ cuff buttons / sleeve links // ~를 채우다 fasten buttons / button (up) (one's coat) // ~를 끄르다 undo [unfasten] buttons / unbutton (a coat) // ~를 달다 put on buttons / sew buttons (on a coat) // ~가 떨어지다 a button comes off[is torn out] // ~를 떼다 take off a button // (엘리베이터의) 7층 ~를 누르다 push the button for the seventh floor // ~는 다 잠겨 있었다 All the buttons were buttoned. // 그녀의 블라우스 ~ 하나가 끌러졌다[없어졌다] One of the buttons on her blouse was unfastened.

● **단춧구멍** a buttonhole; an eye. ¶~을 내다 make a buttonhole // ~을 감치다 work buttonholes.

단축(短軸) [수] the minor axis. ⇨ 짧은지름

단축(短縮) shortening; reduction; contraction; curtailment; condensation; abridg(e)ment; abbreviation. ¶생산 ~ output reduction / a cut[cutback] in production // 조업 ~ reduction[curtailment] of operation // 노동시간의 ~을 요구하다 demand[clamor for] shorter working hours. **단축하다** shorten; reduce; contract; curtail; cut (down); condense; abridge; abbreviate. ¶거리를 200마일 ~ cut the distance by 200 miles // 시간을 ~ reduce the time (of) // 7월 10일부터 수업을 단축하여 실시한다 School hours will be shortened beginning on July 10. // 사고 발생 후 당분간 열차는 횟수를 단축하여 운행했다 For a while after the accident, the trains ran on a curtailed schedule[many of the trains had their runs canceled]. ➔¶수업 시간이 45분으로 단축되었다 The length of a class period was cut to forty five minutes. // 새로운 철도가 생겨 반도 일주 여행이 하루 단축되었다 The new railroad shortened[reduced] the time needed for a tour around the peninsula by one day.

● **단축 수업** shortened school hours.

단출하다 1 (식구가) small; simple. ¶단출한 식구 a small family // 단출한 살림 a simple household[menage] // 우리 집은 세 식구의 단출한 가정이다 I have a small family of three. 2 (일·차림새 등이) simple; handy; convenient; handy-sized; casual. ¶단출한 옷 a handy[convenient] garment // 이 짐은 단출해서 들기가 좋다 This bundle is handy and portable.

단층(單層) a single story[(영) storey]; one story. ¶~의 one-story / one-storied.

● **단층집** a one-story[-storied] house.

단층(斷層) [지] a dislocation; a fault; a throw; a shift; a jump; (의견 등의) a gap[cleavage] (between). ¶~으로 되어 있다 be faulted // ~이 생기다[생기게 하다] fault

● **단층면** a fault plane. **단층 사진** [의] (뢴트겐에 의한) a tomogram. **단층 지진** a dislocation earthquake.

단침(短針) the short[hour] hand.

단칭(單稱) ¶~의 singular.

● **단칭 명제** [논] a singular proposition.

단칸(單—) a single room; a small room.

● **단칸방** a single room; a 6-foot square room. **단칸살림** / **단칸살이** (a poor family) living in a single room; a oneroom household.

단칼에(單—) with one stroke of the sword [knife]. ¶~ 목을 베다 cut off (a person's) head with one stroke (of one's sword) // 나는 ~ 그 사나이를 죽였다 I killed the man with one stroke of my sword.

단타(單打) [야구] a single (hit); a base hit. ¶~를 치다 single / make a base hit / swat a single // 레프트 필드에 ~를 날리다 single to left field.

단타(短打) [야구] chopping. ¶~를 치다 chop (the ball).

단파(短波) a shortwave; a short wavelength. ¶초 ~ a very high frequency(약어 VHF) // ~로 송신하다 shortwave (a message) // 20미터의 ~로 방송하다 broadcast on a short wavelength of 20 meters.

● **단파 무전** a shortwave radio. **단파 방송** a shortwave broadcasting. **단파 송신기** a shortwave transmitter[sender]; a shortwave. **단파 수신** shortwave reception.

단판(單—) a single round[game]. ¶~ 씨름 a single-round *ssireum* // ~에 in a single round / at once / easily / at a breath // ~에 알아맞히다 make a good guess at once / guess right easily.

● **단판 승부** a one-game[-bout] contest decided by a single round.

단판(單瓣) [식] a single petal. ⇨ 홀꽃잎 ¶~의 a single-petaled / unilobed.

● **단판화**(—花) [식] a single flower. ⇨ 홀꽃

단팥죽(—粥) sweet red-bean soup with rice cake.

단편(短篇) a short piece; a sketch; (프) a morceau.

● **단편 소설** a short novel[story]; a novelette; a sketch. **단편 소설가** a (short) storywriter. **단편 영화** a short film; (미국 속어) shortie.

단편(斷片) a fragment; a piece; a shred; a scrap; a snippet; odds (and ends).

단편적(斷片的) fragmentary; scrappy; piecemeal. ¶~으로 in fragments / scrappily / (think) in patches // ~인 지식 fragmentary knowledge // ~인 개혁 piecemeal reforms // ~인 회화가 들렸다 Fragmentary conversation[Fragments of a conversation] could be overheard. // 그는 ~으로 이야기를 했다 He spoke disconnectedly[in fragments]. // 나는 그의 소리를 ~으로 들었다 I heard snatches of his voice.

단평(短評) a short comment[criticism]; a brief review[comment / remark]. ¶시사(時事) ~ brief comments on current events // ~을 하다 criticize briefly / comment briefly (upon) / make a brief comment (on).

단풍(丹楓) (나무) a maple (tree); (잎) red [scarlet-tinged] leaves; yellow[golden] leaves; tinted autumnal leaves; crimson foliage; (색) autumn[autumnal] tints [colors]. ¶~이 들다 turn[red / yellow / crimson] / be tinged with red // ~이 든 산들 autumn-tinted mountains / hills dressed up with red leaves // 단풍나무가 ~이 들었다 The maple leaves have turned red. // ~이 들어 온 산이 불붙는 듯하다 The hill are aflame with autumnal tints. // 설악산은 가을 ~으로 유명하다 Seoraksan(Mt. Seorak) is noted for the glorious tints of its autumn foliage.

● **단풍나무** [식] a maple (tree). **단풍놀이**

단합

maple-tree viewing; an excursion for viewing scarlet maple leaves[autumnal leaves]. ¶내장산으로 ~를 가다 go to Naejangsan(Mt. Naejang) to see the scarlet maple leaves there.

단합(團合) unity; union. ⇨단결
● 단합 대회 a rally to strengthen the unity.

단항식(單項式) [수] a monomial (expression).

단행(斷行) decisive action; resolute enforcement; [실행] carrying out; execution. **단행하다** carry out[through]; carry into effect; effect; execute; enforce. ¶계획을 ~ (resolutely) carry out a plan // 내각 개편을 ~ carry out the reshuffle of the cabinet // 그는 한번 마음먹은 일은 꼭 단행한다 He carries through anything which he has undertaken.

단행범(單行犯) [법] a single offense[(영) offence] (against the law).

단행법(單行法) [법] a special law.

단행본(單行本) a book; a separate volume; an independent volume. ¶일기를 ~으로 출판하다 publish[bring out] one's diaries in book form // 논문을 ~으로 엮다 make[compile] a book out of the articles so far published.

단호하다(斷乎-) [굳다] firm; [결연하다] determined; resolute; decisive; [과감하다] drastic. ¶단호한 거절 a flat[square / obdurate] refusal // 단호한 결의 a firm resolution // 단호한 개혁 a drastic reform // 단호한 태도를 보이다 show a stern attitude // 단호한 조처를 취하다 take a decisive[drastic] measure / take a determined[resolute] step. **단호히** firmly; resolutely; positively; squarely; conclusively; in a determined manner; with a set purpose. ¶~ 부정하다 deny flatly [positively] // 그는 가기를 ~ 거절했다 He positively[flatly] refused to go. // 우리는 개혁에 ~ 반대했다 We stood firmly against the reform. // 그는 그것이 정말이라고 ~ 말했다 He insisted that it was true. // 우리는 파업을 ~ 결행한다 We are determined to go through with the strike. / We will go on strike no matter what.

단화(短靴) (a pair of) shoes; low shoes.

닫다¹ [달리다] (사람이) run; rush; dash; dart; (말이) gallop; canter. ¶전속력으로 ~ run at full speed.

닫다² 1 (문을) shut; close. ¶문을 ~ shut [close] a door // 문을 꼭 ~ keep a door tightly shut // 쾅 ~ slam[bang] (the door) shut / shut (the door) with a bang // 수문을 ~ shut up[close] a sluice // 서랍을 ~ shut a drawer // 닫아 두다 keep (the door) shut [closed] // 문 닫고 들어오시오 Shut[Close] the door after[behind] you. // 그들은 문을 꼭 꼭 닫고 회의 중이다 They are now in conference behind closed doors. // 대문을 닫고 사람을 들여놓지 않았다 They shut the gate to people. // 사용한 후에는 뚜껑을 닫아 주시오 Put the lid back on after you have used it. // 그는 대문을 닫고 보도 관계자를 들여놓지 않았다 He closed the gate upon the reporters. 2 [폐점하다] close a shop; close the door. ¶가게를 ~ close a store(▶ 그날의 영업을 끝냄, 영업을 중지함의 양쪽에 다 씀) / put up the shutters / close up [down] the store / shut up shop // 이 근처의 상점들은 7시에 문을 닫는다 Stores close at seven around here. 3 (입을) close[shut]. ¶입을 ~ close[shut] one's mouth / hold one's tongue.

닫아걸다 fasten[bolt / latch] (a door); lock (자물쇠로). ¶문을 안으로[밖으로] ~ lock [fasten] a door from within[without].

닫치다 close up; shut up. ¶문을 쾅 ~ slam [bang] the door / shut the door with a bang.

닫히다 [닫아지다] be shut; be closed; shut; close. ¶저절로 ~ shut of itself // 대문이 닫혀 있다 The gate is shut[closed]. // 문이 잘 닫히지 않는다 The door won't shut. // 문은 자동적으로 닫힌다 The door shuts automatically. // 내가 도착했을 때 문은 이미 닫혀 있었다 When I arrived the gate was already closed. // 이 문은 제대로 닫히지 않는다 This door doesn't close properly. / This door is ill-fitting.

달¹ [지구의 위성] the moon. ¶~의 이지러짐 wane // ~의 참과 이지러짐 the waxing and waning of the moon // ~의 떠오름 moonrise / the rise of the moon // ~의 뒷면 the other [hidden / dark] side of the moon // ~이 떴다 [졌다] The moon has risen[set]. // 3명의 우주비행사가 ~ 표면에 내려섰다 [발을 디뎠다] Three astronauts touched down on the moon's surface. 2 (달력의) a month. ¶다음다음 ~ the month after next // 한 ~에 한 번 once a month // 두 ~에 한 번 every other month // 석 ~에 한 번 every three months // 매~의 수당 a monthly allowance // 한 ~에 10만 원씩 집세를 물다 pay a rent of 100,000 won per month // 내~에 지불하겠습니다 I'll pay you next month.

달도 차면 기운다(속담) Every flow has its ebb.

달(이) 차다 be in[have gone] her full time. ¶그녀는 달이 차서 여자 아기를 낳았다 Her time came and she had a baby girl. / At (full) term she gave birth to a girl.
● 달 궤도 the lunar orbit.

달가닥 with a rattle[clatter]. ¶부엌에서 ~ 소리가 났다 There was a clatter in the kitchen.

달가닥하다 clatter. ⇨달가닥거리다

달가닥거리다 clatter; rattle; crackle. ¶달가닥거리는 소리 a clatter / clattering / a clack // 바람에 문이 달가닥거린다 A window rattles in the wind. // 수레가 달가닥거리며 지나간다 A wagon is clattering along the road.

달가당 with a clang[clink / bang]. ¶문이 ~ 잠기다 A door is shut with a bang. **달가당하다** clink. ⇨달가당거리다

달가당거리다 clink; clang; rattle; tinkle. ¶달가당거리는 clinking / clangorous // 문고리가 ~ An iron door-ring is clanging.

달각 [부딪치는 소리] clunk.

달갑다 satisfactory; desirable. ¶달갑지 않은 undesirable / unacceptable / objectionable // 달갑지 않은 손님 an unwelcome visitor [guest] // 달갑지 않은 친절 an unwelcome favor // 그것은 별로 달갑지 않네 Thank you for nothing. / That is too much of a good thing. // 우리 집에 그리 달갑지 않은 손님이 들렀다 We[My family] had a guest who was not wholly welcome.

달걀 an egg. ¶~의 노른자[흰자] the yolk[the white] of an egg // 풀어 익힌 ~ scrambled eggs // 생[날] ~ a raw egg // 삶은 ~ a boiled egg // 썩은 ~ an addled[a rotten] egg // 반숙 [완숙] ~ a soft-[hard-]boiled egg // 갓 낳은 ~ a newly-laid egg // ~ 껍데기 an eggshell // ~ 모양의 egg-shaped / oval // ~을 깨다

break[open] an egg// ~을 낳다 lay an egg// ~을 부치다 fry an egg// ~을 휘젓다 beat (up)[whip] an egg// ~을 안다[품다] sit on an egg / brood// 닭에 ~을 안기다 set a hen on eggs.

달걀로 바위[백운대] 치기(속담) You can't tight city hall.; It's no use kicking against the pricks.; It's like banging one's head against a brick wall.

● **달걀말이** an eggroll. **달걀 프라이** a fried egg.

달거리 1 [열병] monthly fever. **2** menstruation; menses. ⇨ 월경(月經)

달견(達見) an excellent idea[views].

달관(達觀) a farsighted view; a philosophic view; philosophic ripeness. **달관하다** take a philosophic view of; take things like a philosopher. ¶인생을 ~ take a philosophical view of life.

달구 [땅 다지는 연장] a ram; a rammer.
● **달구질** ground leveling[(영) levelling]. ¶ ~을 하다 level the ground.

달구경 moon-viewing; enjoying[viewing] the moon.

달구다 heat; make hot. ¶벌겋게 달구어진 쇠 red-hot iron// 부젓가락을 빨갛게 ~ heat a tong red-hot// 오븐을 350도까지 ~ heat the oven to 350 degrees// 번철을 ~ heat up a frying pan.

달구지 a cart; a wagon. ¶소~ an oxcart// ~를 끌다 draw a cart// ~에 싣다 load a cart(with)// 건초를 ~로 농장까지 나르다 cart hay[carry hay in a cart] to the farm.

달그락 with a rattle[clatter]. ¶~ 소리를 내다 clatter / make a clattering sound// 상자를 들어 올리자 ~ 소리가 났다 When I lifted the box, something rattled.

달그락거리다 rattle; clatter. ¶식기를 씻는 달그락거리는 소리 the clink[clinking] of dishes being washed// 빈 깡통이 달그락거리며 굴렀다 An empty can clattered along the road.// 삶은 달걀이 냄비 속에서 달그락거리고 있었다 The eggs were bumping around in the pan as they boiled.

달그랑 [구르거나 부딪치는 소리] with a clink[clang / rattle]. ¶~ 소리가 나다 rattle / clatter// 프라이팬이 ~ 마룻바닥에 떨어졌다 A frying pan clattered to the floor.

달그랑거리다 clang; rattle; tinkle; clink. ¶풍경이 바람에 달그랑거린다 A wind-bell is clanging in the wind.

달다¹ **1** [졸아 들다] be boiled down[dry]; boil down. ¶탕약이 다 달았다 The decoction is parched up.
2 [물건이 뜨거워지다] become (red-)hot; glow(벌겋게). ¶벌겋게 단 red-hot (iron)// 벌겋게 단 숯 glowing charcoal// 벌겋게 단 부젓가락 red-hot[burnt] tongs// 쇠막대가 열로 인해 달아 있다 An iron rod glows with heat.
3 [몸이 뜨거워지다] feel hot[warm]; flush; burn. ¶흥분해서 얼굴이 ~ flush with excitement// 부끄러워서 얼굴이 ~ blush with[for] shame// 열이 있어 몸이 ~ be burning up with fever / feel feverish// 그녀의 얼굴은 불에 빨갛게 달았다 Her face was fire-flushed.
4 (마음이) be[feel] irritated (at / by / with); be fretful; fret[be in a fret] (about / at / over); [안달하다] be[feel] impatient (at / by / for / with). ¶시간이 가지 않아 애가 ~ be impatient for the time to pass / feel that time drags by too slowly// 애인이 보고 싶어 애가 ~ be dying to see one's sweetheart// 직장을 구하려고 애가 달아 돌아다니다 run about eagerly to seek employment// 그들은 결과 발표가 늦어지자 애가 달았다 They became impatient at the delay of the announcement of the results.
5 (코·입 안이) be dried up; be parched. ¶갈증으로 입 안이 ~ be parched with thirst.

달다² **1** [걸다] hang (up); suspend; put up; dangle. ¶태극기를 단 배 a steamer flying the *Taegeukgi*(Korean flag) // 기를 ~ hoist[raise] a flag// 돛을 ~ hoist[spread / put up] a sail// 간판을 ~ hang[put] up a signboard// 플래카드[문패]를 ~ put up a placard[name plate].
2 [부착시키다] fix [affix / attach / tag] (one thing to another); set[put] (one thing on another); fit (up); [연결하다] stick; fasten; join (one thing to another). ¶선반을 ~ fix[make] a shelf// 명찰을 ~ attach[affix] a name tag (to)// 브로치를 ~ put on[wear] a brooch// 머리에 리본을 ~ wear a ribbon in one's hair / decorate one's hair with a ribbon// 손잡이를 ~ put a handle (to)// 훈장을 ~ wear a decoration// 열차에 기관차를 ~ couple an engine to a train// 창문에 커튼을 ~ put up[hang] curtains at a window// 셔츠에 단추를 ~ sew a button on[to] a shirt// 동정을 ~ attach a collar to a coat// 전화를 ~ have a telephone installed// 새집에 전등을 ~ fit up a new house with electric lights// 문에 벨을 ~ fix a bell on the door.
3 [이어 달다] add (something to); [덧붙이다] annex[append] (one thing to another); [기입하다] enter (in a book). ¶단서를 ~ annex a proviso (to a deed)// 주(註)를 ~ add[annex / append] notes (to a book) / annotate// 한자에 한글로 토를 ~ show the reading of a Chinese character in *Hangeul*// 외상을 장부에 ~ enter an account[a bill] in a book// 달아 놓고 물건을 사다 buy a thing on credit// 우리는 툇마루를 이어 달아 넓혔다 We had the verandah [porch] enlarged.// 여백이 모자라면 인쇄된 용지에 종이를 이어 달아 거기에 쓰시오 If you don't have enough space, attach a piece of paper to the printed form and write on that.
4 [이름 등을 정하여 붙이다] give; attach. ¶제목을 ~ give a title (to) / entitle (a book) / attach a headline (to)// 이 책은 과장되 표제를 달았다 This book has a high-sounding title.

달다³ (무게를) weigh (a thing). ¶체중을 ~ weigh oneself (on a weighing machine) / take one's weight// 저울로 ~ weigh (a thing) in the balance[on the scales] / 달아서 팔다 sell (a thing) by weight// 설탕을 5파운드 ~ weigh out five pounds of sugar// 달걀을 저울로 ~ weigh eggs (on a scale)// 나는 저울로 몸무게를 달았다 I weighed myself on the scales.

달다⁴ **1** [달콤하다] sweet; sugary; sweet-flavored. ¶너무 단 홍차 sugary tea// 맛이 ~ have a sweet taste / taste sweet// 설탕으로 달게 하다 sweeten (coffee) with sugar// 이 과자는 너무 달아 내 입에 맞지 않는다 This cake is too sweet for me.
2 [맛있게 먹다] have a good appetite; [맛있다] nice; tasty; toothsome. ¶(음식을) 아주 달

달달 게 먹다 eat with gusto[keen relish].
3 [흡족하다] satisfactory; gratifying. ¶잠 sweet sleep//달게 자다 sleep soundly.

달달¹ **1** [휘젓는 모양] stirringly. **2** [들볶는 모양] importunately; teasingly. **3** [뒤지는 모양] every nook and corner; throughout; ransacking; rummaging. ¶서랍을 ~ 뒤지다 ransack[rummage in] drawers (for).

달달 볶다 1 (곡식을) parch (beans). ¶콩을 ~ parch[roast] beans stirring them / parch beans thoroughly. **2** (사람을) annoy (a person). ¶돈을 (더) 달라고 ~ importune [pester] (a person) for (more) money.

달달² trembling(ly). ⇨<달달¹
달달³ rumbling. ⇨<달달²
달뜨다 grow restless. ⇨<들뜨다³
달라다 〔달라고 하다〕 ask; request; beg; call upon (a person) to (do); pray for; entreat; plead for. ¶해 달라는 대로 at (a person's) request / as requested//도와 ~ ask (a person) for help / call for help//돈을 ~ ask for money//책을 빌려 ~ ask (a person) to lend a book//그는 내 누이를 달라고 말했다 He asked (for the hand of) my sister in marriage.//그에게 있어 달라고 해야겠다 I will have him stay.

달라붙다 〔밀착하다〕 stick (to); 〔서로 들러붙다〕 [stick] close together; be sticky (to); be adhesive (to); be glutinous (to); 〔끈기 있게 찰싹 붙다〕 stick [to]; 〔의존하여 매달리다〕 cling (to). ¶구두창에 껌이 달라붙어 있었다 Chewing gum got stuck to the sole of my shoe.//그의 셔츠가 상처에 달라붙어 있었다 His shirt was stuck to his wound.//해초가 바위에 달라붙어 있었다[자라 있었다] Seaweed was growing on the rock. / Seaweed clung[adhered] to the rock.//두 장의 판자가 접착제로 단단하게 달라붙어 있었다 The two boards were glued tightly together.//라벨이 노트에 달라붙어 안 떨어진다 The label stuck to the notebook and would not some off.//그 게딱지 같은 (낮은) 집은 땅에 달라붙은 것처럼 보였다 The low-built house seemed to cling to the ground.//그 아이는 엄마에게 달라붙어 있었다 The child clung[hold on] to his mother.//그는 뻔뻔스럽게 자기 지위에 달라붙어 있다 He is clinging shamelessly to his position.//우리 팀은 강적에게 끝까지 달라붙어서 싸웠다 Our team put up a good fight and kept close to formidable rivals to the end.//어려운 일에 정면으로 달라붙었다 I tackled[came to grips with] the difficult task squarely.//그는 새 분야의 개척에 달라붙고 있다 He is struggling to develop a new field. / He is engrossed in opening up a new area.//나는 밤새도록 책상에 달라붙어 있었다 I sat at my desk all night.//두 사람은 서로 찰싹 달라붙어 있다 Those two are all over each other[can't keep their hands off each other].//어린아이는 엄마에게 바싹 달라붙어 있었다 The child snuggled up to his mother.//두 부부는 바싹 달라붙어 걸었다 The couple walked along nestling close to each other.//아이들은 그에게 달라붙어 그를 보내려고 하지 않았다 The children followed him about and would not let him go.//그 무서운 목소리가 내 귀에 달라붙어 아직도 윙윙 울리고 있다 The dreadful voice still rings in my ears.

달라지다 〔변화하다〕 change; undergo a change; alter; be altered; shift; turn; vary(여러 가지로); 〔…으로 변형하다〕 change[turn] (into); be turned (into); be transformed [metamorphosed] (into). ¶마음이 ~ change one's mind//주소가 ~ have one's address changed//의견이 ~ veer round in opinion//달라지지 않다 be [remain] unchanged / be [remain] the same (as before) / be constant//세상이 달라졌다 We are now in a different world.//그의 표정은 조금도 달라지지 않았다 His expression remained (quite) unchanged.//값은 사이즈에 따라 달라집니다 The price varies according to size.//서울도 많이 달라졌다 Seoul has undergone a great change.//그 도시는 옛날과 전혀 달라져 있었다 The town is not what it used to be. / The town has changed completely since then.//건폐율은 지역에 따라 달라진다 The building-to-land ratio varies with the district.

달랑 1 〔홀로 있는 모양〕 lonely; alone. ¶혼자만 ~ 남다 be left alone / be left to oneself.
2 〔방울 소리〕 jingle; tinkle; ting.
3 〔놀라서 가슴이 울리는 모양〕. **달랑하다** feel a shock; be shocked (at / by).
4 〔경솔하게 행동하는 모양〕 frivolously; flippantly; rashly; thoughtlessly.
5 〔지닌 것이 적어 홀가분한 모양〕. **달랑하다** 〔돈이 떨어져 가〕 be about to run out. ¶호주머니가 ~ I'm short of money. / I am running out of money.
달랑거리다¹ be restless. ⇨<달랑거리다¹
달랑거리다² tinkle. ⇨<달랑거리다²
달랑달랑하다 1 be restless; tinkle. ⇨<달랑거리다¹,² **2** [돈 등이 거의 다 소비되다] be about to run out; run short[low]; get low.
달래 [식] a wild rocambole.
달래다 1 (좋은 말로) soothe; pacify; calm (down); mollify; 〔가라앉히다〕 appease; placate; comfort. ¶달래기 쉬운 appeasable / placable//달래기 어려운 inappeasable / implacable//성난 사람을 ~ soothe[calm down] an angry person//우는 아이를 ~ soothe[still] a crying child//기분을 ~ get [take] one's mind off (one's sorrow) / divert oneself (by singing)//슬픔을 술로 ~ drown one's grief[sorrows] in drink//달래어서 소동을 가라앉히다 pour oil on[upon] troubled waters//값진 선물로 그의 노여움을 달래려고 했다 I tried to appease[pacify] his anger with valuable gifts.//저런 단순한 사람들은 달래기 수월하다 Such simple people are easily placated[appeased].
2 (살살 꾀어) coax; humor; cajole; wheedle; (비위를 맞추어) fondle; nurse; try to please (a baby). ¶아이를 달래어 약을 먹이다[학교에 보내다] coax a child to take a medicine[to school]//그 아이를 달래어 자게 하였다 The child was coaxed into going to bed [sleep].//가까스로 달래어 돌려보냈다 I had great difficulty in persuading him to return home.

달러 a dollar(기호 $, $); (미국 속어) a buck. ¶1~ 은화 a one-dollar silver coin//5~ 지폐 a five-dollar bill[note] / a fiver//5~ 금화 a half eagle//10~ 지폐 a ten-dollar bill[note] //10~ 금화 an eagle//20~ 금화 a double eagle//1천~ (미국 속어) a grand//미국 ~ U.S. dollar//캐나다 ~ Canadian dollar//홍콩 ~ Hong Kong dollar//~를 많이 버는 상품 a big dollar earner[winner]//~를 벌다

earn dollars∥**~로 지불하다** pay in dollars∥**~를 방위하다** defend the dollar∥~가 1,300원으로 올랐다[내렸다] The dollar has risen [fallen] to 1,300 won.
● **달러 박스** 〔수입원〕 a money box; a cashbox; a strongbox; 〔돈을 벌게 해 주는 사람〕 a gold mine. ¶할리우드의 ~ 배우 a Hollywood box-office star∥그는 스미스 씨를 ~로 삼고 있다 He treats Mr. Smith like his gold mine. **달러 시세** the exchange rate of the dollar. **달러 지역** the dollar area.

달려가다 run [rush / dash / hasten / hurry] (to the spot); run [rush] up to (a person). ¶의사에게 ~ hasten [run] to the doctor's∥차를 몰아 현장으로 ~ rush [hasten] to the scene in a car∥시내까지 ~ take a run to downtown∥〔구령〕 Double march!∥그는 집으로 달려갔다 He ran [hurried] home.∥여러 대의 차가 우리 옆을 달려갔다 Many cars passed us. / Many cars shot past us.(▶ shoot는 재빨리, 휙)∥구조대가 조난 현장으로 달려갔다 The rescue party rushed to the scene of the disaster.

달려들다 go at; pounce upon; fly [spring] at; dart at; spring on; rush at; grapple with. ¶전원이 달려들어 with combined [concerted / united] efforts∥원숭이는 먹이에 달려들었다 The monkey jumped [snatched] at the food.∥사자는 얼룩말에게 달려들었다 The lion pounced [leaped] on the zebra.∥나는 절호의 기회에 달려들었다 I jumped [leaped] on the golden opportunity.∥돈벌이 이야기에 그는 바싹 달려들었다 When he heard of a chance to make money, he jumped at it.∥황소는 몹시 화가 나 맹렬한 기세로 내게 달려들었다 The bull came lunging [charged / rushed] at me furiously.

달려오다 come running; hasten [hurry / rush] to (a place). ¶나는 만사를 제쳐 놓고 이리로 달려왔다 I dropped everything and beat it over here.∥아이들이 달려왔다 The children came running.

달력 (-曆) a calendar; an almanac. ¶걸어 놓는 [매일 찢어 내는] ~ a wall [daily pad] calendar∥~을 넘겨 보다 consult [refer to] the calendar∥~으로는 벌써 여름이다 Officially [According to the calendar], it is already summer.

달로켓 a lunar [moon] rocket; a mooncraft; 〔탐색기〕 a moon probe. ¶~의 발사 launching of a lunar rocket / a moonshot.

달리 〔다르게〕 differently; dissimilarly; 〔갖가지로〕 variously; 〔특수하게〕 distinctively; in a different way; in some other way; 〔따로〕 apart; separately; 〔그 밖에〕 in addition; extra; additionally; besides; 〔각별히〕 particularly; in particular; specially. ¶생각했던 것과는 ~ contrary to one's expectations∥(사람을) ~ 취급하다 give [accord] (a person) special [preferential] treatment∥문장의 의미를 ~ 해석하다 construe the meaning of a sentence differently∥~ 물을 사람이 없다 haven't any other person to ask∥~ 더 효과적인 수단을 취하다 take a more effective step / adopt some other means more effective than this∥~ 할 일이 있다[없다] have something [nothing] else to do∥~ 볼일이 없으면 함께 갑시다 Please come with me, if you are not otherwise engaged.∥~ 갈 곳이 있다 I have another place to go to [visit it].∥~는 설명할 길이 없다 I can't explain it in any other way.∥~ 보면 새로운 방도가 생긴다 I see a new prospect, looking the other way.∥나의 기대와는 ~ 자금을 마련할 수가 없었다 Contrary to my expectations I could not raise the money.∥그녀는 언니와는 ~ 아름답지는 못했다 Unlike her sister she was not beautiful.∥그는 여느 때와는 ~ 일찍 일어났다 He got up unusually early.∥우리 기대와는 ~ 그는 오지 않았다 Contrary to our expectations, he did not come.∥언니와는 ~ 그녀는 몽상가였다 Unlike her sister, she was a dreamer.∥부모의 걱정과는 ~ 그는 자동차 경주에 열중하였다 Ignoring his parents' concern, he became absorbed in auto racing.∥모든 사람이 떠드는 것과는 ~ 그는 소설 읽기에 몰두하였다 Indifferent to everybody's excitement, he went right on reading his novel.

달리기 〔경주〕 a run; a race; a footrace; 〔말의〕 a gallop. ¶~에서 **이기다**[**지다**] win [lose] a race. **달리기하다** run [have] a race (with); race (with).
● **달리기 선수** a runner; a racer; a sprinter 〔단거리의〕.

달리다¹ **1** 〔열매 등이 붙어 있다〕 hang (on / from); hang down (from); dangle; be suspended (from). ¶먹음직한 사과가 나무에 달려 있었다 Juicy apples hung on the tree.∥샹들리에가 천장에 달려 있다 The chandelier is suspended from the ceiling.∥처마에 고드름이 달려 있다 Icicles hang from the eaves.
2 〔…에 의존하다〕 depend (on / upon); hang (on); turn (on); rest (with); hinge (on). ¶그건 네게 달려 있다 It's up to you.∥성패는 너의 노력에 달려 있다 Your success depends on how much effort you make.∥너의 성공 여부는 네 노력에 달렸다 Whether you succeed or not depends on your effort.∥결정하는 것은 네게 달렸다 It rests with [is up to] you to decide.∥계약의 수락 여부는 조건 여하에 달려 있다 The acceptance of the contract hinges upon what the terms are.
3 (우수리가) be tacked on (to a round sum). ¶값은 천 원에 귀가 달린다 The price is a little more than one thousand won.

달리다² **1** 〔붙어 있다〕 be attached; be fixed; be coupled; be appended [fixed / tagged]. ¶큰 거울이 달린 경대 a dressing table with a large mirror∥꼬리표가 달린 트렁크 a trunk with a tag∥책상에 다리가 ~ legs are attached to the table / the table has legs∥이 열차에는 식당차가 달려 있다 There is a dining car attached to this train.
2 〔가설되다〕 be installed; be fitted (up); be set [put] up. ¶전등이 ~ an electric lamp is fixed / be furnished [fitted up] with electric lights∥전화가 달려 있다 A telephone is installed. / The telephone service is operated.
3 〔첨가되다〕 be added [annexed / affixed / appended]. ¶주가 달린 annotated / with notes∥주(註)가 ~ be added [annexed / appended] with notes.

달리다³ **1** 〔부치다〕 be no match [equal] for; be [fall] behind; be inferior to; be not enough. ¶역량이 ~ be beyond one's capacity [power] / be too much for (one)∥실력이 ~ be poor [wanting] of ability∥영어 실력이 ~ be weak in English / be not sufficiently

grounded in English.// 힘이 ~ be not strong enough // 내 능력이 달린다는 것을 잘 알고 있다 I am well aware of my want of ability.
2 [부족하다] (사물이) be insufficient; be in short supply; (사람이) be[come / drop / fall / run] short (of); want; lack; be lacking (in). ¶일손이 ~ be shorthanded / be short of hands // 돈[식량]이 ~ be scant[short] of money[food] // 연료가 ~ run low of fuel // 자금이 달린다 I am pressed for funds. // 그들은 운동 자금이 달렸다 They lacked [were lacking in] campaign funds. // 원료가 달리기 시작하였다 Raw materials are running short. // 석탄[전력]의 공급이 달린다 The supply of coal [electric power] is getting tight.

달리다⁴ **1** [사람·동물 등이 질주하다] run; rush; dash; hurry; dart; (말이) canter(보통 구보로); gallop(전속력으로); (배가) sail; steam(증기로); glide on(매끄럽게); shoot(빨리). ¶전속력으로 ~ run[scoot / dash] at full [top] speed // 한바탕 ~ have a run // 달려 나가다 run[rush] out / run[scamper] off // 밖으로 달려 나가다 run[rush] outdoors / dash out into the street // 그는 빨리 달린다 He runs fast. / He is a fast runner. // 그들은 계단을 달려 올라[내려]갔다 They ran up[down] the stairs. // 역까지 내리 달렸다 I ran all the way to the station. // 거리를 달려서 건너면 안 된다 Don't run across the street. // 그는 학급에서 가장 빨리 달린다 He is the fastest runner in his class. // 역까지는 달려서 5분이오 It's a five-minute run to the station. // 이 배는 시간에 30노트로 달린다 This boat does 30 knots an hour.
2 [몰다] drive (a car); spur on (a horse); urge (a horse) on. ¶전속력으로 자동차를 ~ drive (a car) at top speed // 말을 달리게 하다 ride on horseback // (운동이나 연습을 위해) 말을 ~ exercise a horse // 시속 80마일로 ~ tear along at eighty miles an hour.

달리는 말에 채찍질(속담) urge on a willing person make a person redouble his efforts.

달리아 [식] a dahlia.

달리하다 [다르다] differ (from); be different (from); vary; be dissimilar (in); [차별 두다] discriminate. ¶문화의 수준을 달리하는 사람들 people on various levels of culture // 가치를 ~ be in different social station // 인생관을 ~ view things from a different angle[side] / have a different view of life // 대우를 ~ treat (a person) differently (from others) / discriminate (in favor of against) // 그들은 의견을 달리했다 They differed [were divided] in opinion. // 그들은 신앙을 달리한다 They have different faiths.

달마(達磨) [불] Dharma.

달맞이 enjoying[viewing] the moon; welcoming[viewing] the first full moon. **달맞이하다** welcome[view] the first full moon of the new year.
● **달맞이꽃** [식] an evening primrose.

달무리 the halo of the moon; a ring[circle] around the moon. ¶~가 졌다 The moon has a ring around it.

달문(達文) [세련된 문장] a clearly written composition.

달밤 a moonlight[moonlit] night. ¶~의 moonlit / moonshiny // ~에 산책하다 walk under[in] the moonlight // 우리는 ~에 바닷가를 걸었다 We walked along the beach in the moonlight. // 밝은 ~이다 It is (a) bright moonlight (night).

달변(-邊) [달로 계산하는 이자] a monthly interest.

달변(達辯) eloquence; fluency; a fluent tongue. ¶~의 eloquent / fluent.
● **달변가** a fluent speaker; an eloquent tongue; a glib talker; a good talker.

달빛 moonlight; moonshine; a moonbeam. ¶~ 비치는 under a moonlit night(「달밤」의 시적 표현) // ~ 속에서 in the moonlight // ~이 밝아 나는 그 간판을 읽을 수 있었다 The moon was bright enough for me to read the signboard.

달성(達成) achievement; attainment; accomplishment. ¶세계 평화의 ~ the achievement of world peace // 목표 ~ the attainment of one's goal. **달성하다** achieve; attain; accomplish. ¶목적을 ~ achieve [attain / accomplish] one's aim [object / objective] // 그러한 목적은 도저히 달성할 수 없다 Such a goal is unattainable. → 이리하여 그 위업은 달성되었다 That was how this great work was achieved [accomplished].

달싹거리다 move up and down; be restless. ⇨ 들썩거리다

달싹하다 turned up a little. ⇨ 들썩하다2

달아나다 **1** [빨리 내닫다] speed; scurry (away / off); run off[away]; fly off[away] (새가). run fast. ¶차는 쏜살같이 달아났다 The car sped away.
2 [도망가다] run away[off]; fly; escape(위험·체포 등에서); flee; take flight(추적 등에서). ¶도둑은 허둥지둥 달아났다 The burglar ran away helter-skelter. // 죄수가 감옥에서 달아났다 A convict has escaped from prison. // 사기범은 대만으로 달아난 것 같다 The swindler seems to have fled[(문어) absconded] to Taiwan. // 그녀는 남의눈에 띄지 않게 살며시 달아났다 She slipped [sneaked] away without being seen. // 새가 새장에서 달아났다 The bird flew out of it's cage. // 곰이 우리에서 달아났다 The bear has got(ten) out of [broken loose from] it's pen. // 그는 상점의 매상금을 갖고 달아났다 He ran away [made off /(문어) absconded] with the proceeds of the store. // 정거장에서 누군가가 내 여행 가방을 갖고 달아났다 I had my suitcase stolen at the station. / Someone walked away with my suitcase at the station.
3 [떨어져 나가다] come off[apart]. ¶저고리 단추가 달아났다 A button has come off my coat.

달아매다 **1** [처지게 잡아매다] hang (up); suspend; sling. ¶그네를 ~ put up a swing // 천장에 램프를 ~ swing a lamp from the ceiling // 해먹을 두 나무 사이에 ~ hang a hammock between two trees. **2** [붙들어 매다] bind (a person) to (a stake); tie; fasten.

달아보다 (능력을) size up; evaluate (a person's ability). ¶남을 ~ size a person up // 남의 역량을 ~ size up a person's ability.

달아오르다 **1** [물건이 뜨거워지다] become red-hot; glow; get very hot. ¶달아오른 쇠 red-hot iron. **2** [얼굴이 화끈해지다] feel hot [warm]; burn; flush. ¶빨갛게 달아오른 그녀의 얼굴 her face glowing[aglow] with red / 그녀의 얼굴은 불을 쬐어서 달아올라 있었다 Her face was fire-flushed. // 얼굴이 ~ My face is flushed. // 귀가 ~ My ears are burning.// 목욕을 한 뒤에서 온몸이 달아올랐다 My body was all in a glow[I felt warm all over] after taking bath.

달음박질 running (fast); a run. **달음박질하다** run; rush; dash; dart.

달음질 1 [뛰어 달리는 경주] a race; a running race. **달음질하다** race; run a race. 2 running ⇨ 달음박질

달이다 (간장 등을) boil down; reduce by boiling; (약제를) decoct; infuse; brew. ¶차를 ~ brew tea // 약초를 ~ boil down[brew] herbs // 약을 ~ make a medical decoction // 간장을 ~ boil soy sauce down.

달인(達人) [기예에 숙달한 사람] an expert; a (past) master; a master-hand; [인생을 달관한 사람] a master mind; a philosopher; a farsighted person; a man of wisdom.

달짝지근하다 rather sweet; sweetish; pleasantly sweet.

달창나다 1 [닳다] wear out; be worn out; [해지다] become threadbare; tatter. ¶달창난 구두 a pair of worn-out shoes. 2 [바닥나다] run out; be exhausted; be used up; be all gone. ¶휘발유가 ~ run out of gasoline.

달치다 1 [너무 달다] get too hot; be piping [steaming] hot. 2 [바싹 줄이다] boil (something) hard[dry]; condense (something) by boiling; boil down [away].

달카닥 a click; thump. ⇨ 덜커덕
달카닥거리다 clatter. ⇨ 덜커덕거리다
달카당 clattering(ly). ⇨ 덜커덩
달카당거리다 keep banging. ⇨ 덜커덩거리다
달칵 a click; thump. ⇨ 달카닥

달콤새큼하다 [달콤하고 새큼하다] sweet and sour; sour-sweet. ¶이 귤은 ~ This mandarin orange has a sour-sweet taste.

달콤하다 1 [맛이 달다] sweetish; sweet (flavo(u)red); nicely sweet. ¶달콤한 멜론 a sweet melon // 맛이 ~ taste sweet / have a sweet flavor.
2 (말이) honeyed; sugary; sweet; flattering; smooth; oily; well-oiled. ¶플루트의 달콤한 소리 the sweet tones of a flute // 달콤한 감상(感傷)saccharine sentimentality // 달콤한 연극 a sugary play / (정서에 호소하는) a sentimental[soppy] play // 달콤한 사랑 sweet love / 달콤한 말 sugared words / (알랑거리는) honeyed[fine] words / sweet talk / soft soap / flattery / (사랑을 나타내는) endearing words // 달콤한 말을 하다 say sweet things / talk mush // 달콤한 말로 속이다 deceive (a person) with sweet words // 달콤한 말에 넘어가다 be caught by (a person's) sweet talk / be soft-soaped // 그녀는 달콤한 목소리로 그를 치켜세웠다[달랬다 / 부추겼다] She coaxed him in a sugary voice[a wheedling tone].

달팽이 [동] a snail. ¶식용 ~ an edible snail // ~가 지나간 자국 a snail track // ~처럼 느릿느릿 (proceed / walk) at a snail's pace.
●**달팽이관**(-管) [생] a cochlea.

달포 about a month. ¶그가 미국에 간 지 ~나 된다 It is about a month since he went to America.

달품 [한 달 동안 파는 품] work paid for by the month.

달필(達筆) (솜씨) a ready[facile] pen; a skil(l)ful hand; (글씨) skilful penmanship. ¶저 사람은 ~이다 He writes a good hand. / He has good handwriting. // 메모는 가는 ~로 적혀 있었다 The note was written in a small, skillful hand.
●**달필가** a skilful[good / nimble] penman; a man with a ready pen.

달하다(達-) 1 (수량·정도에) reach; extend (to); cover; range (over); amount to; come (up) to; mount[run] up to. ¶지원자가 천 명에 ~ the number of applicants mounts up to one thousand // 천문학적 숫자에 ~ run into astronomical figures // 절정에 ~ come to the climax // 기준에 ~ come up to the standard // 기준에 달하지 못하다 fall short of the standard // 비용은 1억 원에 달했다 The expenses reached[amounted to] one hundred million won. // 회사의 탈세는 2억 원에 달했다 The company had evaded taxes in the amount [(구어) to the tune] of two hundred million won. // 파티에 초대된 사람은 200명에 달했다 As many as two hundred people were invited to the party. // 그 도시의 인구는 500만 명에 달했다 The population of the city reached five million. // 모금은 아직 목표액에 달하지 못했다 The amount donated still falls short of the goal. // 신제품은 대량 생산 단계에 달했다 The new commodity has reached the stage where it can be mass-produced.
2 [이루다] attain (one's object); gain [secure] (one's end); accomplish [achieve] (one's purpose). ¶목적을 ~ attain one's objective / secure one's end / achieve one's purpose.
3 [도달하다] reach; arrive at[in]; get to[at]; attain; gain. ¶목적지에 ~ reach[arrive at] one's destination.

닭 (암탉) a hen; (수탉) a cock; (미) a rooster; (병아리) a chicken; (거세한 육용) a capon; (산란용) a layer; (집합적) (영) the fowls; (미) domestic[garden] fowls. ¶알을 잘 낳는 [못 낳는] ~ a good[bad] layer // 그는 ~을 기르고 있다 He keeps chickens[fowl]. / (미) He raises chickens.
닭 소 보듯, 소 닭 보듯(속담) look at each other in silence[dumbly].
닭 쫓던 개 지붕 쳐다보듯(속담) be disappointed; be frustrated in one's attempt.
닭고기 chicken; fowl.
닭대가리 〈속〉 [어리석은 사람] a birdbrain; a bonehead; a blockhead.
닭싸움 cockfighting; a cockfight. ¶~을 시키다 fight cocks.
닭의어리 a chicken[hen] coop. ¶병아리를 ~로 덮어 두다 place[put] a coop over chickens / coop chickens.
닭의홰 a perch; a roost; a henroost. ¶~에 앉다 be on the perch.
닭장(-欌) a henhouse; (작은 것) a hencoop; (대규모 사육장) an aviary. ¶~에 넣다 house chickens[fowls].

닮다 be[look] like (another); be alike; resemble; take after (one's father); have a likeness (to); be similar (to). ¶흡사하게 ~ resemble (another)closely / bear a striking [remarkable] resemblance (to) / be quite alike // 용모가 ~ present a personal[facial] resemblance (to) // 닮은 점이 많다 have many points of likeness (to) // 다소 닮은 데가 있다 bear some resemblance (to) / have some similarities (between) // 꼭 ~ be as like as two peas / be the very image (of) / be the exact counterpart (of) // 전혀 닮은 데가

닮음 [수] resemblance; similarity. ¶~의 similar.

없다 do not bear the slightest resemblance (to) / be quite unlike [different from] (another) // 이것과 그것은 모양이 닮았다 This resembles that in shape. // 저 구름은 무엇을 닮았나 What does that cloud look like? // 이 두 잎은 서로 닮았다 These two leaves look alike. / These two leaves resemble each other. // 저 아이는 어머니를 꼭 닮았다 The girl bears a close resemblance [a striking likeness] to her mother. // 이 아기는 누구를 닮았나요 Who(m) does this baby take after? // 누이는 어머니를 닮아 손재주가 많다 My sister takes after our mother in being clever with her fingers. // 그들은 서로 성격이 닮은 데가 많다 They are much alike in character. // 그는 자기 동생과 닮은 데가 조금도 없다 I see no likeness whatever between him and his brother. // 나는 아버지보다 어머니를 많이 닮았다 I take after mother more than father.

닳다 1 [해지다] wear [be worn] out [off]; be rubbed off [down]; (옷이) wear threadbare. ¶닳은 구두 worn-out shoes // 닳은 몽당연필 a pencil stub // 닳아 빠진 붓 a worn-out brush // 전지가 닳았다 The battery went dead. // 이 천은 (오래되어도) 닳는 일이 없습니까 Does this cloth wear well? // 그런 유형의 구두는 쉽게 닳는다 Shoes of that type wear out easily [are soon worn out]. // 내 구두가 [의 창이] 닳아 버렸다 I wore out (the soles of) my shoes. // 그의 양복은 나달나달 닳아 있다 His suit is worn out [threadbare]. // 그의 구두는 뒤축이 닳아 있다 His shoes are run down [worn down] at the heels. // 걸음새가 나쁘기 때문에 구두가 언제나 한쪽만 닳는다 Because I don't walk properly, my shoes wear down unevenly. // 스웨터의 팔굽 부분이 책상에 닳아 얇아졌다 The elbow of my sweater has gotten worn out [has worn thin] from rubbing against the desk. **2** [졸아들다] be [get] boiled down [dry]. ¶국이 다 닳았다 The soup boiled away.

닳고 닳다 [세파에 때 묻다] become sophisticated; be to much a man of the world. ¶닳고 닳은 사람 a sophisticated person // 그녀는 어렸을 때부터 세파에 시달려 닳고 닳아 버렸다 She has suffered such hardships [She has had such a hard time of it] since she was a child that she has become shrewd and sly.

닳리다 1 [해뜨리다] wear away [down]; rub off [down]. ¶구두 뒤축을 ~ have the heels of one's shoes worn down / wear down the heels of one's shoes // wear down one's shoes at the heel // 연필을 ~ wear down the lead of a pencil // 지우개를 ~ rub the eraser off. **2** [졸이다] boil away [off]; boil down (the juice); boil (salt) dry. ¶국물을 ~ boil the soup away // 약을 다 ~ let herb tea boil away.

담 (벽돌 등의) a wall; [울타리] a fence. ¶돌[벽돌]~ a stone [brick] wall // ~을 두른 집 a walled-in house // ~을 넘다 climb over a wall // ~을 두르다 surround (a house) with a wall.

담 (痰) **1** phlegm. ⇨가래³ **2** [담병] congestion; engorgement. ¶~의 congestive // 가슴에 ~이 들다 suffer from the chest congestion.

담 (膽) **1** courage. ⇨담력 **2** [생] the gall. ⇨쓸개

담- (淡) ¶~홍색 pink // ~황색 lemon yellow.

-담 (談) a talk; a story; a tale. ¶성공~ a success story // 모험~ a tale of an adventure // 경험~ a narrative [story] of one's personal experience.

담갈색 (淡褐色) light brown; biscuit; ecru; tan. ¶~의 light-brown.

담결석 (膽結石) a gallstone. ⇨담석(膽石)

담그다 1 (액체 속에) soak [dip / immerse / steep] (in). ¶옷을 물에 오래 담가 두다 give the clothes a long soak // 욕조에 몸을 ~ lower oneself into a bathtub // 더러운 접시를 비눗물에 ~ soak dirty dishes in a soapy water // 그 소녀는 분수에 손을 담갔다 The girl dipped her hand(s) in the fountain. // 비눗물에 10분쯤 더러워진 옷을 담가 두었다 I let the dirty clothes soak for ten minutes in soapy water. **2** (김치 등을) prepare [make] (*gimchi*); pickle (vegetables); (소금에 절이다) salt; preserve with salt [in brine]; (술·장 등을) prepare; brew; ferment. ¶통째로 담근 무 a radish pickled whole // 김치를 많이 ~ get a large quantity of vegetables pickled into *gimchi* (kimchi) // 술을 ~ brew [make] rice wine // 젓갈을 ~ preserve fish with salt // 콩으로 간장을 담근다 Soybean is made into soy.

담금 [화] quenching; tempering; hardening; annealing. ¶~이 잘된 [덜 된] well-[not well-]tempered. **담금질하다** harden; quench; temper; anneal. ¶담금질한 것이 풀리다 lose its temper / the temper is drawn // 달군 강철은 담금질한 후 경화시킨다 We quench hot steel before hardening it.

담기다 1 (그릇에) be filled; be put in; hold; (음식이) be served [helped]; be dished up [out]; (병에) be bottled; (통에) be barreled [casked]; (상자에) be packed (in a case). ¶이 그릇은 물이 많이 담긴다 This vessel holds a lot of water. // 이 병에는 무엇이 담겨 있는가 What is in the bottle? // 이 통에는 술이 얼마나 담기느냐 How much wine can this barrel hold [keep]?

2 [포함되다] be included [comprised] in; be put into. ¶어머니의 정이 담긴 편지 a letter filled with my mother's tenderness // 진심이 담긴 감사의 말 heartfelt words of gratitude // 의미가 담긴 말 words pregnant with meaning // 가을의 정취가 담긴 요리 a dish with the flavor of autumn // 이 짧은 구에 만 가지 뜻이 담겨 있다 This brief phrase is packed with rich meanings. // 그의 말에는 진심이 담겨 있었다 He spoke from the heart. // 그의 일에는 열성이 담겨 있었다 His work was done with enthusiasm. // 그 계획에는 우리들의 온갖 아이디어가 담겨 있다 All our ideas were incorporated into the project.

담낭 (膽囊) [생] the gall bladder. ⇨쓸개
● **담낭관** the cystic duct.

담녹색 (淡綠色) light green.

담다 1 (그릇 안에 넣다) put in; fill; (음식을) serve; help; dish up [out]; (병에) bottle. ¶통에 담은 barreled / in a barrel // 반찬 ~ fill (a dish) half-full // 밥을 사발에 ~ fill a bowl with rice // 밥을 적게 ~ serve small helpings of rice // 샐러드를 모두에게 담아 주다 dish out salad to everybody // 바구니에 과일을 ~ put fruit in a basket // 냄비의 것을 공기에 ~ serve the bowls from the pot // 물을 대야에 담아라 Pour water into the basin. // 좀 더

이 담아 달라고 해라 Ask for a larger helping. **2** (사상이나 감정을) put into; incorporate (in); include; comprise; comprehend. ¶정성을 담은 선물 a gift from (a person) with his best wishes∥자기의 생각을 계획에 ∼ incorporate one's idea in the plan∥RCA는 그 오페라를 LP 2장에 담는 데 성공했다 RCA has managed to get the opera on[onto] two LP records.
3 [말로 나타내다] employ (foul language); speak (ill / foul); mouth (a bad word); say (a thing abusive); have (words of abuse) on one's lips. ¶입에 담지 못할 욕 abusive [foul / ill / scurrilous / uncivil] language∥입에 담지 못할 욕을 하다 abuse [revile] (a person) / call (a person) hard name / give a scurrilous scolding / rate (one's servant) in foul language∥그의 말은 차마 입에 담을 수가 없다 His language won't bear repeating.

담담하다(淡淡−) **1** (물이) clear; (달빛이) bright. ¶밤하늘에 달빛이 ∼ A bright moon shines in the sky. **2** (맛·색채가) plain; light; simple. ¶담담한 맛 plain[light] taste∥담담한 음식 light[plain] food∥담담한 음식을 먹다 take[have] a plain meal / use a simple diet. **3** (마음이) unconcerned; indifferent; disinterested; cool. ¶담담한 심경 a serene [tranquil] state of mind∥담담한 태도 (assume) a disinterested attitude (toward)∥지금의 심경은 담담합니다 Now I am in a serene state of mind.∥그는 명성이나 부에는 아주 담담했다 He is quite indifferent to fame and riches.

담당(擔當) charge; undertaking; one's post. ¶격리 병동 ∼ 간호사들 nurses in charge of the isolation ward∥이 지역 ∼ 판매원 the salesman who covers this district∥그 사건 ∼ 변호사(들) the lawyer(s) in charge of [handling] the case∥각자의 ∼ 부서를 지키다 stand by[stick to] one's post∥∼ 부서를 떠나면 안 된다 You must not desert[leave] your post. **담당하다** take charge (of); be in charge (of). ¶나는 회의장을 담당했다 I took charge of the arrangements for the meeting place.∥저는 이 지역의 판매를 담당하고 있습니다 I'm in charge of sales in this district.∥나는 1학년생의 영어를 담당하고 있다 I teach English to the first-year students[(미) the freshmen].∥그는 고등학교에서 역사 수업을 담당하고 있다 He teaches history in high school.∥나는 2학년을 담당하고 있다 I am in charge of the second-year class.∥그는 회계를 담당했다 He took[had] charge of the accounts. **→담당시키다** give (a person) charge of / put (a person) in charge of / assign (a person for a new task).
●**담당 검사** the prosecutor in charge. **담당 구역** (경관 등의) one's round; one's beat; (외판원의) one's territory; (배달원의) one's walk. ¶∼을 순찰하다 make one's round / (경관이) walk one's beat. **담당 기자** an assignment man. **담당 업무** the business under one's charge; one's duty. **담당자** the person in charge (of).

담대하다(膽大−) daring; bold; plucky; audacious. ¶담대한 태도[노선]를 취하라 Take a tough attitude[a bold line].∥그는 담대한 사람이다 He is a man of great courage.

담력(膽力) courage; pluck; heart; nerve; mettle; (구어) grit; (속어) guts. ¶∼ 시험 a test of a person's courage∥∼이 없다[약하다] be timid[cowardly] / be wanting in pluck∥그는 ∼이 있다 He has steady nerves. / He has guts.∥자네 ∼을 키워야 한다 You must build up your courage.∥∼을 키우려고 우리는 한 사람씩 묘지에 들어갔다 We entered the graveyard one at a time on a dare.

담론(談論) (a) discussion; argument; discourse. **담론하다** discuss; argue; discourse.

담박하다(淡泊−·澹泊−) indifferent; light. ⇨담백하다

담배 tobacco; [식] a tobacco; a cigaret(te)(궐련); a cigar(엽궐련); leaf tobacco(잎담배); cut [pipe] tobacco(살담배); chewing tobacco(씹는 담배); snuff(코담배); (구어) a smoke; (속어) a fag. ¶∼ 한 개비 a cigarette∥∼ 한 갑 a pack of cigarettes / (영) a packet of cigarettes∥사제(私製) ∼ privately manufactured cigarettes∥싸구려 ∼ a cheap cigarette / (영국 속어) a gasper∥필터가 달린 ∼ a filter(-tipped) cigarette∥한 대 ∼를 smoke [fill] of tobacco∥연기 tobacco [cigarette] smoke∥∼를 안 피우는 사람 a nonsmoker∥∼줄을 피우는 사람 a chain smoker∥∼ 연기를 내뿜다 blow smoke from one's cigarette∥∼에 취하다 smoke oneself sick∥∼에 불을 붙이다 light a cigarette∥∼를 물고 with a cigarette in one's mouth∥∼를 **피우다** smoke (tobacco / a pipe) / have [take] a smoke∥∼를 한 대 피우다 have a smoke / smoke a pipe∥∼를 많이 피우다 smoke heavily [hard]∥∼를 몇 모금 빨다 take several pulls on [from] one's cigarette∥∼를 깊이 빨아들이다 draw deeply on one's cigarette∥∼를 빠끔빠끔 피우다 puff at one's pipe[cigar / cigarette]∥∼를 **말다** roll (tobacco into) a cigarette∥∼를 **권하다** offer (a person) a smoke∥∼를 몰래 피우기 시작하다 begin sneaking smokes∥호기심으로 ∼를 시작하다 start smoking out of curiosity∥∼를 **끊다** give up [quit] smoking∥∼ 한 개비 얻을 수 있을까요. Can I bum a cigarette?∥이 ∼는 순하다 [독하다] This tobacco is mild[strong].∥나는 ∼를 피우지 않는다 I am a nonsmoker. / I don't smoke.
●**담배 가게** a cigar store; a tobacconist's (shop). **담배꽁초** a cigarette[cigar] butt [stub / end]; a half-smoked[-consumed] cigarette[cigar]; (미국 속어) a snipe. ¶∼ 줍는 사람 (미국 속어) a sniper / a snipe shooter∥∼를 발로 비비다 grind a cigarette butt under one's foot. **담배쌈지** a tobacco pouch. **담뱃갑** a cigarette case; a tobacco box. **담뱃값** money for tobacco; cigarette money; [약간의 사례금] a small amount of money as reward; a tip. ¶∼도 없다 I haven't even cigarette change. **담뱃대** a pipe; a tobacco pipe. ¶∼를 입에 물고 with a pipe in one's mouth / pipe in mouth∥∼에 불을 붙이다 light a pipe∥∼를 **털다** knock the ashes off one's pipe. **담뱃불** [담배에 붙일 불] a light for one's cigarette[pipe]; [담배에 붙은 불] the light of a cigarette[pipe]. ¶∼을 **붙이다** light (up) a cigarette∥∼을 비벼 끄다 stub out a cigarette∥∼ 좀 빌릴까요. May I trouble you for a light? / Would you give me a light for my cigarette, please? **담뱃재** cigarette ash(es); tobacco ash. ¶∼를 **털다** flick the ashes from a cigarette / knock the ashes

담백하다 off one's pipe.

담백하다(淡白-) **1** (성질이) indifferent; disinterested; candid; frank. ¶담백한 사람 a man of frank disposition // 그 사람은 담백한 성품이므로 사귀기가 수월하다 He is easy to get along with because of his frank disposition. **2** (맛·빛깔이) light; plain; simple. ¶담백한 색 a light color // 담백한 맛의 요리 a lightly seasoned dish / food without much seasoning // 그녀는 담백한 색상의 옷을 입고 있었다 She wore a dress of soft colors.

담벼락 1 (담의 표면) the surface of a wall. **2** [사물을 전혀 이해하지 못하는 사람] a man of dull apprehension; a block; a blockhead.
  담벼락하고 말하는 셈이다(속담) You might as well speak to a stone wall as talk to him.

담보(擔保) (a) security; (a) mortgage(빚의 보증으로 넣는 것); collateral(▶ 융자의 담보 물건). ¶대물 ~ impersonal security // 대인 ~ personal security // 이중 ~ a double mortgage // 제일 ~ the underlying mortgage // 빚의 ~ security for a loan // ~ 없이[무~로] without security / unsecured // 무~로 돈을 빌리다 borrow money without security [collateral] // 빚의 ~로 집을 잡다 take a house as security for a loan // ~를 잡고서 돈을 빌려 주다 lend money on mortgage // 토지를 ~로 하다 [잡히다] mortgage land / offer land as a security // 집을 ~로 돈을 빌리다 borrow money on one's house / borrow money with one's house as collateral // 그 상품들은 모두 ~로 잡혀 있다 All the goods lie [are] in pledge. // 은행은 땅을 ~로 잡고 있다 The bank holds a mortgage on the land. // 그 집은 6백만 원에 ~로 들어가 있다 The house has a mortgage of six million won on it. // 그의 집은 은행 빚의 ~로 들어가 있다 His house has been mortgaged to the bound for [against] a loan. **담보하다** [담보로 잡히다[넣다]] give [lay / put] to pledge [in security]; give [offer] as a security; put up as security; [담보로 잡다] take [receive] (a thing) as security.
  ● **담보 계약** a warranty. **담보권** a security right; a hypothec. **담보금** a security; a margin. **담보 대출** loan on [against] security. **담보물** a security; (a) collateral (security)(근저당). **담보 증서** a warranty deed.

담비 [동] a marten; a Korean sable. ¶흑~ a sable // 흰~ an ermine.

담뿍 plenty; quite a lot. ⇨듬뿍

담색(淡色) a light color [(영) colour]. ¶~의 light-colored.

담석(膽石) a gallstone; a bilestone; a biliary calculus.
  ● **담석증** a gallstones; [의] cholelithiasis.

담세(擔稅) bearing tax.
  ● **담세자** a tax-bearer; taxpayer.

담소(談笑) a chat; chatting; a familiar [friendly] talk; a confabulation. ¶회의는 ~ 속에서 진행되었다 The meeting proceeded through informal discussion [in a relaxed mood]. **담소하다** have a pleasant chat (with); chat (with); talk cheerfully (with); confabulate (with). ¶그들은 밤이 이슥하도록 담소했다 They chatted until late at night.

담수(淡水) fresh water. ⇨민물 ¶염수를 ~로 만들다 turn salt water into fresh water.
  ● **담수어** a freshwater fish. **담수호** a freshwater lake.

담쌓다 1 [담을 두르다] build [set up] a wall; surround (a place) with a wall. **2** [관계를 끊다] break with (a person); break off relations with (a person); (미) be [get] through with. ¶나는 담배와는 담쌓았다 I am through with smoking. // 그와는 담쌓은 지 이미 오래 다 I broke with him long since.

담요(毯-) a blanket; a rug.

담임(擔任) charge; [선생] a teacher in charge. ¶이 학급은 내가 ~입니다 I am in charge of this class. // 그는 새로운 선생에게 2학년 ~을 맡겼다 He placed [put] the new teacher in charge of a second-year class. **담임하다** be in charge (of); take charge (of). ¶민 선생은 지난 학년에 담임했던 반을 새 학년에도 계속 맡았다 Mr. Min is in charge of the same class as last year. // 그녀는 올해 1학년생[학급]을 담임하고 있다 She is in charge of the first graders [a first-grade class] this year. // 그는 내가 담임하는 학생이다 He is a pupil in [under] my charge.
  ● **담임교사** a class teacher; a teacher in charge (of a class); a homeroom teacher; (영) a form master [mistress] (▶ mistress는 여성). ¶그 여자분이 내가 1학년생일 때의 ~였다 She was the teacher in charge of me when I was a first grader.

담자색(淡紫色) light purple.

담쟁이덩굴 [식] an ivy. ¶~에 덮인 벽 an ivy-covered wall // 벽에 ~이 뻗어나게 하다 let ivies creep [trail] on the wall // 벽은 온통 ~로 덮여 있었다 The walls were covered (all over) with ivy.

담즙(膽汁) [생] bile. ⇨쓸개즙(⇨쓸개) ¶~의 bilious / biliary.

담차다(膽-) bold; daring; plucky; full of courage [pluck].

담청색(淡青色) light [pale] blue. ¶~의 light-[pale-] blue.

담판(談判) (a) negotiation; bargaining; a conference; a parley; talks. ¶외교 ~ diplomatic negotiations // ~ 중이다 be under negotiation // 우리는 그들과의 ~에서 실패했다 We failed in our negotiations with them. // ~이 결렬되었다 The negotiations broke down [have failed]. **담판하다** negotiate (with a person about [over / on] a thing); confer [parley] (with); have talks (with). ¶강경하게 ~ press hard / make strong [peremptory] demands // 끈질기게 ~ take a tough [an uncompromising] attitude (in negotiation) // 그와 담판한다는 것은 어려운 일이다 He is a tough customer to negotiate with. // 우리는 안마당의 사용에 대하여 관리인과 담판했다 We negotiated with the manager for the use of the yard. // 그들은 사장과 임금 인상을 담판 했다 They entered into direct negotiations with the president to demand higher wages.

담합(談合) [상담·의논] consultation(s); (a) conference. **담합하다** consult [confer] with. ¶입찰에 관해 ~ confer on the bidding // 그 일로 그들과 담합했다 We conferred with them about [on] that matter.
  ● **담합 입찰** prearranged bidding.

담홍색(淡紅色) pink; rose pink; pale rose color; salmon pink [red]. ¶~의 (rose-)pink / salmon-pink [-red].

담화(談話) [이야기] (a) talk (with); (a) conversation (with); a colloquy; [의견·태도를 밝히는 말] a statement; an informal comment.

¶노변~ a fireside chat // 특별 ~(문) (issue) a special statement // ~ 중이다 be (engaged) in conversation // ~ 형식으로 발표하다 publish in the form of an informal talk // ~를 시작하다 enter[get] into conversation (with) // ~를 나누다 talk together // ~를 계속하다 keep up a conversation. **담화하다** talk [converse] (with); have a talk[chat] (with).
● **담화체** a conversational style; a colloquial style.
담황색(淡黃色) lemon yellow; light yellow; citrine.
답(答) **1** a reply. ⇨ 대답 **2** an answer. ⇨ 회답 **3** a solution (to a problem). ⇨ 해답
답곡(畓穀) grain from the paddy fields; rice.
답농(畓農) cultivation of a paddy field; rice culture; rice farming.
-답다 like; worthy (of); becoming (to); -ly; -like. ¶남자다운 거동 manly behavior // 꽃다운 소녀 a flowerlike girl / a girl as lovely as a flower // 글다운 글 an essay worthy of the name // 신사다운 행위 gentlemanly conduct // 숙녀다운 태도로 in a ladylike manner // 사람답게 살다 live decently / live a life worthy of man[a human being] // 사람답게 행동하다 behave like a human being / act humanly // 나는 인간다운 생활을 하고 싶다 I want live a decent life. // 남자답게 결단을 내리면 어떤가 Why not make up your mind like a man. // 그것은 바로 그녀다운 방식이다 That's just like her. // 그것은 그 사람다운[사람답지 않은] 행동이었다 His behavior was in[out of] character. // 이 고장에는 극장다운 극장이 없다 There is no theater worthy of the name[to speak of / worth mentioning] in this town. // 남의 욕을 하다니 너답지 않다 It is unlike you to speak ill of another person. // 그것은 재판관답지 않은 행위이다 It is an act unworthy of[unbecoming to] a judge. // 그의 연설은 대학 교수답지 않았다 His speech was not worthy of a university professor. // 역시 그 사람~ It is really worthy of him. // 그는 시인다운 시인이다 He is a poet worthy of the name. // 이 근처는 시골~ The place bears [has] a rural character. // 제법 봄다워졌다 The weather has become very springlike. // 공원다운 공원이 없다 There is no park to speak of[worth mentioning]. // 그에게는 학자다운 데가 조금도 없다 There is nothing of the scholar about him. // 그런 짓은 숙녀답지 않다 That's quite an unlady like thing to do.
답답하다 1 (갑갑한) stuffy; close; stifling; suffocating; choking; (옷 등이) tight (coat); (가슴이) (feel) oppressed; heavy. ¶답답한 분위기 an oppressive atmosphere // 답답한 날씨 depressing[gloomy] weather // 답답한 방 a stuffy room // 답답한 느낌 a choking sensation // 답답한 가슴이 들다 feel choky[suffocating] // 가슴이 ~ feel heavy[oppressed] in the chest / feel a pressure on one's chest // 가슴 언저리가 ~ My chest feels as though something were weighing on it. // 이 방은 ~ It is stuffy in this room.
2 (사람됨이) unadaptable; hide-bound; strait [straight-]laced; (말씨 등이) drawling; clumsy; awkward; slow (going); sluggish. ¶답답한 사고방식 a narrow[rigid] view of things // 답답한 사람 an unadaptable[illiberal / intolerant] man / a man of no resources // 말을 답답하게 하다 drawl / speak with a drawl // 그런 것도 몰랐다니 너 참 답답하구나 How dull-witted you are not to have noticed such a thing!
3 (속이) (feel) impatient; irritated; irritable; anxious; restless; uneasy. ¶답답하는 듯이 impatiently / irritatedly // 답답하게 여겨지다 feel irritated[be impatient] (at a person's slowness) // 네가 하는 짓은 참 답답하구나 I get very impatient at the way you do things. // 이 도시의 우편 업무는 느려서 늘 답답할 지경이다 I am always irritated by the slow mail service in this town. / The mail service in this town is exasperatingly[irritatingly] slow. // 그는 답답한 녀석이다 He is irritatingly slow. // (상대방에게 직접 말할 때) (속이) Slow poke! // 보기에도 답답할 지경이었다 It was almost irritating to see it.
답례(答禮) [호의에 대한 인사] a return favor [(영) favour]; a gift in return; a return courtesy; a return call[salute]. ¶…의 ~로 in acknowledgment of ... / in return for ... / 전번에 받은 식사 대접에 대한 ~입니다 This is in return for the meal you treated me the other day. // 선물을 받은 ~로 책을 증정했다 I gave him a book in return for his present. // 대사가 ~로 연회를 베풀었다 The ambassador gave a return banquet. **답례하다** return a favor; (인사에) return[acknowledge / answer / repay] a salute [a call / a visit]; salute in return; salute back; (특히 국가 원수가) take the salute; (예포 등에) answer; (선물로) make (a person) a present in return; make a return present. ¶대령은 소령에게 답례했다 The colonel returned the major's salute.
● **답례품** a return present.
답방(答訪) a return visit. **답방하다** return one's visit; make a return visit.
답변(答辯) an answer; a reply; [변명] an explanation; (피고 측의) a defense; a plea. ¶…의 책임 answerability // …에 대한 ~으로 in answer to ... // ~을 잘하다 be clever in reply // 책임자에게 ~을 요구했다 We demanded an explanation from the person in charge. // 경제 정책에 관한 ~에서 총리는 통계 숫자를 늘어놓았다 In defense of his economic politics, the Prime Minister quoted a long series of statistics. // ~이 막혀 버리고 말았다 I didn't know how to answer[explain]. / I was at a loss what to tell him. **답변하다** answer; reply; make a reply; make (an answer); give on answer; (변호하다) defend[explain] oneself. ¶총리를 대신해 법무 장관이 답변하였다 The Justice Minister replied[stood up to answer] for the Prime Minister.
● **답변서** a written answer[reply / refutation]; (present) a defense(피고의).
답보(踏步) a standstill; pegging. ⇨ 제자리걸음2·3
답사(答辭) an address in reply; a (formal) reply; (미) a valedictory(졸업식의). ¶~를 읽다 read the reply / read a prepared address in reply. **답사하다** give [return] thanks; make a formal reply (to the congratulatory address); (미) deliver a valedictory(졸업식에서). ¶그는 졸업식에서 답사했다 He made an address in reply to the principal's address at graduation. / (미) He delivered the valedictory at commencement.

답사(踏査) a survey; (an) exploration; an investigation; reconnaissance. ¶현지 ~ (make) an on-the-spot survey / (make) a field investigation. **답사하다** survey; make a survey of; investigate; prospect(광산의 가망성을); explore. ¶건설 부지를 ~ make an inspection of the building site // 그들은 이 지방의 식물 상태를 실지 답사했다 They made an on-the-spot survey of the floral ecology of this area. / They made a field investigation of the plant life of this area.
● **답사대**(-隊) an exploring party.

답서(答書) an answer. ⇨ 답장

답습하다(踏襲-) follow in (a person's) footsteps; follow; follow suit. ¶전래의 전통을 ~ follow[stick to] an old tradition.

답신(答信) a reply; an answer; (전신의) a reply-telegram. **답신하다** reply to[answer] a letter; send a reply (telegram).

답안(答案) [해답] an answer; (용지) an examination paper; an answer sheet. ¶백지 ~ a blank paper // 영어 ~ a paper in English // ~을 내다 hand in one's paper // ~을 펜으로 쓰시오 Write your answers with pen and ink.

답장(答狀) an answer; a (written) reply; a reply letter. ¶~을 내지 않다 leave a letter unanswered // 나는 ~을 아직 쓰지 않았다 I haven't written an answer yet. // 그 편지에 ~이 없었다 The letter received no reply. // ~을 기다리겠습니다 I am looking forward to hearing from you.

답전(答電) a reply telegram[message / cable / telex / wire]; an answer to a telegram. ¶나는 승낙하는 ~을 쳤다 I cabled (back) my consent[agreement]. **답전하다** answer[reply to] a telegram; cable[wire / telex / telegram] back; reply by wire[telegram / cable / telex].

답지(遝至) rush; flood; influx; onrush; storming. **답지하다** come with a rush; rush in; throng[rush] to (a place); be flooded [deluged] with; come pouring in; flood; swamp. ¶신청이 ~ be flooded[deluged] with applications // 주문이 ~ have a rush [flood] of orders // 축전[항의]이 답지했다 Congratulations[complaints] came snowing in.

답파(踏破) traveling on foot. **답파하다** traverse; travel on foot; tramp. ¶한라산을 ~ travel across[traverse] Hallasan(Mt. Halla) // 전국을 ~ travel over[through] the length and breadth of the land // 그는 구릉 지대를 1주일에 걸쳐 답파했다 He spent a week tramping through the hills.

답하다(答-) answer; reply; solve. ¶답할 수 없는 질문 an unanswerable question // 편지에 ~ answer[reply to] a letter // 다음 문제에 답하라 Answer the following questions.

닷 five. ¶~ 되[말] five doe[mal].

닷새 1 [5일 간] five days. 2 the 5th day of the month. ⇨ 초닷샛날
● **닷샛날** the fifth (day) (of the month).

닷컴 a dot-com; a dot.com; a dot com; a dotcom; a .com.

당(糖) [화] saccharide. ⇨ 당류

당(黨) [정당] a party; [무리] a group. ¶공화[민주]~ (미) the Republican[Democratic] party // ~의 간부 a party officer // 중진 leaders of a party // ~의 내분 a factional strife in a party // ~의 방침 the party line // ~을 조직하다 form a party // ~에 가입하다 [탈퇴하다] join[leave] a party // ~내에 파벌을 형성하다 form factions within a party // ~을 해산하다 dissolve the party // ~을 대표[재정비]하다 represent[realign] a party.
● **당 총재** the president of the party; the party leader.

당(當) [이] this; [그] that; the said; [현재의] the present; [문제의] in question; at issue. ¶~ 열차 this train // ~ 20세 20 years old (at the time).

-당(當) per ...; (for) each; apiece. ¶1인~ per capita (라)[head] / for each person // 인구 1인~ per head of population // 톤~ per ton // 1페이지~ 낱말 수 the number of words to a page // 1마일~ 7분 seven minutes to the mile // 1일~ 2,000원 2,000 won a[per] day // 한 개~ 100원 a hundred won apiece // 비용은 1인~ 5천 원이었다 The cost come out as five thousand won a head.

당고모(堂姑母) an aunt (who is one's father's cousin).

당구(撞球) billiards; (영국 속어) pills; pool. ¶~ 치는 사람 a billiard player / a billiardist // ~를 치다 play (at) billiards / have a game of billiards // ~에서 이기다[지다] win[lose] a game of billiards.
● **당구장** a billiard room.

당국(當局) the (relevant) authorities; the competent authorities. ¶군[시]~ the military[municipal] authorities // 군 수사 ~ the Army investigation authorities // 학교[경찰] ~ school[police] authorities // 정부 ~ the Government authorities // ~ 사무 the authorities directly in charge // ~에 진정하다 complain[report] to the authorities // ~의 허가를 얻다 obtain the sanction of the authorities // ~의 발표에 의하면 According to the authorities .... / The authorities have announced that .... // ~으로부터의 시달입니다 It is an order from the government [authorities]. // 교섭은 경찰 ~의 탄압으로 중단되고 있다 Because of police suppression the negotiations have come to a standstill. // 경찰 ~의 지시에 의하여 밤 12시에 폐점합니다 We close at twelve midnight by order of the police department. // 그 무렵 노동 운동가는 ~의 주목을 받고 있었다 In those days labor agitators were on the official blacklist. // 관계 ~과 접촉해 보겠다 I will contact the authorities concerned.
● **당국자** a person in authority.

당권(黨權) party hegemony.
● **당권 싸움** a strife for party hegemony.

당규(黨規) party rules[regulations].

당근 [식] a carrot.
● **당근 즙** carrot juice.

당기(當期) the current[present] term. ¶~의 결산 the settlement of accounts for this term.
● **당기 순이익** the net profit of this term.

당기(黨紀) party discipline. ¶~를 문란케 하다 upset[disrupt] party discipline.

당기다[1] 1 [끌다] draw; pull; haul; tug; jerk. ¶턱을 ~ draw in one's chin // 밧줄을 ~ pull (on) a rope // 커튼을 ~ draw the curtains // 방아쇠를 ~ pull the trigger (at / on) / trigger (a rifle) // 소매를 ~ pull[tug] (a person) by the sleeves // 난롯가로 의자를 ~ draw a chair up to the fire // 나는 투망을 당겨

들였다 I pulled [hauled] in the cast net (into the boat).// 이윽고 줄이 당겨지는 것을 느꼈다 (낚시에서) A moment later I felt a tug on the line.// 마른 재목은 불이 빨리 당겨진다 Dry wood is quick to catch fire [catches fire easily].
2 [팽팽하게 하다] stretch (a rope) tight; strain; tighten (a rope). ¶밧줄을 팽팽히 ~ tighten [strain] a rope / stretch a rope tight // 너무 당기면 끊어진다 If you strain it too hard, it will break.
3 [기일을 줄이다] advance; move [carry] (a day) up [forward]; make earlier. ¶7시간째인 국어 시간을 3시간째로 ~ move up the Korean lesson from the seventh hour to the third // 결혼 날짜를 사흘 ~ shift the wedding date three days ahead.

당기다[2] [입맛이] stimulate [whet / provoke / arouse / tempt / appeal to] (one's appetite); (one's appetite) be stimulated. ¶입맛이 당기는 음식 an appetizing food // 입맛이 ~ have a good appetite.

당나귀(唐-) an ass; a donkey. ¶수탕나귀 a male ass / a jackass // 암탕나귀 a jenny donkey / a jennet.

당내(黨內) within the party; (intra)party. ¶~ 사정으로 for internal party reasons // 의 파벌 싸움 intraparty factionalism // ~의 의견을 통일하다 unify opinions inside [within] the party.

당년(當年) [금년] this [the current] year; [그해] that year; [왕년] those years. ¶그는 ~ 20세의 대학생이다 He is a college student, twenty years old this year. // 그녀는 ~ 25세이다 She is twenty-five years old.

당뇨(糖尿) [의] glycosuria; glucosuria.
● **당뇨병** [의] diabetes; (진성) diabetes mellitus. **당뇨병 환자** a diabetic.

당닭(唐-) **1** [동] a bantam. **2** [키가 작고 뚱뚱한 사람] a humpty-dumpty; a short fat man.

당당하다(堂堂-) **1** [번듯하다] stately; [위압하는 듯하다] imposing; [위엄 있다] dignified. ¶당당한 문장 majestic sentences // 당당한 저택 a stately mansion // 풍채가 당당한 남자 a man of majestic bearing // 보무당당한 행진 a grand parade // 그는 당당한 태도로 대답했다 He answered with a dignified attitude [an imposing air]. **당당히** grandly; splendidly; magnificently; majestically; in a dignified manner; with (great) dignity; with an imposing air; with pomp and glory. ¶~ 개선하다 return from a victorious campaign in glory // 시험에 ~ 합격하다 pass an examination with flying colors // 정문으로 ~ 들어가다 enter at the main gate in state // 그는 장관을 상대로 ~ 논진을 폈다 He set forth his argument boldly before the minister.
2 [정대하다] fair; square; open. ¶당당한 권리 a lawful [legitimate] right // 당당한 승부 fair play // 당당한 이론 a fair and square argument // 당당한 이유 a fair [good] reason. **당당히** fairly; justifiably; squarely; openly. ¶~ 얻은 점 [야구] a fairly scored run // ~ 맞서 싸워라 deal squarely (with) // 져도 괜찮으니까 ~ 싸워라 Win or lose, play fair.

당대(當代) **1** [한평생] one's lifetime. ¶그 가게는 ~로 파산해 버렸다 The shop went bankrupt after the death of its founder. **2** [이 시대] (in) the present age; [당시] those days.

¶~의 present / contemporary / of the day / of our time / of the age // ~ 굴지의 지휘자 one of the two or three best conductors of the day // ~의 미술가들 contemporary artists // ~ 제일의 미인 the reigning beauty.

당도(當到) arrival; coming. **당도하다** come (upon); arrive (at / in); get to; reach (목적지에); (기회가) offer [present] itself; occur. ¶목전에 당도한 위험 a pressing [an impending] danger // 시기가 당도했다 The time has [is] come. // 그가 맨 먼저 당도했다 He was the first to arrive. / He was the first arrival.

당도(糖度) sugar content. ¶~가 높은 [낮은] 과일 fruit with a high [low] sugar content.

당돌하다(唐突-) **1** [다부지다] staunch; bold; daring; plucky; spunky. ¶키는 작지만 그는 매우 ~ Though small in stature, he is quite a daring fellow. **2** [무례하다] rude; abrupt; blunt; forward; presumptuous. ¶당돌한 말 an unexpected remark / a remark that takes people by surprise // 그는 당돌하게 입을 열었다 He abruptly spoke up. // 당돌한 말씀이지만 그 일은 제가 해 보겠습니다 It may be presumptuous of me, but I shall try to handle the matter.

당락(當落) the result of an election; success or defeat at the polls. ¶그는 ~ 선상(線上)에 있다 He has a fifty-fifty chance of being elected. // 아직 ~이 판명되지 않은 후보가 많이 있다 There are many candidates whose success or failure in the election is not yet known. // ~은 언제 알 수 있습니까 When will the results of the election be known?

당략(黨略) the policy of a party; (a) party policy.

당론(黨論) the view [platform] of a party; a party; a party platform; a party opinion. ¶~이 …에 기울다 the platform of a party is favorable for … // ~은 정부에 찬성하는 방향으로 기울어져 있다 The platform of the party is favorable for the Government.

당류(糖類) [화] saccharide; sugar.

당리(黨利) the party interests; partisan politics. ¶~를 도모하다 promote [advance] party interests // ~당략에 치우치다 put party interests first // ~당략을 일삼다 play partisan [party] politics.

당면(唐麵) Chinese noodles.

당면(當面) [관형어적] urgent; present; pressing; immediate; impending. **당면하다** face; confront; be confronted [faced] with. ¶당면한 urgent / present / pressing / immediate / impending // 당면한 급선무 the most urgent task // 당면한 일 immediate work / work in hand // 당면한 목적을 달성하기 위하여 to serve a present object // 당면한 과제가 산적해 있다 We face [are confronted with] innumerable problems. // 당면한 문제는 한국의 경제이다 The question of the hour is Korea's economy. // 당면한 해결책으로서 500만 원을 차입하는 길밖에 없다 For the moment the only solution possible is to obtain a loan of five million won.

당목(唐木) Chinese cotton goods; cotton (cloth).

당무(黨務) party affairs [business]. ¶~를 처리하다 manage [conduct] party affairs // ~ 전반을 통할할 책임을 지다 be responsible for supervising [commanding] overall party affairs // 그 당은 원내 대책을 협의하기 위해서

당밀

~ 회의를 소집한다 The party is to call a meeting of its executive committee to discuss the party's floor strategy.
● 당무 위원 an executive member of a party.

당밀(糖蜜) theriac; (미) molasses; (미) syrup; (영) treacle.

당번(當番) [차례] being on duty; being on guard[watch]; [번 드는 사람] a person on duty. ¶청소 ~ one's turn for sweeping // 전화 ~ a person on phone duty // 밤의 ~ (those on) the night shift // ~이다 be on duty // 불[도둑] ~을 하다 watch[keep watch] against fires[thieves] // 오늘은 그가 ~이다 He is on duty today. // 그의 ~을 대신해 주고 있다 I'm doing it[doing duty] in his place. // 누가 내 ~을 대신해 주지 않겠소 Will someone take my return on duty? // 그는 ~에 들어갔다 He went on duty. // 오늘 취사 ~은 나다 It is my turn to cook today.

당부(當付) a request; an entreaty. ¶이 말씀을 전하라는 ~를 받고 왔습니다 I was told to see and tell you this. **당부하다** ask[request / solicit / tell / beg / bid] (a person) to do (something); make a request (for). ¶뒷일을 ~ ask (a person) to take care of future affairs // 한 가지 당부할 일이 있네 I have a favor to ask of you. ➔ ¶당부받다 be told to (do).

당분(糖分) (the amount of) sugar; sugar content. ¶~을 함유한 sugary / saccharated // ~을 함유한 식품 food containing sugar // ~을 삼가다 [적게 하다] cut down on one's sugar intake / [전혀 취하지 않다] do without sugar // 소변의 ~ 검사를 받다 have one's urine examined for sugar // 소변에 가끔 ~이 섞여 나오다 have sugar in the urine off and on.

당분간(當分間) for the present[time being]; for some time (to come); for a while[time]; temporarily. ¶~ 혼자서 이 일을 계속해 보겠습니다 I will continue this work by myself for the present. // ~ 그를 만나지 않겠어요 I won't be seeing him for some time[for a while]. // ~ 비가 오지 않을 것이다 We will have no rain for some time (to come). // 도서관은 ~ 휴관된다 The library is closed for the time being. // ~ 이 집에 살아도 좋습니다 You may live in this house for the time being[for now]. // ~ 이 책상을 이용하십시오 Please use this desk for the time being. // 우리는 ~ 이사하지 않기로 결정했다 We decided to give up the idea of moving for the time being[for now]. // 물가는 ~ 내려가지 않을 것이오 It will be some time before prices go down.

당비(黨費) [당의 유지 비용] party expenditure[expenses]; expenditure[expenses] of a party; [당원비] party fee.

당사(當社) [이 회사] this[our] company [firm]. ¶~의 제품 our company's products / the products of our company.

당사(黨舍) the headquarters of a party.

당사국(當事國) the countries directly concerned[involved].

당사자(當事者) the parties[person] concerned. ¶결혼 ~ the contracting parties in a marriage // 소송 ~ a party to a suit // 학교 ~ the school management // 그는 사건의 ~이다 He is directly involved in[concerned with] the affair. // ~에게 들어보았다 I will ask the person in question. / I will ask the man himself. // 우선 ~의 의향을 타진하시오 Sound him out first. // 누가 뭐라 하든 ~는 조금도 개의치 않는다 He himself doesn't care a bit what other people say.

당선(當選) 1 [선거에 뽑힘] getting[being] elected; winning an election; (의원의) (영) return. ¶무투표 ~ return without voting // ~권에 들다 be[come] within range of being returned / be in the running // ~권 밖이다 be out of the running // 그녀는 ~ 가능성이 있다[없다] She is in[out of] the running. // 그 후보자는 ~이 확실하다 The candidate has been projected to win. // 그의 ~은 무효가 되었다 His election was invalidated[(영) declared void]. **당선하다** be elected; be returned; win[carry] an election. ➔ ¶최고점으로 당선되다 be returned at the head of the poll // 백 표의 차로 당선되다 win the election by a majority of 100 votes // 그는 서대문구에서 국회의원에 당선되었다 He was elected to the Representative from Seodaemun district. (▶ 재선이면 He was returned ...으로 됨) // 그는 무경쟁[절대다수 / 무투표]으로 의장에 당선되었다 He was elected chairman unopposed[by an absolute majority / without a vote].

2 [심사에 뽑힘] winning. **당선하다** win prize; (소설 등이) be accepted. ➔ ¶그는 현상 논문에 1등으로 당선되었다 He won (the) first prize in an essay contest.

● 당선 소설 a prize winning novel. **당선자** (선거의) a successful[an elected] candidate; (심사의) a prizewinner. **당선작** a prizewinner; a prizewinning work.

당세(當世) the present time[day / age]; the day time. ¶~의 modern.

당세(黨勢) the strength[prestige] of a party; party influence. ¶~의 확장 extension of party power[the influence of a party] // 국회에 있어서의 각 당의 ~ the party lineup in the National Assembly // ~가 침체하다 The party is at a low ebb.

당수(黨首) the leader[chief / president] of a party; the party leader[head / boss].

당숙(堂叔) a male cousin of one's father. ⇨ 종숙

당시(當時) at that time; in those days; then. ¶~의 then / of those days[times] / at that time // ~의 대통령 the then President // ~를 **회상하다** recall those days // ~ 나는 어린아이였다 I was only a child then[at that time]. // ~는 차를 갖고 있는 사람이 드물었다 Few people owned cars in those days. // 그 ~로서는 그의 의견은 진보적이었다 His ideas were quite progressive for that day and age. // ~15세에 불과한 그로서는 어쩔 도리가 없었다 Being only fifteen at the time, there was nothing he could do about it. // ~ 나로서는 아무 도리가 없었다 I couldn't do anything about it then[at that time]. // ~ 나는 가난했다 I was poor then[in those days]. // 그 ~ 베풀어 주신 친절에 대해 감사히 여기고 있습니다 Thank you very much for your kindness at that time.

당신(當身) 1 [2인칭의 높임말] you. ⇨ ¹너 2 [옷어른] he; she; himself; herself. ¶이 음식은 ~께서 손수 장만하신 것이다 This food was cooked by my mother herself. 3 (부부 사이의) dear; my dear; (my) darling; (미) (당)

honey.

당연하다(當然-) rightful; proper; fair; reasonable; natural; justifiable; just; 《서술적》 be no wonder. ¶그가 그렇게 말했더면 미움을 받는 게 ~ He deserves to be disliked for having said such a thing.∥그녀가 자식들의 성공을 자랑으로 여겼던 것은 ~ She was justly proud of her children's success.∥그가 땅의 소유권을 주장하는 것은 당연한 이치이다 It stands to reason that he should claim the ownership of the land.∥그가 사과했다고 들었는데, 지극히 당연한 일이다 I hear that he apologized, which was only right.∥당신이 그렇게 말하는 것도 ~ You may well say so. / You are quite right in saying so.∥그렇게 하는 것은 주부로서 아주 당연한 일이다 It is quite natural[reasonable] for a wife to act that way.∥자네가 불평을 하는 것도 ~ Your complaint is understandable[justifiable].∥그녀가 그를 피하는 것에는 당연한 이유가 있다 She shuns him with (good) reason. / She has (a) good reason for shunning him.∥그가 화를 내는 것도 ~ It is natural for him to get angry[that he should get angry].∥너는 사직하는 것이 ~ It is only proper that you should resign (from) your post.∥당신이 화를 내는 것은 당연하오 It is natural that you should be angry. / You have good reason to be angry.∥외투도 입지 않고 추운 밖에 나갔으니 그가 감기 든 것은 당연하지 It is not surprising that he has caught a cold since he was out in the cold without a coat on.∥빚을 갚아야 한다는 것은 당연하지 뭐냐 It is only proper for you to pay your debt.∥그의 말은 아주 당연했다 What he said was most proper[reasonable].∥그가 당연한 일인 듯 나의 허락을 맡으러 왔다 He came to ask my permission as a matter of course. **당연히** justly; properly; naturally; necessarily; deservedly; rightfully; of course; as a matter of course. ¶~ 여기다 take (a thing) as a matter of course / take (a matter) for granted (that)∥~ 받아야 할 것을 받다 get [have] one's due[deserts]∥그는 ~ 해고되었다 He was dismissed as a matter of course. / It's only natural that he was fired. / Of course he was fired.∥그는 ~ 우리에게 전화를 걸어야 한다 He ought to have called us.

당원(黨員) a member of a party; a party man [number]; a partisan. ¶~이 되다 join a party / affiliate oneself with[to] a party.
●**당원 명부** a list of the party members.

당월(當月) 〔이달〕 this[the current] month; 〔그달〕 that month; the said month.

당위(當爲) 〔철〕 what should be; what one should do.

당의(黨議) 〔당의 강령〕 a party policy[principle]; 〔당의 회의〕 a party council; 〔당의 결의〕 a party decision. ¶~에 따르다 abide by the party decision.

당의정(糖衣錠) a sugar-coated pill[tablet].

당일(當日) the day; that day; the appointed day; the day in question; the date named. ¶〔연구 등의〕 ~ 판매하는 표 a ticket sold on the day of performance∥~ 우천 시에는 If it should[In case of] rain on that day ….∥그녀는 결혼식 ~ 병이 났다 She become ill on the very day of her wedding.∥~ 면접에 빠진 사람은 실격이다 Those who do not come for interviews on the appointed day will be disqualified.∥대매출은 ~로 끝났다 The special sale is limited to this[that] one day. / The special sale is on that day only.∥이 차표의 통용은 ~ 뿐입니다 This ticket is valid only for the designated day.
●**당일치기** ¶속리산은 ~가 가능합니다 You can get to Songnisan(Mt. Songni) and back in a day.∥나는 서울에 ~ 출장을 갔다 I came to[am in] Seoul on a day's business trip.

당자(當者) the concerned party; the person concerned[involved / in question]. ¶~들이 하는 대로 내버려 두게 Let them have their own way.

당장(當場) **1** 〔현재〕 the present; the time being; 〔그때〕 that time. ¶지금 ~(은) for the present / for the time being / at present∥~을 모면하기 위해서 얼버무리다 make a temporary excuse∥~에 필요한 돈은 이것으로 족하다 This will take care of[cover] our immediate expenses[our expenses for the moment].
2 〔그 자리에서 즉시〕 on the spot[instant]; in no time; now and here; at once; right away; immediately; promptly; directly. ¶~해야 할 일 business[work] in hand∥나가라 Get out at once!∥~ 자백하라 Own up at once.∥그가 다정히 말을 걸자 그녀는 ~ 돈을 졸라 댔다 When he spoke to her kindly she lost no time in trying to wheedle money out of him.∥그의 말꼬리를 잡고 ~ 질문했다 I jumped on what he said and put a sharp [pointed] question to him.

당쟁(黨爭) interparty strife; faction. ¶~을 일삼다 be given to party squabbles.

당적(黨籍) a party register. ¶공화당에 ~을 둔 사람 a registered Republican∥~을 옮기다 come [go] over to another party∥~을 이탈하다 leave [(문어) disaffiliate oneself from] one's party / give up one's party membership∥그는 ~을 박탈당했다 He was expelled from the party.

당좌(當座) a current account. ⇨~당좌 예금(⇨ 당좌) ¶~를 트다 open a current account with a bank / 〔미〕 open a banking[bank] account∥~에 예금하다 deposit (one's money) on current account.
●**당좌 계정** a current account(약어 a/c). **당좌 대월** (an) overdraft; an overdrawn account. **당좌 대출금** a call loan. **당좌 수표** 〔미〕 a check; 〔영〕 a cheque. **당좌 예금** a current account; 〔미〕 a checking account.

당직(當直) duty; (감시·야경 등의) watch. ¶~을 교대하다 relieve the watch. **당직하다** be on duty[watch] (▶duty는 근무에 임하고 있음, watch는 선원 등이 감시를 하는 것). ¶어젯밤에 당직했다 I was on duty[watch] last night.
●**당직 수당** night duty pay. **당직실** a night duty room. **당직 의사**[간호사] a doctor [nurse] on (night) duty.

당직(黨職) a party post.
●**당직 개편** reorganization of a party's hierarchy; the shake-up of party officials. **당직자** a party executive; an executive staff member of a party; (집합적) the party leadership.

당질(堂姪) a male cousin's son. ⇨=종질(從姪)
당질(糖質) glucide. ¶~의 glucidic.
당질녀(堂姪女) a male cousin's daughter. ⇨=종질녀

당착(撞着) (a) contradiction; (an) inconsistency; a clash; a conflict. ¶자가~ self-contradiction / intellectual suicide∥전후 ~의 이론 an inconsistent theory. **당착하다** be contradictory (to); be inconsistent (with); conflict[collide] (with); be in conflict (with); clash with.

당찮다(當-) [불합리하다] absurd; unreasonable; preposterous; [부당하다] undeserved; unfair; unjust; improper; undue; unjustifiable; un merited. ¶당찮은 생각[말] an absurd[a preposterous] idea[remark] ∥당찮은 요구 an unjustified[unlawful] demand∥당찮은 욕망 an inordinate desire / a wild ambition∥당찮은 처사 unfair measure∥교사로서 당찮은 행동 conduct unworthy of [unbecoming to] a teacher∥당찮은 요구를 하다 make an exorbitant [outrageous] demand∥당찮은 소리 (Stuff and) nonsense! / How absurd! / Don't talk such nonsense. ∥그것은 당찮은 소리다 That's absurd.

당첨(當籤) prize winning; drawing a prize; a prize lot. ¶그는 ~ 운이 있는[없는] 사람이다 He is always lucky[unlucky] in lotteries. **당첨되다** win a prize; draw a winning[lucky] number. ¶당첨된 복권[번호] a winning ticket[number] (in a lottery)∥복권에 당첨되었다 I drew a prize[a winning number].∥1등[100만 원]에 당첨되었다 I won (the) first prize[a million won] in a lottery.∥내가 당첨되었다 The lot fell upon me.∥하와이 여행 추첨에 당첨되었다 I drew a lucky number and won a free trip to Hawaii.∥야아, 당첨되었다 Wow! I won the raffle!
● **당첨 번호** winning[lucky] numbers. **당첨자** a prizewinner; the drawer of the lucky number.

당초(當初) the beginning; the outset; the start. ¶~에는 at first / at the beginning∥~부터 from the first∥~의 계획 one's[the] original plan[intention]∥~의 목표를 달성하지 못했다 We could not achieve our original goal.∥~에 내가 그랬잖아나 Don't you remember I said so at the very beginning?

당칙(黨則) party rules. ⇨**당규**(黨規)

당파(黨派) [붕당(朋黨)] a party; a faction; a junto; [과당] a clique; a league. ¶초~ 외교 supra-party diplomacy∥~적인 party[factious-]spirited / factious / factional∥~색이 없는 nonpartisan (paper) / independent∥~에 속하다 belong to a party[faction] ∥~를 만들다 establish [found] a party / form a clique[faction]∥두 ~로 나뉘다 split into two factions.

당하다(當-) **1** [겪다·만나다] have; encounter; experience; come; arrive; happen; confront; come upon[across]. ¶불행을 ~ suffer [meet with] a misfortune / experience [encounter] a disaster∥상을 ~ have a death in the family / have a sad bereavement in one's family∥모욕을 ~ suffer an insult[affront / indignity] / be insulted∥참패를 ~ suffer an ignominious defeat∥비명의 죽음을 ~ die an untimely death.
2 [맞서다] match[equal / rival] (a person); be a match for; compare with; stand (against / up to); cope with; keep up with (a person). ¶당할 수 없다 be no match for∥그의 독설에는 당해 낼 사람이 없다 No one can stand up to his scathing tongue.∥너에게는 당할 수가 없다 I am no match for you. / I cannot come near you.∥달리기에서는 그를 당할 자가 없다 He has no equal for running.∥이 난국을 당해 내기에는 그는 너무 심약하다 He is too weak-minded to stand up to this difficult situation.∥이렇게 많은 적에게는 당할 재간이 없다 There is no contending against such a heavy odds.∥빈틈이 없는 점에서 그를 당할 사람은 없었다 No one could match him in shrewdness.∥계산에서는 너에게 못 당한다 I am no match for you in calculation.∥햄릿이라면 그를 낭할 사람이 없다 He is unrivaled as Hamlet.∥또 당하겠다는 것을 알자 그들은 도망쳤다 Seeing that the odds were against them, they ran away.
3 [속다] be deceived[cheated / taken in]; [얻어맞다] be struck; receive a blow. ¶감쪽같이 당했다 I was fairly caught. / I was fooled. / I was taken in.∥어른은 때로 아이들에게 꼼짝없이 당하는 경우가 있다 Grownups are crushed by children sometimes.∥나는 그의 꾀에 꼼짝없이 당하여 기가 죽었다 As he had outwitted me, I felt deflated.
4 [사리에 맞다] reasonable; rational; sensible; natural; right. ¶당치도 않은 말을 하다 talk nonsense.

-당하다(當-) ¶거절~ be refused / get turned down∥섬멸~ be annihilated∥구타~ be struck / get licked / receive a blow∥공격~ be attacked∥저격~ be shot (in the head)∥도난~ be stolen / have (a thing) stolen / be robbed (of a thing).

당해(當該) [관형어적] concerned; competent. (▶ competent는 관공서·법원 등에서 쓰고, 관할권이 있음을 의미한다. concerned는 일반적으로 「관계가 있는」을 뜻하는데 명사 뒤에 씀) ¶교통 법규의 ~ 사항을 참조하시오 Refer to the relevant clauses of the traffic regulations.
● **당해 관청** the authorities concerned; the competent[proper] authorities.

당헌(黨憲) the party's constitution.

당혹(當惑) [곤혹(困惑)] perplexity; puzzlement; embarrassment; [진퇴양난] dilemma; [혼란] confusion. **당혹하다** be perplexed [embarrassed / puzzled / baffled / bewildered / nonplussed]; be at one's wit's[wits'] end. ¶나는 어쩌면 좋을지 당혹했다 I was puzzled (over) [at a loss] what to do.

당황하다(唐慌-·唐惶-·惝恍-) be perplexed; be puzzled; be bewildered; be nonplussed(▶ bewildered는 처음의 두 단어보다 뜻이 강함. nonplussed는 뜻밖의 일에 어쩔 바를 모르다); be confused; (문어) be embarrassed; (문어) be discomfited; be flustered; be disconcerted; be flurried; lose one's presence of mind; panic; be upset; (문어) be perturbed; lose one's composure. ¶당황하여 in a flurry / in confusion / in panic / in perplexity∥당황하지 않고 calmly / composedly / cooly∥뜻밖의 질문에 그는 당황했다 The unexpected question threw him off so unexpected that it threw me completely[I was flustered / I was disconcerted].∥당황하지 마라 Take it easy. / Don't panic.∥당황할 것 없다 There is no hurry.∥당황하여 컵을 깨고 말았다 In my agitation[haste] I broke a glass.∥그는 어떤 경우에도 당황하지 않는다 He remains unruffled[cool] on any occasion.∥담배를 피우다가

들켜 소년은 당황했다 Caught smoking, the boy was thrown into confusion[flustered]. // 나는 허를 찔려 당황했다 I was taken by surprise. / I was taken aback. // 어떻게 말해야 좋을지 그는 당황하는 표정이었다 He looked at a loss what to say. // 치러야 할 돈이 모자라서 아주 당황했다 I didn't know what to do [was embarrassed] when I realized that I didn't have enough money to pay the bill. // 그는 조금도 당황하는 기색이 없었다 He showed no sign of confusion[(문어) perturbation]. / He remained perfectly calm [unmoved]. / (미국 구어) He wasn't fazed in the least.(▶ faze는 부정어를 수반함) / 당황해서 대답도 못 했다 I was so flurried that I could not answer. // 수상이 암살당하자 국민은 당황했다 When the prime minister was assassinated, the country was thrown into confusion. // 나는 그들의 연이은 질문을 받고 당황하고 말았다 As they rained questions on me, I got completely flustered [confused]. // 도둑놈은 당황해서 도망치고 말았다 The thief ran away in a panic. // 그는 뜻밖의 소식을 듣고 당황했다 He was thrown off balance by the unexpected news. // 그 사건에 그녀는 아주 당황하여 말도 할 수 없었다 The incident so upset her that she couldn't say word. // 그는 당황하지 않고 가만히 웃고 있었다 He kept smiling calmly without so much as batting an eye. // 사람들은 당황하지 않았다 The people remained calm[kept their heads / kept their presence of mind]. // 나는 갑자기 연설을 요청받아 당황해 버렸다 I got very nervous[(구어) all shook up] when I was suddenly called on to make a speech. // 당황하여 그는 말 한 마디도 하지 못했다 He got stage fright and couldn't say a word. // 그는 뜻하지 않게 아버지를 만나 몹시 당황했다 He was terribly flustered [thrown into confusion / filled with consternation] when he unexpectedly ran into his father. **당황히** perplexedly; confusedly; puzzledly.

닻 an anchor. ¶네가지 ~ a grapnel // ~을 내리다[내리다] weigh[cast / drop] anchor(▶ 관사를 붙이지 않음) // ~이 걸리다 an anchor bites[holds] // (배가) ~을 끌다 drag the anchor // 그 화물선은 앞바다에 ~을 내리고 있다 The cargo ship is (lying) at anchor in the offing.

닻줄 a(n anchor) cable.
닻혀 the fluke (of an anchor); an anchor fluke.

닿다 1 [접하다] touch; come in[into]; contact [touch] with; be close to; get to[at]; attain to. ¶무엇인가가 발에 닿았다 Something touched my foot. / I felt something touch my foot. // 우리가 서로 맞스쳤을 때 그의 팔이 나의 팔에 닿았다 His arm brushed against mine when we passed each other. // 나는 환자의 손이 닿는 곳에 라디오를 놓았다 I put the radio within reach of the sick man. // 그는 키가 얼마나 큰지 거의 천장에 닿을 정도이다 He is so tall that his head almost reaches [touches] the ceiling. // 그의 머리카락은 어깨에 닿아 늘어져 있다 His hair hangs down to his shoulders. // 그녀의 목소리는 멀리까지 닿는다 Her voice carries a long way. // 눈길이 가 닿는 데까지 온통 모래밭이었다 As far as the eye could see, there was nothing but a sandy beach. // 닻이 해저에 닿았다 The anchor touched bottom. // 혼잡한 열차 속에서 누군가의 젖은 우산이 내 등에 닿았다 Somebody's wet umbrella touched my back in the crowded train.
2 [도착하다] reach; arrive at[in / on]; get to. ¶무사히 ~ arrive in safety / (물건이) arrive in good condition[order] / 기차가 정거장에 닿았다 The train arrived at the station. // 배가 목적지에 닿았다 The ship reached its destination. // 짐이 닿았다 Has the baggage turned up? // 8월 4일자의 당신 편지가 어제 닿았습니다 Your letter of August 4[(영)] 4 August] reached me yesterday. / I received your letter of August 4 yesterday. // 그녀가 외출한 후에 그 전갈이 닿았다[왔다] The message arrived[come] after she had left.
3 [연줄이] have a pull (with); have contacts [connections] (with); get in touch (with). ¶서울 시장하고 줄이 ~ have a pull with the Mayor of Seoul // 그 회사와는 줄이 닿는다 I've got a pull with that company.
4 [이치에] hold good; hold water; be consistent with (reason); hang together. ¶조리가 닿는[닿지 않는] 발언 a logical[an illogical] statement // 이치에 ~ stand to[accord with] reason // 방금 네가 한 말은 이치에 닿지 않는다 What you've just said is unreasonable. // 그의 설교는 가슴에 와 닿았다 His sermon came home to my heart.

닿소리 [언] a consonant. ⇨ 자음(子音)
대¹ [식] a bamboo. ¶~를 쪼개다 split a bamboo.
● **대 마디** a bamboo joint[node].
대² 1 [줄기] a stalk; a stem; a pipe; (대나무·버들 등의) a culm; (완두 등의) ha(u)lm; (사탕수수 등의) a cane; [막대] a pole; a staff; a rod; [붓·펜대] a holder; [담뱃대] a pipe. ¶펜~ a penholder // 가로~ a crosspiece / a (cross) bar // ~가 생기는 culmiferous.
2 [줏대] a fixed opinion. ¶~가 센 daring / bold / plucky / audacious // ~가 센 사람 a man of strong convictions // ~가 약하다 be weak kneed / be timid / be fainthearted.
3 [곧고 긴 물건을 세는 단위] a smoke; a puff; a whiff; a cigaret(te); a fill(양). ¶담배 한 ~ a pipeful of tobacco / a cigarette // 담배를 한 ~ 권하다 offer (a person) a smoke // 담배를 한 ~ 피우다 smoke a pipe / have [take] a smoke.
4 [때리는 횟수를 세는 단위] a blow; a stroke; a punch; a hit; (주사의) a shot; an injection. ¶한 ~에 at a[one] blow[stroke] / by a (single) blow // 한 ~ 먹이다 strike[deal / give] (a person) a blow // 몽둥이로 한 ~ 치다 give (a person) a drubbing // 캠퍼를 두 ~ 주사하다 give (a person) two camphor injections[two shots of camphor].

대(大) [큼] largeness; bigness; greatness; [대형] large size; [크기] size. ¶~짜리 large / big // ~·중·소 세 가지 형이 있다 There are[It comes in] three sizes, large, medium and small.

대를 살리고 소를 죽이다(속담) renounce the small in order to secure the great; amputate a limb to save the body.

대(代) 1 [계승의 순위·그 기간] a generation; [치세] a reign; [시대] an age; an era. ¶부모 [자식]의 ~ the parent's[children's] generation // 여러 ~를 이어 오는 명가 a prominent family for many generations // 5~째의 대통령

the fifth President // 제임스 1세의 ~에 in the reign of James I(▶ James the first라고 읽음) // ~를 잇다 succeed (a person) // ~를 끊다 let the family die out // 루스벨트는 몇 ~째의 대통령인가 Where does F.D. Roosevelt stand in the order of American presidents? // 저 가게는 지금 7~째의 주인이 운영하고 있다 The seventh in the line of proprietors runs the store now. // 저 가게는 아들이 ~를 이었다 The son has now taken over that store.
2 [연령·연대의 대강의 범위]. ¶십~의 어린이 a teenager // 그녀는 20~입니다 She is in her twenties. // 그는 50~ 후반[30~ 중반]입니다 He is in his late fifties[in his mid-thirties]. // 2000년~에 in the 2000's[2000s] // 1980년~ 초반[중반] in the early 1980's[mid-1980's].
3 [지] an era; a period. ¶고생~ the Paleozoic (era) // 신생~ the Cenozoic[Cainozoic] era [period.

대(隊) [어떤 목적을 위한 일단] a party(▶ 개개의 구성원을 염두에 둘 때는 복수 취급); [군대] a corps (단수·복수 동형); a company (a of soldiers); a squad; (악대의) a band; [대오(隊伍)] the ranks; a line; formation. ¶~를 짜다 [한 ~를 만들다] form a party / [세로로 정렬하다] form a line[(영) queue] / [가로로 정렬하다] form a row // ~를 짜고 가다 [일단이 되다] go in a body / [행진하다] march in formation.

대(對) 1 [짝] a pair; a counterpart; a parallel; [쌍] a couple. ¶~가 되다 make[form] a pair / form a counterpart[parallel].
2 [상대] versus(약어 V., VS.); against; between; [비율] to; anti-. ¶공~공 미사일 an air-to-air ground // 공~지 미사일 an air-to-ground[-surface] missile // 지~공 미사일 a ground-[surface-] to-air missile // 지~지 미사일 a ground-[surface-] to-ground [-surface] missile // 자본주의 ~ 공산주의 capitalism versus communism // 자이언츠 ~ 타이거스의 야구 경기 a baseball game between the Giants and the Tigers // 타이거스가 5~3으로 이겼다 Tigers won the game (by a score of) 5-3.(▶ 5-3은 five to three로 읽음) // 법안은 380~120으로 부결되었다 The bill was rejected (by a vote of) 380-120.

대(臺) 1 [받침] a stand; a rest; a rack(걸쳐 놓는); a table(탁자); a support(버팀); (비석 등의) a pedestal; [지주] a support; a stool. ¶텔레비전 (받침) ~ a television stand // 발 받침 ~ a foot rest / a footstool // 세면 ~ a washstand // 악보 ~ a music stand // 진열 ~ a display stand[counter] // 나는 의자를 받침~로 삼아 선반 위의 인형을 내렸다 I stood on a chair [I used a chair to stand on] and took down the doll from the shelf.
2 [차·기계 등을 세는 단위] a car; a cart; a plane. ¶텔레비전 3~ three TV sets // 자동차가 한 ~ 지나갔다 A car passed by.

대-(大) [큰] large; great; vast; [거대한] grand; large-scale; wholesale; [뛰어난] great; prominent. ¶~평원 a vast plain // ~사업 a great enterprise // ~가족 a large family // ~승리 a sweeping[great] victory / (선거의) a landslide // ~기업 a large enterprise // ~예술가 a great artist.

대-(對) counter; opposite; equal; versus; anti-. ¶~전차포 an antitank gun // ~북한 방송 프로그램 a radio program beamed at[to] North Korea // ~캐나다 수출 exports to Canada // 중국의 ~일(日) 감정[정책] China's attitude[policy] toward the Japan // ~동남 아시아 무역[관계]을 개선하다 improve trade [relations] with the Southeast Asian countries.

-대(代) [대금] a price; [요금] a charge; a rate. ¶도서~ a book fee // 식사~ food expenses / (the charge for) board(하숙의).

-대(帶) a zone; a region; a belt; a band. ¶삼림 ~ a forest belt // 무풍 ~ the calm belt // 화산 ~ a volcanic zone // 성감 ~ an erogenous zone // 생리 ~ a hygienic band.

-대(臺) a level; a mark. ¶수억~의 자본가 a capitalist with billions // 그는 수학 성적이 항상 80점~였다 He always got eighty something in mathematics. // 금년도의 이익은 2억 원~에 달했다 This year's profit reached the two hundred million won mark.

대가(大家) 1 [거장] a (great) master; a past [passed] master (in / at); a maestro (pl. ~s, -tri); [권위자] an authority; leading figure; (학문의) a great[an eminent / a distinguished] scholar. ¶서예의 ~ a distinguished calligrapher // 음악의 ~ a great musician / a maestro / a virtuoso // 그림의 ~ a master artist[painter] // 문장의 ~ a master of style // 교육계의 ~ a leading figure in the educational world // 그 방면의 ~ an acknowledged authority on the subject[in the field] // ~가 되다 attain eminence[greatness] // 그 방면의 ~로서 인정받고 있다 be an acknowledged[a recognized] authority on the subject.
2 [명문] an illustrious[a distinguished / a great] family; [부호] a wealthy family.
● **대갓집** a distinguished family; a wealthy house.

대가(代價) [희생] a cost. ¶어떤 ~를 치르더라도 단념하지 않는다 I will not give it up no matter what the cost. // 연구를 위해서라면 어떤 ~라도 치를 용의가 있다 I am willing to make any sacrifice for the sake of my research. // 그렇게 무책임한 생활을 하다가는 언젠가 비싼 ~를 치를 때가 올 것이다 Someday you will have to pay a high price [dearly] for your irresponsible way of life.

대가(對價) an equivalent; compensation; prices; [법] consideration.

대가극(大歌劇) a grand opera.

대가다 [목적지에 이르다] arrive on time(정각에); be[arrive] in time (for) (늦지 않게). ¶수업 시간에 ~ arrive at school on time // 약속 시간에 ~ present oneself at the appointed time // 열차 시간에 대갈 수 없었다 We missed[couldn't catch / were late for] the train.

대가리 [머리] the head; (물건의) the top [head / point / tip] (of). ¶생선 ~ the jowl // 소 ~ the head of an ox // 콩나물 ~ the tips of bean sprouts // 망치 ~ a hammerhead // ~를 까다 smash (a person's) skull.

대가연하다(大家然-) pose as[pretend to be] an authority; put on the airs of a great master.

대가족(大家族) 1 [많은 수의 가족] a large family. ¶~을 거느리고 있다 have a large family to support. **2** [복합 가족] an extended family.
● **대가족 제도** an extended family system.

대각(對角) [수] the opposite angle. ¶~의 방

대각거리다 crack; clatter; rattle; keep snapping. ¶그릇이 대각거린다 Dishes are clattering.

대각선(對角線) [수] a diagonal (line). ¶~의 diagonal / cater-corner / cater-cornered // ~으로 diagonally / cater-cornered // ~을 긋다 draw a diagonal (to the opposite angle).

대갈 [편자 못] a horseshoe nail.

대갈마치 1 [작은 마치] a farrier's hammer. 2 [야무진 사람] a person hardened through adversities; a person schooled in [steeled against] adversity.

대갈못 a nail with a big head.

대감(大監) His [Your] Excellency.

대강(大綱) 1 [대체적인 줄거리] an outline; a summary; a gist; substance; general [principal] features. ¶사건의 ~ 줄거리 the (sum and) substance of the case // 강의의 ~ the syllabus of a lecture // ~을 정하다 lay down fundamental principles // ~을 **말하다** outline / give an outline of / sketch out the general features // 외교 정책의 ~을 정하다 formulate main lines of foreign policy // ~을 **가지다** have a general idea (of) // ~을 **나타내다** sketch an outline (of)/줄거리의 ~을 말해 보아라 Summarize [Give the outline of] the story.
2 [대충] roughly; about; approximately; [거의] nearly; [간략하게] briefly; cursorily; [가볍게] lightly; almost; [대체로] generally; in general. ¶~의 견적 a rough estimate // ~ 끝나다 be almost [practically] finished // ~ 어림잡다 make a rough estimate (of) // ~ 이야기하다 give a short sketch (of) // ~의 계획을 세우다 make a general plan // 일을 ~ 하다 do a rough [cursory / passing] job (of it) // 각서의 ~은 다음과 같다 The purport of the memorandum is as follows. // 나는 누가 했는지 ~ 짐작하고 있다 I have a pretty good idea who did it. // 나는 일을 ~ 끝냈다 I have almost finished the work. // 우리는 ~ 합의를 보았다 We have practically come to an agreement. // 네 생각은 내 생각과 ~ 같다 Your idea is about the same as mine. // 나는 그 편지의 요점을 ~ 훑어보기만 하고 찢어 버렸다 I just glanced over the letter and tore it up. // 그 이유에 대해서는 ~ 짐작하고 있다 I can make a rough guess [I have a general idea] about the reason. // 집은 ~ 완성되었다 My house is almost [about] finished.

대강령(大綱領) general rules [principles]; fundamental [first] principles.

대강하다(代講-) teach [give a lecture] for [in place of] (another); act as (a) substitute teacher for (another).

대갚음(對-) return [repayment / requital] in kind; retaliation; tit for tat; measure for measure. **대갚음하다** return [repay / requite] in kind [like for like]; retaliate give [pay] (a person) tit for tat; pay (a person) back in his own coin. ¶은혜를 ~ return a favor / repay (a person) for his kindness / repay (a person's) kindness // 원한을 ~ revenge / avenge / give measure for measure.

대개(大槪) 1 [대부분] most (of); the (a) great part (of); a great [large] portion (of); the majority (of). ¶그 ~는 장식이다 Most of them are ornaments. // 우리 학교 학생들은 ~ 이 읍내에 산다 Most of our pupils live in this town.
2 [개요] an outline; a summary.
3 [대체로] generally (speaking); in general; [대부분] mostly; for the most part; [주로] in the main; mainly; principally; chiefly; [거의] nearly; about; [아마] probably. ¶~의 경우 generally / in most cases // ~ 모두 nearly all / practically all // 나는 ~ 7시에 일어난다 I usually get up at seven. // 그는 아침에는 ~ 산책을 한다 He usually takes a walk in the morning. // 이 병에 걸리면 ~ 죽는다 This disease proves fatal in most cases. // 그들은 ~ 가족 동반으로 소풍 간다 In most cases they go on outings with their families. // 그곳의 거류민은 ~가 중국인이다 The residents there are for the most part Chinese. // 나는 이 거리 ~의 가게 주인을 알고 지낸다 I am known to almost all the shopkeepers in this town. // 2시에 그곳에 가면 ~ 그를 만날 수 있을 것이다 If you go there at two o'clock, you will probably be able to see him. // 미국 사람은 ~ 사교적이다 As a rule, Americans are outgoing. // 이 반은 ~ 이해가 빠르다 This class is on the whole quick to learn. // 우편물은 ~ 10시에 온다 Generally the mail is delivered (at) about 10 a.m. // 나는 휴일에는 ~ 집에 있다 I stay mostly [I usually stay] at home on holidays. // 여기까지 말했으면 너도 ~ 알아들었을 것 같다만 By now I think you know what I'm talking about. // 부모는 ~ 자식을 사랑한다 Parents generally [usually] love their children.

대개념(大槪念) [논] a major concept.

대거(大擧) 1 [한꺼번에 많이] in a body; in (great) force; in large [great] numbers; (프) en masse; [대규모로] on a grand scale. ¶~ 공격하다 attack (the enemy) in full force / take the offensive on a large scale / mass-raid // ~ 적을 공격하다 attack an enemy in full force / 적의 폭격기가 ~ 내습했다 Enemy bombers raided [attacked] (the town) in large [great] numbers. // 그 행사를 보려고 관광객이 ~ 몰려왔다 Hosts of tourists come to watch the event. // 적군이 ~ 침입하여 그 지역을 점령했다 The enemy swept in and occupied the area. 2 [대규모의 거사] a great enterprise; an uprising for a cause.

대거리하다(對-) talk [answer] back; contradict (a person); retort.

대검(帶劍) [총검] a bayonet. ¶~을 꽂다 [빼다] fix [unfix] a bayonet. **대검하다** wear a sword [saber]; be armed with a sword.

대검찰청(大檢察廳) the Supreme Public Prosecutors Office; the Prosecutor-General's Office(약어 PGO).

대견하다 [흡족하다] (be) satisfied; contented; content; [훌륭하다] fine; admirable; praiseworthy; great; [소중하다] valuable; dear; precious. ¶대견하게 여기다 take (a person / a thing) admirable [laudable] / put much importance on / make much [highly] of / be proud of // 결과를 대견하게 여기다 express one's satisfaction at [with] the result / 대견한 일을 해내다 achieve [do] a great thing.

대결(對決) [맞섬] confrontation; a face-to-face meeting; (미) a showdown; [승부] a contest; a match; a game; a bout. ¶(연극의) ~ **장면** a confrontation scene // 백주의 ~ a showdown in broad [open] daylight // 1대 1

의 ~ single combat / a man-to-man fight // 오늘 A와 B의 ~에서는 누가 이길까 Who will win in today's match between A and B? // 이번 선거는 보수와 혁신의 ~이 될 것 같다 The next election will be a confrontation between the conservative and the progressive camp. // 그것은 두 함대에 의한 세기의 ~이었다 The meeting of the two fleets was the showdown of the century [was a critical showdown]. **대결하다** confront (one's accuser); have a showdown (with); stand face to face (with); have a contest[match] (with). ¶대결하게 되다 come to a showdown // 1대 1로 ~ engage in a man-to-man fight / fight man to man. →**대결시키다** confront (a person) with another / bring (a person) face to face with (another).

대경실색하다 (大驚失色-) 〔간담이 서늘하다〕 be astounded; 〔기가 질리다〕 be amazed; turn pale with horror; lose color with astonishment; be greatly startled. ¶그는 말이 안 나올 정도로 대경실색했다 He was speechless with amazement. / He was struck dumb with amazement. / He was dumbfounded. // 그의 갑작스러운 반대에 대경실색했다 I was dumbfounded by his sudden rebuff.

대경하다 (大驚-) be greatly astonished; be startled [astounded / stunned].

대계 (大計) 〔큰 계획〕 a large-scale plan; 〔원대한 계획〕 a long-range plan; a far-reaching policy; a grand plan. ¶백년~ a farsighted (national) policy [program].

대계 (大系) an outline (of history). ¶서양사 ~ An Outline of European History.

대고모 (大姑母) a grandaunt [great-aunt] on one's father's side; a sister of one's grandfather.
● **대고모부** the husband of a grandaunt on one's father's side.

대공 (大公) 〔대공국의 군주〕 a grand duke; 〔스페인·포르투갈의 최고 귀족〕 a grandee; (옛 러시아·오스트리아 등의) the Grand[Great] Prince. ¶룩셈부르크 ~ the grand duke of Luxembourg.
● **대공국** (-國) a grand duchy.

대공 (大功) a great merit; meritorious[distinguished] services; a signal deed. ¶~을 세우다 render meritorious services / achieve great things / distinguish oneself.

대공 (對空) 〔한정어적〕 anti-aircraft; 〔구어〕 anti-air.
● **대공 방어** anti-aircraft defense. **대공 미사일** an anti-aircraft missile.

대과 (大過) a serious error; a grave mistake; a blunder. ¶~ 없이 without (making) any serious errors [mistakes] // ~ 없이 근무하다 serve (for thirty years) without committing any serious mistakes [errors] // 그는 30여 년을 ~ 없이 근무했다 He served creditably for more than thirty years.

대과거 (大過去) 〔언〕 the past perfect tense; the pluperfect (tense).

대관 (大觀) 〔개관〕 a general survey [view]; an overall view; 〔장관〕 a magnificent view. **대관하다** take a large view (of); view broadly; make a general survey (of).

대관 (大官) a high-ranking official; a (governmental) dignitary; high executives of the State.

대관식 (戴冠式) a coronation. ¶~을 거행하다 perform a coronation (ceremony).

대관절 (大關節) (how / what / why) on earth [in the world / the dickens / the blazes]. ¶~ 너는 누구냐 What on earth are you? // ~ 너는 어디에서 왔으며 누구냐 Wherever do you come from and whoever are you? // ~ 어디 갔다 오는 거요 Where the blazes [hell] have you been? // ~ 무슨 일인가 What the deuce is the matter? / Whatever is the matter? // ~ 이건 어떻게 된 거야 What is the meaning of all this? // ~ 무엇을 하고 있었냐 What in the name of hell have you been doing? // ~ 뭘 가지고 싸우시오 What on earth are you quarreling about?

대괄호 (大括弧) a (square) bracket(〔 〕).

대교 (大橋) a large[big] bridge. ¶한강의 ~들 large bridges over the Hangang (Han River).

대구 (大口) 〔동〕 a cod; a codfish; a gadid; a haddock.
● **대구 알** the cod roe; (소금에 절인) salted cod roe.

대구 (對句) 〔문〕 an antithesis (pl. -ses); 〔2행 연구〕 a couplet; a distich. ¶~를 이루다 form [make] an antithesis (to / of).
● **대구법** 〔문〕 antithesis.

대국 (大局) 〔대체의 판국〕 the general [whole] situation; the main issue. ¶~을 잘못 판단하다 take a wrong view of things / miss the main point [issue] of things // 그는 ~을 정확히 파악하고 있다 His grasp [view] of the whole situation is correct.

대국 (大國) 〔큰 나라〕 a large country; 〔위대한 나라〕 a great country [nation]; 〔강대국〕 a big [great] power; 〔전에 우리나라에서 중국을 부르던 말〕 China. ¶경제 [군사] ~ an economic [a military] power.

대국 (對局) (바둑·장기의) a game of baduk[janggi] (with). **대국하다** play (a game of) baduk[janggi] (with); be pitted [set] (against). ¶그는 내일 명인과 대국한다 He has a match with the champion tomorrow.

대국적 (大局的) broad; wide. ¶~으로는 on the whole / generally [roughly] speaking // ~으로 보면 on a broad survey // ~으로 보다 take a wide view of (a matter) / see (something) in perspective // ~으로는 [으로 보아서] 잘되어 가고 있다 On the whole [Generally speaking], things are going well. // ~ 견지에서 그는 상대방에게 양보했다 Taking a broader view of the matter, he yielded to the opposition.

대군 (大君) 〔왕자〕 a (Royal) prince; 〔군주〕 a king; a sovereign.

대군 (大軍) a large [huge] army; a large [vast] force; a host of troops. ¶적의 ~ a large enemy force // ~을 거느리다 lead [command] a large army [vast forces].

대권 (大圈) a great circle.
● **대권 항로** the great-circle track [route].

대권 (大權) 〔최고 권력〕 supreme power; 〔군주의〕 the royal prerogative [authority / power]; 〔통치권〕 the governing power. ¶~의 발동 exercise of the governing power // 병마(兵馬)의 ~ the supreme authority over the army // ~을 침범하다 encroach upon the supreme power // (국가) ~을 장악하다 hold the supreme power (of the state) / reign supreme // ~을 발동하다 exercise the imperial [royal] prerogative.

대궐 (大闕) the royal palace. ⇨궁궐

대규모(大規模) a large[big / grand] scale. ¶~의 large-[big-]scale // ~로 on a large[a big / an extensive / a grand / a gigantic] scale / in a big[large] way // ~의 밀수입 smuggling on a large scale // 마약 밀매자의 ~ 검거 a wholesale roundup of narcotics dealers // ~로 장사를 하다 do business on a large scale // 우리는 ~의 조사를 하였다 We conducted a large-scale survey[investigation].
● 대규모 작전 large-scale (military) operations.

대금(大金) a large[an enormous] sum (of money); a lot of money. ¶강도는 1,000만 원의 ~을 약탈해 갔다 The burglar made away [off] with the huge sum of ten million won.

대금(大笒) a *daegeum*; a large (cross) flute; a large fife.

대금(代金) [산 물건에 치르는 돈] (a) price; (a) cost; (a) charge; the money; a bill; a fee. ¶…의 ~ the price for … // ~을 치르다 pay for (an article) / pay the price (for) // ~을 청구하다 ask (a person) to pay for (a thing) / bill (a person) for (a thing) // 그들은 터무니없는 ~을 청구해 왔다 They charged me an exorbitant [outrageous] price. // ~은 선불하여 주십시오 Please pay in advance. // 자동차 ~으로 100만 원을 지불했다 I paid one million won for the car. // 물품은 ~과 상환으로 내 드립니다 I will hand it over to you on receipt of the money.

대금(貸金) [꾸어 준 돈] a loan; an advance; [돈놀이] money-lending; usury(고리의). ¶~을 회수하다 collect debts / collect[call in] loans.
● 대금업 money-lending business. 대금업자 a money-lender.

대기(大氣) [지구를 둘러싸고 있는 공기] the atmosphere; [공기] the air. ¶~의 atmospheric(al) // 요즘 ~가 불안정하다 Atmospheric conditions have been unsettled for several days.
● 대기권 the atmosphere. ¶~ 내의 핵 실험 nuclear testing[tests] in the atmosphere / the atmospheric testing of nuclear weapons // ~ 밖으로 나가다[로켓을 발사하다] venture [launch a rocket] into outer space. 대기 오염 air pollution. ¶자동차의 배기가스에 의한 ~ atmospheric contamination by exhaust gases[fumes] from automobiles // ~은 대도시에서는 중대한 문제이다 Air pollution is a serious problem in large cities.

대기(大器) [큰 그릇] a large vessel; [인재] a man of capacity[talent]; a great man [talent]; a genius; a man of great caliber.
● 대기만성 Great talents mature late [are slow in maturing]. ¶~형의 사람들 late-bloomers [-developers].

대기(待機) watching and waiting for a chance; standing by. ¶경찰에 ~ 명령을 내리다 alert the police // ~ 상태에 있다 be standing by ready (to do) / be on alert status(함대·공군 등이) // ~ 태세를 취하다 assume a posture of standing by / assume a watch-and-wait attitude // 이 근방에 택시의 ~ 장소가 있습니까 Is there a taxi stand near here? 대기하다 stand ready (for / to do); hold oneself in readiness; stand by; be on standby; be[wait] on call; wait for an opportunity; be on the waiting list. ¶자택에서 ~ stand by at home // 구조대가 대기하고 있다 The rescue party is waiting[standing by] for a chance to help. // 고속도로 순찰대가 상시 대기하고 있다 The highway patrol is on constant alert. // 심부름꾼이 옆방에서 대기하고 있다 The messenger is waiting in the next room. // 병원에서 오래도록 대기하고 있어야 했다 I was kept waiting for a long time at the hospital. // 보도진이 대기하고 있었다 The reporters were waiting[lying in wait] for him. ➔ ¶택시를 대기시켜 놓았습니다 I have a taxi waiting for you.
● 대기 발령 an order of placement on a waiting list. 대기실 a waiting room; an antechamber; an anteroom.

대기업(大企業) a large enterprise[corporation]; a conglomerate(자회사를 거느린); 《집합적》 big business; major companies [firms]. ¶이 회사는 건설업계에서는 ~이다 This is the largest company in the construction business.

대길(大吉) great good luck[fortune]; excellent luck. 대길하다 very luck; very auspicious.
● 대길일(-日) a most auspicious day.

대깍거리다 clatter; rattle. ⇨ 태격거리다

대꼬챙이 a pointed bamboo pole[stick].

대꾸 a retort. ⇨ 말대꾸

대나무 [식] a bamboo. ¶~ 세공 bamboo work.

대낚시 pole-and-line fishing.

대남(對南) [관형어적] against[toward] the South.
● 대남 간첩 an espionage agent against the South. 대남 공작 operations against the South. 대남 방송 broadcasting toward the South.

대납(代納) 1 [대신 납부하기] payment by proxy. 대납하다 pay for (another). ¶그는 아버지 대신 토지대를 대납했다 He paid the land rent for his father. 2 [물납] payment in kind. 대납하다 pay in kind. ¶세금을 물건으로 ~ pay a tax in kind // 상속세를 토지로 ~ pay an inheritance tax in land.

대낮 [백주] broad daylight; [정오] high noon; midday. ¶~에 in broad[full / open] daylight / in the daytime // ~처럼 밝다 be as bright as day[noontime] // ~부터 술을 마시다니 부끄럽지도 않은가 Aren't you ashamed of drinking in the middle of the day [at this time of day]?(▶ at this time of day 는 이런 시간에라는 뜻이 강함) // 그는 ~부터 벌써 취해 있었다 He was already drunk in the middle of the day. // ~에 생긴 일이었다 It occurred in broad daylight / the daytime].

대내(對內) ¶~의 domestic / home / interior.
● 대내 문제 domestic issues. 대내 정책 a domestic[home] policy.

대농(大農) [부농] a wealthy farmer; [큰 농사] large-scale farming.

대뇌(大腦) [생] the cerebrum (*pl.* ~s, -bra); the brain proper.
● 대뇌엽(-葉) a cerebral lobe.

대님 a *daenim*; cloth bands used to tie up the lower ends of trousers; pant-leg ties. ¶양말 ~ garters / 〔영〕 suspenders // ~을 매다 tie ankle bands / tie one's trousers around the ankles.

대다[1] 1 [접촉시키다] put; apply; hold; place; lay; press. ¶수화기를 귀에 ~ hold a receiver to one's ear // 망원경을 눈에 ~ apply one's

대다

eyes to a telescope // 청진기를 가슴에 ~ put a stethoscope to (a person's) chest // 그는 문에 귀를 대었다 He pressed his ear against the door. // 그녀는 내 가슴에 얼굴을 대고 있었다 She cried with her face pressed on my breast. // 나는 문구멍에다 종이를 대었다 I covered the hole in the door with a piece of paper. // 나는 상처에다 손을 대고 있었다 I held my hand against the wound.

2 [닿게 하다] touch; lay [put] one's hand (on / against). ¶이마에 손을 ~ put one's hand to one's forehead / place one's hand against (another's) forehead // 허리를 굽혀 손을 방바닥에 ~ bend down and touch one's hands to the floor [touch the floor with one's hands] // 그것은 손을 대기만 해도 부서진다 The slightest touch will break it. // 손대지 마시오 (게시) Hands off! / Don't touch! // 그는 칼자루에 손을 갖다 댔다 He laid [placed] his hand on the hilt of his sword.

3 [서로 비교하다] compare with; make a comparison with. ¶두 사람의 키를 대보다 compare the heights of the two // 영어 [속도] 에서는 그에 댈 사람이 없다 No one can touch him in English [for speed].

4 [대면·연결시키다] link (together) (with); connect (with / to); bring into contact (with). ¶두 선을 ~ touch the two wires together // A 씨를 대 주십시오 May I talk to Mr. A, please? / Will you get me Mr. A, please? // (전화 교환수가) 잠깐만 기다리세요. 대 드릴게요. One moment, please. I'll get that number for you. // 전화를 3호실에 대 주십시오 Please connect me with Room No. 3. // 경찰 [287국의 5021번]을 대 주십시오 Put me through to the police [to 287-5021]. (▶ two-eight-seven, five-o[ou]-two-one으로 읽음)

5 [세우다] drive [draw / pull] up(차를); put ashore(배를); [시간에 늦지 않다] arrive [be] in time (for); make it. ¶차를 대문 앞에 ~ bring [pull up / draw up] a car to the gate / 기차 시간에 대지 못하다 miss [be too late for] a train / 보트를 기슭에 ~ bring a boat to the shore // 그 운전 기사는 자동차를 문 앞에 댔다 The driver stopped the car [pulled up] in front of the gate. // 나는 막차 [마지막 열차]에 댔다 I was in time for the last train. / I caught the last train. // 나는 근소한 차로 버스 시간에 대지 못했다 I just missed the bus.

6 [향하게 하다] direct; aim. ¶남의 얼굴에 대고 침을 뱉다 spit in a person's face.

7 [의지하다] lean against. ¶등을 벽에 대고 with one's back against the wall.

8 [고용하다] hire; employ. ¶가정교사를 ~ invite [employ] a home teacher.

9 [덧대다] cover (an umbrella); line (a box with tin); apply; fix; put. ¶상처에 거즈를 ~ apply gauze on the wound / 구두에 창을 ~ fix a sole on one's shoes / 코트 안을 털가죽으로 ~ line a coat with fur.

대 오다 come [arrive] on time; get [be] (here) on time. ¶약속 시간에 ~ be on time for an appointment // 9시까지 대 오시오 Please be here by nine.

대다² **1** [물을] draw (water) into; water; irrigate (rice fields). ¶논에 물을 ~ irrigate a rice paddy // 봄에는 논에 물을 댄다 We flood the fields spring. / The paddies are flooded in the spring. **2** [공급·후원하다] supply [provide / furnish / serve] (a person) with. ¶쌀을 ~ supply (the house) with rice // 변호사를 ~ provide (the defendant) with a lawyer // 학비를 ~ furnish a student with his school expenses / supply a student with a fund to pay his school expenses // 일을 대어 받다 be provided with work / be given a job.

대 주다 supply [provide / furnish] (a person with something); find (a person with something); give (rations to). ¶의식(衣食)을 ~ provide (a person) with food and clothing / issue food and clothing (to a person) / feed and clothe (a person) financial aid [pecuniary help] / finance (a person) // 생활비를 ~ assist (a person) in getting a living / support / contribute to (a person's) support // 학자금을 ~ help [supply] (a student) with (his) school expenses // 돈을 ~ furnish [provide] (a person) with money // 남의 장사 밑천을 일체 ~ furnish all the funds necessary to another's business.

대다³ **1** [말하다] speak; tell; inform; (사실대로) tell the truth; speak out; confess. ¶자기 이름을 ~ tell (a person) one's name / name oneself // 증거를 ~ give evidence // 이유를 ~ give a reason (for) / adduce reasons // 바른대로 대라 Tell me the truth. // 내가 알고 있는 것은 모조리 대마 I will tell you all that I know. // 그 일은 워낙 명백해서 증거를 댈 필요도 없다 It is too evident to require proof. **2** [일러주다] tell; show; indicate. ¶가장 가까운 [역으로 가는] 길을 대 드리시오 I will tell you the shortest way [the way to the station].

대다⁴ [동작의 정도가 심함]. ¶웃어 ~ laugh a heavy laugh / laugh oneself to death // 울어 ~ cry one's heart out / cry bitter tears // 먹어 ~ eat heavily / stuff oneself with food // 마셔 ~ drink hard [heavily] // 떠들어 ~ noise about // 찍소리 못하게 해 ~ talk [argue] (a person) down / corner (a person) in argument.

대다수(大多數) a large [great / heavy / crushing / thumping] majority; an enormous majority; the greater part (of); the mass [bulk] (of). ¶압도적 ~ an overwhelming majority // ~를 **차지하다** hold [form] a large majority // ~의 지지를 받다 be supported by the majority // 회의는 온건파가 ~를 차지하고 있었다 The moderates commanded a large majority at the meeting. // 그 법안은 ~의 찬동을 얻었다 The bill was supported by a large majority. // 주민의 ~는 농업에 종사하고 있다 The inhabitants are, for the most part, engaged in farming.

대단원(大團圓) (연극·소설의) a denouement; the (grand) finale; the end; a catastrophe(주로 비극적인). ¶~의 막이 내리다 come to an end // 해피 엔딩으로 ~이 되다 come to [have] a happy ending / turn out happily.

대단찮다 **1** [많지 않다] not (so) many [much]; [크지 않다] not (so) large [huge / big / great]. ¶대단찮은 돈 a small sum of money / 재간이 ~ have little ability [talent] // 대단찮은 집에서 살다 live in a small house // 손해는 ~ There is not much damage. // 도난에 의한 손실은 대단찮은 것이었다 The loss of robbery was not (so) great.

2 [대수롭지 않다] of little importance [value

/ use〕; insignificant; trivial; slight; 〔평범하다〕 ordinary; mediocre. ¶대단찮은 일 a matter of little importance / a trivial matter [affair] / a trifle /대단찮은 사람 a person of no importance / an ordinary man /대단찮게 여기다 think[make] little (of)/용모가 ~ have an ordinary appearance∥그는 대단찮은 학자다 He is not much of a scholar. / He is a third-rate scholar. ∥대단찮은 오해로 평생의 벗들과 틀어지는 일도 있다 Slight misunderstandings may sever lifelong friends.
3 (병 등이) not serious[grave / acute]; slight; mild; trivial. ¶대단찮은 감기[부상] a slight cold[wound] ∥ (병의) 대단찮은 증세 a mild case[form].
4 (추위 등이) not severe[hard / tense]; mild; moderate. ¶추위[더위]가 ~ be not so cold [hot].

대단하다 1 〔수가 많다〕 many; a great[large / good] number of; 〔양이 많다〕 much; a great [good] deal of; 〔엄청나다〕 countless; innumerable; enormous; immense. ¶대단한 금액 a colossal[huge / vast] sum (at)/대단한 비용 enormous[immense] expense / (at) huge[stupendous] cost∥비용이 대단할 것이다 It will cost a lot. / It will be very expensive.∥대단한 인파다 It's a big crowd.∥이처럼 많은 사람들의 식사를 매번 준비한다는 것은 대단한 일이다 It is a lot of trouble[no easy matter] to prepare three meals a day for all these people.∥이만한 서류들을 모두 훑어본다는 것도 대단한 일이다 It is hard work just to look through all these documents.∥그것은 대단한 차이는 아니다 That does not make much difference.
2 〔중대하다〕 important; serious; grave. ¶대단한 일 a serious[an important] matter / a matter of no small consideration / (be) no joke∥그것은 대단한 일이 아니다 That does not make much difference.∥그렇게 대단하게 생각지 않는 것이 좋을 거다 You had better not take it so seriously.
3 〔놀랍다·비상하다〕 horrible; terrible; awful; awesome; dreadful; tremendous; 〔놀랄 만하다〕 wonderful; amazing; (반어적) nice; fine; precious. ¶대단한 부자 a very wealthy man / a man of great wealth /대단한 사람 (반어적) a nice[fine] fellow /대단한 인물 (미국구어) a guy /대단한 여자 (속어) a fox / a knockout / (영) a cracker /초등학생으로서는 대단한 것이다 For a schoolchild, this is quite an achievement. /5천만 원을 저축했다고 정말 대단하군 You're saved fifty million won? That's really something!∥그 녀석은 대단한 놈이다 (속어) He is quite a hotshot. / (미국속어) He is a sharp[smart] cookie. / He's really something else.∥대단한 배짱이로군 What (a) nerve you've got!
4 〔심하다〕 (병 등이) serious; grave; (날씨 등이) severe; intense; violent. ¶대단한 병 a serious[severe] illness[disease] /대단한 추위[더위] severe cold[heat] /대단한 고통[기근] a severe pain[famine] /대단한 아픔 a terrible[an excruciating] pain /대단한 감기에 걸려 있다 have a bad cold∥그의 병은 대단한 것은 아니다 He is not seriously ill.∥그는 대단한 술꾼이다 He is a frightful drinker.∥바람이[비가] ~ It blows[rains] hard.
5 〔뛰어나다〕 great; grand. ¶대단한 학자 a great[an eminent] scholar /대단한 수완가 a person of considerable[great / exceptional] ability∥그는 대단한 학자가 아니다 He is not much of a scholar.∥저 사람은 대단한 예술가다(아니다) He is quite a great artist. [He is not much of an artist].∥그의 음악적 재능은 ~ His talent in music is considerable.∥그는 대단한 집안 출신이라고 한다 He comes from some grand family, I hear. / He is of very good birth, I hear.∥그래 봬도 그는 고향에서는 대단한 사람이다 He is a hero in his hometown.

대단히 very; (very) much; a great deal; greatly; extremely; immensely; highly; seriously; terribly; awfully. ¶~ 비싼 값의 그림 a highly valued picture /~ 예쁜 옷 an awfully pretty dress∥~ 미안합니다 I'm terribly sorry.∥그는 ~ 기뻐하고 있다 He is very[extremely] pleased.∥~ 재미있는 연극이었다 It was a most[highly] interesting play.∥~ 재미있었다 We had a lot of fun.∥그는 ~ 뛰어난 학자다 He is a brilliant student[scholar].∥~ 덥다 It's awfully [terribly] hot.∥~ 죄송합니다 I am very[(구어) awfully] sorry.∥그의 원조 제의는 ~ 환영받았다 His offer of help was very much [deeply] appreciated.∥그는 두뇌가 ~ 명석하다 He is extremely intelligent.∥그는 ~ 훌륭하다 He is truly brilliant.∥그의 연주는 ~ 훌륭했다 He played remarkably well. / His performance was truly excellent.∥~ 맛이 있다 It's deliciously tasty.∥~ 좋은 사람이다 He is such a good man.∥~ 기뻐하였다 He was delighted[pleased] beyond measure.∥~ 당신을 만나고 싶었다 I wanted to see you very badly. / I was dying to see you.∥그는 피아노를 ~ 잘 쳤다 He played the piano very[remarkably] well.∥나는 그것을 ~ 좋아해 I'm very fond of it. / I like it very much.∥나는 ~ 피곤해 I am dead[very] tired.∥그것을 들으니 ~ 기쁘오 I am very[awfully] glad to hear that.∥이것은 ~ 중요하오 This is very[extremely] important.

대담(對談) 〔마주 보고 이야기함〕 a talk; a face-to-face talk; a conversation; a tête-à-tête (*pl.* tête(s)-à-têtes); a colloquy; [회견] an interview. **대담하다** talk with; converse with; have an interview with.

대담하다(大膽―) bold; daring; intrepid; dauntless; fearless; stout-hearted; hardy; adventurous. ¶대담한 기도[계획] a bold [daring] attempt[plan] /대담한 생각[해석] a bold[radical] view[interpretation] /대담한 조치 drastic measures /대담한 행동 a daring act / fearless conduct /대담 무쌍한 dauntless / fearless / daredevil / defying /대담하게도 …하다 be bold enough (to)∥그는 대담한 녀석이다 He has iron nerves[nerves of steel].∥그녀는 대담한 옷차림으로 나타났다 She turned up in a daring dress.∥그 젊은이는 대담하게도 사장을 비난했다 The young man had the audacity [impudence] to lash out as his boss. **대담히** boldly; intrepidly; fearlessly; daringly; courageously; dauntlessly; adventurously; nervily. ¶~ 일을 맞다 face a situation fearlessly /~ 나오다 show[present] a bold front /~ 행동하다 act boldly /~ 처리하다 take drastic steps /~ 말하다 speak out / venture to say∥그들은 ~ 폭풍이 부는 바다로 나아갔다 They ventured out on the

대답(對答) a reply; an answer; a response. ¶~으로서 for an answer // 이도 저도 아닌 ~을 하다 give a noncommittal [vague] answer // 분명한 ~을 하다 have a definite reply // 아무 ~도 하지 않다 make no reply [answer] / answer (a person) nothing // 질문에 대한 ~은 얻었느냐 Have you received a reply to your inquiry? // 여러 번 노크를 해도 ~이 없었다 There was no answer [response] to my repeated knocking on the door. // 그는 나의 질문에 대해 확실한 ~을 하지 않았다 He did not give a definite answer to my question. // 싫건 좋건 확실한 ~을 해 주시오 I should like to have a definite reply, yes or no. **대답하다** reply; answer; make [give] an answer [a reply]; respond (to). ¶거침없이 ~ answer briskly / give brisk answers // 그렇다고 [그렇지 않다고] ~ give an affirmative [a negative] answer / answer in the affirmative [negative] // 뭐라고 대답해야 좋을지 몰랐다 I didn't know how to answer. / I was at a loss for an answer. // 그가 맨 처음으로 대답했다 He was the first to reply. // 이름이 불리면 대답하시오 You must answer when your name is called. // 그녀는 손님의 물음에 재치 있게 대답했다 She dealt skillfully with the customers' inquiries. // 나는 문을 노크했지만 아무도 대답하지 않았다 I knocked on the door, but no one answered.

대대(大隊) (보병·포병의) a battalion; (전차·기병·미국 공군의) a squadron. ¶공병 ~ an engineering battalion // 비행 ~ a squadron.
● **대대장** a battalion commander.

대대(代代) successive generation. ¶~의 hereditary / successive // ~의 신하 a hereditary vassal.

대대로(代代-) generation after generation; for generations. ¶~ 전해 내려오는 물건 a hereditary article // ~ 전해 내려오는 전설 a legend handed down from generation to generation // 저 집은 ~ 학자 집안이다 They have been scholars for generations. // 이 기술은 집안 ~ 이어져 내려오고 있다 This technique has been handed down from generation to generation in the family. // 그들은 ~ 불교를 믿어 왔다 Their hereditary religion was Buddhism.

대대적(大大的) big; extensive; large scale; wholesale; sweeping; grand; immense. ¶~으로 extensively / on a large scale / in a large way // ~인 검거 a wholesale arrest / a roundup // ~으로 선전하다 advertise extensively / place [put in] a large advertisement (in a newspaper) // 그는 여러 군데의 레스토랑을 ~으로 경영하고 있다 He runs many restaurants on a large scale [(구어) in a big way]. // 그 사건은 ~으로 보도되었다 The incident was reported with banner headlines. / The incident was given a lot of coverage.

대도(大道) **1** [큰길] a highway; a main road [street]; a thoroughfare; a public street. ¶~를 활보하다 swagger along [strut on] the road. **2** [큰 도리] a great moral principal; a great cause. ¶박애는 인류의 ~이다 Benevolence is the great principle of humanity.

대도시(大都市) a great [large / big] city; a metropolis.

대독(代讀) reading by proxy. **대독하다** read for [on behalf of] (another). ¶총장의 연설을 대독했다 I read the president's speech for him [on his behalf].

대동(帶同) accompaniment. **대동하다** be accompanied by; take [have] (a person) along (with).

대동단결(大同團結) unity; union; solidarity; grand alliance. **대동단결하다** unite for a common purpose; be (firmly) united. ¶그들은 대동단결하여 적에 맞설 것이다 They will present a united front to their enemies.

대동맥(大動脈) [생] the main artery; the aorta (pl. ~s, -tae). ¶상행 [하행] ~ the ascending [descending] aorta.

대동사(代動詞) [언] pro-verb.

대동소이하다(大同小異-) much [nearly] alike [the same]; almost identical; substantially [practically] the same. ¶양쪽 모두 ~ The two are practically the same. // 방법이 잘못된 점에서는 양쪽이 ~ There is not much difference between the miserable condition of the two roads.

대두(大斗) a ten-*doe* measure; a large (dry) measure. ¶~ 닷 말 five *mal* by large measure.

대두(大豆) a soybean; a soya (bean). ⇨콩.

대두(擡頭) rise (of nationalism). ¶자유 민권 사상의 ~ the rise of the idea of democratic rights. **대두하다** raise [show] one's [its] head; come to the fore [front]; become influential [powerful]; be on the rise. ¶그 무렵 자본주의가 대두하기 시작했다 In those days capitalism was beginning to make its appearance [was on the rise].

대들다 defy; stand against; turn (against / upon); go at; challenge; oppose; rose against; lift a finger against; lash (out) (at); put a chip on one's shoulder. ¶상사에게 ~ snap at one's boss // 상관에게 대들다가 해고되다 be discharged for insubordination // …라고 하면서 ~ challenge (a person) saying that … // 그는 화가 나서 내게 대들었다 He turned upon me in a fury. // 감히 그에게 대들 자는 없다 No one dare lift a finger against him. // 그녀는 내가 자기의 작품을 헐뜯었다고 해서 내게 대들었다 She flared up [flashed out] at me for having spoken unkindly of her work.

대들보(大-) **1** [건] a girder; a crossbeam; a summer. **2** [중요한 사람] a mainstay; a pillar; a prop. ¶집안의 ~ the breadwinner [prop / supporter] of a family // 그는 이 모임의 ~이다 He is the main pillar [mainstay] of this club. // 아버지의 죽음으로 그 가족은 ~를 잃었다 The father's death meant the loss of the family mainstay. / The family was left without support by the father's death.

대등하다(對等-) equal; on an equal status [footing]; even; level. ¶대등하게 equally / on an equivalent basis with // 대등한 관계에 있다 be on an equal footing (with) // 대등한 교제를 하다 associate on an equal footing // 승부 없이 ~ have a game on equal terms / play an even game // 남녀 대등한 조건으로 일하다 work on equal term between sexes // 대등하게 하다 level / even / equalize (a

대뜸 person) to [with] (another) // 대등하게 승부를 겨루다 compete [play] on equal terms // 두 사람의 실력은 ~ The two are equally matched in ability. // 두 사람은 체력적으로 거의 ~ The two are almost equal in (physical) strength. // 그 사람과는 대등한 입장에 서 있다 I am on an equal footing with him.

대뜸 at once; outright; forthwith; on the spot; instantly; promptly; immediately; in no time; offhand; extempore. ¶~ 대답하다 answer immediately / give a ready answer // ~ 승낙하다 give a ready consent / accept (at invitation) immediately // ~ 의견을 말하다 give an offhand opinion (on a matter) // 그는 나를 보자 ~ 멱살을 잡았다 He seized me by the collar the moment [instant] he saw me.

대란(大亂) a serious [great] disturbance; a great commotion [rebellion]. ¶~을 진압하다 suppress [quell] a great rebellion.

대략(大略) **1** [개략] an outline; a summary; an epitome; the gist. ¶~을 말하자면 to sum up / to give a general account of / ~을 말하다 give an outline of / summarize / sum up // ~을 파악하다 have a general [rough] idea (of) // 사건의 ~이 차츰 밝혀졌다 Gradually I got the general idea of what had happened. // 교섭 내용의 ~은 이렇습니다 This is the gist of the negotiations.
2 [대충] about; approximately; nearly; roughly; in the main; cursorily; on the whole. ¶~ 말씀드리면 roughly [broadly] speaking // 손해는 ~ 100만 원으로 예측되고 있다 The damage is estimated at roughly a million won. // 그 시의 인구는 ~ 100만쯤 된다 The population of the city is an approximately one million. // 그의 견해는 ~ 다음과 같다 His views may be summarized as follows.

대량(大量) a large [great] quantity (of); enormous volume; a lot (of); (구어) a pile (of). ¶~으로 in large [great] quantities / in bulk // ~ 수출하다 export (a thing) in large quantities // 식량을 ~으로 사들이다 buy large quantities of food // ~ 구입 시 특가 제공 (게시) Special prices on quantity lots.
● **대량 생산** mass [quantity] production; production on a large scale. **대량 소비** mass consumption. **대량 수요** a large demand. **대량 실업** mass unemployment. ¶당시의 경기 후퇴로 ~이 생겼다 That recession resulted in large-scale unemployment. **대량 주문** bulk [large] order. ¶~으로 값을 싸게 할 수가 있다 We can get lower prices by ordering in bulk. **대량 학살** mass murder; genocide.

대령(大領) (육군·공군) a colonel; (해군) a captain.

대령(待令) waiting for an order [a command]; presenting oneself. **대령하다** wait for an order [a command]; stand ready to carry out an order; present oneself (before an official).

대례(大禮) (국가의) a state ceremony; an august ceremonial; [대관식] a coronation; an enthronement ceremony; [결혼식] a marriage ceremony [service].
● **대례복** full [court] dress; (부인의) (프) robe décolletée; (군인의) a grand gold-laced uniform; a full-dress uniform.

대로 1 […처럼] as; like; [그 모양과 같이] as it is; as it stands; intact; [본떠서] after. ¶종전 ~ as hitherto // 있는 그~의 인생 life as it is // 느낀 ~ 이야기하다 speak just as one feels / 글씨본 ~ 쓰다 write after a model handwriting // 내가 말한 ~지 I told you so! // 어머니 말씀~ 비가 왔다 Mother was right about the rain.
2 […에 따라] as; according to [as]; in accordance with; true to; in pursuance of. ¶약속 ~ as promised // 예정 ~ as scheduled // 규칙 ~ according to the rule // 발이 향하는 ~ 걷다 walk where one's feet lead one // 남이 하라는 ~ 하다 be at another's beck and call [another's bidding] / do whatever one is told // 분부~ 하겠습니다 I will follow your advice. // 내가 하라는 ~ 하면 틀림없다 Follow me, and you will be all right. // 그들은 왕의 명령 ~ 행동했다 They acted according as the king told them to. // 모든 일이 계획~ 진행되었다 Everything went as previously arranged. // 그는 결심한 ~ 실행했다 He did exactly what he had decided to do. // 사장이 말한 ~ 했다 I did as the president told me. // 나는 그가 하고 싶은 ~ 하게 했다 I let him do as he liked [wanted / thought best]. // 시민은 포학한 정복자가 하는 ~ 내맡겨져 있다 The citizens abandoned themselves to the tyranny of the conqueror.
3 [즉시] as soon as; directly. ¶기회가 있는 ~ at [on] the first opportunity // 도착하는 ~ as soon as one arrives / on one's arrival // 형편이 닿는 ~ at one's earliest convenience // 통지를 받는 ~ 즉시 출발할 수 있는 준비가 되어 있다 I am ready to stand at a minute's notice. // 기회가 닿는 ~ 찾아뵙겠습니다 I will call on you at the first [earliest] opportunity. // 도쿄에 닿는 ~ 전보를 치시오 Wire me as soon as you arrive at Tokyo.
4 [원하는 바와 같이] as one pleases; at will. ¶먹고 싶은 ~ 먹다 eat one's fill [to one's heart's content] / eat as much as one likes // 제 하고 싶은 ~ 하다 have everything one's own way // 우리는 무엇이든 하고 싶은 ~ 하고 어디든 가고 싶은 ~ 간다 We do as we like and go where we want to. // 만사가 바라던 ~ 되었다 Everything has turned out just as I wished. // 좋을 ~ 하십시오 Do as you like [please].
5 [할 때마다] every [each] time; each occasion; whenever; as often as. ¶그는 하는 ~ 실패했다 He failed every time he attempted. / He made several attempts and failed as many times.
6 [따로] apart; separately; [자기 나름으로] in one's own way [manner]. ¶그것은 그것~ 두어라 Keep it apart from others. // 나는 나~ 행동을 취했다 I acted in my own way.

대로(大怒) great anger; wild rage; wrath; fury. **대로하다** get angry; rage; be furious. ¶대로하다 in the fury of one's passion.

대로(大路) a highway; a main [principal / broad] street [road]; a highroad; a thoroughfare. ¶~에서 on the street / in the open air.

대롱 a bamboo tube; pipe; (물레의) a spool.

대롱거리다 dangle; swing; sway to and fro; hang loosely. ¶그의 허리께에서 뭔가가 대롱거리고 있었다 Something was dangling at his waist. // 초롱이 바람에 대롱거린다 The lantern is swinging in the wind.

대롱대롱 dangling; dingle-dangle; swaying to and fro. ¶사과 한 알이 가지에 ~ 매달려 있다 An apple is dangling from the branch.

대류(對流) [물] convection current. ¶~시키다 circulate (warm air) by convection/convect.
- **대류권** [기상] the troposphere. ¶~의 tropospheric // (초단파를) ~에서 반사시키다 troposcatter. **대류 전류** a convection current.

대륙(大陸) a continent. ¶신~ the New Continent // 아시아 ~ the Continent of Asia // 암흑의 ~ the Dark Continent // 유럽 ~ the Continent of Europe / the European Continent // ~의 continental // ~ 간 intercontinental // ~화하다 continentalize // 아시아는 모든 ~ 중에서 가장 크다 Asia is the largest of all the continents of the world.
- **대륙 간 탄도탄** an intercontinental ballistic missile(약어 ICBM). **대륙붕** a continental shelf. **대륙성** continentality. ¶~ 기후 continental climate. **대륙 횡단 철도** a transcontinental railway; (미) a coast-to-coast railroad.

대륙적(大陸的) continental; [비유] large-minded; carefree; easygoing. ¶~인 사상 continentalism // 중국인에게는 어딘지 모르게 ~인 기풍이 있다 The Chinese are somewhat continental in their ideas and fancies. // 그에게는 ~인 기풍이 있다 There is something large-hearted[liberal] about his ideas and manners.

대리(代理) [일을 대신하는 행위] representation; agency; proxy; [법] procuration; attorneyship; subrogation; [일을 대신하는 사람] a proxy; a deputy; an agent. ¶과장 ~ a deputy manager / a deputy section chief // 교장 ~ acting principal (of a school) // 의장 ~ a deputy chairman // ~의 acting / vicarious / deputy // ~로(서) by proxy / by deputy / by procuration // 대통령이 입원해 있는 동안 부통령이 ~로 집무했다 The Vice-President acted [stood in] for the President while he was in the hospital. // 그의 ~로 투표했다 I voted on his behalf[as his proxy]. // ~를 세워 투쟁하기로 했다 I decided to retain an attorney and contest the suit. // 나는 아버지 ~로 아저씨 댁에 갔다 I went to my uncle's in my father's place. **대리하다** act (as substitute) for; act in place[behalf] of; act in another's name; stand[be] proxy for; represent (another person); stand in the place of; (구어) deputize for. ¶아버지를 대리하여 회의에 참석했다 I attended the conference in my father's place. / I represented my father at the conference. →¶대리시키다 substitute (a person) for (another) / make (another) one's proxy / [법] subrogate.
- **대리 경작** the cultivation by proxy. **대리 대사** a chargé d'affaires (of an embassy). **대리모**(-母) a surrogate mother. **대리 운전사** a proxy driver. **대리인** a representative; a proxy; an agent; [법] a procurator; (소송의) an attorney. **대리점** ~ a legal representative. **대리점** an agency; an agent. ¶총 ~ the general agent // ~을 설치하다 establish an agency. **대리 투표** voting by proxy.

대리석(大理石) marble. ¶인조[모조] ~ scagliola / artificial marble.

대립(對立) confronting; opposition; antagonism. ¶민족 간의 ~ the antagonism of one race against another // 고용주와 피고용인 간의 ~ antagonism between the employer and the employed // 그 두 파는 ~ 상태에 있다 The two parties stood in opposition[were in a state of confrontation]. // 그것이 노사간의 심각한 ~을 초래케 했다 It brought about [led to] serious antagonism between labor and management. // 주도권을 둘러싼 ~의 연속이었다 There was a constant struggle for the leadership. **대립하다** be opposed to (each other); be pitted against; stand face to face; be antagonistic to (each other). ¶날카롭게 대립한 의견 sharply divided opinions // 여야가 대립하고 있다 The government and opposition parties are pitted against each other. →¶이 문제에 관하여 의견들이 대립되고 있다 There are rival[opposing] opinions on this problem.
- **대립 감정** a feeling of confrontation [rivalry].

대마(大馬) (바둑에서) a large group of stones.
- **대마불사**(-不死) Large groups of stones are seldom captured.

대마(大麻) [식] a hemp (plant). ⇨삼¹
- **대마유** hempseed oil. **대마초** (식물) hemp; (흡연물) a hemp cigarette; hashish; marijuana. ¶~를 상습적으로 피우다 habitually smoke hemp leaf cigarets. **대마초 사범** an offender of the law on hemp control. **대마초 흡연자** a hemp[marijuana] smoker.

대마루 (지붕의) the ridge of the roof.

대막대기 a bamboo stick[pole].

대만원(大滿員) a full house; an overflowing house; a crowded[large] audience; (속은) full up. ¶~의 chock-full / galleryful // ~을 이루다 have a crowded audience / draw a large[crowded] house // 아침저녁의 러시아워에는 모든 교통 기관이 ~을 이룬다 Vehicles of all types are jampacked during the morning and evening rushes. // 극장은 ~이다 There is very good attendance at the theater. / The movie house is packed to capacity. / The theater is bursting with people.

대망(大望) a great ambition; a great desire; an aspiration. ¶~을 품다 be full of ambitions / have[cherish / harbor / nourish] an ambition // ~을 이루다 realize one's supreme ambition / attain the object of one's ambition // 그는 정치가가 되겠다는 ~을 품고 있다 He has an ambition to become a great statesman. // 그는 드디어 ~을 이루었다 He finally realized his ambition.

대망(待望) expectation; anticipation; eager waiting. ¶~의 hoped-for / long-[eagerly-] awaited / eagerly anticipated // ~의 경기 회복 the hoped-for business recovery // ~의 휴전이 마침내 실현되었다 The long-awaited cease-fire finally materialized. // 드디어 ~의 원맨쇼가 열렸다 At long last I was able to hold a one-man show. / I was finally able to fulfill my long-cherished dream of holding a one-man show. **대망하다** wait for eagerly; look forward to; expect. ¶우리 고장에서는 대통령의 내방을 대망하고 있었다 People had long been looking forward to the President's visit to our country.

대매출(大賣出) a special bargain sale. ¶반액[사은] ~ a half-price[thank-you] bargain sale // 연말 ~ a year-end sale // 가구의 ~ a

furniture bargain sale // 저 슈퍼마켓에서는 ~을 하고 있다 The supermarket is holding a big sale // 그 상점에서는 재고 정리 ~을 하고 있다 The store is having a clearance sale.
대맥(大麥) [식] barley. ⇨보리
대머리 a baldhead; a baldheaded person; a baldpate. ¶젊어서 벗어진 ~ a premature baldhead // 일찍 ~가 된 prematurely bald // **~가 벗어지다** become baldheaded // 그는 ~다 He is bald. / (문어·농조) He has a shiny pate.
● **대머리 총각** a bachelor prematurely bald.
대면(對面) an interview; a meeting; [마주 봄] facing; [법] confrontation. ¶첫 ~의 손님 a new[an unfamiliar] customer. **대면하다** meet; see; interview; have an interview (with). ¶동생과 10년 만에 대면할 수 있었다 I was able to meet my brother again after ten years' separation.
● **대면 통행** facing traffic; vis-à-vis traffic; (the system of) walking on the side of the street facing oncoming traffic.
대명(大命) a Royal command[mandate]. ¶~을 받들어 in obedience to the king's command // **~을 내리다** issue a Royal mandate.
대명(待命) pending appointment; awaiting orders; (공무원 등의) being placed on the waiting list. **대명하다** await orders; be placed on the waiting list.
대명사(大名辭) [논] the major term.
대명사(代名詞) [언] a pronoun. ¶부정[의문/관계] ~ an indefinite[an interrogative / a relative] pronoun // 인칭[재귀/지시] ~ a personal[reflexive / demonstrative] pronoun // ~의 pronominal // ~로서 pronominally // 그의 이름은 부자의 ~가 되었다 His name has become synonymous with wealth.
대모(代母) [가] a godmother.
대목 1 [시기] the most important occasion; the height of a certain period; the vital moment; (상의의) a rush period. ¶섣달 ~ the very end of the year // ~을 노리고 물건을 쌓아 두다 stock goods to provide for the rush period // 이제부터 가장 어려운 ~이다 Now we have come to the most difficult part of the work. 2 [글의] a passage; a paragraph. ¶재미있는 ~ an interesting passage // 이 ~의 의미가 애매하다 The meaning of this part [passage] is obscure. // 나는 그 ~을 다시 읽었다 I reread that passage.
● **대목장** a fair preceding a fate day; (연말의) a year-end fair.
대목(臺木) the (parent) stock. ⇨접본(椄本)
대못 [대나무 못] a bamboo peg[nail].
대못(大-) a big[large] nail; a spike (nail). ¶~을 박다 spike (a beam).
대문(大門) a gate; the front[main] gate [entrance]. ¶으리으리한 ~이 있는 집 a house with a stately gate // ~을 걸다 bolt the front gate / close a gate / lock a gate(자물쇠로 잠그다).
대문 밖이 저승이라 (속담) Death keeps no calendar.
대문자(大文字) (로마자의) a capital letter. ¶~로 쓰다 capitalize / write in capitals [capital letters] // 이 말의 첫 글자는 ~로 쓴다 The first letter of this word shall be capitalized.
대문장(大文章) [잘 지은 훌륭한 글] masterful writing; [훌륭한 글을 잘 짓는 사람] a master writer; a great master of (literary)

style.
대문짝(大門-) (문짝) a flap; a (door) leaf; (문) a door; a gate.
대문짝만하다(大門-) huge; conspicuous. ¶(표제 등을) 대문짝만하게 내다 play up (the news) with a banner // 신문에 대문짝만하게 나다 go into headlines // 서울의 모든 신문이 그 기사를 대문짝만하게 실었다 All the Seoul papers bannered the news.
대물(代物) a substitute.
● **대물 변제** payment in substitutes.
대물(對物) objects; reality. ¶~의 real / objective.
● **대물렌즈** an object lens; an objective; a field lens. **대물 담보** security against a thing.
대물리다(代-) hand down; transmit; leave; bequeath. ¶대물린 재산 property inherited from one's parents / a patrimony / a heritage // 손자에게 재산을 ~ bequeath one's property to one's grandson // 아들에게 ~ transmit from father to son.
대미(對美) [관형어적] towards America; with America. ¶~ 수출 자율 규제 voluntary restriction of exports to the U.S.A. // 국민들의 ~ 감정은 보편적으로 좋다 The people have generally favorable feelings toward the United States.
● **대미 관계** relations with America. **대미 무역** trade with America. ¶한국의 ~ Korean trade with the United States. **대미 정책** a policy toward America. ¶우리나라의 ~ our policy toward America / our American policy.
대민(對民) [관형어적].
● **대민 봉사 활동** service for public welfare.
대바구니 a bamboo basket.
대바늘 a bamboo (knitting) needle.
대받다(代-) 1 [상속받다] inherit. ¶재산을 ~ inherit some property. 2 [계승하다] succeed to; continue. ¶아버지의 일을 ~ succeed to one's father's business.
대발 a woven bamboo curtain; a bamboo blind[screen].
대밭 a bamboo thicket[grove].
대번에 [단숨에] at a breath; at a stroke [blow]; at one coup[try]; by a single effort; [곧] at once; immediately; directly; promptly; instantly; [쉽사리] very easily; without difficulty[effort]; readily; [서슴지 않고] without hesitation. ¶~ 알아맞히다 guess right at once // 담을 ~ 뛰어넘다 clear a fence with an easy jump // 나무를 ~ 찍어 넘어뜨리다 fell a tree at a single stroke // 돈을 ~ 다 써 버리다 use up[spend] one's money in no time // 그는 일을 ~ 해치웠다 He finished the work at one standing. // 나는 그곳의 형편을 ~ 알아차렸다 I took in the scene with a single glance.
대범하다(大汎-·大泛-) large-hearted; broadminded; liberal; generous; magnanimous; open-handed; catholic. ¶대범한 태도 an air of magnanimity / loft manners / free and open manners // 그녀는 대범한 사람이다 She isn't fussy about things. / She has no head for details. **대범히** generously; magnanimously; lordly. ¶~ 돈을 쓰다 be liberal [generous / lordly] with one's money.
대법관(大法官) a justice of the Supreme Court; (영국의) Lord (High) Chancellor(약어 L.(H.)C.).

대법원(大法院) the Supreme Court; (영국의) the Supreme Court of Judicature; (프랑스의) the Court of Cassation. ¶~에 상고하다 appeal to the Supreme Court.
● **대법원장** the Chief Justice[President] of the Supreme Court. **대법원 판사** a justice of the Supreme Court.

대법회(大法會) [설법회] a large Buddhist lecture meeting.

대변(大便) [인분] f(a)eces; excrements; stools; dung; evacuation; excreta; motions; movements. ¶~ 보러 가다 go to the lavatory / (미) go to the toilet // ~이 마렵다 want to go to the toilet / have a call of nature // ~을 보다 move[empty] the bowels / go to stool // 오늘은 ~이 나오지 않는다 I haven't had a bowel movement today.
● **대변 검사** an examination of the feces.

대변(代辯) speaking by proxy. **대변하다** speak for; be a mouthpiece for; act as a spokesman (of). ¶아들이 부모의 기분을 대변했다 The son spoke for his parents.
● **대변인** a spokesman; a spokesperson; a press officer; a mouthpiece. ¶민중의 ~ a spokesman for the masses // 신문은 여론의 ~이 되어야 한다 The newspaper must speak for the public.

대변(貸邊) [경] the credit(or)(약어 cr.); the credit side. ¶10만 원을 ~에 기입하다 enter 100,000 won on the credit side.
● **대변 계정** a credit account; accounts of the creditor side.

대변(對邊) [수] the opposite side[edge]; the subtense.

대별(大別) a general[broad] classification. **대별하다** classify[divide] roughly (into); make a general classification. ¶두 종류로 ~ divide into two main classes.

대보다 [비교하다] compare (A with B); measure; balance; make a comparison (between A and B); [대조하다] contrast. ¶…과 대보면 in comparison (with) / as compared (with) // 번역을 원문과 ~ compare a translation with the original // 어느 것이 좋은가 대보자 Let us see which is better.

대보름(大-) daeboreum; the 15th of January by the lunar calendar.

대본(大本) the great foundation; the primal basis; the basic[cardinal] principles. ¶국가[인류]의 ~ the foundation of the state[human morality].

대본(貸本) a book for lending; a book for[on] hire; (미) a rental book; (미) a hired book.

대본(臺本) (연극의) a playbook; a (play) script; (영화의) a (film) script; a scenario (pl. ~s); (오페라의) a libretto (pl. ~s, -ti). ¶방송용 ~ a (radio) script // 회화 ~ a dialogue script // ~에 없는 대사를 말하다 ad-lib // ~ 읽기를 시작하다 get to reading the dialogue of each other's part.
● **대본 작가** (영화의) a scriptwriter; a screenwriter; a continuity writer; a scripter; a scenarist; (가극의) a librettist.

대부(代父) [가] a godfather. ¶우리 아기의 ~가 되어 주시지 않겠습니까 Would you be godfather to our baby?

대부(貸付) loaning. ¶단기 ~ a short(-term) loan // 당좌 ~ a call loan / a loan at call / (미) a day-to-day loan / (영) a demand loan // 부당 ~ a reckless[an improper] loan // 신용 ~ a loan on personal pledge / a personal [credit] loan / an open credit // 은행 ~ a (commercial) bank loan // 일시 [장기] ~ a temporary [time] loan // 장기 ~ a long(-term) loan [credit]. **대부하다** lend; loan; advance; make a loan[an advance]; (속어) tap.

대부분(大部分) [거의 모두] for the most part; most(ly); nearly; practically; on the whole; [전체량에 거의 가까운 수효·분량] the bulk (of); a major[great / large] portion (of). ¶그는 ~의 재산을 탕진했다 He squandered away almost all his property. // 이 등의 ~은 장식용이다 Most of these lamps are for decoration. / These lamps are chiefly[mostly] for decoration. // 옛 친구들은 ~ 죽었다 Most of my old friends were dead (and gone). // 그 보고서는 ~ 비서가 쓴 것이다 The report was written mostly [for the most part] by the secretary. // 건물은 ~ 완성되었다 The building has almost [nearly / practically] been completed. // 작문은 ~ 잘되어 있다 The composition is on the whole well written. // 그의 성공은 ~이 그의 선생 덕택이다 His success is due in large part to his teacher. // 국민의 ~은 그 법안에 반대했다 The majority of the people were against the bill. // 마을 사람들의 ~은 빈곤했다 Most of the villagers were poor. // 그 지방의 ~은 비옥하다 The greater part of the country is fertile. // 참석자는 ~이 젊은 남녀였다 Those present were mostly young men and women. // 그들은 ~이 이민의 후손이다 They are mostly [mainly / for the most part] descendants of immigrants.

대부인(大夫人) your [his / her] (esteemed) mother.

대북(對北) [관형어적] against [toward] the North.
● **대북 방송** broadcasting toward the North.

대분수(帶分數) [수] a mixed fraction.

대불(大佛) a colossal [huge / big] statue of Buddha; a great image of Buddha.

대비(大妃) a Queen Dowager; a Queen Mother.

대비(對比) 1 [대조] contrast; contradiction. ¶색의 ~ color contrast / contrast of colors. **대비하다** contrast (A) with[and] (B); set (A) against (B). ¶…과 대비하여 in contradiction to … // 대비해 보면 as contrasted (with). 2 [비교] comparison; a side-by-side comparison (of A and B). **대비하다** compare; draw (A) into comparison with (B). ¶양자를 ~ compare two things.

대비(對備) [준비] provision (for / against); preparations (for); preparedness (for / against); [방비] defenses. ¶만일의 경우 [불시의 지출]를 위한 ~ provision against emergencies [unforeseen expenses] // ~가 되어 있다 be prepared [ready] (for) // 혹한의 ~는 잘되어 있습니까 Are you well prepared for the severed cold? **대비하다** prepare (for); make preparations (for); provide (for / against). ¶흉년에 대비하여 by way of precaution against a bad year // 장래에 ~ provide [prepare / make provisions] for the future // 노후를 대비하여 저축하다 save money for one's old age // 만일의 경우에 ~ provide [make provisions] against contingencies [emergencies] // 시험에 ~ prepare oneself[get oneself ready] for an examination // 적침에 대비하여 국방력을 강화하다 strengthen the national defense against a possible aggression // 노후에 대비하는 것을 잊지 말아야 한다 We must not forget to provide for our old age. // 전쟁이 일어날 경우에 대비해야 한다 We had better be prepared [ready] in case war should break out. // 그는 경연에 대비하여 밤마다 스피치 연습을 하고 있다 He has been practicing his speech every night for the contest.

대빗 [대나무로 된 빗] a bamboo comb.

대사(大事) 1 [큰 일] a great thing; [큰 사업] a grand enterprise; a great undertaking [task]. 2 [중대사] a matter of grave concern; a serious [grave] affair; [위기] a crisis (*pl.* -ses); an emergency. 3 [대례] a great ceremony; [혼례] a marriage ceremony. ¶~를 치르다 perform a great ceremony / hold a marriage / celebrate (a person's) sixtieth birthday.

대사(大使) an ambassador; an ambassadress(여성). ¶주미[주일] ~ an ambassador to the United States [to Japan] // ~ an ambassador plenipotentiary // 특명 전권 ~ an ambassador extraordinary and plenipotentiary // 순회[이동] ~ a roving ambassador // 대리 ~ (프) a chargé d'affairs // 미국 주재 한국 ~ the Korean Ambassador to America // 주한 이탈리아 ~ the Italian Ambassador to Korea // ~를 파견하다 dispatch a special envoy (to).
● **대사관** an embassy. ¶미국[영국] ~ the American [British] Embassy // 주미 한국 ~ the Korean Embassy at Washington. **대사 부인** an ambassadress.

대사(大師) [불] a saint; a great Buddhist priest; a great teacher of Buddhism. ¶원효 ~ Saint Wonhyo.

대사(大赦) an amnesty; a general amnesty [pardon]; oblivion; [가] (an) indulgence. ¶그는 ~를 받아 출옥했다 He was released from prison on a general pardon [under an amnesty]. **대사하다** proclaim an amnesty; grant a general amnesty to.
● **대사령** a decree of amnesty [oblivion].

대사(代謝) [생] metabolism. ⇨물질대사(⇨물질).

대사(臺詞·臺辭) (배우의) speech; words; one's line. ¶독백 ~ a monolog(ue) / a soliloquy // ~가 없는 역 a walk-on [nonspeaking] role // ~를 말하다 read the lines / speak one's line(s) [part] // ~를 잊다 forget one's line(s) / dry up // ~를 외우다 study one's part // ~를 잘못 말하다 bungle in one's line(s).

대상(大祥) the second anniversary of (a person's) death.

대상(大商) a wealthy [influential] merchant; a merchant prince; a trader.

대상(大喪) death of the king; mourning for the deceased king.

대상(大賞) a grand prize; [프] a grand prix.

대상(代償) 1 [대리 변상] vicarious compensation; [종][심] substitution. **대상하다** compensate on behalf of (another). 2 [딴 것으로 하는] compensation in substitutes. **대상하다** compensate in substitutes.

대상(隊商) a caravan.

대상(對象) [정신 활동의 목적물] the object; the subject; [목표] a target. ¶조사[논의]의 ~ the subject of investigation [discussion] // 비판의 ~ a target [subject] of criticism // 과학적 연구의 ~ an object of scientific study // 과세의 ~ property subject to [liable for] taxation // 동정[선망]의 ~ an object of pity [envy] // 신앙의 ~ the object of worship // 공격의 ~ a target [subject] of attack // 학생을 ~으로 하는 a student-oriented magazine // 비난의 ~이 되다 become the focus of public censure // 조소의 ~이 되다 become a laughingstock [the butt of derision / the joke of the town] // 20대 여성을 ~으로 앙케트 조사를 하다 conduct a questionnaire survey of women in their twenties // 이 법률은 농민을 ~으로 한다 This law applies to the farming population. // 그녀의 소설은 신랄한 비평의 ~이 되었다 Her novel was made the target of harsh criticism. // 그의 행동은 전 국민의 주목의 ~이 되었다 His actions attracted the attention of the whole country [became the focus of the people's attention].

대생(對生) [식] opposition. ⇨마주나기

대서(大暑) 1 [24절기의 하나] *daeseo*; the midsummer-day; "the height of summer" (as one of the 24 seasonal divisions according to the lunar calendar that falls on about 23th of July); midsummer. 2 [심한 더위] an intense (summer) heat.

대서다 1 [뒤따라 서다] stand close behind (a person). ¶대서서 가다 tail after (a person) / follow at (a person's) heels / (차가) tailgate. 2 [대들다] stand against (a person); turn against [upon] (a person); defy.

대서소(代書所) a scrivener's office; a scrivenery.

대서양(大西洋) the Atlantic (Ocean). ¶~의 Atlantic // ~을 횡단하다 cross the Atlantic.
● **대서양 헌장** the Atlantic Charter.

대서특필(大書特筆) a feature (story); a cover story; a wide news coverage; featuring; special mention. **대서특필하다** publish (the news) with heavy headlines; crack the headlines; play up (the event) with a banner; (영) splash the news; headline; banner; feature. ¶대서특필할 만한 (a deed) worthy of special mention // 그 지방 신문들은 대통령의 방문을 대서특필했다 The local newspapers featured the President's visit. // 신문들은 워터게이트 사건을 대서특필하고 있다 The newspapers are headlining a story about the Watergate scandal. // 신문은 호텔의 대화재를 대서특필했다 The newspaper devoted a great deal of space to the big hotel fire. // 최근 신문들은 대규모의 밀수 사건을 대서특필하고 있다 Lately the newspapers have been full of stories about large-scale smuggling.

대서하다(代書-) write [draw up] for (another). ¶나는 늘 할머니의 편지를 대서한다 I always write letters for my grandmother.

대석(臺石) a pedestal (stone); a footstone.

대석하다(對席-) [마주 앉다] sit facing each other; (회견·교섭 등에서) attend together.

대선(大船) a big [great] ship; a large vessel.

대선거구(大選擧區) a major constituency.
● **대선거구제** a major constituency system.

대설(大雪) 1 [많이 오는 눈] a heavy (fall of) snow; a heavy snowfall. ¶[10년래의] ~이다 This is a snowfall such as has not been seen for some [ten] years. / This is

대성

the great[heaviest] snowfall that we have had[seen] for some[ten] years. 2 [24절기의 하나] *daeseol*; "the heavy snowfall" (as one of the 24 seasonal divisions according to the lunar calendar that falls on about 7th of December).
● 대설 주의보 a heavy snow warning.

대성(大聖) a great sage; (공자) Confucius, the Great Sage; [불] a mahatma. ¶~ 소크라테스 the great sage Socrates.

대성공(大成功) a great[big / huge / brilliant] success; a successful[big] hit; a splendid result; (공연 등의) a brilliant performance; (미) a box-office performance. ¶~을 거두다 win[gain] a great success / 이번 연극은 ~이다 The new play is a great success[hit / draw]. / The new play is a big box-office hit. // 그는 쇼에서 ~을 거두었다 He made a big hit in the show. / He was a great success in the show.

대성통곡하다(大聲痛哭−) lament (at the top of one's voice); wail; bemoan; mourn[weep] bitterly.

대성하다(大成−) be crowned with success; attain[come to] greatness. ¶대성할 인물 a man full of promise / a person with the makings of a great man // 그는 앞으로 대성할 것이다 He promises to achieve great things. / He has in him the makings of a great man. // 그는 대성하지 못할 것이다 He will never amount to much. // 그의 사업은 대성했다 His work was crowned with success.

대성황(大盛況) prosperity; flourishing condition; a great success; a boom. ¶~을 이루다 (극장 등) play to the gallery / be a gallery hit // 그 파티는 ~을 이루었다 The party was a great success. / The party went very well. // 박람회는 ~이었다 The exhibition was a great success. / There was a great turnout (of people) at the exhibition.

대세(大勢) 1 [형세·추세] the general trend [drift / situation] (of the times[affairs]); the general tendency (of the world); the general current (of thought). ¶세계의 ~ the general situation of the world / the international situation / the trend of the international affairs // ~에 순응하다 adapt oneself to (the trend of) the times // ~에 따르다 follow the general trend / swim with the tide[stream / current] // ~에 거스르다[역행하다] swim against the tide[stream / current] // ~를 파악하다 grasp [understand] the situation // ~를 결정짓다 bring (a matter) almost to its final issue // ~를 살피다 study the general situation // ~는 우리에게 유리[불리]하다 The general situation[The tide] is in our favor[against us]. / The general situation is[is not] favorable to us. / The tide (of public opinion) has turned in our favor[against us]. // ~는 이미 결정되었다 The final issue is now certain. / The thing[issue] is as good as settled. / (구어) It's all over but[(영) bar] the shouting. // 경기의 ~는 결정되었다 The game is virtually decided. // 세계의 ~는 민주주의로 기울어지고 있다 The tendency toward democracy now holds sway in the world. // 문단의 ~는 신고전주의로 기울어지고 있다 A tendency toward neoclassicism held sway in literary circles.
2 [권세] great power[influence]. ¶~를 잡다 seize[take / assume] power / move into power / come into one's kingdom.
3 (병의) a serious[grave] condition; a critical state[stage]; a crisis.

대소(大小) [대와 소] great and small sizes; [크기] (relative) size; dimensions; magnitude. ¶~의 large and[or] small / of all [many / several / various] sizes // ~의 섬들 islands of various[all] sizes // ~에 따라 according to size // ~에 관계없이 regardless of size / whether large or small // ~의 차가 있다 vary in size // ~를 비교하다 compare the sizes (of two things) // 그것은 ~ 여러 가지를 갖추고 있습니다 We have it in several sizes. // 그것은 ~에 따라 값이 다르다 The price varies according to size. // ~ 함께서 접시 5개에 오천 원에 팔고 있다 They sell a set of five dishes, large and small, for 5,000 won.

대소(大笑) a great[a loud] laughter; a hearty [good] laugh; a burst[roar] of laughter; a convulsive laughter(배꼽을 쥐는). 대소하다 laugh aloud; burst out laughing; roar with laughter; give a bellow of laughter; have a good[hearty] laugh (over / at).

대소(代訴) litigation by proxy. 대소하다 sue [bring suit] on behalf of (another).

대소(對訴) [법] a cross action. ⇨ =반소(反訴)

대소동(大騷動) a great uproar; great trouble [excitement]; a great disturbance[commotion]; a turmoil; [소요] a row; a shindy; a tumult; much ado. ¶~을 벌이다 cause an excitement / cause a great stir[sensation] // 그것 때문에 ~이 벌어졌다 It caused serious trouble. / It created[excited] a considerable agitation. // 모임에서 ~이 벌어졌다 There was a great stir at the meeting. // 온 집안이 ~이다 All is confusion in the house. / The house is topsy-turvy[in a great bustle / in a turmoil]. // 하찮은 일로 어찌 그런 ~을 벌입니까 Why do you make such a fuss about [over / of] nothing?

대소변(大小便) [변] urine and feces; [용변] urination and defecation. ¶~을 보다 relieve oneself[nature] / ease nature.

대소사(大小事) matters great and small; all-sorts of matters; any and every thing. ¶~를 맡기다 leave everything to (a person's) care [discretion].

대소수(帶小數) [수] a number with a decimal.

대소쿠리 a bamboo basket.

대속(代贖) redemption[expiation / atonement] on behalf of (another); atonement for [expiation of] another's sin(s); (예수의) the (Vicarious) Atonement; the Redemption. 대속하다 redeem; atone for (a person); expiate (a person's offence).

대손(貸損) [경] a bad debt; an irrecoverable debt. ¶~이 되다 become irrecoverable.

대수(大數) 1 [큰 수] a great [large / big / high] number. ¶~의 법칙 [수] the law of large numbers. 2 [대운] great fortune; good luck.

대수롭다 important; significant; valuable; useful. ¶대수롭지 않은[사소한] trifling / trivial / insignificant / inconsiderable / of little importance / of no account [consequence] / valueless / unworthy / worthless / useless // 대수롭지 않은 일 a matter of no importance[weight / consequence /

account] / a trivial [trifling] affair [matter] / a trifle // 대수롭지 않은 물건 a trifling thing / a little thing / a trifle / trivial [poor] stuff // 대수롭지 않은 사람 a worthless [an insignificant / a good-for-nothing] fellow / a nobody / a person of no importance // 대수롭지 않은 상처 a slight wound // 대수롭지 않게 여기다 have no regard for / think [make] little [light] of / slight // 대수롭게 여기다 think [make] much of / attach importance to / have a high regard for / hold (a person) in high regard // 생명보다 명예를 대수롭게 여기다 value [prize / esteem / put] honor above life // 그들은 남의 감정 따위는 대수롭지 않게 여긴다 They have no regard for other people's feelings. // 그는 대수롭지 않은 일로 곧잘 화를 낸다 He gets angry over mere trifles [little things]. // 대수롭지 않은 일까지 참견받고 싶지 않다 I don't want you to interfere [interfering] in every little thing.

대수술(大手術) a major (surgical) operation.

대수(학)(代數學) algebra. ¶~적 algebraic(al) // ~적 해법(解法) an algebraical solution / ~로 풀다 solve (a problem) algebraically / work out (a problem) in algebra.

대숲 a bamboo thicket [grove / jungle]; a clump of bamboos; a canebrake.

대승(大乘) [불] Mahayana; the Great Vehicle. ¶~적 견지에서 from a broad(er) viewpoint / from the point of the general good.
● 대승 불교 Mahayanist Buddhism.

대승(大勝) a great [a signal / a decisive / an easy] victory; (선거)의 a landslide [sweeping] victory; a sweep. ¶5대 0의 ~ a great victory with [by score of] five to nothing. **대승하다** gain [win] a great [signal] victory; win big; (선거에서) win a landslide (victory) (over). ¶7대 0으로 대승했다 We won easily by a score of 7:0 (▶ seven to nothing이라고도 읽음).

대승리(大勝利) a great victory. ⇨대승(大勝)

대시 1 [줄표] a dash. ¶b~[b′] [수] (미) b prime / (영) b dash // ~를 붙이다 put a dash (after a word). 2 [역주(力走)] a dash. **대시하다** dash.

대식(大食) 1 [끼니] main meals; breakfast and supper. 2 [많이 먹음] gluttony; voracity; heavy eating. **대식하다** eat much [heavily / voraciously / gluttonously]; gluttonize; gormandize; cram [stuff] oneself; eat like a horse. ¶대식하는 gluttonous / ravenous.
● 대식가 a great [large / big / hearty] eater; a glutton; a go(u)rmand; a large [huge / gross / heavy] feeder; a good trencherman.

대신(大臣) a minister (of State); a State [Cabinet] minister; a Cabinet member; (영) a Secretary (of Labo(u)r). ¶~의 ministerial // ~의 직[자리] a portfolio (pl. ~s) / ministership / a Cabinet position // ~이 되다 become [be appointed] a (State) minister / enter the Cabinet / receive a portfolio.

대신(代身) 1 [대리·대용] substitution; vicariousness; [대용품·대리인] a substitute; [구어] a sub; [대리인] a deputy; a proxy; (미) an alternate; [교대자] a relief. ¶… ~에 in place of / instead of / for / in substitute for / in lieu of / on [in] behalf of / in the name of / as (a) substitute for / in the room of // 가는 ~에 instead of going // ~으로 as a substitute // 쌀 ~에 먹는 식량 a substitute for rice // …의 ~이 되다 serve as [for] … / do duty for … // 버터 ~에 마가린을 쓰다 substitute butter by margarine / substitute margarine for butter // 남 ~에 투표하다 vote in the name of another // 육류 ~에 어류를 먹다 eat fish in the room of meat // 이것은 모자 ~에 쓸 수 있다 This will do for a hat. / This will serve as a hat. // 요즈음은 만년필 ~에 볼펜을 쓴다 We now use ball-point pens instead of fountain pens. // 그 사람 ~ 그 여자가 왔다 She came in his place. // 내 ~ 참석해 주시지 않겠습니까 Will you attend the meeting for me [in my place]? // 남편이 내 ~ 비자를 신청해 주었다 My husband applied for my visa for me [on my behalf]. // 나는 그녀 / 그녀의 아들의 안전을 빌어 주었다 I prayed for her son's safety for her [in her place]. // 자네가 못 가면 그 사람을 ~ 보내게 If you cannot go, let him go instead. // 어떤 자리건 그 사람 ~ 들어앉기는 싫다 I wouldn't be in his shoes for anything. **대신하다** take the place of; act as a substitute; take (a person's) place; be substituted (for a person); [교대하다] relieve (a person). ¶일동을 대신하여 on behalf of the company // 내 아들이 나를 대신할 것이다 My son shall be my proxy. // 형이 아버지를 대신했다 My brother took our father's place. // 그의 외유 중에 누가 그를 대신합니까 Who will take his place while he is abroad? // 좀 대신해 주게 Just take my place, will you? // 기계가 반드시 인력을 대신할 수 있는 것은 아니다 Machinery cannot always take the place of human labor. // 협회를 대신해서 인사 말씀을 드리겠습니다 Allow me to say a few words on behalf of the association. // 클래스 일동을 대신해서 내가 입원 중인 그를 문병했다 I went to see him in [(미) in] the hospital on behalf of the whole class. // 아버님을 대신하여 인사 말씀을 올리겠습니다 Allow me to say a few words of greeting on behalf of my father. // 나는 그를 대신해서 책임을 질 생각이다 I intend to take the blame for [in place of] him. // 서면으로 인사를 대신하겠습니다 Please allow me to send you a letter instead of [in place of] paying you a visit. // 해외여행을 위하여 제트기가 배를 대신하게 되었다 For overseas travel jets have supplanted [taken the place of] ships. // 적자에 쪼들린 단거리 철도선이 폐지되면 버스가 대신하게 되어 있다 After service on the debt-ridden local railway lines is discontinued, bus service will be substituted for it. // 그를 대신할 만한 사람을 구할 수가 없다 We cannot find a substitute for him. // 회계 담당이 그만두었으니 대신할 사람을 찾아야만 한다 As the accountant has resigned, we have to look for someone to take his place.
2 [대상(代償)] compensation; return; [교환] exchange. ¶~에 by way of compensation / in compensation (for) / in return (for) / to make up (for) (벌충하여) / in exchange (for) (교환으로) // 어제 갠 컵 ~에 하나 사 드리겠습니다 I'll replace the cup I broke yesterday. // 톰은 자기가 잃어버린 내 나이프 ~에 새것을 주었다 Tom gave me a new knife to replace my old one, which he had lost. // 네가 브로치를 준다면 ~ 내 시계를 줄게 I'll give you my watch, if you give me your brooch in exchange (for it). // 그녀가 가사를 돌봐 주는 ~ 나는 그녀에게 영어를 가르쳐 주

대심

고 있다 I teach her English in exchange for [in return for] her help with housekeeping. **대신하다** replace. ¶전산 사식이 손으로 하는 식자를 대신하게 되었다 Typesetting by hand has been replaced [superseded] by computerized phototypesetting.
3 [한편] but; though; while. ¶값이 비싼 ~ 품질이 좋다 The quality is good though it is expensive. / It is dear but the quality is good. / 적도 많다 ~에 친구도 많다 I have as many friends as enemies. // 그는 두뇌가 명석한 ~ 몸이 튼튼하지 못하다 He has a sharp mind, but he's not strong physically. // 그 처녀는 인물은 별로 없지만 그 ~에 마음씨가 고왔다 She wasn't very good-looking, but she had a very tender heart to make up for it. // 그는 특별히 재능이 있는 것은 아니나 그 ~ 여간 열심히 노력하는 것이 아니다 He is not particularly talented, but he more than makes up for it with hard work.

대심(對審) [법] [대질] confrontation. ¶내일은 원고와 피고의 ~이 열린다 Tomorrow the accused and his accuser [the plaintiff and the defendant] will confront each other in court. **대심하다** confront (the accused with the accuser).

대아(大我) [철] absolute ego; the higher self; one's larger self; [불] one's true self; [범] Atman.

대안(代案) an alternative plan [proposal]; a substitute (measure / bill). ¶~을 제시하다 make [propose] an alternative plan [measure] // ~할 수밖에 딴 ~이 없다 have [there is] no alternative [option] but to (yield) // 무슨 ~이라도 있습니까 Do you have any alternative proposal?

대안(對岸) the other side (of a river); the opposite bank [shore]. ¶~에 on the other side (of the river) / on the opposite bank [shore] / over [across] (the river).

대안(對案) a counterproposal. ¶~을 제시하다 make a counterproposal // ~을 짜다 work out a countermeasure // 정부의 원안에 대하여 ~을 강구해 냈다 We hammered out a prompt counterproposal to the original bill introduced by the government.

대안렌즈(對眼-) an eyepiece. ⇨ 접안렌즈

대야 a basin; a washbasin; (미) a washbowl.

대양(大洋) an ocean; [시어] the main. ¶~ის oceanic / ~의 한가운데에(서) in the middle of the ocean / in mid-ocean [mid-sea] // ~ 저쪽에 있는 대륙 a transoceanic continent // ~을 가로질러서 half-away across the ocean // ~을 향해하다 sail [plow] the ocean.

● **대양도** an oceanic island. **대양 항로** an ocean line.

대어(大魚) a large [big] fish; a big game fish(특히 낚시꾼의). ¶~를 놓치다 narrowly miss a great chance of winning success // 그는 10파운드짜리 ~를 낚았다 He landed a big fish, a ten pounder.

● **대어 낚시** big-game fishing.

대업(大業) a great achievement [deed]; a great enterprise [undertaking]; great [monumental] work; a great [mighty / gigantic] task. ¶유신 [건국]의 ~ the great work of the Renovation [founding the State] // ~을 맡다 take charge of a great task // ~을 성취하다 achieve a great work.

대여(貸與) lending; a loan. ¶무기 ~법 [법]

(미국의) the Lend-Lease [Lease-Lend] Act // ~를 바라다 ask for the loan of (a thing). **대여하다** lend; give the loan of (a thing); lease; loan; grant the use of. ¶무료로 ~ lend free / loan (a thing) without charge // 그 회사에서는 제복을 대여한다 The firm loans uniforms.

대여섯 (about) five or six.

대역(大役) [임무] an important task [duty]; a heavy trust; an important part [role]; [사명] an important [a great] mission. ¶~을 맡다 undertake [take up / accept] an important part // ~을 완수하다 perform [discharge / accomplish] an important duty // 그 여배우는 ~을 맡기로 되어 있다 The actress is to play an important part. // 그에게 ~이 맡겨졌다 He was charged with an important task. // 그는 ~을 완수했다 He accomplished his important mission.

대역(大逆) [인도에 어그러지는 악행] bestial wickedness.

● **대역죄** treason; high treason; lese majesty; (프) lèse-majesté.

대역(代役) [어떤 역을 대신 맡는 행위] substitution; [역을 대신 맡아 하는 사람] a substitute actor [actress]; a substitute; an understudy; (급할 경우의) a pinch hitter; [영] a stand-in; a double. ¶장군의 ~ 노릇을 하다 act as the double of a general. **대역하다** play as a substitute for; play the part of (another actor); act in (another's) place; [영] double [stand in] for. ¶명배우를 ~ understudy a famous actor // 그 장면에서는 그녀가 주연 여배우를 대역했다 She stood in for the leading actress in that scene.

대역(對譯) a text (of Hamlet) with its (Korean) translation (printed) on the opposite page; a translation printed side by side with original (text). ¶영한 ~ 회화 사전 an English-Korean conversation dictionary // 이 책은 ~본이다 This book is in bilingual. // 이 책은 불한 ~으로 되어 있다 This book has the French original on one page and the Korean translation on the facing page.

● **대역판** a bilingual edition; an interlinear edition.

대열(隊列) [종렬] (a) file; [횡렬] (a) rank.

대엿새 (about) five or six days.

대영 제국(大英帝國) the British Empire.

대오(大悟) spiritual awakening [enlightenment]; great wisdom; [불] divine enlightenment. **대오하다** be spiritually awakened; see the truth; attain divine enlightenment [spiritual awakening]; learn [get] great wisdom; find one's philosophy of life. ¶그 스님은 활연 대오했다 The priest perceived the ultimate [absolute] truth. / The priest attained enlightenment.

대오(隊伍) [대열] the ranks; a line; [진열] an array; formation; [행렬] a procession. ¶~ 정연하게 in regular ranks / in perfect order // ~를 지어 in line [procession] / in regular order / in formation // ~를 짓다 form ranks [a column] / line up // ~를 흩뜨리다 break the line [column / ranks] // 그들은 ~를 정돈했다 [흩트렸다] They straightened [broke] ranks. // 병사들은 ~를 지어 지나갔다 The soldiers filed past us. / The soldiers marched past in ranks [in formation]. // 학생들은 ~를 지어 행진했다 The pupils marched

대왕(大王) [선왕] the late king; [위대한 왕] a great king. ¶세종 ~ Sejong the Great // 알렉산더 ~ Alexander the Great.

대외(對外) [관용어적] foreign; external; oversea(s); abroad; outside.
● 대외 관계 foreign[international] relations; diplomacy. 대외 무역 foreign[overseas / external] trade. 대외 방송 broadcasting abroad; a broadcast beamed overseas. 대외 정책 a foreign[an external / an exterior] policy.

대요(大要) [요약] a summary; a gist; substance; a syllabus; an epitome; a résumé; a précis; an outline; [개요] a general idea. ¶사건 ~ the sum and substance of the matter // 한국사 ~ an outline of Korean history / an outline history of Korea // 그의 논문의 ~ a summary of his dissertation // 질문에 대한 회답의 ~ the general tenor of the answers to a question // ~를 설명하다 describe[give] the outline (of) // …의 ~를 말하다 give a summary[an outline] of / sum up / epitomize / summarize / outline.

대용(代用) substitution. ¶…의 ~으로서 in place of / (in substitution) for // …의 ~이 되다 serve for[as] / can be used as substitute (for) / serve the purpose (of) // 이 상자는 의자 ~이 된다 This box will serve as a chair. / We can use this box as a chair. **대용하다** substitute (A for B); use (one thing) for (another). ¶칠면조 고기가 없으면 닭고기로 대용해도 상관없다 If turkey is not available, you may substitute chicken (for it).
● 대용식 substitute [ersatz] food; (쌀의) a rice substitute. 대용품 a substitute (for); a substitute article [product]; an ersatz (product). ¶플라스틱은 고무의 ~으로 쓸 수 있다 Plastic can be used as a substitute for rubber.

대우(待遇) 1 [취급] treatment; [접대] reception; entertainment. ¶차별 ~ discriminative treatment // 공정한 ~ fair treatment // 극진한 ~를 받다 be kindly treated / be received warmly [cordially] // 신사 ~를 받다 treat (a person) as a gentleman // 전관(前官) ~를 받다 be accorded the treatment due to one's late office // 지위에 상당한 ~를 하다 do (a person) the honor due to his position / do (a person) due honor // 파격적인 ~를 하다 make an exception of one's case [in one's favor] // 모진 ~를 받다 receive a cruel treatment (from) / be cruelly treated (by) // 나는 지위에 상응하는 ~를 기대했었다 I had expected that I would be treated in a way appropriate to my position. // 부사장 ~를 해드리겠습니다 You will receive the same treatment as the vice-president. / You will receive treatment equivalent to that of the vice-president. // 아주 차가운 ~를 받았으므로 다시는 거기에 가지 않겠다 I will never go there again, as I was treated [received] very coldly. **대우하다** treat; receive; entertain. ¶동등히 ~ treat (a person) on the same footing with [as] (another).
2 [급료] pay; salary; remuneration. ¶~를 개선하다 improve labor conditions(조건을) / give (a person) better treatment / raise [increase] (a person's) pay(급료를) // ~가 좋다 (회사가) pay[treat] well / (직원이) be paid well[liberally] // ~가 나쁘다 (회사가) underpay / (직원이) be underpaid / be poorly paid.

대우(對偶) 1 [수] contraposition. 2 [짝] a pair. 3 [논] opposition; antithesis.
● 대우법 [문] antithesis.

대우주(大宇宙) [철] macrocosm; the great universe.

대운(大運) [큰 운수] great fortune; (wonderfully) good luck; [운명] fate; destiny.

대울타리 a bamboo fence [hedge].

대웅성(大熊星) [천] (stars of) the Great bear; Ursa Major.

대웅전(大雄殿) [불] the main[inner] temple; the main building (of a temple).

대원(隊員) a member (of a fire brigade[an expedition team]). ¶등산대 ~ a member of a mountain-climbing party.

대원수(大元帥) the generalissimo (*pl.* ~s); the commander-in-chief(약어 C-in-C) of the Army and Navy.

대원칙(大原則) the broad[dominant] principle.

대월(貸越) (an) overdraft. ⇨"당좌 대월(⇨당좌.

대위(大尉) (육군·공군의) a captain; [영] a flight lieutenant(공군); (해군의) (미) a lieutenant senior; [영] a lieutenant.

대위법(對位法) [음] counterpoint. ¶이중 ~ double counterpoint.

대음순(大陰脣) [생] the labia majora; (구어) the outer lips (of the vulva).

대응(對應) 1 [마주 대함] correspondence. **대응하다** ¶그 한국말에 정확하게 대응하는 말이 영어에는 없다 In English there is no precise equivalent for that Korean word. // 수요와 공급은 1대 1로 대응하는 것이 바람직하다 It is desirable that supply and demand (should) be in a one-to-one ratio.
2 [대처]. **대응하다** ¶우리는 어떤 사태에도 대응할 수 있도록 준비를 갖추고 있다 We are prepared to cope with any situation. // 그는 예기치 못한 진전에 대응하지 못했다 He was unable to deal with [handle] the unexpected development. // 그들의 요구에 대응하여 우리는 새로운 제안을 했다 In response to their demands we made a new proposal. // 우리는 시대에 대응하는 새 대책을 취했다 We adopted new measures suited to the times. // 그들은 새 체제에 대응하지 못했다 They were unable to adapt themselves to the new system.
3 [수] correspondence. **대응하다** correspond to; answer to. ¶2개의 삼각형의 대응하는 변 the corresponding sides of two triangles.
● 대응각 [수] corresponding angles; opposite angles. 대응변 [수] corresponding sides. 대응책 countermove; countermeasure; counterplot; measure devised to deal with (a problem).

대의(大意) [골자] the gist; [취지·의도] the general meaning; (문어) the purport; [개략] an outline; a summary; (문어) the import; [요지] the substance; [논문 등의 요지] a résumé; a synopsis. ¶이 장의 ~를 간략히 설명하시오 Make a brief summary of this chapter. // 말한 그대로가 아니고 ~만을 말씀드리겠습니다 We give the general idea, not the exact words.

대의(大義) [사람의 도리] moral law; justice;

대의 a great moral cause; [충의] loyalty. ¶여성 해방이라는 ~를 위하여 싸우는 여성들 women fighting for the noble cause of women's liberation∥~를 밝히다 recognize one's highest duty (to one's sovereign)∥~에 죽다 sacrifice oneself for justice / sacrifice one's life in the great cause.
 ● **대의명분** a just and great cause; the highest duty; [국민으로서의 본분] one's duty to one's country[lord]. ¶~이 서다 have a good reason (to do)∥~이 서지 않다 cannot be justified / be hardly justifiable∥[억압된 민중의 해방이라는 ~으로 그들은 싸웠다 They fought for (the cause of) the liberation of the oppressed masses.
대의(代議) representation.
 ● **대의원** a delegate; a representative; a member of a delegation. **대의원단** a delegation.
대인(大人) 1 [어른] an adult; a grown-up person. ¶~용 for adult / (남자) for men / (여자) for women∥입장료 ~ 3천 원 Admission: 3,000 won per adult. 2 [거인] a big man; a giant. 3 [덕망이 높은 사람] an upright man; a man of virtue; [도량이 넓은 사람] a magnanimous man; a big[big-hearted / generous / broad-minded] person. ¶그 사람에게는 ~의 풍모가 있다 There is an air[a look] of magnanimity about him. 4 [남의 아버지] your[his] (esteemed) father; [남을 높여 이르는 말] a gentleman.
대인(對人) [관형어적] personnel; personal.
 ● **대인 공포증** anthropophobia. **대인 관계** personal relations[relationship]. ¶그는 ~가 원만하지 않다 His personal relationships are not going well. **대인 방어** man-to-man defense.
대인기(大人氣) great popularity; a great success; a (big) hit. ¶~를 끈 소설 a best seller∥~를 끌다 be very popular / enjoy great popularity / make a great hit / be very successful∥이번 흥행은 ~다 The performance has created a sensation[has a great run].∥그는 학생 간에 ~다 He is very popular[a great favorite] with the students.
대일(對日) [관형어적] towards[with] Japan. ¶한국의 ~ 정책 Korea's policy toward Japan∥한국의 ~ 외교 방침 the orientation of Korea's diplomacy toward Japan.
 ● **대일 감정** the feeling[sentiment] toward Japan. ¶~이 극히 나쁘다 The feeling is very bad toward the Japanese. / The anti-Japanese sentiment is mounting[growing] (in Korea). **대일 관계** relations with Japan. **대일 무역** trade with Japan.
대임(大任) [중대한 일] a great task; [중요한 임무] an important duty; [중요한 직책] an important office; a heavy responsibility; [중대한 사명] an important mission. ¶~을 맡고 있다 be on an important mission∥~을 맡다 undertake an important[difficult] task∥남에게 ~을 맡기다 entrust a person with an important task∥~을 완수하다 complete one's important duty∥~을 띠고 파견되다 be sent on an important mission.
대입(代入) [수] substitution. **대입하다** substitute (A for B).
대자(大字) [큰 글자] a large character; [대자] a capital letter.

대자대비(大慈大悲) [불] great compassion and great mercy. ¶~하신 관세음보살 Avalokitesvara of Great Love and Great Mercy.
대자리 a bamboo mat.
대자보(大字報) (중국의) a big-character paper [poster]; a wall poster[newspaper].
대자연(大自然) nature; (Mother) Nature. ¶~의 품에 안긴 마을 [문어] a mountain village nestled in the bosom of Mother Nature.
대작(大作) [걸작] a masterpiece; a monumental[great] work; [문학 등에서 대규모의 작품] a voluminous work; [대규모의 미술 작품] a large-scale work (of art). ¶그는 1천 페이지 남짓한 ~을 막 탈고했다 He has just completed a voluminous work of over a thousand pages.
대작(代作) 1 [남 대신에 작품을 만드는 행위] vicarious writing; ghostwriting; writing [composing] for (another); [대신하여 만든 작품] a vicarious work. **대작하다** write [compose] for (another); ghostwrite; ghost. ¶그는 유명 작가의 소설을 대작하였다 He ghostwrote a book for a well-known novelist. ∥그의 작품은 언제나 누나가 대작한다 His sister always writes his compositions for him. 2 [농] sowing a substitute plant in a dried rice-paddy. ⇨ 대파(代播).
대작하다(對酌-) drink together; exchange cups (between the two); hobnob (with). ¶우리는 이별의 술잔을 대작했다 We exchanged a few cups of sake[We drank a few cups of sake together] to make our parting.
대장(大將) 1 [육군] a general; (해군) an admiral(▶ 소장·중장에 대하여는 a full general[admiral]이라고 할 때도 있음); (공군) (미) a general; (영) an air chief marshal; a four-star general. 2 [우두머리] a chief; a head; a boss; a master; a captain; (미국 구어) a king pin; (영국 속어) a governor. ¶그의 패거리의 ~ king among his mates / 골목 ~ the king[boss] of the kids[youngsters] of the neighborhood.
대장(大腸) [생] the large intestine.
 ● **대장균** a colon[coliform] bacillus (pl. bacilli).
대장(隊長) [지도자] a leader; a captain; [지휘하는 사람] a commander; (군대의) a commanding officer. ¶소~ a platoon leader∥중[대] ~ company[battalion] commander∥탐험대 ~ the leader of an expedition.
대장(臺帳) [회계 장부] an account book; [원장] a ledger. ¶토지 ~ a land register∥그는 금액을 ~에 기입했다 He entered the sum in the ledger[the account book].
대장간(-間) a smithy; a forge; a blacksmith's workshop.
대장간에 식칼이 놀다 (속담) The shoemaker's son always goes barefoot.; The tailor's wife is worst clad.
대장경(大藏經) [불] the Tripitaka; the complete canon of Buddhist scriptures; a collection of all the sacred writings of Buddhism. ¶팔만~ the Tripitaka Koreana consisting of over 80,000 (wood) blocks[wooden printing blocks].
대장부(大丈夫) a man; a manly[worthy] man; [용사] a heroic[brave] man; [큰 인물] a great man. ¶~다운 manly / manlike / brave / heroic∥~답게 굴어라 Be a man. /

Play the man. / Behave [Act] like a man. // 그것은 ~답지 않은 것이다 It is unworthy of a man. // 그는 너보다 훨씬 ~답다 He is much more of a man than you (are).

대장일 smithery; blacksmith work; forging.

대장장이 a smith; a blacksmith; (농공) a knight of the hammer.

대저(大著) [내용이 방대한 저서] a voluminous work; [명저] a great work. ¶히틀러에 관한 ~ a voluminous work on Hitler // 상·하 두 권의 ~ a bulky two-volume work // 이것은 고금의 ~이다 This was and still remains a great work [a masterpiece].

대저(大抵) generally speaking; in general; on the whole; in the main.

대저울 a beam balance; a steelyard; lever scales.

대적(大敵) [강적] a powerful [great / formidable] enemy; an arch enemy; heavy odds; an invincible [a great] foe; [많은 수의 적] a large group of enemies; a mass of enemies; [경쟁자] a great rival; a formidable opponent. ¶민주주의의 ~ the most deadly foe of democracy // 부주의는 교통안전의 ~이다 Carelessness is a great menace to traffic safety.

대적(對敵) 1 [적과 맞섬] facing [fighting] against; confrontation; hostility; antagonism; contention. **대적하다** turn [fight / contend / face] against; antagonize; confront (one's enemy). 2 [겨룸] rivalry; (a) competition; emulation; a contest; a showdown. **대적하다** [겨루다] rival; vie [contend] (with); compete [strive] (with); [필적하다] be a match for; be (a person's) match; be equal to. ¶너는 그에게 대적할 상대가 안 된다 You are no match for [not a patch on] him. / He is more than a match for you. // 달리기에 있어서는 그에게 대적할 자가 없다 He has no equal for running.

대전(大全) a complete work; a collection; an encyclop(a)edia; a summa (pl. ~s, ~e). ¶「요리법 ~」(책 이름) The Complete Cookbook.

대전(大典) 1 [나라의 큰 의식] a state ceremony. 2 [중대한 법전] a code of laws; (종교의) a canon. ¶불멸의 ~ a canon of everlasting fame.

대전(大戰) a great war; [큰 전쟁] a major [massive] war; [세계 대전] a world war. ¶제1차 세계 ~ the first world war / World-War Ⅰ / the Great War // 제2차 세계 ~ the second world war / World War Ⅱ / the Second War // ~ 전[후]의 prewar [postwar].

대전(帶電) [물] electrification; electrical charge. **대전하다** take a charge; charge with electricity. ¶금속은 대전하기 쉽다 Metal is easily charged with electricity.

대전(對戰) 1 [전쟁] waging war; engagement. **대전하다** be pitched against each other; oppose [confront] (the enemy); take the field (against); meet; engage. 2 (경기·시합 등) competition; a match; a bout. ¶오늘의 가장 흥미있는 ~ the most interesting match today // 그 팀과는 첫 ~이었다 It was the first time that we were matched against [had played] that team. **대전하다** be matched (against); compete (with). ¶적과 ~ confront [face] the enemy // 우리는 홈그라운드에서 상대 팀과 대전했다 We took on our rivals on our home field. // 결승에서 최강 팀과 대전했다 We faced [were matched against] the best team in the finals.

● **대전료** fight money.

대전제(大前提) [논] a major premise [proposition] (of syllogism); a sumption.

대전차(對戰車) [관형어적] antitank.

● **대전차포** an antitank gun.

대접 a (soup) bowl. ¶국 한 ~ a bowl of soup.

대접(待接) [대우] treatment; reception; service; [환대] welcome; entertainment; hospitality. ¶푸짐한 ~ generous treatment // ~을 마시다 drink at another's // 정중한 ~을 받다 be treated with courtesy // 그녀는 손님 ~을 잘한다 She entertains guests very well. / She is very hospitable to guests. // ~이 변변치 못해 죄송합니다 Excuse me for not being a very good host [hostess]. (▶ hostess는 여성의 경우) // 그들은 어디에서나 후한 ~을 받았다 They were given a warm reception everywhere. / They were warmly received everywhere. **대접하다** [대우하다] treat; receive; [환대하다] entertain; show [give] (a person) hospitality. ¶점심을 ~ treat (a person) to lunch / entertain (a person) at [to] lunch // 그는 자주 손님을 불러 맛있는 음식을 대접한다 They are always entertaining guests. / They do a lot of entertaining. // 그들은 진수성찬을 차려 손님을 대접했다 They treated the guest to [entertained the guest with] all kinds of delicacies. // 아무것도 대접해 드리지 못해서 죄송합니다 I'm sorry I could do nothing to entertain you. ➔ 우리는 정중하게 대접받았다 We were treated [received] courteously.

대정맥(大靜脈) [생] the main vein; the vena cava (pl. venae cavae).

대제(大帝) a great emperor. ¶찰스 ~ Charles the Great.

대제(大祭) [큰 제사] a great religious ceremony [service]; [축제] a grand festival; a great fête; a fiesta. ¶종묘 ~ the memorial service for royal ancestors.

대제사장(大祭司長) [종] a high [chief] priest.

대조(對照) [대비] (a) contrast; antithesis; [비교] (a) comparison; [맞추어 보기] (a) collation; check (up). ¶명암 ~ the contrast between light and shade // 교사의 흰 벽과 푸른 하늘이 아름다운 ~를 이루고 있다 The white walls of the school building are in exquisite contrast to the blue sky. // 이들 둘은 좋은 ~를 이룬다 These two set each other off well [beautifully]. // 그는 우리 남편과 좋은 ~를 이룬다 He's the exact opposite of my husband. // 공손한 말씨와는 ~적으로 그녀의 태도는 매우 난폭했다 Her polite words contrasted strikingly with her uncivil manner. / Her polite words and her disagreeable manner were in striking contrast. **대조하다** contrast; compare (A with [and] B); set (A) against (B); check (A) up with (B). ¶나는 그것을 그의 자료와 대조했다 I checked it against his data. // 그들의 진술을 대조해 보니 모두가 부합하였다 On checking [comparing] their statements, I found them all consistent with each other. // 우리는 상품과 견본을 대조했다 We compared the article with the sample. // 나는 교정쇄를 원고와 대조했다 I checked the proof with [against] the

manuscript.// 선생님은 두 답안지를 대조했다 The teacher compared the two papers. // 원본과 대조하시오 Collate it with [check it against] the original.
● 대조 분석 contrastive analysis. 대조표 a calculating table.

대종(大宗) 1 [계통] the lineage of the head [main] family. 2 [주요품] the main items. ¶수출의 ~ the staple article for export / the main export items // 그 ~을 차지하다 form its majority.

대좌(對坐) sitting opposite [face to face]. 대좌하다 sit opposite (each other / to a person); sit face to face (with); sit facing each other.

대좌(臺座) a pedestal; a plinth(원기둥 밑의).

대죄(大罪) a great [high / serious / foul / heinous] crime; a grave offense; a felony; a great [grave / deadly / mortal] sin(종교·도덕상의). ¶~를 범하다 commit a great crime.

대죄하다(待罪-) await the official decision on one's punishment; wait for the judgment.

대주교(大主敎) [가] an archbishop; (수석 대주교) a primate. ¶캔터베리 ~ the Archbishop of Canterbury / the Primate of All England.

대주자(代走者) a pinch runner.

대중 1 [대강 어림함] a rough [rude] estimate [calculation]; an approximate estimate. ¶~이 틀리다 One's estimate is off. 대중하다 estimate [calculate] roughly; make [form] a rough estimation [calculation] (of). ¶집 수리비를 ~ make a rough estimate of the expense for the repair of a house. 2 [표준] a standard; a yardstick. 대중하다 set up a standard. ¶그녀의 말은 대중할 수가 없다 I can't make head or tail of what she says. I can't understand her at all.

대중(大衆) the masses(▶ 약간 경멸적); the mass of people; the multitude; the populace; the general public; the public at large; (속어) grass-roots. ¶근로 ~ the working masses [classes] / the masses of workers / 일반 ~ the general public / the public at large / the mass population // ~ 취향의 popular // ~ 취향의 책 a lowbrow book / a popular book // ~의 지지를 얻다 have a support of the public / have mass support // ~을 우롱하다 fool the public // 그의 작품은 ~의 취향에 맞지 않는다 His works do not appeal to the common taste [are not appreciated by the masses]. // 추상화는 ~적 취향에 들어맞지 않는다 Abstract paintings do not suit the popular taste [are not to everyone's liking].
● 대중가요 a popular song. ¶~ 작가 a songwriter. 대중 교육 popular [mass] education. 대중 사회 mass society. 대중성 popular appeal; popularity. ¶~이 있다 [없다] have [lack] popular [mass] appeal. 대중오락 mass entertainment. 대중 운동 a mass movement; a popular movement. 대중음악 popular music. 대중 집회 a mass rally. 대중화 popularization.

대중없다 [일정치 않다] irregular; variable; unsettled; uncertain; indefinite; unfixed; [변하기 쉽다] inconstant; mutable; changeful; changeable; [줏대 없다] inconsistent; (서술적) be without any fixed principle; have no definite opinion [views] of one's own; have no fixed views of one's own. ¶대중없는 말 inconsistent remarks / a weasel word / a pointless statement // 대중없는 수입 an irregular [incidental] income // 대중없는 대답을 하다 give a vague answer / give a noncommittal answer // 대중없는 행동을 취하다 take an uncertain attitude (toward) // 시작하는 시간은 대중없습니다 There is no fixed rule about the hour of commencement.

대증 요법(對症療法) symptomatic therapy. ¶~을 하다 treat symptoms as they appear.

대지(大地) the earth; the ground; the solid earth; firm ground; (시어) Mother earth. ¶아름다운 ~ this fair earth // ~를 밟다 tread on the ground / stand firm on the ground.

대지(垈地) a lot [plot]; a building [home / residential] site; (a plot of) ground. ¶건축 ~ a building site [lot] // ~의 선정 the selection of a site // ~ 딸린 매가(賣家) a house and lot for sale // 100제곱미터의 ~ 100 square meters of land // ~를 확보하다 secure the location (for) // ~를 물색하다 look for a site (for a building).
● 대지 면적 plottage. 대지 정리 site cleaning.

대지(貸地) land to let [on lease / (미) for rent]; a lot to let [(미) for rent].

대지(臺地) [고원] a plateau (pl. ~s, ~x); a tablelands(▶ 종종 복수형으로 단수 취급); [고대] a height; a rise. ¶용암 ~ a lava plateau.

대지(臺紙) pasteboard; board; ground paper; a (photograph) mount; a mat. ¶~ 없는 사진 an unmounted photograph // 사진을 ~에 붙이다 mount a photograph (on cardboard).

대지(對地) [관청어적] anti-ground. ¶지~ 미사일 a ground-[surface-] to-ground [-surface] missile.
● 대지 공격 an attack from the air; an air raid. ¶공~ an air-to-ground attack.

대지주(大地主) a big [large / great] landowner; a squire; a lord of broad acres.

대진(對陣) [군] camping opposite each other; the confrontation of armies. 대진하다 confront [face] each other; be pitted against each other; take up a position against the enemy; encamp facing each other. ¶양군은 강을 사이에 두고 대진했다 The two armies faced [confronted] each other across the river. // 양군은 서로 대진한 채 공격을 가하지 않았다 The two armies confronted each other without starting an attack.

대질(對質) [법] confrontation; a face-to-face questioning. ¶당사자 상호 간의 ~을 명하다 order witnesses to confront [cross-examine] each other. 대질하다 confront (one's accuser); stand face to face (with). ➔ 피고와 원고를 대질시키다 confront the accused with the accuser / bring the accused face to face with the accuser.
● 대질 심문 (a) cross-examination.

대집행(代執行) [법] execution by proxy.

대짜(大-) [큰 것] a big one [thing]; (사냥·낚시의) big game. ¶~ 못 a big nail // ~ (물고기)를 하나 잡다 catch a big fish // 낚시에서 뭔가 ~가 걸렸다 I have got a bite from something big!
● 대짜배기 a big [gigantic] one [thing]; an awfully big one; a whopper; a jumbo. ¶~로 in [into / with] a big one / on a large [grand / great] scale // ~로 한잔하다 have a drink in a large mug.

대쪽 split bamboo. ¶성미가 ~ 같은 남자 a straightforward[an upright] man / a man of frank disposition / a single-minded man // 그는 ~ 같은 성격이다 He is very straightforward.

대차(大差) a great difference; a big discrepancy[disparity]; a wide[striking] difference. ¶~가 있다 be much[very] different (from) / differ much[a great deal] (from) / a great contrast exists (between) / have a great discrepancy // 버스로 가든 택시로 가든 시간적으로는 ~ 없다 There is no great difference in time whether you go by bus or by taxi. // 어느 쪽이든 ~ 없다 It doesn't make much[It makes little] difference (which you choose). // 상황은 어제와 ~ 없다 The situation is about the same as yesterday. // 여야당의 정책 간에 ~는 없다 The party in power and the opposition do not differ much in their policies.

대차(貸借) (a) loan; (장부상의) debit and credit; (건물 등의) letting and hiring. ¶국제 ~ 결제 the balance of international payments // 사용 ~ loan of use // 소비 ~ loans of consumption // 장부상의 ~ a book account // ~를 대조하다 balance // ~를 차감하다 balance account // ~를 결산하다 strike a balance / sum up the debtor and creditor account // 이것으로 너와는 ~가 없다 Now I am square[even] with you.
● **대차 계약서** (버스 등의) a charter. **대차 대조표** a balance sheet(약어 B/S, b.s.); a statement of assets and liabilities.

대찰(大刹) a large[great / noted] Buddhist temple; a Buddhist cathedral.

대책(對策) [방책] measures; a step; [대항책] a countermeasure; a counterplan; a countermove. ¶비상 ~ an emergency[a drastic] measures / urgent measures // 수해 ~ measures for flood control // 실업 ~ a countermeasures against unemployment // 인플레 ~ a measure to counter inflation / an anti-inflation[a disinflationary] policy // 종합 ~ (work out) comprehensive countermeasures (against) // ~으로서 as a countermeasure // 비상 ~을 쓰다 take[resort] to exceptional[extreme] measures // ~을 강구하다 consider a counterplan / devise a countermove / take a measure to meet the situation / study how to cope with[meet] the situation // 사태의 조치를 위한 ~을 강구하다 take steps[measures] to deal[cope] with the situation(▶ steps는 종종 일련의 대책) // 눈사태[교통사고]에 대한 어떤 ~도 마련되어 있지 않다 No measures have been taken (to guard) against snowslides[traffic accidents].

대처승(帶妻僧) a married (Buddhist) priest.

대처하다(對處-) cope[deal] with; tackle; meet; move against; manage; treat. ¶긴박한 정세에 훌륭히 ~ cope[deal] effectively with a tense situation // 용감하게 난국에 ~ face a difficult situation bravely // 인플레이션 문제에 ~ grapple[wrestle] with the problem of inflation // 긴급 사태에 ~ meet the emergency // 우리는 모두 함께 이 위기에 대처해야 한다 We must all work together to deal with this crisis.

대척(對蹠) (지구 상의) antipodism; [정반대] diametrical opposition. ¶~적인 antipodal / diametrically opposite.
● **대척점** [지] the antipode; the nadir. **대척지** the antipodes.

대천(大川) a large[big] river.

대첩(大捷) a sweeping[great / complete / decisive / signal / sensational] victory. **대첩하다** win a sweeping[great / signal] victory.

대청(大廳) a *daecheong*; the main hall; a hall; the vestibule.

대청소(大淸掃) general (house) cleaning; great[giant] housecleaning; a biannual thorough cleaning; cleaning up; spring-cleaning; (영) a spring-clean. ¶~를 하다 carry out a general cleaning / give one's a thorough turnout / clean the whole house / spring-clean (a room) // 우리는 해마다 한 번씩 ~를 한다 We carry out a general cleaning once a year. / We clean the whole house once a year.

대체(大體) 1 [개요] an outline; a summary; an epitome; an adumbration; the gist; the substance; the drift; the tenor; [취지] the purport; [요점] the principal parts; the main[chief] point(s). ¶사건의 ~ the sum and substance of a case // ~를 말하다 give an[abroad] outline (of) / outline (a case) / give a summary (of) / summarize (a matter). 2 (how / what / why) on earth. ⇨ ☞대관절

대체(代替) substitution; [교체] alternation; replacement (of worn-out parts). ¶~의 법칙 the principle of substitution. **대체하다** substitute (one thing for another); replace (with); alternate (with). →¶대체되다 be replaced (by) // 이 제도는 4월 1일부터 새것으로 대체될 것이다 This system is to be replaced by a new one on April 1. / The new system is to go into effect on April 1.
● **대체물** a substitute; [법] fungibles. **대체 에너지** an alternative energy source. ¶각종 ~ 자원의 개발 exploitation of various substitute energy sources. **대체 효과** [경] substitution effect.

대체(對替) [경] change; changeover; transfer. ¶~로 송금하다 send money by postal transfer. **대체하다** change (a bill); transfer; switch[change] over (to). ¶수수료를 …의 계정으로 transfer a commission to a person's account // 가불금을 손익 계정으로 ~ transfer temporary payments to a profit and loss account // 나는 보통 예금을 신탁 예금으로 대체했다 I changed my ordinary account to a trust deposit. / I moved[transferred] the money in my bank account to a trust deposit.
● **대체 계정** a transfer account. **대체 저금** transfer savings.

대체로(大體-) generally; in general; generally speaking; as a rule. ¶이탈리아 인은 ~ 쾌활하다 Generally (speaking), Italians are cheerful. // 아이들의 건강이 ~ 향상됐다 Children's health has in general improved. // 한국 사람은 ~ 성질이 급하다 Generally speaking, the Koreans are quick-tempered. / The Korean people are on the whole quick-tempered. / The Korean, as a people, are impatient. // 이 지역의 기후는 ~ 따뜻하다 The climate in this area is generally mild. // 결과는 ~ 만족할 만한 것이었다 The results were on the whole satisfactory. // 그들

은 ~ 친절하다 Most of them are kind. / They are mostly [for the most part] kind.

대체적(大體的) general (idea); main (points); rough; loose. ¶~인 뜻 general meaning // ~인 원칙 general principles // ~인 견적 a rough estimate // ~인 개요 a sweeping generalization // ~으로 말해서 generally [broadly] speaking / roughly speaking / in a loose sense of the word / in round [broad] terms // ~으로 보아 on the whole / taken as a whole / all things take together / taken [talking(it)] all in all / in broad outline / at a rough guess [estimate].

대추 [대추나무의 열매] a jujube; a Chinese date.

대추나무 [식] a jujube tree; a Chinese date tree.

대추나무에 연 걸리듯 (속담) be over head and ears in debt.

대출(貸出) (금전의) a loan; lending; (가불) an advance; (물건·책 등의) lending; a loan. ¶부당 ~ an illegal advance [loan] // 비상 ~ emergency advances [loans]. **대출하다** lend; loan; advance; let out on hire. ¶도서는 lend [(미) loan] books // 귀중본은 어느 것도 대출할 수 없음 None of the valuable books may be taken out. → ¶그 책은 대출되어 있습니다 The book is out on loan.
● **대출금** loaned [advanced] money. 대출 금리 the interest on a loan.

대충 approximately; almost; briefly. ⇨ 대강2

대취(大醉) dead drunkenness. **대취하다** get dead [beastly / blind] drunk; (구어) be boozy; (속어) get tanked up.

대치(代置) replacement; succession. **대치하다** replace 《A with B》. ¶석탄불을 가스로 ~ replace coal fires by gas.

대치(對峙) confrontation. **대치하다** stand face to face with; confront [face] each other; stand opposite to each other; be pitted against each other; hold one's own against 《one's antagonist》; hold one's ground against 《the enemy》; take a stand against; hold out against 《the Government forces》; square off (against). ¶대치하고 있는 두 거봉 two lofty peaks facing each other // 양군은 서로 대치했다 The two armies confronted each other.

대칭(對稱) 1 [언] the second person. 2 [수] symmetry. ¶평면 ~ plane symmetry // ~의 symmetric(al) // 선(線)~ line symmetry // 점 ~의 symmetric with respect to a point // 좌우의 무늬 a symmetrical pattern // 이 두 점은 x축에 대해서 ~이다 These two points are symmetric with respect to the x-axis.
● **대칭점** [수] a symmetrical point. **대칭축** [수] an axis of symmetry; (결정의) a symmetry axis.

대타(代打) [야구] pinch-hitting. ¶~로 나서다 pinch-hit / bat for 《a person》.
● **대타자** a pinch hitter. ¶빌이 조지의 ~가 되었다 They put Bill in as a pinch hitter for George. / Bill pinch-hit for George.

대통(-筒) a bamboo tube.

대통(-桶) [담뱃통] the bowl of a (tobacco) pipe.

대통(大統) the Royal line. ¶~을 잇다 succeed to the Royal line [the Throne].

대통령(大統領) [공화국의 원수] a president; the President (▶ 특정한 대통령을 가리킴); the chief [Federal] Executive. ¶고 케네디 ~ the late president Kennedy // ~에 선출되다 be elected President // ~에 지명되다 be nominated for the presidency // ~에 취임하다 be sworn in as President.
● **대통령 경호실**(장) (the chief of) the office of the Presidential Security. **대통령 관저** the Executive [Presidential] Mansion; the Presidential residence; the White House (미국의). **대통령 권한 대행** the acting president. **대통령 당선자** the president-elect. **대통령령** (-令) a Presidential decree; an executive order. **대통령 선거** a presidential election. ¶그는 ~에 출마한다 He will run for the Presidency. **대통령 임기** a presidential term. **대통령 후보** a candidate for the presidency; a presidential nominee [candidate].

대통하다(大通-) go well [right]; be successful. ¶운수가 ~ have a spell of extremely good luck / fortune turns in one's favor / bask in the smiles of Fortune / be in Fortune's lap.

대퇴(大腿) a thigh. ⇨ 넓적다리
● **대퇴골** the thighbone. **대퇴부** the thigh; the femoral region.

대파(大破) 1 [심한 파손] dilapidation; ruin; serious damage; havoc; a great destruction; decay. **대파하다** [크게 깨지다] be greatly destroyed [dilapidated]; be heavily damaged [crippled]; be utterly ruined; (배 등이) be wrecked; (비행기 등이) be smashed. → ¶대파되어 있다 be dilapidated / be in ruins // 소형비행기는 추락하여 대파되었다 The small plane crashed and was completely wrecked. // 3대의 차가 대파되었다 Three cars were badly damaged [totally wrecked / (미국 구어) totaled].
2 [격파] a crushing defeat. **대파하다** [크게 처부수다] defeat utterly; (put to) rout; crush down; smash; rout 《the enemy》 utterly.

대파(代播) [농] sowing a substitute plant in a dried rice-paddy. **대파하다** plant a paddy with (millet); sow in substitution (for). ¶논에 메밀을 ~ sow the paddy with buckwheat in substitution (for rice).

대판(大-) [큰 판국] a large [big / grand / huge] scale; an extensive scale. ¶~ 싸움 《have》 a big quarrel [fight] // ~으로 on a large [an extensive] scale / in a big [large] way.

대패 a plane. ¶널빤지를 ~로 매끈하게 깎다 plane a board smooth.
● **대패질** planing. **대팻밥** (wood) shavings.

대패(大敗) a crushing [complete] defeat; an utterly rout. ¶이 지역의 전투에서 정부군은 ~를 맛보았다 The government forces suffered a crushing defeat [heavy losses] in the battle fought in this area (▶ heavy losses는 다수의 사망자를 내는 것). **대패하다** sustain [suffer / meet with] a crushing defeat; be routed; be put to rout; be beaten hollow. ¶선거에서 ~ be defeated decidedly in an election // 아군은 대패했다 Our side was routed [was put to rout / took to flight]. // 기습을 받고 적군은 대패했다 The surprise attack dealt the enemy a death blow.

대평원(大平原) (미) a prairie.

대포 1 [큰 그릇으로 술을 마시는 일] drinking from a large cup [a goblet]. 2 wine in a large cup. ⇨ 대폿술(↔)대포)

● 대폿술 〔큰 그릇으로 마시는 술〕 wine [liquor] in a large cup. 대폿집 a grogshop; a groggery.
대포(大砲) **1** 〔포탄을 쏘는 병기〕 a gun; (구형의) a cannon (*pl.* ~s, ~); (a piece of) ordnance; 《집합적》 artillery. ¶~ 소리 the roaring[boom] of guns∥일렬로 늘어선 ~ a train of ordnance∥~를 쏘다 fire a gun∥포병대가 ~를 발사했다 The artillery fired their guns.∥~ 소리가 은은히 울려 퍼졌다 The booming of guns resounded all around. **2** 〔거짓말〕 a (big) lie; 〔허풍〕 a brag; tall[big] talk; 《미국 속어》 hot air. ¶~를 놓다 talk big / brag / draw[shoot] a long bow.
대폭(大幅) **1** 〔큰 폭〕 a big jump; a great leap. **2** 〔썩 많이〕 sharply; steeply; by a large margin. ¶~ 삭감 a drastic cut[curtailment] / a sharp cut∥가격의 ~ 인상 a steep raise in prices / a sharp increase / a heavy boost∥월급의 ~ 인상 a big raise in salary∥물가[세금]의 ~ 인하 a sharp reduction prices[taxes]∥~ 하락 a big fall[reduction] / sharp reductions in prices∥지출을 ~ 삭감하다 cut an appropriation sharply∥노동조합은 임금의 ~ 인상을 요구하고 있다 The labor union is demanding a substantial wage hike.
대폭적(大幅的) big; large; substantial. ¶회사에서는 ~인 인원의 해고를 예정하고 있다 The company is planning wholesale dismissals.
대표(代表) **1** 〔여러 사람을 대신함〕 representation; 〔대표하는 사람〕 a representative; a delegate. ¶지역[비례] ~제 regional (proportional) representation∥그들은 회의에 2명의 ~를 보냈다 They sent two delegates[representatives] to the conference. 대표하다 represent; stand[act] for. ¶그는 학급을 대표하여 학생회에 참석했다 He represented his class at the student council meeting. / He attended the student council meeting as the representative of his class.∥그룹을 대표하여 발언하게 해 주시오 Let me speak on behalf of our group.
2 〔전체의 성질·임무 등을 나타냄〕. 대표하다 typify; be typical of. ¶그의 제안은 선거인의 희망을 대표하고 있다 His proposal represents[is representative of] the wishes of his constituents.
● 대표단 a delegation. 대표부 a mission. ¶유엔 한국 ~ the Korean mission to the United Nations. 대표 이사 a representative director. ¶~ 회장 the chairman of a board of directors∥~ 사장 the president-director. 대표자 a representative; (정치적인 회의 등에 파견하는) a delegate; 〔대리역·대의원〕 a deputy. 대표작 a person's masterpiece. 대폿값 〔수〕 representative value.
대표적(代表的) representative; typical (of); (모범적인) model; exemplary. ¶~인 인물 a representative man∥우리 학교의 ~인 학생 a good example of the students at our school∥~인 예 a typical example∥이 그림은 피카소의 초기 작품 중에 ~인 것이다 This picture is typical of[typifies] Picasso's early work.
대풍(大豊) a bumper[heavy / record] crop; a rich[an abundant] harvest; a large yield (of fruit). ¶올해 사과는 ~이었다 This has been a bumper[fruitful] year for apples.∥벼농사는 어느 모로 보든지 ~이다 There is every prospect of a very large rice crop.
대풍(大風) a strong[violent / big / heavy / high] wind; a gale(질풍); a hurricane(폭풍); a typhoon(태풍).
대피(待避) shelter. 대피하다 take shelter (in / under); shunt. ¶사람들은 그 위험 지구로부터 대피했다 The people were evacuated from the danger zone.∥완행열차는 급행의 통과를 위해 대피했다 The local train let the express pass (at the shunting station).
● 대피선 〔철도〕 a (railroad) siding; a siding (track); a sidetrack; a turnout. ¶~에 넣다 sidetrack (a train). 대피소 (도로상이나 철도의) a turn-out; 《영》 a lay-by; (철도 보선원용의) a place of refuge; a safety zone; a shelter. 대피호 a shelter.
대필(代筆) ghostwriting. 대필하다 ghostwrite; write (a letter) for (another); write (a letter) to (another's) dictation. ➔¶그녀의 최근 편지는 분명히 대필되었다 Her last[most recent] letter was obviously written by someone else.
● 대필인 a ghostwriter; a person who writes (a letter) for another.
대하(大河) a big[large] river.
● 대하소설 (프) a roman-fleuve; a saga.
대하(大蝦) 〔동〕 a (Yellow Sea) prawn.
대하다(對－) **1** 〔마주하다〕 face; confront; be opposite to; be over against. ¶적을 ~ confront an enemy / engage[deal with] an enemy∥마주 대하고 앉다 sit opposite (to) / sit face to (with).
2 〔상대하다·대접하다〕 see; face; address; receive; treat. ¶사람을 대하기 싫어하다 don't like to see people∥친절한 태도로 손님을 ~ receive guests with kindness∥남을 후히 ~ treat a person generously∥부드러운 얼굴로 학생에게 ~ address oneself to one's students with a kindly look∥학생들을 대하는 그의 태도는 훌륭했다 His attitude toward(s) the students was admirable.∥이번에 또 실패한다면 친구에게 대할 낯이 없다 How can I face my friends if I fail again.
3 〔대상으로 하다〕. ¶구어체에 대한 문장체 literary style as opposed[in opposition] to colloquial style∥질문에 대한 답 an answer to a question∥친구에 대한 배려 consideration for one's friend∥부모에 대한 의무 one's duty toward one's parents∥국가에 대한 의무 a duty to one's country∥문학에 대한 흥미 interest in literature∥종교에 대한 강연 a lecture on religion∥100에 대하여 20 twenty per hundred∥그는 그 발명에 대하여 500만원의 보수를 받았다 He received a reward of five million won for the invention.∥그는 이성적인 데 대해 그녀는 감정적이다 While he is logical, she is emotional.∥그는 그것에 대해 전혀 무관심했다 He was utterly indifferent to it.∥지난달의 교통사고는 10건인 데 대해 이달은 18건이 있다 We have had eighteen traffic accidents this month as against[compared with] ten last month.∥저는 그분의 학식에 대해 깊은 경의를 갖고 있습니다 I have great respect for his scholarship.∥이웃 나라가 우리나라에 대해 선전 포고를 했다 A neighboring country declared war on [against] us.∥나는 당신에 대해 화를 내고 있는 것이 아닙니다 I'm not angry with you. ∥어린아이들은 가정교사에 대해 반항적인 태도를 보였다 The children took a rebellious

attitude toward(s) their tutor.// 나는 아동 심리학에 대해 많은 흥미를 갖고 있다 I am much interested in child psychology.

대하증(帶下症) [의] leucorrh(o)ea; whites (백대하).

대학(大學) (종합 대학) a university; (단과 대학) a college. ¶서울 ~ (교) Seoul National University // 국립 ~ a national university // 법과[공과 / 농과 / 상과 / 사범 / 미술 / 음악 / 치과 / 약학 / 수의과 / 수산 / 항공] ~ a college of law[engineering / agriculture / commerce / education / fine arts / music / dentistry / pharmacy / veterinary medicine / fisheries / aviation] // 예술 ~ liberal arts college // 전문 ~ a college // 초급 ~ a junior college // 의과 ~ a medical college[school] (▶ school은 대학원)// 시절에 (미) while in college / (영) while at university // ~에 가다 (다니고 있다) (미) go to[be in] college / (영) go to[be at] university // 우리 아들은 ~에 다닌다 My son is a college[university] student.

● **대학교수** a university[college] professor. **대학 교육** a university[college] education; college training. **대학 병원** a university hospital. **대학생** a university[college] student; a college man[woman]; an undergraduate; a collegian. **대학 수학 능력 시험** the government-sponsored scholastic aptitude test (for university education); the national [state-run] academic aptitude test. **대학원** a graduate[postgraduate] school (▶ 미국의 대학에서는 의학부·법학부·상학(商學)부 등은 대학원이라도 a school of medicine[medical school], a school of law[law school], a business school 등으로 말함); the postgraduate course. **대학 학장** a dean; a president.

대학자(大學者) [뛰어난 학자] a great[prominent / profound] scholar; a man of great education; a savant; (박학한 사람) an erudite man.

대한(大寒) 1 [24절기의 하나] daehan; "the height of the winter cold" (as one of the 24 seasonal divisions according to the lunar calendar that falls on about 21st of January); midwinter. 2 [심한 추위] an intense[freezing] cold.

대한(大韓) Korea.
● **대한민국** Daehanminguk; the Republic of Korea(약어 R.O.K.). **대한 적십자사** Korea National Red Cross.

대합(大蛤) [동] a (large) clam.

대합실(待合室) (역 등의) a waiting room; (은행 등의) a lobby. ¶일등 ~ the first-class waiting room.

대항(對抗) [맞겨룸·대립] opposition; antagonism; [대결] confrontation; emulation; rivalry. ¶대학 ~ 럭비 경기 an intercollegiate rugby match // 한·미 ~ 수영 대회 the Korean-U.S. swimming meet // 동·서 ~ 축구 시합 the East-West football game. **대항하다** oppose; confront; face; meet; counter; set up against; (경쟁하다) emulate; rival; cope[vie] with; compete with. ¶…에 대항하여 in opposition to / in rivalry with / against // 대항하는 양파의 세력 the two factions of comparable strength // 힘에는 힘으로 ~ meet[counter] force with force // 체스에서 그에게 대항할 수 있는 사람은 없다 He has no rival[equal] in chess. / No one is a match for him in chess. // 대형 백화점에 대항하여 지방의 상점들이 결속했다 The local stores have united in opposition to the big department store. →¶대항시키다 match[pit / put] (a person) against another / oppose / set (A) (over) against (B).

● **대항책** [대항할 방법] a counterplot; a countermeasure; a countermove. ¶~을 강구하다 take a countermeasure / form a counterplot / promote a rival scheme.

대해(大害) great damage[loss]; great harm; great injury. ¶곡식을 ~를 주다 cause great damage to the grain // 그 태풍으로 말미암아 이들 지방의 벼농사는 ~를 입었다 The typhoon has played dire havoc with[has done much damage to] the rice plants in these regions.

대해(大海) the ocean; the sea; (시어) the deep. ¶망망한 ~ the boundless expanse of water // ~의 한가운데에(서) in the middle of the ocean / in mid-ocean.

대행(代行) vicarious execution. ¶교장[과장] ~ an acting principal[section chief] // 대통령 권한 ~ the acting president. **대행하다** execute (business) for (another); act for (another); execute as proxy (for); act for (a person). ¶그는 대학 총장을 1년간 대행했다 He was the acting president of the university for one year. / He acted (as proxy) for the president of the university for one year. // 우리는 보험 회사의 업무를 대행하고 있다 We handle [(문어) execute] business for an insurance company.

● **대행 기관** an agency. **대행 업무** agency business. **대행자** a proxy; an agent. ¶수출[수입] ~ an export[import] agent.

대헌장(大憲章) [영국 역사] The Magna Charta; The Great Charter.

대형(大型) a large[full] size; oversize. ¶~ 선수의 발굴 discovery of a mammoth[tall-statured] athlete // ~의 large-sized / full-sized / oversize(d) / kingsize(d) / of a large size / big / large // 초~의 extra-large / super-sized / outsize(d) // ~ 선박 a large vessel // ~ 태풍 a large-scale typhoon // ~ 버스 a coach.
● **대형주** a large-capital stock.

대형(隊形) (a) formation; order. ¶밀집 ~ (a) close formation // 전투 ~ (a) battle formation // ~을 정연히 하고 in good formation // ~을 유지하다 keep formation // ~이 흩어져 있었다 The formation was in disarray. // 병사들은 횡렬로 ~을 짰다 The soldiers fell in [formed ranks].

대화(大禍) a great disaster; a calamity; a woe. ¶~를 입다 meet with a calamity [misfortune].

대화(對話) [의견 등의 교환] a dialogue; (미) a dialog; [담화] a conversation. ¶플라톤의 ~편 the Dialogs of Plato // ~가 없는 부부 a couple with nothing to say to each other // 남북 ~ a South-North dialogue // 그 문제에 대하여 ~가 오고 갔다 They carried on a dialogue concerning the program. // 나는 (화제가 궁하여) ~를 계속할 수 없었다 I was unable to keep up the conversation[to keep the (conversational) ball rolling]. **대화하다** have[hold] a conversation (with); talk (with). ¶그들은 프랑스 어로 대화했다 They were talking[speaking] in French.

● **대화극** a dialogue. **대화방** a chat room. **대화체** dialogue (form).

대회(大會) 〔큰 회합〕 a mass meeting; (특정 목적을 위한) a rally; 〔총회〕 a general meeting[assembly]; 〔회의〕 a conference; a convention; (경기의) a meet; a tournament; a tourney. ¶연차 ~ an annual meeting/수영 ~ a swimming meet// 당 ~ a party convention// 교원 노조의 전국 ~ the national assembly[conference] of the teacher's union / ~를 개최하다 hold a mass meeting / 국민 ~ a popular mass meeting / (정당 주최의) (미) a political rally // 기념 ~ a commemoration meeting on a grand scale.
● 대회 신기록 (set) a new meet record.
대회전 경기(大回轉競技) 〔스키〕 the giant slalom.
대흉(大凶) 〔큰 흉년〕 an unusually bad[poor] harvest[crop]; an extremely scanty harvest. ¶올해는 쌀이 ~이다 The rice crop has extremely failed this year.
댁(宅) 1 〔가정〕 a home; 〔주택〕 a house; a residence; 〔상대의 집〕 your home; 〔남의 집〕 a person's home; 〔가족〕 your[his] family. ¶~은 어딥니까 Where is your home? / Where do you live?// ~까지 바래다 드리겠습니다 Let me see you home. // (자동차로) I'll drive you home.// 〔남이나 상대의 집〕 우리 선생님 ~의 정원은 아름답게 꾸며져 있다 The garden of my teacher's home is beautifully designed.// (전화에서) 여보세요, 한 선생 ~인가요 Hello, is this[(영) that] Mr. Han's (home)?
2 〔당신〕 you. ¶~의 부인은 친절한 분이시군요 Your wife is really kindhearted. // 이것은 ~의 것입니까 Is this yours?// 나중에 ~으로 전화드리겠습니다 I will call you up later (at home).
-댁(宅) 〔…의 아내〕 Mrs. ...; the wife of (a person). ¶최 서방~ the wife of Mr. Choe / Mrs. Choe.
댁내(宅內) your family. ¶~가 다 무고하십니까 How are your people? / Are you all getting along well?
댄서 a dancer; a dancing girl.
댄스 a dance; dancing. ¶사교~ a ballroom dance / a social dance// 스퀘어[포크] ~ a square[folk] dance// ~를 하다 dance / have a dance (with) / perform a dance// 다음 차례에 ~ 상대를 해 주시지 않겠습니까 May I have the next dance with you?
● 댄스 교사 a dancing instructor[teacher]; (영) (남자) a dancing master; (여자) a dancing mistress. **댄스 교습소** a dance studio. **댄스파티** a dance; a dancing party; a ball(사교적인 대무도회); a prom(미국의 대학·고교의); (미국 구어) a hop(비공식적인). ¶~를 열다[에 가다] give[go to] a dance// 나는 어젯밤에 ~에 갔다 I went to a dance last night. **댄스홀** (미) a (public) dance hall; (영) a dancing hall[room / saloon]; 〔무도장〕 a ballroom.
댐 a dam. ¶수력 발전용[다목적] ~ a hydroelectric[multipurpose] dam// 저수용 ~ a water-storage dam// 강에 ~을 만들다 build a dam across a river// 강을 ~으로 막다 dam (up) a river.
댓 〔다섯가량〕 about five. ¶~ 권 about five volumes// ~ 사람 about five persons.
댓가지 a branch of bamboo; bamboo branches.
댓돌(臺-) terrace stones.
댓바람 〔단번에〕 all in a breath; at once; immediately; quickly. ¶~ 일을 해치우다 finish (one's) work at a stroke[straight out] // ~ 언덕을 뛰어오르다 go up a hill with one rush[at a dash] // 사고 소식을 듣자 그는 ~ 현장으로 달려갔다 On hearing of the accident, he hurried to the scene at once.
댓새 about five days.
댓줄기 a bamboo stalk[stem].
댓진(-津) tobacco tar accumulated in a pipe. ¶~이 끼다 be chocked with nicotine.
댕 with a clang. ⇨ "땡"²
댕그랑 with a clang(or). ⇨ "땡그랑"
댕그랑거리다 clang; cling. ⇨ "땡그랑거리다"
댕기 a *daenggi*; a pigtail ribbon.
댕기(를) 드리다 wear[put on] a *daenggi*.
댕기다 1 〔불을 옮아 붙게 하다〕 light; kindle; ignite. ¶담뱃불을 ~ light a cigar[cigarette] // 가스에 불을 ~ turn on the gas. 2 〔불이 옮아 붙다〕 catch[take] fire; be ignited; be kindled; spread to. ¶그것은 불이 잘 댕긴다 It catches fire[ignites] easily. / It is easily inflammable. / It is quick of ignition.
더 (수량·정도) more; some more; (시간) longer; (거리) farther; (더욱) still more; further; (부정과 함께) less; still[much] less. ¶나는 딸기를 ~ 먹고 싶다 I want more strawberries. // ~ 빨리 달려라 Run faster. // ~ 긴 밧줄은 없는가 Isn't there a longer rope?// ~ 신중히 생각하고 행동하라 Think more carefully before you act. // ~ 좋은 것은 없는가 Isn't there anything better?// 1주일만 ~ 기다려 주십시오 Please wait another week. / Please give me one more week. // 이 계획을 실행에 옮기려면 시간이 좀 ~ 필요합니다 We need a little more time before we can put the plan to work. // 그는 완쾌하기까지는 좀 ~ 기다려야 한다 He has almost completely recovered. // 2주일 ~ 있으면 기한이 끝난다 The term expires in another two weeks. // 커피를 한 잔 ~ 주십시오 Give me another cup of coffee. // 남보다 ~ 많이 연습했다 I practiced more than others. // 책값을 200원 ~ 지불했다 I paid two hundred won too much for the book. // 나는 한 마디 ~ 덧붙이고 싶다 I should like to add one more word. // 조금만 ~ 올라가면 정상[꼭대기]이다 The summit is only a little farther up ahead. // 이제 아무것도 ~ 말하지 마라 Say no more. // 이제 ~ 참을 수 없다 I can't take it any more[longer]. // 그는 ~ 참을 수가 없었다 He was not able to remain patient. / He was not able to stand it any longer. // ~는 양보할 수 없다 I can make no more concessions. // 이제부터 ~ 추워진다 It's going to get colder (still). // 이와 같은 병이 ~ 있습니까 Do you have any more bottles like this?// 재미있는 이야기가 (이) 밖에도) ~ 있다 I have (many) other interesting stories to tell you (besides this). // 이것이 ~ 좋다 This is still[even] better. // 왜 ~ 빨리 알려 주지 않았니 Why didn't you let me know earlier?// 도와줄 사람이 둘 ~ 필요하다 I need two more people to help.
더구나 in addition; moreover; besides; even [all the] more; at that; furthermore; over and above these; into the bargain; to crown (it) all; (미) on top of that; (설상가상으로) to make matters[things] worse; what is worse. ¶그녀는 아름답고 현명하며 ~ 매우 친절하다 She is beautiful, clever, and very kind besides. // 그녀는 병중임에도 불구하고 순산했

더군다나

으며 ~ 건강한 아이였다 Though she was ill, she was safely delivered of a child, and what was more, it was a healthy baby. // 그는 일도 미숙하고 ~ 게으름쟁이이다 He is unskilled and lazy to boot(▶ to boot는 보통 문장의 끝에 옴). // 그는 학식도 없고 ~ 경험도 없다 He has no scholarship, to say nothing of[not to speak of / muchless] experience.

더군다나 in addition; moreover. ⇨더구나 ¶ 나는 타이프라이터를 쓸 줄 모르며 워드 프로세서는 ~ 모른다 I can't even use a typewriter, much less a word processor.

더그아웃 [야구] a dugout.

더껑이 1 [굳거나 마른 꺼풀] scum; cream; skim; film; an incrustation. ¶죽에 ~가 앉다 a skim forms on the porridge // 우유의 ~를 걷어 내다 skim milk. 2 →더께

더께 encrusted dirt.

-더니 1 since; because; and also. ⇨-니1·2 ¶ 그는 열심히 공부하~ 시험에 일 등으로 합격했다 He studied so hard that he topped the list of successful examinees. // 그는 직무를 태만히 하~ 면직되고 말았다 He lost his position through neglect of duty. // 할 말을 다하고 났~ 가슴이 후련하다 Now that I had my say I feel much relieved. // 일기가 불순하~ 올해에는 돌림병이 유행하고 있다 Owing to the bad weather, infectious diseases are prevalent this year. // 알아봤~ 그는 2년 전에 죽었다 I found out that he has been dead for two years.
2 [회고] used to be ... (but now). ¶그때는 낚시꾼도 드물~ Then there used to be very few anglers (but now ...). // 그전에는 이곳이 연못이~ This used to be a pond.

더덕더덕 [많이 붙어 있는 모양] in clusters. ¶ 우리는 벽에 온통 포스터를 ~ 붙였다 We covered the wall with posters. / We stuck [pasted] posters all over the wall. **더덕더덕하다** clustered.

더듬거리다 1 (손으로) grope; fumble for; feel about[around] for. ¶어둠 속에서 ~ grope about in the dark for (a doorknob). 2 (말을) stammer; falter; stutter; stumble; [우물우물 말하다] mumble; speak indistinctly; mouth one's words. ¶어린애의 더듬거리는 설명으로는 according to the child's faltering explanation // 더듬거리며 읽다 falter over (a passage) // 더듬거리며 말하다 stammer out (an excuse) / speak falteringly // 나는 더듬거리는 영어로 대답했다 I replied in halting[broken] English. // 그는 더듬거리며 고맙다는 인사를 했다 He stammered out his thanks.

더듬다 1 (손으로) grope (for); fumble (in the darkness) for (a thing); feel[grope] about for (a thing); feel after (the handle). ¶회중전등을 찾으려고 ~ grope for a flashlight [(영) torch] // 나는 잔돈이 있는가 하고 호주머니를 더듬었다 I felt about[fumbled / fished] in my pocket for some small change. // 모든 일을 손으로 더듬어서 해야만 했다 I had to do everything by feel[feeling].
2 (말을) stammer; falter; stutter; stumble; be stuck for a word; have an impediment in one's speech. ¶말을 더듬으며 stammering(ly) / stuttering(ly) // 그는 몹시 말을 더듬는다 He stammers badly. // 그는 말을 더듬는 버릇이 있다 He is apt to stutter[falter in speaking].
3 (길을) feel[grope] one's way; pick one's way. ¶(장님 등이) 지팡이로 길을 ~ feel the way with a cane // 그는 어둠 속에서 문 쪽으로 더듬어 갔다 He groped his way to the door in the dark.
4 (근원·기억 등을) trace; retrace; tread; follow (up); pursue; explore. ¶우리가 더듬어 온 길 the path we have followed // 근원을 ~ trace (something) to its origin[source] // 이야기 줄거리를 더듬어 올라가다 trace back a story // 젊은 날의 기억을 ~ retrace[recollect / go over again in memory] the experiences of one's youth // 나는 기억을 더듬어 마침내 그를 확인했다 I finally recognized him by going back over things in my mind.

더듬더듬 1 (손으로) by feel; groping(ly); fumbling(ly). ¶~ 걸어가다 go feeling around / grope one's way along. 2 (말을) stammering(ly); stuttering(ly); faltering(ly). ¶~ 사과하다 stutter out an apology // 그는 ~ 프랑스어를 말했다 He spoke French haltingly.

더듬이[1] a stammerer. ⇨말더듬이

더듬이[2] a feeler; an antenna. ⇨촉각(觸角) ¶ 달팽이가 ~를 내밀었다[움츠렸다] The snail has stuck out[drawn in] its horns.

더디 [늦게] late; dilatorily; behind time [schedule]; [느리게] slow(ly); tardily; sluggishly. ¶~ 걷다 walk slowly[at a slow pace] // ~ 일하다 work slowly[tardily / sluggishly] / be slow in one's work // 목적지에 ~ 닿다 reach one's destination late[behind time].

더디다 slow; tardy; retarded. ¶길음이 ~ be slow[(문어) laggardly] of foot // 진보가 ~ make slow progress // 이해가 ~ be slow to understand[grasp] things / be dull (문어) be slow of understanding // 결단이 ~ be too deliberate in one's decision / take a long to make one's mind.

-더라 [회상·감탄] I found[discovered] that; I noticed that; it has been observed that; it is known that; as we all[I] know; I hear[have been told] that; […이라고 한다] they say; it is said that. ¶그는 앓고 있다~ (I am not sure but) I hear he is sick. // 그녀는 3시에 온다~ I think she said she was arriving at three. // 그는 아까 자고 있~ I found him sleeping a little while ago. / He was noticed to be sleeping a moment ago. // 그는 곧 미국에 간다~ They say[It is said / I have been told] that he is going to America pretty soon.

-더라도 [강한 가정] though; although; (even) if; however; supposing[granting] that; no matter (how); whatever may. ¶설령 그렇~ supposing[admitting] that it is so / even if it were so // 폭풍우가 치~ 우리는 떠나는 겁니까 Are we going to leave even if it is stormy? // 그게 정말이라 하~ 증거가 없다 Even granting[granted] that it is true, there is no evidence. // 틀린 데가 있~ 아주 적다 There are few mistakes, if any. // 그는 그 돈을 전부는 아니~ 절반 이상은 써 버렸다 He has spent more than half the money, if not all. // 아무리 가난하~ 결코 좌절하지 마라 However [No matter how] poor you may be, never lose heart. // 그가 무슨 말을 하~ 들어서는 안 된다 Whatever he may say [No matter what he says], you must not listen to him. // 무슨 일이 있~ 나는 끝장을 볼 거다 Come what may [whatever may happen], I will see it through. // 누가 오~ 문을 잠가 두어라 No matter who comes keep the gate closed.∥몇 번 물어보~ 내 대답은 마찬가지입니다 However often you may ask, my answer will be the same.∥자넨 가지 않~ 괜찮다 You need not go.

-더라면 [과거에 대한 가정] if; if only; if it had been …; if one had done …; provided [supposing] (that); [희망] I wish. ¶노력했~ 해내었을 텐데 You could have done it, if you had tried.∥그 돈이 없었~ 굶어 죽었을 거야 If it had not been for[But for / Without] the money, I would have been starved to death.∥내게 5분만 더 있었~ If I only had had five more minutes!∥부자였~ 좋았을 것을 I wish I had been rich.∥그녀를 문병하러 더 자주 병원에 갔었~ 좋았을 텐데 I wish I'd gone to see her in the hospital more often.

더리[1] 1 [얼마쯤] some; a little; somewhat; to some degree; more or less; [부분적] partially; partly. ¶그 일에 관해서 ~ 알고 있다 I know something about it.∥세상에는 그런 사람이 ~ 있다 There are some people like that.∥너도 그 문제에는 ~ 책임이 있다 You are also more or less responsible for the matter. 2 [때때로] sometimes; occasionally; from time to time; now and then; once in a while; at times; at moments. ¶~ 놀러 오게나 Why don't you come and see us once in a while?∥그런 일이 ~ 생긴다 Occasionally such things happen.

더리[2] […에게] to (a person); toward. ¶어머니께서는 나~ 6시까지 돌아오라고 했다 Mother told me to be home by six.∥그는 나~ 빨리 출발하는 것이 좋다고 권했다 He advised me to start early.∥감히 누구~ 오라 가라 명령이냐 Whom on earth dare you command to get in and out?

더러움 [불결] dirt; uncleanness; filth(iness); impurity; pollution; soil; defilement; contamination; [얼룩·오점] a stain; a blot; a tarnish; a blemish; a smudge. ¶~을 모르는 소녀 an innocent[unsophisticated] girl∥나는 바지의 ~을 뺐다 I cleaned my trousers. / I removed the stains from my trousers.

더러워지다 1 (사물이) become dirty[filthy]; be stained; be soiled; be polluted; be defiled; be blemished[smudged]; be contaminated. ¶더러워진 dirty / unclean / filthy / stained / tainted / defiled∥피로 더러워진 셔츠 a bloodstained shirt∥더러워진 물건을 처리하다 take care of dirty[soiled] things∥이 식탁보는 더러워졌다 This tablecloth is dirty [soiled].∥내 손이 기름으로 더러워졌다 My hands were smeared with grease.

2 (마음 등이) become mean[base / low / sordid / despicable / (미) dirty]. ¶악으로 더러워진 성격 a character stained by vice∥마음이 ~ become mean-spirited[base-minded]∥사람이 ~ become a low[base / mean / dirty] character.

3 (명성 등이) be soiled[tarnished / stained / sullied / dishonored / disgraced]. ¶많은 범죄로 더러워진 명성 a reputation sullied by many crimes∥가명(家名)이 ~ one's family name is disgraced[dishonored / stained].

4 [정조를 잃다] become unchaste; lose one's chastity[purity]; be deflowered. ¶더러워진 여자 an unchaste[a defiled] woman / a woman of stained character∥몸이 ~ lose one's chastity / stain one's virtue.

더럭 [갑자기 많이] all at once; all of a sudden; in[with] a burst. ¶겁이 ~ 나다 be seized with fear[struck with awe] all of a sudden / get into a funk∥화를 ~ 내다 have a fit of anger / fly[get] into a rage∥의심이 ~ 났다 Doubt assailed him. / A doubt rushed into[upon] his mind. / A question burst upon him.

더럼 dirt; uncleanness; a blemish. ⇨더러움 ¶~ 타는 옷 clothes easy to get soiled.

더럽다 1 [불결하다] dirty; filthy; foul; unclean; soiled; squalid; messy; stained; grimy; shabby. ¶더러운 물 dirty[impure] water∥더러운 손수건 a dirty[(문어) soiled] handkerchief∥더러운 변소 a filthy toilet∥누더기 더러운 집들 a row of squalid houses∥옷차림이 더러운 노인 an old man wearing dirty[filthy] clothes∥부엌이 몹시 ~ The kitchen is in a disgusting state.

2 [비열하다] mean; (문어) base; low; dirty; [추잡하다] indecent; obscene; filthy; nasty. ¶더러운 놈 a mean[low] fellow / a dirty guy[dog]∥더러운 화제 a filthy[a ribald / an indecent] talk∥더러운 계집 an unchaste [obscene / impure] woman∥마음이 더러운 사람 a man of low[mean] character∥더러운 생각을 갖다 have a mean idea∥더러운 말을 쓰다 use dirty[filthy] language∥그것은 입에 담기에도 더러운 이야기다 The story is too odious to tell.∥이 더러운 녀석아, 빨리 꺼져 You filthy scum! Out of my sight at once!(▶ 옛날 연극의 대사) / (구어) You dirty sons of bitches[filthy bastard]! Get the hell out of here.

3 [인색하다] stingy; niggardly; sordid; close-fisted; greedy of money. ¶돈에 더러운 사람 a stingy person / a niggard / a miser.

4 [역겹다] disgusting; offensive.

더럽히다 1 [불결하게 하다] make (a thing) dirty[unclean]; stain; soil; foul; defile; blemish; slur; taint; contaminate; pollute (air). ¶옷을 ~ soil one's clothes∥방을 ~ get a room dirty∥하수로 강물을 ~ contaminate a river with sewage∥자동차 때문에 바지를 더럽혔다 A motorcar spattered filth on my trousers.∥많은 공장이 세워지고 그들의 폐기물로 강을 더럽혔다 Many factories were built and their waste polluted the river.

2 (명예 등을) disgrace; dishonor; bring disgrace (upon); sully; defile; tarnish; [모독하다] desecrate (a shrine); profane (a temple). ¶가문을 ~ disgrace the family name / bring disgrace on one's family∥명성을 ~ sully[soil] one's reputation / stain[disgrace] one's name∥조상의 이름을 ~ disgrace the good name[reputation] of one's ancestors∥직업을 더럽히지 않기를 바란다 I hope you will live up to your profession.∥그것은 아버지의 이름을 더럽히는 일이 된다 That would disgrace[stain] my father's name.

3 (여성을) dishonor; outrage; violate; deflower; rape (a woman). ¶(여자가) 몸을 ~ lose her chastity[purity] / stain her virtue∥그녀는 남자에게 몸을 더럽혔다 Her honor fell a sacrifice to the passion of the man.

더미 a heap; a pile; an accumulation; (건초 등의) a stack; a rick. ¶돌[책] ~ a pile of rocks [books]∥쓰레기 ~ a rubbish[trash / dump] heap∥짚 ~ a stack of (rice) straws.

더벅머리 [흩어진 머리] disheveled[unkempt]

더부룩하다 hair; bushy hair; (아이) a lad with disheveled hair.

더부룩하다 1 (머리·수염 등이) tufty; fringy; bushy; thick; unkempt; shaggy; (풀 등이) thick; rank; rampant; luxurious. ¶더부룩한 머리 unkempt hair∥털이 더부룩한 개 a shaggy dog∥그녀는 머리가 더부룩하게 되었다 (구어) Her hair got messed up.∥그는 수염이 더부룩하게 자라나 있었다 He had a bushy head.∥뜰에 풀이 더부룩하게 자랐다 The garden is overgrown with grass[weeds].
더부룩이 (수염·머리 등이) in tufts; tufty; fringy; bushy; thick(ly); unkempt; (풀 등이) thick(ly); rankly; rampantly. ¶(풀이) ~ 자라다 grow thick and wild / be rank∥머리털이 ~ 자랐다 My hair grew thick. / My hair get tufty.
2 (배 속이 시원하지 않다) (서술적) feel stodgy; feel[sit] heavy on the stomach; be heavy; be not easily digested; feel bloated.

더부살이 a resident [living-in] servant; a domestic (servant); (집합적) the domestic staff. ¶~를 살다[하다] become[work as] a domestic help / be hired as a living-in servant

더부살이 환자(患者) 걱정 (속담) worrying about things which are none of one's concern; worrying (oneself) unnecessarily; unnecessary[needless] anxiety.

더불어 1 [함께] together; […과 함께] with; together[along] with; in company with; […에 따라서] as; with. ¶나이와 ~ with (the) years / with one's years / as one grows older∥~ 살다 live together / live under the same roof∥그와 ~ 고락을 같이하다 share joy and sorrow with him∥~ 운명을 같이하다 share one's fate / cast in one's lot (with)∥시대와 ~ 나아가다 keep pace with[abreast of] the times. 2 [한가지로] alike; equally. ¶남녀[노소]가 ~ men and women[young and old] alike.

더블 double. ¶~의 double∥~ 폭의 double-width (cloth).
●**더블베드** a double bed. **더블 스틸** [야구] a double steal. ¶~을 하다 pull off[try] a double steal(▶ pull off는 성공한 경우, try는 시도만 한 경우). **더블 클릭** a double click. **더블 펀치** a double punch. ¶그는 머리에 ~을 먹였다 He dealt a double punch to his opponent's head. **더블 플레이** [야구] a double play. ¶~을 당하다 get a batter to hit into a double play. **더블헤더** [야구] a doubleheader.

더빙 [영] dubbing(-in). **더빙하다** dub. ¶한국어로 더빙한 「햄릿」 Hamlet dubbed in Korean∥미국 영화를 한국어로 ~ dub American films into Korean. ➔¶그 영화는 한국어로 더빙되어 있다 The movie is dubbed in Korean.

더없다 the best; supreme; perfect; ideal. ¶더없는 행복 the supreme happiness. **더없이** (더할 나위 없이) most of all; best (of all); supremely; superlatively; in the last degree. ¶~ 사랑하는 아내 one's most beloved wife∥나는 그 친구가 ~ 그립다 I miss that friend terribly[keenly]. / ~ 화창한 날이었다 It was a very fine day.∥그런 짓을 한다는 것은 ~ 어리석은 짓이다 It is the height of [It is sheer] folly to do such a thing.∥그를 다시 만난다는 것은 ~ 기쁜 일이다 Nothing will give me more pleasure than to see him again.∥그는 무서운 사람은 ~ 착실한 사람이다 He is the most serious man I've ever met.

더욱 [한층 더] more; more and more; still [much] more; all the more; (부정) less and less; still [much] less. ¶~ 중요한 것은 what is more important∥~ 노력하다 make greater efforts∥~ 발전하다 make further progress∥그것은 ~ 돋보일 것입니다 That would look much better. / That would appear to even greater advantage.∥~ 이상한 것은 그의 행동이다 Still, what's strange about it is his behavior. ¶그게 사실이라면 ~ 좋다[나쁘다] If that is true, so much the better[worse].∥그는 지금까지보다 ~ 얌전해졌다 He became even more obedient than before.∥우리는 ~ 그 일을 검토할 필요가 있다 We need to study the matter further. / The matter needs further study.∥그가 시험에 합격하지 못한다면 나는 ~ 가망이 전혀 없소 If even he cannot pass the test, I have very little chance indeed. / If even he can't pass the test, how can I hope to?∥이가 아파지기 시작했다 My tooth began to ache more and more. / My toothache got worse and worse.∥나를 ~ 슬프게 하는 것은 그의 요절(夭折)이다 It makes me grieve anew over his early death.

더욱더 [더욱 많이] more and more; still [even] more; all the more; increasingly; growingly; [더욱 적게] less and less; still [much] less; decreasingly. ¶공부에 대한 흥미가 ~ 강해졌다[적어졌다] I became more and more (or increasingly) [less and less] interested in my studies.∥보면 볼수록 ~ 갖고 싶어 졌다 The more I looked at it, the more eager I became to have it.∥공교롭게 그가 들어와서 일이 ~ 난처하게 되었다 To make matters worse, he came in just then.∥폭풍이 ~ 심해지고 있다 The storm is getting worse all the time[worse and worse].∥그 이야기를 듣고 ~ 불쾌해졌다 Upon hearing that story, I became even more disgusted.∥오지 말라는 말을 들으면 ~ 가고 싶어 진다 When I am told not to come, I become all the more eager to go.

더욱이 besides; moreover; further; furthermore; as well; in addition (to that); particularly; especially; into the bargain; to boot; on top of (that); and that; what's more; also; to; […까지] even. ¶~ 좋은 것은 what is better∥~ 곤란한 것은 to make matters worse / what is worse∥그는 그렇게 말했다. ~ 놀라운 일은 그가 그걸 해낸 것이다 He said it, and what is more surprising, he did it.∥그는 불어를 읽지도 못하고 ~ 쓰지도 못한다 He cannot read French, much less write it.∥그건 영어로 씌어 있다. ~ 서투른 영어로 It is written in English, and poor English at that.

더운물 warm[hot] water.

더워하다 be sensitive to the heat; feel the heat; complain of the heat; feel hot [heat]; suffer from the heat; swelter. ¶몹시도 더워하는구나 How you feel the heat!∥아기가 더워하는 것 같다 The baby seems to feel hot.∥그는 뚱뚱해서 여름에는 유달리 더워한다 Being so fat, he is particularly susceptible to the summer heat.

더위 [더운 기운] heat; warmth; hot weather. ¶찌는 듯한 ~ steamy heat / sweltering heat

// 타는 듯한 ~ scorching [parching / fiery] heat // 숨 막힐 듯한 ~ suffocating [oppressive / stifling] heat // ~에 시달리다 be affected by the heat / suffer from hot weather // ~를 견디다 stand [bear] the heat // ~를 피하다 avoid [escape] the heat // ~가 물러가다 hot weather comes to an end // 나는 ~에 약하다 I am sensitive to the heat. // 나는 ~에는 끄떡 없다 I don't mind the (summer) heat. // ~를 몹시 타시는군요 You seem to feel the heat very much. // 올여름에는 피서지에 가서 ~를 피하겠다 I'm going to summer resort this year to get away from the heat. // 이 ~에 화초가 시들어 버렸다 The plants have drooped in this heat. // 오늘 ~는 유별나다 It is exceptionally hot today. / This is an exceptionally hot day.

더위 먹은 소 달만 보아도 헐떡인다(속담) A scalded cat [dog] fears cold water.; The burnt child dreads the fire.

더위(를) 먹다 suffer from the summer heat; be affected by the heat; be ill from the heat. ¶더위를 먹은 사람 a heat-prostrated person // 대단한 것은 아니야, 더위를 좀 먹었을 뿐이니까 Nothing serious, I'm only feeling the heat.

더치다 1 (병세가) become [grow / get] worse; be seized with a relapse; be aggravated. ¶그의 병이 더쳤다 His illness grew worse [worsened / became more serious]. // 그 사건으로 그의 노이로제가 더쳤다 The incident aggravated his nervous condition [the state of his nerves]. // 그의 감기가 더쳐서 폐렴이 되었다 His cold grew [developed] into pneumonia. 2 offend; give (a person) offense. ⇨덧들이다

더치페이 (×Dutch pay) [각자 부담] Dutch treat. ¶~를 합시다 Let's go Dutch. / Let's split the bill.

더킹 [권투] ducking.

더펄거리다 1 (머리가) bounce [fly] up and down. ¶머리가 ~ one's hair is bouncing up and down. 2 (사람이) act rashly [on impulse / briskly].

더하기 [수] addition; adding up. ¶~를 하다 add up (figures) // 간단한 ~를 하다 do sums in simple addition.

더하다¹ 1 [심해지다] get [become] worse; worsen; grow harder; increase in violence; get serious; gather strength; go from bad to worse; be aggravated; grow in intensity; become intensified. ¶그의 병세는 차차 더해 갔다 His illness is steadily worsening. // 어두워짐에 따라 나의 공포심은 더해 갔다 As it grew darker, my fears deepened. // 태풍은 기세를 더해 갔다 The storm is gathering force. // 그 버릇은 급속히 더해 갔다 The habit rapidly grew upon him. // 망향의 정은 더해 갈 뿐이었다 My nostalgia grew stronger and stronger.
2 [보태어 늘리다] add (up); sum up; add (one number to another); [부족분을 보태어 메우다] make up (for). ¶8에 5를 더하면 13이 된다 Five added to eight makes [is / equals] thirteen. / Eight and five make [are] thirteen. / Eight plus five is thirteen.
3 [늘리다] increase; augment; gain; grow; add to; enlarge. ¶낮은 목소리가 그의 위엄을 더하고 있다 His low voice adds to his dignity. // 그는 나이와 함께 책임감이 더해 감을 느꼈다 He felt his sense of responsibility increasing with age. // 그 파티에 흥을 더할 기획을 생각해 내시오 Please think up some ideas to add to the fun of the party. // 검은 벨벳 옷이 그 부인의 매력을 크게 더했다 The black velvet dress lent great charm to the lady. // 아이들의 존재가 그 모임에 느긋한 분위기를 더했다 The presence of (the) children gave a relaxed atmosphere to the meeting. // 그런 짓을 하면 네 망신만 더할 것이다 That will only add to your shame.

더하다² [(비교하여) 더 많거나 심하다] more; much; all the more [better / worse]. ¶그도 술꾼이지만 그의 아버지는 더한 술고래다 He is (quite) a drinker, but his father is an even heavier drinker. // 혼자 있으니 슬픔이 ~ Left all alone, I feel all the more sad.

더할 나위 없다 the best; supreme; perfect; ideal.

더한층 (-層) still [much] more; all the more; (부정) still [much] less. ¶~ 좋다 [나쁘다] be so much the better [worse] // ~ 노력하다 make greater efforts // 회오리바람은 갑자기 오기 때문에 ~ 무섭다 Cyclones are to be dreaded all the more because they are unexpected.

덕 (德) 1 [미덕] (a) virtue; morality; goodness; moral excellence; a merit. ¶~이 있는 virtuous / respectable // ~을 닦다 cultivate virtue [moral character] // ~을 행하다 practice virtue / do good // ~을 갖추다 [지니다] possess [be invested with] virtue // 온 마을이 그의 ~에 감화되었다 The whole village was influenced by his virtue.
2 [은혜·덕택] favor; good; kindness; mercy; benevolence; indebtedness; [진력] efforts; good offices; [조력] assistance. ¶(남의) ~으로 by (a person's) favor / thanks to / due to / through (a person's) efforts / owing to // 내가 성공한 것은 당신의 ~이오 I owe my success to you. / Thanks to your assistance, I succeeded in the attempt. // 이것도 과학의 ~이다 We are indebted to science for this. // 그는 고아들에게 ~을 베풀었다 He was benevolent to the orphans. / He was good to the orphans.

덕담 (德談) well-wishing [well-meant] remarks.

덕망 (德望) (a) moral influence; a reputation for virtue; high moral repute. ¶~이 있다 have a moral influence (over) / be renowned for (one's) virtues / enjoy good reputation as a man of virtue.
●**덕망가** a man of high moral repute [of fair name].

덕목 (德目) (a) virtue; moral principle.

덕분 (德分) favor; help; support. ⇨덕택

덕성 (德性) moral character; virtue; moral nature. ¶~이 없는 (men) of low moral character // ~을 기르다 [함양하다] cultivate [foster] moral character.

덕스럽다 (德-) virtuous; respectable; estimable; gracious; benignant. ¶덕스러운 사람 a man of virtue / a virtuous man // 덕스럽게 생기다 have respectable features.

덕육 (德育) moral training [culture / education]; character building. ¶~을 중히 여기다 attach importance to moral culture // ~과 지육(智育)은 병행되어야 한다 The cultivation of moral habits should go with that of intellect.

덕의(德義) morality; integrity; probity. ¶~를 중히 여기다 have a high sense of honor / set value on morality.
● **덕의심** moral sense; a sense of honor; probity. ¶~이 높은[강한] 사람 a man of strict morality∥…의 ~에 호소하다 appeal to (a person's) sense of honor.

덕지덕지 layer after layer (of accumulated dirt); thick (with dirt); encrusted. ¶때가 ~ 끼다 be covered thick[encrusted] with dirt.

덕택(德澤) indebtedness; [은혜] favor; grace; patronage; boon; [조력] help; aid; assistance; [후원] support; backing. ¶~으로 thanks to (a person) / thanks to (a person's) patronage / by (a person's) favor [help / aid] / through[by] (a person's) assistance / by (a person's) kind influence / through (a person's) efforts / (이유, 원인) due to / because of / owing to / by[in] virtue of / by grace of∥그녀의 조력 ~으로 나는 성공하였다 Thanks to her assistance I succeeded in the attempt.∥그는 숙부 ~에 일자리를 얻었다 He obtained a job through his uncle's influence[(문어) good offices].∥이 계획이 승인된 것은 그의 노력의 ~이다 The plan was accepted, thanks to his efforts.∥그녀가 시험에 합격한 것은 노력의 ~이다 She passed the examination through hard work.∥그는 사장 ~으로 승진했다 He was promoted thanks to the support of[through the influence of / by recommendation of] the president.∥~으로 모두 잘 있습니다 We are all well and fine, thank you.

덕행(德行) virtuous[moral] conduct; virtue; goodness; welldoing. ¶~을 쌓도록 노력하다 lead a virtuous life / behave oneself well.

-던가 [의문·의심] whether it was (observed to be or happen); (did you notice) was it?; (did you hear or find) was it? ¶걸 어디다 두었~ Where did I leave it? / 길~ 짧~ Was it long or short? / 그래 제주도는 어떻~ How were things at Jejudo? / How did you like Jejudo? ∥ 그가 그렇게 말하~ Did he say so?∥내가 왜 그리 했~ 후회됩니다 I have come to worry over why I did that.

-던걸 [회상·감탄]. ¶굉장한 미인이~ She was a stunning beauty, indeed.∥시시하~ We had a very thin time of it. / That was no fun at all.∥일이 고되~ It was work, I tell you.

-던데 1 [회상] though; although; in spite of; notwithstanding; but. ¶사장이 찾~ 어디 가 있었느냐 Where have you been all this while? The president was looking for you.∥짠 방식은 다른 것 같~ 재료는 같더라 It was the same material, notwithstanding the texture seemed different.∥사람은 젊~ 아주 똑똑하더라 Young though he was, he was very wise.∥어제 보니까 아무도 없~ 누가 이런 짓을 해 놓았을까 I didn't see anybody around here yesterday, so who could have done this?

2 [감탄] I found...; you see[know]; I tell [assure] you. ¶손해는 대단치 않~ The loss was far less than we feared.∥책은 쉽~ I found the book easy.∥아니나 다를까 그는 거기 있~ Sure enough, I found him there.

-던들 [현재의 결과와 반대되는 가정] if only ...; granted that; if it had happened that ...; so long as .... ¶~이 없었~ but for ... / if it had not been for ...∥알고만 있었~ If only I[I only] had known!∥당신의 도움이 없었~ 나는 실패했을 것이다 If it had not been for[But for] your help, I should have failed.∥그가 얼른 팔을 내밀지 않았~ 그녀는 넘어졌을 것이다 She would have fallen but for his sudden arms.

던적스럽다 [비열하다] mean; base; sordid; despicable; [다랍다] stingy; miserly; [추잡하다] indecent; obscene; filthy; foul; dirty. ¶던적스러운 사람 a man of low character[base mind] / a mean-spirited person∥던적스러운 생각 a mean thought∥던적스러운 행실 despicable behavior[conduct]∥던적스러운 이야기 a filthy[an indecent] talk / an obscene[a smutty] story.

-던지 [과거의 회상·의심] whether it was (observed to be or happen). ¶그것이 무엇이었~ 생각이 안 난다 I cannot remember what it was.∥값이 얼마였~ 기억이 안 난다 I don't remember how much it was.

던지다 1 (물건을) throw; hurl; fling; cast; pitch; (창 등을) dart; toss(가볍게). ¶(야구에서) 손을 어깨 위로 올렸다가 내려 던지기 an overhand throw∥개에게 돌을 ~ throw a stone at a dog∥공을 ~ throw[pitch] a ball ∥그는 화가 나서 책을 내게 던졌다 He flung a book at me in a fit of anger.∥그는 개에게 고기 조각을 던져 주었다 He threw a piece of meat to the dog.∥그는 거북에게 돌을 세게 던졌다 He flung[hurled] a stone at the turtle.

2 [투표하다] cast a ballot; ballot (for); (미) cast a[one's] vote (for); poll. ¶깨끗한 한 표를 ~ cast a clean vote∥그에게 한 표를 던졌다 I voted for him.

3 (그림자·빛 등을) cast[throw] (on / over); project; (파문 등을) create; cause. ¶빛을 ~ turn[throw] a light (on a thing)∥석양이 붉은빛을 바다에 던졌다 The setting sun cast a fiery glow over the sea.∥나무들이 지상에 긴 그림자를 던지고 있었다 The trees cast long shadows on the ground.∥그 사건은 교육계에 큰 파문을 던졌다 The incident caused quite a stir in[sent shock waves through] educational circles.∥그는 나에게 불손한 질문을 던졌다 He flung an impolite question at me.∥그는 그 이론에 의문을 던졌다 He threw [cast] some doubt on the theory.

4 (시선 등을) cast (at); send (at). ¶추파를 ~ cast an amorous glance (at) / wink (at).

5 (몸을) throw[cast] oneself (into a river); [비유] enter[launch] (into politics). ¶그녀는 자기 몸을 던지듯 그의 팔에 안겼다 She flung herself into his arms.∥그녀는 바다에 몸을 던졌다 She threw herself in the sea.∥그녀는 여성 해방 운동에 몸을 던졌다 She threw herself into[plunged into / devoted herself to] the women's liberation movement.∥소년은 혁명 단체에 몸을 던졌다 The boy joined a revolutionary group.

6 [그만두다] abandon; throw[give] up. ¶붓을 ~ stop writing / throw down one's pen.

덜 less; incompletely; little; insufficiently. ¶~ 구워진 half-done / underdone / (생선·고기가) half-roasted / (빵이) half-baked∥~ 마른 half-dried / unseasoned (wood / timber)∥~ 취한 half-tipsy / half-drunk∥~ 익은 과일 unripe[green] fruit∥돈이 ~ 드는 방법은 없을까 Isn't there a cheaper[less expensive] way?∥이 쇠고기는 ~ 구워졌다 This beef is too rare for me.// 오늘은 어제보다 ~ 춥다 It is less cold today than yesterday.// 밥이 아직 ~ 되다 The rice is not ready[cooked] yet.

덜거덕 with a rattle. ⇨ 달가닥
덜거덕거리다 clatter; rattle.
덜거덩 with a clang. ⇨ 달가당
덜거럭 with a rattle. ⇨ 달가락
덜그럭거리다 rattle ⇨ 달그락거리다
덜다 1 [빼다] subtract; deduct (from); take off; [적게 하다] decrease; lessen; abate; reduce. ¶3분의 1을 ~ reduce one-third/분량을 ~ decrease the quantity (of)//무게를 ~ reduce[lessen] the weight//10에서 6을 덜면 4가 남는다 Six from ten leaves four. / Ten less[minus] six leaves four.
2 (고통·슬픔 등을) lessen; ease; relieve; allay; alleviate; lighten; mitigate; (돈 등을) save; spare; curtail; cut (down). ¶수고를 ~ save (a person) trouble / save labor//경비를 ~ cut (down)[curtail] expenses//고통[근심 / 슬픔]을 ~ ease[allay] the pain[anxiety / grief]//일의 부담을 덜어 주다 lighten the work load//그녀의 친절한 말을 듣고 나니 내 슬픔이 덜어졌다 Her kind words eased [lessened] my sorrow.//고통을 덜어 줄 무슨 약이 없습니까 Isn't there any medicine that will lessen[relieve / ease] the pain?

덜덜[1] [떠는 모양] trembling(ly); shivering(ly); shaking(ly); quivering(ly). ¶손을 ~ 떨면서 with trembling hands//무서워 ~ 떨다 tremble with fear//추위어 ~ 떨다 shiver with cold//추워서[무서워서] 이를 ~ 떨다 say an ape's paternoster//온몸이 ~ 떨리다 tremble in every limb//손이 ~ 떨려서 글을 쓸 수가 없었다 I could not write as my hand shook.

덜덜[2] [구르는 소리] rumbling; rolling; rattling. ¶~ 굴러 가는 소리 a rumbling sound / a rumble / a rolling noise//(수레가) ~ 굴러 가다 rumble along[up / down].

덜되다 (사람됨이)(서술적) be no good; be wretched[poor / sorry / sad] stuff; be a failure; leave much to be desired; be not up to the mark; be a complete botch. ¶덜된 놈 a good-for-nothing fellow / a greenhorn / a wretched fellow / a silly ass//덜된 수작을 하다 talk nonsense//그는 정치가로서는 덜되었다 He is a failure as a statesman.

덜떨어지다 slow-witted; (서술적) be not all there. ¶나는 때로 그 녀석이 덜떨어진 놈이 아닌가 생각한다 Sometimes I think he's not all there.

덜렁 lonely; jingle; frivolously. ⇨ 달랑1·2·3·4
덜렁거리다[1] (행동이) be restless; conduct [behave] oneself flippantly; act hastily [rashly / carelessly / frivolously]; be always on the go. ¶덜렁거리는 사람 a flighty[hasty] person / a bustling fellow//덜렁거리면서 돌아다니다 hustle[bustle] about / go around restlessly / can't sit still a minute//덜렁거리지 좀 마라 Don't be so hasty. / Calm yourself. / Take it easy.

덜렁거리다[2] (소리가) tinkle; clink; jingle; jingle-jangle.
덜렁덜렁하다[1] be restless. ⇨ 덜렁거리다[1]
덜렁덜렁하다[2] tinkle. ⇨ 덜렁거리다[2]
덜렁이 a restless[careless] person; a flighty [hasty / bustling] person; a scatterbrain; a harum-scarum.

덜리다 1 [덜어지다] be subtracted[deducted]; be taken off[away / from]. 2 [경감·완화되다] be reduced; become less; lessen; decrease; become mild[less severe]; be allayed [eased]; be mitigated[alleviated]. ¶걱정이 덜렸다 My anxiety was eased.//그의 불안이 덜렸다 His misgiving[apprehension] was allayed.//우리의 부담은 많이 덜렸다 We were greatly lightened of our burden.

덜미 the nape; the scruff; the back of one's neck.
덜미를 누르다 call upon (a person to do); give (a person) a hard time (of it).
덜미잡이 grabbing by the back[scruff] of one's neck; grapple. **덜미잡이하다** grab[take / seize] (a person) by the scruff of his neck [by the collar]; grapple with; get a grapple

덜커덕 [단단한 물건이 맞닿아 나는 소리] a click; thump; plump; bump; thud. ¶~ 소리 내며 with a thud[thump] / plump heavily / with a bump[flump] / ~ 떨어지다 fall plump[with a flump] / fall heavily / flump// 창문이 ~ 닫히다 a window shuts with a click. **덜커덕하다** click. ¶문이 덜커덕한다 The door clicks.

덜커덕거리다 keep clattering; clatter; rattle. ¶덜커덕거리는 짐차 소리 the rattling of a cart//덧문이 바람에 덜커덕거린다 The shutter is flapping[slamming] in the wind.

덜커덩 clattering(ly); rattling(ly); clanging(ly); with a clang[bump / bang]. ¶전차가 ~ 멈췄다 The train stopped with a jerk. **덜커덩하다** clatter; rattle; rumble; clang; bang; bump. ¶전차가 덜커덩하더니 움직이기 시작했다 The train lurched and began to move.//문이 덜커덩한다 A door bangs.

덜커덩거리다 keep banging[crashing / rattling / clattering]. ¶미닫이를 덜커덩거리며 닫다 shut the sliding door noisily//기차는 손상된 철교 위를 덜커덩거리며 조심스럽게 지나갔다 The train rattled gingerly over the damaged bridge.

덜컥 1 (갑자기) suddenly; unexpectedly; with a pop. ¶~ 죽다 die suddenly / pop off / drop dead//~ 겁이 나다 be struck with awe [get into a funk] all of a sudden. 2 (가슴이). ¶그의 말에 가슴이 ~ 내려앉았다 His words shocked me.//전보라면 언제나 가슴이 ~ 내려앉는다 A telegram always gives me a turn.

덜하다 [정도가 낮아지다] decrease; diminish; lessen; abate. ¶슬픔[아픔]이 덜해졌다 The grief[pain] has eased.//추위가 덜해졌다 The cold has moderated[let up].//폭발물의 위험이 덜해졌다 The danger of an explosion has lessened.

덤 an addition; a premium; something extra; something thrown in; a throw-in; [경품] a free gift; (미) a giveaway. ¶~을 붙이다 throw in something extra//가구를 샀더니 ~으로 왁스를 주었다 When I bought the furniture, they threw in the wax (for free).//~으로 귤 2개를 드리겠습니다 (구어) I'll throw these two oranges in extra. / I'll give you two oranges into the bargain.

덤덤하다 1 [말이 없다] silent; speechless; closemouthed; mum; (서술적) keep[remain] silent; hold one's tongue; [경품] keep one's mouth shut; keep dumb. ¶덤덤하게 앉아 있다 sit in silence. 2 [차분하다] calm; serene; placid; peaceful; [예사롭다]

덤벙 ordinary; common; (서술적) keep calm [cool]; keep a cool head; do not get excited. ¶덤덤한 마음 a placid [serene / calm] mind // 덤덤하게 지내다 get along as usual. 3 (맛이 싱겁다) plain; flat.

덤벙 splashing; with a plop [dull splash]. ¶강물에 ~ 뛰어들다 plunge [splash] into the river // 물에 ~ 떨어지다 drop in the water with a plop / fall plop into the water. **덤벙하다** plop [flop / plunge / splash] into (the water).

덤벙거리다[1] act frivolously [rashly / flippantly / lightly]; frivol. ¶덤벙거리는 사람 a careless [hasty] person / (구어) a scatterbrain // 덤벙거리며 일을 함부로 하다 do one's work carelessly.

덤벙거리다[2] (물에서) splash; splatter; bespatter; make a splash. ¶진창 속을 덤벙거리며 걷다 go splashing in the mud // 발을 물에 담그고 ~ dabble one's feet in the water.

덤벙덤벙 (경솔히) frivolously; flippantly; rashly; hastily; lightly; carelessly. ¶아무 일에나 ~ 대들다 poke one's nose into everything. **덤벙덤벙하다** act frivolously. ⇨ 덤벙거리다[1]

덤벼들다 1 (대들다) go at; set [pounce] (upon); jump (on); fall on [upon]; turn upon; defy; spring [leap / rush] upon; fly at; challenge (a person to a fight); flare up (at); attack; assault. ¶그는 화를 내며 내게 덤벼들었다 He leapt [sprang] on [at] me in anger. (▶ on은 내게 손질을 했다, at는 나에게 대들었다) / He came at me angrily. // 폭한이 어둠 속에서 덤벼들었다 A thug attacked me in the dark. / I was mugged in a dark place. // 별안간 개가 덤벼들었다 I was suddenly attacked by a dog. // 소년은 그에게 덤벼들려고 주먹을 들어 올렸다 The boy raised his fist to strike at him. // 두 명의 남자가 갑자기 그에게 덤벼들었다 Two men suddenly attacked him.
2 (일에) set [go] about (one's task); get [set / go / fall] to work (on something); get started on (one's work); set oneself to (doing); set [put] one's hand to. ¶모두 덤벼들어 순식간에 일을 끝냈다 All of us tackled the work and finished it in a blink [made short work of it].

덤불 a thicket; a bush; a shrub. ¶가시 ~의 길을 걸어가다 tread a thorny bush.

덤비다 1 (대들다) go at; turn [fall] upon; defy; challenge; strike (out) at (a person); attack; assault; spring [jump / leap / pounce / fly] upon [at]; fling [throw] oneself upon; set upon; rush [fly] at. ¶두 사람이 악당에게 덤볐다 Two of them attacked [made an attack on] the ruffian. // 레슬러는 어린이 몇 명이 덤벼도 꿈쩍도 하지 않았다 The wrestler did not move an inch even with the combined attack of several children. // 자, 덤벼라 Ok, come on!
2 (서두르다) hurry; hasten; be in a hurry; make (undue) haste; be in hot haste; fluster; busy oneself (with); bustle [act helter-skelter] (당황). ¶덤비지 말고 calmly / with calmness [composure] // 덤비지 마라 Get yourself together. / Take it easy. / Steady now. / Keep your shirt on. // 그는 너무 덤비고 있었다 He was in a feverish [tearing] hurry.

덤터기 blame-shifting; (미국 속어) passing the buck. ¶~를 쓰다 have the blame shifted on to oneself // ~를 씌우다 shift the blame on to (another).

덤프트럭 (미) a dump truck; (영) a tipper (lorry [truck]); a tip truck; a dumper (truck).

덤핑 (경) dumping. ¶일시적 ~ sporadic dumping. **덤핑하다** dump (goods). ¶그들은 해외 시장에서 잉여 상품을 덤핑하려 하고 있다 They are trying to dump surplus goods on overseas markets. // 텔레비전을 ~ dump TV sets.
● **덤핑 방지 관세** anti-dumping duties.

덥 hot; warm (▶ hot은 미국에서, warm은 영국에서 흔히 씀); sultry; (서술적) feel hot [warm]. ¶더운 날 a hot day // 더운 여름 a hot summer // 더운 방 a warm [hot] room // 더워지기 전에 before the heat of the day comes on // 더울 때 먹다 eat (food) hot / drink (sul) hot // 몸이 ~ have a fever / have a temperature // 날이 ~ It is hot [warm]. // 더워졌다 It has become hotter [warmer]. / It has got [grown] hot [warm]. // 더워서 죽겠다 I am dying of the heat. / The heat is unbearable. / I can't stand the heat. // 더워서 숨이 막히겠다 It is stifling hot. // 푹푹 찌는 듯이 ~ It is scorching [steaming] hot. // 정말 지독하게 더운 날이로군. 살인적이야 What a sizzler! This is murder! // 대구의 여름은 몹시 ~ Summers are very hot in Daegu. // 지금이 한창 더울 때다 The summer is now at its hottest. // 날씨가 타는 듯이 ~ It is burning [scorching] hot. // 창고 안은 찌는 듯이 더웠다 It was sweltering [sizzling] hot in the storehouse.

덥석 (급히) quickly; suddenly; with a quick movement; all of a sudden; all at once; hastily; (단단히) firmly; tightly. ¶~ 물다 snap at (food) // 개가 그의 팔을 ~ 물었다 The dog sank its teeth into [fastened its teeth on] his arm. // 그는 수박을 ~ 물었다 He bit [sank his teeth] into the watermelon. // 그는 내 두 손을 ~ 쥐었다 He grabbed both my hands with his own.

덧가지 a double branch.

덧거름 (an) additional manuring.

덧걸다 hang (a thing) over [upon / on top of] (another thing).

덧걸리다 be added on. ¶일이 덧걸려 있다 Work piles up.

덧깔다 spread (a thing) over [upon / on top of] (another thing). ¶요 위에 담요를 ~ spread a blanket over the mattress.

덧나다[1] 1 (병이) worsen; become [grow] worse; go from bad to worse; take a bad turn; change [take a turn] for the worse; be aggravated; (종기가) be [get] inflamed; (곪다) form [generate] pus; fester; suppurate. ¶덧난 상처 an inflamed wound // 종기가 덧났다 The boil has gathered [ripened / inflamed]. // 엉터리 약을 먹고 감기가 덧나 폐렴이 되었다 The cold developed into pneumonia due to a quack medicine. 2 (성나다) be offended; get angry; become enraged [indignant]; get into a passion; take offense; lose one's temper; fly off the handle.

덧나다[2] (이가) grow beyond the rest [others]; grow extra; grow from the common root; grow to one side; shoot off; deviate. ¶이가

have a double[side] tooth / grow a snag tooth.

덧날 a wedge (of a plane); back iron. ¶~이 달린 대패 a plane with a back iron∥~을 끼우다 drive the wedge into (a plane).

덧나다 1 (병을) worsen; make worse; cause to take a bad turn; aggravate; (종기 등을) inflame. ¶종기를 건드려 ~ make a boil [tumor] worse by fiddling with it. 2 (사람을) offend; give (a person) offense; anger; drive (a person) into a passion; make (a person) angry; stir[provoke] (a person) to anger; tread[step] on (a person's) toes.

덧니 (미) a snaggletooth (*pl.* -teeth); a snag tooth; a side tooth (grown from the root of another tooth); (겹침) a double tooth; (비스듬히 난) an oblique tooth. ¶~가 나다 cut a snaggletooth / get a snag[double] tooth through.
● **덧니박이** a person with a snaggletooth.

덧대다 put[attach / place] over[upon / on top of] another; add[join] (on a board / a prop / a layer). ¶판자에 판자를 ~ put a board on top of another.

덧들다 (잠이) be hard to get to sleep again; be wakeful after a short sleep.

덧들이다 1 [노하게 하다] offend; give (a person) offense; anger; incense; make (a person) angry; put (a person) out of temper; drive (a person) into a passion; provoke[stir] (a person) to anger. ¶남을 덧들이는 짓을 give provocation to a person∥그는 결코 남을 덧들이는 말을 하지 않는다 He never says anything that might give offense to another. 2 [잠을 덧들게 하다] keep (a person) from getting back to sleep; keep (a person) wakeful after a short sleep.

덧문(-門) an outer[a double] door[window]; a storm[rain] door; a shutter.

덧버선 outer socks.

덧붙다 adhere[attach / stick / cling] to (something) in addition. ¶숙모에게 덧붙어 살다 live[hang] on one's aunt / live with one's aunt (at her expense).

덧붙이다 1 [더 붙이다] add[attach / stick] (one thing to another); append; affix; annex; join[fix] (on top of another). ¶물건에 편지를 덧붙여 보내다 send (a person) a thing with a letter∥벽에 판자를 ~ fix planks of wood on a wall∥"sir"라고 덧붙일 것을 잊지 마라 Don't forget to put in the "sir". 2 (말을) add; say further[in addition]; make an additional remark; (인용구 등을) tag (one's speech) with; tack on[onto]. ¶편지에 추신(追伸)을 ~ add a postscript to a letter∥만약에 대비하여 몇 마디 덧붙여 두겠습니다 Let me add a few more words for caution's sake.∥그는 친구들에게 고맙게 여긴다고 덧붙였다 He added that he was grateful to his friends.∥그녀는 안녕이라고 말한 뒤 즐거웠노라고 덧붙였다 She said good-bye and added that she had had a wonderful time.∥그녀는 사퇴할 생각은 없다고 덧붙여 말했다 She added that she had no intention to resign.∥"기꺼이 가겠습니다." 하고 그는 덧붙였다 "We shall be very happy to come," he added.

덧셈 [수] addition. ¶그는 ~을 잘한다 He is good at addition[doing sums]. **덧셈하다** add up (figures).

덧신 overshoes; galoshes; (고무로 된) rubbers; gumshoes; gums.

덧신다 put on[wear] (a thing) over (one's shoes[socks]); wear overshoes[outer socks].

덧양말(-洋襪) outer socks.

덧없다 1 [속절없다] short-lived; passing; momentary; transient; fugitive; evanescent; fugacious; caducous; transitory; fleeting; (문어)ephemeral; [변덕스럽다] fickle. ¶덧없는 세월 flying[quickpassing] time∥덧없는 세상 an ephemeral world∥덧없는 인생 transient [transitory / evanescent / mutable] life∥덧없는 행복 fleeting[ephemeral] happiness∥덧없는 기쁨 transient[short-lived] joy∥덧없는 마음 a fickle heart∥덧없는 명성 a bubble reputation∥인생은 덧없는 것이다 How brief is the span of (human) life! / Life is but an empty dream. **덧없이** fleetingly; transiently; quickly; ephemerally; evanescently; transitorily; before one knows it; all too soon. ¶세월은 ~ 흐른다 Time flies[passes] fleetingly [before we know it]. ∥한때의 영화도 끝나고 그녀도 ~ 망각 속에 묻혔다 She has had her brief day and gone her short way to oblivion. 2 [공허하다] vain; hopeless; empty. ¶덧없는 노력 vain efforts∥부의 덧없음 the vanity of wealth∥덧없는 희망을 품다 have a vain hope∥속세의 영화란 얼마나 덧없는 것인가 How vain are earthly splendors!∥그것은 덧없는 꿈이었다 That was but an empty dream. **덧없이** vainly; hopelessly; emptily.

덧입다 put on[wear] (a coat) over a garment.

덧저고리 overwear; overalls; a wrapper; a wamus; (미) a duster; (영) a covert coat; (어린이의) a smock (frock).

덩굴 a bine; a vine(포도 등의); a runner [creeper] (땅을 기는); [식] a voluble stem. ¶고구마 ~ (sweet) potato runners[vines]∥포도 ~ a grapevine∥~이 뻗다 a vine creeps [climbs / trails / trains].
● **덩굴손** [식] a tendril; a cirrus (*pl.* -cirri). ¶~이 있는 cirrate∥~ 모양의 cirrose.

덩굴지다 grow creepers; creep; put on vines; run. ¶포도가 덩굴진다 A grapevine grows [puts out] creepers.

덩그렇다 1 [높고 헌거롭다] high and big; stately; imposing. ¶덩그렇게 집을 높이 짓다 build a house tall∥언덕 위에 집 한 채만 덩그렇게 서 있다 A solitary[lonely] house towers high over the hill.∥방에는 큰 책상이 덩그러니 놓여 있었다 A big desk was placed ostentatiously[conspicuously] in the room. 2 [텅 비다] big and hollow[empty]. ¶덩그런 집 a big and empty house.

덩달다 do the same as (a person) does; follow suit; chime in with; echo; tag along; follow (another) blindly. ¶덩달아 웃다 smile in sympathy / laugh following suit∥그가 노래를 부르자 다른 사람들도 덩달아 불렀다 He began to sing and all the rest chimed in.∥큰 아이가 우니까 작은 아이도 덩달아 운다 The elder child is crying, and the younger one pulls the same trick[follows suit].∥저 아이는 친구들이 하자는 대로 덩달아 해 버린다 That child is always ready to follow his friends lead[follow his friends blindly].

덩더꿍 tum-de-dum; tum-tum; tum-tumming.

덩덩 tum-tum; tum-tumming. ¶북이 ~ 울렸

덩실거리다 다 There was a roll of drums.

덩실거리다 dance lively [merrily / cheerfully] (for joy). ¶덩실거리며 dancing for joy / treading on air∥덩실거리며 기뻐하다 dance [jump / leap] for [with] joy / skip about for joy / cut a caper.

덩실덩실 lively; joyfully; merrily; gaily; light-heartedly; cheerfully. ¶~ 춤추다 dance a spirited dance. **덩실덩실하다** dance lively (for joy). ⇨덩실거리다

덩어리 [뭉쳐진 덩이] a lump; a mass; a clod; a gobbet (of meat); (구어) a dollop (of butter). ¶얼음 ~ a lump of ice / pack ice(큰 것)∥흙~ a clod[lump / mass] of earth∥석탄 ~ a lump of coal∥핏~ a lump of blood∥고깃~ a chunk[hunk] of meat∥빵 ~ a chunk[hunk] of bread∥골칫~ a troublesome fellow∥욕심 ~ a very greedy person / a lump of avarice∥~로 만들다 lump (things) together / form into a lump[mass] ∥흙을 ~로 뭉쳐 던지다 fling mud in clumps[lumps].

덩어리지다 lump; mass; cake (on); form a mass; form into a mass[lump]; conglomerate; [엉기다] congeal; coagulate. ¶구두에 덩어리져 붙은 진흙 mud caked on the shoes / 얼음이 ~ ice forms into a mass∥딱딱하게 ~ form a hard mass∥녹말은 너무 급히 끓이면 덩어리진다 Cornstarch will lump if boiled too fast.

덩이 a lump; a cake[chunk]; a clod; a clot; a nugget. ¶쇳~ a lump of metal[iron].
●**덩이줄기** [식] a tuber; a seed(감자 등의). ¶~ 상(狀)의 tuberous.

덩지 →덩치

덩치 physique; frame; build; physical constitution; bulk; mass; size; volume. ¶~가 큰 large(-sized) / big(-bodied) / of imposing [large] build / voluminous∥~가 작은 small(-sized) / short∥~가 큰 사람 a big [bulky] person∥그는 ~만 컸지 아무 쓸모가 없다 He is such a big hulking fellow, but is not yet of any use. / He is like a great tree that is good for nothing but shade.∥이 차는 ~가 커서 다루기가 어렵다 This vehicle is big and hard to handle [drive]. / 그는 ~가 큰 남자다 He is a hulking fellow. / He is a hulk of a man.

덫 a trap; [올가미] a snare; a hook; a gin. ¶쥐 ~ a rattrap / a mousetrap∥~을 놓다 set [lay] a trap[snare] (for)∥~에 걸리다 be caught in a trap / fall into a snare [trap] / be ensnared / be (en)trapped∥~으로 잡다 entrap / snare / gin / ensnare / catch in a trap∥자기가 놓은 ~에 자기가 걸리다 be hoist with one's own petard / be caught in one's own snare∥큰 쥐가 ~에 걸렸다 A big rat was caught in the trap.

덮개 a cover; a covering; a casing; [침구] bedding; bedclothes. ¶~이 있는 covered∥~가 없는 uncovered / bare / open∥~ 없는 차 an open car∥~를 덮다 cover∥~를 벗기다 uncover / bare∥상자의 ~를 열다 take off the lid of a box / open a box∥그 의자에는 ~가 씌워져 있다 The chairs are covered[have covers].

덮다 1 [씌우다] cover (with); put (a thing) on; veil; overspread; overlay; [닫다] close. ¶산꼭대기를 덮은 구름 clouds hanging over the top of the mountain∥냄비에 뚜껑을 ~ put a lid on the pan∥책을 ~ close[shut] a book / turn down a book∥남은 불에 재를 ~ cover the embers with ash∥탁자에 탁자보를 ~ put a tablecloth on the table / cover the table with a tablecloth∥그의 자필 주석이 그 페이지 전체를 덮고 있었다 Notes in his own handwriting covered the whole page.∥그녀는 자는 아이에게 담요[이불]를 덮어 주었다 She spread[put] a blanket[a quilt] over the sleeping child.∥한 그루의 나무가 길 위를 덮고 있다 A tree is hanging over the path.∥들판은 눈으로 엷게 덮여 있었다 The field was lightly covered with snow.
2 [은폐하다] hide; conceal; cover up; keep (a matter) secret; shut one's eyes to; pass over. ¶죄를 덮어 주다 cover up (a person's) crime / keep (a person's) crime secret / shut one's eyes to / pass over∥남의 잘못을 덮어 두다 shut one's eyes to a person's faults / overlook a person's mistakes∥이 사실은 덮어 주시오 Please don't reveal[disclose] this fact. / Please don't tell anybody about this. / Please make it secret.∥이 문제를 덮어 둘 수 없다 I cannot pass over[by] this question in silence.

덮밥 [계란~] a bowl of rice topped with boiled eggs.

덮어놓고 [무조건으로] unconditionally; [무차별로] indiscriminately; [도맷금으로·휩쓸어] wholesale; in a wholesale manner; sweepingly; [일반적으로] reckless of the consequences; thoughtlessly; without asking any reason [explanation]; without any cause [reason]; arbitrarily; out of a clear (blue) sky. ¶~ 때리다 hit (a person) without giving any explanation / up and hit (a person)∥~ 가자고 하다 ask (a person) to go without aim[blindly]∥그들은 ~ 그의 제안에 찬성할 것이다 They will readily agree to his proposal.∥옛 관습은 ~ 불합리하다고는 할 수 없다 We cannot make a wholesale [sweeping] condemnation of all old conventions as unreasonable.∥그는 아들의 말이라면 ~ 믿는다 He believes everything his son says without question[without giving it a second thought].∥수입품이라면 모조리 품질이 좋다고 ~ 믿는 것은 어리석은 일이다 It is absurd to believe that all imported goods are of high quality.∥이번의 실패가 그 사람 때문이라고 ~ 결론을 내려서는 안 된다 You shouldn't jump to the conclusion that he was to blame for the mistake.∥그는 ~ 걷고 있다가 뜻밖에 출구로 나오게 되었다 While he was walking about at random, he came out at the exit before he knew it.

덮어놓고 열넉 냥 금 (속담) give a random judgment.

덮어쓰다 1 [머리에] put on; wear; cover; [머리 위까지·머리가 덮이도록] draw[pull] over.¶담요를 ~ pull a blanket(up) over one's head / 모자를 ~ wear a hat∥그녀는 수건을 덮어썼다 She covered her head with a towel. 2 [누명을 쓰다] take (another's fault) upon oneself. ¶그는 상사의 죄를 덮어썼다 He took his boss's guilt upon himself. 3 [먼지·액체 등을] pour (water) on oneself; be covered with (dust). ¶흙탕물을 온몸에 ~ be covered [splashed] all over with muddy water.

덮어씌우다 1 [가리다·덮다] cover (with); cover over; put (a thing) on; plate (a thing)

bottle of *cheongju* 다시 ~ warm over / reheat∥밥을 다시 데워서 먹다 eat rice made warm over again∥목욕물을 데울까요 Shall I heat the bath?∥스튜를 먹기 전에 그것을 데웠다 I heated the stew before I ate it.∥우유가 난롯불에 데워지고 있다 The milk is warming (up) on the stove.∥술이 다 데워졌소 Is the wine warm enough?

데이비스컵 [테니스] the Davis Cup.
- **데이비스컵전** the Davis Cup tournament [series].

데이터 data (*sing.* datum). ¶…에 대한 ~를 모으다 gather data on …∥논문 작성을 위해 모든 ~를 수집했다 I have collected all the data available to write an article.
- **데이터베이스** a database; a data bank. **데이터 통신** data transmission [communications].

데이트 a date. ¶안면이 없는 남녀간의 ~ a blind date∥~의 상대 one's date∥잭은 제인을 ~에 데리고 갔다 Jack took Jane out on a date.∥그녀는 내 ~ 상대이다 She is my date.∥그는 나에게 ~ 신청을 해 왔다 He asked me to date him. **데이트하다** date (with) (a person); have [make / get] a date (with). ¶자네 또 데이트하러 나가나? 인기가 대단하군 Are you going out on a date again? Aren't you popular? / Another date? You're popular!

데치다 [살짝 익히다] scald; parboil; boil slightly. ¶야채를 끓는 물에 살짝 ~ dip vegetables into boiling water for an instant.

데카당스 [퇴폐적인 문예상의 한 경향] decadence.

데커레이션 케이크(˟decoration cake) a fancy cake.

델린저 현상(─現象) [물] Dellinger fadeout [phenomenon].

도¹ [음] do; C.

도² 1 [및] and; as well as; both … and; [또한·역시] too; also; […도 …이 아니다] not … either; neither … nor …. ¶나~ 그를 알고 있다 I know him, too. / I also know him.∥그는 그 아이에게 용돈~ 주었다 He gave the child some pocket money too [as well].∥바람이 세차게 불고 있었고 비~ 내리기 시작했다 It was blowing hard, and in addition [besides] rain began to fall.∥나~ 보았지만 그녀~ 보았다 I saw it, and so did she.∥"우표를 수집하고 싶다." "나~ 그래." "I want to collect stamps." "So do I."∥"비오는 날은 싫어." "나~ 그래." "I don't like rainy days." "Neither do I." / "I hate rainy days." "So do I."∥나~ 그를 몰라 I don't know him either.∥네가 가지 않으면 나~ 안 가겠네 If you do not go, neither shall I [I will not go, either].∥"배가 고프냐?" "나~ 그래." "Are you hungry?" "So am I."∥"우리는 올여름을 집에서 조용히 보내기로 했다." "우리~ 그러기로 했어." "We have decided to spend this summer quietly at home." "So have we."∥"목이 몹시 마르다." "나~ 그래." "I am very thirsty." "I [Me], too."∥그는 골프~ 하고 테니스~ 한다 He plays not only golf but also tennis.∥그에게는 아내 ~ 있고 아이~ 있다 He has a wife, a child as well. / He has both a wife and a child.∥내가 바보라면 너~ 바보다 If I am a fool, you are another.∥그녀는 내게 옷~ 주고 돈~ 주었다 She gave me money as well as clothes.∥그는 프랑스 어를 읽지~ 쓰지~ 말하지~ 못한다 He cannot read, write, or speak French.∥보고~ 싶었고 보는 것이 겁~ 났다 I was curious to see it and at the same time dreaded seeing it.∥그것은 이득~ 해악~ 되지 않는다 It does neither good nor harm.∥달지~ 않고 시지~ 않다 It is neither sweet nor sour. / It isn't sweet but it isn't sour either.∥너~ 알고 있었지, 안 그래 You knew it, too, didn't you?∥자네~ 거기에 있었나 Were you there also?∥그녀는 똑똑하기~ 하고 친절하기~ 하다 She is as kind as she is wise.∥잊어버리기는 너~ 나와 마찬가지야 You are just as forgetful as I am. / You are no better at remembering things than I am.

2 [조차] even; without so much as. ¶지금~ even now∥원숭이~ 나무에서 때때로 떨어진다 Even monkeys fall from trees occasionally.∥그는 고맙다는 말~ 없이 그것을 받았다 He took it without so much as saying "Thank you."∥그것은 어린아이라~ 안다 It is intelligible even to a child.∥그 사람을 죽이기까지~ 했다 He went so far as to commit a murder.∥5분~ 안 되어 산은 시야에서 사라졌다 The mountain disappeared from our sight within five minutes.∥3만 원~ 들지 않습니다 It won't cost as much as thirty thousand won.∥농담~ 지나치면 못 쓴다 You are carrying your joke too far.∥그런 짓을 하다니 그의 몰상식~ 이만저만이 아니다 It was simply too thoughtless of him to do such a thing.∥지금까지 내게 알리지~ 않았다니 너~ 어지간하다 Why didn't you let me know earlier? I'm surprised at you.∥그는 집에 한 줄의 편지~ 써 보내지 않았다 He hasn't written a single line home.∥그런 곳에는 가고 싶은 생각~ 들지 않는다 I haven't any interest in going such a place.∥한 사람~ 그를 구해 주려고 하는 사람이 없었다 Not a single person made a move to help him.∥아무~ 그 사나이를 모른다 No one knows that man.∥아무것~ 보이지 않았다 There was nothing to be seen.∥아무 데~ 잘못된 곳이 없다 There's nothing wrong with it.

3 [강조]. ¶그는 친절하게~ 돈을 빌러 주었다 He was so kind as [was good enough] to lend me the money.

-도 even if; although. ⇨-이도 ¶어디를 가~ 제 집만 한 곳은 없다 Go where you may, there is no place like home.

도(度) 1 [온도·각도·경도의 단위] a degree. ¶영상 [영하] 7~ seven degrees above [below] zero∥30~의 각 an angle of 30 degrees∥섭씨 15~ fifteen degrees C / 15℃∥북위 25~ 25 degrees [25°] north latitude / latitude 25°N∥동경 24~ longitude 24°E∥네 열은 39~이다 Your temperature is thirty-nine degrees.∥오늘 아침 6시의 기온은 8~였다 The temperature was eight degrees at six this morning.∥그 도시는 북위 30~에 있다 The city is at [in] 30° [thirty degrees] north latitude.

2 [렌즈의 굴절도] a degree; a diopter. ¶10~의 안경 spectacles of 10 degrees∥당신의 안경은 몇 ~ 입니까 What is the degree of your concave lenses?

3 [음정을 재는 단위] a degree. ¶2~ 음정 a second∥장 [단] 3~ a major [minor] third∥3~의 화음 triad / common chord.

4 [알코올 농도의 단위] proof. ¶40~의 위스키 whisky forty percent alcohol by volume /

80 proof whisky(▶ 미국에서는 100% 알코올을 200°, 영국에서는 175°로 나타냄).
5 [정도] a degree; an extent; a measure; [한도] a limit. ¶~를 넘음 excessive / inordinate / immoderate / intemperate // ~가 지나치다 go to excess / go[carry things] too far / break[go beyond] bounds / be immoderate [intemperate] / overstep the bounds / overshoot oneself / exceed the limits // 겸손의 ~가 지나치다 overstep the bounds of modesty // 술은 ~가 지나치면 건강에 해롭다 Excessive drinking impairs one's health. // 무슨 일이든지 ~가 지나쳐서는 안 된다 You mustn't go overboard in anything. // 그의 장난은 ~가 지나치다 He goes too far in his practical jokes. / He carries his jokes too far.

도¹ (道) [행정 구역의 하나] a *do*; a province; a district. ¶~의 provincial / ~내의[에서] inside[in] the province // ~ 당국 the provincial authorities // ~ 행정 provincial administration // 그는 경기~ 사람이다 He comes[(미국 구어) hails] from Gyeonggi-do.

도² (道) **1** [지켜야 할 도리] a duty; [도의] a moral doctrine[principle]; morality; [가르침] teachings; doctrines; [진리] truth; [정의] justice; [도리] reason. ¶~에 어긋난 짓을 하다 misconduct oneself / do wrong / deviate from the path of righteousness // 공자의 ~를 펴다 expound the teachings[doctrines] of Confucius / preach[propagate] Confucianism // ~를 닦다 cultivate one's moral[religious] sense // ~를 깨닫다 perceive a truth / realize a religious truth // ~을 구하다 seek after truth // ~가 트이다 have[get] something down to a science // 그는 접시 닦는 데에 ~가 트였다 He's got his dishwashing down to a science.
2 [기예를 행하는 방법] an art; a craft; an (artistic) accomplishment. ¶궁술~ archery / bowmanship.

-도 (度) [연도] a year (period); a term. ¶금년~ the current year // 내년~ next year.

-도 (圖) [그림·도면] a diagram; a chart; a graph. ¶해부~ an anatomical chart // 설계~ a plan // 풍속~ a genre (painting).

도가니¹ [무릎도가니] the knee bone of cattle; the meat on the knee bone of cattle. **2** [소의 볼기살] rump.

도가니² **1** [공] a crucible; a melting pots. ¶쇠를 ~에 넣고 녹이다 melt metal in a crucible. **2** [들끓는 상태]. ¶정쟁(政爭)의 ~ the whirlpool of political strife // 장내는 흥분의 ~로 변했다 The audience was thrown into a state of feverish[wild] excitement.

도각 (倒閣) overthrowing[unseating] the Cabinet. **도각하다** overthrow[unseat] the Cabinet.

도감 (圖鑑) a picture[a pictorial / an illustrated] book. ¶한국 식물[동물] ~ An Illustrated Guide to Korean Flora[Fauna] // 조류 ~ a bird guide.

도강하다 (渡江-) cross a river.

도개교 (跳開橋) a drawbridge; a bascule bridge; a leaf bridge. ¶~의 개폐부 a draw / a drawspan.

도검 (刀劍) swords; cold steels.

도경 (道警) the provincial police (headquarters).

도계 (道界) the boundary line between provinces; the province limits. ¶경기도와 강원도의 ~ the border of Gyeonggi-do and Gangwon-do.

도공 (陶工) a potter; a ceramist; a porcelain maker; a pottery worker.

도괴 (倒壞) collapse; destruction. ¶가옥 ~로 인해서 부상하다 be injured in the collapse of a house. **도괴하다** collapse; be destroyed; be level(l)ed (to the ground); fall down; tear down; demolish; crumble. ¶1,000호 이상의 가옥이 도괴됐다 Over a thousand houses collapsed[were destroyed]. // 남은 집이 눈의 무게로 도괴했다 The old house fell down [collapsed] under the weight of the snow. // 이 마을에서는 태풍으로 다섯 채의 가옥이 도괴됐다 Five houses in this village were completely destroyed by the typhoon.

도교 (道敎) Taoism.
● **도교 신자** a Taoist.

도구 (道具) **1** [연장] a tool; (비교적 정밀한 것) an instrument; (가사에 쓰는 것) a utensil; (어떤 목적을 위한) an implement(흔히 복수형으로); [설비] equipment; tackle; (작고 편리한) a gadget. ¶청소 ~ a cleaning outfit // 원예용 ~ gardening implements // 생물 실험 ~ instruments for biological experiments // 재봉 ~ a sewing set // 가재~ [가구] furniture / (집합적) household belongings.
2 [수단·방편] a means; a tool; a stepping-stone; an instrument; a vehicle; [앞잡이] a cat's-paw. ¶선전 ~ an instrument of propaganda // 남을 ~로 이용하다 use a person as tool / make a tool of a person // 결혼을 출세의 ~로 삼다 use marriage as a tool for one's advancement // 그 남자는 소년들을 자기의 이익을 얻기 위한 ~로 사용했다 The man used the boys as a tool for his own profit. // 그들은 그 수회 사건을 정쟁의 ~로 이용했다 They made a political issue of the bribery case.
3 (불교의) utensils used in Buddhist services.
● **도구주의** instrumentalism.

도굴 (盜掘) **1** (광물의) illegal[bootleg] mining. **도굴하다** mine by stealth; dig out by stealth. ¶석탄을 ~ dig coal illegally (from another's land). **2** (무덤의) grave robbery. **도굴하다** rob a grave. ¶고분을 ~ rob an ancient tomb. ➔ ¶그 고분은 부장품을 몽땅 도굴당했다 The ancient tomb has been completely pillaged of its grave goods.
● **도굴범** a tomb robber.

도금 (鍍金) (금속의) plating; gilt. ¶금~ gilding / gold plating // 전기~ electric gilding / electroplating // 금[은]~ 접시 gold-plated [silver-plated] dishes. **도금하다** plate (a metal with gold); gild; engild; wash. ¶도금한 숟가락 a plated spoon // 금으로 도금한 반지 a gold-plated ring // 구리에 은을 ~ plate copper with silver // 크롬을 전기로 ~ electroplate with chromium // 그런 도금한 물품은 곧 벗겨진다 Such plated ware will soon rub off.
● **도금액** (-液) a plating solution.

도급 (都給) a contract (for work). ¶~으로 by contract // ~을 주다 put out to contract / give (a person) a contract for [building a house] / contract (a work) // ~을 맡다 take work on contract / contract for // ~으로 일을 하다 have a work done by contract // 주택 건축을 ~ 맡고 있다 have a contract to build a house.
● **도급 공사** contract work; construction

work done on contract.

도기(陶器) 《집합적》 earthenware; pottery; ceramic ware; [사기그릇] crockery; [도자기] china ware. ¶~ 꽃병 a ceramic[an earthenware] vase.

도깨비 [귀신] a *dokkaebi*; an ogre; a goblin; a fiend; [괴물] a monster. ¶~ 같은 여자 a monster of a woman.
도깨비도 수풀이 있어야 모인다(속담) It is necessary to have something to fall back on for a person to achieve anything.

도깨비불 1 [귀화] a will-o'-the-wisp; an ignis fatuous; an elf fire; a jack-o'-lantern(묘지 등의); a corpse candle; a death fire. **2** [원인 불명의 화재] a fire of unknown origin.

도끼 (자루가 긴) an ax(e); a hatchet(손도끼). ¶큰 ~ a big hatchet / a broad-ax/얼음 깨는 ~ an ice ax.
도끼는 날을 달아 써도 사람은 죽으면 그만(속담) A dead man never comes to life again.
● **도끼질** wielding an axe. ¶~을 하다 wield [strike with] an ax. **도낏자루** an axe handle.

도끼눈 glaring [staring] eyes; staring with anger[hatred]. ¶~을 한 사람 an eagle-eyed Person // ~을 하고 보다 glare fiercely at / glower at / look angrily at / scowl at [on] // 그녀는 나를 ~으로 보았다 She looked daggers at me.

도난(盜難) (a) theft; [강탈] (a) robbery; [밤도둑·빈집털이] (a) burglary. ¶~의 피해자 a victim of a theft[robbery / burglary] /차량의 ~ a car theft // ~을 당하다 get[be] robbed (of money) / fall a victim to a theft / (물건이) be stolen / (집이) be burglarized // 그는 수금한 돈을 ~당했다 He was robbed on the street of the money he had collected. // 당하지 않도록 귀중품은 몸에 지녀 주시기 바랍니다 Please carry your valuables with you lest they should be stolen. // ~ 방지를 위해서는 무엇이 가장 효과적입니까 What is most effective in preventing burglaries? /내 저고리를 ~당했다 My coat was stolen. // 요즘 소포의 내용물이 자주 ~당하고 있다 Things have been stolen from a lot of parcels recently.
● **도난 경보기** a burglar alarm. **도난 사건** a (case of) theft; a robbery; a burglary. ¶~이 50건 발생했다 There were fifty cases of robbery.

도내(道內) ¶~의 in[within] the province / provincial // ~에서 throughout the provincial.

도넛 a doughnut. ¶트위스트 ~ a twisted doughnut.

도닥거리다 keep patting. ⇨ °토닥거리다
도닥도닥 knocking repeatedly. ⇨ °토닥토닥
도달(到達) [목적지에 다다름] arrival; reaching; [달성] [문어] attainment. **도달하다** arrive in[at / on]; get to[at]; attain; touch; come to; make it (to). ¶완성 단계에 ~reach[attain] perfection //같은 결론에 ~come to the same conclusion //목적지에 ~ reach the destination // 그 편지는 아직 수취인에게 도달하지 않았다 The letter has not yet reached the recipient. //우리는 결국 같은 결론에 도달했다 In the end we arrived at [reached / come to] the same conclusion. //도달할 수 있는 목표를 세워야 한다 We should set up an attainable[a realizable] goal. // 열차의 소음은 여기까지 도달하지 않는다 The noise of the train does not reach [come up] this far. //우리는 합의에 도달했다 We have reached[come to] an agreement. // 그들은 신제품을 완성하는 데까지 겨우 도달했다 They perfected the new product at long last.

도당(徒黨) conspirators; a band; a gang. ¶~을 지어 (do something) in a gang // ~을 짓다 conspire / (구어) gang up // 그들은 ~을 지어 행인을 습격했다 They ganged up on the passersby. / They banded together[ganged up] to assault passersby.

도대체(都大體) **1** [도무지] (not) in the least; (not) the slightest; (not) at all. ¶~ 알 수 없다 cannot understand (it) at all / be all Greek to (me) / be utterly at sea // 그가 하는 말은 ~ 알 수가 없다 I have no idea of what he means.
2 (how / what / why) on earth[in the world / the dickens / the blazes]. ¶~ 너는 누구냐 What on earth are you! / ~ 어떻게 된 거냐 What the deuce is the matter? / Whatever is the matter! // ~ 나더러 어떻게 하란 말인가 What on earth do you expect me to do? / ~ 그는 영어를 알고 있느냐 Does he know any English at all? / ~ 그 책이 어디 갔는가 Where has the book gone to anyway? / ~ 당신은 내게 무엇을 하라고 설득하려는 것인가 What in the world are you trying to persuade me to do? // ~ 누가 이 가지를 부러뜨렸느냐 Whoever broke this branch? // 어제는 ~ 왜 안 왔니 Why on earth didn't you come yesterday?

도덕(道德) [행동의 바름] morality; [사회에서 받아들여지고 있는 기준에 맞춘 행위] morals. ¶공중 ~ public morals // 교통 ~ traffic manners // 국민 ~ national morality // 사회 [상업] ~ social[commercial] morality // 성의 퇴폐 the corruption of sexual morals // ~의 어지러움 moral decadence // ~이 땅에 떨어졌다 Morality has lost its hold on the people.
● **도덕관념** a moral sense. ¶~이 강한 사람 a person of strict morals / a highly virtuous person. **도덕 교육** moral education. **도덕군자** a gentleman renowned for his virtue. **도덕심** a sense of morality.

도덕적(道德的) virtuous; moral; moralistic; ethical. ¶~인 교훈 a moral lesson / a moral // ~ 감화[기준] moral influence[standard] // ~ 제재 moral restraint // ~으로 설명하다 moralize.
● **도덕적 해이** a moral hazard.

도도하다 arrogant; haughty; proud; overbearing; lordly; toplofty; uppish; puffed-up; (구어) stuck-up. ¶도도한 태도 a haughty [proud] attitude // 그는 아니꼬울 만큼 도도한 녀석이다 He is a provokingly uppish fellow.
도도히 proudly; arrogantly; haughtily; with a lordly air. ¶~ 굴다 behave oneself haughtily / hold one's head very high / ride one's high horse.

도도하다(滔滔-) **1** [물의 흐름이 힘차다] rushing; rapid; swift. **도도히** rapidly; swiftly; with a rush. ¶~ 흘러가는 강 a river in flood // 큰비가 온 뒤의 ~ 흐르는 탁류 a gush of muddy water after a heavy rain // 강물이 ~ 흐르고 있었다 The river flowed swiftly[in torrents]. // 탁류가 ~ 흐른다 The muddy water rushes on in a vast expanse. **2** [말이 거침없]

도독하다

다] eloquent; fluent; flowing; effusive. ¶도도한 웅변 a flood of eloquence / flowing eloquence // 그의 변설은 도도하여 그칠 줄 몰랐다 His tongue went nineteen to the dozen. **도독히** eloquently; fluently; effusively; flowingly.

도독하다 1 [조금 두껍다] thick; heavy. 2 [가운데가 조금 볼록하다] swollen; protuberant; raised; bulgy; convex. **도독이** protuberantly; into a swell.

도돌이표(－標) [음] a repeat mark.

도둑 a thief (pl. thieves); [강도] a robber; [밤도둑] a burglar; [좀도둑] a pilferer; a filcher; a shoplifter; [도둑질] (a) theft; (a) robbery; (a) burglary. ¶일단의 ～ a gang of thieves[robbers] // ～이야 Stop, thief! // 지난번에 우리 집에 ～이 들었다 My house was robbed[broken into] the other day. / A thief broken into my house the other day. // 어젯밤에 여러 곳에 ～이 들었다 There were many burglaries last night. // ～이 매를 든다더니 정말 뻔뻔스럽구나 That's an instance of evil-doer's audacity. // 그 집에 ～이 들었다 He burglarized[robbed] the house.

도둑의 씨가 따로 없다(속담) Thieves are made, not born.

도둑이 제 발 저리다(속담) A thief has a bad conscience and is apt to give himself away.; He that commits a fault thinks that everyone is speaking about it.

● **도둑고양이** a stray[an ownerless] cat; an alley cat. **도둑놈** a thief (pl. -ves). **도둑장가** a secret marriage[consummation]. ¶～를 들다 get married secretly / consummate a marriage secretly. **도둑질** [절도] theft; thievery; stealing; [강도] robbery; burglary; [좀도둑질] pilfering; filching. ¶～을 하다 steal (a thing) from (a person) / commit theft / pilfer / filch / burglarize (the house) / [강탈] rob (a person) of (a thing).

도둑맞다 (사람이) get[have] (a thing) stolen; have (a thing) pilfered[filched]; be relieved [robbed] of (one's purse); (물건이) be stolen. ¶지하철에서 지갑을 도둑맞았다 I had my wallet stolen in the subway. // 겨울옷을 몽땅 도둑맞았다 A thief stole all my winter clothes.

도둑맞고 사립 고친다(속담) Lock[Close] the stable[barn] door after the house is stolen.

도드라지다 conspicuous; swollen. ⇨ <두드러지다

도떼기시장(－市場) an open-air market; a flea market.

도라지 [식] a Chinese[broad] bellflower; a balloon flower. ¶～ 뿌리 platycodon / the root of a broad bellflower // ～를 캐다 dig up the roots of bellflowers.

도락(道樂) 1 [취미] a hobby; a pleasure; a pastime; recreation; relaxation; one's amusement[diversion]. ¶～ 삼아 미술을 공부하다 study the fine arts for pleasure // 헌책방을 뒤지는 것이 그의 ～이다 Old bookstalls are his happy hunting ground. 2 [주색에 빠짐] dissipation; prodigality; debauchery; amorous pursuits. ¶～에 빠지다 be dissipated / debauch oneself / take to loose pleasure / play the prodigal / live a fast life // 그는 나이가 들어도 ～에서 발을 못 빼고 있다 He is an old sinner.

도란거리다 whisper to each other affection-ately; exchange affectionate whispers. ¶소녀들이 도란거리기 시작했다 The girls began to chat in an affectionate undertone.

도란도란 in an affectionate undertone; in affectionate whispers. ¶방에서 ～ 이야기하는 소리가 들린다 The room is all abuzz with affectionate murmur. **도란도란하다** whisper to each other affectionately. ⇨ <도란거리다

도랑 a ditch; [배수구] a drain; (도로의) a gutter. ¶～ 빠지다 fall into a ditch // ～을 치다 [쳐내다] clear a ditch (gutter) // ～을 파다 dig a ditch / ditch // ～을 메우다 fill in a ditch // 진흙으로 ～이 막혔다 The drain [gutter] is stopped[clogged] with mud. // 비가 와서 땅에 ～이 생겼다 The rain has worn channels in the ground.

● **도랑물** ditch water.

도래(到來) arrival; (주요한 사건·인물의) advent; influx; visitation. ¶죽음의 ～ the advent of death // 시기의 ～를 기다리다 wait for an opportunity / bide one's time. **도래하다** come; arrive; present itself; occur. ¶때가 도래하면 in (course of) time // 드디어 궐기하여야 할 때가 도래했다 Now is the time[the time has come] to rouse ourselves to action. // 마침내 좋은 시절이 도래했다 The time has come at last.

도래(渡來) (사람의) a visit; (사물의) introduction; importation; influx. ¶불교의 ～ the introduction of Buddhism // 외국 물건의 ～ the influx of foreign goods. **도래하다** (사람이) come over[across] the sea; cross over (to Korea); visit; (사물이) be introduced (into); be brought over (from).

도량(度量) [너그러운 마음씨] generosity; broad-mindedness; magnanimity; liberality. ¶큰 ～ a mind of great capacity // ～이 넓은 generous / (허용하는) tolerant / (편견 없는) broad-minded // ～이 좁은 narrow-minded [ungenerous] // 그는 ～이 큰 사람이다 He is a broad-minded man.

도량(道場) [불] a seminary for the Buddhist priesthood; a Buddhist seminary.

도량형(度量衡) weights and measures.

● **도량형기**(－器) measuring instruments.

도려내다 (구멍을) bore (a hole through); (날붙이 등으로) scoop[scrape] out; hollow out; excavate; [속을 빼내다] core; (종기를) excise. ¶통나무를 ～ hollow out a log // 사과의 속을 ～ core an apple // 사과의 썩은 부분을 ～ remove[cut out] the bad part from an apple.

도련(刀鍊) trimming; cutting the edge (of paper) even. **도련하다** trim[cut] the edge (of paper) even.

● **도련칼** a paper-trimming knife; a paper cutter.

도련님 1 a bachelor. ⇨ ¹도령 2 [시동생] an unmarried younger brother of one's husband. 3 [주인의 아들] a young master; (호칭) Master; Sonny.

도령 [미혼 남자] an unmarried young man; a bachelor.

도로 1 [되짚어서] back; (over) again. ¶오던 길을 ～ 가다 go back over one's way / go back where one came // 배는 폭풍우로 말미암아 ～ 부산으로 돌아왔다 Owing to the storm the ship put back to Busan.

2 [먼저대로] as before[ever / usual]; as it was. ¶제자리에 ～ 갖다 놓다 put (a thing)

back in its place[where it was] // ~ 건강해지다 become as healthy as before // 그들은 싸웠으나 ~ 친해졌다 They quarrelled but are now friends again. // 두 사람 사이는 ~ 좋아졌다 They have made it up. / The relation between the two has been restored. // 날씨가 ~ 추워졌다 The cold weather has returned. // 태풍이 통과한 뒤 전국적으로 날씨가 더워졌다 After the typhoon passed, the heat reasserted itself nation wide.

도로 아미타불 [애쓴 일이 허사가 됨] a relapse; a setback. ¶~이 되다 be no better than what one used to be / wind up just where one started / have lost all one gained / be back to square one // 나는 재산을 모았으나 전쟁통에 ~이 되고 말았다 I had piled up a fortune but the war reduced me as poor as before.

도로(徒勞) a lost labo(u)r; vain effort; vain [empty] attempt; waste of labo(u)r. ¶~에 그치다 prove abortive[fruitless] / end in a waste of labor / come to nothing // 나의 모든 노력은 ~에 그쳤다 All my efforts were in vain. / All my efforts came to nothing.

도로(道路) [길] a road; [거리] a street; [대로·공로] a thoroughfare; a highway; [코스] the route. ¶고속~ an expressway / (영) a motorway // 환상~ a loop road // ~를 따라서 along the street // ~ 상에서 on the road / on [in] the street // ~의 개통 the opening of a new road // ~ 공사 the Korea Highway Corporation // ~를 건설하다[보수하다] construct[repair] a road // ~를 파헤치다 tear up a road // ~ 수리 중 (게시) Street closed for repairs.
●**도로 공사** road repairing; street improvement. **도로망** a network of roads. ¶~ 확충 expansion[supplementation] of road networks. **도로 표지**(-標識) a road sign.

-도록 1 [목적] (so as) to (do); in order to (do); so [in order] that one may (do); that one may (do). ¶…하지 않~ (so as) not to (do) / that ... may not (do) // 나는 급행열차를 탈 수 있~ 일찍 일어났다 I got up early so as to be in time for the express. // 그가 화를 내지 않~ 말해라 Put it so as not to offend him. // 감기 들지 않~ 그는 언제나 두꺼운 내의를 입고 있다 He always wore heavy underwear for fear of catching (a) cold. // 9시에 조반을 먹~ 해 주시오 Please prepare my breakfast so that I may have it at nine.
2 [···때까지] till; until; to; up[down] to. ¶밤늦~ till late at night // 미치~ 사랑하다 love (a person) to distraction // 목숨이 다하~ 싸우다 fight to the last drop of one's blood // 백살이 되~ 살다 live to (be) a hundred // 그는 9살이 되~ 큰아버지 집에서 자랐다 He was raised at his uncle's up to the age of nine.
3 [가능성] as far as one can; as much as possible; possibly. ¶되~ 빨리 as soon as possible[one can] // 되~ 서두르다 hasten as much as possible / make as much haste as one can.

도롱뇽 [동] a newt; an eft.
도롱이 a straw raincoat.
도료(塗料) paints; paint and varnish; pigments. ¶야광[형광]~ luminous[fluorescent] paint // 벽에 ~를 칠했다 I painted the walls. // 그는 문의 ~를 벗겨 냈다 He scraped the paint off the door.
●**도료 분무기** a paint sprayer; a spray gun. **도료 희석제** a thinner; a paint diluent.

도루(盜壘) [야구] base stealing; a steal; a stolen base; (미국 구어) petty larceny; pilfering. ¶~를 잘하다 be clever at stealing bases // ~에 실패하다 be caught stealing // 그는 ~로 2루에 진루했다 He stole second. // 그는 2루 ~에 실패했다 He was put out trying to steal second. **도루하다** steal a base.

도루묵 [동] a hard-finned sandfish.

도륙(屠戮) massacre; slaughter; butchery. **도륙하다** slay; massacre; slaughter; butcher. ¶일가족을 ~ murder[slaughter] the whole family (in cold blood).

도르다[1] [분배하다] distribute (among / to); pass round; serve out (food); deal out; hand round[out]; [배달하다] deliver; send out [round]. ¶초대장을 ~ send out invitations // 전단[광고지]을 ~ distribute handbills [circulars] // 배급품을 ~ distribute rations // 카드를 ~ deal cards (to the players) // 돈과 먹을 것을 ~ hand out money and food (to the poor) // 선생님은 팸플릿을 학급에 돌렸다 The teacher distributed[handed out] the pamphlets to the class. // 소년은 신문을 도르고 다녔다 The boy went from door to door delivering newspapers.

도르다[2] [변통하다] make shift; tide over; manage (with what one has); contrive; [융통하다] accommodate (a person with money); advance (money to a person); lend. ¶돈을 ~ accommodate (a person) with a loan / advance (money to) / spare (a person money) / make shift[out] to raise money // 소요 금액을 ~ raise money to make up the required sum // 자금을 ~ finance (an enterprise).

도르래 [활차] a pulley; a block. ¶고정 ~ a fixed pulley // 움직 ~ a movable pulley / a running block.

도르르 rolling and round; with a twist; coiling. ¶(종이 등이) ~ 말리다 roll itself // 융단을 ~ 말다 roll up a carpet // 실이 ~ 풀렸다 Thread was twirled off a reel. // 연잎 위의 아침 이슬방울이 ~ 굴러 떨어졌다 The beads of dew on the lotus leaf came rolling down.

도리 [건] (건물의) a beam; (교각 등의) a girder.

도리(道理) **1** [이치] reason; [정당] right; [정의] justice; [진리] truth; [본분] (a) duty. ¶~에 맞는[어긋나는] 대우 reasonable[unreasonable] treatment // ~에 맞는[맞지 않는] 요구 a reasonable[an unreasonable] demand // ~에 벗어난 행동 improper behavior / misconduct // ~에 맞는 생각 right thinking // ~에 어긋나다 stray from the path of righteousness[the right path] // 그것이 자식 된 ~다 That's filial duty. // 나는 ~에 맞는 일이라면 무슨 일이든 하겠다 I will do anything within reason. // 그는 언제나 ~에 맞는 말을 한다 He always speaks reason. // 그는 ~를 모른다 He has no sense of duty.
2 [방도] a way; a method; a process; the ways and means; an alternative. ¶사태가 이 지경이니 딴 ~가 없다 Now that things have come to this, there is no more that can be done. // 없는 것을 내놓을 ~가 없다 You can't get a stocking off a bare foot. / A man cannot give what he hasn't got. // 외국어에 숙

도리깨

달하는 길은 한걸음 한걸음 익혀 가는 수밖엔 ~가 없다 There is no other means of mastering a foreign language but to learn it step by step.

도리깨 a flail; [쇠도리깨] an iron flail.
● **도리깨질** flailing. ¶~을 하다 flail / thresh [thrash] with a flail.

도리다 [베어 내다] cut (out) round; gouge; scoop out; hollow out(구멍을); bore. ¶판자 가운데를 톱으로 ~ cut out a part of a plank with a circular saw.

도리도리 [도리질을 시킬 때의 말] shake (your) head.

도리어 [반대로] on the contrary; instead; [오히려] rather; all the more. ¶이익을 올리는 커녕 ~ 큰 손해를 봤다 It brought us no profit, on the contrary[instead], we incurred a heavy loss.// Far from bringing in a profit, it resulted in heavy losses.// 아이들은 야단을 치면 ~ 더 나빠질 때가 있다 Scolding sometimes does children more harm than good.// 떠들고 논 뒤에는 ~ 맥이 풀린다 After having a spree, I feel all the more depressed.// 포도주보다는 ~ 찬 맥주가 낫다 I'd rather have cold beer than wine.// 택시를 탔더니 전차보다 ~ 시간이 더 걸렸다 I went by taxi but (actually) it was slower than taking the train.// 내가 ~ 미안하오 I should be the one to ask your pardon.// 충고를 했다가 ~ 기분만 상하게 했다 I advised him only to incur his displeasure.// 부정한 수단으로 돈을 버는 것보다는 ~ 가난이 낫다 I would rather be poor than get money by dishonest means.

도리질 shaking head for fun; headshake. **도리질하다** (a baby) keep shaking one's head for fun. ¶아기가 싫다는 시늉으로 도리질했다 The baby shook his head to show he didn't like it.

도립(道立) [관형어적] provincial.
● **도립 병원** a provincial hospital.

도마 a chopping board; a kitchen board. ¶~ 위의 고기 a doomed fish on the dresser / a person who is in a desperate situation.

도마 위의 고기가 칼을 무서워하랴(속담) Nothing is dreadful to a person who is in the jaws of death.

도마 위에 오르다 be an open target.

도마뱀 [동] a lizard.

도막 a bit; a cut; a chop; a fragment; a chip; a slice. ¶나무 한 ~ a chip of wood// 고기 한 ~ a piece[slice / chop] of meat// 그녀는 생선을 여러 ~으로 잘랐다 She cut a fish into several pieces.

도망(逃亡) (an) escape; (a) flight; desertion; decampment; abscondence; elopement. ¶~ 중인 죄인 a criminal on the run// ~을 꾀하다 attempt[make an attempt] to run away / try to escape. **도망하다** fly; flee; run away [off]; get away; escape; desert (a ship); decamp (for / to); abscond[bolt] (from a place); elope (from); take to one's heels; take (to) flight. ¶목숨을 걸고 ~ run[flee] for one's life.
● **도망자** a fugitive; a runaway.

도망치다(逃亡─) fly; flee; run away[off]; get away; escape; desert (a ship); decamp (for / to); abscond[bolt] (from a place); elope (from); take to one's heels; take (to) flight. ¶슬금슬금 ~ sneak away / slink[shirk] off// 허둥지둥 ~ run away in a flurry// 간신히 ~ escape with bare life// 무사히 ~ flee to (a safe distance) / effect[make good] one's escape// 밤을 타서 ~ flee by night / decamp at night / take to moonlight flitting// 아내를 두고 정부와 ~ elope with one's mistress deserting one's wife// 도망치게 하다 let (a person) escape / help (a person) get away// 미처 도망치지 못하다 fail to escape[get off] / be left behind// 우리는 도망치는 적을 추격했다 We chased the retreating enemy.// 그는 외국으로 도망친 것 같다 He seems to have fled abroad.// 범인은 호남 방면으로 도망치고 있다 The criminal is now making his escape toward the Honam district.

도맡다 1 [혼자서 책임지다] undertake alone; take all upon oneself; shoulder (something) alone; take[bear] responsibilities by oneself (for something); run the whole thing. ¶모든 책임을 혼자서 ~ take the whole responsibilities alone// 빚을 ~ hold oneself liable for a debt / shoulder all the debts alone// 도맡아서 판매하다 make an exclusive sale of// 지금은 아들이 장사를 도맡아 하고 있다 The whole business is now in the hands of my son.// 그는 동네의 궂은일을 혼자 도맡아서 한다 He takes on all the troubles in the village.
2 [몰아서 맡다] take over the whole. ¶주택 건축을 ~ have a contract to build a house// 가게의 물건을 ~ take over all the goods in the store.

도매(都賣) wholesale trade. ¶~와 소매(小賣) wholesale and retail.// 물건을 ~로 사다[팔다] buy[sell] goods wholesale// ~로 사서 소매하다 buy wholesale and sell retail. **도매하다** sell (by / (미) at) wholesale; wholesale.
● **도매가격 / 도맷값** a wholesale [trade] price. ¶~으로 드리겠습니다 We will give it to you at wholesale (price). **도매 물가 (지수)** wholesale price (index). **도매상** [도매 영업] a wholesale business[trade]; [도매 가게] a wholesale (rice) store[house / firm]; [도매하는 사람] a wholesale (rice) dealer; a wholesaler. **도매 시장** the wholesale market. **도매업** the wholesale business; the wholesale trade.

도메인 a domain.

도면(圖面) [스케치·도화·선화·그림] a drawing; a sketch; [설계도·겨냥도·평면도] a plan; [청사진] a blueprint. ¶건축 ~ a blueprint// ~을 그리다 draw a plan / make a drawing// 가옥의 ~을 그리다 draw up plans for a house.

도모(圖謀) planning; devising; contriving; designing; scheming. **도모하다** plan; devise; contrive; scheme; plot; [애쓰다] labor[work / strive] (for). ¶자살을 ~ attempt suicide// 공익을 ~ work for the good of the public / serve the public interest// 힘 닿는 데까지 편리를 도모하겠습니다 I will do everything I can[within my power] to help you. // 일을 도모함은 사람이나, 일의 성사는 하늘에 달려 있다 Man proposes, God disposes.

도무지 [전혀] utterly; entirely; quite; altogether; never; (not) at all; (not) in the least. ¶그는 ~ 아무것도 모른다 He knows nothing at all. / He is utterly ignorant.// 그 이야기는 ~ 재미가 없다 The story is not at all interesting. / (구어) The story is a real bore.// 그것은 ~ 문제가 되지 않는다 It is entirely out of the question. // 그것은 ~ 불가능한 일이다 It is by no means possible. // 나는 그것에 대해 ~ 생각이 나지 않는다 I cannot remember a thing about it. / I simply can't remember. / I can't remember at all. // 그가 무엇을 말하고 있는지 나는 ~ 알아들을 수 없었다 I could not make any sense of what he said. / I couldn't understand what he was saying at all. // 그는 최근에 ~ 모습을 나타내지 않는다 I have seen nothing of him lately. // 요즘에 내 영어 성적이 ~ 형편없다 My grades in English recently have been simply awful. // 그는 ~ 거짓말을 못하는 사람이다 He is simply incapable of telling a lie. // 그는 댄스가 ~ 서툴다 He is really an awful dancer. // 그들이 무슨 이야기를 하고 있는지 ~ 알 수가 없었다 I didn't have the slightest [vaguest] idea what they were talking about. // 어디였는지 ~ 기억이 나지 않는다 I don't remember at all where it was.

도미 [동] a sea bream; porgy.

도미 (渡美) going to America; a visit to America. **도미하다** visit [go to] the United States; emigrate to America(이주하다). ¶이달 3일에 도미합니다 I am leaving for America on 3rd instant. // 심씨 일가는 도미했다 The Sims have left for [have gone to] the States.
● **도미 유학생** a Korean student studying in the U.S.

도미노 dominoes. ¶~를 하다 play dominoes.
● **도미노 이론** the domino theory.

도민 (道民) inhabitants [residents] of a province. ¶강원~회 an association [a society] of people from Gangwon Province.

도박 (賭博) 1 [노름] gambling; a game of chance; gaming; a gambling game. ¶사기~ fraudulent [crooked] gambling // ~으로 돈을 벌다 make [earn] money by gambling // 그는 ~에서 돈을 땄다 [잃었다] He won [lost] money in gambling. // 그는 ~으로 돈을 모두 잃었다 He lost all his money in gambling. // 그는 ~으로 재산을 잃어버렸다 He gambled away his fortune. **도박하다** gamble; play for money.
2 [모험적 시도] a speculation; a venture; a hazardous attempt. ¶인생은 ~이다 Life is a game of chance. // 이 투자는 큰 ~이었다 This investment was a major gamble. // 그는 큰 ~을 했다 He ran [took] a great risk. **도박하다** take the risks [a chance / chances]; run a risk; stake one's all (on).
● **도박꾼** a gambler. ¶사기~ a cardsharper / a rook / a swindler. **도박장** a gambling place [room / house / establishment / den]; a gambler's den; a gaming house [room]; a casino (pl. ~s); (미국 구어) a gambling joint. **도박죄** the crime of gambling.

도발 (挑發) provocation; excitement; incitement; stimulation. **도발하다** provoke; arouse; stir up; excite; incite; stimulate; be provocative of. ¶호기심을 ~ excite (a person's) curiosity // 그 소설은 육정을 도발한다 That novel stirs up [stimulates / arouses] sexual desire. // 그 사건은 전쟁을 도발했다 That incident provoked [set off] the war.

도발적 (挑發的) provocative; suggestive (novel); inflammatory (speech); seditious (writings); incendiary (speech). ¶~인 언사 provocative remarks // ~인 소설 a suggestive novel (▶ 성적으로) // ~인 연설 [문장] inflammatory [seditious] speeches [writings] // ~인 행위 a provocative act // ~인 언사를 쓰다 employ provocative language [words] // ~인 태도를 취하다 take a provocative attitude.

도배 (塗褙) papering (of the walls and ceiling of a room); paperhanging. **도배하다** paper [hang paper on] (the walls [ceiling] of a room). ¶방을 새로 ~ repaper a room.
● **도배지** wallpaper.

도벌 (盜伐) the secret felling of trees. ¶산림~ 사건 a forest tree theft scandal. **도벌하다** fell trees in secret. ¶숲의 나무를 ~ cut down forest trees without a license [without permission]. → ¶산림이 빈번히 도벌되었다 Trees were frequently stolen from the forest.

도법 (圖法) drawing. ⇨작도법(⇨작도) ¶정사 [심사] ~ orthographic [gnomonic] projection // 투영~ projection.

도벽 (盜癖) (문어) a propensity for theft; a proclivity to steal; kleptomania. ¶~이 있는 사람 a kleptomaniac // 그녀에게는 ~이 있다 (문어) She has a proclivity to steal. / She is a kleptomaniac. / She is light-fingered.

도보 (徒步) walking; going on foot; pedestrianism. ¶~로 on [by] foot / afoot // ~로 통학 [출근] 하다 walk to school [office] / go to school [office] on foot // 거기까지 ~로 갔다 I walked there. / I went there on foot. // 우리 집은 역에서 ~로 10분이면 간다 It takes ten minutes on foot [It is ten minutes' walk] from the station to my house. // 기차로 갈까 혹은 ~로 갈까 Shall we go by train or on foot?
● **도보 경주** a footrace. **도보 여행** a walking [pedestrian] tour; a walking trip; hiking; a tramp; a hike. ¶~을 하다 travel on foot / make a journey on foot.

도복 (道服) [태권도 등을 할 때 입는 옷] a suit for (taegwondo) practice.

도부 (到付) 1 [공문의 도착] arrival of an official document. **도부하다** arrive. 2 [행상] itinerant hawking; peddling. **도부하다** go around hawking. ⇨「도부(를) 치다(⇨도부)

도부(를) 치다 go around hawking [peddling]; peddle; hawk; engage in an itinerant trade.
● **도붓장사** peddling; itinerant hawking. **도붓장수** a peddler; a hawker; an itinerant vendor [trader].

도사 (道士) 1 [도를 닦은 사람] a man of high moral sense. 2 [불교의 교리를 깨달은 사람·스님] a (Buddhist) priest; [도교 수행자] a Taoist. 3 [숙련자] an expert (at / in). ¶그는 돈 버는 데는 ~다 He is an expert at money-making.

도사리다 1 [웅크리다] sit [squat (down)] cross-legged [tailor-fashion]; sit with one's legs crossed. 2 [뱀 등이] coil itself (up). ¶도사리고 있는 뱀 a snake lying in a coil // (뱀이) 도사리고 있다 be coiled. 3 [마음을] quiet; calm (down). ¶마음을 ~ gather [collect] one's wits [senses] / calm oneself [one's mind]. 4 [생각 등이] lurk (in); be harbored; be rooted. ¶두 사람 사이에 나쁜 감정이 도사리고 있다 There are ill feelings estranging the two.

도산 (倒産) 1 [재산을 잃고 망함] (a) bankruptcy; insolvency; failure. **도산하다** go bankrupt; go under; be bankrupt(ed); become bankrupt [insolvent]. ¶여러 회사가

도살

다같이 도산했다 A number of business concerns went under together. // 그의 회사는 거의 도산할 지경에 이르렀다 (구어) His company is almost broke. 2 [의] cross birth. **도산하다** have a cross birth.

도살(屠殺) slaughter; butchery. ¶밀~ illegal butchery // 밀~ 행위를 적발하다 pick up illegal butchery practices. **도살하다** slaughter; butcher.
● **도살장** a slaughterhouse; a butchery.

도상(道上·途上) 1 [길 위] on the road. 2 [일이 진행되는 도중]. ¶개발~국 a developing country.

도색(桃色) [연분홍빛] rose (color); pink; [색정적임] obscenity; pornography. ¶~의 [연분홍빛의] peach-[rose-]colored / rosy / pink / [색정적인] amorous / [음탕한] lewd.
● **도색 영화** a sex film; (속어) blue movies. **도색 잡지** a pornographic [(구어) girlie] magazine; a yellow journal; a dirty magazine.

도서(島嶼) islands; isles; islets.
● **도서민** an islander; an islesman.

도서(圖書) books; [간행물] publications; [문헌] literature. ¶교양 ~ cultural books / books of cultural studies // 성인 ~ adult books // 수입 ~ imported books // 신간 ~ new books // 아동 ~ children's books // 외국 ~ foreign books // 일반 ~ general books // 전문 ~ special books // 참고 ~ reference books // 학술 ~ scholarly books.
● **도서관** a library. ¶국립 ~ a national library // 국회 ~ the National Assembly Library / (미국의) the Library of Congress // 대학[학교] ~ a university[school] library // 순회 ~ a circulating[travelling] library // ~에서 (책을) 빌려 오다 get (books) out of library. **도서관장** the director[curator] of a library; the (chief[head]) librarian. **도서 목록** a publication list[catalog(ue)]; a catalog of books[publications]. ¶신간 ~ a list of new publications. **도서 전시회** a book exhibition; a book fair; a book show.

도선(渡船) a ferry(boat); [건네 주기] ferrying.
● **도선업** ferriage.

도선(導船) pilotage; piloting; (배) a pilot boat. **도선하다** pilot (a boat).
● **도선사**(-士) a pilot.

도선(導線) a conductor; a conducting wire.

도설(圖說) an explanatory diagram (of insects); a diagrammatic chart; an illustration.

도성(都城) a capital city.

도수(度數) 1 [횟수] (the number of) times; frequency; incidence. 2 (온도·각도 등의) the degree; (렌즈의) a degree; a diopter. ¶안경의 ~ the power of glasses // ~ 없는 안경 (a pair of) plain glasses / plain-glass spectacles // ~가 높은 안경 glasses with thick lenses // 안경의 ~를 높이다 use stronger lenses // 안경의 ~를 맞추다 adjust the lenses to one's eyes // 근시의 ~가 높아졌다 My eyes have grown more nearsighted. // 이 안경은 ~가 맞지 않는다 These lenses do not agree with my eyes. 3 (알코올분의) proof. ¶~가 높은 위스키 high-proof whisky. 4 [수] frequency.
● **도수 분포** [수] frequency distribution.

도수로(導水路) a raceway; a water canal.

도술(道術) Taoist magic; magical arts.

도승(道僧) a Buddhist priest who has attained spiritual enlightenment.

도시(都市) a city; a town; an urban community; towns and cities; (구어) an asphalt jungle. ¶거대 ~ a megalopolis / a megapolis // 공업 ~ an industrial [a manufacturing] town [city] // 과밀 ~ an overpopulated city / a city with an overconcentration of population // 국제 ~ a cosmopolitan city // 대[중/소] ~ a large [mediumsized / small] city // 상업 ~ a business town // 전원 ~ a garden city // 주요 ~ principal [major] cities (of the world) // 중소 ~ small towns // ~의 urban / city // ~풍의 urbane // 인구의 ~ 집중 경향 the cityward tendency of the population // 물의 ~ 베니스 Venice, the city built on water.
● **도시 계획** urban planning; (미) city [(영) town] planning. ¶~하다 시행하다 carry out city planning. **도시 국가** a city state. **도시 생활** city life. **도시인** a city-dweller; a resident of a city. **도시 인구** urban population. **도시 재개발** urban renewal. **도시 지역** an urban area. **도시 행정** municipal administration. **도시화** urbanization.

도시(圖示) illustration; graphic(al) representation. **도시하다** illustrate; show by[in] a diagram; show in a graphic form. ¶호텔이 있는 곳을 ~ illustrate the location of a hotel / sketch a map to show the location of a hotel.

도시락 [음식] (미) a box lunch; (영) a packed lunch (▶ 점심용으로 싸 온, 샌드위치·햄버거 따위의 음식을 가리킨다); [상자 모양의 용기] a lunch box. ¶소풍용 ~ a picnic lunch // ~을 담다 fill a lunch box (with boiled rice) // ~을 갖고 가다 take [carry] a lunch with one // 어머니가 ~을 만들어 주셨다 I had my mother make [prepare] a lunch (for me). // 난 오늘 ~을 싸 왔다 I brought lunch from home today. / I brown-bagged it today.

도식(圖式) [그림] a diagram; a figure; [그래프] a graph; [괘도] a chart. ¶~으로 나타낸 diagrammatic / graphic / schematic.
● **도식화** schematization; diagraming; graphing. ¶~하다 put into the form of a diagram / [그림으로 나타내다] show in a diagram / schematize.

도심(都心) the heart [center] of the Metropolis [the city]; the downtown.
● **도심지** the central area of a town; the downtown [midtown] area.

도안(圖案) a design; an ornamental design; a device; a sketch; a plan. ¶이 ~은 잘되어 있다 This design is well done. **도안하다** design; draw a design (of); make a design (of).
● **도안가** a designer; a patternmaker (직물 등의).

도야(陶冶) training; cultivation; education. ¶인격의 ~ character building. **도야하다** train; cultivate; educate; mo(u)ld; build up. ¶자신의 인격을 ~ cultivate [build up / train] one's character.

도약(跳躍) a jump; a leap; a spring; a skip; a take-off; jumping (경기). ¶한국의 경제적 ~ Korea's economic take-off. **도약하다** jump; leap; spring; skip; prance; (a horse) make [cut] a curvet.
● **도약 경기** jumping. **도약 단계** [경] the take-off stage. ¶경제 발전의 초기 ~에 들어

서 있다 be in the early stage of take-off for economic development. 도약판 a springboard; a leaping board.

도어(倒語) [언] inversion; transposition.

도어맨 a doorman.

도열(堵列) a line (of men). **도열하다** form a line; line up; be drawn up. ¶양쪽에 ~ line [be drawn up on] either side of (the road). ➔¶도열시키다 line (people) along (a street).

도열병(稻熱病) [농] rice blight; rice blast disease.

도예(陶藝) ceramic art; ceramics(▶ 단수 취급); pottery.
● **도예가** a potter; a ceramist.

도외시하다(度外視-) leave (a thing) out of account; neglect; disregard; ignore; slight; overlook. ¶여론을 도외시하고 in disregard of public opinion∥그의 영어는 문법을 아주 도외시한 것이다 His English is quite innocent of grammar.

도요새 [동] a snipe; a longbill.

도용(盜用) **1** [금전의] misappropriation; appropriation; embezzlement; peculation. **도용하다** embezzle; misappropriate; peculate; appropriate. ¶그는 공금을 도용했다 He misappropriated [embezzled] public money. **2** (기타의) surreptitious use; using by stealth; plagiarism. **도용하다** use by stealth; make a fraudulent use of (another's registered design); [표절하다] plagiarize. ¶사인을 ~ use another's private seal by stealth∥그들이 우리 캘린더의 디자인을 도용했다 They stole the design of our calendar.∥그가 내 작품에서 도용한 것은 이 부분이다 This is the passage he plagiarized from my work.

도움 1 [조력] help; aid; assistance; [후원] support. ¶…에게 ~이 되다 be a help to (one) / be of help[service] to / be helpful to ∥~을 **받다** have[receive] help (from)∥남의 ~을 청하다 seek the support of a person∥나는 큰아버지에게서 금전상의 ~을 받았다 I had financial [monetary] help from my uncle.∥우리는 당장 ~이 필요해 We are in urgent need of help.∥그가 틀림없이 당신에게 ~이 될 것으로 나는 생각한다 I'm sure he will be of some help to you.∥그 아이는 남의 ~ 없이는 옷을 입을 수가 없다 The child can't dress without aid[help / assistance].∥간호사의 ~을 빌려 그는 간신히 일어나 앉았다 He managed to sit up supported by[with the help of] the nurse.∥이 사전 덕분에 나는 크게 ~을 받고 있다 This dictionary is a great help to me.

2 [구제·구원] relief; succor; deliverance. ¶수해 지역에서 ~을 청해 왔다 Aid was requested from the flood area.

3 [효용] use; service; utility. ¶~이 되다 be useful[serviceable] / be of use[service]∥~이 되지 않다 be useless[unserviceable]∥개 스널 컴퓨터의 지식이 취직에 크게 ~이 되었다 My knowledge of personal computers proved to be very useful in getting a job.

도움닫기 [체] an approach run.
● **도움닫기 멀리뛰기** a (running) long jump.

도원경(桃源境) a paradise on earth; (a) Shangri-La; Arcadia.

도읍(都邑) the capital. **도읍하다** set up the capital (at); (a dynasty) holds its court (at).

● **도읍지** the seat of government.

도의(道義) morality; morals; moral principles; (principles of) moral justice. ¶~의 퇴폐 moral decadence[deterioration]∥~적으로 보아 from the moral point of view∥~에 어긋나다 be contrary to accepted standards of morality∥그는 ~상의 책임이 있다 He is morally responsible.∥~가 땅에 떨어졌다 Morality has lost its hold on the people. / People have lost their sense of morality.

● **도의심** moral sense; a sense of morality. ¶~이 강한 사람 a man of strict morality.

도일(渡日) a visit[trip] to Japan. **도일하다** visit[go to] Japan.

도입(導入) introduction; induction; invitation; importation; import. ¶외자 ~ introduction of foreign capital. **도입하다** introduce; induce; invite; import; bring in. ¶외자를 한국에 ~ introduce foreign capital to Korea / bring foreign capital into Korea. ➔¶신형 기계가 공장에 도입되었다 A new type of machine was introduced (in)to the factory.

● **도입부** [음] the introduction; the introduction part.

도자기(陶瓷器) ceramic ware; ceramics; china and porcelain; pottery; earthenware.
● **도자기공** a potter; a ceramist.

도작(盜作) [남의 작품을 대강 고쳐서 자기 것으로 만드는 행위] plagiarism; plagiary; literary[artistic] theft; [남의 것을 대강 고쳐서 자기 것처럼 만든 작품] a plagiarism; (구어) a crib. ¶남의 논문의 ~ plagiarism of another person's[somebody else's] essay∥그는 ~의 혐의를 받았다 He was suspected of plagiarism. **도작하다** plagiarize (another's work). ¶남의 시를 ~ plagiarize somebody else's poems.

도장(道場) (무술의) a training[drill] hall; an exercise hall; a gym; a gymnasium (*pl.* ~s, -sia). ¶태권도[유도 / 레슬링] ~ a *taegwondo* [judo / wrestling] hall[school].

도장(塗裝) coating; painting. **도장하다** paint; coat with paint.
● **도장 공사** painting; painter's work.

도장(圖章) [인장] a seal; [소인(消印)·압인] a stamp; a handstamp. ¶인감~ a registered seal∥~을 **찍다** seal / affix[stamp / set / put] one's seal (to) / ~을 **파다** make [engrave] a seal / [새겨 받다] have one's seal cut[engraved]∥문서에 서명하고 ~을 찍다 sign and seal a document∥이 계약서에는 송 씨의 ~이 찍혀 있다 This contract bears the seal of Mr. Song.
● **도장주머니** a seal case.

도저히(到底-) (cannot) possibly; (cannot) by any possibility; (none) at all; not nearly (so); [전혀] utterly; absolutely. ¶~ 비교가 안 되다 cannot for a moment compare with / be beyond all comparison∥…은 ~ 있을 수 없다 It is most unlikely[out of the bounds of possibility] that ….∥해결은 ~ 불가능하다 No settlement is remotely possible. ∥그런 것은 ~ 생각할 수 없다 It is beyond our thinking. / I can hardly think of it.∥그런 일은 ~ 용서할 수 없었다 I couldn't think of allowing it.∥그것은 ~ 말할 수 없다 I cannot tell it to save my life.∥누가 이기는지 ~ 알 수 없다 There is no saying who will win.∥그 시는 ~ 이해할 수가 없다 I cannot understand the poem at all.∥그런 일은 ~

도적(盜賊) a thief (*pl.* thieves). ⇨도둑

도전(挑戰) a challenge; 〔권위 등에 대한 반항〕 defiance. ¶무언의 ~ 〔권위 등에 대한 반항〕 a tacit challenge // ~에 응하다 accept[take up] a challenge / take up the gauntlet[glove]. **도전하다** challenge (a person to a fight); make[give] a challenge; defy; bid defiance (to); call (a person) to combat; fling[throw] down the gauntlet[glove] (to); provoke a battle. ¶세계 기록에 ~ challenge the world record // 그는 100미터 경주에서 존에게 도전했다 He challenged John to a 100 meter race. // 그는 여론에 도전했다 He flew in the face of public opinion [defied public opinion].
● **도전자** a challenger. **도전장** a (written) challenge; a cartel. ¶그는 그들에게 ~을 들이댔다 He thrust a (written) challenge at them.

도전(導電) electric conduction; conduction of electricity.
● **도전체** an electric conductor.

도전적(挑戰的) 〔반항적〕 defiant(ly); 〔자극적〕 provocative(ly); 〔공격적〕 aggressive(ly). ¶~ 태도로 나오다 assume[take] a defiant [provocative] attitude (toward) // 그들은 ~ 인 태도로 나왔다 They assumed a defiant [provocative] attitude.

도정(道程) 〔노정〕 the distance; mil(e)age; 〔여정〕 a journey; an itinerary; 〔과정〕 a process; a route. ¶40킬로의 ~을 하루에 걷다 cover a distance of 40 kilometers in a day.

도정(搗精) pounding; hulling ¶~이 덜 되다 be insufficiently pounded. **도정하다** polish (rice) by pounding.

도제(徒弟) an apprentice. ¶~로 보내다 apprentice / article // ~가 되다 be apprenticed (to) / apprentice oneself (to) / go apprentice / be articled (to) // ~를 두다 take apprentices // 벽돌공의 ~가 되다 become an apprentice brick layer / be apprenticed to a bricklayer // 나는 열세 살 때 소목장이의 ~가 되었다 At thirteen, I was apprenticed to a joiner. // 그는 미장이 밑에서 ~ 기간을 마쳤다 He served out his apprenticeship with a plasterer.
● **도제 제도** apprenticeship; an apprentice system.

도제(陶製) ¶~의 porcelain / ceramic / earthen.
● **도제 파이프** (흡연용의) a clay pipe.

도주(逃走) (an) escape. ⇨도망

도중(途中) ¶~에(서) on the way (to / from) / on one's way (to) / on the road / en route (to / for) / on route (to / from) / in the middle of / in the midst of / in the course of / in transit(운송 중) / (중도에서) halfway / midway // 학교로 가는 ~에 on one's way to school // 집으로 가는 ~에 on one's way [midway] home / en route home // 이야기[식사] ~에 in the middle[course] of a conversation[meal] / midway through a conversation[meal] // ~에 흔히 볼 수 있는 광경 a sight usually seen[met with] on the road // ~에서 돌아가다 turn back halfway[midway] // ~에 들르다 stop off (at) // ~에 그만두다 give up halfway / do not go all the way // 하던 말을 ~에 끊다 break the threads of a talk [story] // 나는 슈퍼마켓에 가는 ~에 우체국에 들르겠다 I'll stop at the post office on my way to the supermarket. // 나는 백화점에 가는 ~에 무엇을 살까 하고 생각하고 있었다 On my way to the department store I was thinking what I would buy there. // ~에 무슨 일이 있었음에 틀림없다 Something must have happened somewhere along the way. // ~ 가는 ~ 날씨는 좋았다 The weather was fine all the way. // 우주선은 달로 비행하는 ~에 궤도를 3회 수정했다 The spacecraft made three midcourse corrections of the orbit in its flight to the moon. // ~에 큰 곤란이 있었다 There lay much difficulty in the way. // 말씀 ~이시지만 지금 몇 시입니까 Excuse me if I interrupt[for interrupting] (you), but what time is it now?
● **도중하차** a stopover; (미) a layover. ¶~를 하다 stop over[make a stopover] (at a way station) / stop off / break one's journey (미) lay over.

도지다¹ 〔병이 재발하다〕 a relapse occurs; (사람이) relapse (into illness); have[suffer] a relapse[return] (of a disease); become serious again; suffer a setback; take a critical[serious] turn. ¶감기가 도졌다 A cold got worse. // 그의 병이 도졌다 He had a relapse. // 그는 늑막염이 도졌다 He has relapsed into [had a relapse of] pleurisy. // 그의 병세가 도졌다 His condition grows worse[takes a turn for the worse]. // 그 열병은 도질 염려는 없다 There is no fear of a return[relapse] of the fever.

도지다² 1 〔심하다〕 severe; extreme; intense. ¶도지게 꾸짖다 scold severely. 2 〔단단하다〕 hard; strained.

도지사(道知事) the governor of a province; a provincial governor.

도착(到着) arrival. ¶~순으로 in order of arrival // 참석자의 이름은 ~순으로 기재되었다 The names of those who came were listed in order of arrival. **도착하다** arrive at[in / on]; 〔도달하다〕 reach; get to; (편지·화물이) come to hand. ¶도착하는 대로 as soon as one arrives / immediately on one's arrival / on [upon] arrival // 서울에 ~ arrive in Seoul // 육지에 ~ reach [gain] land [ground] // 항구에 ~ arrive at[in] a port // 현장에 ~ arrive on the spot // 정각에 ~ arrive on schedule [time] // 무사히 ~ arrive in safety / arrive in good condition [order] (물품이) // 9시 기차로 ~ arrive by[(미) on] the 9 o'clock train // 기차는 정시에 도착했다 The train got in[pulled in] on time[(미) schedule]. // 비행기는 정각

에 도착했다 The plane landed[arrived] on schedule[time]. // 어둡기 전에 우리는 목적지에 도착했다 We reached[got to] our destination before dark. // 이제 모두 도착했다 Everyone has arrived now. // 경찰은 5분 뒤에 현장에 도착했다 The police arrived on the scene five minutes later. // 열차는 아직 도착하지 않았다 The train has not come in yet. // 그분은 언제 서울[호텔]에 도착하십니까 When will he arrive in Seoul[at the hotel]? // 연락선은 오전 9시에 도착할 예정이다 The ferryboat is due at 9 a.m.
 ● **도착역** an arrival station; a destination (station); the receiving station(물품의). ¶이 열차의 ~은 서울입니다 This train is for Seoul. **도착항** a port of arrival.
도착(倒錯) [의] perversion; inversion. ¶성~ sexual perversion[inversion] // 성~자 a (sexual) pervert[invert]. **도착하다** be perverted; be inverted. ➔¶도착된 애정 perverted affection.
도찰(塗擦) embrocation; inunction; smearing and rubbing. **도찰하다** rub in; embrocate.
 ● **도찰제** an embrocation; a liniment.
도처(到處) everywhere. ¶~에 wherever one goes / all over (the world) / throughout (the country) / far and wide[near / nigh] / in every quarter / in all directions / on all sides / on every hand / here, there, and everywhere // 세계의 ~로부터 from all parts of the world // 나는 ~에서 대환영을 받았다 I was warmly welcomed wherever I went. // 그 회사는 거의 전국 ~에 지점이 있다 That company has its branches in almost all parts of the country. // 비슷한 예를 ~에서 볼 수 있다 We find similar instances here and there.
도청(盜聽) (전화의) (wire)tapping; a wiretap; [엿들음] eavesdropping. **도청하다** tap (a telegraph[telephone] wire); listen in (on the enemy's communications line); eavesdrop (on) (a conversation); (미국 속어) bug (a conversation). ¶그는 전화를 도청했다 He tapped the telephone (wires). // 그는 그들의 대화를 도청했다 He listened in on their conversation.
 ● **도청기** (회화의) a concealed microphone; (전화의) a wiretapping device; (벽에 장치한) a wall-snooper; a hidden (electronic) listening device; (미국 속어) a bug. ¶~가 장치되어 있다 be fitted[rigged] with a concealed microphone / be bugged (up) // 범죄 수사에 ~를 쓰다 use a wiretap in detecting a crime. **도청 사건** a wiretap scandal. **도청자** a wiretapper.
도청(道廳) a provincial office[government]; the administration hall[office] of a province.
 ● **도청 소재지** the seat of a provincial office; a provincial seat.
도체(導體) [물] (열·전기의) a conductor. ¶반~ a semiconductor // 부(不)~ a nonconductor // 양~ a good conductor // 불량 ~ a bad conductor.
도축(屠畜) butchery; slaughter.
도출(導出) deduction. **도출하다** draw (a conclusion); deduce (the truth); derive (an idea). ¶이로부터 다음과 같은 결론을 도출했다 From this I drew[deduced] the following conclusion.
도취(陶醉) 1 [거나하게 취함] intoxication. **도취하다** be intoxicated. 2 [감격에 젖음] fascination; rapture. ¶자기 ~ narcissism // 자기 ~자 a narcissist. **도취하다** be fascinated [charmed / carried away] (by); be enraptured (with); be in rapture[ecstasies] (over). ¶자연의 아름다움에 ~ be intoxicated with[fascinated by] the beauty of nature // 승리의 환희에 ~ be intoxicated with[lost in the rapture of] the joy of victory // 그는 그 그림의 아름다움에 도취했다 He was intoxicated with[fascinated by] the beauty of the picture.
도치(倒置) turning upside-down; [언] inversion. **도치하다** invert; reverse; put upside-down. ¶두 단어의 순서를 ~ invert[reverse] the order of the two words.
 ● **도치법** [언] inversion; anastrophe; a hyperbaton (*pl.* ~s, -ta).
도킹 (우주선의) docking; space linkup. ¶~을 풀다 undock (from). **도킹하다** dock (with the command module). ¶아폴로와 소유즈가 도킹했다 The Apollo docked with the Soyuz.
도탄(塗炭) misery; distress. ¶~에 빠지다 fall into[be in] misery / suffer[be in] distress / be reduced to misery // ~에 빠진 백성을 구하다 save the people from distress / rescue the people from misery.
도태(淘汰) [불용물·부적자(不適者)의 제거] selection; weeding out; washing out useless elements. ¶자연 ~ natural selection // 인위 ~ artificial selection // 자웅 ~ sexual selection. **도태하다** select; weed out; screen; sift (the good from the bad). ➔¶환경의 변화에 적응할 수 없는 동물은 도태된다 Animals that cannot adapt to changes in the environment will die out.
도토(陶土) potter's clay; kaoline; porcelain [china] clay.
도토리 an acorn.
 도토리 키 재기(속담) There are all much of a muchness.; There is little to choose[little difference] among them.
 ● **도토리묵** acorn-starch jelly.
도톨도톨 rough(ly); ruggedly. ⇨<두툴두툴
도톰하다 (very) thick. ⇨<두툼하다
도통(都統) 1 [도합] all; [통틀어] in all; all together; totally; all told. 2 [도무지] (not) at all; absolutely. ¶그 사람 일은 ~ 모른다 I know absolutely nothing about him. / I don't know him from Adam. // 요즈음 그녀를 ~ 못 만난다 I have seen nothing of her of late.
도통(道通) spiritual awakening[enlightenment]. **도통하다** be spiritually awakened; attain higher perception[spiritual enlightenment]. ¶그 일에 ~ be well[deeply] versed in the matter / be conversant with the matter.
도판(圖版) [인쇄물을 찍기 위한 그림판] a plate; [책 등의 그림] a figure; an illustration.
도포(塗布) application. **도포하다** apply (an ointment to the skin). ¶소독약을 상처에 도포했다 I applied (an) antiseptic to the wound.
 ● **도포약** an ointment; an endermic liniment.
도포(道袍) *dopo*; Korean full-dress attire (in olden days).
도표(道標) a signpost; a guidepost; a fingerpost; a milestone. ¶길가의 ~ a milestone [signpost] by the roadside // ~를 세우다 set up a guide post[signpost].

도표(圖表) a chart; [도식] a diagram; [그래프] a graph. ¶선~ a line graph // 점~ a scatter[dot] diagram / a scattergram // 통계~ a statistical chart // ~의 diagrammatic(al) / graphic // ~를 만들다 draw a chart [diagram] // ~로 하다[나타내다] put (figures) into the form of a diagram / diagrammatize / chart.

도플러 효과(-效果) [물] the Doppler effect.

도피(逃避) (an) escape; evasion; (a) flight (from the world). ¶현실로부터의 ~ escape from reality // 속세로부터의 ~ an escape from this secular world // 그녀는 남자 친구와 사랑의 ~를 했다 She eloped [ran away] with her boyfriend.(▶ elope는 결혼의 의사가 있는 경우, run away는 결혼 의사가 반드시 있는 것은 아님) **도피하다** escape; fly. ¶사회로부터 ~ seclude oneself from society // 애인과 함께 ~ elope [run away / run off] with one's lover.

● **도피 생활** a life of escape from the world. **도피자** a runaway; a fugitive; a refugee. **도피주의** escapism.

도핑 doping; drug use.

● **도핑 테스트** a dope test; a drug check [test].

도하(都下) the capital; the metropolis.

도하(渡河) the crossing [fording] of a river. **도하하다** cross [ford] a river.

● **도하 작전** a river-crossing [-fording] operation.

도학(道學) 〔유학(儒學)〕 Confucian philosophy; Confucian ethics; [도교] Taoism; [심학(心學)] popularized moral philosophy.

도함수(導函數) [수] a derivative; a derived function.

도합(都合) [모두 합한 것] the total; the sum total; [모두 합해서] in all; all together; all told; in sum; totally. ¶~ 12명의 수행원 a suit of retainers twelve in all // ~ …이 되다 add up to … / reach a total of … / total … // 출석자는 ~ 500명이었다 In all, five hundred people attended. // ~ 30만 원이 된다 It amounts to 300,000 won all told [in all]. // ~ 얼마나 들었습니까 How much did it cost altogether [all together]?

도항(渡航) a passage; a voyage; a sailing; a crossing. ¶자유 ~ an unrestricted passage // ~ 절차를 밟다 arrange passage. **도항하다** make [take] (a) passage (to); make a voyage (to); sail [leave] for (출발하다); go across (to); cross the water. ¶미국으로 ~ go [sail] over to America / take passage for America.

● **도항자** a passenger; a foreign traveler; a visitor. **도항증** a passport for foreign travel.

도해(圖解) an explanatory diagram; a diagrammatic chart; an illustration. ¶곤충 ~ explanatory diagrams of insects // 이 책에는 컬러로 된 ~가 많이 들어 있다 This book has a lot of colored illustrations. **도해하다** illustrate; diagram; show by a diagram [in a graphic form]. ¶도해하면 다음과 같다 It is graphically shown as follows.

도형(圖形) a figure; a device; a diagram. ¶기하학적 ~ a geometrical figure // 평면[입체] ~ a plane [solid] figure // ~으로 나타내다 show in [by] a diagram / figure.

● **도형 기하학** descriptive geometry.

도화(桃花) a peach blossom.

도화선(導火線) 1 [폭약 폭발용 심지] a fuse; a blasting [detonating] fuse; a (powder) train; a train of powder. ¶~에 불을 붙이다 light [fire] the fuse // 폭약에 ~을 연결하다 attach a fuse to an explosive.

2 [직접 원인] a cause; an agency; an impetus; an incentive; an occasion; the origin (of a quarrel). ¶…의 ~이 되다 prove an incentive to … / lead (up) to … / give rise to … / occasion … / touch off … / spark … // 이것이 그 대전(大戰)의 ~이 되었다 This touched off [triggered] the world war. / This led (up) to the Great War. // 학원 소요의 ~이 된 것은 몇 명의 학생에 대한 처벌이었다 The cause of [What led to] the campus riot was the punishment of a few students. // 그의 직무 태만이 참사의 ~이 되었다 His neglect of duty caused a disastrous accident. // 관헌에 의한 시위의 탄압이 혁명의 ~이 되었다 The suppression of the demonstrations by the authorities led to [sparked (off)] the revolution.

도화지(圖畫紙) a drawing paper.

도회(都會) a city; a town. ¶~의 city / town / urban // ~에서 자란[태어난] town-[city-]bred [born].

● **도회 생활** urban [town / city] life; urban [city] living. **도회인** a townsman; townspeople; townsfolk; a city man; a city-dweller; an urbanite; residents in a city; town [city city-dwelling] people. **도회지** urban areas [district]. **도회풍** urban [city] manners; urbanity. ¶~의 urban / urbane / citified / townfied // ~으로 urbanely.

독 a *dok*; an earthenware pot; a crock; a jar(족자리가 없는); a jug(족자리가 있는); an urn(작은 것); a vat(술독 등).

독 안에 든 쥐(속담) be in a fine fix; be quite in a helpless situation; be in a tight box.

독(毒) 1 [유독 물질] (a) poison; poisonous substance. ¶~이 있는 poisonous / virulent / toxic / noxious // ~이 없는 innoxious / innocuous / innocent / harmless // ~이 있는 식물 a poisonous plant // ~이 있는 뱀 a venomous [poisonous] snake // 이 약은 ~을 없애 준다 This medicine neutralizes [counteracts] poison.

2 [독약] poison; a toxicant; [독액] venom. ¶~을 탄 음료 a poisoned drink // ~을 먹이다 administer poison to / poison (a person) // ~을 마시다 take poison // ~이 몸에 당장 퍼졌다 The poison took instant effect.

3 [해독] evil; harm; mischief; virus; poison. ¶~이 되는 (be) harmful / injurious // 젊은이에게 ~을 끼치다 poison the young minds.

4 malice. ⇨독기2

독(이) 오르다 become spiteful [venomous / malicious].

독가스(毒-) poison gas; poisonous [asphyxiating] gas; toxic [noxious] gas. ¶~를 사용하다 use poison gas // ~로 적을 공격하다 gas the enemy // ~를 맡다 be gassed.

● **독가스전**(-戰) (poison-)gas warfare. **독가스탄** a poison-gas bomb [shell]; a gas shell.

독감(毒感) (malignant) influenza; (Spanish) grippe; (구어) flu(e); a bad [nasty] cold. ¶~에 걸리다 be attacked by influenza / contract influenza / catch flu [a bad cold] // ~이 유행하고 있다 There's a lot of flu about.

독거(獨居) solitude; a solitary life. **독거하다** live alone [by oneself]; live in solitude; lead a solitary life.

독경(讀經) sutra-chanting. **독경하다** chant [recite] Buddhist sutras[scriptures / texts]; read a service.

독과점(獨寡占) monopoly and oligopoly.
● **독과점 품목** monopoly-oligopoly (products) items. ¶~으로 지정하다 designate as monopolistic and oligopolistic items.

독극물(毒劇物) toxic chemicals. ¶식품 회사의 ~ 협박범을 엄단하다 deal sternly with extortionists threatening food companies with poison-lacing.

독기(毒氣) 1 [독의 기운] noxious[pestilential] air; poisonous gas[vapor]. ¶~가 있는 poisonous. **2** [악의] malice; spite. ¶~가 있는 malicious / virulent / acrimonious / spiteful // ~가 없는 innocent / harmless / innoxious // ~ 있는 말 a stinging tongue / a malicious[wicked] tongue / a virulent[poisonous] tongue // 그녀의 말에는 ~가 있다 She has a malicious [spiteful] tongue. / Her remarks are poisoned with acrimony. / Her word stings.

독나방(毒—) [동] an oriental tussock moth.

독단(獨斷) 1 [전단(專斷)] arbitrary decision. ¶~의 arbitrary / peremptory // ~으로 at one's own discretion / on one's own authority[judgment / responsibility] / arbitrarily // ~으로 하다 do (it) on one's own authority // ~으로 결정하다 decide for oneself / decide arbitrarily / decide on one's own judgment [responsibility] // 그 일은 내 ~으로 결정할 수 없습니다 I cannot decide the matter myself[on my own responsibility]. **2** [주관적 판단] dogmatism.
● **독단론** a dogma; dogmatism.

독단적(獨斷的) 1 arbitrary; peremptory. ¶~인 말을 하다 lay down the law. **2** dogmatic. ¶~ 발언 a dogmatic assertion // ~으로 dogmatically // ~이어서 남의 의견은 듣지 않다 be too opinionated to listen to what others say.

독려(督勵) encouragement. **독려하다** encourage; urge. ¶부하를 독려하여 일을 서두르다 urge one's men to push[rush] the work // 코치는 더 연습하라고 그들을 독려했다 The coach encouraged[urged] them to practice more.

독력(獨力) one's own efforts; single-handed efforts. ¶~으로 by one's own efforts / for oneself / single-handed(ly) / without help [support] // ~으로 성가(成家)한 사람 a self-made man // ~으로 하다 do (a thing) single-handed / do (a thing) off one's own bat [for oneself].

독립(獨立) 1 [자립] independence; self-help; self-reliance. ¶경제상의 ~ economic independence. **독립하다** become independent (of one's parents); stand on one's own legs [feet]; stand alone; end one's dependence (on); set up for oneself. ¶부모에게서 영업하자 set up business on one's own (account) // 독립하여 가정을 꾸려 나가다 keep house for oneself // 그는 마침내 독립할 수 있었다 He was able to stand on his own two feet at (long) last. // 그는 이제 독립해도 될 나이다 He is old enough to be doing for himself[to be on his own]. → **독립시키다** make (a person) independent / set (a person) on his legs.
2 [자주] independence; freedom. ¶~을 선언하다 declare independence / declare (itself) independent // ~을 인정하다 recognize the independence (of) // ~을 시켜 주다 give [grant] independence (to) // ~을 유지하다 [회복하다 / 획득하다 / 지키다 / 잃다] maintain [recover / gain / safeguard / lose] one's independence. **독립하다** become (free and) independent.
3 [자활] self-support. ¶~ 생계를 영위하다 support oneself / earn one's own living.
4 [분리] separation; [고립] isolation. **독립하다** be separated from; separate (oneself) from; be isolated from. ¶독립하여 separately / in isolation. ¶그 건물은 딴 건물과는 독립되어 있다 The building is separated from the rest.
● **독립가옥** separate houses. **독립 구문** [언] an absolute construction. **독립국 / 독립 국가** an independent state; a sovereign nation. ¶신흥[신생] ~ a newly independent nation [country]. **독립군** an army for national independence. **독립 기념일** (미국의) Independence Day; the Fourth of July. **독립심** an independent spirit; a spirit of independence. ¶~이 없다 lack the spirit of independence. **독립 운동** an independence movement. **독립 채산제** a self-supporting accounting system. ¶~로 on a self-paying basis.

독무대(獨舞臺) 1 [한 사람의 연기가 특히 뛰어난 판] the sole master of the stage[field]. ¶그 연극은 그의 ~였다 In the play he outshone all other actors. **2** [경쟁자가 없음] one's unrivaled sphere of activity; one's monopoly. ¶~ 없이 without a rival // ~다 stand[be] unchallenged[unrivaled / without a rival] // 당시의 정계는 그의 ~였다 At that time the whole political situation was entirely in his hands. / He reigned supreme in the political world then. // 『햄릿』의 연출은 그의 ~다 He stands unrivaled[unchallenged / without a rival] at directing Hamlet.

독물(毒物) 1 [독성 물질] a poisonous[toxic] substance; a poisonous agent; poison. ¶~을 제거하다 remove the poison (from) / detoxify // 위에서는 아무런 ~도 검출되지 않았다 No poisonous substance was detected in the stomach. **2** [악독한 사람] a vicious[ferocious] person.

독미나리(毒—) [식] a water hemlock.

독방(獨房) [혼자 거처하는 방] a single room; a room to oneself; (교도소의) a (solitary) cell; a prison[jail] cell. ¶~에 감금되다 be placed in solitary confinement.
● **독방 감금** solitary confinement.

독백(獨白) a monologue; (미) monolog; a soliloquy. ¶제2막에서 주역이 ~을 한다 The leading actor has a soliloquy in the second act. **독백하다** soliloquize; utter a soliloquy; speak aside.

독버섯(毒—) a poisonous mushroom; a toadstool.

독법(讀法) [읽는 법] (the way of) reading; (해석) (a) reading; (발음) pronunciation.

독보(讀譜) [음] [악보 해독] reading music. ¶그는 피아노는 칠 줄 아나 ~는 못한다 He can play the piano but cannot read music.

독보적(獨步的) unique; matchless; peerless; unparalleled; unequaled; unrivaled; unchallenged. ¶당대의 ~인 시인 the greatest poet of the age[day] // 그는 희극 작가로서 ~인 존

독본 재었다 As a comedian he stood without a peer.
독본(讀本) a reader; a reading book; a textbook. ¶~어 an English reader.
독부(毒婦) a wicked[an evil] woman; a she-devil; a witch.
독불장군(獨不將軍) 1 [따돌림당하는 사람] person left out in the cold; an outcast. 2 [제 주장만 하는 사람] a man of self-assertion; a self-righteous man. ¶그는 ~으로 처신하는 일이 많다 He often behaves self-righteously [in a self-centered way].
독사(毒蛇) a venomous serpent; a poisonous snake; a viper.
독살(毒殺) poisoning; killing by poison. **독살하다** poison; kill[murder] (a person) by [with] poison. ¶그녀는 남편을 독살했다 She poisoned her husband. →그는 독살당한 것 같다 It seems he was killed by poison.
● **독살자** a poisoner.
독살(毒煞) [독한 마음을 품은 모진 기운]. ¶~을 부리다[피우다] act spitefully[malignantly / venomously] / give vent to one's spite.
독살림(獨―) an independent life. **독살림하다** live independently; keep house for oneself.
독살스럽다(毒煞―) venomous; spiteful; malicious; vicious; malignant; acrimonious; bitter; poisonous-looking. ¶독살스럽게 spitefully / malignantly / virulently // 독살스러운 여자 a wicked[spiteful / vicious] woman / a she-devil / a Jezebel // 독살스러운 말을 하다 use spiteful[malicious] language / talk maliciously // 독살스럽게 욕하다 abuse wickedly[viciously].
독생자(獨生子) (Jesus Christ) the only-begotten son (of God).
독서(讀書) reading. ¶~를 좋아하는 사람 a book lover // ~를 좋아하다 be fond of reading // ~삼매경에 빠지다 be buried in books // 그의 ~ 범위는 매우 넓다 His reading is of very wide range. / He is an extensive reader. **독서하다** read (books). ¶독서하지 않는 사람 an unread person / a nonreader // 가을은 저녁에 독서하기에 가장 좋은 계절이다 Autumn is the best season for reading (books) in the evening.
● **독서가** a (great) reader; a well-read person; a person of wide reading. ¶그는 상당한 ~다 He is quite well read. **독서광** a bookworm; a literary glutton. **독서력** reading ability. ¶영어의 ~을 기르다 cultivate [improve] one's reading ability in English. **독서실** a reading room.
독선(獨善) self-righteousness; self-complacence; self-complacency; self-flattery. ¶~과 특권 의식에 사로잡혀 법의 침해를 정당화하다 justify any violation of law out of self-righteousness and sense of privilege.
독선적(獨善的) self-righteous; self-complacent; self-justified; self-flattery. ¶~으로 이야기하다 speak self-righteously.
독설(毒舌) a spiteful tongue; a venomous remark; malicious language; vituperation. ¶~을 퍼붓다 wag one's slanderous tongue (at) / speak with acrimony / speak daggers [venomously] (to).
● **독설가** a malicious person.
독성(毒性) virulence; toxicity. ¶~이 강한 화학 약품 a highly toxic chemical // ~이 있는 virulent / poisonous / toxic / toxicant // 그 약의 ~은 극히 적다 The toxicity of the drug is very low. // 이 식물은 ~이 있다 This plant is poisonous.
독소(毒素) [화] a toxin; poisonous substance. ¶항(抗)~ an antitoxin.
독수(毒手) a vicious clutch; a vicious means; a trick; a trap. ¶악한의 ~에 걸리다[를 벗어나다] fall into[escape from] the clutches of a villain.
독수공방(獨守空房) (남편이 출타 중의) solitude[a lonely life] in one's husband's absence; (별거·사별) a lonely life in separation; a widowed life.
독수리(禿―) [동] an eagle; a vulture.
● **독수리자리** [천] the Eagle; Aquila.
독순술(讀脣術) lip reading. ¶~을 쓰는 사람 a lip-reader // ~로 뜻을 알다 lip-read.
독식하다(獨食―) have[keep] (a thing) all to oneself; monopolize.
독신(獨身) celibacy; a single life; bachelorhood(남자); spinsterhood(여자). ¶~ 아파트 a bachelor apartment house // ~인 숙부 a bachelor uncle // ~인 고모 a spinster aunt // ~의 single / unmarried // ~으로 살다 live [remain] single / lead a bachelor's[spinster's] life // 평생을 ~으로 살다 remain unmarried for life / continue single all one's life.
● **독신 생활** a single[an unmarried] life; celibacy. **독신자** an unmarried person; (남자) a single man; a bachelor; (여자) a single woman; a bachelor girl; (특히 과년한) a spinster. **독신주의** celibacy; bachelorism; (여자의) old-maidism.
독실(獨室) a single room. ⇨ ¯독방
독실하다(篤實―) sincere; faithful; true. ¶독실한 ~인 사람 a man of sincerity / a true gentleman / (집합적) good men and true // 독실한 크리스천 a devout Christian. **독실히** sincerely; faithfully.
독심(毒心) malice; spite; venom. ¶~을 품은 malicious / spiteful / venomous // ~을 품다 be filled with spite.
독심술(讀心術) mind[thought] reading; telepathy. ¶그는 ~에 능하다 He is very good at reading other people's minds.
● **독심술사**(―師) a mind[thought] reader; a telepathist.
독액(毒液) venom(독사 등의); poisonous liquid[juice / sap].
독약(毒藥) poison; a poisonous drug[medicine]. ¶~을 마시다 take poison / poison oneself // ~을 타다 put poison into (food) / mix poison in // ~을 먹이다 poison (a person).
독어(獨語) German. ⇨ ¯독일어(⇨독일)
독일(獨逸) (공식명) the German Federal Republic(▶ 1990년 10월 동독과 서독이 독일 연방 공화국으로 통일됨). ¶~의 German / Germanic.
● **독일어** German; the German language.
독자(獨子) an only son; one's only son [child].
독자(讀者) a reader; [구독자] a subscriber (to a magazine / to a newspaper); (사회 전반의) the reading public. ¶일반 ~ general readership // ~가 많다 (신문·잡지가) have a large circle of subscribers / have a large circulation(▶ circulation은 발행 부수) / (책이) be widely read // 이 잡지는 5만의 ~를 가지고

있다 This magazine has a circulation [readership] of fifty thousand.// 이런 책도 ~가 있을까 I wonder if anyone will read such a book as this?

● **독자란** the reader's column; the correspondence; letters to the editor. ¶~ 투고를 환영합니다 Contributions to the reader's column are most welcome. **독자층** a class of readers. ¶이 잡지들은 제각기 ~이 다르다 Each of these magazines has its own class of subscribers.

독자성(獨自性) [독창성] originality; [그것 자체임] identity. ¶이 계획에는 ~이 없다 This plan lacks originality.// 그 민족은 ~을 유지하고 있다 [상실했다] The race has maintained [has lost] it identity.

독자적(獨自的) 1 [저 혼자인] individual; personal. ¶~ 견해 one's personal views// ~ 행동을 취하다 act independently of others / go [take] one's own way. 2 [독특한] original; peculiar; characteristic of one's own. ¶한국은 다른 나라와는 달리 ~인 길을 가야만 한다 Korea should steer a course independent of other nations.

독작하다(獨酌-) drink alone [without a companion]; drink by oneself; help oneself to wine.

독장수셈 an unreliable account; a fruitless [vain] effort. ¶~을 하다 count chickens before they are hatched / sell the bear's skin before one has caught the bear / run before one's horse to market.

독장치다(獨場-) be the sole master of the situation; stand unchallenged [without a rival]; reign supreme (in the party). ¶정계에서 ~ reign supreme in the political world// 이야기를 독장쳐서 하다 monopolize the talk// 토론회에서 ~ take over a discussion.

독재(獨裁) dictatorship; despotism; autocracy; absolute rule; absolutism. ¶나치스의 ~ the Nazi dictatorship// ~적인 [으로] dictatorial(ly) / despotic(ally) / autocratic(ally). **독재하다** have (a country) under one's despotic rule; hold an absolute rule (over a project); manage [run / operate] (a company) on one's sole authority.

● **독재 국가** a despotic [an autocratic] state. **독재자** a dictator; an autocrat; a despot. **독재 정치** dictatorship; autocracy. **독재주의** dictatorship; despotism; absolutism.

독점(獨占) 1 [독차지] exclusive possession. ¶~적인 monopolistic / exclusive// …의 ~물이 되다 become the exclusive property of …. **독점하다** have [keep] (a thing) to oneself; obtain the exclusive possession of; monopolize. ¶문단은 그가 독점하고 있는 형편이다 It appears that he reigns supreme in the world of letters.// 그녀는 방을 독점하고 있다 She has a room all to herself.// 그는 그 특권을 독점하고 있다 He enjoys that privilege exclusively.

2 [경] a monopoly; monopolization. ¶수요 ~ a monopsony// ~적인 monopolistic// ~적인 지위에 있다 have a monopoly position in the market). **독점하다** monopolize; make [enjoy / hold] a monopoly of (a thing). ¶시장을 ~ monopolize a market// 그들은 시장을 독점할 생각이다 They intend to monopolize the market.

● **독점 가격** a monopoly price. **독점권** (the right to) a monopoly; an exclusive [a sole] right. **독점 금지법** [법] the Antimonopoly [Antitrust] Law. **독점 기업** a monopolistic enterprise [undertaking]. **독점 시장** a monopolistic market. **독점욕** a desire for exclusive possession. ¶~이 강하다 have strong monopolistic desires. **독점 자본** monopolistic capital. **독점 판매** an exclusive sale. ¶~ 계약 an exclusive sales contract.

독종(毒種) [독한 사람] a cold-blooded [malicious / cruel] person; [독한 동물] a fierce animal; [독한 종자] malicious offspring; a bad seed.

독주(毒酒) [독한 술] strong [hard] liquor; spirits; [독을 탄 술] poisoned liquor.

독주(獨走) 1 [혼자 뜀]. **독주하다** run alone. 2 [남보다 훨씬 앞섬]. **독주하다** have a large [sizable] lead [on [over] the others]; be far ahead of (a person); leave (other) far behind. ¶40킬로미터 지점에서 황 선수는 독주하고 있다 (마라톤에서) At the 40-kilometer point, Hwang is way ahead of the others. / Hwang is running by himself at the 40-kilometer mark, having left all the others far behind.

3 [낙승] a walkover; a runaway. ¶다른 팀은 자이언츠 팀의 ~를 허용하고 있다 The other teams just allow the Giants to walk [run] off with the pennant. **독주하다** have a walkover; win in a walk. ¶시장 선거에서 홍 씨는 계속 독주하고 있다 Mr. Hong is expected to win a landslide [runaway] victory in the mayoral election.

4 [제멋대로 행동함]. **독주하다** go one's own way. ¶회의의 논의는 그가 독주함으로써 혼란에 빠지고 말았다 At the meeting he monopolized the discussion and completely disrupted the proceeding.// 이 일에서 그녀가 독주하도록 내버려 두어서는 안 된다 Don't let her have her own way in this matter.

독주(獨奏) a recital; a solo (performance). ¶피아노 ~ a piano solo [recital]. **독주하다** play a solo; play alone.

● **독주곡** a solo. **독주자** a soloist; a solo. **독주회** a recital; a solo.

독지가(篤志家) [자선가] a benevolent [charitable] person; [올선자] a volunteer; a person interested; a supporter (후원자). ¶익명의 ~ an anonymous benefactor// ~의 찬조를 바랍니다 We solicit the support of those who are specially interested in the project.

독직(瀆職) (official) corruption; corrupt practices; bribery; (미) graft. ¶~ 경찰관 a corrupt policeman// 정부 고관의 ~이 발각되었다 Corruption was discovered among high government officials. **독직하다** receive [take] a bribe; practice corruption; (미) graft.

● **독직 사건** a corruption scandal; a bribery [graft / corruption] case.

독차지(獨-) exclusive possession; having [keeping] all to oneself; monopolizing. **독차지하다** have [keep] all to oneself; possess exclusively; monopolize; engross; get the exclusive possession of. ¶유산을 ~ have all the inheritance to oneself// 이익을 ~ take all the profit// 그는 상품을 독차지했다 He carried away all the prizes.// 화제가 아프리카에 이르면 그는 이야기를 독차지한다 When it comes to Africa, he monopolized the conver-

독창(獨唱) a (vocal) solo. **독창하다** sing a solo; give a vocal solo.
● **독창곡** a solo piece. **독창회** a solo vocal recital; a (vocal) recital. ¶~를 **개최하다** hold a (vocal) recital.

독창(獨創) originality. **독창하다** create uniquely; originate. ¶이 방법은 그가 독창한 것이다 This method is original with him.
● **독창력** creative talent[power / faculty]; originality. ¶~이 없다 lack originality [creative faculty] // ~을 보이다 show originality (in). **독창성** originality. ¶~이 있는 original / ~이 없는 unoriginal // 그는 가게의 경영에 ~을 발휘했다 He displayed originality in the management of his shop.
독창적(獨創的) original; creative. ¶~인 복장 original clothes // ~인 연구 a trailblazing study // 이것은 참으로 ~인 아이디어다 This is quite an original idea. // 그녀에게는 ~인 데가 있다 She has an original mind.

독채(獨−) (live in) an unshared[a separate] house.

독초(毒草) [독풀] a poisonous herb; a noxious plant; [쓴 담배] strong tobacco.

독촉(督促) urge; demand; pressing; importunity; [빛의] dun(ning); (세금 등의) a call. **독촉하다** press[prod] (a person for); urge; dun. ¶집주인은 그에게 집세를 독촉했다 The landlord demanded that he pay his rent. / The landlord pressed[urged] him to pay the rent. → 그는 세금을 독촉받았다 He was reminded to pay his taxes. / He received a reminder that his taxes were due.
● **독촉장** a demand note; a reminder a letter demanding payment; a final demand; (차용 금의) a dunning letter[note].

독충(毒蟲) a poisonous[noxious] insect.

독침(毒針) (곤충 등의) a poison sting(er); [독 묻힌 바늘] a poisoned needle. ¶~에 쏘이다 get stung (by a bee) / ~으로 찌르다 prick with a poisoned needle.

독탕(獨湯) a private bath. **독탕하다** take a bath in a private bathroom.

독특하다(獨特−) [고유하다] peculiar (to); [특징이 있다] characteristic; [독자적이다] own; [유일무이하다] unique. ¶그의 독특한 웅변 his inimitable eloquence // 이것은 이 지방의 독특한 습관이다 It is a custom peculiar to this district. // 이 과일에서는 독특한 향내가 난다 This fruit has a characteristic smell. // 누구나가 그녀의 독특한 재능을 인정하고 있다 Everybody appreciates her special[unique] ability. **독특히** specially; uniquely; peculiarly.

독파하다(讀破−) read (through) (a book); read (a book) to the last page; finish reading (a book). ¶수많은 책을 ~ read a world of books.

독판(獨−) the sole master of the stage; one's monopoly. ⇨독무대

독필(毒筆) a spiteful pen; a pen dipped in gall. ¶~을 휘두르다 wield a spiteful pen / dip one's pen in gall / write[attack] with acrimony.

독하다(毒−) **1** [독기가 있다] poisonous; venomous; mephitic; deleterious; toxic; noxious. ¶독한 가스 poisonous air // 독한 가스를 쐬다 be exposed to poisonous air.
2 [진하다] strong; severe; intense; sharp. ¶독한 냄새 a strong[heavy] smell // 독한 술 a strong[potent] wine / a strong[stiff] drink / strong *jeongjong* / hard liquor // 독한 감기 a bad[nasty] cold.
3 [악독하다] malicious; spiteful; bitter; vicious; venomous; atrocious. ¶성미가 독한 여자 a spiteful[wicked] woman / a she-devil // 독한 짓 an infernal[atrocious] deed / an atrocity.
4 [꿋꿋하다] firm; dogged; tough; unflinching; unyielding. ¶독한 마음 a mind of high resolve // 마음을 독하게 먹고 공부하다 study with a firm[unflinching] resolution.

독학(獨學) self-education; self-instruction; solitary studies. ¶~의 self-educated [-taught / -instructed] // 그는 ~으로 대학을 마쳤다 He gave himself a college education. **독학하다** study by oneself; teach[educate] oneself; learn without a teacher. ¶독학한 영어 English self-taught.

독해력(讀解力) ability to read and understand; (reading) comprehension.

독행(獨行) self-reliance; pursuing[taking] a course of one's own choice; going one's (own) way. **독행하다** act independently; pursue[take] a course of one's own choice.

독회(讀會) reading. ¶제1[제2 / 제3] ~ the 1st[2nd / 3rd] reading / the committee [discussion / voting] stage // 의안은 제1~에 회부되었다 The bill was read for the first time. // 의안은 제2~를 생략하고 가결되었다 The bill was passed, the discussion stage having been dispensed with.

독후감(讀後感) (one's) impressions of a book [an article]. ¶(학생의) ~ 리포트 a book report.

돈 1 [금전] money; (속어); juice; (미국 속어) dough; [현찰] cash; [경화] coin; [자금] funds. ¶많은[적은] ~ a large[small] sum of money // 잔~ small money[change] // 부정한 ~ ill-gotten gains / (문어) filthy lucre // 걱정 pecuniary[financial] anxiety // ~ 문제 money[pecuniary] matters // ~의 money / monetary / pecuniary // ~의 유통 the circulation of money // ~의 위력 the power of the purse // ~이 벌리는 일 lucrative[profitable] work / a fat job // ~ 때문에 일하다 work merely for money // ~이 모이다 come to have some money saved // ~이 없어서 …할 수가 없다 want of means prevents (one) from (doing) // ~이 당장 필요하다 need ready money // ~이 달리다 be short of money / be hard up (for money) // ~을 쓰다[절약하다] spend[save] money // ~을 벌다 earn[make] money // ~을 모으다 [모금하다] collect money / [자금을 모으다] raise capital [funds] / [저축하다] save money (for) // ~을 찍어 내다 (동전을) mint a coin / (지폐를) issue paper money // 뼈 빠지게 일해서 ~을 모으다 accumulate money by the sweat of one's brow // ~을 내놓다 hand out money / [지불하다] pay (for) / [자금을] appropriate funds (for) / finance (an enterprise) / [기부하다] donate a fund (for charity purposes) // ~을 낭비하다 waste[lavish / squander] money / make the money fly // ~을 헛되이 쓰다 throw[fool / trifle] away one's money // ~을 갚다 repay / pay back / return money // ~을 은행에 예금하다 put[deposit] money in a bank // ~을 남에게 맡기다 trust a person with money // ~을 묶어 두다 let money lie idle // ~을 걸다 bet money (on) / bet with money // ~을 먹이다 [뇌물을 주다] bribe / grease the hand[palm] of (a person) // 땅을 담보로 ~을 빌려 주다 lend money on land // 아이들의 교육에 ~을 들이다 spend money for [on] the education of one's children // 기업에 ~을 투자하다 sink money in a business venture // 물건을 팔아 ~을 만들다 raise money on things // 증권을 ~으로 바꾸다 sell [(문어) realize] securities // ~으로 지불하다 pay in money // 그는 무슨 일이든 ~의 힘으로 해결하려고 한다 He tries to settle everything with money [through the power of money]. // 그는 ~ 문제로 어려운 처지에 있다 He has money trouble [trouble with money]. // 마침 가진 ~이 없다 I have no money about [with] me. // ~이 아쉽다 I need money badly! / If only I had money enough! // ~이 문제가 아니다 Money is no object. // 너를 위해서라면 기꺼이 ~을 내놓겠다 You are welcome to my money. // 그 땅은 아무리 ~을 많이 주어도 살 수가 없다 No amount of money can buy that land. // 나는 아르바이트를 해서 ~을 벌어야 한다 I have to earn money by (doing) a part-time job. // 그것은 영국 ~으로 약 100파운드이다 It is about 100 pounds in British money [currency]. // 그는 자기 ~으로 집을 지었다 He built the house with his own money. // 그는 ~에 쪼들리고 있다 He is pressed for money. / He is short of money. // ~이 떨어지면 사랑도 멀어진다 Love lasts only as long as the money holds out. // ~ 떨어지면 정분도 떨어진다 When poverty comes in, love flies out. / Money gone, friends gone. // ~이 많으면 근심도 많다 Much coin, much care. // 남의 ~ 천 냥이 내 ~ 한 푼만 못하다 A bird in the hand is worth two in the bush. 2 [물건 값] (a) price; (a) charge; the money; a bill. ¶~을 받지 않고 free of charge [cost] // ~을 치르다 pay for (an article) / pay one's bill (for) (계산서를 받고) // 식당에서 ~을 치르지 않고 도망치다 run away without paying for what one has eaten // 이 책은 아직 ~을 치르지 않았다 This book is not paid for yet. 3 [재산] riches; wealth; fortune. ¶~ 많은 rich / wealthy // ~을 바라고 결혼하는 사람 a fortune hunter // ~ 많은 사람 a rich [wealthy] person / (집합적) the rich // ~과 명예를 바라다 desire for wealth and fame // 그는 ~ 많은 집에서 태어났다 He was born rich.

돈만 있으면 귀신도 부릴 수 있다(속담) Money makes the mare (to) go.

돈이 돈을 번다(속담) Money begets [breeds / draws / gets] money.

돈(을) 굴리다 [투자하다] lay [put] out (one's money); invest in. ¶가장 유리하게 ~ place one's money to the best advantage.

돈을 먹다 ¶그는 돈을 먹고 입을 다물었다 He was bribed into silence. / He was paid to keep his mouth shut.

돈을 물 쓰듯 하다 muddle away money; live it up. ¶그는 돈을 물 쓰듯 했다 He spent money like water.

돈을 뿌리다 lavish [scatter] money; use money freely. ¶돈을 많이 뿌리는 손님 a high-spending client // 그는 술집을 돌아다니며 돈을 뿌렸다 He scattered his money loafing around saloons.

돈(頓) 〈음역〉 a don. ⇨톤
돈가스(豚-) a (deep-fried) pork cutlet.
돈구멍 1 [돈의 구멍] a hole in the middle of a coin. **2** [돈이 생기는 길] a source of income. ¶~을 뚫다 find a way of getting money / ~이 막히다 lose one's source of income.
돈궤(-櫃) a cash [money] box; (상점 계산대의) a till; (금고식의) a strongbox.
돈놀이 moneylending; usury(고리대금업). ¶~꾼 a moneylender / a moneymonger / [고리대금업자] a usurer / a loan shark // 그는 ~로 먹고산다 He earns his living by lending money. **돈놀이하다** run money-lending business; practice usury.
돈더미에 올라앉다 get [become] rich suddenly; gain quick riches.
돈독(-毒) an unhealthy taste for money; mercenariness. ¶~이 오른 사람 a person of mercenary spirit / a moneygrubber // ~이 오르다 become mercenary.
돈독하다(敦篤-) gentle (and sincere); humane; courteous; affable; friendly; amicable. ¶그는 우정이 돈독한 사람이다 He is true to his friends. **돈독히** gently; humanely; friendly. ¶한미 관계를 ~ 하다 promote friendly relations between Korea and America.
돈맛 a taste for money; a love of money. ¶~을 알다 be charmed by money / learn the value [charm] of money // ~을 알면 사람이 인색해진다 One grows stingy when one learns the charm of money.
돈방석에 앉다(-方席-) have plenty of money; be well-off; be rolling in money.
돈벌이 moneymaking. ¶~를 잘하는 사람 a moneymaker. **돈벌이하다** make money; earn money. ¶돈벌이하러 해외로 나가다 go abroad to make money.
돈벼락 맞다 strike a bonanza.
돈복(-福) luck with money; bliss with money. ¶~이 있다 be blessed with a chance to make money // ~이 터지다 hit a source of wealth.
돈사(豚舍) a pigsty; a pigpen.
돈육(豚肉) pork. ⇨돼지고기(⇨돼지)
돈주머니 (a coin) purse. ¶묵직한 ~ a well-lined purse / a plump [fat] purse / ~가 가볍다 have a light purse // ~를 털다 [있는 돈을] 몽땅 쓰다] spend all one's money / empty one's purse to the last penny [cent] / clear one's purse out // 우리 집에서는 아내가 ~를 움켜쥐고 있다 My wife holds the purse strings in my family.
돈줄 financial resources; a source of revenue; [후원자] a patron; a financial backer [supporter]. ¶~을 잡다 [잃다] find [lose] a supplier of funds [a financial supporter] // 그에게는 튼튼한 ~이 있다 He has a good patron [financial backer] / He has a goose which lays golden eggs. // 그의 ~을 추적해 보아야겠다 I'll find out where his money comes from [where he gets his money]. // 누가 그의 ~일까 Who is supporting him financially? / Who is his financial backer?
돈지갑(-紙匣) a (coin) purse; a wallet. ⇨지갑
돈푼 a small sum of money; a small fortune; a snug hoard of money. ¶~깨나 있다고 으스대지 마라 Don't boast yourself of your small fortune. // 그는 ~이나 있는지 모르나 큰돈은 없을 게다 He may have some money but not

돌구다 [높이다] raise; make higher. ¶안경의 도수를 ~ make one's glasses stronger.

돌다 1 (해·달이) come up; rise. ¶해는 동쪽에서 돌아 서쪽으로 진다 The sun comes up[rises] in the east and goes down[sets] in the West.
2 (싹 등이) sprout; bud; come up; shoot. ¶움[싹]이 ~ put forth buds / come into bud / sprout∥장미의 새싹이 돌기 시작했다 The rose has began to put forth new shoots. / 뿌린 씨에서는 아직 싹이 돌아나지 않고 있다 The seeds sowed have not germinated [come up] yet.
3 (피부에) break out; come out; erupt; form. ¶그는 온몸에 두드러기가 돌았다 He has a rash all over the body. / The eruption broke out all over him.∥나는 봄이 되면 여드름이 잘 돋는다 My skin tends to break out when spring comes. / I often get a rash in springtime.

돋보기 1 [노안경] convex glasses [spectacles] for the aged; reading glasses (for the aged). ¶그는 ~를 끼고 책을 보고 있다 He is reading with his reading glasses on. 2 [확대경] a magnifying glass; a magnifier. ¶~로 보다 see through a magnifying glass.

돋보이다 look better (than actually is); set off; make a fine show; look [show] to advantage. ¶돋보이게 하다 show (it) to advantage / set (it) off / make (a thing) look better∥붉은 옷이 그녀를 더욱 돋보이게 했다 The red dress showed her off to advantage.∥검은 배경이 그녀의 흰 살결을 더욱 돋보이게 했다 The dark background brought out her fair complexion [emphasized her fair complexion / made her fair complexion stand out].∥당신이 이 모자를 쓰면 틀림없이 돋보일 것이다 You are sure to look nice [to advantage] in this hat. / This hat will set you off to advantage. / 스테레오가 있으면 방이 훨씬 돋보일 것이다 A stereo will make the room look better.

돋우다 1 [끌어 올리다] raise; turn (a thing) up. ¶그는 스토브 심지를 돋우어 불이 타오르게 했다 He poked up a blaze in the stove.
2 [높이다] make higher; raise; bank. ¶땅을 ~ raise the ground∥길을 ~ bank the road∥베개를 ~ make one's pillow higher / raise one's pillow.
3 (목청을) raise; elevate; lift. ¶목청을 ~ raise [lift] one's voice∥그런 하찮은 일로 목청을 돋울 필요는 없다 You don't have to [need not] shout at such a trifle. / You ought to be more quiet about so small a matter.
4 (용기·힘을) encourage; fan; heighten; inflame; cheer up. ¶기운을 ~ raise (a person's) spirit∥사기를 ~ heighten [stir up] the morale (of troops) / (사물이) give a stimulus to the fighting spirit (of the men)∥용기를 ~ encourage / embolden / give (a person) courage / put (a person) on his mettle∥그녀의 웃는 얼굴이 그의 기운을 돋우어 주었다 The girl's smiling face cheered him up.
5 (입맛을) whet. ¶입맛을 돋우는 한 잔의 포도주 a glass of wine to whet your appetite.
6 (감정·신경 등을) irritate; stimulate; incite; stir (up); gall; provoke; aggravate. ¶화[부아]를 ~ provoke (a person) to anger / make (a person) madder / aggravate (a person's) anger / offend (a person)∥감정을 ~ stimulate [stir up] (another's) sentiment [feelings]∥그녀는 사소한 일에도 신경을 돋운다 Her nerves are set on edge by the merest trifle.

돋을새김 [미] relief. ⇨°양각 ¶~을 하다 emboss.

돋치다 [내밀다] put forth [out / up]; stick out; pop out [forth]; [새로 생기다] grow (out); spring out. ¶가시 돋친 말 harsh language / barbed [stinging] words∥날개가 ~ grow wings∥날개 돋치듯 팔리다 sell [go] off like hot cakes.

돌¹ (천연의) (a) stone; [조약돌] a pebble; (미국 구어) a rock. ~의 stony / lithic∥~로 쌓은 둑 a bank of stone∥~을 잘라 내다 quarry stone∥~을 깨다 break stones∥~을 갈다 dress stone∥~이 되다 turn the stone / petrify∥~을 깔다 pave (the road) with stone∥~을 던지다 throw a stone [rock] (at a dog)∥~에 걸려 넘어졌다 I tripped over [stumbled on] a stone and fell down.∥소년은 그 광경에 ~처럼 굳어있다 The boy petrified at the sight.∥부처 모습이 ~에 새겨져 있다 Images of (the) Buddha are carved in the rocks.
2 [석재] (building) stone. ¶~기둥 a stone pillar.
3 (쌀 등에 섞여 있는) a grit. ¶쌀에서 ~을 골라 내다 pick out grits from rice.
4 [바둑돌] a baduk(go) stone [piece]. ¶~을 놓다 play baduk / have a game of baduk.
5 [라이터돌] a flint. ¶~을 갈아 넣다 change the flint in a lighter.

돌을 던지다 1 [비난하다] criticize unfavorably. 2 [바둑] lose one's game of baduk.

돌² 1 [주년(周年)] an anniversary(기념일); one full year; a full day. ¶창립 30~맞이 기념행사를 하다 observe the 30th anniversary of the opening∥결혼한 지 꼭 세 ~이 된다 It is just full three year since we were married. 2 [첫돌] a baby's first birthday. ¶~을 맞다 mark [celebrate] a baby's first birthday∥우리 아기의 ~이 돌아온다 The first birthday of our baby is coming around.

돌개바람 a whirlwind; a cyclone; an eddy wind; a twister; a tornado.

돌격(突擊) a charge; a rush; a dash; (백병(白兵)의) an assault. **돌격하다** charge (at / on); rush [dash] (at); make a dash at; raid; make an assault upon. ¶적을 향하여 ~ make a dash at [for] the enemy∥적의 진지로 ~ rush [charge] the enemy's position.
●**돌격대** a storming party [corps]; a shock troop; raiders; commandos.

돌계단(一階段) a stone step. ⇨°돌층계

돌계집 a barren [childless / sterile] woman.

돌고드름 [광] a stalactite.

돌고래 a dolphin; (참돌고래 등) a porpoise; a sea hog [pig].

돌공이 a stone pestle.

돌기(突起) a projection; a protrusion; a protuberance; a prominence; [동][식] a process; a boss; [생] a promontory. ¶충양(蟲樣)~ the (vermiform) appendix. **돌기하다** project; protrude; jut out. ¶돌기한 projecting / prominent / protruding.

돌기둥 a stone pillar.

돌기와 a roofing slate; slabs of stone for

roofing.
● **돌기와집** a slate-roofed house.

돌김 [식] laver[sloke] grown on the underwater rock; underwater stone moss.

돌날 a baby's first birthday. ¶오늘은 우리 아기의 ~이다 Today is my baby's first birthday.

돌다 1 [회전하다] turn (round); (축을 중심으로 하여) rotate; (축을 중심으로 빨리) spin; (원 궤도를) revolve; gyrate; (원을 그리며) circle. ¶왼쪽으로 빙빙 ~ turn round and round to the left∥한 바퀴 ~ make a turn / make one revolution (round)∥시곗바늘과 같은 방향으로 ~ turn[revolve] clockwise∥기둥 둘레를 두 바퀴 ~ go around[circle] a post twice∥모터가 돌지 않는다 The motor won't turn over[run].∥팽이가 돌고 있다 The top is spinning.∥달은 지구의 주위를 돈다 The moon revolves around[(영) circle / (문어) about] the earth.

2 [순회하다] go (one's) round; make a round; [주유(周遊)하다] make a tour (of); travel about[around]. ¶유럽의 여러 나라를 도는 1개월간의 여행 a one-month tour of European countries∥산책 삼아 시내를 한 바퀴 ~ go round the city for a walk∥그 순경은 담당 구역을 돌았다 The policeman went the rounds[make his rounds]. / The policeman was (out) on his beat.

3 [방향을 바꾸다] turn (about); go round; make a bend; [전향하다] swing; switch (over). ¶오른쪽으로 ~ turn to the right (hand) / turn right∥뒤로 ~ turn (a) round ∥…의 편으로 ~ swing round in (a person's) favor∥적의 배후로 ~ move around to the enemy's rear∥정부 지지로 ~ swing over to the Administration∥부엌 쪽으로 돌아와 주십시오 Come around[(영) round] to the kitchen.∥바람의 방향이 북쪽으로 돌았다 The wind shifted to the north.∥우리 집은 모퉁이를 돌아서 세 번째입니다 I lived in the third house around the corner.

4 [우회하다] go around; take a roundabout way; round(배 등이); go by[make] a detour; go a long way about; [경유하다] go by way of. ¶친구 집으로 돌아 귀가하다 go around to a friends place on the way home∥유럽에서 미국으로 돌아 귀국하다 come home from via [by way of] America∥도로 공사로 인하여 우리는 길을 돌아 학교에 갔다 Because the road was being repaired, we went a roundabout way to the school.

5 [순환·유통하다] circulate; pass current. ¶돈이 ~ be financed∥돈이 잘 돌지 않다 money is tight[scarce] / be pressed [pinched] for money / be short of money∥돈이란 돌고 도는 것이다 Money will come and go.∥피는 체내를 돈다 The blood circulates through the body.

6 [차례차례 거치다] go around; pass; be passed (around the table); [부배되다] be distributed. ¶회람이 돈다 A circular passes. ∥술잔이 돌았다 The wineglass went around [was passed around].∥모든 사람이 싫어하여 그 역할이 돌고 돌아 그가 떠맡아야만 했다 He had to undertake the role since everybody else had declined to.

7 [기능이 잘 작용하다] work; operate; function. ¶머리가 잘 ~ one's brain works well / be quick-[sharp-]witted∥머리가 잘 돌지 않다 one's brain doesn't work well / be slow-witted[dull]∥혀가 잘 ~ have a glib tongue / be quite a talker / be talkative∥혀가 잘 돌지 않다 be tongue-tied / be inarticulate / lisp∥그 아이는 아직 혀가 잘 돌지는 않는다 The child still speaks with a lisp.∥그가 없으면 우리 회사가 잘 돌지 않는다 Without him our company ceases to function[just stands still].

8 [약·술기운이 나타나다] take effect. ¶기운이 돌기 시작하다 begin to feel the effect (of)∥술기운이 ~ be under the influence of liquor / be tipsy∥그들은 술기운이 많이 돈 상태였다 (구어) They were quite high[tight].∥독기운이 급속히 돌았다 The poison took quick rapid.

9 [현기증이 나다] be[feel] dizzy; get[feel] giddy. ¶눈이 핑핑 ~ feel dizzy[giddy] / one's head reels[swims] / feel[grow] vertiginous∥머리가 핑핑 ~ my head turns[spins] ∥이 바위에 서니 눈이 핑핑 돈다 I feel dizzy [giddy] standing on this rock.

10 [소문이 퍼지다] get about[around / abroad]; circulate; run[be] current; be abroad; be put in circulation. ¶…이라는 소문이 돌고 있다 a rumor is abroad[current] about …∥이 고장에서는 전쟁이 일어날 것이라는 소문이 돌고 있다 Rumors of war are rife in this part of the country.

11 [돌림병이 퍼지다] prevail; be prevalent [epidemic / widespread]. ¶감기가 돈다 A cold is making the rounds.∥전국적으로 독감이 돌고 있다 Influenza is prevailing throughout the country.

12 [미치다] go off one's head[(영) chump]; (속어) go balmy[barmy]; be off one's nut [rocker]; be batty. ¶그는 머리가 좀 돌았다 He is touched in the head. / He's gone off his head.∥그는 틀림없이 머리가 돌았다 He must be crazy[queer in the head].∥머리가 돌 것만 같다 I feel like I'm going to lose my mind[go crazy / (구어) go nuts].

13 [눈물·침 등이 생기다] bear; yield; produce. ¶눈물이 핑 ~ tears comes to [gather in] one's eyes / swim[dim] with tears.

14 [어떤 기운·빛이 나타나다] be tinged with; smack of; partake of. ¶노란색이 도는 파랑 blue with a suggestion of yellow∥회색이 ~ be tinged with gray∥윤기가 ~ be glossy [lustrous]∥얼굴에 화색이 ~ have a good [healthy] complexion / (미) look rosy.

돌다리 a stone bridge.

돌다리도 두들겨 보고 건너라 (속담) Look before you leap.

돌담 a stone wall. ¶~을 두르다 surround with a stone wall / wall round with stone.

돌대가리 [우둔한 사람] a airhead; a blockhead; a dumbbell; a knucklehead. ¶이 ~야, 이런 것도 모르니 You blockhead! Don't you know this?

돌덩이 a piece of stone; a stone; (미국 구어) a rock. ¶~ 같다 be (as) hard as a rock [brick].

돌도끼 [고고] a stone ax(e).

돌돌 1 [둥글게 말리는 모양] into a roll[ball / scroll]. ¶종이를 ~ 말다 roll up a sheet of paper. 2 [구르는 모양] with a twirl[whirl]. ¶물레바퀴가 ~ 돌아가는 소리 the whirl of a spinning wheel.

돌떡 rice cake made for a baby's first birthday.

돌려놓다 change the position (of); change direction; put the other way round; turn (about); shift; veer (round). ¶의자를 ~ rearrange[refix] a set of chairs.

돌려보내다 [도로 보내다] return; give back; send back; [돌아가게 하다] let (a person) go back; release; [법] remand (a case). ¶손님을 ~ see a visitor out / see one's guests off / (만나지 않고) turn away a visitor (at the door) / 심부름군을 ~ send back a messenger // 선생은 학생을 훈계한 다음 돌려보냈다 The teacher dismissed the boy after giving him an admonition. // 이 문서를 총무부로 돌려보내시오 Please send this paper[pass this paper on] to the general affairs department.

돌려쓰다 borrow (a thing from person).

돌려주다 1 [반환하다] return; give back; hand back; pay back. ¶돈을 ~ pay the money back / pay one's debt / return the borrowed money // 빌린 책을 ~ return (a person) a borrowed book // 습득물은 주인에게 돌려주어야 한다 You must restore lost property to its owner. // 그 빚은 3개월이면 돌려줄 수 있다 The debt is repayable in three month. // 습득한 정기권을 잃어버린 사람에게 돌려주었다 I sent the commuter pass that I'd found back to the person who'd lost it.
2 [융통하다] advance; accomodate (a person with a loan); lend; let out. ¶3만 원을 ~ accommodate (a person) with 30,000 won / lend[advance] (a person) 30,000 won // 자금을 ~ finance (an enterprise).

돌리다¹ 1 [회전시키다] turn; spin; trundle; revolve; roll; rotate; wheel; whirl; screw. ¶병마개를 돌려 열다[닫다] screw the top off [onto] a bottle // 꼭지를 돌려 물을 틀다[잠그다] turn the tap on[off] // 볼트를 돌려 침목(枕木)에 고정시키다 screw a bolt into a tie // 시곗바늘을 앞으로[뒤로] ~ set[put] the hands forward[back].
2 [방향을 바꾸다] turn (to); (얼굴을) look (to / toward(s)); turn one's head[face] (toward(s)); veer (around); direct (to / towards); shift; sheer; wheel. ¶강물을 저수지로 ~ divert river water into a reservoir // 등을 ~ turn one's back (to / on) / [변절하다] change about[one's coat] / turn around // 머리를 ~ turn one's head around // 뱃머리를 ~ put[heave] the ship about // 상대방과 이야기하면서 눈길을 딴 데로 돌리는 것은 실례다 It's impolite to turn your eyes away when talking to someone // 그는 기수를 남쪽으로 돌렸다 He swung the plane southwards.
3 [바꾸다] convert[turn] (A into B); change; alter; think better of. ¶마음을 ~ change one's mind / divert one's attention (to) // 마음을 돌려 새사람이 되다 mend one's way / turn over a new leaf // 그는 그 질문으로부터 내 주의를 돌리려 하고 있었다 He was trying to divert my attention from the question. // 그는 갑자기 화제를 돌렸다 He abruptly changed the subject. / He abruptly switched the conversation to another topic. // 그녀는 다른 남자에게 마음을 돌린 것 같다 She seems to have dropped him and fallen in love with.
4 [차례로 전하다] send round (a circular); pass (a thing) round[about]; hand round (on). ¶다음으로 ~ pass on to the next // 회람을 ~ send (out) a circular (letter) / circulate a letter // 술잔을 ~ pass a wineglass around // 돌려 가며 보다 read and pass on / circulate // 돌려 가며 하다 take by spell / take spell and spell // 책을 돌려 보다 pass a book around reading it in turns // 읽고 나면 반 학생들에게 돌려라 When you've read this, hand[pass] it on to your classmates. // 이 통지문을 모든 사람에게 돌려 주시오 Please pass[hand] this notice on to everyone. // 후추 좀 돌려 주시겠어요 Will you pass me the pepper?
5 [도르다] deal out; distribute; deliver; serve out[round]; send out. ¶신문을 ~ deliver newspapers // 크리스마스카드를 ~ send out Christmas cards.
6 [회부하다] send round (a bill to); transmit; [가져가다] refer (a matter to). ¶서류를 담당자에게 ~ send the papers over to the man in charge // 사건을 다른 관청으로 ~ refer a matter to another office // 편지를 이사간 주소로 ~ forward a letter to a person's new address.
7 [빌리다] borrow (a thing from a person); have (money) on loan; [빌려 주다] let out. ¶땅을 담보로 돈을 ~ raise[borrow] money on one's estate // 돈 5만 원을 친구에게서 돌렸다 I obtained an accommodation of 50,000 won from one of my friends. // 돈을 좀 돌려 주실 수 없을까요 May I trouble you for some money?
8 [미루다] postpone; defer; put off; let (a matter) wait[stand over]; hold over. ¶의안의 심의를 뒤로 ~ sidetrack the discussion off a bill // 그건 뒤로 돌리고 이 문제부터 논의합시다 Let us discuss this matter first, leaving that till later on.
9 [원인·책임을 전가하다] attribute to; ascribe (one's failure) to (fate); set[put] down (a matter) to (a person); impute (a crime) to (a person); shift (a responsibility on another's shoulders); lay[throw] (the blame on a person). ¶성공을 행운으로 ~ attribute[credit] one's success to luck // 영광을 하느님께 ~ bring glory to God // 그는 자기 책임을 내게 돌렸다 He shuffled of his responsibility upon[onto] my shoulder. // 너의 실패는 태만의 탓으로 돌려야 한다 Your negligence is responsible for[accounts for] your failure.
10 [전임시키다] transfer. ¶회계과로 ~ transfer (a person) to the accountant section // 총무과로 돌려지다 be transferred to the general affairs section.
11 [충당하다] appropriate (money) to [toward for] something; apply (money) to [toward] something; divert (a thing) to some other purpose; assign (to). ¶학비로 ~ apply (money) toward one's school expenses // 시의회는 5천만 원을 제설기 구입으로 돌렸다 The council appropriated fifty million won for the purchase of a new snowplow. // 그의 기부금은 도서비로 돌리게 되었다 His donation was earmarked for (the purchase of) books. // 혼수 비용으로 얼마나 돌리려고 합니까 How much money are you going to spend on your trousseau?
12 [가동하다] work; operate; run; drive; set [put] in motion. ¶기계를 ~ set a machine

in motion / work[operate] a machine.
13 〔쉬다〕 rest; repose (oneself); pause for breath. ¶잠시 숨을 ~ take[have] a rest[breather] // 한숨을 ~ breathe relief[easier] / breathe easy / get out of a difficult situation // 숨 좀 돌리고 나서 다시 시작하자 Let's have a little rest, and start again.
14 〔간주하다〕 take (as); treat (as). ¶농담으로 ~ take (something) as a joke / treat (a matter) as a joke // 백지로 돌리고 다시 시작하다 start afresh / start / start with a clean slate.

돌리다² 〔고비를 넘기다〕 improve; turn the corner; pass the crisis; take a turn for the better; be over the hump. ¶병이 ~ become[get] better / grow less serious // 열이 내리자 그녀는 병세를 돌렸다 She turned the corner with the fever passed.

돌림 1 〔교대〕 turn; rotation; something passed round. ¶~으로 by turns / alternately / by[in] rotation // ~ 차례로 one after another.(around) in order // ~으로 하는 것이 공평하다 Turn about is fair play. **2** an epidemic disease. ⇨돌림병(⇨돌림) **3** generations of the clan. ⇨항렬(行列)
● **돌림감기** (an epidemic of) influenza; a virus epidemic; (구어) flu(e); grippe. ¶~에 걸리다 suffer from influenza / be attacked by [contract] influenza / have an attack of influenza. **돌림 노래** 〔음〕 a troll; a round. **돌림병** an epidemic (disease). ⇨유행병(⇨유행) **돌림자** a letter of (a person's) given name which is common to the same generation of his kinsfolk.

돌멩이 a stone; (미) a rock; 〔자갈〕 a pebble; a piece of stone.
● **돌멩이질** stone-throwing[-slinging]. ¶~을 하다 stone / sling[throw] a stone (at) / pelt (a person) with stones / pelt at (a person).

돌무더기 a pile[mound / heap] of stones.
돌무덤 a stone grave; a cairn.
돌발(突發) an[a sudden] outbreak; (out-)burst. ¶폭동의 ~ the outbreak of a riot. **돌발하다** break out; occur[happen] suddenly; burst forth.
● **돌발 사고** an unforeseen[unexpected] accident[incident]; a sudden happening; the bombshell. ¶그것은 ~였다 It was an unexpected[unforeseen] accident.

돌발적(突發的) sudden; unforeseen; unexpected; unpredictable(예상할 수 없는). ¶~으로 suddenly / unforeseenly // 그 병은 ~으로 일어나기 때문에 아직 치료법도 알려져 있지 않다 The disease strikes[occurs] suddenly and no remedy is yet know.

돌밭 a stony[gravelly] place.
돌배 〔식〕 a wild pear.
돌변(突變) a sudden change[turn]; an accident. ¶형세의 ~에 놀라다 be amazed at a sudden turn of events. **돌변하다** change suddenly; take a sudden turn; (병세가) take a sudden turn for the worse; take a serious turn. ¶여인숙 주인의 태도가 돌변했다 The innkeeper suddenly changed his attitude.

돌보다 〔보살피다〕 care for; take (good) care of; look[see] after; attend to; tend. ¶어린이를 ~ nurse[look after] a baby / (미) baby-sit // 환자를 ~ care for[nurse / look after / tend to] a patient // 가정을 돌보지 않다 neglect[think little of] one's home // 그녀는 나병 환자를 돌보는 일에 평생을 바쳤다 She devoted her life to the care of lepers. // 그녀는 일에 매여 가정을 돌보지 않았다 She was so absorbed in her work that she neglected her home. // 바빠서 남의 일을 돌볼 겨를이 없다 I am too busy about[pay attention to] others. // 그는 그들을 위해서라면 자기 목숨도 돌보지 않았다 He was ready to risk his life for their sake. // 정원수는 돌보지 않아서 엉망이 되었다 The garden trees were ruined through neglect.

돌부리 a jagged edge[point] of a stone; a jack of rock.
돌부리를 차면 발부리만 아프다(속담) Don't kick against the pricks.

돌부처 1 〔석불(石佛)〕 a stone Buddhist image. **2** 〔감정이 없는 사람〕 a creature [man] with a stony heart; a man deaf to emotional appeals; 〔고집 센 사람〕 a obstinate[stubborn] person. ¶~같이 말이 없다 be as silent[taciturn] as a stone Buddha.

돌비(-碑) a tombstone; a gravestone; a stone monument[tablet / slab].
돌산(-山) 〔돌이 많은 산〕 a stone[rocky] mountain; 〔채석장〕 a quarry.
돌샘 a rock spring; a spring gushing out of stony ground.
돌소금 〔광〕 rock salt. ⇨암염(巖鹽)
돌솜 〔광〕 asbestos. ⇨석면(石綿)

돌아가다 1 〔집·고향 등으로 다시 가다〕 go [come] back (to); return; 〔물러가다〕 leave. ¶집으로 ~ go (back) home // 돌아갈 채비를 하다 prepare (oneself) for going home [back] // 우리는 왔던 길을 (되)돌아가야 했다 We had to go back the way we had come. // 이젠 돌아가야겠습니다 I must be going[be off] home now. / I must say good-bye now. // 그는 상심하여 고국으로 돌아갔다 He went home with a broken heart. // 손님들은 한두 사람씩 돌아갔다 The company dropped away. // 이젠 돌아가도 좋아 You may go [leave] now.

2 (원상태로 되다) return (to); be restored to; turn back; revert (to). ¶(죽어서) 흙으로 ~ fall back to dust // 스프링은 본래대로 돌아갔다 The spring has unwound itself. // 네 자리로 돌아가도 좋다 You may go back to your seat. // 조금 전의 자네 얘기로 돌아가지만 시간을 더 준다는 것에 동의할 수 없다 To return[Getting back] to what you said before, I don't agree that we should allow more time.

3 〔제대로 움직이다〕 work; operate. ¶잘 돌아가지 않다 fail to operate[work] properly / malfunction // 기계는 잘 돌아가고 있다 The machine is working[running] smoothly.

4 〔우회하다〕 go round (a place); make [take] a detour; go by[take] a roundabout way[route]. ¶산을 ~ go around a mountain // 그 길로 가면 멀리 돌아가게 된다 That road goes the long way (around).

5 〔죽다〕 die; be dead; pass away; depart from this life. ¶갑자기 (60세로) 돌아가시다 pass away[die] suddenly (at the age of sixty) // 아버님이 돌아가신 지 3년이 된다 It has been three years since my father died. // 그분은 돌아가셨다 He is no more[dead and gone]. // 돌아가신 아버지를 대신하여 감사드립니다 I thank you on behalf of my deceased [dead] father.

돌아눕다

6 [끝나다] come to; lead to; result[end / terminate] in; arrive at; be reduced to (ashes). ¶수포로 ~ end[go up] in smoke / come to naught[nothing] ~ prove abortive[fruitless] / get nothing for one's pain // 그의 노력은 실패로 돌아갔다 His efforts resulted[ended] in failure. // 하나는 형의 것이 되었으나 나머지는 전부 그의 손으로 돌아갔다 One went into his brother's possession, but all the rest fell into his hands.
7 [차례로 하다] do (a thing) by turns; take turns. ¶돌아가며 일하다[망보다] work[watch] by turns // 우리는 돌아가며 이야기를 했다 We took turns in telling a story.
8 [되어 가다] turn out; develop(발전하다). ¶이 일이 어떻게 돌아갈지 아직 모르겠다 It's further course is still uncertain.
9 [분배되다] go (a)round. ¶음식은 모두에게 돌아갈 만큼 있습니까 Is there enough food to go (a)round?

돌아눕다 turn (over) on one's side; roll. ¶잠결에 ~ turn over[roll] in bed / turn in bed [one's sleep].

돌아다니다 1 [쏘다니다] go[walk] about; wander[roam] about; walk to and fro; get [go / pace] around; (놀러) gad about; (맹수·도둑 등이) be on the prowl; [여행하다] (make a) tour; travel about. ¶이 리저리 ~ wander[tramp] from place to place / gad about // 서울 시내를 ~ go about Seoul // 사냥감을 찾아 숲 속을 ~ range a forest in search of game // 세계를 두루 ~ travel all over the world // 많은 택시가 손님을 찾아 돌아다니고 있었다 Many cabs were cruising about. // 그는 기타를 치며 (구걸하듯) 뒷골목을 돌아다녔다 He strolled about the back streets, playing his guitar (for what he could get). // 그 가난한 연예인은 집집마다 돌아다니며 노래를 불렀다 The poor entertainer sang from door to door.
2 [소문이] go the rounds; get about[abroad / around]; (병이) prevail; be prevalent. ¶…이라는 소문이 돌아다니고 있다 a rumor is abroad[in circulation] about ... // (병이) 돌아다니기 시작하다 become prevalent / break out.

돌아다보다 look back. ☞돌아보다1

돌아들다 come back; return; find one's back (to). ¶저녁이면 새들은 제 둥지로 돌아든다 In the evening the birds return[go home] to their nests.

돌아보다 1 [뒤를] look back (at); turn around; turn one's face[head]; (어깨 너머) look over one's shoulder. ¶홀끗 ~ cast a hasty glance behind[backward] / look back for a second // 그는 회전의자를 움직여서 돌아보았다 He spun about in his swivel.
2 [과거를 다시 생각해 보다] reflect[look back] (upon); recall; recollect; review; retrospect; reflect on[upon] oneself(반성하다). ¶과거를 돌아보면 on looking back upon[into] the past // 돌아보아 후회되는 것이 없다 have no regret for what one has done // 과거의 행복했던 날을 돌아보고 눈물을 흘렸다 Looking back upon past happy days, I shed tears.
3 [돌보다·고려하다] care for; look after; attend to; take notice of; have regard to; take into consideration; pay attention to. ¶그녀는 학생 따위는 돌아보지도 않았다 She wouldn't look twice at a mere student. / She considers mere students beneath her.
4 [살피며 돌다] go one's round; make a round; patrol; walk one's beat. ¶공장을 ~ go[visit] round a factory // (야경이) 밤에 바퀴 ~ go on one's rounds at night.

돌아서다 1 [뒤로 바꾸어 서다] turn away[the other way]; turn one's back on (a person); turn on one's heels; [방향을 바꾸다] turn around (toward); turn about. ¶적을 보고 ~ show one's heels / turn one's back upon / turn tail / beat a retreat // 그는 돌아서서 달아났다 He turned around and ran off. // 그는 갑자기 돌아서더니 강물로 뛰어들었다 He turned around suddenly and jumped into the river.
2 [등지다] turn one's back on; turn against; fall out[quarrel / disagree] with; break up with; become estranged[alienated] (from); dissent. ¶이젠 돌아서기에는 너무 늦다 It's too late to turn back now. // 그녀는 그에게서 돌아섰다 She gave him her back.
3 [(병세가) 나아 가다] improve; get better; take a turn for the better; be progressing favorably.

돌아앉다 sit the other way round; sit with one's back to a person.

돌아오다 1 [제자리로 도로 오다] come[get / be / turn] back; return. ¶돌아올 때에 on one's return / as one returns // 학교에서 돌아오는 길에 on one's way home from school // 제자리로 ~ return to one's seat // 늦게 ~ be late in coming home // 외국에서 ~ return from abroad[from a foreign country] // 오늘은 어느 때보다 일찍 돌아오겠습니다 I'll be [come] back earlier than usual today. // 극장에서 걸어서[차로] 돌아왔다 I walked[drove] home from the theater. // 돌아오는 길에 서점에 들렀다 I dropped in at a bookstore on my way home. // 그는 미국으로 가서 다시는 돌아오지 않았다 He went to America never to return. // 돌아오는 길을 잃었다 I lost my way back. // 9회 초에 두 사람이 돌아와서 동점이 되었다 In the top half of the ninth inning two runners came home[scored] to tie the game.
2 [차례·때가 닥치다] return; come round; come again. ¶차례가 ~ one's turn comes (round) // 노래할 차례가 돌아왔다 My turn to sing came. // 마침내 그의 차례가 돌아왔다 At last his turn came (round).
3 [우회하다] come the round about way (to); make a detour. ¶일부러 ~ make a deliberate detour // 뒷문으로 돌아와 주십시오 Step around to the back door.
4 [결과 등이] fall (up)on; be imposed on; be brought. ¶책임이 ~ a responsibility falls on one's shoulders // 부담은 모두 내게 돌아왔다 I must bear all the expenses.
5 [회복되다] return (to); recover; revert (to). ¶정상으로 ~ return to normal(cy) // 제정신이 ~ come to (oneself) / recover one's senses.
6 [배당되다] fall (to); be allotted [apportioned]. ¶나에게는 이것밖에 돌아오지 않았다 This much has fallen to my lot.

돌연(突然) suddenly; abruptly; unexpectedly; on[all of] a sudden; all at once; without notice[warning]. ¶~ 나타나다 // ~ 슬픈 소식이 날아왔다 The sad news came as a surprise.

돌연변이(突然變異) [생] (a) mutation. ¶~에

의한 mutant // ~를 일으키는 mutagenic.
● 돌연변이설 the theory of mutation.
돌연사(突然死) a sudden death.
돌연히(突然-) sudden; abrupt; unexpected; unlooked-for. ¶돌연한 출발[죽음] an abrupt[a sudden] departure[death] // 돌연한 방문 a surprise visit / a sudden call. **돌연히** suddenly; abruptly. ⇨*돌연*
돌이키다 1 [고개를 돌리다] turn[look] round; turn one's face[head] / face about.
2 (원상으로 돌아가다) get back; regain; recover; restore; retrieve; undo. ¶돌이킬 수 없는 irrevocable / irretrievable / irreparable // 돌이킬 수 없는 과거 the irrevocable past / 건강을 ~ recover[regain] one's health / be restored to (one's usual health) // 돌이킬 수 없는 실수를 저지르고 말았다 I made an irreparable[irrevocable] mistake. // 이미 저지른 일은 돌이킬 수 없다 What is done is done. / We cannot undo the past.
3 [회상하다] look back upon; retrospect; review; [반성하다] reflect on oneself. ¶돌이켜 생각하니 (up)on second thought(s) / on (further) reflection / to look at the matter from a different angle // 과거를 돌이켜 보다 look back upon the past / think back to the past days // 돌이켜 보아 후회될 바가 없다 I have no regret for what one has done // 어제의 내 행동을 돌이켜 생각하니 부끄러운 생각이 들었다 I reflect on[examined] the way I had behaved the day before and felt ashamed.
4 (마음을) change (one's mind); reverse (a decision); make (a person) change (his mind); [재고하다] think better of; reconsider; reflect on. ¶결심을 ~ desist from one's original intention / give up one's resolution
돌입(突入) inrush; a thrust (into). **돌입하다** rush[dash / run] in; charge[plunge] in. ¶적진에 ~ dash[charge] into the enemy's position / (비행기 등이) dive into the enemy's position // 파업에 ~ go[come out] on (a) strike / walk out // 노조는 파업에 돌입했다 The labor union rushed[plunged] headlong into a strike. // 경찰은 그들의 은신처에 돌입했다 The police broke[stormed] into the gang's hideout. // 세계는 놀랄 만한 속도로 전쟁에 돌입했다 The world was rushed [plunged] into war with startling velocity.
돌잔치 a baby's first-birthday party[feast]; the birthday party for one-year-old baby.
돌장이 a (stone) mason. ⇨*석수(石手)*
돌쟁이 [첫돌이 된 아이] a one-year-old baby.
돌절구 a stone mill[mortar].
돌절구도 밑 빠질 때가 있다(속담) Nothing lasts forever.
돌진(突進) a rush; a dash; an onrush; a charge. **돌진하다** rush (at / for / to); (make a) dash (at); make a dart (at); charge (at); storm. ¶돌진하는 차 an onrushing car // 무모하게 ~ rush headlong // 탱크는 돌더미 속으로 돌진했다 The tank smashed[slammed] into the rubble. // 그들은 적진을 향해 돌진했다 They rushed[pushed on] into the enemy camp. // 그 배는 폭풍이 부는 바다로 돌진했다 The ship plowed (its way) through the stormy sea.
돌쩌귀 a hinge; a butt. ¶수톨쩌귀 the pintle of a hinge / a pivot // 암톨쩌귀 the gudgeon of a hinge / a pan.

돌쩌귀에 녹이 슬지 않는다(속담) A rolling stone gathers no moss.; Standing pools gather filth.
돌출(突出) [쑥 내밂] projection; protrusion; [두드러짐] prominence; jutting[popping] out. **돌출하다** project; protrude; jut[pop] out. ¶돌출된 projected / projecting / prominent // 돌출한 바위 protruding[projecting] rock // 돌출한 개구리의 눈 the protruding [protuberant] eyeballs of a frog // 그 지점은 바다에 돌출해 있다 The point juts[sticks] out into the sea.
● **돌출부** a projecting part; a salient (part); [군] a salience; a bulge; (전선의) a perimeter; [동][식] a ramus (pl. -mi); [지] (산·바위 등의) a spur.
돌층계(-層階) (층계의) a stone step(한 단); (a flight of) stone steps; a stone stairway. ¶~를 오르다[내리다] go up[down] the stone steps // ~를 올라가면 공원에 이른다 A flight of stone steps leads (you) to a park.
돌탑(-塔) a stone tower; a pagoda.
돌파(突破) 1 [뚫고 나감] breaking through; a breakthrough. ¶중앙 ~ a frontal breakthrough. **돌파하다** break[smash] through; breach. ¶적의 방어진을 ~ break through the enemy's defenses // 봉쇄를 ~ run a blockade // 우리는 적의 방어진을 돌파했다 We broke through the enemy('s) defenses(▶ 스포츠에서는 the opposition's 또는 our opponents).
2 (곤란 등의) surmounting. **돌파하다** surmount (a difficulty); overcome; get over. ¶입시의 난관을 ~ (successfully) pass a difficult entrance examination (to a college).
3 (수량의) passing; exceed. **돌파하다** pass; exceed; top (..., tons); rise above. ¶5,000 원대를 ~ pass[break] the 5,000 won mark [line] // 금값이 600달러를 돌파했다 The price of gold broke[rose above / passed] the six hundred dollar mark.
● **돌파구** a breach; a breakthrough. ¶~를 만들다 breach (a barrier) / break through / find a way out // 과학자들은 이 발견이 암 퇴치의 일대 ~가 되리라고 믿고 있다 Scientists believe that this discovery will prove a great breakthrough in the fight to conquer cancer.
돌파 작전 [군] breakthrough operations; a breakthrough.
돌팔매 a throwing stone.
● **돌팔매질** stone throwing[slinging]. ¶~을 하다 throw[sling / hurl / fling] a stone (at).
돌팔이 an itinerant trader; a wandering tradesman[semiprofessional].
● **돌팔이 의사** a quack (doctor); a traveling healer.
돌풍(突風) a gust (of wind); a blast. ¶~이 불어서 불은 옆집으로 번졌다 Fanned by the (sudden gusts of) wind, the fire spread to the next house.
돔 [반구형 지붕] dome. ¶철근 ~ an iron dome // 철근 ~ 경기장 a steel-roofed stadium[diamond / bowl / amphitheater].
돕다 1 [조력하다] help (a person with); help (a person (to) do)(▶ 지금은 《영》뿐만 아니라 《미》에서도 특히 구어체에서는 to를 생략함); assist; aid(▶ assist, aid는 help보다 격식 차린 말); give[lend / reach out] a helping hand; lend one's aid (to). ¶남을 ~ help a person // 일을 ~ help (a person) in[with]

돗바늘

his work.// 한 노인이 버스를 타시도록 도와 드렸다 I helped an old man (to) board a bus.(▶ 미국에서는 보통 목적어 to 이하의 부정사를 to를 생략함)//그를 도와 외투를 입혀 주었다 I helped him put his overcoat on.//잠깐만 도와줘 Help me for a minute. / Give me a hand.//무엇을 도와 드릴까요 Is there anything I can do to help you? / Can I do anything to help you? / May I help you? / Can I lend you a hand?//이 무거운 트렁크를 들어 올리도록 도와주세요 Help me lift this heavy trunk.
2 [구제하다] relieve; give relief to; give (a person) a helping. ¶가난한 사람을 ~ relieve the poor / help the needy ¶곤경에 처한 사람을 ~ help a person out of difficulties.
3 [기여·촉진하다] contribute (to); promote; conduce to; be conducive to. ¶생활비를 ~ give [contribute / chip in] some money for living expenses // 성공을 ~ contribute to success // 사회의 발달을 ~ promote the progress of society // 이 운동은 아동의 발육을 크게 돕는다 This sport will greatly promote the physical development of children.// 이 약은 소화를 돕는다 This medicine helps the digestion.

돗바늘 a darning[matting] needle; a darner.

돗자리 a (rush) mat; [짚함석] (rush) matting. ¶꽃~ a figured mat // ~를 깔다 spread a mat (on a floor) // ~를 짜다 make[weave] a mat.

동 1 [조리·이치] reason; logic; coherence; (일관성) consistency. ¶~이 닿는 요구 a reasonable demand ¶그가 말하는 바는 ~이 맞지 않는다 He is not governed by logic. **2** [동안] a period; a term; an interval; a time limit; a span. ¶전기 요금 받으러 오는 것이 이번은 좀 ~이 뜨다 They are later than usual this time in collecting the electricity bill. **3** (옷의) cuffs. ¶끝~ [소맷~] the cuffs of a sleeve. **4** [줄기] a stalk. ¶상추 ~ a lettuce stalk.

동(을) 대다 1 [조리가 서게 하다] make (one's story) consistent[resonable / coherent]; try to give a show of truth; fix (it) up; make (it) look plausible. ¶이야기를 ~ make a story consistent[plausible]. **2** [이어지게 하다] make follow in regular succession. ¶이 쌀을 가지고는 연말까지 동을 댈 수가 없을 것 같다 I am afraid we shall have run out of rice before the end of this year. / The rice won't last until the end of the year.

동(東) east(약어 E). ¶~ 아시아 East Asia // 유럽 East Europe // ~이 틀 무렵에 at the break of dawn / at the first sign of daylight // ~이 튼다 The eastern sky is growing light.

동에 번쩍 서에 번쩍(속담) make frequent appearance here and there; appear in one place and then suddenly appear in another like a flash of lightning.

동(洞) [행정 구역] a *dong*; [마을] a village.

동(銅) copper. ⇨구리 ¶~ 파이프 a copper pipe.

동(棟) [집채의 수를 세는 말]. ¶3~ three buildings[houses] // 1(호)~의 2층 the second[(영) first] floor of building No. 1 // 서울 아파트 7~ 120호 Rm. 120, Seoul Apt. No. 7.

동(同) [위와 같은] the same; the said; [똑같은] equal; [마찬가지의] similar. ¶~ 회사 the same company / (the) said corporation // ~ 세대의 사람들 people of the same generation / one's contemporaries // ~ 대학에서는 in[(미) at] the (above-mentioned) college [college mentioned above].

동가식서가숙하다(東家食西家宿-) lead a vagabond[wandering] life; live as a tramp.

동감(同感) [같은 의견] agreement (in opinion); concurrence; [같은 느낌] the same sentiment; sympathy. ¶그 점은 전적으로 너와 ~이다 I quite agree with you on that point. / You are quite right about that. // 그 점에 대해서는 저도 ~입니다 I agree with you on that. // 그 사건에 관해서는 전적으로 너와 ~이다 I completely share your feelings [I feel exactly the same way] about the incident. **동감하다** [같은 느낌이다] sympathize [think] with; feel the same way (as); share (a person's) feeling; [같은 의견이다] agree (concur) with; be of the same opinion; see eye to eye (with a person over a issue). ¶그것에 대해서는 동감할 수 없다 I can't sympathize[am not in sympathy] with you there [about that].

동갑(同甲) [같은 나이] the same age; [나이가 같은 사람] a person of the same age; (one's) contemporary. ¶우리는 ~이다 We are of the same age. // 나는 당신과 ~이오 I am (of) the same age as you are.
● **동갑내기** one's age-fellow.

동강 a piece; a part. ¶~이 나다 break into pieces[parts] // 칼이 두 ~ 났다 A sword was broken into two pieces. // 그 배는 바위에 부딪혀서 ~이 났다 The ship has gone to pieces on the rocks.

동강동강 into pieces; piece by piece. ¶~ 자르다 cut (a stick) into pieces // (엿가락이) ~ 부러지다 (a rice-candy bar) be broken into pieces.

동거(同居) **1** [함께 삶]. **동거하다** live together [with]; live in the same house [room] (with). ¶나는 숙부 댁에서 동거하고 있다 I live with my uncle[uncle's family]. // 그 집에서는 세 가족이 동거하고 있다 Three families live together in the same house. **2** (남녀의) cohabitation. ¶그는 그녀와 반 년 동안 ~ 생활을 했다 He cohabited[(미국 구어) shacked up] with her for half a year. // 젊은 남녀의 ~ 생활에 대해서 어떻게 생각하십니까 What do you think of cohabitation of young men and women? **동거하다** cohabit (with).
● **동거인** a person living together with one; an inmate; a cohabitant.

동격(同格) **1** [같은 지위] the same rank [status / standing]; an equal footing; equality. ¶그와 ~인 사람 His equal // 그는 송 씨와 ~이다 He is of the same rank as Mr. Song. // 그와 ~으로 대해 주면 좋겠다 I'd like to be treated on an equal footing[basis] with him. **2** [언] apposition. ¶~의 appositive // ~이다 be in apposition with ... // 이 명사는 주어와 ~이다 This noun is in apposition with [to] the subject.
● **동격 명사** [언] a noun in apposition. **동격어** [언] an appositive.

동결(凍結) freezing; a freeze; [물가 [임금]의] a price [wage] freeze / a freeze on prices[wages] // 임금 ~ 정책 a wage-freeze policy // 자산 ~ freezing of assets [credits] // ~을 해제하다 unfreeze. **동결하다**

freeze (up); be frozen. ¶임금과 물가를 90일 간 ~ impose a 90-day freeze on wages and prices // 섭씨 0도 이하에서 물은 동결한다 Water freezes at temperatures of 0℃ and below. → 자산이 동결되었다[자산의 동결이 풀렸다] The assets were frozen[were unfrozen]. // 공공요금이 1년간 동결되고 있다 Public utility charges have been frozen for one year.

동경(東經) the east longitude. ¶~ 180도 동 180th degree of east longitude // 그 도시는 ~ 21도 18분에 위치하고 있다 The city is located at 21 degrees 18 minutes of east longitude.

동경(憧憬) yearning; longing; aspiration; a yen; 〔숭배〕 adoration; admiration. ¶그는 소년들의 ~의 대상이다 He is the object of the boy's adoration. **동경하다** yearn[hanker] after[for]; long[sigh] for(▶ long은 멀리 있는 것, 얻기 어려운 것을 갈망하다, yearn은 다정함·애정으로 그리워하다); aspire after. ¶동경하는 남성 the man of one's dreams // 동경하는 직업 a longed-for[coveted] job // 내가 동경하는 작가 a writer I admire // 도시 생활을 ~ be attracted by town life / yearn after city life // 자유를 몹시 동경하고 있다 have a great yearning[longing] for liberty // 프랑스의 화가들을 ~ admire[be attracted by] French artists // 그녀는 뭇사람이 동경하는 미스 유니버스의 영예를 차지했다 She won the much coveted title of Miss Universe. // 그는 바다를 동경하고 있다 He has a longing for the sea. // 소녀들은 모두 그 테니스 코치를 동경하고 있다 All the girls have a crush on the tennis coach. (▶ 이성에 대하여 long for, yearn for 라고 하면 육체관계를 원한다는 뜻이 됨)

동계(冬季) 〔관형어적〕 winter(ly).
● **동계 방학** / **동계 휴가** the winter holidays [vacation]. **동계 올림픽** the winter Olympics [Olympic Games].

동계(同系) ¶~의 akin / of the same stock / cognate // 이들 부족은 모두 ~이다 All these tribes are of the same descent[stock]. / All these tribes are related to one another.
● **동계 회사** an affiliated company.

동고동락하다(同苦同樂−) share one's lot (with another); share the sweets[pleasures] and bitters[pains] of life (with). ¶우리는 동고동락해 온 사이다 We have been great friends both in joy and sorrow.

동공(瞳孔) the pupil (of the eye). ⇨"눈동자 ¶~이 열려 있다 The pupils of the eyes are dilated.
● **동공 반사** a pupillary reflex. **동공 축소** contraction of the pupil; miosis[myosis]. **동공 확대** dilatation of the pupil; mydriasis.

동광(銅鑛) 〔구리 광산〕 a copper mine; 〔구리를 함유한 광석〕 copper ore; crude copper.

동구(東歐) Eastern Europe. ⇨"동유럽
● **동구권** the East European bloc.

동구(洞口) the entrance[approach] to a village; a village entrance. ¶~ 밖 (on) the outskirts of a village.

동굴(洞窟) 〔산허리 등의 굴〕 a cave; 〔지하의 커다란〕 〔문어〕 a cavern; a grotto (pl. ~s, ~es). ¶~이 많은 산허리 a cavernous hillside // ~에 사는 동물 a cave dweller / a caveman // ~의 입구 a cave mouth // ~을 **탐험하다** explore a cave[cavern] / (미) spelunk.
● **동굴 벽화** a wall painting in a cave. **동굴 탐험** (미) spelunking; (영) potholing.

동궁(東宮) 〔왕세자〕 the Crown Prince; 〔세자궁〕 the palace of the Crown Prince.

동그라미 1 〔원〕 a circle; a circlet(작은). ¶~로 싸다 enclose (a word) with a circle / encircle // ~를 **그리다** draw a circle // 옳은 답에 ~를 치다 mark a correct answer with a circle / mark an answer "Good" // 담배 연기로 ~를 만들다 puff (out)[make] a ring of smoke / blow a smoke ring. 2 〔돈〕 lucre; (속어) chink; (속어) the needful.
● **동그라미표** the circle symbol.

동그랗다 (원형의) round; rotund; (고리 모양의) circular; (공 모양의) globular; spherical. ¶**동그랗게** round / in a circle // **동그란** 눈 round eyes // **동그란** 얼굴 a round[moon] face // 작고 **동그란** 눈깔사탕 small round pieces of candy // **동그랗게** 앉다 sit in a circle // 종이를 **동그랗게** 자르다 cut paper into a circle // 지구는 완전히 **동그랗지는** 않다 The earth is not a perfect sphere.

동그래지다 become round; round.

동그마니 〔홀로〕 lonely; solitarily; alone; lonesomely. ¶강가에 ~ 앉아 있다 sit all alone by the riverside.

동그스름하다 somewhat round[circular]; roundish. ¶**동그스름한** 얼굴 a roundish face.

동글납작하다 round and flat. ¶**동글납작한** 얼굴 a round and flat face // 떡을 **동글납작하게** 만들다 make rice cake round and flat.

동글다 round; circular. ⇨"둥글다

동글동글 ⇨"둥글둥글1

동급(同級) 〔같은 등급〕 the same rank[level]; equality; 〔같은 학급〕 the same class[grade].
● **동급생** a classmate; a classfellow. ¶우리는 ~이다 We are in the same class. / We are classmates. // 그녀는 남자 ~들의 동경의 대상이었다 She was the idol of the boys in her class.

동기(冬期) 〔관형어적〕 winter; wintry.
● **동기 강습** a winter school[class].

동기(同氣) 〔형제자매〕 siblings; brothers and sisters.
● **동기간** sibling relationship. ¶~의 우애 brotherly[sisterly] affection / fraternal love // ~이다 be siblings / be brothers[sisters] / be brother(s) and sister(s).

동기(同期) 1 〔같은 시기〕 the same period. ¶ 작년 ~와 비교해서 매출이 줄었다 Sales have fallen off (as) compared with the corresponding[same] period of last year. // 금년의 1월부터 3월까지는 작년의 ~에 비해서 자동차 사고가 많았다 There were more car accidents in the first three months of this year than in the same period of last year. 2 a classmate. ⇨"동기생(⇨동기)
● **동기생** (같은 반의) a classmate; (같은 해의 졸업생) graduates in the same class[year]. ¶ 우리는 입사 ~이다 We entered the company in the same year.

동기(動機) 1 a motive; an inducement; an incentive. (▶ motive는 심리적·감정적인 자극, incentive는 외부적인 자극을 말하며 특히 보수(報酬)를 의미함) ¶행위[범죄]의 ~ the motive of a deed[crime] // 불순한 ~ a mixed [an ulterior] motive // 부정한 ~ a sinister motive // 개인적[이기적] ~에서 out of[from] personal[selfish] motives // …이 ~가 되어 prompted[motivated / actuated] by … // 금전상의 ~에서 from mercenary motives // 범죄의

동기 ~는 원한이었다 The motive for the crime was a grudge. / The crime was motivated by a grudge.// 어떤 ~로 성냥갑 수집을 시작했습니까 What induced you to begin collecting matchboxes?// 경찰은 범죄의 ~를 조사하고 있다 The police are inquiring into the motive for the crime. **2** [음] a motif.
- **동기 분석 / 동기 조사** [경] motivation(al) research.

동기 (銅器) a copper[bronze] utensil; copperware.
- **동기 시대** the Bronze Age.

동나다 [물건이 바닥나다] be exhausted; be used up; be consumed; be out; [상품이 다 팔리다] sell out; be sold out of stock. ¶식량이 동났다 We have run out of provisions. // 재고품이 동났다 We are cleared of all stock. // 마침 그 물건은 동났습니다 That article is unluckily out of stock. // 휘발유가 동났다 We are getting out of gas[gasoline]. / The gas is running short.

동남 (東南) the southeast. ¶~의 southeast / southeastern // ~으로 southeastward(s).
- **동남아시아** Southeast Asia. **동남향** facing southeast.

동냥 [구걸] begging; mendicancy(탁발승의); [구걸한 돈·물건] an alms; (미) a handout. ¶~ 다니다 go (about) begging / go around as a beggar // ~을 주다 give food[money] to a beggar // ~을 받다 receive food[money] as a beggar. **동냥하다** beg (food, money, etc.); beg one's bread.

동냥은 안 주고 쪽박만 깬다 (속담) only find faults with (a person) without complying with (his) request.
- **동냥아치** a beggar (who is trying to keep up appearances); a mendicant. **동냥질** begging; mendicancy.

동네 [사는 근처] the neighborhood; the (whole) town; the (whole) street; [마을] a [one's] village. ¶큰 ~ a large village // 작은 ~ a hamlet // ~ 어귀에서 on the outskirts of a village // ~의 소문 (a) neighborhood gossip.
- **동네 사람** (단수) a villager; (복수) village folk[people]; (집합적) the whole village. ¶온 ~이 그것을 구경하러 나왔다 The whole village turned out to see it. **동네 어른** elders of one's village.

동네북 a doormat. ¶난 ~인가 보다 I always feel like a doormat.

동년 (同年) [같은 해] the same year; [같은 나이] the same age. ¶그는 2000년 2월에 대학을 졸업하고 ~ 3월에 중학교 교사가 되었다 He graduated from college in February 2000 and became a teacher at a junior high school in March of the same year.
- **동년배** (about) the same age bracket. ¶그녀는 나와 ~이다 She is about as old as I am. / She is about my (own) age. / She is about the same age as me[I am].

동녘 (東−) the east; the eastward. ¶~ 하늘 the eastern sky // ~ 하늘이 밝아 온다 Day [Morning] dawns. / The light of day is peeping in the east.

동댕이치다 1 [내던지다] fling[throw / cast / hurl] (something) at. ¶화가 나서 재떨이[책]를 ~ fling an ash tray[a book] in anger. **2** [그만두다] throw[give] up; (구어) chuck up. ¶하던 일을 중간에서 ~ give up one's work halfway through.

동동 (발을) jumping up and down (from cold / impatience). ¶발을 ~ 구르다 stamp (one's feet) on the ground // 추워서 발을 ~ 구르다 jump up and down from cold // 발을 ~ 구르며 분해하다 stamp with vexation [chagrin].

동동거리다 jump up and down; stamp [(구어) stomp] one's feet (on the ground); beat [thump] one's shoes (on the floor). ¶분해서 발을 ~ stamp with vexation[chagrin] / be hopping mad // 돈을 달라고 발을 ~ ask for money beating one's shoes (on the floor) // 우리는 발이 시려서 동동거리며 기다려야 했다 We had to wait, stamping to keep warm.

동등 (同等) [같음] equality; the same rank(지위가); equivalence; par; parity. **동등하다** equal; coordinate. (▶ equal은 어떤 점에서 완전히 같다는 것을, equivalent는 비교해서 같은 가치가 있다는 것을 뜻함) ¶동등한 권리 equal rights // 동등한 입장에서 on an equal footing // 대학 졸업 또는 그와 동등한 실력을 가진 사람 college graduates and those of equal ability / those with a degree or equivalent qualifications // 동등하게 equally / on the square / coordinately //…과 동등한 조건으로 on equal terms with … // 어른과 어린이를 동등하게 다루다 treat adults and children equally // 이 회사에서는 남녀를 동등하게 취급한다 In this firm men and women are treated equally.

동떨어지다 1 [멀리 떨어지다] be far apart (from); be remote (from); be far[distant] (from); be divorced (from). ¶동떨어진 곳 a remote [an out-of-the-way] place // 인가에서 동떨어진 집 a house far (apart) from a village [in an out-of-the-way place] / a solitary house // 벌판 한복판에 집 한 채만이 동떨어져 서 있었다 There was a house standing all by itself in the middle of the plain. **2** [심히 다르다] be quite different (from). ¶나는 내 취미와 아주 동떨어진 일을 하고 있다 I am engaged in a work quite alien to my taste. // 그의 증언은 진실과는 동떨어져 있었다 His testimony was far removed[quite different] from the truth. // 그 부부는 성격상 아주 동떨어져 있었다 The couple were quite unlike each other in character. // 그의 예측은 결국 전혀 동떨어진 것임이 판명되었다 His estimate proved to be wide of[way off] the mark. // 이 번역은 원문의 뜻과 동떨어져 있다 This translation is much removed from the original meaning.

동떨어진 소리 a statement wide of the mark(거리가 먼); an absurd[a nonsensical] remark(어리석은). ¶자네 얘기는 그것과는 ~야 What you say is irrelevant to it.

동뜨다 1 [뛰어나다] superior; surpassing; outstanding; exceptional; extraordinary; far better[ahead]. ¶동뜨게 by far / by a long way / far[out] and away / outstandingly / exceptionally // 영어를 동뜨게 잘한다 be exceptionally good at English // 이 학급에서 ~ be out and away[by far] the best student in the class // 그는 동뜨게 재간이 있는 사람이다 He has an exceptional[extraordinary] talent. **2** [사이가 뜨다] have a space between; have a longer interval than usual; be few and far between; be far apart. ¶밤

늦어 버스가 동뜬다 The hour is late and the buses are few and far between.

동락하다(同樂-) enjoy together; share one's joy (with); participate in (a person's) joys.

동란(動亂) an upheaval; (agitation; disturbance; commotion; a riot. ¶한국 ~ the Korean War // ~을 일으키다[진압하다] start [put down] a riot [disturbance].

동량(同量) [같은 분량] the same amount [quantity]; an equal amount [quantity]. ¶~의 소금과 설탕 an equal amount of salt and sugar.

동력(動力) [물] electric power; (motive) power; dynamic (force). ¶~으로 움직이는 power-driven (machine) // ~을 공급하다 supply (electric) power (to a factory) // ~으로 움직이다 move under (motor) power.
● **동력계**(-計) (엔진 등의) a dynamometer.
동력선(-船) a power vessel; a powerboat.
동력원(-源) a power source. **동력 전달 장치** a power transmission device.

동렬(同列) 1 [같은 줄] the same line [row] (▶line은 종렬, row는 횡렬). 2 [같은 정도·수준·지위] the same rank. ¶중역과 ~의 사람들 those who are of the same rank as company directors // 그 두 사람을 ~로 다룰 수는 없다 We can't treat those two as equals.

동록(銅綠) green [copper] rust; verdigris; patina (청동기의). ¶~이 슬다 form green rust.

동료(同僚) a colleague; an associate (일과 연관이 있는); a co-worker (함께 일하는); a fellow worker (직장의). ¶그는 직장 ~들과 자주 술 마시러 간다 He often goes drinking with his fellow workers at the office.

동류(同類) [같은 종류] the same kind [class / category]; [비슷한 것] a like (of); [동패] an accomplice; a gang. ¶~의 of the same class / similar // …과 ~다 belong to the same class with / be in the same category as // 그들은 다 ~다 They are all of a sort. // 그도 그 ~에 틀림없다 He must be one of the set [party].

동률(同率) the same percentage [rate]; a tie. ¶우리는 그들과 ~로 선두에 나섰다 We moved into a tie with them for first place.

동리(洞里) ⇨마을1

동마루(棟-) the ridge of a tiled roof.

동맥(動脈) [생] the artery. ¶대~ the main artery // 경(頸)~ the carotid artery // ~의 arterial // 네덜란드에선 수로가 상업의 ~이다 In Holland waterways are the arteries of commerce.
● **동맥 경화증** hardening of the arteries; [의] arteriosclerosis.

동맹(同盟) an alliance; a union; a league. ¶군사 ~ a military alliance // 방위 ~ a defense alliance // 신성 ~ (역사상의) the Holy Alliance // …과 ~을 맺다 conclude [from / enter into] an alliance with … // ~을 파기하다 renounce an alliance. **동맹하다** ally (oneself) with; form [enter into] an alliance with; be allied with; league [confederate] with.
● **동맹국** an ally; an allied power. ¶비~ a nonaligned [an unaligned / an uncommitted] nation [country]; the allies. **동맹 파업 / 동맹 휴업** a (labor) strike; a turnout; (미) a walkout. ¶시한부 [무기한] ~ a strike for a definite [an indefinite] period // 총~ a general strike // ~ 중인 노동자 the workmen on strike. **동맹 파업자** a striker; (영) a turnout. **동맹 휴학 / 동맹 휴교** a strike of students; a school [college] strike.

동메달(銅-) a copper medal (작은); a copper medallion (큰); (경기에서) a bronze medal.

동면(冬眠) winter sleep; hibernation. ¶뱀은 ~ 중이다 Snakes are hibernating [in hibernation] now. // 개구리가 ~에서 눈을 떴다 The frog awoke hibernation. **동면하다** hibernate. ¶동면하고 있다 be in hibernation / lie dormant // 뱀은 동면한다 Snakes hibernate in winter.
● **동면 동물** hibernating [hibernant] animals; hibernants.

동명(同名) the same name. ¶~인 사람 a person with the same name // 이것과 ~인 소설 a novel with the same title as this one.
● **동명이인**(-異人) a person of the same name; a namesake; a homonym. ¶그는 ~이 있음이 밝혀졌다 He was found (to be) a different person of the same name.

동명사(動名詞) [언] a gerund. ¶~의 gerundial.

동무 [친구] a friend; (구어) a pal; (구어) a chum; a mate; a companion. ¶길~ a fellow traveler // 말~ a companion to talk with // ~가 되다 become [make] friends with a person / consider a person a friend // ~를 삼다 make a friend of a person / consider a person a friend // ~가 없다 have no companion [friend] / be companionless / be friendless // ~ 삼아 나도 가겠소 I'll come to keep you company.

동문(同文) [같은 글] (of) an identical text; [같은 문자] the same script. ¶~의 편지를 두 통 보내다 send a message in duplicate // 이하 ~ The following sentences say as the above.

동문(同門) 1 [동창] a fellow pupil [student / disciple]; a classmate; [졸업생] an alumnus (pl. -ni); an alumna (pl. -nae) (여자). ¶~의 학자 scholars who studied under the same teacher. 2 [같은 문중] the same clan; [같은 문중 사람] a clansman; a clanswoman (여자).
● **동문회** an alumni association; an old boys' association.

동문서답(東問西答) an irrelevant answer; an incoherent reply. ¶자네 말은 아주 ~이군 What you say is irrelevant. **동문서답하다** give an irrelevant [incoherent] answer to a question. ¶우리 동문서답하고 있군 I talk of chalk, and you talk of cheese.

동문수학하다(同門受學-) study under the same teacher [master] (with).

동물(動物) an animal; [생물] a (living) creature; [짐승] a beast; [집합적] animal life. ¶고등 [하등] ~ the higher [lower] animals / (개의) ~ a high [low] animal // 육식 [초식] ~ a carnivorous [herbivorous] animal // 태생 ~ a viviparous animal // ~ 취급하다 treat (a person) like a beast // ~을 기르다 [길들이다] keep [domesticate] animals // ~을 애호하다 be kind to animals.
● **동물계** the animal kingdom. **동물성** animal nature; animality; bestiality. ¶~ 단백질 animal protein // ~ 식품 animal food. **동물 애호가** an animal lover. **동물원** zoological gardens; (구어) a zoo; (영업용의) a menag-

동물적

erie. ¶그는 아이들을 ~에 데리고 갔다 He took the children to the zoo. **동물학** zoology. **동물학자** zoologist. **동물화**(-畫) an animal painting.

동물적(動物的) animal; brutal; beastly. ¶~본능 an animal instinct // ~ 충동 a brute impulse.

동민(洞民) the inhabitants of a *dong*; people of a community; the villagers; the village folk.

동바리 (마루의) a supporting post; (갱도의) mine timber; a mine pillar; a pit prop.

동박새 [동] a white-eye; a silver-eye.

동반(同伴) company. ¶~으로 accompanied by ... // 그는 가족 ~이다 He is accompanied by his family. // 그는 부인 ~으로 회합에 참석했다 He attended the meeting, accompanied by his wife. **동반하다** accompany; go (in company) with; go in (a person's) company. ¶부인을 동반해 주십시오 Please bring your wife with you.

● **동반자** one's companion. **동반 자살** (남녀의) a double suicide; a lovers suicide.

동반구(東半球) the Eastern hemisphere.

동방(東方) the east. ¶~의 east / eastern // ~으로 to the eastward // 빛은 ~으로부터 Light from the East.

● **동방예의지국** the country of courteous people in the East; Korea.

동방(東邦) [동쪽 나라] an eastern country; [한국] Korea.

동방화촉(洞房華燭) sharing bed on the bridal [first] night.

동배(同輩) one's equal; a social equal; an associate; a colleague; a comrade. ¶~ 중 뛰어나다 rise above one's fellows // 우리는 ~간이다 We are equals.

동백(冬柏) camellia seeds.

● **동백기름** / **동백유** camellia oil (used to dress hair); **동백꽃** a camellia flower. **동백나무** [식] a camellia.

동병상련하다(同病相憐-) Fellow sufferers sympathize with one another.; Grief is best pleased with grief's company.

동복(冬服) winter clothes[clothing]; winter wear; a winter suit; a winter dress(부인의); a winter jacket(학생의). ¶그는 ~ 차림으로 나타났다 He appeared in winter clothes.

동복(同腹) children born of the same mother. ¶~의 uterine.

● **동복누이** a sister born of the same mother; (아버지가 다른) a half sister. **동복형제** uterine brothers; brothers of the same venter[mother].

동봉하다(同封-) enclose. ¶동봉한 편지 the enclosed letter // 이 편지에 저의 사진을 동봉합니다 I enclose my photograph in this letter. // 2백 달러 수표를 동봉합니다 I send you here with a check for $200. / Enclosed please find a check for two hundred dollars. // 추천장 2통을 동봉합니다 We enclose [Enclosed are] two letters of recommendation.

동부 [식] a (ripe) cowpea; a black-eyed pea; a southern pea.

동부(東部) the eastern part; the east; (미국의) the East. ¶~의 eastern // ~의 여러 주 (미국의) the Eastern States // (미국) ~의 주민 [출신자] an Easterner // ~로 가다 go (to) east // 공장은 시의 ~에 있다 The factory lies in the eastern part of the city.

● **동부 해안** the east coast.

동부인하다(同夫人-) go out with one's wife; take one's wife along[with]; accompany [be accompanied by] one's wife. ¶동부인하여 왕림해 주시기 바랍니다 Please come to see me with your wife. / (의례적) I request the pleasure of your company and that of Mrs. (Han). // 그는 일요일이면 반드시 동부인하여 외출한다 On Sundays he never fails to go out in company with his wife.

동북(東北) the northeast(약어 NE, N.E.). ¶~의 [에 / 으로] northeast / northeastern / northeasterly.

동북동(東北東) east-northeast(약어 ENE).

동분서주하다(東奔西走-) be greatly pressed; busy oneself about [(in) doing]; run[bustle] about. ¶그는 회사를 위해 동분서주하고 있다 He is always on the move doing something for the company.

동사(同社) [같은 회사] the same company; [앞서 말한 회사] the said [afore-said / above(-mentioned)] firm; [그 회사] it; them.

동사(凍死) death from cold [exposure]. **동사하다** die of[from] cold [exposure]; be frozen to death; freeze to death. ¶그 겨울에는 많은 사람들이 동사했다 That winter many people froze to death. // 그는 산속을 헤매다가 동사했다 He was stranded in the mountains and died of exposure [froze to death].

● **동사자** a person frozen to death.

동사(動詞) [언] a verb. ¶규칙 [불규칙] ~ a regular [an irregular] verb // 완전 [불완전] ~ a complete [an incomplete] verb // 자[타] ~ an intransitive [a transitive] verb // ~적 명사 a verbal noun / a gerund // ~의 verbal // ~의 변화 [활용] conjugation.

● **동사구** a verb(al) phrase.

동사무소(洞事務所) a *dong* office; a downblock office.

동산 a hill[hillock] (near a village); (정원의) an artificial [a miniature] hill; a mound.

동산(動産) movable property; movables; personal estate[property / effects]. ¶유체 [무체] ~ corporeal [incorporeal] movables.

● **동산 보험** property insurance. **동산 압류** distraint; distress.

동상(凍傷) frostbite; chilblains. (▶ frostbite가 정도가 심함) ¶~에 걸리다 be [get] frostbitten / get [have] chilblains (on one's hands) // 그는 손과 발이 ~에 걸렸다 He had chilblains on his feet and hands. / His feet and hands were frostbitten. // 그는 귀에 ~을 입었다 He got chilblains on his ears.

● **동상자** a frostbitten person; a case of frostbite.

동상(銅賞) a bronze prize. ¶그는 ~을 받았다 He won third prize.

동상(銅像) a bronze statue; a statue in bronze. ¶~을 세우다 erect [set up] a bronze statue.

동색(同色) the same color; [당파] fellow members of a party; the same faction.

동생(同生) [남동생] one's younger [little] brother; [여동생] one's younger [little] sister. (▶ 영어에서는 우리말 「동생」과 같이 남동생과 여동생을 총칭해서 부르는 말이 없음) ¶막냇~ one's youngest brother [sister].

동서(同壻) [자매의 남편] the husband of one's wife's sister; [형제의 아내] the wife of

one's husband's brother; a sister-in-law.
동서(東西) **1** [동쪽과 서쪽] the east and the west. ¶~로 50마일에 걸쳐 about 50 miles from east to west // 이 거리는 ~로 뻗어 있다 This street runs east and west. // 그 강은 ~로 흐르고 있다 The river flows from east to west.

2 [동양과 서양] the East and the West; the Orient and the Occident. ¶~를 막론하고 in all countries of the world / through the world // 이와 같은 사실은 ~를 불문한다 This is true of any part[all parts] of the world.

3 [공산권과 자유 진영] the East and the West; the Eastern and Western nations. ¶~의 관계[긴장 / 대립] the East-West relations [tensions / confrontation] // ~간의 긴장이 고조되고 있다 East-West tensions are growing.

동서를 모르다 do not know one's right hand from the left; do not know chalk from cheese.

●**동서고금** all ages and countries; all times and places. ¶~을 막론하고 across the ages and in all countries of the world / for all ages and countries[times and spaces]. **동서남북** the (four) cardinal points; north, south, east and west(▶ 영어에서는 이 순서로 말함). ¶그 광장에서 길이 ~으로 뻗어 있다 From the square four roads radiate in the four cardinal directions.

동석자(同席者) those present; the company; a seat companion(탈것의).

동석하다(同席─) sit together; sit in company with. ¶식사할 때 그와 동석했습니다 I sat with him at dinner. // 그 사람과 동석하면 불안하다 I feel ill at ease in his company. // 그 사람과는 동석하고 싶지 않다 I don't like to be in his company.

동선(同船) [같은 배] the same ship; [배를 같이 탐] taking the same ship. **동선하다** take the same ship; sail on[in] the same vessel; be in[on] the same vessel. ¶그와 동선했다 I was[sailed] on the same ship with him. / I took the same ship he did.

●**동선자** a shipmate; a fellow passenger.

동선(動線) the line of flow.

동성(同性) [성별이 같음] the same sex; [동일한 성질] homogeneity; homogeneousness; congeniality. ¶~ 간에 among one's own sex // ~의 homo-sexual / homogeneous / congenial.

●**동성애** homosexuality; homosexual love; (여성끼리의) lesbianism. **동성애자** a homosexual; a gay(주로 남성); (경멸적 속어) a homo; a lesbian(여성).

동성(同姓) the same surname[family name]. ¶그는 나와 ~이다 He has the same surname as myself.

●**동성동본** the same surname and the same family origin.

동소체(同素體) [화] an allotrope.

동수(同數) the same number. ¶귤과 ~의 사과 as many apples as oranges // 찬반이 ~인 경우에는 재투표한다 In case of a tie, there will be another vote.

동숙(同宿) lodging together. **동숙하다** stay at the same hotel; lodge in the same house (with); live[stay] (with). ¶나와 동숙하고 있는 학생 a student who lodges in the same house as I do // 그날 밤은 어느 노부부와 동숙했다 We spent the night in the same hotel as an elderly couple.

●**동숙인** (하숙의) a fellow lodger[boarder]; (호텔의) a fellow guest; the inmates.

동승(同乘) riding together. **동승하다** ride together (with); take the same car[train]; share (a car with). ¶그와 동승해서 부산에 갔다 I went to Busan in the same car with him. // 모르는 사람과 택시를 동승했다 I shared a taxi with a stranger.

●**동승자** a fellow passenger[rider]; (비행기의) a flight companion.

동시(同時) the same time[period]. ~의 simultaneous / current / synchronous / contemporary (with) // ~에 at the same time / simultaneously (with) / (일시에) at a time / at once // ~에 일어난 사건 simultaneous events // ~에 두 가지 일은 할 수 없다 No one can do two things at a time. // 자동차가 기둥에 부딪힘과 ~에 그는 정신을 잃었다 He lost consciousness the moment the car ran into the post. // 우리는 그의 선의는 인정하지만 ~에 그 방법이 서툴렀음을 말하지 않을 수 없다 While we admit his good intentions, we must say that his methods were inappropriate. // 그 운동은 매우 흥미롭지만 ~에 위험하기도 하다 That sport is very exciting, but on the other hand it is also dangerous. // 그의 이야기는 재미있으면서 ~에 유익했다 His speech was at once interesting and instructive. // 아버지가 귀가하시는 것과 ~에 나는 외출했다 I went out the moment father came home. // 내수용과 수출용 자동차를 ~에 제조하고 있다 They manufacture cars for both the foreign and the domestic markets. // 그는 학자인 ~에 예술가다 He is both a scholar and an artist. // 그는 나를 보는 것과 ~에 도망쳤다 The moment he saw me, he ran away. // 지진과 ~에 사방에서 화재가 일어났다 Simultaneously with the earthquake fires broke out fire on all sides.

●**동시 녹음** synchronous recording. ¶~ 촬영 sound shooting. **동시통역** simultaneous interpretation. ¶~을 하다 make simultaneous interpretation.

동시(童詩) children's verse; (a) nursery rime [rhyme].

동시대(同時代) [같은 시대] the same age [period]; [시대를 같이함] contemporaneousness. ¶우리와 ~의 사람은 our contemporaries // ~의 작가들 contemporary[coeval] writers // 그는 콜럼버스와 ~의 사람이었다 He was a contemporary of Columbus. / He lived in the same age[period] as Columbus.

동식물(動植物) animals and plants; (어느 지역·시대의) fauna and flora. ¶그 행성에는 ~이 없다 There is no animal or plant life on that planet.

동실등실 floating light(ly). ⇨동실등실

동심(同心) [같은 마음] the same mind; [마음을 함께 함] like-mindedness; accord; unanimity; concord; agreement; [중심이 같음] concentricity. ¶두 사람은 ~ 일체이다 The two are practically of a mind. **동심하다** share one mind; be of one heart; be of the same mind.

●**동심원** [수] a concentric circle.

동심(童心) the child's mind[heart]; the juvenile mind. ¶~으로 돌아가 회전목마를 즐겼다

I became a child again and enjoyed the merry-go-round.//그는 몇 살이 되어도 ~을 잃지 않았다 He never lost his childlike innocence.//그가 무심코 던진 말 한마디가 ~을 해줬다 His careless words hurt the child's feeling.

동아(東亞) 〔동아시아〕 East[Eastern] Asia; 〔동양〕 the East; 〔극동〕 the Far East. ¶~의 East-Asian / (Far) Eastern//~의 문제 the (Far) Eastern question.

동아리 1 〔부분〕 a part; a portion. ¶윗〔아랫〕 ~ the upper[lower] part. **2** 〔무리〕 a group; faction; companions composed of the people with the same purpose.

동아줄 a rope; a hawser; a stay.

동안 〔명사〕 (a space of) time; a period; a span; a while; 〔간격〕 an interval; a space; 〔부사적〕 in; for (a week / three days); during (the vacation); between; 〔사이〕 in the course of (the dinner); as [so] long as. ¶과거 5년 ~ for the past five years//그~ meanwhile / in the meantime//오랫~ for a long time [while]//살아 있는 ~은 as long as one lives / while one lives//10분 ~을 두고 at intervals of ten minutes//일정 기간 ~에 within a certain [given] period of time//자리를 비운 ~에 during one's absence / while one is out//남이 놀고 있는 ~에 그는 열심히 공부했다 He studied hard while the others were enjoying themselves.//기억이 확실한 ~에 적어 두는 것이 좋다 You'd better write it down while it's still fresh in your memory.//나는 10년 ~ 그를 만난 적이 없다 I haven't seen him (for) these ten years.//이 기간 ~ 나는 숙부님 댁에 머물고 있었다 During this period I stayed with my uncle.//그는 백화점이 열려 있는 ~ 내내 그 안을 왔다 갔다 했다 He walked around the department store during the whole time it was open.//그러는 ~에 저녁 준비가 되었다 In the meantime supper was ready.//내가 살아 있는 ~은 너를 원조해 주지 As [So] long as I live, I will help you.//최근 10년 ~의 과학의 진보는 눈부신 바가 있다 Remarkable progress has been made in science in [for] the last ten years.

동안(童顔) a boyish face. ¶~의 boyish-looking / juvenile-looking//~의 남자 a boyish-looking man//그는 여전히 ~이다 He still has a boyish look.

동액(同額) the same amount [sum] (a money); a like sum. ¶~의 equivalent in amount.//우리의 부담과 ~의 보조금을 받게 될 것이다 We will receive a matching grant [subsidy]. / They will match our expenditures with a grant.//우리 회사의 급료는 남녀 ~이다 Men and women are paid the same salary [paid equally] at our company.

동양(東洋) the Orient; the East. ¶~의 Eastern / Oriental / of the East [Orient]//~화하다 orientalize.
●**동양 문명** 〔미술〕 Oriental civilization [art]. **동양사** Oriental history. **동양 사상** Eastern ideas; Orientalism. **동양인** an Oriental; an Asiatic; the Orientals; 〔속어〕 the gook. (▶ Oriental은 경멸적인 어감이 있는 말이기 때문에, 최근 미국인들은 자국 내에 거주하는 동양인을 완곡하게 Asian American이라고 부르는 경우가 많음) **동양학** Oriental studies. **동양화**(一畵) an Oriental painting.

동업(同業) **1** 〔같은 업〕 the same trade [profession]; the same line of business. **2** 〔사업을 같이함〕. **동업하다** do business in partnership (with); run business together. ¶동업하는 정의(情誼)로 이 일은 비밀로 해 주시오 Please keep to yourself out of professional courtesy.
●**동업자** (의사·변호사·교직 등의) the profession; (상인·직업인의) the trade [craft]; (개인) a person in the same line of business; a fellow trader [businessman]; a colleague (of doctors); a friend; (신문·잡지의) a contemporary; (공동 영업의) a partner; an associate. ¶~ 간의 예의 professional courtesy. **동업 조합** a trade association; a (craft) guild.

동여매다 bind (a person) to (a stake); bind (things) together; tie (a horse) to (a tree); fasten (a rope) to (a post). ¶끈으로 동여맨 꾸러미 a package tied with string//밧줄을 꽉 ~ fasten a rope.

동역학(動力學) 〔물〕 kinetics; dynamics. ¶~의 kinetic.

동영상(動映像) a dynamic image.

동요(動搖) **1** 〔흔들림〕 shake; quake; tremble; (배의) rolling(좌우로); pitching(상하로). **동요하다** tremble; shake; stir; quake; (차가) jolt; (배가) pitch and roll; rock. ¶자동차가 몹시 동요한다 The car jolts badly.//배가 동요한다 The ship rolls [pitches].
2 〔불안〕 restlessness; unrest; disquietude; 〔흥분〕 excitement; agitation; 〔소요〕 disturbance; commotion; (a) tumult; 〔움직임〕 oscillation; fluctuation. ¶그녀는 마음의 ~를 감추고 있었다 She concealed her inward agitation.//금년에는 정계의 ~가 계속되었다 The political world has been very unsettled [turbulent] all this year. **동요하다** be restless; be disturbed; be unsettled; be agitated; oscillate (between); (세상이) be in (a) commotion. ¶그 소식을 듣고 그녀는 몹시 동요했다 She was badly shaken [much agitated] by the news.//그는 동요하지 않고 소기의 목적을 향해 나아갔다 He never wavered from his purpose.

동요(童謠) child verse; a children's song; a nursery rhyme.
●**동요 작가** a child's poet; a writer of children's songs.

동원(動員) mobilization. ¶산업 ~ industrial mobilization//인력 ~ labor [manpower] mobilization//노동력의 ~ labor mobilization//~을 해제하다 demobilize//육군은 일부 ~ 상태로 들어갔다 The army went into a state of partial mobilization. **동원하다** mobilize; set [draw] in motion; (군대 등의 출동) call out. ¶그 쇼는 많은 관객을 동원했다 The show attracted [drew] a large audience.//아이들까지 동원하여 대청소를 했다 Even the children were pressed into service [duty] for the great cleanup.//이 공군 기지의 폭격기는 즉각 언제든지 동원할 수 있다 The bombers from this air base can mobilize immediately at any time. ➔데모에 5,000명의 학생이 동원되었다 Five thousand students were rallied [were called together] for the demonstration.
●**동원령** mobilization orders. ¶제1사단에 그날 ~이 내렸다 Orders for the mobilization of the First Division were issued on that day.

동위(同位) the same rank[position]; the same location; [수]the same digit. ¶~의 coordinate / corresponding.
● **동위각** [수] the corresponding angle. **동위원소** an isotope. ¶방사성 ~ radioactive isotope.
동유럽(東-) Eastern Europe.
동음(同音) the same sound; homophony. ¶Meat와 meet는 ~이다 "Meat" and "meet" are pronounced alike.
● **동음이의어** a homonym(▶ 발음과 철자가 같은 것); a homophone(▶ air와 heir처럼 철자가 다른 것).
동의(同義) synonymy; synonymity; the same meaning. ¶~의 synonymous / synonymic(al).
● **동의어** a synonym; an equivalent. ¶travel과 journey는 ~이다 "Travel" is a synonym of "journey". / "Travel" is synonymous with "journey".
동의(同意) [같은 의견] the same opinion; [승낙·찬성] consent; assent; agreement; approval. ¶그의 ~를 얻어 with his consent // 머리를 끄덕여 ~를 나타내다 nod (one's head) in assent // 그녀는 존과의 결혼에 대하여 양친의 ~를 얻었다 She obtained her parents' approval for her marriage to John. // 나는 그의 ~를 얻었다 I got his OK [consent]. / I got an OK from him. **동의하다** agree with[in / to / upon]; consent[assent] to; approve of; subscribe to; accede; acquiesce. ¶네 의견에 동의한다 I subscribe to your opinion. / I agree with you. // 네 제안에는 동의할 수 없다 I cannot accept your suggestion. // 우리들은 모두 동의하고 있다 We are all of the same opinion. // 우리는 상호 동의하여 그것을 한 것이다 We did it by mutual consent[agreement]. // We both knew what we were doing. // 그에게 끈질기게 설득되어 그녀는 마침내 결혼에 동의했다 He kept after her until she finally agreed to marry him. // 그는 그 제안에 동의했다 He okayed the proposal.
● **동의서** a written consent. **동의자** an assentient; an assenter; an approver.
동의(動議) a motion. ¶긴급~ an urgent motion // A씨의 ~로 on Mr. A's motion // ~에 찬성하다 second a motion // ~를 철회하다 withdraw[reject] a motion // 토론 종결의 ~를 제의하다 move the cloture[closure] // ~가 가결[부결]되었다 A motion was adopted [rejected]. **동의하다** make[bring forward / put] a motion; move; lay a motion on the table.
동이 a[an earthenware] jar. ¶물~ a water jar.
동이다 bind (a box); tie up (in a bundle); fasten; bundle; truss; (끈으로) cord; (사슬로) chain; (가죽으로) strap. ¶끈으로 짐을 ~ tie up a bundle with string // 기둥에 ~ tie [bind] (a person) to a pillar // 경찰관들은 발부림치는 범인의 양팔을 포승으로 옆구리에 동였다 The policemen trussed up the struggling criminal.
동인(同人) **1** [뜻이 같은 사람] people of kindred spirit; fellow members; colleagues; [동료] a comrade; an associate. ¶잡지 「창조」의 ~ a member of the staff of the magazine "Changjo" // 그는 문학 ~의 한 사람이다 He is a member of a literary coterie. **2** [같은 사람] the same person; [그 사람] the said person; the person in question; he.
● **동인잡지** a literary coterie magazine; a little magazine.
동인(動因) a motive; a cause; an inducement. ¶지도자의 체포가 폭동의 ~이었다 The arrest of the leader set off[was the cause of] the riot.
동일(同一) [관형어적]. ¶~ 노동에 대한 ~ 임금 equal pay for equal work. **동일하다** identical; equal; nondiscriminatory; (one and) the same. ¶양자를 동일하다고 보다 consider the two as one and the same thing // 지킬 박사와 하이드 씨는 동일한 인물이다 Dr. Jekyll and Mr. Hyde are one and the same person. // 개와 늑대는 동일한 종류에 속한다 The dog belongs to same family as the wolf. // 그것은 내가 잃어버린 만년필과 동일한 것이다 It is exactly the same as the fountain pen that I lost.(▶ 그러나 잃어버린 그 펜은 아니다) // 영과 혼은 ~ The spirit is one[identical] with the soul. // 나를 그런 사람들과 동일하게 치면 곤란하다 I don't like to be classed with them.
● **동일 개념** an identical conception. **동일화**(-化) identification.
동일시하다(同一視-) identify (a thing) with (another); treat (matters) without discrimination; regard (A) in the same light with (B); put on a par (with); put (a thing) in the same category[class]. ➔¶양자는 도저히 동일시될 수 없다 The two are not to be mentioned in the same breath. / There is no comparison between the two.
동자(童子) a child; a young boy; a youngster. ¶그녀는 옥~를 낳았다 She gave birth to a boy. // 삼척~라도 그것은 안다 Every schoolboy[Even a child] knows it.
● **동자승 / 동자중** a young[boy] monk [bonze]; a priestling; an acolyte.
동작(動作) action; movements; motions; [거동] carriage; bearing; behavior; deportment; demeanor; manners; [몸짓] gestures; an act. ¶우스꽝스러운 ~ a funny gesture // 그는 ~이 기민하다[느리다] His movements are quick[slow]. // 그녀는 우리에게 착석하라는 ~을 지어 보였다 She mentioned us to be seated. // 그녀는 우아한 ~으로 인사했다 She greeted us gracefully[in a graceful manner]. // 그는 ~이 군인답다 He has a soldierly bearing. / He bears himself like a soldier. **동작하다** move; act; bear[carry] oneself.
동장(洞長) the chief of a a *dong* office; a *dong* headman.
동장군(冬將軍) the rigors of winter; General Winter; Jack Frost.
동적(動的) dynamic; kinetic. ¶그는 문장에 ~인 느낌을 잘 나타낸다 He is good at producing a dynamic feeling[sense of movement] in his writing.
동전(銅錢) a copper coin; a copper; (미국 구어) a red. ¶10원짜리 ~ a ten-won coin [piece] // (공중전화의) ~ 넣는 구멍 (drop a coin in) a slot // ~ 교환기 — 가동 중 (게시) Coin change — in operation // ~는 현관 판매대에 준비되어 있습니다 (게시) Coin exchange at cashier's counter in entrance. // 한 푼 안 남기고 돈을 다 써 버렸었다 I had spent my last penny. // 이것은 ~을 넣으면 움직이는 기계다 This is a coin-operated machine.

동절(冬節) winter; the winter season; wintertime.

동점(同點) a tie score; a draw; the same grade[mark / score]. ¶~이 되다 tie with / draw (level) with∥~으로 끝나다 finish (even) in a tie∥시합은 ~ 무승부로 끝났다 The game ended in a tie[draw].∥시합은 4대 4 ~이었다 The game was tied at 4 to 4.∥수학 시험은 그와 ~이었다 I got the same score as he did on the mathematics exam.
● **동점타** the game-tying hit; a score-tying blast.

동정 dongjeong; a collar strip (for a Korean jacket). ¶~을 달다 attach a *dongjeong* onto a *jeogori*.

동정(同情) sympathy; compassion; fellow feeling; pity; commiseration.(▶ pity는 불쌍하게 생각하는 마음, compassion은 불쌍하게 생각함과 동시에 무엇인가 해 주고 싶어 하는 마음) ¶깊은[따뜻한] ~ deep[warm] sympathy∥충심으로부터의 ~ hearty[sincere] sympathy∥~ 어린 행위 considerate deeds∥약한 자에 대한 ~ sympathy for the weak∥~을 끌다 arouse (a person's) sympathy∥~을 사다[받다] win[gain / capture] (a person's) sympathy∥남의 ~으로 살아가다 live on charity / live by alms∥일반의 ~이 그에게 쏠렸다 Public sympathies were centered on him.∥나는 굶주리는 아이들에게 ~을 금치 못했다 I could not help pitying the poor, hungry children.∥그는 화재를 입은 가족들에게 ~을 표시했다 He showed his sympathy for the burnt out family. **동정하다** sympathize with (a person); feel sympathy for (something); have compassion on; be compassionate toward; take pity upon; pity for (a person). ¶남의 불행을 ~ commiserate (a person) on his misfortune∥동정할 만하다 deserve one's sympathy[pity]∥남의 어려운 처지에 ~ have compassion for (a person's) hard lot / sympathize with (a person) in his predicament∥그의 무능은 동정할 만하다 He is pitifully[woefully] incompetent.∥급우 모두가 그녀를 동정했다 All her classmates sympathized with her.∥그녀는 가슴 한구석에서 그를 동정하고 있었다 She kept a corner of her heart for him.∥그에 대해서 동정하는 마음이 우러났다 Sympathy with him swelled up in our hearts.∥그는 나를 조금도 동정하지 않는다 He has not a drop of sympathy with me.∥우리를 좀 동정해 주시오 Have some feeling for us.∥나는 너에게 충심으로 동정한다 You have my hearty sympathy.
● **동정심** a sympathetic feeling; sympathy. ¶~이 있는[없는] sympathetic[unsympathetic] / feeling[unfeeling]∥그녀는 ~이 많다 She is quite considerate. **동정표** a sympathy vote. ¶그에게 ~가 몰렸다 He received a large sympathy vote.

동정(動靜) movements; a state of things; conditions (of the political world). ¶정계의 ~ the development of political affairs∥최근의 교육계의 ~ recent developments[trends] in educational circles∥~을 감시하다 keep watch on (a person's) movement∥적의 ~을 살피다 watch the movements of the enemy∥적은 우리의 ~을 살피고 있는 것 같다 The enemy seems to be spying on our movements.

동정(童貞) virginity; chastity; [수녀] a sister. ¶~을 잃다 lose one's chastity∥~을 지키다 keep one's virginity∥그 사람은 죽을 때까지 ~이었다 He had no carnal knowledge of woman all his life.
● **동정녀** a virgin; [성모] the virgin (Mary).

동조(同調) alignment; [물] tuning; syntony; [영] synchronism; [음] the same key[pitch / tune]. **동조하다** align oneself (with); side [ally oneself] (with); fall in (with); follow suit; act in concert (with). ¶많은 젊은이들이 금진주의에 동조하고 있었다 Many young people were in sympathy with radicalism.∥그는 나의 의견에 동조하지 않았다 He had no sympathy for my view. / He did not accept [go along with] my opinion.∥때로는 대중에게 동조하는 것도 좋은 일이다 It's a good idea to go along with the crowd once in a while.∥그의 설득에 동조하는 사람은 없었다 No one yielded to his persuasion.
● **동조자** a fellow traveler; a sympathizer.

동족(同族) [같은 종족] the same race[tribe]; one's kind; [동포] brethren; fellow countryman; [혈족] the same blood; consanguinity; [일족] the same family.
● **동족상잔** dog-eat-dog; a fratricidal war; devouring one another; an internecine struggle. ¶~의 비극을 겪다 experience the tragedy of fratricidal war. **동족애** brotherly[fraternal] love.

동종(同種) the same kind[sort / description]. ¶~의 kindred / allied / of the same kind∥~의 소책자 similar pamphlets∥~의 식물 allied plants∥이것들은 ~에 속한다 These things are of the same kind.

동지(冬至) [24절기의 하나] *dongji*; the winter solstice; the shortest day of the year. ¶오늘이 ~다 Today is *dongji*.
● **동지설달** the 11th and 12th of the lunar month; the coldest winter month. **동짓달** the 11th month of the lunar calendar.

동지(同志) [뜻이 같음] the same mind; the congenial spirit; a kindred mind; [뜻이 같은 사람] a like-minded person; a friend; a comrade; fellow thinkers. ¶~를 규합하다 muster men under one's banner / rally kindred spirits∥~의 후원으로 클럽을 조직하다 form a club with the support of those (who are) interested in the matter.

동진(東進) marching[proceeding] east; (천체의) easting. **동진하다** march[move] eastward; proceed east.

동질(同質) [같은 성질·품질] the same quality [nature]; [같은 종류임] homogeneity. ¶~의 of the same quality / homogeneous / cognate / coessential∥~의 문화 a homogeneous culture.

동쪽(東—) the east. ¶~의 east / eastern / easterly∥~으로 in the east / to the east∥~으로 가는 나그네 travelers going to[heading toward] the east∥~으로 여행하다 travel (to the) east / travel eastward∥이 마을은 서울 ~ 100킬로 지점에 있다 This town lies a hundred kilometers (to the) east of Seoul.∥집의 ~에 큰 나무가 몇 그루 있다 There are some big trees on the east side of the house.∥~ 하늘이 밝아 온다 The eastern sky becomes light / Day dawns.∥바람은 ~에서 불고 있다 The wind blows from the east.∥해는 ~에서 떠서 서쪽으로 진다 The sun rises

in the east and sets in the west.
동차(同次) ¶~의 homogeneous.
● **동차식** [수] a homogeneous expression.
동참(同參) participation. **동참하다** participate (in); take part (in). ¶나도 그 기획에 동참했다 I participated in the project too. // 지난주의 파업에는 5만 명이 동참했다 There were fifty thousand people who took part in the strike last week.
● **동참자** a participant.
동창(同窓) a fellow student; a schoolmate; a schoolfellow; an alumnus. ¶우리는 ~입니다 We were at school together. / We were classmates at school.
● **동창생** a fellow student; a schoolfellow; a schoolmate; [졸업생] a graduate; an alumnus (pl. -ni); [여자] an alumna (pl. -nae). **동창회** [동창 모임] a graduates' association; an alumni association; an old boys'[pupils'] association; [동기 동창회] a class reunion.
동천(東天) the sky in the east; the eastern sky. ¶이윽고 ~은 붉게 물들었다 By and by the eastern sky was tinged with crimson.
동체(同體) [한 몸] one body; [같은 물체] the same substance.
동체(胴體) (사람·동물의) the trunk; (비행기의) the fuselage; the body; (비행정의) the hull; (조각상의) the torso (pl. ~s, -si). ¶~가 두 동강이 났다 The body was severed in two.
동체(動體) 1 [움직이는 물체] a moving body. 2 [물] a fluid. ⇨유체(流體).
동축 케이블(同軸-) a coaxial cable.
동치(同値) [수] equivalence; equivalent. ¶~의 equivalent.
동치미 dongchimi; watery radish gimchi (kimchi).
동침(-鍼) an slender acupuncture needle.
동침하다(同寢-) sleep together; sleep with (a person); share a bed with (a person).
동태(凍太) a frozen pollack.
동태(動態) movement; dynamic state. ¶인구 ~를 조사하다 investigate the movement of the population / take the dynamic statistics of the population.
● **동태 경제** dynamic economics; mobile economy.
동토(凍土) frozen soil.
동통(疼痛) a sharp pain. ¶가슴에 심한 ~을 느끼다 feel[have] an acute pain in the chest.
동트다(東-) dawn; break. ¶동틀 녘에 at the break of dawn / at the first sign of daylight // 우리는 동틀 녘에 출발했다 We departed at the first gray of dawn.
동티 1 [지신(地神)을 노하게 하여 받는 재앙] retribution from the earth gods. 2 [자초한 말썽] trouble brought on oneself.
동파하다(凍破-) be frozen to burst[rupture].
동판(銅板) sheet copper.
동판(銅版) a copperplate; a copperplate print; a mezzotint.
● **동판 인쇄** (copper) plate printing. ¶~를 하다 print from copperplates. **동판화**(-畵) a copperplate print.
동편(東便) the east[eastern] side.
동포(同胞) [형제] brothers; [같은 겨레] brethren; fellow countrymen; one's countrymen; compatriots; [인류] fellowmen; fellow creature. ¶사해(四海) ~ universal[world] brotherhood // 재일[재미] ~ Korean residents in Japan[the U.S.] // 해외 ~ Koreans abroad // 5천만 ~에게 고함 A word for our fifty million compatriots!
● **동포애** brotherly[fraternal] love; fellow feeling; fraternity.
동풍(東風) an easterly wind; a wind out of [from] the east. ¶마이(馬耳)~ complete indifference / praying to deaf ears.
동하다(動-) 1 [마음이 흔들리다] be shaken [perturbed]; be upset; (감동·욕망 등이) be move[touched]; be[feel] inclined to (do). ¶구미가 동하는 appetizing (dish) / tempting (offer) / attractive (woman) / (마음이) 동하기 쉽다 be (easily) excitable / be easily affected [moved / influenced] / be susceptible (to) / be sensitive (to) // 구미가 ~ (식욕이) feel an appetite (for) / (욕심이) have an itch [desire] (for / to do) / want (to do) / have a (great) mind (to do) // 유혹에 동하지 않다 be proof against temptation. 2 [병이 도지다] become worse.
동해(東海) [동쪽 바다] the eastern sea; (한국의) the East Sea.
● **동해안** the east coast.
동행(同行) going together; traveling together. ¶~ 중 한 사람 one of the party // ~을 잃다 get separated from one's companion // ~은 세 사람이었다 We were a party of three. **동행하다** go (along) with; accompany (a person); go in company with; go in (a person's) company; travel together; [호송] escort. ¶…과 동행하여 (in company) with … / accompanied by … // 경찰서까지 동행합시다 Please come to the police station with me. // 수원까지 동행하겠소 I will go with[accompany] you as far as Suwon.
● **동행인** / **동행자** a fellow traveler; a (traveling) companion.
동향(同鄕) the same native place; the same village[town / district / province]. ¶우리는 ~이다 We are from the same prefecture. // ~의 인연으로 그 사람에게 많은 신세를 지고 있다 He is very kind to me out of goodwill for someone from the same part of the country.
● **동향인** a person from the same town [village].
동향(東向) an eastern exposure[aspect]; facing east; eastward. **동향하다** face east; look toward the east; orient.
● **동향집** a house facing easy.
동향(動向) a tendency; a trend; a movement; an attitude. ¶여론[시세]의 ~ the trend of public opinion[the times] // 세계의 ~ world trends // 금후의 ~을 시사하는 것 a straw in the wind // (정치가가) 세상의 ~에 부단한 주의를 기울이다 hold[keep / have] one's ear to the ground.
동혈(洞穴) a cave; a cavern; a grotto (pl. ~(e)s).
동형(同形) the same shape; [화] isomorphism. ¶~의 잎 leaves of the same shape // 좌우 ~의 symmetrical.
동형(同型) the same type[pattern]; a similar type. ¶내 요트는 네 것과 ~이다 My yacht is (of) the same model as yours. // 이것과 ~으로 색깔이 다른 모자는 없습니까 Do you have a hat of the same style as this but in a different color? // ~의 사기 사건이 빈번히 일어났다 Fraud cases of similar pattern[type]

동호(同好) the same taste. **동호하다** be interested in the same subject; share the same taste[interest].
● **동호인** persons interested in the same subject; a friend of similar tastes. **동호회** an association of like-minded persons. ¶낚시 ~ an amateur anglers' club // 태권도 ~ an amateur *taegwondo* club.

동화(同化) assimilation; [순응] adaptation; [생] anabolism. ¶음의 ~ assimilation of a sound (to another). **동화하다** assimilate (with); adapt oneself to(순응하다). ¶동화할 수 있는 assimilable // 사상이나 문화를 ~ assimilate various foreign ideas // 그들은 쉽사리 미국 문화에 동화하지 않는다 They will not readily assimilate into American culture. ➔ 음식물은 동화되어 유기 조직이 된다 Food is assimilated and converted into organic tissue.
● **동화 작용** 〔영양 물질의 원형질로의 전환〕 assimilation; 〔생물의 물질대사〕 anabolism.

동화(動畵) an animation; a cartoon film; an animated cartoon.
● **동화 제작자** an animator.

동화(童話) 〔어린이를 위한 이야기〕 a children's story; a juvenile story; [옛날이야기] a fairy[nursery] tale.
● **동화극** a juvenile [fairy] play; a play for children. **동화 작가** a writer of children's stories[fairy tales]. **동화집** a collection of fairy tales.

동회(洞會) ➔ 동사무소

돛 a sail; a canvas; (속어) muslin. ¶삼각 ~ a jib // 바람을 가득 안은 ~ a full sail / a sail well taut // 순풍에 ~ smooth[plain] sailing / going well[smoothly / swimmingly] // ~을 달다 set a sail / ~을 올리다 hoist[put up / spread] a sail / ~을 내리다 lower[take down] a sail // ~을 펴다 [감다] unfurl[furl] a sail // 순풍에 ~을 달고 달리다 sail before the wind / be under easy sail // 순풍에 ~을 단 듯 모든 것이 잘되어 간다 Everything goes very well. / It's all plain sailing. // 그 배는 ~을 접고 질주했다 The ship scudded along under bare poles.

돛단배 a sailboat; a sailer; a sailing ship [vessel / boat].

돛대 a mast; a stick. ¶~를 잃은 배 a dismasted vessel.

돛배 a sailboat. ⇨ 돛단배

돛자리 [천] the sail; Vela.

돼다 〔속〕 be good. ⇨ 되다⁴

돼먹지 않다 ¶저 녀석은 돼먹지 않은 놈이다 He is a good-for-nothing person.

돼지 1 [가축] a pig; a hog(▶ (미)에서는 120 파운드 이하의 새끼 돼지는 pig, 어미 돼지는 hog. (영)에서는 hog는 특히 도살용의 거세한 수돼지를 가리키는 경우가 많음. 비유적으로도 씀); [문어] a swine (단수·복수 동형); [수돼지] a sow(sau). ¶새끼 ~ a pigling / a hogling / a piglet / a shoat(한 살 미만의) / a young pig / a piggy // 수~ a porker // ~를 치다 breed pigs / raise hogs // 저 녀석은 ~처럼 처먹는다 He makes a pig of himself. / He eats like a pig. // 그것은 ~ 앞에 진주 격이다 It's like casting pearls before swine(▶ 성서의 말).
2 [뚱보] a fat person; a fatty; [대식가] a greedy person. ¶그는 ~다 [뚱보] He is a fatty. / [대식가] He is a great eater. / He is gluttonous[greedy].
● **돼지고기** pork; hog meat. **돼지비계** lard; hog fat. **돼지우리** a pigsty; a pigpen; (미) a hogpen. ¶~ 같은 집 a shack / a pigpen / a hovel.

되 1 [계량기] a doe; a (one-doe) measure. ¶채용[곡물용] ~ a liquid[dry] measure // 쌀 흠~로 되다 measure rice with a one-*hop* measure // 그녀는 보석을 ~로 될 만큼 가지고 있다 She has a heap of jewels. 2 [계량의 단위] a doe(=0.477 U.S. gallon, 10 *hop*). ¶쌀 넉 ~ four *doe* of rice // ~로 팔다 sell by the measure // ~를 속이다 give short measure // ~를 후하게 주다 give good measure.
되로 주고 말로 받는다(속담) Sow the wind and reap the whirlwind.

되- [다시·도로] re-; again; back; [도리어] reversely; conversely; on the contrary; in return; instead; contrary to what you might expect. ¶~묻다 ask in return // ~돌려 보내다 send (a person) back // ~사다 buy back / repurchase // ~돌아가다 go back / return // ~돌려 주다 return (a person a borrowed book) / give[hand] back // ~씹다 (음식을) chew again and again / chew well / ruminate / (말을) say over again // ~쏘다 shoot back / reflect(빛을).

-되 1 [대립] but; although; (even) though. ¶아름답기는 하~ though (she is) beautiful / 그는 가난하~ 거짓을 모르는 사람이다 Though (he is) poor, he is above telling a lie. // 그 꽃들은 아름답기는 하~ 향기가 없다 The flowers are lovely; only, they have no scent. // 나는 가고 싶기는 하~ 짬이 없다 I should like to come, but I haven't time.
2 [조건] if; when. ¶오기는 오~ 동생을 데리고 와라 If you want to come, bring your brother with you. // 점심을 먹기는 먹~ 빨리 서둘러라 You may have lunch, but hurry over (your lunch)!
3 [부연] and that. ¶그는 그것을 하~ 훌륭하게 해냈다 He did it, and that very well. // 바람이 불~ 지독하게 분다 The wind is blowing, and that terrifically.

되갈다 1 (논밭을) replow; (영) replough; retill; plow[till] again. 2 (가루를) regrind; grind again.

되감다 rewind. ¶테이프를 ~ rewind a tape.

되걸리다 (병에) relapse (into illness); contract (a disease) again; be seized[afflicted] with again; come down with another case (of); be attacked (by a disease) again. ¶감기에 ~ catch[contract] a cold again / be attacked by a cold again / catch more cold // 그는 병이 회복되는 듯싶더니 되걸리고 말았다 He seemed to be getting round but had a relapse[return / second attack] of the disease.

되게 [아주 몹시] very; exceedingly; extraordinarily; heavily; severely; bitterly; extremely; awfully; hard. ¶~ 춥다 [덥다] be very cold [hot] // ~ 무섭다 be quite dreadful // ~ 무식하다 be quite ignorant // ~ 야단맞다 be scolded severely / be given a good scolding // ~ 혼내 주다 give (a person) a good licking / teach (a person) a lesson / defeat one's opponent badly // ~ 아프다 be very[extremely] painful // ~ 비싸다 be very high in price / be very dear // 나는 운이 ~ 좋았다

I had capital luck.//그는 넘어질 때 머리를 ~ 부딪혔다 He got a nasty knock on the head when he fell.

되넘기다 resell; buy an article and sell it again (to). ¶말을 사서 ~ resell a horse / buy a horse and sell it again (to)//사과를 과수원에서 사서 소매상에게 ~ buy apples from an orchard and sell them to a retailer.

되놈 〔중국인〕 a Chinese; 〔경멸〕 a Chinaman; 〔속어〕 a Chink.

되뇌다 retort[talk back] again and again; say over again. ¶강조하기 위해 한 가지 말을 ~ repeat a word for emphasis//같은 소리를 ~ harp on the same string/repeat the same thing//남의 말을 ~ echo[repeat] (a person's) words//죽은 지 2년이 지났는데 아직도 아내는 딸아이 이야기만 되뇌며 지낸다 Two years have passed since our daughter died, but my wife still talks about her all the time[but still her name is always on my wife's lips].

되는대로 〔함부로·마구〕 at random; at haphazard; irresponsibly; 〔아무렇게나〕 carelessly; lukewarmly; half-heartedly. ¶~ 지껄이다 talk irresponsibly[at random] / say whatever comes into one's head//~ 대답하다 answer at[by] haphazard / make a random answer//~ 살다 ride with the tide / live in a happy-go-lucky way / resign oneself to fate //일을 ~ 하다 scamp[fudge/slur over] one's work//그는 ~ 사업을 시작했다 He started business simply on chance.

되다[1] **1** 〔이루어지다〕 be done; be completed; be finished; 〔준비가〕 be ready. ¶일이 다 되었다 The work is finished.//식사 준비가 다 되어 있다 Dinner is ready.//준비가 다 되면 바로 출발하자 Let's start as soon as everything is ready.//시험 준비가 아직 안 되고 있다 I have not prepared for the examination yet. //어떻게 되든 그것을 맞을 준비가 되어 있느냐 Are you ready to accept whatever happens?

2 〔어떤 재료·성분으로 이루어지다〕 be made[manufactured]; 〔세워지다〕 be built [constructed]; 〔구성되다〕 consist of; be composed[made up / formed] of; form. ¶이 책상은 나무로 되어 있다 This desk is made of wood.(▶ of는 재료를 나타냄)//물질은 원자로 되어 있다 Matter is composed of atoms. //물은 수소와 산소로 되어 있다 Water consists of hydrogen and oxygen.//국회는 양원으로 되어 있다 The Congress consists of two houses.

3 〔어떤 신분·위치·상태에 이르다〕 become; get(▶ get은 become보다 더 구어적임); be; grow; form (a part); develop (into); be left (penniless). ¶어른이 ~ grow up / become an adult[a man]//그는 훌륭한 의사가 될 것이다 He will make a fine doctor.//그는 교사직을 그만두고 완전한 저술가가 되어 버렸다 He gave up his teaching job to devote himself full-time to writing.//그런데 그 개는 어찌 되었지요 By the way, what's become of [happened to] the dog?

4 〔인품·행동·글 등이 좋다〕 be good[excellent]; be decent (in conduct); be mature(원만하다); considerate(분별있다). ¶된 사람 a well-cultured person / a person of well-balanced character//이야기가 ~ 〔통하다〕 have an understanding with (a person).

5 〔시작하다〕 begin to (do); come[get] to (do); learn to (do); set in; 〔…으로 발전하다〕 develop into; grow into. ¶감정적이 ~ become emotional//극단적이 ~ go to extremes//그는 범죄를 저지르게 되었다 He took to crime.//너는 곧 알게 된다 You will soon come to understand.//언제부터 담배를 끊게 되었지요 When did you give up smoking?//나는 중학생 시절에 시를 쓰게 되었다 I began to write poetry when I was in junior high school.//그는 최근 훨씬 미남이 되었다 He has grown much more handsome recently.

6 〔결과가 생기다〕 result[end] in; turn out; prove. ¶일장춘몽이 ~ turn out to be a mere dream//쓰이지 않게 ~ fall into disuse//손해가 ~ result in[prove to be] a loss//치명상이 ~ prove (to be) fatal//밥이 잘 안 ~ The food does not turn out very well.//꿈이 현실로 되었다 The dream has come true.//그렇게 되지는 않았다 Things didn't work out that way.//공휴일이 일요일이 되어서 겹쳐 버렸다 The national holiday fell on a Sunday. //그런 짓을 하면 해가 된다 You'll lose by doing that.

7 〔변하다〕 turn[change] into; pass into. ¶이 포도들이 포도주가 됩니다 These grapes are made into wine. / We make wine from these grapes.//그의 전 재산이 재가 되어 버렸다 Everything he had was reduced to ashes.//풀쐐기가 나비가 된다 A caterpillar turns [metamorphoses] into a butterfly.//말다툼이 몸싸움이 되었다 The quarrel developed into a scuffle[fight].

8 〔자라다·흥하다〕 grow; thrive; prosper. ¶이 나라의 이 지방에서는 복숭아가 잘된다 Peaches grow well in this part of the country.//이 농장에서는 촉성 재배의 야채가 잘된다 This farm produces good crops of forced vegetables.//올해에는 벼가 잘되었다 We have had a good crop of rice this year.//장사가 잘됐다〔안 됐다〕 I have done good [poor] business. / Business has been brisk [dull].

9 〔성취되다〕 succeed; be accomplished [attained]. ¶일이 잘 ~ be successful [successfully done] / go well / work [come off] well//잘 안 ~ go badly[amiss / wrong] / be unsuccessful//생각대로 ~ come off to one's expectation//모든 일이 잘되었다 All went well with us.//그것은 잘될 겁니다 I trust it will work out well.//됐다 All right! / Good! / Capital!/ 〔발견 내고서〕 Eureka!// 이번에는 그렇게는 안 될 것이다 I am not so sure of that, this time.

10 〔가능하다〕 (사람이) can (do / write); be able to (do); be capable of (doing); (사물이) be possible. ¶될 수 있는 대로 as ... as possible//만약 된다면 if possible//될 수 있는 대로 정확한 계산 the most accurate calculations available//그 사건을 될 수 있는 대로 철저히 조사해 보았다 I investigated the matter as thoroughly as possible[as I could].//될 수 있는 대로 빨리 오십시오 Please come as soon as possible[as you can].//내 힘으로 될 수 있는 것은 무엇이든지 하겠소 I will do anything in my power[everything I can].//될 수 있는 대로 열심히 노력하시오 Try as hard as possible[you can]. / 〔구어〕 Give it all you've got.//이 기회를 될 수

되다

있는 한 이용하시오 You'd better make the most of this opportunity.
11 […해도 좋다] may (do). ¶자다[가지 않아도] ~ may[need not] go//옆방에서 피아노를 쳐도 됩니까 Do you mind if I play the piano in the next room?//가까이에 살고 있으니깐 가끔은 들러 주셔도 되련만 You'd think he might drop in once in a while, since he lives close by.
12 [충분하다] be enough; be sufficient; will do; answer[serve] the purpose. ¶이것이면 된다 This will do. / This will serve[answer for] my purpose.//이젠 됐습니다[많이 먹었습니다] No more, thank you. / Thanks a lot, but I've had enough[plenty] (of it).//만 원만 있으면 됩니다 Ten thousand won will do [answer the purpose / be enough for the purpose].
13 […에 이르다] come to; amount to; make. ¶17을 5로 나누면 3이 되고 2가 남는다 Seventeen divided by five makes[is] three with two left over[with a remainder of two]. //내 한 달 수입이 100만 원이 된다 My monthly income comes to 1,000,000 won.//우리 5명의 기찻삯은 얼마가 됩니까 How much is the total train fare for the five of us?//지출은 합계 10만 원이 된다 The outlay totals[amounts to] 100,000 won.
14 [혈연관계가 있다] be related to; be a relative. ¶먼 일가가 ~ be a distant relative//그 분과는 어떻게 되십니까 What relation is he to you?//그는 나의 어머니의 시동생이 된다 He is my mother's brother-in-law.//그분은 외가편으로 친척이 됩니다 He is related to [connected with] me on my mother's side.
15 […의 역할을 하다] act as; impersonate; play the role[part] of; serve as[for]. ¶햄릿이 ~ appear as[play the part of] Hamlet / impersonate Hamlet//알코올은 소독약이 된다 Alcohol acts as a disinfectant.//이 지팡이는 무기도 된다 This stick will serve as[for] a weapon.
16 [계절·때가 닥쳐오다] be; come; set in. ¶봄이 되었다 Spring has come.//3월 2일이 되면 학교가 시작하게 된다 School begins on March 2.//곧 새해가 된다 The new year will soon come around.//내 생일이 공휴일이 되었다 My birthday fell on a national holiday. //시간이 거의 다 되었다 Time is nearly up. / It's almost[about] time.//지금 10시쯤 됐을 거야 It must be about ten o'clock now.//아직 4시가 안 됐을걸 I don't think it's four o'clock yet.
17 [경과하다] elapse; pass; it is (a month) since. ¶몇 백 년 된 나무 a tree centuries old //그가 죽은 지도 벌써 5년이나 된다 It is[has been] five years (to a day)[Five years have elapsed] since he died.//1주일이 있으면 만 1년이 된다 Another week will make a full year. / In another week I shall have lived here for a full year.//벌써 그렇게 되었나 Was it so long ago, I wonder?
18 [나이가 되다] attain; reach; turn. ¶서른이 ~ enter upon[attain] one's thirtieth year//그는 40세가 될 말까 한다 He is scarcely forty. //나는 오는 생일에 20세가 됩니다 I'll be twenty years old next birthday.//그는 40이 못 된다 He is under forty. / He is on his side of forty.
19 [없어지다] come to end; run out; be out

[up]; be used up. ¶연료가 다 되었다 The gasoline[fuel] is[has run] out.//계약 기한이 다 되었다 The contract has run out [expired] / The lease is out.//그는 돈이 다 되었다 He has run through all his money. / His money came to an end.//이 자전거도 이제 다 되었다 This bike has seen its day. / This bicycle has done[served] its time.

되어 가다 **1** (일이) go (on); work; progress; advance. ¶잘 안 ~ go badly[amiss / wrong] / come off badly//되어 가는 대로 하다 follow a hit-or-miss method / have the haphazard way of doing everything//되어 가는 대로 내버려 두다 leave (a matter) to take [run] its own course//그는 이제 어른이 되어 간다 He is now on the threshold of adulthood.//일이 그럭저럭 되어 간다 Matters go along somehow. **2** (물건이) be getting finished[completed / attained / accomplished]. ¶동상이 거의 되어 가고 있다 The bronze statue is nearly completed.//연이 다 되어 간다 The kite is being finished. **3** (때가) be getting; be on the verge[brink] of. ¶서른이 다 ~ be close[hard] upon thirty / be on the short side of thirty / be nearing thirty//점심 때가 다 되어 간다 It is almost[well-nigh] noon.//그는 네 살이지만, 다섯 살이 되어 가고 있다 He is four years old — going on five. //그가 미국으로 떠난 지 3년이 되어 간다 It is almost three years since he went to America.

될 대로 되어라 Let it take care of itself.; Go to the devil!; Devil take him!; I don't care a damn about it.

되다² [분량을 헤아리다] measure. ¶말[되]로 ~ measure (rice) with a *mal*[*doe*]//되어 팔다 sell by measure//수북이 되어 주다 give (a person) full[good] measure//빠지게 되어 주다 give (a person) short measure.

되다³ **1** [빡빡하다] hard; thick; stiff; tough. ¶된 죽 thick gruel//되게 반죽하다 give stiff consistency by kneading or churning//나는 밥을 너무 되지 않게 지었다 I cooked the rice a little on the soft side.//풀을 되게 쑤어라 Make the paste thick[stiff].
2 [팽팽하다] tight; taut; tense. ¶줄을 되게 당기다 tighten[tauten] a rope / stretch a rope tight//줄이 ~ A rope is taut.
3 [힘들다] hard; tough; toilsome; laborious. ¶된 생활 a hard life//된 일 hard work / a tough job//일의 된 고비를 넘기다 be through with the hardest part of a job//그 일이 나에게는 ~ The job[task] is very hard for me. / The job is beyond my ability.//등산은 된 일이다 Climbing a mountain is laborious.
4 [심하다] severe; intense; violent; strong; bitter. ¶된 감기 a bad cold//된서리 heavy frost//된 추위 intensely cold weather//된 벌 a severe punishment.

-되다 **1** (동사적 명사에 붙어) be; become; get to be. ¶걱정 ~ be worried[anxious] about// 시작 ~ begin / have a beginning / (병세가) 악화 ~ take a serious turn / change[take a turn] for the worse//완쾌 ~ be completely cured (of a disease) / recover completely // 해결 ~ get solved[resolved]//공인 ~ gain official approval//해고 ~ be[get] dismissed [discharged]//확대 ~ be magnified[scaled up] / (a problem) spread[expand / grow]

자리가 준비되었다 A table was ready.
2 (형용사적 명사나 부사적 어군에 붙어) be. ¶막~ be ill-mannered[-bred] / be wild // 못~ (사람·행동이) be bad-natured / be evil [wicked / bad] // 속~ be vulgar[common] / 참~ be true // 헛~ be false / be in vain / be futile // 망령~ be foolish[unreasonable / silly] / (늙은이가) be senile[doting] / be in one's dotage[second childhood].

되도록 (될 수 있는 한) as ... as possible [practicable]; as ... as one can; (될 수 있으면) if possible[practicable]; if it can be so arranged; if circumstances allow; (부정(否定)) no more than one can help. ¶~ 많이 as much[many] as possible / ~ 빨리 as soon[quickly / promptly] as possible / ~이면 그렇게 하겠습니다 I'll try to do it that way. // ~ 늦지 않도록 하시오 Don't be longer than you can help. // 아침에 ~ 빨리 출발하겠다 I will start as early as possible in the morning.

되돌다 turn back around. ¶그는 되돌아서 달려갔다 He turned around and ran off.

되돌리다 1 (원래의 상태로 놓다) restore. ¶책을 다 읽으면 제자리에 되돌려 놓으시오 When you are through with the books, put them back where they were. // 그걸 네가 주웠던 장소에 되돌려 놓고 오너라 Take it back where you found it. // 한번 파괴된 자연을 원상태로 되돌려 놓기는 어렵다 It is difficult to restore nature to its former condition once it is laid waste. **2** (뒤로 물리다) put[turn] back; back. ¶시계를 두 시간 ~ set back a clock two hours. **3** (각하하다) reject; turn down; dismiss. ¶청원서를 ~ reject a (written) petition.

되돌려 주다 return; give back. ¶돈을 ~ give back the money (one borrowed) // 나는 그가 준 선물들을 모두 그의 면전에서 되돌려 주었다 I'll throw all the presents he gave me right back in his face!

되돌아가다 1 (오던 길을 다시 돌아가다) turn [go] back (to); return (to); retrace one's steps; put back. ¶도중에서 ~ turn back halfway // 온 길을 ~ retrace one's steps[way] / turn back the way one has come // 지갑을 두고 온 것을 깨닫고서 오던 길을 되돌아갔다 Finding that I had left my wallet behind, I retraced my steps[went back].
2 (원래의 상태로 가다) go back(ward); turn back; return (to); revert (to); (병 등이) have [suffer] a relapse. ¶주된 의제로 ~ get back to one's[the main] subject // 나쁜 길로 ~ relapse into vice // 처음으로 되돌아가 계획을 다시 세우자 Let's rethink the plan from the very beginning. // 그 충격 때문에 그는 제정신으로 되돌아갔다 The shock brought him back to his senses.

되돌아보다 look over one's shoulder; turn one's head; turn round; look back[round]. ¶(옛날을) 되돌아보면 in retrospect // 잠깐 ~ cast a hasty glance backward[behind] / look back for a second // 과거를 ~ think back to the past days / think backward / look back upon the past // 자신의 행동을 ~ review one's conduct.

되돌아오다 1 (원래의 상태로 돌아오다) return (to). ¶마치 제2차 세계 대전 당시로 되돌아온 것 같다 It looks as if time had been turned back[backward] to world War Ⅱ. // 그녀는 겨우 제정신으로 되돌아왔다 [제정신을 찾았다] At last she pulled herself together. / (의식을 회복했다) At last she recovered consciousness. / She came to at last. // 종소리가 그녀를 현실로 되돌아오게 했다 The sound of the bell called her back to reality.
2 (다시 돌아오다) be returned. ¶폭풍우 때문에 나는 도중에서 되돌아왔다 I turned back halfway because of the storm. // 버스에 두고 내린 우산은 되돌아왔다 The umbrella I had left on the bus was returned. // 청춘은 다시 되돌아오지 않는다 Your youth will never come back. / You can never regain your youth. // 한 번 더 질문했으나 똑같은 대답이 되돌아왔다 I asked once more but still got the same answer. // 그녀는 막 밖으로 나가려는 그를 불러서 되돌아오게 했다 She called him back just as he was going out. // 그는 부친이 위독하다는 전보를 받고 집으로 되돌아왔다 He was called home by a telegram saying that his father was dangerously ill.

되레 on the contrary; rather. ⇨도리어
되묻다 1 (다시 묻다) ask again; repeat one's question. ¶그는 미심쩍은 얼굴로 되물었다 He asked again[repeated his question] with a doubtful look. **2** (반문하다) ask back; throw back a question. ¶"무슨 말이냐?" 하고 그에게 되물었다 "What do you mean?" I asked back[countered / asked him in return]. // 그러면 너는 어떻게 생각하느냐고 되물었다 I then asked him in return what he thought.

되밀다 push back; bear back; push in return.
되바라지다 1 (그릇 등이 얕다) open; shallow; (눈에 잘 띄다) exposed; conspicuous. ¶되바라진 그릇 a shallow dish[vessel]. **2** (편협하다) narrow-minded; hard; illiberal; intolerant; hidebound. ¶되바라진 사람 a shallow [narrow-minded] person. **3** (지나치게 똑똑하다) precocious; pert; saucy; forward; cheeky; (구어) cocky; (학생) coxy. ¶되바라진 아이 a precocious child / (건방져서) a cheeky[saucy] kid // 저 아이는 어른같은 말을 한다 That boy talks like a grown-up[an adult].

되받다 1 (도로 받다) receive[get] (a thing) back. **2** (꾸짖을 때 반항하다) scold back; defy a scolding.

되부르다 call back; recall.
되살다 1 (먹은 음식이) be not easily digested; be[sit / lie] heavy on the stomach; remain undigested in the stomach; feel uncomfortable because of indigestion. **2** be brought back to life; come back to life. ⇨되살아나다

되살리다 (생명을) raise (a person) from the death; recall[restore] (a person) to life; bring (a person) to life[to (his) senses]; revive; resuscitate; (기억 등을) wake[recall / bring back] (one's memories); call back the memory of; call (something) to mind [memory / remembrance]; (식물 등을) freshen.

되살아나다 be brought back to life; come back to life; be resuscitated; come to oneself [to one's senses]; be restored (from death) to life; return to life; (불이) be rekindled; flame[blaze / burn] up. ¶그는 심장 마사지로 되살아났다 He was revived by heart massage. // 나는 되살아난 듯한 기분이다 I

되새기다

feel refreshed [like a new person].// 새로운 지도자가 나타나 소멸 직전의 그 운동이 되살아났다 The advent of the new leader revived the moribund movement.// 15분가량 인공호흡을 하자 물에 빠졌던 아이가 되살아났다 A quarter of an hour's artificial respiration brought the half-drowned child around [to]. / The half-drowned child came to in a quarter of an hour, thanks to artificial respiration.// 30년 전에 유행했던 드레스가 되살아났다 The dresses that were in vogue thirty years ago have come back.// 옛 기억이 서서히 되살아났다 Memories of the past gradually came back.// 그 광경이 생생하게 되살아났다 I recalled the scene vividly.

되새기다 (음식을) chew over and over again (because of poor appetite); (소 등이) ruminate; chew the cud; (마음속으로) meditate (on / upon); ruminate (about / of / upon / over); relive. ¶자기의 불행을 ~ meditate [ruminate] on one's misfortune// 우리는 선생님이 하신 말씀을 깊이 되새겼다 We thought deeply what our teacher had said.

되새김질 rumination; cud-chewing.

되쏘다 (총 등을) shoot back; [반사하다] reflect; (말로) retort [retaliate] (upon); give [pay] (a person) tit for tat.

되씹다 1 [말을 되풀이하다] repeat; reiterate; tell the same story over again; harp on the same thing. ¶한 말을 ~ repeat oneself// 그는 여전히 똑같은 얘기만 되씹고 있다 He is still harping on the same topic. 2 chew over and over again; meditate (on / upon). ⇨ 되새기다

되알지다 1 [억척손이 야무지다] forcing; coercive; high-handed; pushing; aggressive. 2 [벅차다] beyond one's power; above one's ability; more than one can do.

되잖다 wretched; poor; no good; absurd; nonsensical; worthless; good-for-nothing. ¶되잖은 수작 an absurd remark / silly talk / nonsense/ 되잖은 물건 poor [wretched] stuff// 되잖은 핑계 a poor [lame] excuse// 되잖은 소리를 지껄이다 talk rot [nonsense]// 되잖은 짓을 하다 do wrong / do a dishonest thing [act] / (속어) go [get] on the cross// 되잖은 짓 좀 그만둬라 Don't be absurd.

되지못하다 [건방지다] impudent [conceited / pretentious]; presumptuous [forward / pert / saucy]; (서술적) be no good; be a failure. ¶되지못한 놈 a good-for-nothing / a failure / a wretched fellow / (건방진) a cocky guy / a conceited pup// 되지못하게 굴다 act fresh [smart] / behave badly [indecently] / behave impudently [overbearingly].

되직하다 somewhat thick; a bit too hard; stodgy. ¶되직한 요리 a stodgy [heavy] meal // 밥을 약간 되직하게 짓다 boil rice a little on the firm side// 죽이 ~ The gruel is rather thick.

되질하다 measure (rice) with a *doe* (measure).

되짚어 back; retracing [returning] right away. ¶지나온 인생을 ~ 보다 think back [look back] to the past life// 왔던 길을 ~가다 retrace one's steps [way] / turn back [return] the way one has come / go back over one's way.

되찾다 1 [되돌려 받다] take [get] back. ¶영토를 ~ recover territory// 그는 그녀에게 빌려준 책을 되찾았다 He took back the book he had lent [(미) loaned] her.
2 [회복하다] recover (oneself). ¶침착을 ~ regain [recover] one's composure// 충격에서 제정신을 ~ get over one's shock// 그는 건강을 되찾았다 He recovered his health.// 마을은 평온을 되찾았다 The town was restored to peace and quiet. / The town recovered its normal calm.// 그 팀은 후반에 가서 제 실력을 되찾았다 The team recovered in the second half.// 2, 3일 전 그는 아주 기가 죽어 있었는데 지금은 정상적인 활기를 되찾았다 A couple of days ago, he was really depressed, but he is in much better spirits now [(구어) has pulled out of it now].

되치이다 [당하다] be counterattacked; have the tables turned upon one; [일이 뒤집히다] go for wool and come home shorn; a thing turns out to be contrary to one's hope. ¶일이 되치인 격이로군 It is a case of the biter having been bit.

되풀이 [반복] (a) repetition; a repeat; reiteration. **되풀이하다** repeat; reiterate; do (something) over again. ¶되풀이하여 repeatedly / over again / over and over (again) / again and again// 그는 몇 번이고 되풀이해서 말했다 He said it over and over. / (무의식적으로) He repeated himself many times.// 똑같은 실수를 두 번 다시 되풀이하지 마라 Don't make the same mistake twice. / Don't repeat the same mistake.// 역사는 되풀이한다 History repeats itself. / History is the record of repetition.// 그는 사직할 생각은 전혀 없다고 되풀이하여 말했다 He repeated that he had no intention of resigning.// 그녀는 남편의 편지를 되풀이해서 읽었다 She read her husband's letter again and again.

된똥 hard excrements [feces / stool].

된바람 [강풍] a strong [severe / high / rushing] wind; a gale; a hurricane; [북풍을 의미하는 뱃사람의 말] a north [northerly] wind; (시어) Boreas.

된밥 hard-boiled [overcooked] rice.

된서리 a heavy [hard / severe] frost. ¶그날 밤엔 ~가 내렸다 There was [We had] a hard frost that night.

된서리를 맞다 suffer from a heavy frost; [타격받다] receive a bitter blow; be hard [severely] hit (by); take a stiff beating; be severely affected (by); suffer heavily. ¶소매치기들은 경찰의 일제 검거로 된서리를 맞았다 Pickpockets were hard hit by a police roundup.// 면직물업계는 인플레이션으로 된서리를 맞았다 The cotton industry was seriously affected by inflation.

된서방 (-書房) an overbearing [a domineering / a cruel] husband.

된서방(을) 맞다 be treated harshly [cruelly].

된소리 [언] a fortis (*pl.* fortes).

된장 (-醬) *doenjang*; fermented soybean paste. ¶~을 넣고 끓이다 cook [boil] in *doenjang*// 무를 ~에 절이다 preserve a radish in *doenjang*.

● **된장국** *doenjangguk*; beanpaste potage [soup].

될성부르다 promising. ¶일이 ~ bid fair to succeed.

될성부른 나무는 떡잎부터 알아본다 (속담) Genius displays itself even in childhood.; Sandalwood is fragrant even in seed leaf.

됨됨이 1 (사람의) the man; one's nature [disposition / character / personality]. ¶~가 귀골스럽다 look noble / have the appearance of a high personage // ~가 군인감이다 be made[cut out] for a soldier // 그는 사람 ~가 믿음직하다 He is reliable by nature. // 이것으로 그의 ~를 알 수 있다 This shows what he is made of[what he is (like)]. / This is characteristic of him. // 그는 사람 ~가 변변치 못하다 He is wretched[sorry / poor / sad] stuff. 2 (물건의) make; makeup; structure; workmanship. ¶이 옷장은 ~가 조잡하다 This wardrobe is cheap in make.

됫박 1 〈속〉 a doe. ⇨되 2 [되 대신 쓰는 바가지] a gourd bowl used as a measure. ¶쌀을 ~으로 사다 buy rice by the doe / [조금씩 사다] buy rice in small quantities.

됫술 [한 되쯤의 술] about one doe of liquor; [되로 파는 술] (rice) wine sold by the doe.

두 two; a couple (of). ¶~ 가지 two kinds (of) (종류) / two ways(방법) // ~ 가지로 in two ways / doubly // ~ 가지 견해 two (different) opinions[interpretations / versions] // ~ 내외 a (married) couple / husband[man] and wife // ~ 배 double / two times // ~ 살 난 아이 a child of two / ~서넛씩 by[in] twos and threes / ~잔 잔 two glasses of milk // ~ 가지로 해석되다 can be construed in two ways / admit of two different interpretations.

두(頭) 1 [골치]. ¶아이고 ~야 What a headache[trouble / nuisance]! 2 [네발짐승의 수를 세는 단위] head (단수·복수 동형). ¶50~의 가축 fifty head of cattle.

두각(頭角) [뛰어난 재능] a brilliant talent. ¶~을 나타내다 cut[make] a conspicuous [brilliant] figure (in) / distinguish oneself / stand head and shoulders (above others) / rise into prominence / stand out / lead all the rest // 동료들 사이에서 단연 ~을 나타내다 stand a giant among one's colleagues / tower above one's fellows // 그는 뛰어난 재능으로 ~을 나타내고 있다 He stands out among men for his brilliant mental powers. // 그는 수학에서 ~을 나타내기 시작했다 He began to distinguish himself in mathematics. // 그는 선수 중에서 쿼터백으로서 ~을 나타내고 있다 Among the team members, he stands out as a fine quarterback. // 그는 실업계에서 ~을 나타내고 있다 He cuts a brilliant figure in business circles.

두개(頭蓋) [생] the cranium (pl. ~s, -nia); the skull; the brainpan.

● **두개골** the skull; the cranium (pl. ~s, -nia); the cranial bone.

두건(頭巾) a mourner's hempen hood. ¶~을 쓰다 put on a hempen hood.

두겁 a cap; [붓두껍] a writing-brush cap.

두견(杜鵑) 1 [동] a (common, little) cuckoo. ⇨두견이(⇨두견) 2 [진달래] an azalea.

● **두견이** [동] a (common, little) cuckoo (pl. ~s).

두고두고 [여러 차례] many times; repeatedly; over and over (again); [오래도록] (for) long; for a long time; for a good while; [영원히] forever; eternally; for good (and all); through all eternity[ages]. ¶~ 먹다 keep (something) and eat (it) sparingly // ~ 생각하다 think continually of[about] (something) / turn (a thing) over and over in one's mind // 이 원한은 ~ 잊지 못하겠다 I shall carry the resentment to the grave. // 은혜는 ~ 잊지 않겠습니다 I shall be grateful to you as long as I live. / I shall always remember your kindness to me. // ~ 당신을 잊을 수 없을 겁니다 You will be ever in my mind[thoughts]. // 그것은 ~ 잊혀지지 않는다 The memory haunts me. / It haunts my memory. / I can't shake quite loose of it.

두근거리다 throb; palpitate; pulsate; pulse; beat fast; [불안하다] feel uneasy[nervous] (without any known cause). ¶두근거리는 가슴을 가라앉히다 soothe one's agitation / calm one's agitated breast / compose [collect] oneself / suppress one's agitation / collect oneself // 가슴이 두근거려서 편지 봉투를 뜯지도 못했다 My heart was beating so fast (that) I could not even open the letter. // 가슴을 두근거리면서 차례를 기다렸다 I waited for my turn with a pounding heart. // (걱정 때문에) 가슴이 두근거린다 (구어) I have butterflies in my stomach. // 기쁨에 가슴이 두근거렸다 My heart leaped with joy. // 간밤에는 가슴이 두근거려 잠을 잘 수 없었다 Last night I felt uneasy and could not sleep.

두근두근 pit-a-pat; palpitating; throbbing. **두근두근하다** throb; feel uneasy. ⇨두근거리다

두꺼비 [동] a toad.

두꺼비 파리 잡아먹듯(속담) eat up anything in a twinkling.

● **두꺼비씨름** a tie game.

두꺼비집 [전] a fuse box; a (safety) cutout.

두껍다 thick; heavy; massive. ¶두꺼운 책 a bulky[stout / massive / thick] volume // 두꺼운 웃옷 a heavy coat // 두꺼운 종이 thick paper / a heavy grade of paper // 두꺼운 벽 a heavy[thick / solid] wall // 두꺼운 판자 a thick board // 두껍게 thickly // 낯이 ~ be brazen-(faced)[barefaced] / be shameless [impudent / audacious] // 두껍게 하다 thicken / make (a thing) thicker // (옷을) 두껍게 입다 clothe oneself thickly // 두껍게 [저미다] slice off (a piece) thick // 빵 조각에 잼을 두껍게 바르다 spread jam thick on a slice of bread // 눈이 두껍게 덮여 있다 be thickly covered with snow // 나는 소시지를 두껍게 잘랐다 I sliced the sausage thick.

두께 thickness. ¶5피트의 ~ a thickness of five feet // 3치의 ~로 to a thickness of three chi // ~ 2미터 two meters in thickness / a thickness of two meters // ~가 두껍다[얇다] be thick [thin] // ~가 적당하다 be of moderate thick-ness // ~ 5인치다 be five inches thick [in thickness] / have a thickness of five inches // ~가 얼마입니까 How thick is it? / What is its thickness?

두뇌(頭腦) a head; a brain; brains. ¶인공~ a mechanical brain / 전자~ an electronic brain // 치밀[냉정 / 산만]한 ~ a close [cool / loose] head // 예민한 ~ an acute intellect // 피로한 ~ a weary brain // ~가 명석한 사람 a clear-headed person / a man with a clear head // ~를 명석하게 하는 비결 the secret of a clear head // 보통 ~를 가진 사람 a person of average brains // ~가 모자라다 have a poor[bad / dull] head / have no brains [head] / be dull-brained / be slow-witted // ~가 명석하다 have a clear[good] head / have a good headpiece / have brains (in one's head) / be clear-headed / be bright // ~를 명석히 하다 make one's head clear /

두다

develop a clear-thinking brain // 수학적인 ~를 갖고 있다 have a mathematical brain / have a head for mathematics.

● 두뇌 유출 brain drain; an outflow of brain. 두뇌 집단 a group of brains; a think-tank(er).

두다¹ **1** [놓다] put; place; set; emplace; position; (구어) park; deposit(일정한 장소에). ¶제자리에 갖다 ~ put it back in its place // 나는 돈을 금고에 넣어 두었다 I put [keep] the money in a safe. // 사전을 어디다 두었지 Where did you put the dictionary? // 어디 이것을 둘 자리는 없을까 Is there a place for this [to put this]? // 이 책을 원래의 선반 제자리에 갖다 두세요 Please put the book back on the shelf where you found it [it belongs].

2 [남기다] leave (behind). ¶두고 온 물건 a thing [an article] left behind // 두고 오다 [가다] leave (a thing) behind (one) / leave (a thing) for [with] (a person) / forget (a thing) / forget to bring [take] (something) // 우산을 두고 오다 mislay one's umbrella // 그는 옷짐에 두고 가시오 Leave it next door. // 그는 가방을 책상 위에 둔 채로 갔다 His bag was lying on the desk as he had left it. // 그는 가족을 서울에 두고 부산에 와 있다 He has left his family behind in Seoul, and is living in Busan.

3 [일정한 상태로 있게 하다] leave; allow; let; […하게 두다] keep; have. ¶일을 손대지 않고 ~ leave one's work undone // 내버려 [되어 가는 대로] ~ let (things) slide // 문을 열린 채 ~ leave the door open // 그녀가 하고 싶은 말을 하게 두었다 I let her have her say. // 그를 오랫동안 기다리게 두었다 I kept him waiting for a long time. // 그는 하던 일을 버려두고 외출했다 He went out, leaving the work half done. // 그 제도는 그대로 두기로 하자 Let's leave the system as it is. // 다른 것은 그대로 두고라도 자동차는 안전성이 제일이다 In choosing a car we must think of safety first. // 이 문제는 이대로 둘 수 없다 We cannot let the matter go at this. / We cannot allow matters to rest there. // 나를 그대로 놓아 두세요 Leave [Let] me alone. // 나는 앓아 누운 어머니를 그대로 둘 수는 없다 I can't leave my sick mother unattended [by herself]. // 그들의 무례를 그대로 두어서는 안 된다 You shouldn't leave those boy's bad manners uncorrected.

4 [설치하다] establish; open; set up. ¶도서관을 ~ establish a library // 클럽을 ~ organize a club // 사무실을 ~ have (its / one's) office (in a building) // 교보에 사무실을 두기로 했다 We are going to open an office in Gyobo. // 세계 각지에 지점을 두고 있다 We have branch offices all over the world.

5 [보존하다] keep; hold; store (up). ¶귀중품은 어디에 두나요 Where do you keep your valuables? // 이 고기는 내일까지 둬도 괜찮을까요 Will this fish keep overnight? // 떨어진 사과는 오래 둘 수 없다 Fallen apples do not keep long. // 이렇게 많은 구두를 맡아 둘 장소가 없다 There is not enough room to keep so many shoes.

6 [고용하다] engage; keep; employ; [묵게 하다] lodge; keep. ¶세 명의 하인을 ~ keep three servants // 첩을 ~ keep a mistress [concubine] // 새 비서를 두었다 We employed a new secretary.

7 [배치하다] assign. ¶각 부에 장관을 ~ assign a Minister over each ministry.

8 [주둔시키다] post(초병); station(군대).

9 [사이를 남겨 놓다]. ¶간격을 ~ leave a (wider) space between (the lines) // 2미터의 간격을 두고 at intervals of two meters / two meters apart (from each other) // 같은 간격을 두고 at equal spaces // 이웃 마을은 산을 사이에 두고 그 너머에 있다 The neighboring village is beyond [on the other side of] the mountain. // 두 나라 대표는 테이블을 사이에 두고 마주 앉았다 The delegates of the two nations sat across the table from each other. // 내 집은 그의 집과 두 집을 사이에 두고 있습니다 My house is two doors down from his.

10 [차이·중점을] lay; put; place. ¶차이를 ~ make a difference // 차별을 ~ distinguish (between) / make a discrimination (between) / draw [make] a distinction // 중점을 ~ lay [put / place] emphasis [stress] (on) / emphasize / accent(uate).

11 [(마음속에 어떤 생각을) 지니다] bear; entertain; cherish; set on; hold; harbor; have. ¶의심을 ~ harbor suspicion / entertain a doubt // 마음을 ~ have a mind to / be determined to / fix [set] one's mind on // 염두에 ~ give one's mind [a thought] (to) / bear [have / keep] (something) in mind / remember // 염두에 두지 않다 do not care (about) / give no thought [heed] (to) / take no thought [notice] (to) // 마음에 두고 잊지 않다 hold (the matter) in remembrance / bear in mind // 그는 그런 것을 마음에 둘 사람이 아니다 He is not the type of person who cares about such a thing. // 그는 학자에 뜻 [마음]을 두고 있다 He has set his heart on becoming a scholar.

12 [바둑 등을] play (chess / baduk(go)); move (a chessman / a checker). ¶4점 놓고 ~ accept a four-stone handicap // 체스의 말을 [쓰다] move a piece [a man] on a chessboard // 한 판 두시지 않으시겠습니까 How about (playing) a game?

13 [지칭하다] name; nominate; designate; mean. ¶너를 두고 하는 말이다 It means you.

14 [넣다] put in; add; stuff. ¶밥에 팥을 ~ put red beans in the rice // 이불에 솜을 ~ stuff a quilt with cotton.

두고 보다 [지켜보다] watch (intently); keep (a good) watch (over). ¶두고 보자 (일의 결과를) See how things will shape up. / Watch and wait. / (위협적으로) You will have to pay dearly for it. / There will be the devil to pay. / You shall smart for it. / It will cost you dearly. / You won't get away with this. / 두고 보면 알 거다 Wait and see. / Time will show [tell]. / You shall (soon) see.

두다² [동작의 결과를 지니어 감] do something to get (it) out of the way; get (it) done; do (it) once and for good; get (it) over with; finish up; do (it) thoroughly now (so it will not have to be done again). ¶미리 조사해 ~ examine beforehand / have (it) examined before ... // 내 말을 잘 들어 두어라 Pay attention to what I'm going to say. // 그것도 알아 두면 써먹을 날이 있을 걸세 If you learn how to do it, you would have a chance to make use of it.

두더지 [동] a mole. ¶~가 화단 밑을 팠다 A mole has bored its way under the flower bed.
　두더지 혼인 같다(속담) cherish an empty hope; build a castle in the air.
두덩 (땅의) a bank; a levee.
두두룩하다 swollen; protuberant; raised; elevated; heaved; high. ¶젖가슴이 두두룩한 busty / round-bosomed∥두두룩한 젖가슴 full breasts. **두두룩이** protuberantly; protrusively; into a swell[an elevation]. ¶흙을 ~ 쌓아 올리다 pile[heap] earth up into a small mound.
두둑 (밭 사이의 둑) a bank; a levee; a ridge between fields; [이랑] ridge (in plowed ground).
두둑하다 1 [매우 두껍다] thick; heavy. ¶밖이 꽤 추우니 두둑하게 입고 가거라 It's pretty cold outside, so you'd better bundle up. **두둑이** thickly; heavily.
　2 [풍부하다] plenty; quite a lot; ample; satisfactory. ¶두둑한 사례를 받다 be given a liberal[handsome] reward / be rewarded generously∥돈이 두둑하게 있다 have plenty of money / be flush of money / have a plump purse∥그는 웨이터에게 팁을 두둑하게 주었다 He tipped the waiter handsomely. **두둑이** much; plenty; satisfactorily. ¶돈을 ~ 집어 주다 give plenty of money∥팁을 ~ 주다 tip (a porter) handsomely.
　3 swollen; protuberant. ⇨두두룩하다
두둔하다 back (the weak); shield[screen / shelter] (a person from); support; give support to; stand by; side with; [변호하다] plead[speak up] foe (a person). ¶(싸움에서) 자기 자식을 ~ back one's own child (in a quarrel)∥약자를 ~ stand by the weak [underdog]∥부하를 두둔하여 말하다 talk in favor of[in defense of] one's subordinate∥그를 두둔할 사람은 한 사람도 없었다 No one supported[stood by] / sided with] him.
두둥실 floating gently[lightly]; in an airy manner. ¶하늘 높이 ~ 뜬 기구 a balloon floating on high∥풍선이 ~ 공중에 떠올랐다 A balloon drifted[rose] lazily up into the sky.∥흰 구름이 ~ 하늘에 떠 있다 White clouds are floating in the sky.
두드러기 [의] hives; nettle rash; urticaria. ¶~가 돋다[나다] get nettle rash / have urticaria / form wheals / break out in a rash ∥~가 온몸에 났다[돋았다] A rash broke out over my whole body. / I[My whole body] broke out in a rash all over.∥상한 생선에 중독되어 ~가 났다 Being poisoned by bad fish, I had a breaking-out.
두드러지다 1 [뚜렷하다] conspicuous; prominent (figure); marked (event); remarkable (fellow); notable (person); striking; exceptional; distinct; clear-cut (skyline). ¶(신문에서) 두드러진 사건 a highlighted news event ∥두드러진 인물 a great figure (in history)∥두드러진 성공을 거두고 with remarkable success∥둘 사이에는 두드러진 유사점이 있다 There is a marked[striking] resemblance between the two.∥근년에 지원자 수가 두드러지게 증가했다 The number of applicants has markedly increased in recent years.∥이 저수지의 수위가 두드러지게 내려갔다 The water level of this reservoir has dropped considerably.∥그 사건이 그녀의 치사함을 두드러지게 나타냈다 The incident clearly brought out her meanness. / The incident threw her baseness into relief.∥그는 두드러지게 진전했다 He has made remarkable progress.∥이 학급에는 두드러지게 우수한 학생이 없다 There are no outstanding students in this class.
　2 [불룩하다] swollen; raised; elevated; [내밀다] swell; protuberate; protrude; project; stand out (from the surface); heave (up); raise; become elevated; be embossed. ¶종이에 무늬를 두드러지게 넣다 emboss the paper with a design∥뽀루지가 두드러졌다 A boil was swollen up.∥그는 글자가 두드러져 있는가 보려고 그 위를 손가락으로 더듬었다 He ran his fingers over the letters to see if they had been embossed.
두드리다 [치다] strike; beat; hit; knock; thrash; slap(손바닥으로); rap(똑똑); tap[pat] (가볍게); pound[slog / bang](세게); clap (hands)(마주치다); maul(두드려 상처를 내다). ¶아이의 볼기를 ~ spank a baby∥막대기로 빈 깡통을 ~ tap a stick on an empty can∥손수건으로 눈두덩을 가볍게 ~ dab one's eyes with a handkerchief∥어깨를 톡톡 ~ pat (a person) on the shoulder∥창문을 톡톡 ~ tap against the window∥가슴을 ~ beat the breast(탄식하며) / tap[sound] (a person's) breast(의사가)∥등을 가볍게 ~ clap (a person) on the back∥타이프라이터를 ~ hammer at a typewriter∥북을 ~ beat a drum∥고기를 두드려 부드럽게 하다 pound meat (to make it tender)∥녹초가 되게 ~ beat (a person) to a jelly∥나는 융단을 두드려 먼지를 털어 냈다 I beat the dust out of the carpet.∥우박이 창문을 두드리고 있다 Hailstones are hitting[beating against] the window(s).∥누군가가 문을 두드리고 있다 Someone is knocking on the door.
두들기다 beat; hit; knock. ¶늘씬하게 ~ beat [pommel] (a person) to a jelly∥두들겨 내쫓다 beat and drive out∥문을 두들겨 부수다 batter the door down.
두랄루민 [화] duralumin. ¶~ 판(板) a duralumin plate.
두런거리다 whisper to each other affectionately. ⇨도란거리다
두런두런 in an affectionate undertone. ⇨도란도란
두렁 a ridge between (rice) fields; a levee.
　두렁에 누운 소(속담) a person in easy circumstances.
두레 1 [물 푸는 기구] a scoop (used in irrigation). **2** [농군의 모임] a group of farmers organized for mutual help in the busiest season; a cooperative[help-neighbor] farming team.
두레박 a well bucket. ¶~으로 우물에서 물을 펐다 I drew water from the well with a bucket.
　●**두레박줄** a well rope.
두려움 [공포] fear; (a) terror; dread; horror; [염려] apprehension(s); anxiety; concern; [외경(畏敬)] reverence; veneration; awe. ¶~으로[때문에] out of fear / from[with] fear / driven by fear / in horror[a fright]∥시험에 떨어지지 않을까 하는 ~ a dread of failing in the examination∥~을 지니다 entertain fears[apprehensions / misgivings] / fear / be afraid (of) / be filled with fear∥~을 모르다

두려워하다

be fearless[dauntless / intrepid] / be a stranger to fear // ~으로 부들부들 떨다 tremble like a leaf in terror // ~에 휩싸이다 be seized with fear / be struck with horror // 그는 ~에 말도 할 수 없었다 He could not speak for fear.

두려워하다 1 [무서워하다] fear; dread; be afraid[fearful] of; stand in fear of; be frightened[scared / terrified] at; have a horror [dread] of; be overawed. ¶두려워하여 with fear / in fearfulness / in horror / in a fright // …을 늘 ~ be[live] in constant fear of … / 남을 두려워하게 하다 inspire a person with awe / keep a person in awe // 두려워하지 않다 do not fear; be unafraid (of) / be unterrified // 두려워할 것이 못 되다 be not formidable / there is nothing to fear (in) // 그는 죽음을 두려워하지 않았다 He did not fear[was not afraid of] death.

2 [걱정하다] fear; be afraid of; apprehend; be apprehensive of. ¶…하지 않을까 두려워하여 for fear (of doing / that[lest] … should do) / fearful of (getting infected) // 최악의 사태를 ~ fear the worst // 실패를 두려워하지 말고 하라 Don't be afraid of failing. Just do it. // 아버지에게 꾸지람 들을 일이 두려워 그는 아무 말도 않았다 He said nothing for fear that his father would scold him.

3 [어려워하다] stand in awe of; be struck with awe. ¶두려워하며 우러러보는 마음 a reverential awe // 성스러운 ~ have a holy horror of // 어른을 ~ stand in awe of one's elders / venerate one's elders // 어른을 두려워할 줄 모르다 be defiant of one's elders / do not pay due respect to one's elders // 그는 신을 조금도 두려워하지 않는다 He has no reverence for God.

두렵다 1 [무섭다] fearful; scared; frightened; terrified; (서술적) be afraid of. ¶탄로 날 것이 두려워서 in fear of discovery // …이 두려워서 for fear of (failure) // 두려워서 몸을 움츠리다 shrink for fear // 두려워 떨다 tremble with [shudder for] fear / be in fear and trembling // 나는 그 사람이 ~ I am afraid of him. // 나는 죽는 것이 조금도 두렵지 않다 I am not afraid[scared] of death in the least. / I can look death calmly in the face. // 그 계획을 생각만 해도 두려운 마음이 생긴다 The mere thought of the plan fills me with dread. // 그 아이의 장래를 생각하면 막연한 불안감이 앞서 두려운 생각이 든다 I have vague apprehension about that child's future.

2 [염려스럽다] feared; fearful; apprehended; (서술적) be afraid of; be in danger of. ¶…이 두려워 for fear of (losing money) / lest (one) should / from fear (of punishment) // 그는 실수를 할까 봐 두려웠다 He was fearful of making a mistake. // 위험이 있을까 봐 ~ It is apprehended that there will be some danger.

3 [경외심이 가득하다] awed; awesome; awestricken. ¶두려워서 고개를 못 들다 be too much awed to raise one's head // 그는 그 산의 웅장함에 두려운 감마저 느꼈다 He was awed by the majesty of the mountain. // 소녀는 두려운 기색도 없이 대통령과 악수했다 The little girl boldly shook hands with the President.

두령(頭領) a boss; a chief; a head; a leader; a master; a captain.

두루 [빠짐없이] without exception; thoroughly; [전면적으로] all over; all around; [일반적으로] generally; universally; [널리] widely; extensively; far and wide. ¶~ 찾다 make a wide search / comb // 온 세계에 ~ 알려지다 be known all over the world // 도시를 ~ 안내하다 take (a person) all over city // 전국을 ~ 돌아다니다 go around all over the country // 그것은 세상이 ~ 아는 사실이다 It is a matter of universal[common] knowledge. / The fact is known to the general public. // 그에게 서울을 ~ 구경시켜 주었다 I showed him round[all over] Seoul.

두루마기 a *durumagi*; a Korean topcoat.

두루마리 [둘둘 만 종이] a roll of paper; [족자] a scroll; [편지지] rolled letter paper. ¶~를 펴다[말다] unroll[roll up] a scroll.
● 두루마리 화장지 a toilet roll; a roll of toilet paper.

두루뭉수리 1 [함부로 뭉쳐진 사물] an object of nondescript shape; an indescribable thing; an unshapely thing; a mess. ¶~를 만들어 놓다 make a mess of / put out of shape. 2 [변변하지 못한 사람] a nondescript; a good-for-nothing (fellow); a nobody.

두루미 [동] a red-crested white crane; a Japanese crane; a red-crowned crane. ¶재~ a white-naped crane // 흑~ a hooded crane.

두루치기 1 [둘러쓰기] using a thing for various purposes; alternate use of a thing. ¶~ 일꾼 a servant of all work / a do-all / a factotum. 2 [조갯살 등을 데친 음식] a kind of bouillabaisse.

두르다 1 [둘러싸다] put around; surround (with / by); enclose (with / in); encircle; hem[shut] in. ¶식탁보에 레이스로 테를 두르다[edge] a tablecloth with lace // 줄을 ~ rope in[off] (▶ off는 들어가지 못하게, in은 안에 가두기 위하여) // 산울타리를 두른[둘러친] 집 a house surrounded[enclosed] by a hedge // 정원에 담을 ~ wall in a garden // 프라이팬에 기름을 ~ oil a frying pan // 안전지대는 로프로 둘러져 있었다 The safety zone was roped off. // 그는 집을 산울타리로 둘렀다 He enclosed his house with a hedge.

2 [입다·차다] wear[wrap] about one; engird(le). ¶완장을 ~ wear an armband // 치마를 허리에 ~ wrap a skirt around one's waist // 허리에 띠를 ~ bind a belt about [round] one's waist // 농부는 살을 에는 바람 속에서도 얼굴에 반쯤 수건을 두르고 일하고 있었다 The farmer were working in the biting wind, his face partially covered with a towel.

3 [마음대로 다루다] wield; have (a person) under perfect control; have (a person) well in hand; turn (a person) round one's little finger.

4 [변통하다] make (a) shift (with); shift; contrive; manage to; borrow[raise] (money). ¶돈을 ~ raise[borrow] money / find funds // 돈을 둘러 주다 lend money / accommodate (a person) with money.

5 [속이다] deceive; cheat; swindle; play a trick on; take in (a person).

두르르 1 [말리는 모양] (form) into a roll [scroll]; (wrap) round (on itself). ¶지도 [천]를 ~ 말다 roll up a map[the cloth] // 돛을 ~ 말다 furl the sails of a ship. 2 [바퀴가 구르는 소리] with a rumble. ¶마차가 ~ 굴러

갔다 A carriage rumbled[rolled] along.
두름 a string (of dried vegetables). ¶굴비 한 ~ a string of 20 dried corvinas.
두리번거리다 stare about; look around (restlessly); glance round. ¶눈을 두리번거리며 with unsteady eyes // 두리번거리며 찾다 look around for (something) // 바보처럼 두리번거리지 마라 Don't stare about in that idiotic fashion.
두리번두리번 looking around restlessly [nervously]; with unsteady eyes. 두리번두리번하다 look around (restlessly). ⇨¶두리번거리다
두말 a double tongue; equivocation. 두말하다 [일구이언하다] be double-tongued; break[go back on] one's word[promise]; [이러니저러니 하다] say this or that; raise objection. ¶두말할 것 없이 of course / without saying this or that[anything further] // 두말하지 않는 사람 a man of his word // 두말하지 않고 frankly / honestly / without saying this or that[anything further] / without complaint [grumbling] / without objection[question] // 두말하지 않고 승낙하다 snap (at a bargain) // 한 입으로 ~ keep two tongues in one mouth / speak out of both corners of mouth / tell a lie // 두말하지 않다 keep one's word / mean what one says / be as good as one's word // 나는 두말하지 않는다 When I say "yes," I mean it. // 남아는 두말하지 않는 법이다 A gentleman never goes back on his word.
두말없이 [즉각] readily; without hesitation; without a second thought; [군말 없이] without asking questions; [딱 잘라] point-blank; flatly. ¶~ 승낙하다 consent readily [gladly enough] / give a ready consent // ~ 거절하다 refuse point-blank[flatly] / give (a person) a flat refusal // ~ 거절당하다 meet with a square rebuff // 그는 ~ 동의했다 He was only too glad to consent.
두메 an out-of-the-way mountain village; a secluded village in the mountains; the remote countryside; (미) the backcountry; (미) the backwoods. ¶~에서 살다 live in the backcountry[remote countryside].
두목(頭目) a chief; a head; a boss; a captain; a skipper; a kingpin; a big shot; a mastermind(흑막의); a ringleader(폭동 등의). ¶깡패 ~ a gangleader / (속어) a big gun // 산적의 ~ the head[chief] of the bandits // ~ 기질의 magnanimous // ~급의 big-shot // …을 ~으로 하여 with (a person) at its head // 이 되다 boss it over other people.
두문불출(杜門不出) confining oneself at home; a stay-at-home life; a seclusive life (at home). 두문불출하다 confine oneself at home; lead a stay-at-home life; be in the seclusion of one's own home.
두문자(頭文字) [첫머리에 오는 글자] the first letter (of a word).
두발(頭髮) the hair (of the head).
두벌갈이 [농] plowing[ploughing] for the second time; a second plowing. 두벌갈이하다 make a second plowing.
두부(豆腐) a dubu; bean curd[cheese]. ¶~ 한 모 a cake of dubu // ~ 찌꺼기 dubu refuse.
 두부살에 바늘뼈 (속담) be very delicate [fragile].
● 두부 장수 dubu dealer[seller / maker].
두부(頭部) the head. ¶~의 cephalic // ~에 부상을 입다 be wounded in the head.
두상(頭上) [머리] your[his / her] head; [머리 위] the top of one's head; the crown. ¶~에 on[over] the head.
두상(頭狀) ¶~의 capitate(d).
● 두상화(-花) [식] capitate flowers; a capitulum (pl. -la); a caput (pl. capita); a flower head.
두서(頭書) **1** a preface. ⇨"머리말 **2** [본문 앞에 쓴 글] a superscription.
두서(頭緖) [조리] consistence; coherence; [차례] order. ¶~ 없는 inconsistent / incoherent.
두서너 a few; some; several. ¶~ 번 several times // ~ 마디 a few words // ~ 집 건너 a few doors away // ~ 마디만 말씀드리겠습니다 Allow me to speak just a few words. // 겨우 ~ 사람만이 그 강연에 참석했다 Only a few people attended the lecture.
두서넛 a few. ⇨"두서너
두성(頭聲) [음] head voice.
두세 two or three; a few. ¶~ 번 two or three times / more than once // 어린이가 ~ 명 공원에 있는 것을 보았다 I saw some children in the park.
두셋 two or three. ⇨"두세 ¶~쯤은 당해 낼 수 있다 I can cope with two or three.
두수(頭數) [동물의 마릿수] the number of heads.
두어 [물.가량] about two; a couple of. ¶~ 사람 a couple of people or so // ~ 마리의 소 about two head of cattle // ~ 달 about two months.
두엄 compost; barnyard[farmyard] manure. ¶밭에 ~을 주다 compost[manure] the field.
● 두엄 더미 a compost heap[pile]. 두엄 풀 grass for compost; composted grass.
두운(頭韻) alliteration. ¶ "Might"와 "main"은 ~을 맞춘다 "Might" and "main" alliterate.
두유(豆油) soy(bean) oil. ⇨"콩기름
두유(豆乳) soybean milk; soya milk.
두음(頭音) [언] the initial sound of a syllable (of a word).
두절(杜絶) stoppage; cessation; interruption; suspension(중절). ¶전신의 ~ telegraphic [transmission] interruption. 두절하다 be stopped; be cut off; be interrupted; be blocked; cease; be paralyzed. →¶차량 소통이 두절되었다 The flow of traffic stopped. // 밤이 깊어져서 사람의 왕래도 두절되었다 The night advanced, and the street was deserted. // 이 야기가 두절되어 서먹서먹해졌다 I felt awkward when there was a lull[break] in our conversation. // 갑자기 통신이 두절되었다 Radio communication was abruptly cut off.
두족강(頭足綱) [동] the cephalopod.
두주(頭註) a headnote. ¶~를 달다 put headnotes in a book.
두주(斗酒) kegs of wine. ¶~를 불사하다 be ready to drink gallons of wine / drink like a fish.
두창(痘瘡) smallpox. ⇨"천연두
두텁다 warm; affectionate; kind; cordial; hearty; deep (friendship). ¶두터운 우의 a warm[deep] friendship // 정이 ~ be very friendly / be kind and warmhearted / be cordial (to a friend) // 우의를 두텁게 하다

두통

deepen the friendship.//우리들의 사랑은 날로 두터워 갔다 We loved each other with increasing fervor.//이 지방 사람들은 인정이 ~ These local people have warm hearts. / These local people are warm hearted.

두통(頭痛) (a) headache. ¶편~ (a) migraine (headache)//머리가 깨질 것 같은 ~ a splitting headache//잠을 자서[산책하여] ~을 고치다 sleep[walk] off the headache//조금[몹시]~이 난다 I have a slight[bad] headache.//그는 ~이 잘 일어난다 He is subject to headaches.

● **두통거리** a headache; the source of trouble; a thorn in one's side[flesh]; a nuisance. ¶그에게는 그 문제가 언제나 ~다 That problem is a constant source of brainracking troubles to him.//대기 오염 문제는 아주 ~다 The air pollution problem is a real headache.//게으른 내 아들이 ~다 My lazy son is a source of worry[concern] to me. **두통약** a headache specific.

두툴두툴 rough(ly); ruggedly; lumpily; unevenly. **두툴두툴하다** rough; rugged; lumpy; uneven; (여드름 등이) pimply; pimpled; (조직이나 표면이) granular; granulated. ¶두툴두툴한 표면 a lumpy surface//두툴두툴한 나무 껍질 a rugged bark//여드름이 두툴두툴하게 난 얼굴 a pimpled[pimply] face//두툴두툴하게 만든 가죽 granulated leather//두툴두툴하게 만들다 granulate//길이 몹시 ~ The road is awfully rough.

두툼하다 (very) thick; heavy. ¶두툼한 외투 a thick[heavy] overcoat//두툼한 책 a thick [bulky] book[volume]//두툼한 입술 full lips //두툼한 돈뭉치 a bulky wad[roll] of notes / a thick[massive] stack of bills.

두호(斗護) protection; patronage; favor. ¶…의 ~ 아래 under the patronage of …. **두호하다** protect (the weak); patronize; favor; take (a person) under one's wing. ¶약자를 ~ protect the weak//그가 나를 두호해 주었다 He stood up for me.

둑 1 [제방] a bank; a dike; [호안(護岸)을 위한 제방] an embankment; a levee. ¶강을 따라 ~을 쌓다 build a bank[an embankment] along a river//홍수로 ~이 무너졌다 The flood (waters) broke down the riverbank [levee]. 2 [언덕] a bank; a ridge; a mound. ¶논~ a ridge between rice fields//철롯~ a mound for railroad.

둔각(鈍角) [수] an obtuse angle.
● **둔각 삼각형** [수] an obtuse triangle.

둔감하다(鈍感-) insensible; [감각·감정의 반응이 둔하다] insensitive (to); dull; stolid; obtuse; [무신경하다] thick-skinned; thickheaded. ¶둔감해지다 (사람이) become insensitive / (감각이) become dull//그 여자는 자기에 관한 소문 일체에 ~ She is impervious to all the gossip about her.//그의 피부는 더위에 대해 둔감해졌다 His skin is not very sensitive to heat. / His skin has lost sensitivity to heat.//그는 미(美)에 대하여 ~ He is insensitive[blind / (문이) insensible] to beauty.(▶ insensible은 전혀 반응이 없음)//그는 둔감해서 유머가 통하지 않는다 He is so dull that he fails to see a joke.//그녀는 남의 기분을 이해 못하는 여자가 되었다 She is too thick-skinned to understand other's feelings.

둔갑술(遁甲術) the occult art of transforming oneself (into).

둔갑하다(遁甲-) take the form[shape] (of); turn[change / transform] (oneself into something). ¶사람으로 둔갑한 여우 a fox in the shape of man / a fox in [assuming] human shape[form]. ➔¶요정은 호박을 마차로 둔갑시켰다 The fairy transformed [changed / turned] the pumpkin into a carriage.

둔기(鈍器) a blunt[dull] weapon. ¶~로 때리다 hit[strike] with a blunt instrument [weapon].

둔덕 [두두룩하게 언덕진 곳] a low hill; a (small) mound; a hillock; a knoll. ¶~진 mounded / hillocked / hillocky // ~지다 form [become] a mound.

둔부(臀部) the hips. ⇨엉덩이

둔세(遁世) seclusion[retirement] from the world. ¶출가 ~ monastic seclusion. **둔세하다** retire [seclude oneself] from the world; live secluded [apart] from the world.
● **둔세자** a recluse; a hermit.

둔재(鈍才) [우함] dullness; stupidity; [둔한 사람] a dull-witted [slow-witted] person; a dullard; a dullhead. ¶~의 dull-witted / slow-witted / dull.

둔중하다(鈍重-) be thickheaded; fatheaded; dull; heavy and clumsy; ponderous; logy; heavy; bovine. ¶둔중한 사람 a thickheaded [slow-witted] man//둔중한 동작 slow motion.

둔탁하다(鈍濁-) dull; thick; dead; slow; stupid; dull-witted; thick-witted. ¶둔탁한 소리 a dead sound//뭔가 둔탁한 소리가 났다 We heard a dull thud.

둔통(鈍痛) a dull pain. ¶~이 있다 have a dull pain (in).

둔팍하다(鈍-) thickheaded; slow-witted; stolid; stupid; dull.

둔필(鈍筆) [서투른 글씨] a poor handwriting; [필적이 서투른 사람] a poor hand.

둔하다(鈍-) 1 (성질·머리 등이) dull; slow; stupid; blunt; thickheaded; slow-witted; dull-witted. ¶둔한 사나이 a dull [stupid] fellow / a dolt / a dullard//감각이 ~ be dull-headed / be thick-skinned//그는 머리의 움직임이 ~ He is slow-witted [dull-witted].//그는 신경이 ~ He is slow to notice things. / He isn't very perceptive.//그것을 모르다니 너도 둔한 친구로군 You're stupid if you can't understand that!

2 (동작·상태 등이) slow; sluggish; inactive; inert. ¶둔하게 살찐 사나이 a chubby boy //그녀는 둔하게 두꺼운 스웨터를 입고 있다 She's all wrapped [bundled] up in a heavy sweater.//그는 동작이 ~ He is slow-moving. //그는 운동 신경이 ~ He has slow reflexes.

3 (소리가) thick (sound). ¶둔한 소리 a thick sound.

둔화(鈍化) blunting (of sensibility); slowdown (in the economy). **둔화하다** get[go] dull; slow (down); become[grow] dull; become blunt; weaken(약화)되다. ¶경제 성장률이 둔화했다 The rate of economic growth has slowed. ➔¶감각을 둔화시키다 dull [blunt] the[a person's] senses.

둘 two. ¶~ 다 both//~ 중 하나 one of the two / one between the two//~로 나누다 divide by two / divide in two//책상은 ~ 다 하얗게 칠해져 있었다 Both (of) the desks were painted white.// ~ 다 마음에 들지 않는다 Neither pleases me (will do).// 이 책은 ~ 다 재미있다 These books are both interesting.// 우리 ~ 중 한 사람이 잘못을 범하고 있다 One of us is wrong.

둘도 없다 [오직 하나뿐이다] unique; only; matchless; [아주 소중하다] a most precious; irreplaceable. ¶둘도 없는 친구 a once-in-a-lifetime friend // 창호는 그의 둘도 없는 아들이다 Changho is his one and only son.// 이 자유는 둘도 없는 것이다 Nothing can take the place of the freedom we now enjoy.// 이렇게 쓸모 있는 사전은 ~ This dictionary has no parallel in usefulness.// 그런 괴짜는 ~ You'll never find another person as eccentric as he is. / There is no one so eccentric as he.

둘둘 1 [둥글게 말리는 모양] into a roll [ball / scroll]. 2 [구르는 모양] with a twirl [whirl].

둘러대다 1 [꾸며 대다] give an evasive answer; cook up [concoct] an excuse; explain away; sophisticate. ¶이리저리 둘러대어 그 자리를 모면했다 I managed to get [talk myself] out of trouble for the time being with some excuse or other.// 그녀는 지각한 이유를 그럴듯하게 둘러댔다 She made up a good story to account for her lateness [a clever excuse for being late]. 2 [변통하다] manage to get (a loan); make (a) shift (with). ¶집을 사려고 돈을 ~ swing a loan in order to buy a house.

둘러막다 enclose; surround; environ; shut in; fence (a garden); wall in. ¶둘러막은 곳 an enclosed area / an enclosure // 담으로 땅을 ~ enclose [gird] a place with a fence [wall] // 병풍으로 ~ set up a screen all around.

둘러메다 (lift and) carry (a bag) over (the shoulder); fling (a thing) around one's shoulders. ¶카메라를 둘러메고 with a camera hanging from one's shoulder // 총을 둘러메고 행진하다 march with guns on one's shoulder // 그는 스키를 어깨에 둘러메고 있었다 He was carrying a pair of ski(s) on his shoulder.

둘러보다 look around [about]; take a glance around; make a survey (of); survey. ¶좌중을 ~ survey those present / make a survey of the company // 선생은 교실을 둘러보았다 The teacher looked around the classroom.

둘러서다 stand in a circle. ¶그들은 선생님을 중심으로 둘러섰다 They stood in a circle around their teacher. / They formed [made] a ring [circle] around their teacher.

둘러싸다 1 [주위를] enclose; environ; encircle; surround; [벽·담으로] wall in; [울타리로] fence. ¶그녀를 둘러싼 5인의 남성 the five men around her // 모닥불 [식탁]을 둘러싸고 앉다 sit around the fire [table] // 돌담으로 집을 ~ enclose a house with a stone wall // 못 주위를 좁은 길이 둘러싸고 있다 A narrow path circles the pond.// 그가 도착하자마자 신문 기자들이 그를 둘러쌌다 On his arrival newspaper reporters besieged him.// 경찰관들이 범인을 둘러쌌다 The police encircled [surrounded] the culprit.
2 [어떤 것을 중심 대상으로 하다] surround. ¶…을 둘러싸고 centering [pivoting] around … / in connection with / concerning … // 그의 실종을 둘러싼 비밀 a secret surrounding his disappearance // 그 돈의 출처를 둘러싼 뜬소문 rumors concerning the source of the money // 유산을 둘러싸고 다투다 fight over a legacy.
3 [포위하다] besiege; lay siege (to); invest; surround; envelop. ¶요새를 ~ lay siege to a fortress // 적을 ~ surround the enemy // 적군이 성을 둘러쌌다 Enemy troops besieged the castle.

둘러싸이다 be besieged [invested / surrounded / enclosed / girded]. ¶높은 울로 둘러싸인 집 a house enclosed by a high fence // 바다로 둘러싸인 나라 a country encircled by the sea // 그는 신문 기자들에게 둘러싸였다 He was surrounded by newspaper reporters.// 우리는 한 떼의 아이들에게 둘러싸였다 We were surrounded by a crowd of children. // 한반도는 삼면이 바다로 둘러싸여 있다 The Korean peninsular is surrounded by the sea on three sides.

둘러쌓다 pile (things) up in a circle. ¶집에 담을 ~ enclose a house with a fence / fence round [about] a house.

둘러쓰다 put on; cover with; pour (water) on (oneself); take on oneself. ⇨뒤집어쓰다

둘러앉다 sit round [around]; sit in a circle [ring]; gather around in a circle. ¶식탁 [불가]에 ~ sit [be seated] around the table [fire] // 캠프파이어 주위로 ~ gather around a campfire.

둘러엎다 1 [엎어 버리다] overturn; upset; overthrow; turn upside down. ¶밥상을 ~ overturn a table / throw a table over. 2 [집을 치우다] give up; break up. ¶살림을 ~ do away with a home / break up a household // 그는 가게를 둘러엎고 서울로 나왔다 He closed [shut] down his shop and came to Seoul.

둘러치다 1 [둘러놓다] surround; enclose; encircle. ¶공터에 철조망을 ~ stretch wire entanglements around a vacant lot // 잠자리에 병풍을 ~ surround a bed with screens // 사고 현장에 로프를 ~ rope off the scene of an accident // 침대에 커튼을 둘러쳤다 We drew a curtain around the bed. 2 [내던지다] throw hard; fling; hurl. ¶땅바닥에 ~ hurl [throw] (a person) to the ground. 3 [내리치다] strike (a person) a blow (on the head); bring (a stick) down (on a person's head).
둘러치나 메어치나 매한가지 [매일반] **이다** (속담) It makes no difference which we choose.

둘레 [바깥 언저리] (a) circumference; girth; surroundings. ¶지구의 ~를 돌다 go [move] around [(영) round] the earth // ~가 80센티인 줄기 a trunk eighty centimeters around [in girth] / a trunk with a circumference of eighty centimeters // 집 ~에 울타리를 두르다 build a fence around the house // 경관이 집 ~를 포위했다 The police surrounded the house.// 적이 ~에서 접근해 왔다 The enemy closed in from all around.// "이 연못의 ~는 얼마나 됩니까?" "약 5백 미터입니다." "How big is this pond round?" "It is about 500 meters round."

둘레둘레 (a)round; about; in a circle [ring]. ¶~ 살펴보다 look (a)round / stare around [about] // ~ 앉다 sit (a)round [in a circle].

둘리다 1 (주위를) be surrounded [enclosed / encircled]. ¶높은 산들에 둘린 골짜기 a valley enclosed by high mountains // 성벽에 둘린 고대 도시 an ancient city encircled

둘째

with walls // 그 마을은 사면이 산으로 둘려 있다 The village is surrounded by mountains on all sides. **2** [몸에] be put round; be wrapped (up) in; be worn. ¶허리에 치마가 ~ wear a skirt (round one's waist) // 머리에 수건이 둘러 있다 A towel is worn round one's head. **3** [휘두름을 당하다] be swayed; be wielded; be controlled. ¶남에게 둘리어 under a person's thumb / 남에게 ~ be swayed by a person.

둘째 the second; number two. ¶아래부터 여동생 one's second youngest sister / (미) one's next to youngest sister / 《영》 one's youngest sister but one // 그는 ~다 He is second in his class. // 그는 경주에서 ~로 들어왔다 He was (the) runner-up. / He finished second in the race. // ~로 방을 나간 사람은 누구였더냐 Who was the second to leave the room? // 그는 끝에서 ~로 꼴인했다 He finished [came in] next to last [《영》 last but one]. // 용모는 ~ 문제다 Personal appearance is of secondary importance.

둘째가라면 서럽다 be second to none. ¶그는 가수로서 둘째가라면 서러울 정도였다 As a singer, he was second to none.

● **둘째 손가락** an index finger.

둘하다 [둔하고 미련하다] clumsy; awkward; gawky.

둥¹ [북소리] with a boom. ¶북을 ~ 하고 치다 bang (on) a drum.

둥² […하는 듯도 하고 아니하는 듯도 함]. ¶남의 말을 듣는 ~ 마는 ~ 하다 listen to a person in an absent sort of way / pay little attention to a person's talk // 나는 갈 ~ 말 ~ 한다 I have half a mind to go. // 그들은 찾는 ~ 마는 ~ 하다가 집으로 돌아갔다 After a half-hearted search, they went home. // 비가 오는 ~ 마는 ~ 했다 The rain was only a drizzle. // 나는 아침을 먹는 ~ 마는 ~ 하고 밖으로 나갔다 I went out, taking a hasty breakfast. // 그는 바쁘다는 ~, 아프다는 ~ 하며 약속을 통 지키지 않는다 He never keeps his promises, saying he is too busy, or he is not well, or something. / He keeps breaking his promises on the pretext of pressure of business, ill health or whatnot.

둥그렇다 round; circular. ⇒둥그랗다

둥그레지다 become round; round. ⇒둥그래지다

둥그스름하다 somewhat round. ⇒둥그스름하다

둥근톱 a circular saw; a trepan(외과용); a trephine(자루가 있는).

둥글넓적하다 round and flat. ⇒둥글납작하다

둥글다 (원형의) round; rotund; (고리 모양의) circular; (구형의) globular; spherical. ¶둥근 얼굴 a round [moon] face // 둥근 지붕 a dome // 쟁반같이 둥근 달 a round full moon // 둥근 꽃밭[화단] a circular flowerbed // 둥글게 round / in a circle [ring] // 종이를 둥글게 자르다 cut paper round [into a circle] // 둥글게 앉다 sit in a circle [ring].

둥글둥글 1 [몹시 동그란 모양]. **둥글둥글하다** round; rotund; circular; globular. ¶둥글둥글한 눈깔사탕 round taffies // 둥글둥글한 구슬 round beads // 둥글둥글한 조약돌 round pebbles // 둥글둥글한 귀여운 눈 round, beautiful eyes // 눈이 둥글둥글한 소년 goggle-eyed boy // 감들이 ~ The persimmons are all round.

2 [원만하게] peacefully; amicably; smoothly; harmoniously. **둥글둥글하다** harmonious; amicable; peaceful; (인격이) well-rounded; affable; sociable. ¶둥글둥글한 태도 smooth [bland / suave / affable] manner // 그는 사람이 ~ He has well-rounded corners. // 그녀는 성품이 ~ She is easy to get along with.

둥글리다 round; make round (into a ball); round off(깎아서). ¶눈을 ~ make a ball of snow / make a snowball // 책상의 모서리를 ~ round off the edge of a table.

둥글뭉수레하다 round and blunt-tipped; round at the end.

둥둥¹ [북소리] rub-a-dub; rataplan; tom-tom; boom, boom, boom(큰북 등의). ¶북을 ~ 울리다 beat the big drum.

둥둥² [떠서 움직이는 모양] floating.

둥실둥실 [가볍게 떠서 움직이는 모양] floating light(ly) [buoyant(ly)]. ¶하늘에 흰 구름이 ~ 떠 있다 White clouds are hanging lightly in the sky. // 깃털이 ~ 떠돌고 있었다 Feathers were floating in the air. // 나뭇조각들이 물결 위에 ~ 떠 있었다 Pieces of woods were bobbing between the waves.

둥실둥실하다 round; rotund; plump; corpulent. ¶둥실둥실하게 살찐 돼지들 pigs of marvelous rotundity // 둥실둥실한 얼굴 a round [plumpy] face.

둥우리 [둥지] a nest; [새장] a cage; a coop; a nest [nesting] box(상자형의). ¶닭의 ~ a hencoop.

-둥이 child; one. ¶귀염~ one's dear [precious] child // 막내~ the youngest child [son / daughter] // 바람~ (남자) a playboy / (여자) a flirt // 해방~ a child born in the year of Liberation of Korea in 1945.

둥지 a nest; a roost. ¶새~ a bird's nest // ~에 들다 settle in the nest / nest // ~를 짓다[틀다] build a nest / nest (in a tree).

둥치 [밑동] the base of a tree trunk; the butt. ¶나무 밑 ~를 자르다 cut down a tree (close) at the base / (톱으로) saw off a tree at the root.

둥치다 1 [휩싸서 동이다] tie up together; wrap up. **2** [잘라 버리다] cut off the worthless part.

뒈지다 〈비〉 die; pass away; be gone. ⇒죽다1 ¶뒈져 버려라 Go to hell!

뒤 1 [뒤쪽] the back; the rear. ¶~의 back / rear(▶ back은 일반적인 말, rear는 행렬, 차, 건물의 후부 등에 쓰임) / hind / posterior / backward // ~에 after / behind / back / backward(s) / in the rear / at[on] the back (of) // ~에서 본 모습 one's appearance from the back // 차 바로 ~에 just behind a car // ~로 돌다 (미) about-face / 《영》 about-turn // 그들의 바로 ~를 쫓았다 I followed on their heels. // 집 ~에 시내가 있었다 There was a stream at the back of [behind] our house. // 그는 의자 ~에 서 있었다 He was standing behind the chair. // 그는 ~로 넘어졌다 He fell over backward(s). // 그가 총을 꺼내자 모두들 ~로 물러섰다 They all stepped back when he drew a gun. // 누가 나를 ~에서 밀었다 Someone pushed me from behind. // 그는 행렬의 맨 ~를 걷고 있었다 He brought up the rear of the procession. // 경주를 ~로 하고 부산으로 갔다 We left Gyeongju for Busan. // 배가 섬 ~로 사라졌다 The boat has disappeared on the far side of the island. // 우리

집 ~에는 채소밭이 있다 We have a kitchen garden at the back of[behind] the house.
2 [다음·나중] afterward(s); later. ¶그 ~ since then / ever since / after that // 지금부터 5년 ~에 five years from now // 그 20년에 걸쳐 for twenty years since then // 10년 ~에 after ten years / ten years later // 그가 부자라는 것을 ~에 가서 알게 되었다 I learned later[afterwards] that he was a very rich man. // (그들이 떠난) 돈이 없어진 것을 알았다 I found the money gone after that (after they had left). // 오늘의 날씨는 맑은 ~에 흐리겠다 Today it's going to be clear and then cloudy later on. // 10년 ~에는 이 나무도 상당히 크게 자라날 것이다 This tree will be much taller ten years from now [in ten years / (문어) ten years hence]. // 그것에 대해서는 ~에 의논합시다 We will talk about it another time.
3 [선행한 것의 다음을 잇는 것]. ¶~의 the next / the following / the succeeding / the latter(후자의) // ~로 next / after / ~로 미루다 defer / postpone / put off // ~재난이 이어 일어났다 One calamity followed on the heels of another. // 낮이 지난 ~에는 밤이 온다 Night succeeds [follows / come after] day.
4 [뒷일] future. ¶(여행을 떠나는 사람의) ~를 잘 부탁하오 Please look after my affairs while I am away.
5 [결과] consequences; results; [결말] the end; the conclusion. ¶~는 하늘에 맡기다 leave the consequences[rest] to Heaven // ~는 내가 맡겠다 I will answer for the consequences. // 그런 짓을 하면 ~가 재미없다 You will have to pay dearly for it. // 이 술은 ~가 좋지 않다 This liquor has[leaves] nasty aftereffects. // 그는 성은 잘 내나 ~가 없는 사람이다 He is quick to get angry and quick to get over it. // ~야 어찌 되든 알 바 아니다 I don't care what may come of it. / I don't care for the consequences.
6 [나머지·여타] the rest; the remainder; the others. ¶그 ~는 상상에 맡기겠다 The rest may be left for you to imagine. // N마을까지는 차로 가고 그 ~는 걸어갔다 I went by car as far as N village and walked the rest of the way.
7 [자손] a descendant; a descent; posterity. ¶그 집은 ~가 끊어졌다 The family became extinct. / The family line broke.
8 [후계·후임] succession; a successor. ¶그에게는 ~를 이을 사람이 없다 He has no heir to succeed him. // 그는 아버지의 ~를 이어 사장이 되었다 He became president of the company in succession to his father.
9 [배후] background; the back. ¶말 ~에 숨은 뜻 the hidden meaning of a word / the implication of a word // ~에서 어떤 일이 일어나고 있는지 모른다 There is no knowing what is going on backstage [behind the scenes]. // 그는 ~에서 남의 욕을 한다 He speaks ill of others behind their backs. // ~에서 갖가지 공작이 있었다 There was a great deal of maneuvering behind the scenes. // ~에서 조정하는 자가 있는 것 같다 There seems to be someone pulling strings in the background.
10 [뒷바라지] support; backing. ¶~를 밀어주다 give support to / back (up) / second // 아들을 ~를 대 주어 생활하고 있다 be supported by one's son.
11 [자취·흔적] a trace; a track; a trail. ¶~를 밟다 track[shadow / run after] (a person) / follow in (a person's) track / trail / tail // 형사에게 ~를 밟게 하다 put the detective on (a person's) track // 누가 나의 ~를 밟고 있다 Someone is shadowing[following] me.
12 [똥] f(a)eces; fecal matter; stool. ¶~가 마렵다 have a call of nature / want to go to the toilet // ~를 보다 relieve[ease] nature [oneself] / move the bowels / do one's needs / respond to the call of nature.

뒤노불다 act frivolously[lightly / flippantly]; frolic; rollick. ¶뒤노불지 말고 좀 점잖게 굴어라 Don't be so silly, try to behave like a gentleman.

뒤곁 a back[rear] garden; a backyard. ¶집 ~에서 놀다 play in the backyard.

뒤꽂이 a chignon accessory.

뒤꿈치 the heel. ⇨⇨발뒤꿈치 ¶구두 ~ the heel of a shoe // ~가 높은[낮은] high-[low-]heeled shoes // ~가 떨어지다 be out at (the) heels // 내 구두 ~가 닳았다 My shoes are down at heels. / The heels of my boots are worn out.

뒤끓다 **1** [마구 끓다] seethe; boil up[over]; come to a boil. ¶물이 뒤끓는다 Water is seething. // 주전자의 물이 뒤끓는다 The kettle is boiling.
2 [많은 수효가 같은 곳에서 움직이다] swarm; flock; be infested with; be crowded [jammed] (with people). ¶도둑이 뒤끓는 지방 a country infested with robbers // 그 시장은 연말 손님으로 뒤끓었다 The market place was crowded with year-end shoppers. // 사람들이 공원 둘레에 뒤끓었다 People swarmed around the park. // 교정에 학생들이 뒤끓었다 The campus was crowded with students.
3 [비유] seethe; be in an uproar[a ferment]; stir. ¶흥분으로 ~ seethe[be agog] with excitement (over) // 전쟁이 터질 것이라는 소문으로 국내가 뒤끓었다 Rumors of war caused national ferment.

뒤끝 **1** [일의 맨 나중] a conclusion; an end; [해결] (a) settlement; (a) decision. ¶~이 나다 be settled / come[be brought] to a conclusion[an end] // 그 일은 빨리 ~을 맺어야 한다 The matter demands a speedy settlement. // ~이 어떻게 될까 How will the matter end? **2** [나중에 오는 영향] aftereffects.

뒤끝(을) 보다 bring (a matter) to an end[a conclusion]; complete[finish] (one's work); bring (one's work) to conclusion. ¶그는 일을 벌여만 놓고 뒤끝을 못 본다 He always fails to finish the job he has undertaken.

뒤넘다 [뒤로 넘어지다] fall backward; fall on one's back; [뒤집히다] tumble over; turn over; overturn; upset.

뒤놀다 [흔들리다] shake; sway; totter; reel; be shaky[rickety]; (배가 파도에) roll[pitch] heavily. ¶뒤노는 의자 a shaky[rocky / rickety / crazy] chair // 책상다리가 ~ The legs of a table are groggy. // 물결에 배가 ~ A boat rolls heavily in the waves. **2** [방황하다] wander; roam; rove; (미국 구어) knock around.

뒤늦다 late; tardy; belated; delayed. ¶뒤늦은 경고 a belated warning // 뒤늦게 오다 make a tardy appearance // 뒤늦은 사과를 하다 offer

뒤대다

a belated apology.// 그는 뒤늦게나마 불난 현장에 달려갔다 He ran to the scene of the fire none too soon.// 그녀는 좀 뒤늦게 시작했다 She has begun rather too late in the day.// 뒤늦게나마 당국은 그 사건을 조사하기 시작했다 The authorities began to examine the matter, though it was rather too late.// (편지에서) 뒤늦게나마 감사의 말씀을 드립니다 I would like to offer you my belated thanks. / I'm sorry that I am so late in thanking you. / I should have thanked you sooner.

뒤대다 [대 주다] supply (with); provide (with); assist; help. ¶돈을 ~ supply (a person) with money / give (a person) financial aid // 학비를 ~ supply (a student) with (his) school expenses // 당신에게 계속 사업 자금을 뒤대 주겠소 I will keep you furnished with business funds.

뒤덮다 cover (over / up); overspread; overlay; hang over. ¶산꼭대기를 뒤덮은 구름 clouds hanging over the top of the mountain // 홍수가 온 마을을 뒤덮었다 The flood has spread over the whole village.// 늘어뜨린 머리가 그의 앞이마를 뒤덮고 있었다 A lock of hair hung over his forehead.// 먹구름이 하늘을 뒤덮고 있었다 The sky was overcast with black clouds. / Black clouds obscured the sky.// 그녀는 이불을 뒤덮고 잤다 She pulled [drew] the bed clothes over her head and fell asleep.

뒤덮이다 be covered (all over) (with); veiled; be overspread [overlaid]; be hung over. ¶이끼로 뒤덮인 정원 a garden covered with moss // 꼭대기가 눈으로 뒤덮인 산 a mountain whose top is covered with snow // 눈으로 ~ be blanketed [covered all over] with snow // 봄이 되면 산과 들은 신록으로 뒤덮인다 In spring, the fields and hills are clothed in fresh verdure.// 그 책은 먼지에 뒤덮여 있었다 The book was covered with dust. / The book was dusty all over.

뒤돌아보다 1 [뒤쪽을 돌아보다] look back (at); turn back to see; take a backward glance (at). ¶그녀는 굉장한 미인이라서 지나치는 사람마다 뒤돌아본다 She is such a beauty that everybody turns to look at her when she passes.// 내가 부르자 그는 뒤돌아보았다 He turned when I called.

2 [회고하다] look back on. ¶과거를 ~ think back to the past days / think backward / look back upon the past // 50년 전을 ~ look back over a distance of fifty years // 어린 시절을 뒤돌아보니 고생이 많았다 Looking back on my childhood, I find it was full of hardships.// 나의 일생을 뒤돌아보아 그리 즐겁지 않은 것도 있다 One portion of my life is not very pleasant to look back to.// 그 당시 내가 한 일을 뒤돌아보니 한탄스럽기 짝이 없다 Reflecting on what I did in those days, a feel I deep sense of sorrow.

뒤따르다 1 [뒤를 따르다] follow (along behind); go [run] after (another); [수행하다] accompany; continue; [행렬 등을] bring [close] up the rear. ¶바싹 ~ follow on / run after (a person) closely / run (a person) close // 아들은 아버지를 뒤따라 의사가 되었다 The son followed in his father's footstep [followed his father's example] and became a doctor.// 그가 그것을 하면 급우들이 뒤따를 것이다 If he does it, his classmates will follow suit.// 한 떼의 기마 순경이 뒤따랐다 A group of mounted policemen brought up the rear.// 그녀는 남편을 뒤따라 프랑스로 갔다 She followed her husband to France.

2 [어떤 일에 잇따르다] be followed [succeeded] by; follow; ensue; succeed; go [come / appear] in succession [series]. ¶좋은 일이 있으면 나쁜 일이 뒤따르기 마련이다 Every day has its night, (and) every weal its woe.

뒤떨어지다 1 [뒤에 처지다] be (a long way) behind; [뒤에 남다] leave (behind); remain [stay] behind. ¶혼자 ~ be left (all) alone // 행군에서 ~ fall out while on the march // 모두들 떠났으나 그만이 뒤떨어졌다 All left but he was staying behind.// 그녀는 멀찌감치 뒤떨어져서 그를 따라갔다 She followed a long way behind him.

2 (시대·유행에) get [fall / lag / drop] behind; be in arrear of (the times). ¶시대 [유행] 에 ~ be behind the times [fashion] // 시대에 뒤지지 않도록 하다 keep abreast of the times / keep up with the times // 이 나라의 교육은 아직 뒤떨어져 있다 This country is still backward in education.// 그는 시대에 뒤떨어졌다 He fell behind the times.// 요즘 그런 시대에 뒤떨어진 생각은 어울리지 않아 Such old fashioned [antiquated] ideas are no good nowadays.

3 [학력·지능이] be inferior; be worse than; below; fall behind; be behindhand; drop out. ¶수학이 특히 남보다 ~ be behind the others in mathematics above all // 영어에서 뒤떨어져 있다 be behind the other students in English // 다른 아이들보다 지능이 훨씬 ~ be far beneath the other children in intelligence // 선생님의 열성을 다한 지도에도 불구하고 매년 뒤떨어지는 학생이 많다 In spite of the teacher's enthusiasm [earnest efforts], a lot of students fall [get left] behind every year.// 나는 수학에서는 남에게 뒤떨어지지 않는다 I am second to none in mathematics.

뒤뚱거리다 totter; stagger; falter; waver; be unsteady.

뒤뚱뒤뚱 totteringly; staggeringly; unsteadily. ¶~ 걷다 walk with faltering steps / stagger along. **뒤뚱뒤뚱하다** totter; stagger. ⇨ 뒤뚱거리다

뒤뜰 a back [rear] garden; (미) a backyard.

뒤란 a backyard; the rear [back] of a house.

뒤로돌아 [구령] (미) About face!; (영) About turn!

뒤룩거리다 1 (눈을) glare [goggle] (one's eyes). ¶눈을 뒤룩거리며 with goggling eyes // 눈을 뒤룩거리며 주위를 둘러보다 look around staringly // 그는 눈알을 뒤룩거렸다 He goggled [rolled] his eyes. / His eyes goggled.// 그 노인은 눈을 뒤룩거리면서 휙 둘러보았다 The old man looked around with goggling eyes. 2 (몸을) sway [waddle] (one's body). 3 (성나서) look with glaring eyes; jerk with anger.

뒤룩뒤룩 1 (눈이). **뒤룩뒤룩하다** goggling. 2 (살쪄서). ¶~ 걷다 walk swaying one's body / lump along. **뒤룩뒤룩하다** fatty; fleshy; corpulent. ¶살이 ~ be fat as football [a pig].

뒤미처 soon [shortly] after; right after; at once; immediately; promptly; without delay; close on the heels (of a person). ¶~ 달려오다 hurry to (the place) at the eleventh hour // ~ 쫓아가다 follow (a person) shortly after one has left // ~ 도 사직했다 He too, soon after the other, resigned his post. // 그가 집에 당도하자 ~ 그의 동생도 집에 닿았다 Shortly after he had come back home his brother arrived. // 그는 ~ 도둑의 뒤를 좇았다 He lost no time in pursuing the thief.

뒤바꾸다 reverse; turn around (in position / order); invert; switch; get (it) backwards. ¶순서[자리]를 ~ reverse the order [their positions].

뒤바뀌다 be reversed; change to the opposite; be inverted; be mixed up; be taken[put] in the wrong way; be mistaken. ¶순서가 ~ be topsy-turvy / be out of order // 형세는 우리에게 유리하게 뒤바뀌었다 The tables were turned in our favor. // 상황이 뒤바뀌었다 The situation reversed itself.

뒤밟다 track; shadow; tail; dog (a person's step); follow (in a person's track); follow along[back of] (a person); trail; get on (a person's) tail. ¶남을 뒤밟게 하다 put shadow[tail] on a person // 형사에게 뒤밟게 하다 set a detective on (a person / a person's track) // 뒤밟게 하다 put a dog on the trail // 나는 앞서거니 뒤서거니 하며 그를 뒤밟았다 I shadowed her, now ahead and now behind. // 경관이 도둑을 뒤밟고 있다 A policeman tracks a robber (down). // 비밀경찰이 밤낮 뒤밟고 있다 The secret police are shadowing me night and day.

뒤버무리다 mix (up in); add. ¶나물을 ~ mix up vegetables / toss a salad.

뒤범벅 a jumble; a hotchpotch; a mess; a medley; a muddle; a pell-mell. ¶~이 mixed up / confused // ~을 만들다 jumble (up) together / mix up // 그 기사는 사실과 허구의 ~이었다 That article mixed fact and fiction. / Facts and fiction were jumbled together in that article. **뒤범벅되다** be mixed up; be jumbled (up) together; be in a mess; be confused. ¶그는 기대와 불안이 뒤범벅된 기분이었다 He had mixed feelings of hope and anxiety. // 눈이 뒤범벅되어 내리고 있다 The snow is falling in a whirl. // 그들은 뒤범벅되어 싸웠다 They fought in a confused mass. // 온갖 것이 뒤범벅되어 있었다 All sorts of things are jumbled[mixed] up together.

뒤보다 [용변을 보다] evacuate the bowels; have a bowel motion[movement]; ease [relieve] nature[oneself]; go to stool; do one's needs. ¶뒤보러 가다 go to the lavatory / (미) go to the toilet.

뒤보아주다 take care of; look after; [후원하다] support; back up (a person); help (a person); patronize. ¶불쌍한 고아를 ~ take care of a poor orphan // 장사하는 사람을 ~ help a merchant with funds // 동생의 수학 공부를 ~ help one's brother with his mathematics // 그는 나를 친형제처럼 뒤보아준다 He takes quite a brotherly interest in me. // 자금 융통은 지방 은행이 뒤보아준다 The financing is taken care of by a local bank.

뒤서다 1 [뒤를 따르다] follow (a person); follow[tag] at (another's) heels. ¶뒤서서 가다 go in the rear // 뒤서게 하다 bring to heel // 앞서거니 뒤서거니 하며 now ahead and now behind. 2 fall behind; be backward. ⇨ 뒤지다¹

뒤섞다 [혼합하다] mix (up / together); jumble together; [휘젓다] stir. ¶희극과 비극을 뒤섞은 연극 a drama blended of comedy and tragedy // 여러 가지 꽃씨를 ~ mix (up) the seeds of various flowers // 케이크를 만들기 위해 재료를 ~ mix ingredients to make a cake / 카드짝을 ~ shuffle a pack of cards // 그는 진실과 허구를 뒤섞어 경찰에 이야기했다 He wove truth and fiction together [He mixed facts and falsehood] in the story he told the police.

뒤섞이다 be mixed[jumble] (up / together); be intermixed[mingled / blended]; mix in a confused way; commingle. ¶뒤섞임 a jumble / a hodgepodge / (영) a hotchpotch // 마구 뒤섞인 서류 a jumble // 뒤섞인 감정 mingled feelings // 좋은 것과 나쁜 것이 뒤섞여 있다 The good and the bad are all in a jumble. // 그들 속에는 온갖 민족의 피가 뒤섞여 있다 The blood of all nations is mingling with their own. // 책상 위에는 여러 가지의 서류가 난잡하게 뒤섞여 있었다 Papers of various kinds were jumbled up[in a jumble] on the desk. // 적군과 아군이 뒤섞여 혼전이 되었다 The battle turned into a melee. // 접시 위에는 과일과 과자가 뒤섞여 있었다 Fruit and sweets were heaped on the plate in a jumble. // 이 도시에는 여러 인종의 사람들이 뒤섞여 살고 있다 We find a hodgepodge [medley] of people of various races in this town.

뒤숭숭하다 1 [정신이 어수선하다] nervous; distracted; uneasy; awkward; fidgety; jumpy; restless. ¶마음이 ~ feel[be] nervous [uneasy] / be in a fidget / be ill at ease // 마음이 뒤숭숭해서 아무것도 못하겠다 I am restless and don't feel like doing anything. // 그녀는 아버지의 병환 소식을 듣고 마음이 뒤숭숭했다 She was disturbed to hear of her father's illness.
2 [혼란하다] noisy; troublous; turbulent; troubled; agitated; disturbed; unsettled. ¶뒤숭숭한 세상 troubled[turbulent / unsettled] times // 요즈음 어쩐지 세상이 ~ There is a sign of unrest in the world today. / We live in a dangerous[turbulent / restless] world.
3 [흩어져 있다] confused; messy; untidy.

뒤안길 1 [뒷길] a back street[lane]; [뒷문으로 통하는 길] a passage leading to the back door. 2 [초라하고 쓸쓸한 생활·처지]. ¶인생의 ~을 가다 live a shady life / live outside the mainstream of society // 그는 인생의 ~을 걸어왔다 He has seen the dark[shady] side of life.

뒤얽히다 1 [서로 얽히다] tangle; intertwine. ¶이 털실은 잘 뒤얽힌다 This yarn tangles easily. // 덩굴풀이 뒤얽혀 길이 막혀 있다 The path is blocked by a tangle[an intertwined mass] of vines. 2 [사정 등이 서로 얽힘]. ¶그의 경우, 돈에 명예심마저 뒤얽혀 있다 In his case, desire for fame cannot be separated from (desire for) money. // 사건은 회사의 내분과 뒤얽혀 있다 The case was connected with the company's internal troubles.

뒤엉키다 1 (밧줄·실 등이) get[become] entangled; get[become] entangled; get[become] raveled. ¶뒤엉킨 실을 풀다 untie entangled knots / unravel a thread // 실이 뒤엉켜 있다 The thread is raveled. 2 (이야기 등이) get confused[mixed]; (사건 등이) get complicated; become involved. ¶복잡하게 뒤엉킨 사정 a labyrinthine state of things // 뒤엉킨 문제를

뒤엎다 해결하다 settle a complicated problem.

뒤엎다 1 〔전복시키다〕 upset; overturn; (배를) capsize. ¶찻잔을 뒤엎어 버렸다 I upset [kicked over] the tea cup. 2 〔타도하다〕 overthrow; undermine; subvert; (결정을) overrule; reverse. ¶정설을 ~ explode [overthrow] the established theory // 판결을 ~ overrule a decision / reverse a sentence // 현 정부를 ~ overthrow the present government.

뒤웅박 a gourd; a calabash; a cucurbit.

뒤잇다 follow; succeed; occur in succession; come one after another. ¶뒤이어 continuously / continually / successively / in succession / later on / one after another / following that // 개회사가 끝나고 뒤이어 강연이 시작되었다 The opening address came to an end and then the lecture began. // 뒤이어 M 교수의 연설이 있었다 As the next item on the program, professor M made a speech.

뒤적거리다 ransack; rummage (책 등을) browse; (더듬어서) fumble[feel / fish] (in). ¶ 서류를 ~ rummage among papers // 책을 ~ turn over the leaves of a book / browse through a book // 편지를 찾으려고 서랍을 ~ rummage a drawer for a letter // 책상 위의 서류를 ~ finger the papers on the table // 책을 ~ browse in a book / (이 책 저 책을) browse among the books // 잔돈을 꺼내려고 주머니를 뒤적거렸다 I fumbled in my pockets for change.

뒤적뒤적 rummaging; fumbling; fingering; browsing. **뒤적뒤적하다** ransack; rummage. ⇨ *뒤적거리다*

뒤적이다 ransack; rummage. ⇨ 뒤적거리다

뒤져내다 rummage (out); hunt out; seek [search] out. ¶서랍에서 돈을 ~ rummage [scrounge] money from a drawer // 벽장에 감 춰 둔 과자를 ~ seek out cakes put away in a wall cupboard.

뒤주 a rice chest [bin].

뒤죽박죽 in disorder; pell-mell; in confusion; topsy-turvy; all mixed up; all jumbled up; in a mess. ¶~을 만들다 mix [jumble] up [together] / turn (things) topsy-turvy // ~이 되다 get confused / be jumbled [mixed] up // 세상은 ~이 되었다 Things have become topsy-turvy. // 항목의 순서가 ~이다 The order of entries is utterly without rhyme or reason. // 원고가 방에 흩어져 ~이 되었다 The manuscript sheets are scattered pell-mell all over the room. // 그는 나의 계획을 ~ 으로 만들어 놓았다 He has made a mess of my plans. // 그는 ~으로 흩어진 서류를 정리했 다 He put the papers scattered pell-mell in order. // 모든 것이 ~이다 All is in confusion.

뒤쥐 〔동〕 a shrew; a shrewmouse (pl. -mice); a soricine; a sorex.

뒤지(-紙) toilet paper; a toilet roll; (영국 구 어) bumf.

뒤지다¹ 〔뒤떨어지다〕 fall [drop] behind; fall back; be backward; be behind; be inferior to; (경주에) lose the lead to (one's opponent). ¶지능이 뒤지는 아이 a backward [retarded] child // 문화적으로 뒤진 나라 a culturally backward nation // 시대에 ~ get behind the times [the age] / go out of date / become old-fashioned // 남에게 ~ be outdone by a person // 아무에게도 뒤지지 않 다 yield to none / be second to none // 남에게 뒤질세라 vying [in competition] with one another // 한국은 첨단 기술 분야에서 외국에 뒤져 있지 않다 In the field of modern technology, Korea is not behind other countries. // 그는 눈치 빠르기로는 누구에게도 뒤지지 않 는다 He is second to none in shrewdness. // 이 수족관은 세계의 어느 것에도 뒤지지 않는 다 This aquarium ranks with any in the world. // 회사마다 경쟁사에 뒤지지 않으려고 새 상품을 발표하였다 Each company, in order not to be outdone by [not to get behind] its rivals, announced new products. // 1개월간 입원해 있었더니 학교 공부가 크게 뒤져 있다 I was in the hospital for a month, so I'm far [(구어) way] behind with my school work. // 그 아이는 지능이 뒤져 있다 That child is retarded. // 그는 선두 주자보다 50미터 뒤져 있다 He is fifty meters behind the front runner.

뒤지다² 〔휘젓다〕 rummage (for); 〔찾다〕 ransack; fumble (in); search. ¶책상 서랍을 샅샅이 ~ ransack [rummage in] the desk drawers (▶ ransack은 rummage보다 난폭한 행동이며 정신없이 찾는 경우를 말함) // 서류를 마구 ~ rummage among the papers // 호주머 니를 ~ fumble [feel / fish] in one's pocket (for something) // 남의 몸을 ~ search a person (for a hidden weapon) / (경찰 등이) frisk (a person) // 샅샅이 ~ search thoroughly / rummage / comb (out) (for) // 개가 쓰레기통을 뒤지고 있었다 A dog was rummaging through the garbage can [(영) the dustbin]. // 먹을 것이 없을까 하고 그녀는 부엌을 뒤지고 있었다 She was searching the kitchen for something to eat. // 그는 헌책과 잡지에서 그 사건의 기록을 뒤지고 있었다 He was digging up records [accounts] / of the incident from old books and magazines. / He was raking through old books and magazines for accounts of the incident. // 그녀는 장롱 안을 뒤져서 장갑을 찾았다 She rummaged for her gloves in the chest of drawers. // 경찰은 범인 색출을 위해 그 도시를 샅샅이 뒤졌다 The police have combed (out) the city for the murderer.

뒤져 보다 search [look / hunt] (for); make [prosecute] a search (for); rummage [fumble] (for). ¶돈이 있는지 호주머니 속을 ~ fumble [fish] in one's pocket to see if there is any money // 집 안을 샅샅이 뒤져 보 았으나 그것은 보이지 않았다 I searched all over the house, but I could not find it. // 있을 만한 곳은 모두 뒤져 보았으나 못 찾았다 I hunted in all the likely places, but I failed to find it.

뒤집다 1 〔안팎을 뒤바꾸다〕 turn (a sleeve) inside out; turn the other side; turn wrong side out; turn upside down; reverse; (카드의 겉면을 위로) turn up; (호주머니 등을) turn out. ¶뒤집어 말하면 to put (it) the other way / stated reversely // 뒤집어 생각해 보면 seen the other way around / if you consider it from the opposite point of view // 코트를 뒤집 어 입다 wear a coat inside out // 나는 셔츠를 뒤집어 입고 있었다 I was wearing my undershirt wrong side out [inside out]. // 그의 오만 한 언동은 열등감을 뒤집어 놓은 것이다 He acts arrogantly because he suffers from [has] an inferiority complex. // 안전 제일이라고 그가 말하지만 뒤집어 말하면 할 마음이 없다는 것

이다 He says we must put safety first and proceed cautiously, but the truth of the matter is that he doesn't really want to do anything about it.
2 〖위와 아래를 바꾸다〗 overturn; turn up; capsize; turn over. ¶책을 ~ turn a book over / lay a book facedown // 장돌을 ~ turn up a paving stone // 그녀는 팬케이크를 능숙하게 뒤집었다 She skillfully turned the pancake over. // 한쪽이 구워졌으면 생선을 뒤집어라 Turn the fish over when it is done on one side. // 뒤집지 마시오〔게시〕 This side up. / Don't turn over. // 상자를 뒤집어 놓고 식탁으로 쓰자 Let's set[turn] the box upside down and use it as a table. // 큰 파도가 우리의 보트를 뒤집었다 A big wave upset[overturned] our boat.
3 〖일을 틀어지게 하다〗 reverse; change; overrule. ¶계획을 ~ upset a plan / balk (a person) in his plan / change one's plan // 이제 조금만 다지면 판에 계획이 뒤집어졌다 The plan fell through just as it was about to be completed.
4 〖혼란시키다〗 raise[make] a disturbance; throw into confusion. ¶그 소식은 장내를 발칵 뒤집어 놓았다 The news threw the audience into utter confusion. // 순조롭게 진행되는 회의를 그 혼자서 온통 뒤집어 놓았다 He upset the smooth proceedings of the meeting all by himself.
5 〖체제·제도·학설 등을 뒤엎다〗 overturn; overthrow; upset; turn over. ¶정권을 ~ overthrow a government // 정설(定說)을 ~ disprove an established theory // 대법원은 고등 법원의 판결을 뒤집었다 The Supreme Court overruled[reversed] the decision of the High[District] court. // 그는 종전에 한 말을 뒤집었다 He took back his words.

뒤집어쓰다 1 〖머리에〗 put on; wear; cover. ¶모자를 ~ wear a hat // 그 여자는 수건을 뒤집어썼다 She covered her head with a towel.
2 〖온몸에〗 cover with; put on; draw [pull] over. ¶담요를 ~ be wrapped[wrap oneself] up in a blanket / wrap a blanket about oneself / pull a blanket (up) over one's head.
3 〖가루·액체 등을〗 pour (water) on (oneself); be covered with (dust). ¶물을 ~ pour water upon oneself // 흙탕물을 온몸에 ~ be covered[splashed] all over with muddy water // 나는 물을 머리부터 흠뻑 뒤집어썼다 I doused myself with water. // 그는 머리 위로부터 먼지를 뒤집어썼다 Dust fell all over him. // 그는 머리에 불티를 뒤집어썼다 Sparks rained on his head.
4 〖남의 죄·책임 등을〗 take on[upon] oneself; take a crime on oneself. ¶남의 죄를 ~ take a person's guilt on[upon] oneself // 애매한 죄를 ~ be falsely accused // 그것은 동료의 허물이었으나 내가 뒤집어쓰게 되었다 It was my colleague's fault, but I was left holding the bog.

뒤집어씌우다 〖물건을〗 cover (a thing) with (another thing); put on; 〖죄 등을〗 lay the blame on (a person for something); blame (the accident) on (a person). ¶내 머리에 한 양동이의 물이 뒤집어씌워졌다 A bucket of water was thrown[dashed] over my head.

뒤집히다 1 〖안팎이〗 be turned[turn] inside out; be turned over. ¶우산이 바람에 ~ be blown inside out // 네 옷이 뒤집혀 있다 Your dress is wrong side out. // 널어 놓았던 블라우스가 바람에 뒤집혔다 The blouse I was drying had turned inside out in the wind.
2 〖엎어지다〗 overturn; capsize. ¶보트가 뒤집혔다 The boat capsized[tipped over / overturned]. // 차는 군중에 의해 뒤집혔다 The car was overturned by the mob. // 쟁반이 뒤집혔다 The tray tipped over.
3 〖순서가 바뀌다〗 be reversed; be changed [switched]. ¶순서가 ~ The order is reversed[changed].
4 〖일이 틀어지다〗 be reversed; be overruled; be exploded. ¶계획이 뒤집혔다 The plan was upset. // 그가 결석했기 때문에 예정이 뒤집혔다 His absence upset the (whole) schedule 〔(미국 구어) threw the schedule out of whack〕.
5 〖야단나다〗 be in (an) uproar; be turned topsy-turvy; ferment; throw into confusion. ¶세상이 발칵 뒤집힌 사건 a sensational [much talked about] affair // 그 부정 사건으로 세상이 발칵 뒤집혔다 The scandal created a sensation among the whole nation. // 주인이 죽자 집안은 발칵 뒤집혔다 The master's death threw the whole house into utter confusion.
6 〖체제·제도·학설 등이 뒤엎이다〗 be overturned; be turned over; be upset; be overthrown. ¶뒤집힌 학설 an exploded[overthrown] theory // 지도자의 사망으로 형세가 뒤집혔다 The situation was reversed[The tables were turned] because of the leader's death. // 정권이 뒤집혔다 The government was overthrown. // 현 정부는 곧 뒤집힐지도 모른다 The present government might be tumbled from power before long. // 판결이 뒤집혔다 The decision was overruled [reversed]. // 그의 주장이 뒤집혔다 His claim was disproved.
7 〖속이〗 feel sick[nausea]; (정신이) go[run] mad. ¶눈이 뒤집힌 군중 a frenzied crowd // 속이 ~ have a sick stomach // 눈이 ~ lose one's sober judgement / lose one's mind [wits] // 배가 고파 눈알이 뒤집힐 것 같다 be almost frantic with hunger.

뒤쪽 the backside; the rear. ¶~ 좌석 a back [rear] seat // 집 ~의 호수 the lake to the rear of the house // ~으로 기대다 lean backward // 우리 ~의 산들은 신록에 뒤덮여 있었다 The mountains behind us were covered with fresh green leaves.

뒤쫓다 overtake; catch up with; pursue [chase] (after); go[run / take] after (a person) closely; follow at a person's heels; trail; track; hunt up. ¶범인을 ~ pursue a criminal // 뒤쫓아 가다 run after / chase / pursue / start in pursuit // 뒤쫓아 붙잡다 track down (a criminal) // 경찰관이 도둑을 뒤쫓아 갔다 A policeman chased[pursued] the robber. // 그는 뒤쫓는 주자를 물리치고 골인했다 He finished the race before the next man could catch up with him. / He beat off a challenge by the second-place finisher and crossed the goal line first. // 나는 그를 서울로 올라왔다 I followed him to seoul.

뒤채 〔뒤편의 집채〕 a backhouse; the back wing; a backyard annex.

뒤채다 〔많다〕 be in excess; be superabundant; superfluous; 〔발길에 걸리다〕 get in

뒤처리(-處理) settlement (of an affair); putting (things) to rights[in order]; after adjustment; winding-up. ¶화재 ~를 하다 clear the debris of a fire // 사건의 ~를 하다 settle an affair // 파산한 은행의 ~를 하다 clear[wind] up the affairs of an insolvent bank // 빚의 ~는 자신이 하라 Settle your debts yourself. // 나는 파산 기업의 ~를 부탁 받았다 I was asked to wind up the affairs of a business which had gone bankrupt. **뒤처리하다** settle; set (matters) right; wind up (one's affairs); deal with the aftermath; put (things) in order; dispose of.

뒤척거리다[1] ransack; rummage. ⇨ 뒤적거리다

뒤척거리다[2] [누운 몸을 뒤척뒤척하다] toss [roll] about (in bed); toss and turn. ¶그는 잠을 못 이루어 밤새껏 몸을 뒤척거렸다 He could not sleep a wink and tossed and turned all night long. / He had a sleepless night, rolling[tossing] about on the bed.

뒤척이다 toss about (in bed). ⇨ 뒤척거리다[2]

뒤축 1 (신·양말의) the heel of shoes[socks]. ¶~이 닳아 버린 구두 slipshod shoes // ~이 높은 구두 high-heeled shoes // ~을 대다 put a heel / heel // 구두 ~이 닳아 있다 The heels of my boot are worn out. 2 [발뒤축] the heel.

뒤치다 upset; overturn; turn over. ¶자다가 몸을 ~ turn[heave] (over / round) in sleep / toss about in bed.

뒤치다꺼리 1 [돌봄] taking care of; helping (from behind); looking after; patronage. ¶어린아이의 ~ look after[take care of] a child // 대가족의 ~ provide for a large family. **뒤치다꺼리하다** help (from behind); look after (a person); take care of; provide for; patronize.

2 [뒷수쇄] clearing[winding] up; straightening (out); fixing up. ¶연회의 ~ put things in order after a party // 밥 먹은 ~를 하다 wash up the dishes / clear the (dining) table // 분쟁의 ~를 하다 settle[wind up] a strife / get a trouble straightened // 나는 누이동생이 저질러 놓은 일의 ~를 하게 되었다 I ended up having to straighten out [clean up] the mess my sister had made.

뒤치락거리다 turn over from one side to the other; toss about; roll. ¶몸을 뒤치락거리며 잠을 못 이루다 thrash about in bed unable to sleep.

뒤탈(-頉) after-trouble; later[future] trouble. ¶~이 두려워 for fear of later troubles // ~이 없도록 so as to prevent any trouble that might occur in future / so there will be no future troubles // ~이 없도록 하다 leave no seeds of future trouble // ~이 무서워서 신고 하지 못하다 do not report (a blackmail by hoodlums) for fear of reprisals // 그것 때문에 평생 자네는 ~에 시달릴[벌을 받을] 것이다 You'll be troubled by it[be tormented with it] for life. // 부모의 죄에 대한 ~이 자식에게 미친 것이다 (문어) The sins of the parents were visited upon their children. // 폭주로 나는 위를 망쳤다 I ruined my stomach by drinking too much. / I developed stomach trouble because I drink too much.

뒤통수 the back (part) of the head; [생] the occiput (pl. ~s, -pita).

뒤통수를 얻어맞다 [뜻밖의 일을 당하다] be caught on the wrong foot; be stabbed in the back.

뒤통수치다 [낙담하다] be dejected; get disappointed [dispirited]; lose heart.

뒤통스럽다 [미련하다] stupid; thickheaded; foolhardy; senseless; [서투르다] bungling; clumsy; awkward. ¶뒤통스러운 사람 a bungler / a botcher // 뒤통스런 짓 a blunder // 사람이 뒤통스러워 일을 잘 저지른다 He is such a thick-headed fellow he makes a bungle of everything he does.

뒤틀다 1 [비틀다] twist; wrench; screw; distort; warp. ¶팔을 ~ wrench[twist] (a person's) arm / give a twist to (a person's) arm // 허리를 왼쪽으로 ~ twist[turn] one's hip to the left // 고통으로 몸을 ~ be convulsed with pain / writhe in great agony // 나뭇가지를 뒤틀어 꺾다 wrench a branch off a tree / break off a branch by twisting // 나사를 ~ screw a screw in. 2 (일을) baffle; frustrate; thwart; obstruct; foil. ¶남의 계획을 뒤틀어 놓다 thwart a person's plan // 그의 부주의가 내 계획을 뒤틀어 놓았다 His carelessness frustrated[balked] me in my plan.

뒤틀리다 1 [비틀리다] be twisted; be distorted[wrenched]; grow[become] warped. ¶무릎이 ~ get one's knee wrenched // 목재가 건조 중에 뒤틀렸다 The wood has warped in drying. 2 (마음이) become perverse; get distorted; become crooked; get warped. ¶겹친 불행 때문에 그 여자의 성격이 뒤틀렸다 Her character was warped by repeated misfortunes. 3 (일이) miscarry; fail; be frustrated; be baffled; be upset; be foiled; go wrong [amiss]. ¶그의 계획이 뒤틀렸다 He was thwarted[obstructed / frustrated / foiled] in his plan.

뒤틀어지다 1 [비틀리다] twist; warp; go awry. ¶팔다리가 뒤틀어진다 My limbs twist. 2 (일이) fail; miss; go wrong[amiss]. ¶계획이 뒤틀어진다 A plan misses[fails / goes wrong].

뒤편(-便) 1 [뒤쪽] the backside; the rear. ¶학교 ~에 사과밭이 있었다 There was an apple orchard behind[at the back of] our school. 2 [나중 인편] a later messenger; [편중 차편] (on) a later train.

뒤흔들다 1 [마구 흔들다] shake[swing / sway] violently[hard]; jolt; convulse. ¶천지를 뒤흔드는 큰 음향 a sound loud enough to shake heaven and earth // 지축을 뒤흔드는 쾅음 a deep earthshaking rumble // 과일을 따려고 나무를 ~ shake the tree for fruit // 멱살 [어깨]을 잡고 ~ shake (a person) by the coat collar[the shoulder] // 지진이 그 섬을 뒤흔들었다 An earthquake convulsed the island.

2 [충격을 주다] shock; shake; (마음을) disturb; agitate; stir. ¶세계를 뒤흔드는 대사건 an earthshaking event // 그의 권위를 뒤흔드는 소문 rumors which will undermine his authority // 마음을 ~ disturb (a person's) mind // 세상을 ~ disturb[upset] the world // 정계를 ~ cause a sensation in the political world / jolt[shake up] the political world // 그 발명은 공업계를 뿌리째 뒤흔들어 놓았다 The invention rocked industry to its heels. // 제2차 세계 대전의 발발은 세계를 뒤흔들었다 The outbreak of World War Ⅱ shook the

뒤흔들리다 1 [마구 흔들리다] be shaken [swayed] violently; jolt. ¶바람에 ~ be swayed by the wind/오늘 아침 지진으로 집이 뒤흔들렸다 My house shook hard in the earthquake this morning.//길이 나빠 차가 뒤흔들렸다 The car swayed because of the rough road. 2 [동요되다] be disturbed; waver. ¶그 소식을 듣고서 그의 결심은 뒤흔들렸다 The news shook[upset] his resolution./At the news he wavered in his resolution.//이 정책은 근본부터 뒤흔들리고 있다 This political policy has been shaken from the roots./The whole basis of this policy has become very shaky.

뒷간(-間) a toilet; a water closet(약어 W.C.); a rest room. ¶~ 출입이 잦다 have loose bowels.

뒷간에 갈 적 마음 다르고 올 적 마음 다르다 (속담) Danger past, God forgotten.; Once on shore, we pray no more.

뒷감당(-堪當) [뒤끝을 수습함]. **뒷감당하다** conduct[deal with] the aftergrowth[aftermath]; settle; wind up (one's affairs); straighten up; put in order. ¶뒷감당할 것이 큰일이다 It will be a terrific task to straighten things up.//그는 연회를 뒷감당했다 He put things in order after the party.//나는 내 누이동생의 빚을 뒷감당하게 되었다 I ended up being responsible for my sister's debts.

뒷거래(-去來) backdoor[illegal] dealing [business]. ¶대통령은 야당과 ~를 한 것 같다 President seems to have made a secret deal with the opposition (party).

뒷걱정 after-worries. **뒷걱정하다** worry afterward; worry about an aftermath.

뒷걸음 a backward step.

뒷걸음질 stepping backward; taking backward steps. **뒷걸음질하다** step backward; (약간) step back.

뒷걸음치다 1 [뒤로 물러서다] step[move/walk] backward; step[draw] back; back down. ¶몇 발짝 ~ fall[draw] back a few steps. 2 [퇴보하다] go[move/fall] backward.

뒷골목 an alley; a backlanc; (미) a back street; (미) an alleyway(좁은); a bystreet. ¶~ 인생 a sordid life/a back street existence.

뒷공론(-公論) 1 [일이 끝난 뒤에 쓸데없이 하는 평론] idle discussion after something is over; a futile rehash of an event; a postmortem (debate/discussion). ¶지금은 무슨 말을 해도 ~에 지나지 않는다 At this point, anything you say is no more than hindsight.//~은 제발 그만두시오 Please spare me the after-the-fact commentary! **뒷공론하다** discuss something after it is over; hold a fruitless debate after the event; flog a dead horse. ¶이제 와서 뒷공론해 봐야 소용없다 It is too late now. What is done is done. 2 [험담] backbiting; criticizing[speaking evil of] (a person) behind his back; malicious gossip; scandal; (소문) gossip in private. ¶그에게서 ~ 들을 짓을 하지 마라 Don't give him a handle against you. **뒷공론하다** backbite; criticize[speak evil of] (a person) behind his back[in his absence]; gossip in private; stab (a person) in the back.

뒷구멍 [뒷문] a back door[way]; the kitchen door; a rear entry; backstairs channels; an illegitimate way; an irregular[unfair] way; [부정 수단] unjust[unlawful] means. ¶~으로 하는 계약 a backdoor contract//~으로 도 망치다 escape by the back door//~으로 돈을 대다 give[supply] (a person) money out the back door//~으로 돈을 주다 bribe (a person) with money//그는 ~으로 입학했다 He entered the school through backstairs channel.

뒷귀 [들은 것에 대한 이해력]. ¶~가 먹다[어둡다] be stupid/be dull-[slow-]witted/be slow to understand[catch on]/be unaware.

뒷길¹ 1 [뒤에 있는 길] a back-street; a by-road(샛길). 2 [장래] one's future; prospects. ¶~을 생각하다 think of one's future. 3 [부정적인 수단] unjust[unfair/unlawful] means.

뒷길² (옷의) the back piece of an upper garment.

뒷날 the future; a later day; the days to come; afterdays. ¶~을 위해서 for the future reference(참고)/as a warning for the future(교훈)//~을 생각하다 think of the future/meet the future//~ 후회하지 않도록 해라 Make sure you're not sorry in the future.//그에게는 빛나는 ~이 있다 He has a brilliant [bright] future for him.//~ 다시 봅시다 I'll see you again someday.

뒷다리 a hind[rear] leg. ¶말이 갑자기 ~로 섰다 The horse suddenly rose on its hind legs./The horse suddenly reared.//개가 ~로 흙을 걷어찼다 The dog kicked up the dirt with its hind legs.

뒷다리(를) 잡히다 fall into (a person's) clutches; be caught in a snare; [약점 잡히다] give a handle (to the enemy). ¶그는 내게 뒷다리를 잡혀 있다 He is in my clutches./I have him in my clutches.

뒷담 the wall in back; a back fence.

뒷담당(-擔當) answering[taking responsibility] for the aftermath; taking care[charge] of the rest of (it). **뒷담당하다** answer[take responsibility] for the aftermath (of an affair); take care[charge] of the rest. ¶내가 뒷담당하겠다 I will answer for the consequences[result]./I will handle the rest.//일이 잘못되면 내가 뒷담당하겠다 If anything goes wrong, I will deal with it.

뒷대문(-大門) a back[rear] gate.

뒷덜미 the nape; the scruff; the back of one's neck. ¶~를 잡다 seize[take/grasp] (a person) by the nape of the neck.

뒷돈 [자금] capital; funds; stakes; [비상금] reserve funds; extra funds. ¶장사의 ~을 대다 finance a business/provide money for a business//노름의 ~을 대다 supply (a person) with gambling stakes//~을 대지 못해 사업이 중단되었다 The enterprise was abandoned owing to lack of funds.

뒷동산 a hill at the back (of a house/of a village).

뒷마당 a backyard; a backgarden; ground at the back of a house; a rear garden.

뒷말 1 [계속되는 이야기] the sequel (of a story); [나머지] the rest. ¶그는 고개를 끄덕이고 ~을 재촉했다 He nodded me on.//~은 하지 않아도 알겠다 The rest needs no telling. 2 [뒷공론의 말] backbiting.

뒷맛 (an) aftertaste. ¶싸운 후의 개운찮은 ~

뒷머리 1 (물건의) the back part (of); the back end. ¶책상의 ~ the back end of a table. 2 (행렬의) the rear; the end. ¶줄의 ~ the rear [end] of a row // 행렬의 ~ the rear of a procession. 3 [머리 뒤쪽의 머리털] back hair(여자의); the back of the head. ¶모자를 ~에 얹어 쓰다 wear hat on the back of one's head / hitch one's hat back. 4 the back (part) of the head. ⇨ ˚뒤통수

뒷면 (-面) 1 [이면] the reverse [other] side; the back (side); [내면] the inside. ¶사진의 ~에 on the back of the picture // 레코드의 ~을 올려놓다 play the other side of a record // 표지의 ~에 약어표가 있다 A list of abbreviations is given on the back of the cover [on the inside of the cover]. // 2번의 답은 답안지의 ~에 쓸 것 Write the answer to the second question on the back [opposite side / reverse side] of the paper. ¶~을 보시오 (게시) Please turn over.(▶ (영)에서는 P.T.O.로 약(略함)) / (미) Over.
2 (화폐의) tails(▶ 보통 복수형. 앞면은 heads. 단, heads, tails는 동전을 던져서 승부를 결정할 때밖에 쓰지 않음); the reverse (of a coin / a note). ¶(동전을 던져서) 앞면이 나오면 네가 이기고, ~이 나오면 내가 이긴다 Heads you win, tails I win. // 국명은 화폐의 ~에 있다 The name of the country is on the reverse side of the coin.

뒷모습 the sight [appearance] of one's back; one's back [rear] view; one's retreating [receding] figure [back]. ¶~을 보다 catch sight of (a person's) back // ~이 꼭 형과 같다 look just like one's brother from behind // 뛰어가는 그의 ~이 보였다 I caught sight of his back as he ran along. // 그의 ~을 줄곧 바라보았다 I gazed after him. // 톰은 ~이 짐과 꼭 닮았다 When seen from behind, Tom looks exactly like Jim.

뒷모양 (-貌樣) the sight of one's back. ⇨ ˚뒷모습

뒷문 (-門) 1 [후문] a back door [gate]; a back entrance [way]; a rear [postern] gate. ¶성(城)의 ~으로 쳐들어가다 storm into a castle from behind [the rear] // 그들은 모두 ~으로 들어왔다 They all entered by the back door. 2 [부정한 수단] unjust [unfair / unlawful] means. ¶~으로 하는 영업 a backdoor [an illegal] business // ~으로 도망가다 escape [run away] by the back door [gate] // 그는 ~으로 입학한 것 같다 He seems to have bought his way into the school.

뒷물 bathing one's private parts; a hip bath; a sitz bath. **뒷물하다** bath one's private parts; take a sitz bath.

뒷바라지 looking after; giving aids; a help; taking care of; care. ¶그 여자는 애들의 ~에 바쁘다 She is busy with the care of her children. **뒷바라지하다** look after; help (out); take care of; care for; provide for. ¶환자를 ~ attend [wait on] a patient // 아들의 살림을 ~ provide one's son with daily necessaries / help one's son's family out // 내가 그 아이를 뒷바라지하게 되었다 The baby came into my care. / The baby was left in my care.

뒷바퀴 the back [rear] wheel(s). ¶자동차 ~ a rear [back] wheel of a car.

뒷받침 [지지] backing; backup; support; [증명] proof (of / that); evidence (of / that / to do); substantiation; [보증] guarantee; endorsement; [기반] foundation. ¶증거의 ~이 없는 자백 a naked [an uncorroborated] confession // 그는 내 사업에 ~이 되어 주었다 He backed me up in my business. **뒷받침하다** back (up); support; endorse; substantiate; prove; give substance to (words); add support to (the rumor). ¶태양 에너지 설비를 뒷받침하는 과학 기술 the technology behind solar energy systems / the technology that makes solar energy systems feasible // 그는 그의 이론을 뒷받침할 자료를 모으고 있다 He is collecting data to support [back up] his theory. // 상황 증거 외에는 그의 범행을 뒷받침할 만한 것이 없었다 There was only circumstantial evidence to prove his crime. // 그는 변명을 거짓말로 뒷받침하고 있다 He uses lies to support his excuses. // 이 서류는 그가 정당한 상속인이라는 것을 뒷받침한다 This document proves that he is the rightful heir.

뒷발 [네발짐승의 뒤에 달린 두 발] a hind foot; a heel; a hind leg(다리). ¶~로 차다 kick with one's heel // ~로 흙을 파헤치다 scratch up the dirt with (its) hind legs.

뒷방 (-房) a back [an inner / a rear] room; a room at the back.

뒷배 backing; support; helping from behind. ¶~를 부탁하다 ask [come upon] (a person) for help [support] // ~를 보다 support / back up (a person) / stand behind (a person) // ~ 봐 주는 사람 a supporter / a backer.

뒷벽 (-壁) a back wall.

뒷북치다 fuss about belatedly; pother after the event. ¶미련한 놈 뒷북친다 Fools are wise after the event.

뒷산 (-山) the mountain [hill] at the back of [in the rear of / behind / back of] one's house [a village].

뒷소문 (-所聞) gossip about some past event; rumors in the wake of an event; later tidbits (of news [information]); an aftertalk.

뒷손[1] [사양하는 체하며 뒤로 슬그머니 받는 손] acceptance (of something) on the sly; illegal [false] reach; dirty hand (for money); getting a bribe. ¶~을 벌리다 [내밀다] demand [a thing] under a counter / be ready to accept on the sly / be open to bribery.

뒷손[2] [뒷수쇄를 하는 손]. ¶~이 없다 careless [loose / slipshod] about finishing things up / negligent / (서술적) leave things unfinished // 그는 무슨 일에나 ~이 없다 He lets everything slipshod get past him. / He never finishes what he starts doing.

뒷손가락질하다 point after (a person); point a finger of scorn at (a person); talk about (a person) with scorn. ➔**뒷손가락질받다** have depreciating words uttered behind one's back / be talked of (in contempt) / be an object of social contempt // 남에게 뒷손가락질 당하지 않도록 해라 Keep yourself above suspicion. // 나는 결코 남에게 뒷손가락질받을 만한 일은 않겠다 I shall never do anything

뒷수쇄(-收刷) putting things in order; setting matters right; clearing up; rearrangement; readjustment; later adjustment; winding-up. **뒷수쇄하다** put things in order; rearrange; clear up; settle; wind up; readjust; dispose of; take remedial measures.

뒷수습(-收拾) settlement (of an affair). ¶사건의 ~을 하다 settle an affair∥네 잘못의 ~은 안하겠다 I'm not going to make up for your mistakes[cover up your blunders / clean up your mess for you]∥나는 그의 보증인이었으니 그의 빚의 ~을 하지 않을 수 없었다 Since I was his guarantor, I was made to clean up his debts for him.

뒷심 1 〔조력〕 help[aid / assistance] from behind; backing-up; support; protection. ¶~이 든든하다 have a good backing∥~이 있다 have (a person) at one's back∥삼촌의 지위가 사업에 적잖게 ~이 된다 The social position of my uncle makes no little help to my business activities. 2 〔끝에 가서 회복하는 힘〕 strength[power] that is restored at the end; 〔저력〕 latent[potential] energy[power].

뒷이야기 a sequel to the story. ¶사건의 ~ a sequel to the event.

뒷일 1 〔뒤의 일〕 the aftermath of an event[affair]; the rest; the sequence; later happening. ¶소송의 ~을 처리하다 dispose of the aftermath of a lawsuit∥~을 부탁합니다 See (to it) that all is well after my departure. ∥~은 네게 맡기겠다 I'll leave the rest to you.∥~은 책임질 수 없다 I will not take responsibility for what may happen later on. 2 〔장래에 생길 일〕 future affairs; (사후의) affairs after one's death. ¶~을 부탁하다 entrust (another) with future affairs / ask (another) to look after one's affairs while one is away / give (another) the charge of the affairs after one's death∥먼 ~을 생각하다 have future in view of posterity at heart∥친구에게 애들의 ~을 부탁하다 entrust the care of one's children to a friend / entrust a friend with the care of one's children.

뒷자리 the[a] back seat; a seat at[in] the back. ¶~에 앉다 take a back seat / sit in the back seat.

뒷전 1 〔뒤쪽〕 the back; the rear. ¶멀리 ~에 앉다 sit far back.
2 〔나중의 차례〕 negligence. ¶~으로 돌리다 lay aside (one's work) / neglect[ignore] (one's studies) / leave (something) out of account[consideration] / pay no attention (to)∥공부를 ~으로 돌리다 neglect[ignore] one's studies∥그것은 ~으로 돌려도 된다 That can wait. / You can do it later.∥그 문제는 ~으로 미루어졌다 The question was deferred for future discussion.
3 〔배후〕 the back. ¶~에서 (남이 없는 데서) in (a person's) absence / (배후에서) behind the scene / (몰래) in secret∥~에서 남을 헐뜯다 speak ill of a person behind his back∥backbite a person∥~에 앉아서 조정하다 pull the wires[strings] from behind.
4 (굿의) the last of 12 stages of an exorcism.
● **뒷전풀이** performance of the last stage of an exorcism.

뒷정리(-整理) arrangements for the conclusion[end]; after adjustment; clearance work; winding-up. **뒷정리하다** arrange to end[conclude]; put (things) in order; set (matters) right; wind up (one's affairs); clear away(청소); dispose of(처리); clear the table(식사의).

뒷조사(-調査) a detailed[secret] investigation[inquiry]. **뒷조사하다** investigate secretly[in secret]; make secret[confidential] inquiries into (a matter).

뒷줄 1 the row behind; a back[rear] row. 2 (배후 세력) a patron; a backer; a pull.

뒷질하다 pitching; rocking. **뒷질하다** (a ship) pitch; (a boat) rock back and forth. ¶폭풍우 속에서 배가 마구 뒷질하였다 The ship pitched about in the storm.

뒷짐 ~을 지다 clasp one's hands behind one's back∥~을 지우다 make (a person) clasp his hands behind his back / (결박 짓다) tie (a person's) arms behind his back.

뒷집 the house behind; a house in[at] the back of one's own; the house right back of one's own.

뒹굴다 1 〔누워서 구르다〕 roll[tumble] about[over]; throw oneself down; (고통으로) writhe. ¶잠자리에서 ~ toss[tumble] about in one's bed∥잔디 위에 ~ roll about on a lawn / throw oneself down on the lawn. 2 〔빈둥빈둥 놀다〕 idle[loaf] one's time away; be on the loaf; (미) loaf around; live at ease; eat the bread of idleness. ¶일요일은 집에서 뒹굴며 지내다 pass sundays idly at home∥그는 아무것도 않고 뒹굴고 있다 He leads an idle life. 3 〔여기저기 널려 있다〕 be spread[scattered] all over.

듀스 〔체〕 deuce. ¶~가 되었다 The game went to deuce.
● **듀스 어게인** deuce again.

듀엣 〔음〕 duet; 〔발레〕 a pas de deux. ¶왕자와 공주의 ~ a pas de deux between a prince and a princess∥~으로 노래하다 sing a duet∥~으로 춤추다 dance a duet / dance with a partner / perform a pas de deux.

드나들다 1 〔출입하다〕 come in and go out; go[come] in and out; (자주 가다) go often; frequent (a house); make frequent visits (to). ¶드나드는 배 ships going in and out∥드나드는 관광객 in-and-out tourists∥술집에 자주 ~ hang out[around] a bar / frequent a pub∥마음대로 ~ have free adit∥자주 드나들며 오랜 시간을 보내다 be a constant visitor (at)∥항구는 드나드는 배들로 북적거렸다 The harbor was thronged with departing and arriving ships.∥나는 그곳에 자유롭게 드나들고 있읍니다 I have free access to the place. ∥그 집에는 드나드는 사람이 많다 They have many visitors.
2 〔들쭉날쭉하다〕 zigzag; crooked; bent; indented; go in and out.

드날리다 1 (이름이) (one's name) resound[echo] far and wide; come to fame; become famous[popular]. ¶이름을 온 세상에 ~ be known all over the world∥명망이 전국에 ~ be popular throughout the country∥그의 명성이 전국에 드날렸다 His name echoed throughout the country.
2 (이름을) have one's name up; make[win] a name for oneself. ¶온 세상에 이름을 ~ gain a worldwide reputation / achieve [enjoy] worldwide fame∥그는 그 작품으로 이름을 드날렸다 He established distinction by the

드넓다

work. / The work gained him a reputation. ¶그는 지금 한창 명성을 드날리는 문단의 거장이다 He is the most influential[the foremost] figure in literary circles today.

드넓다 spacious; wide; large; open; extensive; vast. ¶그는 드넓은 들판에서 말을 달렸다 He galloped his horse in open field.

드높다 high; tall; lofty; eminent. ¶하늘에 드높이 high in the air / (미) way up in the sky / 정부를 비난하는 소리가 ~ The government is loudly attacked. / 대학 교육을 개혁하라는 소리가 ~ There are loud cries demanding a reform of university education.

드디어 at last; finally; eventually; at length; after all; in the end; in the long run; ultimately. ¶그는 ~ 성공했다 At last he got a success. // 그는 열심히 공부하더니 ~ 합격했다 He had been studying hard and finally passed the examination.

드라마 a drama; a play. ¶라디오 ~ a radio play / 인간 ~ a human drama / 텔레비전 연속 ~ a television serial drama.

드라마틱하다 dramatic.

드라이 dry.
● **드라이아이스** dry ice(▶ 원래는 상표명). **드라이클리닝** dry cleaning. ¶외투를 ~ 보내다 send one's overcoat to the (dry) cleaner's / have one's overcoat dry-cleaned // 이걸 ~ 해 주십시오 Will you have this dry-cleaned, please?

드라이버 1 [나사돌리개] a screwdriver. 2 [장거리용 골프채] a driver.

드라이브 a drive; motoring; a motor ride; a joyride. ¶~ 가다 go for a drive / ~에 좋은 날씨 ideal weather for motoring[a drive] / 그들은 자동차로 ~ 나갔다 They went for a drive in a motorcar. **드라이브하다** take[have] a drive (in); take a spin. ¶내 차로 파로 호까지 드라이브했다 I took a drive to Paro Lake in my car.

드라이어 a drier; a dryer. ¶~로 머리를 만지다 do one's hair with a hair drier[dryer].

드래그 [컴] [끌기] drag.

드래프트제 (-制) the draft system.

드러나다 1 [표면에 나타나다] come into view; come out; appear; crop out (광맥이); emerge (from); be exposed; be bared. ¶어깨가 ~ one's shoulders are exposed // 광맥이 ~ a mineral vein crops out[appears].
2 (성질·표정이) reveal[show] itself; be revealed; come in evidence; be expressed. ¶마각이 ~ show the cloven hoof // 그녀의 얼굴에 기쁜 빛이 드러났다 Joy was (written) in her face. // 술에 취하면 사람의 본성이 드러난다 Wine reveals the true character of a man. // 그의 얼굴에는 개전의 빛이 드러났다 Repentance was written upon his face.
3 (비밀이) be found (out); be disclosed; be exposed; be detected; be laid bare; come to light; be brought to light. ¶그의 거짓말이 드러났다 His lie was detected. / His falsehood was found out. // 비밀이 드러났다 The secret got out. // 그의 악행이 드러났다 His evil doings came to light[were discovered]. // 그의 정체가 드러났다 His identity was revealed [was discovered]. // 시험 결과 그의 실력이 바닥이 드러났다 As a result of the examination his pretense to knowledge was found false. // 두 사람 사이의 대립은 완전히 드러났다 The conflict between the two has become quite open[public].
4 [유명해지다] be known to; become known [prominent / conspicuous / famous]. ¶드러나게 prominently / preeminent / conspicuously // 세상에 ~ become famous in the world / 업적이 ~ one's achievements become known.

드러내다 1 [노출하다] expose; lay bare [open]; bare; uncover; disclose. ¶드러낸 naked / bare / uncovered // 가슴을 ~ expose [bare] one's breast / 넓적다리를 ~ expose one's thigh / 양팔을 ~ lay one's arms bare // 이를 드러내고 웃다 grin (at a person) / bare one's teeth in a grin / smile a toothy smile // 염천에 몸을 ~ be exposed to the heat of the burning sun // 그녀는 맨살을 드러내 놓고 침대 의자에 누워 있었다 She was lying on a couch naked[in the nude / without any clothes on] // 개가 이를 드러내고 으르렁거렸다 The dog growled, baring [showing] its teeth.
2 (공공연히) bring (a matter) before the public; make (a matter) public; bring (a matter) to light. ¶드러내 놓은 open / public // 드러내 놓고 반대하다 oppose publicly / offer an open opposition.
3 [보이다] show; indicate; display; exhibit; manifest; [입증하다] prove; speak for; bespeak. ¶정직함을 ~ speak for one's honesty // 차이를 ~ bring out the differences // 이 일은 그의 현명함을 드러냈다 This matter proved his sagacity. // 그는 있는 재간을 다 드러내어 보였다 He displayed all his talents[skills].
4 (성질·본성을) show; reveal; betray; express; disclose. ¶본심을 ~ disclose one's real intention / reveal one's real motive // 자기의 무지(無知)를 ~ betray one's ignorance // 정체를 ~ throw off the mask[one's disguise] / unveil[reveal] oneself // (상대에게) 속셈을 ~ show[reveal] one's hand / put one's cards on the table // 성난 빛을 ~ betray one's anger // 그는 무심코 본성을 드러냈다 He has betrayed himself. / He has shown his true colors.
5 [폭로하다] reveal[disclose / divulge] (a secret); expose[betray] (one's ignorance); lay bare (one's scheme). ¶비밀을 ~ reveal [divulge / spill] a secret // 흉계를 ~ lay bare one's evil design // 회사의 내막을 ~ disclose the inside story of a company // 잘못을 ~ expose one's fault[mistake].
6 (명성을) distinguish; make famous. ¶이름을 ~ distinguish oneself / become famous / make one's name // 전투에서 이름을 ~ distinguish oneself in the battle.

드러눕다 lie down; lay oneself down; throw down; lie on one's back; stretch oneself. ¶길게 ~ lie at full length (on) / stretch oneself (on) // 반듯이[모로] ~ lie on one's back[side] // 병으로 ~ be laid up with illness / be confined to one's bed / keep one's bed / be ill[sick] in bed // 그는 풀밭 위에 드러누웠다 He lay[threw himself] down on the grass.

드럼¹ [북] a drum. ¶~을 치다 beat a drum.

드럼² [통] a drum. ¶~통 a drum (can) // 석유 두 ~ two drums of petroleum[(미) gasoline].

드렁드렁 snoring (loudly). ⇨ "드르릉드르릉

드레스 a dress. ¶~를 입은 여성 a woman in dress.

드로잉 drawing.

드르렁거리다 keep snoring (loudly); snore. ¶코를 ~ be snoring away∥드르렁거리기 시작하다 fall to snoring.

드르렁드르렁 snoring (loudly / terribly). ¶~ 코 고는 소리 a tremendous rattling snore∥그는 ~ 코를 골고 있었다 He was snoring loudly[terribly]. **드르렁드르렁하다** snore. ⇨ 드르렁거리다

드르르[1] 1 [미끄럽게] smoothly; slipperily; rolling along. ¶~ 미끄러져 내려가다 slide down∥(문이) ~ 열리다 open smoothly. 2 [떠는 모양] trembling(ly); shivering(ly). ¶~ 진동하다 tremble (all over) / shiver∥폭풍 때문에 유리창이 ~ 흔들렸다 The explosion made the windowpanes tremble.

드르르[2] [거침없이] smoothly; swimmingly; without a hitch; fluently; without any difficulty. ¶글을 ~ 읽다 read a passage smoothly∥~ 외다 say by heart without a single break∥어려운 문제를 ~ 풀다 solve a hard question easily∥일이 ~ 진행되었다 The matter went on very smoothly[on swimmingly].

드리다[1] 1 [주다] give; offer (up); present (one's compliments); make a present (of); dedicate; serve. ¶기도를 ~ offer[put up] prayers (to God)∥축하를 ~ give[offer] one's congratulations∥윗사람에게 물건을 ~ present a thing to the superior∥어머니께 진지를 ~ serve one's mother with dinner∥무엇을 드릴까요 (식당 에서) Can I offer you anything?∥이것을 드리겠습니다 This (gift) is for you.∥커피 좀 드릴까요 Will you have some coffee?
2 [팔다] sell; let (a person) have; offer. ¶무엇을 드릴까요 (가게에서) What can I do for you? / May I help you?∥싸게 드리겠습니다 I will let you have it very cheap.∥3만 원이면 드리겠습니다 You can have it for three thousand won.

드리다[2] (곡식을) winnow away[off] the chaff from the grain.

드리다[3] [꼬다] braid; plait; twist (into a rope); twist together; twine; entwist. ¶실을 ~ entwist threads∥댕기를 ~ intertwine one's hair with ribbon into a pigtail∥이 밧줄은 여러 가닥으로 드린 것이다 This rope is twisted from many threads.

드리다[4] [방·마루 등을 만들다] set; put in; make; construct; arrange. ¶마루를 ~ make a floor / floor∥방을 ~ set a room∥벽에 창을 ~ furnish a wall with windows.

드리다[5] (윗사람에게) do as a favor for a superior. ¶알려 ~ inform (a person) of / tell (a person)∥보여 ~ submit a thing for (a person's) inspection∥이 점 통지해 드립니다 I wish to inform you that.∥댁까지 모셔다 드릴까요 Shall I see you home?∥그분께 길을 가리켜 드렸다 I have shown the gentleman the way.

드리블 [구기] a dribble; dribbling. **드리블하다** dribble.

드리우다 1 [아래로 늘어뜨리다] hang down; suspend; overhang; let (hang) down. ¶발을 ~ let down a bamboo blind∥처마에 매달아 풍경을 ~ hang a wind-bell from the eaves∥드리워지다 be hung (with)∥창문에는 커튼이 드리워져 있다 There is a curtain hanging at the window.∥구름이 하늘에 낮게 드리워져 있었다 Clouds hung low in the sky. / The sky was covered with low-hanging clouds.∥지금 우리 집에 어두운 그림자가 드리워지고 있다 A dark cloud is[Dark clouds are] hanging over[threatening] my family now.∥버드나무 가지가 땅에 바짝 드리워지고 있었다 The willow branches hung[dropped] down close to the ground.
2 [가르침을 주다] give (to an inferior); grant; confer; bestow (on / upon). ¶교훈을 ~ give a (moral) lesson.
3 [후세에 남기다] hand down; leave; bequeath. ¶이름을 후세에 ~ leave one's name to posterity / immortalize one's name / win immortal fame.

드릴 1 [천공기·송곳] a drill. ¶전기 ~ an electric drill∥~로 문에 구멍을 내다 drill a hole in the door. 2 [연습] a drill.

드맑다 very clear. ¶드맑은 하늘 a bright, blue sky.

드문드문 1 (시간적으로) once in a (long) while; at (rare / long) intervals; from time to time; occasionally; now and then. ¶~ 찾아오다 come once in a while / show up from time to time∥그런 일이 ~ 있다 Such a thing happens from time to time.∥그의 소식을 ~ 듣는다 I hear from him now and then. 2 (공간적으로) at intervals; here and there; sporadically; sparsely; thinly; scatteredly. ¶나무를 ~ 심다 plant trees at intervals[here and there]∥들에 집이 ~ 있다 The field is sparsely dotted with houses.∥그 산에는 나무가 ~ 나 있다 The hill is sparsely wooded.

드물다 [진귀하다] rare; uncommon; unusual; [수효가 적다] scarce; few; (few and) far between; [특이하다] unique. ¶드물게 rarely / seldom / uncommonly / on rare occasions / at rare intervals∥아주 드물게 very rarely / once in a long while∥드문 일 a rare[an uncommon] occurrence∥보기 드문 미인 a rare beauty / a woman of rare[extraordinary] beauty∥그가 일찍 일어나는 것은 드문 일이다 It is rare[unusual] for him to get up early.∥그녀가 집에 있는 일은 ~ We seldom find her at her home.∥그러한 성공은 드문 일이다 Such a success is quite phenomenal.∥물론 사고도 일어나지만 그것은 아주 드문 일이다 Accidents might occur, of course, but they are few and far between.∥그것은 하등 드문 일이 아니다 It is no rare thing. / There's nothing unusual about it.∥그는 드물게 보는 웅변가다 He is a man of rare eloquence.∥그런 사건은 드물게 일어난다 Such an incident seldom occurs.

드새다 pass the night (at an inn). ¶하룻밤 ~ stay overnight / get accommodation[take a lodge] for the night∥하룻밤 드새기를 청하다 ask (a person) for a night's lodging.

드세다 (사람이) wild (nature); savage (disposition); violent (temper); (일이) rough; tough; difficult. ¶성질이 드센 여자 a woman of violent temper∥드센 일 a stiff task / a tough job / heavy work∥그는 고집이 몹시 ~ He is extremely stubborn.

드잡이 [격투] a grapple; grips; handgrips; a scuffle; a wrestle; a grappling; a scrimmage; a rough and tumble fight. ¶말다툼이 끝내는 ~가 되었다 Their quarrel ended in a fist [rough-and-tumble] fight. 드잡이하다 grapple (with); come to grapples [handgrips/grips] (with); scuffle. ¶서로 ~ grapple with each other / come to grips with each other // 두 아이들이 드잡이하고 있다 The two children are fighting [grappling (with each other)].

득(得) [이득] (a) profit; (a) gain; interest(s); [유리] advantage; benefit. ¶~이 되는 profitable / advantageous / gainful / paying / economical // ~이 되다 turn [prove] to one's profit (to) / do (a person) good // ~을 보다 profit / gain / gain profit / benefit / do well [nicely] out of (a war) // ~을 보면 봤지 손해는 보지 않는다 You have everything to gain and nothing to lose. // 그 사업으로 가장 ~을 보는 사람은 누구일까 Who will benefit [gain] the most from that project? // 손해 보는 사람이 있으면 ~을 보는 사람도 있다 It is an ill wind that blows nobody any good. // 그것을 당장 팔아 버리는 것이 훨씬 ~이 될 겁니다 It would be much profitable to sell it at once. // 그렇게 하는 것이 ~이 될 겁니다 It would be advantageous [to your advantage / in your interest] to do so. // 지름길로 가면 1마일 ~을 본다 You save a mile by taking a shortcut.

득남(得男) delivery of a baby boy. 득남하다 have a baby boy; beget a baby boy(남성에 대하여 말함). ¶그녀는 득남했다 She had a (baby) boy. / She became the mother of a baby boy.

득녀(得女) delivery of a baby girl. 득녀하다 have a baby girl; beget a baby girl(남성에 대하여 말함).

득달같다 [지체하지 않다] prompt; quick; ready; (서술적) be right on time. 득달같이 promptly; without delay; at once. ¶~ 대령하다 present oneself promptly.

득도(得道) attainment of Nirvana; spiritual awakening [enlightenment]. 득도하다 attain Nirvana; achieve spiritual enlightenment [awakening].

득세하다(得勢-) 1 [세력을 얻다] gain [acquire / obtain] power [influence]; become influential [powerful]. ¶그의 의견이 점점 득세하고 있다 His view is gaining ground. 2 [형세가 좋아지다] turn to one's advantage; get an opportunity. ¶그는 하는 일마다 득세했다 Everything turned to his advantages [profits].

득시글득시글 in swarms; swarming. ¶벌레가 ~ 끓고 있다 There are swarms of insects. 득시글득시글하다 be swarming (with); be crowded [teeming] (with); be alive (with); (벌레 등이) squirm [wriggle about] in a swarm. ¶구더기가 ~ swarm with maggots / maggots swarm // 옷에 이가 ~ The clothes are covered with lice all over.

득실(得失) [얻음과 잃음] gains and losses; [이익과 손해] profits and losses; [성패] success and failure; [장단점] merits and demerits; advantages and disadvantages [shortcomings]. ¶~을 떠나서 leaving [without considering] the personal interests // ~을 따지다 weigh [ponder on] the merits [relative advantages] / 제출된 안(案)의 ~을 논하다 discuss the advisability of the proposal // ~이 거의 반반이다 The gains and losses are about even [about on a par].

득실득실 in swarms. ⇨득시글득시글

득의(得意) pride; triumph; elation. ¶~의 웃음을 띠고 [머금고] with a smile of triumph [self-satisfaction].

득의만면하다(得意滿面-) (서술적) be proud (of); pride [plume] oneself (on); take a pride (in). ¶득의만면하여 elatedly / triumphantly / in triumph / with self-satisfaction / with a proud air // 소년은 득의만면하여 10킬로의 길을 끝까지 걸었다고 말했다 The boy told us triumphantly [with a look of triumph] that he had walked the whole course of ten kilometers. // 그는 득의만면하여 낚아 올린 고기를 보여 주었다 He was beaming with triumph as he showed us the fish he had caught.

득의양양하다(得意揚揚-) (서술적) be as happy as a king; be as proud [pleased] as a peacock [Punch / turkey]; be on (a) cockhorse; be all set up; be in the skies. ¶득의양양한 얼굴 [태도] a triumphant air / a complacent look // 득의양양하여 proudly / in triumph / triumphantly / with a triumphant air // 그녀는 더없이 득의양양했다 She is feeling extremely happy and proud of herself. // 그는 성공하여 득의양양했다 He was puffed up [elated] by his success.

득점(得點) the marks obtained; (경기의) the points made; the runs scored; a score; scoring; [야구] runs [R]. ¶대량 ~ a large score / 팀 [개인] ~ a team [an individual] score // 무 ~ 경기 [야구] a runless game // ~이 없다 score nothing / be [go] scoreless // 한국은 일본에 6대 0의 큰 ~ 차로 이겼다 Korea won against Japan by the lopsided score of 6 to 0. 득점하다 score (a point); make [earn] a score. ¶대량 ~ score many points / make a good record / [야구] score a lot of runs // 한 점 ~ gain a point (over) / score a point (against) // 그들은 5회에 3점을 득점했다 They scored three runs in the fifth inning.
● 득점자 a scorer. 득점판 (야구 등의) a scoreboard. 득점표 a points table; a scorecard.

득표(得票) [최고] the highest poll // 법정 ~ 수 the legally required minimum number of votes [polls] // 최고 ~를 얻다 poll the largest number of votes // 최고 ~로 당선되다 be elected (to the assembly) with the highest poll / be elected polling the largest number of votes / head the list of successful candidates / (미) lead the ticket // ~ 운동을 하다 canvass for votes // 그의 ~는 20만 표였다 He polled 200,000 votes. 득표하다 poll [get / gain / obtain / win] votes. ¶대량 ~ poll a large vote // 남보다 많이 [적게] ~ get more [less] votes than another / (미) run ahead of [behind] another's ticket.
● 득표 전략 vote-getting tactics. 득표 차 plurality [majority] over one's rival candidate.

든 either ... or; even. ⇨~든지
-든 even if; or. ⇨-든지

든든하다 1 [굳세다] robust; healthy; stout; strong; hardy; sturdy. 든든히 strongly; robustly; stoutly; firmly; solidly; steadily. ¶집을 ~ 짓다 build a house durable // 지반을 ~ 쌓다 firmly establish one's sphere of influence.
2 [단단하다] firm; solid; secure; steady. ¶든든한 기초 a solid foundation // 재정이 든든한 회사 a solid company // 든든한 담보 a gilt-

edged[good] security // 방비가 ~ be strongly [heavily] fortified // 방비를 든든하게 하다 strengthen the defenses. 든든히 firmly; solidly.
3 [미덥다] secure; confident; reassuring; encouraging; reliable; safe. ¶든든한 사람 a reliable person // 든든한 자리 a safe position // 마음 든든한 말 encouraging words // 든든한 백이 있다 have a good backing // 마음이 ~ feel reassured[confident / safe / secure] / be inspired with confidence // …을 들으니 마음이 ~ it is heartening[encouraging] to hear that … // 그가 있어 주는 것만으로도 나는 마음 든든하였다 His mere presence reassured me [made me feel confident]. / His mere presence gave me courage[confidence]. // 당신이 계시니 내 마음이 든든합니다 Your presence reassures[encourages] me. / It's reassuring to have you with me. / I feel reassured since you are with me. // 당신이 도와주신다니 마음이 아주 든든합니다 Your help will greatly embolden[encourage] me. 든든히 securely; safely; reassuring; confidently; reliably. ¶마음 ~ 생각하다 feel reassured[confident / safe / secure] / be inspired with confidence / feel emboldened.
4 [배가 부르다] full; replete. ¶배가 ~ have a full stomach[belly] / have the stomach full // 배가 든든하지 않으면 일을 할 수가 없다 One cannot work on an empty stomach. / A full belly counsels well. 든든히 fully; to repletion. ¶밥을 ~ 먹다 take a full meal.

든지 1 [무엇이나 가리지 아니함] either … or; whether … or. ¶사과~ 배~ either apples or pears // 정말이~ 거짓말이~ whether (it be) true or not // 이거~ 그거~ 둘 중 하나를 가져라 Take one of the two, either this one or that one. **2** […까지도] even; even if [though]; -ever. ¶내가 할 수 있는 일이라면 무엇이~ 하겠다 I am willing to do everything in my power to help you. // 대학이라면 어디~ 좋다 If it is a university, any one will do[I don't mind which]. // 언제~ 좋을 때 오시오 Come whenever[(at) any time] you like. // 언제~ 좋소 Any time will do.
-든지 1 […더라도] even if; although; though; no matter (who / what / when / where / how). ¶무엇을 하~ whatever (it be found that) one does // 누가 뭐라고 하~ whatever others may say (about / of) // 어떻게 해서~ at all costs / at any cost / by any means // 얼굴이야 어떻게 생겼~ regardless of what (a person) looks like // 어디들 가~ 내 집보다 좋은 곳은 없다 Go where you may, there is no place like home. // 어떤 일이 있~ 오늘 밤에는 밖에 나가지 마라 Don't go out tonight no matter what will happen.
2 [무엇이나 가리지 않고] or; either … or; whether … or. ¶비가 오~ 안 오~ 간에 whether it may rain or not / rain[wet] or shine // 그가 죽~ 살~ 나는 모른다 I don't care whether he lives or dies. // 그녀에게 전보를 치~ 편지를 하~ 해야 한다 You must either wire or write to her. // 펜으로 쓰~ 연필로 쓰~ 좋도록 해라 You may write it either with a pen or a pencil. // 가~ 오~ 마음대로 하게 Come or go, whichever you please.

든직하다 grave; serious; sedate; imposing; dignified. ¶든직한 인물 a man of substance / a sedate[grave] man // 든직한 태도 a grave and serious attitude // 그는 든직하여 믿을 만하다 He is a man of substance and very reliable.

듣다[1] [방울져 떨어지다] drip; trickle; dribble; fall in drops. ¶처마에서 낙숫물이 듣는다 Raindrops are falling[dripping] from the eaves.

듣다[2] **1** [효험이 있다] be effective; be efficacious (against fever); have an effect (on); be good (for a cold); act[work / tell] (on). ¶잘 듣는 약 a very efficacious medicine / a medicine of marvelous efficacy / a drug of great virtue // (약 등이) 놀랄 정도로 잘 ~ work wonders // 뇌물에 ~ [안 ~] be susceptible to bribery[be proof against bribes] // 듣지 않다 fail to work / be no good (for) / have no effect (on) // 이 약은 아주 잘 듣는다 The medicine acts marvelously well. // 이 약은 듣지 않았다 The medicine had no effect on me. // 이 약은 두통에 잘 듣는다 This medicine works well[is good] for headaches. // 약이 듣지 않게 되었다 The drug has lost its effect on me.
2 [정상적으로 움직이다] work; act. ¶오른손이 말을 안 ~ lose the use of one's right arm / one's right hand is out // 몸[수족]이 말을 안 ~ be disabled / cannot help oneself / be helpless // 이 열쇠가 말을 안 듣는다 This key won't work any more. / Something is wrong with this key. // 브레이크가 안 듣는다 The brake refuses to act[work].

듣다[3] **1** (소리를) hear (music); listen to; give ear to; lend an ear to; heed. ¶남이 듣는 데서 in the audience of a person / in a person's audience // 라디오를 ~ listen to[on] the radio // 연설을 ~ hear a speech / hear an address (from) / hear (a person) speak / listen to a speech // (연속) 강의를 ~ hear a course of lectures // 비 오는 소리를 ~ listen to it rain // 음악을 ~ listen to music // 귀를 기울여 ~ listen attentively[carefully] (to) / listen with pricked ears (to) / strain one's ears // 잘 주의해서 ~ listen to (a speech) attentively / be all attention[ears] // 열심히 얘기를 ~ hang on (a person's) words // 건성으로 ~ hear (a person) inattentively[with half an ear] // 처음부터 끝까지 ~ hear (a person) out // 잘못 ~ hear amiss / mishear / be misinformed (about) // 듣기 거북하다 be offensive[unpleasant / harsh] to the ear // 듣기 어렵다 be hard[difficult] to hear // 듣기 좋다 be agreeable[pleasant] to the ear // 듣기 좋은 소리를 하다 say pleasant[agreeable] things / flatter / tickle (a person's) ear // 듣기 싫은 소리를 하다 say a disagreeable [spiteful] thing (to) // 듣지 못하다 fail to hear / leave (something) unheard // 참고로 들어(만) 두다 hear (it) for one's information // 들으려 하지 않다 turn a deaf ear (to) // 그는 내가 하는 말 뭐던 들으려고 하지 않는다 He won't listen to me. / He turns a deaf ear to me. // 내 말을 귀담아들으세요 Mark my words. / Hear[Listen to] me. / Listen [Give heed] to what I say[I am going to say]. // 조용히 들어 주십시오 Attention, please. / Please be quiet and listen. // 귀하의 의견을 듣고자 합니다 I'd like to hear your opinion. // 조속한 대답을 들을 수 있기를 바랍니다 Please give me your answer as soon as possible. / Would you please give me a prompt

듣다못해 reply?//집안 사람에 대한 욕은 듣기 거북한 것이다 It's unpleasant to hear nasty things said about one's relatives.//그가 영어를 하는 것을 들으면 영국인으로 착각할 정도다 To hear him speak English, one would take him for an Englishman.//그가 듣는 데서 그런 소리 하지 마라 Don't say things like that in his hearing.//그 사람이 잘못 들은 거다 He didn't hear me right[correctly]. / He misheard me.//그는 언제나 듣는 편이 된다 He always takes the role of listener.//듣기 싫다 I don't want to hear about it!//듣기 좋은 이야기도 한두 번이다 The best fish smells after three days.
2 (소식·소문 등을) hear of; be informed[told] of[about]; learn (something from[of] a person); understand; (사물이) come to one's ears[knowledge]. ¶많이 들어 본 이름 a familiar name//별로 들어 보지 못한 unfamiliar / strange / new//듣는 바에 의하면[듣자하니 / 듣기로는] from what I hear / I hear[we learn] (that ...) / I'm told (that ...)//소문으로 ~ hear of (a matter) / hear say of / learn (something from[of] a person)//풍문에 ~ learn[have it] by hearsay / get wind of//그런 얘기는 들어 본 적이 없다 I never heard of such a thing.//그것[그 사람]에 대해서는 들었다 I have heard about it[him].//당신에 관해서는 요즘 많이 듣고 있습니다 I have been hearing about you for some time now. / I have heard a lot about you.//여기 유명한 불상이 있다고 들었어요 I was told that[I hear] there's a famous statue of the Buddha here.//나는 그 소식을 듣고 놀랐다 I was surprised when I heard the news.//그 회사가 도산한다는 소문을 들었다 I heard a rumor that the company was going bankrupt.//내가 서울에 와 있다는 말은 그녀에게서 들었다 She told me[I heard from her] that you were in Seoul.//처음 듣는 얘기다 This is news to me.//하이잭에 관해서는 현지로부터 아직 아무것도 듣지 못했다 We have no on-the-spot information yet about the hijack.//듣자하니 아이가 아프다면서요 I hear that your child is sick.//그는 듣자하니 곧 사임한다고 한다 I don't know for certain, but they say he is going to resign.//그녀는 내가 들던 것보다 훨씬 미인이었다 She was even more beautiful than I had heard.
3 (칭찬·꾸지람을). ¶칭찬을 ~ be praised[admired / extolled / applauded] (by) / catch[get] it (from dad) / catch[have / get] a scolding//칭찬 듣고 화낼 사람은 없다 Nobody feels offended at compliments.//그따위 짓을 하면 꾸지람을 듣는 정도로 그치지 못할걸 If you do a thing like that, you can't get away with a mere scolding.
4 (이르는 말 등을) obey; follow; take (a person's) advice; listen to; mind; (부탁을) grant (a person's request); (요구 등을) comply with[accede to] (a demand); (호소를) hear. ¶말을 잘 듣는 어린이 an obedient child / a child who listens to[does] what he is told//말을 안 듣는 어린이 a disobedient child / an unreasonable[a willful / a naughty] child//부모의 말을 ~ obey one's parents / mind what one's parents say//충고를 ~ follow[take] (a person's) advice//남의 말을 안 ~ will not listen to what others say / will not take advice from others / will give no ear[heed] to (others)//아버지의 말을 안 ~ defy one's father//청을 들어주다 grant a request[favor] / comply with (a person's) request//그녀의 남편은 그녀의 말을 잘 듣는다 She has a great influence over her husband.//이 아이는 부모의 말을 잘 듣는다 This child obeys his parents. / This child minds[does] what his parents tell him.//나는 그의 충고를 듣고 담배를 끊었다 Following [Taking] his advice, I gave up smoking.//부탁을 들어 드리지요 I will attend to your wishes.//이번에는 네 청을 들어주겠다 I will grant your request this time.//어머니는 내 청을 들어주시려 하지 않았다 My mother wouldn't do what I asked[wouldn't listen to my request].

들으면 병이요 안 들으면 약이다(속담) Listeners hear no good of themselves.; What the eye sees not the heart rues not.; Ignorance is bliss.

듣다못해 (being) unable to hear (a person) out[to the end]; (being) unable to hear with indifference; (being) tired[sick] of hearing. ¶~ 화를 냈다 I got tired of listening to him and blew up.//마누라의 바가지를 ~ 그는 밖으로 나가 버렸다 Fed up with his wife's nagging, he went out.

들¹ a field; (전답) the fields; (평야) a plain. ¶~에도 산에도 in the mountains as well as on the plains//넓게 펼쳐진 ~ a stretch[an expanse] of plains//~ 가운데의 외딴집 a lone[solitary] house in the middle of a plain//~로 일하러 나가다 go to work in the fields//~에 나가 일하다 work in the fields.

들² (등등) and so on[forth]; and others[other things] (of the same kind); and[or] the like; and what not; et cetera(약어 &c., etc.). ¶책상 위에 노리개부 책 ~이 많이 놓여 있었다 The table was loaded with toys, books, and what not.//동물원에 가서 코끼리, 범, 사자, 곰 ~을 보았다 We went to the zoo and saw elephants, tigers, lions, bears, and the like.

들³ ¶얘~야 Hey you people[you folks / you all]!//잘~ 했습니다 You all did well.//이리~ 오너라 You boys[girls / people / folks] come here.//빨리~ 갔다 We left fast.//놀러~ 갑시다 Let's all go out to play.//다~ 갔느냐 Has everybody gone?//먹기에~ 바쁘다 They're all busy eating.//먹지~ 마시오 Don't eat it, anybody!//들어~ 오시오 Come in, you people.

-들 ¶우리~ we / us//사람~ people / other people / others//어린이~ children//이분~은 우리 회사 사람~입니다 These are my colleagues in the company.

들개 a cur; an ownerless[a homeless] dog; stray dog; (쏘다니는 사람) a gadabout. ¶~의 무리 a pack of ownerless dogs.

들것 a stretcher; a litter. ¶~으로 나르다 carry (a person) on a stretcher//~에 싣다 put (a patient) on a stretcher.

들고나다 1 (참견하다) intrude; obtrude; interfere; (inter)meddle; poke one's nose into. ¶공연스레 ~ intrude where one is not wanted[asked]//그녀는 무슨 일에든지 들고나는 여자다 She meddles with everything.//남의 일에 들고날 것 없다 There's no need to stick your nose into another's business. / This is no business of yours. / Mind your own business. **2** (팔려고 가지고 나가다)

carry out (one's household goods) for sale.
들고뛰다 〈속〉 run away[off]; fly. ⇨달아나다
들고튀다 〈속〉 run away[off]; fly. ⇨달아나다
들국화(一菊花) a wild chrysanthemum [aster / erigeron].
들기름 perilla oil.
들길 a path[track] across a field; a field path.
들까부르다 1 [키질하다] winnow [fan] briskly. 2 [위아래로 흔들다] move (something) up and down briskly; (아기를) dance; dandle. ¶우는 아이를 ~ dandle a crying baby.
들까불다 1 winnow briskly; dandle. ⇨들까부르다 2 [경망하게 굴다] act flippantly [lightly / frivolously / rashly].
들깨 [식] perilla; perilla seeds(씨).
들꽃 a wild [field] flower.
들꿩 [동] a hazel hen [grouse].
들끓다 1 [많이 모이다] swarm (about / in / with); gather (round); crowd; (특히 해충·도둑 따위가 설치다) infest. ¶쥐가 들끓는 집 a house infested with rats // 거지가 ~ (장소가) swarm [be overflowing / be crowded] with beggars // 구더기가 ~ be infested with maggots // 도둑이 들끓는 산 mountains infested with robbers // 그 집에는 바퀴벌레가 들끓고 있다 The house is infested with cockroaches. // 읍내에 들끓는 폭력단끼리의 다툼이 끊이질 않는다 There is constant strife between the gangs who infest [have their bases in] the town. // 파출소 앞에는 사람들이 들끓고 있다 There is a big crowd of people about the police box.
2 [흥분하다·술렁거리다] be excited; seethe; ferment; be in an uproar. ¶들끓는 군중 a boiling [an excited] crowd // 들끓는 소동 an uproar / a ferment // 그 문제로 온 나라가 들끓었다 The whole country seethed [was in a ferment] over the question.
들녘 an open field; a plain; a flat; a flat country(지방).
들놀이 a picnic; an outing. ¶~ 가다 go (out) on a picnic / go picnicking. **들놀이하다** picnic; have a picnic; be on a picnic.
들다¹ 1 [날씨가 개다] clear (up); become clear; [안개가 걷히다] lift; clear away [off]; break away; [비가 그치다] hold up; stop [leave off] raining; cease to rain. ¶날이 든다 It [The weather] clears up. / It stops raining. // 날이 들 것 같다 It looks as if it will [would] clear up. / It is going to be fine. / The weather looks promising. 2 [많이 멎다] ease; stop. ¶많이 ~ stop sweating.
들다² (날 등이) cut (well); be keen; be sharp. ¶잘 드는 [잘 안 드는] 칼 a sharp [dull] knife // 칼이 잘 드는지 시험해 보다 test the sharpness of a sword // 이 칼은 잘 든다 This knife cuts well. / This knife is sharp. // 이 칼은 잘 안 든다 This knife won't cut. // 이 칼은 들지 않게 되었다 This knife has become dull.
들다³ (나이가) grow older [in years]; get on [up] in years; take [put] on years; advance in age [years]. ¶나이가 듦에 따라 one grows old(er) / with advancing years // 나이 든 사람 an old [aged] person / (집합적) the aged [old] / old people // 그녀는 나이가 훨씬 들어 보인다 She looks much older than her age. / She looks quite old for her age. // 그는 나이가 들어도 젊어 보인다 He wears [carries] his years well. // 나이가 들면 지혜가 생긴다 Wisdom comes with age. / Years bring wisdom.
들다⁴ 1 [입주하다] settle (at / in); move in(이사하여); [투숙하다] put up (at); stop (at). ¶새집에 ~ settle in a new house // 셋방에 ~ rent [take] a room // 호텔에 ~ put up [stop / stay] at a hotel / register at [check in] a hotel // 손님이 ~ have a visitor [guest / lodger] // 그 집엔 누가 들어 있느냐 Who is the occupant of the house? // 그 집에는 지금 아무도 들어 있지 않다 The house is not occupied. / The house is vacant [empty / unoccupied] now.
2 [들어가다] go in [into]; get in [into]; come in [into]. ¶방 안에 ~ enter a room / walk into a room // 잠자리에 ~ go to bed // 사정거리 안에 ~ come within range (of fire) // 병상에 들어 있다 be confined to one's bed / be laid up // 자, 안으로 드십시오 Please step [come] in.
3 [포함하다] hold; contain; be contained; be included; [부류에 들다] come [fall] under (the category of); [수용하다] accomodate; admit. ¶병에 든 물 water in a bottle // 3천 원이 든 지갑 a purse with 3,000 won in it // 그 호텔에는 5백 명의 손님이 들 수 있다 The hotel can accommodate 500 guests. // 지갑에는 돈이 많이 들어 있었다 The wallet had a lot of money in it. // 잡비도 계산 속에 들어 있다 The miscellaneous expenses are included in the account. // 그 병은 두 홉이 든다 The bottle holds two hop or so. // 이 상자는 많이 든다 This box holds a great deal. // 편지 속에 몇 장의 사진이 들어 있었다 The letter contained some pictures. / Some pictures were enclosed in the letter. // 그들 중에 나도 들어 있다 I am among [one of] them. // 이 정제에는 비타민 C가 들어 있다 This tablet contains vitamin C.
4 [가입·가담하다] join; enter; go into; associate oneself (with); [합격하다] enter (a school); pass into. ¶보험에 ~ insure oneself / take out (a policy of) insurance (on) / carry (10,000,000 won) insurance (on one's life) // 클럽에 ~ enter [join] a club / become a club member // 대학에 ~ enter a college // 시험에 ~ pass [succeed in] an examination // 조합에 ~ join an association // 나는 생명 보험에 들었다 I have taken out life insurance (on myself).
5 [염색되다] dye; be dyed; take (up) color; [감염하다] be stained [tainted / infected]. ¶검게 물이 ~ be dyed black // 물이 잘 ~ [들지 않다] dye well [badly] // 나쁜 물이 ~ be tainted with vice / sink in vice.
6 [소요되다] take; want; need; require; cost; [(사물이) 필요하다] be necessary [needed]; be required. ¶돈이 얼마가 들더라도 at any cost / regardless of expense // 공든 세공 elaborate workmanship // 돈이 ~ take [cost] money // 시간이 ~ take [require] (a lot of) time // 힘이 ~ be hard [toilsome / tough / trying] / require much effort // 비용이 많이 ~ cost a great deal / be (very) expensive // 얼마 들었소 How much did it cost you? // 이것은 만 원 가까이 들었다 This cost me a little less than 10,000 won. // 집을 수리하는 데 100만 원이 들었다 It cost (me) one million won to have my house repaired. // 딸의 결혼식에 상당히 많은 돈이 들었다 I paid a

들다

considerable sum of money for my daughter's wedding. // 이 기관차는 기름이 많이 든다 This engine consumes much oil. // 그런 생활방식으로는 돈이 많이 들 것이다 Your way of living is costly, isn't it?

7 [어떤 상태가 되다·생기다] become; get; grow; [때가 되다·접어들다] come round; set [close] in; begin; approach. ¶8월 들어 (곧) (early) in August // 멍이 ~ get bruised // 버릇이 ~ get [fall] into a habit (of) / get in the way (of doing) / acquire [pick up] a habit (of) // 잠이 ~ go to sleep / fall asleep // 재난이 ~ suffer [be visited by] a calamity // 정신이 ~ come to oneself / come to (one's senses) / recover [regain] one's senses // 철이 ~ get [come to have] some sense / become sensible / cut one's eyeteeth [wisdom teeth] // 정이 ~ become attached to [grow fond of] (a girl) / fall in love // 풍년 [흉년] 이 ~ have a bumper [lean] year / have a good [bad] harvest // 생각이 ~ come across [into] one's mind / come into one's head / occur to one / hit [strike] one // 잠님이 ~ be lost in idle thoughts // …이라는 느낌이 ~ give a feeling of [that] ... / have a feeling that ... // 문득 … 이라는 생각이 들었다 It flashed through [on / across] my mind that …. / It occurred to me that …. // 담배 피우는 버릇이 ~ contract [fall into] the habit of smoking / take to smoking // 나는 밤늦게까지 안 자는 나쁜 버릇이 들었다 I got into the bad habit of staying up late. // 금년에는 윤달이 들어 있다 A leap month sets in this year. // 장마가 들었다 The rainy season has set in. // 이달 들어 몹시 추워졌다 The weather has been extremely cold since the beginning of this month. // 새해 들어 갓 스무 살이 되었다 I have just entered my twentieth year this January.

8 [침입하다] visit; attack; break in [into]; force an entrance [one's way] into (a house). ¶어젯밤 우리 집에 도둑이 들었다 A burglar broke into my house last night. / My house was broken into last night.

9 [만족스럽다] be pleased [satisfied] (with); be satisfactory; be acceptable to (a person); [마음에 들다] suit [catch / take / capture / strike] (a person's) fancy; suit (a person's) taste; be in (a person's) favor. ¶마음에 드는 집 a house to one's taste / a house one likes // 마음에 드는 여자 a woman after one's heart // 마음에 들도록 to one's satisfaction / (so as) to please (a person) // 마음에 ~ suit [catch / take] one's fancy / suit one's taste / be in [gain] (a person's) favor // 마음에 들지 않다 (사람이) do not like / be dissatisfied [displeased] with / (사물이) be against [not to] (a person's) taste [liking] / be unsatisfactory // 누구의 마음에나 다 들기는 어렵다 It is hard to suit everybody. // 저 그림이 마음에 든다 That picture appeals to my taste. / I take a fancy to that picture. // 이것이 제일 마음에 든다 This suits my taste best. / I like this best. // 놈의 하는 짓이 통 마음에 들지 않는다 I hate the way he behaves.

10 [병이 생기다]. ¶병이 ~ fall [get / be taken] ill [sick] / be attacked [seized] with a disease / be affected by a disease // 감기가 ~ catch (a) cold // 폐병이 ~ get a lung disease [consumption] / suffer from tuberculosis [T.B.] // 감기가 들었다 I have a cold. // 감기가 들면 입맛이 없다 A cold dulls one's taste.

11 [뿌리·열매가 굵어지다] become big. ¶뿌리가 ~ take root / the root becomes big // 씨가 ~ go [run] to seed.

12 [맛이 알맞게 되다]. ¶맛이 ~ become good [pleasant] to the taste / [익다] get [become] ripe [mellow] // 사과가 맛이 ~ an apple gets some flavor (in it) // 술맛이 ~ wine mellows // 김치 맛이 들었다 The gimchi (kimchi) has ripened.

13 [햇볕 등이] come [shine] in [into]; pour in [into]. ¶저녁 햇살이 드는 방 a room open to sunshine from the west // 이 방은 별이 잘 든다 This room gets a lot of sun. // 이 방은 햇볕이 거의 들지 않는다 This room gets very little sun [sunshine].

14 [어떤 일·행동을 하다]. ¶중매를 ~ act as (a) go-between [middleman] / arrange a match [marriage] (between A and B) // 역성 (을) ~ side (with a person) / take sides (with) / stand up for // 시중을 ~ wait upon / attend on.

들다[5] **1** [위로 올리다] raise; lift (up); put [set] up; hold up; heave; hoist. ¶돌을 ~ lift (up) a stone // 얼굴을 ~ raise one's face / look up // 머리를 ~ raise [lift up] one's head // 손을 ~ raise [lift] a [one's] hand / hold up one's hands / (찬성하여) show one's hand // 모자를 들어 인사하다 raise one's hat in greeting // 나는 놀라 얼굴을 들었다 I looked up in surprise. // 얼굴을 좀 더 들어요 Please look up [lift your face] a little more. // 이 상자는 너무 무거워서 들 수가 없다 This box is too heavy to lift. // 찬성하는 사람은 손을 들어 주십시오 Those in favor, raise your hands. // 우리 뒤에서 "손들어!" 하고 누군가가 말했다 "Hands up!" said someone behind us.

2 [손에 쥐다] hold (a book in one's hand); take hold of; have (a thing) in one's hand; [휴대하다] take [have / carry] (a thing) with [about] one. ¶칼을 빼 들고 with a naked sword [blade] in one's hand // 지팡이를 들고 with a stick in one's hand // 펜을 ~ take a pen in one's hand / write // 손에 책을 들고 산책하다 take a walk, book in hand [with a book in one's hand] // 들고 다니다 carry about (one) // 들고 나오다 take [bring] out / carry out [away] // 그는 손에 책을 들고 있다 He has a book in his hand. // 그녀는 손에 양동이를 들고 있었다 She was carrying a bucket. // 그는 큰 손가방을 들고 왔다 He came carrying a large bag with him. // 가방을 들어 드리겠습니다 Let me hold the bag. // 그것은 제가 들어 드리지요 Let me give you a hand with that. // 강도는 식칼을 들고 있었다 The burglar was armed with a kitchen knife. // 그들은 우승기를 높이 들고 행진했다 They marched with their pennant held high.

3 [예증하다] give (an example); mention (a fact); produce (evidence); [인용하다] quote (a passage from a book); cite (an instance). ¶예를 들면 for instance [example] // 예를 ~ cite [give] an instance [example] // 증거를 ~ adduce [give] evidence // 이유를 ~ adduce reasons / state a reason // 남의 이름을 ~ mention [give] a person's name // 비슷한 예를 두셋 더 ~ give a few more similar examples / (문어) cite a few more similar cases // 그는 그들 국회의원의 이름을 들었다 He mentioned those National Assembly members by name.

//알고 있는 꽃 이름을 들어 봐라 Name the flowers that you know.//경찰은 상황 증거밖에 들 수 없었다 The police could produce only circumstantial evidence.//이와 꼭 같은 경우를 하나 더 들 수 있느냐 Can you cite another case at all like this one?//예를 들면 한이 없다 Examples are too many to be cited.

4 [먹다·마시다] take; help oneself to; have; eat; drink. ¶아침을 ~ take (one's) breakfast //그는 어제부터 아무것도 들지 않았다 He hasn't touched food since yesterday.//케이크를 좀 드십시오 Please help yourself to the cake.//커피를 드시겠습니까 Will you have a cup of coffee?//뭣 좀 드시지요 Won't you have something to eat?//자 듭시다 Let us fall to.//더 드시지요 Will you take another helping?//차를 한 잔 드시지요 How about a cup of tea?//좀 들어 보시지요 Won't you have a bite?//마음껏 드십시오 Please help yourself to it.

들어 올리다 raise; lift (up); give (a stone) a lift; heave; elevate; hold[put / boost] up; (구어) up. ¶물건을 어깨에 ~ lift a thing onto one's shoulder//그는 양손을 머리 위로 들어 올렸다 He lifted up[held up / raised] his hands over his head.

들들 stirringly; importunately; ransacking. ⇨＝달달¹

들뜨다 1 [붙은 것이 틈이 생겨 일어나다] come off[undone]; get loose[free]; become unfastened. ¶장판이 들떴다 The layer of oil paper came off the floor.
2 (살이) sallow and swell. ¶누렇게 들뜬 얼굴[피부] a sallow and swollen[bloated] face [skin].
3 [마음이 들썽거리다] grow restless[giddy / unstable / unsteady / fickle]; be in high spirits; treat[walk] on air. ¶휴가를 눈앞에 두고 학생들은 아주 들떠 있었다 As the vacation was just around the corner, the pupils were very animated.//그는 마음이 들떠 있었다 He was quite distracted.//봄이 되면 왠지 마음이 들뜬다 When spring comes, I get somewhat light-headed.//그날 아침 일어날 때부터 그녀는 마음이 들떠 있었다 That morning she had been high spirits since getting up.//좋은 소식으로 마음이 들떴다 The good news cheered me.//그의 얼굴을 보자 마음이 들떴다 The sight of his face made my heart leap for joy.//전화 목소리가 들떠 있었다 The voice on the phone was full of excitement.//그 말은 그녀의 허영심을 들뜨게 했다 The words tickled[flattered] her vanity.//마음이 들뜨는 봄날의 하루였다 It was an exhilarating spring day.

들락거리다 frequent. ⇨＝들랑거리다
들락날락하다 go in and out frequently; make frequent entrance and exit[egress and ingress]; frequent. ¶아이들은 노상 들락날락한다 Children are always popping in and out.//저 집엔 무시로 많은 사람들이 들락날락한다 The house is frequented by many visitors.//쥐가 들락날락하며 밤을 다 물어 갔다 Going in and out, back and forth, the rats carried away all the chestnuts.

들랑거리다 keep going in and out; frequent.
들러리 1 (신랑의) a groomsman; a best man(▶ groomsman의 대표); (신부의) a bridesmaid; a matron of honor(▶ bridesmaid의 대표가 기혼 여성일 때); a maid of honor(▶ bridesmaid의 대표가 미혼 여성일 때). ¶~를 서다 serve as a best man[bridesmaid]. **2** [비유] a setoff; a foil. ¶~가 되다 serve as a setoff (for) / act as a foil (for).

들러붙다 1 [부착하다] stick to; cling to; adhere to; cleave to. ¶찰싹 ~ stick fast (to) //젖은 옷이 몸에 들러붙었다 The wet clothes clung to my body.//눈이 들러붙어서 떠지지 않는다 I cannot open my eyelids. They are glued together.//거머리가 발에 들러붙었다 Leeches clung[stuck] to my feet.//내 발이 땅에 들러붙은 것 같았다 My feet seemed to be nailed to the ground.//햄버거 고기를 들러붙게 하는 데는 계란을 한 개 쓰십시오 Use an egg to make the hamburger meat stick together.
2 (사람이) stick[cling / adhere / cleave] (to). ¶귀찮게 ~ hang about (a person) / pester (a person) to death//그 소녀는 밤새 어머니에게 들러붙어서 떨어지지 않았다 The girl remained glued to her mother the whole night.//그는 거머리처럼 들러붙어서 떨어지지 않는다 He clings (fast) to me like a leech.
3 [일에 열중하다] stick[adhere] to (one's work); stick at (a piece of work). ¶끝까지 일에 들러붙어라 Stick to the task until it is finished.//온 가족이 모내기에 들러붙었다 The whole family stuck to[at] bedding out young rice plants.

들려오다 catch[fall on / reach] one's ears; come into hearing.

들려주다 [알리다] tell; inform (a person of [about] a matter); let (a person) hear [know] (of); (읽어서) read (a thing) (out) to (a person); (연주하여) play for (a person); give (a person) a tune. ¶노래[음악]를 ~ sing[play] for a person//이야기를 ~ tell (a person) a story//시를 ~ read a poem to (a person)//이것은 아이들에게 들려줄 이야기가 못 된다 This story must not be told to[is not fit for the ears of] children.//그에게 들려주려고 한 것은 아니다 It was not meant for his ears.//자세한 이야기를 들려주십시오 Tell me all about it. / Let me hear all about how it happened.

들르다 [방문하다] call at (a house); step at (a place); drop[stop] in for a short visit; [지나가다] drop in (on a person / at a place); drop into (an office); look (a person) up; stop[come] by; (미) go by (a house); (배가) call[touch / stop] at. ¶책방에 ~ drop into a bookstore[(영) bookshop]//부디 우리에게 들르시오 Please come and see us.//Please drop in on us.//다른 데에 들르지 말고 바로 귀가해라 Go straight home (without stopping on the way).//그는 자주 그 클럽에 들렀다 He visited the club frequently[very often].//집으로 돌아가시는 길에 잠시 내 집에 들러 주십시오 Please drop[look] in at my house on your way home.//그 가게에 잠시 들러 보자 Let's have a peep[look in] at the shop.//이쪽으로 올 때에는 들러 주십시오 Look us up when you get down[come] our way.//숙모 가게에 들렀다 I dropped by my aunt's store.//그는 또 우리 집에 들르지 않고 지나갔다 He passed our house again without dropping in.//대전에 들르지 않고 곧장 부산으로 갔다 I went straight[directly] to Busan without stopping off at Daejeon.//돌

들리다

아가는 길에 그것을 가지러 들르겠다 I shall call for it on my way back.

들리다¹ 1 〔자연히 귀에 들어오다〕 (사람이) (can) hear; catch; (소리가) be heard; be audible; reach [fall on] one's ear; meet [greet] the ear. ¶잘 들리지 않는 difficult [hard] to hear∥들리는[들리지 않는] 데서 in [out of] one's hearing range (of)∥부르면 들리는 곳에(서) within call [hearing / earshot] (of)∥회장의 구석구석까지 잘 들리는 목소리 a voice which carries to the farthest corners of the hall / a voice which can be heard all over the hall∥이상한 소리가 들렸다 I heard a strange sound.∥내가 하는 말이 들립니까 Can you hear me [what I'm saying]?∥시끄러워서 텔레비전 소리가 들리지 않는다 It's so noisy I can't hear the television.∥그가 아무리 크게 소리를 질러도 들리지 않았다 No matter how loudly he yelled, we couldn't hear him.∥소음으로 강사의 목소리가 들리지 않았다 The noise drowned out the lecturer's voice.∥요즘 귀가 잘 들리지 않는다 I've been going deaf recently. / My hearing has become worse recently.∥나는 선천적으로 왼쪽 귀가 들리지 않는다 I am naturally deaf in my left ear.∥개가 짖는 소리가 들렸다 I heard a dog bark.∥그녀의 목소리는 잘 들린다〔쩌렁쩌렁하다〕 Her voice carries well. / She has a resonant [a clear] voice.∥부르면 들리는 곳에 있게 Stay within earshot [call].∥그의 발소리가 멀어져 들리지 않았다 The sound of his footsteps faded away into the distance.∥강사가 감기에 걸려 목소리가 잘 들리지 않았다 The lecturer had a cold and it was hard to hear him.∥방송 중에 잘 들리지 않은 부분이 있었기에 사과를 드립니다 We apologize for the poor sound quality of the broadcast.∥전화 소리가 멀어서 잘 들리지 않았다 The voice on the phone was faint and difficult to hear [catch].∥(전화에서) 안 들립니다 I cannot hear (from) you.
2 〔생각되다·의미가 이해되다〕 sound; ring; seem. ¶역설적으로 ~ sound paradoxical∥이 말이 이상하게 들립니까 Does this expression sound strange?∥그 말은 별스럽고 재미있게 들렸다 The words sounded quaint.∥이상하게 들릴지 모르지만 그 말은 신용할 만하다 Strange as it may sound, the story is credible.∥네 이야기는 좀 수상하게[의심스럽게] 들린다 Your story sounds a bit fishy.∥그가 하는 말은 빈정대는 말처럼 들린다 What he says sound ironical.∥솔깃하게 들리는 이야기에 끌려 100만 원을 출자했다 It sounded so good that I took the bait and put up a million won.
3 〔소문 등이〕 be said [told]; be rumored; come to one's ears [knowledge]. ¶들리는 바에 따르면 according to the report [rumor] / I am told that … / it is said that … / from what I have heard …∥내 소문에 ~ be talked [gossiped] about∥네 소식이 종종 들렸다 I've often heard of you.∥그녀가 돈을 많이 모았다는 소문이 들린다 They say [It is said] that she has made a lot of money.∥그 뒤로 그의 소문은 들리지 않는다 He has not been heard of since.∥들리는 바에 따르면 그는 인격자라고 한다 He is said to be a man of character.

들리다² 〔귀신 등이 들러붙다〕 be possessed (by / with); be obsessed (by); be bewitched. ¶사람들은 그 여자에게 악마가 들렸다고 생각했다 People thought the woman was possessed by a devil.

들리다³ (병에) catch; contract; be taken [fall] ill; be attacked [affected] by (a disease); be seized [afflicted] with (a disease); be infected with (the plague); suffer from. ¶감기에 ~ catch [take / get / contract] (a) cold / have an attack of flu∥그녀는 중병에 들렸다 She is suffering from a serious illness.

들리다⁴ 〔고갈되다〕 be exhausted [drained / used up / consumed]; run out; be out of stock; be (all) gone. ¶밑천이 ~ come to the end of one's money / be out of money [funds].

들리다⁵ 〔올려지다〕 be lifted (up); be raised; 〔올리게 하다〕 (a person) raise [lift (up)] (something); let (a person) heave [elevate]. ¶책상 다리가 들렸다 The legs of the desk were lifted.∥그는 몸이 공중에 들렸다 He got lifted up in the air.

들리다⁶ 1 〔갖게 하다〕 let (a person) have [take / hold]; put (a person) in possession of (something). ¶그 사람 손에 들려 주면 무딘 칼도 날카로워진다 A dull blade becomes a sharp weapon in his hands. 2 〔운반시키다〕 get (a person) to take [carry] (a thing). ¶하녀에게 선물을 들려 보내다 send [offer] a present by the maid.

들먹거리다 1 〔물체가〕 move up and down; be raised and lowered; shake. ¶책상 다리가 ~ the leg of a table shakes∥바위가 ~ a rock shakes [jolts] / a rock moves up and down.
2 〔물체를〕 move (a thing) up and down; raise and lower (a thing); shake (a thing). ¶바위를 ~ shake a rock.
3 〔몸이〕 (one's shoulders [buttocks]) move up and down; (가슴·심장이) go pit-a-pat; throb; thump; flutter; pound; (마음이) become restless; be excited [tempted] (to do); be inclined (to do); be eager (to). ¶궁둥이가 ~ one's buttocks move up and down / become restless∥어깨가 ~ one's shoulders twitch [move up and down] / become restless∥그녀는 가고 싶어서 들먹거리고 있다 She is impatient [all eagerness] to go.∥한 대 치고 싶어서 팔이 들먹거렸다 My hands itched to deal him a blow.
4 (몸을) move (one's shoulders [buttocks]) up and down; (마음을) make (a person) restless; stir up; incite; instigate; fan; egg on. ¶어깨를 ~ move [twitch] one's shoulders restlessly∥마음을 ~ make (a person) restless / excite (a person) / make (a person) eager to / fire (a person) interest∥민중을 들먹거려 폭동을 일으키다 incite [instigate / excite / goad] people to violence∥그의 영화 이야기가 마음을 들먹거려 놓는다 His talk about the movie has made me eager to see it.
5 〔언급하다〕 mention; speak of; refer to; specify by name. ¶그녀까지 들먹거릴 필요야 없지 않느냐 You don't have to mention her name.

들먹들먹 〔아래위로 움직이는 모양〕 moving up and down; shaking; (마음이) buoyantly; excitedly; restlessly. **들먹들먹하다** move up and down; mention. ⇨들먹거리다 ¶어린이들은 흥분하여 들먹들먹하고 있었다 The children were all tingling with excitement.

들보 [건] a (cross) beam; a girder(대들보).
들볶다 annoy; tease; harass; torment; pester; nag at; make it tough[rough / hot] for (a person); be hard[rough / severe / tough] on (a person); be cruel[hard] to (a person); urge (a person to do); press (a person for a thing). ¶못 견디게 ~ make it too hot [warm] for (a person) / huff (a person) to pieces// 며느리를 ~ be cruel to one's daughter-in-law/ 돈을 내라고 ~ press (a person) for payment (of money) / pester (a person) for money// 그이가 들볶아요 He is very mean about me[hard on me].
들볶이다 be teased ; be tormented; be hounded; be pestered. ¶빚쟁이에게 ~ be tormented[hounded] by a pressing creditor.
들부수다 break up. ⇨ˇ들이부수다 ¶닥치는 대로 ~ destroy whatever[anything that] one can lay hands on// 파도가 배를 들부수었다 The waves dashed the boat to pieces.
들새 a wild bird; (집합적) wild fowl.
들소 a bison (단수·복수 동형); a wild ox (*pl.* wild oxen); (미국산의) a buffalo (*pl.* ~, ~(e)s); (유럽산의) a wisent.
들숨 inspiration; inhalation; air breathed in; air that is being inhaled. ¶~ 날숨 inhalation and exhalation / breathing.
들숨 날숨 없다 be in a fix[quandary]; be bogged down.
들썩거리다 1 [움직이다] move up and down; rise and fall. 2 [마음이] be restless[nervous / fidgety]; be in a flutter[fidget]; [충동하다] stir up (to). ¶그 소식에 가슴이 들썩거렸다 The news made my heart fall into a flutter.
들썩하다 1 [그럴듯하다] plausible; specious; verisimilar; fair-spoken; glittering (propaganda). 2 [떠들어 있다] turned up[lifted (up) / raised / tilted] a little[a bit / slightly]. ¶책 귀가 ~ The corner of the book is a bit turned up. 3 noisy; troubled. ⇨ˇ떠들썩하다¹·²
들썽거리다 be impatient (for); be anxious [eager] (for / to do); be irritated; be nervous; be spoiling (for); ache (to do); itch [have an itch] (for action). ¶가고 싶어서 마음이 ~ be impatient[all eagerness] to go// 그녀는 사실을 말하고 싶어서 들썽거렸다 She was burning to tell the truth.
들쑤시다 sting; stir up; dig up. ⇨들이쑤시다
들쓰다 1 [이불·외투 등을 덮어쓰다] put on (something) all over oneself; pull up (something) all over oneself. ¶이불을 들쓰고 자다 sleep under a coverlet / sleep with the bedclothes[quilt / bedspread] (pulled) over one's head.
2 [물 등을 온몸에 받다] be poured on; pour [dash] (water) on[upon / over] oneself; be covered with. ¶차는 먼지를 들쓰고 있었다 The car was thickly covered with dust.
3 [모자 등을 되는대로 쓰다] wear[put on] (a cap) casually; cover (one's head with a hat) casually. ¶모자를 들쓰고 나서다 go out with a hat on casually.
4 [책임·허물 등을 떠맡다] take (responsibility / blame) upon oneself; be charged (with a crime). ¶남의 허물을 ~ take upon oneself another's fault[blame].
들씌우다 [들쓰게 하다] 1 (이불 등을) pull up (something) all over (a person); put (something) on; cover (with). ¶머리에 이불을 ~ pull the bedclothes[bedspread] over (a person's) head.
2 (물 등을) pour[throw] (water) all over (a person); cover (a person) all over with (dust).
3 (모자 등을) put (a hat) on (a person's) head casually. ¶어린이에게 모자를 들씌워 데리고 나가다 take a child out with a hat pulled over his head.
4 (허물 등을) impute (a crime to another); lay (the guilt upon / a blame at another's door); shift[shuffle off] (a responsibility on another's shoulders); charge[fix / put] (a guilt on another); (속에) pass the buck (to). ¶죄를 남에게 ~ lay the guilt on another.

들어가다¹ 1 [안으로 가다] enter (a room); go [get / come] in; go[get / come] into (a house); walk[step] in; walk[step] into (a room); turn in; make one's entry into (a place); find one's way into; set foot inside (a house); let oneself in. ¶창으로 ~ enter by [through] a window// 물[수영장]에 ~ enter [go into] the water [swimming pool]// 기어 ~ creep[crawl] into[under] // 적진으로 깊숙이 ~ cut one's way into the enemy's position// 들어가게 하다 let (a person) enter / allow (a person) to get into (a building)// 들어가 있다 be in (a room)// 몰래 방에 ~ steal[slip] into a room// 붐비는 회장에 억지로 ~ force one's way into a crowded hall// 들어가도 좋습니까 May I come in?// 들어가지 마시오 (게시) No admittance.// 들어가십시오 (수위의 말) Please pass on.// 안으로 들어가 주십시오 Move[Step] back to the rear, please.// 우리는 안내를 받아 서재로 들어갔다 We were shown[ushered] into the study.// 우리는 마음대로 그의 방에 들어갈 순 없다 We can't enter[go into] his room without permission.// 우리는 미궁에 들어가서 헤매었다 We wandered into a maze.// 집은 큰길에서 조금 들어간 곳에 있다 The house is a little way off the main street.
2 [틈·속·사이로] go through; enter; penetrate; be inserted; be lodged. ¶뚫고 ~ penetrate into// 군중 속을 밀어제치고 ~ thrust oneself into a crowd// 바늘귀에 실이 들어간다 A thread goes through the eye of a needle. / A needle is threaded. // 총알이 벽을 뚫고 들어 간다 A bullet penetrates [is lodged in] a wall.// 상처에 세균이 들어갔다 The wound got infected.// 그 단어는 이 두 단어 사이에 들어간다 The word goes[is to be inserted] between these two words.
3 [움푹 패다] sink; sag; be hollow; cave[fall] in; be sunk(en). ¶깊숙이 들어간 만 a landlocked bay// 쑥 들어간 눈 deep-set[retreating] eyes// 배가 고파서 내 눈이 들어갔다 My eyes grew hollow with hunger.
4 [모임·단체 등의 구성원이 되다] join; enter; go into; associate oneself with (a society); (회사 등에) join; go to work for (a firm); find [take] service in[with]; be employed (by); (학교에) enter (a school); pass into (Harrow). ¶클럽에 ~ join[enter] a club / be enrolled in a club / become a club member // 대학에 ~ enter [pass into / get into] a college / register[make one's registration] at a college // 그는 이번에 노동부에 들어갔다 He was appointed to the staff of[got a job in]

들어가다

the Ministry of Labor.// 그는 실업계[정계]에 들어갔다 He went into business[politics]. / He entered the business[political] world.// 그는 군대에 들어가 있다 He is in the army.// 그 녀석 좋은 자리에 들어갔군 What a good berth he has got!

5 [포함되다] contain; hold; include; enter; go into; be included[contained]. ¶나도 거기에 들어가 있었다 I was among[one of] the number.// 인명사전에는 그의 이름도 들어가 있었다 The biographical dictionary contained his name.// 잡비도 계산 속에 들어가 있다 The miscellaneous expenses are included in the account.// 그것은 이 항목에 들어간다 It comes[falls / is included] under this heading. / It belongs in[under] this category.

6 [수용 능력이 있다] hold; accommodate; house. ¶이 회관은 1,500명 들어간다 This hall seats[can accommodate / hold] 1,500 people.// 전원이 들어갈 수 없습니다 There is not enough room for all of you.// 이 병은 얼마나 들어갈까 How much will this bottle hold?

7 [소유가 되다] fall into (a person's) hands [power]. ¶…의 손에 들어가 있다 be in the hands of …// 중요한 서류가 경찰의 손에 들어갔다 An important document fell into the hands of the police.

8 [비용이] cost; be spent; be consumed; be put in; be sunk. ¶집을 짓는 데 많은 돈이 들어갔다 Much money has gone into building the house.// 이 사업엔 돈이 막 들어간다 This enterprise eats money. / This is a very costly enterprise.

9 [시작되다·시기가 되다] begin; set in; enter (into / upon). ¶새 생활로 ~ enter upon a new life// 내일부터 신학기에 들어간다 The new semester begins tomorrow.// 장마철에 들어갔다 The rainy season has set in.// 시합은 연장전으로 들어갔다 The game went into extra innings.

들어가다² [가져가다] pilfer; filch; purloin; (속어) hook; (속어) swipe; take[carry] away; take[bear] off; make away[off] (with); catch away. ¶주인의 돈을 ~ run[go / walk] away with one's master's money// 누군가가 내 우산을 들어갔다 Somebody has taken away my umbrella.// 좀도둑이 들어 몇 가지 가재도구를 들어갔다 A petty thief swiped some of our household goods.

들어내다 1 [밖으로 내놓다] remove; lift out; take[bring / carry / get] out; whip out; (을 피하려고) save; rescue. ¶몰래 ~ smuggle (something) out of (the house)// 돈을 궤짝에서 ~ take some money out of a box / take out some money from a box// 뜰에 책상을 들어내었다 I brought a desk out into the garden.// 불이 나면 이 상자들부터 들어내어야 한다 In case of fire, these cases must be removed for safety first of all.// 불이 빠르게 번져서 아무것도 들어내지 못했다 The fire spread so fast that we could not rescue [save] anything.

2 [쫓아내다] expel; turn[get / put / drive] out; kick[run] (a person) out (of the house); (속어) boot out; (해고하다) dismiss; discharge; (미국 구어) fire; (영국 구어) sack; (속어) bounce; (적위에서) oust [expel / dislodge] (a person from a position); (셋방 등에서) eject[evict] (a tenant from the house). ¶자네 말로 안 나가면 들어내겠네 If you won't go yourself, I shall turn [rush] you out.// 저놈을 들어내라 Out with him!// 나를 억지로 들어내지는 못해 I am not going to be forced[kicked] out.

들어맞다 1 [적합하다] fit; fit in (with); be fit (for); suit; be suited (to); go on(신발 등이). ¶꼭 들어맞는 옷 a perfect fit// 몸에 잘 들어맞는 옷 a well-fitting suit// 몸에 들어맞지 않는 옷 an ill-fitting[a badly fitting] suit// 꼭 ~ fit perfectly[neatly] / fit like a glove / be an exact fit// 몸에 잘 ~ [들어맞지 않다] fit (a person) well[ill] / suit well[badly] // 이 모자는 너에게 꼭 들어맞는다 This hat is a fit for your head.

2 [일치하다] fit together; agree (with); be in accord (with); coincide (with); tally (with); square[conform] (with); answer to; meet. ¶그들의 이야기가 들어맞는다 Their accounts tally[square] with each other.// 우리 의견은 늘 들어맞지 않는다 Our opinions never agree.// 용의자는 인상서와 들어맞았다 The suspect met[answered (to)] the description. // 외양과 실제가 들어맞는 경우는 좀처럼 없다 Appearance and reality seldom correspond.

3 [정확하다] be correct; be right; (계산 등이) balance. ¶계산이 꼭 들어맞는다 The accounts are quite correct.// 총계가 1,000원이 들어맞지 않는다 The total is 1,000 won out.

4 [적중하다] hit (the mark); tell; catch; make a good hit; (명이) hit it (right); hit the (right) nail on the head; (말이) guess right; hit the truth; (예상이) prove (to do) right; come[turn out] true; come off; (계략이) take; work. ¶총알이 전부 들어맞았다 All shots told.// 화살이 과녁에 들어맞았다 The arrow hit the target.// 계획이 잘 들어맞았다 My plan worked well. / My plan had the desired effect. / 네 예상이 들어맞았다 You were right in your conjecture. / Your conjecture turned out true. / You guessed right.// 그녀의 예언이 들어맞았다 Her prediction has come true.

5 [적용되다] apply (to); go (for); be applicable (to); be valid (for); be true (of); hold true (of); hold good (of / for); [해당하다] come[fall] under (the heading); conform (to); be in conformity[accordance] (with). ¶이것은 그 경우에 꼭 들어맞는 말이다 This is the exact[very] word[just the word] for it. // 그 규칙은 이느 경우에나 들어맞는다 The rule covers[applies to] every case.// 그것에 들어맞는 영어 표현은 없다 There is no corresponding expression (for it) in English. / There is no English for it.

6 [충족시키다] meet; fulfill. ¶그의 요구에 들어맞는 것은 아무것도 없다 There is nothing which meets his requirements.// 이 조건에 들어맞는 사람을 찾아 주시오 Find a man who fulfills these conditions.

7 [맞추어지다]. ¶이 문은 들어맞지 않는다 This door does not fit in.

들어먹다 1 [탕진하다] squander; exhaust; drain; eat (a person / oneself) out[up]; use up; go[run] through (one's fortune); spend all (one's money); clean out. ¶가산을 ~ run through one's fortune / play ducks and drakes with[make ducks and drakes of]

one's fortune // 밑천을 도박으로 모두 ~ run through all one's money [lose one's shirt] // 도박으로 가산을 ~ drink [gamble] away one's fortune // 돈을 다 들어먹고 한 푼도 남지 않았다 I had spent my last penny.
2 [남의 것을 차지하다] pocket; peculate; misappropriate; embezzle; appropriate (to oneself); divert (another's money) into one's own pocket. ¶공금을 ~ appropriate public money to one's private [own] use // 남의 것을 들어먹으려고 꾀하다 figure out a way to get (something) away from a person.

들어박히다 1 [들어가 박히다] fall [plunge / stick / slip / sink] into; be stuck; (못 등이) be driven (in / into); (별·보석 등이) be studded [set / inlaid]; (총알 등이) be lodged; (물건들이 빽빽이) be packed; be stuffed; be chock-full. ¶끝까지 들어박힌 못 a nail driven home // 머리에 들어박힌 탄환 a bullet lodged in (a person's) brain [head] // 책이 가득 들어박힌 서가 a shelf closely packed with books // 진창에 ~ be caught [stuck / bogged] in the mud // 하늘에 별이 총총히 들어박혀 있다 The sky is all studded [jeweled] with stars.
2 [꼭 붙어 있다] stay in [indoors / at home]; be confined indoors [to one's home]; keep [confine oneself] indoors; shut oneself up; seclude [immure] oneself in; remain in seclusion. ¶집에만 들어박혀 있는 사람 a homekeeper / a home-immured person / a stay-at-home // 시골에 ~ retire into the country / live in rural retirement // 서재에 ~ shut oneself up in one's study // 감기로 들어박혀 있다 be laid up with a cold // 병으로 ~ keep to one's bed / be confined to one's bed // 하는 일 없이 집에 ~ stay at home without a job.

들어붓다 1 (비가) fall [rain] heavily; pour down; rain cats and dogs; rain in torrents; rain (in) buckets. ¶들어붓는 비 a pouring [heavy / driving] rain / a pelting rain [shower] / a downpour (of rain) / (미) a cloudburst // 비가 사뭇 들어부었다 It rained hard [heavily / in torrents]. / It rained cats and dogs.
2 (물 등을) pour (water) into [on / out of] (something). ¶솥에 물을 ~ pour water into an oven // 주전자의 물을 ~ pour water out of a kettle // 남에게 물을 ~ pour [throw] water upon [over] a person / douse a person with water.
3 (술을) quaff; guzzle; drink heavily; drink like a fish; (구어) swig; swill. ¶술을 들어붓는 사람 a soaker / a guzzler / a deep drinker // 술을 단숨에 ~ empty (the glass) at a draught / quaff (the glass) to the dregs / drain (the up) at one gulp.

들어서다 1 (안으로) enter; step [tread] in; set foot inside; come [go / get] into. ¶마당 [집 안]에 ~ step [walk] a garden [a home] // 구내에 ~ enter the premises.
2 [자리 잡다] occupy; hold; take (up); [꽉 차다] be full (of); be filled (with); be crowded (with). ¶나무가 빽빽이 들어선 산 a woody [bosky] hill a thickly-[well-]wooded hill // 제시간에 ~ come in [arrive] on time // 이 근처는 집이 잔뜩 들어서 있다 The neighborhood is crowded [packed] with houses. // 변화가에 는 큰 건물들이 쭉 들어섰다 Many great buildings stood in a row on the busy street. // 이제는 그곳도 집이 많이 들어서 있다 The place is much built up now.
3 [계통을 잇다] succeed (a person, to a position, etc.); accede [come] to (a place); occupy [take] (a position). ¶대신 ~ replace / supplant / take the place of / step in another's shoes.
4 [접어들다] begin; set in. ¶노년기에 ~ arrive at senescence / become senescent / reach old age // 장마철에 들어섰다 The rainy season has set in.
5 [대들다] stand [rise] against; put [set] oneself against; stand up to.

들어앉다 1 (안쪽으로) get [come] in and sit; step [walk] in and sit; [다가앉다] sit closer [nearer] (to). ¶화롯가로 들어앉으시오 Come in and be seated nearer [closer] to the fireplace. // 좀 더 가까이 들어앉게 Come (in) and sit down a little bit closer.
2 [위치하다] lie; be situated [located]. ¶길거리에서 들어앉은 집 a house which stands back [apart] from the street // 솔밭 중앙에 들어앉은 학교 a school situated in the middle [center] of a pine wood.
3 [나오지 않다] keep [stay] indoors; confine oneself in one's house; shut oneself up; live in seclusion; [은퇴하다] retire (from); go into retirement; sever oneself (from active life); resign (an office). ¶시골에 ~ retire into the country // 사업을 그만두고 ~ retire from business // 연금을 받고 ~ retire on a pension [an annuity].
4 [지위를 차지하다] take office; take up (a position); engage in (an occupation); get [obtain] (a position); settle down; [후임으로] succeed (a person in his post); sit in (a person's) place; replace (a person); step into (a person's) shoes. ¶장관 직에 ~ take office as a State Minister // 그녀가 죽자 그 여자가 그의 아내로 들어앉았다 Upon her death the woman became his second wife.

들어오다 1 (안으로) enter; come [get] in; come [get] into; walk [step] in [into]; turn in; let oneself in; set foot inside; (도둑 등이) burgle; burglarize; break in [into]; enter (a house) by force. ¶항구에 ~ enter [make] port / come into port // 바람이 틈새로 ~ blow in through the crevices // 들어오십시오 Please come in [(미국 구어) Come on in]. / Step in(side), please. // 여기는 외풍이 들어온다 It's drafty [(영) draughty] here. // 열차는 10시에 들어올 예정이다 The train is scheduled to arrive [come in / pull in] at ten. // 배는 항구에 내일 들어옵니다 The steamer will be in tomorrow. // 바다가 육지로 깊숙이 파고 들어와 있다 An arm of the sea runs deep into the land. // 햇빛이 방 안으로 비쳐 들어왔다 The sunlight found its way into the room. // 주문한 책이 들어왔다 The book you ordered has come in [arrived]. // 바람이 들어오게 창문을 열어라 Open the window to let in air. // 용무가 없는 사람은 들어오지 마시오 (게시) No admittance except on business. // 내 우산으로 들어오세요 Won't you come under my umbrella?
2 [입회하다·참가하다] join; come into; enter; participate [take part] in; take a hand in. ¶우리 클럽에 ~ join our club / be enrolled in

들어주다

our club // 사원 한 사람이 새로 들어왔다 A new member has joined our company. // 너도 카드놀이에 들어와 Won't you play cards with us?
3 (사이에) come in (between); be inserted. ¶이것이 두 말 사이에 들어올 말이다 This comes [is to be inserted] between these two words.
4 (수입 등이) have; get; receive; make. ¶월 30만 원 들어온다 I get [have an income of] 300,000 won a month. // 뉴스가 들어왔다 A piece of news came in. // 그녀에게 혼담이 들어왔다 An offer of marriage was brought to her.
5 [시작되다] begin; set in. ¶20세기에 들어서 곧 early in the twentieth century // 이달에 들어와서부터 몹시 덥다 It has been very hot since the beginning of this month.
6 [이용이 가능한 상태다] be laid on; be installed. ¶텔레비전의 전원이 들어와 있다 [있지 않ది] The TV is [is not] plugged in. // 우리 집에는 수도, 가스, 전기가 들어와 있다 Water, gas, and electricity are laid on in my house.
7 (눈에) come into sight [view]; be seen; greet [meet] the [one's] eye; (귀에) reach [come to] one's ears; come to one's knowledge. ¶눈에 들어오는 것은 무엇이든 내게는 신기했다 Everything I saw was new to me. // 회사 내에서 일어나는 일은 무엇이든 내 귀에 들어온다 Whatever happens in this company never fails to reach [come to] my ears.

들어주다 (요구·부탁을) comply with (a person's request); grant (a request / a favor); entertain (a person's request); concede [listen to] (a request); accede [assent] to (a proposal); hear [answer] (a person's prayer); (충고 등을) take [follow] (a person's advice). ¶부탁 [청]을 ~ grant [allow / comply with] (a person's) request // 부탁을 들어주지 않다 turn a deaf ear to a person's request // 부디 제 청을 들어주십시오 Please grant my request. // 하느님은 꼭 소원을 들어주실 거다 I'm sure God will hear [answer] my prayer.

들어차다 fill (with); become full (of); be filled [replete] (with); be packed; be stuffed; be jammed; be jam-packed; teem [swarm] (with); overflow (with); be overflowing (with). ¶꽉 ~ be packed to the full / be chock-full (of) // 스탠드에는 관중이 꽉 들어차 있었다 The stands were overflowing [packed to capacity] with spectators. // 난민들이 그 방에 꽉 들어찼다 The refugees were packed into the room. // 이 지역에도 상당한 집이 들어찼다 This area has been built up quite a bit.

들여가다 1 [안으로 가져가다] bring [take] in (a thing); carry (a thing) into (a room). ¶빨래를 ~ take in washing // 땔나무를 집에 ~ carry firewood into one's house. 2 [사들이다] purchase; buy (in); take in. ¶쌀을 대량으로 ~ make a large purchase of rice / lay in a large stock of rice // 사과 좀 들여가세요 Won't you buy (in) some of the apples?

들여놓다 1 (물건을) take [bring / get / carry] in (and put down). ¶방에 책상을 ~ bring a desk in a room // 짐을 차 안에 ~ take [carry / bring] one's baggage into a car.
2 (발을) set foot (in / on); put one's foot (in / on); step into (a bog); tread (on). ¶위험한 곳에 발을 ~ tread on dangerous ground // 이 숲 속에는 아무도 발을 들여놓은 적이 없다 No one has so much as set foot in this forest.
3 [사들이다] purchase; buy (in) (books); take in (a fresh supply of fuel); lay in (a stock). ¶월동용으로 식량과 연탄을 ~ lay in provisions and briquets for the winter // 책을 잔뜩 ~ make a considerable purchase of books.
4 [진출하다] go into; enter. ¶정계에 발을 ~ go into politics / enter the political world.

들여다보다 1 (안을) look in [into]; peep [peek] into (a room); peep through (a hole); snoop into (a home). ¶현미경으로 ~ look through a microscope // 구멍 [열쇠 구멍 / 틈]으로 ~ peep through a hole [a keyhole / an opening] // 창문으로 ~ look [peek] in at the window // 누군가가 창 유리를 통해서 방 안을 들여다보았다 Someone peered into the room through the windowpane. // 그녀는 하루에 몇 번이나 거울을 들여다본다 She looks into the mirror many times a day.
2 (빤히) gaze (at / on); stare (at); look hard [fixedly] (at); fix [fasten] one's eyes (on). ¶얼굴을 빤히 ~ stare (a person) in the face / keep one's eyes fixed upon (a person's) face // 그가 빤히 들여다보아서 그녀는 홍당무가 되었다 She blushed under his gaze.
3 (자세하게) look [go] over; look [inquire] into; examine closely [carefully]. ¶서류를 ~ look over [dig into] the documents // 사건의 전말을 ~ examine an event in detail.
4 [들르다] look [drop / call / pop] in; look (a person) up. ¶가게를 ~ pop in at a store / show one's nose in a shop // 귀갓길에 입원한 그녀를 들여다보았다 On my way home I dropped in the hospital to see her.

들여다보이다 be seen through; be exposed to view; be in sight. ¶빤히 들여다보이는 거짓말 a feeble [transparent / palpable] lie // 울타리 사이로 아름다운 정원이 들여다보인다 A beautiful garden can be seen through the hedge. // 그는 속이 빤히 들여다보이는 거짓말을 했다 He told an obvious lie.

들여보내다 send (a person / a thing) into; let (a person) in [into]; allow to enter; allow in; admit. ¶남을 집으로 ~ send a person in(to) the house // 어린이를 학교에 ~ send [put] a child to school // 선물을 ~ send in a present // 통행증을 가진 사람만 ~ admit those only who have a pass // 창문은 빛과 공기를 방으로 들여보낸다 Windows admit light and air to the room. // 비서는 그의 방에 나를 들여보내지 않았다 His secretary wouldn't let me into [admit me to] his room.

들여앉히다 1 [외출을 막다] keep (a person) from going out; let (a person) refrain from outing; confine (a person) to [in] (a room). 2 (여자를) have [make / let] (a woman) settle down in her home. ¶첩으로 ~ keep [set up] (a woman) as a mistress [concubine] // 회사에 다니던 아내를 ~ have one's wife stay at home and give up her office job.

들여오다 1 [밖에서 안으로] bring in; carry in; take in. ¶음식물을 호텔에 ~ bring [take] food and drink into a hotel // 상을 ~ carry in the dinner table // 이 짐을 들여온 사람이 누구냐 Who brought [carried] this baggage in?

2 [사들이다] buy; get (in); [주문하다] order; (우편·주문 판매로) send (away) for; [수입하다] import. ¶오스트레일리아에서 양모를 ~ import wool from Australia // 그녀는 모퉁이의 채소 가게에서 채소를 들여온다 She gets vegetables from the greengrocery at the corner. // 이 책은 미국에서 들여온 것이다 I ordered the book from the States.

들은풍월(-風月) knowledge [information] acquired [picked up] by listening to others; learning by ear; manners [ideas] picked up here and there. ¶~로 많은 노래를 알고 있다 I know many songs which I have picked up by hearing others sing.

-들이 (capable of) holding ...; containing. ¶10정~ 갑 a package containing ten pills // 2리터~ 병 a two-liter bottle / a bottle capable of containing 2 liters.

들이다 1 (안으로) let [allow] in; admit; show [usher] in. ¶손님을 응접실에 모셔 ~ usher [show] a guest into the drawing room // 아무도 방에 들이지 않다 admit no one to one's room / keep people out of one's room // 그가 와도 우리 집에는 들이지 않겠다 He shall not be received at my house.

2 [입회시키다] let join [participate]; enlist; receive; admit; let in. ¶새 회원을 ~ admit a new member // 당에 사람을 ~ range a person into a party.

3 [자본·시간·비용·노력 등을 쓰다] invest (capital); lay out [sink] (capital in some venture); spend (money on clothes / time in toilet); expend (time on); consume; make efforts. ¶많은 시간을 들여서 with a great sacrifice of time // 힘을 ~ put in effort / throw oneself into // 그는 가구에 큰돈을 들였다 He laid out a great deal of money on his furniture. // 매일 영어 청취력 연습에 30분씩을 들이고 있다 I spend 30 minutes every day [put in half an hour every day] trying to improve my aural comprehension in English. // 그는 5,000만 원을 들여서 집을 지었다 He spent fifty million won to build a house. / He had a house built at the cost of fifty million won. // 그는 그 책을 쓰는 데에 3년의 노력을 들였다 It took him three years' hard work to finish the book. / The book cost him three years' labor. // 나는 정성을 들여 장미를 기르고 있다 I put the utmost care into growing my roses.

4 [고용하다] employ; engage; take (a person) into one's service; (양자를) adopt; take into the family. ¶요리사를 새로 ~ engage [hire] a new cook // 조카를 양자로 ~ adopt a nephew as one's son // 가정교사를 ~ engage [have] a tutor.

5 [들여놓다] take [bring] in; carry in [into]. ¶볏섬을 뜰에 ~ bring rice bags into the yard // 피아노를 집에 ~ carry a piano into the house.

6 [맛을 붙이다] get [acquire] a taste (for); take to. ¶여자에 맛을 ~ take to running after women // 돈에 맛을 ~ get a taste for money.

7 [염색하다] dye. ¶검정 물을 ~ dye (a thing) (in) black // 무슨 물을 들일까요 What color shall I dye it? // 머리를 갈색으로 물들였다 I have my hair dyed brown.

8 [땀을 멈추게 하다] cause (sweat) to subside; cool off [oneself]; catch one's breath; rest; take [have] a rest. ¶땀 좀 들이고 다시 하자 Let's have a little rest, and start again. // 계곡의 개울물에서 땀을 들였다 I cooled off in the mountain stream.

들이닥치다 draw [come] near; be close [near] at hand; descend upon; raid; rush in; make a rapid approach to; storm (a place); fall on. ¶눈앞에 들이닥친 위험 an imminent [a pressing] danger // 뜻하지 않은 손님이 ~ be visited by unexpected guests // 파멸이 그의 코앞에 들이닥쳤다 Ruin stared him in the face. // 추격병이 곧 들이닥칠 것이다 The pursuers will be upon us in a moment. // 폭풍이 들이닥칠 것 같다 There are signs of an approaching storm. // 어느 날 저녁 경찰은 경고도 없이 그 여관에 들이닥쳤다 One evening the police descended, without warning, on the hotel.

들이대다 1 [바싹 가져다 대다] thrust (a thing) before (a person); put [place] under (a person's) nose; point (a gun) at [to / toward]. ¶권총을 ~ point [aim] a revolver at (a person) // 단도를 들이대고 협박하다 threaten (a person) with a dagger // 증거를 ~ bring forward evidence / thrust proofs before (a person) // 남에게 터무니없는 요구를 ~ force [thrust] an unreasonable demand on a person // 우리는 그에게 증거를 들이대어 자백시켰다 We thrust the evidence at him and made him own up. // 그들은 칼[총]을 들이대고 나를 협박했다 They threatened me at knifepoint [gunpoint].

2 [대들다] resist openly; defy; protest; go at; challenge. ¶윗사람에게 ~ set oneself against one's superior // 진상을 밝히라고 ~ press (a person) to disclose the truth // 그는 월급을 올려야 한다고 사장에게 들이댔다 He protested to his president that his salary ought to be raised.

3 [공급하다] supply continuously; provide constantly. ¶장사 밑천을 ~ keep (a person) supplied with business fund

들이덤비다 go at (it) hard; set upon [attack / assault] furiously; fall [turn] upon (a person); challenge; flare up (at). ¶맹렬한 기세로 ~ spring at (a person) with tiger-like ferocity // 상관에게 ~ challenge one's superior // 그는 …이라고 말하면서 나에게 들이덤볐다 He challenged saying (that) .... // 여럿이 들이덤벼서 겨우 범인을 잡았다 The offender was caught at last by the combined efforts of many men.

들이마시다 (기체를) breathe in; inhale; draw [take] in; (액체를) suck in; drink in; gulp down. ¶담배를 깊이 ~ take a deep pull [drag] at a cigarette // 산소를 들이마시고 탄산가스를 내쉬다 inhale oxygen and exhale carbon dioxide // 수프를 소리 내어 ~ slurp one's soup // 술 한 병을 단숨에 ~ drink up a bottle of liquor at one gulp // 그는 신선한 공기를 가슴 깊이 들이마셨다 He took [drew] a deep breath of fresh air. // 그녀는 독가스를 들이마시고 죽었다 She died from inhaling poison gas.

들이맞추다 get [put / let] in; fit (into). ¶담뱃대를 대통에 ~ fix the stem of a pipe into the bowl // 미닫이에 유리를 ~ fit a pane in a sliding door

들이몰다 (안으로) drive in; (마구) drive violently; make [let] run; [책하다] blame

들이몰리다

heavily; call to account; censure; reproach. ¶닭을 닭장에 ~ shoo chickens into the coop // 막다른 골목으로 ~ drive (a thief) into a blind alley // 궁지로 ~ drive (a person) into a corner // 차를 ~ hasten [drive fast] (to a place) in a motorcar // 책임을 등한히 했다고 ~ scold [blame] (a person) for neglecting his duty.

들이몰리다 1 (안쪽으로) be driven in; be shoved in. 2 (호되게) be called to account; be taken to task; be roundly scolded. ¶책임을 등한히 했다고 ~ be scolded for neglecting one's duty // 수상은 여야 쌍방으로부터 몹시 들이몰렸다 The Prime Minister came under heavy fire from his own party as well as from the opposition.

들이밀다 1 (안쪽으로 밀다) push [thrust / force / shove] in; (마구 밀다) push [thrust] hard. ¶주먹을 창으로 ~ thrust one's fist through a (paper) window // 들이밀면 2명쯤은 더 들어간다 If we squeeze them in, there is still room for about two more. // 너무 들이밀어서 바구니의 밑이 빠졌다 The basket was so crammed that its bottom burst. // 한 남자가 뒤에서 나를 들이밀었다 A man gave a violent push behind me.

들이밀리다 1 (안으로) be pushed [thrust / shoved] in (to). ¶방구석에 ~ be pushed into the corner of a room // 인파에 들이밀려 이야기도 못했다 We could not even speak with each other because of the press of people. 2 (한곳으로) gather [flock] (together); crowd; swarm; (구어) gang up; make [rush] for. ¶(행락지의) 사람이 들이밀리는 곳 a favorite haunt (of) / a pleasure resort // 그곳은 여름만 되면 사람이 많이 들이밀린다 In summer the place attracts many visitors. // 예금자들이 은행에 들이밀렸다 The depositors besieged the bank.

들이박다 drive [pound / press / strike] (it) in; ran down (a stake); (쐐기 등을) wedge in. ¶못을 ~ drive [hammer] a nail into (a wall).

들이받다 run [bump / strike / knock / hit] against; run into; butt; bunt hard. ¶자동차로 담벼락[전주]을 ~ run [crash] a car into a wall [an electric pole] // 소가 뿔로 ~ a bull bunts (a person) with its horns // 머리를 벽에 ~ knock [bump] one's head against the wall // 남의 배를 ~ butt a person in the stomach.

들이부수다 break [take] (a thing) to pieces [into fragments]; break up; smash. ¶낡은 집을 ~ tear down a house // 낡은 담을 ~ knock an old wall down // 차를 ~ wreck a car.

들이불다 (바람이 안으로 불다) blow this way; blow in; (바람이 세차게) (a wind) blow hard; sweep along [over]; rage. ¶사흘 동안 계속 폭풍우가 들이불었다 For three days the tempest raged unceasingly.

들이붓다 (쏟아 넣다) pour into; (계속해서) keep pouring; pour continuously. ¶독에 물을 ~ pour water into a jar.

들이비치다 (안으로 비치다) shine in; (세차게 비치다) shine hard. ¶해가 들이비치지 않는 방 a room that gets no sun // 창문을 통해 해가 들이비치고 있다 The sun is shining in through the window. // 이 방에는 저녁 햇살이 들이비친다 This room is open to the afternoon sun.

들이빨다 (안으로 빨아들이다) suck in; inhale; imbibe; (힘 있게 빨다) suck hard. ¶담배를 ~ inhale the smoke of a cigarette // 젖을 ~ suck [draw] the breast hard // 해면이 물을 들이빤다 A sponge sucks up water. // 나는 연기를 들이빨지 않고 담배를 피운다 I puff [suck] cigarettes without inhaling the smoke.

들이세우다 1 (안에) take [bring / carry] (a thing) in and stand (it) up. ¶우산을 방에 ~ bring an umbrella into a room and stand it up. 2 (지위에) place; install (a person in a position); establish (a person as governor). ¶과장을 ~ install (a person) as a section chief // 새 교장을 ~ appoint a new principal for the school.

들이쉬다 breathe in; inhale; inspire; draw (a breath). ¶급히 숨을 한 번 들이쉬고 with a rapid intake of breath // 숨을 크게 ~ breathe deeply / draw a deep breath.

들이쌓다 pile [heap] (up). ¶창고에 상품을 ~ put [deposit] goods in a warehouse / warehouse [store] goods.

들이쌓이다 lie in a heap; heap [be heaped] up; collect; accumulate. ¶창고에 쌀이 들이쌓인다 Rice lies heaped up in a warehouse. // 눈이 바람에 들이쌓여 있었다 The snow was piled in drifts. // 책상 위에 먼지가 들이쌓인다 Dust collects [is thick] on the table.

들이쑤시다 1 (마구 쑤시다) sting; tingle [smart / throb] with pain; rankle; ache; have an acute pain. ¶온몸이 ~ have a severe pain throughout one's body // 이가 들이쑤신다 My tooth stings. // 골마디가 들이쑤신다 My head aches on and off. // 갑자기 옆구리가 들이쑤셨다 I felt an acute [a sharp] pain in my side. 2 (남을 들쑤시다) instigate; incite; needle; stir up. ¶허영심을 ~ inflate the vanity (of a person) // 들이쑤셔 싸움을 붙이다 stir up a fight. 3 (뒤지다) dig up; rummage [rout] (in a drawer); poke and pry (into). ¶남의 비밀을 ~ poke and pry into another's secret.

들이치다¹ (바람 등이) blow in [into]; (비 등이) drive into [through]. ¶비가 들이치지 않도록 하다 shut out the rain // 바람이 불면 비가 들이친다 When it's windy it rains in. // 창문으로 비가 들이친다 It is raining into the room through the window. / Rain is coming into the room through the window.

들이치다² (침입하다) attack; assault; storm; raid. ¶적진을 ~ attack the enemy's position // 경관이 도박장을 들이쳤다 Policemen raided [made a raid on] a gambling den.

들이켜다 drink (down); drink deep; gulp; take [have] a pull at (liquor); toss [quaff] off. ¶물을 꿀꺽꿀꺽 ~ gulp down water // 단숨에 ~ empty (one's glass) in one draft // 쭉 ~ take a long pull / drink (a glass) dry // 그는 단숨에 맥주를 들이켰다 He gulped down the beer.

들이키다 (안쪽으로 다그다) bring (a thing) near (to); tug [draw / take / pull] in. ¶발을 ~ draw in one's legs // 나무를 담 가까이 들이켜 심다 plant trees closer to a wall.

들이퍼붓다 (그릇에) pour (water) hard; (욕설 등을) heap [shower / rain] (abuses) upon; asperse (a person) with (bitter reproaches); (쏟아지다) rain [snow] hard on; bombard hard. ¶(야구에서) 맹타를 ~

들일 farm work[labor]; work in the fields; field[farm] labor. ¶~을 하다 do farm work / work on the farm// 아버지는 ~을 하러 나가셨습니다 My father is working out in the fields.

들입다 recklessly; frantically; forcibly; ceaselessly; like mad; blindly; [지나치게] extremely very much. ¶~ 패다 beat (a person) hard// ~ 공부하다 study hard (without let-up) / (속에) dig into one's subject / ~ 일하다 work hard [away] / work like a horse[tiger]// ~ 조르다 entreat (a person) to do.

들장미(-薔薇) [식] a wild[multiflora] rose.

들쥐 [동] a field[meadow] mouse.

들짐승 wild animals.

들쩍지근하다 rather sweet. ⇨달짝지근하다

들쭉날쭉 jaggedly; ruggedly; unevenly. **들쭉날쭉하다** jagged; indented; notched. ¶가장자리가 들쭉날쭉한 잎 a notched leaf / a leaf with a serrated margin// 들쭉날쭉한 해안선 an indented coastline// 들쭉날쭉한 이 uneven teeth// 톱니가 ~ The teeth of a saw are notched.

들창(-窓) a window set in high in the wall; a skylight.
● **들창코** an upturned nose(코); a person with an upturned nose(사람).

들추다 1 [폭로하다] disclose[let out] (a secret); uncover; reveal; expose; dig up [into]; bring to light. ¶남의 잘못을 ~ expose a person's fault// 남의 과거를 ~ rake up a person's past// 회사 내정을 ~ make public disclosure of the inside affairs of a company// 남의 조상을 들추어 말하다 take a dig at another's ancestors. 2 [뒤지기] search; ransack; rummage (in). ¶호주머니 속을 ~ fumble in one's pocket (for)// 연필이 있나 하고 서랍을 ~ rummage in a drawer for a pencil.

들추어내다 expose; disclose; lay bare; unmask. ¶다른 사람의 흠을 ~ find fault with other people / pick holes in others// 남의 불미스러운 과거를 ~ dig up a person's disreputable past// 남의 사생활을 ~ lay bare another's private life.

들치기 [날쎄게 훔치는 행위] (shop)lifting; [날쎄게 훔치는 사람] a (shop)lifter; [미국 속어] a booster. **들치기하다** shoplift; lift. ¶들치기하다가 잡히다 be caught lifting (something)// 그는 들치기하다가 잡혔다 He was caught in the act of shoplifting. →역에서 여행 가방을 들치기당했다 I had my suitcase stolen at the station. / Someone walked away with my suitcase at the station.

들치다 raise; lift; hold up (the end of). ¶담요를 ~ hold up an end of a blanket.

들키다 [발견되다] be found (out)[discovered / detected / caught] (doing / in the act of doing); come out. ¶들킬까 봐 lest it should be found out / for fear of detection// 장난하다 선생님에게 ~ be caught up to some mischief by the teacher// 그들은 용케 들키지 않았다 They managed to escape notice.// 그의 잘못은 누구에게도 들키지 않고 지나갔다 His error passed unnoticed.// 그에게 들키지 않고 책상 속을 조사했다 Without attracting his attention, I inspected the contents of his desk.// 그는 도둑질 현장을 들켰다 He was caught red-handed stealing.

들통(-桶) a pail; a bucket.
들통 나다 be detected[revealed / disclosed]; be brought[come] to light; get found out. ¶그의 거짓말이 들통 나고 말았다 His lie was discovered[exposed].// 그들의 비밀이 들통 났다 Their secret has come[leaked] out.(▶ come out은 드러나다, leak out은 누설되다) // 그들의 부정행위가 들통 났다 Their dishonest act came to light.// 그 비밀은 들통 나지 않도록 해라 Don't let the cat out of the bag.

들판 [들을 이룬 벌판] a plain; a field. ¶~ 한 가운데 서 있는 외로운 소나무 a lone[solitary] pine tree in the middle of a field.

듬뿍 plenty; much; quite a lot; to the brim; to the full. ¶돈이 ~ 들은 지갑 a purse full of money// ~ 벌다 make a killing[a bundle] / rake in the money// 물건을 ~ 사들이다 buy things in large quantities// 빵에 잼을 ~ 바르다 spread a lot of jam on the bread// 먹물을 붓에 ~ 먹이다 allow a brush to absorb all the ink it can// 그는 웨이터에게 팁을 ~ 집어 주었다 He tipped the waiter generously.// 그는 상을 ~ 받았다 He was well rewarded. // 그는 돈을 ~ 내놓았다 He generously plunked down a huge sum of money.// 그는 생선에다 소스를 ~ 부었다 He poured sauce all over the fish. / He drowned the fish in sauce. **듬뿍하다** full; brimful.

듬성듬성 sparsely; thinly; scatteredly; sporadically; here and there. ¶털이 ~ 나다 hair grows thinly// 나무를 ~ 심다 plant trees sparsely// 거기에는 인가가 ~ 있다 There are scattered cottages there.// 그 언덕에는 나무가 ~ 심어져 있다 The hill is sparsely wooded. **듬성듬성하다** sparse; thin; scattered; sporadic.

듬쑥 full; greedily. ¶과자를 ~ 손에 그러쥐다 grasp of greedy handful of cake// 그는 동전을 한 주먹 ~ 움켜쥐었다 He seized all the coppers that his fist can hold.

듯 ¶… ~ 마는 ~ 하다 it hardly seems one way or the other / it hardly feels as if / one hardly knows whether// 일을 할 ~ 하면서 아니하다 look about to do the work but never do it// 밥이 적어서 먹은 ~ 만 ~ 하다 There was so little rice I hardly feel as if I had eaten any.// 비가 올 ~ 말 ~ 했다 I was not sure if it would rain or not.// 어젯밤은 모기에 물려 자는 ~ 마는 ~ 했다 I was bitten by mosquitoes so much that I got hardly any sleep last night.// 짙은 안개로 보일 ~ 말 ~ 했다 We could scarcely see through the thick fog.// 그는 대답을 할 ~ 한 ~ 하다가 아니했다 He kept looking as if he were going to come up with an answer but then he never did.

듯싶다 […인 듯 생각되다] seem; it seems (to me) that; […일 것 같다] be likely (to); probably. ¶그는 학생인 ~ He looks like a student.// 벼슬이라도 한 듯싶은 모양이구나 You act as if you had become a government official or something.// 비가 올 ~ It looks like rain.// 그는 아무래도 아픈 ~ He seems to be ill.// 주인인 듯싶은 사람이 나왔다 A man, apparently the master of the house, came out.// 금시라도 비가 올 듯싶은 날씨다

듯이 It looks as though it might start to rain at any moment.∥부인인 듯싶은 사람이 전화를 받았다 A woman, apparently his wife, answered the phone.∥슬퍼서 가슴이 메어지는 듯싶었다 My heart was almost burst with grief.∥없을 때 그가 찾아온 ~ He called in my absence, apparently.∥종이가 좀 남을 ~ It looks as though he'll have more than enough paper.

듯이 as if; as though; like; giving the appearance of. ¶그는 네가 생각하~ 그렇게 대학자는 아니다 He is not such a great scholar as you think.∥그는 중국인이지만 미국인이 영어를 말하~ 영어를 한다 He is a Chinese, but he speaks English like an American.∥녹이 쇠를 부식하~ 근심은 마음을 좀먹는다 As rust eats away iron, so does care eat away the heart.∥눈물이 비오~ 쏟아진다 Tears pour down like rain.∥삶이 있~ 죽음이 있다 As a man lives, so he dies.∥음식이 몸을 기르~ 독서는 정신을 기른다 Reading is to the mind what food is to the body.

등 the back. ¶의자의 ~ the back of a chair / 벽에 ~을 대고 backing on the wall∥~을 펴다 straighten one's back / stretch (oneself) / ~을 돌리다 turn one's back (on)∥~을 맞대고 앉다 sit back to back∥~을 구부리고 앉다 sit with one's back hunched up∥국민의 신망은 ~에 업다 be backed by the confidence of the people∥~을 웅크리다 hump [hunch] up one's back∥그는 ~에 타박상을 입었다 He got a bruise on his back.∥그는 내게 ~을 돌린 채 대답을 하지 않았다 He sat [stood] with his back to me and didn't reply.∥고양이가 ~을 꼬부렸다 The cat arched its back. ∥그녀는 화를 내어 ~을 돌렸다 She got angry and turned her back on me.∥그는 적에게 ~을 보이고 도망쳤다 He fled in the face of the enemy. / He turned tail and ran away from the [his] enemy.∥그는 우리의 원조 제의에도 ~을 돌렸다 He turned his back on our offer of help.

등(이) 달다 get all hot and bothered; fret [stew] (about); be upset; be irritated [impatient]; chafe (under). ¶사업의 진행이 여의치 않아 그는 등이 달아 있다 He is quite nervous because his undertaking is not making satisfactory progress.∥그는 꾸어 준 돈을 받지 못해 등이 달아 있다 He is all hot and bothered because he can't collect the money he lent out.∥그는 손실을 회복하려고 등이 달아 있었다 He was impatient [eager] to make up (for) the loss.

등(이) 닿다 have backing; be supported; lean on; depend on; shelter oneself under [rely upon] (the man of influence). ¶그는 서울에 등이 닿는 친척이 있어 몸을 의지하러 갔다 He has a relative to depend upon in Seoul and has gone there to live him.

등을 대다 〔남의 세력에 의지하다〕 lean [depend / rely] on (a person's) authority [power / influence]; turn [look] to (a person's) power. ¶미국에 등을 댄 정권 the U.S.-backed regime∥직권에 ~ hide behind one's authority∥아버지의 위세에 등을 대고 뽐내다 give oneself airs under the shelter of one's father's influence∥그는 정부에 등을 댈 만한 유력자 몇 사람이 있다 He has several men of influence he can count on in the government.

등(等) 1 〔등급·석차〕 a class; a grade; a degree; a rank. ¶1~ the first class [grade]∥3~으로 떨어지다 drop to [slip into] third place∥그는 경주에서 2~이 되었다 He finished [came in] second in the race. / He was the runner-up.∥네 성적은 반에서 몇 ~이냐 How do you stand in your class? 2 〔…따위〕 and the like; and so forth [on]; et cetera (약어 etc.); and such like (things); and what not. ¶한국, 중국, 일본 ~의 나라에서 in these three countries of Korea, China, and Japan∥모자, 장갑, 신발 ~ hats, gloves, shoes, etc∥그는 그림, 음악, 수학 ~을 배웠다 He studied painting, music, mathematics, and the like.∥수업이니 저술이니 ~으로 조금도 틈이 없다 Between [What with] teaching and writing, my time is wholly taken up.

등(燈) a light; a lamp; a lantern. ¶~이 켜져 있지 않은 방 an unlighted room∥~을 켜다 light a lamp / light up (a room) / (전등을) turn [put] on the light∥~을 끄다 put out [extinguish] the light [lamp]∥~이 켜 있다 The light is on.∥~이 꺼졌다 The light has gone out [is out].

등(藤) 〔식〕 rattan; cane. ¶~가구 rattan [cane] furniture / ~의자 a rattan [cane] chair∥~으로 엮다 weave with rattan.

등가(等價) 〔화〕 equivalence; equivalency; 〔경〕 parity (of exchange). ¶~의 equivalent∥당시의 1,000원은 현재의 1만 원과 ~이다 One thousand won in those days was equivalent to ten thousand won now.
● **등가물** an equivalent.

등각(等角) 〔수〕 equal angles. ¶~의 equiangular.
● **등각 삼각형** 〔수〕an equiangular triangle.

등거리 a sleeveless jacket; a lady's fur.

등거리(等距離) equal distance; equidistance. ¶~의 equidistant∥~에 at equal distances.
● **등거리 외교** equidistance diplomacy. ¶~정책 a policy of dealing equally (with A and B) / equal distance diplomacy.

등걸 a stump; a stub. ¶나뭇~을 캐내다 dig up the stump of a tree.

등걸잠 sleeping with one's clothes on [without changing dress]. ¶~을 자다 sleep with one's clothes on / sleep without changing.

등겨 chaff(왕겨); rice bran [husks] (겨).

등고선(等高線) a contour line. ¶지도에 ~을 그리다 provide a map with contour lines / draw contour lines on a map.
● **등고선 지도** a contour map.

등골 1 〔등줄기〕 the line of the backbone; the hollow along the spine. ¶~에 땀이 나다 be given a hard time / be awfully ashamed. 2 〔생〕 the spinal cord. ⇨척수(脊髓) 3 the backbone. ⇨등골(⇨등골).

등골(이) 빠지다 suffer extremely; have a very hard time of it. ¶등골이 빠지는 일 a laborious [toilsome] task / a tough job / heavy work∥등골이 빠지게 일하다 work very hard.

등골(을) 뽑다 squeeze [wring / extort] money out of (a person); exploit; fleece [bleed / soak] (a person) (of his money). ¶고용주는 고용인의 등골을 뽑았다 The employer sweat his worker.

등골(이) 오싹하다 feel a chill run down one's spine. ¶등골이 오싹해지는 광경 a spine-chilling sight∥나는 등골이 오싹했다 I felt a

cold chill pass through me. / A shiver ran through my limbs. // 무시무시한 이야기를 들으니 등골이 오싹했다 A cold shiver[chill] ran down my spine when I heard the weird story. / The weird story sent a chill up my spine.
●**등골뼈** the backbone; the spine; the spinal column.

등과하다(登科-) pass the higher civil service examination.

등교(登校) attending school; school attendance. ¶그는 불미한 행위로 인하여 1주일간 금지가 되어 있다 He is suspended from school for a week for bad conduct. **등교하다** go to[attend] school. ¶지원자는 오전 9시까지 등교해야 한다 The applicants [examinees] are requested to be at school before 9:00 a.m.

등귀(騰貴) a rise (in prices); (시세·평가액의) appreciation. ¶땅값[원]의 ~ the appreciation of land value[the won]. **등귀하다** rise; go up; advance; (급등하다) soar. ¶땅값이 등귀하고 있다 Land values are on the increase [rise].

등극(登極) accession (to the throne); enthronement. **등극하다** ascend[accede] to the throne; come to[mount] the throne.

등긁이 a back scratcher.

등급(等級) a class; a grade; a rank; a degree; (별의) magnitude. ¶술의 ~은 어떻게 매기죠 How do you grade[rank] liquor? // 이 아이들은 수영 솜씨에 따라 ~이 1에서 5까지 붙는다 These children are ranked from 1 to 5 according to their swimming skill. // 그 극장의 좌석에는 몇 가지 ~이 있었다 There were several classes of seats in that theater. // 급여의 ~이 한 계단 올랐다 I had my salary raised one step. // 유스 호스텔에는 ~의 구별이 없다 There are no distinctions among youth hostels based on rankings.

등기(登記) registration; registry. ¶국내 [국제] ~ domestic [international] registration // 변경 ~ registration of an alternation // 선적 ~ registration of nationality (of a ship) // ~필의 registered // 가옥 ~를 말소하다 cancel the registration of a house. **등기하다** register; effect[make] registration; have (a thing) registered. ¶정식으로 ~ register in proper form // 최근에 산 토지를 등기했다 I had my newly-bought land registered.
●**등기 말소** cancellation of registration. **등기부** a register (book). **등기소** a registry (office). **등기 우편** registered post [(미) mail]. ¶~으로 부치다 send (a letter) registered[by registered mail]. **등기필증** a registration certificate.

등나무(藤-) [식] (a) wisteria; rattan; cane.

등단하다(登壇-) 1 [단 위에 오르다] take[go on / proceed to / ascend] the platform; take [mount] the rostrum. 2 [등장하다] start; enter upon; make one's debut. ¶문학계에 ~ start one's literary career.

등대(等待) waiting. **등대하다** wait for; await; be[get / stand] ready for (an order).

등대(燈臺) a lighthouse; a light tower; a beacon; (시어) a pharos. ¶월미도 ~ the Wolmido Light.
●**등대지기** a lighthouse keeper; a lighthouseman; a lightkeeper. **등댓불** a beacon lamp.

등덜미 the upper part of the back; [뒷덜미] the nape; the scruff (of the neck). ¶~를 치다 pat (a person) on the back // ~를 붙잡다 seize[take] (a person) by the nape[scruff] of the neck.

등등(等等) and so on; and so forth; and all that sort of thing; and what not; et cetera(약어 etc.). ¶우리는 물통, 냄비, 접시 ~을 샀다 We bought buckets, pots, plates, etc[and so forth / and so on]. // 그는 인생, 사랑, 죽음 ~에 대해서 이야기를 했다 He talked about life, love, death, and so on[forth].

등등하다(騰騰-) [서슬 푸르다] mighty; powerful; influential; [의기양양하다] triumphant; exultant; on one's high horse; riding high. ¶기세가 ~ show one's spirit [nerve] / be in high spirits[feather] // 노기가 ~ be filled with fury and anger // 살기가 ~ reek of murder / be all in a truculent mood.

등락(騰落) rise and fall; ups and downs; fluctuations. ¶주가의 ~ the ups and downs [rise and fall / fluctuations] of stock prices.

등량(等量) an equal amount[quantity]; equivalent; equivalence. ¶~의 equivalent // ~의 소금과 설탕 an equal amount of salt and sugar // ~으로 (처방전에서 약을) ana(▶ aa로 줄어 씀).

등렬(等列) [같은 항렬] the same rank.

등록(登錄) registration; (경기·단체 등에의) entry; enrollment. ¶사전(事前) ~제 an advance registration system // 상표[실용신안 / 의장 / 판권] ~ registration of trademark [utility model / design / copyright] // 선적(船籍) ~ registration of nationality // 주민 ~ the resident registration // 유권자의 ~ the registration of voters // 금전 ~기 a cash register // 미~의 unregistered (trademark). **등록하다** register; be registered (with); put on record; enter; make an entry; enroll. ¶판권 [상표]을 ~ register a copyright[trademark] // 직업소개소에 ~ register oneself with[at] the unemployment office // 신입생을 ~ register[enroll] new students // 경기 참가자 명부에 ~ enter one's name for a race.
●**등록금** a registration fee; (학교의) university expenses; school fees. **등록 상표** a registered trademark. **등록세** a registration tax. **등록증**(-證) a certificate of inscription. **등록필** (게시) Registered.

등롱(燈籠) (걸어 놓는) a hanging[a garden] lantern; (들고 다니는) a hand lantern; (신전의) a dedicatory lantern. ¶석(石)~ a stone lantern // ~에 불을 켜다 light a hanging lantern.

등마루 the ridge of the spine; the spinal column; (산의) a ridge. ¶산 ~ the ridge [summit] of a mountain // 지붕 ~ the ridge of a roof.

등반(登攀) climbing. ¶그들은 히말라야 ~을 계획 중이다 They are planning to climb the Himalayas. **등반하다** climb up; scale (a wall, a cliff, etc.); make the ascent of.
●**등반대** a climbing party.

등받이 (의자의) the back of a chair.

등변(等邊) [수] equal sides. ¶~의 equilateral.
●**등변 삼각형** an equilateral triangle. ⇨정삼각형

등본(謄本) a (certified) copy; a transcript; a duplicate; [법] a tenor. ¶~을 신청하다 apply for a copy // ~을 떼다 obtain[get] an attest-

등분 ed [a certified] copy / make an attested copy.

등분(等分) an equal division; division into equal parts. ¶삼~ trisection / 사~ quadrisection. 등분하다 divide equally[in equal parts]; share equally. ¶이익을 등분하자 Let's share the profits equally.

등불(燈-) a light; a lamplight; an electric light(전등). ¶~을 켜다[끄다] (전등의) turn [switch] the light on[off] / (램프의) light[put out] the lamp // 램프의 ~을 켜다 light a lamp // ~ 아래서 글을 읽다 read by lamplight // 실험실에는 ~이 환히 밝혀져 있었다 The laboratory was brightly lit up. // ~이 하나씩 꺼져 갔다 The lights went out one by one.

등비(等比) [수] (an) equal ratio; geometric ratio. ¶~로 in equal ratio.
●등비급수 [수열] [수] a geometric series [sequence].

등뼈 the backbone. ⇨등골뼈(⇨등골)

등사(謄寫) [베껴 씀] copy; transcription; [등사판 인쇄] mimeographing. 등사하다 copy; transcribe; (등사판으로) mimeograph.
●등사기(-機) a mimeograph. 등사 원지 a stencil; stencil paper. ¶~에 쓰다 cut a stencil.

등산(登山) mountain climbing; mountaineering; hiking. (▶ mountain climbing과 mountaineering은 장비를 갖춘 전문 스포츠를 가리키고, hiking은 특별한 장비 없이 가볍게 산을 오르거나 시골길을 걷는 것을 가리킴) ¶~ 안내자[짐꾼] a mountain guide[carrier]. 등산하다 climb a mountain; go up a mountain; go hiking. ¶한라산을 ~ climb[ascend] Hallasan(Mt. Halla) // 이번 주말에 등산합시다 Let's go hiking this weekend.
●등산가 a mountaineer; an alpinist; a cragsman(암벽의). 등산로 a path up a mountain. 등산화 mountain-climbing boots.

등살 the flesh[muscle] of one's back. ¶~이 꼿꼿하다 be in a fix / be in a quandary.

등성이 1 (동물의) the line[ridge] of the spine. 2 (mountain) ridge. ⇨산등성이 ¶해가 ~로 넘어갔다 The sun set behind the mountain ridge.

등속(等速) [물] uniform velocity.
●등속 운동 uniform motion.

등속(等屬) and so forth[on]; and[or] the like; and such like; et cetera(약어 &c., etc.). ¶보리, 밀 ~ barley, wheat, and such like.

등수(等數) [등급에 따라 정한 차례] a grade; a rank; a rate. ¶~를 매기다 grade / graduate / rate / rank // 반에서의 그의 ~는 5등 이내였다 He ranks among the top five in his class. // 그의 ~가 10등 올라갔다[내려갔다] His rank[standing] in the class has risen [fallen] ten places. / He has gone up [come down] ten places in his class.

등식(等式) [수] an equality. ¶절대적 [조건부] ~ an absolute [conditional] equality.

등신(等神) a fool; a dunce; a blockhead; a noodle; (구어) a stick. ¶~ 같은 foolish / silly / stupid // ~ 같은 짓을 하다 do a foolish [silly] thing / make a fool[an ass] of oneself / play the fool // 이 ~아 You fool[noodle / stupid thing]! // 이런 ~은 본 적이 없다 I've never come across such a fool in my life.

등신대(等身大) life size. ¶~의 life-size(d) / as large as life // ~의 동상 a life-size bronze statue // ~의 초상화를 그리다 paint a life-size portrait.

등신상(等身像) a life-size statue.

등심(-心) sirloin; meat around the backbone of cattle.

등심(燈心) [심지] a wick.

등쌀 annoying; annoyance; bothering; harassing; pestering; molesting; needling. ¶어젯밤에는 모기 ~에 혼이 났다 I was pestered by[with] mosquitoes last night. // 그녀는 시어머니 ~에 견디지 못하고 친정집으로 쫓겨 왔다 She couldn't take her mother-in-law's nagging, so she left her husband and came home.

등압선(等壓線) an isobar; an isobaric line.

등에 [동] a horsefly; a gadfly; a breeze.

등온선(等溫線) an isothemal line; an isotherm.

등외(等外) a failure; (구어) an also-ran. ¶~의 (경기 등에서) unplaced / (품질이) offgrade / below standard // ~인 사람[말] an also-ran // ~로 떨어지다 fail to win a prize / win no place[prize] / fall under the regular grades(품질에서) // 그는 아깝게도 ~였다 Regrettably, he failed to place[finish among the best six]. (▶ place는 (미)에서는 「2등」, finish among the best six는 「6등 안에 들어가지 않다」의 뜻)

등용(登用) [임용] appointment; assignment; [승진] elevation; promotion; advancement. ¶공무원 ~ 시험 a civil service examination // 인재 ~의 길을 열다 open up opportunities for the talented // 신인의 ~을 방해하다 obstruct the rise of new talent. 등용하다 appoint[assign] (a person to a position); [승진시키다] promote[advance] (a person to a higher position); elevate. ➔ ¶그는 법관으로 등용되었다 He was appointed (as a) judge. / He was raised to the bench. // 그는 간부로 등용되었다 He was promoted to an executive post.

등용문(登龍門) an opening to honors; the gateway to success (in life). ¶문단의 ~ a gateway to the literary world[to success as a novelist] // 우리나라에서는 공무원 시험이 관리의 ~이다 In our country, civil service examinations alone open government careers to people[are the only way to careers in government].

등원(登院) attendance at the House. ¶~ 일수가 적은 사람 those whose attendance record is poor. 등원하다 attend a session of the House.

등위(等位) 1 a class; a grade. ⇨등급 2 [같은 위치] the same rank.
●등위 접속사 [언] a coordinate conjunction.

등유(燈油) lamp oil; kerosene; (영) paraffin oil.

등자(鐙子) a stirrup; a footstall(여자용).

등잔(燈盞) an oil cup for a lamp; a lamp-oil container.

등잔 밑이 어둡다(속담) The beacon does not shine on its own base.; At the foot of the candle it is dark.; One has to go abroad to get news of home.
●등잔불 a lamplight; a lantern light.

등장(登場) 1 [무대에 나타남] (an) appearance (on the stage). ¶햄릿 ~ (▶ 각본 용어) Enter Hamlet / Hamlet enters. 등장하다 come on (the) stage; enter the stage; appear

on (the) stage; make a stage appearance. **2** [출현] advent(신병기 의의); appearance. ¶신무기의 ~ the advent of new weapons. **등장하다** appear; show up; make an appearance; put in one's appearance. ¶갑자기 ~ burst on the scene // 그녀는 혜성처럼 연예계에 등장했다 She made a comet-like appearance in the world of entertainment. // 때마침 명탐정이 등장하여 사건을 단번에 해결했다 A timely appearance by [The timely arrival on the scene of] the great detective solved the case in no time.
● **등장인물** (문학 작품의) the characters (in a novel); (연극의) (라) dramatis personae; persons connected (with an affair).

등재(登載) registration; record. **등재하다** register; record.

등정(登頂) ¶일행은 ~에 성공했다 The party succeeded in reaching the summit. // 그들은 몽블랑의 첫 ~을 이룩했다 They accomplished the first ascent of Mont Blanc. **등정하다** gain [reach / climb to] the summit.

등정(登程) departure; starting [setting out] on a journey. **등정하다** depart; start [go] on a journey; set off; leave (for).

등줄기 the line of the backbone. ¶~에 식은 땀이 흘렀다 I felt a chill go down my spine.

등지(等地) (and) like places. ¶서울·부산 ~ Seoul, Busan and like [other] cities.

등지느러미 [동] the dorsal fin.

등지다 1 [틀어지다] fall out (with a person about trifles); become estranged [alienated] (from); break [split] (with). ¶…과 등지고 살 be on bad terms with (a person) / be at odds with (a person) // 형제가 서로 등진 지 오래다 It has been a long time that the two brothers are at odds. // 사소한 오해로 평생의 친구와 등지게 되는 일이 있다 Slight misunderstanding may sever lifelong friends. // 그것이 원인이 되어 우리는 서로 등지게 되었다 That caused [produced] a breach of friendship between us.
2 [배반하다] rise [turn] against [on / upon]; betray; [돌아서다] turn one's back on; [떠나다] leave. ¶나라를 ~ turn against one's country / leave one's native country // 친구를 ~ turn against one's friend // 세상을 등지고 살다 live apart from the world / live in isolation // 아직 젊은 나이에 세상을 등지고 여승이 되었다 Though still young, she renounced the world and became a nun.
3 [등 뒤에 두다] (one's back) lean against. ¶관중을 등지고 with one's back to the audience // 그는 산을 등지고 사진을 찍었다 He had a photo taken with the mountain in the background. // 서울은 북악산을 등지고 있다 Seoul lies with Bugaksan(Mt. Bugak) at the back.

등질(等質) homogeneity. ⇨"균질(均質)

등짐 a pack [burden] carried on one's back. ¶~을 지다 carry a burden on one's back / backpack.
● **등짐장수** a peddler.

등차(等差) [같은 차] (an) equal difference.
● **등차급수** [**수열**] [수] an arithmetic series [sequence].

등창(-瘡) an abscess [a tumor] on one's back.

등청(登廳) attendance at office. **등청하다** go to one's (government) office; attend the office.

등촉(燈燭) a lamplight and a candlelight; a (lighted) lamp.

등치다 [빼앗다] extort (money from a person) (by intimidation [threats]); blackmail; pinch; squeeze; wring [screw / pull / scare] (money out of a person); (미국 속어) racketeer. ¶등쳐 먹는 사람 a blackmailer / (미국 속어) a racketeer // 등쳐 먹고 살다 live by racketeering.

등치고 간 내먹다(속담) do harm to (a person) under the pretense of friendship [kindness].

등치고 배 문지른다(속담) treat (a person) with threats and coaxings.

등판하다(登板-) [야구] take the plate [mound]; go to the mound [(미국 속어) hill]; (구원 투수로) come in [up] to pitch. ¶오늘 경기에는 홍길동이 등판할 예정이다 Hong Gildong is to take the plate [mound] in today's game. // 그는 25시합에 등판했다 He pitched in twenty-five games.

등피(燈皮) (세로의) a (lamp) chimney; (구형의) a globe. ¶램프에 ~를 씌우다 put a chimney on a lamp // 램프에는 ~가 씌워져 있었다 There was a chimney [A chimney had been placed] on the lamp.

등하불명(燈下不明) The beacon does not shine on its own base.

등한시(等閑視) negligence; neglect; disregard. **등한시하다** neglect (one's job); be neglectful of; be negligent in; overlook; slight; make light of; disregard. ¶그는 가정을 등한시했다 He took no heed of [paid little attention to] his family. // 그 문제는 등한시할 수 없다 The problem cannot be disregarded [made light of].

등한하다(等閑-) negligent; neglectful; careless. **등한히** negligently; neglectfully; carelessly. ¶~ 하다 neglect / slight / disregard // 문제를 ~ 하다 overlook [neglect] a problem // 경고를 ~ 한 사람들이 참화를 입었다 Those who ignored [disregarded] the warning met with disaster.

등허리 [등과 허리] the back and the waist; [허리의 등쪽] the small of the back.

등화(燈火) a light; a lamplight. ⇨"등불 ¶~가 친(可親)의 계절이 되었다 The good season for reading is on.
● **등화관제** control of lights; control over lighting; a blackout; a brownout; a dimout. ¶~하(下)의 도시 a blacked-out city // ~를 하다 black [brown / dim] out // ~가 해제되었다 The blackout was up. **등화 신호** a light signal; signaling by a flashlight.

디데이 (the) D-day.

디디다 1 [밟다] step on; tread (up)on. ¶외국 땅을 ~ step [set foot] on foreign soil // 한 발짝 내어 ~ take a step forward // 첫발을 내어 ~ make the first step (toward) // 발을 내어 ~ enter into politics / enter upon a political career // 방에는 책이 흩어져 있어 발 디딜 곳도 없었다 The room was strewn with books, and there was no place to stand. **2** (누룩·메주를) tread malted flour paste into cakes.

디딜방아 a treadmill (pestle); a mortar (worked by treading).

디딤돌 [디디고 오르내리는 돌] a stepstone; [수단] a stepping stone; a springboard. ¶남

디밀다

을 ~ 삼아 출세하다 improve one's position at the expense of another // 장차 출세하는 ~이 되다 serve as a stepping stone for future success // 실패를 성공의 ~로 삼다 make one's failure stepping stone to success.

디밀다 push in; push hard. ⇨들이밀다

디브이디 a DVD(▶ digital versatile [video] disc의 약어).

디스카운트 (a) discount.

디스켓 a diskette; a floppy (disk).

디스코 [유] (미) disco.
● **디스코텍** a disco(theque). ¶오늘 밤엔 ~에서 춤추자 Let's go and dance at the disco tonight.

디스크¹ a disc; a disk. ¶콤팩트 ~ a compact disc.
● **디스크자키** [방송] a disc[disk] jockey; (속어) a deejay.

디스크² [의] hernia of an intervertebral disk; a reptured disk; a slipped disk. ¶목 ~ a slipped disk in the neck.

디스토마 [동] a distome; flukes. ¶간~ (라) distoma hepaticum // 폐~ pulmonary distomiasis.

디스플레이 [컴] a display.
● **디스플레이 장치** a display unit.

디자이너 a designer. ¶복식(服飾) ~ a dress designer // 상업[공업] ~ a commercial[an industrial] designer // 인테리어 ~ an interior designer [decorator].

디자인 a design; designing. ¶그래픽 ~ (a) graphic design // 상업[공업] ~ a commercial [an industrial] design // 인테리어 ~ interior design [decoration] // 기발한 ~의 가구 furniture of striking design. **디자인하다** design. ¶드레스를 ~ design a dress. ➔특별히 디자인된 블라우스 a specially designed blouse.

디저트 (a) dessert. ¶~로 아이스크림이 나왔다 Ice cream was served for dessert.

디제이 a D.J.(▶ disc jockey의 약어).

디젤 기관차(-機關車) a diesel locomotive.

디젤 엔진 a diesel engine.

디지털 ~의 digital.
● **디지털시계** a digital clock[watch]. **디지털 통신** digital communications.

디프테리아 [의] diphtheria. ¶~ 예방의 antidiphtheritic // ~에 걸리다 suffer from diphtheria.
● **디프테리아 혈청** diphtheria serum.

디플레이션 deflation. ¶~을 악화시키다[막다] aggravate[prevent] deflation.
● **디플레이션 정책** a deflationary policy.

딜러 a dealer. ¶그가 ~였다 He was the dealer.

딜럭스 [관형어적]. **딜럭스하다** deluxe.
● **딜럭스 모델** a deluxe model. **딜럭스판**(-版) a deluxe edition.

딜레마 a dilemma. ¶~에 빠지다 be in a fix / be on the horns of a dilemma / be caught between the devil and the deep blue sea[(문어) between Scylla and Charybdis] / come up against a dilemma // ~에 빠뜨리다 force (a person) into a dilemma // 의리와 인정 간의 ~에 빠지다 be torn between one's sense of duty and one's feelings // 남을 ~에 몰아넣다 put a person in a dilemma // 나는 ~에 빠졌다 I am on the horns of a dilemma.

딩굴다 →뒹굴다

딩크족(-族) dink; DINK(▶ double income no kids의 약어).

따갑다 1 hot; heated. ⇨'뜨겁다 2 [쑤시다] prickly; pricking; smarting. ¶벌한테 쏘인 데가 ~ The spot stung by the bee is tingling.

따귀 a cheek. ¶그의 ~를 때려 주었다 I slapped him on the cheek. // 양쪽 ~를 맞았다 I got slapped on both cheeks.

따끈따끈하다 warmly. **따끈따끈하다** warm; hot. ¶따끈따끈한 감자 steaming[piping] hot potatoes / potatoes hot from the oven // 커피가 ~ The coffee is piping hot. // 이렇게 추운 날은 따끈따끈한 국수 생각이 간절하다 On a cold day like this, I long for a bowl of steaming hot *guksu*.

따끈하다 hot; heated. ¶따끈한 커피 hot coffee // 음식은 따끈한 것이 좋다 I like my food hot. // 이 요리는 따끈해서 좋다 The dish is nice and warm. // 따끈한 스튜 요리가 나왔다 The stew was served hot from the pot. **따끈히** warmly; hot; good and hot. ¶우유를 ~ 데우다 scald milk warmly // 물을 ~ 끓이다 boil water good and hot // 방을 ~ 하다 heat the room / make the room warm.

따끔거리다 smart; prick; prickle; tingle; sting. ¶따끔거리는 상처 a sore cut // 따끔거리는 아픔 a smarting pain // 눈이 ~ have a tingling pain in one's eye // 상처는 아직 따끔거린다 The wound smarts still. // 이 내의는 따끔거린다 This undershirt scratches.

따끔따끔 pricking; stinging; tingling. ¶눈이 ~ 아프다 have a throbbing pain in one's eye // 바늘로 ~ 찌르다 prick with a needle. **따끔따끔하다** smart; prick. ⇨따끔거리다 ¶따끔따끔한 아픔 a smarting pain // 등이 ~ My back smarts. // 상처를 소독했더니 따끔따끔했다 It smarted[stung] when I put some disinfectant on the wound. // 상처가 아직 ~ The wound still smarts. // 연기 때문에 눈이 ~ The smoke makes my eyes smart. // 상처가 따끔따끔해서 잠을 이루지 못했다 The smart of [pain from] my wound kept me awake. // 이 약을 바르면 좀 따끔따끔합니다 The medicine stings when you apply it.

따끔하다 1 [아프다] prickly; pricking; prickling; stinging; tingling; piercingly painful. ¶따끔하게 찌르다 prick (with a needle) // 따끔하게 아프다 have a prick // (모기가) 따끔하게 물다 bite (one's leg). 2 [호되다] severe; harsh; sharp; caustic; vitriolic. ¶따끔한 비평 (a) harsh[caustic] criticism (on) // 따끔한 맛을 보다 [혼나다] have a bitter experience [a hard time of it] / [야단맞다] have [get / receive] a good scolding // 따끔한 맛을 보여 주다 make (a person) smart (for it) / give (a person) a lesson [a good licking].

따님 (your / his) daughter. ¶아기는 아드님입니까 ~ 입니까 Is your baby a boy or a girl[is he or a she]?

따다¹ 1 [잡아떼다] pick; pluck; nip; clip; trim; [모으다] gather; cull. ¶꽃[딸기]을 ~ pick flowers[strawberries] // 꽃을 따러 가다 go gathering flowers // 악의 싹을 봉오리 때에 따내다 nip evil in the bud // 찻잎을 ~ pick tea leaves // 어떤 아이가 꽃봉오리를 딴 것 같다 Some child must have broken[pulled] off the buds. // 그녀는 내게 포도 한 송이를 따 주었다 She plucked a bunch of grapes off the vine for me. // 장미꽃 봉오리를 따지 마라 Don't pull the buds off the rose bushes. // 어머니는 아이를 지나치게 감싸 독립성의 싹을 따 버리고 말았다 The mother pampered her

child and nipped his spirit of independence in the bud.
2 [터뜨리다·뜯다] open; lance; cut out (affected parts). ¶브랜디 병을 ~ open a new bottle of brandy / 병마개를 ~ pull out a top [bung] / unstopper / uncork a bottle / 종기를 ~ open an abscess [a boil].
3 [인용·발췌하다] quote; make selections; pick out; extract; sum up; summarize; epitomize. ¶시에서 마음에 든 표현[구절]을 ~ select [pick out] one's favorite expressions [phrases] from poems // 남의 글귀를 ~ steal another's words / plagiarize / 요점을 ~ pick out the main points / sum up.
4 [노름·내기 등에서 얻다] gain; get; win (in gambling). ¶속임수로 돈을 ~ rook (a person) / 노름에서 돈을 많이 ~ gain much money in gambling.
5 [얻다·받다] get; obtain; gain; take; receive. ¶백 점[만점]을 ~ get [score] full marks // 금메달을 ~ be awarded a gold medal (at an exhibition) // 박사 학위를 ~ get a doctor's degree // 면허를 ~ take out a license / 그는 수학에서 80점을 땄다 He got an 80[(영) 80 marks] in mathematics.

따다² **1** [만나 주지 않다] pretend not to be in; pretend to be out; be not at home (to a caller); feign absence; refuse to see (a caller pretending to be away from home). ¶신문 기자가 와도 그는 따 버렸다 He refused an interview with the pressman pretending to be out. **2** [따돌리다] leave (a person) out; get rid of (a person); reject; exclude; (미행자 등을) give (a person) the slip; shake off (a person following one); throw [put] (a detective) off the scent. ¶그들은 나를 따 버리고 자기들끼리 소풍 갔다 They all went off on a picnic alone, leaving me out.

따돌리다 leave (a person) out (in the cold); leave (a person) severely alone; put (a person) on one side; exclude; disdain; shun; (사회적으로) ostracize; blackball. ¶따돌림을 받는 사람 a black sheep / a person left out in the cold / (사회의) an [a social] outcast // 남의 따돌림을 당하다 be shunned by all / be ostracized // 전과자를 사회에서 ~ brand an ex-convict as a social outcast // 거짓 약속으로 남을 ~ fob a person off with empty promises // 마을에서 따돌림을 받다 be ostracized in the village / be boycotted by the villagers // 미행자를 ~ shake off one's shadow / give one's shadow the slip // 나는 동생을 따돌리고 친구와 영화를 구경하러 갔다 I gave my brother the slip and went out with friends to see a movie. // 누구나 따돌림 받기 싫어한다 No one likes to be left out. // 그녀를 용케 따돌려 버렸다 I slipped away from her. / I succeeded in getting rid of her.

따듯하다 warm; mild; genial. ⇨ 따뜻하다

따뜻하다 **1** [온도가 알맞다] warm; mild; genial; hot. (▶ 음식물에는 hot을 쓰는 일이 많음. warm은 「미지근하다」라는 느낌이 됨) ¶따뜻한 밥 hot rice // 따뜻한 커피 hot coffee // 따뜻한 기후 a warm [mild / genial] climate // 따뜻한 방 a warm room // 따뜻한 겨울 a soft [mild / green] winter // 점점 따뜻해지다 get [become] warm / warm up / grow warmer / (몸을) 따뜻하게 유지하다 keep oneself warm // 이달은 ~ It is warm this month. / We are having warm weather this month. // 방에 난로를 놓아 따뜻하게 했다 I heated the room with a stove. // 이 집은 쉽게 따뜻해지지 않는다 This house does not get warm easily. // 난로가 전혀 따뜻하지 않다 The fireplace gives out no heat. // 햇빛이 들이비치자 방 안은 점점 따뜻해졌다 With the sun shining in, the room gradually grew warmer [warmed up]. // 이 물은 아직 따뜻한 기운이 남아 있다 This water is still a little warm. / There is some warmth left in this water. **따뜻이** warm(ly); hot; mild(ly). ¶방을 ~ 하다 heat the room / make the room warm / 몸을 ~ 하다 keep oneself warm / dress warmly // 커피를 ~ 데우다 warm up coffee.
2 [정답다] kindly; genial; cordial; heartwarming (kindness). ¶따뜻한 환영 a cordial [hearty] welcome / a warm reception // 마음이 따뜻한 사람 a person of a genial disposition / a warmhearted [kindhearted / warmnatured] person // 따뜻한 마음 a warm [kindly / feeling] heart // 부모[형제]의 따뜻한 정을 모르다 be a stranger to parental [fraternal] affection // 그녀는 (손님에게) 따뜻한 환대를 베풀었다 She extended warmhearted [warm] hospitality (to her guests). // 그는 인간적으로 정말 따뜻한 사람이었다 There was a lot of human warmth in him. // 그는 행복한 가정의 따뜻함을 모른다 He has never known the warm atmosphere of a happy home. // 그들은 그에게 따뜻한 동정을 나타냈다 They were warmly sympathetic to him. // 그녀의 따뜻한 애정은 그에게 격려가 되었다 Her warm [tender] affection gave him the strength to go on. **따뜻이** warmly; kindly; heartily; cordially. ¶~ 맞아들이다 welcome warmly [with warm affection] / receive (a person) with warm hands.

따라가다 **1** (뒤에) follow; (함께) go [come] with; accompany; go in the wake of. ¶길을 ~ follow a path // 나는 너를 따라가고 싶다 I'd like to go [come] with you. // 딸의 졸업식에는 아내가 따라가기로 되어 있다 My wife is going to accompany our daughter to her graduation ceremony. // 계류의 둑을 따라갔더니 작은 호수에 다다랐다 I went up along the bank of the mountain stream and came to a small lake. / Following the course of the mountain stream, I came upon a small lake.
2 [쫓아가다] keep up with; catch up with [to]. ¶따라가 따라잡다 catch up and pass (another) // 전혀 따라가지 못하다 lag way behind (another) // 한 달 동안 학교를 쉬었더니 수학 공부를 따라갈 수 없게 되었다 I was absent from school for a month, so now I can't keep up with my mathematics[(구어) math] class.
3 [겨루다] compete with; be a match for; equal; rival. ¶따라갈 사람이 없다 be peerless / be without a peer // 수학에 있어서 그를 따라갈 사람은 없다 No one can compete with him in mathematics.
4 [쫓아 하다] obey; follow; act upon; bow to. ¶남이 시키는 대로 ~ bow to another's will.

따라다니다 follow (a person) about [around]; shadow; dangle about [after] (a woman). ¶따라다니는 사람 a hanger-on (*pl*. hangers-on) // 그 아이는 엄마를 귀찮게 따라다녔다 The child tagged after her mother. // 어떤 젊은 불량배가 언제나 그녀를 따라다니고 있었다 A young hoodlum was always hanging

따라붙다

around her.// 불안감이 나를 따라다니고 있다 I am haunted by uneasiness.// 그의 주위에는 항상 가십[뜬소문/후문]이 따라다니고 있었다 There was always some gossip about him.// 그는 그 처녀의 꽁무니를 끈질기게 따라다녔다 He persistently chased[ran after] the girl.// 그는 언제나 윤 씨 곁을 따라다닌다 He follows Mr. Yun around like a shadow.

따라붙다 overtake; catch up with[to]; get [come / draw] up with; fetch [close] up with; come level with; (점점) close in upon. ¶후발 메이커가 우리 회사를 바싹 따라붙고 있다 Another manufacturer, who got a later start than we did, is really putting the pressure on us.

따라서 so; accordingly; consequently; therefore; hence; for that reason; (so) that. ¶~ 이상과 같다 (증서의 문구) Therefore as above. / Such is the purpose of the document.// 품질이 좋으니 ~ 값도 비싸다 The article is of fine quality, and consequently the price is high.// 그가 맨 처음에 왔다. ~ 좋은 자리를 잡았다 He came first. Therefore [So / That's why] he got a good seat.

따라오다 1 (뒤에) follow; (함께) come with; accompany; keep up with. ¶개가 집의 문까지 따라왔다 The dog followed[tagged along after] me to the gate of our house.// 따라와 Come (along) with me! / Follow me!/ 정원이 입구까지 따라와서 공손히 인사를 했다 The clerk accompanied us to the entrance and made a very deep bow[bowed deeply].
2 (남이 하는 대로) follow (suit); do likewise [the same]; catch up. ¶그는 우리를 따라오느라고 애를 썼다 He had a hard time catching up with us.
3 [겨루다] compete; rival; equal; be a match for. ¶따라올 사람이 없다 have no equal [match] / be without a match[peer]// 학급에서 영어 실력으로 나를 따라올 사람은 없다 There is no one in our class who can match me in ability in English.

따라잡다 (앞선 것을) catch up (with); overtake. ¶그녀의 차는 내 차를 곧 따라잡고 말았다 Her car easily overtook mine.// 두 번째 주자가 앞 주자를 방금 따라잡았다 The second runner is now overtaking the first runner.// 서구의 수준을 ~ attain[reach] the Western level// 상대 팀을 (동점으로) ~ catch up[pull even] with the other team// 이 품목은 생산이 수요를 따라잡을 것 같지 않다 Production is unlikely to catch up with the demand for this article.// (능력상) 그를 따라잡을 사람은 없다 There is nobody like him. He is beyond comparison[compare].// 세계의 인구 증가율은 식량 생산의 증가율을 곧 따라잡을 것이다 The world population growth will soon catch up with the increase in food production.

따라지 [노름의 한 끗] one point; the lowest point[hand] (in a card game). 2 [보잘것없거나 하찮은 존재] a miserable existence. ¶~ 생활을 하다 live[lead] a wretched life.
● **따라지목숨** a slavish life; a life in bond; a life lived under another's thumb.

따로 1 [별개로] separately; apart; independently. ¶…과는 ~ apart[aside] from … / ~ 살다 live separately// ~ 두다 keep[set] (a thing) separately[apart] / put by / lay aside [by / away / off]// 이 문제를 개인의 이해와는 ~ 생각해 보자 Let's consider this problem apart from personal interests.// 이 섬들은 본토와는 ~ 통치되었다 The islands were governed independently of the mainland.
2 [여분·추가로] extra; additionally; in addition; besides. ¶방세는 9천 원이고 식비는 ~ 치른다 Lodging costs 9,000 won and board extra[board is an extra].// 더 좋은 좌석을 원하시면 ~ 돈을 내야 합니다 You have to pay extra for a better seat.
3 [특별히] particularly; in particular; specially. ¶~ 볼일은 없다 I've nothing very special to attend to.// 그밖에 ~ 이유는 없다 There is no other special reason.

따로나다 set up a branch family; create a new family. ¶내 동생은 따로났다 My younger brother moved out and started[set up] a branch family.

따로내다 make (a person) set up a branch family; make (a person) establish a separate home. ¶아들을 ~ have[let] one's son set up a branch home.

따로따로 [떼어서] separately; apart; [각각으로] each; severally; respectively; individually. ¶~인 (별개의) separate / separated / (흩어진) scattered / (각자의) each / several / respective / ~인 소비자 단체를 통합하다 unite separate[independent] consumer associations// ~ 흩어진 소를 휘몰다 round up scattered cattle// 둘이는 군중 속에서 ~ 흩어졌다 The two got separated (from each other) in the crowd.// 아이들은 부모와 ~ 살고 있다 The children live away[apart] from their parents.// 그들은 ~ 요구하고 있다 They are making their demands independently.// 이것을 하나씩 ~ 싸 주시오 Please wrap each of these separately[these one by one].// 그 목격자들은 ~ 소환되었다 The witnesses were summoned one at a time[one by one].

따르다[1] 1 (뒤를) follow; go after (a person); follow at (another's) heels; track; shadow; dog (a person); (구어) tag along. ¶유행을 ~ follow[run after] the fashion // 시세에 ~ go with the stream// 이야기의 줄거리를 ~ follow the plot of a story// 형사를 따르게 하다 set a detective on (a person / a person's track)// 모두 나를 따르라 Follow me, men.// 영어에서 나를 따를 사람은 없다 No one can come near me in English.// 장관의 뒤를 따라 차관도 사임했다 The Vice-Minister resigned, following the Minister's suit.// 저는 어머니를 따라왔습니다 I tagged along and came with my mother.// 산꼭대기에 이르는 작은 길을 따라갔다 I followed the path that led to the top of the mountain.// 그는 언제나 이기는 쪽을 따른다 He always takes the winning side.// 그들은 범인의 자취를 따라가 그를 찾아냈다 They traced the criminal's tracks and found him.// 내 희미한 기억에 따르면 여기에 샘이 하나 있었다 Going back through my faint memories[Retracting my vague memories], I recall that there was a well here.
2 [본뜬다] follow; follow suit; tread in (a person's) steps; follow in the wake of; [모방하다] imitate; model (after); copy after [from]. ¶전례를 ~ follow[copy after] a precedent// 본을 ~ follow a model// 남의 예를 ~ follow another's example// 옛날 식을 ~ follow the old style// 다른 대도시도 이를

따르고 있다 The practice is being taken up in other large towns.∥프랑스가 찬성하면 유럽의 다른 나라들도 따를 것이다 If France agrees, other European states will follow suit.
3 [입각·의거하다] be based [founded / grounded] on (something); depend [turn / hang / hinge] on (something). ¶사실에 따른 이야기 a story based upon fact∥따라야 할 기준 a rule to go by / an authoritative rule∥그의 권고에 따라 on his advice∥관례에 따라 in conformity with [according to] custom∥귀하의 부탁에 따라 at your request / in compliance with your request∥교칙 제5조에 따라 under [in pursuance of] Art. 5 of the school regulations∥진급은 근무 연수에 따른다 Promotion goes by length of service.∥순서에 따라 설명해 주십시오 Please explain them in order.∥그 나라의 급속한 공업화에 따라 대학 지망자가 늘어났다 With the rapid in industrialization of the country, the number of college applicants has increased.∥한불 양문(兩文)에 차이가 있을 경우에는 불문에 따른다 The French version will prevail if discrepancies exist between it and the Korean version.∥선생님의 가르침에 따라 열심히 노력하라 Respond to your teacher's instruction by working hard.∥보수는 작업량에 따라 지불된다 You will be paid according to the amount of work you do.∥수입에 따라 세금이 부과된다 We are taxed in proportion to our income.∥음악회에 가느냐 안 가느냐는 프로그램에 따라서이다 Whether I go to the concert or not depends on the program.
4 [수반하다] accompany; follow; be followed by; attend on; be attended [accompanied] by; be consequent upon. ¶…에 따르는 폐해 the evil effects attendant upon …∥…에 따르기 마련이다 always accompany [go with] …∥곤란이 따를 것이다 be attended with [by] difficulties∥죄악에는 불행이 따른다 Miseries are attendant upon vice.∥여자에게는 허영이 따르기 마련이다 Vanity is a vice peculiar [common] to women.∥전쟁에는 여러 가지 나쁜 일이 따른다 War brings many evils in its train.∥등산에는 커다란 위험이 따른다 Mountain climbing involves great risks.∥권리에는 (당연히) 의무가 따른다 Rights come together with duties. / Rights are accompanied by duties. / Rights and responsibilities go hand in hand.∥돈벌이에는 위험이 따르게 마련이다 We cannot make money without taking risks.
5 [복종·준수하다] obey; follow; yield; submit [give in]; conform (oneself) to; act on [upon]. ¶충고를 ~ take [follow] (a person's) advice / heed [listen to] a warning∥규칙을 ~ comply with the rule∥남의 뜻을 ~ submit [resign] oneself to another's will / yield [bow] to another's will∥교칙을 ~ obey school regulations∥대세에 ~ conform to the times∥관례를 ~ observe a custom∥그는 이치에 따르는 사람이다 He is open to conviction.∥우리는 판결에 따를 수밖에 없다 We have no choice but to abide by the verdict.∥정부의 방침에 따라 에너지를 절약하려고 한다 We are trying to conserve energy in accordance with Government policy.
6 [좋아하여 붙좇다] take (kindly) to (a person); love; like; be fond of; be attached to

(a person); be tamed. ¶따르게 하다 make [get] (another) attached to one / win (a person's) heart∥그 아이는 아버지를 따른다 The child is fond of his father.∥아이들은 모두 그녀를 잘 따랐다 All the children were attached to her. / She was loved by all the children.∥그녀는 아주 매력적이어서 뭇 남성들이 따랐다 She was so attractive that a great many gentlemen used to court her.∥남자 아이들은 새로 온 선생님을 이내 따랐다 The boys soon took [became attached] to the new teacher.∥그의 개는 사람을 잘 따른다 His dog likes people.∥그 개는 좀처럼 나를 따르지 않았다 It took a long time for me to win the dog over. / The dog didn't take to me easily.

따르다² pour (in / out); fill (a cup with coffee). ¶차를 ~ pour tea∥유리컵에 물을 ~ fill a glass with water∥컵에 우유를 ~ pour milk into a cup∥술을 잔에 반쯤 ~ [fill] a cup half full of wine∥술을 ~ pour out wine / fill a glass with wine / serve wine∥제가 따르겠습니다 Let me serve.∥그녀는 손님으로 온 사람에게 차를 따라 드렸다 She poured (out) a cup of tea for each of the guests.∥찬물을 좀 더 따라 주십시오 Please pour in some more cold water.∥한 잔 더 따를까요 You want a refill?∥그녀는 수프를 접시에 따라 내놓았다 She served the soup in a soup plate.

따르르 1 [구르는 모습] rolling; rumbling. ¶~ 굴리다 roll (a glass bead) over (the floor)∥~ 구르다 roll over and over. **2** [벨 등의 소리] tinkle; jingle. ¶초인종이 ~ 울렸다 The doorbell rang.∥전화가 ~ 울리고 있다 The telephone [phone] is ringing.∥시계가 ~ 울리며 9시를 알렸다 The clock tinkled out the hour of nine.

따름 only; just; merely; simply. ¶…일 ~이다 It is just [only] that ….∥나는 그녀를 만났을 ~이다 I just saw her.∥나는 다만 시간을 물어보고 싶었을 ~입니다 I only wanted to ask you the time.∥내 의무를 다했을 ~입니다 I have done nothing but my duty.∥그는 일개 학생일 ~이다 He is a mere student. / He is nothing but a student.∥당신은 당연한 일을 했을 ~이다 You simply have done what you ought to do.

따리 [아첨] flattery; a salve; sycophancy; bowing and scraping; toadyism.
따리(를) 붙이다 flatter; toady; curry favor with; fawn upon; bootlick.
● **따리꾼** a flatterer; a toady; a sycophant; a bootlicker.

따먹다 1 (장기·바둑 등에서) take; catch; get; seize. ¶(장기에서) 이런, 이 차가 따먹히겠는데 Oh, this cha is in danger of being captured. **2** 〈속〉 (여자를) defile [trifle with] (a girl's) chastity; seduce [dishonor / ruin] (a girl); make a toy of (a woman). ¶그는 여자 따먹기로 유명하다 He plays havoc among girls.

따분하다 1 [지루하다] bored; tedious; tiresome; wearisome. ¶따분한 일상생활 an insipid daily life∥따분한 여행 a tedious [monotonous] journey∥따분한 사람 a dull [tedious] fellow∥따분한 문체 an enervated style∥따분한 책 [강연자] a stodgy book [lecturer]∥따분한 연극 공연 a lifeless performance of a play∥따분한 세상(살이) the dreary world / wearisome life∥따분해 보이다

따스하다

look bored∥따분하게 살다 lead a wretched [an unhappy] life∥따분해 죽겠다 I am bored to death∥세상살이가 따분해졌다 I have got sick (and weary) of life.∥Life seems hollow to me.∥그의 귀국을 기다리다니 따분한 이야기다 It's a slow business waiting for him to return from abroad. **따분히** tediously; tiresomely; wearisomely.
2 [맥없다] weak; feeble; languid; (서술적) feel tired [exhausted / enervated / worn out / done in]. ¶따분한 오후 a slack afternoon∥따분한 날씨 enervating weather∥따분해지다 become weary [tired] (of)∥날씨가 더워서 ~ The heat makes me feel languid. **따분히** weakly; languidly; spiritlessly; in low spirits. ¶~ 앉아 있다 sit exhausted.

따스하다 warm; mild; genial. ¶따스한 스웨터 a warm sweater∥따스한 겨울 a soft [mild / green] winter∥난로가 조금도 따스하지 않다 The fireplace gives out no heat.∥나날이 따스해지고 있다 It is getting warmer day by day.∥왔다 갔다 하여 몸을 따스하게 하였다 I kept myself warm by pacing back and forth.

따습다 comfortably warm; nice and warm.
따오기 [동] a Japanese crested ibis.
따옴표(-標) quotation marks.
따위 1 [등등] and so on [forth]; and [or] the like; and such like; et cetera(약어 etc., &c)(▶ 보통 생략형으로 참고서나 상업문에서 씀. 문중에서는 보통 et cetera라고 읽음. 앞에 콤마를 찍고 and는 붙이지 않음). ¶예를 들면 … ~ such as … / … for example∥케이크나 빵 ~ cakes, bread, and the like∥장난감 ~ toys or the like∥펜이나 잉크 ~ 의 필기도구 writing materials, such as pens, ink, and so on∥그들은 내 나이, 이름 ~를 물었다 They asked my age, my name, and so on.∥그는 그림이며 산수며 음악 ~를 배웠다 He studied painting, arithmetic, music, and the like.
2 [얕잡아 일컫는 데]. ¶그~ 것 such a thing / that sort of thing∥너 ~ 바보 such a fool like you∥이~ 물건 an article of this kind [sort]∥난 돈 ~는 필요 없어 I want no money.∥너 ~가 참견할 일이 아니야 It's none of your business. / You keep out of this.∥너 ~가 할 수 있을 것 같아 You never could do it.∥너 ~는 알 수 없지 You wouldn't understand.∥나에게는 예복 ~는 없다 I do not possess such a thing as a dress coat.∥야구 ~를 하기보다는 책을 읽고 싶다 I would rather read a book than play baseball or anything like that.

따지다 1 [시비를 가리다] distinguish [discriminate] (between right and wrong). ¶잘 잘못을 따지지 않고 (whether) right or wrong / without discussing the rights and wrongs of the case.
2 [조사하다] inquire [investigate / dig] into; [추궁하다] cross-examine; question [examine] closely; inquire severely; demand an explanation of; press (a person) about [for]; [비판하다] criticize; find fault (with); blame (a person) (for). ¶근원을 ~ inquire into the origin∥사건의 배후 관계를 ~ investigate who is pulling the wires∥끝까지 ~ probe (a matter) to the bottom∥호되게 따지고 들다 pass severe criticism (on)∥미심스러운 점을 ~ have a doubtful point explained (by someone)∥그는 따지기를 아주 좋아한다 He is a really inquisitive man.∥조합원은 그녀의 해고 이유를 부장에게 따져 물었다 The union members demanded an explanation of her dismissal from the director.
3 [숫자를 헤아리다] calculate; reckon; count; compute; figure up. ¶대충 따져서 on a liberal calculation∥비용을 ~ calculate expenses∥손익을 ~ reckon [calculate] the profits and losses∥이자를 ~ compute [reckon] interest.

딱 1 [마주치거나 부러질 때 나는 소리] with a bang [crack / crash / smash / pop]. ¶머리를 ~ 부딪히다 bump one's head against (a wall) / crack one's head on (a post)∥~ 부러지다 break with a snap / snap / crack∥노가 ~ 부러졌다 Snap went an oar.∥그의 머리를 ~ 때렸다 I gave him a whack on the head.
2 [갑자기] suddenly; abruptly; unexpectedly. ¶~ 마주치다 meet by chance / meet [stand] face to face with (a person) / (미) run up against (a person)∥~ 멈춰 서다 stop suddenly [short] / come to a standstill∥대답이 ~ 막혔다 I was at a loss for an answer.∥그녀와 길에서 ~ 마주쳤다 I ran against [across] her on the street.∥내 앞에서 차 한 대가 갑자기 ~ 멈춰 섰다 A car stopped suddenly right in front of me.∥시계추가 ~ 섰다 The pendulum came to a dead stop.
3 [단호히] definitely; decisively; positively; resolutely; flatly. ¶~ 잘라 거절하다 refuse flatly [positively] / give a flat [point-blank] refusal∥~ 잘라 말하다 speak flatly∥~ 잡아떼다 [부인하다] give a flat denial∥~ 결심하다 make a grim [firm] resolution / make up one's mind definitely∥그는 내 부탁을 ~ 거절했다 He flatly refused my request.∥그는 ~ 잘라서 대답했다 He gave a definite [decisive] answer.∥그를 ~ 단념했다 I gave up on him completely [entirely].∥그녀는 그 계획을 ~ 단념했다 She gave up the plan with no regrets.∥그녀는 그 남자의 제의를 ~ 거절했다 She flatly declined the man's offer.
4 [활짝 벌어진 모양] wide-open. ¶입을 ~ 벌리고 with one's mouth wide-open / (어안이 벙벙하여) agape∥놀라서 입을 ~ 벌리다 be gape with wonder [surprise]∥두 눈을 ~ 부릅뜨다 open one's eyes wide∥가슴이 ~ 벌어지다 have a broad chest / be broad of chest∥그저 입을 ~ 벌리고 있었다 We simply gaped at it.
5 [정확히] exactly; just; precisely; to a T. ¶~ 맞는 옷 a well-fitting suit∥~ 5시간 five hours to a minute / exactly five hours∥~ 7시에 at seven o'clock sharp∥~ 들어맞다 fit nicely / suit (one) to a T / (말이) fitly apply (to)∥구두가 발에 ~ 맞았다 The shoes fitted my feet just right. / My shoes were an excellent fit.∥계산은 ~ 들어맞는다 The accounts are quite correct.∥그는 내가 생각하고 있던 일을 ~ 들어맞혔다 He guessed exactly what I was thinking.
6 [완전히] perfectly; completely; entirely. ¶담배를 ~ 끊다 give up [quit] smoking once for all∥그 후 그는 발길을 ~ 끊었다 It was his last visit.∥양념이 ~ 알맞다 It is perfectly seasoned.∥(우는 아이에게) ~ 그쳐 Stop crying!∥아첨은 ~ 질색이다 I hate flattery.∥비가 ~ 멎었다 The rain has stopped.

//편지가 ~ 끊겼다 The correspondence ceased entirely. / The letters stopped coming once and for all.//아내가 죽은 후에 그는 담배를 ~ 끊었다 After his wife's death he never smoke again[he completely gave up smoking].

7 [찰싹] close(ly); tight(ly). ¶~ 들러붙다 stick fast (to)//~ 붙어 앉다 sit closely together / sit close to each other//그 아이는 엄마에게 ~ 달라붙어 있었다 The child clung to his mother.

8 [꼭] only; just; but. ¶~ 한 번 only[but] once//~ 한 마디만 하다 say just a word//~ 한 잔만 더 마시다 have just one more glass (of wine).

9 [굳세게 버티는 모양] firmly; stubbornly. ¶~ 버티고 서다 stand firm (against) / won't yield[budge] a step[an inch].

딱따구리 [동] a woodpecker.

딱따기 1 [야경 돌 때 치는 나무토막] wooden clappers. ¶~를 치다 beat[strike] (wooden) clappers. **2** [나무토막을 치며 야경 도는 사람] a night watchman.

딱딱 1 [마주치는 소리] with claps[crashes / cracks / bangs]; plop, plop. ¶손뼉을 ~ 치다 clap one's hands. **2** [부러지는 소리] with snaps[cracks]; snappingly. ¶~ 부러지게 snap in[to] pieces//손가락 마디를 ~ 소리내다 crack (the joints of) one's fingers//그는 공포로 이를 ~ 부딪쳤다 His teeth chattered with fear.//돌을 ~ 부딪쳐 신호를 했다 I gave a signal by knocking[hitting] stones together.

딱딱거리다 〔을러대다〕 speak harshly [roughly / snarlingly / roughly]; be strict [severe] with. ¶…에게 ~ snap at a person / nag (at) a person//딱딱거리면서 snappishly//너무 딱딱거리지 마라 Don't speak so harshly.//우리 주인은 노상 딱딱거리기만 한다 Our master is always nagging and scolding.

딱딱하다 1 [단단하다] hard; solid; tough; stiff; rigid. ¶딱딱한 침대 a hard bed//가죽처럼 딱딱한 비프스테이크 a beefsteak as tough as leather//말라서 딱딱해지다 be dried and hardened//이 연필은 ~ This pencil has hard lead[is hard].
2 [엄하다] strict; severe; (표정 등이) stern; rigid; [융통성이 없다] hard-boiled; hidebound; leathery. ¶딱딱한 표정 a stern look //딱딱한 관습 rigid customary practices//그는 그 말을 듣더니 표정이 딱딱해졌다 His expression hardened[stiffened] when he heard it.//그의 딱딱한 태도에 기가 죽있다 I winced at his rude[rough / overbearing] manner(▶ overbearing은 고압적인 태도).//그는 미인 앞에서는 흥분해서 딱딱해진다 He become nervous and stiff[(구어) get all tied up in knots] in the presence of beautiful women.
3 [문어적·형식적이다] bookish; stiff; formal; serious; [진지하다] grave; sober; ceremonious; (미국 구어) stuffy. ¶딱딱한 문체 a stiff [bookish] style//딱딱한 관청 용어 (formal) officialese//딱딱한 얼굴을 하다 look grave [solemn]//그는 어지간히 딱딱한 사람이다 He is very punctilious.//그가 쓴 글에는 딱딱한 표현이 많다 His writings are full of bookish expressions.//그가 말하는 영어는 ~ He speaks in bookish English.//딱딱한 이야기는 그만두자 Let's not talk about serious matters[Let's talk about lighter topics].//그렇게 딱딱하게 생각지 마세요 Please take it easy.

딱부리 a lobster-[bug-]eyed person; a person with huge and bulging eyes; a person with goggle[pop] eyes.

딱새 [동] a redstart.

딱성냥 a lucifer match; a friction match. ¶~을 긋다 strike[light] a match.

딱정벌레 [동] a ground beetle.

딱지¹ **1** (부스럼의) a (dried) scab; a crust; a slough. ¶부스럼에 ~가 앉았다[퇴자] A scab formed over the boil. //~가 덜 떨어졌다 The scab peeled away[went off / has come off]. **2** [종이의 티] a fleck in paper. **3** [게·소라·거북 등의 껍데기] a shell; a carapace. ¶게 ~ a carapace//거북의 등~ (a) tortoise[turtle] shell//소라의 ~ the shell of a turban shell. **4** (시계의) a (watch) case. ¶금~ 시계 a gold watch / a watch in a gold case//시계의 뒤~ the back of a watch case.

딱지² 〔거절〕 rejection; refusal; (퇴짜) a setdown; a rebuff. ¶~를 놓다 refuse / reject / snub / give (a person) a rebuff / (구혼자에게) give (a suitor) the mitten / kick (a person's proposal)//~를 맞다 be rejected / suffer[meet with] a rebuff / get a snub / (구혼자가) get the mitten / be kicked//그녀는 나에게 ~를 놓았다 She gave me a rebuff.

딱지 (-紙) **1** [종잇조각] a card; a label; a tag; a sticker; a stamp. ¶우표~ a postage stamp //~를 붙이다 label / put a tag (on an article)//~가 붙어 있는 여행 가방 a suitcase with stickers on//그 가방에는 「취급 주의」라고 ~가 붙어 있었다 The trunk was labeled "Handle with care."
2 [악평] a bad[an evil] reputation; ill fame; notoriety. ¶~ 붙은 notorious / regular//~ 붙은 깡패[사기꾼] a notorious scoundrel [swindler]//그에게는 부정직하다는 ~가 붙어있다 He has a bad reputation of being dishonest.
3 (교통 위반의) a (traffic) ticket. ¶주차 위반 ~ a parking ticket//~를 떼다 ticket (a traffic offender)//~를 떼이다 get a traffic ticket.
4 (딱지치기의) a picture card used in a children's game.

딱총 (-銃) a popgun; [폭죽] a (fire) cracker; a squib.

딱하다 1 [가엾다] pitiable; pitiful; poor; miserable; [안됐다] sorry; regrettable; too bad. ¶딱한 사정 a pitiable circumstance//딱하게도 sorry[sad] to say//딱한 사정을 호소하다 appeal for another's sympathy / plead for mercy//…이라니 ~ it is a (great) pity that //부모가 갑자기 돌아가셨으니 남아 있는 아이들이 ~ The plight of the children, left alone in the world by their parents' sudden death, is heartrending[enough to bring tears to the eyes].//아들의 행방을 찾아다니는 그녀의 모습은 참으로 딱했다 She made a truly tragic[pathetic] sight, searching for her lost son.
2 [난처하다] embarrassing; awkward; troubled. ¶딱한 처지에 놓이다 be in an awkward situation / be in a nice[bad] fix//딱하게도 내게 돈이 없다 The trouble is that I have no money.//일이 딱하게 되었다 Things have

come to a pretty pass(▶ pass는 사람이 주어일 때는 쓰지 못함).

딱히 [분명히] clearly; distinctly; [확실히] certainly; surely; [정확히] (not) exactly. ¶그는 믿을 수 없는 사람이지만 ~ 무능하지는 않다 He is unreliable but not necessarily incompetent.//그것은 어려운 일이나 ~ 불가능하지는 않다 It is difficult but not altogether impossible.//그의 논리는 결함이 있으나 ~ 틀렸다고는 할 수 없다 His reasoning is flawed but not exactly wrong, either.

딴[1] [다른] another; other; different; else; separate. ¶~ 데 (긍정문에서) some other place / (의문·부정·조건문에서) any other place // ~ 방법 another [different] method(s) // ~ 사람 a different person / another person / someone else // 언젠가 ~ 날 some other day // ~ 때에 at another time // 또 가 보실 ~ 곳이 있습니까 Have you any other places to visit? / Are there any other places that you have to visit? // 어디 ~ 곳을 찾아보자 Let's look somewhere else. // 우리 대학의 하기 강습에는 ~ 데 강사를 몇몇 초빙하고 있다 We invite a number of lecturers from outside to [A number of outside lecturers come to speak at] our university's summer seminar. // 누구 ~ 사람에게 물어봐라 Ask somebody [someone] else. // ~ 사람 아닌 네 일이니까 애써서 보겠다 I will do my best for your particular sake. // 이 작품의 연주는 한 씨와 그의 그룹의 ~ 회원들이었다 This piece was performed by Mr. Han and the other members of his group. // ~ 사람들의 결정이야 어떻든 나는 송 씨를 지지하다 Whatever the others decide, I will support Mr. Song. // 무슨 ~ 질문은 없습니까 Do you have any other questions?

딴[2] […으로서는] as; as for (oneself); in one's own way; on one's parts; in one's own estimation. ¶우리들 ~에는 in our own eyes // 내 ~에는 in my thought / as for myself / on my part // 내 ~에는 농담을 한 셈이었다 I intended it to be a joke. / I meant it as [for] a joke. // 내 ~엔 최선을 다한다고 한 것이 이렇게 되었다 Poor as the job is, I have done my best. // 그녀는 제 ~에는 미인이라고 생각하고 있다 She fancies herself beautiful. / She is beautiful in her own conceit.

딴것 another one [thing]; something else; a different thing; (둘 중에서) the other; [다른 여러 개] the others; the rest. ¶~은 젖혀 놓고 before everything else / first of all // ~ 좀 봅시다 Show me another, please. // 이것말고 ~으로 몇 개 보여 주시오 Please show me some others. // 나는 수학 시간에 ~을 하다가 선생님께 들켰다 Our teacher caught me doing something else in the mathematics class. // ~은 아무것도 모른다 I know nothing else.

딴마음 [다른 생각] any other intention; [배반하는 마음] duplicity; a double heart; treachery. ¶~이 있는 double-faced / double-dealing / treacherous // ~이 없는 single-hearted / sincere / devoted // **~이 있다** have an ax to grind / have an ulterior motive // ~을 품다 have two faces / play (a) double game // ~이 있어 그렇게 말한 것은 아니다 I meant no harm in saying that. // 당신에 대해서 ~이 없습니다 I am faithful [loyal] to you.

딴말 **1** [관계없는 말] an irrelevant [improper] remark. ¶~을 하다 digress [wander] from the main subject // ~ 말고 이야기를 계속하라 Keep to the point! // 넌 ~을 하고 있군 You are talking nonsense. / You are getting off on a tangent. **2** [번복하는 말] duplicity; double-dealing. ¶~을 하다 break [go back] one's word [promise] / be double-tongued // 그렇게 굳게 약속했으니 ~은 하지 않겠지 After his solemn promises he cannot back down now. // ~은 안 할 테니 안심해요 You may rest assured that I shall honor my commitment.

딴맛 [본디의 맛에서 달라진 맛] a different taste; a changed taste; [색다른 맛] a particular [peculiar] taste. ¶이 술은 어쩐지 ~이 난다 This liquor tastes changed. // 토마토에는 그 나름의 ~이 있다 Tomato has a peculiar taste of its own.

딴사람 [전과 달라진 사람] a different [new] being; a changed man. ¶그는 ~이 되었다 He was a different [completely changed] man. // 그는 수염을 깎더니 아주 ~이 되었다 He looked quite a different person after shaving off his beard. // 그녀는 완전히 ~이 된 것 같다 She seems to be quite another person now.

딴살림 [따로 삶] living apart; a separate living [livelihood]; [부부의 별거] a separation; limited divorce; [첩을 둠] concubinage. **딴살림하다** live in a separate house; live separately; live apart (from); [첩을 두다] keep [set up] a mistress [concubine]. ¶그 형제는 딴살림하고 있다 The brothers have their own homes.

딴소리 an irrelevant remark; duplicity. ⇨ ¤딴말

딴은 [하기는] indeed; really; well (yes); I see; it is true; to be sure; so you say; [그렇기는 하지만] (It is) true, but ...; though. ¶~ 그렇다 So it is, to be sure. // ~ 네 말이 맞다 Indeed, you are right. / Indeed, so it is. // ~ 네 말이 그럴듯하다 Hearing what you say, it sounds quite reasonable. // ~ 대단한 일은 아니지만 It does not count much, though.

딴전 [관계없는 언동] irrelevant remarks; an irrelevant matter [act]; quite another business; [언행 불일치] an inconsistent behavior; [화제의 일탈] digression; deviation. ¶~을 보다 do another work / neglect one's duty / be negligent of one's duties // ~을 부리다 make irrelevant [unrelated] remarks / miss [get off] the point / digress / speak of a different subject / feign [pretend] ignorance (of) / say what one does not mean // ~을 부려 봐야 소용없어 You can't fool me.

딴채 a house [building] separate [detached] from the main building; an outbuilding; (집) an outhouse.

딴청 irrelevant remarks; quite another business. ⇨ ¤딴전

딴판 [다름] complete difference; dissimilarity; [불일치] disagreement; discord(ance). ¶(아주) ~이다 be quite [completely / entire] different (from) / differ entirely (from) / do not bear comparison with / disagree with // 생각 [의견]이 ~이다 differ completely (from a person) in opinion / have quite different opinion // 그는 사람이 옛날과는 ~이다 He is quite another man now. // 그 읍은 대도시와는 ~으로 조용했다 The town was quiet in con-

딸 a daughter. ¶막내[첫]~ one's last[first] daughter // 큰~ the eldest[oldest] daughter // ~을 시집보내다 marry off one's daughter.

딸가닥 with a rattle. ⇨딸가닥
딸가닥거리다 clatter; rattle. ⇨딸가닥거리다
딸강 with a clang. ⇨딸강
딸강거리다 clink; clang. ⇨딸강거리다
딸그락 with a rattle. ⇨딸그락
딸그랑 with a clang; rattle. ⇨딸그랑거리다
딸기 a strawberry; a raspberry(나무딸기).
● **딸기밭** a strawberry bed[patch]. **딸기 잼** strawberry jam.
딸깍발이 a penurious scholar (who has to wear wooden shoes all the time).
딸꾹질 a hiccup; a hiccough. ¶ 일반적으로 ~로 쓰이며 단수 취급을 함) ¶~을 참다 catch a hiccup // ~을 멎게 하다 stop one's hiccups // 아무리 해도 ~이 멈추지 않았다 No matter what I tried I could not get rid of my hiccups[hiccoughs]. // ~이 나면 숨을 참아 보세요 If you have hiccups, you should hold your breath. **딸꾹질하다** hiccough; hiccup; have the hiccups.
딸리다 [부속되다] be attached[annexed] to; belong to; go with. ¶가스·수도가 딸린 셋집 a house with gas and water // 가구 딸린 방 a furnished room // 5퍼센트의 이자가 딸린 공채 bonds bearing 5 percent interest // 이 책장에는 서랍이 두 개 딸려 있다 This bookcase has two drawers. // 이 상품에는 경품이 딸려 있다 This article comes[is sold] with a free gift. // 국회의원 한 사람에게는 2명의 비서가 딸린다 A member of the National Assembly is provided with two secretaries. // 환자에게 간호원이 딸렸다 A nurse tended the patient.
딸림음(-音) [음] dominant; dominante.
딸림화음(-和音) [음] dominant chord.
딸자식(-子息) my daughter.
땀[1] (흘리는) sweat; perspiration(▶ 사람의 땀을 말할 때 perspiration은 sweat보다 딱딱한 말); (말의) lather; foam. ¶구슬 ~ beads of sweat // 식은 ~ a cold sweat[perspiration] // ~에 젖다 be soaked[dripping] with sweat // ~을 흘리다 sweat / break into a sweat / perspire // ~을 흘리고 있다 be in a sweat / be perspiring // ~을 몹시 흘리다 sweat[perspire] profusely // 몹시 ~이 나다 perspire [sweat] profusely[copiously / heavily] / sweat freely // 구두를 신고 있으면 ~이 난다 My feet get sweaty in my shoes. // 줄줄 ~이 났다 I sweated profusely. / I was streaming with sweat. // ~내는 요법 sweating treatment // 이불을 쓰고 (한바탕) ~을 내다 work up a sweat covering oneself with bedclothes // ~를 내어 감기를 낫게 하다 sweat out a cold // 그는 얼굴의 ~을 닦았다 He wiped the sweat[(the) perspiration] off[from] his face. // ~을 뻘뻘 흘리며 일한 뒤에 마시는 맥주 맛은 각별하다 After you've been working, drenched with sweat, beer tastes especially delicious. // 운동을 조금 했더니 ~이 뺐다 A little exercise made me perspire a bit [slightly sweaty]. // 테니스를 치고 한바탕 ~을 흘렸다 I worked up a good sweat playing tennis. // ~ 흘려 일해서 번 돈을 도둑맞았다 The money I earned by the sweat of my brow was stolen. // 셔츠가 온통 ~에 젖었다 My shirt was thoroughly soaked with sweat. // 우리는 도로 공사에 ~을 흘렸다 We sweated at the road construction work. // 그의 옷은 ~으로 흠뻑 젖어 있었다 His clothes were soaking wet with sweat[perspiration]. // 그는 ~이 비 오듯 했다 He was dripping with sweat. / He was wringing wet with perspiration. // 그들은 ~에 흥건히 젖어 있었다 They were soaked[bathed] in sweat. / They were all sweaty. // 그는 갑자기 ~이 났다 He broke into a sweat[broke out in perspiration]. // 목욕탕에서 ~을 씻고 나니 개운했다 I felt refreshed after washing my sticky [sweaty] body in the bath. // 그는 ~ 흘려서 벌어 먹고 살았다 He lived[earned his living] by the sweat of his brow. // 우리는 손에 ~을 쥐고 경기를 구경했다 We watched the game in breathless excitement[with breathless attention].
땀(을) 빼다 [수고하다] sweat (with heavy work, etc.); [애먹다] suffer severely; sweat (it out); have a hard time of it. ¶일하느라 ~ have a hard time in doing a job / 그 문제를 푸느라고 ~ take great pains to solve the problem / have a hard time in solving the problem / 아버지한테 꾸중을 듣느라 땀을 뺐다 I had to sweat through a lecture from my father.
땀[2] (바느질의) a stitch.
땀기(-氣) a bit[trace] of sweat; a slight sweat. ¶~가 있다 be a little bit in sweat / have a bit of sweat (in one's palm).
땀나다 [몹시 힘들거나 애가 쓰이다] be hard [toilsome]; take pains. ¶땀나는 일 a hard [an onerous] job / a thing hard to bear / a horrible sweat / 그 숙제는 정말 땀나더라 The homework was really a horrid sweat.
땀내 the smell of sweat. ¶~ 나는 옷 clothes stinking with[of] sweat // ~ 나다 smell [stink] of sweat / 그에게서 ~가 났다 He smelled of sweat. // 내 운동복에서 ~가 난다 Your sportswear smells sweaty[reeks of sweat].
땀띠 prickly heat; (미) (a) heat rash; [의] miliaria. ¶~ 나다 have (an attack of) prickly heat / suffer from prickly heat / 목덜미가 H으로 끈적거리더니 ~가 났다 My neck got sticky with perspiration, and it developed heat rash. // 갓난아기가 ~가 났다 The baby is suffering from prickly heat.
● **땀띠약** prickly heat powder; baby powder; talcum powder.
땀받이 a sweat shirt; (속옷) an undershirt; underwear; (모자 안쪽에 댄) a sweatband; (말의 안장 밑의) sweat clothes.
땀방울 beads[drops] of sweat. ¶그의 이마에 ~이 맺혀 있었다 Beads[Drops] of sweat stood out on his forehead. / The sweat stood in beads on his forehead.
땅[1] 1 (대지) the earth; [지면] the ground; [육지] land. ¶하늘과 ~ heaven and earth // ~ 끝 the end(s) of the earth // ~에서 3미터 위에 three meters above the ground // ~을 파다 dig in the ground // ~을 고르다 roll [level] the ground / grade the ground // ~에 묻다 bury (a thing) in the ground // ~이 꺼졌다 The ground gave way[collapsed / sunk]. // ~ 파 봐라, 돈이 나오나 Do you think money

땅 grows on trees? 그는 ~이 꺼지라고 한숨을 내쉬었다 He gave[let out] a deep sigh. **2** [토지] land; ground; a piece[lot / plot] of land; a landed property. ¶개인 ~ privately-owned land // 부자가 great land owner // 넓은 ~ a large tract of land / broad acres // 좁은 ~ a small piece[a patch] of land // 금싸라기 같은 ~ ground which is worth its weight in gold // 35만 평방피트의 ~ land covering 350,000 square feet // ~을 가지다[팔다 / 사다 / 빌리다] own[sell / buy / lease] a lot[a piece of land] // ~을 놀려 두다 keep land idle.

3 [토양] soil; earth; land. ¶메마른 ~ poor [barren] soil // 기름진 ~ fertile[rich] soil // ~을 갈다 till the soil[ground] / cultivate land // ~을 걸우다 enrich[fertilize] the soil // ~이 벼농사에 적당치 않다 The soil is not fit for rice culture.

4 [영토] (a) territory; a land. ¶~을 넓히다 extend one's territory // 이국~에서 죽다 die in a strange land[a foreign country] // 그는 1940년에 처음으로 한국의 ~을 밟았다 He first set foot on Korean soil in 1940.

5 [고장] a district; an area; [장소] a place. ¶인삼은 금산 ~의 명물이다 Insam(Ginseng) is the principal product in Geumsan area. // 그들은 안주할 ~을 찾아서 헤매었다 They wandered searching for a place where they could live peacefully.

땅 짚고 헤엄치기(속담) a walk in the park; a piece of cake; as easy as pie.

땅² bang; with a clang. ⇨ 탕
땅강아지 [동] a mole cricket.
땅개 1 [키가 몹시 작은 개] a dog having short legs. **2** [작고 뚱뚱하며 잘 싸다니는 사람] a dumpy[short and plump] gadabout.
땅거미 [저녁 어스름] dusk; twilight; crepuscule. ¶~ 진 twilight / crepuscular // ~가 질 무렵에 at the dusk of the evening / in the gathering dusk / at dusk[twilight] // ~가 졌다 The dusk gathered. / Dusk fell.
땅굴 (-窟) **1** [땅속으로 길게 뚫린 굴] a tunnel; an underground way[passage]. ¶~을 파다 build[bore / excavate] a tunnel (through a mountain). **2** [땅을 깊숙이 파서 만든 구덩이] a dugout.
땅기다 be cramped; have a cramp[stitch]. ¶옆구리가 ~ have a stitch in the side // 그는 다리의 근육이 땅겼다 He had a cramp in his leg.
땅꾼 a snake catcher[dealer].
땅덩이 [지구] land; the earth; [국토] a territory; [대륙] a continent. ¶넓은 ~ a large [big] tract of land // 한국은 인구가 많고 ~좁은 나라다 Korea is a narrow, overpopulated country.
땅딸막하다 thickset; short and thick; fat and short; pudgy; stocky; stodgy; chunky. ¶땅딸막한 사내 a stocky man // 그녀는 ~ She is a dumpy[short and plump] woman.
땅딸보 a pudge; a stocky[dump] man; a chunky fellow.
땅땅거리다 1 [호화롭게 살다] live in a grand [an extravagant] style; live like a prince; be quite well off; live on the fat of the land; enjoy great prosperity. ¶그녀는 이제 큰 저택을 사서 땅땅거리며 산다 Now she has bought a mansion and is living on the fat of the land. **2** [큰소리치다] talk big[tall / high-handedly / high and mighty]; swagger. ¶그는 대학에 들어갈 자신이 있다고 땅땅거리고 있다 He is bragging that he is confident to pass the college entrance exam.

땅뙈기 [구획된 토지 조각] a patch of land; [얼마 안 되는 논밭] a small plot[piece] of land[field].
땅마지기 a few acres of field.
땅문서 (-文書) a land registration certificate.
땅바닥 [땅의 맨바닥] the (bare) ground; [땅의 거죽 부분] the surface of the earth [land]. ¶~에 주저앉다 sit[squat] on the (bare) ground // ~에 눕다 lie on the bare earth // ~은 아직 젖어 있다 The ground [surface of the land] is still wet.
땅버들 [식] a pussy willow. ⇨ 갯버들
땅벌 [동] a (digger) wasp; a mud dauber.
땅벌레 [동] a grub; the larva of a ground beetle.
땅볼 [야구] a grounder; a ground ball. ¶내야 ~ an infield grounder // ~을 치다 hit [ground ball] (to short) // ~ 안타를 치다 hit into the dirt // 그는 3루~로 아웃이 되었다 He grounded out to third.
땅속 ¶~의 underground / subterranean // ~에 in[under] the ground / underground // ~에서 사는 동물 an earth animal // ~에서 파내다 dig out of the ground / unearth(보물을) // ~에 매몰되어 있다 be buried in the earth [ground].
땅임자 a landowner; a landholder; a landlord.
땅콩 [식] a peanut; (영) a monkey nut; (미) a groundnut.
땋다 braid (one's hair); plait. ¶머리를 땋은 소녀 a girl in her braid / a pigtailed girl // 머리를 한 가닥으로 ~ plait hair into a pigtail // 머리를 땋아 늘이다 wear one's hair in a plait [pigtail / queue / tail / in (two) braids].

때¹ 1 [시간·시각] time; an hour; a moment. ¶~를 알리는 종소리 an hour bell // ~가 되면 [오면] in due course of time / in (due) time / with time // (하루의) 이맘~에 at this time (of day) // 아침은 공부하기에 가장 좋은 ~다 Morning is the best time for study. // 그러다 보면 알게 된다 Time will tell. // 비가 뿌리기 시작했을 ~마침 택시가 지나갔다 It had just begun to sprinkle when luckily a taxi came by. // 내가 막 자려고 할 ~ 전화가 걸려 왔다 There was a telephone call just when I was getting ready for bed. // 식사 ~에 방문해서는 안 된다 You should not call on a person at mealtime.

2 [경우] a case; an occasion; time; a conjuncture. ¶어느 ~라도 at all times / at any time / under all circumstances // 급할 ~는 in case of (an) emergency // ~와 장소에 따라서는 should time and circumstances permit and place // ~와 장소를 가리지 않고 without the least respect[regardless] of time and place // ~에 따라서는 as occasion requires [demands] / as the case may be // 무슨 일이 있을 ~는 should emergency arise / in case [time / the hour] of need // 마침 좋은 ~ just at the right moment / just in time (for) // 다음에 상경할 ~는 함께 가자꾸나 Let's go together the next time I go to Seoul. // 그에게 비밀을 털어놓을 ~는 바로 지금이다 Now is the time to confide in him. // 이제 슬슬 은퇴할 ~가 아닌가 Isn't it about time you retired? // 그것은 ~와 경우에 달렸다 That depends (on the time and the situation).∥~가 ~이니만큼 언행을 조심하시오 As the situation is delicate, you should be careful of what you say and do.∥~를 가리지 않고 전화를 걸어 온다 He calls me whenever [at any hour] he likes.∥이 마을은 태풍이 지나갈 ~마다 큰 피해를 입는다 Every[Each] time a typhoon hits the town, there is great damage.∥울고 있을 ~가 아니다 This is no time for tears.∥이 옷은 어느 ~라도 입을 수 있다 This dress can be worn on all occasions.

3 [기회] an opportunity; a chance; [시기·계절] (a) time; season; time of the year; [순간] a moment. ¶추수 ~ the harvest time∥~를 못 만난 영웅 an unappreciated hero∥아주 좋은 ~ a golden opportunity∥~를 기다리다 wait[bide] one's time / wait for a favorable chance∥~를 놓치다 miss an opportunity∥~를 만나다 have a favorable opportunity / have one's day[time of prosperity] / have luck / get a chance / find an opportunity∥~를 타다 avail oneself of on opportunity∥~가 좋지 못하다 It is not a favorable moment [time].∥지금은 배꽃이 만발할 ~다 It is the height of the pear blossom season now.∥~는 8월 한여름이었다 It[The time] was August in the middle of summer.∥그는 ~가 오면 운이 트일 거라고 믿고 있었다 He was sure better times were coming.∥모든 것은 다 ~가 있는 법이다 There is a time for everything.∥이제 ~가 왔다 Now is our chance.∥우리는 ~를 기다리고 있다 We are waiting on the lookout for an opportunity.

4 [시대·당시] the times; the time; the day. ¶아직 젊었을 ~ when I was still young∥전쟁 ~에는 in wartime / in time of war∥그가 떠날 ~는 건강한 모습이었다 He looked well when he left.∥그 무렵은 어려운 ~였다 Times were hard then. / Those were hard times.∥그는 젊었을 ~는 엉뚱한 짓도 했었다 He did reckless things in his day[when he was young].

5 [끼니] a meal; mealtime. ¶~를 거르다 go without a meal∥간신히 ~를 잇다 eke out a scanty livelihood∥두 ~ 굶다 miss[skip / do not have] two meals∥하루 한 ~밖에 못 먹었다 I had only one meal a day.

때 아닌 [제 때가 아닌] unseasonable; untimely; inopportune; out of season; [뜻하지 않은] unexpected. ¶~ 꽃 a blossom out of season / off-season flowering(꽃이 핌)∥~ 손님 an unexpected visitor∥~ 폭풍 an unseasonable storm∥그녀의 ~ 죽음 her untimely death∥~ 시각에 at an unseasonable hour / [한밤중이나 새벽의] at an ungodly hour.

때 없이 [아무 때나] (at) any (old) time; regardless of the time; at irregular intervals; irregularly. ¶~ 밥을 달라다 ask for food at any old time∥~ 나갔다 들어왔다 하다 go in and out regardless of the time.

때² 1 [더러움] dirt; filth; grime; [물때] scale. ¶~투성이의 dirty / filthy / ~ 묻은 옷 soiled [dirty] clothes∥~가 끼다 become dirty / become filthy[soiled]∥~를 밀다 wash off the dirt / wash oneself∥흰 장갑은 ~를 잘 탄다 White gloves soil easily.

2 [메부수한 티] unrefinedness; [촌티] rusticity. ¶~ 묻지 않은 소녀 an innocent [unsophisticated] girl∥~를 벗은 refined / elegant / chic / smart / polished / (취미가) in good taste / (시골티를 벗은) free from boorishness∥~를 못 벗은 unpolished / unrefined / uncouth / rustic∥아직 ~ 묻지 않은 양심 a conscience as yet clear∥~ 묻은 정치가 a tainted politician∥조금도 ~ 묻지 않은 생활을 하다 lead a life pure from any blemish∥그녀는 시골에서 온 지 얼마 안 되기 때문에 아직 ~를 벗지 못했다 The maid hasn't yet got the hayseed out of her hair.

3 [누명] a false[an unjust] charge; [오명] a slur; a stain; a blot; disgrace; dishonor. ¶도둑의 ~를 벗다 clear oneself of a false charge of theft.

때까치 [동] a bullheaded shrike; a butcher-bird.

때깔 the color and charm (of cloth); the colorful pattern (of cloth).

때꾼하다 (눈이) be sunken[hollow] (from exhaustion). ¶그는 눈이 ~ His eyes have sunken.

때늦다 too late. ¶때늦게 핀 꽃 late-blooming flowers∥때늦게 발표된 성명 a belated statement which is now too late∥때늦은 감이 있지만 당국은 그 사건에 손을 댔다 The authorities began to examine the matter, though it was rather too late.

때다 [땔감 등을 태우다] burn; kindle; [불을 붙이다] make[build] a fire; stoke(보일러 등에). ¶석탄[장작]을 ~ burn coal[wood]∥난로를 ~ make a fire in the stove∥방에 불을 ~ heat a (hypocausted) room∥땔거리가 없다 have nothing to make a fire with / run out of fuel / have no fuel∥불을 ~ light a fire.

때때로 [가끔] sometimes; (every) now and then[again]; occasionally; [이따금] once in a while; [드문드문] at intervals. ¶맑은 후 ~ 흐림 Fair, occasionally cloudy.∥흐린 후 ~ 비 Cloudy, with occasional rain.∥~ 그에게서 편지가 온다 I hear from him once in a while[at intervals].∥~ 시골에 간다 Sometimes I go to the country.∥그는 ~ 나를 찾아온다 Occasionally[Every now and then] he drops in on me.

때때옷 a colorful dress for children.

때때중 [나이 어린 중] a young Buddhist monk.

때려눕히다 knock[strike / batter] (a person) down; floor (a person) (with a fist); beat (a person) to pulp; stretch (a person) on the ground. ¶여지없이 ~ pommel (a person) to a jelly∥여럿이 함세하여 ~ make a combined attack on (a person)∥나는 화가 나서 그 녀석을 때려눕히고 싶을 정도였다 I was so furious I could have beaten him to a pulp.

때려죽이다 knock[strike / beat] (a person) to death.

때려치우다 give[throw] up; quit; abandon; relinquish. ¶학교를 ~ give up[withdraw from] school∥장사를 ~ quit one's business∥직장을 ~ throw up one's job∥법률 공부를 때려치우고 미술 공부를 하다 abandon law for art∥그녀는 무대 생활을 때려치웠다 She abandoned her stage career.

때로 according to circumstance; on occasion; sometimes; in some cases; occasionally; once in a while. ¶그도 ~ 실수를 한다 Even he makes a mistake once in a while[at

때리다 [후려치다] beat; strike; knock; hit; thrash; give [deal / deliver] (a person) a blow; punch; (손바닥으로) slap; (몽둥이로) drub; club. ¶뭅시 ~ give a beating [whipping] (to a naughty child) / (엉덩이를) spank (a child) // 얼굴을 ~ hit a person in the face // 머리를 ~ hit a person on the head // 멍이 들도록 ~ beat a person black and blue // 아버지는 말을 듣지 않는 아들의 귀싸대기를 때렸다 The father boxed his unruly son's ears. // 어린이의 머리를 때려서는 안 된다 You mustn't hit kids on the head. // 그의 뺨을 한 대 때려 줘라 Give him a slap on the cheek. // 비[바람]이 창을 세차게 때렸다 The rain[wind] lashed [raged] against the window. // 그는 오늘 공을 잘 때리고 있다 He is hitting the ball well today. // 선생님은 개구쟁이 소년의 엉덩이를 세게 때렸다 The teacher gave the naughty boy a good spanking. // 파도가 해안을 때리고 있었다 The waves were pounding against the shore. **2** [비난하다·공격하다] attack; charge; criticize; denounce. ¶신문에서 ~ attack [pound / traduce] (a person) in the press // 신문은 그녀의 스캔들을 호되게 때렸다 She was attacked [criticized] severely in the newspaper for causing such a scandal.

때려 부수다 smash up [in / down]; shatter; break [tear] down. ¶낡은 담장을 ~ knock an old wall down // 집을 ~ tear down a house.

때마침 opportunely; seasonably; timely; in the very nick of time; in good time; [때에 알맞게] fortunately; luckily; as good luck would have it. ¶~ 나타나다 make a timely [an opportune] appearance // ~ 내린 비로 야구 경기는 중단되었다 As it started raining, the baseball game was called off. // ~ 그가 왔다 He happened to come just then. // ~ 전화벨이 울렸다 Just then [At that very moment] the telephone rang.

때맞다 [기회가 좋다] timely; seasonable; opportune; well-timed. ¶때맞은 비 a timely rain // 때맞은 원조 timely aid // 때맞은 말 a seasonable [an opportune] remark // 그 제안은 때맞게 제출되었다 The suggestion came at a seasonable time.

때문 ¶~에 because (of) / on account of / owing to / by [for the] reason of / as / since / for / due to / thanks to // 무엇 ~에 for what reason / on what grounds [account] // …이 없기 ~에 for want [lack] of // 우천 ~에 소풍이 연기되었다 The excursion has been postponed because [on account] of the rain. // 짙은 안개 ~에 그들은 착륙하지 못했다 Owing to the dense fog, they were not able to land. // 너 ~에 창피를 당할 뻔했다 Thanks to you, I almost humiliated myself. // 그가 저지른 큰 실수 ~에 우리 계획은 수포로 돌아갔다 Owing to his blunder, our plan fell through. / His bungling upset our plans. // 최근의 물가 상승 ~에 사람들이 시달리고 있다 People are suffering as a result of the recent rise in prices. // 그가 경솔했기 ~에 우리는 큰 곤경에 빠졌다 His rashness caused us a great deal of trouble. // 그는 단지 그 한 문제를 풀지 못했기 ~에 낙방했다 He failed simply [just] because he couldn't solve that one problem. // 바로 그 ~에 그가 부산에서 서울로 올라온 것이다 For that very reason he came to Seoul from Busan. // 내가 일찍 일어난 것이 이 ~이었다 It was for this purpose that I got up early. // 그가 병이 든 것은 틀림없지만 성공하지 못하는 것은 그 ~만은 아니다 He is certainly sickly, but it is not only on that account that he never succeeds. // 그는 여러 마일의 거리를 걸었기 ~에 그 이상 걸을 수 없었다 He had walked so many miles that he was unable to walk any more. // 마을 사람들이 친절히 돌보아 주었기 ~에 그 길손은 곧 건강을 되찾았다 Owing to [Thanks to] the kindness of the villagers the traveler soon recovered his health. // 그는 어리기 ~에 이해하지 못하는 것이다 He can't understand it because he is too young.

때우다 **1** [땜질하다] solder; tinker; braze; [깁다] patch (up) (the trousers); darn (stockings); put [add] a patch on (a coat); sew (in) a patch. ¶솥을 ~ solder [braze] a pot. **2** [대강 넘기다] make shift (with); make (a thing) do [serve the purpose]. ¶…없이 ~ dispense with … / do without … // 도넛으로 점심을 ~ substitute doughnuts for regular lunch / make a lunch of doughnuts // 저녁을 국수로 ~ dine off a bowl of noodle. **3** [액운을 ~]. ¶액운을 ~ forestall a disaster with a lesser sacrifice.

땔감 [땔거리] fuel; firewood(장작). ¶~을 절약하다 save [economize] fuel // 난로의 ~이 떨어졌다 No fuel is left for the stove.

땔나무 [장작] firewood; [섶] brushwood. ¶~를 하러 가다 go firewood gathering.
● **땔나무꾼** a firewood gatherer; [소박한 사람] a simple [naive] person.

땜¹ tinkering; a patchwork; a makeshift. ⇨땜질

땜² [액운] an escape (from). **땜하다** forestall (a disaster) with a lesser sacrifice.

땜납 (─鑞) solder; pewter.

땜장이 a tinker; a tinsmith.

땜질 **1** [때우는 일] tinkering; soldering. **땜질하다** tinker; solder; mend (kettles). ¶이 쇠주전자의 금간 데를 땜질해 주시오 Please solder the cracked spot of this iron pot. / Please mend this iron pot. **2** (옷 등의) a patchwork. **땜질하다** patch up (a paper screen). **3** [미봉책] a makeshift; a patchwork; a stopgap. **땜질하다** temporize.

땟국 dirt; filth; soil. ¶~이 흐르는 옷 soiled [dirty] clothes // 얼굴에 ~이 끼다 have dirt on one's face.

땟물 **1** [자태] a figure; form; one's appearance. ¶~이 휜하다 have a good [graceful] figure / be fair of form / be smart. **2** [더러운 물] dirty [filthy / foul] water; dirt.

땡¹ **1** (노름에서) two cards of the same denomination; a pair. ¶~을 잡다 hold a pair. **2** [행운] (a stroke of) good fortune; (미) a lucky [good] break falling with a windfall; meeting with an unexpected good fortune; having a stroke of good luck.

땡² [종소리] with a clang. ¶종을 ~ 치다 clang a bell.

땡감 [떫은 감] an unripe and puckery [astringent] persimmon.

땡그랑 with a clang (or); clangorously. ¶~

땡그랑거리다 clang; cling; ring; jingle; tinkle. ¶빈 깡통이 땡그랑거리며 굴러 갔다 An empty can went clattering along the road. // 종이 땡그랑거렸다 The bell clanged. // 풍경이 땡그랑거리기 시작했다 A wind bell began to tinkle.

땡땡 ding-dong; clang-clang. ¶(종소리가) ~ 울리다 peal // 망루의 종을 ~ 울리다 ring [clang] the bell of a watch tower // 종이 ~ 울린다 The bell is ringing. // 시계가 ~ 친다 The clock is chiming. // 벽시계가 ~ 쳤다 The clock chimed [went "bong, bong"].

땡땡이 〈속〉 laziness. ⇨게으름

땡땡이중 a mendicant priest who goes around hitting a gong.

땡땡이치다 〈속〉 play hooky; bunk off classes [lessons]; skip [gip / cut] classes.

땡땡하다 hard; tight; taut; compact. ¶땡땡한 근육 a hard muscle // 배가 땡땡해지도록 먹다 stuff [load] one's stomach with food / stuff [gorge] oneself with food / eat one's fill // 암소의 젖이 부풀어 ~ The udders of the cow are bursting with milk.

땡잡다 make a lucky [big] hit; strike a bonanza; (미) hit the jackpot; (구어) make a killing. ¶그는 그 사업에 투자하여 땡잡았다 He had invested in the business and made a killing. // 듣자 하니 증권에서 땡잡았다면서 I hear you've pulled off a nice pile on the stock market.

땡추(중) a priest only in name.

떠가다 float [fly] away. ¶하늘에는 흰 구름이 떠가고 있었다 White clouds are drifting across the sky.

떠꺼머리처녀(-處女) an old maid with a pigtail.

떠꺼머리총각(-總角) an old bachelor with a pigtail.

떠나다 1 [출발하다] start (off); start out; set off [out]; leave; (구어) pull up stakes and move); depart (from); go away [off]; quit; (기차 등이) pull out; (비행기가) take off. ¶여행을 ~ start [set out] on a journey // 그는 중국으로 여행을 떠났다 He started an a trip to China. / He left for China. // 내일 여기를 떠나 서울로 갑니다 I am going to pull up stakes and go to Seoul tomorrow. // 내일 서울로 떠날 예정입니다 I plan to leave for Seoul tomorrow. // 5시에 떠날 예정이오 We are planning to leave [start] at five. // 열차가 역에서 떠났다 The train left the station. // 그 사나이는 나에게 즉시 떠나라고 말했다 The man told me to leave at once. // 그의 떠나가는 뒷모습이 잊혀지지 않는다 I will never forget the sight of his back as he walked away. // 그는 다시는 돌아오지 않겠다면서 파리를 떠났다 He left [(문어) quit] Paris, intending never to return. // 떠나는 사람을 붙잡지 않는다는 것이 내 주의다 I make it a rule never to try to detain a person who wants to leave. / I believe in letting people have the freedom to leave if they want to. // 떠난 사람과는 차츰 사이가 멀어진다 [보지 않으면 소원해진다] Out of sight, out of mind.

2 [있던 곳을 뜨다] separate; part from [with]; fall apart. ¶고국을 멀리 ~ leave one's native land far behind // (새가) 보금자리를 ~ leave the nest // 제자들은 실사회로 떠났다 My pupils went out [set forth] into the world. // 돈이 떨어지니 친구들이 그에게서 떠났다 When his money was gone, his friends drifted away (from him).

3 [물러나다] resign (from) 〔one's post〕; leave [quit] 〔one's post〕; relinquish 〔one's post〕. ¶집[부서]을 ~ leave home [one's post] // 그녀가 무대를 떠난 지 3년이 된다 It has been three years since she left [quit / retired from] the stage. // 지금은 정계를 떠나 있다 I have left [I have nothing to do with] politics now. // 그는 교단을 떠났다 He resigned from [quit] his teaching job.

4 [벗어나다] be estranged from; cut oneself off [from]. ¶마누라가 자기를 떠나 버리니 그는 자포자기의 상태였다 He was in a desperate mood, having been deserted by his wife. // 그 사업은 이젠 내 손에서 떠났다 The undertaking is out of my hands now.

5 [사라지다] fade away; disappear; vanish. ¶그 광경이 내 마음에서 떠나지 않는다 The sight haunts [is always present in] my mind. / I can't forget the sight. // 그날의 비참했던 광경이 머리에서 떠나지 않는다 I cannot forget the cruel sight of that day.

6 [죽다] die; pass away [on]; be gone. ¶내 부친은 2년 전에 세상을 떠나셨다 My father died [passed away] two years ago.

떠내다 1 [액체를] scoop up; dip up; ladle out. ¶국물을 ~ ladle [spoon up] soup // 물고기를 그물로 ~ scoop fish with a net. 2 (나무 등을) scoop up; (돌을) quarry (out). ¶뗏장을 ~ scoop up a chunk of sod [turf].

떠내려가다 be washed [swept / carried] away; drift away [down]. ¶하류로 ~ be carried down the river // 바다로 ~ be washed out to sea // 그 다리는 떠내려갔다 The bridge was carried [washed] away.

떠넘기다 leave [commit] 〔a matter〕 to 〔a person's〕 care. ⇨떠맡기다

떠다니다 1 (공중·하늘을) float (about); fly (about) (공중을); drift (about)(표류하다). ¶하늘을 떠다니는 구름 a floating [drifting] cloud // 배는 물결치는 대로 밤새 떠다녔다 The ship drifted about all night at the mercy of the waves. 2 wander; roam. ⇨떠돌다1

떠다밀다 push; thrust; leave 〔a matter〕 to 〔a person's〕 care. ⇨떠맡기다

떠돌다 1 [방랑하다·헤매다] wander; roam; rove; tramp (abroad). ¶그는 농장에서 잡일로 돈을 벌면서 여기저기 떠돌아다녔다 He wandered from farm to farm doing odd jobs for money. // 그는 30년 동안이나 여기저기 떠돌아다녔다 He drifted from place to place for thirty years.

2 (물 위에) drift (about); be adrift; (뜨다) float; (공중에) float (in the sky); hover. ¶물 흐르는 대로 ~ drift with the current // 매가 공중에 훨훨 떠돌고 있었다 A hawk was circling [wheeling] in the sky. // 연이 바람 부는 대로 떠돌고 있었다 A kite was drifting about at the mercy of the wind. // 작은 배는 나뭇잎처럼 파도에 밀려 떠돌고 있었다 The boat was being tossed about like a leaf by the waves.

3 [소문 등이 퍼지다] get about [abroad / around]; go the rounds; get [take] air. ¶1주일 후에 큰 지진이 일어난다는 뜬소문이 떠돌고 있다 There's a rumor [A rumor is afloat] that there will be a great earthquake in a week. // 그런 소문이 떠돌고 있소 Is there

떠돌이

such a rumor going around?∥괴문서가 그 도시에 떠돌고 있다 A mysterious [strange] document is being circulated throughout the town.

떠돌이 a vagabond; a drifter; (직장을 옮기는) a job-hopper(▶특히 급료가 좋은 자리에); a wanderer; a waif; a tramp; (미) a hobo. ¶~ 노동자 a wandering [migratory] laborer∥그에게는 다소 ~ 기질이 있다 He has a dash [touch] of the Bohemian in him.

● **떠돌이별** [천] a planet. ⇨°행성

떠들다¹ 1 [시끄럽게 하다] make a noise; raise a clamor; be boisterous [uproarious / clamorous]; clamor; [지껄이다] gaggle; gabble [talk] boisterously [clamorously / wildly]; wag one's tongue [jaw] noisily; [외치다] cry; shout; give [utter] a cry. ¶술을 마시고 ~ drink and make merry∥그렇게 떠들면 꾸중 듣는다 You'll catch it, if you make so much noise.∥아이들이 떠들며 [즐겁게] 뛰놀고 있다 The children are romping about [making merry].∥그녀는 떠들기를 좋아한다 She likes to talk. / (사교적인) She is gregarious.

2 [술렁거리다] kick up a row; raise a dust; make a disturbance; [법석대다] make much ado; bustle (about); (make a) fuss (about). ¶하찮은 일로 떠들지 마라 Don't make a fuss about little things.∥이제 와서 떠들어야 아무 소용이 없다 It's no use making a fuss about it now.∥사람들이 이 문제로 떠들고 있다 Public excitement runs high about this question.∥주간지는 흔히 사소한 일로 떠들어 댄다 Weekly magazines often make a great fuss about trifles [(미국 구어) raise a ruckus over nothing].

3 [소문이 크게 나다] be rumored; gossip [talk] about; be in everybody's mouth; create a (public) sensation. ¶학교 전체가 그 화제로 떠들고 있었다 It was the sole topic of conversation at the school.∥그 회사는 망할 거라고들 떠들고 있다 A rumor is current [afloat / in the air] that the firm is failing.

떠들다² [덮인 것을 걷어 쳐들다] turn up [lift / raise] an edge of (an object); lift [take off / undo] (the lid). ¶모기장을 떠들고 자는 애를 들여다보다 lift up an edge of the mosquito net and look at the sleeping baby∥전화 번호부를 떠들어 보다 find out [look for] (a person's) telephone number in the telephone book.

떠들썩하다¹ 1 [시끄럽다] noisy; boisterous; uproarious; clamorous; vociferous; tumultuous (crowd). ¶떠들썩한 웃음소리 gay [merry] laughter∥떠들썩한 여인네들 a gaggle of women∥떠들썩하게 noisily / boisterously / clamorously / uproariously∥군중 속에서 떠들썩한 소리가 들려왔다 There was a stir [commotion] among the crowd.

2 [어수선하다] turbulent; troubled; disturbed; unquiet; agitated. ¶이웃을 떠들썩하게 만들다 disturb the neighborhood∥세상이 ~ We are living in troubled times.

3 [소문이 자자하다] sensational; much discussed; noised about; making the rounds (of); (be) abroad; [야단스럽다] excited; agog; agitated. ¶온 마을이 떠들썩한 소문 a rumor making the rounds of the village∥온 도시를 떠들썩하게 하다 alarm [electrify] the whole town / set the whole town agog∥그 사건은 세상을 온통 떠들썩하게 했다 The affair caused a great sensation [was quite sensational].

떠들썩하다² [떠들려 있다] slightly lifted [raised]. ¶이불 끝이 좀 ~ The end of the quilt is slightly raised.

떠들추다 (비밀을) reveal; disclose; divulge; expose; lay bare; unmask; dig up. ¶사기꾼의 정체를 ~ show (a person) up for a charlatan∥회사의 기밀을 ~ make a public disclosure of the inside affairs of a company.

떠들치다 lift up one side of (an object). ¶이불을 ~ lift up an end of a quilt.

떠듬거리다 stammer; falter. ⇨°더듬거리다2

떠듬떠듬 stammering(ly); stuttering(ly). ⇨°더듬더듬2

떠름하다 1 [약간 떫다] somewhat astringent [puckery / rough]. ¶떠름한 감 a puckery [an astringent] persimmon∥떠름한 포도주 rough wine. 2 [내키지 않다] indisposed; uninterested (in); reluctant; [심드렁하다] sullen; sulky; glum; [미심쩍다] doubtful; suspicious; questionable; unreliable; untrustworthy. ¶떠름한 얼굴을 하다 make a glum [wry] face / look grim [sullen]∥떠름하게 승낙하다 give a reluctant [an unwilling] consent∥떠름하게 대답하다 give a half hearted answer. 3 confounded; confused; flurried. ⇨°얼떨떨하다

떠맡기다 leave [commit] (a matter) to (a person's) care; entrust (a person) with (a task); saddle (a person) with; (가짜 물건 등을) impose (a matter) on [upon] (a person); pass upon. ¶부채를 남에게 ~ saddle one's debts upon another∥일을 강제로 ~ force [thrust / shove (off)] work on (a person)∥나쁜 물건을 ~ palm [impose] a bad article upon (a person)∥나에게 온통 떠맡기지 마라 Don't leave everything to me. / (구어) Don't pass the ball [buck] to me.

떠맡다 1 (일을) undertake; assume; take on (a task); (보호·관리를) be charged with; be saddled with; take charge of; (사업을) take over (another's business); succeed to (a business). ¶큰일을 ~ take a heavy task upon oneself∥(변호사가) 사건을 ~ undertake [be entrusted with] a case∥그토록 많은 일을 떠맡으면 몸을 해친다 If you take on so much work, you will injure your health.∥성가신 일을 떠맡고 말았다 I have a troublesome problem on my hands.∥그가 결근했기 때문에 그의 일도 내가 떠맡게 되었다 Because of his absence I have been saddled with his work on top of mine.∥그가 죽은 뒤에는 누가 그 책임을 떠맡을 것인가 When he is gone, who will take over his responsibilities?

2 [책임지다] answer for; be responsible for; hold oneself responsible for. ¶네가 손해를 보면 내가 떠맡겠다 I'll answer [make up] for your possible losses.∥그는 어떻게 해서 동생의 빚을 떠맡게 되었는가 How did he come to shoulder his brother's debts?∥좋아, 이 싸움은 내가 떠맡겠다 All right, I'll make this my quarrel.

떠메다 lift (a thing) up and shoulder (it); carry [take / bear] (a thing) on the shoulder. ¶한국의 장래를 ~ bear the destiny of future Korea on one's shoulders.

떠밀다 1 [세게 밀다] push; thrust; shove; force aside. ¶문을 ~ push [give a push] at the door // 남을 떠밀어 물에 빠뜨리다 push a person into the water // 어깨로 사람들을 떠밀며 나아가다 shoulder one's way through a crowd. **2** leave [commit] (a matter) to (a person's) care; entrust (a person) with (a task); saddle (a person) with; (가짜 물건 등을) impose (a matter) on [upon] (a person); pass upon.

떠받들다 **1** [받치어 쳐들다] lift up; raise up; hold up; hoist; (구어) boost. ¶떠받들어 담을 넘게 하다 give (a person) a hoist [a boost] over a wall [fence] / boost [hoist] (a person) over a wall [fence] // 그는 그 돌을 한 손으로 떠받들었다 He lifted the stone with one hand.
2 [공경하다] respect; revere; look up to; [섬기다] serve faithfully; take good care of; [추대하다] set up; set (a person) on pedestal; back [bolster] up (a person). ¶남편을 ~ be devoted [attentive] to one's husband / be [make] a good wife // 신(神) [조상]을 ~ worship God [one's ancestors] // 스승으로 ~ look up to (a person) as one's teacher // 우리는 그를 대표로 떠받들었다 We persuaded him to be [to serve as] our representative. // 죽은 후 그는 신으로 떠받들어졌다 After his death, he was deified [was worship(p)ed as a god].
3 [소중히 하다] make [think] much of; take good care of; care much for; hold (a person) dear; pay (one's) attentions to (a person).

떠받치다 support; bolster; prop [shore] up. ¶벽을 기둥으로 ~ support a wall with a post // 지붕을 ~ give support to a roof / hold up the roof // 지팡이로 몸을 ~ support oneself with a stick // 그녀는 창밖을 내다보고 있었다 She was looking out of the window, resting her chin on her hand(s).

떠버리 [수다쟁이] a rattler; a prattler; a chatterbox; a babbler; a gossip(monger); (속어) a chatterbug; [허풍선이] a braggart; (속어) a gasbag.

떠벌리다 [과장하다] exaggerate; brag; blow; talk big [tall]; draw a long bow; [수다떨다] wag one's tongue [jaw(s)]; talk volubly; rattle on [away / off]. ¶그는 자기를 백만장자라고 떠벌리고 다닌다 He advertises himself as [brags about being] a millionaire. // 그는 자랑스럽게 아들의 성공을 떠벌리고 다녔다 He boasted to everyone about [of] his son's success.

떠보다 **1** [무게를 달아 보다] weigh (a thing); check the weight. **2** (사람됨을 ~) measure; try [test] (a person's) character [personality / caliber]; size up (a person). ¶사람의 능력을 ~ put a person through his paces // 사람을 외모로 떠보기란 불가능하다 A man's character cannot be measured by his appearance. **3** (속뜻을) sound; fathom; feel. ¶남의 속을 ~ sound (out) [feel] a person [a person's views] (on a matter) / on tap a person's opinion / fathom a person's thoughts // 의향을 ~ sound (a person's) inclination / sound (a person) on (his) intention.

떠오르다 **1** (공중에) rise (up); be up; float up; rise to [in] the sky. ¶풍선이 하늘에 가볍게 떠올랐다 A balloon rose lightly into the sky. // 해가 떠오르고 있다 The sun is coming up. / The sun is rising above the horizon.
2 (물 위로) rise [come up] to the surface; surface; break the surface; float; float to the top. ¶잠수함이 우리 눈앞에 떠올랐다 A submarine surfaced right in front of us. // 폐수가 못에 흘러들어 물고기가 떠올랐다 Fish came floating to the surface dead because of the waste water that had flowed into the pond.
3 (생각 등이) come [flit / flash / shoot] across [into] one's mind; come into one's head; occur to one; hit [strike] one; burst [dawn] upon one. ¶좋은 생각이 떠올랐다 A good idea occurred to me. / I've got [hit on] a good idea! // 좋은 생각이 떠오르지 않았다 No good ideas occurred to me. / I could think of no bright idea. // 멋진 생각이 퍼뜩 머리에 떠올랐다 A wonderful idea flashed into my mind [(문어) upon me]. / I hit upon [I had] a wonderful idea.
4 [얼굴에 어떤 표정이 나타나다]. ¶그 소식을 듣고 냉소가 그의 입가에 떠올랐다 A cynical smile played about his lips when he heard the news.
5 [존재를 나타내다]. ¶수사선상에 ~ appear on the network of police search.

떠오르는 (샛)별 a rising star; a whizz-kid; a new kid on the block.

떡¹ [음식] *tteok*; (a) rice cake. ¶가래~ *garaetteok* / a long and slender rice-cake // 구운~ roast [toasted] rice cake // 쑥~ *ssukttoek* / a rice-flour cake flavored with mugwort // ~을 빚다 shape dough for cakes.

떡 줄 사람은 꿈도 안 꾸는데 김칫국부터 마신다(속담) Catch the bear before you sell his skin.; First catch your hare (then cook him).

떡 해 먹을 집안(속담) a troubled [trouble-ridden] family.

떡 주무르듯 하다 lead (a person) by the nose; turn [twist] (a person) round [around] one's (little) finger; have (a person) well in hand. ¶영리한 여자라면 너쯤은 떡 주무르듯 할 것이다 Any smart woman can twist you around her finger.

떡² **1** wide-open; exactly; close(ly); firmly. ⇨떡4·5·7·9 **2** [의젓하거나 여유 있는 모양] with a grand air; with dignity; composedly; with great composure.

떡가래 a stick [bar / roll] of rice cake.
떡가루 rice flour (for making rice cakes). ¶~를 빻다 pound rice into flour // ~를 반죽하다 knead dough // ~를 찌다 steam rice flour.
떡갈나무 [식] an oak (tree). ¶~의 quercine / oak // ~의 열매 [도토리] an acorn // ~의 재목 oak.
떡갈잎 leaves of an oak (tree).
떡고물 bean flour (for rice cake).
떡국 *tteokguk*; rice-cake soup (prepared with slices of rice cake, beef, eggs, etc.). ¶~ 한 그릇을 먹으면 한 살 더 먹는다 Every bowl of *tteokguk* means a year to your age.
떡메 (a) paste bait; paste.
떡밥 (a) paste bait; paste.
떡방아 a rice-flour mill. ¶~를 찧다 pound rice into flour / make rice flour.
떡볶이 a seasoned bar rice cake.
떡잎 [식] a seed leaf; a cotyledon; [싹] a bud; a sprout.
떡집 a rice-cake shop.
떨거덕거리다 clatter; rattle. ⇨덜거덕거리다

떨거지 one's folk; one's relatives.
떨구다 →떨어뜨리다
떨기 (한 송이) a bunch; a cluster; (한 그루) a root; a plant. ¶한 ~ 꽃 a bunch of flowers // 한 ~ 장미꽃 a cluster of roses.
떨다¹ (몸을) tremble; quiver; quake; shiver; (진율하다) shudder; thrill; (목소리를) wobble; (진동하다) vibrate. ¶사지를 ~ tremble in every limb // 무서워 덜덜 ~ tremble with fear // 추워서 덜덜 ~ shiver with cold // 방정맞게 무릎을 ~ jiggle one's knee (compulsively) // 현수교를 덜덜 떨면서 건넜다 I was shaking all over as I crossed the suspension bridge. // 그는 입술을 떨며 화를 냈다 His lips trembled in anger. // 그는 목소리를 떨었다 His voice shook [quavered].
떨다² 1 (먼지 등을) sweep[brush] off; shake down; (담뱃재를) knock off. ¶먼지를 ~ dust (furniture) / shake [beat] off the dust // 담요를 ~ shake [beat] a mat [blanket] // 담배 파이프의 재를 ~ knock the ash off one's pipe. 2 [공제하다] deduct; take off[away]; cut off. ¶월급에서 세금을 ~ take tax off one's pay. 3 [팔다 남은 것을 몽땅 팔다] sell off[out]; clear out [off]; close out (a stock of shoes); trade away; dispose of. ¶재고품을 ~ clear out a stock / have a clearance sale. 4 (주머니·돈을) empty. ¶가산을 ~ squander one's fortune // 주머니를 ~ empty one's purse.
떨다³ (애교·엄살을) display; do; show; pretend. ¶극성을 ~ grow impatient / get upset // 애교를 ~ display one's charm / turn on the charm / be profuse of one's smiles // 수다를 ~ wag one's tongue / rattle on // 엄살을 ~ pretend to be in pain.
떨떠름하다 1 (맛이) astringent; puckery. ¶이 감은 ~ This persimmon has a very puckery taste. 2 [내키지 않다] indisposed (to do / for); reluctant; unwilling. ¶그는 우리와 함께 가는 것이 떨떠름한 모양이다 He seems to feel indisposed to come with us. 3 [꺼림칙하다] uneasy; concerned; anxious; nervous; (서술적) weigh on one's mind; lie at one's heart. ¶일은 해결되었으나 뒷맛이 ~ The matter was brought to a settlement but it makes me uncomfortable.
떨떨하다 1 [천하다] mean; shabby; unbecoming; indecent. ¶옷맵시가 ~ be shabbily [poorly] dressed. 2 [내키지 않다] disinclined; indisposed; reluctant; unwilling; (서술적) be in no mood[humor] (to do); have no inclination (to do). ¶그 음식은 먹기가 ~ I don't feel like eating the food. // 거기에 가기가 ~ I'm not very keen on going there. 3 bewildered; puzzled. ⇨얼떨떨하다
떨리다¹ (몸이) shake; tremble; shiver; quake; quiver(가늘게); (목소리 등이) wobble; waver; (현악기 등이) vibrate. ¶무서운 광경을 보고) 공포로 ~ shudder with fear (at the terrible sight) // 추위로 ~ shiver with [from (the)] cold // 분해서 몸이 ~ tremble with anger // 내 손[다리]이 떨렸다 My hands[legs] were trembling [shaking]. // 나뭇잎이 바람에 떨리고 있다 The leaves are trembling in the wind. // 그녀의 목소리는 흥분으로 떨렸다 Her voice shook [trembled / quivered] with excitement. // 나는 온몸이 떨렸다 I trembled all over. // 현(絃)이 떨렸다 The string vibrated. // 화면의 글씨가 떨리고 있다 The letters on the screen are dancing about. // 내 무릎이 부들부들 떨렸다 My knees were knocking together.

떨리다² 1 [먼지 등이 떨어져 나오다] be shaken off; be beaten [thrown] off; fall [come] off; be brushed off. ¶담요의 먼지가 잘 떨리지 않는다 The dust in the blanket won't come out. 2 [떨려 나다] be excluded [plucked / eliminated / removed / left out]. ¶채용 시험에서 떨려 나다 be plucked in the examination for service // 공직에서 떨려 나다 be removed[ousted] from public office / be purged from public life // 품행이 방정치 못하여 학교에서 떨려 나다 be expelled [(것)/ fired] from school for one's misconduct.

떨어뜨리다 1 [아래로 내려지게 하다] drop; throw down; let fall; dump; (고개를) hang [drop] (one's head); droop. ¶다리 위에서 돌을 ~ drop a stone from a bridge // 크림에 바닐라에센스를 몇 방울 ~ add a few drops of vanilla essence to the cream // 고사포로 적기를 ~ shoot [bring down] an enemy plane with antiaircraft guns // 나무를 흔들어 밤을 ~ shake chestnuts off a tree // 컵을 마루에 떨어뜨렸다 I dropped a glass on the floor. // 그녀는 고개를 푹 떨어뜨렸다 Her head slumped forward.
2 [놓치다] miss (one's hold); let slip; drop. ¶공을 ~ miss a ball / fail to catch a ball / fumble (a grounder) // 받았던 공을 ~ muff.
3 [빠뜨려 흘리다] drop; lose. ¶돈[지갑]을 ~ have lost one's money[wallet] // 손수건을 떨어뜨렸어요 You dropped your handkerchief.
4 (지위를) debase; abase; degrade; reduce; lower; (가치 등을) depreciate; detract (from one's merit); take from (the value). ¶선수를 제2군으로 ~ drop a player to the farm team // 가치를 ~ detract [impair] the value / depreciate // 값을 ~ lower [slash / put down] the price // 신용을 ~ lose one's credit (with) / lower [diminish] credit // 위신을 ~ lose one's prestige // 인기를 ~ (사물이 주어) detract from one's popularity // 화폐 가치를 ~ devaluate [devalue] currency / lower the monetary value // 품질을 ~ lower in quality / deteriorate // 식품의 품질을 ~ adulterate food.
5 (속도 등을) lessen; decrease. ¶차의 속력을 ~ slow down a car.
6 (시험에서) reject (a candidate); fail; sift out; eliminate; weed out; throw[bolt] out. ¶시험을 쳐서 ~ screen (candidates) through a test // 지원자의 반수를 ~ fail half the candidates // 시험관은 필기시험에서 지원자의 3분의 2를 떨어뜨렸다 The examiners failed two third of the applicants on the written paper.
7 (경주에서) leave behind; outstrip; outrun; get[pull] ahead of; outsail (another ship). ¶경주에서 다른 선수를 ~ outrun [get ahead of] the other runners in a race // 결승점에서 그를 떨어뜨렸다 I outstripped him near the goal.
8 [해어뜨리다] wear out[down]. ¶옷을 ~ wear out one's clothes.
9 [달리게 하다] exhaust; run out; use up; run through[short]. ¶쌀을 ~ use the rice up / have run out of rice // 재고품을 ~ be out of stock.
떨어지다 1 [낙하하다·추락하다] fall; drop; get [have] a fall; come [go] down; be down; (비

행기 등이) crash; (액체가) drip. ¶굴러 tumble down // 2층에서 ~ fall downstairs // 말[사다리]에서 ~ fall off[from] one's horse [a ladder] // 자전거에서 ~ fall off a bicycle // 배에서 물속으로 ~ fall overboard // 컵이 손에서 떨어졌다 The cup fell[dropped] from my hand. // 마루에 100원짜리 동전이 떨어져 있었다 A hundred won coin lay[had fallen] on the floor. // 헬리콥터가 떨어졌다 The helicopter crashed[fell to the ground]. // 나무에 벼락이 떨어졌다 Lightning hit[struck] the tree. // 화산재가 머리 위로 떨어졌다 Volcanic ash fell[came down] on our heads. // 빗방울이 가지 끝에서 떨어지고 있었다 Raindrops were falling from the tip of the branches.

2 [(해·달이) 지다] set; sink; go down. ¶해가 서산에 떨어졌다 The sun went down behind the (western) mountains. // 해가 지평선에 떨어지고 있다 The sun sinks[dips] below the horizon.

3 [실패하다] fail[get plucked] (in the exam); lose[fail] (in an election); (구어) flunk. ¶그는 면접시험에서 떨어졌다 He failed to pass the oral test. // 이번 시험에 떨어지면 퇴학당할 것 같다 If I fail[flunk] this exam, I will probably be expelled from school. // 1차 시험에는 합격했으나 2차 시험에서 떨어졌다 I was successful in the first screening, but failed (in) the second[to pass the second] examination.

4 (성적이) go down. ¶그는 성적이 떨어졌다 His grades[(영) marks] went down. // 2학기는 학교 성적이 떨어졌다 I got poor grades at school in the second term.

5 [분리되다] separate; part from[with]; fall apart. ¶외부 연료통은 우주 왕복선에서 탈없이 떨어져 나갔다 The outer fuel tank was successfully detached from the space shuttle.

6 (붙었던 것이) come off; come apart; be off; become disjoined. ¶저고리의 단추가 떨어졌다 A button has come off my coat. // 이 두 우표는 들러붙어서 떨어지지 않는다 These two stamps are stuck together and won't come apart[separate].

7 (사이가) be estranged[distant] from; cut oneself off[from]. ¶민심은 이미 현 정부에서 떨어져 나갔다 Public opinion is estranged from the Government. // 돈이 없어지자 친구들은 그에게서 떨어져 나갔다 When his money was gone, his friends drifted away (from him).

8 (거리가) be (a long way) off; (간격이) keep off. ¶그는 서울에서 100킬로미터 떨어진 곳에 살고 있다 He lives 100 kilometers away[at a distance of 100 kilometers] from Seoul. // 그의 집에서 100미터 떨어진 곳에 내 집을 지었다 I built my house a hundred meters away from his. // 두 사람은 멀리 떨어진 곳에 살고 있다 The two live far apart. // 나무가 2미터씩 떨어져서 서 있다 The trees stand at intervals of two meters. / The trees have been planted two meters apart. // 이 그림은 조금 떨어져서 보면 더 잘 보인다 This picture looks better if you stand back a short distance.

9 [손에 들어오다] fall into; be carried away. ¶그 그림은 경매에서 50만 원에 내 손에 떨어졌다 The picture was knocked down to me at an auction for 500,000 won.

10 [하락하다] go down; fall; drop; (기력 등이) decline; break down; crack up; (미국 구어) go downhill. ¶그녀의 인기는 완전히 떨어지고 말았다 She has lost her popularity. // 그 건으로 그의 신용은 땅에 떨어졌다 That affair ruined his reputation. // 시세가 뚝 떨어졌다 Market prices suffered a serious decline. // 속력이 떨어졌다 The speed dropped. // 판매고가 날로 떨어지고 있다 Sales are falling off day by day.

11 [열등하다] be inferior (to); [미달하다] do not come up to; fall short of; [뒤떨어지다] fall[drop / lag / hang] behind; be backward in; yield to (another). ¶값싼 연필은 질에서 떨어진다 The cheaper pencils are inferior in quality. // 그 점에서는 남에게 안 떨어진다 I'm sure I'm equal to anyone in that respect. // 그의 수입은 표준보다 떨어진다 His income does not come up to the standard.

12 [함락되다] fall (to / into); be reduced. ¶마침내 도시는 적의 수중에 떨어지게 되었다 The town finally fell into enemy hands[was finally captured by the enemy / finally fell to the enemy].

13 [남다] be left (over / behind) (from); remain; [꼭 나뉘다] be divisible; can be divided (by). ¶그 빚을 갚고도 상당한 돈이 떨어졌다 There was a considerable[sizable] sum left over after paying the debts. // 12는 3으로 나누어떨어진다 Twelve is evenly divided by 3.

14 (가격이) fall; drop; go down; decline; sag; depreciate. ¶값이 ~ fall in price.

15 (열·온도가) drop; fall; go down. ¶그는 열이 떨어지지 않는다 There is no abatement in his fever.

16 [해지다] be worn out[through]; wear threadbare; become seedy. ¶떨어진 옷 seedy [ragged / worn out / threadbare] clothes // 사전이 너덜너덜 떨어졌다 The dictionary has been worn to tatters.

17 [바닥나다] (사람이 주어) run[get] out of; be[run] short of; be out of; (매진되다) be sold out; be out of stock. ¶쌀이 떨어졌다 Rice has run out[run short] of rice. // 수중에 돈이 떨어졌다 I have no money in my wallet. // 그 물건은 재고가 떨어졌다 That article is out of stock. // 자전거의 기름이 떨어졌다 My bicycle needs oiling. // 약이 떨어지니 열이 또 났다 My fever returned once I ran out of medicine. // 저희 가게에서는 이 품목이 떨어졌습니다 We are out of stock of this item. / This item is out of stock.

18 [속아 넘어가다] fall into; be deceived; be taken in. ¶계략에 ~ fall into a snare / be entrapped / be ensnared.

19 (병·버릇 등이) be gone; be got rid of; be got over; be shaken off. ¶감기가 여간해서 떨어지지 않는다 I can't shake off[get over] my cold. // 감기가 절로 떨어질 때까지 기다려라 Wait till your cold wears itself out.

20 [유산하다] abort; miscarry; (사람이) have a miscarriage. ¶애가 ~ have an abortion[a miscarriage].

21 [끝나다] be finished; be completed. ¶내일이면 일이 다 떨어진다 The work will be finished tomorrow.

22 [터지다] be broken; be punctured; be torn; pierce; split; rend. ¶귀청이 떨어질 것

떨이

같은 ear-splitting[-piercing] / deafening // 귀청이 떨어질 것 같다 rend[burst on] one's ears.

23 (숨·감각 등이) ¶숨이 ~ breathe one's last / expire / die // 숨이 떨어지려는 사람 a person at the point of death[at death's door / in his last moments] / a dying man // 입맛이 ~ lose one's appetite.

24 (명령 등이) be given; be issued. ¶진전 명령이 떨어졌다 We were ordered to march.

떨이 cut-price[sacrifice] goods; a bargain; goods for clearance[rummage] sale; remaining articles offered at market-down[knocked-down / reduced] prices. ¶~로 팝니다 Surplus stock for sale at a (great) sacrifice.

떨치다[1] 1 [널리 알려지다] be widely felt[known]; become well known; be wielded. ¶그녀의 명성은 전 세계에 떨쳤다 Her fame spread all over the world. / She won[enjoyed] a world wide reputation. // 독감이 전국에서 맹위를 떨치고 있다 Influenza is raging all over the country.

2 [널리 드날리다] make well known in the world; wield (power, influence, etc.). ¶그는 악명을 천하에 떨치고 있다 He is notorious throughout the country. // 그는 피아니스트로서 명성을 떨쳤다 He won fame as a pianist. // 장군은 용맹을 떨쳤다 The general was renowned for his bravery. // 일찍이 호족이 이 고장에서 세력을 떨치고 있었다 Once a powerful clan held sway over this district. // 그 곡은 그의 명성을 전 세계에 떨쳤다 That piece made his name known all over the world.

떨치다[2] (흔들어) shake off; beat. ¶그는 몸을 떨쳐 자리에서 일어났다 He tore himself away from the seat.

떫다 astringent; puckery; rough. ¶떫은 차 strong[bitter] tea // 떫은 포도주 rough wine // 이 감은 ~ this persimmon has a puckery[an astringent] taste.

떫은맛 astringency; a puckery[rough] taste. ¶감의 ~을 없애다 remove the astringency of persimmons / sweeten persimmons.

떳떳하다 [버젓하다·당당하다] honorable; respectable; fair; aboveboard; open; [정당하다] right; rightful; righteous; just; [깨끗하다] upright; clean; pure; [합법적이다] lawful; legal; legitimate. ¶떳떳한 행동 an honorable deed[act] / right conduct // 떳떳한 일 what is right / a right thing // 떳떳하지 못한 거래 a shady deal // 떳떳한 길을 걷다 follow[tread] the path of virtue / pursue an honest career // 양심에 비추어 ~ have an easy[a clear / a clean] conscience / feel no prick of conscience // 저 가족은 떳떳하지 못한 과거가 있다 The family has a dark secret. / The family has a skeleton in the cupboard. // 나는 떳떳하지 못한 점은 하나도 없다 I have nothing to hide. / I have a clear conscience. // 그들은 떳떳하게 부부가 되었다 They were legally[formally] married. // 그는 일을 처리하는 데에 있어 어딘가 떳떳하지 못한 데가 있다 There is something underhand(ed) in the way he goes about his work. // 아들이 살인 사건에 관련되어 있어서 떳떳하지 못하다 I can't hold my head high when my son's involved in a murder case. // 떳떳하지 못한 일은 하지 않았다 I have done nothing to be ashamed of. **떳떳이** [버젓하게·당당하게] honorably; in a honorable way; fairly; openly; with an easy[a clear / a clean] conscience; [정당하게] right(ly); justly; righteously; aright. ¶~ 행동하다 play fair / act fair and square // ~ 이기다 win a game fairly // ~ 해라 Do fair play[business]. // 말할 것이 있으면 험담하지 말고 ~ 말해 봐라 If you have anything to say, say it out to my face instead of backbiting.

떵떵거리다 live in a grand style; live like a prince. ⇨ 땅땅거리다1

떼[1] [무리] a group; a troop (of schoolchildren); (사람의) a crowd; a throng; a knot(한 덩어리); a multitude(다수의); (짐승의) a herd(말·소 등의); a flock(양의); a pack(이리·사냥개의); a troop(원숭이의); a rookery(물개·펭귄 등의); a pod(고래·작은 새 등의 적은 떼); a drove(몰려가는 가축의); a string(한 줄로 이동 중인); (새의) a flock; a flight(날고 있는); a bevy; a covey; a gaggle; a wisp; a skein; a raft; (물고기의) a school; a shoal; a run(이동 중인); (벌레의) a swarm; a cluster; a cloud(메뚜기 등의). ¶소 ~ a herd of cattle // 양[새] ~ a (large) flock of sheep[birds] // 물고기 ~ large schools of fish // 메뚜기 ~ a (vast) swarm of locusts // ~를 지어 in groups / [crowds / packs / flights / swarms / flocks] // ~를 지어 사는 동물 a gregarious[herd] animal // 날아가는 기러기 ~ a flight of wild geese // ~를 짓다 form groups / cluster[group] together // ~로 몰려오다 swarm like locusts // 진달래꽃이 ~ 지어 피어 있다 Azaleas are blooming in clusters. // 그들은 ~를 지어서 왔다 They came in a group. // 우리는 삼삼오오 ~를 지어 출발했다 We started in groups of four or five. // 실업자가 ~를 지어 모여들었다 Jobless people gathered in crowds.

떼[2] [잔디] sod; turf. ¶~를 뜨다 cut out sod / cut[tear] turfs (from) // ~를 입히다 sod / turf // 그는 들에서 ~를 몇 장 떠서 잔디밭의 벗어진 곳에 입혔다 He cut some turfs from a field and covered a bare spot in the lawn with them.

떼[3] [뗏목] a raft. ¶~를 만들다 make a raft (of) // ~를 타고 가다 travel by raft / cross[go down] (a river) by raft / cross[go down] (a river) by raft // ~를 띄워 보내다 send a raft along the stream.

떼[4] [억지·고집] an impossible[an unreasonable / an importunate / an insistent] demand[claim / assertion]; keeping at (a person) for something; insisting on. ¶~가 늘다 grow in waywardness / grow selfish all the more.

떼거지 [떼를 지어 다니는 거지] a bunch of beggars; [이재민] a great number of victims of a natural calamity.

떼구루루 rolling; rumbling. ⇨ 데구루루
떼굴떼굴 rolling continuously. ⇨ 데굴데굴
떼그럭거리다 clatter; rattle.
떼꾼하다 be sunken (from exhaustion). ⇨ 떼꾼하다
떼다 1 (붙은 것을) take away[off]; remove; strip[tear] off; bare (it of its covering). ¶선반을 ~ remove a shelf / take a shelf down // (기관차에서) 차량을 ~ uncouple a train (from a locomotive) // 포스터를 ~ clear (a pole) of bills // 달력을 한 장 ~ tear off a leaf

from a calendar // 옷의 장식을 ~ rip trimming off a garment.
2 [분리하다] part; separate; disconnect; divide; isolate; (사이를) keep (one thing) from (another); detach; space (the lines). ¶…과 떼어서 separately from … / apart from … / independent(ly) of … // (일정한) 사이를 떼고 at (regular) intervals / sparsely // 행간을 ~ leave spaces between lines / space the lines // 그에게서 눈을 떼지 마라 Don't take your eyes off him. // 그 꼬마 녀석은 아주 장난꾸러기여서 눈을 떼서는 안 된다 The little boy is so naughty, so we must keep an eye on him. // 이 문제는 저 문제와는 떼어서 생각해야겠다 I will consider this matter separately [apart] from that one. // 10그루의 나무가 3미터씩 떼어서 심어졌다 Ten trees were planted three meters apart [at intervals of three meters]. // 그 둘은 뗄 수 없는 사이[친구]다 The two are inseparable (friends).
3 [봉한 것을 뜯다] open [break / take off] the seal; cut (a letter) open. ¶함부로 봉을 ~ tamper with the seal.
4 [빼다·제하다] subtract (from); deduct [subduct / detract] (from); take away [off]. ¶세금[비용]을 떼고 80만 원의 수입 an income of 800,000 won after tax [expenses] // 봉급에서 ~ deduct (a sum) from one's salary / take (a sum) off one's pay // 그는 이자를 미리 떼고 돈을 빌려 준다 He loans money with the interest deducted in advance.
5 (문서 등을) issue [draw / write out / make out] (a check); tear off (a chit). ¶전표를 ~ sign [give / write out] a chit / issue a voucher [a payment slip] // 나는 그에게 100만 원짜리 수표를 떼어 주었다 I have issued a check for one million won in favor of him.
6 [말문을 열다] break the silence; open the conversation. ¶입을 ~ open one's mouth to talk.
7 (병을) cure (a disease). ¶학질을 ~ cure malaria / get rid of malaria.
8 [유산시키다]. ¶아이를 ~ commit feticide / have an abortion / have an (artificial) abortion performed.
9 [끊다] quit [stop / give up] (drinking / smoking); abstain [refrain] from (drinking / smoking); cut (smoking) altogether. ¶젖을 ~ wean a child // 버릇을 ~ (자기의) get rid [break oneself] of a habit / overcome [get over] a habit / (남의) cure (a person) of a habit / get (a person) out of a habit.
10 [끝내다] finish up. ¶책[소설]을 ~ read [get] through a book [novel] / finish (reading) a book [novel] / have done with a book [novel].
11 (장기에서 말을) play [have a game] with a handicap. ¶마를 떼고 두다 play without *ma* [knight] as a handicap.
12 (화투·카드 등을) cut (the cards).

떼어 놓다 [갈라놓다] part; separate; detach; disconnect; keep apart; keep (one thing) from (another); cut off [apart]; [격리하다] isolate; [이간하다] estrange (people); alienate (a person) from (another); make strife. ¶싸우는 사람들을 ~ pull combatants apart / part quarreling persons // 애인 사이를 ~ separate the pair of lovers // 부부 사이를 ~ sever husband and wife / cut a husband from his wife // 어린 아이를 부모에게서 ~ take a little child away from its parents // 나는 싸우는 사내아이들을 떼어 놓았다 I parted [separated] the fighting boys. // 그것을 더 떼어 놓아라 Move it further away. // 우리는 그 두 마리 개가 서로 싸우기 때문에 떼어 놓았다 We keep those two dogs apart for they fought with each other. // 좀 더 멀리 떼어 놓게 Keep it further away.

떼도둑 a group [gang] of robbers; a pack of thieves.

떼돈 ¶~을 벌다 hit the jackpot / make a clean up / (구어) rake in the money / (미국구어) make a killing / [폭리를 취하다] profiteer (▶ 특히 전쟁 중에 생필품을 매매하여) 그들은 땅을 여러 번 매매하여 1억 원의 ~을 벌었다 They made a killing of a hundred million won by passing the land from hand to hand in dubious deals.

떼먹다 cheat by failing to pay (one's debt); evade payment of (a bill). ⇨ 떼어먹다

떼밀다 thrust [push / shove] aside [away]; force [push] aside [out of the way]; elbow (a person) out (팔꿈치로); (안으로) push (it) in; (이리저리) push (a person) around [about]. ¶떼밀고 들어가다 force one's way into // 팔꿈치로 군중을 떼밀고 지나갔다 I jostled along [elbowed my way] through the crowd. // 떼밀지 마라 Don't push me so much. / Stop shoving. // 바위를 떼밀어 낭떠러지에서 떨어뜨렸다 I pushed a rock over [off] a cliff.

떼쓰다 ask for the impossible; fret; badger [pester] (a person to do); tease [press / importune] (a person for something); make an unreasonable demand of (a person). ¶아이는 아이스크림을 달라고 떼썼다 The child cried for ice cream. // 나는 돈을 더 달라고 어머니에게 떼썼다 I importunately asked my mother for more money. // 그는 틀린 것을 옳다고 떼쓴다 He stands firm in his error. // 그는 어머니에게 떼써서 카메라를 샀다 He teased his mother into buying him a camera. // 그는 그녀를 꼭 만나야겠다고 떼썼다 He insisted on seeing her.

떼어먹다 bilk [jump] (a bill / a person); cheat by failing to pay (one's debt); cheat (a person) out of a loan; evade [shirk] payment of (a bill); eat and beat (식당 등에서); (속어) welsh on (a debt). ¶술값을 ~ shirk paying for one's drink / bilk a bar bill // 빚을 떼어먹고 도망치다 bolt without paying one's debts / run away leaving one's debts unpaid // 그가 내 돈 만 원을 떼어먹었다 He has cheated [bilked] me out of ten thousand won. // 그는 장사꾼의 돈을 예사로 떼어먹는다 He defrauds tradespeople without scruple. // 그는 음식 값을 떼어먹고 자취를 감추었다 He disappeared without paying the restaurant bill. // 그는 노무자의 임금에서 20퍼센트를 떼어먹었다 He took a cut of 20 percent on the laborer's wages.

떼이다 be cheated (of a debt); be welshed [welched] on; be bilked. ¶떼인 빚 a dishonored debt / 떼인 외상값 a bill left unpaid // 외상 판매에서 ~ suffer a loss on a credit sale // 빚을 떼였다 A debt was dishonored.

떼치다 1 [떼어 물리치다] shake oneself loose [free] from (a person's grasp); release oneself (from); break loose (from); tear oneself away (from); (떼밀어) push away

뗏목 [aside]; thrust away[aside]; brush[force] aside; [떼어 놓다] leave (a person) behind. ¶그의 손을 ~ pull free from his grasp / break his grasp∥그는 애원하는 여자의 손을 뗴쳤다 He thrust[threw / pushed] the woman's imploring hands aside. **2** [잘라 거절하다] refuse[brush aside] (a request); decline; reject (a demand); spurn (an offer); turn down; repel (a plea). ¶돈 달라는 것을 ~ refuse (a person) money.

뗏목(-木) a raft. ¶~ 사공 a raftsman∥~ 다리 a raft bridge∥~을 만들다 make a raft (of)∥~을 타고 강을 내려가다 go down the river on a raft∥그들은 목재를 ~에 실어 나른다 They transport the timber on floats.

뗏장 a sod; a turf; a piece of sod[turf]. ¶~을 새로 입힌 무덤 a newly sodded grave∥~을 뜨다 cut[tear] turfs (from a field).

뗑그렁 with a clang(or). ⇨땡그랑

뗑그렁거리다 clang; cling. ⇨땡그랑거리다

뗑뗑 ding-dong. ⇨땡땡

또 1 [다시] again; once more[again]; [반복해서] repeatedly; [계속해서] in succession. ¶승리 ~ 승리 victory after victory∥~ 일을 시작하다 begin one's work again / resume one's work / be back at work∥간밤에는 ~ 지진이 있었다 There was another earthquake last night.∥그 같은 사람이 ~ 있을까 Shall we ever see the like of him again?∥~ 놀러 오세요 Come and see me again.∥다음에 ~ 뵙겠습니다 I will call again some other time.∥그럼 ~ 만납시다 See you later [tomorrow / next week] (▶ later는 같은 날에).

2 [다시 더] and; more; moreover; besides; further(more); what is more. ¶~ 한 마디 one more word∥~ 1년 another year∥그는 달리고 ~ 달렸다 He ran and ran.∥그는 수완도 좋고 ~ 돈도 많다 He has ability and plenty of money to go with it.∥게다가 ~ 감기까지 걸렸다 What is worse, I have a bad cold.∥그는 대학자인데다가 ~ 강의도 잘한다 He is a great scholar, and what is better, a good teacher. / He is a good teacher as well as a good scholar.∥그는 정치가요 ~ 시인이다 He is a statesman and poet.

3 [한편] on the other hand; in turn; while. ¶형은 공부하기를 싫어하는데 동생은 ~ 책을 매우 좋아한다 The elder brother does not like study, while on the other hand the younger brother is very fond of reading.∥형은 언제나 게으른데 동생은 ~ 그렇게 열심이다 The elder brother is always idle, while the younger brother is such a hardworking man.

4 [기타]. ¶난 ~ 누구라고 Well, It is you (I thought it was somebody else).

또는 or; either ... or; otherwise; [바꾸어 말하면] in other words. ¶이것 ~ 저것 (either) this or that / whether this or that∥편지를 내든지 ~ 전보를 치든지 해야 한다 You must either wire or write to him.∥일요일 ~ 월요일에 돌아가겠다 I'll come home on Sunday or Monday.∥소금 ~ 간장으로 맛을 들이다 season (food) with either salt or soy sauce.

또다시 [한 번 더] once more[again]; over again; [재차] for the second time; [두 번] again; twice; a second time; [새로이] afresh. ¶~ 일어나다 recur / renew∥~ 시작하다 repeat / do over again∥한 번 거짓말을 하면 ~ 하게 된다 One lie leads to another.∥폐를 끼치게 되어 죄송합니다 I am sorry to put you to repeated troubles.

또닥거리다 keep patting. ⇨"토닥거리다 ¶등을 ~ pat[clap] (a person) on the back∥어머니는 나의 어깨를 연방 또닥거렸다 Mother went pat, pat on my shoulder.

또닥또닥 knocking repeatedly. ⇨"토닥토닥

또랑또랑하다 clear; distinct; vivid; plain; explicit. ¶또랑또랑한 목소리로 the clear voice[tone] ∥아이들의 또랑또랑한 목소리가 들렸다 I heard the clear, vivid voices of children.∥그녀는 눈이 ~ She is bright in the eye.

또래 (나이의) (of) the age; (사물의) (of) the size. ¶네 ~의 소년 a boy about your age∥내가 너희 ~였을 때에는 when I was your age∥모두 그 ~다 All of them are of the same age[size].∥그 ~의 것을 몇 개 더 보여 주오 Show me a few more that size.

또렷또렷 all vividly[clearly / distinctly]. ¶글씨를 ~ 쓰다 write a clear hand∥~ 설명하다 [진술하다] explain[state] explicitly. **또렷또렷하다** all clear[distinct / vivid / plain / explicit]. ¶또렷또렷한 이목구비 clear-cut [well-defined] features∥정신이 ~ be sane / be wide awake / look alive∥옛일이 또렷또렷하게 생각난다 Old memories come vividly to mind.

또렷하다 distinct; evident. ⇨'뚜렷하다

또바기 [한결같이] always; regularly; without fail. ¶인사를 ~ 잘하다 greet[salute] whenever to see[meet].

또박또박¹ struttingly. ⇨뚜벅뚜벅

또박또박² 1 [정확히] exactly; correctly; accurately; punctually. ¶시간을 ~ 지키다 be punctual (to the moment)∥글씨를 ~ 쓰다 write a letter exactly[correctly]∥~ 발음하다 pronounce correctly. **2** [거르지 않고] regularly; with regularity. ¶매월 ~ 빚을 갚다 pay back regularly every month.

또한 [게다가] and; besides; moreover; what is more; further(more); [동시에] and at the same time; [역시] also; too; likewise; as well; either; (부정 구문에서) neither; nor; not ... either. ¶그의 연설은 재미도 있고 ~ 고무적이었다 His speech was both[at once] interesting and stimulating. / His speech was stimulating as well as interesting.∥그는 과학자이며 ~ 시인이기도 하다 He is a poet as well as a scientist. / He is both[at once] a scientist and a poet.∥그녀는 아름답고 ~ 총명하다 She is bright as well as beautiful. / She is as clever as she is gorgeous.∥그는 영어 회화도 잘하려니와 ~ 작문도 잘한다 He speaks English, and writes it as well.∥시간도 늦었고 ~ 바깥도 몹시 춥다 It's late, and besides[moreover] it's very cold outside.∥그도 ~ 진정한 모험가다 He is a real adventurer, too. / He is likewise a real adventurer.∥나도 ~ 같소 That is also the case with me. / (구어) Same here.∥아버지도 ~ 당근은 싫어하신다 My father does not like carrots, either.∥그의 양친도 ~ 연회에 초대받았다 His parents, too, were invited to the banquet. / His parents also were invited to the banquet.∥그녀는 거기에 가지 않았으며 나도 ~ 가지 않았다 She didn't go there, neither did I.∥그는 약속을 했으며 ~ 그것을 지켰다 He made a promise and kept it. /

Besides making a promise, he kept it.

똑[1] with a snap; with a thump; with a tap. ⇨ 뚝[1]·2·4

똑[2] 〔정확히〕 exactly. ¶~ 닮다 be the exact image[likeness] (of).

똑같다 just[exactly] alike; absolutely identical (with); exactly the same (as); equal (to); 〔닮다〕 be the exact image[likeness] (of). ¶똑같은 날에 on the very same day // 똑같은 말을 몇 번이고 되풀이하다 say the same thing again and again / harp on the same string // 똑같은 잘못을 되풀이하다 repeat the same sort of mistakes // 높이가 ~ be of the same height // 수〔길이 / 넓이〕가 … 과 ~ be as many[long / wide] as … // 어제 들은 이야기와 ~ It is the same story that I heard yesterday. // 나는 이와 똑같은 우산을 갖고 있다 I have an umbrella identical with this one. // 이와 똑같은 쿠키를 먹어 본 일이 있다 I have eaten cookies of the same kind (as these) before. // 나도 당신과 똑같은 생각이오 Your thoughts echo mine. // 자매가 ~ The sisters are exactly alike. // 그는 얼굴 생김새가 그의 아버지와 ~ His face is his father's to a T. / His face notably resembles his father's. // 남자나 여자나 모두 똑같은 대우를 받고 있다 Men and women are treated equally[without discrimination]. **똑같이** equally(평등하게); evenly(한결같이); impartially(공평하게); 〔indiscriminately(차별 없이); 〔마찬가지로〕 alike; similarly; in the same way; likewise. ¶~ 보이다 look alike // ~ 분배하다 divide (money) equally[into equal parts] // 높이를 ~ 하다 make all of uniform height // 남녀를 ~ 취급하다 treat men and women equally // 비용을 ~ 부담하다 share the expenses equally with (a person) // 그 두 사람은 ~ 명배우다 The two are equally great actors. // 그는 재산을 자식들에게 ~ 나눠 주었다 He divided his property equally among his children.

똑딱거리다 〔시계가〕 ticktack; ticktock; tick; 〔타자기 등이〕 click, click, click …; 〔딱딱한 물건이〕 click; clatter; patter. ¶시계가 똑딱거리고 있다 The clock is ticking (away) (the time). // 똑딱선이 똑딱거리며 지나간다 The motorboat is chugging along.

똑딱단추 a snap fastener. ¶~를 채우다 close a snap fastener.

똑딱똑딱 ticktack; ticktock; tick-tack; click-clack. ¶〔시계가〕~ 가다 tick away[off] the time // 낡은 시계가 여전히 ~ 정확히 가고 있다 The old clock still ticks off the hours accurately. **똑딱똑딱하다** ticktack; click. ⇨ "똑딱거리다

똑딱선(－船) a motorboat; a motor-powered boat; a motor ship.

똑똑 dripping; with snaps; rapping. ⇨ <뚝뚝

똑똑하다 1 〔분명하다〕 clear; distinct; plain; definite; vivid; explicit; sharp. ¶똑똑한 발음 clear[articulate] pronunciation // 똑똑한 글씨 clear handwriting // 똑똑한 구별 a sharp [clear / clear-cut] distinction // 〔텔레비전의〕 똑똑한 화면 (get) distinct picture // 똑똑한 인쇄 clear printing // 똑똑한 목소리로 in a clear[distinct] voice[tone] // 이 사진은 똑똑하지 않다 This photograph has not come out clear. **똑똑히** clearly; distinctly; vividly; plainly; explicitly; definitely. ¶~ 말하다[발음하다] speak[pronounce] distinctly / articulate (a syllable) // ~ 들리다 (사물이) hear (a voice) distinctly / 〔사물이 주어〕 be heard distinctly / be clearly heard // 나는 그의 얼굴을 ~ 기억하고 있다 I remember his face very distinctly. // 달빛 아래에서 키가 큰 사람의 모습을 ~ 알아볼 수 있었다 I could make out [〔문어〕 discern] a tall figure clearly in the moonlight.

2 〔영리하다〕 clever; bright; brainy; wise; intelligent; 〔빈틈이 없다〕 shrewd; smart. ¶ 똑똑한 아이 a bright child / a clever boy [girl] // 똑똑한 체하는 사람 a knowing chap // 똑똑한 체하다 try to appear smart / pretend to be wise / behave like a wise man // 똑똑해 보이다 look brainy[intelligent] / have an intelligent face // 그는 똑똑하지 못하다 He lacks sense. // 그는 똑똑한 사람이니까 그런 짓은 안한다 He is too wise to do such a thing. / He knows better[has more sense] than to do so. **똑똑히** wisely; cleverly; brightly; intelligently; 〔빈틈없이〕 shrewdly; smartly. ¶~ 행동하다 act wisely[sensibly] // 일처리를 ~ 하다 dispose of a matter intelligently.

똑바로 1 〔곧게〕 straight; in a straight line; in a beeline; 〔곧추〕 (bolt) upright; erect; 〔수직으로〕 perpendicularly; vertically; 〔직행으로〕 straight; direct. ¶~ 앞을 보다 look straight ahead // ~ 앉다 sit upright[erect] // ~ 서다 stand upright[erect] // ~ 걷다 walk straight // ~ 가다 go[keep] straight on / make straight (toward / for) / follow one's nose // ~ 놓다 set (something) upright // ~ 집으로 가다 go home straight[direct] // 자세를 ~ 하세요 Hold yourself straight[erect]. // 나는 역으로 갔다 I went directly[straight] to the station. // 모퉁이를 돌지 말고 ~ 가십시오 Go straight without turning at that corner.

2 〔바른 대로〕 honestly; frankly; straightforwardly; candidly; 〔옳게〕 right(ly); 〔틀리지 않게〕 correctly; exactly. ¶~ 말하자면 to tell the truth / to be frank[honest] with you / candidly[frankly] speaking // ~ 대다 frankly [candidly] confess (to a fact / that …) / make an honest[a frank] confession (of) // ~ 처신하다 go straight / act on the square / behave properly[correctly] // ~ 발음하다 pronounce correctly // ~ 살아가다 live straight / lead an honest life / pursue an honest career.

똑바르다 1 〔곧다〕 (dead) straight; (as) straight as an arrow; direct; 〔직립하다〕 upright; erect. ¶똑바른 길 a straight road // 똑바른 기둥 an upright post // 똑바른 자세로 in a correct posture / sitting[standing] erect. 2 〔올바르다〕 right; (as) right as nails; righteous; just. ¶똑바른 행동 right conduct // 행실이 ~ behave properly[correctly].

똑소리 나다 be smart as a whip; 〔영〕 be (as) bright as a button; 〔영〕 be (as) keen as mustard; be mustard keen. ¶따님이 똑소리 나네요 Your daughter is smart as a whip.

똘똘 1 into a roll; with a twirl. ⇨ 돌돌 2 〔굳게〕 ~ 뭉치다 be closely banded together / be strongly united.

똘똘이 a bright child; a clever boy.

똘똘하다 clever; bright; smart. ¶똘똘한 사내아이 a bright[clever] boy. **똘똘히** cleverly; brightly; smartly.

똘마니 〈속〉 a henchman. ⇨ 부하(部下)

똥 excrement(s); ordure; f(a)eces; 〔속어〕 shit;

똥값

똥 (소·말의) dung; droppings(조류의); guano(바닷새의). ¶~ 구덩이 a manure pit // ~ 푸는 사람 a night-soil man[carrier] // ~을 누다 have a bowel movement / evacuate[move] the bowels / ease[relieve] nature / relieve oneself / (개 등이) dung / (속어) shit // ~이 마렵다 feel a motion / feel like defecating / feel one's bowels urge / (구어) be taken short(갑자기) // ~을 푸다 dip up night soil // ~이 무서워 피하랴 Shun bad people as you would filth.

똥 누러 갈 적 마음 다르고 올 적 마음 다르다 (속담) Once on shore, we pray no more.; The danger past and God forgotten.

똥 묻은 개가 겨 묻은 개 나무란다(속담) The pot calls the kettle black.

똥(을) 싸다 [매우 힘들다] have a hard[bad] time; have a hell of time; be put to it.

똥줄(이) 나게[빠지게] very hastily[urgently]; in haste; in a hurry[rush].

똥줄(이) 당기다 be frightened out of one's wits; be scared to death; be scared shitless.

똥값 a nominal price; a dirt-cheap price. ¶~으로 팔다 sell for almost nothing // ~이다 be dirt-cheap[dog-cheap] // 그런 것은 팔아 봐야 ~이다 That would fetch only a small price.

똥개 [잡종의 개] a mongrel (dog); a dog of nondescript breed.

똥거름 night soil; dung-manure; manure [muck] (농장에서 얻는). ¶~을 주다 apply dung-manure to (land) / dung[manure] the ground.

똥구멍 the anus; the anal passage[orifice].

똥구멍이 찢어지게 가난하다(속담) be as poor as a church mouse.

똥끝 the tip(s) of excrement. ¶~이 타다 feel anxious[uneasy] very much / be fidgeted (about) / worry oneself (sick).

똥독(-毒) poison[virulence] in excrement(s); rash caused by excrement(s). ¶~이 오르다 get[have] a rash from touching excrement.

똥똥하다 fat; stout. ⇨뚱뚱하다

똥바가지 a dung dipper.

똥배 a potbelly; a (prominent) paunch; a portly belly.

똥싸개 a child who is too young to control his bowel movements; a pants-soiler.

똥오줌 feces and urine; human waste; excretions.

똥차(-車) **1** [똥을 실어 나르는 차] a night soil wagon[car(t)]; (속어) a honey cart. **2** [고물 차] a rattletrap; a rickety[ramshackle] vehicle.

똥칠하다(-漆-) [똥을 묻히다] smear dung; [명예를 더럽히다] disgrace. ¶그는 부모 얼굴에 똥칠했다 He disgraced his parents[besmirched his parents name]. // 내 얼굴에 똥칠하지 마라 Don't bring disgrace on me.

똥통(-桶) [인분 저장용] a manure[dung] tub; [인분 수거용] a manure pail; a honey bucket.

똥파리 a bottle-green fly; a dung fly.

똬리 a ring-shaped[coiled] pad (put on the head by women to ease the weight of a headload); a headload pad.

뙈기 1 [논·밭의 작은 한 구획] a patch[plot / lot / section] (of a field[paddy]). ¶한 ~의 땅 a patch[piece / plot] of land[ground] / a lot (of land) / a plot // 밭[논] 한 ~ a patch of field[paddy] // 그는 논밭 ~나 가졌다 He has a few fields. / He is an owner of some farmland. **2** [이불·담요 등의] a piece; a sheet; a mat. ¶~자리 a mat // 이불 ~ a bedquilt.

뙤약볕 the scorching[blazing] sun; dazzling [broiling / burning] sunshine. ¶~을 받으며 under the burning sun // 한여름의 ~ the burning sun in midsummer // ~을 쬐다 expose oneself to strong[scorching] sunshine / be under the full sun.

뚜껑 1 [덮개] a cover(커버); a lid(상자·솥 등의); a cap(병·만년필 등의); a flap(호주머니의); a case(시계의); an apron(대포의 포구의); a hood(배의 승강구 등의); [동][식] an operculum (pl. -la, ~s). ¶깡통의 ~ a cover to a can / 우유병의 ~ the cardboard top of a milk bottle // 술통 ~ a barrelhead // ~이 있는[달린] covered / lidded // ~이 있는 그릇 a covered vessel[receptacle] / a dish with a lid // ~이 없는 lidless / open / open-faced(시계 등의) / (a saucepan) without a top // ~을 연 채로 with the lid off // ~이 닫혀 있다 be covered / have a lid on // 술통의 ~을 뽑다 take out the barrelhead / open a barrel // ~을 닫아 두다 keep (a thing) covered / [비밀로 하다] keep (a matter) (a) secret. **2** 〈속〉 a cap; a hat. ⇨모자(帽子)

뚜껑(을) 열다 open; uncover; lift the lid [cover]; [발표하다] make public; lay (a matter) before the public. ¶뚜껑을 열기 전에는 승부를 알 수 없다 It's impossible to tell ahead of time[No one can forecast] who will win. // 뚜껑을 열어 보기 전에는 무엇이라 말할 수 없다 No one can make any prediction before it becomes an actuality.

뚜덕거리다 keep patting. ⇨˝투덕거리다

뚜드리다 strike; pat. ⇨˝두드리다

뚜들기다 beat; hit. ⇨˝두들기다

뚜뚜 toot-toot; hoot-hoot ¶~ 소리 (기적 등의) a hoot / (자동차의) a honk / a toot // ~ 소리 내다 (자동차가) give off its 'honk-honk' / (나팔·피리 등의) too-too // 경적을 ~ 울리며 달리다 run with honks / run honking.

뚜렷하다 [분명하다] clear; plain; distinct; vivid; definite; [자명하다] evident; obvious; apparent; patent; manifest; explicit; [두드러지다] striking; conspicuous; remarkable; marked; distinguished. ¶뚜렷한 사실 a plain truth / an obvious fact / a patent fact // 뚜렷한 증거 clear[positive] evidence / an evident proof // 뚜렷한 이유 a definite reason // 둘 사이에는 뚜렷한 차이가 있다 There are distinct differences between the two. // 그가 그곳에 있었다는 뚜렷한 증거가 있다 There is clear evidence that he was there. **뚜렷이** [똑똑히] distinctly; vividly; clearly; in bold[strong] relief; [두드러지게] strikingly; conspicuously; remarkably. ¶~ 만족한 빛을 띠고 with an evident air of satisfaction / with visible satisfaction / visibly satisfied // ~ 인쇄하다 print clearly // ~ 보이다 show clearly // 눈을 인 몽블랑이 푸른 하늘에 ~ 보인다 Snow-capped Mont Blanc stands sharply outlined [in bold relief] against the blue sky. // 그것이 그의 얼굴에 ~ 나타나 있다 It can be seen on his face. / It is written visibly in[on / over] his face.

뚜벅거리다 swagger; strut; walk gingerly[in affected manner].

뚜벅뚜벅 struttingly; with a strutting gait. ¶~ 걷다 strut / swagger // 구두 소리가 ~ 들

뚜벅뚜벅하다 swagger; strut. ⇨뚜벅거리다
뚜쟁이 a procurer(남자); a procuress(여자); a pimp; a pander. ¶~노릇하다 pimp / pander / procure / act as a pander for.
뚝¹ 〔부러지는 소리·모양〕 with a snap. ¶~ 부러지다 snap[break] short.∥노가 ~ 부러져 있다 Snap! went an oar.∥지팡이가 ~ 부러져 있다 A stick is broken with a snap. / A stick is snapped.
2 〔물방울 등이 떨어지는 소리·모양〕 with a thump[thud / whack / plump]. ¶땅에 ~ 떨어지다 drop with a thud on the ground.∥잉크 한 방울이 노트에 ~ 떨어졌다 A blob of ink dripped down on the notebook.∥홍시[연시]가 땅에 ~ 떨어졌다 A ripe persimmon plopped down on the ground.
3 〔성적 등이 갑자기 떨어지는 모양〕 ¶학교 성적이 ~ 떨어졌다 My grades really fell[did a nose dive].∥시세가 ~ 떨어졌다 The bottom nearly fell out of the market.∥그는 최근에 성적이 ~ 떨어졌다 His performance has really fallen off recently.∥경기가 ~ 떨어졌다 Business suddenly dropped off.
4 〔한 번 두드리는 소리〕 with a tap[rap].
5 perfectly; completely. ⇨딱⁶
뚝뚝¹ 〔액체가 떨어지는 모양·소리〕 dripping; in drops; pattering; dropping one by one; trickling (down / out / along). ¶눈물을 ~ 떨어뜨리다 shed teardrops.∥눈물이 ~ 떨어지다 tears fall in drops.∥그의 얼굴에서 땀이 ~ 떨어지고 있었다 His face was dripping with sweat.∥내 이마에서 땀방울이 ~ 떨어졌다 Perspiration[Sweat] trickled off my forehead.∥마루에는 피가 ~ 떨어져 있었다 There were big blotches of blood on the floor.∥비가 ~ 떨어지기 시작했다 It began to sprinkle[to rain a little].∥그녀는 닭똥 같은 눈물을 ~ 떨어뜨렸다 Her tears fell in big drops.
2 〔부러지는 모양·소리〕 with snaps; with creaks; snappingly. ¶손가락 마디를 ~ 소리내다 crack (the joints of) one's fingers.∥나뭇가지가 ~ 부러졌다 The branches were broken with snaps.
3 〔두드리는 소리〕 rapping; knocking. ¶그는 계속 문을 ~ 두드렸다 He kept knocking at the door.∥그는 지팡이로 보도를 ~ 두드리며 갔다 His cane went rapping[tapping] along the street.
뚝뚝하다 **1** 〔굳다〕 hard; tough; stiff; rigid. **2** (성질이) harsh; rough; tough; unaffable; rude; unsociable; blunt. ¶뚝뚝하게 bluntly / curtly.∥뚝뚝한 응대 a stiff reception.∥뚝뚝한 사람[성질] an unsociable person[nature].∥그는 태도가 ~ He is blunt in his bearing.
뚝배기 a *ttukbaegi*; an earthen(ware) bowl.
뚝배기보다 장맛이 좋다 (속담) Appearances are often deceptive.; You can't tell a book by its cover.
뚝심 great physical power[strength]; brute force; 〔버티는 힘〕 staying power; endurance. ¶~이 센 사람 a man of mighty sinews.∥~이 있다 be endowed with brute force / be persevering.∥그는 ~이 있다 He is very firm[unbending / resolute / persevering].
뚤뚤 into a roll; with a twirl. ⇨돌돌
뚫다 **1** 〔구멍을 내다〕 dig through; bore (a hole / a well); drill(▶ dig는 괭이, bore는 드릴이나 송곳으로, drill은 드릴로 구멍을 뚫다); perforate; 〔관통하다·난관 등을 극복하다〕 penetrate; pierce (through); go through; break through; shoot through(탄환이); (길을) bore; cut; excavate; build; open (up). ¶산을 뚫어서 만든 터널 a tunnel dug through a mountain.∥산에 터널을 ~ bore[dig] a tunnel through a mountain.∥판자에 구멍을 ~ punch a hole in the cupboard.∥벽에 구멍을 ~ make[bore] a hole in the wall.∥숲 속을 뚫고 나오다 pass through a wood.∥하수구를 ~ clear the drain[sewer] / improve the drainage.∥천장을 ~ go through the ceiling.∥그는 군중 속을 뚫고 나왔다 He made his way through the crowd.∥작은 구멍 속을 간신히 뚫고 나왔다 I just squeezed through the small hole.∥어둠을 뚫고 번갯불이 번쩍 빛났다 Lightning flashed through the darkness.∥그는 곤경을 뚫고 나갔다 He found a way out of his troubles.∥허다한 난관을 뚫고 나왔다 I have come through[overcome] all kinds of hardships.∥못이 판자를 뚫었다 The nail went through the board.∥총탄이 그의 가슴을 뚫었다 A bullet pierced his[hit him in the] chest.∥그들은 철도를 놓으려고 산을 뚫었다 They cut through a mountain to construct the railway.∥그들은 숲을 뚫고 길을 냈다 They cut a way through the forest.∥그들은 빽빽한 덤불을 뚫고 길을 만들었다 They cut[cleared / hacked / hewed / opened] a path through the thick under growth.∥그는 많은 고난을 뚫고 제 갈길을 열었다 He carved a way for himself through many hardships.
2 〔방도를 알아내다〕 find a way. ¶돈구멍을 ~ find a way to get money.∥일자리를 ~ look for a job / seek a job.
3 〔법망·감시 등을〕 evade; slip past; elude (the law). ¶감시망을 ~ elude the vigilance of the guard.∥포위망을 ~ fight[cut] one's way through the enemy.∥그는 법망을 뚫고 국외로 도망쳤다 He gave the police the slip and fled across the border.∥나는 감시의 눈을 뚫고 그와 연락을 취했다 Avoiding the watchful eye of the guard, I managed to make contact with him.∥그들은 적의 포위를 뚫고 길을 열었다 They cut their way through the besieging army.∥범인은 비상선을 뚫고 달아났다 The guilty man[criminal] slipped through the police cordon and escaped.
4 〔이치를 깨닫다·통찰하다〕 get at; master; penetrate; pierce. ¶마음속을 뚫어 보다 read (a person's) inmost thoughts / see through (a person's) intention.
뚫리다 **1** (구멍 등이) be pierced[bored / perforated / drilled / penetrated]. ¶구멍이 ~ a hole is made.∥터널이 ~ a tunnel is made[bored / excavated].∥길이 ~ a road[path] is made[open] / a way is found.∥"이 골목은 뚫렸습니까?" "아니, 막혔습니다." "Can you pass through the alley?" "No, it is a blind alley." **2** (이치가) be attained; be mastered. ¶학문의 깊은 이치가 뚫린다 The secrets of learning are mastered[penetrated].
뚫어지다 be bored[drilled / pierced / perforated]. ¶이 송곳은 잘 안 뚫어진다 This drill won't bore.∥이 펀치는 안 뚫어진다 This punch doesn't work[pierce].∥험한 산에 긴 터널이 힘들게 뚫어졌다 A long tunnel in a

똥딴지 steep mountain has been laboriously excavated[driven out]. // 네 양말에 구멍이 뚫어져 있다 There is a hole in your sock.

똥딴지 1 〔우둔하고·무뚝뚝한 사람〕 a blunt and dull person; a dunce; a blockhead. 2 〔전〕 an insulator. ⇨ 애자(礙子) 3 〔식〕 a Jerusalem artichoke.

똥딴지같다 too fantastic[preposterous]; outrageous; farfetched; extraordinary. ¶똥딴지 같은 생각 a wild idea / a fantastic notion // 똥딴지같은 말을 하다 make a preposterous [an absurd] remark / say extraordinary things.

똥땅거리다 keep drumming and twanging [twangling]. ¶똥땅거리며 놀다 have a hilarious[riproarious] time / hold high jinks / go on a spree / (미) whoop it up.

똥똥보 a fatty. ⇨ 똥뚱이
똥뚱이 a fatty[corpulent / stout / plump] person; a fatty.

똥똥하다 fat; stout; corpulent; fatty; fleshy; plump; (미국 구어) corn-fed; (농조) well-padded. ¶똥똥한 부인 a stout lady[matron] // 똥똥한 남자 a man with a lot of fat on him // 똥똥한 신사 a gentleman of ample proportions // 좀 똥똥한 stoutish / fattish // 똥똥해지다 fatten / grow[get] stout[fat] / grow corpulent / become fat / fat (up) // 배가 ~ be potbellied / have a full stomach // 너무 똥똥해져서 이젠 외투가 안 맞는다 This overcoat is too small for me now, I have grown stouter. // 스웨터를 두 벌이나 껴입고 있으니까 똥똥하게 보일 수밖에 없다 You look bundled up[well padded] because you're wearing two sweaters.

똥보 1 〔똥한 사람〕 a sulky[sullen / glum] person. 2 a fatty. ⇨ 똥뚱이

똥하다 1 〔성질이〕 taciturn; reticent; incommunicative. ¶성질이 똥한 사람 a taciturn person / a man of few words. 2 〔시무룩하다〕 moody and taciturn; sullen; sulky; sour; glum. ¶똥하니 sullenly / in moody[sulky] silence / in sullen taciturnity // 똥하게 있다 look sullen / be in the sulks // 똥하니 말이 없다 keep a sullen[moody / sulky] silence.

뛰놀다 〔뛰어다니며 놀다〕 romp (about); frisk (about); kid around; frolic; rollick; gambol; caper. ¶뛰놀기 좋아하는 larksome / gamesome / frolicsome / frolicky / larky // 아이들은 눈 속에서 뛰놀고 있었다 The children were frolicking in the snow. // 새끼 양들이 들에서 뛰놀고 있다 Lambs are skipping about in the field.

뛰다¹ 1 〔두근거리다〕 throb; thump; beat; palpitate; pound; pulsate. ¶맥이 ~ pulsate / one's pulse beats // 그 소식을 듣고 내 가슴은 뛰었다 My heart beat quick at the news. 2 〔(물가 등이) 오르다〕 rise; advance (in price); go[run] up; jump (abruptly); shoot up. 3 〔속〕 run away; fly. ⇨ 달아나다₂

뛰다² 1 〔빨리 달리다〕 run; dash; rush. ¶뛰기 시작하다 start running / begin to run / break into a run // 갑자기 뛰어 들어오다 make a sudden rush into (a room) // 역까지는 뛰어서 5분이다 It is five minutes' run to the station. // 개가 뛰어 들어왔다 A dog burst in[came rushing in]. // 오늘은 경기장에서 죽어라고 뛸 작정이다 We're going to run wild [wreak havoc / run all over them] on the field today. // 우리가 방에서 이야기하고 있는 데 이상한 사람이 뛰어 들어왔다 A strange man jumped into the room where we were talking.

2 〔도약하다〕 jump; leap; spring; bound; (한 발로) hop. ¶뛰어서 with a jump / in a leap // 깡충 ~ make a leap[bound] / give a spring // 가볍게 ~ take a slight jump / leap lightly // 그는 그 경기에서 15미터를 뛰어 우승했다 He won the event on[with] a leap[jump] of 15 meters.

3 〔차례 등을 거르다〕 skip (over); jump (over); omit. ¶5등에서 1등으로 ~ jump from the fifth place to the top // 10페이지에서 15페이지로 ~ skip[jump] from page 10 to 15.

4 〔단호한 태도를 보이다〕 be firm[decisive]. ¶펄쩍 뛰며 부인하다 deny (it) emphatically [flatly / hotly].

뛰는 놈 위에 나는 놈 있다 (속담) Talent above talent.

뛰다³ 1 〔그네를〕 swing (on a swing); have a swing; rock back and forth (a swing); propel (a swing). 2 〔널을〕 seesaw; play seesaw [teeter-totter].

뛰어가다 run (to); rush (for); dash; dart; go running. ¶전속력으로 ~ run[dash] at full [top] speed // 단숨에 ~ dash in a breath [with one breath] // 그는 학교까지 쭉 뛰어갔다 He ran all the way to school. // 잠깐 뛰어가서 택시를 불러 오마 I will run and call [get] a taxi. // 그는 군중 속을 뚫고 뛰어갔다 He ran through a crowd.

뛰어나가다 (밖으로) run out; rush[burst] out; barrel out; start forward[out]. ¶거리로 ~ run out into the street // 방에서 ~ rush [run / dash / dart] out of the room // 집을 ~ dart[dash] out of a house // 그는 맹렬한 기세로 뛰어나갔다 He dashed off[away] wildly [at a furious pace]. // 그는 얼른 방을 뛰어나갔다 He popped out of the room.

뛰어나다 〔탁월하다〕 outstanding; remarkable; 〔우수하다〕 excellent; 〔유명하다〕 noted; (서술적) be superior to; stand high above the others. ¶뛰어난 연주 a superb performance // 뛰어난 업적 an outstanding[a brilliant] achievement // 뛰어난 사람 an outstanding person // 뛰어난 재간 a distinguished talent / rare[unusual] ability // 뛰어나게 out[far] and away / by far / preeminently / out of the ordinary / prominently / conspicuously // 뛰어나게 좋은 물건 an article far superior to others / an extra-fine article // 영어 회화에 뛰어난 사람 a good [fluent] speaker of English // 검술에 ~ be proficient in fencing // 수예에 ~ be skilled in handicrafts // 스포츠에 ~ excel in[at] sports / excel as an athlete // 뛰어난 솜씨를 보여 주다 perform[pull off] a masterful trick // 그녀는 요리에 ~ She is good at cooking. / She is an excellent cook. // 그녀는 노래를 뛰어나게 잘 부른다 She is by far the best singer. / She is head and shoulders above the others in singing. // 그는 수학에 뛰어난 소질이 있다 He has exceptional mathematical talent. / He has the makings of an exceptionally fine mathematician. // 그녀의 아름다운 목소리는 그 그룹에서 뛰어났다 She was outstanding in the group for her sweet voice. // 꽃병은 만든 솜씨가 ~ This vase is of excellent[superb] workmanship. // 그녀는 뛰어난 기억력을 가지고 있다 She has an extraordinary memory. / Her memory is out of the ordinary[(구어) something else].∥그의 영업 실적은 뛰어났었다 His sales figures were prominent[stood out].∥그는 펜싱에서 남달리 뛰어났다 He excelled in fencing.∥그는 뛰어난 연기로 유명하다 He is famous for his skilled[excellent] performances.∥그는 뛰어난 프랑스 어 실력은 정평이 있다 He is generally acknowledged to have an excellent command of French. / He has an established reputation for his ability in French.∥이 아이는 뛰어난 인물이 될 것이다 This boy will make something of himself[is going to amount to something].∥This boy will be a success.∥한 씨는 재계에서 뛰어난 존재였다 Mr. Han was an outstanding figure in the financial world.∥그녀는 문장이 ∼ She is good at[(문어) excels in / is proficient in] writing. / She has a talent for writing.∥그는 장사에 대한 재간이 ∼ He is shrewd in business. / He is a shrewd businessman.∥그는 그 점에서 남보다 ∼ He is superior to (the) others in that respect.

뛰어내리다 jump[leap / spring / hop] down [off]. ¶2층[창문]에서 ∼ leap down from a second story[out of a window]∥달리는 열차에서 ∼ jump off[out of] a moving train∥그 소녀는 달리는 말에서 뛰어내렸다 The girl jumped off[leaped from] the running horse.∥그녀는 5층에서 뛰어내려 자살했다 She leaped to her death[committed suicide by leaping] from the fifth floor.

뛰어넘다 1 (장애물 등을) jump[leap / spring] over; clear (a fence); vault over (a gate). ¶담을 ∼ clear[jump over] a fence∥장애물을 ∼ clear[leap] a hurdle∥6피트를 쉽게 ∼ clear six feet with an easy jump∥그는 바[가로장]를 깨끗이 뛰어넘었다 He cleared the bar.∥그 소년은 웅덩이를 뛰어넘었다 The boy jumped [hopped / leaped] over a puddle. 2 (순서를) skip[jump] (over). ¶5페이지를 ∼ skip five pages∥한 계급 뛰어넘어 승진되다 be jumped one grade in rank∥2학년을 뛰어넘어 3학년이 되다 skip the second grade and enter the third∥그는 선배를 뛰어넘고 승진했다 He was promoted over his seniors.

뛰어다니다 1 [경중경중 뛰면서 돌아다니다] jump[bounce / frisk] about; cavort. ¶뛰어다니며 놀다 romp / gambol / frolic / wanton∥그 개가 방 안을 뛰어다녔다 The dog ran [romped / raced] about the room.
2 [바삐 돌아다니다] run about[round]; rush about; fly about; hustle[bustle] about; dash; (미국 구어) cut around; (구어) kick up one's heels; (말을 타고) ride about. ¶일 때문에 ∼ rush about on one's job∥이곳저곳을 뛰어다니다 I searched for it high and low[everywhere], but in vain.∥그는 취직 자리를 찾아 분주하게 뛰어다니고 있다 He is busy hunting for employment[a job].∥내 부친은 항상 여러 외국을 뛰어다니신다 My father is always hopping from one foreign country to another.∥어머니는 돈을 마련하려고 여기저기 뛰어다니셨다 My mother rushed about[was busy] trying to raise money.∥그는 어려운 사태를 수습하기 위해 바삐 뛰어다녔다 He worked busily trying to resolve the difficult situation.

뛰어들다 1 (몸을 던지다) jump[spring / plunge / leap / dive] in[into]. ¶뛰어들기 a plunge(▶ 단수형으로 씀) / [수영의 다이빙] diving / a dive∥바다에 ∼ jump into the sea∥물속으로 ∼ go[plunge] into the water∥철도로 ∼ throw oneself on a track∥품속으로 ∼ fly to[into] (a person's) arms∥창문을 통해 방으로 ∼ jump into a room through the window∥그녀는 피난하기 위해 내 집으로 뛰어들었다 She rushed into my house seeking refuge.∥어머니는 어린아이를 구하기 위해 불타는 집 속으로 뛰어들었다 The mother rushed into[entered] the burning house to rescue her child.∥그들은 방공호로 뛰어들었다 They ran into an air-raid shelter for refuge.∥개구리가 못에 뛰어들었다 A frog jumped[leaped / (영) leapt] into the pond.∥불청객이 뛰어들었다 An unwanted fellow [(구어) A gate-crasher] butted in(▶ gate-crasher는 특히 파티에의 난입자).
2 [갑자기 들어가다]. ¶자동차가 인도로 뛰어들었다 The car ran onto the pavement.∥경찰이 도박장으로 뛰어들었다 The police raided [made a raid on] the gambling den.
3 [참견하다] thrust oneself into (the scene of dispute); thrust one's nose in; butt into; [관련을 가지다] involve oneself in. ¶남의 가정 문제에 ∼ involve oneself in a person's family affair.

뛰어오다 come running; come at a run. ¶집에서 여기까지 줄곧 뛰어왔다 I have run all the way from home.∥어린애가 우리들 서 있는 데로 뛰어왔다 A child came running to where we were standing.

뛰어오르다 1 (위로) jump[spring / leap] up; start[leap / jump] to one's feet; bounce; bound; (말이) prance; [껑충 뛰다] hop; (달리는 자동차에) jump into (a moving car); (달리는 말 등에) jump on (a running horse). ¶연단에 ∼ spring up on a platform∥개구리가 30cm가량 공중으로 뛰어올랐다 The frog leaped[jumped] about thirty centimeters into the air.∥급류에서 고기가 뛰어올랐다 A fish jumped (up) in the rapids.∥달리는 열차에 뛰어올라 타는 것은 위험하다 It is dangerous to jump onto a moving train.∥그 사람은 달리는 열차에 뛰어올라 탔다 The man swung [leaped] aboard the moving train.∥그 소녀는 안장 없는 말에 뛰어올라 탔다 The girl leaped bareback onto the horse.∥갑자기 메뚜기가 잎에서 뛰어올랐다 Suddenly a grasshopper jumped[hopped] from the leaf.
2 (가격·지위 등이 갑자기 오르다) rise suddenly; jump; soar; skyrocket; rise; go up. ¶물가가 뛰어오르다 Prices take a jump.∥100원에서 1000원으로 뛰어올랐다 The price was suddenly raised from 100 won to 1000 won.∥시세가 어제 뛰어올랐다 The market jumped yesterday.

뜀뛰기 [경기] jumping; leaping; skipping.
● **뜀뛰기 선수** a jumper. **뜀뛰기 종목** a jumping event.

뜀박질 1 running (fast). ⇨**달음박질** 2 jumping.

뜀틀 a (vaulting) horse; a buck. ¶∼을 하다 (체조의) perform on the (long) horse∥∼을 **뛰어넘다** vault (over) a horse / vault a (long) horse.

뜨개바늘 a knitting needle. ⇨**뜨개질바늘**(⇨뜨개질)

뜨개질 knitting; knitwork; crochet(코바늘의).

¶~을 시작하다 take up one's knitting. **뜨개질하다** knit; do knitting; crochet. ¶뜨개질하는 사람 a knitter.
● **뜨개질바늘** a knitting needle; a knitting pin[stick]; [코바늘] a crochet hook.

뜨거워지다 become[get] hot; grow[get] warm. ¶햇살이 뜨거워지기 전에 before the heat of the day comes on // 뜨거워지기 쉬운 금속 metals that get hot easily // 모터가 뜨거워졌다 The motor has gotten hot. / The motor has overheated.

뜨거워하다 feel (it) hot; find (it) hot. ¶어린애가 국을 뜨거워한다 The child finds the soup too hot.

뜨겁다 1 [열이 높다] hot; heated; burning. ¶뜨거운 국[물] hot soup[water] // 뜨거운 커피 piping hot coffee // 뜨겁게 하다 heat / warm / (영국 속어) hot // 햇볕이 ~ The sun is hot. // 부끄러워 얼굴이 ~ My face burns with shame. // 나는 뜨거운 음식을 좋아한다 I like my food hot. // 음식이 너무 뜨거워서 못 먹겠다 The food is too hot to eat. // 환자의 몸은 열이 나서 뜨거웠다 The patient was hot with fever.
2 [열렬하다] hot; passionate; burning. ¶뜨거운 사랑 a passionate[burning] love // 뜨거운 눈물을 흘리다 shed[weep] hot tears // 뜨거운 박수를 보내다 give a big hand (to) / clap and shout (to) // 그들은 서로 뜨거운 사이다 They are sweet on each other. / They are deeply[passionately] in love with each other.

-뜨기 one; guy; thing; fellow. ¶사팔~ a cross-eyed[squint-eyed] person // 시골~ a hick / a country bumpkin // 칠~ a moron / an idiot.

뜨끈뜨끈 warmly. ⇨ 따끈따끈
뜨끈뜨끈 hot. ⇨ 따끈하다
뜨끔거리다 smart; prick. ⇨ 따끔거리다
뜨끔뜨끔 pricking; stinging. ⇨ 따끔따끔
뜨끔하다 prickly; severe. ⇨ 따끔하다

뜨내기 1 [방랑자] a wanderer; a vagabond; a tramp; a hobo; [먼 곳에서 온 사람] a stranger; a man from another part of the country. ¶~ 일꾼 a wandering laborer / an itinerant. 2 [어쩌다가 간혹 하는 일] an odd [a casual] job; a job done off and on. ¶~ 직업 an unstable occupation / a precarious trade // ~로 행상하다 go around peddling off and on / hawk on and off.
● **뜨내기손님** a chance[casual / stray] customer; a chance comer; a transient guest. ¶~을 받는 호텔 a transient hotel. **뜨내기장사** a casual[temporary] business; a business done off and on. ¶~를 하다 do business temporarily[off and on].

뜨다¹ 1 (물·하늘에) float; buoy; fly; keep afloat. ¶비행기가 뜨다 An airplane flies in the sky. // 물거품이 떠 있다 Bubbles float on the water. // 나뭇조각이 물 위에 떠 있다 A piece of wood is floating on the water. // 둥근 척이 물 위에 떠 있었다 A boat was riding on the water. // 나는 잠시 내 몸이 공중에 뜨는 것을 느꼈다 I felt my body rise into the air for a moment. // 구름 한 점이 하늘에 떠 있었다 A cloud was sailing in the sky. // 공중에 연이 떠 있었다 A kite was flying in the sky.
2 (해·달이) rise; come up. ¶이곳은 해가 일찍 [늦게] 뜬다 The sun rises early[late] here. // 달은 오후 6시에 뜬다 The moon rises at 6:00 p.m. // 보름달이 중천에 떠 있다 The full moon is high up in the sky.
3 [틈이 생기다] get[break] loose; come off[a part]; be detached; be disjoined. ¶장판이 ~ floor paper comes off the floor // 그는 잇새가 떴다 There are gaps between his teeth.
4 [빌려 준 것을 받지 못하다] be lost for good; go up in smoke. ¶그에게 빌려 준 돈이 떠 버려 손해 보았다 I suffered a loss because the money I lent him was dissipated.

뜨다² 1 [발효하다] ferment; undergo fermentation; [썩다] become stale; grow moldy; go musty and fusty; turn bad (from heat). ¶날씨가 더워서 창고의 쌀이 떴다 The rice stored in the warehouse has become stale due to the hot weather. 2 [얼굴이 누렇게 살갗이 부은 것처럼 되다] become[grow] sallow. ¶누렇게 뜬 얼굴 a sallow face // 집에만 틀어박혀 있어서 네 얼굴이 떴다 Since you have shut yourself in the house all the time, your face has grown all sallow.

뜨다³ 1 (자리를) leave; quit; go away (from); depart (from); resign; (옮기다) move; clear out. ¶자리를 ~ leave one's seat // 관직을 ~ resign[retire from] office // 고향을 ~ bid good-bye to one's native land[country] // 그는 슬그머니 자리를 뜨고 없었다 He had slipped out of the room unnoticed. // 그는 지금 자리를 뜨고 없습니다(전화 등에서) I'm sorry, but he seems to have stepped out. / He is not at his desk just now. 2 [죽다] die; depart. ¶세상을 ~ depart from this world (to the eternity) / pass away / die.

뜨다⁴ 1 [일부를 떼어 내다] cut off[out]; shovel off. ¶잔디를 ~ cut sod // 구들장을 ~ cut a floor-slab stone // 강에서 얼음을 ~ cut out ice blocks from a river // 그들은 흙을 삽으로 떠냈다 They shoveled up clods of earth.
2 (물·국 등을) scoop up; ladle (out); dip up; spoon up[out]. ¶물고기를 그물로 ~ scoop up fish with a net // 국자로 수프를 ~ ladle (up) soup / spoon up soup // 저녁을 한 숟갈 ~ have a bite of supper / have a spot of dinner // 샘물을 손으로 떠서 마셨다 I scooped up water from the spring with my hands and drank it.
3 (고기를) (meat) into slices. ¶고기포를 ~ cut meat into slices (to be dried).
4 (각을) cut up. ¶소를 잡아 각을 ~ cut up a slaughtered cow.
5 (옷감 등을) cut out[buy] a piece of cloth (from a bolt to make clothes). ¶장에 가거든 옷감을 한 감 떠다 주시오 When you go to the market place, get me a piece of cloth for making my dress, please.
6 (종이를) shape; make. ¶종이를 ~ make paper.

뜨다⁵ 1 (눈을) open (one's eyes). ¶눈을 크게 뜨고 with one's eyes wide open // 눈을 ~ open one's eyes / wake up / awake // 졸려서 눈을 뜰 수가 없다 I can't keep my eyes open because I'm so sleepy. 2 (귀를) hear; begin to hear; prick up (one's ears). ¶음악에 귀를 ~ come to appreciate[understand] music // 아기가 귀를 떴다 A baby began to hear.

뜨다⁶ 1 [그물을 짜다] net; weave; (뜨개바늘로) knit; crochet. ¶그물을 ~ make[weave] a net / net // 성기게 [촘촘하게] ~ knit with loose[tight] stitches // 털실로 스웨터를 ~

knit a sweater out of woolen yarn / knit a wool sweater. **2** [마느질하다] stitch; sew. ¶터진 곳을 한두 바늘 ~ put one or two stitches in a rip / sew up a rip with one or two stitches∥실로 이름의 머리글자를 ~ work one's initials (on a handkerchief). **3** [문신하다] tattoo (a design on). ¶등에 용의 문신을 ~ have a dragon tattooed on one's back.

뜨다[7] **1** (남의 본을) follow suit; model (oneself) (on / upon / after); copy after (precedents); imitate. ¶아버지의 본을 ~ imitate one's father / follow one's father's example. **2** (도면 등을) copy; trace; draw; facsimile. ¶사본을 ~ copy / make a copy (of)∥버선본을 ~ copy a pattern of socks from the original model∥본을 떠서 그리다 paint from a copy.

뜨다[8] (뜸을) cauterize (the skin) with moxa; apply cauterizing [moxa-cautery]. ¶머리에 뜸을 ~ cauterize the top of one's head (with moxa).

뜨다[9] **1** [느리다] slow. ¶템포가 뜬 음악 music in slow tempo∥걸음이 ~ be slow-footed [-paced] / be slow of foot. **2** [둔하다] dull; slow; slow-[dull-]witted. ¶눈치가 ~ be slow[dull] in sensing[catching] a situation∥깨우침이 ~ be slow at understanding. **3** [말수가 적다] taciturn; reticent; slow of speech. ¶입이 뜬 사람 a man of few words∥입이 ~ be taciturn / be tight-lipped. **4** [무디다] dull; blunt; (물매가) gentle ¶날이 뜬 칼 a knife with a blunt edge∥물매가 뜬 지붕 a gently sloping roof / a roof which has an easy slope. **5** (시간·공간이) have an interval (of time / of space); be at a distance (from); be distant [apart] (from). ¶마을에서 멀리 뜬 곳 the place far from the town∥10년 ~ be at an interval of 10 years∥역에서 너의 집까지는 거리가 얼마나 뜨냐 How far is it from the station to your house?

뜨듯하다 warm; mild. ⇨²뜨듯하다
뜨뜻미지근하다 lukewarm; tepid; disagreeably warm. ¶뜨뜻미지근한 대책 a halfway [lukewarm] measure∥난폭 운전사에 대한 단속이 ~ We ought to be harder on reckless drivers.
뜨뜻하다 warm; mild; genial; hot. ¶뜨뜻한 옷 warm clothes∥뜨뜻한 날씨 warm weather∥날씨가 뜨뜻해서 불을 땔 필요가 없다 The weather is too warm for fires. **뜨뜻이** warm(ly); hot; mild(ly).
뜨락 →뜰
뜨물 the washing water of rice; water from the (first) washing of rice.
뜨스하다 warm; mild. ⇨²따스하다
뜨습다 comfortably warm. ⇨²따습다
뜨음하다 infrequent. ⇨²뜸하다
뜨이다 1 (눈이) be opened; awake(잠에서); (귀가) prick up; come to know [understand]. ¶아침 일찍 눈이 ~ awake early in the morning∥현실에 눈이 ~ awake to the realities of the society∥성에 눈이 ~ be awakened to sex / be sexually awakened∥그림에 눈이 ~ begin to appreciate painting∥음악에 귀가 ~ begin to understand[appreciate] music∥그 소식을 들었을 때 귀가 번쩍 뜨였다 My ears pricked up with surprise on hearing the news. **2** (눈에) be seen; be visible; be in sight [view]; [발견되다] be found; catch the eye; arrest [attract] the attention; [돋보이다] be prominent; be conspicuous; be remarkable. ¶눈에 뜨이는 attractive / prominent / conspicuous∥눈에 뜨이지 않는 unnoticeable / unattractive / inconspicuous∥눈에 뜨이는 특징 conspicuous characteristics∥눈에 뜨이는 미인 an attractive beauty / a woman of striking [dazzling] beauty∥눈에 뜨이는 대로 at [on] sight∥눈에 뜨이게 conspicuously / strikingly / remarkably / noticeably / markedly∥눈에 뜨이지 않게 in a quiet [a modest / an inconspicuous] way / so as not to attract attention∥우연히 눈에 ~ come across [upon] / happen [stumble] upon∥눈에 뜨이는 곳에 게시하다 put up a notice in a conspicuous place∥그는 눈에 뜨이게 쇠약해졌다 His health has declined noticeably. ∥그녀는 눈에 뜨이게 향상됐다 She has made remarkable success. ∥오는 길에 책을 떨어뜨렸는데 혹 눈에 뜨이지 않던가 Did you happen to see a book along the way by any chance? I seem to have dropped one. ∥사진기를 들고 나가다가 아버지 눈에 뜨였다 I was taking the camera with me when I was detected by my father.

뜬구름 1 [떠다니는 구름] a cloud drift; a floating [drifting] cloud. **2** [덧없음] transience; transitoriness; evanescence; ephemerality. ¶~ 같은 transient / transitory / evanescent / ephemeral∥~ 같은 인생 transient [ephemeral] life / mutable life∥인생은 ~ 같다 How brief is the span of (human) life. / Life is but an empty dream.
뜬구름(을) 잡다 [허황된 일을 하다] chase a rainbow; (영) build castles in the air.
뜬눈 unsleeping eyes. ¶~으로 밤을 새우다 cannot get a wink of sleep / do not sleep a wink / remain awake all night / pass a sleepless [wakeful] night∥우리는 하룻밤을 ~으로 새웠다 We passed [spent] a sleepless night.
뜬세상(-世上) the transitory world; transient [fleeting] life; the earth; this weary world.
뜬소문(-所聞) a groundless [wild] rumor; an unfounded report; a canard. ¶…이라는 ~이 돌다 a groundless rumor is abroad [current / in circulation] about … / an unfounded rumor is going round that … ∥그것은 ~이다 There is no foundation for the rumor.
뜯기다[1] **1** [물리다] be bitten. ¶벼룩에게 뜯긴 자리 a fleabite∥모기한테 ~ be bitten by a mosquito. **2** [빼앗기다] have (a thing) bitten off; be plucked [fleeced] (of); be exacted [extorted / squeezed] (by). ¶낚시 미끼를 ~ have a bait bitten off / lose one's bait∥돈을 ~ be fleeced (of money) (by sharpers) / be squeezed out of one's money∥그들의 임금은 청부업자들에게 뜯기기 쉽다 Their wages are subject to a rakeoff by the contractors. **3** [머리털 등이 뽑히다] be plucked; be pulled out; be torn out [off]. ¶머리털을 ~ One's hair is torn [pulled] out by the roots. ∥공작이 깃을 뜯겼다 A peacock is plucked of his feathers.
뜯기다[2] (마소에게 풀을) graze (cattle); put (cattle) to grass; put (cattle) (out) to pasture; pasture. ¶들의 풀을 ~ graze a

뜨다 field.

뜯다 1 (풀·털 등을) pluck[pick / pull / tear] (off). ¶닭의 털을 ~ pluck[pick] a chicken / pick feathers from a chicken // 풀을 ~ pluck grass / pluck up weeds / weed (a garden) // 담요의 보풀을 ~ pick at the blanket.
2 [떼어 먹다] bite; graze; pasture. ¶벼룩이 ~ a flea bites // 소가 풀을 ~ the cattle graze [pasture] // 불갈비를 ~ eat roast ribs of beef // 닭고기를 뜯어 먹다 nibble on a chicken // 소가 목장에서 풀을 뜯어 먹고 있다 The cattle are feeding in the pasture.
3 [떼다·찢다] tear off [up / down]; tear [take] apart; take off; remove; disassemble; break up; disjoint. ¶마루의 널을 ~ tear up the floorboards // 지붕을 ~ strip the roof of tiles / unroof a house // 달력의 한 장 ~ tear off a leaf from [a sheet of] a calendar // 편지를 ~ open a letter / cut a letter open // 공장을 ~ dismantle a factory // 고기를 ~ tear meat apart (into shreds) // 기계를 ~ take a machine apart [to pieces] / break up a machine / strip a machine down // 시계를 ~ take a watch apart [to pieces] // 그녀는 성급하게 그 봉투를 뜯었다 Impatiently she tore the envelope open.
4 [꿰맨 것을] unsew; unstitch. ¶옷의 솔기를 ~ unsew clothes [a dress] // 뜯어진 솔기를 꿰매다 mend an open seam.
5 [빼앗다] pluck [fleece] (a person of his money); extort (money from a person).
6 (노름에서) gain; get; receive. ¶(노름판에서) 개평을 ~ take a (free) cut of the winnings / receive a tip from each gambler.
7 [(현악기의 줄을) 퉁겨서 소리를 내다] play (on); pluck [touch] (the strings of); thrum (on) (a mandoline); pick (a guitar). ¶가야금을 ~ play (on) the Korean harp.

뜯어고치다 1 [해체하여 고치다] tear [take] apart and mend [repair]; [개조하다] reconstruct; rebuild; remodel; adapt (문장 등을). ¶옷을 ~ remake one's clothes // 집을 ~ alter a house // 방을 ~ remodel a room. 2 [검토하여 수정하다] look over and change [alter]; examine and improve; revise. ¶원고를 ~ revise a manuscript // 법령을 ~ revise an ordinance.

뜯어내다 1 (붙인 것을) take off [away / down]; tear off [up / away / down]; pick [pluck] (off). ¶달력 한 장을 ~ tear off a leaf from a calendar // 옷에서 실밥을 ~ remove waste thread from clothes // 옷의 안감을 ~ rip off [out] the lining // 잡풀을 ~ pluck up weeds // 마루 판자를 뜯어내니까 거기에 작은 단지 하나가 있었다 When they tore up the floorboards, they found a pot.
2 [분해하다] disjoint; dismantle; disassemble; disintegrate; take [pull] (a thing) to pieces; take (a machine) apart [down]. ¶(술통 등의) 밑바닥을 ~ rip off the bottom // 기계를 ~ take a machine to pieces // 지붕을 ~ strip the roof of tiles / unroof a house.
3 (재물을) extort; pluck; fleece. ¶남편한테서 돈을 ~ pluck one's husband of his money / tease [importune / press] one's husband for money.

뜯어말리다 separate (two fighting persons); pull [draw] (fighters) apart; stop (a fight). ¶싸움을 ~ draw [pull] combatants [quarreling persons] apart / put down a fight // 맞붙어 싸우는 아이들을 ~ pull the grappling boys apart // 나는 두 사람의 싸움을 뜯어말렸다 I pulled the two men who were fighting apart.

뜯어먹다 [졸라서 얻어먹다] squeeze; pinch; sponge (off a person); hang on (a person); act like a leech on (a person) // 남을 뜯어먹고 살다 live [prey] on a person / victimize a person // 그는 노상 뜯어먹을 궁리만 하고 있다 He is always thinking of sponging on another.

뜯어보다 1 (봉한 것을) open (a thing) [tear (a thing) open] and look at (it). ¶편지를 ~ open a letter [tear a letter open / cut open a letter] and read it. 2 [자세히 살피다] scrutinize; scan; look closely (at); examine (a thing) narrowly [closely]; inspect [examine] carefully [in detail]. ¶사람됨을 ~ scrutinize the caliber [quality] of (a person) // 얼굴을 ~ scrutinize [study] (a person's) face / get a good look into (a person's) face // 집을 이모저모로 ~ look a house over thoroughly. 3 [간신히 읽다] read [construe] with difficulty; falter (in reading).

뜰 [정원] a garden; [안마당] a courtyard; a yard. ¶뒤~ a backyard // 앞~ a front garden [yard] // ~ 안의 초목들 the trees and flowers in the garden // ~에 나무를 심다 plant a garden (with trees) // ~을 손질하다 trim (up) a garden.

뜸[1] [한] moxa cautery; moxibustion. ¶~ 자국 a mark // ~을 뜨다 cauterize (the skin) with moxa / burn moxa (on the skin).

뜸[2] [열에 익힌 것을 얼마간 그대로 두어 속속들이 익힘] being well-steamed [-cooked]. ¶밥이 잘 ~ 들었다 The rice has been fully steamed.

뜸(을) 들이다 (일을) give a necessary interval of time; give a pause; give time (enough). ¶일을 뜸 들여 하다 allow enough time to get a job done / give a pause [break] in doing a job.

뜸부기 [동] a water cock; a mud [marsh] hen.

뜸질하다 cauterizing with moxa; moxibustion. 뜸 질하다 cauterize with moxa; apply a heat treatment.

뜸하다 infrequent; (서술적) have a rather long interval; be in a lull [break] (비·바람 등이). ¶(바람 등이) 뜸한 사이 a lull [break] (in the rain / in a storm) // 뜸해지다 hold [let] up / abate / subside / become light // 집 소식이 ~ have not heard from home for quite a long time // 이웃집의 싸움이 좀 ~ The next-door people don't quarrel as often as they used to these days. // 비가 뜸해졌다 The rain is letting up a little. // 적의 포화가 뜸해졌다 The enemy's fire slackened a little.

뜻 1 [의미·의의] meaning; sense; significance; [취지] the import; the purport; the effect; a point; [내포된] implication. ¶깊은 ~ a deep [profound] meaning // ~의 미묘한 차이 a delicate shade of meaning // 숨은 ~ a latent [hidden] meaning // 애매한 ~ an ambiguous [obscure] meaning // 어떤 ~에서는 in a (certain) sense / in a way // ~을 곡해하다 pervert [twist] the meaning // 좋은 ~으로 해석하다 take it in a favorable way / take (it) well // 여러 번 읽고 또 읽으면 그 ~을 절로 이해하게 된다 If you read it over and over again, you will understand what it

says.∥그 의식의 진정한 ~을 아는 사람은 적다 Few people can understand the true meaning of this ceremony.∥내가 참석하지 않으면 모임은 ~이 없다 The meeting will mean little without your attendance.∥이 구절은 여러 가지 ~으로 해석된다 The passage may be read in various ways.∥이것은 무슨 ~이오 What does this mean?∥나쁜 ~으로 말한 건 아니다 I meant no ill will / My meaning was quite innocent.∥별로 깊은 ~이 있어서 그렇게 말한 것은 아니다 I did not mean anything serious when I said so.∥내가 그런 ~의 말을 했을지도 모른다 I may have said something to that effect.∥잘 있다는 ~의 편지를 받았다 I received a letter to the effect that he is getting along well.∥내가 한 비유를 그는 글자 그대로의 ~으로 해석하여 격분했다 Taking literally what I only meant to be a metaphor, he flew into a rage.∥그는 ~이 없는 말을 중얼거리고 있다 He is muttering meaningless sounds.
2 〔의지〕 will; 〔의향〕 intention; a motive; a design; 〔마음〕 a(one's) mind; an idea; a thought; a wish. ¶일이 ~과 같이 되지 않다 be baulked in one's designs∥~이 서로 통하다 come to[arrive at] understanding∥(일 등이) ~에 맞다 meet (a person's) wish/ suit (a person's) fancy∥~을 밝히다 speak one's mind∥남의 ~을 떠보다 sound a person's views∥~을 거역하다 act against (a person's) will∥그것은 다시는 안 와도 좋다는 ~이 아닐까 I guess that was a hint that he didn't want me to come anymore.∥이것은 하느님의 ~임에 틀림없다 This must be the will of God[God's will].∥나는 그의 유족에게 애도의 ~을 표했다 I expressed my condolences to his bereaved family.∥모든 것이 자기 ~대로 된다고 생각한다면 큰 잘못이다 You are mistaken if you think that you can have your own way in everything[have everything your own way].∥그녀는 부모의 ~을 어기고 그 남자와 결혼했다 She married him against her parents' wishes.∥교장은 일선 교사들의 ~에 따라 학교 규칙의 개선에 착수했다 The principal began to reform the school rules in compliance with the teachers' wishes.∥일이 ~대로 되지 않았다 Things[Everything] went wrong with her.∥내 희망[의도]과는 반대 방향으로 일이 되었다 Things turned contrary to my hopes[intentions].∥아버님 ~에 따라 가업을 이었다 In obedience to[Following] my father's wishes, I took over the family business.∥이번에는 내 ~을 관철했다 I had my way this time.∥그는 ~은 있으나 가난해서 공부를 하지 못한다 He has a desire to study but can't because he is so poor.∥~ 있으신 분들의 참석을 환영합니다 Those interested are welcome to attend.∥우리가 만난 것은 신의 ~이다 It is divine will that has brought us together.
3 〔목적〕 an object; an aim; a purpose; 〔대망〕 ambition; aspiration; 〔지망〕 wish; desire; hope. ¶굳은 ~을 지닌 사람 a man of strong will[resolution]∥높은 ~을 품다 aim high / hitch one's wagon to star∥그는 인생의 큰 ~을 품고 집을 나섰다 He resolved on his path in life and left home.∥그는 20살 때에 의사가 되겠다는 ~을 세웠다 He conceived an ambition to become a doctor when he was twenty.∥마침내 그는 자기 ~을 이루었다 He attained[accomplished] his aim [purpose] at last. / He finally realized his aspiration[goal].∥그는 ~을 이루지 못하고 죽었다 He died before he could realize his aspiration.

뜻이 있는 곳에 길이 있다(속담) Nothing is impossible to a willing mind.; Where there's a will, there's a way.

뜻(이) 맞다 1 〔의기 상통하다〕 congenial; likeminded; (서술적) be of congenial temper; be of a mind; see eye to eye (with); be united in spirit; hit it off (with). ¶뜻이 맞는 친구 congenial friends∥그 둘은 뜻이 맞는 사이다 They are like-minded. / There is a great affinity between them.∥우리들은 서로 뜻이 맞지 않는다 We cannot temperamentally agree with each other. **2** 〔마음에 들다〕 suit one's taste[fancy]; accord with one's will; be in one's favor; satisfactory; acceptable. ¶뜻이 맞지 않다 be not to one's liking / be undesirable / go against the grain∥좀처럼 뜻이 맞는 사람을 구할 수 없다 It's hard to find a man to suit me.

뜻글자(-字) an ideograph. ⇨"표의 문자(⇨표의)

뜻대로 just as wished[hoped / intended / meant]; as one likes[pleases / desires / wished]; at one's pleasure; in one's own way. ¶만사가 ~ 된다면 if I could have everything my own way∥~ 되지 않는 세상 life full of vexations∥~ 하다 have[get] one's (own) way (in a matter)∥그는 만사를 자기 ~ 하려고 했다 He wanted to have things his own way.∥계획이 ~ 되었다 The plan worked as desired.∥사정은 그들의 ~ 되지 않았다 Circumstances were hardly such as to give them their way.∥세상만사는 ~ 안 된다 If wishes were horses, beggars would ride. / Life is full of troubles.∥일이란 좀처럼 ~ 되는 것이 아니다 Things seldom come up to our expectations.

뜻밖 〔생각 밖〕 unexpectedness; a surprise. ¶~의 unexpected / unlooked-for / unanticipated / unsuspected / surprising / unthought-of∥~의 손님 an unexpected visitor ∥~의 일이었기 때문에 더욱 당황했다 The suddenness of it confused us all the more.∥그의 결혼은 아주 ~이었다 His marriage was utterly unexpected.∥내가 실패하다니 나로서는 정말 ~이었다 Your failure upsets me. / (구어) I don't understand how you could have muffed it!∥나는 ~의 장소에서 그를 만났다 We met where I had least expected to see him.∥그의 ~의 제의에 깜짝 놀랐다 I was surprised at his completely unexpected offer.∥그것은 전혀 ~의 사태였다 It was a totally unexpected development.

뜻밖에 〔의외로〕 unexpectedly; accidentally; surprisingly; by accident[chance]; beyond expectation; suddenly. ¶정말 ~ 마지막 순간에 형세가 역전되었다 Quite unexpectedly, the tables were turned at the last moment.∥그 나이에 ~ 그는 정정하였다 I found him unexpectedly hale and hearty for his age.∥~ 그는 내 이야기를 들어 알고 있었다 Unexpectedly, he had heard of me.∥어느 날 그가 ~ 찾아왔다 One day I received[had] an unexpected visit from him. / One day he called on me unexpectedly.∥역에서 ~ 그를 만났다 I happened to meet[bumped into] him at the station.∥~ 두 사람은 같은 결론

뜻있다 에 도달했다 Quite unexpectedly, the two came to the same conclusion.

뜻있다 [의미 있다] significant; [유익하다] useful; [가치 있다] worthwhile; [함축성 있다] meaningful. ¶뜻있는 생애 a life worth living / a well-spent life∥뜻있는 미소를 띠다 with a meaningful smile∥뜻있게 사용하다 put (a thing) to a good use∥그 사업은 그의 생활을 뜻있게 해 준다 The work makes his life worth living[significant].∥그 모임은 매우 뜻있었다 The meeting proved very significant. / They had much sense in holding the meeting.

뜻하다 [계획하다·의도하다] plan; intend (to do); aim at; purpose; have an ambition (to); aspire to[after] (fame / honor); hope; set one's heart[mind] on; [결심하다] determine (to rise in the world); make up one's mind (to go to sea). ¶나는 고교 때부터 외교관이 되려고 뜻하고 있었다 I aspired to a diplomatic career[I wanted to be a diplomat] ever since I was in high school.∥나는 그가 뜻하고 있는 바가 무엇인지 이해할 수 없다 I can not guess what he is driving at.
2 [의미하다] mean; signify; imply; connote. ¶그것은 무엇을 뜻하느냐 What does it mean [signify]?∥그녀의 미소는 우리를 용서하였음을 뜻했다 Her smile implied that she had forgiven us.∥침묵은 때때로 동의를 뜻한다 Silence often implies consent.

띄다 1 be opened; be seen; be found. ⇨ 뜨이다 2 space. ⇨ 띄우다³

띄어쓰기 spacing words.

띄엄띄엄 1 [사이가 벌어진 모양] sparsely; thinly; scatteredly; [사이를 두고 하는 모양] at intervals; intermittently. ¶그는 ~ 말을 했다 He spoke with pauses between his words.∥그녀는 ~ 어머니를 놓친 사연을 설명했다 She brokenly explained how she had lost sight of her mother.∥그녀는 어릴 때 들은 이야기를 ~ 이야기했다 She told snatches of a story she had heard as a child. **2** [느릿느릿한 모양] slowly; sluggishly.

띄우다¹ 1 (공중에) fly; let fly; make fly. ¶연[모형 비행기]을 ~ fly a kite[a model plane]∥풍선을 ~ fly[send up] a balloon∥비행기를 ~ fly an airplane / launch an airplane into the air. **2** (물 위에) float; set (a ship) afloat; sail (a toy boat); [진수시키다] launch. ¶배를 ~[진수시키다] set a ship afloat / [달리게 하다] sail a boat∥보트를 띄우고 호수에서 하루를 즐겼다 We enjoyed the day, riding around the lake in a boat[rowing a boat on the lake].∥그들은 재목을 하루로 띄워 보냈다 They floated the timber downstream.

띄우다² [발효시키다] ferment; leaven; sweat(담뱃잎을). ¶누룩[메주]을 ~ ferment malt[boiled soybean lumps]∥술을 ~ brew wine.

띄우다³ (사이를) space; leave a space (between); leave an interval. ¶사이를 띄워서 at intervals / sparsely∥행과 행 사이를 ~ leave space between the lines∥25미터씩 띄워서 나무를 심다 plant trees with the space of 25 meters.

띄우다⁴ [보내다] send; dispatch. ¶편지를 ~ send[address] a letter (to a person) / post [(미)] mail] a letter∥파발을 ~ send an express messenger (to).

띠¹ **1** [허리띠] a belt; a (waist) band; a girdle; a sash; (띠 종류) belting. ¶가죽 ~ a leather belt[girdle]∥검정 ~ [유도·태권도] (wear) a black belt∥~를 매다[풀다] tie [untie] a belt∥~를 조르다 tighten one's belt / adjust [fix] one's belt. **2** (아기 업는) a baby-carrying band[strap]. **3** (물건을 매는) a (drawing) string; a tape; a binder twine.

띠² **1** [탄생한 해의 지지(地支)를 상징하는 동물명] the zodiac(al) sign under which one was born. ¶그녀는 말~ 태생이다 She was born in the Year of the Horse. **2** (화투 패의) a five-point card in the flowery card game.

띠³ [식] a cogon (grass); an alang-alang; an alang grass.

띠다 **1** [두르다] put on; do up; tie. ¶띠를 ~ do up[put on]. a belt[sash] / tie a girdle / girdle[belt] oneself.
2 [지니다] wear; bear; carry; be armed with.
3 [사명 등을 가지다] be charged with; be entrusted with; be invested [clothed] with. ¶공무를 띠고 on official business[duty]∥중대한 사명을 ~ be charged[entrusted] with some important mission∥그는 사명을 띠고 아프리카로 날아갔다 He flew to Africa on some mission or other[on an official mission].
4 [빛·기색 등을 조금 나타내다] have; wear; assume; take on. ¶붉은 기를 띤 노란색 reddish yellow∥우수 띤 얼굴 a sorrowful [melancholy] face∥그녀는 노기 띤 눈으로 나를 보았다 She looked at me with angry eyes.∥그녀의 빰이 홍조를 띠었다 A flush came over her cheeks. / She blushed.∥그녀는 만면에 미소를 띠고 무대에 나타났다 She appeared on the stage all smiles.∥그녀는 얼굴에 근심의 빛을 띠고 있었다 She wore a sorrowful look.∥너는 주기(酒氣)를 띠고 있다 You have been drinking.∥이 문제는 점차 정치적 성격을 띠기 시작했다 The issue has gradually taken on[assumed] a political character.

띵하다 (아픔이) dull; obtuse; (정신이) muddled. ¶띵한 머리 a muddled head∥머리가 ~ My head is buzzing[humming]. / [욱신거린다] I have a splitting headache.∥수면 부족으로 머리가 ~ I feel my brains muddled owing to want of sleep.

ㄹ

-ㄹ 1 [일반적 사실]. ¶할 일 things to do // 잘 시간 the time to go to bed // 팔 집 a house for sale // 그 책을 살 돈 money to buy the book with // 마실 것 something to drink // 그는 나를 버릴 남자가 아니다 He isn't the man to desert me. // 그는 외출할 때면 언제나 개를 데리고 나선다 When he goes out he always takes his dog with him.
2 [미래의 일]. ¶그것을 할 작정이다 I expect to do it. // 그는 그곳에 갈 작정이다 He intends going[to go] there. // 나는 그를 꼭 찾아볼 생각이다 I'll certainly go and see him. // 내일은 날씨가 갤 것이다 It will be fine tomorrow. // 그는 내일 서울에 도착할 예정이다 He is expected to be in Seoul tomorrow.

-ㄹ걸 1 [후회]. ¶그를 찾아가 볼걸 I should have called on him. 2 [추측] I dare say; I should say; perhaps; probably; maybe; possibly; I suppose; I think; I presume; I guess. ¶아마 그럴걸 It may be so. / I should think so. // 이것으로 충분할걸 This will probably be enough. // 그는 40세 정도 될걸 I guess him to be about 40 [I guess that he is about 40].

-ㄹ게 [행동의 약속]. ¶잠깐 다녀올게 I will be [come] back soon. / (미국 구어) I'll be right back. // 내일 아침 눈뜨자마자 전화할게 I'll call you first thing tomorrow morning. // 역까지 바래다줄게 I will see you to the station.

-ㄹ까 1 [의문·추측]. I wonder; I am afraid; I fear. ¶저 사람은 누구일까 I wonder who that man is. // 도대체 무슨 일일까 I wonder what happened. // 그게 사실일까 I wonder if [whether] it can be true. / Can it be true? // 내일 비가 올까 I wonder whether[if] it will rain tomorrow. // 도대체 그가 그것을 어떻게 할 작정일까 What can he mean by that, I wonder? // 저 환자는 곧 좋아질까 Will the patient get well soon?
2 [제의]. ¶산책할까 How about taking a walk? / Let's go out for a walk, shan't we? // 이렇게 하면 어떨까 How[What] about doing this? // 걸어서 갈까 What do you say to going on foot? // 내일까지 기다려 보면 어떨까 Suppose we wait till tomorrow. // 내가 노래를 부를까 Shall I sing a song?
3 [부탁]. ¶부탁 하나 드릴까요 Would you do me a favor? // 들어가도 될까요 May I come in? // 소금 좀 집어 주실까요 May I trouble you to pass me the salt? / Would you please pass me the salt? // 담배를 피워도 될까요 Mind[Do you mind] if I smoke?

-ㄹ까 말까 1 [망설임] hesitatingly; with hesitation. ¶나는 안으로 들어갈까 말까 망설이고 있었다 I was balancing in my mind whether to go in or not. // 그녀는 초대에 응할까 말까 망설였다 She hung between refusing or accepting the invitation. 2 [미달] less than; not more than; scarcely; barely. ¶일 년이 될까 말까 해서 in less than a year // 생후 15개월이 될까 말까 한 아기 an infant less than fifteen months old // 그 회의의 참석자는 30명이 될까 말까 했다 There were scarcely thirty people present. // 그녀는 겨우 15살이 될까 말까 하다 She is barely[scarcely] fifteen.

-ㄹ까 보다 1 [의구심]. ¶체포될까 봐 도망치다 run away for fear of being arrested // 어머니는 딸이 볼까 봐 그것을 감추었다 Mother hid it lest her daughter should see it. 2 [불확정한 자기 의사]. ¶당신 고용주에게 당신 행동에 대해 말해 버릴까 보다 I've half a mind to tell your employer about your behavior. // 당신과 런던으로 갈까 보다 I have a good mind to go to London with you. // 오늘 밤에는 외식이나 할까 보다 I feel like eating out tonight. // 굴욕을 당하느니 차라리 죽어 버릴까 봐 I would rather die than suffer disgrace. / I had rather die than live in dishonor.

-ㄹ는지 [불확실한 추측] if ...; whether ... (or not); I wonder .... ¶비가 오는지 안 오는지 (모르겠다) I can't tell whether it will rain or not. // 그가 언제 올는지 (알 수 없군) I don't know when he will be here.

-ㄹ라 [염려]. ¶조심해라, 넘어질라 Be careful, lest you fall down. / Be careful, or you will fall down. // 과로하지 마라, 병날라 Don't overwork yourself, you might get sick[ill].

-ㄹ라치면 [가정] when; whenever; if. ¶나는 서울에 갈라치면 언제나 아저씨 댁에서 머문다 Whenever I go to Seoul, I stay with my uncle. // 그는 외출할라치면 꼭 우산을 잃어버리고 온다 He never goes out without losing his umbrella. / He loses his umbrella every time he goes out. // 나는 그가 필요할라치면 언제나 벨을 울립니다 If I want him, I ring.

-ㄹ락 말락 [간신히] barely; hardly; scarcely; [거의] almost; [미달] less than; not more than; short of. ¶들릴락 말락 [보일락 말락] hardly (to be) heard [seen] // 잠이 들락 말락 하다 be half asleep // 안개 속에서 그 섬이 보일락 말락 했다 We could see the island dimly [had a vague view of the island] through the haze. // 기부금은 모두 합쳐서 백만 원이 될락 말락 했다 The subscriptions were short of one million won in total.

-ㄹ망정 [비록 그러하지만 그러나] (even) though; although; (even) if; (and) yet; nevertheless; however; but. ¶가난할망정 poor as one is / though (one is) poor // 그는 몸은 약할망정 의지는 굳다 He may be weakly but he has a strong mind. // 그는 가난할망정 자신의 처지에 만족하고 있다 Though he is poor, yet he is (nevertheless) satisfied with his situation.

-ㄹ밖에 cannot (choose) but (do); cannot help (doing); cannot do otherwise than; have no choice but (to do). ¶그렇게 할밖에 (다른 수가 없다) There is nothing for it but to do so. / It's the only thing we can do. / There is [we have] no choice [alternative] but to do so. / That's the only course open to us. // 돈이 없으니 빚을 낼밖에 Since I am broke, I've got to get a loan. // 그의 충고에 따를밖에 I have no choice but to [cannot

-ㄹ뿐더러 [뿐만 아니라 다른 일이 더 있음] not only[merely] ... but (also); as well as. ¶그녀는 용모가 아름다울뿐더러 총명하기도 하다 She is not only beautiful but also intelligent.∥그는 지식도 있을뿐더러 경험도 있다 He has experience as well as knowledge.

-ㄹ세 you know; I (can) tell you; I assure you. ¶나는 화가가 아닐세 I am not a painter, you know.∥쉬운 일이 아닐세 It is not soft job, I (can) tell you.

-ㄹ세라 [우려] lest (should); for fear (that). ¶그는 들킬세라 달아났다 He ran away lest he should be seen.∥그녀는 갓난아기를 깨울세라 우리더러 조용히 해 달라고 부탁했다 She asked us not to be noisy, for fear of waking the baby.

-ㄹ수록 [어떤 일이 더하여 감] the more [less] ..., the more[less]. ¶싸면 쌀수록 좋다 The cheaper, the better.∥생활 수준이 높아질수록 지출도 늘어난다 Expenses will increase as the standard of living rises.∥빠르면 빠를수록 좋다 The sooner, the better.∥그는 볼수록 그녀가 마음에 들었다 The more he looked at her, the more he liked her.∥가지면 가질수록 욕심이 더 난다 The more one gets, the more one wants.

-ㄹ이만큼 →-ㄹ만큼

-ㄹ지 [추측으로 의심을 나타냄] whether (... or); if. ¶내가 가야 할지 모르겠다 I wonder whether I should go (or not).∥그가 올지 어떨지 I wonder whether he will come.∥어떻게 하면 거기에 빨리 도착할지 나는 생각하고 있었다 I was wondering how to get there quickly.∥무슨 일이 일어날지 아무도 모른다 There is no saying[No one can say] what may happen.∥지금 저축하는 습관을 길러라 안 그랬다간 노후에 곤란해질지 모르니까 Learn to save now, otherwise you may want in old age.∥회의가 언제 끝날지 모르겠다 I don't know when the meeting will be over.

-ㄹ지나 [마땅히 … 할 것이지만] though ... must[should] ...; must[should / ought to] (do), but .... ¶그의 죄는 죽어 마땅하나 his crime deserves certain death, but ....

-ㄹ지니라 [당연히 … 할 것이니라] must; should; ought to (do); shall (2, 3인칭). ¶거짓말은 하지 말지니라 You must not tell a lie.∥어버이를 공경할지니라 Parents ought to be honored.∥살인하지 말지니라 [성] Thou shalt not kill.

-ㄹ지라도 [비록 …하더라도] though; even if [though]; no matter (who / what / when / where / how). ¶무슨 일이 생길지라도 whatever may happen / come what may / 설사 이것이 사실이라고 할지라도 granting this to be true[that this is true]∥그가 아무리 영리하다 할지라도 아직 어린아이에 불과해 Even though he is clever[Clever though he may be], he is still only child.∥그녀와 결혼한다 할지라도 2년 후의 일이야 Even if I marry her, it won't be for two years.∥그에게 동정하는 사람이 있다 할지라도 극소수이다 There are few people, if any, who sympathize with him.∥그렇다 할지라도 그 사람이 너무 늦는걸 Even so, he is quite late.∥그가 큰 부자일지라도 반드시 기부금에 응한다고는 할 수 없다 Just because he is very rich it doesn't necessarily follow that he will agree to donate money. / He may not be willing to donate money though he is very rich.∥그 사람일지라도 자신이 한 일에 대해 후회하는 일이 있는 게야 Even he regrets some of the things he has done.∥명의(名醫)일지라도 모든 병을 다 고치지는 못한다 The best doctor cannot cure every illness.∥우리가 아무리 돈을 절약할지라도 집을 살 만큼의 돈은 마련하지 못할 것이다 Even if we save every penny, we won't even have enough money to buy a house.∥그가 비록 가난할지라도 탐하지는 않는다 Poor though he is, he is not greedy.∥어린아이일지라도 그의 이름을 알고 있다 Even a small child[Every small boy] knows the man's name.∥영웅일지라도 공포를 느끼는 순간이 있다 Heroes experience moments of fear, too.

-ㄹ지어다 must; should. ⇨-ㄹ지니라

-ㄹ지언정 even if[though]; rather [sooner] than. ¶실패를 할지언정 한번 해 보겠다 Though I might fail, I will attempt it.∥나는 청빈한 가난뱅이가 될지언정 부정한 부자가 되고 싶지는 않다 I prefer honest poverty to dishonest richness.

-ㄹ진대 [조건] if; in case; suppose; supposing; provided; on condition that ...; [-ㄹ 것 같으면] judging from. ¶어차피 입신양명 못할진대 돈이나 벌겠다 If I couldn't rise to eminence, I would rather amass a fortune.∥내가 볼진대 그는 승산이 없다 From what I know of him[In my opinion] the chances are against him.

라 [음] 1 [음명] re; D. ¶~단조[장조] D minor [major]. 2 [제6계명] la.

-라¹ 1 [서술]. ¶인명은 재천이~ Life and death are providential.∥그것은 신사가 할 짓이 아니~ It is not proper for a gentleman to do such a thing. 2 [원인·병렬]. ¶그는 아직 어린애~ 그 말을 이해할 수 없다 Since he is a child, he can not understand it. / He is too young to understand it.∥낯선 사람들 앞이~ 나는 당황했다 I was embarrassed by[in] the presence of strangers.∥그는 정직한 사람이 아니~ 악당이다 He is not an honest man, but a villain.

-라² [명령형]. ¶그리 서둘지 마~ Don't be in such a hurry!∥이 문을 열지 마~ You mustn't[must never] open this door.∥잔디밭에 들어가지 마~ Keep off the grass.∥편지 부치는 것 잊지 마~ Don't forget to mail the letter.∥빨리 하~ Be quick.

라고¹ 1 [직접적인 인용]. ¶그는 "너는 가장 좋은 친구야."~ 말했다 He said, "You are my best friend."∥그는 "그건 말도 안 돼."~ 말했다 He said, "That's ridiculous!" 2 [예외가 아님을 나타냄]. ¶젊은이라면 누구나 군대에 가야 하는데 너~ 예외는 아니다 Every young man has to go to army, you are no exception.∥누구나가 참고 견디지 않으면 안 된다, 나~ 예외는 아니다 Everyone must be patient, not excepting me. 3 [얕잡아 지적하는 투]. ¶잡지~ 샀더니 읽을 것이 하나도 없다 I bought that so-called "magazine" and can't find a thing in it to read.

-라고² 1 [명령]. ¶그에게 들어오~ 할까요 Shall I ask him in?∥그녀는 아버지에게 도와 달~ 소리쳤다 She called to her father for help.∥그는 나에게 말을 중단하~ 신호했다 He sig-

naled me to stop talking.// 그에게 일어서~ 해라 Tell him to stand up.
2 [인용]. ¶사람들이 그를 부자~ 한다 They [People] say he is rich. / He is said to be rich.// 그들은 그를 거짓말쟁이~ 한다 They label him a liar.// 누구시~ 여쭐까요 Who shall I say, sir?// 네 실언이 취중이었기 때문이~ 하여 빠져나갈 수는 없다 You can't get away with your slip of the tongue by saying you'd been drinking. / You cannot blame your irresponsible remark solely on alcohol.// 그 사람이 아침 식사로 먹고 싶은 것이 무엇이~ 하더냐 What did he say it was that he wants to have for breakfast?
3 [반문]. ¶그녀가 기혼자~ What? She got married?// 그가 시인이~? 설마 (구어) Him a poet? What a joke!

라놀린 [화] lanolin(e).

-라는 [...라고 하는]. ¶그린 씨~ 분 a certain Mr. Green// 동호~ 소년 a boy named [called] Dongho / a boy, Dongho by name// 부산이~ 도시 the city of Busan//...~ 이름 [상호]의 상사 a firm under the style of ...//...~ 제목의 책을 출판하다 publish a book titled ... [under the title of ...]// 우리에게는 애덤스~ 좋은 지도자가 있다 We have a good leader in Adams.// 나는 한국의 명승지~ 명승지는 빼 놓지 않고 거의 다 가 보았다 I have visited almost every single beauty spot in Korea without exception.// 개~ 충실한 동물은 인간의 가장 좋은 친구이다 The dog, a faithful animal, is a man's best friend.// 외출 중에 최 ~ 사람이 찾아왔었다 While you were out, a Mr. Choe [a person named Choe] called.// 송 씨~ 분이시지요, 이리로 오십시오 Mr. Song — that's your name, I understand. — Please come this way.// 말~ 대로 하라 Do as you are told.// 나는 사직하~ 통고를 받았다 I received a notice that I should retire [resign] from office.// 그는 나에게 그곳에 가지 말~ 충고를 했다 He advised me not to go there.

-라니 [...라고 하니]. ¶이 집을 나가~ 나가겠소 I will get out of this house as you told me to. **2** [의문·의외]. ¶벽화~, 어느 벽화 말인가 By murals, what kind of murals do you mean?// 그 사람이 스파이~ To hear that he is a spy! / That he should be a spy!

-라니까 1 [...라고 하니까]. ¶그녀에게 들어오~ 싫다고 했다 I asked her in, but she refused. // 자네가 그녀를 만나~ 내가 만나기는 하겠다 I will see her for you, since you want me to do.// 그에게 집에 가~ 가더라 I told him to go home and he did. **2** [상대방에게 다시 일러 줌]. ¶집에 가~ Go home, I tell you.// 나를 따라오지 말~ Did I not tell you [I told you] not to follow me?

라니냐 [태평양 적도의 해수면 온도가 낮아지는 현상] La Niña.

라도 if; even if [though]; though; although; however; any. ¶언제~ 오십시오 You may come any time [day].// 누구~ 그런 비평에는 화를 낼 것이다 Anyone would get mad at such criticism.// 우리는 지금이~ 해낼 수 있다 We can still make it.// "그렇게 고민하고 [병을 앓고] 싶지 않아." "누구~ 그래." "I don't want to suffer like that." "Nobody does."// 얼마~ 좋으니 모금에 협력해 주십시오 Please subscribe to the fund-raising, no matter how small your contribution may be.// 언제

~ 좋습니다 Any time will do.

라돈 [화] radon(기호 Rn).
라듐 [화] radium(기호 Ra). ¶~을 쬐다 give radium treatment (to).
● **라듐 요법** [의] radium treatment. **라듐천** (一泉) a radium spring.
라드 lard. ¶~유 lard oil.
라든지 [나열] and; or; and so on [forth]; etc.; and the like [all that]; and what not; [선택] either ... or. ¶잉크~ 종이~ 책이~ 하는 여러 가지 것들 ink, papers, books, and various other things [and what not].
-라든지 or; whether [either] ... or; otherwise. ¶그에게 그 일을 하~ 말~ 결정을 해 줘야 한다 We must decide whether to make him do the work or not.
라디안 [수] radian.
라디에이터 radiator.
라디오 [방송 프로그램] (미) radio(▶ 종종 the radio); (영) wireless; [수신기] a radio; a radio [wireless] set. ¶~ 중국어 강좌 a radio course in Chinese//~를 통한 연설 an address through radio / a radio address (to the nation)//~를 켜다[끄다] turn on [off] the radio / switch on [off] the radio//~의 다이얼을 맞추다 tune in//~ 소리를 크게[작게] 하다 turn up [down] the radio / turn a radio up [down] / raise [lower] the volume of the radio//~를 듣다 listen to the radio//~로 음악을 듣다 listen to music over [on] the radio //~로 연설[뉴스를 방송]하다 speak [broadcast news] over the radio// 지금 ~에서 무엇을 하고 있습니까 What's on the radio now? // 이 ~로 외국 방송을 들을 수 있습니까 Can we get foreign stations on this set?
● **라디오 뉴스** the news on the radio; radio news. **라디오 방송** radio broadcasting; a radio broadcast(1회의). ¶~을 하다 (방송국이) broadcast / radiocast / send [put] on the air / (방송자가) go on the air / speak over the radio. **라디오 방송국** a radio (broadcasting) station. **라디오 송신기** a (radio) transmitter; (자동차용) (미) an autoradio. **라디오 수신기** a (radio) receiver; a radio (set). **라디오 아나운서** a radio announcer. **라디오 (전국) 중계** a (country-wide) relay; (미) a (nationwide) hookup. **라디오존데** [기상] (독) Radiosonde. **라디오 청취자** a radio listener; a wireless listener. **라디오 해설자** a radio commentator.
라르고 [음] largo. ¶~로 연주하는 곡 a largo.
라마[1] [불] a lama. ¶달라이 ~ the Dalai [Grand] Lama// 판첸 ~ the Panchen Lama.
● **라마교** Lamaism. **라마교도** a Lamaist; a Lamaite. **라마 사원** a Lamasery.
라마[2] [동] a llama; a lama.
라마르크설 (一說) [생] Lamarckism.
라면 ramen; Japanese instant noodles.
-라면[1] [가정·조건] if; in case; suppose; supposing; provided; [관례어는] as for; for. ¶나 ~ 그것을 내 자신이 할 텐데 (If I were you) I would do it for myself.// 아침이~ 좋겠는데 I wish it were [(구어) was] morning.// 그 사람이라면 몰라도) 저 자~ 두 번 다시 만나고 싶지 않다 As for that man, I never hope to see him again.// 경치~ 한국만 한 곳도 없다 For [As for] scenery, there is no country like Korea.
-라면[2] [...라고 하면]. ¶하~ 해라 Do as you are told.// 그가 달~ 주지 If he asks, I shall

라벤더

give it.// 고마움을 나타내기 위해서~ 무슨 일이든지 하겠습니다 I would do anything in the world to show my gratitude.// 너를 위한 일이~ 뭐든지 하겠다 I would do anything for you.// 2킬로 이내~ 나는 역까지 기꺼이 걸어가겠다 I would be willing to walk to the station, if it weren't more than two kilometers.

라벤더 [식] lavender.
● **라벤더유**(-油) lavender water.

라벨 a label. ¶병에 ~을 붙이다 label a bottle.// 가스 기구에 「사용 금지」라는 ~이 붙어 있었다 The gas appliance was labeled "Don't use."

라비 [유대교] a rabbi.

라서 [감히·능히] indeed. ¶뉘 나를 이기리요 Who indeed can beat me? / Who would dare to beat me? // 그가 어디에 있는지 누구~ 알리요 Heaven knows where he is. / Nobody can know where he is.// 뉘~ 그걸 믿어 주겠소 Try and make anybody believe it!

-라서 [원인·근거]. ¶그는 그 아이를 막내~ 더욱 귀여워한다 He loves the child all the better because it is the youngest.// 비가 온 뒤~ 강물이 흐려 있었다 The river looked thick[turbid] after the rain.

-라손 치더라도 (even) though; (even) if. ⇨ -ㄴ다손 치더라도 ¶그것이 사실이~ granting it to be true[that it is true] / granted it is true.

라스트 the last.
● **라스트 스퍼트** [체] last spurt. ¶~를 내다 put on a last spurt. **라스트 신** [연][영] the last scene. **라스트 이닝** [야구] the last inning.

라야(만) only; alone; not ... until. ¶너~ 그 일을 할 수 있다 Only you[You alone] can do it. / None[No one] but you can do it.// 사람은 건강을 잃고 난 뒤에~ 그 고마움을 안다 People do not know the blessing[value] of health until they lose it.// 그 일은 저녁 늦게~ 끝난다 The work will not be finished until late in the evening.

-라야(만) only; not ... until. ¶기혼녀가 아니~ 입회가 허가된다 Only an unmarried girl shall be admitted a member.

라운드 [권투·골프] a round. ¶10~의 권투 시합 a boxing-match of ten rounds // 18홀 1~ an 18-hole round // 제1~ 2분 30초 만에 at 2:30 of the first round // 코스를 원 ~ 하다 [골프] go round a course // 그는 3~에서 녹아웃당했다 He was knocked out in the third round.

라운지 a lounge.

라이거 [동] a liger.

라이너 1 [야구] a liner; a line drive. ¶~를 치다 hit[drive] a liner. 2 [코트 안감] (a) liner.

라이노타이프 [인] a linotype.

라이닝 1 lining. 2 [안감을 댐] lining; [안감] cloth[material] for lining.

라이덴병 (-瓶) [물] a Leyden jar[bottle].

라이벌 a rival. ¶좋은 ~ a rival who spurs one to give one's best / a close competitor who keeps one up to the mark // ~ 회사 a rival company[firm] // 상업상의 ~ rivals in trade / business rivals // 사랑의 ~ a rival in love // 그는 내 지위를 노리는 나의 ~이었다 He was my rival for the post.
● **라이벌 의식** a sense of rivalry; a competitive sense. ¶~이 강하다 have a strong sense of rivalry / be full of competitive spirit.

라이선스 a license.

라이스페이퍼 rice paper.

라이온스 클럽 Lions Club(▶ Lions is liberty, intelligence, our nation's safety of rival).

라이카판 (⑬Leica判) (a) 35 millimeter[35-mm] film.

라이터 (cigarette) lighter. ¶~를 켜다 strike a lighter / snap a lighter into flame / click a lighter to flame // 가스 ~ a (butane) gas lighter // 다 쓰고 버리는 ~ a throwaway lighter // 로 담뱃불을 붙이다 light a cigarette with a lighter // ~ 가스를 넣다 refill a gas lighter // ~가 안 켜진다 The lighter won't work.
● **라이터 기름** lighter oil[fluid]. **라이터돌** lighter flint. ¶~을 갈다 change the flint in a lighter.

라이트 [조명등] a (car) light. ¶~를 켜다[끄다] switch on[off] a light / switch a light on [off].

라이트 윙 (위치) right wing; (선수) a right wing.

라이트 필더 [야구] a right fielder.

라이트 필드 [야구] right field.

라이프 사이클 a life cycle.

라이플(총) (-銃) a rifle.

라인 a line. ¶공이 ~ 밖으로 나갔다 The ball went out of bounds.
● **라인 아웃** line out.

라인업 [체] (출전 선수들의 진용) a lineup. ¶선발(先發) ~을 발표하다 announce the starting lineup.

라일락 [식] a lilac.

라임라이트 the limelight.

라켓 (테니스의) a racket[racquet]; (탁구의) a bat; a paddle. ¶나는 ~의 줄을 갈았다 I had my racket restrung.// 나는 탁구 ~의 고무판을 갈았다 I had my table-tennis paddle resurfaced.

라켓볼 racquetball.

라텍스 [화] latex.

라틴 [관형어적] Latin.
● **라틴 문학** Latin literature. **라틴 민족** the Latin peoples[races]. **라틴 어** the Latin language. **라틴 음악** Latin music.

-락 [동작이나 상태의 되풀이]. ¶비가 오~가~ 하다 rain off and on // 정신이 오~가~ 하다 (one's mind) wander[stray].

락타아제 [화] lactase.

락토오스 [화] lactose; milk sugar. ⇨ 젖당

락산 (-酸) [화] lactic acid.

란 1 […라고 하는 것은]. ¶날씨~ 알 수 없는 것이다 There is no telling about the weather.// 진리~ 무엇인가 What is truth? // 사고~ 일어나게 마련이다 Accidents will happen.// 여자~ 어쩔 수 없어[어쩔 수 없는 것이 여자야] Women are[will be] woman.// 여자~ 말이 하고 싶은 법이다 Women will be talking. 2 […라고 하는). ¶이 지역에서는 학교~ 학교는 다 독감으로 문을 닫았다 In this area all the schools are closed because of an influenza epidemic. // 아이~ 아이가 다 온순하다고는 할 수 없다 Not all children are obedient.// 길이~ 길은 사람으로 꽉 메워졌다 Every street was filled with people.

-란 1 […라고 하는). ¶나를 보고 어떻게 하~ 말입니까 What do you want me to do? // 나를 보고 가~ 말이냐 Do you mean that I should go? 2 […라고 한). ¶부하에게 전진하~ 명령을 내린 사람은 사령관이다 It is the Commander

란제리 (프) lingerie.
-람¹ 1 [못마땅함]. ¶그가 무슨 상관이~ That's none of his business! // 그것이 그녀의 인격을 증명하고 있다 — 인격은 무슨 인격이~ It's a testimony to her character. — Character nothing. 2 [비난·난처함]. ¶내가 가야 할 게 뭐~ Why should I go of all things? // 하필이면 그가 생일날에 병으로 쓰러질 게 뭐~ Just imagine his falling ill on his birthday of all days!
-람² if; in case; as for. ⇨ -라면¹
랑 and; or; and so on [forth]; etc.; [함께] (together) with. ¶너~ 나~ you and me // 친구~ 산책 나가다 go for a walk with a friend // 그는 돼지~ 소~ 개 등등을 사육하고 있다 He raises pigs, cattle, dogs, and so on [forth]. // 그는 동료~ 함께 왔다 He came, together with a companion.
랑데부 a rendezvous (*pl.* -vous(▶ 복수에서는 s를 [z]로 발음함)); (구어) a date. ¶~의 장소 a rendezvous // ~의 상대 one's date. 랑데부하다 (우주선이) (have a) rendezvous (with); (남녀가) (구어) date [have a date] (with).
-래 […라고 해] they say; I hear. ¶그의 아버지는 교사~ I hear that his father is a teacher. // 그가 뭐~ What did he say? // 그녀가 자네 보고 조용히 하~ She told you to be quiet.
래드 [물] [방사선 흡수량의 단위] a rad.
-래서 […라고 해서]. ¶그 소년은 어머니에게 오천 원을 달~ 책을 샀다 The boy asked his mother for 5,000 won and bought a book. // 그가 그 책을 달~ 주었다 I gave him the book because he asked it.
-래서야 […라고 해서야]. ¶한 달 안에 그에게 그만두~ 되겠소 It is unreasonable that you should ask him to quit within a month. // 그렇게 턱없이 달~ 누가 그것을 사겠나 Nobody would buy it if you ask so much for it.
래커 lacquer. ¶~를 칠하다 lacquer / coat (a thing) with a lacquer.
랜싯 [의] a lancet.
랜턴 a lantern.
램 [컴] RAM(▶ random access memory의 약어). ¶128메가바이트 ~ 128 megabytes of RAM.
램프¹ a lamp. ¶석유~ an oil [a petroleum / a kerosene] lamp // 알코올~ an alcohol [a spirit] lamp // ~의 심지 lampwick // ~를 켜다 [끄다] light [put out] a lamp // ~의 심지를 돋우다 [줄이다] turn up [down] a lamp // ~의 불 밑에서 편지를 쓰다 write a letter by lamplight.
램프² [인터체인지와 고속도로를 접속하는 경사진 부분] a ramp.
랩 [체] a lap.
● 랩 타임 one's lap time. ¶800미터의 ~ one's 800 meter lap time.
랩소디 [음] a rhapsody.
랭크되다 rank. ¶그는 학급에서 2위로 랭크되어 있다 [상위 10퍼센트에 랭크되어 있다] He ranks second [among the top ten percent] in his class. // 그 가수는 베스트 10에 랭크되어 있다 The singer placed among the best ten.
랭킹 ranking. ¶국내 [국제] ~ national [international] ranking // 올해 ~ 1위의 기사(棋士) the *baduk*(go) player who has been ranked (by experts) [ranks] first this year // ~ 1위를 차지하다 take the first ranking.

who ordered his men to advance.

-랴 1 [반어]. ¶그 사람말고 누가 그것을 쓰~ Who should write it but himself? // 그것이 어찌 스스로 부러지~ It cannot break of itself. / How can it break of itself? 2 [문의]. ¶돈을 주~ Shall I give you some money? / Do you want some money? // 무얼 해 주~ Tell me what you want? // 이제 공부를 시작하~ Shall I begin the lesson now? / Do you want me to begin the lesson now?
량(輛) [열차·전철 등의 칸을 세는 단위]. ¶객차 8~ 편성의 열차 a train made up of eight cars [(영) carriages].
량(量) [분량·수량] volume; quantity; (an) volume. ¶교통~ traffic volume / the volume of traffic / traffic // 생산~ an output (of a factory) // 원자 [분자] ~ atomic [molecular] weight // 호흡~ breathing [vital] capacity.
-러 [목적] for the purpose of; in order to. ¶수영하~ 가다 go for a swim // 낚시하~ 가다 go fishing // 데이트하~ 나가다 go out on a date // 다음 일요일에 놀~ 오너라 Come and see [Come to see] me next Sunday. // 책을 가지~ 보내라 Send and fetch a book. // 나는 의사를 부르~ 그를 보냈다 I sent him for a doctor. // 그는 방금 점심 식사하~ 나갔다 He just stepped [went] out for lunch.
러너 1 (육상 경기에서) a runner. ¶장거리 ~ a long-distance runner // 단거리 ~ a sprinter. 2 [야구] a (base) runner.
러닝 a running (race).
● 러닝머신 (*running machine*) a treadmill. 러닝메이트 a running mate. 러닝셔츠(*running shirt*) [속옷] (미) an undershirt; (영) a vest; [운동용] an athletic shirt. 러닝슈즈 (a pair of) running shoes; spiked shoes. 러닝 호머 (*running homer*) [야구] an inside-the-park homer. ¶만루 ~를 치다 hit an inside-the-park grand slam home run.
러브 [테니스] [무득점] love.
● 러브 게임 [테니스] love game.
러브스토리 love story.
러브신 love scene.
러셀차 [一車] [제설차] a Russel [wedgetype]; snowplow [(영) snow-plough].
러시 [쇄도·급증] a rush. ¶골드 ~ the gold rush.
러시아워 the rush hour(s). ¶아침저녁의 ~ the morning and evening rush hours // ~에 during [in] the rush hours / at rush hour(s) // 이 역은 아침 7시부터 8시까지 통근~이다 This station is jammed with commuters from seven to eight in the morning.
러일 전쟁 (-日戰爭) the Russo-Japanese War.
러키세븐 [야구] the lucky seventh.
러키 존 [야구] the lucky zone.
럭비(풋볼) rugby (football); Rugby; (영국 속어) rugger. ¶~를 하다 play rugby.
● 럭비공 a rugby ball; (구어) an oval.
럭스 [조도(照度) 단위] a lux (*pl.* ~es, luces). ¶~계 a luxmeter.
럼주(-酒) rum.
레가토 [음] legato.
레그혼 [동] a leghorn.
레늄 [화] rhenium.
레닌주의(-主義) Leninism.
● 레닌주의자 a Leninite; a Leninist.
레모네이드 lemonade.
레몬 [식] a lemon.
● 레몬산 citric acid. 레몬수 lemonade. 레몬

레버 a lever.
레벨 [표준·수준] a level. ¶~이 높다[낮다] be on a high[low] level // ~을 높이다 raise the level (of) // 높은 ~에 이르다 attain a high level.
레스토랑 a restaurant.
레슨 a lesson. ¶피아노 ~ a piano lesson / a lesson in piano // 음악 ~을 받다 have[take] music lessons.
레슬러 a wrestler.
레슬링 wrestling.
● 레슬링 선수 a wrestler; (미국 속어) a matman. 레슬링 시합 a wrestling match [tournament].
레위기(-記) [성] (the Book of) Leviticus(약어 Lev.).
레이 [하와이의 화환] a lei. ¶~를 목에 걸다 hang a lei (a)round a person's neck.
레이더 radar(▶ radio detecting and ranging의 약어).
● 레이더 기지 a radar base[site / station]. 레이더망 a radar fence[screen / network]. 레이더 장치 a radar device[set / system].
레이디 퍼스트 Ladies first.
레이스¹ [수예 편물] lace; lacework. ¶~를 달다 trim with lace.
레이스² [경주] a race.
레이아웃 a layout.
레이온 rayon.
● 레이온 펄프 rayon pulp.
레이저 [물] laser(▶ light amplification by stimulated emission of radiation의 약어).
● 레이저 광선 a laser beam. 레이저 통신 laser communication.
레인지 a (kitchen) range; a cooking stove. ¶가스~ a gas range // 전자~ an electronic[a microwave] oven.
레인코트 a raincoat; (벨트가 달린) a trench coat; a waterproof; (고무를 입힌) a mackintosh; (구어) a mac; (미) a weather-all(청우(晴雨) 겸용); (미) a slicker.
레일 a rail; (a railway) line; (미) a (railroad) track(궤도). ¶~ 위를 달리다 run[move] on the rail // ~에서 벗어나다 go off the rail / get derailed / leave the track[metals] // ~을 깔다 lay rails.
레저 leisure; leisure time amusement.
● 레저 붐 a leisure boom. 레저 산업 the leisure industry.
레즈비언 a lesbian.
레지(*register) (다방의) a tearoom waitress.
레지스탕스 resistance (activity).
레커차(-車) [구난차] a wrecker; a wrecking car; a tow car[truck].
레코드 [음반] a (phonograph / gramophone) record; a disk; a disc; an album. ¶어학 ~ a Linguaphone // 엘피 ~ an LP[a long-playing] record // ~를 틀다 put a record on the player / play a record // ~에 녹음하다 cut a record // ~에 취입하다 disc (one's singing) / record (one's speech) on a disk // 이 ~은 낡아서 긁히는 소리가 난다 This record has been worn to scratchiness.
● 레코드 수집가 a discophile. 레코드 음악 recorded[disk] music; (속어) a canned music. ¶~ 시간 [라디오] a disk hour // 해설자 [라디오] a disk jockey. 레코드 콘서트 a record concert; a disk [phonographic]

recital. 레코드플레이어 a record player; a phonoplayer.
레크리에이션 (a) recreation.
레터링 [글자의 도안화(圖案化)] lettering.
레테르(⑩letter) a label; (미) a sticker. ¶가짜 ~ forged label // 성냥의 ~ a match label // ~가 붙은 병 a bottle with a label // 빨갱이[무능자]라는 ~가 붙다 be branded[labeled / ticketed] as a Red[good-for-nothing] // ~를 붙이다 label (a bottle) / attach[affix] a label to (a bottle) / put[place] a label on (a bottle).
레토르트 [화] a retort.
레퍼리 (게임의) a referee; (구어) a ref. ¶~를 맡아보다 act as referee / referee (a match) // 그 시합은 ~ 스톱이 되었다 The referee stopped the fight.
레퍼토리 a repertory; a repertoire. ¶~에 들어 있는 곡목 a repertory piece[item] // 저 악단은 모던 재즈를 ~로 하고 있다 The repertoire of the band is modern jazz.
레프트 윙 (위치) left wing; (선수) a left wing.
레프트 잽 a left jab.
레프트 필더 [야구] a left fielder.
레프트 필드 [야구] left field.
렌즈 a lens (pl. ~es). ¶교환 ~ an interchangeable lens // 광각 ~ a wide-angle lens // 대물 ~ an objective / an objective lens // 망원 ~ a telephoto lens // 어안(魚眼) ~ a fisheye lens // 오목[볼록] ~ a concave [convex] lens // 접안(接眼) ~ an eyepiece / an ocular lens // 줌 ~ a zoom lens // 표준 ~ a standard[normal] lens // 합성[확대] ~ a compound[magnifying] lens // ~의 중심 the optical center // 도수 높은 ~ a powerful [strong] lens // ~를 들이대다 [향하게 하다] direct the lens to // ~를 맞추다 train the lens on // ~를 갈다 grind a lens // ~를 닦다 clean a lens.
렌치 [틀거나 죄는 공구] a wrench.
렌터카 a rent-a-car; a rental car.
-려 with the intention of (doing). ⇨ -려고
-려고 [의도] with the intention of (doing); with a view to (doing); [목적] in order to (do); in order that ...; for the purpose of .... ¶시험에 합격하~ in order to pass the examination // 구조하~ 오다 come to the rescue // 임무를 다하~ 노력하다 try to do one's duty // 그를 찾아 나가~ 내가 일어섰을 때 마침 그가 나타났다 He turned up just when[as] I stood up to go to look for him.
-려기에 [...려고 하기에] on account of; owing to; as; because; since. ¶날이 어두워지~ 이내 돌아왔다 As it was getting dark, we soon turned back. // 그녀가 사직하~ 내가 말렸다 I dissuaded her from resigning. // 그녀가 식사를 하~ 나는 자리를 떴다 She was going to begin eating[to eat], so I left there.
-려나 [...려고 하나] I wonder (if, whether, what, who, where, when, etc.). ¶누가 오~ I wonder who will come. // 내일은 비가 오~ I wonder if it will rain tomorrow. // 언제 오~ When will you come and see me? // 이 편지를 부쳐 주~ Post this letter for me, will you? // 이렇게 멀리서도 들리~ Will they be able to hear at such a distance? // 내가 내일 죽는다면 어쩌하~ If I were to die tomorrow, what would you do?
-려네 [...려고 하네] I will (do); I intend [mean / purpose] to (do); I am going to (do). ¶이것을 가지~ I will take this one. //

나는 교사가 되~ I purpose to become a teacher.// 오전에 돌아오~ I expect to come back before noon.// 그를 만나 보~ I am going to see him.// 나는 내년에 외국에 가~ I intend[mean] to go abroad next year.

-려느냐 […려고 하느냐]. ¶무엇을 하~ What do you intend[are you going] to do?// 이것을 가지~ Will you take this?// 커피를 좀 더 마시~ Do you care for some more coffee?// 한국에는 얼마나 체류하~ How long are you going to stay in Korea?// 차 한 잔 더 하~ Won't you take one more cup of tea?// 천 원만 꾸어 주~ Would you mind lending me 1,000 won?

-려는 […려고 하는]. ¶만나~ 분이 누구요 Who(m) do you want? / Who(m) are you going to see?// 너를 해치~ 생각은 없었다 I didn't intend[had no mind] to hurt you.// 이 책을 보~ 학생이 참 많다 There are many students who want to read this book.// 목적은 사고를 방지하~ 데에 있다 The idea is to prevent accidents.

-려는가 […려고 하는가]. ¶지금 떠나~ Are you going to leave now?// 자네는 언제 떠나~ When are you going to leave? / When do you intend to leave?// 얼마 동안 이곳에 머무르~ How long do you plan to remain here?// 자네는 무엇을 하~ What are you going to do?

-려는데 […려고 하는데]. ¶내가 자리를 뜨~ 그녀가 왔다 She came as I was leaving.// 그가 막 길을 건너~ 요란한 폭음이 들려왔다 Just as he was going to cross the road, there was a loud explosion.

-려니 [속으로만 하는 추측]. ¶세상은 그런 것이~ 생각하라 Take the world as it is.// 나는 그가 오~ 생각했다 I expected him to come.// 그가 사직하~ 생각했다 I should have thought that he would resign.// 나는 그가 기쁜 소식을 가져오~ 하고 기다렸다 I waited hoping that he would bring a good news.

-려니와 [또한] not only ... but; as well as; and; moreover; besides; in addition to that. ¶그는 키도 크~ 잘생겼다 He is tall and handsome.// 너도 너~ 나 역시 골치 아픈 일이 있다 Not only you but also I am in trouble.// 그는 정치가도 아니~ 학자도 아니다 He is neither a politician nor a scholar.// 나는 그 일을 알지도 못하~ 알려고 하지도 않는다 I neither know nor care to know it.// 나는 부자도 아니~ 또 되고 싶지도 않다 I am not rich, neither do I wish to be.

-려다가 […려고 하다가]. ¶고향에 내려가~ 말다 give up[abandon / relinquish] the idea of going home// 날씨가 너무 추워서 그는 사냥을 가~ 그만두었다 It was so cold that he gave up an attempt to go hunting[an idea of going hunting].// 나는 그 다음 날 떠나~ 생각을 달리했다 I was planning to leave the next day, but I changed my mind.

-려면 […려고 하면]. ¶내가 하~ 할 수는 있는데 I could do so, if I would.// 사전을 만들~ 많은 시간과 노력이 든다 Making a dictionary costs much time and care.

-려무나 [제 뜻대로 하라] be pleased to ...; may; you had better (do). ¶마음대로 하~ Do as you please[like].// 가고 싶으면 가고 말고 싶으면 말~ You may as well go (as not).// 이제 가서 자~ You had better go to bed now.// 내 사전을 쓰고 싶으면 쓰~ You may use my dictionary if you like.// 여기 열쇠가 있으니 언제든지 들어오~ Here is the key, you may enter at will.

-려야 […려고 하여야]. ¶어찌하~ 할 도리가 없다 It can not be helped. / It's all up with me.// 더 견디~ 견딜 수가 없었다 I couldn't stand it any longer.

-려오 […려고 하오]. (I) will (do); intend to (do); have a mind to (do). ¶내일 여행을 떠나~ I will start on a journey tomorrow.// 당신이 가면 나도 따라가~ If you go, I will accompany you.// 다시는 그런 짓을 안 하~ I will never do such a thing again.// 언제 여기 오~ What time will you be here?

-력(力) [힘] power; strength; might; [능력] ability; capability; capacity; competence. ¶경제~ economic power[strength / might]// 구매~ purchasing power// 이해~ the comprehensive faculty / the power to understand / sense// 접착~ adhesive strength// 정치~ political power[influence].

-련 ⇨ -려느냐

-련다 […려고 한다]. ¶나는 내일 가~ I'm going to go tomorrow.// 실패하더라도 한번 더 해 보~ If[Even if] I should fail, I would try again.

-련마는 […한 듯한데] ¶그는 전기 기사도 아니~ 전기에 대해서 아는 것이 많다 He does not seem to be an electrician, but he knows much about electricity.

-렴 be pleased to .... ⇨ -려무나

-립니까 1 [요청·권유]. ¶커피를 더 드시~ Do you care for some more coffee?// 내가 여기 있다고 그에게 전해 주시~ Would you tell him that I am here? **2** […려고 합니까]. ¶기차로 가시~ Are you going by train?// 세 시에 댁에 계시~ Shall you be at home at 3 o'clock?

-립니다 […려고 합니다]. ¶나는 의사가 되~ I purpose to become a doctor.// 무슨 일이 있어도 나는 가~ Whatever happens, I will go.

-렷다 [당연한 추측·다짐·명령] be sure[bound / agreed] to happen; will surely happen; will likely[probably] happen; probably be. ¶그들은 한 시 안으로 도착하~ They should arrive by one o'clock, I think.// 네가 어제 전화를 건 그 아이~ You are[must be] the boy who called me yesterday, aren't you?// 자식된 자는 어버이의 말에 따르~ Children should obey their parents.// 내일쯤은 비가 오~ I expect[suspect] it will rain by tomorrow.

-령(令) an order; a decree. ¶금지~ a prohibition order.

-령(領) [영토] a dominion; a domain; a territory; a possession; [봉토] a fief. ¶영(국)~ 보르네오 British Borneo// 한국~에서 in Korean territory// 이 섬은 네덜란드~이다 This island belongs to the Netherlands. / This island is Dutch territory.

로 1 [수단·기구·방식] by; by means of; with; in; on. ¶기계~ 짠 양탄자 a rug woven by machine// 자전거~ by[on a] bicycle// 육로~ 가다 go by land// 월급제~ 일하다 work by the month// 다스~ 팔다 sell by the dozen// 외모~ 남을 판단하다 judge a person by his appearance// 영어~ 이야기하다 speak in English// 1,000원짜리 지폐~ 지불하다 pay with 1,000 won notes// 피아노~ 소나타를 치다 play a sonata on the piano// 그의 새 차~ 드라이브하러 갔다 We went for a drive in his

new car.// 그녀는 노래~ 생계를 꾸려 가고 있다 She earns her living by singing.// 그는 베풀어 준 친절에 대한 감사의 표시~ 그들을 초대했다 He invited them as a token of his gratitude for their kindness.// He invited them in return for their kindness.// 그는 생일 선물~ 시계를 받았다 He was given a watch for his birthday.// 그녀는 고운 목소리~ 노래하고 있다 She is singing in a lovely [pretty] voice.
2 [방향·목적지] for; to; toward; into; in. ¶해변가~ 가다 go to the seaside // 교회~ 들어오다 enter [come into] the church // 다음 모퉁이에서 좌~ 도시오 Turn (to the) left at the next corner.
3 [재료] of; [원료] from. ¶나무로 만든 상자 a box made of wood // 밀크~ 치즈를 만들다 make cheese from milk // 우리는 종이~ 여러 가지 물건을 만든다 We make many things with [out of] paper.// 석유~ 여러 가지 물건을 만들 수가 있다 Lots of things can be made out of petroleum.
4 [원인·동기] because of; owing to; of; at; with; from; through. ¶그는 티푸스~ 죽었다 He died of typhoid fever.// 그는 자신의 의사~ 사직했다 He resigned of his own free will.// 그는 과로~ 병이 났다 He fell ill from [through] overwork.// 그는 심한 공포~ 말을 하지 못했다 He was so terrified that he was unable to speak.// 그는 분노~ 미칠 것만 같았다 He was almost insane with anger.// 그는 부주의~ 사고를 일으켰다 He caused an accident through his carelessness. / The accident was due to his carelessness.// 그는 사기죄~ 체포되었다 He was arrested for fraud.// 이 호수는 아름답기~ 유명하다 This lake is noted for its beauty.
5 [지위·신분] as; for. ¶맏이~ 태어나다 be born eldest.
6 [변화·결과] into; to. ¶젤리 상태~ 굳다 harden into jelly // 우리말을 영어~ 번역하다 put [turn] Korean into English.
7 [시간·경과] by; at. ¶소년은 7월 2일~ 15세가 된다 The boy will be fifteen years old come [on] July 2.// 내일~ 원서 접수가 마감된다 The deadline for applications is tomorrow.

-로(路) a route; a street; a road; (미) an avenue. ¶교통~ a traffic route // 십자~ a cross-roads.

로가리듬 [수] a logarithm. ⇨ 로그

로고스 [철] logos.

-로구나 [감탄]. ¶그 여자 정말 미녀~ She is a beauty indeed! // 벌써 12시~ It is already 12 o'clock! // 정말 구경거리~ What a sight it is! // 그것 참 좋은 생각이~ It's a really good idea. // 이 진주는 전부 가짜~ These pearls are all shame.

-로구먼 ⇨ -구먼 ¶참 좋은 책이~ This is a nice book indeed.

로그 [수] a logarithm. ¶자연 [상용]~ natural [common] logarithms.
● **로그표** a table of logarithms. **로그 함수** [수] a logarithmic function.

로그인 [컴] login; log-in.

로나 [비행기~ 가면 몰라도 다른 걸로 타면 제 시간에 닿을 수 없을걸 You would not get there in time by anything but a plane.

로는 1 [⋯을 가지고는]. ¶영어~ 「사람」을 뭐라고 하느냐 What is the English for "saram"? / What do you call "saram" in English? // 눈으로는 보고 귀~ 듣는다 We see with our eyes, and hear with our ears.
2 [⋯에 있어서는]. ¶어떤 의미~ 이 말이 맞다 In a way this statement is true.
3 [⋯에 의하면]. ¶내 시계~ 약 5시다 It is about five by my watch. // 들리는 바~ 그녀가 프랑스에 간다고 합니다 I hear [understand] she is going to France.
4 [⋯에는]. ¶나는 그 후~ 한 번도 그녀를 못 보았다 I have never seen her since then.
5 [⋯으로서는]. ¶그 손실은 승리의 대가~ 너무나 비싼 것이었다 Such losses were too high a price to pay a victory.

-로다 ⇨ -로구나

로데오 a rodeo (pl. ~s).

-로되 [⋯이긴 하나]. ¶그는 학자~ 조금도 학자답지 않다 He has nothing of the scholar in him.

로듐 [화] rhodium.

로드 게임 [원정 경기] a road game.

로드 쇼 [영] a road show.

로드워크 (운동선수의) roadwork; a road run.

로마 ¶~의 Roman.
로마는 하루아침에 이루어지지 않았다 (속담) Rome was not built in a day.
● **로마 가톨릭** (교) Roman Catholi-cism; (경멸) Romanism. **로마 교황** the Pope; the Holy Father. **로마 교황청** the Vatican (palace). **로마서** (一書) (성) (Pauline) Epistle to the Romans. **로마 숫자** Roman numerals. **로마자** Roman characters [letters]; the Roman [Latin] alphabet. ¶한글을 ~로 표기하다 Romanize Korean. **로마 제국** the Roman Empire.

로마네스크 Romanesque (architecture).

로망 (roman) a novel.

로맨스 a romance; a love affair; [연애 사건] affairs of the heart; a love story. ¶~가 많은 romantic / full of romance // 너의 ~를 들려다오 Tell me your love story.

로맨스그레이 (*romance grey) a fine elderly gentleman with gray hair.

로맨티시스트 [낭만주의자] a romanticist; [공상가] a visionary; a daydreamer.

로맨틱하다 romantic. ¶로맨틱한 생애 a romantic [checkered] career // 로맨틱한 생각에 잠기다 indulge in romantics.

로봇 [인조인간] a robot; [꼭두각시] a puppet. ¶산업용~ an industrial robot // 신임 지배인은 전임자의 ~에 지나지 않는다 The new manager is a mere puppet of his predecessor.

로부터 [⋯에서부터] from; out of. ¶서울~ 부산까지 from Seoul to Busan // 이~ 몇 달 동안 for a few months ahead [from now] // 이~ 3년 후에 three years hence // 그리스~ 유래된 말 a word derived from Greece // 멀리 있는 친구~ 온 편지 a letter from a friend far away // 이것은 예~ 전해 오는 이야기다 This story dates back on ancient times. // 이 상태는 이~ 몇 년 동안 계속될 것이다 Things will go on like this for a few years. // 이~ 많은 문제가 생겼다 Out of this many troubles arose. // 이~ 그의 모험이 실패하기 시작했다 Hence his failure in the adventure.// 그 풍습은 우리 선조~ 전해 내려온 것이다 The custom has come down to us from our ancestors.// 아버지~ 엄한 꾸중을 들었다 My father gave me a good scolding. / I got scold-

ing from my father.
로비 a lobby.
● 로비 활동 lobbyism. ¶~을 하다 lobby (in UN).
로비스트 a lobbyist.
로빙 [테니스] lobbing.
로서 1 [지위·신분·입장·자격을 가지고] as; for; in the capacity of; in[under] the character of. ¶학자~ as a scholar∥부모~의 의무 one's duty as a parent∥부부~ 어울리지 않는 쌍 an ill-mated pair∥…~ 통하다 figure [be regarded / pass] as / go by the name of. ∥나~는 찬성도 반대도 않는다 As for me, I am neither for nor against it.∥그는 정치가~ 보다는 소설가~ 더 잘 알려져 있다 He is better known as a novelist than as a statesman. 2 from; out of. ⇨⁼로서*
로션 (a) lotion. ¶헤어~ hair lotion.
로스¹ [손실] (a) loss.
● 로스 타임(*loss time) added time; injury time; lost time.
로스² roast (meat). ⇨⁼로스트
로스트 roast (meat).
● 로스트비프 roast beef.
로스트 제너레이션 [문] the lost generation.
로써 [도구] with; [수단] by; by means of; through. ¶전기(電氣)~ by electricity∥석유~ 재산을 모으다 make one's fortune in oil∥이~ 판단하건대 judging from this∥이~ 나의 인생은 끝장이다 This will ruin me. / This will be the end of me.∥이~ 내가 얼마나 어리석 었는가를 알았다 Now I realize how foolish I was.∥그 아름다움은 말~ 표현할 수가 없다 Words cannot express its beauty. / It is too beautiful for words.∥이 나라에서는 주류 판매가 법률~ 금지되어 있다 The sale of liquor is prohibited by law in this country.
로열박스 (극장·경기장 등의) a royal box.
로열 젤리 royal jelly.
로열티 a royalty.
로이드안경(-眼鏡) tortoise-shell[horn-rimmed] spectacles.
로이터 통신사(-通信社) the Reuter News Agency; Reuter's Ltd.
로제타석(-石) the Rosetta stone.
로진 백 [야구] a rosin bag.
로케(이션) [영] a location; a location scene. ¶~ 가다 go on[out for] location∥~ 중이다 be on location.
로켓 [비행체] a rocket. ¶~ (추진)식의 rocket-powered∥달[우주]~ a moon[space] rocket∥3단[다단]식 ~ a three-stage [multistage] rocket∥역추진 ~ a retro-rocket∥증속(增速)~ a booster[retarding] rocket∥행성 ~ an interplanetary rocket∥~으로 날다 fly by rocket (to) / rocket (to the moon).
● 로켓 연료 rocket fuel. 로켓탄 a rocket bomb. 로켓포 a rocket gun; (보병용) a rocket launcher.
로코코 [건][미] rococo.
● 로코코식 건축 rococo architecture.
로큰롤 [춤·곡] rock-'n'-roll; rock and roll. ¶~에 열중하 있는 젊은이들 youngsters rock-'n'-rolling frantically.
로터리 a rotary; a traffic circle.
● 로터리 클럽 a Rotary club. ¶국제 ~ Rotary International∥~ 회원 a Rotarian.
로테이션 rotation. ¶~으로 (do something) by[in] rotation∥~에서 빠지다 be put out of rotation.
로프 (a) rope; (a) cord. ¶…을 ~로 동이다 rope (a trunk / a man to a tree).
로힐 low-heeled[flat] shoes.
록 [음] rock. ¶~을 연주하다 play the rock type of music.
록클라이밍 rock-climbing.
-론(論) 1 [논의] (an) argument; (a) discussion; a discourse; a dispute; (a) controversy; (a) debate(토론). ¶추상~ an abstract argument∥증세(增稅)에 반대[찬성]~을 펴다 argue against[for / in favor of] a tax increase. 2 [이론] a theory; a doctrine. ¶유심~ spiritualism∥진화~ the theory of evolution. 3 [논설] an essay; a treatise; [평론] a comment. ¶예술~ an essay on art∥여성~ [견해] a view of women / [논문] an essay on women. 4 [문제] a question; a problem. ¶한자(漢字) 제한~ the question of limiting the use of Chinese characters.
론도 [음] a rondo (pl. ~s).
론 테니스 lawn tennis.
롤러 a roller; a roll; a runner; (땅을 고르는) a roller; a road roller[leveler]; a packer; [사진] a squeegee. ¶(땅을 다지는) 중기 ~ a steam roller∥~로 고르게 하다 smooth (a field) with a roller / bulldoze (a field).
롤러스케이트 (놀일) roller skating; (구두) (a pair of) roller skates. ¶~를 타다 roller-skate / skate on wheels.
롤링 rolling; a roll.
롤빵 a roll of bread.
롬 [컴] [판독 전용 메모리] ROM(▶ read only memory의 약어).
-롭다 be; be characterized by. ¶새~ new / fresh∥해~ harmful (to) / injurious (to) / do harm / have an injurious effect (on)∥향기~ fragrant / sweet-scented / aromatic∥호화~ gorgeous / splendid / luxurious.
롱런 [연] a long run. ¶그 연극은 20개월이나 ~을 했다 The play had a long run of twenty months.
롱스커트 a long skirt.
롱플레잉 레코드 a long-playing record(약어 LP).
뢴트겐 Roentgen.
● 뢴트겐 검사 an X-ray examination. 뢴트겐 사진 a Roentgen[an X-ray] photograph; radiogram; radiograph. 뢴트겐선 Roentgen rays; X-rays.
-료(料) 1 [요금] a charge; a rate; a fee. ¶입장 ~ an admission fee∥전화~ a telephone charge∥배달~ delivery charges∥진찰~ a (doctor's) consultation fee. 2 [재료] a material. ¶조미~ a seasoning.
루블 [소련의 화폐 단위] a rouble.
루비 1 [광] a ruby. ⇨⁼홍옥₁ ¶~색(의) ruby. 2 [인] (미) an agate; (영) ruby.
● 루비 반지 a ruby ring; a ring set with ruby.
루주 rouge. ¶~를 바르다 rouge∥새빨갛게 ~를 칠한 입술 thickly rouged[painted] lips.
루트¹ [수] a root. ¶~ 4는 2다 The root of 4 [Root 4] is 2. / The square[second] root of 4 is 2.
루트² [경로] a route; a channel. ¶불법[암(暗)]~ an illegal channel∥판매[distribution] channels∥구입 ~를 조사하다 trace the channels of purchase.
루프 a loop.

●**루프 안테나** a loop antenna.
루피 [인도·파키스탄의 화폐 단위] a rupee(약어 R, Re).
룰 a rule. ¶~을 어기다 be against the rules // 기본 ~ a ground rule // ~대로 하다 do what the rules prescribe.
룰렛 1 [도박] (play) roulette; [그 도구] a roulette. 2 [양재용] a roulette.
룸메이트 a roommate.
●**룸바** r(h)umba. ¶~를 추다 (dance the) rumba.
룸서비스 room service.
룸펜 [부랑자] a loafer; a tramp; a (street) bum; (미국 속어) a hobo (*pl.* —(e)s); a vagrant; [실업자] a jobless[an unemployed] man.
룻기 [一記] [성] the Book of Ruth(약어 Ruth.).
-류(流) 1 [형(型)] a style; a fashion; a type; a mode; a form; a way; a manner. ¶자기~의 방식으로 in one's own way // 영국~의 인사 an English bow // 미국인~의 사고방식 an American mode[way] of thinking // 그는 마티스~의 그림을 그렸다 He painted a picture after[in the style of] Matisse. 2 [유파] a school; a style; a system. ¶추사~ 서체 Chusa school of calligraphy. 3 [등급] a class; a rate; an order; a rank; a grade. ¶상[중]~ 계급[사회] the upper[middle] classes // 일~ 시인 a poet of the first order.
-류(類) [종류] a sort; a kind; a variety; a class; a genus (*pl.* genera); a description; a type; a species. ¶거미~ a genus of spider // 내복~ underwear / underclothes // 밀감~ a kind[variety] of orange.
류머티즘 [의] rheumatism; (구어) the rheumatics; rheumatic trouble. ¶급성[만성 / 관절 / 근육] ~ acute[chronic / articular / muscular] rheumatism // ~이 일어나다 / ~에 걸리다 have a touch[an attack] of rheumatism // 어깨에 ~이 생기다 develop rheumatism in one's shoulder(s).
륙색 a rucksack; knapsack. ¶~을 메다 carry a rucksack (on one's back).
르네상스 the Renaissance; the Renascence. ¶~는 근대 문명의 여명이다 Renaissance is the dawn of modern civilization.
르포르타주 (do / write) reportage; a report (on); a documentary. ¶윤색을 하지 않은 ~도 하나의 문학이다 Straightforward reportage is also a branch of literature.
를 ¶자전거~ 타다 ride a bicycle // 시계~ 주다 give (a person) a watch // 부(富)~ 소유하다 possess[be possessed of] wealth // 나에게 일자리~ 구해 주다 find me a job // 곧 회복하기~ 바라다 hope that one will recover soon // 학교~ 결석하다 stay away[absent oneself] from school // 나는 그~ 노려보아 무안하게 만들었다 I looked him to shame. // 누구~ 기다리느냐 Who(m) are you waiting for?
리(理) reason; possibility. ¶…일 ~가 없다 cannot be / must not be / It is hardly possible (that) // 그것이 사실일 ~가 없다 It cannot be true. // 그럴 ~가 있나 How can it [that] be? / It cannot be true, I'm sure. / (가능성) It's absolutely impossible! / Impossible! // 늦을 ~가 없다 There is no reason for delay. // 그가 서울에 있다니 그럴 ~가 없지 He's in Seoul? He can't be. // 그가 그랬을 ~가 없다 He cannot have done such a thing. / It is impossible[inconceivable] that he should have done such a thing.
리(里) [거리의 단위] a ri(=0.4km).
-리(裏) in; amid(st). ¶극비~에 with absolute secrecy / 암암 ~에 secretly / covertly / 갈채~에 단(壇)을 내려오다 leave a platform amidst [in] the applause of the audience.
리골레토 [음] rigoletto.
리그 a (baseball) league. ¶메이저[마이너]~ the Major[Minor] League.
●**리그전**(一戰) a league game[match]; the league series. ¶고교 야구 ~ the High-School Baseball League // 야구[테니스]의 ~ a league baseball game[tennis match].
리넨 linen.
리놀륨 linoleum.
-리다 1 […하겠소] I will. ¶알려 드리~ I will let you know. // 내가 하~ I'll be glad to do it. // 당신에게 도움이 된다면 뭐든지 기꺼이 하~ I shall be glad to do what I can to help you. // 손해를 보신다면 내가 책임지~ I'll answer for your possible losses. 2 [추측·경고]. ¶더 열심히 공부하지 않으면 시험에 떨어지~ Unless you work harder, you will never pass the examination.
리더 [지도자] a leader. ¶그는 ~가 될 그릇이 아니다 He does not have the ability to lead others[to be a leader]. / He is not of leadership caliber.
●**리더십** leadership. ¶~을 발휘하다 take the lead / act as a leader.
리드¹ 1 [앞섬] a lead. ¶~를 빼앗기다 lose the lead (to). **리드하다** lead (a person in a race); take the lead; go into the lead; get ahead (of). ¶경주에서 ~ gain the lead in a race / 근소한 차로 ~ have[hold] a slight [narrow] lead (over) // 세계를 ~ lead the world (in) // 우리 팀이 3점 리드하고 있다 Our team has a three-point[-run] lead.(▶run은 야구에서) // 그는 스타트에서부터 리드했다 He was in the lead from the start. // 이 나라는 과학 기술에 있어서 유럽 여러 나라를 리드하고 있다 This country is ahead of the European countries in technology.
2 [지휘·인도] lead; leading; leadership. **리드하다** ¶파트너를 ~ lead one's partner // 잘못 ~ fail to lead (a person) properly // 클럽을 ~ lead[take the lead in] a club // 여자를 리드하여 왈츠를 추다 lead a woman in a waltz. 3 [야구에서 주자가 베이스를 떠남] a lead. **리드하다** take a lead; lead off (first base).
리드² (악기의) a reed.
●**리드 오르간** a reed organ.
리드미컬하다 rhythmical. ¶리드미컬하게 rhythmically // 리드미컬하게 말하다 speak rhythmically.
리듬 (a) rhythm. ¶~ 있는 rhythmic / rhythmical // ~에 맞추어 (dance) to the rhythm // 빠른 ~으로 to a fast tempo[beat].
리라 [이탈리아 화폐 단위] a lira (*pl.* lire)(약어 L).
-리라 1 [추측] may[might] (be / do); must; would; I think[suppose]. ¶아마 그러~ It may be so. / I suppose so. // 그녀는 틀림없이 성공하~ She will certainly succeed. / She is sure to succeed. 2 [의지] I will[shall]; I would; I am going to. ¶그녀를 위해서라면 무엇이든지 하~ I will do anything for her. // 실패하더라도 한번 더 해 보~ If I should fail, I would try again.
-리만큼 […할 정도로] enough to (do); so ...

that; so much as to (do). ¶그 집은 우리 식구가 모두 살기에 충분하~ 크다 The house is large enough for all of us.∥그는 그것도 모르~ 바보가 아니다 He is too wise not to know it.∥나는 아직 영어로 연설을 하~ 영어에 능통하진 못하다 I don't know English well enough yet to make a speech in it.

리모컨 a remote (control); (미국 구어) a zapper. ¶~이 어디 있지 Where's the remote control?

리모트 컨트롤 remote control. ¶~의 텔레비전 a remote-control TV set∥~로 모형 비행기를 띄우다[조종하다] fly[operate] a model plane by remote control.

리무진 [자동차] a limousine.

리바운드 a rebound. ¶평균 7, 8개의 ~를 따내다 pull down an average of 7-8 rebounds.

리바이벌 (a) revival (of). **리바이벌하다** revive. ¶묵은 연극을 ~ revive an old play. → ¶옛 노래를 리바이벌시키다 revive an old song.

리버럴하다 liberal. ¶나는 이 대학의 리버럴한 학풍에 끌렸다 I was attracted by the liberal traditions of this university.

리베이트 (*rebate) (미국 구어) a kickback; [뇌물] a bribe(▶ rebate는 '환불'의 뜻). ¶그는 제조업자로부터 20퍼센트의 ~를 받았다 He took a kickback of 20 percent from the manufacturers.∥공무원들은 업자로부터 ~를 받았다 The officials had accepted a bribe from the dealers.

리벳 a rivet. ¶~을 박다 rivet∥철판을 ~으로 고정시키다 rivet iron plates together / fasten iron plates with rivets.

리보솜 [생] a ribosome.

리보 핵산(-核酸) [생] ribonucleic acid(약어 RNA).

리본 a ribbon; (모자의) a band. ¶모자의 ~ (남자의) a (hat) band / (여자의) a hat ribbon [band]∥타자기의 ~ a typewriter ribbon∥장미 매듭 ~ a bow of ribbon∥~으로 매다 tie[bind] with a ribbon∥~을 달다 put on a ribbon∥옷에 ~을 달다 trim a dress with ribbons∥머리에 ~을 매다 wear a ribbon in one's hair.

리볼버 [연발 권총] a revolver.

리비도 [심] [성(性)적 욕망] libido.

리빙 룸 [거실] a living room.

리사이틀 [음] a (vocal / piano / Chopin) recital. ¶~을 **열다** give[have] a recital (of Schubert songs).

리서치 [조사·연구] research. ¶마케팅 ~ marketing research∥~를 **하다** conduct research (on).

리셉션 a reception. ¶~을 **열다** hold[give] a reception.

리스 a lease. ¶이 토지는 30년 ~로 빌렸다 We have a thirty-year lease on this land.

리스트 a list. ¶~에 기재된 이름 listed names∥~를 **작성하다** make[compile / draw up] a list (of) / list∥~에 올리다 put (a person) on the list∥병명별로 환자의 ~를 작성하다 make a list of patients broken down by [according to] disease∥그의 이름은 후보자 ~에 있다[없다] His name is[is not] on the list of candidates.

리시버 (*receiver) earphones.

리시브 [체] receiving. **리시브하다** receive (the served ball).

리아스식 해안(-式海岸) [지] a rias coast.

리어카 (*rear car) a handcart; a pushcart.

리얼리즘 realism.

리얼리티 reality.

리얼한 [현실적이다] real; [사실이다] realistic. ¶인생의 리얼한 묘사 a realistic depiction[presentation] of life.

-리요 [자문·탄원]. ¶어찌 하~ What am I to do now? / What shall I do?∥이 고마움을 무슨 말로 다 표현하~ I do not know how to express my thanks. / I cannot find words to thank you.

리졸 (상표명) Lysol.

리치 [권투] reach. ¶~가 긴 복서 a boxer with a long reach∥~가 **길다** have a long reach.

리케차 [생] a rickettsia (pl. -ae, ~s).

리콜제(-制) the recall system.

리큐어 [혼성주의 일종] a liqueur.

리타르단도 [음] ritardando.

리터 [용량 단위] (미) a liter; (영) litre(기호 l, lit.).

리튬 [화] lithium(기호 Li).

리트 (⑤Lied) [가곡] a lied (pl. lieder).

리트머스 litmus.
● **리트머스 시험지** [화] litmus paper.

리포터 a reporter.

리포트 1 [보고] a report. 2 [과제] a paper; an essay. ¶그는 제정 러시아에 관한 역사 ~를 작성했다 He did a history paper on Imperial Russia.

리프트 (스키장의) a (ski) lift; (의자를 매단) a chair lift. ¶~로 올라가다 go up (a slope) by lift.

리허설 a rehearsal. ¶카메라 ~ a camera rehearsal∥드레스 ~ a dress rehearsal∥~에 많은 시간을 들이다 have much rehearsal time∥「햄릿」은 지금 ~ 중이다 Hamlet is in rehearsal now.

린네르 → 리넨

린스 a rinse.

린치 a lynching; lynch (law). ¶~를 **가하다** lynch (a traitor).

릴 a reel. ¶낚싯줄을 ~에 감아 넣다[~에서 풀어내다] reel in[out] a fishing line.

릴레이 a relay (race). ¶400미터 ~ 400-meter relay.

림프 [생] lymph.
● **림프관** a lymphatic vessel[duct]. **림프샘**·**림프선**(腺) a lymphatic gland; a lymph node. ¶~이 **붓다** develop swollen lymphatic glands. **림프액** lymph.

립스틱 a lipstick; a lip pencil.

링 1 (권투·레슬링 등의) the ring. ¶~ 밖으로 나가다 step over the edge of the ring / step out of bounds. 2 [체조] (the) flying rings; the rings. 3 [반지] a ring. 4 [피임용] an intrauterine (contraceptive) device(약어 IU(C)D).

링거(액)(-液) [의] Ringer's solution[fluid].

링거 주사(-注射) (give) an injection of Ringer's solution.

링사이드 (sit at) the ringside.

링크[1] [경] a link.
● **링크 제도** [경] a link[grouping] system; a linked purchase system. ¶~로 **하다** place (something) on a link system.

링크[2] [컴] a link.

링크[3] [스케이트장] a (skating / roller-skating) rink.

ㅁ

-ㅁ세 I will gladly (do it for you); I shall be glad to (do); let me. ¶내 나중에 감세 I'll be along later. // 내 곧 감세 I'll be there right away. // 도움이 된다면 무엇이든 도와줌세 I shall be glad to do what I can.

마¹ [식] a yam.

마² [음] mi; E. ¶~음 E // 내림[올림]~ E flat [sharp] // ~장조[단조] (a symphony in) E major[minor] // ~ 플랫 장조 E flat major.

-마 I will gladly (do); I shall be glad to (do). ¶내 꼭 다시 오~ I promise (you) to come again. / I promise you (that) I will come again.

마(麻) [식] flax; a flax plant. ⇨삼¹

마(魔) [악마] a demon; a devil; an evil spirit; evil influence; [불길함] ill[bad] luck. ¶~의 해협 a channel where disasters are apt to happen[occur frequently] // ~의 교차점 dangerous[fatal] crossing[crossroads] // ~의 금요일 Black Friday // ~가 들다 be tempted by a devil / be possessed by [come under the influence of] an evil spirit / be jinxed // 일에 ~가 끼어 있다 My plan is jinxed. // 그녀가 ~에 걸리려 하고 있다 She is about to fall under some evil influence [fall a victim to temptation]. // 그런 말을 하다니 내게 ~가 들었음에 틀림없다 I must have been possessed by some evil spirit to have said such a thing. / I can't imagine what made me say such a thing.

마(碼) a yard. ⇨야드 ¶한 ~에 얼마로 팔다 sell (a fabric) by the yard.

마가린 margarin(e); (영국 구어) marge; (미) oleo. ¶식물성 ~ nut margarine // 빵에 ~을 바르다 spread margarine on bread.

마가목 [식] a mountain ash; a rowan (tree).

마가복음(-福音) [성] (the Gospel of) Mark; The Gospel according to St. Mark.

마각(馬脚) [말의 다리] a horse's legs. **마각을 드러내다** show the cloven hoof[foot]; reveal one's true character; betray oneself. ¶결국 그는 마각을 드러냈다 In the end he revealed his true character[gave himself away].

마갈궁(磨羯宮) [천] the Goat; Capricorn; Capricornus.

마감 conclusion; a close; an end; a finish; (기한 등의) closing; closure. ¶끝 ~ the last finish // 모집 ~ (기부 등의) the close of the subscription // 장부 ~ the closing of books // 편집의 ~ editorial deadline / the time for going to press / the final editing // ~ 후에 도착한 원고 late[belated] manuscripts // ~ 후의 기사 late news // ~에 대다 make[meet] the deadline // ~이 다가오고 있다 The deadline is approaching. **마감하다** end; close; finish; drop (a matter); bring (a matter) to an end[a close]; put an end to. ¶계산을 ~ close the account // 일을 ~ finish a job // 원고를 ~ accept no more manuscripts / go to press with the manuscripts on hand // 신청은 10일에 마감합니다 We will close applications on [The deadline for application is] the 10th. ➔그 건은 그날 밤에 마감되었다 The subject was closed [dropped] for the evening. ●**마감날** the closing day; the final day (for); the time limit (for); (미) the deadline (for). ¶응모의 ~은 3월 20일이다 The deadline [last day] for applications is March 20. // 오늘이 리포트 제출의 ~이다 Today is the closing day [final day / deadline] for turning in the paper. **마감 시간** a closing time; (신문 기사의) the time limit for a copy. ¶~에 대다 make[meet] the deadline.

마개 (병 등의) a stopper; a stop; a stopple; a cork(코르크로 된); (금속제의) a crown cap. ¶귀~ an earplug // 병~ a cork / a stopper // ~를 막다 plug (up) (a hole) / close (a bottle) with a stopper / cork (a bottle) // ~를 뽑다 [따다] uncork[unstop(per)] (a bottle) / extract a cork (from a bottle) // 귀에 ~를 하다 block one's ears // 병에 단단히[느슨히] ~를 하다 cork a bottle tightly[loosely] // 그 통은 ~가 달려 있다 The cask is on tap. (▶ on tap은 「꼭지가 달려 있는」의 뜻의 관용구)

마고자 a *magoja*; a Korean jacket worn over one's upper garment.

마구 1 [몹시] hard; much. ¶욕을 ~ 해 대다 heap abuses on (a person) // 아기가 ~ 울어 대기 시작했다 The baby began to cry wildly. // 비가 ~ 온다 It is raining hard[cats and dogs].
2 [함부로] recklessly; blindly; carelessly; haphazardly; at random; roughly; in a disorderly way; without discretion [discrimination]; slapdash; hit-or-miss; happy-go-lucky; wantonly. ¶돈을 ~ 쓰다 spend money freely [extravagantly] / lavish money / spend money fast [recklessly] // 홧김에 ~ 먹어 대다 eat madly to ease one's frustration // (실망하여) ~ 마셔 대다 drink with a vengeance (in one's despair) // 일을 ~ 하다 do a half-baked [slapdash] job of it // 종이를 ~ 쓰다 waste paper // 사람을 ~ 다루다 handle (a person) roughly / (속어) manhandle // 초콜릿을 ~ 먹다 stuff oneself with [gorge oneself on] chocolate // (미국 구어) eat chocolate like crazy // 찬물을 ~ 마시면 배탈이 난다 Drinking too much cold water will affect your stomach. // 범인은 총을 ~ 쏘아 댔다 The criminal fired his gun blindly [at random]. // 그렇게 공치사를 ~ 늘어놓지 말게 Stop dishing out flattery so lavishly. // ~ 이 되지 마라 Don't be so lavish with your compliments. // 그는 감탄사를 ~ 내뱉는다 His speech is full of exclamations. // 그녀는 돈을 ~ 쓴다 She spends money like water. // 그는 여기저기서 ~ 돈을 빌렸다 He borrowed money here, there and everywhere. // 그렇게 돈을 ~ 쓰지 마라 Don't spend your money so freely. // 그녀는 ~ 지껄여 댔다 She kept rattling away [on].

마구(馬具) harness; horse gear [equipment];

saddlery; trappings(장식한 것). ¶~를 단 harnessed // ~를 **달다** harness (a horse) / put harness on (a horse) // ~를 **풀다** unharness (a horse) / remove the harness from (a horse).
● **마구상** 〔마구를 파는 사람〕 a harness maker; a saddler; 〔마구를 파는 상점〕 a harnessry; a saddler's shop; a saddlery.

마구(간) (馬廐間) a stable; (미) a (horse) barn. ¶~에서 일하는 사람 a stableman / a stabler // ~에 **넣다** stable (a horse) / put [lodge] in a stable.

마구리 〔물건의 양쪽 면〕 an end; an end face; 〔덮어 끼우는 물건〕 caps (on both ends).

마구잡이 (행동) careless [haphazard / random] behavior; (선택) random choice. ¶~로 blindly / senselessly / indiscriminately / recklessly / at random // 일을 ~로 하다 do one's work carelessly / do a slapdash job of it // 책을 ~로 읽다 read (books) at random // ~의 거짓말을 하다 tell an irresponsible lie.

마굴 (魔窟) 1 〔마귀의 소굴〕 a lair of devils. 2 〔악한들이 모인 곳〕 a den; an underworld hangout. 3 〔갈보집〕 a brothel; a house of ill fame; (미국 구어) a good-time house; 〔홍등가〕 a red-light district; a white-slave market.

마권 (馬券) a pari-mutuel ticket.

마귀 (魔鬼) 1 〔잡귀〕 an evil spirit; a devil; a demon; evil influence. ¶~ 같은 devilish / fiendish / diabolic // ~를 **쫓아내다** avert evil influence / keep evil spirit away. 2 〔기〕 a Satan; the Devil. ¶~ **들리다** (사람이) be tempted by a Satan / be possessed by [come under the influence of] the Devil / ~를 **쫓다** drive out the Satans / exorcise Satans (from a person [place]).
● **마귀할멈** a witch; a hag; a harridan; an ogress.

마그나 카르타 〔역〕 the Magna Carta [Charta].

마그네사이트 〔광〕 magnesite.

마그네슘 〔화〕 magnesium(기호 Mg); (사진의) flash powder. ¶탄산 / 염화 / 수산화 / 황산 ~ magnesium carbonate [chloride / hydroxide / sulphate].

마그네시아 〔화〕 magnesium oxide. ⇨산화마그네슘(⇨산화(酸化)) ¶탄산~ magnesium carbonate / magnesia alba / carbonate of magnesia // 황산~ sulphate of magnesia.

마그마 magma.

마나님 〔나이 많은 여자〕 an elderly lady; an old woman; (호칭) madam; (구어) ma'am; Mrs ...; your good lady.

마냥 1 〔끝없이〕 endlessly; ceaselessly. ¶그는 ~ 지껄였다 He would go on talking forever. // 비가 ~ 내린다 It is raining endlessly. // 그녀는 ~ 눈물을 흘렸다 Her tears fell fast. / She shed copious tear. 2 〔실컷〕 till full; to satiety; to one's heart's content. ¶~ 즐기다 enjoy oneself to the full // ~ 먹다 eat as much as one wants // 불평을 ~ 늘어놓다 grumble one's fill.

마네킹 a mannequin; a manikin; a dummy.

마녀 (魔女) 〔마법사〕 a witch; a sorceress; a hex; 〔여자 악마〕 a she-devil; a she-demon.

마노 (瑪瑙) agate.

마누라 one's wife; one's better half; (구어) one's old woman; (호칭) my dear; honey; darling. ¶~를 **얻다** get [take] a wife / get married // 그는 ~ 없이는 하루도 못 사는 사람이다 His wife is everything [is all in all] to him.

마는 〔그러하지마는〕 but; though; although; while; only. ¶나는 가난하지~ 행복하다 I am poor but happy. / I am happy though poor. // 나는 가고 싶지~ 바빠서 못 간다 I should like to go only I'm too busy. // 달려갔지~ 대지 못했다 I ran, but I could not make it.

마늘 〔식〕 a garlic; 〔향료〕 garlic. ¶~ 한 조각 a clove of garlic // ~ 냄새가 나는 garlicky / smelling of garlic.
● **마늘장아찌** pickled garlics. **마늘종** the stalk [stem] of a garlic.

마니교 (摩尼教) Manich(a)eism; Manich(a)eanism.
● **마니교도** a Manich(a)ean; a Manichee.

마니아 〔열광하는 사람〕 a maniac; a fan; (미국 구어) a buff. ¶재즈 ~ a jazz maniac // 영화 ~ a film buff.

마님 1 madam; ma'am; (호칭) Milady; My lady. ¶안방~ the mistress (of a house). 2 Your [His] Excellency; My Lord. ¶대감[영감]~ My Lord.

마다 〔낱낱이〕 each; every; all. ¶밤~ every evening / every night // 5시간~ every five hours / at intervals of five hours // 2일 ~ every other day // 사흘~ every three days / every third day // 집집~ every door // 거의 밤 ~ almost every night // 밤~ 의 목욕 a nightly bath // 그를 만날 때~ 그는 용돈을 달라고 조른다 Each [Every] time I see him, he pesters me for pocket money. // 그는 나를 만나러 자주 오는데 그때~ 꽤 오래 머무른다 He often comes to see me, and stays for a long while every [each] time. // ~가는 곳~ 나는 대환영을 받았다 I was warmly welcomed everywhere [wherever] I went. // 밤~ 9시에 뉴스가 방송된다 There is a newscast at nine every evening. // 그들은 밤~ 그 일에 대해서 토론했다 They discussed it night after night. // 인구가 해~ 증가하고 있다 The population keeps on growing with the years. // 그 테니스 선수가 어려운 공을 되받아칠 때~ 관객이 환성을 질렀다 Each [Every] time the tennis player returned a difficult ball, the spectators gave a cheer. // 그는 미국에 갈 때~ 미시간에 있는 친구를 찾았다 Whenever he visited the U.S., he went to call on his friend in Michigan. // 나는 매년 프랑스에 가는데 그때~ 딸을 데리고 간다 I go to France every year and each time I take my daughter with me. // 그는 외출할 때~ 레코드를 사 온다 Whenever he goes out, he comes back with a new record. // 그녀는 나를 만날 때~ 미안하다고 한다 She apologizes whenever she meets me. // 그 여자 아이는 볼 때~ 커 가고 있었다 The child had grown taller every time I saw her. // 그에게서 계절~ 편지가 온다 He writes to me each season. // 1,000원~ 50원의 할인이 있다 There is a discount of fifty won on each thousand won. // 주차료는 1시간~ 2,000원입니다 The parking rate is 2,000 won per [an] hour. // 내가 그에게 전화를 할 때~ 그는 외출 중이었다 Every time I phoned [called] him, he was out. // 5분~ 열차가 도착한다 A train arrives every five minutes.

마다하다 1 〔싫어하다〕 dislike; hate; loathe; detest. ¶나는 어떤 일도 마다하지 않겠다 I

마담 don't mind doing any job.// 찬 바람도 마다하지 않고 그는 아침마다 조깅을 한다 He jogs every morning, not minding[paying no heed to] the cold wind.// 그것을 손에 넣기 위해서라면 나는 노고[출비]를 마다하지 않겠다 I would go to any amount of trouble[pay anything] to get it. **2** [싫다고 거절하다] refuse; decline. ¶마다할 수가 없다 have no words to decline / do not know how to decline// 나는 그것을 선뜻 마다할 수가 없었다 I hesitated to refuse it. / I could not find it in my heart to refuse it.

마담 a madam (*pl.* mesdames); (프) madame; [요정 등의 주인] the proprietress. ¶다방 ~ the manageress of a coffee shop[tea room]// 얼굴 ~ the manageress (of a tea room)// 유한 ~ a rich[wealthy] woman of leisure// ~ 버터플라이 Madam Butterfly / Mrs. Butterfly// 그녀는 음식점의 ~이다 She is the proprietress of[She runs] a restaurant.

마당 1 [뜰] a yard; a court; a garden. ¶안~ a courtyard / a[an inner] court// 앞[뒷] ~ a front[rear] garden// ~을 빌리다 hold a wedding ceremony in the bride's house. **2** [타작 마당] a threshing ground; the yard for threshing. **3** [경우] an instance; a case; [때] the moment. ¶이 ~에 on this occasion / at this time[juncture]// 궁한 ~에 무엇을 가리랴 Beggars should not be choosers.// 이 ~에 무슨 군소리냐 The case does not allow of saying such a thing. **4** [판소리 등의] an episode. ¶봉산 탈춤 일곱 ~ 중의 하나 one of the seven episodes of the *Bongsan Talchum*.

● **마당발** a flatfoot; a splayfoot (*pl.* -feet). **마당질** threshing [flailing] in the yard. ¶~을 하다 thresh[flail] (rough rice) in the yard.

마대 (麻袋) a gunny bag[sack]; a jute bag; a sandbag; a burlap bag.

마도로스 (⑩matroos) a sailor; a seaman.
마도요 [동] an Indian curlew; a sabrebill.
마돈나 [성모] the Madonna.
마드리갈 [음] a madrigal.

마들가리 1 [가지 없는 줄기] a branch without twigs; [땔감의 잔가지] twigs of firewood; dead branches. **2** [해진 옷의 남은 솔기] seams of a worn-out garment. **3** [흙킨 마디] a tangle of strand in a rope[thread].

마디 1 [관절] a joint; [손가락 관절] a knuckle.
2 (나무의 옹이) a knot; a knob; a lump; a nod; [실 등의 매듭] a knot. ¶나무의 ~ a knar / a gnarl// 대나무의 ~ a bamboo joint / a node[joint] of a bamboo// 실의 ~ a knob / a burl// ~투성이의 full of knots / knotty (timber) / knobby / gnarled(줄기).
3 [체절(體節)] a ringlike segment; a segment; (곤충 등의) an annulus.
4 (말의) a word; a phrase; (노래의) a snatch; a tune; a melody; [소절] a bar; a measure. ¶(노래의) 첫째 ~ the first measure / measure 1// 몇 ~ 말하고 나서 after making a brief remark// 한 ~ 부르다 sing a tune// 한두 ~ 인사말을 나누다 exchange a word or two of greeting (with).

마디다 durable; enduring; long-lasting; long-wearing. ¶마디게 쓰다 make (food) keep long / add to the life (of).

마디마디 1 (식물의) all the joints[nodes]; every joint[node]. **2** (뼈의) the joints; every joint (of the body). ¶몸의 ~가 아프다 My joints ache[hurt]. **3** (말의) (all) the words [phrases]; every word[phrase]. ¶~에 깊은 뜻이 있다 All the words are pregnant with meaning.

마디지다 [마디가 있다] gnarled (trees); bony; knuckly[strong-jointed] (finger); knotty (hand). ¶늙어 마디진 손 old knotty hands.

마디충 (-蟲) [동] a rice borer; a pear; a pearl moth.

마디풀 [식] a knotgrass; a knotweed.

마따나 [말한 대로] as; like; just as (a person) say; according to (a person). ¶자네 말~ 이 책은 따분하더군 This is really so dull to read as you told me about it.// 자네 말~ 그의 말이 옳았다고 내가 생각할 날이 올지도 모르겠다 As you say, I may be convinced some day of the justice of his remark.

마땅하다 1 [적합하다] becoming; befitting; right; proper; appropriate; suitable; apposite; [상당하다] fair; reasonable. ¶마땅한 자리 a suitable position// 마땅한 인물 a competent person / a person qualified (for the task) // …에게 마땅한 경의를 표하여 with due respect[regard] to[for]// 마땅한 값에 사다 buy at a reasonable price// 마땅한 예를 들다 give a good[an appropriate] example// 그렇게 해야 ~ That is the right[proper] way to go about it.// 마땅한 조치를 취하겠습니다 I will act at my discretion in your favor.

마땅히 suitably; adequately; appropriately; properly; reasonably. ¶값을 ~ 부르다 bid a reasonable price.

2 [마음에 들다] good; satisfactory; pleased; gratifying. ¶마땅치 않은 일 an undesirable thing / a dislikable[an unwanted / a dissatisfactory] thing// 마땅잖은 얼굴을 하다 look displeased with[at] / turn glum// 이 물건은 아무래도 마땅치가 않다 These goods are by no means satisfactory.// 이것이 가장 ~ This suits my taste best.

3 [당연하다] justifiable; warrantable; rational. ¶죽어 마땅한 범죄 a serious crime deserving of death// 부모의 말에 순종해야 ~ You ought to obey your parents.// 내가 그만큼 그를 돌보아 주었으면, 그도 내게 감사하다고 말했어야 ~ Since I gave so much assistance to him, he should[ought to / might at least] have thanked me.// 그런 사람은 엄벌을 받아 ~ Such a man deserves to be punished severely. **마땅히** properly; naturally; exactly; justly; necessarily; of necessity; deservedly; of course; as a matter of course. ¶~ …해야 하다 ought to (do) / it is (just and) proper that (one) should (do)// ~ 그래야 한다 That must be expected. / That's the natural thing to be expected.// 너는 ~ 벌을 받아야겠다 You deserve punishment.// 그는 지금쯤은 ~ 목적지에 도착해 있어야 한다 He ought to have arrived at his destination by now.

마뜩찮다 dissatisfactory; disagreeable; offensive. ¶마뜩찮은 소리를 지껄이다 say something disagreeable[offensive]// 그 식당의 음식은 마뜩찮은 것뿐이다 None of the foods and dishes at the restaurant can be served to my taste and satisfaction.

마뜩하다 satisfactory; agreeable; acceptable.
마라톤 a marathon (race); (운동을 위한) long-distance running. ¶~을 하다 (경기) take part in a marathon race / (운동을 위한) run long distance.
● **마라톤 선수** a marathon runner; a marathoner.
마량(馬糧) horse feed; fodder. ⇨ 말먹이
마력(馬力) horsepower(약어 HP, hp). ¶공칭 ~ nominal horsepower // 실 ~ actual horsepower // 유효 ~ effective horsepower // 정격(定格) ~ rated horsepower // 축 ~ brake horsepower // 100~의 모터 a 100 HP motor // ~을 올리다 push the power up // 그 발동기는 2백 ~이다 The motor develops [has a capacity of] 200 HP.
마력(魔力) 〔이상한 힘〕 magical powers; supernatural powers; spell; 〔매력〕 the power to charm; fascinating power; charm. ¶사랑〔활자〕의 ~ the magic of love [the printed word] // ~에 걸려들다 fall under [be bound by] a magic spell / find oneself under the charm (of) // 그는 그녀의 ~에 매혹되었다 He fell under the spell of [was fascinated by] her charms.
마련 1 〔준비〕 preparation; provision; arrangement; 〔계획〕 (a) plan; 〔설비〕 furnishing. ¶혼자 살아갈 만한 ~은 되어 있는 몸이오 I've got what it takes to be able to go it alone. **마련하다** prepare (seats); provide; arrange; furnish; get ready (for); make ready for; plan. ¶술자리를 ~ hold a banquet // 사무실을 ~ set up [establish / open] an office // 규정을 ~ lay down rules / 규약에 예외를 ~ constitute [set up] an exception to the rules // 구실을 ~ make an excuse // 혼담을 ~ arrange a marriage // 기회를 마련하여 내가 그 두 사람을 만나게 하겠다 I will provide an opportunity for them to meet. →¶저쪽에 좌석이 마련되어 있습니다 A seat has been prepared for you over there. // 대통령을 위한 특별기가 마련되었다 A special plane was prepared for the President.
2 〔변통〕 contrivance; management; makeshift; arrangement. **마련하다** contrive; manage; make shift; arrange. ¶자금을 ~ raise funds // 나는 간신히 돈을 마련했다 After a struggle, I managed to raise the money. // 내주까지 500만 원을 마련해야 한다 I have to raise five million won by next week. // 나는 내 결혼에 필요한 물품을 마련해 놓았다 I purchased the things necessary for my wedding.
3 〔당연〕. ¶겨울 등산은 위험하기 ~이다 Mountain climbing in winter is always risky. // 설교란 지루하기 ~이다 A sermon is meant to be boring. / Sermons are boring by definition. // 아기란 울기 ~이다 It is a baby's job to cry.
마렵다 feel an urge to urinate [defecate]; have a call of nature; want to relieve oneself. ¶똥이 ~ have to defecate / feel like going to stool // 오줌이 ~ have a desire to urinate [pass water] // 마렵지 않다 feel no urge to ease nature // 엄마, 오줌〔똥〕 마려워 (구어) Mammy, I want to do my needs.
마로니에 (프) marronnier; a horse chestnut (tree).
마루¹ 〔집의〕 a (wooden) floor; a flooring. ¶집에 ~를 깔다 floor a house // ~를 떼어 내다 tear up the floor.
● **마루 운동** 〔체조〕 floor exercise. **마루청** a floorboard; 〔집합적〕 flooring. ¶모자이크 무늬의 ~을 깐 방 a room with mosaic flooring / 집에 ~을 깔다 lay flooring in a house / floor a house. **마룻바닥** the floor. ¶~에 앉다 sit on the floor // ~이 꺼졌다 The floor fell through.
마루² **1** (지붕·산의) a ridge. ¶산~ the ridge of a mountain // 용~ the ridge of a roof // 지붕~ the ridge of a roof. **2** (일의) the final [most important] part of an event.
마루터기 the top; the summit; a peak; a ridge. ¶고갯~ the summit of a pass // 산~ the ridge of a mountain // 지붕 ~ the ridge of a roof.
마르다¹ **1** 〔건조하다〕 dry (up); get [become] dry; (목재가) be seasoned; (초목이) wither; be withered. ¶마른 수건 a dry towel // 물이 바싹 마른 강 a dried-up river // 셔츠가 말랐다 The shirt has dried. // 이 천은 빨리 마른다 This cloth dries fast. // 그녀는 눈물이 마를 겨를도 없었다 She experienced one sorrow after another. // 그는 아직 머리에 피도 마르지 않았다 He is still not dry behind the ears. // 논의 물이 바싹 말라 타들어 간다 Rice paddies all have been dried up and now are burning in the summer sun. // 가뭄이 들면 풀이나 나무들이 말라 죽는 수가 가끔 있다 Droughts sometimes blast [dry up] the grasses and trees. // 대개의 소는 약 열 달이면 젖이 마른다 Most cows run dry in about ten months.
2 〔목·입술이〕 물기가 적다〕 be thirsty; parch; be parched (up). ¶바싹 마른 입술 parched lips // 목이 ~ be thirsty / have a dry throat.
3 〔야위다〕 become lean [thin]; grow gaunt [slim]; lose (one's) weight; (병으로) lose flesh; (사랑·근심으로) pine away. ¶마르는 약 an antifat remedy / a fat [flesh] reducer // 마른 사람 a thin [lean / skinny / scrawny / scraggy] person // 빼빼 마른 사람 a dry-bones // 걱정으로 ~ worry oneself into a frazzle // 못 먹어 ~ be wasted with hunger / be underfed // 마르기 위해 운동을 하다 take weight-reducing exercises // 전보다 많이 말랐군요 You have got much thinner than you were. / You appear to have lost flesh.
4 〔고갈되다〕 run out; become exhausted; be used up. ¶돈이 ~ have no money left / be cleaned out / money is tight [scarce / in short supply] // 호주머니가 ~ have a cold purse / feel the draught / be low in (one's) pocket // 그의 상상력은 마르는 일이 없다 His imagination is never exhausted [never runs dry].
마르다² (옷감 등을) cut out; make by cutting. ¶마르는 일 cutting / design setting [cutting] // 옷을 ~ cut out clothes // 재목을 재어 ~ cut lumber to measure.
마르크 〔독일의 화폐 단위〕 a mark.
마르크스주의(-主義) Marxism.
● **마르크스주의자** a Marxist.
마른걸레 a dry cloth [duster]; a dry mop. ¶~질하다 wipe [clean up] (the floor) with a dry mop [cloth].
마른국수 〔말린 국수〕 dried noodles; 〔걷거나 비비지 않고 삶아 놓은 국수〕 uncooked noodles.

마른기침 a dry cough. ¶연거푸 나오는 ~ a hacking cough. **마른기침하다** have a dry [hacking] cough; clear one's throat.

마른날 a fine [clear] day.

마른반찬(-飯饌) dried meat or fish eaten with rice as side dishes.

마른밥 [국 없는 밥] a meal of boiled rice not accompanied by soup. 2 [주먹밥] balled rice.

마른버짐 [한] psoriasis; a kind of ringworm.

마른번개 lightning across[in] the blue sky.

마른안주(-按酒) an assortment of dried meat and fish served with drinks; a "bar snack".

마른옴 [한] the itch; scabies.

마른일 housewife's chores done without wetting her hands. **마른일하다** do one's dry-handed housework.

마른입 [국물을 마시지 않은 입] a thirsty mouth after a soupless meal.

마른천둥 thunder in the clear blue sky.

마른하늘 the clear (blue) sky; the cloudless sky.

마른하늘에 날[생]벼락(속담) a bolt from the blue; a thunderbolt; a bombshell.

마른행주 a dish towel; (영) a dishcloth.

마름¹ [이엉을 말아 놓은 단] a roll of thatch.

마름² [식] water caltrop [nut / chestnut]; curly pondweed.

마름³ [소작지 관리인] the supervisor of a tenant farm; an estate agent.

마름모꼴 a lozenge; diamond shape; [수] a rhombus (pl. ~es, -bi). ¶~의 lozenge-shaped / rhombic / diamond-shaped.

마름쇠 a caltrop; a caltrap.

마름자 [마름질에 쓰는 자] a tailor's yardstick.

마름질 cutting (out). ¶~을 시작하다 begin to cut (cloth) // ~이 바느질보다 어렵다고 한다 Cutting is said to require more skill than tailoring. **마름질하다** cut out (a garment).

마리 a head (단수·복수동형); the number (of animals). ¶두 ~의 개 [곤충 / 뱀] two dogs [insects / snakes] // 다섯 ~의 새끼 고양이 five kittens // 물고기 세 ~ three fishes.

마리화나 [환각제] marijuana; (속어) grass.

마마¹(媽媽) 1 [한] (the) smallpox; variola. **마마하다** have smallpox; be attacked by [suffer from] smallpox. 2 [별성마마] plague.

● **마마꽃** pox pustules. **마마자국** a pock; a pit; a pockmark. ¶그는 얼굴에 ~이 있다 His face is pitted with smallpox [is marked by smallpox]. / His face is pockmarked.

마마²(媽媽) [경칭] Your [His / Her] Majesty [Highness]. **대전**[상감]~ His Majesty the king / Your Majesty // **동궁**~ His (Royal) Highness the Crown Prince / Your Highness // **중전**~ the Queen / Her Majesty [Highness].

마마보이 (미) a mama's boy; (영) a mummy's boy; a mother's boy.

마멋 [다람쥣과의 동물] a marmot.

마멸(磨滅) wear (and tear); defacement; abrasion. ¶이 재질은 ~에 강하다 This material is durable [resistant to wear]. **마멸하다** be worn out [away / down]; wear out [away]; be defaced. →¶마멸된 구두 뒤축 worn-down heels (of shoes) // 도장이 마멸되었다 The stamp has become defaced. // 돌계단이 마멸되고 있다 The stone steps are wearing away.

마모(磨耗) wear (and tear); abrasion. ¶이 재질은 ~에 견딘다 This material resists abrasion. **마모하다** be worn away. →¶이 기계는 상당히 마모되어 있다 This machine is badly worn.

마무르다 1 [끝손질하다] give [put / add] the final [finishing] touch; touch up; do up; finish off. ¶멍석을 ~ give the final touches to [finish up] a straw mat // 바느질을 ~ make [sew] the final stitches. 2 [일의 끝을 맺다] settle; bring (a matter) to a finish; finish (off / up); complete; conclude; get through with. ¶문장을 솜씨 있게 ~ round off a sentence // 분쟁을 원만히 ~ settle a dispute peacefully // 일을 ~ finish [get through with] (one's) work.

마무리 [완성] finishing; completion; conclusion; [마지막 손질] the finish; the finishing touches [strokes]; (벽 시멘트칠의) a setting [finishing] coat. ¶~는 숙련공이 했다 The finishing was done by a skilled worker. // 화가는 마지막 ~로 두세 군데 손질을 했다 The artist gave the picture a few finishing touches. // 이 테이블은 마호가니로 ~를 했다 This table has a mahogany finish. // 그 여배우는 화장의 ~를 했다 The actress finished (up) her makeup. // ~가 중요하다 All's well that ends well. **마무리하다** settle; arrange; finish; complete; conclude; get through with. ¶정교하게 마무리된 조각 a sculpture with a fine finish // 이젠 토론을 마무리할 때가 되었다 The time has come to bring the discussion to a conclusion. // 일을 서둘러 마무리하자 Let's hurry up and finish the job. // 밀주된 물품을 내일까지 마무리해 주시오 Please supply the article ordered by tomorrow. →¶두 나라의 통상 조약이 마무리되었다 A trade pact [treaty] was concluded between the two countries. // 이번 일이 마무리되면 여행을 가겠습니다 After I finish this job, I am going to take a trip.

마물(魔物) [마성의 것] a demon; a devil; an evil spirit; [마귀] a goblin.

마바리(馬-) [짐 실은 말] a horse carrying a burden packhorse; (말에 실은 짐) a horse load [burden]; a pack.

● **마바리꾼** a packhorse driver; a packhorse man; a packhorse peddler.

마법(魔法) magic; sorcery; black art; witchcraft(여자의); wizardry(남자의). ¶~의 지팡이 a magic wand // ~의 나라 a magic land // ~으로 by magic / magically // ~의 힘으로 by (the influence of) magic // 남에게 ~을 걸다 cast a spell on a person // ~에 걸리다 be bound by a spell // ~을 풀다 break a spell / free a person from a spell // 나는 어떤 ~에 걸리기라도 한 듯이 꼼짝할 수가 없었다 I was as unable to move as if I had been under some sort of magic.

● **마법사** a magician; a sorcerer; a wizard; a necromancer. ¶여자 ~ a witch / a sorceress.

마부(馬夫) (역마차의) a cabman; a coachman; a driver; (짐마차의) a carter; a wagoner.

● **마부석** the driver's box; the coach box.

마분지(馬糞紙) strawboard; pasteboard; millboard.

마비(痲痺) paralysis; palsy; numbness; [의] monoplegia; stupor(정신의); an(a)esthesia

(약에 의한). ¶뇌성 ~ cerebral palsy/대(對) ~ paraplegia/부전(不全) ~ paresis/partial paralysis//소아~ infantile paralysis//심장 ~ heart failure//안면 ~ facial paralysis//전신[국부] ~ general[local] paralysis//진행성 ~ progressive paralysis/(매독에 의한) general paresis[paralysis]//교통 ~ a traffic jam//도의심의 ~ moral paralysis. **마비되다** be paralyzed[(영) paralysed]; (특히 추위·냉함 등으로) be numb(ed); (약 등으로) (미) be anaesthetized; (영) be anaesthetised[anaesthetised]. ¶수족이 마비되어 있다 My limbs are paralyzed.//추위로 발이 마비되었다 The cold numbed my feet.//그의 양심은 마비되어 있다 He is dead to conscience./His conscience is benumbed.//충격으로 사고력이 마비되어 버렸다 The shock has paralyzed my ability to think.//태풍으로 모든 교통 기관이 마비되어 있다 All transportation facilities have been paralyzed by the typhoon.

마사(馬事) horse affairs[matters]. ¶한국 ~ 회 the Korean Horse Affairs Association.

마사지 (give) a massage; a rubdown. ¶근육 ~ a massage of the muscles//얼굴 ~ a face massage/(미국 구어) a facial//전기 ~ electromassage. **마사지하다** massage[rub down] (a person); give (a person) a massage[rubdown]. ¶얼굴을 ~ have a facial massage.
● **마사지사**(-師) a massagist. **마사지 요법** massotherapy.

마삯(馬-) the fee for hiring a horse; the pay for a hired horse.

마상(馬上) horseback. ¶~에서 on horseback//~에서 소리치다 call out (to another) from one's horse.

마상1 [작은 배] a small boat; a skiff. 2 [통나무배] a canoe; a dugout (canoe); a pirogue.

마성(魔性) devilishness; fiendishness. ¶~의 devilish/diabolic(al)//~을 지닌 사람[것] an evil spirit/a demon//~을 지닌 여자 a vampire/a temptress/an enchantress(매혹적인)/a devilish woman(마귀 같은)/a woman who uses wiles to lead men astray(유혹하는).

마세 [당구] (프) a massé (shot).

마셜 플랜 the Marshall Plan.

마소 horses and oxen[cattle]. ¶~처럼 부리다 work (a person) like a beast of burden.

마손(磨損) wear and tear; friction loss; (기계 등의) abrasion; attrition; (활자의) batter. **마손하다** wear; be worn (away).

마수 1 [그날 장사의 운수] the business luck of the day[the prospect of the day's business/the day's business outlook] predictable by the first sale[transaction]. ¶~가 좋다[나쁘다] make a good[bad] start in sale/the first sale bodes well[ill] for the day's business. 2 the first break of the day's business. ⇨ 마수걸이(⇨마수)

마수(를) 걸다 make the first sale of the day; make the first lucky break of the day's business.
● **마수걸이** the first break of the day's business; the first sale of the day; [개점의 첫 거래] the first transaction of a new business. ¶~로 팔다 sell (an article) as the day's [firm's] first sale//~를 하다 make the first sale[transaction] of the day/break the ice in the day's business//당신이 ~를 하면 오늘 내 재수가 좋을 텐데 If you are my first customer, I shall have good luck for the day.

마수(魔手) an evil hand; evil power[influence]. ¶~에 걸려들다 fall a victim (to)/be caught in (a person's) claws//살인귀의 ~에 걸리다 fall victim[prey] to a devilish killer//음모단의 ~가 그에게 뻗011 왔다 The plotters have begun to reach out toward him.

마술(馬術) horsemanship; horseback riding; (the art of) riding; [곡마술] equestrian art. ¶고등 ~ high school/(프) haute école//종합 ~ (올림픽의) the three-day events//~의 명수 a master horseman//~에 능하다 be at home in the saddle/be a good horseman [horsewoman].
● **마술 경기** an equestrian [riding] event. **마술 교사** a riding master.

마술(魔術) [마력을 부리는 술법] magic; [사악한 마법] witchcraft; the black arts; [악령의 도움을 빌려 행하는 술법] sorcery. ¶말의 ~ the spell of words//~을 부리다 practice magic[witchcraft/the black arts sorcery]//남에게 ~을 걸다 cast a spell on[upon/over] a person//~로 망령을 불러내다 conjure up a spirit//여기 아무런 감추어진 ~도 없습니다 There is no secret trick to this./I have no tricks up my sleeve.//~의 정체를 보여 드리죠 I'll show you how the trick is done.
● **마술사** [마법사] a magician; (악령의 힘을 빌린) a sorcerer; a black magician; (여자의) a sorceress; [요술쟁이] a magician; a conjurer.

마스카라 mascara. ¶속눈썹에 ~를 칠하다 apply mascara to one's eyelashes.

마스코트 a (good-luck) mascot.

마스크 1 [얼굴을 가리는 것] a (face) mask; a face guard. ¶데스 ~ a death mask//방독 ~ a gas mask//산소~ an oxygen mask//~를 쓰다 wear a mask. 2 [용모] looks; features.

마스터베이션 [수음(手淫)] masturbation. ¶~의 masturbatory//~을 하다 masturbate.

마스터키 a master key.

마스터플랜 [기본 계획] a master plan.

마스터하다 [기술 등을 충분히 익히다] master. ¶외국어를 ~ master a foreign language.

마스트 a mast. ¶~가 셋인 배 a three-masted ship/a three-master.

마시다 1 (액체를) drink; have; take; [삼키다] swallow(▶"약을 먹다"의 경우는 일반적으로 take). ¶차를 ~ drink tea//커피를 한 잔 ~ drink a cup of coffee//수프를 ~ eat soup/(컵으로 직접) drink soup//홀짝홀짝 ~ drink in little sips//양동이의 물을 ~ drink water from a bucket//뭐 마실 것 좀 주세요 Give me something to drink.//그는 먹지도 마시지도 않고 산속을 헤맸다 He wandered through the mountains without food or drink.//그들은 차를 마시면서 이야기했다 They talked over a cup of tea.//가서 한잔 마시자 Let's go and have a drink.//그는 술을 마시고 잠들어 버렸다 He downed[(구어) knocked back] a drink and then fell asleep.
2 (기체를) breathe in; inhale; inspire; draw (air) into (the lungs). ¶신선한 공기를 마시기 위해 창문을 열다 open the window to let

마신(魔神) a malevolent deity; an evil spirit; Satan; a devil.

마신(馬身) a horse's length. ¶그 말은 3~의 차로 이겼다 The horse won by three lengths.

마애불(磨崖佛) a Buddha image on a cliff; a rock cliff Buddha.

마야 문명(-文明) Mayan civilization[culture].

마약(痲藥) a narcotic; a drug; (미국 구어) a dope. ¶~을 쓰다 take a drug / administer an anaesthetic // ~을 피우다 inject[inhale / sniff] a narcotic.
● 마약 단속 a dope check; narcotic control. **마약 밀매** drug traffic[trade / business]; (구어) dope peddling; traffic in drugs. **마약 상습자** a drug addict; a narcotic; (구어) a junkie. **마약 중독** drug addiction(▶ 마약도 포함하여 약물 중독의 뜻); [의] narcotism. ¶~이 되다 (미국 속어) go[be] hooked (by the morphine habit) / become addicted to (the use of) narcotics.

마왕(魔王) the Devil; Satan; Lucifer; the Prince of Darkness[Evil]; [불] an evil spirit.

마요네즈 mayonnaise. ¶감자에 ~를 치다 dress the potatoes with mayonnaise.

마우스 [컴] a mouse.
마우스패드 [컴] a mousepad.
마우스피스 a mouthpiece.

마운드 [야구] the mound; the pitcher's plate. ¶~에 서다 take the mound / be on the mound / pitch (an inning) // ~를 내려오다 leave the mound / (구어) get knocked out (▶ 언어먹고) / 주전 투수가 ~에서 내려와 경기의 흐름이 달라졌다 The course of the game changed when the ace pitcher got knocked out[left the mound].

마을 1 [동네] a village; a hamlet; a rural community. ¶이웃 ~ a neighboring village // 새~ 운동 the *Saemaeul*[New Community] Movement // 고립된 ~ an isolated village. **2** [나들이] a visit to (one's) neighborhood (for a chat); go out for a chat with (one's) neighborhood. **3** [옛 관청] a government office.
마을(을) 가다 [이웃에 놀러 가다] visit one's neighboring village[neighborhood] (for a chat); go out for a chat with (one's) neighborhood.
● 마을금고 a village fund. **마을 사람** (한 사람) a villager; (집합적) the village; village people[folk].

마음 1 [정신] (the) mind; spirit; [생각] an idea; (a) thought; [심성] mentality. ¶~과 몸 the mind and the body // 불순한 ~ an impure heart // 어리석은 ~ (one's) foolish idea // 어린 ~ young ideas / a juvenile [puerile] mind // ~의 양식 food for thought / spiritual[mental] food // ~의 탓 (mere) fancy / a trick of senses // ~의 평화 peace of mind // ~이 고운 tender-hearted // ~이 따뜻한 warmhearted // ~이 더러운 dirty-minded // ~이 좁은 small[narrow-] minded / ungenerous // ~이 좋은 good-natured // ~이 큰[넓은] big-hearted / broad-minded / generous / liberal // ~이 맞는 친구 a likeminded company // ~이 젊은 사람 a man of youthful spirit(s) // ~을 합쳐 with one accord / in one mind // ~에 들지 않는 놈 a disagreeable fellow // ~이 끌리다 be attracted (by) / take (an) interest (in) // ~이 기쁘다 be glad (at heart) // ~이 놓이다 be[feel] relieved / feel at ease / be assured // ~이 변하다 have (one's) mind changed / (남녀간에) grow out of love (with) // ~이 부풀다 feel excited[encouraged] // ~이 산란해지다[헷갈리다] be distracted with the thought (of) // ~이 쓰이다 be worried[concerned / anxious] about // ~이 차분[침착]하다 have presence of mind / be self-possessed // ~이 커지다 become emboldened / lose (one's) timidity // ~에 걸리끼다 have an uneasy conscience // ~에 걸리다 (사람이) be anxious[nervous] (about) / feel uneasy (about) / (사물이) weigh (up)on (one's) mind / worry (a person) // ~에 그리다 picture[image] to oneself / draw a mental picture (of) // ~에 든든하다 feel safe[secure / reassured] // ~에 떠오르다 (사물이) occur to (a person) / spring[come] to mind / come across[to] one's mind // ~에 새기다 print [engrave] (a fact) on one's mind[memory] / take (the advice) to heart // ~에 거리낄 것이 없다 have a clean conscience // (…하려고) ~에 정하고 있다 have one's heart[mind] set on doing // ~을 가라앉히다 collect[calm / compose] oneself // ~을 고쳐먹다 reform (oneself) / turn over a new leaf // ~을 피롭히다 trouble one's mind // ~을 끌다 attract / allure / appeal to (one's) curiosity // ~을 긴장시키다 strain one's nerves // …이라고 생각하여 ~을 달래다 salve (one's) conscience by the thought that … // ~을 쓰다 concentrate on / put[pour] one's heart (and soul) into // 남의 ~을 읽다[살피다] read another's mind // ~을 정하다 make up one's mind / resolve (to) // ~을 합하다 be united / act in concert (with) / cooperate in harmony // 회사에 ~이 좀 끌리는 사람이 있다 There's someone I'm kind of interested in[(영) someone I fancy] at work. // 그녀와는 어쩐지 ~이 잘 맞지 않는다 Somehow she and I just don't hit it off very well. // ~이 훗훗해지는 이야기다 It is a heartwarming story. // ~이 산란해지니 조용히 해라 Be quiet. I can't concentrate. // 그녀는 나이에 비해 ~은 젊다 Her heart is young for her age. // ~은 젊지만 몸이 말을 듣지 않는다 Though I'm young at heart, I am not so lively as I used to be. // 그는 어쩐지 ~에 들지 않는다 I just don't like him. // 그의 안색이 나쁜 것이 ~에 걸린다 I cannot forget how pale he was. // 그녀의 병이 ~에 걸린 Her illness weighs on my mind. // ~을 굳게 가져라 Don't let yourself get [be] discouraged. // 그는 ~을 바꾸었다 He changed his mind. // ~을 가다듬고 나는 처음부터 다시 시작했다 Pulling myself together [Collecting myself], I started again. // 그는 몸도 ~도 건강하다 He is sound in mind and body. / He is mentally and physically sound. **2** [심정] (the) heart; [감정] sense; feeling; [기분] mood; frame of mind; humor. ¶어머니의 ~ a mother's feeling[love] / maternal affection // 존경하는 ~ (a feeling of) respect // ~이 변덕스러운 사람 a man of moods // ~이 울적하다 be in a low mood / be low-spirited // ~이 상하다 one's heart breaks // ~이 편하다 feel easy / find (oneself) more at ease // ~이 편치 않다 feel ill at ease / feel constrained[awkward] // ~에 사무치다 go to one's heart // ~을 모질게 먹다 harden[steel] one's heart[oneself] (against pity) // ~을 빼앗다 charm / bewitch / fascinate / captivate // (남의) ~을 움직이다 move (a person) / touch (a person's heart) // ~을 주다 trust oneself (to) / share one's confidence (with) // ~을 털어놓다 open[bare] one's heart (to) / unbosom oneself (to) // 나는 자책하는 ~이 들었다 I had a guilty conscience. / I felt remorse for what I had done. // 나는 불안한 ~에 사로잡혔다 I was seized with (a sense of) uneasiness. // 나는 ~이 울적하고 짜증만 났다 I was depressed and irritable. // 그의 일을 생각하니 ~이 무겁다 My heart is heavy when I think of him. // 그것을 듣고 ~이 편해졌다 It's a relief to hear that. // 오늘은 도무지 일할 ~이 나지 않는다 I don't feel like working today. / I'm in no mood[humor] for working today.

3 [진심] sincerity; heart; wholeheartedness. ¶~의 벗[친구] a cordial friend / one's bosom friend // ~으로부터의 감사 warm [cordial / heartfelt] thanks / thanks from the bottom of one's heart // ~에 품다 cherish / entertain / harbor // ~을 담다[쏟다] give one's whole mind (to) // ~을 터놓고 이야기하다 speak frankly / be frank with (a person) / talk heart to heart (with) // 여자에게 ~을 주다 give oneself to a woman. // 그와는 ~을 터놓고 지내는 사이다 He is a very close friend of mind.

4 [사려] thought; [인정] consideration; sympathy; tenderness. ¶~를 쓰다 be considerate / be kind to (a person) // (남의) ~을 헤아리다 feel for / sympathize with / enter into another's feeling // 그는 아내의 ~을 헤아릴 수 없었다 He could not enter into his wife's feelings. // 그는 그녀의 슬픈 ~에 동정했다 He sympathized with her in her sorrow.

5 [의지] will; [의향] mind; design; inclination; intention. ¶~이 있다 have a mind (to do) / have an idea of (doing) / have a fancy (for a woman) // ~이 없다 have no mind (to do) / have no heart (for study) // ~을 떠보다 probe[try to find out] (a person's) mind // 불현듯 ···하고 싶은 ~이 생기다 have a sudden desire to (do) // ~에 없는 말을 하다 say what one does not mean / say what is not in one's mind // 정말로 갚을 ~만 있으면 갚을 수 있는 금액이다 The debt is small enough that he could pay it back if he really intended[wanted] to. // 그는 저 처녀에게 ~이 있는 것 같다 He seems to be interested in[to have taken a fancy to] that girl.

6 [취미·기호] fancy; taste; mind; liking; heart. ¶~에 드는 favorite / darling / pet / after one's fancy[heart] / to one's taste [liking] // ~에 들도록 to one's satisfaction / (so as) to please (a person) // ~에 드는 모양 a pattern that suits one's taste / a pattern that takes one's fancy / a pattern one likes [to one's liking] // ~에 들다 be pleased [delighted / satisfied] (with) / suit[please / catch] (a person's) fancy / suit[flatter] (a person's) taste // 나는 그 사람[일]이 ~에 들지 않는다 I don't like him[that job]. // 그의 계집애 같은 태도가 내 ~에 들지 않는다 His sissy attitude gets on my nerves. // 사람들의 ~이 사치로 흐르고 있다 People are inclined to extravagance.

마음(이) 내키다 feel inclined (to do); feel like (doing); be willing (to do); be in the mood (for doing / to do). ¶마음 내키는 대로 as one feels inclined / as fancy dictates [leads] one / as the humor takes one // 마음이 내키지 않다 be in no mood[humor] (to do / for doing) / be reluctant (to do) / have no inclination (to do) / feel diffident // 그를 방문할 마음이 내키지 않는다 I am reluctant to go and see him. // 마음 내키는 대로 여행을 떠났다 I set out intending to travel as fancy led me. // 마음 내키면 전화해 주십시오 Please call me up whenever you feel like it. // 도무지 그 일을 할 마음이 내키지 않는다 I'd rather not do that work. / I don't feel like doing that work.

마음(을) 놓다 1 [안심하다] set one's heart [mind] at ease[rest]; take it easy; relax. ¶마음 놓고 without worry[anxiety] / with mind at ease / free from care / with (a sense of) relief / freely // 마음 놓고 살다 have[lead] a carefree life / live with security // 잘 있으니 마음 놓으십시오 Please set your heart at ease because I am getting along well. // 마음 놓고 있을 수 없다 I can't afford to take it easy. / I cannot remain idle. // 우리는 밤잠도 마음 놓고 잘 수 없다 We can't even get [enjoy] a good night's sleep. / We can't even have sleep in peace at night. // 그 사람이면 마음 놓고 돈[일]을 맡길 수 있다 You must trust him with money[to do the work for you]. // 언제든지 마음 놓고 들르시오 Feel free to drop in anytime. 2 [방심하다] relax one's attention; slacken[let up in] one's effort; be off one's guard; be negligent; be inattentive. ¶마음을 놓지 않다 be on (one's) guard / be wide awake / have (all) one's wits about one / be on the lookout.

마음(이) 든든하다 feel secure[safe / reassured]; be secure; (사물이) be encouraging [reassuring]. ¶마음 든든한 reassuring / encouraging / ···을 들으니 ~ It is heartening[encouraging] to hear that ···. // 그와 함께 있으면 마음이 든든했다 His presence was reassuring[made me feel better]. // 그런 말씀을 들으니 마음 든든합니다 That is a very reassuring remark. / Your words give me great relief[are very encouraging to me].

마음(이) 들뜨다 feel excited[elated]; be in a buoyant spirit. ¶남의 마음을 기대에 들뜨게 해 놓고 계획을 중지하다니 그도 너무 심하다 It's awful of him to cancel the plan after having given me so much reason to hope.

마음(을) 쓰다 1 [유의·걱정하다] give heel (to); pay attention (to); worry[care] (about); mind. ¶마음 쓰는 일 work which strains one's nerves[needs all one's attention] / a nerve-racking job // 그가 하는 말에 마음 쓸 것 없다 Don't mind what he says. // 세상 소문에 마음 쓰지 말게 Don't mind what the world says (about you). 2 [배려해 주다] think of; be thoughtful of[for]; [동정하다] sympathize with.

마음에 두다 mind; take (something) to one's heart; bear[keep / fix] (something) in mind; be mindful of. ¶마음에 두지 않다 do not mind / do not care (about[for]).

마음은 굴뚝 같다 have a great mind to; be

마음(을) 졸이다 be anxious [uneasy / nervous] about; trouble oneself; worry oneself (about). ¶마음을 졸이며 하다 bother / worry / keep (a person) in suspense // 나는 시험에 실패할까 봐 마음을 졸였다 I was anxious to know whether I failed the exam or not.

●**마음가짐** [마음의 자세] a mental attitude; the attitude [a frame] of mind; [각오] determination; resolve; resolution. **마음결** a cast [turn] of mind; temper; nature; grain; disposition. ¶~이 고운 good-natured / good-tempered / kind-hearted // ~이 사나운 [고약한] ill-natured / bad-tempered / cross (-minded) // ~이 사나운 [고약한] 사람 an ill-natured man / a man of coarse grain // ~이 곱다 be tender-hearted / be sweet-tempered / be of gentle disposition. **마음보** [심보] nature; temper; disposition; a cast of mind; spirit. ¶~가 고약한 [나쁜] 녀석 fellow // ~가 사나운 여자 a (scratch) cat / a she-devil / a shrew / a witch. **마음속** one's inmost feelings; (deep within) one's heart; the bottom of one's heart; one's innermost thoughts; one's bosom. ¶~에서 우러나오는 말 words flowing out of one's heart // ~ 깊이 사무치다 go to one's heart / sink deep into one's heart // ~에 묻어 두다 keep (the story) to oneself // ~을 꿰뚫어 보다 read (a person's) inmost thoughts / see through (a person's) intention / see (a person's) inside and out // ~을 털어놓다 speak one's inmost mind [thoughts] / unbosom oneself (to) // ~으로 그는 그들을 경멸했다 Inwardly [At heart], he despised them. // 나는 그녀가 그녀의 ~을 언뜻 보여 준 것 같은 생각이 들었다 I thought I had a glimpse of what she was really thinking [her true feeling / her real intentions]. **마음씨** (a) nature; (a) temper; (a) disposition; a turn [cast] of mind. ¶~가 고운 tender in sentiment / sweet-tempered / well-disposed // ~가 나쁜 ill-natured / ill-[bad-]tempered / cross // ~가 더러운 [비루한] mean / base / dirty // ~가 고운 아이 a child with a kind disposition // 그녀는 ~가 곱다 She is kind-hearted [tenderhearted] (▶ (영)에서는 kind-hearted, tender-hearted와 같이 하이픈을 넣음). / She has a good heart.

마음껏 [실컷] to one's heart's content; to the utmost [hilt]; as much as one likes [pleases]; all on wants. ¶~ …하다 give free play to / give rein to // ~ 먹다 [마시다] eat [drink] one's fill // ~ 울다 weep oneself out / cry one's heart // ~ 상상력을 ~ 발휘하다 give full pay to one's imagination // ~ 인생을 즐기다 enjoy life to the full // 나는 그를 ~ 때려 주었다 I hit him as hard as I could. // ~ 즐거운 시간을 보내십시오 Enjoy yourself fully to your heart's content. // ~ 음식을 드십시오 Eat as much as you like. // 그는 세계 최고의 바이올린 주자로서의 명성을 ~ 누렸다 He enjoyed the reputation of being the greatest violinist in the world. // 나는 라디오 음악에 ~ 귀를 기울였다 I listened to music on the radio to my heart's content.

마음대로 [하고 싶은 대로] as one pleases [likes / wishes]; at one's pleasure; [독단으로] at one's (own) discretion; on one's own authority; [자유 의사로] at (one's own) sweet will; freely; [무단으로] without leave [permission]. ¶~ 하다 have one's (own) way (in everything) // ~ 되지 않다 be beyond one's control // 남의 것을 ~ 쓰다 make use of another's things // 남을 ~ 주무르다 have a person at one's beck and call / get a person under one's thumb // 권력을 ~ 휘두르다 abuse one's authority / usurp power // ~ 해도 좋아요 Do as you please. / Have [Take] your own way. // 그렇게 ~ 안 될걸 You are counting without your host. // ~ 과자를 먹어라 Please help yourself to the cookies. // 이 사전을 ~ 쓰셔도 좋습니다 You are free to use this dictionary. // 어디로든지 내 ~ 갈 수 있다 I can go wherever I like. // 표를 사든 사지 않든 네 ~다 It's up to you whether you buy a ticket or not. // 가건 말건 네 ~ 해라 You are at liberty to go or stay.

마음먹다 1 [결심하다] make up one's mind; make a resolution; be determined [resolved] (to do). ¶…하려고 단단히 마음먹고 with a full [firm] determination to (do, get, etc.) / 굳게 ~ be firmly determined // 마음먹은 대로 하다 act up to one's resolution // 하려고 마음먹으면 못할 일이 없다 Where there is a will, there is a way. / A resolute will makes the goods give way. // 그것은, 네가 마음먹기에 달렸다 It rests with you to decide. / All [Everything] depends upon your decision. // 굳게 마음먹으면 안 되는 일이 없다 Nothing is impossible to a determined mind. // 그는 한 번 마음먹으면 여간해서 번복하지 않는다 Nothing could dissuade him from his resolution. // 단단히 마음먹고 내가 다시 한번 해 보겠다 I will give it just one more determined try. // 그는 큰 과학자가 되려고 마음먹고 있다 He is firmly determined to become a great scientist. // 그 글을 쓰려고 마음먹었지만 아직 쓰지 못하고 있다 I have been intending to write the article, but I just haven't gotten around to it yet.

2 [의도하다] intend to; plan [want] to; have a mind to; be going to. ¶만사가 마음먹은 대로 되었다 Everything turned out as I wished.

마음잡다 take hold of oneself; get [keep] a firm grip on oneself; settle (down); keep the presence of mine; recover one's composure. ¶마음잡고 일을 시작하다 settle (down) to work // 마음잡고 올바르게 살다 amend one's way of living.

마의 (麻衣) hemp clothes.

마이너 [음] minor.

마이너 리그 (미국 프로 야구의) a minor [bush] league. ¶~ 선수 a minor leaguer.

마이너스 1 [수] minus. ¶~ 5도 minus five degrees / five degrees below zero // 10 ~ 6은 4 Ten minus six is [equals] four. 2 [음전하 (陰電荷)]. ¶~ 전기 a negative charge of electricity / a negative electric charge. 3 [손실·적자] a deficit; deficiency. ¶~를 분을 메우다 cover [make up] the deficit // 적자를 ~였다 It showed a great loss. // 가계는 8만 원의 ~였다 Our household budget is 80,000 won in the red. // 음악회의 수지는 플러스 ~ 제로였다 We just broke even on the concert. 4 [불리한 점] a handicap; a disadvantage. ¶그에게는 그것이 ~가 된다 It will be a disadvantage to him. / It'll hurt him.

●**마이너스 성장** negative growth. ¶~률 a negative growth rate.

마이동풍(馬耳東風) utter indifference; praying to deaf ears. ¶~이다 turn a deaf ear to (another's advice) // ~으로 흘러버리다 turn a deaf ear (to) // 아무리 내가 말해도 그는 ~이었다 All my words fell on deaf[heedless] ears. / All my words fell flat upon [were unheeded by] him. / All my advice was just so much sound to him.

마이신 [약] streptomycin. ⇨~스트렙토마이신

마이크 a microphone; (구어) a mike. ¶~ 앞에 서다 speak at the microphone / stand before[at] a microphone // ~로 이야기하다 speak over[through] a microphone // ~를 향하다 take[come] to a microphone // 아, 아, 시험 중입니다 One-two-three-four-testing! Testing!

마이크로미터 a micrometer; micrometer callipers.

마이크로버스 a microbus.

마이크로컴퓨터 a microcomputer.

마이크로파(-波) [물] a microwave.

마이크로폰 a microphone. ⇨~마이크

마이크로필름 a microfilm. ¶~에 찍다 microfilm (a newspaper).

마일 a mile(=1.6km). ¶반 ~ half a mile / a half mile // 시속 50~로 달리다 run at the rate[speed] of fifty miles per hour / run 50 mph[m.p.h.].

마일리지 a mileage.

마작(麻雀) mah-jongg; mah-jong. ¶~의 패 a tile.
● **마작꾼** a mah-jong player.

마장 [십 리나 오 리가 못 되는 거리] a *majang*.

마장(馬場) [경마장] a racecourse; a race track.

마장수 a peddler with a packhorse.

마저¹ [남김없이] without leaving any; with everything else; with all the rest. ¶~ 듣다 hear the last of it // 재고품을 ~ 팔아 치우다 sell off all the stock left over // 이것도 ~ 먹어라 Take[Eat] this last one up, too.

마저² [까지도] besides; what is more; even; also; on top of; to the length[extreme / extent] of; so far as; into the bargain; in addition to. ¶빚 ~ 내어 even going to the extent of incurring debt // 도둑질~ 하다 go to the length[extent] of committing theft / go so far as to commit theft // 비~ 내리기 시작했다 On top of that[everything], it began to rain. // 형제~ 그를 배신했다 Besides [What is more], he was betrayed (even) by his own brothers. // 나는 아침부터 메스꺼웠는데 배~ 아파 왔다 I had felt nauseated since morning, and then I got a stomachache into the bargain[to boot].

마적(馬賊) (mounted) bandits; mounted thieves[brigands].

마전 bleaching. **마전하다** bleach.

마전(-廛) [곡식을 마질하는 곳] a grain-measuring place (in the market).

마제형(馬蹄形) horseshoe shape. ¶~의 horseshoe-shaped / U-shaped.

마젤란운(-雲) [천] the Magellanic clouds.

마조히즘 masochism.

마주 face to face; facing each other; (right / directly) opposite; vis-à-vis; tête-à-tête; just across (from each other). ¶~ 보다 face each other / look at each other // ~ 서다 stand face to face / stand right opposite // ~ 앉다 take a seat opposite to (a person) / sit face to face with (a person) // ~ 잡다 take each other / hold[take] together // ~ 바라보다 look each other in the face / confront [face] each other // 놀라서 서로 ~ 보다 exchange looks of astonishment // 손에 손을 ~ 잡고 hand in hand (with) // 탁자를 ~ 잡아 lift a table together // 그는 나를 ~ 보고 앉았다 He sat opposite me. // 호텔은 역을 ~ 보고 있다 The hotel faces[is opposite] the station. // 그들은 테이블을 가운데 놓고 서로 ~ 보았다 They faced each other across the table. / They sat across the table from each other. // 그는 그녀와 ~ 앉았다 He sat face to face with her. // 나는 그와 ~ 앉아 이야기를 나누었다 I had a tête-à-tête with him. // 그 두 사람은 ~ 앉아 술을 마시고 있었다 The two men were drinking, seated across from each other.

마주나기 [식] opposition. ¶~의 opposite (-leaved) / adverse // 이 식물의 잎은 ~이다 This plant has opposite leaves. / The leaves of this plant are in opposing pairs.

마주르카 [음] maz(o)urka.

마주치다 1 [충돌하다] crash together[against / into]; collide (with); knock[bump / dash] against; run against[into]. **2** [우연히 만나다] happen to meet; chance[hit] upon; come [fall / run] across; fall[drop] in with; meet with. ¶딱 ~ come[be brought] face to face with (a person) // 막다른 골목에서 원수와 ~ confront an enemy in a blind alley // 그놈이 싫은데 또 마주치지 않았으면 좋겠다 I hate that fellow and hope I shall never cross his path again.

마주하다 put[be] opposite. ¶책상을 마주하고 앉다 sit opposite the table.

마중 meeting; going[coming] out to meet (a person); reception(영접). ¶~을 나가다 go to meet a person // ~을 나오다 come for a person // ~을 받다 be met[greeted] (at the airport) // ~ (…을 위해) 차를 ~ 보내다 send a car[an automobile] to meet (a visitor) // 많은 친구들이 정거장에 나를 ~ 나왔다 Many friends came down to see me at the station.

마중하다 meet (a person); receive; greet; go [come] (out) to meet (a person) on arrival.

마지기 *majigi*(=a Korean measure of farmland, equal to 0.12-0.16 acre or 5-6 ares); a patch of field requiring one *mal* of seed. ¶논 한 ~ a patch of rice paddy.

마지노선(-線) the Maginot line.

마지막 [맨 끝] the last; [결말] the conclusion; the end. ¶~ 날 the last[closing / concluding / final] day (of a show) // ~ 승리 the final[ultimate] victory // ~ 역 (미) a terminal station / (영) a terminus // ~ 저항 a last-ditch resistance // ~ 점검 a last-minute checkup // ~으로 도착한 사람 the last person to arrive // 이 책의 ~ 두 페이지 the last two pages of[in] the book // ~까지 싸우다 fight to the last (drop on one's blood) / fight it out / fight to a finish[to the end] // 오늘이 내 (생애의) ~ 날이다 This is my last day alive[on earth]. // 그를 만난 것도 그것이 ~이었다 That was the last I saw of him[my last sight of him]. // 그가 맨 ~으로 왔다 He was the last to come. // 이것이 술을 끊는 나의 ~ 술잔이다 This is the last cup of drink I'll ever drink. / With this cup, I'm giving up drink forever.(▶ 술을 끊겠다) / This will be my last cup (of drink). // ~에는 싸움이 되고 말았다 It ended in a quarrel.

마지못하다 《서술적》 be obliged[forced / compelled] to; cannot help[but]; be under the necessity[compulsion] of; be driven by dire necessity to. ¶마지못해 [부득이하여] unavoidably / inevitably / out of necessity / [마음에도 없이] reluctantly / unwillingly / against one's will[wish] // 마지못해 맺어진 인연 an unfortunate but inescapable relationship / 〔문어〕 a fatal bond // 마지못해 …하다 be compelled[obliged / forced] to (do) / be hard put to it to (do) // 마지못해 진상을 말하다 speak the truth reluctantly / be reluctant to speak the truth // 그는 마지못해 승낙했다 He consented unwillingly[reluctantly / with bad grace]. / He gave unwilling[reluctant] consent. // 그녀는 마지못해 건달 남편에게 붙어살고 있다 She is hopelessly tied to a good-for-nothing husband. // 그녀는 싫은데 마지못해 상자 속을 들여다보았다 She peered into the box with squeamish reluctance. // 그는 마지못해 그 제안에 찬성하지 않을 수 없었다 He had to agree to the proposal against his will.

마지아니하다 can never (thank) enough. ¶몹시 기다려 마지아니하던 비 the long-waited-for[long awaited] rain // 축하해 ~ offer one's sincerest congratulation // 극구 칭찬해 ~ extol / applaud highly.

마직물(麻織物) hemp cloth.

마진 a margin (of profit). ¶~ 거래 a margin transaction // ~제(制) the margin system // 약간의 ~ a slim [thin / narrow / small] margin // 폭이 큰 ~ (with) a large[wide] margin // ~이 많다 [적다] have a wide [narrow] profit margin // ~을 줄이고 매상을 늘렸다 We cut down the profit margin[We allowed ourselves only a small profit margin] and expanded sales.

마질하다 measure with a *mal* measure.

마차(馬車) a (horse-drawn) carriage; a coach; a (horse) cab; (짐 싣는) a cart; a wagon. ¶사륜 ~ a four-wheeler / a wagon // 쌍두 [사두] ~ a carriage and pair[four] // 무개(無蓋) ~ an open carriage // 유개(有蓋) ~ a close carriage / [덮개] a covered wagon // 한 필이 끄는 ~ a one-horse carriage // ~를 타다 ride in [(미) on] a carriage // ~로 가다 go by carriage / drive (in a carriage) to (a place).

● **마차꾼** a cabman; a carter. ⇨마부

마차부자리(馬車夫-) 〔천〕 the Charioteer; the Wagoner; Auriga.

마찬가지 the (very) same; sameness; the selfsame; one and the same; 〔유사〕 likeness; similarity. ¶~의 [동일한] the same / [유사한] like / similar (to) / [동등한] equal (to) / equivalent (to) / uniform / [동류의] of the same kind[sort] // ~로 equally / similarly / alike / likewise / in like manner / as ever / in the same manner[way] // ~다 be the same / be equal / be equivalent / be identical / be like / be similar / be alike // ~ 것 the same thing // 거의 ~인 much the same // 앞과[위와] ~로 like the preceding / ditto // ~가 되다 come to the same thing // 둘 다 ~다 The two are much the same. / There is nothing to choose between the two. // 그의 병의 상태는 어제와 ~다 His condition is the same as (it was) yesterday. // 아버지께서 나를 의절한 거나 ~다 My father as good as disinherited me. // 형은 스포츠를 싫어했는데 나도 ~였다 My brother did not like sports, and neither did I. // 이 기계는 저것과 ~로 버튼 하나로 조작할 수 있다 This machine is operated by pushing a button, in the same way as[just like] that one. // 그도 ~로 몸이 허약했다 He was delicate, too. // 그는 가난한 사람에게나 부자에게나 ~로 친절하다 He is equally kind to the rich and the poor. // 우리 아버지는 아이들에게 엄격했다. 어머니도 ~로 엄격했다 My father was very strict with us children. So was my mother. // 그와 ~로 나도 그것을 몰랐다 I knew no more about it than he did. // 너와 ~로 나도 그 계획에는 마음이 내키지 않는다 I like the plan no better than you do. // 그의 솜씨는 종전과 ~였다 His skill remained the same.

마찰(摩擦) 1 [비벼대기] rubbing; chafing. ¶냉수[건포(乾布)] ~ a rubdown with a wet [dry] towel. **마찰하다** rub (against / with); chafe (the skin). ¶나뭇조각을 마찰하여 불을 일으키다 make fire by rubbing together two pieces of wood. ➔전선과 나뭇가지가 마찰되면 위험하다 It is dangerous for the electric wire to rub against the branch.

2 [접촉 면의 저항] friction. ¶~의 frictional // 공기 ~ air friction // 회전 ~ 〔물〕 rolling friction // 금속과 나무의 ~ friction between metal and wood // ~을 막다 prevent friction / minimize the effect of friction // ~을 적게 하다 reduce[diminish] friction.

3 [불화·알력] (a) discord; (a) trouble; friction. ¶좌파와 우파 사이의 ~ conflict[friction] between the left and right wings // ~을 일으키다 produce friction / raise [make] trouble // ~을 피하다[없애다] avoid [remove] friction // 그들 사이에 끊임없이 ~이 있다 There is constant trouble between them.

● **마찰 계수 / 마찰 상수** 〔물〕 the coefficient of friction. **마찰력** frictional force; friction. **마찰음** a frictional sound; [언] a fricative (sound); a fricative consonant; [동] (귀뚜라미 날개 등의) a stridulating sound. **마찰 전기** [전] frictional electricity.

마천루(摩天樓) a skyscraper.

마철(馬鐵) a horseshoe. ⇨말편자

마초(馬草) horse-fodder. ⇨말꼴

마취(痲醉) an(a)esthesia; narcotism. ¶국부 [전신 / 척수] ~ local [general / spinal] anesthesia // 에테르 ~ etherization // ~에서 깨어나다 come out from under the anesthetic. **마취하다** put (a person) under anesthesia; anesthetize; narcotize. ¶수술은 클로로포름[에테르]으로 마취하여 실시됩니다 The operation is performed under chloroform [ether].

● **마취과** the anesthesia department. **마취법 / 마취 상태** [의] narcosis. **마취 요법** narcotherapy. **마취의**(-醫) an anesthetist. **마취제**/ 마취약 an anesthetic; a narcotic.

마치[1] [장도리] a small [claw] hammer.

마치[2] [음] a march. ¶웨딩 ~ the wedding march.

마치[3] [꼭] just; just[exactly] like; [흡사 (…과 같이)] like; as; just as; as if [though]; as it were. ¶~ 나가라는 듯이 as if to say "get out" // ~ 죽은 사람 같다 look as if dead / be more dead than alive // ~ 거미와도 같이 벽을 기어오르다 scale the wall just like a spider // 그는 ~ 모든 것을 알고 있는 것처럼 지껄여 댔

다 He talked away as if he knew everything.∥나는 ~ 천둥소리 같은 꽝음을 들었다 I heard a roaring sound like that of thunder.∥도시 전체가 ~ 대학 같다 It seems as if the entire town were a university.∥그는 ~ 지겹도록 보았다고 말하고 싶은 것 같은 표정을 짓고 있다 He looked as if he wanted to say that he had seen similar things too often.

마치다[1] **1** 〔막히다〕 be struck; be obstructed; be stuck; 〔닿다〕 hit. ¶말뚝이 바위에 마치어 들어가지 않는다 The stake has hit a rock and won't drive in any deeper. **2** 〔결리다〕 have a pain [stitch]; feel an acute pain; pinch. ¶옆구리가 ~ have a stitch in the side ∥구두에 발이 ~ one's feet are pinched by one's shoes.

마치다[2] 〔끝내다〕 end; finish; get[be] through (with); make an end of; complete; conclude; 〔수행하다〕 accomplish; 〔졸업하다〕 graduate (from). ¶하루 일과를 마치고 after a day's work∥그가 아직 말을 마치기도 전에 before he could finish his sentence∥일을 ~ finish [be through with] one's work [task] / get one's work done∥세상을 ~ finish up∥그는 복무 연한을 마쳤다 He has served out his time in the army.∥그는 주(州) 지사로서의 4년 임기를 마쳤다 He completed his four-year term as governor.∥그는 5년 전에 학업을 마쳤다 He finished school [college] five years ago.∥그녀는 춤을 마치자, 무대에서 사라졌다 When she finished her dance, she vanished from the stage.

마침 〔운 좋게〕 luckily; fortunately; as good luck would have it; 〔시기에 맞게〕 in the very nick of time; in good time; just in time [season]; opportunely; seasonably; 〔그때에〕 just at the time; just then. ¶~ 오다 [지나가다] happen to come [pass] by∥~ 가지고 있다 happen to have on hand / have on hand / have with [about] one∥~ 잘 왔어 You came by at just the right moment [time].∥~ 잘됐어 How timely!∥~ 편지를 쓰려는 참이다 I'm going to write a letter.∥~ 세수하고 있을 때 전화벨이 울렸다 The telephone rang just as [when] I was washing my face.∥~ 떠나려는 참이다 I'm (just) about to leave.∥~ 사고 현장에 있었다 I happen to be at the scene of the accident.(▶ 사고 발생 시에) / I happen to come upon the scene of the accident.(▶ 사고 발생 직후에)∥물에 빠진 아이는 ~ 지나가던 사람에게 구조되었다 The drowning child was saved by a man who just happened to be passing by.

마침가락 〔우연의 일치〕 a strange coincidence; 〔안성맞춤〕 a right fit (for); the very thing [person] wanted; the right thing [person]; just the thing [person].

마침내 〔드디어〕 at (long) last; finally; at length; 〔결국〕 after all; in the end; ultimately; in the long run; 〔오랜 시간이 지나〕 at length. ¶~ 승리를 거두다 gain the final victory∥~ 이해하게 되다 come to understand at length∥그들은 ~ 파업에 들어갔다 They went on strike at last.∥나는 ~ 그 문제를 풀었다 I solved the problem at last. / I finally came up with the answer to the problem.∥나는 ~ 논문을 완성했다 〔구어〕 At long last I finished my thesis.∥그는 ~ 재기 불능이 되었다 In the end his condition deteriorated to such a degree that recovery was impossible.∥그 결과 그는 ~ 자기 스스로를 파멸시키게 되었다 As a result he finally brought ruin upon himself.

마침표(-標) a period; a full stop. ¶~를 찍다 put a period (to).

마카로니 (이) macaroni.
● **마카로니웨스턴**(×⑩macaroni+western) a spaghetti western; an Italian western.

마케팅 marketing.
● **마케팅 리서치** marketing research.

마크 〔표〕 a mark; 〔레터르〕 a label; 〔상표〕 a trademark; 〔휘장〕 a badge. ¶이 물건에는 제조 회사의 ~가 없다 There is no manufacturer's label [mark] attached to this article.∥이 회사 제품에는 고양이 ~가 들어 있다 This company's products bear the mark of a cat. / This company uses a cat as its trademark. **마크하다** mark 〔guard / (미) check〕 (a certain player). ¶한국 신기록을 ~ 〔달성하다〕 set a new Korean record∥그를 마크하라 Keep your eyes on him.∥상대 투수가 특히 그를 마크하고 있다 The opposing pitcher is being particularly careful with him.

마키아벨리즘 Machiavellism; Machiavellianism. ¶~의 Machiavel(l)ian.

마 태 복 음 (-福音) 〔성〕 (the Gospel of) Matthew(약 Matt.).

마파람 〔남풍〕 the south wind; a souther.

마파람에 게 눈 감추듯(속담) eat up in a moment [in no time at all].

마판(馬板) 〔바깥에 말 매어 두는 곳〕 a horse paddock; 〔마구간의 널빤지〕 floorboards of a stable.

마포(麻布) hemp cloth; flax. ⇨ ¹삼베

마피(馬皮) horsehide.

마피아 〔미국의 범죄 비밀 결사〕 the Maf(f)ia.
● **마피아 단원** a Mafioso (pl. -si).

마필(馬匹) a horse. ⇨ ¹말¹

마하 〔물〕〔항〕 a Mach (number) (약어 M). ¶~ 2.5의 신예 전투기 a powerful new jet fighter that can fly at Mach 2.5∥~ 3으로 비행하다 fly at Mach 3.

마호가니 〔단향과의 교목〕 mahogany; 〔그 재목〕 mahogany.

마호메트교(-教) 〔이슬람교〕 Islam; Mohammedanism. (▶ 정식 명칭은 Islam. Mohammedanism이란 말은 신자에게 불쾌감을 주는 말)

마흔 forty.

막[1] 〔방금〕 just; just[right] at the moment; just now. ¶~ …하려 하다 be about to (do) / be ready to (do) / be on the point [edge / verge] of (doing)∥~ 시작하다 be going [about] (to do) / begin (to do / doing)∥내가 책을 ~ 읽기 시작하자 그가 들어왔다 Just as I began [was beginning] to read a book, he came in.∥열차는 ~ 출발하려 하고 있었다 The train was about to leave [on the point of leaving].∥물속으로 내가 ~ 가라앉으려 할 때 구조되었다 I was rescued just as I began to sink into the water.∥우리가 ~ 떠나려는데 전보가 왔다 Just as we were leaving, we received the telegram.∥벚꽃은 ~ 피기 시작했을 뿐이다 The cherry blossoms have only just begun to bloom.∥내가 ~ 아침 식사를 하려고 할 때 전화벨이 울렸다 Just as I was going to have breakfast, the telephone rang. / I was just about to have [I was on the point of having] breakfast, when the telephone rang.∥나는 그것을 지금 ~ 끝냈다 I have just finished it. / I finished it just now.

막² hard; recklessly. ⇨ 마구

막(幕) **1** [임시로 지은 집] a temporary shed [shelter]; a booth; a shack; a hut; a shed. ¶원두~ a look-out shed // ~을 짓다 put up a booth[shed].
2 [장막] a curtain; a hanging screen; hanging; [천막] (set up / fold up) a tent. ¶~을 치다 stretch a curtain // ~을 열다 (위로) raise the curtain / (옆으로) draw the curtain (aside) // ~을 닫다 (아래로) drop the curtain / (옆으로) close the curtain // ~을 올리다 [내리다] raise [lower / let down] a curtain // ~을 거두다 fold up a tent // ~을 옆으로 당기다 pull [draw] aside a curtain // 3시에 ~이 열린다 The curtain rises at three o'clock. // 마지막 ~이 내렸다 The curtain fell on the last scene.
3 [연극의 단락] an act. ¶제1~ 제2장 Act I, Scene 2 / 3~ 6장의 (a play) in three acts and six scenes // 제2~이 방금 시작되었다 The second act has just begun.
4 [끝장] an end; a close; a conclusion. ¶전쟁의 ~을 내리다 put an end to the war // 연극은 슬픈 장면에서 ~이 내렸다 The play ended with a sad scene. // 이것으로 3개월간에 걸친 노동 쟁의가 ~을 내렸다 This ended a labor dispute extending over three months. // 그 긴 이야기도 마침내 ~을 내렸다 The long story has at last come to an end [been played out].

막(膜) [점막] a membrane; (물갈퀴의) webbing; [얇은 층] a film. ¶~ 모양의 membran(e)ous / filmy // 표면에 ~이 생겼다 The surface was covered with a film. / A film has formed on the surface. // 우유를 데웠더니 ~이 생겼다 When I heated the milk, a skin formed on it.

막가다 [막되게 행동하다] behave rudely [rambunctiously]; misbehave oneself.

막간(幕間) (미) (during) an intermission; (영) an interval (between the acts [scenes]). ¶15분간의 ~에 가벼운 식사를 하다 eat a light meal between acts [during an intermission].
● **막간극** an interlude; a middle piece; a skit between acts.

막강하다(莫強-) mighty; having [of] the greatest power; enormously powerful. ¶막강한 군사적 강함 great military strength // 막강한 전함 a mighty battleship // 당시 그 사나이는 아무도 대항할 수 없던 막강한 세력자였다 The man was so powerful at the time that no one dared defy him.

막걸리 makgeolli; raw [unrefined] rice wine; home brew.

막내 the lastborn; the youngest of the family.
● **막내둥이** the lastborn. ⇨ 막내 **막내딸** the last [youngest] daughter. **막내며느리** the wife of one's last [youngest] son. **막내아들** the last [youngest] son. ¶얘가 내 ~입니다 This is my youngest son. **막냇사위** the youngest son-in-law.

막노동(-勞動) rough work; toil. ⇨ 막일

막다 1 [닫다] close; shut; [채우다] stop up (a hole); fill (up) (a hole); fill (up) (a crevice); clog (a pipe); block (up). ¶병 아가리를 ~ stop (up) [seal] a bottle // 쥐구멍을 ~ stop up a rathole // 귀를 ~ wad [fill / stop / stuff] one's ears (with cotton) / place one's hands over one's ears (손으로) // 구멍을 종이로 ~ close up an opening with paper // 병마개를 ~ stop [cork / cap / put the stopper on] a bottle.
2 [둘러막다] wall (up); fence (round); enclose. ¶집을 돌담으로 ~ enclose a house with a stone wall.
3 [가로막다] block up (장애물로); [방해하다] obstruct; hinder; [저지하다] stop; check; interrupt (the progress); hold in check. ¶(자신의) 입을 ~ hold a hand over one's mouth / (남의) cover (a person's) mouth / gag (a person) / (비밀이 새지 않게) silence (a person) / buy (a person's) silence // 길을 ~ block one's path / obstruct one's way // 소리를 ~ absorb [muffle] noises // 강 [흐름]을 ~ dam up a river [a stream] // 교통의 흐름을 ~ stop the traffic [flow of cars] // 입구를 ~ stop up the doorway / block (the way to) the door // 인플레이션의 진행을 ~ stem the tide of inflation / check inflation // 소문을 ~ hush up a rumor // 자기 귀를 ~ cover [hold] one's ears // 손수건으로 자기 입을 ~ hold a handkerchief over one's mouth // 두꺼운 벽이 거리의 소음을 완전히 막았다 The thick walls deadened the noise from the street. // 사람들의 입을 수는 없다 You can't shut people's mouth. / We cannot stop gossip. // 소방차가 제때에 와서 화재의 연소를 막았다 The fire engine arrived in time to stop the spread of the fire. // 그들은 성의 입구를 커다란 바위로 막았다 They blocked (up) the entrance to the castle with big rocks.
4 (칸을) screen off; partition; compart. ¶방의 칸을 ~ partition a room // 휘장으로 칸을 ~ screen off part of a room.
5 [방어하다] defend (oneself against the enemy); protect (from / against); [저항하다] resist; [접근을 시키지 않다] keep [hold] off; keep [hold] (the enemy) at bay; [방지하다] keep away [out / off / back]; hold in check; ward off (danger); [예방하다] prevent; guard against. ¶적의 공격을 ~ stop the enemy's attack // 그들의 침입을 ~ prevent them from invading / stop their invasion // 파리를 ~ keep away the flies // 강의 범람을 ~ keep the river from overflowing // 외풍을 ~ keep out the draft // 청소년의 비행을 미연에 ~ prevent wrongdoing by juveniles before it happens // 이 약은 구토를 막아 준다 This medicine prevents vomiting. // 소금과 설탕은 식품의 부패를 막는다 Salt and sugar preserve food (from decay). // 도둑을 막기 위해 문단속을 엄중히 한다 Fasten the doors securely to protect against burglary. // 비바람을 막을 만한 것은 아무것도 없었다 There was nothing to protect [shield] them from the wind and rain.

막다르다 dead-end (street); blind (alley); (a street) closed at one end; [비유의] final (최후의); deadlocked (정체된). ¶막다른 길 the dead end of a road // 막다른 판에 at the last [critical] moment / at the eleventh hour // 막다른 지경에 이르다 come to [reach] a deadlock // 막다른 지경을 타개하다 break a deadlock // 그의 방은 막다른 낭하 끝에서 두 번째입니다 His room is the second from the far end of the corridor. // 우리는 이 막다른 궁지에서 벗어나지를 못하게 되었다 We can find no way out of this difficulty. / (구어) We're in a fix.

막다른 골 〔절박한 경우〕 a standstill; a (tight) corner. ¶~에 몰리다 be driven into a corner [to the last extremity] / be cornered // ~에 몰아넣다 drive a person into a corner // 협상은 ~에까지 가고 말았다 The negotiations have come to[have reached] a deadlock.

막다른 집 a house at the end of a blind alley [dead-end street].

막대그래프 〔수〕 a bar graph.

막대기 a stick; a rod; a bar; a staff; a club(곤봉); a baton(지휘봉). ¶쇠 ~ an iron bar // 금속 ~ a metal bar // 대 ~ a bamboo stick // 그는 ~로 개를 때렸다 He hit a dog with a stick.

막대자석(-磁石) 〔물〕 a bar magnet.

막대패 a jack plane; a fore plane. ¶~질 jack-planing / ~질하다 use a fore plane.

막대하다(莫大-) vast; huge; immense; colossal; enormous; tremendous; fabulous. ¶막대한 빚 a vast debt // 막대한 돈 a huge[an enormous] sum of money // 막대한 비용 enormous[immense] expense // 막대한 재산 an immense wealth[fortune] // 벼농사에 막대한 피해를 입었다 A vast damage was done to the rice crop. // 수해로 우리는 막대한 손해를 입었다 We suffered an enormous loss from the flood. // 오랜 불경기로 실업계는 막대한 타격을 받고 있다 Business suffers greatly from a long-continued depression.

막도장(-圖章) a private seal. ¶~을 찍다 stamp with one's private seal.

막동이 →막둥이

막되다 ill-bred; ill-mannered; rude; boorish; wild; outrageous; lawless. ¶막된 놈 an ill-bred fellow / an ill-mannered person / a wild guy / a boor // 막된 여자 a loose woman // 막되게 굴다 behave rudely / be rude to (a person) // 이 애는 막되어 먹었다 This child has no manners.

막둥이 1 the last[youngest] son. ⇨"막내아들 (⇨막내) 2 〔잔심부름꾼〕 a boy servant; a handy boy; a page.

막론하다(莫論-) go without question; be a matter of course; be needless to say; there is no need to speak (of). ¶~을 막론하든 not to speak of / to say nothing of / as a matter of course // 남녀를 막론하고 regardless of sex / (no matter) whether in man or woman / 지위의 고하를 막론하고 irrespective of rank // 결과의 여하를 막론하고 no matter what the consequences may be // 불법으로 침입한 자는 누구를 막론하고 사살한다 (게시) Anyone who trespasses be shot.

막료(幕僚) 〔참모들〕 the staff; (한 사람) a member of one's staff; a staff officer. ¶사령관과 그 ~ a commander and his staff.

막막하다(寞寞-) 〔적막하다〕 lonely; lonesome; desolate; dreary; deserted; 〔의지가 없다〕 forlorn; helpless. ¶막막한 밤 a dreary [hushed] night // 막막한 생활 a desolate life.

막막하다(漠漠-) vast; boundless; extensive. ¶막막한 벌판 a vast plain // 막막한 황야 a vast[boundless] wilderness // 막막한 사하라 사막 the vast and boundless Sahara Desert // 막막한 초원[바다] a vast expanse of grass [water] / a boundless grassland[ocean].

막 말 〔통명스러운 말〕 a blunt remark [speech]; 〔막된 말〕 harsh[vulgar / foul] language; rude[rough] talk. ¶~로 to put it bluntly[roughly] / in foul[bad] language // 그는 걸핏하면 ~을 한다 He is apt to be rough of speech. **막말하다** speak roughly; talk at random; talk wild; put (it) bluntly; talk without thinking.

막무가내(莫無可奈) ¶~로 stubbornly / doggedly / obstinately / resolutely / firmly / ~로 들어주지 않다 refuse flatly / will not listen to / turn a deaf ear to // 그렇게 ~로 굴지 마라 Don't be so obstinate. // 그에게 아무리 사정을 하여도 ~였다 I tried very hard to persuade him, but he won't listen.

막바지 1 〔끝〕 the bottom (of a street); the very[dead] end. ¶언덕 ~ the top of a hill // 골목 ~ the end of the alley // 길 ~ the dead end of a road // 똑바로 가면 길 ~에 그 집이 있습니다 Keep straight on, and you will find the house at the end of the road. 2 〔극한〕 (the last) extremity; 〔절정〕 a climax; 〔고비〕 the last moment; 극도의 절박한 상태 a terrible pinch. ¶~에 몰리다 be driven to the last extremity[moment] // ~에 몰아넣다 drive (a person) to bay // 선거 운동도 ~에 이르렀다 The election campaign has reached [gone into] its last[final] stages. // 나는 이제 ~에 있다 (구어) I'm in a real fix[bind].

막벌이 earning wages as a day laborer. **막벌이하다** earn wages as a day laborer.
● **막벌이꾼** a day laborer; an odd-jobber.

막사(幕舍) a barracks; a camp; quarters.

막사리 tidewater (before it is frozen).

막살다 lead a rough[careless / haphazard / reckless] sort of life; lead a nondescript [drab / grubby] life. ¶산골에 있을 때에는 한동안 막살았다 I really roughed it for a while in the mountain village.

막상 〔급기야〕 ultimately; really; actually; in reality; after all. ¶~ 일이 닥치면[다급해지면] at the last moment / at a pinch / when one is put to the push / when the moment arrives / 〔만부득이하면〕 if compelled[forced] / when occasion demands // ~ 일을 해 보면 꽤 어려운 법이다 When one comes to doing it, one finds it rather difficult. // ~ 내가 당해 보니 상상과는 아주 달랐다 I found the reality quite different from what I had imagined. / 일이란 ~ 당해 보지 않으면 모르는 것이다 The proof of the pudding is in the eating.

막상막하(莫上莫下) nothing better and nothing worse. ¶~로 equally (well) / as ... as (the other) / (경기 등에서) (run) neck to [and] neck / (미국 구어) nip and tuck // ~의 열전 a nip and tuck race / an evenly-matched contest. **막상막하하다** equal (to); well-matched; evenly-matched; (서술적) be on a par (with); stand even. ¶두 형제는 똑똑하기가 ~ The two brothers are equally clever. // 쌍방이 막상막하한 시합을 벌였다 The two sides played an evenly-balanced game. // 두 선수의 실력이 ~ (팽팽하다) The two are evenly matched. / They are even in ability[skill / strength].

막서다 〔함부로 대들다〕 face; defy; stand up to; lift[raise] a[one's] hand (to); turn upon [against]; become hostile (to).

막소주(-燒酒) bootleg distilled liquor.

막심하다(莫甚-) extreme; immense; enormous; tremendous; serious; heavy. ¶막심한 손해 serious damage / a heavy[tremendous]

막역하다

loss // 막심한 타격을 받다 suffer a hard blow // 후회가 ~ I regret it very much. // 무역의 불경기가 오늘보다 막심한 적이 없었다 Never before has trade experienced such heavy depression. // 당시는 취직난이 지금보다 막심했다 The difficulty of securing employment was then more keenly felt than now.

막역하다(莫逆-) intimate; familiar; close. ¶막역한 사이 intimate relations // 막역한 친구 a close[an intimate] friend / a steadfast and trusted friend / a sworn[devoted / bosom] friend // 막역하게 지내다 be intimate [friendly] (with) / be on intimate [good / friendly] terms (with) // 두 사람은 막역한 친구다 They are Damon and Pythias[David and Jonathan]. / They are hand and glove with each other.

막연하다(漠然-) vague (idea); obscure (meaning); ambiguous (attitude); hazy (notion); misty (conception / recollection); dim (memory); indefinable (word); nebulous (idea). ¶막연한 말을 하다 speak in general terms // 이 점에 대한 그의 대답은 막연했다 His answer was rather hazy on this point. // 그의 생각은 막연하고 요령부득이다 His ideas are vague and pointless. // 그녀로부터 막연한 대답이 왔다 A vague[An indefinite] reply came from her. **막연히** vaguely; obscurely; hazily. ¶나는 …에 대해 ~ 알 따름이다 I have only a vague idea of it. // 나는 그때의 일을 ~ 기억하고 있을 뿐이다 I have but a faint remembrance of those days.

막일 rough work; physical labor; toil; heavy [rough] work; (미국 속어) a roughnecking job. **막일하다** be engaged in rough work.
● **막일꾼** a manual[physical] laborer; an odd jobber.

막자 a (medicine) pestle.
● **막자사발** a mortar.

막잡이 1 [막쓰는 물건] a crude[rough] article for careless use; [잡동사니] odds and ends; sundries. 2→마구잡이

막장 [광] 1 [채벽] a blind end[front] in a mine gallery; [광석 등의 채굴 현장] a (working) face. ¶석탄의 ~ a coal face. 2 [채굴 작업] mining; digging; exploitation. ¶~일을 하다 mine / engage in mining operations.
● **막장꾼** a miner; a digger; a pitman.

막중하다(莫重-) [귀중하다] very precious; priceless; invaluable; [중요하다] very important; of great account. ¶막중한 시간 valuable time // 막중한 책임 a weighty[heavy] responsibility // 막중한 사명(使命)을 띠다 be charged with very important mission.

막지르다 1 [앞질러 막다] interrupt; stand in one's way; confront; block; bar. ¶말을 ~ interrupt (a person) / cut (a person) short. 2 [냅다 지르다] thrust[jab / stab / push / kick] at random[with force].

막차(-車) the last train[bus]. ¶~를 놓쳤다 I missed the last bus.

막치 [조제품] a coarse[crude] article; poor stuff; coarse manufactures; (미국 구어) junk.

막판 1 [마지막 판] the last round; the final scene[stage]; [위기] the last[critical] moment; the eleventh hour. ¶~에 가서 at the last moment / at the eleventh hour // ~에 접어들다 be on the last stage of (doing). 2 [뒤범벅판] a haphazard[chaotic] scene; a mess.

막후(幕後) the rear; the background. ¶~에서 조정하다 pull the wires[strings] // ~에서 활약하다 play an active part in the background // ~에 무엇인가 있다 There is something behind the scenes. // 협상은 ~에서 진행되었다 The negotiations were conducted behind the scenes.
● **막후 인물** a man behind the scene; wire-puller; (미) a mastermind. **막후 흥정**[협상] (정치의) behind-the-scenes dealing[negotiation].

막히다 1 (구멍 등이) be stopped[plugged] up; be[get] clogged; be obstructed; be choked. ¶숨이 ~ be choked / be suffocated / be stifled // 목이 ~ be choked (with) // 소변이 ~ have trouble (in) urinating // 병의 주둥이가 막혔다 The mouth of the bottle is clogged [stopped up]. // 하수구가 막혀 버렸다 The ditch got clogged. // 파이프가 흙으로 막혀 있다 The pipe is clogged[blocked / stopped up] with dirt. // 코가 막혔다 My nose is bunged[stuffed] up. // 바람이 전혀 불지 않아 숨이 막힐 것 같다 There was no wind at all and the air was stifling[suffocating]. // 굴뚝이 검댕으로 막혀 버렸다 The chimney is choked with soot.
2 (길 등이) be blocked (up); be barred; be obstructed; be interrupted; be suspended; stop. ¶앞이 막힌 골목 a blind[dead] alley [lane] // 통행이 ~ be held up (for a few minutes) // 앞길이 ~ be at the end of a road // 차량으로 교통이 막혀 앞으로 나아갈 수 없다 We can not move because the traffic is blocked. // 도로는 휴가로부터 돌아오는 사람들의 차들로 막혀 있다 The road is jammed [clogged] with the cars of people returning from holiday. // 사업이 자금 부족으로 막혔다 The business came to a standstill for lack of funds.
3 (말·생각 등이) stick (in one's speech); get tongue-tied; be at a loss for (an answer); be driven to one's wit's end; come to the end of one's tether. ¶막힌 사람 a blockhead / a thickhead / a halfwit // 말문이 ~ be stuck for a word / be at a loss for words / stumble at one's words // 대답이 막혔다 I did not know what to answer. / I was at a loss for an answer. // 그녀는 노래 도중에 막혀 버렸다 She stumbled in the middle of her song. // 추궁을 당하여 나는 말문이 막혔다 Questioned closely, I didn't know what to say[I was at a loss for words].
4 [구획되다] be partitioned; be compartmented; [가로놓임] lie across. ¶벽으로 ~ be partitioned with a wall // 앞에 강이 ~ a river lies across the path ahead / have a river ahead // 뒤에 산이 ~ be walled in from behind by a mountain / have a mountain behind // 방들이 칸막이로 막혔다 The rooms were partitioned[compartmented] with screens.

만¹ [시간의 경과] after the lapse of …; interval. ¶2년 ~에 after the lapse[an interval] of two years // 3년 ~에 귀향하다 come home after three years' absence // 10년 ~에 형을 만나다 see one's brother after ten years' separation // 그가 태어난 지 3년 ~에 그의 어머니가 돌아가셨다 His mother died three years after he was born. // 이것은 10년 ~의 더위다

This is the warmest weather we have had for[in] ten years.

만² 1 [단지·다만·뿐] only; alone; merely; just; [한도·범위] as many[much] as; as[so] far as. ¶한 번 ~ only once // 한 번 ~ 더 just once again // 이번[그때] ~은 for this[that] once / on this[that] particular occasion // 사람은 빵~으로 살아갈 수 있는가 Can man live by bread alone? // 음악~이 그에 대한 위안이었다 Listening to music was his only [sole] consolation. // 너~이 이것을 할 수 있다 You alone[Nobody but you / You are the only one who] can do this. // 오전 중에~ 이것을 빌릴 수 있겠습니까 May I[Could] I borrow it just for the morning? // 그것은 신문뿐~ 아니라 주간에도 실려 있었다 It was reported not only in the newspapers but also in the weekly magazines. // 서울에서~도 그런 사건은 10건이나 있었다 There were ten such cases in Seoul alone. // 나는 네가 사과의 말 한 마디~ 했더라면 한다 I wish you had said just[even] one word of apology. // 그것을 제안[보기]~ 한 것으로 그는 화를 냈다 The mere suggestion[sight] of it made him angry. // 그것을 잠간 보여 주기~ 하면 됩니다 You have only to let me have a glance at it. // 그것~이 내게 만족을 준다 That alone gives me satisfaction. // 그것~을 희망으로 삼고 나는 살아왔다 I have lived with that sole hope. // 거대한 부(富)도 그것 ~으로는 내게 매력이 되지 못한다 Great wealth, as such, does not appeal to me. // 그 생각~ 해도 나는 가슴이 설렌다 The mere thought of it excites me. // 그를 놀리려고 해 보기~ 해도 넌 혼난다 Just try making fun of him, and you'll be sorry. // 정직~으로 성공을 기대할 수는 없다 One cannot hope to succeed by honesty alone. // 그는 만화~ 읽는다 He reads only comics. // 그는 아침부터 밤까지 푸념~ 늘어놓는다 He does nothing but complain from morning till night. // 그는 늘 남의 책~ 빌리고 있다 He is always borrowing other people's books. // 그는 이름~ 화가다 He is an artist in name only. // 아이들뿐~이 아니라 어른들도 소풍을 즐겼다 Not only the children but also the adults enjoyed the outing. / The adults as well as the children enjoyed the outing. // 사람은 정직~을 자랑할 일이 아니다 Uprightness is not the only thing people should boast of. // 그들은 그들~ 있기를 바랐다 They wanted to be alone. // 네가 해 보아도 좋지만 한 번~이다 I'll let you try just once. // 이번~ 가르쳐 주지 I will teach you this time only[(for) just this once]. // 음악을 좋아하는 것은 너~이 아니다 You are not the only one who loves music. // 그~은 그런 짓을 할 사람이 아니다 He would be the last person to do such a thing. // 그날 ~은 그가 정각에 오지 않았다 He never failed to come at the fixed time except on that particular day. / That was the only day when he didn't come at the fixed time. // 제가 가야 합니까[저보고 가라고 하시는 것입니까]? 그것~ 은 못 하겠습니다 You mean I have to go? I will do anything but that!
2 [적어도] at least. ¶나는 한 달에 10만 원~ 은 저금하고 싶다 I want to save at least a hundred thousand won every month. // 나는 아들은 고등학교~은 보낼 셈이다 I will give my boy a high school education at least.
3 [비교] as ... as. ¶네 키는 너~ 하다 I am as tall as you (are). // 새알~ 하다 be the size of a bird's egg / be as small as a bird's egg.

만³ but; though. ⇨ 마는

만(卍) [불교의 표시] the Buddhist cross; the Buddhist emblem; [글자] a fylfot; a gammadion (*pl.* -dia); a swastika. ¶~기 the swastika flag(나치스 독일의).

만(萬) ten thousand; [다수] a myriad; many; all. ¶수~ tens of thousands // 수십~ hundreds of thousands // 10~ a hundred thousand // 100~ a million / one million // 1천~ ten million // ~분의 1 a ten-thousandth // 몇 ~이나 되는 사람 tens of thousands of people // ~에 하나라도 by any chance // 그런 일은 ~에 하나도 일어나지 않을 것이다 There isn't a chance in a million that such a thing will happen.

만에 하나 be very rare.

● 만 리 길 a journey of ten thousand miles; a long way to go.

만(灣) a bay(작은); a gulf(큰). ¶멕시코 ~ the Gulf of Mexico // 울산 ~ Ulsan Bay / the Bay of Ulsan // ~ 안 inside the bay // ~을 이루다 form a gulf[bay].

만(滿) just; full; fully; to a day. ¶~ 한 시간 (for) a full[good] hour / (for) one solid hour // ~ 3일간 (for) a full[whole] three days / for fully three days / for three days solid // 나이를 ~으로 세다 count (a person's) age in full // 나는 ~ 스물셋입니다 I have turned twenty-three. / I'm twenty-three (years old). (▶ 구미에서는 나이는 당연히 「만」으로 세기 때문에 「만」을 특별히 나타내지 않음) // 아내가 죽은 지 ~ 3년이 됩니다 It's been three full years since my wife died. // 거기 가는 데는 ~ 이틀이 걸린다 It takes fully two days[all of two days] to get there. // 그는 이 달 10일에 ~ 20세가 되었다 He became twenty years old on the 10th of this month. // 그가 한국을 떠난 지 ~ 2년이 된다 It is a full two years since he left Korea.

만가(輓歌) a dirge; an elegy; a lament; [상여를 메고 갈 때 하는 소리] a funeral song.

만감(萬感) a flood[crowd] of emotions. ¶~이 북받쳐 가슴을 메웠다 A thousand emotions crowded in on my mind. // ~이 북받쳐 말이 나오지 않았다 My heart was too full for words. / I could not utter a word with a heart full of feeling.

만강(滿腔) a full heart; full-heartedness; whole-heartedness. ¶~의 hearty / heartfelt / wholehearted // ~의 경의를 표하다 express one's wholehearted[most sincere] respect (for / to) // ~의 축의를 표하다 offer one's hearty congratulations.

만개(滿開) full bloom. ⇨ 만발

만경(晚景) 1 [저녁 경치] an evening scene. ¶파로 호의 ~ an evening view of Lake Paro. 2 [늦경치] a scene behind the season.

만경(萬頃) vastness; enormousness; extensiveness; boundlessness; immensity.

● 만경창파(一蒼波) the boundless expanse of water.

만고(萬古) [옛] all antiquity; remote antiquity; time immemorial; [영원] eternity; perpetuity. ¶~에 유례없는 unique for all generations // ~의 영웅 a hero for all ages // ~로부터 from immemorial antiquity.

● 만고불멸 immortality; imperishability;

만곡하다

everlastingness; eternity; perpetuity. ¶~의 immortal / undying / imperishable / deathless / permanent / eternal. **만고불변** permanence; constancy; being unchangeable. ¶~의 진리 immutable truths / eternal laws. **만고절색** an unsurpassed beauty; a (woman of) peerless beauty; the fairest of the fair; the loveliest of all. **만고절창** an unparalleled singer(가수); a superb song unequalled in its beauty(노래); a poem unexcelled in its beauty throughout the annals of literature(시). **만고풍상** all kinds of hardships and privations; long trials. ¶~을 겪다 suffer hardships and privations / undergo [experience] all sorts of hardships and privations.

만곡하다 (彎曲−) curved; crooked; bent; bowed; sinuous; bandy(무릎이); tortuous.

만국 (萬國) all nations; the nations of the world; all countries on earth; the world. ¶~의 international / universal.
● **만국기** the flags of all nations; (집합적) bunting. ¶~로 꾸며져 있다 be decked with bunting. **만국 박람회** an international exposition; (미) a world fair.

만군 (萬軍) 1 [많은 군사] a myriad soldiers. ¶~은 얻기 쉬워도 일장(一將)은 얻기 힘들다 Workers are earlier[easier] found than masters. 2 all things (under the sun). ⇨ **만유**(萬有).

만권 (萬卷) [수많은 책] many books; a large library.

만근 (萬斤) [무거운 무게] great weight. ¶그의 말은 우리에게는 ~의 무게가 있다 His word carries great weight with us.

만금 (萬金) [많은 돈] ten thousand pieces of gold; an immense sum of money. ¶~으로도 바꿀 수 없다 be invaluable / be priceless // ~을 투자하다 invest an immense sum (in).

만기 (滿期) expiration (of a term); expiry (of a contract); (어음의) maturity(약어 mat.). ¶~전에 before the full term is up / prior to the expiration of the period // ~의 matured / time-expired // ~가 되다 (임기가) expire / (어음이) mature / fall[be / become] due / (복역이) serve out one's time / 계약이 ~가 되었다 The contract has expired. / 이 어음은 앞으로 3개월[이달 25일]이면 ~가 된다 The note is due in three months[on the 25th of this month]. // 그의 보험은 3월 말로 ~가 된다 The term of his insurance expires on the last day of March. // 그의 형기는 ~가 되었다 He served out his time[sentence].
● **만기 배당** [보험] a maturity dividend. **만기 상환** redemption at[on] maturity. **만기 석방** release (of a prisoner) on the expiration of the period of punishment. **만기 어음** a matured bill. **만기일** the expiration date; the date of maturity. **만기 제대** discharge on expiration of term of service.

만끽하다 (滿喫−) [마음껏 마시고 먹다] have [eat / drink] one's fill (of); eat[drink] to one's heart's content; do ample justice to (the dinner); [마음껏 즐기다] enjoy fully[to the full]. ¶그들은 봄의 따뜻한 햇빛을 만끽하고 있었다 They were enjoying the warm spring sunshine to the full. / They were thoroughly enjoying the warm spring sunshine.

만나다 1 [얼굴을 대하게 되다] see; meet; [맞닥뜨리다] come across; run into; [면회하다] see; interview; have an interview (with). ¶우연히 ~ come across / [재회하다] meet again by chance // 어디서 만날까 Where shall we meet? // 이 공원은 젊은 두 사람이 언제나 만나는 장소였다 This park was the young couple's usual rendezvous[where the young couple always met]. // 이 도시에 살고 있으면서 내게는 여러 부류의 사람과 만날 기회가 있다 Living in this town, I have the chance to meet[I come across] various sorts of people. // 그 후에는 그를 한 번도 만난 적이 없다 I never (once) saw him again after that. // 그와 역전에서 만나기로 했다 I arranged to meet him in front of the station. // 좀 이야기할 것이 있는데 잠깐 만나 주시겠소 Can I have a few minutes? I have something to talk to you about. // 그를 만나게 해 주십시오 Please let me see him. // 그가 특별히 만나고 싶어 했던 사람은 그곳에 없었다 The person he particularly wanted to see was not there. // 서로 만나면 그들은 고개를 끄덕여 인사를 주고받았다 When they met, they nodded to each other. // 이틀 뒤에 나는 우연히 또 그를 만났다 I happened to meet him again two days later. // 큰길 모퉁이에서 나는 뜻밖에 선생님과 만났다 I ran into my teacher at the street corner. // 그녀는 오랜 세월에 걸쳐 행방을 모르고 있던 자식을 다시 만났다 She was reunited with her long-lost child.
2 [일·때를 당하다] meet with (an accident); encounter (the enemy); come upon[across]; suffer (a calamity); experience (hardship); be confronted by (a crisis). ¶재난을 ~ suffer[be visited by] a calamity / meet with a misfortune // 폭풍우를 ~ (사람이) be caught in[overtaken by] a storm / (장소가) be visited[struck / hit / swept] by a storm // 화재를 만나 그의 장서는 대부분이 타 버렸다 He had the greater part of his library burnt in the fire.
3 [알게 되다] become[get] acquainted (with); contract[strike up] an acquaintance (with); come to know (a person); come in contact (with). ¶나는 그녀를 우연히 만나 결국 결혼했다 I picked an acquaintance with her and succeeded in marriage.
4 (사물이) join; cross; interest. ¶두 선이 만나는 점 the point of intersection of two lines // 두 길은 거기서 만난다 The two roads join[unite] there. // 그곳에서 본류와 지류가 만난다 The main stream and a branch meet[converge]. / There a branch flows into the main stream. // 만남은 곧 헤어짐이다 That which has been joined shall one day be parted.

만난 (萬難) thousand and one difficulties; innumerable difficulties; all obstacles [hindrances]. ¶~을 무릅쓰고 at all costs [risks / hazards] / through thick and thin / …, come hell and high water // ~을 무릅쓰다 [극복하다] surmount[overcome] all difficulties // ~을 무릅쓰고 그것을 나는 해내겠다 I will carry it out at any cost[at all costs].

만날 (萬−) every day; all the time; always; constantly. ¶그는 ~ 부모에게 걱정만 끼친다 He is a constant source of anxiety to his parents. // 이런 일은 ~ 있는 것이 아니다 Such things do not occur every day. // ~ 비가 온다 It rains continuously. // ~ 그들은 서로 싸운다 They quarrel with each other all the time.∥나는 ~ 네 생각뿐이다 Not a day passes without my thinking of you.

만년(晚年) one's later [latter / last / declining] years; the latter part of one's life; the close [evening] of one's life [days]; one's closing days. ¶~에 접어들다 enter the twilight of one's life∥그는 ~을 불우하게 보냈다 He lived the rest of his life in obscurity.∥그 림은 그의 ~의 작품이다 He painted this picture in his later years.∥그는 ~이 되어 겨우 성공했다 It was only late in life that he achieved success.

만년(萬年) [영원성] eternity; perpetuity.
● **만년설** perpetual [permanent] snow (field); (높은 산의) an icecap. ¶극지(極地)의 ~ polar icecaps. **만년 처녀** a fadeless beauty; a perennially youthful woman. **만년 청년** a man of perennial [ageless] youth. **만년 후보** a candidate who always fails of election.

만년필(萬年筆) a fountain pen; a self-feeding pen. ¶자동(自動)식 ~ a self-filling (fountain) pen∥~에 잉크를 넣다 fill [refill] a fountain pen∥~에 잉크가 떨어졌다 The fountain pen has run out of ink.∥이 ~은 잘 써진다 This fountain pen writes smoothly.

만능(萬能) omnipotence; being almighty; having an all-round capability. ¶~의 [전능의] all-powerful / almighty / omnipotent / [다재한] all-round / (미) all-around / 기계 ~의 시대 the age of machinery / 황금 ~의 세상 Money is everything. / Money makes the world go round.
● **만능선수** (경기의) an all-round [(미) all-around] player [athlete]; (전문가에 대하여) a generalist.

만다라(曼陀羅·曼荼羅) [불] a mandala; Buddha's picture.

만단(萬端) everything; all; [방법] every possible means. ¶~의 준비가 다 갖추어있다 Every preparation is made. / Everything is ready [(미) O.K.].
● **만단설화**(一說話) all sorts of stories; various stories. **만단수심**(一愁心) all kinds of worries; lots of worries; manifold vexations.

만담(漫談) a comic chat [monologue]; a gag; a joke. ¶한 차례 ~을 하다 give [deliver] a comic monologue / tell a comic story (to an audience)∥코미디언의 ~에 관중이 폭소를 터뜨렸다 The comedian's gags made the audience laugh. **만담하다** gag; joke.
● **만담가** a comic storyteller; a gagster; a gagman; a comic chat artiste.

만당(滿堂) [공간에 사람이 가득 참] the whole house [hall / company]; [가득 찬 사람들] all the audience; the whole assemblage.

만대(萬代) all ages; all generations; eternity. ¶~에 for all ages / forever / everlastingly / eternally∥(위업이) ~에 전해지다 be remembered for ages to come / live forever on the lips of people∥그의 이름은 ~에 전해질 것이 다 His name shall endure for ages.

만돌린 [음] a mandolin(e). ¶~을 타다 play the mandolin.

만동(晚冬) late winter. ⇨늦겨울

만두(饅頭) a steamed (bean-jam) bun; a bun; a dumpling. ¶고기~ a meat bun / 군~ a fried dumpling / 물~ a dumpling served in soup∥찐~ a steamed dumpling∥팥~ a bun with a bean-jam filling / a bean-jam bun.
● **만두 가게** a bun shop. **만둣국** dumpling soup.

만득(晚得) [늦게 낳은 자식] a child begotten in one's later years; [늦게 자식을 낳음] begetting a child in one's later years. **만득하다** beget [procreate] a child in one's later years.

만들다¹ 1 [창조하다] make; create. ¶태초에 하느님이 천지를 만드시니라 In the beginning God created (the) heaven and (the) earth. 2 [제작·제조하다] make; (기계 등을 사용하여 대규모로) manufacture; [급히 만들다] knock up. ¶잘[서투르게] 만든 물품 a well-made [poorly-made] article / an article of fine [poor] make∥잘[서투르게] 만든 양복 a well-cut [a poorly-cut] suit∥이것은 훌륭히 [형편없이] 만들어졌다 This is wonderfully well [badly] done.∥유리는 모래로 만든다 Glass is made from sand.∥책은 종이로 만든다 Books are made of paper.(▶ 원료의 질이 바뀌지 않을 경우는 of, 바뀔 경우는 from)∥나는 과일즙과 설탕으로 시럽을 만들었다 I made syrup with [out of] fruit juice and sugar.∥버 터는 우유로 만든다 Butter is made from milk.∥이 천으로 스커트 둘을 만들 수 있다 This cloth will make two skirts.∥이 장남감은 정교하게 만들어졌다 This toy is elaborately designed [delicately made].∥당신이 그 양복을 다 만드는 데 몇 시간이나 걸립니까 How many more hours will it take you to finish the suit?∥이 공장에서는 들통[물통]을 만들고 있다 This factory produces buckets.∥내 공장에서는 기계를 사용하여 물품을 대량 으로 만든다 My factory manufactures goods in large quantities by using machines.∥이런 종류의 열쇠를 만들기 시작한 것은 그가 처음 이었다 He was the first to make this type of key. 3 [양조하다] make [brew] (beer); distill (whisky). ¶쌀로 막걸리를 ~ make makgeolli from rice. 4 [작성하다] make; frame; make out; draw up(서류 등을). ¶책을 ~ make [write] a book∥초고를 ~ make [prepare] a draft∥계약서 를 ~ draw up a contract [an agreement]. 5 [주조하다] coin; cast; strike; mint. ¶주화를 ~ strike [mint] coins / coin money. 6 [건조하다] make; build; erect; construct; fit up. ¶보금자리를 ~ build a nest∥이 다리 는 튼튼하게 만들어졌다 This bridge is solidly built. 7 [형성하다] form; make. ¶열(列)을 ~ form in line / form a line / 4열을 ~ form fours. 8 [조직하다] constitute; form; organize; found; set up; establish. ¶학교를 ~ found [establish] a school∥회사를 ~ set up a company∥클럽을 ~ organize a club. 9 [양성하다] foster; cultivate; build (up). ¶인 물[선량한 사람]을 ~ build up [train] a man of talent [good citizens]. 10 [마련하다] make; get. ¶규칙을 ~ make [lay down] a rule / 전례(前例)의 ~ establish [set] a precedent∥그를 만날 기회를 네게 [너 희에게] 만들어 주겠다 I will make an opportunity for you to meet him.∥나는 그에게 말을 꺼낼 계기[기회 / 실마리]를 만들기에 고심 했다 I had difficulty (in) finding an occasion to talk to him.∥그는 텔레비전 드라마에 새 로운 형식을 만들어 냈다 He created [origi-

만들다

nated] a new style in T.V. drama.∥그는 새로운 시스템[장치]을 만들어 냈다 He invented[devised] a new system.

11 [상처 등을 내다] wound; injure. ¶예쁜 얼굴에 상처를 ~ disfigure[mar] the beautiful face.

12 [조작하다] make up; invert; fabricate; concoct; (구어) cook up. ¶만든 이야기 a made-up[an invented] story.

13 [조리하다] prepare (food); cook; bake; (도시락을) (미) fix (a lunch). ¶스튜 요리를 ~ make (a) stew∥맛있는 것을 만들어 드리겠어요 I'll prepare something nice for you. / I'll get you something nice.∥이 수프를 잘 만들었다 This soup is well made[very good].

14 […이 되게 하다] make; [···으로 바꾸다] change[turn / convert] (into). ¶황무지를 개간하여 밀밭을 ~ turn barren land into wheat fields∥그들은 플라스틱으로 가지가지의 용기를 만들었다 They made plastic into various kinds of containers.∥저 여자를 구슬러서 내 것으로 만들어 보여 주겠다 I'm going to make her mine — you'll see.∥나는 내 아들을 의사로 만들 셈이다 I want to make my son a doctor[make a doctor out of my son].∥열은 물을 증기로 만든다 Heat turns water into vapor.∥우리는 헛간을 어린이 방으로 만들었다 We converted the storeroom into a children's room.

만들다² […하게 하다] make[have / let] (a person do); get[induce / cause / force] (a person to do). ¶가게[믿게] ~ make (a person) go[believe (in)]∥서명하게[서명하도록] ~ force (a person) to sign (the paper).

만듦새 [만들어진 본새] make; workmanship. ¶~가 좋은[나쁜] of fine[poor] workmanship∥~가 최고급인 코트[웃옷] a coat of (a) first-class make∥~가 좋지 않다 The make is poor. / It is of poor make.

만료(滿了) expiration[expiry] (of a term); termination (of office). ¶계약 ~ the termination of an agreement∥기한 ~ the expiration of the term[period]∥기한 ~ 일 the expiration date∥임기 ~ the termination of one's office. **만료하다** expire; fall[become] due; complete. ¶그의 임기는 만료했다 His term of office expired[was completed].

만루(滿壘) [야구] loaded bases. ¶~가 되어 with the bases loaded∥투 아웃으로 ~ 다 The bases are loaded with two outs.

● **만루 홈런** (hit) a bases-loaded home run; a grand-slam homer. ¶그의 ~으로 승패가 역전됐다 His bases-loaded[grand slam] home run turned the tide of the game.

만류하다(挽留-) detain; keep[hold] back (a person from fighting). ¶소매를 잡으며 detain (a person) by the sleeve∥싸우지 말라고 ~ hold (a person) from wrangling / dissuade (a person) from fighting∥더는 만류하지 않겠습니다 I won't keep you any longer.∥그의 상사가 그의 사직 의사를 만류했다 His boss persuaded him to stay.∥그녀는 우중에 외출하려는 아들을 만류했다 She stopped her son from going out in the rain. / She persuaded her son not to go out in the rain.

만리장성(萬里長城) the Great Wall of China.

만만하다 **1** [부드럽다] soft; tender; pliable; supple; yielding. **만만히** softly; tenderly; (so it is) soft[tender].

2 [다루기 쉽다] easily manageable; easy to deal with; tractable; docile. ¶만만한 사람 (미국 속어) an easy mark / (미국 속어) a pushover∥그는 만만찮은 아이였다 He was an unyielding boy.∥그는 만만찮은 사람이다 He is very difficult to deal with. / He is quite a hard man to manage. / (구어) He is a tough customer.∥그 여자는 만만치 않은 여자다 She is a formidable woman.∥나를 만만하게 보지 마라 Don't see green in my eye. **만만히** easily; readily. ¶그 여자가 ~ 떨어지지는 않을 게다 The girl won't readily let you go.

3 [대수롭지 않다] negligible; slight; insignificant; trivial; of little importance; of no account. ¶만만찮은 적 no common enemy / a formidable adversary∥그는 만만찮은 학자다 He is no mean scholar.∥우리는 적이 만만찮다는 것을 알았다 We found in them no despicable foes. **만만히** negligently; slightingly. ¶~ 보다[여기다] make light of / undervalue / hold (a person) cheap / don't make very much of (a person)∥그것은 ~ 여길 일이 아니다 That is not a matter to be slighted[to be taken lightly].∥약한 적이라 하더라도 ~ 여기지 마라 Don't despise a weak enemy.

만만하다(滿滿-) full of (ambition); brimming with (vigor); filled with (courage). ¶야심이 ~ be full of ambition / be highly ambitious∥자신이 ~ be full of self-confidence∥패기가 ~ be highly ambitious / be full of go [(미) pep].

만면(滿面) the whole face. ¶그는 ~에 웃음을 띠면서 들어왔다 He came in with a broad smile (on his face)[with a beaming face]. **만면하다** (서술적) be full of[with full of]. ¶그는 희색이 만면했다 His pleasure showed clearly on his face. / His pleasure was written all over his face.

만무하다(萬無-) (서술적) be impossible [unbelievable]; cannot (be); it is utterly impossible that …; it is not likely at all that …; it is out of the question that …; there is no reason why …. ¶그럴 리 ~ It is impossible. / It cannot be so.∥그녀가 그런 짓을 했을 리 ~ She can't have done such a thing.∥네가 그것을 모를 리 ~ I cannot believe that[There is no reason why] you know nothing about it.∥그것이 저절로 깨질 리가 ~ It cannot break of itself.

만문(漫文) [마음 내키는 대로 쓴 글] random notes; [웃음고 재미있게 쓴 글] a causerie.

만물(萬物) all things (under the sun); [하느님의 창조물] all creation. ¶천지[우주] ~ all things in the universe / everything under the sun∥인간은 ~의 영장이다 Man is the lord of creation.∥~은 유전(流轉)한다 All things change.∥~이 죽은 듯한 정적이었다 It was as quiet as if all creation were dead.

● **만물박사** a well-informed person; a walking dictionary; a pantologist. **만물상** a convenience store; a general store[shop]; a grocery (store).

만민(萬民) the whole nation; all the people. ¶~의 안녕을 빌다 wish for the well-being of the whole nation[all the people].

만반(萬般) all things; all sorts (of matters). ¶~의 all / every∥~의 준비[태세]를 갖추다 make full[thorough] preparations / get

만발(滿發) full bloom. **만발하다** be in full bloom[blossom / flower]; bloom all over [in profusion]. ¶벚꽃이 만발해 있다 The cherry blossoms are in full bloom[at their best].// 공원에는 봄꽃들이 만발해 있다 In the park, the flowers of spring are in all their glory.

만방(萬方) all directions; every way; all possible means. ¶~으로 손을 쓰다 try all[every] means available / exhaust all possible means // ~으로 진력하다 make every effort / exert oneself to the utmost.

만방(萬邦) all the countries of the world; all nations on earth.

만백성(萬百姓) all the people; the whole nation.

만병(萬病) all (kinds of) diseases[maladies]. ¶감기는 ~의 원인 A cold may lead to all kinds of diseases. / A cold may develop into all kinds of illness.
● **만병통치약** a cure-all; a panacea; a universal remedy.

만보(漫步) a ramble; a stroll; a saunter. **만보하다** ramble; saunter; stroll.

만복(萬福) blessedness. ¶~을 빕니다 I wish you every happiness in the world.

만복(滿腹) a full stomach[belly]; satiety.
● **만복감** a feeling of fullness[plenitude] (after a meal). ¶그는 ~으로 기분이 좋았다 He was feeling comfortably full.

만부당하다(萬不當-) utterly[entirely / absolutely] unjust; unlawful; unreasonable; absurd. ¶만부당한 말 an absolutely[utterly] unreasonable remark.

만부득이(萬不得已) unavoidably; inevitably. ⇨ "부득이"

만분지일(萬分之一) [아주 적음]. ¶입은 은혜의 ~이라도 갚을 수 있었으면 좋겠습니다 I wish I could do even a little to repay your kindness.

만사(萬事) everything (in the world / under the sun); all things[affairs / matters]; all (sorts of things). ¶~ 오케이 All's well. / (미) Everything's O.K.// ~ 잘돼 간다 All goes well[favorably] (with me).// ~가 들어졌다 Everything went wrong with us.// ~를 잘 부탁한다 See that all is well.// 요즈음은 ~가 돈으로 좌우된다 Money is everything nowadays.
● **만사태평** [일이 잘됨] all going well; [무관심] nonchalance; indifference; carelessness. ¶그는 ~이다 He is perfectly carefree. / It looks as if there were nothing to trouble him.

만사형통하다(萬事亨通-) all goes well; be prosperous in everything; everything turns out as one wished. ¶우리는 만사형통했다 Lucky was with us and everything went well. / Fortune smiled on us.

만삭(滿朔) [출산이 임박함] parturiency; [해산할 달] the last month of pregnancy; the month of parturition. ¶~의 여인 a parturient woman / a woman near her time // ~이 되다 come to one's time (of parturition) // 그녀는 지금 ~이다 Her time is near. / She is near her time (of childbirth).

만산(滿山) the whole hill[mountain]; all the hills. ¶단풍이 ~에 덮여 있다 The whole hill is covered[dressed up] with red leaves. **만산하다** (blossoms) cover the whole hill [mountain].

만상(萬象) all kinds of phenomena; all things in the universe.

만생(晩生) a child begotten in one's later years; begetting a child in one's later years. ⇨"만득"

만석꾼(萬石-) a person who owns fields yielding ten thousand *seok* of rice; a wealthy [millionaire / many-acred] landlord.

만성(慢性) [의] chronicity; being chronic. ¶~적 실업 chronic unemployment // ~화하다 become chronic // 내 위병은 ~입니다 I am a chronic dyspeptic.// 그의 거짓말은 ~이 되어 버렸다 He is a habitual liar.// 그는 노름을 좋아하더니 ~이 되었다 He is a confirmed gambler.// 불경기는 ~화되고 있다 The bad economic situation is becoming chronic.
● **만성병** a chronic disease. **만성 위장병** inveterate[confirmed] dyspepsia. **만성 인플레** chronic inflation. **만성 전염병** a chronic infectious disease.

만세(萬世) all ages[generations]; [영겁] eternity. ¶~에 이르도록 through all ages to come // ~에 전하다 be transmitted to all ages // 그의 업적은 ~에 길이 남을 것이다 His great achievements will be remembered for all ages to come.

만세(萬歲) 1 [만년] all ages; eternity. 2 [외치는 소리] a hurrah; hurray; rah; cheers; cheering. ¶그들은 ~를 불렀다[외쳤다] They hurrahed. // 그들은 ~를 삼창했다 They gave three cheers[shouted "Hurrah!"] three times].// 그는 ~ 소리를 받으며 떠났다 He was sent off to cries of "Hurrah".// 우리는 이 졌다. ~ We won. Hurray!// ~! 나는 해냈다 Hurray! I've finished it!// 여왕 폐하 ~ Long live the Queen!

만세력(萬歲曆) a perpetual calendar; a perpetual almanac.

만수(滿水) ¶~가 되다 be filled (to the brim) with water.

만수무강(萬壽無疆) a long life; longevity. ¶~을 빕니다 Long life to you! **만수무강하다** live long; enjoy longevity; live to a great age.

만숙(晩熟) late (sexual) maturity; late ripening. ¶~의 late-maturing / late-ripening.

만시지탄(晩時之歎) a belated regret; an afterthought; repenting (of) one's missing a chance.

만신(滿身) the whole body. ¶~에 all over (the body) / from head to foot // ~의 힘을 기울여 with all one's might[strength] / with might and main.
● **만신창이** being covered all over with wounds.

만안하다(萬安-) peaceful; tranquil; secure; healthy; well; 《서술적》 be in good health.

만약(萬若) if; (an) emergency. ⇨"만일"

만연(蔓延·蔓衍) spread; diffusion. ¶발진 티푸스의 ~을 막다 prevent[check] the spread of typhus. **만연하다** [널리 퍼지다] grow thick(ly); spread; prevail; diffuse; be prevalent; be widespread. ¶이 거리에는 악(惡)이 만연해 있다 Vice thrives in this town. // 그 나라에 질병과 빈곤이 만연하고 있었다 Disease and poverty were rampant in the country. // 경기 지방에 독감이 만연하고 있다 Influenza [The flu] is sweeping the Gyeonggi district. // 공업 지구에 오염이 만연하고 있다 Pollution is widespread in industrial area.

만연하다(漫然-) aimless; rambling; desultory. **만연히** aimlessly; desultorily; in a rambling[desultory] way.

만열(滿悅) great delight; ecstasy; satisfaction. **만열하다** be much delighted[satisfied]; feel ecstatic; be in ecstasy[rapture].

만용(蠻勇) [함부로 날뛰는 용맹] daredevil courage; brute[animal] courage; savage valor; barbaric vigor; foolhardiness; recklessness; [완력] (physical) force. ¶~을 부리다 use[resort to] force / show reckless valor // 그는 ~을 부려 단신으로 적진에 뛰어들었다 With reckless valor[a reckless show of valor] he marched into enemy territory alone.

만우절(萬愚節) All Fools' Day; April Fools' Day.

만원(滿員) no vacancy; a full[capacity] house(극장의); congestion(교도소 등의). ¶자리는 ~입니다 All the seats are taken[sold out]. / There are no seat left. // 호텔은 ~이었다 There was no room[vacancy] at the hotel. // 열차는 초~이었다 The train was crowded beyond capacity[jammed full]. // 극장은 ~이다 The theater is filled to capacity. / All the seats in the theater are occupied. / The theater is full[packed]. // ~ 사례 (극장의 게시) Full House. / (열차 등의 게시) Car Full.
● **만원 버스** a jam-packed bus.

만월(滿月) a full moon. ¶~의 밤에 on a night with a full moon.

만유(萬有) all things (under the sun); the creation; all things in the universe; the whole of creation.
● **만유인력** [물] universal gravitation. ¶~의 법칙 the law of universal gravitation.

만유(漫遊) a (pleasure) tour; a (leisurely) trip. **만유하다** make a tour (of / through); tour (a country). ¶세계를 ~ make[go on] a (leisurely) tour of the world / tour the world // 국내를 ~ travel in[about] the country.

만유신론(萬有神論) pantheism. ⇒범신론

만인(萬人) all (sorts of) people[men]; everybody. ¶~에게 알맞다 suit[meet] all taste / suit everybody // 이것은 ~이 인정하는 진리이다 This is a universal truth.

만인(蠻人) a savage; a barbarian.

만일(萬一) 1 [만약] if; in case (of) (…의 경우에는); provided[supposing] (that) (조건); by any chance(만에 하나라도). ¶~ 비가 오면 [in case] it rains / in case of rain // ~ 필요하다면 if (it is) necessary // ~ 내가 실패하면 if (by any chance) I should fail / in case I fail // ~ …이 없었더라면[아니었더라면] if it were not[had not been] for ... / were it not[had it not been] for ... / but for ... // ~ 내가 너라면 그런 짓은 안 한다 If I were you, I would not do such a thing. // ~ 그를 만나면 나한테 오라고 해 주시오 If you meet him, tell him to call on me. // ~ 내가 그 자리에 있게 되면 이러쿵저러쿵 말이 많을 게다 If I should [Should I] be there, it would be talked about. // ~ 내일 죽는다면 너는 어떻게 하겠느냐 If you were to die tomorrow, what would you do? // ~ 병이라도 나면 어떻해 What if you should be taken ill? // ~ 나에게 돈만 있다면 If only I had money! // ~ 그때 알기만 했더라면 If I had only known! // ~ 그가 오지 않으면 어떻게 하지 Supposing he doesn't come, then what are you going to do? / What if he doesn't turn up?
2 [뜻하지 않은 일] (an) emergency; a rare possibility; an unlikely event. ¶~의 경우에는 in (case of) emergency / should emergency arise / in case[time] of need / if anything[the worst] should happen // ~의 경우에 대비하다 provide[make provision] against (the) time of need[a rainy day / an emergency] / prepare for the worst // ~을 위해 다시 한 번 말씀드립니다 Allow me to repeat it by way of precaution[for precaution's sake]. // ~을 위해 그에게 직접 물어보시오 Ask him in person to satisfy yourself. / ~을 위해 레인코트를 입고 가시오 Wear your raincoat just in case. // ~의 경우에는 백부한 테 가거라 Go to your uncle in time of need.

만입(灣入) [지] embayment; (해안선의) an indentation. **만입하다** curve in; (the sea) penetrate (into the land); push a bay (into the land). ¶바다는 육지에 깊이 만입해 있다 An arm of the sea penetrates far into the land.

만자(卍字) a fylfot; a gammadion (*pl.* -dia); a swastika.
● **만자 무늬** a fylfot pattern.

만장(萬丈) [무척 높음] unfathomable height. ¶~의 계곡 a ravine of unfathomable depth // 홍진 ~ a cloud of dust // ~의 산 a very high mountain // ~의 기염을 토하다 give full vent to one's feelings / [호언하다] talk big [tall] / make a grand splurge / [의기양양하다] be in all one's glory // 그는 기염 ~이었다 He had an overabundance of enthusiasm. // 조금만 바람이 불면 이곳은 홍진~의 지역으로 변한다 When it blows a little, this area is covered with a cloud of yellow dust[becomes a sea of yellow dust which seems to reach the sky]. // 그는 팀을 위해 ~의 기염을 토했다 He raised the name of his team sky-high.
● **만장봉** a lofty[high] peak; an alp.

만장(滿場) [공간에 꽉 들어참] the whole house[company]; [꽉 들어찬 사람들] the whole audience[assembly]. ¶그의 연기는 ~의 갈채를 받았다 His performance brought the house down[won the applause of the whole house]. // ~은 그의 노래에 황홀하게 귀를 기울였다 The whole audience listened to his songs with rapt attention.
● **만장일치** unanimity (of the whole assembly). ¶~로 unanimously / by unanimous [universal] consent / by a unanimous vote / with a unanimous approval / (문어) with one consent[accord] // 의안은 ~로 통과되었다 The bill was passed unanimously [without dissent]. // 그는 ~로 회장에 선출되었다 He was elected president by a unanimous vote. / He was unanimously elected president.

만재(滿載) the loaded[full load] condition; (at) full load. **만재하다** (배·차가) be loaded to capacity (with); be fully loaded[laden] (with); be loaded down (with); carry a full load (of); (신문·잡지가) be full (of articles); be filled with (stories). ¶야채를 만재한 트럭 a truck carrying a full load of vegetables / a truck loaded to capacity with vegetables // 배는 수출용 자동차를 만재하고 있었다 The ship was carrying a full cargo of cars for export. // 이 잡지는 컬러 사진을 만재하고 있다 This magazine is full of color photographs.

●**만재 흘수선**(-吃水線) a load line [waterline]; the Plimsoll line [mark] (▶ 이 표시가 잠길 정도로 적재하지는 못함).

만전(萬全) perfectness; perfection. ¶~의 safe / perfect / [튼튼한] secure / [틀림없는] infallible // ~을 **기하다** make perfection more perfect / make assurance doubly sure / see that all is of 100.

만점(滿點) **1** [규정된 점수의 가장 높은 점] full marks; a perfect score. ¶역사에서 ~을 받다 get a perfect score in history / (영) gain [win] full marks in history // 수학을 200점 ~으로 채점하다 mark mathematics examination papers on a maximum scale of 200 points // ~을 **주다** give full marks [the full number of points] (to) // 나는 100점에 40점밖에 못 받았다 I got only 40 points out of 100.
2 [만족할 만한 정도]. ¶~의 [인] perfect / quite satisfactory // 영양 ~의 음식물 very nourishing food // 스릴 ~의 롤러코스터 타기 a perfectly thrilling roller coaster ride // 서비스가 ~이다 The service is quite satisfactory. // 그의 응대하는 태도는 ~이었다 His manner of receiving people was perfect. / There was nothing to be desired in his way of receiving people.

만조(滿潮) a high [full] tide; high water. ¶~때에 at high tide // 지금이 ~다 The tide is full now. / The tide is in now. // ~ 시각이 오후 2시다 The tide is full at 2 p.m.

만족(滿足) [흡족함] satisfaction; contentment; gratification(욕망의); complacency; complacence. ¶자기 ~ self-contentment [-satisfaction] / self-complacency / self-sufficiency // 결과에 대하여 ~의 뜻을 표하다 express one's satisfaction at [with] the result // 행복은 ~에 있다 Happiness lies in contentment. **만족하다** satisfactory; gratifying; (서술적) be satisfied (with); be gratified (with / by); be contented [content] (with); content oneself (with); find satisfaction [contentment] (in). ¶만족하여 contentedly / in contentment // 크게 ~ be amply satisfied (with) // 나는 그 소식을 듣고 크게 만족했다 I heard the news with great [much] satisfaction. // 모두가 만족하도록 사건을 해결하기란 어렵다 It is difficult to settle the matter to the satisfaction of all. ➔¶그 방정식을 만족시키는 x의 값 the value of x that satisfies the equation // 만족시키다 satisfy / gratify / give (a person) satisfaction // 호기심을 만족시키다 gratify one's curiosity. **만족히** satisfactorily; with satisfaction; in a satisfactory way [manner].
●**만족감** (a sense of) satisfaction; (a feeling of) fulfillment [contentment].

만족스럽다(滿足-) satisfactory; gratifying; (서술적) be satisfied (with); be gratified (with / by); be contented [content] (with); content oneself (with); find satisfaction [contentment] (in). ¶만족스러운 듯이 contentedly / with an air of satisfaction // 만족스럽게 satisfactorily / in a satisfactory way [manner] // 그의 설명은 결코 만족스러운 것이 못 되었다 His explanation was far from satisfactory.

만종(晩鐘) an evening bell; a curfew (bell); a bell at sunset.

만좌(滿座) the whole company [assembly]. ¶~의 사람들 the whole assembly / the company present // ~ 중(中)에서 나는 매도당했다 I was called names before the whole group [in public]. // 그는 ~의 웃음거리가 되었다 He was laughed at by all those present [everybody there].

만지다 touch; feel; (미) feel of; handle; (호트러진 머리를) comb [smooth] down; dress; [가지고 놀다] play with; (손가락으로) finger. ¶손으로 ~ feel a thing with one's hand // 피아노의 건반을 ~ finger the keyboard of a piano // 목걸이를 ~ [만지작거리다] play [toy] with a necklace // 골동품을 ~ dabble in curios // 정원을 만지는 것이 취미입니다 Pottering about in the garden is my hobby. // 내 타이프라이터를 만지지 말아 주게 Don't tamper [(속어) mess] with my typewriter. // 만지지 말 것 (게시) Hands Off. / Don't Touch. // 약간 만지기만 해도 그것은 부서진다 It will break at the slightest touch. // 이 천을 만져 보고 확인하십시오 Feel this cloth.

만지작거리다 (손가락으로) finger (a button); fumble [fiddle] with [at / about] (a key); (구어) paw(서투르게); touch(건드리다); [갖고 놀다] play [toy] with (fire); tamper [tinker] with (a machine); monkey [fool] (about / around) with (a tool); meddle with (papers). ¶그는 수염을 만지작거리며 말하는 버릇이 있다 He has a habit of twirling [playing with] his mustache while he talks.(▶ twirl은 머리, 수염 등의 경우에 자주 쓰임) // 그녀는 이야기를 하면서 자기 목걸이를 만지작거리고 있었다 She was playing [toying] with her necklace while she talked.

만질만질하다 smooth (to the touch); soft; velvety; downy. ¶만질만질한 모피 a glassy fur // 만질만질한 표면 a smooth surface.

만찬(晩餐) dinner; supper. ¶가짓수가 많은 ~ a many-course dinner // 최후의 ~ the Last Supper // ~ **연설** a dinner speech / an after-dinner speech // ~에 **초대하다** ask [invite] (a person) to dinner / entertain (a person) at [to] dinner.
●**만찬회** a dinner party; (공식의) a banquet. ¶…을 주빈으로 ~를 열다 give a dinner for [in honor of] (a person).

만천하(滿天下) the whole world. ¶~에 in the whole world / throughout the realm / under the sun // ~의 사람들 people all over the world // ~를 **다스리다** reign over the whole country / [정복하다] conquer the whole country // 그의 이름은 ~에 알려져 있다 His name is known to the whole world.

만초(蔓草) (땅을 기는) a vine; a creeper; a trailing plant; (담장 등을 기어오르는) a vine; a climbing plant; a climber.

만추(晩秋) late autumn; the latter part of autumn; (미) late fall. ¶~에 in late fall / late in autumn // ~의 of [in] late autumn.

만춘(晩春) late spring; the latter part of spring.

만취(漫醉) dead drunkenness. **만취하다** get dead [beastly / blind] drunk; be fuddled [muddled] with drink; (속어) get tanked up. ➔¶그는 만취됐다 He is dead drunk. // 그는 만취되어 있었다 He had drunk himself into a stupor. / (속어) He was really plastered. / He was dead drunk.

만큼 1 [정도] an extent; a degree; a measure. ¶어느 ~ to what extent [degree] / how

만판 far(거리) / how long(시간) ¶나는 그것을 싫증이 날 ~ 먹었다 I have eaten it so much [often] that I am sick of it. // 그는 큰 집을 지을 ~ 돈이 없다 He doesn't have money enough to build a big house. // 그는 버는 만큼의 돈을 저축한다 He saves as much as he earns. // 네가 필요한 ~의 돈을 내가 꾸어주마 I will lend you any sum you may need. // 나도 먹고 지낼 ~의 수입이 필요하다 I must have income enough to live on.
2 [원인·근거] because (of); since; as; for. ¶기대하지 않았던 ~ 우리는 더욱 기뻤다 We were all the more delighted because we had not expected it.
3 [비교] like; as; as ... as; so ... as; equal to; [부정] not so[as] ... as; less ... than. ¶···할 때~ 즐거운[처량한] 때는 없다 at no time is one so happy[miserable] as when .... // 눈은 입~ 말을 할 수 있다 The eyes can say as much as the mouth. / The eye is as eloquent as the tongue. // 금년은 작년~ 춥지 않다 This year is not so[as] cold as last year. // 자기 집~ 좋은 곳은 없다 There is no place like home. // 그것~ 좋은 것은 없다 Nothing is better than that. // 남은 너~ 못하는 줄 아느냐 Do you think anyone can't do as well as you? // 이~ 재미있는 책은 없다 No book is more interesting than this one. // 오늘날~ 문명이 발달한 시대는 없었다 At no time has civilization made so great advance as at present. // 당신은 나이~ 늙어[젊어] 보이지 않습니다 You don't look your age.

만판 1 [마음껏] to one's heart's content; to one's satisfaction; heartily; as much as one likes[wishes]; to the full; to the utmost [hilt]; without reserve; unreservedly. ¶~ 먹다[마시다] eat[drink] one's fill[to one's heart's content / as much as one likes]. **2** [마냥] entirely; wholly; solely; exclusively; merely; simply; only; always. ¶~ 놀기만 하다 be always playing[idle] / do nothing but idle[play] / spend one's time (in) doing nothing.

만평(漫評) [생각나는 대로 비평함] a rambling [desultory] criticism; literary gossip; [만화로 비평함] making a caricature of; a satirical cartoon. ¶시사 ~ rambling criticism on current events[topics]. **만평하다** (글로) criticize ramblingly[desultorily]; gossip (on literary works); (만화로) make a caricature of.

만필(漫筆) stray[random / rambling] notes; random jottings; causeries (신문·잡지의).

만하(晩夏) late summer; the last[latter] part of summer.

만하다 1 [가치가 있다] be worth; be worthy of; deserve (of); merit; claim; be entitled to. ¶볼 만한 것 a sight / a spectacle / an attraction // (미) highlight // ~가 볼 만한 곳 a place worth visiting // 믿을 만한 정보 trustworthy information // 주목할 ~ be worthy of note // 볼 만하기도 하고 들을 만하기도 하다 be both worth seeing and worth hearing // 가 볼 ~ be worth[worthy of] a visit // 참 볼 만했다 It was something to see[watch]. / It was a thing worthy of seeing. / (비꼬아서) It was a sight to see. // 그의 얼굴은 볼 만했다 His face was a comical[perfect] study. // 그녀는 의논 [상의]을 할 만한 친구가 없었다 She had no friend to consult. // 그는 믿을 만한 사람이다 He is a trustworthy man. // 그의 행위는 칭찬할 ~ His deed deserves[is worthy of] praise. // 그 계획은 검토할 ~ The plan is worth considering. // 그 사람이라면 이 직책을 맡을 ~ He has the ability[what it takes] to fill this position.
2 [가능하다] be likely (to do); be probable; be in all likelihood[probability]; [적절하다] be fit (for service); be fitted (to); be suited (to); be suitable (for one's purpose); (족하다] be sufficient (to do); be ... enough (to). ¶~ be fit for use / can be used // 먹을 ~ be good to eat / be fit for eating / be fit to be eaten // 내가 회답을 늦춘 것은 그럴 만한 이유가 있었던 것이다 I had a good reason for delaying my answer. // 그는 매우 열심히 일했고 그 노력에 어울릴 만한 성과를 올렸다 He worked very hard and achieved results matching[(문어) commensurate with] his efforts. // 나는 코트를 놓아둘 만한 장소를 찾아보았다 I looked for a place to put my coat.

만학(晚學) a late education; studying late in life. **만학하다** get a late education; study late in life.
● 만학자 a late learner.

만학천봉(萬壑千峯) deep valleys and craggy peaks.

만행(蠻行) barbarity; savagery; brutality; cruelty; an atrocity; a savage deed; an outrage. ¶~을 저지르다 commit an act of brutality // 그들의 ~을 규탄하다 impeach them for their brutalities.

만혼(晚婚) (a) late marriage; (a) marriage late in life. **만혼하다** get married late; marry late in life. ¶저 부부는 만혼했다 The couple married late (in life).

만화(漫畵) comics; [풍자·시사만화 등] a cartoon; [풍자적인 회화] a caricature; [이야기를 그림과 문장으로 엮은 극화] story comics. ¶불량 ~ substandard comic books // 연재 ~ serial comics // 토막 ~ (몇 장면의) a comic strip / (영) a strip cartoon // 한 토막 ~ a single-frame cartoon // 네 토막 ~ a four-frame comic strip // 소년[소녀] ~ comics for boys[girls] // ~를 그리다 draw a cartoon // 돈키호테를 ~로 그리다 turn Don Quixote into a cartoon / make a cartoon out of Don Quixote // 나는 그것을 ~로 만들어 보겠다 I will make a caricature of it.
● 만화가 a cartoonist; (풍자만화가) a caricaturist; a comic artist. **만화 영화** a cartoon film; a movie cartoon; an animated (film) cartoon. **만화 잡지** a comic magazine. **만화책** a comic book.

만화경(萬華鏡) a kaleidoscope. ¶~ 같은 kaleidoscopic (changes).

만회(挽回) retrieval; recovery; restoration; revival. ¶야당 측의 세력 ~가 기대된다 It is hoped that the opposition parties will stage a comeback[make a recovery / recoup their losses]. **만회하다** retrieve (one's fortune / credit); restore[redeem] (one's honor); recover (one's good reputation); revive (activity in the market); regain. ¶세력을 ~ regain one's strength / 2회전에서 그는 만회했다 He made a comeback[rallied] in the second round. // 페넌트 레이스의 종반 가까이에서 그 팀은 세력을 만회하기 시작했다 Toward the end of the pennant race, the team began to regain lost ground. // 야당은 세력을 만회했다 The opposition parties

많다 (수가) many (things / persons); (문어) many a (thing / person) (▶ 단수 취급); a good[great] many; a large number of (things / persons) (▶ 복수 취급); (구어) lots of (things / persons); (양이) much; plenty of; a good[great] deal of; a large quantity of; (구어) lots of. (▶ 다음에 이어지는 명사는 불가산 명사, 단수 취급, 구어로는 many, 특히 much는 흔히 긍정문에는 쓰이지 않고, 부정문, 의문문, 조건문 등에 쓰임. 긍정문에서는 대신 (양수) a lot of, lots of, plenty of; (양) a great deal of; (수) a large number of를 씀. 긍정문에서도 주어를 수식하는 경우나, as, so, too 등에 이어질 경우에는 much, many가 쓰임) ¶많은 사람들 a great number of[a great many] people / numbers[scores / crowds] of people / a great crowd[throng] of people // 많은 지식 a great store[stock / wealth] of knowledge / a mine of information // 친구는 많습니까 Do you have many[a lot of] friends? / 나는 될 수 있는 대로 많은 책을 읽고 싶다 I want to read as many books as I can. // 이 산에는 많은 야생 원숭이가 있다 This mountain is full of wild monkeys. / There are a great many[a lot of / a large number of] wild monkeys on this mountain. // 이 저자에 대해서는 많은 것이 언급되어 있지는 않다 Not much has been said about this author. // 오늘의 숙제가 ~ We have a lot of homework today. // 아직 시간이 ~ We have plenty of time yet. // 음식물이 ~은 ~ We have plenty of food[time]. // 우리는 많은 이익을 얻기를 바랍니다 We expect a large[substantial] profit. // 그는 많은 돈을 저축하고 있었다 He had hoarded up a large sum of money. // 나는 많은 잔소리를 들었다 I got a good scolding. // 나는 집에서 지내는 시간이 ~ I spend most of my time at home. // 대학 생활을 즐기지 않는 학생이 많아졌다 An increasing number of students are finding university life dull. // 많아야 3일 걸릴 집이다 It'll take three days at the longest[most]. // 올 사람은 많아야 50명이 될 것이다 We expect fifty people at most.

많이 〔다수〕 in large[great] numbers; (미) aplenty; 〔많이〕 plentifully; in plenty; amply; abundantly; in abundance; in profusion; in large quantities; in a large amount; in full measure; 〔그만큼〕 ~ as much as that / (구어) that much[many] // ~ 있다 be abundant[plentiful] / abound in[with] / be full of // ~ 사다 buy (lavatory paper) in bulk // 담배를 ~ 피우다 smoke heavily[too much / to excess] // 돈을 ~ 벌다 make[amass] a fortune / coin money / (속어) make a pile (of money) / make money in cartloads // 올 여름에는 비가 ~ 왔다 We had a copious rainfall this summer. // 나는 아침밥을 ~ 먹지 않았다 I didn't eat much for breakfast. // 너무 ~ 마시면 몸에 해롭다 Too much drinking is bad for your health. // ~ 먹었습니다 (상대가 음식 등을 권했을 때) Thank you I've had plenty. / No more, thank you. // ~ 드십시오 Eat your fill. / Help yourself to as much as you like. // 그는 상스러운[더러운 / 천한] 말을 ~ 쓴다 He uses a lot of bad[dirty] language. // 그 물에는 소금이 ~ 포함되어 있었다 The water contained a large quantity of salt.

맏- firstborn; first; eldest; oldest.
맏딸 the eldest daughter; the first daughter.
맏며느리 the eldest daughter-in-law; the wife of the eldest son.
맏물 〔그해 맨 처음 생산된 것〕 the first fruits; the earliest produce[crops / fruits] of the season; the first product of the season; the first supply (of bonito[tomatoes]); the first crop (곡식·과일); the first cut(채소 등). ¶~ 사과 apples from the first crop / the first apples of the season / early apples // ~만 찾는 사람 a novelty seeker // ~ 딸기를 먹다 eat early strawberries.
맏배 the firstborn (of animals); the first batch [hatch / litter].
맏사위 the husband of one's firstborn[eldest] daughter; one's eldest son-in-law.
맏상제 (-喪制) the chief mourner; the eldest son of the deceased.
맏손녀 (-孫女) one's firstborn granddaughter by one's eldest son.
맏손자 (-孫子) one's firstborn grandson by one's eldest son.
맏아들 the firstborn[eldest] son.
맏이 the firstborn (son); the eldest (child). ¶~로 태어나다 be born first / be the eldest // 내가 ~오 I am the eldest.
맏잡이 〔맏아들〕 one's eldest son; 〔맏며느리〕 one's eldest daughter-in-law; the wife of one's eldest son.
맏형 (-兄) one's eldest[(미) oldest] brother.

말¹ 〔동〕 a horse; (암말) a mare; (종마) a stallion; a stud; (새끼 말) a foal; (새끼 수말) a colt; (새끼 암말) a filly; (조랑말) a pony. ¶경마용 ~ a race horse / a racer // ~을 타다 ride a horse / mount[get on] a horse // ~ 타고 가다 go on horse-back / ride horseback // ~에서 내리다 dismount / alight from[get off] a horse // ~에서 떨어지다 fall off[be thrown from] one's horse // ~에서 내동댕이쳐지다 be thrown off a horse // ~을 길들이다 break in [train] a horse / bust a bronco // ~을 달리다 gallop a horse / spur a horse on // 그는 안장 없는 ~도 잘 탄다 He can ride a horse well bareback, too. // 그는 (말고삐를 당겨) ~을 세웠다 He reined in his horse. // 젊은 아가씨가 ~을 붙잡고 있었다 A young girl was holding the horse.

말 갈 데 소 간다(속담) One goes where one shouldn't.
말 타면 경마 잡히고 싶다(속담) The more one has, the more one wants.

말² (장기의) a pondweed; algae (sing. alga); 〔수초〕 a waterweed. ¶바닷~ seaweed.
말³ (장기의) a chessman; a piece; a man; (체커의) a checker; (영) a draughtsman. ¶~을 움직이다 move a piece / make a move.
말⁴ **1** 〔계량기〕 a measure containing about 18 liters. **2** 〔계량의 단위〕 a unit of measure.
말⁵ 〔언어〕 language; speech; 〔단어〕 a word; a term; 〔집합적〕 wordage; (두 단어 이상의) an expression; a phrase; (글로 쓴) a written word; parlance(어법); 〔표현〕 phraseology; diction; wording; an expression; 〔언어〕 a language; a tongue; 〔방언〕 a dialect; 〔진술〕 a statement; a remark; 〔언사〕 what one says; a remark; a statement; an observa-

말

tion; [담화] a talk; (a) conversation; a chat; [연설] a speech; an address. ¶한국~ Korean / the Korean language // 자기 나라 ~ one's native tongue [language] / one's mother tongue / one's own language / the vernacular (language) // 외국~ a foreign language // 상~ vulgar speech // 서울~ Seoul speech // 시골~ a local dialect / dialect speech / country [rustic / rural] speech // 표준~ the standard language // 진부한 ~ a stereotyped phrase [expression] / 악의에 찬 ~ a malicious statement [remark] // 동정의 ~ a word of sympathy // 혀가 잘 돌지 않는 [발음하기 어려운] ~ a tongue twister / a jawbreaker // 입에 발린 ~ lip homage // 가시가 돋친 ~ harsh language / stinging [barbed] words / cynical words / a caustic remark // 달콤한 ~ honeyed [sweet / cajoling] words // 이별의 ~ one's parting words / farewell speech / a valediction // 인사~ a greeting // 하는 ~과 하는 행동 saying and doing / words and deeds // 하고 싶은 ~ what one wants [has] to say // ~의 장벽 a language barrier // ~의 묘미 a figure of speech // ~이 많은 사람 a wordy [talkative / garrulous / loquacious] person / a controversialist / a man of many words // [수다쟁이] a gossiper / a chatterbox / a gibberer / ~이 적은 사람 a man of few words / a silent [a taciturn / a tight lipped / an uncommunicative] person // 교묘한 ~로 with honeyed [sweet / cajoling] words // 조용한 ~로 in a calm [quiet] tone // 다른 ~로 말하면 in other words / to put it another way // ~로는 표현할 수 없는 아름다움 inexpressible [indescribable] beauty // ~을 잘하는 사람 a fluent [glib] talker // ~을 꺼내기 어려운 일 a matter hard to broach // ~이 거칠다 be rough of speech / be rough-spoken // ~이 막히다 be at a loss for a word [words] // ~이 서투르다 be a poor speaker / be poor at talking // ~이 통하다 make oneself understood / a language is spoken // ~이 틀리다 a remark does not tally / talk a different story / be a horse of a different color // 대답할 ~이 없다 have no word in reply / words fail (one) to reply // ~에 궁하다 be at a loss for words // ~을 나누다 talk with a person // ~을 걸다 address (a person) // ~을 삼가다 mind one's language / watch what one says // ~을 흐리다 speak ambiguously [evasively] / do not commit oneself // 남의 ~을 막다 interrupt a person / break in while a person is talking // 어떤 나라의 ~을 알다 know the language of a country // ~을 꺼내다 begin to talk / start a talk / broach a subject / break the ice // ~을 꾸미다 use fine language / use fair words / adorn one's words / euphemize / talk in fine language // ~을 돌리다 switch the conversation / change the subject // ~을 꺼내기를 망설이다 hesitate to speak out // 감정을 ~로 표현하다 express [describe] (one's) feelings in words // …라고 해도 지나친 ~이 아니다 It is not too much to say that …. // 약속을 지키지 않은 것에 대해 어떤 할 ~이 있느냐 What is your excuse for not keeping your promise? // 나도 거기에는 할 ~이 있다 I have an objection to that. / I have a complaint to make in that connection. // ~ (이) 없는 대중의 목소리를 들어라 Listen to the silent majority. // 총탄 자국이 난 자동차는 그 비극에 대한 ~ 없는 증인이었다 The bullet-marked car bore mute witness to the tragedy. // 술이 들어가니 그는 더욱 ~이 많아졌다 Liquor made him even more talkative [(문어) loquacious]. // 네 ~이 옳아 Well said! / What you say is to the point. // 그의 ~에는 모가 나 있다 He talks sarcastically [bitingly]. // 그녀의 ~에는 사투리가 섞여 있다 She speaks with an accent. // 그는 ~에 힘을 주며 그 계획을 예정대로 실행하겠다고 단언했다 He declared emphatically that he would carry out the plan. // 프랑스 ~로 ~이 통했다 I was able to make myself understood in French. // 그 느낌은 ~로 표현할 수 없다 The sensation is beyond expression [description]. / The sensation is indescribable [inexpressible]. // ~로는 형언할 수 없는 고통이었다 The pain was beyond words [description]. // 그는 ~을 이리저리 돌리며 후원자의 이름을 밝히려 하지 않았다 He used excuses and evasions to avoid giving the name of his sponsor. / He equivocated [beat around the bush] and would not give the name of his sponsor. // 내가 온갖 ~을 다해서 설명했는데도 그는 이해하지 못했다 He still didn't understand even after so much explanation (and reasoning). // 그녀는 ~을 잘할 줄 모른다 She does not know how to say [how to speak] things properly. // 그녀는 기쁨에 벅차서 무슨 ~을 해야 할지 몰랐다 She was so overcome by [with] joy that she was at a loss for words [she didn't know what to say]. // 마루의 핏자국을 보고 나는 ~을 잃었다 My voice failed me when I saw the blood on the floor. // 그는 화가 나서 며칠 동안 내게 ~을 하지 않았다 He was angry and wouldn't speak to me for days. // 그녀는 한번 ~을 꺼내면 물러설 줄 모른다 Once she has said something, she will never take back her words. / Once she has spoken her mine, she will stick to it. // 그가 경주에 가자고 ~을 꺼냈다 He suggested that we go to Gyeongju. // 그녀는 남이 하는 ~을 경청한다 She is a good listener. // 나는 그의 ~을 잊을 수가 없다 His words [remarks] still linger in my mind. / I cannot forget what he said. // 그는 고별의 ~을 했다 He made a farewell address [speech]. // 그 사람은 말을 더듬는 버릇이 있다 He is apt to stutter [falter in speaking]. // 그의 ~을 빌리면 그녀는 달의 여신이다 To borrow his expression [As he puts it / In his phrase], she is a Diana. // 이렇게 말하고 그는 ~을 맺었다 With these words he concluded [finished] his speech. // 아버지는 어머니를 잘 보살펴 드리라는 ~을 내게 남기고 런던으로 부임했다 Telling me to take good care of Mother, Father left to take up his job in London. // 나는 무엇인가 ~을 빠뜨린 것만 같다 I have the feeling there's something I forgot to mention. // 그 사람의 ~을 들어 보자 Let him have his say! // 네가 하고 싶은 ~을 해 보아라 Speak your piece. / Let's hear what you have to [want to] say. // 그의 칭찬은 ~뿐이다 His praise is just so much talk. // 그는 ~과 마음이 다를 때가 있다 He doesn't always say what he means. // 그 따위 ~은 듣고 싶지 않아 I won't listen to such words. / Don't you dare say such a thing to me. // 그들이 하는 일이란 ~뿐이고 아무런 실

천도 하지 않는다 All they ever do is talk; they never do anything.∥그게 그가 입버릇처럼 외는 ∼이다 That's his favorite saying[pet line].∥그를 현대의 갈릴레오라고 말하는 것은 지나친(과장된) ∼이다 It is an overstatement [exaggeration] to call him a modern Galileo. ∥그것은 지나친 ∼이 아닌가 Aren't you putting it rather strongly?∥지구가 돈다는 ∼을 맨 처음 한 사람이 누구냐 Who was the first to say that the earth rotates?∥죽은 사람은 ∼이 없다 Dead men tell no tales.
2 [속담] a (common) saying; a proverb; a say; an adage; [금언] a maxim; an apo(ph)thegm. ¶옛 ∼에도 있듯이 as the proverb says[goes / has it].
3 [꾸중·잔소리] (a) scolding; a rebuke; a lecture; faultfinding; [속어] a talking-to; a nagging. ¶∼ 많은 여편네 a termagant wife ∥그는 늘 ∼을 듣는다 He is a constant victim of nagging.
4 [소문] a rumor; a report; gossip; common talk; a story; a whisper. ¶밑도 끝도 없는 ∼ a groundless rumor / an unfounded report / a canard∥∼이 퍼지다 be talked[gossiped] about / become the talk (of) / be in everybody's mouth∥그 사람에 대해서는 항간에 ∼이 많다 Various rumors are abroad about him.∥나에 대한 항간의 ∼ 따위에 나는 신경을 쓰지 않는다 I do not care what people say about me.
5 [전갈] a (verbal) message[communication]; word (of mouth). ¶∼을 전하다 deliver [give] a (verbal) message / send word[a message] (to).
6 [주장] one's say; what one has to say; one's claim[point / case]. ¶그의 ∼에 의하면 according to him∥양쪽 ∼을 듣다 hear both sides (of the story) / listen to the cause of either party∥그에게도 할 ∼이 있다 He too has a case.∥내 ∼이 그 ∼이야 That's my point. / That's what I'm saying. / You can say that again. / You said it.
7 [명분·이름]. ¶∼뿐인 insincere / specious / nominal / in name only / titular / token (concession)∥그는 그녀의 ∼뿐인 변명을 꿰뚫어보았다 He saw through her specious excuse.∥그들은 여성의 지위에 대해 ∼로만 경의를 표하고 있다 They only pay lip service to women's status.
8 [뜻] (a) meaning; a sense. ¶도대체 무슨 ∼인지 모르겠다 I can't make out what it is all about. / I can't make head or tail of it.
9 [이유·원인] (a) reason; (a) cause; ground(s). ¶무면허로 운전을 하다 남을 치다니 참으로 ∼도 안 되는 행위다 It is perfectly outrageous to drive a car without a license and hit somebody.
말은 적을수록 좋다(속담) The less said, the better.; (The) least said, (the) soonest mended.
말 한마디에 천 냥 빚도 갚는다(속담) One should be wary of one's words.; Your tongue can make or break you.
말(이) 나다 1 [이야기에 오르다] be brought into conversation; be talked about; become the topic[subject] of a talk[conversation]; be broached; be proposed; be taken up. ¶말난 김에 by the way / in passing / incidentally / in the course of conversation. **2** [소문나다] be gossiped about; become the talk (of); be in everybody's mouth; be in the air; be rumo(u)red; (비밀이) come[be] out; leak (out); be disclosed[revealed]; come [be brought] to light; transpire. ¶말이 날까 두려우니 아무한테도 이야기 말게 Don't tell anybody about it. — I'm afraid of its leaking out.
말(을) 내다 1 [이야기에 올리다] begin to talk about; broach (a subject) bring into conversation; propose (a plan); advance [put forth / offer] (an opinion). ¶이야기 중에 장사에 관한 일을 ∼ bring[(구어) lug] business matters into conversation∥누가 말을 냈는지 모르지만 근거 없는 이야기이다 I don't know who started the story, but it is entirely groundless. **2** (비밀 등을) tell to others; divulge; blab; reveal; let out; disclose; betray. ¶말을 내지 않다 keep (a matter) (a) secret / keep silent (about a matter) / keep (a secret) (closely) to oneself / lock (a secret) in one's breast∥말을 내지 않겠다고 맹세하다 swear[vow] secrecy.
말(이) 되다 [이치에 맞다] stand[conform / be conformable] to reason; be reasonable; accord with reason; be logical. ¶말도 되지 않다 be unreasonable / do not stand[be contrary] to reason.
말(이) 뜨다 slow-spoken; slow in one's speech.
말(이) 아니다 1 [이치에 맞지 않다] absurd; outrageous; unreasonable; ridiculous; preposterous; nonsensical. ¶말이 아닌 요구 a preposterous[an unconscionable] demand ∥말이 아닌 소리를 하다 speak[talk] through (the back of) one's neck∥그건 말도 아니다 What's a thing to say! / Absurd! / Impossible! / Far from it! / That's (glorious) nonsense! **2** [형편없다] miserable; wretched; pitiful; (서술적) be in bad shape; be in very poor condition. ¶옷차림이 ∼ be shabbily [poorly] dressed∥체면이 ∼ utterly lose one's face[prestige]∥생활이 ∼ lead a miserable[wretched] life∥형편이 ∼ be in a piteous plight∥그 사람의 요즈음 건강이 ∼ He is in pretty bad shape[very poor health] these days.

말(末) **1** [끝·마지막] the end[close] (of). ¶9월 ∼에 at the end of September∥8월 ∼경에 귀성합니다 I'll go home in late August. **2** [야구] the second[lower / last] half; the bottom. ¶양키즈는 3회 ∼에 2점을 얻었다 The Yankees scored two runs in the bottom half of the third inning.
말갈기 a horse's mane.
말갛다 clear; clean; limpid; pure. ¶말간 물 clear[crystal] water∥말갛게 하다 clear / make clear / clarify.
말개지다 become clear; clear; clarify; get clean.
말거리 1 the cause[source] of trouble. ⇨ 말썽거리 ¶∼를 일으키다 raise[make] / cause trouble / lead to a dispute / raise [kick up] a dust / have a[get into] trouble (with). **2** [화제] a subject (of talk); a topic (of conversation). ¶∼가 동이 났다 We have no more topics to talk about. / We have emptied the bag.
말거머리 [동] a horseleech.
말경(末境) **1** [끝판] an end; a close; a conclusion; a termination; a finale; a denouement.

2 [말년] old [advanced] age; senescence; one's declining years.

말고기 horsemeat; horseflesh; horse beef.

말고삐 a bridle; reins; ribbons. ¶~를 잡다 hold [lead] a horse by the bridle / handle the reins // ~를 늦추다 slacken the reins // ~를 잡아당기다 draw rein / rein in (a horse) / check (a horse) with reins // ~를 잡아당겨 말을 멈추다 rein up [back] a horse.

말공대(-恭待) addressing in honorifics; respectful address. **말공대하다** use polite expressions; address in honorifics.

말괄량이 a hussy; a minx; a flapper; a hoyden; a tomboy; a tomboyish girl; a kitten; a romp; a romping [bouncing] girl; a giglet; a giglot; (구어) a filly; a shrew. ¶~ 같은 [사내아이 같은] tomboyish / romping / bouncing / pert / forward / saucy.

말구유 [말먹이를 담는 그릇] a manger; a crib; a horse trough.

말구종(-驅從) a groom; a footman; an ostler; (영) a horseboy.

말굴레 a headstall; a headgear; a bridle; a halter.

말굽 a horse's hoof; a horseshoe(편자). ¶~ 모양의 horseshoe-shaped / U-shaped // ~을 대다 [박다] shoe a horse.
● **말굽 소리** the sound of a horse's hoofs; the clatter of a horse's hoofs; hoofbeat. **말굽자석** [물] a horseshoe magnet.

말귀 [말뜻] the import [meaning] of the words; [알아듣는 총명] hearing; understanding; catching on; an ear (for words). ¶~ 밝다 be quick of hearing / be quick-eared / have long ears / be able to distinguish delicate shades of meaning // ~가 어둡다 be dull [weak] of hearing / have a bad ear / be slow in understanding what (a person) says // ~가 빠르다 be quick to understand what (a person) says / catch on quick // ~를 못 알아듣다 can't make out what (a person) says / ~를 알아듣다 understand the meaning / make sense (of).

말기 (末期) the end; the close; the last period [years / days / stage]; the late stage(s). ¶~ 증상의 환자 a terminal patient / a patient in the terminal stage // 전쟁의 ~ the last stage of the war // 빅토리아조 ~에 in the last years of the Victorian age / in the late Victorian age // ~ 암 terminal cancer // 19세기 ~에 at the close of the 19th century // ~ 증상을 보이다 show signs of a downfall.

말꼬리 the end of words [speech]. ⇨ 말끝

말꼬리(를) **잡다** pounce on a person's words. ¶남의 말꼬리를 잡고 늘어지다 pick [cavil] at a person's words / trip a person up / find fault with a person's remark.

말꼬투리 a fault on a person's words. ¶~를 잡다 pounce on a person's words / find fault with a person's remark.

말꼴 horse-fodder; provender [forage (grass) / hay / feed] for horses. ¶~을 주다 fodder [give fodder to] a horse / feed (green grass) to a horse.

말꾸러기 1 [잔말이 많은 사람] a prattler; a tattler; a chatterbox; a babbler; (속어) a chatterbug. **2** a troublemaker; a mischief-maker. ⇨ 말썽꾼(⇨말썽)

말끄러미 with a blank [vacant] look. ⇨ 물끄러미

말끔 clean; all; utterly; completely; entirely; thoroughly; totally; wholly. ¶빚을 ~ 갚다 clear oneself of one's debts / pay [repay] all one's debts // 세간을 ~ 치우다 carry off all the furniture // 문제를 ~ 해결하다 settle the question once (and) for all.

말끔하다 clean(ly); clear; neat and tidy; pretty; comely; fair; fine; graceful. ¶말끔한 집[방] a neat house [room] // 말끔한 옷차림을 하다 dress oneself cleanly / be finely dressed / (미국 속어) be dolled up. **말끔히** clean(ly); clearly; neatly. ¶~ 쓸어 내다 clean [clear] out // ~ 닦다 wipe (a thing) clean // 수염을 ~ 깎다 shave closely / be clean shaven // 방을 ~ 치워 두다 keep a room clean (and tidy) / keep a room in good order.

말끝 the end of words [speech]; concluding remarks; the ending [termination] of a word. ¶~을 흐리다 slur the end of one's words [sentence] / leave one's statement vague / give a vague answer // ~을 맺다 conclude one's speech // 그는 ~마다 욕을 한다 He never opens his lips without curse and swear.

말년 (末年) **1** (일생의) one's later [latter / last / declining] years; the latter part of one's life; the close [evening] of one's life [days]; one's closing days. ¶~의 톨스토이 Tolstoy in his later years // ~에 접어들다 enter the twilight of one's life. **2** the end; the close. ⇨ 말기

말다¹ [돌돌 감다] roll (paper); roll (a thing) up (in paper). ¶돛을 ~ furl [hoist] a sail // 담배를 ~ roll a cigarette // 장막을 말아 올리다 gather up a curtain // 말아 넣다 roll [wrap] (up) in / enfold // 종이[지도]를 ~ roll (up) a piece of paper [a map].

말다² (물이나 국에) put (boiled rice) into soup [water]; mix (food) with (soup / water). ¶국에 밥을 ~ put rice into soup // 국수를 ~ put noodles into soup / prepare noodles.

말다³ [그만두다] stop; cease; discontinue; break [leave / lay / call] off; give [throw] up; quit; abandon; cut off; desist from (doing). ¶먹다 만 바나나 a half-eaten banana // 피우다 만 담배 a half-smoked cigarette // 하다 만 일을 하다 do an unfinished task // 일을 (하다 가) ~ leave [knock] off work / lay aside [cease] one's work / (구어) chuck one's job // 이런 이야기는 맙시다 Let's drop [have done with] the subject. // 비가 오다 말다 It started to rain and then stopped. // 먼저 쓰다 만 편지를 마치게 해 주시오 Let me first finish the letter I have been writing. // 그는 일을 하다 말고 나가 버렸다 He went out leaving his work unfinished [half done]. // 그 사람 말고 그의 부인이 왔었다 It was his wife, not he, that came. // 너 말고 누가 그런 짓을 하겠느냐 Who would do such a thing but you? // 그 말고는 믿을 사람이 아무도 없다 There is no one to rely on but [except] him. // 이것 말고는 달리 방법이 없었다 We had no alternative. / There was no way but this. // 보나 마나 그 기도는 실패할 것이 뻔하다 The attempt is necessarily foredoomed to failure.

말다⁴ **1** [금지] don't; keep [refrain] from (doing). ¶잊지 마라 Don't forget. // 가지 말자 Let's not go. // 마음을 놓고 말게 Don't fall asleep at the switch, now. // 서슴지 말고 전화 해 주십시오 Don't hesitate to telephone me.

//진열품에 손을 대지 마시오 Do Not Touch. / Please Do Not Touch the Exhibits.// 잔디밭에 들어가지 마시오 Keep Off the Grass.// 허가 없이 들어오지 마시오 No Entry To Unauthorized Persons.
2 [필경] end up (doing); finally do; get around to (doing). ¶그는 술 때문에 죽고 말았다 Drink ended him.// 필경 싸움이 벌어지고 말겠구나 I am afraid there will be a fight after all.// 그는 그 일을 너무 생각한 나머지 미치고 말았다 He took the matter too much to heart, until (at last) he went mad.// 이 일을 꼭 해 놓고야 말겠다 I will get this job done if it kills me!

말다툼 [말싸움] a (verbal) quarrel; [논쟁] an argument; a dispute; a wordy conflict [battle]; a row; a wrangle; an altercation; bickering(s); (exchange of) high words; a brawl; a rhubarb; a fracas; a jangle. ¶두 사람이 만나기만 하면 ~이 시작된다 Whenever the two meet, there is an exchange of fiery words [they get into a bitter argument].// 나는 가게(家計) 문제로 아내와 ~을 했다 I got into a quarrel with my wife about our family budget.// 하찮은 일로 두 사람 사이에 ~이 벌어졌다 A dispute arose between them over a trifle. / They began to quarrel [bicker / argue] over a trifle. **말다툼하다** quarrel (with); have a quarrel [dispute] (with); dispute [argue] (with a person about something); have (angry / high / hot / warm / sharp) words (with); altercate; bicker; wrangle. ¶사소한 일로 남과 ~ quarrel with a person over [about] a small matter// 그는 아버지와 장래의 일로 말다툼했다 He had a quarrel [an angry dispute] with his father about his future.// 나는 집의 소유권 관계로 그들과 말다툼했다 I argued with them about the ownership of the house.

말단(末端) the end; the tip. ¶행정 기구의 ~ a government office in direct contact with the public / the smallest unit of the administrative organization// ~까지 전해지다 reach the rank and file // 중앙 지도부의 의도가 ~에까지 철저하다 The aims of the central leadership were carried out at even the lowest level(s).
●**말단 공무원** a petty [minor] official; an understrapper; 《영》 a humble placeman. **말단 기관** terminal offices [organs]. **말단 사원** a minor clerk.

말대꾸 a retort; a back talk; (give) a back answer; answering [talking] back; contradiction; (미국 속어) a crack. **말대꾸하다** answer (a person) back; talk [speak] back (to a person); contradict (a person); retort; give (a person) a retort [back talk]; (속어) sass. ¶손윗사람한테 ~ talk back to one's superiors // 아들은 꾸중을 듣자 아버지의 말이 무리라고 말대꾸했다 Scolded, the boy retorted [shot back] that his father was being unreasonable.// 말대꾸하지 마라 Don't talk back.

말대답(-對答) a retort; a back talk. ⇨"말대꾸

말더듬이 a stammerer; a stutterer. ¶그는 심한 ~ He stammers badly.

말동무 a conversational partner. ⇨"말벗

말똥 horse dung [droppings]; stable manure.

말똥가리 [동] a common buzzard.

말똥거리다 roll (one's eyes) vacantly. ¶누운 채 눈을 말똥거리며 천장만 바라보다 lie with a vacant stare at the ceiling.

말똥말똥 ¶~ 얼굴을 쳐다보다 stare a person in the face / look [stare] hard at a person / gaze steadily at a person. **말똥말똥하다** (잠이 안 와서) wakeful; wide-awake. ¶시계가 두 시를 쳤는데 눈은 더욱 말똥말똥했다 The clock struck two, and my wakefulness increased.

말뚝 a stake; a post; a pile; a picket(울타리 등의). ¶~치기 piling / pile driving// ~ 박는 기계 a pile driver / a piling gin // ~을 박다 drive in a stake [a post] // ~을 뽑다 extract a pile [post] // 경계선을 따라 ~을 박다 plant stakes along a boundary line// 부지 입구에 ~ 두 개를 세웠다 I set up two stakes at the entrance to the lot.

말뜻 the meaning of a word; acceptation.

말라기서(-書) [성] (The Book of) Malachi(약어 Mal).

말라깽이 a skinny [very lean / scrawny] person; a (living) skeleton; a bag of bones.

말라리아 [의] malaria. ¶~에 걸린 malarial / malarian / malarious // ~에 **걸리다** contract [be stricken with] malaria.
●**말라리아열** malaria fever. **말라리아 환자** a malarial patient.

말라붙다 (액체 등이) dry up; be dried up. ¶고양이의 말라붙은 시체 the dried-up corpse of a cat // 말라붙은 레몬 a shriveled lemon // 이 더위에 꽃이 말라붙었다 The flowers have shriveled [dried up] in this heat. // 오랜 가뭄으로 논이 말라붙었다 A long drought made the rice fields dry up. // 샘[강]이 말라붙었다 The well went [The river ran] dry.

말랑거리다 be soft [plastic / tender].

말랑말랑하다 soft; spongy; tender; plastic; squashy(과일 등이 너무 익어서). ¶말랑말랑한 군고구마 nice and soft sweet potatoes (hot from the oven) // 말랑말랑한 사람 a person easy to deal with / a softy / a sissy // 만져 보니 ~ feel soft / be soft to the touch // 빵이 말랑말랑하게 구워졌다 The bread has been baked nice and soft.

말려들다 [연루되다] be implicated in; be involved [entangled] in; get mixed up in; be concerned with. ¶싸움에 ~ get entangled in [(구어) be dragged into] a quarrel // 범죄[음모]에 ~ be implicated in a crime [plot] // 전쟁에 ~ be dragged [drawn] into a war // 사건에 ~ be involved in [get dragged into] an affair // 기계에 ~ be caught in a machine // 나는 그의 교활한 질문에 말려들었다 I was taken in [fooled] by a tricky question he asked me.// 그는 파벌 싸움에 말려들었다 He was entangled [caught up] in factional strife.

말로(末路) one's last days; the end; the fate. ¶영웅의 ~ the last phase of a heroic career / the last days of a hero // 인생의 ~ the end of one's career // 그의 ~는 뻔하다 I can see his finish. // 그는 비참한 ~를 보냈다 He spent his last days in misery. / He had a miserable end.

말리다¹ (감겨서) be rolled [curled] (up). ¶치맛자락이 ~ the end of a skirt is rolled.

말리다² **1** [만류하다] (try to) stop [keep / prevent / (문어) dissuade] (a person from doing something); (try to) persuade (a person not to do). ¶그는 아이들이 새끼 고양

말리다

이를 괴롭히는 것을 말렸다 He stopped the children from teasing the kitten.// 그는 그 언쟁을 말렸다 He stopped the quarrel.// 나는 사직하려는 그를 설득하여 말렸다 I persuaded him not to resign. / I dissuaded him from resigning.// 그는 감시원이 말리는 것도 듣지 않고 물이 불어난 강에서 헤엄치기 시작했다 He began to swim in the swollen river, in spite of the watchman's warning.// 나를 말리지 마라 Don't you try to stop me! / Don't start telling me not to do it.
2 [금지하다] forbid (a person to do); prohibit (a person from doing); debar[prevent] (a person from doing). ¶나무를 못 하게 ~ prohibit (people from) cutting the forest trees.

말리다³ [마르게 하다] dry; make[let] dry; weather; (식물을) let die; (목재를) season; (우물·재원 등을) exhaust; draw off (water); drain off[away]; air(빨래를). ¶충분히 말린 목재 well-seasoned wood// 고등어를 말린 것 a mackerel pike which has been cut open and dried// 빨래를 햇볕에 ~ dry the washing in the sun// 젖은 옷을 불에 ~ dry wet clothes by the fire// 젖은 옷을 ~ hang up[out] wet clothes to air// 돗자리를 ~ air mats// 연못을 ~ dry up a pond// 물 주는 일을 잊고 화분을 말려 버렸다 I forgot to water the potted plant and let it die.// 어떤 세균은 식물을 말려 버리는 경우도 있다 Certain bacteria cause blight in plants.// 그들은 지하자원을 마구 채굴하여 말려 버렸다 They exhausted their underground resources by mining them indiscriminately.

말림 1 conservancy [protection / restriction] (of forest / pasture). **말림하다** reserve (a forest); conserve. 2 a reserved forest. ⇨ 말림갓(⊕말림)
● **말림갓** a reserved forest; a forest reserve.

말마디 a bit[piece] of speech; a talk; a speech; a phrase; a clause. ¶그 사람은 ~나 할 줄 안다 He knows how to put a talk over. / He is quite a good speaker.

말막음 [입막음] hushing[shutting up; avoiding[forestalling] (another's) words. ¶나는 그에게 ~으로 십만 원을 줬다 I paid [gave] him 100,000 won hush money. / I bought his silence for 100,000 won. **말막음하다** hush up; shut (a person) up; stop (a person's) mouth; forestall another's word; allay; appease; get around[avoid] (a person's) words.

말머리 1 [말의 첫머리] the beginning of one's speech[talk]; introductory remarks; opening words; one's first few words. 2 [화제] the subject of one's speech. ¶~를 돌리다 change the[one's] subject / change the topic[subject] of conversation / shift the conversation.

말먹이 horse feed; fodder; hay; forage (grass); feed stuff; provender.

말몰이꾼 a pack-horse driver; a road-horse man.

말문 (-門) one's mouth when speaking.

말문(을) 열다 open one's case; open the conversation; break the silence. ¶그녀는 갑자기 말문을 열어 말을 쏟아 놓았다 She suddenly began to speak volubly. / Words suddenly began to pour from her lips as though a dam had broken.

말문이 막히다 be at a loss for words; not know what to say[answer]; be dumbfounded; be struck dumb (with surprise); be speechless; be agape (with wonder). ¶나는 그것을 보고 말문이 막혔다 I was dumbfounded at that[it]. / Words failed me at that.

말미 (a) leave of absence; (a) furlough; a vacation. ¶~를 주다 grant (a person) a leave of absence[furlough] // ~를 얻다 get [obtain / secure] a leave of absence / have a furlough // (사흘) day off / (반어적)~를 얻어 고향에 돌아가다 go home on furlough // 사흘간의 ~를 주셨으면 합니다 I should like to get three days' leave[day off] / Would you please give me three days' leave[furlough]?

말미 (末尾) the end; the close; the tip. ¶~의 last / final // 보고서의 ~에 at the end of a report // 그 단어의 ~의 문자가 빠져 있었다 The final letter of the word was missing.

말미암다 come from; arise from; be derived from; be owing to; be due to; be caused by; be in consequence of. ¶말미암아 owing to / because of / in consequence of / due to / in accordance with // 병으로 말미암아 on account of illness // 운전 부주의로 말미암은 사고 an accident due to careless driving // 감기로 말미암아 오지 못했다 Cold kept me from coming. // 그의 실패는 태만으로 말미암은 것이다 His failure is due to negligence.

말미잘 [동] a sea anemone; a seaflower.

말밑 the etymology[origin] of a word.

말발굽 a horse's hoof. ⇨ 말굽 ¶~ 소리가 들렸다 We heard the clatter of hooves[a horse's hoofs]. / The clatter of hoofs was heard. / Hoofbeats were heard.

말버릇 one's manner of speaking; one's way of talking. ¶고약한 ~ a mean[low] expression // ~이 나쁘다 have a foul tongue / be rude in speech[address] // ~ 좀 고쳐 봐라 Mind your speech! // 무슨 ~이 그러냐 How dare you talk to me like that? / (반어적) That's nice way to speak to me. // 그는 그것을 ~처럼 말하고 있다 He never opens his mouth without saying it. // 그것은 윗사람에게 하는 ~이 아니다 That is no way to talk to your superiors. / You should not use that kind of language with your superiors.

말버짐 [한] ringworm; psoriasis; fungus.

말벌 [동] a (ground) wasp; a kind of hornet; a yellow jacket.

말벗 a conversational partner; a friend to talk with; a companion to chat with. ¶좋은 ~ a boon companion / a crony / a pal // ~이 되다 keep (a person) company // ~이 없다 have no one to talk to[chit-chat with] // ~이 있으면 좋겠다 I want to have company to talk together with.

말보 talkativeness from a usually taciturn person. ¶~가 터지다 begin to talk freely / break the ice.

말복 (末伏) the last 10-day period of the dog days; the last phase of the dog days [midsummer heat].

말본 grammar. ⇨ 문법

말불버섯 [식] a puffball; a smut ball.

말뼈 [성질이 거센 사람] a wild fellow; a rough; a rowdy; (미) a tough.

말사 (末寺) a branch[subordinate] temple.

말살 (抹殺) [있는 것을 아주 없앰] liquidation; annihilation. **말살하다** kill; get rid of; liquidate; annihilate. ¶공산주의를 ~ liquidate communism// 프랑스 혁명은 귀족 계급을 말살했다 The French Revolution liquidated the nobility.

말상(-相) a horseface; an extremely long face. ¶~의 여자 a woman with a horseface [a long horse's face] / a horse-faced woman.

말석(末席) the lowest seat; the bottom; a back seat. ¶~을 차지하다 [출석하다] have the honor of being present at (a meeting) / [회원이다] have the honor of being a member (of)// 나는 언제나 학급의 ~입니다 I'm always at the bottom of the class.

말세(末世) the end of the world; [타락한 세상] a degenerate [corrupt] age; these latter days; the hopeless world; [최후의 심판일] the doomsday; the judgment day. ¶세상은 ~다 The world is going to the dogs. / It is indeed an age of decadence we live in. / 이쯤 되면 세상도 ~다 With things going on like this, the world has fallen on evil days. // ~에 살아서 무슨 낙이 있겠는가 What pleasure can I find, living in such a degenerate world?

말소(抹消) erasure; effacement; cancel; obliteration; blot; writing-off. ¶등기의 ~ cancellation of registration // ~회사 a defunct company. **말소하다** erase; efface; cancel; obliterate; blot out; strike [cross] out [off]; write off. ¶소송을 ~ withdraw a suit // 명부에서 이름을 ~ cross (a person's) name off [from] a list. ➔ 저 선수는 등록이 말소되었다 That player was taken off the active list. / (부상 때문에) That player was placed on the disabled list.

말소리 a voice; (속삭임) a whisper; a murmur. ¶~가 높다 have a loud voice / talk in a loud voice // ~가 들리다 hear (a person) talk // 옆방에서 사람들의 ~가 들렸다 I heard several voices talking in the next room.

말속 the implied meaning of one's words; the true intent; what is behind one's words; the implication of a remark; one's intention. ¶~을 모르다 miss the implication of what (a person) is saying / can't understand (a person's) intention.

말솜씨 one's way of speaking; eloquence. ¶~가 좋다 be good at speaking [talking] / be eloquent / be a good [glib] talker / have a ready [glib] tongue // ~가 없다 be poor at speaking [talking] / be a poor speaker // ~가 보통이 아니군 That's very nice way of putting it. / I'm quite flattered(알랑거리는 말을 듣고).

말수(-數) the number of words one speaks; words; speech. ¶~가 적은 사람 a taciturn [reticent] person / a man of few words // ~가 많은 사람 a talkative person / a chatterbox / a prattler // ~가 적다 be taciturn [reticent / laconic / terse] / be (a man) of few words / be reserved in speech // ~가 많다 be talkative [loquacious / voluble / verbose / wordy] // ~가 적다 He does not have a glib tongue. / He is a taciturn [reticent] person.

말술 a mal of wine; [많은 술] kegs of wine. ¶(술을) ~로 마시다 be capable of downing kegs [gallons] of wine / drink like a fish.

말승냥이 1 [동] [늑대] wolf (pl. wolves). 2 [키크고 사나운 사람] a tall [lank], wild person; (미) a gangling and violent-tempered fellow.

말실수(-失手) a tongueslip; a slip of the tongue; a slip [mistake] in speaking; a verbal lapse; an impropriety in speech. **말실수하다** make slip [lapse] of the tongue; make a slip [mistake] in speaking; use improper language [words]; commit an impropriety in speech; one's tongue slips. ¶말실수한 것을 사과하다 apologize for one's impropriety in speech // 말실수를 힐책하다 blame (a person) for his improper language.

말썽 trouble; difficulties; complaint; criticism; a dispute (분쟁); complication (분규). ¶~ 없이 without making complaints / without any objection // ~이 나 있다 be in trouble (with) // ~을 일으키다 cause trouble / lead to a dispute / rock the boat // 그는 동료들과 ~을 빚고 있다 He has gotten [(영) got] into trouble with his colleagues. // ~을 일으키지 않도록 조심해라 Be careful not to cause trouble. // ~이 일어날 것 같다 Trouble seems to be brewing. // 그 문제로 ~이 생긴 일이 있다 There has been a dispute over the matter. // 그는 그 계획에 ~을 일으켰다 He threw cold water on the plan. // 그와 아내와의 사이에 ~이 그치지 않는다 There is constant friction between him and his wife. // 그 녀석은 내가 하는 일마다 ~을 부린다 He finds fault with whatever I do.

●**말썽거리** the cause [source] of trouble; a matter for complaint; a source of dissatisfaction; the origin of a dispute; a bone of contention; an apple of discord; a cause of anxiety. ¶~가 되다 become a source of trouble [a matter for complaint] // ~를 만들다 sow (the seeds of) trouble [discord] / give rise to a quarrel // 그 정당 내부에 ~가 있는 것 같다 There seems to be internal trouble in the party. / There seems to be discord within the party. **말썽꾸러기** a troublemaker; a mischief-maker. ⇨ =**말썽꾼**(⇨**말썽**) **말썽꾼** a troublemaker; a mischief-maker; a black sheep; a grumbler; a burden; a nuisance; a pest. ¶집안의 ~ the black sheep of the family // 저 아이는 정말 ~이야 That child is a perfect pest. // 그의 가족은 그를 ~으로 치고 있다 His family treats [regard(s)] him as a burden [nuisance].

말쑥하다 clean; neat; smart; tidy; neat and clean; trim. ¶말쑥한 방 a neat and clean room // 옷차림이 말쑥한 사람 a neatly-dressed person // 검소하지만 말쑥한 옷차림을 하고 있다 be plainly but neatly dressed // 말쑥하게 하다 trim / smarten / make trim // 이발을 하고 나니 말쑥하구나 You look sharp after a haircut. **말쑥이** clean; neatly; smartly; tidily. ¶옷을 ~ 차려입다 spruce oneself up / dress oneself up smartly // 방을 ~ 치우다 tidy one's room up neatly.

말씀 speech; speech; talk; saying; language. ¶~대로 at your [his] word / as you say // 친절한 ~ your kind words // 인사 [사례의] ~을 드리다 express [tender / offer] one's thanks // ~ 중에 죄송합니다만… Excuse me for interrupting you, but .... // ~만 하십시오 [대로 하겠습니다] I am completely at your service. / I shall obey your orders. // 옳은 ~입니다 You are right. / What you say is quite right. // 아버님께 ~ 좀 전해 주시겠습니까 (전화로) Can you take [May I leave] a message for your

말씀드리다

father? / ~을 통 이해할 수 없습니다 I find no sense in what you say. **말씀하다** ¶뭐라고 말씀하셨지요 I beg your pardon? / What did you say? // 말씀하세요 (전화에서) Go ahead, please. // 도와 드릴 수 있는 일이 있으면 말씀해 주십시오 If there is anything I can do (for you), just let me know. // 이쪽은 홍길동. 말씀하세요 (무선 전화에서) This is Hong Gildong speaking. Over.

말씀드리다 state; mention; tell; say; relate; inform; report (to a high personage). ¶일전에 말씀드린 대로 as I told you the other day.

말씨 1 [말하는 버릇·태도] one's way [manner] of speaking; use of words; (표현) wording; expression; diction; grammar(문법). ¶점잖은 ~ refined diction // 야비한 ~ a mean [low] expression // ~가 거칠다 be rough in speech / use harsh[violent] language // ~에 조심하다 watch one's language // 그녀의 ~는 세련되어 있다 She is clever[good] at choosing words. // 그는 ~가 부드럽다 He always expresses himself mildly. // 남에게 충고할 때는 ~를 조심해야 한다 When you are giving advice, be careful how you put it. // 그는 ~가 지나치게 솔직하다 He speaks too bluntly. // 내 ~가 서툴러서 오해가 생겼다 I expressed it poorly, and that led to a misunderstanding. // 그는 마치 백만장자 같은 ~를 쓴다 He talks as if he were a millionaire. // 그녀의 ~로는 아직 마음을 작정하지 않은 것 같다 Judging from the way she talks, she doesn't seem to have made up her mind yet.

2 [어조] a dialect; a brogue; an accent. ¶경상도 ~ the Gyeongsangdo dialect / a Gyeongsangdo accent // 약간 서울 ~로 말하다 speak with a trace of the Seoul accent // 나는 그의 ~로 그가 이 고장 사람이 아니라는 것을 알았다 I knew he was an out-of-towner by his accent.

말없이 [조용히] in silence; silently; dumbly; without saying anything; without a word [comment]; [이의 없이] without objection; without question; [말썽 없이] without causing any trouble; without ado; [무단으로] without leave[permission]; without notice. ¶~서 있다 stand mum [tongue-tied] // ~ 보고 있다 be looking in silence // ~ 돈을 치르다 pay a bill without asking questions // 그는 가족들 아무에게도 ~ 외출했다 He went out without telling anyone in his family. // 그는 ~ 결근했다 He absented himself without leave[without notice]. // 그 부부는 ~ 잘산다 The couple are getting along well without any trouble between them. // 그는 책을 ~ 가져갔다 He walked off with the book.

말엽(末葉) the end; the close; the last [closing] days. ¶19세기 ~ toward(s) the end[close] of the 19th century.

말일(末日) the last day; the end. ¶4월 ~ the end[last day] of April.

말장난 a play upon words; a pun. **말장난하다** play upon words; make puns.

말재주 a talent for words [language]; eloquence; (구어) the gift of (the) gab. ¶~가 있다[좋다] be gifted with eloquence / have the gift of gab / have a talent for languages // ~가 없다 be awkward in speaking / be a poor speaker / be slow in speech / be no speaker // 그는 ~는 있지만 듣는 재주는 없다 He is a good talker, but a poor hearer.

말쟁이 [말수가 많은 사람] a talkative [wordy] person; a chatterbox; a prattler; a prater; a tattler; a gossip(monger); a glib talker.

말절(末節) the last part; the last paragraph(문장의); the last stanza(시의); trifles.

말조심(-操心) care in speaking. **말조심하다** be careful in one's speech [of one's language]. ¶말조심해 Watch your tongue [mouth].

말주변 talking ability; tact in speech; oratorical skill [talent]; the gift of gab. ¶~이 좋은 (능변의) eloquent / (유창한) fluent / (수다스러운) talkative / (입심 좋은) glib / (말이 많은) voluble // ~이 없는 inarticulate / clumsy in speaking // ~이 좋은 사람 a glib [facile / ready / tactful] talker // ~이 없는 사람 a poor talker / an inarticulate person // ~ 좋게 설득하다 persuade (a person) with a honeyed tongue // 그는 ~도 좋고 일 처리도 잘하는 수완가다 He is a good talker and efficient worker who gets things done. // 그는 ~이 없어 곧잘 오해를 받는다 He speaks so poorly [is so awkward with words] that he is often misunderstood.

말죽(-粥) boiled forage [feed] for horses.

말직(末職) the lowest post[position]; a petty office[position].

말질 1 [남의 말] tale-telling; gossiping; criticism. ¶~을 잘하는 사람 a tell-tale / a gossip(monger) / a busybody / a tale-bearer. **말질하다** tell tales about others; gossip; criticize. 2 [말다툼] a quarrel; a dispute; an altercation; an argument; (exchange of) high words. ¶두 사람 사이에 심한 ~이 오고갔다 High words were exchanged between the two. **말질하다** quarrel with a person (about / for / over); have a quarrel (with); dispute; altercate; have an argument (with).

말짜(末-) [가장 나쁜 물건] (mere) trash; garbage; an inferior article; goods of poor [inferior] quality; [버릇없는 사람] a good-for-nothing (fellow); a worthless [shiftless] fellow; an ill-mannered [unmanly] fellow; a low character; the dregs of society [humanity].

말짱하다 1 [흠이 없다] flawless; faultless; spotless; sound; free from blemish [damage]; perfect; [온전하다] whole; complete; intact; [깨끗하다] clean; tidy; neat. ¶말짱한 옷 spotless [clean] clothes // 말짱한 그릇 a dish in perfect condition / a whole [an unbroken] dish // 말짱한 거짓말이다 [날조된] be made out of whole cloth / [완전한] be a downright [an outright] lie // 말짱한 것이라고는 하나도 없다 None is without defect in the whole lot. // 나는 방을 말짱하게 치웠다 I kept a room clean (and tidy). // 승객들은 말짱하였다 The passengers were unhurt. **말짱히** safely; intactly; without a flaw [blemish]; in perfect shape.

2 [(정신이) 또렷하다] 《서술적》 be in one's senses; be in one's right mind; (술 취하지 않고) be dead [cold] sober; be not drunk. ¶말짱한 때에 in one's sober times / when (one is) not drunk // 말술을 마시고도 정신이 ~ remain quite sober after drinking a gallon of wine // 나는 말짱한 정신으로는 그것을 말할 수 없다 I can't talk about it in (all) soberness.

말참견(-參見) [남의 말에 끼어드는 일] interference; meddling; officiousness; meddlesomeness; [끼어들어 하는 말] an impertinent remark[comment]; gratuitous advice. ¶~을 좋아하는 사람 a meddlesome person / a man who has something to say about everything. **말참견하다** interfere; intervene in; meddle in[with]; put in a word; make an uncalled-for remark; break[cut / butt] in; make comment (on); put[shove] in one's oar; poke[thrust] one's nose. ¶남의 일에 말 참견하지 말아 주시오 Don't meddle in[interfere in / stick your nose into] other people's affairs. ∥남의 이야기에 말참견하지 말게 Don't interrupt[cut into] my talk. ∥그는 매사에 말참견한다 He has a word to say about practically everything. ∥두 사람이 이야기하고 있을 때 그가 옆에서 말참견했다 While the two were talking, he rudely cut[broke] in.

말채찍 a (horse) whip; a (riding / hunting) crop(끝에 가죽 끈 고리가 달린 것).
● **말채찍질** whipping[lashing] (a horse). ¶~을 하다 whip[lash] a horse / trail one's whip across the horse(가볍게).

말초(末梢) [가지 끝으로 갈리어 나간 가는 가지] the tip of a twig; [말단] a tip; an end; [생] the periphery.
● **말초 기관** an end-organ. **말초 신경** [생] a peripheral nerve.

말초적(末梢的) nonessential; trifling; trivial; insignificant; minor. ¶~인 일에 구애받지 be meticulous.

말총 horsehair.

말치레 a compliment; flattery; using fair[fine / pretty / honeyed] words; making a specious remark. ¶~로 with flattery / by fine words / in a honeyed tongue∥잘못을 ~로 얼버무리다 gloss over one's errors. **말치레하다** pay compliment; flatter; use fair[fine / pretty / honeyed] words; say nice[pretty] things; make a specious remark.

말캉말캉 softly; squashily. ⇨물컹물컹

말코[1] [베틀의] a loom roller.

말코[2] [말코 같은 코를 지닌 사람] a horse-nosed person.

말투(-套) one's way[manner] of talking [speaking]; delivery; turn of words. ¶강경한 ~ (in) strong language∥야비한 ~ a mean [low] expression∥독특한 ~ one's peculiar way of speaking / one's peculiarity in speech ∥날카로운 ~로 in a harsh tone / harshly / sharply∥센 ~로 말하다 speak emphatically [with emphasis]∥그는 불안스런 ~였다 He sounded discontented.∥그는 이상한 ~를 쓴다 He speaks in a peculiar way.∥그녀의 ~에서 나는 모든 것을 짐작했다 I could guess everything from the way she spoke.∥그는 모든 것을 다 알고 있는 듯한 ~였다 He sounded as if he knew everything.∥그의 ~로 보아 그의 성공이 틀림없는 것으로 생각되었다 From the way he talked, it seemed he was headed for certain success.∥그는 당장이라도 사직할 것 같은 ~였다 He talked as if he would resign any moment.∥그녀는 선생의 ~를 흉내 내어 모두를 웃겼다 She made everyone laugh by impersonating their teacher.∥무슨 ~가 그러냐 How impertinent! / What words to use! / What a thing to say!

말판 a game board; a dice board.

말편자 a horseshoe. ¶~형의 horseshoe-shaped / U-shaped∥~를 박다 shoe a horse / horseshoe.

말하다 1 [말을 꺼내다] say; speak; talk(▶ say는 어떤 사람이 하는 말을 전하거나 그 내용을 전하다. speak는「말을 하다, 어떤 말을 하다, 연설하다」 등의 뜻. talk는 speak와 거의 같은 뜻이나, 보다 허물없는 대화를 뜻하는 경우가 많음); [이야기하다] tell(▶「정보·이야기·진실·거짓 등을 전하다」의 뜻. tell은 say와 마찬가지로 직접·간접 화법에 모두 쓰이나, 간접 화법의 경우는 I told George[him] I'd go.처럼 인명이나 대명사가 없으면 불가); converse; have a talk[chat] with. ¶말하기 어려운 듯이 hesitantly / falteringly∥말하기 어려운 일 a delicate matter∥솔직히 ~ talk frankly [without reserve] (to)∥…하자고 ~ talk of (doing)∥엉터리 프랑스 어를 ~ speak in broken French∥경험을 ~ tell about[(문어) relate] one's experiences∥나는 아내와 전화로 말했다 I spoke with[talked to] my wife on the[by] phone.∥우리 꼬마 녀석이 이제 꽤 말한다 Our little boy talks a lot now.∥나는 진지하게 말하고 있어요 I am talking seriously now! / I'm serious.∥"저는 학생입니다." 라고 톰은 말했다 Tom said, "I'm a student."(▶ 대명사일 때 said he[she]처럼 said를 앞에 내놓는 것은 진부한 표현임에 주의. he[she] said라고 하든지 이름을 사용하는 것이 보통.)∥그는 어제 서울에 왔다고 말했다 He said[told me] (that) he had come to Seoul the day before.∥다시 한 번 말해 주시지 않겠습니까 Would you mind saying that again[repeating that]? / I beg your pardon.(▶ 약간 억양을 높여 말함)∥말하기는 쉽고 행하기는 어렵다 Easier said than done.∥뭐라 말해야 좋을지 모르겠다 I don't know what to say.∥그녀는 하고 싶은 말을 말했다 She had her say. / She spoke her mind.∥그가 작은 목소리로 말했기 때문에, 나는 듣지 못했다 As he spoke in a low voice, I could not catch his words.∥내가 말했다고 말하지 말아 주게 Don't tell anybody I said so. / (정부 관계자 등이) Don't quote me.∥그 사람은 거짓[진실]을 말했다 He told a lie[the truth].∥그녀는 그 광경에 놀라 한마디도 말할 수 없었다 She was dumbfounded[struck dumb / struck speechless] with astonishment at the sight. ∥나는 그런 말을 그에게 말하기가 어려웠다 I hesitated[found it hard] to say such a thing to him.∥나는 하지 않았어야 할 이야기를 말해서 큰 실수를 했다 I made a blunder by saying what I should not have said.∥입에 음식을 가득 물고 말하는 것은 예절에 어긋난다 It is bad manners to talk with your mouth full.∥내가 흥분한 나머지 쓸데없는 말을 한 것 같다 In my excitement, I seem to have said something stupid.∥그는 처음부터 끝까지 한마디도 말하지 않았다 He did not say a word from beginning to end.

2 [알리다] tell; say; speak of; relate; narrate; recite; [언급하다] mention; refer (to); [뜻하다] mean. ¶간단[간략]히 ~ tell[relate] briefly∥상세히 ~ go[enter] into the details (of) / give a full account (of)∥좋게[나쁘게] ~ speak well[ill / evil] of (a person) / say good[bad] things about (a person)∥고쳐 ~ improve one's expressions[wording] / correct oneself / correct one's misstatement ∥위에 말한 바와 같이 as said[stated / described / shown] above∥내가 말하는 대로

말하다

하시오 Do as I tell you. // 아무에게도 말하지 말게 Don't tell it to anyone. / Keep it strictly to yourself. // 잠깐 말할 게 있다 I'd like to have a word with you for a minute. // 그곳이 어떤 곳인지 좀 말해 주시오 Would you just give me an idea of what the place is like? // 나중에 전부 말해 줄게 I'll let you know all about it later on. // 나는 네가 말하는 것을 이해하지 못하겠다 I don't understand you. / I can't follow you. // 그는 가지 못하게 될 것이라고 말했다 He said he would not be able to go. // 그 비밀은 누구에게도 말해서는 안 된다 You must not let out [divulge] the secret to anybody. // 성함과 주소를 말해 주시오 Please give your name and address. // 다들 의견을 말해 주십시오 Everybody speak up, please. // 누구를 말하는 거냐 Who(m) do you mean? / Who(m) are you speaking of? // 진심으로 말하는 것입니까 Do you mean it? // 틀리다고 말하는 거냐 Do you mean to say that that is not the case?

3 〔명령하다〕 tell; order; 〔의뢰하다〕 ask; beg; wish; hope; request. ¶그는 내일 이곳에 오라고 내게 말했다 He told me to come here tomorrow. // 그는 우리에게 당장 물러가라고 말했다 He ordered us to leave at once. // 그는 이 편지를 타이프해 달라고 말했다 He asked me to type this letter. // 놀러 오라고 그에게 말해 주십시오 Please ask him to come and see us. // 그는 때릴 수 있으면 때려 보라고 내게 말했다 He dared me to hit him. // 그녀에게 결혼해 달라고 말했다 I asked her for her hand. / I asked her to marry me. // 나는 돈을 빌려 달라고 말하기가 거북했다 I found it rather awkward to ask for money. // 딸에게 말하여 그 계획을 포기하도록 해 주시오 Would you tell my daughter to give up the plan?

4 〔생각 등을 말로 나타내다〕 remark; state(▶ remark는 생각한 것, 느낀 것을 말하다, state는 격식 차린 사항에 대해서 분명하게 말하다의 뜻); declare; pronounce; 〔시인하다〕 admit; acknowledge; 〔단언하다〕 affirm; swear; 〔주장하다〕 insist; claim; assert; 〔호소하다〕 complain of (a pain); 〔고백하다〕 confess; 〔변명하다〕 explain oneself; 〔제의하다〕 propose; offer. ¶그는 그 진술이 거짓이라고 말했다 He declared the statement to be false. // 그는 자기의 잘못이라고 말했다 He acknowledged [owned] himself in the wrong. // 남자답게 졌거라 말해 Acknowledge your defeat with good grace! // "그의 일이 뜻대로 진행되지 않는 것 같아요."라고 그녀는 말했다 "His work doesn't seem to be going well," she remarked. // 수상은 가까운 장래에 감세(減稅)는 없을 것이라고 말했다 The Prime Minister stated that there would be no tax cut in the near future. // 아내는 존스 부부를 저녁 식사에 초대하는 것이 어떻겠느냐고 말했다 My wife suggested that we (might) invite Mr. and Mrs. Jones to dinner.

5 〔비평하다〕 make a comment (on); 〔조언하다〕 advise; 〔꾸짖다〕 scold; give (a person) a scolding. ¶그는 그것에 대해서 아무것도 말하지 않았다 He made no comment on it. / He said nothing about it. // 아주 훌륭합니다 아무것도 말할 것이 없습니다 That's perfect. It leaves nothing to be desired. // 가정의(家庭醫)는 전문의의 진찰을 받아 보는 것이 좋겠다고 내게 말했다 Our family doctor advised me to see a specialist. // 내가 말하는 것을 들어주십시오 Take my advice. // 그 사람에게 아무리 말해도 소용없다 It is no use telling him anything [giving him any advice]. // 그것 봐라! 내가 뭐라고 말했더냐 There! What did I tell you? [I told you so!] // 그 애가 말을 듣지 않으니 한번 단단히 말해 주시오 I want you to give the boy a sound scolding, he is so disobedient.

6 〔표현하다〕 express; describe; utter; set [put] forth. ¶나는 영어로 내 생각을 말할 수 있다 I can express myself in English. // 이것은 걸작이라고 말할 수 있다 It can safely be said [It is not too much to say] that this is a masterpiece. // 그는 자기 의견을 말할 기회가 없었다 He had no chance to express himself [his opinion]. // 넌 좋은 의견을 말했어. 그렇잖니 You have expressed [given] a fine opinion, haven't you? // 그는 연극에서 과장된 대사를 말했다 He delivered a high-flown speech. // 그 작가에 대해서는 아무리 많이 이야기해도 다 말할 수 없다 It is impossible to run out of things to say about that writer. // 이 복잡한 사정을 5,000어(語) 정도로는 다 말할 수 없다 It is impossible to give a full account of these complicated circumstances in five thousand words or so. // 당신의 친절에 감사한 마음은 이루 다 말할 수 없습니다 I cannot thank you enough for your kindness. / No words can fully express my gratitude for your kindness. // 그 경치의 아름다움은 이루 다 말할 수 없다 The beauty of the scenery is beyond description.

7 〔나타내다〕 show; indicate; prove. ¶돈이 말하는 사회 a society where money talks [counts (for everything)] // 이 사실은 그의 견실한 성격을 잘 말해 주고 있다 The fact tells a great deal about [speaks volumes for] his steadfast character. // 의자의 온기가 조금 전까지 그가 앉아 있었다는 것을 말해 주고 있다 The warmth of the chair shows that he was sitting on it until a moment ago.

말하자면 〔…으로 [하게] 말하면〕 if we are to speak (about); if we must say; speaking [talking] of ...; it reminds me ...; 〔이를테면〕 so to speak [say]; so to call it; as it were; in a manner (of speaking); in a way [sense / kind / sort]; as one might put it; in a word(한 마디로 말해); say. ¶다시 ~ in other words / that is (to say) / to put it (in) another way // 일반적으로 [대충 / 엄밀히] ~ generally [roughly / strictly] speaking // 그분은 ~ 우리 아버지와 같다 He is, so to speak, just like my father. // 그녀는 ~ 새장의 새와 같다 She may be likened [compared] to a caged bird. // 그것은 ~ 사기다 It amounts to fraud, as a matter of fact. / It is practically a fraud. // 나의 인생은 ~ 실패의 연속이었다 My life has been, as it were, a succession of failures.

말할 것도 없다 ¶말할 것도 없이 (as a matter) of course / needless to say / it goes without saying / …은 말할 것도 없이 not to mention [speak of] / to say nothing of / not only ... (but) // …은 ~ it is a matter of course that ... / it is needless to say that ... // 그들이 매우 기뻐한 것은 ~ It is needless to say [It goes without saying] that they were very delighted. // 그는 영어는 말할 것도 없고 프랑스 어도 (말)한다 He speaks

French, let alone English.∥그는 위스키는 말할 것도 없고 맥주도 안 마신다 He does not drink beer, to say nothing of whisky.∥말한 것도 없이 열파(熱波)의 엄습을 받은 지역에서는 수확에 타격을 받았다 Of course [Needless to say], the crops were hard hit in the regions affected by the heat wave.

말할 수 없이 indescribably; inexpressibly; unutterably; beyond description [words]. ¶그 경치는 ~ 아름답다 The beauty of the view is beyond words [expression].

말향(抹香) incense powder; incense.

맑다 1 (물·소리 등이) clear; clean; limpid; pure; transparent; fresh; crystal; lucid. ¶맑은 공기 fresh [limpid] air∥맑은 물 clear [transparent] / (문어) limpid] water∥맑은 하늘 a clear [serene] sky∥맑은 색 a clear color∥맑은 눈 clear [bright / shining] eyes∥맑은 마음 a tranquil mind∥맑은 종소리 the clear sound of a bell∥맑아지다 (액체 등이) become clear [transparent] / (소리 등이) become clear∥맑게 하다 make clear∥그는 맑은 목소리로 이야기했다 He spoke in a clear voice.∥얼어붙은 밤공기에 종소리가 맑게 울려 퍼졌다 The sound of the bell reverberated clearly in the freezing night air.∥우리는 여과기로 흐린 물을 맑게 했다 We cleaned [purified] the polluted water with a filter.

2 (날씨가) fine; clear; fair. ¶맑은 날씨 fine [fair] weather∥맑 날 a fine [clear] day∥맑은 아침 a fine [beautiful] morning∥(날씨가) 맑아지다 clear (up) / become clear∥날씨가 맑아질 것 같다 It is going to be fine. / The weather looks promising.∥날씨도 맑아 포근한 겨울날이 되었다 The weather cleared to a mild winter day.

3 (마음·기분 등이) clear; fresh; pure; refreshing. ¶맑은 마음 a pure heart [soul]∥맑은 심경으로 with a clean [clear] conscience / in a serene frame of mind / serenely∥머리가 맑아지다 have a clear head∥기분이 맑아지다 feel [be] refreshed [cheerful / lighthearted] / feel fine∥내 기분이 맑아졌다 My mind has started to click.∥오늘은 자네 머리가 맑고 또렷또렷하군 그래 You're really sharp [on the ball] today!∥간밤에는 머리가 맑고 초롱초롱하여 밤새껏 잠을 자지 못했다 I was wide awake all night last night.

4 (처세·생활 등이) clean; honest; innocent; clear; pure; [청렴하다] poor (but honest). ¶맑은 사람 a man of integrity∥맑은 살림 a meager living∥맑은 생활을 보내다 live an honest [a pure] life / lead an immaculate life.

맑은 물에 고기 안 논다(속담) A man of too much integrity is politely shunned by others.

맑디맑다 very clear; perfectly clear; be as clear as can be [as crystal].

맑은소리 [언] a voiceless [an unvoiced] sound. ⇨안울림소리

맑은술 refined [filtered] rice wine.

맑은장국 (-醬-) clear [thin] meat soup; bouillon; (프) consommé.

맑히다 [맑게 하다] make clear [clean]; purify; clean; clarify; settle; cause to become clear; cleanse. ¶물을 ~ clear the water∥정신을 ~ refresh one's mind / make one's mind fresh.

맘 (the) mind; (the) heart; sincerity; thought; will; fancy. ⇨마음

맘껏 to one's heart's content. ⇨마음껏

맘마 〈소아〉 boiled [cooked] rice. ⇨밥¹

맘모스 →매머드

맘보 [라틴 아메리카의 춤] the mambo. ¶~의 리듬으로 in mambo rhythm∥~를 추다 dance the mambo / mambo.

●**맘보바지** drainpipe trousers [pants].

맙소사 Oh, no!; Good God [Lord / me]!; Good gracious [heavens]!; Gracious Heaven [goodness]!; Gracious!; Goodness!; Save us!; My eye(s)!

맛¹ 1 (음식의) taste; flavor; savor. ¶뒷~ aftertaste∥특이한 ~ a peculiar flavor∥매운~ a hot [biting / spicy] taste∥신~ a sour taste∥~이 좋은 [있는] nice / tasty / palatable / savory / delicious / toothsome∥~이 나쁜 [없는] ill-tasting / untasty / unsavory / unpalatable∥~이 있다 [좋다] taste good [nice / delicious] / have a good taste∥~이 없다 [나쁘다] taste bad [flat] / be unsavory [unpalatable] / be unpleasant to the taste∥…의 ~이 나다 taste [savor] of (Lemon, apple, etc.)∥~이 변하다 become stale / (시어지다) turn sour∥~을 보다 try (the flavor of) / (간을) taste (something) to see how it is seasoned∥~을 내다 season (food with salt) / flavor (a drink) / add seasoning (to)∥~을 좋게 하다 improve (its) flavor∥~을 버려 놓다 spoil the taste∥과자는 아주 ~이 좋다 [나쁘다] This cake has wonderful [doesn't have much] flavor.∥레몬은 홍차에 ~을 더해 준다 Lemon adds flavor to tea.∥이 커피는 ~이 없다 [싱겁다] This coffee is tasteless [insipid].∥수프 ~이 어떻습니까 How do you like the soup?∥이 수프는 좀 이상한 ~이 나지 않느냐 Can you taste anything strange in this soup?∥고기 ~을 좀 봐 주시오 Please see how the meat is doing?∥나는 생선회의 ~을 모른다 I just can't appreciate [don't enjoy] the taste of raw fish.∥~이 든 수박 watermelon ripe enough to eat∥술이 ~이 들었다 The wine is properly aged.∥이 요리는 차게 먹어야 더 ~이 있다 This dish tastes better eaten cold.∥어떤 ~이 납니까 What does it taste like?∥마늘 ~이 납니다 This has the flavor of garlic.∥I (can) taste garlic in it.∥이 술은 ~이 좋아 나는 자칫 과음한다 This rice-wine goes down so easily that I tend to drink too much of it.

2 [묘미] relish; taste; zest; gusto; aroma; charm. ¶돈 ~ a taste for money∥여자 ~ an interest in women∥…의 ~을 알다 [붙이다] get [acquire] a taste for / take a liking for [to] …∥그의 문장은 독특한 ~이 있다 His writing has a charm all its own.

3 [만족스러운 느낌] satisfaction. ¶꼭 오늘이어야만 ~이냐 Why need it be today?∥하필 오늘 가야 ~이냐 Why do you have to choose to go today necessarily?

4 [혼나기] ¶~을 보여 주다 teach (a person) a lesson / give (a person) a raw deal / put (a person) under disciplinary punishment∥어디 ~ 좀 봐라 Wait and see. / See what I will do. / You shall have your due in time. / You will have to pay for this. (어디 두고 보자)∥그런 놈은 ~ 좀 봐야 돼 A little discipline would do him a world of good. / He needs correction.

맛(을) 들이다 [재미를 붙이다] get [acquire] a taste (for); take a liking for [to] …; be interested (in); find pleasure (in). ¶돈에 ~ get a taste for money // 도박에 ~ take to gambling // 주색에 한번 맛 들이면 좀처럼 헤어나지 못한다 Once you pick up a taste for wine and women, you will find it very hard to give up. // 투기에 한번 맛을 들이면 여간해서 그만둘 수가 없다 Once you are successful in speculation, it is hard to leave off.

맛² [동] a solen; a razor clam [shell].

맛깔스럽다 1 [입에 맞다] agreeable [pleasing] to the taste; pleasant-tasting; palatable; toothsome; suit [be to] one's taste [palate]; be nice to the palate. ¶맛깔스러운 음식 [맛] an agreeable food [taste]. 2 [마음에 들다] agreeable to one's taste; palatable; pleasing; please [catch / suit / capture / take / strike] one's fancy; flatter [suit] (one's) taste; be in (one's) favor.

맛나다 [맛있다] tasty; delicious; sweet; savory; palatable; [맛이 돌다] taste good [nice]; have a good flavor (of). ¶맛난 요리 a delicious [palatable] dish // 아, ~ It tastes good. / (미) Goody!

맛난이 1 [화학조미료] sauce; a flavoring; a seasoning; a condiment; something to bring out the flavor. 2 [맛있는 음식] delicious [dainty] food; a (table) delicacy; a tidbit; (미 국 속어) good eats.

맛보기 tasting; sampling; foretaste; prelibation; degustation.

맛보다 1 [시식하다] taste; get [have] a taste of; sample; try (the flavor of); foretaste; degust. ¶간을 ~ taste (a dish) to see how it is seasoned with salt // 소스를 ~ taste [take a taste of] the sauce // 특별한 요리를 ~ enjoy [relish] a special dish // …을 쬐금 ~ have a (small) taste of (cake) // 맛보아 주십시오 Just try [taste] it. / Please see how it tastes. // 이 포도주를 한 모금 맛보시지 않겠어요 Won't you have a taste of this wine? // 우리는 파티에서 여러 가지 진미를 맛보았다 We enjoyed various kinds of delicacies at the party.
2 [경험하다] taste; know; experience; go through; undergo; learn. ¶슬픔의 쓴잔을 ~ drain [drink] the cup of sorrow to the bottom // 여행의 재미를 ~ enjoy one's journey // 그는 세상의 쓴맛 단맛을 다 맛보았다 He has tasted [experienced] the bitter and the sweet [the sorrows and joys]. // 그것은 인생의 쓰라림을 맛본 사람만이 쓸 수 있는 책이다 It is a book that could be written only by a man who has tasted [experienced] the bitter side of life.

맛부리다 behave insipidly [disgracefully / indecently]; behave in an insipid manner; make a sight of oneself.

맛살 the flesh of a razor clam; razor clam flesh.

맛없다 1 (음식이) tasteless; unsavory; unpalatable; untasty; ill-tasting; flavorless; insipid; flat; (서술적) taste bad. ¶맛없는 음식 unsavory [tasteless] food // 맛없어 보이는 unappetizing / uninviting // 그것은 ~ It doesn't taste good. / That is bad eating. // 보기에도 맛없는 요리였다 The dish was uninviting even to look at. // 이렇게 맛없는 저녁은 난생 처음이다 This is the worst dinner I've ever had. 2 [재미가 없다] dull; flat; uninteresting; insipid; dry; vapid; irksome; wearisome. ¶맛없는 세상 the dreary world / wearisome life // 맛없이 살아가다 lead a dull life.

맛있다 (음식이) tasty; delicious; palatable; dainty; savory; sweet; nice; flavorous. ¶맛있게 보이는 appetizing / delicious-looking / tempting // 맛있는 요리 a tasty dish // 이 케이크는 ~ This cake is good [tasty]. // 저 가게의 스튜는 ~ They serve delicious stew at that restaurant. // 그 요리는 아주 맛있고 훌륭했다 The food was lip-smacking good [chop-licking good]. // 그는 맛있는 음식을 늘 [습관적으로] 먹고 있다 He is used to delicacies. / He is accustomed to eating well. // 정말 맛있는데 Tastes good! / How delicious! // 맛있어요? [맛이 어때요?] How does it taste? / Do you like it? (▶ "Is it delicious?"라고는 하지 않음) // 맛있어 보이는 요리가 나왔다 Appetizing dish were served. // 나온 요리마다 그는 맛있게 먹는 듯했다 He seemed to enjoy every dish that was served. // 나는 밥을 맛있게 먹었다 I made a good dinner of it. / I dined with a good appetite.

맛적다 [재미가 적다] unenjoyable; disagreeable; unpleasant.

맛조개 [동] a razor clam [shell]; a pen shell.

망¹ (望) [동정을 살핌] watch; lookout; observation; vigilance; guard; surveillance; vigil. ¶~을 세우다 set [post] a lookout (for) / place a guard (at the door) / keep guard (over the house).

망² (望) 1 [만월] a full moon. 2 [음력 보름날] the fifteenth day of a lunar month.

망 (網) 1 [그물] a net; (집합적) netting. ¶머리~ a hairnet // 어~ a fishing net // 투~ a casting net // ~에 걸리다 be trapped [caught] in a net / be netted // ~을 치다 stretch [set] a net / ~을 뜨다 make a net / net // ~으로 새를 잡아 넣다 net a bird / catch a bird in a net. 2 [조직] a network. ¶법~ the net [grip / clutches / toils / meshes] of the law / justice // 방송~ a radio network // 철도 [통신]~ a railway [communication] network // 수사~ the police dragnet // 수사~을 치다 [펴다] spread [drop] the dragnet // 법~을 빠져나가다 evade (the clutches of) the law / slip from the grip of the law.

망가뜨리다 [부수다] break (down); destroy; demolish; [손상하다] injure; damage; ruin; [고장 내다] put [get] (a watch) out of order; [찌그러뜨리다] crush; smash. ¶모자를 ~ smash [squash] a hat // 기계를 ~ break up a machine // 그는 마분지 상자를 짓밟아 망가뜨렸다 He crushed the cardboard box under his feet. // 그들은 소나무를 베어 쓰러뜨려 아름다운 경치를 망가뜨렸다 They destroyed the beautiful scenery by cutting down the pine trees.

망가지다 [부서지다] break; be broken; be wrecked; be demolished; be ruined; fall to ruin; [파손되다] be damaged / be destroyed / break [come] down; [고장 나다] get out of order; [찌그러지다] be crushed; be smashed. ¶망가진 우산 a broken umbrella // 망가진 차 a damaged [disabled] car // 망가지기 쉬운 easily breaking / easy to break / brittle / fragile / frail // 산산조각으로 ~ be broken to fragments [pieces] / be smashed

망각(忘却) lapse of memory; oblivion; forgetfulness; obliteration. ¶그는 ~의 사람이 되어 버렸다 He has fallen into obscurity. **망각하다** forget; be forgetful[oblivious] of; consign (something) to oblivion[limbo]. ¶사실을 ~ lose sight of the fact // 취해서 앞뒤를 ~ become utterly befuddled with drink // 자식으로서의 본분을 ~ forget one's filial duty // 공무원으로서의 의무를 ~ neglect one's duty as a public servant. →¶세상에서 망각되다 be buried in oblivion.

망간 [화] manganese(기호 Mn).
● **망간강**(-鋼) manganese steel.

망건(網巾) a *manggeon*; a headband made of horsehair. ¶~ 쓰고 세수하다 do things in reverse order / put[get / set] the cart before horse.

망건 쓰자 파장(속담) muddle[dally] away one's opportunity.

망고 [식] a mango (*pl.* ~es, ~s).

망구다 ruin; spoil; destroy; wreck. ¶계획을 ~ spoil[ruin] a plan / 신세를 ~ ruin oneself / bring ruin upon oneself // 나라를 ~ ruin [destroy] a nation.

망국(亡國) [나라의 멸망] national ruin[decay]; the ruin of one's country; [망한 나라] a ruined[doomed] country. ¶~적 문학 antipatriotic literature // 그는 ~적인 사상의 소유자였다 He harbored ideas ruinous to his own country. / He held treasonable opinions. **망국하다** ruin[destroy] one's country.
● **망국지민**(-之民) a ruined people; a homeless race. **망국지탄**(-之歎) lamentation [grief] over the national ruin.

망그뜨리다 →망가뜨리다
망그러지다 break; be damaged. ⇨ 망가지다
망극하다(罔極-) immeasurable; inestimable; inscrutable; great; immense. ¶망극한 은혜 a great favor[benefit] of one's parents[king] // 성은이 망극하옵니다 Your minister thanks you. // 얼마나 망극하십니까 Please let me offer my condolence to you on this sad event.

망꾼(望-) a watchman; a lookout; a guard; a keeper; [보초] a sentry; a sentinel.

망나니 1 [참수인] an executioner; a head cutter. 2 [못된 사람] a rough-and-tumble man; a hard-boiled egg; a rascal; a rough; a rowdy. ¶찰~ a real bastard[stinker] // ~짓을 하다 play the gangster // 예이 ~ 자식 You damn son-of-a-bitch!

망녀(亡女) [죽은 딸] one's deceased daughter.

망년(忘年) 1 [송년] speeding the old year. 2 [나이를 잊기] indifference to age.
● **망년회** a year-end (dinner) party[social gathering]. ¶~를 열다 give a year-end party / celebrate the outgoing year.

망대(望臺) a watchtower. ⇨ 망루(望樓)
망동하다(妄動-) act blindly[on impulse]; behave rashly.

망둥이 [동] a goby.

망라하다(網羅-) [모든 것을 포함하다] include[comprehend / contain] all …; [남김없이 모으다] collect all …. ¶모든 것을 망라한 comprehensive / all-inclusive / exhaustive // 모든 사실을 ~ cover[include] all the facts // 이 사전은 미국의 현행 속어를 망라하고 있다 This dictionary contains all current American slang. // 이것은 모든 문제점을 망라하고 있다 This covers all the questions. →¶그 모임엔 사회 각층의 인사가 망라되어 있다 Every class of society is represented at the meeting.

망령(亡靈) [망혼(亡魂)] a departed spirit [soul]; the spirit of a dead person; [유령] an apparition; a ghost; a specter.

망령(妄靈) dotage; senility; anility; second childhood. ¶~ 든 늙은이 a dotard / an old man in his dotage[second childhood] / a befuddled old man // ~이 나 있다 be in one's dotage / be childish with age / be in one's second childhood // ~이 들다 dote / get [grow] senile[weak in mind from old age] / fall into one's dotage / become[grow] senile / become childish with age // ~을 부리다 behave like a child / behave unreasonably [foolishly] // ~ 들지 않았다 have one's mental faculties unimpaired // ~ 들었군요 You're gone gaga. // 그는 늙어 ~이 들기 시작하고 있다 He is getting quite silly in his old age.

망령되다(妄靈-) foolish; silly; absurd; unreasonable. ¶망령된 말 an absurd remark.

망루(望樓) a watchtower; an observation tower; a lookout (tower).

망막(網膜) [생] the retina (*pl.* ~s, -nae).
● **망막 세포** a retinal cell; a retinula (*pl.* -lae). **망막염** retinitis.

망막하다(茫漠-) 1 [광막하다] vast; boundless; extensive. ¶망막한 바다 a boundless expanse[stretch] of water // 망막한 평원 a vast stretch of lowland. 2 [막연하다] vague; obscure. ¶망막한 장래의 전망 vague prospects.

망망대해(茫茫大海) a vast expanse of water; a boundless ocean.

망망하다(茫茫-) vast; boundless; extensive.
망망하다(忙忙-) (서술적) be very busy; have much[many things] to do.

망명(亡命) flight from one's own country; exile. ¶정치적 ~을 요구하다 ask for[seek] political asylum (in France) // 정치적 ~을 허용하다 grant[give] (a person) political asylum (in) // 소련의 피아니스트가 미국에 ~을 요청했다 A Russian pianist sought asylum[refuge] in the United States. **망명하다** flee from one's own country (for political reasons); exile oneself; seek[take] refuge (in a foreign country). ¶미국에 ~ come to the United States as an exile[a refugee] / seek[take] refugee in the United States. // 그는 북한에서 망명했다 He defected from North Korea.
● **망명객** a political exile. **망명 생활** (a) life in exile. ¶~을 하다 live in exile. **망명자** (특히 정치상의 이유로 국외로 망명한) a (political) refugee; an exile; (적국으로의) a defector. **망명 정부** a refugee government; a government in exile.

망모(亡母) one's deceased[late] mother.

망발(妄發) a reckless remark; thoughtless words; an absurd[unreasonable] speech; (행위) an ignominious behavior. ¶그 말은 ~이었다 That remark was a bad slip of the tongue. **망발하다** make reckless[thoughtless] remarks; use absurd [unreasonable] language; behave ignominiously.

망보다(望-) keep watch (for / against / on); be on the watch [lookout] (for); watch; keep an eye on; picket.

망부(亡父) one's deceased [late] father.

망부(亡夫) one's deceased [late] husband.

망부석(望夫石) the stone on which a faithful wife stood waiting for her husband until she perished.

망사(網紗) gauze.

망상 (妄想) a fancy; a wild [vagrant] fancy; a fantasy; a fantastic idea; an impossible idea; [의] a delusion. ¶과대～증 insanity of grandeur / megalomania / 피해～증 a delusion of persecution / persecution mania // ～에 빠지다 [잠기다] be lost in wild fancies / spin a daydream / indulge in woolgathering // ～에 시달리다 suffer from delusions // 그는 ～에 잠겨 있다 He is given to [is lost in] wild fancies.

망상 (網狀) net shape; reticulation. ¶～의 netlike / reticular / reticulate(d) ～을 이루다 reticulate.

망설이다 hesitate; waver; hang [hold] back; vacillate; shilly-shally; think twice (about); jib [balk] at; be irresolute. ¶망설이면서 hesitatingly / waveringly // 망설이지 않고 without hesitation [flinching] / unhesitatingly // 망설이지 않고 …하다 have no hesitation in doing / make no scruple to do [of doing] / 확실한 답변을 ～ hesitate to give a definite answer // 나는 망설이지 않고 대답할 수 있었다 I was able to answer without hesitation. // 그는 조금도 망설이지 않고 상사의 욕을 한다 He speaks ill of his boss without any hesitation (whatsoever). / 그는 조금도 망설이지 않고 브라질로 가서 살기로 결정했다 He had no hesitation about going to live in Brazil. // 그는 그것을 말하기를 망설였다 He hesitated to say that. // 그는 위험을 무릅쓰기를 망설였다 He was hesitant about taking the risk. // 그는 홀에 들어가기 전에 잠시 망설였다 He hung back momentarily before entering the hall. // 내가 왜 망설이는지 아시겠소 Do you know why I am wavering? // 할까 말까 하고 나는 망설이고 있다 I am hesitating [in two minds] as to whether I shall undertake it or not. // 나는 그에게 말을 할까 말까 하고 망설이고 있다 I am in [(미) of] two minds about telling him.

망신(亡身) shame; disgrace; dishonor; infamy; ignominy; humiliation; loss of reputation. ¶～을 주다 put (a person) to shame / cause (a person) to feel ashamed / humiliate / bring (a person) into contempt / put (a person) out of countenance // 집안 ～을 외부에 드러내다 wash dirty linen in public // 그는 우리 집안의 ～감이다 He is a disgrace [dishonor] to our family. / He is a blot on our family name. // 그는 과음하여 ～을 샀다 He made a fool of himself by drinking too much. // 그의 비행은 집안의 ～이 될 것이다 His misdeeds will bring disgrace on his family. **망신하다** bring shame on oneself [one's family]; disgrace oneself in public; make an ass [a fool] of oneself; humiliate oneself. ➔그는 여러 사람 앞에서 나를 망신시켰다 He disgraced me in public.

● **망신살** a bad luck to bring shame (on oneself).

망신스럽다(亡身-) dishonorable; shameful; disgraceful. ¶그런 복장을 하다니 자넨 정말 망신스럽네 You look really disreputable [disgraceful / crazy] in those clothes. / You look an absolute disgrace in those clothes.

망실(亡失) loss. **망실하다** lose; miss.

망아지 [작은 말] a pony; [말새끼] a colt (수컷); a filly (암컷); a foal (통성).

망양지탄(亡羊之歎) lamenting one's inability [incapacity]; a feeling of hopelessness [total incapacity].

망언 (妄言) a reckless remark; thoughtless words; a slip of tongue; a blunder; [못된 말] abusive language. **망언하다** make reckless [thoughtless] remarks; use abusive language.

망연자실(茫然自失) abstraction; stupefaction; entrancement. **망연자실하다** (서술적) be stupefied [abstracted] (with grief); be dazed [stunned] (by the news); be distraut; be at one's wit's end; feel all at sea. ¶망연자실하여 with an air of complete abstraction / abstractedly / absentmindedly // 아버지가 돌아가셨다는 소식을 듣고 그녀는 망연자실했다 She was stunned by the news of her father's death.

망연하다(茫然-) 1 [넓고 아득하다] vast; wide; extensive; boundless. 2 [멍하다] vacant; blank; abstracted; absentminded; dazed; stupefied. ¶망연한 얼굴로 with an absentminded [a vacant] look on one's face // 망연하여 어쩌할 바를 모르다 be quite at a loss what to do. **망연히** vacantly; blankly; abstractedly; absentmindedly; in a daze.

망외(望外) ¶～의 unexpected / unlooked-for / unanticipated // ～의 성공 [결과] an unlooked for success [result] / 그것은 ～의 성공이었다 The success exceeded my most sanguine hopes. / I was agreeably surprised by a success greater than my expectations.

망울 1 [덩어리] a lump; a mass; a ball; a bulb. ¶～지다 get lumpy / have a lump. 2 a flower bud. ⇨꽃망울 3 [임파선종] an induration; [의] lymphadenoma. ¶젖～ a lump in the breast / ～ 서다 have lymphadenoma / have a swollen (lymph) glands.

망원경(望遠鏡) a telescope; a spyglass (소형의); [쌍안경] a binocular; field glasses. ¶천체 ～ an astronomical telescope // 태양 관측용 ～ a helioscope // 광학 ～ an optical telescope // 전파 ～ a radio telescope // 반사 ～ a reflecting telescope / a reflector // 굴절 ～ a refracting telescope / a refractor // 조준 ～ a sighting telescope / 지상 ～ a terrestrial telescope // ～으로만 보이는 별 telescopic stars // ～으로 보다 look (at the moon) through a telescope // ～을 눈에 맞추다 adjust a telescope to one's eye // ～을 들여다보다 look in the telescope.

망원 렌즈(望遠-) a telephoto(graphic) lens; a telelens.

망원 사진(望遠寫眞) a telephoto(graph).

망월(望月) a full moon (on the fifteenth night). ⇨보름달 ⇨보름).

망은(忘恩) ingratitude; unthankfulness. **망은하다** be ungrateful; lose one's gratitude.

망인(亡人) the dead person; the deceased; (집합적) the dead.

망일(望日) a full-moon day; the 15th day of

망자(亡者) the dead person. ⇨망인(亡人)
망조(亡兆) a sign [an omen] of ruin. ¶~가 들다 show signs of ruin / be a sign of ruin / be ominous of ruin.
망종(亡終) the last hour of one's life; one's last moments; the end of one's life; the hour of death.
망종(亡種) 〔행실이 못된 사람〕 a rogue; a villain; a scoundrel; a regular rascal; a good-for-nothing (fellow); a scamp.
망종(芒種) 1〔까끄라기가 있는 곡식〕 awned [bearded] grain. 2〔24절기의 하나〕 *mang-jong*; "the barley harvest season" (as one of the 24 seasonal divisions according to the lunar calendar that falls on about 6th of June).
망주석(望柱石) a pair of stone posts in front of a tomb.
망중한(忙中閑) leisure in intervals of one's business; a moment of relief (snatched) from pressure of business; a break in the pressure of one's (official) work.
망지소조하다(罔知所措-) be at a loss what to do; do not know what to do.
망집(妄執) a mistakenly held obsession; a deep-seated [-rooted] delusion.
망처(亡妻) one's deceased [late] wife.
망측하다(罔測-) 〔불쾌하다〕 offensive; disgusting; 〔상스럽다〕 low; abominable; mean; lascivious; indecent (talk); 〔추잡하다〕 nasty; vicious; 〔꼴사납다〕 ugly; bad-looking; unsightly; shabby. ¶망측한 소리[이야기] an indecent [a low] talk / spicy conversation // 망측한 꼴을 보이다 cut an unsightly figure / expose oneself to ridicule // 여자에게 망측한 소리를 하다 say ugly [improper] things to a girl / make an obscene remark to a girl.
망치 a hammer (쇠망치); a mallet (나무망치); (큰 망치) a maul; a sledge (hammer) (대장간의); (의장이나 경매인의) a gavel. ¶돌 깨는 ~ a stone hammer // ~로 치다 hammer / strike with a hammer // ~로 못을 박다 drive in a nail with a hammer / hammer a nail (into) // 의장은 ~로 탁자를 두드렸다 The chairman rapped on the table with his gavel.
● **망치질** hammering. ¶~을 하다 hammer.
망치다 spoil; mar; ruin; destroy; damage; work [play] havoc with; make a mess [muddle] (of). ¶일생을 ~ blast one's career / make a wreck of one's life / be ruined for life // 계획을 ~ frustrate [upset] a plan / throw a wet blanket over a project // 몸을 ~ ruin [degrade] oneself / go wrong // 난봉으로 몸을 ~ ruin oneself by dissipation // 비가 벚꽃을 망쳤다 The rain spoiled the cherry blossoms. // 뇌우가 농작물을 심하게 망쳤다 The thunderstorm has badly damaged [has done a great deal of damage to] the crops. // 개들이 꽃을 망쳐 놓았다 Some dogs wrought havoc with flowers. // 그 간판이 경치를 망치고 있다 That signboard ruins the scenery. // 술을 너무 마시면 건강을 망친다 Too much drinking will ruin your health. // 그는 술을 너무 마셔 몸을 망쳤다 He ruined himself [[미국 구어]] did himself in] by drinking too much. // 그는 방탕한 생활로 몸을 망쳤다 He ruined himself by fast living. // 단 한 번의 실수로 그는 일생을 망쳤다 His one mistake ruined his career [him for life]. // 아주 작은 잘못된 판단으로 인하여 그는 장래를 망치고 말았다 A small miscalculation ruined [wrecked] his future. // 그는 여자 때문에 신세를 망쳤다 Women brought him to ruin. // 곡물이 냉해로 완전히 망쳐졌다 The crops were completely ruined by cold weather. // 비로 경기가 망쳐졌다 The game was rained out.

망태기(網-) a net [mesh] bag.
망토 a mantle; a cloak; a cape(어깨 망토). ¶~를 몸에 걸치다 fold one's cloak about one.
망판(網版) 〔인〕 a halftone; a halftone plate [block].
망하다(亡-) 1 〔멸망하다〕 perish; cease to exist; die out; meet with destruction; 〔영락하다〕 be ruined; go [come] to ruin; go to the bad [the dogs / the devil]; 〔파산하다〕 go [become] bankrupt. ¶망한 실업가 a bankrupt businessman // 망한 집안 a reduced family // 망해 가는 민족 a dying race // 거지가 되다 be reduced to beggary // 일족이 ~ a clan dies out // 나라가 ~ a country perishes // 집안이 ~ a family goes down // 회사가 ~ a company fails // 술로 ~ go to the dogs with drink // 함께 ~ fall [be ruined] together / share the same fate // 그의 사업은 망하기 직전에 놓여 있다 His business is on the verge of collapse. // 그 회사는 망해 버렸다 The company has passed out of existence [gone (out)]. // 난 망했다 I'm finished. / I'm washed-up. / I'm done for. // 망할 놈의 말같을 가 줘야지 What can I do with the wretched nag — it is so slow!
2 〔고약하다〕 be wretched; be hard to deal with. ¶그 책은 읽기 ~ The book is hard to read.
망향(望鄕) homesickness; nostalgia. ¶~병에 걸리다 become homesick [nostalgic] / yearn [long] for the sight of one's home.
망혼(亡魂) a spirit; a soul. ¶이승에 떠도는 ~ a spirit lingering in this world [on earth] // ~을 달래다 solace [pacify] the departed soul // 전사자의 ~을 달래다 pray for the souls of fallen soldiers.
맞- 〔마주〕 opposite; face-to-face; 〔서로〕 mutual; reciprocal; each other; 〔함께〕 together; jointly. ¶~대면 a face-to-face interview // ~부딪치다 hit each other // ~앉다 sit face to face with (a person) / sit opposite (a person).
맞갖지 않다 unsatisfactory [unacceptable / distasteful / disagreeable] (to); (서술적) do not suit [please] (a person's) fancy [taste]; be against (a person's) taste [liking]. ¶맞갖지 않은 음식 a disagreeable food // 맞갖지 않은 놈 a disagreeable fellow // 맞갖지 않은 일 an uncongenial piece of work / a job not to one's liking [taste] // 맞갖지 않은 소리를 하다 say something disagreeable [unpleasant / offensive].
맞걸다 1 〔마주 걸다〕 interlock; lock [link] together. 2 (노름판에서) bet [stake] the same amount (of money) as the other party.
맞걸리다 be interlocked; be locked [linked] together; interlock. ¶차량 연결기가 맞걸려 있다 The couplers of the cars are interlocked [engaged].
맞고소(-告訴) a cross action; a counteraction; a counterclaim; a counter-suit. **맞고소하다** counterclaim (against a person for a

matter); plead a counterclaim; bring a cross action (against a person for a matter). ¶최씨가 윤 씨를 수회죄로 고소하자 윤 씨는 최씨를 명예 훼손으로 맞고소하였다 Mr. Choe charged Mr. Yun with bribery, and Mr. Yun counter-charged Mr. Choe with slander.
●**맞고소인**(-人) a counterclaimant.

맞구멍 a hole (made) through (a thing); a perforation.

맞꼭지각(-角) [수] vertically opposite angles; vertical angles.

맞다¹ **1** [영접하다] meet; go (out) to meet; receive; greet. ¶반가이 ~ welcome / make (a person) welcome / receive (a person) with delight // 따뜻이 ~ give (a person) a warm reception // 현관까지 나가서 손님을 ~ come out to the door to receive [greet] a visitor // (…을) 역에 나가 ~ meet (a person) at the station / go to the station to meet (a person) // 두 팔을 벌려 ~ open out one's arms to (a person) // 손님을 응접실에 맞아들이다 receive a guest and show him to the drawing room // 집주인은 그를 따뜻이 맞았다 The master of the house was very hospitable to him. / He was well received by the host.
2 [받아들이다] invite; engage. ¶아내를 ~ take a wife / get married // 사위를 ~ take a son-in-law into one's family / find a husband for one's daughter // 새 선생님을 ~ have a new teacher come // 양자로 ~ adopt (a child) (as one's son) / receive (a nephew) into one's family as a son.
3 [어떤 때를] ¶새해를 ~ greet [hail] the New Year // 묵은해를 보내고 새해를 ~ see the old year out and the new year in // 48세의 생일을 ~ see one's 48th birthday come round // 드디어 서력 2000년을 맞았다 Today we enter upon the 2000th year of A.D.
4 [(적 등을) 상대하다] meet [confront] (the enemy). ¶적을 맞아서 싸우다 meet [engage / receive] the enemy / fight to repulse the attack of the enemy.
5 [비·바람 등을] be exposed to; expose oneself to. ¶비를 ~ be exposed to rain / be caught in a rain // 비바람을 ~ be open to wind and rain / be exposed to the weather // 밤이슬을 ~ be exposed [expose oneself] to the night dew // 선풍기의 바람을 ~ [쐬다] sit in the current of an electric fan // 취기에서 깨기 위해 찬 바람을 ~ air oneself to take off the effects of drink // 밤이슬을 맞아 나는 감기가 들었다 I caught cold from exposure to the night dew.
6 [어떤 일을 당하다] meet with; encounter (a difficulty); come upon [across]; suffer. ¶도둑을 ~ be stolen by (a thing) / (물건이) be stolen // 퇴짜를 ~ be rejected / get a snub / get snubbed // 야단을 ~ get [catch] a scolding / be scolded [reproved] / (구어) catch it (from) dad // 위기를 ~ be confronted by a crisis.
7 [매·총 등을] get a blow; be struck; be beaten; be knocked; be lashed; be whipped; (총에) be shot. ¶빰을 ~ be boxed on the ears / be slapped across the face // 종아리를 ~ be whipped on the calves // 볼기를 ~ be spanked [flogged] (on the buttocks) // 머리를 ~ be struck on the head // 콧등을 ~ be hit in the nose // 호되게 ~ be struck hard / receive a hard blow // 회초리로 10대를 ~ receive 10 strokes of the lash // 벼락을 ~ be struck (dead) by lightning // 배에 총을 ~ get shot in the stomach / take a bullet [slug] in the guts // 나는 따귀를 맞았다 I was slapped on the cheek. // 그는 다리에 총을 맞았다 He was shot in the leg. // 공이 그의 머리에 맞았다 The ball hit him on the head. // 화살이 과녁의 한가운데에 맞았다 The arrow hit the bull's-eye. // 돌이 유리창에 맞았다 The stone hit [struck] the windowpane.
8 (주사를) get [have] (an injection); take (a needle); (도장·검인을) receive (a seal [a stamp] of approval). ¶팔에 모르핀 주사를 ~ get [have] a morphine shot in [on] the arm // 장티푸스 예방 주사를 ~ be inoculated against typhoid.
9 (점수를) get; receive; gain; take. ¶90점을 ~ get a 90 percent rating // 시험에서 만점을 ~ get [score] full marks in an exam // 영점을 ~ get zero (in English) / receive a zero marking [mark] // 너는 모든 학과에서 80점 이상을 맞아야 한다 You must get more than 80 marks in all subjects.

맞다² **1** [옳다] be right; be correct; (시계가) keep good time; (계산·장부가) balance. ¶맞는 답 a correct [right] answer // 시간이 잘 맞는 [맞지 않는] 시계 a good [bad] timekeeper // 맞게 (대)답하다 give a correct answer / answer right // …이라는 것은 맞는 말이다 It is rightly said that …. // 계산이 딱 맞았다 The calculation came out exactly right. // 네 말이 맞는다 You may well say so. / You are right. // 맞았어 You are right. / That's right. / That's what it is. / To be sure! / (셈을 마치고) All right!
2 [적합하다] suit (one's taste); answer [serve] (the purpose); meet (one's wishes); come (measure) up to (one's expectations); befit. ¶입에 맞는 [맞지 않는] 음식 an agreeable [a disagreeable] food // 체질에 맞는 음식 food suitable to one's constitution // 도리에 맞는 행위 conduct accordant [conformable] to reason // 마음에 맞는 after one's fancy [heart] // 마음에 맞는 여자 a woman after one's heart // 그녀의 이상에 맞는 청년 a youth who represented her ideal // 취미에 맞는 직업 an occupation to one's liking // 마음에 ~ suit one / suit [please / catch / take / capture / strike] (a person's) fancy / suit [flatter] (a person's) taste // 이상에 ~ meet one's ideal / measure up to the ideal // 취미에 ~ suit one's taste / be to one's liking // 그는 장사꾼으로는 맞지 않는다 He is not of a business turn. / He isn't cut out for business [a trader]. / He won't do for [isn't suited to be] a businessman. // 내 가족 전원의 마음에 맞는 집을 구하기란 어렵다 It is difficult to find a house which suits every member of my family.
3 [일치하다] agree (with); accord (with); be in accord (with); be consistent (with); conform (to); [부합하다] coincide (with); correspond (with); tally (with); square (with); be in concordance (with). ¶사실과 맞지 않다 conflict with the facts // 의견이 맞지 않다 differ [vary] in opinion / opinion varies // 말이 사실과 맞는다 The statement squares with the facts. // 그의 말과 행동은 맞지 않는다 His deeds do not match his

words. // 두 사람의 말이 서로 맞는다 Their accounts tally with each other. // 그의 의견은 나와 맞지 않는다 His opinions clash [(문어) are at variance] with mine. // 그 남자는 실물이 인상서(人相書)와 꼭 맞았다 The man met [answered (to)] the description. // 그것은 내 계획과 잘 맞는다 It fits in well with my plan. **4** [조화를 이루다] go (with); match (with); harmonize (with); be in harmony (with); be in tune (with); [어울리다] become. ¶맞는 harmonious / symmetrical / well-matched / 장단이 ~ be in tune // 장단이 맞지 않다 get out of tune / be out of tune (with) // 옷이 아무에게 ~ [맞지 않다] become [do not become] a person // (남녀의) 눈이 ~ become intimate (with) / take up with (a girl) // 그 넥타이는 너의 웃옷에 잘 맞는다 The tie matches your coat well. // 그 저 배우는 손발 [장단]이 잘 맞는다 The two actors agree in tune.

5 (몸 등에) fit; suit; be suited (to); (뚜껑 등이) fit on. ¶몸에 잘 맞는 양복 a well-fitting suit // 잘 맞지 않는 옷 an ill-fitting suit // 맞지 않는 구두 ill-fitting shoes / (짝이) 맞지 않은 구두 an unmatched pair of shoes // 몸에 꼭 (딱) ~ fit perfectly [neatly] / fit like a glove / fit to a T [nicely] / 몸에 잘 ~ [맞지 않다] fit (a person) well [ill] / sit well [badly] / 쐐기가 구멍에 ~ a wedge fits in a hole // 이 옷은 내게 딱 맞는다 This suit fits me perfectly [to a T]. // 이 구두는 나한테 아주 잘 맞는다 These shoes fit me very well [are very comfortable]. // 맞나 안 맞나 한번 입어 보겠다 I will try it on for size. // 열쇠가 자물쇠에 꼭 맞는다 The key fits the lock.

6 [적중하다] hit (the) mark; tell; catch; (예상 등이) prove (to do) right; come true; come off. ¶예언이 ~ a prophecy comes true [comes to pass] / 짐작이 ~ one's guess is right / make a good guess / guess right // 화살이 과녁에 ~ an arrow hits the mark // 총알이 모두 맞았다 All shots told. // 총알이 맞지 않았나 The shot missed [went aside of] the mark. // 그의 추측은 맞았다 [맞지 않았다] He guessed right [wrong]. / He hit [missed] the mark. // 네 말이 꼭 맞았다 You hit the nail on the head. // 탄알이 목표물 복판에 맞았다 The bullet hit the target right in the center. // 맞았어 You have guessed right. / You've hit it. / Good shot! // 그녀의 예언이 딱 맞았다 Her prediction hit the nail on the head. // 오늘 일기 예보는 맞았다 Today's weather forecast proved right.

맞닥뜨리다 meet (with); (미국 구어) meet up with; encounter (the enemy); come across; face; be confronted by [with]. ¶딱 ~ come face to face with // 난관에 ~ face [be brought face to face with / run up against] a difficulty / be confronted by difficulty // 막다른 골목에 ~ run [come] right into a dead end // 길에서 사람을 ~ come across (a person) on the street // 외나무다리에서 원수와 ~ encounter an enemy on a log bridge // 우리는 뜻하지 않은 난관에 맞닥뜨렸다 We ran into an unforeseen difficulty. // 모퉁이를 돌자 인호와 딱 맞닥뜨렸다 Going round the corner, I bumped into Inho. // 이 길을 1마일 쯤 가면 고속도로와 맞닥뜨리게 됩니다 If you follow this road about a mile you will hit the expressway.

맞담배 ¶~를 피우다 smoke to (a person's) face / smoke in the presence of one's superior [elder].

맞당기다 pull [drag / tug] (a rope) from both sides. ¶줄을 ~ tug a rope from both sides // 줄이 맞당겨 끊어졌다 A rope was pulled apart.

맞닿다 come in touch [contact] (with); touch each other. ¶땅과 하늘이 맞닿은 지평선 the horizon where the land and (the) sky seem to meet // 하늘과 바다가 ~ sky and water merge into each other // 그들의 손과 손이 맞닿았다 Their hands met.

맞대다 1 (마주 대다) bring [put] (them) into contact (with each other); [마주 대하다] face (with). ¶맞대고 face to face / vis-à-vis / to (a person's) face / in the presence (of a person) / …과 얼굴을 ~ come [be] face to face with … // 무릎을 ~ sit knee to knee face to face with (a person) / sit opposite each other // 얼굴을 맞대고 앉다 sit face to face [vis-à-vis] (with) // 이마를 맞대고 의논하다 lay [put] (their) heads together / (구어) go into a huddle // 음극을 양극에 ~ put the cathode in contact with the anode // 맞대고 욕하다 [칭찬하다] abuse [praise] (a person) to his face [in his teeth] // 나는 그와 매일 얼굴을 맞대고 일하고 있다 I work face-to-face with him every day. **2** [대면시키다] bring (one person) face to face with (another); confront (a person) with (another). ¶살 사람과 팔 사람을 ~ bring parties to a sale together // 피고와 원고를 ~ bring the accused face to face with the accuser / confront the accused with the accuser // 우리는 양 당사자를 맞대어 의견을 물었다 We brought the two parties concerned together face to face and asked their opinions.

맞대면 (-對面) a face-to-face interview [meeting]. **맞대면하다** interview [confront] face to face; meet face to face.

맞대하다 (-對-) face [confront] each other. ¶맞대하고 앉다 sit face to face (with) / sit vis-à-vis (with) / sit opposite (each other) // 용의자는 수사관과 맞대하게 앉혀졌다 The suspect was seated facing [opposite (to)] the criminal investigator.

맞돈 [spot] cash; ready money; cash [spot] payment. ¶~으로 지불하다 pay in cash / pay (cash) down / pay on the spot // ~으로 사다 [팔다] buy [sell] for (spot) cash // ~으로 거래하다 deal (things) in cash.

맞들다 1 (마주 들다) lift (up) together; hold up together. ¶책상을 ~ lift a desk together. **2** [힘을 합하다] cooperate; unite [join] efforts; join forces (with).

맞뚫다 bore [penetrate] (a tunnel) from both sides.

맞먹다 1 [상당하다] be equal [equivalent] to; be worth; be worthy of. ¶석 달치의 봉급에 맞먹는 보너스 a bonus equivalent to three month's pay // 그 시대의 10원은 지금의 천 원에 맞먹는다 Ten won of those days is worth one thousand won now. // 1달러는 1,200원에 맞먹는다 One dollar is equivalent to 1,200 won. / One thousand two hundred won goes

맞물다 to a dollar.
2 [필적하다] be a match for; match; be as good as; be equal to; rival; stand comparison with. ¶맞먹을 자가 없다 have no equal [match / parallel] / be without a match [peer] / be unrivaled / be peerless // 학급에서 영어 실력으로는 그에게 맞먹을 자가 없다 There is no one in our class who can match him in his ability in English. / He has no equal [is unrivaled] in English in our class. // 두 사람은 기술면에서 거의 맞먹는다 The two are nearly equal in their skill.

맞물다 (기어가) gear (into / with); be in gear (with); engage (with); mesh (with); [치과] occlude(위아래의 이가). ¶두 기어가 맞물고 있다 The two cogwheels engage each other. / The teeth of one gear engage with teeth of another.

맞물리다 go[be] in gear (with). ¶맞물려 있다 [있지 않다] be in[out of] gear // 기어가 잘 맞물린다 The cogs gear smoothly. // 톱니바퀴가 잘 맞물리지 않는다 The gears do not mesh [engage] smoothly. // 윗니와 아랫니가 잘 맞물린다 The upper teeth and lower teeth meet[occlude] well(▶ occlude는 치과 용어).

맞바꾸다 barter (A for B); exchange (one thing for another); (미) trade; truck. ¶시계와 카메라를 ~ exchange a watch for a camera // 쌀과 기계를 ~ barter[trade] rice for machines.

맞바둑 an unhandicapped match of *baduk*; *baduk* players of equal skill. ¶~을 두다 play *baduk* on an equal footing // ~으로 두다 have the first move in alternate games.

맞바람 a head wind; a contrary [an adverse / a foul] wind. ¶배가 ~을 받아 잘 가지 못한다 The ship is held back by a head wind. // 바람은 ~이다 The wind is against us.

맞받다 **1** (정면으로) receive[face] head-on [directly]. ¶햇빛을 ~ receive the sunlight directly. **2** [들이받다] crash head-on (into); collide head-on (with). ¶이마를 ~ bump [knock] heads together / bang heads with each other / bump against[into] each other. **3** [응수하다] give[pay] (a person) tit for tat; make a retort. ¶상대방의 악담에 그도 지지 않고 맞받아 주었다 Undaunted by his opponent's abuse, he retorted as sharply.

맞받이 the opposite[other] side. ¶그 언덕은 우리 집의 ~에 있다 The hill stands just opposite (to) my house.

맞배지기 (씨름의) counter-lifting.

맞벌이 working together (for a living); working in double harness; the joint breadwinning (of husband and wife). ¶그들은 아이린애가 생기기 전에 ~를 하고 있었다 Both of them were working to make a living) before the baby was born. **맞벌이하다** work together for a living; earn a livelihood together; work[run] in double harness. ¶부모가 맞벌이하는 집안의 아이 a door-key child / a latchkey child[kid / boy / girl].
● **맞벌이 가정** a dual-income[two-income] family. **맞벌이 부부** a two-paycheck couple; a working couple. ¶그들은 ~다 They bring home the bacon.

맞벽 (-壁) [건] the outer part of a double wall.

맞보기 plain glasses.

맞보다 face[look at] each other.

맞부딪치다 run[bump / hit / dash] against; run[crash] into; collide with. ¶머리를 ~ bump each other's head // 버스와 트럭이 맞부딪쳤다 A bus collided with a truck. / A bus and a truck ran into each other.

맞붙다 **1** (한데) stick [cling] together. ¶그 두 점포는 서로 맞붙어 있다 The two shops stand close to each other. // 둘은 밤낮 맞붙어 돌아다닌다 They always stick together. // 종이가 맞붙어 떨어지지 않는다 The two pieces of paper are stuck so hard they won't come apart.
2 [격투하다] wrestle[grapple / close] with; be matched against. ¶맞붙어 싸우다 fight hand to hand / come to grips with each other // 그는 도둑과 맞붙었다 He grappled with the burglar. // 이 씨름 선수는 내일 천하장사와 맞붙는다 This wrestler is matched [pitted] against *Cheonhajangsa* tomorrow.

맞붙들다 catch[hold] together[each other]; grapple with each other; get a clinch of each other. ¶어깨를 양쪽에서 ~ hold (a person) by both shoulders // (레슬링 등에서) 맞붙들고 있다 be in holds / be at grips.

맞붙이 **1** [맞대면] a face-to-face interview [meeting]; a direct negotiation. **2** [겹옷] a lined but unwadded[unpadded] garment.

맞붙이다 **1** (물건을) stick [plaster / glue / fix] (things) together. ¶고무 풀로 종이 두 장을 ~ stick[put] two sheets of paper together with 'gum // 나는 접착제로 깨진 찻잔을 맞붙였다 I glued the broken teacup together. // 나는 두 장의 판자를 못을 박아 맞붙였다 I nailed two boards together. **2** (사람을) bring (them) together[into contact]; (경기 등에서) match one competitor with [against] another; pit one against another. ¶저 두 사람을 맞붙이면 누가 이길까 If those two were set against each other, which (do you think) would win?

맞붙잡다 seize[grasp] each other.

맞상대 (-相對) a man-to-man fight; a single (-handed) combat[fight]; a straight fight.

맞서다 **1** [마주 서다] stand face to face (with); face each other; be opposite (to); confront.
2 [대항하다] stand against[up to]; rise against (one's lord); oppose; turn against [upon]; defy; [필적하다] be a match for; stand comparison with. ¶…에[과] 맞서 in opposition to / in rivalry with // 맞서 싸우다 fight against each other // 힘에는 힘으로 ~ meet[counter] face with face // 어른에게 ~ defy one's elders [superiors] / turn upon one's elders // 주인에게 ~ lift a hand against one's master / turn on one's master // 적과 ~ defy [engage] the enemy / face [fight against / stand up to] enemy // 그는 운명에 맞섰다 He fought against fate. // 그들은 주인에게 맞섰다 They turned on[rose against] their master. // 그들은 잔인한 폭군에 맞섰다 They rose against the cruel tyrant. // 사회당은 격렬하게 정부에 맞섰다 The socialist party strongly opposed the Government. // 그에게 맞서는 사람은 아무도 없었다 No one offered him any resistance[opposition]. // 그에게 나는 맞설 수가 없다 I am no match [rival] for him. / He is too much for me. // 영어에서는 그와 맞설 사람이 없다 There is no one who can match him in English.

맞선 a (formal) meeting with a view to marriage; a marriage meeting. ¶~을 보다 be formally introduced to a prospective marriage partner / see each other with a view to marriage / have an interview with one's prospective bride[bridegroom].

맞소송(-訴訟) a counteraction; a counterclaim; a counter-suit.

맞수(-手) a good match[rival]. ⇨＊맞적수

맞아들이다 receive; invite[ask] (a person) in; show[usher] (a person) into (a house). ¶외국인 관광객을 ~ receive foreign tourists // 아내를 ~ take a wife.

맞아떨어지다 tally; be correct. ¶계산이 ~ a calculation is correct / the figures tally // 꼭 ~ exactly correspond to / correspond point for point // 이것은 자네 말과 맞아떨어진다 This fall in with your story. // 내 계산은 네 계산과 맞아떨어진다 My figures tally[check] with yours.

맞욕(-辱) counter-abuse; answering back with abusive language; calling (a person) names right back. **맞욕하다** abuse[curse / inveigh] back; call (a person) names back; answer back with abuse; use abusive language back.

맞은편(-便) [반대쪽] the opposite side [place]; the other side; [상대편] the opposite[other] party; one's opponent party; the opposing team. ¶~ 집 the house opposite [over the way / across the street] // 내 ~에 앉아 있는 사람 the person in the seat facing me[directly across from me] // 이 집 ~의 가게 the shop directly opposite[just in front of] this house / 강 ~에 across the river / on the opposite[other] side of the river // ~에서 오다 come from the opposite direction // 그 호텔은 역 바로 ~에 있다 The hotel is just across from the station. // 그는 우리 집 ~에 살고 있다 He lives opposite our house [across the street from us]. // 회의석상에서 그들은 서로 ~에 앉아 있었다 They were sitting vis-à-vis at the conference.

-맞이 meeting; greeting; welcoming; reception. ¶손님~ reception of guests.

맞이하다 [영접하다] meet; go (out) to meet; [접대하다] receive; play host to; [환영하다] welcome; make (a person) welcome; greet; hail; [맞아들이다] invite; engage; (때를) meet; face; be confronted (by); [즈음하여] be on the eve of (a general election). ¶역에 나가 ~ go to the station to meet (a person) / meet (a person) with a smile / smile a welcome to (a person) / 60세의 생일을 ~ see one's 60th birthday come round / mark [attain] one's 60th birthday // 아내를 ~ take a wife / get married // 따뜻이 ~ give (a person) a warm reception / receive (a person) with warm hands // 그는 현관으로 나와서 나를 맞이했다 He came out to welcome[greet] me at the door. // 주인 부부가 홀에서 손님을 맞이했다 The host and hostess received their guests in the hall. // 아버지는 조용히 죽음을 맞이했다 My father met his death calmly. // 군중은 환호성으로 영웅을 맞이했다 The crowd received the hero with cheers. // 결혼해서 두 번째의 봄을 맞이했다 The second spring after our marriage came around. // 새해를 맞이하여 만복을 빕니다 (A) Happy New Year (to you).

맞잡다 take each other; take[hold] together. ¶탁자를 맞잡아 들다 lift a table together.

맞잡이 a good match; an equal; a peer. ¶씨름 [장기]의 ~ a good match in wrestling [chess].

맞장구치다 [남의 말에 동조하다] give responses that make a conversation go smoothly; echo (another's words); make agreeable responses; chime in (with others); flatter [ingratiate oneself with] a person. ¶남의 이야기에 ~ throw in words of agreement[encouragement] while a person is speaking.

맞장기(-將棋) even-match *janggi*; an unhandicapped *janggi* game. ¶~를 두다 play a game of *janggi* with no handicap / play *janggi* on even terms.

맞적수(-敵手) a good match[rival]; a worthy opponent; a lively competitor; an equal; a peer.

맞절 mutual bowing. **맞절하다** bow to each other; greet each other; exchange bows (with). ¶공손하게 ~ bow deeply at each other.

맞접다 fold together; fold on itself.

맞줄임 [수] abbreviation. ⇨＊약분(約分)

맞추다 1 [대조하다] compare (with); check (with); collate (with); verify; tally (with). ¶원장과 ~ compare with[refer to] the ledger // 그는 재고를 목록과 맞추어 보았다 He checked the stock with[against] a list. // 번역문을 원문과 맞추어 보아라 Compare the translation with the original.

2 [조립하다] assemble; fix up; put[fit / piece] together. ¶시계를 분해했다가 다시 ~ reassemble [overhaul] a watch // 부품을 맞추어 완제품을 만들다 assemble the parts into a complete unit.

3 [맞게 하다] set[fit / adjust / adapt / conform / square / gear] (one thing to another); tune (something to the purpose); bring (a thing) into line (with another). ¶피아노[테이프에 녹음된] 반주에 맞추어 노래하다 sing to piano[taped] accompaniment // 보조를 ~ keep[fall into] step (with) // 수지를 ~ make[gain] a profit / profit (from the sale) // 미터를 영(零)에 맞추시오 Set the meter at zero. // 나는 시계를 매일 아침 라디오의 시보에 맞춘다 I set my watch by the time signal on the radio every morning. // 나는 바이올린의 선율을 피아노에 맞추었다 I tuned the violin to the piano. // 라디오를 KBS의 FM에 맞추어 주게 Tune the radio in to KBS FM. // 나는 6시 반에 자명종을 맞추어 놓았다 I set the alarm for six thirty. // 우리는 음악에 맞추어 춤을 추었다 We danced to the music. // 그녀는 멜로디에 맞추어 몸을 흔들었다 She swayed to the melody. // 나는 피아노에 맞추어 플루트를 불었다 I played the flute to the accompaniment of the piano.

4 [적응시키다] fit; adapt; accomodate; meet; [조화시키다] match (colors). ¶세인의 기호에 ~ suit[hit] the taste of the public / hit [capture] the popular fancy // 비위를 ~ curry favor with (a person) / ingratiate oneself with (one's master) / flatter / fawn upon // 몸에 맞추어 드레스를 줄이다 take in a dress to fit[to make it fit] a person // 넥타이를 옷에 ~ make a match of tie with one's suit // 이 장소에 맞추어 탁자를 만들어 주십시

오. Make a table to fit into this space.
5 [접합시키다] join (one thing to another); piece on (one thing to another); piece[put] (broken pieces) together. ¶뼈를 ~ set a fracture[a broken bone] // 뼌 데를 ~ set a dislocation.
6 [마주 대다] touch. ¶입을 ~ kiss (a girl on the mouth) / press one's lips against // 볼에 입을 ~ kiss (a person) on the cheek.
7 [주문하다] give an order (for an article to a maker); order (an article from a maker); place an order (with a maker). ¶백화점에서 맞춘 양복 a suit made to order[custom-made] at a department store // 새로 맞춘 드레스 a newly-made[brand-new] dress // 구두를 ~ have a pair of shoes on order // 코트를 새로 맞추었다 I had a new coat made. // 그는 맞춘 옷을 입고 있다 He is wearing a custom-made suit. / The suit he is wearing was made to order. // 그녀는 옷을 모두 맞추어서 입는다 She has all her dresses made to order. // 무엇으로 맞추겠습니까 What about the order, please? // 그는 15만 원에 양복을 맞추었다 He gave an order for a suit at 150,000 won. // 당신은 옷을 어디서 맞춥니까 Who is your dressmaker?(▶ dressmaker는 여자 옷의 경우) / Where do you have your dresses[suits] made?

맞춤 [주문] an order; [주문품] an article ordered; a thing made to order; an order. ¶~의 ordered / custom-[tailor-]made / custom-tailored // ~으로 짓다 make (a suit) to order.
●**맞춤옷** a suit made to measure[order]; a tailor-[custom-]made suit; a (custom-)tailored suit; [미] a custom suit.
맞춤법(-法) orthography; the rules of spelling; orthographical rules. ¶한글 ~ the spelling system of *Hangeul* / the rules of Korean spelling[orthography] // 현행 ~ the current[present] spelling system // ~에 맞추어 쓰다 spell correctly according to the rules of orthography // ~을 익히다 learn to spell correctly / learn a correct spelling.
●**맞춤법 통일안** a draft for unified spelling system.
맞혼인(-婚姻) a marriage with equal share of expenses between the two families.
맞흥정 face-to-face bargaining[chaffering]; a first-hand[direct] deal. **맞흥정하다** make a direct[buyer-to-seller] bargain; bargain [chaffer] (with a tradesman) directly; make a deal without a broker.
맞히다 **1** (목표에) hit (the mark). ¶잘 ~ make a good hit // 못 ~ miss the mark // 과녁에 화살을 ~ shoot an arrow into the target / hit the mark with an arrow // 과녁의 중심을 ~ hit the bull's-eye / hit[make] a bull's-eye on the target.
2 (옳은 답을) guess right; make a good guess [hit]; hit the truth; hit the nail on the head. ¶답을 ~ answer right / give a right[correct] answer // 맞히지 못하다 miss one's guess / make a wrong guess // 바로 맞혔다 That's (exactly) it. / You hit the mark. / You have guessed right. / You have it the nail on the head. / That's the very thing.
3 (비·바람 등을) expose (to); subject (to). ¶비[바람]를 ~ expose to[leave out in] the rain[air] // 비를 맞히지 않도록 하다 protect [keep] (a thing) from the rain.
4 (주사 등을). ¶주사를 ~ have (a child) get an injection // 장티푸스 예방 주사를 ~ get (a child) inoculated against typhoid.

맡기다 **1** [보관시키다] entrust[trust] (a person with a thing / a thing to a person); deposit[leave] (a thing with a person [in a bank]); place[leave] (a thing) in (a person's) charge[hands]; put (a thing) in charge of (a person); leave [check] (a thing) with (a person); give (a thing) into (a person's) keeping[custody]. ¶돈을 ~ entrust a person with one's money / trust one's money to a person // 돈을 은행에 ~ put[deposit] money in a bank / keep one's money in a bank // 귀중품을 남에게 ~ place valuables in a person's custody / entrust jewels to[with] a person // 짐을 ~ (미) check one's baggage / (영) book one's luggage // 집을 이웃 사람에게 ~ leave one's house in charge of a neighbor // 귀중품은 보관소에 맡겨 주십시오 Check your valuables at the checkroom, please. // 그 보석함은 그에게 맡겨 놓고 있다 The jewel case is in his keeping. / The jewel case has been left with him. // 이 서류를 맡기겠소 I will leave these papers with you. // 그 코트를 휴대품 보관소에 맡기는 게 어떻습니까 Why don't you leave that coat with the check girl?
2 [위임하다] assign; entrust (a matter) to (a person); entrust (a person) with (a task); leave (a matter) (up) to (a person); leave (a person) with (a matter); trust (a person) with (something); commit[leave] (something) to (a person's) care; delegate (a task) to (a person). ¶임무를 ~ charge (a person) with a duty / assign (a person) to a task[job] / place a duty upon (a person) // 책임을 ~ place[put / thrust] the responsibility (for something) on (a person) / saddle (a person) with responsibility (for) // 싸움의 중재를 ~ leave a quarrel for (a person) to settle // 모든 것을 너에게 맡긴다 I leave everything to you. / I leave everything in your hands. // 그에게 이 일을 맡길 수 없다 I cannot trust him with[to do] this task. / He cannot be entrusted with this task. // 최근에 그에게 중요한 책임이 맡겨지고 있다 These days he is being given important responsibilities. // 그에게 보안 요원의 임무를 맡기자 Let's assign him to the maintenance crew. // 주역이 내게 맡겨졌다 The main role was assigned to me.
3 (사람을) put (a child) with (a person); leave (a child) in the care of (a person); place (a child) under (a person's) care; give (a person) charge of (a child). ¶환자를 의사에게 ~ leave a patient to the doctor's care // 나는 어린아이를 누님에게 맡겼다 I left my child in my sister's care[charge] // 아이의 후견인 역은 그에게 맡겨졌다 The boy was placed under his guardianship.
4 [방임하다] leave (a person to do something); let (a person do something). ¶운을 하늘에 ~ leave it to chance / trust to luck [chance] // 본능이 이끄는 대로 몸을 ~ act according to the dictates of one's instinct // 상상에 맡기겠다 I'll leave it to your imagination.

맡다¹ **1** [보관하다] keep; receive (a thing) in

trust[custody]; take charge of (a thing); take (a thing) in charge; take (a thing) under one's charge; have the custody of (a thing); be entrusted with (a thing); take over. ¶맡은 돈 money left in one's keeping // 고아를 맡아서 기르다 take charge of[take in] an orphaned child and bring him up // 돈을 가지고 돌아올 때까지 이 시계를 맡아 주시오 Here's my watch to keep until I come back with the money. // 출발 2시간 전까지 이 항공표를 맡아 두겠습니다 We will hold the ticket until two hours before flight time.

2 (책임지다·담당[감독]하다) undertake; take on; take[have] charge of; be in charge of (a class); take in hand; take (it) upon oneself (to do); charge oneself (with the work); have (a boy) under one's charge [care]; assume the care of (children); take (a person) in charge. ¶그 사무를 맡은 사람 a man in charge of the business // 일을 ~ undertake a job / take a job on oneself // 의장직을 ~ accept[take on] post of chairman // 사건의 처리를 맡기로 하다 agree to take care of an affair // 주문을 맡다 accept an order // 노인 역을 맡아 하다 act[play] the part of an old man // 그녀는 아동 도서실을 맡아 돌보고 있다 She takes charge of the children's library. / The children's library is under her charge. // 부부가 여행하는 동안에 내가 그들의 집을 맡아 보았다 While the couple were away on a trip, I took care of their house. // 그가 한번 일을 맡으면 사건은 깨끗이 해결된다 Once he takes charge of them, cases are settled[cleared up] at once. // 이 일은 내가 맡겠다 I'll handle[undertake / manage] this job. // 저분은 어떤 직책을 맡고 있습니까 What office does that gentleman hold? // 선장은 수천 명의 생명을 맡고 있다 The captain has the safety of thousands of lives in his keeping. // 그는 판매원으로 이 지역을 맡고 있다 He covers this district as a salesman. // 그는 환영회에서 주역을 맡아 했다 He played the leading role at the reception. // 나는 2학년을 맡고 있다 I am in charge of the second-graders[second-year student]. (▶ second-year students는 중학생 이상의 경우) // 내가 심판을 맡았다 I acted as referee. // 내가 그 일을 맡기로 정해졌다 It was decided that I should take on the job[undertake the responsibility].

3 (허가 등을) get; obtain; receive; be given; have; take out (a license). ¶허가를 ~ obtain[be granted] permission / get a permit // 면허를 ~ get[obtain / secure] a license / be licensed // 여기서 사진을 찍으려면 당국의 허가를 맡아야 한다 You must apply to the authorities for permission to take a photograph here.

맡다² **1** (냄새를 느끼다) smell; scent; (개 등이) sniff. ¶냄새를 잘 맡는 사람 a person sensitive to odor / a person of sensitive nostril // 냄새를 ~ smell (at) (a flower) / take a smell (at) / have a smell (of) // 이 꽃 냄새를 맡아 봐 Smell at this flower. // 개는 누군가가 바닥에 떨어뜨린 손수건의 냄새를 맡았다 The dog sniffed at the handkerchief somebody had dropped on the floor. // 불고기 냄새를 맡으니 나는 배가 고파졌다 The smell of the roasted meat made me hungry.

2 (냄새를 알다) scent; get wind of; smell a rat; smell out (a secret); detect a secret; (미) get wise; (속어) smoke out. ¶계략의 낌새를 ~ sniff out[get wind of] a trick[plot] // 여기 있는 것을 어떻게 냄새 맡았나 How did you learn that I was here? / How did you dig me up out here?

매¹ **1** (막대 끝에 가죽 끈·노끈을 매단) a whip; (가죽으로 된) a lash; (막대 모양의) a rod; (교사용의) a pointer. ¶~를 **때리다** lash / flog / whip / swish / cane / switch (a boy with a cane) / (구어) tan / give (a person) the rod [a caning / a thrashing] // ~를 **맞다** be whipped / be lashed / be caned / get the cane / be flogged // 죄인을 ~로 50번 때리다 give a criminal fifty lashes // 또 ~를 맞고 싶으냐 Do you want another thrashing? // 그런 짓을 하면 ~ 맞는다 If you do such a thing, you will get licked. // 훗날에 아버지의 사랑의 ~를 고맙게 생각했다 Later in life I appreciated my father's loving severity.

2 whipping; lashing. ⇨매질

매² **1** a (stone) hand mill. ⇨맷돌 **2** a wooden hand mill for hulling rice. ⇨매통

매³ (동) a hawk; (매 사냥용의) a falcon. ¶~ 같은 hawkish // ~의 발톱 a hawk's talons.

매⁴ (양·염소의 울음소리) baa; bleat. ¶염소가 ~ 울었다 The goat bleated.

-매 (모양) a shape; a form; (외양) appearance; (모습) figure. ¶눈~ a look (in a person's eyes) / an expression of the eyes // 몸~ one's figure[shape] / one's physique.

매 (枚) a sheet (of paper); a leaf (of a book). ¶80원짜리 우표 10~ ten 80-won stamps.

매 (每) every; each; apiece. ¶~ 월요일 every monday // ~ 페이지마다 every page / page after page.

매가 (買價) (사는 값) a purchase[buying] price; (경) the price on demands.

매가 (賣家) selling a house; a house for[on] sale. **매가하다** sell a house.

매가 (賣價) (파는 값) a sale price; a selling price; a labeled price.

매가오리 (동) an eagle ray.

매각 (賣却) sale; disposal (by sale). **매각하다** sell (off); dispose of (by sale). ¶그는 집을 매각했다 He sold his house.

● **매각인** a seller; a vendor. **매각 조건** terms of sale. **매각 처분** disposal[disposition] by sale.

매개 (일이 되어 가는 형편) the course (of events); the development (of an affair); the progress (of inquiries); (추이) the turn (of events). ¶~를 **보다** watch the development [course] of events / wait and see how things will turn out / wait for the turn of events.

매개 (媒介) intermediation; intervention; mediation; agency; (논)(철) mediacy. ¶…의 ~에 의하여 through the medium[agency / instrumentality] of … / by[through] the good offices[the instrumentality] of … // 말라리아는 모기의 ~로 전파된다 Malaria is carried[conveyed] by the mosquito. **매개하다** (inter)mediate[intervene] (between two parties); act as (an) intermediary; serve as a medium; (전파하다) carry (germs). ¶모기는 종종 전염병을 매개한다 The mosquito is often a carrier[vehicle] of infectious disease.

● **매개물** a medium; an agency; (병균의) a carrier; a vehicle. ¶전염병의 ~ a vehicle of infection. **매개 변수** (수) parameter.

매개념(媒概念) [논] the middle concept [term].

매고르다 [비슷하다] all alike; much[nearly] the same; [가지런하다] even; uniform; regular.

매관매직(賣官賣職) corruption in the government personnel administration; trafficking of official posts; [엽관 제도] spoils system. **매관매직하다** traffic in government positions; practice payoff deals for appointive offices.

매국(賣國) selling one's country; betrayal of [treachery to] one's country. **매국하다** sell [betray] one's country; be treacherous to one's country.
● **매국노** a traitor (to one's country); a betrayer (of one's country); a quisling.

매기(每期) [기간] each[every] period [term]; [회기] each[every] session[sitting]; [지불의] each[every] quarter.

매기(買氣) a bullish[buying] sentiment [tone]; buying enthusiasm[disposition]. ¶~가 있다 be in the buying mood // ~가 붙다 [떨어지다] get[lose] buying[bullish] support // ~가 활발하다[침체하다] The buying is brisk[dull].

매기다 [정하다] decide; set; put; fix. ¶값을 ~ price / mark the price on (an article) / set [put] a price on (an article) // 등급을 ~ classify / grade // 점수를 ~ score / give marks // 눈금을 ~ graduate (a thermometer) / mark with degrees // 이 물건은 비싼 값을 매길 수 있겠다 I can give a good price for this.

매끄럽다 [반드럽다] smooth; sleek; velvety; glassy; [미끄럽다] slippery; greasy; [언] lenis; [생] glabrous. ¶매끄럽게 smoothly / [막힘없이] without a hitch // 매끄러운 바닥 [표면 / 피부] a smooth floor[surface / skin] // 매끄러운 모피 a glassy fur // 매끄러운 종이 sleek[slick] paper // 매끄럽게 하다 smooth / make (the surface) smooth // 그의 문장은 매끄러운 맛이 없다 There is no easiness in his style. // 길이 ~ The streets are as slick as glass. // 보트는 매끄럽게 나아갔다 The boat glided forward.

매끈거리다 feel smooth; be slippery. ⇨<미끈거리다

매끈매끈하다 greasy; clammy. ⇨미끈미끈하다

매끈하다 sleek; slender. ⇨미끈하다

매나니 1 [맨손] a bare[an empty] hand (in doing something). ¶~로 with empty[bare] hands / empty-handed. 2 [맨밥] a meal without (proper) side dishes; a simple [a plain] diet.

매너 manners. ¶테이블 ~ table manners // ~가 좋은[나쁜] 사람 a well-mannered[an ill-mannered] person / ~가 좋다 have good manners // 그는 ~가 돼먹지 않았다[없다] He has no manners. // 그 가수는 무대 ~가 좋다 The singer bears[handles] himself well on the stage.

매너리즘 a mannerism. ¶~에 빠지다 become stereotyped / fall into mannerism // 최근에 노동 운동은 ~화되고 있다 The labor movement has become stereotyped recently. // 년간 같은 자리에 앉아 있으면 ~에 빠지기 쉽다 If you stay in one position for many years, you tend to get into a rut. // 그는 젊은 화가들에게 ~에 빠지지 않도록 주의시켰다 He cautioned the young painters to avoid the pitfalls of mannerism.

매년(每年) every year; yearly; annually; per year. ¶~의 annual / yearly // ~의 행사 annual [yearly] events // ~ 이맘때쯤 at this time every year / at this time of the year // ~ 1회 once a[every] year // ~ 이 지방에는 홍수가 진다 Flood is practically an annual occurrence in this district. // 나는 ~ 설악산에 간다 I go to Seoraksan(Mt. Seorak) every year. // ~ 물가가 오른다 Prices rise year after year.

매니저 a manager; (프로 복싱 등의) a handler; (흥행의) an impresario (*pl.* ~s, -ri); proprietor. ¶여자 ~ a female manager / a manageress // 호텔의 ~ the manager of a hotel // 무대 ~ a stage manager.

매니큐어(*manicure) [손톱 물감] (미) (a) nail polish; (영) (a) nail varnish. (▶ manicure는 손과 손톱을 다듬는 일을 가리킴) ¶~ 지우개 a nail-polish remover // ~를 바르다[칠하다] (스스로) manicure / do manicuring / (남을 시켜서) have[get] a manicure // ~를 지우다 remove the nail polish[(영) nail varnish].

매다¹ 1 [동여 묶다] tie (up); fasten (together); bind; lash; lace; [매듭을 짓다] make[tie] a knot; (높은 곳에) hang oneself (on a tree / down from a tree branch). ¶뒤로 매는 혁대 a back-tied belt / 단단히 ~ tie securely [hard] / tie[bind / make] fast // 구두끈을 ~ tie a shoestring[shoelace] / lace (up) one's boots / tie one's shoes // 넥타이를 ~ tie a necktie // 허리띠를 ~ fasten [put on] a belt / use one's belt around one's waist / tie [wear / use] a belt // 실의 끝을 ~ knot the end of the thread // 목을 매어 죽이다 strangle (a person) to death // 이 밧줄은 잘 매어지지 않는다 This rope won't tie. // 그는 오늘 넥타이를 매고 왔다 He came wearing [in] a tie today. // 그는 구두끈을 단단히 매었다 He tied [fastened] his shoestrings tightly.
2 [묶어 두다] tie; fasten; chain; last; (말을) hitch; tether; (배를) moor; tie up; keep on (a) leash (개 등을). ¶말을 (나무에) ~ tie [fasten / hitch] a horse (to a tree) // 개를 나무에 ~ tie a dog to a tree // 개를 가죽 끈으로 매어 두다 keep[have / hold] a dog on a leash // 배를 부둣가에 ~ tie up a boat alongside the quay // 부표에 배를 매어 두다 moor a boat to a buoy // 돛을 돛대에 ~ fasten sails to the mast // 배들이 밧줄로 매어져 있다 The boats are tied with a rope.
3 [묶어 만들다] bind; make. ¶책을 ~ bind a book // 선반을 ~ make a shelf / fix a shelf (to a wall) // 붓을 ~ make a brush.
4 [치다] stretch; extend; string. ¶밧줄을 ~ stretch a rope (between) // 빨랫줄을 ~ stretch a clothesline.
5 (베를) paste the threads of hemp (to stiffen for weaving).

매다² [풀을 뽑다] weed (out). ¶김을 ~ sweep off weeds / weed out // 논을 ~ sweep off [weed out] a rice paddy.

매달(每-) every[each] month; monthly. ¶~ 지불 monthly payment [installments] // ~의 monthly // ~ 한 번 once a month / monthly // ~ 두 번 twice a month // 그는 ~ 진찰받는다 He consults[sees] a doctor every month.

//나는 수입에서 ~ 얼마씩 저축한다 I save some portion of my income every month.

매달다 [달아매다] hang (up); suspend; swing; sling; dangle. ¶사슬로 ~ hang by a chain//실로 ~ suspend (a ball) with a string//고양이의 목에 방울을 ~ attach a bell to a cat / bell a cat//천장에 모빌(각종 조각들에 실·철사를 꿰어 매다는 조형물)을 ~ hang[suspend] a mobile from the ceiling//대들보에 목을 ~ hang oneself from a beam of one's house//노인은 목을 매달아 죽었다 The old man hanged himself.(▶ 이 뜻의 hang은 규칙 동사)

매달리다 1 [달리다] hang down (from); be hung (down); be suspended (from); dangle; swing. ¶공중에 ~ hang in the air[midair]//귤이 나무에 주렁주렁 매달려 있다 Oranges are dangling all over the orange tree.//램프가 천장에 매달려 있었다 A lamp was suspended[hanging] from the ceiling.//그는 공중의 밧줄에 매달려 있었다 He was hanging by a rope in midair. / He was dangling from a single rope in midair.
2 [붙잡다] cling to; hang on; hold on to (a person); take[catch / get] hold of (a rope). ¶팔에 ~ cling to a person's arm//(전철 등의 가죽) 손잡이에 ~ hang on[hold on to] a strap//결사적으로 ~ hold on to (a rope) for dear life[like grim death]//제인은 항상 엄마에게 작별어 있었다 Jane was always clinging to her mother.//그녀는 여러 사람 앞에서도 자기 보이프렌드에게 매달린다 She hangs onto her boyfriend even in public.//아이들은 산타클로스에게 매달렸다 The children clung to Santa Claus.//그들은 전복된 보트에 매달렸다 They hung on[clung] to the capsized boat.//나는 밧줄에 매달려 암벽을 내려왔다 I went down the rocky cliff cling[hanging on] to a rope.//그녀는 그의 어깨에 매달려 울었다 She wept on his shoulder.//그는 매달리는 처자에게 작별을 고하지 않을 수 없었다 He had to bid farewell to his wife and children, who had thrown their arms around him.//그는 두꺼운 판자에 매달려 구조를 요청했다 Hanging on [Clinging] to a plank, he cried for help.//그는 헬리콥터에서 내려진 밧줄에 매달렸다 He caught[took / got] hold of the rope lowered from the helicopter.
3 [달라붙다] hold on to; stick (fast) to; adhere to; cling to. ¶…에 매달려 있다 be devoted to … / give one's whole[full] time to … / devote all one's energies to … / be given up to …//일에 매달려 있으면 어떻게든 살아갈 수 있다 As long as I stick to[at] my work, I can earn a living somehow or other.//아이들 치다꺼리에 매달려 나는 텔레비전도 못 본다 I am too busy with [taking care of] my children even to watch TV.//밤새도록 나는 그 보고서에 매달려 있었다 I devoted myself to the report throughout the night.//그 일에는 세 사람이 매달려 있다 The job takes three person's time and energy.//아들이 살아 있을지도 모른다는 가냘픈 희망에 매달려 나는 허둥지둥 달려왔습니다 I hurried here hoping against hope[clinging to a faint hope] that my son might be alive.
4 [의지하다] depend [rely / lean] on[upon]; place [put] dependence on; place [put] reliance on[in]. ¶매달린 식구 family dependents//아들에게 ~ depend upon one's son for support / lean on one's son//그에게는 매달린 식구가 많다 He has a big family to support. / He has many mouths to feed.//이제는 내게 매달리지 말고 자립하게 Now get yourself to stand alone from me. / Don't depend upon me any longer.

매대기 smearing [daubing] all over (with); besmearing.
매대기(를) 치다 bedaub; besmear; daub all over. ¶그의 몸에는 진흙이 매대기 쳐져 있었다 He was all besmeared with mud.

매도(罵倒) denunciation; condemnation; scathing [severe] criticism; abuse; raillery.
매도하다 denounce; condemn; abuse; decry; criticize severely; hurl abuse (at); rail (at); cry down; call (a person) hard names.

매도(賣渡) sale and delivery. **매도하다** sell (something) over to (a person); negotiate (a bill); sign away (one's property, one's rights, etc.).
● **매도 계약** a contract for selling. **매도인** a seller; [법] a vendor[a vender]. **매도 증서** a bill of sale; a sales note(매도 계약서).

매독(梅毒) [의] syphilis; (미국 속어) a secret disease; (비어) pox. ¶**선천성** ~ congenital syphilis//**양성** ~ florid syphilis//**유전성** ~ hereditary syphilis//**음성** ~ latent syphilis//~**성의** syphilitic / luetic//**제1[2 / 3]기** ~ primary[secondary / tertiary] syphilis//~**에 걸리다** contract[catch / get] syphilis / become syphilitic / suffer from syphilis.
● **매독 환자** a syphilitic (person).

매듭 1 (끈의) a knot (in a rope); a tie; [해] a bend. ¶**나비** ~ a bowknot / a rosette(리본)//**당기면 풀리는** ~ a running knot//~**을 풀다** unknot / untie[undo] a knot / pick a knot apart//~**을 꽉 죄다** tighten a knot//~**을 늦추다** loosen a knot / make a knot loose//~**이 풀렸다** The knot has come untied [undone].//끈의 ~이 느슨해졌다 The knot in the string loosened.//그 ~이 단단해서 푸는 데 시간이 걸렸다 It took me some time to undo the hard knot. **2** [일의 해결] a settlement; [결말] a conclusion; an end; [합의] an agreement.

매듭짓다 [결말짓다] settle; fix (up); finish; conclude; bring (a matter) to an end[a conclusion]; put an end to; (미) be through with; (미) close up (one's affairs). ¶**매듭지어지다** [결말이 나다] be settled[fixed] / be concluded / be finished / be completed / be brought to completion / (타협되다) reach [arrive at / come to] an agreement / be brought to an agreement / be arranged//무사히 매듭지어지다 be settled in peace / come to peaceful settlement//문제를 ~ settle a matter (with a person) / 연구를 ~ round off (one's) researches//논문[과제 작품]을 ~ put a conclusion to (one's) theme//일을 ~ bring (one's) work to an end / finish (one's) work//쌍방이 만족하게 일을 ~ arrange a matter to the satisfaction of both parties//네가 어떻게든 일을 매듭지어 주어야겠다 I want you to settle [fix] the matter somehow.//나는 일을 벌여 놓고 매듭지을 줄을 모른다 I am ready to start a job but never gets it done.//우리는 협상을 매듭짓지 못했다 We could not bring the negotiations to a successful conclusion. / Negotiations fell through.//조속히 일을 매듭지어 주십시오 I should like to have

매력 the matter brought to a speedy settlement. // 이젠 이 문제를 매듭지었으면 한다 I'd like to put the matter to rest [bring the matter to a conclusion] now. // 그 일은 이미 매듭지어졌다 The matter has already been settled. // 이 일은 빨리 매듭지어져야 한다 The matter demands a speedy settlement. // 이 문제는 좀처럼 매듭지어지지 않는다 This matter is proving rather hard to settle.

매력(魅力) (a) charm; a bewitching [spellbinding] power; (a) fascination; glamo(u)r; attractiveness; (an) appeal; an allure; a lure. ¶~ 없는 unappealing / unattractive // 성적(性)인 ~ a sex appeal / a lure to the other sex / (속어) "it" // 여성적인 ~ feminine attraction / ~ 있는 여자 a glowingly attractive woman / ~ 없는 여자 a plain [homely] woman / 관광지로서 ~ 있는 나라 a land of travel lure // ~이 있다 appeal (to) / have an appeal [a fascination] (to) / have an allure (for) / have something attractive // ~이 없다 do not appeal (to) / have [offer] no appeal (to) / have no charms (for) / have nothing attractive // ~을 느끼다 be charmed [fascinated] (by) // ~을 잃다 lose (one's [its]) appeal / lose (its) glamor // …에 ~을 느끼지 않게 되다 grow [become] disenchanted with … // 파리는 관광객에게 아주 ~ 있는 곳이다 Paris has a great charm for tourists. / 그에게는 뭔가 사람을 끌어당기는 ~이 있다 There is something engaging [attractive] about him. / 그녀의 아름다운 눈에 ~을 느꼈다 I was fascinated [charmed / attracted] by her beautiful eyes.

매력적(魅力的) charming; fascinating; attractive; appealing. ¶~인 개성 a magnetic personality / ~인 여자 a glowingly attractive woman / 아버지는 ~인 남성이었다 My father was a man of charm.

매료하다(魅了-) charm; fascinate; captivate; cast a spell (on); hold (the audience) spellbound. ¶그의 연기는 관객을 매료했다 His performance hold the audience spellbound. → 그는 경치의 아름다움에 매료되었다 He was fascinated [captivated] by the scenic beauty of the spot.

매립(埋立) (land) reclamation; filling-up. ¶해안 ~ reclamation of the foreshore. **매립하다** fill in (a moat); fill up (a pond with earth); reclaim [gain] (land from the sea); recover. ¶그들은 바다를 매립하여 공업 지대로 만들었다 They reclaimed land from the sea and made it into an industrial area.

● **매립 공사** reclaiming [reclamation] work. **매립지** a reclaimed [filled / filled-up / filled-in] land [ground].

매만지다 adjust (one's dress); tidy [do] up; tend; trim; groom; care for. ¶곱게 매만진 머리 well-groomed hair / one's hair slicked neat // 머리를 ~ fix [arrange] one's hair / smooth one's hair down / give a smooth to the hair // 옷매무새를 ~ adjust oneself [one's dress] / straighten one's dress [clothes] / tidy oneself / (미) fix oneself // 정원을 ~ tend trees and plants in the garden / engage in horticulture // 나는 헝클어진 머리를 급히 손가락으로 매만졌다 I hastily smoothed my hair back [down] with my fingers.

매맛 the bitters of a whip. ¶~을 보이다 lash / flog / whip / switch (a boy) (with a cane) / (구어) give (a person) a hiding // ~을 보다 be whipped [lashed] / get the cane / (구어) get a hiding // ~을 알아야 게으름 피우지 않겠지 I'll flog laziness out of you!

매매(賣買) buying and [or] selling; purchase and [or] sale; [거래] trade; dealing; transaction; a bargain; traffic (in furs, in narcotics, etc.); (속어) a deal. ¶견본 ~ a sale by sample / a sale by pattern // 부정 ~ an illegal [illicit] bargain // 선물(先物) ~ a future sale [trading] / a forward bargain // 예약 ~ a sale by subscription // 위장 ~ a wash sale // 위탁 ~ consignment sales and purchases // 인신 ~ human traffic // 직접 ~ a direct sale // 투기 ~ a sale on contingent / speculative trade / 현물 ~ a spot sale [transaction] // 현찰 ~ a cash sale // 국제적인 무기 ~ the international traffic in arms // ~를 약정하다 strike [close] a bargain / close a contract [deal] // ~를 확인하다 confirm a sale / ~를 취소하다 cancel a contract [deal] // 증권 거래소에서는 약 20만 주의 ~가 있었다 About 200,000 shares changed hands on the Exchange. **매매하다** buy [purchase] and sell; deal [trade] (in); traffic (in); market; handle (취급하다). ¶토지를 ~ deal in land // 어음 [증권]을 ~ negotiate a bill.

● **매매 가격** sale price. **매매 계약** a sales contract; a bargain. **매매 조건** sales terms; terms of sale [transaction / bargaining]. **매매 증서** a bill of sale; a contract note.

매머드 1 [동] a mammoth. 2 [거대한 것] a mammoth.

● **매머드 기업** a mammoth enterprise. **매머드 도시** a huge city; a megalopolis; a megacity.

매명(賣名) self-advertisement. ¶~을 위하여 for publicity's sake / as a publicity stunt / from motives of self-advertisement. **매명하다** seek [court / strive for] publicity; publicize [advertise] oneself.

매목(埋木) lignite; fossil wood; bogwood.

매몰(埋沒) burying. **매몰하다** bury (in / under). → 그 산사태로 집이 매몰되었다 The house was buried under the landslide.

매몰스럽다 heartless; cold; pitiless; unkind; callous; hard; hard-[cold- / stony-]hearted; cruel. ¶매몰스럽게 heartlessly / cold-heartedly / pitilessly / coldly / harshly / cruelly // 매몰스러운 사람 a cold-hearted [stony-hearted] person // 매몰스럽게 굴다 treat (a person) coldly [in a cold way] / deal harshly with (a person) / give [show / turn] the cold shoulder to (a person) / be hard upon (a person) / behave coldly toward (a person) // 매몰스럽게 거절하다 give a point-blank [flat] refusal // 그 여자를 버리다니 너도 ~ It is heartless of you to abandon her. // 그녀는 정말 매몰스러운 사람이다 She has a heart of stone.

매몰차다 very cold; very unkind; hard; harsh; heartless; merciless. ¶그런 짓을 하다니 그도 매몰차구나 It is cruel of him to do such a thing.

매무새 the appearance [outward look] of one's dress; elegance of one's clothes. ¶~가 단정하다 [단정치 못하다] be neatly [slovenly] dressed // ~를 고치다 adjust one's dress [attire] / tidy (up) oneself.

매무시 primping; dressing up. ¶~가 단정하다

look neat and tidy. **매무시하다** trim; tidy; adjust; primp. ¶단정하게 ~ keep oneself neat and trimmed / make oneself look neat and tidy / be careful[attentive] about one's outward appearance.

매문(賣文) literary journeywork[hackwork]; selling of writing. **매문하다** be engaged in literary journeywork; sell one's writing; make a living with one's pen.

매물(賣物) an article for[on] sale; offerings. ¶(증권에서) ~ 회소 light offerings // ~로 내놓다 put (a thing) on the market / offer[put up] (a thing) for sale / place (a thing) on sale // ~ (게시) For sale. ¶이것은 ~이 아니고 견본입니다 This is not for sale, just for show. // 현재 시장에는 ~이 많이 나돌고 있다 The market is now flooded with sales[offerings].

매미 [동] cicada (pl. ~s, -dae); a cicala; a harvest fly; a balm cricket; (미) a locust. ¶~ 소리 the chirp of a cicada // ~의 허물 the cast-off shell of a cicada // ~가 울고 있다 A cicada is singing.

매번(每番) each[every] time. ⇨번번이 ¶그는 ~ 똑같은 말을 한다 He says the same thing every time. // 만나러 갈 때마다 그녀는 ~ 집에 없었다 Every time I went to see her, she was not at home.

매복(埋伏) ambush; [군] ambuscade; [치과] impaction. ¶대상(隊商)은 ~ 습격을 당했다 The caravan fell into an ambush. **매복하다** ambush; waylay; lie in wait (for); lie [hide] in ambush (for); conceal oneself in ambush; perform ambush. ¶나무 뒤에 ~ ambush oneself behind a tree // 후퇴하는 적을 매복하여 기다리다 ambush[lie in ambush for / lie in wait for] the retreating enemy.

● **매복치**(-齒) an impacted tooth.

매부(妹夫) one's sister's husband; one's brother-in-law.

매부리¹ [매를 부리는 사람] a falconer; a hawker.

매부리² [매의 부리] a hawk's beak[bill]. ¶~ 같은 hawk-billed.

● **매부리코** [매부리 같은 코] a hawk nose; a hooknose; an aquiline nose; a hooked nose; [그런 코를 지닌 사람] a hawk-nosed[hooknosed] person.

매사(每事) [일] each[every] affair[matter]; [사업] every business[undertaking]; [계획·시도] each step[attempt / plan]; [상황] every circumstance. ¶그는 ~에 관대하다 He is generous in everything. // 그녀는 ~에 있어서 내게 반대한다 She opposes[goes against] everything I say and do. // 계모(시어머니)는 ~에 내게 심하게 대했다 My stepmother [mother-in-law] was hard on me in every way.

매사는 불여(不如)**튼튼이라** Success in every business comes from constant preparedness.

매사냥 falconry; hawking. **매사냥하다** hawk; go hawking; hunt with a hawk.

● **매사냥꾼** a falconer; a hawker; a falcon hunter.

매사불성(每事不成) failure in every attempt [undertaking]. **매사불성하다** fail in every attempt [undertaking].

매상(賣上) 1 [상품을 팖] sale; selling. 2 (gross) earnings; the sales (amount). ⇨매상고(⇨매상) ¶수입품의 ~이 오르고 있다 The sales of imported goods are on the increase [going up]. // 어제는 20만 원의 ~을 올렸다 The sales of yesterday amounted to[totaled] 200,000 won.

● **매상고** (gross) earnings; the sales (amount); the amount sold; the proceeds (of sales); the returns; the receipts (from sales); the turnover; the takings. ¶총~ gross sales [proceeds] // 평균[월] ~ average [monthly] sales // 금주에는 ~가 올랐다[내려갔다] Sales were up[down] this week. // 이 가게의 하루 ~는 20만 원이다 This shop takes in two hundred thousand won a day.

매석(賣惜) an indisposition to sell. **매석하다** hold[hoard] goods (for future sale); hold back; be indisposed[unwilling] to sell; hoard. ¶그들은 머지않아 값이 오를 것을 내다보고 물건을 매석하고 있다 Anticipating a rise in prices in the near future, they aren't eager to sell [are holding] their goods (now).

매설(埋設) laying. **매설하다** lay (under the ground). ¶수도관을 ~ lay water-pipes under the ground // 케이블을 ~ lay cables underground // 지뢰를 ~ lay[charge] a (land) mine.

매섭다 strict; fierce; violent; severe; sharp; acute; stern. ¶매서운 공격 a severe attack / [비난] a bitter criticism // 매서운 눈초리 hard eyes // 매섭게 생기다 look sharp / look fierce // 매섭게 노려보다 glare fiercely (at) / scowl (at).

매수(枚數) the number of leaves[sheets]. ¶엽서의 ~를 세다 count (the number of) postcards.

매수(買收) 1 [사들임] purchase; buying up [off]. **매수하다** purchase; buy up; take over. ¶회사를 ~ buy up a company // 정부는 고속도로 건설을 위하여 토지를 매수했다 The government bought[purchased] the land for the construction of superhighways.

2 [금품으로 꾀기] buying over[off]; corruption. **매수하다** buy off[over]; win over (by bribery); corrupt. ¶매수할 수 있는 bribable / corruptible / accessible to bribery // 매수할 수 없는 incorruptible / inaccessible to bribery // 유권자를 ~ manipulate a voter // 국회의원을 ~ corrupt[buy off] some members of the Assembly // 그는 반대파를 매수하여 표를 모았다 He gathered votes by bribing the opposing faction. ➔ 경영자 측에 매수당하다 be bought over to the management // 그는 돈으로 매수될 수 있다 He can be bought [bribed]. // 돈에 매수될 내가 아니다 Money can't buy me.

● **매수 가격** a purchase price. **매수 계획** a purchasing plan. **매수세** a desire to buy; an interest in buying; (증권 시장의) bullish sentiment. ¶~가 있다 be in the buying mood. **매수자** a fixer. **매수 행위** (선거 때 등의) corrupt practices.

매수(買受) (a) purchase; buying (over); acquiring by purchase. **매수하다** buy[take] over; acquire (a thing) by purchase. ¶상품을 전부 ~ buy up all the goods // 토지를 ~ purchase[buy] an estate / (문어) acquire an estate by purchase.

● **매수인** a purchaser; a buyer; (특히 부동산에 관한 법률 용어) a vendee.

매스 게임 [집단 체조] mass calisthenics.

매스껍다 sickening; disgusting. ⇨ 메스껍다
매스 미디어 the mass (communication) media (▶ 원래는 복수형이지만, 오늘날에는 단수형으로 취급되는 일도 많음).
매스컴 [대량 전달] mass communications; [전달 수단] the mass media. ¶ ~을 타다 be in the news / be on the air // ~을 타고 싶이 하다 seek press publicity // ~에서 떠들어 대다 [을 타지 못하다] receive much [little] publicity from the press // ~ 분야에서 일하고 싶습니다 I would like to work in the field of mass communications. // 그 사건은 ~을 크게 떠들썩하게 했다 The case attracted much attention from the mass media.
매시 (每時) every hour; per hour. ¶ ~ 200킬로 [마일]의 속도로 at a speed of 200 kilometers per hour [200-mph / 200 m.p.h.].
매식 (買食) [사 먹는 식사] a paid meal; [사 먹는 행위] eating at a restaurant [an inn]. **매식하다** eat out; take [have] a meal at a restaurant; eat at a restaurant.
매실 (梅實) a Japanese apricot.
● **매실주** Japanese apricot brandy.
매싸리 a twig of the bush clover for a whip.
매씨 (妹氏) your [his] esteemed sister.
매암쇠 (맷돌의) a rind [rynd] (of a millstone); a millrind.
매약 (賣約) a sales contract. ¶ ~필 (게시) Sold. **매약하다** make a sales contract; contract to sell; contract for sale; bargain.
매약 (賣藥) a patent medicine; a drug. **매약하다** sell a patent medicine.
● **매약상** (영) a chemist; (미) a druggist.
매양 each [every] time. ⇨ 번번이
매연 (煤煙) [연기] sooty smoke; smoke; [검댕] soot; [자동차의 배기가스] automobile exhaust fumes; exhaust gas. [~는] smoky [smokeless] // ~을 뿜어내다 fume out exhaust gas // ~에 그을러 시커멓다 be dark with soot and smoke // 자동차의 ~이 스모그 현상의 주요 원인의 하나로 꼽히고 있다 Automobile exhaust fumes are blamed as one of the major causes of smog.
● **매연 공해** smoke pollution. **매연 차량** a vehicle [car / bus] that discharges exhaust fumes. ¶ 경찰은 시민의 보건을 해치는 ~을 엄중 단속하고 있다 Police exercise strict control over vehicles with faulty exhausts that produce fumes harmful to citizens' health.
매염 (媒染) mordanting; color-fixing by means of a mordant. **매염하다** mordant (something); treat (something) with a mordant.
● **매염 염료** mordant dyes [dyestuffs]. **매염제** a mordant; a fixative.
매우 very; greatly; excessively; very much; awfully; terribly; remarkably; extraordinarily. ¶ ~ 재미가 있는 책 a most [a very / an extremely] interesting book // ~ 아름다운 여인 a very beautiful woman // ~ 빨리 much too fast // ~ 놀랍게도 to one's great surprise // ~ 크다 be extremely large // ~ 피곤하다 be very tired // ~ 곤란을 겪다 be hard pressed // ~ 감사하고 또 much be much obliged (to you) // 그는 ~ 엄숙히 판결문을 읽었다 He read the sentence very solemnly. // 그는 ~ 간단하게 그 수수께끼를 풀었다 He solved the riddle very easily [with no difficulty whatsoever]. // 그들은 ~ 친했다 They were great friends. // 네가 없으면 나는 ~ 외롭다 I miss you very much. // 우리는 ~ 재미있었다 We had a very [rattling / ripping] good time (of it). / It was great fun. // 그는 ~ 기뻐했다 He was much [greatly / highly] delighted. // 그는 몸이 ~ 좋아졌다 His health has been very much improved.
매우 (梅雨) the long spell of rain in early summer.
● **매우기** (-期) the rainy [wet] season.
매운바람 a biting [piercing / cutting] wind.
매운탕 (-湯) a *maeuntang*; a pepper-pot soup; a hot chowder.
매움하다 rather hot [spicy / sharp / pungent].
매워하다 find (it) hot [spicy / sharp / pungent]; feel (it) too hot. ¶ 고추를 많이 치지 않았는데도 그는 국을 매워한다 Although I didn't put much red pepper in the soup, he finds it too hot.
매월 (每月) every [each] month. ⇨ 매달
매음 (賣淫) prostitution; harlotry. ¶ ~을 주선하다 pimp / pander. **매음하다** prostitute; practice prostitution; sell oneself for money; walk the streets; (미국 구어) work as a hooker.
● **매음굴** a brothel; a whorehouse; a bawdy house; a house of prostitution. **매음부 / 매음녀** a prostitute; a whore; a street walker. **매음 행위** (an act of) prostitution. ¶ ~를 하다 prostitute oneself / practice prostitution.
매이다 1 (끈 등으로) be tied; be fastened; be bound. ¶ 구두끈이 ~ shoelaces are fastened / one's shoes are tied // 나뭇가지에 목이 ~ be hanged on the branch of a tree // 풍선이 실에 매여 있다 The balloon is on a string. // 그 말은 말뚝에 매여 있다 The horse is tethered to a stake.
2 [구속되다] be bound [fettered / tied / restricted]. ¶ 시간에 ~ be restricted by time // 규칙에 ~ be bound by a rule // 일에 ~ be chained [tied down / fettered] to one's business [work] // 주부는 가정에 매이게 마련이다 It's the way of housewives to be held to the works for their family. // 나는 직장에 매인 몸이다 I am an organization man [a workaholic]. // 나는 시간에 매이는 것을 싫어한다 I hate to be bound [restricted] by time.
매인 목숨 not being one's own boss; [하위 신분] being an underling [a slave]; [노예의 신분·상태] slavery; bondage; servitude; [하위 직원] an underling; [노예] a slave. ¶ ~이라 시간이 자유롭지 않다 Since I am not my own boss, I have no time to myself at all. // 직장에 ~이라 일요일밖에는 틈을 낼 수가 없다 I have only Sundays to myself as I am busy with my office work.
매인 (每人) every [each] person. ¶ ~당(當) for each person / per head / per capita // ~당 2개씩 주어라 Give them two apiece.
매일 (每日) every day; daily; day after day; day by day. ¶ ~ 밤 every night [evening] / nightly / night after night // ~ 오전 [오후] every morning [afternoon] // ~의 일 one's daily works [duties] // ~ 있는 일 daily happenings [events] // ~같이 almost every day // ~ (~) 비가 내렸다 It rained day after day. // 그는 ~ 바쁜 사람이다 His days are full. // 이런 일은 ~ 일어나지 않는다 Such things do not happen every day. // 그들은 ~같이 싸움을 한다 They quarrel with each other day after day [almost every day].

매일반(一般) sameness. ¶둘러치나 메치나 ~이다 It's six of one and half-a-dozen of the other.// 오늘 출발하나 내일 출발하나 ~이다 It makes little difference whether I set out today or tomorrow.

매입(買入) 〔사들임〕 buying; purchase; stocking; laying in; (공사채 등의) a subscription. ¶고본(古本) ~ (게시) "Second-Hand Books Bought."// 골동품 고가 ~ (게시) Curios bought at high prices.// 지금은 겨울옷의 ~ 시기이다 It is time to stock winter clothes.// 상사들은 밀의 ~에 전념하였다 The firms went all out to buy in wheat. **매입하다** buy; purchase; make purchases; lay in. ¶대량으로 ~ make a large purchase of (rice) / lay in a large stock of (coal)// 원자재를 ~ purchase raw materials// 지금은 주식을 매입할 시기이다 Now is the time to lay in a stock.
● **매입 가격** the purchase price. **매입 상환**〔경〕 redemption [repayment] by purchase. **매입 원가** first [original / prime] cost; the price paid; the cost price. **매입 환율** a buying rate of exchange; a buying exchange quotation.

매자나무 〔식〕 the Korean barberry.

매잡이¹ 1 〔매듭의 단단한 정도〕 tightness of a knot. 2 〔일의 마무리〕 the finishing touches [strokes].

매잡이² 1 〔행위〕 hawk [falcon] hunting. **매잡이하다** hunt falcons [hawks]. 2 〔사람〕 a falcon [hawk] hunter.

매장(埋葬) 1 (시체의) (a) burial; 〔문어〕 (an) interment. ¶가~ (a) provisional burial [interment]// 이 끝났다 The earth closed over him. **매장하다** bury; 〔문어〕 inter; lay (a person's body) to rest; entomb. ➔¶그는 정중히 매장되었다 He was given a respectful burial. / He was buried [interred] with dignity [due ceremony]. 2 (사회적인) social ostracism. **매장하다** ostracize; oust [expel] (a person) from society. ➔¶매장되다 be ousted from society / be ostracized// 그런 사람은 사회에서 매장되어야 한다 That sort of man ought to be ostracized from society.

매장(埋藏) 1 〔문어서 감춤〕 burying underground. **매장하다** hide underground; bury in the ground. ¶매장해 두었던 보석 jewels buried in the ground. 2 (광물의) deposits (of minerals). **매장하다** have (oil) deposits underground.
● **매장량** reserves; (광물의) deposits. ¶석유의 ~ oil deposits / oil reserves// 석탄의 ~ coal reserves / (the estimated amount of) coal deposits. **매장물** (광물의) a deposit; 〔금전·금은 등 땅속이나 기타의 장소로부터의 발굴물〕 a treasure trove.

매장(賣場) 〔파는 장소〕 a counter; a sale(s)-room; 〔점포〕 a shop; a store. ¶문방구 [장난감] ~ the stationery [toy] counter// ~의 여자 점원 a girl behind the counter// (백화점의) 신사화 ~ the men's shoes department.

매점(買占) (주식·상품 등의) a corner; cornering; 〔전부 삼〕 buying up. ¶시장 ~ market cornering// 주식 ~ a bull corner. **매점하다** 〔전부 사다〕 buy up; (주식·상품 등을) corner. ¶부근의 토지를 ~ buy up all lands in the neighborhood// 시장 제고의 밀을 ~ corner the stock of wheat on the market// 콩을 ~ make a corner in soybeans / have a corner on soybeans / corner the soybean market [supply].
● **매점 매석** cornering and hoarding. ¶~을 단속하다 crack down on practices of cornering and hoarding.

매점(賣店) a stand; a stall; a booth; 〔공원·역 등의 간이매점〕 a kiosk; 〔공원·극장·백화점·슈퍼마켓 등에서의 대여 판매 코너〕 a concession stand. ¶학교 ~ (미) a school store// 협동 소비조합 ~ a co-op store// 회사 ~ a company store// 역의 ~ a station stall// ~을 내다 install a booth / set up a stand [stall].

매정스럽다 heartless; cruel; unfeeling. ⇨매정하다

매정하다 〔무정하다〕 heartless; hard-hearted; 〔냉혹하다〕 cruel; merciless; 〔인정이 없다〕 unfeeling; pitiless. ¶매정한 사람 a cruel man / a hard-hearted [cold-blooded] person// 매정한 말 cruel [unkind] words// 매정하게도 heartlessly / cruelly / be cold-hearted enough to// 매정하게 거절하다 give a point-blank [flat] refusal// 매정하게 대하다 treat (a person) coldly / behave coldly toward (a person)// 이런, 이렇게 매정할 수가 있나 Good God! This is too cruel [bad]. // 아픈 사람에게 그런 말을 하다니 그는 참 매정하였다 It was heartless of him to say such a thing to the sick man. // 매정하게도 그는 병든 아내를 저버렸다 He cold-heartedly abandoned his sick wife.// 그에게 말해 주지 않으면 그는 자네를 매정한 사람이라고 생각할 걸세 If you don't tell him, he will think you are cold [standoffish / lacking in frankness].

매제(妹弟) one's younger sister's husband; one's brother-in-law.

매조미쌀(糙米-) unpolished rice.

매주(每週) every week; weekly; week in week out. ¶~의 weekly// ~ 수요일에 every Wednesday// ~ 1회 once a week// ~ 목요일 밤에 every Thursday night.

매주(買主) a buyer; a purchaser; 〔법〕 a vendee; 〔증권〕 a bull; a bull operator. ¶~가 나타나지 않다 have no demand// 그는 ~가 없이 농장을 세놓았다 Failing a purchaser, he rented the farm.// 그 물건에 몇 명의 ~가 났었다 Several offers were made for the article.

매주(賣主) a seller; a vendor; a bargainer; 〔증권〕 a bear; 〔법〕 a bargainor. ¶중고차의 ~ the seller of a used car.

매죽(梅竹) a Japanese apricot and a bamboo.

매직(*magic) a marker (pen). ⇨매직펜(⇨매직)
● **매직펜**(*magic pen) a marker (pen). ¶~으로 쓰다 write with a marker.

매진(賣盡) a sellout; being sold out. ¶금일 ~ All sold out for today.// ~ (품절의 게시) Out of stock.// 전 좌석 3월 20일까지 ~ (게시) All seats booked until March 20. **매진되다** be sold out; be out of stock. ¶오늘분은 매진되었습니다 Everything sold out for today.// 그 연극은 입장권이 매진되었다 The play was a sellout.// 좌석이 매진되었다 Every seat is booked.// 재고품이 금방 매진되었다 We sold out [sold off / exhausted] the whole stock in no time. / The stock was soon sold out.

매진(邁進) pushing on; dash. **매진하다** push on [forward]; dash on [forward]; struggle on; 〔노력하다〕 strive (for). ¶일에 ~ get on with

매질 one's work // 진리 탐구에 ~ strive for the truth // 우리 모두 새 한국의 건설을 향해 매진하자 Let all of us strive to build up (a) new Korea.
매질 whipping; lashing; flogging; flagellation. **매질하다** whip; lash; flog; swish; cane; beat. ¶매질해서 철들게 하다 whip sense into (a child).
매질(媒質) [물] a medium (pl. ~s, -dia).
매체(媒體) a medium (pl. ~s, -dia). ¶광고 ~ a medium of advertisement / 대중 ~ the mass (communications) media / the mass media (of communication) // 공기는 소리를 전달하는 ~이다 Air is the medium that conveys sound. // 에테르는 전파의 가상(假想) ~이다 The ether is a supposed medium for radio waves.
매초(每秒) every second; per second. ¶~ 10 미터의 속도로 at a speed of 10 meters a [per] second.
매축(埋築) (land) reclamation; filling-up. **매축하다** fill up (a pond with earth); reclaim [gain] (land from the sea).
● 매축 공사 reclaiming [reclamation] work. **매축지** a reclaimed land [ground]; [간척지] a polder.
매춘(賣春) prostitution; harlotry. ⇨매음
● 매춘부(-婦) a prostitute; a whore. ⇨매음부(⇨매음) **매춘 생활** a life of prostitution; street-walking. **매춘업자** a vice racketeer.
매출(賣出) (a) sale; selling. ¶연말 대~ a year-end bargain sale // 염가 대~ a bargain sale / a special sale / (재고 정리의) a clearance sale. **매출하다** sell; offer (articles) for sale; put (articles) on sale; dispose of.
● 매출 가격 a selling [an offering] price.
매치 1 [시합] a match. ¶타이틀[리턴 / 태그] ~ a title [return / tag] match. 2 [조화]. **매치하다** match (with); go well (with). ¶그녀의 모자가 옷에 잘 매치한다 Her hat matches [goes with] her dress well.
매캐하다 1 [연기 냄새가 나다] smoky. ¶매캐한 냄새 a smoky smell. 2 [곰팡내가 나다] musty; moldy; fusty; frowzy.
매콤하다 hot (to the taste); pungent; peppery; sharp. ¶매콤한 냄새가 코를 찌른다 A peppery smell is offensive to the nose.
매큼하다 hot (to the taste). ⇨매콤하다
매통 a wooden hand mill for hulling rice.
매트 a mat. ¶바닥에 ~를 깔다 spread a mat on the floor.
● 매트 운동 mat exercises.
매트리스 a mattress.
매파(-派) [강경파] the hawks; a hard-liner. ¶~의 hawkish // 의회의 비둘기파와 ~ the doves and the hawks of the Congress.
매파(媒婆) an old woman go-between.
매판 an under mat (for a handmill).
매판 자본(買辦資本) comprador capital. ¶한 나라의 경제적 독립을 위해서는 ~이 민족 자본으로 전환되어야 한다 National capital must replace the comprador capital if a country is to attain its economic independence.
매팔자(-八字) easy living; easy circumstances. ¶~이다 lead an easy life / be in easy circumstances.
매표(賣票) selling of tickets. **매표하다** sell tickets.
● 매표구 / 매표창구 a ticket window. ¶~에서 매표를 시작했다 The ticket window is open.
매표소 a box office; (미) a ticket office; (영) a booking office. **매표원** (미) a ticket agent [girl]; (극장의) a box-office girl; (영) a booking clerk.
매품(賣品) an article for sale; (게시) For sale. ¶비~ Not for sale.
매한가지 sameness. ¶~인 the same / all the same / much the same // 오늘 가건 내일 가건 ~다 It makes little [no] difference whether I go today or tomorrow. // 잘못은 우리 둘이 ~다 We are both to blame [at fault]. // 내가 거짓말쟁이라면 너도 ~다 If I'm a liar, so are you. // 귀찮은 것은 내게도 ~다 It annoys me [It's a nuisance to me] too, you know!
매향(梅香) a fragrance of Japanese apricot blossoms.
매혈하다(賣血-) sell blood for money.
매형(妹兄) one's elder sister's husband; one's brother-in-law.
매호(每戶) each [every] house [household].
매호(每號) every number [issue].
매혹(魅惑) (a) charm; (a) bewitchment; captivation; fascination. **매혹하다** charm; bewitch; fascinate; enchant; captivate; throw [cast] a spell over [on] (one's audience). ¶매혹하는 미모[미색] captivating [fascinating] beauty. →¶매혹되다 be charmed / be fascinated / be bewitched / be enchanted // 여자의 미모에 매혹되다 fall under the spell of a girl's charms / fall victim to a woman's charms // 달콤한 말과 미색(美色)에 매혹되다 be carried away by her honeyed words and radiant beauty // 그는 그 여인에게 매혹되었다 He was captivated by [infatuated with] a woman. // 그녀는 보석의 아름다움에 매혹되었다 She was captivated [fascinated] by the beauty of the gem.
매혹적(魅惑的) charming; fascinating; captivating; bewitching. ¶~인 미소 a killing [bewitching] smile // ~인 여자 a glamorous woman // ~인 미소를 띠고 with a rapt smile.
매화(梅花) [매실나무] a Japanese apricot tree; [그 꽃] a Japanese apricot flower [blossom].
매회(每回) each [every] time; (권투의) each [every] round; (야구의) every [each] inning. ¶저 팀은 ~ 주자[러너]를 내보냈다 That team had men on base in every inning.
맥(脈) 1 pulsation; the pulse. ⇨맥박 ¶부정~ an irregular pulse // ~이 없는 pulseless // ~이 뛴다 The pulse beats. // ~이 빠르다 The pulse goes [beats] rapidly. / The pulse is quick [fast / rapid / sharp]. // ~이 느리다 The pulse is slow [long]. // ~이 약하다 The pulse is weak [feeble]. // ~은 보통이다 The pulse is normal [regular]. // ~도 모르고 침통 흔들다 try to do [cope with] something without knowing anything about it // 환자의 ~은 약하다 This patient has a weak [feeble] pulse. // 나의 평소 ~은 74이다 My normal pulse rate is 74. // ~이 끊겼다 The pulse has ceased to beat.
2 a blood vessel. ⇨혈맥₁
3 a vein of ore; a lode. ⇨광맥 ¶~을 뚫다 open up a vein of ore.
4 (a line of) connection. ⇨맥락₂
5 [기운·힘] spirit; vigor. ¶남자는 여자의 눈물을 보면 ~을 못 쓴다 Men are a pushover for women's tears.

6 (풍수지리의) a topographically favorable location (where the well-wishing spirits of dragons are believed to converge).
맥(을) 못 추다 ¶여자 앞에서는 ~ get weak-kneed in the presence of a woman.
맥(을) 보다 feel[take / examine] (a person's) pulse; have one's fingers on (a person's) pulse; 〔살피다〕 sound out (a person); feel out (a situation).
맥(이) 빠지다 be discouraged; be disappointed; be dejected; be damped; be dispirited; be disheartened. ¶그는 맥 빠진 표정을 하고 있었다 He had a listless expression on his face.∥딸의 결혼식이 끝나자 나는 갑자기 맥이 빠졌다 When my daughter's wedding was over, I suddenly felt exhausted.∥시험 결과를 보고 나는 맥이 빠졌다 I felt greatly disappointed at the result of the examination.∥이 보고를 듣고 그들은 맥 빠진 기분이었다 This report came as a disappointment to them.∥맥이 쭉 빠져서 나는 그것을 할 생각이 없어졌다 I am so discouraged that I've lost the will to do it.∥맛있는 음식을 만들려고 하고 있었는데 그가 못 온다는 말을 듣고 나는 맥이 빠져 버렸다 It was a letdown to learn that he could not come, for I was just going to prepare a good dinner for him.
맥(이) 풀리다 lose one's energy[vigor]; fall into low spirits; be dispirited; lose interest. ¶이래서는 맥이 풀린다 This is very disappointing. / This takes all the fun[meaning] out of it.∥어린이들은 맥 풀린 얼굴이었다 The children looked disappointed.
맥고모자(麥藁帽子) a boater; a straw hat.
맥농(麥農) barley farming. ⇨ =보리농사(⇨보리)
맥동(脈動) pulsatory motion; pulsation; pulsebeat.
맥락(脈絡) **1** 〔생〕 the veins; the system of veins. **2** 〔연결〕 (a line of) connection; coherence; logical connection. ¶~이 있는[없는] 이야기 a coherent[an incoherent] account∥~을 통하다 be in collusion with (a person) / secretly communicate with each other∥그는 그때까지의 이야기와 아무런 ~도 닿지 않는 내용을 이야기하기 시작했다 He began to speak on a subject that had no connection with what he had been saying.∥양자 간에는 한 가닥 ~이 있다 A thread of connection links the two.∥그의 이론에는 ~이 없다 His argument is not coherent.
● **맥락막** 〔생〕 the choroid; the chorioid; the chorioidea; the choroid coat[membrane].
맥류(麥類) barley, wheat, rye, oats, etc.
맥맥이(脈脈-) continuously; unbrokenly. ¶~ 이어 오는 전통 an unbroken tradition∥애국심이 그 민족의 피 속에 ~ 흐르고 있다 Patriotism throbbed ceaselessly in the people's veins.∥평화 운동의 정신은 ~ 이어질 것이다 The spirit of the peace movement will live on.
맥박(脈搏) pulsation; the pulse; the stroke of the pulse. ¶〔결체성(結滯性)〕 ~ intermittent pulse∥약하고 빠른 ~ a thready pulse∥정상적 ~ a regular[normal] pulse∥~이 120으로 올라갔다 The pulse mounted to 120.∥~이 정상인지 아닌지 세어 보았다 I counted my pulse to see whether the beat was normal (or not).
● **맥박계** a pulsimeter; a sphygmometer. **맥박수** (a) pulse frequency; a pulse[heart] rate.
맥반(麥飯) boiled barley (and rice). ⇨ =보리밥(⇨밥)
맥분(麥粉) **1** 〔밀가루〕 wheat flour. **2** 〔보릿가루〕 barley flour.
맥석(脈石) 〔광〕 gangue; veinstone; veinstuff.
맥소(脈所) 〔맥이 짚이는 곳〕 the places (on a human body) where the pulse can be felt [observed]; 〔급소〕 a vital point.
맥시 a maxi; a maxiskirt.
맥아(麥芽) malt.
● **맥아당**(-糖) maltose. ⇨ =엿당
맥암(脈巖) 〔광〕 a dike rock.
맥없다(脈-) 〔기운이 없다〕 weak; feeble; feel tired[exhausted / enervated / worn out / done in]; 〔풀이 죽다〕 dispirited; dejected; 〈서술적〉 be in low spirits; be in the dumps; feel blue. ¶길고 맥없는 하품 a long, drawn-out yawn∥맥없어 보인다 You look gloomy.
맥없이[1] weakly; spiritlessly; in low spirits. ¶~ 앉아 있다 sit exhausted / sit dejected [disappointed]∥~ 쓰러지다 fall down helplessly∥~ 의자에 주저앉다 sink[slump] into a chair / sit wearily[limp(ly)] in a chair∥그는 ~ 내게 쓰러졌다 He fell limply against me.∥그녀는 지칠 대로 지쳐서 ~ 늘어졌다 She was limp with fatigue. / She was dead tired[〔영〕 fagged out].∥내가 그를 발견했을 때 그는 ~ 바닥에 쓰러져 있었다 When I found him, he was lying helplessly on the floor.∥그는 전염병으로 ~ 죽었다 He died feebly of a contagious disease.∥나는 ~ 지고 말았다 I was easily beaten.
맥없이[2](脈-) 〔까닭 없이〕 without any reason; for nothing; groundlessly. ¶~ 벌 받다 be punished for nothing[without cause]∥~ 울다 start crying at the least little thing.
맥작(麥作) barley farming. ⇨ =보리농사(⇨보리)
맥주(麥酒) beer; ale; lager(저장 맥주).(▶ ale은 〔미〕에서는 보통 맥주보다 검은빛을 띠며 알코올 도수가 높음. 〔영〕에서는 흡이 들어가지 않고 맛이 담백한 맥주를 가리키며 beer보다 고상한 표현임) ¶통 ~ canned beer∥병 ~ bottled beer∥생 ~ draft[〔영〕 draught] beer / beer on tap[draft]∥저장 ~ lager / stock beer∥흑 ~ dark beer / stout∥~ 한 조끼[병] a jug[bottle] of beer∥~의 거품 froth on beer∥거품이 잘 이는 ~ grassy beer∥김빠진 ~ stale[flat] beer∥김빠진 ~ 같다 be as insipid as stale beer∥~의 거품이 인다 The beer is up.∥~ 거품이 컵에서 흘러넘쳤다 The head[froth] on the beer spilled over the glass.∥~ 한잔 드시겠어요 Would you like a (glass of) beer?
● **맥주병** 〔맥주를 담는 병〕 a beer bottle; 〔수영이 서툰 사람〕. ¶수영이라면 그는 ~이다 He cannot swim at all[even a stroke]. **맥줏집** a beer hall; a beerhouse; a beer parlor[saloon].
맥진(驀進) a dash; a rush. **맥진하다** dash (forward); rush (onward); dart; run at full speed; hightail.
맥쩍다 **1** 〔무료하다〕 boring; wearisome; tiresome. ¶맥쩍어 for want of occupation / because one has nothing to do∥할 일이 없어 ~ With nothing to do, I am bored to death.∥정말 맥쩍은 하루였다 The day

맥추

dragged on. 2 [대할 낯이 없다] shameful; (서술적) be ashamed of oneself. ¶자네를 만나기가 맥쩍네그려 I'm ashamed to see you. // 그에게 다시 청하기에는 ~ I cannot with any grace make further request to him. // 돈을 더 꾸어 달라기가 ~ I am afraid to ask for more money.

맥추(麥秋) the time of barley harvest (in early summer); the barley harvest season.

맥파(脈波) a pulse wave.

맨[1] [가장] most; extreme; the very. ¶~ 왼쪽의 leftmost // ~ 꼭대기에 on (the) top (of) // ~ 끝 the (very) end [last] / the terminal // ~ 나중의 the very last [end] // ~ 먼저 at the very first // ~ 밑 [아래] the very bottom // ~ 앞 the head / the van / the foremost / the (very) front // ~ 위 the top / the summit / the peak / the apex / [최고] the maximum / [최상] the best // ~ 처음 the first / the outset / the beginning // ~ 나중 the very last [end] / the tail (end) // ~ 꼴찌다 be at the end [bottom] (of a class) // ~ 앞의 차 the foremost car // ~ 앞에 서서 가다 go at the head of (a party) / lead the way // ~ 처음에 오다 come first / be the first to come // 줄의 ~ 뒤에 서 있다 be at the tail of a queue // 소설을 ~ 끝까지 읽다 read a novel through [to the end] // ~ 나중에 나가다 go out (of a theater) after all the others // 복도 ~ 끝에 있습니다 It's way down at the end of the hall. // ~ 먼저 무엇을 할까 What shall we do first? // ~ 먼저 그가 달려왔다 He was the first to arrive on the scene. // 아침에 일어나면 ~ 먼저 나는 정원수에 물을 준다 First thing in the morning I water the plants. // 그의 이름이 ~ 밑에서 두 번째에 있었다 His name was second from the bottom of the list. // 그의 이름이 ~ 앞에 나와 있다 His name leads the list. // 왜 ~ 처음에 그렇게 말하지 않았는가 Why didn't you say so at the outset?

맨[2] [오로지] exclusively; nothing but; just; full of. ¶그 화가의 그림은 ~ 초상화뿐이다 The artist confines himself to portrait-painting. // 구경거리는 없고 ~ 사람뿐이다 There is nothing to see but a crowd of people.

맨- bare; naked; nothing but; just; unadulterated. ¶~발 bare feet // ~손 bare [empty] hands // ~밥 just rice (without any side dishes).

맨드라미 [식] a cockscomb.

맨땅 bare ground. ¶~에 앉다 sit on the bare ground.

맨머리 1 [아무것도 쓰지 않은 머리] a head without a headgear [hat]; a bare head. ¶~로 나가다 go out bareheaded / go out without putting on a hat. 2 [낭자를 하지 않고 쪽 찐 머리] a hairdo done without any false hair.

맨몸 1 [알몸] a naked body; nakedness; nudity; a nude. ¶~으로 in the nude / with nothing on / in one's birthday clothes // ~이 되다 become naked / strip / strip oneself naked // ~에 와이셔츠를 입다 wear a shirt next [close] to the skin // ~으로 자다 sleep naked / sleep in the raw. 2 [무일푼] pennilessness. ¶~의 penniless // ~이 되다 become penniless / (속어) go (clean) broke.

맨바닥 the bare floor [ground].

맨발 a bare [naked] foot. ¶~의 barefoot / barefooted / [신을 신지 않은] unshod // ~인 어린이 a barefooted child // ~로 걷다 walk barefoot(ed) / go [walk] with bare feet // ~이 되다 [~을 벗다] become barefooted // 그 여자는 ~에 샌들을 신고 있었다 The woman was wearing sandals without any stockings. // 그는 ~로 도망쳤다 He fled without (putting on) his shoes. // 그는 뜨거운 모래사장을 ~로 걸었다 He walked on the hot (beach) sand with bare [naked] feet.

맨밥 (boiled) rice without any side dishes. ¶~을 먹다 eat rice alone / eat rice without any side dishes at all.

맨살 bare [naked] skin. ¶그녀의 등은 온통 ~이 드러나 있었다 Her back was entirely bare.

맨션 (*mansion) [고급 아파트] an apartment (of a better class); (영) a flat (of a better class); (건물) an [a ferroconcrete) apartment house; (영) a block of flats; (분양식의) a condominium. (▶ 영어의 mansion은 대저택을 뜻하지만 mansions로 써면 한국어의 맨션에 가까운 뜻으로도 쓰임). ¶고급 ~ a luxury apartment [apartment house] / (영) a luxury flat / a block of luxury flats.

맨손 1 [손에 아무것도 갖지 않음] an empty [a bare] hand. ¶~으로 [아무것도 갖지 않고] with one's bare hands / with empty hands / [무기 없이] unarmed // ~으로 싸우다 fight unarmed // ~으로 적과 맞서다 face the enemy with bare hands // ~으로 찾아가다 call on (a person) with empty hands / visit (a person) without bringing a present. 2 [수단·기술·자본을 갖지 않음]. ¶~으로 without art or craft / without capital / empty-handed // ~으로 장사를 시작하다 start a business with practically no capital // ~으로 엄청난 돈을 벌다 make a fortune starting from scratch.

● **맨손 체조** free gymnastics; (경기 종목) free standing exercises.

맨송맨송하다 1 [털이 없이 반반하다] hairless; bald; bare. ¶턱이 ~ be beardless / have no beard / have a bald chin. 2 [나무나 풀이 없다] treeless; bald; bare. ¶맨송맨송한 산 a treeless mountain. 3 [술 마셔도 정신이 말짱하다] sober; not drunk; unintoxicated. ¶맨송맨송한 때에 in one's sober times // 맨송맨송한 기분으로는 말하기 거북하다 I haven't the nerve to say it when sober [in (all) soberness].

맨입 1 [아무것도 먹지 않은 입] an empty mouth. 2 [공짜] free of charge. ¶~으로는 일 하지 않겠다 I won't work for nothing.

맨주먹 a naked fist; an empty fist; a bare [an empty] hand. ¶~의 barefisted / empty-handed / with one's bare [naked] hands [fists] / barehanded // ~으로 싸우다 fight with naked fists // 거의 ~으로 장사를 시작하다 start a business with practically no capital // ~으로 범을 잡다 kill a tiger with one's naked fist // ~으로 막대한 재산을 쌓아 올렸다 He built up an enormous fortune out of nothing.

맨투맨 man-to-man. ¶코치와 선수는 ~으로 연습하고 있다 The coach and the athlete are practicing one-to-one.

● **맨투맨 디펜스** (구기에서) a man-to-man defense [(영) defence].

맨틀 (지구의) a mantle.

맨홀 a manhole.

● **맨홀 뚜껑** a manhole cover.

맴돌다 1 [돌다] spin oneself round; turn round[in circular]; whirl. 2 [발전이 없다] remain in obscurity. ¶만날 평사원으로 ~ remain[live the humdrum life of] a mere clerk.

맴돌리다 1 (제자리에서) spin[turn] (a person) round; make (a person) turn round [in circular]. 2 (이곳저곳으로) lead (a person) a chase[dance]; pull about; send (a person) on a wild-goose chase.

맴돌이 전류(-電流) [전] an eddy current.

맴맴 chirping. ¶매미가 ~ 운다 A cicada is singing. / A locust is chirping.

맵다 1 [혀를 쏘는 듯하다] hot; [자극성이 있다] pungent; [후추 같다] peppery; sharp; spicy. ¶매운맛 a sharp[pungent] taste∥매운 조미료 a pungent condiment∥매운 소스 a hot[pungent] sauce∥매운 음식 [spicy / pungent] food∥이 요리는 ~ This dish is hotly seasoned. / 매운 몹시 ~ This tastes hot[pungent]. ∥샌드위치의 겨자가 너무 ~ The mustard in the sandwich is too hot.∥이 카레라이스는 너무 ~ This curry and rice is too hot (for me). 2 [혹독하다] severe; intense; inclement. ¶참 추위가 맵군요 How intense the cold is!

맵시 shapeliness; smartness; figure; form; appearance; a style. ¶몸~ one's figure [carriage] ∥옷~ a style of dressing / the cut of one's clothes∥~ 있는 smart / stylish / shapely / well-cut / chic∥~ 없는 ungainly / awkward / shapeless / gangling / ill-shaped[-formed] / clumsy∥~ 있는 몸매 a handsome[graceful] figure∥~에 온통 정신이 쏠려 있는 소녀 a girl whose major interest in life is her appearance∥~가 있다 be nicely turned out / look stylish[smart]∥옷~ 있게 입다 wear one's clothes stylishly / dress oneself in good shape∥그녀는 ~가 있다[없다] She has a good[poor] form.

맵싸하다 pungent; acrid; peppery; tongue-tingling.

맷돌 a maetdol; a (stone) hand mill; a set of millstones; a millstone. ¶~로 곡물을 갈다 grind corn in a hand mill.
● **맷돌질** grinding grain in a stone mill.

맷방석(-方席) a round straw mat which is spread under the millstone.

맷손 [맷돌 손잡이] the handle of a quern.

맹-(猛) ¶~연습 strenuous[hard] training∥~반격 a terrific counterattack.

맹견(猛犬) a fierce dog.
● **맹견 주의** 《게시》 Beware of The Dog.; Beware ― Fierce Dog.

맹공격(猛攻擊) a violent attack; a severe [heavy] attack. ¶~을 받다 come under heavy attack∥우리 팀은 상대 팀에게 ~을 가했다 Our team made a merciless attack on our opponents. **맹공격하다** make a vigorous attack (on); attack violently.

맹그로브 [식] a mangrove; a red mangrove.

맹금(猛禽) a bird of prey; a raptorial bird; a predatory bird. ¶~성의 hawklike / accipitral.
● **맹금류** birds of prey.

맹꽁이 1 [동] a small round frog. 2 [맹추] a birdbrain; a simpleton; a blockhead; an idiot; a moron.

맹도견(盲導犬) 《미》 a Seeing Eye dog(▶ 상표명인 Seeing Eye에서 본뜬 것.특별히 훈련을 받은 개); a guide dog (for the blind); a blind-man's dog.

맹독(猛毒) (a) deadly[virulent] poison; (동물의) deadly venom. ¶~성의 fatally poisonous∥~의 뱀 a very poisonous[highly venomous] snake∥~이 있다 be virulently poisonous.

맹동(孟冬) 1 early winter. ⇨ˇ초겨울 2 [음력 10월] October of the lunar calendar.

맹랑하다(孟浪-) 1 [허망하다] false; untrue; [믿을 수 없다] incredible; unbelievable; [근거 없다] groundless; unfounded; unreliable; [터무니없다] absurd; fabulous; nonsensical; unreasonable. ¶맹랑한 사람 an unreliable[a disappointing] person∥맹랑한 이야기 an incredible story∥맹랑한 소문을 퍼뜨리다 set wild rumors afloat∥일이 맹랑하게 됐다 My plan was unexpectedly frustrated. / My plan got spoiled so easily.∥누가 그런 맹랑한 소리를 하더냐 Whoever told you such a silly story as that?
2 [허술히 볼 수 없다] tougher than one had expected; harder to tackle than one had expected; not negligible. ¶맹랑한 아이 a shrewd child∥맹랑한 일 a stiff task∥일이 ~ This is a little too hard to solve.

맹렬하다(猛烈-) violent (storm); vehement (wind); furious (anger); fierce (hatred); keen (competition). ¶맹렬한 더위 intense heat∥맹렬한 충격 a severe[violent] shock∥맹렬한 공격 a fierce[furious] attack∥맹렬한 경쟁 fierce competition∥맹렬한 폭풍 a violent storm∥맹렬한 연습 heavy[vigorous] training[practice] / hard training∥그는 맹렬한 스피드로 모퉁이를 돌았다 He rounded the corner at breakneck speed. **맹렬히** violently; fiercely; furiously; vehemently; intensely. ¶~ 공부하다 study hard[intently]∥~ 싸우다 fight desperately[hotly]∥내 부친은 그것에 ~ 반대하셨다 My father was absolutely opposed[adamant in his opposition] to it.∥그 매는 먹이에게 ~ 덤벼들었다 The hawk swooped down fiercely on its prey.∥그는 ~ 그들을 비난했다 He criticized them vehemently.∥그는 그 계획에 ~ 반대했다 He opposed the plan passionately.∥병사들은 적을 ~ 공격했다 The soldiers made a furious assault on the enemy.

맹맹하다 (코가) stuffy; (서술적) be bunged up; be stuffed up.

맹목(盲目) 1 a blind eye. ⇨ˇ먼눈¹ 2 [이성이 없음] (spiritual) blindness.
● **맹목 비행** a blind flight; blind[instrumental] flying.

맹목적(盲目的) blind; reckless. ¶~ 사랑 blind love∥~ 모방 blind[servile] imitation∥~ 숭배 blind devotion∥~ 시도 a venture made blindly / a leap in the dark∥~으로 blindly / recklessly∥~으로 사랑하다 love blindly / dote on (a child).

맹물 1 [물] plain[tasteless] water; insipid [flat] stuff; dishwater(싱거운 음료). ¶이것은 맥주가 아니고 ~ 이다 This isn't beer ― it's dishwater!∥이 수프는 ~ 같다 This soup is mere wash. 2 [야무지지 못한 사람] a dull[uninteresting] person; a dull drink of water; a drip. ¶그 사람은 ~이다 He is a dull drink of water.

맹방(盟邦) an ally; an allied power; a confederate (state); a league (of allies).

맹성(猛省) grave [serious] reflection [reconsideration / self-contemplation]. ¶우리는 부패한 국회의원의 ~을 촉구한다 We urge corrupt National Assemblymen to do some serious soul-searching. **맹성하다** reflect seriously [gravely] on oneself.

맹세(盟誓) an oath(▶ 성경에 손을 얹고 하는 것과 같은; a vow; a pledge; a promise(약속). ¶~를 지키다[어기다] keep[break] one's vow [oath]. **맹세하다** (하느님 등을 두고) swear; (엄숙하게) vow; make a vow; [선서하다] take an oath(▶ 종종 성경에 손을 얹고); [약속하다] promise [pledge] (to do)(▶ pledge는 굳게 약속하다. ¶신 앞에 ~ swear by God [Heaven] / swear before [to] God ∥ 충성을 pledge one's loyalty (to) ∥ 하느님을 두고 나의 결백을 맹세합니다 I swear by God that I am innocent. ∥ 그는 금주를 맹세했다 He swore to give up drinking. ∥ 나의 비밀을 누구에게도 말하지 않겠다고 맹세하겠소 Will you promise me [give me your word of honor] that you will not tell my secret to anyone? ∥ 그 둘이는 서로 결혼하기로 맹세하고 있다 They have promised to marry each other. ∥ 아버님은 금연을 맹세하셨다 My father made a vow [vowed] not to smoke. ∥ 그는 절대 도박을 하지 않겠다고 맹세했다 He swore [vowed] to stop gambling.

맹세코(盟誓—) upon my oath [word / honor / life]; by God [Jove / Jupiter].

맹수(猛獸) a fierce [ferocious] animal; a savage beast; (육식의) a predatory animal; a beast of prey. ¶~를 부리는 사람 a tamer of wild beasts / a wild animal trainer [tamer].
● **맹수 사냥** big-game hunting; a safari(동부 아프리카의). ¶~꾼 a big-game hunter ∥ ~을 하다 shoot big game / go big-game hunting.

맹습(猛襲) a vigorous [furious / heavy / hot] attack; a violent assault; an onslaught. **맹습하다** make a fierce [savage / ferocious] attack (on the enemy); attack fiercely [furiously].

맹신(盲信) a blind belief; overcredulity. **맹신하다** believe unquestioningly; be overcredulous. ¶국민은 수상이 하는 말을 맹신했다 The people swallowed whole [blindly accepted / accepted without question] what the Prime Minister had said.

맹아(盲啞) a blind and dumb person; (집합적) the blind and dumb; [소경과 벙어리] the blind and the dumb.
● **맹아 교육** education for the blind and dumb. **맹아 학교** a school for the blind and the dumb.

맹아(萌芽) 1 [새로 트는 싹] a bud; a germ; a sprout. 2 [사물의 시초]. ¶이 나라의 정치 정세 불안의 ~는 인종 문제에서 나왔다 The political unrest in this country sprang from [originated in] racial problems.

맹약(盟約) [서약] a pledge; [협정] a pact; a covenant; a compact; [동맹] an alliance; a confederacy; a league. ¶~을 맺다 conclude a pact (with) / form an alliance (with). **맹약하다** confederate; form a league.

맹연습(猛練習) hard [intensive] training; heavy [vigorous] practice. **맹연습하다** do hard training; carry out vigorous practice [exercises].

맹우(盟友) a sworn friend.

맹위(猛威) fierceness; fury; ferocity. ¶~를 떨치다 (폭풍우 등이) be furious / rage / be rampant / (사람이) exercise an overwhelming influence (over others) ∥ 폭풍우가 하루 종일 ~를 떨쳤다 The storm raged all day. / 유행성 감기가 그 고장 전체에 ~를 떨쳤다 Influenza was rampant throughout the town.

맹인(盲人) a blind person; (집합적) the blind.
● **맹인 교육** blind education; education of the blind. **맹인 학교** a school for the blind.

맹자(孟子) [맹자의 언행록] the Works [the Discourse] of Mencius.

맹장(盲腸) [생] the c(a)ecum (pl. -ca); the blind gut. 2 →충수
● **맹장염** [의] appendicitis. ⇨충수염(⇨충수) ¶급성 ~ acute [an attack of] appendicitis ∥ ~ 수술을 받다 be operated on for appendicitis.

맹장(猛將) a strong general; a brave general; a dauntless leader; a veteran fighter; an expert (in judo, in fencing, etc.). ¶저 팀에는 ~들이 수두룩하다 That team is full of fierce [(구어) tough] players.

맹점(盲點) a blind spot [point]; [생] a scotoma (pl. ~s, -mata). ¶법 [한국인]의 ~ a blind spot in the law [the Korean mind] / 법의 ~을 이용하다 take advantage of a blind [weak] point of law / make an illicit use of law / take advantage of a loophole in the law ∥ 그들은 내 이론의 ~을 공격했다 They attacked the weak point in my theory.

맹종(盲從) blind obedience [submission]. **맹종하다** follow [obey / submit] (a person) blindly [without question]; follow like (a) sheep; be led by the nose.
● **맹종자** a blind [thoughtless] follower.

맹주(盟主) the leader (of confederate states); the leading power. ¶그는 그 운동의 ~가 되었다 He became the leader [assumed the leadership] of the movement.

맹진(猛進) a dash; a drive; a thrust. **맹진하다** dash [make a bold dash] forward; push forward vigorously; advance furiously. ¶저돌적으로 ~ dash forward recklessly / make a mad dash forward.

맹추 a fool; a simpleton; a dunce; a blockhead; a thickheaded person; a dullard.

맹추(孟秋) 1 early autumn. ⇨초가을 2 [음력 7월] July of the lunar calendar.

맹춘(孟春) 1 early spring. ⇨초봄 2 [음력 정월] January of the lunar calendar.

맹타(猛打) a heavy [hammer] blow; [야구] slugging. ¶~를 퍼붓다 [가하다] [야구] hit hard / pump out hits / [권투] make a punching bag out of (one's opponent) ∥ 타이거즈는 라이온스에게 ~를 가했다 The Tigers rained a shower of hard hits on the Lions. / The Tigers unleashed a furious batting attack on the Lions. ∥ 그는 상대에게 ~를 가했다 (복싱에서) He landed a flurry of heavy blows on his opponent. **맹타하다** hit severely [hard]; give a heavy hit; hammer the pitcher; slug (a ball).

맹탕(—湯) 1 [싱거운 국] insipid [watery] soup; flavorless soup; unseasoned soup. ¶이 국은 ~이다 This soup is mere wash. 2 [싱거운 사람] a dull [an uninteresting] person; an empty person; an insipid person.

맹폭(盲爆) unscrupulous [blind] bombing. 맹

맹폭하다 bomb[bombard] blindly.
맹폭(猛爆) intensive bombing; heavy bombing; an intensive air raid. **맹폭하다** make an intensive bombing raid (on enemy positions); bomb[bombard] heavily; strafe.
맹풍(猛風) a violent [vehement] wind; a furious wind; a storm; a hurricane; a typhoon; a gale.
맹하(孟夏) **1** early summer. ⇨초여름 **2** [음력 4월] April of the lunar calendar.
맹호(猛虎) a fierce[ferocious] tiger.
맹화(猛火) [세차게 타는 불] raging[roaring] flames. ¶~ 속에 뛰어들다 rush[plunge] into the raging flames // ~에 휩싸이다 be enveloped in raging fire.
맹활동(猛活動) vigorous activity[action]. **맹활동하다** take[play] a very active part (in); be in full activity[swing]. ¶사회 개혁가로서 ~ be actively engaged as a social reformer.
맹훈련(猛訓鍊) hard[intense] training. **맹훈련하다** carry out intense training; train hard.
맹휴(盟休) **1** a strike of students. ⇨동맹 휴학(⇨동맹) **2** a (labor) strike. ⇨동맹 휴업(⇨동맹)
맺다 1 (끈·매듭을) tie (up); knot. ¶구두끈을 ~ tie one's shoes / lace one's boots.
2 (끝을) conclude; close; finish; end (off); wind up. ¶토론의 끝을 ~ close a debate // …이라고 말하고 말을 ~ conclude by saying … // 그는 고맙다는 말로 연설의 끝을 맺었다 He concluded his speech with a few words of thanks.
3 (계약·관계를) form (a connection / a relationship); make (a contract); close (a bargain); conclude (a treaty). ¶동맹을 ~ form an alliance (with)/인연을 ~ form a relationship (with) / [결혼하다] marry // 우정을 ~ cultivate[contract / form] friendship with (a person) // 의형제를 ~ become sworn brothers // 계약을 ~ enter into a contract / 협정을 ~ conclude an agreement // 매매 계약을 ~ conclude a sales contract (with a company) // 그들은 사랑으로 맺어졌다 They were bound together by love.
4 (열매를) bear; produce. ¶열매를 ~ bear [produce] fruit.
맺고 끊는 데가 없다 [결단성이 없다] indecisive; wishy-washy; spineless; namby-pamby.
맺음말 a conclusion. ⇨결론
맺히다 1 (열매가) come into bearing; fruit; go to seed.
2 (매듭이) be tied; be knotted; get tied into knot.
3 (눈물·이슬이) form. ¶눈물이 맺힌 눈 be dewed eyes / eyes filled with tears // 이슬이 맺힌 dewy / moist[sprinkled] with dew // 이슬방울이 토란 잎에 맺혔다 Dewdrops have formed on the taro leaves. // 창문 턱에 이슬방울방울 맺혀 있었다 Drops of dew stood on the window sill.
4 (원한이) be pent up; smolder. ¶가슴에 맺힌 원한 a grudge smoldered in one's heart // 원한이 ~ have a long-smoldering grudge.
5 (피가) gather (in one part of the body); (피부에) be bruised.
머금다 1 (입 안에) keep[hold] 《something》 in one's mouth(음식물). ¶물을 머금고 with one's mouth full of water. **2** [함유하다]

673　　머리

contain; comprise; hold; have. ¶물을 흠뻑 머금은 땅 waterlogged ground // 눈물을 ~ have tears in one's eyes // 이슬을 ~ have dew on 《it》 / be wet with dew // 웃음을 ~ have a smile on one's lips / wear a smile.
머나먼 1 (거리가) faraway; very far[distant]. ¶~ 곳 a faraway place / a place far far away // ~ 길을 오시느라 수고가 많으셨소 It is very kind of you to come all this distance. **2** (시간적으로) remote. ¶~ 옛날 the remote ages / the far-off days // ~ 옛날을 생각하다 think of the days long past.
머루 (열매) wild grapes; (식물) a wild vine.
머리 1 [두부(頭部)] the head. ¶~의 끝 the crown of the head // ~에서 발끝까지 from head to foot / from top[crown] to toe // ~ 위의[에] over[above] one's head / overhead // ~가 어질어질하다 feel dizzy[giddy] / have a giddy head // ~를 똑바로 세우다 hold up one's head / hold one's head erect // 창에서 ~를 내밀다 put[stick] one's head out of a window // ~를 움츠리다 duck 《one's head》 // 아이의 ~를 쓰다듬다 pat a child on the head / pat a child's head // ~를 들다 raise [lift] one's head // ~를 낮게 수그리다 bend [bow] one's head low // ~를 부딪치다 butt heads with 《another》 // 양손으로 ~를 감싸다 bury[hold] one's head in one's hands // ~를 맞대고 의논하다 lay[put] 《their》 heads together // ~를 갸우뚱하다 incline one's head (as if in doubt) // ~를 흔들어서 정신을 차리다 shake one's head clear // 나는 ~가 무겁다 I feel heavy in the head // 내 ~ 위에 밤송이가 떨어졌다 A chestnut bur fell on my head. // 나는 ~를 주먹으로 한 대 얻어맞았다 I took a blow to the head. // "안 된다" 하며 그는 ~를 가로저었다 He shook his head and said "no". // 그는 ~를 끄덕였다 He nodded his head in agreement. // ~가 조금 아프다 I have a slight headache. / My head aches a little. // 숙취로 나는 ~가 무겁다 My head feels heavy because of a hangover. // ~ 조심 (게시) (낙하물에 대하여) Danger Overhead. / (부딪히지 않도록) Watch[《영》 Mind] Your Head.
2 [끝·꼭대기] the top; the head; the point; the tip; the end (part). ¶책상~ the top of a table / 기둥~ the top of a pillar / 끝~ the end (part) / the end piece // ~에 눈을 이고 있는 한라산 Hallasan(Mt. Halla) capped with snow / snowcapped Hallasan.
3 [시작] the beginning. ¶말~ introductory remarks // 일~ the beginning of a job // (첫) ~에서 세 번째의 the third from the head.
4 the chief; the head. ⇨우두머리2
5 [두뇌] a head; a brain; brains; one's mind; [지력(知力)] intelligence. ¶명석한 ~ a clear head // ~의 회전이 빠른 사람 a quick-thinking person // ~를 쓰는 일 mental labor / brainwork // ~가 좋은 학생 a quick[bright] pupil // ~가 나쁜 학생 a poor[dull] pupil // ~가 잘 돌다[돌지 않다] have a quick[slow] mind / be quick-[slow-] witted / be fast-[slow-] thinking // ~가 모자라다 lack[want] brains // ~를 혹사하다 overtax one's brain // ~를 쉬게 하다 rest one's mind // ~에 그리다 [떠올리다] picture 《something》/ imagine / envisage 《something》 // ~에 넣어 두다 have 《something》 in mind / make a mental note of 《something》 // (생각이) ~에 스치다 flash

across one[one's mind] / flash into one's mind // 너무 바빠 ~가 돌 지경이다 I'm having a hectic time of it. / I'm so busy that my head seems to be spinning. // 그는 ~가 모자라는[잘 돌지 않는] 것 같다 He seems to be dull-witted[be lacking in brains]. // 그는 ~가 좋다 He has a fine brain[mind]. / He has brains. / He is bright. // 그는 ~가 명석하다 He is clearheaded. / He has a clear head. // 그는 ~가 흐릿해졌다 He went soft in the head. / (구어) He went gaga. // 이 일을 하는 데는 ~가 필요하다 It requires brains[intelligence] to do this work. // 어머니의 병이 늘 머릿속에 있었다 I was thinking about my mother's illness all the time. / I had my mother's illness on my mind all the time. // 좋은 생각이 ~에 떠올랐다 A good idea occurred to me. / A good idea came into my mind.

6 [머리털] hair (▶ 대체로 불가산 명사로 쓰이는 말이나, 털을 낱개로 셀 때에는 가산 명사로도 쓰임). ¶~ 한 가닥 a lock of hair // 빳빳한[부드러운] ~ stiff[soft] hair // 짧게 깎은 ~ close-cut[close-cropped] head / a crew cut / (미) a flattop // 숱이 많은[적은] ~ thick [thin] hair // 흰 ~[백발] silver[white] hair // 희끗희끗한 ~ gray hair // 금발 ~의[~가 빨간] 여자 a fair-haired[redheaded] woman / 블론드[브루넷] ~ (여성) blonde[brunette] hair // (남성) blond[brunet] hair // 헝클어진 ~ untidy[disheveled] hair // 고수 ~ curly [frizzy / wavy] hair (▶ 보기 좋게 곱슬곱슬한 것이 curly, 보기 흉하게 곱슬곱슬한 것은 frizzy 또는 kinky) // 가지런히 자른 ~ evenly cut hair // ~를 땋다[빗다] braid[comb] one's hair // ~를 뒤로 묶다 bind one's hair at the back // ~를 풀어 내리다 let down one's hair // ~를 감다 wash one's hair / have a shampoo / shampoo (one's hair) // ~를 깎다 get[have] a haircut / have[get] one's hair cut [trimmed] // 할아버지의 ~가 세었다 My grandfather's hair turned gray[(영) grey]. // 나는 절박한 문제로 ~를 쥐어뜯고 있다 Pressing problems have me tearing my hair out. / I am tearing my hair out over urgent problems. // 그는 ~를 가운데서[오른쪽에서] 가르고 있다 He parts his hair in the middle [on the right side]. // 나는 ~를 짧게 깎았다 I had my hair cut[cropped] short[close]. // 그녀는 ~를 길게 기르고 있다 She wears her hair long. // 나는 (미용사에게) ~를 매만지게 했다 I had my hair dressed[done up]. // 요즘에 ~숱이 적어진다 I am losing my hair.

머리가 돌다 go off one's head; become[go] mad[insane]; lose one's mind[wit / reason]. ¶그는 ~ 돌았다 He is crazy[mad]. / He is off his head[out of his mind]. // 가엾게도 그녀는 기어이 머리가 돈 것 같다 It seems that the poor thing finally lost her mind [went crazy].

머리가 수그러지다 ¶그의 노력에는 머리가 수그러진다 I take off my hat to him for his effort. / I admire him for his effort.

머리(를) 굽히다 [숙이다] submit[surrender / yield / succumb / give in] (to). ¶저 녀석에게만은 절대로 머리를 굽히고 싶지 않다 He is the one person I couldn't bear to give in to.

머리(를) 깎다 1 [중이 되다] become a bonze; shave one's head in order to enter the priesthood. **2** [교도소에 복역하다] be sent to jail; serve a prison term.

머리(를) 들다 ¶회원들 사이에 불만이 머리를 들기 시작했다 Discontent began to show itself among the members.

머리(를) 식히다 ¶머리 좀 식히고 하렴 Why don't you take a break and do the rest later? // 그는 머리를 식히러 여행을 떠났다 He went on a trip to refresh himself.

머리(를) 쓰다 think; view (a matter) from every angle; use one's head[brains].

머리(를) 얹다 1 put[turn] up one's hair; do one's hair in a chignon. **2** (기생이) lose one's virginity; be deflowered. **3** [시집을 가다] get married; attain womanhood.

머리에 피도 안 마르다 be wet behind the ears.

머리(를) 쥐어짜다 cudgel[rack] one's brains; puzzle; think hard (of / about). ¶그들은 사고 방지를 위해 머리를 쥐어짜고 있다 They are racking[cudgeling] their brains for ways of preventing accidents. // 그들은 그 대책에 머리를 쥐어짜고 있다 They are racking their brains over how to deal with the matter. // 그는 답을 내리고 머리를 쥐어짰다 He racked his brains[beat his brains out] to find the answer.

머리(를) 흔들다 1 [거절하다] refuse; decline. **2** [부인하다] deny; negate.

● **머리글자** the first[initial] letter of a word; an initial. ¶나는 반지에 이름의 ~를 새기게 했다 I had my initials inscribed on the ring. **머리끄덩이** the lock[clump] of one's hair. ¶남의 ~를 잡다 grab a person by the hair. **머리끝** [머리털의 끝] the ends of one's hair; [정수리] the crown (of the head). ¶~에서 발끝까지 from the crown of the head to the tip of the toes // ~까지 부아가 치밀어 있다 be in hot anger[a fume] / (미) get mad with anger. **머리띠** a headband; a hairlace (여자용); a fillet (가느다란); a frontlet (장식 있는). **머리말** a preface; an introduction; a foreword. (▶ preface는 저자가 쓰는 머리말, 본문의 목차나 내용을 언급하는 foreword는 보통 저자 이외의 사람이 쓰는 간단한 머리말, introduction은 본론의 예비적 해설) ¶책의 ~을 쓰다 write a preface to a book // 책에 ~을 달다 preface a book. **머리맡** one's bedside [pillowside]. ¶~에 붙어 있다 be[watch] at[by] (a person's) bedside. **머리쓰개** a headpiece; headgear; headdress; a hood; a kerchief; a veil. **머리 염색** hair dyeing. ¶~을 하다 dye one's (gray) hair black. **머리 염색약** hairdye. **머리채** a long tress of hair. **머리카락** a hair (of one's head). ¶굵은 ~ a coarse[thick] hair // ~을 뽑다 pull out a hair // ~ 뒤에서 숨바꼭질하다 try to pull the wool over a person's eye // 그 무시무시한 광경에 내 ~이 곤두섰다 My hair stood on end at the frightful sight. **머리칼** a hair (of one's head). ⇨ **머리카락** (⇨) **머리털** hair. ¶~을 쥐어뜯다 tear[rend] one's hair. **머리통** the size of one's head. ¶~이 크다 have a big head. **머리핀** a hair pin. **머릿골** ⟨속⟩ a brain; a cerebrum. ⇨ **뇌** **머릿기름** hair oil; hair cream; (고형의) pomade. ¶~을 바르다 apply hair oil [pomade] to one's hair. **머릿수** the number of persons; a head count; numerical strength; (의회의) quorum. ¶~를 세다 count the number of persons / count heads // 이익을 ~대로 나누다 share the profits equally /

(영) go shares in the profits.∥~를 늘리다[줄이다] increase[decrease] the number.∥~가 2명 부족하다 We are two men short of the required number. 머릿수건 a head kerchief; a babushka.

머릿돌 a foundation stone; a cornerstone.

머무르다 1 [정지하다] stop; halt; come to a halt[standstill].

2 [그대로 있다·유숙하다] stay (at / with); remain. ¶돌아가려는 그를 우리는 말려 머무르게 했다 As he was leaving, we stopped [detained] him.∥아이를 집 안에 머물러 있게 하다 keep a child inside the house∥사직하려는 그를 우리가 머물러 있도록 말렸다 We persuaded [(문어) prevailed on] him not to resign. / We persuaded him against resigning.∥자네를 현직에 머물러 있게 하겠다 We will retain[keep] you in your present position.∥이 이상 더 억지로 머무르게 하지는 않겠습니다 I won't keep you any longer.∥그는 사장 자리에 머무를 작정이다 He is going to stay[remain] in office as president.∥그들은 그날 밤에 대천의 여관에 머물렀다 They stayed[put up] at an inn in Daecheon that night.∥그는 기껏 계장 자리에 머무르게 된다 He'll be lucky if he makes it to subsection chief.∥나는 이 도시에 머물러 있고 싶지 않다 I don't want to stay in this city.∥그는 현직에 머물렀다 He remained in his present office.

3 [어떤 범위에 한정되다]. ¶그 회의는 문제점을 지적하는 일에 머물렀다 The conference did no more than point out some problems [list some points at issue]. / The conference confined itself to listing some points at issue.∥그가 저지른 못된 짓은 여기에 머무르지 않는다 His evildoing does not stop here.∥그의 호기심은 머무를 줄을 모른다 There are no bounds to his curiosity.∥물가의 상승은 머무르지 않는다 Prices keep on rising.

머무적거리다 hesitate; waver; falter; shilly-shally. ¶그는 매사에 머무적거린다 He can't ever make up his mind. / He shilly-shallies [hems and haws] about everything.∥그녀는 수줍어 머무적거리며 대답을 하지 못했다 She was bashful and hesitated to answer.∥머무적거리며 그는 이야기를 시작했다 Hesitantly he began to talk.

머무적머무적 hesitantly; diffidently; in a hesitant[diffident] manner. **머무적머무적하다** hesitate. ⇨˝머무적거리다

머물다 stop; stay (at / with). ⇨˝머무르다
머뭇거리다 hesitate; waver. ⇨˝머무적거리다
머스크멜론 [식] a muskmelon.
머스터드소스 mustard sauce.
머슴 [농가·농장의 일꾼] a farmhand; a farm servant; a farmer's man. ¶~을 살다 become [serve as] a farmhand∥~을 두다 keep a farmhand.

● **머슴살이** serving[working] as a farmhand; the life of a farmhand. ¶~를 하다 work as a farmhand / take service as a farm laborer.

머쓱하다 1 [키가 크다] lank(y); spindly; gangling; rangy. ¶머쓱한 사나이 a lanky man / a gangling fellow∥그는 키가 머쓱하니 크다 He is tall and lanky. **2** [열없다] awkward; shy; ill at ease; self-conscious; (서술적) feel small.

머위 [식] a butterbur; a bog rhubarb.
머저리 a half-wit. ⇨˝어리보기
머줍다 dull; slow; sluggish; tardy.

머지않아 [이윽고] soon; presently; before long; in a short time; by and by; [때가 되면] in due course of time; in due course [time]; [불원간] some [one] day; at no distant date. ¶그들은 결혼할 것이다 Their wedding is in the offing.∥그 문제는 ~ 해결될 것이다 The problem will solve itself in course of time.∥~ 눈도 다 녹을 것이다 The snow will melt away soon[before long].∥~ 선거가 있을 것이다 There will be an election before long[in the near future].∥~ 좋은 소식을 듣게 될 것이다 You will hear good news soon [shortly].∥~ 그는 그것을 이해하게 될 것이다 He will come to understand it before long [in due time].

머츰하다 stop[cease] for a while. ¶비가 ~ 한다 It stops raining for a while. / It lets up for the moment. / The rain is letting up a little.∥열이 ~ The fever abates.

머큐로크롬 (상표명) Mercurochrome.
머플러 1 [목도리] a muffler. ¶~를 목에 두르고 with a muffler around one's neck∥~를 두르다 wear a muffler. **2** [소음기] (미) a muffler; (영) a silencer.

먹 1 an ink stick. ¶~ 한 자루 a cake[stick] of Chinese ink∥~을 갈다 rub an ink stick back and forth (to make ink). **2** India(n) ink; Chinese ink. ⇨먹물1

먹고살다 live (on / by); subsist (on); feed on (grass); earn[make] one's living. ¶월급으로 ~ live on one's salary∥먹고살 길을 강구하다 find some means of living∥먹고살기 어렵다 find it hard to make a living / be badly off∥먹고살기에 걱정이 없다 have enough money to live on / be in independent circumstances∥남이 번 것으로 ~ live on (a person's) earning∥나 혼자 먹고살기가 바쁘다 It's all I can do to feed[support] myself.∥나는 그를 먹고살게끔 해 주었다 I have put him in the way of earning his own bread.∥4인 가족이 월 20만 원으로는 먹고살 수가 없다 A family of four cannot live on two hundred thousand won a month.∥그는 붓으로 먹고산다 He lives by his pen.

먹구렁이 [동] a blacksnake.
먹구름 dark[black / ugly] clouds; brewing. ¶하늘은 ~으로 덮여 있다 The sky is covered with dark clouds.

먹그림 a contour picture drawn in India ink.
먹다[1] **1** (음식을) eat; have; take. ¶쌀을 주식으로 ~ eat rice as a staple food∥조금씩 ~ have a bite∥밖에서 ~ [외식하다] eat out∥허겁지겁 ~ gobble (up)[bolt] food∥잔뜩 입에 넣고 ~ fill[stuff / cram] one's mouth (with food)∥먹이를 ~ (동물이) feed∥사자는 고기를 먹는다 Lions eat meat.(▶ 진행형으로 쓰지 않음)∥이 버섯은 먹을 수 있다 This mushroom can be eaten[is edible].∥이 버섯은 먹을 수 있습니까 Is this mushroom edible[good to eat]?∥아침은 먹었니 Have you had your breakfast?∥그의 요리는 먹을 만하다[나쁘지 않다] His cooking is edible[is not so bad]. / [꽤 맛있다] His cooking is pretty good.∥잔뜩 밥을 입에 넣고 먹고 있었으니 바로 말이 나오지 않았다 My mouth was full of rice, so I couldn't say anything right away.∥이 나무의 열매는 먹을 수 있다 You can eat the fruit of this tree. / The fruit of this tree is edible.∥이 조개는 살이 질겨서 못 먹겠다 This shellfish is too tough to eat

먹다

[chew]. / I can't eat this shellfish because it's too tough. // 저 여자 아이는 아직도 연애 소설보다 먹기를 더 좋아한다 That girl still prefers eating to romance. // 음식이라고는 아직 조금도 먹지 못했다 I haven't had a bite to eat [a morsel of food] yet. / I haven't eaten a bite yet. // 음식을 잘못 섞어 먹어서 배탈이 났다 The strange mixture of food upset my stomach. // 나는 속이 좋지 않아 아무것도 먹지 못한다 My stomach is out of order, and so I can't eat anything. // 그녀는 아무것도 먹으려고 하지 않았다 She would not eat anything. // 그러면 잘 먹겠습니다 Then I'll go ahead and help myself. // 대단히 맛있게 먹었습니다 I really enjoyed this [meal / cake]. / It was very delicious. // 아닙니다. 많이 먹었습니다 No (more), thanks. I've had plenty (enough). // 자, 먹을까요 Shall we start (eating)? // 사양하지 않고 먹겠습니다 I'll help myself, thank you.
2 (물·술·약 등을) drink; have; take. ¶술을 ~ drink (wine) // 약을 ~ take medicine(s) // 알약을 ~ take [swallow] a pill // (아이가) 젖을 ~ suck milk / suck the breast // 우물물을 ~ drink [get a drink] at [from] a well // 술을 먹으면 취하는 것이 당연하다 If we drink, we are drunk, no wonder.
3 (남의 것을) pocket; embezzle; appropriate (to oneself); seize upon. ¶은행[남]의 돈을 ~ embezzle money from a bank [person] // 공금을 ~ embezzle [misuse] public funds // 뇌물을 ~ take [accept] a bribe / (미국 구어) graft.
4 (욕·겁을) receive; undergo; get; suffer. ¶욕을 ~ [꾸지람을 듣다] be scolded [reproved / rebuked] / [비난을 받다] be blamed [criticized] / 겁을 ~ be struck with awe / get into [be in] a funk.
5 (마음을) fix (up); decide; determine; mark. ¶마음을 ~ make up one's mind / be determined (to do) / put one's heart (into) / set [keep] one's mind (on).
6 (나이를) grow (older); get on [up] in years. ¶나이 먹은 사람 a man of years / an old man // 나이를 먹어 감에 따라 with advancing years / with growing age // 보기보다는 나이를 먹지 않다 be not so old as one looks // 그는 꽤 나이를 먹었다 He is well on in years.
7 (더위를) be affected (by the heat). ¶더위를 ~ be affected by the (summer) heat / suffer from hot weather / have [suffer] sunstroke.
8 (이문·구전을) get; receive; have. ¶이문을 먹지 않고 without profit // 매상에 대해 5퍼센트의 구전을 먹기로 하고 at [for] a commission of 5% on sales // 구전을 ~ get a commission [fee].
9 (판돈·상금을) win [bear away] (a prize, wager, etc.). ¶10만 원의 상금은 그 사람이 먹었다 The 100,000 won prize went to him.
10 (주먹을) be hit (by); be shot (in the head); receive a blow. ¶비유 여지없이 나는 한 방 먹었다 I was fairly caught. / I was fooled. / I was taken in.

먹어 치우다 eat up [off]; consume; devour; put away; polish off. ¶그는 접시의 음식을 모조리 먹어 치웠다 He ate up [polished off] all the food on the plate. // 우리는 순식간에 식탁 위의 음식을 먹어 치웠다 We ate up all the food on the table in an instant. // 이만한 음식은 세 사람이 도저히 먹어 치우지 못한다 It is simply impossible for three people to eat up [consume] all this food. // 메뚜기의 대군은 농작물을 순식간에 다 먹어 치웠다 A swarm of locusts ate up the crops in no time. // 그는 여러 접시의 요리를 차례로 먹어 치웠다 He ate up [devoured] one plate of food after another.

먹다[2] **1** [도구가 제 기능을 발휘하다] saw; bite; cut (well); grind (well); gin (well). ¶이 톱은 잘 먹는다 This saw bites [cuts] well. // 이 대패는 잘 먹지 않는다 This plane doesn't bite [cut] well. / This plane is blunt. // 씨아가 잘 ~ The cotton gin gins well.
2 (물감·풀·화장품 등이) dye (well); soak in (well). ¶풀이 잘 먹은 well-starched (cloth) / starchy (sheet) // (물감이) 잘 ~ [먹지 않다] dye [take dye] well [badly] // 이 광택지는 잉크가 잘 먹지 않는다 This glossy paper does not absorb ink well. / Ink does not take on this glossy paper. // 이 분은 잘 먹지 않는다 This powder does not stick well. // 이 크림은 피부에 잘 먹는다 The skin absorbs this cream well.
3 (휘발유·돈 등이) cost; consume; spend. ¶이 차는 기름을 많이 먹는다 This car consumes much oil.
4 (벌레 등이) eat into; be worm-eaten; be decayed. ¶좀 먹은 책 a moth-eaten book // 벌레 먹은 이 a decayed tooth // 옷에 좀이 먹는다 A garment is moth-eaten.

먹다[3] (귀가) become deaf; lose one's hearing; go deaf; be deafened. ¶귀가 ~ become deaf / be hard [slow / thick] of hearing // 그는 한쪽 귀가 먹었다 He is deaf of [in] one ear. // 그는 귀가 아주 먹었다 He is stone-deaf. / He is as deaf as door.

먹도미 (동) a black porgy. ⇨ ˮ감성돔

먹똥 1 [먹물 찌꺼기] dried sediment of India [Chinese] ink. **2** [먹물 자국] a black ink spot.

먹먹하다 deaf; deafened; stunned; deafening. ¶귀가 먹먹해지는 굉음 a deafening [an ear-rending / an ear-splitting] roar // 귀가 ~ be hard [dull] of hearing / have difficulty [be weak] in hearing // 그는 몹시 얻어맞아서 귀가 먹먹해졌다 He was boxed on ears so violently that his hearing was affected.

먹물 1 [먹을 간 물] India(n) ink; Chinese ink. ¶~로 쓰다 write in Indian ink // 나는 붓을 ~에 담갔다 I dipped my brush in the ink. **2** [검은 물] inky [black] water.

먹보 a glutton; a gourmand. ⇨ ˮ식충이(⇨식충)

먹빛 a shade of India(n) ink; an ink(y) black. ¶하늘은 ~이 되었다 The sky turned as black as ink [pitch-black].

먹성 (-性) appetite; how to eat; [먹는 양] one's eating capacity. ¶~이 한창때인 아이들 boys with a hearty appetite // ~이 좋다 have a good [large] appetite [stomach] / be omnivorous.

먹실 [먹물을 칠한 실] a string stained with ink; a string dyed black.

먹실(을) 넣다 tattoo; apply tattoo. ¶팔뚝에 ~ tattoo one's arm / have one's arm tattooed.

먹음새 [식사 태도] the way of eating; table manners. ¶~가 좋은 사람 (구어) a hearty [big] eater / a trencherman.

먹음직스럽다 delicious-looking; appetizing;

tempting. ¶먹음직스러워 보이다 look delicious / be tempting[appetizing] / make one's mouth water∥탁상에는 요리가 먹음직스럽게 차려졌다 Dishes were served appetizingly on the table.∥이 참외는 꽤 ~ This melon looks very tempting.

먹음직하다 delicious-looking. ⇨먹음직스럽다
먹이 food; feed; a prey(맹수의); meat(개의); a bait(물고기의). ¶물고기의 ~ fish-bait∥~로 하다 (습성으로서) prey on[upon]∥…의 ~이 되다 become the prey of (wolves) / fall a prey to∥~가 떨어지다 run out of provisions∥~에 길들다[~를 먹기 시작하다] begin to eat food / begin to feed / take to feeding∥낚시에 ~를 달다 bait a (fish-)hook∥개에게 ~를 주다 feed a dog∥말의 ~로 건초를 주다 feed a horse on hay∥금붕어에게 ~를 주었느냐 Have you fed[given food to] the goldfish?∥동물에게 ~를 주지 마시오 Please do not feed the animals.∥고양이는 쥐를 ~로 한다 Cats prey on[upon] mice.
● **먹이 사슬 / 먹이 연쇄** [생] food chain.

먹이다¹ 1 [사육하다] raise (sheep, hogs, etc.); rear; keep (a cat); feed (cattle on hay); [양육하다] support. ¶소를 ~ raise a cow∥이 땅은 40마리의 양을 먹이기에 충분하다 The land will depasture 40 sheep. 2 [때리다] give; deal; administer. ¶나는 녀석에게 주먹을 한 대 먹였다 I punched the guy. / I gave him a knuckle sandwich.∥저 놈은 건방지니까 한 대 먹여 줄까 보다 That fellow is such a smart aleck, I think I'll bust him in the mouth.∥그는 상대의 턱에 멋진 어퍼컷을 먹였다 He landed to the opponent's jaw a beautiful uppercut.

먹이다² 1 (음식을) let (someone) eat[drink]; feed (an animal on); serve (a person with); treat (a person to); entertain (a person) with. ¶굶주린 아이들을 ~ feed hungry children∥아기에게 모유를 ~ feed a baby with [on] its mother's milk / breast-feed[nurse] a baby∥남에게 약을 ~ give medicine to a person∥이 물고기는 작은 지렁이를 먹이면 된다 You can feed this fish on small earthworms.∥그녀는 아이들을 배불리 먹였다 She let the children eat their fill.∥아이들에게 무엇을 좀 먹여라 (구어) Give the kids something to eat. / Feed the kids.
2 (뇌물을) bribe with; grease[oil] a person's palm (with). ¶돈을 ~ bribe (a person) / slip money into (a person's) hands∥먹여서 입을 막다 bribe (a person) into secrecy / by (a person's) tongue∥먹인 보람이 있다 The bribe has worked.
3 (피해·접·욕을) make (a person) suffer with; inflict (on a person). ¶남을 욕~ let a person get a scolding / cause a person to the abuses∥겁을 먹여 승낙[복종]케 하다 intimidate[threaten] (a person) into compliance[submission].
4 (풀을) starch; (초를) wax; (기름을) oil. ¶풀 먹인 종이 wax paper.∥풀을 너무 먹인 셔츠 a stiffly starched shirt∥장판에 기름을 ~ oil floor paper∥실에 초를 ~ wax a string.
5 (기계에) put (a thing) in; feed (a thing) at[with]. ¶씨아에 솜을 ~ feed a gin with cotton / feed cotton to a gin∥작두에 풀을 ~ feed a hay cutter with hay∥인쇄기에 종이를 ~ feed paper to a printing press.

먹여 살리다 [부양하다] support; feed; provide for; keep; maintain. ¶가족을 먹여 살리는 것은 쉬운 일이 아니다 It is not an easy task to support a family.∥그녀가 그를 먹여 살리고 있다 He's living off her.

먹자 a carpenter's square (for drawing ink lines).

먹자판 1 [향락주의적 생각] epicurism; hedonism; a pleasure-loving way of life. 2 [먹고 마시는 자리] a spree; a scene of riotous eating.

먹장구름 black clouds; an inky cloud. ¶~이 빨리 움직이고 있다 Black clouds are moving fast.

먹줄 1 [먹통 줄] a string attached to an inkpot and stained with ink for drawing lines. 2 [먹통 줄로 그은 금] a carpenter's inkline. ¶~을 치다[띄우다] stretch out an inking line∥곧기가 ~ 같다 be straight as a carpenter's inkline.

먹줄 친 듯하다 (속담) be straight and even.

먹지 (-紙) carbon paper; copying paper.

먹칠 (-漆) coating[smearing] with Chinese ink. **먹칠하다** smear[coat] with Chinese ink; (명예) disgrace; discredit; dishonor; stain[sully] (a person's) good name. ¶인격에 ~ impair one's dignity∥가문에 ~ bring disgrace on one's family∥명성에 ~ smear one's reputation with infamy / tarnish one's reputation / cast a slur on one's fame.

먹통 (-桶) (목수의) an[a carpenter's] inkpad; [먹물 그릇] an inkwell; an inkpot.

먹황새 [동] a black-headed stork.

먹히다 1 [먹음을 당하다] be eaten (up); get eaten; be swallowed[gulped]; be devoured; be consumed. ¶먹느냐 먹히느냐의 싸움 a life-and-death struggle / a struggle without quarter∥개구리가 뱀한테 먹혀 버렸다 A frog was swallowed by the snake.
2 [먹게 되다] can be eaten[drunk]. ¶밥이 많이 ~ have a keen[hearty] appetite∥술이 먹히지 않다 be in no mood[humor] to have [for having] a drink / do not feel like having a drink.
3 [재료·노력 등이 들다] take; require; cost. ¶이 달걀은 한 개에 130원 먹힌다 These eggs cost 130 won apiece.∥그것을 다스(12개)로 사면 싸게 먹힌다 If you buy them by the dozen, you can get them cheaper.∥이 구매품은 결국 비싸게 먹혔다 The purchase did not pay in the long run.∥그것은 예상보다 비용이 훨씬 싸게 먹혔다 It was far less expensive than expected.∥이 사업은 돈이 많이 먹힌다 This enterprise eats money. / This is a very costly enterprise.
4 [받아들여지다] be accepted; go over. ¶그의 연설은 청중들에게 먹혀 들지 않았다 His speech didn't go over with the audience.
5 (화장품이 얼굴에). ¶그녀의 얼굴에는 분이 잘 먹히지 않았다 The powder did not stick to her face properly.

먼눈¹ [소경] a blind eye.
먼눈² [멀리 보는 눈] a far-off[faraway] look in one's eyes.

먼동 the eastern sky of an early morning; the dawning sky. ¶~이 틀 때 at the break of dawn / at the crack[peep] of dawn / at the first sign of daylight∥~이 트기 전에 before it is morning[light]∥~이 틀 때부터 해 질 녘까지 from dawn till dust / (미) from sunup to sundown∥~이 트기를 기다리다 wait for

먼발치 the light of day // ~이 튼다 Day breaks [dawns]. / Morning[It] dawns.

먼발치 a somewhat distant place; a spot far-off. ¶~에 at some[a] distance // ~에서 보면 in a distant view / (when) seen from a distance // ~에서 보다 have a distant view (of).

먼빛으로 from afar; from far away. ¶~ 보아 (when viewed) from a distance / to a gaze at a distance / in a distant view // ~ 보다 view from a distance.

먼일 distant[future] events; events to come. ¶~을 예상하다 anticipate what is to come // ~을 생각하다 think of the future / look forward into the future // 그렇게 ~까지는 생각지 않았다 I didn't think so far ahead.

먼저 **1** [앞서서] first; ahead. ¶~ 가다 go first / go before others / go ahead / take precedence // ~ 먹다 take[eat] first / eat before others // ~ 실례합니다[갑니다] Excuse me, but I must be going. / Please excuse me for going on ahead of you[, but I'll go ahead]. // 내가 그보다 ~ 왔다 I came earlier than he did. / I arrived before he did. // 그가 맨 ~ 일어섰다 He was the first to stand up. // ~ 가십시오 Please go first. / Let me follow you. // 그것보다 이것을 ~ 해야 한다 You must do this before that.
2 [우선] first of all; above all; before anything else. ¶우선 무엇보다 ~ first of all / before everything else / first / to begin with / (문어) at the outset // 무엇보다 ~ 집을 사다 buy a house first of all // ~ 우리 국민성에 대해서 말하겠다 I shall begin with the national character of our people. // ~ 빚을 갚아야겠다 I have to pay my debts before anything else. // ~ 부모님께 알려 드리세요 First of all[Before anything else], you must let your parents know about it.
3 [전에] (sometime) ago; previously; before; formerly. ¶~ 말한 바와 같이 as previously stated / as noted[said] above // ~ 말한 바로 미루어 judging from the foregoing // ~ 상태로 돌아가다 return to the previous condition // ~ 그렇게 말한 일이 있지 않은가 Didn't you say that sometime ago?

먼저께 the other day; some time[a few days] ago; [요즈음] lately; in the recent past; recently. ¶~의 recent / late // ~ 당신에게 말한 바와 같이 as I told you previously

먼지 dust; dirt; [티끌] a mote. ¶~투성이의 full of dust / covered with dust // ~투성이의 거리 a dusty street // ~가 일다[나다] be dusty // ~가 끼다 be covered with dust // ~를 일으키다 raise[stir up] dust // ~를 털다 brush away[beat off] dust / dust (a coat) / brush (a hat) // ~를 가라앉히다 lay the dust // 차서 ~를 일으키다 kick up dust // 테이블의 ~를 털다 dust a table // 가구의 ~를 털다 dust the furniture // 차가 ~투성이다 Your car is covered with dust. // 내가 한 발씩 걸을 때마다 ~가 일었다 Dust rose with each step I took. // 일단의 트럭이 ~ 구름을 일으키며 달려갔다 A convoy of trucks [(영) lorries] rolled past, raising a cloud of dust. // 물을 뿌려 ~가 일지 않게 해라 Sprinkle some water to settle[lay] the dust. // 나는 온통 ~를 뒤집어썼다 I got dusty all over.
● **먼지떨이** a duster.

멀거니 blankly; vacantly; absentmindedly; stupidly; with a blank[far-off] look; with an abstracted air. ¶~ 바라보다 look[gaze] vacantly[blankly] (at) / moon (over) // ~ 생각에 잠기다 be in a brown study / be lost in reverie[in the clouds] // ~ 앉아 있다 be sitting absentmindedly.

멀건이 an absentminded person; (미국 속어) a goofer.

멀겋다 **1** [흐릿하게 맑다] dull; lusterless; dim; leaden; (애체 등이) milky. ¶멀건 하늘 a leaden[gray] sky / a gloomy[an overcast] sky // 멀건 눈 glazed[glassy] eyes / clouded [fishy] eyes. **2** [묽다] sloppy; weak[watery] (tea / beer); thin (coffee, porridge, paste, etc.); (wishy-)washy (milk). ¶멀건 우유 washy milk // 멀건 죽을 홀짝이다 sip thin [watery] gruel // 이 수프는 너무 ~ This soup is mere wash.

멀게지다 [흐릿하게 맑아지다] become dull [milky / dim]; [묽어지다] become watery [(wishy-)washy / sloppy]; thin; become thin.

멀구슬나무 [식] a chinaberry (tree); a bead tree; a bastard cedar.

멀다[1] **1** (거리가) far; distant; remote; far-off; faraway. ¶먼 곳 a distant place // 먼 곳의 distant / remote // 먼 곳에 far away / in the distance // 먼 앞마당에 far out in the offing // 그는 먼 곳에서 왔다 He came from far away [a distant place]. // 먼 곳을 와 주셔서 감사합니다 You are very kind to come so far[all this way]. // 이 학교에서 그리 멀지 않은 곳에 오래된 절이 하나 있다 There is an old temple not too far (away) from our school. // 우체국은 여기서 멉니까 Is the post office far from here? // 시청은 버스 정류소에서 꽤 ~ The city hall is quite a long way from the bus stop. // 먼 곳으로 이사 가신다지요 I hear you are moving a long way off. (▶ 거리를 나타내는 far는 보통 의문문·부정문에서 쓰고, 긍정문에는 a long way off, far, very far 등을 흔히 씀) // 그것은 어떤 먼 나라에서 일어난 일이야 It happened in some far-off[distant] country. // 먼 산골에 들어가고 싶다 I wish I could go deep into the mountains.
2 (시간적으로) remote. ¶그 전설은 먼 옛날부터 전해 내려오고 있다 The legend has been handed down from ancient times[the remote past]. // 그것은 먼 옛날에 일어난 일이었다 It happened a long time[while] ago. / That's something that happened in the distant past. // 나는 먼 앞날을 예견할 수 없다 I cannot foretell the remote future. // 먼 장래를 생각해 봅시다 Let's look far (ahead) into the future. // 이리로 이사 온 것이 먼 옛날처럼 느껴진다 It seems to me as if it were ages ago when I moved here[I had lived here for ages]. // 그가 임원으로 승진하는 것도 그리 멀지 않다 It will not be long before he is promoted to director. // 그는 사흘이 멀다 하고 내게 전화를 한다 He calls me at least once every three days. // 그의 일이 완성되기까지는 아직 멀었다 He has a long way to go before he finishes his work.
3 (관계가) distant. ¶그는 먼 친척이다 I am distantly related to him. / He is one of my distant relatives. // 어제 먼 친척 한 분이 찾아왔다 A distant relative of mine called on me yesterday. // 두 사람의 사이가 점점 멀어졌다 Gradually they became estranged from each other. / Gradually a gulf grew up

between them.∥그는 친구들로부터 멀어지게 되었다 His friends began to avoid [keep away from] him.
4 (정도가) be no match (for); be far inferior (to); (미숙련) poor; unskilled. ¶그녀는 미인하고는 거리가 ~ She is far from beautiful. / She can't be called beautiful.∥수상의 발언은 서민의 감정과는 거리가 먼 것이었다 The premier's remarks showed little understanding of the feelings of ordinary people.∥그녀는 예술가의 수준에는 아직 멀었다 She is far from artistic. / She is not in the least artistic.

먼 사촌보다 가까운 이웃이 낫다(속담) A good neighbor is better than a brother far off.

먼 길 a long way; [긴 여행] a long journey; [장거리] a long distance. ¶~을 가다 make a long journey / go a long way∥~을 오시느라고 수고하셨습니다 Thank you for coming all that way [from such a great distance / from so far away].

멀다² **1** (눈이) become [go] blind; become sightless; lose [be deprived of] one's (eye) sight. ¶한쪽 눈이 ~ be blind of an eye∥눈이 ~ be [become] blind∥(비유) 돈에 눈이 ~ be blinded by money. **2** become deaf; lose one's hearing. ⇨²먹다³

멀뚱멀뚱 [멀거니] blankly; vacantly; absent-mindedly; with a blank look. ¶~ 바라보다 gaze [look] vacantly [blankly] (at) / moon (over)∥~ 보고만 있다 remain an idle spectator. **멀뚱멀뚱하다** absentminded; vacant; blank; (미국 속어) moony. ¶멀뚱멀뚱한 눈 a vacant stare [look] / glassy [remote] eyes∥멀뚱멀뚱한 얼굴 a vacant look / a vapid face / (미국 속어) a moony face.

멀리 far; far away [off]; afar; a long way off; in the distance; at a distance. ¶~ 떨어져 있는 마을 a far-off [distant] town∥교회의 첨탑이 ~서도 잘 보인다 The spire of the church can be seen very well from afar [from a distance].∥~서 사이렌 소리가 들린다 There is a siren blowing in the distance.∥대포 소리가 ~서도 들렸다 The report of the guns could be heard even at a distance.∥승리의 소식이 ~ 퍼졌다 The news of the victory spread far and wide.∥그는 ~ 바다 건너에서 왔다 He came all the way from abroad.∥이웃 읍에서 왔는데도 나는 ~서 온 것 같은 느낌이 들었다 I felt as if I had come from afar, though I came only from the neighboring town.∥우리는 정상에서 들과 산을 ~ 바라볼 수 있다 We can have a distant view of mountains and fields from the summit.∥~ 설악산이 보인다 We can see Seoraksan (Mt. Seorak) in the distance.

멀리뛰기 (미) a broad jump; (영) a long jump. ¶제자리 ~ a standing broad jump.

멀리하다 [경원하다] keep (a person) at a (respectful) distance [at an arm's length]; give a wide berth (to); keep away from (a person); shun (a person); avoid; alienate; eschew; [절제하다] abstain (from); keep off. ¶단것을 ~ avoid sweets∥저런 사람은 멀리하는 것이 좋다 It is wiser for you to keep your distance from [give a wide berth to] such a person.∥그동안에 그는 절친한 친구도 멀리하였다 He cut himself off from [avoided / kept away from] even his best friend during the period.∥마이크를 좀 멀리해 주세요 Please move the microphone a little further away.∥그는 친구를 모두 멀리하고 있었다 He kept all his friends at a distance [at arm's length]. / He didn't let anyone get close to him.∥그녀의 부모는 그녀를 그로부터 멀리하려고 했다 Her parents tried to keep her away from him [make her break off with him].∥분쟁을 멀리하는 것이 현명하다고 생각한다 I think it's wiser to keep out of the dispute.

멀미 **1** [메스꺼운 증세] (motion) sickness; nausea; queasiness. ¶뱃 ~ seasickness∥비행기 ~ airsickness∥차~ carsickness. **멀미하다** feel [be] sick. **2** [싫증] an aversion; dislike; disgust; a repugnance (to / for); being fed up (with); being sick (of). ¶~가 나다 be sick (and tired) (of) / be fed up (with) / feel a repugnance to [for]∥인제 이 일에는 ~가 난다 I am getting [growing] tired of this job.
● **멀미약** preventive medicine for travel sickness.

멀쑥하다 **1** clean; neat; smart. ⇨²말쑥하다 **2** (키가) lean and tall; lanky; long and skinny; spindly; (구어) gangling. ¶키가 멀쑥한 사내 a lanky man.

멀어지다 [거리가] become more distant; [멀리 사라지다] grow distant; become far off [distant]; get away; recede (from view); (소리가) die [trail] away (in the distance); grow faint. ¶발소리가 점점 멀어져 갔다 The footsteps gradually faded away.∥기적 소리가 멀어져 갔다 The whistle faded [died] away in (to) the distance. **2** (관계가) be [become] estranged [alienated] (from); fall away (from); drift apart (from each other). ¶저 집안과는 사이가 멀어졌다 We no longer have any contact with that family.∥얼마 안 가서 두 사람의 사이는 멀어지고 말았다 Soon they were estranged from each other.

멀쩡하다 **1** [온전하다] flawless; faultless; spotless; free from blemish; sound; perfect; [다친 데가 없다] unhurt; uninjured; unwounded; (정신이) sane; sober. ¶정신이 ~ be in one's right mind / be in one's senses∥그는 정신이 ~ He is sane enough. / (취하지 않았다) He's quite sober.∥멀쩡한 정신으로 하는 소리냐 Do you say so in earnest? **2** [뻔뻔스럽다] impudent; shameless; hypocritical; cheeky; bold; barefaced. ¶멀쩡한 놈 a brazen-faced fellow / a brassy one / a guy as bold as brass∥멀쩡한 거짓말 a barefaced lie∥멀쩡한 놈이로군 What nerve [What a cheek] he's got!

멀찍멀찍 far apart; at distant intervals (between); at a good distance; some distance apart. ¶~ 떨어져 앉다 take seats some distance apart∥나무를 ~ 심다 plant trees at a good distance from each other.

멀찍하다 pretty far; rather distant; far-off; remote; some distance away [apart]. **멀찍이** pretty far; rather distant; far apart; far enough. ¶~ 보이는 산 a mountain in the distance / a distant mountain∥~ 사이를 두다 leave a pretty long interval (between)∥나무를 집에서 ~ 심다 plant a tree rather far from the house∥우리 집은 길에서 ~ 떨어져 있다 Our house is quite a way off the street.

멀티미디어 [컴] [다중 매체] multimedia.

멈추다 **1** [멎다] stop; cease; (폭풍 등이)

멈칫거리다

subside; calm [die] down; come to an end. ¶소음이 갑자기 멈추었다 The noise stopped suddenly.//열차가 역에 멈추었다[멈추고 있었다] The train pulled up[stopped] at the station.//자동차가 갑자기 멈추었다 The car came to a sudden stop.//자동차의 엔진이 멈추고 움직이지 않는다 The engine (of the car) stalled[went dead] and won't start (again).//눈 때문에 열차의 운행이 멈춰지고 있다 The trains are not running owing to the snow.//그는 포스터 앞에 아주 멈추어 섰다 He came to a full stop[halted / stood still] in front of the poster.//그 말은 장애물 앞에서 갑자기 멈추어 섰다 The horse balked in front of the hurdle.//치통은 멈추었느냐 Is your toothache gone?//정전으로 열차가 멈춰 버렸다 The train stopped[halted / came to a standstill] because of a power failure.//잿불을 부치고 있던 손이 갑자기 멈춰졌다 The hand fanning the embers suddenly paused.//선생님이 오시는 것을 보고 그녀는 멈추었다 She stopped when she saw her teacher approaching.//독감의 전염력은 멈출 줄을 모른다 The spread of influenza knows no bounds.//대기 오염의 증가는 멈출 줄을 모른다 There is no end to the increase in air pollution.
2 [멎게 하다] stop; cease; put a stop [an end] to; bring to a stop[standstill]; hold up [on]. ¶출혈을 ~ stop the bleeding//시계를 ~ stop a clock / (전기 시계를) turn off a clock//통증을 ~ kill the pain//나는 눈물을 멈출 수가 없었다 I could not keep[hold] back my tears. / I could not help weeping.//그는 발을 멈추고 지도를 보았다 He stopped to take a look at his map.//그는 깃발을 흔들어 열차를 멈추었다 He flagged down the train. / He stopped the train by waving a flag.//택시를 멈추어 주시오 Flag (down) a cab[taxi] for me.//그는 끽 소리를 내며 차를 멈추었다 He brought his car to a screeching halt.//걸음을 멈추지 마시오 Keep moving please. / Move along, please.

멈칫거리다 hesitate; waver; hang[hold] back; vacillate; falter; dally; dawdle; linger; dilly-dally; shilly-shally; pause; mark time; be dilatory. ¶멈칫거리지 않고 without hesitation[flinching] / unhesitatingly / without scruple[wavering] / straight off / without (further) delay//들어갈까 말까 ~ balance in one's mind whether to go in or not//멈칫거리면서 분명한 대답을 않다 hesitate to give a definite answer//멈칫거리지 말고 네 생각을 말해라 Out with it! Never stand shilly-shally.

멈칫멈칫 hesitatingly; hesitantly; waveringly; dilatorily; lingeringly. ¶~ 자리에서 일어나지 않다 be slow to leave one's seat / (잠자리에서) dally in bed//~ 말하다 speak in a halting way / speak hesitatingly / drawl. **멈칫멈칫하다** hesitate; waver. ⇨ **멈칫거리다**

멈칫하다 [갑자기 멈추다] stop abruptly (for a moment); break (off); be interrupted; [주저하다] hesitate. ¶그녀는 무엇인가 말을 하려다가 멈칫했다 Half-formed words died on her lips.

멋 1 [고상한 운치] relish; taste; zest; gusto; aroma; flavor, savor; interest; delight; pleasure; (속어) kick. ¶인생의 ~ the zest of living / a kick out of life//~을 아는 사람 a man of taste//~을 모르는 사람 one who doesn't appreciate elegance and taste//~을 알다 have a taste (for) / relish / appreciate (the fun, beauty, etc.) / be in the know / get what is going on//~을 모르다 have no taste [relish] (for) / have no appreciation (of) / do not delight (in)//세상 ~을 알다 have been around / have been through the mill / have seen the world.
2 [맵시] dudism; dandyism; foppery. ¶~으로 show하는 사람 a fop / a dandy//~을 부리다[내다] smarten[preen] oneself / dress smartly / brush up//그는 ~과는 거리가 먼 사람이다 He is quite free from dandyism.//나는 ~으로 카메라를 메고 다니는 것이 아니다 I am not carrying a camera about with me merely[just] for show.//그는 ~으로 안경을 쓴다 He wears glasses for show[for appearance's sake].

멋대가리 〈속〉 relish; taste; dudism. ⇨ 멋

멋대로 as one pleases[likes / wishes]; [자유의사로] freely; of one's own accord; of one's (own) free will; [독단적으로] at one's (own) discretion; arbitrarily; [무단히] without leave[permission]. ¶~ 굴다 act as one pleases / have everything one's own way//입에서 나오는 대로 ~ 지껄이다 talk without thinking / say the first thing that[say whatever] comes into one's head / speak off the top of one's head//그가 ~ 하게 내버려 두시오. Let him do as he pleases. / Let him go his own way.//그것은 내 ~ 할 수 없는 일이다 That is not up to me (to decide).//그것은 그가 ~ 결정한 일이다 He decided it without consulting anyone.//거리에서는 불량배들이 ~ 놀아나고 있다 In the town the hoodlums have everything their own way.//거기에 도착하면 여러분은 어떤 행동이든 ~ 해도 좋습니다 When you arrive there, take whatever action you think appropriate.//나는 ~ 저녁 거리를 거닐었다 I walked about the evening streets as my fancy led me.//당신이 그를 ~ 하게 내버려 두면 난처하게 될 것이오 It will lead to trouble if you let him have his (own) way[let him do as he likes].//그는 두 사람의 관계를 ~ 상상해 보았다 He speculated freely[let his imagination run wild] about the relationship between the two.//그렇게 해서는 안 된다 Don't be so selfish.//~ 해 봐라 Do it your own way. / Do as you please [like].

멋들다 be captivating; get interesting; be beautiful.

멋들어지다 wonderful; splendid; stylish; grand; excellent; capital; exciting; dramatic; delightful; captivating; fascinating; dashing; (구어) great; (구어) swell. ¶멋들어진 노래 a song full of gusto / a fascinating song//멋들어진 생각 a capital[good] idea//멋들어진 풍채(風采) commanding presence / imposing appearance//멋들어지게 with gusto[zest] / interestingly / fascinatingly//멋들어지게 춤추다 dance with gusto / dance beautifully//수양버들이 멋들어지게 늘어져 있다 A weeping willow droops gracefully.//그는 연설을 멋들어지게 끝맺었다 He concluded his speech on just the right note.

멋모르다 do not know; know nothing; be ignorant (of); have no idea[conception] (of); be innocent (of); be quite unconscious [unaware] (of). ¶멋모르는 사이에 before one is aware (of it) / without one's knowledge // 멋모르고 달려들다 try to go at somebody [something] without knowing anything about him[it] // 멋모르고 떠들지 마라 Don't poke your nose without the least knowledge of it.

멋없다 unrefined; unstylish; inelegant; tasteless; flat; unsavory; prosaic; unromantic; boorish; rustic; uncouth; senseless; awkward; vulgar; lacking in polish. ¶멋없는 사람 a man of uncouth tastes // 멋없는 농담 a joke that falls flat // 그녀는 멋없는 스카프를 두르고 있었다 She wore a dowdy[an unfashionable /(미) a tacky] scarf. // 그것 참 시시하고 멋없는 일이다 That's too ordinary (to be interesting). / That's trite and uninteresting. // 그는 멋없는 사람이다 He lacks delicacy [good taste]. / He is a boorish [an unpolished] man. // 정말 멋없는 질문이군 What a thoughtless question to ask!

멋있다 [풍치 있다] tasty; tasteful; elegant; fine; (프) chic; [맵시 있다] fashionable; stylish; smart; smartish; gallant. ¶멋있는 너석[자] (구어) a cool[groovy / neat] guy[car] // 멋있는 옷 chic dress // 멋있는 디자인 a smart[stylish] design // 멋있는 농담 a clever [witty] joke // 멋있는 생각 a bright [an ingenious] idea // 멋있는 말 a topping remark / a witty saying // 멋있는 인품 an interesting personality // 멋있는 장식 tasteful decoration // 멋있는 표현 an apt expression / a nice turn of phrases // 그녀는 언제나 멋있는 옷차림을 하고 있다[옷을 멋있게 입는다] She is always stylishly [fashionably / smartly / attractively] dressed.

멋쟁이 a dandy; a gallant; a swell; a smart [fashionable] dresser; (미) a dude; a beau (pl. ~x, ~s). ¶빨간 나비넥타이를 맨 ~ a dandy wearing a red bow tie // ~는 겨울에도 두꺼운 옷을 입지 않는다 A dandy does not wear heavy clothes even in cold weather.

멋지다 [근사하다] fairly good; very smart [(미국 속어) cute]; [훌륭하다] fine; splendid; nice; neat; (맵시·태도 등이) stylish; smart; polished; foppish; dandyish; (미국 속어) swell; high-toned; (영국 속어) posh; (솜씨가) skillful; dexterous. ¶멋진 드레스 a stylish dress // 멋진 생각 a splendid idea // 멋진 여자 a smart[stylish] woman // 멋진 집 a stylish [tasteful] house // 취미가 ~ have refined tastes // 멋진 옷차림을 하고 있다 be smartly dressed // 그것 참 멋지겠다 That would be marvelous[(구어) great]. // 나는 멋진 소녀를 만났다 I met a wonderful girl. // 참 멋진 정원이군요. What a lovely [charming] garden! // 우리는 파티에서 멋지게 지냈다 We had a wonderful [splendid / (구어) great] time at the party. // 그녀는 옷차림이 ~ She is stylishly dressed. // 그녀는 검은 옷차림이 오히려 멋지게 보였다 She looked all the more chic in black. // 그는 콧수염이 아주 ~ He looks really nice with a mustache.

멋쩍다 [쑥스럽고 어색하다] awkward; embarrassing; (서술적) embarrassed; feel uncomfortable; feel ill at ease. ¶멋쩍은 듯이[멋쩍게] awkwardly / embarrassedly // 멋쩍어하다 feel awkward [nervous / strained] / become self-conscious / be [feel] ill at ease // 멋쩍은 듯이 웃다 smile sheepishly // 자리가 비어 있는데도 서 있는 것은 멋쩍은 짓이다 There is no sense in standing when there are seats available.

멍 1 [피부에 맺힌 피] a bruise; a contusion; a black eye(눈 언저리의). ¶~이 들다 be bruised / be black and blue // 그는 얻어맞아 눈가에 ~이 들었다 He has a black eye from the blow. // 그는 싸움 끝에 온몸에 ~이 들었다 He was black and blue all over after the fight. 2 [일의 속으로 생긴 탈] something wrong; a hitch; an obstacle; a (deep-rooted) trouble; an impediment; a snag. ¶가혹한 말이 그녀의 마음에 ~이 들게 했다 Harsh words bruised her feelings.

멍게 [동] an ascidian; a sea squirt.

멍군 [장기] a defensive move against a checkmate; "out of check". ¶장군 ~이다 be hard to tell which of the two is wrong.

멍들다 1 [마음 등이] be hurt [ruined / marred / spoiled]. ¶남의 감정을 멍들게 하다 hurt [lacerate / injure / bruise] (a person's) feelings / hurt (a person). 2 [일의 탈이 생기다] go wrong (with); develop trouble; get mixed up; be spoiled; suffer a serious hitch [setback] / run into a real snag[an insuperable obstacle].

멍멍 [개 짖는 소리] bowwow. ¶~ 짖다 bow-wow / bark (at).

멍멍개 〈소아〉 a bowwow; a doggie.

멍멍하다 deafened (by the din); stunned [dazed]. **멍멍히** as if stunned; blankly; absentmindedly; vacantly.

멍석 a straw mat; (집합적) straw matting. ¶~을 깔다[짜다] spread [plait / weave] a straw mat.

멍에 a yoke (bar). ¶사랑의 ~ the yoke of love // ~를 지다 bear the cross / carry an albatross around the neck / be a millstone around one's neck // ~를 벗다[벗어던지다] throw [cast / shake] off the yoke (of) / [비유] free oneself from restraint // 소에 ~를 메우다 put a yoke on oxen / yoke oxen / put an ox to the yoke // ~를 벗어던지고 자유롭게 살아라 Throw off your yoke and be free.

멍울 a lump; a mass; an induration. ⇨°망울1·3 ¶나는 오른쪽 유방에 ~이 있다 I have a hard lump in the right breast. / A hard lump has formed in my right breast.

멍청이 a fool; an idiot; (속어) an ass; a donkey; a blockhead; a dunce; a dolt; a fathead; a half-wit; a careless [thoughtless] person; a dull-witted person; (구어) a dim-wit; (미국 속어) a goofer. ¶그런 절호의 기회를 놓치다니 너는 정말 ~구나 How stupid of you to miss such a good opportunity!

멍청하다 stupid; foolish; silly; idiotic; dull-[half- / slow-]witted; thickheaded; stolid. ¶멍청한 사람 [부주의한 사람] a careless person / [멍한 사람] an absentminded [inattentive] person // 멍청한 얼굴로 with a stupid[blank] look of amazement // 멍청하게 보이는 얼굴 a stupid-looking face // 멍청한 짓을 하다 do a thoughtless thing // 그런 말을 하다니 나도 참 멍청했다 It was really careless of me to say such a thing. / How silly [stupid] of me to have said such a thing! // 그는 멍청하게 서 있었다 He was standing there absentmindedly [looking blank]. **멍청히** absentmindedly; vacantly; blankly. ¶~ 바라보다 look blankly [vacantly].

멍텅구리 1 a fool; an idiot. ⇨°멍청이 2 [한 되

멍하니 들이의 못생긴 병) an ill-shaped bottle (holding a bit more than a doe).

멍하니 [방심하여] blankly; vacantly; absentmindedly; with a blank look; as if stunned. ¶~ 생각하다 be in a brown study / be lost in reverie / lose oneself in the clouds // 바라보자 look[gaze] vacantly[blankly] (at) // ~ 서[앉아] 있다 stand[sit] idle // ~ 돌아다니다 mope about // ~ 보고만 있다 remain an idle spectator // ~ 서 있지만 말고 좀 거들어라 Don't just stand around like a fool. Do something to help. // 그는 방 한구석에 ~ 서 있었다 He was standing absently[vacantly] in a corner of the room. // 그는 ~ 허공만 바라보았다 He simply gazed into space absent-mindedly[with a blank look on his face].

멍하다 absentminded; abstracted; vacant; blank; apathetic; (미국 속어) moony; [상심하다] stunned; stupefied; (귀가) deafened. ¶멍한 얼굴로 with an absentminded[a vacant] look on one's face // 멍해지다 be absentminded[abstracted / stupefied / dazed] / 귀가 ~ be deafened (by a noise) // 정신이 ~ be in a daze / be stunned // 그녀는 나를 멍한 눈으로 보았다 She looked at me with vacant eyes. // 그는 아직도 멍한 상태이다 He is still in a state of apathy. // 잠이 모자라 머리가 ~ I'm groggy from lack of sleep. // 연휴 때문에 머리가 ~ My mind isn't functioning after these consecutive holidays. // 지금은 시차 때문에 머리가 ~ At the moment my mind isn't quite clear because of jet lag. // 나의 비서는 월요일 아침에는 늘 멍해 있다 (구어) My secretary's just not with it on Monday mornings. // 그는 내 잔소리를 멍하게 듣고 있었다 He listened to my scolding with an absentminded air[absentmindedly]. // 열심히 이야기했지만 그는 멍해 있었다 I talked to him earnestly, but his mind was somewhere else.

멎다 [멈추다] stop; [그치다] (문어) cease; come to a stop[an end]; (바람 등이) die down; (소리 등이) die away. ¶바람이 멎었다 The wind has died down. // 음악은 어느새 멎어 있었다 The music had stopped[ceased] before we were aware of it. // 지진은 수 초 만에 멎었다 The earthquake died away in a few seconds. // 열차가 역에 멎었다[멎어 있었다] The train pulled up[was stopped]. // 자동차가 갑자기 멎었다 The car came to a sudden stop.

메[1] [나무나 쇠토막에 자루를 박은 망치] a mallet(목제); a hammer(철제); (대장간의) a sledge hammer; a maul(큰 것); a beetle(큰 것). ¶~로 치다 hammer / strike[beat] with a hammer.

메[2] [메꽃(의 뿌리)] (the root of) a bindweed [convolvulus].

메[3] [제삿밥] rice offered to the gods[to departed spirits].

메- [차지지 않은] nonglutinous; not sticky. ¶~떡 cake made of nonglutinous grain // ~조 nonglutinous millet.

메가사이클 [물] a megacycle(약어 Mc, mc).

메가톤 a megaton(약어 MT). ¶~급의 (a hydrogen bomb) in the megaton range.

메가폰 megaphone. ¶~으로 알리다 announce by (a) megaphone.

메가폰을 잡다 ((영화)감독을 맡다) direct; undertake the charge of a (film) director.

메가헤르츠 [주파수의 단위] megahertz(약어 MHz).

메기 [동] a catfish; a bullhead; a horned pout; (큰 것) a wels (pl. ~es).
● **메기입** a big (long) mouth; a catfish-like mouth.

메기다[1] 1 [소리를] lead (a song / a chant). 2 [톱질에서] take the lead (on a two-man saw).

메기다[2] 1 (화살을) fix; put. ¶화살을 ~ fix[fit] an arrow in one's bow / put an arrow on the string[to the bow] / notch an arrow (upon the bow). 2 (윷을) move a yut piece.

메꽃 [식] a convolvulus (pl. ~es, -li); a (field) bindweed.

메뉴 a menu; a bill of fare; a (menu) card. ¶~에 있다 be on the menu[bill / card] // ~에 있는 요리밖에 안 됩니다 We serve only the dishes on the menu.

메다[1] (어깨에) shoulder (a gun); carry[bear / take] (a load) on one's shoulder. ¶총을 메고 행진하다 march with guns on one's shoulder // 그는 항상 어깨에 총을 걸어 메고 있다 He always has a rifle slung over his shoulder.

메다[2] 1 [막히다] be[get] choked [filled / stopped / plugged] (up); be[get] blocked; get clogged; be glutted; be obstructed. ¶목이 멘다 My throat is choked. // 굴뚝이 메었다 A chimney was foul[choked up]. // 목이 메게 울다 be choked with tears / sob // 그 말을 들으니 가슴이 멘다 It depresses me to hear it. // 그는 가슴이 메어 말도 못했다 His heart was too full for words. // 코가 메었다 My nose is stuffed[bunged] up. 2 →메우다[1]

메다[3] put a hoop on (a tub); put on; fix; yoke. ⇨메우다[2]

메달 a medal; a medallion(대형의). ¶[은 · 동] ~ a gold[silver / bronze] medal / ~권에 들다[~권에서 탈락하다] enter[drop out of] the range of winning a medal // ~을 획득하다 win a medal (in[for] the horizontal bar) // 그는 100m 경주에서 ~을 획득했다 He won [was awarded] a medal in the 100-meter dash.

메달리스트 a medalist. ¶금~ a gold medal winner / a gold medalist.

메들리 [음][체] a medley.

메뚜기 [동] (집합적) a grasshopper; [벼메뚜기] a locust.

메리야스 (⑩medias) knit[knitted] fabric [goods]; knit work.

메마르다 1 [땅이 건조하다] very dry; dried-up; arid; parched; [땅이 기름지지 못하다] sterile; barren; meager; infertile. ¶메마른 땅 barren[poor / sterile / unproductive] soil [land] / wasteland // 메마른 날씨 dry weather // 메마르게 되다 (땅이) become sterile / become impoverished // 이 땅은 몹시 메말라 있다 This soil is so sterile. 2 [피부 등이] shriveled; withered; shriveled; rough. ¶메마른 살갗 a dry[parched] skin // 메마른 손 a dry, rough hand. 3 [마음이] hard(-hearted); cold(-hearted); harsh; severe. ¶메마른 마음 a cold [a hard / an unfeeling] heart / a heart of stone.

메모 a memorandum (pl. ~s, -da); a memo (pl. ~s). ¶~ 없이 설명하다 explain without[(문어) recourse to] notes // 그는 ~를 보고 이야기했다 He spoke from notes. **메모하다** take a memo; take notes (of / on); jot

메모리 [컴] a memory.

메밀 [식] (common) buckwheat.
● 메밀가루 buckwheat (flour). 메밀국수 buckwheat noodles[vermicelli]. 메밀묵 buckwheat paste[jelly].

메벼 nonglutinous rice plants.

메부수수하다 rustic; rusticated; boorish; countrified; countryish.

메스 (@mes) [수술용 칼] a scalpel; a (surgical) knife. ¶…에 ~를 가하다 plunge a scalpel into / probe (a matter) to the bottom / dig into … / 환자에게 ~를 대다 operate on a patient (for a tumor) // 문제에 ~를 가하다 apply a scalpel of sharp criticism (to) / 부패 정치에 ~를 가하다 [분석하여 밝히다] investigate and expose political corruption / [근본적 해결을 도모하다] reform[clean up] corrupt politics.

메스껍다 1 [토할 것 같다] sickening; nauseous; nauseating; (영국 구어) sick. ¶메스꺼워지다 feel sick[nausea / queasy] / feel like vomiting // 메스꺼운 냄새 a sickening smell / 속이 ~ be sick at the stomach // 나는 ~ I feel nauseated [sick]. / 차멀미로 메스꺼웠다 I got carsick. / 그 냄새를 맡았더니 메스꺼웠다 The smell made me sick. 2 [아주 불쾌한] disgusting; abominable; loathsome; offensive; revolting; sickening. ¶메스꺼운 아첨 nauseating[sickening] flattery // 메스껍게 굴다 act[behave] disgustingly // 그의 위선적인 태도에는 메스꺼워진다 His hypocrisy nauseates me.

메슥거리다 feel sick[queasy / nauseated]; be sick at the stomach; feel like throwing up [vomiting]. ¶속이 좀 ~ get sickish.

메슥메슥하다 feel sick[nausea]; feel like vomiting. ¶보기만 해도 속이 메슥메슥해진다 The mere sight of it makes me sick.

메시아 [구세주] the Messiah. ¶~의 Messianic.

메시지 a message. ¶축하의 ~를 보내다 send one's congratulations // 그에게 ~를 전해 주시오. Please deliver my message to him. / Please give him my message.

메신저 a messenger.

메아리 an echo; echoes. ¶~가 울려왔다 Echoes resounded [reverberated]. / 내가 외친 소리가 ~가 되어 돌아왔다 My call was echoed back.

메아리치다 echo; resound; be echoed; reverberate. ¶여자의 비명이 긴 복도에 메아리쳤다 A woman's scream echoed through the long passage.

메어치다 throw (a person) over one's shoulder; throw (a person) to the ground; get [knock] (a person) down. ¶그는 상대방을 메어쳤다 He threw his opponent over his shoulder.

메우다[1] 1 (틈·구멍 등을) fill up[in]; plug (up); fill [cover] in; stop up; (모래 등이) choke up; (바다·호수 등을) reclaim; (군중 등이) jam. ¶구멍을 ~ fill[block / stop] up a hole / stop a gap // 바다를 ~ reclaim a foreshore / recover land from sea // 여백을 ~ fill up (in) a blank // 벽의 구멍을 시멘트로 ~ fill up a hole in the wall with cement // 여백을 메울 기사를 좀 써 주세요. Please write something to fill up the space. // 여백을 삽화로 메우시오 Let's fill (up) the blank space with an illustration. // 다음 문장의 여백을 메우시오 Fill in the blanks in the following sentences. // 구멍은 토사로 메워져 있다 The hole has filled up [is filled] with earth and sand. // 그들은 경음악을 두 프로그램 사이를 메우는 데 썼다 They used a piece of light music as a filler between the two programs. // 그들은 바다를 메워 공업 지대로 만들었다 They reclaimed land from the sea and made it into an industrial area. // 공원은 사람들로 메워져 있었다 The park was overflowing with people. / A capacity crowd filled the park. 2 [보충하다] compensate for; make up [amend] for; atone for; make good; supplement. ¶부족액을 ~ replenish a shortage / make up a deficit // 손실을 ~ make up [compensate] for the loss // 적자는 아직 메워지지 않았다 The deficit has not been made good[covered] yet.

메우다[2] 1 (테를) put a hoop on (a tub). ¶(통에) 테를 ~ hoop (a tub) / bind with hoops. 2 (북통에 가죽을) put on; stretch. ¶북 테를 ~ make a drum / put a drumhead [skin / cloth] on a drum. 3 (쳇바퀴에 쳇불을) fix. ¶체를 ~ fix a sieve net on its frame / make a sieve. 4 (멍에를) yoke. ¶소에 멍에를 ~ yoke an ox / put an ox to the yoke.

메이데이 May Day.

메이저 [음] major.

메이저 리그 the Major League; (미국 속어) the majors; (구어) the big leagues.

메이커 a maker; a manufacturer. ¶~ 제품 name-brand goods // ~의 것이 아닌 off-brand // 우리 가게는 일류 ~의 제품만 취급합니다 We handle only the best brands of articles.

메이크업 makeup. ¶~을 지우다 remove [clean off] one's makeup // 그녀는 ~을 하지 않는다 She has no makeup on. 메이크업하다 make (oneself) up; put on makeup; use makeup. ¶메이크업한 여배우 an actress in her makeup // 노파 역으로 ~ make oneself up for the part of an old woman.

메조 [식] nonglutinous[regular] millet.

메조소프라노 [음] mezzo-soprano.

메조 포르테 [음] mezzo forte(약어 mf).

메조 피아노 [음] mezzo piano(약어 mp).

메주 meju; fermented soybeans. ¶~를 쑤다 boil meju.
● 메주콩 (malt) soybeans. 메줏덩이 a ball [block] of meju.

메지 [일단락] the end of work; the conclusion of a job; a pause; a conclusion; a settlement.

메지(가) 나다 (a matter) come to a conclusion[an end]; be fixed; be settled.

메지(를) 내다 bring (a matter) to a conclusion; fix; settle.

메지다 [끈기가 없다] nonglutinous; not sticky.

메질 hammering; pounding. 메질하다 hammer; pound; strike with a hammer.

메추라기 [동] a quail. ¶~ 알 a quail egg.

메치다 throw (a person) over one's shoulder.

메카 1 [이슬람교도의 순례지] Mecca. 2 [동경의 땅·중심지] a mecca. ¶그곳은 프랑스 영화 애호가들의 ~라고 할 수 있다 It can be called

메커니즘 (a) mechanism.
메케하다 smoky; musty. ⇨메캐하다
메타포 (a) metaphor. ⇨은유
메탄 [화] methane.
● 메탄가스 methane (gas); marsh gas.
메탄올 [화] methanol; methyl[wood] alcohol.
메트로놈 [음] a metronome.
메트로폴리스 a metropolis.
메틸 [화] methyl.
● 메틸알코올 [화] methanol. ⇨메탄올
멘델의 법칙(-法則) Mendel's[Mendelian] laws (of heredity); Mendelism.
멘스 [생] menstruation; (문어) the menses(▶단수·복수 취급).
멜대 a carrying pole[stick]. ¶~로 메다 carry (something) on a pole.
멜라닌 [생] melanin.
멜로드라마 a melodrama; a soap opera. ¶~같은 melodramatic.
멜로디 [음] a melody; a tune.
멜로디언 [음] a melodion.
멜론 [식] a melon.
멜빵 (바지의) (영) suspenders; (영) braces; (총의) a sling; (짐의) a shoulder belt[strap].
멤버 a member. ¶정규 ~ a regular member // 게임을 하기에는 ~가 한 사람 부족하다 We have to get one more person to have a game.
● 멤버십 membership. ¶~을 갖다 hold membership / belong to (a club).
멥새 [동] a meadow bunting. ⇨멧새2
멥쌀 nonglutinous[regular] rice.
멧닭 [동] a black grouse; (수컷) a blackcock; (암컷) a gray hen.
멧돼지 [동] a (wild) boar. ¶~ 고기 boar meat / (영) brawn.
멧부리 the top of a mountain; the peak; the summit.
멧새 1 (산새) a mountain bird[fowl]. 2 [동] a meadow bunting.
멧종다리 [동] a mountain hedge sparrow.
며 (둘 이상의 사물 열거) and. ¶사과~ 복숭아~ 기타 여러 과일 apples, peaches and many other fruits.
-며 1 (사물·동작·상태의 열거) and; or. ¶그의 어머니는 얼굴도 고우~ 품행도 얌전하다 His mother is both good-looking and well-behaved. 2 (동작·상태의 진행) ... ing; (…면서 (동시에)) while; as; between; during; over; with; at the same time (that) ... ¶미소하~ with a smile // 울~ 말하다 tell between sobs // 한잔하~ 이야기하다 talk over a bottle of wine.
며느리 a daughter-in-law (pl. daughters-in-law). ¶~를 보다 take a daughter-in-law into one's family // ~에게 못되게 굴다 be unkind to one's daughter-in-law.
며느리가 미우면 손자까지 밉다 (속담) He who hates Peter harms his dog.; Love me, love my dog.
며느리발톱 (닭의) a spur; (말 등의) a fetlock; [생] a calcar (pl. -caria).
며루 [동] the larva of a crane fly[mosquito].
며칠날 the date. ⇨며칠1
며칠 1 the date; what day of the month. ¶오늘은 ~입니까 What's the date today? / What date is (it) today? / What day of the month is it today?(▶ "What day is it today?"는 "오늘은 무슨 요일입니까?"라는 뜻임) / (미) What date (is it) today? // ~에 출발합니까 When are you starting?
2 (일수) how many days; how long; (수일) several days; a few days. ¶~ 동안 for (a few) days // ~ 전 a few days ago / the other day // ~이건 as long as one likes // ~이고 for (many) days / (계속해서) for days on end // 그와는 ~ 만나지 못했다 I haven't seen him for several days [(for) the last few days]. // ~ 전에 눈이 왔다 It snowed several days ago. // ~ 후에 와 주십시오 Come again after a few days [in three or four days]. // 그녀는 ~ 동안 고열이 계속되고 있다 She has had a high temperature for the past few days.
멱¹ [목] a throat; a gullet. ¶돼지 ~ 따는 소리 a squeak / a squeal / a squealing sound // ~을 그러잡다 grip (a person's) throat / grasp (a person) by his throat // ~을 따다 cut (a fowl's) gullet / stick (a pig).
멱² bathing; a bath. ⇨미역 ¶~을 감다 take [have] a bath (in a river) / bathe in water.
멱³ [장기] the path of a horse's [an elephant's] move (in janggi).
멱(冪) [수] involution. ⇨거듭제곱
멱근(冪根) a radical root. ⇨거듭제곱근(⇨거듭제곱)
멱살 the flesh of the throat; the throat; [멱 부분의 옷깃] a collar; a lapel. ¶~을 잡다 seize [grab / take] (a person) by the collar[lapels].
멱수(冪數) an exponent.
멱통 the throat.
-면 if; unless; when; whenever. [가정적 조건]. ¶비가 오~ 산에 오를 수 없다 If it rains [should rain], we won't be able to climb the mountain. // 네가 달아날 수 있다고 생각하~어서 그렇게 해 봐 If you think you can run away, go ahead and try it. // 다들 모이~ 사진을 찍자 When everyone gets here, we will take a picture. // 한 군이라고 말하~ 그 사건이 생각난다 Han's name reminds me of that incident. // 버둥거리~ 버둥거릴수록 더욱 깊숙이 진창으로 빠져 들어갔다 The more I struggled, the deeper I sank in the mud.
면¹(面) 1 (표면) the surface; the face; (다면체의) a facet; a face. ¶육면체에는 6~이 있다 A cube has six sides[faces].
2 (국면) an aspect; a side; (방면) a field. ¶인생의 어두운 ~ the dark side of life // 경제 ~에서 in the economic respect // 어느 ~으로 보나 in every respect // 사물의 밝은 [어두운] ~을 보다 look on the bright [dark] side of things // 그는 모든 ~에서 훌륭하다 He is splendid in every respect. // 이 문제를 다른 ~에서 검토해 보자 Let us consider this problem from another side[angle]. / Let's consider another aspect of this problem.
3 (체면) dignity; prestige; face; honor.
4 (지면) a page. ¶제1~ the front[first] page // 사회 ~ the local[city] news page.
면²(面) (행정 구역) a myeon (as a subdivision of a gun); a township; a subcounty.
면(綿) cotton. ¶이 모직에는 ~이 조금 섞여 있다 This woolen cloth contains some cotton.
면각(面角) [수] a face angle.
면경(面鏡) a hand mirror; a small looking-glass.
면관하다(免官-) dismiss (a person) from a government [an official] post. ¶그는 자진해서 의원 면관되었다 He was relieved of his official post at his own request.

면구스럽다(面灸-) abashed; shamefaced. ⇨ 면구하다

면구하다(面灸-) abashed; shamefaced; (서술적) feel ashamed; feel awkward [embarrassed].

면나다(面-) [체면이 서다] get credit; gain [win] honor; be honored; be glorified.

면내다(面-) [체면을 세우다] bring honor [credit] (to); save (a person's) face; do (a person) proud [credit]; win [gain] (a person) honor.

면담(面談) an interview. ¶상세한 것은 ~ 후 결정 [광고] Particulars to be arranged personally. / Apply in person for particulars. **면담하다** have an interview [a conversation] (with a person); meet and talk (with); talk personally (with). ¶이 건에 대해 면담하고 싶다 I'd like to talk over this matter with you.

면대(面對) facing; a (face-to-face) confrontation. **면대하다** face; meet [come] face to face; confront [face] each other. ¶면대하여 face to face / to (a person's) face / vis-à-vis // 그에게 면대하여 그런 말을 할 수 있는 사람은 우리들 중에 아무도 없다 None of us will dare to say it openly [right] to his face.

면도(面刀) 1 [수염을 미는 일] shaving. ¶~용 크림 shaving [shave] cream. **면도하다** shave (oneself); (남에게 시켜서) get [have] a shave; get oneself shaved (by). ¶깨끗이 면도한 얼굴 a clean-shaven face // 면도하지 않다 go unshaven // 그는 콧수염을 면도하였다 He shaved off his mustache. →¶(면도사에게) 면도시켰다 I got [had] a shave. 2 a razor. ⇨ 면도칼(⇨면도)

● **면도날** a razor's edge; (안전면도기의) a razor blade. ¶~같이 날카로운 as keen as razors // ~을 세우다 sharpen [strap] a razor blade. **면도칼** a razor. ¶~을 갈다 sharpen a razor / (혁지(革砥)로) strop a razor.

면려(勉勵) industry; endeavor; exertion; assiduity. **면려하다** be industrious; exert oneself; work hard; apply oneself (to).

면류(麵類) noodles.

면류관(冕旒冠) a (royal) crown; a diadem. ¶가시 ~ the crown of thorns.

면마(綿馬) [식] a male fern; an aspidium.

면면하다(綿綿-) [끊이지 않고 이어지다] continuous; unbroken; [끝없는] unceasing; endless. ¶면면한 정서 a lingering emotion. **면면히** continuously; ceaselessly. ¶이 가게는 11세기부터 ~ 이어오고 있다 The line of this family has been unbroken since the eleventh century.

면모(面貌) (얼굴의) looks; features; (문어) a countenance; (일의) aspect; appearance. ¶~를 일신하다 put [take] on quite a new aspect / be completely changed / undergo a complete change [reformation] // 도시의 ~를 일신하다 change the entire face [look] of a city // 새로운 ~를 띠다 assume a new aspect [phase].

면목(面目) 1 [체면] face; countenance; honor; (영) honour. ¶~을 세우다 [손상시키다] raise [harm] one's reputation / rise [fall] in public estimation / earn a high reputation [lose one's dignity] // ~을 유지하다 preserve one's honor // 그는 그 일로 ~이 섰다 The work did him credit. / The work won [gained] him honor. // 그 계획에 실패하면 그는 ~을 잃게 된다 He will lose face if he fails with the project. // 당신이 내 제안에 동의를 표명해 주신다면 내 ~이 설 텐데요 If you would express your approval of my proposal, it would save my face.

2 [겉모습·상태] features; an appearance; an aspect. ¶~을 일신하다 undergo a complete change // 도시의 ~을 일신하다 change the entire face [look] of a city.

면목(이) 없다 be ashamed of oneself; be put out of countenance; have no face to show. ¶면목 없는 짓을 하다 do a shameful [disgraceful] thing // 면목이 없습니다 I am (deeply) ashamed of myself. // 퇴학당하는 것은 정말 면목 없는 일이다 It is really shameful [a disgrace] to be expelled from school.

면밀하다(綿密-) [세밀하다] minute; detailed; close; nice; [정확하다] exact; [빈틈없다] careful; [세심하다] scrupulous; meticulous; elaborate. ¶면밀한 관찰 minute observation // 면밀한 계획을 세우다 make a detailed plan. **면밀히** minutely; closely; carefully; scrupulously; elaborately. ¶~ 조사하다 make a close [careful] investigation (of) // 이것은 주도 ~ 작성된 계획이다 This is a carefully worked-out plan.

면바르다(面-) (생김새 등이) well-featured; clear-[clean-]cut; [반듯하다] even; level.

면박(面駁) refutation to (a person's) face. **면박하다** refute [confute / reproach] to (a person's) face; cast [throw] the fault in (a person's) teeth.

면방적(綿紡績) cotton spinning.

면벽(面壁) [불] meditation facing the wall (of a cave).

면봉(綿棒) [치료용 막대] a cotton [(영) cotton wool] swab (on a stick); (상표명) a Q-tip.

면분(面分) a nodding acquaintance; knowing by sight. ¶~이 있다 be a nodding acquaintance / know by sight.

면사(綿絲) cotton thread; cotton yarn. ⇨ 무명실(⇨무명)

면사무소(面事務所) a myeon [township] office.

면사포(面紗布) a wedding [bridal] veil; a face veil.

면상(面上) the face. ¶~에 흉이 있다 have a scar on the face // ~을 치다 strike (a person) in the face.

면상(面相·面像) a look; (문어) a countenance; features; physiognomy. ¶질투에 날뛰는 그녀는 마녀의 ~이었다 In her jealous rage she looked like a female demon.

-면서 1 [동작·상태의 진행] ...ing; [···하면서(동시에)] while; as; between; during; over; with; at the same time (that). ¶가난하게 살~ while living in poverty // 울~ 이야기하다 tell (a story) between sobs // 수상한 자가 주위를 둘러보~ 그 집으로 숨어들었다 A suspicious-looking man looked around carefully and stole into the house. // 식사를 하~ [포도주를 마시~] 이야기합시다 Let's talk over our meal [a bottle of wine]. // 그는 눈을 반짝이~ 선생님의 말에 귀를 기울였다 He listened to the teacher with shining eyes.

2 [···이지만] though; [···에도 불구하고] but; yet; still; in spite of; for [with] all. ¶싫어하~(도) against one's will / reluctantly // 몸에 해로운 줄 알~ 담배를 끊을 수 없다 I cannot

면세 (免稅) exemption from taxation; tax [duty] exemption; immunity from taxes; remission of taxes. ¶~의 tax-[duty-]free / tax-exempt // ~이다 be free of tax / be exempt[immune] from taxation // 이 물건은 ~이다 The article is exempt from taxation.
면세하다 exempt (a person, land, etc.) from taxation; (관세를) free (foods) from (customs) duties. ¶피아노에 ~ exempt a piano from taxation. →¶면세되다 be exempted from taxation[a tax] / be let off taxes.
● **면세 수입품** (duty-)free imports; free goods. **면세점** a duty-free shop. **면세품** a tax-[duty-]free article; an article exempt from taxation.

면소 (免訴) acquittal[discharge / release] (of a prisoner); (각하(却下)에 의한) dismissal (of a case). **면소하다** acquit [discharge / release] (a case); dismiss (a case). →¶면소되다 be acquitted / be discharged / be released / have one's case dismissed // 그 사건은 증거 불충분으로 면소되었다 The case was dismissed for lack of evidence.

면수 (面數) [책의 페이지 수] the number of pages [leaves].

면식 (面識) acquaintance. ¶~ 있는 사람 an acquaintance // 그 사람과는 ~이 있다 I am acquainted with him. // 그와는 전혀 ~이 없다 He is a perfect stranger to me. // 그녀와는 언제부터 ~이 있습니까 When did you get[become] acquainted with her?

면실 (棉實) cottonseed.
● **면실유** cottonseed oil.

면양 (緬羊·綿羊) [동] a sheep (단수·복수 동형).

면업 (綿業) the cotton industry.

면역 (免役) 1 (부역의) exemption from public labor. **면역하다** be exempted [relieved / spared] from public labor. 2 (병역의) exemption[immunity] from military service. **면역하다** be exempted from military service.

면역 (免疫) (병원균 등에 대한) immunity (from a disease). ¶~이 되다 become [be rendered] immune (to / against / from) // ~이 되어 있다 be immune (to / against / from) / [비유] be callous to (public censure) / be not affected by (adverse criticism) // 예방 주사를 맞았기 때문에 독감에는 ~이 되어 있다 Thanks to an injection, I am immune to influenza. // 백신 접종을 맞으면 소아마비에 ~이 된다 Vaccination immunizes us against polio. // [비유] 그의 혹평에는 ~이 되어 있다 I am impervious[immune] to his scathing criticism. **면역하다** confer immunity; render immune; immunize.
● **면역 기간** a period of immunity. **면역 반응** an immune reaction[response]. ¶자가 ~ an auto-immune reaction. **면역성** immunity. ¶후천 ~ acquired immunity. **면역 요법** immunotherapy. **면역원**(-原) [생] an antigen. ⇨*항원(抗原) **면역자** an immune person. **면역제** an immunizing agent. **면역 주사** (a protective) inoculation. **면역체** [생] an antibody. ⇨*항체(抗體) **면역학** immunology. **면역 혈청** an immune serum; an antiserum.

면작 (棉作) [목화 농사] cotton cultivation [culture]; cultivation of cotton; the cotton harvest[crop] (수확).

면장 (免狀) 1 a license; a permit. ⇨*면허장(⇨면허) 2 a letter of pardon. ⇨*사면장(⇨사면(赦免))

면장 (面長) the head [chief] of a myeon [township].

면적 (面積) (an) area; square measure; size (of land); [수] superficial content(s); [바닥넓이] floor space. ¶경작 ~ area under cultivation // 총~ the gross area // 땅의 ~ the area of land / superficial measure of land // 삼각형의 ~ the area of a triangle // ~이 100 제곱미터다 cover an area[a space] of 100 square meters / be 100 square meters in area // ~을 구하다 square // 이 공원의 ~은 10제곱킬로미터다 This park is 10 square kilometers in area.

면전 (面前) presence. ¶…의 ~에서 in the presence of (a person) / under one's (own) eyes / before (a person) // 사람들 ~에서 in the presence of others / before [in] company / in public // 그는 양친의 ~에서 소년을 구박하였다 He scolded the boy before his parents.

면접 (面接) 1 [만나 봄] an interview. ¶개인 ~ an individual interview. **면접하다** interview; see; receive; have an interview. ¶한 사람 한 사람 면접하여 앙케트 조사를 했다 I interviewed each person to collect information for a questionnaire. 2 an oral test [examination]. ⇨*면접시험(⇨면접)
● **면접시험** an oral test [examination]; an interview; (구어) orals. ¶~을 받다 undergo an oral examination [an interview].

면제 (免除) (an) exemption; immunity; impunity; discharge; excuse; remission; release. (▶ exemption은 의무나 이행 등으로부터 해방되는 것. immunity는 의무·속박·벌·고통 등으로부터 해방 보호되는 것. impunity는 벌을 면제받는 것) ¶수업료[병역] ~ exemption from school fees [military service] // 일부 ~ partial exemption // 입학금 ~ exemption of the entrance fee // 전부 ~ total exemption. **면제하다** exempt (a person from taxation); release [relieve] (a person from obligation); excuse [remit] (a person from a task); discharge (a person from a debt). ¶벌금을 반액 ~ remit a fine to half the amount. →¶조세[시험]를 면제받다 be exempted [freed] from taxation [an examination] // 징집[병역]이 면제되다 be exempted from draft [military service] // 이달에 입학하는 사람은 입학금이 면제된다 Applicants are admitted free of entrance fees this month.

면제품 (綿製品) cotton goods [stuff].

면죄 (免罪) acquittal; remission of sin; (가톨릭에서) a papal indulgence; pardon. **면죄하다** acquit; remit (a sin); pardon. →¶그는 면죄되었다 He was acquitted of the charge.
● **면죄부** an indulgence.

면지 (面紙) the reverse [inside] of the (front / back) cover (of a book); an endpaper; an endleaf; an endsheet.

면직 (免職) dismissal [removal] from office; deprivation of office; discharge. **면직하다** dismiss [remove / eject] (a person) from office; discharge (a person) from (his) duties; relieve (a person) of (his) office [post]. →¶나는 면직되었다 I have been relieved of my post. / I've been dismissed. / (구어) I've been fired. ∥ 그는 무단결근을 거듭하여 면직되었다 He was dismissed for repeated unexcused absences from work.

면직물(綿織物) cotton fabrics [textiles / cloth / tissue]; cotton; cotton stuff; cotton piece goods.

면책(免責) immunity [exemption] from responsibility. **면책하다** be exempted [discharged] from responsibility. ➔¶면책되다 receive immunity from responsibility / become immune from obligation.
● **면책 특권** the privilege of exemption from liability.

면책(面責) personal reproof. **면책하다** reprove (a person) to (his) face; reprimand (a person) personally.

면치레(面-) a face-lifting. **면치레하다** face-lift; save [keep up] appearances; save (one's) face; put up a good front; put a good face on the matter.

면포(綿布) cotton (cloth). ➪ ˝무명

면하다(免-) **1** [모면하다] escape (danger, arrest, conscription, etc.); be saved [rescued] from (drowning). ¶죽음을 ~ escape death / be saved from death ∥ 위기를 ~ get through a crisis / tide [get] over a crisis ∥ 부상을 ~ get off unhurt ∥ 처벌을 ~ escape punishment / go scot-free ∥ 화재를 ~ be saved from the fire ∥ 아슬아슬하게 ~ have a narrow [hair breadth] escape (from death) ∥ 모호한 대답으로 곤란한 처지를 ~ get out of the (awkward) situation by giving a vague answer ∥ 목숨이 있는 자는 죽음을 면하지 못한다 Life is subject to decay. / Man is mortal. ∥ 나는 다른 버스를 탔기 때문에 사고를 면했다 As I was in another bus I missed the accident.
2 [회피하다] escape (responsibility); evade (one's duty); elude (taxation); get round (the law); excuse oneself from (responsibility). ¶책임을 면하려고 하다 shirk [shift off] one's responsibility.
3 [면제되다] be exempt(ed) from (taxation); be immune from (draft); be released from (pain); be relieved of [have relief from] (pain); get [be] rid of (a nuisance). ¶병역 [징집]을 ~ be exempted from military service [draft].

면하다(面-) face (on); front on; look toward [on / on to]; look out on [on to / into]. ¶바다에 면한 집 a house facing [fronting (on)] the sea ∥ 뜰에 면한 창문 a window that opens on the garden ∥ 호수에 면한 호텔 a hotel on the lake / a lakeside hotel ∥ 그 집은 남쪽에 면해 있다 The house faces the south. ∥ 그 호텔은 항구에 면해 있다 The hotel fronts on [looks out upon] the harbor. ∥ 그 집은 큰길에 면해 있다 The house stands on the main street.

면학(勉學) study; academic pursuit; pursuit of knowledge. ¶~을 위하여 for study ∥ 그는 ~에 힘쓰고 있다 He is studying hard. **면학하다** study (hard); prosecute one's studies; pursue knowledge.
● **면학 분위기** the studious atmosphere on campus; the campus atmosphere fit for study. ¶~를 조성하다 create an academic atmosphere.

면허(免許) permission; license. ¶제조 ~ manufacturing license ∥ ~가 있는 [없는] licensed [unlicensed] ∥ 운전~ 시험 an auto-license examination [test] ∥ 의사 개업 ~ a license to practice medicine ∥ ~를 받다 [얻다] obtain [secure] a license ∥ 그는 교사 ~를 취소당했다 He had his teacher's certificate [license] canceled. **면허하다** permit; license; authorize.
● **면허 기간** a term of license. **면허 영업** a licensed business. **면허장 / 면허증** a license; (영) a licence; a certificate (증명서); a permit (허가증); a charter (특허장). **~가 ~** a temporary license / (영) a provisional license ∥ 운전 ~ (자동차의) (미) a driver's license / (영) a driving licence ∥ ~을 교부하다 award a license / grant [issue] a license [certificate] ∥ ~을 가지고 있다 hold a license ∥ ~을 압수하다 forfeit a license.

면화(棉花) a cotton (plant). ➪ ˝목화(木花)

면회(面會) [만나 봄] a meeting; [회견] an interview. ¶~를 요청하다 ask (a person) to see (one) / ask for [request / seek / solicit] an interview (with) ∥ ~를 거절하다 refuse an interview (with) / decline to see / excuse [deny] oneself to (a caller). **면회하다** [만나서 이야기하다] see; [협의 등을 위해 만나다] meet; [회견하다] have an interview (with). ¶아무도 환자와 면회할 수 없었다 No one was able to see the patient. ∥ 어찌어찌해서 대통령과 면회하였다 I managed to meet [have an interview with] the President.
● **면회 사절** (게시) No Visitors. ¶작업 중 ~ (게시) Interviews declined during working hours. **면회 시간** visiting hours; office hours. **면회실** (교도소 등의) an interview room. **면회인** a visitor; caller.

멸공(滅共) rooting up communists; eradication of communism.
● **멸공 정신** the anti-Communist spirit; the "Defeat Communism" spirit.

멸구 [동] a (green) leaf hopper.

멸균(滅菌) sterilization; pasteurization. ➪ ˝살균

멸망(滅亡) [절멸] extinction; [몰락] a fall; a downfall; ruin; collapse; destruction. ¶로마 제국의 ~ the fall of the Roman Empire ∥ 민족의 ~ the extinction of a race ∥ ~에 직면하다 be on the brink [verge] of ruin ∥ ~의 길을 걷다 be on the road to collapse [ruin / doom]. **멸망하다** [절멸하다] perish; die out; [몰락하다] be ruined; go to ruin; cease to exist; be destroyed. ¶그 종(種)은 오천 년 전에 멸망했다 The species became extinct [died out] five thousand years ago. ∥ 그 나라는 기원전에 멸망했다 The country was ruined before the Christian era. ➔ 멸망시키다 [괴멸시키다] destroy / (구어) wipe out ∥ 그들은 적을 멸망시켰다 They overthrew [destroyed] their enemies. ∥ 원주민은 백인에 의해 멸망되었다 The natives were exterminated by the whites.

멸사봉공(滅私奉公) self-annihilation for the sake of one's country; selfless devotion to one's country.

멸시(蔑視) contempt; disdain; disregard. ¶그는 동료들의 ~를 견딜 수 없었다 He could not bear the contemptuous [scornful] looks of his colleagues. ∥ He could not endure his colleagues' looks of contempt [scorn]. **멸시하다** regard (a person) with contempt; despise; disrespect; disregard; disdain; hold

멸족하다 (a person) cheap; make light [little] of; slight; neglect. ¶그런 짓을 하면 세상 사람들이 너를 멸시한다 That will lower you in public estimation. // 가난한 사람들을 멸시하지 마라 Don't despise [look down upon] poor people. → ¶멸시당하다 be held in contempt [irreverence] // 멸시당했다는 생각에 늘 사로잡히다 be always the victim of a sense of neglect [the feeling of being neglected].

멸족하다 (滅族-) [멸망시키다] exterminate (a person's) whole family [kinsfolk]; wipe [put / blot] a tribe out of existence; [멸망하다] (a family / a tribe) be exterminated.

멸종 (滅種) extermination of a stock [race]. **멸종하다** [멸망시키다] exterminate a stock [race]; [멸망하다] (a stock / a race) be exterminated. ¶공룡은 이미 멸종한 동물이다 The dinosaur is an extinct animal.

멸치 [동] an anchovy.
● **멸치젓** salted [pickled] anchovies.

멸하다 (滅-) [멸망하다] go to ruin; perish; [멸망시키다] ruin; destroy; exterminate. ¶나라를 ~ ruin [destroy] a nation // 적을 ~ destroy [conquer] an enemy.

명 (名) [사람 수] a man; a person; persons. ¶20~ twenty persons [people] // 모두 열 ~ ten in all.

명 (命) 1 life. ⇨목숨 ¶~이 길다 live long / last on / have a long life // 제~에 죽다 live out a natural life / die a natural death // 그 아이는 ~이 짧았다 The child had only a short life. // 그는 ~이 긴 녀석이다 He has nine lives like a cat. // 이래서는 제 ~대로 못 살겠다 This will make me die before my time [bring me to an early grave]. 2 an order (to do). ⇨명령1 ¶(당국의) ~에 의하여 by order (of the authorities) / under government orders // ~을 따르다 [거역하다] obey [disobey] (a person's) orders. 3 (a) fate; (a) destiny. ⇨운명(運命)

명 (銘) (비석 등의) an inscription; an epitaph (묘비명).

명- (名) [유명한] famous; noted; [탁월한] excellent; celebrated; distinguished; [현명한, 슬기로운] wise; judicious. ¶~선수 a star player // ~감독(영화의) a celebrated director / (야구 등의) a famous manager // ~연주 an excellent performance // ~판사 an able judge / a Daniel.

명가 (名家) 1 [이름난 가문] a good family; a prestigious family. ¶그는 ~ 출신이다 He comes of an old, prestigious family. 2 [명성이 있는 사람] an eminent personage; [대가(大家)] a great master.

명가수 (名歌手) a famous [reputable / distinguished] singer; a great singer.

명견 (名犬) a good [fine] dog.

명경지수 (明鏡止水) ¶내 심정은 ~와 같다 My mind [mental state] is as serene as a polished mirror (and still water).

명곡 (名曲) a famous tune [piece of music]; a musical masterpiece. ¶~을 감상하다 appreciate an excellent piece of music // 이 노래는 ~이다 This song is beautifully composed.

명공 (名工) a master craftsman; a master hand; an expert (artisan); a skillful workman.

명관 (名官) a renowned [celebrated] magistrate [governor].

명구 (名句) a famous [an apt] phrase [saying]; a fine expression; a wise saying; a well-known adage.

명군 (明君) a wise ruler [king]; an enlightened monarch.

명궁 (名弓) [활 잘 쏘는 사람] an expert archer; a famous bowman; [이름난 활] a noted bow.

명금 (鳴禽) [잘 지저귀는 새] a songbird; a songster.

명기 (名妓) [이름난 기생] a gisaeng famed for her beauty; (제주가 뛰어난) a talented gisaeng; a gisaeng of great talent [artistic gifts].

명기 (名器) [이름난 기구] a rare [famous] utensil; [이름난 악기] a famous instrument. ¶스트라디바리우스의 ~ a (famed / famous) Stradivarius.

명기 (鳴器) [동] the syrinx (pl. -ringes. ~es).

명기하다 (明記-) write clearly; write expressly; (조문 등에 명확하게) specify. → ¶규칙에 명기되어 있다 be specified [defined clearly] in the regulations // 내 답변은 편지에 명기되어 있다 I wrote my answer clearly [expressly] in my letter. // 신앙의 자유는 헌법에 명기되어 있다 Freedom of religion is spelled out [specifically guaranteed] in the Constitution.

명년 (明年) next year. ⇨내년

명단 (名單) a register [list] of names. ¶초청객의 ~ a list of guests invited // 찬동자로서 그의 이름이 ~에 올라 있다 His name is on the list of supporters.

명단 (明斷) a clear judgment; a judicious decision. **명단하다** pass [make] a clear judgment (on).

명담 (名談) a wise [golden] saying; a witty [felicitous / famous] remark.

명답 (名答) [올바른 대답] the right answer; the correct answer; [교묘한 대답] a clever answer. ¶~이오. You said it. / You've hit it.

명답 (明答) [분명한 답] a definite [decisive] answer. **명답하다** answer [reply] definitely; give (a person) a definite answer.

명당 (明堂) 1 [좋은 묏자리] a propitious site for a grave; [좋은 터] a very good place. ¶붕어낚시의 ~자리 a superfine spot for crucian (carp) fishing. 2 [무덤 앞 평지] the graveyard lawn. 3 [정전(正殿)] the king's audience [presence] hall.

명도 (明渡) [법] evacuation; quitting. ¶세든 사람에게 ~를 요구하다 give a tenant a notice to quit [move]. **명도하다** vacate [quit] (a house); clear out of (a house); evacuate. ¶집을 ~ vacate [quit] a house.
● **명도 신청** a petition for eviction.

명도 (明度) [미] brightness; luminosity; value (of color).

명도 (冥途) Hades; the other [nether] world; the region beyond the grave.

명란 (明卵) spawn [roe] of a (walleye) pollack.
● **명란젓** salted pollack roe.

명랑하다 (明朗-) clear; bright; cheerful; gay; sunny; sunshiny. ¶명랑한 소녀 a cheerful [sunny-natured] girl // 명랑한 사람 a man of sunny disposition // 명랑한 성격 an open character // 명랑한 목소리로 in a clear [sonorous / gay] voice // 명랑한 웃음소리가 옆방에서 들려왔다 Gay peals of laughter in the next room reached my ears. // 그녀는 명랑한 얼굴로 나타났다 She appeared with a radiant face. // 여주인은 우리를 명랑한 미소로 맞아 주었다 The hostess greeted us with a beaming smile.// 그는 애써 명랑한 태도를 취해 보였다 He tried to behave as cheerfully as possible. **명랑히** cheerfully; merrily; with a light heart; in a gay spirit. ¶~ 웃다 laugh merrily / smile brightly.

명령(命令) **1** an order (to do)(▶ 흔히 복수형으로); [권위자의 절대적 명령] a command; [지시] directions; instructions; a fiat; bidding. ¶전투[전투 중지] ~ a combat [cease-fire] order // 작전 ~ an operation order // ~대로 하다 act upon (a person's) orders / do (a person's) bidding / do as one is told // 남의 ~을 받다 take orders from a person // ~에 따르다[거역하다] obey [refuse to carry out] an order [a command] // ~조로 말하다 speak in a commanding [(문어) a peremptory / an authoritative] tone // 그들은 적정(敵情)을 정찰하라는 ~을 받고 출발했다 They set out under orders to reconnoiter the enemy's movements. // ~대로 하시오 Do as you are told. // 대령은 공격 ~을 내렸다 The colonel gave the command to attack. // 그 배는 출범 ~을 받고 있다 The ship is under sailing orders. // 나는 그렇게 하는 것이 싫지만 ~이므로 할 수가 없다 I hate to do that, but an order is an order. // 우리는 당신의 ~은 듣지 않겠소 We will not be dictated by you. // 내일 출발하라는 ~이 내렸다 Orders have gone [run] out that we are to start tomorrow. // 내일 아침 공격 개시의 ~이 내려져 있다 We have orders [The orders are] to begin an attack tomorrow morning. **명령하다** order; tell; instruct (a person to do); command; give orders [a command / instructions]; decree; direct; dictate. ¶그는 부하들에게 그것을 즉시 하라고 명령했다 He ordered his men to [He gave orders to his men that they should] do it at once. // 지배인은 비서에게 잇달아 용건을 명령했다 The manager was giving his secretary orders one after another. // 경찰은 그들에게 철거할 것을 명령했다 The police ordered them to vacate the place. ➔¶학생들은 교정에 정렬하라고 명령받았다 The pupils were directed [received directions] to line up in the schoolyard.
2 [법원의 지시] a decree.
● **명령 계통** a chain of command. **명령문** [언] an imperative sentence. **명령서** an order; [법] a warrant; a precept. **명령 위반** violation of an order. **명령형** [언] an imperative form (of a verb).

명론(名論) an excellent opinion; a sound [well-founded] argument [theory].

명료도(明瞭度) [통신] articulation.

명료하다(明瞭-) clear (meaning); plain (language); obvious (reason); evident (fact); distinct [articulate] (pronunciation); lucid (style); perspicuous (expression).

명류(名流) a celebrity; a man of note. ➪ ☞ **명사**(名士).

명리(名利) fame and wealth; name and fortune; riches and honor. ¶~에 초연하다 be above (concern for) riches and honor // ~에 급급[대맹]하다 be intent on [be indifferent] to fame and wealth [fortune].
● **명리심**(-心) worldly aims [interests]; carnal ambition. ¶~이 있는[없는] worldly- [unworldly-] minded.

명마(名馬) [우수한 말] a fine horse; [유명한] a famous horse.

명망(名望) reputation; renown; popularity. ¶~ 있는 reputed / renowned / popular // ~을 얻다 gain [win] fame // ~을 잃다 lose one's reputation [popularity].
● **명망가** a man of renown [high repute]; a popular man; a man high in public esteem. ¶이제 그는 상당한 ~이다 He now enjoys a fairly high reputation.

명맥(命脈) life; the thread of life. ¶간신히 ~을 이어 가다 barely keep (itself) in existence / maintain (its) slender existence // ~을 유지하다 survive / keep alive / keep the fire going // 그의 회사는 겨우 ~을 유지하고 있다 His company is barely surviving. / His company is barely keeping its head above water.

명멸(明滅) glimmering; blinking. **명멸하다** [깜박깜박하다] flicker; [켜졌다 꺼졌다 하다] blink. ¶명멸하는 등불 a flickering light // 네온사인이 명멸하고 있다 A neon light is flickering. // 청신호가 명멸하기 시작했다 The green light [signal] began to blink. ➔¶건널목지기는 램프를 명멸시켜서 열차를 정차시키려고 했다 The flagman tried to stop the train by blinking his signal light.
● **명멸 신호** a blinking signal.

명명(命名) christening; naming. **명명하다** name; (세례하여) christen; give a name (to); call; designate; denominate. ¶본회를 「상우회」라 명명한다 This society shall be called [designated as] "Sanguhoe". // 그들은 그 아이의 이름을 할아버지의 이름을 따서 해럴드라 명명하였다 They named the baby Harold after [(문어) for] his grandfather.
● **명명식** a christening; a naming ceremony.

명명백백하다(明明白白-) as clear as day [daylight]; as plain as a pikestaff.

명목(名目) a name; a title; an appellation; [구실] a pretext. ¶~상의 ostensible // ~에 지나지 않다 be just nominal / be in name only // 무슨 ~이든 만들어 on [upon] some pretext or other // 그는 ~상의 사장이다 He is a president in name only.
● **명목론** [철] nominalism; terminism. **명목 임금**[가격] nominal wages [prices].

명문(名文) [뛰어난 글] a beautiful [superb] passage; a fine piece of writing; (구어) some great writing; [유명한 글] a literary gem. ¶~이다 be well written / be high in literary merit // 이 구절들은 대단한 ~이다 These passages are very well composed [written].

명문(名門) a noble [distinguished] family. ¶사학(私學) ~ one of the leading private schools [universities] (in Korea) // ~의 자제 children born of a good family // 그는 ~ 출신이다 He comes from [(문어) of] a noble [distinguished] family.
● **명문교** a celebrated [distinguished / prestigious] school. ¶럭비의 ~ a school famous for its excellent rugby team.

명문(明文) **1** [조문] an express provision [statement / words]; a specific proviso. **2** [증서] a bond; a deed; a written contract.
● **명문화** stipulation. ¶~하다 stipulate / put in a statutory form // ~되어 있다[되어 있지 않다] be [be not] provided for in the law / be [be not] expressly stipulated in the text.

명문(銘文) an inscription.

명물(名物) **1** [어떤 특색으로 이름난 것] a feature; an attraction. ¶이 식당은 냉면이

명민하다

이다 This restaurant features *naengmyeon*. **2** [명산물] a noted[special] product; a local specialty[(영) speciality]. ¶대구의 ~인 사과 the apple which is a special product of Daegu[for which Daegu is noted]// 이 지방의 ~은 무엇입니까 What is this locality noted for? **3** [남다른 특징으로 유명한 사람] a popular figure; institution. ¶그 마을의 ~ a popular figure in the village// 그는 이 도시에서 ~이다 He is quite an institution of this town.

명민하다(明敏−) sagacious; perspicacious; intelligent; clear. ¶그는 ~ He has a clear head[an incisive mind]. / He is clearheaded.

명반(明礬) [화] alum.

명백하다(明白−) [분명하다] obvious; [애매하지 않다] clear; [확실히 알 수 있다] plain; [틀림없다] unmistakable[positive / undeniable]; [상황으로 보아 확실하다] evident; apparent; manifest; explicit; distinct; patent; (미국 구어) open-and-shut; indisputable[indubitable]. ¶명백한 사실 an obvious[a clear / a plain / a clear-cut / an incontrovertible] fact// 명백한 증거 positive [undeniable / indisputable] evidence// 아주 명백한 (as) clear as day(light)[noonday / a map / a whistle]; (as) plain as a pikestaff [as print / as the nose on one's face]// 그가 거짓말하고 있는 것은 ~ It is obvious that he is lying.// 그것에 대한 명백한 증거가 있다 I have positive proof of it.// 그의 결백은 ~ His innocence is evident. **명백히** clearly; plainly; evidently; obviously; manifestly; distinctly; explicitly; expressly; unmistakably. ¶~ 하다 make clear / clear up / clarify / manifest// ~ 진술하다 state clearly[plainly].

명복(冥福) heavenly bliss; happiness in the other world. ¶~을 빌다 pray for the repose of (a person's) soul / pray for the souls of the departed / bless (a person's) memory// 그의 ~을 빕니다 I pray his soul may rest in peace. / May he[his soul] rest in peace!

명부(名簿) a register[list] of names; a nominal; [등록부] a register; a nominal list [register / roll]. ¶선거인 ~ a pollbook / a voting[voter] roll / a voters' list// 신입생 ~ a register of new students[freshmen]// 직원 ~ a register of the staff// 학급 ~ a class list // 회원 ~ a membership list / a list of members// 이름을 ~에 넣다 put[enter] a person's name on a list / register a person's name// ~에 실려 있다 be on the list / be listed// ~에서 이름을 지우다[빼다] put a person's name off a list / remove[erase / cancel] (a person's) name from the list / cross (a person's name) off[out] from the list.

명부(冥府) Hades; the other world. ⇨명도(冥途)

명분(名分) [본분] one's moral duty[obligations]; [정당성] (moral) justification; justice; [이유] a just cause. ¶~이 서는 just // ~이 서지 않는 행동 an unjustifiable act// ~을 세우다 justify oneself[one's conduct] / ~을 밝히다 clearly define one's moral obligations / fulfill one's specified duty / uphold the cause of loyalty// 야심만으로는 전쟁의 ~이 서지 않는다 Mere ambition does not justify (the making of) war.

명사(名士) a celebrity; a man of note; a notable; a man of distinction; a distinguished[celebrated / prominent] person; a prominent figure; (구어) a big name; (구어) a swell. ¶당대의 ~ prominent men[figures] of the time / distinguished people of the time / (영) the lion of the day[moment] // 문단의 ~ a famous[noted] writer / a big name in literary circles / notabilities in literary circles / a writer of distinction// 정계의 ~ a prominent figure in politics / a noted politician// 만찬 석상에서 이 도시의 몇몇 ~들이 연설을 했다 Several men well-known in the city made speeches at the dinner.

명사(名詞) [언] a noun; a (noun) substantive. ¶물질[추상 / 보통 / 고유 / 집합] ~ a material [an abstract / a common / a proper / a collective] noun// ~의 nominal.
● **명사구**[절] a noun phrase[clause].

명사(名辭) [논] a term; a name. ¶매(媒)[중] ~ the middle[mean] term// 대[소] ~ the major[minor] term// 절대 ~ the absolute term// ~의 terminal.

명산(名山) a noted[celebrated] mountain.
● **명산대찰** noted mountains and large Buddhist temples.

명산(물)(名産物) a noted[special] product; a speciality. ¶이 지방의 ~은 복숭아이다 Peaches are a special[noted] product of this district. / This district is noted for its excellent peaches.

명상(冥想) meditation; contemplation. ¶~적인 meditative / contemplative// 그는 ~에 잠겨 있었다 He was lost[sunk] in meditation.

명상하다 meditate (on); contemplate. ¶그는 철학 문제를 놓고 명상하고 있다 He is meditating on[contemplating] a philosophical problem.
● **명상가** a meditator; a contemplator.

명색(名色) a name; a title; an appellation. ¶~뿐인 학자 a scholar in name only// ~뿐인 보수 a nominal fee// ~뿐인 자유를 얻다 have only the shadow of freedom// ~이 남자라면 그런 짓이 어울릴 리가 없다 It cannot be becoming in any man worthy of the name.// ~이 학생이라면 학생답게 해라 If you are anything of a student, behave like one [as such].

명석하다(明晳−) clear; bright; lucid; distinct. ¶명석한 두뇌의 소유자 a clearheaded person // 두뇌가 ~ have a clear head// 그는 늙었지만 머리는 ~ Though he is old, he has a clear head.

명성(名聲) fame; (a) reputation; (문어) renown; (구어) a kudos(단수·복수 동형). ¶~있는 음악가 a celebrated[noted / renowned] musician// ~ 높은 용사 a renowned soldier // 세계적 ~의 과학자 a scientist of worldwide fame / a world-famous scientist// ~이 올라가다 rise in fame// ~을 얻다 win[gain / earn / acquire / attain] fame / gain / obtain[attain] renown / win one's renown / win[gain / earn / make / achieve / acquire] a reputation / make a name for oneself// ~이 떨어지다 lose one's reputation// ~을 더럽히다 tarnish one's reputation / cast a slur [stain] on one's fame[reputation] // ~을 손상하다 hurt[injure / damage / impair / affect] one's reputation / bring discredit on one's name// 그는 수재로 ~이 높다 He has a reputation for brilliance.// 그 사건으로 그는

~을 잃었다[높였다] The affair damaged [enhanced] his reputation.// 그는 용맹한 장군이라는 ~을 온 세계에 떨쳤다 He gained world-wide fame as a daring general.// 그의 ~은 온 나라 안에 자자했다 His fame spread throughout the country.// 그는 ~을 전 세계에 떨쳤다 He has become world-famous. / His fame has spread throughout the world. // 그의 ~은 국내외에 자자하다 His name is known both at home and abroad.// 그 작가는 참신한 작품으로 ~을 얻었다 The writer gained fame[made a name for himself] with his original style.

명성(明星) the morning star; venus. ⇨ *샛별₁
명세(明細) particulars (on / about); details (on / about). **명세하다** minute; particular; detailed. ¶명세한 회계 보고 A full statement of account / an accounting // 사건의 명세한 보고서를 작성하다 make a minute[detailed] report on[of] a case // 이 기획에 관한 더 명세한 사항은 나중에 알려 드리겠습니다 I will give you further details[particulars] on [about] this project later. **명세히** minutely; in every particular; in detail; fully. ¶~ 적다 set down[state] in detail[fully].
●**명세서** a detailed[full] statement; details; specifications; a minute description; a list of particulars; a detailed account(계산서). ¶내용 ~ a detailed statement of contents // 지출 ~ a bill of expenditures // 별첨 ~와 같이 as per specifications attached.
명소(名所) [유서 깊은 곳] a noted place; a place of interest[note]; a celebrated locality; sights (to see); [사적지] a place rich in[with many] historical associations; [명승지] a beauty[scenic] spot; a picturesque site; a place of scenic interest. ¶관광 ~ a tourist attraction // 옛 도시의 ~를 구경[관광]하다 see[do] the sights of an old city // ~를 안내하다 take (a person) to places of note / conduct (a person) over places of interest // 진해는 벚꽃의 ~이다 Jinhae is noted [famous] for its cherry blossoms.
명수(名手) a master hand (at); a famous hand (at); an expert (in / at / with); an adept (in / at); a talented[an accomplished] performer[player]; a crack (at cards); (구어) a dab (at games); a master. ¶사격의 ~ a dead[a crack] shot / a first-rate shot // 펜싱의 ~ a fencing master / an expert fencer / a master of fence // 장기의 ~ an adept in *janggi* / a masterful player of *janggi* // 카드놀이의 ~ a card shark // 그는 통소의 ~이다 He is an accomplished[a master / an expert] player of the *tungso*.// 그는 연애의 ~이다 He is quite a fast worker (with woman).// 그는 검술의 ~이다 He is a good swordsman.
명수(名數) 1 [인원수] the number of persons. 2 [수] a denominate[concrete] number.
명승(名勝) scenic beauty; picturesque[noted] scenery.
●**명승고적** scenic spots and places of historic interest; (famous) places of natural [scenic] beauty and historic interest. ¶~을 돌아보다 visit places of natural beauty and historic interest. **명승지** a place of[noted for] scenic beauty; a beauty[scenic] spot; a famous sight; a place of interest.
명승(名僧) a distinguished[noted / celebrated] priest.

명시(明示) clear statement; elucidation. **명시하다** express[describe] clearly; specify; state plainly[clearly / expressly]; clarify. ¶자기 의사를 ~ express one's wishes clearly // 돈의 용도를 ~ account for the money spent // 허가증을 명시할 것 The licence must be displayed where it can be clearly seen. ➔ ¶비용은 청구서에 명시되어 있다 The expenses are specified on the bill.// 남녀 평등은 헌법에 명시되어 있다 (문어) It is clearly[expressly] stipulated[stated] in the Constitution that men and women are equal.
명시(明視) clear vision. **명시하다** see (a thing) clearly.
●**명시 거리** [물] the range of clear vision.
명신(名臣) a renowned[celebrated / distinguished] subject[retainer]; a great[an eminent / a prominent / an illustrious] statesman.
명실 공히(名實共一) both nominally and virtually[really]; both in name and reality; in fact[really] as well as in name. ¶이 팀은 ~ 한국 제일이다 This team is Korea's best, both in name and reality. / This team is Korea's best in fact[reality] as well as in name.
명실상부하다(名實相符一) be true to the name; be up to (its) reputation. ¶명실상부한 대정치가 a great statesman worthy of his reputation[the name] // 그것은 명실상부하지 않다 The reality does not agree with[falls short of] the name. / It is a misnomer.
명심하다(銘心一) bear[keep] (something) in mind; take (the advice) to heart; have (something) stamped[engraved] on one's mind; impress (a fact) on one's mind. ¶명심해야 할 일 things that should be remembered[borne in mind] // 이것을 명심하시오 Bear[keep] this in mind.// 나는 선생님의 훈계를 명심했다 I took my teacher's warning to heart.// 지각하면 안 된다는 점을 명심하라 Keep[Bear] it in mind that you must not be late for work.// 하신 말씀을 명심하겠습니다 I will bear your words in mind. / I will treasure up your words.
명아주 [식] wild spinach; a goosefoot; a pigweed.
명안(名案) a good[capital / brilliant] idea; a good[splendid] plan. ¶~이 떠오르다 hit on [upon] a good plan[idea] / have a good [capital] idea // 그에게 ~이 떠올랐다 A bright idea occurred to him.
명암(明暗) light and darkness[shade]. ¶~이 뚜렷하지 않은 사진 a flat picture // 이 그림은 ~이 뚜렷하다 [~을 잘 나타내고 있다] This painting shows a clear contrast between light and shade. / This painting shows fine effects of light and shade.// 그것은 바로 인생의 ~을 말해 주고 있다 It shows clearly the bright and dark sides of life.
●**명암법** [미] [명암의 배합을 기조로 하는 화법] chiaroscuro; [묘영(描影) 화법] shading; clear obscure.
명약관화하다(明若觀火一) as clear[plain] as day[daylight]; as plain as the sun[the nose on your face]; as plain as a pikestaff; as plain as plain can be. ¶그의 무죄는 ~ His innocence is as clear as day.
명언(名言) [사리에 맞는 훌륭한 말] a wise

명언 [witty] remark; [유명한 말] a famous [well-known] saying; a wise [golden] saying. ¶고래의 ~ an old saying // ~을 하다 make wise [witty / apt] remark // 그것 참 ~이다 That's well [aptly / wisely] said.

명언(明言) declaration; a definite statement; assertion. **명언하다** declare; say [state] positively [definitely]. ¶그는 그것이 사실이라고 명언하였다 He said definitely [declared / asserted] that it was true.

명역(名譯) [뛰어난 번역] an apt [an excellent / a sterling / a happy] translation; [유명한 번역] a famous translation.

명연기(名演技) a fine [an excellent] performance.

명예(名譽) [영예] honor; (영) honour; glory; [명성] fame; reputation; distinction; renown; [신망] credit. ¶~로운 지위 an honorable position // 나라의 ~ the pride of [a credit to] a country [nation] / the glory of a country / national glory [honor] // ~에 관한 문제 a point of honor // ~를 존중하는 사람 a man of honor // ~로운 전사를 하다 die a glorious death in battle / die an honorable [a heroic] death in action // ~를 얻다 gain [win / achieve / attain] honor // ~를 주다 award honor to (a person) / bestow [confer] honor on (a person) / accord (a person) honor // ~를 중히 여기다 [존중하다] value [prize] honor / prize [value] one's good name // ~를 회복하다 restore [retrieve] one's honor / vindicate [redeem] one's honor // ~가 되다 be a credit [an honor] to / do [bring] honor [credit] to / be to one's honor [credit] / reflect honor [credit] upon // ~를 걸고 …하다 be upon one's honor to ... / make it a point of honor to ... // …의 ~에 관계되다 […의 ~가 걸려 있다] affect [reflect on / compromise] the honor of ... / cast a reflection on ... / one's honor be at stake / concern one's honor // …을 ~로 여기다 [생각하다] esteem [deem] it an honor to (do) / feel it an honor to (do) // 가문의 ~를 회복하다 retrieve the family credit // ~를 더럽히다 [손상하다] bring [invite] disgrace on (a person) / stain [hurt / impair / injure / sully / blight] (a person's) honor / discredit [dishonor] (a person) // 그의 행위는 그의 ~를 훼손하는 것이 결코 아니다 His deed are no discredit to him [his name]. // 이것은 우리들의 ~에 관한 [~가 걸린] 문제이다 This is a point of honor with us. // 그가 이 대업을 완수한 것은 그의 부모에게도 ~가 된다 It brings honor to his parents as well that he should have completed this great task. // 그러한 학생은 학교의 ~가 된다 [~이다] Such a student is an honor [a credit] to the school. // ~를 걸고 당신을 지키겠소 I will make it a point of honor to protect you. // ~를 걸고 꼭 하겠다 Upon my honor, I will do it. / I will make it a point of honor to do it.

●**명예 교수** an emeritus [honorary] professor; a professor emeritus (pl. professors emeriti). ¶~의 칭호를 받다 be granted the title of emeritus professor. **명예시민** an honorary citizen. **명예심** [명예를 얻으려는 마음] (a) desire for fame; [명예를 중요시하는 마음] a sense of honor. **명예욕** love of fame; a desire for fame; aspiration for fame. ¶~이 강하다 have a strong desire to win fame / have an ardent passion for fame. **명예의 전당** the Hall of Fame. **명예직** an honorary post; an honorary office; a post without pay. **명예퇴직** voluntary resignation; quitting one's job voluntarily; (정년에 가까운 경우) voluntary retirement (before the retirement age). **명예혁명** [영국 역사] the Glorious [Bloodless] Revolution; the English Revolution. **명예 훼손** defamation of character.

명왕성(冥王星) [천] Pluto.

명운(命運) (a) fate; (a) destiny; doom. ⇨운명(運命)

명월(明月) a bright moon; (추석날의) the harvest moon; [보름달] a full moon.

명의(名義) 1 [이름] a person's name. ¶~상의 nominal / titular // ~상으로는 nominally / in name / titularly // ~상의 당총재 the nominal head of a party // …의 ~로 in [under] the name of // ~를 변경 [이전] 하다 change the holder / transfer (property) to (another) // 남의 ~를 사칭하다 assume a false [another's] name // A 씨 ~로 이전하다 transfer (property) to the name of Mr. A // 자기 ~의 사용을 허용하다 allow the use of one's name // ~상으로는 그가 책임자이다 He is, nominally, the person in charge. // 나의 토지를 아들 ~로 변경하였다 I transferred my land to my son. 2 one's moral duty; justice. ⇨명분(名分)

●**명의 변경** transfer (of the title) (약어 trans.); entry of a change of holders; [증권] transfer.

명의(名醫) [뛰어난 의사] a skilled physician [doctor]; an excellent physician; [유명한 의사] a noted doctor.

명인(名人) a master (of / in / at); an expert (in); a master hand (at). ¶춤의 ~ a master at dancing // 바둑의 ~ a grand master of baduk(go) / an expert baduk player / the champion baduk player (국수(國手)) // ~이 되다 [~의 경지에 이르다] master (an art) / become a master hand [past master] / make oneself master (of) / attain consummate skill (in).

●**명인전**(一戰) (장기의) the professional chess players' championship series.

명일(名日) a festive [gala] day; a national holiday.

명일(明日) tomorrow.

명작(名作) a masterpiece; a fine piece (of literature); a fine work (of art); a masterwork.

●**명작 소설집** a collection [an anthology] of famous stories.

명장(名將) a great commander; an illustrious [a renowned] general [admiral] (▶ admiral은 제독).

명장(名匠) a master craftsman; a skilled [skillful / (영) skilful] workman [artisan / artist]; a master hand.

명저(名著) [유명한 저서] a famous book; [훌륭한 저술] a fine [great] book [work]; a masterpiece.

명절(名節) a festive day; a national holiday; a gala [fête] day. ¶실상 ~ 기분은 그믐날 밤부터 시작된다 In reality, the festive mood begins on the eve of the New Year's Day.

명제(命題) 1 [논] a proposition; a position; a thesis. ¶가언 ~ a hypothetical [conditional] proposition // 긍정 ~ an affirmative proposition // 단칭[특칭 / 전칭] ~ a singular [particular / universal] proposition // 부정 ~ a negative proposition // 정언(定言) ~ a categorical [an absolute / a predicative] proposition. **2** [제목] a given subject (for a composition); [제목을 정함] giving a subject (for).

명조(明朝) **1** [내일 아침] tomorrow morning. **2** [명나라] the Ming dynasty.
● **명조체** Ming(-style) type.

명주(明紬) silk.
● **명주실** silk (thread). **명주 천** silk fabric.

명주(銘酒) high-quality liquor; liquor of a superior [special / noted] brand; choice liquor.

명주잠자리(明紬-) [동] an ant lion.

명중(命中) a hit. **명중하다** hit (the mark); tell. ¶과녁에 ~ hit the target // 명중하지 않다 miss (the mark) / go wide (of the mark) // 아녁 한복판에 ~ hit the bull's eye / hit [make] a bull's-eye on the target // 탄알이 표적에 명중했다 The bullet hit the mark // 눈 뭉치가 그의 눈에 명중됐다 The snowball hit him in the eye. // 탄환은 모두 명중했다 Every shot told.

명찰(名札) [이름표] a name card; (미아 등의) an identification tag; a nameplate [tag]; (좌석의) a place card. ¶~을 달다 attach [affix] a name tag (to) // 왼쪽 가슴에 ~을 달고 있다 have a name card on one's left lapel.

명찰(名刹) a famous [noted] temple with a long history.

명찰(明察) [똑똑히 살핌] discernment; [통찰] perception; insight; penetration; clear judgment. **명찰하다** discern; have an insight (into); see through. ¶그는 남의 감정을 명찰하는 능력이 있다 He has keen insight into people's feelings.

명창(名唱) [잘 부르는 노래] a well-sung song; [뛰어나게 잘 부르는 사람] a well-known [celebrated / great / gifted] singer; a master singer.

명철하다(明哲-) wise; sagacious. ¶명철한 사람은 화를 피한다 A wise man keeps himself from harm.

명충(螟蟲) [동] a pearl-moth. ⇨"이화명나방

명치 the pit of the stomach; (구어) the solar plexus; the wind.
● **명치뼈** the bone above the pit of the stomach.

명칭(名稱) [이름] a name; a title; a term; a designation; an appellation; (종파·화폐 단위 등의) a denomination. ¶법률상의 ~ a legal name // ~을 붙이다 name / give a name (to) / designate // ~을 바꾸다 change the name / rename / retitle // 이 협회의 ~은 무엇입니까 What is the name of this society?

명콤비(名-) (form) an ideal combination; (make) an excellent [a good] pair.

명쾌하다(明快-) clear; lucid; explicit. ¶명쾌한 발언 a clear statement // 설명이 참으로 ~ The explanation is quite clear [lucid / to the point]. // 명쾌한 대답이 나왔다 An explicit answer was given. **명쾌히** clearly; lucidly; explicitly.

명태(明太) [동] a walleye [an Alaska] pollack.

명패(名牌) [이름 등이 기재된 책상에 놓는 패] a nameplate.

명품(名品) [훌륭한 물건] a fine article; a gem; [뛰어난 작품] a masterpiece.

명필(名筆) [잘 쓰는 글씨] (a) superb [skilled / masterful] (piece of) calligraphy; an excellent handwriting; [글씨를 잘 쓰는 사람] a master [famous / noted] calligrapher; a master of calligraphy.

명하다(命-) **1** order; tell; command. ⇨"명령하다(⇨명령) **2** appoint (a person to an office). ⇨"임명하다(⇨임명)

명함(名銜) (개인용) a calling card; a visiting card; (영업용) a business card. ¶~을 내놓다 hand [present / give] a person one's calling [visiting / business] card / send in [up] one's card(들여보내다) // ~을 주고받다 exchange cards // ~을 두고 가다 leave one's card.
● **명함판 사진** (프) a carte de visite; a card-size photograph.

명화(名花) [아름다운 여자·기생] a celebrated beauty [courtesan]; [이름난 꽃] a celebrated flower.

명화(名畫) [탁월한 그림] a masterpiece (of painting); a beautiful [masterful] drawing [painting]; [유명한 그림] a famous [celebrated / great] picture; [훌륭한 영화] an excellent film; a noted film. ¶서양의 ~ masterpieces of Western painting.

명확하다(明確-) clear; [확실하다] definite; [정확하다] precise. ¶명확한 대답 a definite answer // 명확한 발음 clear pronunciation // 그의 설명은 명확하지 못하다 His explanation lacks clarity [precision]. / His explanation is ambiguous. **명확히** definitely; precisely. ¶~하다 make clear / clear up / clarify / define // 공사(公私)를 ~ 구별하다 draw a distinct line [make a clear distinction] between public and private matters // 이 점을 ~ 할 필요가 있다 It is necessary to make this point clear.

몇 1 [부정의 수] some; a few; several. ¶일 년 ~ 개월 one year and some months // 20 ~ 마일 twenty and some miles // ~ 십만 [~ 백만]의 사람들 hundreds of thousands [millions] of people // 10 [20 / 300] ~ 권의 책 ten-odd [twenty-odd / three hundred-odd] books // 그는 서른 ~ 살에 죽었다 He died somewhere in his thirties [at the age of thirty-odd years]. // 나는 그것을 3천 ~ 원에 샀다 I paid three thousand some won [three thousand something] for it. // 그것은 ~ 주일 [~ 백 년] 전의 일이었다 It happened a few weeks [several hundred years] ago. // 그는 1980 ~ 년에 귀국했다 He came home in nineteen eighty something. // 지금은 서울 부산 간을 다니는 데 ~ 시간밖에 걸리지 않는다 Now it takes only a few hours to travel between Seoul and Busan. // 연은 ~ 백 미터 높이까지 올라갔다 The kite rose to a height of many hundreds of meters. // 그것을 하는 데는 ~ 가지 방법이 있다 There are several methods of doing it. // 저기에 상자가 ~ 개 있다 There are some boxes over there.

2 [의문] how many (days / weeks / months)(수); how much(양·금액); how far(거리); how long(시일); how old(연령); what time(시간). ¶가족은 ~ 명입니까 How many people [members] are in your family? // 오늘은 ~ 십 [백 / 천 / 만] 명쯤 왔습니까 About how many people came today?(▶ 영어에서는 이러한 수를 구별할 적당한 표현이 없음) // 그때 당신은 ~ 살이었습니까 How old were you then? // 그것은 ~ 원이치였습니까 How much was it in won? / How much did it

몇몇

cost? // 결혼식은 ~ 년 ~ 월 며칠이었습니까 What was the year and date of the wedding? // 책은 ~ 권이나 가지고 있느냐 How many books do you have? // 자제분은 ~ 살입니까 How old is your child? // 이 상자 안에 사과가 ~ 개 들어 있습니까 How many apples are there in this box? // (온도계는) ~ 도를 가리키고 있습니까 How many degrees does the thermometer read [register]? / What's the temperature? // 그것을 끝내는 데 ~ 날이나 걸리겠습니까 How many days will it take you to finish it?

몇몇 ¶ ~의 a few / some / several // ~ 사람 some people // ~ 그룹만이 그 회의에 나왔다 Only a few groups turned up at the meeting. // 그들 중 ~은 버스로 갔고 나머지는 걸어서 갔다 Some of them went by bus and others on foot.

모¹ 1 [벼의 싹] rice sprouts; sprouts of rice; a rice seedling. ¶ ~를 내다 [심다] transplant rice seedlings / set [bed] out rice plants. 2 a seedling; a sapling. ⇨ ˚모종

모² 1 [각(角)] an angle; [모서리] an edge; a corner. ¶ ~가 난 angular / angled // 세~꼴 a triangle // 네~꼴 a quadrangle / a quadrilateral / a square. 2 [사물의 측면] the side. ¶어느 ~로 보나 every inch / to all appearance / from top to toe. 3 [성깔이나 가탈] angularity; stiffness; harshness. ¶ ~가 나게 말하다 speak harshly // 여러 사람과 사귀면 ~가 없어질 것이다 Mix with people and you will become more affable.

모³ [두부·묵의 수효] a cake; a piece. ¶두부 두 ~ two pieces [cakes] of dubu.

모⁴ [윷놀이] the 5 points made by throwing the four yut sticks so that all four faces are down.

모(毛) 1 [털] hair; wool; fur. 2 [십진급수의 단위] a mo (=one-tenth of a ri).

모(母) (one's) mother.

모(某) 1 [어떤 사람] a certain person; Mr. X; (이름을 모를 경우) Mr. So-and-so; somebody; Mr. ―. ¶손 ~ (씨) a certain (Mr.) Son / a man called Son / a [one] Mr. Son / ~ 박사 Dr. X / Doctor So-and-so / Doctor What's-his-name. 2 [어떤 사물] one; a; certain. ¶작년 ~ 월 ~ 일 [~시] 에 on a certain date [time] last year // ~ 신문 a certain newspaper.

모가지 1 〈속〉 a neck. ⇨ ˚목 2 [면직·파면] dismissal; discharge; (미국 속어) kiss-off.

모감주나무 [식] a goldenrain (tree); a Chinese bladdernut.

모개로 all together; in the lump; in (the) gross; in bulk; (프) en masse. ¶(돈을) ~ 치르다 pay in a lump sum [in one sum] // ~ 사다 buy (things) in a lot [mass] // ~ 보내다 send (things) together // ~ 흥정하다 make a package deal [wholesale dealing]

모개흥정 wholesale dealing; a package deal.

모계(母系) the maternal line; one's mother's side; the uterine descent; the matrilineal descent. ¶ ~의 maternal / on the maternal [mother's] side / umbilical / matronymic // 그의 ~에는 음악가가 많다 There are many musicians on his mother's side of the family.

● **모계 제도** matriarchy. **모계 (중심) 사회** a matrilineal [matricentric] society.

모골(毛骨) hair and bone.

모골이 송연하다 feel one's hair stand on end; be frightened from the tips of one's hair to the marrow of one's very bones.

모공(毛孔) pores (of the skin). ⇨ ˚털구멍

모과(木瓜) [식] the fruit of a Chinese quince.

● **모과나무** a Chinese quince.

모관(毛管) [물] a capillary tube. ⇨ ˚모세관₁

모교(母校) (미) one's alma mater (▶ 주로 고교·대학을 말함); one's (old) school. ¶당신의 ~는 어디입니까 Which school did you graduate from? / Where did you go to school?

모국(母國) one's mother [native] country; the [one's] homeland. ¶재외 한국인의 ~ 관광단 a tourist party of Koreans living abroad on a visit to their homeland.

● **모국어** one's mother tongue. ¶외국어를 ~로 하는 사람에게 배우다 learn a foreign language from a native speaker // 그는 영어를 ~처럼 말한다 He speaks English as if it were his native language.

모권(母權) mother's authority; maternal rights; matriarchy. ¶ ~을 신장하다 raise the status of motherhood.

모근(毛根) a hair root [bulb]; the root [bulb] of hair. ¶ ~을 이식하다 implant a hair.

모금 (액체의) a draft [drought]; a gulp; (뜨거운 차 등의) a sip; (담배의) a puff; a whiff. ¶물 한 ~ a draft [drought] of water // 담배를 한 ~ 피우다 have a smoke / have a puff / take a whiff // 그 후로 그는 술을 한 ~도 안 마셨다 He has not tasted a drop of wine since.

모금(募金) fund-raising; collection [invitation] of subscriptions; collection of contributions [donations]. ¶가두 ~ the collecting [collection] of contributions on the street / a street collection of subscriptions // 자금 ~ 파티 a fund-raising party. **모금하다** raise money; raise [invite] subscriptions (to a fund); collect contributions. ¶기금을 ~ raise [collect] funds // 이것은 우리 급우들한테서 모금한 돈입니다 This is the money we collected from our classmates. // 우리는 미술관 건립을 위해 모금하고 있다 We are raising funds to build an art museum.

● **모금 운동** (start) a fund-raising campaign; a drive to raise [obtain] funds; a canvass for subscriptions. **모금함** a collecting [collection] box.

모기 [동] a mosquito (pl. ~s, ~es). ¶ ~ 떼 a swarm of mosquitoes / a column of swarming mosquitoes // ~가 많은 곳 a mosquito-ridden place // ~에게 물린 자국 a mosquito bite // ~를 쫓다 drive away mosquitoes / fan out [away] mosquitoes // (부채로) ~를 쫓아내다 / smoke out mosquitoes (연기로) // ~를 (때려) 잡다 swat [slap] a mosquito // ~에 물렸다 I was bitten [stung] by a mosquito. // ~ 한 마리가 귓전에 앵앵거린다 A mosquito is whining [buzzing] near my ear.

모기 보고 칼 빼기 break a butterfly on the wheel; much ado about nothing.

● **모기장** a mosquito net [curtain / tent / (미) bar]; mosquito netting. ¶ ~을 치다 put [set / hang] up a mosquito net (ting) // ~을 걷다 take down a mosquito net (ting) // ~을 치고 자다 sleep under a mosquito net. **모기향** a mosquito-repellent (incense); a mosquito coil [stick]. ¶ ~을 피우다 burn mosquito-repellent (incense). **모깃불** smudge; a mosquito-fumigator; a mosquito-smoker; (미) a mosquito[smudge] fire. ¶~을 피우다 make a smoke to drive away mosquitoes.

모기둥 [건] an angular[a square] pillar.

모나다 1 (물건이) angle; be angular; be angulated; be angled; (뾰족하게) be pointed; be sharp. ¶모난 angled / square / square-built / angulated / angular / sharp // 모난 얼굴 an angular[a squarish] face // 모난 글씨를 쓰다 write in a square hand.
2 (성격·행동이) be angular[stiff / harsh / severe]; be unsociable[unaffable / uncompromising]. ¶모난 성격[사람] an unaffable character[person] // 모난 행동 odd behavior // 모나지 않은 사람 an affable[a sociable] person // 모난 태도로 in an intransigent [intractable] manner // 모나게 굴다 act [behave] harshly.
3 (쓰임새가) make something valuable [useful]. ¶돈을 모나게 쓰다 spend money usefully[effectively / well].

모난 돌이 정 맞는다 (속담) Those who push themselves forward can expect to take a beating.; A tall tree catches much wind.

모내기 rice planting; rice transplantation. ¶~로 바쁘다 be busy planting the rice. **모내기하다** transplant rice seedlings; plant rice. ¶이 지방에서는 6월 중순경에 모내기한다 In this district they plant rice in the middle of June.
● **모내기 철** the rice planting season.

모내다 [모를 심다] transplant rice seedlings.

모녀 (母女) mother and daughter. ¶~간 between[the relation of] mother and daughter.

모년 (某年) a certain year.

모노그램 [두 글자 이상을 합친 도안 글자] a monogram.

모노드라마 [연] a monodrama.

모노레일 [철도] a monorailway; monorail system; [궤도] a monorail. ¶현수식[승마식] ~ a suspended[mounted] type monorailroad // 공항으로는 ~로 갈 수 있다 You can take the monorail to the airport. / You can go[get] to the airport by monorail.

모노타이프 [자동 주조 식자기] a monotype.

모놀로그 [독백] a monologue; soliloquy.

모눈종이 graph paper; squared[sectional] paper; plotting paper. ¶3밀리 ~ paper ruled into 3-millimeter squares.

모니터 a monitor. ¶텔레비전 프로그램의 ~를 하다 monitor a TV program.

모닝콜 a wake-up call; a morning call. ¶내일 아침 6시에 ~을 해 주세요 Give me a wake-up call at 6 tomorrow morning, please.

모닥불 a bonfire; a fire in the open air; (야영의) a campfire. ¶~을 피우다 build a bonfire // 낙엽을 그러모아 ~을 피우다 rake up the fallen leaves to make a fire.

모더니스트 a modernist.

모더니즘 modernism.

모던하다 modern. ¶그것이 당시로서는 모던한 복장이었다 It was a fashionable dress in those days. // 나는 이런 모던한 그림을 좋아하지 않는다 I don't like modernistic pictures like this.

모데라토 [음] moderato. ¶알레그로 ~ allegro moderato.

모델 1 [모형·본보기·본] a model (of honesty).
2 (그림·소설 등의) a model; a sitter. ¶패션 ~ a fashion model // 화가의 ~ an artist's model // …을 ~로 하여 그린 초상화 a portrait painted from sittings given by … // ~이 되다 act as a model / model for an artist / pose for an artist[a picture] // 실제 인물을 ~로 하여 쓰다[그리다] work[draw] from a living model // 나는 세 번 그의 ~이 되어 주었다 I sat[posed] for him three times.

모뎀 [통신을 보낼 때의 변복조 장치] a modem(▶ modulator와 demodulator의 합성어).

모독 (冒瀆) [신·신성한 것을 더럽히기] profanity; [독신(瀆神)적인 욕] blasphemy; [신성한 것·장소를 더럽히기] sacrilege; [신성한 것의 악용·남용] desecration; [존경하지 않기] disrespect. ¶그것은 인간성에 대한 ~이다 That is disrespect of humanity. // 그런 행위는 법에 대한 ~이다 Such deeds amount to a desecration of the law. **모독하다** profane; desecrate; defile; blaspheme (against); do not respect. ¶신을 ~ blaspheme (against) the Gods / profane the name of God // 존엄성을 ~ debase (a person's) dignity / impair a person's dignity // 이런 해석은 원작을 모독하는 것 같다 It seems to me such an interpretation degrades[is a profanation of] the original work.

모두 all(▶ 사람은 복수 취급, 사물은 원칙으로 단수 취급); [모든 사람] everyone; everybody(▶ 단수 취급); [모든 사물] everything (▶ 단수 취급); in all; in a body; all together; one and all; altogether; without an exception; in the gross. ¶우리 ~ all[every one] of us // 아이들은 ~ all the children // 7명[개] seven in all // 빚을 ~ 갚다 pay [repay] all one's debts // 준비를 ~ 마치다 make every preparation (for) / be all set [ready] (for) // 우리 ~ 함께 가자 Let's all go together. // 그의 친구, 지인 ~가 그의 귀향 환영회에 모였다 All his friends and acquaintances came to the party to welcome him home. // 이 아이들은 ~ 시골에서 자랐다 Every one of these children is[All these children are] country-bred. // 책이 10권 있는데 ~ 내 것이다 There are ten books. All are mine. // ~ 앞에 나온 복수 명사를 받아서 all은 복수 취급) 그들은 ~ 전사했다 They were killed to a man. // ~ 피살됐다 None escaped death. // 온 마을 사람들이 ~ 축제를 즐겼다 The whole village enjoyed the festival. // 그들은 그 계획에 ~ 찬성했다 They agreed to the plan without a single exception[unanimously]. // 저분들은 ~ 독신이다 They are bachelors without exception. // 우리 ~가 간 것은 아니다 Not all of us went there. // 그의 형제는 ~ 키가 크지 않다 None of his brothers are tall. // 그는 병의 우유를 ~ 마셨다 He drained the bottle of milk to the last drop. // 그는 그 책을 이틀 만에 ~ 읽었다 He read the book through[the whole book] in only two days. // 얼마입니까 How much is it altogether? // ~ 합해서 5만 원이다 It comes to fifty thousand won in all. // ~ 합해서 8만 원이 들었다 It cost 80,000 won altogether[in all]. // 나는 이 책들을 ~ 읽었다 I have read all these books. // ~가 순조롭게 진행되었다 Everything went smoothly. // 그녀는 용돈을 ~ 써 버렸다 She has spent the last penny of her pocket money. // 나는 하는 일마다 ~ 실패했다 In everything I undertook I failed. // 계산이(서비스료를 포함하여) ~ 이겁니까 Does this bill include everything? // 송료 포함

모두 해서 ~ 얼맙니까 How much will it be shipping[freight charges] included?

모두(冒頭) the beginning; the outset; the opening (of a composition / speech); the head (of a column); the opening paragraph. ¶연설의 ~에 at the outset of one's speech // ~에 싣다 give (an article) at the beginning // 그 책의 ~에는 다음과 같이 씌어 있다 We find the following in the opening sentences of the book.
● **모두 진술** opening statement; [법] arraignment.

모드 [유행] the mode; (a) fashion; [음] a mode; [수] a mode. ¶금년의 ~ this year's fashion(s) / the style this year.

모든 all; every(▶ every 뒤에는 가산 명사의 단수형. all은 가산·불가산 명사의 어느 것이나 쓰임); each; each and every. ¶~ 이에게 to everyone / to all (persons) // ~ 경우에 있어서 in all cases / on every[any] occasion // ~ 종류의 물건 all kinds[sorts] of things // ~ 각도에서 검토하다 discuss the matter from every angle // ~ 수단을 다하다 try every possible means // 나는 ~ 것을 잃었다 I lost everything[my all]. // ~ 비용은 회원의 회비로 충당된다 The whole[entire] cost is covered by membership fees. // ~ 경비가 7만 원이 되었다 The total expenses amounted to seventy thousand won. // ~ 것을 말해 주겠다 I will tell you everything[all I know]. // ~ 것이 순조롭게 진행되었다 Everything went smoothly. // 그것으로 ~ 것이 명백해졌다 That tells the whole story. // ~ 사람은 자기를 지킬 권리가 있다 Everybody has a right to protect himself.
모든 길은 로마로 통한다(속담) All roads lead to Rome.

모들뜨기 a cross-eyed person; a convergent squinter.

모들뜨다 look with both eyes turning toward the nose; take a cross-eyed look.

모라토리엄 [지급 유예] a moratorium (pl. ~s, -ria).

모락모락 rapidly; well; thickly; densely. ⇨ <무럭무럭>

모란(牡丹) [식] a (tree) peony.
● **모란꽃** a peony blossom.

모란채(牡丹菜) [식] a cauliflower.

모래 sand; grit(굵은). ¶~ 한 알 a grain of sand // ~가 많은 sandy // ~를 씹는 것 같은 insipid [tale] / tasteless (food) / flat (speech) / dull (life) // ~ 속으로 스며 들어가다 sink into the sand // 바닷가의 ~알처럼 한없이 많다 be as numberless as the grains of sand on the seashore // ~로 거르다 filter through sand // 눈에 ~가 들어갔다 Some sand got in my eye. / I have got some sand in my eye. // 그들은 얼어붙은 도로에 ~를 뿌렸다 They sanded[sprinkled sand over] the icy[frozen] road.
● **모래땅** a sandy place[soil]; the sands. ¶~에서 사는[자라는] living[growing] in sandy places. **모래무지** [동] a false[goby] minnow. **모래밭** the sands; a sandpit(모래 채취장); a sandbox(놀이터); a sandy-soil field(모래밭). ¶아이들이 ~에서 놀고 있다 The children are playing on the sands. **모래사장** a sandy[river] beach. ⇨ °모래톱(⇨모래) **모래시계** a sandglass; (1시간짜리) an hourglass. **모래주머니** a sandbag; [군] an earth bag; [동] (새의) a gizzard. **모래찜질** a (hot) sand bath. ¶~을 하다 take a sand bath. **모래톱** a sandy[river] beach; the sands; (강 가운데의) a sandbank in a river. **모래흙** sandy soil.

모래집 [생] the amnion. **모래~**양막

모략(謀略) strategy; a stratagem; an artifice; a trick; a scheme; a plot. ¶~을 꾸미다 devise a stratagem / concoct[work out] a plot // ~에 걸려들다 fall into a snare / be caught in a trap // 그는 적의 ~에 빠졌다 He fell into the snare set by his opponents. // 그들은 교묘한 ~을 꾸미고 있다 They are devising[contriving] a clever trick[subtle stratagem].
● **모략가** a schemer; a scheming man. **모략선전** tricky propaganda.

모럴 [도덕·윤리] morals; ethics; moral sense.

모럴리스트 a moralist.

모레 the day after tomorrow.

모로 [비스듬히] diagonally; obliquely; half right[left]; (옆으로) sideways. ¶~ 줄을 긋다 draw a line obliquely // ~ 걷다 sidle (through a crowd) / walk sideways // ~ 누워 자다 sleep on one's side // 그는 ~ 쓰러졌다 He fell on his side.

모로 가도 서울만 가면 된다(속담) It doesn't matter which way you take to reach your destination.; The end justifies the means.

모롱이 (산·언덕의) a spur of a mountain[hill].

모루 an anvil.
● **모루채** a hammer; a sledge (hammer).

모르다 1 [알지 못하다] do not know; be ignorant of; (구어) be innocent of. ¶아무것도 모르고 unknowingly // 모르는 말 a word [language] one does not know // 그런 줄은 모르고 without knowing it // 모르는 사이에 without one's knowledge [knowing it] / without knowing / before one knows it // 글을 ~ be unlettered [illiterate / ignorant] // 전혀 ~ know nothing (about) / have no idea [conception] (of / how) // 모르고 있다 remain ignorant [in ignorance] (of) / be unaware of // 모른다고 우기다 stoutly maintain one's ignorance // 모르는 것은 모른다고 하다 make no secret of one's ignorance // 하나만 알고 둘은 ~ know only one side (of the matter) // 나는 그것에 대해 아무것도 모른다 I know nothing about it. // 나는 그것을 오늘 아침까지 몰랐다 I did not hear of it until this morning. // 어떻게 해야 좋을지 모르겠다 I don't know what to do. / I am at my wit's end. // 확실히는 모른다 I don't know for certain. // 나는 독일어를 조금밖에 모릅니다 My German is very limited. // 그가 그런 범죄를 저지른 것을 나는 전혀 몰랐다 I had no idea he had committed such a crime. // 모른다고 시치미 떼어도 소용없다 It's no use feigning ignorance. // 나는 그것에 대해 아무것도 모른 체했다 I pretended not to know anything about it. / (문어) I assumed an air of [feigned] ignorance about it.
2 [이해하지 못하다] do not understand; have no idea of; (사물이) be above [beyond / past] one's comprehension ¶글의 뜻을 ~ do not understand the meaning of a sentence // 조금도 ~ do not understand at all / do not have the slightest idea [inkling] of // 나는 네가 무슨 말을 하는지 모르겠다 I don't know what you are talking about. / You are talking over my head. / You've lost me. / I've

lost you.// 나는 그것은 도저히 모르겠다 It is beyond me[my comprehension].// 당신의 논리를 나는 모르겠다 I cannot follow your reasoning[logic / line of thinking].
3 [인식하지 못하다] have no understanding (of); be ignorant (of); do not recognize [appreciate]; ignore; disregard (of). ¶돈을 ~ do not appreciate the value[power] of money / be indifferent to money// 중요성을 ~ do not appreciate the importance (of)// 그는 시를 모른다 He cannot[doesn't] appreciate poetry.// 나는 음악을 모른다 I have no ear for music.// 나는 도자기는 잘 모른다 I am no judge of ceramics.// 저를 모르시겠습니까 Can't you recognize me?// 그가 누군지 모르겠다 I can't recognize who he is.// 피해자의 신원은 아직 모른다 The victim's identity is still unknown[not yet known]. / The victim has not yet been identified.// 그녀는 길에서 나를 만나도 모른 체했다 She cut me dead [pretended not to recognize me] when we met on the street.
4 [안면이 없다] be not acquainted with; be unfamiliar; be a stranger. ¶모르는 얼굴 a strange[an unfamiliar] face / a stranger// 잘 모르는 곳 an unfamiliar[a strange] place// 나는 이 근방은 전혀 모른다 I am a complete stranger here.// 모르는 사람 사이에서는 늘 수줍어진다 I am always shy with strangers.
5 [깨닫지 못하다] be unaware (of); be unconscious (of); do not come under one's notice. ¶그는 자신도 모르게 우산을 바꾸어 가지고 갔다 He carried off another person's umbrella by mistake. / He carelessly walked off with the wrong umbrella.// 나도 모르게 눈물이 나왔다 Tears had gathered in my eyes before I knew it.// 나도 모르게 경솔한 말을 하여 미안하다 I'm sorry I made that thoughtless remark.// 나도 모르게 소리 지르고 말았다 I shouted in spite of myself.// 그는 자기의 약점을 모른다 He is not conscious [aware] of his own weakness.// 사람들은 자기의 결점은 잘 모른다 We are blind to our own shortcomings.// 매일 10분씩 연습하면 모르는 사이에 숙달이 된다 If you practice just ten minutes a day, you will improve without even realizing it.
6 [느끼지 못하다] be insensible (of / to); do not feel; be impervious (to); be dead (to). ¶염치를 ~ be shameless// 인정을 ~ be heartless// 은혜를 ~ be ungrateful// 그녀는 동정이라는 것을 모르는 여자다 Pity is a word that has no place in her vocabulary.
7 [추측하지 못하다] cannot tell; be past conjecture; be hard to foresee[foretell / forecast]. ¶그라면 할는지도 모른다 I wouldn't be surprised if he did it. / (구어) I wouldn't put it past him.// 그는 무슨 짓을 할지도 모른다 He would stop at nothing.// 그가 제시간에 올지 정말 모르겠다 I am not quite sure (whether) [It is doubtful whether] he will come on time.// 목소리만 들어서는 누가 누군지 모르겠다 I could not tell them apart by their voices.// 우리는 이런 불행이 닥쳐올 것을 몰랐다 We did not foresee that such a misfortune was awaiting us.// 재해란 언제 닥쳐올지 모른다 There can be a disaster at any moment. / There is no telling[you never can tell] when a disaster may strike[occur].// 이 계획이 잘될지 어떨지 아직 모른다 It remains [is yet] to be seen whether this plan will work or not.
8 [경험이 없다] have no experience; be ignorant of. ¶세상을 ~ know nothing of the world / be ignorant of the world / be a mere babe in the ways of the world// 나는 등산은 모른다 I know nothing about[I have no experience in] mountain climbing.// 그것은 내가 전혀 모르는 세계의 일이다 That is entirely outside my experience.// 그녀는 이 세상의 쓰라린 맛을 모른다 She has not experienced[is inexperienced in] the troubles of this world.
9 [기억하지 못하다] do not remember; forget. ¶그 당시의 일은 전혀 모르겠다 I cannot remember anything of those days at all.
10 [관계가 없다] have no relation (with); have nothing to do (with); be not concerned (with). ¶나는 그 일은 모른다 I have nothing to do with it. / It's no concern of mine.// 나는 모른다, 네 마음대로 해라 Just do[go] as you like, it's none of my business.

모르모트 [동] a guinea pig.
모르몬교(-敎) Mormonism.
●**모르몬교도** a Mormon.
모르타르 mortar. ¶~를 바른 집 a mortared [stucco] house// 집 외벽에 ~를 바르다 mortar[plaster / stucco] the outside of a house.
모르핀 morphia; morphine.
●**모르핀 중독** morphine poisoning; (만성의) morphinism; morphine addiction.
모름지기 necessarily; by all means. ¶아이들은 ~ 부모를 따라야 한다 Children should obey their parents.// 네 나이면 ~ 분별이 있어야 한다 At your age you ought to know better [reasonable] way.// 우리는 ~ 인명을 존중해야 한다 It is essential that we (should) have respect for human life.
모리(謀利·牟利) profiteering. ¶~를 **단속하다** control profiteering. **모리하다** profiteer (in); make an unfair profit.
●**모리배** a profiteer.
모멘트 **1** [물] a moment. ¶~의 momental// 힘의 ~ the moment of a force / torque// 관성 ~ moment of inertia. **2** a chance; an opportunity. ⇨ˇ계기(契機)
모면(謀免) escape; evasion; avoidance; shirking; elusion. **모면하다** escape; avoid; evade; shirk; elude; excuse oneself from (responsibility). ¶모면할 수 없는 unavoidable / inescapable / inevitable / ineluctable// 그는 언제나 입에 발린 소리를 하여 곤경을 모면한다 He always gets through difficult situations by saying what is expected of him.// 수상은 아무것도 모르는 체하며 그의 날카로운 질문을 모면했다 The Prime Minister parried [evaded] his sharp questions by pretending ignorance.// 그는 책임을 모면하려 했다 He tried to evade[avoid taking] the responsibility.// 그들은 어떤 형태로든 처벌을 모면할 수 없을 것이다 They cannot escape[avoid / get off without] some form of punishment.// 다행히 내 차는 사고를 모면했다 Fortunately my car missed being involved in the accident.
모멸(侮蔑) contempt; disdain; scorn. ¶~적인 언사 a word of contempt. **모멸하다** despise; disdain; scorn; abase; (문어) contemn; look

모모 698

down on[upon] (a person).
모모(某某) unspecified[unnamed] persons; so-and-sos.
● **모모인**(-人) a certain number of persons; Messrs. So-and-sos.
모모한(某某-) worthy of mentioning; notable; well-known; celebrated; distinguished. ¶~ 인사 somebody / anybody / a respectable citizen / [저명인사] a man of distinction / a notable / a wellknown person.
모반(母斑) [의] a n(a)evus; a birthmark.
모반(謀叛) [군주·국가에 대한 반역] treason; [대규모의 반란] a rebellion; [격렬한 폭동] a revolt; [비조직적인 반역] an insurrection. ¶정부에 대한 젊은 장교들의 ~ a rebellion [revolt] of young officers against the government // 국왕에 대하여 ~을 꾀하다 plot treason against the king // ~을 일으키다 rise in revolt (against) / start an insurrection (against). **모반하다** revolt; rebel; conspire; plot treason; plot against; rise in revolt (against).
모발(毛髮) [집합적] hair (of the head); [털 하나] a hair. ¶~이 빠지다 hair falls out[off].
● **모발 영양제** a hair tonic.
모방(模倣) imitation; copying; mimicry. ¶~ 가능성 imitability // ~을 잘하다 be a clever imitator. **모방하다** imitate [가능한 한 정확히 흉내 내다] copy (from / after); model after [on]; pattern (after); follow an example (of). ¶모방한 것 an imitation / a copy / an echo (pl. ~es) / [가짜] a sham // …을 모방하여 after the model[manner] of ... / in imitation of ... // 모방하여 만들다 make (a thing) on the model of (another) / model (a thing) after (another) // 그것은 포드를 모방한 것이다 It is a copy of a Ford. // 그의 독특한 필치는 남이 도저히 모방할 수 없다 His unique style defies imitation. // 그들은 서양 문화를 모방하기에 바빴다 They were busy copying Western culture. // 이것은 저것을 그대로 모방한 것이다 This is an exact copy[a very close imitation] of that.
● **모방 본능** the instinct of imitation. **모방성** imitative nature. **모방 예술** imitative arts. **모방자** an imitator; a copier; (구어) a copycat.
모범(模範) a model; a (good) example; a pattern; a paragon. ¶~적인 model / exemplary / typical // ~으로 삼아야 할 사람 a model of what a man ought to be // ~이 되다 be a good example (to others) / become an example (of) // ~으로 삼다 pattern[model] after (a person) / take pattern[example] by (a person) / follow the example[model] of (a person) // 그는 예의범절의 ~이다 He is a model of good manners. // 그는 우리 학교의 ~적인 학생이다 He is the model student at our school. // 이 방법은 미국에서 사용되는 것을 ~으로 삼은 것이다 This method is modeled after[on] that used in America. // 스승은 제자들에게 ~을 보여야 할 것이다 A teacher should set a good example for his pupils.
● **모범생** a model[an exemplary] student. **모범수**(-囚) a model[well-behaved] prisoner.
모법(母法) a mother law; a parent law.
모병(募兵) recruiting; conscription; enlistment of soldiers[sailors]; (미) drafting. **모병하다** recruit (troops); (미) draft.
모본단(模本緞) damask (silk); satin damask.

모빌 [미] a mobile.
모사(毛絲) woolen[(영) woollen] yarn [thread]; knitting wool.
모사(模寫) copying; a copy(모사물); a reproduction(미술 작품); a facsimile; a replica.(▶ facsimile는 「치수는 다를지 모르나 정확한 모사 복사」, copy는 가장 일반적인 말로「원물의 복사」이며 흔히 「근사한 모방」의 뜻으로도 쓰임. reproduction은 「원물에 극히 가까운 모사」로서 재료·크기·성질이 다른 것에 쓰임) ¶「모나리자」의 ~ a reproduction of the Mona Lisa. **모사하다** copy (out); trace; reproduce; facsimile; hit off. ¶피카소의 그림을 ~ copy from[make a copy of] a painting by Picasso.
모사(謀士) (좋은 뜻으로) a tactician; a strategist; an adviser; a man of resources; (나쁜 뜻으로) a schemer; a machinator. ¶정계의 ~ a wily politician.
모사(謀事) planning; scheming; maneuvering. **모사하다** plan; make a plan; scheme; plot (against); device a stratagem; lay[form] a plan.
● **모사꾼** a schemer.
모살(謀殺) premeditated[deliberate / willful] murder. **모살하다** murder; kill (a person) with malice of forethought. ¶그는 동업자를 모살하였다 He murdered his partner.
● **모살 미수**(-未遂) attempted murder; an attempt to kill[murder]. **모살범** (the crime of) murder; petit treason(주인·남편에 대한).
모색(暮色) [저무는 풍경] (evening) twilight [dusk]; the shades[gray] of evening. ¶~이 짙어 가고 있다 Evening dusk is fast gathering. / The shades of evening are closing in.
모색(摸索) [더듬어 찾음] groping. ¶암중 ~ groping in the dark. **모색하다** grope (for); fumble (for). ¶모색하여 in search of (a better solution) // 문제의 해결책을 ~ try to find a solution to a problem // 살인 사건의 단서를 ~ grope for some clue to the murder.
모서리 1 a corner; an edge; an angle. ¶책상 ~ the corners of a desk // 뾰쪽한 바윗돌 ~ the sharp edges of a rock // ~를 죽이다 round off the angles. **2** [수] an edge.
모선(母船) a mother ship[vessel]; a depot ship; (우주선의) a mother craft; a command ship(사령선). ¶포경(捕鯨) ~ a (whaling) factory ship / a mother ship.
모성(母性) motherhood; maternity. ¶그녀에게는 ~의 자각이 없다 She has no sense of responsibility as a mother.
● **모성 본능** a maternal instinct. **모성애** motherly[maternal / mother's] love[affection].
모세관(毛細管) **1** [물] [가는 관] a capillary tube. **2** [생] a capillary. ⇨ 모세 혈관
모세 혈관(毛細血管) [생] a capillary; a capillary vessel.
모션 a motion. ¶~이 큰 투수 a pitcher with a big motion // ~하려는 ~을 쓰다 make a motion (to) // ~을 취하다 [작용을 시도하다] try to influence[work on] a person / [먼저 말을 붙이다] make advances to a person / make a pass at a person // 그 투수는 제1구의 ~을 취했다 The pitcher is winding up for the first pitch.
모손(耗損) [닳아 없어짐] wearing out; friction loss; wear (and tear); abrasion. **모손하다** wear out; undergo friction loss; abrade.
모순(矛盾) (a) contradiction; contradictori-

ness; (an) inconsistency; an antinomy; (a) discrepancy; a conflict (of evidence). ¶그의 말은 ~투성이다 What he says is full of inconsistencies. **모순되다** 〔반대이다〕 be contradictory (to); 〔일관성이 없다〕 be inconsistent (with); 〔양립하지 않다〕 be incompatible (with); 〔대립하다〕 conflict (with). ¶「전쟁 없는 군대」란 모순된 말이 아닐까 Isn't "an army without war potential" a contradiction? // 당신은 모순된 말을 하고 있다 You contradict [are contradicting] yourself. // 그런 행동은 자치 정신과 모순된다 Such an action is inconsistent [incompatible] with the spirit of self-government. // 외무 장관의 답변은 총리의 연설과 모순된다 The Foreign Minister's answer is in conflict with the Premier's speech.
● **모순 개념** 〔논〕 a contradictory concept [idea]. **모순 대당** (一對當) 〔논〕 a contradiction; a contradictory (opposition). **모순성** contradictoriness.

모숨 a handful (of grass); a lock (of straw).

모스 부호 (一符號) the Morse code [alphabet / signals]; the Morse. ¶~로 **통신하다** signal [communicate] in Morse (code) / (드물게) Morse.

모스크 〔회교 사원〕 a mosque.

모슬린 〔직물〕 (muslin) delaine; (프) mousseline (delaine).

모습 1 〔몸의 모양〕 a figure; a form; 〔얼굴 모양〕 features; (outward) looks. ¶죽은 누님의 ~을 생각하다 remember one's (dead) sister's look [face] // 그녀는 우아한 ~을 하고 있다 She has a graceful figure. // 그녀의 눈에는 아버지의 생전의 ~이 지금도 생생하게 떠오른다 She still sees her deceased father vividly in her mind's eye. // 그녀는 아버지의 ~을 잘 기억하고 있다 She can still recall her father's image vividly. // 그는 그의 아버지의 ~을 많이 닮았다 He looks quite a bit like his father. / He reminds me of his father.
2 〔외관〕 appearance; 〔옷차림〕 guise; dress. ¶이상한 ~을 한 사나이 a funny-looking man / a man with a strange appearance // 처량한 ~ a sad appearance // 탁발승으로 ~을 바꾸다 disguise oneself as a begging friar // 그 아이는 초라한 ~을 하고 있었다 The child was shabbily dressed.
3 〔상태〕 a state; a condition; 〔양상〕 an aspect; a phase; a picture. ¶인생의 여러 가지 다른 ~ diverse aspects of human life // 옛 ~을 회복하다 restore (a thing to) its former appearance // 젊은이가 떠나고 난 이 마을은 이미 옛 ~이 아니었다 Young people have deserted the village, and it is no longer what it used to be. // 이 뒷골목은 옛 ~을 간직하고 있다 This back lane looks just as it did in the old days.
4 〔자취〕 a trace; a track. ¶속리산이 구름 사이로 ~을 드러냈다 Songnisan(Mt. Songni) appeared from between the clouds. // 곧 호수가 ~을 드러냈다 Soon the lake came into view [sight]. // 어제저녁의 모임에는 팀의 ~이 보이지 않았다 I didn't see Tim at the party last night. // 짐은 아직 ~을 나타내지 않았다 Jim has not turned [shown] up yet. // 그의 ~은 아무 데도 보이지 않았다 He was nowhere to be seen. // 그런 짓을 해 놓고 내가 어떻게 남 앞에 ~을 나타낼 수 있겠는가 How can I show myself [appear] in public after having done such a thing. // 그 이후로 그는 ~을 감추어 버렸다 We have seen nothing of him since. / That was the last we saw of him. // 그의 목소리는 들리는데 ~은 보이지 않는다 He can be heard but not seen. / We can hear him, but we can't see him.

모시 1 〔옷감〕 *mosi*; ramie fabric [cloth]; a grass cloth. 2 〔식〕 a Chinese silk plant. ⇨ 모시풀(⇨모시)
● **모시옷** clothes of *mosi*. **모시풀** 〔식〕 a Chinese silk plant; a ramie [ramee]; a China grass.

모시 (某時) a certain [an undisclosed / an unidentified] hour [time]. ¶모일 ~에 at a certain day and hour.

모시다 1 〔섬기다〕 attend [wait] (upon) (a person); be in attendance on (a person); minister to (a person); serve; take service under (a person). ¶부모를 ~ have one's parents with him / serve [support] one's parents / wait upon one's parents // ···을 모시고 in attendance upon (a person) / accompanying (a person) // 병든 아버지를 모시고 있다 have one's sick father to attend to // 그는 어머니를 극진히 모신다 He shows great devotion to his mother. / He is faithful to his mother.
2 〔신령으로 받들다〕 deify; worship as a god; (사당 등에) enshrine. ¶사당을 세워 ~ dedicate [consecrate] a shrine to (a deity) // 조상의 영혼을 ~ celebrate [hold] a (requiem) mass for the repose of the souls of one's forefathers / perform memorial rites in honor of one's ancestors // 사후에 그는 신으로 모셔졌다 After his death, he was deified [worship(p)ed] as a god.
3 〔인도하다〕 show [usher / conduct] (a person) in [into]. ¶선생님을 상좌에 ~ seat the teacher at the head / give the teacher the place [seat] of honor // 역까지 제가 모시고 가겠습니다 I will go to the station with you. // 당신을 모시러 사람이 왔습니다 A man has come to fetch you. // 당신을 모시러 10시에 차를 보내겠습니다 A car will be sent to pick you up at ten.
4 〔초청하다〕 invite; ask. ¶의사를 모시러 보내다 send for a doctor // 선생님을 모임에 ~ invite one's teacher to a meeting // 사장을 모시고 with one's president in attendance.
5 〔추대하다〕 have (a person) over (a society); be presided by. ¶모임은 K 씨를 회장으로 모시고 있다 The society is under the presidency of Mr. K.

모시조개 〔동〕 a corbicula. ⇨가무락조개
모심기 rice-planting. ⇨모내기

모양 (模樣) 1 〔형상〕 (a) shape; (a) form; make; 〔외관〕 appearance. ¶도끼 ~의 흉기 an ax-shaped weapon // 코 ~의 the shape of one's nose // 잘 생긴 ~ a fine [well-proportioned] figure // 이 색다른 집 a house with a strange appearance [shape] // 사자 ~을 한 바위 a rock shaped like a lion // 달걀 ~을 한 in the shape of an egg / egg-shaped // U자 ~의 골짜기 a U-shaped valley // ~이 여러 가지다 be various [vary] in form [shape] / be of varied forms [shapes] // ~보다 내용을 중히 여기다 value substance above form // 케이크는 ~이 흐트러져 버렸다 The cake lost its shape. // 이 상자와 저 상자는 ~이 같다 This box has [is] the same shape as that one. // 논

모양내다

문이 마침내 ~을 갖추기 시작했다 My thesis is finally beginning to take shape.
2 [차림새·맵시] appearance; a look; an air. ¶~꾼(여자) a woman fond of finery / (남자) a dandy / a fop∥그녀는 그 옷을 입으니까 ~이 우습다 She looks funny in that dress.∥나는 ~ 따위는 아무래도 좋았다 I didn't care how I looked.
3 [상태] the state[aspect / phase / situation / position] of affairs [things]; circumstances. ¶살아가는 ~ (living) circumstances∥이 ~으로 나가면 if things go like this∥일이 되어 가는 ~을 보다 see the run of events / see which way the wind blows [the cat jumps]∥그의 당황하는 ~을 보았어야 하는 건데 You should have seen how upset he was.
4 [방식] a way; a manner; a style. ¶이런 ~으로 in this way[manner] / like this.
5 [체면] face; honor; dignity; prestige. ¶~이 말이 아니다 lose (one's) face / be put out of countenance∥그걸 말해 버리면 내 ~은 뭐가 되겠나 What about my disgrace if you tell him about that?
6 [짐작·추측]. ¶…할 ~이다 it seems [appears] that … / look like …∥하늘을 보니 눈이 내릴 ~이다 It is likely to snow from the look of the sky. / The sky[It] looks like snow.∥아무래도 그가 오지 않을 ~이다 It looks as though[(이) like] he's not coming.∥화성에는 생물이 없는 ~이다 There is no sign of[There doesn't seem to be any] life on Mars.∥저 애가 이 애의 형인 ~이다 He seems to be this boy's older brother.∥이의가 있는 ~이다 There seems to be an objection.∥쌀값이 또 오를 ~이다 There are indications that the price of rice will advance [go up].

모양(이) 사납다 look ugly[uninviting]; be unpleasant in appearance; make a sorry [poor] show.

모양(이) 아니다 look out of shape.

모양(이) 있다 look nice[well / graceful]; cut a brilliant figure; be good-[nice-]looking; be personable.

●**모양새** [모양의 됨됨이] (a) shape; (a) form; (a) figure; an appearance; [체면] face; dignity; reputation. ¶겉 ~ the outward appearance∥~가 예쁘다 be nice-looking / look nice [pretty] / be shapely / be well-shaped / be well-formed∥~가 나쁘다 be ill-shaped / be shapeless / look poor.

모양내다 (模樣―) dress[smarten] oneself up; adorn[preen] oneself; deck oneself out[up]. ¶오늘은 굉장히 모양냈군그래 You are quite dressed up today, aren't you?

모양체 (毛樣體) [생] (눈의) a ciliary body. ¶~의 ciliary.

모어 (母語) [자기 나라 언어] one's mother tongue; [언] [모체가 되는 언어] a parent language. ¶한국어의 ~는 무엇인가에 관한 논쟁 a controversy about the origins[roots] of the Korean language∥라틴 어는 근대 로망 어의 ~이다 Latin is the parent of the modern Romance languages.

모여 [구령] Fall in!; Rally!

모여들다 gather[flock] (together); assemble; come[get] together; meet[throng / draw] together. ¶주위에 ~ gather[cluster] about [around]∥사방에서 ~ flock from all quarters∥책상 둘레에 ~ draw (together) around a table∥구경꾼이 운동장에 모여들었다 Spectators crowded into the playground.∥벌 떼가 꽃에 모여들었다 Bees clustered around the flowers.∥쓰레기통에 파리가 모여들고 있다 The garbage can in swarming with flies.∥잉어 떼가 연못 한가운데에 모여들었다 The carp have formed a school in the center of the pond.∥여름이 되면 이곳에 많은 사람이 모여든다 In summer the place attracts many visitors.∥지나가던 사람들이 노인의 둘레에 모여들었다 Passersby crowded round the old man.

모역 (謀逆) **1** [반역] treason; conspiracy(음모); plotting treason. **모역하다** plot treason (against); conspire (against). **2** [종묘 파괴죄] (the crime of) devastating royal tombs [palaces]. **모역하다** devastate royal tombs [palaces].

모욕 (侮辱) insult; affront(▶insult는 상대에게 창피를 주려 하는 언동, affront는 맞대고 하는 무례한 언동); contempt; indignity; slight; outrage. ¶[법정] ~죄 contempt of court∥~적인 말[언사] insulting[affronting] remarks∥~을 주다 offer (a person) an insult[affront]∥~을 참다 swallow an insult [affront] / bear an affront / brook[pocket] an insult∥~을 당하다 suffer an insult / be insulted / be slighted∥그는 법정 ~죄로 고발당했다 He was charged with contempt of court.∥그의 ~적인 언사에 참을 수 없었다 I could not stand his insulting remarks.∥나는 손님들 앞에서 ~을 당했다 I was put to shame in the presence of the guests.∥그는 동료들한테 ~을 당했다 He was insulted by his colleagues.∥그런 ~은 참을 수 없다 I can't bear[endure] such an insult. **모욕하다** insult; affront; throw contempt on; put a slight on; subject (a person) to insult. ¶그는 남들 앞에서 나를 모욕했다 He insulted me in the presence of other people.

모월 (某月) a certain month. ¶~ 모일 a certain day of a certain month.

모유 (母乳) mother's milk; breast milk. ¶~로 자란 아이 a breast-fed child / a child reared at the breast∥~을 먹이다 give the breast to (a baby)∥~로 키우다 feed (a child) on mother's milk∥~ 먹여 키우기 계몽 운동을 강화하다 strengthen enlightenment campaigns stressing breast feeding.

모으다 1 (사물·인원을) gather; get[bring / put] together; collect; make a collection of; round up (scattered cattle). ¶여러 가지 과일을 한데 모은다 get an assortment of fruit∥그러 ~ scrape together∥자료를 ~ gather [collect] data∥재산을 ~ make a fortune∥운동 자금을 ~ raise funds for a campaign∥모아서 묶다 gather and bundle∥기부금을 ~ solicit[call for] contributions / make an appeal for contributions / take up a collection∥기금을 ~ raise[collect] funds∥회원을 ~ invite people to join (a club) / issue an invitation for new members∥그들은 입을 모아 그를 낯선 사람이라고 말했다 They all said that he was a stranger.∥국무총리는 전 각료의 사표를 한데 모았다 The prime minister collected[gathered] the resignations of all the ministers.∥그는 두 손을 모아 기도하고 있었다 He was praying with his hands together.∥짐을 모두 모아 두어라 Put all the

baggage together.//그 책은 그가 남긴 수필을 모은 것이다 The book is a (posthumous) compilation of his essays.//누이동생이 그의 편지를 모아 출판했다 His sister compiled [edited] and published his letters.//그는 제자들을 전국에서 모았다 He collected [gathered together] disciples from all over the country.//그는 민화를 모아 책으로 만들었다 He collected folktales into a book.//아이들을 모아서 야구를 하자 Let's gather the children [get the children together] and play baseball.//그는 자금을 모으기에 바쁘다 He is busy raising funds.//그는 희귀한 나비를 50종 이상이나 모았다 He has collected over fifty kinds of rare butterflies.//그는 책이라면 덮어놓고 모은다 He just accumulates books without discrimination.//우리는 그를 기소하는 데 충분한 증거를 모았다 We have gathered enough evidence to prosecute him.//여러 종류의 꽃을 모아 꽃다발을 만들었다 I combined several kinds of flowers in a bouquet. / I put together an assortment of flowers and made a bouquet.//그는 희귀 우표를 많이 모으고 있다 He has a large collection of rare stamps.//그 아이는 예쁜 조약돌 모으기를 좋아하였다 The child liked collecting [gathering] beautiful pebbles.//전부 한데 모아 보내는 편이 낫다 You'd better send them all together.
2 [집중시키다] focus (on); concentrate (one's energy on something, rays of light into a focus, etc.). ¶정신[힘]을 ~ concentrate one's attention [strength] on (one's work)//광선의 초점을 ~ concentrate rays of light into focus.
3 [끌다] attract; draw; catch; arrest; win. ¶세인의 이목을 ~ attract public attention//중망(衆望)을 한 몸에 ~ have public hopes centered upon one//극장마다 관중을 모으는 데 고심한다 Every theater is trying hard to attract as many people as possible.//교향악단은 어디서나 많은 청중을 모았다 The orchestra attracted [drew] large audiences everywhere.//그는 모든 동료의 신망을 모으고 있다 He is admired by all his colleagues.
4 [저축하다] save; lay [put / set] by; store; lay up; accumulate; amass. ¶어렵게 모은 돈 one's hard-saved money // 돈을 ~ save [accumulate] money//(저수지 등에) 물을 모아 두다 store [impound] water (in a reservoir)//내일의 경기를 위해 힘을 모아 두다 save one's energy for tomorrow's race//다람쥐는 나무 열매를 모아 둔다 A squirrel stores away nuts.

모음(母音) [언] a vowel (sound). ¶단 ~ a monophthong // 반 ~ a semivowel // 비(鼻) ~ a nasal vowel // 이중 ~ a diphthong // 전설(前舌) ~ a front vowel // 중성 ~ a mixed [neutral] vowel // 후설 ~ a back vowel // ~화하다 vocalize.
● **모음 변화** vowel gradation; mutation; modification. **모음조화** vowel harmony.
모의(模擬·摸擬) imitation; copy. ¶~의 imitation / sham / mimic / mock.
● **모의국회** a mock assembly. **모의 법정** a moot [mock] court. **모의시험 / 모의고사** a trial run of an examination; a sham [trial] examination. **모의전**(-戰) a sham fight [battle]; (a) mock [mimic] battle; a dry run.

모의(謀議) conference; consultation; deliberation; conspiracy(음모). ¶공동 ~ (a) joint conspiracy//정부를 전복하려는 ~가 발각되었다 A plot to overthrow the government was uncovered [brought to light]. **모의하다** plot [conspire] together; confer; consult together; [의논하다] hold counsel; deliberate on [over] (a matter). ¶반란을 ~ conspire to rise in revolt//그들은 대통령 암살을 모의했다 They conspired [plotted] to assassinate the President. / They plotted the assassination of the President.

모이 feed. ¶닭 ~ chicken feed//새 ~ bird feed / birdseed(식물의 씨)//암탉에게 ~를 주다 feed hens.
● **모이주머니** [동] a crop; a craw.
모이다 1 [몰려들다] gather [flock] (together); come [get] together; crowd; swarm; cluster. ¶…의 둘레에 ~ gather [crowd / flock / swarm / cluster] about [around] …//구석에 옹기종기 ~ huddle up in a corner//그 다방은 학생들이 자주 모이는 곳이다 The coffee shop is a favorite haunt of students.//학생들은 한데 모여서 승차해야 한다 Pupils should get on the train [bus] together.//사고 현장에 사람들이 모여 있었다 A crowd gathered [collected] at the scene of the accident.//자동차 주위에 많은 사람들이 모여 있다 There is a crowd of people around the car.//문 앞에 모이지 마세요 Don't gather [crowd] around the doorway.//그들은 각자 그 사건의 정보를 수집하여 한곳에 모였다 They got together, each bringing some information about the incident.//아이들이 놀이터에 모였다 The children gathered on the playground.//모여서 그것을 의논하자 Let's get together and discuss it.//대표들은 회의실에 모였다 The delegates met [assembled] in the conference room.//모인 사람들은 모두 그 제안에 찬성했다 Those present were all in favor of the proposal.//많은 사람들이 광장에 모였다 A large number of people massed in the square.
2 [회동하다] meet; assemble; congregate. ¶회의하려고 ~ meet [assemble] for a meeting//모인 사람이 많다 have a large attendance//어디로 모일까 Where shall we meet?
3 [걷히다] be collected [gathered]. ¶모인 돈 the collected money / the money collected//모금으로 모인 돈이 20만 원이었다 The money collected [Contributions] amounted to 200,000 won. / Two hundred thousand won was collected through the campaign.
4 [쌓이다] be saved [accumulated]; accumulate. ¶돈을 모으려고 해도 모이지 않는다 Although I try to save money, it just won't accumulate.
5 [집중되다] center (on / in / at); focus (on / at). ¶세상의 이목이 그에게 모였다 All eyes were turned on him. / He was the focus [center] of public attention.//인구는 도시에 모이는 경향이 있다 Population tends to concentrate in cities.//정부 기관들은 서울에 모여 있다 Government offices are concentrated in Seoul.

모인(某人) a certain person; Mr. So-and-so.
모일(某日) a certain day; one day. ¶~ 모시에 on a certain hour of a certain day.
모임 [회합] a meeting; [회동] a gathering; [집단] a group; (동호인의) a set; [파티] a

모자

party; [비공식적인 회합] a get-together(스포츠 등의); (미) a meet; (영) a meeting; an assembly; a congregation; a party. ¶첫 ~ the first meeting / 가족의 ~ a family gathering // 식후의 ~ an after-dinner get-together // 동급생의 ~ a class meeting[reunion] (▶ reunion은 졸업 후의) // 새 임원의 ~ a meeting of the new members of the board // 원예 애호가의 ~ a group of amateur gardeners / 요트 동호인의 ~ the yachting set / ~이 있다 hold a meeting / A meeting will be held.

모자(母子) mother and child. ¶~의 정 maternal and filial affection / ~가 다 건재하다 Mother and child are doing well.
● **모자 보건법** the Mother and Child Health Law.

모자(帽子) a hat(테 있는); a cap(챙 달린); a bonnet(여자용); a hunting[sporting] cap(사냥모); a derby (hat)(중산모); a soft[felt] hat; (영) a bowler; (집합적) headgear. ¶~의 테 the brim of a hat / 테가 넓은 ~ a broad[wide-] brimmed hat / ~을 손에 들고 hat in hand // ~를 쓰다 don[put on] a hat / get a hat on // ~를 벗다 take off[doff / remove] one's hat / unhat / uncap / uncover // ~를 써 보다 try on a hat / ~를 씌우다 hat [cap] (a person) / ~를 쓴 채로 있다 keep one's hat[cap] on / ~를 벗고 남에게 인사하다 raise [lift / take off] one's hat to a person // ~를 벗기다 unhat[uncap] (a person) / ~를 쓰지 않고 있다 be bareheaded / be without a hat / ~를 삐딱하게 쓰다 cock one's hat / wear one's hat on one side / ~를 젖혀 쓰다 wear one's hat on the back of one's head // ~를 푹 눌러 쓰다 wear one's hat deep / pull one's hat down over one's eyes // ~를 벗으시오(주의시키는 말) Off with your hat. / Please remove hats. / Take hats off. / Hats off. / 노부인에게 ~를 벗고 인사했다 I raised his hat to the old lady. // 그는 ~ 도 쓰지 않고 나가 버렸다 He went out bareheaded [without his hat].
● **모자걸이** a hat hanger; a hat rack; (벽에 붙어 있는) a hatrail; a hatstand; a hat tree; [못] a hat peg[hook].

모자라다 1 [부족하다] be not enough; be insufficient[deficient]; lack; want; be lacking[wanting / short of]; [만족스럽지 못하다] (사물이) be unsatisfactory; be not gratifying; be not (good) enough; (사람이) dissatisfied (with); be discontented (with). ¶역량이 ~ be wanting in ability / be incapable / 일손이 ~ be short of hands / be short-handed // 지식이 ~ have only a poor [scanty] knowledge // 돈이 모자라게 될 것 같다 We may run short of money. // 는 1만 원이 모자란다 I am ten thousand won short. // 요즘 공장에서는 일손이 모자란다 These days factories are shorthanded [are short of help]. / 한 달에서 3일이 모자란다 It is three days short of a month. // 나는 요구하는 연령에 2개월이 모자란다 I am two months under the required age. // 의자가 2개 모자란다 We need two more chairs. / 너는 경험이 모자란다 You are lacking in experience. / You don't have enough experience. / 이 작품에는 뭔가 모자라는 데가 있다 This work leaves something to be desired [lacks something]. // 우리 서로 모자라는 것을 보충해서 함께 일합시다 Let's work together, each of us making up for what the other lacks. / We ought to complement each other's efforts. // 그는 상상력이 모자라는 사람이다 He is lacking[wanting] in imagination. / He has very little imagination. // 그는 교사로서 조금 모자라는 데가 있었다 He lacks something as a teacher. // 그의 답은 약간 모자란 데가 있었다 His answer left something to be desired. / His answer was not entirely satisfactory. // 능력이 모자라는 학생은 그의 강의를 따라가지 못한다 Students without much ability cannot follow his lectures. // 이것은 1그램 모자란다 This is one gram short. // 그는 인내심이 모자란다 He lacks[is lacking in] patience. // 그는 대학자이긴 하나 일상의 일에는 좀 모자란 데가 있다 Though he is a great scholar, he is childish [something is missing up there] when it comes to everyday matters. // 그는 90점에서 조금 모자라는 점수를 땄다 His mark was a little short of ninety.

2 [지능이 낮다] dull-[half-] witted; stupid; dull(-brained).(▶ dull은 이해력·사고력이 부족하며, stupid는 지능이 떨어짐의 의미) ¶좀 모자란 사람 a dull[slow-witted] person // 그는 좀 모자란다 He is a little wanting [somewhat weak] in the head.

모자반 [식] a gulfweed; a sargasso (weed).
모자이크 a mosaic. ¶~식의 건물 바닥 a mosaic floor.
모작(模作) an imitation; an imitation work. ¶피카소의 ~ an imitation of Picasso[Picasso's work].
모정(母情) maternal love[affection]; a mother's love.
모정(慕情) longing (for); yearning (for / after); love; affection. ¶그녀는 선생님에게 아련한 ~을 품고 있었다 She was slightly infatuated with[rather fancied] her teacher. / She had a slight infatuation for her teacher.
모조(模造) [모방하여 만듦] imitation. ¶~의 imitation / counterfeit / faked(-up) / sham / artificial(인조의). **모조하다** imitate; copy (from); reproduce (from); counterfeit; fake.
● **모조 보석** imitation jewelry; fake(d) stones. **모조지** imitation vellum; vellum (paper). **모조 진주** an imitation pearl. **모조품** an imitation; a sham; a counterfeit; a fake; a replica; (미국 속어) a phon(e)y (pl. -nies, -neys). ¶이 다이아몬드 반지는 ~이다 This diamond ring is a fake.
모조리 all; without exception; to the very last; wholly; altogether; thoroughly; completely. ¶~ 가져가다 take away everything (one can lay hands on) // ~ 검거하다 make a wholesale arrest (of the gangsters) // ~ 털어놓다 make a clean breast of (a matter) // 나는 보석을 ~ 도둑맞았다 All my jewels were stolen. // 값나가는 것은 ~ 도난당했다 Everything of value was stolen. // 홍수로 집이고 작물이고 ~ 유실되었다 Houses and crops were all washed away by the flood. // 그는 생각하고 있는 것을 ~ 이야기했다 He told everything he had been thinking. / He spoke all his thoughts [his whole mind]. // 나는 그녀가 몰래 결혼한 사실에 대해 ~ 이야기했다 I passed on every last bit of news about her secret marriage. // 집 안에 있는 물건을 ~ 도

둑맞았다 The burglar stole [cleaned out] everything in the house. / Every single thing in the house was stolen.∥네가 꺼림칙하게 생각하는 것을 ~ 이야기하면 기분이 후련해질 것이다 You will feel easier if you make a clean breast of it.

모종(-種) [농] a seedling; (나무의) a sapling; a young plant [tree]; a nursery tree. ¶**고구마 ~** a sweet potato cutting∥**토마토 ~** a tomato seedling. **모종하다** plant [transplant] a seedling; bed out seedlings; plant out. ¶팬지를 ~ plant pansy seedlings.
● **모종삽** a (garden) trowel.

모종(某種) a certain kind. ¶**~의** a certain / some / unnamed∥**~의 이유로** for a certain reason∥**~의 혐의를 받고 있다** be [lie] under some suspicion.

모주(母酒) 〔찌꺼 술〕 crude [raw] liquor; 〔재강〕 lees; dregs.
● **모주망태** a (confirmed) drunkard; a heavy [hard] drinker; a souse; a (drunken) sot.

모지다 1 angle; be angular. ⇨ *모나다* 1·2 ¶ 그는 모지지 않은 사람이다 He has well-rounded corners. 2 → 모질다

모지랑붓 a worn-out writing brush.
모지랑비 a worn-out [stumpy] broom.
모지랑이 something worn to a stump; a stump.

모직(물)(毛織物) woolen stuff [goods]; (천) woolen fabric [cloth]. ¶~을 입고 있다 be dressed in woolen.

모질다 1 〔잔인하다〕 ruthless; cruel; atrocious; harsh; hardhearted; merciless; wicked; pitiless; brutal. ¶모진 사람 a wicked / a wicked man / a hardhearted [coldblooded] person∥모질게 대하다 treat (a person) badly [harshly] / be hard [rough / severe] on (a person)∥마음을 모질게 먹고(다시는 그런 짓을 하지 않도록) 귀여운 아들을 호되게 벌주었다 I hardened [steeled] myself and punished my dear son severely (so that he wouldn't do the same thing again).
2 〔억세다〕 patient; persevering; tenacious; unremitting; long-suffering. ¶모진 목숨 one's contemptible life / one's wretched [miserable] life / one's hard [heavy] lot∥모진 목숨을 어쩌지 못하다 have to bear one's wretched life / cannot escape one's contemptible existence∥불행을 모질게 견디다 bear one's misfortune with stoical fortitude ∥이가 아픈 것을 모질게 참다 bear (the) toothache patiently∥모진 목숨이 아직도 붙어 있소 I am still prolonging this damned life of mine.
3 〔매섭고 사납다〕 violent; strong; fierce; furious; hard; bitter. ¶모진 비바람 a violent [heavy] storm∥모진 추위 severe [intense / bitter] cold.

모집(募集) 1 (군인 등의) levy; enlistment; recruitment; recruiting. ¶~**에 응하다** enlist (as a volunteer) / respond to [answer] the call for recruits∥그는 군인 ~에 응했다 He enlisted as a soldier. **모집하다** levy; enlist; enroll; recruit; muster.
2 (지원자 등의) invitation; collection; registration(학생의). ¶~**에 응하다** respond to an invitation / apply for the position offered∥**~을 마감하다** close the list∥**학생 ~을 시작하다** [마감하다] open [close] registration of students∥**타자원 ~** 《광고》 Wanted: Typists. / Typists Wanted.∥**점원 ~** 《광고》 Clerks wanted. / Wanted: (store) clerks.∥**학생 ~** 《광고》 New students invited.∥**회원 ~** 《광고》 New members asked [invited] to join.∥**현상 논문의 ~은 내일 시작된다** [마감된다] They will open [close] the essay contest tomorrow. **모집하다** invite; collect; raise; advertise for(광고를 내어). ¶**사무원을 ~** invite applications for the position of clerk∥**입찰자를 ~** invite fresh bidders∥**회원을 ~** collect [raise] members∥**현상 소설을 ~** open a prize list for novels / start [run] a prize contest for stories∥**그의 일은 클럽의 새 회원을 모집하는 일이었다** His task was to recruit new members for the club.∥**우리 학교에서는 입학 지원자를 모집하고 있다** Our school is accepting applications for admission.
3 (공채(公債) 등의) flotation (of a public loan); subscription (for). ¶**주식의 ~에 응하다** subscribe for shares [stocks]∥**공채의 ~에 응하다** take up a loan / apply [subscribe] for a loan∥**공채를 ~ 중이다** Subscriptions are invited. **모집하다** float; raise; place (for subscription). ¶**총액 …의 공채를 ~** invite subscriptions for a loan to the amount of ….
● **모집 광고** advertisement; (개개의) a want ad. ¶**점원 ~** an advertisement for shop clerks [《영》 assistants]. **모집 인원** a volume of recruitment; the number (of students) to be admitted [accepted].

모집단(母集團) 〔수〕 a population; a universe.
모채(募債) loan flotation; the flotation [raising] of a loan. **모채하다** float [raise / issue] a loan.
● **모채 가격** the issue price. **모채액** the amount of a loan.

모처(某處) a certain [an undisclosed] place; somewhere. ¶**서울의 ~에서** somewhere in Seoul.

모처럼 1 〔오래간만에〕 after a long time [interval / silence / absence / separation]; (고대했던) long-awaited; much-awaited. ¶**~ 맞은 좋은 날씨** the first fine day in a long time / fine weather after a long spell of rain ∥**~의 휴일** the first holiday in a long time / a long-awaited holiday∥**~ 찾아오다** take the trouble to pay a visit after a long interval ∥**~ 오는 것이니 이번에는 좀 더 쉬었다 가게** Stay a little longer this time, as you do not come often.∥**~ 맞은 휴일인데 비 때문에 망쳤다** The rain spoiled the much-awaited holiday.∥**그녀는 비 때문에 ~의 나들이옷이 엉망이 되었다** The rain spoiled her best clothes, which she had put on especially for the occasion.∥**~의 기회를 이용하는 것이었는데** You should have taken advantage of such a rare opportunity.
2 〔벼른 끝에〕 at great pains(수고스럽게); especially(특별히); with (much) trouble [effort]; (각별히) specially; on purpose; expressly. ¶**그가 ~ 한 일이 실패로 끝나다니 정말 안됐다** What a pity that he should have failed after such great labor!∥**친구가 ~ 권하여 승낙했다** I agreed at the pressing insistence of my friend.∥**~ 그가 찾아왔는데 공교롭게 내가 집을 비웠다** He had come all the way to see me but unfortunately I was out.∥**~ 여기까지 왔으니 정상까지 오르자** Since we have come this far, let's climb up to the summit.∥**그의 실책으로 ~ 애쓴 일이**

모체

헛수고가 되었다 All our efforts came to nothing because of his blunder.

모체(母體) [어머니의 몸] the mother's body; the mother; (주체) the parent body; the parent; (이끼·균류의) a matrix. ¶선거의 ~ an electorate / (미) the electoral college(대통령의)//~를 보호하기 위하여 for the health of the mother//태아를 꺼내지 않으면 ~가 위태롭다 Unless the fetus is extracted, the mother's life is in danger.//이 협회는 ~에서 선출된 멤버로 구성되어 있다 This association is made up of members selected from the parent organization.

● **모체 발아**(一發芽) [식] viviparity. **모체 전염** hereditary transmission.

모춤 [농] a bunch of rice seedlings; bundled rice seedlings.

모충(毛蟲) a hairy caterpillar; a wooly bear (caterpillar).

모친(母親) a mother; a female parent. ¶~께서는 안녕하십니까 How is your mother?

● **모친상** mourning for one's mother; one's mother's death. ¶~을 당하다 have one's mother die / lose one's mother / be bereaved of one's mother.

모태(母胎) the mother's womb[uterus]; (발생·생성의) the matrix. ¶~ 내에서의 발육 불충분 defective intrauterine development//~내의 생명 an antenatal life//서민 문화의 ~ the matrix[wellspring / cradle] of popular culture of the common people.

모터 a motor; [발동기] an engine. ¶~를 돌리다 [멈추다] start[turn off / stop / cut off] a motor//~가 돌고 있다 The motor[engine] is running.

● **모터보트** a motorboat; a powerboat(▶ 강력한 모터가 붙어 있는 것). **모터사이클** a motorcycle.

모텔 [자동차 여행자용 숙박소] a motel; an auto court.

모토 [신조·좌우명·표어] motto (pl. ~s, ~es). ¶…하는 것을 ~로 하다 make it one's motto to do//그의 ~는 인내다 Patience is his motto.

모퉁이 a corner; a turn; a turning. ¶~의 가게 a corner shop / a shop at[on] the corner//~ 땅 a corner lot//~를 돌아서 세 번째 집 the third house round the corner//~를 돌다 turn[take / go round] a corner / round the corner//그 집은 ~에 있다 The house stands on the corner.//세 번째 ~에서 왼쪽으로 돌아가시오. Turn (to the) left at the third corner. / Take the third turning to the left.//~에서 두 번째 집이 한 씨의 집이다 The second house around[from] the corner is Mr. Han's.//~에 공중전화가 있다 There is a (public) telephone booth at the corner.

● **모퉁잇돌** [건] a corner[an angle] stone.

모티프 [예][음] a motif; a motive.

모판(一板) [농] a rice seedbed; a nursery; a seed plot.

모포(毛布) a blanket; a rug. ⇨ 담요

모표(帽標) a cap-badge; the badge on a cap.

모피(毛皮) a fur(부드러운); a fell; a skin(거친); a pelt(생가죽). ¶~로 만든 외투 a fur(-lined) overcoat / a mink coat//~ 외투를 입은 부인 a lady in furs / a fur coated lady//그녀는 ~ 옷을 입고 있다 She is wearing a fur. / She is wrapped in furs.

● **모피상** a furrier; a fur trader. **모피 외투** a fur coat; a fur-lined overcoat. **모피 제품** a fur piece; (집합적) furs.

모필(毛筆) [붓] a writing brush; [화필] a paint brush; a hairbrush; a hair pencil(수채화용).

● **모필화** a hair-pencil picture; a wash drawing.

모함(謀陷) false incrimination; a plot to entrap (a person). ¶~에 빠지다 fall into a trap (snare) / be entrapped[ensnared] / be caught in a trap. **모함하다** intrigue against (a person); falsely incriminate; frame (up); entrap; ensnare. ¶남을 모함하려다가 자기가 판 함정에 빠지다 be caught in one's own trap / be hoist with one's own petard//그는 나를 기회 있을 때마다 모함하려 했다 He never lost an opportunity to set a trap for me.

모항(母港) a (ship's) home port.

모해(謀害) a plot[scheme] to do harm. **모해하다** plot to do harm (to a person).

모험(冒險) an adventure; a venture; a risky [hazardous] attempt; a hazard; a risk. ¶연속 ~ a cliff-hanger//~을 좋아하는 사람 an adventurous person / a lover of adventure//~ 삼아 해 보다 take[try] one's chance / venture in (an enterprise)//목숨을 걸고 ~을 하다 risk one's life//그건 좀 ~이 아닐까 걱정이 된다 I'm afraid that is rather risky[hazardous].//나는 ~을 할 생각이 나지 않았다 I didn't feel like taking a chance [running the risk].//그것은 ~이라고 생각하지 않나요 Don't you think it's a little too hazardous?//다소의 ~이 필요하다 Some risk must be run. **모험하다** venture; risk; run a risk[hazard]; make a venture; take chances[a chance]. ¶목숨을 걸고 ~ stake [venture] one's life / risk one's neck.

● **모험가** an adventurer. **모험담** a tale of adventure; an adventure story. ¶~을 늘어놓다 relate one's adventure. **모험 소설** an adventure novel[story]. **모험심** an adventurous[a venturesome] spirit; the spirit of adventure.

모험적(冒險的) adventurous. ¶~ 정신 an adventurous[a venturesome] spirit//~인 adventurous / risky / hazardous//~으로 adventurously / at a venture//~인 사업 a hazardous enterprise / [투기] a speculation.

모형(母型) (활자의) a matrix (pl. -trices).

모형(模型) a model; (기계 등) a pattern; (주조의) a mold. ¶…의 석고 ~ a gypsum model of …//인체의 ~ a model of the human body / (화가·재단사의) a lay figure//소(小)~ a miniature//실용 ~ (기계의) a working model//축척 ~ a scale model//실물 크기 ~ a life-size model / a (full-scale) mock-up//~을 만들다 make a model (of).

● **모형도** a model picture. **모형 비행기** a model plane. **모형 지도** a relief map; a (three-dimensional) model map.

모호하다(模糊─) dim; vague; faint; obscure; ambiguous; equivocal. ¶모호하게 dimly / obscurely / indistinctly / in a haze//모호한 태도 a dubious[an uncertain] attitude//모호한 말을 하다 speak ambiguously / use ambiguous expression[language]//모호하게 대답하다 give a vague[dubious] answer//모호한 태도를 취하다 take an equivocal [dubious] attitude//그는 일부러 모호하게 대

답했다 He deliberately gave an evasive [a vague] answer.∥그것에 대해서는 모호한 기억밖에 없다 I have only a dim [hazy] recollection of it.

모회사(母會社) a parent company [corporation].

목 1 [모가지] a neck. ¶길고 가느다란 ~ a long, slender neck∥굵고 짧은 ~ a thick bullneck∥~이 굵은[가는] thick-[thin-]necked∥가는 ~ a delicate neck [bullneck]∥**~이 뻣뻣하다** have a stiff neck∥**~에 매달리다** hang on (a person's) neck∥**~을 끌어안다** throw both arms round (a person's) neck∥**~을 자르다** cut off (a person's) head/behead∥**~을 조르다** grip (a person's) throat/strangle (a person) to death∥**~을 졸라 죽이다** strangle (a person) to death∥**~을 비틀다** wring (a fowl's) neck/wring the neck (of a chicken)∥**~을 찌르다** stab[jab] in the throat/pierce (a person's) neck (with a spear)∥죄인의 ~을 치다 behead [decapitate] a criminal∥그는 행렬을 보려고 ~을 길게 뺐다 He stretched [craned] his neck to see the procession.∥그는 그녀의 ~을 졸라 죽였다 He strangled her.∥그는 ~을 매어 죽었다 He hanged himself.∥그는 ~이 졸려 죽었다 He was strangled to death.∥너를 ~이 빠지도록 기다리고 있다 I have been waiting for you for ages.∥그녀는 그의 ~에 매달렸다 She threw her arms around [She hung on] his neck.∥그는 갑자기 창밖으로 ~을 내밀었다 He popped his head out of the window.∥그녀는 ~을 움츠렸다 She shrugged her shoulders.

2 [직책·목숨]. ¶**~이 떨어지다** be dismissed/(미국 구어) be fired/(영국 구어) get [receive] the sack∥그 녀석은 아직 ~이 붙어 있다 He has not been dismissed [fired] yet.

3 a throat; a gullet. ⇨**²목구멍** ¶**~이 메다** be choked (with)∥**~이 쉬다** get [become] hoarse [husky/harsh]∥**~을 따다** cut one's throat∥**~을 축이다** appease [quench] one's thirst/(구어) wet one's whistle [lips]∥물로 ~을 축이다 quench one's thirst with water∥**~이 마르다** I am [feel] thirsty.∥**~이 아프다** I have a sore throat.∥**~이 쉬었다** I've lost my voice.∥**~에 가시가 걸렸다** A bone struck in my throat.∥**~이 메어 물을 마셔야겠다** I am choking. I'll have to drink some water.∥나는 급히 밥을 먹어 ~이 멨다 I swallowed the rice so hurriedly that I choked [that it stuck in my throat].

4 [물건의] the narrow part; the throat. ¶병~ the bottleneck/the neck of a bottle∥버선~ the ankle of a sock∥길~ a narrowing [squeeze/bottleneck] in a road/a key position (on the road)/a strategic point∥여울~ the narrow throat of a stream.

5 [요소] an important point [place]; a strategic point. ¶~이 좋아야 장사가 잘된다 The locality brings a great deal of business.

목에 핏대를 세우다 [노하다·흥분하다] be angered [enraged/offended]; get [become] angry (with/at); be excited; be highly strung.

목에 힘을 주다 mount one's [the] high horse; act high and mighty.

목이 날아가다 [파면되다] be dismissed [discharged]; get the boot; get the sack; be fired. ¶목이 날아가지 않도록 노력하다 make effort to retain [preserve/remain in] one's employment.

목(을) 자르다 [면직하다·해고하다] dismiss; (미국 구어) fire; (영국 구어) give a person the sack; sack.

목(이) 잘리다 (미) get fired; get a pink slip; get one's walking papers; (영) get the sack.

목(이) 잠기다 get [become/grow] hoarse [husky/harsh]; hoarsen; lose one's voice. ¶목이 잠기도록 말하다 talk oneself hoarse∥너무 소리 질러 ~ shriek oneself hoarse.

목(目) **1** [항목] an item; a subitem; a division; a class; [분류학상의 단위] an order. ¶같은 ~의 동물[식물] co-ordinal animal [plant] (▶ 식물학에서는 -ales, 동물학에서는 -acea를 붙여 목을 표시함). **2** (바둑의) a piece (돌); a cross (집). ¶10~ 이기다[지다] win [lose] by ten crosses∥5~ 놓다[놓게 하다] take [give] odds of five crosses.

목가적(牧歌的) pastoral; bucolic. ¶~ 풍경 pastoral scenery.

목각(木刻) **1** [나무에 새김] wood carving; woodcraft; [그 작품] a wood carving. **목각하다** carve [engrave] wood; make a woodcarving [woodcut]. ¶목각한 곰 a bear carved in wood/a wooden bear. **2** a woodcut. ⇨**²목각화**(⇨목각) **3** a block letter. ⇨목각 활자(⇨목각)

● **목각술** woodcraft. **목각 인형** a wooden doll; a doll carved in wood. **목각화**(-畫) a woodcut; a wood-block print; a wood print; a wood engraving. **목각 활자** a block letter.

목간(沐間) a bathroom. ⇨**²목욕간**(⇨목욕)

● **목간통** a bathtub; a bath basin.

목걸이 a necklace; a necklet; a rivière(보석); a choker (목에 꼭 끼는 짧은 것); (개의) collar. ¶진주~를 두르다 wear a pearl necklace.∥~를 달다 put a collar on (a dog).

목검(木劍) a singlestick; a wooden sword (for practice).

목격(目擊) observation; witnessing; sighting. **목격하다** witness; see with one's own eyes; observe. ¶나는 끔찍한 광경을 목격했다 I witnessed [was a witness to] a horrible scene.∥나는 그들의 참상을 목격했다 I witnessed their misery.∥나는 두 사나이가 싸우고 있는 것을 목격했다 I witnessed the two men fighting.∥나는 그가 호주머니에서 권총을 꺼내는 것을 목격했다 I saw him take a revolver out of his pocket with my own eyes. ➔**목격되다** come under one's yes [notice/observation].

● **목격자** an eyewitness; a witness; an observer. ¶~의 이야기 an eye-witness's(') account/a firsthand account∥~의 대질(경찰에서의) an identification parade/a choice of faces/a lineup.

목공(木工) woodwork(공예); a woodworker(사람); (목수) a carpenter.

● **목공 기술** carpentry; woodcraft. **목공소** a carpenter's shop [plant]; a woodworking plant. **목공품** woodwork.

목관(木棺) [나무로 짠 관] a wooden coffin.

목관 악기(木管樂器) a woodwind (instrument); (집합적) the woodwind.

목구멍 a throat; a gullet(식도); a windpipe(기관). ¶**~이 아프다** have a sore throat∥**~이 막히다** be choked (with)∥그 말이 ~까지 나왔었다 The word was (just) on [at] the tip of my tongue.∥**~에 가시가 박혔다** A bone

stuck in my throat.∥그녀는 너무 상심하여 밥을 ~을 넘어가지 않았다[식욕을 잃었다] She was so heartbroken[dejected] that she lost her appetite.∥너무 빨리 먹어서 음식이 ~에 걸린 것 같았다 I ate too fast and the food felt as if it was stuck in my (o)esophagus.
  목구멍이 포도청이다(속담) The hungry belly has no ears.; A full belly counsels well.
  목구멍에 풀칠하다 barely make (both) ends meet; live from hand to mouth.
목금(木琴) a xylophone. ⇨실로폰
목기(木器) a wooden container; a vessel made of wood; wooden tableware.
목다리(木—) (a pair of) crutches; a crutch. ¶~를 짚고 걷다 walk[go] on crutches.
목단(牧丹) [식] a (tree) peony. ⇨모란
목덜미 the nape[back / scruff] of the neck. ¶고운 ~ a charming nape∥~를 붙잡다 seize [grab] (a person) by the collar∥~가 춥다 The back of my neck feels cold.∥그는 소년의 ~를 잡았다 He seized the boy by the scruff of his neck.
목도 carrying (a weight) with a pole[poles] jointly shouldered by two[four] persons. **목도하다** shoulder (a weight) by the use of poles.
목도(目睹) observation; witnessing. ⇨목격
목도리 a (neck) scarf; a muffler; (긴 털실로 만든) a comforter; a (neck) wrap; a boa; a neckerchief; (모피의) a neckpiece. ¶~를 하고 with a muffler (a)round one's neck∥~를 하다 wear a muffler.
목돈(뭉칫돈) a (good) round sum; a sizable [tidy] sum[amount] (of money). ¶~으로 백만 원 a (good) round sum of one million won∥~을 좀 만들다 scrape together some money∥~을 만들 수가 없다 I can't make up the sum.∥천만 원의 ~으로 만들어 주마 I will make it up to 10,000,000 won.
목동(牧童) a young ranch hand; a cow boy; (미) a cowpuncher; a herdboy; (양의) a shepherd boy; (소의) a young cowherd.
목련(木蓮) [식] a (lily) magnolia; a cucumber tree. ¶백~ a white magnolia.
목례(目禮) a nod; nodding. ¶~를 주고받다 exchange nods. **목례하다** nod (to); give (a person) a nod; recognize; greet with one's eyes.
목로(木櫨) a long and narrow table in a public house; a counter; a bar; a stand.
  ● **목로주점 / 목로술집 / 목롯집** a tavern; a bar; a public house; (영국 구어) a pub.
목록(目錄) (상품·장서(藏書)의) a catalog; (영) a catalogue; (재산·상품의) an inventory. ¶물품 ~ a list of articles∥재산 ~ an inventory∥신간 서적 ~ a list[catalog(ue)] of new books[publications]∥카드식 ~ a card catalogue∥~을 만들다 make a list[an inventory] (of articles) / list / catalog / (영) catalogue∥장서의 ~을 만들다 catalogue a library∥~에 올리다[싣다] catalogue (articles) / put[place] (an item) on[in] the catalogue∥~작품 ~을 만들다 make a list of one's works / list one's works.
목마(木馬) 1 [목제의 말] a wooden horse; [흔들 목마] a rocking horse; a hobbyhorse. [회전 ~] a merry-go-round / (영) a roundabout / (미) a carousel. 2 (기계 체조용) a vaulting horse. ¶~를 타다 vault a horse.

목마르다 1 [갈증 나다] thirsty; (서술적) be [feel / get] thirsty; have a dry throat. ¶나는 ~ I am[feel] thirsty.∥산책을 하고 나니 목말랐다 I felt dry after my walk.∥그는 탈 듯이 목말랐다 He was parched with thirst. 2 [갈망하다] be thirsty after[for / of] (knowledge); have a thirst for (money, knowledge, etc.); thirst[crave / yearn] for (money); hunger for (knowledge, affection, etc.). ¶목마르게 기다린 비 long-awaited rain / the long-looked-for rain∥목마르게 기다리다 wait for (news) on tiptoe / be on the tiptoe of expectation / look forward to (something) with impatience.
목말 ¶~을 타다 ride on (another's) shoulders / ride pickaback (on a person)∥~을 태우다 mount[have / hold] (a child)[give (a child) a ride] on one's shoulders / have (a child) pickaback∥~ 태우고 가다 carry (a child) on one's shoulders / ride[carry] (a child) pickaback[piggyback]∥아버지의 ~을 탔던 일을 기억하고 있다 I remember riding on my father's shoulders.∥그는 아이를 ~ 태우고 갔다 He carried the child on his shoulders[piggyback / (영) pickaback].
목매달다 (남을) hang (a person); (스스로) hang oneself. ¶나무에 ~ hang oneself on a tree[down from a tree branch]∥대들보에 목매달아 죽다 hang oneself from a beam of one's house∥노인은 목매달아 죽었다 The old man hanged himself.∥그녀는 밧줄로 목매달아 죽어 있었다 She was hanging with a rope round her neck.
목메다 be choked[stifled / suffocated] (with / by). ¶목메어 우는 소녀 a sobbing girl / a girl choked with tears∥목메어 울다 sob / be choked with tears∥그녀는 목메어 울면서 이야기했다 She told her story with tears in her voice.
목면(木棉) 1 [식] a cotton plant. 2 cotton (cloth). ⇨무명
  ● **목면사** cotton yarn; cotton (thread).
목물 [흔부 목욕] a bust bath. **목물하다** take a bust bath.
목민(牧民) government (of people); governing the people. **목민하다** govern the people.
  ● **목민관** a governor; a magistrate.
목발(木—) a crutch. ¶~을 짚고 걷다 walk on crutches.
목본(木本) a tree; a woody plant; [식] an arbor (pl. -bores).
목부용(木芙蓉) [식] a cotton rosemallow.
목불인견(目不忍見) ¶~이다 cannot bear [endure] to see / be unable to bear[stand] the sight of / be too pitiful to look upon∥~의 참상이다 be too miserable[cruel] to look at / present a gruesome sight(살인 현장 등이)∥그 참상은 ~이었다 The tragic sight was simply appalling.
목뼈 the neck bone; the cervical vertebrae.
목사(牧師) a clergyman; (집합적) the clergy; [영국 국교의 교구 목사] a rector; a vicar; a curate; a pastor; (영국 국교 이외의 신교의) a minister (of the Gospel); a churchman; a cleric; [종군 목사] a chaplain. ¶~가 되다 become a clergyman / enter the ministry / (가톨릭·영국 국교에서) take (holy) orders / enter the Church∥그는 ~다 He is in holy orders.
목상(木像) a wooden image[statue / idol]; [목

우(木偶)] a wooden figure[doll]; a dummy.
목석(木石) [나무와 돌] trees and stones; [생명이 없는 물건] inanimate objects; stocks and stones. ¶~이 아니다 be sentient / be a sentient being〃나는 ~이 아니다 I am not a stock nor a stone. / I am made of flesh and blood.
목석같다(木石-) have no more feeling than a stone; be lost to sense. ¶목석같은 [무감각한] unimpressionable / insensible / unsusceptible / impassive / callous〃목석같은 사람 an unfeeling[a callous] person / stocks and stones〃그는 목석같은 사람이다 He is as unfeeling as a stone. / He has a heart of stone.
목선(木船) a wooden vessel[ship].
목성(木星) [천] Jupiter.
목소리 a voice; a tone (of voice). ¶가는 ~ a thin voice〃굵은 ~ a deep[full] voice〃큰 ~ a loud voice〃낮은 ~ a low voice / a whisper / a murmur〃아름다운 ~ a sweet [beautiful] voice〃맑은 ~ a clear[silvery / ringing] voice〃낭랑한 ~ a resonant [sonorous] voice〃쉰 ~ a husky[hoarse] voice〃새된[카랑카랑한] ~ a shrill [high-pitched] voice〃성난 ~ an angry voice〃듣기 싫은 ~ an ugly[a discordant] voice〃걸걸하고 귀에 거슬리는 ~ a harsh, grating voice〃~가 큰[부드러운] loud[soft-] spoken〃~가 들리는[들리지 않는] 곳에 within[out of / beyond] hearing[earshot]〃작은[낮은] ~로 in a low voice / in a quiet tone / in an undertone / in whispers〃(talk) low〃슬픈 ~로 in a sad voice / in accents of grief〃큰 ~로 in[with] a loud voice / in a high voice / loudly / loud〃우레 같은 ~로 in a voice of thunder / in a very loud[[문어] stentorian / thunderous] voice〃한~로 in unison[chorus] / with one voice〃상냥한 ~로 in a tender[sweet] voice / in a soft [gentle] tone〃한껏 큰 ~로 at the top of one's voice〃~를 낮추어서 in whispers / under one's breath〃~가 좋다 have a sweet [fine / musical] voice〃~가 나쁘다 have a poor voice〃~가 안 나오다 one's voice fails / lose one's voice / be out of voice〃~가 쉬다 one's voice becomes husky[hoarse]〃~가 쉬도록 외치다 shout oneself hoarse〃큰[낮은] ~로 말하다 speak in a loud[low] voice〃떨리는 ~로 in a quivering[trembling / quavering / tremulous] voice〃떨리는 ~로 노래하다 sing in a tremulous[quavering] voice〃~를 높이다 raise[lift] one's voice〃~를 낮추다 lower[drop / sink] one's voice〃~를 쥐어짜다 strain one's voice〃~를 삼키다 swallow one's voice〃~를 트이게 하다 improve[cultivate] one's voice〃남의 ~를 알아듣다 recognize another's voice〃그녀는 ~가 곱다 She has a sweet[pleasant] voice.〃그 여자는 전화 ~가 곱다 She has a sweet[melodious] voice on the phone.〃그는 ~가 상냥하다[거칠다] He is gentle[rough] in voice.〃그녀의 ~는 잘 들린다 Her voice carries well.〃아들 녀석의 ~가 변하기 시작했다 My son's voice has begun to change.〃무서워서 ~가 나오지 않았다 My voice was frozen with horror.
목수(木手) a carpenter. ¶도~ a master [boss] carpenter〃엉터리 ~ a hack [novice / clumsy / bungling] carpenter〃배 만드는 ~ a ship's carpenter.

목수가 많으면 집을 무너뜨린다(속담) Too many cooks spoil the broth.
●**목수 일** carpenter's work; carpentry; carpentering. ¶~을 하다 carpenter / do carpentering.
목숨 life. ¶귀한 ~ one's most precious life / one's dear(est) life〃천한 ~ one's abject life / one's wretched[dammed] life〃모진 ~ / 초로 같은 ~ a dewdrop-like[transitory] life [existence] / a frail life〃~이 붙어 있는 한 as long as one lives[life lasts]〃~ 다음으로 소중하다 be next to one's life[heart] / be heart's blood〃~이 끊어지다 breathe one's last / be dead〃~이 질기다 have nine lives〃~이 붙어 있다 one's life is spared / still live〃~이 다할 때까지 싸우다 fight to the last drop of one's blood〃~이 아깝다 one's life is dear (to one) / hold one's life dear〃~이 위태롭다 be in peril of one's life〃~을 건지다 escape[get away / get out] alive[with one's life] / escape death / be saved (from death) / survive(살아남다)〃위기일발에서 ~을 건지다 have a narrow escape from death / escape narrowly[barely] with one's life〃~을 잃다 die / lose one's life〃~을 버리다 throw away[lay down] one's life / give (up) one's life (for) / die (for)〃~을 빼앗다 take (a person's) life / kill〃~을 빼앗기다 be [get] killed〃남의 ~을 구하다 save a person's life / save a person from death〃남의 ~을 살려 주다 spare a person's life〃~을 아까워하다 hold one's life dear〃~을 돌보지 않다 disregard one's life / set one's life at naught〃~을 부지하다 sustain[maintain] life〃~을 가볍게 여기다 slight one's life〃~을 소중히 여기다 value one's life / hold one's life dear〃~을 노리다 seek (a person's) life / plot (a person's) death / make an attempt on (a person's) life〃~을 이어 가다 support one's life / keep body and soul together / keep on living / subsist (on)〃~을 위태롭게 하다 endanger[imperil] (a person's) life〃~을 단축시키다 shorten one's life[days]〃그는 교통사고로 ~을 잃었다 He lost his life[was killed] in a traffic accident.〃사람의 ~은 이슬처럼 덧없다 Man's life is as transient as dew.〃그는 술 때문에 ~을 잃었다 Drinking was the cause of his death. / He lost his life because of drinking.〃그는 ~만은 살려 달라고 했다 He pleaded for his life.〃제발 ~만은 살려 주십시오 For mercy's sake spare me!〃그 사고로 열 사람이 ~을 잃었다 Ten people were killed[Ten lives were lost] in the accident.〃그는 겨울 산에서 ~을 잃었다 He lost his life in the mountains in winter.〃아버지는 뇌일혈로 쓰러지셨으나 겨우 ~만은 건지셨다 My father had a stroke and narrowly escaped death[but somehow he survived].〃어린이는 유괴되어 ~이 위태롭다 The child has been kidnapped and his life is in danger.〃그 남자는 대통령의 ~을 노리고 있었다 The man was planning to take the President's life. / The man was plotting to assassinate the President.〃그는 식당의 잔반으로 ~을 부지하고 있었다 He kept himself alive[sustained himself] on leftovers from restaurants.〃나는 이 그림을 내 ~ 다음으로 소중히 여긴다 I value this picture next to my life.〃의학의 발달로 사람의 ~이 연장되고 있다 Because of progress in science, our life

목쉬다

expectancy is lengthening. ¶~이 있는 한 회망이 있다 While there is life, there is hope.

목숨(을) 걸다 risk[hazard] one's life; risk one's neck. ¶목숨을 걸고 at the risk [hazard] of one's life / neck or nothing [naught] / desperately /목숨을 건 (a matter) of life and death / [필사의] desperate (efforts) / deadly (combat) /목숨을 건 사랑 love at the risk of one's life /목숨을 걸고 구하다 risk life and limb to save /목숨을 걸고 맹세하다 swear on[upon] one's life /그는 목숨을 걸고 당국의 결정에 항의했다 He protested against the authorities' decision at the risk of his life. /목숨을 걸고 비밀을 지킬 것을 맹세합니다 I swear on my life that I will keep the secret.

목숨(을) 끊다 (남의) take (a person's) life; kill; (스스로) take one's own life; kill oneself.

목숨(을) 바치다 offer[lay down / sacrifice] one's life. ¶나라를 위해 ~ offer[lay down / sacrifice] one's life for one's country / die for one's country /그들은 조국을 위해 목숨을 바쳤다 They gave their lives for their country.

목숨을 거두다 die; lose one's life.

목쉬다 become[get / grow] hoarse[husky / harsh]. ¶목쉰 소리 a hoarse[husky] voice / 목쉰 소리로 말하다 speak in a husky [hoarse] voice /목쉬도록 외치다 scream oneself hoarse (for help) /목쉬도록 지껄이다 talk oneself hoarse /당신 목쉬었군 You sound hoarse.

목양(牧羊) sheep-breeding[-farming / -raising]. **목양하다** raise[breed] sheep.

목양말(木洋襪) cotton socks[stockings].

목어(木魚) **1** [동] a hard-finned sandfish. ⇨도루묵 **2** a wooden fish (used by Buddhist priests). ¶~를 두드리다 sound[beat] a wooden fish. **3** [불] a (wood) block (in a Buddhist temple). ⇨목탁1.

목요일(木曜日) Thursday(약어 Thur(s).). ¶내주 [지난주] ~ next[last] Thursday / Thursday week.

목욕(沐浴) a bath; bathing; ablution. ¶~을 좋아하다 be fond of bath. **목욕하다** have [take] a bath; bathe; (영) bath; wash oneself; wash up; clean up; have a tub. ¶대충 [빨리] ~ have a short[quick] bath /천천히 ~ have a long bath /서둘러 ~ have a dip (in a bath) / take a hurried bath /(목욕탕에) 목욕하러 가다 go to the (public) bath / go to a bathhouse / go to take a bath /목욕하십시오 Take a bath, won't you? ➔**목욕시키다** give (a baby) a bath / bathe[(영) bath] (a baby).

●**목욕간** a bathroom. **목욕물** water for bath; bath (water). ¶~을 데우다 heat the bath / prepare a bath / get a bath ready // ~이 준비되었습니다 The bath is ready. // ~이 뜨겁다 The bath is too hot. // ~이 미지근하다 The bath is not warm enough. // ~이 상태가 어떻습니까 How is the bath? **목욕재계**(─齋戒) ablutions; a purification ceremony. **~하다** bathe one's body and purify oneself / perform[make] one's ablutions / ~하고 기도하다 offer prayers after purifying oneself [performing purification rites / performing one's ablutions]. **목욕탕** a bath; a bathhouse. ¶대중~ a public bath[bathhouse] // ~의 때밀이꾼 a bathhouse attendant / bath man[boy] // ~에 가다 go to the (public) bath. **목욕통** a bathtub. ¶~에 들어가다 soak in a bathtub / sink into a (hot) bath.

목자(牧者) **1** [양치기] a shepherd; [산양치기] a goatherd. **2** [가] a pastor; [성] [성직] a shepherd (of souls)(신자를 양으로 보고). ¶선한 ~ [성] the Good Shepherd(그리스도).

목작약(木芍藥) [식] a (tree) peony. ⇨모란

목장(牧場) a stock farm; [방목장] a pasture (ground); a pasturage; [목초지] a meadow; (미) a ranch. ¶~의 일꾼 a ranch hand / a cowhand // ~에 풀어 놓다 put[send / turn (out)] (cattle) to pasture // ~에서 일하다 work on a ranch[stock farm] // 소가 ~에서 풀을 뜯고 있다 Cows[Cattle] are grazing in the pasture.

●**목장주** the owner of a stock farm; a stock farmer; (미) a rancher.

목장갑(木掌匣) (a pair of) cotton work gloves.

목재(木材) wood; (건축용) (house) timber; (미) lumber; (집합적) timbering. ¶이 집은 수입한 ~로 건축되어 있다 This house is built with imported timber.

●**목재상** a lumberman; a timber[lumber] merchant. **목재소** a sawmill; a timber [lumber] mill. **목재 펄프** wood pulp.

목적(目的) a purpose; an object; an end (in view); [의도] a design; an intention; [목표] a goal. ¶주~ the[one's] central aim // 확고한 ~ a fixed[set] purpose / 공동의 ~ a common cause / 인생의 ~ an aim in[of] life // ~ 없는 purposeless / aimless // ~이 있는 purposeful / purposive (action); telic(al) // ~ 없이 for no purpose / without aim // …할 ~으로 with the object of doing / with a view[an eye] to doing / with the view of doing / for the purpose of doing // 이 ~으로 for this purpose / to this end / with this (end) in view / with this view / 군사상의 ~으로 for military purposes // 오로지 …을 ~으로 하여 with the sole object of ... / 무슨 ~으로 what for? / for what purpose / to what end? // ~에 걸맞다[합당하다] answer[fit / be fit for] the purpose / serve one's purpose / suit one's end[purpose] // ~에 걸맞지[합당하지] 않다 be unfit[inapposite to] the purpose // ~을 ~으로 삼다 aim (at) / have (something) for one's object // ~을 가지고 있다 have an end in view // ~에서 벗어나다 wander from one's purpose // ~을 바꾸다[바꾸지 않다] change[stick to] one's purpose // ~을 정하다[세우다] set up a purpose // ~을 달성하다[이루다] accomplish [achieve / gain / attain] one's object [purpose / end] / effect[secure / carry out / succeed in] one's object / effect /realize / bring about] one's purpose / achieve[carry out] one's aim // ~을 이루지 못하다 miss one's object[purpose] // 본 협회의 ~은 …에 있다 The object of the association shall be .... / The association has for its object .... // 최초의 ~은 그를 설득하는 것이었다 My original intent was to persuade him. // 그는 외국에 갈 ~으로 영어 공부를 열심히 하고 있다 He is studying English hard with the intention of going abroad. // 양국의 친선이 이 회합의 ~이다 Friendship between the two countries is the aim[object] of this meeting. // 그것은 ~과 다르다 It is unfit for the purpose. // 그는 한국 역사를 연구할 ~으로 한국에 왔다 He came to Korea with the intention[with

the aim / for the purpose] of studying Korean history.// 그는 뚜렷한 ~ 없이 미국으로 갔다 He went to the United States without any definite object.// 그는 이렇다 할 ~도 없이 집을 떠나 뉴욕으로 왔다 He left home and came to New York without any specific purpose.// 그녀를 속이려고 한 ~은 무엇이었나 What was your motive in trying to deceive her?// 그는 확고한 ~이 있어 한 것은 아니다 He did not do it on set purpose.// 인생의 참된 ~은 무엇인가 What is the real aim of life?// 무슨 ~으로 여기에 왔는가 What was your purpose in coming here?/ What have you come here for?// 무슨 ~으로 이런 짓을 하였는가 What is your purpose in doing this?// 이것은 세상에 발표할 ~으로 쓴 것은 아니다 This is written with no eye for publication.// 정치의 ~은 모든 국민이 평화스럽게 살 수 있도록 하는 것이다 The aim [object] of administration is to let all the people live a peaceful life.// ~을 위해서는 수단 방법을 가리지 않아도 된다고 생각하는 사람들도 있다 Some think that the end justifies the means.// 그가 여기에 온 데는 무슨 ~이 있다 He has some object [an axe to grind] in coming here. **목적하다** aim (to); have (something) in one's mind [for one's object]. ¶목적한 부락에 도착하기 전에 날이 저물었다 Night had fallen before I reached the village which was my destination.
● **목적격** [언] the objective (case). **목적론** [철] teleology. **목적물** the object; the objective; the aim; the game. **목적성** [철] finality. **목적어** an object (to a verb). ¶직접 [간접] ~[언] a direct [an indirect] object. **목적지** one's destination; the end of one's journey; the goal. ¶~에 **도달하다** reach [arrive at] one's destination / reach the end of one's journey.
목전(目前) ¶~의 before [under] one's eyes / immediate / imminent / impending // ~의 위험 an imminent danger // …의 ~에서 in (the) ~ face of ... / in the presence of ... // ~에서 일어난 사건 an event which happened under one's eyes // 시험 [선거]을 ~에 두고 with the examination [election] coming soon [just before one / close at hand] // ~의 이익만을 꾀하다 seek [look to] immediate gain / take a short-sighted policy // ~의 이익에 정신 팔리다 be tempted by the prospect of [blinded by the desire for] immediate gain // ~의 사태에 눈을 감다 [를 모르는 척하다] ignore what is before one's eyes / shut one's eyes to what is in front of one // ~에 닥치다 be near [close] at hand / be imminent / be just ahead // ~의 일밖에 생각 못하다 take only a short-sighted view of things // 그 사고는 그의 ~에서 일어났다 The accident took place under his (very) nose [right before his eyes]. // 그의 죽음이 ~에 닥쳐왔다 Death stared him in the face.
목젖 [생] the uvula (pl. -lae, ~s).
목제(木製) wooden construction [structure]. ¶~의 wooden / made of wood.
● **목제품** wooden goods; wooden ware [manufactures]; wood products; woodwork. ¶~ 공업 the wooden article industry.
목조(木造) wooden construction. ⇨ᵀ목제
● **목조 가옥** [건물] a wooden [(미) frame] house [building].

목조(木彫) [나무에 조각을 함] wood carving; woodcraft; [그 작품] a woodcarving. ¶~의 (a doll) carved in [out of] wood.
목질(木質) ¶~의 woody / ligneous.
● **목질부** [식] the xylem. ⇨ᵀ물관부(⇨물관)
목질 섬유 woody fiber.
목차(目次) (a table of) contents.
목책(木柵) a fence stake. ⇨ᵀ울짱1
목청 1 [후두 중앙부의 발성 기관] the vocal c(h)ords [bands]. ¶~을 울리다 vibrate the vocal chords. 2 [목소리] one's voice; one's tune (of voice). ¶~껏 at the top of one's voice [lungs] / at the pitch of one's voice // ~이 좋다 have a sweet [fine / lovely / musical] voice // ~이 나쁘다 have a poor voice.
목청(을) 돋우다 raise [lift (up)] one's voice; raise one's pitch.
목초(牧草) grass; pasture; pasturage. ¶암소들이 ~를 뜯고 있다 The cows are at grass [pasture]. / The cows are grazing in the field [meadow / pasture].
● **목초지** a pasture; a pasturage; pastureland; grassland; a meadow; meadowland.
목축(牧畜) (live) stock-farming; cattle breeding [raising]; pasturage(방목). ¶이 지방은 ~이 성하다 Cattle breeding is a big business in this area. **목축하다** raise [rear] cattle; ranch.
● **목축업** stock-farming; cattle-breeding [-raising]. ¶우리나라의 ~은 아직 초보적 단계에 있다 The stock-farming in our country is still primitive [in an early stage]. **목축 지대** cattle land [country].
목측(目測) eye measurement. ¶~을 잘못하다 make a mistake in measuring the distance with the eye. **목측하다** measure (the distance) with the eye [by (the) eye].
● **목측 거리** distance measured with the eye.
목침(木枕) a wooden pillow.
목탁(木鐸) 1 [불] a (wood) block (in a Buddhist temple). ¶~을 두드리다 sound [beat] a wood block. 2 [지도자] a leader; a guide of the public; [식자] a man of light and learning; a herald of justice and culture. ¶사회의 ~인 신문 the press that should lead the public.
목탄(木炭) 1 charcoal. ⇨ᵀ숯 2 [미] a charcoal pencil; fusain.
● **목탄 가스** charcoal gas. **목탄지** charcoal paper. **목탄화** a charcoal (drawing); a fusain.
목판(木板) (음식 담는) a wooden platter [tray]; a trencher; [널조각] a board; a plank.
목판(木版) a (printing) block; a wood (printing) plate; a woodcut; an engraved woodblock; an engraving block. ¶~으로 인쇄하다 make a print from a wood block / make a wood-block print.
● **목판본** a block [xylographic] book. **목판 인쇄** wood-block printing. **목판화** a (wood-) block print; a woodcut; a wood engraving; a woodprint; a wood-block print.
목표(目標) 1 [표지] a mark; a landmark; a sign. ¶~을 ~로 하여 advance with ... for a guide // 그들은 그 별을 ~로 삼아 나아갔다 They went on with the star as their guide. // 우리 집에 올 때 학교를 ~로 삼으면 쉽사리 찾을 수 있다 If you use the school as a landmark, you won't have any

trouble finding my house.
2 [표적] a target; a mark. ¶공격 ~ the target for[of] an attack // 군사 ~ (bomb) a military target // 매상 ~ a sales target // 중간 ~ [군] an intermediate objective // 쉬운 공격 ~ an easy target for attack / a sitting duck // 좋은 ~가 되다 present a fat target (for).
3 [목적] a goal; a target; an object; an objective; an aim; [표준] (a) standard. ¶학습의 ~ the aim of a lesson // 어학 학습의 ~ the object of language study // 정부의 새 정책의 제일 ~ the first(-priority) objective of the new Government policy // 인생의 ~를 정하다 set one's goal in life // ~에 **도달하다** reach [attain] the goal // ~에 도달하지 못하다 be short of goal // 살아가는 ~가 있다 have something to live for // 1할 증산을 ~로 하다 set[fix] a goal of ten percent increase in production // ~를 **세우다** set up a standard // 우리는 생산 배가를 ~로 하고 있다 We are aiming at doubling production. // ~에 도달하려면 아직 멀었다 The goal is far off. / We are far from the goal. **목표하다** aim at; have (something) as[for] one's object; set the goal at.
● **목표액** a target figure. ¶월 생산 ~ the target for monthly output // 저축[수출] ~ a savings[an export] target // ~에 **도달하다** realize[hit] the target / reach the targeted level // ~을 돌파하다 pass[exceed] the target [targeted level]. **목표 지점** [군] the target spot; the aiming[objective] point.
목피 (木皮) [나무껍질] bark (of a tree). ¶초근 ~ roots and barks / herbs(약초).
목하 (目下) now; (문어) at present; at the present moment; currently; presently. ¶~의 present / existing / current // ~ 고려 중인 사항 a matter now under consideration // ~의 급선무 the urgent necessity of the day.
목형 (木型) a wooden form; a (wooden) pattern. ¶구두의 ~ (일정한 모양을 잡는) a shoe stretcher[tree] // [구둣골] a last.
목화 (木花) a cotton (plant); raw cotton; cotton wool. ¶~를 **따다** pick cotton (from a cotton plant) // ~를 **틀다** gin cotton.
● **목화꽃** a cotton flower. **목화솜** cotton; cotton wool. **목화씨** cottonseed. **목화 재배** cotton growing.
목회 (牧會) pastoral duties; cure of souls; pastorate. **목회하다** take the spiritual care of a congregation of christians; shepherd a flock of souls.
몫 a share; a portion; an allotment; a quota; (속어) a whack; (미국 구어) a cut; (미국 속어) a rake-off; a split; a divvy; [수] the quotient(약어 q.). ¶**자기 ~** one's share / one's winnings // 세 ~으로 나누다 divide [split] into three portions // 자기 ~을 요구하다 claim one's share (in the profit) // A의 ~으로 남겨 두다 reserve[leave aside] (something) for A // 남의 ~까지 먹다 eat another's part [portion] as well as one's own // 부당하게 큰 ~을 차지하다 take an excessive share [a lion's share] // 자기 ~을 받다 get one's share / receive one's quota // 내 ~을 다오 Give me my share. / Snacks! // 이것이 네 ~이다 This is for you. / This is your share (of it). // 이만큼이 내 ~이다 This much has fallen to my lot. // 이것은 내 ~으로 갖겠다 I will take this as my share. // 저마다 제 ~을 받았다 A share was allotted to each. // 네 ~으로 1할을 주겠다 (미국 구어) I'll cut you in for 10 percent. // 그의 ~의 재산은 많았다[적었다] His portion[share] of the property was large[small]. / He received a large[small] share of the estate. // 6 나누기 2의 ~은 얼마냐 What is the quotient of 6 divided by 2? // 그는 세 사람 ~의 일을 했다 He did the work of three men.
몫몫이 each[every] share[portion / quota]; into shares[portions / quotas]; share by share. ¶~ **차지하다** take each one's own share / take one's respective shares // (공평하게) ~ **나누다** divide into (equal) shares [portions] / allot shares (equally).
몬순 a monsoon.
몰각 (沒却) [없앰] effacement; [무시] disregard. **몰각하다** ignore; disregard; efface; forget. ¶원칙을 ~ disregard the principle.
몰골 (unshapely) figure[features]. ¶~**이 초라하다** cut a poor figure // 이런 ~로는 남에 나설 수가 없다 I am not fit to be seen. / I am not presentable.
몰골사납다 unshapely; shapeless; misshapen; unsightly; indecent. ¶몰골사나운 짓 unseemly[improper / unbecoming / mean] behavior // 몰골사나운 차림새 unsightly appearance / a shabby dress // 몰골사나운 복장을 하다 be shabbily dressed (in).
몰년 (沒年) [죽은 해] the year of (a person's) death; [죽은 해의 나이] a person's age at death.
몰다 1 [마소·차 등을 운전하다] drive. ¶차를 ~ drive a car // 말을 ~ drive a horse / spur one's horse // 소를 시장으로 몰고 가다 drive cattle to market // 양을 목장으로 ~ drive sheep to a meadow // 차를 몰고 …으로 가다 drive to … // 차를 몰고 현장에 급히 가다 rush [hasten] to the scene in a car // 자동차를 몰고 시내를 돌아다니다 motor[drive] about the town / ride about the city (streets) in a motorcar // 그들은 차를 몰고 왔다 They drove up. / They came by car. // 그는 차를 몰아 그녀의 집으로 갔다 He drove to her house.
2 [쫓다] pursue[chase] (after); give chase to; go[run / take] after; hunt up; course. ¶토끼를 ~ chase[hunt up] a hare // 물고기 떼를 그물로 ~ chase a school of fish into a net // 짐승을 몰고 있다 be on the track[trail] of an animal // 개들이 사슴을 산 위로 몰았다 The dogs chased the deer up the mountain.
3 (궁지에) drive[chase] (into); corner. ¶궁지에 ~ corner / drive into a (tight) corner / drive[push] to the wall.
4 [죄인 등으로 다루다] charge (a person with a crime); lay (the blame on a person); impute (a crime to a person); accuse (a person of a crime); brand (a person as an imposter); call (a person as thief). ¶사람을 역적으로 ~ denounce[brand] a person as a traitor // 도둑으로 ~ call (a person) a thief.
5 [한곳으로 모으다] gather (up); push to one side. ¶몰아 (한꺼번에) (all) in all / all together / one and all / in a body / in a lump / in the aggregate / collectively / en masse // (돈을) 몰아서 지불하다 pay in a lump sum [in one sum].
몰아 받다 1 [한꺼번에 받다] receive[get] (it) all at one time[in a lump]. ¶3개월분 급료를 ~ receive three months' pay in a lump // 빚

몰두(沒頭) devotion (to); absorption (in); immersion (in study). **몰두하다** be immersed in; be absorbed [lost / engrossed] in; immerse oneself in; be devoted to; devote oneself to; give oneself up entirely to; bury oneself in; be up to the eyes [neck / elbows] in (one's work). ¶그는 연구에 몰두해 있다 He is absorbed [immersed] in his studies. // 그녀는 미국 문학 연구에 몰두해 있다 She is absorbed in the study of American Literature. // 나는 새로운 소설의 구상에 몰두해 있었다 I was so deep in my plans for a new novel. // 그녀는 일에 몰두하려 했으나 허사였다 She attempted vainly to lose herself in work. / She attempted to lose [bury] herself in work, but it was in vain.

몰라보다 fail to recognize; cannot [do not] recognize; [무시하다] ignore; fail to appreciate; show no appreciation of (the kindness). ¶친구를 ~ fail to recognize one's friend / neglect [disregard] one's friend // 수고를 ~ fail to appreciate (a person's) trouble // 몰라볼 만큼 달라지다 be altered [transformed] beyond [out of] recognition / change beyond [out of] recognition / look as if (he / it) were another person [thing] // 그 소년은 몰라볼 만큼 컸다 The boy had grown so tall that I could hardly recognize him at first. // 당신은 몰라보게 달라졌다 You have changed almost beyond recognition. / You have changed so much that I hardly recognized [knew] you. // 이 근처는 몰라볼 만큼 근대화되었다 This neighborhood has been modernized beyond [past] all recognition. // 몰라뵈어 죄송합니다 I am sorry not to have recognized you.

몰락(沒落) [파멸] ruin; fall; collapse; downfall; wreck; [파산] bankruptcy. ¶로마 제국의 ~ the fall of the Roman Empire // 탄광업의 ~ the decline of the coal [mining] industry. **몰락하다** fall; go to ruin; be ruined; be wrecked; go to the dogs; [파산하다] become [go] bankrupt. ¶몰락한 귀족 ruined peers // 그 사건으로 그의 가족은 몰락했다 The incident brought about the ruin of his family. // 그 사건으로 그는 완전히 몰락했다 The event completed his ruin. // 그는 몰락하여 거지가 되었다 He was reduced to beggary. // 그는 지금은 몰락했지만 한때는 날렸다 He is now down-and-out, but he has seen better days. // 그가 그렇게까지 몰락했으니 그를 구할 길이 없다 Now that he has fallen that low, there's no saving him. // 토지 개혁으로 많은 지주들이 몰락했다 Many a landowner has become bankrupt due to the land reform. / Many landed proprietors were ruined due to the land reform. ➡¶몰락시키다 ruin / bring [reduce] to ruin / put the skids under.

몰래 stealthily; by stealth; quietly; secretly; in secret; privately; surreptitiously; imperceptibly; furtively; in a stealthy way; on the quiet; clandestinely. ¶집안 사람들 ~ without the knowledge of one's people [folks] // ~ 빠져나가다 slip out / sneak out // ~ 방에 들어가다 [방에서 빠져나오다] slip into [out of] the room // ~ 눈짓하다 give a furtive wink // ~ 도망하다 steal away / slip off [away] // ~ 뒷문으로 빠져나가다 slip out by the back door // ~ 뒤를 밟다 shadow (a person) stealthily // ~ 만나다 have a clandestine meeting / meet secretly [clandestinely] // ~ 보다 cast stealthy [furtive] glances (on) / steal a look [glance] (at) // ~ 재미보다 take one's pleasure on the sly // ~ 조사하다 spy out (the land) // ~ 읽다 read (a letter) surreptitiously [by stealth] // ~ 결혼식을 올리다 have a quiet wedding // 기차를 ~ 타다 steal a ride on a train // 그는 ~ 사슴에게 다가갔다 He approached the deer stealthily. // 그는 ~ 뒷문으로 나갔다 He went out by the back door unobserved. // 그는 ~ 서류를 복사했다 He copied the document secretly [on the sly / stealthily]. // 무슨 일을 나 ~ 꾸미고 있느냐 What are you plotting behind my back? // 그들은 계획을 ~ 짜고 있었다 They were shaping their plan secretly [in secret]. // 그는 화병을 ~ 훔쳐 냈다 He stole a vase without being noticed. // 가족 ~ 나는 집을 나올 수 있었다 I was able to leave the house [get away] without attracting my family's notice [unnoticed by my family]. // 방에서 ~ 빠져나가자 Let's slip [steal / sneak] out of the room. // 나는 그 두 사람을 ~ 훔쳐보았다 I stole a glance at the two. // 그들은 매주 ~ 만나고 있다 They meet secretly [in secret] every week. // 그 소년은 ~ 담배를 피웠다 The boy smoked in secret. // 그는 매일 밤 ~ 애인을 찾아갔다 He stole his way to his girl friend every night. / He paid a secret visit to [sneaked in to see] his girl friend every evening. // 그는 한밤중에 ~ 실험을 계속했다 He continued his experiments secretly in the middle of the night. // 나는 부모님 ~ 나이트클럽에 간 적이 있다 I once went to a nightclub without my parent's knowledge. // 아버지한테는 자주 야단을 맞았지만 어머니는 아버지 ~ 격려해 주셨다 I was often scolded by my father, but my mother supported me behind his back. // 그녀는 선생님 ~ 친구들에게 쪽지를 돌렸다 She passed notes to her friends behind the teacher's back. // 나는 그의 행적을 ~ 조사해 보았다 I have investigated his conduct on the sly [(구어) on the quiet]. (▶ on the sly는 부당한, 또한 음험한 느낌이 있음)

몰려가다 crowd [flock] (to); throng (to) (a place); storm (a theater); go in groups; besiege. ¶응원하러 ~ turn out (in droves) to cheer [support] (a team) // 연극의 초연을 보려고 ~ throng to see the premiere of a new play // 초대도 받지 않고 ~ call on (a person) uninvited / invite oneself to (a place) / (구어) crash [gate-crash] (a party) // 승객들은 문으로 몰려갔다 The passengers thronged toward the doors. // 휴가가 시작되면 사람들은 산과 바다로 몰려간다 People flock to mountains and beaches when vacation starts. // 송년회가 파하자 남은 사람들은 술집으로 몰려갔다 After the year-end party broke up the people left behind streamed into a bar.

몰려나다 be expelled [turned / put / sent / driven] out; (속어) be booted out; (직장에서) be ousted [dislodged] (from a position); (셋집 등에서) be evicted [ejected] (from a

몰려나오다

몰려나오다 go out in groups [crowds / swarms / flocks]; turn out en masse; sally forth. ¶야구장에서 많은 군중이 한꺼번에 몰려 나왔다 A big crowd surged out of the baseball stadium. // 사람들이 홀에서 몰려나왔다 People thronged [swarmed] out of the hall.

몰려다니다 walk in groups [crowds / swarms / flocks]; throng about [round]. ¶아이들이 몰려다니며 놀고 있었다 Children were playing about [around] in groups [clusters / bunches]. // 이리는 먹이를 찾아 몰려다닌다 Wolves hunt in large packs.

몰려들다 come in groups [crowds]; crowd [flock / swarm] in. ¶해안으로 ~ flock to the seaside // 방으로 ~ storm in a room // 그곳에는 여름에 많은 사람들이 몰려든다 In summer the place attracts many visitors. // 아이들이 열차 속으로 몰려들었다 Children poured [swarmed] into the train. // 새 떼가 나무에 몰려든다 Birds flock to a tree. // 실업자가 몰려들었다 Jobless people gathered in crowds. // 그 유명한 배우를 보기 위해 사람들이 몰려들었다 People thronged [flocked] to see the famous actor.

몰려오다 come in crowds [flocks / groups]; flock; throng; storm (a place). ¶우르르 ~ come swarming about / storm [stampede] (a place) // 개미 떼처럼 ~ come on in great [overwhelming] numbers // 시위대가 몰려왔다 The demonstrators drew near [were approaching]. // 해변에 사니까 여름에는 별의 별 사람들이 나에게 몰려온다 I get all sorts of people crashing in on me in the summer, as I live by the sea. // 관광객이 경주로 몰려왔다 Gyeongju was deluged with tourists. // 수많은 외국 기자들이 서울에 몰려왔다 Hordes of foreign reporters poured into Seoul.

몰리다¹ 1 [밀리다] be driven; be pressed; be pushed. ¶일이 ~ be pressed with work / be driven by business // 일과에 ~ be overtasked [too busy] with one's daily work // (바둑에서) 초기에 ~ be pressed by countdown.
2 (궁지에) be driven to a corner; be cornered; [궁해지다] be hard up; be pressed for (money); [난처해지다] be at a loss for (an answer); be driven to one's wit's end. ¶대답에 ~ be at a loss [be embarrassed] for a reply // 궁지에 ~ (구어) be placed in fix / be in a tight corner / stand [be] at bay / be pushed to the wall / be driven into a corner // 자금에 ~ be hard up for capital // 돈에 ~ be pinched [pressed / hard up] for money // 나는 궁지에 몰렸다 I was cornered. / (구어) I was in a fix. // 그는 토론 중에 궁지에 몰렸다 He was driven into a corner during the argument. // 만사가 뜻대로 되지 않아 나는 막다른 골목에 몰렸다 Everything went against me, and I was driven to a corner.
3 [한쪽으로 쏠리다] gather [flock] (together); come [get] together; crowd; swarm; cluster; throng. ¶돈이 한곳으로 ~ money flows into one place / money is poorly distributed // 청중은 방 한쪽에 몰려 앉아 있었다 The audience had clustered on one side of the room.

몰리다² 1 [쫓기다] be pursued [chased] (after); be trailed [hunted up]. ¶도둑이 몰려서 골목으로 뛰어들었다 The hunted robber rushed in an alley. 2 [좋지 않은 사람으로 다루어지다] be accused of; be charged with; be blamed for. ¶역적으로 ~ be accused of [charged with] treason / be arraigned for treason.

몰리브덴 (ⓓMolybdän) [화] molybdenum (기호 Mo).

몰매 beating in a group; mob violence. ¶~를 때리다 join in drubbing (a person) / gang up on (a person) / mob (a person) // ~를 맞다 be under subjected to a pelting rain of blows.

몰사(沒死) annihilation; extinction; dying out. **몰사하다** be annihilated; become extinct; be wiped [stamped] out; die to the last man.

몰살(沒殺) extermination; annihilation; (무차별의) (a) total slaughter; (무저항자에 대한) a massacre; (국민·민족 등에 대한) genocide. **몰살하다** kill (the enemy) to a man; massacre; annihilate; exterminate; wipe out. ¶온 가족을 ~ murder the whole family // 적을 ~ annihilate the enemy // 군인들은 부녀자와 어린아이들까지도 몰살했다 The soldiers massacred even the woman and the children. →¶마을 사람들은 몰살당했다 All the villagers were murdered. / The whole village was killed to a man. / The whole village was wiped out [annihilated].

몰상식하다(沒常識—) absurd; preposterous; thoughtless; (서술) have no common sense. ¶아주 몰상식한 utterly absurd / ridiculous // 그건 몰상식하기 짝이 없는 짓이다 That's a sheer absurdity. // 그는 ~ He has no common sense [sense of how to behave]. / He is wanting in [lacks] common sense. // 그거야말로 몰상식한 이야기다 It simply shows your lack of common sense. / Nothing could be more absurd than that. // 그런 짓을 하다니 그 사람이야말로 ~ It was foolish [stupid / thoughtless] of him to do such a thing. // 그의 행동은 너무 몰상식했다 His behavior showed his lack of common courtesy [decency].

몰수(沒收) confiscation; (과실·죄 등에 대한 벌로서의) forfeiture; (압수) seizure. **몰수하다** take away; forfeit; (직권으로) confiscate; seize; impound. ¶선생님은 학생의 만화책을 몰수했다 The teacher took away [confiscated] the student's comic book. →¶몰수되다 be confiscated / be forfeited (to the government) // 그는 이 범죄 때문에 재산을 몰수당했다 He forfeited his property by this crime. // 그의 토지와 소유권이 몰수되었다 His lands and titles were forfeited. // 그의 재산 일부는 국가에 의해 몰수되었다 Part of his property was confiscated by the state.
●**몰수 경기 / 몰수 게임** a forfeited game.

몰식자(沒食子) [식] a gall; a gallnut.

몰아(沒我) self-effacement; self-renunciation; selflessness. ¶~의 경지에 이르다 transcend oneself / rise above oneself / attain a state transcending oneself.

몰아가다 1 [몰아서 데리고 가다] drive (away). ¶소를 풀밭으로 ~ drive cattle (out) to pasture. 2 [휩쓸어 가다] take away in a lump [in bulk / by the gross / in one lot / en

몰아내다 [내쫓다] turn[get / put / send / drive] out; kick[run] (a person) out (of the house[company / army]); (지위에서) oust [expel] (a person from a position); (셋집에서) evict (a tenant from the house). ¶적을 도시에서 ~ drive the enemy from the town // 왕을 왕위에서 ~ dethrone (a king) // 나쁜 생각을 마음에서 ~ purge the mind of [from] false notions // …의 이유로 남을 클럽에서 ~ exclude a person from the club for … // 나는 그를 그 직위에서 몰아내었다 I ousted him from his office. // 나는 집요한 외판원을 집에서 몰아냈다 I sent the persistent salesman packing.

몰아넣다 1 [들어가게 하다] drive[chase / push] in[into]. ¶돼지를 우리 안에 ~ drive a pig into the pigpen // 그는 소를 우리 안으로 몰아넣었다 He drove the cattle into an enclosure [a corral]. 2 (궁지에) corner (a person); get[drive] (a person) into a (tight) corner; drive[push / thrust] to the wall; (구어) put (a person) in a fix[hole]. ¶궁지에 ~ corner (a person) up / drive (a person) into a corner // 자살로 ~ drive a person to (commit) suicide. 3 (휩쓸어) put[push / press] all into (a place). ¶학생들을 한 교실에 ~ put [cram] all the students into one classroom.

몰아대다 1 [마구 해 대다] drive (a person) into a corner; give (a person) a setdown; refute; blame; reproach; criticize. ¶직무 태만에 대해 ~ denounce (a person) for his neglect of duty. 2 [재촉하다] hurry (up); hasten; press; urge on; rush; bustle. ¶일을 빨리 하라고 ~ press (a person) to make a quick job of it[to speed up the work] // 돈 내라고 ~ press (a person) for payment of money // 말을 ~ urge[spur] a horse on.

몰아들이다 1 [몰아서 들어오게 하다] drive [chase] in[into]; push[press] into. ¶여우를 굴속으로 ~ chase[pursue] a fox into its earth // 죄수들을 노역장으로 ~ drive[push] prisoners into a workhouse[labor house] // 방목지의 소를 ~ (미국 서부·오스트레일리아 등지에서) round up the cattle on the range. 2 [있는 대로 모두 들어오게 하다] take in all together; take all in a mass[in bulk]; buy (up) in a lot[mass]. ¶시장의 쌀을 ~ buy up all the rice on the market.

몰아붙이다 1 [한쪽으로 몰다] push[put / thrust / press] all to one side; [그 이상 달아날 수 없는 곳까지] run down. ¶수사슴을 막다른 곳까지 ~ drive[bring] a stag to bay // 호랑이를 막다른 곳까지 몰아붙여 놓치지 않다 hold[have] a tiger at bay // 의자를 방구석에 ~ put the chairs to a corner of the room. 2 [꼼짝 못하게 하다] drive (a person) into a corner; give (a person) a setdown.

몰아세우다 scold away; rate (a person) roundly; take (a person) roundly to task; (구어) blow up (a person) roundly. ¶잘못했다고 ~ give (a person) a hard time (of it) over his mistake // 빚을 갚지 않는다고 ~ berate (a person) for the delay in paying his debt // 그는 우리에게 증거를 대라고 몰아세웠다 He demanded that we give him some proof.

몰아오다 1 [한꺼번에 몰려오다] come all at once[one time]; come all together. ¶오랜 가뭄 끝에 큰비가 몰아왔다 There was a heavy rain all at one time after a long spell of dry weather. 2 [휩쓸어 가져오다] take[bring / buy up] the whole lot; [몰고 오다] drive [chase / pursue] along. ¶그는 서점의 책을 죄다 몰아와서 서재를 꾸몄다 He bought up all the books in a bookstore, and furnished his study with them.

몰아주다 (한꺼번에) give[pay] in a lump[in one lot / by the gross]; give[pay] all at once [at a time]. ¶1년 생활비를 ~ give (a person) the living expenses for one year in a lump sum.

몰아치다 1 [몰아닥치다] make[rush] for; (비바람이) storm; (파도가) surge[rush] upon. ¶눈이 몰아쳤다 It was snowing thick and fast. // 온종일 비바람이 몰아쳤다 It stormed all day. 2 [급히 서두르다] do[work] all at once; speed up (one's business); make short work (of it); bundle off in quick[short] order. ¶밀린 일을 ~ get caught up on one's work in one big push // 시험공부를 몰아쳐서 하다 cram[get crammed] for an examination // 몰아쳐서 미안합니다 I'm sorry to hurry you up. / Excuse me, but I must ask you to be more quick.

몰염치하다 (沒廉恥-) impudent; shameless; (서술적) be without shame; have no shame. ¶몰염치하게도 shamelessly / unblushingly / in a shameless manner / ignominiously // 몰염치하게도 …하다 have the impudence to do.

몰이 (사냥의) chasing; hunting; beating; running (after).
● **몰이꾼** a beater; a chaser.

몰이해하다 (沒理解-) lacking in understanding; ununderstanding; unfeeling; heartless; unsympathetic.

몰인정하다 (沒人情-) nonhuman; inhuman; cruel; unkind; unfeeling; heartless; ruthless; merciless. ¶몰인정한 사람 a heartless [an unfeeling] person / a man cold as a stone // 그는 몰인정한 짓을 했다 What he did was inhuman.

몰입 (沒入) [몰두] immersion; devotion; absorption. **몰입하다** be immersed [absorbed] in (one's work); get oneself absorbed in (one's study). ¶황홀경에 ~ lapse into a state of ecstasy // 그는 자기 일에 몰입해 있다 He is absorbed[immersed] in his work. // 나는 사색에 몰입해 있었다 I was lost in thought.

몰지각하다 (沒知覺-) thoughtless; indiscreet; senseless; ill-advised.

몰취미하다 (沒趣味-) tasteless; out of taste; insipid; dull; dry (as dust). ¶몰취미한 [세련되지 않은] unrefined / [촌스러운] rustic / boorish / [무뚝뚝한] blunt // 몰취미한 사람 a rustic / an unpolished [unsophisticated] person // 몰취미한 생활 a commonplace [vapid] life // 그는 ~ He doesn't have any particular pastimes. // 그들은 모두가 몰취미한 사람들뿐이었다 They were all such uninteresting[dull / boring] people.(▶ dull, boring은 무미건조한, 지루한)

몸 1 [신체] the body; [체격] physique; build;

몸

constitution(체질); frame(뼈대); [신장] stature; [크기] size; [모습] figure. ¶사람의 ~ the human body / 좋은 ~ a robust [fine] physique / 허약한 ~ a delicate constitution // ~의 구조 the bodily structure // ~에 맞는 옷 well-fitting clothes // ~도 마음도 body and soul // ~이 큰 large(-sized) / big-bodied / of imposing[large] figure // ~이 큰 남자 a man of large build // ~이 작은 small(-sized) / short // ~이 가냘픈 thin / slim-figured / slender (girl) // ~이 튼튼한[약한] 사람 a man of strong[weak] constitution[frame] // ~이 튼튼하다[약하다] have a strong[weak] constitution // ~이 나다[수척해지다] gain [lose] weight / put on [lose] flesh // ~이 건강하다[호리호리하다] be of sturdy [slender] build // ~에 걸치다 put on / wear / be wrapped in (a shawl) // 분노에 ~을 떨다 shake with anger // ~을 단련하다 build up one's body // ~을 꼿꼿이 세우다 hold oneself erect // ~을 편하게 하다 make oneself comfortable / ease oneself // 그 애는 ~만 컸지 아직 아무것도 모른다 He is such a big hulking fellow, but is not yet of any use. // 그녀는 ~을 구부려 마룻바닥의 책을 주웠다 She bent [stooped] over to pick up the book on the floor. // 그는 발을 뻗어 ~을 편하게 했다 He stretched out his legs and made himself comfortable. // 이 옷은 ~에 맞지 않는다 This suit doesn't fit me. // 아이가 자라서 바지가 ~에 맞지 않는다 The child has outgrown his trousers. // 그 사나이는 ~이 멍투성이였다 The man was black and blue all over. // ~이 두 개라도 모자라겠다 If I cut myself into four quarters, they would not be sufficient. // 비록 ~은 떨어져 있어도 마음만은 너와 함께 있다 Though absent in body, I am with you in spirit. // 그는 ~을 아끼지 않고 일했다 He worked without sparing himself.

2 [몸통] the body; the trunk (of the body); the torso. ¶여자 머리에 사자 ~을 가진 스핑크스 the sphinx with a women's head and lion's body.

3 [건강] health. ¶~이 좋아지다 get well / improve in health // ~이 약해지다 become weak / be run down // ~이 나빠지다 break down in health // ~이 회복되다 be well [all right] again / be restored to health // ~에 좋다 be good for the health / do (a person) good / be healthful [healthy / wholesome] / ~에 나쁘다 be bad for the health / be unhealthful [unwholesome] // ~에 해롭다 hurt [affect / ruin] one's health // ~에 도움 (a person) harm // ~을 조심하다 take (good) care of oneself / be careful of one's health // 나는 ~의 상태가 좋다 [나쁘다] I am in good [poor] health. // 그는 타고난 건강한 ~이다 He has a very healthy constitution. // 이 음식은 ~에 좋다[해롭다] This food is good [bad] for the health. // 그는 과음으로 ~을 망쳤다 He injured his health by drinking too much. // 더 이상 ~을 지탱할 수 없을 것 같다 I'm afraid I can't keep this up any longer. // 담배는 ~에 아주 해롭다 Smoking is fatal to the health. // ~이 감당할 수 있겠소 Can you stand the strain? // 저렇게 일을 많이 하면서 용케도 ~이 배겨나는군 I wonder how he manages to keep himself well with so much work to do. // 오늘은 ~의 상태가 아주 좋다 (환자가) I'm much better today. / (선수가) I'm in the best form [condition].

4 [일신] self; one's self; oneself. ¶자유로운 ~이다 be one's own master [mistress] / be a free man [woman] // ~에 지니다 have [keep] (a thing) on one's person // ~을 숨기다 conceal [hide] oneself / tuck oneself at (a person's) disposal / put oneself into (a person's) disposal // 이럴 때는 누구나 자기 ~부터 생각하는 법이다 At such a moment every body thinks of self first.

5 [신분] one's situation in life; one's social status; [처지] one's circumstances; [자리] one's position[place]. ¶노예[종]의 ~ a person the status as a slave / a slave // 천한 ~ a person of humble condition [birth / social standing] // 귀하신 ~ a person of high rank / a distinguished [an important] figure // 미천한 ~으로 입신하다 rise from obscurity / make [win] one's way up from the bottom of the (social) ladder.

6 menstruation. ⇨ 몸엣것

7 (도자기의) unglazed pottery; bisque; biscuit (ware).

몸(이) 나다 put on [gain] weight; get fat; fatten; grow [get] stout [plump / fleshy]; fat (up).

몸(이) 달다 fidget (about); have [be in] the fidgets [a fidget]; (미) jitter (about); fret (oneself to death); be too eager [anxious] (for / to do); be in a bustle. ¶애인을 못 만나서 ~ be all hot and bothered to be kept from seeing one's sweetheart // 영화 구경을 가지 못해 몸 달아 하다 be all hot and bothered because one wants to go [because one can't go] to the movies.

몸(을) 던지다 throw oneself (into a river).

몸(을) 두다 stay [live] in; find shelter with (a relative); stay with (one's uncle). ¶몸 둘 곳이 없다 have no place to live [stay] in / have no place for one // 몸 두어 일할 곳을 구하다 look for a place to work in.

몸 둘 바를 모르다 do not know what to do with oneself. ¶(부끄러워) 몸 둘 바를 모르겠습니다 I am deeply ashamed of myself. / I really don't know where to look.

몸(을) 망치다 shatter one's constitution; (건강이) fall into ill health; injure [lose] health.

몸(을) 붙이다 ¶나는 몸 붙일 곳이 없다 I have no place to go to [no friend to turn to] for help.

몸(을) 아끼다 spare oneself (the trouble). ¶그는 몸을 아끼지 않고 일했다 He worked without sparing himself.

몸에 배다[익다] be [get] used (to); grow [become] accustomed to; grow familiar (with). ¶아직 몸에 배지 않은 기술 a half-learned skill // 그의 기예는 아직 몸에 완전히 배지 않았다 He has not yet made the art entirely his own. // 밥벌이할 기술을 몸에 익혀 두어야 한다 You ought to acquire some art [craft / skill] useful in making a living.

몸을 가지다 1 [임신하다] become [be] pregnant; be expecting; (문어) be with child; be in the family way; conceive. ¶몸을 가진 지 6개월이다 be six months pregnant [gone with child] / be in the six months of pregnancy. 2 [월경하다] have the menses [monthlies]; see the flowers.

몸을 더럽히다 lose one's virginity [cherry].

몸을 허락하다 give herself to (a man). ¶마음

내 그녀는 몸을 허락했다 She finally let him sleep with her[went to bed with him]. // 그녀는 그에게 몸을 허락하지 않았다 She refused to give herself to him.

몸이 근질근질하다 be itching[dying] (to do); be dying (for something). ¶그는 스키 타러 가고 싶어 몸이 근질근질했다 He was itching to go skiing.

몸(을) 팔다 sell oneself for living ; give oneself (for money); prostitute oneself for living. ¶그녀는 몸을 팔아 병든 남편을 부양했다 She supported her sick husband by selling herself.

몸(을) 풀다 1 [워밍업하다] warm up; get the kinks out of one's body. 2 [해산하다] give birth to (a baby); be delivered of (a baby).

몸가짐 [태도] demeanor, (영) demeanour; [거동·행동거지] manners; (a) carriage; movements. ¶~이 조용한 신사 a gentleman with a self-possessed manner // 친절한[상냥한]~으로 in a kindly manner // 우아한~ elegant[graceful] movements[manners] // 가벼운 ~ an easy carriage / light movement // 그녀는 ~이 차분하다 She has a quiet demeanor. // 그녀는 ~이 우아하다 She is graceful (in her movements). / She has graceful manners[carriage].

몸값 [화대] money paid for prostitution; (포로 등의) ransom; price of redemption; the money[price] for flesh traffic (for a slave). ¶노예의 ~ the money[price] for a slave // ~을 지급하다 pay the ransom (for) // ~을 노리고 감금하다 hold (a person) prisoner for ransom // 많은 ~을 치르고 빼내다 ransom (a person) at a heavy price // ~을 받다 exact a ransom (for a prisoner / from another) // 그는 ~을 5천만 원이나 지불하고 아들을 찾아왔다 He paid a ransom of fifty million won to get his son back.

몸단장(―丹粧) adornment (of one's person). ⇨ ˝몸치장 ¶그는 ~을 너무 소홀히 한다 He is too careless about his appearance.

몸담다 employ oneself[be employed] in; work for.

몸뚱이 [몸의 덩치] the body; frame. ¶~가 크다 be huge of limb / have a bulky frame // ~가 작다 be small of frame / be short of stature.

몸매 one's figure; one's shape; one's form. ¶날씬한 ~ a slender figure // 균형 잡힌 ~ a well-proportioned figure[form] // ~가 좋다 have a good figure / be fair of form // 그 형제는 ~가 비슷하다 The brothers are exactly like each other in build. // 그녀는 옷을 입으면 (실제보다) 말라 보이는 ~다 She has the type of build that makes her look thinner (than she really is) when she's dressed. // 무용을 하면 ~가 예뻐진다 Dancing improves one's figure[carriage].

몸부림 1 [버둥거림] writhing; squirming; a (violent) struggle. **몸부림하다** struggle; writhe. ⇨ ˝몸부림치다 2 [잠자리에서의 몸을 뒤치는 짓] turning over in bed; tossing about in bed. **몸부림하다** turn (over / round) in sleep. ⇨ ˝몸부림치다2

몸부림치다 1 [버둥거리다] struggle; writhe; flounce; wriggle; flounder; squirm. ¶괴로워서 ~ writhe in agony // 경관의 손에서 벗어나려고 ~ try to struggle loose[twist away] from the grip of the policeman // 아무리 몸부림쳐 봐야 소용없다 It's no use struggling and wriggling. // 그는 괴로움에 몸부림쳤다 He writhed in agony. // 그는 물 위로 떠오르려고 필사적으로 몸부림쳤다 He struggled desperately to come to the surface. // 그는 비참한 처지에서 어떻게든 벗어나려고 몸부림쳤다 He struggled[strove] to break out of the miserable circumstances he was in.

2 [잠자리에서] turn[heave] (over / round) in sleep; toss[roll] about in bed.

몸살 illness from fatigue; general[great] fatigue. ¶~로 눕다 take to one's bed from fatigue.

몸살(이) 나다 […하고 싶어 못 견디다] be anxious[eager / impatient] to do; be dying for[to do]. ¶그가 보고 싶어 몸살 나겠다 I am dying to see him.

몸서리 1 [무서워서 다시는 하고 싶지 않은 마음] a shudder; a quiver; a thrill; a quake; a tremble; a shiver; quivering; shuddering; trembling; shivering. 2 [지겨움] weariness, tiresomeness.

몸서리나다 1 [무섭다] shudder (at); shiver; tremble (for fear); quiver (with emotion). ¶ 몸서리나는 terrible / terrifying / shocking / hair-raising // 무서워 ~ tremble with fear // 나는 피를 보고 몸서리났다 I shuddered at the sight of the blood. // 그것은 듣기만[생각만] 해도 몸서리난다 I shudder at the mere mention[thought] of it. // 전쟁이란 말만 들어도 몸서리난다 The mere mention of a war makes me shake[shiver] in my shoes. // 그는 무서워 몸서리났다 A terrible quaking fear seized upon him. // 그 광경을 보고 무서워서 몸서리났다(사물이) The scene made my hair stand on end[made my blood curdle]. / (사람이) I shuddered[was horrified] at the scene.

2 [지겹다] be sickened (of); be sick[quite tired] (of); (구어) be sick and tired (of); be bored (with / by). ¶…에 ~ keenly realize the wretchedness of … / be[get] quite sick of … // 이 일에는 이제 몸서리난다 I have become utterly disgusted with this work. // 가난한 생활에는 몸서리난다 I am tired of my humble life. // 세상살이에 몸서리난다 I am quite sick of life.

몸서리치다 shudder (at); be sickened (of). ⇨ ˝몸서리나다

몸소 personally; in person; (do it) oneself. ¶ ~ 시찰하다 make a personal inspection (of) // ~ 방문하다 make a personal call (on / at) // ~ 지휘하다 take[assume] personal command (of) / be in personal command (of) // 그는 부하에게 모범을 보였다 He personally set an example to his inferiors. // 할아버지께서 ~ 뜰을 쓰신다 My grandfather himself sweeps the garden.

몸수색(―搜索) a body search; (옷 위로 하는) a frisk. **몸수색하다** search[frisk] (a person for concealed weapons); rub down. ¶흉기를 숨기고 있는지 ~ search (a person) for concealed weapons // 밀수품을 갖고 있는지 ~ search (a person) for smuggled goods.

몸엣것 [월경] menstruation; the menses; [그 피] menstrual blood.

몸져눕다 take to one's bed; be ill in bed; lie in one's sickbed; (구어) be laid up (with a cold); keep one's bed. ¶그는 폐병으로 몸져누워 있다 He is laid up with consumption.

몸조리 (-調理) taking care of one's health; (병후의) recuperation. ¶산후 ~ postpartum care // ~를 안 하다 be careless of[neglect] one's health. **몸조리하다** take care of one's health; (병후의) recuperate (oneself); recruit (oneself). ¶몸조리하기 위하여 for (the good of) one's health / for recuperation.

몸조심 (-操心) 1 [몸조리] care of one's health. ¶출산할 때까지는 ~을 잘해야 한다 You must take good care of yourself until the baby is born. **몸조심하다** take (good) care of one's health; be careful of one's health. ¶부디 몸조심하십시오 Please take good care of yourself. // 병에 걸리지 않도록 몸조심하라 Take care not to make yourself ill. // 몸조심하시오 I wish you a good journey. 2 [언행을 삼감] prudence; discretion; behaving oneself. **몸조심하다** behave oneself prudently; be prudent [use prudence] in action. ¶그 사건 이후 나는 매우 몸조심하고 있다 The accident has rendered me very cautious. // 이런 문제에는 몸조심하는 것이 제일이다 One must observe caution in these matters.

몸종 a lady's maid; a handmaid [slave girl] (to Mrs ...); a body maid.

몸집 the stature; one's build; the frame. ¶~이 작은 small-sized // ~이 작은 여자 a woman of small stature[build] / a small woman // ~이 큰 소년 a boy big for his age // ~이 큰 여자 a large woman / a woman of large build / a big-boned woman // ~이 큰[작은] 사람 a big[small] man // ~이 실팍한 사나이 a well-built man // ~이 호리호리한 소녀 a girl of slender frame // ~**이 통통하다** be pudgy // 그는 나이에 비해서 ~이 크다 He is big (-bodied) for his age. // 그는 ~이 작다 He is a small man. / He is of slight build.

몸짓 a gesture; (a) gesticulation; (an) action; (a) motion. ¶~에 의한 의사 전달 gestural communication // 과장된 ~ an exaggerated [a dramatic / an extravagant] gesture // ~**으로 나타내다** show by a gesture / express (oneself) by gesture // ~으로 일어서도록 신호하다 motion (a person) to get up // ~으로 찬성[불찬성]의 의사를 표시하다 make a gesture of assent [dissent] // 그녀는 우아한 ~으로 차를 따랐다 She poured the tea with graceful movements. // 어린이는 ~으로 목이 마르다고 어머니에게 호소했다 The child gestured to his mother that he was thirsty. // 그녀는 돌아갈 듯한 ~을 했다 She made motions as if to leave. **몸짓하다** make a gesture (of despair); gesticulate; motion; pose. ¶몸짓하며 가며 말하다 accompany one's speech with gesture // 그는 조용히 하라고 몸짓했다 He gestured for me to be quiet.

몸차림 adornment (of one's person). ⇨ ᇃ몸치장 ¶그는 늘 ~이 단정하다 He always looks neat and tidy.

몸채 (집의) the main house [building].

몸치장 (-治粧) adornment (of one's person); dressing (oneself) up; decking oneself out; trimming oneself up. **몸치장하다** (옷으로) dress (oneself) up; be gaily [gaudily] dressed; be dressed up; (장식물로) ornament [adorn / deck] oneself (with). ¶야하게 ~ be gaudily dressed / overdress (oneself) // 보석으로 ~ deck oneself up[out] with jewels / bejewel oneself // 그 여자는 말쑥이 몸치장했다 She trimmed herself up.

몸통 the trunk; the body; the bulk of one's body; girth. ¶~이 굵다 have a thick [big] trunk [waist] // ~**이 길다** be long-waisted // ~이 절구통 같다 be fat as a mortar barrel // 그는 ~이 40인치나 된다 He measures 40 inches around the waist [in girth].

몹시 1 [대단히] very (much); exceedingly; excessively; extremely; greatly; immensely; terribly; highly. ¶~ 기뻐하다 be highly [much] pleased // ~ 바쁘다 be very busy / be terribly busy // ~ 아름답다 be strikingly beautiful // ~ 감동하다 be deeply touched // ~ 가난하다 be awfully poor // ~ 서두르다 be in a great [deadly] hurry // ~ 어둡다 be pitch-dark / be (as) dark as midnight // 나는 ~ 목이 마르다 I am terribly thirsty. // 나는 그 소리에 ~ 시달리고 있다 I am greatly annoyed by the noise. // 나는 ~ 집이 그립다 I am overwhelmingly homesick. // 그 사람을 만나고 싶다 I am dying to see him. // 그는 그 소식을 듣고 ~ 놀랐다 He was very much surprised at the news. // 그 여자를 ~ 만나고 싶다 I badly want to see her. // 그녀의 인정 어린 말에 ~ 감명을 받았다 I was deeply impressed by her considerate words. // ~ 기쁘다 I am extremely glad. // 방 안이 ~ 덥다 It's terribly hot in the room. // 간밤에는 개가 ~ 짖는 바람에 잠을 잘 수가 없었다 I wasn't able to sleep last night, because a dog was barking terribly. // 오늘은 ~ 졸린다 I'm very [terribly] sleepy today. // 오늘은 ~ 덥지 It's awfully hot today, isn't it? // 오늘 밤은 ~ 피곤하다 I am dead tired tonight. 2 [심하게] severely; violently; intensely; heavily; badly. ¶~ 아프다 feel [suffer] a severe pain // ~ 울다 cry bitterly / cry bitter tears // ~ 취해 있다 be heavily [beastly / dead] drunk // 머리가 ~ 아프다 have a severe [terrible] headache / have a devil of a headache // ~ 부려 먹다 drive (a person) hard / sweat (a servant) // 피를 ~ 흘리다 bleed badly // …이 없어서 ~ 곤란을 겪고 있다 be badly in want of ... / be hard up for (money) // 그는 독감을 ~ 앓고 있다 He is suffering from a severe attack of influenza. // 그 광경을 보고 그녀는 ~ 불쾌해졌다 The sight excited strong disgust in her. // 그는 ~ 화가 났다 His anger knew no bounds. // 그는 ~ 취해 있었다 He was dead drunk. // 집이 ~ 헐었다 The house is badly dilapidated. // 그는 종아리를 ~ 맞았다 He received a nasty blow on the leg.

몹쓸 1 [나쁜] bad; evil; ill; immoral; sinful; [사악한] wicked; ill-natured; malicious; villainous; roguish. ¶~ 놈 a wicked man / a rascal // ~ 짓을 하다 do (a person) harm [an ill turn] / do a cruel thing to (a person) // ~ 친구와 어울리다 keep bad company // 그렇게 순진한 여자를 속이다니 너도 참 ~ 놈이다 How wicked you are to deceive such an innocent girl! // 부부 사이를 갈라놓다니 ~ 사람이군 How awful of him to come between a husband and wife! 2 (악성의) malignant (influenza); virulent (disease); nasty. ¶~ 병 a virulent disease.

못[1] (금속으로 만든) a nail; (대못) a spike; [나무못] a peg. ¶나무 ~ a wooden peg [nail] // 장식 ~ an ornamental stud // ~대가리 a nailhead // ~ 제조소 a nailery // ~통 a nail keg // 둥근 ~ (보통 쓰는 것) a wire nail // 박는 기구 a riveting[nailing] machine // ~에 찔린 상처 a nail wound[puncture] // 기둥에 ~을 박다 drive a nail into a pillar // 상의를 ~에 걸다 hang a coat on a peg // 발을 ~에 찔리다 run a nail into one's foot // ~을 박다 nail / drive a nail / ~을 뽑다 extract[pull out / draw out] a nail / unnail (a box) / ~을 빼고 뚜껑을 벗기다 remove a nailed cover // 옷이 ~에 걸렸다 The nail caught her dress. // ~을 박아 상자 뚜껑을 닫았다 I nailed the box shut. // ~이 빠져나왔다 The nails have come out. // 태풍에 대비해서 창을 ~으로 고정시켰다 We nailed down the windows in preparation for the typhoon. // 이 문은 ~으로 고정되어 있다 This door is nailed shut. // ~이 단단히[헐겁게] 박혀 있다 The nail is fast[loose].

못(을) 박다 1 〔마음에 상처를 입히다〕 wound a person's feelings. 2 〔다짐하다〕 assure; pledge; make sure; give one's pledge. ¶그는 다음 달까지 빚을 갚겠다고 못을 박았다 He gave his word that he would pay the debt by next month. // 누구에게도 말하지 말라고 그에게 못 박아 두었다 I made it clear to him that he mustn't tell anyone.

못² (손발 등의) a corn; a callus; a callosity.

못(이) 박이다 become callous; have[get] a corn. ¶못이 박인 발가락 a toe with a callosity // 못이 여러 개 박인 손 a hand with callous places // 발에 ~ have[get] a corn on the feet // 귀에 못이 박이도록 듣다 be sick [tired] of hearing (something) / hear more than enough of (something) // 오른발에 못이 박였다 I have a corn[callus] on my right foot. // 그 얘기라면 귀에 못이 박이도록 들었다 I have heard about that so often that I'm sick of it.

못³ a pond; a pool(작은 웅덩이). ¶연 ~ a lotus pond // ~가에서 by a pond / by the pondside // ~에서 헤엄치다 swim in a pond / ~을 파다[메우다] dig[fill in] a pond / ~에 얼음이 두껍게 얼었다 Ice was thick on the pond.

못⁴ 〔불가〕 (definitely) not; won't; 〔불능〕 cannot (do); unable (to do); incapable (of doing). ¶어두워서 ~ 읽겠다 It is too dark to read. // 교내에서는 담배를 ~ 피우게 되어 있다 Smoking is prohibited within the school bounds. // 나는 그 영화를 ~ 보았다 I missed that picture.

못 본 체하다 (보고도) pretend not to see[to have seen] (something); (관대하게) overlook; look over; pass over (a matter) in silence; let (it) pass[go]; connive (at). ¶잘못을 보고도 ~ overlook[slur (over)] (a person's) fault / 길에서 만나도 ~ cut (a person) (dead) in the street // 곤경에 처한 친구를 ~ leave one's friend in the lurch / fail a friend in his need // 그의 파렴치한 행동을 못 본 체할 수 없다 I cannot shut[close] my eyes to his shameful conduct. // 그는 나를 못 본 체하고 지나갔다 He looked the other way and walked past me. / He walked past, pretending not to see me.

못나다 1 〔못생기다〕 plain; ugly; bad-[ugly-/ plain-]looking; ill-favored; (미) homely (-looking); uncomely. ¶못난 여자 a plain[an ugly / (미) a homely] woman // 지지리 ~ awfully ugly-looking // 그녀는 얼굴이 못났다 She looks plain[homely]. 2 〔어리석다〕 foolish; stupid; silly; dull; witless; fatuous; asinine; (미국 구어) daffy; zany. ¶못난 짓을 하다 do a foolish[stupid] thing / act the fool [ass] / make an ass of oneself // 못나게도 foolishly enough // 이 못난 녀석아 You big fool! / What a scoundrel! // 그런 짓을 하다니 그녀도 꽤나 못났군 It is very silly of her to do such a thing.

못난이 1 〔바보〕 a simpleton; a fool; a half-wit; a ninny; a dunce; a loggerhead; a blockhead; a thickhead; a fathead; a gull; a goose; an ass; (구어) a moron; (구어) a silly; (속어) a poop; (속어) a pinhead; (미국 속어) a boob(y); (미국 속어) a dumb clock. 2 〔추남·추녀〕 an ugly.

못내 〔그지없이〕 immeasurably; incalculably; 〔잊지 않고〕 unforgettably; 〔늘〕 always; ever. ¶이별을 ~ 아쉬워하다 be deeply sorry to part from (a person) // 돌아가신 어머니를 ~ 그리워하다 sorely miss one's dead mother // ~ 잊지 못하다 never forget / hold (a person's) memory ever dear / be ever present in one's mind // 그녀는 ~ 아쉬운 듯 뒤돌아보며 떠나갔다 She went her way, looking back wistfully again and again.

못되다 〔나쁘다〕 bad; evil; wrong; 〔사악하다〕 wicked; ill-natured; malicious; criminal. ¶못된 생각 an evil intention / a mistaken idea // 못된 놈 a wicked man / a bad egg / a rascal // 못된 장난 mischief // 못된 짓 a wrong / an evil deed / a misdeed / a vice / (주색잡기) evil [loose / coarse] pleasures // 못된 짓을 하다 do wrong / commit a sin[crime] // 남에게 못된 짓을 하다 do something malicious to a person // 못되게 굴다 misbehave oneself / conduct oneself[behave] improperly[in an immoral fashion] // 그는 술만 마시면 못되게 군다 He turns vicious when he drinks. // 못된 농담은 그만두어라 Don't make such nasty [cruel / vicious] jokes.

못된 송아지 엉덩이에 뿔 난다(속담) The lean weed lifts its head high.; An ill-bred boy behaves rudely.

못마땅하다 〔사물이〕 마음에 안 들다〕 disagreeable[offensive / distasteful / unacceptable] (to); not to (a person's) liking; unsatisfactory; undesirable; 〔불만스럽다〕 displeased[dissatisfied] (with something). ¶못마땅한 녀석 a disagreeable guy // 못마땅한 말을 하다 say something disagreeable[unpleasant / offensive] // 못마땅한 얼굴을 하다 scowl / glower / look displeased[glum] / wear a grave look // 못마땅한 표정이다 look sour[grim] // 못마땅하게 여기다 be displeased [dissatisfied] with (something) // 나는 그 녀석의 말이 ~ His words cut me to the quick [get on my nerves]. // 그 조건이 못마땅하여 거절했다 I declined it as the terms were unsatisfactory. // 무엇이 그렇게 못마땅한가 What makes you so unhappy? // 나는 정부의 에너지 정책이 ~ I am impatient with[at] the government's energy policy.

못뽑이 a nail puller[extractor]; a claw hammer; (a pair of) pincers.

못살다 1 〔가난하게 살다〕 live in poverty; be in needy circumstances. ¶못사는 가정 a needy family. 2 〔기를 못 펴다〕 cower; shrink (with fear); be timid. ¶못살게 굴다 persecute / oppress / torment / be hard (up) on (a person) / be cruel to (a dog) / (구어) ride (a

못생기다

person) (hard) / (장난삼아) tease / annoy / (신입생 등을) (미) haze / (속어) rag / 강아지를 못살게 굴다 torment a small dog / be cruel to a puppy // 그녀는 며느리를 못살게 군다 She is hard on her daughter-in-law. // 그는 고양이를 못살게 굴었다 He treated the cat very cruelly. // 나를 그렇게 못살게 굴지 마시오. Don't be so hard on me.

못생기다 〔잘나지 못하다〕 ugly; (용모가) bad-looking; (특히 여자가) plain; (미) homely(▶ homely, plain은 완곡한 표현임). // 못생긴 코 an unshapely nose // 그녀는 자신의 못생긴 코 굴을 걱정하고 있었다 She worried about her plain features [looks]. // 그녀는 얼굴은 못생겼지만 마음씨는 곱다 She is plain, but sweet-tempered.

못쓰다 〔쓸모없다〕 be useless; be worthless; be unfit for use; bad; (금지) must not (do); shall not (do) (2, 3인칭에); ought not to (do); should not (do). ¶못쓰게 되다 become useless [worthless] / become spoilt / spoil / be rendered useless / (사람이) (a person) get bad [worse] / (a person) become poor in health(병으로) / 그런 짓을 하면 못쓴다 You must not do such a thing. // 그렇게 말하면 못쓴다 Don't talk like that. // 그 사람을 만나면 못써 You must never see him. // 이 봉투는 너무 작아 못쓰겠다 This envelope won't do because it's too small.

못자리 1 〔농〕 a rice seedbed; a nursery; a seed plot. 2 〔씨 뿌리는 일〕 sowing rice seed.
못자리하다 sow rice; seed on the beds.

못줄 〔농〕 a guideline[guide rope] for orderly-spaced planting of rice seedlings.

못지않다 no less (than); just as good (as); not inferior (to); by no means inferior (to); equal (to). ¶남자 못지않은 여자 아이 a strong-minded girl // 남 못지않게 like the common run / like others [other people] / like most people // 그는 나 못지않게 힘이 세다 He is just as strong as I am. // 오늘도 어제 못지않게 춥다 Today is just as cold as yesterday was. // 그는 기타 솜씨가 누구 ~ (문어) He is second to none in playing the guitar. / He is the best guitar player there is. / (구어) Nobody can beat him at playing the guitar. // 그녀는 배짱이 어떤 남자 아이 ~ She is as brave[bold] as any boy. / (구어) When it comes to guts, she can hold her own against any boy. // 그는 돌아가신 그의 선친 못지않게 친절한 사람이다 He is just as kind as his late father used to be. // 오락은 일 못지않게 필요하다 Recreation is no less necessary than work.

못질하다 nail (up) (a box); nail down (a lid); fasten with nails.

못하다[1] 〔일정한 수준에 못 미치다〕 be bad [poor / weak]. ¶…을 ~ be bad [not good / bad hand] at (drawing) / be weak in (arithmetic).

못하다[2] 〔할 수 없는 상태가 되다〕 fail to (do); miss (doing). ¶승진하지 ~ fail to be promoted // 알아맞히지 ~ guess wrong [amiss] // 그가 설명하는 끝 부분을 듣지 못했다 I missed the last part of his explanation. // 나의 진짜 목적은 아버님께 말씀드리지 못했다 I failed to tell my father of my true purpose [motive]. // 우리는 폭풍우 때문에 떠나지 못했다 The storm prevented us from starting. // 너무 바빠 연락을 드리지 못해서 죄송합니다 I'm sorry I was so busy that I failed[forget] to get in touch with you. // 가져가지 못함 (게시) Not to be taken out. / Not to be removed from the premises.

못하다[3] 〔뒤떨어지다〕 inferior [second] to (another); worse than; below; unequal to; not as good as; not on a level [par] with. ¶약간 ~ fall (a little) behind (another) / be a cut below (a person) // 훨씬 ~ be far beneath (another) // …보다 못해 보이다 compare unfavorably[poorly] (with) / cannot stand [bear] comparison (with) / cannot compare (with) / be not so good (as) // 이 점에서 나는 그만 ~ I am inferior to him in this respect. / I fall behind [below] him in this respect. // 그는 짐승보다 못한 녀석이다 He is worse than an animal. // 그의 두 번째 작품은 기대만도 못했다 His second work fell short of [failed to live up to] expectation. // 이것은 내 구성에 있어서 결코 저것만 못하지 않다 This is no less durable than that.

못하다[4] 〔일정한 상태에 미치지 않다〕 not. ¶빛깔이 곱지 ~ The color is not fine. // 그는 유능하지 ~ He is lacking in ability.

몽글다 (곡식이) clean (grain).

몽글리다 1 (곡식을) clean (grain); make (threshed rice) clean. 2 〔단련하게 하다〕 inure; habituate; accustom; make (a person) used [accustomed / inured] to (something). 3 (옷매시를) dress [smarten] oneself up; adorn [preen] oneself; deck oneself up; spruce (oneself) up.

몽글몽글하다 soft; pulpy; flaccid; mushy.

몽니 perverse character [nature]; vicious temper; perversity; obstinacy. ¶~를 부리다 behave perversely / act in perversity.

몽니(가) 굳다[사납다] very perverse [vicious / obstinate].

● **몽니쟁이** a perverse fellow; (구어) a cross-patch.

몽달귀신(-鬼神) 〔총각 귀신〕 the ghost of a dead bachelor.

몽당붓 a stubby [stubbed] writing brush.
몽당비 a stubby [stubbed / stumpy] broom.
몽당이 a stubby [stubbed / stumpy / blunted] thing; (실뭉치) a ball of string [thread].

몽당치마 a skirt worn cut short.

몽둥이 a stick; a club; a cudgel. ¶~를 휘두르다 wield a club // ~로 때리다 beat (a person) with a club / club [cudgel] (a person) // ~로 얻어맞다 get beaten with a club / be clubbed [cudgeled] // ~로 때려죽이다 club (a dog) to death.

● **몽둥이세례**(-洗禮) beating with a stick; clubbing; cudgelling. ¶~를 주다 beat with a stick / club / cudgel // ~를 받다 get beaten with a stick / be clubbed.

몽땅 (one and) all; everything; entirely; wholly; completely; in its entirety; in a body. ¶있는 대로 ~ all that there is [that one has] // 나는 소지품을 ~ 도둑맞았다 My personal effects were all stolen. // 홍수로 집들과 농작물이 ~ 떠내려갔다 House and crops were all washed away by the flood. // 값나가는 물건은 ~ 도둑맞았다 Everything of value was stolen. // 빚을 갚았더니 월급이 ~ 없어졌다 Paying my debts really wiped out my paycheck. // 밤새워 술을 마셨더니 번 돈이 ~ 없어졌다 I drunk all night long, and all my earnings have gone down the drain.

몽롱하다(朦朧−) dim; indistinct; vague; faint; fuzzy; obscure; opaque; hazy; cloudy; misty; foggy. ¶의식이 몽롱한 상태 a condition of clouded consciousness / [의] fugue // 몽롱하게 dimly / mistily / indistinctly / vaguely / faintly / fuzzily / obscurely / like smoke / like a phantom // 의식이 몽롱해 get fuzzy // 그는 의식이 몽롱한 상태에 있다 He is only half conscious. // 그때는 과음하여 몽롱해 있었다 At that time I was fuddled because I had had too much to drink.

몽매(夢寐) (during) one's sleeping hours. ¶~간에도 잊지 못하다 do not forget (something) even in sleep [even while one is asleep / even of a moment] // 그 사람의 일은 ~간에도 잊지 못하겠다 He is ever in my mind. / His memory haunts me night and day.

몽매하다(蒙昧−) unenlightened; (completely) ignorant; benighted; uncivilized. ¶무지몽매한 백성 uncivilized [unenlightened] people.

몽상(夢想) a dream; a vision; a fancy; a daydream; a fantasy. ¶~에 잠기다 fall into [be lost in] (a) reverie / be given to daydreaming. **몽상하다** dream (of / that); fancy; see visions; indulge in reveries. ¶그것은 내가 몽상하지도 못했던 일이다 I little dream of it. / I never even dreamed [dreamt] of it.
●**몽상가** a (Utopian) dreamer; a visionary; an idealist.

몽실몽실 plumply; fleshly. ¶~ 살진 아기 a chubby baby // ~ 살이 찌다 be [grow] plump. **몽실몽실하다** lumpy; plump. ¶몽실몽실한 젖가슴 an ample [a rich] breast / a well-rounded bosom // 몽실몽실한 얼굴 a full face.

몽유병(夢遊病) [의] sleepwalking; somnambulism. ¶~의 somnambulant.
●**몽유병자** a sleepwalker; a somnambulist.

몽정(夢精) a nocturnal pollution [emission]; seminal loss during a lascivious dream; a wet dream. **몽정하다** have a nocturnal pollution [emission]; have a wet dream.

몽치 a cudgel; a club; a truncheon. ¶쇠~ an iron cudgel.

몽타주 (a) montage.
●**몽타주 사진** (make) a composite picture [photograph]; a composite; (compose) a montage picture [photo]; a photomontage.

몽혼(朦昏) an(a)esthesia; narcotism. ⇨˝마취

몽환(夢幻) dreams and phantasma; (a) fantasy; visions. ¶~적 dreamlike / dreamy / phantasmal.
●**몽환곡** [음] a nocturne.

뫼 1 a grave; a tomb. ⇨˝무덤 **2** feed. ⇨˝모이

뫼(를) 쓰다 bury at [in]. ¶선산에 ~ bury in the family cemetery.

묏자리 a grave site; a site for a grave; a burial site. ¶~를 잡다 select [choose] a grave site / determine a burial site.

묘(妙) a mystery; a miracle; a wonder; [교묘] cleverness; adroitness. ¶조화의 ~ the mystery of nature [creation] / the wisdom of the creator // ~를 **터득하다** have a knack (for) / be clever (at / in) / be skillful (in).

묘(墓) a grave; a tomb. ⇨˝무덤

묘계(妙計) a capital [clever] scheme. ⇨˝묘책

묘기(妙技) [기술] wonderful skill; [곡예] a miraculous [wonderful] feat; (연예 등에서의) a wonderful performance; (야구 등에서의) a fine play. ¶공중 ~ an aerial stunt // ~를 부리다 perform a (miraculous) feat // 그 개는 여러 가지 ~를 할 수 있다 The dog can do many tricks.

묘령(妙齡) youth; the flower [prime] of youth; young [early] womanhood. ¶~의 여성 a young lady.

묘리(妙理) the abstruse [cardinal] principle; the profound law; [비결] the secret; the (subtle) point. ¶~를 **터득하다** apprehend the profound principle [law] / get the knack (of) / know the secret (of).

묘목(苗木) a (young) plant; a nursery tree; a sapling; a seedling. ¶장미[토마토]의 ~ a young rose [tomato] plant.

묘미(妙味) exquisiteness; charm; beauty; a nicety; a nice point. ¶거기에 등산의 ~가 있다 That's the attraction of mountain climbing. // 이 시의 ~를 알 수 있는가 Can you appreciate the exquisite flavor of this poem?

묘박(錨泊) anchoring; anchorage. **묘박하다** anchor.

묘방(妙方) **1** [신묘한 처방] a wonder-drug [secret] prescription. **2** a capital [clever] scheme. ⇨˝묘책

묘법(妙法) **1** [교묘한 방법] an excellent method; a clever way [means]; [비결] the mystery; the secret. **2** (부처의) the supreme [marvelous] law of Buddha.

묘비(墓碑) a tombstone; a gravestone; a funerary slab; a mortuary monument. ¶~를 세우다 set up a tombstone / place a tombstone (over a grave).
●**묘비명**(−銘) an epitaph; an inscription on a tombstone.

묘사(描寫) (a) description; (인물·풍물의) a portrait; (문어) (a) depiction; delineation; representation. ¶감각적 ~ a sensational description // 사실적 ~ realistic description // 성격 ~ character delineation [portrayal] // 실물 ~ model drawing // 심리적 ~ a psychological description // 인물 ~ character portrayal / characterization // 인상 ~ an impressionistic description. **묘사하다** describe; portray; (문어) depict; delineate; represent; picture. ¶유명한 해전을 묘사한 그림 a picture representing [a painting depicting] a famous sea battle // 빈민가의 생활을 묘사한 소설 a novel depicting slum life // 정경을 생생하게 ~ give a vivid description of a scene // 그는 그 정경을 생생히 묘사했다 He described the scene vividly. / He gave a vivid description of the scene.

묘상(苗床) [농] a seedbed; a seed-plot; a seed tray; [묘목밭] a nursery.

묘석(墓石) stonework set before a tomb. ⇨˝석물

묘소(墓所) a graveyard; a burial ground [place].

묘수(妙手) **1** [명수] an expert. **2** [장기 등의 뛰어난 수] a clever move; excellent skill.

묘안(妙案) a happy [bright] idea; an excellent [ingenious] plan [scheme]. ¶~을 생각해 내다 hit on [be struck with] a capital idea / a bright idea strikes one // ~이 떠올랐다 A bright [good] idea came to me.

묘안석(猫眼石) [광] (a) cat's-eye.

묘약(妙藥) a miracle [wonder] drug [cure]; [특효약] a specific medicine [remedy].

묘역(墓域) a graveyard.

묘연하다(杳然-) (거리가) far away; remote; [기억이 흐릿하다] dim; vague; indistinct; (소식이) unknown; missing. ¶그의 소식이 ~ Nothing whatever has been heard of him. / His whereabouts are [still remain] utterly unknown. / No clue to his whereabouts has been found.∥그의 행방이 ~ No one knows his whereabouts.

묘제(墓祭) ancestral rites held before the grave.

묘지(墓地) a graveyard; a burial ground [place]; (공동묘지) a (public) cemetery; (교회 부속의) a churchyard; God's acre. ¶공원~ a cemetery park∥국립~ the National Cemetery∥무연고(無緣故) ~ a potter's field∥유엔 ~ the U.N. Memorial Cemetery.

묘지기(墓-) a grave keeper.

묘책(妙策) a capital [clever] scheme; an ingenious plan. ¶~을 생각해 내다 hit on a clever method [idea].

묘판(苗板) [농] a rice seedbed. ⇨못자리1

묘포(苗圃) [농] a seedbed; a nursery (garden).

묘하다(妙-) **1** [기묘하다] strange; curious; odd(▶ strange는 낯설고 불가사의한, curious는 호기심을 돋우는, odd는 보통과 다른 기묘함); queer; funny; singular; (속어) rum. ¶묘한 것 a curious thing / an oddity∥묘한 사람 a queer (kind of) person / an odd fish / an oddity / (구어) a curiosity / (구어) a caution / (구어) a case∥묘한 버릇 a peculiar [an eccentric] habit∥묘한 얼굴 a funny face / [찌푸린 얼굴] a grimace / (속어) a mug∥~이라니 묘한 일이다 it is strange that ... / it is a curious thing that ...∥묘하게도 curious [strange] to say [relate] / strange to tell / strangely [curiously / funnily] enough / the strange thing is ...∥묘하게 들리다 [보이다] sound [look] strange [funny]∥일이 묘하게 되었다 It had an unexpected outcome. / It had unexpected [strange] consequences.∥어제 묘한 일이 생겼다 A curious thing happened to me yesterday.∥그 지방에는 묘한 풍습이 있다 There is an odd custom in the area.∥그것을 듣고 그는 묘한 얼굴을 했다 On hearing it, he made a queer face(▶ queer는 사람에게 쓰면 구어에서 동성 연애를 의미하기 때문에 쓰지 않는 것이 바람직함). **2** [절묘하다] exquisite; subtle; marvelous; wonderful; excellent.

묘혈(墓穴) [시체 묻는 구덩이] a grave; a tomb; a pit (for a dead body). ¶스스로 ~을 파다 dig one's own grave / bring about one's own ruin / be one's own funeral∥그렇게 하는 것은 스스로 ~을 파는 거나 같다 It would be suicidal to do that.∥지금 정책을 변경하는 것은 스스로 ~을 파는 거나 마찬가지다 Changing our policy now would be like digging our own grave [would be disastrous / would ruin us].

무 [식] a radish; an icicle radish.

무 밑동 같다 be all alone in this world.

무(武) [군사] military [material] affairs; [무예] military arts; the science of war. ¶~를 **닦다** train oneself in warlike arts / encourage military arts.

무(無) [없음] nothing; naught; nil; nihility; nullity; zero. ¶~가 되다 [로 돌아가다] come [be brought] to naught [nothing] / go for [to] nothing / be in vain / be wasted / be lost / be thrown away / be expunged / fall through∥~에서 유는 생기지 않는다 Nothing comes of [from] nothing.∥일체가 ~다 All is vanity.∥나의 모든 노력이 ~로 돌아갔다 All my efforts came to nothing [went for nothing / were wasted].

무-(無) no; none; un-; in-. ¶~관심 indifference / unconcern.

무가당(無加糖) ¶~의 unsweetened / sugarless / sugar-free∥~ 오렌지 주스 sugarless orange juice∥~ 요구르트 unsweetened yog(h)urt∥~ 연유 unsweetened condensed milk.

무가치하다(無價値-) worthless; valueless; of no value; useless.

무간하다(無間-) intimate; familiar; friendly. ¶무간한 친구 a good [a close / an intimate] friend∥무간하게 지내다 associate on friendly [cordial] terms (with)∥무간한 사이다 be on intimate terms (with) / be friends (with).

무감각(無感覺) **1** [감각이 없음] insensibility; senselessness; [마비되어 있음] numbness; [무감동] apathy; impassiveness; callousness; callosity. **무감각하다** insensible (to pain); anesthetic; numb; apathetic; callous; thick-skinned; dead (to pity); (서술적) have no feeling. ¶무감각하게 되다 become numbed / be benumbed∥고통에 대해서 ~ be insensible to pain∥추위 때문에 발가락이 무감각해졌다 My toes are numb with cold. **2** [감수성이 둔함] insensitivity; [무신경] callousness. ¶미에 대한 ~ a lack of sensitivity to beauty. **무감각하다** insensitive (to); (문어) insensible (of); callous. ¶남의 고생에 대하여 ~ be callous [apathetic] to the sufferings of others∥그는 치욕 [모욕]에 대해서 ~ He doesn't seem to feel shame [insults] at all.∥그는 남의 괴로움에 대해 ~ He is indifferent to other people's sufferings. / He is callous [unfeeling] about the sufferings of others.∥요즘엔 거리의 소음에 대해서 나는 무감각하게 되었다 Recently I have become insensitive [immune] to street noise.

무개(無蓋) ¶~의 open / uncovered.
● **무개차** an open car. **무개화차**(-貨車) (미) an open freight car; (영) an open wagon; (긴 물건 수송용의) (미) a flatcar.

무겁다 1 [무게가 많다] heavy; weighty. ¶무거운 발소리 a clamp / a heavy tramp∥무거운 짐 a heavy load∥무겁게 하다 make heavy∥무거워지다 become heavy [heavier]∥이 문은 ~ This is a heavy door.

2 [입이] taciturn; uncommunicative; reticent; quiet; reserved (in speech); (행동이) prudent; serious; grave; ponderous. ¶입이 무거운 사람 a taciturn [reticent / discreet / tight-lipped] person∥그는 입이 ~ He's very discreet. / He can keep a secret.

3 [머리·기분·분위기가] heavy; depressed; dull; languid. ¶무거운 분위기 an oppressive atmosphere∥무거운 마음으로 with a heavy heart∥마음이 ~ have a heavy heart / be depressed in spirits / weigh on one's spirits∥그의 말이 내 마음을 무겁게 짓눌렀다 What he said depressed me [weighed (heavily) on my heart].∥오늘은 왠지 머리가 ~ Somehow my head feels heavy today.∥기분이 ~ I feel depressed [(구어) down].∥아버지가 돌아가신 후 우리 집에는 무거운 분위기가 감돌았다 After my father's death, there was

gloom hanging over our house.
4 [병이 심하다] serious; critical; [죄가 크다] grave; grievous; [벌이 심하면] severe. ¶무거운 벌 a heavy [severe] punishment // 무거운 죄 a grave crime / (a) felony // 무거운 병 a serious [severe] illness [disease] / a disease of a serious nature // 친구의 병이 ~ My friend is seriously ill. / My friend's illness is serious.
5 [중요하다] important; weighty; momentous; grave. ¶무거운 직책 an important position [post] / a position of trust // 무거운 책임 a heavy [grave] responsibility // 무거운 사명을 띠고 있다 be charged with an important mission // 이번 임무는 대단히 ~ This mission involves very heavy responsibilities.

무게 1 [중량] weight; (미) heft. ¶실의 ~ the weight of thread // 대단한 ~ a heavy [lumping] weight // ~로 내려앉다 collapse [give way] beneath [under the weight of] (the people) // ~를 지탱하다 bear the weight // 자신의 몸~를 달아 weigh oneself // ~가 많이 [적게] 나가다 be heavy [light] // 달걀을 ~로 팔다 sell eggs by weight // 요새 내 몸~가 줄었다 I have lost weight recently. // 저 정육점에서는 쇠고기의 ~를 넉넉하게 [모자라게] 달아 판다 They sell beef at good [short] weight at that store. // 이 애는 몸~가 30킬로그램이나 나간다 The child weighs all of 30 kilograms. // 이 수박이 ~가 더 나간다 This watermelon is heavier than the other one.
2 [중요성] weight; importance; [위엄] dignity; [가치] worth; value. ¶~ 없는 unimposing / undignified / (an opinion) of no weight // ~ 있는 사람 a man of dignified presence // ~ 있는 말 a remark carrying weight [authority / conviction] // ~를 더하다 gain in dignity // 그녀의 말에는 ~가 있었다 Her words carried weight. // 교장 선생님은 ~ 있는 분이다 The principal is a very dignified person.
●**무게 중심**(-中心) [물] the center [(영) centre] of gravity.

무경험(無經驗) inexperience; lack [want] of experience; greenness. ¶~의 inexperienced / unexperienced / untrained / raw / green.
●**무경험자** an inexperienced person; a green [an untrained] hand; (구어) a greenhorn. ¶~ 환영 (광고) Help wanted. Experience not necessary.

무계획(無計劃) ¶복지에 대한 정부의 ~에는 어처구니가 없다 The government's total lack of a consistent plan for welfare is simply appalling. **무계획하다** unplanned; haphazard; [무모하다] reckless. ¶무계획한 토지 개발 haphazard [unplanned] land development // 그녀는 무계획하게 돈을 쓴다 She spends her money recklessly.

무고(誣告) [거짓으로 꾸며 고소함] a false accusation [charge]; [법] a malicious prosecution; (문서에 의한) a libel; a slander; a calumny (구두의). ¶…에 대한 절도죄의 ~ a false accusation of theft against (a person).
무고하다 slander; calumniate; make a false accusation [charge] (against a person); accuse (a person) falsely (of theft).
●**무고죄** calumny; libel; a false accusation [charge].

무고하다(無故-) [무사하다] safe and sound; (서술적) nothing is the matter (with); be all right; [건강하다] be (quite) well. ¶무고하게 지내다 get along well [all right] // 댁내 무고하신지요 Have all of you been well? // 온 가족이 ~ Everyone in my family is getting along well.

무고하다(無辜-) [사실과 다르다] false; [결백하다] innocent; guiltless. ¶무고한 죄 a false charge // 무고한 백성 innocent people // 무고함이 밝혀지다 have one's innocence established / be proved innocent / be cleared from the charge // 무고한 절도죄로 고발당하다 be falsely accused of theft // 무고한 죄로 투옥되다 be put into prison on a false charge // 그는 탈세라는 무고한 죄를 뒤집어썼다 He was falsely [unjustly] charged with [accused of] tax evasion.

무곡(舞曲) [음] a dance music. ⇨춤곡

무골충(無骨蟲) [뼈 없는 벌레] a (boneless) worm; [줏대 없이 무른 사람] a spineless [backboneless] fellow; an invertebrate.

무골호인(無骨好人) the meekest of men; an excessively good-natured person; (미국 속어) a come-on.

무공(武功) military achievements [merits / exploits / feats]; distinguished military services. ¶~을 세우다 distinguish oneself in war [action] / render distinguished military services // ~을 세워 훈장을 받다 be awarded a medal for outstanding [meritorious] military services.
●**무공 훈장** the Order of Military Merit. ¶화랑 [태극] ~을 받다 be awarded the Order of Military Merit *Hwarang* [*Taegeuk*].

무과(武科) the military service examination (for the royal army).

무과실 책임(無過失責任) [법] strict [absolute / no-fault] liability; liability without (any) fault.

무관(武官) an officer; a military [naval] officer.

무관(無冠) ¶~의 uncrowned // ~의 제왕 an uncrowned king [monarch] / a king without a crown.

무관심(無關心) indifference; unconcern; nonchalance; apathy; callousness; lacking interest (in). ¶정치적 ~ political apathy // 교육에 대한 일반인의 ~ the indifference of the general public toward education. **무관심하다** indifferent (to); unconcerned (about / with); apathetic; nonchalant; callous (to); uninterested (in); careless (about / of). ¶무관심한 대답 an indifferent response / a half-hearted answer // 무관심한 태도 an air of indifference // 무관심하게 with an air of casualness [nonchalance] / in a casual manner / casually // 남의 감정에 ~ have no regard for the feelings of others // 그녀는 옷차림 [머리형]에는 ~ She is unconcerned [careless] about her clothes [hairdo]. // 그는 음식에는 무관심한 것 같다 He seems indifferent to food. // 그는 자신의 평판에 전혀 ~ He is totally indifferent to [unconcerned about] his own reputation. // 그는 그 문제에 전혀 무관심한 체하고 있다 He is assuming an air of total indifference to the matter. // 그는 거기에 대해서 전혀 무관심한 것처럼 행동했다 He acted quite unconcerned about it. // 학생의 대부분은 국제 문제에 무관심했다 Most of the students were indifferent to [showed little interest in] international problems. // 그들은 다른 사람이

무관하다 받은 부당한 처우에 대해 무관심했다 They were apathetic to the injustice done to others.∥이제 와서 우리는 그 문제에 무관심할 수는 없다 We can no longer remain unconcerned about the problem.

무관하다(無關-) unconnected; unconcerned; unrelated; indifferent; (서술적) have no connection (with); have no relation (to / with); have nothing to do (with); be not connected (with); be not concerned (in / with); be independent (of); be irrelevant (to). ¶문제에 무관한 사항 a matter foreign [extraneous] to the question∥그것은 나와는 전혀 ~ That does not concern [regard] me at all.∥나는 그 사건과 ~ I have nothing to do with [I am not concerned in] the case. / I have no part in the affair.∥그가 무엇을 하든 나와는 ~ It matters little to me whatever he may do.∥그것은 지금 논의 중인 문제와는 ~ That is irrelevant to the topic under discussion.∥이 것은 주민의 생활 향상과 전혀 ~ This has no bearing whatever on the betterment of the living conditions of the inhabitants.∥그의 인생은 예술과 무관했다 His life had nothing to do with art.∥그는 세상사와 ~ He stands aloof from the world.∥나는 그들과 ~ I do not associate with them.∥국민 감정과는 무 관하게 정치적 거래가 이루어지고 있다 Political maneuvering is being carried on regardless [quite independently] of the people's feelings.

무교육자(無敎育者) an uneducated person.

무구하다(無垢-) pure; spotless; innocent; (문어) immaculate.

무국적(無國籍) statelessness; a loss of nationality. ¶~ 피난민 a stateless refugee∥~의 stateless.
● **무국적자** a stateless person; a denationalized person. ¶~가 되다 lose one's nationality [citizenship] / be denationalized.

무궁무진하다(無窮無盡-) infinite; endless; boundless; inexhaustible. ¶그 지방에는 철광이 무궁무진하다 The region has inexhaustible deposits of iron ore.

무궁하다(無窮-) eternal; infinite; everlasting; immortal; endless; boundless. **무궁히** eternally; infinitely; forever; immortally.

무궁화(無窮花) mugunghwa; a rose of Sharon; an althea.

무궤도(無軌道) lacking tracks; aberration; recklessness; rashness. ¶~의 railless / unrailed / trackless. **무궤도하다** [상궤를 벗어나다] aberrant; wild; eccentric; extravagant; unprincipled. ¶무궤도한 행동 erratic [unprincipled] behavior∥무궤도한 생활 a reckless [loose / dissipated] life∥무궤도한 행동을 하다 be eccentric in behavior∥그의 무궤도한 짓에 모두가 골머리를 앓고 있다 All of us are annoyed by his eccentricities [wild behavior].
● **무궤도 전차** a trackless tram; a trackless trolley car.

무균(無菌) [의] asepsis. ¶~의 aseptic / germfree / without bacilli [germs]∥~의 수술 기구 aseptic surgical instrument.
● **무균 사육** (동물의) germ-free feeding.

무극(無極) 1 [무한] endlessness; limitlessness; boundlessness. ¶~의 endless / limitless / boundless. 2 [물] [전극이 없음]. ¶~의 [무전극의] without poles / lacking poles / nonpolar.
● **무극성 분자** a nonpolar molecule.

무근하다(無根-) groundless; baseless; unfounded; false. ¶전혀 사실무근한 이야기 a pure fabrication∥그 보도는 사실 ~ The report is unfounded [a pure fabrication]. / There is no foundation for the report.

무급(無給) ¶~의 unpaid / unsalaried / gratuitous / honorary∥~으로 without pay [salary] / for nothing / gratuitously∥~의 의사[일] an unpaid doctor [job]∥~의 서기(단체 등의) an honorary secretary∥~으로 일하다 serve without pay / work for nothing∥그 직책은 ~이다 The post carries no pay.

무기(武器) 1 [전투에 쓰이는 기구] a weapon; (집합적) arms; weaponry; ordnance; armament. ¶대항 ~ a counterweapon∥재래식 ~ conventional weapons∥핵~ a nuclear weapon∥~와 탄약 arms and ammunition∥~의 불법 소지 illegal possession of arms∥조국을 위해 ~를 들다 take up arms for one's country∥~를 휴대하다 carry [bear] arms∥~를 버리고 나와라 Lay [Throw] down your weapons [arms] and come out.
2 [(일정 목적을 이루는 데 쓰이는) 힘]. ¶달변이 그가 믿는 ~였다 Eloquence was his most trusted weapon.∥눈물은 여자의 ~다 Tears are a woman's weapon.∥그녀는 미모라는 ~를 갖고 있었다 She was armed with beauty.
● **무기고** an armory; ordnance stores; (미) an ordnance department.

무기(無期) an indefinite period. ⇨무기한
● **무기 공채** a perpetual public loan. **무기수**(-囚) a lifer. **무기 연기** (an) indefinite postponement. ¶~가 되다 be postponed [put off] indefinitely [for an indefinite period]. **무기정학** suspension from school. ¶그는 ~ 처분을 받았다 He was suspended from school for an indefinite period. **무기 징역** [종신 징역] imprisonment for life; (판결) a life sentence [term]. **무기형** imprisonment for life.

무기(無機) ¶토양의 ~ 성분 the mineral content of the soil∥~의 (화학에서) inorganic / unorganized / (광물의) mineral.
● **무기물** inorganic matter; an inorganic substance; a mineral. **무기질** [무기물] inorganic matter; [광물질] mineral matter. **무기화학** inorganic chemistry; a biochemistry. **무기 화합물** an inorganic compound.

무기력하다(無氣力-) spiritless; enervate; nerveless; lethargic; languid; leaden; flabby. ¶무기력한 외교 weak-kneed diplomacy∥무기력한 복종 tame submission∥무기력하게 하다 enervate / emasculate / weaken∥그렇게 무기력해서 어떻게 하겠는가 What can you do if you are so weak-kneed [(구어) gutless]?

무기명(無記名) ¶~의 unregistered / (무서명의) unsigned / (주식·채권 등의) blank / uninscribed / ~식의 (배서 등의) blank / general / (지참인 지불의) (a check) payable to bearer / bearer (check).
● **무기명 공채** [사채 / 증권] an unregistered [a bearer] bond [debenture / security]. **무기명 투표** a secret ballot; a secret vote; secret voting.

무기음(無氣音) [언] unaspirated sounds.

무기한(無期限) an indefinite period; no time limit. ¶~의 limitless / indefinite / without a time limit∥~으로 indefinitely / for an indef-

inite period[time] / without time limit // 회담을 ~ 연기하다 postpone a meeting indefinitely[for an indefinite period] // 이 티켓은 ~ 유효하다 This ticket is valid[good] at any time.
● 무기한 파업 a no-time limit strike. ¶~에 돌입하다 go on strike for an indefinite period.

무김치 radish *gimchi*(kimchi)[pickles]; pickled radish.

무난하다(無難-) **1** [쉽다] easy; simple; not difficult. **무난히** easily; without (any) difficulty[trouble]; with ease; readily. ¶그것은 ~ 끝났다 It was finished successfully. // 나는 그들 모임에 ~ 가입했다 I had no trouble (in) joining their circle. / I joined their circle without any difficulty[trouble].
2 [안전하다] safe; secure; free from danger. ¶무난한 정책 a safe policy / 무난한 화제로 이야기하다 chatter away on safe[harmless] topics // 만일의 경우에 대비하는 것이 무난할 것이다 It will be safe for you to prepare for emergency. **무난히** safely; securely; uneventfully. ¶그날 밤은 ~ 지나갔다 The night passed uneventfully[without accident]. / Things were quiet that night.
3 [무던하다] fairly good; moderate; passable; acceptable; flawless; free from fault. ¶무난한 작품이 적었다 There were few passable [tolerable] works. // 그만하면 그저 ~ This is tolerable[passable]. / This may pass. / This may be acceptable. // 이 사진이면 ~ This photo may pass[will probably do]. / (구어) You can probably get away with this photo.

무남독녀(無男獨女) an[the] only daughter; a daughter and only child (of).

무너뜨리다 break down; pull down; tear down; destroy; (문어) demolish. ¶돌담을 ~ tear[pull] down a stone wall // 산을 ~ level a hill / 적진을 ~ put an enemy force to rout // 정부를 ~ overthrow[unseat / topple] the government // 낡은 탑을 무너뜨렸다 We tore [pulled] down the old tower.

무너지다 1 [붕괴하다] crumble; go[fall] to pieces; collapse; break; give way; be destroyed; come down; [함몰하다] cave in. ¶무너져 가는 crumbling (wall) / ruinous (hut) // 금방이라도 무너질 것 같은 오두막 a tumbledown shack // 짐 더미가 무너졌다 The piles of cargo crumbled. // 비가 와서 벼랑이 무너졌다 The rain caused a landslide. // 눈의 무게로 지붕이 무너졌다 The roof collapsed [caved in] under the weight of the snow. // 현수교가 무너졌다 The suspension bridge gave way. // 갱도의 천장이 무너져 세 명의 광부가 갇혔다 Three miners were trapped by the collapse of the tunnel roof.
2 [질서 등이 파괴되다] break; give way; be thrown into disorder[confusion]; be routed. ¶군대가 무너졌다 The army gave away[was routed]. // 면밀한 계획이 사소한 실수로 무너지고 말았다 My carefully made plans collapsed due to a small mistake.

무녀(巫女) an exorcist; a (female) shaman. ⇨무당

무념무상(無念無想) [불] freedom from all ideas and thoughts. ¶~의 경지 (enter) a state of impassivity / free from all ideas and all thoughts // ~이 되다 rid oneself of all worldly thoughts / attain a perfect serenity of mind.

무념하다(無念-) (서술적) be in a frame of mind void of all ideas and thoughts; be free from all distracting thoughts.

무능(無能) incompetency; inefficiency; lack of ability; inability; incapacity; inadequacy; inequality (to a task). ¶경찰의 ~을 비난하다 criticize the inefficiency of the police. **무능하다** incompetent; inefficient; incapable; ineffective; talentless; lacking in ability[efficiency]; good-for-nothing. ¶무능한 사람 an incompetent (man) / a man of no ability / a good-for-nothing (fellow) // 무능한 정권 an inefficient regime // 그 사람은 ~ He is good for nothing. / He has nothing (good) in him. // 그는 무능해서 해고되었다 He was dismissed (merely) for incompetence.

무능력(無能力) inability (at / in / to do); lack of ability; [법] incompetence; incapacity (for / to do); disability. ¶~화 incapacitation // ~화하다 incapacitate / disable (a person for work) / cripple. **무능력하다** incompetent; inefficient; incapable; lacking in ability. ¶재정상 무능력해지다 be financially crippled.
● **무능력자** an incompetent[incapable] (person); a person without (legal) capacity.

무늬 a pattern; a figure(▶ figure는 반복되는 작은 무늬); a design(▶ 모양이나 색채를 다루는 방법이나 배열 등을 강조함); (털·깃 등의) (a) marking. ¶유행하는 ~ the pattern in fashion[vogue] // 복잡한 ~ an intricate design // ~가 있는 figured / patterned // 줄~ stripes / a striped pattern // 물방울 ~ polka dots // 꽃 ~ floral design / flower patterns // 손으로 그린 ~를 넣은 찻잔 teacups with hand-painted designs // 나비를 날개의 ~로 구별하다 distinguish butterflies by the markings on their wings // ~를 넣다 figure / pattern / decorate with a pattern / make designs[patterns].

무단(武斷) militarism; enforcement(강행); highhandedness.
● **무단 정치** military government[rule]; government by the bayonet; an iron rule. ¶~를 하다 govern by the bayonet / rule one's people with the rod of iron.

무단(無斷) **1** [예고 없음]. **무단히** without (pervious) notice; without warning; unannounced. ¶부모에게 알리지 않고 ~ 여행을 떠나다 go on a trip without the knowledge of [without saying so to] one's parents. **2** [허가 없음]. ¶~출입 금지 (게시) No trespassing. // ~ 흥행 금지 (게시) All rights of performance reserved. **무단히** without permission [leave]. ¶~ 차용하다 borrow (something) without the owner's permission // 남의 것을 ~ 사용하다 make free use of another's possessions.
● **무단결근** an unauthorized absence; being absent without permission[due notice]; absence without leave[(due) notice]. ¶~을 하다 be absent without leave[without (due) notice] / stay from work without leave. **무단결석** (school) truancy. ¶~을 하다 absent oneself (from school) without notice / stay away (from school) / play truant / cut a class / (미) play hook(e)y. **무단 사용** illegal use.

무담보(無擔保) ¶~의 unsecured / naked / without collateral[security] // ~로 대부하다

무당 grant (a person) a loan without security.
● 무담보 대출금 an unsecured loan. 무담보 사채 an unsecured [a naked] debenture.
무당 a mudang; an exorcist; a (female) shaman; a sorceress; a witch; [영매] a (psychic) medium (pl. ~s).
무당벌레 [동] a ladybird (beetle); a lady cow; [미] a ladybug; a lady beetle.
무당새 [동] a yellow bunting.
무대(舞臺) 1 (연극의) the stage; the boards. ¶원형 ~ [미] a theater-in-the-round // 회전 ~ a revolving [rotative] stage // ~에 서다[나가다] appear on the stage [before the footlights] / make stage appearance / play the stage role / [배우가 되다] go on [come on / follow] the stage / take to the stage // 각본을 ~에 올리다 stage a play / put a play on the stage [boards] / present [produce] a play // ~에서 물러나다 go [come] offstage / [은퇴하다] retire from the stage // 그녀는 6살 때 첫 ~를 밟았다 She made her début [her first appearance] on the stage at the age of six. // 거기서 ~가 바뀐다 The scene changes [shifts] there. // 그는 작년에 ~를 떠났다 He left [retired from] the stage last year. // 그는 ~에 복귀할 희망을 갖고 있다 He hopes to come back to the stage.
2 (활동의) the sphere [field] (of activity); the arena; the stage; theater. ¶경쟁 ~ the arena of competition // 활동 ~ one's sphere of activity / one's field of action / the stage of one's operations // 세계를 ~로 하여 with the whole world as one's stage // 국제 ~에 서다 appear on the international stage // 이 소설은 서울을 ~로 하고 있다 The story is laid in Seoul. // 여기가 그의 활동 ~이다 This is his realm [sphere]. / There is his theatre of activity. // 그는 세계를 ~로 하여 활약하고 있다 The wide world is his stage. // 이야기의 ~는 전국 시대이다 [로 옮아간다] The story is set in [The scene of the story shifts to] the age of civil wars. // 그는 정치 ~에 화려하게 등장했다 He made a dazzling début [appearance] on the stage of politics [on the political scene].
● 무대 감독 stage management(일); a stage director [manager] (사람). ¶~을 하다 stage-manage. 무대 경험 stage experience. 무대극 a stage play [drama]; the speaking stage. 무대 예술 theatrical art. 무대 의상 stage [theatrical] costume. ¶~을 입은 배우 an actor in costume. 무대 장치 stage setting; decor; (프) mise-en-scène. ¶~ 담당자 a sceneshifter / a sceneman / a grip(조수) / (소도구의) a property man [master] // ~를 하다 set the stage. 무대 조명 stage illumination; stage lighting. 무대 효과 stage effect; scenic effects.

무더기 a pile; a heap; a deposit; a lot; a mound. ¶사과 한 ~ a pile of apples // 돌~ a pile [heap] of stones // 고철 ~ a heap of iron scrap // 그들은 한 ~에 2,000원에 사과를 팔고 있었다 They were selling apples at 2,000 won per basket. // 쓰레기가 여기저기 ~로 널려 있었다 Debris lay in heaps here and there. // 사람들이 ~로 죽었다 People died in piles [a mass].

무더위 sultriness; hot and humid weather; (high) humidity; sultry weather; sweltering heat. ¶대단한 ~다 be oppressively hot and humid / be awfully sultry [sweltering].

무던하다 1 (정도가) serviceable; passable; satisfactory. ¶그만하면 ~ That will serve the purpose. // 그만한 돈이면 그에게는 ~ Such an amount of money surely will do for him. 무던히 [어지간히] quite; fairly; fairly; considerably. ¶~ 애쓰다 make considerable efforts // 오늘은 ~도 추운 날이다 It's awfully cold today. 2 (성질이) generous; broad-minded; liberal; quite good [nice]. ¶무던한 사람 a good-natured man // 무던한 마음씨 generosity / magnanimity // 그는 사람됨이 ~ He is good-natured. / He is quite a nice man. / He is broad-minded.

무덤 a grave; a tomb; a graveyard; a cemetery; (남) a sepulcher. (▶ grave는 땅을 파고 만든 일반적인 묘, tomb는 규모가 아주 큰 묘, graveyard는 교회의 묘지, cemetery는 교회에 딸리지 않은 공동묘지를 가리킴) ¶합장한 ~ a twin grave for man and wife // A 씨의 ~ (묘비명) "Sacred to the Memory of Mr. A" // ~파는 사람 a gravedigger / a sexton // ~에 묻다 bury (the body) in a grave / entomb / consign (the body) to the grave // ~에 잠들다 lie in one's grave / be under the sod // ~에 꽃다발을 바치다 place [lay] a wreath [bunch of flowers] on [at] the grave (of) // ~을 파다 dig a grave // ~을 만들다 build a tomb / set up a tombstone // 스스로 ~을 파다 dig one's own grave / bring about one's own ruin / be one's own funeral // 그것은 스스로 ~을 파는 격이다 It is suicidal [tantamount to digging your own grave] to take such a step.

무덥다 sultry; sweltering; muggy; close and hot; hot and damp; steaming; humid. ¶무더운 날씨 muggy [sultry] weather // 무더운 방 a close and hot room // 무더워 잠 못 자다 cannot sleep well on account of the oppressive heat // 오늘은 무더워 못 견디겠다 It is unbearably hot and humid today.

무도(武道) [예] (the) martial arts [science]; [무사도] chivalry; knighthood; the precepts of a warrior.

무도(舞蹈) [춤] a dance; [춤추기] dancing; footing; (속어) hop; (프) pas. ¶죽음의 ~ the dance of death // ~의 상대 a (dance) partner. 무도하다 dance; perform a dance; (속어) shake a leg; (미국 속어) hop (it).
● 무도곡 dance music. 무도장 (미) a dance hall; a dancing hall. 무도회 a ball; a dancing party; a dance. ¶가면 [가장] ~ a masked [fancy dress] ball / a masquerade // ~용 드레스 a ball dress // ~를 열다 give a ball [dance].

무도병(舞蹈病) [의] St. Vitus's dance; chorea; the jumps.

무도하다(無道−) wicked; evil; atrocious; inhuman; immoral; brutal; cruel; heartless; outrageous. ¶무도한 짓을 하다 act brutally [cruelly] toward (a person) / be cruel (to).
무도히 wickedly; evil; atrociously.

무독하다(無毒−) 1 [무해하다] nonpoisonous; innoxious; innocuous; nonvenomous (snake). ¶무독한 뱀 a harmless [nonpoisonous] snake. 2 [성질이 온순하다] gentle; tender; soft; mild; suave; quiet.

무두장이 a tanner.
무두질 1 (가죽의) tanning; tannage; tawing; dressing skin. 무두질하다 tan (hide); dress; taw. ¶무두질한 가죽 tanned leather // 무두질

할 수 있는 tannable // 무두질하지 않은 an untanned [raw] (hide) // 가죽을 ~ tan [dress] a hide. **2** [고통] a grinding [pricking / burning / gnawing / piercing / stabbing] pain (in stomach). 무두질하다 grind; burn; gnaw; prick; pierce; stab. ¶배 속에서 ~ have a gnawing pain in one's stomach.

무드 [기분] a mood. ¶~를 조성하다 create [set] a mood.
● 무드음악 mood(y) music.

무득점(無得點) ¶~의 scoreless / [야구] runless // 시합은 ~으로 끝났다 The game ended in a scoreless tie. // 투수는 7회까지 그들을 ~으로 막았다(야구에서) The pitcher held them scoreless for seven innings. // 우리는 상대방을 ~으로 눌렀다 We shut out our opponents. // 그때까지의 ~은 8회에서 깨졌다 The string of goose eggs was broken in the eighth inning.

무디다 **1** [날이 예리하지 못하다] dull; blunt; obtuse; pointless; edgeless. ¶무딘 면도날 a dull razor blade // 칼날이 ~ This blade is blunt[dull]. // 가위 날이 무디어졌다 The scissors have become dull[blunt]. / The scissors don't cut well any more.
2 [둔하다] dull; slow; thickheaded; slow-witted; dense. ¶무딘 사람 a dull [dense] person / a dullard / a dolt / a slow coach // 감각이 무디어지다 get dull of one's sense // 그는 운동 신경이 ~ He has slow reflexes. // 잠시 동안 연습을 하지 않았기 때문에 내 기술이 무디어졌다 Since I haven't practiced for some time, my skill has dulled. / (구어) Being out of practice, I've been rather rusty.
3 [말이 무지하고 뚝뚝하다] blunt; curt; short; brusque; rough; impolite; uncourteous. ¶무디게 말하다 talk bluntly [shortly / slowly] / be blunt of speech / have a rough manner of speaking.

무뚝뚝하다 [퉁명스럽다] blunt; brusque; abrupt; short; [붙임성 없다] unsociable; [멋없다] curt; [쌀쌀맞다] cold. ¶무뚝뚝한 사람 a blunt [brusque] person // 무뚝뚝한 말투 a brusque way of talking // 무뚝뚝한 대답 a curt [short / blunt] answer // 무뚝뚝하게 bluntly / curtly / brusquely // 무뚝뚝하게 말하다 speak with asperity / talk bluntly [shortly] // 무뚝뚝하게 대답하다 reply in a monosyllable / answer shortly / give a curt [blunt] answer // 그는 무뚝뚝한 태도로 손님을 대했다 He treated the visitor in an unfriendly[a cold] manner. // 그는 정말 무뚝뚝한 사람이다 He makes no effort whatsoever to be agreeable.

무람없다 impolite; discourteous; rude; impudent. 무람없이 impolitely; discourteously; rudely; impudently; without ceremony.

무량하다(無量-) immeasurable; infinite; incalculable; inestimable; beyond measure. ¶감개 ~ My heart is full.

무럭무럭 **1** [자라는 모양] rapidly; well; perceptibly; quickly. ¶~ 자라다 grow up quickly [rapidly] / (키가) become taller with rapidity [day by day] // 나무는 ~ 자랐다 The tree grew taller and taller. **2** [냄새·연기가] thickly; densely; heavily; in thick clouds. ¶김이 ~ 나다 puff steam // 연기가 ~ 난다 Smoke rises up in thick clouds. // 굴뚝에서 연기가 ~ 나왔다 Plumes of smoke rolled lavishly from the chimney.

무려(無慮) [자그마치] to the prodigious [vast] number of; as many as; no less than. ¶~ 5천 명 as many as five thousand // 71%의 지지표를 얻다 win a surprising 71% of vote (in) // ~ 2만 원을 주고 이 책을 샀다 This book cost as much as twenty thousand won. // ~ 2만 명의 청중이 모였다 The audience was about [approximately] twenty thousand strong. // ~ 1만 명의 구명을 탄원했다 No fewer than [as many as] ten thousand people petitioned for his life.

무력(武力) military force [power]; armed might [force]; force of arms; the sword [saber]; the mailed fist. ¶~으로 by (force of) arms / at the point of the bayonet [sword] // ~에 의하지 않고 without an appeal to arms // ~에 호소하다 appeal [resort] to arms [the sword] / use force // ~으로 굴복시키다 keep (people) in submission by the saber [sword] // ~으로 해결하다 settle (an affair) by force [the sword] // ~을 쓰다 use armed force // ~을 과시하다 make a show of force / demonstrate muscles // 그는 ~으로 천하를 평정하였다 He subjugated the whole nation by force (of arms).
● 무력간섭 armed intervention [interference]. 무력 도발 an armed [a military] provocation. 무력전 armed hostility. 무력행사 the use of armed force. ¶우리는 ~도 불사한다 We are ready to use armed force [resort to force].

무력감(無力感) a feeling of helplessness [ineffectualness].

무력하다(無力-) powerless; helpless; impotent; weak; feeble; incompetent; incapable. ¶무력한 부녀와 아이들 helpless women and children // 무력한 군대 ineffective troops // 무력하게 하다 incapacitate / debilitate / neutralize (enemy defense) // 적의 기습을 받아 수비대는 전혀 무력했다 The guards were utterly helpless in the face of the surprise attack by the enemy.

무렵 [때] time; [즈음] about; around; toward(s); [···할 즈음] about the time when .... ¶~에 at the time / on the occasion / when / as // 메밀꽃 필 ~ a buckwheat-flower season // 벚꽃이 필 ~에 in the cherry blossom season / when the cherry blossoms are in bloom // 해 질 ~에 toward evening / at sunset [sundown] // 그 ~에 in those days / at that time / then // 날이 밝아 올 ~에 toward daybreak // 매년 이 ~에(는) at this time of (the) year // 그 ~까지는 by that time // 19세기가 끝날 ~에 toward the end of the 19th century // 그 ~은 좋았었다 Things were much better in those days. / (감회에 젖어서) Those were the days! / Now the great times are done! // 그 ~과는 세상이 많이 달라졌다 Things have changed since those days. / Things are not what they used to be.

무례(無禮) [실례] impoliteness; rudeness; discourtesy; disrespect; [불손] insolence; impertinence. ¶저의 ~를 용서해 주시기 바랍니다 I humbly apologize for my lack of courtesy. / Please forgive my rudeness [bad manners]. 무례하다 impolite; rude; discourteous; disrespectful; indecent; uncivil; insolent; impertinent. ¶무례한 놈 an insolent [an impertinent / a rude] fellow / an insolent // 무례한 젊은이 an ill-bred young man // 무례

무뢰한

한 말을 하다 say rude things / use abusive language (to) / 무례한 태도를 취하다 be rude (to) / act disrespectfully (to) // 그런 말을 묻는 것은 무례한 일이다 It is impolite [bad manners] to ask such a question. // 나는 그런 무례한 질문에는 대답할 수 없다 I can't answer such impertinent questions. // 그 젊은이는 무례하게도 내 딸과 결혼할 것을 청해 왔다 That young man had the impudence to ask for my daughter's hand in marriage. **무례히** impolitely; rudely; discourteously; impertinently. ¶그는 ~ 그녀를 팔꿈치로 밀어제쳤다 He was rude [impolite] enough to elbow her aside.

무뢰한(無賴漢) a rogue; a villain; a scoundrel; a bum; a ruffian; a hooligan; a rowdy; a vagrant; (속어) a hoodlum; (구어) a roughneck; a desperado; a rascal; an outlaw.

무료(無料) no charge; free of charge. ¶~의 free (of charge) / gratuitous // ~로 free / free of charge / gratis // ~로 for nothing / without pay [fee] // ~로 제공되다 be offered free [without cost] // ~로 봉사하다 serve for nothing / work without pay // 배달은 ~입니다 It will be delivered free of charge. / There is no delivery charge. // 견본은 ~로 드립니다 You may have a sample free [for the asking]. (▶ for the asking은 「청구하는 대로」의 뜻) // 이 서비스는 일체 ~다 There is no charge whatever for this service. // 수화물은 20킬로그램까지는 ~다 Each passenger is allowed 20kilograms of baggage free. // 6세 미만 (게시) Admission free for children under six. // 상품 포장 ~ (게시) Case [Packing] free. / No charge for case. // 운임 ~ (게시) Freight free. // 입장 ~ (게시) Admission (is) free. / No charge for admission. // ~ 증정 (게시) Free gift. // ~ 통화 (게시) No charge for call. ●**무료 관람권** a complimentary [free] ticket. **무료승차권** a free pass (over a subway). **무료 진료소** a free clinic; a dispensary.

무료(無聊) [심심함] tedium; ennui; wearisomeness; dullness; [열없음] awkwardness. ¶~를 달래다 beguile the tedium / while away [kill] the time // 음악을 들으며 ~를 달랬다 I relieved my ennui [tedium / boredom] by listening to music. // 그는 잡담으로 ~를 달래려고 하였다 He tried to disguise his embarrassment by talking familiarly. **무료로다** tedious; wearisome; dull; boresome; tiresome; awkward; (서술적) suffer from [be overcome with] ennui. ¶무료하여 for want of occupation / because one has nothing to do // 혼자서 술을 마시면 무료하기만 하다 There is no pleasure in drinking alone.

무르녹다 1 [잘 익다] ripen; get fully ripe; mature; mellow; be at its best (꽃 등에). ¶무르녹은 과일 fruit with a mature softness / overripe fruit // 과일이 무르녹는다 Fruits get their full ripe.

2 [그늘이 매우 짙어지다] deepen; become deeper [verdurous]. ¶신록이 무르녹는다 The fresh green becomes deeper. / The woods are bright [glistening] with fresh verdure. // 여름이 다가옴에 따라 녹음이 무르녹았다 The green shade deepened toward summer.

3 [일이 한창때에 이르다] be ripe for (action); ripen; mature. ¶기운이 무르녹기를 기다리다 wait for a ripe opportunity // 때가 무르녹았다 The time is ripe for it. / The opportunity has matured. / It is high time (now).

무르다¹ 1 (익어서) soften; get soft; become tender. ¶복숭아가 물렀다 The peach has got soft. 2 (요리되어) be well cooked [done]; get soft; become tender. ¶무른 감자 a well-cooked potato // 알맞게 ~ be done to a turn // 지나치게 ~ be overdone / be boiled to a pulp // 잘 물렀습니까 Is it cooked well? / Is it well done? // 이건 아직 안 물렀다 This is only half boiled [half done]. / This is underdone.

무르다² 1 (산 것을) take back [redeem] money cancelling a purchase; get a refund; (판 것을) give back [return] money cancelling a sale; give a refund. ¶대금을 ~ refund the price paid // 샀던 시계를 ~ return the watch one (has) bought and get the money back // 팔았던 시계를 물러 주다 accept [receive] the watch one (has) sold and refund the price paid // 마음에 들지 않거든 언제든지 물러 드리겠습니다 We will refund your money at any time should you find it unsatisfactory. 2 (장기·바둑에서) turn around; retreat; go back; withdraw; retract a move.

무르다³ 1 (연하다) soft; tender; flabby; flaccid; mushy; pulpy; limp; weak (foundation); frail (structure). ¶무른 고기 tender meat // 무른 살 soft muscles / loose flesh // 무른 감 a soft [squashy] persimmon // 무르게 하다 soften / make soft / (고기 등을) tenderize // 이 연필은 매우 ~ This pencil is very fragile [easily broken].

2 [약하다] weak; feeble; infirm; frail; limp; delicate; [유순하다] submissive; pliant; yielding; facile; [관대하다] indulgent; fond; spoon(e)y (on girls); indulgent (with women). ¶아내에게 무른 남편 an uxorious [a doting] husband // 자식에게 무른 어머니 an indulgent [a permissive] mother // 무른 성질 yielding disposition [temper] // 정에 ~ be easily moved (to tears) / be tenderhearted // 그는 생활 태도가 ~ He does not take life seriously enough. // 그는 여자에게 ~ He has a weakness [soft spot] for women. / He is spoony on a woman. // 한 선생은 ~ (규율 등이) Mr. Han is not strict with us. / [채점 등이 후하다] Mr. Han is a lenient grader. // 내 남편은 아이들에게 ~ My husband indulges [pampers] the children. // 그는 사람이 물러서 좀처럼 「싫다」는 소리를 못한다 He is a weak sort of person unable to say "No" on most occasions.

무르익다 1 (과일 등이) ripen; mellow; mature; become [get] ripe; come to maturity. ¶무르익은 ripe / mellow / mature // 무르익은 감 a fully ripened persimmon // 무르익은 술 mellow [well-mellowed] wine / rich wine. 2 (시기나 일이) be ripe for; (음도 등이) come to a head. ¶기회가 무르익기를 기다리다 wait for a ripe opportunity [moment] / wait till the time is ripe (for) // 때는 무르익었다 It is high time (now). // 혁명의 기운이 무르익었다 The time was ripe for a revolution. // 계획이 무르익기 전에 실행하지 마라 Do not put your plan into action until it has matured.

무르춤하다 halt; start back; hold back one's steps; stop short; shrink back (at / from); pull back; recoil (from); flinch (from); hesitate. ¶뱀을 보고 ~ stop short at the sight of a snake // 그들은 밀려오는 적의 대군을 보고 나서 무르춤했다 They flinched before the great force marching against them.

무르팍 〈속〉 a knee; a lap. ⇨무릎

무름하다 rather soft [tender]; quite weak [infirm].

무릅쓰다 risk; defy [face] (a danger); venture; dare; run (a risk, a hazard, etc.). (▶ brave는 「각오하고 견디어」라고 하는 느낌에 대해 defy는 「건방지게 무시한다」는 느낌) ¶…을 무릅쓰고 in spite of / despite / at the risk of / in defiance of / in the face [teeth] of // 만난을 무릅쓰고 in defiance [face] of all difficulties / at all hazards [risks] // 위험을 brave [dare / risk / defy / face] a danger / run [face] a risk // 바람을 무릅쓰고 나아가다 advance against [in the teeth of] the wind // 죽음을 무릅쓰고 항거하다 face death to resist // 백 번이나 죽음을 무릅썼다 I braved death a hundred times. // 그는 그녀를 구하기 위해 생명의 위험을 무릅썼다 He tried to save her at the risk of his life. // 그는 폭풍을 무릅쓰고 외출했다 He went out in spite of [braving] the storm. // 항의 시위자들은 경비원의 제지를 무릅쓰고 법정에 난입했다 The protesters burst into the courtroom, defying the orders of the guards. // 그것은 생명의 위험을 무릅쓰고 할 가치가 있는 일인가 Is it worth doing at the risk of your life? // 구조대는 태풍을 무릅쓰고 출발했다 The rescue party set out in the face of the storm.

무릇[1] 〈식〉 a squill; a scilla.

무릇[2] generally [broadly] speaking; as a (general) rule; in general; on the whole. ¶~ 역사는 되풀이되는 것이다 As a whole history repeats itself. // ~ 신랄한 비평은 적의를 사게 된다 As a general rule, cutting comments create hostility.

무릉도원(武陵桃源) an Arcadia; a Utopia; the Happy Valley. ¶~의 꿈 a Utopian dream.

무릎 a knee; a lap; a genu (pl. -nua). ¶~까지 내려오는 스커트 a skirt of knee length / a knee-length skirt // ~까지 물에 잠겨 up to the knees in (the) water // ~을 크게 벌리고 with knees spread wide // ~을 드러내고 with one's knees fully exposed // 두 ~을 세우고 with bent one's knees drawn up // ~으로 기다 go on one's knees // ~을 꿇다 kneel (down) / fall [go down / throw oneself] on one's knees / (예배하려고) genuflect // ~을 꿇고 기도하다 kneel in prayer / pray on one's knees // 한쪽 ~을 꿇다 kneel down on the knee / fall [go] on a knee // ~을 꿇고 간청하다 [빌다] implore [beg pardon] on one's knees // ~을 꿇게 하다 bring (a person) to his knees // ~을 구부리다 [굽히다] bend one's knees // ~을 세우다 draw up one's knees // 한쪽 ~을 세우고 앉다 sit [squat] (on the floor) with one knee (drawn) up // 남의 ~을 베다 lay [rest / pillow] one's head on [in] a person's lap // ~ 위에 앉다 sit on (a person's) lap // 아이를 ~에 앉히다 hold a child in [on] one's lap // ~을 마주 대고 앉다 sit knee to knee (with) // ~을 마주 대고 이야기하다 have a familiar [heart-to-heart] talk (with) / talk face to face // 무서워 내 ~이 덜덜 떨렸다 My knees shook under me with fear. // 바지의 ~이 불룩하다 [반들거린다] My trousers are baggy at the knees [shiny in the knees]. // 그녀는 애견을 ~ 위에 올려놓고 있었다 She had a pet dog in her lap. // 눈이 ~까지 빠질 정도로 쌓여 있었다 The snow lay knee-deep. / The snow was more than knee-deep. // ~에 힘이 빠져 버렸다 My knees were weak under me. / I've got weak knees. // 그녀는 ~을 꿇고 애원했다 She entreated me on her knees. // 그들은 그의 ~을 꿇렸다 They brought him to his knees. // 산허리에는 잡초가 ~까지 자라나 있었다 Weeds grew knee-high on the hillside. // 이 바지는 ~이 닳았다 These trousers are worn thin [are threadbare] at the knees.

무릎(을) 꿇다 〔굴복·항복하다〕 bow the knee to; yield to. ¶그는 권력 앞에 무릎을 꿇었다 He bowed [yielded] to authority.

무릎(을) 치다 slap one's lap (with glee or admiration).

● **무릎마디** a knee joint. ⇨슬관절 **무릎 반사** [의] a knee jerk; a patellar reflex.

무릎맞춤 a confrontation; a face-to-face meeting. **무릎맞춤하다** confront; have a confrontation (with).

무릎치기 1 〔짧은 바지〕 shorts; knee breeches; knickers. 2 〔씨름〕 a knee-whack.

무리[1] 1 〔도당〕 a company; a party; a group; a circle; a coterie; a gang(주로 악한의); a band(무장자·도둑 등); a set; a lot; a tribe; persons; gentry; 〈구어〉 a crowd; a bunch. ¶인정사정없는 ~ a heartless lot // 불량배의 ~ a gang of rogues // ~를 짓다 form a party [circle / group] / band together / gang up // 나쁜 ~에 끼이다 get into a bad company / get among bad people [companions]. 2 〔떼〕 a group; a crowd; a throng; (짐승의) a herd(소·말 등); a flock(양·토끼 등); a pack(사냥개·이리·고래 등); a shoal [school](물고기의); a swarm(벌레의). ¶사람의 ~ a crowd of people // 고등어의 ~ a school of mackerel // 열 스물씩 ~를 지어 in groups of ten to twenty // ~를 짓다 form groups / flock / form groups / band together // 학생들이 ~를 지어 다가왔다 The students approached in a group. // 승객들이 ~를 지어 개표를 기다리고 있었다 The passengers were waiting at the gate in a cluster.

무리[2] 〔생산물의 성수기〕 the season (of prevalence for fish). ¶청어 ~ the herring season // 굴은 지금이 ~다 Oysters are now in season. / It is the season for oysters now.

무리[3] 〔해·달의〕 a halo (pl. ~es); a ring; a corona; a burr; a circle(달의). ¶〔행〕 the halo of the moon [sun] // 달가 저 있다 There is a halo [ring] around the moon.

무리(無理) 1 〔도리에 어긋남〕 unreasonableness. ¶~ 없는 〔이치에 맞는〕 reasonable / 〔지당한〕 justifiable / 〔자연스러운〕 natural / 〔받아들일 수 있는〕 excusable / pardonable // ~가 없는 자세 a natural posture / a logical position // 그가 화내는 것도 ~는 아니다 He has a good reason to be angry. / It is natural that he should resent it. // 그가 화난 것도 ~가 아니다 It's no wonder he got angry. // 네가 웃은 것도 ~는 아니다 Now I see why you laughed. / No wonder you laughed. // 네가 그렇게 말하는 것도 ~는 아니다 You may well say so. / It is natural for you to say so. // 더 이상 바라는 것은 ~다 You can't reasonably wish for more. // 그것을 내 탓으로 돌리는 것은 ~다 It is unreasonable for you to blame it on me. **무리하다**

unreasonable; unjustifiable; unwarrantable; unnatural. ¶무리한 값 an unreasonable [exorbitant] price∥무리한 요구를 해서는 안 된回 You cannot make unreasonable demands.
2 [불가능] impossibility. 무리하다 impossible; beyond one's power. ¶무리한 일을 하려고 하다 attempt the impossible / try to do something beyond one's power∥너는 무리한 짓을 하고 있다 You are trying to do the impossible.
3 [강제·억지] compulsion. 무리하다 compulsory; forcible; forced. ¶무리하게 by force / perforce / forcibly / compulsorily / under compulsion / against one's will∥무리하게 당기다 pull by force∥무리하게 먹이다 force-feed (a person)∥무리하게 …시키다 compel [force] (a person) to (do) / force [drive / bludgeon] (a person) into (doing).
4 [과도] excessiveness; immoderation; [과로] overstrain; overwork. ¶아무런 ~ 없이 without the smallest strain. 무리하다 excessive; immoderate. ¶무리한 운동 immoderate exercise∥무리하지 말게 Take it easy.∥무리했다가 몸살이 났다 Overwork began to tell on my health.
5 [힘에 겨움]. ¶이 돌을 들어 올리는 것은 어린이에게는 ~다 This stone is too heavy for a child to lift.∥그 일은 혼자서는 ~다 The job is too much for one person.∥부탁이 ― 일는지 모르지만 … I may be asking too much of you, but ….
● 무리 방정식 [수] an irrational equation. 무리수 [수] an irrational [a surd] number.

무마(撫摩) [달램] (a) consolation; (a) solace; soothing, pacification. 무마하다 (노여움을) appease; pacify; (싸움 등을) suppress; quell; put down. ¶무마하기 쉬운 appeasable / placable∥무마하기 힘든 inappeasable / implacable∥남의 노여움을 ~ pacify [allay] a person's wrath [rage] / calm [soothe] down an angry person∥무마하여 체념시키다 coax (a person) to give it up [into giving it up]. →¶소동을 겨우 무마시켰다 We had much difficulty in putting down the sedition.
무말랭이 dried slices of radish.
무망중(無妄中) [뜻하지 않게] unexpectedly; unawares.
무면허(無免許) ¶~의 unlicensed / without a license / unqualified∥~로 자동차를 운전하다 drive a car without a license∥~로 병원을 개업하다 practice medicine without a license.
● 무면허 운전자 an unlicensed driver. 무면허 의사 an unlicensed doctor [physician / medical practitioner].
무명 cotton; cotton cloth. ¶~ 같은 cottony.
● 무명실 cotton thread; cotton yarn (직물용).
무명옷 cotton clothes [garments]; cottons.
무명(武名) military fame [renown]; renown in arms. ¶~을 펼치다 obtain military distinction / win military fame.
무명(無名) 1 [이름이 없음] being nameless. ¶~의 nameless / unnamed∥~의 섬 a nameless [an unnamed] islet. 2 [유명하지 않음] obscurity. ¶~의 obscure / unknown / ignoble / nameless.
● 무명씨 an anonym; an anonymous person; Mr. Unknown. 무명용사 an unknown soldier. ¶~의 묘 the Tomb of the Unknown Soldier(s) (미국 워싱턴의). 무명작가 an obscure [a nameless] writer. 무명지(―指) the third finger. ⇨°약손가락 무명지사 an obscure individual; a person of no distinction [reputation / name].
무명(無明) ignorance; spiritual darkness; illusion. ¶~의 ignorant / dark / lightless∥~의 어둠 속에서 헤매다 grope in spiritual darkness.
무명조개 [동] a (large) clam. ⇨°대합(大蛤)
무모증(無毛症) [의] atrichia; atrichosis.
무모하다(無謀―) [사려가 없다] thoughtless; inconsiderate; imprudent; incautious; [경솔하다] rash; reckless; wild; [무작정하다] foolhardy. ¶무모한 녀석 a reckless fellow / a daredevil∥무모한 계획 an ill-advised [a reckless] plan / a wild scheme∥무모한 짓을 하다 act recklessly / do a reckless [thoughtless] thing∥저런 악천후에 등산을 하다니 그들은 얼마나 무모했던가 How rash they were to go mountain climbing in that stormy weather!∥그는 무모한 운전을 하여 경찰에 붙잡혔다 He was arrested by the police for reckless driving.∥그는 무모한 녀석이다 He is ready to dare the devil. / He is a care-for-nothing. / He is foolhardy [recklessly daring]. 무모히 thoughtlessly; recklessly; rashly; [맹목적으로] blindly; [무작정하게] foolhardily. ¶돈을 아주 ~ 쓰다 spend money with absolute recklessness∥그는 충분히 생각하고 않고 ~ 결정을 내리고 했다 He decided impulsively [hastily] without thinking the matter over.∥군부 지도자들은 ~ 전쟁으로 치닫으려고 했다 The military leaders were ready to plunge recklessly into war.
무문근(無紋筋) [생] a smooth muscle. ⇨°민무늬근
무미건조하다(無味乾燥―) dry (as a chip); dry-as-dust; dusty; (flat and) insipid; uninteresting; dull; vapid; jejune; tasteless; prosaic. ¶무미건조한 해설 a matter-of-fact [prosaic] explanation∥무미건조한 문체 a bald style∥무미건조한 강의 a dull [dry-as-dust] lecture∥그의 연설은 무미건조했다 His speech was dull [boring].
무미하다(無味―) tasteless; flavorless; vapid; insipid; flat; trite; dry; uninteresting; dull. ¶무색 ~ 무취의 액체 a colorless, tasteless, and odorless liquid.
무반(武班) the military nobility.
무반동(無反動) ¶~의 recoilless / with no recoil.
● 무반동총 a recoilless rifle [gun]. 무반동포 a recoilless cannon [gun].
무반주(無伴奏) ¶~의 [음] unaccompanied (cello sonata).
● 무반주 합창 a cappella (choir).
무방비(無防備) ¶~의 defenseless [(영) defenceless] / unfortified / open / [무장하지 않은] unarmed∥마을은 이제 ~ (상태)다 The town is now in a defenseless state.∥그 진지는 완전히 ~다 The position lies quite uncovered.
● 무방비 도시 an open [a naked] city.
무방하다(無妨―) [서술적] [해가 되지 않다] do (one) no harm; be harmless; [지장 없다] be no obstacle [hindrance / impediment]; [이의가 없다] have no objection; [상관없다] do not matter; make no difference; [해도 좋

다] may; can; be allowed to (do); be all right; [없어도 좋다] can do without. ¶무방하다면 if it suits your convenience / if you don't mind / if you have no objection // 산책은 좀 해도 ~ A little walk will do you no harm. // 네가 외출해도 ~ You may [can] go out. // 자네가 없어도 ~ I can do without you.

무배당 (無配當) [이익 배당이 없음]. ¶~의 without paying a dividend / non-dividend paying // ~으로 하다 suspend payment of dividends / declare no dividend // 이 주는 ~이다 This stock pays no dividends. // 그 종목의 우량주는 ~으로 되었다 That blue chip stock became a non-dividend payer. // 그 주식은 지난 수년간 ~이 계속되고 있다 No dividend has been paid on that stock for the past several years.
● **무배당주** a non-dividend payer.

무법 (無法) [불법] injustice; unlawfulness; outlawry; wrongfulness; outrage; violence; [이치에 어긋남] lawlessness; unreasonableness; absurdity. **무법하다** [불법적이다] unjust; unlawful; wrong(ful); outrageous; violent; [이치에 어긋나다] lawless; unreasonable; absurd. ¶무법한 행동을 하다 act unlawfully / commit outrage [an unlawful act] / do wrong.
● **무법자** an outlaw; an outrageous fellow; (구어) a hellion. **무법 지대** a lawless area [district]. **무법천지** a lawless world; a state of extreme disorder.

무변 (無邊) [무이자] being free of interest; bearing no interest.

무변하다 (無邊-) limitless; boundless; infinite. ¶광대무변한 vast and boundless.

무병하다 (無病-) healthy; sound; well; (서술적) be in sound [good] health; be free from diseases [illness]; be hale and hearty (노인이).

무보수 (無報酬) nonpayment; no compensation; no pay. ¶~의 unpaid / unsalaried / gratuitous // ~로 without recompense [pay / remuneration] / [무료로] gratuitously / gratis / free of charge / for nothing / without a fee [reward] // ~의 일 a non-paying [gratuitous] job // ~로 일하다 work without pay / give one's service free // 그녀는 아이들에게 ~로 영어를 가르치고 있다 She teaches English free [for nothing] to children. // 나는 ~로 이 일을 하고 있다 I am not paid for this job. // 나는 ~로 아이를 돌보아 주었다 I looked after the child without pay [for nothing].

무복 (巫卜) shamans and soothsayers; exorcists and fortuneteller; mediums and diviners.

무분별하다 (無分別-) indiscreet; thoughtless; imprudent; rash; reckless; injudicious; ill-considered [-judged]. ¶무분별하게 indiscreetly / imprudently / thoughtlessly / recklessly / rashly // 무분별한 행위 a misconduct / a folly [misdemeanor] / an indiscreet act // 무분별한 사람 an imprudent [indiscreet] person / a misguided [misdirected] person / 무분별한 짓을 하다 act indiscreetly [imprudently / rashly] / commit a rash act / do something rash // 환자에게 그런 말을 한 것은 무분별했다 It was thoughtless of you to say such a thing to sick person. // 무분별하게도 그는 폭풍 속에 배를 저어 나갔다 He rashly rowed out in the storm. // 혼잡한 거리에서 그런 속력으로 차를 몰다니 그도 무분별하기 짝이 없다 How reckless of him to drive at such a speed in crowded streets! // 비밀을 누설할 정도로 자네가 무분별하지는 않다 Surely you know better than to talk about our secret. // 그녀는 무분별하게도 모르는 남자에게 자기 주소를 알려 주었다 She was indiscreet enough to give the stranger her address. // 그는 가족을 부양할 능력이 없으면서 무분별하게도 결혼했다 He imprudently married before he was able to support a family. // 무분별한 행동을 하지 마라 Don't act rashly. / Don't go and do something silly.

무불간섭 (無不干涉) meddlesomeness; officiousness; unnecessary [indiscreet] meddling in everything; indiscreet interference. **무불간섭하다** never fail to meddle with [in]; constantly poke [put / stick / thrust] one's nose into (another's affair); always nose into.

무비 (無比) incomparableness; peerlessness. ¶~의 matchless / peerless / incomparable / unparalleled / unexampled / unequaled / unsurpassed / unrivaled / unique / unchallenged / without a parallel [a peer / an equal] // 세계 ~인 unique [unparalleled] in the world / having no equal in the world // 그는 당대(當代) ~의 문호다 He stands unchallenged in the present literary world.

무비판적 (無批判的) uncritical; indiscriminate. ¶~으로 uncritically / indiscriminately // ~으로 채택하다 adopt (a textbook) without due consideration [reflection] // 신문 기사를 모두 ~으로 받아들여서는 안 된다 We should not swallow everything the papers say uncritically [without question].

무사 (武士) a warrior; a soldier; a knight (기사).
● **무사도** chivalry; knighthood; the code of the warrior.

무사 (無死) [야구] no out [down]; none out.
● **무사 만루** full bases with no outs. ¶~의 핀치를 벗어나다 get out of a bases-loaded no-out jam // ~다 The bases are full [loaded] with no outs.

무사고 (無事故) ¶~로 without any trouble [an accident] // 저는 5년 동안 ~ 운전입니다 I have had a perfect driving record for five years.

무사주의 (無事主義) the principle of conceding anything to avoid trouble; a peace-at-any-price principle. ¶만사 ~로 나가야겠다 I will abide by the principle of peace-at-any-price in everything.

무사태평하다 (無事太平-) peaceful; tranquil; easy; easygoing; carefree; happy-go-lucky. ¶무사태평한 얼굴 a carefree face // 무사태평하게 지내다 lead an easy life / live in a happy-go-lucky fashion // 그는 무사태평한 성질이다 He is of an easygoing disposition.

무사하다 (無私-) unselfish; selfless; disinterested. ¶공평무사한 판정 a fair and disinterested judgment.

무사하다 (無事-) [안전하다] safe; secure; [평온하다] peaceful; quiet; calm; uneventful; [탈 없다] (quite) well; doing well [nicely]. ¶무사하기를 빌다 pray for (a person's) safety // 그렇게 하는 편이 무사할 것이다 It would

무산

be safer to do so. // 불이 났을 때 금고는 무사했다 The safe remained intact in the fire. **무사히**(無事-) 〔안전하게〕 safe(ly); in safety; 〔평온하게·사고 없이〕 peacefully; in peace; uneventfully; without accident [incident / hindrance / mishap]; without a hitch; without any trouble [misadventure]; 〔성공적으로〕 successfully; 〔탈 없이·건강하게〕 well; all right. ¶~ 끝나다 pass [go] off without mischance / go on smoothly [without a hitch] / be carried out all right // ~ 돌아오다 come back safe [whole] // ~ 지내다 live peacefully // 나는 서울역에 ~ 도착했다 I arrived at Seoul Station safely. // 간밤에 ~ 댁에 돌아가셨습니까 Did you get home all right last night? // (여행을 떠나는 사람에게) ~ 다녀오십시오 Bon voyage! / Have a nice trip! // 전원이 ~ 피난했다 All of them escaped unhurt. // 소포가 ~ 도착한 것 같다 The parcel seems to have reached its destination in good condition. // 당신이 ~ 돌아오시기를 저는 빕니다 I pray that you'll come back safely [safe and sound]. // 우리는 그럭저럭 ~ 끝낼 수 있었다 Somehow we finished it [got it finished] without any trouble. // 그날이 ~ 지나갔다 The day passed uneventfully [without incident]. // 수뇌 회담은 ~ 끝났다 The summit conference went off without a hitch. // 양친께서는 ~ 지내고 계십니까 How are your parents getting along?

무산(無産) 〔관형어적〕 propertyless; without property; unpropertied.
● **무산 계급** the propertyless [unpropertied] (class); the proletariate(e); proletarians. **무산 대중** the proletariat(e); proletarians; 〔구어〕 have-nots. **무산자** a person without property; a proletarian; 〔구어〕 have-nots.

무산(霧散) 〔흩어져 없어짐〕 dispersion; dissipation; dissipating [vanishing] like the mists. **무산하다** disperse; dissipate; vanish (like mist); be dispelled [dispersed].

무산증(無酸症) 〔의〕 anacidity; achlorhydria.

무상(無上) ¶~의 기쁨 the greatest [supreme] pleasure / the greatest [sweetest] joy / perfect joy / unequaled pleasure // 이 상을 받은 것은 ~의 영광입니다 I feel [deem] it the highest honor to be awarded this prize. **무상하다** supreme; superlative; consummate; the best; the greatest; the highest.

무상(無常) 〔변하기 쉬움〕 mutability; 〔덧없음〕 uncertainty; vanity; transiency; impermanency. ¶인생의 ~을 절실히 느끼다 feel keenly the precariousness [capriciousness] of life / feel deeply the pathos of life // 그는 세상의 ~을 깨닫고 불문에 들어갔다 Realizing the vanity [evanescence] of life, he became a Buddhist monk. **무상하다** mutable; evanescent; transient; uncertain; vain; transitory. ¶인생이란 모두 ~ Man's life is transitory. / Nothing is certain [lasting] in life [in this world].

무상(無償) no compensation. ¶~의 gratis / gratuitous / for nothing / 〔법〕 nude / 〔법〕 voluntary / 〔법〕 without consideration / without cost / without compensation / free of charge // ~으로 gratuitously / voluntarily / for nothing / without compensation [consideration / pay] / without [free of] cost / free of charge // ~의 사랑 selfless love // 사회를 위한 ~의 봉사 voluntary [gratuitous] service on behalf of society // 이 일을 나는 ~으로 했다 I did this work gratis. // 초등학교 교과서는 ~으로 배포된다 Elementary school textbooks are distributed (to children) free of charge.
● **무상 계약** a gratuitous [naked] contract; a nude contract [pact]. **무상 대출** a free [an interest-free] loan. **무상 배급** free distribution. **무상 원조** a grant; grant-type aid. **무상주** a stock dividend.

무상출입하다(無常出入-) frequent; go in and out constantly; have free access to (a person's house); visit freely.

무색(-色) 〔물감을 들인 빛깔〕 dyed color. ¶~옷 dyed clothes / clothes made of colored cloth // 그런 자리에는 ~옷은 피하는 게 좋다 You should avoid wearing brightly colored clothes on such an occasion.

무색(無色) 〔빛깔이 없음〕 colorlessness; lack of color. ¶~의 colorless / achromatic // ~투명한 액체 a colorless, transparent liquid // ~렌즈 an untinted lens // ~으로 하다 make (a thing) colorless / achromatize.

무색하다(無色-) 〔서술적〕 feel shame; be ashamed (of). ¶무색한 얼굴 an ashamed [abashed] look // 무색케 하다 put (a person) to shame / bring shame to (a person) / make (a person) feel ashamed [blush with shame] / 〔빛을 잃게 하다〕 outshine [overshadow] (a person) / put (a person) in the shade / cast [put / throw] (a person) into the shade / make (a person) small in comparison // 전문가를 무색케 하는 연기 acting which outshines that of a professional // 그는 요리 솜씨가 좋아서 전문가도 무색케 할 정도다 She is such a good cook that even a professional would be put to shame. // 그의 바이올린 연주는 전문가를 무색케 할 정도이다 He plays the violin so well that he puts even professionals to shame.

무생물(無生物) a lifeless thing; an inanimate object.
● **무생물계**(-界) the inanimate world. **무생물 시대** the azoic age [era].

무서리 the first frost of the year. ¶~가 내렸다 We have had the first frost of the year.

무서움 fear; fearfulness; dreadfulness; formidableness; ferocity; terror; horror; frightfulness; terribleness. ¶~이 없다 [~을 모르다] have [know] no fear / be fearless / fear nothing // ~을 타다 be easily frightened // ~을 참다 bear one's fear // 그는 ~을 모른다 He does not know what fear is. // 그녀는 ~을 잘 탄다 She is a coward [timid person]. / She is easily frightened.

무서워하다 fear; be afraid (of); be frightened (at / by); be scared (at); be in fear (of); be in a fright; be timid (of); be nervous (about). (▶ be afraid는 일반적인 말로 항상 무서워하고 있는 데 대해, be frightened는 놀람을 동반한 두려움, be scared는 be frightened와 거의 같은 경우에 쓰이나 구어적, fear는 걱정을 수반함) ¶무서워하게 하다 frighten / scare // 뱀을 몹시 ~ fear [dread] snakes very much / have a mortal fear of snakes // 아무것도 무서워할 것 없다 You have nothing to fear. / There is nothing to be nervous about. // 그 어린이는 가면을 쓴 남자들을 무서워했다 The child was afraid of the masked men. // 그녀는 꾸중 들을 것을 무서워하여 아

무 말도 하지 않았다 She did not say a word for fear of being scolded.

무선(無線) radio; 〔영〕 wireless. ¶선박 ~ marine[ship's] radio.

● **무선국** a radio[wireless] station. **무선 방송** radio broadcasting; 〔미〕 radiocasting. **무선 전신** radiotelegraphy; wireless telegraphy. ¶~을 보내다 radio / wireless / telegraph by wireless // ~을 받다 pick up a wireless message. **무선 전화** radio-telephony; wireless telephony. ¶이 섬에 ~가 개통되었다 A radiophone service has been inaugurated on this island. **무선 전화기** a radio[wireless] telephone; radiophone. ¶휴대용 ~ a walkie-talkie. **무선 조종** radio control. **무선 중계** radio relay. **무선 통신** radio[wireless] communications. **무선 표지** a (radio) beacon; a radiophare. **무선 표지국** a radio beacon station. **무선 호출기** a beeper [pager].

무섭다 1 〔끔찍하다〕 fearful; frightful; terrible; dreadful; dread; frightening; horrible; horrific; awful; 〔구어〕 scary(▶ fearful은 걱정이 섞인 두려움, dreadful은 fearful보다 강한 두려움, frightening은 놀람이 따름, horrible은 혐오감을 불러일으키는 강한 두려움); 〔으스스하다〕 grim; uncanny; weird; 〔사납다〕 fierce; ferocious; truculent; savage; villainous; 〔상대하기에 접나다〕 formidable; 〔두렵다〕 be afraid (of / that); be apprehensive; be scared[frightened]. ¶무서운 영화 a horror [scary] film // 무서운 이야기 a dreadful [terrible] story // 무서운 맹수 a fierce [ferocious] wild beast // 무서운 얼굴 a stern look / a grim[threatening] face // 무서운 폭풍우 a fearful[terrific] storm // 무서운 병 a horrible disease // 무서운 광경 a frightening sight // 무서운 상대 a formidable [〔문어〕 redoubtable] opponent // 무서운 비행기 사고 a terrible [dreadful / ghastly] airplane accident // 무서운 것을 모르는 개구쟁이 a fearless imp // 마약 [각성제] 중독의 무서운 실태 the terrifying realities of drug addiction // 무서움 나머지 for[from / out of] fear / in horror[a fright] / with fear[fright] // 무서운 얼굴을 하다 look fierce[threatening] // 무서워서 울다 cry for [in] fear // 무서워서 도망치다 run away through fear // 무섭게 노려보다 glare at (a person) fiercely // 무서워지다 be seized with fear / get frightened[scared] (at) // 암이 얼마나 무서운가를 나는 처음으로 알았다 I knew for the first time how dreadful cancer is. // 나는 무서워서 말도 못 했다 I was struck dumb with fright. // 암살자의 무서운 마수가 희생자에게 다가가 있다 The terrible[dreadful] hand of the assassin draws near its victim. // 무서워서 나는 덜덜 떨었다 I shuddered with dread[fear]. // 무서운 일을 당했다 I had a dreadful[frightful / horrible] experience. // 〔섬뜩했다〕 〔구어〕 I got a fright[was scared to death]. // 그렇게 무서운 눈으로 보지 마라 Don't look[glare] at me so fiercely[with such a fierce look]. // 무서워라 You scare me. / I'm scared. / Don't frighten me. // 그것은 무서운 정도가 아니다 Fearful is no word for it. // 그 지역은 무서운 곳이니 가까이 가지 마라 As that area is dangerous, keep away from it. // 사소한 부주의가 무서운 사고를 불러일으킨다 Slight carelessness can lead to a terrible accident. // 죽는 것이 나는 조금도 무섭지 않다 I am not afraid[scared] of death in the least. / I can look death calmly in the face. // 그녀는 무서워 죽을 뻔했다 She was scared to death. // 그는 정계에서 무서운 사람이 없다 He fears no one in the political world. // 나는 뱀이 ~ I am afraid of snakes. // 개가 내게 짖어서 무서웠다 I was frightened[scared] when a dog barked at me.

2 〔대단하다·지독하다〕 awful; very; frightful; terrible; horrible; tremendous; wonderful; marvelous; prodigious; stupendous. ¶무섭게 awfully / terribly / frightfully / horribly / wonderfully / very // 무서운 구두쇠 an awful miser // 무서운 기세 stupendous force // 거대한 운석의 무서운 에너지 the awe-inspiring [enormous / tremendous] energy in gigantic meteorites // 무섭게 춥다 be terribly[awfully] cold // 무서운 속도로 차를 몰다 drive at (a) tremendous speed // 습관이란 ~ A habit is something not to be lightly treated.

무성(無性) 〔관형어적〕 sexless; nonsexual.

● **무성 생식** 〔생〕 asexual reproduction; monogony; monogeny; agamogenesis; agamogony; agamy; 〔식〕 blastogenesis; blastogeny.

무성(無聲) 〔소리가 없음〕. ¶~의 silent / noiseless / dumb / voiceless / 〔언〕 voiceless / unvoiced / breathed / aphonic.

● **무성 영화** a silent film[(motion) picture / movie]. **무성음** 〔언〕 a voiceless[an unvoiced] sound. ⇨ˮ안울림소리 ¶~으로 발음하다 unvoice // (유성음을) ~화하다 devoice / devocalize.

무성의(無誠意) insincerity; bad faith. **무성의하다** insincere; unfaithful; false; fickle. ¶무성의하게 insincerely / unfaithfully // 무성의한 답변[정책] a haphazard reply[policy] // 네 행위는 ~ Your conduct betrays want of sincerity.

무성하다(茂盛-) thick; dense; luxuriant; exuberant; profuse; rank; rampant; close-grown.(▶ rank는 바람직하지 않은 식물에 사용) ¶무성한 잡초 rank weeds / a tangled growth of wild grass // 잡초가 무성한 정원 a garden overgrown[rank] with weeds // 나무가 무성한 숲 a luxuriant[thick] forest // 잎이 무성한 나무 a leafy tree / a leaf-heavy tree / a tree thick of leaves / a tree with luxuriant foliage // 풀이 ~ be thick[densely covered] with grass // 그 오두막은 무성한 덤불 속에 있었다 The hut stood amid a riot of bushes. // 그곳에는 닭의장풀이 무성했다 The dayflowers luxuriated[grew abundantly] there. // 뜰에 들장미가 ~ Wild roses have spread all over [have taken] the garden. **무성히** thickly; densely; luxuriantly.

무세(無稅) 〔세금이 부과되지 않음〕. ¶~의 free / tax-free / untaxed / taxless / 〔관세〕 free // ~ 수입을 허가하다 allow the free entry (of goods) / admit 《goods》 free of duty 《custom free》.

● **무세품** duty-free goods; goods free of duty [tax].

무소 〔동〕 a rhinoceros. ⇨ˮ코뿔소

무소득(無所得) no income[gain / benefit]. **무소득하다** without any income[gain / benefit]; 〔서술적〕 gain[get] nothing 《from / by》; get[derive] no[little] benefit 《from》; be little benefited 《by》.

무소부지(無所不知) omniscience; infinite

무소불위 [universal] knowledge. **무소부지하다** omniscient; know everything; have infinite knowledge.

무소불위(無所不爲) omnipotence; almightiness. **무소불위하다** omnipotent; almighty; all-powerful.

무소속(無所屬) ¶~의 independent / unattached / affiliated with no party / neutral / ~의 후보자 an independent (candidate) // ~이다 be independent / (미국 속어) be not a party man // 그는 ~으로 입후보했다 He ran for election independently of any party. // 저 배우는 ~이다 That actor doesn't belong to any theatrical company [group].
●**무소속 의원** an independent (Assemblyman [member]); an Assemblyman without party affiliation; a nonpartisan representative.

무소식(無消息) no news (from a person). ¶~이다[하다] hear nothing from (a person) / have no news from / receive no words from // 그 후로 그는 영 ~이다 Nothing has been heard from him since.

무소식이 희소식(속담) No news is good news.

무쇠 cast iron; iron. ¶~ 같은 의지[의지를 지닌 사람] an [a man of] iron will.

무수(無水) ¶~의 anhydrous.
●**무수물** an anhydride.

무수리[1] (동) an adjutant; an adjutant bird [crane / stork].

무수리[2] (궁중의) a maid in charge of the water for the court ladies to wash their faces.

무수하다(無數-) numberless; innumerable; incalculable; countless. ¶무수한 예를 들다 give no end of examples. **무수히** innumerably; countlessly; without [out of] number; in unmeasured numbers; beyond count. ¶이 문제에 관한 책이 ~ 있다 Books upon this subject are legion.

무숙자(無宿者) a homeless wanderer; a tramp; a vagrant; a vagabond; (미국 구어) a bum; (미국 속어) a hobo (pl. ~(e)s).

무순(無順) ¶~의[으로] without order / in random [unalphabetical] order / in no particular [special] order.

무술(巫術) shamanism.

무술(武術) the military [martial] arts. ¶~에 다소 조예가 있다 have some military accomplishment.

무스탕(*mustang) a sheepskin coat; a lambskin coat.(▶ mustang은 미국 남서부에 사는 야생마)

무슨 [의문] what; what kind [sort] of; [어떤] some; some kind of. ¶~ 일 [의문] what / [어떤 일] something / [만사] everything // ~ 일로 on what business // ~ 일이나 in everything / in all matters [things] // ~ 까닭으로 why / for what reason // ~ 일이 있으면 if anything [the unexpected] should happen (to a person) / in case of emergency [need] // ~ 일이 있어도 at any cost [price / risk] / at all costs [hazards] / by all means // 그 일이 있어도 그것을 마쳐라 Finish it by all means [whatever may happen]. / (미국 구어) Get it over blow high, blow low. // 나는 ~ 일이 있어도 목적을 관철해 보이겠다 I will move heaven and earth to attain my end. / I will go to any [all] lengths to gain my end. / Nothing shall hinder me from accomplishing my purpose. // 그런 짓은 ~ 일이 있어도 하지 않겠다 I wouldn't do that on any account. // ~ 말씀이셨지요 I beg your pardon. / Pardon.(▶ 끝을 올려 말함) // 내가 그 사람을 만나러 가서 ~ 소용이 있나 What is the use of me [my] going to him? // 내가 ~ 이야기부터 해야 할지 모르겠다 I don't know where to begin. // 요즘 ~ 일이라도 있나 보지요 Something is wrong [seems to be the matter] with you these days. // ~ 일이지요 What's the matter? / (구어) What's up? // ~ 일로 오셨어요 What brought you here? / May I help you?(▶ 손님을 맞는 사람의 입장에서) // ~ 수를 써 수가 있겠소 Couldn't you do something? // 그에게 ~ 충고를 해 주어라 Give him some advice. // 환자의 상태에 ~ 변화가 생기면 알려 줘 Please let me know if there is any change in the patient's condition. // 이렇게 조용하다니 도시 ~ 일일까 What does this silence mean? // ~ 일이든지 조심해서 해라 Be careful in everything you do. // 그는 (내가 잘 모를) ~ 이유로 나를 피하는 것 같다 He seems to be avoiding me for some reason. // 여자 아이를 울리다니 ~ 짓이냐 Shame on you for making a little girl cry! // ~ 방법을 써서라도 나는 성공하고 싶다 I want to succeed no matter what means I have to use. // ~ 일이 일어나더라도 당황해서는 안 된다 No matter what happens [whatever happens], try not to loose your head. // 안색이 나쁜데 ~ 일이냐 What's the matter (with you)? You look pale.

무승부(無勝負) a drawn game; a tie; a draw (in a game); an undecided match. ¶~로 끝나다 end in a tie [draw] / be drawn / tie [draw] (with) // 시합은 ~가 되었다 The game ended in a draw [tie].

무시(無視) disregard (for rules); neglect (of consequence). **무시하다** disregard; ignore; defy; discount; neglect; take [make] no account (of); set (the rules, etc.) at naught [nothing]. ¶무시해도 좋을 정도의 미량(微量) a negligible quantity // 개인의 의사를 전혀 무시하고 in total disregard of the wishes of the individual // …을 무시하고 in disregard of … / without regard for / in defiance of … // 남을 ~ slight a person / look down (up)on a person // 규칙을 ~ disregard the rules // 불합리한 요구를 ~ take no account of an unreasonable demand // 사고는 운전사가 신호를 무시했기 때문에 일어났다 The accident occurred because the driver ignored the traffic lights. // 경고를 무시하면서 그는 강에서 수영을 했다 Disregarding [ignoring] the warning, he swam in the river. // 매달 30만 원의 가외 수입은 무시하지 못할 금액이다 An extra three hundred thousand won a month is not a sum to be sneezed at. → ¶그의 의견은 무시되었다 His opinion was ignored [made light of].

무시로(無時-) [수시로] any time at all; irregularly; (at) any time; [언제나] at all times [hours]; all the time; always.

무시무시하다 frightful; [송장 같다] ghastly; [초자연적이다] weird; [불가사의해서 기분 나쁘다] uncanny; (구어) [귀신같다] spooky; [소름 끼치다] (구어) creepy; horrible; cruel; brutal; dismal; terrible; dreadful; fearsome. ¶무시무시한 사건 a ghastly [horrible] incident∥무시무시한 얼굴 표정으로 with a ghastly look (on one's face)∥무시무시한 소리 a terrible[terrific] sound∥무시무시한 폭풍 a frightful[an awful] storm∥무시무시한 광경이었다 It was a frightful sight.∥그것은 무시무시한 사고였다 It was a dreadful[terrible / horrible] accident.∥그는 무시무시한 표정으로 나를 노려보았다 He glared at me with a threatening[terrible] look.∥정말 너무나 무시무시한 사건이었다 The incident was simply too awful.

무시험(無試驗) no[without] examination. ¶중학교 ~ 추첨 제도 the lottery system instead of written examinations in enrolling freshmen at middle schools∥~의 free of examination∥~ 입학 자격이 있다 be entitled to admission without examination∥~으로 입학하다 be admitted into a school without examination.

무식(無識) ignorance; illiteracy. ¶~을 드러내다 betray[expose] one's ignorance / display one's lack of knowledge∥그는 자신의 ~을 부끄러워한다 He is ashamed of his illiteracy.
무식하다 ignorant; [읽고 쓰지 못하다] illiterate; (문어) unlettered; [교육받지 못하다] uneducated. ¶무식한 탓으로 due to ignorance∥무식해도 유분수다 What an ignorant fellow he is!
● **무식쟁이 / 무식꾼** an ignorant[illiterate] person.

무신경하다(無神經-) apathetic; indifferent; stolid; dull; [둔감하다] insensitive; [냉담하다] callous; [뻔뻔스럽다] thick-skinned. ¶그는 이웃 사람의 고통[비탄]에 대하여 ~ He is callous[unfeeling] about the distress of his neighbors.∥나는 그의 무신경함에 화가 치밀었다 I grew resentful of his lack of sensitivity[delicacy].∥이런 으슥한 밤에 그렇게 큰 소리로 떠들다니 얼마나 무신경한가 How inconsiderate to talk in such a loud voice at this late hour!∥그는 어떤 핀잔을 들어도 전혀 ~ He is so thick-skinned that irony doesn't bother him at all.

무신론(無神論) atheism. ¶~적(인) atheistic.
● **무신론자** [무신론 주장자] an atheist; [신앙심이 없는 사람] an unbeliever.

무실점(無失點) ¶~으로 without losing a point∥~을 기록하다 record no losing point [score].

무심결에(無心-) unintentionally. ¶그는 ~ 웃음을 터뜨렸다 He burst out laughing in spite of himself[against his will].

무심중에(無心中-) unintentionally. ⇨"무심결에

무심코(無心-) [아무 생각 없이] unintentionally; involuntarily; [문득] casually; by chance; accidentally; [부주의하게] carelessly; [저도 모르게] unconsciously; in spite of oneself. ¶나는 ~ 있다가 정류장을 세 곳이나 지나쳐 갔다 I was daydreaming and[My thoughts were elsewhere and I] was carried three stops beyond my destination.∥나는 ~ 형님의 책을 가지고 왔다 I brought my brother's book by mistake.∥나는 ~ 아무 데나 두었다가 초청장을 잃어버렸다 I inadvertently misplaced my letter of invitation.∥나는 ~ 본심을 실토하고 말았다 In an unguarded moment I revealed my true intentions.∥나는 ~ 있다가 그들의 이야기를 엿듣고 말았다 I happened to overhear[accidentally overheard] their conversation.∥~ 한 말이 그의 감정을 상하게 했다 My careless [thoughtless] remark hurt him.

무심하다(無心-) innocent; casual; [관심 없다] unconcerned; [인정 없다] heartless; hard; inconsiderate. ¶무심한 행동 an involuntary action. **무심히** unintentionally; undesignedly; [문득] casually; in a casual way; incidentally; accidentally; [부주의하게] carelessly; unguardedly; [자기도 모르게] unconsciously; in spite of oneself; [뜻하지 않게] unexpectedly; (all) unawares; [순진하게] innocently. ¶~ 말하다 speak lightly∥~ 바라보다 look ahead casually∥~ 한 말이 친한 친구의 사이를 벌어지게 하는 수가 있다 A few light words sometimes estrange the closest friends.

무쌍하다(無雙-) matchless; peerless; unexampled; unparalleled; unequaled; incomparable; unrivaled; unchallenged; unsurpassed. ¶용감무쌍한 사람 a man of great prowess∥변화무쌍한 일생 an eventful[a dramatic / a colorful] career[life].

무아(無我) self-effacement; self-renunciation; annihilation of self; selflessness. ¶~의 경지에 이르다 attain a spiritual state of perfect selflessness / rise above self / go into an impersonal state.
● **무아경**(-境) ecstasy; transport; rapture; exaltation.

무악(舞樂) a court dance and music.

무안(無顔) shame; disgrace; dishonor. ¶~을 당하다 be put to shame / disgrace oneself / bring disgrace upon oneself. **무안하다** ashamed; feel shamed at; lose face; humiliate oneself by; blush with shame. ¶무안에서 고개를 떨구다 hang one's head with shame∥그는 몹시 무안해했다 He was filled with shame.
무안을 주다 put (a person) to shame[the blush]; put (a person) out of countenance.

무어 1 what; which. ⇨"무엇 ~ 맛있는 것 something nice to eat∥~ 제가 잘못한 게 있습니까 Did I do anything wrong?∥이건 대체 ~야 Whatever is this object?∥~ 먹을 것 있습니까 Have you anything to eat?∥저 친구가 하긴 무얼 해 What can he do? / I am blessed if he can do anything.∥그건 자네가 알아서 무얼 해 What is that to you?
2 [놀라움] what!; huh!; why! ¶~, 다시 한번 말해 봐 What[Huh]! Say it again.∥~, 내가 미쳤다고 What! I am mad[crazy]?∥~, 얼마라고 What! How much did you say it is?∥ "~?" 하며 그녀는 의아스러워 하는 표정을 지었다 "What?" She said with a questioning look on her face.
3 [어리광·강조] but; but anyway; somehow or other; just. ¶누워서 떡 먹기지 ~ Why nothing is easier.∥돈이 여간 들어야지 ~ You know it costs a lot of money. / It's so expensive, you see.∥세상이란 이런 거지 ~ This[Such] is the way of the world.

무어니 무어니 해도 say what you will. ⇨"뭐니 뭐니 해도(⇨뭐)

무언(無言) silence; muteness; reticence; taciturnity. ¶~의 silent / [말이 없는] dumb / (과묵·암묵 속의) tacit∥~의 고행(苦行) the ascetic practice of silence∥두 사람 사이에는 ~의 이해가 있었다 There was a tacit understanding between the two.∥그녀의 ~의 저

항이 나의 신경을 건드리기 시작했다 Her mute resistance began to tell on my nerves. ∥우리는 ―중에 양해가 되었다 We came to a tacit understanding.
● **무언극** a pantomime; a dumb show.

무엄하다(無嚴―) 〔삼가지 않다〕 imprudent; indiscreet; 〔버릇없다〕 presumptuous; forward; impudent; impertinent. ¶무엄한 언동 indiscreet words or actions∥이렇게 아침 일찍 찾아오다니 그 녀석 참 무엄하구나 How rude of him to come visiting so early in the morning!∥그는 무엄하게도 우리들의 대화를 가로막고 끼어들었다 He had the impudence [(구어) cheek] to interrupt our conversation. **무엄히** imprudently; indiscreetly; impudently; presumptuously; impertinently.

무엇 what; which; something; anything. ¶~이든 anything / whatever / everything∥이것은 ~입니까 What's this?∥다음에 ~을 하면 되는지 가르쳐 주세요 Please tell me what to do next.∥그런 것을 내가 알 게 ~이냐 How would I know (such a thing)?∥그 사람은 ~을 하는 사람입니까 What does he do?∥~ 때문인지 그는 갑자기 달리기 시작했다 We don't know why, but he suddenly began to run.∥~ 때문에 네가 울고 있느냐 What are you crying for?∥Why are you crying?∥~ 때문에 네가 그런 거짓말을 했느냐 What did you lie like that for? / Why did you tell such a lie?∥한국말의 「모자」는 독일어로 ~이라고 합니까 What is the German for the Korean word "moja"?∥이 새는 영어로 ~이라고 합니까 What do you call this bird in English?∥글쎄, ~이라고 하면 ~일세 Let me see, how shall I express[say] it!∥~이라고 감사를 드려야 할지 모르겠습니다 I cannot find words to thank you. / I do not know how to express my thanks. ∥~이든 그들이 말하고 싶은 대로 말하게 내버려 두라 Let them say whatever[anything] they like.∥더위고 ~이고 다 잊어버리고 나는 일에 열중했다 I completely forget the heat and everything else and threw myself into my work.∥그의 소설 가운데서 ~이 가장 좋으냐 Which of his novels do you like best?∥~이 일어나고 있는지[~인지] 나는 도무지 알 수가 없었다 I hadn't the faintest[slightest] idea what was going on[what it was all about].∥~을 숨기랴, 내가 바로 주모자[두목]였단 말이다 To tell the truth[To be frank with you], I was the ringleader.∥~을 하든 간에 세상에서는 머리만 있으면 다 된다 Brains are everything in this world.∥~이라고! 또 자네가 지각을 했어 What! Were you late again?∥~, 아무렇지도 않아 Oh, I don't care a bit!∥~, 괜찮아요 Why, it's all right. / Why, never mind.∥~인가 우리가 할 수 있는 일이 틀림없이 있을 것이다 There must be something we can do.∥그는 손에 ~인가 검은 것을 가지고 있었다 He had something black in his hand.∥그가 계단인가 ~인가에서 떨어졌다고 한다 I hear he fell from the staircase or something.∥~ 보다도 건강에 주의하여라 Above all, be careful of your health.∥손자들이 찾아오는 일이 ~보다도 그녀에게 큰 위안이었다 Nothing gave her greater consolation than a visit from her grandchildren.

무엇하다 〔부적절하다〕 improper; incongruous; unbecoming; 〔어색하다〕 awkward; embarrassing; 〔불만스럽다〕 unsatisfactory.

¶이렇게 말씀드리기가 좀 무엇합니다만 excuse me for my frankness, but ... / it may be rude to say so, but ...∥내가 그런 것을 물어보면 좀 무엇하지 않을까 Would it be quite proper for me to ask him such a question?∥그는 신사라기에는 좀 ~ He isn't quite a gentleman.∥자신이 이렇게 말하기가 무엇하지만 if I may be permitted to say so ... / though I say it who shouldn't ...∥이렇게 말하면 무엇하지만, 그도 나이를 먹었구먼 I hate to say this, but he has aged, hasn't he?

무역(貿易) trade; commerce. ¶가공 ~ processing trade∥구상[바터] ~ compensation [barter] trade / trade on a barter system∥국제[세계] ~ international[world] trade∥대미 ~ Korea's trade with America / commerce between Korea and America∥대일 ~ Korea's trade with Japan∥보세 가공 ~ bonded processing trade∥보호 ~ protective trade∥보호 ~주의 protectionism∥삼각 ~ triangular trade∥수출 ~ export trade∥연안 ~ coastwise[intercoastal] trade∥외국[해외] ~ foreign trade / seaborne[overseas] trade /(영) oversea trade∥자유 ~ free trade∥중계 ~ transit trade∥편(片) ~ unilateral [lopsided / one-way] trade∥해상 ~ floating trade∥~의 확대 trade expansion∥우리나라의 대미 ~ our trade with America [the U.S.A.]∥~에 종사하다 engage in foreign trade∥~을 시작하다 open (up) trade (with) / establish trade (with)∥~을 육성하다 foster trade∥~을 촉진[진흥]하다 promote foreign trade∥~을 증진하다 increase foreign trade∥~을 자유화하다 liberalize (external) trade∥~을 재개하다 reopen trade∥미국의 연간 ~액은 굉장하다 The annual amount of trade done by the U.S.A. reaches very big figures.∥한국은 그 나라와 ~ 관계가 없다 Korea has no trade relations with that country. **무역하다** trade (with); conduct [carry on] trade. ¶중국과 ~ trade with China.
● **무역량** the volume of trade. **무역 마찰** trade friction; trade conflicts. **무역 박람회** a trade fair. **무역 불균형** (a) trade imbalance. **무역상** a trader; a trading merchant; an importer(수입상); an exporter(수출상). ¶~을 경영하고 있다 be in the export-import business. **무역 상사** a trading company[firm]. **무역선** a merchant ship[vessel]; a trader. **무역 수지** the balance of trade. **무역 신용장** a trade credit[L/C]. **무역업** trade[trading] business. **무역 역조** an adverse trade balance; an unfavorable balance of trade. **무역 외 거래** invisible trade. **무역 외 수지** an invisible trade balance; invisible exports and imports. **무역 자유화** liberalization of trade. **무역 장벽** a trade barrier. **무역항** a trade [treaty] port. ¶자유 ~ a free port. **무역 회사** a trading company[firm]. **무역 흑자[적자]** a trade surplus[deficit].

무역풍(貿易風) a trade wind; monsoon. ¶겨울[여름] ~ dry[wet] monsoon.

무연(無煙) ~의 smokeless.
● **무연 연료** smokeless fuel. **무연탄** anthracite (coal); smokeless[hard / blind] coal; stone coal; glance coal.

무연(고)(無緣故) ¶~의 indifferent / unrelated / 〔연고자가 없는〕 without relations / having no surviving relatives.

●**무연묘지** a cemetery for those who left no relatives behind. **무연분묘** an unknown person's grave; [연고자 없는 묘] a neglected [deserted] grave.

무연하다(憮然-) [낙담하다] disappointed; disheartened; dejected; [놀랍다] surprised; astonished; startled. **무연히** [낙담하여] disheartenedly; in disappointment; dejectedly; disappointedly; [놀라서] surprisingly; in astonishment [surprise]. ¶그는 깨진 항아리를 ~ 바라보고 있었다 He was gazing sadly at the broken pot.

무예(武藝) military [martial] arts; feats of arms. ¶~에 능한 사람 a master of martial arts∥~를 닦다 practice military arts∥~에 능하다 be skilled in the military arts.

무욕하다(無慾-) unselfish; generous; disinterested; unavaricious.

무용(武勇) bravery; valor (in arms) (특히, 전투에서의); military prowess.
●**무용담** a tale of bravery [heroism]. ¶~을 늘어놓다 fight one's battle over again (in one's talk).

무용(舞踊) [춤을 춤] dancing; [한 차례의 춤] a dance. ¶민속 ~ a folk dance∥한국 ~ Korean dance∥~의 동작 movements in dancing∥~을 배우다 take lesson in dancing [dancing lessons]∥그녀는 ~을 잘한다 She is a good dancer. / She dances well. **무용하다** dance; perform a dance.
●**무용가** a dancer. **무용극** a dance drama [play]. **무용단** (프) a corps de ballet. **무용수** a dancer; a dancing girl; (발레의) a ballet dancer; a ballerina (*pl.* ~s, -ne).

무용지물(無用之物) a useless thing [person]; a good-for-nothing.

무용하다(無用-) **1** [쓸모없다] useless; of no use; good for nothing; unnecessary; needless. ¶무용한 토론 useless discussion. **2** [용무가 없다] without business.

무우 [식] →무

무운(武運) the fortune(s) of war. ¶~이 없다 be unfortunate in war∥~이 다하여 그는 전사했다 Fortune was against him, and he was killed in action.∥~을 빕니다 I wish you good luck in the war. / May fortune be with you in battle!

무운시(無韻詩) blank verse; an unrhymed poem.

무월경(無月經) [의] amenorrh(o)ea.

무위(武威) military prestige [glory / power]; armed might. ¶~를 떨치다 raise [exalt] military prestige / achieve martial glory.

무위(無爲) [아무 일도 않거나 이루지 못함] doing nothing; idleness; inactivity; inaction; quietism; faineancy. ¶~의 생활 a life of ease / an idle life∥~의 do-nothing (government)∥~로 끝나다 come to nothing∥그는 ~로 날을 보내고 있다 He is idling his time away. **무위하다** idle; inactive. ¶무위하게 idly / leisurely / inactively / in idleness.
●**무위도식**(-徒食) an idle life. ¶~하다 live an idle life / eat the bread of idleness / idle one's time away.

무위무탁(無依無托) having no place to turn to; having no one to depend on. **무위무탁하다** forlorn; helpless; homeless; (서술적) have no one to turn [look] to; have no one to depend [rely] on. ¶무위무탁한 고아 a helpless orphan.

무의미하다(無意味-) [뜻이 없다] meaningless; insignificant; pointless; [부질없다] worthless; useless. ¶무의미한 토론 a meaningless argument∥무의미한 노력 efforts to no purpose / wasted effort∥인생을 무의미하게 보내다 waste [fritter away] one's life∥무의미한 말을 입 밖에 내다 talk nonsense∥그런 시험을 하다니 정말 ~ There's no point in giving tests of that sort.∥너의 수고는 무의미하지만은 않았다 You have not gone to all this trouble for nothing. / Your efforts were not vain.

무의식(無意識) unconsciousness; involuntariness; [정신 분석] the unconscious. ¶~의 [으로] unconscious [unconsciously] / [의지에 따르지 않은 [않고] involuntary [involuntarily] ∥~의 상태 (중병 등으로) an unconscious state / [방심] a state of unawareness∥그는 ~적으로 담뱃갑을 꺼냈다 He mechanically took out his cigarette case.
●**무의식 상태** an unconscious state [condition]; (lapse into) unconsciousness.

무의식중에(無意識中-) without realizing it; unconsciously; [자신의 뜻에 반하여] in spite of oneself; [본능적으로] instinctively. ¶~ 한숨이 나오다 sigh unconsciously∥웃음을 터뜨리다 laugh in spite of oneself∥차가 부딪히려고 하는 순간, 나는 ~ 눈을 감았다 I shut my eyes instinctively just as the car was about to crash.∥그녀는 파리에 오랫동안 살고 있어서 이제 프랑스 어가 ~ 튀어나오게끔 되었다 She has lived in Paris for years, and her French has become automatic.∥~ 나는 그의 기분을 상하게 하는 말을 하고 말았다 Without realizing it, I said something which hurt him.

무의촌(無醫村) a doctorless village; a village without a doctor.

무의탁(無依託) having no one to depend [rely] on.
●**무의탁 노인** a senior citizen who does not have dependents; an old man without dependents.

무이자(無利子) no interest; without interest; interest-free. ¶~의 free of interest / bearing no interest / [법] passive∥~로 without interest / free of interest / interest-free∥~로 돈을 빌리다 borrow money without [free of] interest.
●**무이자 공채** [채무] passive bonds [debt].

무익하다(無益-) useless; futile; unavailing; unprofitable; no good; fruitless. ¶무익한 살생 wanton destruction of life∥유해~ do more harm than good∥고소해 봤자 무익한 일이다 It's no use [no good] going to court [the police]. ∥그런 무익한 언쟁은 그만두시오 Stop that useless quarreling.

무인(武人) a soldier; a warrior; a military man.

무인(拇印) a thumbmark. ⇨지장(指章)

무인(無人) [관형어적] manless; unmanned; uninhabited; desert.
●**무인 건널목** an unattended [unguarded] (railroad) crossing. **무인고도**(-孤島) a desert islet; an uninhabited and isolated island. **무인도** a desert island; an uninhabited island. ¶그 섬은 ~이다 The island is uninhabited. **무인 비행기** a pilotless [radio-controlled] airplane. **무인 위성** an un-

manned satellite. 무인지경 an uninhabited [a vacant] region; no-man's-land. ¶~을 가듯 전진하다 carry[sweep] everything before (one) / advance with irresistible force. 무인 판매대 (신문 등의) a self-service stand.

무일푼(無--) pennilessness. ¶~의 penniless / (구어) broke // ~이 되다 become penniless / (속어) go (clean) broke // 나는 오늘 ~이다 I don't have a penny today. / (구어) I'm clean broke today. // 그는 돈을 다 써 버려 ~이 되었다 He spent his last penny. // 그는 화재를 만나 ~이 되었다 He lost everything in the fire. // 그는 ~으로 사업을 시작했다 He started his business with practically nothing.

무임(無賃) ¶~으로 free / free of charge / charge-free / carriage-free(화물이).
●무임 승객 a free passenger; (구어) a deadhead. 무임승차 a free ride; (구어) deadheading. ¶~를 하다 ride free / (부정으로) cheat (the railway) / (미국 구어) steal a ride / pinch a free ride.

무자각하다(無自覺-) insensible (of); blind (to); unconscious (of one's responsibility).

무자격(無資格) disqualification; [법] incapacity; incompetence. ¶~의 disqualified / incompetent / [면허의] unlicensed / uncertificated / [허가가 없는] unqualified / ~으로 만들다 [법] disqualify / incapacitate.
●무자격 간호사 [의사 / 안마사] an unlicensed nurse [doctor / massagist]. 무자격 교사 an unlicensed teacher. 무자격자 an unqualified[unlicensed] person; [법] an incompetent.

무자맥질 diving; ducking. ⇨ 자맥질

무자본(無資本) ¶~의 [으로] without capital [funds] / with nothing to start with.

무자비하다(無慈悲-) merciless; ruthless; cruel; pitiless; heartless; hard-hearted. ¶무자비한 짓을 하다 do a cruel thing / 그들의 탄원을 그는 무자비하게 거절했다 He pitilessly [coldly] rejected their plea. // 그는 참 무자비한 놈이로군 What a merciless[pitiless] tyrant he is! // 그들은 무자비하게도 그 남자를 죽였다 They murdered the man in cold blood.

무자식(無子息) childlessness. 무자식하다 childless; heirless; 《서술적》 have no children[issue].

무자식 상팔자(속담) Love of children is an eternal encumbrance.

무자위 [물을 자아올리는 기계] a water pump. ¶~로 물을 푸다 pump up water (from).

무작위(無作爲) ¶~의 unintentional / unintended // ~로 [아무 생각 없이] unintentionally / [임의로] at random // 그는 명단에서 ~로 세 사람을 골랐다 He chose three names at random from the list.
●무작위 추출법 a random sampling method. 무작위 표본 a random sample.

무작정(無酌定) [미리 정한 것이 없음] lack of any definite plan; lack of definite view in mind; recklessness; rashness; [무턱대고] with no particular plan[view] in mind; without any goal in mind; recklessly; blindly. ¶~ 남이 하는 대로 하다 imitate [follow] (a person) blindly / 그녀는 ~ 상경했다 She went up to Seoul with no definite object. 무작정하다 planless; unplanned;

rash; aimless; reckless; haphazard.

무장(武將) a military commander; a general; a warlord.

무장(武裝) arms; (국가의) armament; (병사의) equipment. ¶비~ 지대 a demilitarized zone(약어 DMZ) // 완전 ~ (in) full kit // ~을 해제하다 disarm / demilitarize / dismantle. 무장하다 arm (a person, a ship, etc.); equip (an army); (스스로) equip[arm] oneself (with rifle); bear[take up] arms. ¶무장한 armed / under[with] arms // 병사는 갑옷 무기로 무장하고 있었다 The soldiers were clad in armor from head to foot. // 그들은 라이플을 으로 무장했다 They armed themselves [were armed] with rifles.
●무장간첩 an armed spy[agent]. 무장 경찰 / 무장 경관 an armed policeman. 무장 공비 an armed Red bandit; an armed communist guerilla. 무장봉기 rising in arms; an armed uprising. ¶그들은 마침내 정부에 대해 ~를 하였다 They finally took up arms[rose up in arms] against the government. 무장 시위 행렬 armed demonstration. 무장 해제 disarmament; demilitarization(국가의); dismantlement(군함·포대의).

무장지졸(無將之卒) a leaderless army.

무재(無才) lack of ability; being untalented; incompetence. 무재하다 lacking in ability; talentless; untalented; incompetent.

무저항(無抵抗) nonresistance. ¶~의 nonresistant / unresisting // ~의 저항 passive resistance.
●무저항주의 the principle of nonresistance. 무저항주의자 a nonresistant.

무적(無敵) invincibility. ¶~의 matchless / unrivaled / unequaled / invincible // 그 팀은 천하~이다 The team is unrivaled throughout the nation.
●무적함대 [역] (에스파냐의) The Invincible Armada.

무적(無籍) absence of a registered domicile; lack of a record. ¶~의 without a registered domicile.
●무적자 a person without a registered domicile[fixed address]; [부랑자] a vagabond; a vagrant.

무적(霧笛) a foghorn; a fog siren. ¶~을 울리다 sound a foghorn.

무전(無電) 1 radiotelegraphy. ⇨ 무선 전신(⇨무선) 2 radio-telephony. ⇨ 무선 전화(⇨무선) ¶~기를 장비한 자동차 a radio car / a telecar // ~으로 by wireless[radio] // ~을 치다 (미) radio / (영) wireless / send a message[telegraph] by radio[wireless] // 런던발 ~에 의하면 according to a radio[wireless] message from London // ~ 장치가 있다 be fitted with radio[wireless] installations.

무전여행(無錢旅行) a penniless trip; a vagabond journey.

무절제하다(無節制-) immoderate; intemperate; incontinent; 《서술적》 commit excesses. ¶무절제한 시장의 확장 uncontrolled[unsystematic] market expansion // 무절제한 생활을 하다 lead an intemperate life.

무정란(無精卵) a wind egg; an unfertilized egg.

무정부(無政府) [관형어적] anarchic; anarchical.
●무정부 상태 a state of anarchy. ¶~에 있다 be in a state of anarchy / be in an anarchi-

무정하다(無情-) [인정 없다] heartless; hard-hearted; cold-hearted; inhuman; cruel; [무자비하다] merciless; pitiless. ¶무정한 비 pitiless rain // 무정한 마음 a cold[stony] heart / a heart of stone // 무정하게도 그는 나에게 물을 주지 않았다 He was so heartless [hard-hearted] that he would not even give me water. // 그의 무정한 말이 내 가슴을 찔렀다 His heartless[cruel] words pierced me to the heart.

무정형(無定形) shapelessness; amorphousness. ¶~의 shapeless / formless / [비결정체인] amorphous.
● **무정형 물질** an amorphous substance. 무정형 탄소 amorphous carbon.

무정형(無定型) ¶~의 formless.
● **무정형 시** blank verse; formless verse.

무제(無題) no title. ¶~의 without a title / untitled // ~ (그림 등의 제목) No title.

무제한(無制限) ¶~의 unrestricted / unlimited // ~으로 without any[with no] restriction / freely / without reserve // ~으로 입장을 허락하다 admit people without any restriction.

무조건(無條件) ¶~의 unconditional / absolute / unqualified // ~(으로) unconditionally / unqualifiedly / without condition [reservation] // ~ 승낙하다 give unqualified consent // ~으로 조약에 조인하다 sign a treaty without any conditions // ~ 찬성입니다 I agree with you absolutely[unconditionally]. // 나는 ~ 그의 초청을 거절했다 I flatly refused his invitation. / I refused his invitation point-blank. // 그는 ~ 딸을 그 사나이에게 시집보냈다 He forced[compelled] his daughter to marry the man. // 그 청년은 ~ 경찰에 연행되었다 The young man was taken to the police station by force.
● **무조건 반사** [심] an unconditioned reflex. **무조건 항복** unconditional surrender.

무족목(無足目) [동] Apoda; Apodes; Apodia.

무좀 athlete's foot; dermatophytosis. ¶~에 걸리다 have athlete's foot.

무종교(無宗教) lack of religion; irreligion; no religion. ¶~의 irreligious / atheistic.
● **무종교자** a person without religion; an atheist; an unbeliever.

무죄(無罪) innocence; guiltlessness. ¶~를 선고하다 declare[find] (a person) not guilty // ~ 선고를 받다 be given a verdict of "not guilty" // 피고는 ~를 주장했다 The defendant pleaded not guilty. // 그녀는 ~가 되었다 She was found innocent. **무죄하다** innocent; not guilty; guiltless.
● **무죄 석방** acquittal (and discharge). ¶~이 되다 be found innocent and acquitted. **무죄 판결** a judgment of acquittal; a decision of "not guilty". ¶그는 ~을 받았다 He was found innocent.

무주의(無主義) lack of principle. ¶~의 without any principle / unprincipled.
● **무주의자** a person without definite principle.

무주택(無住宅) ¶~의 homeless / houseless.
● **무주택 서민(층)** the homeless masses. **무주택자** a houseless[homeless] person; houseless people.

무중력(無重力) zero gravity; weightlessness; zero G; nongravitation.
● **무중력 비행** a weightless flight. **무중력 상태** (a state of) weightlessness; a weightless state; a gravity-free state. ¶~가 되다 become weightless.

무지(無地) plain color [(영) colour]. ¶~의 plain / unfigured / solid (black) / of solid color // ~의 스커트 a plain-colored skirt.

무지(無知) [모름] ignorance; [문맹] illiteracy; [어리석음] stupidity. ¶자신의 ~를 드러내다 betray one's ignorance / display one's lack of knowledge // ~를 깨우치다 enlighten (people, a person's mind, etc.). **무지하다** ignorant (of); illiterate; stupid; silly. ¶무지한 백성 unenlightened[uncivilized] people // 정치에 관해서 그녀는 매우 ~ She is quite ignorant of politics.

무지(拇指) the thumb. ⇨엄지손가락(⇨엄지)

무지각(無知覺) insensibility; indiscretion. **무지각하다** insensible; senseless.

무지개 a rainbow. ¶쌍~ a coupled[double] rainbow // ~를 쫓는 사람 a rainbow chaser // ~ 다리 the rainbow's arch // ~가 하늘에 떴었다 There is a rainbow in the sky.
● **무지갯빛** rainbow[spectral] colors. ¶~의 rainbow-colored / [무지개처럼 빛이 변하는] iridescent.

무지근하다 (서술적) feel heavy[dull]. ¶머리가 ~ have a slight[dull] headache / feel heavy in the head // 다리가 ~ have a heavy [uncomfortable] feeling in one's leg // 뒤가 ~ My bowels are stuffy[constipated].

무지러지다 get stumpy[blunt]; wear down to a stump; wear out; be worn out; be stumped. ¶무지러진 비 a stumpy broom // 붓이 무지러졌다 The writing brush is worn to a stump.

무지렁이 [어리석은 사람] a lout; a dunce; a moron; a stupid person.

무지르다 cut off[away]; break (off); snap. ¶나뭇가지를 ~ cut branches off a tree / cut away branches from a tree.

무지막지하다(無知莫知-) ignorant and uncouth. ¶무지막지한 행동을 하다 act rudely / be wild / commit an outrage.

무지몰각(無知沒覺) ignorance and lack of understanding. **무지몰각하다** utterly ignorant; know nothing.

무지몽매하다(無知蒙昧-) unenlightened; ignorant. ¶그 섬의 토인은 ~ The inhabitants of the island are in an uncivilized state [in the darkest ignorance].

무지무지하다(無知無知-) horrible; awful; rough; rude. ⇨무지하다2·3

무지하다(無知-) 1 [지식이 없다] ignorant; illiterate. 2 [놀라울 만큼 대단하다] horrible; awful; awesome; dreadful. ¶무지한 부자 a very wealthy man / a man of great wealth // 무지하게 많은 빚[부채] staggering debts // 무지한 혼란 tremendous[awful] confusion // 무지하게 덥다 be awfully hot. 3 [우악스럽다] rough; rude; wild; violent. ¶무지하게 굴다 behave rudely / play it tough // 무지한 짓을 하다 act outrageously / commit an outrage.

무직(無職) inoccupation. ¶~의 without (an) occupation / [실직한] out of work[a job] / unemployed / jobless // 우리 아버지는 관직을 물러난 뒤로 줄곧 ~입니다 Since his retirement from government service, my father has had no regular employment. // 그는 지금 ~이다 He is unemployed[out of work] at

무직하다

the moment.
● 무직자 a person without a regular occupation; [실업자] an unemployed[a jobless] person; [집합적] the unemployed.

무직하다 feel heavy. ⇨무지근하다

무진장(無盡藏) ¶ 그에게는 돈이 ～ 있다 He is rolling in money.// 기운을 내게! 여자는 ～ 있어 Cheer up! There are lots more women in this world. 무진장하다 inexhaustible; unlimited; limitless; infinite; unfailing. ¶ 무진장한 천연자원 inexhaustible natural resources// 그들은 자금을 무진장하게 갖고 있다 They have inexhaustible[unlimited] funds.

무진히(無盡–) endlessly; infinitely; boundlessly.

무질서(無秩序) disorder; confusion; absence of order; disorderliness; chaos. 무질서하다 disordered; lawless; confused; chaotic. ¶ 무질서하게 without any order[system] / randomly // 교실 안은 무질서한 상태였다 The classroom was in disorder. // 모임의 무질서한 운영이 재정난을 초래했다 The lax management of the society led to financial difficulties. // 그 부대는 무질서하게 후퇴했다 The troops fled in disorder.

무쪽같다 be ugly[ill-favored] / look plain [homely].

무찌르다 1 [마구 죽이다] kill off; wipe out; mow[cut] down. ¶ 수천의 적군을 ～ mow down thousands of the enemy. 2 [공격하다] attack; assault; launch an attack (on); fall upon; set upon; [유린하다] devastate; overrun; conquer. ¶ 적의 성을 ～ assault [devastate] an enemy castle.

무차별(無差別) indiscrimination; nondiscrimination. 무차별하다 indiscriminate; equal. ¶ 무차별하게 indiscriminately / equally // 무차별하게 다루다 treat equally[indiscriminately] // 그 무법자[산적]는 무차별하게 마구 총을 쏘아 댔다 The bandit fired his gun indiscriminately.
● 무차별 곡선 [경] an indifference curve. 무차별 폭격 indiscriminate bombing.

무착륙(無着陸) ¶ ～의 nonstop / without alighting.
● 무착륙 비행 (make) a nonstop flight.

무참하다(無慘–) cruel; atrocious; pitiless; ruthless; merciless. ¶ 무참한 광경 a tragic scene // 무참한 죽음을 당하다 die a terrible death / meet with[come to] a tragic end // 사고 현장은 실로 무참한 광경이었다 The scene of the accident presented a horrible [dreadful] spectacle. 무참히 cruelly; pitilessly; mercilessly; without pity[mercy]. ¶ 우리 희망은 ～ 깨어졌다 Our hopes were sadly crushed.

무참하다(無慚–) 《서술적》 feel quite ashamed (of / for); be overwhelmed with shame; feel mortified. 무참히 shamefully; disgracefully; shyly; bashfully.

무채색(無彩色) an achromatic color.

무책임(無責任) [책임(감)이 없음] irresponsibility; lack of a sense of responsibility. 무책임하다 irresponsible. ¶ 무책임하게 irresponsibly / without a due sense of responsibility // 무책임한 발언 irresponsible remarks // 그는 아주 무책임했다 He has no sense of responsibility whatever. // 무책임한 대답은 그만두어라 Stop giving random[irresponsible] answers. // 그는 언제나 무책임한 말을 한다 What he says is never reliable. / He always says whatever comes into his head. // 그는 무턱대고 무책임한 짓을 했다 He rushed blindly into an irresponsible act.

무척 very; extremely; greatly; highly; exceedingly. ¶ ～ 오랫동안 나는 집을 비워 두고 있었습니다 I have been away from home for a very long time. // 올해는 ～ 추운 겨울이었다 It has been awfully cold this winter. // 그가 ～ 기뻐했을 것이다 He must have been extremely pleased. // ～ 더운 날이었다 It was a very hot day.

무척추동물(無脊椎動物) an invertebrate animal.

무청 the green part of radish.

무취(無臭) ¶ ～의 odorless / (영) odourless / unscented / scentless / inodorous // 무색～의 colorless and odorless.

무취미하다(無趣味–) tasteless; insipid. ⇨ 몰취미하다

무치다 season; dress (vegetables) with (some condiment). ¶ 나물을 ～ season vegetable.

무턱대고 [무분별하게] recklessly; needlessly; indiscreetly; [준비(까닭) 없이] without any preparation[reason]; [닥치는 대로] haphazardly; at random; [무차별하게] indiscriminately; blindly. ¶ ～ 돌진하다 rush forward blindly[recklessly] // ～ 추측하다 make reckless guesses // ～ 행동하다 act rashly // ～ 시험을 치다 take an examination cold[without any preparation] // 그렇게 ～ 해 보았자 아무 소용이 없다 There is no sense in doing things so haphazardly.

무테(無–) ¶ ～의 rimless / frameless / unframed / brimless.
● 무테안경 (a pair of) rimless glasses.

무통(無痛) painlessness; [의] indolence. ¶ ～의 painless / free from pain / [의] indolent.
● 무통 분만 (a) painless delivery; (마취를 한) delivery in twilight sleep.

무투표(無投票) ¶ ～로 without vote[voting] // 그는 ～로 의장에 선출되었다 He was chosen to be chairman without a vote.
● 무투표 당선 return without voting.

무패(無敗) no defeat; a clean record. ¶ ～의 undefeated // ～를 유지하다 maintain one's undefeated record // ～의 전적이다 have a record of all wins and no defeats / have a clean slate with no mark of defeat // 이 팀은 과거 2년간 ～를 기록했다 The team has not suffered a single defeat for the last two years.

무표정하다(無表情–) expressionless; blank; wooden. ¶ 무표정한 얼굴 an expressionless face / [무표정을 가장한 얼굴] a poker face // 그녀는 무표정하게 꼼짝 않고 서 있었다 She was standing stock-still with a blank look on her face.

무풍(無風) 1 [바람이 없음]. ¶ ～의 calm / windless // ～ 상태 a (dead) calm. 2 [평온함]. ¶ ～ 상태의 시세 a featureless[trendless] market // 노사 관계는 현재 ～ 상태이다 At present there is no dispute between labor and management. / At present all is quiet on the labor front.
● 무풍대 the calm belt[latitude]. ¶ 적도 ～ the equatorial calm / the doldrums.

무학(無學) illiteracy; illiterateness; ignorance. ¶ ～의 unlettered / uneducated / illiterate /

ignorant.
무한(無限) infinity; [영구] eternity. **무한하다** limitless; infinite; boundless; [무진장하다] inexhaustible; [영원하다] eternal. ¶무한한 공간 infinite space∥무한한 천연자원 inexhaustible natural resources∥인간의 욕망은 ~ Human desires know no bounds. **무한히** infinitely; endlessly; eternally. ¶수요는 ~ 증대할 것이다 The demand will increase to an unlimited extent.
● **무한궤도** an endless track; a caterpillar [tread]. **무한급수** [수] an infinite series. **무한대** infinitude; an infinite magnitude. ¶~의 infinite / infinitely great. **무한소** the infinitesimal. ¶~의 infinitesimal / infinitely small. **무한 집합** [법] an infinite set. **무한 책임** [법] unlimited liability.
무한정(無限定) [한정이 없음] infinity; unlimitedness; [한정 없이] unlimitedly; boundlessly; without limit[end]; endlessly. ¶~기다릴 수는 없다 I can't wait (for him) indefinitely [forever].
무해(無害) harmlessness; innocence; innocuousness; innoxiousness. **무해하다** harmless; innocent; inoffensive; innocuous; innoxious; (서술적) do (a person) no harm; produce no ill effects. ¶무해한 약품 a harmless drug ∥이 약은 인체나 가축에 ~ This drug is harmless to men and farm animals. ∥이 나무의 열매는 먹어도 ~ Even if you eat it, this nut will do you no harm.
무허가(無許可) no permit. ¶~의 [무인가·무면허의] unlicensed (doctors) / [무등록의] unregistered (brokers) / [무자격의] unqualified∥그는 ~로 약을 팔고 있다 He sells medicine without a license.
● **무허가 건물** an unauthorized[unlicensed] house[building]. **무허가 판매[제조]** nonlicensed sale[production].
무혈(無血) ¶~의 bloodless / without bloodshed.
● **무혈 전쟁** a white war (of propaganda). **무혈 쿠데타** a bloodless coup d'état. **무혈 혁명** a bloodless revolution. (1688년 영국의) the Glorious Revolution.
무혐의하다(無嫌疑-) clear (of suspicion); unsuspected; (서술적) be free from suspicion.
무협(武俠) [관형어적] chivalrous; heroic; chivalric.
● **무협 정신** a chivalous spirit.
무형(無形) ¶~의 [형체가 없는] formless / shapeless / [비물질적인] immaterial / [만질 수 없는] intangible / [정신적인] spiritual / moral∥지식은 ~의 재산이다 Knowledge is a moral asset.∥오늘의 그가 있은 것은 친구들의 유형 ~의 지원 덕분이다 He owes what he is to his friends' support, both material and spiritual [moral].
● **무형 문화재** an intangible cultural asset. **무형 재산 / 무형 자산** intangible[immaterial] property[assets].
무화과(無花果) [열매] a fig; (나무) a fig tree.
무효(無效) [실효] invalidity; nullity; [통용되지 않음] unavailability; [보람이 없음] ineffectiveness; futility; [경] no effects. ¶~인 invalid ineffectual / unavailable / ineffective / effectless / fruitless / vain / ¶~가 되다 become null [void / ineffective / unavailable] / be invalidated / lose effect / [법] lapse /

prove futile∥~로 하다 invalidate / annul / [법] void (a check)∥도중하차하면 이 차표는 ~가 된다 If you break your journey, the ticket will not be valid thereafter.∥이 투표들은 ~이다 These votes are invalid.
● **무효투표** (행위) invalid voting; (그 표) an invalid vote.
무훈(武勳) military achievements. ⇨=**무공**
무휴(無休) ¶~이다 have no holiday∥~로 일하다 work without taking a day off∥연중 ~ (게시) Open throughout the year. / Open through Dec. 31. / Open all year.∥3개월간 ~로 일했다 I have worked for three months without a holiday [having no holiday].
무희(舞姬) a dancing girl; a female dancer; a ballet-girl; a ballerina; (프) a danseuse.
묵 muk; jelly. ¶녹두~ green-pea jelly∥도토리~ acorn jelly∥메밀~ buckwheat jelly.
묵객(墨客) an expert in calligraphy and ink drawing.
묵계(默契) a tacit agreement[promise]; a tacit [secret] understanding; an implicit agreement. ¶~하에 (do something) on a tacit understanding∥그 두 사람 사이에는 ~가 있다 There is a tacit understanding between the two of them. **묵계하다** agree tacitly [implicitly]; make a tacit agreement (with).
묵과(默過) connivance. **묵과하다** overlook; look over; pass over (a matter) in silence; let (it) pass; let (a person) go unchallenged [unpunished]; connive [wink] (at). ¶묵과할 수 없는 모욕 an intolerable insult∥과실을 ~ overlook [slur (over)] (a person's) fault∥이대로 묵과할 수는 없다 I cannot pass it over in silence.
묵념(默念) 1 a silent [tacit] prayer. ¶희생자들에게 잠시 ~을 올립시다 Let us offer a moment of silent prayer for the victims. **묵념하다** pray silently; offer a silent prayer (to). ¶전몰자에 대해 1분간 ~ pay one minute's silent tribute to the war dead / offer one minute's silent prayer for repose of the souls of the war dead. 2 (a) meditation. ⇨=**묵상**
묵다[1] [오래되다] become [get / grow] old; become antiquated [outdated / outmoded / out of date / old-fashioned]. ¶묵은 관습 an old custom / a worm-eaten custom∥묵은 물건 an old article∥묵은 서랍장 an old chest of drawers∥묵은빚 an old debt / a debt of long standing∥묵은 빵 stale bread∥묵은 김치 stale *gimchi*(kimchi)∥묵은 쌀 old rice∥케케~ be hackneyed / be threadbare / be stale. 2 [유급하다] stay back in the class; remain in the original class. 3 [논밭이] be not in use; lie idle. ¶묵고 있는 밭 a field lying idle / an idle field.
묵다[2] [숙박하다] stay (at / in / with); lodge (in / with); put up [stop] (at a hotel); register (at a hotel). ¶호텔에 ~ put up [stay] at a hotel∥그날 밤은 호숫가의 어관에 묵었다 I put up at a lakeside hotel for the night.∥우리 집에 손님이 두 사람 묵고 있다 We have two guests staying with us.∥나는 절대로 밖에서 묵는 일이 없다 I never stay out overnight.∥그 호텔에는 200명이 묵을 수 있다 The hotel accommodates two hundred guests.∥나는 백부 댁에 묵고 있다 I am staying with my uncle.∥나는 하룻밤을 묵으러 숙부님 댁으로 갔다 I went to stay

overnight with my uncle.//나는 친구를 하룻밤 묵게 했다 I gave a friend a night's lodging.//그들은 자택에 피난민을 묵게 했다 They put the refugees up[gave the refugees lodging] in their own homes.

묵도 (默禱) a silent prayer. ⇨"묵념1

묵독 (默讀) silent reading. 묵독하다 read (a book) silently.

묵례 (默禮) a bow; a nod; nodding. 묵례하다 bow (to); make a bow (to); bow in silence; nod (to). ¶서로 ~ exchange bows[nods] // 학생들은 교장 선생님에게 묵례하였다 The pupils bowed to the principal in silence.

묵묵하다 (默默-) silent; mute; dumb. 묵묵히 silently; in (stony) silence; mutely. ¶그들은 ~ 행진했다 They marched in silence.//그녀는 (아무 불평도 없이) ~ 일을 잘해 주었다 She served me well without uttering any complaints[unobtrusively and well].

묵비권 (默祕權) the right of silence; (미) the Fifth Amendment. ¶~을 행사하다 stand mute (of malice) / use[exercise] the right of silence / (미) take the Fifth Amendment.

묵살하다 (默殺-) take no notice of; pass (over) (a matter) in silence; treat (it) with silent contempt; ignore (by keeping silence). ¶그는 모두의 반대를 묵살하고 여행을 떠났다 He ignored everyone's opposition and left on a trip. / Disregarding everyone's opposition, he set out on a trip. ➔묵살되다[당하다] be ignored / meet with disregard // 우리의 항의는 묵살되었다 Our protest was treated with silent contempt[was completely ignored].

묵상 (默想) (a) meditation; contemplation. ¶~에 잠기다 be lost in contemplation[reflection] / (a) reverie / be absorbed[buried] in meditation. 묵상하다 meditate (on / upon); muse (on).

묵시 (默示) 1 [계시] revelation. 묵시하다 reveal. 2 [은연중에 생각을 나타내기] implication. ¶~의 tacit / implied // 명시 또는 ~의 계약 an agreement expressed or implied.
● **묵시록** [성] The Book of the Apocalypse of St. John. ⇨요한 계시록

묵시 (默視) a silent watching. 묵시하다 [간과하다] overlook; wink [connive] at; [방관하다] remain a passive spectator. ¶그 사실은 묵시할 수가 없다 I cannot shut my eyes to the fact.

묵약 (默約) a tacit agreement[promise]. ⇨"묵계

묵언 (默言) silence; muteness. 묵언하다 keep silent; utter no words.

묵연하다 (默然-) silent; mute; tacit. 묵연히 silently; without saying anything; mutely; speechlessly.

묵은해 the old year; the year gone by; last year. ¶~와 새해 the old year and the new year // ~를 보내고 새해를 맞이하다 ring out the old year and ring in the new year // "올드 랭 사인"을 노래하면서 우리는 ~가 가는 것을 지켜보았다 We saw the old year out singing "Auld Lang Syne."

묵음 (默音) ¶~의 silent / [언] mute.

묵인 (默認) tacit[silent] approval[consent]; tacit admission; (나쁜 짓의) connivance (at / with); toleration. ¶~ 가격 a permitted price / …의 ~하에 with (a person's) connivance. 묵인하다 permit tacitly; tolerate; connive[wink] at. ¶그것은 감독자도 묵인하고 있는 실정이다 The supervisor (knows but) just winks at it.//그것을 묵인한 사람에게도 책임이 있다 Whoever let it pass[let him get away with it] is to blame, too. ➔이런 부패가 묵인되다니 참 한탄할 노릇이다 It is matter for sincere regret that such corruption should be overlooked.

묵정이 an old thing; old stuff; stuff that has been laid aside for a long time.

묵종 (默從) passive obedience; acquiescence. 묵종하다 obey passively; acquiesce (in); submit tamely[unprotestingly] (to).

묵주 (默珠) [가] a (Roman Catholic) rosary.

묵중하다 (默重-) taciturn; reticent; reserved. 묵중히 taciturnly; reticently.

묵직하다 1 (무게가) heavy [massive / weighty]. ¶묵직한 스웨터 a heavy[bulky] sweater // 묵직한 단지 a heavy pot // 묵직한 상자 a heavy box // 그 금화 자루는 묵직했다 The bag full of gold was heavy[weighed heavily] in my hands.//그의 지갑은 ~ He has plenty of money. / (구어) He has a nice fat wallet. 묵직이 heavily. ¶짐을 ~ 싣다 load a heavy cargo / pack a weighty load. 2 (언행이) serious; grave; solemn; imposing; dignified. ¶묵직한 발걸음으로 with a heavy [leaden] step / with a dignified step // 입이 ~ be rather taciturn. 묵직이 seriously; gravely; solemnly; with due solemnity. ¶입을 ~ 열다 talk in a grave[serious] manner.

묵척 (墨尺) a carpenter's square (for drawing ink lines). ⇨먹자

묵허 (默許) tacit permission[consent]; (나쁜 짓의) connivance (at / with). 묵허하다 allow; give tacit permission (to); connive[wink] (at); pass over.

묵화 (墨畵) (화법) monochromatic ink painting; (그림) an India(n)-ink picture [drawing]. ¶~의 산수(山水) a landscape drawn in India ink / an India-ink landscape.
● **묵화가** a chiaroscurist; a painter in India ink.

묵흔 (墨痕) ink marks; handwriting(필적). ¶~이 선명하다 be written vividly / be written in bold strokes.

묵히다 leave unused[wasted]; let (a thing) lie idle; keep (money) idle. ¶팔다 남은 스키복을 다음 해까지 ~ keep[hold over] unsold ski wear till the following year // 우리는 땅을 1년간 묵혔다 We let the soil [land] lie fallow for a year.//그처럼 많은 돈을 두 달이나 묵힐 수는 없다 We can't (afford to) leave such an amount of money idle for two months.

묶다 1 (매다) tie up; bind(▶ 묶어서 움직이지 못하게 하는 데는 tie도 bind도 쓸 수 있으나 개를 기둥에 묶는 경우에는 tie를 씀); fasten; bundle; tie up in a bundle; cord(끈으로). ¶볏단을 짚으로 ~ tie up [bind] sheaves of rice with straw // 헌 신문을 끈으로 ~ tie up old newspapers with rope // 볏짚을 묶어 세우다 bind straw into sheaves // 밧줄로 ~ tie up (a box) with a rope // 밧줄로 단단히 ~ tie fast with a rope // 우리는 그 개를 기둥에 묶어 놓았다 We tied the dog to a post.//그들은 나의 양다리를 묶었다 They tied [bound] my legs together.//열쇠를 끈으로 허리띠에 묶었다 I fastened the key to my belt with a string.//그들은 도둑을 단단히 묶었다 They tied up the thief.//그녀는 머리를 뒤로 묶어 놓고 있다 She has her hair tied at the back.

2 [속박하다] bind; fetter; tie; restrict; restrain; chain. ¶낮은 수준으로 묶어 놓은 임금 wages pegged at a low level∥우리는 규칙에 꽁꽁 묶여 있다 We are tied down by the rules.∥나는 돈에 묶여 있다 I'm bound with money.∥그들은 낡은 관습에 묶여 자유롭게 행동할 수 없었다 Fettered by old customs, they were unable to act freely.

3 [일괄하다] collect; put[bring / get] together. ¶문장 속의 괄호로 묶은 부분은 생략할 수 있다 The parts of the sentence enclosed in parentheses can be omitted.

묶음 a bundle; (같은 종류의 것의) a bunch; (볏단 등의) a sheaf (*pl.* sheaves); (장작 등의) a faggot; (건초 등의) a truss. ¶볏짚[막대기] 한 ~ a bundle of straw[sticks]∥장작 한 ~ a fagot[(영) faggot] (of firewood)∥서류 한 ~ a sheaf[bundle] of papers∥꽃 한 ~ a bouquet[bunch] of flowers∥~으로 만들다 bundle up / pack into[make] a bundle∥~으로 팔다 sell by the bundle∥그는 헌 신문지를 여러 ~으로 묶어 쌓아 올렸다 He tied the old newspapers in bundles and piled them up.

●**묶음표** parentheses; brackets. ⇨˝괄호

묶이다 1 (사람·물건이) be bound[tied / fastened / trussed / sheaved]; be chained [fettered / tied up / bound together / restricted / screwed down]. ¶두 손이 뒤로 묶여 with one's hands tied behind∥손발이 묶여 with one's hands and feet tied up∥꽁꽁 ~ be tightly[securely] bound∥포로의 팔은 옆구리에 묶였다 The captive's arms were pinioned to his sides.∥범인은 손발이 묶였다 The criminal was tied up[bound] hand and foot.∥그는 저항도 하지 않고 오라에 묶였다 He didn't resist as he was bound with (a) rope. / He was arrested without resistance.

2 [속박되다] be tied[fettered / restricted] by; be bound by (a rule). ¶시간에 ~ be restricted by time / be not the master of one's time∥규칙에 ~ be screwed down to a rule / be bound by a rule∥의리에 ~ be fettered by a sense of duty∥많은 여자들이 가정에 묶여 있다 Many women have home ties.∥나는 무슨 일에나 묶이기는 싫다 I am impatient of any restraint. / I don't like to be ruled by anything.∥그 함대는 지중해에 묶여 있다 The fleet is bottled[tied] up in the Mediterranean (Sea).∥그 파업으로 2만 명의 통근자의 발이 묶였다 The strike prevented twenty thousand people from getting to work. / The strike deprived twenty thousand commuters of their means of transportation.∥수도 요금은 당분간 현행대로 묶일 것 같다 The water rate is likely to be left as it is for some time.

문(文) **1** [문장] writings; a composition; (문법 상의) a sentence; [본문] the text; [문체] style. **2** [문학] literature; letters. ¶~은 무(武)보다 강하다 The pen is mightier than the sword. **3** [신발 크기의 단위] about 2.64cm. ¶9~의 신발 size 9 shoes / shoes of about 23cm sole.

문(門) **1** (방문) a door; (장지) a sliding door; (창문) a window; (대문) a gate(way); (회전문) a revolving door. ¶~의 들여다보는 구멍 a peephole∥~의 손잡이 a doorknob∥두 짝 ~ a two-leaved door∥출입~(정원·통로 등의) a wicket (gate)∥정원 출입~ a (wooden) garden gate∥좁은 ~ the strait gate (to Heaven)∥~을 열다 open a door∥~을 닫다 shut[close] a door∥~을 두드리다 knock on [at] the door∥~을 잠그다[~에 자물쇠를 채우다] lock the door∥좁은 ~으로 들어가라 Enter at the strait gate!∥~을 꼭 닫아 주시오 Don't leave the door open.∥그는 쾅 하고 ~을 닫았다 He slammed the door.∥이 ~은 밖으로[안으로] 열린다 This door opens outward[inward]∥그 ~은 서재로 통해 있었다 The door opened into a study.∥그는 ~을 열어 주지 않았다 He shut the door on us.∥~을 닫고 들어오시오 Close the door after you.∥교회는 천당으로 들어가는 ~이 아니다 The church is not a gateway to heaven.

2 [생물 분류학상의 단위] [동] a phylum (*pl.* -la); [식] a division. ¶~의 phyletic

3 [대포를 셀 때의 단위] a cannon. ¶대포 5~ five pieces of ordnance / five guns [cannons].

문(問) [물음·문제] a question; a problem. ¶제 1~ the first question.

문간(門間) the door; the gate; the entrance; the gateway; [현관 앞] the doorway. ¶손님을 ~까지 전송하다 see a visitor off to the gate∥~에 누가 있다 Someone is at the gate.∥~까지 배웅하겠습니다 I will see you to the door[gate].

●**문간방** a room beside the entrance[gate]; the vestibule.

문갑(文匣) a box[case] for letters; a stationery case.

문경지교(刎頸之交) [생사를 같이하는 사람] inseparable friendship; sworn[devoted / fast] friendship. ¶그와 나는 ~의 벗이다 He and I are devoted friends. / He is a friend who would die with me.

문고(文庫) **1** [서고] a library; [문방구 함(函)] a stationery box; [책장] a bookcase; a book chest. ¶마을~ a village library∥가죽~ a leather case[box]. **2** [상당한 규모의 장서] a collection of books. **3** [총서(叢書)] a library. ¶펭귄~ the Penguin Library.

●**문고본**(-本) a pocket[paperback] edition; a paperbacked book; a paperback. ¶이 소설은 ~으로 나와 있다 There is a paperback edition of this novel.

문고리(門-) an iron-ring handle (attached to a door); a door fastener; a doorpull; a catch(미닫이의). ¶~를 걸다 lock[latch / fasten] a door.

문과(文科) **1** the liberal arts; (대학의) the school[college] of liberal arts. ¶~의 학생 a student in the school of liberal arts / (미) a liberal arts major. **2** [문관 선출을 위한 과거(科擧)] the civil service examination under the kingdom. ¶~에 급제하다 pass the civil service examination.

●**문과 대학** a liberal arts college; a college of liberal arts.

문관(文官) a civil official[officer / servant]; a civilian; (집합적) the civil service.

문구(文具) **1** stationery. ⇨˝문방구 **2** rhetorical embellishments. ⇨˝문식

문구(文句) a passage; a paragraph; a sentence; words; a phrase; a clause; [표현] an expression. ¶편지의 ~ the wording of a letter∥재치 있는 ~를 쓰다 use a witty expression.

문구멍(門-) a rip in a door[window].

문기둥(門-) a gatepost. ⇨'문설주
문단(文段) 〔문장을 크게 나눈 단락〕 a paragraph.
문단(文壇) 〔문학계〕 the literary world; literary circles; the world of letters. ¶기성 ~ existing literary circles∥기성 ~인 a writer [an author] of established reputation∥~의 경향 literary trends∥한국의 ~ the Korean literary circles[scene]∥~의 거성 a literary magnate / the most prominent figure in the literary world∥~의 총아 a popular writer∥~에 데뷔하다 make one's debut as a writer / start one's literary career∥~에 명성을 떨치다 win literary fame / become a famous writer.
문단속(門團束) fastening[locking] the doors. ¶밤에 ~을 하다 lock up for the night∥~을 단단히 하다 fasten the doors securely∥~이 되어 있는가 보러 돌아다니다 go around to see whether the door are fastened∥도둑이 들지 않도록 ~을 철저히 하시오 Bolt your door fast against possible burglary. **문단속하다** lock up; lock[fasten / make fast] the doors; secure[fasten the door securely.
문 답(間答) questions and answers; a dialog(ue)(대화); catechism(문답식 교수). ¶소크라테스의 ~법 the catechetic(al) method of Socrates∥~식으로 catechetically / using [in the form of] questions and answers. **문답하다** exchange questions and answers (with); hold a dialogue[discussion].
● **문답식 교수법** the interrogatory method of teaching.
문대다 rub (in / into); scour. ⇨'문지르다
문덕문덕 in lumps; into pieces. **문덕문덕하다** fall apart (from deterioration).
문도(門徒) a disciple; a follower; an adherent; a believer.
문둥병(-病) 〔의〕 leprosy; lepra. ⇨"나병
문둥이 a leper.
문드러지다 (썩어서) rot; decay; disintegrate; decompose; (익어서) be overripe; (상처·피부가) be sore; be inflamed; (곪다) fester; ulcerate. ¶문드러진 잇몸 an ulcerated gum∥썩어 문드러진 시체 a decomposed body∥문드러진 토마토 an overripe tomato∥문둥병으로 얼굴이 ~ have one's face disfigured by leprosy.
문득 〔갑자기〕 suddenly; 〔우연히〕 by chance [accident]; casually; accidentally; unexpectedly(생각지 않게). ¶~ 생각나다 occur to (one) / flash across one's mind∥나는 ~ 창 밖을 내다보았다 I chanced to look out the window.∥~ 좋은 생각이 머리에 떠올랐다 Suddenly a good idea occurred to me.∥나는 ~ 그 생각이 떠올랐다 That idea crossed my mind[occurred to me].∥~ 어떤 생각이 그에게 떠올랐다 An idea struck[flashed into] his mind.
문득문득 suddenly; unexpectedly recurring (on several occasions). ¶~ 돌아가신 어머님 생각이 난다 The memory of my late mother revives unexpectedly from time to time.
문뜩 suddenly; by chance. ⇨'문득
문란하다(紊亂-) disordered; disorderly; confused; corrupt; loose; lax. ¶문란한 가정 a disorderly household∥문란하게 하다 disturb (public peace) / derange (social order) / corrupt (public morals)∥문란해지다 fall into disorder / be confused∥문란한 풍기를 바로잡다 correct the deplorable state of public morals∥풍기가 몹시 ~ Public morals are very lax[sadly decayed].∥교내의 풍기가 극도로 문란해지고 있었다 The school was completely lacking in discipline.

문례(文例) an example; a model sentence. ¶편지의 ~집 a collection of model sentences for letter-writing∥~가 풍부하다 be full of illustrative examples∥~를 들다 give an example.
문루(門樓) a gatehouse; a gate tower.
문리(文理) 1 〔문과와 이과〕 liberal arts and science(s). 2 〔문맥〕 the construction[style] of classical Chinese; the context. 3 〔조리〕 the line of thought.
● **문리과** department of liberal arts and science(s). **문리과 대학** the College of Liberal Arts and Science(s).
문맥(文脈) the context (of a passage); the line of thought. ¶~으로 뜻을 파악하다 grasp the meaning (of word) from the context∥이 산만하다 The writing is incoherent [jerky]. ∥그 ~에서는 그런 뜻을 읽을 수 없다 We cannot read[get / derive] such a meaning from the context.
문맹(文盲) 〔글을 모름〕 illiteracy; 〔문맹자〕 an illiterate[uneducated] person. ¶~의 illiterate / unlettered / ignorant / uneducated.
● **문맹률** (lower) the illiteracy rate. ¶이 나라는 ~이 높다 The illiteracy rate is high in this country. **문맹 퇴치 운동** a crusade against illiteracy; a campaign to abolish illiteracy.
문머리(門-) the upper frame of a gate[door].
문면(文面) the contents [text wording] of a letter. ¶그 서류의 ~상으로는 on the face of the document∥나는 내 제의를 거절한다는 ~의 그의 편지를 받았다 I received a letter saying that he declined my offer.
문명(文名) literary fame[reputation]. ¶~을 떨치는 작가 a famous[an eminent] writer∥~을 떨치다 win literary fame / make a name for oneself as an author∥그는 이 작품으로 ~을 떨쳤다 With this work, he made his name[a name for himself] as a writer. / This work made him a famous writer.
문명(文明) civilization; 〔문화〕 culture. ¶물질 [기계] ~ material [mechanical] civilization∥~서양 Occidental [Western] civilization∥원시 ~ primitive culture∥고도의 ~ a high level of civilization / high civilization∥~의 이기(利器) modern conveniences / a weapon of civilization∥~의 산물 a gift[product] of civilization∥~의 붕괴 the destruction of civilization∥고대 ~의 발상지 the birthplace [(문어) cradle] of ancient civilization∥~이 발달함에 따라 with the advance of civilization∥~이 발달하다 progress in civilization∥외국의 ~을 받아들이다 adopt [introduce] the foreign civilization∥이 ~의 세상에서도 고칠 수 없는 병이 있다 Even in this civilized age[age of civilization] there are incurable diseases.∥우리는 ~의 이기에 둘러싸여 있다 We are surrounded by modern conveniences.
● **문명국** a civilized country[nation]. **문명병** diseases incidental to civilization. **문명사회** civilized society. **문명인** a cultured person.
문묘(文廟) a shrine[temple] of Confucius.

문무(文武) [문학과 무도] literary and military arts; the pen and the sword; [문사(文事)와 무사(武事)] civil and military affairs. ¶그 사람은 ~ 양쪽에 능하다 He is skilled in both literary and military arts. / He is distinguished both as a scholar and a soldier.
● **문무백관** civil and military officials.

문물(文物) the products of civilization. ¶서양 ~ Occidental civilization / things Western // 한국의 ~을 외국 국민에 소개하다 introduce Korean culture to the people of foreign countries // 서양의 ~을 받아들이다 adopt the products of Western civilization.

문민(文民) a civilian.

문밖(門-) **1** [문의 바깥] the outside of a house. ¶~에(서) out of doors / outdoors // ~ 출입을 하지 않다 keep[remain] indoors. **2** [성문 밖] the outside of a castle.

문방구(文房具) stationery; writing materials.
문방사우(文房四友) the four precious things of the study.

문벌(門閥) [가문] lineage; birth. ¶~이 좋은 사람 a man of a distinguished family[high birth] / a man of renowned[good] lineage // 그는 ~도 재산도 없다 He has neither birth nor money. // 그는 훌륭한 ~ 출신이다 He is of high birth. / He was born of an aristocratic[a good / a distinguished] family.

문법(文法) grammar; rules of composition. ¶규범 ~ prescriptive grammar // 기술(記述) ~ descriptive grammar // 비교[일반] ~ comparative[general / universal] grammar // 학교 ~ school grammar // ~상의[적인] grammatical // ~상으로[적으로] grammatically // ~상의 오류 a grammatical mistake / an error in grammar // 영~ English grammar // ~에 맞다 be grammatically correct / be grammatical // ~에 맞지 않다 be ungrammatical / violate grammar // ~에 맞추다 grammaticize // ~에 맞는[맞지 않는] 어법을 쓰다 use good [bad / poor] grammar // ~에 구애되다[구애되지 않다] adhere to[be free of] grammar // 그는 ~상의 잘못이 많았다 He made many grammatical errors. / He made many mistakes in grammar. // 이 문장은 ~적으로 맞다 This sentence is grammatically correct.
● **문법 책** a grammar (book).

문병(問病) a visit to a sick person; an inquiry after a sick person. **문병하다** inquire[ask] after a sick person; visit (a person) in his sickbed. ¶나는 친구를 문병하러 갔다 I visited my sick friend.

문빗장(門-) a latch; a bar; a bolt. ¶~을 지르다[빼다] latch[unlatch] the door.

문사(文士) a literary man; a man of letters; a writer. ¶신진 ~ an up-and-coming young writer / a new literary light // 삼문(三文)~ a hack writer.

문살(門-) the ribs of a lattice door.

문상(問喪) [조상(弔喪)] condolence; [조문(弔問)] a visit of condolence. ¶~을 받다 receive callers for condolence // ~을 가다 make a call of condolence / call at (a mourner's) home to offer one's condolence // 나는 그의 아버지의 ~을 갔다 I called on him to express my condolences[sympathy] on his father's death. **문상하다** condole with (a person on his bereavement); offer one's condolence to (a person on a sad event). ¶유족을 ~ pay a visit to express one's sympathy [condolences] to the bereaved family.
● **문상객** a condoler; a condolence caller.

문서(文書) [서류] a document; [기록] a record; archives; [통신] letters; notes. ¶불온 ~ dangerous[inflammatory] literature / subversive documents // 외교 ~ a diplomatic note // 항복 ~ an instrument of surrender // 공[사] ~ an official[a private] document // ~의 형식으로 in written form / in[by] writing // ~화하다 commit to[put in] writing // ~로 지령을 내리다 issue written instructions // 생각하고 있는 것을 ~화하다 commit one's thoughts to writing // ~로 신청해 주십시오 Please send in your application in writing. // 그는 대답을 ~화하여 제시했다 He presented his answer in written form.
● **문서 위조** forgery (of documents); falsification. **문서 위조죄** forgery (of documents).

문선(文選) **1** [선집] a selection of literary works; an anthology. **2** [인] type-picking. **문선하다** pick type; select literary works; set (up) type.
● **문선공**(-工) a compositor; a typesetter.

문설주(門-柱) a gatepost; a doorpost.

문수(文數) a size; shoe sizes. ¶~ 5의 신발 size five shoes / shoes of size 5.

문식(文飾) rhetorical embellishments[flourishes / ornaments].

문신(文臣) a civil minister[vassal].

문신(文身) [먹물로 살갗에 그림 등을 새김] tattooing; [무늬] a tattoo (pl. ~s); tattoo marks. ¶등에 용의 ~을 하고 있다 have a dragon tattooed on one's back // 그는 왼팔에 새겨 넣은 닻의 ~이 있다 He has an anchor tattooed on his left arm. **문신하다** tattoo. ¶등에 ~ tattoo (a flower) on (a person's) back / (남을 시켜) have one's back tattooed.

문안(門-) [성내]. ¶~ 사람 a city dweller; townsfolk // ~에 살다 live in the city limits (of).

문안(文案) (미) a draft; (영) a draught; a sketch; an outline. ¶광고 ~을 작성하다 draft [prepare a draft of] an advertisement.

문안(問安) an inquiry[asking] after (a person's) health; sending kind regards. ¶~ 말씀 an expression of one's sympathy (for) // 복중 ~ a call[letter] of inquiry after (a person's) health in the hot season // 환자에게 ~을 드리다 express one's concern for a sick person // 입원 중인 선생님께 우리 모두 병~을 갔었다 We went together to visit our teacher in the hospital. **문안하다** inquire [ask] after (a person's) health; send one's kind[best] regards to (a person); pay one's respects to (a person). ¶문안하러 가다 visit [call on] (a person) to inquire after (his) health // 나는 은사를 문안하러 댁으로 찾아갔다 I called on my old teacher at his home to see how he was doing.
● **문안 편지** (계절에 따른) a letter conveying the compliments of the season; a letter of inquiry[sympathy]. ¶더위에 ~를 보내다 write a letter to a person to inquire after his health in the hot season.

문약하다(文弱-) effeminate.

문어(文魚) [동] an octopus (pl. ~es, -pi). ¶~ 단지 an octopus trap.

문어(文語) [문장어] written[literary / classical] language; [문어의 한 단어] a literary word. ¶~로 쓴 책 a book written in literary

문예

language // 이 말은 ~로만 쓰인다 This word is used only in literary writing.
● 문어체 literary [book] style. ¶~의 영어 literary English // ~로 쓰다 write in a literary [dignified / formal] style.

문예(文藝) 〔문학과 예술〕 the arts; literature [learning] and the arts; 〔문학〕 literature; 〔학예〕 liberal arts. ¶~에 조예가 깊다 be well versed in art and literature.
● 문예가 a literary man; a man of letters. 문예 기자 a literary writer. 문예부 the literary section. 문예 부흥 the revival of learning; (유럽의) the Renaissance. 문예 사조 literary thoughts; trends in literary theory. 문예지 a literary magazine. 문예 평론 literary criticism; a book review.

문외한(門外漢) 〔직접적인 관계가 없는 사람〕 an outsider; 〔전문이〕 아닌 사람〕 a layman; an amateur. ¶~의 의견 a lay [layman's] opinion / an outsider's opinion // 그는 전혀 ~이다 He is a rank outsider. // 나는 그 학문에는 ~이다 I know nothing about that branch of science.

문우(文友) a literary friend [associate]; a fellow writer.

문의(文義·文意) the meaning (of a passage); the effect [purport] (of a writing [phrase]). ¶이 문장의 ~가 애매하다 This [The meaning of this] sentence is ambiguous [not clear]. // 나는 이 절(節)의 ~를 파악할 수 없다 I can't make out what this passage is supposed to mean.

문의(問議) an inquiry; a reference; a request for information. ¶전화 ~ a telephone inquiry // 전화 ~는 삼가십시오 Please refrain from making inquiries by telephone. // 우리는 홍콩으로부터 피아노에 관한 거래 ~를 받았다 We received inquires about [request for] pianos from Hong Kong. 문의하다 make inquiries (about); inquire; check; ask. ¶우리는 마감 일자를 문의했다 We inquired [made an inquiry] about the deadline. // 그 사람들에게 편리한 날을 문의합시다 We will ask what would be a convenient date for them. // 문의해 보았더니 마을에 최한수라는 이름의 인물은 없었다 On inquiry, we found no one by the name of Choe Hansu in the village. // 상세한 것은 인사부에 문의하여 주십시오 For particulars please apply to [inquire at] the Personnel Office.
● 문의처 a reference.

문인(文人) a literary man; a man of letters; (집합적) the literati.
● 문인 협회 the Literary Men's Association.

문인화(-畫) a painting in the literary artist's style.

문자(文字) 1 〔글자〕 a letter; a character(한자 등). ¶그리스 ~ Greek letters // 표음 ~ an ideograph // 표음 ~ a (Korean) phonetic letter // ~를 읽을 줄 아는 [모르는] 사람들 literate [illiterate] people // ~ 다중 방송 teletext // ~에 구애되다 adhere to the letter (of the law). 2 〔글귀〕 a maxim; (idiomatic) phrase] from the Chinese classics; a pedantic expression. ¶~를 잘 쓰다 be much given to using idiomatic phrases from the Chinese classics / talk like a book.

문자 그대로 literally; to the letter; in literal sense of the word. ¶그의 얼굴은 ~ 창백하게 되었다 His face literally turned white. // 그 아이는 ~ 내 지시에 복종한다 The child obeys my words to the letter. // 나는 ~ 무일푼이다 I am literally penniless. / I haven't got a red cent to the letter.

문자반(文字盤) a dial (plate); the face (of a clock); the clockface.

문장(文章) 〔글월〕 writing; 〔작문〕 a composition; 〔문체〕 (a) style; 〔논문〕 an article [essay]; 〔산문〕 prose. ¶에머슨의 ~ Emerson's style // 뛰어난 ~ master writings // ~ 능하다 [서투르다] write a good [bad] style / write cleverly [poorly] // ~을 짓다 write [make] a composition // ~을 다듬다 polish (up) one's style // 「21세기의 한국」에 관하여 ~을 지으시오 Write a composition [an essay] on "Korea in the Twenty-First Century." // 그 ~은 썩 잘되었다 It is well written. // 그는 최남선의 ~투를 흉내 내고 있다 He models his style on Choe Namseon's. // 나는 이 ~의 뜻을 모르겠다 I don't understand (the meaning of) this sentence.
2 〔문(文)〕 a sentence. ¶간결한 [복잡한] ~ a crisp [complicated] sentence // 세련된 [서투른] ~ a polished [clumsy / poor] sentence // 완전한 ~ a complete sentence // 그 이야기 시작의 [첫] ~ the first sentence [beginning passage] of the story // ~을 고치다 [고쳐 쓰다] correct [rewrite] a sentence // ~을 분석하다 analyze a sentence.
3 a good writer; an essayist. ⇨ 문장가(⇨문장)
● 문장가 a good [fine / clever] writer; 〔수필가·평론가〕 an essayist; a stylist(문체가). ¶선생님은 대단한 ~다 My teacher is quite a writer. 문장 구조 the sentence structure. 문장론 〔언〕 syntax.

문장(紋章) a crest(▶ 방패 위쪽에 투구를 본뜬 모양인데 of arms와 같은 뜻으로 쓰일 때도 많음); a (heraldic) device; family insignia; a coat of arms. ¶기(旗)에는 공작 가문의 ~이 붙어 있었다 The banner bore the arms of the Duke(▶ 방패꼴이라는 인상이 강함).

문재(文才) 〔글재주〕 literary talent [ability]. ¶~가 있는 사람 a person of [gifted with] literary ability // ~를 발휘하다 display [show] a talent for writing.

문전(文典) a grammar; a grammar book.

문전(門前) ¶~에 before [in front of] a gate / at the gate [door] // ~ 걸식하다 beg one's bread from door to door / go out begging // ~ 성시를 이루다 have many visitors / be thronged with callers // 그녀는 나를 ~에서 내쫓았다 She turned me away at the door. / She shut [slammed] the door in my face. / She refused to see me.

문제(問題) 1 〔답을 구하는 질문〕 a question; (해답에 계산·작도(作圖) 등을 필요로 하는) a problem. ¶시험 ~ an examination question [paper(전체)] // 주어진 ~ a given question [problem] // 머리를 짜내도록 애먹이는 ~ a puzzling question [problem] // ~에 답을 내다 answer a question // ~와 씨름하다 attack [tackle / grapple with] a problem // ~를 내다 set [give] a question / set (a student) a paper // 수학 ~를 풀다 solve a problem in mathematics // 네게 ~ 하나를 내겠다 Let me put a question to you. // 역사 시험에 어려운 ~가 많이 나왔다 We had a lot of difficult questions on [(영) in] the history exam. //

는 수학 시험에서 두 ~밖에 풀지 못했다 I was able to solve only two problems on [(영) in] the math exam.
2 [해결해야 할 일] a question; a problem; [쟁점] an issue; [과제] a subject. ¶연구 ~ a subject of [for] inquiry [study] // 경제 [사회 / 식량 / 정치] ~ an economic [a social / a food / a political] problem [question] // 인도주의적인 ~ a humanitarian question // 아직 아무도 손을 대지 않은 ~ an untouched subject // 이 ~에 관한 저서 works on this subject // 가장 중요한[부차적] ~ a matter of prime [secondary] importance // 긴급한 ~ a pressing [burning] question // 중대한 ~ a matter of grave concern // 당면한 ~ the question [point] at issue // 해결해야 할 ~ a problem awaiting solution // 그 ~는 덮어 두고 putting aside the question // ~시하지 다 take no notice [account] of / pay no heed (to) // ~에 봉착[직면]하다 meet [confront] a problem // ~가 되다 become an issue [a subject of discussion] / be at issue / come into question // 큰 ~이 되어 있다 be in serious question // ~가 되지 않다 be out of the question / [대수롭지 않다] do not matter [figure] / matter little / [하찮다] be insignificant / be negligible / count for nothing // ~로 삼다 call (a matter) to account / put (a matter) in question // 정치상의 ~로 삼다 make a political issue of (a matter) // 남의 능력을 ~로 삼다 call a person's ability into question // ~를 해결하다 solve a problem / settle a question // ~를 제기하다 pose a problem (to) // ~를 다루다 handle [treat] a problem [question] // 이 두 논문은 같은 ~를 다루고 있다 These two treaties treat of the same subject. // ~는 그것을 여하히 확보하느냐에 있다 The question is how to secure it. // 그 사건은 소년법에 새로운 ~를 제기하게 되었다 The incident raised new questions about the law on juveniles. // 교과서 개정은 정치 ~가 되었다 They made a political issue (out) of the revision of textbooks. // 성공은 단지 시간 ~다 Success is only a question [matter] of time. // 그런 제안은 ~가 되지 않는다 Such a proposal is out of the question [isn't worth considering]. // 그 일에 대해서는 ~ 삼지 않아도 된다 That matter may be left out of consideration. / That matter doesn't have to be brought up. // 그 ~에 있어서 우리의 의견이 크게 갈라졌다 Our opinions differed greatly on the subject. // 그런 거래는 생각해 볼 ~다 Such a deal is questionable. // 지금 그들에게 그것을 알리는 것은 생각해 볼 ~이다 We had better not tell them now. // 그는 ~없이 당선될 것이다 His success in the election is beyond question. / There is no doubt that he will win the election. / He will win the election without any trouble. // 그가 언제 돌아오느냐는 ~가 아니다 It does not matter when he comes back. // 자네가 그렇게 하거나 안 하거나 ~될 것이 없다 It won't matter whether you do it or not. // 경찰은 그의 동기를 ~시하고 있다 The police regard his motives as questionable. // 그 ~는 아직 해결 안 된 채로 있다 The question remains untouched. // 그 problem remains unsolved. // 이 ~를 불문에 붙일 수는 없다 We cannot pass this question in silence. // 그것은 지엽적인 ~다 That is only a peripheral issue. // 집보다 빵 ~가 급하다 The question of food precedes that of housing. // 이런 것은 큰 ~가 아니다 This is a small matter. // 이 건에 있어서 금전은 ~가 아니다 In this affair money is no consideration. // 그런 것은 ~시할 것도 못 된다 It is beneath our notice. // 그 점은 ~ 삼지 않아도 된다 That point may be left out of consideration. / It's mere child's pay. / (미국 속어) No sweat! // 그것은 ~다 That's serious!
3 [물의] public discussion [comment]. ¶~의 인물 the person in question / a controversial figure // ~의 영화 the film in question // ~가 많은 작품 a controversial work // ~를 일으키다 cause [give rise to / bring on] public discussion // 그의 실언이 ~가 되었다 His slip of the tongue brought on much criticism. // 그의 연설은 교육계에 ~을 일으켰다 His speech has given rise to a controversy in the educational world.
4 [관련된 일] a matter; a question; an affair. ¶시간 ~ a question [matter] of time // 금전상의 ~ a money matter / a monetary affair // 양심의 ~ a case [point] of conscience // 풍기(風紀) ~에 있어서 우리 학교는 상당히 엄격하다 With respect to [In matters of] discipline, our school is very strict.
5 [말썽] trouble. ¶~를 일으키다 cause [arouse / make / give rise to] trouble // 그는 또 여자와의 일로 ~를 일으켰다 He has caused a problem with a girl. // 그것이 오히려 ~를 크게 만들었다 It only aggravated [magnified] the trouble.
● **문제극** a controversial play; a play which causes a furor [raises an uproar]; a problem play. **문제 소설** a controversial novel; a novel which causes a furor [raises an uproar]; a problem novel. **문제아** a child who needs special care; a problem child. **문제 의식** (have) a critical mind. 그들은 세계 정세에 ~을 갖고 있다 They are very much aware of the world situation. **문제점** the point at issue; a controversial [an open / a moot / (미) a mooted] point. ¶몇몇 ~을 제기하다 raise several questions [points at issue] // 그의 설에는 약간의 ~이 있다 There are a few disputable points in his theory. // 이 논설은 현대 사회의 몇몇 ~을 지적하고 있다 The article points out several problems concerning modern society. **문제집** a collection of problem.

문죄(問罪) (an) accusation; indictment; arraignment. **문죄하다** accuse (a person of a crime); indict (a person) for [on a charge of] (a crime).

문주란(文珠蘭) [식] a crinum.

문중(門中) a family; a clan; one's kinsfolk; one's relatives.

문지기(門−) a gatekeeper; (현관의) a doorkeeper; a gateman; (호텔·클럽 등의) a doorman; a (house) porter; (호텔 등의) a commissionaire; a concierge.

문지르다 [무엇에 대고 비비다] rub (in / into); scour; scrub. ¶광내는 가루로 주전자를 ~ scour a kettle with polishing powder // 소금으로 오이 한 개를 ~ rub a cucumber with salt / (엷게 썬 오이를) crush slices of cucumber in salt // 손에 묻은 먼지를 헝겊에 ~ rub (off) the dirt from one's hands onto a cloth // 마른 헝겊으로 문질러 광을 내다

문지방(門地枋) the threshold; the (door) sill. ¶~을 넘다 cross[pass] the threshold // ~이 닳도록 찾아가다 make frequent visits to (a person) // 다시는 내 집 ~을 넘지 마라 Don't you ever set foot in my house again!

문진(問診) ¶증상에 대해 환자에게 ~을 하다 ask a patient detailed questions about his condition.

문집(文集) a collection of works; [한 작가 또는 같은 형식에 의한 여러 작가의 선집] an anthology. ¶헉슬리 ~ The Collected Works of Aldous Huxley.

문짝(門-) (a leaf[flap] of) a door. ¶~을 열어 젖뜨리다 push[pull] the door open.

문채(文彩·文采) 1 [문장의 멋] a trope; tropes; rhetorical flourishes; literary embellishments. 2 a pattern; a design. ⇨무늬

문책(問責) (문어) (a) censure; (a) reproof; reprehension. **문책하다** (문어) censure; reprimand; reprehend; reprove; rebuke. ¶남의 실수를 ~ censure a person for his blunder. →¶**문책받다** be reprimanded[rebuked / censured] // 그는 태만을 문책당했다 He was censured[(문어) rebuked] for being lazy. // 그 장관은 실책을 문책당했다 The minister was reprimanded for his mistake.

문체(文體) a (literary) style; a style; a style of writing; language. ¶고(古)~ an antiquated style // 평이한[공들인] ~ a plain[an ornate] style // 명쾌한 ~ a clear style // 화려한 ~ a flowery[florid] style / fine language // 세련된 [거친] ~ a polish[rough] style // 힘찬 ~ a vigorous[powerful] style // 짜임새 없는[있는] ~ a slovenly[crisp] style // 간결한 ~ a pithy [concise] style // 지드의 ~를 모방하여 쓴 소설 a novel written in the style of Gide // 쉬운 ~로 쓰여 있다 be written in an easy[a plain] style // 자기만의 ~를 만들어 내다 make[cultivate] a style of one's own // 그의 ~는 간단하고 명쾌하다 He has a simple, lucid style. // 이 수필은 그의 독특하고 유려한 ~로 쓰여 있다 This essay is written in a fluent style of his own.

문초(問招) questioning (a criminal); (cross-)examination; an inquiry; an interrogation. ¶심한 ~를 받다 be subjected to[be put through] a severe cross-examination // 경찰의 ~를 받다 be examined[questioned] by the police // ~를 받고 있다 be under examination. **문초하다** question (a criminal); (cross-)examine; interrogate. ¶죄인을 ~ examine a criminal // 엄중히 ~ subject (a person to) a close examination.

문치(門齒) an incisor (tooth); an incisive; a foretooth.

문치(文治) civil administration; administration by civilians.

문치적거리다 dilly-dally; vacillate; act shilly-shally; dawdle; waver. ¶문치적거리다가 기회를 잃다 dally away one's opportunity // 문치적거리지 말고 네 생각을 말해라 Out with it! Never stand shilly-shallying.

문턱(門-) a threshold; a doorsill. ¶~을 넘다 cross[step over] the threshold // ~에 걸터앉다 sit on a doorsill // 다시는 그 집 ~을 넘어 서지 마라 Never show your face again at that house. / Never cross his threshold again.

문투(文套) a (literary) style; a literary form. ¶자기 나름의 ~로 in a style of one's own // 남의 ~를 흉내 내지 말고 자신의 ~을 개발하게 Don't copy anybody's style, develop your own.

문틀(門-) the framework of a door; a door-frame.

문틈(門-) a crack[chink] in door. ¶~으로 들어오는 바람 a draft / (영) a draught // **~으로 들여다보다** peep in through a chink in the door // ~으로 들어오는 바람을 막다 cut off the drafts.

문패(門牌) a doorplate; a nameplate. ¶~를 **달다** put up a nameplate (at the gate) / peg one's nameplate (at).

문풍지(門風紙) a weather strip; (집합적) weather stripping. ¶~를 **달다** seal up (a window) / weatherstrip (the joints of a window) // ~를 달아 한기를 막다 paper out the cold wind.

문필(文筆) literary art[work]; writing. ¶~의 재능이 있다 have a talent for writing / ~로 먹고살다 live by one's pen / make a profession of literature // 그는 ~에 종사하고 있다 He is doing literary work. / He is following a literary career. // 그는 ~ 작업에 열중하고 있다 He is involved in literary pursuits. // 그는 ~로 생활하고 있다 He writes for a living. / (문어) He lives by his pen. // 그녀는 ~ 활동을 계속했다 She continued his literary activity.

●**문필가** a literary man; a man of letters; a writer. **문필업** the literary profession[occupation / pursuits]. ¶~에 **종사하다** follow [engage in] the profession of letters.

문하(門下) being under (a person's) instruction[guidance / tuition]; studying under (a person). ¶~에 들어가다 become a pupil of ... // 그는 홍 선생의 ~에서 배운다 He is a pupil[disciple] of Mr. Hong's. / He studies under Mr. Hong. // 그의 ~에 2명의 노벨상 수상 화학자가 있다 Among his students are two Nobel Prize winning chemists. // 방방곡곡의 수재들이 그의 ~에 모여들었다 Men of talent from all parts of the country flocked to his institution.

●**문하생** one's[a young] pupil[disciple / follower]; (집합적) one's following. ¶그는 대학에서 나의 ~이었다 He was a student under me at the university.

문학(文學) literature; letters. ¶~적 literary / ~적으로 [~상] literarily // 고전[근대] ~ classical[modern] literature // 낭만[자연]주의 ~ romantic[naturalistic] literature // 대중[기록 / 국민] ~ popular[documentary / national] literature // 비교 ~ comparative literature // 순~ serious[polite / pure] literature / (프) belles lettres // 한국 ~ Korean literature // ~의 소양이 있다 have a knowledge of literature.

●**문학 개론** a literary survey; a survey of literature; an introduction to literature. **문학계** the literary world; literary circles; the world of letters. **문학 박사** (사람) a doctor of literature[Letters] / (학위) Doctor of Literature [Letters] (약어 Litt. D.). **문학사**(-士) (사람) a bachelor of Arts / (학위) Bachelor of Arts(약어 B.A.). **문학사**(-史) the history of literature. **문학상** a literary award. **문학소녀** a young lady of literary interests. **문학자** a man of letters; a literary man. **문학 작품**

literary work[writing / production]. **문학잡지** a literary magazine.
문헌(文獻) (어떤 주제에 관한) literature; [기록자료] documents. ¶참고 ~ literature cited / books for reference / [목록] a bibliography // 많은 ~ a large[voluminous] literature // 이 문제에 관한 ~은 아주 적다 The literature on the subject is very scanty. // 나는 영어로 된 의학의 ~을 조사했다 I referred to[looked up] the medical literature written in English. // 이 연구에는 풍부한 ~이 있다 There is abundant literature for this research.
● **문헌학** philology. ¶~적인 philological.
문형(文型) a sentence pattern. ¶기본 ~ a basic sentence pattern.
문호(文豪) a great[distinguished] writer[man of letters]; a literary lion.
문호(門戶) the door. ¶외국에 ~를 개방[폐쇄]하다 open[close] the door to foreign countries.
문화(文化) culture; [문명] civilization. ¶세종 ~ 회관 the Sejong Cultural Center // ~가 높은[낮은] 나라 a nation with a high[low] cultural level / a nation with an advanced[a primitive] culture // 한국 ~의 전통 Korean cultural tradition // **~가 뒤떨어지다** be backward in civilization / be at a low level of culture.
● **문화 관광부** the Ministry of Culture and Tourism. **문화 교류** cultural exchange. ¶국가 간의 ~를 도모하다 promote cultural exchange[interchange] between[among] nations. **문화 국민** a cultured nation; a nation of culture; civilized citizens. **문화권**(-圈) a cultural area. **문화부** (신문사의) the culture desk. **문화사**(-史) cultural history. ¶한국 ~ the cultural history of Korea / the history of Korean culture. **문화 사절** a cultural envoy[delegate / mission]. **문화생활** a civilized[(영) civilised] life; a cultural [cultured modern] life. **문화 수준** the cultural level; the level of culture; the standard of culture. ¶이 나라의 ~은 높다[낮다] This nation has a high[low] level of culture. **문화 영화** a cultural[an educational] film. **문화유산** cultural inheritance. **문화인** [교양을 갖춘 사람] a cultured[cultivated] man; a man of culture; [학문이나 예술을 직업으로 삼고 있는 사람] a person in an academic or artistic career. **문화재** cultural assets[properties]. ¶무형 ~ intangible cultural assets // 인간 ~ human cultural assets // 주요 ~로 지정되다 be designated as important cultural property. **문화제**(-祭) a cultural festival. **문화 혁명** (중국의) the (Great Proletarian) Cultural Revolution.
문후(問候) inquiring (by letter) after another's well-being; paying one's respect to (a person) (by letter). **문후하다** write a letter (to).
묻다[1] 1 [질문하다] ask; [조사하다] inquire (of a person about a thing) (▶ ask보다 격식 차린 말). ¶무엇인가 묻고 싶은 듯한 표정 a questioning look // 그는 길을 잘못 물었다 He did not ask the way properly. // 자세한 것은 도서관원에게 물어 주시오 For further information, please ask[see] the librarian. // 말씀 좀 묻겠습니다 May I ask you a question? // 전문가의 의견을 묻는 것이 좋다 You had better ask for a specialist's opinion. // 이 문제에 관한 귀하의 의견을 묻고 싶다 I would like to ask your opinion concerning this problem. // 그것에 대해서 좀 더 자세한 것을 묻고 싶다 I would like[Give me] more information about it.
2 [따지어 밝히다]. ¶죄를 ~ accuse (a person) of some crime / charge (a person) with some crime // 책임을 ~ call (a person) to account / charge (a person) with irresponsibility.
3 [문제를 삼다] (부정문에서) care. ¶…을 묻지 않고 no matter (how / what / when / where) / whether or not // 승패는 묻지 않는다 It doesn't matter whether we win or lose. // 경험은 묻지 않음 (광고에서) Experience unnecessary. / No experience (is) necessary [required].
4 (안부·소식을) ask[inquire] after (a person, a person's health, etc.); inquire about. ¶소식을 ~ ask how (a person) is getting along[on] / ask for news about (a person) / ask about (a person's) news // 그녀가 당신의 건강 상태[안부]를 물었다 She asked[inquired] after you. / She asked how you were.
묻다[2] [들러붙다] stick (to); adhere (to); be stuck; be covered; (더럼·때 등이) be stained [smeared] (with). ¶피가 묻은 옷 bloodstained clothes // 옷에 잉크가 묻었다 My dress was stained with ink. // 네 구두에 진흙이 묻었다 Your shoes are muddy. / There's some mud on your shoes. // 그 용의자의 셔츠에 피가 묻어 있었다 The suspect's shirt was bloodstained. // 옷깃에 묻은 때가 지워지지 않는다 The dirt clinging to the collar can't be washed out.
묻다[3] 1 [파묻다] bury (in / under); inter; inhume; cover (up). ¶시체를 ~ bury a corpse[body] // 나는 그 병을 땅속에 묻었다 I buried the jar in the ground. // 나는 이 땅에 뼈를 묻을 작정이다 I mean to die[be buried] here. // 그녀는 내 가슴에 얼굴을 묻었다 She buried her face against my chest. // 그 아이는 커다란 베개에 머리를 묻었다 The child sank his head into the big pillow. 2 [숨기다] hide [conceal / keep] (a matter from a person); keep (a matter) secret (from). ¶살인 사건을 비밀로 묻어 두다 keep a case of murder (a) secret // 그것을 나는 내 마음속에만 묻어 두었다 I have kept it to myself.
묻히다[1] [매장되다] be buried (in); [숨겨지다] be hidden[concealed] (from a person); be kept secret (from). ¶무덤 속에 묻혀 있다 be buried in the ground / lie beneath a grave // 비밀 속에 ~ be kept secret[back / dark] // 고향에 묻히고 싶다 I wish to be buried in my native country. // 그 오두막은 눈에 묻혀 있었다 The hut was buried under the snow. // 그는 책 속에 묻혀 살고 있다 He lives entirely surrounded by his books. // 산사태로 무너진 토사 밑에 5명의 어린이가 묻혀 있다 Five children are buried under the landslide. // 그 사건은 어둠 속에 묻혔다 The matter was hushed.
묻히다[2] [묻게 하다] stain; smear; cover. ¶신발에 흙을 ~ get mud on one's shoes / have one's shoes muddy // 펜에 잉크를 ~ dip a pen in ink // 우표에 물을 ~ moisten a stamp // 탈지면에 소독약을 ~ soak absorbent cotton with disinfectant // 나는 양복에 페인트

를 묻혀 버렸다 I got paint on my suit.

물¹ 1 (일반적인) water. ¶단~ fresh water // 짠~ salty[salt] water / seawater // 더운~ hot water // 찬~ cold water // ~의[같은] watery // ~을 탄 브랜디 한 잔 a glass of brandy and water // ~을 긷다 draw water (from a well) // ~을 끼얹다 dash[sprinkle] water (over a person's face) // ~을 끼얹어 불을 끄다 put out a fire with water // (논에) ~을 대다 draw water into[irrigate] a paddy // ~을 뒤집어쓰다 pour water on oneself // (배가) ship[take] water // ~을 뜨다[푸다] draw water (from) / scoop[dip] water // ~을 빼다 drain off (a pool) // ~을 뿌리다 sprinkle water (on the dusty street) / water (the garden) // 나무 뿌리에 ~을 주다 sprinkle water at the root of a tree // ~을 채우다 fill (a tub) with water // ~을 타다 add water (to) / dilute (whisky) with water // ~이 새지 않다 be waterproof / be watertight // ~이 새지 않게 하다 make (it) watertight // ~에 담그다 soak[dip] in the water // ~에 행구다 cleanse[rinse] with water // ~로 희석하다 water down // ~로 행구다 rinse with water // ~은 낮은 곳으로 흐른다 It is in the nature of water to run downward. / Man is helpless in the face of the strength of nature. // 수도에서 ~이 나오지 않는다 No water comes from the tap. // 연못의 ~이 말랐다 The pond has gone dry[dried up]. // 지난 일은 ~에 흘려보내고 의좋게 지내자 Let bygones be bygones and let us be friends.
2 [홍수] a flood; an inundation. ¶~에 잠기다 be flooded[swamped] / be submerged // ~이 나다 have a flood / be flooded // 논이 ~에 잠겼다 The rice field is flooded. / The rice field is under water. // 집 두 채가 ~에 떠내려 갔다 Two houses were carried away by the flood. // 처마 끝까지 ~이 찼다 The water came as high as the eaves. / The house was flooded up to the eaves.
3 [액체·즙] liquid; [유동체] fluid; extract; (과실의) juice; (초목의) sap; soup. ¶나무에 ~이 오르기 시작하다 the sap begins to flow (in a tree) // 그는 팔꿈치의 관절에 ~이 괴었다 Fluid accumulated on his elbow.
4 [조수] the tide. ¶~이 써고 있다 The tide is ebbing[on the ebb].

물에 빠지면 지푸라기라도 잡는다(속담) A drowning man will catch at a straw.

물(을) 내리다 [물을 치면서 체질을 하다] resift rice flour on a loose sieve while pouring water over it.

물(이) 내리다 [기운이 빠지다] lose one's strength[sap / vitality]; become weak (due to an illness, agony, etc.); be sapped; be devitalized.

물 쓰듯 쓰다 spend (money) like water; be a free spender; spend (money) unsparingly. ¶여자에게 미쳐서 돈을 ~ spend money freely on a woman // 그는 돈을 물 쓰듯 한다 He is quite a spendthrift. / He plays ducks and drakes with his money.

물에 빠진 생쥐 같다 look like a drowned rat; be drenched to the skin.

물² [빛깔] dyed color; dye. ¶~을 빼다 take the color out / bleach // ~이 날다 the color fades // ~이 잘 들다[들지 않다] dye[take dye] well[badly].

물³ 1 (빨래의) a period between one wash and another; the number of times clothes have been washed; a wash. ¶새 [첫] ~ new clothes that have yet to be laundered // 한 ~ 빤 옷 clothes that have been washed once. 2 (과일·해산물의) the season; a crop; a flush. ¶막~ 사과 the first (crop of) apples in its season // 끝~ 조기 yellow corvina caught in the last of its season. 3 (누에의) a hatch [batch] of silkworms. ¶첫 ~ 누에 the first hatch of silkworms.

물가 (강변) a riverside; a riverbank; [바다·호수의 가장자리] a shore; [연안] the coast; the beach; the waterside; the water's edge. ¶강 건너편 ~에 on the other bank[side] of the river // 배가 표류하여 ~로 다가왔다 A vessel drifted inshore[toward the shore]. // 부서진 배가 ~로 밀려 올라왔다 A broken boat was washed ashore. // ~에서 떨어진 곳에 섬이 있다 There is an island offshore. // 모터보트는 ~를 따라 전진했다 The motorboat advanced along the coast.

물가(物價) price(s). ¶소비자 ~ the consumer('s) price // 주요 ~ prices of staple commodities // ~의 현실화 price rationalization // 소비자 ~에 맞춘 승급(昇給) a cost-of-living adjustment in wages // ~가 오르다 prices rise[go up] // ~가 계속하여 뛰어오르다 prices keep on soaring // ~가 내리다 prices fall[come down] // ~를 올리다 raise [advance] prices // ~를 내리다 lower[bring down / reduce] prices // ~를 현실화하다 rationalize the price structure // 모든 ~이 싸다[싸다] Prices are high[low]. // ~의 변동이 크다 Prices fluctuate widely. // 이달에는 ~가 올랐다[내렸다] This month prices have gone up[gone down]. // ~는 오름세에 있다 Prices are tending upward(s). // ~는 환시세의 변동에 따라 변한다 Prices are liable to alteration in accordance with the fluctuations of exchange.
● **물가고**(-高) high prices of commodities; the increased cost of living. **물가 등귀**(-騰貴) a rise[an advance] in prices; a price rise. **물가 변동 / 물가 파동** price fluctuation. **물가 안정** a price stabilization. **물가 인하** a price reduction. **물가 지수** a price index. **물가 하락** a fall in prices.

물갈래 [지류] a branch[fork] of a river; a tributary (of); [분기점] the fork[crotch] of a river[stream].

물갈이 [농] plowing[[영] ploughing] a paddy with water in it. **물갈이하다** plow a paddy with water in it.

물갈퀴 (물새·개구리의) a web; (수영용의) a fin; a flipper. ¶~이 있는 오리의 발 the webbed feet of a duck.

물감 1 [염료] dyestuffs; dyes; colors; stain. ¶합성[인조] ~ synthetic[artificial] dyes. 2 paints; colors. ⇨ 그림물감

물개 [동] 1 a fur seal. 2 an otter. ⇨ 수달

물거미 1 [동] a water spider. 2 [동] a water strider.

물거품 1 [물의 거품] bubbles(▶ 보통 복수형); a foam; froth. ¶~ 같은 foamy / frothy / bubble // ~처럼 사라지다 burst like a bubble / end[go up] in smoke // 배가 ~을 일으키면서 가라앉았다 The boat sank, leaving a trail of bubbles[giving off a great mass of bubbles].

2 [덧없는 것] transience. ¶~ 같은 vain / evanescent / ephemeral / fleeting // ~ 같은 명성 a bubble reputation // ~ 같은 사랑 a short-lived love // 모든 나의 노력은 ~이 되고 말았다 All my efforts were fruitless [wasted / in vain]. / (구어) All my efforts went down the drain. / All my efforts came to nothing [(문어) naught]. // 평생을 바친 그의 사업도 자금난으로 ~이 되고 말았다 The business to which he had devoted his whole life vanished like a dream amidst financial difficulties.

물건(物件) [물체] a thing; an object; [물품] an article; goods; [재료] material; stuff; [재고품] stock; [소유물] a possession; [품질] quality. ¶과세 ~ an object of taxation / a taxable object // 증거 ~ material evidence / ~을 탐내다 lust for [after] things // ~이 떨어지다 be out of stock / run out (of) // ~이 풍부하다 [적다] be well- [ill-] stocked // ~이 좋다 be of good [fine] quality // ~이 나쁘다 be of bad [coarse / poor] quality // 이 종류의 ~은 재고가 떨어졌습니다 Articles of this kind are out of stock. // ~이 부족해지고 있다 Goods are running short.

물걸레 a damp [wet] floorcloth [mop]. ¶~로 닦다 wipe with a damp cloth [wet duster].

물결 a wave. ¶거친 ~ wild waves / a rough sea // 밀려오는 ~ a surf / a comber // 부서지는 ~ a breaker / 잔 ~ a ripple / 큰 ~ a billow // 하얗게 부서지는 ~ whitecaps / white horses // ~의 꼭대기 the crest of a wave // ~이 일다 the sea gets up / waves rise // ~이 자다 the sea goes down / waves subside // ~에 휩쓸리다 be washed [carried] away by the waves // ~을 타다 ride on the waves // ~이 높다 The waves are high. / The sea is rough. // ~이 잔잔해졌다 The waves have subsided. / The sea has calm down. // 노 1개가 ~에 휩쓸려 갔다 One of the oars was washed away by the waves. // 그 배는 ~에 뒤덮여 가라앉았다 The boat was swallowed up by [in] the waves. // 그 배는 ~을 헤치며 나아갔다 The ship plowed through the waves. // 통나무가 ~에 떠돌고 있다 A log is drifting on [being carried this way and that by] the waves. // ~이 바닷가에서 출렁거리고 있었다 The waves were lapping the shore.

물결치다 move in waves; undulate; surge; swell; roll; billow(크게). ¶물결치는 머리카락 wavy hair / 물결치는 바다 a rolling sea / 물결치는 벼 이삭 waving heads of rice / 물결치는 대로 at the mercy of the waves / 바람에 ~ waves rise in the wind // 파도는 크게 물결치면서 배를 밀어 올렸다 The waves surged high and lifted the ship.

물결표(-標) a swung dash (~).

물경(勿驚) surprisingly [startlingly / astonishingly] (enough); to one's surprise; you would be surprised but ...; it will surprise you but .... ¶그녀는 ~ 만 권의 책을 수집했다 She made a marvelous collection of ten thousand volumes.

물계(物界) [물질의 세계] the material [physical] world.

물고(物故) **1** [저명인사의 죽음] death of a celebrity. **물고하다** die; decease. **2** [죄인의 죽임·죄인의 죽음] putting [being put] to death. **물고하다** kill (a person); die.

물고(가) 나다 be put to death.

물고(를) 내다 put (a criminal) to death; kill (a person). ¶그놈 물고를 내어라 Put him to death. / Kill him.

물고기 a fish (*pl.* ~, ~es)(▶종류를 말할 때는 fishes); [어유] fish. ¶~ 떼 a school [shoal] of fishes // ~ 뼈 a fish bone // ~를 낚다 fish / angle (for fish) // ~를 손으로 잡다 catch a fish with one's hands // ~ 비린내가 나다 smell of fish / have a fishy smell.

물고기 밥이 되다 drown; be drowned; become food for fishes.

●**물고기자리** [천] the Pisces; the Fishes.

물고동 →수도꼭지(↔)수도(水道))

물곬 a drainageway; a drainage channel [ditch]; a drain. ¶~을 내다 make a drain // ~이 메어 있다 A drain is stopped up.

물관(-管) [식] a vessel; a trachea (*pl.* -cheae).

●**물관부** [식] the xylem.

물구나무서기 [체] a handstand; (머리를 바닥에 대는) a headstand.

물구나무서다 stand on one's hands [head]; do a handstand [headstand]. ¶물구나무서서 걷다 walk on one's hands.

물구덩이 a (stagnant) pool; a (mud) puddle; a water hole; a plash. ¶~가 많은 puddled / sloppy // 길의 군데군데에 ~가 생겼다 The road was pitted with puddles.

물굽이 a bend [curve] in a river [stream]. ¶~가 지다 bend / curve / wind / (a river) has a bend / meander.

물권(物權) [법] a real right. ¶~의 설정 [이전] the creation [transfer] of a real right.

●**물권법** the Law of Reality [Realty].

물귀신(-鬼神) a water demon [spirit / monster]. ¶~(이) 되다 drown / be drowned / find a watery grave.

물그릇 a water bowl.

물긋하다 [묽다] somewhat thin [washy / watery].

물기(-氣) [수분] water; [습기] moisture; dampness; wetness; [액즙] juice. ¶~가 있는 watery / moist / damp / wet / (과일의) juicy / succulent // ~가 없는 dry / husky / parched / drained (channel) // ~가 많은 오렌지 a juicy [succulent] orange // 두부의 ~를 빼다 drain (the water off) the *dubu*[bean curd] // 이 반죽은 ~가 너무 많다 This dough is too moist. // 이 배는 ~가 적다 This pear is too dry.

물기둥 a column of water. ¶그 비행기는 큰 ~을 솟구쳐 올리며 바다로 추락했다 The plane crashed into the sea, sending up a huge column of water.

물길 a water course; a waterway; a water route. ¶~을 따라 항해하다 sail along a waterway // ~로 가다 go by sea [ship / water].

물김치 watery plain [flat] *gimchi*(kimchi).

물까마귀 [동] a pale Pallas's dipper.

물까치 [동] an azure-winged magpie.

물꼬 an irrigation gate; a sluice gate.

물끄러미 with a blank [vacant] look; staring (with fixed eyes). ¶~ 쳐다보다 stare (a person) in the face / gaze at (a person's) face / look hard [steadily] at (a person's) face // 그는 그 그림을 ~ 쳐다보았다 He gazed [looked intently] at the painting. // 그는 보이지 않을 때까지 그녀를 ~ 쳐다보았다 He gazed after her until she was out of

물난리(-亂離) 1 [홍수] a flood disaster. ¶~가 나다 have a flood disaster / suffer from a flood. 2 [식수난] the shortage of water supply; a water famine.

물납(物納) payment in goods[kind]. ¶세금 ~ payment of tax in kind. **물납하다** pay (taxes) in kind.
● **물납세** a tax in kind.

물너울 swell on the sea; rolling of the waves; a surge.

물놀이 1 [잔물결 침] wrinkling of water; rippling. **물놀이하다** wrinkle; ripple. 2 [물장난] dabbling in water. **물놀이하다** play [disport oneself] in the water; splash water playfully. 3 [물가에서의 휴양] a waterside vacation. ¶~를 가다 go to a summer resort / go swimming (to the seaside).

물다¹ 1 [개 등이] have a bite (at); bite[snap] (at). ¶다리를 ~ bite (a person) in the leg// 목을 꽉 ~ sink one's teeth deep in the throat// 물어 죽이다 bite to death// 물어서 끊다 bite off / cut[gnaw] off with the teeth// 고양이가 쥐를 물어 죽었다 A cat bit[sank its teeth into] the rat and killed it.
2 [물고기가] bite[nibble] (at); take a bite. ¶미끼를 ~ take[rise to] the bait[fly] / snap at the bait// 물고기가 미끼를 물었다 The fish latched onto the bait. / I've got a bite.// 오늘은 고기가 잘 문다 The fish are biting [taking] well today.
3 [벌레가] bite; sting. ¶벼룩이 문 자리가 부어 올랐다 The bite of a flea has swollen up.
4 [입에 머금다] hold[put] in one's mouth; hold[have] between one's teeth. ¶담배를 물고 일하다 work with a cigarette in one's mouth// 고양이가 생선을 물고 달아났다 The cat ran away with the fish in its mouth.// 그는 찬 멜론 조각을 입에 물었다 He bit into a chilled slice of melon.
5 [사람·이권을 차지하다] get; catch; obtain; find. ¶계집이 사내를 ~ a woman gets a man.

물고 늘어지다 (약점 등을) hang[hold] on to; stick to; cling to; get a firm grip on (one's rival); (미국 속어) latch on to. ¶끝까지 ~ stick to one's last // 말꼬리를 ~ catch (a person) in his own words / cavil at (a person's) word// 질문 공세로 ~ harass (a person) with repeated interpellation[questions].

물다² 1 [돈을 치르다] pay; repay. ¶벌금을 ~ pay a fine / pay one's penalty [forfeit] // 빚을 ~ pay[repay] one's debt// 자기 돈으로 ~ pay for (a thing) out of one's own pocket // 집을 사면 세금을 물게 된다 A tax is imposed when you buy a house.// 그는 주차 위반으로 벌금을 물었다 He was fined for illegal parking. 2 [배상·보상하다] compensate; make up for; make good; indemnify; reimburse. ¶손해 배상을 ~ make good[make up for] the loss / reimburse (a person) for damages caused him// 손해는 당신이 물어야겠소 I must ask you to make reparation for the damages.

물어 주다 pay (for); compensate; reimburse; make good; make up for. ¶비용을 ~ compensate (a person) for (the) cost// 잃어버린 책값을 ~ pay[compensate] for the book one has lost // 아들 빚을 ~ pay[settle] one's son's debt.

물덤벙술덤벙 blindly; aimlessly; thoughtlessly; at hazard[random]; naively. **물덤벙술덤벙하다** act blindly[naively]; go it blind.

물독 a water jar [jug / pot].

물동이 a water jar [pitcher].

물들다 1 [빛깔이 들다] dye; get dyed; take (up) color. ¶파랗게 ~ be dyed blue // 잘 [물들지 않다] dye well[badly] // 피로 ~ be stained[smeared] with blood // (하늘이) 붉게 ~ glow / burn / be aglow (with the setting sun) // 하늘은 저녁노을로 빨갛게 물들어 있었다 The sky was tinged with red by the setting sun.
2 [초목이 빛깔을 띠다] color; become[be] colored[tinged]; (단풍 등이) turn red [crimson]. ¶감이 물들기 시작했다 The persimmons are turning orange.// 봄이 되면 초목은 초록색으로 물든다 In spring plants put on fresh green colors.// 올해는 나뭇잎이 예년보다 일찍 물들기 시작했다 This year the leaves have turned red[have changed color] earlier than usual.
3 [감염되다] be imbued[infected / contaminated / stained / tainted] (with); be influenced (by); be steeped (in); catch. ¶서양[미국] 풍조에 물든 사람 a Europeanized [an Americanized] person who affects a European[an American] manner // 도시의 폐풍에 물들지 않은 전원 지방 a country area not poisoned[contaminated] by the bad customs of the city // 악에 ~ be affected by evil influences / (문이) be steeped in [tainted with] vice // 악습에 ~ get into [be infected with] the evil habit (of) // 그는 마르크스주의에 물들었다 He has become infected Marxism.

물들이다 1 [물들게 하다] dye. ¶검게 ~ dye (a thing) (in) black // 그녀는 희끗희끗한 머리를 검게 물들였다 She dyed her gray hair black. / She had her gray hair dyed black. 2 [채색하다] color; tint; paint; tinge. ¶손톱을 빨갛게 ~ tint[paint] one's nails with carmine[red] polish // 저녁노을이 그 절을 붉게 물들였다 The setting sun bathed the temple in red light.

물때¹ [간만 시간] tide time; [밀물 때] high tide; the time when the tide begins to rise [flow in]. ¶~를 기다리다 wait for the high tide [the favorable tide] //~를 놓치다 miss the high [flood / full] tide // 출범하기에는 지금이 알맞은 ~인 것 같다 I think the tide now is just favorable for us to set sail.

물때² [물속의 더러운 것으로 인해 끼는 때] fur; (boiler) scale; (an) incrustation; scum; slime. ¶~ 낀 보일러 a boiler covered with scale [fur] //~가 끼다 fur (forms) (on) / be covered with fur [scale] / scale //~를 벗기다 clean fur (from) / scrape off the fur // 보일러에 ~가 꼈었다 Fur has formed in the boiler. // 나는 주전자의 ~를 긁어냈다 I scrubbed [scraped] the mineral deposit out of the kettle.

물때까치 [동] a Chinese great grey shrike.

물똥 liquid stool; splashing waterdrops. ⇨물찌똥

물똥싸움 splashing water on each other. ⇨물싸움²

물량(物量) the amount[quantity] of materials [resources]. ¶~의 우세 material odds /

physical superiority // ~의 힘을 과시하다 let one's material superiority tell on (the enemy) // ~으로 압도하다 overwhelm (the enemy) with material superiority // 적은 ~을 앞세워 공격을 개시했다 The enemy opened an attack on us on the strength of their material superiority [advantage]. // 우리가 그들에게 도저히 당할 수 없다 We are no match for them in material resources.

물러가다 1 [뒷걸음쳐 가다] move backward; draw [fall / pull] back; back; retrogress; recede; retreat. ¶한 발짝 물러가서 생각해 보면 전체 상황이 더 잘 보이게 된다 You can see the whole situation better if you step back a little.
2 [떠나다] retire; leave; withdraw (from); take a leave. ¶사람들을 물러가게 하다 make all people leave the room // 만찬 후 부인들은 다른 방으로 물러갔다 After dinner the ladies withdrew [retired] to another room. // 그만 물러가겠습니다 I must be off [be going] now. / 물러가라 Begone! / Away with you (from my presence)!
3 [더위 등이] be over; be gone; come to an end. ¶더위가 물러갔다 The hot weather is over [gone].

물러나다 1 [후퇴하다] retreat; withdraw (from); leave; recede; move [go] backward; back. ¶옆으로 ~ step [move] aside // 급히 ~ beat a hurried [hasty] retreat / retire hurriedly // 3보 뒤로 물러나 주시오 Move back three steps.
2 [사임하다] retire (from service); withdraw. ¶직위에서 ~ leave office / resign one's post in an office // 그는 아직 정계의 일선에서 물러날 나이가 아니다 He is not old enough yet to withdraw [retire] from the front line of political activity. // 그렇게 쉽사리 물러날 그가 아니다 He won't back down [give up] that easily. // 그는 사임을 밝히고 무거운 마음으로 회의실에서 물러났다 He announced his resignation and withdrew from the meeting room with a heavy heart.
3 [틈이 벌어지다] come loose; come out [off]; fall off. ¶턱뼈가 ~ get one's jaw out of joint // 책상 다리가 물러났다 A leg of the table came loose.

물러서다 1 [뒤로 나서다] step [stand] back; back; [후퇴하다] retreat; recede; [길을 내어 주다] make way (for a person); get out of the way (of). ¶거리에서 멀찌감치 물러서 있는 집 a house (standing) for [well] back from the street // 그는 한 걸음 뒤로 물러섰다 He took a step backward. // 그는 좀처럼 물러설 사람이 아니다 He is very stiff-necked fellow. // 이제 물러서기에는 너무 늦었다 We have gone too far to retreat. / It is too late to back out of it now.
2 [사임하다] retire; resign; withdraw. ¶정계에서 ~ retire from the political world // 대학의 자리에서 물러서기로 나는 작정했다 I decided to resign from my university post.

물러앉다 1 [자리를] draw [move] one's seat back; sit back. ¶그는 아버지 앞에서 물러앉았다 He gave the seat of honor to his father. 2 (관직 등에서) retire; resign; leave. ¶직위에서 물러앉게 하다 dismiss (a person) from office / relieve (a person) of his post [office / duty].

물러오다 come back; retrace one's step;

retreat; recede; retrogress. ¶도중에서 ~ turn back halfway / turn back on the way out.

물러지다 1 [무르게 되다] soften; become tender. ¶감이 물러진다 A persimmon softens up. 2 soften; become conciliatory. ⇨ 누그러지다3

물렁팥죽(―粥) 1 (사람) a softy; a milksop; a sissy; a pushover. 2 (물건) soft stuff.

물렁하다 1 (물건이) soft; tender; squashy; juicy; overripe. 2 (성질이) yielding; soft; weak-kneed; compliant; flabby; flaccid.

물레 a spinning wheel.
● **물레질** spinning; making yarn.

물레방아 a *mullebanga*; a waterwheel; a water mill. ¶ ~를 돌리다 operate a *mullebanga* // ~에 곡식을 찧다 grind grain in a *mullebanga*.

물려받다 [넘겨받다] take over; (양도 증서에 의해) obtain by transfer; succeed to (the throne); [상속하다] inherit. ¶부모에게서 물려받은 재산 property inherited from one's parents // 사업을 ~ take over a business // 부모의 재산을 ~ inherit [succeed to] one's parents' property // 그녀는 남편에게서 주식을 물려받았다 She obtained the stocks from her husband by transfer. // 나는 아버지의 성급한 성질을 물려받았다 I inherited [got] my quick temper from my father. // 그녀의 파란 눈은 어머니에게서 물려받은 것이다 She got [inherited] her blue eyes from her mother.

물려주다 turn [hand / make] over; transfer; [남겨 주다] leave (왕위를) abdicate; (동산을) bequeath; (부동산을) devise. ¶정권을 ~ hand over the reins of government [power] // 자식에게 사업을 ~ turn the business over to one's son // 소유권을 ~ yield [transfer] ownership (of something to a person) // 왕자에게 왕위를 ~ abdicate the throne in favor of his son // 전 재산을 아내에게 ~ make [hand] over all one's property to one's wife.

물력(物力) 1 [물건의 힘] material power. 2 [재료와 노력] materials and efforts. ¶그 집을 짓는 데 많은 ~이 들었다 It took a lot of labor and materials to build the house.

물론(勿論) of course; to be sure; undoubtedly; naturally; needless to say. ¶…은 ~이다 it goes without saying that … / it is a matter of course that … // ~ 당신이 옳다 Of course, you are right. // 그녀는 영어는 ~이고 프랑스어도 말할 수 안다 She speaks French, not to mention English. / She speaks French as well as English. / She speaks not only English but also French. // 남의 것을 훔쳐서는 안 된다는 것은 ~이다 Needless to say, [It goes without saying that] you should not steal. // ~ 당신이 알고 있을 것으로 나는 생각했다 I took it for granted that you knew it. // 자넨 ~ 이 책을 읽어 보았겠지 I'm sure [No doubt] you've read this book. // ~이다 Of course! / That [It] goes without saying. // 나는 그리스 어는 ~이고 영어조차 잘 모른다 I don't understand even English well, to say nothing of Greek. // 그는 학식은 ~이고 경험도 많다 He has experience as well as knowledge. // 예외가 있는 것은 ~이다 It goes without saying that there are exceptions.

물리(物理) 1 [사물의 이치] the law of nature; physical laws. 2 physics. ⇨ 물리학(⇨물리)
● **물리 요법** physiotherapy; physical therapy

물리다

[treatment]; physical medicine. **물리학** physics; physical science. ¶~적 physical // **실험** ~ experimental physics // 응용[이론] ~ applied [theoretical] physics // 정신 ~ psychophysics // 지구 ~ geophysics // 핵~ nuclear physics. **물리학자** physicist; a natural philosopher.

물리다[1] [싫증 나다·따분하다] be bored (by / with); [진저리 나다] (구어) be fed up (with); get[grow] tired (of); get sick (of); lose interest (in); want nothing more to do (with); (음식에) be sick[tired] of eating; be satiated[sated] (with); have enough (of). ¶물리도록 to satiety / to one's heart's content // 물리게 하다 satiate / surfeit / feed up // 물리도록 먹다 eat to satiety / eat one's fill // 물릴 줄 모르는 greedy[insatiate / insatiable] // 단것도 자주 먹으면 물린다 Sweets served too often cloy the palate. // 나는 영화에 물렸다 I have lost interest in movies. // 그 노래는 물리도록 들었다 The song has been sung to death. // 나는 잔소리에 물렸다 I have heard enough of scolding. // 점심도 저녁도 생선을 먹어 물려 버렸다 I ate fish for lunch and dinner, and so I am tired[sick] of it. // 나는 그의 장황한 이야기에 물렸다 I was bored (to death) by his long lecture. // His long lecture bored me to death. // 자네의 자기 선전에는 이제 물려 있네 I'm fed up with your self-advertisement.

물리다[2] [푹 익히다] cook soft[tender]; do (meat) well[thoroughly]. ¶고기를 ~ cook meat tender.

물리다[3] 1 [연기하다] put off; postpone; defer. ¶기한을 ~ extend the term (from ... to ...) // 회의 날짜를 ~ postpone (the date of) a meeting // 하루하루 ~ put off from day to day.
2 [옮겨 놓다] change direction; turn; shift; switch over; remove; get around. ¶의자를 ~ push back a chair // 차를 ~ pull a car back // 책상을 1미터가량 ~ pull[push] back the desk a meter or so // 자동차를 조금 더 물리시오 Back up your car a little more.
3 [물려주다] hand over; leave; bequeath; transfer; yield; convey; (지위·권리) abdicate. ¶소유권을 아우에게 ~ yield one's right of possession to one's little brother // 그녀는 언니가 차례로 물린 드레스를 입고 있었다 She was wearing a dress that descended from sister to sister in her family.
4 [다른 데로 옮겨 가게 하다] put[take] away; clear away. ¶밥상을 ~ clear the table // 사람을 방 밖으로 ~ clear the room of people // 그는 사람을 방 밖으로 물리라고 일렀다 He ordered the room to be cleared of people.
5 [잡귀를 쫓아내다] exorcise; expel; dispel; drive away[out]. ¶악귀를 ~ exorcise evil spirits (from / out of) // 굿으로 집안의 악귀를 ~ drive evil spirits out of a household with shaman rites.

물리다[4] [곤충·동물 등에] be[get] bitten. ¶물린 상처투성이의 얼굴 a face covered with stings // 벼룩에 ~ be bitten by a flea // 개에게 다리를 ~ be[get] bitten in the leg by a dog // 독사에 물려 죽다 die from a viper[an adder] bite // 모기에 물렸다 I was bitten by a mosquito. // 지퍼에 천이 물렸다 The cloth has gotten caught in the zipper.

2 [물게 하다]. ¶남에게 (수건으로) 재갈을 ~ gag a person // 젊은 어머니는 어린아이에게 젖꼭지를 물렸다 The young mother nursed her baby[gave her baby the breast]. // (이와 이를) 마주 ~ clench[set] (one's teeth) // 톱니바퀴를 마주 ~ engage a gear / put (a machine) in gear.

물리다[5] [배상시키다] make (a person) compensate[indemnify / reimburse / repair]. ¶깨뜨린 그릇 값을 ~ make (a person) pay for a broken dish // 농작물에 끼친 손해를 ~ make (a person) pay compensation for the damage done to one's crops.

물리적(物理的) ~인 성질 physical properties // ~으로 불가능한 physically impossible // ~ 법칙 a physical law // ~ 변화 a physical change // ~ 현상 a physical phenomenon.

물리치다 1 [거절하다] refuse; turn down; reject. ¶뇌물을 ~ spun a bribe // 선물을 ~ decline a gift // 요구[신청]를 ~ refuse [reject] (a person's) request[application] // 충고를 ~ ignore[disregard / repulse] (a person's) advice // 그들은 그의 의견을 물리쳤다 They rejected[refused to adopt] his opinion. // 그는 단호히 유혹을 물리쳤다 He resolutely thrust the temptation from him.
2 [격퇴하다] drive[turn / send] away; beat off; repel; expel; [멀리하다] keep away. ¶좌우를 ~ send the servants out of the earshot [the guards to leave] // 사람을 물리치고 밀담하다 have a closed door conference (with) / meet[hold consultation / talk] behind closed door // 그들은 적의 공격을 물리쳤다 They beat off[repelled / repulsed] the enemy's attack. // 경찰은 데모대를 물리쳤다 The police pushed[forced] the demonstrators back.
3 (승부에서) defeat; beat. ¶선거에서 다른 후보를 ~ defeat another candidate in an election // 그는 콘테스트에서 강적을 물리쳤다 He beat[defeated] a powerful rival in the contest.

물마개 (병 등의) a stopper; (코르크로 만든) a cork; (수도 등의) a stopcock; (구멍을 막는) a peg; a plug; (배 밑바닥 등의) a bung.

물만두(~饅頭) a stuffed bun served in water.

물망(物望) popular expectations[prospects]. ¶후보 ~에 오른 사람 (미) a (Democratic) prospect / a prospective candidate // ~에 오르다 be popularly[widely] expected // 그는 국무 장관 ~에 올라 있다 He is expected to be nominated as Secretary of State.

물망초(勿忘草) [식] a forget-me-not.

물매[1] [매질] hard whipping[lashing / flogging]. ¶~를 맞다 be whipped hard.

물매[2] [과실을 따려고 던지는 몽둥이] a slingshot; a sling (for throwing stones). ¶~로 과일을 따다 knock off fruits with a slingshot.

물매[3] [경사] a slope; (an) inclination; a slant; (지붕의) a pitch. ¶지붕의 ~ the slope[slant] of a roof // ~가 싸다 The roof has a steep enough slant to it. // ~가 뜨다 The roof is not steep enough. // 이 지붕의 ~는 30도이다 This roof has an inclination of 30 degrees.

물맴이 [동] a whirligig beetle.

물목 1 [물이 넘나드는 어귀] the point at which the water flows in or out; the fork of a river[stream] (물갈래); a narrow(해협 등의). ¶~을 지키다 stand watch at the fork [crotch] of a river. 2 (사광에서) the spot where gold dust pans thickest.

물목(物目) a catalog of goods; a list of articles. ¶~별로 item by item.

물물 교환(物物交換) barter; bartering truck; (미) dicker; dickering. ¶이 가능한 물건 barterable goods∥~으로 by barter / on the barter system∥거래는 ~으로 행해지게 되었다 They decided to trade with each other using the barter system.∥그들은 원주민들과 무기와 식량을 ~ 했다 They bartered weapons for food with the natives.

물미 a ferrule; a spike.

물밀다 (조수가) rise; flow; come in. ¶물밀 때 the time of the flowing tide∥물밀듯 밀려오는 군중 a surging crowd of people∥물밀듯이 밀어닥치다 surge forward in crowds / be deluged (with tourist) / rush like a flood.

물밀 협상(-協商) secret negotiations.

물바가지 a gourd for dipping water.

물바다 ¶마을은 홍수로 ~가 되었다 The village was flooded. / A flood swept over the village.∥강이 범람하여 밭이 ~가 되었다 The river overflowed and submerged[inundated] the field.∥집 주변은 온통 ~였다 The house was surrounded by floodwater.

물받이 a waterspout; a drainspout; a gutter.

물방개 [동] a diving beetle.

물방아 a waterwheel; a water mill. ⇨물레방아

물방울 a drop of water; (a) spray; (뒤긴) a splash; [이슬] a dewdrop. ¶나뭇잎에서 ~이 똑똑 떨어졌다 Drops of water fell[Waterdrops fell / Water dripped down] from the leaves of the tree.∥~이 방울방울 떨어졌다 The water trickled[dribbled] down in drops.∥거미줄에 ~이 맺혀 있었다 Beads of water had formed on the cobweb.∥그는 ~을 튕기면서 물속으로 뛰어들었다 He jumped[dove] into the water with a splash.∥~이 우리에게 떨어졌다 The spray fell on us. / we were splashed with water.

● **물방울무늬** polka dots. ¶~의 스커트 a polka-dot skirt.

물뱀 [동] a sea snake; a water snake.

물벌레 a water insect; a water beetle.

물베개 a water pillow [cushion].

물벼락 splashing[dashing] water (on a person) all of a sudden; dousing (a person) with water. ¶~을 맞다 get doused[a dousing] / be suddenly poured over with water∥지나가던 버스가 우리에게 ~을 안겼다 The bus spattered us with muddy water [spattered muddy water on us] as it passed.

물벼룩 [동] a water flea.

물병(-甁) a water jar[jug / flask / bottle]; a pitch; [불] a water bottle dedicated to the image of Buddha. ¶유리 ~ a carafe.

● **물병자리** [천] the Water Bearer; Aquarius.

물보라 a spray (of water); a splash. ¶폭포수의 ~ the spray[smoke] of a waterfall∥~를 일으키다 raise[throw up] spray / send up [toss] up clouds[a cloud] of spray∥파도는 ~를 일으키면서 바위에 부딪혔다 The waves struck the rocks, raising[throwing up] a cloud of spray.

물부리 (담뱃대의) a mouthpiece; (궐련의) a cigarette tip[filter / holder]. ¶~가 달린 궐련 담배 a filter-tipped cigarette / a filter tip.

물불 water and fire.

물불을 가리지 않다 go through fire and water; stick to it through thick and thin; move heaven and earth (to do). ¶우리는 목적을 달성하기 위해 물불을 가리지 않을 각오였다 We were prepared to face any hardship [danger] in order to achieve our goal.∥그를 위해서라면 물불을 가리지 않겠다 I will go through fire and water[thick and thin] for his sake.

물비누 liquid soap; soft soap.

물비린내 a fishy smell of water.

물빛 1 [물의 빛깔] the color of water; [남색] a sky[light] blue; a turquoise. 2 [물감의 빛깔] a dye color; a dyed color.

물산(物産) a product; (주로 농산물의 총칭) produce. ¶~이 풍부하다 be rich in products.

물살 the force[speed / velocity] of flowing water[a current]. ¶~에 떠내려가다 drift with the current∥~을 거슬러 가다 swim [sail / row] against the current∥강 중류는 ~이 세다 The current is swift in the middle of the river.∥이 강은 ~이 세다[약하다] This river has a swift[gentle] current.∥그는 그 강의 세찬 ~에 떠내려갔다 He was swept away by the strong current of the river.

물상(物象) (사물) an inanimate object; (현상) a material phenomenon (pl. -na, ~s); (학과) the science of inanimate nature.

물상(物相) the shape of an object.

물새 1 [물과 관련된 새] a waterfowl; an aquatic[a water] bird; a swimming bird. 2 a common Indian kingfisher. ⇨물총새

물색(物色) 1 [물건의 빛깔] the color of a thing; [물들인 빛] a dyed color. 2 [까닭·형편] (a) reason; (a) cause; ground(s); the matter; the case. 3 [풍경] scenery; a landscape; a scene; nature. 4 [찾음] looking for; [고름] selecting. **물색하다** [찾다] look for; search for; cast about for; hunt up; [고르다] select; pick[single] out. ¶후임을 ~ look for a successor∥아내감을 ~ look for a wife∥일자리를 물색해 주마 I'll help you hunt for a job.∥우리는 대회의 후보지를 물색하는 중이다 We are looking[searching] for a suitable place to hold the general meeting.

물색없다 irrational; illogical; unreasonable; absurd; extraordinary. **물색없이** irrationally; unreasonably; absurdly; illogically.

물샐틈없다 watertight (plan); strict (watch); rigorous (guard). ¶물샐틈없는 경계 closed guard∥(야구에서) 물샐틈없는 수비 airtight fielding∥물샐틈없는 경계망을 펴다 throw a tight cordon[net] around.

물성(物性) properties of matter; physical properties.

물세례(-洗禮) 1 [기] baptism (by immersion). 2 splashing water (on a person) all of a sudden. ⇨물벼락

물소 [동] a water buffalo.

물소리 the sound of flowing[running] water; murmurs of a stream.

물속 ¶~의 underwater∥~에 in the water / under water / below the surface of the water / ∥~에 가라앉다 sink under water[below the surface of the water]∥~에 처박다 give (a person) a ducking∥(실수로) ~에 퐁당 빠지다 get a ducking∥~으로 뛰어들다 jump [plunge] into the water.

물수건(-手巾) a wet towel; a steamed[hot]

물수란 towel; a moist [steaming hot] hand towel.
물수란(-水卵) a poached egg.
물수리 [동] an osprey; a fish hawk; an ossifrage.
물수세미 [식] a water milfoil; a parrot's-feather.
물수제비뜨다 skip a stone (on the surface of the water); play ducks and drakes. ¶물수제비뜨는 돌 a duckstone/내가 던진 돌이 물수제비치고 나갔다 The stone [pebble] I threw skipped [I skipped a stone] on [along] the surface of the water.
물시계(-時計) a water clock; an hourglass; a clepsydra (*pl.* ~s, -drae).
물신 숭배(物神崇拜) fetishism; fetishistic religion. ¶~자 a fetishist.
물실호기하다(勿失好機-) do not miss [lose / let slip] a chance.
물심양면(物心兩面) ¶~으로 both materially and morally / physically and spiritually/나는 ~으로 그에게 많은 신세를 지고 있다 I owe him a great deal both practically and emotionally [materially and spiritually].
물싸움 1 (논물의) an irrigation [a water-rights] dispute. **물싸움하다** dispute about the water rights. **2** splashing water on each other; a water fight. **물싸움하다** splash water on each other.
물써다 [조수가 빠지다] ebb; go out; be on the ebb. ¶물썰 때에 at low tide.
물쑥 [식] a kind of wormwood; an artemisia.
물씬 [냄새가 심하게 코를 찌르는 모양]. ¶냄새가 ~ 풍기다 (일반적으로) smell strongly (of) / (지독한 악취가) stink (of)/나는 향수 냄새를 ~ 풍기는 한 부인을 만났다 I met a woman who reeked of perfume.//그 방은 ~풍기는 꽃향기로 가득 차 있었다 The room was filled with the fragrance of flowers.//그는 술 냄새를 ~풍기고 있다 He reeks [stinks] of alcohol.
물씬물씬하다 1 [물렁물렁하다] soft; tender; pliant. **2** (냄새가) (서술적) smell strongly [prodigally]; give off a strong smell; (악취가) reek (of); stink (of fish). ¶그녀가 지나갈 때 향수 냄새가 물씬물씬했다 She passed along, leaving a strong scent behind her.//그에게서는 언제나 술 냄새가 물씬물씬한다 He always reeks of wine.
물아(物我) [철] (external) objects and self; the ego and the non-ego; the subjective and the objective; [물질계와 정신계] the material world and the spiritual world.
물안개 a wet fog; a rain-fog.
물안경(-眼鏡) swimming goggles; (a pair of) (diver's) goggles.
물약(-藥) **1** [액체로 된 약] a liquid medicine; (미) a liquor. **2** [광] a shot of dynamite.
물어내다¹ [변상하다] pay for; compensate; indemnify; make good.
물어내다² (몰래) smuggle (something) out of (the house); [누설하다] let [leak] out (a family secret). ¶쥐가 밤을 물어내고 있다 A rat is carrying off chestnuts in its mouth.
물어넣다 [축낸 것을 갚아 넣다] pay back; repay; refund; reimburse; compensate for. ¶유용한 회사 돈을 ~ repay misappropriated company funds.
물어뜯다 gnaw on; bite (hard); bite [snap] off; bite (at); tear off with one's teeth. ¶코를 ~ bite (a person's) nose//물어뜯어 죽이다 bite to death//서로 ~ bite each other//그는 커다란 커틀릿을 물어뜯었다 He bit into the big cutlet.//개 두 마리가 서로 물어뜯고 있다 The two dogs are biting (at) [fighting with] each other.//개가 밧줄을 물어뜯고 달아났다 The dog bit through the leash and ran away.//그는 고기를 두 토막이 나게 물어뜯었다 He bit the meat in two.
물어보다 [묻다] ask; inquire; question; query; [조회하다] make inquiries (about); refer to; apply to; [확인하다] ascertain (by inquiry). ¶길을 ~ ask the way (to) / inquire for the way/귀찮게 ~ plague (a person) with questions/안부를 ~ ask [inquire] after (a person)/좀 물어볼 말이 있는데 There is something I'd like to ask you.//지난 일을 물어봐야 아무 소용없다 There's no point in blaming me for what I did in the past.//그는 심문 중에 물어봐도 불지 않다가 무심결에 스스로 실토했다 He kept the secret stubbornly while being interrogated [questioned], but, in an unguarded moment, he let it slip out (of his own accord).//그에 대한 소식을 물어봤지만 아무도 몰랐다 I asked [(문어) inquired] after him [I asked for new about him], but nobody knew anything.
물억새 [식] a common reed.
물여우 [동] a caddis worm.
물역(物役) [건축 재료] building [construction] materials.
물엿 starch syrup; glucose.
물오르다 1 [초목에 물이 오르다] rise. ¶봄이 되어 나무에 물오르기 시작한다 Spring has come and the sap of trees begin to rise. **2** [잘 살게 되다] get rich; make; make money; get ahead (in life); rise.
물오리 [동] a wild duck; a mallard duck; (수컷) greenhead.
물외 a cucumber.
물욕(物慾) worldly [earthly] desires [ambitions]; love of gain. ¶~에 사로잡힌 사람들 materialistic worldly-minded people//~에 눈이 멀다 be blinded by worldly desires.
물위 the upper reaches [courses] of a river; an upper stream [course].
물유리(-琉璃) [화] water [liquid / soluble] glass.
물음 a question; a query; an inquiry; an interrogation. ¶다음 ~에 답하시오 Answer the following question(s).
●**물음표** a question [an interrogation] mark.
물의(物議) public criticism [censure]; public discussion [comment]; trouble. ¶자주 ~을 일으키는 사람 a stormy petrel//~을 빚다 [일으키다] arouse [evoke] criticism / give rise to public discussion / bring on public criticism / raise a scandal/신 박사의 연설이 교육계에 ~를 일으켰다 The speech made by Dr. Sin elicited much criticism in educational circles.//수상의 실언은 커다란 ~를 일으켰다 The careless remarks made by the prime minister caused a lot of fuss [criticism].
물이끼 [식] (a) sphagnum (*pl.* -na); bog moss. ¶~가 많은 sphagnous.
물자(物資) [공급물] supplies; [물품] goods; [상품] commodities; [자원] materials; resources. ¶구호 ~ relief goods//생활 ~ subsistence goods / daily commodities//소비 ~ consumer goods//필수 ~ essentials / necessities//~의 공급 a supply of goods//

의 부족 a shortage[famine] of materials [goods] // ~를 확보하다 secure the supply of goods // ~를 보급하다 supply goods (to) / furnish supplies (to) // ~를 아낍시다 (게시) Save supplies. // 그들에게는 ~가 부족했다 They were running short of supplies. // 우리는 빨리 ~를 재보급해 주기를 바란다 We want to be resupplied[have our supplies replenished] immediately. // 이 나라는 ~가 풍부하지 않다 This country is not rich in (natural) resources.
● **물자 수급** supply and demand of goods.
물자동차(-自動車) **1** a sprinkler (truck). ⇨ˆ 살수차 **2** a water-supply wagon. ⇨ˆ급수차(⇨급수(給水))
물잠자리 [동] a damselfly.
물장구 [장단] drumming on gourd vessels turned over on the water. **2** (헤엄칠 때) the beating; the flutter kick; the thrash. ¶~를 **치다** make flutters[flutter kicks] / swim with the thrash.
물장난 1 dabbling in water; playing with water. **물장난하다** play[dabble] in the water; play with water. **2** [홍수의 재앙] a flood disaster.
물장사 [물 판매업] water-selling; [술집 영업] a gay trade. ¶~를 하는 여자 a woman of the gay world / a gay lady / ~ 집에서 일하는 여자 a woman working in a bar or a cabaret.
물장수 a water-seller; water-bearer.
물재배(-栽培) hydroponics; water[hydroponic / soilless] culture; aquiculture; tray agriculture; tank farming.
물적(物的) [물질적] material; (감지할 수 있는) physical.
● **물적 담보** a secured mortgage; a real security. **물적 자원** material resources. **물적 증거** real evidence; physical evidence; material evidence.
물정(物情) **1** [사물의 정상] the condition of things; the state of affairs. **2** [세상의 형편] (the condition of) the world; worldly matters; [세상 인심] public feeling. ¶세상 ~을 모르는 젊은이 an ingenuous youth // 세상 ~에 밝다 know much of the world / be a man of the world // 세상 ~에 어둡다 be ignorant of the world / know little of the world // 그는 세상 ~도 모르고 혼자 잘난 체한다 He is in blissful ignorance of the world.
물주(物主) **1** [자본주·전주] a financier; a financial supporter. **~가 되다** finance / become a financier (of) // 친구들이 그의 새 사업의 ~가 되었다 His friends financed his new business. **2** [노름판의] the banker.
물주머니쥐 [동] a water rat[vole / muskrat].
물줄기 1 [흐름] a stream (of water); a (water) current; a watercourse; a flow. ¶그 ~가 두 갈래로 갈라졌다 The water branched off into two streams. **2** (내뿜는) a spout[gust / gush / jet] of water. ¶~가 세게 뻗쳐 나온다 Water spouts[gushes] out.
물증(物證) real evidence. ⇨물적 증거(⇨물적)
물지게 a water-carrying yoke; a water-toting device (strapped to the back). ¶그 사람은 두 양동이의 물을 ~로 날랐다 The man carried two buckets of water on a yoke.
● **물지게꾼** a water carrier.
물질(物質) (정신에 대하여) matter; [물체를 이루는 본바탕] substance; [재료] material. ¶단단한 ~ solid matter // 반(反)~ [물] anti-matter // 이 세계를 구성하고 있는 ~ the matter of which this world consists / the matter which constitutes this world // 그것은 어떤 반투명의 ~로 되어 있었다 It was made of some translucent material.
● **물질계** the material world. **물질대사** [생] metabolism. **물질 명사** [언] a material noun. **물질문명** material civilization. **물질 불멸의 법칙** the principle of conservation of matter. **물질주의** materialism. ¶~적인 materialistic.
물질적(物質的) material; physical; objective. ¶~인 생각 a materialistic view // ~으로 physically / materially // ~으로 풍부하다 be well off // ~으로 곤란을 받고 있다 be badly off / be in needy circumstances // 그의 생각은 너무나 ~이다 He is very materialistic in his ideas. // 그는 ~ 혜택을 받고[받지 못하고] 있었다 He was well[badly] off. // 그에게는 ~인 원조가 필요하다 He needs material assistance. // 그는 ~인 쾌락만을 추구하고 있다 He is only after physical pleasures.
물집¹ (피하의) a blister. **~이 생긴 손** a blistered hand // **~이 생기다** blisters form[rise] / get[have] a blister (on one's foot) / blister // ~투성이가 되다 be (all) covered with blisters // ~이 터졌다 The blister broke.
물집² [염색업을 하는 곳] a dye house; a dye shop.
물쩡하다 [성질이 무르다] soft; weak-willed; (서술적) be a milksop; have no spirit [backbone]; lack nerve.
물찌똥 1 [묽은 똥] liquid[loose] stool. ¶~을 **싸다** have loose bowels. **2** [물덩이] splashing waterdrops.
물차(-車) a water-supply wagon. ⇨ˆ급수차 (⇨급수(給水))
물참 the high tide.
물체(物體) [물건의 형체] an object; (물리에서) a body; [고체] a solid (body); [법] a material object. ¶미확인 비행 ~ a UFO(▶ an unidentified flying object의 약어).
물총(-銃) a water pistol[gun]; a squirt (gun). ¶~**으로 쏘다** shoot (a person) with a water pistol / squirt a water pistol (at).
물총새(-銃-) a common Indian kingfisher.
물침대(-寢臺) a water bed.
물컥하다 spoil; fester. ⇨ˆ물크러지다
물컥(물컥) with a strong stink[stench]; stinking(ly). ¶생선 썩은 냄새가 ~ 나다 stink of rotten fish // 거기에 들어서자 고약한 냄새가 ~ 코를 찔렀다 A nasty smell greeted my nose as I entered there.
물컹거리다 be very soft[pulpy / squashy / mushy]. ¶나는 어둠 속에서 무엇인가 물컹거리는 것을 밟았다 I stepped on something soft[mushy] in the dark.
물컹물컹 softly; squashily. **물컹물컹하다** soft; squashy. ¶해삼은 물컹물컹해서 나는 좋아하지 않는다 I don't like sea slugs because they are so slimy and amorphous.
물컹이 [물컹한 물건] soft[overripe] stuff; something squashy[mushy]; [약한 사람] a softy; a milksop; a weakling; a sissy.
물컹하다 squashy; pulpy; mushy. ¶물컹한 땅 squashy ground.
물쿠다 (찌는 듯이 덥다) be[become] sultry [sweltering / steaming hot]. ¶물쿠는 날씨 sultry weather // 날이 몹시 물쿤다 It is steaming hot.
물크러지다 (과일이) spoil; rot; (종기가) fester;

물큰(물큰) ulcerate; decompose.

물큰(물큰) with a strong smell; piquant; pungent; (악취가) stinking; reeking. ¶향수 냄새가 ~ 풍긴다 The pungent smell of perfume hits one's nose. ∥커피향이 ~ 났다 The aroma of coffee greeted my nose.

물탕(-湯) a hot-spring bathing place; a hotbath.

물통(-桶) a (water) pail[bucket]; a water tank; a cistern. ¶~에 가득 찬 물 a bucketful of water.

물편 rice cakes in general except steamed ones.

물표(物標) [라벨] a label; [꼬리표] a tag; a tally. ¶물건에 ~를 달다 put a label[tag] on an article / label[tag] an article.

물푸레나무 [식] an ash tree.

물풀 a water[an aquatic] plant. ⇨ =수초(水草)

물품(物品) [물건] an article; [상품] a commodity; goods(▶ 복수 취급; 수사(數詞)를 붙이지 않음). ¶~의 수량 the number of articles∥~의 종류 items of merchandise∥부족 shortage of goods∥이 가게에는 ~의 수가 많다[적다] (수량) This shop has a large [small] stock of goods. / (품종) This shop has a rich[limited] assortment of goods. ∥~은 교환할 수 없다 This article cannot be exchanged.
●**물품 목록** a list of goods; a catalog; (재고 조사의) an inventory. ¶~을 작성하다 itemize.

물품세 a commodity tax; an excise tax. ¶모든 상품에 ~를 부과하다 impose an excise tax on everything.

물행주 a (wet) dishrag[dishcloth]; a wet (table) napkin.

물화(物貨) goods; commodities; merchandise.

물활론(物活論) [철] hylozoism; animism.

묽다 1 (농도가) watery; washy (milk); thin (coffee, porridge, paste, etc.); sloppy (food). ¶묽은 수프 thin soup∥묽은 차 weak tea∥물을 타서 풀을 묽게 하다 thin paste with water∥국물을 묽게 하다 dilute the broth [soup]∥수프에 물을 타서 묽게 하다 dilute soup with water∥이 수프는 아주 ~ This soup is mere wash.∥커피는 조금 묽은 것이 나는 좋다 I like my coffee a little weaker.∥이 풀은 너무 진하니까 좀 묽게 하는 편이 낫다 This paste is took thick. You'd better thin it down. 2 (사람이) weak; feeble; weak-spirited; faint-hearted. ¶묽은 사람 feeble person / a softy.

뭇¹ [큰 작살] a large harpoon.

뭇² [묶음] a bundle; a bunch; [볏단] a sheaf (pl. sheaves); [장작] a faggot. ¶생선 두 ~ twenty fish / 장작 한 ~ a bundle of firewood ∥ 짚 한 ~ a bundle of straw / a sheaf of straw / 한 ~에 200원 200 won a bundle.

뭇³ [여러] many; various; all; every; all kinds [sorts] of; every sort[kind] of. ¶~ 사내[계집] all sorts[kinds] of men[women] ∥ ~ 사내의 노리개가 되다 be made a plaything of all men.

뭇나무 firewood in bundles; a faggot. ¶나무를 ~로 팔다 sell firewood by the bundle.

뭇매 beating in a group. ⇨몰매

뭇발길 1 [많은 사람의 발길질] kicking in a group. ¶~에 채다 get[be under / be subjected to] a pelting rain of kicks (by a gang). 2 [여러 사람의 공박] an attack from all quarters.

뭇사람 [온갖 사람] people of all sorts and conditions; [여러 사람] company; society; the public; the world. ¶~ 앞에서 in public / in company∥~ 앞에 나서다 go into society / appear in public∥~ 앞에서 꾸짖다 scold (a person) before others[in public]∥~들이 다 그를 칭찬한다 All the people praise him.

뭇시선(-視線) everyone's eyes [gaze]; public gaze. ¶~을 모으다 attract public gaze.

뭇입 the popular voice; the public cry; popular criticism; public rebuke. ¶~을 두려워하다 fear what people will say∥~을 막기는 어렵다 It is hard to defend oneself against criticism from all sides.

뭉개다 1 [짓이기다] crush; smash; squash; mash(감자를); (일을) make a mess of. ¶밟아 ~ smash[crush] (a thing) by treading on / flatten (a thing) under one's feet∥모자를 깔고 ~ sit on a hat (and mash it in)∥꽃을 구두 뒤축으로 ~ squash the flower under (one's) heel∥일을 ~ make a mess of a matter. 2 [꾸물거리다] linger; dawdle (over); idle about; dally away. ¶이불 속에서 ~ dally in bed∥뭉개고 앉아서 시간을 보내다 dally away one's time.

뭉게구름 [기상] a cumulus. ⇨ =적운(積雲)

뭉게뭉게 in (thick) clouds; thickly; densely. ¶~ 피어오르는 연기 volumes [billows] of smoke∥~ 피어오르는 김[증기] thick vapors / bursts of white steam∥구름이 ~ 피어오르다 clouds appear one after another.

뭉그러뜨리다 demolish; pull down; destroy; level (down). ¶돌담을 ~ demolish a stonewall∥벼랑[언덕]을 ~ level a cliff [hill].

뭉그러지다 crumble; go [fall] to pieces; collapse; break; give away; be destroyed; come down. ¶비바람을 맞아서 ~ fall to pieces as the result of exposure to wind and rain∥돌담이 뭉그러졌다 The stone wall fell down.

뭉그적거리다 linger; dawdle (over). ¶한자리에서 ~ dawdle in one place∥면회 시간이 지났는데도 ~ linger on past visiting hours∥모임이 끝났는데도 ~ dawdle after a meeting.

뭉그적뭉그적 slowly; sluggishly; tardily; idly. ¶~ 나아가다 go[proceed] at a snail's pace / crawl.

뭉근하다 low but steady (fire); (burn) slow; simmering. ¶뭉근한 불 a low[slow] fire / a simmering fire∥뭉근한 불에 끓이다 stew / cook over a slow fire. **뭉근히** low but steady; simmeringly. ¶불을 ~ 때다 keep a low fire going steadily.

뭉글뭉글하다 soft; pulpy. ⇨ 몽글몽글하다

뭉긋하다 [비스듬하다] gently-sloping; gentle; easy; [휘우듬하다] slightly bent; gently curved. ¶뭉긋한 고개 an easy[a gentle] slope.

뭉기다 [아래로 추어내리다] pull down; [뭉그러지게 하다] demolish; destroy.

뭉떵뭉떵 lump after lump; chunk after chunk; in [by] the lump; in chunks; in big lumps. ¶떡을 ~ 썰다 cut a rice cake into big chunks.

뭉뚝하다 blunt; stumpy; stubby. ¶뭉뚝한 연필 a stubby pencil∥뭉뚝한 끝 a blunt point [edge] ∥뭉뚝한 손가락 stubby fingers.

뭉뚱그리다 1 [대강 싸다] wrap[pack / do] up (a parcel) in a slipshod way; throw together hastily; bundle up crudely. ¶짐을 ~ bundle up a package crudely. 2 [총괄하다] lump

뭉실뭉실 plumply; fleshly. ⇨ 몽실몽실

뭉치 1 [덩이] a bundle; a roll; a lump; a clod. ¶실[털실] ~ a ball of string[wool] // 편지 한 ~ a bundle of letters // 지폐 한 ~ a bundle [roll / wad] of bank notes / a roll of (paper) money. 2 [소의 볼기 아래에 붙은 살] beef round.

뭉치다 1 [단결하다] unite; stand [hold / hang / band] together; be banded [leagued] together; combine. ¶뭉쳐서 in union / in one united body / in a body // 굳게 ~ be closely banded together / be strongly united // 뭉쳐서 …에 대항하다 be united against … // 뭉쳐서 일어서다 rise in unity (against) // 투철한 애국심과 확고한 역사 의식으로 굳게 ~ be firmly united with patriotic spirit and perspectives regarding history // 국가의 위기에 모든 정당이 한데 뭉쳤다 All the political parties stood together [closed ranks] in a national crisis. // 뭉치면 살고 흩어지면 죽는다 United we stand, divided we fall.
2 [덩어리가 되다] lump; mass; cake; conglomerate. ¶풀이 뭉친다 Paste lumps. / Paste forms a hard mass.
3 [덩어리로 만들다] make a lump; lump; mass; conglomerate; press together. ¶눈을 ~ press snow into a lump / make a snowball // 종이를 ~ crumple paper into a ball // 흙을 뭉쳐서 덩어리로 만들다 harden earth into a mass // 손수건을 뭉쳐 호주머니에 쑤셔 넣다 Wad up a handkerchief and put [shove] it in one's pocket.

뭉크러지다 1 crumble; collapse; fall down. 2 (종기 등이) break; (궤양으로) ulcerate. ¶뭉크러진 잇몸 an ulcerated gum // 문둥병으로 얼굴이 ~ have one's face disfigured by leprosy // 물집이 뭉크러져서 생살이 나왔다 The blisters broke and the skin became raw.

뭉클하다 1 (먹은 것이) (feel) heavy on the stomach. ¶속이 뭉클하고 내리지 않다 oppress the stomach / sit [lie] heavy on the stomach / remain undigested in the stomach. 2 (가슴이) be choked (with grief); be filled (with emotion); feel a lump in one's throat. ¶슬퍼서 가슴이 뭉클했다 My heart was choked with sorrow. // 가슴이 뭉클해서 아무 말도 나오지 않았다 My heart was too full for words. / I was so filled with emotion that I could hardly say a word.

뭉텅 in lumps.
뭉텅뭉텅 lump after lump. ⇨ 뭉떵뭉떵
뭉텅이 a lump; a bundle; a package; a wad. ¶지폐 ~ a bundle [roll / wad] of bank notes / a bundle of (paper) money // 헝겊 [종이 / 솜 / 머리카락] ~ a wad of cloth [paper / cotton / hair].

뭉툭하다 blunt; stumpy. ⇨ 몽똑하다
뭍 1 land; the shore. ⇨ 육지 ¶~에서 on land [shore] / ashore // ~에서 멀리 떨어져서 far away from land / far off the coast (of). 2 [섬에서 본 본토] the mainland; the country proper.
뭍바람 [지] a land wind [breeze]. ⇨ 육풍
뭍사람 [육지인] a landlubber; a landsman; [본토인] natives; mainlanders.
뭍짐승 a land animal.

뭐 what; what!; but. ⇨ 무어 ¶너 ~ 좀 먹어야지 Surely you have to eat something, don't you? // ~ 맛있는 것 없느냐 Have you not anything nice to eat? // ~라고 하기만 하면 운다 She cries at every trifle. // ~ (고쳐 물을 때) Eh? / What? // ~라고 I beg your pardon. / Excuse me. / What did you say? // ~가 뭔지 통 모르겠다 We don't know what's what. // ~ 그렇게 할 필요가 있을까 Why should I do it? / What is the use of doing such a thing? // ~ 그렇게 화낼 것 없지 않아 You have no reason whatever to be so angry. // ~! 그 사람이 죽었어 What! Is he dead?

뭐니 뭐니 해도 say what you will; whatever one may say; when all is said and done; all things taken together; after all; indeed. ¶~ 정계에서는 그 사람이 최고다 After all he is the greatest star [figure] in the political world.

뭣 what; which. ⇨ 무엇
뮤지컬 a musical.
뮤직 비디오 a (music) video.
뮤직홀 a music hall.
뮤추얼 펀드 [회사형 투자 신탁] 《미》 a mutual fund; 《영》 (a) unit trust.

-므로 [까닭으로] on account of; owing to; as; because (of); since. ¶그는 몸이 허약하~ 심한 육체노동은 할 수가 없다 He cannot do hard muscular labor because of his delicate health [because he is weak in health].

미 [음] mi.
미¹ (美) [아름다움] beauty; the beautiful; grace; charm. ¶남성 ~ masculine [manly] beauty // 여성 ~ womanly [female / feminine] charms // 육체 ~ physical beauty / bodily charm // 자연의 ~ natural beauty / beauty in nature / the beauties of nature // 운율의 ~ rhythmical charm // ~의 감각 a sense of beauty [the beautiful] // ~를 알다 [보는 눈이 있다] have an eye for the beautiful / can appreciate beauty.

미² (美) the United States (of America). ⇨ 미국

미- (未) un-; in-; not yet. ¶~발표 작품 an unpublished work / a work not yet published // ~완성의 incomplete / unfinished // ~결정의 undecided / undetermined / unsettled / pending.

미가 (米價) the price of rice. ⇨ 쌀값
● **미가 정책** the rice price policy. **미가 조절** control [regulation] of the rice market [price].

미각 (味覺) the (sense of) taste; the palate; the gustation. ¶~의 가을 autumn which brings with it the pleasures of the table // ~을 돋우는 tempting / inviting / appetizing // ~을 돋우는 음식 tempting [inviting / appetizing] food / food tickling the palate // ~이 발달되어 있다 have a delicate palate // ~에 맞다 suit one's palate / be (agreeable) to one's taste // ~을 만족시키다 please one's palate / ~을 돋우다 tickle one's palate / tempt the appetite / make one's mouth water // 맛있는 냄새가 ~을 돋웠다 The smell was very appetizing.
● **미각 기관** a taste organ. **미각 세포** a taste [gustatory] cell. **미각 신경** a gustatory nerve.

미간(未刊) ¶~의 unpublished / not yet published // ~ 소설 an unpublished novel.

미간(眉間) the space of the eyebrows; the brow; the glabella (pl. -lae); the glabellum (pl. -la). ¶~의 상처 a scar between the eyebrows // ~을 찌푸리다 knit [gather / bend] one's brows / frown.

미간지(未墾地) uncultivated land. ⇨ 미개간지(⇨미개간)

미감(味感) the (sense of) taste. ⇨ 미각

미감(美感) a sense of beauty; an aesthetic sense [feeling]. ¶~이 결여되어 있다 lack a sense of beauty [the beautiful] / be insensible to beauty.

미개(未開) 1 [발전이 없이 문화 수준이 낮음] ¶반~의 semibarbarous / semibarbarian / semicivilized // ~ 상태에 있다 be in a state of nature. 미개하다 uncivilized; benighted; savage; barbarous; wild. 2 [꽃이 피지 않음]. 미개하다 be not in blossom; be unbloomed [unblossomed].
● 미개국 an uncivilized [savage] country. 미개 사회 (a) primitive society. 미개인 a barbarian; a savage; (종족) a savage [primitive] people [race]; an uncivilized tribe. 미개지 [개명되지 못한 지역] a savage [barbaric] land; [개발되지 않은 지역] a backward region; undeveloped land.

미개간(未開墾) ¶~의 uncultivated / wild.
● 미개간지 uncultivated land; land in grass; land in its natural state; wilds; virgin soil.

미개발(未開發) ¶~의 undeveloped (region) / unexploited (district) / untapped (resources) / wild (land).
● 미개발 지역 an undeveloped area.

미개척(未開拓) ¶~의 undeveloped / unreclaimed / unexploited / untapped / wild / (학문 등의) unexplored.
● 미개척 분야 an unexplored field. ¶과학의 세계에는 아직 ~가 많다 There are still vast regions to be explored by scientists. 미개척 시장 a potential market. 미개척지 undeveloped [unreclaimed / waste] land; untapped territory; virgin [maiden] soil; wilds.

미거(美擧) a praiseworthy act [undertaking]; a commendable [laudable] act; good work. ¶근래에 보기 드문 ~이다 It is the most praiseworthy [laudable] act that we have heard of in recent years.

미거하다(未擧—) [생각이 모자라다] thoughtless; imprudent; indiscreet; [아둔하다] foolish; unwise; silly. ¶미거한 생각 a foolish [childish] idea / a short-sighted view.

미결(未決) 1 pendency. ¶~의 undecided / pending / open / unsettled / unconvicted(죄인의) // ~ 2개월 통산 1년 6개월의 금고 imprisonment for one year and six months [18 months] with credit for two months served prior to conviction // ~로 남아 있다 be left unsettled / be held in abeyance // 그 문제는 아직 ~이다 The question is still open [unsettled]. // 그는 ~로 3개월 구류 중에 있다 He has been in detention for three months pending trial. 2 a house of detention. ⇨ 미결감(⇨미결) 3 an unconvicted prisoner. ⇨ 미결수(⇨미결)
● 미결감(-監) a house of detention. 미결 구류 detention pending trial [judgment]; unconvicted detention. 미결수 an unconvicted [under trial] prisoner; a prisoner under trial. 미결안 an unsettled bill; an undecided matter; a pending case.

미결산(未決算) ¶~의 unsettled (debt) / [미불의] unpaid.
● 미결산 계정 an open account(약어 OA); an unbalanced [outstanding] account.

미결제(未決濟) ¶~의 [미결산의] unsettled / outstanding / [미불의] unpaid.
● 미결제 거래 an incomplete transaction. 미결제 계정 a suspense [an outstanding] account.

미경지(未耕地) uncultivated land; an area not yet brought under cultivation.

미경험(未經驗) ¶~의 inexperienced / unexperienced / green / raw.
● 미경험자 an inexperienced person; a green hand; a novice; (구어) a greenhorn. ¶~ 환영 Welcome the inexperienced.

미곡(米穀) rice.
● 미곡 도매상 a rice factor; (미) a rice commission merchant. 미곡상(-商) (사람) a rice dealer; (가게) a rice store; (장사) dealing in rice. 미곡 시장 the rice market.

미골(尾骨) [생] the coccyx. ⇨꼬리뼈(⇨꼬리)

미관(美觀) a fine [pretty / lovely] view; a fine [beautiful] sight; a charming [beautiful] spectacle; beauties(보통 복수형). ¶자연의 ~ the beauties of nature // ~을 이루다 present a fine spectacle // ~을 해치다 spoil [injure] the beauty (of) // 거리의 ~을 해치다 mar the appearance of the streets // 여기저기 붙은 포스터가 거리의 ~을 해치고 있다 The posters put up here and there spoil the appearance of the streets [make the streets look bad].

미관(微官) a petty [minor] official; (영) a humble placeman.

미광(微光) a faint light; a gleam; a glimmer (of light); a shimmer. ¶어둠 속에서 ~을 발하는 것이 있었다 We saw something glimmering in the darkness.

미구에(未久—) soon; shortly; before long; in the near future. ¶그는 ~ 완쾌될 것이다 It will not be long before he gets well. // 그는 ~ 도미할 것이다 He will leave for the United States in the near future [in the not too distant future].

미국(美國) the United States (of America)(약어 U.S., U.S.A.); America; the Union; (구어) the States. ¶~의 American / U.S. / Yankee // ~제 자동차 an American-made car / a car made in U.S.A.
● 미국 국기 the American flag; the Stars and Stripes; the Star-Spangled Banner. 미국 말 the American language; American. 미국 문학 American literature. 미국 문화원 the U.S. [American] Cultural Center. 미국인 / 미국 사람 an American; (전형적인) Uncle Sam; (북부나 New England 지방의) (속어) a Yankee; (집합적) the Americans. 미국 중앙 정보국 the Central Intelligence Agency(약어 CIA, C.I.A.).

미군(美軍) [미국 군대] the U.S. armed forces; the U.S. Army [Navy / Air Force]; American forces; [미국 병사] an American soldier [sailor / airman]; a GI. ¶주한 ~ the U.S. Forces (stationed) in Korea.

미궁(迷宮) a labyrinth; a maze. ¶~에 빠진 살인 사건 an unsolved murder mystery [case] // (사건 등이) ~에 빠지다 become shrouded [be wrapped] in mystery / become [prove] impossible of solution // 사건은 ~에 빠졌다 The case went unsolved.

미급하다(未及-) be unattainable; do not reach; fall short (of); be beyond one's tether. ¶미급하지만 도와 드리자요 I will help though in a humble measure. / I will do what little I can.

미기(美技) 〔훌륭한 연기〕 a brilliant[beautiful / neat] performance; a stunt; (운동 경기에서) (make) a fine play.

미꾸라지 〔동〕 a loach; a mudfish.
미꾸라지 한 마리가 온 웅덩이를 흐려 놓는다 (속담) One ill weed mars a whole pot of pottage.; The rotten apple injures its neighbor.
미꾸라지 같다 ¶미꾸라지 같은 놈 a slippery [an eely] fellow // 그는 늘 애매한 대답만 하는 미꾸라지 같은 사람이다 He is an elusive person who always gives noncommittal [evasive / vague] answers.

미끄러뜨리다 〔활주하게 하다〕 let slip; slide; glide; 〔낙방시키다〕 fail. ¶발을 ~ miss one's footing / slip.

미끄러지다 1 〔활주하다〕 slide; glide; slip; skid. ¶미끄러지듯이 glidingly // 얼음 위를 ~ slide on the ice // 바나나 껍질에 ~ slip on a banana peel // 미끄러져 내려가다 slide down (a slope) // 미끄러져 넘어지다 slip and fall // 얼음판에서 미끄러져 넘어지다 slip and fall on the ice // 계단에서 미끄러져 떨어지다 slip [slither] down the stairs // 미끄러지기 시작하다 start sliding / begin to slide [slip] // 발이 미끄러졌다 My foot slipped. // 계단에서 미끄러져 바닥으로 떨어졌다 I slipped on the stairs and fell to the bottom. // 미끄러지지 않도록 조심하라 Watch your steps so as not to slip. // 체조 선수가 착지했을 때 왼발이 미끄러졌다 When the gymnast landed, his left foot slipped. // 카누는 호수 위를 미끄러져 나갔다 The canoe glided over the lake.
2 〔낙방하다〕 fail (in) an examination; (영국구어) get plucked in an examination. ¶나는 대학 입시에서 미끄러졌다 I failed my university entrance examinations.

미끄럼 sliding; slipping; a slide; a slip. ¶~을 타다 (얼음 위에서) skate on the ice / do skating / (눈 위에서) slide over the snow (in a sleigh) // (차바퀴의) ~을 **방지하다** prevent (a wheel) from slipping // 얼음이 얇아서 ~을 탈 수가 없다 The ice is not thick enough to skate upon. // ~ 주의 (게시) Slippery.
● 미끄럼틀 / 미끄럼대 a (playground) slide. ¶~에서 미끄럼을 타다 slide[play] on a slide / take a slide.

미끄럽다 slippery; slithery; greasy; 〔반드럽다〕 smooth; sleek. ¶미끄러운 길 a slippery road // 미끄러운 종이 sleek[slick] paper // 몹시 ~ be as slippery as an eel // 비가 와서 길이 ~ The path is slippery with the rain. // 땅바닥은 이끼가 끼어서 미끄러웠다 The ground was slippery with moss.

미끈거리다 1 〔반들거리다〕 feel smooth; be smooth to the touch. ¶미끈거리는 smooth / sleek / velvety. 2 〔미끌대다〕 be slippery; be slimy; be greasy (기름으로). ¶미끈거리는 액체 a slimy liquid // 땀으로 미끈거리는 이마 a forehead clammy with sweat // 미꾸라지는 미끈거리기 쉽다 Loaches are slippery.

미끈미끈하다 greasy; clammy; slimy; slippery; slithery. ¶뱀장어는 미끈미끈해서 잡기가 어렵다 Eels are so slippery that we can't hold them.

미끈하다 1 (사물이) sleek; slick; smooth; streamlined. ¶미끈한 자동차 a streamlined motorcar. 2 (사람이) slender; slim; (옷맵시가) neat; gay; flashy. ¶미끈한 얼굴 a sleek face / a good-looking face // 미끈한 여자 a beautiful girl, slender as a lily // 미끈하게 생기다 be good-looking / be handsome / have nice features // 미끈하게 차리다 be flashly dressed / be well-dressed.

미끼 1 〔낚시용 먹이〕 a bait. ¶낚시 ~ a fish bait / a bait for fish // 떡밥 ~ (a) paste bait / paste (이겨서 만든) // 산 ~ a live bait // 낚시에 ~를 꿰다 bait[put a bait on] an angling hook / bait up // ~를 물다 take a bait // ~를 갈다 replace one's bait / put on a fresh bait // ~를 떼이다 lose the bait (to the fish) // ~ 없이는 고기를 낚을 수 없다 Without bait no fish can be caught.
2 〔유혹물〕 a bait; a decoy; a lure; an allurement. ¶~에 걸려들다 be lured / get decoyed // 처녀를 ~로 쓰다 use a girl as a decoy // 물건을 사게 하기 위해 경품을 ~로 쓰다 use presents to tempt a person to buy a thing // 돈을 ~로 여자를 낚다 decoy[lure] a woman with money // 여자를 ~로 돈을 옭아내다 get money from (a person) using a woman as a bait // 닭을 ~로 여우를 잡다 catch a fox with a hen for a decoy // 그는 돈을 ~로 나를 유혹하려 했다 He tried to entice me by offering me money. / He tempted me with money.

미나리 〔식〕 a dropwort; a Japanese parsely.
미나리아재비 〔식〕 a buttercup; a goldcup.
미남(美男) a handsome[good-looking] man; an Adonis; an Apollo.
미납(未納) (make) default in payment; nonpayment. ¶~은 unpaid / in arrears / back / outstanding // 그의 수업료는 아직 ~이다 His tuition has not yet been paid. // 그는 세금 ~으로 처분을 받았다 He was penalized for failure to pay his taxes [defaulting on his taxes]. **미납하다** leave (a thing) unpaid; be in arrears.
● **미납세** unpaid[back] taxes; arrears of taxes. **미납액 / 미납금** the amount in arrears; the amount outstanding; arrearages. **미납자** a person in arrears; a (tax) defaulter. **미납 처분** punishment for failure to pay[of payment].

미네랄 (a) mineral. ¶이 음식은 ~이 풍부하다 This food is rich in minerals.
● **미네랄워터** mineral water; (영) minerals.

미녀(美女) a beauty; a belle; a good-looking girl; a beautiful woman; (미국 속어) a knockout. ¶절세의 ~ a rare beauty / a woman of matchless[peerless] beauty / the fairest of the fair.

미농지(美濃紙) (a kind of) rice paper.
미뉴에트 〔음〕 a minuet; a menuet.
미늘 (낚시 등의) a barb (of a fishhook).
미니 a mini.
● **미니스커트** a miniskirt.
미니멈 a minimum.
미니어처 (그림·모형의) a miniature. ¶서브관 a subminiature tube.
미다 〔구멍을 내다〕 tear a hole in (paper, leather, etc.); get torn; rip (open). ¶미인 곳 〔구멍〕 a tear (in the coat) // 잘못해서 종이를 ~ tear a hole in the paper by mistake.

미닫이 a sliding door [window].

미달(未達) shortage; lack; deficiency; insufficiency. ¶체중 ~ underweight // 연령 ~의 underage // 정원 ~로 for want [in the absence] of a quorum // 아직 정원 ~이다 The number limit has not been reached. // 투표 결과 과반수에서 5표 ~이다 The vote lacks five of being a majority. **미달하다** be short (of); be deficient (in); be less than; be under; lack; want. ¶정족수에 ~ lack [want] a quorum.

미담(美談) a praiseworthy [fine / laudable / commendable] anecdote [episode]; a moving story; an impressive tale. ¶그가 ~의 주인공이었다 He was the hero of the moving tale. // 이 이야기는 아직도 ~으로 전해지고 있다 The story is still told with undiminished admiration.

미답(未踏) ¶~의 [발을 들여놓지 않은] untrodden / [손대지 않은] unexplored // 전인(前人) ~의 빙원 an ice field never trodden by man / a virgin ice field.

미대(美大) a college of fine arts.

미덕(美德) a virtue; a noble attribute; a grace (of character); a good trait; a good deed(선행). ¶자선의 ~ a virtue of charity // ~을 지닌 사람 a man of virtue / a virtuous man // ~을 행하는 사람 the doer of a good deed / ~을 **발휘하다** display the virtue of humility [unselfishness].

미덥다 reliable; trustworthy; sure-footed; (장래가) hopeful; promising. ¶미더운 사람 a reliable [trustworthy] person // 장래가 미더운 사람 a promising person / a person (full) of promise / a person with a great [rosy] future // 미덥지 못한 unreliable / untrustworthy / not to be depended upon / undependable / unpromising / …을 크게 미더워하다 repose [place] great trust in (a person) / hope [expect] much from (a person) of good credit / 미더운 자리에 딸의 혼처를 정하다 get one's daughter engaged to a dependable person // 그는 미더운 사람이다 He is to be depended upon [a reliable man].

미동(美童) **1** [잘생긴 사내아이] a handsome [good-looking] boy. **2** [비역 상대] a catamite.

미동(微動) a slight shock; a tremor; a quiver. ¶~도 않다 do not budge [stir / move] an inch / stand as firm as a rock.

미들급(-級) the middleweight. ¶~의 middleweight (wrestler).
● 미들급 선수 a middleweight.

미들 헤비급(-級) the middle heavyweight.

미등(尾燈) (자동차의) a tail light [lamp]; a rear light.

미등(微騰) a fractional [marginal] advance. **미등하다** inch up.

미디 [미니와 맥시의 중간] a midi.
● 미디스커트 a midiskirt.

미라(@mirra) a mummy. ¶~로 하다 [만들다] mummify / embalm.

미락(微落) [증권] a fractional [marginal] decline. **미락하다** inch down. ¶주가가 미락하고 있다 Stock prices are slipping [eroding].

미란(靡爛) [염증] inflammation; [궤양] ulceration; fester; erosion; [썩어서 문드러짐] decomposition. ¶시체는 지독한 ~ 상태에 있었다 The corpse was in a fearful state of decomposition. **미란하다** be inflamed; ulcerate; fester; be decomposed; decompose(시체 등이). → ¶남자의 미란된 사체 the decomposed body of a man.

미란다 원칙(-原則) Miranda rule.

미래(未來) **1** [다가올 앞날] (the) future; time [days] to come. ¶~의 future / coming / to come / prospective / in (the) future / in days to come / in the womb of time // ~의 남편 [아내] one's future [prospective / intended] husband [wife] / the husband-[wife-]to-be // ~의 일 future [coming] events / ~에 살다 live in the future / ~를 **예상하다** anticipate what is to come // ~의 계획을 세우다 form a plan for one's future / 그녀는 ~의 스타이다 She is a future star [a star-to-be]. // 그는 ~의 내 남편이다 He is my future [intended] husband. // 그는 건축가로서 ~가 촉망된다 He is a promising architect. / He has a bright future as an architect.
2 a better world. ⇨내세
3 [언] the future tense.
● 미래사(-事) future [coming] events [affairs]. 미래상(-像) an image of the future. ¶이 책은 사회의 ~을 그리고 있다 The book describes what society will be like in the future. 미래 완료 [언] the future perfect tense. 미래파 (학파) futurism; Futurism; (사람) a futurist; a Futurist. 미래학 futurology.

미량(微量) a very small amount; extremely small quantities. ¶~의 독물이 검출되었다 A very small amount of poison was detected.
● 미량 분석 [화] microanalysis. 미량 천칭 / 미량 저울 a microbalance; a delicate balance.

미레자 a carpenter's square (for drawing ink lines). ⇨먹자

미레질 reverse [back-hand] planing.

미려하다(美麗-) beautiful; pretty; lovely; fine; graceful; elegant. **미려히** beautifully; finely; gracefully; elegantly.

미력(微力) [능력] poor ability; the little one can do; [자력(資力)] slender means; [세력] little influence; [노력] one's pigmy effort. ¶~이나마 in spite of one's poor ability // ~을 **다하다** do one's bit / do what (the little) one can / exert oneself to the full / contribute one's mite (to).

미련 stupidity; dullness; silliness; asininity. **미련하다** stupid (as an owl); dull; thickheaded; weak-headed; soft-[dull-]witted; imbecile. ¶그렇게 행동하다니 내가 미련했어 It was stupid of me to behave like that.
● 미련쟁이 a dullard; a soft-[dull-]witted person; a stupid; an ass; a blockhead. 미련퉁이 a dullard; a stupid. ⇨미련쟁이

미련(未練) [애착] lingering attachment [affection]; [섭섭함] regret; reluctance to give (it, a person, etc.) up. ¶~이 (남아) **있다** be still attached (to) / have a lingering affection [love] (for) / have a lingering regret (for the past) / feel (some) regret // ~이 **없다** have nothing to regret / have nothing to look back on with regret // 그는 아직도 그 여자에게 ~이 남아 있다 Still he cannot give her up. // 이제 그에게 더 이상 ~은 없다 I'm no longer interested in him. / I don't care [I feel no attachment] for him any longer. // 나는 아직 그 지위에 ~이 있다 I still retain a lingering desire for the position. // 도시 생활에 ~을

없다 I do not regret giving up city life.∥최선을 다했으니 ~은 없다 I did my best [everything I could], so I have no regrets.∥지금 학교를 그만두기에는 ~이 남는다 I feel reluctant to leave school now.∥이제 죽어도 ~은 없다 Now I can die happy [without regrets].

미로(迷路) a maze; a labyrinth. ¶~ 같은 labyrinthine / labyrinthian∥~에서 빠져나가다 go [find one's way out] through a labyrinth / thread a maze∥나는 ~에 빠졌다 I was lost in a maze. / I was at a loss what to do.

미료(未了) ¶~의 unfinished / unfulfilled / unexecuted.

미루나무 [식] a poplar.

미루다 1 [연기하다] put off; postpone; defer; [기한을 연장하다] prolong; extend; protract; [지연시키다] delay; hold off. ¶미루어지다 be moved [put] back (차례로 늦어지다) / be postponed (예정보다 늦어지다)∥출발을 한 시간 ~ move [put] the departure time back an hour∥시합 일정이 뒤로 미루어졌다 The schedule for the tournament has been moved back.∥회의를 내주의 수요일로 미루자 Let's postpone [put off] the meeting until next Wednesday.∥그들은 출발을 이틀 동안 미루었다 They delayed [put off / postponed] their departure for two days.∥자금 부족으로 그 계획이 얼마 동안 뒤로 미루어졌다 Because of [Owing to] a lack of funds, the plan was postponed [put off] for a while.∥그 목수는 이런저런 구실을 내세워 우리 가옥 건축의 착공을 하루하루 미루었다 The carpenter put off starting to build our house from day to day on one pretext after other.∥저의 지불 기일을 미루어 주십시오 Please let me defer the payment [pay later].∥당신이 그것을 언제까지나 미룰 수는 없어요 You can't put it off [procrastinate] forever.
2 [전가하다] lay [throw] (the blame on a person); shift [shuffle off] (a responsibility on another's shoulders); [속어] pass the buck (to). ¶일을 남에게 ~ shift one's work on (another) / force [thrust / shove off)] work on (a person) / (강제로) urge [compel / constrain] (a person) to undertake (a task)∥책임을 남에게 ~ push the responsibility off into a person / (구어) pass the buck to a person∥책임을 서로 ~ shift the responsibility back and forth / keep passing the buck∥자기 잘못을 남에게 ~ lay one's mistakes at another's doorstep.
3 [추측하다] infer [deduce / gather] (from); conclude; judge (by / from); [억측하다] guess; surmise; conjecture; suppose. ¶그의 말로 미루어 judging from his statement∥여러 가지 사정을 미루어 생각건대 all things taken together / all things considered∥이 일로 미루어 보아 과열이 원인인 것 같았다 From this, I suppose [gather] (that) overheating was the cause.∥여러 가지 정황으로 미루어 보아 그의 사임은 불가피하다 Considering the circumstances, I assume he has to resign.∥나머지는 미루어 알 수 있다 The rest may better be imagined than described. / From this one may judge the rest. / The rest you can easily imagine. / The rest may be inferred.

미륵(彌勒) 1 [불] Maitreya (bodhisattva). ⇨ 미륵보살(⇨미륵) 2 [돌부처] a stone Buddhist image.
●**미륵보살** [불] Maitreya (bodhisattva).

미리 beforehand; in advance; previously; in anticipation; ahead of time. ¶남에게 ~ 알려주다 let a person know beforehand [ahead of time]∥파티의 회비를 ~ 내다 pay the fee for a party in advance∥재학 중인 학생을 ~ 채용하다 recruit (new employees) before they graduate from school [college]∥~ 모든 준비가 갖춰져 있었다 Everything had been previously arranged.∥things had been arranged beforehand.∥내가 뉴욕에 도착한다는 것을 그들에게 ~ 알려야 한다 You should notify them of your arrival in New York in advance.∥그는 항상 ~ 손을 쓴다 He always makes early preparations [gets ready early].∥그 일을 자네 부인에게 ~ 알려 두는 것이 좋을 걸세 You'd better tell your wife about it beforehand [in advance].∥~ 적의 배후로 돌아 공격하여 선수를 쳐라 Forestall the enemy by attacking them in the rear.

미립(微粒) a small [fine] grain; a granule.
●**미립자** [물] a minute [an ultrafine] particle; a corpuscle. ¶~의 corpuscular. **미립체** [생] a microsome.

미만(未滿) ¶~의 under / below / less than∥10분 ~ in less than ten minutes∥18세 ~ 입장할 수 없음 (게시) No admittance to those under eighteen years of age.∥1000원 ~은 잘라 버릴 것 Amounts less than [Figures below] one thousand won are to be disregarded.∥그녀의 급료는 50만 원 ~이었다 Her salary was short of [less than] five hundred thousand won.

미만하다(彌滿─·彌漫─) [퍼져 있다] prevailing; prevalent; diffused; widespread; [들끓다하다] nearly [almost] full.

미망(迷妄) an illusion; a delusion; a fallacy. ¶~ 상태에 빠져 있다 be in a state of spiritual darkness∥~에서 깨어나다 be disillusioned / be undeceived / come [be brought] to one's senses / awake [wake up] from a delusion [an illusion]∥그의 망령이 아직 깨닫지를 못하고 ~ 상태에서 헤매고 있다 His ghost is still haunting the area.∥우리는 그의 영혼이 ~에서 벗어나 편히 쉬도록 기도했다 We prayed that his soul would rest in peace. **미망하다** be misguided; labor under a delusion; remain in darkness.

미망인(未亡人) a widow. ¶존슨 씨의 ~ Mr. Johnson's widow / the wife of the late Mr. Johnson∥전쟁 ~ a war widow / a war-bereaved wife∥~이 된 내 누님 my widowed sister∥~이 되다 lose one's husband / become a widow.

미맥(米麥) [쌀과 보리] rice and barley.

미명(未明) the gray of the morning; early dawn. ¶~에 before daylight / before dawn [daybreak] / in the grey of the morning.

미명(美名) a good [fair] name; fame; a high reputation. ¶…의 ~하에 in the name of ... / under the cloak [veil] of (charity) / under the good name of ...∥조사라는 ~ 아래 그는 회사의 비밀을 캤다 He pried into the secrets of the company under the pretext of making a survey.∥그들은 전도 사업이라는 ~하에 원주민의 땅을 약탈했다 They deprived the aborigines of their land under the cloak of doing missionary work.

미모(美貌) good [attractive] looks; pretty fea-

미모사

tures; a beautiful[handsome] face; a fair face; personal beauty; beauty of person; charming personal attraction. ¶눈부실 정도의 ~ a radiant[dazzling] beauty∥~의 미망인 a beautiful widow∥그녀는 드물게 보는 ~의 여인이다 She is a woman of rare beauty.∥~가 화근이었다 Her beauty was her ruin[downfall].

미모사 [식] a mimosa; a sensitive plant.

미목(眉目) features; looks; a face. ¶~이 수려한 청년 a handsome young man∥~이 수려하다 have a handsome face[clean-cut features].

미몽(迷夢) an illusion; a delusion; a fallacy. ¶~에서 깨어나게 하다 disillusion (a person) / dispel (a person's) illusions / bring (a person) to (his) senses[reason] / open (a person's) eyes∥그는 ~에서 깨어났다 He awakened from his illusions.

미묘하다(美妙-) fine; sweet; elegant; graceful; exquisite. ¶미묘한 음악 소리 exquisite music.

미묘하다(微妙-) subtle; delicate; fine; nice.(▶ subtle은 식별이 어려운, 포착하기 어려운 미묘함, delicate는 미세한 문제 등이 세심한 주의를 요하는 등의 느낌을 가짐. fine은 delicate 정도는 아니지만, 겨우 알 수 있다는 정도의 사소함을 나타냄. nice는 문어적인 말로 더욱 복잡하고 미묘한 느낌을 나타냄) ¶미묘한 뜻의 차이 delicate[fine] shades of meaning∥이것과 그것과는 미묘한 점에서 차이가 있다 This is different from that in delicate[subtle] way. / This differs subtly from that.∥정세는 ~ It's a touch-and-go situation.∥이 시에는 사춘기의 미묘한 감정이 나타나 있다 The subtle[delicate] feelings of adolescence are captured in this poem.

미문(美文) flowery[elegant] prose; fine writing.
  ●**미문체** a flowery[an ornate] style; a florid prose style.

미물(微物) [미생물] a microorganism; a microscopic organism; a microbe; [하찮은 것] a trifle.

미미하다(微微-) [근소하다] slight; [빈약하다] meager[(영) meagre]; [하찮다] trifling; [중요하지 않다] insignificant; unimportant. ¶미미한 증가(감소) an immaterial increase [decrease]∥미미한 수입 a meager income∥그에게는 그러한 사건은 미미한 일처럼 생각되었다 Such an event seemed insignificant[of little importance] to him.

미발표(未發表) ¶~의 unpublished / not yet made public∥~ 작품 an unpublished work∥결과는 아직 ~이다 The results have not yet been made public[published / publicized].

미발행(未發行) ¶~의 unissued / not yet issued.

미복잠행하다(微服潛行-) travel incognito [incog]; pay a private[surreptitious] visit (to); visit (a place) incognito.

미봉(彌縫) patching up; temporizing; time-serving. **미봉하다** patch[tinker] up (a matter); temporize; make (a) shift; gloss over (a fault). ¶임시 ~ patch (things) up for the moment / temporize / make shift (for the present) / (그럭저럭) muddle[rub] on.
  ●**미봉책** a makeshift; a stopgap[temporary] measure. ¶~을 쓰다 adopt a stopgap

measure / resort to a temporary expedient.

미부(尾部) [꼬리 부분] the tail; (비행기 등의) the tail (section); the empennage.

미분(微分) 1 [수] differential; differentiation. **미분하다** differentiate. 2 differential calculus. ⇨미분학(⇨미분)
  ●**미분 방정식** a differential equation. **미분적분학** differential and integral calculus. **미분학** [수] differential calculus.

미분자(微分子) an atom; a particle; a corpuscle; a molecule.

미불(未拂) nonpayment; [체납] default; arrears; arrearage. ¶~의 unpaid / unsettled / not yet paid / outstanding∥아직 ~인 채이다 It's still unpaid.∥그 청구서는 아직 ~이다 The bill hasn't been paid[settled] yet.
  ●**미불금** an account not yet paid; (the amount in) arrears; arrearages.

미불(美弗) American currency. ⇨미화(美貨)

미비(未備) [불완전·불충분] imperfection; insufficiency; defectiveness; inadequacy; [부족] lack; deficiency; [미비점] a defect; an imperfection; a loophole(법률 등의). ¶제도상의 ~ an institutional inertia∥하수도의 ~ lack of an adequate sewage system∥그는 법의 ~를 악용하여 큰 부자가 되었다 He abused legal loopholes and became very rich. **미비하다** defective; faulty; deficient; imperfect; incomplete; lame(이론 등의). ¶미비한 점은 용서하십시오 Please forgive any oversight on our part. / Please overlook our inadequacies.∥서류가 미비하여 각하당했다 The papers were incomplete and were rejected.

미쁘다 reliable; dependable. ⇨믿음직하다

미사(가)(라) Missa; (a) mass; Mass. ¶장엄 ~ Solemn Mass / (라) Missa Solemnis∥진혼 ~ a requiem mass∥추도 ~ mass for the dead∥~를 올리다 hold a mass∥~를 드리다 (성직자가) read[say] Mass.

미사여구(美辭麗句) fine phrases; florid language. ¶~를 늘어놓다 utter strings of flattering compliments / pay one flattering compliment after another∥그는 온갖 ~를 늘어놓고 그녀의 비위를 맞추려고 했다 He tried to please her with all sorts of flowery words.

미사일 a missile. ¶공대공 ~ an air-to-air missile(약어 AAM)∥공대지 ~ an air-to-surface missile(약어 ASM)∥공중 발사 탄도 ~ an air-launched ballistic missile(약어 ALBM)∥다핵탄두 ~ a multiple independently targeted re-entry vehicle(약어 MIRV)∥대륙 간 ~ an intercontinental missile∥대전차 ~ an antitank missile∥열 추적 ~ a heat-seeking missile∥유도 ~ a guided missile(약어 GM)∥전략용 ~ a strategic missile(약어 SM)∥중거리 ~ an intermediate range missile∥지대공 ~ a surface [ground] (-to-)air missile(약어 SAM)∥탄도탄 요격용 ~ an antiballistic missile(약어 ABM)∥핵 ~ a nuclear missile∥대(對) ~ 방위 antimissile defense∥육군 ~ 부대 an army missile unit∥장[단]거리 ~ a long-[short-]range missile∥전술 ~ 부대 a tactical missile forces∥~을 발사하다 fire[launch] a missile.
  ●**미사일 기지** a missile base[station]. **미사일 발사 기지** a missile launching site.

미삼(尾蔘) rootlets[root hairs] of ginseng.

미상(未詳) ¶~의 [불명의] unknown / [미확인의] unidentified / not exactly known∥작자

[필자] ~의 of unknown authorship / anonymous // 신원 ~의 시체 an unidentified corpse // 사고로 인한 부상자의 성명, 연령 등은 ~이다 The man injured in the accident is still unidentified. / Nothing is yet known about the identity of those injured in the accident.

미상불(未嘗不) as a matter of fact; in reality; sure enough; really; indeed; certainly.

미상환(未償還) ¶~의 outstanding / unredeemed // ~액 outstanding issues.
● **미상환 채무** an unpaid [outstanding] debt.

미색(米色) pale yellow; straw yellow; bran.

미색(美色) 1 [아름다운 색깔] a beautiful color. 2 [미인] a beauty; a belle; a beautiful woman; [(여자의) 아름다움] beauty (of a woman); loveliness; charms.

미생물(微生物) a microbe; a microorganism; a microscopic organism; a germ. ¶~의 microbial / microbic.
● **미생물학** [생] microbiology. ¶~(상)의 microbiological.

미성(未成) ¶~의 unfinished / uncompleted / incomplete / halffinished (picture).

미성(美聲) a sweet [beautiful] voice; a silvery [ringing] voice.

미성년(未成年) minority; nonage; (legal) infancy. ¶~의 minor / infant / under age // ~이다 be under age / be not yet of age.
● **미성년자** a minor; a person under age; [법] an infant. ¶~의 흡연을 금하다 prohibit minors from smoking.

미성숙(未成熟) immaturity; unripeness. **미성숙하다** unripe; immature; green.

미세스 →미시즈

미세하다(微細−) [아주 작다] minute; fine; nice; infinitesimal; microscopic; [세밀하다] minute; detailed; full; particular. ¶미세하게 in detail / minutely / fully // 미세한 사항 the minor details // 미세한 점 minute details.

미션 스쿨 a mission [missionary] school.

미소(美蘇) American and the Soviet Union. ¶~의 American-Soviet / Russo-[Soviet-]American // ~의 군비 경쟁 [냉전 / 해빙] arms race [cold war / détente] between the U.S. and the Soviet Union.
● **미소 공동 위원회** the U.S.-Soviet Joint Commission.

미소(微笑) a smile. ¶~ 짓는 얼굴로 with a smile // 예쁘게 ~ 짓는 소녀 a girl with a beautiful smile // ~를 짓다 smile // 억지로 ~를 짓다 force a smile // 그녀는 부드럽게 [슬프게] ~ 지었다 She smiled tenderly [sadly]. // 그는 수수께끼의 ~를 흘렸다 He smiled a mysterious smile. // 할머니는 만면에 ~를 띠고 계셨다 Grandmother was all smiles. // 아련한 ~가 그녀의 입가에 떠올랐다 A faint smile played around her lips. // 그는 손자의 귀여운 몸짓에 ~ 짓지 않을 수 없었다 He could not help smiling [repress a smile] at the innocent behavior of his grandchild. // 나라는 것을 알아보고 그 소녀는 환히 ~ 지었다 Recognizing me, the girl smiled [broke into a smile]. // 그는 그 소식을 듣자 환한 ~가 얼굴에 떠올랐다 His face broadened into a smile at the news. // 그녀는 남 앞에서 ~를 거두는 일이 없다 She is always smiling when in the presence of others. / There is always a smile on her face when she is in the presence of others. // 어린이는 어머니에게 ~ 지어 보였다 The child smiled at its mother. // 그녀는 승낙의 의사 표시를 했다 She smiled her consent. **미소하다** smile (at a person); crack a smile; beam (upon a person). ¶그 낯선 부인은 미소하면서 나에게 다가왔다 The strange woman came smiling toward(s) me. / The strange woman came toward(s) me with a smile on her face.

미소년(美少年) a handsome [good-looking] boy [young man / (문어) youth].

미소하다(微小−) minute; microscopic; infinitesimal. ¶미소한 입자 a fine particle // 인간은 우주 속에서 미소한 존재에 지나지 않는다 Man is but an insignificant being in the universe.

미소하다(微少−) very little.

미송(美松) [식] a Douglas fir [pine]; an Oregon pine [fir].

미수(未收) ¶~의 accrued / outstanding / receivable / unearned / deferred // 그의 세금은 ~로 되어 있다 He is in arrears with his taxes. / His taxes remain unpaid.
● **미수금** an uncollected [outstanding] amount.

미수(未遂) ¶방화 ~ attempted arson // 살인 ~ an attempted murder / a murder attempt // 자살 ~ an attempt to kill oneself / (an) attempted suicide // 자살 [암살] ~자 a would-be suicide [assassin] // ~의 attempted / unconsummated // ~로 끝나다 fall [end] in the attempt // 음모는 ~에 그쳤다 The plot ended in failure [failed / was abortive].
● **미수범** [법] a would-be criminal.

미수(米壽) 88 years of age. ¶~를 축하하다 celebrate a person's eighty-eighth birthday.

미숙련(未熟鍊) [관형어적] unskilled; unskillful; inexpert.
● **미숙련공** an unskilled worker [laborer]; a green hand; (집합적) unskilled labor.

미숙아(未熟兒) a premature baby.

미숙자(未熟者) an inexperienced person; a greenhorn.

미숙하다(未熟−) (과실이) unripe; [익숙하지 않다] immature; [경험이 없다] inexperienced; [숫되다] naive; [구어] green. ¶미숙한 문장 an immature [awkward] style // 그들의 생각은 ~ Their ideas are [Their thinking is] immature. // 이 일에는 그가 아직 ~ He is still green at this job. // 그의 운전은 ~ He lacks experience as a driver.

미술(美術) art; (the) fine arts (▶ 회화·건축·조각·공예를 가리킴; 영어에서는 그 밖에 음악·시 등을 포함하는 경우도 있음). ¶응용 ~ applied art // 장식 ~ decorative art // 조형 ~ formative [plastic] arts // ~적인 artistic(al) // ~적으로 artistically // 동양 [서양] ~ Oriental [Western] art // 20세기 ~ twentieth-century art // 상업 ~ commercial art // ~적 관점에서 말하자면 그것은 졸작이다 From an artistic point of view [As art], it is rubbish.
● **미술가** an artist. **미술 감독** [영] an art director. **미술관** an art museum; an art gallery. ¶국립 현대 ~ the National Museum of Modern Art. **미술 교육** art education. **미술 대학** a college of fine arts. **미술 전람회** an art exhibition [show]. **미술품** a work of art; an art object [piece / work]; an object of art; an objet d'art (pl. objets d'art). **미술 ~수집** ~ an art collection. **미술 학교** an art school [academy]; a school of fine arts.

미숫가루 *misutgaru*; powder of roast grain [rice / barley].

미스¹ [미혼 여성의 성 앞에 붙이는 호칭] Miss; [미혼의 여성] an unmarried girl [woman]. ¶~ 코리아 Miss Korea // 유니버스로 뽑히다 be elected Miss Universe / win the Miss Universe title // 그녀는 아직 ~다 She is still unmarried. / She still remains single.

미스² a mistake. ¶식자 ~ a printer's error / a misprint.

미스터 Mister(약어 Mr. (*pl.* Messrs.)).

미스터리 1 [이상한 일] (a) mystery. ¶그것은 여전히 ~이다 It's still a mystery. **2** a detective story. ⇨추리 소설(⇨추리(推理))

미스프린트 a misprint. ¶이 팜플렛은 ~투성이다 [~가 없다] This pamphlet is full of [is free from] misprints.

미시 경제학(微視經濟學) [경] microeconomics.

미시적(微視的) microscopic. ¶~인 관찰 microscopic observation.

미시즈 [기혼 여성의 성 앞에 붙이는 호칭] Mrs.; (영) Mrs (*pl.* Mrs., Mesdames); [기혼 부인] a married woman. ¶~ 스미스 Mrs. Smith // ~ 스미스와 ~ 블랙 Mrs. [Mesdames] Smith and Black.

미식(美式) (in) an American way [manner]; (in) the American fashion; Americanism. ¶~의 American-style.

● **미식 영어** American English. **미식축구** American football.

미식(美食) dainty [delicious] food; a lavish [rich] diet. **미식하다** live on dainty food; eat good [fancy] food; live well [high / highly]; be an epicure.

● **미식가** an epicure; a gourmet; a gourmand; a gastronome(r); a good [high] liver; (프) a bon vivant (*pl.* bons vivants).

미신(迷信) (a) superstition; a superstitious belief. ¶허황된 ~ an absurd [a vain] superstition / an old wives' tale // ~적인 superstitious // ~을 타파하다 break down [do away with] superstitions // ~을 믿습니까 Are you superstitious? // 사다리 아래를 지나가면 재수가 없다는 ~이 있다 There is a superstition that walking under a ladder brings bad luck. // ~을 너무 믿지 마라 Don't be so superstitious.

● **미신가** a superstitious person.

미심스럽다(未審-) doubtful; suspicious. ⇨미심쩍다

미심쩍다(未審-) [의심스럽다] doubtful; open to doubt; dubious; [수상하다] suspicious; questionable. ¶미심쩍은 점 a doubtful [suspicious] point // 미심쩍은 데가 있다 have one's doubts // 미심쩍은 생각을 없애다 dispel (a person's) doubts / explain doubtful points // 미심쩍은 데가 있습니까 Is there any doubt about it? // 좀 미심쩍은 데가 있는데요 I have a question to ask.

미싱 a sewing machine. ⇨재봉틀

미아(迷兒) a stray [lost / missing] child. ¶~가 되다 be lost / [길을 잃다] lose one's way // ~를 찾다 search for a missing child // ~를 안내 말씀 드리겠습니다 We have a child here looking for his [her] parents. // 한 아이가 ~가 되었다 A child is missing.

● **미아보호소** a home for missing children.

미안(美顔) a beautiful [handsome / fair] face; pretty features; good looks.

● **미안수** a beauty wash [lotion]. **미안술** facial care; beauty treatments (for the face); facial culture.

미안쩍다(未安-) sorry; regretful; ashamed. ¶그의 초대에 응하지 못하여 몹시 ~ I am awfully sorry that I couldn't accept his invitation.

미안하다(未安-) regrettable; sorry. ¶미안하지만 (…해 주시겠습니까) I'm sorry to trouble you, but ... / may I trouble you to (do) / do you mind (doing) // 미안합니다 I'm sorry. / Excuse me. / I beg your pardon. (▶ I'm sorry는 대개의 경우 쓸 수 있음. Excuse me나 I beg your pardon은 중대한 실수에 대해서는 사용하지 않고, 우연한, 가벼운 일에 대해서만 사용함) // 당신께 많은 폐를 끼쳐 미안합니다 I am sorry to have put you to so much trouble. // 그 초대를 수락하지 못해 미안한 생각이 든다 I feel bad about not being able to accept the invitation. // 미안합니다. 물건이 다 팔리고 없습니다 I'm sorry. It's out of stock. // 그런 일을 해서 정말 미안합니다 I'm awfully sorry for having done such a thing. // 미안해, 그렇지만 오늘은 바빠서 너를 만나지 못해 I'm sorry, but I'm too busy to see you today. // 미안하지만 물 한 컵만 주시오 Give me a glass of water, please. // 미안해서 그 돈을 받을 수가 없다 I can't, in conscience, accept the money.

미약하다(微弱-) feeble; weak; faint. ¶미약한 반응을 나타내다 make a faint [feeble] response / react slightly // 미약하지만 도움이 되실 것으로 생각합니다 I trust that I can be of some slight help to you.

미어(美語) American (English).

미어뜨리다 tear a hole in (paper / leather); rend; rip.

미어지다 be [get] torn; tear; rip (open); be rent; rend; wear [be worn] out. ¶가슴이 미어질 듯한 heart-rending (sorrow) / heart-breaking (sorrow) // 그의 부음에 접하여 나는 슬픔으로 가슴이 미어졌다 I was crushed with grief at his death.

미역¹ [물로 몸을 씻기] bathing; a bath; [수영] a swim; a dip; (영) a bathe. ¶내에서 ~을 감다 swim in a river / have a dip [(영) bathe] in a river // 우리는 내에 ~ 감으러 갔다 We went bathing in the river.

미역² [식] a brown seaweed. ¶~을 따다 gather brown seaweeds.

미역국 *miyeokguk*; brown-seaweed soup.

미역국(을) 먹다 [시험에 떨어지다] fail (in) [flunk] an examination; [해고당하다] be [get] dismissed [discharged; (미국 구어) fired]; (미국 구어) be sacked; (영국 구어) get [be given] the sack.

미연에(未然-) before (it) happens; beforehand; previously. ¶~ 방지하다 prevent (a war) / obviate (a disaster) / prevent [keep] (it) from occurring / nip (a plot) in the bud / check (it) in the egg // 사고를 ~ 방지하다 prevent an accident from happening / take precautions against possible accidents.

미열(微熱) a slight [low] fever [temperature]; febricula(원인 불명의). ¶~이 있는 것 같군 You look a little feverish. // 나는 저녁때가 되면 ~이 난다 I develop [get] a slight fever in the evenings.

미온(微溫) tepidity; lukewarmness.

●미온수 tepid[lukewarm] water.
미온적(微溫的) 〔철저하지 않은〕 lukewarm; tepid; 〔좋지도 나쁘지도 않은〕 indifferent; half-hearted. ¶지금까지 너무 ~인 정책을 펴 왔다 Up to this point, the measures we have taken have been too lukewarm.∥그렇게 ~인 단속으로는 범죄를 예방할 수가 없다 Such lax controls[indifferent restraints] cannot prevent crime.

미완(未完) incompletion. ⇨°미완성 ¶~의 incomplete / unfinished∥~의 소설 an unfinished novel∥~의 일 halffinished work.

미완성(未完成) incompletion. ¶~의 〔미완료의〕 unfinished / 〔불완전한〕 incomplete∥~의 작품 an unfinished work (of art) / a torso (pl. ~s, -si) (미술·음악의)∥저 건물은 ~이다 The building is not yet finished.
●미완성 교향곡 the Unfinished Symphony.

미용(美容) beauty culture. ¶~과 건강을 위해 조깅을 한다 I jog for the sake of my health and figure.
●미용사 a hairdresser; a hairstylist; a beautician(▶ beautician은 머리뿐 아니라 피부 관리 등도 전문으로 하는 사람임). 미용술 cosmetology; beauty art[culture]. 미용식(-食) a food for beauty. 미용원 a beauty salon. ⇨°미장원(⇨미장(美粧)) 미용 체조 calisthenics; aesthetic gymnastics.

미우(眉宇) the brow(s).

미욱하다 〔어리석고 미련하다〕 stupid (as an owl); dull; weak-headed; thickheaded; soft-[dull-]witted; half-[dim-]witted; imbecile. ¶미욱한 사람 a stupid person / a fool / an ass / a simpleton∥미욱한 짓을 하다 do a stupid thing / make a fool of oneself / bungle∥그녀가 그런 짓을 하다니 정말 미욱했다 It was very stupid[silly] of her to do such a thing.

미움 hatred; hate; enmity; animosity; rancor; bad[ill] blood; 〔밉살스러움〕 hatefulness; 〔불쾌〕 displeasure; disfavor; disgrace. ¶~받는 사람 an object of hatred / a hated person∥~을 받다 be hated[detested / disliked] (by)∥~을 사다 incur (a person's) enmity / become an object of loathing∥그녀는 어디를 가나 - 을 받는다 She is an unwelcome guest everywhere.∥저 사람한테서 ~을 살 만한 짓을 한 적이 없다 I don't remember having done anything to incur his hatred.

미워하다 hate; detest; abhor; abominate; have a hatred (for); have a spite (at / against); ¶서로 ~ hate each other / be hateful to one another∥…를 미워하는 나머지[…을 미워하여] to spite (a person) / out of hatred (for) / in hatred of (a person)∥아직도 그를 미워하고 있느냐 Do you still hate [feel a hatred for] him?∥죄는 미워하되 사람은 미워하지 마라 You must hate the offense [sin], not the offender[inner].

미음(米飮) thin rice gruel; water gruel; rice water. ¶~을 쑤다 prepare thin rice gruel.

미의식(美意識) a sense of beauty; (an) aesthetic sense.

미이다 get torn; be tattered; be worn out; split; burst.

미이라 →미라

미익(尾翼) 〔비행기의 꼬리 날개〕 the tail assembly. ¶수직 ~ a vertical tail (plane)∥수평 ~ a horizontal tail plane.

미인¹(美人) 〔용모가 아름다운 여자〕 a beauty; a belle; a beautiful[lovely] woman[lady]; a pretty girl; 〔구어〕 a lovely; 〔미국 속어〕 a good-looker; a peach; 〔미국 속어〕 a pin-up (girl); 〔구어〕 a bombshell. ¶당대의 으뜸가는 ~ the reigning beauty∥굉장한 ~ a stunning beauty / 〔미국 구어〕 a god's gift to men / 〔미국 속어〕 a knockout / a cute little number∥절세의 ~ a woman of unsurpassed beauty∥서울 ~ a Seoul belle.
●미인계 (미) a badger game. ¶~를 쓰다 pull a badger game(▶ 영국에는 이에 해당하는 말이 없음). 미인 대회 a beauty contest. 미인박명 Beauty and good fortune seldom go hand in hand.

미인²(美人) an American. ⇨°미국인(⇨미국)

미작(米作) 〔벼농사〕 rice cultivation[growing]; 〔벼 수확〕 a rice crop[harvest]. ¶금년의 ~은 순조로울 전망이다 A good rice crop is expected this year. / The prospects for this year's rice crop are favorable.
●미작 지대 a rice-producing district.

미장(美匠) (도안 등의) a decorative[an artistic] design.

미장(美粧) beauty treatment; beauty art [culture]; (미) cosmetology.
●미장원 a beauty parlor[shop]; a beauty salon[studio]; (미) a beauty parlor[shop].

미장이 a plasterer.

미적(美的) aesthetic(al). ¶~으로 aesthetically∥그것은 ~ 견지에서 말해서 아무런 가치도 없다 From an aesthetic point of view, it has no value.
●미적 가치 aesthetic value. 미적 감각 (an) aesthetic sense; a sense of beauty.

미적거리다 1 〔조금씩 앞으로 내밀다〕 push [shove] forward inch by inch[by inches]. 2 〔자꾸 미루다〕 prolong; protract; delay; draw [drag/spin] out. ¶미적거리다가 기회를 놓치다 dally away one's opportunity∥일을 ~ delay one's work.

미적분(微積分) 〔수〕 differential and integral.
●미적분학 〔수〕 differential and integral calculus.

미적지근하다 1 〔미지근하다〕 tepid; lukewarm. ¶미적지근한 물 tepid[lukewarm] water. 미적지근히 tepidly; lukewarmly. 2 〔비유〕 indecisive; vague; dubious; lukewarm; irresolute; undetermined; shilly-shally. ¶미적지근한 대답 a dubious[vague] reply / a noncommittal reply∥미적지근한 방법 weak [easy-going] measures∥미적지근한 태도를 취하다 assume a lukewarm[an indecisive / an undecided] attitude (toward). 미적지근히 irresolutely; indecisively; reluctantly.

미전(美展) an art exhibition. ⇨°미술 전람회(⇨미술)

미점(美點) a merit; a virtue; a beauty (of something); a charm; a good point. ¶그의 ~은 인정이 많다는 데 있다 He has the virtue of being warmhearted.

미정(未定) suspense; pendency. ¶~의 undecided / unfixed / unsettled / pending / uncertain(확실치 않은)∥~제목 ~ subject [title] undecided∥~이다 remain unsettled [undecided] / be in abeyance∥그들의 결혼식 날짜는 ~이다 The date of their wedding has not yet been fixed[decided]. ∥연제(演題) ~ (게시) Subject undecided.∥출범일은 ~이다 The date of sailing is not yet fixed.

미제(未濟) ¶~의 unfinished / outstanding / unsettled / to be settled / pending / unpaid.

미제(美製) ¶~의 American[U.S.]-made / of American make / made in U.S.A.
• 미제 상품 American-made goods; articles [goods] made in U.S.A.

미조(美爪) manicure.
• 미조사(-師) a manicurist. 미조술 a manicure(손의); a pedicure(발의).

미조직(未組織) ~의 unorganized.

미주(美洲) the continent(s) of America.

미주 신경(迷走神經) [생] a vagus[pneumogastric] nerve; a vagus (pl. -gi); a pneumogastric.

미주알고주알 inquisitively; overcuriously. ¶~ 캐는 inquisitive / overcurious / prying / curious / nos(e)y // ~ 캐묻다 ask persistently / keep asking questions // 그렇게 ~ 캐묻지 마라 Don't be so inquisitive. // 나는 그녀의 계획을 сraw하서 ~ 캐어물었다 I catechized her (to the last detail) about her plan.

미즈 [기혼·미혼 불문의 여자의 성 앞에 붙이는 경칭] Ms. ¶~ 송 Ms. Song.

미증유(未曾有) ¶~의 unprecedented / without precedent / unexampled / unheard-of / record-breaking // ~의 대풍작 a record crop // ~의 대지진 the greatest earthquake on [upon / in] record / the most disastrous earthquake that has ever been experienced // ~의 사건 an unprecedented[unheard-of] event // 이것은 이 나라 역사상 ~의 사건이다 This is absolutely unexampled in the history of this country.

미지(未知) ¶~의 unknown / strange / unacquainted (with) // ~의 땅 a strange land // ~의 사람 a stranger // ~의 세계 the unknown world // ~의 세계를 탐험하다 explore the unknown world // ~의 세계로 들어가다 venture into the unknown.
• 미지수 [수] an unknown quantity; the unknown. ¶승패는 전혀 ~이다 The match is a very open one. // 문단에서 그녀는 아직 ~다 She is still an unknown quantity in the literary world.

미지근하다 1 [온도가 낮다] tepid; lukewarm; not warm enough. ¶미지근한 물 tepid [lukewarm] water // 미지근한 방 a room not warm enough // 미지근하게 tepidly / lukewarmly // 목욕물이 ~ The bath is not warm enough. // 이 차는 미지근해서 못 마시겠다 The tea is too tepid to drink. 2 [철저하지 못하다] slack; lax; mild; lenient; not strict[severe] enough. ¶미지근한 조치 a halfway measure // 미지근한 대책 halfhearted[lukewarm] measures // 미지근한 태도를 취하다 adopt a lukewarm attitude (toward) / show little enthusiasm // 학생들을 너무 미지근하게 다루다 be too easy[lax] with one's students.

미진(微塵) an atom; a modicum; a particle; a bit; a mite; an insignificant thing.

미진(微震) a slight shock (of an earthquake); a faint earth tremor; microseism(지각의). ¶어젯밤에 ~이 있었다 There was a weak earth tremor last night.

미진하다(未盡-) [끝내지 못하다] unexhausted; incomplete; unfinished; [흡족하지 못하다] unsatisfied. ¶마음에 미진한 데가 있다 have an unsatisfied feeling / miss something // 그녀의 설명만으로는 ~ Her explanation does not give us entire satisfaction.

미착(未着) unarrival; nonarrival. ¶~의 not yet arrived / [미배달의] not yet delivered / undelivered // 그 물품은 ~이다 The article has not yet arrived. / [미배달되었다] The article has not yet been delivered.

미착수(未着手) ¶~의 not yet started.
• 미착수 공사 construction work not yet started.

미처 yet; before; as yet; up to now; so far; hitherto; to this day. ¶~ 손 쓰기 전에 (die) before we[a doctor] come to (one's) aid // ~ 상상도 못할 beyond the stretch of imagination // 거기까지는 그가 ~ 생각 못 했다 He was not far-sighted enough to think of that. // 나는 그걸 ~ 몰랐다 I didn't know that before. // 바빠서 ~ 모임의 준비를 하지 못했다 I was too busy to arrange things for the meeting in advance. // 그는 ~ 피하지 못해 타 죽었다 He failed to escape and was burnt to death. // 온 지 ~ 한 시간도 못 되어 그는 집에 돌아가고 싶어 졌다 He had hardly been there an hour before he wanted to return home.

미처분(未處分) ¶~의 unfinished / undisposed (articles).

미천하다(微賤-) lowly; humble; ignoble; obscure; of humble origin. ¶미천한 몸[신분] a man of obscure birth / a person in humble station // 미천하게 태어나다 be base born / be of humble origin // 미천한 신분에서 입신하다 rise from obscurity / rise from the gutter [ranks] // 그는 미천한 몸으로 입신양명했다 He rose from obscurity to fame.

미추(尾椎) [생] the coccyx (pl. ~es, -cyges); the tailbone.

미추(美醜) beauty or ugliness; personal appearance(용모).

미추룸하다 [한창때 건강미가 있다] healthy and handsome; healthy and fair; [서술적] shine with health; have the glow of health.

미취학(未就學) [관형어적] not (yet) attending school; preschool.
• 미취학 아동 a preschool child; child not attending school; a preschooler.

미치광이 1 [광인] a madman; a madwoman (여자); a lunatic; an insane[a crazy] person; a crackbrain. ¶반~의 half-mad. // ~ 짓 (an act of) madness / an insanity // ~같이 like mad / madly / frantically // ~ 짓을 하다 behave like a madman / act crazy[frantic] // ~가 되다 become mad[insane] / go mad [insane] / lose one's reason[senses] / madden // ~가 아닌 이상 그런 짓은 하지 않을 것이다 No one in his right mind would do such a thing. 2 [열광자] a maniac; (미) a fan; a fanatic; a buff. ¶춤 ~ a dance maniac // 그는 영화 ~다 He is crazy about the movies.

미치다¹ 1 [정신 이상이 되다] go mad[out of one's mind]; become[go] insane[crazy]; lose one's head[wits / mind]; (속어) go crackers[nuts]. ¶미친 mad / crazy / insane / crackbrained / (구어) cracked // 미친 듯이 frantically / frenziedly / (구어) like mad [crazy] / madly // 미친개 a mad[rabid] dog // 미친 사람 같은 행동 mad[crazy] conduct // 사랑에 미쳐서 madly[wildly] in love (with) // …하고 싶어서 ~ be unable to contain oneself / be dying (to do / for) // 미친 듯이 물을 찾다 be mad for water // 미치게 하다 drive [send] (a person) mad[crazy] / unhinge (a

person's) mind[brain]. // 미쳐 날뛰다 run amuck / rush about wildly / rush about in a frenzy // 질투로[화가 나서] 미칠 것 같다 be mad with jealousy[rage] // 도시의 미칠 듯한 소음에서 벗어나다 escape from the maddening noise of the city // 네가 신열이 있는데도 나가는 것은 미친 짓이다 It's madness to go out in the snow when you have a fever. // 그는 미친 듯이 자기 머리털을 쥐어뜯었다 He tore at his hair in a frenzy. // 그녀는 미칠 듯이 그 사내에게 홀딱 빠져 있었다 She loved the man to distraction. // 자기 자식을 잃은 그 어머니는 미쳐 죽었다 The mother who had lost her child died mad [crazed] with grief. // 어머니의 갑작스런 죽음이 그를 미치게 했다 His mother's sudden death drove him mad. / He became insane when his mother died suddenly. // 그 소식을 듣고 그녀는 미친 듯이 좋아했다 At the news she was mad[she was beside herself] with joy. // 그녀는 실연하여 미쳤다 Losing his love drove her mad. // 그는 분해서 미칠 것만 같았다 He nearly went mad[He was beside himself] with mortification. // 그녀는 미친 듯이 소리를 질렀다 She yelled and screamed frantically[(구어) like mad]. // 젊은이들은 밤새도록 미친 듯이 춤추었다 They young people danced like mad[like crazy / in a frenzy] all night long. // 그녀의 미모는 남자들을 미치게 했다 Her beauty nearly drove men mad. // 그는 미칠 듯이 그녀를 사랑하고 있었다 He was madly in love with her. / He was nearly out of his mind with love for her.
2 [열중하다] be absorbed[engrossed] (in); be devoted (to); be given up (to); [열광하다] be crazy (about); be a fanatic. ¶그는 여자에게 미쳐 있다 He is infatuated with[He has lost his head over] a woman. // 그는 장기[경마]에 미쳐 있다 He is crazy about *janggi* [horse racing]. // 그는 추리 소설에 미쳐 있다 He can't keep away from detective stories. / (구어) He's a detective story buff.

미치다² 1 [이르다] reach; attain to; amount to; come to; come up to (the standard); [걸치다] extend (to / over); stretch; range over (the whole country, wide subjects, etc.). ¶손이 미치는 곳에 within one's reach // (화제가) 어떤 사건에 ~ turn on some subject // (설명 등이) 상세한 점에 ~ go[enter] into details (particulars) // (품질 등이) 표준에 ~ come up to standard // 미치지 못하다 be unattainable / do not amount (to) / do not reach / fall short (of) // 기대에 미치지 못하다 do not come up to one's expectations // 생각이 ~ 할 만큼 clever[alert / farsighted] enough to think of // 이런 외딴 시골에도 시대의 물결이 미친다 The current of the times reaches even a remote country place like this. // 그 영향은 전국에 미쳤다 The effect extended over the whole country. // 나는 힘이 미치는 한 엄격한 훈련을 견디었다 I endured the hard training as best I could. // 완력에 있어서는 그에게 미칠 자가 없다 He has no equal[No one can match him] in physical strength. // 부모의 눈길이 아이에 가까이 미치지 못한다 His parents can't keep close eye on the child. // 태풍은 논밭에 막대한 피해를 미쳤다 The typhoon did great damage to the fields. // 그것은 그들에게 좋은[나쁜] 영향을 미쳤다 It exerted[exercised] a favorable[bad] influence upon them. // 담배는 건강에 나쁜 영향을 미친다 Cigarette smoking is dangerous [hazardous] to one's health.
2 [닥치다] visit; befall (a person); happen to (a person). ¶그에게 재난이 미쳤다 A misfortune befell him. / An accident happened to him.
3 [필적하다] match; equal; be a match for; rival (another) in; come up with; (힘이) lie in one's power[ability]. ¶힘이 미치는 한 as much as lies in one's power / to the best of one's power // 힘이 미치지 못하다 (일이) be beyond one's power[ability / capacities] / (사람이) be unequal (to the task) / be incompetent (to do / for doing) // …에 못 ~ be inferior to / be no match[equal] for / be [fall] behind // 훨씬 못 ~ be far behind (another) / fall (by) far short of (another) // 나 따위는 그에게 도저히 미치지 못한다 I don't even come close to him. / I couldn't possibly be compared with him[compete with him]. / (구어) I'm nowhere near as good as him. / I'm not in the same class with[(영) as] him. // 나는 빈틈없는 점에 있어서는 그에게 도저히 미치지 못한다 I am no match for him in shrewdness. // 아무도 그의 역량에 미치지 못한다 No one can even remotely rival him. / Nobody can in any equal him.

미칭(美稱) [아름답게 일컫는 말] a euphemism.

미크론 [전] a micron (*pl.* ~s, -cra) (기호 μ). ¶밀리 ~ a millimicron(기호 mμ).

미터 a meter[(영) a metre]. ¶100~ 경주 the hundred-meter dash.
● **미터기**(-器) a meter; (택시의) a taximeter; gauge. ¶~에 나온 숫자 the meter reading // ~를 속이다 tamper with a meter // ~를 검사하다 (고장의 유무를) examine a meter / (사용량을) inspect[read] a meter // 가스[전기 / 수도]의 ~를 알아보다 read a gas [an electric / a water] meter // (택시의) ~를 바로 세우다[꺾다] put up the flag[turn the flag down] (on the taximeter). **미터법** the metric system.

미토콘드리아 [생] mitochondria.

미투리 hemp-cord sandals.

미트 [야구] a mitt. ¶캐처[퍼스트] ~ a catcher's[first baseman's] mitt.

미팅 1 [회합·회의] a meeting. 2 [모르는 남녀 간의 만남] a blind date.

미풍(美風) a laudable[beautiful / fine / good] custom.
● **미풍양속**(-良俗) established social morals and good manners[customs]. ¶한국에서는 윗사람의 의견을 따르는 것이 ~으로 되어 있다 In Korea it is considered proper to go along with the ideas of one's superiors. // 그것은 전통적 ~에 해를 끼칠 우려가 있다 It is feared that it will have a harmful effect upon our long-established and fine custom.

미풍(微風) a breeze; a gentle [light / soft] wind; a breath of air; (시어) (a) zephyr. ¶상쾌한 ~ a lively[refreshing] breeze // ~이 불고 있다 The wind blows gently.

미필(未畢) [아직 끝내지 못함] incompletion. ¶~ 원고 an unfinished manuscript // 심의 의안 a pending bill / ~의 unfinished / unfulfilled / incomplete / unexecuted // 병역 ~자 a person who has not yet completed his military duty. **미필하다** have not finished

미필적 고의 [fulfilled].

미필적 고의(未必的故意) [법] willful [advertent / conscious] negligence; (라) dolus eventualis.

미학(美學) aesthetics. ¶~적 aesthetic // ~견지에서 말하면, 그 그림은 삼류이다 From an aesthetic point of view, it is a third-rate painting.

미합중국(美合衆國) the United States (of America). ⇨ 미국

미해결(未解決) ¶~의 unsolved / unresolved / unsettled / pending / outstanding // ~의 문제 an unsolved problem / an unsettled [a pending] question // ~인 채로 두다 leave (a matter) unsettled [outstanding] / leave (an issue) open // 그 살인 사건은 ~인 채로 있다 The murder case [was still] unsolved. // 쟁의는 ~인 채로 있다 The trouble has been unsettled.

미행(美行) a laudable [good] conduct; a good deed.

미행(微行) incognito traveling. ¶~의 왕자 a prince incognito // ~으로 방문하다 pay an incognito visit (to). 미행하다 travel incognito; pay a private visit (to); visit (a place) incognito.

미행자(尾行者) a tail; a shadow. ¶나는 ~를 에써 따돌릴 수 있었다 I managed to shake off the tail.

미행하다(尾行-) follow (up); shadow; trail; (after) (a person); dog (a person's step). ¶미행하는 형사를 따돌리다 ditch a shadow / give a shadowing detective the slip // 우리는 사람을 시켜 그를 미행하도록 했다 We decided to put a shadow [a tail] on him. → 그는 형사에게 미행당했다 He was tailed [shadowed] by a detective. // 나는 끈질기게 미행당했다 I was shadowed [tailed] tenaciously. // 그는 최근 사립 탐정에게 미행당하고 있다 He is being followed around [(구어) tailed / (영) followed about] by a private detective these days.

미혹(迷惑) 〔홀림〕 (a) delusion; (an) infatuation; 〔갈팡질팡함〕 perplexity; bewilderment. 미혹하다 〔홀리다〕 be deluded; be infatuated; be bewitched; be captivated; 〔갈팡질팡하다〕 be perplexed; be bewildered; be at a loss. ¶낭설을 퍼뜨려 인심을 ~ seduce the public by spreading false rumors. → ¶여자에게 미혹되다 be infatuated by a woman // 헛소문에 미혹되다 be carried away by rumors.

미혼(未婚) ¶~의 single / unmarried // 그녀는 아직 ~입니다 She is still single.
● 미혼모 an unmarried [unwed] mother. 미혼자 an unmarried person.

미화(美化) beautification; idealization(이상화). 미화하다 beautify (a city); make (the look of the town) beautiful; landscape (경으로); idealize (death) (이상화하다). ¶젊은이는 죽음을 미화하는 경향이 있다 Young people are apt to romanticize death.
● 미화 운동 a beautification [clean-up] drive [campaign]. ¶도시 〔국토〕 ~ a city [land] beautification movement.

미화(美貨) American currency [money]; the U.S. dollar. ¶~로 in American currency [money] // 1달러당 1,200원 1,200 won per a U.S. dollar // ~로 지불하다 pay in U.S. dollars.

미확인(未確認) ¶~의 not yet confirmed / unconfirmed.
● 미확인 보도 news from an unconfirmed source. 미확인 비행 물체 an unidentified flying object(약어 UFO).

미확정(未確定) ¶~의 not yet decided / unsettled / pending.

미흡하다(未洽-) (사람이) unsatisfied (with); dissatisfied (with); (사물이) insufficient; unsatisfactory; unsatisfying; inadequate. ¶미흡한 점 one's faults / one's shortcomings [failings] // 미흡한 점이 많다 [없다] leave much [nothing] to be desired // 미흡한 감이 들다 feel not quite satisfied / feel something wanting / miss something // 그의 설명으로는 ~ His explanation does not give us entire satisfaction. // 혹 미흡한 점이 있으면 말해 주십시오 Please remind us if there is anything amiss on our part. // 미흡하나마 도와 드리겠습니다 I will do what (little) I can to help you. / In my small way I will do what I can to help you. // 미흡하나마 열심히 하겠습니다 I'll do the work to the best of my ability.

미희(美姬) a beautiful maiden [girl]; a beauty.

믹서 1 〔과일 가는 기계〕 a blender; (영) a liquidizer. 2 〔음성 조정 장치〕 a mixer.

-민(民) 〔인민〕 the people; 〔국민〕 a nation; a people; 〔민족〕 a race. ¶자유~ children [sons] of liberty // 유목~ a nomadic race // 이재~ the sufferers (from) / the afflicted people / the victims (of).

민가(民家) a private house; a commoner's house.

민간(民間) ¶~의 (공(公)에 대하여) private / nonofficial / nongovernmental / (군에 대하여) civilian / civil / nonmilitary // ~에서 among the people / in nongovernmental circles // ~에서 선출된 대표 delegates chosen from among ordinary [private] citizens / nongovernment delegates // ~에 맡기다 leave (it) to private hands // 그 미신이 ~에 만연되고 있다 That superstition is widespread among the people. // 그것은 오랫동안 ~에 전해 내려오는 치료법이다 That is a care which has long been handed down among the common people.
● 민간 방송 a commercial [sponsored] broadcast. 민간 신앙 a popular [folk] belief. 민간 외교 nongovernmental [people-to-people] diplomacy. 민간요법 folk remedies. 민간인 a non-official civilian; a nongovernment person. 민간 항공 civil aviation.

민감성(敏感性) susceptibility; sensitiveness; sensibility. ¶이상 ~ 〔의〕 allergy // 이상 ~에 allergic.

민감하다(敏感-) sensitive; susceptible; susceptive. ¶지나치게 민감한 oversensitive / oversubtle // 극도로 민감한 hypersensitive / supersensitive // 열에 민감한 sensitive to heat // 민감한 사람 a sensitive person // 허약하고 민감한 아이 a delicate and sensitive child // 나는 더위와 추위에 ~ I am sensitive to heat and cold. // 그는 색에 ~ He has a keen sensibility to color. // 그들은 유행에 ~ They are susceptible to changes in fashion. // 정치가는 여론에 ~ A politician is easily swayed [influenced] by public opinion. // 나의 어린이 양육론은 민감한 어머니들에게 큰 반향을 불러일으켰다 My essay on how to bring up children created a great sensation among impressionable mothers.//이 기구는 진동에 아주 ~ This instrument is very sensitive to vibrations. **민감히** sensitively; susceptibly. ¶어린이는 어머니의 애정을 ~ 느낀다 A child is very sensitive to its mother's love.//그의 만화는 세태를 ~ 그려 냈다 His cartoons are an acute reflection of the state of the world.

민국(民國) a republic; a democratic country [nation]; a democracy. ¶대한~ the Republic of Korea(약어 ROK)//중화~ the Republic of China.

민권(民權) civil rights; the people's rights. ¶~을 유린하다 trample on the people's rights //~을 옹호[신장/주장]하다 defend[extend/assert] the people's rights.
● 민권 (수호) 운동 a civil right movement; a movement for the protection[defense] of civil right. 민권 운동가 (미국 구어) a civil righter.

민꽃식물(-植物) a cryptogam; a flowerless plant. ⇨ 은화식물

민날 the bare blade of a dagger[sword]; a naked dagger[sword].

민낯 a woman's unpainted face; a face with no make up on it; a naked face.

민단(民團) a settlement corporation. ⇨ 거류민단(⇨ 거류)

민도(民度) [문화의 정도] the cultural[moral] level of the people; [생활의 정도] the standard of living of the people. ¶~가 매우 높다[낮다] The people's standard of living is very high[low].//형편없는 후진국으로서 그 ~는 말이 아니다 It is a fearfully backward country and the low state of its people surpasses description.

민둥민둥하다 bald; bare; deforested; treeless (hill). ¶민둥민둥한 산 a bare[bald] mountain.

민둥산(-山) a bald[bare] mountain.

민들레 [식] a dandelion. ¶~의 깃털 the pappus (pl. -pi) of a dandelion / the (fluffy) tuft of a dandelion.

민란(民亂) a riot[revolt] of the people; an uprising[insurrection] of the people. ¶~을 일으키다 raise[start / get up] a riot[an insurrection] / rise in revolt[rebellion] //~을 진압하다 suppress an insurrection of the people //~이 일어났다 A riot broke out. / A revolt started[occurred].

민망(民望) [백성의 희망] public desire; popular expectation; [백성의 신망] public confidence[trust]; popular favor. ¶~을 얻다 enjoy public confidence.

민망하다(憫惘) 1 [측은하다] pitiable; pitiful; piteous; miserable; sad; sorry. ¶민망한 생각이 들다 feel pity[compassion / for / toward]. **민망히** pitiably; pitifully; piteously; miserably; sorrily. 2 [열없다] awkward. ¶나는 가진 돈이 적어 민망했다 I felt awkward to find myself short of cash.//거 참 민망하군요 That's very embarrassing.//방 안에 혼자 남게 되었을 때 내가 얼마나 민망했을까 상상해 보시오 Imagine my embarrassment upon being left alone in the room. **민망히** awkwardly.

민머리 1 [벼슬 없는 사람] a person holding no office. 2 [대머리] a bald head; (속어) a cue-ball head. 3 [쪽 안 진 머리] undone hair.

민며느리 a young girl taken into one's family as a future daughter-in-law.

민무늬근(-筋) [생] a smooth muscle; an unstriated muscle.

민물 fresh water.
● 민물고기 a freshwater fish. 민물낚시 freshwater fishing.

민박(民泊) a home-stay. **민박하다** lodge at a private house.

민방위(民防衛) civil defense[(영) defence]; civilian defense.
● 민방위대 the Civil Defense Corps. 민~ 본부 the Civil Defense Corps Headquarters. 민방위 훈련(의 날) (the day designated for) Civil Defense training.

민법(民法) 《집합적》 civil law; (협의의) the Civil Law Act; the Civil Code(법전).

민병(民兵) a militiaman(남자); a militiawoman(여자).
● 민병대 a militia corps.

민복(民福) national[public] welfare; the well-being[welfare] of the people. ¶~을 도모하다 promote the public welfare.

민본주의(民本主義) democracy.

민사(民事) civil affairs[matters]; a civil case[action]. ¶~(상)의 civil.
● 민사 사건 a civil case. 민사 소송 a civil suit[action]. ¶~을 제기하다 bring a civil action[civil proceedings to bear] (against). 민사 재판 a civil trial.

민생(民生) the livelihood of the people [nation]; public welfare. ¶~의 안정 the stabilization of the people's livelihood.
● 민생고 the people's economic plight[difficulties].

민선(民選) [관형어적] elected by popular vote; popularly elected.
● 민선 의원 an Assemblyman elected by the people[by popular vote].

민성(民聲) the voice of the people; people's voice; public opinion. ¶~에 따르다 obey the dictates of public opinion / act in accordance with public opinion.

민속(民俗) folk[ethnic] customs; folkways. ¶국립 ~ 무용단 the National Folk Ballet Troupe.
● 민속 공예 folkcraft; folk handicraft; folk [native] art. 민속극 a folk drama[play]. 민속 무용 a folk dance. 민속 박물관 a folklore museum. 민속음악 folk music. 민속 음악 →민속악(⇨민속) 민속촌 the Folk Village. 민속학(-學) folklore.

민속하다(敏速-) quick; active; prompt; swift; agile. **민속히** quickly; promptly; swiftly; agilely. ¶~ 행동하다 be prompt in action / act promptly//사무를 ~ 처리하다 transact business with dispatch.

민수(民需) [민간에서 필요하여 얻고자 함] private[civilian] demands[requirements]. ¶정부는 국유지의 일부를 ~용으로 돌렸다 The authorities released some government [nationally-owned] land to meet private [civilian] demand.
● 민수 산업 civilian industry. 민수품 civilian goods; consumer's goods; goods for non-governmental use[consumption].

민수기(民數記) [성] (The Book of) Numbers(약어 Num., Numb.).

민숭민숭하다 hairless; treeless; sober. ⇨ 맨송맨송하다

민심(民心) popular feeling; public[popular] sentiment; the mind of the people. ¶~의 안정을 꾀하다 work to prevent popular unrest // ~을 동요시키다 disturb[arouse] the feelings of the people // ~을 잃다 lose popularity [the support of the people] // ~에 역행하다 go against public sentiment // ~을 선동하다 stir up[inflame] the popular passion // ~이 동요하고 있다 Restlessness prevails among the people. // 독직 사건의 속출로 ~은 정부로부터 멀어져갔다 The series of corruption cases cost the Government popular support.

민심은 천심(속담) The people's voice is the voice of God.

민약설(民約說) the theory of social contract. ⇨사회 계약설(⇨사회(社會))

민어(民魚) [동] a sciaenoid fish; a croaker.

민영(民營) private management[operation]. ¶~의 privately-managed[-operated] / private / nongovernment(al) // ~이다 be under private management / be run by private management // ~으로 하다 place under private management / commit (an enterprise) to private hands // ~으로 되다 fall into private hands / come under private management.

● **민영 사업** a private enterprise[undertaking / business]. **민영 아파트** a privately-built apartment house; an apartment house built by the private sector.

민예(民藝) folk handicraft; folk entertainment.

● **민예품** a folkcraft.

민완(敏腕) [관형어적] able; capable; competent; shrewd; sharp; (문어) astute.

● **민완가** an able man; a man of ability; a highly competent man. **민완 형사** a competent detective.

민요(民謠) a folk song; a popular ballad.

● **민요 가수** a folk singer.

민원(民怨) public resentment[grievance]; popular discontent.

민원(民願) a civil appeal[petition]; a civil application.

● **민원 공무원** a civil affairs official. **민원 사무** civil affairs administration. **민원 상담소** a civil affairs office. **민원 창구** a window for civil petitions.

민유(民有) private ownership; the people's possession. ¶~의 privately-owned / in private possession / private.

● **민유지** private land. **민유 철도** a privately-owned railway.

민의(民意) the will of the people; [여론] public opinion. ¶~의 표시 a manifestation of the popular will // ~를 존중[반영]하다 respect[reflect] the will of the people // ~를 묻다 seek[appeal to] the judgment of the people / consult the will of the people // ~를 무시하다 disregard the will of the people // 이 안은 ~를 반영한 것이다 This plan reflects the opinion of the people.

민의원(民議院) [하원] the Lower House; (미) the House of Representatives; (영) the House of Commons; (프) the Chamber of Deputies.

민정(民政) civil administration[government]; [민주 정치] democracy; democratic government. ¶~을 실시하다 establish a civil government // 점령지에 ~을 펴다 establish (a) civil government in an occupied territory / place an occupied region under civil administration // 나는 정부가 ~에 더 한층의 노력을 기울이기를 바란다 I wish the Government would work harder to promote public welfare.

민정(民情) 1 [백성의 사정·생활 형편] the condition of the people; the realities of the people's life. ¶~을 살피다 see how the people live / observe the conditions of the people // ~에 밝다 be familiar[be well acquainted] with the life of the lower classes // 국무총리는 ~을 시찰했다 The Prime Minister traveled about to observe how people lived. 2 popular feeling. ⇨민심

민족(民族) a race; a nation; a people; a nationality; an ethnic group. ¶다~ 국가 a multinational[multiracial] country // 소수~ a minority race // 유대 ~ the Jewish nation // 지배 ~ a master race // (나치가 제창한) the Herrenvolk // ~의 화합 national reconciliation // ~적(인) 편견 racial prejudice // ~의 동질성 national homogeneity // 앵글로·색슨 ~ the Anglo-Saxon race // 그들은 모두 독일 ~이다 They are all Germans by race.

● **민족 감정** a race feeling; a national sentiment (toward). **민족 국가** a nation-state. **민족 문화** national culture. **민족성** racial characteristics[traits]; the character of a people. **민족 운동** a national movement (for independence). **민족의식** national[racial] consciousness. **민족 자결주의** the principle of self-determination of peoples. **민족 자본** native capital; national capital. **민족정신** racial[national] spirit. **민족주의** [국민주의] nationalism; [인종주의] racialism. **민족학** ethnology; ethnography.

민주(民主) democracy. ¶반~ 세력 the anti-democratic forces (in a country).

● **민주 공화국** a democratic republic. **민주 국가** a democratic state; a democracy. **민주 정치** democratic form of government; democratic government. **민주 제도** the democratic system; democracy. ¶대의[절대] ~ representative[absolute] democracy. **민주주의** democracy; democratism; democratic principles. ¶의회[사회 / 인민 / 대중] ~ parliamentary[social / peoples / mass / national / guided] democracy // 직접[간접] ~ direct [indirect] democracy. **민주주의자** a democrat; a democratist; an advocate of democracy. **민주화** democratization.

민주적(民主的) democratic. ¶비~인 undemocratic // ~으로 democratically // 이 회사는 ~인 운영이 이루어지고 있다 This company is run democratically. // 여왕의 ~ 태도가 국민에게 친근감을 주었다 The Queen's democratic ways made her dear to her people.

민중(民衆) the people; the mass of people; the masses; the public; the populace; people in general; the multitude. ¶~적인 popular / democratic // 그의 생각은 일반 ~에게는 받아들여지지 않았다 His idea was not popularly accepted.

● **민중 예술** popular arts. **민중 오락** popular amusements. **민중 운동** a popular movement. **민중화** popularization. ¶~하다 popularize.

민지(民智) the intellect[intellectual level] of the people; the public intellect.

민짜 a plain thing. ⇨ˮ민패
민첩하다(敏捷-) quick; prompt; nimble; agile; smart; shrewd. ¶민첩한 남자 a shrewd man / (속어) a spanker ¶고양이는 ~ Cats are agile. ∥그는 행동이 ~ He is quick [nimble] in action. **민첩히** quickly; promptly; nimbly; with alacrity [agility / promptitude]. ¶그는 ~ 기회를 포착했다 He was alert in seizing [quick to seize] the opportunity.
민틋하다 even and slant; gently-sloping; smoothly-sloping. ¶민틋한 비탈 a gentle [an easy] slope.
민패 a plain [simple] thing; an artless [undecorated] article.
민폐(民弊) public harm [damage]; an abuse suffered by the public; a public nuisance(대중 상대의); a private nuisance(특정인 상대의); [금전의 갈취] extortionate practices by public officials; (공직자의 비행) a malpractice. ¶~를 끼치다 cause a nuisance to the people / cause inconvenience to the general public / make trouble for the people.
민하다 senseless; thoughtless; stupid; silly; foolish; slow- [dull-]witted; awkward.
민화(民話) a folktale; a folk story.
민화(民畵) (a piece of) folk painting.
민활하다(敏活-) quick; prompt; active; nimble; agile. ¶민활한 조치를 취하다 take prompt action. **민활히** quickly; promptly; briskly; with alacrity [dispatch]. ¶~ 행동하다 [기회를 잡다] be quick in action [to seize opportunities] ∥그는 정세 변화에 ~ 대응했다 He responded to the change in the situation with alacrity.
믿다 1 [의심치 않다] believe; put belief in; credit; give credit [credence] to; put credit in; accept (a thing) as true; be convinced of (a fact); be persuaded (of / that). ¶믿을 수 있는 credible / believable ∥믿을 수 없는 이야기 an unbelievable [incredible] story / a story that passes belief ∥내가 믿는 바로는 in my opinion / to the best of my belief / my belief is (that) ∥굳게 ~ firmly believe (that) / have a firm belief (that ...) ∥정말로 ~ take (a thing) for truth / accept (a remark) (as true [truth]) / believe (a statement) (to be true) ∥남의 말을 (그대로) ~ believe what a person says / take a person at his word ∥남의 말을 잘 ~ be credulous / be ready to believe anything one hears ∥남의 말을 잘 믿지 않다 be incredulous (of / about) / be skeptical (about) ∥나는 그가 말하는 것을 믿는다 I believe him [what he says]. ∥내가 믿기로는 그것은 정말이다 To the best of my belief, it's true. ∥그녀는 남의 말을 쉽게 믿어 버린다 She is very credulous. / She readily takes people at their word. ∥그 문제는 믿기 어려울 정도로 복잡하였다 The matter was complicated beyond all belief. ∥믿건 말건 난 여왕님을 만난 거야 Believe it or not, I met the Queen. ∥그 당시에는 지구가 평평하다고 사람들이 믿고 있었다 In those days it was believed that the earth was flat [the earth was believed to be flat]. ∥그의 말을 믿을 수 없다 I cannot believe him. / I can't give credit to his statement. ∥나는 도무지 믿어지지 않는다 I'm rather inclined to doubt it. ∥그가 죽었다고는 도저히 믿을 수 없다 I cannot persuade [convince] myself that he is dead [of his death]. ∥그녀는 믿을 수 없다는 몸짓을 했다 She made an incredulous gesture.
2 [신뢰하다] trust; trust [believe / confide] in; have confidence in; put trust [faith] in; [의지하다] rely on; depend upon; trust to; place reliance on; look [turn] to (a person) for help; lean [reckon / calculate] on; [기대하다] expect. ¶믿을 만한 reliable / trustworthy / dependable / (a person) to be relied [depended] upon / authentic (report) / authoritative ∥믿을 만한 소식통 a reliable source ∥믿을 만한 보도에 의하면 according to reliable [trustworthy] information ∥믿을 수 없는 unreliable / undependable / untrustworthy / (a person) not to be trusted / (a person) not to be relied [depended] upon / unauthentic / unauthoritative ∥믿을 수 없는 사람 an unreliable [untrustworthy] person / a dishonest person ∥자신의 능력을 지나치게 ~ be overconfident of one's ability / place too much confidence in one's ability ∥다수의 힘을 ~ rely on [trust to] numbers ∥아들을 집안의 기둥으로 ~ rely on one's son as the prop and stay of the family ∥그는 믿을 만한 친구다 He is a reliable friend. / He is a friend in deed. ∥나는 남편을 믿어요 I trust [have faith in] my husband. ∥믿을 만한 증거를 내놓으시오 Produce reliable evidence. ∥그는 믿을 수 없다 He is not to be trusted [relied upon]. ∥이젠 넌 못 믿겠다 I know now that you're not to be counted on. / I don't have confidence in you any more. ∥여기 날씨는 믿을 수 없다 You never know about the weather here. ∥누구도 믿어서는 안 돼 Don't trust anyone. ∥자네를 믿고 부탁하네 I make this request with full confidence in you. ∥당신을 믿고 이 일을 맡긴다 I will trust to you for the performance of the task. ∥나는 가장 믿었던 사람에게 배반당했다 I was betrayed by the man I had trusted most [more than anybody else]. ∥그들은 다수임을 믿고 하고 싶은 짓을 다했다 Relying on numbers [Made confident-by the safety of numbers], they did whatever they liked. ∥그를 너무 믿지 말게 Don't expect too much of him.
3 [확신하다] be sure of; be confident of. ¶나는 성공하리라 믿고 밤낮으로 최선을 다했다 I did my best day and night in the belief that I would succeed. ∥그들은 자기들의 승리를 굳게 믿고 있다 They were confident of their victory. / They were confident that they would win a victory. ∥지식은 힘이라고 나는 믿고 있다 It is my firm belief that knowledge is power.
4 [신앙하다] believe (in); have belief [faith] (in); embrace; profess; confess faith (in). ¶신을 믿는 사람 a devout person / a religious-minded person ∥불교를 ~ believe [profess] in Buddhism ∥하느님을 ~ believe in God / have faith in God ∥아무 종교도 믿지 않다 profess no religion ∥나는 귀신 따위를 믿지 않는다 I don't believe in ghosts.
믿는 도끼에 발등 찍힌다(속담) Stabbed in the back [Betrayed] by one's trusted friend.; Bite the hand that feeds you.
믿음 1 [믿는 마음] trust; confidence; credit; reliance; credence. ¶~을 얻다 be trusted by (a person) / get (a person's) credit [trust] /

믿음직하다

be in (a person's) confidence[trust] // ~을 잃다 lose credit (with) / lose the confidence // ~을 저버리다 betray (a person's) trust [confidence]. **2** faith; belief. ⇨신앙 ¶~이 없는 사람 an impious person / an infidel // ~이 두텁다 be pious / be devout / have a strong[deep] faith // ~을 갖게 되다 get religion / become pious // ~을 버리다 forsake[give up / renounce / abjure] one's faith // 그는 ~이 강하다[약하다] He is strong[weak] in faith. // 나는 ~이 깊은 편이 못 된다 I'm not one for religion. // 그는 ~이 깊은 가정에서 자랐다 He was brought up in religion.

믿음직하다 reliable; dependable; trustworthy; authentic; authoritative; (유망하다) hopeful; promising. ¶믿음직한 친구 a steadfast friend // 믿음직한 성품 staunch character // 믿음직한 솜씨[기술] dependable workmanship // 믿음직하지 못한 unreliable / untrustworthy / not to be depended upon / unpromising // …을 퍽 믿음직하게 생각하다 repose[place] great trust in (a person) / hope[expect] much from (a person) // 그는 믿음직한 사람이다 He is to be depended upon[a reliable / a trustworthy] man. // 그것 참 믿음직한 말이오. Those are hopeful words.

밀¹ [식] wheat. ¶~을 뿌리다 sow[plant] wheat // ~ 농사를 짓다 grow[raise] wheat.

밀² beeswax; (yellow) wax. ¶~ 먹인 waxed // ~ 먹인 종이 wax paper.

밀가루 wheat flour.
● 밀가루 반죽 dough; (버터를 섞은) puff paste; (우유·버터·달걀을 섞은) batter. ¶된 ~ stiff dough // ~을 만들다 knead dough.

밀감(蜜柑) [식] a mandarin orange; a tangerine (orange). ¶~ 껍질 an orange peel // ~밭 a tangerine orchard[plantation].

밀계(密計) a secret plan[design / plot]; an intrigue; a conspiracy. ¶~를 꾸미다 plot secretly / frame[weave] a secret plot / make [form] a secret plan / conspire.

밀고(密告) secret information (against); an anonymous report[notice]; betrayal; (구어) a tip-off; a tip. ¶익명의 사람으로부터 그가 여기에 있다는 ~을 받았다 We received information[a tip] from an anonymous person that he was here. / We were informed[tipped off] by an anonymous person that he was here. **밀고하다** inform against[on]; lay [lodge] information (against); turn informer (on a person); (속어) peach[squeal] (on a person); (구어) tip off (about / that); (속어) blow the gaff (to the police); snitch (on). ¶자기 친구를 ~ inform[squeal] on one's friends // 누구인지 경찰에 내 일을 밀고했다 Somebody informed the police against[on] me. / Somebody tipped off the police about me.
● 밀고자 an informer; a betrayer; an informant; (속어) a snitch(er); (속어) a squealer; a rat; (영국 속어) a sneak(학생).

밀교(密敎) [불] Esoteric[Tantric] Buddhism.

밀국수 wheat vermicelli; wheat-flour noodles; noodles.

밀기울 (wheat) bran; pollard(밀가루가 들어 있는).

밀다 **1** [힘을 주어 앞으로 나아가게 하다] push; shove; thrust; jostle; give a push; elbow(팔꿈치로); bunt(머리나 발로); bob(약간). ¶한 번 ~ give a thing a push[a shove] // 짐수레를 ~ push a cart // 계획을 밀고 나가다 go[move] ahead with a plan // 자기 생각을 밀고 나가다 persist in one's opinion / adhere[hold on] to one's belief // 대담하게 밀고 나가다 brave[breast] it out // 밀어 넘어뜨리다 push down // 밀어젖히다 push aside // 밀어 올리다 push[thrust] up / give a boost to (a person, a thing, etc.) (up) // 문을 밀어 열다 push the door open // 밀고 들어가다 force oneself[one's way] into // 등 뒤에서 ~ push (a person) from behind // 서로 ~ jostle one another // 낭떠러지[기차]에서 남을 밀어 떨어뜨리다 thrust[push] a person over a cliff[off a train] // 승객을 만원인 전차에 밀어 넣다 squeeze passengers into a (crowded) train // 작은 방에 많은 사람을 밀어 넣다 crowd a lot of people into a small room // 지갑에 지폐를 밀어 넣다 stuff one's wallet with bills / stuff bills into one's wallet // 옷가방에 옷을 마구 밀어 넣다 cram one's clothes into a suitcase // 밀고 밀리는 대혼잡이다 be overflowing with people / be packed to overflowing / be crowded[jammed] with people // (만원 버스 등에서) 너무 밀지 마라 Don't push me so much! / Don't press me, you all.
2 [깎다] shave; plane; [문지르다] rub; scrub; [눌러 펴다] press; roll. ¶턱수염을 ~ shave off one's beard // 때를 ~ wash off the dirt // 등을 ~ wash[rub] down one's back / scrub one's back // 대패로 판자를 ~ plane a board // 파이 반죽을 ~ roll out pie dough // 머리를 밀고 중이 되다 take the tonsure (to be a monk).
3 [추천하다] recommend; propose; nominate(지명하여); [지지하다] support; back (up); (미) boost. ¶후진을 ~ help one's juniors to get ahead / give (a person) a lift / look after one's juniors // 한 배우를 아낌없이 ~ patronize an actor munificently // 우리는 그를 의장으로 밀었다 We recommended [backed] him for the post of chairman. // 그는 많은 신인 가수를 텔레비전 분야에 밀고 있다 He is pushing a lot of young singers to the television people.
4 →미루다

밀담(密談) a private[secret] conversation; a confidential talk. ¶그들은 지금 ~ 중이다 They are talking behind closed doors. **밀담하다** talk secretly[behind closed doors] (with).

밀도(密度) **1** [조밀의 정도] density. ¶~가 높은 dense (metal) / of high density // 인구 ~ the density of population. **2** [내용의 충실의 정도]. ¶~가 높은 토의 a debate full of substance / a meaty discussion. **3** [물] density.
● 밀도계 a densimeter; a densitometer. 밀도측정 densimetry.

밀도살(密屠殺) secret[clandestine] slaughter (of cattle); illegal butchery. ¶~ 행위를 적발하다 pick up illegal butchery practice. **밀도살하다** slaughter (cattle) clandestinely[in secret]. ¶소를 ~ butcher a cow unlawfully.

밀떡 wheat plaster[paste] (to be applied to a wound).

밀뜨리다 push[shove] (a person) off; thrust; give a shove. ¶사람을 절벽에서 ~ thrust [push] a person over a cliff.

밀랍(蜜蠟) beeswax. ⇨밀²

밀레니엄 a millennium.

밀려나다 be pushed [thrust / forced] out; be elbowed [hustled] out; (씨름에서) be pushed out (of the ring); (지위 등에서) be ousted [expelled / dislodged] (from); be squeezed [shoved] out of; (아래로) be relegated (to). ¶사람이 많아서 홀에서 ~ be crowded out of a hall // 사장 자리에서 ~ be squeezed out of the president's seat // 회사에서 ~ get shoved [pushed] out of one's job with the company // 그 나라는 세계열강 중에서 제2위로 밀려났다 The country was relegated to (the) second place amidst the Great powers of the world. // 미국은 세계 조선계의 2위의 자리에서 밀려나고 말았다 The U.S. has been nudged out of second place in world shipbuilding. // 그는 주역에서 밀려났다 He was removed from the leading role. / He had the leading role taken away from him.

밀려들다 advance on (a castle). ⇨ 밀려오다

밀려오다 [밀어닥치다] advance [come / press] on (a castle); make [rush] for (the door); rush [surge / crowd] into; besiege (one's house); (파도가) surge [beat / rush] upon (the shore). ¶밀려오는 파도 advancing [surging] waves // 밀려오는 적 the surging [advancing] enemy // (한 떼가) 입구로 ~ make a rush for the door // 떼 지어 ~ storm [stampede] (a place) / crowd [pour] in(to) (a house) // 주문이 ~ have a rush [flood] of orders // 사인을 받으러 …에게로 ~ storm [crowd around] (a person) for autographs // 해일이 바닷가로 밀려왔다 The tidal wave swept toward the beach. // 예금자들이 은행으로 밀려왔다 The depositors besieged the bank. / The bank had a rush of depositors. / There was a rush (of depositors) on the bank. / There was a run on the bank. // 군중은 회관 안으로 한꺼번에 밀려왔다 The crowd surged into the hall. // 이런 외딴 시골에도 시대의 물결은 밀려온다 The current of the times reaches even a remote country place like this.

밀렵(密獵) poaching. **밀렵하다** poach (for) (pheasants); steal game; trespass on game [fish]; take game [fish] by illegal method. ¶꿩을 ~ poach for pheasants // 남의 수렵지에서 ~ poach upon another's preserves.
● **밀렵꾼** a poacher.

밀리그램 a milligram (me) (약어 mg, mgm, mgrm).

밀리리터 a milliliter (약어 ml).

밀리미터 a millimeter (약어 mm).

밀리다 1 [일이 쌓이다] be left undone; be delayed [retarded]; be piled up; be accumulated; be in arrears (with). ¶밀린 일 piled up work / arrears of work / work still waiting to be done // 주문이 ~ orders pile up // 나는 지금 일이 많이 밀려 있다 I have a lot of work on my hands [left unfinished]. / I have much pressing work. / I am pressed with work. // 나는 밀린 사무를 해치워야 한다 I have some unfinished work to dispose of. // 일이 산더미처럼 밀려 있다 There is a good deal of work left undone. / There are heaps of work in arrears. // 나는 일이 많이 밀려 그 모임에 가지 않았다 I had so much work left to do that I did not go to the meeting.
2 (지불이) fall into arrears; be in arrears (with); be left unpaid; be overdue; be outstanding. ¶밀린 돈 arrears / arrearages // 밀린 이자 an interest on arrears // 밀린 봉급 back pay [salary] // 밀린 집세 back rent / rent in arrears // 지불이 많이 ~ have many unpaid bills / run up bills // 그의 지불 청구서가 밀려 있다 His bill is overdue. // 그는 집세가 2개월분이 밀려 있었다 He was two months behind [(문어) in arrears] with the rent.
3 [떠밀리다] be pushed; be shoved; be thrust. ¶밀고 밀리는 경쟁 [싸움] a ding-dong race [fight] / a seesaw struggle [battle] // 인파에 ~ be jostled in the crowd / be swept along in the crowd // 물결에 이리저리 ~ be tossed about by the seas / be at the mercy of the waves / drift on the waves // 파도에 밀려 바닷가에 닿다 be cast ashore / be washed up on the beach // 인파에 밀려 나는 그를 잃어버렸다 Jostled in the crowd, I lost sight of him. // 남자의 시체가 해변으로 파도에 밀려 올라왔다 The body of a drowned man was washed ashore [up on the beach]. // 많은 사람들이 방에서 밀려 나왔다 Many people were crowded out of the room.
4 [깎이다] get shaved; shave (면도기로); (대패로) get planed; plane. ¶수염이 잘 ~ one's beard shaves well / have an easy beard (to shave) // 이 판자는 잘 밀린다 [밀리지 않는다] This board planes well [poorly].

밀림(密林) a dense [thick] forest; a jungle; a close thicket (관목의). ¶~의 왕자 the king of the jungle.
● **밀림 지대** a jungle area.

밀매(密賣) an illicit sale (of); illicit traffic (in); smuggling; (주류의) (미) bootlegging. **밀매하다** sell secretly; deal secretly (in); smuggle; practice smuggling; bootleg (주류를). ¶그는 밀수품을 밀매하고 있다 He illegally sells smuggled articles.
● **밀매자** a secret [an illicit] dealer; a smuggler; (미) a runner; (주류의) a bootlegger; (마약의) (속어) a pusher. **밀매품** smuggled [contraband] goods.

밀매매(密賣買) illicit traffic (in). **밀매매하다** engage in illicit traffic (in); deal secretly (in).

밀매음(密賣淫) illegal [unlicensed] prostitution. **밀매음하다** prostitute illegally; practice [engage in] unlicensed prostitution.
● **밀매음녀** an unlicensed prostitute.

밀모(密謀) a plot; an (underhand) intrigue; (공모) a conspiracy; (비밀회의) a secret conference [consultation]. **밀모하다** plot; conspire; hold a secret conference; have a secret consultation (with).

밀무역(密貿易) smuggling. **밀무역하다** smuggle (in / out). ¶헤로인을 ~ smuggle heroin (into the country).
● **밀무역업자** a smuggler.

밀물 the inflow [rising] of the tide; (조수의) flowing [rising / high] tide. ¶~ 때에 at high tide // ~을 기다리다 wait for the tide to come [flow] in // ~이 들어온다 The tide is rising [coming in]. / The tide is on the flow. // ~이 쓰기 시작한다 The tide begins to ebb.

밀방망이 a rolling pin (to flatten dough).

밀밭 a wheat field.

밀범벅 wheat-and-pumpkin pudding.

밀보리 1 [밀과 보리] wheat and barley. 2 [식] rye. ⇨ 쌀보리

밀봉(密封) sealing up; sealing tightly. **밀봉하**

밀봉하다 seal hermetically; seal up. ¶밀봉한 편지 a sealed letter∥병을 ~ bottle up[in].
● **밀봉교육** secret[clandestine] training.
밀봉(蜜蜂) a honeybee. ⇨꿀벌
밀사(密使) a secret envoy[messenger]; an emissary. ¶~로 보내다 send (a person) on a secret mission / send (a person) as a confidential agent (to).
밀생(密生) dense[thick] growth (of grass). 밀생하다 grow thick[luxuriantly in clusters]; be thickly wooded. ¶이 골짜기에는 양치류가 밀생해 있었다 The valley was thick[was densely covered] with ferns. / Ferns grew thick in the valley.
밀서(密書) a secret letter[note]; a confidential message. ¶~를 지니다 bear[carry] a secret message.
밀선(密船) a smuggling vessel[boat]; a smuggler; (미) a runner.
밀선(蜜腺) [식] a nectary. ⇨꿀샘
밀송하다(密送-) send[dispatch] secretly [in secret].
밀수(密輸) smuggling; contraband (trade). 밀수하다 [밀수입하다] smuggle (goods) in(to) (the country); import through illegal channels; [밀수출하다] smuggle (goods) abroad [out of the country]; export (an article) unlawfully; (미) run. ¶금제품을 ~ run contraband goods.
● **밀수단** a smuggling ring[gang]. ¶대규모 ~ a large-scale smuggling ring∥5인조 ~ a five-man (gold) smuggling ring. **밀수선** a smuggling vessel[boat]; a smuggler. **밀수품** smuggled goods; contraband articles (미) run goods.
밀수입(密輸入) smuggling; contraband trade.
밀수제비 a piece[dish] of flour dough boiled with soup; wheat-flour dough boiled in soup.
밀수출(密輸出) smuggling (goods) out [abroad].
밀실(密室) a secret room[chamber]; a closet. ¶~에 감금하다 keep (a person) in solitary [close] confinement / confine a person in a room∥~에서 이야기하다 closet oneself with (another) / be closeted together.
● **밀실 회의** a closed-door[secret] session.
밀약(密約) [약속] a secret promise[understanding]; [협약] a secret agreement[treaty]. ¶~을 맺다 conclude[enter into] a secret treaty / contract a secret pact / make a secret promise∥두 나라 사이에는 ~이 이루어져 있다 A secret understanding exists between the two countries.∥그들 사이에는 ~이 있었다 There was a secret agreement [understanding] between them. 밀약하다 make a secret promise; make a secret agreement (with).
밀어(密漁) poaching (for fish). 밀어하다 poach for fish; trespass on fish; take fish by illegal method.
밀어(密語) a confidential[private] talk.
밀어(蜜語) (애인 사이의) lover's whispers. ¶~를 속삭이다 talk in whispers.
밀어내다 push[press] out[forward]; push (a thing) out; thrust out; force out; squeeze out; crowd out; elbow[hustle] out. ¶의자를 앞으로 ~ thrust a chair forward∥저 회사는 우리 회사 제품을 시장에서 밀어내려 하고 있다 That company is trying to push our products off the market.∥그는 선배를 밀어내고 출세했다 He was promoted ahead[at the expense] of his senior colleagues. / He elbowed his way past his older colleagues on the ladder to success.
밀어붙이다 push[drive] (a person) to; push [thrust] against; pin against(움직이지 않도록); hold against; (힘있게) press hard. ¶벽쪽으로 ~ drive (a person) to the wall∥상대방을 링 가장자리로 ~ push one's opponent to the edge of the ring∥책상 위의 잡동사니를 한쪽으로 ~ brush[push] the odds and ends on a desk to one side∥경기를 계속 밀어붙였다 We were constantly on the offensive[were constantly threatening to score] in that game.
밀어젖히다 push away[aside / by]; thrust aside[away]; force aside[out of the way]; crowd[squeeze] out; shove[brush] aside; elbow (a person) out[aside / to one side] (팔꿈치로). ¶사람을 ~ push people aside∥군중을 밀어젖히고 나아가다 elbow[push / force] one's way through a crowd∥그는 나를 밀어젖히고 앞으로 나섰다 He shoved me aside[pushed me out of his way] and stepped forward.
밀월(蜜月) a honeymoon. ¶온양에서 ~을 보내다 honeymoon[spend the honeymoon] at Onyang.
● **밀월여행** a honeymoon (trip). ¶~을 하다 make a honeymoon trip / honeymoon.
밀의(密議) a secret conference[consultation]; a conclave; a chamber council; (구어) a huddle. 밀의하다 confer in private (with); have a private consultation (with); hold a secret conference; (구어) go into a huddle (with). ¶머리를 맞대고 ~ lay heads together in secret consultation∥장시간 ~ have long discussions behind closed doors[in camera].
밀입국(密入國) illegal entry into a country; smuggling oneself into (a country); stowing away. 밀입국하다 smuggle oneself into (a country); enter[slip into] a country secretly [illegally]; stow away. ➔¶간첩을 밀입국시키다 smuggle a spy into a country∥멕시코 국경을 통하여 미국으로 밀입국시키다 smuggle (a person) into the United States over the Mexican border.
● **밀입국자** an illegal entrant; [밀항자] a stowaway.
밀장지(-障-) [옆으로 밀어서 여닫는 장지] a sliding door[screen]; a sliding partition.
밀전병(-煎餠) a grilled wheat cake.
밀접하다(密接-) close (to); intimate (with); near. ¶밀접한 관계 a close relationship [connection] (between) / (사항의) a close correlation∥수요와 공급의 밀접한 관계 an intimate relationship between supply and demand∥밀접한 관계가 있다 be closely connected[related] (with) / be in close connection (with) / have a close relation (with) / be brought closer together∥그것과 이것은 밀접한 관계가 있다 It is closely related to this. / The two are closely related.∥양국의 관계는 더욱 밀접해졌다 The two countries have come even closer together. **밀접히** closely; intimately; nearly.
밀정(密偵) a spy; a secret[confidential] agent; an emissary; an undercover man

밀조(密造) illicit manufacture; (술의) unlawful brewing; illicit distilling; (미국 속어) bootlegging [moonshining]. **밀조하다** manufacture [brew] clandestinely [secretly / illicitly]; brew [distill] unlawfully; (미국 속어) moonshine. ¶술을 ~ produce liquor illegally / distill (whisky) illicitly.

밀주(密酒) home-brewed wine; home brew; (미국 속어) moonshine; bootleg; bathtub liquor; illegally brewed liquor. ¶~를 담그다 brew [distill] illicitly [secretly / clandestinely] / (미국 속어) moonshine.

밀집(密集) massing; concentration. ¶가옥의 ~ 지대 a(densely) built-up area // 인구 지역 a densely populated district / a congested district [area]. **밀집하다** crowd; swarm; close up [together]; aggregate densely; cluster together; from in close order. ¶밀집해 있는 close / massed / crowded / thick / congested / compact // 광장에는 사람들이 밀집해 있었다 The square was crowded with people. // 그 지역은 작은 주택이 밀집해 있는 곳이다 In that area small houses are clustered [stand] close together.

밀짚 (wheat) straw.
● **밀짚모자** a straw hat. ¶그는 ~를 쓰고 있었다 He was wearing a straw hat.

밀착(密着) [꼭 붙음] close adhesion. **밀착하다** stick (fast) to; adhere closely to; be glued (together / to). ¶밀착시키다 stick (A) fast to (B) / weld (together) // 붕대가 상처에 밀착되어 떨어지지 않는다 The bandage is stuck to the wound and will not come loose.
● **밀착법** [사진] contact printing. **밀착 인화** a contact print [copy].

밀초(蜜-) a wax candle.

밀치다 push; shove; thrust; give a push [thrust]; push [thrust] away [aside]. ¶서로 ~ jostle [push / hustle / crowd / elbow] one another // 옆으로 ~ push [thrust] aside [away] / force out of the way // 군중을 밀치고 나아가다 force [elbow / push] one's way through the crowd // 출입구에서 서로 밀치는 바람에 여러 사람이 다쳤다 There was a jam at the exit, and many were injured.

밀치락달치락 hustling and jostling. **밀치락달치락하다** hustle and jostle; push and shove; push one another. ¶밀치락달치락하는 군중 a milling crowd [throng] / a jostling crowd // 폭도들은 서로 밀치락달치락했다 The rioters pushed and shoved [jostled] one another. // 사람들은 밀치락달치락하며 앞으로 나아갔다 People elbowed and pushed their way on. / People went forward crowding against one another. // 그와 밀치락달치락하고 있는 동안에 그녀는 낭떠러지에서 떨어졌다 While struggling with him, she fell from the cliff. // 군중이 경기장 둘레에서 밀치락달치락하고 있었다 A crowd of people milled around the stadium. // 폐점 세일은 사람들이 밀치락달치락하는 대성황이었다 That shop's going-out-of-business sale was a booming success [attracted a large crowd].

밀크 (cow's) milk.
● **밀크세이크** milk shake. **밀크 커피** white coffee; (프) café aulait.

밀타승(密陀僧) [화] [일산화납] litharge; lead monoxide.

밀탐(密探) spying; espionage; secret investigation. **밀탐하다** spy (on a person / into a secret); be engaged in espionage; do detective work; make secret inquiries into (a matter); investigate secretly. ¶적의 움직임을 ~ spy upon the enemy's movement // 회사의 내정을 ~ investigate the inside affairs of a company.

밀통(密通) 1 [간통] an illicit intercourse [amour]; adultery; misconduct; a liaison; an intrigue. **밀통하다** commit adultery (with); make an illicit love (to); misconduct oneself (with); carry on an intrigue (with a woman); be intimate (with). 2 [내통] secret communication; a secret understanding. **밀통하다** communicate secretly (with); have a secret understanding (with); (구어) tip (the enemy) off (on a matter). ¶적과 ~ communicate secretly with the enemy / betray (us) to the enemy.

밀펌프 a forcing [force] pump.

밀폐하다(密閉-) shut tight(ly); cover [close] up tight; seal hermetically; make [keep] airtight; seal [glue] up. ¶밀폐한 상자 an airtight box / a hermetically sealed box // 뚜껑을 ~ cover tightly with the lid // 용기를 밀폐해 두면 내용물이 꽤 오래갑니다 If the receptacle is made airtight, the contents will keep for quite a long time. → ¶밀폐된 용기 an airtight container.

밀항(密航) a secret passage; stowing away; smuggling oneself. **밀항하다** attempt [try to] stow away on a cargo boat // 샌프란시스코로 ~을 기도하다 attempt to go over to San Francisco as a stowaway (on a steamer). **밀항하다** stow away (on a steamer); steal a passage (to); smuggle oneself (into); go as a stowaway; sail in secret.
● **밀항선** a smuggler. **밀항자** a stowaway.

밀행(密行) a prowl; going secretly. **밀행하다** prowl (about); go secretly [stealthily] (to); travel incognito; (경관이) patrol in plain clothes.

밀회(密會) a clandestine [secret] meeting; a (romantic) rendezvous. ¶…과 ~의 약속이 있다 have an assignation with …. **밀회하다** have a clandestine [secret] meeting (with); meet (a person) secretly [in secret]; rendezvous.
● **밀회 장소** a place of assignation; a place of secret meeting; a secret rendezvous; a tryst.

밉다 [싫다] hateful; disgusting; detestable; odious; [가증스럽다] abominable; cursed; [심술궂다] spiteful; [얄밉다] provoking. ¶미운 사람 an odious person / a detestable [hateful] fellow // 미운 짓 spiteful conduct // 밉지 않은 innocent / artless / naive // 주는 것 없이 ~ have an antipathy [a prejudice] (against) // 밉게 굴다 behave [act] detestably [abominably] // 저 놈이 ~ I hate [detest / loathe] that man. // 예닐곱 살 때는 한창 미운 짓만 한다 A boy of six or seven is really mischievous. // 그가 그녀를 밉지 않게 생각하고 있는 것 같다 He seems to be attracted by [have a liking for] her.

미운 오리 새끼 [귀찮은 존재] an ugly duckling.

밉살맞다 hateful; detestable. ⇨밉살스럽다

밉살스럽다 [싫다] hateful; detestable; disgusting; [지긋지긋하다] abominable; cursed;

밉상

odious; horrible. [심술궂다] spiteful; [얄밉다] provoking; offensive. ¶밉살스럽게 spitefully / maliciously / hatefully / provokingly // 밉살스러운 짓 spiteful conduct / abominable cruelty // 밉살스러운 얼굴 a forbidding [repulsive] countenance / a hateful look // 밉살스러운 녀석 a detestable [odious] fellow // 밉살스러운 말을 하다 say spiteful things (to) / talk spitefully [provokingly] // 밉살스럽게 웃다 smile a malicious smile // 참 밉살스러운 놈이군 What a repulsive [an odious] wretch he is! // 그 녀석은 밉살스럽도록 침착했다 He remained provokingly cool [calm]. // 그의 눈에는 아마 내가 밉살스럽게 비치겠지 Probably I appear hateful [detestable] to him.

밉상(-相) [미운 얼굴] a repulsive [disgusting] countenance [face / appearance]; [미운 행동] spiteful conduct. ¶그다지 그녀가 ~은 아니었을 테지 You have a fancy for her, haven't you?

밋밋하다 [굴곡이 없다] flat; even; plane; plain; smooth; smooth and flat; [곧고 길다] slender and tall; straight and long. ¶밋밋한 나무 a slender and upright tree // 밋밋한 언덕 a soft [gently-sloping] hill / (헐벗은) a bare [bald / treeless] hill // 얼굴이 ~ have a smooth expressionless [blank] face.

밍근하다 [좀 미지근하다] lukewarm; tepid.

밍밍하다 tasteless; flat; insipid; weak [watery] (tea); thin (porridge); washy (milk); mild (tobacco); light (liquor). ¶밍밍한 국 thin soup // 밍밍한 술 flat wine / washy liquor / sloppy drink.

밍크 [동] a mink (pl. ~(s)).
● 밍크 목도리 a mink stole. 밍크코트 (wear) a mink coat.

및 and; also; as well as; in addition to; besides; both ... and. ¶영어 ~ 수학에 있어서 in mathematics as well as in English // 이 법령은 부산 ~ 인천에서 실시되고 있다 This ordinance is in effect in Busan and Incheon.

밑 1 [아래쪽] the lower part; the foot; the base; the bottom. ¶~의 under / lower // 바로 ~의 directly [just / right] under // ~으로 down / downward // 책상 왼쪽 ~의 서랍 the lower left drawer of a desk // ~에 under / beneath / below / underneath (바로 밑에) // 산 ~에 at the foot [base] of a mountain // 계단 ~에 at the foot [bottom] of the stairs // 눈 ~에 under the eye // 나무 ~에 under a tree // ~에서 다섯째 줄에 in the fifth line from the bottom // ~에 놓다 put [lay / set] down // ~에서 받치다 support (a thing) from below // 나무 ~에서 하늘을 올려다보다 look up at the sky from under a tree // ~으로 내려가다 go [come] down / go [come] downstairs(아래층으로) // ~으로 떨어지다 fall down / fall to the ground(지상으로) // 지평선 ~으로 지다 sink below the horizon // ~을 보다 look down / lower one's eyes // 그것은 이 돌 ~에 묻혀 있다 It is buried beneath this stone. // 그는 ~에서 당신을 기다리고 있습니다 He is downstairs waiting for you.
2 [하위]. ~의 lower / subordinate / (이하의) below / under // ~에서 두 번째 아이 the second youngest of one's children // 그는 나보다 세 살 ~이다 He is three years my junior [younger than I]. // 대위는 소령보다 한 계급 ~이다 A captain is one rank below a major. // 그의 학교 성적은 자기 반에서 맨 ~이다 He is [stands] at the bottom [foot] of his class. / He is the last boy in his class.
3 [조건·환경]. ~에 under / on // 지휘 [지도 / 감독] ~에 under the command [direction / supervision] of ... / under ... // 부모 ~에서 (grow up) under one's parental roof // 부모 ~을 떠나다 leave one's parental roof / run away from one's parents // 선생 ~에서 바이올린을 배우다 study violin under a teacher // 그는 홍 씨 ~에서 일하고 있다 He works under Mr. Hong. / He plays second fiddle to Mr. Hong.
4 the anus; the vulva. ⇨ 밑구멍2
5 the lower part. ⇨ 밑동 ¶나무 ~ the base of a tree // ~이 들다 form a root [bulb].
6 [바닥] the bottom (of a bottle); the bed (of a river). ¶바다 ~에 가라앉다 sink [go down] to the bottom of the sea // ~에 닿다 (닿이) find bottom / (발이) touch bottom // ~을 떼어 내다 knock the bottom (of a box) out // 상자의 ~이 쏙 빠졌다 The bottom came [fell clean] out of the box. / The bottom of the box has come out. // 그는 ~ 빠진 수렁에 빠져들고 있다 [비유] He is getting hopelessly bogged down.
7 [근본] the root; the source; the origin; the foundation; the basis. ¶~도 끝도 없는 소문 a groundless rumor / an unfounded gossip // ~도 끝도 없는 말 a pure fabrication [invention].
8 [수] a base; a radix.

밑 빠진 독에 물 붓기(속담) be like throwing water on thirsty soil; be nothing more than a drop in the bucket.

밑(이) 구리다 feel smell [guilty]; be ashamed (of); have a bad conscience.

밑도 끝도 없이 suddenly; all of a sudden; out of the blue; without any warning.

● 밑 화장 a makeup base; a foundation. ¶~으로 크림을 바르다 use some cream as a makeup base.

밑각(-角) [수] a base angle.

밑거름 manure given at sowing [planting] time; initial [base] manure. ¶~이 되다 [비유] make a sacrifice of oneself (for).

밑구멍 1 [밑으로 뚫린 구멍] a hole at the bottom; a bottom hole. 2 [항문] the anus; [여자의 음부] the vulva.

밑그림 a rough sketch; a draft; a design; (프) a dessin. ¶자수의 ~ a design for embroidery // ~에 따라 조각하다 carve on a design // ~을 그리다 make a rough sketch (of) / make a design (of) / design / draft.

밑넓이 [수] the base area.

밑돌다 do not amount (to); fall short (of); be less [lower] than; be [fall] below (the average); be a fraction (of). ¶(결과가) 예상을 ~ fall short of one's expectation(s) // 그는 100미터 경주에서 10초를 밑돌았다 He ran [did] 100 meters in under [less than] 10 seconds. / He broke [beat] the ten second mark in the 100-meter race. // 그들은 가방을 원가를 밑도는 값으로 팔고 있다 They are selling the bags below cost.

밑동 the lower part; the base; a root; a stump. ¶기둥~ the lower part [base] of a column // 잎꼭지 [잎자루]의 ~ the butt (of a petiole) // 벌목한 큰 나무의 ~ the stump of a large felled tree // ~을 다듬다 take off the roots (of vegetables) // 나무를 ~에서 자르다

cut down a tree (close) at the base / (톱으로) saw off a tree at the root.
밑둥치 the root (of a tree).
밑머리 original hair. ¶~를 치다 thin one's hair.
밑면(-面) [수] the base plane (of a geometrical figure).
밑면적(-面積) [수] the base area. ⇨=밑넓이
밑바닥 1 [물건의 바닥] the bottom; the base; the bed (of a river). ¶구두의 ~ the sole of a shoe // 냄비의 ~ the under surface of a saucepan // ~에 쌓인 물건 the lower layer of goods // ~이 이중으로 된 double-bottomed (trunk / ship) // ~이 없는 bottomless // 상자의 ~이 빠졌다 The bottom came[fell clean] out of the box. // 나의 트렁크는 ~에 깔려 있었다 My trunk was at the bottom of the heap. // 냄비의 ~에 구멍이 하나 뚫려 있다 There is a hole in the bottom of the pan. // 수조의 ~에 물고기가 보인다 I see a fish at the bottom of the tank. // 강 ~은 자갈로 덮여 있다 The riverbed is covered with pebbles.
2 [최하층] the bottom; the depths; the abyss; the nadir (of one's fortune). ¶~에 있는 사람들 people at the very bottom of society[lowest level of society] // 그는 ~ 인생을 살고 있다 He is at the bottom of the pecking order. // 언젠가는 ~ 인생에서 벗어날 테다 I'm determined to raise[lift] myself out of obscurity someday.
3 (마음의). ¶마음의 ~ (in) one's inmost thoughts[desire] / one's real intention [motive] // 네 마음속 ~이 드러나 보인다 I can clearly see through your intention. / Your motive is apparent. / I can read your inmost thoughts.
● **밑바닥 생활** a life of penury[extreme poverty]; a life in the slums; a poverty stricken life; an obscure life. ¶~을 하는 사람들 the submerged tenth / the scum of society a person of low rank / (집합적) the lower classes.
밑바탕 1 [본질] essence; [기초] the foundation; the basis; the groundwork; the ground. ¶서구 민주주의의 ~ the basic ideas of western democracy // 이 주의가 그 학설의 ~이 되어 있다 This doctrine underlies the theory. 2 [본성] the original nature; the inherent character; one's true colors. ¶~이 좋다 [나쁘다] be good[bad] by nature // ~이 천하다 be of low birth.
밑반찬(-飯饌) side dishes pickled, salted, or preserved by other means for longer duration to go with rice as meals.
밑받침 1 [밑에 까는 것] an underlay; [책받침] a celluloid board[cardboard]. ¶~을 받치고 글씨를 쓰다 write on a paper with a board beneath it. 2 [버팀] a support; a prop; a stay. ¶기둥의 ~ a stay at the base of a pillar // 담의 ~ a support at the base of a wall.
밑밥 (낚시질의) ground bait.
밑변(-邊) [수] the base; the bottom side of a polygon; the base line. ¶삼각형의 ~ the base of a triangle.

밑불 [불씨] kindling[live] charcoal[coal] to make a fire; (항상 점화해 두는) a pilot flame [light / burner].
밑살 1 [미주알] the anal sphincter; the sphincter ani. 2 [소의 볼깃살] beef around the anus.
밑씨 [식] a germinal vesicle; an ovule.
밑씻개 toilet paper; (영국 속어) bumf.
밑알 a nest egg.
밑조사(-調査) [예비 조사] a preliminary investigation; spadework.
밑줄 an underline. ¶~을 친 부분 an underlined[underscored] part // …에 ~을 치다[긋다] underline / underscore (a line).
밑지다 lose on the cost[price]; do not cover the first cost; [손해 보다] lose (over); suffer [incur] a loss; do not pay. ¶밑지고 팔다 sell with loss on cost / sell below cost (price) / sell to[at a] disadvantage // 본전을 밑지고 팔다 sell at a price lower than the original cost / 그러면 밑집니다 That's below (the) cost. / Then I shall be unable to cover the cost. // 이 거래에서 천 원 밑지고 있다 I am 1,000 won out of pocket by this transaction. // 이번 일이 안 되더라도 밑져야 본전이다 If I fail in this attempt, I shall be none the worse for it.
밑져야 본전(속담) Trying wouldn't hurt[do any harm].
밑지는 장사 a losing business[transaction].
밑짝 the under piece (of a 2-part object).
밑창 the bottom piece; the outsole (of a shoe); the base piece. ¶구두 ~ the sole of a shoe.
밑천 [자본] capital; funds; stock; [원금] the principal; [원가] the cost[prime] price; (도박의) a stake. ¶장사 ~ business funds // 한 잡다 [장만하다] amass[pile up] a fortune / (구어) make a pile // ~이 들다 cost much / be expensive // 적은 ~으로 사업을 시작하다 start business on a small capital // 돈벌이의 ~으로 삼다 turn (something) to account make capital(out) of (something) // 적은 ~으로 큰 이익을 얻으려 하다 throw a minnow to catch a whale // ~을 들이다 lay out money (on) / put[sink] money (in) / invest capital (in an enterprise) // ~을 건지다 earn as much as the capital invested / recover one's investment / get one's money's worth // ~을 건지지 못하다 fail to return the original investment // 그가 ~을 대 주겠다고 한다 He offers to finance the business[to supply us with business]. // 건강[건강한 몸]이 ~이다 Health[A healthy body] is like money in the bank. // 아름다운 용모만이 그녀의 ~이었다 Her beauty her only asset. // 그는 5천만 원의 ~으로 상점을 열었다 He opened a store with capital of fifty million. // ~이 말려서 사업이 중단되었다 The enterprise was abandoned owing to lack of funds. // 이러면 ~도 못 건질 것이다 This will not cover my original outlay. // 그가 그만한 경험을 쌓는 데는 상당한 ~이 들었을 것이다 He must have paid a high price for his experience.
밑층(-層) the lower floor. ⇨=아래층(=)아래)
밑판(-板) the bottom board.

ㅂ

-**ㅂ니까** [의문] are (you / they) ...?; is (he / it) ...?; do (you) ...? ¶지하철로 통학합니까 Do you go to school by subway?//댁의 이름은 무엇입니까 What is your name?

-**ㅂ니다** [동작이나 상태의 서술] be; do; have. ¶봄입니다 It is spring.//학교에 걸어서 갑니다 I go to school on foot.

-**ㅂ디까** [상대방이 겪은 바를 물음] did you hear[notice] that ...?; have you been told that ...?; have you found that ...?; be it known that ...? ¶사람들이 나에 대해서 무어라고 합디까 What do they say of me?//그는 언제 귀국한답디까 When did he say he would return home?

-**ㅂ디다** [자신이 겪은 바를 알림] they say; it is said that; I hear[am told] that; it is known that; as it is found that. ¶그는 약혼했다고 합디다 He was engaged, I hear.//그는 백만장자라고 합디다 They[People] say that he is a millionaire.//그는 그림을 잘 그린다고들 합디다 He is said to be a good painter. / They say[It is said] that he is a good painter.//당신 나라는 아름답다고 합디다 I've heard that your country is beautiful.

-**ㅂ시다** 1 [같이 행동하기를 권함] let us (do); we will (do). ¶차 마십시다 Come and have tea with me!//차로 드라이브하러 나갑시다 Let's have the car out for a drive. 2 [청하거나 허락을 구함]. ¶그의 말을 들어 봅시다 Let him have his say.

바¹ [음] fa; F. ¶~장조[단조] F minor[major]//올림[내림]~ F sharp[flat].

바² [줄] a (straw or hemp) rope; (마소용의) a tether; (가는) a cord; (계선용의) a hawser. ¶~를 치다 rope off (a place) / stretch a rope (around a place).

바³ 1 [방법] a way; means; how (to do). ¶어찌할 ~를 모르다 be at a loss what to do / be at one's wits'[wit's] end//위에서 말한 ~와 같이[동일하게 / 마찬가지로] as stated [mentioned / remarked] above / as aforesaid//당연히 기대되는 ~와 같이 as is naturally expected//그것이 바로 내가 바라던 ~다 That's just what I have wished for.

2 [일] a thing; what. ¶그가 하고자 하는 ~를 거의 알 수가 없었다 I could hardly understand what he wanted to do.//그것은 당신이 알 ~가 아니다 That's none of your business. / It is no concern of yours.//그 사람이 실패하건 말건 내가 알 ~ 아니다 He may fail for all[anything / what] I care.

3 [범위] extent. ¶내가 아는 ~로는 so far as I know / to the best of my knowledge / from what I know / to the best of my knowledge//들리는 ~로는 그가 다시 입후보한다더군요 I hear he's going to run for election again.//그가 말하는 ~에 의하면 그것은 사실이 아니다 According to him, it is not true.//내가 생각하는 ~로는 그는 미쳤다고 생각했음에 틀림없다 The way I see it, he must have thought I was crazy.

4 [...하였는데] and (then). ¶우리 몇 사람이 그 모임을 후원하였던 ~ 의외로 번창하였다 We few people sponsored the society and it has prospered beyond our expectations.

바⁴ 1 [서양식 술집] a bar; a barroom; a bar parlor; (미) a saloon; (영) a public house; (영국 구어) a pub. ¶~의 여급[~걸] a barmaid / (미국 속어) a B-girl//~의 단골 (미국 구어) a barfly. 2 [높이뛰기·축구 골문의 가로장] a crossbar. 3 [물] a bar.

바가지 a gourd (dipper); a calabash. ¶~로 물을 푸다 scoop[dip] water with a gourd.

바가지 긁다 nag[snap / (속어) yap] (at); speak crossly (to); grumble (at). ¶바가지를 긁는 아내 a nagging wife / a Xanthippe//심하게 바가지를 긁는 여자 a nag / a nagger//밤늦게 온다고 ~ yap at (husband) for being late at night.

바가지(를) 쓰다 get ripped off; be overcharged; be charged high; (be made to) pay through the nose; pay exorbitantly. ¶나는 어제 식당에서 바가지를 썼다 Yesterday I was paid through the nose at a restaurant.//그 부인은 리본 하나에 엄청나게 바가지를 썼다 They rushed the lady shockingly for a ribbon.

바가지(를) 씌우다 rip (a person) off; charge an exorbitant price; overcharge; demand [sell out] extortionate prices; ask an unreasonable[a fancy] price; make undue [indecent] profits; give a tall order; (구어) soak; (미국 속어) tuck[put] it on (to); (영국 속어) rush. ¶바가지를 씌우는 하급 레스토랑[카바레] clip joint//그 택시 기사는 나에게 바가지를 씌우려 했다 The taxi driver tried to rip me off.//그는 중고차 대금을 나한테 바가지를 씌웠다 He charged me an unreasonable price. / I got taken by him on that used car.

● **바가지요금** an exorbitant price[fare].

바라 creaking; squeaking; grating. **바라하다** creak; squeak; grate.

바겐세일 [염가 판매] a bargain sale.

바곳 an awl[a gimlet] with a side-handle.

바구니 a basket; (집합적) basketry; a crate(큰 것). ¶대~ a bamboo basket//고리버들(잔가지 세공의) ~ a wicker basket//장~ a shopping basket//딸기 한 ~ a basketful of strawberries / a basket of strawberries//~를 짜다 weave[make] a basket.

바구미 [동] a rice weevil; a black weevil; a grain weevil.

바그르르 (물이) (boil) simmering; (거품이) bubbling; foaming. **바그르르하다** simmer; bubble; foam.

바글거리다 1 (물이) boil; seethe; simmer; come to a boil. ¶물이 바글거린다 The water is boiling briskly. 2 (거품이) bubble up; rise in bubbles. ¶비누 거품이 바글거린다 Suds are bubbling up. 3 (많이 모여) be crowded (with); crowd (together); flock together; swarm[teem] (with). ¶거지가 ~ (장소가) swarm[be overflowing / be crowded] with

바꾸다

beggars // 광장에는 군중이 바글거렸다 The public square was crowded with people.
바글바글 1 (물이) boiling (briskly). ¶~ 끓다 boil (over) / simmer. **바글바글하다** boil; seethe; simmer; come to a boil. 2 (거품이) bubbling; foamily. **바글바글하다** bubble up; rise in bubbles. 3 (많이 모여서) in swarms [crowds]. **바글바글하다** crowd (together); be crowded (with); throng; swarm[teem] (with); flock together. ¶사람이 바글바글하는 아파트 an enormous human warren of tenements // 땅에는 벌레들이 바글바글했다 The ground was simply crawling with worms.
바깥 [바깥쪽] the outside; [옥외] the out-doors; out-of-doors; the open (air); [겉면] the exterior. ¶~의 outer / outside / external / exterior / outward / outdoor // ~의 소음 outside noises // ~ 면 the exterior surface // ~에서 outside / out of doors / outdoors // ~에서 놀다 play outdoors / play in the open // ~에서 식사하다 dine[eat] out // ~에서 기다리다 wait outside[without] // ~으로 나가다 go out (of doors) / go out into the open air [the street] // ~에서 잠을 자다 sleep outdoors / ~을 내다보다 (창문에서) look out (of) the window / (창 너머로) look out through the window // ~은 날씨가 차다 It is cold outside. // 차가 ~에서 대기하고 있다 The car is waiting outside. // ~은 차차 어두워지고 있다 Outdoors it is growing dark. // ~의 모든 시간을 ~에서 지냈다 Farm workers spend most of their time outdoors. // 그는 좀처럼 ~출입을 하지 않는다 He is a stay-at-home [home-keeping-man].
● **바깥사돈** the father of one's son-in-law [daughter-in-law]. **바깥소식** news; the news of the town; [해외 소식] foreign news; information from overseas. ¶~에 어둡다 have but little information of the world / be unfamiliar with what is going on in the world. **바깥양반** your master; your husband. **바깥일** [주로 남자들이 하는 일] the job[work] of one's husband; a man's work[job]; [집 밖의 일] outdoor work; [세상일] the affairs [occurrences / happenings] in the world. ¶~을 하다 work in the yard[garden / field] // 집 안에만 있어서 ~은 모른다 I always stay at home, so I don't know what happens in the streets. **바깥쪽** the outside; the outer side; the exterior. ¶~의 outer / outside / exterior / [식][동] external // ~으로 outward / to the outside // ~에서 from without [the outside] // 문의 ~ the outside of a gate // ~에서 문을 열다 open the door from (the) outside // 그 집은 ~이 녹색으로 칠해져 있다 The house is painted green outside[on the outside]. // 그것은 ~이 빨간 종이로 싸여 있다 It is covered on the exterior with red paper. **바깥채** an outhouse; an outbuilding; an annex.
바꽃 [식] an aconite; a wolfsbane; a monkshood.
바꾸다 1 [교환하다] exchange [change / barter] (one thing for another); [전환하다] convert [change / turn] (one thing for another). ¶수표를 현금으로 ~ cash a check // 원을 달러로 ~ exchange won for dollars / convert won into dollars // 1,000원짜리 지폐를 100원짜리 동전으로 ~ change a 1,000 won note for 100 won coins / change [(구어) break] a 1,000 won bill into 100 won coins // 증권[토지]을 팔아 돈으로 ~ realize securities [an estate] // 카메라를 팔아 돈으로 ~ convert [change] a camera into money // 남과 자리를 ~ change places [seats] with a person // 물건과 물건을 ~ trade [barter / swap] one thing for another // 불량품은 바꾸어 드립니다 We will replace defective articles. // 조니는 자전거를 빌리의 새 손목시계와 바꾸었다 Johnny swapped his bike for Billy's new watch. // 천 원짜리 지폐를 잔돈으로 바꿔 주겠니 Can you break a thousand won (bill) for me? / Can you give me change for this 1,000 won? // 이것을 딴것으로 바꿔 주시겠습니까 Will you give me something else in exchange of this? / Would you exchange this for something else? / 나는 자리[근무 시간]를 그와 바꾸었다 I changed seats [shifts] with him. // 이 반지를 돈으로 바꾸고 싶다 I'd like to exchange this ring for money. / I'd like to turn [(문어) convert] this ring into cash. // 저 여인에게 자리를 바꾸자고 해라 Ask that woman to change seats with you. // 그녀는 목숨과 바꾼다 해도 그것을 놓치지 않았을 것이다 She would not have parted with it for the life of her. // 어떤 것도 목숨과 바꿀 수는 없다 Nothing can take the place of life. / Life is all in all to us. / Life is everything to us.
2 [변경하다] change; (문어) alter(▶ 보통 change는 전면적 변경을, alter는 부분적 변경을 나타냄); switch; (방향을) turn; shift; veer (round); wheel; change (direction of); (놓는 장소를) change (the location of); change [shift / move] (a thing from A to B); (배열을) rearrange; [고치다] reform, revise; amend; (새것으로) replace (one thing) with (new ones). ¶주소를 ~ change address // 직장을 여러 번 ~ change jobs many times // 계획을 일부 ~ alter a part of the plan // 갑자기 태도를 ~ suddenly change one's attitude / show a sudden change of attitude // 생각을 ~ change one's mind // 역사의 흐름을 ~ change[turn] the course of history // 피아노의 위치를 ~ move a piano // 키의 방향을 ~ shift the helm // (의론의) 입장[논거]을 ~ shift one's ground // 배의 방향을 ~ turn a ship from her course // 제도를 ~ reform a system // 헌 타이어를 새것으로 바꾸어 끼우다 replace a worn tire by [with] a new one // 커튼을 ~ renew curtains // 책상과 책장을 바꿔 놓았다 I switched around the desk and the bookshelf. // 방법을 바꿔 보자 Let's change [(문어) alter] out method. / Let's try a different method. // 한 자를 미터법으로 바꾸면 약 33센티미터가 된다 If expressed in the metric system, a *ja* is about 33 centimeters. // 먼저 네 사고방식을 바꿔라 Change your way of thinking first. // 그는 이야기를 좀 더 진지한 화제로 바꾸었다 He switched the conversation to a more serious subject. // 열차가 선로를 바꾸었다 The train was shunted from one track to another. // 그 책을 읽고 나는 인생관을 바꾸었다 Reading the book changed my outlook on life. // 정부는 불공평한 세제를 바꿀 의향은 전혀 없었다 The government had no intention of reforming the unfair taxation system. // 일단 결정을 내렸으니 마음을 바꾸지 않겠다 I will not change my mind once I have decided. // 이제는 예정을 바꿀 수

바꿈질

없다 We cannot change[alter] the schedule now.∥그는 토지[주식]를 아들 명의로 바꾸었다 He transferred the land[stocks] to his son.
3 [대체하다] substitute (one thing for another); replace (one thing with another). ¶버터 대신 마가린으로 바꿔 보지 그래 Why don't you substitute margarine for butter?∥낡은 기계를 새 기계로 바꿀 필요가 있다 The old machines need to be replaced by[with] new ones. / We need to replace old machines with new ones.
바꿔 말하면 in other words; that is (to say); to put it (in) another way. ¶쉬운 말로 ~ put it in simpler terms.

바꿈질 (an) exchange; barter; swap(ping); swop. **바꿈질하다** make an exchange (with another); swap[swop / exchange] (one thing) for (another); swap off (one thing) for (another).

바뀌다 [변하다] change; be[get] changed; undergo a change; alter; be altered; shift; turn; [풍향이] shift (round) (to); turn; veer; come around[about]; work round; [개정되다] be revised; be amended; [개선되다] be improved; be bettered; [교정되다] be corrected; be reformed; [대체되다] be replaced; [새로워지다] be renewed. ¶철이 바뀔 때 a change in the season∥세기가 바뀔 무렵에 at the turn of the century∥조수가 바뀔 때 at the turn of the tide∥텔레비전 프로가 바뀌었다 The TV program was changed.∥그는 임시에서 정식 직원으로 바뀌었다 His employment status was changed from temporary to permanent.∥그는 학년이 바뀔 때에 학교를 옮겼다 He changed schools at the end of the school year.∥출발은 3일로 바뀌었다 The day of departure has been changed to the third.∥이 집은 주인이 두 번 바뀌었다 This house has changed hands twice.∥해가 바뀌었다 A new year began. / The new year has arrived[has come around].∥바람이 남풍으로 바뀌었다 The wind shifted (around) to the south. / The wind turned into the south. / The wind veered round to the south.∥비가 눈으로 바뀌었다 The rain has turned to snow.∥그의 주소가 바뀌었다 He has (moved to) a new address. / He has his address changed.∥요즘은 그녀의 관심은 개인적인 일에서 사회의 문제로 바뀌었다 Recently her interest has veered from personal affairs to social problems.∥언젠가는 석유 대신 태양에너지로 바뀔 것이다 Eventually oil will probably be replaced by solar energy.∥열차 시간표가 바뀌었다 The train schedule was changed.∥그 계획은 바뀔 가능성이 있다 There is a possibility that the plan may change[be changed / be altered].∥진열품이 새롭게 바뀌었다 (상품이) New articles are on display. / (배열이) The articles on display have been rearranged.∥그의 가방과 내 방이 바뀌어 놓여 있었다 Someone had switched the position of his bag and mine.∥장면이 바뀐다 The scene shifts.

바나나 a banana. ¶~ 껍질 a banana skin∥~ 껍질을 벗기다 peel (off the skin of) a banana.

바나듐 [화] vanadium(기호 V).

바느질 needlework; sewing. ¶마무리 ~ the final sewing∥~로 살아가는 여자 a needlewoman∥~이 얌전하게[꼼꼼하게] 되어 있다 be carefully sewn∥~을 잘하다 be clever with one's needle / be good at needlework / be a good needlewoman∥그녀는 ~로 살림을 꾸려 갔다 She made a living by doing needlework. **바느질하다** do needlework; sew. ¶~으로 ~ sew by hand∥재봉틀로 ~ sew (something) on[with] a (sewing) machine.
● **바느질거리** sewing; needlework; a dress to be made. ¶~가 있다 have clothes to make. **바느질삯** sewing charges. **바느질품** needlework[sewing] as a means of living.

바늘 1 (바느질의) a (sewing) needle. ¶뜨개질 ~ a knitting needle / a crochet hook∥실을 꿴 ~ a needle and thread / a thread and needle∥~에 실을 꿰다 thread a needle / pass a thread through the eye of a needle∥~에 손가락을 찔리다 prick one's finger with a needle.
2 (낚시의) a hook; (시계의) a hand (on the clock); (측음기의) a needle; (레코드의) a stylus (pl. -li, -es); (주사기의) a needle; (기계 등의) an index (pl. -es, -dices); an indicator; a pointer; [핀] pin. ¶나침반의 ~ the needle of a compass∥~에 미끼를 달다 bait a hook.
3 [한 바늘·한 코·한 땀] a stitch. ¶~ 코를 빠뜨리다 drop a stitch∥옷을 한 ~ 깁다 put a stitch in a garment∥상처를 세 ~ 꿰맸다 It took three stitches to close up the wound.
바늘 가는 데 실 간다(속담) be inseparably related (to each other).
바늘 도둑이 소도둑 된다(속담) He who steals a pin will steal an ox.
● **바늘겨레** a pincushion; a needle pad. **바늘귀** the eye of a needle; a needle eye[hole]. **바늘밥** thread remnants. **바늘방석** a pincushion; a needle pad; [비유] a bed of thorns. ¶난 ~에 앉아 있는 기분이었다 I felt as if I were sitting on thorns. **바늘쌈** a packet of needles.

바늘구멍 a hole made by a needle; a pinhole.
바늘구멍으로 하늘 보기(속담) be narrow-minded; have a narrow view of things.
바늘구멍으로 황소바람 들어온다(속담) A draught is cold, that comes in through a chink.

바니시 [화] varnish.

바닐라 [식] vanilla.

바다 the sea; [대양] the ocean(▶ 성구(成句) 외에는 보통 정관사를 붙임). ¶거친 ~ a rough[stormy] sea∥~ 냄새 the tang of sea air / the smell of sea∥~ 경치[그림 / 사진] a seascape∥~의 사나이 a seaman / a sailor / a mariner / a seafaring man∥~의 요정 a sea-nymph / a sea fairy∥~의 산물 products of the sea / marine products∥~로 둘러싸인 나라 a country surrounded by the sea / (문어) a seagirt[seabound] country∥~같이 큰 은혜 one's deep obligation (to a person)∥~로 나가다 go out to sea / put (out) to sea / sail out to sea∥~에 나와 있다 be out at sea [on the sea]∥~가 잔잔하다 The sea is calm. ∥~가 거칠다 The sea is rough[troubled / raging].∥나는 올여름에도 ~로 간다 I'm going to the seaside again this coming summer.
바다는 메워도 사람의 욕심은 못 채운다(속담) Covetousness is always filling a bottomless vessel.

● **바다거북** [동] a sea[marine] turtle; a turtle. **바다낚시** sea fishing. **바다뱀** [동] a sea snake[serpent]. **바다사자** [동] a Steller's sea lion. **바다코끼리** a walrus; an elephant seal; a sea elephant. **바다표범** [동] a seal; an earless[a true] seal; a hair seal. **바닷개** [동] a fur seal. ⇨"물개1 **바닷게** a sea crab. **바닷말** seaweeds. ⇨해조(海藻) **바닷물** seawater; saltwater; brine. ¶~이 들어오는 강 a tidal river. **바닷물고기** a sea fish; a saltwater fish. **바닷바람** a sea wind. ⇨해풍 ¶~을 쐬다 enjoy the (cool) breeze that comes from the sea.

바닥 1 [평면을 이룬 부분] the broad; the flat. ¶방~ a floor (of the room)// 손~ the palm [flat / broad] of a hand// 땅~에 앉다 sit on the (bare) ground.
2 [물체의 밑부분] the bottom; the sole; the bed. ¶강~ a riverbed// 암초[모래] ~ the rocky[sandy] bottom// 이중 ~으로 된 배 a ship with double bottom// ~시세가 되다 reach[touch] bottom// 값이 ~으로 떨어졌다 The price has hit bottom.// 물이 얕아서 발이 ~에 닿는다 The water is so shallow that I can touch the ground[bottom].
3 [피륙의 짜임새] texture; weave; fabric. ¶~이 고운[거친] of fine[coarse] texture [weave].
4 [지역] an area; a district; a place. ¶서울 ~ the Seoul area// 장~ a marketplace.
5 [일·물건이 다 없어진 끝] the end of one's resources; exhaustion.
바닥(을) 보다 [밑천이 다 없어지다] run out of capital[fund]; [끝장을 보다] see the end [conclusion] of.
● **바닥짐** ballast.

바닥나다 be exhausted; be used up; be consumed; run out; be gone; come to an end; give out. ¶우리의 자금이 바닥나고 있다 We are running out[short] of funds. / The funds are running low.// 적의 식량 보급품이 바닥났다 The enemy soldiers have come to the end of their food supplies.// 가물철에는 저수지의 물이 바닥날 때가 있다 In the drought season the (water in the) reservoir sometimes dries up.

바닥내다 allow (a thing) to run out; run out of. ¶술을 ~ let wine out of stock / run [be] out of wine.

바동거리다 (kick and) struggle; squirm. ⇨ 〈버둥거리다

바둑 (the game of) *baduk*; go(▶ "go"는 일본어에서 온 말임). ¶~의 명수 an expert in the game of *baduk* / a master of *baduk*// ~을 두다 play *baduk* / have a game of *baduk*.
● **바둑돌** a *baduk* stone[piece]. **바둑무늬** a pattern with black and white spots; a speckled pattern. **바둑판** a *baduk* board; a checkerboard. ¶길이 ~처럼 뻗어 있다 The streets are laid out in a grid pattern[at right angles].

바둑이 a black and white dog; a dog spotted with black and white.

바드득 with a grinding[grating / creaking] sound. **바드득하다** grind; grate. ⇨"바드득거리다

바드득거리다 grind; grate; grit; creak.

바득바득 persistently; obstinately. ⇨〈부득부득

바들바들 tremblingly. ⇨〈부들부들

바디 a reed; a yarn-guide.

바라 [음] small cymbals. ⇨"자바라

바라다 1 [원하다] wish (for / to do / that); desire (to do / that); want (to do / that); long[crave / yearn] for; seek; care for; [기대하다] hope (for / to do / that); expect (to do / that); look for; look forward to. ¶성공을 ~ hope for success// 세계 평화를 ~ wish [pray] for world peace// 간절히 ~ greatly desire / earnestly wish (for) / long for// 평화를 간절히 ~ long for peace// 요행을 ~ hope against hope / trust to luck[chance] // 그는 명성을 바란다 He is desirous of fame.// 당장 가 주기를 바란다 I wish[desire] you to go at once.// 그녀는 그가 무슨 말인가를 해 주기를 간절히 바랐다 She longed for him to say something.// 당장 내가 주기를 바란다 I want you to go out of here at once.// 성공하시기 바랍니다 I wish you success. / I hope you will succeed.// 앞으로도 계속 애호해 주시기 바랍니다 (문어) I look forward to the continued enjoyment of your favor.(▶ 영어에서는 별로 쓰지 않음)// 그것이 바로 내가 바라는 바다 I could ask nothing better. / That's exactly what I wanted[desired]. / That is just the thing.// 여러분이 전력을 다해 주기를 바랍니다 I'd like you to do your best.// 우리 팀이 우승하기를 바란다 I wish our team would[I hope our team will] win the championship.// 이것은 더 바랄 수 없는 좋은 기회이다 You couldn't ask for a better chance than this.// "하느님이시여, 바라옵건대 그를 불쌍히 여기소서." "I pray you, God, to take pity on him." / "May God take pity on him!".// 바라옵건대 남편이 곧 무사히 돌아오게 해 주십시오 I pray my husband will soon came back safely.// 그는 모두가 출석하기를 바랐다 He wanted that everybody should be present.// 바랐던 대로 되지 않는 일이 많다 Many things fall short of our expectations.// 간절히 바라옵건대 사람들에게 평화를 주시옵소서 We pray that there may be peace among men.// 평화야말로 우리가 오랫동안 바라던 바다 Peace is exactly what we have wanted for a long time.
2 [요청하다] beg; ask; request (to do / that); require (to do / that); [간청을 하다] implore; (문어) entreat (to do). ¶방세를 꼬박꼬박 치러 주기 바랍니다 You are required to pay the rent regularly.// 지각하지 않도록 해 주기 바랍니다 You are requested not to be late.// 당신의 조언을 바랍니다 Would you be good[kind] enough to give me some advice? / Could I ask you to give me some advice?// 즉시 출석을 바랍니다 Your presence is requested immediately.// 제발 사실대로 말씀해 주시기 바랍니다 I beg that you will tell the truth.
3 [선택하다] prefer; choose. ¶불명예보다는 차라리 죽음을 ~ choose death before dishonor.

바라문 〈婆羅門〉 〈음역〉 Brahman. ⇨브라만
● **바라문교** Brahmanism. ⇨"브라만교(⇨브라만)

바라보다 1 [건너다보다] look at; watch; see; [응시하다] gaze at[on]; stare at; [관망하다] take[get] a view (of); view; look over. ¶그림

바라보이다

을 ~ look at a picture // 그녀를 ~ look toward her // 풍경을 ~ view the landscape // 먼 곳을 ~ look into the distance / look afar / gaze off far into the distance // 별을 가만히 ~ gaze up at the stars // 멍하니 [우두커니] ~ look absentmindedly (about) / moon (over) // 뚫어지게 ~ look hard [fixedly] at // 천장을 ~ look up at the ceiling // 마루를 ~ look down at the floor // 남의 얼굴을 ~ look into [gaze at] a person's face / study a person's face // 나는 들어온 사람을 바라보았다 I looked at the man who had come in. // 그 호수는 여기서 바라보아야 가장 아름답다 The lake seen from here is most beautiful. // 그는 나를 오래 바라보았다 He gave me a long look. // 이 방에서 한라산의 멋진 경치를 바라볼 수 있다 This room commands a splendid view of Hallasan(Mt. Halla).

2 [방관하다] look on; sit back [tight] and watch; remain a spectator. ¶남이 싸우는 것을 바라보기만 하다 remain a spectator to others' quarrel.

3 [바라다] expect; hope [look] for; look forward to; count on [upon]; reckon on [upon]. ¶그 사업에서 많은 이익을 ~ look for much profit from the business.

4 [그 나이에 근접하다] be close [hard] upon; be getting on for [to]. ¶나이 50을 ~ be getting on for fifty // 그녀는 나이 30을 바라본다 She is close to thirty.

바라보이다 be looked over; overlook; command. ¶바다가 바라보이는 언덕 a hill overlooking the sea // 남쪽으로 호수가 바라보이는 집 a house facing a lake to the south // 그 언덕에서 바라보이는 바다 경치가 장관이다 The hill commands a splendid prospect of the ocean. // 우리 집에서 만의 경치가 바라보인다 My house commands a view of the bay. // 이 창문에서 바다가 바라보인다 This window overlooks [looks out on] the sea.

바라지 [여러 가지로 돌봐 주는 일] attentive care; looking after; provision. **바라지하다** take care of; care for; look after. ¶자식들을 ~ look after [take care of] one's children.

바라지다[1] **1** [갈라지다] split off; be separated. **2** [넓게 열리다] widen; open (out); be wide open. ¶틈이 바라진다 A gap [An opening] widens. // 봉오리가 바라지기 시작하고 있었다 The buds were beginning to open.

바라지다[2] **1** (몸이) short and fat; thick-set; have a stocky build. ¶딱 바라진 남자 a stocky man // 어깨가 딱 ~ be broad-shouldered / have broad of chest. **2** (그릇이) shallow. ¶바라진 대접 a shallow soup bowl. **3** [야무지다] saucy; cheeky; pert; perk; (구어) uppish; (미국 구어) fresh; forward. ¶바라진 아이 a forward child // 바라진 말을 하다 say a cheeky thing. **4** [도량이 좁고 편협하다] narrow-minded; illiberal; intolerant.

바라크 (⑨baraque) a shack; a makeshift hut; a temporary shelter; a barrack(많은 사람이 사는).

바락 (shout) suddenly; abruptly. ⇨`버럭

바락바락 desperately; frantically; doggedly; (구어) like hell. ¶~ 기를 쓰다 make desperate efforts / struggle [strive] frantically.

바람[1] **1** [공기의 움직임] a wind; (미풍) a breeze; (외풍) a draft; (영) a draught; (돌풍) a blast [gust] (of wind); (폭풍) a storm; (외기) air; a current(선풍기 등의). ¶부드러운 ~ a breath of air / a gentle breeze // 살을 에는 듯한 ~ a cutting [piercing / biting / nipping] wind // 얼어붙는 듯한 ~ a freezing wind // ~이 세게 부는 [없는] 날 a windy [windless] day // ~이 잘 통하는 방 an airy [a well-ventilated] room // ~이 통하지 않는 방 an unaired room // 일진의 [한바탕의] ~ a blast [gust] of wind / a blast // ~이 불어 가는 쪽에 [under] the lee / leeward // ~을 세게 받는 ~ a rattling wind // ~을 심하게 받는 산허리 a wind-swept mountainside // 시원한 ~ a cool [refreshing] breeze // ~이 통하지 않는 windtight / airtight // 선풍기 ~을 쐬면서 in the current of an electric fan // 방 안에 ~을 들이다 [통하게 하다] let some fresh air into a room / admit air into a room / air a room / give a room airing // ~이 세다 blow hard / (장소가) be windy / be wind-swept // ~을 안고 [거슬러] 나아가다 walk [sail] against the wind [in the wind's eye / in the teeth of the wind] // ~을 등지고 가다 go before the wind / (돛단배가) sail [run] before [with] the wind / have a free wind / square away // ~이 들어오지 않도록 하다 prevent the admission of wind / [찬 바람의 유입을 막다] keep out cold air // ~에 나부끼다 [펄럭이다] flutter [flow / flicker / flap / fly] in the wind // 오토바이를 타고 ~을 가르며 나아가다 go flying along on a motorcycle // ~이 일었다 A wind has risen [sprung up]. // ~이 그쳤다 The wind died away [went down / died down / fell / dropped]. // 밤까지는 ~이 그칠 것이다 The wind will die down [blow itself out] by nightfall. // ~이 불고 있다 The wind is blowing. // 대단한 ~이다 There is a strong wind (blowing). // 우리 집은 ~이 불어 가는 쪽에 있었지만, 다행히 화재를 면했다 Our house lay to the leeward, but luckily it escaped the fire. // ~의 동쪽으로 방향이 바뀌었다 The wind has shifted [changed / veered] to the east. // 어느 쪽에서 ~이 불어오고 있느냐 Which direction is the wind blowing from? // ~이 (새어) 들어온다 I feel a draft. / There is a draft. // 나는 모자를 ~에 날렸다 My hat was blown off by the wind. / I had my hat blown off. // 삼나무 향기가 ~에 풍겨 왔다 The aroma of cedar trees wafted in on the breeze. // 불길은 ~을 타고 옆집으로 번졌다 Fanned by the wind, the fire spread to the next house. // ~ 한 점 없었다 There was not a breath [stir] of air. / The air was breathless. // 돛이 ~을 안고 있었다 The sail was filled with the wind [billowed in the wind]. / The sail filled. // 화살은 ~을 가르고 날아갔다 The arrow flew through the air. // 이 집은 북쪽 ~을 심하게 받는다 The wind blows strongly against the north side of this house. // 이 해안은 항상 ~이 심하다 This coast is always windy.

2 [공·타이어 등의 공기] air. ¶~을 넣다 fill (a football) with air / pump up (a tire) // ~을 빼다 deflate (a tire) / let the air out of (a football).

3 [들뜬 마음] inconstancy; fickleness; [들뜬 행동] an amour.

4 [허풍] gas; a big [tall] talk; a shopping lie; (미국 속어) hot air. ¶~이 센 친구 a gas-bag / a boaster / a braggart / (미국 속어) a blow-hard // 그는 ~이 세어 믿을 수 없다 He talks too big to be trusted.

5 〈속〉 nervous diseases. ⇨풍병
6 [일시적 유행] (the) fad; (the) fashion; (the) vogue. ¶여자들 사이에 미니스커트 ~이 불고 있다 Miniskirts are in vogue with girls.
7 [비유]. ¶**정치** ~ a political storm∥재계에 새~을 불어넣다 send a breath of fresh air through economic circles∥무슨 ~이 불었는지 그 유명한 구두쇠가 나에게 식사 대접을 했다 I don't know what got into him, but that notorious cheapskate treated me to a meal. ∥이렇게 일찍 일어나다니 무슨 ~이 불었느냐 Whatever made you get up so early?∥무슨 ~이 불어 여기까지 왔느냐 What (stroke of fortune) has brought you here? / What (good) wind has blown you here? / How does it happen that you're here?

바람(이) 나가다 [공·바퀴 등의 바람이 빠지다] leak; escape; get[find] vent; be[have gone] flat; [융성한 기운이 없어지다] grow [become] dull; slacken; wane; become insipid. ¶바람 나간 풍선 a flat[deflated] balloon∥이 타이어는 바람이 나갔다 This tire is flat[has gone flat].
바람(이) 들다 (무 등이) get porous[spongy / full of pores]; [탈이 생기다] be hindered [impeded / balked]; meet with a setback; go wrong. ¶바람 든 무 a porous[spongy] radish.
바람(을) 쐬다 (기분 전환으로) air oneself; take an airing; take the air.
바람(이) 자다 1 [바람이 그치다] calm[die / go] down; fall (calm); drop; pass; lull; abate; blow over. ¶바람이 차차 잔다 The wind is abating[slowly dying down]. **2** [들떴던 마음이 가라앉다] calm down; quiet down; become calm.
바람(을) 잡다 1 [마음이 들떠 돌아다니다] indulge in[be given to] dissipation [debauchery]; take up a wild[fast] life; lead a fast[dissolute] life; burn[light] one's candle at both ends. **2** [허황한 짓을 꾀하다] conceive a wild hope[scheme]; be lost in wild fancies; indulge in woolgathering; spin a daydream. ¶바람 잡는 계획 a wild-goose chase / a chimerical project / a visionary [wildcat] scheme.
● **바람개비** [바람에 돌게 만든 장난감] a pinwheel; [풍향계] an anemoscope. ¶바람에 뱅뱅 도는 ~ a pinwheel whirling in the wind ∥~를 돌리다 spin a pinwheel. **바람기**(一氣) [바람이 불 듯한 기운] the feel[force] of wind; [이성에 대해 들뜬 마음] a flirtation; fickleness; wantonness; (a) wanton temperament. ¶~가 있는 여자 a woman of loose morals[easy virtue] / a wanton woman / a flirt∥~ 있는 사내 a man with a roving eye. **바람둥이** (남자) a playboy; a licentious man; a Don Juan; an inconsistent lover; (문어) philanderer; (여자) a flirt; a fickle [wanton] woman; a woman of easy virtue; a light-o'-love. ¶그는 이미 70대이지만 아직도 ~이다 He is already in his seventies, but he's still quite a playboy[but he still has quite an eye for women]. **바람막이** a windbreak; a shelter from the wind; a protection from[against] the wind; an air screen. ¶이 나무들이 교정의 ~가 된다 These trees help to protect[shelter] the schoolyard from the wind. / These trees serve as a shelter from the wind. **바람받이** a place exposed[open] to the wind; a wind-swept place; a wind-blown place; a windy[bleak] place. ¶언덕의 ~에 있는 집 a house in an exposed position on the hill / a house exposed to the winds on the hill.

바람[2] **1** [어떤 일에 따른 기세] conjunction; process; result; consequence; outcome; influence; effect; impetus; motive. ¶~에 in conjunction (with) / in the process of / as a result of / as a consequence of / in consequence of / under the influence of / on account of / owing to / as / due to∥그 경기는 비가 오는 ~에 연기되었다 The game was put off on account of rainy weather. ∥폭설이 내리는 ~에 기차가 연착했다 Owing to a heavy snowfall the train was delayed.∥그가 병이 난 ~에 당신을 찾아뵐 수 없었습니다 I couldn't call on you in consequence of his illness. / As[Since / Because] he was taken ill, I could not call on you. / His illness prevented me from (my) calling on you. / I couldn't call on you because of[on account of] his illness. ∥화가 나는 ~에 그랬어 I did it in a fit of anger.
2 [차림새]. ¶셔츠 ~으로 in one's shirt sleeves / without one's coat on∥파자마 ~으로 in pajamas only / without one's trousers on∥그녀는 버선 ~으로 거리로 뛰어나갔다 She ran out into the street without her shoes on.

바람결 1 [바람의 움직임]. ¶~에 on the wind ∥~에 썰매 소리가 들려왔다 The sound of sleds was carried to me on the wind. ∥~에 삼나무 향기가 풍겨 왔다 The aroma of cedar trees wafted in on the breeze. **2** [풍문] a rumor; hearsay. ¶~에 들으니 the wind brought the news that ... / a little bird told me that ... / there is a rumor that / rumor has it that ... / it has come to my ear that ... / (구어) as I hear tell / I've heard through the grapevine / the rumor runs that ...∥~에 들으니 자네가 새 일자리를 구했다던데 It has come to our ears that you have got a new job.

바람나다 1 [이성 관계로 마음이 들뜨다] become fickle[flippant / dissipated]; take to fast living; take to amours; have a secret love affair. ¶바람난 fickle / wanton / flirtatious. **2** [능률이 한창 나다] warm up; get warmed up; get into the swing of (one's work); be the best of form; be up to the mark; hit[strike / get into] one's stride.
바람맞다 1 [중풍에 걸리다] be stricken [smitten] with paralysis; have a stroke of paralysis. ¶그는 바람맞아 좌반신을 못 쓴다 He is paralyzed on his left. **2** [헛기다리다] wait[be kept waiting] for (a person) in vain. ¶여자에게 바람맞은 남자 a rejected lover[suitor] ∥ 여자에게 ~ be rebuffed [spurned] by a girl.
바람맞히다 [헛기다리게 하다] keep a (person) waiting in vain; break[fail to keep] an appointment; (미국 구어) stand up. ¶그는 나를 바람맞혔어 He stood me up.
바람직하다 desirable; advisable; [환영할 만하다] welcome. ¶바람직한 법률 a desirable law ∥바람직하지 않은 일 an undesirable thing / a matter to be deprecated∥바람직한 사람 a desirable person / (라) a persona grata∥바람직하지 않은 사람 an undesirable person /

바람피우다

(라) a persona non grata.// 전원이 식에 참석하는 것이 ~ It is desirable that all of you (should) attend the ceremony.// 그들에게 알리는 것은 바람직하지 못하다 It is undesirable[It is not to be desired] that they should be told.// 일 주일에 두 번 교습을 받는 것이 ~ It is desirable[to be desired] that you should take lessons twice a week.// 자네는 지체 말고 전지 휴양을 하는 것이 ~ It is advisable that you go for a change of air at once.// 그는 바람직한 동업자가 아니다 He is not a desirable partner.// 가는 것이 바람직하다고 보십니까 Do you think it advisable to go?

바람피우다 have an affair[a flirtation] (with)(▶ affair는 성적 관계를 의미한다. flirtation은 더 가벼운 뜻); play with love; be an unfaithful wife[husband]; take to amours; have an amour[a secret love affair] (with another man[woman]); play the wanton; wanton; be unfaithful in love. ¶바람피우지 않다 be faithful[true] to a man[woman]// 그녀는 남편이 바람피워 속이 상해 있다 She is worried over her husband's fickleness.// 그는 또 바람피우기 시작했다 He's started to play around with another woman again.// 그는 절대로 바람피우지 않는다 He is entirely faithful to his wife.

바랑 [중이 등에 지고 다니는 자루] a holdall; a (pilgrim's) scrip; a beggar's bag; a wallet.

바래다¹ 1 [빛이 변하다] (물건이) lose[cast] color[(영) colour]; discolor[(영) discolour]; be discolored[(영) discoloured]; get washed out; (물건 또는 빛깔이) fade (away); (빛깔이) go[come] off. ¶바래기 쉬운 빛깔 a color which fades easily / a fugitive color// 바래지 않는 빛깔 a fast[a fadeless / an unfading / a standing] color// 색이 바랜 커튼 a faded [discolored] curtain// 페인트 색이 바랬다 The paint is discolored.// 이 색은 바래지 않는다 This color is fast. / This color does not fade.// 이 모직물은 빨아도 색이 전연 바래지 않는다 The color of this woolen clothe [material] washes very well[stands wash].// 빨간 T셔츠가 바래서 엷은 분홍색이 되어 버렸다 The red T-shirt faded into a light pink.

2 [희게 하다] bleach; blanch; fade; wash out (dye). ¶햇빛에 ~ bleach (a thing) in the sun// 무명을 ~ bleach cotton.

바래다² see (a person) off. ⇨ "배웅하다(⇨배웅)

바래다주다 see[take] (a person to a place); escort; see (a person) off[leave]. ¶집까지 ~ see (a person) home / (자동차로) take (a person) home (in one's car) / drive[motor] (a person) home// 문까지 ~ see[show / follow / accompany (a person) to the door// 내가 역까지 바래다주겠다 I will see you to the station. / Let me go as far as the station with you. / (자동차로) I will drive you to the station. / I will take you to the station in my own car.// 어머니들은 아침마다 아이들을 유치원까지 바래다준다 Every morning the mothers see[accompany] their children to the kindergarten.// 나는 자동차로 그녀를 집까지 바래다주었다 I gave her a ride[(구어) lift] to her home. / I drove[motored] her home.

바로 1 [굽지 않고 바르게] right; straight; upright; erect; [정당하게] justly; rightly; properly; duly; [정확하게] correctly; accurately; [진실되게] truly; honestly; truthfully; straightforwardly. ¶~ 앉다 sit properly / sit up straight// 자세를 ~ 하다 stand[sit] up straight / straighten one's posture / straighten up// 그것을 책상 위에 ~ 놓아라 Put it right on the table.// 모자를 ~ 써라 Put your hat on straight.// 상관을 보자 그는 ~ 앉았다 When he saw a senior official, he straightened himself[sat up properly].// 넥타이를 ~ 매십시오, 비뚤어져 있어요 Straighten[Adjust] your tie — it's crooked.// ~ 맞혔다 You've hit upon the very thing [right answer]. / That's exactly right. / You've guessed right.

2 [지체 않고 곧] at once; directly; immediately; right now[off]; promptly; without (a moment's) delay[hesitation]; (미국 구어) right[straight] away. ¶저녁 식사 후 ~ right after dinner// 답장 주십시오 Please reply by return mail.// 우리는 그들에게 ~ 전보를 쳤다 We cabled them immediately.// 그가 돌아오면 ~ 전화드리도록 하겠습니다 As soon as he comes home I will have him call you back.// 그는 고등학교를 마치자 ~ 대학에 들어갔다 He entered college directly after finishing high school.// 그는 귀가하자마자 ~ 잤다 Immediately he returned home, he went to bed.

3 [곧장] straight; directly. ¶학교에서 ~ 집으로 가다 come straight home from school// 뉴욕으로 ~ 가다 go direct to New York// ~ 사무실로 가거라 Go straight to the office.// 나는 ~ 역으로 갔다 I went directly[straight] to the station.

4 [다른 것이 아니라 곧] the very ...; (just) the same; in itself; [꼭·정확히] just; right; precisely; exactly; [확실히] surely; certainly; [정말로] really; truly; [불과] only; but; [의심할 바 없이] beyond any doubt[question]. ¶~ 위[아래]에 right above[under] / ~ 머리 위에 just above one's head / right overhead// ~ 가까이에 hard[close / near] by / close at hand / quite near (the house) / close to [by] / in the immediate neighborhood (of)// ~ 그때 just then / just at that moment / at the very moment// ~ 오늘 this very day / ~ 이곳에서 right here// ~ 맞은편에 right opposite// ~ 저기 있는 집 the house right[just] over there// 그는 ~ 내 앞에 섰다 He stood right before me.// 나는 ~ 어제 그것을 들었다 I heard it only yesterday.// ~ 이웃에서 불이 났다 There was a fire in the immediate neighborhood.// 조카는 ~ 가까이에 살고 있다 My nephew lives nearby[close at hand].// 식전에서 ~ 내 옆에 앉았던 사람을 알고 있습니까 Do you know the man who sat next to me at the ceremony?// 빨간색 차가 ~ 우리 뒤를 따라왔다 A red car was following close behind us. / A red car followed us closely.// 저는 학교 ~ 옆에 살고 있습니다 I live close by the school.// 그의 집은 ~ 이웃입니다 His house is right next door (to ours).// ~ 그렇다 That's perfectly right. / Exactly so.// 그것이 ~ 내가 하고 싶은 말이다 That is exactly what I want to say.// 그는 ~ 한국의 피카소다 He is indeed the Picasso of Korea.// 그가 ~ (그것을 한) 최초의 사람일 것이다 He will be the first (to do it).// 그 아이의 모습은 ~ 순진 그대로였다 The child

looked like innocence itself[personified]. // 누군가 했더니 ~ 너였구나 Oh, it is you! / Why! Is that you? // 사진에 있는 사람은 ~ 제 남편입니다 The man in the picture is surely my husband (and none other). / There is no doubt that the man in the picture is my husband. // 내가 추측한 대로이다 It is just as I conjectured. // 녹음된 목소리는 어제 내가 전화로 들은 ~ 그 목소리다 The tape-recorded voice is the very same voice I heard over the phone yesterday. // 그것은 ~ 내 눈앞에서 일어났다 It happened under my very eyes [right under my nose].
5 [원래의 자세로 돌아가라는 구령] As you were! // 우로 봐, ~ Eyes right! — Eyes front!

바로미터 **1** [기압계] a barometer. **2** [추정 기준] a barometer; an index; an indicator. ¶신문은 종종 여론의 ~가 된다 Newspapers are often barometers of public opinion. // 신문은 여론의 ~로서 믿을 만한 것이 못 된다 The newspaper is unreliable as an indication of public opinion.

바로잡다 **1** [굽은 것을 곧게 하다] straighten; make straight[right]; (나뭇가지 등을) set up again; train. ¶나뭇가지를 ~ train a twig / 굽은 등뼈를 ~ straighten one's bent backbone.
2 [잘못된 것을 고치다] correct; redress; reform (evil practices); remedy; rectify (an error); cure; set right; set[put / bring] to rights; straighten. ¶잘못을 ~ correct a mistake // 옷차림을 ~ tidy oneself up / adjust one's clothes // 남의 나쁜 버릇을 바로잡아 주다 cure a person of a bad habit / correct a person's bad habit // 사람을 ~ reform a person / (구어) straighten a person out // 미스프린트를 ~ correct misprints // 자기 행동을 바로잡고 새 출발을 하다 mend one's ways and make a fresh start // 빨간 잉크로 쓴 부분이 선생님이 바로잡은 곳이다 The parts in red ink are the corrections made by the teacher. // 현행 교육 제도는 바로잡아야 한다 The present educational system has to be put to rights.

바로크 baroque.
●**바로크 건축** baroque architecture. **바로크 음악** baroque music.

바륨 [화] barium (기호 Ba).

바르다¹ **1** [붙이다] (종이 등을) stick; paste; plaster; affix; put; post; (장지문 등을) paper (a sliding door). ¶벽에 전단을 ~ stick [paste up] a bill on the wall // 천장을 ~ put up a ceiling // 장지를 ~ paper a sliding door // 벽지를 다시 ~ repaper the wall.
2 [칠하다] apply (one thing to another); paint (칠을); spread (on); plaster (회반죽 등을); daub; bedaub; coat (그림 물감·옻 등을); varnish (바니시를); lacquer (옻칠을); rub (in) (문질러서); use; put on make up (화장품을); powder one's face (분을); glaze (유약을). ¶새빨갛게 바른 입술 lips painted bright red // 빵에 버터를 ~ spread butter on bread / spread bread with butter / butter bread // 모기에 물린 자리에 연고를 ~ apply ointment to a mosquito bite // 입술연지를 ~ put on [apply] lipstick // 얼굴에 분을 ~ put face powder on / powder one's face (분을); 도자기에 유약을 ~ glaze[enamel] pottery // 나는 다친 무릎에 약을 발랐다 I applied some medicine to [put some medicine on] my injured knee.

바르다² [발라 내다] open[split] (and take out the inside of); split[scrape / strip] off; cleave; shell; husk. ¶(생선) 가시를 ~ bone [fillet] fish // 복숭아에서 ~ remove the stone [pit] from a peach / pit a peach.

바르다³ **1** [곧다] straight; erect; upright. ¶바른 자세 good posture // 바른 길 a straight road // 바른 자세로 in an erect[upright] position[posture] / sitting[standing] erect [upright] // 자세를 바르게 해라 Hold yourself straight[erect].
2 [참되다] honest; upright; true; straight; [솔직하다] straightforward; frank; [옳다] right; true; just; [정확하다] correct; accurate; exact. ¶마음이 바른 righteous / righthearted / right-minded / upright / honest // 바른 방법 the proper way / the correct method // 바른말을[옳은 말을] 하다 tell [speak] the truth / tell what is right / [입바른 말을 하다] speak straight out [frankly] / in a straightforward manner // 바른 일만 한다면 겁낼 것이 없다 If you are upright in all your actions, you need not fear anything. // 네가 훔쳤다고 바른대로 말해라 Be honest and tell me[Make a frank confession] that you have stolen it.
3 sunny. ⇨양지바르다.

바르르 **1** [끓어오르는 모양·소리] seething; bubbling; in bubbles; boiling; hissing; fizzing. ¶~ 끓기 시작하다 come to a bubbling boil. // 물이 ~ 끓는다 The water comes to a bubbling boil.
2 [사소한 일에 성을 내는 모양] in a fit of anger[passion]; in hot blood; in a huff. ¶~ 성이 나다 flare up in anger / boil up // 그는 화가 나서 ~ 떨었다 He trembled with anger. // 그 광경을 보고 그는 ~ 성냈다 The sight made his blood boil[him boil over].
3 [불이 가볍게 타오르는 모양] in a (sudden) burst of flame. ¶~ 타오르다 flare up (into flames).
4 [떠는 모양] trembling; shivering; quivering. ¶추위에 ~ 손을 떨면서 with trembling hands with cold // 무서워서 ~ 떨다 tremble for fear / shiver with fright / shudder at (the sight, etc.) // 그는 추워서 ~ 떨었다 He shivered with cold.

바른길 **1** [곧은길] a straight way[road]. **2** [옳은 길] the path of righteousness[virtue / duty]; the straight path; the right track. ¶~로 되돌리다 guide (a person) back to the right path // ~을 가다 tread the path of righteousness / follow the path of virtue / pursue the honest career / be just / keep to the right path // ~에서 벗어나다 stray from the right track[the path of righteousness].

바른말 [옳은 말] a right[proper / reasonable] word; truth; [직언] plain speaking; a straight talk; a candid[frank / straightforward] remark; outspoken advice. ¶~을 하는 사람 a plain-[free-]spoken person / an outspoken person // 상사에게 ~을 하다 speak plainly[frankly / without reserve] to one's boss // ~은 귀에 거슬린다 Outspoken advice is[sounds] harsh to the ear. / Unpleasant advice is a good medicine. / A good medicine tastes bitter[is bitten to the taste].

바리¹ **1** [여자의 놋쇠 밥그릇] a woman's brass rice bowl. **2** [불] a wooden rice bowl used by temple priests. ⇨바리때

바리² [짐을 세는 단위] a pack; a load; a horse-load. ¶이 모래는 말 한 ~의 짐에 불과하다 This sand makes only a horse-load.

바리때 [불] a wooden rice bowl used by temple priests.

바리캉 (㉘ bariquant) (a pair of) hair [barber's] clippers; a hair[barber's] clipper.

바리케이드 a barricade. ¶~를 치다[쌓다] set up a barricade / barricade (a place) // ~를 돌파하다 break through a barricade.

바리톤 [음] [테너와 베이스 사이의 음역] barytone; baritone; [그 음역의 가수] a barytone (singer). ¶~의 baritone // 힘찬 ~으로 노래하다 sing in a vigorous baritone.

바림 [미] shading off; shade.

바바리(코트) a trench coat; (상표명) a Burberry (coat).

바베큐 → 바비큐

바벨 [역기] (lift) a barbell.

바벨탑(-塔) the Tower of Babel.

바보 a fool; a simpleton; an ass; a donkey; a goose; [멍청이] a stupid fellow; a dunce; a blockhead; a thickhead; a cabbagehead; a fathead; a dunderhead; a dullard; a dolt; a minny; a dolt; a ninny; a booby; a chump; (미국 속어) a dumb-bell; a nut; [백치] an idiot; an imbecile. ¶~짓 a foolish act / a fooly / a foolery / a tomfoolery // ~의 [~ 같은] foolish / silly / stupid / weak-minded / dull-witted // ~ 같은 얼굴 a stupid look [face] // ~짓을 하다 do a foolish [silly] thing / commit a folly / make a fool [an ass] of // 이 ~ 녀석아 You idiot! // 그는 ~ 같은 짓만 한다 Everything he does is stupid. // 뭐야, ~같이 Nonsense! // 이 무슨 ~ 같은 짓이냐 What a foolish [silly] thing you have done! // 저 아이는 ~다 That kid is not all there. / That kid has a screw loose. // 저 사람은 늘 ~ 같은 소리만 한다 That man is forever saying dumb [stupid] things. // 10만 원을 흘리다니 [잃다니] 정말 ~스런 짓이다 How stupid [What bad luck], losing a hundred thousand won! // 그는 정말 ~다 He is a real dolt. // 그런 ~ 같은 말은 들어 본 적이 없다 I have never heard of such a stupid [an absurd] thing. / Such stupidity is unheard of. // 전동차를 잘못 타다니 내가 정말 ~였어 What a fool I was [How stupid of me] to take a wrong train! // ~는 죽을 때까지 ~다 A fool remains a fool until he dies. // ~에는 약도 없다 There's no medicine that can cure a foolish head. // ~는 불행을 자초한다 A fool hunts for misfortune. // ~와 가위는 쓰기 나름이다 Even fools and blunt scissors can be useful in the hands of a clever person. // ~는 한 가지 얻어 배우면 아무 때나 써먹으려 한다 A fool always tries to show off the only thing he knows.

바비큐 [통구이] a barbecue. ¶~로 하다 barbecue (meat).

바쁘다 1 [겨를이 없다] busy; (서술적) be occupied; be engaged; be all tied up; be not free. ¶바쁜 사람[몸] a busy person // 바쁜 생활[하루] a busy life [day] // 이 바쁜 시대에 in these bustling times // 바쁜 몸에도 불구하고 despite the claims of a busy life // 눈이 핑핑 돌 정도로 ~ live in a whirl of business / be in a rush // 공무로 바빠서 by [on account of] stress [pressure] of official business // 일 때문에 ~ I am busy with my work. // 나는 여행 준비로 바빴다 I was busy getting ready for my journey. // 나는 오늘 몹시 바빴다 I've had a hectic time today. // 여러 가지로 바빠서 편지를 쓸 수 없다 I have so many things to do that I have no time to write letters. // 이달 말까지는 계속 ~ I'm fully occupied [(문어) engaged] until the end of this month. // 우리는 바쁜 일정으로 읍에서 읍으로 뛰어다녔다 Our schedule was full [tight], and we were rushed from one town to another. // 바쁘신데 죄송합니다 I'm sorry to trouble [intrude on] you when you are so busy. // 손님이 오시는 날이면 어머니는 아침 일찍부터 바쁘시다 Whenever we have visitors my mother is busy [hard at work] from early in the morning. // 나는 자질구레한 일로 몹시 ~ I am very busy with odd jobs. // 그는 노는 데 ~ He is always busy seeking pleasure. // 선생님은 시험지 채점하시느라 바쁘시다 The teacher is busy marking papers. // 바쁘신 데 와 주셔서 감사합니다 Thank you very much for coming right in the middle of your day. **바삐** busily; like a busy bee. ¶~ 지내다 lead [live] a busy life // ~ 일하다 work busily / be hard at work.

2 [급하다] pressing; urgent; immediate; hurried; hasty. ¶바쁜 걸음으로 at a quick [brisk] pace / with hurried [hasty] steps // …하기에 ~ be intent [bent] on (doing) / be eager [anxious] to (do) // …하기가 바쁘게 […하자마자] no sooner ... than / hardly [scarcely] ... when [before] // 아버지는 바쁜 일로 읍에 가셨다 My father has gone to town on urgent [pressing] business. // 뭐가 그리 바쁘냐 What's the hurry? // 그것은 바쁜 것은 아니다 There is no hurry about it. // 요전에는 너무 바빠서 실례했습니다 I was in such a hurry the other day that I'm afraid I was impolite to you. // 가장 바쁜 일을 먼저 마치겠다 I'll finish the most pressing work first. **바삐** in a hurry; in a hurried manner; hurriedly; in haste; hastily; in a rush; [즉시] at once; without delay [loss of time]; immediately. ¶~ …하다 hasten to (something) in a hurry / lose no time in (doing) // ~ 집으로 돌아오다 hurry (back) home // ~ 타다 [내리다] hurry on [off] // ~ 걷다 walk hurriedly [briskly / with hurried steps] / go with (all) speed / make the best of one's way / (미) rush along // ~ 굴다 behave hurriedly / hurry (up) / make haste / rush / bustle (about) // ~ 서둘러라 Hurry up! / Make haste! / Be quick! / (속어) Jump to it!

바삭 [잎 등의] with a rustle [a rustling sound]; rustlingly; (깨물 때의) with a crunch. **바삭하다** give a rustle; rustle; crunch; crack.

바삭거리다 rustle; crinkle; crunch (again and again). ¶나뭇잎이 밤바람에 바삭거렸다 The leaves rustled in the night breeze. // 가랑잎이 발밑에서 바삭거린다 The fallen leaves crunch under my foot.

바삭바삭 rustlingly; with a rustling sound; with a rustle [crinkle / crisp sound]. ¶~ 소리를 내며 꾸러미를 열다 undo wrapping with a rustling noise // 이 과자는 ~ 소리가 난다 This rice cracker is crisp [crunchy]. // 낙엽이 ~ 소리를 냈다 The fallen leaves rustled. **바삭바삭하다** rustle. ⇨ 바삭거리다

바셀린 vaseline.

바소 [침] a lancet.
바소쿠리 a wicker basket[dirt-carrier].
바수다 break (into pieces). ⇨부수다
바순 [목관 악기의 하나] a bassoon.
● 바순 연주자 a bassoonist.
바스대다 [자꾸 움직이다] stir[move] restlessly; be restless; be fidgety; fidget; be never still. ¶바스대는 아이 a restless [fidgety] child // 바스대지 말고 가만히 있어 Be still and don't fidget!
바스락 with a rustle[rustling sound]; faint(ly); indistinct(ly); stealthily; with a low [soft / muffled] sound. ¶~ 소리에 놀라다 be surprised by a rustling sound // ~ 소리도 들리지 않았다 Not a stir was there[heard]. / 방구석에서 쥐가 ~ 소리를 냈다 A rat made a rustling noise in the corner of the room. **바스락하다** rustle. ⇨바스락거리다
바스락거리다 rustle; make a rustling sound. ¶바람에 낙엽이 바스락거렸다 The fallen leaves were rustling in the wind. / The wind rustled the fallen leaves. // 그녀는 종이 봉지에 손을 넣어 바스락거리며 뭔가를 찾고 있다 She is rummaging for something in a paper bag with a rustle. // 쥐가 헛간에서 바스락거리며 돌아다니고 있다 Rats[Mice] are scurrying [rustling] about in the barn.
바스락바스락 rustlingly; with a rustling sound; with a rustle. **바스락바스락하다** rustle. ⇨바스락거리다
바스러뜨리다 break (into pieces); crumble; crush; shatter.
바스러지다 1 [부서지다] break; be broken [smashed / crushed / shattered]; go[tear] to pieces; go smash; crumble. ¶빵이 ~ bread crumbles // 바스러지기 쉬운 easy to break[crumble] / fragile. 2 [얼굴이 쪼그라지다] get thin[lean] (for one's age); get emaciated. ¶바스러진 얼굴 a haggard[gaunt] face // 근심 걱정으로 바스러진 얼굴 a care-worn face.
바스켓 a basket.
● 바스켓볼 [농구] basketball; [농구공] a basketball.
바심[1] [재목을 다듬는 일] trimming lumber. **바심하다**[1] trim[dress / shape / smooth] lumber.
바심[2] 1 harvesting grain before it is ripe. ⇨풋바심 2 [이삭을 떨어 낟알을 거둠] threshing. **바심하다**[2] thresh.
바싹 1 [물기가 없게] (dried up) completely; in a parched manner; bone-dry; scorched; [타 버리게] burnt up[off]. ¶~ 말라붙은 도랑[우물] a dried-up ditch[well] // ~ 마르다 dry up / be dried up / run dry(우물 등이) // ~ 타고 재만 남다 be (completely) burnt to ashes // 목이 ~ 마르다 I am parched. / My throat is as dry as dust. // 이런 날씨에 빨래가 ~ 마른다 In this weather the washing dries very quickly[nicely]. / 튀김은 튀겨야 맛이 있다 Fried food tastes best when it is fried crisp.
2 [밀착하여] closely; close to; side by side; hard (by). ¶~ 붙어 앉다 sit closely together / sit close to each other // …의 뒤를 ~ 따라가다 follow close(ly) on the heels of (a person) / dog the heels of (a person) // 차를 길 오른쪽의 ~ 대다 bring a car to the very [extreme] edge of the right hand side of the road.
3 [짧게] short; close; [최소한으로] to the minimum. ¶손톱을 ~ 깎다 cut one's nails close / cut a nail to the quick.
4 [단단히] firmly; tightly; fast. ¶~ 동여매다 bind fast.
5 [여위어] leanly; haggardly; emaciatedly. ¶~ 마른 사람 a skinny[lean and scrawny] person // a living skeleton // 몸이 ~ 마르다 become[get / grow] emaciated / be reduced to a shadow[skeleton] // 그는 ~ 말랐다 He is terribly skinny.
6 [완강히] stubbornly; resolutely; obstinately; [거침없이] quickly; remarkably; markedly. ¶~ 늘다 increase markedly // ~ 우겨 고개를 저으며 with an obstinate toss of one's head // 그는 그의 계획을 더욱 ~ 해치울 것을 결심했다 He decided to finish his plan more quickly.
바야흐로 1 [한창] at the height (of); in full swing[operation]; [바로] just; really; truly. ¶~ 봄이다 Spring is really here. / We are now in the midst of spring. // ~ 딸기 철이나 Strawberries are now in season. // 가 보니 ~ 싸움이 한창이었다 I found them at the height of quarrel. 2 [이제 곧] (be) about to (do); on the point[brink / verge] of (doing); almost; nearly. ¶해가 ~ 지려고 하고 있다 The sun is about to sink[set]. // 꽃봉오리가 ~ 벌어지려고 한다 The buds are just ready to burst. // ~ 승리를 위해 나아갈 순간이다 This is the moment to go for victory.
바운드 [공이 튀어 오름] bound; bounce. ¶공을 원 ~로 잡다 catch a ball on the first bounce. **바운드하다** bound; bounce. ¶(야구에서) 공이 불규칙하게 ~ take a bad hop.
바위 a rock; a crag(울퉁불퉁한); a reef(암초). ¶흔들~ a rocking stone / a log(g)an (stone) // ~투성이의 // ~가 많은 rocky / cragged / craggy // ~처럼 단단하다 be as firm as a rock.
바위를 차면 제 발부리만 아프다(속담) If one kicks a rock, it only hurts one's own foot.; If you act on impulse, you will make an awful mess of[shall have to pay for] it.
● 바위솔 [식] a houseleek; a sengreen. 바위옷 (rock) moss; lichen. ¶~이 끼다 be covered with moss / be mossy. 바윗돌 a rock block; a block of rock.
바음자리표 (-音-標) [음] the bass clef. ⇨낮은음자리표
바이러스 a virus. ¶~(성)의 viral // 인플루엔자 ~ an influenza[a flu] virus.
바이블 the Bible. ¶~에 맹세하다 swear on the Bible.
바이스 [공] (미) a vise; (영) a vice.
바이애슬론 biathlon.
● 바이애슬론 선수 a biathlonist.
바이어 a buyer; a buying agent from abroad.
바이올렛 1 [식] a violet. 2 [보랏빛] violet.
바이올리니스트 a violinist.
바이올린 a violin; [구어] a fiddle. ¶~의 명수 a master violinist // 제1[2] ~ (play) the first [second] violin[fiddle] // ~을 켜다 play the violin.
바이킹 [역] a Viking.
바이트[1] [절삭 공구] a bite.
바이트[2] [컴] a byte.
바자 [자선시] a bazaar; (미) a bazar; a rummage sale. ¶자선 ~ a charity bazaar // ~를 열다 open[hold] a bazaar.

바작바작

바작바작 1 [씹거나 타는 소리] with a sizzling; crackling. ¶~ 소리 내다 crack / crackle / make a crackling sound / snap // ~ 타다 burn crackling // 숯이 ~ 불꽃을 튀겼다 A piece of charcoal crackled. // 밥이 솥에서 ~ 탄다 The rice is sizzling in the pot. **2** [마음 죄어드는 모양] fretfully; nervously; anxiously; in a state of apprehension [anxiety]. ¶속이 ~ 타다 be full of anxiety / be devoured by anxiety // 마음을 ~ 죄다 be impatient / be held in suspense / feel anxious (about).

바장이다 walk idly back and forth. ⇨ 버정이다

바장조(-長調) [음] F major.

바주카포(-砲) a bazooka (gun).

바지[1] (a pair of) trousers; (미) pants(▶ pants는 (영)에서는 속바지); (윗옷과 한 벌로 되어 있지 않고 스포티한) slacks; (주로 짧은 것) breeches.(▶ 모두 복수형으로 쓰임) ¶반- breeches / short pants / (무릎 위까지 오는, 남녀가 입는 (Bermuda) shorts // 속~ (미) (under-)shorts / (영) pants / drawers / 솜- wadded [cotton-padded] trousers // 승마~ riding breeches / peg tops // **양복**~ trousers // **여자**~ slacks // **작업**~ overalls // **나팔**~ bell-bottom(ed) trousers / bell bottoms (영국 속어) bags // 여벌의~ spare pants // ~를 걷어 올리다 roll up one's trousers [trouser legs] // ~ 단추를 채우다 button up one's trousers // 몸에 착 붙는 ~ closefitting trousers // ~를 벗다 take off trousers // ~ 단추가 끌러져 있다 Your trousers are unbuttoned.

바지[2] [배의 일종] a barge.

바지락(조개) [동] a short-necked clam; a baby-necked clam; a littleneck clam.

바지랑대 a laundry pole; a washline pole.

바지저고리 trousers and coat; [비유] a man of no guts; a good-for-nothing; (미국 속어) no-good; [무실권자] a figurehead; a dummy. **바지저고리만 다닌다**(속담) He has no backbone.; He is a straw man [a man of straw].

바지지 with a hiss [rip]. **바지지하다** give [let out] a hiss [rip]; hiss; rip.

바지직 with a hiss [rip]. ⇨ 바지지

바지직거리다 hiss (and hiss); keep ripping; fizz.

바짝 (dried up) completely; closely; short; firmly; leanly; stubbornly. ⇨ 바싹

바치다[1] **1** [드리다] give (to a superior); present; make a present (of); dedicate(저서·음악 등을); offer (to a god); make an offering (to); consecrate (to). ¶제단에 양초를 ~ offer candles on the altar // 남에게 저서를 ~ dedicate a book to a person // 돌아가신 아버님께 바칩니다 (저서의 헌사) Dedicated to the memory of my late father. // 나는 단에 꽃을 바쳤다 I offered flowers at the altar. // 나는 단에 꽃을 바쳤다 I laid [placed] flowers on the altar (as an offering). **2** [진력하다] devote; [희생하다] sacrifice. ¶일신을 ~ devote [dedicate / give] oneself to (a cause) // 목숨을 ~ sacrifice [immolate] oneself (for one's country) / give [lay down] one's life (for one's country) / die (for a cause) // 의학에 일생을 ~ devote one's life to medicine // 그는 모든 시간과 정력을 저술에 바쳤다 He devoted all his time and energy to writing. // 그는 그녀에게 사랑을 바쳤다 He offered his love.

3 [납입하다] pay; [납품하다] supply; serve; deliver; purvey. ¶세금을 ~ pay one's taxes // 뇌물을 ~ bribe (a person) / offer a bribe. **4** [윗분께 …해 드리다] do (a thing) for someone superior. ¶선생님께 숙제를 해 ~ hand in one's homework to one's teacher.

바치다[2] [지나치게 즐기다] be addicted to; be overly fond; be preoccupied with; have an excessive liking for; be mad [crazy / wild] about. ¶계집에 ~ be wild about women / be sex-mad // 술을 ~ be crazy about liquor [alcoholic drinks] / indulge in wine.

바캉스 (a) vacation; holidays; (프) vacances.

바코드 a bar code.

바쿠스 [로마 신화의 주신](酒神) Bacchus.

바퀴[1] **1** [수레바퀴] a wheel; a rundle; (무거운 가구 등에 다는) a caster. ¶자전거 ~ wheels of a bicycle // 앞 [뒷] ~ the front [rear] wheel // ~ 달린 재봉틀 a sewing machine on casters // ~를 **달다** fix a wheel // ~를 멈추게 하다 brake / apply [put on] the brake // 차~는 회전한다 The wheel turns round. **2** [도는 횟수] a round; a turn; [회전] a turn; a revolution; a rotation. ¶매초 두 ~씩 도는 바퀴 a wheel that makes two revolutions a second // 한 ~ 돌다 (둘레를) make a round [circuit] (of) / (담당 구역 등을) go [make] one's rounds / [산책하다] take a turn [round] / (바퀴가) make a revolution // 연못을 한 ~ 돌다 walk around [(영) round] a pond // 세계 [지구]를 한 ~ 돌다 travel round the world // 경비원은 빌딩을 한 ~ 돌았다 The (security) guard made his rounds of the building.
●**바퀴살** a spoke (of a wheel). **바퀴통** the hub (of a wheel); a nave. **바큇자국** a rut; a (wheel) track; a furrow; the print of a wheel. ¶~을 남기다 (make a) rut.

바퀴[2] [동] a croton bug; (일반적) a cockroach; a roach; a black beetle. ¶~가 날뛰는 roach-ridden (kitchen).

바탕[1] **1** [성질] nature; (a) disposition; temperament; temper; character; [재질] endowments; gifts; ability; talent; [소지·소질] an inclination; the making; [체질] (physical) constitution. ¶~이 좋은 사람 a man of good disposition // 그는 음악가가 될 ~이다 He has the making of a musician. **2** [물건의 바탕] (the) ground; field; (직물의) texture; weave. ¶검은 ~에 흰 무늬 a white pattern [design] on a black ground // 푸른 빛깔을 ~으로 한 실내 장식 an interior decorating scheme based on blue [with blue as its basic theme]. **3** [기초] foundation; groundwork; basis (pl. bases). ¶…에 ~을 두다 be based [founded] on ... // ~이 되어 있다 have a grounding (in Latin) // 이 계획은 현실에 ~을 두고 있지 않다 This plan is not based on the realities of life. // 그들의 행동은 이 이론에 ~을 두고 있다 Their behavior is based on this theory.

바탕[2] [활의 사정거리] a bowshot (=about 300 meter).

바터 [물물 교환] barter.
●**바터 무역** barter trade; (미) give-and-take trade. **바터제** the barter system [basis].

바텐더 (미) a bartender; a barman; a barkeep(er).

바통(⊕baton) **1** a baton. ⇨ 배턴 **2** [비유]. ¶~을 물려받다 succeed to / take over (a task).

바통을 넘기다 hand over (to …).

바투 near[close] (by); closely; close at hand. ¶~ 앉다 sit close[closely] // 손톱을 ~ 깎다 cut one's nails close[to the quick] // 좀 더 ~ 오시오 Come a little closer.

바특이 [조금 바투] a little bit close(ly); close to; right by. ¶책을 ~ 놓다 put[place] books close together.

바특하다 [국물이 적다] thick; not watery; rather dense. 바특이² thick(ly). ¶국물을 ~ 끓이다 boil down the soup / make the soup a bit thick(er).

바티칸 the Vatican.
●바티칸 궁전 the Vatican (Palace).

박¹ 1 [식] a gourd; a calabash. 2 a gourd (dipper). ⇨ 바가지 ¶쪽~ a small gourd (dipper) // ~을 타다 split a gourd in two.

박² 1 [긁거나 가는 소리] with a vigorous rasp [grate / scrape / grind]. 2 [찢는 소리] with a rip.

박(拍) [음] a beat.

박(箔) [금속을 얇게 편 것] (metal) foil; leaf(▶leaf 쪽이) 얇음); gilt(칠한). ¶금[은/석(錫)] ~ gold[silver / tin / lead] leaf // 금속을 ~으로 하다 beat metal into foil // 금[은]을 입히다 put gold[silver] leaf (over).

박(泊) stay. ¶4~ 5일의 여행 a five-day trip // 1~ 2식(食)에 3만 원 thirty thousand won a night including two meals // 1~을 하다 stay [(미) stop] overnight.

박격포(迫擊砲) a trench mortar; a mine thrower; a bomb-gun.

박공(膊栱) [건] a gable.

박꽃 a gourd flower.

박다 1 [말뚝 등을] drive[strike / knock]; ram down (a stake); wedge in(쐐기 등을). ¶말뚝을 ~ drive in a stake[a post] // 기둥에 못을 ~ drive a nail into a pillar // 상자 뚜껑을 못으로 박아 붙이다 nail the cover on a box // 우리는 새 말뚝을 박았다 We drove in a new stake. // 나는 비를 걸기 위해 못을 박았다 I hammered a nail to hang a broom from.
2 [음식에 소를 넣다] fill (rice cake) with (savory matter); stuff with. ¶만두에 소를 ~ stuff a bun (with bean jam) / fill a bun with stuffing / put stuffing[filling] in a bun.
3 [촬영하다] take (a photograph); [인쇄하다] print; put (a book) in print; impress; run [print / strike / work] off. ¶명함을 ~ have one's cards printed // 사진을 ~ take a picture[photograph] // 1,000부를 ~ print [strike] off one thousand copies.
4 [찍어 내다] make[cut out] (cookies) in a shape; shape.
5 [재봉하다] sew (by backstitch). ¶재봉틀로 커튼의 가장자리를 ~ stitch the edge of a curtain on one's sewing machine.
6 [상감하다] inlay; set; stud; enchase; gem(보석을); mount(금은 등을). ¶다이아몬드를 박은 왕관 a crown set with diamonds // 작은 진주를 박아 넣은 드레스 a dress studded with seed pearls // 반지에 다이아몬드를 ~ set a ring with a diamond.

박달(나무) [식] a kind of birch.

박대(薄待) unkind treatment. ⇨푸대접

박덕(薄德) scanty virtue; lack[want] of virtue. 박덕하다 (서술적) be scanty of virtue; be scant in virtue.

박동(搏動) (a) pulsation; (a) beat. ¶나는 심장의 ~을 느낄 수 있었다 I could feel the beat of my heart. 박동하다 pulsate; beat.

박두(迫頭) pressure; urgency; impendence. 박두하다 draw near; press; impend; be near [close] at hand; be imminent. ¶박두한 위험 a pressing[an impending] danger // 약속한 날짜가 박두했다 The appointed day is now close at hand[is just ahead]. // 시간이 박두했다 We are pressed for time.

박람(博覽) 1 [많이 읽음] wide reading; extensive knowledge. ¶~강기(強記)한 사람 a man of erudition and strong memory / a scholar well-informed and retentive in memory. 박람하다 read widely or extensively. 2 [널리 봄] getting a broad view. 박람하다 get a broad view of.
●박람회 an exhibition; (미) an exposition; a fair. ¶만국 ~ an international exhibition / (미) a world('s) fair.

박래품(舶來品) an imported[a foreign-made] article; (집합적) foreign[imported] goods.

박력(迫力) force; power; drive; wallop. ¶~ 있는 strong / powerful / able / convincing / forcible // ~이 없는 문체 an enervated[a washy] style // ~이 모자라다 be lacking in drive // ~이 약하다 be not aggressive enough // 그의 말엔 별로 ~이 없다 There is not much punch in his remarks.

박리(薄利) small profits; a narrow margin (of profits). ¶~로 팔다 sell at small profits.
●박리다매(多賣) small profits and quick returns(약어 S.P.Q.R.); quick sales at small profits; a nimble penny.

박멸(撲滅) eradication; extirpation; extermination; destruction; suppression; annihilation. 박멸하다 eradicate; extirpate; exterminate; destroy; suppress; annihilate; wipe out (of existence); make an end of; put down; stamp[wipe] out. ¶해충을 ~ destroy [annihilate / exterminate] vermin.

박명(薄命) [불운] a sad[hapless] fate; unhappiness; misfortune; [단명] a short life. ¶미인 ~ Beautiful women die young. / Beauty is often inconsistent with luck. / Beauty and luck seldom go hand in hand. 박명하다 unhappy; unfortunate; short-lived.

박물(博物) [넓은 견문] wide knowledge.
●박물관 a museum. ¶과학~ a science museum // 국립 ~ the National Museum // 대영 ~ the British Museum. 박물학 natural history; the study of nature.

박박¹ 1 [긁는 소리] (grate / rasp / scrape) hard[roughly / vigorously / with a vengeance]. ¶통을 ~ 문지르다 rub a tub hard / give a tub a good scrub // 셔츠를 ~ 비벼 때를 벗기다 scrub the dirt out of a shirt // ~ 씻다 wash roughly[vigorously] // 나는 수건으로 몸을 ~ 문질렀다 I rubbed myself hard with a towel. // 나는 벽에 붙은 오래된 껌을 ~ 긁어 냈다 I scraped some old gum off the wall.
2 [찢는 소리] with a sound as of tearing cloth to pieces; ripping up; shredding. ¶그는 그 편지를 ~ 찢었다 He tore the letter to pieces.
3 [짧게 깎은 모양] close; short. ¶~ 깎은 중대가리 a closely shaven head // 머리를 ~ 깎다 have one's hair closely cropped.

박박² [얽은 모양] (pockmarked) all over (the face); solid (with pockmarks). ¶그의 얼굴은 ~ 얽었다 His face is pitted with the ravages

박복 of smallpoxes.

박복(薄福) misfortune; ill luck; unhappiness; sad[hard] fate. **박복하다** unfortunate; unlucky; unhappy; ill-starred[-fated]. ¶박복한 사람 an unfortunate[ill-fated] person / a man out of luck // 박복하게 태어나다 be born under an unlucky star // 그는 자신의 박복함을 슬퍼했다[한탄했다] He grieved over his ill [tough] luck.

박봉(薄俸) a small[slender / meager / scanty / low] salary; poor pay; a pittance. ¶~자 a low-salaried person // ~으로 일하다[생활하다] work at[live on] small pay[salary] // ~에 만족하다 never complain of one's small salary[income] // 나는 ~에 쪼들리고 있다 I starve on (my) scanty pay.

박빙(薄氷) a thin coat of ice. ⇨ˆ살얼음

박사(博士) [대학의 가장 높은 학위를 지닌 사람)] a doctor; [정통한 사람] an expert; [학자·식자] a learned man. ¶A ~ Dr. A / 만물~ a well-informed person / a walking[living] dictionary // 문학[철학 / 의학 / 법학 / 신학] ~ a doctor of literature[philosophy / medicine / law / divinity].
● **박사 과정** the doctor's course (in law). ¶~을 하고 있다 be enrolled in a doctoral course [(미) program]. **박사 논문** a thesis for a doctorate; a doctoral thesis (dissertation). **박사 학위** a doctor's degree; a doctorate. ¶~를 수여하다 confer a doctorate on (a person).

박살 [조각조각 깨짐]. ¶~이 나다 be shattered / go to smash[pieces] // ~을 내다 shatter / smash / knock (a thing) to pieces / break (a thing) up // 유리창 ~이 났다 The glass was broken[smashed] to pieces[(구어) to smithereens]. // 충돌하여 차의 유리 창문이 ~났다 The windshield was shattered by the collision.

박살(撲殺) [때려죽임] clubbing[beating] (a person) to death. **박살하다** club[beat / knock / strike] (a person) dead[to death].
→ **박살당하다** be beaten to death.

박새[동] a (Korean) great tit; a titmouse.

박색(薄色) an ugly look[face]; a plain [homely(-looking)] woman. ¶천하에 없는 ~ be ugly enough to stop a clock.

박수[남자 무당] a *baksu*; a male divine [shaman]; a sorcerer.

박수(拍手) hand clapping; (a) clapping of hands; a handclap. ¶~를 보내다 give (a person) a clap / clap (a person) // ~로 맞이하다 receive a person with applause // 그가 모습을 나타내자 우레 같은 ~가 터졌다 A storm of hand clapping arose at his appearance. // 손님에게 ~를 보냅시다 Let's give our guest a big hand [a round of applause]. // 우레와 같은 ~ 속에 막이 내렸다 The curtain fell amid thunderous applause. **박수하다** clap (one's hands in applause).
● **박수갈채** cheers; cheering and clapping; applause; plaudits. ¶~로 환영하다 greet (a person) with loud applause.

박스 a box.

박식하다(博識-) erudite; learned; well-informed; knowledgeable. ¶박식한 사람 a well-informed[knowledgeable] person // 박식한 체하는 표정으로 with a knowing look / 박식한 체하는 사람 (구어) a know-it-all / a smart-alec // 그는 아주 ~ He has a wide knowledge of many things.

박애(博愛) love of mankind; philanthropy; [자선] charity; benevolence; humanity. ¶~의 philanthropic / benevolent / humane / charitable // 우리는 사람들의 ~ 정신에 호소했다 We appealed to the philanthropic spirit of the people. **박애하다** love (mankind); engage in philanthropy.
● **박애주의** philanthropism. **박애주의자** a philanthropist.

박약(薄弱) infirmity; feebleness; weakness. **박약하다** feeble; weak; flimsy; (근거·신용이) shaky; insufficient. ¶정신이 ~ be weak-minded // 근거가 ~ be based on insufficient evidence // 증거가 ~ have shaky evidence / be based on insufficient evidence // 의지가 ~ have a weak will / be weak-willed / be infirm of purpose.

박은이 [인쇄한 사람] a printer; a typographer.

박음질 sewing; sewing-machine stitches; a backstitch. **박음질하다** backstitch.

-박이 an inlaid one. ¶덧니~ a person who has a side[double] tooth.

박이다¹ 1 (속에) get stuck in[embedded]; run (a thorn) into; (마음에) sink deeply into one's mind. ¶못이 박인 손가락 a finger with a callosity // 그 일이 머릿속에 박여 잊혀지지 않는다 It sticks in my memory like a burr. 2 [몸에 배다] get[fall] into a habit (of); form [pick up] a habit (of). ¶인이 박이는 약 a habit-forming drug // 담배를 피우면 인이 박여 끊기 어렵다 Once smoking becomes a habit, you can hardly give it up. / The smoking habit stays with you.

박이다² [박게 하다] (인쇄물을) let[put into] print; (사진을) have one's picture taken. ¶책을 ~ put a book into print.

박자(拍子) time; rhythm; measure; beat; timing; [음] a musical time pattern. ¶2[3 / 4]~ duple[triple / quadruple] time // 4분의 2[3]~ two-four[three-four] time // 4분의 4 ~로 in four-four[common] time[measure] // ~를 맞추다 keep time with // 손가락으로 ~를 맞추다 beat [keep] time with one's finger // 왈츠는 4분의 3~ 음악이다 A waltz is a piece of music in three-four time. // 그녀의 노래는 ~가 맞지 않는다 Her singing is offbeat. / She can't keep time when she sings.
● **박자표 / 박자 기호** [음] a time signature.

박작거리다 bustle; be crowded. ⇨ˆ북적거리다

박장대소(拍掌大笑) applause mingled with laughter. **박장대소하다** engage in applause mingled with laughter; laugh aloud clapping one's hands.

박절기(拍節器) [음] a metronome. ⇨ˆ메트로놈

박절하다(迫切-) heartless; unfeeling; cold-hearted; hardhearted; cruel; indifferent; unkind. ¶박절한 처사 cold treatment // 박절한 사람 a heartless person // 박절한 말을 하다 speak cruelly[heartlessly] / say a harsh thing // 박절하게 거절하다 give a point-blank [flat] refusal.

박정하다(薄情-) unfeeling; heartless; cold-hearted; hardhearted; stonehearted; cruel.

박제(剝製) (행위) stuffing; mounting; (물건) a stuffed[mounted] specimen. ¶동물의 ~ a stuffed animal. **박제하다** stuff[mount] (a bird). ¶박제한 새 a stuffed bird.

●박제사(-師) a taxidermist. 박제술 taxidermy.
박주가리 [식] a milkweed.
박쥐 [동] a bat; a flittermouse; an aerial mammal.
●박쥐구실 opportunism; a wait-and-see policy; a seesaw policy.
박진감(迫眞感) truthfulness to life; verisimilitude. ¶~이 있는 true to life[nature] / realistic / lifelike∥그의 ~ 있는 연기 his (compellingly) realistic acting∥이 초상화는 ~이 있다 This portrait is drawn to life.∥그 연기는 ~이 없다 The performance is not very convincing[true to life].
박진하다(迫眞-) 《서술적》 be true to life[nature]; be lifelike; be realistic.
박차(拍車) a spur; a rowed spur(톱니가 달린); [촉진] speeding up; acceleration.
박차를 가하다 (말에) set[put] spurs to one's horse; spur (on) one's horse; [비유] spur [put] (a person) (to do / into action); accelerate; give impetus to. ¶마라톤 선수는 마지막 박차를 가했다 The marathon runner put on a last[final] spurt.∥그 사건은 교육 논쟁에 박차를 가했다 The incident added fresh fuel to the educational controversy.
박차다 [발길로 차다] kick away[off]; give a vigorous kick; kick out hard; [거절하다] reject (a request); turn down (a proposal). ¶그는 자리를 박차고 회의실을 나갔다 He stamped out of the conference room.∥대사는 자리를 박차고 나갔다 The ambassador walked out in protest.
박치기 butting; (서로의) bumping of heads. ¶남에게 ~를 먹이다 give a person a butt of head / butt a person. **박치기하다** give (a person) a butt of head; (서로가) bump into [against] each other; bump heads together.
박탈(剝奪) (권리 등의) deprivation; forfeit; forfeiture; (관직의) divestiture; (명예 등의) deplumation. ¶공민권의 ~ the deprivation [forfeit] of civil rights. **박탈하다** deprive [strip] (a person) of (his office); divest (a person) of (his rank). ➔박탈당하다 forfeit (one's civil rights) / be deprived of (one's rank) / be stripped of (all one's government and party posts)∥특권을 박탈당하다 be shorn of one's privilege∥그는 재산을 박탈했다 His property was forfeited.∥그는 관직을 박탈당했다 He was divested[deprived / stripped] of his office.∥그는 변호사 자격을 박탈당했다 He was disqualified as a lawyer.
박테리아 [생] a bacterium (*pl.* -ria).
박테리오파지 a bacteriophage.
박토(薄土) barren[poor] soil; sterile[infertile] land.
박편(薄片) a thin leaf[layer]; a scale; a flake.
박피(薄皮) (식물 등의) a thin skin; a pellicle; [피막] a membrane.
박하(薄荷) [식] mint; peppermint.
●박하뇌 menthol (crystals). **박하사탕** peppermint (candy). **박하정**(-精) mint camphor; essence of mint.
박하다(薄-) 1 [인색하다] illiberal; stingy; niggardly; tight; hard; (점수가) severe[strict] in marking; (인정이) inhuman; unfeeling; tough. ¶인심이 박한 세상 a hard[tough] world to live in∥점수가 ~ be strict[severe] in marking / be chary of marks∥박하게 굴지 마라 Don't be so stingy. 2 [소득 등이 적다] scanty; meager; little. ¶그 장사는 이가 박했다 The business yielded only small profits.
박학(博學) erudition; extensive learning; wide [encyclop(a)edic] knowledge. **박학하다** erudite; learned; well-read; well. ¶박학한 사람 a man of erudition∥그는 박학한 체한다 He pretends to know much.
●박학다식(-多識) being erudite and well-informed. ¶~한 사람 a well-informed man with broad vision.
박해(迫害) persecution; oppression; torment. ¶~의 희생자 victims of oppression∥종교상의 ~ religious persecution∥많은 신도들이 ~를 당했다 Many believers suffered persecution[were persecuted]. **박해하다** persecute; oppress; torment.
●박해자 a persecutor; an oppressor; a molester.
박히다 1 [들어가 꽂히다] stick; be stuck; run into; get stuck[imbedded / driven in]. ¶탄환이 벽에 박혔다 The bullet lodged in the wall.∥내 손에 가시가 박혔다 I have a splinter in my hand. 2 [찍히다] be taken(사진이); be printed(인쇄물이). ¶사진이 잘 박혔다 The photo came out good. 3 [한곳에 들어앉아 있다] be confined in; remain indoors. ¶그녀는 온종일 방 안에 박혀 있다 She keeps her room all day long.

밖 1 [바깥쪽] the outside; [외부] the exterior; [옥외] the outdoors; the open (air). ¶당선권 ~에 있다 be out of the running (in an election)∥창문 ~을 내다보다 look out of the window∥~에서 조금 운동을 하다 get some outdoor exercise∥울타리 ~에서 발걸음 소리가 나는 것을 들었다 I heard footsteps outside the fence.∥이 창문은 ~으로 열린다 This window opens outward.∥그는 방 ~으로 뛰어나갔다 He rushed out of the room.∥나는 ~에서 문을 잠갔다 I locked the door from the outside.∥술 취한 그 자를 ~으로 내쫓아라 Throw the drunk out.∥~에 나가 놀아라 Play outdoors[out of doors].∥~의 온도는 몇 도냐 What is the outdoor temperature?∥오늘은 ~에서 식사를 한다 I'm eating[(문어) dining] out today.
2 [이외] another; the other; the rest; outside of (a limit); with the exception of; [다른] else; [다만 …뿐] only; but; no more than; merely; barely. ¶이 ~의 장미는 모두 붉다 All the rest of the[All the other] roses are red.∥이 ~의 사람들은 모른다 I know nobody but these people.∥이 ~에 한 씨 부부도 참석했었다 Besides, Mr. and Mrs. Han were there.∥그는 이 ~에 체험담을 이야기해 주었다 In addition, he told us about his experiences.∥이 ~에 필요한 것은 없느냐 What else do you need?∥20명은 제1교실에서, 그 ~의 사람은 음악실에서 대기해 주시오 Twenty of you are to wait in classroom No. 1, and the others in the music room.∥그녀는 피아노, 바이올린, 그 ~에 여러 가지 악기를 가지고 있다 She has a piano, a violin, and various other instruments.∥그는 인생, 사랑, 죽음, 그리고 그 ~에 여러 가지 일에 대해서 이야기했다 He talked about life, love, death, and so on[forth].∥거기는 덥지만, 그 ~의 모든 방은 시원하다 It is hot there, but all the other[rest of the] rooms are cool.∥그 ~에 무엇을 원하느냐 What else do you want?∥그 ~에 무엇을 그가 주더냐 What else did he

give you?// 아이들에게 책이랑 그 ~의 많은 것을 주었다 I gave the children books and many other things.// 그 ~에 그는 그들의 다음 기획에 대해서 우리에게 설명했다 In addition, he explained to us about their next project.// 그 ~로 책으로 내 관심을 끈 것은 하나도 없었다 That was the only book I was interested in. / I was not interested in the rest of the books[the other books].// 그것은 문제 ~이다 That is out of the question.// 그 문제는 나의 전문 분야 ~이다 That subject is out of[not in] my line.

밖에 [이외에] another; the other; the rest; outside of (a limit); with the exception of; [다른] else; [다만 …뿐] only; but; no more than; merely; barely. ¶나는 이것~ 가지고 있지 않다 This is all I have. / I have nothing but this. / I have only this.// 나는 그와 한 번 ~ 만나지 않았다 I have met him only [(문어)] but] once.// 나는 그의 행위가 배신으로~ 생각되지 않았다 I could not help regarding his conduct as a betrayal.// 그 곡을 그렇게 잘 부를 수 있는 사람은 그 사람~ 없다 No one else can sing that tune as well as he. / He alone can sing that song so well.// 설탕이 그것~ 남아 있지 않느냐 Isn't there any more sugar left?// 그는 그것~ 말하지 않았다 That was all he said.// 나는 잠자코 참는 수~ 없었다 I had no choice[There was nothing for it] but to endure in silence.// 돈은 이것~ 없다 I have only this much money. / This is all the money I have.// 그는 언제나 이것~ 주지 않는다 This is all he ever gives me. / He never gives me any more than this.// 나는 그이~ 아는 사람이 없다 I know nobody[no one] but him.// 그것을 할 수~ 도리가 없다 There is nothing for it[We have no choice / There is no other way] but to do that.// 나는 그것을 듣고 쓴웃음을 지을 수~ 없었다 I could not help smiling a bitter smile when I heard of it.// 아버지에게 경제적 도움을 청하는 수~ 없었다 There was nothing for it but to ask my father for financial help.// 그 사람~ 적임자가 없다 He is the only one who [No one else] is fit for the post.

반(反) [철] the antithesis (pl. -ses).

반(半) 1 [절반] (a) half. ¶양동이에 물을 ~만 채우다 fill half a bucket with water / fill a bucket halfway with water// 수박을 ~으로 자르다 cut a watermelon in half// 50의 ~은 25이다 Half of 50 is 25.// 이 딸기의 ~은 썩었다 Half (of) the strawberries are rotten.(▶ 동사는 half (of) 뒤의 명사의 수와 일치함)// 내 숙제는 아직도 ~밖에 끝나지 않았다 My homework is only half done.// 이익이 ~으로 줄었다 The profit fell fifty percent.// 그들은 재산을 ~씩 나누었다 They divided the fortune into equal halves.// 그는 ~은 무의식[농담]으로 그렇게 말했다 He said so half without thinking[half in jest].// 일은 ~은 끝났다 The work is half done.// 그 이야기의 ~은 거짓말이었다 Half of his story was false.// 이 책장의 책의 ~은 사전이다 Half the books on this shelf are dictionaries. **2** [중앙] the middle; the center; [중도] halfway. ¶인생의 ~을 지나다 pass the middle milepost of life// 이미 ~은 왔다 We have already covered half the distance. **3** [반쯤·거의]. ¶그는 ~은 포기하고 있었다 He had half[nearly] given up. **4** [중간 정도·거의 비슷한] half; semi-; demi-; hemi-. ¶~장화 half boots// ~영구적인 semipermanent.

반(班) **1** [집단] a party; a company; a group; a set; a team; a unit; [학급] a class; [군] a section; a squad. ¶상급[하급] ~ the senior [junior] class// 회화 ~ a conversation class// 수사 ~ a criminal investigation squad// 학생을 세 ~으로 나누다 divide the students into three classes// 신 선생님이 우리 ~의 담임이시다 Miss Sin is our class[(미) homeroom] teacher. / Miss Sin is in charge of our class. **2** [행정 구역] ban; a neighborhood association. ¶~상회 a (monthly) meeting of a neighborhood association.

반-(反) anti-. ¶~민주주의의 antidemocratic.

반가공품(半加工品) semimanufactured [semiprocessed] goods.

반가부좌(半跏趺坐) [불] sitting with one's legs half-crossed as in Buddhist statues.

반가워하다 be[look] glad[pleased / delighted] about (meeting); rejoice[be rejoiced] (in / over); take pleasure in. ¶소식을 듣고 ~ be overjoyed at (hearing) the news// 성공을 ~ be pleased with (a person's) success / rejoice in (a person's) sucess// 이 선물은 누구든지 반가워할 것이다 This gift would be acceptable to anyone.

반감(反感) (an) antipathy; animosity; ill feeling; an antagonistic feeling; a feeling of revolt; (a) revulsion of feeling. ¶~을 일으키는 repellent (action) / provoking (attitude)// ~을 사다 rouse (a person's) antipathy / antagonize (a person) / ~을 품다 harbor [nurse] ill feeling against (a person)// ~을 나타내다 show one's antipathy / jib against (another's act)// 소년은 엄격한 부친에게 ~을 가지고 있었다 The boy was antipathetic toward his strict father. / The boy felt hostile toward his over bearing father.// 과대광고는 사람들의 ~을 산다 The overdue advertisement arouse resistance(s) in the public.

반감(半減) a reduction[cut] by half. **반감하다** [줄이다] reduce[cut] by half[50 percent]; halve; (가격을) take off half the price; [줄다] be halved; be cut in half; be reduced by half; decrease to half. ¶그는 인플레이션으로 실수입이 반감했다 His real income was cut in half by the inflation.// 가치가 반감했다 Half of its value is gone[lost].// 불경기로 수출이 반감하였다 Exports were cut in half[halved] by the recession.

●**반감기** [물] a half-life; half(-life) period. ¶생물학적 ~ a biologic half-life// 방사능의 ~ a half-value period// 이 동위 원소의 ~는 23분이다 This isotope has (a) half-life of twenty-three minutes. / The half-life of this isotope is 23 minutes.

반갑다 glad; joyful; joyous; happy; welcome; delightful; pleasant (to see). ¶반가운 소식 glad[welcome / happy / joyful] news[(문어) tidings] // 반가운[반갑지 않은] 손님 a welcome[an unwelcome] guest// 반가워서 어쩔 줄을 모르다 / in one's joy// 반가워 반가운 일은 없다 Nothing gives us so great a pleasure as this. / Nothing can give greater pleasure than this. / Nothing is more gratifying than this. // 우리는 반갑지 않은 회답을 받았다 We received an unfavorable answer.// 오랜 가뭄 뒤에서 비가 ~ The rain is welcome after long spell of drought[dry weather] we've had.∥만나 뵈어 반갑습니다 Nice to meet you. / Glad to know you. **반가이** gladly; delightedly; joyfully; with pleasure[delight]; with[for] joy; happily. ¶~ 맞이하다 welcome (a person) / receive (a person) with great joy[with open arms].

반값(半-) half the price; a half price. ¶~으로 at half price / at half the (usual) price / half-price / at 50% off the regular price∥~에 사다 buy a thing for half the price[at half price]∥~으로 내리다 reduce the price to half∥~으로 깎아 주다 take off half the price / give a 50% discount.

반개(半開) 1 (문의) being half[partly] open; being ajar. **반개하다** be half open; be ajar. 2 (꽃의) being half in bloom; being half out. **반개하다** be half in bloom; be half out. 3 (문화의) being semi-civilized; being semi-barbarous. **반개하다** be half-[semi-] civilized.

반거들충이(半-) a half-baked[half-educated] person; a smatterer; a dilettante (pl. ~s, -ti); a sciolist; a man of half[superficial] knowledge. ¶~의 superficial / half-learned.

반격(反擊) a counterattack; a responsive attack; a counteraction; a counteroffensive; a counterdrive; a counterblow; a counterbuff. ¶~에 나서다 launch a counterattack. **반격하다** make a counterattack; counterbuff; strike[fight / beat / hit] back. ¶그는 바로 반격했다 He struck right back. / He gave as good as he got. / He countered[retaliated] boldly.∥적은 반격했다 The enemy made a counterattack (on us).
● **반격 작전** counterattack operations.

반경(半徑) ➡**반지름**
반고리관(半-管) [생] semicircular canals.
반골(反骨・叛骨) an uncompromising [a defiant] attitude of mind. ¶~의 unyielding / proud.
● **반골 정신** a spirit of defiance; an unyielding spirit.

반공(反共) anti-Communist; anti-Communism. ¶~의 anti-Communist∥~ 사상을 고취하다 infuse[instill] strong anti-Communist idea[spirits / sentiment] (into the mind of the public). **반공하다** oppose communism.
● **반공 교육** anti-Communist education. **반공정신** anti-Communist spirit. **반공주의** anti-Communism. **반공주의자** an anti-Communist.

반공(反攻) a counteroffensive; a counterthrust.
반공일(半空日) [토요일] Saturday; [반휴일] a half-holiday.
반관반민(半官半民) semi-governmental management. ¶~의 semiofficial / semi-government.
반구(半球) a hemisphere. ¶동[서]~ the Eastern[Western] Hemisphere.
반국가적(反國家的) antinational; antistate (activities).
반군(叛軍) a rebel army. ⇨**반란군**(⇨**반란**)
반기(半期) a half term[year]; a semester. ¶상[하]~ the first[latter] half of the year / 전[후]~ the first[second] half year / ~의 half-yearly / semiannual∥상[하]~ 무역 trading during the first[latter] half of the year.

반기(反旗・叛旗) a standard[banner] of revolt [rebellion].
반기를 들다 raise the standard of revolt; rise in revolt[rebellion] (against); take up arms (against); be up in arms (against). ¶그들은 정부에 대해 반기를 들었다 They revolted [rose in revolt / took up arms] against the government.(▶ took up arms는 무기를 들고 일어남)
반기(半旗) a flag at half-mast. ¶~를 게양하다 fly [hoist / hang out] a flag at half-mast [staff] / half-mast a flag.
반기다 be[look] glad (about); be pleased [delighted] (at / with); rejoice [be rejoiced] (in / at / over / to do); [환영하다] greet; welcome. ¶손님을 ~ be delighted to see a guest∥옛 친구를 ~ receive one's old friend with great joy[with open arms].
반기생(半寄生) [생] hemiparasitism. ¶~의 hemiparasitic / semiparasitic.
● **반기생 생물** a hemiparasite; a semiparasite.
반나절(半-) a quarter of a day; half the morning; several hours of the day. ¶~을 독서로 보내다 spend a few hours [half the morning] in reading.
반나체(半裸體) a half-naked body; seminudity. ¶~의 half-naked / seminude / semi-naked∥~의 시체 a half-naked dead body / ~의 사진 a seminude photograph.
반날(半-) half a day; (미) a half day.
반납(返納) return; restoration. **반납하다** return; give[send] back; restore. ¶우리는 이미 받은 특별 수당을 반납했다 We returned the special allowances that we had received.∥그들은 여름휴가를 반납하고 그 일을 마쳤다 They gave up their summer vacation[(영) holiday] in order to finish the work.
반년(半年) half a year; (미) a half year. ¶~마다 half-yearly / semiannually∥~마다의 결산 semiannual settlement of accounts∥이 잡지는 ~마다 간행된다 This magazine is published semiannually[every six months].
반닫이(半-) a clothes chest with a hinged front flap.
반달(半-) 1 [반원형의 달] a half moon; a dichotomy. 2 [한 달의 반] a half month. ¶~치[분]의 semimonthly (pay) ∥~마다 내는 정기 간행물 a semimonthly[biweekly / (영) fortnightly] (publication). 3 [의] [속손톱] a lunule; a lunula (pl. -lae).
반달가슴곰(半-) an Asiatic black bear; a Himalayan[Tibetan] bear; a moon bear.
반대(反對) 1 [위치・내용상의] the reverse; the inverse; the opposite; the contrary. ¶~의 opposite (direction) / contrary (opinion) / reverse (side) / adverse (wind) / ~로[거꾸로] 하다 (상하를) turn (a thing) upside down / (순번을) reverse the order∥연필을 ~로 쥐다 hold a pencil by the wrong end∥1,000을 ~로 세다 count from one thousand backward∥내가 그 상자를 ~로 놓았기 때문에 속에 든 것이 쏟아졌다 As I set the box wrong side up[upside down], the contents fell out.∥사실은 그 ~이다 Just the reverse [contrary] is true.∥나는 그 ~의 소문을 들었다 I heard a rumor to the contrary.∥단어의 순서가 ~이다 These words are in the wrong[opposite] order.∥그는 신사이기는커녕

반도

그 ~다 He is quite the opposite of gentleman.∥일반적인 예상과는 ~로 그는 선거에서 이겼다 Contrary to general expectations, he won the election.∥그는 ~ 방향으로 갔다 He went in the opposite direction.∥나는 핸들을 ~로 돌려 버렸다 I turned the wheel the wrong way.∥만사가 ~로 되어 버렸다 Everything went against me [wrong].∥그들의 입장(위치)이 ~가 되었다 Their positions have been reversed.∥그 ~입니다 It's the other way around!(▶ 상대방이 반대되는 말을 했을 때)∥그 아이는 신발을 좌우 ~로 신고 있었다 The child had the wrong shoe on the wrong foot.∥내가 그를 우리 편으로 끌어넣으려고 했는데 ~로 내가 그쪽에 끌려 들어가게 되었다 I meant to bring him over to our side, but instead I was persuaded to join his party.

2 (의견·행동상의) opposition; resistance; antagonism; hostility; (속어) kick; [이론] objection; dissension. ¶~의 opposite / contrary / hostile∥~를 위한 ~를 하다 oppose for opposition's sake [for the sake of opposition]∥그는 ~ 의견을 말했다 He made an objectionable comment.∥그의 계획은 친구들의 강한 ~에 부딪혔다 His plan met with strong opposition from his friends.∥그는 아내의 ~를 물리치고 투기에 손을 댔다 He went in for speculation in spite of his wife's opposition. **반대하다** oppose; be opposed (to); offer opposition (to); object (to); take exception (to); raise [make / have] an objection (to); take a stand (against); stand (against); antagonize. ¶…에 반대하여 in opposition to … / in defiance of … / against … / 끝까지 ~ stubbornly [tenaciously] oppose (a scheme) / hold out (against a person's order) / 여론에 ~ defy public opinion / 의안에 ~ vote against the bill∥그의 부모는 그 혼담에 극력 반대한다 His parents are strongly opposed to the match.∥그들은 내가 하는 일에는 무엇이든 반대한다 They are all against me whatever I do.∥그에게 반대한 사람들은 해고되었다 Those who were opposed to him were fired.∥우리는 전쟁에 강력하게 반대했다 We strongly objected to [opposed] the war.∥자네가 어느 편을 택하든지 나는 반대하지 않겠네 Whichever you may take, I will not object to it.

●**반대 개념** a contrary concept. **반대급부** a consideration. **반대 세력** counterforce; counterpressure. **반대 신문** [법] cross-examination. ¶~을 하다 cross-examine / cross-question. **반대어** an antonym; an opposite. **반대파** the opposing party; a dissident group; one's rival faction.

반도 (半島) ~의 peninsular∥한~ the Korean Peninsula.

반도 (叛徒) rebels; insurgents. ¶~를 소탕하다 mop up [clean up] the rebels.

반도체 (半導體) [물] a semiconductor.

반동 (反動) reaction; counteraction; (총 등의) kick; recoil; (탄력체의) resilience. ¶무~ 총 [포] a recoilless rifle [cannon]∥~적인 reactionary∥~으로서 as a reaction∥이 총은 ~이 거의 없다 This gun kicks only slightly.∥이 총은 ~이 세다 This rifle has a powerful kick [recoil].∥그들은 보수 ~이다 They are right-wing reactionaries. **반동하다** react; (총 등이) kick; recoil; rebound; (탄력체가) resile; spring back. ¶총은 발사 후 반동했다 The gun recoiled after I fired.

●**반동력** reaction. **반동분자** reactionary elements. **반동 세력** reactionary forces. **반동주의** reactionism. **반동주의자** a reactionary; a reactionist.

반드럽다 **1** [윤기가 나고 매끄럽다] smooth and shiny; glossy; sleek; slick; glazed; velvety. ¶반드러운 마루 a slippery [smooth] floor / 반드러운 볼 a smooth cheek∥반드러운 머리카락 sleek hair∥반드럽게 하다 smooth / make smooth∥이 종이는 감촉이 ~ This paper is smooth to the touch. **2** [약삭빠르다] sleek; slick; shrewd; smart; sharp; alert. ¶반드러운 녀석 a smart [shrewd] guy [fellow] / a slicker∥반드럽게 굴다 be keen after one's interests / be wide-awake (to one's own interests).

반드르르 smoothly; glossily; lustrously; sleekly. ¶~ 윤기 나는 머리카락 glossy [lustrous] hair∥~ 윤기 나는 얼굴 a bright [blooming] complexion. **반드르르하다** smooth; glossy; lustrous; sleek. ¶마루를 얼음장처럼 반드르르하게 닦다 polish a floor as smooth as a sheet of ice.

반드시 **1** [꼭] certainly; surely; infallibly; positively; upon one's life; by God; [틀림없이] without fail; [기필코] by all (manner of) means; at any cost; at all costs. ¶~ 필요하다 be positively necessary∥~ …하다 be sure [certain] to (do) / be bound to (do) / never fail to (do)∥그는 ~ 실패한다 He is bound [certain / sure] to fail. / (미) He'll never make it [succeed], I bet.∥식사 전에는 ~ 손을 씻어라 Be sure to wash your hands before a meal.∥내일은 ~ 비가 올 것이다 It is sure [certain] to rain tomorrow. / It will certainly rain tomorrow.∥그녀는 아들이 언젠가는 ~ 돌아올 것으로 믿고 있었다 She believed that her son would surely come back some day.∥그가 한 말은 ~ 실현될 것이다 What he said will undoubtedly [certainly] be realized.∥그는 아침 식사 전에 ~ 한 시간 산책한다 He never fails to take an hour's walk before breakfast.

2 [항상] always; invariably; habitually; (습관적으로); [필연적으로] necessarily; inevitably; of necessity. ¶~ …하다 make a point of (doing) / make it a rule to (do)∥~ …하지는 않다 [~ …하다고는 할 수 없다] not always [necessarily] … / not all … / not altogether … / not every … / not entirely [completely] …∥나는 아침마다 ~ 조깅을 한다 I make it a rule to go jogging every morning.∥그들은 만나기만 하면 ~ 싸운다 They never meet without quarreling. / They quarrel whenever they meet.∥그가 크다고 해서 ~ 강건하다고는 할 수 없다 A big man is not always robust. / Not all big men are robust.

반듯 with a flash. ➪**번듯**

반들거리다 **1** [윤이 나다] shine; have a gloss; get glossy [lustrous]. ¶의자가 낡아서 반들거린다 The chair is shiny with use. **2** [약게 굴다] be shrewd [smart / alert]. **3** [게으름 피우다] idle; lounge; loaf.

반들반들 **1** [윤나게] smoothly; glossily; lustrously; shiningly. ¶~ 곱게 갈아놓는 재료 materials with a good gloss. **반들반들하다** smooth; glossy; lustrous; shiny. ¶소매가 닳아 반들반들한 상의 a coat worn shiny in the sleeves. 2 [약게] shrewdly; smartly; alertly. **반들반들하다** shrewd; smartly; alert. 3 [게으르게] idly; lazily; slothfully. **반들반들하다** idle; lazy; slothful.

반듯하다 1 [곧다] straight; upright; erect; [고르다] even; square and level. ¶반듯한 길 a straight road // 반듯한 기둥 an upright post // 네모반듯한 종이 a perfectly square sheet of paper. **반듯이** straight; upright; in an even form. ¶~ 앉다 sit straight [erect squarely] // ~ 서다 stand straight [upright] // ~ 눕다 lie on one's back / lie face up // 연필을 ~ 쥐다 hold a pencil right // 그는 기둥을 ~ 세웠다 He set a post upright. // 자세를 ~ 하시오 Keep yourself in an erect posture. 2 [흠없다] flawless; decent; [단정하다] neat; tidy; [정연하다] orderly; regular; in good order [shape]. ¶반듯한 집안 a decent [respectable] family // 반듯한 옷차림을 한 사람 a well-groomed [neatly-dressed] person // 책상을 반듯하게 정리해 두다 keep a desk in (good) order. **반듯이** orderly; in good order [shape]. ¶구두를 ~ 놓다 put one's shoes squarely. 3 [반반하다] comely; well-shaped; clear-cut; nice-looking. ¶반듯한 용모 finely-chiseled features // 그녀는 용모가 ~ She has comely [classical] features. **반듯이** comelily; finely.

반등(反騰) a reactionary rise [advance]; a rebound; a rally; a regain. **반등하다** rally; rebound; rise in reaction. ¶반등한 값으로 팔다 sell on a rally.

반딧불 the glow [glimmer] of a firefly; glowfly light. ¶~같이 희미한 빛 a light as faint as the glow of a firefly.

반딧불로 별을 대적하랴(속담) Can a firefly cope with a star in brightness?

반딧불이 [동] a firefly; a glowfly.

반라(半裸) a half-naked body. ⇨ **반나체**

반락(反落) [증권] a reactionary fall (in stock prices); a fall in reaction. ¶주가의 ~ a reactionary fall in stock prices // 시세는 ~ 상태였다 The market fell as a reaction. **반락하다** fall [drop] in reaction; fall [slip] back. ¶철강주가 반락했나 Steel stocks have fallen in reaction.

반란(叛亂·反亂) a rebellion; a revolt; (an) insurgency; [폭동] an insurrection; [봉기] a rising; an uprising.(▶ rebellion은 무력에 의한 조직적인 반역으로 보통 실패로 끝남. revolt는 성패의 결과가 바로 나타나는 폭동) ¶~을 일으키다 rise in revolt [insurrection] / revolt [rise / rebel] (against) // ~을 진압하다 get under [put down / suppress / pacify] a revolt (against) // 국왕에 대한 ~이 일어났다 A rebellion broke out against the king. // 대령이 이끄는 일단이 대통령에 대하여 ~을 일으켰다 A force led by the colonel revolted [started a revolt] against the President. // 정부는 ~을 진압했다 The government put down the revolt. **반란하다** revel [revolt / rise] (against).

● **반란군** a rebel army; insurgent [mutinous] troops. **반란자** a rebel; an insurgent.

반려(伴侶) a companion; an associate; a comrade; a mate; a partner; (집합적) company. ¶평생의 ~ a companion for life / a life partner / one's spouse(배우자) // 이 책은 나와 같이 여름을 날 좋은 ~이다 This book is my best companion to pass the summer with.

반려(返戾) return; restoration; giving back; retrocession. **반려하다** give back; return; restore; retrocede. ¶사표를 ~ turn down [reject] a person's resignation.

반론(反論) a refutation; a counterargument; an opposing argument; a polemic (against). ¶그 정책에는 여러 가지 ~이 있다 There are all kinds of opposing arguments [counterarguments] against that policy. // 이 논의에는 ~의 여지가 없다 This argument admits of no refutation. **반론하다** refute; object to; bring forth [build up] a counterargument. ¶그의 말에 반론하는 사람은 아무도 없었다 Nobody objected to what he said.

반만년(半萬年) five millenniums [millennia / millenaries]; 5,000 years. ¶~ **역사** a 5,000 year-old history.

반말(반-) impolite speech; the low forms of speech. **반말하다** talk roughly [slovenly]; speak impolitely; use the low forms of speech (to); practice familiarism.

반면(反面) the other side; the reverse; the opposite. ¶~에 on the other hand / on the other side / while // 그는 점잖은 ~ 대담한 데가 있다 Though he is gentle, he also has a bold streak in him. // 이 도시는 물가가 싼 ~ 공공시설이 빈약하다 Prices are low in this town, but on the other hand, there aren't many public facilities, either. // 그는 재능도 있지만 그 ~에 결점도 없지 않다 He is able, but on the other hand he is not without fault.

반면(半面) (얼굴의) half the face; a half face; a profile(옆얼굴); (사물의) one side; a half. ¶달의 ~ the moon's disc // 문제의 ~을 보다 look on [upon] one side of a question // 그의 성격에는 그러한 ~도 있다 His character has such a phase, too.

반모음(半母音) [언] a semivowel.

반목(反目) [서로 싫어하고 미워함] enmity; antagonism; variance; hostility; enmity; feud. ¶두 정당 간의 ~ antagonism [hostility] between the two political parties. **반목하다** feud (with); be antagonistic [hostile] (to); be in antagonism (with); be at odds [variance / defiance] (with); be at feud [enmity] (with); be at loggerheads (with). ¶서로 ~ be hostile to each other // 서로 반목케 하다 set (a person) at odds with (another) / set (one class) against (another) // 두 집안은 서로 반목하고 있었다 The two families were feuding [at odds] with each other.(▶ feud는 오랫동안 앙심을 품고 있음을 나타냄)

반문(反問) [되받아물음] a return question; [반대 신문] a cross-question [-examination]. ¶검사의 ~은 엄격했다 The public prosecutor's cross-examination was relentless. / The public prosecutor put the witness through a rigorous cross-examination. **반문하다** [되받아묻다] ask a question in return; [반대 신문] cross-question; cross-examine. ¶나는 "누구 탓이냐?"라고 반문하고 싶었다 I would have liked to ask back, "Who to blame?"

반문(斑紋) a spot; a speckle. ¶~이 있는 spotted / speckled / mottled // ~을 찍다 spot / speckle.

반미(反美) [관형어적] anti-American [-U.S.].

●반미 감정 an anti-American sentiment. ¶국민들 사이에 ~이 흐르고 있었다 There was anti-American sentiment[feeling] among the people. 반미 운동[활동] anti-U.S. movement [activities].

반미개(半未開) semi-barbarism.
●반미개인 semi-barbarous people; a semi-barbarian.

반미치광이(半-) a slightly mad[crazy] person; a half-mad[-crazed] person.

반민주적(反民主的) antidemocratic. ¶~ 단체 an antidemocratic organization.

반바지(半-) knee trousers[pants]; knee[short] breeches; knickers; knickerbockers.

반박(反駁) (a) refutation; confutation; disputation; contradiction; disproof; retort; [법] rebuttal(원고의 반증에 의함); rebutter(피고의 반증에 의함). ¶~의 여지가 없는 irrefutable //그의 말은 ~의 여지가 없다 His statement is irrefutable. / There's no denying what he says. **반박하다** refute; confute; contradict; dispute; disprove; rebut; answer[shoot / talk / argue] back; take issue (with). ¶정면으로 반박하여 with a frontal rebuttal.

반반(半半) [반과 반·절반] half-and-half; fifty-fifty. ¶~으로 half-and-half / in half[halves] //~으로 하다 [나누다] halve / go halves / divide[cut] into halves / split fifty-fifty //~로 섞다 mix half-and-half //~으로 하자 I will go halves with you. / Let's go fifty-fifty. //그가 남긴 업적의 공과는 ~이다 He left behind a mixture of[both] benefits and damage. //그는 자기를 버린 어머니에 대해 사랑과 증오심이 ~이었다 He has mixed[ambivalent] feelings of love and hatred for his mother, who abandoned him. //찬성과 반대의 의견이 ~이었다 There were an equal number of assenting and dissenting opinions. //그들이 성공할 가능성은 ~이다 Chances are about even that they will succeed. / There's a fifty-fifty chance that they'll succeed. / They have a fifty-fifty[an even] chance of succeeding. //두 형제는 유산을 ~씩 나누었다 The two brothers divided the legacy equally[evenly]. //우리는 이익을 그와 ~씩 나누었다 We split the profits (fifty-fifty).

반반하다 1 [고르다] smooth; even; level; flat. ¶반반한 길 a level road //반반한 표면 a smooth surface. 2 [예쁘장하다] comely; pretty; handsome; attractive; charming; nice-looking. ¶반반한 집 a neat[snug] house //반반한 계집애 a pretty lass[girl] / a nice-looking girl / a cute little girl //그 여자 얼굴 반반한데 She is good to look. / She looks good. 3 [지체가 있다] decent; respectable; good. ¶집안이 ~ be of high[noble] birth / come of[from] good family.

반발(反撥) 1 [되받아 퉁김] repulsion; [되퉁겨짐] rebounding; a backlash. **반발하다** repel; repulse; bound[spring] back; rebound. ¶자석의 양극(陽極)끼리는 서로 반발한다 The two positive poles repel each other. 2 [반항] opposition; resistance; rebellion. ¶그와 같은 말에는 ~을 느낀다 I find such a remark repulsive. **반발하다** oppose; resist; defy; rebel (against). ¶아버지가 엄격했기 때문에 자식들은 반발했다 As their father was strict with them, the boys rebelled.
●반발력 repulsive[repelling] power; repulsive[repellent] force.

반백(半白) 1 [흑백이 반반씩 섞인 머리털]. ¶~의 gray-haired / gray / grizzled / grizzly / half-white //~의 사나이 a gray-haired man. 2 [현미와 백미가 반씩 섞인 쌀] polished rice mixed half-and-half[evenly] with unpolished one.

반벙어리(半-) a half-mute; a mumbler; a stammerer; one who lisps.

반병신(半病身) 1 [반불구자] a half-cripple; a semi-paralytic; a partially deformed [disabled / handicapped] person. 2 a half-wit. ⇨반편이.

반복(反復) (a) repetition; a repeat; iteration; reiteration; [음] epistrophe; anaphora(악절 의); (시·노래의) a refrain; a burden. ¶~적인 repetitious / repetitive //그가 말하는 방법은 달라도 같은 것의 ~에 지나지 않는다 He is only repeating himself, though in different terms. //이 노래는 ~이 너무 많다 There is too much repetition in this song. **반복하다** repeat; iterate; reiterate; do over again. ¶반복하여 repeatedly / over again / again and again //세 번 반복하여 읽다 read (a story) three times over //역사는 반복한다 History repeats itself.
●반복 기호 [음] a repeat mark. ⇨도돌이표

반봉건(半封建) semi-feudalism.

반분(半分) [반의 분량] (a) half; [반으로 나눔] halving; an equal division; taking equal shares; halves. **반분하다** halve; go halves [snacks / fifty-fifty] (with a person in something); divide (something) into equal shares[halves]; cut in[into] halves. ¶이익을 ~ go fifty-fifty on the profit / divide[share / distribute] the profit equally / split the profit //이 돈을 둘이 반분하자 Let's divide this money equally between us. / Let's share in this money.

반비(反比) [수] an inverse ratio.

반비례(反比例) [수] an inverse proportion; a reciprocal proportion. **반비례하다** be in inverse proportion (to); be inversely proportional (to). ¶~에 반비례하여 in inverse proportion to ... / inversely proportional to ... // X는 Y에 반비례한다 X is in inverse proportion to Y.

반사(反射) reflection; (영) reflexion; reverberation. ¶난~ diffused reflection //전~ total reflection //조건 ~ a conditioned reflex [response] //햇볕의 ~로 매우 따뜻하다 be very warm through the reflection of the sunshine. **반사하다** reflect; reverberate; throw [flash] back; (비추다) image; mirror (in). ¶물은 빛을 반사한다 Water reflects light. //달은 태양 광선을 반사하여 빛난다 The moon shines by the reflected light of the sun. //이 벽은 열파를 반사한다 This wall reflects heat waves.
●반사각[선] an angle[a line] of reflection. 반사경 a reflecting mirror; a reflector. 반사광[열] reflected light[heat]. 반사 광선 reflected rays. 반사 운동 a reflex movement. 반사 작용 [물][심] a reflex (action).

반사적(反射的) reflecting; reflective; reflexive. ¶~으로 reflectively / reflexively //그는 ~으로 공을 피했다 He dodged the ball reflexively [instinctively]. //"정말이야?" 하고 그는 ~으로 물었다 "Is it true?" he shot back instantly.

반사회적(反社會的) antisocial. ¶~ 집단 an

antisocial group // ~ 행위 antisocial action.

반상회(班常會) a neighborhood meeting; a monthly neighbor's meeting.

반색하다 show great joy; rejoice (in / at / over / to do); be delighted (in); light[brighten] up with joy; be all smiles; smile a welcome (to). ¶반색하며 승낙하다 give one's hearty approval / consent with pleasure // 그녀는 기다리고 기다리던 애인을 보자 반색하였다 She was rejoiced at[by] seeing the long-awaited man. / She received the long-awaited man with great joy[with open arms].

반생(半生) half one's life; half a lifetime. ¶전[후]의 the former[latter] half of one's life / ~을 보내다 spend half a lifetime.

반석(盤石·磐石) [큰 바위] a huge rock; a crag; [견고함] firmness. ¶~ 같은 as firm as a rock / adamantine / ~ 위에 지은 집 a house built on the rock // 국기(國基)를 ~같이 튼튼하게 하다 place one's country on a stable foundation / place the state in a position of perfect security.

반설음(半舌音) a semi-lingual (sound). ⇨ =반혓소리

반성(反省) self-examination; reflection; introspection; reconsideration(재고). ¶~적 심리 reflective psychology / ~을 촉구하다 ask [urge] (a person) to reconsider (the matter) / call for grave reflection. **반성하다** examine oneself; reflect (on); search one's heart[soul] (on a matter); introspect; reconsider. ¶자신의 행위를 ~ reflect on one's conduct // 반성하여 보면 on reflection / on second thought(s) // 반성하여 부끄러움이 없다 have an easy conscience // 내가 말한 것을 모두 반성해 보게 Reflect upon all I have said to you.

반성 유전(伴性遺傳) [생] sex-linkage.

반세기(半世紀) half a century. ¶4~ a quarter century.

반소(反訴) [법] a cross action; a counteraction; a counterclaim; a countersuit; a countercharge. ¶손해 배상의 ~ a counterclaim for damages // 그는 명예 훼손으로 ~를 제기하였다 He brought a cross action[a countersuit] for libel. **반소하다** counterclaim (against a person for a matter); countercharge (a person with a matter); plead a counterclaim (against a person for a matter); bring a cross action (against a person for a matter). ¶손 씨가 최 씨를 수회죄로 고소하자 최 씨는 손 씨를 명예 훼손으로 반소했다 Mr. Son charged Mr. Choe with bribery, and Mr. Choe countercharged Mr. Son with slander.

반소(半燒) partial destruction by fire. ¶~된 half-burnt / partially-burnt. **반소하다** be partially destroyed by fire. ➔¶화재로 창고가 반소되었다 The warehouse was partially destroyed by [in] a fire.

반소경(半-) **1** a one-eyed person. ⇨ =애꾸눈이(⇨)애꾸) **2** [시력이 약한 사람] a half-blind person; a person of purblind [blurred / dimmed] eyes. ¶~의 half-blind / purblind / dim-eyed / dim-sighted. **3** [글을 모르는 사람] an unlettered person; an illiterate; an ignoramus. ¶~의 unlettered / illiterate.

반소매(半-) a half(-length) sleeve. ¶~ 블라우스 a blouse with short sleeves / a short-sleeved blouse.

● **반소매 셔츠** a shirt with half-length sleeves.

반송(返送) sending back[home]; repatriation. **반송하다** return; send back. ¶선편으로 ~ ship back // 소포를 발송인에게 ~ return a package[send a package back] to the sender.

반송(搬送) conveyance. **반송하다** convey; carry.

반송장(半-) a half-dead person; a person who is as good as half-dead (from age and infirmity); a person who has one foot in the grave; a good-for-nothing old person. ¶그의 아버지는 ~이나 다름없다 His father is a little better than a corpse. / His father has one foot in the grave.

반수(半數) half the number; half (of the members). ¶위원의 ~ 개선(改選) the reelection of half the committee // ~를 넘다 be more than half the number / show[hold] a majority // 참석자의 ~는 대학생이었다 Half of the members were college students.

반숙(半熟) [반쯤 익힘]. ¶~의 half-[soft-]boiled / half-cooked / half-done. **반숙하다** boil (an egg) soft[lightly]; be half-boiled [half-done].

● **반숙란** a half-done egg; a half-boiled egg.

반식민지(半植民地) a semicolony. ¶~의 semicolonial.

● **반식민지 국가** a semicolonial state. **반식민지 상태** semicolonialism.

반신(半身) (상하의) half body; half-length; (좌우의) one side of the body. ¶상[하] ~ the upper [lower] half of the body // 오른쪽 ~이 마비되다 be paralyzed on the right side of the body.

● **반신불수** paralysis of one lateral half of the body; hemiplegia. ¶그는 ~가 되었다 He became paralyzed on one side. **반신상** a portrait of a person from the waist up(그림의); a half figure(조각의); a bust(흉상의).

반신(返信) a reply; an answer; (전신의) a reply telegram. ¶국제 ~ 우편 an international reply coupon // ~으로 in reply [response] to a letter. **반신하다** reply to a letter; answer a letter; send a reply (telegram).

● **반신료** ➔회신료(⇨)회신)

반신반의(半信半疑) ¶~의 incredulous / half in doubt / dubious. **반신반의하다** be half in doubt; throw some doubt on; do not quite believe; have[entertain] a doubt about; be doubtful[suspicious / distrustful] of. ¶반신반의하여 half in doubt / doubtfully / dubiously // 그녀는 그 기쁜 소식을 반신반의했다 She could not quite believe the good news.

반신반인(半神半人) a demigod.

반암(斑巖) [광] porphyry.

반액(半額) a half amount[sum]; half the amount [sum / price / fare]. ¶~으로 at half the price [fare] / at half price // ~으로 하다 reduce the price [fare] by half // ~을 환불[할인]하다 repay [discount] half the sum // 12세 미만의 어린이는 ~입니다 Children under twelve are allowed half rates. // 어린이는 ~임 (버스 등이) Half fare for children. / (입장료 등이) Half price for children. // ~에 드리겠소 You can have it for[at] half price. / I'll sell it to you at a fifty percent discount.

반야(半夜) **1** midnight. ⇨ =한밤중 **2** [반밤]

half a night.

반양성자(反陽性子) [물] an antiproton.
반어(反語)(비꼬기); a rhetorical question(수사적 의문); a word in reverse(역어(逆語)). ¶~적 표현 an ironical expression // ~를 쓰다 speak ironically.
반역(反逆·叛逆) (high) treason; breach of faith[allegiance]; treachery; (an) insurrection; (a) rebellion; (a) revolt; insurgency; mutiny; insubordination. ¶대~ heinous treason // ~적인 treasonous / treasonable / treacherous / traitorous / rebellious // ~을 꾀하다 conspire (against) plot treason (against). **반역하다** turn traitor; (권위에 대해) revolt[rebel] (against); rise in revolt [mutiny] (against).
● **반역자** a traitor; an insurgent; a rebel; a plotter; a mutineer. ¶~의 낙인이 찍히다 be branded with the disgraceful name of a rebel. **반역죄** (high) treason.
반열(班列) (a) rank; order. ¶…의 ~에 들다 rank[be ranked / attain a rank] among … / take one's place among … // 귀족의 ~에 들다 be raised on[to] the peerage.
반영(反映) reflection; [영향] influence. ¶민의의 ~ a reflex of the will of the people. **반영하다** reflect; influence; be reflected; be reflective of. ¶이 소설은 현대의 사회상을 반영하고 있다 This novel reflects contemporary social standing. → 외국인의 눈에 반영된 한국 Korea as she appears to foreign eyes / Korea as foreigners see it / Korea through foreigners' eyes // 국민의 여론은 국회에 반영된다 Public opinion is reflected in the National Assembly.
반영(半影) [천] a penumbra (pl. -brae, ~s); a partial shadow. ¶~의 penumbral.
반영구적(半永久的) (being) semipermanent. ¶~인 건물 a semipermanent building.
반올림(半─) rounding off to the nearest integer. **반올림하다** round; round (off) to the nearest whole number; count fractions of 5 and over as a unit (and cut[cast] away the rest). ¶11.3572를 소수점 이하 네자리에서 반올림하면 11.357이 된다 11.3572 rounded to the three decimals becomes 11.357. // 45.758을 소수점 이하 세자리에서 반올림하면 45.76이 된다 If 45.758 is rounded off to the second decimal place, it becomes 45.76.
반원(半圓) a half circle; a semicircle. ¶~의 semicircular / half-round // ~을 그리다 make [draw] a half circle / describe a semicircle.
● **반원형** a semicircle; a hemicycle. ¶~으로 앉다 sit in a semicircle.
반월(半月) a half moon. ⇨ **반달**1
반유대주의(反Judea主義) anti-Semitism. ¶~의 anti-Semitic.
반유동체(半流動體) [화] a semifluid; a semiliquid.
반음(半音)(半音程) [음] a (chromatic) semitone; a halftone; a half step. ¶~을 올리다 sharp (a note) by halftone // …보다 ~ 높다[낮다] be a half tone higher [lower] than ….
● **반음계** a chromatic scale.
반응(反應) [작용·감응] counteraction; [반향] a response; [효과] an effect; [화] a reaction. ¶거부 ~ (a) rejection // 알칼리성 ~ an alkaline reaction // 양[음]성 ~ a positive [negative] reaction // 연쇄 ~ a chain reaction // 투베르쿨린 [알레르기] ~ a tuberculin [an allergic] reaction // 핵~ a nuclear reaction // ~이 있는 responsive / effective / telling // ~이 없는 irresponsive / ineffectual / submissive / yielding // **~이 있다** react (to) / take[have] effect (on) // **~이 없다** show no reactions / have no effect (on) // **~을 일으키다** act on[upon] // 산성 ~을 나타냈다 It showed an acidic reaction. // 이 물질은 금속에 어떤 ~을 일으키는가 How does this substance react on metals? // 그의 제안에 대해 큰 ~이 있었다 There was a lot of response to his proposal. // 나는 그가 그 소식에 대해 어떤 ~을 보였는지 알고 싶었다 I wanted to know how he reacted to the news. // 진지하게 충고했지만 아무 ~이 없었다 I found in him nothing responsive to my earnest advice. // 이 제안에 대해서 위원들의 ~이 전혀 없었다 The proposal fell flat on the committee members. / The committee members showed no interest in the proposal at all. **반응하다** react (to / on); act (upon / on); respond (to); effect. ¶그 개의 귀는 어떤 작은 소리에도 반응했다 The ears of that dog reacted [responded] to the slightest sound. // 그들은 선생의 태도에 민감하게 반응했다 They were very sensitive to their teacher's attitude.
● **반응 물질** [화] reactant. **반응 속도** reaction rate. **반응열** heat of reaction.
반의반(半─半) half of a half; a quarter; one fourth. ¶사과의 ~이 썩었다 One fourth of the apples are rotten.
반의식(半意識) [심] subconsciousness.
반의어(反義語·反意語) an antonym. ¶「위」의 ~는 「아래」이다 "Down" is the antonym [opposite] of "up."
반일(半─) (하루 일의) half of a daywork; a half day('s) work; a half-time job; (어떤 일의) half of a work.
반일(反日) [관형어적] anti-Japanese.
● **반일 감정** anti-Japanese sentiment[feeling].
반일(半日) half a day; (미) a half day.
반입하다(搬入─) carry[bring / take] in. ¶전람회를 위해 그림을 반입했다 They carried in the pictures for exhibition.
반자성(反磁性) [물] diamagnetism. ¶~의 diamagnetic.
● **반자성체** [물] a diamagnetic (substance).
반작용(反作用) [물] (a) reaction; (효과를 상쇄하는) (a) counteraction. ¶~의 reactive / counteractive // 작용과 ~ action and reaction // ~을 일으키다 cause a reaction // 작용이 있으면 ~이 따르게 마련이다 Action is inevitably followed by reaction.
반장(班長) a squad [section / party / group] leader; (학급의) a monitor; a class president; (직공의) a foreman; (동네의) the head of a neighborhood association.
반장화(半長靴) half boots; short boots. ¶~를 신다[벗다] put on [take off] one's short boots.
반전(反戰) opposition to war; renunciation of war. ¶~ 안티war // ~을 부르짖다 cry against war / advocate peace.
● **반전론** opposition to (the) war(반전주의); pacifism(평화주의). **반전론자** a pacifist; a dove. **반전 운동** an antiwar movement.
반전(反轉) 1 [반대로 구름] revolution in the opposite direction; [기] reverse. **반전하다** reverse; turn[revolve] in the opposite direc-

tion. 2 [뒤바뀜] turning over; reversal; [수][화] inversion. **반전하다** [거꾸로 돌다] turn reversely [the other way round]; [거꾸로 되다] be reversed; [거꾸로 되게 하다] reverse; invert; [거꾸로 돌아오다] reverse its [one's] course. ¶이 버튼을 누르면 차바퀴가 반전한다 Press this button and the wheel will turn the other way.
● **반전 기어** a reversing gear.

반절(半折) a half. ⇨ '절반'
반절(半切·半截) (전지를 2등분한 것) a half sheet of paper; half size.
반점(斑點) a spot; a speck; a speckle; a dot; a fleck. ¶둥근 ~ 무늬 (a towel with) a spotted pattern // ~이 있는 spotted / specked / speckled / fleckered // ~이 있다 be covered with spots / be speckled.
반정부(反政府) [관형어적] antigovernment; antiministerial. ¶~ 활동으로 기소되다 be accused of antigovernment activities.
반제(反帝) anti-imperialism. ⇨ '반제국주의'
반제(返濟) payment; repayment; reimbursement; refundment; redemption; return(물품의). ¶그에게 빌려 준 돈의 ~를 청구했다 I demanded (re)payment of the money I had lent him. / I demanded that he repay [pay back] the money I had lent him. // 그 빚의 ~ 기한은 6월 30일이다 The debt falls due on June 30. // 빚의 ~ 기한은 지난 지 오래다 The debt is long overdue. **반제하다** pay (back / off); repay; reimburse; refund; redeem; return(물품을). ¶빚을 ~ pay back one's debt [what one owes] / settle a debt // 이달 안에 반제하겠다 I will pay back by the end of this month.
반제국주의(反帝國主義) anti-imperialism.
반제품(半製品) semimanufactured goods; semiprocessed goods; semimanufactures; half-finished goods.
반주(半周) a semicircle; a hemicycle.
반주(伴奏) an accompaniment. ¶민소희 ~ Accompanied by Miss Min Sohui // 관현악 ~ an orchestral accompaniment // 즉석 ~ a vamp // ~에 맞추어 to the accompaniment of ... / 자신의 ~에 맞추어 노래하다 accompany oneself (on the guitar) / sing to one's own (stringed) accompaniment // 피아노 ~로 노래하다 sing to a piano (accompaniment) / sing accompanied by piano // 피아노로 바이올린의 ~를 하다 accompany the violin on the piano // 그들은 피리와 북의 ~를 받으며 춤을 추었다 They danced to the accompaniment of pipes and drums. **반주하다** accompany (a person); play (a person's) accompaniment; play music; [장단을 맞추다] keep [beat] time.
● **반주자** an accompanist.
반주(飯酒) liquor taken at a meal. ¶저녁의 ~ 한 잔은 나쁘지 않다 A glass of wine at supper is not amiss. // 아버지는 저녁 식사 때 ~를 하신다 My father drinks with his supper.
반주그레하다 [보기에 반반하다] rather nice-looking; seemingly attractive.
반죽 dough; paste (of bread). **반죽하다** knead dough; mo(u)ld (clay).
반죽(이) 좋다 [노여움·부끄러움이 없다] impudent; brazen; rudely bold; have a nerve.
반죽음(半-) half death. ¶나는 ~을 당했다 I was nearly killed (by them). // 그들은 그를 때려서 ~의 지경에 이르게 했다 They beat him nearly to death [to within an inch of his life].
반증(反證) (a) proof to the contrary; disproof; counterevidence. ¶~을 들다 produce counterevidence / disprove // 진술의 ~으로 증거를 제시하다 offer evidence against [in disproof of] a statement // 그에 대한 ~이 없다 There is no evidence to the contrary. // 이 증언에 대한 ~을 제시해 주기 바란다 I would like you to produce evidence against [which contradicts] this testimony. **반증하다** disprove; prove against.
반지(半指·斑指) a (finger) ring. ¶결혼[약혼] ~ a wedding [an engagement] ring // 금~ a gold ring // 루비 ~ a ring gemmed with rubies // 보석 ~ a ring set with a jewel / a jewel ring // ~를 낀 손가락 a ringed finger // ~를 끼다 put [slip] a ring on one's finger // ~를 뽑다 slip a ring off one's finger.
반지르르 1 [미끄럽고 윤이 나는 모양] glossily; sleekly; lustrously; lubricously. **반지르르하다** greasy and smooth; slippery; lubricous; glossy; sleek; lustrous. ¶반지르르한 마루 a glistening floor // 머리에 기름을 반지르르하게 바르다 oil one's hair till it shines // 그는 머리를 포마드로 반지르르하게 발랐다 He slicked down his hair with pomade. **2** [겉만 그럴듯한 모양] deceptively; showily; tawdrily; gaudily. **반지르르하다** deceptive; showy; tawdry; gaudy; flashy. ¶겉보기만 ~ be not so good as it looks / be deceptive // 그는 말은 반지르르하나 신뢰할 수 없다 He is smooth-tongued but untrustworthy.
반지름(半-) [수] a radius; a semidiameter.
반지빠르다 1 [얄미울 만큼 눈치 빠르다] (self-)conceited; audacious; cheeky; impertinent; snobbish; pert; presumptuous; saucy. ¶반지빠른 녀석 an impertinent [a saucy] fellow / a conceited pup / a snob // 반지빠르게도 ⋯하다 be impudent enough to do / have the cheek to do. **2** [이중되다] noncommittal; insufficient [unsuitable] either way; not perfectly fit.
반직업적(半職業的) semi-professional. ¶~인 운동선수 a semi-professional athlete.
반짇고리 a workbasket; a workbox; a workbag; a needle case; a housewife; a hussy.
반질거리다 [매끈거리다] be slippery; be smooth; be glossy; be sleeky; be oily. ¶사나이들의 얼굴은 비지땀으로 반질거리고 있었다 The men's faces were shiny [gleaming] with grease. // 새로 니스를 칠한 마루 표면이 반질거린다 The newly varnished floor shows glossy surface. **2** [게으름을 피우다] be idle; be lazy; idle away.
반질반질 1 [매끈하게] sleekly; glossily; smoothly; in an oily [slippery] fashion. **반질반질하다** sleek; glossy; smooth; slippery. ¶반질반질한 머리 sleek [glossy / lustrous] hair // 반질반질한 안색 a blooming complexion. **2** [게으르게] idly; lazily. **반질반질하다** idle; lazy.
반짝 1 [빛나는 모양] with a flash. **반짝하다** give out a flash; flash. **2** [정신이 드는 모양] suddenly; with a start; strongly. **3** [들어 올리는 모양] (수월하게) lightly; easily; without (any) effort; (높이) aloft; high.
반짝거리다 glitter; twinkle. ⇨ '번쩍거리다'

반짝반짝 with a flash; lightly. ⇨ˇ번쩍번쩍

반짝이다 glitter; glisten; sparkle; gleam; glimmer; glint; twinkle; (순간적으로) flash; glance; glimpse; wink.(▶ shine은 빛나다, 빛을 내다, twinkle은 별이나 먼 물빛이 반짝이다, glitter는 눈부시게 반짝거리다, sparkle은 반짝반짝 빛나거나 눈 등이 생기가 넘치도록 반짝거릴 때도 씀) ¶반짝이는 like the twinkling stars/ 눈을 반짝이면서 with sparkling[twinkling] eyes(▶ sparkling은 열심·발랄함을 나타내고 twinkling은 장난기 등을 나타냄)/ 별이 반짝이고 있었다 Stars were twinkling[glittering]./ 보석이 그녀의 손가락에서 눈부시게 반짝이고 있었다 A jewel was glittering on her finger./ 신부는 반짝이는 다이아몬드 반지를 끼고 앉아 있었다 The bride was sitting with her diamond ring glittering [sparkling]./ 멀리서 등불이 반짝이고 있다 A light is glimmering from afar./ 이슬이 햇볕에 반짝였다 The dewdrops glistened[sparkled] in the sunshine./ 어두운 밤하늘을 가로질러 번개가 반짝였다 The lightning flashed across the dark sky.

반쪽(半一) (a) half. ¶사과 ~ the[one] half of an apple.

반찬(飯饌) a (side) dish; dishes served to go with rice; subsidiary articles of diet. ¶고기~ a meat dish/ 보잘것없는 ~ a poor side dish/ 도시락 ~은 뭐가 좋으냐 What would you like in your box lunch?

● **반찬 가게** a grocery (store); a grocer's (shop). **반찬거리** groceries; materials for making side dishes.

반창고(絆創膏) a sticking plaster; an adhesive plaster; (테이프 모양의) an adhesive tape; (상표명) (미) a Band Aid; (영) an Elastoplast. ¶고무~ a rubber adhesive plaster/ 테이프 ~ adhesive tape/ ~를 붙이다 apply a sticking plaster (to the wound)/ 나는 벤 상처에 ~를 붙였다 I applied an adhesive plaster to the cut.

반체제(反體制) ¶~의 antiestablishment.

● **반체제 운동** an antiestablishment movement. **반체제 인사** a dissident.

반추(反芻) rumination. **반추하다** ruminate; chew the cud. ¶나는 그의 말을 여러 번 반추하여 보았다 I thought over his remark again and again./ 그녀는 그때의 감격을 반추하였다 She ruminated over[pondered] the thrill she had felt on that occasion.

● **반추 동물** a ruminant. **반추위** the ruminant stomach.

반출(搬出) carrying[taking] out. ¶외화의 국외 ~은 금지되어 있다 Foreign currency cannot be taken out of the country./ 도서 외부 ~ 금지 Books may not be taken [checked] out of the library. **반출하다** carry[(구어) lug] (a thing) out; take out. ¶중요한 서류를 ~ carry[take] out important documents.

반취(半醉) half-drunkenness; slight intoxication. **반취하다** get half-drunk [-tipsy]; be half-seas over; be slightly drunk.

반측하다(反側一) [뒤척거리다] turn (over); toss about; toss and turn.

반칙(反則) (a) breach of regulations; (an) infringement[violation] of rules; an irregularity; [체] (a) foul play; a foul. ¶~의 foul/ against the rules / contrary to the regulations/ ~으로 퇴장당하다 foul out of the game// 너의 행위는 ~이다 Your conduct is against the rule.// 그는 시합 중 두 번 ~을 범했다 He committed two fouls during the game.// 그는 ~을 너무 많이 해서 퇴장당했다 He fouled out of the game. **반칙하다** violate [act against] the rules; (play) foul; commit a foul.

● **반칙자** an offender; a transgressor.

반코트(半一) a car coat; a three-quarter coat.

반타작(半打作) tenancy on half-and-half shares. **반타작하다** share the crop equally; share equally[half-and-half] with the landowner.

반투막(半透膜) [물][화] a semipermeable membrane.

반투명(半透明) semitransparency; translucency. ¶~ 유리 semitransparent[translucent] glass. **반투명하다** semitransparent; translucent.

● **반투명체** a translucent; a semitransparent body.

반파(半破) partial destruction. ¶~되다 be partially[partly] destroyed.

반편(이)(半偏一) a half-wit; a fool; a simpleton; a blockhead; (구어) someone who isn't all there. ¶~ 같은 짓을 하다 do a stupid [foolish] thing.

반포(頒布) 〔공포〕 proclamation; promulgation; (a) public announcement; 〔발표〕 publication. **반포하다** proclaim; promulgate; announce publicly; make public[known]; publish.

반포(反哺) requital of parental love. ⇨ˇ안갚음

반품(返品) returned goods; an article sent back; returns. ¶~ 사절 (게시) All Sales Final. **반품하다** return[send back] articles [goods] (to the manufacturer). ¶불량품은 반품할 수 있다 You can return the goods if they are defective.// 이 물건을 반품하고 싶은데요 I'd like to return this.

반하다 1 〔연모하다〕 fall in love (with); be enamored (of); be attached (to); take a fancy (to); lose one's heart (to); (구어) be taken (with her / by her beauty); (구어) be keen (on); (구어) fall for; (속) be mashed on. ¶첫눈에 ~ fall in love (with a girl) at first sight / take a fancy (to a person) at first meeting/ ~ be madly in love with // 그는 그 여자에게 반해[미쳐] 있다 He is infatuated with[(구어) crazy about] that woman.// 그는 최 양한테 홀딱 반한 것 같다 He seems to be pretty gone on Miss Choe.// 두 사람은 서로를 홀딱 반했다 The two are deeply in love with each other.// 그는 그녀에게 홀딱 반했다 He is quite keen on her. / He is quite taken with her. / He's head over heels in love with[crazy about] her.// 그는 자기가 반한 여자와 결혼했다 He was married to the woman of his heart.// 그녀는 그 남자한테 반해 있다 She is soft about[on] that boy.

2 〔감탄하다〕 admire; be charmed; [넋을 잃다] forget oneself; be entranced [enraptured] (by / with). ¶아름다운 목소리에 ~ be entranced with (a person's) sweet voice/ 나는 그녀의 아름다운 목소리에 반했다 I was fascinated[charmed] by his beautiful voice.// 나는 그녀의 인품[됨됨이]에 반했다 I was captivated[charmed] by her personality.// 나는 그의 인품에 홀딱 반해서 그에게 장사를 모두 맡겼다 Deeply impressed with his character,

I left my business entirely in his charge.

반하다(反-) **1** [반대되다] oppose; be opposed to.
2 [어긋나다] be contrary (to); go against; run counter (to); be contradictory (to); (규칙 등에) violate (a law); infringe (a rule); break (the regulations). ¶그들의 행위는 이 운동의 취지에 반한다 Their action goes against[is out of step with] the aim(s) of this movement.// 그는 아버지의 희망에 반하여 그녀와 결혼했다 He married her against his father's wishes.// 형이 착한 데 반하여 잭은 대단히 심술궂었다 In contrast to his brother's good-heartedness, Jack was quite ill-tempered.// 그것은 시류에 반하는 의견이다 It is an opinion that goes against the times.

반합(飯盒) a messtin; a mess kit(군인용); a (soldier's) canteen.

반항(反抗) [저항] resistance; insubordination; recalcitrance; recalcitrancy; [권위 등의 무시] defiance; [대항] opposition; [적대] hostility; antagonism; [반역] rebellion; revolt; mutiny(병사의). **반항하다** [저항하다] oppose; resist; offer resistance (to); [복종하지 않다] disobey; be insubordinate (to); [권위를 무시하다] defy; bid defiance (to); [적대하다] antagonize; be antagonistic (to); rebel (against); turn upon (a person); lift[raise] one's hand to[against] (a person). ¶…에 반항하여 in opposition to / in defiance of / in the teeth of / 군주에게 ~ turn against (one's) lord / bite the hand that feeds one // 권력에 ~ rise against[oppose / stand up against] those in power // 내게 반항할 작정인가 Do you mean to disobey me?// 그들은 점령군에게 반항하였다 They resisted the occupation army.// 일부 학생들은 체제에 반항하려 하였다 Some students tried to defy the Establishment.

● **반항기** the period of contrariness; the negative phase. **반항심** a spirit of insubordination[contradiction]; a rebellious spirit.

반항적(反抗的) rebellious; defiant; antagonistic; hostile. ¶~ 태도를 취하다 take[assume] a defiant[hostile] attitude (toward) // 그는 선생님에게 ~ 태도를 취했다 He took a defiant attitude toward the teacher.

반향(反響) **1** [울림] an echo (*pl.* ~es); reverberation.
2 [영향] repercussions; influence; [반응] reflection; an echo (*pl.* ~es); a response; (a) reaction. ¶~이 없다 have no response (to) //~이 있다 have [receive / find] an echo [a response] (in) / be echoed (abroad) / be reflected (on) //~을 불러일으키다 evoke[call forth] an echo[a response] (in) / be responded to (by) / meet with a reaction // 현지 보고는 큰 ~을 불러일으켰다 The on-the-spot report created a great sensation. // 대통령의 선언은 국제적으로 큰 ~을 불러일으켰다 The president's declaration had major repercussions all over the world.

반혁명(反革命) a counterrevolution. ¶~의 counterrevolutionary.

반혓소리(半-) a semi-lingual [-lateral] (sound).

반환(返還) return; restoration; repayment(돈의); retrocession(영토의); rendition(토지·사람의); restitution(정당한 소유주로의). ¶토지 ~ 소송 a suit for the eviction of a tenant // 영토의 ~을 요구한다 We demand the return[the restoration] of our territory.// 그 책은 ~ 기한이 지났다 That book is overdue. **반환하다** return; repay; pay back; refund; restore; retrocede; give back; send back; replace. ¶정부가 소유자에게 집을 반환하였다 The government returned[restored] the house to its owner.// 내가 빌려 준 돈을 언제 반환해 주겠습니까 When are you going to pay back the money you owe me?// 이 돈은 10년 이내에 반환해야 한다 This money has to be returned[paid back] within ten years.// 클럽을 그만두려면 회원증을 반환해야만 한다 You have to turn in your membership card if you leave the club. → ¶등록금은 반환될 수 있음 The enrollment fee is refundable.

● **반환점** (마라톤의) (at) the turn; the turning point.

받다¹ **1** [수령하다] get; have; receive; take; obtain; be given; be presented (with); [받아들이다] accept; [수여되다] be awarded. ¶물건을 고맙게 ~ accept a thing gratefully // 호평[갈채]을 ~ win popularity[applause] // 2일간의 휴가를 ~ take a two-day holiday // 뇌물을 ~ take[receive] a bribe // 포화의 세례를 ~ be under fire // 그는 쏟아지는 칭찬의 소리를 온몸에 받았다 He had praise heaped [showered] on him.// 칭찬을 받아 송구스럽습니다 I am honored[overwhelmed] by your praise./ I do not deserve such praise.// 그는 이익의 분배를 받았다 He had a share in the profits.// 그는 노벨상을 받았다 He was awarded a Nobel prize.// 그에게서 전보를 받았다 We have received a telegram from him. // 변변치 않은 것입니다만 감사의 표시로 받아 주십시오 Please accept this as a slight token of my gratitude.// 귀하의 서신을 오늘 받았습니다 Your letter reached me today. / I recéived[got] your letter today. // 그는 꾸준히 노력하여 우리의 신뢰를 받게[얻게] 되었다 He won[gained / earned] our trust by constant effort.// 당신 편지를 아직 받지 못했소 I have not received your letter yet.// 일금 1백만 원을 정히 받았음 Received, the sum of one million won.// 수험표는 원서를 받으면 보내 드립니다 An admission ticket for the examination will be sent on[upon] receipt of your application (form).// 그것을 받으시면 (받았다고) 알려 주십시오 Kindly[Please] acknowledge receipt of it.// 그녀는 일 주일에 두 번 오르간 교습을 받고 있다 She takes organ lessons twice a week.// 그는 자기 딸에게 좋은 선생의 지도를 받게 하였다 He had his daughter study with[under] a good teacher. // 결혼 피로연의 예약은 이 방에서 받습니다 Reservations for wedding banquets are taken in this room.// 저 선수의 서브는 받아내기 어렵다 That player's serves are hard to receive.// 그는 대학에서 장학금을 받고 있다 He receives[gets] a scholarship from the university.// 나는 초과 근무에 대한 특별 수당을 받았다 I got extra pay for overtime.// 대통령은 그 도시 사람들로부터 열렬한 환영을 받았다 The President was given an enthusiastic welcome[was welcomed enthusiastically] by the people of the town.// 한국에서는 총을 소지하려면 허가를 받아야 한다 In Korea you must get[obtain] permission to own a gun. // 이 사업은 국가로부터 보조를 받고 있다 This enterprise is subsidized by[gets a

받다

subsidy from] the state. // 그는 그 소설로 동인상을 받았다 He was awarded the Dongin Prize for that novel. // 집 수리의 대금 청구(서)를 받았다 I received the bill for the repairs on the house. / I was asked to pay for the repairs on the house. // 수표는 어제 받았습니다 I received your check yesterday. // 친구로부터 그의 아들의 교육에 관한 상의를 받았다 A friend asked me for advice about his son's education. / I was consulted by a friend about his son's education. // 잘 때에는 창문을 열어 놓지 말도록 주의를 받았다 I was warned not to leave[against leaving] the windows open when I went to bed.

2 (급료·대금 등을) be paid; be given; take; receive; accept; (세금을) collect (taxes); (요금을) charge; ask. ¶그들은 식비로 그에게 월 10만 원을 받는다 They charge him one hundred thousand won for his board. // 저 사람한테서는 회비를 받을 수 없다 We cannot collect[get] his dues from him.

3 (꾸어 준 것을) recover (a debt); be recovered; be paid back. ¶받을 수 있는[없는] 빚 a good[bad] debt // 돈을 빌려 주면 이자를 받을 수 있다 You can earn interest by lending money.

4 (당하다) receive (an insult); suffer; incur (a loss); be subjected[exposed] to (an insult). ¶그는 절도 혐의를 받았다 He was suspected of theft. // 뜻밖에 나는 그들의 오해를 받았다 To my surprise, they misunderstood me. // 그의 신작 오페라는 혹평을 받았다 His new opera was harshly criticized[(문어) subjected to scathing criticism].

5 (치료·수술 등을) undergo (an operation); go through. ¶그들은 1년에 두 번 건강 진단을 받는다 They undergo[have] a medical examination[(구어) checkup] twice a year. // 전문의의 진찰을 받는 것이 좋다 You should consult[see] a specialist.

6 (공 등을) catch; stop; receive. ¶그는 공을 한 손으로 받았다 He caught the ball with one hand. // 그는 모자로 그 공을 받았다 He caught the ball in his cap.

7 (그릇 등에 담다) put[take / bring] in. ¶물을 두 통 ~ pour water into two buckets / get water in a bucket twice // 자루에 쌀을 ~ put rice into a sack[bag].

8 (우산 등을) put up[raise / hold] (an umbrella). ¶우산을 ~ put up one's umbrella // 내 우산을 같이 받읍시다 Won't you share my umbrella?

9 (모개로 사다) buy (things) in a mass [lot]; buy (by / (미) at) wholesale. ¶받아다 팔다 retail / sell at retail // 사과를 받아다가 동네에서 팔다 buy apples by the gross and sell them in the neighborhood // 도매상에서 받아다 팔다 buy wholesale and sell retail.

10 (접객업자가) admit; show in. ¶내일은 손님을 받지 않습니다 We (will) suspend business[close our shop] tomorrow.

11 (응답하다) answer. ¶전화를 ~ answer the phone / come to the phone / pick up a telephone / (미) take a call // 보통은 내가 전화를 받습니다 Usually I answer the telephone.

12 (아기를) deliver (a woman of a child). ¶아기 받는 사람 a midwife (pl. -wives).

13 (바람·햇볕 등을) bask; be bathed (in); catch. ¶그 탑의 지붕은 지는 해의 빛을 받아 반짝반짝 빛났다 The roof of the tower caught the rays of the setting sun and glistened brightly. // 이 곳은 강한 서북풍을 정통으로 받고 있다 This promontory is hit directly by the strong northwesterly wind. // 달빛을 받아 그 절은 한층 장엄하게 보였다 Bathed in moonlight, the temple looked all the more solemn.

14 (뿔·머리 등으로) butt; gore; beat[bump] (one's head) against[on] (the door). ¶머리로 벽을 ~ dash one's head against the wall // 염소가 그의 배를 받았다 The goat butted him in the stomach.

받다² [음식이 잘 먹히다] agree with (a person); suit one's taste[palate]; be to one's taste. ¶몸에 받는[받지 않는] 음식 an agreeable[a disagreeable] food // 요즈음 나는 음식이 잘 받지 않는다 I have lost my appetite[I have a poor appetite] these days.

-받다 ¶주목~ receive attention // 우리는 성찬을 대접받았다 We were treated to a grand feast. / We were given a big dinner[meal]. // 나는 그의 생일 파티에 초대받았다 (초청받다) I was invited to his birthday party. / (초대장을) I received an invitation to his birthday party. // 그녀는 한 어린애를 점지받았다 She was blessed with a child.

받들다 1 (공경하다) respect; revere; esteem; venerate; hold (one's teacher) in esteem [reverence]; pay respect to (a person); (모시다) serve; work under[for]. ¶신(神)을 ~ serve God // 부모를 ~ be dutiful to one's parents. **2** (지지하다) hold up; uphold; support; (보좌하다) assist; aid; help; (추대하다) have (a person) over; (따르다) obey; follow; (신봉하다) believe in[embrace] (Christianity). ¶총재로 ~ install (a person) as the president / (받들고 있다) be under the presidency of (a person) // 정부를 ~ support the government. **3** (받아 올려 들다) lift (up); hold up; uphold; raise.

받들어총(-銃) [구령] Present arms!

받아넘기다 parry (a blow / a question); dodge; make a ready reply; sing (after another) readily. ¶챔피언은 도전자의 맹공격을 가볍게 받아넘겼다 [피했다] The challenger's thrusts were evaded by the champion. / The champion ducked out of the way of the challenger's onslaught. // 상대방의 최초의 공격을 받아넘겼다 I warded[fended] off my opponent's first attack. // 총리는 기자 등의 질문을 가볍게 받아넘겼다 The prime minister lightly eluded[parried] the reporters' questions. // 그는 우리들의 추궁을 가볍게 받아넘겼다 [가볍게 응답했다] He treated our questions lightly. / [가볍게 피했다] He easily dodged[parried / evaded] our questions.

받아들이다 [영수하다] accept; receive; [동의하다] assent[agree / consent] to; [들어주다] grant (a person a request); listen to; comply with; [승인하다] accept (a newly independent nation into the UN); [따르다] follow [take] (a person's advice); [포용하다] tolerate; comprehend; [도입하다] introduce; [채택하다] adopt. ¶널리 받아들여지고 있는 생각 an idea widely received // 망명자를 ~ taken in[accept] refugees // 소수파의 의견을 ~ accept[adopt] minority opinions // 충고를 ~ listen to[accept] a person's advice // 그는 호의를 받아들이지 않았다 He did not appreciate my kindness.//나는 그것을 받아들일 수 없다 I cannot accept[take] it.//나는 그 조건들을 받아들일 수 없다 I can't accept[agree to] those terms.//그의 말은 액면대로 받아들일 수 없다 I cannot take what he says at face value.//그렇게밖에 받아들일 수 없다 I cannot view[interpret / take] it (in) any other way.//나[내가 한 일]를 나쁘게 받아들이지 말기를 바라오 Please do not think ill of me[for what I have done].//제이는 내 말을 그대로[에누리없이] 받아들인 것 같다 Jay seems to have taken my words literally[with a grain of salt].//그 문제를 너는 어떻게 받아들이느냐 How are you going to respond to [deal with] the problem? / What is your reaction to the problem?//그녀는 이 문제를 냉정하게 받아들였다 She faced this problem calmly. / She gave a calm attitude toward this problem.//중국은 서양 문화를 받아들이고 있다 China has been receptive to Western culture.//일본은 서양의 기술을 신속하게 받아들였다 Japan introduced[adopted] Western technology quickly.//회사는 종업원의 요구를 받아들였다 The company complied with the employees' requests. / The company agreed to the employees' demands.//그의 주장은 받아들여지지 않았다 His assertions[claims] were not accepted[were rejected].//그 병원은 그 사고의 부상자 30명을 받아들였다 That hospital admitted fifty people injured in the accident.//우리는 새 회원을 받아들일 준비가 되어 있지 않다 We are not yet ready to receive[accept / take in] new members.//그들은 외부로부터의 제의도 기꺼이 받아들였다 They willingly accepted the outside proposal.//아버님은 완고하셔서 남의 말을 받아들이지 않으신다 My father is so stubborn that he will not listen to anybody.//환자는 너무나 쇠약해서 이젠 약도 받아들이지 못한다 The patient is so weak that he can no longer even take medicine.

받아쓰기 a dictation; writing to dictation. ¶~시험 a dictation test//학급의 학생에게 ~를 시키다 give a dictation to the class. **받아쓰기 하다** have dictation.

받아쓰다 write down; (구술을) take dictation. ¶연설을 속기로 ~ take down a speech in shorthand//그녀는 환자의 말을 받아썼다 She took down what the sick man said.//그는 비서에게 편지를 받아쓰기 했다 He dictated a letter to his secretary.

받을어음 a bill receivable(약어 BR, B/R, b.r.); a note receivable.

받치다 1 [우산 등을 받다] hold up (an umbrella); hold (an umbrella) over one's head; put up[raise] (an umbrella).
2 [괴다] prop[bolster / shore](up); support (with a prop); underpin; hold up. ¶기둥으로 ~ support (a wall) with a post//바지랑대로 빨랫줄을 ~ prop the clothesline with a stick//글쓰는 데 받칠 것 좀 주시오 Give me something to lay under writing paper.
3 [언] (자음을) place a consonant under a vowel.
4 [배기다] be hard; pinch; squeeze. ¶이 의자는 궁둥이가 받친다 This seat is hard under my buttocks.
5 [먹은 것이] sit[lie] heavy on one's stomach; remain undigested in the stomach; be stodgy.
6 [치밀어 오르다] surge; feel a surge[gush] (of anger); well up (in one); (사물이) fill one's heart.

받침 1 [지주] a prop; a stay; a support; a strut; a shore; a fulcrum (pl. ~s, -cra); underpinnings; (앉는) a stand; a pedestal; (앉는) a mat; a pad. ¶책~ a celluloid board [cardboard] (laid under writing paper)//꽃병 ~ a flower-vase stand//~을 괴다 prop [shore] up / strut / put a support (under)//지렛대 밑에 ~을 괴다 put a fulcrum under a lever. **2** [언] a consonant placed under a vowel.
● **받침대** a prop; a support; a strut. **받침 접시** a saucer.

받히다 [부딪히다] be butted; butted; be gored; be struck; be hit; be bumped. ¶소에게 ~ be gored by a bull//트럭에게 ~ be run [struck] against by a truck.

발[1] **1** a foot (pl. feet); a paw(고양이 등의 발톱이 있는); (오징어·낙지 등의) a tentacle; an arm; (굽이 있는 동물의) a hoof (pl. ~s, hooves). ¶~ 아래의[에] at one's feet//~이 아프다 be footsore / have a sore foot//~이 저리다 one's feet have gone to sleep / one's foot is asleep / one has pins and needles in one's foot//~을 다치다 get hurt in the foot / injure one's foot//~(목)을 삐다 sprain one's ankle[foot] / have one's ankle sprained//~을 벌리다 spread one's legs (apart)//~을 걸다 trip (a person) up//~로 박자를 맞추다 keep[beat] time with feet//그는 ~이 크다 He has big feet.//내 ~이 저린다[마비되었다] My feet are numb[asleep].//나는 지친 ~을 질질 끌고 걸었다 I dragged my weary foot on.//누군가가 내 ~을 밟았다 Somebody stepped on my foot.//나는 ~을 헛디더 계단에서 넘어졌다 I slipped and fell down the stairs. / I lost my footing on the stairs and fell.//그는 넘어져서 왼~이 부러졌다 He fell down and broke his left leg.
2 [걸음] walking; walk; [보조] a step; [걷는 속도] pace; speed. ¶~이 빠른[느린] 사람 a quick[slow] walker//~이 빠르다[재다] be quick[swift] of foot / be light-[quick-]footed / be a fast[quick / good] walker//~이 느리다 be slow of foot / be a slow walker//~가는 대로 걷다 walk as one's legs lead[carry] one / walk at random//~을 멈추다 stop / halt / stay//한 ~ 나서다[물러서다] take a step forward[backward]//그는 ~을 멈추었다 He stopped (walking).
3 [기물의] a foot; a leg. ¶~이 셋인 의자 (세발 의자) a three-legged stool//테이블의 ~ the leg of a table.

발 없는 말이 천 리 간다(속담) Give a lie twenty-four hours' start, and you can never overtake it.

발(을) 구르다 stamp[stomp] (one's feet) (on the floor). ¶분하여 ~ stamp with vexation [mortification / chagrin].

발(이) 넓다 know a lot of people; have a wide[large circle of] acquaintance; can call everybody by his first name; be well-connected; (미) get around. ¶그 사람은 재계에 ~ He has many acquaintances in the financial world. / He knows a lot of financiers.

발(을) 들여놓다 set foot (in); put one's foot (into / inside). ¶다시는 우리 집에 발을 들여놓지 마라 Never darken my door[cross the

발
threshold of my house] again.
발 디딜 틈이 없다 be packed (like sardines in a can). ¶러시아워에 지하철은 ~ The subways are packed like sardines during rush hour.
발(이) 맞다 fall into step; be in step. ¶발이 맞지 않다 be[get] out of step / break step.
발(이) 묶이다 be deprived of means of transit; be stranded; be tied up. ¶철도 파업으로 발이 묶인 통근자들 commuters deprived of their transport by the railway workers' strike // 주자는 1루에서 발이 묶였다 The runner was left stranded on first base.
발 벗고 나서다 throw oneself into (a matter) with eagerness[enthusiasm]; jump in with both feet. ¶남 돕는 일에 ~ devote oneself to helping others.
발(을) 빼다 wash one's hands of (an affair); sever connections with; break (off) with; break away from; withdraw oneself (from). ¶그는 암흑 세계에서 발을 빼고 살아가기로 결심했다 He decided to sever his connections with[to wash his hands of] the underworld and go straight.

발² a bamboo[rattan] blind. ¶~을 걷다[내리다] roll up[let down] a bamboo blind // ~이 걷혀[내려져] 있다 The bamboo blind is up [down].

발³ [두 팔을 벌린 길이] a fathom; the length of outstretched arms. ¶밧줄 두 ~ two fathoms of ball cartridge // ~로 밟다 span (it) (off) // ~이 크다 have a large arm span.

발⁴ [직물의] texture; weave. ¶~이 성기다[촘촘하다] be loose[close] in weave // ~이 곱다[거칠다] be fine[rough / coarse] in texture.

-발 [죽죽 내뻗는 줄·기운] lines; streaks; rays; impression. ¶빗~ streaks of rain.

발(發) 1 [탄환 수] a round(소총의); a shot(소총·대포의); a cartridge(소총·엽총의); a shell(대포의); [발사 횟수] a round; a shot. ¶20~의 탄환 rounds of ball cartridge // 6~쏘다 fire six rounds[shots]. 2 [발동기 수] a motor; an engine. ¶쌍~의 bimotor(ed) / twin-engine(d) / twin-motor(ed).

-발(發) 1 [출발] departure. ¶서울역 6시 20분~ 기차 the train leaving Seoul at 6:20 / the 6:20 train from Seoul // 부산~ 급행 an express (train) from Busan // 5월 10일 인천~ 기선으로 by steamer leaving Incheon on May 10 // 김포~ 8시 10분 칼기로 출발한다 I am taking a KAL flight from Gimpo at 8:10. 2 [발신] sending. ¶AP통신~ an AP dispatch // 3월 9일~ 전보 the cable dated March 9 // 파리~ 보도 a piece of news under a Paris dateline.

발가락 a toe; a digit; [동] a dactylus. ¶새끼~ the little toe // ~이 보이는 (디자인의) 구두 peep-toe(d) shoes // ~을 구부리다 curl one's toes.

발가벗기다 strip (a person) bare[to the skin]; strip (a person)(down) naked; denude; [죄다 뺏다] strip[rob] (a person) of all he has.

발가벗다 strip oneself of all one's clothes; strip oneself bare[stark-naked]; take off one's clothes; undress.

발가숭이 a naked body; a penniless person. ⇨벌거숭이

발각(發覺) detection; revelation; discovery; disclosure; exposure. **발각하다** find out; discover; detect. ➔¶발각되다 be detected[revealed / discovered / disclosed / exposed] / be found out / come[be brought] to light // 발각될까 봐 lest it should be found out / for fear of detection // 사기는 발각되지 않았다 The fraud escape detection. // 음모는 사전에 발각되었다 The plot was detected before it was carried out.

발간(發刊) publication; issue. **발간하다** publish; bring out; issue; start (a magazine); launch (a newspaper). ➔¶발간되다 be published / come out // 그 책은 언제 발간되느냐 When will the book come out? // 이 소설은 2002년에 발간되었다 This novel was published[came out] in 2002.

발갛다 red; crimson. ⇨빨갛다
발개지다 turn red; redden. ⇨빨개지다
발걸음 a step; a pace; a tread. ¶~이 빠르다[느리다] walk[run] fast[slowly] // 무거운[가벼운] ~으로 걷다 walk with a heavy[light step] // ~을 빠르게 하다[늦추다] quicken[slacken] one's step[pace] // ~ 닿는 대로 걷다 walk where[wherever] one's legs carry one / wander (about) without a particular destination // 그는 ~을 멈추었다 He stopped (walking). // 어른의 ~으로 거기까지 20분 걸린다 An adult can get there in twenty minutes on foot. / It takes a grown-up person twenty minutes to walk there. // 행진의 ~이 흐트러졌다 The marchers broke step. // 날이 점점 어두워졌으므로 우리는 ~을 재촉했다 As it was getting dark, we quickened our pace[step]. // 그는 흐트러짐이 없는 ~으로 다가왔다 He approached with steady steps. // 그의 ~은 빨라졌다 His step grew quicker.

발걸이 [발 놓는 데] a foothold; a footrest; (책상 등의) a footrail; (의자 등의) a rung; (자전거의) a pedal.

발견(發見) discovery; revelation; [발각] detection. ¶과학상의 대~ brilliant discoveries in science // 획기적 ~ an epoch-making discovery // 미 대륙의 ~ the discovery of America. **발견하다** discover; make a discovery; find (out); detect; spot; (우연히) chance (up)on (a thing); light upon (a fact); strike out (a theory). ¶잘못을 ~ find a mistake // 표류선을 ~ discover a drifting ship // 물건에서 하자를 ~ detect a flaw in an article // 나는 이 일을 우연히 발견했다 I discovered this matter by chance. // 나는 그의 거처를 발견했다 I found out where he was. // 마침내 그 사실을 발견했다 I finally discovered that fact. ➔¶조사 결과 놀랄 만한 사실이 발견되었다 The inquiry has revealed a surprising fact. // 그는 시체가 되어 숲 속에서 발견되었다 He was found dead in the woods. // 강에서 익사체가 발견되었다 A drowned body was found in the river.
● **발견자** a discoverer; a finder; a detector.

발광(發光) luminescence; radiation. ¶태양의 ~ the emission[radiation] of light by the sun. **발광하다** radiate; emit[give forth] light. ¶발광하는 luminous / photogenic / radiant // 이 물질은 발광한다 This substance emits light[give off light / is luminescent].
● **발광기** [생] a luminous organ. **발광체** a luminous body; a luminary; an illuminant; [전] a glower.

발광(發狂) 1 [미침] madness; craziness; dis-

traction; insanity; lunacy; mental derangement; (mental) alienation. **발광하다** go[run] mad; become insane[lunatic / crazy]; become mentally deranged; be cracked; lose one's head[mind / reason / wit / senses]; go out of one's mind[head / senses]. ¶발광한 mad / insane / lunatic // 발광한 사람 an insane[a mentally deranged] person // 발광하게 하다 drive (a person) mad[crazy] / craze / derange.
2 (미친 듯이 날뜀) a crazy act; a wild action; an insanity. **발광하다** be beside oneself; act [behave] like mad. ¶그는 절망하여 발광하였다 In an excess of despair he lost his reason [(구어) went off his head].

발군(拔群) 〔여럿 속에서 훨씬 뛰어남〕. ¶~의 preeminent / conspicuous / distinguished / outstanding // ~의 성적으로 졸업하다 graduate from (school) with (unprecedented) honors[distinction] // ~의 공을 세우다 serve with distinction / distinguish oneself by extraordinary exploits // 그는 언어 연구에서 ~의 업적을 이룩했다 He distinguished himself in linguistic research.

발굴(發掘) (an) excavation; (시체의) exhumation. ¶석유 ~권 an oil concession // 나는 고분[시체]의 ~에 입회하였다 I took part in the excavation of an ancient tomb[exhumation of a dead body]. // 나는 인재 ~에 성공했다 I succeeded in finding a capable man. **발굴하다** dig (out / up); excavate; unearth; turn up; (시체를) exhume; disentomb; untomb; disinter. ¶탤런트를 ~ scout for talent / pick out (young) talent // 폐허를 ~ excavate [dig out / unearth] the ruins. ➔ ¶묘에서 시체가 발굴되었다 A corpse was exhumed from the grave. // 그는 여러 단역 배우들 중에서 발굴되어 주역이 되었다 He was singled[picked] out from among many bit actors to be the star.
●**발굴자** an excavator; a digger. **발굴지** the digs; (발굴품이 발견된) a findspot; a find place. **발굴품 / 발굴물** an excavation; a find.

발굽 a hoof (*pl.* ~s, hooves); an unguis (*pl.* -gues). ¶~ 자국 a hoofprint // 말에는 ~이 있다 Horses are hoofed[ungulate] (animals). / Horses have hoofs.

발권(發券) the issue of banknotes; note issuing.
●**발권 은행** a bank of issue.

발그레하다 reddish; tinged with red; (안색이) ruddy; rubicund; aglow; reddened; flushed; (서술적) be aglow. ¶발그레한 뺨 ruddy cheeks // 그는 기뻐서 얼굴이 ~ His face is flushed with joy. // 그녀의 볼이 (포도주를 마셔서) 발그레해졌다 Her cheeks were slightly flushed (with wine).

발그림자 a footmark; a trail; a trace; a shadow.
발그림자도 아니하다 cease to visit; never come; do not appear. ¶그 후 그는 발그림자도 아니했다 Since then, there has been no trace of him.

발그스레하다 reddish. ⇨ 발그스름하다
발그스름하다 reddish; somewhat red; light red. ¶그는 술을 마셔서 얼굴이 ~ He is flushed with alcohol. // 먼동이 트면서 하늘이 발그스름해졌다 The sky began to lighten [grew gray] just before daybreak.

발급하다(發給-) issue. ¶어권을 ~ issue a passport.

발긋발긋하다 marked with red spots[speckles]; red in spots[here and there].

발기(勃起) (음경의) (an) erection. ¶~성의 erectile. **발기하다** (사람이 주어) have an erection; (음경이 주어) stand erect; become stiff.
●**발기 부전**(-不全) impotence; impotency.

발기(發起) 〔계획〕 projection; 〔제의〕 a proposal; a suggestion; instance; a proposition; (사업의) promotion; 〔출선〕 initiation; 〔주최〕 auspices. ¶...의 ~로 at the proposition [proposal / suggestion] of ... / at the instance of ... / under the auspices [sponsorship] of .... **발기하다** propose; project; suggest; promote; initiate. ¶무역 회사의 설립을 ~ promote a new trading firm // 이 사업은 한 씨가 발기한 것이다 This project is promoted[originated] by Mr. Han.
●**발기인** (계획의) a projector; an originator; a sponsor; (회사 등의) a promoter; 〔제안자〕 a proposer.

발기다 open (up); crack (open) (a chestnut); split (open); shell (peas); tear (away / off / out).

발기발기 in[to] pieces; in strips; (tear) into [in / to] shreds. ¶~ 찢다 tear (a letter) up [to pieces].

발길 1 〔차는 힘〕 (the force of) a kick. ¶~로 차다 give (a person) a kick / kick (a person). **2** 〔걸음〕 a step; 〔왕래〕 coming and going. ¶~이 닿는 대로 가다 go where one's feet lead one // ~을 되돌리다 turn[go] back // ~이 잦다 frequent (a place) / make frequent calls (on a person, at a place, etc.) // 우리는 학교를 향해 ~을 돌렸다 We turned [directed] our steps toward the school.
발길에 채다 〔걷는 사람의 발에 채다〕 be given a kick; be[get] kicked (by a horse).
발길이 멀어지다 come[visit] less frequently (than before). ¶그녀는 삼촌 댁에서 발길이 점점 멀어졌다 Her visits to her uncle's have grown less frequent.
●**발길질** kicking. ¶~을 하다 give (a person) a kick / kick out at (a person) / kick.

발깍 1 〔갑자기 성내거나 힘쓰는 모양〕 all of a sudden; in a sudden outburst; with a burst. ¶~ 화를 내어 in a rage // 문을 ~ 열다 jerk a door open. **2** 〔소동이 나는 모양〕 topsy-turvy; in a great bustle; in a turmoil[hubbub / mess]; in utter confusion; pell-mell; (미국구어) every which way. ¶온 집안이 ~ 뒤집혔다 All is confusion in the house. / The house is all torn up. / The whole house was in a terrible confusion. // 회의장이 ~ 뒤집혔다 The chamber was thrown into an uproar.

발깍거리다 1 〔담근 술이 몹시 괴어오르다〕 bubble up; rise in bubbles. ¶술이 ~ be brewing a hubble-bubble / be brewing a bubble / be bubbling a brew. **2** 〔진흙 등을〕 자꾸 주물러 비어저 나오게 하다〕 knead (dough, mud, etc.) to squash[squish]; make mud squash underfoot.

발꿈치 the heel.

발끈 in hot blood; (get angry) on a sudden (at[about] trifles); with a burst; in a fit of passion; in a (fit of) rage. ¶~ 성을 내다 fly into a rage // 그는 ~ 성을 내며 일어섰다 He stood up in a rage. // 그는 ~ 성을 내며 나에게 자를 내던졌다 He threw a ruler at me in a

발끈거리다

발끈하다 fly[fall] into a passion; flare[flash] up (in anger); fly into a (great) rage. ¶발끈하기 쉬운 성질 (a man with) an explosive temper.

발끈거리다 be roused to anger easily (at trifles); be irascible[irritable]; be quick to flare[flame / flash / burn] up (at the drop of a hat); easily fall[fly / burst] into a passion.

발끈발끈 in fits of anger; aflame (at); with flares of temper. **발끈발끈하다** be roused to anger easily (at trifles). ⇨발끈하다

발끝 the tip of a toe; a tiptoe; a toe(구두·양말 등의). ¶~으로 서다 stand on tiptoe // ~으로 걷다 tiptoe / walk on tiptoe // 그녀는 머리끝에서 ~까지 나무랄 데 없는 옷차림이었다 She was perfectly dressed from head to toe.

발놀림 [스포츠] footwork.

발단(發端) 〔일이 벌어짐·일의 첫머리〕 the origin; the opening; the start; the beginning; the commencement; the outset; the inception. ¶사건의 ~ the origin of an affair // 그것이 사건의 ~이 되었다 That was how it all started. // 그 일의 ~부터 말하겠다 I'll tell you about it from the very beginning. // 그것의 ~은 무엇이었습니까 What started it? / How did it start? **발단하다** originate (from / in / with); be originated; start (from); begin; commence.

발달(發達) 〔성장〕 development; growth; 〔진보〕 progress; advance; advancement. ¶지식[학문 / 과학 / 예술]의 ~ the advancement of knowledge[learning / science / art] // 근대 언어학의 ~ the advance of modern linguistic // …의 ~을 돕다[늦추다 / 저해하다] promote[retard / arrest] the development[growth] of ... // 비타민 부족은 신체의 ~을 방해한다 Lack of vitamins prevents physical growth[development]. **발달하다** develop; grow (up); progress; make progress; advance. ¶크게[잘] 발달한 highly-[well-]developed // 저 아이는 정신도 육체도 아직 발달하지 않았다 The child is underdeveloped both in mind and body[has not fully developed in mind or in body]. // 이 동물의 엄니[청각]는 매우 발달해 있다 This animal has highly-[well-]developed fangs[ears].

- **발달 심리학** developmental psychology.

발돋움하다 stand on (one's) tiptoe(s). ¶발돋움하여 책을 선반에서 내리다 take[reach] down a book from a shelf on tiptoe // 그는 내가 발돋움해도 닿지 않을 키가 크다 He is taller than I even if I stand on my tiptoes.

발동(發動) 〔법적 권력의 행사〕 exercise; 〔동력을 일으킴〕 motion. ¶사법권의 ~ an operation of judicial power. **발동하다** exercise; invoke(법·규약 등을); move; put in motion. ¶강권을 ~ take strong measures / appeal to legal action // 규약 제9조를 ~ invoke Article 9 of the covenant // 대통령은 강권을 발동하여 파업을 중지시켰다 The President took legal action to stop the strike. → ¶사법권이 발동될 것이다 The judicial power will be put in action.

- **발동기** a motor; an engine. ¶백 마력의 ~ a 100-horsepower[100 h.p.] motor // 공랭식[수랭식] ~ an air-cooled[a water-cooled] engine // 가솔린 ~ an oil[a gasoline] engine.

발동기선(-船) a motorboat; an autoboat; a motor ship(디젤 엔진에 의한). **발동력** motive power.

발뒤꿈치 the heel.

발뒤꿈치도 따를 수 없다 be no match for (a person). ¶너 같은 건 그의 ~ You are no match for him. / You cannot stand comparison with him.

발뒤축 the heel.

발등 the top side of the foot. ¶~을 밟다 step[tread] on (another's) foot // ~에 불이 떨어졌다 I am pressed by urgent business. / I got so I had to do something about it quickly. // 그는 ~에 불이 떨어져야만 일을 한다 He gets for leaving his work until someone lights a fire under him[until he is really pressed].

발등(을) 찍히다 be betrayed by (a person).

발딱 〔급히 일어서는 모양〕 suddenly; with a jerk[start]; quickly; rashly; abruptly; 〔자빠지는 모양〕 on one's back; with the face upward; flat; supinely.

발라내다 shuck (corn); hull (peas); crack (a chestnut); remove. ¶생선의 가시를 ~ clean[bone] a fish // 닭고기의 뼈를 ~ bone a chicken // 살구 씨를 ~ remove stone[pit] from an apricot / pit an apricot // 뼈에 붙은 살을 깨끗이 ~ pick a bone bare.

발라드 a ballad.

발라맞추다 〔알랑거리다〕 flatter; adulate; coax; butter (a person) up; curry favor (with one's superior); court (a person's) favor; 〔구슬리다〕 cajole; wheedle. ¶슬을 발라맞추어 돈을 뺏다 wheedle[cajole] (a person) out of money.

발라먹다 (남의 재물을) cajole (a person) out of (something); coax[wheedle] (something) out of (a person).

발랄하다(潑剌-) lively; sprightly; animated; fresh; vivid. ¶발랄한 소녀 a perky[jaunty] girl // 재기 발랄한 사람 a man of keen intellect // 생기 ~ be full of vigor[go / vim / vitality / animation] / be vivid with life / 《미국 속어》 be peppy / be full of pep // 그는 생기 ~ He is full of life.

발랑 on one's back. ⇨벌렁

발레 ballet. ¶수중 ~ water ballet // 창작 ~ a balletic creation // ~를 가르치다[배우다] give[take] ballet lessons.

발레단 (프) a corps de ballet.

발레리나 a ballerina (pl. ~s, -rine); a female ballet dancer.

발렌타인데이 →밸런타인데이

발령(發令) 〔명령을 내림〕 giving an (official) announcement of appointment; 〔반포〕 (an) official announcement; proclamation (of law, of a decree, etc.); 〔영〕 gazetting. ¶~을 받다 receive an official announcement of appointment // 그는 대구 지점으로 ~이 났다 His appointment to the Daegu branch was announced officially. // 그의 새 직위는 오늘 ~ 난다 His appointment to a new post will be announced today. **발령하다** give an order; announce (a person's appointment) officially; issue (regulations, a warning, etc.).

- **발령장** a written appointment; a warrant[writ / letter] of appointment.

발로(發露) (an) expression; (a) manifestation; exhibition. ¶애국심의 ~ an expression[a manifestation / an outburst] of patriotism // 우정의 ~ a manifestation[an expression] of friendship. **발로하다** manifest[express / reveal] itself; become manifest.

발록거리다 quiver; idle away one's time. ⇨`벌룩거리다`
발록발록 quivering. ⇨`벌룩벌룩`
발론(發論) a motion; a proposal; a suggestion. **발론하다** move; propose; suggest. ¶발론할 것이 있다 have a proposal to make.
발룸거리다 quiver. ⇨`벌름거리다`
발름하다 partly open. ⇨`벌름하다`
발리 [테니스] a volley.
발맞추다 keep pace (with); fall[get] into step (with); (행동을) act in concert (with). ¶발맞추어 걷다 walk[march] in step[line] (with) / walk with measured steps.
발매(發賣) sale. ¶(상품이) ~ 중이다 be on sale[the market] // ~ 중 (게시) On Sale / Available. **발매하다** sell; put (books) on the market[on sale]; release (a new record). → ¶발매되다 be put on sale / be put on the market / appear on the market // 그 책은 곧 발매된다 The book will be put on sale soon. // 새 사전은 내달에 발매된다 The new dictionary will be out next month.
● 발매 금지 prohibition of sale[circulation]; suppression (of a book); (게시) "Sale Prohibited." ¶그 잡지는 ~ 되었다 The sale of the magazine was prohibited. / The magazine was banned. 발매일 the date of issue. 발매처 a sales[selling] agent.
발명(發明) 1 [신고안] invention; contrivance. ¶~의 천재 an inventive genius // 그는 ~의 재능이 있다 He has an inventive mind. // 그의 ~이 최근에 실용화되었다 His invention has lately been put to practical use. **발명하다** invent; device; contrive. ¶그가 발명한 새 장치 the new device of his invention // 이 장치는 그가 발명한 것이다 This device is his invention. 2 [변명] vindication; exculpation; explanation; defense; a plea; justification. **발명하다** vindicate (oneself, one's innocence, etc.); exculpate[clear] oneself (from a charge); explain oneself (for).
● 발명자 / 발명가 an inventor. 발명품 an invention; [신고안품] a contrivance; a device.
발목 the ankle. ¶~을 삐다 sprain one's ankle.
발목(을) 잡히다 (일에) be tied to (a steady job); be chained[fettered] to (one's business); be pressed with (business); be very busy with (work); [약점을 잡히다] have one's sore spot found; give a handle to the enemy.
발문(跋文) an epilogue; a postscript[an afterword] (to a book).
발밑 ¶~에 at one's feet / close to one's feet // ~에도 미치지 못하다 be far inferior (to) / be no match (for) / cannot hold a candle (to) // ~을 조심해라 Watch your step(s). / Watch [Look] where you are going. // 어두워서 ~이 보이지 않는다 It is too dark to see where I am treading. // 나는 수학에서는 그의 ~에도 못 따라간다 I am not nearly so good at mathematics as he is.
발바닥 the sole[bottom] of the[one's] foot. ¶~에 티눈이 생기다 get a corn on the sole of one's foot.
발바리 [동] a pug dog; a spaniel (dog); a Peking(g)ese (dog)(중국 원산의).
발발 tremblingly. ⇨`벌벌`
발발(勃發) outbreak; outburst; sudden occurrence. ¶전쟁의 ~ the outbreak of war. **발발하다** break[burst] out; flare up; occur suddenly. ¶반란이 발발했다 A revolt broke out.
발버둥이 치다 flutter one's feet; squirm. ⇨=발버둥 치다
발버둥질 fluttering one's feet; squirming; wriggling; useless[fruitless] struggling. **발버둥질하다** flutter one's feet; squirm. ⇨=발버둥 치다 ¶필사적으로 발버둥질했으나 그는 기진맥진해서 물속으로 가라앉았다 After desperate, futile struggling, he sank exhausted into the water.
발버둥 치다 (아이가) flutter one's feet; (kick and) struggle; do not sit still; be restless; [몸부림치다] squirm, wriggle; struggle; [헛애를 쓰다] make vain effort; make a useless struggle. ¶붙잡힌 범인은 도망가려고 발버둥 쳤다 The captured criminal struggled to escape. // 그는 도망치려고 발버둥 쳤으나 허사였다 He struggled in vain to escape. // 이제 와서 발버둥 쳐야 소용없다 It's no use struggling now.
발병(-病) a foot disease[trouble]; footsoreness; a pain in the foot. ¶~이 나다 have a sore foot / be footsore.
발병(發病) an attack (of a disease); the outbreak of one's illness. **발병하다** be attacked with a disease; contract a disease; be taken ill; become[get / fall] ill[(미) sick]; (잠복기를 지나서) show the symptoms (of a disease). ¶그는 귀국하자마자 발병하였다 Soon after he came home, he fell[was taken] ill.
발본(拔本) 1 [원인을 뽑아 버림] eradication. **발본하다** eradicate; root up[out]; uproot. 2 [밑천을 뽑음]. **발본하다** restore[get back] one's capital (from an investment).
발본색원하다(拔本塞源-) eradicate sources (of evil); lay the ax to the root of (evil).
발부리 the tip of a toe; tiptoe; a toe(신발·양말 등의). ¶돌에 ~를 채다 trip on[against] a stone.
발붙이다 [의지하다] rely[depend / lean / count] (on / upon); place[put] reliance (on / in). ¶발붙일 곳 없는 lonely / helpless / forlorn // 발붙일 (만한) 사람이 없다 have no one to depend on / have no one to turn to for help.
발뺌 an excuse; a pretext; a pretense; evasion; a subterfuge; a put-off; (미국 구어) an alibi (pl. ~s). ¶~을 잘하다 be good at subterfuge [finding excuses] / be skillful in evading[dodging] // 그것은 ~에 불과하다 That is only a pretext. // 그런 ~은 안 통한다 Such an excuse won't do. // 그는 정말이지 ~을 잘한다 He is awfully good at making excuses[evading the issue]. **발뺌하다** make [find / invent] an excuse[a pretext] (of); find excuses; talk oneself out of (difficulty); evade; shirk (one's duty). ¶책임을 안 지려고 ~ shirk[evade] one's responsibility.
발사(發射) [총포 등을 쏨] discharge; firing; shooting; (로켓의) launching; blast-off; lift-off. ¶~ 10초 후[전]에 ten seconds after [before] launch // 로켓의 ~에 성공했다 The rocket successfully blasted off. / The launch of the rocket went successfully. // 그 우주선은 ~ 준비 중이었다 The spacecraft was being readied for launch. **발사하다** discharge

발산

[fire / let off] (a gun); shoot (a rifle / a bullet from a rifle); launch[blast off / put up] (a guided missile); emit; emanate; radiate; send forth. ¶권총을 ~ discharge [fire] one's revolver // 일제히 ~ fire a volley / fire by volleys // 인공위성을 ~ launch [blast off / put up] an artificial satellite. →¶ 오늘 밤 인공위성이 발사될 예정이다 Tonight a (man-made) satellite is going to be launched.
● **발사대** (로켓 등의) a launch(ing) ramp [pad]; a launch platform. **발사 시간** the lift-off time; T-time. **발사 장치** a launcher (of a guided missile). **발사 지점 / 발사 기지 / 발사장** a launch(ing) site[point].

발산(發散) 1 [밖으로 퍼져 흩어짐] exhalation(증기·냄새 등의); radiation; emanation (빛·열 등의); diffusion(확산). **발산하다** give forth[out / off]; send forth; emit; exhale (from). ¶불이 발산하는 열과 연기 heat and smoke emitted by fire // 향기를 ~ give out [diffuse] fragrance // 악취를 ~ emit a foul odor // 이 동물은 독한 냄새를 발산한다 This animal emits[gives off] a strong scent. // 이 물체에서 광선이 발산한다 Light radiates from this object.
2 [정력 등의] explosion. **발산하다** give vent (to); let off; release. ¶매력을 ~ display one's charms // 분노를 ~ blow[let] off (the) steam // 그는 넘치는 정력을 등산으로 발산하였다 He worked off his excess energy by mountain climbing.
3 [수|물] divergence; divergency. **발산하다** diverge.

발상(發想) [착상] conception; [음] expression. ¶~이 뛰어나다 be cleverly conceived / be a good idea // 그의 ~은 현실과 동떨어져 있다 He does not fit his ideas to real condition. // 그것은 재미있는 ~이다 That's an interesting idea[conception]. // 그것은 전형적인 한국인적 ~이다 It's a typically Korean way of thinking.

발상지(發祥地) [나라를 세운 임금이 난 땅] the native place of the founder of a dynasty; [요람] the cradle (of civilization); the birthplace (of jazz music). ¶고대 문명의 ~ the birthplace[(문어) cradle] of ancient civilization.

발상하다(發喪-) commence wailing; set up cries of lamentation.

발생(發生) [발현(發現)·생김] occurrence; (an) outbreak; [창생] origination; genesis; birth; creation; [출현] appearance; (생물·열·전기 등의) generation; production; [생물] growth; [생] development. ¶자연 ~ spontaneous generation // 개체 ~ ontogeny // 문명의 ~ the dawn of civilization // 사건의 ~ the occurrence of an event[an accident] // 콜레라의 ~ an outbreak of cholera // 모기의 ~을 막다 prevent[stop] the growth of mosquitoes // 이 약은 해충의 ~을 막는다 This chemical prevents the appearance of harmful insects. **발생하다** [일어나다·생기다] occur; happen; take place; spring[crop] up; break out; come into existence [being]; appear; be generated; be produced; originate (from); come (from); spring (from); [생육하다] grow; [번식하다] breed; [생] develop. ¶장차 무슨 일이 발생할지 모른다 One cannot tell what may happen in the future. // 근처에 콜레라가 발생했다 A case of cholera has broken out in the neighborhood. // 남쪽 해상에 태풍이 발생하였다 A typhoon has formed[appeared] in the southern sea. // 이 건널목에서 사고가 발생하였다 An accident occurred[happened / took place] at this crossing.
● **발생기**(一期) a developmental stage; [화] a nascent state[condition]. **발생 생리학[심리학]** genetic biology[psychology]. **발생학** (생) embryology.

발설(發說) disclosing; divulging; revealing; announcement; publication. **발설하다** disclose; tell; mention; reveal; divulge; announce; publish; make known; give out. ¶비밀을 ~ let out[divulge] a secret.

발성(發聲) utterance; speaking; vocalization; phonation; exclamation; ejaculation. ¶~을 공부하다 study voice // 너는 ~이 좋지 않다 You vocalize poorly[have poor vocalization]. **발성하다** make voice; utter; speak; exclaim; ejaculate.
● **발성법** [음] vocalization; [언] enunciation. **발성 연습** vocal exercises.

발소리 the sound of footsteps[feet]; a footstep; a footfall; a footbeat; a step; a tread. ¶~를 내고 with sounding footsteps // ~를 내지 않고 with silent steps / softly // ~를 죽이고 with stealthy steps / stealthily / on one's noiseless shoes // ~를 내다 make a sound as one walks // ~가 들리다 hear (the sound of) (a person's) footsteps // 사람의 ~가 났다 Footsteps were heard. / Steps sounded. // 밖에서 ~가 들렸다 We heard (foot) steps outside. / We heard someone walking outside. // 우리는 ~를 죽이고 걸었다 We walked stealthily[with stealthy steps]. // 그는 ~를 죽이고 방에 들어왔다 He stole into the room with stealthy steps.

발송(發送) sending; forwarding; dispatch; (미) shipping. **발송하다** send out[forth]; forward; dispatch; (미) ship; (우편물을) (미) mail out; (영) post. ¶통지서를 ~ send out notices // 역에서 하물을 3개 ~ send out three pieces of baggage at the station // 주문하신 물건은 2, 3일 안으로 발송하겠습니다 Your order will be dispatched in a few days. // 초청장은 발송하였습니다 I have mailed [posted] the invitation.
● **발송계**(원) a forwarding clerk; (미) a shipping clerk; a mail clerk(우편물의). **발송인** a sender; a consignor(출하주); a remitter(송금자).

발신(發信) [편지를 내기] dispatch[despatch] of a message[letter]; [전신을 보내기] sending[dispatch of] a telegram. **발신하다** send (a letter / a telegram); dispatch (a message); telegraph; cable(해외로).
● **발신국** the sending office[station]. **발신음** (전화의) a dial tone; (무전 등의) a signal. ¶~이 떨어지지 않는다 I don't get a dial tone. **발신인** (편지의) an addresser; (전신 등의) the sender (of a telegram).

발아(發芽) germination; sprouting; budding; gemmation. **발아하다** germinate; be germinant; sprout (out); bud (out); pullulate; put forth buds.

발악(發惡) [욕] abusive language; revilement; [모진 짓] infernality; atrocity. ¶최후의 ~ the last-ditch fight. **발악하다** use abusive language; abuse; revile; rail (at); rave; inveigh (against); do infernal things; kick and struggle.

발안(發案) 1 [발의] a suggestion; a proposition; a proposal; [고안] an idea. ¶그의 ~으로 at his suggestion [initiative] // 그것은 그의 ~이었다 It was his idea. / The idea originated with him. **발안하다** suggest; make a suggestion; propose; [고안하다] devise; [발명하다] invent. ¶이것은 B 씨가 발안한 계획이다 This plan originated with Mr. B. 2 [동의] a motion. **발안하다** move.
● **발안자** a proposer; an originator; an inventor.

발암(發癌) carcinogenesis; the production of cancer. ¶~성의 carcinogenic (chemicals) / cancerogenic / cancer-causing [-forming / -producing] (substance / agent).
● **발암 물질** a carcinogenic [cancerogenic] substance; a carcinogen.

발언(發言) (an) utterance; speaking; (a) speech; [제언] a proposal. ¶~의 기회를 잃다 lose the opportunity of speaking // ~을 취소하다 retract one's words // ~을 금지하다 prohibit (a person) from speaking // ~을 허용하다 allow (a person) to speak // ~을 허락받다 be allowed to speak // ~ 시간을 제한하다 limit on questioning time / limit time on questioning (in the House) / set a time limit on questioning // 정 의원의 ~은 인정합니다 (의장이) Mr. Jeong has the floor. **발언하다** speak; utter; open one's mouth; take the floor(의원이); [제언하다] propose. ¶그는 회의 중에 한마디도 발언하지 않았다 He remained quite silent [He said nothing] throughout the conference.
● **발언권** the right to speak [of speaking]; (the right to) a voice. ¶~이 있다[없다] have a [no] voice (in a matter) / (구어) have a [no] say (in a matter) // (의원이) ~을 얻다 get [obtain] the floor / catch the Speaker's eye. **발언자** a speaker.

발연(發煙) emitting smoke; fuming. **발연하다** smoke; emit [give off] smoke; fume.
● **발연제** a fumigant; a smoke generating agent. **발연탄** a smoke shell [bomb].

발열(發熱) 1 [열을 냄] generation of heat; calorification. **발열하다** emit [generate] heat. 2 [체온이 높아짐] (an attack of) fever; pyrexia; febrility. **발열하다** become feverish; be attacked with fever; have an attack of fever; have [develop] (a) fever; run a fever.
● **발열기**(一期) a pyrogenetic [hot] stage(말라리아의). **발열량**[력] calorific value [power].

발염(拔染) discharging. **발염하다** discharge.
● **발염제** a discharge printing agent.

발원(發願) offering a prayer (to a god). **발원하다** offer a prayer (to a god); make a petition [vow] (to a deity).

발원(發源) 1 (물의) the source; the fountainhead; the head. **발원하다** rise [flow / come] (from a lake, from a spring, etc.); take (its) rise [source] (from a mountain). ¶강은 그 산에서 발원한다 The river rises among the hills. 2 (사물의) the origin; the beginning. **발원하다** originate (in); have (its) origin (in); take (its) rise (in).

발육(發育) growth; development; progress. ¶~이 늦은 아이 a retarded child // ~이 빠르다 [늦다] grow rapidly [slowly] // ~이 좋다 be well grown // ~이 나쁘다 be undergrown / be underdeveloped // ~을 방해하다 check the growth (of) / arrest [retard] the development (of) // ~을 돕다 promote the growth (of) // 아이들은 ~이 빠르다 Children grow rapidly. **발육하다** grow; develop. ¶완전히 발육한 full-grown / fully developed // 한창 발육하는 아이 a growing child // 발육하지 않다 fail to develop / abort.
● **발육 부전** incomplete development; abortion; (의) atel(e)iosis; hypoplasia.

발음(發音) [언] pronunciation; enunciation; articulation(음절로 나누어서의). ¶~대로 phonetically // 또렷한 [정확한] ~ clear [correct] pronunciation // 틀린 ~ mispronunciation // ~대로의 철자 phonetic spelling // ~이 명확한 사람 an articulator // 이 좋다 [나쁘다] have a good [bad] pronunciation / one's pronunciation is good [bad]. **발음하다** pronounce; enunciate; articulate(음절로 나누어). ¶올바르게 ~ pronounce correctly // 그의 이름을 잘못 발음하였다 I mispronounced his name. // 이 낱말은 어떻게 발음합니까 How do you pronounce this word? // 그것은 두 번째 음절에 악센트를 주어 발음한다 It is pronounced with an accent on the second syllable.
● **발음 기관** a speech organ; a sound-producing organ. **발음 기호 / 발음 부호** a phonetic symbol [sign / alphabet].

발의(發議) a proposal; a suggestion; [동의] a motion. ¶A 씨의 ~로 at the instance of Mr. A / on the motion of Mr. A / at Mr. A's suggestion [proposal] // ~가 있다 have a proposal to make // 그의 ~로 비밀 투표가 채결되었다 His motion for a secret vote was accepted. **발의하다** propose; suggest; move. ¶휴회를 발의합니다 I move that the meeting be adjourned.
● **발의권** [정] the initiative. **발의자** a proposer; a mover; an introducer.

발인(發靷) the departure [starting] of a funeral procession (toward a graveyard). ¶오전 11시 ~ The funeral cortege leaves the residence at 11 a.m. **발인하다** (a funeral procession) leave for a cemetery.

발자국 a footprint; a footmark; a spoor; (미) a track; [행방] a trace. ¶눈 위에 뚜렷이 남은 ~ footmarks printed off distinctly in the snow // ~을 남기다 leave one's footprints / (미) track (a floor) // ~을 따라가다 follow up (a person's) footsteps / trace (a person's) footmarks // 길 위에 ~이 남아 있었다 There were large footprints [footmarks / tracks] on the path. // 우리는 사냥개가 남긴 ~을 따라갔다 We followed the tracks left by the hounds.

발자취 1 [발자국] a footprint; a footmark; (미) a track; [종적] a trace. ¶발전의 ~ signs [traces] of progress // ~를 남기다 leave one's mark (in history) // 경찰은 범인의 ~를 뒤쫓고 있다 The police are tracing the footsteps [movement] of the culprit [offender]. // 경찰은 여기까지[현재까지]는 도둑의 ~를 추적했다 The police have traced the thief [the thief's movements] this far. 2 [더듬어 온 길] a course. ¶지난 20년간의 ~를 회고하다 think of [recollect] the course one has followed for twenty years.

발작(發作) a fit; a spasm; a paroxysm; an

발작적

access; an ictus (*pl.* ~(es)). ¶격렬한[가벼운] ~ a violent[mild] fit[stroke] (of apoplexy) // ~을 **일으키다** have a fit[spasm / paroxysm] // 그에게 격심한 통증의 ~이 일어났다 He had a spasm[a paroxysm] of intense pain. **발작하다** have a fit[spasm / paroxysm]; go into a fit.

발작적(發作的) spasmodic; paroxysmal; convulsive; fitful. ¶~ 정신 이상 a temporary derangement of the mind // ~으로 spasmodically / paroxysmally / fitfully / by fits (and starts) // ~으로 울다[웃다] have fits of weeping[laughter] / cry[laugh] hysterically.

발장구 the beating; the flutter kick; the thrash. ¶~를 **치다** [발질하다] beat / kick / flutter one's feet / thrash / [태평하게 지내다] lead an easy life / pass one's days in indolence.

발장단 ¶~을 **치다** beat[mark] time (to the music) with one's foot[feet].

발재봉틀 (−裁縫−) a pedal-operated[treadle / foot] sewing machine.

발전(發展) [뻗어 나감] expansion; extension; enlargement; development; growth. ¶공업의 ~ industrial growth // 도시의 급격한 ~ the rapid growth of cities // 산업의 ~을 꾀하다 foster (the growth of) industry // ~을 저해하다 hamper[arrest] the growth (of trade) // 사건의 ~을 지켜보다 watch the development of an event // 이 지역의 ~은 괄목할 만하다 The growth of this area is amazing. **발전하다** develop; grow; expand; extend. ¶발전하는 도시 a developing city[town] // (도시가) 교외로 ~ expand over the surrounding country // 해외로 ~ make overseas expansion[development] // 형세는 유리하게 발전했다 The situation has developed favorably[in our favor]. // 사태는 급속히 발전하였다 The situation changed rapidly. // 이야기가 의외의 방향으로 발전됐다 The conversation took[moved in] an unexpected turn. →¶사업을 발전시키다 develop one's business.

● **발전도상국** a developing country. ⇨*개발도상국*(⇔개발(開發)) **발전성** possibility of future growth; possibilities; [잠재 능력] potential. ¶~이 있는 promising / (a company) with (bright) futures.

발전(發電) [전기의 발생] the generation of electricity; the production of electric power. ¶원자력 ~ atomic (power) generation // 자가 ~ home generation of electricity. **발전하다** generate electricity; produce electric power. ¶10만 킬로와트의 ~ generate 100,000 kilowatts of power.

● **발전기** a[an electric] dynamo (*pl.* ~s); a (power) generator; an electric generator. ¶교류[직류] ~ an alternating[a direct] current dynamo / an A.C. [a D.C.] generator // 수력[화력] ~ a hydro[thermal] generator // 원자력 ~ an atomic power generator. **발전소** a power plant[station]; a powerhouse; a generating plant[station]. ¶수력 ~ a hydroelectric power plant[station] / a hydropower plant[station] // 원자력 ~ an atomic (nuclear) power station[plant] / a nuclear plant // 화력 ~ a thermoelectric [steam] power plant[station].

발전적(發展的) expansive; developmental; growing.

발정(發情) sexual excitement; [동] (o)estrus; heat(암컷의); rut(수컷의). **발정하다** come into heat; get on heat; go to (the) rut; rut. ¶발정한 개 a dog in [(영) on] heat // 발정하지 않은 [동] anoestrous // 발정하고 있다 (동물이) be in [on / at] heat[rut].

● **발정기** (the age of) puberty; (동물의) the mating[rutting] season; the season of heat.

발족(發足) (사업·조직·기관 등의) inauguration. **발족하다** start; make a start; be inaugurated. ¶새로 ~ start afresh / make a new start (in) // 새로운 협회가 3월에 발족하기로 되어 있다 The new association is to start functioning in March.

발주(發注) [주문함] placing an order; ordering. **발주하다** place[send out] an order (for an article); order. ¶새 가구를 발주하였다 I have ordered new furniture from the manufacturer.

발진(發進) (비행기의) departure; take-off; (로켓의) launching; blast-off; lift-off. ¶군함에 ~ 명령이 내려졌다 An order was issued for the warship to set sail. **발진하다** take off; scramble. ¶육상 기지에서 발진하는 land-based (fighters) // 비행기는 기지에서 발진하였다 The plane took off from the base.

발진(發疹) [의] (an) eruption; (an) efflorescence; [부스럼] a rash; an exanthem (*pl.* ~ata, ~s). ¶~성의 eruptive // 그의 가슴에 ~이 생겼다 A rash appeared[came out] on his chest. **발진하다** break out (in a rash); come out (in spots); erupt; effloresce.

● **발진 티푸스** typhus (fever); eruptive[spotted] fever.

발진기(發振器) [전] an oscillator.

발짝 a step; a pace. ¶한 ~ 한 ~ step by step // 두 ~ 앞으로 나오다[뒤로 물러서다] take two steps forward[backward].

발차(發車) the starting (of a train); departure; (차장의 신호) All aboard! ¶~를 **알리다** call a train. **발차하다** start (from); leave (the station); depart; pull out (of the station). ¶열차는 3번 선에서 발차했다 The train started from track No. 3. // 버스는 몇 분마다 발차합니까 How often does the bus leave? // 열차는 25분마다 발차한다 A train leaves every 25 minutes.

● **발차 시간** the time for departure. **발차 신호** a starting signal.

발착(發着) departure and arrival. ¶비행기의 ~ 시간 departure and arrival time for airplanes. **발착하다** arrive and depart.

● **발착 시간표** a timetable; a (railroad) schedule.

발췌(拔萃) [뽑아냄] extraction; excerption; selection; [뽑아낸 것] an extract; an excerpt; [적요] an abstract; a summary; [선집] a selection. ¶신문의 ~ newspaper cuttings[(미) clippings]. **발췌하다** [골라내다] extract (from); excerpt (from); select[cull] (from); pick up; make an abstract (of). ¶편지의 한 구절을 ~ transcribe[quote] a passage from the letter // 이 절은 그의 논문에서 발췌한 것이다 I excerpted this paragraph from his essay.

● **발췌곡** a (musical) selection.

발치 [발의 방향] the area where the feet lie; the foot (of one's bed); [말단] an end; a tip; the tail end; the lower end. ¶무덤의 ~ the foot of a grave // ~에(서) at one's feet.

발칙하다 [무법하다] lawless; [무례하다]

발칙 insolent; rude; outrageous; [용서할 수 없다] inexcusable; unpardonable. ¶발칙한 놈 an insolent [a rude] fellow∥발칙한 언사 an impertinent [insolent] remark∥발칙한 짓을 하다 misbehave / do wrong / commit an outrage∥발칙하게 굴다 behave impertinently [improperly / outrageously] / (남에게) take liberties (with)∥발칙하게 (남에게) 그런 말을 하다니 (a person) culpable∥이 따위 편지를 보내다니 발칙한 녀석이다 What an insolent fellow he is to write me!∥어른에게 그런 말을 하다니 발칙한 놈이다 It is extraordinarily rude [insolent] of him to make such a remark to his superiors.∥이런 발칙한 놈이 있나 How I detest you!

발칵 all of a sudden; topsy-turvy. ⇨ '발끈

발코니 a balcony. ¶~로 나가다 go out on the balcony∥~로 나가 시원한 바람을 쐬다 enjoy the cool air out on the balcony.

발탁(拔擢) selection; choice. **발탁하다** select; pick [single / sift] out; choose (out of / from among many); draw (from). ¶백 명 중에서 3명을 ~ choose three out of 100. →¶많은 사람 가운데서 발탁되다 be picked out from among many others∥그는 중역으로 발탁되었다 He was selected [chosen / singled out] for a director ship.∥그는 재능이 있어 곧 발탁되었다 His abilities soon marked him for promotion.

발톱 (사람의) a toenail; (짐승의) a claw; (독수리·매 등의) a talon. ¶~이 있는 clawed / ungual∥~이 빠지다 have one's toenail off [peeled]∥~으로 할퀴다 claw / scratch with the claws∥그 고양이는 ~으로 내 손을 할퀴었다 The cat scratched my hand. / The cat fastened [plunged / buried] its claws into my hand.∥새끼 고양이가 ~으로 그물을 친 창을 할퀴고 있다 The kitten is clawing the screen door.

발파(發破) blasting. ¶~ 장치를 하다 set dynamite (to). **발파하다** blast; set dynamite; blow (it) up with dynamite. ¶바위를 ~ blast [dynamite] a rock / blow up a rock with dynamite.
● **발파공** a blaster. **발파 약** a bursting charge; a shot.

발판(－板) **1** [발돋움 받침] a step; a stool; a footstool; [발판 사다리] a stepladder. ¶~에 오르다 climb [get] up on a stool.
2 [건축 공사용] scaffolding; a scaffold. ¶공중에 매단 a flying scaffold∥~을 놓다 set up [erect] a scaffolding.
3 (열차 등의 승강용의) a footboard; a step; (피아노·자전거의) a pedal.
4 [발을 의지하는 곳] a foothold; a footboard; a toehold.
5 [출세 등의 수단·기반] a footing; a foothold; a stepping-stone; a springboard. ¶~을 얻다 gain [obtain] a footing (in society) / secure a foothold∥~을 잃다 lose one's footing∥장래의 ~이 되다 serve as a stepping-stone [a springboard] for future success∥남을 ~으로 하여 출세하다 improve one's position at the expense of another∥그는 동료를 ~ 삼아 출세하려고 했다 He made his colleague a stepping-stone towards his own promotion. / He tried to achieve distinction at the expense of his colleague.
6 (제조·육상·수영의 도약용의) a springboard.

발포(發布) promulgation; proclamation; issue. **발포하다** promulgate; proclaim; issue; publish; announce. →¶새 헌법이 발포되었다 A new constitution was promulgated.

발포(發砲) firing; the discharge of a gun. **발포하다** ~를 삼가다 hold [fire off] a gun. **발포하다** fire (upon); open fire (on); discharge [fire off] a gun. ¶우리에게 ~ fire (a revolver) at us / open fire on us∥그는 통행인에게 발포하였다 He fired (his gun) [shot] at passersby.∥어느 쪽이 먼저 발포하였느냐 Which side fired [opened fire] first?∥그들은 저쪽에서 발포하면 이쪽도 발포하라는 명령을 받고 있다 They were under orders to fire if fired upon.

발포(發泡) foaming; foamy effluence; effervescence. **발포하다** foam; froth; effervesce. →¶고무를 발포시키다 foam rubber.
● **발포제** a foaming [blowing] agent.

발표(發表) [공표] (an) announcement; publication; [성명(聲明)] a statement; a communiqué; (정견 등의) (a) manifestation; [표현] expression. ¶정식 ~ a formal announcement∥결과 ~ an announcement of the results∥중간 ~ an interim announcement [report]∥미 작품 an unpublished work∥~를 보류하다 withhold an announcement∥경찰은 희생자 명단의 ~를 보류하였다 The police withheld the names of the victims. **발표하다** announce; make public; publish; make (something) known; give out; lay (a matter) before the public; issue (a statement); express; release; present (the results of study). ¶정견을 ~ air [make a declaration of / set forth] one's political views∥성명서를 ~ announce a statement∥연구를 (출판물로) publish the result of one's research / (학회 등에서) read a paper (on a subject) / 당의 방침을 ~ publish a party line∥정부는 중대한 성명을 발표했다 The government issued an important statement. ∥학교에서는 응모 조건을 발표하였다 The school announced the requirements for applying.∥그는 새 소설을 잡지에 발표하였다 He published a new novel in a magazine. ∥당국은 전사자 명단을 발표하였다 The authorities released the casualty list.∥주저하시 말고 의견을 발표하시오 Don't hesitate to express your opinion. →¶시험 성적이 발표되었다 The results of the examination have been announced.

발하다(發－) **1** [피다] bloom; come out.
2 [발산하다] issue forth [out]; emit; give out [forth]; (소리를) utter; (빛·열 등을) emanate; radiate. ¶개똥벌레는 몸의 끝에서 빛을 발한다 A firefly emits light from the end of its body.
3 [펴서 드러내다] issue; give; publish; send [give] out. ¶명령을 ~ give [issue] orders.
4 [떠나다] leave (a place) for; depart for.
5 [일으키다·생기게 하다] cause to rise; give rise to.

발한(發汗) sweating; perspiration; hidrosis; diaphoresis. **발한하다** perspire; sweat. →¶발한시키다 induce perspiration / sweat (a patient) / throw (a person) into a sweat.
● **발한제** a diaphoretic; a sudorific; a sudatory.

발행(發行) **1** (도서·잡지의) publication; issue. ¶매월 [월 2회] ~의 잡지 a monthly [a semimonthly] (magazine)∥~을 정지 [금지] 하다 prohibit [suspend] publication∥~이 정지되다 be placed under the ban / be suppressed.

발행하다 publish; issue; bring out; put into circulation. ¶잡지를 ~ publish[start] a magazine∥우리는 주로 아동 도서를 발행하고 있다 The main items on our publication list are books for children.
2 (채권·지폐·증명서 등의) issue; flo(a)tation. **발행하다** float (a loan); issue (banknotes). ¶화폐[채권/증명서]를 ~ issue money[a bond/a certificate].
3 (어음·수표의) drawing; issue; draft; draught. ¶~국 (어음의) a selling office (of money orders) / an office of issue. **발행하다** write a check; draw; issue. ¶어음을 ~ draw a bill[draft] (upon a person for a sum)∥나는 그에게 10만 원의 수표를 발행했다 I wrote a check for hundred thousand won for him.
● **발행 가격** an issue price; (증권 등의) an issue par. **발행고** (一高) (the amount of) circulation; (공채·지폐 등의) the amount of issue. **발행 부수** the circulation (of a magazine). ¶~ 백만 부의 잡지 a magazine with a circulation of one million (copies)∥~가 많은[적은] 잡지 a mass-[limited-]circulation magazine∥국내 최고의 ~를 가진 신문 the paper with the heftiest circulation in the land. **발행인** a publisher; a drawer (of a bill); a remitter (of a money order); an issuer (of a check). **발행일** the date[day] of issue[publication]. ¶~을 늦추다 shift[move down] the date of issue (to). **발행 정지** prohibition[suppression / suspension] of publication.

발헤엄 treading water. **발헤엄하다** tread water.

발현(發現) revelation; manifestation. **발현하다** (드러나게 하다) reveal; manifest; (드러나 보이다) be revealed[manifested]; manifest itself.

발호(跋扈) (권세·세력을 휘둘러 함부로 날뜀) rampancy; prevalence; domination; predominance. ¶군의 ~ the domination of the military men. **발호하다** (횡행하다) be[run] rampant (among people); prevail; (세도를 부리다) be dominant; dominate; domineer over; reign supreme; lord it over; ride triumphantly. ¶온갖 악덕이 발호하고 있다 Vice of all kinds are rampant over.

발화(發火) (불이 일어남) an outbreak of fire; ignition. ¶자연 ~ spontaneous combustion ∥~의 원인 the origin[cause] of a fire. **발화하다** fire; ignite; catch[take] fire. ¶…에서 ~ the fire starts from …∥맨 앞의 객차에서 발화했다 The fire originated in the first car of the train.
● **발화 장치** an igniter; an ignition device. **발화점** the ignition[combustion] point; (기름의) the burning[firing / flash] point.

발효(醱酵) fermentation; zymosis. **발효하다** ferment; undergo fermentation. ¶발효하고 있다 be in ferment. →¶발효시키다 ferment / leaven / sweat.
● **발효소** (화) ferment; yeast; leaven. **발효 작용** zymolysis; fermentation; zymosis.

발효(發效) coming into effect; effectuation; effectiveness. ¶평화 조약의 ~에 따라 with the effectuation of the peace treaty. **발효하다** become effective; take effect; come into effect[force / operation]. ¶이 법은 8월 1일부터 발효한다 This act will come into effect on and after August 1.∥그 조례는 아직 발효되지 않았다 The ordinance is not yet in effect.

발휘(發揮) demonstration; display; manifestation; exhibition. **발휘하다** display; exhibit; show; demonstrate; make manifest. ¶재능을 ~ display[exhibit / show / demonstrate] one's ability∥요리 솜씨를 ~ show off [display / exhibit] one's ability in cooking∥그는 상상력을 십분 발휘했다 He used his imagination to the full.∥그는 실무가로서의 재간을 발휘했다 He demonstrated[displayed] his ability as a businessman.∥그 문제는 그가 실력을 발휘할 기회가 되었다 The problem gave him a chance to show what he could do.

발흥(勃興) (갑자기 일어나 번창해짐) a sudden [meteoric] rise; a sudden increase in the power (of). ¶고구려의 ~ the rise of Goguryeo∥로마 제국의 ~ the rise of the Roman Empire. **발흥하다** rise suddenly; rise into power; make a sudden rise. ¶그 무렵에 중산 계층이 발흥하기 시작했다 At about that time, the middle class began its rise to power.

밝기 [밝은 정도] luminosity. ¶전등의 ~ the brightness of an electric bulb.

밝다¹ [날이 새다] dawn; break. ¶날이 밝기 시작한 하늘 the dawn sky / the sky at dawn∥날이 밝기 전에 before dawn∥날이 밝는다 It dawns. / It gets light. / Day[morning] breaks.∥주위가 점점 더 밝아졌다 It became lighter (and lighter) around us.∥5시에 날이 밝는다 The day breaks[dawns] at five.∥새해가 밝았다 A new year has begun.

밝다² **1** [광선이 충분하다] light; (조명이 충분하다) (well-)lighted; [빛나고 있다] bright; [빛을 발하다] luminous. ¶밝게 brightly / brilliantly / with brightness∥밝은 곳에서 in the light∥밝은 동안에[어둡기 전에] while it is (still) light / before (it gets) dark∥밝은 달 bright moon∥밝은 방 a well-lighted room∥밝은(빛나는) 물체 luminous body∥대낮처럼 ~ be as bright as day∥밝은 거리로 가다 go by[take] (well-)lighted streets∥하늘이 밝아[맑아]지고 있다 (흐린 하늘이) The sky is brightening [lightening]. / (새벽에) It is getting light.∥태양이 밝게 빛나고 있다 The sun is shining bright(ly).∥밖은 아직 ~ It is still light outside.∥이 전구는 ~ This bulb gives a good light.∥별들이 밝게 빛나고 있다 The stars are shining brightly.∥동쪽 하늘이 밝아 오기 시작한다 The eastern sky is growing light.
2 [빛깔이 산뜻하다] light. ¶밝은 녹색 bright green∥밝은 색 a bright[clear / vivid] color [(영) colour]∥밝지 않은 빛깔 a dull[somber] color∥밝은 색과 어두운 색 a bright color and a dark one.
3 [눈·귀가 좋다] sharp; acute; keen; quick. ¶밝은 눈[귀] acute vision[hearing] / sharp eyes[ears]∥귀가 ~ have a sharp[quick] ear / be quick-eared∥그는 귀가 매우 ~ He has a very sharp ear.
4 [정통하다] well acquainted (with); well informed[versed] (in); expert (in / at); familiar (with). ¶정계의 사정에 ~ be well informed on[about] political affairs∥한국 사정에 ~ be well acquainted with the affairs of Korea∥이 근처의 지리에 ~ know one's way around here∥사무에 ~ be well versed in business methods∥세상 물정에 ~ know

much of the world / be a man of the world // 그는 중국 사정에 ~ He is posted up in things Chinese. // 그는 회사의 내부 사정에 ~ He is acquainted with [well informed about] what goes on inside the company. // 그는 컴퓨터 분야에 ~ He is well versed [an expert] in computer science. // 그는 프랑스 문학에 ~ He is well read in French literature.

5 [표정·분위기가 유쾌하다] cheerful; spirited. ¶밝은 얼굴 a cheerful face [look] // 밝은 성격이다 be of a cheerful disposition // 오늘은 자네의 얼굴이 밝지가 않네 You look depressed today. // 그 소식을 듣고 그의 얼굴이 밝아졌다 His face lighted up at the news. // 그녀는 이전만큼 밝지 않았다 She was not so cheerful as she used to be.

6 [유망하다] bright; promising; rosy. ¶밝은 장래 a bright future // 우리의 미래는 밝지 않다 We have a dark future before us. // 이것은 우리의 계획 사업에 있어서 밝은 소식이다 This is encouraging news for our project.

7 [공정하다] clear; clean. ¶밝은 사회 a community in peace and prosperity // 밝은 정치 clean politics // 밝은 선거 a fair and honest election.

밝을 녘 daybreak; dawn; the early hours of the morning. ¶~에 at daybreak / at dawn // ~까지 공부하다 study into the early morning hours.

밝히다¹ [밝게 하다] light up; brighten; lighten. ¶불빛[등불]을 ~ turn up the light / make the lamp brighter // 그 거리는 네온등으로 밝혀져 있었다 The street was lit up with neon lights.

밝히다² **1** [분명히 하다] make (a matter) clear [plain]; clear (up) (the cause); clarify [define] (one's attitude); [공개하다] bring (a matter) to light; make (a matter) public; [파헤치다] dig up; bare [uncover / discover] (the truth / the mystery); disclose [reveal / divulge] (a secret); [뚜렷하게 하다] throw [cast / shed] light on (the meaning); [확인하다] ascertain (a matter); verify. ¶계획을 ~ lay the scheme bare [open] // 사리를 ~ reason with (a person) // 신분을 ~ prove [disclose] one's identity // 심중을 ~ open [bare] one's heart (to) / unbosom oneself (to) // 이름을 ~ disclose one's name // …의 뜻을 ~ explain the meaning (of) // 태도를 ~ clarify one's attitude / make one's position clear // 밝혀지다 become clear [plain] / be ascertained / come [be brought] to light / prove [turn out] (to be) / be identified (as) // 화재의 원인을 밝혀내다 pinpoint [(문어) ascertain] the cause of a fire // 사건을 ~ bring a matter to light / disclose a matter / make a matter public [known to the public] // 동기를 ~ clarify (a person's) motives // 사고의 원인을 ~ determine the cause of an accident // 그는 자기가 거기에 갈 수 없는 이유를 밝혔다 He explained why he could not go there. // 그는 그의 야심적인 계획을 내게 밝혔다 He disclosed his ambitious plan to me. // 그는 이 논문에서 자기의 입장을 밝혔다 He defined his position in this thesis. // 당신의 의도를 밝히시오 Will you explain your motive? // 총리는 그의 외교 방침을 밝혔다 The Prime Minister made known [public] his foreign policy. // 두 사람 [가지]의 관계를 밝혀내는 일은 어렵다 It is difficult to find [put one's finger on] the connection between the two. // 독직 사건이 밝혀졌다 A case of graft has come to light [has been brought to light / has been disclosed]. // 돈이 어떻게 쓰여졌는지 밝혀지지 않았다 How the money had been spent was not accounted for.

2 [밤을 새우다] sit [stay] up all night [the whole night]; keep [remain] awake all night; keep vigil; see the dawn in; pass [spend] (a night). ¶독서로 밤을 ~ sit up all night reading [over a book] // 이야기로 밤을 ~ talk the night away // 하룻밤을 눈물로 ~ pass a whole night in tears / weep all night // 술로 하룻밤을 ~ make a night of it / spend a night in debauchery.

밟다 1 [디디다] step on; tread upon [on] (with the feet); [짓밟다] trample (on); stamp. ¶밟아 다져진 길 a beaten path // 밟아 다지다 (흙을) tread down (the earth) / level (the earth) by treading down / (길을) beat (a path) // 밟아 다져진 눈 snow trodden hard // 땅을 밟아 다지다 stamp (on) the ground until it is firm / stamp the ground flat // 힘껏 밟고 서다 stand firmly // 한 발짝한 발짝 밟고 나아가다 step forward with caution / move forward a step at a time // 액셀러레이터를 꽉 ~ push the accelerator of one's car down to the floor / floor the gas pedal suddenly [strongly] // 브레이크를 꽉 ~ press [stamp] on the brake / hit the brakes // 남의 발을 ~ step on a person's foot // 페달을 ~ pedal // 외국 땅을 ~ step [set foot] on foreign soil // (차를 더 빨리 운전하라는 뜻으로) 더 밟아 Step on it! // 잔디를 밟지 마시오 (게시) Keep off the grass. / Don't tread [step] on the grass.

2 [수속 등을 거치다] go through (formalities); undergo; [마치다] finish; complete. ¶절차를 ~ go through formalities / take proceedings // 정규 과정을 ~ complete a regular course.

3 [뒤를] follow; track; shadow; tail. ¶몰래 남의 뒤를 ~ follow a person secretly / shadow a person // 형사로 하여금 뒤를 밟게 하다 set [put] a detective on (a person's) track.

4 [되풀이하다]. ¶전철(前轍)을 ~ make [repeat] the same error [mistake].

밤¹ night; [저녁] evening.(▶ evening은 일몰이나 저녁 식사 때부터 취침 시까지, night는 일몰에서 태양이 비추지 않는 시간을 가리킴) ¶오늘 ~ tonight / this evening (▶ 주로 일몰에서 취침 때까지) // ~마다 every night / night after night / nightly / at nights // ~ 7시에 at seven in the evening // 오늘 ~ 텔레비전의 일기 예보 the weather forecast on TV tonight // 8월 16일 ~에 on the evening [night] of August 16 // ~의 파리 Paris by [at] night // ~에만 나오는 동물이 많이 있다 Many animals come out only at night [by night]. // ~이 깊었다 (과거에) The night grew late. / (현재에) It's grown very late. // ~을 틈타 도망쳤다 I escaped under cover of darkness [night]. / 우리는 그 나무 밑에서 ~을 새웠다 We spent the night under the tree. // ~이 되기 전에 끝내자 Let's finish this before it gets dark [before night falls]. / 나는 ~이 되면 열이 오른다 My temperature rises in the evening [at night]. // 나는 토요일 ~에 영화를 보러 갔다 I went to the movies on Saturday night. // 그는 아침부터 ~까지 책을 읽고 있었다 He was

밤

reading books from morning till night.∥오늘 ~안에 일을 끝낼 작정이다 I intend to finish the job tonight.∥~ 안으로 파업이 중지될 것 같다 The strike is likely to be called off in the course of the night.∥나는 작년의 오늘 ~ 처음으로 서울에 왔다 I came to Seoul for the first time exactly a year ago this evening.∥나는 오늘 ~에 호텔에서 묵겠다 I'll stay at this hotel for the night[tonight].∥오늘 ~의 식사는 매우 맛있었다 The dinner this evening was very good.∥오늘 ~은 날씨가 맑을 것입니다 It will be clear tonight[this evening].∥그녀는 매일 ~ 두세 시까지 앉아 있다 She stays up till the small hours every night.∥그는 ~마다 그 술집에 갔다 He went to the bar night after night[every night].∥환자의 간병으로 ~을 꼬박 새웠다 I stayed up all night watching the patient.∥그는 ~을 꼬박 새워 일을 끝냈다 He stayed up all night to finish the work.

밤² [밤나무의 열매] a chestnut. ¶~을 주우러 가다 go chestnut gathering∥~ 까다 crack a chestnut.

밤거리 night streets; the town at night. ¶~의 여인 a lady of the night / a streetwalker / a street girl / a woman of the streets∥~를 걷다 walk the street at night.

밤길 a night journey[walk / trip]. ¶~을 가다 go[travel] by night / walk out at night / make a night journey[trip]∥나는 급한 볼일로 이웃 읍까지 ~을 갔다 I made a night journey[I walked after dark] to the next town on an urgent errand.

밤꽃 a chestnut blossom.

밤꾀꼬리 [동] a nightingale. ⇨나이팅게일

밤나무 [식] a chestnut tree.

밤 낚시 fishing at night; night fishing [angling]. ¶~를 하다 angle at night∥~를 하러 가다 go fishing at night.

밤낮 [밤과 낮] day and night; night and day; (언제나) day and night; constantly; always; all the time; day in, day out; (문어) day in and day out. ¶~을 가리지 않고 around[((영) round] the clock / night and day / by day and by night / all the time∥그는 ~ 레코드만 듣고 있다 He listens to records at all hours.∥그는 ~을 가리지 않고 공부하고 있다 He studies day and night.∥그들은 지진에 대비하여 ~으로 경계 태세를 취하고 있다 They are constantly[always] on the alert for an earthquake.∥그들은 철도의 복구를 위하여 ~을 가리지 않고 작업을 계속했다 They worked around the clock to reopen the railroad.

밤낮없이 day and night; night and day; (a)round the clock. ¶~ 일하다 work night and day[day and night]∥그들은 ~ 걸었다 They walked on and on night and day.∥그는 ~ 책만 읽고 있다 He does nothing but read books all the time[day in, day out]. / He is always reading books.

밤눈 [야간의 시력] night vision. ¶~이 밝다 have good sight in the dark / have the eyes of a cat∥~이 어둡다 be blind at night / be night-[moon-]blind∥~에도 잘 보인다 be clearly seen even in the dark.

밤늦다 late at night. ¶밤늦게 late at night / when night is advanced∥밤늦게까지 till late at night / far into the night∥밤늦게까지 자지 않고 있다 sit up till late[at night]∥밤늦게까지 공부하다 work until[till] late at night / burn the midnight oil∥아침 일찍부터 밤늦게까지 일하다 work early and late∥제인은 밤늦게까지 공부한다 Jane studies till late at night[far into the night]. / Jane sits up studying till late at night.∥그는 밤늦게 여기 도착했다 He got here late at night.∥밤늦은 거리에는 사람의 그림자를 찾아볼 수 없었다 At that late hour of the night there was no one in the streets.∥밤늦게까지 자지 않는 것은 건강에 좋지 않다 Staying up late[Keeping late hours] is bad for the health.∥그들은 매일 밤늦게까지 마작을 했다 Every night they sat up till late playing mah-jong(g). / (오전 두세 시까지) Every night they played mah-jong(g) until the small hours of the morning.

밤바람 the evening wind; a night wind [breeze]. ¶~을 쐬어 감기에 걸렸다 After being exposed to the (chilly) evening breeze, I caught a cold.

밤비 rain in the night; nightly rain; the evening[night] rain.

밤사이 the nighttime; (부사) during [in] the night. ¶~ 맹위를 떨친 폭풍우로 on account of the storm that has been raging overnight∥~ 내린 호우로 언덕이 무너졌다 There was a landslide owing to the heavy rain that had been falling throughout the night[since the previous night].∥~에 도둑이 들었다 My house was broken into during the night.∥~ 잘 주무셨습니까 Did you sleep well (last night)?

밤새 the nighttime; during[in] the night. ⇨밤사이

밤새껏 all night long[through]; through the whole night; all the night through; through [through out / all through] the night. ¶~ 마시다 make a night of it∥~ 울다 keep crying all night∥그는 ~ 눈을 붙이지 못했다 He lay awake all night.∥그녀 밤 나는 ~ 고열이 계속되었다 I had a high temperature all that night.∥그녀는 ~ 일했다 She kept working all night.∥간밤은 ~ 한잠도 못 잤다 I lay awake all last night. / I didn't sleep a wink last night.∥~ 그와 이야기했다 I talked with him the whole night through.∥개가 ~ 짖어 댔다 The dog howled all night (long)[all night through / all through the night].∥그녀는 ~ 환자 곁에 있었다 She kept an all-night vigil by the side of the patient.

밤새우다 pass a night without sleep; sit[stay] up all night; keep[stay] awake all night. ¶독서로 ~ sit up all night reading [over] a book∥울며 ~ weep all night∥흥청대며[방탕한 놀이로] ~ make a night of it / spend a night in debauchery∥이야기로 ~ talk the night away / talk all night∥뜬눈으로 ~ cannot get a wink of sleep / pass a sleepless night∥도둑을 지키느라고 ~ keep vigil against the thieves∥그는 밤새워 시험 준비를 했다 He sat up all night preparing himself for the examination.

밤새움 sitting up all night. ⇨밤샘

밤색 (-色) ¶~의 chestnut / nut brown / maroon∥짙은 ~ dark brown.

밤샘 sitting[staying] up all night; an all-night vigil[sitting]; (초상집의) a corpse watch; a death watch. **밤샘하다** stay[sit] up all night;

keep vigil.
밤소경 a night-[moon-]blind person.
밤손님 a thief; a robber. ⇨=도둑
밤송이 a chestnut bur(r).
밤안개 a night fog[mist]. ¶골짜기에는 ~가 끼어 있었다 The valley lay hidden in a night fog. / A night fog hung over[(문어) enveloped] the valley.
밤알 a chestnut. ¶~을 줍다 gather chestnuts.
밤이슬 the evening[night] dew; nightly dew. ¶~을 맞다 expose oneself to the night damp.
밤일 1〔밤에 하는 일〕 night work; a night shift(교대 작업의 야근). **밤일하다** work at [by] night; do night work; work into the night(밤까지); work on the night shift(야근으로); (공장이) operate at night. **2** (sexual) intercourse. ⇨=성교
밤잠 night sleep; sleeping at night.
밤중(-中)〔밤의 한가운데〕(in) the middle of the night; (in) the dead of night; 〔자정〕 (at) midnight. ¶~에 ~에 in the middle of the night // 이 ~에 무슨 볼일인가 What do you want of me at this time of night? / 나는 ~에 몇 번 잠을 깼다 I awoke several times in the night[during the night]. // 이 ~에 무엇을 먹느냐 What do you think (you're) eating at this time of night?
밤차(-車)〔야간 열차〕a night train; (미) an owl train. ¶~를 타다 board a night train.
밤참 a nighttime meal; a night snack. ¶~을 먹다 have a night snack.
밤톨 a chestnut. ¶~만 한 혹 a wen as big as a chestnut // ~만 하다 be a chestnut size.
밤하늘 a night[nocturnal] sky. ¶은하수가 ~ 높이 걸려 있었다 The Milky Way hung high in the night sky.
밥[1] **1**〔쌀밥〕 boiled[cooked] rice;〔잡곡밥〕 any boiled cereal. ¶~ 한 그릇 a bowl of boiled rice // ~을 내놓다 serve rice // ~을 사발에 담다 fill a bowl with rice // ~을 짓다 boil[cook] rice // ~을 공기에 푸다 serve [dish up] rice in a bowl // (레스토랑에서) ~을 곁들인가요 Would you like (some) rice, too? // ~을 몇 공기나 먹었나 How many bowels of rice did you eat?
2〔식사〕 a meal; food. ¶~ 때 mealtime / dinner time // ~을 먹다 take[have / eat] a meal // ~을 함께 먹다 eat[dine] together / eat off the same trencher // 하루에 ~을 세 끼 먹다 take three meals a day // ~이 다 되었어요 Breakfast is ready! // 아직 이 되었나 Isn't breakfast[lunch / supper] ready yet?
3〔먹이〕 food; feed; a bait;〔희생물〕 prey; a victim.〔돼지〕 ~ hog feed //〔고기〕 ~ fish food // ~이 되다 fall a prey[victim] to // ~으로 삼다 exploit (a person) / prey upon / make a victim of (a girl) / make a sucker out of (a person) // 그는 쉽사리 고용주의 ~이 되었다 He was[became] an easy prey to his employer.
밥[2]〔부스러기〕(a) waste; chips; waste material produced in cutting. ¶가윗~ scraps of cloth[paper] // 끌~ chisel dust // 대팻~ shavings // 실~ bits of thread // 톱~ sawdust.
밥값(식당의) the charge for food; (가정의) table expenses. ¶그는 ~도 못 한다 He is a good-for-nothing. / He cannot earn his keep.

밥그릇 a rice bowl. ¶~에 밥을 반만 담다 fill a bowl half-full with rice.
밥맛 1〔밥의 맛〕 the taste of boiled rice. **2** appetite. ⇨=식욕
밥물 1〔밥 짓는 물〕 water for boiling rice. **2**〔밥이 끓어 넘치는 물〕 rice-water. ¶~이 넘는다 The rice-water is boiling over.
밥벌레 a drone; a good-for-nothing (fellow); a useless mouth. ¶그 여자는 ~다 She is not worth her salt.
밥벌이 (a means of) living; breadwinning; livelihood; one's bread and butter. ¶~를 못 하다 be unable to earn one's bread / cannot make a living // ~를 시켜 주다 put (a person) in the way of making a living // 이 장사는 ~가 안 된다 This business doesn't pay. **밥벌이하다** earn one's bread; make a livelihood[living]. ¶겨우 ~ eke out a scanty livelihood / make a bare living.
밥상(一床) a (dining) table. ¶~ 앞에 앉다 sit down at the table (to eat) // ~을 올리다 set [lay] a meal before (a person) // ~을 치우다 clear the table / remove[take away] the cloth // 어머니는 ~을 차렸다 My mother has prepared a meal. / My mother has set[laid] the table. // ~을 치우자 Let's clear the table.
밥솥 a rice cooker; an iron pot. ¶전기~ an electric rice cooker.
밥술〔밥의 몇 술〕 a few spoonfuls of (boiled) rice;〔밥을 먹는 숟가락〕 a rice spoon. ¶~이나 얻어 먹으려고 일을 하다 do the job just to keep oneself alive.
밥알 a grain of cooked[boiled] rice.
밥장사 the boiled rice trade; restaurant business. **밥장사하다** run a restaurant; sell meals; run an eating house; trade in boiled rice.
밥장수 a boiled rice trader; an eating house keeper; one who sells meals.
밥주걱 a rice spatula.
밥줄 1〔속〕 an occupation. ⇨직업 **2**〔생〕 the gullet. ⇨=식도(食道)
밥줄이 끊어지다 lose one's means of livelihood[job]. ¶이 일을 못 하게 되면 나는 밥줄이 끊어진다 If I lose this job, I will[(영) shall] starve.
밥집 an eating house; a chophouse; a cheap restaurant.
밥통(一桶) **1**〔밥을 담는 그릇〕 a container for boiled rice. ⇨¹위(胃) **3**〔무능자〕 a good-for-nothing (fellow); a useless mouth.
밥투정하다 grumble at[about / over] one's food; complain about the inadequacy of one's food. ¶우리 애는 늘 밥투정하고 있다 My boy is always whining about his food.
밥풀 1〔풀 대신 쓰는 밥알〕 rice paste. **2** a grain of cooked rice. ⇨=밥알
밥하다 boil[cook] rice; prepare food.
밧줄 a rope; a line; a stay. ¶교수형용 ~ the rope // 세 가닥으로 꼰 ~ a three-ply rope // ~로 당기다 pull with a rope // ~을 잡아당기다 pull at a rope // ~로 짐을 묶다 tie a package with a rope / rope a package // ~을 치다 stretch a rope / rope // ~을 타고 내려오다 climb down a rope // 그들은 공터의 둘레에 ~을 쳤다 They put up a rope around the vacant land. // 경찰이 ~을 치고 사람들의 출입을 금지시켰다 The police have roped off the area to keep the crowd out.

방(房) a room; a chamber. ¶빈~ a vacant [an unoccupied] room // 어린이 ~ a children's room // 햇볕이 잘 드는 ~ a sunny room // 이 다섯 있는 집 a five-room house / a house with five rooms // 3제곱미터의 ~ a room three meters square // 셋~ a room for rent [(영) to let] // 하인의 ~ a servant's room / servants' quarters // ~의 할당 assignment of rooms [lodgings] // 여섯 칸짜리 ~ a six-*kan* room // ~을 세내다 rent a room // ~을 세놓다 rent [(영) let] a room (to a person) // ~을 예약하다 reserve a room (at a hotel) // ~을 비우다 vacate a room / leave a room // 이 ~은 나의 서재입니다 This room serves for my study.

방(榜) 1 [과거 급제자의 성명록] the list of successful candidates. 2 [포고문] a placard; a public notice.

방(放) a round; (소총의) a shot; (대포의) a shell. ¶대포 세 ~ three volleys of the cannon // 한 ~의 포성 a roar of cannon // 사슴에다 한 ~ 쏘다 fire a shot at a deer // 여섯 ~을 쏘다 fire six rounds.

방갈로 [긴] a bungalow.

방개 [동] a diving beetle. ⇨ 물방개

방계(傍系) a collateral line [family]. ¶~의 collateral / oblique / (모회사에 대하여) subsidiary.
● **방계 비속** [존속] a collateral descendant [ascendant]. **방계 친족** a collateral relation. **방계 회사** a subsidiary company; a subsidiary (of a company); an affiliated company.

방고래(房-) the flue of an *ondol* [a hypocaust]. ¶~를 켜다 [놓다] lay a system of flues in the floor of a room // ~가 메었다 The flue of a hypocaust was clogged up.

방공(防共) defense [(영) defence] against communism. ¶~의 anticommunist(ic). **방공하다** fight [defend against] communism.

방공(防空) air defense [(영) defence]; air armament; anti-aircraft defense. ¶한국 ~ 식별 구역 Korean Air Defense Identification Zone(약어 KADIZ).
● **방공 시설** air defense facilities; anti-air raid establishments. **방공호** an air-raid shelter; a bomb shelter; a dugout. ¶~에 들어가다 shelter oneself in a dugout. **방공 훈련 / 방공 연습** (민간의) an air-raid drill; (군대의) air-defense maneuvers [(영) manoeuvres]. ¶민~ a civil air defense drill.

방과(放課) dismissal of a class. ¶~ 후 after school / after-school hours // ~ 후까지 기다려라 Wait until school is over [out]. // 그는 ~ 후에는 도서관에서 시간을 보내는 일이 많았다 He spent many of his after-school hours in the library.

방관(傍觀) onlooking; looking on as a spectator; standing idle by [aside]. ¶~적 태도를 취하다 assume the attitude of an onlooker / assume an indifferent attitude. **방관하다** look on; (문어) remain a spectator [an idle onlooker]; sit [stand] by and watch; be on the hedge. ¶수수~ look on with folded arms / remain an unconcerned spectator // 그는 싸움을 방관하고 있었다 He stood by and watched the fight. // 그들은 그저 방관할 따름이었다 They just looked on without doing anything. / They just remained spectators. // 친구의 곤경을 방관하고 있을 수는 없다 I cannot be indifferent to the distress of my friend. // 이대로 방관하고 있을 수는 없지 않은가 You can't get away with sitting on the fence forever [(영) for ever].
● **방관자 / 방관인** an onlooker; a bystander; a looker-on (*pl.* lookers-on); an idle spectator; a sideliner. ¶그는 어느 정도 인생을 초탈해서 ~의 입장에서 바라보게 되었다 He became somewhat detached from life and came to see things more as a bystander.

방광(膀胱) [생] the (urinary) bladder; the urinary cyst.
● **방광염** cystitis; inflammation of the bladder.

방구석(房-) [방 속] the interior of a room; [방의 구석] a corner of a room. ¶~에 in a room / indoors // ~에 틀어박혀 있다 keep (in) one's room all day long // ~에서 뭘 하느냐 What are you doing in the room?

방귀 wind; (비어) a fart. ¶~를 뀌다 fart / break wind / pass gas.

방귀가 잦으면 똥 싸기 쉽다(속담) Coming events cast their shadows before.; Repeated small irregularities lead to serious consequences [trouble].

방귀 뀐 놈이 성낸다(속담) get angry at others for one's own mistakes.

방그레 smilingly; beamingly; with a sweet [gentle] smile. ¶~ 웃다 smile sweetly (at a person) / smile a sweet smile / beam (upon a person).

방글거리다 smile radiantly (at). ⇨ 벙글거리다

방글방글 (smile) with a broad smile. ⇨ 벙글벙글

방금(方今) a moment ago; just now; right now. ¶~ 말씀드린 대로 as I have just said // 그녀는 ~ 돌아왔다 She has just come home. // 그는 ~ 산책 나갔습니다 He just (now) went out for a walk. // 그들은 ~ 떠났다 They have just left. // 그는 ~ 외출했다 He went out a moment ago. // ~ 이 편지가 도착했습니다 This letter came just now. / This letter has just arrived.

방긋 1 [웃는 모양] smilingly; beamingly; with a (bland) smile. ¶~ 웃다 smile sweetly (at a person) / beam (upon a person) / break into a smile // ~ 웃으며 인사하다 greet a person with a smile. **방긋하다** beam (upon); smile radiantly (at). 2 [열린 모양]. ¶그녀는 문을 ~ 열고 들여다보았다 She opened the door gently and peeped in. **방긋하다** (서술적) be ajar; be slightly [partly] opened.

방긋방긋 (smile) with a broad smile; smilingly.

방긋이 smilingly. ⇨ 방긋

방년(芳年) the sweet age (of a young girl); sweet sixteen(▶ 영어에서는 16세를 처녀의 한창 꽃다운 나이로 삼음). ¶~ 17세의 처녀 a girl of seventeen summers [of sweet seventeen].

방뇨(放尿) urination; micturition; (속어) pissing. ¶~ 금지 (게시) No urinating. **방뇨하다** urinate; make [pass] urine [water]; discharge urine; relieve oneself; (속어) piss; pee.

방담(放談) a random talk; a free [an unreserved] talk. ¶총리와 대통령의 차내 ~ a frank informal talk on the train between the prime minister and the president.

방대하다(厖大-·尨大-) bulky; massive; vast; voluminous; copious; extensive; enormous; stupendous; colossal; fabulous; mammoth; huge; gigantic; enormous. ¶방대한 계획 a grand plan // 방대한 생산 과잉 enormous overproduction // 방대한 예산 a budget of staggering proportions // 방대한 우주여행 계획 a colossal space flight project // 방대한 자료 massive material // 방대한 작품 a work on a grand scale // 방대한 저술 a voluminous work // 3천 단어로 된 방대한 문서 a bulky document of three thousand words // 그가 여태껏 행한 연설들을 모으면 방대한 책이 될 것이다 The speeches he has delivered would fill a big volume. **방대히** massively; vastly; voluminously; copiously.

방도(方途·方道) a way; a method; a means; a measure. ¶돈 버는 ~ how to make money / the art of making money // 문제 해결의 ~ a way to solve [a means of solving] a problem // 적절한 ~를 취하라 take proper measures // 달리 무슨 ~가 있었을 텐데 You might have done it in some other way. // 이것 말고는 달리 ~가 없다 There is no alternative for it. / There is nothing for it but to do so. // 이 궁지에서 벗어날 ~가 없다 There is no way out of this dilemma. // 돈 벌 ~가 달리 있을지도 모른다 There may be some other means [ways] of earning money.

방독(防毒) keeping away poisonous substances; protecting oneself from poison. **방독하다** keep away poisonous substances; protect oneself from poison.
● **방독면 / 방독 마스크** a gas mask [helmet]; an antigas mask; (영) a respirator.

방둥이 [길짐승의 엉덩이] the rump; the buttock of an animal.

방랑(放浪) wandering; roaming; roving; a Bohemian life. ¶~길에 오르다 start on a wandering [roving] journey. **방랑하다** wander about; roam; rove; tramp; lead a Bohemian life. ¶세상을 두루 ~ (구어) wander [knock / roam] about the world / go gypsying about the world.
● **방랑벽** vagrant habits; vagabondism. ¶~이 있다 be of a rambling [roving] disposition. **방랑자** a wanderer; a vagabond; a vagrant; a hobo; a tramp; an exile.

방류(放流) discharge. **방류하다** (물을) discharge; (물고기를) stock [plant] (a river) with (fish); release (fish) into (a river). ¶그들은 해마다 강에 잉어 새끼를 방류한다 They stock the river with carp fry every year. → ¶팔당 댐의 물은 조심스럽게 방류되고 있다 The water from Paldang Dam is carefully discharged.

방만(放漫) looseness; laxity; indiscretion. **방만하다** loose; lax; careless; reckless. ¶방만한 재정 a lax [an irresponsible] financial policy // 그의 방만한 경영으로 회사는 도산했다 Owing to his careless [irresponsible] management, the company went bankrupt. **방만히** loosely; laxly; carelessly; recklessly.

방망이 a club; a billy (club)(경찰관의) a cudgel(무기로 쓰는). ¶다듬잇 ~ (a pair of) wooden fulling sticks // 빨랫 ~ a wooden laundry paddle // 야구 ~ a (baseball) bat / (미국 속어) a willow / a stick // 도깨비 [요술] ~ a mallet of luck / a horn of plenty fulling sticks.

● **방망이질** beating with a club [paddle] (in washing, smoothing clothes). ¶~을 하다 beat with a club [paddle] / (가슴이) (one's heart) beat fast / palpitate / go pit-a-pat.

방매(放賣) (a) sale; selling. ⇨ᐧ매출

방면(方面) 1 [방향] a direction; a side; a way; [지역] a quarter; a district. ¶서울 ~ Seoul districts // 각 ~에서 [으로부터] from all quarters // 각 ~으로[에] in all directions [quarters] // 어느 ~에서 폭발 소리가 났습니까 From which direction did you hear the explosion? // 그 차는 신촌 ~을 향하고 있다 The car is heading for Sinchon. // 백조는 시베리아 ~으로 날아가 버렸다 The swans flew away toward(s) Siberia. // 종로 ~의 교통이 마비되고 있다 Traffic is congested in the Jongno area. // 호남 ~에 오시게 되면 알려 주십시오 Let me know when you come to the Honam district.

2 [분야] a field; a sphere; a line; [각도] an angle; [국면] an aspect; a phase. ¶각 ~에서 (견지·각도) from every point of view / from all angles // 문화 [스포츠] ~에서는 in the field of literature [sport] // 문제를 모든 ~에서 고찰하다 consider a question in all its bearings [aspects] / discuss a question from all angles // 새로운 ~으로 돌입하다 enter a new field / enter upon a new phase // 그 ~은 나의 전문이 아니다 I am no expert in that field [line]. // 여러 ~의 사람들이 모여 있었다 People of different walks of life were gathered there. // 각 ~에서 문의가 있었다 Inquiries came from all [various] quarters. // 그 문제는 여러 ~에서 검토해 봅시다 Let's look at the question from various angles. // 그들은 각기 여러 ~에서 이름을 날리고 있다 They have made a name for themselves in various spheres of activity.

3 [네모난 얼굴] a squarish face.

방면(放免) [용서하여 놓아 줌] release from custody; discharge; liberation; [무죄 석방] acquittal. ¶훈계 ~ dismissal with a caution / release after admonition // 무죄 ~의 선고 acquittal by a court of law // 그는 무죄 ~이 되었다 He was acquitted of the charge. **방면하다** release; discharge; liberate; set (a person) free; let go (a person); acquit (a person of the charge). ¶무죄 판결을 받은 사람을 ~ release an acquitted person from custody // 형기를 마친 복역수를 ~ release a convict who has completed his sentences.

방명(芳名) [남의 이름] your (honored) [(영) honoured] name; [명성] a good [fair] name [fame / reputation]. ¶~은 익히 알고 있습니다 I have often heard of you. / Your name is very familiar to me.
● **방명록** (방문객의) a visitor's book [register / list]; a list of names [acquaintances].

방모(紡毛) [털실을 뽑음] carding wool; spinning wool.
● **방모기** a carding machine. **방모사** spun woolen [(영) woollen] yarn.

방목하다(放牧) grazing; pasturing. **방목하다** graze (cattle); put [turn out] (cattle) to grass; pasture. ¶소를 ~ put the cattle out to pasture // 소는 방목하고 있습니다 The cows are at pasture. // 여름에는 고지에서 소를 방목한다 In summer they take their cattle up to high ground and turn them out to pasture.
● **방목지** grazing land; a pasture.

방문(房門) a door (of a room).
방문(訪問) a call; a visit; an interview. ¶가정 ~ a call at a student's home (by a teacher) // 첫 ~ the first visit / 공식 ~ a formal visit / an official call / 〈국가 원수의〉 a state visit // ~ 중에 while one is at (a person's) home / 인사차 ~ a visit of courtesy // ~을 받다 receive [get] a call [visit] (from a person) / 그는 일요일에는 ~을 받지 않는다 He does not receive visitors [see people / allow people to visit (his house)] on Sundays. // 대통령은 동남아 여러 나라의 ~ 길에 올랐다 The President set off on a visit to [a tour of] various Southeast Asian countries. **방문하다** visit; call on (a person); call at (a place); pay (a person) a visit. ¶친구의 집을 ~ call at a friend's home / 내일 8시에 방문하겠습니다 I'll call on [come and see] you tomorrow at eight o'clock.
● **방문객** a caller; a visitor; a guest. ¶~이 있다[없다] have a [no] visitor to receive. **방문단** a group [team] of visitors. ¶재미 동포 모국 ~ a group of Korean residents in U.S.A. who are visiting their fatherland.
방물 fancy goods; 〈미〉 notions; 〈영〉 haberdashery; women's merchandise items.
● **방물장사** selling women's items from door to door. **방물장수** a notions dealer; a haberdasher; a peddler of women's items.
방미(訪美) visit to the United States. ¶~ 길에 오르다 leave for the United States.
방바닥(房−) the floor of a room; the room floor. ¶~이 눅눅하다 The floor is wet [damp].
방방곡곡(坊坊曲曲) everywhere throughout the country; all over the country; every nook and corner [cranny] of the land. ¶~에 throughout the length and breadth of the land / in all parts of the country // ~에서[으로부터] from every quarters / from every nook and corner (of the land) // ~에 알려지다 be [become] known far and wide [all over the country].
방백(傍白) an aside; a stage aside.
방범(防犯) prevention of crimes; crime prevention. ¶그곳 주민의 긴밀한 유대가 ~에 기여하고 있다 The close bonds between the residents help to prevent crime in the neighborhood. **방범하다** prevent crimes; take preventive measures against crimes.
● **방범대원** a night [security] guard; a (night) watchman.
방법(方法) 〔목적을 이루기 위해 취하는 방식〕 a way; 〔체계적인 방법〕 a method; 〔방책〕 a plan; a system; 〔…식·양식〕 a manner; 〔수단〕 a means; 〔책략〕 a scheme; a device; a program; 〔조치〕 a step; a measure; 〔과정〕 a process; 〔절차〕 a procedure; 〔처방〕 a recipe; a formula (pl. ~s, -lae). ¶현대적인 어학 교육 ~ modern methods of language teaching // 유일한 ~ the only way / 최선의 ~ the best method // …하는 ~ how to (make / swim) / 같은 ~으로 in the same way / in like manner // 일정한 ~으로 in a certain way / on a fixed plan / 올바른[틀린] ~으로 하다 do (a thing) in the proper [wrong] way // ~을 생각해 내다 figure out a way (to do) / devise [think out] a method [plan / way] / ~을 강구하다 devise means / take measures [steps] to (do) // ~을 정하다 fix upon a plan // 다른 ~을 써 보다 try another tack // 원자핵 분열의 ~을 발견하다 discover the procedure for splitting an atom // 그것은 어떤 ~으로 했는지 알 수 없다 I have no idea how it was done. // 좋아하는 ~으로 하시오 Do it (in) your own way. // 그 문제는 몇 가지 ~으로 풀 수 있다 We can solve the problem by several methods [in several ways]. // 그 지역 사회에서는 독특한 ~으로 의사가 결정된다 In this community decisions are made in a unique [peculiar] manner. // 과감한 ~을 쓰지 않는 한 환경 보존은 불가능하다 Conservation of the environment is impossible unless some drastic measure is taken. // 그는 파리를 잡는 좋은 ~을 고안해 냈다 He invented a good device for catching flies. // 그 ~이 좋다 That's a good way of doing it. // 이 곤경에서 헤어날 ~이 없다 There is no way out of this dilemma. // 그 밖에는 달리 ~이 없다 There is no alternative [other way].
● **방법론** methodology.
방벽(防壁) a protective [defensive] wall; a barrier; a barricade; a bulwark. ¶옛날에 중국인은 거대한 ~을 쌓았다 The Chinese built a great defensive wall in ancient times.
방부(防腐) preservation from [against] decay; prevention of [against] putrefaction; antisepsis; 〈시체의〉 embalmment. ¶~성의 antiseptic / aseptic (operation) // 목재의 ~ 보존 preservation of timber against decay // 식품의 ~에는 여러 가지 방법이 있다 There are many methods of preserving food [keeping food from going bad]. // 그들은 왕의 시체에 ~를 위해 향유를 발랐다 They embalmed the king's body. **방부하다** preserve from decay; prevent putrefaction; embalm(시체를).
● **방부제** an antiseptic (substance [solution]); 〈식품용의〉 a preservative. ¶합성 ~ 첨가 (표시) synthetic preservatives added // ~ 처리를 하다 apply antiseptic treatment (to) / 〈시체에〉 embalm / preserve.
방불하다(彷彿−) closely resemble; be alike; 〈서술적〉 bear a close resemblance (to). ¶실전을 방불케 하는 대연습 the maneuvers reminding the spectators of actual warfare // 방불케 하다 remind (one) of (something) / indicate faintly / adumbrate / visualize (the scene).
방비(房−) 〔방을 쓸기 위한 비〕 an indoor broom.
방비(防備) 〔방어〕 defense; defensive preparations [works]; 〔방어공사〕 defense works; fortifications. ¶무~의 defenseless / unfortified / open // ~가 없는 defenseless / unguarded / undefended / unfortified / unarmed // 외적의 침입에 대비하여 국가의 ~를 공고히 하다 strengthen [fortify] the country's defenses against invasion by a foreign enemy // 그들은 만전의 ~를 하고 있다 They are making full defensive preparations. // 그들은 국경 ~를 강화했다 They strengthened their border defenses. / They fortified the border. **방비하다** make defensive preparations; guard; defend; fortify; secure. ¶그들은 방비하기 쉬운 지점에 진을 쳤다 They pitched camp in a defensible position.
방사(房事) sexual intercourse; what occurs in the privacy of the bedroom[behind closed doors]. ¶~ 과도 sexual intemperance. 방사

하다 have sexual intercourse.
방사(放射) 1 (빛·열의) emission; (라듐 등의) emanation. **방사하다** emit; radiate; emanate. ¶방사하는 radiant (rays) /열을 사방으로 ~ radiate heat on all sides /이 기기는 열을 사방으로 방사한다 This apparatus radiates heat on all sides. 2 [물] radiation. ⇨ **복사**(輻射)
● **방사기** an ejector. **방사능** radioactivity. ¶인공 [자연 / 잔존 / 대기 중의] ~ artificial [natural / residual / atmospheric] radioactivity // ~ 검출 radioactivity readings // ~이 있는 radioactive (rain) / ~이 없는 not radioactive / radio-inert // ~ 낙진을 맞다 [~에 오염되다] be affected [contaminated] by radioactive fallout. **방사능 오염** radioactive contamination. ¶~ 물질 a radioactive contaminant. **방사상** a radial shape. ¶~ 도로 roads radiating [branching off] in all directions / radial roads // ~의 radiate(d) / radial // ~으로 in a radial manner / radiately / radially. **방사선** radiation; (방사능 광선) radioactive rays; (복사 광선) radiant [radiant] rays. ¶~ 누출 a radiation leak // ~의 강도 radiation intensity // ~을 쐬다 be exposed to radiation(폭격으로) // ~ 치료를 받다 undergo radiological treatment. **방사선과** the department of radiology. **방사선 요법** radiotheraphy. **방사성** radioactivity. ¶~ 탄소에 의한 연대 측정 radiocarbon dating. **방사성 동위 원소** a radioactive isotope; a radioisotope. **방사성 물질** a radioactive substance; a radiation material; 《구어》 a hot material. ¶의약용 ~ atomic cocktail. **방사성 원소** a radioactive element; a radioelement. **방사성 폐기물** radioactive waste; hot soup. **방사열** a radiant heat. ⇨ **복사열**(복사(輻射))
방사(紡絲) (실) a (weaving) thread; a strand; [방적] spinning; [방적사] spun cotton [silk / wool]; yarn.
방사(放飼) pasturage; grazing. **방사하다** pasture [graze] 《cattle》; put 《cattle》 to grass; leave 《a dog》 at large; keep 《a pig》 loose.
방사림(防沙林) an erosion control forest; trees for sand arrestation.
방산(放散) dispersion; scattering. **방산하다** disperse; scatter.
방생(放生) the release [setting free] of living creatures from captivity (as an act of Buddhist virtue).
방석(方席) a (Korean) cushion. ¶수(繡)~ an embroidered cushion // ~을 깔다 [~에 앉다] sit [seat oneself / be seated] on a cushion.
방선균(放線菌) [생] actinomycetes; ray fungi.
방설(防雪) protection from [against] snow.
● **방설림** (a stand of trees that serves as a) snowbreak; a snow forest [wood].
방세(房貰) a room rent. ¶~를 올리다 raise the (room) rent / ~는 얼마입니까 How much do you charge for the room? / What is the rent for the room?
방세간(房-) room furniture; furnishings.
방송(放送) (텔레비전·라디오의) (TV / radio) broadcasting; (1회의 라디오 방송) a radio broadcast; (1회의 텔레비전 방송) a television broadcast; a telecast. ¶뉴스 ~ a newscast / newscasting // 민간 [국영] ~ a commercial [national] broadcast / a broadcast by a commercial [government-run] station // 생 ~ a live broadcast / (텔레비전의) a live telecast // 전국 중계 ~ broadcasting over a nationwide hookup [network] // 제1 [2] ~ (a broadcast on) the First [Second] Program // 음성 다중 ~ (2개 국어의) a bilingual broadcast // 중계 ~ rebroadcasting / rebroadcast // 해외 ~ an overseas broadcast // ~을 끝마치다 (방송국이) sign off // ~을 듣다 listen to the radio broadcast / listen in (on the radio) // ~ 중이다 [중이 아니다] be on [off] the air / 라디오 ~을 듣다 listen to the radio / listen to a radio broadcast / listen in (to a speech) on the radio / 텔레비전 ~을 보다 watch television / watch a TV program // 야구 ~을 듣다 listen to the broadcast of a baseball game / 대통령은 오늘 밤에 라디오 ~을 하기로 되어 있다 The President is going to speak on [over] the radio this evening. **방송하다** (방송국이) broadcast; put (the news) on the air; telecast; televise; (사람이) appear [go] on television; speak over the radio. ¶KBS는 전국 중계로 야구를 방송한다 KBS broadcasts [televises] baseball games over a nationwide network [(미) hookup] (▶ televise는 텔레비전으로).
● **방송국** a broadcasting [radio / TV] station. ¶중앙 [지방] ~ a key [local] station. **방송극** a radio drama; a TV drama; a broadcast play. **방송 기자** a radio [TV] reporter [newsman]; a network reporter [journalist]; a (network) reporter on camera. **방송망** a radio [TV] network [circuit]. ¶이 (방송) 프로는 중앙 방송국에서 36개소 지방 방송국의 ~으로 방송해 드리고 있습니다 This program is being sent out over the network to thirty-six stations from the Central Broadcasting Station. **방송실** a (radio / TV) studio (pl. ~s); a broadcasting room; (항공사의) a public address booth; an announcement room(안내 방송의). **방송 종료** sign-off. **방송 중단** (속어) dead air; a dead spot. **방송 통신 대학** [고등학교] the Air and Correspondence College [High School].
방수(防水) 1 (스며드는 물의) waterproofing. ¶~의 waterproof / watertight. **방수하다** waterproof; watertight; make 《cloth》 watertight. 2 (넘쳐흐르는 물의) flood control; prevention of flood. **방수하다** prevent [control] flood.
● **방수복** a waterproof clothes. **방수 시계** a watertight watch. **방수제** a waterproof agent; waterproof stuff. **방수포** waterproof cloth; (배) tarpaulin; oilskin.
방수(放水) (물의 배출) (water-)drainage; a discharge (of water from a dam). **방수하다** drain water off; drain (water).
● **방수관** a drainpipe; an offlet; (분수의) a (d)jutage. **방수로** a (drainage) canal; a drain; a flood control channel; a sluiceway.
방술(方術) 1 (방법과 기술) method(s) and technique(s); arts. 2 (신선의 술법) necromancy; Taoist magic (arts).
방습(防濕) ¶~의 dampproof / moistureproof.
● **방습제** a desiccant; a desiccating agent.
방식(方式) (공식) a formula (pl. ~s, -lae) [형] a form; [양식] a manner; a mode; [방법] a method; a way; a system(계통적); [절차] formalities; [관례] usage. ¶사고 ~ one's way of thinking // 교통 정리의 새로운 ~

방식 system of traffic control // 대로 in proper [due] form // 일정한 ~으로 in an established [a regular] form // 자기 ~대로 하다 do (something) in one's own way // ~에 따르다 [어긋나다] follow [run counter to] the established form [usage] // 나는 내 ~으로 하겠다 I'll do it my way [in my own way]. // 그 회사의 영업 ~은 건실하다 The business methods of that company are sound. // 우리는 그것을 하는 ~이 각각 다르다 Each of us has a different way of doing it. // 너는 너대로 독자적 ~을 취해도 된다 You may do things in your own way. / Feel free to take your own way. / Feel free to take your own course [line]. // 그 결혼식은 재래 ~에 따라 거행되었다 The wedding was performed in the traditional manner [way]. / 그는 이력서를 소정의 ~대로 썼다 He wrote his personal history [curriculum vitae], following the accepted [standard] form.

방식 (防蝕) corrosion protection. ¶~의 corrosion-proof [-resistant].

● **방식제** (一劑) [화] an anticorrosive.

방실거리다 smile sweetly [radiantly]; beam with a smile.

방심 (放心) 1 [부주의] carelessness; inattention; [대비 없음] unpreparedness. ¶~은 금물이다 Carelessness [Overconfidence] is our greatest enemy. (▶ overconfidence는 자신 과잉) **방심하다** [부주의하다] be careless about; [경계를 게을리 하다] be off one's guard (toward); be unwatchful; relax one's attention. ¶방심하고 있다 be off one's guard // 방심하지 않고 있다 be on one's guard / be attentive [alert] / have one's eyes wide off one's guard // 방심하게 하다 put [throw] (a person) off his guard // 그 사람은 언제나 방심하지 않는다 He is always on his guard. // 방심하지 말고 일해라 Don't be negligent [careless] in your work. / Be careful in your work. // 방심한 사이에 감쪽같이 속았다 Caught off guard, I fell for the trick completely. // 저 남자에게 방심하지 마라 Don't take your eye(s) off that man. / Be careful of that man. / Keep a watchful eye on that man. // 방심하면 또 병에 걸린다 If you aren't careful, you'll get sick again. // 방심한 틈에 지갑을 소매치기당했다 I had my pocket picked in an unguarded moment [when I was off my guard]. // 방심한 것이 사고의 원인이었다 Being caught off guard was the root of the whole disaster. // 방심했기 때문에 그런 실수를 한 것이다 You made such a blunder because you were careless [not attentive enough].

2 [걱정 없이 마음 편하게 지냄] relief [freedom] from care or anxiety. **방심하다** feel easy (about); feel [be] relieved; feel at rest [ease]. ¶그 일에 대해서는 아무쪼록 방심하세요 Please don't trouble yourself [Please set your mind at rest] about that matter.

방아 a mill; a mortar. ¶물~ a water mill // 디딜~ a treadmill.

● **방앗간** a mill. **방앗공이** a pestle; a pounder. ¶~로 찧다 pound (rice) with a pestle.

방아깨비 [동] a grasshopper; an Oriental longheaded locust; a click beetle; a snapping beetle.

방아쇠 the trigger (of a gun). ¶~를 당기다 pull [press] the trigger / trigger (a rifle) // 그는 그녀에게 총을 대고 ~를 당겼다 He pointed the gun at her and pulled the trigger.

방안 (方案) a plan; a program; a scheme; a device. ¶~을 세우다 draw up [formulate] a plan / lay out [frame] a scheme.

방안지 (方眼紙) graph paper. ⇨ °모눈종이

방약무인 (傍若無人) [뻔뻔스러움] audacity; effrontery; outrage; [불손함] insolence; defiance; [뻐김] overbearance; arrogance. **방약무인하다** audacious; outrageous; insolent; overbearing; arrogant. ¶방약무인하게 (do)다 have the cheek to (do) // 방약무인하게 행동하다 behave outrageously // 그의 방약무인한 태도를 참을 수 없다 I cannot put up with his arrogance [insolence].

방어 (防禦) defense [(영) defence]; protection; safeguard. ¶공세 ~ active defense / an offensive defense // 밀집 ~ tight defense // 지역 ~ zone defense // 해안 ~ coast defense // ~가 튼튼한 [없는] well-fortified [unprotected] // 공격에 대비한 ~ a defense against an attack // ~에 나서다 stand on the defensive // ~ 태세를 취하다 assume a posture of defense // 공격은 최선의 ~이다 Offense [Attack] is the best defense. **방어하다** defend; protect; safeguard; bulwark; shield. ¶그들의 격렬한 공격에 대하여 방어할 길이 없었다 There was no defense [We could not defend ourselves] against their violent attack.

● **방어망** a torpedo net. **방어선** a line of defense. **방어율** [야구] an [a pitcher's] earned run average(약어 ERA). **방어전** a defensive war. ¶~을 하다 fight a defensive battle / take the defensive // 우리 팀은 시종 ~에 급급했다 Our team was on the defensive throughout the game.

방언 (方言) (표준어에 대하여) a dialect; [그 지방 특유의 말·표현] a provincialism. ¶계급 ~ class dialect // 사회 ~ social dialect // 지역 ~ a regional [local] dialect // ~의 dialectal / provincial.

● **방언학** / **방언 연구** dialectology. **방언학자** / **방언 연구가** a dialectologist.

방언 (放言) a wild [random / reckless] talk; irresponsible [indiscreet] remarks. **방언하다** talk wildly [big / recklessly].

방역 (防疫) the prevention of epidemics [infectious diseases]; communicable diseases control; disinfection; quarantine. ¶~에 힘쓰다 strive hard for the prevention of epidemics. **방역하다** prevent an epidemic of; take preventive measures against (epidemics).

● **방역 대책** anti epidemic measures.

방연석 (方鉛石) [광] galena.

방열 (放熱) [발산되는 열] radiant heat; [열의 발산] the radiation (of heat). **방열하다** radiate heat.

● **방열기** a radiator.

방염 (防焰) fire prevention.

방영 (放映) televising (a movie); television broadcasting. ¶그 프로는 현재 ~ 중이다 The program is now being telecast [on the air]. **방영하다** televise (a movie); broadcast on television; telecast. → ¶우주 왕복선이 착륙하는 광경이 전 세계에 방영되었다 The landing of the space shuttle was televised [seen on television] all over the world. // 대통령의 연설은 텔레비전으로 전국에 방영되었다 The President's speech was televised throughout the nation [on a nationwide program].

방울 1 [쇠방울] a (small) bell. ¶~을 달다 bell (a cat) / ~을 tie [attach] a bell / ~을 울리다 ring [tinkle] a bell / ~을 흔들다 shake a bell.
2 [둥근 액체 덩이] a drop. ¶눈물~ drops of tears // 물~ waterdrops // 빗~ raindrops // 굵은 빗~ large drops of rain // 이슬~ dewdrops // 나뭇잎 끝에서 두세 ~의 물이 떨어졌다 Two or three drops of water slowly fell from the tip of the leaf. // 술은 한 ~도 안 마신다 I don't drink [I never touch] a drop of alcohol. / I don't drink at all. // 목마른 소년은 주스를 마지막 한 ~까지 마셨다 The thirsty boy drank the juice to the last drop. // 땀~이 그의 얼굴에 흘러내렸다 Beads of sweat ran down his face.

방울방울 drop by drop; in drops; dribbling; dripping. ¶~ 떨어지다 drip [drop] (from) / fall in drops.

방울뱀 [동] a rattlesnake; a rattler.
방울벌레 [동] a (bell) cricket.
방울새 [동] (참샛과(科)의) an Oriental greenfinch.
방울지다 form a drop. ¶방울져 떨어지다 drop / drip / fall in drops / dribble / trickle.
방울토마토 a cherry tomato.

방위(方位) a point of the compass; a compass direction [bearing]; a direction; a course; [천] azimuth. ¶진(眞)~ [항] the true heading [bearing] // ~를 정하다 find one's bearings [position] // ~를 확인하다 get [take] one's bearings.
● **방위각** [천] [물] an azimuth (angle); [편각] a declination. **방위 나침반** an azimuth compass. **방위표** (배의) a traverse table.

방위(防衛) defense [(영) defence] (against); protection; safeguard. ¶국토~ national defense // 달러 ~ defense of dollar // 자주~ self-defense // 전면 안전 ~ an exclusively defensive security system // 정당~ (legitimate) self-defense / legal defense // ~ 자세를 취하다 put oneself in the posture of defense // ~를 강화하다 build up [strengthen] one's defenses // ~선을 펴다 stretch a defensive cordon (against). **방위하다** defend (against / from); protect; safeguard; shield. ¶국토를 ~ defend one's land [country] // 그들은 도시를 적의 공격으로부터 방위하기 위해 일치단결했다 They united to defend their city against the enemy's attack.
● **방위력** a defensive capacity. **방위비** defense costs; the defense budget. **방위 산업** the defense industry. **방위세** a defense tax. **방위 소집** the defensive call-up; defense call; defensive mobilization.

방음(防音) soundproofing; sound insulation [absorption / arresting / isolation]. ¶~의 soundproof / soundproofed. **방음하다** (make it) soundproof; absorb [arrest] sound.
● **방음벽** a soundproofed wall; sound absorbing walls. **방음 유리** soundproof glass. **방음 장치** soundproofing; a soundproof device; an isolator; (총의) a silencer.

방임(放任) noninterference; nonintervention; do-as-you-please; (프) laissez faire. ¶자유~ 정책 (외교의) a noninterference [nonintervention] policy / (경제의) a laissez-faire policy.
방임하다 [간섭하지 않다] do not interfere (with); [내버려 두다] let [leave] (a person) alone; [본인에게 맡기다] leave (a person) to himself; leave (a matter) to take its own course. ¶당국은 그 사건을 방임했다 The authorities let the matter run [take] its course. // 그 사태는 방임할 수 없다 The course [state] of things cannot be left to itself.
● **방임주의** a hands-off [let-alone / noninterference / permissive] policy; (경제적) a laissez-faire policy [principle]; liberalism.

방자(房子·幇子) [지방 관청의 남자 심부름꾼] a servant; a footman; a valet; [궁중의 작은 일을 돌보던 시녀] a woman [maid] servant of the royal household.

방자하다(放恣-) impudent; self-indulgent; uppish; licentious; willful; selfish.(▶ willful 은 남의 말을 무시하고 제멋대로 함, selfish는 남을 무시하고 이기적임) ¶방자하게 willfully / selfishly // 방자한 사람 a person who does as he pleases // 방자하게 굴다 behave as one pleases.

방장(房帳) **1** [방에 두르는 휘장] a room curtain. **2** → 모기장(→).

방재(防材) (a wooden) boom; (교각(橋脚) 등의) a fender.

방재(防災) protection [prevention] against [of] disasters. ¶이 도시는 ~에 힘을 쏟고 있다 This city is making an effort to protect itself from natural disasters. **방재하다** prevent [fend off] disasters.

방적(紡績) (cotton) spinning.
● **방적견사**(-絹絲) spun silk. **방적 공장** a spinning mill; [면사 공장] a cotton mill; a spinnery. **방적업 / 방적 공업** the spinning industry.

방전(放電) [물] an electric discharge; discharge of electricity. ¶공중 [불꽃 / 진공] ~ atmospheric [spark / vacuum] discharge. **방전하다** discharge (electricity).
● **방전관** a discharge tube.

방점(傍點) a side dot [mark]. ¶강조하는 단어에 ~을 찍다 put dots [marks] alongside the words to show emphasis.

방접원(傍接圓) [수] an escribed circle; an excircle.

방정 [경망스러운 말·행동] light-headedness; flightiness; levity; frivolity; whimsy; giddiness; a rash act. ¶~을 떨다 behave rashly / act imprudently.

방정맞다 1 [경망스럽다] light-headed; flighty; frivolous; rash; giddy; unreliable. **2** [불길하다] ill-omened; ominous; inauspicious; (서술적) invite the wrath of God. ¶그런 방정맞은 소리 하면 못써 Don't say in such an ominous way. / Don't talk such an ill-omened thing.

방정식(方程式) [수] an equation. ¶고차 ~ an equation of higher degree // 대수 [화학] ~ an algebraic(al) [a chemical] equation // 미분 ~ a differential equation // 연립 ~ simultaneous equations // 2항 ~ a binominal equation // 1 [2 / 3 / 4]차 ~ a simple [quadratic / cubic / biquadratic] equation / an equation of the first [second / third / fourth] degree // 지수 ~ an exponential equation.

방정하다(方正-) upright; good; irreproachable; correct; excellent. ¶품행이 방정한 사람

a man of irreproachable conduct / an upright person.
방제(防除) (해충 등의) prevention of the breeding and extermination (of flies); control (of insect pests). ¶이 약은 초목의 병해 ~에 도움이 된다 This chemical helps prevent disease in plants.
방조(幇助) assistance; backing; aid; help; (범죄의) aiding and abetting. ¶자살 ~ aiding and abetting suicide / helping (a person) commit suicide. **방조하다** assist; back up; aid; help; (범죄를) aid and abet. ¶그녀는 남편의 문서 위조를 방조했다 She abetted her husband in forgery.
● **방조자** an aider and abettor[abetter]; a backer; a supporter.
방조제(防潮堤) a tide embankment; a sea wall; a sea dike.
방종(放縱) self-indulgence; (미) license; (영) licence; (방탕) dissoluteness; dissolution; debauchery. ¶자유와 ~ liberty and license // ~에 흐르다 be given to dissolution[self-indulgence] // 자유를 ~으로 착각하지 마라 Don't take the liberty for the license. // 그들은 ~에 흐르기 쉽다 They are given to dissolution[self-indulgence]. **방종하다** self-indulgent; licentious; dissolute; unrestrained; loose; unbridled. ¶방종한 생활을 하다 lead a wild[fast / dissipated / loose] life / (예술가의) lead a Bohemian life.
방주(方舟) an ark. ¶노아의 ~ Noah's ark.
방주(旁註) marginal[side] notes; marginalia. ¶본문에 ~를 달다 add[append] marginal notes to the next.
방죽 a bank; an embankment; a dike[dyke]; (미) a levee. ¶~을 쌓다 construct[build (up)] a bank (for) / embank (a river) // ~이 무너졌다 The bank gave way.
방증(傍證) [법] supporting evidence; circumstantial evidence; corroboration. ¶…의 ~으로서 as a supporting evidence (of) / in corroboration (of) // ~을 굳히다 corroborate (one's case) // 이 전설은 거기서 전투가 있었다는 견해의 ~이 된다 This legend provides some support for the theory[idea] that a battle was fought there. // 변호인 측은 ~수집을 끝냈다 The defence has finished collecting supporting[collaborating / collateral] evidence.
방지(防止) prevention; check; preclusion; keeping off. ¶소년 범죄의 ~ the prevention of juvenile crimes. **방지하다** prevent; check; hold in check; stave off; head off; fend off; keep off; preserve (something from decay); nip in the bud(미연에). ¶방지할 수 있는 preventable (~을 방지하기 위해 [법] in bar of … // 사고를 ~ prevent an accident // 충분히 [효과적으로] ~ prevent[check] effectively / impose an effective check (on) // 음식이 썩는 것을 ~ preserve foods from decay // 유행병을 ~ prevent the plague from spreading // 교통사고를 방지하려고 노력하다 make an effort to prevent traffic accidents // 청소년의 비행을 미연에 ~ nip juvenile delinquency in the bud.
● **방지책** a preventive measure. ¶인플레 ~ an anti-inflation policy // 전쟁 ~ a preventive of war.
방직(紡織) spinning and weaving. **방직하다** spin and weave.

● **방직 공업** the textile[weaving] industry.
방진(方陣) 1 [군] a square (formation); a phalanx. ¶~을 치다 form a square // ~을 풀다 break a square. 2 [수] a magic square.
방진(防塵) ¶~의 dustproof / dust-tight.
방책(方策) [피하기·계략] a plan; a device; [계획·음모] a scheme; [정책] a policy; [방법·수단] a measure; a step. ¶만전의 ~ a sure [(구어) sure-fire] measure / an infallible plan // ~을 세우다 [강구하다] devise a scheme / frame a plan / take steps // 아무런 ~도 쓸 도리가 없다 Nothing can be done. // 그들은 기금을 모을 ~을 강구하고 있다 They are working on a plan to raise funds.
방책(防柵) [군] a palisade; a paling; a stockade. ¶~을 두르다 enclose (a place) with a palisade / palisade.
방첩(防諜) [군] counterespionage; counterintelligence; prevention of espionage.
● **방첩 부대** Counterintelligence Corps(약어 C.I.C.).
방청(傍聽) hearing; attendance. ¶~이 금지된 회의 a meeting closed to the public / a closed-door meeting // ~을 금지[허가]하다 (일반적으로) exclude[open to] the public / (법정에서) try a case with closed[open] doors // ~ 금지로 재판하다 try (a case) in camera // ~ 무료 (게시) Admission Free. // 그 사건의 공판에는 일반의 ~이 허용되었다 The public were admitted to the court when the case was tried. **방청하다** hear; listen to; attend (a lecture). ¶국회를 ~ visit the National Assembly in session / attend a sitting of the National Assembly // 나는 그 재판을 방청하였다 I was in the courtroom to hear the trial. // 그 회의는 방청할 수 있다[없다] The meeting is open[closed] to the public.
● **방청객 / 방청인** a hearer; an auditor; (집합적) an audience; the public. **방청권** an admission ticket; (의회의) an order. **방청석** seats for the public; (의회·법정 등의) the (public / visitors') gallery.
방추(紡錘) a spindle. ¶~형의 spindle-shaped / fusiform.
방추형(方錐形) a square pyramid. ¶~의 pyramidal.
방축(防縮) shrink-proofing. ¶~의 shrink-proof.
● **방축 가공** non-shrink treatment; shrink-resistant finish.
방출(放出) 1 (저장 물자 등의) release. ¶정부 보유미[비료]의 ~ the release of government-stock rice[fertilizer]. **방출하다** release. ¶군에서 방출하는 army-surplus (coats). 2 [배출] discharge; (폐수의) effluence. ¶유해 폐기물의 ~ effluence of poisonous waste (from a chemical factory). **방출하다** discharge (water); exhaust; (물고기가 알을) spend. 3 emission; radiation. **방출하다** emit; radiate; give off (energy).
● **방출 물자** released goods[commodities].
방충(防蟲) protection against insects [moths].
● **방충망** a mosquito net. **방충제** an insecticide; mothballs(좀약).
방취(防臭) deodorization. **방취하다** deodorize.
● **방취제** a deodorizer; a deodorant; (가스의) an odorant.
방치(放置) leaving[letting] (a thing) alone;

letting (a thing) as it is [stands]; [등한시] negligence. **방치하다** [상관 않다] leave [let] (a thing, a person, etc.) alone; leave (a matter) as it is [stands]; leave (a matter) to chance; leave (a thing) to take its own course; [등한히 하다] neglect (one's work); lay aside. ¶수도꼭지를 튼 채로 ~ leave a tap on // 부상자를 ~ leave an injured person behind // 상황은 방치할 수 없을 만큼 악화되어 있다 The situation has become so aggravated that it can no longer be ignored [that some action must be taken]. // 우리는 이 문제를 방치해 둘 수는 없다 We cannot leave the matter unsettled. / The matter cannot wait any longer. // 병든 모친을 방치해 둘 수는 없다 I can't leave my sick mother unattended [by herself]. → ¶저 차는 3일 전부터 저곳에 방치되어 있다 That car has been sitting there for three days. // 수사 방침이 바뀌어 사건은 그대로 방치되었다 Because of a change in policy, the investigation of the case was laid aside.

방침 (方針) [일을 처리해 나갈 방향] a course; a line; a tack; [정책] a line (of) policy; [계획] a plan; [주의] a principle; [목적] an aim; an object (in view); a purpose. ¶근본 ~ a fundamental policy // 시정 [교육 / 외교] ~ an administrative [an educational / a foreign] policy // 영업 ~ a business policy [plan] // 행동 ~ a course of action // 일정한 ~ a definite policy / a definite object in view // 이런 ~으로 with this object in view // **이 없다** have no definite [fixed] plan [policy] // 일정한 ~에 따라 나아가다 proceed on a certain definite line / pursue [follow] a definite policy // 선임자의 ~에 따르다 act on the same lines as one's predecessor / tread in the steps of one's predecessor // 당의 ~에 따르다 toe [hew to] the party line // …을 ~으로 삼다 make a point of (doing) / make it a principle [rule] (to do) // ~을 세우다 frame a plan / map out one's course / formulate one's policy [aim] / decide on one's policy / orientate (a foreign policy) // 장래의 ~을 세우다 shape one's course for the future // 강경한 ~을 취하다 take [follow] a hard [harsh / strong / tough] line (on / over / toward) / ~**을 변경하다** change [shift] one's course / change [alter] one's plan [policy] / do (a thing) in a new [different] way / adopt a new line // 독자적 ~을 취하다 take one's own line [course] // ~이 확정되지 않았다 The policy is not definitely fixed. // 그들은 외국에 대하여 문호 개방의 ~을 지켰다 [결정했다 / 채택했다] They followed [decided on / adopted] an open-door policy toward foreign countries. // ~대로는 되지 않았다 It didn't go according to plan [as planned]. / 우리는 박리다매의 ~을 취하고 있습니다 It is our policy to hold down our profit margin and sell as much as possible.

방탄 (防彈) protection against bullets. ¶~의 bulletproof / bombproof / shellproof / proof against shells [bombs]. **방탄하다** protect against shells [bombs].

● **방탄유리** bulletproof glass. **방탄조끼** (미) a bulletproof vest [(영) a bulletproof waistcoat]; (군대의) a flak jacket.

방탕 (放蕩) dissipation; profligacy; prodigality; debauchery; dissoluteness; vicious courses; loose habits; riotous [dissolute] living. ¶~**에 빠지다** indulge in debauchery / give oneself up to dissipation // 그의 아내는 그의 ~ 때문에 그의 곁을 떠났다 His wife left him because of his infidelity [immoral conduct]. **방탕하다** dissipated; dissolute; prodigal; profligate. ¶방탕한 자식 (문어) a profligate [prodigal] son // 방탕한 생활을 하다 live [lead] a fast [dissipated / wild] life / take [be given] to dissipation // 방탕한 나날을 보내다 lead a life of debauchery / (미국 구어) live life in the fast lane // 그는 방탕한 생활을 시작했다 He has taken to fast living. // 그는 방탕한 생활을 하다가 망했다 He ruined himself by dissipation [debauchery]. **방탕히** dissipatedly; dissolutely; prodigally.

● **방탕아** a fast liver; a libertine; a prodigal; a debauchee; a rake.

방파제 (防波堤) [건] a breakwater; a bulwark; a mole. ¶~**를 쌓다** build a breakwater.

방패 (防牌) [창·화살을 막는 데 쓰던 무기] a shield; a buckler (둥근 방패); a screen (작은); an escutcheon (문장(紋章)이 있는); (고) a targe (작고 둥근). ¶법을 ~ 삼아 on the strength [authority] of law // …을 ~로 삼다 use (something) as a shield (against) / screen oneself behind / shield [cover] oneself behind (a thing) // 그 회사는 어느 폭력단의 ~(막이)가 되어 있었다 That company provided a cover [front] for a gang.

방편 (方便) [수단] an expedient; a shift; a means (단수·복수 동형); an instrumentality; [도구] an instrument. ¶생활의 ~ a means of living / 목적을 위한 ~ a means to an end // 일시적 ~ a temporary expedient / a makeshift / a stopgap / a makeshift [stopgap] measure // ~**으로 쓰이다** be used as an instrument / be made a cat's-paw of // 거짓말도 ~이다 Circumstances may justify a lie. / A lie is sometimes expedient. // 우리는 일시적인 ~으로서 그 방책을 채택했다 We adopted the measure as a temporary expedient [means].

방풍 (防風) protection against wind.

● **방풍림** a windbreak; (미) a shelter belt.

방학 (放學) the school vacation [holidays]. ¶**서울 [여름] ~** the winter [summer] vacation / ~ **동안** during [through] the vacation // ~ **중이다** be on vacation // 학교는 내주부터 여름 ~이다 (미) School closes for summer vacation next week. / (영) School breaks up for the summer holidays next week. // 언제부터 겨울 ~인가 When are you to break up for the winter vacation? **방학하다** close [break up] the school (for a vacation); go on vacation; be free from school; have holidays.

방한 (防寒) protection against the cold. ¶~**용으로는 확실히 모피가 제일이다** For keeping out the cold, fur is certainly best. **방한하다** protect against the cold; keep out the cold.

● **방한모** a winter cap. **방한복** winter [arctic] clothes; heavy winter clothing. **방한화** arctic boots [shoes].

방한 (訪韓) a visit to Korea. ¶~ **중인 외교 사절** a foreign envoy who is now in Korea // ~ **미국 무역 사절단** an American trade mission to Korea. **방한하다** visit Korea.

방해 (妨害) [훼방] disturbance (잠·행동 등의); obstruction (진행·통행 등의); block; (간섭)

방해석 interruption; interference; check; prevention; trouble; (전파의) jamming; [장애·지장] a hindrance; an obstacle; an impediment; a barrier; an inconvenience; an encumbrance. ¶공무 집행 ~ an unlawful interference with an officer in the execution of his duty.//교통 ~ traffic obstruction//의사(議事) ~ a filibuster//치안 ~ the disturbance of public peace/~가 되는 사람 a nuisance/(문어) an encumbrance//그것이 그의 출세에 ~가 되었다 It was an obstacle [a hindrance] to his getting ahead./It stood in the way of [hindered] his advancement.//그는 경찰관에 대한 공무 집행 ~죄로 고발되었다 He was charged with obstructing a police officer in the performance of his duties. **방해하다** disturb; interrupt; interfere with; intrude (oneself) (upon); obstruct; hinder; hamper; prevent; check; clog (up); retard; block; encumber; preclude; bar; debar; arrest; (전파를) jam. ¶비행기 소음이 안면[잠]을 방해했다 My sleep was disturbed by the noise of the airplane.//그들은 의사 진행을 방해하려고 기도하고 있다 They intend to obstruct the proceedings./(길게 연설을 계속하여) (미) They are planning a filibuster.//누군가가 전파를 방해해서 방송 프로가 나오지 않는다 Someone is jamming the program we broadcast on that frequency.//상호 이해의 부족이 순조로운 교섭을 방해하고 있다 Lack of mutual understanding obstructs smooth negotiations.//사막은 도시의 성장을 방해하였다 The desert hindered [stood in the way of] the growth of cities.//그들은 주주 총회를 방해하러 왔다 They came to create a disturbance at the stockholders's meeting.//방해해서 미안합니다만 누가 와서 뵙자고 합니다 Excuse me for interrupting you, but someone is here to see you.//내가 이야기를 하는데 방해하지 마라 Don't interrupt me when I am talking./Don't interrupt our conversation. ➔¶그는 청중의 야유에 방해받아 이야기를 계속할 수가 없었다 His speech was interrupted by the hooting of the audience.//자전거를 거기에 두면 통행에 방해된다 If you put the bicycle there, it will block [obstruct] the way.

● **방해물** [장애물] an obstacle; [진행을 방해하는 것] a hindrance; an impediment; a check; an encumbrance; a drag. ¶~을 제거하다 remove [get rid of] an obstacle/get obstacles out of the way//~이 되다 become a drag (on a person)/(미국 구어) be underfoot. **방해 방송** jamming. **방해자** an obstructor; an obstructionist (특히 의사 진행 등의).

방해석(方解石) [광] calcite; calcspar.

방향(方向) 1 [향하는 쪽] a direction; (one's) bearings; a quarter; a situation; a way; a point of the compass; (어떤) a course; a line. ¶무선 ~ 탐지 radio-direction-finding(약어 R.D.F)//조류의 ~ the drift of a current//옳은 ~ the right direction [course]//틀린 ~ the wrong direction [course]//~이 바뀌다 (바람·조류 등의) turn/shift (to the west)/sheer(배가)/veer (round)/wheel (about/around)/come round [about]//반대 ~에 in a contrary [an opposite] direction//…의 ~으로 in the direction of …/toward(s) …/같은 ~으로 in the same direction//~을 바꾸다 change direction/change [shift] one's course/turn to a different direction//~을 잃다 lose one's bearings/cannot find one's way//오른쪽으로 ~을 바꾸다 turn to the right//~을 취하다 [유지하다] take [hold] one's course//~을 잘못 잡다 go in the wrong direction/go in a different way/(배가) take the wrong course//그 차는 해안 으로 달려갔다 The car drove off in the direction of [toward] the coast.//그 총소리는 어느 ~에서 들려왔습니까 Which direction [Where] is the shot coming from?//나도 그 ~으로 갑니다 I'm going that way, too.//공원은 어느 ~입니까 Which way is the park? 2 [뜻이 향하는 곳] one's course [aim/object]. ¶장래의 ~을 정하다 decide on [map out/choose] one's future course//~을 바꾸다 change one's object [course].

● **방향 감각** a sense of direction; bearings. ¶~이 예리하다 [둔하다] have a good [poor] sense of direction//어둠 속에서 ~을 잃다 lose one's bearings in the dark. **방향 전환** change [shift] of direction; a change of principle [policy/object]; a turnabout; a switch. ¶~을 하다 change [shift] one's course (in life)//차를 ~을 시키다 turn a car around. **방향타**(-舵) a (vertical) rudder. **방향 탐지기** a radar; a direction finder. ¶무선 ~ a radio compass//자동 ~ (항공기의) an automatic direction finder(약어 A.D.F.).

방향(芳香) (a) perfume; (a) fragrance; (an) aroma. ¶~이 있는 fragrant/aromatic/sweet-smelling//~을 풍기다 give out fragrance/smell sweet/diffuse aroma/spread fragrance//장미꽃이 ~을 내뿜고 있다 The roses are giving off [forth] a fragrance [sweet scent].

● **방향제** an aromatic.

방형(方形) a square. ¶~의 square(-shaped).

방호(防護) protection; custody; guard. ¶~용 마스크 a protective mask. **방호하다** protect; have custody of; guard. ¶통행인을 낙하물로부터 방호하는 그물 a net to protect passerby from falling objects.

방화(防火) [화재를 미리 막음] fire prevention; fireproofing; prevention against fires.

● **방화벽** a fire wall. **방화사**(-沙) fire prevention sand. **방화수** fire-fighting water. **방화전**(-栓) a (fire) hydrant. ⇨ *소화전* (≒) 소화(消火)) **방화 훈련** a fire drill.

방화(邦畵) a Korean film [movie].

방화(放火) [불을 지름] incendiarism; arson. ¶그 화재는 ~였다 The fire was caused by arson. **방화하다** set fire to (a house); set (a house) on fire; raise a fire; commit incendiarism [arson]. ¶그는 건물에 방화했다 He set fire to a building.

● **방화광** an incendiary maniac; a pyromaniac; (미국 속어) a firebug; a torch. **방화범** an incendiary; an arsonist; an arsonite. **방화죄** arson; incendiarism.

방황(彷徨) wandering. **방황하다** (길을 잃고) lose one's way (in darkness, in a wood, etc.); [정도(正道)에서 벗어나다] go astray; swerve [stray] from the right path; wander [roam/stray/knock/hang] about; rove; hover (about)/stray. ¶방황하는 사람 a wanderer/a vagabond/a tramp/(미) a hobo//방황하는 양 a lost [stray] sheep//낯선 도시에서 ~ stray about in a strange city//이곳저

곳 ~ wander from place to place // 숲 속을 정처 없이 ~ stray aimlessly through the wood // 그는 오랫동안 여기저기를 방황한 끝에 이곳에 정착했다 He finally settled down here after years of roaming (about).

밭 a (dry) field; a farm; a patch; a garden; an orchard. ¶감자~ a potato plot // 딸기~ a strawberry field[patch] // 배추~ a cabbage patch // 채소~ a kitchen garden // ~작물 dry crops / field products // ~에 나가다 go (out) into the field // ~에 씨를 뿌리다 sow seeds in a field // ~을 갈다 till[cultivate] the soil / plow[(영) plough] the soil[field] // ~에 나가 일하다 work out in the fields.

밭갈이하다 plow[(영) plough / till] a field.

밭고랑 a furrow. ¶~을 짓다 make furrows (in) / furrow.

밭곡식(-穀食) a field crop; dry crops. ¶~이 잘 [안]되다 have a good [bad] dry crop.

밭농사(-農事) dry-field farming. **밭농사하다** do dry-field farming.

밭다¹ [체에 거르다] strain; drain; filter; filtrate; leach; percolate; pass (a liquid) through a filter. ¶술을 ~ strain (rice) liquor // 커피 찌꺼기를 밭아 내다 strain coffee to remove the grounds / leach out grounds from coffee.

밭다² 1 [시간·공간이 매우 가깝다] very[too] close[near]; tight; near[close] at hand; [길이가 짧다] short. ¶사이가 너무 ~ be too short between // 시간이 ~ time is pressing / be pushed[pressed] for time // 책상 사이가 밭으니 좀 떼어라 The desks are too close together, leave some more space between them. 2 [인색하다] stingy; niggardly; mean; closefisted; tightfisted. 3 (기침이) dry; hacking.

밭도랑 a drain in a field. ¶~을 내다 make drains in a field.

밭두둑 a ridge; a rib.

밭둑 an embankment around the end of a field.

밭매기하다 weed a dry field.

밭머리 an end of a field.

밭문서(-文書) the (title) deed for[to] a dry field.

밭벼 a dry-field rice plant; rice[a rice plant] grown in a dry field.

밭은기침 a dry cough; a hack; a hacking cough(계속해서 하는). ¶~을 하다 have a dry [hacking] cough // ~을 자주 하다 have a frequent hack.

밭이다 be[get] strained[filtered / filtrated] through.

밭이랑 a row in a dry field; a ridge; a rib.

밭일 field labor; work in the fields; farm work [labor]. **밭일하다** work (out)[labor] in the fields; do farm work; work on the farm.

밭장다리 a bow-[bandy-]legged person; [의] valgus. ¶~의 bow legged / bandy-legged / valgus / X-legged // ~로 걷다 toe out / walk the toes turned out[outward].

밭치다 strain; drain. ⇨밭다¹

배¹ 1 [복부] the abdomen; the belly; (구어) one's side; [위] the stomach; [장(腸)] the bowels; [생] the ventral side. ¶~의 ventral / abdominal / [의] alvine // ~ 속 the inside of the stomach // ~가 나온 potbellied / bigbellied / fat-bellied // ~가 쑥 들어간 empty-bellied // ~에 힘을 주다 apply a strain to the stomach / put one's (whole) strength in the abdomen / bear down // ~가 나오다 develop a potbelly / (속어) get a fat tummy // ~가 크다 [나와 있다] have a big paunch / be paunchy / (중년에) be thick in the middle [midsection] // ~가 거북하다 feel heavy in the stomach // ~가 꾸르륵거리다 make one's empty stomach churn / have belly-throbbing[grunts of bombs] // ~를 든든히 채워 두다 fortify oneself with a meal (against something) / take a meal (preparatory to taking up one's work) // ~ 속이 편치 않다 have a disordered stomach / (위가) have a stomach trouble // ~ 속이 비다 have an empty stomach // 내 ~ 속이 좀 이상하다 Something is wrong with my stomach. // 나는 ~가 땡땡하다 I feel bloated[gassy]. // 그는 ~가 나왔다 He has a potbelly. // 나는 ~가 아프다 I have (a) stomachache. / I feel a pain in my stomach. // 한창 자라나는 아이들은 이것으로는 ~가 차지 않는다 This isn't enough for growing children. // 나는 요새 ~가 나오기 시작했다 I'm starting to get a spare tire[some flab around my middle].

2 [긴 물건 가운데 볼록한 부분] the bulging part; the belly (of); the bilge. ¶통의 ~ the belly of a cask.

3 [물] an antinode; a loop.

4 [새끼 낳는 횟수] a birth; a litter. ¶한~에 at a birth[litter] / at one birth[litter].

배보다 배꼽이 크다(속담) It's like the tail wagging the dog.

배(를) 내밀다 [남의 요구에 응하지 않다] reject (a person's offer) haughtily; snub (a person's offer).

배(가) 맞다 1 [남녀가 남몰래 서로 몸을 허락하다] have illicit intercourse (with); commit adultery (with). 2 [나쁜 짓에 서로 뜻이 통하다] conspire (with); be in cahoots (with).

배(가) 아프다 [남이 잘되어 심술이 나다] be green with envy; feel intense jealousy (toward). ¶배 아파하다 be jealous[envious] (of another's success) / envy (a person's good fortune) / feel envy (of a person) // 그는 배가 아파서 하는 소리다 He says such things out of envy. // 왜 배가 아픈가 Why, are you jealous?

배(를) 채우다 [불리다] satisfy one's appetite [the inner man]; appease one's hunger; steady one's stomach; stuff out the belly.

배² a boat(작은 배·기선); a vessel(대형의); a ship(노를 쓰지 않는 대형의); a steamer(기선); a liner(정기 항로의); a barge(바닥이 평평한 짐배); [집합적] shipping; (water) craft. ¶놀잇~ a pleasure boat / a barge // ~로 on board a ship / (go) by ship / (travel) by sea // ~ 안에서 in a ship / on board (a ship) / aboard // 미국 가는 ~ a ship bound for America // 오징어잡이 ~ a ship to angle for cuttle-fish // 항구를 떠난 ~ a ship free [outside] of the harbor // 둘이 젓는 ~ a two-oared boat // ~가 떠나다 sail / leave (a) port / take off (from) // ~가 항구에 닿다 arrive in port / put in a port / reach port // ~에 타다 get on board a boat[ship] // ~에서 내리다 get off[leave] a boat // ~를 젓다 row a boat // ~로 제주도에 갔다 I went to Jejudo by ship [boat / sea]. / I took a ship[boat] to Jejudo. // 그 ~에는 승객이 없었다 There were no passengers aboard[on board] the ship.

배³ [배나무 열매] a pear. ¶서양~ a western pear.// 지금은 ~가 나돌 철이다 The pear is now in season.
배 먹고 이 닦기(속담) Killing two birds with one stone.

배(胚) [생] an embryo (pl. ~s); (포유류의) a f(o)etus; [발생] a germ.

배(倍) **1** [갑절] two times; twice; double; twofold. ¶~의 double / twice / twofold// …~의 양[수] twice as much[many] as … / twice[double] the quantity[number] of … / ~의 값을 받다 charge double prices // ~의 값을 치르다 pay as much as twice / pay double[twice] the price // 크기[길이]가 ~다 be twice as large[long] as / be twice size [length] of // 이건 전의 값의 ~다 This costs double what it did before. // 무게가 ~로 된다 The weight doubles. / The weight is[gets / becomes] doubled. // 그의 재산은 나의 ~가 된다 His fortune doubles mine. // 적은 우리의 ~가 되는 군대를 동원했다 The enemy mobilized a military force twice as great as ours. // 이 끈의 두 ~의 길이로 해 주시오 Make it twice as long as[two times the length of] this string. // 그의 방은 내 방의 ~나 넓다 His room is twice as large as[twice the size of] my room. // 그 기계를 사용하면 일을 ~나 할 수 있다 We can do double the work by using that machine.
2 [곱] times; -fold. ¶1~ once /(미) one time // 1~ 반 one and a half times[time and a half] (as … as) // 2~ double / twice / twofold // 3~ three times / treble / thrice / threefold // 4~ quadruple // 5~ quintuple // 6~ sextuple // 7~ septuple // 8~ octuple // 9~ nonuple // 10~ decuple // 100~ centuple // 몇 ~나 many times over // 1천 5백 ~의 현미경 a microscope of 1,500 magnifications // 수[양]를 10~로 하다 increase the number [quantity] (by) ten times // 남보다 ~로 일하다 work twice as hard as others // 이것은 저것의 3~의 크기다 This is three times[threefold] larger than that. // 24의 3~는 얼마입니까 What is 24 multiplied by 3? // 10년 동안에 그의 수입은 3~가 되었다 His income has trebled in ten years. // 5를 몇 ~하면 100이 되는가 What times 5 is 100? // 이 나무는 저 나무의 2.5~의 높이이다 This tree is two and a half times as tall as that one[two and a half times the height of that one]. // 그녀는 언니보다 몇 ~ 아름답다 She is several times more beautiful than[several times as beautiful as] her sister.

배가하다(倍加─) double; double itself; be doubled; increase double [twofold]. ¶노력을 ~ redouble one's efforts // 인구가 3년 동안에 배가하였다 The population doubled in three years. ➔ // 수송력이 배가되었다 Transport capacity was redoubled. // 딸의 결혼에다가 아들의 승진으로 양친의 기쁨이 배가되었다 Together with their daughter's wedding, their son's promotion brought the parents double[twofold] joy.

배갈 kaoliang(=a Chinese alcoholic drink).

배격(排擊) rejection; denunciation. **배격하다** reject; denounce; show strong disapproval of; drive out. ¶공산주의[파시즘]를 ~ oppose[reject / denounce] the Communism [Fascism]. ➔ 그는 이단자로서 배격당했다 He was denounced[condemned] as a heretic.

배경(背景) **1** [배후] a background; a backdrop. ¶우리는 산을 ~으로 해서 사진을 찍었다 We had our picture taken with hill for a [in the] background. // 아름다운 한라산의 모습이 푸른 하늘을 ~으로 하여 서 있다 The graceful figure of Hallasan(Mt. Halla) stands out clear against the blue sky.
2 [무대의] scenery; a setting; a scene. ¶고대 한국을 ~으로 한 영화 a movie with ancient Korea as its setting / a movie set in ancient Korea // ~을 바꾸다 shift the scenes // ~을 그리다 paint scenes.
3 [배후 세력] backing; (미국 속어) pull. ¶정치적 ~ political backing[affiliations / connections / support / pull] // 유력한 ~ strong backing / a strong backer[supporter] (사람) // ~이 없다 have no "pull" behind (one) // ~이 되다 back up / support / give support to / be at a person's back // 나는 유력한 정치적 ~이 있다 I have an influential politician backing behind me.
● **배경 음악** background (music).

배고프다 hungry; sharp-set; (서술적) feel[be / get] hungry. ¶배고픈 김에 마구 먹다 indulge one's appetite to excess // 배고파하다 complain of hunger // 배고파 죽겠다 I'm starving[famished] (to death). / I am dying of hunger. / I'm famished. / I'm terribly hungry. / I am ravenous. // 우리 아이들을 배고프게 할 수는 없다 My children must not go hungry. // 배고플 때에는 맛없는 음식이 없다 Nothing is unpalatable[comes amiss] to a hungry man[person]. / Hunger is the best sauce. // 배고파서는 일을 할 수가 없다 One cannot work[There is nothing doing] on an empty stomach. / A full belly counsels well.

배곯다 starve; have an empty stomach. ¶그는 언제나 배곯고 지낸다 He always goes hungry. // 가족을 어떻게 배곯게 할 수 있겠는가 How can I let my family go hungry?

배관(配管) pipe arrangement[laying]; (집합적) piping; [배관 공사] piping work; plumbing. **배관하다** lay[arrange] pipes.
● **배관공** a plumber.

배교(背教) renegation; apostasy; lapse from faith. **배교하다** apostatize; abjure[renounce] one's religion.
● **배교자** a renegade; an apostate; a backslider.

배구(排球) volleyball.
● **배구 경기** [코트] a volleyball game[court]. **배구공** a volleyball.

배금(拜金) the worship of money; money worship; mammonism.
● **배금주의** mammonism. **배금주의자** a mammonist; a mammonite; a money worship(p)er.

배급(配給) distribution; supply; rationing(식량의). ¶~을 타다 draw one's rations // ~ 대상에서 제외되다 come off the ration list // 우리에겐 쌀의 ~이 없었다 We had no rations of rice. **배급하다** distribute; supply; deal out; (식량을) ration. ¶그들은 수재민에게 식량을 배급했다 They supplied food to the flood sufferers. ➔ // 10일분의 쌀이 배급되었다 Ten days' ration of rice was distributed.
● **배급소** a distributing[supply] station [point]; a distribution[ration] point[cen-

ter); (미) a ration board. 배급자 a distributor. **배급제도** a distribution[rationing] system. **배급품** rationed goods.

배기(排氣) 〔공기를 밖으로 뽑아냄〕 exhaust; 〔물〕 exhaustion; evacuation; 〔배출된 가스 등〕 used steam; exhaust (steam/gas); 〔통풍〕 ventilation.
● **배기가스** waste[exhaust] gas; exhaust fumes; (engine) exhaust. **배기관 / 배기 파이프** an exhaust[eduction] pipe. **배기량 (piston) displacement.** ¶∼ 2,000cc의 차 a two thousand cubic centimeter displacement car. **배기 밸브** a cutout; an exhaust [eduction] valve. **배기펌프** an air pump.

배기다¹ 〔몸 밑에 단단한 것이 받치는 힘을 느끼게 되다〕 be hard on; pinch; squeeze; press so as to hurt. ¶등이 ∼ feel[be] hard on one's back.

배기다² 〔견디다·참다〕 bear up (under); endure; suffer; put up with; persevere; tolerate; bear; 〔지탱하다〕 stand; hold out; withstand. ¶…하지 않고는 못 ∼ cannot help [keep from] (doing) / cannot but (do) // 배길 수 있는 bearable / endurable / sufferable / tolerable // 배길 수 없는 unbearable / unendurable / insufferable / intolerable / beyond endurance [one's perseverance] / past [beyond] bearing // 일이 고되어서 배길 수 없다 I cannot stand the strain of the work. // 이런 생활은 더 이상 배겨 낼 수 없다 (구어) I can't go this life any more. // 그 방은 무더워서 더 이상 배겨 낼 수 없었다 The room was so hot and stuffy that I could stay in it any longer.

배꼽 1 〔생〕 the navel; the umbilicus (pl. -bilici); the omphalos (pl. -li); (속어) the bellybutton. ¶내민〔불거진〕 ∼ a protruding navel // 오목한 ∼ a deep[sunken] navel // ∼이 빠지도록 웃다 laugh like anything / laugh oneself into convulsions // 이것이 걸작이라니, ∼이 웃겠다 You call this a great work? What a joke! // 그의 몸짓은 ∼을 쥘〔뺄〕 정도로 우스웠다 His funny gestures threw us into a fit of laughter. 2 (열매의) the eye [basin] (of an apple).

배나무 a pear tree.
배낭(胚囊) 〔식〕 an embryo sac.
● **배낭 세포** 〔식〕 an embryo sac cell.
배낭(背囊) (미) a backpack; (영) a rucksack; 〔낡〕 a knapsack. ¶∼을 꾸리다 pack (things) in a backpack / pack a backpack with (things) // ∼을 벗다 take off a backpack // ∼을 지다〔메다〕 strap on a backpack / carry a backpack on one's back.
● **배낭여행** backpacking. ¶∼을 떠나다 go backpacking.

배내똥 (갓난아이의) meconium; the first faecal excretion of a newborn baby.
배내옷 baby clothes[clouts]; swaddling[long] clothes; clothes for a newborn baby.
배냇니 a milk tooth. ⇨젖니
배냇병신(一病身) a congenital cripple [deformity]; a person born with a deformity.
배냇짓 (an) infant's sleeping spasms.
배뇨(排尿) 〔의〕 urination; miction; micturition; excretion of urine. **배뇨하다** pass urine [one's water]; urinate; micturate.
배다¹ 1 (물기 등이) soak (through/into); permeate; infiltrate; sink (into); penetrate. ¶…이 배어 있다 be saturated with ... // 책에 냄새를 배게 하다 soak a book with a scent // 배어나다 ooze (out) / exude / come out in drops[beads] // 셔츠에 땀이 배어 있다 My shirt is soaked through with perspiration[is wet with sweat]. // 과자마에 땀이 배어 있다 The sweat soaked my pajamas. // 흰 식탁보에 잉크가 배었다 The ink spread through the white tablecloth. // 연기 냄새가 집 안에 배었다 The odor of smoke permeated[penetrated] the house. // 그의 셔츠에 피가 약간 배어 있다 His shirt is slightly bloodstained [stained with blood]. / A little blood has seeped into his shirt. // 잉크가 압지에 배었다 The ink sank into the blotting paper.
2 (버릇·일이) be[get] accustomed to; be[get] used to; be[become] habituated to; get in the way (of doing); be experienced (in). ¶몸에 밴 일 a familiar work / a job one is experienced in / one's accustomed work // 음주의 습성이 몸에 ∼ fall into[get / contract] the bad habit of drinking // 몸에 배어 있다 be at home (in) / be thoroughly in one's element (with) // 그는 평소의 버릇이 몸에 배어 있다 He is very much wedded to his mannerisms. // 질투는 인간의 본성에 깊이 배어들어 있다 Jealousy is deeply ingrained in human nature.

배다² 〔아이·알 등을 배 속에 가지다〕 conceive; become pregnant; bear in the womb. ¶그 여자는 아이를 뱄다 The woman is pregnant. / The woman is in the family way. // 그녀는 그의 아이를 배고 있었다 She was pregnant with his child. / She was carrying his child. // 암소가 새끼를 뱄다 The cow is heavy with calf. // 그 물고기는 모두 알을 배었다 The fish are all full of eggs[roe]. // 그는 그 여인에게 아기까지 배게 했다 He even got the woman pregnant.

배다³ 〔촘촘하다〕 (옷감의 올·결 등이) close; compact; close-grained; (간격이) close together; 〔조밀하다〕 dense; thick. ¶올이 밴 옷감 cloth of a close texture // (글씨를) 배게 쓰다 write close // 씨를 배게 뿌리다 sow seeds thickly // 나무를 배게 심다 plant trees closely together / plant trees densely.

배다르다 (born) of a different mother; half-blood(ed). ¶배다른 형제 a half brother / a brother born of a different mother / a brother of the half blood // 그들 형제〔자매〕는 ∼ They are half-brothers[-sisters].

배다리 a pontoon bridge. ¶(강에) ∼를 놓다 build a pontoon bridge (across a river).

배달 (the earliest name for) Korea.
● **배달민족 / 배달겨레** the Korean people [race].

배달(配達) delivery (service); distribution. ¶무료 ∼ free delivery // 시내[특별] ∼ local [special] delivery // ∼품 〔배달할 물품〕 an article to be delivered // 신속 ∼ (게시) Quick delivery. **배달하다** deliver. ¶신문〔우유〕을 ∼ deliver[carry] newspaper[milk] to (houses) // 음식을 ∼ supply[deliver] dishes to order // 시내는 무료로 배달합니다 Delivery is free within the city limits. // 매일 아침 우유를 두 병씩 배달해 주십시오 Please deliver two bottles of milk every morning. // 대금은 배달할 때 지불해 주세요. Please pay on delivery. ➔그 편지는 잘못 배달되었다 The letter was delivered at the wrong address. // 우편은 하루에 두 번 배달된다 Mail is delivered twice

배달료 a delivery [an express] charge. ¶저 가게에서는 ~를 받는다 That store charges for delivery. **배달원** a delivery man [boy]; a distributor; (신문의) a newsman; newsboy; (우유의) a milkman; (우편의) a postman; (미) a mailman; a letter [mail] carrier. **배달증명 우편** certified mail.

배당(配當) (an) apportionment; (an) allotment; a share; (주식의) a dividend; (보험의) a disbursement (to a policyholder); (인원수의) a quota; distribution. ¶무~ non dividend (약어 non div.) / 우선~ a preferred dividend / 주식~ stock dividend / 이익 없는 ~ a bogus dividend (paid out of fictitious profits) / 높은 ~ (주식의) high [good] dividends / a high rate of return (on a stock [shares]) / ~이 많은 주식 a high-yielding stock / a stock [(영) shares] yielding good dividends / 저 회사는 5%의 ~을 준다 That company pays a dividend of 5% (on its stock). / 그 회사의 주식은 계속해서 ~이 많다 That company continues to pay good dividends. / The return on that company's shares remains good. **배당하다** apportion (to); allot (to); divide; share; (배당금을) pay a dividend. ¶여러 가지 일에 시간을 ~ apportion time to several tasks. →¶이익을 **배당받다** share [participate] in the profits.

● **배당금** a dividend. ¶특별 ~ an extra dividend (on stocks) / a bonus (on stocks). **배당률** dividend rate. **배당 소득** income from (stock) dividends. **배당주** a dividend yielding stock.

배덕(背德) immorality; demoralization; corruption; a lapse from virtue. ¶~의 immoral / corrupt. **배덕하다** immoral; corrupt.

● **배덕자** an immoral [a corrupt] man.

배돌다 [한데 어울리지 못하다] keep aloof from others; avoid mixing with people; keep [live] to oneself; love one's own company; be unsociable.

배드민턴 badminton. ¶~공 a bird / a shuttlecock.

배때기 the abdomen. ⇨ ¹배

배란(排卵) [생] ovulation. **배란하다** ovulate.

● **배란기** an ovulatory phase.

배럴 [용량 단위] a barrel.

배려(配慮) consideration; solicitude; care; concern; (진력) trouble; (알선) effort; good offices. ¶세심한 ~ thoughtful consideration / scrupulous care // …의 ~로 through the good offices of … / 상사의 ~로 나는 제주도로의 전근을 모면했다 Thanks to the kindhearted help of my boss, I escaped being transferred to Jejudo. // 그녀는 아이들에게 어머니로서의 ~가 부족한 것 같다 It seems she doesn't give as much care to her children as a mother should. // 그녀는 남을 위한 자상함과 ~가 없다 She lacks delicacy and consideration for others. **배려하다** take care; give consideration (to); take the trouble. ¶배려해 주셔서 감사합니다 I am obliged to you for your (kind) consideration. / Thank you very much for your trouble [your concern]. // 제 아들에 대해 배려해 주셔서 감사합니다 I appreciate your thoughtfulness toward(s) my son. // 지연되지 않도록 배려해 주세요 Please see to it that there is no delay.

배례(拜禮) a salutation; a salute; worship. **배례하다** bow down; salute; worship.

배롱나무 a crape myrtle; an Indian lilac.

배리(背理) unreasonableness; irrationality; absurdity; paralogism; unnaturalness. ¶~의 unreasonable / irrational / absurd / contrary to reason / unnatural.

배면(背面) the rear; the back. ¶적의 ~을 공격하다 attack the enemy in the rear.

● **배면 공격** an attack from the rear; a rear attack.

배명하다(拜命-) 1 [명령을 받다] receive orders (from); (미) get the word. 2 [임명되다] receive an (official) appointment; be appointed (to the post of …).

배물교(拜物教) fetishism; fetichism.

배반(背反·背叛) 1 [저버림] (a) betrayal; (a) perfidy. ¶이율~ [철] antinomy / 그것은 우리 주의에 대한 ~이다 It is treachery against our principles. / It is a betrayal of our principles. **배반하다** [동료의 약속 등을 깨다] betray (a person's trust, one's master, etc.); play (a person) false [foul]; sell (one's friends); (미) double-cross (a person); [변절하다] change front; turn one's coat. ¶친구를 ~ betray one's friend / betray [rebel against] one's lord // (여자가) 남자를 ~ jilt a man / 그는 나에 대한 약속을 배반했다 He broke his promise to me. / He went back on his word. // 나는 그가 나를 배반하리라고는 생각지 않았다 I never thought he would play me false. // 그녀는 남편을 배반했다 She was unfaithful to her husband. // 그는 자기 친구들을 배반하여 살해당했다 He was killed for having double-crossed [sold out] his friends. // 그는 세상 사람들의 기대를 배반했다 He failed to live up to the people's expectations. →¶그는 아내에게 배반당해 자포자기가 되어 있다 He is in a desperate mood, having been deserted by his wife.

2 [반역] rebellion; revolt; (an act of) treachery. ¶그것은 국가에 대한 ~이다 It is high treason (against) the nation. **배반하다** turn traitor; revolt [rebel] (against). ¶나라를 ~ betray [turn traitor to] one's country.

● **배반자** a traitor; a betrayer; [밀고자] an informer; [파업 방해자] a strikebreaker; (속어) a scab; [변절자] a turncoat; a quisling; (속어) a rat.

배반(胚盤) [생] the germinal disk; the embryo disk; the blastodisk.

배배 windingly. ⇨ ²비비

배변(排便) the action [movement] of the bowels; a bowel movement; (의학에서) an evacuation; defecation. ¶나는 ~이 규칙적이다 I have regular bowel movements. // 나는 3일간 ~이 없었다 I have been constipated for three days. / I have had no (bowel) movement for three days. // ~을 하게 하다 loosen [move] the bowels / ~이 잘되게 하다 improve the action [movement] of one's bowels. **배변하다** open [move / empty / evacuate] the bowels.

배본(配本) (구매자에게) distribution of books; (소매점에) delivery of (new) books to retail bookstores. ¶제1권은 ~이 끝났다 The first volume has already been distributed [delivered] to subscribers. **배본하다** distribute books.

배부(配付) distribution. **배부하다** distribute (blankets to the poor); pass out (papers to

배부르다 1 [양이 차다] full [cloyed / satiated] (with food); [서술적] have a full stomach; have the stomach full. ¶배부르게 먹다 eat one's fill / eat heartily / have enough [plenty] / eat to one's heart's content / make a good square meal / be satiated with / do ample justice (to a dinner) / (속어) make [have] a hearty meal of // 저는 배불러요 I'm (so) full. / I've eaten [had] my fill. / My stomach is full. / I've had enough. / I'm stuffed. **배불리** heartily; abundantly; [실컷] to one's heart's content. ¶~ 먹었습니다 I have had more than enough. / I've had enough. / I'm full.
2 [배가 불룩하다] bigbellied; paunchy; potbellied; (임신하여) big (with child). ¶배부른 여자 a woman big with child // 그녀는 ~ 다 She is expecting a baby. / She is pregnant [in the family way].
3 [넉넉하다] rich; affluent; well-off; well-fixed.

배분(配分) distribution; division; apportionment; allotment. ¶휘발유의 공정한 ~ a fair allocation of gasoline. **배분하다** distribute (to / among); divide (among); share; portion out; apportion (to); allot (to). ¶이익은 두 사람에게 배분하였다 The profits were shared [divided / apportioned] between the two.
● **배분 법칙** [수] the distributive law. ⇨"분배 법칙(⇨분배)

배불뚝이 a potbellied [paunchy] person; a person with a potbelly; a potbelly.

배사(背斜) [지] an anticline. ¶~의 anticlinal.

배상(拜上) Yours sincerely [truly / faithfully / respectfully / cordially]; Sincerely [Respectfully / Cordially] yours.

배상(賠償) reparation; indemnity; compensation; recompense; remedy; redress; indemnification; restitution; satisfaction. ¶금전 [현물] ~ reparation in cash [kind] // …의 ~ 으로서 in reparation of … / in compensation for … // ~을 청구하다 demand reparation [compensation] (for) / claim (against a company) for compensation / seek redress // ~을 받아 내다 take [obtain / exact] reparations [indemnities] // 그를 상대로 손해 ~ 소송을 제기하다 bring an action for damage against him. **배상하다** indemnify; [변상하다] compensate; recompense (for); make reparation (for); give compensation (for); make [give] satisfaction (for); make restitution; make good (a loss); make up for (a loss). ¶손해를 ~ pay for damage (done) / indemnify (a person) for damage // 이 손실에 대해서 당신에게 배상하겠다 I will compensate you for this loss.
● **배상금** indemnities; reparations; damages; a tender. ¶~을 지불하다 pay indemnities [reparations] // 기액의 ~을 요구하다 demand a large indemnity / claim heavy compensation // ~을 받다 recover damages. **배상 문제** (discuss) reparations problems. **배상 요구** a claim for compensation. **배상 청구권** the right to demand compensation.

배색(配色) a color scheme [arrangement]; coloring; coloration. ¶빨간 모자 및 이에 ~이 맞는 옷 a red hat with a coat to tone // 이 그림은 ~이 좋지 않다 The coloring of this picture is not satisfactory. // ~이 좋다 [나쁘다] The colors (don't) match well. **배색하다** match colors; arrange colors; do the colors [coloring / color scheme].

배서(背書) (an) endorsement; (an) indorsement. ¶~가 있는 [없는] endorsed [unendorsed] // 공동 ~ a joint endorsement. **배서하다** endorse [indorse / back] (a bill). ¶어음에 ~ endorse (one's name on) a bill. ➔¶서류에 (서명이) 배서되어 있다 The document is endorsed.
● **배서 수표** an endorsed note [bill]. **배서인** an endorser; an indorser. ¶피~ an endorsee / an indorsee.

배석(陪席) sitting (with one's superior). ¶A씨의 ~하에 with Mr. A attending [in attendance]. **배석하다** sit with (one's superior). ¶두 나라 정상의 회의에 나도 배석했다 I had the honor of attending the summit conference between the two countries.
● **배석자** an attendant. **배석 판사** an associate judge; a puisne (judge).

배선(配線) [전선을 끌어 장치함] wiring; [전선] a service wire. ¶전기의 ~ electric wiring // 전화선의 ~이 아직 끝나지 않았다 The telephone wires have not been installed yet. / The telephone wiring has not been completed yet. // 이 건물은 ~이 잘되어 있다 The building is well wired. **배선하다** wire (a house).
● **배선 공사** wiring work. **배선도** a wiring diagram.

배설(排泄) excretion; evacuation; discharge; dejection. ¶~을 촉진하는 evacuant. **배설하다** excrete; evacuate; purge; discharge; eject; egest.
● **배설기 / 배설 기관** an excretive [excretory] organ. **배설물** excrement; discharges; excretions; body wastes; ejection; dejection; evacuation; ejecta; evacuated matter; (신진 대사에 의한) output. **배설 작용** the excretory process; evacuation.

배속(配屬) assignment; attachment. **배속하다** assign; attach (an officer). ➔¶배속되다 be attached (to) / get posted // 나는 연구소에 배속되었다 I was assigned to the research center. // 그녀는 간호사로서 야전 병원에 배속되었다 She was sent to a field hospital as a nurse.
● **배속 장교** a military officer attached to a school.

배수(拜受) acceptance. **배수하다** receive (a thing / a gift) with thanks; accept; be grateful to receive.

배수(配水) supply [distribution] of water; water supply [service]. ¶시 당국은 시간제 ~를 지시하였다 The city authorities issued an order restricting the hours of water supply. **배수하다** distribute [supply] water.
● **배수관** a water [conduit] pipe; a conduit. **배수지**(-池) a water(-supply) reservoir; a distributing reservoir.

배수(倍數) 1 [수] a multiple. ¶공~ a common multiple // 6은 2와 3의 ~이다 Six is a multiple of both two and three. 2 [갑절] a double number.

배수(排水) 1 [물을 빼내기] draining; drainage; pumping out; bailing. ¶급수 및 ~의 설비 (건물 내의) plumbing equipment / plumbing // 급수 및 ~ supply and drain water // 욕실의 ~가 잘되게 하다 improve the drainage of a bathroom.∥이 땅은 ~가 잘된다[잘되지 않는다] This land drains well [badly].∥이 택지는 ~ 시설이 불완전하다 The sewage[sewerage] arrangements at this housing site are incomplete[inadequate]. 배수하다 drain (off); dike(도랑으로); pump out(펌프로); bail(배에 괸 물을). 2 [물을 밀어내기] displacement. 배수하다 displace (200 tons of water).

● 배수관 a drainpipe; a watershoot. 배수구(-口) (건물의) a beak; an overflow; a drainage hole; outlet. ¶이 ~는 물이 잘 빠지지 않는다 Water doesn't run off well. 배수량 displacement. ¶그 배는 ~이 2만 톤이다 The ship has a displacement of twenty thousand tons. / The ship displaces twenty thousand tons. 배수로 / 배수구(-溝) a waterway; a drainageway. 배수펌프 a drain(ing) pump.

배수진(背水陣) a position taken up with a river behind the troops; burning the bridges [boats] (behind one). ¶~을 치다 burn one's boats[ships] / burn one's bridges (behind one) / fight with one's back to the wall[sea]∥우리는 ~을 치고 회사의 재건을 도모했다 We staked everything on the reconstruction of our company.

배신(背信) betrayal; infidelity; (a) breach of trust[confidence / faith]. ¶~적인 unfaithful / treacherous. 배신하다 betray (a person's) confidence; break faith with (one's friend). ¶당신은 나를 배신하였다 You have betrayed my trust. / You have broken faith with me.

● 배신자 a betrayer; a turncoat(변절자).

배심(陪審) (a) jury. ¶~ 구성의 절차 the proceedings of composing a jury / ~은 유죄 평결을 내렸다 The jury brought in a verdict of guilty. 배심하다 hold (a) jury; participate in a trial as juryman; serve[sit / be] on a jury; do jury duty.

● 배심원 (집합적) a jury; (개인) a juryman; a jurywoman; a juror(남·녀). ¶대~ a grand juror / 소~ a petty juror∥~의 평결 a verdict∥~을 선임하다 impanel a jury∥~이 되다 serve[sit / be] on a jury∥그는 ~이 되어 있다 He is (sitting) on a jury.∥~은 피고를 유죄로 평결했다 The jury found the accused guilty. 배심 재판 trial by jury. 배심 제도 the jury system.

배아(胚芽) an embryo bud; a germ.

● 배아미(-米) whole rice; rice with germs; rice with embryo buds.

배알 1 [창자] the intestines; the bowels; the guts(동물의). 2 [배짱] self-confidence; boldness; audacity; nerve.
배알이 꼴리다 ¶그것을 보니 배알이 꼴린다 My gorge[stomach] rises at it.

배알(拜謁) an audience (with the King). ¶그는 여왕의 ~을 허락받았다 He was received in audience by Her majesty. / He was granted an audience with Her Majesty. 배알하다 have an audience (with the King); make one's curts(e)y to (the Queen).

배앓이 a stomachache; a bellyache; colic; gripe(s). ¶~를 앓다 suffer from[have] a stomachache / have colic.

배양(培養) cultivation; nurture; culture. ¶세균 ~ germiculture / cultivation of bacteria∥시험관 ~ test-tube culture∥인공 ~ artificial culture∥조직 ~ tissue culture∥이 과수는 ~에 의해 이렇게 큰 열매가 열리게 되었다 Cultivation has made this tree yield such big fruit.∥그 나라의 역사적 풍토는 민주주의의 ~에 적합하다 The historical background of the country made it suitable for the growth of democracy. 배양하다 cultivate; culture; nurture; breed; raise; grow. ¶세균을 ~ culture[cultivate] bacteria.

● 배양 균 cultured bacteria; cultures. 배양액 a culture fluid[solution / medium].

배역(配役) the cast (of a play). ¶~을 정하다 cast a play / assign parts to (actors) / cast (an actor) for a part[role] / cast[assign] the parts (of a play to the actors) / ~을 바꾸다 alter the cast∥그 여배우를 주역으로 한 것은 ~의 잘못이었다 The actress was miscast in the role of[as] the heroine.∥이 연극은 ~이 좋다[좋지 않다] The play is well cast[miscast]. 배역하다 cast.

배역(背逆) betrayal; rebellion. 배역하다 betray; rebel against; turn against[upon].

배열(配列·排列) arrangement; disposition; disposal. 배열하다 arrange; dispose; put [place / set] in order; array; set in array. ¶소나무와 국화의 그림을 배열한 호화로운 병풍 a magnificent screen with a picture of pines and chrysanthemums on it∥ABC순으로 ~ arrange (words) alphabetically[in alphabetical order / in ABC order]. →¶이름은 가나다 순으로 배열되어 있다 The names are arranged according to the Korean syllabary.

배엽(胚葉) [식] a germinal[germ] layer; a blastoderm.

배영(背泳) the backstroke. ¶~을 하다 swim on one's back / swim[do] the backstroke.

● 배영 선수 a backstroke swimmer.

배외(排外) ¶~의 antiforeign / antialien.

● 배외사상 antiforeign ideas; an antiforeign spirit; antialienism.

배우(俳優) a player; [남자 배우] an actor; [여배우] an actress(▶ actor는 일반적으로 남자 배우를 뜻하나, 때로 남녀 구별 없이 사용되기도 하며, 많은 여성들은 성 차별을 배격하는 뜻에서 여배우가 actress보다는 actor로 불리기를 원함); a performer; (집합적) people of the stage. ¶무대[연극] ~ a stage actor[actress]∥아마추어 ~ an amateur actor∥인기 ~ a star / a star actor[actress]∥영화 ~ a movie [cinema / film / screen] actor[actress]∥극장 전속 ~ an actor[actress] attached to a theater∥영화~ 지망자 an aspirant to a screen career∥~가 되다 become an actor [actress] / (무대에 서다) go on[take to] the stage / appear before the footlights∥~를 그만두다 retire from[go off] the stage / leave the boards[stage].

● 배우 학교 a school of acting.

배우다 learn; be taught; take lessons (in); study; [연습하다] practice; [교훈을 얻다] draw a lesson[(much) instruction] (from). ¶선생에게 ~ study under[with] a teacher∥미국인에게 영어를 ~ learn English from [study English under] an American∥하버드 대학에서 ~ study[be educated] at Harvard∥책에서 ~ learn from books∥철저히 ~ learn thoroughly / master∥많은 것을 ~ learn many things∥나는 수영을 배웠다 I learned[was taught] how to swim.∥수학은 저 선생에게 배웠다 That teacher taught me mathematics. / I learned mathematics from that teacher.∥당신은 누구에게서 영어를 배웠

습니까 Who did you learn English from? / Who taught you English? // 나는 어렸을 때 스키를 배웠다 I learned (how) to ski when I was a child. // 그녀는 한 씨 부인에게서 무용을 배웠다 She was trained in dancing under Mrs. Han. // 내 딸은 발레를 배우고 있다 My daughter studies ballet. // 나는 일 주일에 두 번 춤을 배운다 I take dancing lessons twice a week. // 나는 꽃꽂이를 배운 적이 없다 I have never studied flower arrangement. // 이 아이는 빨리 배운다 This child learns quickly. // 그녀는 예의범절을 꼼꼼하게 배웠다 She was given careful training in manners. // 나는 그것이 나쁘다고 배웠다 I was taught that it is wrong. // 나는 컴퓨터를 조작하는 법을 그에게 부탁해서 배웠다 I got him to show [teach] me how to use the computer. / I got him to give me instructions for using the computer.
배운 도둑질 같다(속담) be like second nature (to a person).
배우자(配偶子) [생] a gamete.
배우자(配偶者) a spouse; a consort; a life partner; a companion for life; a partner in life; a wife(아내); a husband(남편). ¶~가 없는 spouseless / mateless // 적당한 ~를 고르다 choose a suitable match (for one).
배웅 seeing (a person) off; a send-off. ¶성대한 ~을 받다 be given[receive] a good send-off // 역까지 ~ 나가다 go to a station to see (a person) off. 배웅하다 see (a person) off; send (a person) off; give (a person) a send-off. ¶배웅하러 온 사람 a person who has come to see someone off / 배웅하는 사람들 persons present for a send-off // 손님을 대문까지 ~ accompany (a person) to the gate / see the visitor to the gate // 공항에서 성대히 ~ give a person a royal send-off at the airport // 많은 사람들이 K 씨를 배웅하러 나왔다 Many people came to give Mr. K a send-off.
배위(配位) [화] coordination.
● 배위 결합 a coordinate (covalent) bond; a coordinate covalence.
배유(胚乳) an albumen. ⇨배젖
배율(倍率) [광] magnification; magnifying power. ¶~ 10의 렌즈 a lens with a magnifying power of 10 / 15~의 쌍안경 field glasses of fifteen magnifications / an 15-power binocular / 고(高)~의 (a telescope) of high power / ~을 높이다[낮추다] raise[lower] the power.
배은망덕(背恩忘德) ingratitude; ungratefulness. 배은망덕하다 be ungrateful; lose one's gratitude (to); forget kindness[benefits] received. ¶배은망덕한 짓을 당하다 be bitten by the mouths that accepted one's charity / be returned evil for good // 그는 배은망덕한 놈이다 He is an ungrateful wretch[an ingrate].
배음(倍音) [물] harmonics; [음] an overtone; a harmonic (overtone).
배일(排日) ¶~의 anti-Japanese.
● 배일 감정 an anti-Japanese sentiment [feeling].
배일성(背日性) [식] negative heliotropism; apheliotropism.
배임(背任) breach of trust[faith]; malpractice; defalcation; misappropriation(횡령). ¶업무상 ~ dereliction of duty // 죄로 고발당하다 be charged with breach of trust[with misfeasance in office].
배자(胚子) [생] an embryo.
배자(褙子) a (women's) waistcoat.
배전(倍前) ¶~의 more than ever / all the more / ~의 노력을 하다 redouble one's exertions / make redoubled efforts // ~의 지원을 부탁드립니다 We request you to redouble your efforts to help us.
배전(配電) supply of electric power; electric [power] supply; power distribution; distribution of electricity. ¶~을 중지하다 cut off the electric supply. 배전하다 supply electricity; distribute power.
● 배전반 a distributing board[panel]; a switchboard. 배전선 a service wire; a distribution line. 배전소 a power distribution station.
배점(配點) distribution[allotting] of marks. 배점하다 allot (20 points) to (a question).
배정(配定) assignment; allotment; allocation; apportionment; quota. 배정하다 assign; allot; allocate; apportion; parcel[map] out. ¶방을 ~ assign rooms (to persons) / 역(役)을 ~ assign a role (to each actor) / cast the parts (to the actors).
배젖(胚—) an albumen; an endosperm. ¶~이 있는 albuminous.
배제(排除) exclusion; removal; elimination; [법] abatement. 배제하다 make[do] away with; exclude; remove; eliminate. ¶…을 배제하고 to the exclusion of ... // 정실을 ~ put aside personal considerations / eliminate favoritism // 회의에서 정치 문제를 ~ eliminate politics from the conference // 과학자로서 나는 억측을 배제하고 싶다 As a scientist, I should like to exclude conjectures.
배종(陪從) accompanying[following] one's superior; waiting upon[attending on] one's superior. 배종하다 wait upon[attend on / accompany / follow] one's superior.
배주(胚珠) [식] a germinal vesicle. ⇨밑씨
배주룩하다 projecting a bit. ⇨비주룩하다
배죽 poutingly. ⇨비죽
배중률(排中律) [논] the principle of the excluded middle.
배증(倍增) doubling; growing double. 배증하다 double; be doubled; grow[increase] double.
배지 〔휘장〕 a badge. ¶학교 ~ a school badge.
배지느러미 [동] the ventral fin.
배지성(背地性) [식] negative geotropism; apogeotropism.
배진(背進) backing; [철수] withdrawal. 배진하다 fall back; retire; withdraw.
배짱 1 [마음속의 뜻] one's inmost thought(s); one's real intention. ¶그는 외상값을 떼어먹을 ~이다 He has the intention of bilking the bill. // 그의 ~은 알 수 없다 Who can guess at his hidden motives[at what he's really thinking]?
2 [버티는 힘] courage; nerve; (구어) guts; self-confidence; boldness; audacity; hardihood; assurance. ¶~이 있는 (용기가 있는) brave / plucky / (대담한) daring // ~이 없는 timid / cowardly / gutless // 그는 ~이 있다 He is a man of courage[guts]. / He has plenty of guts. // ~ 한번 좋군 What a nerve [chutzpah]! / Such nerve! // 나에게는 도저히

배차

그를 거역할 ~이 없다 I don't have the courage[nerve] to oppose him.// 그녀가 ~이 좋은 데는 놀랐다 I was surprised at her daring[pluck].// 이렇게 되면 ~을 부리는 수밖에 없다 There is no other way than to push forward.

배짱(이) 맞다 congenial; (서술적) be united in spirit; hit it off (with).

배차(配車) operation[allocation] of cars. **배차하다** operate[run] cars; allocate cars.
● **배차원** a (train) dispatcher.

배척(排斥) rejection; expulsion; exclusion; ostracism; boycott. **배척하다** drive out; reject; exclude; expel; proscribe; ostracize; boycott; (속어) pip. ¶그녀는 간사해서 모두 그녀를 배척하고 있다 She's crafty so everyone shuns her. → 모두에게 배척당하고 있다 be scorned[shunned/left] by all// 그의 이기주의 때문에 그는 모두에게 배척받고 있다 He is shunned[given the cold shoulder] by everyone because of his selfishness.// 전체주의는 그 나라에서 배척받았다 Totalitarianism was rejected in the country.
● **배척 운동** an expulsion agitation. ¶일본인 ~ anti-Japanese movement.

배추 a Chinese[white] cabbage.
● **배추김치** cabbage *gimchi*(kimchi); pickled cabbage.

배추흰나비 [동] a small[cabbage] white; a cabbage butterfly.

배출(排出) discharge; exhaust; excretion(배설). ¶공기의 ~ deflation of air. **배출하다** draw off; discharge; transpire; exhaust; issue; egest; eliminate. ¶노폐물을 체외로 ~ eliminate waste matter from the system.// 자동차는 유독 가스를 배출한다 Cars emit noxious fumes.
● **배출구** (물의) an outlet; (감정의) a vent; an outlet. ¶분노의 ~를 찾아내다 give vent to one's anger.

배출하다(輩出-) come forward in succession; appear one after another; produce a large[great] number of (scholars). ¶그 고장은 인재를 많이 배출했다 The place has produced many men of distinguished talent [has turned out a great many talented men]. → 그 시대에는 위인이 계속 배출되었다 The age was productive of many great men.

배치(背馳) contrariety; inconsistency; contradiction. **배치하다** be contrary (to); run counter (to); contradict (each other). → ¶그것은 법의 정신에 배치된다 It would run counter to the spirit of the law.// 이것은 사실과 아주 배치된다 This is utterly opposed to the fact.// 갓 도입된 이런 풍습은 우리 전통적인 것에 배치된다 These customs and manners just introduced run counter to our traditional ones.

배치(配置) arrangement; disposition; stationing; posting; placement; [군] deployment. ¶공격 [방어] ~ offensive[defensive] disposition// 부대 ~ troop disposition// 인원 ~ disposition of men// ~가 잘되어[잘못되어] 있다 be well[badly] arranged. **배치하다** arrange; distribute; make distributions for; dispose; [군] deploy; (부서에) post; station; detail. ¶나는 돌을 정원에 배치했다 I arranged the stones in the garden.// 그들은 인원을 요소에 배치했다 They placed[positioned] members of the staff at important points. → ¶연도에 경찰관이 배치되었다 Policemen were placed[posted/stationed] along the route.// 거기에는 경찰관이 상시 배치되어 있다 There are always policemen stationed[on duty] there.
● **배치 계획** block planning(도시 계획 등); [건] plot planning. **배치도**(-圖) an arrangement plan; [건] a plot plan; a block plan.

배코 the place right under the topknot where the hair is cut off.

배코(를) 치다 cut off the hair under the topknot; [머리를 면도로 밀다] shave the head; tonsure.

배타(排他) exclusion (of others). ¶~적(인) exclusive / clannish / cliquish. **배타하다** exclude; expel; debar.
● **배타주의** exclusivism; exclusionism. **배타주의자** an exclusivist; an exclusionist.

배탈(-頉) a stomach disorder[trouble / upset]. ¶~이 나다 have a stomach ache / have a pain in the stomach / suffer from indigestion// ~을 일으키다 put the stomach out of order / disorder[upset / spoil] the stomach// 나는 과식하여 ~이 났다 I've my stomach by eating too much.

배태(胚胎) [임신] pregnancy; germination; [기인·기원] origin; germ. **배태하다** [임신하다] become pregnant; [···에서 기원하다] originate (in); have (its) origin[genesis] (in); arise (from); result (from). ¶그것은 심장 질환에서 배태한다 It originates in some disorder of the heart.

배터리 1 [야구] the battery. ¶~ 간의 사인 a battery sign. 2 [축전지] a battery. ¶자동차의 ~ a car battery// 내 차의 ~가 나갔어요 My car battery is dead.

배터 박스 [야구] a batter's box.

배턴 a baton. ¶~을 이어받다 receive the baton (from the starting runner)// ~을 넘기다 hand over[pass] the baton (to the next runner).
● **배턴 터치**(*baton touch) a baton pass.

배토하다(培土-) earth up; hill (potatoes).

배트 [야구] a (baseball) bat; a willow (미국 속어); a stick. ¶~를 휘두르다 swing one's bat// ~를 길게[짧게] 잡다 hold one's bat long[short]// 공에 가볍게 ~를 대다 bat a ball lightly.

배틀다 twist; thwart. ⇨비틀다

배틀배틀 totteringly; staggeringly. ⇨비틀비틀

배팅 [야구] batting.
● **배팅오더** the batting order.

배편(-便) shipping service. ¶~으로 by ship [steamer / water / sea]// ~이 있는 대로 곧 보내다 send (things) by the first available ship[vessel]// 다음 ~을 기다리다 wait for the next boat// 그 섬으로 가는 ~이 있습니까 Is there (a) steamer service to the island?

배포(配布) (wide) distribution; division; apportionment. **배포하다** distribute (among / to); deal out; divide (among); apportion (to).

배포(排布·排鋪) 1 [머리를 써 계획함] mapping out[drawing up] a plan; scheming; [계획] a plan[scheme] (in one's mind). ¶가슴에 딴 ~가 들어 있다 have some plot in one's mind / have an axe to grind. 2 [마음가짐] a mental attitude; a frame of mind.

배포(가) 크다 be magnanimous; think on a large scale; have big idea.

배필(配匹) a spouse; a consort; a life partner; a life's companion; a companion for life; a mate; a wife[husband]; one's better half. ¶좋은 ~ a good wife[husband]∥천생~ a well-matched couple∥적당한 ~을 고르다 choose a suitable match (for one).

배합(配合) 1 [조화] match; harmony. ¶색의 ~ the combination[arrangement] of colors / a color scheme[harmony]∥~이 잘 안 된 well-matched / harmonious∥~이 잘 안 된 ill-matched / inharmonious∥그 회색과 핑크의 ~이 좋다 That combination of gray and pink is nice. **배합하다** match; harmonize; tone(색을). 2 [혼합] mixture; blending. **배합하다** mix; compound; blend. →배합되다 get mixed[compounded].

● **배합 비료** compound fertilizer. **배합 사료** assorted feed.

배행(陪行) 1 [윗사람을 모시고 따라감] accompanying[following] one's superior. **배행하다** attend[accompany / go with] (one's superior). 2 seeing (a person) off. ⇨배웅

배화교(拜火敎) fire-worship; a Zoroastrianism; Parsiism.

● **배화교도** a fire worshiper; a Zoroastrian; a Parsi.

배회(徘徊) loitering (about); sauntering; hovering (about); knocking about; rambling about; wandering[roaming] about; (미) hanging around. **배회하다** loiter (about); saunter; hover (about); (미) hang around [about]; wander [roam / ramble / knock] about; (도적이) prowl (about). ¶여기저기를 ~ wander from place to place / (미) go places∥숲 속을 정처 없이 ~ stray aimlessly through the wood.

배후(背後) the rear; the back. ¶~에 behind / at the rear[back] (of) / back of ...∥~에서 조종하다 pull (the) wires[strings] from behind / maneuver from behind the scenes [in the background]∥적의 ~를 찌르다 attack the enemy in the rear[from behind]∥~ 관계를 조사하다 inquire into the hidden circumstances that led up to the case / (극막을) investigate who is pulling the wires∥이 사건은 분명히 누군가가 ~에서 조종하고 있다 Somebody must be maneuvering at the bottom of this affair.

● **배후 인물** / **배후 조종자** a wirepuller; a man behind the scenes.

백[1] 1 [뒤] back.
2 [후원] backing; protection; support; [후원자] a backer; a supporter; a seconder; a protector; a patron; a friend at court; [연줄] an intermediary; an introducer; a medium (*pl.* ~s, -dia); connections; relations; (미국 속어) pull. ¶든든한 ~ strong pull∥~을 쓰다 pull strings / use one's connections∥나는 ~이 없다 I have no connections. / I have no strings to pull.∥경찰에 ~이 있다 have pull with the police∥~이 되어 주다 back up / support / be at (a person's) back∥~이 든든하다 have a good backing∥~으로 출세하다 ride on a person's coattails∥그에게는 든든한 ~이 있다 He has a powerful supporter[good backing].
3 [후위] a back.

백[2] [휴대용 가방] a bag.

백(白) 1 [흰빛] a white color. 2 a white *baduk* stone. ⇨백지

백(百) a[one] hundred. ¶3~ three hundred∥~ 번째의 the hundredth∥~분의 1 a [one-] hundredth / one percent∥~ 번째의 사람 the hundredth person∥~ 살 먹은 사람 a centenarian∥~ 명 중 3명이 낙제했다 Three students out of a hundred failed.

백-(白) white. ¶~설탕 white sugar.

백건(白鍵) [흰건반] a white key; a natural.

백계(百計) all[every] means; all resources. ¶~를 다 쓰다 try every[all] means available [conceivable] / try every possible means / leave no stone unturned / exhaust all resources[means] / be at one's wit's end / come to the end of one's rope.

● **백계무책**(-無策) helplessness.

백곡(百穀) all kind(s) of grain[(영) corn].

백골(白骨) 1 [송장이 썩고 남은 흰 뼈] a bleached[white] bone; a skeleton(해골). ¶은혜는 ~난망이옵니다 I shall never forget your kindness[what you have done for me]. 2 [옻칠하기 전의 목기류] wooden articles before lacquering.

백곰(白-) [동] a white bear. ⇨흰곰

백과(百科) all branches of knowledge.

● **백과사전**(-事典) an encyclopedia[(영) an encyclopaedia]. ¶~적 encyclopedic[(영) encyclopaedic].

백관(百官) all the government officials. ¶문무 ~ civil and military officials / all the officials of both services.

백구(白鷗) [동] a sea mew. ⇨갈매기

백군(白軍) 1 (경기에서) the white team; the white(s). ¶~이 이겼다 The white team won. / The whites won. 2 [역] the White Russian Army (at the time of the Russian Revolution).

백그라운드 the background.

백금(白金) white gold; [화] platinum.

백기(白旗) a white flag; [항복을 나타내는 기] a flag of surrender[truce]. ¶~를 내걸다 raise a white flag / [항복하다] signal that one is surrendering.

백기를 들다 [굴복하다] wave a white flag.

백난(百難) all obstacles[difficulties]; all sorts of trouble. ¶~을 극복하다 surmount[overcome / tide over] all difficulties.

백날(百-) 1 one hundredth day. ⇨백일(百日) 2 [아무리 애써도·아무리 오래 걸려도]. ¶~ 해 봐야 마찬가지다 It is no use[There is no use in] making any efforts.∥바다 경치는 ~ 봐도 좋군 I never get tired of looking out over the sea.

백납(白-) [한] leucoderma; vitiligo (*pl.* ~s).

백납(이) 먹다 have leucoderma.

백내장(白內障) [의] a cataract (in the eye). ¶노인성 ~ senile cataract / cataracta senilis∥선천성[후천성] ~ congenital[acquired] cataract∥~에 걸린 눈 an eye affected with cataract.

백넘버(*back number) [운동선수의 등번호] a uniform number(▶이 의미로 흔히 사용하는 back number의 실제적인 영어상의 의미는 간행물의 지난 호·시대에 뒤진 것[사람]을 뜻함). ¶~ 5번의 선수 the player wearing uniform number 5.

백네트(*back net) [야구] a backstop.

백년가약(百年佳約) a conjugal[matrimonial] tie; a marriage bond. ¶~을 맺다 tie the

백년대계 (百年大計) a farsighted (national) policy [program]. ¶국가의 ~를 세우다 draw up [devise] a grand [long-term / long-range] strategy for the nation / formulate a far-sighted national policy.

백년초 (百年草) [식] a cactus. ⇨˝선인장

백년해로 (百年偕老) (husband and wife) sharing the years happily together. ¶~의 가약을 맺다 be united as man and wife (for weal and woe) / swear to become on flesh / promise to live together till death parts them. **백년해로하다** be man and wife [life together in happy union] till parted by death.

백단향 (白檀香) [식] (Indian) sandalwood.

백당 (白糖) [흰 빛깔의 설탕] white [refined] sugar.

백대 (百代) [오랜 세월] long time; a long stretch of time; many years.

백대서 a background dancer.

백도 (白桃) a white peach.

백랍 (白蠟) [초의 원료] white [refined] wax; [백랍벌레의 집] insect wax.

백랍 (白鑞) solder. ⇨˝땜납

백련 (白蓮) [흰 연꽃] a white lotus (flower); [흰 목련] a white magnolia.

백로 (白鷺) [동] a white heron.

백로 (白露) [24절기의 하나] *baengno*; white dew; one of the 24 seasonal divisions of a year.

백로지 (白露紙) pulp paper. ⇨갱지(更紙)

백리 (白痢) [한] dysentery with diarrhea that becomes white with mucus.

백마 (白馬) a white horse.

백만 (百萬) 1 a [one] million. ¶~분의 1 a [one] millionth // 수~ 명의 사람들 millions of people // ~ 번 a million times // 이~ 달러 Two million dollars. 2 [수가 매우 많음]. ¶네가 참가해서 ~의 대군을 얻은 것 같다 Your participation makes me feel as if I had gained a host of supporters.
● **백만장자** (-長者) a millionaire.

백면서생 (白面書生) a pallid student of books; a callow student.

백모 (伯母) an aunt; the wife of one's father's older brother.

백목련 (白木蓮) [식] a yulan; a Chinese magnolia.

백묵 (白墨) chalk. ⇨˝분필

백문불여일견 (百聞不如一見) Seeing is believing.; A picture is worth a thousand words.; The proof of the pudding is in the eating.; To see for oneself is worth all the books of travel.; There's nothing like seeing for oneself.

백미 (白米) polished [cleaned / faced / hulled] rice.
백미에 뉘 섞이듯 (속담) be very rare.

백미 (白眉) the finest (example) (of); the best [pick] (of); the prince [monarch] (of). ¶영국 소설 중의 ~ one of the best British novels // 장서 중의 ~ the gem of one's library // 저서 중의 ~ the outstanding masterpiece among one's works.

백미러 (*back mirror) a rearview [rear-vision] mirror. ¶~로 보다 watch through the rearview mirror.

백반 (白斑) 1 [흰 반점] a white spot. ¶~이 있는 white-spotted. 2 [천] a facula (*pl.* -lae). 3 [의] [백반증] (피부의) leucoderma; leukoderma; vitiligo; albinism in patches; a piebald skin; a white macula (in the skin); (각막의) leucoma.

백반 (白飯) boiled [cooked] rice.

백반 (白礬) [화] alum.

백발 (白髮) white [gray] hair; snowy [snow-white / hoar(y)] hair. ¶~의 white-haired / white-headed / hoar(y) // with white hair // ~이 되다 (머리가) turn gray / (사람이) grow gray // 그는 ~이 성성한 70노인이다 He bears the snow of seventy years on his head.
● **백발노인** a gray-headed [-haired] old man.

백발백중 (百發百中) 1 (단환이) hitting [making] the bull's-eye one [a] hundred percent. ¶~이다 Every shot told. // 그는 ~의 명사수이다 He [His shot] never misses the mark. / He is an ace marksman. / He is a dead [crack] shot. **백발백중하다** never miss the target [mark]. ¶(총알이) 백발백중했다 Every shot told. // 그의 화살은 백발백중한다 His arrow never misses the target [mark]. 2 [틀리지 않음]. ¶~이다 be infallible // 금주의 일기 예보는 ~이었다 The weather forecasts for this week were all correct [right on target].

백방 (百方) 1 [온갖 방법] various ways; every way. ¶~으로 힘쓰다 make every effort / exert oneself to the utmost // 우리는 ~으로 손을 써서 그의 행방을 찾았다 We tried all [every] possible means to find out where he had gone. / We left no stone unturned in seeking his whereabouts. 2 [여러 방향] every direction; all sides. ¶~으로 사람을 구하다 look all round [all over] for a person.

백배 (百拜) ¶~사례하다 bow one's thanks a hundred times / offer a thousand thanks // ~사죄하다 bow a hundred apologies / make a humble apology. **백배하다** bow a hundred times; bow many times.

백배 (百倍) [비교도 안 될 만큼] beyond [past] comparison; far and away. ¶둘 중에서 이 ~ 낫다 This is far and away the better of the two.

백배하다 (百倍-) gather strength; grow in intensity; become intensified. ¶그는 자기 편을 얻어 용기가 백배했다 He is much more cheerful now that he has found some friends.

백병전 (白兵戰) hand-to-hand fighting; a hand-to-hand fight; a close combat; fighting at close quarters; fighting with swords and bayonets. ¶~을 벌이다 fight hand to hand (with). **백병전하다** fight hand to hand (with).

백부 (伯父) an uncle; one's father's [dad's] older brother; 《문어》 an older paternal uncle.

백분 (白粉) 1 [흰 가루] white powder; flour. 2 [화장용 분] (face) powder.

백분비 (百分比) (a) percentage. ⇨˝백분율

백분율 (百分率) (a) percentage.

백사 (白沙) white sand.
● **백사장** a white sandy plain; a white (sandy) beach.

백사 (百事) all kinds [sorts] of matters [things]; everything.

백산호 (白珊瑚) white coral.

백삼(白蔘) white ginseng.

백색(白色) 1 [흰빛] a white color; white. ¶~의 white / of white color / white-colored. 2 [우익] the white[right] wing.
● **백색 인종** the white race; Caucasians.

백서(白書) a white paper (on); a white book (on). ¶경제 ~ (publish / issue) an economic white paper.

백석(白石) a white stone.

백선(白癬) [백선균에 의한 피부병] a ringworm; [의] the tinea; [머리의] favus.

백선(百選) ¶명곡 ~ a hundred pieces of famous music.

백설(白雪) (white) snow. ¶~로 덮인 산 a snow-capped mountain // ~ 같은 snowy / snow-white / white as snow.

백설기(白-) baekseolgi; steamed rice-cake.

백설탕(白雪糖) white[refined] sugar; castor sugar.

백성(百姓) [인민] the (common) people; [국민] the nation; [민중] the public; the populace. ¶온 ~ all people / an entire people.

백세(百世) [오랜 세대] all ages[generations]; eternity.

백수(百獸) all kinds of animals. ¶~의 왕 the king of beasts // 사자는 ~의 왕이다 The lion is (the) king of beasts.

백수건달(白手乾達) a penniless bum[tramp]; a good-for-nothing; an out-and-out libertine; a debauchee; a ne'er-do-well.

백숙(白熟) meat[fish] boiled in water. ¶영계 ~ chicken boiled with rice.

백신 [접종용 면역 약물] (a) vaccine.

백씨(伯氏) [민중] your[his] eldest brother.

백악(白堊) 1 [백악계의 석회질 암석] chalk; chalkstone. 2 white clay. ⇨백토(白土).
● **백악계**(-系) [지] the Cretaceous system. **백악기**(-紀) [지] the Cretaceous (period). **백악층** chalk bed.

백악관(白堊館) [미국 대통령 관저] the White House.

백안시하다(白眼視-) look coldly on[upon / at] a person; look on[upon] a person with disapproval; that a person coldly; have a prejudiced view (of); affect a detached irony.

백야(白夜) nights with the midnight sun.

백약(百藥) sundry medicines[remedies]; all sorts of medicine. ¶~이 무효다 All medicines prove useless. // 술은 ~의 으뜸이다 Wine is the best of all medicines.

백양(白羊) a white sheep[goat].
● **백양궁** [천] the Ram; Aries.

백양(白楊) [식] a (white) poplar; a white asp [aspen].

백업 [야구] backup; [컴] backup. ¶~을 하다 back up / support.

백여우(白-) 1 [동] a white[silver] fox. 2 [요사스러운 여자] an uncanny[capricious] woman.

백연석(白鉛石) white lead ore; cerusite.

백열(白熱) 1 [높은 온도] white heat; incandescence; white glow. ¶~화하다 become white-hot / be incandescent / glow white. 2 [열정이 최고조에 달함] enthusiasm; the climax(경기 등의). ¶~화한 논쟁[토론] a heated controversy[discussion] // ~화하다 grow[get] excited / (토론 등이) become heated / (영) hot up.
● **백열등** an incandescent; electric lamp[light]; a glow lamp. **백열전** hot fighting; (경기의) a close contest[game]. ¶~을 벌이다 put on a blistering race[game].

백엽상(百葉箱) a box housing for outdoor meteorological instruments.

백옥(白玉) a white gem; a white precious stone.

백운(白雲) a white[woolly / fleecy] cloud.

백운모(白雲母) [광] white[common] mica; muscovite.

백운석(白雲石) [광] dolomite.

백의(白衣) 1 [흰옷] a white robe[dress]; (간호사 등의) a white overall; a white (hospital) frock. ¶~의 in white / ~를 입고 있다 be dressed in white. 2 (포의(布衣)) a scholar without office; a commoner. ¶~종군하다 serve in a war as a commoner. 3 [불] [승려가 아닌 일반인] a layman; a man of the world; (집합적) the laity.

백의의 천사 an angel in white; a ministering angel[nurse]; a white-clad[-robed] nurse.
● **백의민족** the white-clad[-robed] race; Korean people.

백인(白人) a white man; a Caucasian; (속어) a white. ¶~ 여자 a European woman[lady] / a white woman // ~에 의한 지배 white domination (in Africa).
● **백인종** the white race; the whites.

백일(白日) broad daylight; a bright day; the daytime; the light of day. ¶~하에 드러나다 be brought to light / be exposed to the light of day.
● **백일몽** a daydream; a walking dream; a revery. **백일장** a literary writing contest; an essay contest. ¶주부 ~ an essay contest for housewives.

백일(百日) [생후 백 번째가 되는 날] one hundredth day.
● **백일기도** prayer for a hundred days. **백일잔치** a party given to a hundred-day-old baby. **백일천하** a hundred-day reign; a very brief reign.

백일해(百日咳) [의] whooping[hooping] cough; pertussis.

백일홍(百日紅) [식] a zinnia.

백자(白瓷·白磁) baekja; white porcelain.

백작(伯爵) a count; (영) an earl; (프) a comte.
● **백작 부인** a countess; (프) a comtesse.

백장 a butcher. ⇨=백정

백전노장(百戰老將) a veteran; an old timer; an old campaigner.

백전백승(百戰百勝) an ever-victorious record; invincibility. ¶~의 ever-victorious / invincible / unbeaten // ~의 군대 an invincible army. **백전백승하다** win every battle (that is fought); be ever victorious. ¶아군은 백전백승하였다 Our army was unbeaten[victorious in every battle].

백절불굴(百折不屈) ¶~의 정신 an indomitable spirit. **백절불굴하다** indefatigable; unbending; unflinching; indomitable.

백정(白丁) a butcher; (미국 구어) a meat-man. ¶~의 개 a dog catcher[killer].

백정이 버들잎 물고 죽는다(속담) The leopard cannot change its spots.

백조(白鳥) [동] a swan(고니); a cob (swan)(수컷); a pen(암컷); a cygnet(새끼).
● **백조자리** [천] the Swan; Cygnus.

백주에(白晝-) in broad[open] daylight; in

the day time. ¶~ 도둑이 활보하다 Thieves stalk about at noonday.

백중(百中·百衆) the Buddhist All souls' Day(=July 15th of lunar month).

백중(伯仲) 〔맏형과 그다음〕 one's eldest brother and second eldest brother.

백중하다(伯仲−) 〔우열이 없다〕 〔서술적〕 be equal (to); be even (with); be on a par (with); be evenly-matched; be well contested; match (each other). ¶백중한 시합 an evenly balanced game∥그들의 힘은 서로 ~ They are well balanced in strength. / They are equal in strength. ∥양팀의 실력은 백중한 The two teams were perfectly matched.

백지 a white *baduk*(go) stone. ¶~를 쥐다 occupy the superior side of board.

백지(白紙) **1** 〔흰 종이〕 white paper; Korean paper made from mulberry fiber. ¶얼굴이 ~장 같다 look as white as a sheet / look pale. **2** 〔공지(空紙)〕 a blank sheet of paper. ¶~의 blank // ~에 답안을 내다 give [hand] in blank paper // 내 일기는 아직 ~ 그대로이다 The leaves of my diary are still virgin white. // 그의 답안지는 완전히 ~이다 His examination paper is completely blank. **3 a** clean state. ⇨백지상태(⇨백지) ¶~로 돌리다 call off / nullify / cancel / start afresh / start with a clean state / make a fresh start / go (all) over it again.

백지장도 맞들면 낫다(속담) Cooperation makes work easier.; Two heads are better than one.

● **백지상태** a clean state; a mind free from prejudice[preconception]. ¶나는 서양 음악에 대해서는 ~이다 I know nothing about Western music. **백지 수표** a blank check. **백지 위임장** a blank power of attorney; 〔프〕 a carte blanche. ¶~을 주다 give (a person) the carte blanche.

백차(白車) a (police) patrol car; a squad [cruise / prowl] car; 〔미국 구어〕 a cruiser.

백척간두(百尺竿頭) the last[critical] extremity; extremities; the eleventh hour. ¶~에 서다 be in a dire extremity / be driven [reduced] to the last extremity ∥~에서 진일보하다 go a step farther.

백청(白淸) 〔희고 질 좋은 꿀〕 white honey of good[fine] quality.

백출하다(百出−) arise[appear / pop up] in great numbers. ¶그 문제로 의론이 백출했다 The matter became the subject of heated discussion. // 어려운 문제가 백출했다 A variety of difficult problems arose one after another.

백치(白癡·白痴) 〔상태〕 idiocy; imbecility; 〔사람〕 an idiot; an imbecile; a moron. ¶~의〔~와 같은〕 idiotic.

● **백치 미인** a beautiful fool.

백탄(白炭) fine charcoal; charcoal of fine quality.

백태(白苔) 〔의〕 **1** 〔혀의〕 the fur[coat] (on the tongue). ¶~가 끼었다 The tongue is coated. **2** 〔눈의〕 a morbid coating on the eyeball that interferes with vision.

백태(百態) various phases. ¶이 만화는 봉급생활자의 ~를 묘사하고 있다 These comic strips depict white-collar worker in various situations.

백토(白土) white clay[earth]; 〔라〕 terra alba.

백통 nickel; white brass; cupronickel.

● **백통돈** / **백통전** / **백통화** a nickel (coin).

백팔번뇌(百八煩惱) the hundred-and-eight torments of mankind; the 108 passions (a) man is subject to.

백팔십도(百八十度) 〔정반대〕 the exact opposite; 〔정반대로〕 in direct opposition to. ¶~ 전환을 하다 do a complete about-face / make a complete[radical] change / perform a hundred-and-eighty degree turn / reverse one's course[opinion].

백팔 염주(百八念珠) a Buddhist rosary of 108 beads.

백포도주(白葡萄酒) white wine; (라인산의) Rhine wine; hock; (남에스파냐산의) sherry.

백학(白鶴) 〔동〕 a red-crested white crane. ⇨두루미

백합(百合) 〔식〕 a lily. ¶~같이 아름답다 be as fair as lily.

백해(百害) all (sorts of) evils.

백해무익하다(百害無益−) be very harmful; be utterly destructive; do more harm than good. ¶그것은 내게는 ~ It is more injurious than beneficial for me.

백핸드 〔테니스·탁구〕 backhand; a backhand drive. ¶~로 on backhand // 그는 ~를 잘 친다 He has a good backhand.

백혈구(白血球) 〔생〕 a white corpuscle; a leukocyte; a leucocyte. ¶~의 leukocytic.

백혈병(白血病) 〔의〕 leuk(a)emia; leukosis; leucosis.

백형(伯兄) one's eldest brother. ⇨맏형

백호주의(白濠主義) the "White Australia" principle.

백화(白話) colloquial[spoken] Chinese.

● **백화문** written colloquial Chinese. **백화 문학** literature in colloquial Chinese.

백화(百花) all sorts[varieties] of flowers. ¶들에는 ~가 만발해 있다 The field is alive [bright] with all shorts of flowers.

백화점(百貨店) a department store; (영) the stores; an emporium.

백화 현상(白化現象) 〔동〕 albinism.

밴대질 lesbianism; sexual practice between women. **밴대질하다** practice lesbianism.

밴댕이 〔동〕 a large-eyed herring.

밴둥거리다 loaf one's time away. ⇨빈둥거리다

밴드¹ 〔띠·끈〕 the band; a (wrist) strap; 〔머리장식〕 a bandage; 〔혁대〕 a (leather) belt; 〔접착 밴드〕 〔미〕 (a) Band-Aid(상품명); 〔영〕 (a) (sticking) plaster. ¶양복 바지의 ~ the belt rungs of one's trousers // 고무 ~ a rubber band // 헤어 ~ a hairband // ~를 매다 put one's belt around one's waist / wear a belt / use a belt // ~를 죄다〔늦추다〕 tighten [loosen] one's belt // ~를 고쳐 매다 adjust one's belt // ~를 끄르다 undo one's belt.

밴드² 〔악단·악대〕 a (music(al)) band; a band of musicians; a brass band(취주악대). ¶재즈 ~ a jazz band // 행진곡을 연주하고 있는 ~ a band playing a march.

● **밴드마스터** a bandmaster.

밴들거리다 be idle; loaf; loiter; lounge; idle [loaf / laze / fiddle] one's time away; lead an idle life.

밴들밴들 idly; lazily; doing nothing. **밴들밴들하다** be idle. ⇨밴들거리다

밴조 〔음〕 a banjo (*pl.* ~(e)s).

● **밴조 주자** a banjoist.

밴텀급(−級) the bantamweight class.

● 밴텀급 선수 a bantamweight.
밸런스 〔균형〕 balance. ¶~가 잡혀 있다[있지 않다] be well[ill] balanced // ~를 잡다 balance/poise oneself.
밸런타인데이 Saint Valentine's Day(2월 14일).
밸브 a valve. ¶안전 ~ a safety[relief] valve // 배기[흡입] ~ an exhaust[intake] valve // ~를 열다[닫다] open[close] a valve.
● 밸브 장치 valve gear.
뱀 〔동〕 a serpent(구렁이). ¶~ 가죽 (a) snakeskin // ~ 가죽 벨트 a snakeskin belt // ~ 같은 snakelike / snaky / (모양) serpentine // ~의 독 snake venom // ~ 부리는 사람 a snake charmer // ~처럼 구불구불한 강 a serpentine river // ~에 물려 죽다 die from a snake bite / die of the bite of a snake.
뱀딸기 〔식〕 an Indian[mock] strawberry.
뱀자리 〔천〕 the Serpent; the Snake.
뱀장어 (-長魚) 〔동〕 an eel. ¶민물 ~ a freshwater eel.
뱁새 〔동〕 a Korean crow-tit.
뱁새가 황새를 따라가면 다리가 찢어진다(속담) People ruin themselves by trying to ape their betters.; You must cut your coat according to your cloth.
● 뱁새눈 tiny downward-slanted[narrow / slitted] eyes.
뱃가죽 〈속〉 the skin of the belly. ⇨뱃살
뱃고동 a boat whistle.
뱃구레 the abdomen.
뱃길 a (ship's) course; a waterway; a channel(해협); a fairway(항구·강구 등의); 〔항로〕 a sea route; a seaway; a passage. ¶사흘 걸리는 ~ a three days passage[crossing] // ~로 가다 go by ship[water] / take[go on board a] ship (to) // ~의 안전을 빕니다 I wish you a safe passage. / Bon voyage!
뱃노래 a sailor's[boatman's] song; a boating song; a chant(e)y[shanty]; a barcarol(l)e. ¶베니스의 ~ a Venetian gondolier's barcarol(l)e // ~를 부르다 sing a boating song.
뱃놀이 a boating (excursion); (미) a boat ride; yachting(요트의); a row(보트 젓기). 뱃놀이하다 enjoy boating[a boat ride]. ¶뱃놀이하는 사람 a boater // 호수에서 ~ enjoy boating on a lake // 뱃놀이하러 가다 go boating[rowing] / (미) go for a boat ride / go for a row.
뱃놈 〈속〉 a shipowner; a sailor. ⇨뱃사람
뱃대끈 1 〔여자의〕 a drawstring (for a woman's drawers). 2 〔마소의〕 a bellyband; a (saddle) girth; a surcingle; (미) a cinch. ¶~을 조르다 tighten the girth.
뱃머리 the bow; the prow; the head (of a boat). ¶~ 쪽으로 fore / forward // ~부터 가라앉다 sink by the head // ~를 향하다 head (for) // 배는 부두로 ~를 돌렸다 The ship headed for the pier.
뱃멀미 (qualms of) seasickness; nausea; (프) mal de mer. ¶~를 잘하다 be apt to get seasick / be a bad[poor] sailor. 뱃멀미하다 get[become] seasick; feed the fishes(토하다). ¶뱃멀미하는[뱃멀미하지 않는] 사람 a poor[good] sailor // 나는 자주 뱃멀미한다 I often get seasick.
뱃밥 oakum; pledget; ca(u)lking. ¶~을 만들다 pick oakum // ~으로 메우다 ca(u)lk (a seam / a boat) / stop up (a seam) with oakum // 뱃사람은 배를 ~과 타르로 메운다 Sailors calk boats with oakum and tar.
뱃병 (-病) stomach trouble; intestinal upsets. ¶~이 나다 have stomach trouble / have a stomach upset / have a disordered stomach.
뱃사공 (-沙工) a boatman; a skipper; a waterman; the master of a junk; a ferryman(나룻배의).
뱃사람 1 〔선주〕 a shipowner. 2 〔선원〕 a sailor; a seaman; a crewman; a mariner; a seafarer. ¶노련한 ~ an old sailor[salt] // ~의 생활 seafaring life / a sailor's life // ~이 되다 become a sailor / go to sea // ~의 말씨를 쓰다 talk sailor.
뱃삯 〔승선료〕 passage (fare / money); boat fare; 〔도선료〕 ferriage; ferryboat charge; 〔화물 운임〕 freight (rates); 〔용선료〕 charterage. ¶~ 대신 배에서 일하며 미국에 건너가다 work one's passage to America // 1등 ~은 얼마입니까 What is the charge in the first cabin?
뱃살 the skin[flesh] of the belly[abdomen]; abdominal muscle. ¶~을 잡다 hold[shake / burst] one's sides with laughter / have a side-splitting laugh / be convulsed with laughter // ~을 잡아야 할 만큼 우습다 It's so funny you have to hold your sides. // 우리는 모두가 ~을 잡고 웃었다 We all shook[held our sides] with laughter.
뱃소리 a boatman's song; a chanty.
뱃속 〔마음속〕 (a) heart; (a) mind; (an) intention. ¶~을 떠보다 probe[try to find out] (a person's) intention / fathom (another's) thoughts / sound (a person on a matter) // ~을 터놓고 이야기하다 speak frankly / be frank (with a person) / come out frankly (and tell ...) / talk heart to heart (with).
뱃속이 검다 blackhearted; evilhearted; malicious; wicked; crafty; scheming.
뱃심 1 〔버티는 힘〕 push; pertinacity; 〔배짱〕 courage; pluck; brazen effrontery; impudence; mettle; (속어) guts. 2 〔속셈〕 one's inmost thought[idea]; what one has in mind. ¶그의 ~을 모르겠다 I don't know what he has in mind. // 무슨 ~으로 자네가 그런 말을 했나 In[With] what spirit did you say so?
뱃심이 좋다 pushing; pushy; persistent; sticky; strong-willed. ¶뱃심이 좋은 사람 a man of push and go // 이렇게 되면 뱃심 좋게 밀고 나아가는 수밖에 없다 There is no other way than to push forward.
뱃일 work on board (a ship). 뱃일하다 work on board (a ship); work aboard.
뱃장사하다 peddle (small) merchandise with a boat[bumboat].
뱃장수 a bumboat man.
뱃전 the sides[edge] of a boat[ship]; a gunwale; a ship's side the broadside. ¶~을 헛딛다 slip off the gunwale (of a boat) / fall overboard // ~이 기울어진다 A boat tips [lists] to one side.
뱃짐 a (ship's) cargo; a freight; freightage; a lading; load. ¶~을 싣다 take in cargo / load a ship // ~을 부리다 discharge cargo / unload a ship // ~을 풀다 break bulk.
뱅 1 〔한 바퀴 도는 모양〕 round; (미) around. ¶~ 돌다 turn around / wheel about. 2 〔둘러싼 모양〕 (all) round; in a circle. ¶사면이 바다로 ~ 둘러싸인 나라 a country girded by

뱅그레 the sea on all sides. 3 [아찔해지는 모양]. ¶머리가 ~ 돌다 get dizzy[giddy] / one's head swims[spins] / be stunned(얻어맞고).

뱅그레 with a smile. ⇨빙그레

뱅그르르 (turn / skate / glide) around smoothly. ¶~ 돌다 turn round[around] / wheel about / whirl[spin] around // 얼음판 위를 ~ 돌다 skate smoothly in a circle on the ice // 한쪽 발뒤꿈치로 ~ 돌다 spin on one's heel.

뱅글뱅글 [도는 모양] round and round smoothly. ¶소년은 팽이를 ~ 능숙하게 돌렸다 The boy skillfully spun the top.

뱅뱅 round and round. ⇨빙빙

뱅어 [동] a whitebait; an icefish.
● 뱅어포 dried slices of seasoned whitebait.

-뱅이 a person; a fellow; one. ¶가난 ~ a poor man / a have-not / a pauper // 비렁 ~ a beggar / a tramp / a hoho / a mendicant / (미국 구어) panhandler // 주정 ~ a bad drunk / a drunken brawler.

뱅충맞다 clumsy; dull-witted. ⇨빙충맞다

뱅충이 a thick-witted person. ⇨빙충이

뱉다 1 [입 밖으로] spew; spit out; expectorate; salivate. ¶침을 ~ spit (on) / eject saliva / expectorate // 가래를 ~ cough out[bring up] phlegm // 뱉어 내다 spit / spit out // "바보같이!" 하며 그는 뱉어 내듯이 말했다 "Nonsense!" he said disdainfully[he spat at me]. // 그놈한테 나는 침이라도 뱉어 주고 싶었다 I would have spat on[at] him. // 바닥에 침을 뱉지 마시오 (게시) No spitting on the floor. 2 [차지했던 것을 도로 내놓다] disgorge; surrender; give up; spew; spue; vomit. ¶그는 횡령한 돈[100만 원]을 뱉어 놓았다 He disgorged[surrendered] the embezzled money[one million won].

버걱 creaking; squeaking; grating. **버걱하다** creak; squeak; grate.

버겁다 uncontrollable; unmanageable; (서술적) be beyond one's capacity[control]; be too much for (one); be too big[thick / bulky] to handle. ¶이 일은 나에게 ~ This work is beyond my capacity. / I am not equal to the task. // 그는 내게 버거운 사람이다 He is an awkward[ugly] customer to deal with.

버그러뜨리다 1 [빠개다] split; cleave; [벌어지게 하다] loosen; make loose; [못쓰게 만들다] break up[down]; demolish. ¶의자를 ~ break a chair / 자물쇠[문]를 버그러뜨리고 열다 force open a lock[gate]. 2 [일을 틀어지게 하다] upset; spoil; frustrate; break up; rupture. ¶계획을 ~ frustrate[upset] a plan / throw a wet blanket over a project // 혼담을 ~ break up a proposed marriage.

버그러지다 1 [빠개지다] split apart; cleave; [벌어지다] widen; [못쓰게 되다] break; be broken; be demolished. ¶틈이 버그러진다 A split[crack] gets wider. // 마른나무보다 생나무가 잘 버그러진다 Green wood splits more easily than dry. 2 [일이 틀어지다] be upset [frustrated / spoiled]; fall through; be broken off; be ruptured. ¶모든 일이 버그러지기만 했다 Everything went against me. / Nothing came up to my expectations. // 그 혼담은 버그러지고 말았다 The match was ~ break up a proposed marriage.

버그르 (물을) (boil) simmering; (거품이) bubbling; foaming. ¶물이 ~ 끓다 Water simmers. **버그르르하다** simmer; bubble; foam.

버글거리다 boil; bubble up; be crowded (with). ⇨바글거리다

버글버글 boiling (briskly); bubbling; in swarms. ⇨바글바글

버금가다 be in the second place; be second to; come second; rank next to. ¶뉴욕에 버금가는 대도시 the greatest city next[second only] to New York / the largest city after [ranking only after] New York // 작가로서 밀턴은 셰익스피어에 버금간다 As a writer, Milton is placed after Shakespeare.

버금딸림화음 (-和音) a subdominant chord.

버너 a burner. ¶가스 ~ a gas burner // 석유 ~ an oil burner.

버둥거리다 (kick and) struggle; squirm; wriggle; writhe; flounder (in the mud); [말 등이] paw the ground [air] . ¶고통으로 ~ writhe in pain // 살려고 ~ struggle to make a living // 경관의 손에서 빠져나가려고 ~ try to struggle loose[to twist away] from the grip of the policeman // 그는 어떻게든 출세해 보려고 버둥거렸다 He strove hard to rise in the world. // 버둥거리면 버둥거릴수록 밧줄이 살을 파고들었다 The harder I tried[struggled] to break loose, the deeper the rope cut into my flesh. // 아무리 버둥거려도 소용없다 It is no use struggling and wriggling.

버둥질 fluttering one's feet. ⇨발버둥질

버드나무 [식] a willow. ¶늘어진 ~ 가지 long drooping branches of a willow tree.

버드러지다 1 (밖으로) project; protrude; push [jut] out. ¶버드러진 projecting / protruding / protuberant // 버드러진 이 a projecting [prominent / protruding] tooth / a bucktooth. 2 [굳어서 뻣뻣해지다] stiffen; get stiff; become rigid. ¶버드러진 stiff / rigid / stark and stiff.

버들 [식] a willow. ⇨ 버드나무 ¶~ 같은 허리 a slender waist.
● 버들개지 a pussy; a catkin; a cattail.

버들치 [동] Moroco oxycephalus(학명).

버디 [골프] a birdie.

버라이어티 쇼 (영) a variety (show); (미) a vaudeville.

버러지 〈속〉 an insect; a bug. ⇨벌레

버럭 [갑자기] (shout) suddenly; abruptly; (all) of a sudden; outright; on a sudden. ¶~ 화를 내다 be roused to anger / fly into a passion / burst into a passion / explode with rage / burn up / (구어) see red // ~ 소리를 지르다 cry[shout] suddenly // 그는 라디오를 끄라고 소리를 질렀다 "Turn the radio off!" barked he.

버럭버럭 desperately. ⇨바락바락

버력¹ [천벌] Heaven's vengeance; divine punishment [retribution]; curse.
버력(을) 입다 be punished by Heaven; be visited with Heaven's judgment; incur the wrath of God. ¶이 버력 입을 놈 같으니 The deuce[devil] take you! / Go to the devil! / Bad luck to you!

버력² [광] muck; debris. ¶감돌과 ~ ore rock and muck.

버르장머리 〈속〉 (good) manners; etiquette. ⇨버릇²

버르적거리다 writhe; struggle; wriggle; squirm; flounder. ¶아파서 몸을 ~ writhe in a desperate agony / writhe in (the agony) of

//그는 어려운 고비에서 헤어나려고 버르적거렸다 He wriggled out of a difficulty.// 나는 사슬에서 빠져나오려고 버르적거렸다 I struggled to free myself from my bonds.

버르집다 1 [헤집어 펴다] push a dent out; cut open; cut and enlarge; open up; draw apart. ¶상처를 ~ open up a wound (for treatment) / draw apart the lips of a wound // (닭이) 흙을 버르집어 벌레를 찾다 scratch the ground for worms. 2 [숨은 일을 들추어내다] disclose [divulge / let out] (a secret); expose; lay bare; dig up (scandal). 3 [작은 일을 크게 떠벌리다] exaggerate; render more serious; aggravate. ¶일을 버르집어 놓다 make too much of the matter / carry the matter to a foolish extent.

버름하다 1 [틈이 벌어져 있다] slightly [partly] open; loose; creviced; loosely fitted. 2 [마음이 맞지 않아 서먹하다] differing; disagreeing; discordant; at variance (with).

버릇 1 [습관] a (personal) habit [way]; a customary practice; a habitual practice; an acquired tendency; [성벽] a propensity; an idiosyncrasy (체질적인); a characteristic; a peculiarity; a peculiar way. ¶말 ~ one's peculiar way of speaking // 아침 일찍 일어나는 ~ the habit of early rising / 고질적인 ~ an inveterate [a deeply ingrained] habit // 거짓말하는 ~ a tendency to tell lies // 나쁜 ~이 생기다 fall into [get into / acquire] a bad habit / 눈을 깜짝이는 ~이 있다 have a way of blinking // ~이 고쳐지다 be cured of a habit / get out of a habit // ~이 되다 grow into a habit with (one) / (선례가 되다) become a precedent // ~을 들이다 form [cultivate] a habit (of) / be [get] accustomed [used] to (something / doing) // ~을 고치다 (남의) cure (a person) of a habit / get (a person) out of a habit / (자기의) get rid [break oneself] of a habit / overcome a habit // 일단 ~이 들면 고치기 힘들다 Once you get the habit, it will stay with you. // 그에게 돈을 빌려 주면 ~이 되니까 안 빌려 주는 것이 좋다 You'd better not lend him money or it may become a habit. // 나는 밤늦게까지 자지 않는 것이 ~이 되었다 I have fallen into the habit of staying up late at night. // 평소의 ~으로 그는 넥타이를 만지작거리기 시작했다 Out of habit, he began to fumble with his tie. // 퇴근길에 한잔하는 것이 그의 ~이다 He is in the habit of stopping for a drink on the way home from the office. // 또 그의 투덜대는 ~이 시작되었다 He's started on his usual grumbling again. // 그는 가게 물건을 슬쩍하는 ~이 있다 (상습의) He is an inveterate shoplifter. // 그는 자기의 나쁜 ~을 고친 것 같다 He seems to have cured himself of his bad habit. // 그는 연필을 씹는 나쁜 ~을 고쳤다 He broke himself of the bad habit of chewing on his pencil. // 그는 남의 허물을 캐는 ~이 있다 He has a propensity for finding faults with others. 2 [예의] (good) manners; etiquette; breeding; courtesy; propriety; decorum; politeness; civility; behavior; respectful deportment. ¶~ 들이기 teaching manners / (home) discipline // ~을 가르치다 give (a person) lesson in manners [etiquette] / teach (a person) manners // ~이 나쁘다 be ill-mannered [ill-behaved] / be of bad behavior // ~이 없어지다 lapse from good manners / grow impudent [insolent] / be spoilt // 이 아이들은 ~이 없다 This children have no manners. // 그는 부모가 너무 귀여워만 줘서 ~이 없어졌다 He is spoiled by his fond parents.

버릇없다 ill-mannered; ill-behaved; ill-bred; unmannerly; impertinent; rude; mannerless; uncivil; uncourteous; discourteous; impolite; churlish; boorish; (서술적) be badly brought up. ¶버릇없는 아이 a spoilt child / an ill-bred boy // 버릇없는 말을 하다 say a rude thing / make an insulting remark / use abusive language // 그것은 버릇없는 짓이다 It is bad manners [form] to do so. / That isn't nice. **버릇없이** rudely; discourteously; impolitely; impertinently. ¶~ 굴다 behave rudely / be [show oneself] rude (to).

버릇하다 be [get / grow] accustomed [used] to; be habituated to; be in the habit of (doing); form a habit. ¶가 ~ visit frequently / be familiar with // 먹어 ~ be accustomed [used] to eat // 써 ~ be accustomed to use [to the use of] // 일찍 일어나 ~ accustom oneself to early rising / 규칙적인 생활을 해 ~ accustom oneself to a regular life / 밖에 나가 ~ get the habit of going out often / (어린애가) get the desire to be taken out.

버릇다 [파서 헤집어 놓다] scatter; kick [scratch] about; dig open; cut open.

버리다[1] 1 [내던지다] throw [fling / chuck / cast] away; (쓰레기 등을) dump. ¶쓰레기를 ~ dump refuse // 필요 없는 것을 ~ drop [throw] a useless thing into the discard // 한 번 쓰고 ~ use (something) only once and then throw (it) away // 헌신짝처럼 ~ throw away [cast aside] like an old shoe [hat] // 아직 쓸 수 있는 것을 버리지 마라 Don't throw away anything you can still use. // 이 강에 쓰레기를 버리지 말 것 (게시) No dumping of Rubbish in This River. // 나는 물통의 물을 버렸다 I emptied the bucket.
2 [종사하던 직업을 그만두다] give up; abandon; resign; (돌보지 않다) desert; leave; discard; forsake; renounce; turn one's back upon; lay [set] aside. ¶현관에 버려진 갓난아이 a baby left on the doorsteps // 세상을 ~ renounce [forsake] the world / 낡은 생각을 ~ dismiss [discard / scrap] old ideas // 그는 지위 [희망]을 버렸다 He gave up his position [hope]. // 많은 젊은이가 나라를 위하여 목숨을 버렸다 Many young men laid down their lives for their country. // 그는 세상을 버리고 은둔 생활을 했다 He renounced the world and lived in seclusion. // 그 문제는 중대해서 버려둘 수 없다 The problem is too serious to be left unattended to [undealt with]. // 그녀는 남편을 버리고 애인 곁으로 갔다 She left the husband and went to live with her lover.
3 [망치다] spoil; mar; ruin; (해치다) harm; injure; impair; (더럽히다) soil; stain. ¶건강을 ~ injure [ruin / destroy] one's health // 옷을 ~ spoil one's clothes // 매를 아끼면 아이를 버린다 Spare the rod and spoil the child. // 독서로 눈을 버렸다 Reading impaired his sight. // 상처를 동여매는 데 나는 손수건을 여러 장이나 버렸다 In my effort to bind up the wound, I spoiled [ruined] a lot of handkerchiefs.

버리다

4 [제외하다] omit; discard; cut off; cast away. ¶소수 둘째 자리 이하를 ~ omit the figures below the second place of decimals // 백 원 미만의 우수리는 버린다 Any fractional sum (of) less than a hundred won shall be discarded.

버리다² [끝내다] finish; get through; do completely; get (it) done; dispose of (a job). ¶다 써 ~ be used up / be exhausted / spend out // 다 마셔 ~ drink up[off] / drink to the dregs // 그는 지쳐 버렸다 He is tired out. / He is exhausted. // 나는 돈을 다 써 버렸다 I have spent all my money. // 그는 거지 신세가 되어 버렸다 He was reduced to begging for a living. / 1주일 내에 내가 이 책 5권을 다 읽어 버릴 수 있을까 I wonder if I can read these five books in a week. // 다 먹어 버릴 수 없을 많은 음식이 나왔다 There was too much of a feast to eat it all up.

버림받다 be abandoned; be left behind; be forsaken[deserted]; be jilted; be marooned. ¶남편에게 ~ be discarded[deserted / left] by one's husband // 사회에서 ~ be cast out from society // 세상에서 ~ die from the memory of the public // 그는 친구에게 아주 버림받았다 He was the despair of his friends. // 그는 하느님에게 버림받았다 He was lost before God.

버무리 food mixed (with).

버무리다 mix together[up]; dress (vegetables) with (other condiment); compound. ¶나물을 ~ mix[dress] a salad // 김장 속을 ~ mix stuffings for pickled vegetables.

버석 with a rustle. ⇨바삭

버석거리다 rustle; crinkle. ⇨바삭거리다

버석버석 rustlingly. ⇨바삭바삭

버선 a *beoseon*; Korean socks; sweat socks. ¶겹[홑]~ lined[unlined] socks // 꽃~ embroidered socks // 솜~ wadded[padded] socks // 한 켤레 a pair of socks // ~을 벗다[신다] take off[put on] one's socks.
●**버선목** the ankle of a sock. **버선발** one's feet with socks on; stocking feet. ¶그는 ~로 나갔다 He went out in stocking feet.

버섯 a mushroom; a fungus (*pl.* -gi); a toadstool(유독한). ¶독~ a poisonous mushroom // 원폭~ a mushroom cloud in an A-bomb explosion // ~을 따다 gather [pick (up)] mushrooms // ~을 따러 가다 go mushroom gathering / (미) go (out) mushrooming.

버성기다 **1** [틈이 있다] loose-fitting; loose; creviced; loosely fitted. **2** [두 사람 사이가 탐탁하지 않다] estranged; alienated. ¶두 사람 사이가 버성기어졌다 The two became estranged from each other[had a break in their friendship].

버스 a (motor) bus (*pl.* bus(s)es); an autobus; (미) a motor coach. ¶관광~ a sightseeing bus / a rubberneck bus // 장거리 ~ a long distance bus // 통근 ~ a commuter [commuting] bus // 통학 ~ a school bus // ~로 가다 go (to a place) by bus / take a bus (to) / (구어) bus (to) // ~를 놓치다 miss a bus / [비유] miss the bus // ~에 타다 take a bus / take a bus ride // 이 근처에는 ~ 편이 없다 There is no bus service[no bus running] around here. // 그곳까지 ~ 편이 있다 A bus service is available as far as there. / You can get there on the bus[by bus]. // 고장으로 학교에 늦었다 I was late for school on account of the bus breakdown.
●**버스 요금** bus fare. **버스 정류장** a bus stop; a coach station(장거리 버스의). **버스 종점** a bus terminal.

버스러지다 **1** [표면이 벗겨지다] come[fall] off; peel[scale] off; be worn off; [까지다] be grazed[abraded]. ¶페인트칠이 군데군데 버스러져 있다 The paint has peeled[fallen] away. **2** [벗나가다] exceed; be in excess of; go beyond. ¶(정도(正道)에서) ~ stray from the right path // 물건 값이 생각했던 값에서 버스러진다 The price is more than I expected.

버스럭 with a rustle. ⇨바스락

버스트 a bust. ¶그녀의 ~는 36인치다 Her bust measurement is 36 inches. / She has a 36-inch bust.

버썩 (dried up) completely; closely; short; firmly; stubbornly. ⇨바싹 1·2·3·4·6

버저 a buzzer. ¶~를 울리다 buzz // ~를 누르다 press a buzzer.

버적버적 with a sizzling; fretfully. ⇨바작바작

버전 a version.

버젓하다 respectable; decent; stately; fair and square; good. ¶버젓한 직업 a respectable occupation // 버젓한 태도 a stately manner // 버젓한 집안 a respectable family // 그는 그런 일을 하고도 버젓했다 He did it, and yet with a good conscience. // 그는 면허장도 없이 버젓하게 병원을 차리고 있다 He poses as a doctor though without a license. **버젓이** fairly; in the open; openly; overtly; with a good[clear] conscience. ¶~ 말하다 say openly // 도둑은 ~ 앞문으로 들어왔다 The thief entered the house through the main gate in state. // 그 범행은 백주에 ~ 행해졌다 The crime was committed (openly) in broad daylight.

버정이다 walk idly back and forth; stroll [saunter] aimlessly.

버지다 **1** [날붙이에 베어지다] get a shallow cut (from a sharp edge); [긁히다] get [receive] a scratch. ¶칼에 손가락이 ~ cut one's finger with a knife. **2** [찢어지다] fray; be frayed; be worn out; wear out. ¶소매가 버졌다 The cuff was frayed[became threadbare].

버짐 ringworm; pityriasis(진버짐); psoriasis (마른버짐).

버찌 a cherry; a cherry-bob(꼭지가 붙은).

버캐 [찌꺼기·더껑이] an incrustation; (a) crust; (고기 끓일 때의) scum; crystallized substance. ¶소금[오줌] ~ salt[urine] incrustations // 육즙[고기 국물]의 ~를 건지다 skim the broth.

버클 a buckle. ¶구두의 ~ a shoe buckle // 벨트를 ~로 잠그다 buckle a belt.

버킷 a bucket.

버터 butter. ¶~를 바른 빵 bread and butter // 인조~ margarine / oleomargarine // 빵에 ~를 바르다 butter one's bread / spread butter on bread.

버터플라이 수영법(-水泳法) the butterfly (stroke).

버튼 a button.

버티다 **1** [맞서다] resist; oppose; do not give in; stand up to; hold one's ground; hold out [firm]; stand out[fast / firm]; be unyielding; (주장을) insist (on / upon); persist (in). ¶끝까지 ~ persist to the last / hold out to the

end / stand it out / stick to one's own opinion(의견을) / carry one's point(주장을) 굴하지 않고 ~ hold one's ground undauntedly // 떡 버티어 서다 stand in one's way / confront // 그 여성 단체는 임금 인상을 요구하며 굳게 버티었다 The women's group held out[held fast] to the end in its demand for higher wages. // 다시 한번 맞서서 버티어 보십시오 Please make another effort[give it another try]. // 그는 마지막까지 반전론자[평화주의자]로 버티었다 He remained opposed to war[held his own as a pacifist] to the end. // 사복 경찰이 입구에 버티고 있어서 나는 안에 들어갈 수 없었다 I could not get in because plainclothesmen were guarding the door zealously. // 두 씨름꾼은 서로 버티었다 The two wrestler exchanged violent arm thrusts. // 자넨 그렇게 완고하게 버티지 말아야 하네 You shouldn't insist on having your way so obstinately[stubbornly]. // 쌍방이 다 자기 설을 주장하며 버티었다 The two contending parties remained adamant in asserting their own opinions.
2 [견디다] endure; bear up (under); stand up (to); hold (out / on / up); maintain; keep. ¶버티어 나가다 endure through / persevere // 공격에 ~ hold out against an attack // 모든 어려운 일에 버티어 가다 stand all hardships // 더 버티지를 못하다 cannot hold out any longer // 버틸 힘이 없다 lack tenacity // 그들은 증원 부대가 올 때까지 버티었다 They held out[hung on] till reinforcements arrived. // 버티어라 Stick with[to] it! / (구어) Hang in there! / 끝까지 버티어 내겠다 I'll stick it out! // 이만큼의 식량이 있으면 내가 두 달 동안 버틸 수 있을 것이다 This much food will last me two months. // 그 환자는 버티어 내어 위기에서 벗어났다 The patient hung on and came through the crisis. // 하룻밤 버티어 생명을 유지하면 그는 고비를 넘길 것이다 If he lives through the night, he will be out of danger. // 나뭇가지는 눈의 무게에 간신히 버티고 있었다 The branches could hardly bear the weight of the snow. // 우리 팀은 끝까지 버터 마침내 시합에 이겼다 Our team never gave up[(구어) Our team hung in there] and finally won. // 그는 참 잘도 버틴다 How well he sticks to it! // 홍차 한 잔으로 그는 두 시간 버티었다 He lingered[stayed] for (all of) two hours over one cup of tea. // 버틸 대로 버티어 보았지만 나는 어쩔 수 없었다 I failed in spite of all my stubborn efforts.
3 [괴다] prop (up); bolster [shore] up; support (a thing) with a prop. ¶기둥으로 ~ support (a wall) with a post // 바지랑대로 빨랫줄을 ~ prop the clothesline with a pole // 막대기로 나무를 ~ prop up a plant with a stick // 경첩이 빠진 문을 우리는 막대기로 버티었다 We propped up[supported] the door which had come off its hinges with a stick.

버팀목(-木) a prop; a stay; a strut; a support. ¶~으로 받치다 prop (up) (a pillar) / support (a wall) / stick(식물에) // ~으로 나무를 버티다 prop up the tree with a wooden support.

버팅 [권투] a butt; butting.
벅벅 **1** [긁는 소리] (grate / rasp / scrape) hard [roughly / vigorously / with a vengeance]. **2** [찢는 소리] with a sound as of tearing cloth to pieces; ripping up; shredding. **3** [짧게 깎은 모양] close; short.

벅적거리다 bustle; be crowded; be thronged; throng. ¶거리는 몹시 벅적거렸다 The street was full of bustle. // 그 백화점은 손님들로 벅적거렸다 The department store was crowded with customers.

벅적벅적 in a bustle; bustlingly; uproariously; tumultuously. **벅적벅적하다** bustle. ⇨ 벅적거리다

벅차다 1 [힘에 겹다] beyond one's power [capacity]; above one's ability; too much for (one). ¶벅찬 일 work beyond[that surpasses] one's power / a stiff[formidable] task // 그는 내게 ~ He is too much for me. // 나 혼자서는 ~ I cannot manage it alone. // 이것은 내게 ~ This is more than I can handle. / This is beyond[too much for] me. // 장난꾸러기 아이들은 선생에게 벅찼다 The teacher was not able to control the mischievous boys. // 그 일은 내게는 너무 ~ The job is too hard[difficult / much] for me.
2 [넘칠 듯이 가득하다] full; overflowing. ¶나는 가슴이 벅차서 말도 나오지 않았다 My heart was too full for words. // 나는 기쁨으로 가슴이 벅찼다 My heart was overflowing with joy.

번(番) **1** [당번] duty. ¶돈[난] ~ on[off] duty // ~을 서다 keep a watch / be on a night watch.
2 [횟수] a time. ¶두 ~ twice / two times // 두세 ~ two or three times // 세 ~ three times / (문어) thrice // 대여섯 ~ five or six times // 한 ~ 더 once more[again] // 여러 ~ many times / many a time // 다시 한 ~ once more[again] / (구어) one more time // 첫[두] ~째 the first[second] // 두 ~째 결혼 one's second marriage // 두 ~에[2회째] for the second time / [또다시] for a second time // 한 해[달]에 두 ~ 나오는 잡지 a semiannual [semimonthly] magazine // 그녀는 두 ~ 비명을 질렀다 She gave two screams. // She screamed twice. // 두 ~째는 그가 성공했다 On the second try he was successful. // 그가 책을 낸 것이 이것이 두 ~째다 This is the second time that he has published a book. / This is the second book he has published. // 복어요리를 먹은 것은 이것이 두 ~째다 This is the second time I have eaten globefish. // 그는 두 ~ 상을 탔다[죄를 범했다] He is a two-time prizewinner[offender]. // 이런 기회는 두 ~ 다시 오지 않는다 You'll never have such a good chance again. / This is a golden opportunity. // 이 장미는 한 해에 두 ~ 꽃이 핀다 These roses bloom twice a year. // 정원의 철쭉은 두 ~째 꽃이 피고 있다 The azaleas in our garden are blooming for the second time this year. // 두 ~ 다시 오지 않도록 필요한 서류를 전부 가지고 오시오 Bring all the necessary documents so that you will not have to come again. // 우리는 몇 ~이나 항의했다 We protested again and again. // 거기에는 몇 ~ 갔느냐 How many times have you been there? // 몇 ~ 말해야 알아듣겠나 How many times do I have to tell you (before you understand)? // 그 시를 외울 때까지 몇 ~이고 읽어라 Read the poem again and again until you know it by heart.
3 [번호] a number(약어 No.). ¶1~ 타자 [야구] the leadoff batter[man] // 시벨리우스의 작품 1~의 2 Sibelius opus 1, No. 2 // 번호표

번갈아

1~을 가진 사람은 앞으로 나오시오 Whoever has ticket No.1, please step forward.∥내 등록 번호는 824~이다 My registration number is No. 824.∥"댁의 전화번호는 몇 이죠?" "230의 5211~입니다." "What is your telephone number?" "230-5211."(▶ two three oh[zero], five two one one 이라고 읽음) ∥마지막 열차는 2~ 홈에서 출발합니다 The last train will start from platform No. 2.

번을 갈다 relieve (a person); alternate (with another).

번을 들다 be[go] on duty[watch]; be on shift(교대로로).

번갈아(番) alternately; by turns; in turn; by spells; in rotation (with). ¶~ 하다 take by spell / take spell and spell∥~ 근무하다 do duty by turns∥~ 일하다 work in shifts ∥~ 감시하다 keep watch by turns∥통증과 구토가 ~ 일어났다 Pain alternated with nausea.∥자매는 ~ 환자를 간호했다 The sisters nursed the patient by turns.∥그들은 여덟 시간마다 ~ 일한다 They work in eight-hour shifts.∥그들은 나를 ~ 찾아왔다 They came to see me by turns.

번갈아들다(番—) alternate; take turns.

번개 (a flash of) lightning. ¶~가 쳤다 There was a flash of lightning. / ~가 번쩍인다 Lightning flashes.∥~ 같은 솜씨 a lightning trick∥~같이 like (a flash of) lightning / in a flash / at[with] lightning speed / as quick [fast] as lightning∥그 생각이 ~같이 마음에 떠올랐다 The thought flashed across [into] my mind.

번개가 잦으면 천둥을 한다(속담) Coming events cast their shadows before.

번갯불 lightning; a flash[streak] of lightning. ¶~이 번쩍했다 Lightning is flashing.

번갯불에 콩 볶아 먹겠다(속담) be quick [nimble] in action.

번거롭다 **1** [복잡하다] complicate; complex; intricate; [어수선하다] entangled; confused; [귀찮다] troublesome; [성가시다] annoying; cumbersome. ¶번거로운 규칙 vexatious rules∥대도시의 번거로운 생활 the complex life of a great city∥번거로운 절차 red-tape formalities∥법률상의 번거로운 절차 the cumbersome processes of the law∥사전을 찾아보는 번거로움을 싫어하다 spare oneself the trouble of consulting a dictionary∥외국으로 송금하는 일은 참 ~ It's troublesome [You have to go to a lot of trouble] to send money abroad.∥그것은 일을 더욱 번거롭게 만들 것이다 That would only complicate matters.
2 [수선스럽다] noisy; boisterous; turbulent; clamorous; tumultuous.

번뇌(煩惱) worldly desires[passions]; affliction; anguish; agony; pangs; [불] evil passions; earthly desires[passions]; lusts; carnal desires. ¶~를 씻다 rarefy one's earthly desires∥~에 시달리다 be harassed by passions∥아무리 해도 ~를 떨쳐 버릴 수가 없다 The earthly passions would return each time they are driven away. **번뇌하다** agonize oneself; be in anguish; be harassed by worldly passions.

번다하다(煩多—) troublesome; onerous; vexatious. **번다히** onerously; vexatiously.

번데기 a pupa (*pl.* -pae, ~s); a chrysalis (*pl.* -lises, -lides). ¶~의 pupal∥~가 되다 become a pupa / pupate∥이 벌레는 지금 ~ 시기[상태]에 있다 This insect is in the pupal stage now.

번드럽다 smooth and shiny; slick. ⇨반드럽다

번드르르 smoothly. ⇨반드르르

번득 with a flash. ¶그들이 자객이 아닌가 하는 의심이 그의 머리에 ~ 들었다 The suspicion flashed across him[his mind] that they might be assassins. **번득하다** flash; scintillate. ⇨번득이다

번득거리다 flash; flicker; glitter. ¶저 멀리 등댓불이 번득거리고 있었다 A lighthouse was flashing in the distance.

번득이다 (번개 등이) flash; fulgurate; (빛이) glitter; (재치 등이) scintillate; flash; sparkle. ¶그녀의 말에는 지성의 번득임이 있었다 A gleam of intelligence was evident in what she said.∥그는 재기가 번득이는 사람이다 He is a brilliant person[a man scintillating with wit].

번들거리다 shine; be shrewd; idle. ⇨반들거리다

번들번들 smoothly; shrewdly. ⇨반들반들

번듯하다 straight; flawless; comely. ⇨반듯하다

번뜩 with a flash. ⇨번득

번론(煩論) troublesome[vexing / complicated] arguments.

번문욕례(繁文縟禮) red tape; red-tapism; officialism; circumlocution; bureaucracy; an inefficient way of doing things.

번민(煩悶) [걱정] worry; [고민] anguish; agony; suffering(s); (an) affliction. ¶~을 잊으려고 술을 마셨다 I took drinking to drown my agony[mental anguish].∥그는 일에 대한 ~을 나에게 털어놓았다 He confided his anxiety[worries] about his job to me. **번민하다** be worried[troubled]; worry[fret] oneself (about); be troubled in mind. ¶그는 그것 때문에 번민한다 It causes him mental anguish.∥그는 사업의 실패로 번민하고 있다 He is shattered by[is in anguish over] the failure of his business.

번번이(番番—) each[every] time; each occasion; whenever; as often as. ¶서울에 올 때마다 ~ every time I come to Seoul∥~ 폐를 끼쳐 죄송합니다 I am sorry to trouble you so often[frequently].∥몇 차례 해 보았지만 실패했다 I made several attempts and failed as many times.

번번하다 smooth; comely; decent. ⇨반반하다

번복하다(飜覆—·翻覆—) change; turn; reverse; upset. ¶그는 앞서 한 발언을 번복했다 He changed his former opinion. / He ate [went back on / took back] his words.∥범인은 자백을 번복했다 The criminal reversed [repudiated] his former confession.

번분수(繁分數) [수] a compound fraction.

번서다(番—) go[be] on duty[watch]; stand guard[watch].

번성(蕃盛·繁盛) (자손의) prosperity; thrift; abundance; (수목 등의) luxuriance of growth; exuberancy. **번성하다** flourish; prosper; (초목이) grow wild[vigorously / rank]; thrive; luxuriate; gad. ¶번성한 thick / luxuriant / exuberant (foliage) / rampant [rank] (weeds)∥집안이 ~ have a prosperous[thriving] family.

번수(番手) [실의 굵기] (yarn) count. ¶20~의 면사 No. 20 count cotton yarn.

번식(繁殖·蕃殖) propagation; breeding; reproduction; multiplication; increase(증식); [배양] culture. ¶박테리아의 ~ the propagation of bacteria // 세균의 ~ the propagation of germs // 인공 ~ artificial fecundation [spawning]. **번식하다** propagate [reproduce] itself; breed; multiply; proliferate(동물이); increase; cultivate. ¶소나무는 씨로 번식한다 Pine trees propagate by seed.
● **번식기** a breeding season. **번식력** propagation power. ¶~이 왕성하다 be prolific. **번식률** a breeding coefficient.

번안(翻案) [작품을 본국에 맞게 고침] an adaptation. ¶이것은 「리어 왕」의 ~이다 This is an adaptation of King Lear. // 그 희곡은 다른 소설로부터의 ~이다 That play is an adaptation from another novel. **번안하다** adapt. →¶그 소설은 작가 자신에 의해 무대용으로 번안되었다 The novel was adapted for the stage by the novelist himself.
● **번안 소설** an adapted story.

번역(翻譯·飜譯) (a) translation; rendering; a version. ¶원문에 충실한 ~ a translation faithful to the original // 명쾌한 ~ a lucid translation // 서투른 ~ a poor translation // 그는 ~으로 생활한다 He makes a living by doing translations. // 그는 ~을 잘한다[잘하지 못한다] He is a good[poor] translator. // 이 ~은 잘됐다[서투르다] This is a good[bad/poor] translation. // 이것은 ~ 잘못됐다[잘못된 ~이다] This is mistranslated[(a) mistranslation]. // 나는 포(E.A. Poe)를 ~으로 읽었다 I read Poe in translation. // 시의 ~은 어렵다 Poetry does not translate easily. // 본서의 ~ 복제(複製)를 불허함 [판권 표시] "All rights of translation of this book are reserved." **번역하다** translate (into); put (into); render (into); turn into; (암호를) decipher; decode. ¶영어로 ~ translate [render] (Korean) into English // 잘못 ~ mistranslate // 이 영문을 한국어로 번역할 수 있습니까 Can you translate[put] these English sentences into Korean? // 이 말은 잘 번역할 수 없다 This word does not translate well. // 이 책은 유명한 프랑스의 소설을 영어로 번역한 것입니다 This book is an English translation[version] of a famous French novel. // 다음 우리말을 영문으로 번역하라 Translate [Put] the following Korean into English. →¶그의 작품은 현대 작가 가운데서 가장 많이 번역되어 있다 He is the most translated of modern writers.
● **번역가 / 번역자** a translator. **번역권** the right to translate; translation rights. ¶~을 얻다[갖고 있다] secure[be given] translation rights. **번역료** a charge[fee] for translation. **번역물 / 번역판** a translation; a (Korean) version.

번영(繁榮) prosperity; flourish. ¶~의 prosperous / flourishing / thriving // 국가의 ~ the prosperity of nation / national prosperity // 이 도시에서는 ~의 자취는 찾아볼 수 없다 This town retains no trace of its past prosperity. **번영하다** prosper (▶ 특히 금전적으로); thrive; flourish. ¶번영하는 prosperous / flourishing / thriving // 그 나라는 더욱더 번영했다 The country became more and more prosperous. // 악인은 망하고 선인은 번영한다 The wicked fall and the good prosper.

번잡(煩雜) [번거로움] troublesomeness; [복잡함] complexity; complicatedness; intricacy; [혼잡] confusion. **번잡하다** troublesome; complicated; complex; intricate; crowded; confused. ¶번잡한 형식 complicated formalities // 번잡한 거리 a thronged[crowded] street.

번족(蕃族·繁族) [번성한 집안] a prosperous [thriving] family.

번주그레하다 rather good[nice] in appearance.

번죽거리다 say something spiteful; make sarcastic[cynical] remarks; say something to hurt another's feeling; talk[behave] insidiously[snakily]; act craftily[trickily].

번지(番地) a house[lot / street] number; the number (of an address). ¶같은 ~에 살다 live at the same number // 댁은 몇 ~입니까 What is the street number of your house? // 이 편지는 ~가 틀렸다 This letter is wrongly addressed.
● **번지수** ¶나에 대한 그의 공격은 ~가 틀렸다 His attack on me was misdirected[out of place].

번지다 1 (잉크 등이) spread; run; blot. ¶빨아도 번지지 않는 물감 dyes that do not run in washing // 이 종이에는 잉크가 번진다 Ink blurs on this paper. // 잉크가 번져서 읽을 수 없는 글자가 있다 Some of the letters are blurred and illegible. // 잉크가 번졌다 The ink has run[spread]. // 편지에는 잉크가 번져 있었다 The ink was blurred in the letter.
2 (질병 등이) spread; prevail; diffuse; be prevalent. ¶독이 온몸에 번졌다 The poison has passed into his system. // 홍역이 이웃 마을로 번졌다 Measles spread to a neighboring village.
3 (불·전쟁 등이) spread; expand; become serious. ¶화재는 이웃 동네로 번졌다 The fire spread to the neighboring town. // 우리는 전쟁의 불길이 이 이상 더 번지기를 원치 않는다 We seek no wide[no escalation of] war.
4 (소문 등이) get about[abroad / around]; go the rounds. ¶그 소문은 날이 갈수록 번져 가고 있다 The rumor is spreading[getting abroad] every day.

번지르르 1 [미끄럽고 윤이 나는 모양] glossily; sleekly; lustrously; lubricously. **번지르르하다** greasy and smooth; slippery; lubricous; glossy; sleek; lustrous. 2 [겉만 그럴듯한 모양] deceptively; showily; tawdrily; gaudily. **번지르르하다** deceptive; showy; tawdry; gaudy; flashy.

번지 점프 a bungee jump; bungee jumping. ¶~를 하다 do[make] a bungee jump.

번질거리다 be slippery; be idle. ⇨**반질거리다**

번질번질 1 [매끈하게] sleekly; glossily; smoothly; in an oily[slippery] fashion. **번질하다** sleek; glossy; smooth; slippery. 2 [게으르게] idly; lazily. **번질번질하다** idle; lazy.

번쩍 1 [빛나는 모양] with a flash. ¶그의 눈이 ~ 빛났다 His eyes glittered. **번쩍하다** give out a flash; flash. ¶눈에서 불이 ~ see stars. 2 (감관·의식에 들어옴) suddenly; with a start; strongly. ¶눈이 ~ 뜨이는 (미국 구어) eye-catching // 귀가 ~ 뜨이다 strike[catch] one's ears // 눈에 ~ 뜨이다 catch[strike] one's eye / be attractive[conspicuous] // 정신

이 ― 들다 come to oneself with a start. **3** [들어 올리는 모양] (수월하게) lightly; easily; without (any) effort; (높이) aloft; high. ¶두 손을 ~ 들고 with one's hands high up / (stand) with upraised hands // 나는 큰 돌을 ~ 들어 올렸다 I lifted a huge rock with agility.

번쩍거리다 (보석·샹들리에 등이) glitter; glisten(▶ glitter는 금속적인 것의, glisten은 젖은 것의 반짝임을 나타내는 경우가 많음); twinkle(별 등); (섬광) glare; flash; sparkle(보석 등). ¶번쩍거리게 닦은 구두 well-polished shoes // 잎사귀 위의 물방울이 햇빛에 번쩍거리고 있었다 The drops of water on the leaves were shining[sparkling / glistening] in the sun. // 그녀의 눈에서 눈물이 번쩍거렸다 Tears glistened in her eyes. // 잘 닦은 구리 주전자가 번쩍거리고 있었다 The well-polished copper kettle was glistening[sparkling].

번쩍번쩍 1 [빛나는 모양] with a flash. **번쩍번쩍하다** (섬광이) flash in rapid succession; (반사광이) glitter; shine; sparkle. ¶번쩍번쩍하는 보석 a glittering[dazzling] jewel // 번개가 번쩍번쩍했다 Lightning played in the sky. / Lightning flashed in the sky in rapid succession. **2** [들어 올리는 모양] lightly; easily; aloft; high. ¶그는 쌀가마니를 ~ 들어 올렸다 He lifted up rice sacks easily[lightly] in rapid succession.

번쩍이다 glitter; glisten. ⇨″반짝이다

번차례(番次例) an order; a turn. ¶~로 alternately / by turns / in turn / turn and turn about // ~를 **기다리다** wait for [await] one's turn // ~로 파수 보다 keep watch by turns.

번창(繁昌) prosperity; flourish; success. **번창하다** prosper; flourish; thrive; succeed (in / as); be successful; do well. ¶번창하게 하다 make prosperous // 사업이 크게 ~ (상인이) drive a prosperous[thriving] trade / (의사 등이) have[enjoy] a large practice // 철도의 부설로 역에 인접한 상가가 번창했다 The construction of a railroad brought prosperous to the adjoining shopping districts. // 저 가게는 번창하고 있다 That store has a lot of customers. / That store is doing a good business. / 이 지방에서는 제철업이 번창하고 있다 The iron industry is prospering[doing very well] in this district.

번철(燔鐵) (전(煎) 등을 부치는) a frying pan; (요리용의) a frypan; a salamander; (과자 굽는) a griddle; (오븐에 넣는) a shallow pan; a (baking) sheet.

번트 (야구) a bunt; bunting. ¶드래그 ~ a drag bunt // 희생 ~ a sacrifice bunt // 자세를 취하다 pose to bunt // 다음 타자는 ~로 주자를 진루시켰다 The next batter advanced the runner with a bunt. **번트하다** bunt (the ball). ¶2루 쪽에 ~ bunt down the second-base line.

●**번트 히트** a bunt hit.

번호(番號) a number. ¶수험 ~ an examinee's (seat) number // 자동 ~ 날인기 an automatic numbering machine // 등록 ~ a registration number // 순서대로 in numerical order // ~가 낮은[높은] low-[high-]numbered // ~가 없는 unnumbered / numberless // ~를 붙이다 number / give a number // ~를 매기다[격다] number / assign[give] a number (to) // (전화)~를 돌리다 dial a number // ~가 틀렸습니다 (You've got the) wrong number. // ~ [점호의 구령] Number[Count] off!

●**번호판** a license[number] plate; a registration number plate. **번호표** a number ticket[check].

번화가(繁華街) [상점가] business[shopping] quarters; [붐비는 곳] the busiest quarters; a bustling place; [환락가] an amusement quarter; downtown; the downtown area.

번화하다(繁華-) prosperous; flourishing; thriving (town); bustling (street); busy. ¶번화한 거리 a thriving town // 번화한 마을 a lively[busy] town // 번화해지다 prosper / thrive // 이 근처는 ~ The traffic is busy around here.

벗가다 go astray[wild]; deviate[swerve / go away] from the right path; digress. ¶이 나이 또래의 소년은 벗가기 쉽다 A boy at this age is apt to go astray.

벋나다 grow outward; stretch out.

벋다[1] protruding (tooth); protrudent; projecting. ¶벋은 이 a protruding tooth.

벋다[2] spread; stretch. ⇨″뻗다[1]

벋대다 hold out; oppose. ⇨″뻗대다

벋디디다 (힘주어 디디다) stand firmly; [내어 디디다] step out of bounds. ¶그는 두 발을 벋디디고 연설을 시작했다 He stood squarely on his two feet and started speaking.

벋정다리 a stiff leg. ⇨″뻗정다리

벌[1] [들] a field; the green(초원); [평야] a plain; the plains; (미) a prairie(대초원); (영) a moor. ¶황량한 ~ a wilderness // 언덕에 둘러싸인 ~ a hill-girt plain / a plain girded by [girt with] the hill.

벌[2] (짝) a set (of cups); a pair (of); a suit (of clothes). ¶옷 2~ two suits / (여성의) two dresses // 찻단[식기] 한 ~ a tea[dinner] set // 골프 도구 한 ~ a golf set / a set of golf clubs // 상하 한 ~의 옷 a suit of clothes // 세 가지 한 ~의 옷 a three piece suit // 한 ~의 찻그릇 a set of tea things / a tea service // 이 유리컵은 6개가 한 ~입니다 These six glasses make a set. // 나는 입고 나갈 만한 옷 한 ~이 없다 I haven't got[don't have] any clothes fit to go out in.

벌[3] [동] [꿀벌] a (honey) bee; [참벌] a wasp; [말벌] a hornet; [땅벌] a ground wasp; a bumblebee. ¶~의 침 a bee's sting // ~에 쏘이다 be stung by a wasp[bee] // ~들이 윙윙거린다 Bees hum[buzz].

●**벌 떼** a swarm of bees. ¶~ 같은 swarms [great numbers] of (insects) / multitudinous / multitudes of // ~같이 밀어닥치다 come on in swarms[in great force] / surge (round).

벌(罰) (a) punishment; penalty; (문어) chastisement; [천벌] divine punishment. ¶가벼운[무거운] ~ a light[heavy] punishment // ~을 주다[과하다] inflict punishment [a penalty] (on) / impose[amerce] a penalty (upon) / deal[mete] out punishment (to) // ~을 모면하다 escape punishment / go scot-free[unpunished] // ~을 달게 받다 submit to punishment // ~을 받지 않고 넘어가다 escape punishment / go unpunished / go scot-free / get away with it // 그런 일을 하면 ~을 받는다 Heaven will punish for it. // 그는 강도죄로 (금고형의) ~을 받았다 He was punished for robbery (by imprisonment). //

탐관오리에게 ~을 받게 하자 Let's bring the corrupt officials to justice.//어머니는 ~을 주기 위해 그에게 아침 식사를 주지 않았다 The mother made him go without breakfast as a lesson[to teach him a lesson].//우리는 개구쟁이 소년들에게 따끔한 ~을 주었다 We inflicted severe punishment on the mischievous boys. / The mischievous boys were severely punished.//그런 짓을 하면 (반드시) ~을 받는다 You will pay dearly for it. / You will suffer for it. / You cannot do such a thing and get away with it[with impunity].

벌거벗기다 strip (a person) bare[to the skin]; strip (a person) (down) naked; denude; (죄다 뺏기) strip[rob] (a person) of all he has. ¶어린아이를 ~ undress a young child//산을 ~ denude a hill / deforest a mountain.

벌거벗다 strip oneself of all one's clothes; strip oneself bare[stark-naked]; take off one's clothes; undress. ¶벌거벗은 산 a bare [bald] mountain[hill] // 벌거벗고 with nothing on / stark-naked / in the nude / in one's bare skin / (구어) in the altogether / 벌거벗고 헤엄치기[헤엄치다] skinny-dip // 겨울 산은 벌거벗은 모습이었다 The winter mountain was completely bare.//나 벌거벗고 있어 I'm naked. / I'm in the raw. / I'm in my birthday suit(▶ 익살스러운 표현).

벌거숭이 1 [알몸뚱이] a naked body; a nude. ¶~의 naked / bare / unclothed / undressed / nude // ~가 되다 (스스로) become naked / strip to the skin / strip oneself naked / (남에게 당하여) be stripped naked // ~로 만들다 unclothe / divest / uncover / denude / strip (a person) naked. **2** [흙이 드러나 보일 만큼 나무가 없는 산]. ¶그 산은 ~다 The hill is bald[is stripped of all vegetation]. **3** [빈털터리] a penniless person. ¶그녀는 노름을 하여 ~가 되었다 She gambled away all her fortune.
● **벌거숭이산** a bald[bare] mountain.

벌겋다 red; crimsom. ⇨"뻘겋다
벌게지다 turn red; redden. ⇨"뻘게지다
벌그스레하다 reddish. ⇨"벌그스름하다
벌그스름하다 reddish.

벌금(罰金) a (monetary) penalty; (위약금) a forfeit; a penalty. ¶10만 원 이하의 ~ a fine not exceeding a hundred thousand won // ~을 과해야 할 finable / punishable with[by] a fine // ~을 **과하다** fine (a person) / punish (a person) with a fine / impose [inflict] a fine on (a person) // ~으로 **때우다** get off[be let off] with a fine // ~을 **물다** pay a fine / pay one's penalty[forfeit] // ~을 **면제하다** remit a fine // 그것을 행하는 자는 누구든지 ~에 처해진다 Anyone doing that is liable to a fine.
● **벌금형** a monetary penalty; [법] amercement.

벌꺽 1 [갑자기 성내거나 힘쓰는 모양] all of a sudden; in a sudden outburst; with a burst. ¶~ 성내다 fall[get / fly] into a passion / flare up (in anger). **2** [소동이 나는 모양] topsy-turvy; in a great bustle; in a turmoil [hubbub / mess]; in utter confusion; pell-mell; (미국 구어) every which way.

벌꿀 honey; mel(l)(약용의).
벌끈 in hot blood. ⇨"발끈
벌다[1] [틈 등이 생기다] get wider; spread. ¶사이가 벌었다 The crack spreads[got worse]. **2** [맞닿은 자리가 벌어지다] split [burst] open. ¶밤송이가 벌었다 A chestnut burst open.

벌다[2] **1** [돈을 얻다] make[earn / gain / (구어) clean up] (money); find one's account (in); cash in (on); come off a gainer; [이익을 얻다] profit (by); make[get / obtain / realize / derive] a profit (from). ¶에서 번 돈 hard-earned money // 생활비를 ~ earn[make] one's living // 머리를 써서 돈을 ~ coin one's brains // 그녀는 한 달에 80만 원 번다 She makes[earns] 800,000 won a month. // 그는 경량 렌즈를 고안하여 큰돈을 벌었다 He made a fortune by inventing lightweight lenses. // 그는 그 거래에서 큰돈을 벌었다 He made a large profit on the deal. // 나는 역까지 걸어가 600원 벌었다 I saved 600 won by walking to the station. // 이 장사를 하면 떼돈을 벌 수 있다 The money just rolls in this business. **2** [자초하다] bring[draw] upon (oneself); incur; court; invite. ¶매를 ~ incur[invite] whipping // 욕을 ~ bring slander upon oneself.

벌다[3] [몸피가 가로퍼지다] be too big (for something to hold).

벌떡 [갑자기 일어서는 모양] suddenly; with a jerk[start]; quickly; rashly; abruptly; [자빠지는 모양] on one's back; with the face upward; flat; supinely. ¶~ 일어서다 spring to one's feet / get up with a jump // ~ 자빠지다 fall (flat) on one's back // 의자에서 ~ 일어서다 jump up from one's chair // "불이야!" 하는 소리에 모두 ~ 일어났다 At the cry of "Fire!" everyone sprang[leaped] to his feet.

벌떡거리다 1 (심장 등이) go pit-a-pat; palpitate; throb; thump; pound; beat. ¶벌떡거리는 가슴 a beating[palpitating] heart // 장시간의 등산으로 가슴이 벌떡거렸다 The long climb made my heart throb. **2** [들이마시다] gulp down; quaff; guzzle; swig; swill. ¶물을 벌떡거리며 마시다 gulp down a glass of water.

벌떡벌떡 1 [심장 등이 뛰는 모양] pit-a-pat.
벌떡벌떡하다 go pit-a-pat. ⇨"벌떡거리다1 **2** [들이마시는 모양]. ¶~ 마시다 quaff / take draughts (of) / swill / swig / guzzle / drink heavily[in large draughts] // 술을 ~ 마시다 swig[swill] wine / (영) knock back wine // 물을 ~ 마시다 gulp water down / [단숨에] drink a glassful of water at one draft [draught](▶ draft는 (미), draught는 (영)) // 그 사나이는 맥주를 ~ 마셨다 The man really guzzled (down) the beer. **벌떡벌떡하다** gulp down. ⇨"벌떡거리다2

벌렁 on one's back. ¶~ 드러눕다 lie down on one's back / lie face up // 그는 해변에 ~ 누웠다 He threw himself down on the beach. // 그는 집에 돌아오자마자 ~ 누웠다 He flopped down on the bed as soon as he came home.

벌렁거리다 [가볍고도 재빠르게 움직이다] behave lightly; act nimbly; move agilely [smartly / briskly]; be smart[quick] in action.

벌렁벌렁 [민첩히] nimbly; agilely; quickly; smartly; briskly. **벌렁벌렁하다** behave lightly; act nimbly. ⇨"벌렁거리다

벌렁코 a flat nose with flared nostrils; a flaring[snub] nose.

벌레 [곤충] an insect; a bug; a grub[ground

벌룩거리다

beetle] (땅벌레); a beetle (딱정벌레 등); a cricket (여치 등); a moth (나방 등); (송충이 등) a caterpillar; (구더기 등) a worm; [해충] vermin (집합적); [유충] a larva (pl. -vae). ¶우는 ~ a singing insect∥우는 소리 the singing [chirping] of insects∥~ 먹은 worm-[moth-]eaten / mothy∥~ 먹은 이 a decayed [carious] tooth∥~ 먹은 밤 a worm-eaten [wormy] chestnut∥~에 물리다[쐬다] be bitten [stung] by an insect∥~가 꾀다 (초목에) be infested with (noxious) insects [vermin] / become verminous / suffer from an insect pest (벼 등에)∥~에 잘 물리다 be stung on the arm∥벼에 ~가 끓는다 The rice-plant is infested with noxious insects.∥이런 종류의 과일에는 ~가 잘 꾄다 This kind of fruit often becomes wormy. / Worms often get into this kind of fruit.

벌룩거리다 1 quiver; palpitate; inflate and deflate alternately. ¶코를 ~ quiver [twitch] one's nostrils∥코가 벌룩거린다 My nostrils quiver. 2 [놀며 다니다] idle away one's time.

벌룩벌룩 quivering; palpitating; inflating and deflating alternately. **벌룩벌룩하다** quiver; idle away one's time. ⇨벌룩거리다

벌름거리다 swell and subside alternately; quiver.

벌름하다 partly open; half-open [-opened]. ¶입을 벌름하게 벌리고 with one's mouth half-opened.

벌리다¹ [돈·재물이 벌어지다] be profitable [gainful]; yield profits; pay; be paying. ¶벌리는 장사 a profitable [lucrative / paying] business∥돈이 벌리는 투자 a money-making investment∥이 장사는 돈이 벌린다 [벌리지 않는다 / This business is [is not] profitable. / This business pays [does not pay].

벌리다² 1 [열다] open (up); unfold. ¶입을 벌리고 with an open mouth / with one's mouth open / open-mouthed / agape∥굴이 입을 벌렸다 The oyster gaped.∥우리는 입을 크게 벌리고 웃었다 We roared with laughter.∥입을 좀 더 크게 벌리세요 Open your lips more. / Open your mouth wider. / Your lips are not open wide enough.
2 [넓히다] leave space; widen; [펴다] stretch; outstretch; spread. ¶다리를 ~ set one's legs apart∥팔을 ~ open [spread] one's arms∥가랑이를 벌리고 with one's legs spread out [wide apart / outstretched] / straddle-[spraddle-]legged∥그녀는 두 팔을 벌려 우리를 마중했다 She welcomed us with open arms.∥그는 2위와의 차이를 크게 벌렸다 He increased his lead over the runner-up.
3→벌리다

벌목(伐木) felling; cutting; logging; (미) lumbering; (영) timbering. ¶~이 금지된 산 a mountain where timbering is prohibited. **벌목하다** cut down; cut over; fell (trees); lumber ((in) a valley); log.
● **벌목꾼** a logger; (미) a lumberman; a lumberjack; (영) a timberman; a timberjack. **벌목 작업** felling operation.

벌물 [마구 마시는 물] water that is swilled.

벌물 켜듯 (속담) drink heavily [in large draughts]; take draughts (of); swill; swig.

벌바람 wind on an open field; a field wind.

벌벌 tremblingly; shiveringly; shakingly. ¶~ 떨다 tremble / shiver / shake∥무서워 ~ 떨다 shake [tremble] for fear / shiver [tremble] with fright∥나는 추워 ~ 떨고 있었다 I was shivering with cold.∥내 손이 ~ 떨려 글씨를 제대로 쓸 수 없었다 My hands were shaking so badly that I could not write well.∥그는 얼음 위를 ~ 기어갔다 He trod his way cautiously over the ice.

벌부(筏夫) a rafter; a raftsman.

벌서다(罰~) stand in the corner.

벌써 [오래전에] long ago [since]; [이미] already; yet (의문문에서); [어느새] so soon. ¶~ 정오다 It is already noon.∥~ 그 책을 다 읽으셨습니까 Have you already finished the book?∥그 편지는 ~ 오래전에 가 닿았어야 하는 건데 The letter should have arrived a long time ago.∥나는 그 일을 ~ 오래전에 잊어버렸다 I had long since forgotten all about it.∥~ 12시가 지났다 It was well past twelve.∥그런 말은 ~ 했어야 했는데 You should have said that long ago.∥그들은 ~ 두 아이를 가졌다 They now have two children.

벌쐬다 be [get] stung by a bee [wasp]. ¶벌쐰 사람 같다 be like a man stung by a bee / beat a hasty retreat / make a hurried departure / hurry away [off].

벌어먹다 earn one's livelihood [bread]; gain [earn / make] a livelihood; support [maintain] oneself. ¶문필로 ~ make [earn] a living [livelihood] by literary work / live by one's pen∥정직하게 ~ eat one's honest bread / live honestly∥식구를 벌어먹이다 support [maintain] one's family∥하루하루 벌어먹고 살다 eke out a bare existence from day to day∥그는 행상을 해서 벌어먹는다 He earns his daily bread by peddling.

벌어지다 1 [틈이 생기다] crack (apart); become open; [넓어지다] widen; become wider; [가지 등이] split [burst] open; crack. ¶(꽃봉오리가) 벌어지기 시작하다 begin to open [bloom] / peep [come] out∥그녀는 좋아서 입이 벌어졌다 Her mouth cracked [broke into] a smile.
2 [소원해지다] be estranged [alienated] (from); fall away (from). ¶(두 사람) 사이가 ~ be alienated [estranged] from each other.
3 [일이 발생하다] arise; happen; take place; come up [about]; turn up. ¶일이 크게 벌어졌다 The matter has become serious.∥무슨 일이 벌어질 것만 같다 Something is likely to happen. / There is something in the wind.
4 [차이가 나다] have a (wide) margin; differ (from). ¶(차이가) 크게 ~ differ greatly [a great deal] (from) / (경기에서) have a long lead (on)∥그와 2등의 차는 2미터로 벌어졌다 He was two meters ahead of the runner-up.
5 [몸이 가로퍼지다] become strong [stout / sturdy]. ¶딱 벌어진 체격 a robust constitution / a stout build∥어깨가 딱 ~ be broad-shouldered / have broad shoulders.

벌이 moneymaking; income; earnings; gainings; pay. ¶~가 되다 [안 되다] pay [do not pay] / be profitable [unprofitable]∥~가 좋다 earn a good [comfortable] income / have [earn / draw] a large income∥~가 시원치 않다 earn a poor [small] income / have [draw] a small income∥그녀는 하루 3만 원 ~를 한다 She earns [makes] thirty thousand won a day. **벌이하다** work for one's living; earn one's bread [living]; (돈을) earn [make] (money). ¶벌이하러 나가다 go to work // 벌이하러 객지로 가다 work away from home.

벌이다 1 [시작하다] begin; open; start; [착수하다] set about; enter into [upon]; take to. ¶가게[식당]를 ~ open a store [restaurant] / 사업을 ~ start [get launched on] an enterprise // 전쟁을 ~ enter into a war // 그는 부산에 가게를 벌이고 있다 He runs a store in Busan. // 동생은 따로 살림을 벌였다 My brother has set up his own home [started up a home of his own].

2 [베풀어 놓다] hold; give; (미국 속어) throw (a banquet). ¶잔치를 ~ hold [give] a banquet / give a feast // 퍼레이드를 ~ parade (a street) / march in parade // 오늘 밤에는 잔치를 벌이자 Let's have a feast and celebrate tonight.

3 [늘어놓다] arrange (goods); display (goods); show (samples); exhibit; (음식을) spread (dishes). ¶가게에 물건을 벌여 놓다 arrange [put] goods in a show window.

벌임새 (상품 등의) the look [mode] of display [arrangement] (of goods). ¶~가 훌륭하다 be attractively exhibited.

벌잇줄 a means of (earning a) living; a livelihood; one's job. ¶~이 끊어지다 lose one's means of livelihood.

벌전(罰錢) [위약금] a forfeit; a penalty; [벌금] a fine; a (monetary) penalty.

벌점(罰點) black [demerit] marks. ¶~을 주다 give black marks.

벌주(罰酒) a penalty cup (of wine); the wine forced on (a person) to drink as punishment.

벌주다(罰-) punish; inflict punishment (on).

벌집 [벌이 생활하는 집] a beehive; a hive; a honeycomb; a comb. ¶탄환으로 ~처럼 만들다 riddle (a person's body) with bullets // ~을 건드리다 stir up [arouse] a hornets' nest [a nest of hornets] // 장내는 ~을 쑤신 듯 발칵 뒤집혔다 The audience in the hall was thrown into utter confusion. // ~을 건드리지 마라 Let sleeping dogs lie.

● **벌집위**[생] the reticulum (pl. -la).

벌쭉거리다 keep on opening slightly and shutting (one's mouth).

벌쭉하다 half open; slightly parted.

벌채(伐採) felling; lumbering; deforestation. **벌채하다** cut down; cut over; fell (trees); lumber; log. ¶산림을 ~ exploit [work / cut down] a forest.

● **벌채량** a fall. **벌채자** a feller; a logger; (미) a lumberman; a woodcutter.

벌책(罰責) reproof; rebuke; reprimand; censure; admonishment. ¶~을 받다 receive a rebuke / be reprimanded (for) / be subjected to reprimand. **벌책하다** rebuke; reprove; reprimand; censure; admonish. ¶잘못을 ~ censure (a person) for a fault.

벌초(伐草) mowing; cutting the weeds [mowing the grass] around a grave. **벌초하다** mow; cut the weeds [mow the grass] around a grave.

벌충 amends (a) compensation; reparation; an offset (to); [보충] a supplement; (임시변통의) a stopgap. **벌충하다** make up [amends] for (a loss); make good; compensate; supplement. ¶손해를 ~ recover [offset / make up for] a loss // 잃어버린 돈은 어떻게든 벌충하겠다 I will make up for the money I lost somehow. // 그는 장부상의 결손을 벌충하려고 주식에 손을 댔다 He dabbled in stocks to (try to) make up the deficit in the accounts.

벌칙(罰則) penal regulations [clauses]; punitive provisions. ¶~에 저촉되다 infringe the penal regulations // ~에 의거 처벌하다 punish (a person) according to the penal regulations // 이 법률에는 엄한 ~이 있다 This law carries stiff [severe] penalties.

벌컥 all of a sudden; topsy-turvy. ⇨'벌꺽'

벌통(-桶) a beehive; a hive.

벌판 [평야] a field; a plain; [초원] a green; [대초원] (미) a prairie; [황야] a wildness; (영) a moor. ¶황량한 ~ a vast wilderness / a vast expanse of bleak plain.

벌하다(罰-) punish; penalize; visit (a person) with punishment; visit [amerce] a penalty (upon); subject (a person) with punishment; subject (a person) to punishment [a penalty]; mete out punishment (to); bring (a person) to justice. ¶벌해야 할 행위 punishable conduct / conduct deserving punishment // 죄를 ~ punish (a person) for his crime // 벌하지 않고 두다 let go unpunished.

범 a tiger; a tigress (암컷). ¶새끼 ~ a tiger kitten [cub] / 사냥 ~ a tiger shoot // ~을 풀어 놓다 let a tiger run loose // ~을 길러 화를 입다 nourish a serpent [warm a snake] in one's bosom.

범굴에 들어가야 범을 잡는다(속담) Nothing venture, nothing gain [win].; You cannot go swimming without getting your feet wet.

범 없는 골에 토끼가 스승이라(속담) When the cat's away, the mice will play.; In the kingdom of blindmen the one-eyed is king.

범(犯) [형벌을 받은 횟수] ¶전과 5~의 사나이 a man with five previous convictions.

범-(汎) Pan-. ¶~아시아주의 Pan-Asianism // ~태평양 회의 the Pan-Pacific Conference.

-범(犯) [범행] an offense; [범인] an offender; a criminal; a culprit. ¶강력~ a violent offense [criminal] // 절도~ a larcener.

범고래 [동] an orc; a grampus; a killer (whale).

범과(犯過) a fault; a wrong; wrongdoing. **범과하다** commit a fault; do a wrong.

범국민적(汎國民的) pan-national; nationwide(전국적인). ¶~ 운동을 벌이다 conduct [carry on] a nation-wide campaign [drive] (for / against).

범나비 [동] a swallowtail (butterfly). ⇨'호랑나비'

범람(汎濫·氾濫) [넘쳐흐름] inundation; flooding; overflow; a deluge; [홍수] a flood; (영) spate; [마구 쏟아져 나와 나돎] a flood; oversupply. **범람하다** overflow; flow [run] over (the banks); flood; be inundated. ¶호우로 강이 범람했다 The river flooded [overflowed its banks / overran its banks] after the heavy rain(s). // 강이 범람하여 온 마을이 물에 잠겼다 The river flooded the whole village. / The whole village was inundated by the flooding of the river. // 외국 제품이 범람하고 있다 There is an oversupply [a flood] of foreign goods on the market. // 도시에 에로 잡지가 범람하고 있다 There is a flood of

obscene magazines in the city.
범례(凡例) introductory[explanatory] notes [remarks].
범미주의(汎美主義) Pan-Americanism.
범민(凡民) a commoner; the common people; a plebeian.
범벅 1 [된풀처럼 쑨 음식] mixed-grain porridge. **2** [여러 사물이 뒤섞인 상태] (utter) confusion; a muddle; a jumble; a mess; a pell-mell. ¶모든 것이 ～이 되었다 All things are mixed up. / Things are all in a muddle. / Things are at sixes and sevens.
범범하다(泛泛-) careless; heedless; inattentive; absent-minded. ¶범범한 사람 a careless man.
범법(犯法) lawbreaking; violation of the law; an offense (against). **범법하다** break [violate] the law; commit an offense; go against the law; offend against; transgress.
● **범법자** a lawbreaker; an offender (against the law). **범법 행위** an illegal act; (공무원 등의) an irregularity; a malfeasance.
범부(凡夫) **1** [보통 사람] a common[an ordinary] man. ¶그것은 ～의 약점 때문에 일어난 것이다 That is due to the weakness of an average man.∥그는 ～가 아니다 He is no ordinary man. **2** [불] an unenlightened person.
범사(凡事) **1** [모든 일] all matters; all things; everything. **2** [범범한 일] a commonplace; an ordinary matter.
범상하다(凡常-) ordinary; usual; common; mediocre; average; commonplace; of ordinary type. ¶범상한 사람 an ordinary[average] person / (집합적) the common run of men∥범상한 일을 하다 do as other people do∥범상치 않다 rise above mediocrity[the common herd] / be out of the common∥그에게는 범상치 않은 데가 있다 There is something extraordinary[peculiar] about him.
범서(凡書) a mediocre book; an ordinary book.
범서(梵書) **1** [범어로 된 글] writings in Sanskrit[Pali]; a book written in Sanskrit [Pali]. **2** the Buddhist scriptures. ⇨불경(佛經)
범선(帆船) a sailboat. ⇨돛단배
범속하다(凡俗-) common; ordinary; commonplace; humdrum; mediocre; vulgar; worldly. ¶범속한 사람 a common[an ordinary / a mediocre] person∥범속한 생각 a commonplace idea.
범신론(汎神論) pantheism. ¶～적인 pantheistic.
● **범신론자** a pantheist.
범실(凡失) [야구 등에서의 평범한 실수] a stupid error.
범심론(汎心論) panpsychism.
범아귀 the space between the thumb and the forefinger.
범안(凡眼) unprofessional eyes; a layman's eyes; ordinary intelligence. ¶～에는 그렇게 비칠지도 모른다 It may look so to the uninitiated[untrained] eye.
범애(汎愛) love of mankind. ⇨박애
범어(梵語) Sanskrit. ⇨산스크리트 어
범연하다(泛然-) careless; heedless; remiss; inattentive; inadvertent; incautious; sloppy; indifferent. **범연히** carelessly; heedlessly; inattentively.

범용 컴퓨터(汎用-) a general-purpose computer.
범용하다(凡庸-) mediocre; common; commonplace; ordinary. ¶범용한 사람 an ordinary person∥범용한 솜씨의 화가 a painter of mediocre[indifferent] ability.
범위(範圍) an extent; a scope; a sphere; an ambit; (the) limits[bounds / confines] (of); the province (of); the purview (of); [통계] a range. ¶세력 ～ the sphere[range] of influence / the domain∥활동 ～ the sphere [field] of activity∥그의 지식의 ～ the breadth of his knowledge∥문학의 ～ the realm[province] of literature∥…의 ～ 안에 within the limits[scope / range / sphere] of …∥…의 ～ 밖에 beyond the limits[scope] of …/ beyond the compass of (imagination) ∥인간 경험의 ～ 밖에 있다 be outside the range of human experience∥～를 제한하다 set limits[bounds] (to) / fix the limits (of) / limit / bound / circumscribe∥아마추어의 ～ 를 넘어서다 pass[go beyond] the confines of amateurism∥인지(人智)의 ～를 넘어서다 be beyond the boundary of human knowledge ∥교제 ～가 좁다 have a small circle of acquaintance(s)∥그의 독서 ～는 넓다 His reading is of a very wide range.
범의(犯意) intention of committing an infraction; a criminal[guilty] intent; malice. ¶～가 있는 malicious∥～를 인정하다 recognize one's criminal intent.
범의귀 [식] a creeping[strawberry] saxifrage.
범인(凡人) [보통 사람] an ordinary person; an ordinary mortal; (집합적) the common [ordinary] run of men; [범용한 사람] a (man of) mediocrity; a mediocre person. ¶그 것은 ～의 힘으로는 할 수 없다 It is beyond the power of a common mortal.∥～의 재주밖에 없었으므로 나는 그의 책략을 꿰뚫어 볼 수 없었다 Being no genius, I could not see through his designs.
범인(犯人) a criminal; a culprit; an offender; a convict(기결수); a suspect(피의자). ¶상습 ～ a habitual criminal∥살인 ～ a murderer ∥～을 은닉하다 harbor a criminal∥～을 쫓다 track down a criminal∥～은 아직 잡히지 않았다 The criminal is still at large.∥그 사람이 ～일 것으로 나는 생각했다 I suspected him.
● **범인 은닉** concealment of an offender.
범자(梵字) Sanskrit (writing); Sanskrit characters.
범작(凡作) [평범한 작품] a common place [mediocre] work. ¶그의 최근의 시는 모두 ～ 이다 His recent poems are all mediocre.
범재(凡才) [평범한 재주] common[ordinary] ability; mediocrity; [평범한 인재] a person of common[average] ability; a (man of) mediocrity; a mediocre person.
범절(凡節) etiquette; proprieties; decorum; (good) manners; form; deportment. ¶저 사람은 ～을 아는[모르는] 사람이다 He is a well-bred[an ill-bred] man. / He has good[bad] manners.
범종(梵鐘) the bell of a Buddhist temple; a (Buddhist) temple bell.
범죄(犯罪) an offense; a crime; [법] (a) delict; guilt. ¶～(상)의 criminal∥～의 소추 criminal prosecution∥우발성 ～ an occasional crime∥소년 ～ a juvenile delinquency∥집단

~ an organized crime(조직적인) / a group crime(조직적 단체가 아닌) // ~을 저지르다 commit a crime // ~를 폭로하다 disclose a crime.
● **범죄 과학** criminalistics. **범죄 수사** (a) criminal investigation. **범죄 심리학** criminal psychology. **범죄 예방** crime prevention. **범죄자** an offender; a criminal; a culprit(미결의); a convict(기결의). ¶도피 수배 중인 ~ a criminal at large / a fugitive from justice // 상습 ~ a habitual criminal // **소년** ~ a juvenile delinquent // **전쟁** ~ a war criminal. **범죄 조직** a criminal syndicate. **범죄학** criminology. **범죄 행위** a criminal act. **범죄 현장** the scene of a crime.

범주(範疇) a category; a class. ¶문법적 ~ a grammatical category // …의 ~에 넣다 place (something) under the category of … // …의 ~에 들다 fall under[come within] the category of ….

범천(왕)(梵天王) [불] Brahma.

범칙(犯則) (an) infringement[(a) violation / breach] of regulations; transgression of the law; default; infraction. **범칙하다** violate [infringe] the regulations; transgress; default.
● **범칙금** a fine. **범칙물자** illegal materials [goods]; a smuggled article(밀수품). **범칙자** an offender; a transgressor; a defaulter.

범칭(汎稱·泛稱) a general title[term]; a popular name.

범타(凡打) [야구] [평범한 타격] an easy out; [플라이·땅볼] an easy fly[grounder]. ¶~ 그치다 prove poor at bat // 2번 타자는 ~로 끝났다 The second batter was put out easily. **범타하다** hit an easy fly[grounder] (to).

범퍼 (자동차의) a bumper.

범포(帆布) sailcloth; canvas.

범하다(犯一) 1 [잘못 등을 저지르다] commit; perpetrate; sin against (morality). ¶과오를 ~ commit[make] a fault[an error] / err // 벌이 무서워서 죄를 범하지 않는 사람이 많다 The fear of punishment deters many people from crime. 2 [규칙·법률 등을 어기다] violate; infringe; break; offend against; transgress; trespass against. ¶교칙을 ~ break the school regulations / 금령을 ~ violate the ban[interdict]. 3 [무시하다] defy; make little of; disregard. ¶그는 어딘지 범하기 어려운 데가 있다 He has something that commands respect. 4 [정조를 빼앗다] attack; assault; violate; outrage; rape.

범행(犯行) a criminal act; a crime; an offense. ¶잔인한[대담한] ~ an atrocious[a bold] crime // (현장 검증 때의) ~의 재연 a reenactment of the crime // (법정에서) ~을 시인하다 plead guilty // ~을 부인하다 deny one's having committed the crime / refuse to admit one's crime / (법정에서) plead not guilty // ~을 자백하다 confess one's crime // ~이 발각되다 have one's offense detected.
● **범행 현장** the scene of an offense.

법(法) 1 [법칙] a law; a rule; [법률] the law; (집합적) the legislation; an act; a regulation(조례) ; a rule(법규); [법전] a code (of laws); [사법] justice. ¶~의 정신 the spirit of the law // ~에 맞는 lawful / legal // ~에 벗어난 unlawful / illegal // 나라의 ~에 따라 according to[in obedience to] the state law // ~에 어긋나다 be against[contrary to] the law // ~에 맞다[합치하다] conform to the law // ~에 따라 행동하다 act on[upon] the regulation // ~에 호소하다 appeal to the law / invoke (the power of) the law / bring (a person) to justice(재판하여) // ~에 저촉되지 않도록 하다 stay on the right side of the law // ~을 고치다[개정하다] revise[alter] the law // ~을 지키다 observe[keep / obey] the law // ~을 어기다 infringe[break / violate] the law / go against the law // ~을 시행하다 enforce a law / put a law in force / carry a law into effect // ~을 제정하다 legislate / enact a law / establish regulations[a law] / ~을 집행하다 administer[deal out] justice // 그는 ~ 없이도 살 사람이다 He is a straight arrow. / He is as straight as a die.
2 [방법] a method; a way; a manner; [과정] a process; [기술] an art; technique(예술상의). ¶교수~ a method of teaching / a teaching method // **장수**~ a recipe for long life // 공부하는 ~ a method of study // **수영**~ a way of swimming / how to swim // 요리~을 가르치다 teach (a person) how to cook // 글쓰는 ~을 가르치다 teach writing / teach a person how to write // 너는 공부하는 ~이 틀렸다 You are studying in the wrong way. // 그녀는 절하는 ~도 모른다 She does not even know how to bow (properly). // 저 사람이 말하는 ~이 서툴다 His way[manner] of talking is awkward. / He speaks awkwardly. // 그는 사람들의 환심을 사는 ~을 알고 있다 He knows how to please people[win people's regard / get himself into people's good graces].
3 [예법] etiquette; manners; good form; [도리] reason. ¶그런 ~은 없다 That's against reason. / That's unreasonable[absurd / outrageous]. // 그런 ~이 어디 있느냐 Where do you find get that way! // 그렇게 말하는 ~이 어디 있소 How can you say that! / You shouldn't talk like that. // 일을 하다가 말면 못쓰는 ~이다 You ought not to leave a matter unsettled. // 어른한테 그렇게 말하는 ~이 아니다 You shouldn't speak like that to your elders.
4 Buddhism. ⇨ **불법**(佛法)
5 [언] the mood (of a verb). ¶**서술**~ the indicative mood // **명령**~ the imperative mood.

법은 멀고 주먹은 가깝다 Where drums beat, laws are silent.

법계(法系) a legal system; a code of law; law. ¶**로마** ~ Roman law // **중국** ~ Chinese law / the Chinese legal system.

법계(法界) [불] [불법의 범위] the universe; the realm of Buddhism; [불교도의 사회] the world[society] of Buddhists.

법과 대학(法科大學) a law college; a college [school] of jurisprudence.

법관(法官) a judicial officer; a judge; (집합적) the judiciary; the bench.

법권(法權) a legal right.

법규(法規) law and regulations; legislation. ¶**교통 관계** ~ traffic regulations // **현행** ~ the laws in force // 상거래에 관한 ~ regulations concerning[regarding] business transactions // ~ 에 legally / according to the regulations // **현행** ~를 지키다 observe the laws in force // **현행** ~를 무시하다 neglect the laws in force // ~상의 절차를 밟다 go through the legal formalities // ~에 따라 처벌하다 punish

법당 (a person) according to the law.

법당(法堂) [불] a Buddhist sanctum.

법도(法度) a law; a rule; a regulation. ¶~를 어기다 violate[infringe] the law.

법등(法燈) [불법] the light of Buddhism; the teachings of Buddha; [전통] Buddhistic heritage[tradition]; [부처 앞에 올리는 등불] a light offered to the Buddhist altar.

법랑(琺瑯) (porcelain) enamel. ¶~을 칠한[입힌] enameled // ~을 입히다 enamel / cover with enamel.
- **법랑철기** enameled ironware.

법령(法令) a law; an ordinance; 〈집합적〉 a statute; laws and ordinances. ¶~에 의하여 by law / according to (the) law // ~에 의하여 규정되어 있다 be provided for[be specified] in the law.
- **법령집** a complete collection of laws and regulations.

법례(法例) the law governing the application of laws. ¶~의 규정에 따라 according to the rules concerning the application of laws.

법률(法律) a law; 〈집합적〉 (the) law; legislation. ¶~을 금하는 ~ a law prohibiting [against] (opium smoking) // ~의 legal / juridical // ~지식이 있는 사람 a person who has legal knowledge // ~상 legally / from a legal point of view // ~에 호소하다 have recourse to law // ~로 금하다 prohibit[interdict] (smoking)by law // ~을 지키다 observe [obey / keep] the law // ~을 어기다 break [violate] the law // ~을 제정하다 [만들다] enact[make] a law / legislate // ~을 실시하다 put a law in force / bring a law into force / put a law into effect[operation] / enforce a law // ~을 집행하다 administer [deal out] justice // ~을 폐지하다 repeal[rescind / (문어) abrogate] a law // 그것은 ~에 규정되어 있다 It is provided[specified / ordained / prescribed] by law. // 그 분쟁은 ~에 호소하지 않고도 해결되었다 The dispute was settled without recourse to the law. // 그는 ~에 정통하다 He is a legal expert. / He is well acquainted with the [well versed in] law. // 그 행위는 ~로 인정[금지]되어 있다 The act is authorized [prohibited] by law. // 세금의 납부는 ~이 명하는 바이다 The law requires us to pay taxes. // 만인은 ~상 평등하다 All people are equal before [in the eye(s) of] the law. // ~은 만인에게 공평히 시행되어야 한다 The laws should be carried out with justice to everybody.
- **법률가** a lawyer; a jurist. **법률 고문** a legal adviser[counsel]. **법률 사무** law[legal] business. **법률 상담** legal advice. **법률 상담소** a legal information center; (영) a legal advice centre. **법률안** a legislative bill; a draft of a proposed law. **법률 용어** a legal[law] term. **법률 제도** the legal system. **법률학** jurisprudence; the science of law. **법률 행위** a juristic act; a legal action.

법리(法理) [법률의 원리] a principle of law; legal principles.
- **법리학** jurisprudence; the science of law; [법철학] philosophy of law.

법망(法網) the net [grip / clutches / toils / meshes] of the law; justice. ¶~에 걸리다 fall into the meshes[clutches] of the law / be picked up by the law / be brought to justice / come within the grip of the law // ~을 피하다 [빠져나가다] evade [avoid / dodge / elude] the law / slip from the grip of the law / escape the meshes [long arm] of the law // 그 악명 높은 사기꾼이 마침내 ~에 걸렸다 That notorious swindler at last fell into the clutches of the law.

법명(法名) [불] [속명을 대신한 승려의 이름] a Buddhist name; [불가의 망자에게 붙이는 이름] a posthumous Buddhist name.

법무(法務) 1 [법률 사무] judicial affairs. 2 [불] a clerical duty.
- **법무관** a law officer; a judiciary; [군] a judge advocate. **법무부** the Ministry of Justice; (미) the Justice Department. **법무부 장관** the Minister of Justice; (미) the Attorney General. **법무사**(-士) [법무 서류를 대리로 작성해 주는 직업인] a judicial scrivener.

법문(法文) 1 [법령의 문장] the text [letter / wording] of the law. ¶~에 명시 [규정] 되어 있다 be specified [provided for] in the law. 2 [불경의 글] Buddhist writings.

법문(法門) [불] (the gate to) Buddhism. ¶~에 들어가다 embrace Buddhism.

법복(法服) 1 (법관의) a judge's robe; a gown; (변호사의) a lawyer's robe; a barrister's gown. 2 a vestment. ⇨ ˚법의(法衣)

법사(法師) [설법승] a Buddhist priest [monk]; a bonze; [법주] the teacher of a Buddhist priest.

법석 a noise; a hubbub; a clamor; an uproar; fuss; ado; bustle. ¶손님을 맞느라고 ~을 부리다 make much ado to receive a guest / lionize a guest // 웬 ~이냐 What a babel! / What's all this noise? **법석하다** make [raise] a great uproar; make a fuss (about); fuss (about); make a noise; make much ado. ¶공연한 일로 ~ make a great fuss [much ado] about nothing // 술을 마시며 ~ go on a spree.

법선(法線) a normal (line).

법식(法式) 1 [법도·양식] a rule; a law; a regulation. ¶~에 따르다 [어긋나다] follow [run counter to] the formalities // ~대로 증서를 쓰다 draw up a deed in proper form. 2 a formula; a form. ⇨ ˚방식(方式) 3 [불교의 법요 의식] Buddhist ritual; formalities of a Buddhist ceremony.

법안(法案) a bill; a measure. ¶~을 제출하다 introduce [bring in / submit] a bill // ~을 가결 [부결] 하다 pass [reject / throw out] the bill // 그 ~은 국회를 통과했다 The bill passed the National Assembly. // ~은 국회를 통과해야 법률이 된다 A bill becomes a law when it has passed the National Assembly.

법어(法語) [불교에 관한 말] a Buddhist sermon; [불교에 관한 글월] Buddhist literature [writing]; [불교 용어] Buddhistic terms; a Buddhist term.

법열(法悅) 1 [설법을 듣고 마음속에 일어나는 큰 기쁨] religious exultation. 2 [참된 이치를 깨달았을 때의 황홀감] an ecstasy; rapture; a transport. ¶~에 잠겨 있다 be in ecstasies (over).

법요(法要) [불] a Buddhist service.

법원(法院) a court of justice [law]; a law-court; a courthouse. ¶가정 ~ a family court / (미) a domestic relations court // 고등 ~ the High Court / (영) the Court of Appeal / a court of appeal / an appellate court // 대

the Supreme Court // 지방 ~ a District Court // 지방 ~ 판사 a district judge // 항고 [상고] ~ a court of complaint [revision] // ~에 출두하다 come into court / appear in court.
● 법원 서기 a court clerk. 법원장 the president [presiding officer] of a court.
법의(法衣) [중이 입는 옷] a vestment; a sacerdotal [priest's] robe; priestly vestments; canonical dress; (in full) canonicals.
법의(法意) the spirit [intent] of the law.
법의학(法醫學) legal [forensic] medicine; medical jurisprudence. ¶~의 medicolegal.
법익(法益) the benefit and protection of the law.
법인(法人) [법] a juridical [juristic / legal] person; an artificial person; a corporation; a body corporate. ¶공개 ~ an open corporation // 국내 ~ a domestic corporation // 단독 ~ a corporation sole // 사단 ~ a corporation aggregate // 재단 ~ a (juridical) foundation / (미) a nonprofit corporation // 영리 ~ a business corporation // 외국 ~ a foreign corporation // ~의 corporative.
● 법인 과세 taxation on juridical persons. 법인 단체 a body corporate. 법인세 a corporation tax. 법인 소득 the income of a corporation. 법인 조직 a corporate organization.
법적(法的) legal; legalistic. ¶~ 수단 legal procedure [steps / action / proceedings] // ~ 수단을 취하다 take legal steps [action] / institute legal proceedings // ~으로는 legally (speaking) / in the eye of the law // 우리에게는 ~으로 알 권리가 있다 We have a legal right to know. // 네 요구는 ~ 근거가 없다 Your demand has no legal basis. // 안락사는 ~으로 인정되지 않고 있다 Euthanasia is not legally recognized.
● 법적 근거 a legal basis (*pl.* bases).
법전(法典) [법] a code (of laws); a body of law. ¶현행 ~ the code in force // ~을 제정하다 establish a code // ~을 편찬 [집성] 하다 codify laws.
법정(法廷) a (law) court; a court of justice [law]; a courtroom; a tribunal; a judgment hall; the bar. ¶대 [소] ~ a Grand [petty] Bench (of the Supreme Court) // ~ 밖에서 out of court // ~에 서다 stand at the bar // ~에 출두하다 appear in court / come [go] into court // ~에서 다투다 go to law (with) / bring a suit [an action] (against) / (쟁점을) contest [contend] (a point) at law / litigate (a point) // ~을 개정하다 hold a court / (사건을) ~으로 끌고 가다 bring a matter before the court [to court] // 죄인을 ~에 끌어내다 drag a criminal into court // ~은 4월 1일부터 개정된다 Court will convene on April 1. // 지금 ~이 개정 중이다 The court is now in session. / The court is sitting now. // 그는 내일 ~에 출두한다 He will appear in court tomorrow. // 그들은 그 사건을 ~까지 가지 않고 해결했다 They settled the affair out of court. // 우리는 그와 ~에서 싸웠다 We took him to court. / We brought a suit [an action] against him. // 그 사건은 ~에서 해결되었다 [계쟁 중이었다] The case was resolved [pending] in court.
● 법정 모욕죄 (criminal) contempt of court. ¶~로 기소되다 be charged with contempt of court. 법정 투쟁 court struggle; (영) a liti-

gating struggle.
법정(法定) [관형어적] legal; statutory; designated by law.
● 법정 가격 a legal price. 법정 관리 (be under) legal management. 법정 권한 legal authority. 법정 기간 a legal term [period]. 법정 대리인 a legal representative. 법정 이율 the legal rate of interest. 법정 전염병 an infectious disease designated by law; a legal epidemic. 법정 통화 / 법정 화폐 legal tender; lawful money. 법정 휴일 (미국의) a legal holiday; (영) a bank holiday.
법제(法制) legislation; laws.
● 법제사 annals of legislation; a history of laws. 법제처 the Office of Legislation; the Legislative Office.
법조(法曹) the legal profession; [사법관] a judicial officer [official]; [변호사] a lawyer; (미) an attorney.
● 법조계 legal [judicial] circles; the judicial world; the bench and bar. ¶~의 원로들 leaders of the law.
법철학(法哲學) philosophy of law.
법치(法治) constitutional government.
● 법치 국가 a constitutional state; a law-governed country. 법치 사회 a community of law; a law-abiding society. 법치주의 legalism; constitutionalism.
법칙(法則) a law; a rule. ¶자연 ~ a law of nature / a natural law // 경제상의 ~ economic laws // 수요 공급의 ~ the law of supply and demand // 옛날에 사람들이 우연이라고 본 것 중에서 오늘 우리는 ~을 발견한다 Where formerly men saw chance we now see laws.
법통(法統) [불] a religious tradition. ¶~을 잇다 receive the mantle (of the preceding abbot) / succeed to the abbacy [abbotcy] (in a temple).
법하다(法-) [가능·추측] (서술적) it seems likely (that); be likely (to); be probable; may. ¶그녀가 왔을 ~ She must have arrived. // 이 성공할 ~ It seems likely to succeed. // 비가 올 ~ It looks like rain. // 대학생이라면 알 법한 일인데 A college student ought to know it. // 적어도 그가 작별 인사쯤 하러 왔을 법한데 He ought at least to have come to me to say goodbye. // 그렇게 무엇이든 잘 할 수 있는 사람은 달리 있을 법하지가 않다 There's not likely to be anyone with such all-round talents.
법학(法學) law; jurisprudence.
● 법학도 a law student. 법학 박사 (사람) a doctor of laws; (학위) Doctor of Laws(약어 LL. D). 법학부 the law school [department]; the faculty of jurisprudence [law]. 법학자 a jurist; a lawyer; a legal scholar.
법화(法貨) legal tender. ⇨법정 통화(⇨법정(法定))
법화경(法華經) the Lotus Sutra.
법회(法會) [재를 올리는 모임] a Buddhist mass; a Buddhist memorial service; [설법회] a Buddhist lecture meeting. ¶고 법사의 추도 ~ a memorial service for [a service in memory of] the late priest // ~를 열다 hold a mass / hold a Buddhist service [mass] for the dead / hold a memorial [religious] services (for the dead).
벗 a friend; a companion; a comrade; (구어) a pal; (구어) a chum; company. ¶친한 ~ a

벗겨지다

close [an intimate] friend / a chum // 참다운 ~ a true [tried] friend // 믿을 수 없는 ~ a fair-weather friend // 신앙의 ~ a brother [sister] in faith // 오랫동안 사귄 ~ an old friend / a friend of many years' standing // 평생의 ~ a lifelong friend / a companion for life // 가난한 사람들의 ~ a friend of[to] the poor // ~이 없는 friendless // …의 ~이 되다 become[make] friends with a person // 책을 ~ 삼다 have books for companions / make companions of books // 자연을 ~ 삼다 converse [hold converse / commune] with Nature // 그는 책을 ~ 삼아 인생을 즐기고 있다 He is enjoying life with books as his companions. // 우리는 학문상의 ~이었다 We were fellows in our studies. // ~을 잃는 것은 쉽지만 얻기는 어렵다 A friend is easier lost than found.

벗겨지다 1 (옷·신 등이) come off; be taken [stripped] off; get undressed; slip off [down / out]; (단추 등이) be unbuttoned [unzipped]. ¶구두가 벗겨지지 않는다 My shoes will not come off. // 내 장갑이 좀처럼 벗겨지지 않는다 My gloves won't come off.
2 (칠·비늘 등이) fall[come] off; (가죽·껍질 등이) get stripped off; peel off [away]. ¶래커칠이 군데군데 벗겨져 있다 The lacquer is (worn) off in places. // 도금이 벗겨지고 있다 The gilt is coming off. // 칠이 벗겨지기 시작하고 있다 The paint is peeling [scaling / flaking] off. // 화강암 대좌의 표면이 군데군데 벗겨져 있었다 The surface of the granite pedestal has flaked off in spots.
3 (덮개 등이) get removed; be taken off. ¶걸쇠가 벗겨졌다 The hook came undone. // 대문의 빗장이 벗겨져 있었다 The gate was unbolted. // 마침내 그의 가면이 벗겨졌다 At last he revealed his true nature [he was unmasked].

벗기다 1 (옷 등을) unclothe; undress; strip (a person) of (his clothes); take off (a person's clothes). ¶옷을 ~ unclothe [undress / disrobe] (a person) / strip [divest] (a person) of his clothes // 발가~ strip (a person) to the skin // 외투를 벗겨 주다 help (a person) off with his overcoat / help (a person) out of his overcoat // 좀도둑은 그의 옷을 벗겨 호주머니를 뒤졌다 The thief stripped him and searched his pockets.
2 (껍질 등을) chip [slice / flake] off; peel (an orange) (손가락으로); pare (an apple) (칼로); shuck (corn); hull (peas); (가죽을) skin (off) (an animal); strip off; flay (a rabbit); (곡식을) husk. ¶때를 ~ wash off the dirt // 나무껍질을 ~ strip a tree of its bark / strip the bark from a tree / unbark (a tree) // 감자 껍질을 ~ peel [pare] potatoes // 바나나 껍질을 ~ strip the skin from a banana / peel off the skin of a banana // 콩깍지를 ~ shell [pod] peas // 페인트칠을 ~ peel the paint off (a wall).
3 (떼어 내다) remove; take off; (드러내다) uncover (덮은 것을). ¶담요를 ~ remove the blanket // 빗장을 ~ unbar [unbolt / unlock / unlatch] (the gate) // 가면을 ~ unmask [take off the mask of] (a villain) / show up (a person's) hypocrisy / debunk // 녹을 ~ get the rust off // 통의 테를 ~ unhoop a barrel / take off hoops // 나는 상자의 뚜껑을 벗겼다 I removed the lid from the box. / I took the lid off a box. / I uncovered a box.

벗나가다 go beyond the bounds; deviate [swerve] (from); go astray; go [run] off the rails.

벗다 1 (옷 등을) take [peel / leave / shuck] off (one's coat); strip [divest] oneself of (one's shirt); remove (one's hat); (스르르) slip off (one's clothes); (훌렁) fling [throw] off (one's boots); (잠아당겨서) pull off (one's gloves). ¶황급히 ~ rush out of (one's nightgown) // 모자를 ~ take off [remove] one's hat // 안경을 ~ remove [take off] the glasses // 옷을 ~ disrobe [undress / unclothe] (oneself) / get out of one's clothes // (차서 던지듯이) 신발을 ~ kick off one's shoes // 웃통을 벗고 일하다 work bare to the waist // 그녀는 양장을 벗고 잠옷을 입었다 She undressed and put on a pajamas. // 그는 셔츠를 훌훌 벗어 던졌다 He flung off [threw away] his shirt. // 신발을 벗을까요 Shall I take off shoes? // 모자를 벗으시오 Off with your hat.
2 (책임·의무를) be freed from one's duty; get rid of one's responsibility; shift off one's duty; (짐·부담을) unload; unburden oneself of. ¶어깨의 짐을 ~ ease one's shoulder // 나는 그것으로써 나의 책임을 벗게 된다 I will be relieved of my responsibility with it.
3 (티·때 등을) get rid of (uncouthness / vulgarity / rusticity); get refined [polished]. ¶시골티를 ~ get citified [polished / sophisticated] / get smart / (구어) get the hayseed out of one's hair // 어린 티를 ~ grow out of childhood // 그녀는 아직 어린 티를 벗지 못했다 She has not yet emerged from infancy.
4 (누명을) clear [divest] oneself of (a false charge). ¶오해를 ~ remove the misunderstanding // 그는 수뢰의 누명을 끝내 벗지 못했다 He was never able to wipe away [clear himself of] the suspicion of bribery.
5 (허물을) slip out of (its skin); cast (off) (the skin); change (its skin); leave the cocoon (곤충의). ¶뱀이 허물을 벗었다 A snake sloughed its skin [cast aside its slough].

벗어나다 1 [···에서 헤어나다] get out of (difficulties); get rid of; be relieved of (trouble); escape from (danger); free oneself from [from] (a bondage); break away from [rid oneself of] (a bad habit). ¶벗어날 수 없는 unavoidable (disasters) / inevitable (fate) // 가난에서 ~ overcome poverty // 구속 [빚 / 속박]에서 ~ free oneself from bondage [debt / fetters] // 위기에서 ~ circumvent a crisis // 궁지를 ~ get out of difficulty [trouble] // 법망을 ~ get out of the clutches of the law / evade the law // 오랜 편견[습관]에서 ~ slough off old prejudices [habits] // 악습에서 ~ break oneself [get rid] of a bad habit // 죽음에서 ~ escape death / be saved from death / be snatched from the jaws of death // 질곡에서 ~ shake off fetters / cast off the yoke (of) // 슬럼프에서 ~ pull oneself out of the slump // 마침내 무거운 책임에서 벗어났다 At last I was relieved of my heavy responsibilities. // 궁지에서 벗어날 수 있는 좋은 방법이 있다 There is a good way out of [means of escape from] the difficulty. // 그 사람들은 아직 야만적인 상태를 벗어나지 못했다 The people are little removed from barbarism.
2 [눈에 들지 못하다] be out of (a person's)

favor; incur [fall under] (a person's) displeasure; lose (a person's) favor. ¶그녀는 하는 짓이 남의눈에서 벗어난다 Her ways fail to find favor in the eyes of another.// 그는 하는 일마다 사장 눈에서 벗어났다 Everything he did displeased his employer.// 왜 그가 그녀의 눈에서 벗어났는지 모르겠다 I wonder why he lost her favor.

3 [어긋나다] be contrary to; be against; (정도(正道)를) depart from; deviate [swerve] from. ¶도리에 ~ be contrary to reason// 정도(正道)에서 ~ stray from the right path / take a wrong step// 규칙에 ~ be against rules [law / regulations] // 예의범절에 ~ transgress the bounds of decency / get against etiquette// 관습에서 ~ deviate from the custom// 인정에 벗어난 짓을 하다 swerve [deviate] from the path of humanity// 무슨 일을 하든 정도(正道)에서 벗어나지 않도록 주의해라 Whatever you do, take care not to deviate [stray] from the normal course of action.

4 [범위·한계 밖으로 나가다] miss the mark; go wide; stray (from); deviate (from a course). ¶과녁을 ~ miss the target / go wide of the mark// 침로(針路)에서 ~ swerve from the course / sheer (off) / yaw (특히 항공기가) // 상궤(常軌)를 ~ be aberrant / deviate from the normal routine// (이야기가) 본제(本題)를 ~ wander [digress] from the subject / go astray [diverge] from the main subject// 그 질문은 요점을 벗어났다 The question was beside the point.// 인공위성이 예정 궤도를 벗어났다 The satellite went off the planned orbit [failed to orbit properly].

벗어부치다 1 (옷을) slip off one's clothes. ¶웃통을 벗어부치고 일하다 work bare to the waist// 그는 저고리를 벗어부치고 일을 시작했다 He threw off his coat and started work. **2** [비유] go at (it) taking off the gloves [with might and main]. ¶그는 벗어부치고 장사에 나섰다 He dared by himself to engage in business taking off the gloves.

벗어지다 1 (몸에 걸친 것이) come off; slip off [down]. ¶치마가 자꾸 벗어진다 My skirt keeps slipping off.
2 (머리가) become [go / grow] bald; be [get] bold (in front); lose one's hair. ¶이마가 벗어진 bald at the forehead// 벗어진 이마 a bald forehead// 아직 이른 나이에 머리가 ~ become baldheaded prematurely [before one's time] // 요즘 머리가 벗어지기 시작했다 I have been getting bald [losing hair] recently. / My hairline is receding.// 그의 이마는 벗어져 있었다 His hair retreated way back leaving forehead bald.
3 (거죽면 등이) peel (off); come [strip] off; be worn off; (상가죽이) get [be] skinned. ¶햇볕에 너무 타서 등가죽이 벗어졌다 The skin of my back peeled off with too much exposure to the sun.// 층계에서 떨어져 무릎이 벗어졌다 I fell down the steps and skinned off my knee.

벗트다 achieve a first-name friendship (with); arrive at terms of slangy intimacy (with).

벗하다 1 [벗으로 삼다] associate (with); make a friend [friends] (with); make a companion [companions] (with). **2** achieve a first-name friendship (with). ⇨벗트다

벙거지 [모자] headgear; a hat; (옛 군인의) a soldier's hat [helmet].

벙글거리다 smile radiantly (at); beam (upon); be all smiles; look happy; wear a smile (on one's face). ¶기뻐서 ~ beam with delight [joy]// 어린애가 그의 손을 잡고 쳐다보며 벙글거렸다 The child took his hand and beamed up at him.

벙글벙글 (smile) with a broad smile; smilingly. ¶~ 웃는 얼굴 a smiling [beaming] face / a radiant look// ~ 웃다 smile radiantly (at) / beam with a smile.

벙긋 smilingly. ⇨방긋

벙긋벙긋 (smile) with a broad smile. ⇨방긋방긋

벙벙하다 stunned; tongue-tied; dumbfounded; perplexed; puzzled; bewildered; quite embarrassed; (서술적) be at a loss; do not know (what to do / how to say). ¶어안이 ~ be stunned [dum(b)founded] / stand aghast (at the sight)// 어안이 벙벙하여 in blank [mute / utter] amazement / with a vacant look of amazement// 벙벙하여 말이 안 나오다 be (struck) dumb with amazement// 그녀는 잠시 어안이 벙벙했다 She was nonplus(s)ed for a moment. / She kept quiet without a word for a while.// 나는 벙벙하여 대답을 못했다 I was at my wit's end for an answer. **벙벙히** dumbfoundedly; perplexedly.

벙실거리다 smile sweetly. ⇨방실거리다

벙어리 (말 못하는) a mute; a dumb person; a dummy; [농아] a deaf-mute. ¶~의 dumb / mute// ~처럼 잠자코 in stony silence// ~ 시늉을 하다 play dumb / play the dummy// ~가 되다 become [fall] dumb// 그녀는 태어나면서부터 ~ 다 She has been dumb from birth.
벙어리 냉가슴 앓듯 (속담) suffer in silence.
●**벙어리장갑** (a pair of) mittens. **벙어리저금통** a saving box; a (piggy) bank (돼지 저금통).

벙커 1 [골프] a bunker; a sand trap. **2** [배의 석탄 창고] a bunker.
●**벙커시유** bunker C oil.

벚꽃 cherry blossoms [flowers].
●**벚꽃놀이** cherry blossom viewing; [행락] a picnic under the cherry blossoms.

벚나무 [식] a cherry tree.

베 1 hemp cloth. ⇨삼베 **2** (일반적으로) cotton cloth. ¶~ 짜는 사람 a weaver// ~를 짜다 weave.

베개 a pillow; [긴 베개] a bolster. ¶공기 ~ an air cushion// ~를 베고 (sleep) with one's head on a pillow// ~를 베다 use a pillow / lay [rest] one's head on the pillow.
●**베갯머리** one's bedside. ¶~에 앉아 시중들다 sit up by [at] (a person's) bedside. **베갯밑공사**(-公事) a wifely advice; a curtain lecture. ¶~에 넘어가지 않는 남자 없다 No one can fail to comply with his wife's private entreaties. **베갯속** the stuffing of a pillow. **베갯잇** a pillowcase; a pillow slip [sham].

베고니아 [식] a begonia.

베끼다 1 [옮겨 쓰다] copy; take a copy (of); transcribe. ¶원고를 ~ make a copy of a manuscript// 노트에 ~ copy into a notebook // 책에서 문제를 ~ copy (out) a problem from a book// 참고서에서 그대로 ~ copy information word for word from a reference book// 그의 리포트는 백과사전을 한 자 한 자 그대로 베낀 것이었다 His report was copied from the encyclopedia word for word. **2** [모사

베네룩스 Benelux. ▶ Belgium, Netherlands 및 Luxembourg 3국의 총칭.

베니어 veneer.
● **베니어판** a veneer board; a plywood board(합판). ¶~을 댄 문 a veneered door∥~을 대다 veneer (a wall). **베니어합판** plywood.

베다¹ (베개 등을) rest[lay] one's head on (a pillow / a thing). ¶팔베개를 ~ pillow one's head on one's arm∥베개를 베고 자다 sleep with one's head on the pillow.

베다² 1 [자르다] cut; chop; hash(잘게); slice(얇게); slash; hack (to pieces) (토막 내다); saw(톱으로); shear; clip(가위로); fell; hew; cut down(나무를); mow(풀을); reap; gather in; harvest(곡식을). ¶깊이 ~ cut deep into∥잘게 ~ chop up / cut into pieces / hack to pieces / hackle / hash / mangle∥얇게 ~ cut (the meat) in slices∥둘로 ~ cut (a thing) in[into] two∥나무를 ~ fell [cut down] a tree / cut wood / hew timber∥목을 ~ cut off (a person's) head / behead (a person) / decapitate a person.
2 [상처를 내다] cut; wound; inflict a wound (on); injure; scratch. ¶손가락을 ~ cut one's finger (on a knife)∥칼로 베어 죽이다 put (a person) to the sword∥면도할 때 얼굴을 베지 않도록 조심하라 Mind you don't cut your face when you're shaving.

베어 먹다 cut off and eat; take a slice and eat it; take a bite out of. ¶사과를 한 입 ~ take a bite out of an apple∥그는 빵의 귀퉁이를 베어 먹었다 He bit off the heel of the bread.

베드 신 a bed room scene.
베드로 전서(-前書) [성] The First Epistle of St. Peter; I Peter(약어 I Pet.).
베드로 후서(-後書) [성] The Second Epistle of St. Peter; II Peter(약어 II Pet.).
베란다 a veranda(h); (미) a porch; a gallery.
베레(모)(-帽) (프) béret; a beret (cap). ¶그는 ~를 비스듬히 눌러 쓰고 있었다 He had a beret pulled on sidewise above his face.
베르무트 [리큐어의 일종] vermouth.
베를린 장벽(-障壁) the Berlin Wall.
베릴륨 [화] beryllium(기호 Be).
베스트 [최선·전력] best. ¶~를 다하다 do one's best[utmost]∥~을 다해라 Do your best. / Do the best you can.
베스트셀러 a best[top] seller; a best-selling book. ¶그의 책이 금주 ~의 톱을 차지했다 His book was at the top of the best seller list this week. / His book was this week's number one best seller.
● **베스트셀러 작가** a best-selling author [writer].
베실 hemp thread[yarn]; linen thread.
베어링 [공] a bearing. ¶롤러 ~ a roller bearing∥볼 ~ a ball bearing.
베옷 hemp[hempen] clothes.
베이다 cut oneself; get (it) cut; get a cut (on). ¶칼에 손가락을 ~ get a cut on the finger with a knife∥그는 정강이를 베였다 He received a cut on the shin.∥그는 얼굴에 베인 상처가 있다 He has a scar from a cut on his face.
베이스¹ [야구] a base; a base bag; (미국 속어) a sack. ¶1[2/3]루 ~ first[second /

third] base∥홈 ~ home base[plate]∥~에 미끄러져 들어가다 slide into the base∥(주자가) ~에 있다 be on the base / hold the base∥~를 떠나 있다 be off the base∥~를 밟다 step on a base / reach a base(도달하다)∥풀 ~이다 The bases are loaded.
● **베이스 온 볼** [야구] a base on balls; a walk; a pass. ¶~로 일루에 진출하다 get a base[walk to first] on balls.
베이스² [음] 1 [남자 목소리의 가장 낮은 음역] bass; [그 음역의 가수] a bass (singer). ¶굵은 ~ 목소리 a deep bass voice. 2 a contrabass. ⇨**콘트라베이스**.
베이스캠프 [등산] a base camp.
베이식 [컴퓨터 초급 언어] BASIC(▶ Beginner's All-purpose Symbolic Instruction Code 의 약어).
베이지(색)(-色) [밝은 갈색] beige. ¶~의 beige∥~ 수트 a beige suit.
베이징 원인(北京原人) [고고] a Sinanthropus; Peking[Pekin] man.
베이컨 bacon. ¶~ 세 조각 three strips [slices] of bacon∥~에그 bacon and eggs / eggs and bacon.
베이클라이트 [화] bakelite. ¶~ 제품 bakelite goods.
베이킹파우더 baking powder.
베일 a veil. ¶신부의 ~ a bridal veil∥~을 쓰고 under the veil of∥~을 쓰다[~로 얼굴을 가리다] veil one's face / muffle one's face in a veil∥~을 벗다 unveil / reveal oneself∥~을 올리다 lift[raise] a veil∥~을 내리다 lower [drop] a veil∥신비의 ~에 싸여 있다 be veiled[wrapped] in mystery∥그 여자는 얼굴에 ~을 쓰고 있었다 The woman was wearing a veil[had a veil over her face].
베짱이 [동] a long-horned grasshopper; a katydid.
베크렐선(-線) [물] Becquerel rays.
베타선(-線) [물] β-rays; beta rays.
베타 입자(-粒子) [물] beta particles.
베테랑 a veteran; [숙련자] an expert. ¶~ 조종사 a veteran pilot∥~ 조율사(調律士)의 ~ an expert piano tuner∥외교의 ~ an adept in diplomacy∥그는 이런 일에 있어서는 ~이다 He is an old hand at this sort of thing.
베틀 a loom. ¶~로 짜다 weave (fabric) on a loom.
베풀다 1 (잔치 등을) give[have] (a party); hold (a banquet[meeting]); (미국 영어) throw (a party, a banquet, etc.). ¶홍 씨의 귀국 축하연이 베풀어졌다 A dinner was given in honor of Mr. Hong who had recently returned from his journey abroad.∥당신을 위하여 연회를 베풀고자 합니다 I'd like to give a party in your honor.
2 (자비심·동정·사랑 등을) have mercy (on); [은혜를 누리게 하다] do a person a kindness; [자선 금품을 주다] give alms (to the poor); bestow (a favor on a person). ¶자선을 ~ give alms / render aid (to a person)∥자비를 ~ have mercy (on) / show (a person) mercy∥동정을 ~ have[take] pity on (the poor)∥남에게 호의를 ~ give[hand out] favors to others∥먹을 것을 베풀어 주십시오 Please give me something to eat.∥신이여 자비를 베푸소서! God have mercy on us!
벡터 [수][물] a vector. ¶~의 장(場) a vector field.
벤 다이어그램 [수] a Venn diagram.

벤젠 [화] benzene; benzol.
벤처 기업 (一企業) a venture business.
벤처 캐피털 [경] (a) venture capital; (영) (a) risk capital.
벤치 [긴 의자] a bench; [스포츠에서 선수 대기소] the (player's) bench; [야구장의] a dugout. ¶정원 ~ a garden bench∥~을 지키다 be bench warmer / warm the bench∥선수를 ~로 불러들이다 bench a player.
벤치워머 a bench warmer.
벨 a bell; a doorbell; a front-bell; a buzzer. ¶비상~ an alarm bell∥~ 소리 the sound of the bell∥~을 울리다 ring[touch] the bell / ring at the bell∥~을 누르다 press[push / touch] the bell[(bell) button]∥~을 울려 하인을 부르다 ring for a servant∥~이 울리고 있다 The doorbell is ringing. / There does the doorbell.∥내가 ~을 울리자 노파가 문을 열었다 An old woman opened the door in response to my ring.∥전화~ 소리가 울리고 있다 The telephone is ringing.∥볼일이 생기면 이 ~을 울려 주십시오 Please push this button if you want anything. / (가게 등에서) Ring this bell for service.
벨벳 (a) velvet. ¶~ 같은 velvety / velvet-like∥~처럼 매끄러운[부드러운] velvety / velvet / as smooth as velvet.
벨트 [띠] a belt; a waist belt; [피대] a belt; belting. ¶그린 ~ a green belt∥안전 ~ a safety[seat] belt∥~가 달린 상의 a belted coat∥~를 매다 fasten[buckle (on)] a belt / ~를 죄었다[늦추었다] I tightened [loosened] my belt.∥그는 ~를 죄면서 밖으로 나갔다 He went out fastening his belt.∥그녀는 허리에 넓은 ~를 하고 있었다 She wore a wide belt around her waist.
벼 [식] a rice plant; (열매) unhulled rice; a grain of (unhusked) rice(낟알). ¶~를 심다 plant rice∥~를 베다 reap[harvest] rice / mow[cut down] rice (plants)∥~가 잘되고 있다 The rice is doing well.
● **벼 베기** rice reaping; mowing of rice plants. **벼 타작** rice threshing.
벼농사 (一農事) (재배) rice growing[farming]; (수확) a rice crop. ¶올해는 ~가 잘되었다[잘 안 되었다] This year's rice crop is good [poor]. **벼농사하다** do[engage in] rice farming.
벼락 a thunderbolt; a thunderstroke; a stroke of lightning. ¶날 ~ a bolt from[out of] the blue∥~ 치는 소리 a peal[roar / roll] of thunder / cracks of thunder∥~이 떨어지다 be hit by a thunderbolt / be struck by lightning / [비유] (상관으로부터) be scolded severely / get a scolding∥소나무에 ~이 떨어졌다 The pine tree was struck by lightning.∥근방에 ~이 쳤다 The thunderbolt fell close by.
벼락 치는 하늘도 속인다(속담) You can fool anybody if you want to.
벼락(을) 맞다 suffer a quite unexpected mishap[calamity]; [야단맞다] be scolded severely. ¶자네 그런 짓 하면 벼락 맞네 If you do that, there will be hell to pay.
● **벼락감투** (생각지도 않은) an unexpected government position given overnight; (배경·정실에 의한) an official post given to an undeserved man through backing[pull / influence]; a government position given to a person as a political favor. ¶~를 쓰다 become a government official overnight / get promoted suddenly to a higher position (through favoritism) / be appointed to a position quite unexpectedly. **벼락공부** cramming; bolting (for an examination); [구어] cram. ¶~를 하다 cram (up) / get up / swot (at) (a subject). **벼락부자** an upstart; a new rich; (프) a nouveau riche; (프) a parvenu; (집합적) the new rich. ¶~가 되다 become very rich suddenly / strike it rich / gain sudden wealth∥그는 미친 듯이 엄청난 ~가 되었다 He rose from obscurity to immense wealth. **벼락출세** ¶~를 하다 rise suddenly in the world. **벼락치기** hasty preparation; hasty[hurried] job; a stopgap. ¶~ 공부 cramming∥~로 만든 초안 a hastily prepared[an improvised] draft∥~로 만든 위원회[팀] a scratch committee[team].
벼락같다 [요란하다] thunderous; [빠르다] quick; rapid; prompt. ¶벼락같은 소리 a thunderous[an ear-splitting] roar∥벼락같은 소리를 지르다 thunder out / cry in a thunderous voice. **벼락같이** ¶아버지는 아들에게 ~ 호통쳤다 The father thundered at his son.
벼랑 a cliff; a precipice; a bluff(바닷가의); palisades(강가의). ¶~ 끝 the edge[brink] of a precipice∥~을 기어오르다 climb[scale] a cliff / go over a precipice∥~에서 떨어지다 fall over a precipice / tumble down a precipice∥~에서 아래를 내려다보다 look over a precipice.
벼랑에 몰리다 [궁지에 몰리다] have one's back to the wall; be behind the eight ball.
● **벼랑길** a ledge.
벼루 (먹을 가는) an ink stone; an ink slab. ¶~에 먹을 갈다 rub an ink stick on the ink stone.
● **벼룻돌** (stone used as) an ink stone. **벼룻집** (연갑·연상·硯箱) an ink stone case; [연상(硯床)] a stationery cabinet.
벼룩 a flea. ¶~ 약 flea[insect] powder∥~에 물린 자국 a fleabite∥~에 물린 팔 a fleabitten arm∥~에 물리다 be bitten by a flea∥~에 시달리다 be tormented by fleas∥~에 물린 데가 가렵다 The fleabite itches.
벼룩의 간을 내먹는다(속담) skin a flea for its hide (and tallow).
● **벼룩시장** a flea market.
벼르다[1] [미리 마음을 먹다] plan; design; aim (at); intend (to do); contemplate (doing); be intent[bent] (on); have (something) in mind; keep both[one's] eyes wide open (for); look forward (to); be determined (to do); be eager (for / to do). ¶기회를 ~ watch for a chance / be on the lookout for an opportunity∥그는 사장 자리를 벼르고 있다 He has kept his eyes wide open on the presidency of the company.∥마침내 그는 오랫동안 벼르던 책을 샀다 At last he bought the book he had wanted so long[for a long time].∥"어디 두고 보자." 하고 그는 벼르며 나갔다 He left, saying "We shall see."
벼르다[2] [여러 몫으로 나누다] distribute; apportion; divide[share] equally; deal out (to / among); portion out. ¶사과를 세 몫으로 ~ divide an apple into three shares.
벼리 1 (그물의) a head rope. 2 [뼈대] a general plan; the skeleton (of a poem).
● **벼릿줄** a head rope. ⇨ ²벼리1

벼리다 reforge [retemper] the blade (of an old knife [sword]); put a edge on (a knife by forging). ¶부엌칼을 ~ reforge [retemper] the blade of a kitchen knife.

벼슬 a government [an official] post [position]; official rank. ¶~이 높은 사람 a high(-ranking) official [officer] // ~이 높다 [낮다] be high [low] in official rank / be of high [low] government position // ~이 오르다 rise in official rank / …보다 ~이 위이다 outrank (a person) / be above [over] (a person) in official rank / ~을 얻다 [잃다] obtain [lose] a government position // ~을 그만두다 leave [resign / quit] one's public office [government service] / resign office // ~에 있다 be in the government service / be at service as an official / hold an official position / …의 ~을 내리다 confer upon (a person) the title of … // 지금 어떤 ~에 계십니까 What office do you hold? **벼슬하다** take up a public office; enter the government; enter into government service; hold an office [appointment] under [in the] government.
● **벼슬길** the way (to get) into government service [public office / officialdom]; government employ [service]. ¶~에 나서다 [오르다] enter [go into] government service / start one's career as an official. **벼슬살이** an official life [career]; life as an official. ¶~를 하다 lead an official life / serve as a government official. **벼슬아치** a government [public] official; (영) a civil servant. ¶~가 되다 become a public [civil] servant / take up a public office / enter into government service.

벽(壁) a wall; [칸막이] a partition (wall). ¶~이 없는 wallless // ~으로 칸막이하다 [막다 / 두르다] wall off [up / in] // ~을 바르다 plaster a wall // ~에 기대다 lean against the wall // ~에 그림을 붙이다 fix a picture to the wall // ~을 사이에 두고 이야기하다 talk (with a person) with a wall between / talk (to a person) on the other side of the wall // (남에게) ~을 두다 deep (people) at a distance [at arm's length] / be reserved // 9초의 ~을 깨뜨리다 crack the 9 second barrier (for 100 meters) / ~을 깨다 break the sound barrier // 달력을 ~에 걸었다 I hang the calendar on the wall. // ~에 구멍이 (나) 있다 There is a hole in the wall.
벽에도 귀가 있다 (속담) Walls have ears.
벽에 부딪히다 [난관에 부딪히다] come up against a brick wall; run into [hit] a blank wall; reach a deadlock; be deadlocked.

벽(癖) 1 [치우치게 즐기는 성벽] a craze (for); a mania (for). ¶수집~ a mania for (stamp) collecting / a collecting mania. 2 [버릇] a (personal) habit; a (peculiar) way; a peculiarity; a trick; a quirk; a vice(나쁜).
벽개(劈開) [광] cleavage. **벽개하다** cleave.
벽걸이(壁-) wall decorations; a wall tapestry. ¶~ 전화기 a wall telephone set.
벽계(碧溪) a blue [bluish] stream.
벽공(碧空) the blue [azure] sky; the azure.
벽난로(壁暖爐) a fireplace. ¶~ 바닥 a hearth.
벽돌(甓-) a (piece of) brick. ¶공동(空洞) (a) hollow brick / 내화 ~ (a) firebrick / 방화 ~ (a) fireproof brick // 붉은 ~ (a) red brick // ~ 굽는 가마 a brickkiln // 구멍 난 ~ (a) perforated brick // ~색 brick-red / bricky // ~로 포장한 도로 a brick-topped road // ~로 짓다 build (a house) of brick [with bricks] // ~을 쌓다 lay bricks // ~을 굽다 bake [burn / fire / make] bricks.
● **벽돌공** [벽돌 쌓는 사람] a bricklayer; a mason; [벽돌 만드는 사람] a brick maker; a brick burner. **벽돌담** a brick wall. **벽돌집** a brick house; a building in brick.

벽두(劈頭) [글의 첫머리] the opening [beginning] (of a writing); [일이 시작된 맨 처음] the first [start]; the outset. ¶~에 at the outset [very beginning] / in the first place / to start [begin] with / first of all / first and foremost / ~부터 from the start [outset] // ~에 그녀의 이름이 있다 Her name heads the list.

벽력(霹靂) a thunderbolt. ⇒**벼락**. ¶청천 ~ a bolt from the blue // ~같이 소리 지르다 roar [thunder] (at) // 내게는 그야말로 청천의 ~이었다 For me it was a veritable bolt from the blue. / I was flabbergasted [thunderstruck].

벽면(壁面) (the surface [face] of) a wall.
벽보(壁報) a poster; a placard; a bill; a wall newspaper; (게시) a notice. ¶괴~ a strange [mysterious] poster / an illegal bill // ~를 붙이다 put up a poster [placard / bill] / stick [paste up] a bill / post a notice // 금연이라는 ~가 있었다 There was a notice prohibiting smoking. // ~ 붙이지 말 것 (게시) Post No Bills. / No Posters.

벽서(壁書) a writing on a wall; [벽보] a bill; a poster; a placard. **벽서하다** write on a wall.
벽시계(壁時計) a wall clock.
벽신문(壁新聞) a wall newspaper.
벽안(碧眼) blue eyes. ¶~의 사람 a blue-eyed person / [서양인] a Westerner.
벽오동(碧梧桐) [식] a Chinese parasol (tree); a Phoenix tree.
벽옥(碧玉) [광] jasper; green jade.
벽장(壁欌) a (wall) closet; a built-in closet; a wall cupboard.
벽지(僻地) a remote [secluded] place; an isolated area; an out-of-the-way place; an outlying region; backcountry; (口) back country; (구어) the sticks. ¶~의 어린이들 children in a remote part of the country // ~에 살다 live far away from a city [civilization] / live in an out-of-the-way place.
벽지(壁紙) wallpaper. ¶~를 바르다 wallpaper / paper a wall.
벽창호(碧昌-) an obstinate [incorrigible] person; a pigheaded person; a hardhead; a blockhead.
벽촌(僻村) a remote village; an out-of-the-way hamlet; the remote countryside. ¶나는 강원도의 ~에서 태어났다 I was born in a secluded village in Gangwondo.
벽토(壁土) plaster; stucco; wall mud. ¶~를 개다 prepare plaster [wall mud].
벽해(碧海) the blue sea; emerald [blue] water.
벽화(壁畵) a wall painting; [프레스코 화법에 의한 것] a fresco (pl. ~es, ~s); a mural. ¶고분 ~ mural paintings in a tumulus / the ancient tomb mural.

변 a jargon; an argot; a lingo (pl. ~es, ~s); a cant; secret language. ¶도둑의 ~ the patter of thieves / thieves' Latin // ~을 써서 이야기하다 talk in secret language.
변(便) [대소변] excreta; excrement; [대변]

f(a)eces; stool(s); motions; movements. ¶된 [묽은] ~ hard[loose] feces//~이 통하다 have a motion (of the bowels)//~을 보다 evacuate the bowels / have a bowel motion [movement] / obey[respond to] the call of nature / (고) stool//~이 통하다 My bowels move[act / are open].

변[1](邊) (한자의) the left-hand side[radical] of a Chinese character. ¶(한자를) ~으로 찾다 look up (a Chinese character in a dictionary) under its radical//이 글자는 옷의 ~으로 해야 한다 This letter should have the clothing radical.

변[2](邊) **1** (다각형의) a side; [수] a member; a latus (*pl.* latera). ¶밑 ~ the base/삼각형의 세 ~ the three sides of a triangle. **2** (바둑의) the side area of a *baduk* board. **3** (과녁의) the fringe[periphery] of the bull's-eye of a target. **4** [가장자리] a side; an edge; a verge. ¶강~ a riverside / a river bank / an edge of a river.

변[3](邊) interest (on a loan). ⇨변리(邊利) ¶싼 [비싼] ~으로 at low[high] interest.

변(變) [돌발사] a sudden happening; an unexpected occurrence[event]; [사고] an accident; a mishap; [재앙] a calamity; a disaster; a misfortune; [비상사] an emergency; a contingency; [난리] a disturbance; an uprising; an agitation. ¶~이 나다 an accident[incident] happens[occurs]//~을 당하다 have a mishap / meet with an accident[a disaster]//~을 일으키다 cause[bring about] an accident.

변격(變格) (an) irregularity. ⇨변칙

변경(邊境) a frontier (area); a border area; a remote region; an outlying district. ¶~의 도시 a frontier town / a town on the frontier/~을 침범하다 violate a frontier//~의 수비를 공고히 하다 fortify (the defenses of) the frontier.
●**변경 개척자** a frontiersman.

변경(變更) (전체 또는 부분적인) (a) change; (부분적인) (an) alteration; [수정] (a) modification; (an) amendment. ¶동의의 ~ modification of a motion//~을 가하다 make a change (in) / make alterations (in) / make an amendment (to)/예정에 ~이 없다 The schedule remains unchanged[unaltered]. / There have been no changes[alterations] in the schedule. **변경하다** alter; change; modify; amend; shift. ¶변경할 수 있는 changeable / alterable//변경할 수 없는 unchangeable / unalterable//날짜[일자]를 ~ change the date (of). →¶식비는 예고 없이 변경될 수 있다 Charges for board are subject to change without notice.//시(市) 청사의 모양이 완전히 변경되었다 The city hall was completely remodeled.//토지 개발 계획은 시민 공원 건설로 모양이 변경되었다 The development plan for the land was changed [altered] to provide for a public park.

변고(變故) [재난] a calamity; a disaster; a disastrous event; a misfortune; [사고] an accident; a mishap; happening; [말썽거리] trouble. ¶거듭되는 ~ a series of misfortunes//~ 없이 지내다 get along with no trouble(s)[without any trouble]//~을 당하다 meet with trouble / suffer a calamity / have a mishap/그 ~를 듣고 나는 현장에 달려갔다 Hearing of the disaster, I rushed to the spot.

변곡점(變曲點) [수] an inflection[(영) inflexion] point; a point of inflection.

변광성(變光星) [천] a variable star.

변괴(變怪) [재변] an unusual[extraordinary] calamity[disaster]; [악행] an outrageous deed; an extraordinary misdeed; an atrocity.

변기(便器) a toilet bowl; (침실용) a chamber pot; (환자용) a bedpan; (벽에 설치한 남자용) a urinal.

변놀이(邊—) moneylending. ⇨돈놀이

변덕(變德) (a) caprice; capriciousness; a (passing) whim; fickleness; a change of mind. ¶일시적 ~ the caprice[whim] of the moment//~이 없는 사람 an even-tempered [equable] person//~을 부리다 behave capriciously//그녀는 ~이 심하다 She is inconstant. / She is always changing her mind.//날씨가 ~을 부리고 있다 We are having crazy weather.
●**변덕꾸러기** / **변덕쟁이** a capricious[whimsical / moody / fickle] person; a person who flits from one thing to another; a weathercock.

변덕스럽다(變德—) inconstant; changeable; capricious; whimsical; fitful; (주로 여자가 남자에 대해) fickle. ¶변덕스럽게 capriciously / whimsically / at whim / by fits and starts//변덕스러운 성격 an inconsistent[a whimsical] character//변덕스러운 (가을) 날씨 changeable[unstable / fickle] (autumn) weather//사랑은 변덕스러운 것 Love is erratic. / You can't rely on love.//그는 변덕스러운 사람이었다 He was a capricious [moody] man.//그녀는 변덕스러워서 남자 친구를 자주 바꾼다 She is fickle[capricious] and is always switching boyfriends.//그는 여자 관계에서 ~ He never sticks to one woman for long. / (문어) He is inconstant in love.//무슨 변덕스런 생각에서 내가 그녀와 교제하고 있는 것은 아니다 I'm not going out with her out of some capricious whim[(구어) just for kicks].

변돈(邊—) money lent[put out] at interest; a loan.

변동(變動) (a) change; (an) alteration; (시세 등의) (a) fluctuation. ¶무~ 임금 a pegged wage/대~ a violent[radical] change/계절적 ~ seasonal fluctuation//물가의 ~ fluctuations in prices//~이 심한 물가[시황] fluctuating prices[markets]//~ 없는 unchanged / unaltered / stationary / firm//~을 보이다 show a change//우리는 사회의 격심한 ~을 따라갈 수 없었다 We could not keep up with the rapid changes in society.//물가에 격심한 ~이 있었다 There was a sharp fluctuation in prices.//내각의 ~이 예상되고 있다 A reshuffle of the Cabinet is (being) predicted. **변동하다** (undergo a) change; fluctuate; alter; vary. ¶물가가 격심하게 변동하고 있다 Prices are fluctuating sharply.//온도는 25도와 30도 사이에서 변동한다 The temperature varies[ranges] between 25 and 30 degrees.
●**변동 소득** fluctuating income. **변동 폭** the range of fluctuation (in prices). **변동 환율 (제)** floating exchange rate (system); the free-exchange rate (system).

변두리(邊—) **1** [교외] the outskirts[environs] (of a town); a suburb. ¶~의 suburban//서

울 ~에 on[in / at] the outskirts of Seoul // 그는 ~에서 가게를 내고 있다 He has[runs] a store (situated) away from the center of the city[business center]. / His shop is located off the beaten track. // 그는 마을 ~에 살고 있다 He lives on the outskirts of town. // 마을 ~에서 사고가 있었다 There was an accident at the edge of the town. // 이 거리의 ~에 작은 성당이 있다 There is a small shrine just off this street. **2** [가장자리] the outer edge; the brim; the rim; the margin; [주위] the circumference.

변란(變亂) a (social) disturbance; an upheaval; [반란] an uprising; a rebellion; [내란] a civil war; [전란] a war.

변량(變量) [수] a variable; a variate; variable quantities. ¶**표준 ~** a canonical variate.

변론(辯論) **1** [논쟁] discussion; argument; controversy; disputation; [토론] debate. **변론하다** argue; discuss; debate. **2** [법정의] pleading; oral proceedings[pleadings]; debate; argument; a forensic speech. ¶**구두 ~** oral proceedings // **법정 ~의** forensic // **~에 들어가다** enter upon debates / open the oral proceedings // **~을 개시[재개]하다** open [reopen] the oral proceedings // **~을 종결하다** conclude one's argument. **변론하다** proceed orally; argue; plead (at the bar / before the court). ¶변호인이 피고를 위해 변론했다 The defense attorney[counsel] pleaded[argued] for the accused.
● **변론가** a debater; a controversialist; an orator.

변류기(變流器) [전] a converter; a current transformer; a rheotrope.

변리(辨理) management; conduct; disposition; dealing. **변리하다** manage (a matter); conduct (business); dispose of (a matter); deal with (an affair).
● **변리 공사**(-公使) a minister resident (*pl.* ministers resident). **변리사**(-士) a patent attorney[lawyer / agent].

변리(邊利) interest (on a loan). ¶**~ 없이** free of interest // **싼[비싼] ~로** at low[high] interest // **~가 붙다** yield[bear] interest (at 5 percent).

변말 a cant phrase; a slang; a jargon; a lingo (*pl.* ~(e)s); secret language. ¶**~을 쓰다** speak the jargon of one's society.

변명(辨明) an explanation; an excuse; [정당화] (a) justification; [항변] a defense[(영) defence]. ¶**궁색한 ~** a lame[sorry / poor] excuse // **서투른 ~** a clumsy excuse // **~적인 explanatory / vindicatory** // 우리가 납득할 수 있는 ~을 할 수 있겠니 Can you give us a convincing explanation? // 그녀는 자신의 행동에 대해서 ~ 같은 말은 한마디도 하지 않았다 She didn't say anything in justification of her conduct. // 그는 나를 위해 많은 ~을 해 주었다 He said much in my defense. // 당신의 행동은 ~의 여지가 없다 What you have done is inexcusable. / Nothing can excuse your action. // 그런 ~은 통하지 않아 Such excuses will not serve you. / We can not accept such an excuse. // 그런 짓을 하고 ~을 할 수 있는가 Do you think your action admits of any excuse? / How can you justify what you have done? **변명하다** explain; explain oneself (for); vindicate (oneself, one's honor, etc.); excuse oneself (for doing something); make an excuse; justify oneself; defend oneself; plead one's case. ¶그는 지각하여 선생님에게 변명했다 He made an excuse to his teacher for being late. // 그가 아무리 변명하려고 해도 그의 혐의는 풀리지 않는다 However hard he tries to explain [defend] himself, he cannot clear himself of suspicion. // 그녀는 그 주(州)의 법률을 몰랐다고 변명했다 She pleaded ignorance of the laws of that state. // 나에게도 변명할 기회를 주게 Give me a chance to defend myself.

변명(變名) [이름을 바꿈] changing one's name; [그 이름] an assumed name. **변명하다** change one's name; assume an other name.

변모(變貌) (a) transfiguration; (a) transformation; a change in one's looks[of appearance]; a metamorphosis (*pl.* -phoses). **변모하다** change; undergo a complete change; be transformed[transfigured]; assume a different aspect. ¶나는 그 마을이 어쩌나 변모해 보이는지를 알고서 놀랐다 I was astonished to see how entirely transformed[changed / different] the village looked. // 한국인의 사상은 6·25 전쟁 후에 변모했다 The ideas of the Korean have changed since Korean War.

변모없다(變貌-) [융통성 없다] inflexible; unadaptable; simple and honest; [말·행동을 마구 하다] unscrupulous; forward; rude.

변박(辯駁) refutation; confutation; contradiction; disproof; rebuttal. **변박하다** refute; confute; contradict; disprove; rebut. ¶사실을 들어 논적(論敵)을 ~ confute one's opponent with facts.

변발(辮髮·編髮) a pigtail; a queue. **변발하다** queue; plait one's hair into a pigtail. ¶**변발한** pigtailed.

변방(邊方) **1** [가장자리 쪽] the outer area; edges; sides. **2** a frontier (area). ⇨**변경**(邊境)

변방(邊防) the frontier defenses.

변변하다 1 [생김새가] (fairly) good-looking; handsome; comely; pretty. **변변히** comelily; pretty. ¶**~** 생기다 be good-looking / look comely[handsome / pretty].
2 (사람·사물의 질·내용 등이) fairly good; tolerable; passable; fair; decent; respectable; proper. ¶그는 영어로 변변한 편지 한 장 못 쓴다 He can't write a letter in English properly. / He can't write a decent letter in English. // 나는 변변한 봉급도 받지 못하고 있다 I am miserably[poorly] paid. // 그녀의 남편은 변변한 책이 없다 Her husband has no books to speak of[worth mentioning]. // 이 고장에는 변변한 음식점이 없다 There are no restaurants to speak of in this town. **변변히** [잘] well; [충분히] enough; sufficiently; much; [만족스럽게] satisfactorily; [알맞게] decently; properly. ¶**~** 생각해 보지도 않고 without due consideration // 그와 ~ 이야기할 시간도 없다 I have hardly time enough to talk with him. // 그는 너무 소심해서 사람들 앞에서는 ~ 말도 못 한다 He is so timid that he scarcely opens his mouth in public.

변별(辨別) discrimination; distinction. ¶**~적인** distinctive / discriminative / [언] obviative. **변별하다** discriminate[tell / distinguish] (A from B / between A and B). ¶그는 옳고 그름을 변별할 줄 안다 He has the capacity to discriminate between right and

wrong.
- **변별력** discrimination; judgment.
- **변보**(變報) news[a report] about an accident [a disaster / a calamity]; (a piece of) bad news.
- **변복**(變服) (a) disguise. ¶~으로 in disguise / incognito. **변복하다** disguise[dress] oneself (as); be disguised (as). ¶그는 순례자[여자]로 변복했다 He disguised himself as a pilgrim [woman].
- **변비(증)**(便祕症) [의] constipation; obstipation; costiveness. ¶~로 고생하는 사람 a constipated person // ~에 걸리다 be constipated / be costive // suffer from constipation // ~를 고치다 relieve constipation // 1주일 동안 ~에 걸려 있다 I have been constipated for a week. // 이 약은 ~에 좋다 This medicine loosens[opens] bowels.
- **변사**(辯士) [연사] a speaker; [웅변가] an eloquent speaker; an orator; [무성 영화의 해설자] a silent-film narrator; a film interpreter; a movie talker.
- **변사**(變死) an unnatural[accidental] death; [비명횡사] a violent death. **변사하다** meet (with) an unnatural[a violent] death[end]; die by violence; die with one's boots on[in one's boots]; be killed by[in] an accident.
  - **변사자** a person who has met[died] an unnatural death; a person accidentally killed. **변사체** the body of a man who died an unnatural death.
- **변상**(辨償) compensation; indemnification; reparation; reimbursement. **변상하다** compensate; indemnify; reimburse; repair; make up for; make good; pay for (damage). ¶손해는 그 사람 대신 제가 변상하겠습니다 I will compensate you for your loss on his behalf.
  - **변상금** an indemnity; (a) compensation; reparations.
- **변색**(變色) 1 [빛깔의] (a) change of color[(영) colour]; discoloration[(영) discolouration]; fading. **변색하다** change color; [색이 바래다] fade; [색이 칙칙하게] discolor; become discolored. ¶변색하지 않는 빛깔 a fast color // 변색한 옷 a faded dress // 염색한 것이 변색하지 않도록 그늘에서 말리다 dry dyed goods in the shade to keep the color from fading // 청색 천은 변색하기 쉽다 Blue cloth discolors easily. // 이 천은 변색하지 않는다 The colors [dyes] in this cloth are fast. →¶천을 변색시키다 allow cloth to discolor // 커튼이 매우 변색되어 있었다 The curtains were badly discolored. / The color of the curtains were badly faded.
  2 [안색의] change of countenance. **변색하다** change (one's) countenance.
- **변설**(辯舌) tongue; speech; eloquence. ¶유창한 ~ fluent speech / an eloquent tongue / lucid[beautiful] eloquence // ~을 늘어놓다 speak eloquently[fluently] / exert one's oratorical power // ~이 유창하다 have a fluent [ready] tongue / be fluent in speech.
- **변성**(變成) (a) rebirth; (a) regeneration; (a) metamorphosis (*pl.* -phoses). **변성하다** regenerate; metamorphose.
  - **변성암** [광] a metamorphic rock.
- **변성**(變性) [의] degeneration; [화] denaturalization. **변성하다** degenerate; be[get] denatured; [바꾸다] denaturalize; denature. →¶변성시키다 denature / denaturalize.
- **변성**(變聲) the change[breaking / cracking] of voice. **변성하다** (one's voice) change [break / crack]. ¶소년은 사춘기가 되면 변성하여 목소리가 굵어진다 A boy's voice changes and becomes deeper at puberty.
  - **변성기** the period when a boy's voice changes[breaks]; the age of the change of voice.
- **변성명**(變姓名) [성과 이름을 고침] changing one's (surname and given) name. **변성명하다** change one's name. ¶그는 홍길동으로 변성명하고 있었다 He had changed his name to Hong Gildong.
- **변소**(便所) a lavatory; a water closet(약어 W.C.); a privy; (영) a convenience; a latrine(공장·학교 등의); (미) a toilet (room); a washroom; (욕조 등이 있는) a bathroom; (영국 속어) a loo; (회사·은행·역 등의) a ladies'[men's] room; (미) a rest room; (배·군함의) the head; the john; (미국 속어) the can. ¶공동 ~ a communal lavatory[closet] / 공중 ~ a public lavatory[toilet / rest room] / (미) a comfort station // 남자[여자] ~ men's [ladies'] room / (게시) Men[Women] / Gentlemen[Ladies] // 수세식 ~ a flush toilet / a water closet // ~ 치는 사람 a night-soil man // ~에 가다 go to the toilet[bath / bathroom / closet] / go to stool / (완곡하게) go to wash one's hands / get a wash.
- **변속**(變速) a change of speed. ¶5단 ~ 자동차 a car with five gears. **변속하다** change speed; change[(미) shift] gears.
  - **변속기** a gearbox; a transmission.
- **변수**(變數) [수] a variable; a fluent.
- **변신**(變身) 1 disguise.
  2 transformation; metamorphosis. ¶화려한 ~ transforming oneself in a conspicuous [an eye-catching] way. **변신하다** change (into); turn (into); be transformed[metamorphosed] (into); transform oneself (into). ¶동화에서는 흔히 동물이 사람으로 변신한다 In fairy tales animals very often transform themselves into human beings. // 그는 10년 동안에 아주 화려하게 변신했다 He has transformed himself in a most magnificent way in ten years' time. // 그는 회사에서는 점잖지만, 집에 돌아오면 폭군으로 변신한다 Though he is polite in the office, he turns into a tyrant when he gets home. // 그는 보수에서 혁신으로 변신했다 He changed [switched] from a conservative to a progressive.
- **변심**(變心) [마음의 변함] a change of heart [mind]; [배반] betrayal; treachery; [변덕] fickleness. **변심하다** [마음을 달리 먹다] change one's mind; have a change of heart; [배반하다] turn traitor; betray (a person). ¶여자들은 변심하기 쉽다 Women are fickle. // 그는 변심하여 적에게 투항했다 He turned traitor and went over to the enemy. // 그녀는 이제 그에게서 변심해 버렸다 She has lost interest in him.
- **변압**(變壓) [전] transformation. **변압하다** transform (a current) (in potential).
  - **변압기** a (current) transformer; a potential transformer.
- **변온 동물**(變溫動物) a cold-blooded animal; a poikilothermic animal; a poikilotherm; a hematocryal animal.
- **변위**(變位) [물] displacement.

변이

●**변위 전류** [물] a displacement current.
변이(變異) **1** [생] variation; a rogue(열등한). ¶돌연~ (a) mutation. **2** an accident. ⇨ˇ이변(異變)
●**변이설** the variation theory.
변이(變移) (a) change; (a) shift; (an) alteration; (a) mutation; (a) transmutation; [화] a conversion. **변이하다** change; mutate.
변장(變裝) (a) disguise. **변장하다** put on a makeup; disguise oneself (as); be disguised (as); wear a disguise; make up (as); [가장하다] masquerade (as). ¶그는 구두닦이로 변장했다 He disguised[dressed] himself as a shoeblack.∥그는 누더기를 입고 변장했다 He wore rags as a disguise.∥그는 경관으로 변장하고 도망쳤다 He got away in[under] the disguise of a policeman.∥그는 농부 차림으로 변장하고 도망쳤다 He fled[ran away] dressed like[in the disguise of] a farmer.∥그는 농군으로 변장하여 무사히 검문소를 통과했다 Disguised as[In the disguise of] a peasant, he passed the checkpoint safely.∥그는 가발을 써서 변장했다 He disguised himself with a wig.
●**변장술** the art of disguise[camouflage].
변재(辯才) oratorical talent[skill]; 《속어》 the gift of (the) gab; eloquence. ¶~가 있다 be gifted with eloquence / have an oratorical talent / have a fluent[ready] tongue∥~가 없다 be awkward in speaking / be a poor speaker.
변재(變災) an accident; a calamity; a disaster.
변전(變轉) (a) change; vicissitudes; mutation. ¶인생의 ~에 참고 견디다 bear up under the vicissitudes of life. **변전하다** change; mutate. ¶끊임없이 변전하는 세태 ever-changing social conditions∥사태가 어지럽게 변전함에 따라 as a result of the quick changes in the situation.
변전소(變電所) a substation.
변절(變節) [절개를 바꿈] treachery; betrayal; [주장을 바꿈] (a) defection; apostasy; tergiversation. **변절하다** betray; change[turn] one's coat; change about; turn traitor to (one's country); turn against (a person); change sides; apostatize; tergiversate; desert one's cause[principles / colo(u)rs]; go over [(미) flop] to (the other party).
●**변절자** (당·주의 등의) a renegade; a turncoat; a traitor; (종교상·주의상의) an apostate.
변제(辨濟) repayment; payment; [결제] settlement; [청산] liquidation. **변제하다** repay; pay off; settle; liquidate.
변조(變造) [개조] (an) alteration; [위조] (a) forgery; falsification. **변조하다** alter; forge; falsify; (미) raise (a check). ¶변조한 1만 원권 an altered[a forged / a falsified / (미) a raised] 10,000 won note∥수표를 ~ 하다 raise a check[(영) cheque].
●**변조자** a forger; a falsifier; a (check) raiser. **변조 화폐**[지폐] a counterfeit[false] coin[note]; an altered coin[note].
변조(變調) **1** [음] modulation. ⇨ˇ조바꿈 **2** [물] modulation. ¶주파수 ~ frequency modulation(약어 FM, F.M., f.m., f-m)∥진폭 ~ amplitude modulation(약어 AM, A.M., a.m., a-m). **변조하다** modulate. **3** [불규칙] irregularity; [이상(異常)] abnormality; anomaly. ¶~를 일으키다 become irregular[abnormal] / show strange symptoms[signs] / go[get] out of order.
●**변조기** [물] a modulator.
변종(變種) [생] [원종에서 변화한 것] a variation; a variety; [돌연변이종] a mutation; a mutant; a sport; [기형] a freak; a monster. ¶장미의 새 ~ a new variety of rose.
변주(變奏) [음] (a) variation. **변주하다** play a variation (on a tune, on a theme, etc.).
●**변주곡** a (musical) variation.
변죽(邊─) [그릇·세간들의 가장자리] a rim; a brim; an edge.
변죽(을) 울리다 hint (at / that); intimate; insinuate; suggest; allude to (a fact); give [drop] a hint (to a person); give an inkling of (a fact); beat about[around] the bush. ¶그는 담화에서 오직(汚職) 문제에 대해 변죽을 울렸다 His speech alluded to the problem of corruption.
변증(辯證) demonstration. **변증하다** demonstrate.
●**변증법** [철] dialectic. ¶~적인 dialectic(al) ∥유물론적 ~ materialistic dialectic∥헤겔의 ~ the Hegelian dialectic.
변질(變質) [성질이 변하기] change in quality; [품질 등의 악화] deterioration; [의] degeneration; (연금술의) transmutation. ¶식품의 ~을 방지하다 prevent spoilage of food. **변질하다** change in quality; deteriorate; degenerate; transmute; (음식물이) go bad. ¶더운 날씨에는 음식이 변질하기 쉽다 Food goes bad quickly in hot weather.
변천(變遷) a change; [추이] (a) transition; (인생·처지 등의) vicissitudes; ups and downs. ¶많은 ~ 끝에 after many changes∥그때 나는 시대의 ~을 느꼈다 I felt then the change of the times.∥우리는 대부분 시대적 ~을 겪으며 살아왔다 Many of us have lived through the ups and downs of the times. **변천하다** change; undergo a change. ¶시대는 변천했다 Times have changed.
변칙(變則) [불규칙] (an) irregularity; [예외] an anomaly.
●**변칙 동사** [언] an irregular verb. ⇨ˇ불규칙(ˇ불규칙)
변칙적(變則的) [불규칙적] irregular; [이례적] anomalous; [비정상적] abnormal. ¶~인 방법 (an) irregular procedure / an irregular way of doing things.
변태(變態) **1** [생] (a) metamorphosis (pl. -ses). ¶~의 metamorphic∥구더기에서 파리로의 ~ the metamorphosis of a maggot into a fly∥완전[불완전] ~ a complete[an incomplete] metamorphosis. **2** [비정상] abnormality. ¶~의 abnormal.
●**변태 성욕** sexual perversion; abnormal sexuality[sexual desire]. **변태 심리** [심] abnormal mentality.
변통(便通) action of the bowels; a (bowel) movement; a motion; a passage; an evacuation.
변통(變通) contrivance; management; makeshift; shifting; arrangement. ¶임시 ~ a temporary[rough] makeshift. **변통하다** contrive; manage (with); shift; arrange; (미국 구어) make out (to do); make shift (with); make do (with). ¶돈을 ~ (manage to) raise money∥그들은 이리저리 돈을 변통해서 집을 샀다 They managed somehow or other to

buy a house.∥돈을 변통할 길이 없다 I cannot find any way of raising the money.∥어떻게든 제가 변통해 보겠습니다 I will see to it somehow.

변하다(變-) change; undergo a change; make a change; become different; alter; be altered; shift; vary; (풍향이) come round [about]; work round; shift; […으로 변형하다] change[turn] (into); be turned (into); be transformed (into); be metamorphosed (into). ¶변하지 않다 be [remain] unchanged / be [remain] the same (as before) / be constant / stay put∥마음이 ~ 하다 change one's mind∥시대는 변했다 Times have changed.∥어린이의 관심은 빨리 변한다 Children's interests shift[change] quickly.∥이 물질은 가열하면 기체로 변한다 When heated, this substance changes[turns] into gas.∥사내아이는 보통 10대에 목소리가 변한다 Usually a boy's voice breaks[changes / cracks] when he is in his teens.∥그녀는 아주 변해 버렸다 She is not the same woman I used to know. / She is quite another woman now.∥그의 분노는 차츰 체념으로 변했다 His indignation gradually changed[faded] into resignation.∥세상도 이젠 변했다 We are now in a different world.∥그녀는 많이도 변했더군 How changed she is!∥(십수 년 만에 만난 사람에게) 하나도 변하지 않았네요 You haven't changed a bit.

변혁(變革) a change; [개혁] a reform; a reformation; [대변혁] a revolution; an upheaval. ¶대~을 가져올 만한 발견 revolutionary discoveries∥전기 기구의 보급은 가사에 큰 ~을 가져왔다 The wide use of electrical appliances has revolutionized house work. **변혁하다** change; reform; revolutionize.

변형(變形) [모양·형태를 바꿈] transformation; variation; modification; metamorphosis; deformation; [바꾼 모양] a variety; a modification; a deformity(기형). **변형하다** [바꾸다] change; transform; metamorphose; [바뀌다] transform (into); change (into); turn (into); be transformed [metamorphosed] into. ¶선인장의 가시는 잎이 변형된 것이다 Cactus thorns are metamorphosed leaves.

변호(辯護) 1 [변명] defense; (영) defence; exculpation; vindication; justification; explanation. ¶자기 ~ self-justification∥그의 행위는 ~의 여지가 없었다 What he did was indefensible. / There was no justification for his behavior. **변호하다** defend; advocate; vindicate; justify; speak in defense of (another); speak for [in favor of]; explain (a person's conduct) in (his) vindication. ¶그 교수는 자신의 이론을 변호했다 The professor spoke in defense of his own theory.∥엄마가 동생을 꾸짖을 때마다 순희는 그를 변호했다 Whenever her mother scolded her brother Sunhui defended him [came to his defense / (구어) stood up for him].
2 [법] (법정에서의) defense(피고의); pleading(원고 및 피고의). ¶~를 **의뢰하다** employ [approach] a lawyer / (영) take one's case to an advocate / (영) brief∥…의 ~를 맡다 take a brief for (a person) / undertake to plead for (the defendant). **변호하다** defend; plead for [in favor of]; argue [plead] the case; hold a brief (for). ¶나는 피고를 변호하기로 했다 I decided to defend the accused [defendant].∥변호사는 유창하게 피고를 변호했다 The lawyer spoke eloquently in defense of the accused.

●**변호사** a lawyer; (미) an attorney [a counselor] (-at-law); counsel; (법정 변호사) (영) a barrister; (사무 변호사) (영) a solicitor; (집합적) the bar [Bar] (▶ 미국에서는 법정 변호사와 사무 변호사의 구별이 없음. 미국의 법정 변호사는 a trial attorney라고도 하나 이 명칭은 자격을 나타내는 것이 아님). ¶**국선** ~ a court-appointed lawyer∥개업 ~ practicing lawyer / ~가 되다 enter the law [legal profession] / ~를 **대다** get [retain / employ / engage / approach] a lawyer [(a) counsel]∥~에게 사건을 의뢰하다 give a brief to counsel / (영) take one's case to an advocate∥~ 자격을 박탈당하다 be disbarred∥그는 ~ 자격을 취득했다 He was admitted to the bar. / (영) He was called to [before] the bar. **변호사 사무소** a law office; a lawyer's office. **변호사업** the practice of a lawyer; the legal profession. **변호 의뢰인** a client. **변호인** a counsel; a pleader; a defender; an advocate; (집합적) the counsel. ¶원고 측 ~ the plaintiff's lawyer / the counsel for the plaintiff∥**특별** ~ a special counsel∥**피고 측** ~ the defense counsel / the counsel for the defense. **변호인단** the (defense) counsel (composed of several attorney-at-law).

변화(變化) 1 [바뀜·바뀜] (a) change; (a) variation; [변경] (an) alteration; [변천] (a) mutation; [변천] a transition. ¶계절의 ~ a change of season / seasonal changes∥날씨의 ~ changes in the weather∥사회적 ~ social changes∥태도[정책]의 ~ a shift in attitude [policy]∥풍향의 ~ a shift of wind / a change of wind direction∥**상황** ~ a change in one's circumstances∥온도의 ~ a variation of temperature∥~ 없는 정책 a changeless [an unchanging] policy∥~무쌍한 인생 the kaleidoscope of life / the shifts and changes of life∥유아에서 소년으로의 ~ 시기에 있는 어린아 a child in the transition period from infancy to boyhood∥시대의 ~에 응하다 respond to the change of the times / respond to the changing times∥틀에 박힌 일상사에서 ~를 찾다 long for a variation in one's routine∥환자의 병세에는 아무 ~도 없다 The condition of the patient remains the same.∥뜻밖의 사태 ~에 우리는 당황했다 We were thrown off balance by the unexpected turn of events.∥인간의 마음의 ~는 매우 미묘한 것이다 The workings of the human heart are very subtle. **변화하다** change; make [undergo] a change; turn (from / into / to); shift (into); alter; vary. ➔ ¶더 이상 변화될 여지가 없다 No further alterations [changes] can be made.
2 [다양] variety; diversity. ¶~를 주기 위해 for the sake of variety∥~가 많은 일생 an eventful [a dramatic / a colorful] career / a varied [checkered] life∥그는 ~가 많은 생애를 보냈다 He lived an eventful [a checkered] life.∥그의 소설에 등장하는 여성 인물들은 거의 ~가 없다 The women in his novels lack diversity [are almost all the same type].
3 [문법] (격의) declension; (동사의) conjugation; (명사·동사 등의) inflection; [언] (모음의) mutation; [음] (음·목소리·리듬의) modula-

tion. ¶라틴 어는 ~가 많다 Latin is a highly inflected language. **변화하다** decline; conjugate; inflect.
● **변화구** [야구] curve (ball); [슈트] a shoot. ¶~를 던지다 throw a breaking pitch∥~를 서브하다 [배구] use a spin serve.

변환(變換) 1 change; [전환] conversion. **변환하다** change; convert. ¶방침을 ~ change one's policy. ➔¶열에너지로 변환되다 be transformed into heat energy. 2 [수] (도형·식의) transformation. 3 [물] transmutation; transformation. **변환하다** transmute; transform. 4 [컴] (2종의 코드의) conversion. **변환하다** convert.

별 1 [천] a star; (집합적) the stars; (이칭) the eyes of heaven [night]. ¶~빛 starlight / stellar light∥~의 stellar / astral∥~이 빛나는 밤 a starlit [starlight] night∥~이 총총한 밤하늘 the starry [star-spangled / star-flecked] sky / the starry heavens∥~이 반짝반짝 빛나고 있었다 Stars were twinkling.∥~도 없는 어두운 밤이었다 It was dark, starless night. 2 [군인의 계급장] a star; (표지) a mark. ¶~이 셋인 장군 a three-star general / a lieutenant general∥~표 an asterisk / a star∥(군인이) ~을 달다 become a general.

-별(別) ¶학생들은 남녀 [연령] ~ 그룹으로 나뉘었다 The pupils were divided into groups according to their sex [age].∥서류는 연도~로 분류되어 있었다 The documents were classified by year.

별개(別個) [구별이 되는 딴 것] a different thing; another thing; a separate [distinct] one; exception; a special case. ¶그의 수법은 나의 수법과는 전혀 ~의 것이다 His technique is quite different from mine.∥이것은 ~의 문제다 This is another [a separate] problem [question].∥말하기와 행하기는 전혀 ~의 일이다 To say is one thing, to do is quite another.∥웨일스 어는 영어와는 ~의 것이다 Welsh is distinct from English. / Welsh and English are distinct.∥그것은 ~의 이야기다 That is another story.

별거(別居) (부부의) (a) separation; limited divorce; (법률상의) legal [judicial] separation; [법] divorce a mensa et thoro. ¶~ 중의 남편 [아내] a separated husband [wife] / a grass widower [widow]. **별거하다** live in a separate house; live separately; live apart (from); set up separate residences; separate. ¶그녀는 남편과 별거하기를 원한다 She wants a separation [to separate] from her husband.∥양친은 별거하고 있습니다 My parents are living apart.(▶ 단순히 따로 살고 있다는 뜻)

별것(別-) 1 [드물고 이상스러운 물건] a rarity; a curious [peculiar / special] thing; an oddity. ¶그의 조직력은 ~ 아니다 His ability to organize is not very great. / He is not very good [(구어) not so hot] at organizing.∥예금의 이자는 ~ 아니다 The interest on deposits is negligible [(구어) not worth bothering about].∥이 영화는 ~ 이 아니다 This film is nothing special.∥저 여배우는 소질이라고 해야 ~ 아니다 That actress has no talent to speak of [worth mentioning]. 2 [다른 물건] another thing; a different thing.

별고(別故) 1 [특별한 사고] an accident; a mishap; an untoward event; a hindrance; a hitch. ¶~ 없이 [건강하여] quite [very] well / in good health / [무사히] safe(ly) / in safety / without mishap [an accident / a hitch] / without any incident∥~ 없으신지요 How are you? / How are you getting along? / (속어) How goes [fares] it (with you)?∥다들 ~ 없이 잘 지내고 있습니다 All of us are getting along [on] very well. 2 [다른 까닭] a special [particular] reason; another reason.

별관(別館) an annex; (영) an annexe; a dependency; (미) an extension; an outhouse; an outbuilding. ¶박물관의 ~ an annex to the museum / the museum annex.

별궁(別宮) 1 [역] the palace of the new bride queen [the wife of the heir apparent (to the throne)]. 2 [따로 지은 궁전] a detached palace; a royal villa.

별기(別記) a separate paragraph [notation]. **별기하다** write in a separate paragraph; make a separate notation (of). ¶별기한 바와 같이 그는 파리에서 공부를 했다 As stated elsewhere [As stated in a separate paragraph] he studied in Paris.

별꼴(別-) an eyesore; offense to the eye; an offensive [obnoxious] figure [person, thing, sight, spectacle, etc.]. ¶~이야 What an eyesore! / What a sight [spectacle]!

별꽃 [식] a chickweed.

별나다(別-) eccentric; quaint; queer; peculiar; out of the usual [ordinary]; unusual; odd; singular; uncommon; bizarre; novel; (구어) viewy; wacky; extraordinary. ¶별난 것 an unusual article / a novelty / an eccentricity / a bizarre [strange] thing / (음식) freak [bizarre / strange] food∥별난 취미 bizarre taste / a liking for things that normally put people off / a taste for odd things∥별난 음식을 찾아 먹는 사람 an eater of unusual [bizarre] food / a man of eccentric taste in food / a gross feeder∥별난 데가 전혀 없는 글 씨체 writing with no strange peculiarities∥별난 버릇 peculiar habits∥별난 것을 좋아하다 be fond of novelty [the unusual] / be eccentric∥별난 사람들과 사귀다 associate with different sorts of people∥별난 짓을 하다 do extraordinary things∥새 코치는 조금 별난 데가 있는 분이다 The new coach is a different type of man.∥그는 교사로서는 별난 경력의 소지자이다 He has an unusual background for a teacher.∥그는 자신이 별난 사람임을 보여 주려고 저런 짓을 하고 있는 것이다 He does things like that in order to show how different he is.∥그런 일을 하다니 자네는 참으로 별난 사람이군 What a whimsical person you are to do such a thing!∥그가 그런 별난 음식을 먹고도 (탈이 나지도 않고) 아무렇지 않다니 놀랍네 I am surprised that he survives such weird food (without even getting sick).∥그날따라 그는 별나게도 걸어서 집에 돌아갔다 That day he came home on foot, which he normally did not do.∥그는 별나게 빠른 주자였다 He was an uncommonly [extraordinary / unusually] fast runner.

별나라 the star land; the land of the stars; the stellar world.

별납(別納) 1 [따로 더 바침] an extra [a special] payment [offering]. **별납하다** make an extra [a special] payment [offering]. 2 [따로 바침] separate payment [delivery]. ¶요금 ~ postpaid [(영) post-free] ¶나는 요금 ~ (우편)으로 소포를 보냈다 I mailed the package postpaid. **별납하다** pay [deliver] separately. ¶요금을 ~ pay a charge separately.

별다르다(別-) particular; special; extraordinary; exceptional. ¶별다른 일 something particular∥별다른 명시[지정]가 없는 한 unless otherwise specified∥별다른 이유 없이 for no particular [special] reason / without any particular [special] reason∥별다른 일 없이 잘 지냅니다 I am getting along all right. / I'm getting along as usual with nothing particular happening. / Nothing is wrong with me.∥정세에 별다른 변화는 없었다 There has been no particular change in the situation.∥그가 별다른 생각 없이 맡았던 일이 나중에 알고 보니 아주 골치 아픈 일이었다 The work he had taken on with a light heart [so lightly] proved to be quite troublesome.

별달리 otherwise; differently; particularly. ¶내 말을 ~ 생각지는 마시오 Don't take my words amiss [ill]. / Don't take my words in ill [bad] part.

별당(別堂) 〔딴채〕 a separate house; an outhouse; a detached building; 〔딴방〕 a detached [separate] room; an annex(e).

별도(別途) 1 〔딴 방면〕 a separate way; another way; 〔추가〕 addition; extra. ¶~로 [별개로] separately / apart / 〔추가로〕 extra / additionally / in addition / besides / else / ~로 돈을 치르다 pay extra∥…에 관해서는 ~로 정하다 the specifications as to … will be given elsewhere [will be specified elsewhere]∥이 일에는 ~의 수당이 붙는다 I am paid extra for this work.∥나는 그들에게 ~로 1달러를 더 지불해야 했다 They charged me an extra dollar.∥그림과는 ~로 붓글씨도 전시되었다 In addition to the paintings, works of calligraphy were on display too.∥~로 이 문제도 거론되었다 Besides [In addition], this question was also taken up.∥이 두 문제는 각각 ~로 생각해야 한다 The two problems have to be considered separately.∥나는 ~의 수입이 있다 I have a second [an additional] income [other sources of income].∥서비스료는 ~로 받습니다 Attendance is charged extra.

2 〔딴 용도〕 a separate [special] use. ¶~로 for a special purpose [use]∥돈을 ~로 남겨두다 reserve [put aside / put by] money for a special use [purpose]∥그 돈은 ~의 목적으로 쓰였다 That money was used for a different purpose.

별도리(別道理) another way [means]; an alternative; a better way [measure / remedy]; a choice. ¶이제는 떠날 수밖에 ~가 없다 We have no choice [There is no alternative] but to leave now.∥~가 없다 It cannot be helped.

별동대(別動隊) a detached force [corps]; a detachment.

별똥돌 a meteorite. ⇨ˉ운석

별똥(별) a shooting star. ⇨ˉ유성(流星)

별로(別-) in particular; particularly; specially; especially; (not) very; (not) much. ¶오늘은 ~ 바쁘지 않다 I am not particularly busy today.∥"뭐, 필요하신 게 있습니까?" "아니요, ~ 없습니다." "Do you want anything?" "Nothing in particular."∥그는 ~ 상처를 입지는 않았다 He received no noticeable injuries.∥그것 외에는 ~ 이렇다 할 이유가 없습니다 There is no other special reason.∥"배가 고프니?" "아뇨, ~." "Are you hungry?" "No, not very."∥그의 용태는 ~ 좋지 않다 His condition is not very good.

별리(別離) separation. ⇨ˉ이별

별말(別-) an extraordinary [unexpected / uncalled-for] remark; an unreasonable [an absurd / a preposterous]. ¶~ 다 한다干 듣겠네] What a thing to say! / What an absurd idea! / That's preposterous. / Nonsense! / None of your nonsense! / Be reasonable!

별말씀(別-) ¶(감사를 받고) ~ 다 하십니다 Oh no, not at all. / Never mind! / Oh! don't mention it. / (답) You're welcome.

별명(別名) 1 〔남들이 지어 부르는 이름〕 a nickname; a byname. ¶~을 붙이다 give (a person) a nickname / fasten a nickname upon (a person) / nickname (a person) / dub∥남을 그의 ~으로 부르다 call a person by his nick name∥그녀에게「현대판 잔다르크」라는 ~이 붙었다 She was nicknamed "the modern Joan of Arc."∥고교 시절에 그의 ~이「교수」였다 In high school he was nicknamed "professor." 2 〔본명 외의 이름〕 another name; an alias; a pseudonym. ¶(본명은) 디킨슨, ~은 팰컨 Dickinson, alias Falcon.∥그는 많은 ~으로 불린다 He is called by a number of names.

별문제(別問題) another [a different] question [problem / matter / thing / story / case]. ¶이것은 ~로 생각하자 Let's consider this problem separately.∥이 경우, 성공하느냐 못하느냐는 ~이다 Under the circumstances, it is irrelevant [it doesn't matter] whether we succeed or not.∥그것은 ~다 That is another story. / It is beside the question. / That is aside from the subject. / That is a horse of another color. / That is another pair of shoes [boots].

별미(別味) 〔특별히 좋은 맛〕 delicate [exquisite] flavor [taste]; 〔특별히 좋은 음식〕 a (choice) delicacy; a tidbit; a dainty.

별반(別般) in particular. ⇨ˉ별로

별별(別別) of various [different] and unusual sorts. ¶~ 음식 all sorts of rare dishes∥~ 일 all sorts [kinds / manner / shades] of unusual matters [affairs]∥~ 수단을 다 쓰다 try every means available / try every possible [imaginable] method∥거기에는 ~ 사람이 다 모여 있다 You will find a motley assembly of people [all sorts of people (in all conditions of life)] there.

별봉(別封) 〔따로 싸서 봉함〕 separate cover; 〔그 편지〕 a letter under separate cover; the accompanying letter [document].

별빛 starlight. ¶~의 starlit / starlight∥~으로[아래] in (the) starlight∥~ 찬연한 밤이었다 It was a clear [bright] starry [starlit] night. / It was a starlight [starlit] night.

별사건(別事件) (특별한) some particular event; (다른) an another event.

별사람(別-) a queer (kind of) person; an oddity; an eccentric (person); a queer fish [bird / card / customer]; an odd fish; 《미국 속어》 an oddball. ¶~도 다 있군 I have never seen such a case [crank] as him. / How odd [curious] he is! / I have never seen such a mess of a man.

별석(別席) 〔따로 베푼 자리〕 another [different] seat; 〔특별히 베푼 자리〕 a special seat. ¶그를 위해 ~이 마련되어 있다 There is a

별세(別世) decease; demise; passing (away). **별세하다** die; decease; pass away; depart this world.

별세계(別世界) 1 [이 세상 밖의 다른 세상] another world [planet / sphere]; a different [new] world. ¶그는 ~에서 온 사람 같다 He looks as if he came from another [a different] world. / (지구 밖에서) He looks like something from outer space [another planet]. 2 [경치 등이 아주 좋은 곳] a fairyland.

별소리(別−) an extraordinary remark. ⇨ ˭별말 ¶~ 다 한다 The things you say! // 오래 살다 보니 ~를 다 듣는군 Now I've heard everything.

별송하다(別送−) send by separate post [under separate cover].

별수(別) 1 [달리 어떻게 할 방법] a special [an effective] means [way]; a secret key [method]; the secret; the mystery; a magical formula; a capital [brilliant / particular] idea. ¶이젠 ~ 없다 There is no help for it at this late date. / It's too late to do anything about it. / Now we are the end of our tether [resources]. // ~가 없으면 내가 돈을 내겠다 I will pay for it, if nothing else can be done about it [if there's no other way]. // 그런다 해도 ~ 없다 That's terribly inefficient way to do it. // 아이들이 조르는 통에 ~ 없이 동물원에 데리고 갔다 Since my children were so persistent in asking, I had no choice but to take them to the zoo.
2 [여러 방법] every means; all resources. ¶~를 다 쓰다 try every means available / try every possible [imaginable] method.

별수(別數) [특히 좋은 운수] special luck; extraordinary good fortune; (미) a very lucky [good] break. ¶~가 나다 come plump upon [run into] unexpected good fortune / hit [strike / open] the jackpot / make a big [smash] hit / be blessed with a very good thing.

별스럽다(別−) eccentric; quaint. ⇨별나다

별실(別室) 1 [다른 방] another room; a separate room; [특실] a special room. ¶나는 ~에서 그와 이야기를 했다 I talked with him in another room. 2 a mistress. ⇨ ˭작은집2

별안간(瞥眼間) [눈 깜짝할 동안] in the twinkling [blink] of an eye; before one can bat an eyelash; quick as a wink; in a flash; in an instant; [갑자기] suddenly; on [all of] a sudden; abruptly; [느닷없이] unexpectedly; without the slightest notice [warning]. ¶~에 일어난 일이라서 나는 놀랐다 It surprised me, as I had not expected it. // ~ 하늘이 깜깜해졌다 Suddenly [All of a sudden] the sky became overcast. // 그는 ~ 웃기 시작했다 He abruptly began to laugh. / He burst into laughter. // ~ 거리로 뛰어들면 위험하다 It is dangerous to dash out into the street suddenly. // 상대방은 ~ 그에게 덤벼들었다 His opponent made a sudden lunge at him. // 그는 ~ 벌떡 일어섰다 He sprang to his feet. / He stood up abruptly.

별의별(別−別) of various and unusual sorts. ⇨ ˭별별

별일(別−) [특별한 일] a particular thing [event]; an unusual event; [별별일] all sorts [kinds / manner / shades] of unusual matters [affairs]; [이상한 일] an odd thing; a strange thing. ¶~ 없으면 내일 가겠습니다 I'll come tomorrow unless something serious happens. // 여행 중에는 ~ 없었습니다 I returned from my journey safe and sound [without any trouble]. // ~ 없습니까 How are you (getting along)? // ~ 다 보겠네 Ridiculous! / Nonsense! // ~ 없어야 할 텐데 There might be something wrong, I'm afraid. / I'm afraid it may lead to something serious.

별자리 [천] a constellation; an asterism.

별장(別莊) (대규모의) a villa; a country house; (소규모의) a cottage; (산중의) a cabin; (여름의) a summer house. ¶해변의 ~ a seaside villa.
● **별장지기** a caretaker of a country house.

별점(−占) horoscope.

별정직 공무원(別定職公務員) officials in special government service.

별종(別種) 1 [다른 종자] a distinct species; a variety. ¶이 장미는 그것과는 ~이다 This rose is a different kind from that one. 2 [다른 종류] another [a different] kind [sort / description]. ¶그에게는 ~의 수입이 있어 He has other [another source of] income. / He has an additional source of funds. 3 an eccentric person. ⇨ ˭별짜1

별주(別酒) 1 [특별한 방법으로 빚은 술] a specially prepared [brewed] liquor. 2 a farewell drink. ⇨ ˭이별주(⇨이별)

별지(別紙) a separate sheet of paper; an annexed [attached / enclosed] paper; an accompanying sheet; an annex. ¶~에 기재된 바와 같이 as stated in the accompanying sheet // 명세는 ~에 기재되어 있음 Details are given on the attached [a separate] sheet of paper. // 해답은 ~에 쓰시오 Write your answers on another [a separate] sheet.

별짜(別−) 1 [별스러운 사람] an eccentric [a cranky / a crotchety / an unusual] person; an eccentric. 2 [별스럽게 생긴 물건] a strange [a curious / a peculiar / a singular / an odd] thing.

별채(別−) a house separate from the main building. ⇨딴채

별책(別冊) a separate volume; a supplement; a supplementary volume (to); (잡지 등의) an extra number [issue]. ¶지도가 ~으로 되어 있다 The maps come in a separate volume.
● **별책 부록** a separate-volume supplement.

별천지(別天地) another world; a fairyland. ⇨별세계 ¶폭서의 서울에서 와 보니 이곳은 ~이다 After the scorching heat of Seoul, this is a paradise. // 그곳은 아주 ~다 The place makes a world of its own. / It is a world in itself.

별칭(別稱) another name. ⇨ ˭별명2

별편(別便) separate post; (미) separate mail; another post.

별표(−標) a star; an asterisk; a pentagram. ¶~ 4개가 붙은 우수 영화 a 4 star movie // ~를 붙이다 mark with an asterisk / put an asterisk (on / at) / asterisk / star.

별표(別表) an annexed [attached] list [sheet]; an attached table [chart]. ¶작년도 회계는 ~ 참조 See the attached table [chart] for last year's accounts.

별항(別項) a separate paragraph; another clause [provision / section]; (under) special heading. ¶상세한 것은 ~에 기재되어 있다 Details are given in a separate paragraph [section / chapter / clause]. // 이 사항은 ~으로 잡혀 있다 This matter comes under a different [separate] heading.

별행(別行) another line; a new [separate] line. ¶~을 잡다 begin a new line // 이름은 ~에 쓰십시오 Write your name on a separate line.

별호(別號) 1 a pen name. ⇨ ⇒호(號)4 2 a nickname. ⇨ ⇒별명1

볍씨 seed rice.

볏¹ (새의) a cockscomb; a comb; a crest (of a fowl).

볏² (쟁기의) a moldboard; (영) a mouldboard.

볏가리 a stack [shock] of rice straw; a rick.

볏단 a rice-sheaf; a sheaf of rice.

볏섬 a straw rice-bag; a sack of rice.

볏자리 the part of a plow to which a moldboard is attached.

볏짚 rice straw. ¶~을 단으로 묶다 bundle rice straw / tie up rice straw in sheaves // ~을 엮다 plait rice straw // ~을 깔다 spread rice straw / (마구간에) litter (a stall) down.

병(丙) (등급의) third class; C; [제3자] the third person [party].

병(病) 1 (일반적으로) (미) sickness; (영) illness; (특정의 병) a disease; a malady; an affection; (가벼운) an indisposition; an ailment; (부적인) a trouble; a complaint; a disorder. ¶눈~ eye trouble // 발~ footsoreness / a sore foot // 심장~ heart trouble // 위장~ stomach trouble // 정신~ mental trouble // ~이 든 [난] (미) / (미) sick (※ (영)에서는 보통 한정 용법에서만, 술어적으로는 ill, unwell을 씀) // ~으로 누워 있다 be ill in bed // ~에 걸리다 fall [get / be taken] ill [sick] / contract a disease / take a disease / be attacked [affected] by a disease // ~에 듣다 [효험이 있다] be of medicinal value // ~으로 고생하다 be afflicted [troubled] with a disease // ~으로 죽다 die of sickness [illness] / die of [from] a disease // ~을 앓다 suffer from a disease // ~을 고치다 cure a disease [an illness] / cure (a person) of a disease [an illness] // ~을 치료하다 treat a disease // ~을 치료받다 undergo [receive] medical treatment // ~을 예방하다 prevent [stave off] a disease // ~을 전염시키다 transmit [communicate] one's illness [disease] to (another) / infect (another) // 어머니는 ~으로 한 달이나 누워 있다 My mother has been ill [sick] in bed for a month. // 그는 ~ 때문에 학교를 쉬었다 He was absent from school on account of sickness [illness]. // 그는 ~으로 직장을 쉬고 있다 He is on sick leave. // 그는 로마에서 ~이 들었다 He fell [was taken] ill in Rome. // 저 아이는 걸핏하면 ~이 든다 The boy gets ill easily. // 형[동생]의 ~이 그에게 옮은 것 같다 He seems to have caught the disease [it] from his brother. // 그는 ~을 무릅쓰고 일하러 나갔다 He went to work in spite of his illness [being sick]. // ~이 쾌차하시기 바랍니다 I hope you will get well [get over your illness / recover from your illness] soon. // 그는 정체를 알 수 없는 ~을 앓고 있다 He was afflicted [seized] with a strange disease. // 그는 귀국하자 곧 ~이 났다 He fell ill soon after he returned from abroad.

2 a weakness. ⇨ ⇒병집 ¶거짓말을 하는 것이 그의 ~이다 His failing [weakness] is that he tells lies.

3 [고장] trouble (with a thing); malfunction; a breakdown. ¶기계에 ~이 생기다 have trouble with a machine.

병(瓶) a bottle; (아가리가 큰) a jar (▶ 포도주용의 마개를 뽑는 유리병은 a decanter, 포도주 등을 넣는 큰 병, 또는 자루·뚜껑·부리가 있는 식탁용의 목이 가는 술병은 a flagon, 유리제의 작은 병, 특히 약병은 a vial 또는 a phial이라고 함). ¶맥주~ a beer bottle // 포도주의 ~ a wine bottle // 한 ~의 위스키 a bottle of whisky // ~의 부리 the mouth of a bottle // 나는 딸기잼을 ~에 넣었다 I put some strawberry jam in a jar. // 이 ~은 2리터 든다 This bottle has a capacity of two liters. // 이 ~의 용량은 어느 정도인가 How much does this bottle hold?

병가(病暇) sick leave. ¶~ 중이다 be on sick leave.

병객(病客) a sick person. ⇨ ⇒병자(病者)

병결(病缺) absence (from school / from work) on account of illness. **병결하다** be absent [absent oneself] due to illness.

병고(病苦) the pain [torment] of sickness; suffering from illness. ¶~에 시달리다 suffer acutely from one's illness.

병골(病骨) a sickly person; a weak person.

병과(兵科) an arm (of the army); a branch of the service.

병과(兵戈) 1 a weapon. ⇨ ⇒무기(武器)1 2 war; warfare. ⇨ ⇒전쟁

병구(病軀) a sick body; a sickly constitution. ¶그는 ~를 무릅쓰고 우중에 나섰다 He went out in the rain in spite of his poor health.

병구완(病-) nursing; tending (a sick person); care (for the sick). ¶극진한 ~ careful nursing. **병구완하다** nurse; tend; care for; attend on. ¶밤새도록 ~ sit up with (a patient) / attend on (a sick person) all through the night // 그는 정성껏 병구완한 보람도 없이 어젯밤에 죽었다 He died last night, all the care taken of him proving of no avail.

병권(兵權) military power [authority]. ¶~을 잡다 possess [assume] military power.

병균(病菌) a disease germ; a bacillus (pl. -li). ● **병균 보유자** a germ carrier.

병근(病根) [병의 근원] the cause [origin] of a disease; a morbific agent; [화근] the root [cause] of an evil. ¶~을 없애다 exterminate the germs of a disease / strike at the root of an evil.

병기(兵器) a weapon; arms; (집합적) ordnance. ¶공격~ an offensive weapon // 화학[생물]~ a chemical [biological] weapon. ● **병기고**(-庫) an armory; (영) an armoury.

병나다(病-) 1 [병이 생기다] fall [get / be taken] ill [sick]; suffer from a disease; take a disease; be affected by a disease. ¶과식하여 ~ make oneself ill by overeating // 어머니는 슬픔에 지쳐 병나셨다 Overcome with grief, my mother fell ill. 2 [고장이 나다] get [be] out of order; (something) go wrong (with).

병내다(病-) 1 [병들게 하다] cause [bring on] illness; make (a person) sick. 2 [고장 나게 하다] put [get] (something) out of order; make (something) go wrong [break (down)].

병독(病毒) a disease germ. ¶~을 퍼뜨리다

병동 spread infection[a disease] // ~에 감염되다 be infected / be tainted.
병동(病棟) a ward; a pavilion. ¶격리 ~ an isolation[quarantine] ward // 일반 ~ a general ward // 외래[입원] ~ outpatients' [inpatients'] ward.
병들다(病−) fall ill. ⇨＝병나다1
병란(兵亂) a war; a (military) disturbance.
병략(兵略) strategy. ⇨＝군략(軍略)
병력(兵力) military power[force]; force of arms; (군사 面의) the strength (of an army). ¶5만의 ~ an army fifty thousand strong // 300만의 전시 ~ a war effective of three million // 1개 중대[대대] ~ 으로 in company [battalion] strength // 아군은 ~의 반수 이상을 잃었다 We lost more than half of our army.
● **병력 감축** a troop cut; a reduction in the armed forces.
병력(病歷) a case[clinical] history; the history of a case. ¶나는 심장병의 ~이 있다 I have a history of heart trouble.
병렬(竝列) arranging in a row[line]. ¶~의 parallel. **병렬하다** stand in a row[in rows]; line up; [병렬시키다] arrange in a row; line up.
● **병렬 회로** [전] a parallel circuit.
병리(病理) pathology.
● **병리학** pathology. **병리학자** a pathologist.
병리 해부학 morbid[pathologic(al)] anatomy.
병립(竝立) compatibility; coexistence; standing side by side. **병립하다** stand side by side (with); stand together; coexist (with); be consistent[compatible] (with). ➔ ¶당시 두 조정(朝廷)이 병립되어 있었다 Two Imperial courts coexisted at the time.
병마(兵馬) 1 [병사와 군마] soldiers and (war) horses. 2 [군대] an army; troops; [군력] military strength; [군사(軍事)] military affairs; [싸움] a battle. ¶~를 동원하다 raise [mobilize] an army / appeal to arms // ~의 대권을 잡다 assume supreme military power.
병마(病魔) the demon of ill health; the curse of a disease; a disease. ¶~가 덮치다 be seized with an illness / be attacked by a disease // ~에 시달리다 labor under one's disease // ~에 쓰러지다 succumb to a disease / come down with an illness.
병마개(瓶−) a bottle cap[top / stopper / cork]; a cork; a stopper. ¶~를 뽑다 uncork a bottle / pull out a stopper // ~를 하다 stopper a bottle / put a stopper in a bottle / cork a bottle / put a cap on a bottle.
병명(病名) the name of a disease. ¶~을 알 수 없는 병 an unidentified disease // 의사는 ~이 무엇인지 분간할 수 없었다 The doctor was unable to identify the disease[make a diagnosis].
병목(瓶−) the bottleneck; the neck of a bottle.
병무(兵務) military[conscription] affairs.
● **병무청** the Office of Military Manpower Administration.
병발(竝發·倂發) 1 [여러 가지 병이 동시에 생김] a complication. **병발하다** supervene on (a shot wound); have a complication; be complicated by (another disease). ¶다른 병이 병발하지 않는다면 그는 곧 회복될 것이다 He will recover soon provided there are no complications. // 그는 맹장염에 걸렸는데 복막염이 병발했다 He was suffering from appendicitis, which developed into peritonitis. 2 [동시에 일어남] concurrence; coincidence. **병발하다** concur; coincide; synchronize; break out at the same time.
● **병발증** a complication; an intercurrent disease; a deuteropathy.
병법(兵法) [구체적인 전술] (military) tactics; [대국적인 전략] (military) strategy.
● **병법가** [전술가] a (military) tactician; [전략가] a (military) strategist.
병사(兵士) a soldier; a private.
병사(兵舍) barracks(▶ 보통 복수형으로 단수·복수 취급). ¶서둘러 ~가 세워졌다 A barracks was hastily erected.
병사(兵事) military affairs.
병사(病死) death from an illness. ¶~자가 20명 이상 되었다 More than 20 persons died of illness. **병사하다** die of an illness.
병사(病舍) 1 [병원 건물] a hospital; (hospital 보다 소규모의) an infirmary. 2 a ward. ⇨＝병동
병살(倂殺) [야구] a double play. **병살하다** execute[pull off] a double play; (구어) get two; make a double play. ➔ ¶병살당하다 hit into a double play / be doubled up / have[be victims of] a double play.
병상(病床) a sickbed. ¶그는 작년부터 죽 ~에 누워 있다 He has been bedridden[sick in bed] since last year. // 그는 폐렴으로 ~에 누워 있다 He is laid up with pneumonia.
병상(病狀) the condition of a disease [patient]. ¶그의 ~이 갑자기 악화했다[좋아졌다] His condition[He] took a sudden turn for the worse[better]. // 환자의 ~에 이렇다 할 변화는 보이지 않았다 There was no particular change in the patient's condition.
병색(病色) a sickly complexion; sickly appearance.
병서(兵書) [전략서] a book on military strategy; [전술서] a book on military tactics.
병서하다(竝書) write the same (consonant) characters laterally attached.
병석(病席) a sickbed. ¶~에 눕다 take to one's bed // ~에서 일어나다 leave one's (sick)bed / rise from a sickbed.
병선(兵船) a warship; a military vessel; an armed vessel.
병설(竝設·倂設) establishment as an annex. **병설하다** establish (a primary school) as an annex (to the college). ¶그들은 공장에 연구소를 병설했다 They established a research center attached to the factory. // 그들은 법학과와 경제학과를 병설하였다 They established both a department of law and a department of economics.
병세(病勢) the state of a disease. ¶다음 날 그의 ~가 더욱 나빠졌다 He got worse the next day. / The next day, his condition took a turn for the worse. // 그 소식을 듣고 그녀의 ~는 악화되었다 The news aggravated her illness[condition].
병세(兵勢) military force; the number of soldiers; an army; a force.
병소(病巢) [의] a focus (pl. foci, ~es); a nidus (pl. -di); a hotbed of disease. ¶~를 찾아내다[적출하다] detect[extract] a focus.
병술(瓶−) bottled liquor; liquor sold by the

bottle.

병신(病身) **1** [불구] deformity; malformation; disfigurement; [불구자] a deformed [maimed] person; a deformity; a cripple(다리 병신). ¶~을 만들다 deform / disfigure / maim / cripple // ~으로 태어나다 be born deformed // 평생 ~이 되다 be crippled [maimed / disabled] for life // 해마다 교통사고로 수천 명이 ~이 된다 Traffic accidents maim thousands of people every year.
2 [병든 몸] a sick body; a sickly constitution; [만성병자] a chronic invalid.
3 [바보] a fool; a stupid (person). ¶~ 같은 소리 silly talk / nonsense // ~ 같은 짓을 하다 do a foolish[stupid] thing / act foolishly / make an ass[a fool] of oneself // 이 ~아 You fool[stupid thing]! / You stupid [idiot]!
4 [온전치 못한 물건] a defective[misshapen / damaged] thing; an odd set. ¶영화가 검열에서 잘려 ~이 돼 버렸다 The censor mutilated the film.

병실(病室) a sickroom; (병원의) a hospital room; a (hospital) ward; (배의) a sick bay. ¶~을 한 바퀴 돌다 make a round of the ward.

병아리 a chicken; a chick. ¶~를 까다 hatch chickens.
● **병아리 감별사** a chicken sexer.

병약자(病弱者) a sickly (and suffering) person.

병약하다(病弱-) (constitutionally) weak; weakly; sickly; invalid; infirm; (서술적) have a weak[delicate] constitution. ¶병약한 아이 a sickly child / 병약한 사람 a sickly person / an invalid // 그녀는 ~ She has a weak [sickly] constitution. / She is very delicate. // 그 아이는 태어날 때부터 병약했다 The child was born weak. / The child was sickly from birth.

병어 [동] a harvest fish; a silver pomfret.

병역(兵役) military service. ¶~을 필한 자 a person who fulfilled one's military service // ~에 복무하다 serve in the army / do [undergo] military service / bear [carry] arms // ~을 면제하다 exempt a person from military service // ~의 의무가 있다 be liable to military service [to serve in the army].
● **병역 기피** evasion of military service. **병역 면제** exemption from military service. **병역 의무** obligatory [compulsory] military service; (미) selective service.

병영(兵營) barracks. ⇨ 병사(兵舍) ¶~ 생활 army life / life in the barracks.

병용하다(並用-·併用-) use jointly[in combination] (with); use (two things) at the same time. ¶두 가지 방법을 ~ use both methods(jointly) // 두 가지 약을 병용하는 것은 위험하다 It is dangerous to take the two medicines together[at the same time].

병원(兵員) [군사 인원·수효] the strength of an army; the number of soldiers.

병원(病院) a hospital; [진료소] a clinic; (미) a doctor's office; [학교·공장 등의 부속 진료소] an infirmary.(▶ hospital은 입원·수술 등의 시설을 갖춘 큰 병원을 가리키고, clinic은 hospital의 일부로서 특정의 진료를 하는 곳을 가리키며, doctor's office는 개인 병원을 가리킴) ¶가축~ a veterinary surgeon's / (《영국구어》) a vet's / 격리 ~ an isolation hospital // 외과 ~ a surgical hospital // 이비인후과 ~ an ear, nose, and throat hospital // 소아과 ~ a children's clinic // 정신 ~ a mental hospital // 적십자 ~ a Red Cross Hospital // 종합 ~ a general hospital / a polyclinic // 부인과 ~ a gynecological hospital / (영) a gynaecological clinic / (영) a gynaecologist's // 야전 ~ a field hospital // 개인 ~ a private hospital // 후송 ~ an evacuation hospital // ~에 가다 go to the doctor's (office)(▶ 가벼운 병으로 갈 때 쓰는 표현으로, 입원·수술 등을 하기 위해 병원을 갈 때에는 "go to the hospital"을 씀) // ~에 입원하다 go to (the) hospital / enter (the) hospital(▶ 입원·퇴원 등에 관하여 (영)에서는 관사를 붙이지 않으나, (미)에서는 관사를 붙이는 것이 보통) // 그는 ~에 입원하고 있다 He is in (the) hospital. // 그는 팔에 부상을 입고 ~에 실려 갔다 He was sent [taken] to (the) hospital with an injured arm. // 나는 매일 ~에 다니고 있습니다 I go to (the) hospital [the doctor's] every day.
● **병원장** the director of a hospital.

병원(病原·病源) [의] the cause[origin] of a disease; an etiological cause. ¶~ 불명의 병 a disease of unknown etiology.
● **병원균** disease-causing germs [bacteria]; a bacillus (*pl.* -li). ¶~을 박멸하다 destroy germs. **병원체** a pathogenic organism.

병인(病人) a sick person. ⇨ 병자

병인(病因) the cause of a disease. ¶그의 ~은 술이다 Wine is at the bottom of his illness.

병자(病者) a sick person[man]; an invalid; a patient(환자); (집합적) the sick. ¶~용의 식사 a diet for the sick // ~ 같다 look sickly // ~를 간호하다 nurse the sick // 금년에는 ~가 많다 The sick rate is heavy this year.

병작(並作) tenancy on half-and-half shares. **병작하다** tenant (a farm) on half-and-half shares.

병장(兵長) (미 육군의) Private 1st Class; (미 해군의) Seaman; (미 해병의) Lance Corporal; (미 공군의) Airman 1st Class; (영 육군의) Lance Corporal; (영 해군의) Leading Seaman; (영 공군의) Senior Aircraftman(지상 정비원).

병적(兵籍) **1** [군인의 신분] military status. **2** a muster roll. ⇨ 병적부(⇨병적) ¶~에 있다 be in military service // ~에 들다 enlist in the army.
● **병적부** a muster roll.

병적(病的)(변태적). ¶~인 생각 a morbid idea // 그는 ~으로 신경질적이다 He is abnormally nervous. // 그는 ~으로 의심이 많은 사람이다 He looks upon everything with morbidly suspicious eyes.

병정(兵丁) a soldier.
● **병정개미** [동] a soldier ant; a dinergate.

병존(並存) coexistence. ¶양자의 ~은 불가능하다 The two are incompatible. / The two cannot coexist. **병존하다** coexist (with); be coexistent (with); exist together.

병졸(兵卒) a (common) soldier. ⇨ 군사(軍士)

병종(丙種) the third class[grade].

병주머니(病-) a person with many (chronic) disease; a bag of woes.

병중(病中) ¶~임에도 불구하고 in spite of one's illness / though one is ill [sick] // 그의 ~에 어머니를 별세하셨다 His mother died while he was ill [during his illness].

병증(病症) the nature[symptoms] of a

병진하다(竝進-) keep abreast of (a person); keep pace with (a person); advance side by side.

병집(病-) [결점·나쁜 버릇] a weakness; a fault.

병참(兵站) [군] communications; impedimenta; supply trains.
● **병참 기지** a supply base. **병참 장교**(미) a quartermaster; a commissary.

병창하다(竝唱-) sing together [in chorus].

병추기(病-) a sickly person; an invalid. ¶이 아이는 ~이다 This child is weak. / This child becomes sick easily.

병충해(病蟲害) damage from disease and harmful insects. ¶작물은 심한 ~를 입었다 The crop was heavily damaged both by disease and harmful insects.

병치하다(倂置-) [나란히 두다] put [place] (two things) side by side; juxtapose (with / to); [부가하다] attach (to).

병칭하다(竝稱-) rank [class] (a person) with (another). → ¶병칭되다 be ranked [classed] (with).

병탄(竝呑·倂呑) annexation. **병탄하다** annex; take possession of.

병폐(病弊) evils; ills; evil practices. ¶사회적 [도시의] ~ social [urban] ills // 전(前) 정권 [정치 체제]의 ~를 단절하다 do away with the evils of the former regime.

병풍(屛風) a byeongpung; a folding screen. ¶여섯 폭 ~ a six-panel [six-leaved folding] screen // 우리는 방 한구석을 ~으로 칸막이했다 We screened off a corner of the room. // 산들이 ~을 두른 듯 험준하게 뻗쳐 있다 A range of mountains stretches away as precipitously as walls.

병학(兵學) military science; [병술] military strategy.

병합(倂合) union; (a) combination. ⇨ 합병

병해(病害) crop damage (due to disease); disease damage to crops. ¶담뱃잎에 ~가 퍼지고 있다 Damage caused to tobacco leaves by disease is spreading.

병행(竝行) 1 [나란히 감]. **병행하다** go side by side; go abreast (of); keep pace (with); run parallel (to / with). ¶전동 열차와 급행열차가 병행하여 달려갔다 An electric train and an express train sped away side by side. 2 [동시에 행함]. **병행하다** do [perform / practice] (two things) simultaneously [at the same time]. ¶두 가지 일을 ~ do two things at the same time / 실업률은 불경기와 병행하고 있었다 Unemployment kept pace with the business recession.

병화(兵火) a fire caused by war. ¶중요 문화재가 ~에 파괴될 위험이 있다 There is danger that important cultural properties might be destroyed by the fires of war.

병환(病患) a disease; (영) illness; (미) sickness. ¶누님의 ~은 어떠하신지요 How is your (sick) sister?

병후(病後) convalescence; the convalescent stage. ¶~의 간호 [치료] aftercare // 그녀는 ~에 시력이 약해졌다 Her eyesight weakened after her illness. // ~에 무리를 해서는 안 됩니다 You must take it easy during your convalescence.

볕 the heat of the sunbeams. ⇨ 햇볕

보¹ [건] a (cross) beam. ⇨ 들보

보² a small bowl of porcelain. ⇨ 보시기

보(步) 1 walking. ⇨ 걸음 2 [거리를 재는 단위] a measure of length (= 6 ja).

보(洑) 1 [저수지] a dammed pool for irrigation; a reservoir. 2 dam (water). ⇨ 봇물

보(褓) (덮는) a cloth-covering (for a table); a cloth cover; (싸는) a (cloth) wrapper; a wrapping cloth. ¶책 ~ a cloth for wrapping books // 상 ~ a tablecloth.

보(保) [법] 1 (a) security. ⇨ 보증 ¶~를 세우다 find security [surety] (for). 2 a guarantor. ⇨ 보증인(⇨ 보증)

-보(補) [보좌관] assistant. ¶서기~ an assistant clerk // 외교관 ~ a probationary diplomat // 차관 ~ an assistant undersecretary [vice-minister].

보각(補角) [수] a supplementary angle. ¶~의 supplementary.

보각거리다 bubble. ⇨ 부걱거리다

보감(寶鑑) 1 [본보기가 될 만한 사물을 적은 책] a handbook; a manual; a thesaurus (pl. ~es, -ri); a treasury. 2 [모범] a paragon; a mirror; an exemplar.

보강(補强) reinforcement. **보강하다** reinforce (a bridge); strengthen. → ¶졸업생이 몇 명 가담해 준 덕택에 육상부가 현저하게 보강되었다 The track and field club was strengthened remarkably by a number of graduates joining it. // 이 건물은 철근으로 보강되어 있다 This building is reinforced with iron staples.
● **보강 공사** reinforcement work.

보강(補講) a supplementary lecture; a makeup lesson. ¶~을 받다 take supplementary [makeup] classes [lectures]. **보강하다** give supplementary [makeup] classes [lectures].

보건(保健) preservation of health. ¶국민 ~운동 a national fit movement // 세계 ~ 기구 the World Health Organization(약어 WHO) // 이 읍에서는 주민 ~에 힘을 쓰고 있다 This town is making an effort to preserve [keep / protect] the health of its inhabitants.
● **보건 복지부** the Ministry of Health and Welfare. **보건소** a (public) health center.

보검(寶劍) 1 [의장용 칼] the sword of state [honor]. 2 [보배로운 검] a treasured [choice / fine] sword.

보결(補缺) 1 [부족분을 메우기] supplementing; filling a vacancy. ¶그는 고등학교의 ~ 합격자 안에 들어 있었다 He was placed on the waiting list by the high school admissions office. **보결하다** fill (a vacancy); supplement. 2 [결점을 보충함] supply of deficiency. **보결하다** supply [make up] a deficiency.
● **보결생** a student for filling a vacancy; a supplementary student; a standby student.

보고(報告) 1 [말·글 등으로 알리는 것] a report; an account; (미) (a) briefing; information(▶단수형이며 부정 관사를 붙이는 일 없음); a statement; returns(계수(計數)의). ¶연차 [연례] ~ an annual report // 중간 ~ an interim report // 최종 ~ the final report // 국세 조사 ~ census returns. **보고하다** report; make [submit] a report (of / on); inform (a person) of (an accident); give an account of (an affair); (미국 구어) brief (a person) on (a matter); read a paper(학회에서). ¶나는 그 사건에 대해 요약해서 보고했다 I made [gave] a summary report of the incident. 2 a

●보고서 a (written) report; (공식 답신(答申) 동의) findings 〔of a Presidential commission〕; (학회의) a paper; a memoir; (계수(計數)의) returns(▶ 보통 복수형); (협회 등의) a journal; transactions(▶ 이 뜻으로는 복수형); 〔기사〕 a record; a brief; a briefing. ¶~를 작성하다〔쓰다〕 make a report (on)// ~를 제출하다 send in[file] a report. 보고자 a reporter; an informer; a person giving a report; (학회·세미나 등에서의) a person who reads [presents] a paper.

보고(寶庫) 1〔보물을 넣어 두는 창고〕 a treasure house; a treasury. ¶지식의 ~ a treasure house of knowledge / a mine [storehouse] of information. 2〔훌륭한 재원이 묻혀 있는 땅〕. ¶천연자원의 ~ a district rich in natural resources// 바다는 광물과 식량의 ~다 The sea is a treasure house of minerals and food.

보관(保管) custody; charge; keeping; safekeeping; (a) deposit; storage. 보관하다 keep; take custody[charge] (of); take (a thing) into one's custody; keep (a thing) (in custody); hold (money) on deposit. ¶예금 통장을 금고에 보관해 두어야겠다 I will keep the bankbook in the safe.// 보석은 내가 보관하고 있다 I have the jewels in my custody [keeping].// 창고의 열쇠는 그가 보관하고 있다 He is in charge[has charge] of the key to the warehouse.// ¶보관되어 있다 be in one's safekeeping// 서류는 안전한 곳에 보관되어 있다 The documents are in safekeeping.
●보관료 charges for custody; 〔창고료〕 storage fee. 보관물 / 보관품 an article in custody; a thing on deposit. 보관소 a depositary.

보교(步轎) a kind of sedan (chair); a palanquin.

보국(報國) patriotism; service(s) to one's country; national service. 보국하다 serve one's country; do much for one's country; place oneself in the service of one's country; render service (to one's country); lay down one's life (for one's country). ¶목숨을 바쳐 ~ offer[sacrifice] one's life for one's country.
●보국안민(-安民) national and public welfare. ¶~하다 promote the interests of the nation and provide for the people.

보궐(補闕) supplementing. ⇨보결(補缺)1
●보궐 선거(-미) a special election; 〔영〕 a by-election. ¶스미스 씨의 서거에 따라 국회의원의 ~가 실시되었다 A local by-election was held to fill the vacancy created[caused] by Mr. Smith's death.

보균자(保菌者) a germ[bacteria / disease] carrier; a carrier. ¶콜레라 ~ a cholera carrier// 그는 콜레라 ~의 혐의로 격리되었다 He was quarantined on suspicion of carrying cholera vibrios.

보균하다(保菌-) carry germs[bacteria]; be infected.

보그르르 boiling briskly; bubbling. ⇨ᵇ부그르르

보글거리다 boil (over); bubble. ⇨ᵇ부글거리다·2

보글보글 boiling briskly; bubbling. ⇨ᵇ부글부글·2

보금자리 a nest; a roost; a home. ¶사랑의 ~ a love nest// ~에 들다 settle in the nest / nest// ~를 떠나다 leave the roost// 날아서 ~로 돌아가다 fly home to roost.

보금자리(를) 치다 build (and settle in) a nest; nest.

보급(普及) diffusion; spread; propagation; extension(확장); 〔대중화〕 popularization. ¶의학 지식의 ~에 따라 전염병이 격감했다 With the spread[diffusion] of medical knowledge, infectious diseases have decreased remarkably. 보급하다 (지식·병 등을) spread; (학문·문화 등을) diffuse; (사상·소식 등을) propagate; extend; make popular; 〔대중화시키다〕 popularize. ➔¶그는 학문을 보급시키는 데 몸을 바쳤다 He devoted himself to the spreading[(문어) dissemination] of learning.// 그는 불교를 보급시킨 사람 중의 한 사람이다 He is one of the men who propagated Buddhism.// 교육이 전 국민에게 보급되었다 Education spread[diffused] throughout the whole nation.// 이 사상은 서구 제국에 보급되어 있다 The idea prevails[is widespread] in Western nations.// 새로운 가치관이 젊은이 전부에게 보급되어 있는 것은 아니다 The new sense of values has not yet been accepted by all the younger generation.// 각종 전기 기구가 거의 모든 가정에 보급되어 있다 All sorts of electric appliances have spread to[found their way into] almost every household.// 세탁기는 농촌의 구석구석까지 보급되어 있다 Washing machines have spread even to[are in common use even in / have even found their way into] remote farming villages.
●보급소 an agency; a distributing agency [agent]; a distributor. ¶신문 잡지 ~ an agent for newspapers and magazines. 보급판 a popular[cheap] edition.

보급(補給) supply; replenishment. ¶영양 ~ the furnishing of nutrition// 그 지역의 분쟁으로 석유의 ~이 일시 중단되었다 Because of fighting in the region, the oil supply was temporarily cut off. 보급하다 supply; replenish. ¶비행기에 연료를 ~ refuel an airplane // 어린이 캠프에 식량을 ~ supply children's camps with food.
●보급관〔군〕 a quartermaster; a supply officer. 보급 기지 a supply base[depot]. 보급로 a supply route. 보급선 a supply ship.

보기¹ 〔예〕 an example; an instance; a case; an illustration. ¶~를 들면 for example [instance] // ~를 들다 draw [quote] an instance (from) // 그 사람을 ~로 들다 take the person as an example // 이것이 좋은 ~ 다 This is a case in point. // 다음의 ~와 같다 It is as in the following examples. // ~를 들어 설명하면 간단하다 It is simple to explain by giving examples.

보기² 〔골프〕 a bogie; a bog(e)y. ¶2번 홀에서 ~를 내다 bogie the second hole.

보꾹 〔건〕 the inner part of a roof; the ceiling.

보나 마나 to be sure; needless to say; undoubtedly; obviously; in all probability.

보내기(状-) making irrigation ditches.

보내기 번트 a sacrifice bunt. ⇨희생 번트(⇨희생)

보내다 1〔물건·사람 등을 다른 곳으로 가게 하다〕 send; dispatch; forward; transmit; (상품을) consign; (배·차로) ship; 〔송금하다〕 remit. ¶보낼 곳 the receiver's address the

보너스

destination // 서울로 보낼 부품 parts to be sent to Seoul // 차례로 증원군을 ~ send out more and more reinforcements // 답장을 ~ send a reply // 소포를 ~ send (a person) a parcel / send a parcel to (a person) // 특사[사자]를 ~ send an emissary [a messenger] // 아이를 컴퓨터 학원에 ~ send children to computer school // 다달이 (50만 원씩) 보내 주는 돈으로 생활하다 live on a monthly allowance (of five hundred thousand won) // 2, 3일 동안 하인[가정부]을 보내 주실 수 있겠습니까 Would you lend us your helper for two or three days? // 언제든지 자제분을 수영하러 우리 수영장에 보내 주십시오 Your child is welcome to come and swim in our pool any time. // 잭이 심부름꾼으로 보내졌다 Jack was sent as a messenger. // 부인회가 국제 대회[회의]에 대표를 보냈다 The women's club sent a delegate to the international conference. // 그는 네 아들을 대학에 보냈다 He sent his four sons to college. // 그는 그녀에게 꽃다발을 보냈다 He sent her a bouquet of flowers. // 그는 서류를 가져오도록 비서를 보냈다 He sent his secretary for the papers. // 두 아들을 대학에 보내는 것은 그에게는 쉬운 일이 아니었다 It was not easy for him to send his two sons to college. // 나는 시계를 고치러 보냈다 My watch has been sent to be repaired. // 우리는 재해 지구에 급히 구호물자를 보냈다 We rushed emergency aid to the disaster area. // 주문도 하지 않았는데 그들이 잡지를 보내 왔다 They sent me a magazine which I had not ordered. // 우리 회사는 전 세계에 제품을 보냅니다 We ship our products all over the world. // 부품을 즉시 차 편[철도 편 / 우편 / 항공 편]으로 보내겠습니다 We will dispatch the parts by car [rail / mail / airmail] immediately. // 즉시 돈을 보내시오 Remit [Send] the money at once. // 이 통지서를 전달 순서대로 보내시오 Please pass this notice on. // 답안 용지를 한 장씩 갖고 나머지는 뒤로 보내시오 Take one answer sheet and pass the rest to the back. // 우리는 의사를 부르러 급히 사람을 보냈다 We sent quickly for the doctor. // 내가 그의 편에 안내장을 보내 드리겠습니다 I will have him bring you an invitation. // 아버지는 아들에게 학자금을 보내 주셨다 The father provided his son with [sent his son money for] his school expenses. // 나는 딸이 보내 줄 돈을 기대하고 있다 I count on the money my daughter sends me.

2 [시간이나 세월을 지나가게 하다] pass (time); pass away (one's time); kill time; spend (one's time); live [lead] (a life); while [dawdle] away. ¶그 젊은 미망인은 매일 눈물로 보냈다 The young widow did nothing but weep night and day. // 나는 텔레비전을 보면서 (시간을) 보냈다 I spent [passed] my time watching television. // 그날 밤 우리는 그의 집에서 즐거운 시간을 보냈다 We had a good time at his place that evening. // 나는 제주도에서 한 달을 보냈다 I spent a month in Jejudo. // 그는 평범한 일생을 보냈다 He lived an uneventful life. // 시간을 헛되이 보내지 마라 Don't waste [idle away] your time. // 그는 자신의 말년을 조용히 보냈다 He lived [spent] the last years of his life quietly [in peace]. // 나는 아주 바쁜 나날을 보내고 있다 I'm leading a very busy life. / I'm very busy every day. // 퇴직한 후로 아버지는 하는 일 없이 시간을 보내고 있다 My father is simply idling away his time since retirement.

3 [신호·뜻을 전달하다]. ¶그 감독은 투수에게 사인[신호]를 보냈다 The manager gave the pitcher a signal. // 그는 그녀에게 윙크를 보냈다 He winked at her. // 그녀의 훌륭한 연기에 모두가 갈채를 보냈다 Everyone applauded her excellent performance.

4 [그냥 가게 하다] let (it) go; [야구] let a pitch go by. ¶공을 그대로 ~ (야구에서 타자가) let a pitch go by (without swinging) / (외야수 등이 홈런을) watch a ball sail over one's head into the stands // 나는 버스에 사람이 너무 많아 한 대 그대로 보냈다 I let one bus go by (without getting on) because it was so crowded.

보너스 [상여금] a bonus.
보늬 the inner skin (of a chestnut).
보닛 1 (모자) a bonnet. **2** [자동차 엔진 위의 덮개] (미) a hood; (영) a bonnet.
보다¹ **1** (일반적으로) see; look (at); watch (▶ see는 눈에 보이기 때문에 보는 것을 뜻하는 데 반해, look at와 watch는 의도적으로 관심을 가지고 보는 것을 뜻함. 한편, watch는 look at에 비해 상대적으로 긴 소요 시간을 전제로 하며, 특히 대상이 움직이는 것일 때 씀); get (a) sight (of); (속어) set [lay] eyes (on); [목격하다] witness. ¶언뜻 봄 a glance / a glimpse // 자주 보는 광경 a common scene // 자주 보는 얼굴 a familiar face // 흘긋 glance (at) / [언뜻 눈에 들어오다] catch a glimpse (of) // 주의 깊게 ~ watch / 빤히 ~ stare [gaze] (at) // 잘 ~ look carefully (at) / have a good look (at) // 오른쪽을 ~ face right / 위[아래]를 ~ look up [down] // 보지 못하다 miss // 신호를 잘못 ~ misread the signal // 보라 Look! / See [Have] a look (at it)! // 자 봐라 눈이 온다 Look! It's started to snow. // 저 사람은 역에서 자주 보는 사람이다 I often come across that man at the station. // 며칠 전에 나는 도서관에서 그녀를 보았다 I happened to see her in [at] the library a few days ago. // 어디를 보아도 아름다운 꽃뿐이었다 I saw beautiful flowers everywhere [on all sides]. // 내가 보기에는 그에게 아무 일도 없다 As far as I can see, there is nothing the matter with him. // 어쩐지 이 옷은 보기에 좋지 않다 Somehow this dress doesn't look good. // 보시다시피 저는 건강해졌습니다 As you see I am now well and strong. // 당신을 뵐 면목이 없습니다 I'm too embarrassed to see you. // 나는 표제어를 언뜻 보았을 뿐이다 I have only glanced [taken a brief look] at the headlines. // 내가 잘못 본 것일까 (아니, 그럴 리가 없다) Did my eyes deceive me? // 그들은 의심스러운 눈으로 나를 봤다 They regarded me with suspicious eyes. // 그들은 청중을 보고 연단 위에 자리 잡고 있었다 They were seated on the platform, facing the audience. // 나는 게시를 못 보았다 I missed (seeing) the notice. / I failed to see the notice. // 그는 보기만 해도 메스꺼워지는 놈이다 Just one glance tells you [You can see at a glance] that he is a repulsive man. // 그런 꼴은 보기에 좋지 않다 You are not fit to be seen like that. // 가족끼리의 싸움은 보기 좋은 것이 아니다 A family quarrel is not a pleasant thing to watch. // 그녀는 한복이 보기 좋다 She looks better in a hanbok. // 이것 봐 Look (and see). // 누군지 가 보겠지 I'll go and see

who it is. // 저런 무서운 광경은 본 적이 없다 That was the most horrible sight I have ever seen [witnessed]. // 그 광경은 차마 볼 수가 없었다 I could not bear to look at the sight. // 그는 꼴도 보기 싫다 I hate [can't bear] even the sight of him. // 그가 화내는 것을 본 적이 없다 I have never known him to get angry. (▶ (영)에서는 부정사 to가 없어도 됨) // 비장의 미술품을 좀 보여 주십시오 Please let me see your art collection.

2 [관찰하다] observe; look (at); view; see; [시찰하다] inspect; visit. ¶미국 체류 중에 본 것 what one observed during one's stay [while] in America // 외국인이 본 한국 Korea as foreigners see it [as seen by foreigners] // 나는 영어 수업을 보러 갔다 I visited an English class. // 기회를 보아 나는 그를 방문할 작정이다 When I have a chance, I'll call on him. / (문어) If an opportunity arises [offers], I will call on him. // 형편이 어떻게 돌아가는가를 본 후에 행동을 취하자 Let's see which way the wind is blowing before we take action.

3 [구경하다] see the sights (of); [구경가다] visit (a museum); do (a town). ¶볼 만하다 be worth seeing [visiting] / be visitable // 영화 [연극]을 ~ see a movie [play] / 텔레비전에서 영화를 ~ watch [see] a movie on TV // 이 도시에는 별로 볼 것이 없습니다 There are not many sights to see in this town.

4 [어떤 일을 맡아보다] attend to (business); manage; take; conduct. ¶사무를 ~ do [attend to] business // 일을 ~ conduct affairs / do one's job / work // 직무를 ~ perform the duties of an office / attend to one's official duties // 내 아내가 집안일을 본 다 My wife manages the household.

5 [돌보다] take care of; look after; watch; [간호하다] attend to; [밥상 등을 차리다] set. ¶상을 ~ set the table // 어린아이를 잘 ~ take good care of a baby // 내가 없는 동안 아이를 보아 주시오 Please look after my son in my absence. // 내가 없는 동안 가게를 잘 보아라 Keep an eye on the store while I am away.

6 [읽다] read; see; (대충) look through [over]. ¶서류를 대충 ~ look [run one's eyes] over the papers // 오늘 신문 보았습니까 Have you read today's paper? // 어제 신문에서 그 기사를 보았다 I saw that story in yesterday's newspaper. // 나는 그의 이름을 때때로 신문에서 본다 I sometimes see his name in the newspaper.

7 [조사·검사하다] look over [into]; look over [into]; examine; [참고하다] refer to (a dictionary). ¶당신의 솜씨가 어떤지 한번 봅시다 (게임에서) Let's (have a game and) see how good you are. // 2층 난로를 내가 껐는지 보고 오겠다 I'll go and see if I turned off the stove upstairs. // 내 시계의 어디가 고장인지 보아 주시오 Please take a look and see what's wrong with my watch.

8 [판단하다] judge; [추정하다] presume; [간주하다] regard (as). ¶나는 그 사태를 중대하다고 본다 I regard the situation as serious. // 나는 그를 잘못 봤다 I misjudged him. // 그는 그녀를 명문 출신으로 보았다 It was his guess [He guessed] that she came from a noble family. // 내가 보는 눈이 틀림없다 My judgment never errs. / It is just as I thought. // 외관으로 보아 그렇게 나쁘지는 않다 Judging by [from] its appearance it is not so bad. // 나는 그를 좋은 집안의 출신으로 보았다 I judged him to be from a respectable family. // 내가 보기에 그 손해를 회복할 수는 거의 없었다 In my opinion [As I see it], the loss incurred is almost irrevocable. // 조난자의 대부분은 사망한 것으로 보인다 It is presumed that most of the victims are dead. // 그들은 당신이 어떻게 볼지는 몰라도 [어느 모로 보나] 이상적인 한 쌍이다 No matter how you look at it, they are an ideal couple. / They are an ideal couple in every respect. // 그는 그것을 쓸모없는 것으로 보고 있었다 He regarded it as useless. // 역까지 30분 걸린다고 보면 충분하다 If you allow thirty minutes, you'll have plenty of time to get to the station.

9 [경험하다] encounter personally; experience; undergo; go through; suffer; enjoy. ¶손해를 ~ suffer [sustain] a loss / suffer damage // 두고 보자 You'll be sorry for this! // 그것 봐 I told you so! / There! Didn't I tell you? // 따끔한 맛을 보여 주겠다 I'll show [teach] him a thing or two. // 휴강이 되어 나는 덕을 좀 보았다 It was a bit of luck [a windfall] that the lecture was canceled. // 숙부님이 나를 학교까지 차로 데려다 주셔서 덕을 보았다 I was lucky because my uncle gave me a lift to school.

10 [치르다] take [sit for] (an examination). ¶시험을 ~ take [undergo] an examination / sit (for) an examination // 시험을 보지 않고 입학하다 be admitted into a school without examination.

11 [배설하다] relieve oneself [nature]. ¶소변을 ~ urinate / make [pass] water // 나는 변을 보고 싶었다 [화장실에 가고 싶어 졌다] I needed to go to the bathroom. / (미국 구어) I needed to go to the john [(영국 구어) loo]. (보통 회화에서는 이와 같은 완곡한 말씨를 쓰지만, 의사한테 설명하거나 할 때는 I felt the need to urinate [defecate]라고 한다)

12 [장에서 물건을 사거나 팔다] buy [sell] (in the market). ¶장을 ~ deal in the market / do one's [the] marketing // 장 보러 가다 go to market / go shopping [marketing].

13 [값을 평가하다] price; offer (a price); name [bid] a price (for). ¶그의 시계 값을 5천 원밖에 보지 않다 make an offer of only 5,000 won for his watch // 나는 비용을 100만 원으로 보고 있다 I would put the cost at a million won. / I imagine the cost will be about one million won.

14 [새 식구를 얻거나 맞다] get; have. ¶며느리 [사위]를 ~ get a daughter-[son-]in-law // 손자를 ~ have [get] a grandson [grandchild] // 자식을 ~ get a child / beget [father] a child.

15 [바람피우다] have a secret (love) affair with. ¶계집을 ~ keep a mistress // 샛서방을 ~ cuckold [deceive] one's husband / have a secret lover.

16 [참다] bear; stand; put up with. ¶보자 보자 하니 그가 너무 거만하여 참을 수 없다 I can no longer put up with his arrogance. / His arrogance has almost exhausted my stock of patience.

17 [관상·운을 살피거나 헤아리다] tell; read; have one's fortune told. ¶관상을 ~ tell one's

face read (by a phrenologist) // 손금을 ~ read (in) one's palm / tell (a person's) hand / (보게 하다) have one's palm read (by) // 나는 점쟁이에게 운수를 보게 했다 I had my fortune told by a fortuneteller.
18 [맡아 보다] take[have] charge of; deal with; undertake; act as. ¶사회를 ~ preside at [over] (a meeting) / take the chair / (방송 등의) act as master of ceremonies (for) / (미국 구어) emcee (a show).

보기 좋은 떡이 먹기도 좋다(속담) Names and natures do often agree.

보다 못해 unable to stand by (any longer). ¶~ 나는 그들의 싸움을 말렸다 Unable to stand by, I drew the combatants apart.

보란 듯이 for show[display]; flauntingly; boastfully; braggingly; proudly; demonstratively; ostentatiously. ¶~ 행동하다 act demonstratively / (미국 속어) cut around / 장난감을 ~ 친구에게 자랑하다 show off a toy to one's friend // ~ 그는 불룩한 지갑을 꺼냈다 He took out his fat purse as of to show it off. // 젊은 부부가 ~ 팔짱을 끼고 걸어간다 The young couple are walking arm in arm as of to attract others' attention [to show themselves off].

볼 낯(이) 없다 be ashamed to see (a person); lose (one's) face; be unable to face (one's sweetheart). ¶나는 ~ I am ashamed of myself.

볼 장(을) 다 보다 have done with (a thing); be ruined. ¶그걸 못하면 넌 볼 장 다 본다 If you make a botch of it, it'll be the curtains for you. // 그 사람은 이젠 볼 장 다 봤다 It is all up[over] with him. / He is beyond hope.

보다² **1** [시험 삼아 하다] try; have a try (at); test. ¶해 ~ try / have a try (at / for) / 코트를 입어 ~ try on a coat / try a coat on // 이 모자를 써 보아라 Try this hat on. // 할 테면 해 보아라 Go ahead and try if you dare. // 한번 해 보자 Let's have a try at it. // 한 입 먹어 보시오 Have a bite and see how it tastes. / Try a bite of it. // 가는 데까지 가 보지 그래 Why don't you just go, anyway? // 이 편지를 죽 읽어 보아 주시겠어요 Will you look through this letter?
2 [경험] ¶달에 가 보고 싶다 I wish I could visit the moon. / I'd like to visit the moon.
3 […해 보니(결과); …해 보면(조건)]. ¶정신이 들고 보니 모든 사람들이 나를 쳐다보고 있었다 When I came to [recovered consciousness] I found everyone (was) looking at me. // 그의 입장이 되어 보면 자네에게 얻어맞고 그가 얼마나 화가 났을지 알 수 있을 것이다 If you put yourself in his place, you will see how angry he was when you struck him.
4 [전제] (even) if[though] …; granting[supposing] that …. ¶밑져 보았자 even if one loses / 당신이 지금 가 보았자 그를 만나지는 못한다 Even if you start now, you will not be able to see him. // 불평해 보았자 소용없다 It is no use complaining. // 비싸다고 해 봤자 기껏 5천 원 정도일 거다 It will cost you five thousand won at (the) dearest.

보다³ **1** [추측] it seems (to one) that; I guess. ¶그런가 ~ I guess[suppose] so. // 비가 오는 가 ~ It seems to be raining. // 그는 친구가 많은가 ~ He appears to have a lot of friends. **2** [확고하지 않은 의지]. ¶그만둘까 ~ I should give it up.

보다⁴ **1** [한층 더] more; still[much] more. ¶~ 힘드는 일 (much) harder work / ~ 정확히 말하면 to be more exact / to speak more precisely // ~ 중요한 것은 what is more important / 이쪽이 ~ 낫다 This is still better. **2** [비교] than; to. ¶… ~ 못하다 [낫다] be inferior [superior] to / be worse[better] than … / A와 B를 합친 것 ~ 크다 be bigger than A and B both together.

보답(報答) (a) repayment; (a) return; reward; (a) recompense; (a) requital. ¶…의 ~으로서 in recompense[return] for / 너의 ~는 나는 그의 친절에 충분한 ~을 하고 싶다 I would like to repay[return] his kindness in full. / 그 웨이터는 이전의 팁의 ~으로 내게 맥주 한 잔을 서비스했다 Out of gratitude for past tips, the waiter served me an extra glass of beer. // 착한 일을 하면 반드시 ~을 받는다 A good deed never goes unrewarded. **보답하다** repay; return; requite; recompense. ¶남의 은혜에 ~ repay a person's kindness // 수고에 ~ recompense (a person) for (his) trouble [services] // 노력에 ~ recompense (a person) for (his) labor // 남의 사랑에 ~ return a person's love.

보도(步道) a footpath; a footway; (미) a sidewalk; (영) a pavement. ¶횡단~ a pedestrian crossing.

보도(報道) news; a report; information. ¶~의 자유 freedom of the press // 신문 ~에 의하면 according to the paper[the newspaper reports] / The newspaper says that … // ~에 접하다 receive the news (of) // 대통령 사망의 첫 ~는 어젯밤 늦게 들어왔다 The first report of the President's death was received last night. // 소녀 납치의 ~는 경찰에 의해 금지되었다 The news of the girl's kidnapping was suppressed by the police. / The police prevented the girl's kidnapping from being made public. // 이 신문의 ~는 광범위에 걸쳐 있다 This newspaper provides [has] wide coverage. // 이 신문의 ~는 편파적이다 This newspaper carries [contains] biased reports. / There are biased reports in this newspaper. **보도하다** report; inform [notify] (a person) of; let (a person) know. ¶크게 [큰 표제로] ~ give prominent coverage (to) / headline / 잘못 ~ make a false report (of) / give out a false news / misreport. ➡¶이미 보도된 바와 같이 as previously [already] reported [announced] // 신문에 자세히 보도되다 get full coverage in the papers.
● **보도 관제** [보도의 정지] news blackout; [보도의 검열] news censorship. **보도 기관** an information[a news] medium (pl. -a); the press; news organs. **보도전(-戰)** a reportorial warfare; a news competition. **보도진** a news front; (미) a press corps; (영) the pressmen.

보도(輔導·補導) guidance; direction; a protection and guidance. ¶직업[학생] ~ vocational [student] guidance // 청소년의 ~ the protection and guidance of young people. **보도하다** guide; direct; lead.

보동보동 ⇨ᵛ포동포동
보드득 with a grinding. ⇨ᵛ부드득
보드랍다 soft; tender. ⇨ᵛ부드럽다¹
보드상자(-箱子) a cardboard box.
보드카 [러시아산의 증류주] vodka.
보들보들하다 very soft [tender / velvety /

smooth]. ¶보들보들한 살결 a very tender skin.
보디 a body.
● **보디가드** a bodyguard; a guard. **보디 블로**〔권투〕 a body blow. **보디빌딩** body-building; 〔구어〕 pumping iron. ¶~을 하다 work out with weights / 〔구어〕 pump iron.
보따리(褓−) a bundle; a package; a parcel. ¶책[빨래] ~ a package of books[laundry] // ~를 싸다 bundle (clothes) / do up in a bundle.
● **보따리장수** a peddler; a packman.
보라매 a young hawk (tamed for hawking).
보라(색)(−色) violet.
● **보랏빛** violet. ⇨¨보라 ¶연~ lavender / orchid.
보람 1 〔효과〕 (an) effect; fruit; worth; benefit. ¶~ 있는 worth (while) / fruitful / effective // 말한 ~이 있는 worth mentioning // 말한 ~이 없는 not worth mentioning // ~ 있는 〔남의 욕을 돋우는 일〕 a challenging job / 〔애쓸 만한 일〕 a worthwhile job / work worth doing // ~ 없는 일 a thankless task // ~도 없이 in vain / to no purpose / without result / uselessly / fruitlessly // ~**이 없다** be in vain / be useless / be of no use[avail] / go for nothing // ~**이 있다** be worth while (to do) / be worth (doing) / be rewarded / be of use // 사는 ~이 있다[없다] have something[nothing] to live for / be [be not] worth living // 사는 ~을 느끼다 find one's life worth living / find this world worth living in // 효과가 나타나 우리는 ~을 느꼈다 We felt encouraged as the results began to show. // 자네가 그에게 무슨 말을 해도 말한 ~이 없게 될 것이다 Whatever you say to him, you will be simply wasting your breath. / Whatever you say, your words will be lost on him. // 이런 소식을 기다린 ~이 있었다 This news was well worth waiting for. // 노력한 ~이 있어 그가 1등을 차지했다 His efforts were fully rewarded, for he won the first prize. // 모두가 극진히 간호한 ~도 없이 그는 숨을 거두었다 He passed away in spite of their excellent care. // 그녀는 노후에 무엇인가 생(生)에 ~이 되는 것을 하고 싶어 졌다 She wanted something to live for in her old age. // 나는 내가 ~ 없는 생활을 하고 있는 듯한 느낌이 든다 I feel I am leading a useless life.
2 〔약간 드러나 보이는 표적〕 an indication; a sign; a mark; a symptom.
보령(寶齡) the age of the King.
보로통하다 swollen; sullen. ⇨부루퉁하다
보료 a decorated pouf; a fancy mattress (used as cushion).
보루(堡壘) a fort; a fortress; a rampart; a fortification; a battery; a stronghold. ¶해안 ~ a seacoast fortification // 청교도의 ~ a stronghold of puritanism // ~를 **구축하다** fortify / raise [construct] a fort / construct defense works.
보루(*board) a carton. ¶담배 한 ~ a carton of cigarettes.
보루박스 ⇨보드상자
보류(保留) reservation; 〔중지〕 suspension; 〔법안 등의〕 pigeonholing; shelving. **보류하다** reserve; defer; withhold. ¶한 가지만 보류하는 조건부로 찬성합니다 I agree, but with one reservation. →그 결정은 보류되었다 The decision was deferred [put off / held over]. // 출발은 보류되었다 Our departure has been postponed [put off]. // 감세 법안은 보류되었다 The tax reduction bill has been shelved [deferred / (미) tabled] (▶ 〔영〕에서 table은 심의에 붙인다는 뜻). // 그 계획은 당분간 보류될 것이다 The plan will be laid [set / put] aside for some time. // 보상의 지급이 보류되었다 Compensation payments were suspended. // 그 법안은 보류되었다 The bill has been shelved [pigeonholed]. // 그 문제는 보류되었다 The question was shelved.
보름 1 〔열닷새 동안〕 fifteen days; a half month. ¶~ 안에 within fifteen days [half a month] / within a fortnight // ~만에 돌아오다 come home after a fortnight's absence. **2** the fifteenth day of the (lunar) month. ⇨¨보름날 (⊙날)
● **보름날** the fifteenth day of the (lunar) month. ¶정월 ~ the 15th of the first lunar month [of January]. **보름달** a full moon (on the fifteenth night).
보리 〔식〕 barley; rye(라이 보리). ¶볶은 ~ parched barley.
● **보리농사** barley farming. **보리밥** boiled barley (and rice); boiled rice with barley. ¶~에는 고추장이 제격이다 Like goes well with like. / Like matches (with) like. **보리밭** a barley field. **보리쌀** polished barley. **보리차** barley tea. **보릿고개** the farm hardship period; spring cessation to the peasant; the spring austerity; the barley hump. ¶~를 넘기다 get over the barley hump // ~가 지났다 The barley hump is over.
보리(菩提) 〔불〕 **1** 〔지혜〕 Bodhi; the Supreme Enlightenment [Wisdom]. **2** 〔불과(佛果)〕 달성의 길〕 (attainment of) Buddhahood.
● **보리수**(−樹) 〔식〕 a bo tree; a pipal (tree); a sacred fig; (유럽의) a linden tree; a lime (tree).
보리새우 〔동〕 a prawn.
보린(保隣) mutual help [assistance] among neighbors. **보린하다** aid [help / assist] one another among neighbors.
보링 〔천공〕 boring.
● **보링 머신** a boring machine.
보막이하다(洑−) build [make] a dammed pool.
보매 〔언뜻 보기에〕 apparently; seemingly; judging from the appearance. ¶언뜻 ~ at the first glance [sight] // ~ 그는 장사치 같았다 The man was apparently a merchant. / He looked like a merchant. // 언뜻 ~ 좋다 It looks good enough at first sight. // ~ 그는 40살쯤 되겠다 He looks about forty. // 그는 ~ 정직한 것 같지만 실은 그렇지 않다 He is not so honest as he looks [he apparently is].
보모(保姆) a (dry) nurse; a nursery governess. ¶보육원의 ~ a nursery school teacher.
보무당당하다(步武堂堂−) swaggering; strutting. ¶보무당당하게 in fine array // 보무당당하게 나아가다 march [advance] in fine array / go on proudly.
보무라지 〔종이·헝겊·실 등의 잔 부스러기〕 tiny scraps (of paper, cloth, etc.); tiny bits of thread; lint. ¶실 ~ short pieces of waste thread [yarn] / thrums / ravelings.
보물(寶物) a treasure; a highly prized article; valuables.
● **보물선** a treasure ship. **보물섬** a treasure

보배
island. **보물찾기** treasure-hunting; a treasure hunt.

보배 [재보] (a) treasure; riches; (집안 대대의) an heirloom; (매우 귀중한 것) valuable [precious] things. ¶숨은 ~ hidden [burried] treasure // 집안[나라]의 ~ a family[national] treasure // 젊음이 ~로다 Youth is a treasure. // 어린이는 나라의 ~다 Children are the treasure of the country.

보배롭다 precious; valuable. ¶이번에 새로 들어온 조수는 보배롭기 이를 데 없다 Our new assistant is quite a treasure.

보병(步兵) (부대) infantry; foot; (사병) an infantryman; a foot soldier; (미국 속어) a dogface. ¶경~대 light infantry(약어 L.I., Lt. Inf.).
● 보병 중대[대대 / 연대] an infantry company[battalion / regiment]. **보병 학교** an infantry school.

보복(報復) revenge; retaliation(▶ retaliation 은 같은 방법으로 보통 즉각 보복하는 일); (a) reprisal(국가간의); retortion; requital. ¶대량 ~ a massive retaliation // …의 ~으로 in retaliation[revenge] for ... / in[by way of] reprisal for ... ¶나는 ~으로 그의 책을 감추었다 I retaliated by hiding his book. **보복하다** revenge (oneself on); retaliate; take [exact] revenge; get even with; make[carry out] a reprisal (on). ¶상대가 한 대로 똑같이 ~ repay him in the same coin // 나는 그에게 보기 좋게 보복해 주었다 I got my revenge on him. / (구어) I got even with him. / 두고 봐라! 꼭 보복해 줄 테다 I'll get even with you [I'll get my revenge]! Just you wait! // 게릴라는 동료의 처형에 보복하여 정부 요인을 납치했다 The guerrillas avenged their executed comrades by kidnapping government VIPs.
● 보복 관세 retaliatory[retaliative] duties.

보부상(褓負商) a pedlar; a peddler; a packman. ¶~을 하다 peddle / hawk.

보빙(堡氷) [지] barrier ice; the (Antarctic) barrier.

보살(菩薩) 1 [보리살타] a Bodhisattva; a Buddhist saint. 2 [보살승] the Bodhisattva vehicle. 3 [나이 많은 여신도] an old female believer in Buddhism.

보살피다 [뒤를 돌보아 주다] take care of; look[see] after (a person); have (a person) under one's charge; have[take] charge of; see to. ¶집안일을 ~ look after[mind] the household affairs / manage household matters // 환자를 ~ attend to[on] the sick // 그녀는 어머니처럼 어린 동생을 보살펴 주었다 She took care of her younger sister like a mother. // 그 늙은 모친은 아들이 보살피고 있다 The old woman is looked after by her son. // 그 선생은 학생들을 힘껏 잘 보살핀다 That teacher does whatever he can for his students. // 장례는 부친의 회사 동료들이 보살펴 주었다 My father's colleagues at the firm took care of[looked after] the funeral. // 이 아이는 아직도 많은 보살핌이 필요하다 This child still needs a lot of looking after. // 나의 수호신이 나를 보살펴 주실 것이다 My guardian angel will watch over me. // 그녀는 어머니를 3년 동안 보살폈다 She nursed [took care of] her mother for three years.

보상(報償) compensation; consideration; remuneration. ¶…의 ~으로서 in[as] compensation for ... // 내 노력은 충분한 ~을 받은 것으로 생각한다 I feel more than recompensed for my efforts. // 그녀는 자신의 노력에 대해 충분한 ~을 받았다 She was fully rewarded for her efforts. / Her efforts were fully rewarded. **보상하다** recompense; remunerate; reward.

보상(補償) compensation; (문어) indemnification; reparation. ¶수출 ~ export compensation // 전면 ~ (demand) full[complete] compensation // ~을 요구하다 demand [make] reparation (for) // 그는 작업 중의 부상에 대하여 회사에 ~을 요구했다 He demanded compensation from the firm for the injury he received at work. // 자네 책을 더럽힌 ~으로 내가 새 책을 사 왔다 I bought a new book for you as[in] compensation for the one I got dirty. // 그는 자네에게 ~을 하고 싶어 한다 He wants to make it up[make amends / make reparation] to you. // 우리는 그의 노고에 ~을 해야겠다 We will compensate[(문어) recompense] him for his trouble. **보상하다** compensate (for); make reparation (for); make up (for); (문어) indemnify (a person for injuries). ¶손해를 ~ indemnify losses[damages] / make compensation[reparation] for a loss // 국가는 원고의 소송 비용을 보상해야 한다 The state should compensate the plaintiff for his court costs.
● 보상금 compensation payment; an indemnity; (문어) remuneration; (문어) (a) recompense. ¶~을 받다 receive the compensation money (from) // ~을 지급하다 pay compensation to (a person for) // 그들은 그 손해에 대해 ~을 청구했다 They demanded compensation[an indemnity] for the damage.

보색(補色) [미] a complementary color[(영) colour].

보서다(保-) [보증을 서다] go[give / stand] security (for).

보석(步石) 1 [디딤돌] a stepping-stone. 2 a stepping-stone. ⇨섬돌

보석(保釋) [법] bail; bailment. ¶~이 되다 be allowed bail / be released[liberated] on bail // ~으로 출감 중이다 be out on bail // 판사는 ~을 허락하지 않았다 The judge refused bail.
보석하다 let (a person) out on bail.
● 보석 bail. ¶~을 내다 give[furnish] bail (for) // 그는 500만 원의 ~을 내고 석방되었다 He was released on five million won bail[bail of five million won].

보석(寶石) a jewel; a precious stone; (연마한) a gem; (시계의) a ruby; (집합적) jewelry [(영) jewellery]. ¶~을 박은 시계[반지] a jeweled watch[ring] // ~을 갈다 polish a jewel[precious stone] // ~으로 장식하다 jewel / bejewel / adorn[bedeck] with jewels [gems] // 반지에 ~을 박다 [끼워 넣다] set gems[a jewel] in a ring / [장식하다] set a ring with jewels.
● 보석상 (장수) a jewel(l)er(▶ 팔기도 하고 세공도 하며 또 시계의 수리 등도 함); a gem dealer; (가게) a jewel(l)er's (store). **보석 세공** jewelry; (영) jewellery.

보선(保線) [철도 선로의 유지·수선] maintenance of tracks; railroad[track] maintenance. **보선하다** keep[maintain] the tracks in good condition.
● 보선공 a line(s)man; (미) a tracklayer; (영) a platelayer.

보선(普選) a popular election. ⇨보통 선거

보선(補選) a special election. ⇨보궐 선거(⇨보궐)

보세(保稅) ¶~의 in bond / bonded.
● **보세 가공** bonded processing. **보세 창고** a bonded warehouse. ¶~에 맡기다[넣다] bond / store (goods) in bond. **보세품** bonded goods.

보송보송하다 1 [잘 말라서 물기가 없다] dry; dried up[out]; parched; waterless. ¶보송보송한 빨래 the dried out wash. 2 [살결 등이 곱고 보드랍다]. ¶보송보송한 살결 soft and moistureless skin.

보수(步數) [걸음의 수] the number of steps. ¶~를 세다 count one's steps[paces].

보수(保守) [재래 풍습 등을 지키기] conservatism; conservativeness.
● **보수당** a conservative party; (영국의) the Conservative Party. **보수주의** conservatism; Toryism. **보수주의자** a conservative (person); a Tory. **보수파** the conservatives; the old liners.

보수(補修) repair; mending. ¶그 다리는 ~ 중이다 The bridge is under repair. **보수하다** repair (the road); mend (a broken fence); (미국 구어) fix.
● **보수 공사** repair[maintenance] work.

보수(報酬) [봉급] pay(▶ 일반적인 말); (a) salary; [임금] wages; remuneration; a recompense; [대가] a reward; an honorarium (pl. ~s, honoraria); (의사·변호사 등의) a fee. ¶~를 받지 않고 without consideration[pay / fee / remuneration / recompense] / for nothing // ~의 …로서 in consideration [requital] (of) … / in recompense[reward / return] for … // ~가 좋은 일 a good-paying [lucrative / profitable] job // ~가 박한 일 a badly[poorly] paid job // ~를 주다 recompense[remunerate / reward / pay] (a person for his labor) // ~를 받고 가르치다 teach for pay[a consideration] // ~를 받고 수고에 대한 ~를 드리겠습니다 I will pay you for your trouble. // 그들은 노력에 대해 좋은 ~를 받는다 They receive a good return for their efforts. // 일은 어려웠는데 ~는 얼마 되지 않았다 I got very little by way of reward[received little remuneration] for my hard work. // 도둑맞은 가방의 정보 제공자에게는 5만 원의 ~를 드립니다 A reward of fifty thousand won is offered for information about the stolen suit case.

보수적(保守的) conservative; old-guard; unobtrusive; (미국 구어) square. ¶~인 방법 [생각] a conservative method[idea] // ~인 사람 an old-fashioned[a conservative] person // ~인 생각을 가진 사람 a person with [holding] conservative view // 그의 사업 방식은 아주 ~이다 His business methods are quite conservative.

보스 [우두머리·정계의 영수] a boss; a boss man. ¶재계의 ~ the boss of the business world.

보스락 with a rustle. ⇨부스럭

보슬보슬 [눈·비가 내리는 모양] gently; softly. ¶비가 ~ 내리고 있다 It is drizzling. / The rain is gently falling.

보슬비 a drizzling rain; a drizzle; a misty rain. ¶~가 내리다 It is drizzling.

보습 a plowshare; a share.

보습(補習) supplementary lessons; (미) refresher training. ¶영어 ~ 수업을 하다[받다] give[receive] supplementary tuition [lessons] in English. **보습하다** supplement (education).
● **보습 교육** continuation[supplementary] education.

보시(布施) [남에게 베푸는 일] almsgiving; charity; [절에 바치는 돈이나 물건] an alms (단수·복수 동형); an offering (to a priest). ¶절에 ~를 바치다 make an[a monetary] offering to a temple // ~를 청하다 beg[ask] (a person) for (an) alms. **보시하다** give alms (to).

보시기 a small bowl of porcelain.

보신(保身) self-protection. ¶그가 그런 행동을 취한 것은 전적으로 ~을 위해서였다 He acted on that way only because he did not want to lose his position[solely for the purpose of protecting his own interests]. **보신하다** [이해관계를 지키다] protect[defend] one's own interests; [지위를 유지하다] maintain [preserve / retain] one's position[place].
● **보신책** the ways[techniques] of self-protection.

보신(補身) nurturing; tonicking. **보신하다** improve[build up] one's health by taking tonics.
● **보신탕** dog soup.

보신하다(補腎–) recruit vitality[invigorate oneself] by taking tonics.

보쌈김치(褓–) wrapped-up gimchi(kimchi).

보아주다 overlook; wink at. ⇨봐주다

보아하니 so far as my observation goes; so far as the appearances go; to all appearance; apparently. ¶~ 점잖은 분이 왜 이러시오 You look like a gentleman-you should behave yourself better.

보아한들 however hard one may think; by any reckoning; to the best of one's judg(e)ment.

보안(保安) the preservation[maintenance] of public peace[security]. ¶국가 ~법 the National Security Law.
● **보안 경찰** peace preservation police. **보안관** a peace officer; (미국의) a sheriff; a marshal. **보안등** a security light. **보안 사범** national security violators; a public security offender.

보약(補藥) a restorative; a tonic (medicine); an invigorant.

보양(保養) [건강을 보전하고 활력을 기름] preservation of one's health; (병후의) recuperation. ¶~을 위해 for one's health / for recuperation // 병후에는 ~을 잘 하지 않으면 안 된다 You must take good care of your health after illness. **보양하다** take a rest for one's health; (병후에) recuperate. ¶그는 산장에서 병후의 몸을 보양하고 있다 He is trying to recover his health at a mountain cottage.
● **보양지** a health resort.

보얗다 1 (빛깔이) milk-white; pearly; frosty; cream-colored; opaque. ¶살결이 ~ have a pearly skin. 2 (안개·연기 등으로) hazy; misty; heavy (in the air). ¶숲에 안개가 보얗게 끼어 있다 The woods are veiled in mist. // 방 안이 담배 연기로 ~ The room is heavy with tobacco smoke. // 하늘이 먼지로 ~ The sky is hazy with dust.

보얘지다 get misty; become hazy. ⇨부예지다

보어(補語) [언] a complement. ¶주격 [목적격] ~ a subjective[an objective] complement.

보온(保溫) keeping warm; heat[thermal] insulation. ¶~이 잘되는 옷 warm clothes∥~을 위해서 for keeping warmth / to keep (a thing) warm∥이 내복은 ~성이 좋다 This underwear is (good for keeping) warm. **보온하다** keep (a thing) warm[hot]. ¶두꺼운 커튼은 방을 보온하는 데 좋다 Heavy curtains help (to) keep a room warm.
- **보온병** a vacuum bottle; a thermos bottle [flask / jug]; (상품명) Thermos. ¶이 ~은 보온이 잘된다 This thermos bottle keeps liquids hot for a long time.

보완(補完) supplementation; (a) complement. **보완하다** complement; supplement; make up for. ¶현행 입시 제도의 약점을 ~ make up for the weak points in the current entrance examination system.

보우(保佑) protection; help. **보우하다** protect; guard; help.

보위(保衛) [보전] integrity; preservation; [방위] protection; defense. **보위하다** preserve the integrity (of); preserve (one's country) intact; defend.

보위(寶位) [제왕의 자리] the throne; the crown. ¶~에 오르다 accede to the throne / ascend[come to / mount] the throne / throne∥~를 잇다 succeed to the throne.

보유(保有) possession; retention; maintenance. ¶영토의 ~ the maintenance of territory∥현재 ~ 병력 current military[troop] strength∥현재 ~ 의석 a party's seats / the seats held by a party / a party's current strength (in the National Assembly)∥원자재 materials on[at] hand / the raw materials that (a company) has (in stock)∥핵 ~국 a nuclear state. **보유하다** possess; hold; keep; retain; maintain. ¶그는 원반던지기의 세계 기록을 보유하고 있다 He holds a world record of the discus throw.∥우리 회사는 현재 제트 여객기 80대를 보유하고 있다 Our company now owns eighty jetliners.∥현재 그 나라는 항공모함 3척을 보유하고 있다 At present, the country has[possesses] three aircraft carriers.
- **보유고 / 보유량** holdings; holding amount [volume]; capacity. ¶적정 외환 ~ an adequate amount of foreign exchange holding∥금 ~ gold holdings. **보유자** a holder. ¶기록 ~ a record holder.

보유(補遺) a supplement (to a dictionary); an appendix (pl. ~es, -dices). (▶ supplement는 보통 별책, appendix는 권말에 붙음) ¶~의 supplementary. **보유하다** add a supplement[an appendix] to (a main work).

보육(保育) childcare; nurture; upbringing. ¶아동 ~ childcare / [유아 교육] children's education. **보육하다** nurture; take care of (a child); nurse (an infant); bring up; rear; foster.
- **보육기**(-器) an incubator. **보육원** [고아원] an orphanage; an orphan asylum; (미) a day nursery; (영) a nursery school.

보은(報恩) repayment of kindness; gratitude. ¶은사에 대한 ~으로 in return[gratitude] for one's teacher's kindness / (in order) to repay[(문어) requite] one's teacher's kindness. **보은하다** repay[return] (a person's) kindness; requite (a person's) favors.

보응(報應) retribution; nemesis. **보응하다** be requited[repaid / rewarded].

보이 (호텔의) a bellboy; a porter; (식당의) a waiter; (여객선의) a cabin boy; (객선·열차 등의) a steward; (침대차 등의) (미) a porter; (영) a steward.

보이다¹ (눈에) see; catch sight of; (사물이) be seen; be visible; show; be in sight; be open to the view. ¶보이지 않는 눈 a sightless eye∥잘 보이는 자리 a good seat from which to watch (the stage / the game)∥예술가처럼 보이는 남자 a man who looks like an artist∥잘 ~ easy to see∥보이지 않다 be not seen / be out of sight[view] / be invisible∥보이지 않게 되다 (사물이) go[pass] out of sight / (사람이) become blind / lose one's eyesight / lose sight of∥보이게 되다 come in sight[into view] / appear (in sight)∥한국인처럼 보이지 않다 do not look like a Korean∥그녀는 늘 우울하게 보인다 She always looks gloomy.∥그는 앓고 있는 것처럼 보인다 He seems (to be) ill. / It seems that he is ill. / He appears to be ill.∥그는 실패한 것처럼 보인다 He appears[seems] to have failed.∥그 사람은 교사같이 보인다 He looks like a teacher.∥이 것은 이상하게[익살맞게] 보인다 This looks funny.∥그는 목적을 달성한 것처럼 보인다 He appears[seems] to have attained his object.∥왼쪽 눈이 안 보이다 be blind in the left eye∥그녀는 수술받고 나서 눈이 보이게 되었다 After the operation she regained her eyesight.∥그의 눈이 점점 안 보이게 되어 가고 있다 His eyesight is failing.∥내 웃옷이 안 보인다 I cannot find my coat. / My coat is missing.∥금성은 어디 있지? 아, 저기 보인다 Where is Venus? Oh, there it is!∥무엇이 보이느냐 What do you see?∥나무 사이로 바다가 보였다 The sea showed[was sighted] through the trees.∥회원 배지는 보이는 곳에 달아야 한다 Members' badges must be worn visibly.∥고양이는 어둠 속에서도 눈이 보인다 Cats can see in the dark.∥보이지 않게 될 때까지 우리는 그를 전송했다 We watched him until he was out of sight.∥내가 앉아 있던 곳에서는 시합이 전혀 보이지 않았다 From where I sat I could see nothing of the game.∥나무 꼭대기 쪽에 새의 둥지가 보인다 A bird's nest can be seen toward the top of the tree.∥지붕 위에서 도시가 잘 보인다 We have a good view of the town from the roof.∥네 슬립[속옷]이 보인다 Your slip is showing.∥세균은 육안으로는 보이지 않는다 Germs are invisible to the naked eye.∥우리는 비행기가 보이지 않을 때까지 바라보았다 We watched the plane until it was out of sight[till we lost sight of it].∥자동차 열쇠가 안 보인다 I can't find my car keys. / My car keys are missing.∥방의 번호는 잘 보이는 곳에다 붙여 놓으시오. Put up the room number where it can be easily seen.∥그녀가 창가에 있는 것이 보였다 I caught sight of her sitting by the window.∥그녀의 스커트 밑에서 속옷[슬립]의 일부가 삐죽이 나와 있는 것이 보인다 Her slip is showing[peeping out] from under her skirt.∥그의 바지 주머니에서 지폐 다발의 일부가 삐죽이 나와 있는 것이 보인다 A wad of bills was sticking out from his trouser(s) pocket.∥노여움이 그의 얼굴에 나타나 보였다 His anger shows immediately on his face.

보이다² [보게 하다] show; let (a person) see [look at]; [전시하다] display; exhibit; evince; (감추진 것을) disclose (to view);

reveal. ¶다른 것을 ~ show (a person) another kind // 모범[표준]을 ~ set (a person) an example [standard] // 실력을 ~ show [display] one's ability // 의사에게 ~ consult [see] a doctor / be examined by a doctor // 개찰구에서 정기권을 ~ show a commuter pass at the ticket (collector's) gate // 소녀는 새 가방을 친구들에게 자랑스레 보였다 The girl show off her new bag to her friends. // 좀 보여 주세요 Let me have a look at it. // 차표를 보여 주십시오 Ticket [Show your ticket], please. // 어떻게 하는지 보여 주시오 Please show me how to do it. // 이것을 당신에게 보일 생각은 아니었습니다 This was not intended for your eyes. // 실례를 하나 보여 드리지요 I will give [Here is] an example. // 그는 신분증명서를 나에게 보였다 He showed me his identification card. // 그 흰 장갑을 보여 주세요 Let me see those white gloves.

보이다³ [···인 것 같다] look (like); seem; appear. ¶젊어 보이는 사람 a youthful appearing man // 정직해[우스워] ~ look honest [funny] // 그는 시종 슬퍼[울적해] 보였다 He looked sad [depressed] from beginning to end. // 이 사진으로는 그가 너무 늙어 보인다 This portrait makes him too old. // 그 여자는 마흔 살쯤 되어 보인다 She looks about forty.

보이 소프라노 (성부) (boys') soprano; (사람) a boy soprano.

보이 스카우트 the Boy Scouts.

보이콧 [불매 동맹] a boycott; boycotting. ¶통상(通商) ~ a trade boycott // ~을 선언하다 declare a boycott. 보이콧하다 boycott [taboo] (goods); stage a boycott. ¶그 가게에 대해 보이콧하기로 결정하다 decide on a boycott of that store // 수업을 집단으로 ~ cut (professor Brown's) class en masse // 우리는 그 회사의 제품을 보이콧할 생각이다 We are going to boycott that company's products.

보이프렌드 a boyfriend (▶ 우리말 「보이프렌드」가 주로 10대 소녀의 남자 친구를 가리키는 데 반해, 영어 "boyfriend"는 그 뜻 외에 성 관계를 맺고 있는, 성인 여자의 남자 애인을 가리키기도 함).

보일러 a boiler. ¶석탄[기름](을 때는) ~ a coal- [an oil-] fired boiler // ~를 때다 stoke (up) the boiler.

●**보일러실** a boiler room.

보자기 a wrapping cloth; a kerchief. ¶~에 싼 것 a parcel wrapped in a cloth / a cloth-wrapped bundle.

보잘것없다 worthless; valueless; trifling; beneath notice; trivial; useless. ¶보잘것없는 녀석 a nobody / a man of straw // 보잘것없는 일 a trifle / a triviality // 보잘것없는 작품 a work of low [small] merit // 보잘것없는 일을 가지고 법석을 떨다 make a fuss about trifles // 보잘것없는 것이나마 받아 주십시오 Kindly accept this little trifle. // 그의 공헌이래야 ~ His contribution is insignificant [not worth mentioning].

보장(保障) [보증] guarantee; [확보] security. ¶자유의 ~ the securing of liberty // 사회 ~ social security // 생활 ~ daily life security // 안전 ~ 조약 a security pact // 안전 ~ 이사회 (유엔의) the Security Council // 집단 안전 ~ collective security // 머리가 좋다고 해서 출세한다는 ~은 없다 Intelligence is no guarantee of [does not guarantee] success in life. **보장하다** guarantee; secure; assure. ¶평화를 ~ secure peace // 남의 생활을 ~ guarantee a person's living [livelihood] // 1할의 배당을 ~ guarantee a dividend of 10% // 경찰은 당신의 안전을 보장해 줄 겁니다 The police will guarantee your safety. // 비행기가 정시에 도착할지 어떨지는 보장할 수 없다 The punctual arrive of airplanes cannot be guaranteed. // 아드님은 반드시 돌아옵니다. 보장합니다 Your son is sure to come back. Depend on it. // 그의 성실성을 내가 보장합니다 I will vouch for [I assure you of] his earnestness. ➔그에게 사장 자리가 보장되어 있다 The presidency is guaranteed to him.

보전(保全) integrity; preservation; conservation; (기계 등의) maintenance. ¶국토 ~ conservation of national land // 영토 ~ territorial integrity // 증거 ~ perpetuation of evidence // 국립공원 삼림의 ~ the conservation of forests [woodlands] in national parks // 그는 항상 자기 지위 ~에 힘썼다 He always strove to protect his position [to keep his position secure]. **보전하다** preserve [safeguard] the integrity (of); preserve [keep] (one's country) intact; keep (a machine) in good condition; maintain. ¶민간 전승[영토]을 ~ preserve folklore [the nation's territorial integrity] // 재산을 ~ keep one's property intact.

보전(寶典) 1 [귀중한 법전] an important [a highly prized] code. 2 [귀중한 책] a thesaurus (pl. ~es, -ri); a treasury (of words and phrases); a precious book.

보정(補正) [보충과 바로잡음] revision; [물] correction; compensation. **보정하다** revise; correct; compensate (a pendulum).

보제(補劑) [보양] a restorative; a tonic; [보조약] an adjuvant; a synergist; (염색의) an auxiliary agent.

보조(步調) 1 [걸음걸이의 모양·속도 등의 상태] (a) pace; (a) step; cadence. ¶~가 맞다[맞지 않다] be in [out of] step (with) // ~를 맞추다 keep [mark] step [pace] / get [fall] into step (with) / keep (in) step (with) // ~를 맞추어 행진하다 march at attention [in step] / walk with mcasured tread // 그들은 갑자기 ~를 빠르게 했다[늦추었다] They suddenly quickened [slackened / slowed] their pace. // 그들은 ~를 맞춰 행진하고 있었다 They were marching in step. // 나는 그의 ~에 맞춰 걸었다 I kept in step with him. // ~ 맞추어[발 맞추어] 가 Mark time!

2 [일·행위 등에서 상호 간의 일치 상태] pace. ¶~를 맞추어 행동하다 act [work] in concert (with) // 시대의 진보에 ~를 맞추다 keep up [keep pace] with the times // 이 일에서는 그에게 ~를 맞추는 것이 최선의 방책이다 In this matter, the best thing is to act [work] in concert with him.

보조(補助) 1 [원조] assistance; help; aid. ¶~의 assistant // ~로서 as assistant / in aid (of) // 그는 누구의 ~도 받지 않고 이 사업을 이룩했다 He carried out this project entirely on his own. // 그녀는 딸한테서 전적으로 생활비의 ~를 받고 있다 She depends entirely on her daughter for her living expenses. // 이 연구는 국고의 ~를 받고 있다 This research [project] is subsidized by the government [from public funds]. **보조하다** assist; help; aid; subsidize. ¶재정적으로 ~ give financial

보조개 aid [assistance] (to).
2 [보충] supplement. ¶～의 supplementary / auxiliary / subsidiary. 보조하다 supplement. 수동 브레이크는 제동 장치의 기능을 보조하고 있다 The hand brake supplements the function of the main braking system.

● 보조금 a subsidy; a bounty; a grant-in-aid (*pl.* grants-in-aid); a grant of money. ¶생활 ～ a supplementary living allowance // 정부 ～ a government subsidy [protection] // 정부는 이 연구소에 5,000만 달러의 ～을 주었다 The government granted a subsidy [made a grant] of fifty million dollars to this institute. 보조 기관(一機關) a donkey engine; (일반적인) a subsidiary organ. 보조 기억 장치 an auxiliary storage [memory]; a secondary storage [memory]. 보조 동사 [언] an auxiliary verb. 보조원 a supplementary member; an assistant.

보조개 a dimple. ¶한쪽 ～ a dimple on one cheek // ～가 있는 얼굴 a dimpled face // ～가 생긴다 [없어진다] Dimples appear on [disappear from] the cheeks. // 그녀가 웃으면 한쪽 볼에 ～가 생긴다 A dimple appears in her cheek when she smiles.

보조적(補助的) 1 [원조] assistant. 2 [보충] supplementary; auxiliary; subsidiary. ¶～인 수단 a supplementary means // 그들은 그 혁명에서 ～인 역할을 한 것에 불과하다 They played only a minor role in the revolution.

보족(補足) [보태어 넉넉하게 함]. ¶～의 supplementary / complementary / additional. 보족하다 complement; supplement; supply (a want).

보존(保存) preservation; storage; maintenance; (새와 짐승·하천·천연자원 등의) conservation. ¶그 사적은 ～ 상태가 좋다 [나쁘다] The historic site is in a good [bad / poor] state of preservation. 보존하다 preserve; conserve; keep; maintain; retain. ¶냉장고에 보존하면 이것이 1개월은 간다 This can be preserved [will keep] for a month in the refrigerator. // 이 지역은 아직도 전원(田園)의 아름다움을 잘 보존하고 있다 This district retains its pastoral beauty. ➔ 잘 보존되어 있다 [유지되어 있다] be well preserved / [수리가 잘 되어 있다] be kept in good repair.

● 보존림(一林) a forest reserve [preserve].

보좌(補佐) assistance; aid. ¶～ 역할을 하다 act as (an) adviser (to). 보좌하다 aid; assist; help; (구어) backstop; [조언하다] counsel; give advice (to a person). ¶그는 총장을 잘 보좌했다 He assisted the president (of the university) very capably.

● 보좌관 an assistant; (미) an aide. ¶대통령 ～ a presidential aide.

보좌(寶座) (왕의) (royal) throne; (부처님의) the seat of Buddha's image; the place where Buddha sits. ¶～에 앉히다 set (a person) on the throne.

보증(保證) (품질·내용 등의) a guarantee; a warranty; [법] (a) security. ¶신원 ～ (고용인의) fidelity guarantee // 은행 ～ bank guarantee / banker's guarantee / 빚으로서 집을 담보로 잡히다 borrow money with one's house as security // ～을 서다 go [give / stand] security (for) / stand [go] surety (for) // ～을 세우다 find [give] security [surety] (for). 보증하다 guarantee; warrant; assure; ensure; answer for; vouch for; certify; endorse. ¶신원을 ～ vouch for (a person's) character / guarantee (a person's) character / stand [go] surety for (a person) // 품질을 ～ guarantee [warrant] the quality (of an article) // 그 물건의 질은 보증할 수가 없다 We cannot guarantee the quality of that article. // 그녀의 인품은 내가 보증합니다 I will vouch for her character. // 그의 능력은 내가 보증합니다 I will answer for [vouch for / guarantee] his competence. // 내가 그녀의 신원을 보증했다 I vouched for her.

● 보증금 security (money); guaranty money. ¶～ 없이 without a deposit // ～을 내다 pay security [guaranty] money / deposit money as security // ～을 걸다 make [give] a deposit (of 500,000 won on a car) / pay earnest money. 보증서 a (letter of) guarantee; (인물·기량 등의) a reference; (장사의) a warranty. ¶재정 ～ an affidavit of support. 보증 수표 a certified check [(영) cheque]. 보증인 [법] a guarantor; (채무의) a surety; a reference (신원 조회처). ¶연대 ～ a joint surety / a surety liable collectively [jointly and severally] // 신원 ～ a (personal) guarantor // 그는 조카의 빚을 얻는 데 ～이 되었다 He stood [went] security for his nephew's debt.

보지 a vagina (*pl.* ～s, -nae); [생] a vulva (*pl.* ～s, -e); (금기) a cunt; (금기) a pussy; (금기) a twat.

보지(保持) maintenance; preservation; retention. 보지하다 maintain (public peace); preserve; retain; sustain; keep; hold (a world record). ¶선수권을 ～ hold the championship.

보지(報知) information; news; a report. 보지하다 inform (a person) of (a matter); communicate (a fact) to (a person); let (a person) know; report.

보직(補職) assignment to a position; appointment. 보직하다 assign [appoint] (a person to the post of). ➔ ¶보직되다 be assigned [appointed] (to the post of).

보채다 fret; be fretful [peevish]; beg [whine / tease] for (things); importune; grizzle. ¶보채는 아기 a fretful baby // 보채는 아이를 달래다 humor [soothe] a fretful child // 등에 업힌 젖먹이가 자꾸 보채고 있다 The baby on her back is fretting [peevish]. // 이 아이가 보채는 것은 졸리기 때문이다 He is so fretful because he is sleepy. // "엄마, 이것 사 줘!" "보채면 안 돼요." "Mama, buy me this!" "Don't be difficult."

보철(補綴) [치과] dental prosthesis; prosthetic dentistry; prosthetics; prosthodontia. ¶부분 [전체] ～ a partial [full] denture.

보첩(譜牒) a genealogy; a pedigree. ⇨ 족보

보청기(補聽器) a hearing aid; (상표명) an Acousticon. ¶～를 끼면 잘 들립니다 I can hear all right with [If I wear] a hearing aid.

보초(步哨) a sentry; (문어) a sentinel; [군] a guard. ¶～를 서다 stand [keep] sentinel / stand sentry / be on sentry duty // ～를 세우다 post a sentry / picket (soldiers) // ～를 교대시키다 relieve a sentry.

● 보초 근무 sentry duty. 보초병 a guard; a sentry.

보충(補充) [보태어 채우기] replenishment; [추가] supplementation; [보태어 넉넉하게 함] (a) supplement; (교체에 의한) replacement; recruiting (병력의). 보충하다 supplement; replenish; replace; fill up; supply; recruit(병력을). ¶결원을 ~ fill (up) a vacancy/식량을 ~ lay in a supply of food/새 회원을 ~ bring in a new member/탱크에 기름을 ~ replenish a tank with oil// 나는 깨진 컵을 보충했다 I replaced the broken cups with new ones.//그는 부족분을 빚으로 보충했다 He made up the deficit with a loan.//용지를 보충해야겠다 We must have a new supply of forms.//그는 가정교사를 해서 생활비를 보충했다 He supplemented his regular income by working as a tutor.//부족액은 임시비로 보충했다 The deficit was made up with[covered by] money from the contingencies[incidental expenses].

● **보충병** a reservist; a (new) recruit; (집합적) reserve conscripts. **보충 수업** supplementary lessons. ¶영어의 ~을 하다[받다] give[receive] supplementary tuition[lessons] in English.

보칙(補則) [법] [법령 규정 보충을 위한 규칙] supplementary rules.

보컬 a vocal (performance). ¶남성[여성] ~ male[female] vocals.

보컬리스트 [성악가] a vocalist.

보크 [야구] a ba(u)lk. ¶~를 범하다 commit a balk/투수의 ~로 1루 주자는 2루로 진루했다 The first-base runner advanced to second on a balk.

보크사이트 [광] bauxite.

보타이 [나비넥타이] a bow tie.

보태다 1 [더하다] add (A to[and] B). ¶보태어 말하다 exaggerate a story / make one's story tall[high] /3에 4를 보태면 7이다 Three and four make[are] seven. / Four added to three makes[equals] seven. / Three plus four is seven.//약속한 금액에 1만 원을 더 ~ add ten thousand won to the agreed amount / give an extra ten thousand won//그는 규정된 요금에 조금 더 보태어 지불해 주었다 He paid me a little more than the regular amount.

2 [보충하다] make up (for); make good; supply; supplement. ¶모자라는 것을 ~ make[fill] up the deficiency//그는 부업을 하여 수입에 보탰다 He supplemented his income by doing odd jobs.

보탬 [도움] help; aid. ¶~이 되다 go (far) toward / help / do much to help//실용에 아무 ~이 되지 않다 be of no practical use//언젠가 그것이 어떤 ~이 될 것이다 It will be of some use[help] someday.

보통(普通) **1** [예사로움] commonness; normality; the common run. ¶~의 [평소의] ordinary / commonplace / [흔한] common / [평균의] average / [중간치의] medium / [범상의] mediocre(▶ 대수롭지 않다는 뜻을 포함하는 경우가 있다) / decent / ~ 이상의 out of the ordinary / uncommon//~으로 생긴 여자 woman of ordinary appearance//~의 물건 a common article//~ 회원 a regular member //~ 제품의 만년필 a fountain pen of common[ordinary] make//~이 아닌 extraordinary / uncommon / ~ 정도의 생활을 하다 lead an ordinary life//그의 ~으로 하는 방법이다 That's the usual way of doing it.//그는 ~ 배우가 아니다 He is no common [ordinary] actor.//그의 학업 성적은 ~[~ 이상 / ~ 이하]이다 His school record is average[above the average / below the average]./ 그는 ~ 아버지가 아니다 He is not a usual[he is no ordinary] father.//그녀는 ~ 비서와는 다르다 She is not a run-of-the-mill secretary./She is different from the common run of secretaries.//나는 오늘 ~때의 건강 상태가 아니다 Today I am not in a normal state of health. / (구어) I am not feeling up to par today.//그것은 ~ 수단으로는 해결되지 않는다 It cannot be settled by ordinary means.//그 음료를 마셔 보니 ~ 설탕물이었다 I tasted the drink and found it was merely sugared water.//그들은 ~ 사이가 아닌 것 같다 They seem to be more than just friends.

2 [일반적으로] usually; commonly; ordinarily; normally; on the average; as a general [usual] thing. ¶조문할 때는 ~ 그런 말은 하지 않는다 That is not a usual expression of sympathy. / We usually don't use such words[wording] in expressions of sympathy.//장례식에는 ~ 검은 옷을 입는다 Black is generally worn at funerals.//그런 일은 ~으로 일어난다 That sort of thing occurs very commonly.//그런 사고는 ~은 일어나지 않는다 That is no everyday accident.

● **보통내기** [평범한 사람] an ordinary [a common] man; a mediocrity; the common run of man. ¶~가 아니다 be not an ordinary man / be very hard to manage[deal with]. **보통 명사** (名詞) [논] a common noun. **보통 사람** an ordinary[average] person. **보통 선거** a popular election; universal suffrage. **보통 예금** an ordinary deposit; (계좌) an ordinary account. **보통 우편** ordinary mail[post].

보퉁이(褓−) a bundle; a package. ¶옷 한 ~ a bundle of clothes//~를 싸다[꾸리다] make a bundle [package] / bundle (clothes)//~를 풀다 unpack / undo a package[bundle].

보트 a (rowing) boat; a rowboat; a shell (1인승 경기용); (군함에 부속된) a cutter; a gig(선박에 부속된). ¶고무 ~ a rubber raft//~에 타다 take a boat/~를 내리다 launch a boat / lower a boat(배에서)//~ 놀이를 가자 Let's go boating[go for a row].//우리는 호수에서 ~를 저었다 We rowed a boat on the lake.

● **보트 레이스** a boat race; (미) a regatta; (옥스퍼드 대 케임브리지 대학 대항 경기) the Boat Race. **보트피플** [선상 난민] boat people.

보편(普遍) universality; generality; ubiquity(편재).

● **보편성** universality. **보편주의** universalism. **보편타당성** universal validity. **보편화** generalization.

보편적(普遍的) universal; omnipresent; ubiquitous; all-pervasive. ¶~으로 universal(ly) / general(ly)//신은 ~으로 존재한다 God is omnipresent.//그것은 ~으로 인정된 진실이다 That is a universally acknowledged truth.

보폭(步幅) a step; a pace; (길게 잡은) a stride. ¶그녀는 ~이 짧다[길다] She walks with short [long] steps.//그는 ~을 늘려 금방 일행을 따라잡았다 Lengthening his stride, he caught up with the party in no time.

보표(譜表) [음] a staff (pl. staves); a score; a stave.

보푸라기 nap; shag. ⇨ **보풀**

보풀 (옷감 등의) nap; shag; (모직물 등의) fuzz; fluff; (우단·융단 등의) pile. ¶~이 선

보풀다 nappy / fluffy / ~을 일으키다 nap / fluff / raise a nap (on a fabric) // 스웨터에 ~이 일었다 This sweater has started to pile.

보풀다 become fluffy [nappy]; have a slight nap (on a fabric); have fuzz (on the surface of paper).

보풀리다 raise a nap on; fluff.

보풀보풀 with a (rough) nap; with fuzz. 보풀보풀하다 nappy; fluffy; downy; fuzzy.

보필(輔弼) assistance (to the throne). 보필하다 assist; advise; counsel (one's lord); give advice [counsel] (to).

보하다(補-) 1 [원기를 돋우다] strengthen (with); tone up; invigorate. 2 [관직을 맡기다] appoint; assign. ¶도지사에 ~ appoint (a person) (to the post of) governor.

보학(譜學) (the study of) genealogy.

보합(步合) [비율] rate; ratio; [백분율] percentage.

보합(保合) [경] [시세의] steadiness; no change; flat [sideways] movement. ¶~세를 나타내다 《the prices of stocks》 show a steady tone / be firm in tone // 시세가 ~ 상태이다 Prices are [remain] steady [stationary]. // 지방의 수요 때문에 가격은 ~ 시세를 유지하고 있다 Prices are firmly maintained owing to provincial demands. // 환시세는 ~ 상태를 유지하고 있다 There are no fluctuations in the exchange rates.

보행(步行) 1 [걸어감] (a) walk; walking; ambulation. ¶~의 자유를 잃다 be crippled // ~이 어렵다 find it hard to walk / have difficulty in walking // ~ 규칙 위반자를 적발하다 crack down on jaywalkers // 그는 병후 ~이 곤란해졌다 He had difficulty in walking after his illness. // 이 구두는 험한 길의 ~에 견디지 못한다 These shoes are not made for walking over rough roads. 보행하다 walk; go on foot. 2 [심부름] an errand (to a distant place).

●**보행기**(-器) (유아의) a baby-walker. 보행 위반 traffic violation by a pedestrian. 보행자 / 보행인 a walker; a pedestrian; a foot passenger. ¶~가 우선이다 Pedestrians [Walkers] should be given priority over vehicular traffic. / Pedestrians have the right of way.

보험(保險) insurance; (영) assurance (보통 생명 보험). ¶~에 든 insured / (영) assured // 생명 ~ life insurance // 건강 [상해 / 자동차 / 항공 / 양로 / 실업 / 손해 / 사회] ~ health [accident / automobile / aviation / endowment / unemployment / damage / social] insurance // 화재 [해상] ~ fire [marine] insurance // 의료 ~ medical insurance // 간이 ~ postal life insurance // 재 ~ reinsurance // 단체 [종신 / 상호] ~ group [whole life / mutual] insurance // 강제 [임의] ~ obligatory [voluntary] insurance // 피~자 an insured person / a policyholder / (집합적) the insured // ~에 들어 [가입되어] 있다 carry [be covered by] insurance // 도난 ~에 들다 insure one's property against burglary [theft] // ~에 가입하다 take out an insurance / buy insurance // ~ 가입을 권유하다 canvass a person for insurance // 나는 그 ~을 해약했다 I canceled the insurance policy. // 이 집은 보험 회사에 5천만 원의 ~에 계약되어 있다 This house is insured for fifty million won with an insurance company.

●**보험금** insurance money; the insurance; [급부금] benefits. ¶사망 ~ a death benefit // 가옥의 화재로 많은 ~을 받다 receive a large insurance for a house burnt // ~을 노리고 자기 집에 방화했다 He set fire to his own house in order to collect the insurance. 보험료 a premium; an insurance bill. 보험 약관 insurance clauses [terms]. 보험업 insurance business; underwriting. 보험 증권 an insurance policy. 보험 회사 an insurance company.

보헤미안 [방랑적이고 자유분방한 생활을 하는 사람] a Bohemian.

보혈(寶血) [기] the precious blood (of Jesus).

보혈제(補血劑) [약] a h(a)emati(ni)c; an antian(a)emic (agent).

보혈하다(補血-) nourish the blood.

보호(保護) [지키기] protection; (경찰에 의한) protective custody; shelter; safeguard; harborage; guardianship; [돌봄] care; [보존·유지] preservation; conservation (▶ 국가 등에 의한 자연보호에 쓰이는 일이 많음). ¶야생 동식물의 ~ preservation of wildlife // 삼림 ~ conservation of forests // 문화재 ~ (the) preservation of cultural assets // …의 아래 under the protection [care / guardianship] of … // 이것은 법률의 ~를 받고 있다 This is under the protection of the law. / This is legally protected. // 정치범이 미국 대사관에 ~를 요청했다 A political offender applied to the U.S. Embassy for protection [sought asylum in the American Embassy]. **보호하다** protect; [주로 교회가 비호하다] give sanctuary (to); [돌보다] take care of; [보존·유지하다] preserve; conserve. ¶생명과 재산을 보호하기 위하여 for the protection of lives and property // 보호해 주다 provide protection for (a person) / provide shelter // 국내 산업을 ~ protect home industries // 경찰은 피의자의 신병을 보호했다 The police took the suspect into protective custody. / The police took the suspect into custody to protect him. // 그 교회는 전쟁 고아들을 보호해 주었다 The church gave sanctuary to war orphans. → ¶이 절은 폭풍우로부터 보호되어야 한다 This temple needs protection against the weather.

●**보호 관세** a protective tariff. 보호 관찰 [법] probation. ¶~ 중인 사람 a person who is on probation // 그 비행 소년들은 ~에 처해졌다 The juvenile delinquents were put on probation. 보호망 protective netting. 보호 무역 protective trade. 보호 무역주의 protectionism. 보호색 apatetic coloration; protective coloring [coloration]; a protective color. 보호자 a protector; a guardian; a patron; a patroness(여자); a conservator(금치산자의). 보호 정책 a protective policy.

보화(寶貨) a treasure. ⇨ 보물(寶物)

복 [동] a swellfish; a globefish; a blowfish; a puffer; a balloonfish. ¶~의 독 swellfish poison / tetrodotoxin(복의 독성분).

복 치듯 하다 strike [beat] (something) roughly [at random].

복(伏) dog days. ⇨ 복날 ¶말~ the end [last] of the dog days / the last period of the dog days // ~중 the middle (period) of the dog days // ~초 the beginning of the dog days / the first period of the dog days.

복(福) fortune; good luck; blessing; bliss;

happiness. ¶~의 신(神) the god of wealth // ~을 받은 blessed / felicitous / happy // ~이 있다 be fortunate / be in luck // ~이 없다 be out of luck / be unfortunate // ~을 주다[받다] bless[be blessed] (with a good thing) // ~을 빌다 invoke a blessing (upon a person) // ~을 가져다주다 bring (a person) good luck // 마음이 가난한 자는 ~이 있나니 [성] Blessed are the poor in spirit. // 새해　많이 받으십시오 Happy New Year!

복-(複) double; compound; composite; multiple; bi-.

-복(服) a suit; a garment; clothes; clothing. ¶ 신사~ men's clothing.

복각(伏角) [물] a dip (of the compass); a magnetic dip; an inclination.

복간(復刊) republication; reissue; revived publication. ¶~ 잡지 제1호 the first number of a revived magazine. **복간하다** reissue; revive the publication (of). ➔¶그 책은 복간되었다 That book was reissued [published again].

복강(腹腔) the abdominal cavity.
● **복강 임신** abdominal pregnancy.

복고(復古) [옛것대로 돌아감] (a) restoration; revival (of the ancient regime); [손실의 회복] recovery. ¶왕정~ the restoration of the Royal Regime / the Restoration (영). **복고하다** restore; recover.
● **복고조**(-調) the trend to return to old days; the nostalgia[revival] boom[trend]; a revival mood; [복고적인 경향] a reactionary tendency. **복고주의** reactionism.

복교(復校) returning to school. ⇨복학

복구(復舊) rehabilitation; recovery; restoration; restitution. ¶중앙선의 ~ 작업을 서두르다 hasten to restore service on the Jungang [Seoul-Gyeongju] Line // 도로의 ~는 시간이 걸릴 것이다 It will be a long time before the road is reopened. **복구하다** return to the former condition; be restored (to the original state); be rehabilitated; restore. ➔¶파손된 건물을 훌륭히 복구되었다 The damaged building was beautifully restored. // 호남선은 10시간 이내에 복구될 전망이다 The Honam [Daejeon-Mokpo] Line will resume normal service in ten hours.
● **복구공사** restoration[repair] work. ¶~ 중이다 be under repair // ~에 착수하다 get[set] to repair work.

복굴절(複屈折) [물] double refraction; birefringence.

복권(復權) restoration of (civil) rights; reinstatement; rehabilitation. **복권하다** be rehabilitated; be reinstated. ¶한번 지위에서 쫓겨나면 복권하기는 어렵다 Once you are ousted from your position, it is difficult to be reinstated[to regain your rights].

복권(福券) a lottery ticket. ¶~의 당첨 번호 a lucky number // ~ 판매인 a seller of lottery tickets // ~이 당첨되다 win (a prize) in a lottery // ~을 사다 buy a lottery ticket // ~ 추첨에서 공치다 win nothing in a lottery // ~이 판매되고 있다 They are running a lottery. / Lottery tickets have gone on sale. // 그는 ~ 추첨에서 1억 원[1등]에 당첨되었다 He won one hundred million won[first prize] in a public lottery.

복귀(復歸) a return; a comeback; reinstatement. **복귀하다** return (to); come back (to politics); be restored (to); [법] rebert (to). ¶ 그전 직위로 ~ be reinstated in one's former position // 영화계로 ~ find one's way back into the screen // 원대 ~ rejoin one's regiment // 사회로 ~ (make) a comeback to normal life // 무대로 ~ return to the stage // 천하 장사 자리로 ~ regain the rank of *Cheonhajangsa* // 그녀는 무대에서 일단 은퇴했다가 2년 후에 복귀했다 She retired from the stage once, but made a comeback two years later.

복근(腹筋) an abdominal muscle. ¶~ 운동 exercise to strengthen the abdominal muscle.

복날(伏-) dog days.(▶ 우리말 「복날」은 여름 중 가장 더운 「초복·중복·말복」의 사흘을 가리키나 영어 "dog days"는 7월 3일부터 8월 11일까지의 연중 가장 더운 날들을 가리키므로, 엄밀히 말해 같은 개념은 아님)

복날 개 패듯(속담) hit[clog / beat] (a person) as if he were a beast.

복대(腹帶) (임부의) an abdominal bandage; abdominal binder; a maternity band[belt / binding] (worn for support[protection] after pregnancy); [배를 싸 덮도록 만든 띠] a health[stomach] band.

복대기(광) residue left after gold is panned; slag; the dross of gold.

복대기(를) 삭히다 extract gold from slag.

복대기다 1 [떠들어 대다] make a great fuss (about); be noisy[in a bustle]; bustle. ¶복대기는 교실 a noisy classroom. 2 [정신 못 차리다] be tossed about; be jostled around. ¶나는 두 시간이나 사람들 속에서 복대기었다 I was jostled in the crowd for two hours.

복더위(伏-) the midsummer heat. ⇨삼복더위(⇨삼복)

복덕방(福德房) a house[real estate] agent; (미) a realtor; a house-finding agency.

복도(複道) a passage (way); a corridor; a gallery; (미) a hallway; a lobby(극장 등의).

복되다(福-) [복을 받아 즐겁고 기쁘다] blessed; happy.

복류(伏流) an underground[a subterranean] stream[river].

복리(福利) welfare; well-being. ⇨=복지(福祉)

복리(複利) compound interest. ¶~로 계산하다 calculate[reckon] at compound interest.

복마(卜馬) [짐을 싣는 말] a pack[draft / cart] horse.

복마전(伏魔殿) 1 [마귀가 숨어 있는 집이나 굴] an abode of all the demons; a pandemonium. 2 [비밀리에 나쁜 일을 꾸미는 사람들이 모이는 곳]. ¶저 파벌은 정계의 ~이다 That faction is a hotbed of political intrigue.

복막(腹膜) [생] the peritoneum (*pl*. -nea).
● **복막염** peritonitis.

복면(覆面) a mask; a veil; (문어) a vizard. ¶ ~의 masked / vizarded // ~을 벗다 unmask oneself. **복면하다** veil oneself; muffle (up) [cover] one's face; have one's face masked. ¶강도는 복면하고 있었다 The burglar wore a mask[was masked].
● **복면강도** a masked burglar[robber].

복명(復命) a report. **복명하다** report to (a person on one's work); report one's mission (to); report to (one's superior) on the mission one has carried out.

복모음(複母音) [언] a diphthong.

복무(服務) (public) service. ¶육군[해군]에 ~

중이다 be in the army[navy] // 현역에 ~ 중이다 be on active service // 그는 ~ 중이다 He is on duty. **복무하다** serve; [복무 중이다] be in (public) service. ¶보병[수병]으로 ~ enter military service as a soldier[sailor] / serve in the army[navy] // 군대에 오래 ~ see much (military) service // 그는 경찰관으로 20년간 복무했다 He served as a policeman for twenty years.
●**복무연한** the term of (public) service; the tenure of office.

복문(複文) [언] a complex sentence.

복받치다 [솟아나오다] well up; gush out [forth]; [감정이 치밀어 오르다] be filled [seized] (with); have a fit (of); (사물이) fill one's heart. ¶복받쳐 오는 슬픔 the sorrow welling up within one // (감동하여) 뜨거운 것이 가슴에 ~ feel a lump rise in one's[the] throat // 나는 분노가 복받쳐 올랐다 Indignation surged up within me. // 그녀는 눈물이 복받쳤다 Tears came into her eyes.

복벽(腹壁) [생] the abdominal wall.

복병(伏兵) an ambush; an ambuscade; troops in ambush. ¶~을 만나다 fall into an ambush / ~을 배치하다 lay[make / plant] an ambush / ambuscade // 적은 ~을 배치해 놓고 있었다 The enemy lay[was waiting] in ambush.

복복 with a scraping sound. ⇨북북

복복선(複複線) [철도] a four-track line; a quadruple track.

복본위제(複本位制) the double[bimetallic] standard; bimetallism. ¶금은 ~ gold and silver bimetallism.

복부(腹部) [의] the abdomen; the belly; the abdominal region. ¶~의 abdominal // 그는 자주 ~의 압박감을 호소하고 있다 He often complains of an oppressive sensation about his abdomen.

복부인(福夫人) a wealthy housewife (chasing after the speculative benefit); women speculators swarming to a place of bidding.

복부호(複符號) [수] a double sign.

복비(複比) [수] a compound ratio.

복비례(複比例) compound proportion; the double rule of three.

복사(伏射) prone shooting[firing]. **복사하다** fire while lying prone; fire from a prone position.

복사(複寫) [원본을 베끼는 것] copying; duplication; [복제] reproduction. **복사하다** copy; [복제·모조하다] reproduce; duplicate; manifold; take[produce] a copy of; make a duplicate[copy] of; transfer (a picture); facsimile; reprint. ¶원고를 ~ copy[manifold] a manuscript // 사진을 ~ reproduce [take copies of] a photograph // 편지를 ~ copy [make a copy of] a letter // 원물대로 ~ reproduce in facsimile.
●**복사기** a duplicating[reproduction] machine; a duplicator. ¶편지를 ~로 복사하다 run a letter through a photocopying machine. **복사물** a copy; a reproduction; a duplicate; a facsimile. **복사지** copying paper; carbon paper.

복사(輻射) [물] radiation. ¶~의 radial / radiant. **복사하다** radiate; be radiative.
●**복사광[파]** radiant light[wave]. **복사선** a radiant ray. **복사열** a radiant heat; radiation. ¶태양[지구] ~ solar[terrestrial] radiation.

복사뼈 the ankle (bone); [생] the malleolus (*pl.* -li); [생] the talus (*pl.* -es, tali); the astragalus (*pl.* -il).

복상(服喪) wearing mourning. **복상하다** wear mourning; go into mourning.

복색(服色) [빛깔·차림새] the colour and style of a uniform[an official dress].

복서 [권투 선수] a boxer.

복선(伏線) preparation; foreshadowing; a foreshadow. ¶~을 깔다 (소설 등에서) give [provide] a hint which is to be developed later / foreshadow / [미리 준비하다] make contingency plans.

복선(複線) 1 a double track. ⇨'복선 궤도(⇨복선). ¶~이 double-tracked // 이 철도는 ~이 되어 있지 않다 This railway is not double-tracked[has only a single track]. 2 [겹줄] double lines.
●**복선 궤도** a double track; a two-track line.

복성(複姓) a two-character[compound] surname.

복성(複星) [천] a multiple star.

복성스럽다(福星-) happy-looking; fat and well-looking. ¶복성스런 얼굴 a fat and well-looking face / a full face // 그녀의 얼굴은 ~ She has a cherubic face.

복소수(複素數) a complex number.

복속(服屬) subjection; subjugation. **복속하다** be subject(ed) (to); be subjugated.

복수(復讐) revenge; [격렬한 복수] vengeance; vendetta; [보복] retaliation; requital. ¶…에 대한 ~로 in revenge for[of] … / in revenge against (one's father) // ~를 꾀하다 seek vengeance (upon) // ~를 맹세하다 swear revenge (on / against). **복수하다** revenge oneself (on a person for something); take revenge (on a person for a murder); avenge (a person's death on someone); avenge (a (dead) person). (▶ revenge는 개인의 감정에 의한 것이고 avenge는 부정 등에 대한 당연한 갚음으로써 벌을 줄 때 쓰이는 일이 많음) ¶이 일에 대해 네게 꼭 복수하겠다 You shall pay for this. // 언젠가는 복수하겠다 I will avenge myself[get even] someday.
●**복수극** a revenge tragedy. **복수심** revengeful thought. ¶~이 있는 revengeful / vindictive / ~에 불타다 burn with revengeful thoughts[the desire for revenge]. **복수전** an avenging battle; a vengeful war; a war of vengeance; a battle of revenge; (경기의) a return match.

복수(腹水) [의] (증상) abdominal dropsy; ascites; hydroperitoneum.

복수(複數) [언] the plural (number). ¶~의 plural // ~ 하다 pluralize // "man"의 ~는 무엇인가 What is the plural (form) of "man"?
●**복수 명사** a plural noun. **복수형** the plural (form).

복수초(福壽草) [식] a pheasant's eye; an Amur Adonis.

복술(卜術) the art of divination; the mantic art.

복숭아 [열매] a peach.
●**복숭아꽃** a peach blossom. **복숭아나무** a peach (tree). **복숭아빛** peach (color).

복스럽다(福-) happy-looking; fat and well-looking (face). ¶그녀는 살이 쪄서 복스러워 보이는 노파였다 She was a plump and happy-looking old woman.

복슬복슬하다 plump and shaggy.
복습(複習) [a] review; [영] [a] revision. **복습하다** review; go over[through] (one's lesson); [영] revise. ¶영어를 ~ review one's English lessons / brush up one's English.
복승식(複勝式) [경마] ¶~으로 걸다 bet (one's money) on a horse to place.
● **복승식 마권** a place ticket.
복시(複視) [의] diplopia; diplopy; double vision. ¶~의 diplopic.
복식(服飾) 1 [옷의 꾸밈새] the style of a dress. 2 [옷과 장신구] dress and its ornaments. ¶여성용 ~ ladies' trimmings.
복식(複式) 1 [둘 이상으로 겹치는 방식] multiple forms[formulae]. 2 bookkeeping by double entry. ⇨복식 부기(⇨복식) 3 ⇨복승식 4 a double match. ⇨복식 경기
● **복식 경기** a double match. **복식 부기** bookkeeping by double entry; the double entry system; double-entry bookkeeping.
복식 호흡(腹式呼吸) abdominal breathing [respiration]; the abdominal type of respiration. ¶~을 하다 breath from the abdomen.
복신(福神) the God of Wealth; Billiken; a luck-bringer.
복싱 boxing. ¶새도~ shadowboxing // 프로 ~ professional boxing.
복안(腹案) [마음속으로 품고 있는 계획] a plan[scheme] (in one's mind); an idea. ¶~을 세우다 map out[draw up / formulate] a plan // 무슨 ~이 있습니까 Have you a plan ready?
복안(複眼) [동] compound eyes. ⇨겹눈
복약(服藥) taking medicine. ⇨복용1
복어(-魚) a globefish; a swellfish; a puffer. ¶~에 중독되다 be poisoned by swellfish.
복역(服役) 1 [징역] (penal) servitude. **복역하다** serve time[a sentence]; serve a prison [jail] term. ¶그는 교도소에서 5년간 복역했다 He served a five-year sentence[five years] in prison. 2 [병역] military service. **복역하다** serve (one's time[term]) in the army[navy].
● **복역 기간** (징역의) the term of a sentence. **복역수** a convict.
복엽(複葉) [겹잎] a compound leaf.
● **복엽기 / 복엽 비행기** a biplane.
복용(服用) 1 [약을 먹음] taking medicine; internal use[application]. **복용하다** take (medicine); use[apply] internally. ¶주의: 1회 2정 이상 복용하지 말 것 Warning: Do not take more than two tablets at a time. ➔복용시키다 give (medicine) // 키니네를 복용시키다 dose (a boy) with quinine. 2 [옷을 입음] wearing (clothes).
● **복용량** dosage; dose.
복원(復元·復原) [원래대로 회복함] restoration; restitution; rehabilitation; [재건] reconstruction. ¶옛 성의 ~ the restoration [reconstruction] of an old castle. **복원하다** restore; reconstruct.
● **복원력** restitutive force; [배의] stability; strength of stability; force[power] of restitution; restoring force.
복위(復位) restoration; reinstatement; rehabilitation; reinstallment. **복위하다** be restored [rehabilitated / reinstated / reinstalled]. ¶왕이 복위했다 The king was restored to the throne.
복음(福音) 1 [희소식] glad tidings; [반가운 소식] good[welcome] news. 2 [그리스도의 가르침] the gospel. ¶선교사들은 마을 사람들에게 ~을 전파했다 The missionaries preached the gospel to the villagers.
● **복음서** the (four) Gospels; Gospels. **복음전도** evangelism; evangelization; mission; evangelical preaching(설교); evangelical work(전도 사업).
복음(複音) [언] [복합된 음] a compound sound; (하모니카의) a compound note (on a harmonica).
복자(卜者) a diviner. ⇨점쟁이
복자(福者) [복이 많은 사람] a fortunate [blissful] man; [가] Blessed ...; (집합적) the Blessed.
복자(覆字) (해당하는 활자가 없는 경우) a turn (in set type); an upside-down (letter). ¶검열에 걸린 글자는 ~로 했다 The censored words were represented by a series of x's.
복작거리다 bustle; boil (over). ⇨북적거리다
복작복작 in a bustle. ⇨북적북적
복잡하다(複雜−) complicated; complex; intricate. ¶복잡한 기구 complex[complicated / intricate] machinery // 복잡한 문제 a complicated question / a knotty problem(엉클어진 문제) // 복잡한 사건 a complicated[an intricated / an involved] case / 인생의 갖가지 복잡한 일 the complexities of life // 복잡해지다 get confused / get mixed up / (사건 등이) get complicated // 나는 머리가 좀 ~ I am getting a little confused. / 이야기가 복잡하여 잘 이해할 수 없다 The conversation is too mixed up[involved] for me to understand. // 사태가 점점 더 복잡해졌다 The situation[matter] has become more and more complicated. // 문제는 점점 더 복잡해졌다 The matter is getting more and more complicated. // 그의 설명은 문제를 더욱 복잡하게 만들 것이다 His explanations will complicate the issue all the more. // 사장이 그만둔 후 회사는 복잡해졌다 The firm was thrown into confusion after the president resigned. // 나는 복잡한 사정이 있어 그 제의를 거절하지 않을 수 없었다 I had to decline the offer on account of complicated circumstances. // 그것은 복잡하게 만들어져 있다 It is elaborately contrived. // 복잡한 사정이 있어서 그렇게 된 거야 It is as it is because of intricate circumstances behind it. // 그들의 관계는 대단히 ~ Their relationship is very complex. // 그것을 들으니 기분이 복잡해진다 Hearing it arouses mixed feelings in me.
복장(腹臟) [가슴의 한복판] the center of the chest.
복장(이) 타다 be nervous (about); be anxious[worried] (about / for); be in suspense; be on tenterhooks; be in a stew; be impatient. ¶병이 낫질 않아서 그는 복장이 타고 있다 He is fretting because he does not get better.
복장(服裝) dress; clothes; (집합적) clothing; (풍속으로서의) costume. ¶고려 시대의 ~ the dress of the Goryeo Dynasty period // 서구풍의 ~ western-style clothes / the western way of dressing // 경찰관의 ~ a policeman's uniform // ~을 단정히 하다 tidy oneself up // 그녀는 ~이 훌륭하다[초라하다] She is well [poorly] dressed. // 외출할 만한 ~을 하고 있지 않습니다 I am not dressed to go out. // 어머니는 ~에 별로 신경 쓰지 않는다 My

복적하다

mother does not pay much attention to her clothes. ¶~은 임의 Dress optional(▶ 초대장의 후기).
●**복장 검사** a dress inspection; (군인의) a kit inspection.

복적하다(復籍-) return to one's original domicile[own family].

복제(服制) **1** [복장에 대한 규정] dress regulation. ¶~를 정하다 adopt a definite[special] uniform. **2** (상복의) the traditional system of mourning attire.

복제(複製) (facsimile) reproduction; duplication; reprinting; [복제물] a reproduction; a replica(▶ 종종 원작자의 손에 의함); a facsimile(▶ 크기가 다를 경우도 있음); [똑같은 것] a duplicate. ¶명화의 ~ a reproduction of a famous painting. **복제하다** reproduce (a picture); reprint. ¶원본 그대로 ~ reproduce with complete fidelity // 아주 귀중한 원본에서 복제한 삽화 illustrations reproduced from priceless originals.
●**복제 불허** All rights reserved. **복제 인간** a human clone. **복제품** a reproduction; a duplicate; a replica.

복족강(腹足綱) Gastropoda.

복종(服從) obedience; submission; subordination; [묵종] acquiescence. ¶절대~ absolute obedience / complete submission // 맹목적 ~ blind obedience // ~을 강요하다 inculcate obedience (upon a person) // 부모에게는 절대~입니다 We obey our parents absolutely. // 국법에는 ~이 요구된다 We are subject to the law of our country. **복종하다** [명령에 따르다] obey; be obedient (to); [항복하다] submit oneself (to); [묵종하다] acquiesce (in); [굴복하다] yield (to). ¶부모의 명령에 ~ obey one's parents' orders // 하느님의 권위에 ~ submit to divine authority // 그녀는 언제나 시어머니에게 복종했다 She always yielded[submitted] to her mother-in-law. ➔¶복종시키다 subordinate / subdue / subjugate / get hold of / have[hold] under one's girdle / hold (a person) in subjection // 위협하여 복종시키다 scare (a person) into submission.
●**복종심** obedience; a submissive spirit.

복죄(服罪·伏罪) acceptance of one's sentence. **복죄하다** accept a sentence; submit to a sentence; plead guilty (to a crime).

복중(伏中) (the period of) the dog days; midsummer; the hot season.

복지(服地) suiting; cloth; stuff.

복지(福祉) welfare; well-being. ¶국민 ~ 연금 (제도) the national welfare pension (system) // 국민의 ~를 증진하다 promote a nation's welfare.
●**복지 국가** a welfare state. **복지 사업** welfare (work). ¶아동 ~ child welfare (work). **복지 사회** a welfare society. **복지 시설** welfare facilities. **복지 후생** a welfare program.

복직(復職) [원래의 지위에 다시 오름] reinstatement; reinstal(l)ation; resumption of office; [재임명] reappointment; rehabilitation. ¶학생들은 신 선생의 ~을 요구했다 The students demanded the reappointment of Mr. Sin. **복직하다** resume office; be reinstated[reinstal(l)ed] (in one's post[former office]); be restored[come back] to one's former position; be reappointed[rehabilitat-ed]. ➔¶병이 회복되면 그를 복직시킬 작정이다 I will reinstate him in[restore him to] his former position on his recovery.

복창(復唱) repetition. **복창하다** repeat (an order).

복채(卜債) the fee for having one's fortune told.

복통(腹痛) a stomachache; a bellyache; an abdominal pain; a pain in the stomach [guts]; [의] gastralgia; colic(급성의); (미국 구어) cramps(경련 특히 월경 시의); gripes(간헐적인); tormina(심한); (미국 속어) mulligrubs. ¶~으로 고생하다 suffer from [have] a stomachache / have (the) gripes(격통) / be badly griped // ~을 호소하다 complain of a stomachache // ~이 가라앉다 be cured of stomachache.

복판 1 [한가운데] the (very) middle; the center; the heart. ¶~의 middle / central // ~에 right[just] in the middle[center] (of) / midmost (of) // 방 ~에 in the middle [center] of the room // 상가 ~에 in the heart of the business district // 과녁의 ~에 맞다 hit the target right[fairly] in the center // 길의 ~을 걷지 마라 Don't walk in the middle of the road. **2** (고기의) middle part of her(s) [shank / beef from around the knee bone].

복학(復學) returning to school. ¶~을 허가하다 allow (a boy) to return to school / readmit (a boy) into school // ~을 허락받다 be readmitted into school // 그는 ~이 허용되었다 He was allowed to return to school. // 이 대학에서는 휴학 후 5년이 지나면 ~이 허용되지 않는다 At this university students are not allowed to reenroll[to return] after five years' absence. **복학하다** be reinstated (at school); return to school.

복합(複合) composition; compositeness; [의] complex. ¶~의 composite / compound(▶ compound는 합성해서 일체가 된 것을, composite은 각 요소가 독자성을 잃을 때까지 긴밀히 결합한 것을 나타냄) / mixed / complex / multiplex / manifold. **복합하다** compound; pound together; unite; be united; mix; be mixed.
●**복합 명사** a compound noun. **복합 비료** composite[compound / complex] fertilizer. **복합어** a compound (word). **복합 영농** [농] combined agriculture. **복합체** a complex (body).

복화술(腹話術) ventriloquism. ¶~을 쓰다 [~로 말하다] use ventriloquism / ventriloquize.

볶다 1 (커피콩·땅콩 등을) roast; (콩·곡식 등을) parch; scorch; singe; pan-broil. ¶볶은 콩 parched[roasted] beans[peas] // 땅콩을 ~ roast peanuts // 깨를 ~ toast sesame seeds // 기름에 ~ fry in oil // 우리는 양파를 볶았다 We fried the onions. **2** [성가시게 굴다] tease; pester; annoy; plague; harass; torment. ¶과자를 사 달라고 어머니를 ~ tease[pester] one's mother for candy // (남에게) 무엇을 달라고 볶아 대다 pester (a person) for something // 그는 돈을 더 달라고 어머니를 볶아 댔다 He importunately asked his mother for more money.

볶은 콩에 꽃이 피랴(속담) Don't cry over spilt milk.

볶아치다 hasten; hurry; press[urge / goad] on; spur (to do / to / into); rush; precipitate. ¶일을 제시간에 끝내려고 ~ rush around frantically trying to finish one's work on time∥일은 볶아친다고 되지는 않는다 It's no good rushing things.

볶음 pan-broiled[roasted] food; a roast; a broil. ¶닭~ chopped roast chicken∥떡~ broiled rice cake.
- **볶음밥** bokkeumbap; fried rice.

볶이다 1 [불에] be roasted. 2 [성가심을 당하다] be pestered[annoyed]. ¶빚쟁이에게 ~ be harassed by creditors.

본¹(本) 1 a lesson; an example. ⇨ 본보기 ¶~을 보이다 set an example (for the children). 2 (옷의) a pattern. ¶드레스의 ~을 뜨다 cut out a pattern for a dress. 3 a place of origin. ⇨ =본관(本貫) ¶~이 어디십니까 Where did your family originate? 4 capital; fund. ⇨ 본전²

본²(本) [이] this (year); [우리] our; [당면한] the present. ¶~ 협약 the present agreement.

본-(本) 1 [중심의] main; chief; principal; head. ¶~점 a head office∥~무대 a main srage. 2 [진짜의] real; [정식의] regular. ¶~명 a person's real name∥~회의 a regular [full] session.

본가(本家) one's principal residence. ⇨ =본집

본값(本-) the (prime[original]) cost; the cost price. ¶~에 팔다 sell (something) at cost (price) / sell at prime cost.

본거지(本據地) a base (of operations). ⇨ =근거지(⇨)근거) ¶…을 ~로 하여 with ... as the base of operations∥…의 ~를 꾸미다 establish one's base of operations[headquarters] at (a place) / make (a place) the base of operations.

본건(本件) this case[affair / matter]; the matter in question[at issue]; the matter under consideration; the case (lying) before us. ¶~에 관하여 in this connection / as to this matter / concerning this connection / as to this matter / in regard to this matter.

본격(本格) fundamental rules; a regular style. ¶~화하다 become serious / get into (its) stride.

본격적(本格的) [진짜의] genuine; real; [정통적인] orthodox; [표준적인] standard; [충분한 자격이 있는] full-fledged; [전면적인] full-scale. ¶~인 여름[겨울] a real summer [winter]∥~인 경기 a game played in real earnest[(구어) for keeps]∥~으로 일에 착수하다 set to work in earnest∥탐험의 준비가 마침내 ~으로 시작되었다 Preparations for the expedition have now begun in earnest.

본견(本絹) pure silk. ¶~의 스카프 a scarf of pure silk.

본고장(本-) a home; a habitat. ⇨ 본바닥

본과(本科) a regular course.

본관(本官) 1 (임시 관직에 대해) a permanent office; (겸직에 대해) the principal official post. 2 (관리의 자칭) the present official; I.

본관(本貫) a place of origin; one's ancestral home; family origin.

본관(本管) a main[principal] (pipe); a (supply) main.

본관(本館) (별관·분관에 대하여) the main building.

본교(本校) (분교에 대하여) the principal [main] school.

본국(本局) (분국·지국에 대하여) the head [main] office; [중앙 전화국] (미) the central (office); (영) the exchange; [중심이 되는 방송국] a key station. ¶~ 500번 Central 500.

본국(本國) [자기의 국적이 있는 나라] one's own country; one's home[native] country; [모국] one's mother country; [조국] one's fatherland; [고향] one's fatherland; one's home. ¶~으로 돌아가다 go[return] home∥밀입국자들은 ~으로 강제 송환되었다 The smugglers were forcibly returned to their own country.
- **본국 송환** repatriation.

본남편(本男便) [본디의 남편] one's (real) husband; one's legal[lawful] husband(법적인); [전남편] one's ex-husband.

본능(本能) (an) instinct. ¶~에 의하여 by instinct∥~에 따라 행동하다 act on instinct ∥~에 따르다 follow one's primitive instincts ∥자기 보존의 ~을 가지다 have[possess] the instinct of self-preservation∥~을 만족시키다 satisfy one's instinct∥동물은 ~으로 위험을 알아차린다 Animals sense danger by instinct.

본능적(本能的) instinctive; instinctual. ¶~으로 instinctively / instinctually∥~으로 좋아 [싫어]하다 have an instinctive taste for [horror of] (a thing)∥그는 거의 ~으로 엎드렸다 He threw himself down almost instinctively.

본당(本堂) [불] the main[inner] temple; the main building[hall / sanctuary] (of a temple); [가] a parish church.

본대(本隊) [본부가 있는 부대] the main body of troops; the main force; [자기가 소속는 부대] the main body to which one belongs; one's regular outfit.

본댁(本宅) 1 one's principal residence. ⇨ 본집 2 one's lawful[legal] wife. ⇨ 본댁네(⇨본댁)
- **본댁네** one's lawful[legal] wife.

본데없다 ill-mannered[-bred]; inexperienced; (have) no manners.

본드 [접착제] bond (glue) (상표명).

본디(本-) [본래·원래] originally; primarily; [처음부터] from the outset[beginning / first]; [나면서부터] by nature; naturally; [본질적으로] essentially; intrinsically. ¶~의 original / primary∥~부터의 타고난 장사꾼 a born merchant∥그는 ~ 서울 토박이다 He was born and raised in Seoul.∥그는 ~ 사람이 좋다 He is a good man through and through.∥그는 ~ 악인은 아니다 He is not really a bad man.∥그것은 ~ 중국에서 건너온 것이다 Originally it was introduced from China.∥이 철도는 ~ 철광석을 운반하기 위해 부설되었다 This railroad was originally built for the transportation of iron ore.∥이 학교는 ~ 여성을 위한 고등 교육 기관이다 This school has been an institution for the higher education of women from its very beginning. ∥그는 ~ 게으름뱅이다 Really, the problem is that he is lazy by nature.∥그것은 ~ 한국인이 발명한 것이다 It was originally invented by a Korean.∥그는 ~ 그들을 도와줄 생각은 없었다 From the outset[beginning] he had no intention of helping them.∥그것은 제가 ~부터 알고 있었습니다 I have known that from the beginning[first].∥그는 ~부터 바보는 아니다 He is not a complete fool.∥나는 ~ 잊어 먹기를 잘한다 I have always been forgetful. / I was forgetful

본때 to begin with.∥그는 ~ 호기심이 강하다 He is by nature curious.

본때(本-) 〔본보기〕 a model; a pattern; an example; things that can be modeled [patterned] after.

본때를 보이다 teach (a person) a lesson; make an example [a lesson] (of). ¶저 녀석은 건방지니까 본때를 좀 보여 주자 Let's teach that smart aleck a lesson.∥두고 봐, 본때를 보여 줄 테니 Look here, buddy [(¶) mate], I'm gonna [I'll] show you a thing or two.

본때(가) 있다 〔본받을 만하다〕 exemplary; typical; 〔멋있다〕 stylish; smart; splendid; excellent. ¶본때 있는 행동 (an) exemplary conduct∥본때 있게 잘하다 do a splendid job of it∥본때 있게 해치우다 come off with flying colors.

본뜨다(本-) 〔원형·모형을 만들다〕 cut out a pattern (for one's socks); model [pattern] (on / after); 〔모방하다〕 imitate; copy (from); 〔본보기로 삼다〕 follow the example [model] of (a person); take example [pattern] by (a person). ¶…을 본떠 after / after the model [example] of ... ∥…을 ~ follow a person's example∥그것은 새를 본뜬 것이다 It is (made) in the shape of a bird.∥이 정원은 오산에 있는 어느 절의 정원을 본떠서 만든 것이다 This garden is modeled on that of a temple in Osan.∥나는 이 집을 송 씨 집을 본떠서 지었다 I modeled this house on Mr. Song's.∥너는 그의 나쁜 점이 아니고 좋은 점을 본떠야 한다 You should copy his good points, not his weak points.

본뜻(本-) **1** 〔의도·목적〕 one's original purpose; one's (real) intention [will / motive]. ¶그 제의를 거절했지만 내 ~은 아니었다 I declined the offer, with some reluctance. **2** 〔본래의 의미〕 the original [primary] meaning; the original import; the true [basic / literal] meaning [sense / conception]. ¶그 말의 ~을 모르겠다 I can't make out the original meaning of the word.

본래(本來) originally; primarily. ⇨본디

본령(本領) 〔특색〕 a special character; a feature; a characteristic; one's specialty; 〔본분〕 the proper province [function]; one's duty; one's business. ¶문학의 ~ the proper function of literature∥경찰관의 ~은 공공질서를 유지하는 일이다 The proper function of the police is to maintain public order.

본론(本論) the main discourse [issue / subject]. ¶~에서 벗어나다 digress from one's [the] main subject / get off the subject (of one's talk)∥이야기를 ~으로 돌리면… Getting back to our main subject ... ∥~으로 돌아가서 to return to our subject∥~으로 들어가자 Let's get to the point.∥그러면 ~으로 들어가겠습니다 Now let us proceed to the main subject [issue].∥~으로 들어가기 전에 두세 가지 분명히 해 둘 일이 있습니다 Before taking up the main subject [issue], we have to clarify a few things.

본루(本壘) a home base. ⇨홈 베이스
● **본루타** 〔야구〕 a home run. ⇨홈런

본류(本流) the main course (of a river); the mainstream.

본마음(本-) one's right mind; one's senses.

본말(本末) 〔처음과 끝〕 the beginning and the end; 〔경중〕 the important and the trivial. ¶~을 전도하다 confuse the order of things / fail to put first things first / put the cart before the horse∥제도의 결함을 무시하고 개인의 실수를 비난하는 것은 ~을 전도하는 것이다 It is getting things backwards to blame individuals, disregarding the defects of the system itself.

본명(本名) **1** one's real name; 〔필명·예명에 대하여〕 one's autonym. ¶~으로 under one's real name∥~으로 쓴 저서 an autonym∥~을 대다 give one's real name. **2** a baptismal [Christian] name. ⇨세례명(⇨세례)

본무대(本舞臺) ¶정치의 ~에 뛰어들다 make a sudden debut into the world of politics / make a sudden entrance onto the political stage.

본문(本文) 〔주문(主文)〕 the text (of a book / of a contract); the body (of a letter); (삽화에 대하여) (영) the letterpress.

본문제(本問題) 〔본래의 문제〕 the original problem [question].

본밑천(本-) capital; stock; funds.

본바닥(本-) 〔본디의 산지〕 a home; a habitat; the (best) place (for); the (productive) center(중심지); 〔본디부터의 거처〕 a native place; the place of origin. ¶~ 사람 a native / an indigene∥서울 ~ 사람 a native of Seoul / an indigenous Seoulite∥~ 영어 English as it is spoken by its native speakers∥~의 비단 genuine brocade∥~의 스카치위스키 genuine [real] Scotch whisky∥귤 [커피]의 ~ the home of the tangerine [coffee]∥~의 native / indigenous / genuine∥외국어를 ~에서 배우다 learn a foreign language in the country where it is spoken (by its native speakers)∥그의 프랑스 어는 ~에서 배운 것이다 He learned his French while he was in France.∥금산은 인삼의 ~이다 Geumsan is one of the famous ginseng-growing centers of Korea.∥영국은 의회 정치의 ~이다 England is the birthplace of the parliamentary government.

본바탕(本-) 〔본질〕 essence; (real) substance; intrinsic [true] nature; essential quality; one's disposition; one's true colors [quality]; 〔밑바탕〕 the ground; (도자기의) the body. ¶~ 그대로의 plain / undisguised / simple∥~이 정직한 naturally honest / honest by nature∥그는 ~은 썩 좋은 사람이다 He is a very good fellow at heart [bottom].

본받다(本-) imitate; follow; model oneself (on / after); make (a person) one's model; take pattern by (another); follow the example [model] of (a person). ¶…을 본받아 after / after the example [model / fashion / style] of / in [after] the manner of / on [along the lines of / in imitation of∥네가 그를 본받는 것도 당연하다 You may well follow his example.∥아랫사람은 윗사람을 본받기 마련이다 Like master, like man. / As is the master, so are his men.

본보기(本-) 〔교훈〕 a lesson; 〔모범〕 an example; 〔경고〕 a warning; a model; a pattern. ¶~로 as an example∥앞으로의 ~로 as a warning for the future (to others)∥~로 삼다 make (it) an example [a lesson] / ∥~가 되다 serve as a lesson∥행동의 ~가 되다 be a model of (good) behavior.

본봉(本俸) the regular salary [pay]; 〔기본급〕 the basic salary; the base pay. ¶~과 여러

본부(本部) the head[main / front] office; the headquarters; the seat(연맹의); the ministry proper(정부 부처의). ¶대학 ~ the administrative building of a university // 참모 ~ the General Staff Office // 그들은 시 경찰국에 수사~를 설치했다 They set up the investigation headquarters in the Metropolitan Police Office.

본분(本分) one's duty; one's part. ¶자기의 ~을 다하다 do[discharge / fulfill] one's duty // ~을 게을리 하다 neglect[fail in] one's duty / fail to do one's duty // 자식으로서의 ~을 잊다 forget one's filial duty // 사람으로서의 ~을 다하다 discharge one's full duty as man // 그의 행위는 공무원의 ~에 어긋난다 His conduct is unworthy of a public servant.

본사(本寺) [불] 1 [처음 출가하여 승려가 된 절] the temple at which one became a bonze[Buddhist priest]. 2 [자기가 있는 절] our[this] temple. 3 [통할하는 큰 절] the main[head] temple.

본사(本社) (지사에 대하여) the head[main] office. ¶~ 근무로 되다 be assigned [transferred] to the head office.

본산(本山) [불] the temple at which one became a bonze; our temple. ⇨ 본사(本寺)1·2

본새(本-) 1 [본디부터의 생김새] looks; features; appearance. 2 [됨됨이] nature; quality; character; sum of attributes. ¶~가 사납다 have a foul nature.

본색(本色) 1 [본디의 특색·정체] one's real character; one's characteristic; one's true colors; one's true quality. ¶~이 드러나다 show one's true colors / come out in one's true colors // ~을 드러내다 show the cloven hoof / show one's true colors / reveal one's true character / betray one's true self // ~을 숨기다 wear[put on] a mask / disguise oneself // 그것이 그 여자의 ~이다 That's what she really is. 2 [본디의 빛깔] the original color; the true[natural] color. 3 [본디의 생김새] the original looks.

본서(本書) (부본(副本)에 대하여) the text; (사본에 대하여) the script; this[the present] work.

본서(本署) the principal office; headquarters; (경찰서의) the chief police station; police headquarters.

본선(本船) [모선] a mother ship; a depot ship.
● **본선 인도** free on board(약어 F.O.B., f.o.b.)(수출항에서); ex ship(수입항에서). ¶~ 가격 free on board price / F.O.B. price / the price ex ship.

본선(本線) a trunk (line). ⇨ 간선(幹線)

본선(本選) [최종 선발] the final selection. ¶~에 참가한 사람은 10명이었다 There were ten entries in the final contest[competition].

본성(本性) [본래의 성질] one's true character [colors]; one's real nature. ¶~을 드러내다 reveal one's true character / betray [unmask] oneself / show[come out in] one's true colors / throw off one's mask // 그것이 그의 ~이다 It is in his nature. // 잔인한 것이 그의 ~이다 He is cruel by nature.

본소송(本訴訟) [법] an original suit(원소송); a main action(반소(反訴)에 대하여).

본숭만숭하다 glance[run one's eyes] over (a letter); run over; take a cursory view of; skim over[through]; (미국 구어) give (a thing) the once-over.

본시(本是) originally; primarily. ⇨ 본디

본시험(本試驗) the final examination.

본실(本室) one's lawful[legal] wife. ⇨ 본처(本妻)

본심(本心) [진심] one's real intention(s); [속마음] one's heart. ¶~을 드러내다 bare one's heart // ~을 털어놓다 give oneself away / disclose one's real intention[motive] // 그의 ~을 이해할 수 없다 I cannot understand what he really wants[intends]. // 그렇게 하시는 당신의 ~을 말해 주시죠 Please tell me your real intention[motive] in behaving like that. // 나는 그가 ~으로 그렇게 말한다고는 생각하지 않는다 I don't think he really means it. / I don't think he is saying what he really thinks.

본안(本案) [원안] the original bill[draft]; the original plan.

본얼굴(本-) [본디의 얼굴] one's original [unchanged / unpainted] face. ¶~을 보이다 let one's unpainted face seen (by) / [비유] lift one's visor.

본업(本業) one's regular [principal / main] occupation[profession]. ¶~ 외의 일 a side business [job / line] // ~에 힘쓰다 attend to one's business // 그는 시인으로서 유명하지만 ~은 엔지니어[기사]다 Though famous as a poet, he is an engineer by profession.

본연(本然) ¶~의 [자연적인] natural / [나면서부터의] inborn / innate / inherent / proper / ~의 자세 the way that one[it] should be // 이것이 나의 ~의 모습이다 This is my true self.

본원(本源) [주장이 되는 근원] a source; an origin; a fountain; the root (of). ¶사물의 ~을 밝히다[캐다] study the origin of a thing / trace a thing to its source.

본위(本位) [기본] a standard; [기초] a basis (pl. bases); [주의] a principle; a line. ¶자기 ~의 사람[사고방식] a self-centered person [way of thinking] // 우리는 응모자의 학력보다도 인물 ~로 생각해야 한다 We should pay more attention to the applicant's personal character than to their academic backgrounds. // 그는 흥미 ~로 모든 일을 생각한다 Amusement is his first consideration. / His guiding principle is amusement. // 그는 품질 ~의 방침으로 사업에 성공했다 His "quality first" policy brought him success in business.
● **본위 화폐** a standard money[coin / currency]; legal tender.

본의(本意) one's original purpose; one's real intention[will / motive]. ¶~ 아닌 reluctant / unwilling // ~ 아니게 reluctantly / unwillingly / against one's will // 그것은 내 ~와는 동떨어져 있었다 It was far from my true intention. // 그건 네 ~가 아니었지 You didn't really mean that, did you? // 나는 ~ 아니게 그것을 단념했다 I gave it up against my will. // ~가 아닌 말을 드린 것을 용서하십시오 Please forgive me, for I did not mean what I said. // 나는 ~ 아니게 아들에게 호통을 쳐 버렸다 I shouted at my son without really meaning to.

본의(本義) the main object; the true aim. ⇨ 본지(本旨)

본인(本人) 〔나〕 I; 〔(문제의) 당사자〕 the person himself[herself]; the subject; the said person; the person in question; the principal(대리인에 대하여). ¶만약 내가 ~이라면 if I were in his position[place] // **~이 출두하다** present oneself (at a court) // 나는 그 ~을 만났다 I saw the man himself. // 그는 ~ 자신이 그것을 인정하고 있다 He admits it himself. // ~ 자신이 신청할 것 Apply in person. // ~에게서 들은 말이므로 사실임에 틀림없다 I have the news at first hand, so it must be true. // 우리 모두가 걱정하고 있는데도 불구하고 ~ 자신은 천연덕스러운 얼굴을 하고 있다 Though all of us are worried about him, he himself looks quite indifferent. // 우리가 말하고 있던 ~이 바로 지금 도착했다 The very man we were talking about arrived at this point. // ~은 아무것도 모르고 있었다 He himself[The person most directly concerned] knew nothing about it. // ~이라는 것을 나타낼 증명서를 갖고 오시오 Bring some identification (papers) with you.

본적(本籍) one's legal residence; one's permanent domicile; 〔본적지〕 one's legal domicile. ¶그의 ~은 부산 동래다 He is domiciled in Dongnae Busan. // 나는 ~을 부친의 고향에서 나의 현주소로 옮겼다 I transferred my domicile from my father's hometown to my present address.

본전(本錢) 1 〔원금〕 the principal. 2 〔밑천으로 들인 돈〕 capital; fund; a stake(노름의); 〔원가〕 the (prime[original]) cost; the cost price(원가). ¶이 장사는 ~도 못 뽑는다 This business doesn't pay. // 기껏 잘 보아야 ~이다 If I succeed, I'll come out even on it. // 그가 거절한다 해도 우리는 ~이다 Even if he refuses, we will be none the worse off.

본점(本店) (지점에 대하여) the head[main] office[shop / store]. ¶백화점의 ~ the main branch of a department store.

본제(本題) 〔중심이 되는 제목〕 the main question[issue]; the main subject; 〔본래의 제목〕 the original topic[subject]. ¶~로 돌아가서 to return (to our subject) // ~로 들어가다 enter into the main question / go on to [take up] the main subject[theme] / get down to business.

본존(本尊) 〔불〕 the principal image; the principal object of worship (at a temple).

본줄기(本-) the main line; (흐름 등의) the main current; the mainstream; (산맥의) the main mountain range.

본지(本旨) 1 〔본래의 취지·의미〕 the main [principal] object[purport]. ¶...의 ~에 맞다 serve[answer] the purpose of .... 2 〔참 목적〕 the true aim; the object in view; the spirit.

본지(本紙) our paper; these[our] columns; this[our] newspaper. ¶~의 애독자 our readers / one of our readers // 이미 ~에 보도된 바와 같이 as already reported in these columns[in our paper] // ~의 기자 our correspondent[reporter].

본지(本誌) this[our] journal[magazine].

본직(本職) 1 〔본업〕 one's (regular) occupation[profession]; one's principal[main] business; one's regular work[job]; one's line. ¶~ 이외의 일 a side job // ~을 소홀히 하다 neglect one's regular[main] work // 그의 ~은 변호사다 He is a lawyer by profession. 2 〔관리의 자칭〕 I; me; myself.

본질(本質) 〔근본적인 요소〕 essence; 〔실질〕 (real) substance; true nature; essential [intrinsic] qualities. ¶현상의 배후에 있는 ~을 포착해야 한다 We must go behind the outward form to grasp the inner meaning of the phenomenon.

본질적(本質的) essential; substantial; substantive; intrinsic (value). ¶민주주의의 ~ 요소 the essentials of democracy // ~으로는 자네 말에 찬성하지만 세부에 들어가서는 동의할 수 없다 I agree in substance with what you say, but we differ on some minor points.

본집(本-) one's principal residence; one's (own) house; one's town[city] house[home] (별장에 대하여).

본처(本妻) one's lawful[legal] wife; one's wedded wife. ¶(관계가 있었던) 제인을 ~로 삼다 make an honest woman of Jane.

본청(本廳) 〔지청에 대한 중앙 관청〕 the central government office.

본체(本體) 1 〔철〕 the substance; the noumenon (*pl.* -na); the entity; the thing in itself; 〔불〕 reality; the real thing. 2 〔참모습〕 a true form. ¶…을 ~로 하다 attach primary importance to … / make (it) a primary object to (do) // ~이 무엇인지를 알 수 없다 have no idea of (its) true character. 3 〔기계 등의 중심 부분〕 the body.

본초(本草) 〔약재〕 medicinal stuff; 〔약학〕 pharmacy; pharmaceutics.

본초 자오선(本初子午線) 〔지〕 the prime[first] meridian.

본토(本土) the mainland; the country proper. ¶~에서 멀리 떨어져 있는 섬 an island far from the mainland / a remote island // 중국 ~ the Chinese mainland / China proper // 영국 ~ the British Isles.

● **본토박이** a native; an aborigine. ¶~ 서울 사람 a Seoulite born and bred. **본토인** natives; mainlanders.

본회담(本會談) a full-dress[full-fledged / full-scale] talk; the main conference.

본회의(本會議) (국회의) a plenary session; (회의의) a full session. ¶국회[하원]의 ~ a plenary session of Congress[the House of Representatives].

볼¹ 1 〔빰의 한복판〕 a cheek. ¶~이 붉은 red [rosy-]cheeked // 포동포동한 〔통통한〕 plump cheeks // ~을 붉히다 blush / redden // ~을 비비다 press[nestle] one's cheek against another's // 그는 불만으로 ~을 부루퉁하게 부풀렸다 He puffed out [up] his cheeks in dissatisfaction. 2 〔물건의 너비〕 the width of a long and narrow object. ¶~이 넓은 발 a broad foot // ~이 좁다 be narrow. 3 (버선의) a patch. ¶버선에 ~을 대다 [받다] put patches on the sole of a Korean socks at the front and rear.

볼² 1 a ball; a handball. ⇨**공**¹ 2 〔야구〕 〔스트라이크가 아닌 투구〕 a ball. ¶심판은 ~을 선언했다 The umpire called the pitch a ball. // 그는 ~인데 배트를 휘둘렀다 He swung at a ball.

● **볼 카운트** 〔야구〕 the count. ¶~는 원 스트라이크 스리 볼이다 The pitcher has one strike and three balls on the batter. / The count is three and one.

볼가심 〔아주 적은 음식으로 시장기를 면하는 일〕 a morsel of food; a bite; (a) bite and (a)

불가심하다 have [take / eat] just a bite of food to appease one's hunger; allay [alleviate] one's hunger with a bit[morsel] of food. ¶불가심할 것도 없다 do not have a bite to eat.
볼각거리다 chew away; scrub. ⇨불각거리다
볼거리 [한] parotitis; mumps(단수 취급).
볼그레하다 reddish. ⇨볼그레하다
볼그스름하다 reddish. ⇨볼그스름하다
볼기 the backside; the rump; (문어) buttocks; (구어) the bottom(▶ 주로 소아이); the rear; (구어) the behind; (미국 속어) the ass; (영국 속어) the arse. ¶~를 맞다 get spanked / be flogged on the buttocks[hip] // ~를 치다 spank // 그는 아들의 ~를 때렸다 He spanked his son. / He smacked his son's bottom [his son on the behind].
●**볼깃살** (소의) the rump.
볼꼴 outward appearance; show; look. ¶~이 사납다 be unsightly[ungainly / unseemly / shabby / ugly / indecent / improper / mean] // ~ 사나우니 그만두게 Stop it for decency's sake. / Stop doing things like that. It's a shame. // 참 ~ 사납다 What a sight! / Shame on you!
볼레로 [여자의 짧은 윗옷] a bolero (pl. ~s); [에스파냐의 무용·무곡] bolero (pl. ~s).
볼록거리다 swell and subside. ⇨볼록거리다
볼록 거울 a convex mirror.
볼록 렌즈 a convex lens[glass]; a convex.
볼록하다 swollen; baggy. ⇨볼록하다
볼륨 1 [양감(量感)] volume. ¶~ 있는 사전 a bulky dictionary // 그녀는 ~이 대단하다 [뚱뚱하다] She's really fat. / [글래머이다] She has some [quite a] build. 2 [음량] volume. ¶~ 있는 목소리 a very powerful[loud] voice // 라디오의 ~을 높이다 [낮추다] turn up [down] the radio.
볼링 bowling. ¶~ 처러 가다 go bowling.
●**볼링장** a bowling alley.
볼멘소리 sullen [grouchy] words. ¶~로 in angry tone // ~로 대답하다 give a sullen answer / grumble (out) an answer.
볼모 1 [전당품] a pawn; a pledge. 2 a hostage. ⇨인질 ¶~을 잡다 take[hold] (a person) (as a) hostage / ~로 잡히다 be taken[held] (as a) hostage.
볼셰비즘 Bolshevism.
볼셰비키 a Bolshevik (pl. ~s, -viki); a Bolshevist.
볼썽사납다 indecent; unseemly; ungainly; unsightly.
볼일 business; affairs; [할 일] things to do; an engagement; work; (심부름의) an errand. ¶~로 on business / (심부름으로) on an errand // 부득이한 ~이 있어서 owing to an unavoidable engagement // ~이 있다 have something to do / be engaged (in) // ~이 없다 have nothing to do / be free // ~이 남아 있다 have something more to do // ~을 보다 do one's business / perform [transact / get through / carry through] business / ~을 마치다 [끝내다] finish [settle] one's business / have done with (something) // 나에게 무슨 ~이냐 What do you want with [of] me? / What is your business with me? / What can [may] I do for you? / ~이 있어서 가지 못했습니다 Business prevented me from going there. // 그에게 급한 ~이 있다 I have urgent business with him. // 오늘은 특별히 ~이 없다 I don't have anything in particular to do today. // 그는 급한 ~로 부산에 갔다 Urgent business called him away to Busan. / He has gone to Busan on urgent business. // 이제 ~은 다 봤다 I have done all the work assigned to me.

볼트[1] [나사못] a bolt; a screw bolt. ¶~로 죄다 (up) / fasten with a bolt // ~를 죄다 tighten a bolt.
볼트[2] [전] [전압의 단위] a volt; voltage(볼트수). ¶220~의 전류 a 220-volt current.
볼펜 a ball-point (pen); (영) a biro (pl. ~s) (상표명).
볼품 (outward) appearance; show; looks. ¶~이 있다 look nice[fine / well] / be pleasing in appearance / be attractive // 방을 ~ 있게 꾸미다 make a room look nice.
볼품없다 do not look nice; make a poor show; have a bad appearance; be unattractive [vulgar]. ¶볼품없는 사람 a man who makes a poor impression.
봄 spring; [봄철] springtime. ¶올 ~ this spring // ~의 따뜻한 햇살 a soft, warm spring sun(shine) // ~에 입는 카디건 a cardigan for spring (wear) // ~이 되면 as spring comes round / in (the) spring // 이른 [늦은] ~에 early[late] in spring / in early [late] spring // ~이 한창이다 Spring is in all its glory. / We are at the height of spring now. // ~에는 나무들이 움튼다 Trees put forth new leaves [buds] in (the) spring.
봄(을) 타다 suffer from [get / succumb to] spring fever; fall away in spring.
봄갈이 spring plowing [(영) ploughing]. ¶봄갈이하다 do the spring plowing [ploughing].
봄기운 a feel[an air] of spring. ¶~을 느끼다 feel a breath of spring.
봄날 a spring day; spring weather. ¶화창한 ~ the mild days of spring.
봄내 all through [throughout] the spring.
봄눈 spring snow. ¶~ 슬듯 하다 disappear [vanish] into thin air / (음식)이 melt in one's mouth / digest [go down] smoothly.
봄맞이꽃 [식] a rock jasmine.
봄바람 a spring wind [breeze].
봄볕 spring sun(shine).
봄비 (a) spring rain [drizzle].
봄빛 [봄 경치] spring scenery; a spring view; [봄기운] a feel of spring.
봄옷 spring wear [clothes].
봄철 spring; springtime; the spring season.
봅슬레이 (썰매) a bobsleigh; a bobsled; (경기) bobsledding.
봇논 (洑−) a paddy field watered by a reservoir.
봇도랑 (洑−) an irrigation ditch [conduit].
봇돌 1 (아궁이의) a support stone on either side of the fireplace. 2 (지붕의) stone weights over a roof.
봇둑 (洑−) a dam; levees surrounding a reservoir.
봇물 (洑−) dam (water); water of reservoir; irrigation water.
봇짐 (褓−) a pack carried on one's back; a bundle; a backpack. ¶~을 짊어지다 carry a bundle on one's back / shoulder bundle // ~을 풀다 undo a bundle [package].
●**봇짐장수** a peddler who carries his wares

봉 on his back.

봉 (메우는) a solder patch; (이의) filling; (충치 구멍의) plugging; a plug; stopping. ¶치아에 ~을 해 박다 plug[stop] a tooth / fill a tooth (with).

봉(封) a pack(age) (of). ⇨봉지2

봉(鳳) **1 a** (Chinese) phoenix. ⇨봉황 **2 a** male phoenix. **3** (만만한 사람) a victim; a prey. ¶~으로 삼다 make a sucker out of (a person)/그들은 행락지에서 ~을 찾고 있었다 They were looking for an easy mark in the holiday resort.//그는 사기꾼의 좋은 ~이 되었다 He fall an easy victim[prey] to the swindler.

봉건(封建) **1** [봉건 제도] feudalism. **2** [봉함] setting up (a person) as a feudal prince; enfeoffing.
● **봉건사상** a feudalistic idea; feudalistic thinking[thought]. **봉건 사회** a feudal society. **봉건 제도** feudalism; the feudal system[regime]. **봉건주의** feudalism.

봉건적(封建的) feudalistic; feudal; (보수적) conservative; old-fashioned; (중세적) medieval; (전제적) despotic; (인습적) conventional. ¶우리 아버지는 ~이시다 My father is an old fogy.

봉곳하다 swollen; loose. ⇨봉긋하다

봉급(俸給) (a) salary; pay; wages. ¶높은 ~ high pay / a high salary // 낮은[적은] ~ small pay / a low[small] salary // 높은 ~을 받는 사람 a highly[well-paid] employee // 월 80만 원의 ~ a salary of 800,000 won a month // ~을 지급하다 pay[give] a salary / pay for (a person's) regular work[services] // ~을 받다[타다] receive a salary / get paid // ~을 올리다[내리다] get a raise[cut] in one's salary / have one's salary raised [reduced] // ~이 많다[적다] be well[ill / poorly] paid // 높은 ~을 주고 고용하다 employ a person at a high salary // ~으로 생활하다 live on one's salary / ~ 인상을 요구하다 demand an increase[a raise / (영) a rise] in salary // ~생활을 그만두고 자립하다 become self-employed // 그녀는 나보다 ~를 더 받고 있다 She makes[draws / pulls in] a higher salary than I do. // 그는 회사로부터 ~을 받고 있다 He draws a salary from the company. / He is in the pay[on the payroll] of the company. // 그 회사는 ~이 많다 The company pays good salaries.
● **봉급생활자** a salaried man; (미국 속어) a white-collar worker. **봉급일** a payday (▶ 단 Tomorrow is payday.에서는 관사가 붙지 않음). **봉급쟁이** a salaried man. ⇨봉급생활자 (⇨봉급)

봉기(蜂起) an uprising; a revolt; (an) insurrection. ¶농민 ~ a peasant uprising. **봉기하다** rise in revolt[rebellion / arms] (against); rise[revolt] (against).

봉납(奉納) dedication; offering; presentation (to a deity); oblation. **봉납하다** dedicate; offer; present; consecrate.
● **봉납물** an offering; a votive offering.

봉당(封堂) an unfloored[dirt-floored] area between two rooms.

봉독(奉讀) reading reverentially [deferentially]. **봉독하다** read with reverence.

봉돌 a (fishing) sinker; a (fishing) weight; a weight of stone[lead] on a fishline. ¶~을 달다 weight a line / tie a weight on a fishing line.

봉두난발(蓬頭亂髮) shaggy[unkempt / disheveled] hair; a rat's nest.

봉랍(封蠟) (sealing) wax.

봉밀(蜂蜜) honey; nectar. ⇨꿀

봉변(逢變) [변을 당함] meeting with a mishap; a mishap; an insult; humiliation. **봉변하다** [변을 당하다] meet with a mishap; [망신을 당하다] be insulted[humiliated]; have bitter experiences; have a hell of a time; have a hard time of it.

봉분(封墳) a (grave) mound. **봉분하다** mound (a grave); build a mound over a grave.

봉사 [소경] a blind person.

봉사(奉仕) (고객에 대한) service; (국가에 대한) (a) public duty [service]; [시중들기] attendance; [근무하기] (a) service. ¶근로 ~ labor service // 사회 ~ public service / service to society // 그는 ~ 정신이 희박하다 He lacks [is wanting in] public spirit. **봉사하다** serve; attend; render service(s) (to). ¶나라에 ~ place oneself at the service of one's country / serve the nation // 사회에 ~ serve the public[community].

봉사(奉事) [섬김] service; attendance. **봉사하다** serve; attend; wait on.

봉살(封殺) [야구] a force-out. ⇨포스 아웃

봉서(封書) a sealed letter.

봉선화(鳳仙花) [식] a touch-me-not; a (garden) balsam.

봉쇄(封鎖) [출입을 막음] a blockade; blocking; bottling up. ¶경제 ~ an economic blockade[boycott] // 직접[간접] ~ a direct [cruising] blockade // 해상 ~ a naval[sea] blockade // 항구의 ~를 풀다[뚫다] lift[break] the blockade of a port. **봉쇄하다** blockade; block (up); [가두다] confine; [봉쇄 정책을 취하다] contain. ¶성의 입구를 ~ block the entrance to the castle // 적은 항구를 봉쇄했다 The enemy blockaded the harbor entrance. // 정부는 야당의 반대를 봉쇄하는 데 성공했다 The government succeeded in silencing [suppressing] opposition to its policies.
● **봉쇄 구역** a blockade zone. **봉쇄 정책** a blockade policy.

봉술(棒術) the art of using a stick as a weapon; the art of fighting with a cudgel [staff]; the art of stick fighting.

봉안(奉安) enshrinement. **봉안하다** enshrine.

봉양(奉養) supporting[serving] one's (grand)parents. **봉양하다** support one's (grand)parents; serve one's (grand)parents faithfully.

봉오리 a (flower) bud; a button. ⇨꽃봉오리 ¶피어나는 ~ bursting buds // ~마다 all the buds / all in bud(s) // ~가 나오다 bud / put forth[shoot out] buds // ~가 맺혀 있다 be in bud // 복숭아나무의 ~가 부풀어 있다 The peach trees are budding[are in (full) bud].

봉우리 a (mountain) peak. ⇨산봉우리 ¶소백산맥의 ~를 타다 walk along the ridges of the Sobaek mountain chain.

봉인(封印) a (stamped) seal; sealing. ¶~을 떼다 unseal (a letter) // ~을 뜯다 break[take off] a seal. **봉인하다** seal (a letter); put (a letter) under seal; put the seal (up)on. ¶봉인한 편지 a sealed letter. ↪¶서랍은 봉인되어 있었다 The drawer was sealed (up).

봉정(奉呈·捧呈) dedication; presentation (to a superior). **봉정하다** dedicate; present;

봉제(縫製) needlework; sewing (by machine); dressmaking. **봉제하다** make[sew] (a dress) with a sewing machine.
● **봉제공** / **봉제사** a needleworker; a worker in a sewing factory; a dressmaker. **봉제완구** stuffed toys.
봉지(封紙) 1 [종이 주머니] a paper bag [sack]. ¶~에 가득한 과자 a paperful of biscuits. 2 (셀 때) a pack(age) (of). ¶약 한 ~ a packet of medicinal herbs / a (packaged) dose of medicine // 약 한 ~를 먹다 take a dose of medicine.
봉직(奉職) government[public] service. **봉직하다** serve (at / in); hold an office (at / in); work (for); have a post[position] (in). ¶아버지는 20년간 고등학교 교사로 봉직하고 계신다 My father has been on the staff of a (senior) high school for twenty years.
봉착하다(逢着-) encounter; confront; face (with); meet (with); come upon[across]. ¶그는 마침내 생사의 문제에 봉착했다 He was finally confronted with the problem of life and death.
봉창(封窓) [봉한 창] a sealed window; sealing (up) a window(봉하기); [뚫은 창] an opening in the wall; a small blind window.
봉축(奉祝) celebration (of an occasion). **봉축하다** celebrate; commemorate. ¶석가 탄신을 ~ celebrate the birth of Buddha.
봉토(封土) 1 [제후를 봉하여 내준 땅] a feudal estate; a fief; a feud. 2 [흙을 쌓아 올린 것] an earthen mound; (무덤의) a burial[grave] mound.
봉투(封套) an envelope. ¶각[양]~ a side-opening envelope / 반신용 ~ a return envelope // 편지 ~ a letter envelope // ~를 뜯다 open[break open] an envelope / cut (a letter) open // ~를 봉하다 seal / wafer (a letter) // 편지를 ~에 넣다 put a letter in an envelope.
봉하다(封-) 1 (봉투·문을) seal (a letter); seal up (a window); glue up; fasten. ¶봉한[봉하지 않은] 편지 a sealed[an unsealed] letter // 봉하여 보내다 send (a thing) under seal // 봉하지 않은 채 부치다 send (a letter) unsealed. 2 (구멍을) close[stop] up (a hole). ¶창구멍을 ~ cover a hole in a paper window. 3 (입을) shut (one's mouth); seal. ¶입을 봉하고 말이 없다 keep one's lips tight / keep one's mouth shut / keep silent. 4 (봉토를) invest (a person) with a fief; enfeoff; (작위를) confer a peerage.
봉함(封緘) a seal; sealing. ¶~을 뜯다 break [open] the seal[envelope]. **봉함하다** seal. ¶봉함한 sealed // 단단히 봉함하여 in a tight cover // 봉함하지 않고 with[under] a flying seal.
● **봉함엽서** a letter card.
봉합(縫合) [의] (a) suture; (a) seam; (a) raphe. **봉합하다** suture (a wound); stitch (up) (a wound) together; seam. ¶의사는 상처를 봉합했다 The doctor sewed[stitched] up the wound.
봉행하다(奉行-) obey (a person's) orders; do in obedience to (a superior's order); carry out (an order).
봉헌(奉獻) offering; dedication; presentation; consecration. **봉헌하다** offer up; dedicate [consecrate] (a thing) to (a superior / shrine).
봉화(烽火) a signal fire; a beacon; a (signal) rocket.
봉화(를) 올리다[들다] 1 raise a beacon fire. ¶그들은 봉화를 올려 그들의 위치를 알렸다 They made known their position by lighting a signal fire[by lighting a beacon / by firing a rocket]. 2 start (a campaign). ¶그들은 반핵 운동의 봉화를 올렸다 They started [launched] a campaign against nuclear weapons.
봉황(鳳凰) a (Chinese) phoenix.
● **봉황새자리** [천] the Phoenix.
봐주다 [눈감아 주다] overlook; wink at; turn a blind eye to. ¶부정행위를 ~ wink at[turn a blind eye to] dishonest acts // 제발 좀 봐주세요 Give me a break[chance], please. / Have a heart, please. // 제발 이번만 봐주십시오 Please let it pass[go] just this once.
뵙다 see[meet]; have an audience[interview] with. ¶처음 뵙겠습니다 How do you do? // 이렇게 뵙게 되니 참 반갑습니다 It's good[nice] to see you here. / I am very glad to have the opportunity of meeting you. // 그럼 내일 또 뵙겠습니다 Well then, I (shall) come tomorrow.
부(父) a father. ⇨ ゠아버지1
부(否) no; nay; negation. ¶가(可)~ aye and no / pro and con // 그의 대답은 ~였다 He answered[His reply was] in the negative. // ~가 다수였다 The noes have it.
부(部) 1 [부분] a part; a portion; a section. ¶중심~ the central part // 제1~ section I / 「헨리 4세」 제1~ the first part of King Henry the fourth // 2~로 된 소설 a novel in two parts // 그의 전기는 2~로 되어 있다 His biography consists of two volumes [is divided into two parts].
2 [부서] a ministry; (미) a department (▶ 우리나라 회사의 「부」에 해당. 「과(課)」는 a section); a bureau; a division; [클럽] a club. ¶경리~ the accountants' department // 국방~ the Ministry[Department] of National Defense // 그는 회사의 판매~에서 일하고 있다 He works in the sales department of the company. // 그녀는 연극~에 들어갔다 She joined the theatrical club[the drama club / the dramatic society].
3 (책을 셀 때) a copy (of a book, magazine, etc.); [권] a volume. ¶3[4]~작 a trilogy [tetralogy] / a three-[four-]volume work // 1~에 3천 원 three thousand won a[per] copy // 주간지 2~ two copies of the weekly / 초판 천 ~ a first edition of one thousand copies // 「톰 존즈」 5~를 보내 주세요 Please send me five copies of Tom Jones.
부(富) riches; wealth; a fortune; [풍부] opulence. ¶~의 분배 distribution of wealth [riches] // 일국의 ~ a nation's wealth // ~를 쌓다 make[build up / pile up / accumulate / amass] a fortune / gather wealth.
부-(不) not; non-; un-; im-; ir-; il-; dis-. ¶~도덕 immorality // ~정기 irregularity.
부-(副) assistant; vice-; deputy; sub-; under-; adjutant; substitute; accessory; (미) alternate. ¶~통령 a vice president // ~지배인 an assistant manager // ~작용 a side[secondary] effect.
-부(附) 1 [작성·발송한 시일] dated; under the date of. ¶8월 15일~의 편지에 대해 감사

드립니다 Thank you for your letter of [dated] August 15. // 그것은 며칠~의 편지였습니까 What was the date of the letter? // 그는 4월 1일~로 부장으로 승진했다 He was promoted to department head as of [effective / (영) from] April 1. 2 [소속·부속) attached (to); belonging (to); in attendance (upon); bearing. ¶그는 주영 대사관~로 발령되었다 He was attached to the Korean Embassy in London.

부가(附加) addition; supplement; annexation. ¶~의[적] additional / annexed / supplementary / accessory / extra(여분의). **부가하다** [덧붙이다] add (to); make additions to; [보충하다] supplement (with / by); [첨부하다] append; annex; [추가하다] subjoin.
● **부가 가치** value added; added value. ¶~가 높은 제품 high value-added products.

부각 fried kelp.
부각(俯角) [수] a dip. ⇨ 내려본각
부각(浮刻) relief; relievo; embossed carving. **부각하다** emboss; raise; [새기다] carve in relief. ➜¶부각되다 be embossed / stand out in bold relief / [비유] be brought to the fore / be highlighted // **부각시키다** bring (a thing) into relief // 그 사건으로 그녀의 비천함이 부각되었다 The incident clearly brought out her meanness.

부각(腐刻) [인] etching.
부강하다(富强-) rich and powerful (nation). ¶부강한 나라를 세우다 found a rich and powerful country [nation].

부걱 with a bubble [pop].
부걱거리다 bubble; pop (in fermentation).
부걱부걱 bubbling; popping; hubble-bubble (소리). **부걱부걱하다** bubble. ⇨ 부걱거리다

부검(剖檢) a postmortem examination; an autopsy. **부검하다** examine (a corpse) to determine the cause of death.

부결(否決) (a) rejection; negation; voting down. **부결하다** reject; (투표에서) vote down; vote against; throw out; kill; veto. ➜¶부결되다 be rejected [voted down / thrown out] / get voted [killed] // 읍장의 불신임안은 읍 의회에서 17대 15로 부결되었다 The town assembly rejected [voted down] a nonconfidence motion [a motion of nonconfidence] against the mayor by a vote of 17 to 15.
● **부결권** the right of veto; a veto; a negative voice.

부계(父系) the paternal side [line]; the male line; the patrilineage. ¶~의 paternal / patrilineal / on the paternal [father's / spear] side / agnate / [로마 법] consanguinean // 나에게는 ~의 숙부가 세 분 계신다 I have three uncles on my father's side.
● **부계 사회** a patrilineal society.

부고(訃告) an announcement of (a person's) death; an obituary (notice); an obit. ¶그의 ~를 받고 깜짝 놀랐다 I was thunderstruck at the news of his death.

부과(賦課) (세금 등의) (a) levy; (의무·책임 등의) imposition; assessment; incidence. ¶자동 ~(세)제 taxation-by-schedule system // 재~ reimposition. **부과하다** levy [impose] (on); lay (a tax on an article); assess (in / at so much). ➜¶내 집에 5만 원의 고정 재산세가 부과되었다 A fixed property tax of fifty thousand won was imposed [levied] on my house.

● **부과금** (세관 등의) dues; a levy.
부관(副官) an adjutant; an aid(e)-de-camp (pl. aid(e)s-de-camp). ¶**고급** ~ a senior adjutant // **전속** ~ an aid(e)-de-camp / an aide.
부광(富鑛) a rich ore; a rich mine.
부교(浮橋) a floating [pontoon] bridge.
부교감 신경(副交感神經) [생] a parasympathetic (nerve).
부교수(副教授) an associate professor.
부교재(副教材) an auxiliary textbook.
부국(部局) a department.
부국(富國) 1 [부유한 나라] a rich country. 2 [나라를 부유하게 함] national enrichment.
● **부국강병** (a policy for) enhancing the wealth and military strength of a country.
부군(夫君) a [one's] husband.
부권(父權) paternal rights.
● **부권 사회** a patriarchal society.
부권(夫權) the husband's rights; marital authority.
부귀(富貴) wealth and rank; riches and hono(u)rs. **부귀하다** wealthy [rich] and noble. ¶부귀한 사람 a noble and wealth man // 부귀한 집에 태어나다 be born to a life of position and wealth.
● **부귀영화** wealth and prosperity.
부그르르 1 [물이 끓는 모양] boiling briskly; simmering. ¶물이 ~ 끓는다 Water simmers [boils]. // 주전자의 물이 ~ 끓고 있다 The (water in the) kettle is boiling. **부그르르하다** boil briskly; boil (up); simmer. 2 [거품이 이는 모양] bubbling; frothing. ¶거품이 ~ 일어난다 Suds bubble up. **부그르르하다** bubble up; foam; froth.
부근(附近) [근처] the neighborhood; the vicinity; environs; a part(지역). ¶서울 ~ the vicinity [environs] of seoul / Seoul and (its) neighborhood / Seoul and (its) vicinity / in and around Seoul // ~의 neighboring / nearby / adjacent // ~의 상가가 a neighboring [nearby] shopping center // 이 ~ 일대에 all around here // 이 ~에 파출소가 있습니까 Is there a police box near here [in this neighborhood]? // 나는 이 ~의 뒷거리를 잘 알고 있다 I am quite familiar with the back streets in this neighborhood [area]. // 서울의 이 ~이 가장 땅값이 비싸다 The land rent is highest in this part of Seoul. // 이 ~은 전혀 모릅니다 I am quite a stranger in these parts [in this neighborhood]. // 우리 집 ~에 공회당이 있다 There is a public hall in the neighborhood [vicinity] of our home.

부글거리다 1 (물이) boil (over); seethe; come to a boil; simmer. ¶주전자의 물이 부글거린다 The kettle is singing. / 내 배 속이 부글거렸다 My belly growled. / The bowels rumbled. 2 (거품이) bubble; foam; froth; rise in bubble. ¶거품이 부글거리며 솟아 흘러내렸다 Bubbles oozed and foamed along. 3 (마음이) fret (and fume); be fretful; become impatient. ¶…에 가슴이 ~ be fretful over (something) // 그는 하찮은 일에도 속이 부글거린다 He frets about [over] trifles. 4 (사람·벌레 등이) be crowded [thronged] (with beggars); swarm.

부글부글 1 [끓는 모양] boiling briskly; with a seething sound. ¶~ 끓다 boil (over) / seethe / come to a boil // ~ 끓이다 simmer / stew / boil (▶ simmer와 stew는 약한 불로 서서히 끓이다, boil은 센 불로 끓이다) // 스튜를

~ 끓이다 simmer stew // 냄비 속에서는 콩이 ~ 끓고 있다 The beans are simmering (away) in the pot. **부글부글하다** boil (over); seethe. ⇨**부글거리다**1
2 [거품이 이는 모양] bubbling; foamily; [소리] hubble-bubble. ¶~ 솟아나는 온천 a bubbling[gurgling / burbling] hot spring // 거품이 ~ 일다 bubble up / rise in bubbles. / ~ 가라앉다 sink leaving a trail of bubbles. **부글부글하다** bubble; foam. ⇨**부글거리다**2
3 [마음이 언짢은 모양]. ¶(화가 나서) 속이 ~ 끓다 be convulsed with anger / boil with rage. **부글부글하다** fret (and fume); be fretful. ⇨**부글거리다**3
4 [많이 모여 복잡하게 움직이는 모양] in swarm. **부글부글하다** be crowded (with beggars). ⇨**부글거리다**4
부금 (賦金) an instal(l)ment; a premium(보험의). ¶이달 치 ~ this month's instal(l)ment // ~을 내다 pay in [by] instal(l)ments / pay one's share (in a mutual aid society) by instal(l)ments // 생명 보험의 ~으로 매달 2만 원씩 내고 있다 Every month I pay a premium of twenty thousand won on my life insurance.
부기 (附記) an addition; an additional remark; a supplementary note; a postscript(약어 P.S., p.s.). **부기하다** add; write in addition; append a note (to); add a postscript (to a letter).
부기 (浮氣) dropsy; dropsical swelling; anasarca(전신 부종). ¶~가 가라앉았다 The swelling has subsided[gone down]. // 그의 눈 가장자리의 ~가 가라앉았다 The puffiness around his eyes was gone.
부기 (簿記) bookkeeping. ¶가계 ~ domestic bookkeeping // 단식 [복식] ~ bookkeeping by single [double] entry // 상업 [공업 / 은행] ~ commercial [industrial / bank] bookkeeping // 행렬 ~ matrix bookkeeping // ~를 하다 keep books / keep accounts.
●**부기장** an account book.
부기우기 [음] boogie-woogie; boogie. ¶~를 부르다 sing a boogie-woogie song.
부꾸미 a kind of cake made by mixing various flours.
부끄러움 shame; (feeling of) shyness. ⇨**부끄럼**
부끄러워하다 1 [수줍어하다] be[feel] abashed; be bashful; be coy. ¶부끄러워하여 shyly / bashfully // 부끄러워하지 말고 의견을 말하시오 Don't be shy about giving your opinion. // 그 소년은 칭찬을 받자 부끄러워하는 것 같았다 He looked abashed when he was praised. **2** [창피해하다] be ashamed (of); feel shame (at); consider something shameful [a shame]. ¶부끄러워하는 얼굴 an ashamed look // 가난한 ~ be ashamed of one's being poor // 가난은 부끄러워할 것이 못 된다 Poverty is no disgrace.
부끄럼 1 [창피] shame; disgrace; dishonor; humiliation; ignominy. ¶~을 아는 사람 a man of honor / ~을 모르는 사람 a shameless person // ~을 **알다** have a sense of shame / be sensible to shame // ~을 **모르다** have no sense of shame / be dead [lost] to (all sense of) shame / be shameless // ~을 **당하다** disgrace oneself / humiliate oneself / be put to shame // ~을 알라 For shame! / Shame on you! / What a disgrace! // 그는 ~도 모르고 거짓말을 한다 He lies shamelessly. // 나는 ~을 무릅쓰고 그에게 청했다 I stooped to ask a favor of him.
2 [수줍음] (feeling of) shyness; bashfulness; coyness. ¶~을 잘 타는 사람 a shy [bashful] person // ~을 **타다** feel shy / be bashful [coy] // 그 소녀는 ~을 타서 말도 제대로 못한다 The girl is too shy to speak [coy of speech]. // ~ 타지 말고 노래 하나 불러라 Don't be bashful, sing a song for us.
부끄럽다 1 [창피하다] shameful; disgraceful; dishonorable; be ashamed (of); feel shame (at). ¶부끄러운 행위 disgraceful [dishonorable / shameful] behavior [conduct] // 부끄러운 얘기지만… to my shame I must confess [I am ashamed to say] that ... // 어디에 내놓아도 부끄럽지 않은 인물 a worthy person / a noble character // 신사로서 부끄럽잖은 행동을 하다 act as a gentleman / do a thing worthy of a gentleman // 부끄러워 얼굴을 붉히다 blush [flush] with shame // 부끄러워 고개를 숙이다 hang one's head for shame // 그는 부끄러운 줄을 모른다 He has no sense of shame [honor]. // 부끄러운 줄 알아라 You ought to be ashamed. / For shame! // 이런 큰 실수를 보여 드려서 부끄럽기 짝이 없습니다 I am deeply ashamed of myself for committing such a serious blunder in your presence. // 그는 약속을 잊은 것을 부끄럽게 생각하고 있다 He is ashamed of himself for having forgotten [He is ashamed that he forgot] his promise. // 이런 부끄러운 일에서 손을 떼겠다 I am going to wash my hands of this shameful job. // 나는 부끄러운 짓은 아무 것도 하지 않았다 I have done nothing to be ashamed of. // 이런 짓을 저질러 놓고 부끄럽지도 않으냐 Aren't you ashamed of having done such a thing? // 부끄럽게 생각할 필요는 없습니다 There's no need for you to feel small. // 칭찬해 주시니 도리어 부끄럽습니다 Your praises put me to shame.
2 [수줍다] shy; bashful; coy; abashed. ¶부끄러운 듯이 bashfully / coyly / shyly // 어쩐지 ~ be [feel] ashamed somehow or other // 그녀는 부끄러워 말도 못한다 She is too shy to speak. // 그 소녀는 부끄러워서 두 손으로 얼굴을 가렸다 The little girl covered her face with her hands from bashfulness. // 남들이 보면 ~ I am [feel] shy when people are watching me. // 나는 부끄러워졌다 Shyness came over me. // 그녀는 부끄러워서 낯선 사람에게 말을 걸지도 못한다 She is too shy to speak to strangers. // 칭찬을 듣자 그녀는 부끄러워했다 She looked abashed when she was praised.
부나비 [동] a garden tiger moth. ⇨**불나방**
부낭 (浮囊) **1** [구명용 기구] a lifebuoy; a life belt; a life preserve [jacket]; (수영용) an inner tube; (미) a (tire) tube; (영) water wings; (수영 초보자용) a float; a rubber ring. **2** [물고기의 부레] an air bladder; a swim(m)ing bladder; a (gas) bladder.
부녀 (父女) father and daughter.
부녀(자) (婦女子) a woman; [집합적] womenfolk(s); the fair [weaker / gentle / softer / tender] sex. ¶~ 폭행범 a rapist // ~를 **괴롭히다** bully the fair sex.
부농 (富農) a rich [wealthy] farmer; a farmer who is well-off.

부닥치다

부닥치다 1 [만나다] face; encounter; confront; meet with; be faced[confronted] with; come upon[across]; come face to face with. ¶난관에 ~ encounter[be faced with] difficulties // 벽에 ~ run into a blank wall / reach a deadlock // 위험에 ~ get into danger // 반항에 ~ meet with hostility (from) // 부닥쳐 보다 have a try / [맞서 보다] face up (to) // 나는 많은 어려운 문제에 부닥쳐 있다 I am confronted with many difficult problems. // 그는 마침내 생사의 문제에 부닥쳤다 He was finally confronted with the problem of life and death. // 죽든 살든 부닥쳐 보아라 Take your chance. / Make an attempt anyhow.
2 [충돌하다] run[knock / hit / bump / collide / dash] against; run[crash] into; strike. ¶사람과 ~ bump into a man // (자동차 등이) 기차에 ~ run[smash] into a train.

부단하다(不斷-) constant; ceaseless; incessant; continual; persistent; perpetual; steady. ¶부단한 발전 continuous development // 부단한 노력이 그의 성공을 가져오 았다 His constant[persistent] effort brought him success. **부단히** constantly; continually; continuously; incessantly; ceaselessly; unremittingly. ¶~ 노력하다 continue one's unremitting exertions / make sustained [constant] efforts // ~ 감시하다 keep a constant watch (over) / be always on the watch (over) // 살아 있는 언어는 ~ 변화한다 A living language changes constantly.

부담(負擔) a burden; a charge; a load; responsibility(책임); obligation(의무); liability(채무); defrayment(지출); incidence(조세의). ¶각자 ~ an equal split / paying each for his own account / (회식 등의) a Dutch treat[party] // 자기 ~으로 at one's own expense[charge] / out of one's own pocket // ~이 되다 be a burden[strain] (on) / weigh (on) // ~을 주다 impose[lay] a burden on (a person) // ~을 덜다 lighten[lessen] a burden // ~이 크다 have too many things on one's hands // 과중한 ~에 시달리다 groan under a heavy burden // 세금의 ~을 경감하다 ease the tax burden / reduce taxes // ~에 견디지 못하다 cannot stand one's burden / be unable to bear a burden // 가족을 부양하는 것은 그 소년에게는 과중한 ~이었다 Supporting his family was too heavy a burden for the boy. / The effort[attempt] to support his family was too much for the boy. // 그러면 너의 ~이 과중해진다 That would make the burden too heavy for you. **부담하다** bear; take upon oneself; shoulder (a burden); (일부를) share (in). ¶비용을 ~ bear[shoulder / stand] the expense // 손해를 ~ account for the loss incurred // 비용은 각자가 부담했다 Each bore a part of the expense. // 여행 비용은 누가 부담합니까 Who is to pay[bear / shoulder] the travel expenses? ➔¶**부담시키다** charge (expenses) to (a person) / make (a person) bear[pay] (the expenses).
● **부담액** an amount to be borne; one's share (in expenses); an allotment; a share.

부당(不當) [관형어적]. **부당하다** unjust; unfair; unreasonable; wrongful; improper; unwarrantable; [지나치다] excessive; unmerited; undue; undeserved; exorbitant. ¶부당한 요구 an excessive demand // 부당한 조치 an unfair dealing / an injustice // 부당한 값 an unreasonable price // 부당한 구금 unwarranted[illegal] detention // 부당한 이익을 취하다 make unfair profits // 부당한 짓을 하다 act unreasonably // 부당한 대우를 받다 be given an unfair treatment // 부당한 벌을 받다 receive an undeserved punishment // 죄 없는 아이를 꾸중하는 것은 ~ It is wrong [unjust] to scold an innocent child. **부당히** unreasonably; unjustly; unlawfully; lawlessly. ¶남을 ~ 대우하다 do a person wrong / do wrong to a person.
● **부당 거래** an unfair[unconscionable] bargain. **부당 이득** an undue[unreasonable / excessive] profit; [법] unjust enrichment. **부당 해고** [법] unfair[wrongful] dismissal.

부대(附帶) [관형어적] incidental; attendant; collateral; accessory. **부대하다** accompany; be incidental[accessory / appendant] to; be attached[annexed] to. ➔¶부동산의 소유에 부대되는 권리와 의무 the rights and duties incident(al) to owning real estate.
● **부대 비용** incidental expenses. **부대사업** a subsidiary enterprise. **부대 상황** collateral [attendant] circumstances. **부대조건** a collateral[incidental] condition. ¶~이 없는 (원조) (aid) with no strings attached / no-strings-attached (aid) // ~이 있는 (원조) (aid) with strings attached.

부대(負袋) a (burlap) bag; a (gunny) sack; a bale. ¶밀가루 한 ~ a sack of flour // ~에 담다 put into a sack / sack.

부대(部隊) 1 a (military) unit; a corps (단수·복수 동형); (구어) an outfit; a party; a detachment(파견대); a squad(분대); troops. ¶보병의 대[소] ~ a large[small] infantry unit // 기갑 ~ armored troops // [미] forces] / an armored unit[column] // 기계화 ~ a mechanized unit // 기동 ~ mobile troops / a task force // 전투 ~ a fighting unit // 지상 ~ ground troops // 후방 ~ rear guards // (전함의) 전열 ~ a fighting squadron // 외인 ~ a foreign legion. 2 [행동을 함께 하는 일단] a corps (단수·복수 동형); [집단] a group.
● **부대장** the commanding officer(약어 C.O.); a commander.

부대끼다 1 [시달리다] be pestered (by); be harassed (by / with); be annoyed (by). ¶빚쟁이에게 ~ be worried by creditors // 만원 버스에서 ~ be violently jostled in a crowded bus // 아이한테 부대끼어 장난감을 사 주다 be pestered by one's child to buy a toy for him. 2 [괴로움을 당하다] suffer (from); be troubled (with); be afflicted (with). ¶속이 ~ feel uncomfortable with one's stomach loaded with heavy food // 더위에 ~ suffer greatly from the heat // 나는 자주 복통으로 부대낀다 I am often troubled with stomach ache. / I suffer from frequent stomachache.

부대하다(富大-) fat; corpulent; plump; obese; (미) fleshy; stout.

부덕(不德) [덕이 없음] (a) lack[want] of virtue; unworthiness. **부덕하다** short of virtue; unworthy; (서술적) lack virtue. ¶그는 모든 것이 자신이 이런 소치라고 체념했다 Blaming only himself, he resigned himself to it. // 모두 저의 부덕한 소치입니다 I am solely to blame for it. / All is due to my lack of discretion.

부덕(婦德) womanly [female] virtues. ¶~의 귀감 a model [mirror / paragon] of female virtues [womanhood] // ~을 쌓다 cultivate womanly [female] virtues // ~을 갖추다 possess [be invested with] female virtues.

부도(不渡) dishonor; nonpayment.
● **부도 수표** a dishonored [bad] check; (속어) a rubber check. ¶~를 **남발하다** pass a bad check. **부도 어음** a dishonored [bad] bill. ¶~을 **발행하다** draw a dishonored bill / pass a bad draft.

부도(附圖) an appended [attached] chart [map / diagram].

부도(婦道) womanhood; the duty of a woman.

부도나다(不渡-) be dishonored. ¶그의 수표가 부도났다 His check was dishonored [bounced].

부도내다(不渡-) dishonor [fail to pay] a bill [check]. ¶부도내지 않다 manage to honor a bill [check] // 우리는 사업이 잘 안 되어 어음을 부도냈다 Our business has collapsed to the point where we have dishonored a bill.

부도덕(不道德) (an) immorality; lack of morality; bad morals; vice. **부도덕하다** immoral; unvirtuous; wicked; vicious; dissolute; licentious; depraved; profligate. ¶부도덕한 행위 an immoral conduct // 부도덕한 사람 a man lost to virtue / a reprobate / an unprincipled person // 부도덕한 짓을 하다 act immorally / commit an immoral act / be guilty of immorality // 부도덕하기 짝이 없다 It is a flagrant breach of morality.

부도체(不導體) [물] a nonconductor; a nonconducting substance. ¶열[전기]의 ~ a nonconductor of heat [electricity].

부동(不動) immovability; firmness; stability; immobility. ¶~의 immovable / firm / stable / immobile // ~의 결의 immobile resolution // ~의 신념 firm belief // ~의 지위 an indisputable [unshakable] position // 우리 방침은 ~이다 Our policy remains unshakable. // 송씨는 작가로서 ~의 명성을 유지하고 있다 As a writer Mr Song's reputation is unassailable.
● **부동산** real [fixed / immovable] property [estate]; immovables; realty; a landed estate. ¶~을 **매매하다** deal in real estate // 그는 3억 원 상당의 ~을 갖고 있다 He holds three hundred million won in real estate. / He has real property worth three hundred million won. // 그는 부모에게서 많은 ~을 물려받았다 He inherited from his parents extensive real estate holdings. **부동산 거래** a real estate transaction. **부동산 등기** real estate registration. **부동산 중개업자** a realty dealer; (미) a realtor; a real estate agent [broker]. **부동산 투기** speculative investment in real estate. **부동자세** an immobile posture; [군] the position at attention. ¶군인들은 ~를 취했다 The soldiers came to [stood at] attention.

부동(浮動) [유동] floating; [변동] fluctuation. **부동하다** float (in the air); be afloat; (냄새 등이) waft; be wafted; (시세 등이) fluctuate. ¶부동하는 floating / fluctuating / unsettled / unsteady // 부동하는 물가 fluctuating prices.
● **부동표** a floating vote; a swing vote. ¶그는 ~ 획득에 애를 썼다 He tried hard to attract floating votes.

부동액(不凍液) an antifreezing solution.

부동하다(不同-) lacking in uniformity; unequal; uneven; dissimilar; irregular; diverse. ¶표리가 부동한 double-dealing / double-faced / treacherous / unfaithful / dishonest // 표리가 부동한 성격 a disingenuous character // (행동에서) 표리가 ~ carry two faces under one hood / play a double game.

부동항(不凍港) an ice-free port; a nonfreezing port.

부두(埠頭) a wharf (pl. wharves, ~s); a quay; a pier; a jetty. ¶(배가) ~를 **떠나다** move away from the quayside // ~에 배를 대다 bring [moor] (steamer) alongside the quay // 그녀는 인천 ~에서 그를 만났다 She met him on the wharf at Incheon.
● **부두 노동자** a stevedore; a longshoreman; a wharf man; a dock laborer. **부둣가** the wharfside; the quayside.

부둥켜안다 embrace; hug; give (a person) a hug. ¶어머니는 자식을 꼭 부둥켜안았다 The mother embraced [hugged] her child tightly. // 나는 아기를 품 안에 부둥켜안았다 I clasped [held] the baby in my arms. // 자매는 서로 부둥켜안았다 The sisters embraced [hugged] each other. // 둘은 부둥켜안고 울었다 The two threw themselves into each other's arms and wept. / They wept in each other's arms.

부드드하다 grasping; stingy; niggardly.

부드득 with a grinding [grating / creaking] sound. **부드득하다** grind; grate. ⇨ **부드득거리다**

부드득거리다 grind; grate; grit; creak. ¶이를 부드득거리며 갈다 grind [grate / grit / gnash] one's teeth.

부드럽다 1 (촉감이) soft; tender; (빛 등이) mellow; subdued; gentle. ¶부드럽게 softly / tenderly // 부드러운 가죽 soft [pliable] leather // 어린이의 부드러운 손발 the supple limbs of a child // 부드러운 햇살 soft sunlight / soft [gentle] rays of the sun // 비단처럼 부드러운 살결 skin soft as silk // 감촉이 ~ feel soft / be soft to the touch // 바람이 부드럽게 불고 있다 The wind is blowing softly [gently]. // 불에 쬐니 고무가 부드러워졌다 Heat softened the rubber. // 엷은 빛이 요란한 벽 색깔을 부드럽게 하고 있었다 A faint light softened [toned down] the gay color of the walls. // 나는 가구 색은 부드러운 것이 좋습니다 I like furniture in mellow [soft] colors. // 부드러운 햇빛이 나무 위에 비치고 있었다 Soft [Mild] sunshine was showering on the trees.
2 (성질·태도가) gentle; tender; soft; mild (mannered); suave; smooth; meek. ¶부드러운 미소 a gentle [soft] smile // 부드러운 태도로 in a gentle manner / with a friendly [domestic] attitude // 부드럽게 softly / gently / mildly // 부드러운 목소리로 말하다 speak in a soft [gentle] voice // 마음씨가 ~ have a soft [tender] heart / be tender-[gentle-]hearted // 부드럽게 이야기하다 talk in easy terms / speak in a familiar tone // 그녀의 눈매는 ~ She has gentle eyes. // 그가 부드러운 태도로 나왔기 때문에 나는 맥이 빠졌다 His affability in manner and speech simply disarmed me. // 그의 완강한 태도가 부인의 간청으로 부드러워졌다 His obstinate attitude was softened by his wife's urging.

부드레하다 rather soft[tender]; very gently [mild / meek]; subdued.

부득부득 persistently; obstinately; stubbornly; doggedly; importunately; tenaciously. ¶~ 조르다 importune (a person for money) / ask (a person) importunately for (money) // ~ 우기다 persist in [stick to] one's opinion(s) // ~ 고집을 부리다 stick doggedly to one's idea.

부득불(不得不) [하지 않을 수 없이] unavoidably; inevitably; necessarily; (out) of necessity; from necessity; under compulsion; [마지못해] reluctantly; against one's will. ¶~ …하다 be compelled [forced / obliged] to (do) / be hard put to it to (do) / be driven by dire [sheer] necessity to (do) // ~ 최후 수단을 쓰다 be driven [impelled] to extreme measure // 나는 ~ 단념하기로 했다 I reluctantly [unwillingly] decided to give up. // ~ 거짓말을 했다 I lied out of necessity. // ~ 그렇게 하지 않으면 안 되었다 Necessity obliged him to that action.

부득이(不得已) unavoidably; inevitably; of [from / out of] necessity; unwillingly. ¶만~ out of sheer necessity // 그녀는 ~ 상사의 지시에 따를 수밖에 없었다 She was forced [compelled] to obey her boss's instructions. // 그는 ~ 상대방의 제안에 동의했다 Unwilling [Reluctant] as he was, he had no choice but [he was obliged] to agree to the other party's proposal. **부득이하다** unavoidable; necessary; inevitable; obligatory; compelling; pressing; (서술적) can not be helped. ¶부득이한 사정으로 as a result of unavoidable [uncontrollable] circumstances / owing to circumstances beyond one's control // 사정이 부득이한 경우에는 in an unavoidable case / if necessary / when circumstances compel [require] it // 부득이한 경우가 아니면 나는 가지 않겠다 Unless absolutely compelled [compelled by absolute necessity], I will not go. // 나는 부득이한 용무가 있어서 갈 수 없었다 I had unavoidable business and couldn't go. // 부득이한 이유 외에는 그것이 허용되지 않습니다 It is not permitted unless there is a compelling [an imperative] reason. // 어느 정도의 손실은 부득이했다 Some losses could not be helped [avoided]. // 부득이한 사정으로 갈 수 없었다 Unavoidable circumstances prevented me from going.

부들부들 [몸을 떠는 모양] tremblingly; quiveringly; shiveringly. ¶~ 떨다 tremble all over [like an aspen leaf] / shiver like a jelly / flutter // 그는 공포[분노]로 ~ 떨고 있었다 He was trembling with fear [anger]. // 나는 추위로 ~ 떨고 있었다 I was shivering with cold. // 그는 술을 너무 마셔 손을 ~ 떤다 His hands tremble from over-drinking. // 그는 입술을 ~ 떨면서 그녀에게 나가라고 말했다 With quivering lips he ordered her to leave. // 나는 손이 ~ 떨려 제대로 쓸 수 없었다 My hands were shaking so badly that I could not write well.

부들부들하다 very soft. ⇨보들보들하다
부듯하다 tight; brimful. ⇨"뿌듯하다
부등변 삼각형(不等邊三角形) a scalene (triangle); an inequilateral triangle.
부등식(不等式) [수] an (expression) of inequality.

부등하다(不等—) unequal; incongruent.
부등호(不等號) [수] an inequality sign.
부디 [꼭] by all means; without fail; at any cost; at all costs; in any case; [바라건대] (if you) please; pray; kindly; I beg. ¶~ …해 주십시오 have the goodness to (do) // ~ 한번 들러 주십시오 Please drop in by all means. / Do come and see us. // ~ 알려 주십시오 Please let me know. // ~ 행복하게 사십시오 I wish you will live a happy life. / I wish you every happiness. / God bless you! // ~ 부모님께 안부 전해 주십시오 Please give my best regards [remember me] to your parents. // ~ 그렇게 해 주십시오 I hope you will do so.

부딪다 strike; hit. ⇨"부딪치다1
부딪뜨리다 crash [smash / bump] (into / against / together); knock (against); dash (against). ¶몸을 문에 ~ dash [throw] oneself against the door // 그는 머리를 기둥에 부딪뜨렸다 He knocked [bumped] his head against the post. // 술 취한 사람이 자동차를 가로수에 부딪뜨렸다 A drunk ran [rammed] his car into a roadside tree.

부딪치다 1 [맞다] strike; hit; [충돌하다] run against [into]; collide with; run foul of (배가); crash into [against / together]; knock [bump / dash / strike / butt] against. ¶남과 ~ bump into a person // 파도가 바위에 부딪치고 있다 The waves are dashing against the rocks. // 그는 차를 전신주에 부딪쳤다 He bumped his car into a telephone pole.
2 [해 보다] try; risk; chance; [담판하다] negotiate directly with. ¶운을 하늘에 맡기고 부딪쳐 보다 run [take] a risk [chance] / chance [risk] it // 직접 부딪쳐 보자 Let's go and see for ourselves. / (되든 안 되든) 부딪쳐 봐라 Take your chance. / Make an attempt anyhow. // 그를 좋아한다면 한번 부딪쳐 보지 그래 If you like him, why don't you have a go at him [let him know]?

부딪히다 1 [부딪음을 당하다] be bumped [crashed] into; be bumped [run] against; be collided with. ¶자동차에 ~ be run over [knocked down] by a car / be hit by a car // (자동차 등이) 열차에 ~ run [smash] into a train // 나는 머리를 벽에 부딪혔다 I bumped [struck / knocked] my head against the wall. // 나는 이마를 쾅 부딪혔다 I bumped my forehead hard. // 배가 바위에 부딪혔다 A boat was dashed against a rock.
2 [직면하다] face; face up to; be confronted by. ¶난관에 ~ face [run up against] a difficulty / be confronted by a difficulty // 우리는 뜻하지 않은 어려움에 부딪혔다 We met [ran into] unforeseen difficulties. // 교섭은 마침내 벽에 부딪혔다 The negotiations finally came to a deadlock [standstill]. / The negotiations finally reached an impasse. / 그의 이론은 벽에 부딪혔다 His theory led him to a dead end. // 그 회사는 마침내 벽에 부딪혔다 The enterprise finally ran up against a brick wall.

부뚜막 a cooking fireplace; a kitchen range; cooking range.
부뚜막의 소금도 집어넣어야 짜다(속담) No pains, no gains.; Nothing ventured, nothing gained.; No mill, no meal.
부라리다 glare (at); scowl (at); frown (at); look sharply; look angrily [fiercely]. ¶눈을

look with glaring eyes.//그는 눈을 부라리고 나를 노려보았다 He shot an angry look at me. / He glared angrily at me.//그는 그녀에게 눈을 부라렸다 He glared[stared] at her.//그가 눈을 부라리면 모두는 찍소리 못한다 They shrink beneath his withering glance.

부락(部落) a village(마을); a (village) community(공동체로서의); a hamlet(작은 마을); a settlement. ¶농촌 ~ a farming settlement // ~ 단위로 with a village as a unit.
● **부락민** people of the (village) community; village folk; villagers.

부란(孵卵) incubation; hatching. **부란하다** hatch (out) (an egg); incubate.
● **부란기**(-器) an incubator; an incubator house; a hatcher. ¶~로 알을 까다 hatch eggs in an incubator.

부랑(浮浪) vagrancy; wandering; vagabondage. **부랑하다** wander[stray] about; vagabondize; tramp; roam; lead a vagrant [hobo] life.
● **부랑배** roughnecks; toughs; hoodlums; hooligans; the scum of the street; a vagrant tribe. **부랑아** a juvenile vagrant; a waif; a guttersnipe; a street Arab. **부랑자** a vagabond; a loafer; a tramp; (미국 속어) a hobo; a bum; (속어) a vag;《미국 속어》a gold brick.

부랴부랴 in haste; in a hurry; hurriedly; hastily. ¶~ 떠나다 make a hurried departure// ~ 상경하다 hurry up to Seoul without a moment's delay// ~ 기차에 타다[내리다] hurry on[off] a train// 일을 ~ 해치우다 hurry through one's work//나는 ~ 병원으로 달려갔다 I dropped everything and rushed to the hospital. / I immediately hastened to the hospital.//그는 ~ 상경했다 He hurried to Seoul.//손님이 온다고 해서 ~ 청소를 했다 Because guests were coming we did the cleaning in a fluster.//그 소식을 듣고 그녀는 ~ 귀국길에 올랐다 Receiving the news, she speeded homeward from abroad.

부러 purposely; on purpose; deliberately; intentionally; knowingly(알면서).

부러뜨리다 break (off); snap(딱 소리를 내며); fracture(뼈를). ¶나뭇가지를 ~ break off a branch / break a branch off a tree//목을 ~ break one's neck//이를 하나 ~ have a tooth knocked out//막대기를 딱 하고 ~ snap a stick / break a stick with a snap//무릎에 대고 ~ break (a stick) across one's knee//나는 오른팔을 부러뜨렸다 I broke my right arm.

부러워하다 envy; be envious[jealous] of; feel envy of. ¶남의 성공을 ~ be[feel] envious of another's success / envy a person his success//~ 눈시로 ~ (구어) to green with envy//부러워하지 않다 (구어) feel no envy (at)//그는 친구의 승진을 부러워하고 있다 He envies his friend his promotion. / He is envious[jealous] of his friend for being promoted.//그는 학교 성적이 좋아서 반 친구들이 그를 부러워하고 있다 He is envied by his classmates for his good school record. / He is the envy of his classmates because of his good school record.//그는 결코 부자를 부러워하지 않는다 He is never envious of the people for their wealth.//그때위 지위는 부러워할 것이 못 된다 Such a position is not to be envied.//우리 아버지의 직업은 모두가 부러워할 만한 것이다 My father's job is an enviable one. / Everyone is envious of my father's job.

부러지다 break; be[get] broken; give way; snap(딱 하고); fracture(뼈가). ¶잘 부러지지 않는 막대기 a tough stick//한가운데가 똑 ~ break in half//노가 딱 하고 부러졌다 The oar broke with a snap.//그는 말에서 떨어져 팔이 부러졌다 A fall from the horse resulted in a broken arm. / He fell off his horse and broke his arm.//이 쇠는 잘 부러진다 This lead is easy to break. / This lead breaks easily.//태풍으로 많은 소나무가 부러졌다 Many pine trees were snapped[broken] off by the typhoon.

부럼 a *bureom*; [민] nuts eaten on the 15th of January of the lunar calendar (to guard oneself against boils for a year).

부럽다 enviable. ¶부러운 듯이 enviously / with envy / with envious eyes//부럽지 않다 be not to be envied / be unenviable//네가 부럽구나 How I envy you!//나는 그의 성공이 부러웠다 I envied (him)[I was envious of] his success. / I was filled with envy at his success.//나는 그의 행운도 부럽지 않았다 I felt no envy at his good luck. / His good luck aroused[excited] no envy in me.//참 부러운 지위에 계십니다 You are really in an enviable position.

부레 1 (물고기의) an air bladder; a fish bladder; a (gas) bladder; a float. 2 fig. made from air bladders. ⇨부레풀(⇨부레)
● **부레풀** glue made from air bladders; fish glue; isinglass.

부력(浮力)〔물〕 buoyancy; buoyance; floatage; buoyant force; (비행선의) lifting power; lift. ¶~이 있는 buoyant//~의 중심 the center of buoyancy.

부령(部令) a ministerial ordinance; an order [a decree] from a government ministry.

부록(附錄) a supplement; an appendix (pl. -dixes, -dices); extra; an addendum (pl. -da); a postscript(발문). ¶잡지의 ~ a supplement[an appendix] to a magazine// 별책 ~ a separate booklet appended to a magazine// ~을 붙이다 add an appendix to (a book) / append a supplement//그 잡지의 가을 ~은 꽤 재미있다 The autumn extra to that magazine is highly interesting.

부루퉁하다 1 (부어서) swollen; bloated; bulging; dropsical. ¶얼굴이 ~ have a swollen[bloated] face. 2 (불만스러워서) sullen; sulky; cross; mumpish; peevish; sour; pouty. ¶부루퉁한 얼굴 a sulky look [face] / a sullen look//부루퉁해 있다 be in the sulks[sullen] / look sulky[cross]//부루퉁하여 입을 비죽거리다 pout / thrust out the lips in displeasure[sullenness]//그는 부루퉁하니 말이 없었다 He kept a sullen silence.

부룩소 a small bull.

부류(部類) a class; a head(ing); a group; a category; an order; a division. ¶…의 ~에 들다 come [fall] under the head [group / heading / category] of …//…에 ~에 넣다 classify [group / catalogue] (a thing) with [as] …//다른[같은] ~에 속하다 belong in a different [the same] classification//이것은 산문시의 ~에 들어가야 한다 This should be classed under [be put in the category of] prose poems.//그의 노래는 민요 ~에 든다

His song comes [falls] under the head [heading] of folk music.

부르다[1] **1** [소리 내다] call; call out (to); hail; call after(뒤에서); invoke(신(神)을). ¶부르면 들리는 곳에 within call [hail / earshot] // 불러도 들리지 않는 곳에 out of call [hail] // 야성이 부르는 소리 the call of the wild // 남의 이름을 ~ call a person by name // 택시를 ~ hail a taxi // 큰 소리로 ~ shout out to (a person) // 나는 "이봐!" 하고 불렀다 "Hey!" I called. // 뒤에서 누가 나를 부르는지 뒤돌아보았다 I looked back as someone called me from behind.
2 [오게 하다] call (a person) to one; summon; (사람을 보내어) send for [after]; call in; (연예인 등을) engage; hire. ¶전화로 ~ telephone for (a person) // 전문가를 ~ engage the service of an expert // 종을 울려 하인을 ~ ring for the servant // 손뼉을 쳐서 ~ clap one's hands for (a servant) // 손짓하여 ~ beckon with the hand / wave (a person) on to [into] (a place) // 머리맡으로 ~ call (a person) to one's bedside // 다시 ~ recall / call back // 부르러 가다 go for / go to fetch / 불러 모으다 call [gather] together / assemble / summon (together) // 전화로 택시를 불러 주시오 Please ring for [call] a taxi. / Would you telephone a taxi, please? // 사장님께서 부르십니다 The president wants [needs] you. // 의사를 부를까요 Shall I call you a doctor? / Shall I call a doctor for you?
3 [청하다] invite; ask; [끌어들이다] attract; draw over. ¶잔치에 손님을 ~ invite guests to a feast // 저녁 식사에 ~ invite (a person) to dinner // 손님을 ~ (식당 등에서) attract customers / draw custom // 저녁 식사에 스미스 씨 내외를 불렀다 We are having [inviting] the Smiths over for supper.
4 [일컫다] call; name; christen; style; term; designate. ¶…이라고 ~ call (it) ... / give (it) the name of // 악당이라고 ~ call (a person) a rascal // 그 아이를 존이라고 ~ call the boy John // 이것을 남대문이라고 부른다 This is called Namdaemun(the South Gate). // 그를 선동자라고 부르는 것은 부당하다 It is unjust to label him as an agitator.
5 [값을 말하다] quote; (경매에서) bid (for an article); make a bid (for). ¶부르는 값 the (first) price asked [named] // 값을 ~ make [give] a price // 비싼 [싼] 값을 ~ quote a high [low] price (on a house) // 집 값을 ~ ask a high [low] price (for a house) // 5달러를 ~ be quoted at $5 // 부르는 값에 사다 buy (an article) at the first price asked // 값을 싸게 ~ bid [name] a low price // 얼마를 불렀습니까 How much did you bid for it?
6 [외치다] cry; shout. ¶만세를 ~ cry "Hurrah!" / give (three) cheers.
7 [노래하다] sing; chant; recite; carol. ¶노래를 ~ sing a song // 피아노에 맞추어 노래를 ~ sing to the piano // 노래를 부르기 시작하다 break [burst] into song.
부르는 게[것이] 값이다 (the article) be beyond pricing; be above [beyond / without] price.

부르다[2] **1** (배가) full; satisfied. ¶배가 부르게 먹다 eat heartily / eat one's fill / eat to one's heart's contents / have a hearty meal // 이젠 배가 부릅니다 I have my stomach full. / I've a full stomach. / I have had enough. / I'm (so) full. // 보기만 해도 배가 ~ Just a look at it is enough to make me feel satisfied. // 생선과 고기를 배가 부르게 먹고 우리는 잘 잤다 We slept soundly after eating [having] our fill of fish and meat. // 나는 배가 부르게 먹으면 공부가 잘되지 않는다 I can't study well on a full stomach. // 배가 부르자마자 졸음이 왔다 As soon as I got full, I felt sleepy.
2 (임신하여) pregnant; big with (child). ¶배가 잔뜩 부른 암소 a cow big with calf // 그녀는 배가 ~ She is expecting a baby. / She is pregnant [in the family way].
3 (항아리 등이) bulgy; swollen; bulging. ¶배가 부른 항아리 a big-bellied jar // 그 통은 배가 ~ The barrel swells in the middle.

부르르 seething; in hot blood; in a (sudden) burst of flame; trembling. ⇨바르르

부르릉 with a burr; roaring.

부르릉거리다 burr; roar; make a whirring sound. ¶프로펠러의 부르릉거리는 소리 the burr of a propeller // 오토바이의 부르릉거리는 소리 the 'jug-jug-spat' of a motorcycle // 액셀러레이터를 밟아 엔진을 마구 부르릉거리게 하다 press on the accelerator, savagely roaring the engine // 프로펠러 비행기는 부르릉거리는 소리를 내며 이륙하였다 The prop plane roared and took off.

부르주아 [중산 시민] a bourgeois (pl. ~); a man of means; [집합적] the bourgeoisie; [유산 계급] the moneyed [propertied] class(es). ¶그녀는 ~ 출신이다 She is [comes] from a bourgeois family. // 그것이 소위 ~ 근성이라는 것이다 That is what we call the bourgeois mentality.

부르쥐다 [(주먹을) 힘들이어 쥐다] tighten [clench / double] (one's fists). ¶주먹을 ~ clench [double up] one's fist // 그는 두 주먹을 부르쥐고 싸울 자세를 취했다 He stood up, ready to fight, with his hands closed in a tense fist.

부르짖다 **1** [소리치다] cry; shout; shriek; let out a yell; exclaim; ejaculate; scream; utter [give] a cry. ¶큰 소리로 ~ cry [call] out // 성나서 ~ shout [roar] with rage // 목이 쉬도록 ~ shout oneself hoarse // 이구동성으로 ~ shout as with one voice // 사람 살리라고 ~ cry [call out / scream] for help // "불이야!" 하고 ~ shout "Fire!"
2 (사회에 대해서) cry (for); clamor (for); advocate; set forth. ¶개혁을 ~ cry (loudly) for reform // 임금 인상을 ~ cry for a raise in pay / clamor for higher wages // 남북통일을 ~ cry out for the unification of Korea // 산아 제한을 ~ advocate birth control // 평화 [주전론(主戰論)]를 ~ advocate peace [war].

부르트다 blister; rise in blisters; form vesicles [blebs] (on); get [have] a blister (on). ¶발바닥이 ~ get [have] a blister [blisters] on (one's) foot // 새 구두를 신어서 발뒤꿈치가 부르텄다 My new shoes have made blisters on my heels.

부름 a summons; a call. ¶~에 응하여 in response to the call [summons].

부릅뜨다 (눈을) make (one's eyes) glare; glare fiercely; goggle. ¶눈을 부릅뜨고 with one's eyes wide open // 눈을 ~ look with glaring eyes (at) / stare with bulging eyes (at) // 그는 눈을 부릅뜨고 나를 노려보았다 He glared at [on / upon] me with hot angry eyes.

부리 1 [새의 주둥이] a bill; (특히 갈고랑이 모양의) a beak. **2** [물건의 뾰족한 끝] the tip; the end; the nozzle (of a hose). ¶발~ the tips of the toes // 총~ the muzzle (of a gun).

부리나케 hurriedly; in a (great) hurry; in (great) haste; hastily; speedily; at great speed; with flying feet. ¶~ 가다 hurry (to) / rush (to) / hotfoot (it) // ~ 도망가다 flee in all haste.

부리다[1] **1** (사람·동물을) manage; handle; use; keep; employ. ¶사자 부리는 사람 a lion tamer // 하인을 ~ keep a servant / work a servant // 말을 부릴 줄 알다 know how to manage a horse // 사람을 소나 말처럼 ~ work[drive] a person hard like a beast of burden / make a person drudge // 사람을 몹시 ~ work one's men hard / sweat one's employees // 그 공장에서는 6백 명의 직공을 부리고 있다 The plant gives employment to 600 hands. / Six hundred hands are employed by[in] the plant. // 그는 내 마음대로 부릴 수 있다 He is at my beck and call. // 그는 부하를 잘 부릴 줄 안다 He is good at handling[managing] his men.
2 (기계를) manage; work; operate; handle; control. ¶기계를 ~ handle[operate] a machine // 자동차를 ~ drive a car.
3 (꾀·재주 등을) play; practice; do. ¶마술을 ~ juggle / do conjuring tricks // 재주를 ~ exercise one's talent / perform a trick.
4 [행사하다] wield; exercise; [일부러 하다] do (a thing) intentionally. ¶욕심을 ~ be greedy[(문어) avaricious] // 허세를 ~ make a display[show] // 소년은 끝까지 고집을 부렸다 The boy remained obstinate to the last. // 그는 추태를 부렸다 He acted the fool [made a fool of himself].

부려 먹다 work (a person) hard[like a horse]; drive (a person) hard; keep (a person) trotting[on the trot]; keep[hold / put] another's nose[face] to the grindstone; have (a person) at one's beck (and call). ¶부려 먹는 사람[주인] a hard taskmaster [master] // 싼 임금으로 ~ underpay and sweat one's workers // 남을 제 마음대로 ~ have a person at one's beck (and call) / turn a person round one's (little) finger // 사주가 그들을 호되게 부려 먹었다 The boss drove them hard. / Their boss worked them very hard. // 그는 사람을 너무 부려 먹는다 He works his men hard. / He's hard[rough] on his men. / He is a hard taskmaster. / (구어) He's a slave driver.

부리다[2] [실었던 짐을 풀어 내려놓다] unload [discharge] (a ship / cargo from a ship); unburden. ¶트럭에서 짐을 ~ unload a truck / unload goods from a truck // 육지에 ~ land (cargo) // 그 배는 짐을 부리고 있다 The ship is unloading.

부리부리하다 big and bright; flaring. ¶부리부리한 눈 big bright eyes / big eyes full of fire.

부마(도위) (駙馬都尉) a son-in-law of the king.

부모(父母) [양친] parents. ¶~의 parental // ~가 없는 parentless / orphaned // ~의 사랑 [위엄] parental love [authority] // ~ 없는 아이 a parentless child / an orphan // ~와 교사의 모임 the Parent-Teacher Association (약어 P.T.A., PTA) // ~를 잃다 lose one's parents // ~를 부양하다 support one's parents // ~ 슬하에서 살다 live with one's parents // ~를 박대하다 ill-treat one's parents // 그의 ~가 누구인지 모른다 His parentage is unknown. // 자식에게 이런 짓을 하게 하는 ~가 어떻게 생겼는지 보고 싶다 I want to know what kind of parents allow their children to do such a thing. // ~에게 효도해야 한다 You should be respectful toward parents. // 그녀는 어려서 ~를 여의었다 She lost her parents early in her life.
부모가 자식을 겉 낳았지 속 낳았나 (속담) It is a wise father that knows his own child.
● **부모 형제** one's parents, brothers and sisters; one's nearest relatives; the next of kin.

부목(副木) [의] a splint. ¶~을 대다 splint (an arm) / apply a splint (to an arm).

부문(部門) [분류] a class; [범주] a category; [구분] a section; a department; [방면] a branch; a field. ¶생활의 모든 ~ every phase of life // 이 작품은 전기 ~에 속한다 This work falls[comes] under the heading [falls in the category] of biography. // 이 학문은 세 ~으로 나누어진다 This field of study is divided into three areas. // 업계의 여러 ~에서 최고위급 인사들이 모였다 The top people assembled from various branches[fields] of industry.

부복(俯伏) prostration. **부복하다** prostrate oneself (before); lie prostrate (before); fall prostrate[flat] (on the ground).

부본(副本) [원본과 동일한 보관용 서류] a duplicate (copy); [사본] a copy; (어음·영수증 등에 붙은) (미) a stub; (영) a counterfoil. ¶이 서류의 정본과 ~ 두 통을 보관하시오 Keep the original document and a copy.

부부(夫婦) husband and wife; man and wife [woman]; a (married) couple; a (wedded) pair. ¶~의 conjugal // ~노~ an old couple // 젊은 ~ a young couple // 신혼 ~ a newly married couple / (미) the newlyweds // 강 씨 ~ Mr. Gang and his wife / Mr. and Mrs. Gang // 어울리는[어울리지 않는] ~ a well-[an ill-]matched pair[couple] // 맞벌이 ~ a couple working together for a living / a husband and wife who both have jobs // ~ 동반으로 with one's wife[husband] // ~가 화합하여 in connubial harmony // ~로서 지내다 share bed and board (with) // ~의 인연을 맺다 plight oneself[one's troth] (to) / contract a marriage (with) // 마치 ~처럼 행동하다 behave just like (a) husband and wife // 두 사람은 ~가 되었다 They became man and wife.
부부 싸움은 칼로 물 베기 (속담) Nothing is so unpalatable as a lover's quarrel.
● **부부 생활** married life; wedlock; cohabitation. ~을 하다 live a married life / share bed and board (with) / live together / cohabit. **부부 싸움** a quarrel[fight] between husband and wife; a marital quarrel. **부부애**(-愛) conjugal love.

부분(部分) a part; a portion; a section (▶ part 는 가장 일반적인 말, portion은 할당된 부분, section은 전체 중에서 다른 것과 다른 부분); a percentage. ¶~을 보고 전체를 미루어 알다 infer the whole from a part // 이것은 전체 가운데 작은 ~에 불과하다 It is only a small part[portion] of the whole. // 그 일화에는 꾸며 낸 ~이 있다 That anecdote is partly ficti-

부빙

tious[made-up]. / Part of the anecdote is fictitious.// 이 집의 한 ~은 나무로, 다른 한 ~은 돌로 되어 있다 This house is built partly of wood and partly of stone.// 이 이야기는 세 ~으로 나뉘어 있다 This story is divided into three sections[parts].// 이 작품은 ~적으로만 뛰어나다 This work is superior only in parts.
● **부분 부정** [논] partial negation. **부분 압력** [물] partial pressure. **부분 월식** [천] a partial lunar eclipse. **부분 일식** [천] a partial solar eclipse. **부분 집합** [수] a subset. ¶A는 B의 ~이다 A is a subset of B. / A is contained in B.

부빙(浮氷) [떠다니는 얼음덩이] drift[floating] ice; a[an ice] floe(평원 같은); an ice pack(극지의 부빙군); pack ice(총빙(叢氷)).

부사(副詞) [언] an adverb. ¶~의 adverbial / 양태의 ~ an adverb of manner.
● **부사구**[절] an adverbial[adverb] phrase [clause].

부사관(副士官) (주로 육군) a noncommissioned officer; (해군) a petty officer.

부사장(副社長) a vice-president.

부산물(副産物) a by-product; an outgrowth. ¶학습의 즐거움은 교육의 매우 중요한 ~이다 Pleasure is a very important by-product of education.

부산하다 1 [바쁘다] (noisily) busy; restless; bustling. ¶부산한 거리 a bustling[busy] street // 늘 부산한 사람 a restless person / a bustler // 일로 ~ bustle (up) with one's work. **부산히** restlessly; bustlingly. ¶~ 돌아다니다 bustle about // 그는 ~ 카메라로 사진을 찍고 있었다 He was busy with his camera. 2 [떠들썩하다] noisy; boisterous; clamorous; (서술적) be in a bustle. **부산히** boisterously; noisily; clamorously; bustlingly. ¶~ 굴다 be noisy[boisterous] / make [kick up] a shine.

부삽 a fire shovel; (영) a fire pan.

부상(負傷) an injury; a wound (▶ injury는 사고 등에 의한 부상, wound는 구타나 칼에 의한 부상 등을 말함); a cut(벤 상처); a bruise(타박상). ¶가벼운 ~ a slight injury // 심한 ~ a serious injury[wound] // 아버지는 공습 때의 ~으로 돌아가셨다 My father died from a wound received during the air raid. **부상하다** get[be] injured; be wounded; get hurt; hurt oneself. ¶그는 교통사고로 오른쪽 어깨에 부상했다 His right shoulder was injured[hurt] in the traffic accident.
● **부상자**[병] a wounded[an injured] person [soldier]; (집합적) the wounded; the injured.

부상(副賞) a supplementary prize.

부상하다(浮上―) 1 [물 위로 떠오르다] rise (to the surface); surface(잠수함이). ¶잠수함이 부산 먼 바다에 부상했다 A submarine surfaced off the coast of Busan. 2 [갑자기 유명한 처지로 올라서다] leap into (fame). ¶무명이었던 사진가 일약 제일선으로 부상했다 An unknown cameraman suddenly leaped into prominence.

부서(部署) one's post; one's station; one's place of duty. ¶자기 ~로 가다 take up one's post[station] / (승무원이) take up one's quarters // ~를 지키다 remain at one's post [station] // ~로 To stations!

부서(副署) countersignature. **부서하다** countersign.

부서지다 break; be broken; crack; be cracked; smash; be smashed; pulverize; [파손되다] be destroyed; break[come] down; go out of repair(집 등이). ¶부서진 broken / destroyed / damaged // 부서지기 쉬운 easily breaking / easy to break / brittle / fragile / frail / delicate // 부서지기 쉬운 물건 a fragile article // 그것은 부서지기 쉽다 It breaks easily. / It is fragile.// 그의 차는 충돌해서 엉망으로 부서졌다 His car was badly smashed up[(미)] was totaled] in the crash.// 지진으로 많은 집들이 부서졌다 Many houses were destroyed[demolished] by the earthquake. // 파도가 바위에 부서지고 있었다 The waves were breaking on the rocks.// 유리그릇이 바닥에 떨어져 산산이 부서졌다 The glass container fell to the floor and broke into (little) pieces.// 자동차는 금방이라도 부서질 듯이 삐걱거렸다 The car was rattling as though it might come apart at any moment.// 그녀의 꿈은 산산이 부서졌다 Her dreams were shattered.// 소년의 꿈은 산산이 부서졌다 The boy's dream was shattered.

부석(浮石) [광] a pumice stone; a floatstone.

부석부석하다 (slightly) swollen[bloated]. ¶얼굴이 ~ have a swollen[bloated] face // 그녀의 얼굴은 수면 부족으로 부석부석했다 Her face was puffy from lack of sleep.

부설(附設) attachment; annexation; adjunct. **부설하다** attach(annex(e)] (a thing to another). ¶대학에 연구소를 ~ establish a research institute attached to a university.
● **부설 기관** an auxiliary organ; an attached [affiliated] organization.

부설(敷設) [건설] construction; [설치함] laying. **부설하다** lay (down); build; construct. ¶철도를 ~ lay[build / construct] a railway // 해저 전선을 ~ lay a submarine cable // 부설하는 중이다 be under construction.

부성(父性) paternity; fatherhood; the father (in a person).
● **부성애** father's[paternal] love. ¶그는 차츰 차츰 ~에 눈떴다 The father gradually came into his heart.

부속(附屬) 1 [딸려서 붙음] attachment; affiliation; addendum. ¶~적인 adjunctive / incidental / subsidiary / subordinate / secondary // ~의 attached to / annexed to / affiliated to / belonging to / associated with / adjunctive / accessory / subordinate / incidental / dependent / appendant. **부속하다** be attached[annexed] to; belonging to; go with. 2 an accessory; fittings. ⇨ 부속품(⇨부속)
● **부속물** belongings; a thing attached (to); an appendage; an appurtenance; an accessory; an adjunct. ¶교실의 책상과 다른 ~ desks and other appurtenances of a classroom. **부속 병원** a hospital in affiliation. **부속품** an accessory; fittings; a gadget; appurtenances. ¶전기 청소기의 ~ attachments for a vacuum cleaner // 기계와 그 ~ a machine and its fittings.

부수(附隨) an accompaniment. **부수하다** be annexed (to); [수반하다] accompany; go with; follow; attend[be attendant] (on / upon); be collateral (with); be incident(al) (to); come in the train[wake] (of).

- **부수 서류** appended papers [documents]; annexes.
부수(部數) 〔책 등의 수효〕 the number of copies; 〔발행 부수〕 a circulation. ¶~가 많이 [적게] 나가다 sell in big [but in small] figures // ~에 제한이 있다 The number of copies [The edition] is limited. // 그 월간지는 발행 ~가 5만이다 The monthly (magazine) has a circulation of fifty thousand.
부수다 (산산이) break (into pieces); smash; crush(▶ 특히 smash는 세게 내던져서, crush 는 짓누르듯이 하여 부수다); 〔파괴하다〕 destroy; demolish; 〔파손하다〕 damage; (갈아서) grind up; (빻아서) pound. ¶흙덩이를 잘게 부수어 보드라운 흙으로 만들다 break up clods into fine soil // 장난감[창문]을 ~ break a toy [window] // 건물을 ~ (화재나 사고로) destroy a building / (새로 짓기 위해) pull [tear] down a building // 그는 일격에 그 값비싼 단지를 때려 부수었다 With one blow, he smashed [shattered / broke] the valuable vase into [into] pieces. // 그들은 미술품을 거칠게 다루어 부수었다 They damaged the art object by rough handling.
부수 식물(浮水植物) duckweeds; floating weeds.
부수입(副收入) (가외의) (a) side income; extra benefit; 〔음성 수입〕 a perquisite; 〔구어〕 a perk. ¶그는 그의 지위에서 여러 ~이 있다 He enjoys various benefits [perks] in his position. // 그는 월급 이외에 뭔가 ~이 있다 He has some income besides his salary.
부수적(附隨的) accompanying; attendant; 〔따르기 마련인〕 incidental. ¶~ 비용 incidental expenses.
부숭부숭하다 dry; dried up [out]. ⇨보송보송하다1
부스대다 stir [move] restlessly. ⇨바스대다
부스러기 broken pieces; fragments; scraps; ends; crumbs; chips; odds and ends. ¶고기 ~ scraps of meat // 나무 ~ chips of wood / wood chips // 빵 ~ bread crumbs.
부스러뜨리다 break (into pieces). ⇨바스르뜨리다
부스러지다 break; be broken. ⇨바스러지다1
부스럭 with a rustle [rustling sound]; faint(ly); indistinct(ly); stealthily; with a low [soft / muffled] sound. **부스럭하다** rustle. ⇨부스럭거리다
부스럭거리다 rustle; make a rustling sound.
부스럼 a swelling; 〔발진〕 a rash; 〔종기〕 a boil; 〔종양〕 a tumor [〔영〕 tumour]. ¶얼굴에 난 ~ a furuncle on the face // 이 나다 have a rash // 봄이 되면 ~이 잘 난다 My skin tends to break out when spring comes. / I often get a rash in springtime.
부스스 1 〔느리게 슬그머니〕 gently; slowly; quietly. ¶잠자리에서 ~ 일어나다 sit up slowly in one's bed. 2 〔머리털 등이 헝클어진 모양〕. **부스스하다** disheveled; unkempt; shaggy; untidy. ¶부스스한 얼굴 an unshaven face / a hairy face // 부스스한 머리 disheveled [unkempt] hair.
부슬부슬 gently; softly. ⇨보슬보슬
부슬비 a drizzling rain. ⇨보슬비
부시 (a) steel (for striking sparks from flint). **부시(를) 치다** strike fire [sparks] with [out of] flint (and steel); make sparks with steel on flint; strike a flint.
부시다[1] 〔씻다〕 rinse (out); wash (lightly); clean out. ¶부신 물 rinsings // 그릇을 ~ rinse (out) dishes // 물을 부어 ~ swill out (a dish).
부시다[2] (눈이) dazzling; glaring; blinding (flash) (전등) 의. ¶자동차의 헤드라이트에 눈이 ~ My eyes are blinded by the headlights. // 눈이 부셔서 뜰 수가 없다 The light is so bright that I cannot keep my eyes open. // 조명이 ~ The lights daggle me. // 강한 불빛에 눈이 ~ I am daggled by the bright light.
부시장(副市長) a deputy mayor.
부식(扶植) implantation. **부식하다** plant; implant; (확립하다) establish. ¶자기의 세력을 ~ establish [extend] one's influence // 그는 당원들 사이에 자기의 세력을 부식하려 했다 He tried to extend his influence over the party members.
부식(腐植) humus. ¶그 토양은 ~질(質)이 풍부하다 The soil is rich in humus.
- **부식토** humus (soil).
부식(腐蝕) corrosion; (주로 물이나 바람에 의한) erosion; 〔썩음〕 rot; decay; 〔녹〕 rust. ¶~성의 corrosive / erosive / 〔의〕 caustic // 내성의 corrosion-resistant (alloy) / anticorrosive. **부식하다** corrode; erode; eat (into); 〔녹슬다〕 rust [eat] away. ¶부식하지 않는 incorrodible / rustless // 함석 지붕이 부식하기 시작했다 The tin roof began to corrode. // 산류는 금속을 부식한다 Acids eats into metals.
- **부식 작용** corrosive [erosive] action; corrosion; erosion. **부식제** a corrosive (agent); a corroder; 〔의〕 a caustic.
부식(물)(副食物) a side dish; a subsidiary food [article of diet]; dishes other than staple food.
부신(副腎) 〔생〕 an adrenal gland; a (supra) renal gland (capsule); a suprarenal; adrenal / suprarenal. ¶~의 adrenocortical hormones / an adrenal cortex hormone.
- **부신 피질** the adrenal cortex. ¶~ 호르몬 adrenocortical hormones / an adrenal cortex hormone.
부실기업(不實企業) an insolvent enterprise; an improperly-run enterprise.
부실하다(不實-) 1 〔허약한〕 weak; delicate; infirm; sickly; feeble; 〔서술적〕 be not strong. ¶몸이 ~ be poor [delicate] in health / be in poor health / be weak. 2 〔부족하다〕 insufficient; wanting; lacking; deficient; short. ¶양식이 ~ be scant [short] of food // 볏섬이 ~ The sack of rice is a little short. 3 〔미덥지 못하다〕 unreliable; untrustworthy; undependable; shaky; shifty. ¶부실한 남편 [아내] an unfaithful [a faithless] husband [wife].
부심(副審) 〔축구·크리켓 등의〕 an assistant umpire; (권투·럭비 등의) an assistant judge.
부심하다(腐心-) take pains; be at pains (to do); tax one's ingenuity; rack one's brains; be bent [intent] on; think and think (about). ¶그는 아들의 교육에 부심하고 있다 He is taking great pains [a great deal of trouble] over his son's education. // 그는 어떻게든 주어진 임무를 다하려고 부심하고 있었다 He was anxious to accomplish what he was required to do.
부싯깃 tinder; touchwood; amadou.
부싯돌 (a) flint; (a) firestone. ¶~과 부시 (a) flint and steel.
부썩 stubbornly; resolutely. ⇨바싹6
부아 1 〔생〕 the lungs. ⇨=폐(肺) 2 〔분한 마음〕

부양 resentment; indignation; [화] anger; rage; passion; wrath. ¶부앗김에 in a fit of temper [anger] / borne away by anger // ~통이 터지다 burn[flash / be furious] with anger / be [get] red-hot (with anger) / flash crimson with anger // ~가 나다[돋다] be exasperated / be indignant (at / over) / be angry (with / at) / feel sore (at) // 그는 ~가 나서 참을 수가 없었다 He couldn't help his hackles rising.

부양(扶養) support; maintenance. **부양하다** keep up; support; maintain. ¶양친을 ~ support one's parents // 그는 대가족을 부양하고 있다 He has a large family to keep [support / provide for]. // 그는 가족을 부양할 의무가 있다 It is up to him to feed and clothe[provide for] his family. // 그는 부양할 네 명의 식구가 있다 He has a family of four to support.
● **부양가족** a (family) dependent; [딸린 식구] (family) ties; encumbrances; relatives and in-laws. ¶~이 5명 있다 have five people to support // 그는 ~이 없다 He has no dependents. / He is unencumbered by family ties. // 그는 ~이 많다 He has a large family. / He has many mouths to feed. // ~이 몇이냐 How many dependent do you have? **부양의무** the duty of supporting (one's family). **부양자** a supporter; a sustainer.

부양(浮揚) floating; flo(a)tage; flo(a)tation. **부양하다** float (off); be buoyant; (침몰선을) be refloated. ¶기구를 ~ release[send up] a balloon.
● **부양책** a pump-priming policy. ¶경기 침체에 대처하여 부분적 ~을 쓰다 take partial pump-priming measures to cope with the business slowdown.

부언(附言) a postscript(약어 P.S.); an additional remark. **부언하다** add (that); say in addition; make an additional remark. ¶편지에는 그가 내주에 온다고 부언하고 있었다 There was a postscript to the letter saying that he was coming to see me next week.

부업(副業) a side job; a by-job; a sideline; a side business; subsidiary work; an auxiliary [a minor / a sideline] occupation. ¶가내 ~ piecework done at home // ~으로 하는 수공업 handiwork one takes in on the side // ~으로 양계를 하고 있다 We raise poultry as a sideline. // 그는 민예품 제작을 ~으로 하고 있다 He is engaged in folk art to supplement his income. // 그는 ~으로 빌딩의 경비를 한다 He guards a building as an extra job. // 그는 번역을 ~으로 하고 있다 He takes on translation as a sideline. // 그는 낮에는 회사에서 일하고, 밤에는 바텐더를 ~으로 하고 있다 He works at a company by day and moonlights as a bartender.

부엉부엉 tu-whit(t); tu-whoo. ¶~ 울다 hoot / whoop / ululate.

부엉이 [동] a Korean scops owl; an owl. ¶~가 운다 The owl hoots.

부엌 a kitchen. ¶~과 거실을 겸한 방 a living room with a kitchen(ette) attached // ~과 식당을 겸한 방 a dining-kitchen / a (combination) kitchen-dinning room // 요리 교습용 간이 ~이 갖추어진 소형 트럭 a van with a kitchenette used for cooking lessons // ~에서 아낙네들이 분주히 일하고 있다 The women are working busily in and about the kitchen.
● **부엌데기** a kitchen maid. ⇨ˮ식모 **부엌살림** kitchen utensils[appliances]; (집합적) kitchenware; kitchen equipment. **부엌일** (do) kitchen work. ¶~을 하다 do scullery work. **부엌칼** a kitchen knife. ⇨ˮ식칼

부여(附與·賦與) 1 [가지거나 지니게 해 줌] grant; bestowal; allowance. **부여하다** give; (요청에 의해) grant; (권리 등을) invest. ¶권리[권력 / 재산]를 ~ vest rights[authority / property] in a person // 대학은 그에게 명예박사를 부여하였다 The university conferred [bestowed] an honorary doctorate on him. / The university gave him an honorary doctorate. → 그는 사장으로부터 대임을 부여받았다 He was assigned[given] a great responsibility by the president.
2 [나눠 줌] endowment. **부여하다** endow [gift] (a person) with; bless (a person) with; gird[endue] (a person) with(보통 수동태로 써서). ¶하늘이 부여한 재능 innate [natural / inborn] talent. → 그는 훌륭한 음악적 재능을 부여받았다 He was endowed [blessed] with splendid musical talent.

부여잡다 take[catch / grab / lay] hold of (a thing); (단단히) clutch; clutch hold of.

부역(附逆) complicity in treason. **부역하다** join[take the side of] the rebel army; take sides[a side] with the rebels.
● **부역자** a traitor; a betrayer.

부역(賦役) slave labor; compulsory[statute] labor; compulsory service; corvée. ¶~을 시키다 put (a person) to slave labor / press (a person) into service / exact statute labor [corvée] from (people).

부연(敷衍) expatiation; amplification; enlargement; dilatation. **부연하다** expatiate [dilate / enlarge / dwell / elaborate] on; amplify; extend; expand; develop. ¶이 문제에 대해서는 부연하지 않겠습니다 I will not go into[enlarge upon] this problem any further. // 부연해서 설명하라 Explain at length[in full detail].

부엽토(腐葉土) humus; leaf mold[(영) mould].

부영사(副領事) a vice-consul.

부옇다 1 (빛깔이) milk-white; pearly; frosty; cream-colored; opaque. 2 (안개·연기 등으로) hazy; misty; heavy (in the air). 3 [희미하다] blurred; dim; indistinct; blurry. ¶달빛이 부옇게 비추고 있었다 The moon was giving off pale light.

부예지다 get misty; become hazy; haze. ¶하늘이 ~ The sky turns hazy.

부용(芙蓉) 1 [식] [아욱과의 낙엽 관목] a cotton rose; a Confederate rose. 2 a lotus flower. ⇨ˮ연꽃2

부원(部員) (전체) a staff; (개인) a person on the staff; a member (of a department[club]); a staff member.

부위(部位) [의] a part; a region. ¶심장 ~ the region of the heart.

부유(浮遊·浮游) floating; [물] suspension(고체 입자의). **부유하다** waft; float. ¶솜털 같은 먼지가 공중에 부유하고 있었다 Fluffy dust was floating in the air.
● **부유물** a floating[suspended] matter; (티끌) floating particles of dust. **부유 생물** [생] plankton. ⇨ˮ플랑크톤

부유스름하다 somewhat pearly[frosty / misty]; milky; creamy.

부유층(富裕層) the wealthy classes; the well-to-do; the high-income bracket; (a shop for) the carriage trade.

부유하다(富裕-) rich; wealthy; opulent; affluent; well-heeled; (미) well-fixed. ¶부유한 사람 a person of wealth / a well-to-do person // 부유하게 살다 live in opulence [affluence] / be well-off [well-to-do] / live in easy circumstances // 부유한 집에 태어나다 be born rich / be born of a rich family // 그들은 부유하게 살고 있다 They are well-off [living in affluence]. // 그녀는 어려서 부유한 환경에서 자랐다 She was brought up in affluent [easy] circumstances.

부음(訃音) an announcement of (a person's) death. ⇨ 부고(訃告)

부응하다(副應-) meet; satisfy; gratify; fulfill(기대 등에); answer(희망 등에). ¶현실에 부응하는 교육 education based on reality / education adopted to meet the demands of reality // 부모의 희망에 ~ comply with [satisfy / obey] a parent's wishes // 시대의 요구에 부응하도록 새 정책이 채택되었다 A new policy was adopted to meet the needs of the times.

부의(賻儀) (offering) condolence money [goods]; a monetary token of condolence; an obituary gift; a condolatory present.(▶ 영미(英美) 풍속에는 없음)

부의장(副議長) a vice-president [-chairman]; a deputy speaker.

부의하다(附議-) bring (a matter) before (a conference); submit (a measure) to (a council); place (a bill) on the agenda; refer to. ¶그들은 그 제안을 위원회에 부의했다 They referred the proposal to a committee.

부이 a buoy. ¶구명 ~ a life buoy [(미) preserver].

부익부 (빈익빈)(富益富貧益貧) The rich get richer (and the poor get poorer).

부인(夫人) 1 [남의 아내] a wife (*pl.* wives); [기혼자] a married lady; a dame; a matron. ¶한 씨 ~ Mrs. Han // 한테 충실한 남편 a faithful [devoted / devoting] husband // 이 파티에는 ~ 동반으로 참석해 주십시오 Please bring your wife to the party.
2 (경칭) Mrs.; Madam(e)(▶ 보통 Mrs.를 쓰지만 드물게 특히 존경의 뜻을 나타내어 Madam을 씀. Madame은 Madam과 마찬가지로 특히 존경을 나타내어 Madam보다 많이 쓰이는데 보통 영어의 native speaker 아닌 여성에게 쓰임. Madam(e)으로 불리는 여성은 주로 대통령, 수상, 대사 등의 부인, 또는 예술가 특히 음악가임). ¶대처 ~ Mrs. Thatcher / Madame Thatcher.

부인(否認) denial; negation; nonrecognition; disaffirmance; disaffirmation; (문어) repudiation. ¶사실의 ~ denial of the truth (of something). **부인하다** deny; negate; disavow; disown; disclaim; repudiate; say nay(to); disaffirm. ¶부인할 수 없는 사실 an undeniable fact // 자기의 행위를 ~ disavow one's own action // 그는 그 사실을 부인했다 He denied it. // 그는 그 아이가 친아들임을 부인했다 He denied that the child was his. // 우리 편의 패배를 더 이상 부인할 수 없다 We can no longer deny the fact of our defeat. // 피고는 자백을 부인했다 The defendant repudiated his confession.

부인(婦人) a (married) woman; a lady(신분·교양이 있는). ¶중년 ~ a middle-aged [an elderly / a matronly] woman.

● **부인과**(-科) gynecology. **부인병** a woman's disease; a female disorder. **부인회** a women's society [association]. ¶애국 ~ the Ladies' Patriotic Society.

부임(赴任) starting for one's new post. ¶~ 길에 오르다 start for post. **부임하다** start [leave / go] for one's new post; proceed to one's post. ¶새로 부임해 온 교사 a new teacher // 내가 맨 처음 부임한 곳은 부산 지점이었다 I was first sent [assigned] to the branch office in Busan. / My first assignment was the branch office in Busan.

● **부임지** one's new post; the place of one's assignment.

부자(父子) father and son.

부자(富者) a rich [wealthy] person; a man of wealth [means / property]; rich folk(s); (집합적) the rich; the moneyed class. ¶큰 ~ a millionaire / (미국 속어) a plute // ~가 되다 become [get / grow] rich / make a fortune [(구어) a pile] // 대단한 ~다 have a mint of money / roll in riches // ~ 라고 반드시 행복한 것은 아니다 The rich are not always happy.

● **부잣집** [부유한 가정] a rich [wealthy] family; [부호] a rich man's house. ¶~ 딸 a bourgeois girl // ~에 태어나다 be born rich / be born to an ample fortune / be born with a silver spoon in one's mouth // ~에 장가들다 marry a fortune [rich heiress] // 그는 부잣집에 태어났다 He was born rich [into a rich family].

부자연스럽다(不自然-) unnatural; against nature; artificial; factitious; (…이 체하는) a forced smile [style]. ¶부자연스러운 태도 affected manners // 그는 부자연스러운 목소리로 말을 한다 He speaks in an affected voice. // 그는 부자연스러운 문체로 글을 쓴다 He writes in an affected style.

부자유스럽다(不自由-) not free; disabled. ⇨ 부자유하다 ¶손[다리]이 ~ have trouble in the hand [leg] / have lost the use of one's hand [leg] // 몸이 ~ be physically handicapped // 그는 다리가 ~ He has lost the use of his legs.

부자유하다(不自由-) not free; restricted; inconvenient; uncomfortable; (몸이) disabled. ¶몸이 부자유한 사람들 disabled men.

부작용(副作用) a (usually adverse) side [secondary] effect (on). ¶약의 ~을 일으키다 produce ill effects [a bad reaction / unfavorable side effects] / cause harmful side effects // ~이 없다 have no side effects / be free from harmful side effects // 이 약은 ~이 없다 This medicine produces no [is free from] harmful aftereffects.

부장(部長) the head [chief / director] of a department [division]; a department manager [head / chief]. ¶경리[인사]부 ~ the chief of the accountants' [the personnel (affairs)] department // 영업부 ~ the sales manager.

부장품(副葬品) grave goods; burial accessories; the favorite possessions of the dead person which are to be buried with him.

부재(不在) absence. ¶인간 ~의 교육 dehumanized education.

● **부재자** an absentee. **부재중** (게시) Out. ¶~에 during [in] one's absence // 아버지는 ~

부적 입니다 My father is not at home [not in/out]. // 그는 부산에 가서 지금은 ~입니다 He is away in Busan at the moment. **부재 증명** an alibi.

부적(符籍) a charm; an amulet; a phylactery. ¶액막이 ~ an amulet to avert evils / a charm against evils.

부적격(不適格) disqualification; unqualifiedness; unfitness. ~의 disqualified (for) / unqualified (for) / unfit (for).
● **부적격자** a person disqualified for [unacceptable to] a position.

부적당하다(不適當-) unsuitable; unfit (for); inappropriate (to / for); inadequate; impertinent; out of place; improper; ineligible; inapplicable. ¶소풍에 부적당한 날씨 unfavorable weather for picnic // 이 책은 학교에서 쓰기에는 ~ This book is unfit [unsuitable / inappropriate] for school use. // 이 땅은 목축에는 ~ The land is unfit for raising stock. // 이런 실내 장식은 한옥에는 ~ Interior decoration of this type is unsuitable for [out of place in] a Korean-style house. // 그는 의사로서 ~ He is not cut out to be a doctor. / He doesn't have what it takes to be a doctor. // 너는 상인으로는 ~ You will never do as a merchant. / You'll never make a merchant. // 그 옷은 이와 같은 자리에는 ~ The clothing is not proper for an occasion like this.

부적응(不適應) maladjustment (to one's social environment). ¶~의 maladjusted.

부적임(不適任) unfitness; unsuitableness; inadequacy; incompetency.
● **부적임자** an unqualified [incompetent] person; an unfit [incompetent]. ¶그녀는 그 일에 ~다 She is unfit [unsuited] for the job. / She is not the right person to undertake the job. // 그 영어 실력으로는 그녀는 영어 교사로서 ~다 With that sort of English, she is not qualified to be an English teacher.

부적합(不適合) incongruence. **부적합하다** incongruent.

부전(不全) imperfection; incompletion. ¶~의 (불완전한) incomplete / imperfect / [부분적인] partial // 발육 ~ underdevelopment / undergrowth // 발육 ~의 개 an undergrown dog.
● **부전 마비** partial paralysis; paresis.

부전(附箋) a tag; a slip; a label. ¶~을 붙이다 tag / label / put a tag on. // 편지는 「주거지 부재」라는 ~이 붙어 돌아왔다 The letter was returned with a tag which said, "Not at this address."

부전공(副專攻) a minor. **부전공하다** minor (in). ¶수학을 ~ minor in math.

부전나비 (동) a hairstreak; a gossammer wing; a lycaenid.

부전승(不戰勝) (싸우지 않고 이김) an unearned win; (상대의 불참함에 의한) a victory [win] by default. **부전승하다** win by default; be credited with a win by forfeit of the opponent; (추첨으로) draw a bye.

부전자전(父傳子傳) transmission from father to son. ¶~이다 Like father, like son. / Like breeds like. **부전자전하다** transmit from father to son.

부절제(不節制) intemperance; excesses; immoderation. **부절제하다** be intemperate [immoderate]; commit excesses.

부점(附點) [음] a dot; a prick.
● **부점음표** a dotted note.

부접 못하다(附接-) 1 [접근 못하다] cannot approach [come near to]; be kept from approaching; be denied approach [access]. ¶부접을 못하게 하다 keep oneself inaccessible [unapproachable] / keep (a person) away from (one / a thing). 2 [한곳에 붙어 있지 못하다] cannot [be unable to] stay at [in] (one's house); be too warm [hot] (for a person); cannot bear [stand / endure]. // 그 여자의 집에는 가정부가 부접을 못한다 Her house seems to be too warm for any kitchenmaid. / Kitchenmaids do not stay long in her house.

부젓가락 (a pair of) tongs; metal chopsticks for handling live charcoals. ¶벌겋게 단 ~ (a pair of) red-hot tongs.

부정(不正) [불공정] injustice; unfairness; iniquity; [비행] wrong; unrighteousness; [위법·불법·무법] illegality; unlawfulness; [부정직] dishonesty; obliquity; [부당] impropriety; venality (금전상의). ¶~을 바로잡다 redress [remedy] injustice. **부정하다** bad; unjust; unfair; foul; wrong; unrighteous; iniquitous; (위법인) illegitimate; unlawful; illegal; improper (부당한); (허위의) false; fraudulent. ¶부정한 돈 dirty [tainted] money / ill-gotten money / filthy lucre / (미국 구어) graft (특히 정치 관계의) // 부정한 벌이 dirty gains // 부정한 사람은 the unjust // 부정한 거래 oblique dealings / (구어) a queer transaction // 부정한 짓을 하다 do a dishonest thing [act] / commit an injustice [irregularities] / do wrong / (경기에서) play foul / (시험에서) cheat [crib] (in [(미)on] an examination) // 부정한 방법으로 이기다 win unfairly.
● **부정부패** illegality and corruption; abuse of power and graft (공무원 등의). **부정 축재** accumulation of wealth [making a fortune] by illicit means. ¶그는 ~를 했다 He amassed an immorally acquired fortune. / He made money immorally [by immoral means]. **부정행위** an unfair [a corrupt] practice; a dishonest [an improper / a wrongful] act; irregularities; (관료 등의) misconduct; (경기 중의) cheating; cribbing; (경기 중의) foul play. ¶~를 하다 misbehave / do something irregular // 시험에서 ~를 하다 cheat [crib] in an examination // 경기에서 ~를 하다 play foul.

부정(不定) uncertainty; indefiniteness; incertitude; indeterminateness; mutability. ¶주소 ~의 사람 a man of no fixed abode / a vagrant / a tramp / (집합적) the homeless. **부정하다** unsettled; uncertain; indefinite; unfixed; undetermined; undecided; unsure; indeterminate; [수] arbitrary; (변하기 쉬운) inconstant; mutable; variable; changeful; changeable. ¶주거가 부정한 having no fixed abode / homeless / wandering.
● **부정 관사** [대명사] [언] an indefinite article [pronoun].

부정(不貞) unchastity; unfaithfulness; inconstancy; incontinence; incontinency; infidelity. **부정하다** unchaste; unfaithful; faithless; false (to one's husband); wanton. ¶부정한 아내 an unfaithful wife // 남편에게 부정한 짓을 하다 deceive [be unfaithful to] one's husband // 나는 아내에게 부정한 짓을 했다 I was unfaithful to my wife.

부정(不淨) 1 〔불결〕 uncleanliness; dirtiness; filthiness; impurity; defilement. **부정하다** unclean; dirty; filthy; (종교적으로) unholy; impure. ¶부정한 돈 unclean money / ill-gotten money〔gain〕/ (미) tainted money. 2 (꺼려서 피할 때의) happening of an evil event (during one's unlucky day). 3 〔민〕 the first stage of a shamanist rite.

부정을 타다 suffer an evil〔a bad luck〕; have〔meet with〕a misfortune.

부정(否定) (a) denial; (a) disavowal; (a) disclaimer; (a) contradiction; negation. ¶이중 ~ 〔논〕 a double negative∥~의〔~적인〕 negative. **부정하다** deny (a fact); negative〔a statement〕; negate; gainsay; say no (to); disown; disavow; contradict. ¶부정할 수 없는 undeniable / incontestable / indisputable∥부정할 수 없는 사실 an undeniable fact∥그것을 부정할 수 없다 It cannot be denied. / There is no denying the fact.∥당국은 어디까지나 이 사실을 부정하고 있다 The authorities are positive in denying the fact.

● **부정문** 〔언〕 a negative sentence. **부정어** 〔언〕 a negative.

부정기(不定期) irregularity. ¶~의 〔불규칙한〕 irregular / unfixed / indeterminate / nonscheduled∥이 잡지는 ~적으로 간행된다 This magazine is published irregularly.

● **부정기선** a tramp(er); a nonregular liner.

부정당하다(不正當–) unjust; wrong; unfair; improper; unrighteous; unlawful; illegitimate.

부정맥(不整脈) 〔의〕 arrhythmia; an irregular pulse.

부정사(不定詞) 〔언〕 an infinitive.

부정직하다(不正直–) dishonest; untruthful. ¶부정직한 행위〔사람〕 a dishonest act〔person〕∥부정직한 진술 an untruthful〔a dishonest〕statement.

부정확(不正確) inaccuracy; incorrectness; inexactness; uncertainty; imprecision. **부정확하다** inaccurate; incorrect; uncertain; inexact; imprecise. ¶부정확한 번역 a loose translation∥부정확하게 inaccurately / incorrectly / inexactly∥그의 계산은 ~ His calculations are inaccurate.

부제(副題) a subtitle; a subhead(ing).

부조(父祖) (one's) father and grandfather.

부조(不調) (건강·기운 등의) a bad condition; a disorder; a slump; (날씨 등의) unseasonableness; unfavorableness; irregularity. **부조하다** (날씨 등이) unseasonable; unfavorable; irregular; (건강 등이) (서술적) be in a bad condition; be in disorder; be out of form(운동가가); be out of sorts; be not one's usual self.

부조(扶助) (결혼 때의) making〔sending〕a wedding〔congratulatory〕gift; contribution to the expenses of a wedding; (상가에 대한) offering condolence money〔goods〕; making〔giving〕a donation to help out a bereaved family; 〔조력〕 aid; help; assistance. ¶상호 ~ mutual aid / interdependence∥부모의 ~를 받다 depend on one's parents for support / receive financial help〔support〕from one's parents. **부조하다** offer goods〔money〕to help (a person) (to) perform a marriage〔funeral〕service; aid; help; render (a person) assistance.

부조는 않더라도 제상이나 치지 마라(속담) Don't put a spoke in my wheel.; Don't put your finger into my pie.

● **부조금** congratulatory money(결혼 때의); a solatium〔condolence money〕; a monetary token of condolence. ¶나는 그의 결혼 ~으로 2만 원을 냈다 I gave him twenty thousand won as a wedding gift.

부조(浮彫) 〔미〕 relief; relievo; embossed carving. ¶얕은〔높은〕 ~ low〔high / grand〕 relief / bas-〔alto-〕relief. **부조하다** emboss; carve〔sculpture〕in relief. ¶그는 부친의 옆얼굴을 부조했다 He carved a relief of his father's profile.

부조리(不條理) absurdity; irrationality; unreasonableness; improperness; (프) 〔철〕 absurde. ¶~를 제거하다 eliminate improperness / put (things) straight∥사회의 ~를 제거하다 eliminate social absurdities∥회사 경리상의 ~를 제거하다 put the accounting of a company on a fair-and-square basis. **부조리하다** irrational; unreasonable.

부조화(不調和) inharmoniousness; inharmony; disharmony; discord; discordance; incongruity; disparity; disagreement; dissonance; dissonancy. ¶색의 ~ inharmoniousness〔disharmony〕of colors. **부조화하다** do not harmonize〔match〕(with).

부족(不足) 1 〔불충분〕 insufficiency; 〔모자람〕 shortage; deficiency; deficit(특히 금전의); 〔결핍·고갈〕 want; lack; scantiness; scarcity; dearth; famine (of coal〔water〕). ¶공급 ~ failure in supply / shortage in〔of〕supply / short supply∥수면 ~ want〔lack〕of sleep / insufficient sleep∥식량 ~ a scarcity〔shortage〕of food / insufficiency of provisions∥칼슘 ~ calcium poverty∥물자의 ~ a scarcity of goods∥교원의 ~ a scarcity of teachers∥셋집의 ~ a shortage of houses for rent∥아이디어의 ~ a paucity of ideas∥수면 ~으로 for want〔lack〕of sleep∥자금 ~으로 인하여 because of〔owing to〕a lack of funds∥~을 매우다 make good〔make up (for)〕a deficiency / supply〔meet / cover / fill up / remedy〕the shortage short / deficient / wanting / lacking / scanty / 〔결손을 매우다〕 supply〔stop〕a gap∥~으로 수입의 ~을 메우다 eke〔help〕out one's income with (odd jobs)∥주택 ~은 심각하다 The housing shortage is serious. **부족하다** insufficient; short; deficient; wanting; lacking; scanty; (사물이) be in short supply; fail; (사람이) be〔come / drop / fail / run〕short (of); want; lack; be lacking (in); be in want〔need〕(of). ¶상상력이 부족한〔결여된〕사람들 those who lack〔are lacking in〕imagination / unimaginative persons∥천 원 ~ be one thousand won short / be short by a thousand won∥일손이 ~ be shorthanded / be short of hands∥돈〔식량〕이 ~ be scant〔short〕of money〔food〕∥부족해지다 prove deficient〔insufficient〕/ run short of∥(비행기 등의) 연료가 부족해지다 run low of fuel∥우리는 식량〔일손〕이 부족했다 We were short of food〔hands〕.∥연료가 부족해지고 있다 We are running short of fuel.∥비누가 ~ Soap is running short〔is scarce〕. / We have run short of soap.∥일자리가 매우 ~ There are very few jobs available. / Jobs are scarce〔few and far between〕.∥이 나라에는 석유가

부족

~ Oil is scarce in this country.∥올해는 비가 크게 ~ We are in great want of rain this year.∥두 명이 사직해서 우리 과는 인원이 ~ Two people have resigned and our section is short-handed[undermanned].∥그 아이는 영양이 ~ The child is undernourished.
2 [불만족]. **부족하다** dissatisfied; discontented; [불완전하다] imperfect; [부적당하다] inadequate. ¶부족한 점이 없다 leave nothing to be desired∥부족한 듯한 얼굴을 하고 look dissatisfied∥아직도 부족한가 Are you still dissatisfied?∥그 사람이라면 상대로서 부족하지 않다 I find a worthy opponent in him. / He is worthy of my steel[metal].
● **부족액** shortage; (미) wantage; a deficiency; a deficit; (구어) a shortfall; shorts; a difference(차감 계정의).

부족(部族) a tribe. ¶~의 tribal∥~ 간의 싸움 a tribal war / tribal warfare.

부존자원(賦存資源) natural resources. ¶~의 부족(을 메우다) (make up for) the shortage of natural resources∥~이 많다 be blessed with natural resources.

부종(浮腫) dropsy; dropsical swelling; anasarca; [의] (o)edema (*pl.* -mata).

부주의(不注意) carelessness; heedlessness; incautiousness; inadvertence; want of care [attention]; inattention; negligence. ¶운전 ~ careless driving∥~로 through (one's) carelessness∥~로 인한 잘못[실수] a careless mistake∥운전 ~로 인한 사고 an accident due to[caused by] careless driving∥~로 일어나다 arise from carelessness∥그는 운전 ~로 사고를 일으켰다 His careless driving caused the accident.∥저의 ~를 사과드립니다 I apologize[am very sorry] for my carelessness.∥그는 순전히 ~로 그녀에게 소식을 전하는 것을 깜박 잊어버렸다 Out of sheer carelessness he forgot to give her the message. **부주의하다** be careless (in); be heedless (of); be inattentive (to). ¶부주의한 careless / heedless / inattentive / unmindful (of one's duty) / inadvertent / incautious / negligent∥부주의하게도 당신의 편지를 잃어버렸습니다 I inadvertently mislaid your letter.∥나는 부주의하게도 그것을 간과하고 말았다 I carelessly passed it by. / I was so careless that I passed it by.∥그는 부주의하게도 비밀을 입 밖에 내 버렸다 He had the imprudence to[He was so imprudent as to] let the secret out[(구어) let the cat out of the bag].

부지(不知) ignorance. ¶~의 진술 a plea of ignorance / a declaration of ignorance of fact. **부지하다** do not know; be ignorant of; (구어) be innocent of.
● **부지기수**(一其數) being numberless[innumerable / countless].

부지(敷地) a (building) site; (a plot of) ground; a plot; a lot. ¶건축 ~ a building site[lot]∥~를 물색하다 look for a site (for)∥~를 선정하다 select a site (for)∥~를 확보하다 secure the location (for).
● **부지 선정** the selection of site (for an exhibition).

부지깽이 a poker.

부지런 diligence; industry; hard work; assiduity. ¶~을 떨다[피우다] display diligence / work hard[diligently / like a bee]. **부지런하다** diligent; industrious; assiduous; studious; sedulous. ¶부지런한 사람 a diligent[an industrious] person / a hard worker / a laborious man / a wheel horse∥이렇게 밤늦게까지 일을 하시다니 정말 부지런하시군요 You are really industrious to be working until so late at night. **부지런히** diligently; assiduously; hard; industriously; (자주) frequently. ¶~ 일하다 work diligently [hard / assiduously] / work like a bee∥~ 공부하다 work hard / apply oneself closely to one's studies∥~ 다니다 frequent (a saloon) / visit (a place) frequently∥그녀는 날마다 ~ 일한다 She works diligently every day.

부지불식간(不知不識間) ⇨ 부지중

부지사(副知事) a vice-governor; a deputy[(미) lieutenant] governor.

부지중(不知中) ¶~에 [자기도 모르게] unconsciously / unwittingly / unknowingly / unawares / instinctively / in spite of oneself / before one knows (it) / [뜻하지 않게] unintentionally∥~에 눈물이 고였다 Tears had gathered in my eyes before I knew it.∥하루에 10분만 연습하면 ~에 향상될 것이다 If you practice just ten minutes a day, you will improve without even realizing it.

부지하다(扶持・扶支) hold (out / on / up); last; endure; bear; stand (the strain); maintain; keep up. ¶목숨을 ~ sustain[maintain / preserve] one's life∥그런 식사로는 몸을 부지하지 못할 것이다 You cannot keep yourself in good health on such a diet.

부지하세월(不知何歲月) ¶~이다 do not know when (a thing) will be completed∥건물이 언제 완공될지 ~이다 Nobody knows[can tell] when the building will be completed.

부직(副職) an additional post.

부진(不振) dullness; depression; inactivity; stagnation; a slump. ¶거래 ~ [증권] lack of interest[enthusiasm]∥수출 ~ inactivity [a poor showing] of the export trade∥사업의 ~ business depression / stagnation of trade / a slump[slack] in business∥사업의 ~으로 아버지는 실직하셨다 A slump in business caused my father to lose his job. **부진하다** be dull[inactive / depressed / stagnant / flat / slack]; be at a low ebb[in (a) bad shape / in a bad condition / in a poor way / in a slump / out of form]. ¶식욕이 ~ have a poor[weak] appetite / lack appetite (for food)∥부진해지다 go[fall] into a slump∥왠지 건강 상태가 ~ I don't seem to be in very good physical condition. / Something seems to be wrong with me[my health].∥사업이 ~ Business is slack[slow].∥시장은 거래가 ~ [증권] The market is stagnant[dull / inactive].∥나는 수학 성적이 ~ I am not doing very well in mathematics.∥저 투수는 ~ The pitcher is not up to the mark[is not in good form].∥이 타자는 ~ This batter is in a slump.∥어제 그 팀은 매우 부진했다 The team made a very poor showing[played very badly] yesterday.

부진(不進) no progress; poor progress. **부진하다** make no[little / poor] progress. ¶지지 ~ make very slow progress / progress at a snail's pace.

부질없다 idle; vain; useless; unprofitable; futile; trivial. ¶부질없는 이야기 a useless [silly] talk / idle gossip∥부질없는 생각 an idle[a useless] thought // 부질없는 짓을 하다 do a useless[foolish] thing // 부질없는 소리를 하다 talk nonsense / utter an absurdity. **부질없이** idly; uselessly; fruitlessly; to no purpose; in vain. ¶~ 시간을 보내다 spend one's time away // ~. 돈을 쓰다 spend one's money uselessly[to no purpose] / trifle away one's money.

부집게 (a pair of) (iron) tongs.

부쩍 (dried up) completely; closely; short; firmly; leanly; stubbornly. ⇨ 바싹

부차(副次) secondary.

부착(附着·付着) sticking; adhesion(점착); bond(ing); cohesion(고착); agglutination; conglutination(딱 달라붙음). **부착하다** adhere[stick / attach / cling] to; agglutinate; conglutinate.

부창부수(夫唱婦隨) a way of life in which the wife follows the lead set by her husband. ¶가정의 행복을 유지하는 데는 ~가 제일이다 The best way to maintain domestic happiness is for the wife to follow the husband's lead[to do as her husband wishes].

부채 a *buchae*; a fan. ¶~ 을 부치다 a folding fan // ~를 부치다 *buchae* oneself / use a *buchae* // 그는 창가에서 ~를 부치고 있었다 He was fanning himself by the window.

● **부채꼴** fan shape; (기하에서) a sector. ¶~의 fan-shaped // ~로 펼치다[펴기다] fan out. **부채춤** a *buchaechum*; a dance with a fan [fans]; a fan dance. **부챗살** the ribs of a fan.

부채(負債) a debt; liabilities; dues. ¶고정[미상환] ~ fixed[outstanding] liabilities // 유동 ~ floating liabilities // 장부상의 ~ a book debt // ~가 있다 be in debt / be indebted to (a person) // ~가 없다 be clear[free] from debts / be out of debt // ~가 생기다 [~를 지다] get[run / fall] into[in] debt / put oneself in debt // ~를 갚다 repay[clear off / pay off] a debt / liquidate one's liabilities // ~를 면제하다 cancel a debt / release a person from [forgive a person] his debt // ~를 남기다 leave debts // 자넨 ~가 얼마나 되는가 How much do you owe? / What is the extent of your liabilities? // 그는 내게 50만 원의 ~를 지고 있다 He owes me five hundred thousand won.

● **부채 상환** debt redemption. **부채액** the amount of debts; indebtedness; liabilities.

부채질하다 1 (부채로) fan; fan oneself(자기를); use a fan. **2** [선동하다] instigate; stimulate; stir[work / key] up; agitate; (감정 등을) kindle; inflame. ¶허영심을 ~ inflate the vanity (of a person) // 교통 혼잡을 더욱 ~ fan the traffic jams even further.

부처 [불타] Buddha; Gautama[Gotama] Buddha; [성인] a Buddhist saint; [비유] a saint of a man; a saintly person; [불상] an image of Buddha; the Buddha. ¶그는 ~님 같은 사람이다 He is a saint of a man. / He is a merciful man.

부처님 가운데 토막(속담) a man too saintly to be true; a saint; a little tin Jesus.

부처님한테 설법(속담) Teach your grandmother to suck eggs.

부처(夫妻) husband and wife. ⇨ 부부 ¶브라운 씨 ~ Mr. and Mrs. Brown / the Browns.

부척(副尺) ⇨ 아들자

부초(浮草) a floating weed. ¶그는 ~ 같은 생활을 하고 있다 He leads a precarious life.

부촌(富村) a rich[wealthy] village.

부총리(副總理) a deputy prime minister; a vice-premier.

부총재(副總裁) a vice-president.

부추 [식] a leek; a scallion.

부추기다 stir up; instigate; incite; urge[egg] on; abet; (개 등을) set (a dog) on[at] (a person); set on (a dog). ¶부추겨서 …시키다 incite[instigate] (a person to an action[to do]) / cajole[wheedle] (a person into doing) / egg (a person on to an act[on to do]) // 부추겨서 싸움을 시키다 egg (a person) on to fight with (another) // 그들은 민중을 부추겨 반정부 데모를 일으켰다 They incited the people to an antigovernment demonstration. // 저 사람이 파업을 하도록 부추겼다 That man instigated[put them up to] the strike. // 그는 학생들을 부추겨 수업을 거부하게 했다 He incited the students to go on strike. // 그 자는 소년들을 부추겨 식품점을 처들어가게 했다 The man instigated the boys to break into a grocery. // 폭동을 부추긴 사람은 누구냐 Who instigated the riot?

부축하다 help (a person) by holding (his) arms; help; support; give one's arm to (a person). ¶부축하여 일으키다 help (a person) to his feet / help (a person) up // 노인을 집까지 부축해 가다 help an old man to walk home // 부인을 차에서 부축해 내리다 help a lady off a car / hand a lady down from[out of] a cab // 나는 노인을 부축해서 차에 태워 드렸다 I helped an old man(to) board a bus. // 이 환자는 이제 남이 부축하지 않아도 걸을 수 있게 되었다 This patient is now able to walk without being supported (by anybody) [without anyone's help].

부츠 [장화] boots. ¶~를 신은 booted // ~를 신은 여자 a woman in[wearing] (a pair of) boots.

부치다[1] [힘이 모자라다] be beyond[out of] one's capacity[power / strength]; be too much for (one). ¶힘에 부치는 일 work beyond one's power[capacity / ability / skill] // 이 일은 내 힘에 부친다 This work is beyond my capacity. / The work is too much for me. / I am not equal to the task. // 나는 내가 착수한 사업이 내 힘에 부친다는 것을 알게 되었다 I found myself unequal to what I had undertaken.

부치다[2] [부채·풍구로 바람을 일으키다] fan; use a fan. ¶불을 ~ fan a fire // 석탄 불을 부쳐서 불길이 오르게 하다 fan coals into a blaze // 파리를 부채로 부쳐 쫓다 fan away flies // 신문지로 ~ fan oneself with a newspaper // 매우 더워서 그녀는 분주히 부채를 부쳤다 As it was very hot she fanned herself busily.

부치다[3] [물품 등을 보내다] send; forward; transmit; consign(상품을); ship(배·차로); [발송하다] dispatch; [송금하다] remit; [우송하다] (미) mail; (영) post; send[forward] (something) by post[mail]. ¶남에게 소포를 ~ send a person a parcel / send a parcel to a person // 소포로 책을 ~ send a book by parcel post // 기차로 상품을 ~ ship goods by rail // 편지를 항공편으로 ~ mail a letter by air mail // 우편환으로 돈을 ~ remit money by money order // 나는 그 소포를 속달로 부쳤다 I sent the package by express (mail).

부치다[4] [경작·재배하다] cultivate; farm;

부치다 grow. ¶논[밭]을 ~ cultivate a paddy [a field].

부치다[5] [음식을 지지다] griddle; fry; cook [bake] in a greased pan [on a griddle]. ¶달걀을 ~ fry an egg / ¶빈대떡을 ~ cook lentil [green gram] pancake.

부치다[6] **1** [회부하다] refer; put; commit; submit; hand over to(넘기다). ¶표결에 ~ put [submit] (a bill) to a vote [ballot] // 심의에 ~ refer (a matter) to discussion // 공판에 부쳐지다 be brought to trial / come on before the judge (for trial / for hearing). **2** [어떤 취급을 하기로 하다]. ¶불문에 ~ overlook; pass over. **3** [심정을 의탁하다] convey one's feelings in (verse); liken [compare] (one's feelings) to (flowers and birds).

부칙(附則) additional rules; an additional clause; a supplementary provision; a subsidiary law; (의안·계약서 등의) a rider.

부친(父親) one's father.
● **부친상** mourning for one's father; one's father's death. ¶~을 **당하다** have one's father die / lose one's father.

부침(浮沈) [떠올랐다 잠기었다 함] sinking and floating; rise and fall; ebb and flow; [성쇠] vicissitudes (of life [fortune]); ups and downs (of life); prosperity and adversity. ¶회사의 ~에 관계되는 거래 business transactions vital to the prosperity of the company // ~을 같이하다 cast [throw] in one's lot (with another) / stand or fall (with [by] another / together) / share the smiles and frowns of fortune (with another) // 나는 인생의 온갖 ~을 경험했다 I have gone through all sorts of ups and downs in life. **부침하다** bob (up and down); sink and float (to the surface); rise and fall; ebb and flow; fluctuate; have ups and downs.

부침개 fried food; a fried dish; a fry.

부탁(付託) **1** [당부] a request; a favor; [간청] a solicitation. ¶친구의 간곡한 ~ (at) the pressing request of a friend / ···의 ~으로 at the request of (someone) / at (a person's) request / by a request from (a person) // ~을 **들어주다** comply with [accede to] another's request / grant a request / do (a person) a favor / oblige (a person) // ~을 들어주지 않다 [거절하다] turn down [refuse / decline] another's request / refuse (a person) a favor // ~**이 있다** have a favor to ask of (a person) / wish to make (a person) a request / wish to ask a favor of (a person) / ~이 있는데요 I have a favor to ask of you. / I need a favor from you. // ~ 좀 들어주시겠어요 Would [Will / Could] you do me a favor? / May [Can] I ask you a favor? / May [Can] I ask a favor of you? / 나는 그의 ~으로 그렇게 했다 I did so at his request. // 우리들의 ~을 들어주었다 Our request was granted. // 나는 그가 오늘 밤 10시에 도착한다는 것을 네게 알려 달라는 ~을 받았다 I was asked to let you know that he is arriving at ten tonight. // 나는 송 씨로부터 이 꾸러미를 당신에게 전해 달라는 ~을 받았습니다 Here is a parcel Mr. Song asked me to give to you. // 제발 ~이니 나를 좀 혼자 있게 해 주오 Leave me alone, for a favor. // 가지 마십시오, ~입니다 Don't go away, I implore you. **부탁하다** ask; beg; request; make (a person) a request; ask a favor (of a person); [간청하다] beseech; entreat; implore; solicit. ¶···에게 부탁하여 through (the courtesy of) (a person) // 도움을 ~ ask (a person) for help [assistance] / look [turn] to (a person) for help / 연설을 ~ ask [call upon] (a person) for a speech / 돈을 꾸어 달라고 ~ ask for a loan // 자동차에 편승을 ~ ask for a lift // 부탁하러 오다 come to (a person) for (something) / 그에게 그것을 해 달라고 부탁했다 I asked him to do it. // 편지 [전갈]를 전해 달라고 그에게 부탁했다 I asked him to deliver a letter [message]. // 그가 부탁하면 나는 거절하지 못한다 I cannot turn him down. / I can't say no if he asks me. // 그녀에게는 아무것도 부탁하고 싶지 않다 I don't feel like asking any favors of her. // 그가 부탁하면 난 안 할 수 없겠지 I'll probably have to do it if he asks me (to). // 이런 상황에서는 그 사람밖에 도움을 부탁할 사람이 없다 I have no one but him to look to for assistance in this situation. / He is the only person I can ask for help in this situation. // 잘 부탁합니다 (손님에게) We solicit your patronage.

2 [맡김] charge; trust; entrusting; committal; commitment. ¶그 일은 모두 당신께 ~을 드립니다 I leave the matter entirely in your hands [to your discretion]. **부탁하다** entrust (something to a person / a person with something); charge (a person to do); place (something) under a person's charge [care]; commit (a child) to a person's care. ¶남에게 일을 ~ charge [entrust] a person with a commission // 편지 [전언]를 ~ charge (a person) with a letter [message] // 선생님께 아이의 교육을 ~ place one's child under the care of a teacher // 친구에게 재산 관리를 ~ entrust a friend with the care of one's property // 그녀는 어린 아들을 숙부에게 부탁했다 She committed [entrusted] her little boy to the care of his uncle. // 톰에게 부탁해서 당신에게 차를 조금 보내 드립니다 I am sending you some tea by Tom. // 한 군을 잘 부탁합니다 I hope you will kindly look after Mr. Han. // 부재중 [사후에] 뒷일을 네게 부탁하고 싶다 I'd like to ask you to look after my affairs while I'm away [after my death].

부탄 [화] butane.

부터 1 [시간] from; at; on; in; since(이래) on and after(어느 날 이후). ¶3월 1일~ on and after March 1 / 아침~ 밤까지 from morning till night / 2시~ 4시까지 from two to four / 언제~ since when // 신학기는 3월~ 시작된다 The new term begins in march. // 수업은 8시 ~ 시작된다 School begins at eight o'clock. // 다음~ 좀 더 조심하시오 You must be more careful from now on. // 회의는 8월 1일~ 10일까지 열릴 예정이다 The conference is to be held from the 1st of August to the 10th [from August 1-10]. // 작년~ 여기서 살고 있다 I have lived [been] here since last year. // 그녀는 어릴 때~ 부지런했다 She has been hardworking from her girlhood. // 그는 그때 ~ 줄곧 앓고 있습니다 He has been ill since then. // 승차 요금이 5월 1일~ 인상된다 The fares will be raised on and after May 1st. // 원서는 2월 10일~ 접수함 Applications will be accepted starting February 10. // 집무 시간: 오전 9시~ 오후 5시까지 Business hours: 9 a.m.—5 p.m. // 이 법률은 2002년 1월 1일 ~ 시행한다 This law shall come into force

on [as from] January 1, 2002.
2 [순서] beginning with; first; starting from. ¶역사~ 공부하다 study beginning with history / study history first // 무엇~ 시작할까요 what shall I begin with? // 이것~ 시작하자 Let's do this first. // 우선 방~ 치우세 Let's start by getting the room cleaned up.
3 [장소] from; out of; off; through; by; with; at; in; on; down. ¶20페이지의 9행~ 시작하다 begin at page 20, line 9 // 제2장~ 시작하다 begin with the second chapter // 이 책의 10페이지~ 읽기 시작하자 Let's begin reading on page ten of this book.
4 [범위] "… ~ …까지의 (ranging) from … to…. ¶~ 처음 ~ 끝까지 from beginning to end // 대체로 3만 원~ 5만 원 사이 all the way from 30,000 won to 50,000 won // 10세~ 15세까지의 어린이 children (ranging) from ten to fifteen years // 초봉은 25만 원~ 30만 원까지이다 The commencing salary ranges from 250,000 to 300,000 won.

부통령(副統領) a vice-president(약어 V.P.).
부티르산(-酸) [화] butyric acid.
부팅 a booting.
부패(腐敗) **1** [썩음] decomposition; rot(tenness); putrefaction; decay; [의] sepsis. (▶ decay는 decayed teeth처럼 자연히 조금씩 썩는 경우, rot(tenness)는 부패 현상을 강조하며 동식물에 쓰임. decomposition은 원래의 구성 요소로 분해되는 경우에 쓰임). ¶~를 **막다** preserve[keep] (a thing) from decay[rotting].
부패하다 rot; become rotten; putrefy; be decomposed; be vitiated; decay; go bad; be spoilt. ¶부패한 rotten / decomposed / putrid / decayed / bad / addled (egg) / tainted (meat) / turned (milk) // 부패하기 쉬운 corruptible / perishable / putrescible // 부패하기 쉬운 음식 perishables // 이 햄은 부패했다 This ham has gone bad[spoiled]. // 날씨가 더우면 우유는 부패한다 Warm weather turns [sours] milk. // 부패하기 쉬운 음식은 냉장고에 넣어 두어라 Put perishables in the refrigerator. // 부패하기 쉬움 — 열을 멀리할 것 (게시) Perishable — keep from heat.
2 [타락] corruption; degeneration; depravity; deterioration; taint. ¶사회적[도덕적] ~ social[moral] decay[disintegration] / dry rot / 도덕의 ~ moral taint[corruption] / gangrene // 정치의 ~ political corruption / corruption in politics // 공무원의 ~ corruption of government officials // 이 나라에서는 공무원의 ~ 행위가 당연한 것으로 되어 있다 In this country corrupt practices are quite common among government officials. **부패하다** corrupt; become[grow] corrupt[degenerated / deteriorated / vitiated]; degenerate; deteriorate. ¶부패한 corrupt(ed) / degenerate / vitiated // 부패한 공무원 a corrupt government official // 부패한 정신 a vitiated mind.
● **부패균** putrefying[saprogenic] bacteria.
부평초(浮萍草) [식] a (great) duckweed. ➪개구리밥
부표(否票) a negative vote[ballot]; a "nay" vote; a vote "no". ¶~를 **던지다** vote against [in opposition to] ….
부표(浮漂) floating; floatage. **부표하다** float; drift about.
● **부표 식물** duckweeds. ➪부수 식물
부표(浮標) [항로 표지] a (marker) buoy. ¶계선(繫船) ~ a mooring buoy.
부푸러기 nap; fuzz; pile. ➪부풀
부풀 (옷감 등의) nap; shag; (모직물 등의) fuzz; (솜·융단 등의) pile.
부풀다 1 become fluffy[nappy]. ➪보풀다 **2** (살가죽 등이) swell; become swollen. ¶살가죽이 부푼다 The skin swells (up). **3** (물건이) swell out; get big; [팽창하다] expand; be inflated; rise(만두 등의). ¶빵이 잘 부풀었다 The bread rose well. // 풍선이 부풀었다 The balloon was inflated. // 빵이 잘 부풀지 않는다 The bread will not rise. **4** (희망 등으로) be buoyant; be lighthearted; be cheered up. ¶좋은 소식으로 가슴이 ~ be buoyed up by good news // 희망에 가슴이 부풀어 있다 I am full of hope. / My breast swelled with hope. // 그들은 희망에 부푼 가슴으로 결혼했다 They were married full of[filled with] hope.
부풀리다 1 raise a nap on. ➪보풀리다 **2** (사물을) swell (out); fill out; bulge; expand; dilate(펴 넓히다); (가스·공기 등으로) inflate (with gas); puff; (불어서) blow up; (효모로) raise. ¶풍선을 ~ inflate a toy balloon // 공기베개를 ~ plump up a pillow // 가슴을 ~ heave one's breast // 빵을 ~ raise bread / let bread rise // (새가) 깃을 ~ fluff out its plumage // 바람이 돛을 부풀렸다 The wind swelled the sails.
부품(部品) (machine) parts; spare parts; components. ¶텔레비전의 ~ parts for a TV set // ~을 조립하여 완성품으로 만들다 assemble the parts into a complete unit.
부프다 1 [부피가 크나 가볍다] bulky; voluminous. ¶부픈 짐 a bulky package // 그것은 부프나 가볍다 It is bulky but light. **2** [성급하다] hasty; impatient; rash. ¶그는 성미가 부픈 사람이다 He is a rash person.
부피 bulk; size; volume; cubage. ¶~가 있는 [큰] bulky / voluminous / unwieldy // ~가 큰 물건 an article of great bulk // ~가 큰 꾸러미 a bulky package[bundle] // 이것은 ~는 크지만 가볍다 This is light in spite of its bulk. // 이 가방은 ~가 너무 커서 들 수가 없다 This bag is too bulky[unwieldy] to carry.
부하(負荷) **1** [짐을 짐] carrying[bearing] a burden; [짐] a burden. **부하하다** carry [bear] a burden[load]; be loaded. **2** [전] (원동기에서 내는 에너지를 소비하는 것] load. **부하하다** load.
● **부하율** a load factor.
부하(部下) a subordinate; a follower; (폭력단 등의) a henchman; (경멸) an underling; (집합적) one's men; a person's following. ¶두목과 ~ a boss and his henchmen[followers] // ~ **병사** men under one's command // 믿을 수 있는 ~ a henchman // 두목에 대해 ~로서 충성을 맹세하다 pledge loyalty to one's boss // ~로 **삼다** place (a person) under one's orders // ~가 **되다** place oneself under (a person's) orders.
부하다(富-) **1** [부유하다] rich; wealthy. **2** [뚱뚱하다] fat; fatty; corpulent; fleshy.
부합(符合) [일치] coincidence; [상응함] correspondence. **부합하다** coincide with; agree with; accord with; correspond with; conform with; tally with; check up with. ¶그의 진술은 증거와 부합하지 않는다 His statement contradicts the evidence. / What he says is inconsistent with[contradictory to] the evidence. ➔¶네 이야기는 그의 이야기와 부합된

다 What you say coincides [agrees / corresponds] with his account of it. / Your story agrees [corresponds / tallies] with his.

부형(父兄) [아버지와 형] one's father and elder brothers; [보호자] guardians.

부호(符號) **1** [기호] a mark; a symbol. ¶강세~ [언] a graphic accent.∥X표[별표]를 붙여 주십시오 Mark with an "X" [an asterisk]. **2** [수] a sign. ¶양[음]의 ~ a plus [minus] sign. **3** [코드] a code. ¶~화하다 code.

부호(富豪) a rich [wealthy] man; a man of wealthy; [백만장자] a millionaire; a billionaire. ¶대~ a multimillionaire∥그는 굉장한 ~다 He is as rich as Croesus [a Jew]. / He is rolling in gold.

부화(孵化) hatching; incubation. ~artificial incubation. **부화하다** be hatched; hatch; incubate. ¶오리 새끼가 부화했다 The ducklings have hatched.∥병아리가 세 마리 부화했다 Three chicks were hatched.∥알이 부화했다 The eggs have hatched.
● **부화기** an incubator. ⇨**부란기**(⇨부란)

부화뇌동(附和雷同) blind following. **부화뇌동하다** follow others blindly (and uncritically).

부활(復活) [재생] (a) revival; [재흥] restoration; (그리스도의) the Resurrection. ¶구제도의 ~ the revival [return] of the old system∥군국주의의 ~을 막다 prevent the rebirth of militarism. **부활하다** revive; come to life again; resurrect; be restored (to the original state). ¶옛 유행이 부활했다 That old style [fad] has come back into fashion. →¶부활시키다 revive / resuscitate / restore (to life).
● **부활절** Easter; [그 축제일] Easter Day [Sunday]; [철] Eastertide. ¶~ 전날 Easter eve∥~ 다음 날 Easter Monday∥~ 주간 (Easter Sunday로부터 1주일간) Easter week.

부회장(副會長) a vice-chairman; a vice-president.

부흥(復興) [재흥] (a) revival; restoration; rehabilitation; [재건] reconstruction. ¶경제~ economic revival / an economic comeback∥문예 ~ the Renaissance / the Revival. **부흥하다** [재흥하다] revive (the economy); [재건하다] reconstruct. ¶서울은 잿더미 속에서 부흥했다 Seoul rose from the [its] ashes.
● **부흥회** a revival (service).

북¹ [베틀의] a spindle; a shuttle.

북² a drum. ¶큰~ a big drum / (오케스트라용) a low [bass] drum∥작은~ a high drum / (오케스트라용) a side [snare] drum∥~을 치다 beat a drum∥~을 울려 어린이들을 모으다 drum up children.
북은 칠수록 소리가 난다(속담) Don't waste argument on such a person.

북³ [흙] soil that covers roots; a hill (over [around] roots).
북을 주다 earth up; hill (potatoes).

북⁴ [소리가] with a scratching sound; with a rip. ¶~ 긁다 scratch∥헝겊을 ~ 찢다 rip a piece of cloth.

북(北) the north(ward). ⇨**북쪽**

북괴(北傀) (communist) north Korea; the north Korean puppet regime; the north Korean Communists.

북구(北歐) North [Northern] Europe. ⇨**북유럽**

북구라파(北歐羅巴) North [Northern] Europe. ⇨**북유럽**

북극(北極) the North Pole. ¶~의 arctic / polar∥~을 경유하여 via [by way of] the North Pole.
● **북극곰** [동] a white [polar] bear. ⇨**흰곰**
북극광 the aurora borealis; the northern lights. **북극권** the Arctic circle [zone]. **북극성** [천] the polar star; the polestar; Polaris; the North Star; the lodestar. **북극 지방** the Arctic [polar] regions. **북극해 / 북극양** the Arctic Ocean.

북녘(北-) the north(ward); the northern part [district].

북단(北端) the northern extremity [end]; the northernmost extreme.

북대서양(北大西洋) the North Atlantic Ocean.
● **북대서양 조약 기구** the North Atlantic Treaty Organization(약어 NATO).

북데기 waste straw.

북돋다 enliven; raise. ⇨**북돋우다**

북돋우다 [원기·힘을] enliven; [쪽]으로 stimulate; encourage; cheer up; strengthen; invigorate. ¶허영심[흥미]을 ~ excite [stir up] a person's vanity [interest]∥나의 호기심을 더욱 북돋우었다 My curiosity was stimulated all the more.∥위로의 말만으로는 그의 사기를 북돋우어 주지 못한다 We won't be able to cheer him up [encourage him] with mere words of consolation.∥제1회전에 이김으로써 팀의 사기가 북돋우어졌다 Winning the first game bolstered the teams' spirits [gave the team a life].

북동(北東) (the) northeast(약어 NE). ¶~(쪽)의 northeast / northeastern∥~(쪽)으로 (to the) northeast / northeastward∥배는 ~쪽으로 나아가고 있다 The ship is sailing northeast [toward the northeast]. / The ship is on a northeasterly course.∥나는 서울의 ~쪽에 살고 있다 I live in [to] the northeast of Seoul.(▶ to는 서울 바깥쪽)
● **북동풍** a northeasterly wind; a northeaster.

북두칠성(北斗七星) [천] (미) the Big Dipper; the Plow [(영) Plough]; the Great Bear; the Ursa Major.

북류하다(北流-) flow north.

북면(北面) [북향] facing (the) north; [북쪽에 있는 면] the north side [face]. **북면하다** face (the) north.

북미(北美) North America. ⇨**북아메리카**

북반구(北半球) [적도에서 북쪽 부분] the northern hemisphere.

북받치다 well up; gush out [forth]. ⇨**복받치다**

북방(北方) **1** the north(ward). ⇨**북쪽 2** [북쪽 지방] a northern district.
● **북방 민족** a northern race. **북방 정책** a northward policy.

북벌(北伐) [북쪽 지역을 치는 것] the subjugation [conquest] of the northern areas. **북벌하다** subjugate [conquer / attack] the north.

북부(北部) the northern part; the north. ¶~의 northern.

북북 [긁는 소리] with a scraping sound; [찢는 소리] (rip) to pieces. ¶다리를 ~ 긁다 scratch one's leg roughly∥그림을 ~ 찢다 rip a picture to pieces∥벽을 ~ 긁다 scratch [scrape] (against) the wall∥이를 ~ 갈다 gnash [grind] one's teeth furiously.

북북동(北北東) (the) north-northeast(약어 NNE). ¶키를 ~으로 잡다 steer north-northeast.

북북서(北北西) (the) north-northwest(약어 NNW). ¶바람은 ~에서 불어오고 있다 The wind is blowing north-northwest.

북빙양(北氷洋) the Arctic Ocean. ⇨북극해(⇨북극)

북상(北上) going north; northing. ¶태풍이 ~중이다 The typhoon is moving northward. **북상하다** go (up) north.

북새통 ¶~에 in the confusion / during the commotion // ~에 아이를 잃다 lose one's child in the hustle and bustle // ~에 도둑질하다 steal something in the midst of [taking advantage of] the confusion // ~에 한몫 보다 fish in troubled waters.

북서(北西) (the) northwest(약어 NW). ¶~으로 northwest / northwestern // ~로 (to the) northwest / northwestward.
● **북서풍** a northwesterly wind; a northwester.

북송(北送) [북으로 보냄] repatriation to the north. **북송하다** repatriate to the north.
● **북송선** a repatriation ship to the north.

북슬북슬하다 plump and shaggy.

북아메리카(北 -) North America. ¶~의 North American.

북안(北岸) the northern coast.

북양(北洋) [북쪽의 바다] the north sea [ocean]; the northern waters.
● **북양 어업** the northern-sea fishery.

북어(北魚) [마른 명태] a dried pollack [pollock].

북위(北緯) [적도 이북의 위도] the north latitude(약어 N.L.). ¶~ 38도 38 degrees [38°] North Latitude // 서울은 ~ 37도 33분에 있다 Seoul is situated in lat. 37°33′N.

북유럽(北 -) North [Northern] Europe; Scandinavia. ¶~의 North [Northern] European / Scandinavian.

북적거리다 1 [사람이 들끓다] bustle; crowd; be crowded [thronged] (with people); be bustling [in a bustle]; be congested (with). ¶북적거리는 거리 a crowded street // bustling street // 장은 사람들로 북적거렸다 The fair was thronged with people. 2 [술 등이 끓어오르다] boil (over); come to a boil; bubble up; be in ferment.

북적북적 in a bustle; bustlingly; uproariously; tumultuously. **북적북적하다** bustle; boil (over). ⇨북적거리다

북진하다(北進 -) go [march] north; sail northward.

북쪽(北 -) the north(ward). ¶~의 north (ward) / northern / northerly // …의 ~에 to the north of / [방향에] in the direction of north / [북부에] in the north part of / [경계를 접하여] on the north side of // ~으로 northward(s) / north / toward(s) north / in a northerly direction // 서울의 ~ 20마일에 at 20 miles north of Seoul // 우리나라는 ~으로 만주와 접한다 On the north Korea borders on Manchuria.

북채 a drumstick; a stick.

북천(北天) the northern sky; [천] the sky north of the zodiac.

북춤 a drum dance; a dance with a drum. ¶~을 추다 perform a drum dance.

북측(北側) the north(ward). ⇨북쪽

북통(- 筒) the (wooden) body of a drum; a drum frame; a drum. ¶~ 같다 be potbellied.

북풍(北風) a north [northerly] wind. ¶차디찬 ~ a freezing [biting / piercing] north wind // ~이 살을 엘 듯이 차다 The north wind cuts like a blade.

북한(北韓) North Korea; (공식명) the Democratic People's Republic of Korea. ¶~ 문제 전문가 an expert on North Korea affairs.

북해(北海) [영국 북쪽의 바다] the North Sea.

북향(北向) a northern aspect [exposure]. **북향하다** face (the) north.
● **북향집** a house facing (the) north.

북회귀선(北回歸線) the tropic of Cancer.

분 a personage; a worthy; a gentleman; a lady. ¶이 [저] ~ this [that] gentleman [lady] // 손님 네 ~ four customers [guests] // 여러 ~ ladies and gentlemen / everybody / all of you // K라는 ~ a gentleman named K / a (certain) Mr. K.

분(分) 1 (10분의 1) one-tenth; a tenth; (100분의 1) percent. 2 [시간의 단위] a minute. ¶15~간 for fifteen minutes [a quarter of an hour] // 한 시 30~ (미) half after one / (영) half-past one / one thirty [1:30] // 30~ 후에 제가 전화를 드리겠습니다 I will call you back in thirty minutes [half an hour] // 한 시 15 ~ 전입니다 It is a quarter to one. / 세 시 20 ~입니다 It is twenty minutes past three. / It is three twenty. 3 [각도의 단위] a minute. ¶북위 32도 10~ 32 degrees 10 minutes north latitude(약어 32°10′ N. Lat). 4 one's lot; one's place. ⇨분수²

분(憤·忿) [분한 마음] indignation; resentment; ire; exasperation; anger; rage; wrath. ¶~을 풀다 vent one's anger [spite] (on) // (남의) ~을 돋우다 fan (a person's) anger / add insult to injury // 참았던 나의 ~이 폭발했다 My repressed anger [indignation] exploded. // 그는 그 같은 부당한 조치에 ~을 참을 수 없었다 He could not contain his anger [(문어) wrath] in the face of such an unjust measure.

분(盆) a pot; a flowerpot. ¶~에 꽃을 가꾸다 grow a flower in a pot.

분(粉) (face) powder. ¶물~ liquid powder // 얼굴에 ~을 바르다 powder one's face.

-분(分) 1 [나눔] division; [부분] a part. ¶2~의 1 one half / a half // 3~의 1 one third / a third (part) // 4~의 3 three quarters // 3과 8~의 6 three and six eighths // 247~의 162 a hundred and sixty-two over two hundred and forty-seven // 5만~의 1의 지도 a map on the scale of 1:50,000 [▶ one to fifty thousand라고 읽음] // 1시간의 4~의 1은 15분이다 A quarter of an hour is fifteen minutes. // 나는 숙제의 4~의 3을 끝냈다 I have finished three quarters of my homework. // 이것을 3~해 주십시오 Please divide this into three.
2 [분량] an amount; quantity; a ration(식량의); [몫] a share; a portion. ¶2일~의 약 medicine for two days // 1주일~의 식료품 a week's supply of food // 그는 2인~을 먹었다 He ate enough for two persons. // 그는 3인~일을 한다 He does the work of three men. // 한 달~ 방세와 식대는 얼마죠 How much is room and board per month?
3 [물질의 구성 요소]. ¶이 과자는 당~이 많다 This cake contains a lot of sugar.

분가(分家) a branch family; a cadet family;

an offshoot. **분가하다** establish[set up] a branch[separate] family. ¶내 동생은 분가하였다 My younger brother moved out and started[set up] a branch family.

분간(分揀) distinction; discrimination. **분간하다** distinguish[discriminate] 《A from B / between A and B》; know[can tell] 《from》. ¶분간하기 어려운 indistinguishable // 분간할 수 없을 정도로 beyond[our of] recognition ; indistinguishably // 향기[와인]를 ~ smell incense[taste wine] to judge[test] the variety // 진짜 진주와 가짜 진주를 ~ distinguish real pearls from[between real pearls and] imitation pearls // 저 쌍둥이를 분간할 수 있겠니 Can you tell those twins apart?

분갑(粉匣) a (powder) compact; a puff case [box].

분개(分介) journalizing. **분개하다** [경] journalize.
● **분개장**(一帳) a journal (book). ¶~에 기입하다 enter in a journal.

분개(憤慨) indignation; anger; resentment. ¶위선에 대한 ~ impatience of hypocrisy. **분개하다** be angry 《at》; be enraged 《by / at》; resent; be indignant 《at / over》; burn with indignation; chafe 《at》. ¶분개하여 in a rage / in resentment[indignation] // 자넨 나를 분개하게 만든다 You make me very angry. // 그는 친구의 배신에 분개하고 있었다 He was indignant at[He resented] his friend's betrayal. // 그는 분개하여 방을 뛰쳐나갔다 He rushed[flung] out of the room in indignation. // 그는 개에게 돌을 던진 아이들에 대해 분개하고 있었다 He was indignant[furious] with the children for throwing stones at his dog.

분격(憤激) exasperation; resentment; wrath. **분격하다** exasperate 《at / against》; get enraged; be infuriated.

분견(分遣) [갈라서 내보냄] detachment; detail. **분견하다** detach; detail; draft; tell off.
● **분견대** a detachment; a detached force; a contingent.

분계(分界) [한계] delimitation; demarcation; [경계] the boundary; the border.
● **분계선** a boundary line; a line of demarcation. ¶한반도의 군사 ~ the Military Demarcation Line on the Korean Peninsular // ~을 긋다 draw a line between 《the two》.

분골쇄신하다(粉骨碎身一) do one's best; make one's best exertion; exert oneself to the utmost; devote one's energies 《to》. ¶분골쇄신하겠습니다 I will do my best. / I will exert myself to the utmost.

분과(分科) a department; a branch; a section; a course (of study). ¶대수학은 수학의 한 ~다 Algebra is a branch of mathematics.
● **분과 위원회** a subcommittee.

분과(分課) a subdivision (of a section); a section of a bureau; a section; a branch. **분과하다** divide (an office); divide (a bureau) into sections.

분관(分館) an annex; (영) an annexe; a detached building; (도서관의) a branch library.

분광(分光) a spectrum (pl. -ra, ~s).
● **분광계** a spectrometer. **분광기**(一器) a spectroscope; a spectral apparatus. **분광 사진** a spectrogram; a spectrograph. **분광학** spectroscopy.

분교(分校) a branch school. ¶S교의 ~ a branch[an annex] of the S school.

분국(分局) a branch office[bureau].

분권(分權) decentralization of power[authority]. ¶지방 ~ decentralization. **분권하다** decentralize power[authority].
● **분권주의** decentralism.

분규(紛糾) [뒤얽힌 말썽] complication(s); entanglement; tangle; confusion; disorder; a trouble. ¶~를 **일으키다** cause[make] trouble // 세 사람 사이에 일어난 ~는 한층 심해졌다 The relations among the three became even more complicated. // ~ 사태는 점점 더 심화되었다 The situation grew more and more entangled[involved]. // 회의에서 그 일을 둘러싸고 회원들이 ~에 휘말렸다 The members got into an imbroglio over the matter at the meeting.

분극(分極) [전] polarization. ¶~화(化) polarization // ~하다 polarize.

분근(分根) [뿌리를 나눔] root division; [나눈 뿌리] a divided root. **분근하다** part[divide] the roots (of a plant) for transplanting.

분기(分岐·分歧) [나뉘어 갈라짐] divergence; ramification; forking. **분기하다** diverge (from a center[a main course]); branch off (away); turn off; fork; ramify. ¶여기서 선로가 간선으로부터 분기한다 Here the track diverges[branches off] from the trunk line.
● **분기선** a branch (line); a spur track; a turnout track. **분기점** a turning point; (선로의) a junction; (도로의) a crossroads. ¶그 역은 철도의 ~이었다 That station was located at a junction (point). / The tracks branched off in various directions at that station. // 그는 인생의 ~에 서 있었다 He was standing at the turning point[crossroads] of his life.

분기공(噴氣孔) (화산의) a fumarole; a vent.

분기하다(奮起一) rouse (oneself) (to action); be stirred up; bestir[rouse] oneself; brace one's energies[nerve]. ¶그의 성공담을 듣고 분기하여 나는 시험을 위해 재수할 생각을 하게 되었다 His story of success stirred me to try the examination again. ➤¶남을 분기시키는 설교 an inspiring sermon // 남을 분기시키다 rouse a person into activity.

분김(憤一) in a fit of anger[rage]; in (one's) mortification[resentment / indignation]; out of vexation. ¶그는 ~ 그 편지를 갈기갈기 찢었다 He tore the letter into pieces in a fit of anger.

분꽃(粉一) a four-o'clock; a marvel-of-Peru (pl. marvels-of-Peru).

분납(分納) payment in[by] installments; installment payment. **분납하다** pay in[by] installments. ¶나는 세금을 4회에 분납했다 I paid my taxes in four installments.

분내(粉一) the smell of face powder.

분노(憤怒·忿怒) anger; (a) rage; (a) fury; (문어) wrath; resentment; indignation. ¶~에 찬 목소리 an angry voice // ~에 불타오르다 burn with anger / rage / be furious // 남의 ~를 유발하다 [가라앉히다] arouse[calm] a person's anger // ~가 머리끝에 오르다[폭발하다] fly into a rage[fury] / explode in anger // 나는 ~에 자제력을 잃었다 I forgot myself in anger. / I was carried away by anger. I was beside myself with anger. // 나는 ~에 못 이겨[정신이 나가] 그를 때렸다[주먹으로 쳤다] Blind with rage[In a fit of anger], I hit him.

¶그런 부당한 처사에 대해 나는 ~를 참을 수 없었다 I was unable to repress my indignation at such injustice.∥국민의 ~에도 불구하고 정부는 중세를 부과할 계획이었다 Ignoring the people's anger [(문어) wrath], the government planned to impose heavy taxes on them.∥그의 얼굴에 ~의 빛이 짙어졌다 The look of anger deepened on his face. **분노하다** get [become] angry; get into rage; be exasperated [indignant / enraged]; flare [fire] up. ¶나는 마음속으로 분노했다 I felt resentment in my heart.

분뇨(糞尿) excrementitious matter; human waste; excretions; feces and urine; night soil. ¶~를 **치다** remove [dip up] night soil.
● **분뇨차** a dung cart; a honey wagon.

분단(分團) a branch; a chapter.

분단(分斷) dividing into sections; division; partition. ¶국토 ~ division of territory / national division / division [partitioning] of the country / 한반도의 ~ the partition of the Korean peninsula. **분단하다** divide (into sections); partition (into).
● **분단국가** a divided [partitioned] country [nation / state].

분담(分擔) assignment; allotment; share; division of works(분업). ¶손해 ~ apportionment of a loss∥내 ~은 이것뿐입니다 This is my allotted share of the work. / This is the work assigned to me. **분담하다** 〔일 등을 나누다〕 divide; 〔공유하다〕 share; 〔할당하다〕 assign. ¶각자 일을 분담하자 Let's divide [split] up the work among us.∥자네와 비용을 분담하겠네 I will share the expenses with you.

분당(分黨)〔당파를 가름〕 secession (from a political party); 〔가른 당파〕 a split [splinter] party. **분당하다** secede (from a political organization).

분대(分隊)〔소대의 구성 단위〕〔육군의〕 a squad; 〔해군의〕 a division.
● **분대장**〔육군의〕 a squad commander.

분대질 making [raising] trouble; meddling(참견); disturbance(소란); botheration; nuisance(폐 끼침). **분대질하다** bother; upset; disturb; meddle; make [raise] trouble; make a nuisance of oneself; kick up a dust.

분도기(分度器) a protractor. ⇨각도기(⊕각도)

분동(分銅) a weight; a counterweight; a counterpoise.

분란(紛亂) disorder; confusion; trouble(s). ¶정치적 ~ a political disturbance∥가정 ~ a family trouble [strife]. **분란하다**〈서술적〉 be in confusion [disorder]; be in a tangle.

분량(分量)〔계량할 수 있는 것의 양〕 a quantity; 〔총량〕 an amount; (약의) a dose. ¶(수)화물의 ~ the quantity [amount] of baggage [luggage]∥소금의 ~을 줄이다〔배로 하다〕 reduce [double] the amount [quantity] of salt∥~을 정확하게 재다 measure the quantity [amount] exactly∥약의 ~을 잘못 알다 make an error in dosage.

분력(分力)〔물〕 a component (of a force); a component force.

분류(分流) a distributary; a branch; a tributary. **분류하다** branch from (a larger river).

분류(分溜)〔화〕 fractional distillation; fractionation; fraction. **분류하다** fractionate; crack.

분류(分類) assortment; (조직적인) classification; grouping; 〔생〕 diagnosis. ¶인위〔자연〕 ~법 artificial [natural] classification∥제목에 의한 책의 ~ classification of books by subject. **분류하다** sort; (문어) assort; (계통적으로) classify. ¶쓰레기를 ~ separate rubbish [(미) garbage] according to type [according to whether it should be burned or not]∥달걀을 크기로 ~ sort eggs according to size∥쌓인 서류를 ~ sort out accumulated files∥그림을 수채화와 유화로 ~ classify paintings into water color and oil paintings∥이 슈퍼마켓에서는 원하는 물건을 쉽게 고를 수 있도록 분류해 놓고 있다 This supermarket has arranged items in such a way that it is easy to choose what one wants. ➔¶우편은 행선지에 따라 분류된다 Mail is sorted according to destination.
● **분류표** a classification table. **분류학** taxonomy; taxology; the science of classification. **분류학자** a taxonomist; a systematist.

분류(奔流)〔세찬 물줄기〕 a torrent; a rapid [rushing] stream. ¶~에 **떠내려가다** be swept away by the torrent. **분류하다** rush; flush; run with rapidity; dash along.

분리(分離)〔나뉘어 떨어짐〕 separation; secession; disunion; severance; disjunction; division; split; 〔이탈〕 detachment; 〔절연〕 isolation; (인종 간 등의) segregation. ¶정치와 교육의 ~ separation of politics and education∥인종 간〔백인과 흑인〕의 ~ segregation of races [of blacks and whites]∥재산 ~ separation of property∥정경 ~ separation of political and economic affairs. **분리하다** 〔떼어 놓다〕 separate (from); secede; disjoin; disconnect; split; detach; sever; isolate; 〔떨어지다〕 be separated (from); be divided (from); be isolated (from); secede [sever] oneself (from); split off. ➔¶인종에 의해 분리된 교육 [버스] segregated education [buses].
● **분리 과세** separate taxation. **분리기** a separator. ¶원심 ~ a centrifuge. **분리대**〔중앙 ~〕(미) a median strip / (영) a central reserve. **분리수거** separate collection.

분립(分立)〔분리〕 separation; 〔독립〕 independence. ¶입법, 행정, 사법권의 ~ the separation [independence] of legislative, administrative and judicial authority. **분립하다** set up independently; become independent (of).

분만(分娩) (a) childbirth. ⇨해산(解産)
● **분만실** a delivery room. **분만 휴가** maternity leave.

분말(粉末) powder; dust. ⇨가루

분망하다(奔忙−) busy; bustling; 〔서술적〕 be occupied (with business); be heavily engaged (in). ¶회의 준비에 ~ be very busy preparing for a conference.

분매하다(分賣−) sell (things) separately [singly]. ¶땅을 ~ sell land in lots / parcel out land.

분명하다(分明−) clear; obvious; evident; plain; unquestionable; distinct. ¶분명한 사실 an obvious fact∥분명한 증거 positive [unquestionable] evidence∥그 둘 사이의 분명한 차이 a clear distinction between the two∥분명하지 않은 어린 시절의 기억 indistinct memories of childhood∥분명한 발음 distinct [clear] pronunciation∥문장의 뜻이 분명하지 않다 The meaning of the sentence is ambiguous [not clear].∥그 뜻은 아주 ~ The meaning is quite clear.∥그녀는 말없이

가만히 있었지만 그것을 싫어하고 있다는 것이 분명했다 Though she remained silent, it was clear[plain] to me that she did not like it.// 그의 말끝은 분명하지 않다 He does not pronounce the last syllable of words distinctly. // 그의 진술에는 분명하지 않은 점이 있다 His statement has something ambiguous about it.// 그의 대답에는 분명하지 않은 데가 있다 There is some ambiguity in his reply.// 불을 보는 것처럼 ~ It is as clear as day.// 그에게서 아무런 원조도 바랄 수 없다는 것은 ~ It is clear[plain] that we can expect no help from him.// 그가 그것을 훔쳤다는 것은 ~ It is obvious[evident] that he stole it.// 그것의 효과는 아직 분명하지 않다 Its effectiveness has not been proved yet.// 그의 태도는 분명하지 않다 His attitude is ambivalent.// 분명한 대답을 해 주십시오 Give me a definite answer. **분명히** clearly; distinctly; plainly; obviously; evidently; [확실하게] definitely; certainly; undoubtedly. ¶문제의 요점을 ~ 하다 make the point at issue clear / clarify the point at issue // 자네는 ~ 그것을 알고 있겠지 You evidently[obviously] know about it, don't you?// 이것은 ~ 피카소 그림이다 This is unquestionably a painting of Picasso's.// 그는 악의가 없었다는 것을 ~ 했다 He showed clearly[plainly] that he meant no harm.// 그는 이 논문에서 자기 입장을 ~ 했다 He defined his position in this thesis.// 그는 자신의 가설이 옳았다는 것을 ~ 했다 He proved that his hypothesis was correct.// 당신의 의도는 ~ 해 주시오 Will you explain your motive?// 수상은 자기의 외교 방침을 ~ 했다 The Prime Minister made known[public] his foreign policy.// 그는 ~ 말했다 He spoke out[up].// 이 그림은 그의 대표작이다 This painting is beyond a doubt[unquestionably] his best work.// 그의 승리였다 His victory was absolute. / He won a clear[clear-cut] victory.// 이것과 저것은 ~ 구별된다 We make a sharp[clear-cut] distinction between this and that.// 내 눈으로 ~ 보았다 I saw it distinctly[clearly] with my own eyes.// ~ 약속했지 You've made a firm promise, right?// 좀 더 ~ 말씀해 주시겠습니까 Will you speak more plainly?// 이름을 ~ 써 주십시오 Please write your name legibly[clearly]// 선생님의 목소리는 ~ 들린다 I can hear the teacher's voice clearly [distinctly].// 이제 나는 내가 바보였다는 것을 ~ 알았다 Now I see clearly that I was a fool.// 난 이 점을 ~ 해 두고 싶다 I'd like to make this point clear.// 이 사건에 대해서는 ~ 기억하고 있다 I have a vivid recollection of that incident.// ~ 말하면 너는 모든 사람에게 귀찮은 존재다 To be plain[frank] (with you), you are a nuisance to everybody.// 그는 매사에 ~ 말하는 사람이다 He is an outspoken person.

분모(分母) [수] a denominator. ¶공(公)~ a common denominator.
분묘(墳墓) a grave; a tomb. ⇨ 무덤
분무(噴霧) [화] atomizing.
  ● **분무기** a spray(er); a spray gun; a vaporizer; a pulverizer; (향수용) an atomizer; (의료용) a nebulizer. ¶~로 천에 물을 뿌리다 spray water on cloth with a sprayer.
분문(噴門) [생] the cardia; the esophageal [cardiac] orifice (of the stomach).

분받침(盆-) a flowerpot saucer.
분발(奮發) strenuous exertions[efforts]; a spurt. **분발하다** strain[exert] oneself; make strenuous efforts; put forth one's efforts; spurt; stir up oneself. ¶분발하여 일하다 work at top speed / put all one's energies into one's work // 우리는 좀 더 분발해야 한다 We must try a little harder. → 남을 분발시키다 inspire a person with courage / rouse a person (into activity).

분방하다(奔放-) wild; unrestrained; free; [예술가 등이 전통에 얽매이지 않다] bohemian. ¶분방하게 wildly / without inhibitions // 자유분방하게 행동하다 have one's (own) way / behave as one pleases // 자유분방하게 살다 lead a free and uninhibited[unrestrained] life.

분배(分配) [배급] distribution; [나누어 줌] division; [할당] allotment; allocation. ¶이익 ~ division of profit / profit sharing // 부의 ~ distribution of wealth // 나는 이익 ~를 받지 못했다 I was not able to share in[(구어) get a cut of] the profits. **분배하다** distribute (among / to); divide (among / between); share (out) apportion; portion (out); allocate; allot. ¶난민에게 식량을 ~ distribute food to refugees. → 그가 남긴 돈은 세 형제에게 동등하게 분배되었다 The money he left was divided equally among his three brothers.
  ● **분배 국민 소득** the national income distributed. **분배 법칙** [수] the distributive law.

분별(分別) 1 [구분] division; [분리] separation; [차별] distinction; discrimination; [분류] classification; assortment. **분별하다** [구분하다] classify; assort; [화] fractionate. ¶분별할 수 있는[없는] distinguishable [indistinguishable] // 목소리를 ~ recognize (a person's) voice // 분별할 수 없다 cannot distinguish (between things / A from B) / cannot tell (A from B) // 그는 술이 취하면 사람을 분별하지 못한다 He loses all distinction of people when he gets drunk.
2 [세상사에 대한 바른 판단] discretion; prudence; judgment; wisdom (지혜); good sense (직관적인). ¶~(이) 있는 discreet / prudent / sensible / thoughtful / wise / judicious / considerate // ~ 없는 indiscreet / imprudent / thoughtless / injudicious // ~이 있어 보이는 여자 a prudent-looking woman // ~이 생길 나이 the age of wisdom[discretion / discernment] // ~이 있다 be sensible / have discretion[good sense] / know where one stands // ~을 잃다 lose one's wits[mind] / lose control of oneself // 그는 ~이 있는 사람이다 He is a man of sense. / He knows right from wrong.// 내가 그렇게 경솔히 행동한 것은 ~없는 짓이었다 It was thoughtless of me to act so rashly. **분별하다** judge; discern; discriminate; use[exercise] discretion.

분봉하다(分蜂-) hive off; swarm; split the hive.
분부(分付·吩咐) [명령] an order; a bidding; a command; [지시] directions; instructions. ¶~대로 하다 do as one is bidden[told] / act according to orders[commands] / follow the instructions // ~를 **받다** have orders (to do) // ~를 어김없이 거행하다 carry out instructions to the letter // 부모님의 ~를 거역하다

disobey one's parents // ~대로 하겠습니다 I am completely at your service. / I shall obey your orders. // 무슨 일이든 ~만 내리십시오 We are ready to comply with your request. / We are ready to carry out your orders. **분부하다** tell [order / command / direct / instruct / charge] (a person to do something); bid (a person do something); give [send] (a person) an order (for); place an order (for).

분분하다(紛紛-) [소란하다] tumultuous; [어수선하다] complicated; scattered; pell-mell; [다르다] diverse; divergent; various; conflicting. ¶이 문제에 대해서 의견이 ~ There are various opinions about [Opinion is divided on] this question. / There is a diversity [divergence] of opinion on this point. / There are conflicting opinions on this question. **분분히** confusedly; pell-mell; in confusion.

분비(分泌) [생] secretion. ¶내 ~ internal secretion // ~를 촉진하는 secretive [secernent] // 위액의 ~ the secretion of gastric juices. **분비하다** secrete. ¶이 선(腺)은 타액을 분비한다 These glands secrete saliva.

● **분비물** a secretion; an exudate; excreta(선(腺) 분비물). **분비선 / 분비샘** a secreting gland. **분비 세포** a secreting cell. **분비액** secreting fluid; juice.

분사(分詞) [언] a participle. ¶현재 [과거] ~ a present [past] participle.

● **분사 구문** a participial construction.

분사(噴射) jet; spray; injection. **분사하다** jet (water); shoot (water) at [into]; shoot out (water); eject.

● **분사 추진 기관** a jet-propelled engine. **분사 추진식 비행기** a jet (plane). ➪ 제트기(⑤제트)

분사하다(憤死-) die of indignation [resentment]; die in a fit of anger.

분산(分散) 1 breakup; dispersion; decentralization; divergence. ¶인구 ~책 the population decentralization policies. **분산하다** break up; scatter; disperse; decentralize (industries). ¶인구는 ~ disperse the population // 그들은 분산하여 목적지로 향하였다 They dispersed and headed for their destination. ➜ ¶공장을 지방으로 분산시키는 것이 바람직하다 It is desirable that factories be dispersed around the country. 2 [물] dispersion. ¶빛의 ~ dispersion of light. 3 [수] variance.

● **분산매**(-媒) dispersion media.

분서갱유(焚書坑儒) [역] burning books on the Chinese classics and burying Confucian scholars alive.

분석(分析) analysis (pl. -ses); (금속의) assay(ing). ¶미시적 [거시적] ~ a microscopic [macroscopic] analysis / microanalysis [macroanalysis] // 소득 [가격] ~ income [price] analysis // 스펙트럼 ~ spectrum analysis // 정량 [정성] ~ quantitative [qualitative] analysis // 정신 ~ psychoanalysis // 중량 ~ gravimetric analysis // 한계 ~ [경] marginal analysis // 분석적 analytic(al) // ~적 사고 analytic thinking // ~에 의하여 그것이 세 요소로 이루어져 있음이 판명되었다 Analysis showed [It was proved by analysis] that it consisted of three elements. **분석하다** analyze; resolve; assay (a drug / an alloy); make an analysis; reduce (a thing) to its element; take apart. ¶분석할 수 없는 unanalyzable / indecomposable // 실패의 원인을 ~ analyze the cause of failure // 광석의 견본을 ~ assay an ore sample // 그는 음식을 분석하여 독이 들어 있는 것을 알아냈다 He analyzed the food and found it contained poison.

● **분석 비평** analytical criticism. **분석표** an analysis table. **분석학** analytics. **분석 화학** analytical chemistry.

분설(分設) establishment of a branch; separate establishment [installation]. **분설하다** establish [set up] a branch; install a branch (of); install separately.

분손(分損) [경] partial loss.

분쇄(粉碎) pulverization; trituration; [건] grinding. **분쇄하다** [가루로 만들다] pulverize; comminute; reduce to powder; [부수다] crush; break into pieces [fragments]; shatter [smash] to pieces [smithereens]; reduce into splinters; (기도 등을) frustrate [baffle] (a plan); (적군을) crush; annihilate; smash. ¶적군을 ~ crush [annihilate] the enemy // (상대의) 주장을 ~ tear (a person's) argument to pieces // 음모를 ~ crush [smash] a plot. ➜ ¶반란군은 당장에 분쇄되었다 The rebel forces were crushed in no time.

● **분쇄기** a grinder; pulverizer; a crusher; powdering machine; a mill(수동식).

분수¹(分數) 1 [사려 분별] discretion; propriety; discrimination; discernment; good sense. ¶~를 아는 discerning / discreet / sensible // ~를 모르는 undiscerning / indiscreet / imprudent / unreasonable.

2 [분한(分限)] one's lot; one's place; one's status; one's social station [position / standing]. ¶~를 모르고 forgetting one's place / without regard for one's position // ~를 알다 know one's station [place] / know oneself // ~를 모르다 fail to know oneself [one's place] / be self-conceited // ~를 잊다 forget oneself / (구어) get above oneself // ~를 지키다 keep to one's sphere in life / keep one's place / keep within one's bounds [own province] // ~에 맞게 행동하다 behave in accordance with one's station in life // 그는 ~에 맞는 생활에 만족하고 있었다 He was content to live within his means. // ~에 넘치는 욕망을 버려라 Give up ambitions that are beyond your reach. // ~에 넘치는 욕망 같은 것은 없다 I have no inordinate desires. // 너는 ~를 모른다 You don't know your place. // 그는 ~를 모른다 He does not know his place. // 왜 참견했어? ~도 모르고 Why did you butt in (like that)? Remember your place. // ~에 넘치는 칭찬의 말씀입니다. Thank you very much for such undeserved praise.

분수²(分數) [수] a fraction; a fractional number. ¶가~ an improper fraction // 기약~ a irreducible fraction / a fraction reduced to its lowest terms // 대(帶)~ a mixed fraction // 번~ a complex fraction // 부분~ a partial fraction // 진~ a proper fraction // ~의 fractional / fractionary.

● **분수 방정식** a fractional equation. **분수식** a fractional expression.

분수(噴水) a fountain; [분출하는 물] a jet [squirt] (of water). ¶~에서 물을 내뿜고 있다 Water is spouting [spraying] from the foun-

분수공(-孔) a jet; a spout. ¶고래의 ~ the blowhole[spout (hole)] of a whale.

분수령(分水嶺) [분수계가 되는 산맥] a watershed; a divide; [전환점] a turning point. ¶이 산맥은 이 나라의 ~을 이루고 있다 This mountain range forms the watershed of the country.

분승하다(分乘-) ride separately. ¶그들은 3대의 자동차에 분승하여 출발했다 They set out in three different cars.

분식(粉食) flour-based meals. ¶~을 장려하다 encourage the use of flour for food. 분식하다 eat foods based from ground grains; have a diet based on flour[meal].

분식(粉飾) 1 [거짓 꾸밈] makeup; furbelows; showy ornaments; toilet. 분식하다 make up (one's face); make one's toilet. 2 [겉만 발라 꾸밈] embellishment; gilding; adornment. 분식하다 embellish; adorn.

분신(分身) 1 [불] an incarnation of the Buddha. 2 [제2의 나] the other self; one's alter ego; [주체에서 갈려 나온 것] a branch; an offshoot. ¶그는 그 소년에게서 자신의 ~을 발견하였다 He found his alter ego in the boy.

분신자살(焚身自殺) suicide[self-immolation] by fire; self-burning; burning oneself to death. ¶~을 기도하다 make an attempt to burn oneself to death.

분신하다(焚身-) set fire to oneself; burn oneself (to death).

분실(分室) [관청의] a branch[detached] office; an annex; [병원의] an isolated room [ward].

분실(紛失) loss; losing. 분실하다 [잃어버리다] lose; miss. ¶도장을 분실하여 은행에 신고했다 I reported the loss of my seal to the bank. → ¶분실되다 be lost / be missing // 시계가 분실되었는데 찾을 수가 없다 I can't find my watch. // 그 책은 분실되었음이 틀림없다 The book must have got lost.

●**분실물** a lost[missing] article; lost property. ¶~ 습득자 the finder of a lost article. 분실(물) 신고 a report of the loss of an article.

분압(分壓) [물] partial pressure. ⇒"부분 압력(分압력)"부분.

분야(分野) a field; a sphere; a division; a realm; a branch; one's speciality[line]. ¶연구 ~ a field[an area] of study // ~가 다른 사람들 men of different fields // 수학의 여러 ~ various branches of mathematics // 음악 ~에 종사하는 사람 a career[professional] musician // 다른 ~로 진출하다 move in another sphere // 그는 그 ~에서 전문가다 He is an expert in the field. // 화학은 내 ~가 아니다 Chemistry is not in[is out of] my line. // 그녀는 여성 활동의 새 ~를 열었다 She opened up a new field[sphere] of activity to women. // 그는 조각 ~에서는 제일인자다 He is second to none in the world of sculpture. // 그것은 내 전문 ~가 아니다 It's not in my line[field]. / That's out of my line[field].

분양(分讓) sale (of land) in lots[parcels]. 분양하다 sell (land) in lots[parcels]; divide (one's estate) into lots[parcels] and sell; lot out; parcel out.

●**분양 주택** a house built for sale in parcels. [맨션] a condominium.

분업(分業) division of labor[(영) labour]; [경] specialization. ¶국제 ~ international division of labor // 의약 ~ separation of the dispensary from the doctor's office[clinic / (영) surgery] // 우리는 일을 ~으로 했다 We each took responsibility for one aspect of the work. 분업하다 divide work (among); specialize (in). ¶셋이 분업하자 Let's divide the work among us three.

분연하다(憤然-·忿然-) indignant; wrathful. 분연히 angrily; indignantly; in anger; in a rage. ¶~ 일어나다 spring up[get to one's feet] in a rage // 그는 ~ 방을 나갔다 He left [flung out of] the room in anger[indignation / a rage].

분연하다(奮然-) resolute; strenuous; vigorous. ¶재해에 직면해서도 분연한 그들의 정신은 가상하다 The determined spirit they have shown in the face of the disaster is admirable. 분연히 resolutely; courageously; vigorously; with one's determination. ¶아군은 ~ 적군을 공격했다 Our army vigorously [courageously] attacked the enemy. // 그는 ~ 일에 대처했다 He resolutely tackled the problem.

분열(分裂) division; dissolution; dismemberment; disintegration; disunion; (사람이나 당파 간의) split; (종파 등의) schism; (세포의) segmentation; disorganization. ¶핵 ~ nuclear fission / (생물의) nuclear division // 유사[무사] ~ [생] mitosis[amitosis] // 감수 ~ [생] meiosis / reduction division // 다수 ~ [생] multiple division // 사상적 ~ an ideological division // 세포 ~ cell division // 급진파와 반동파의 ~ a schism between radicals and reactionaries // 그 사건은 당내에 ~을 초래했다 The affair brought about a split in the party. 분열하다 split; segment; disunite; break up; be split[disunited]; be disrupted; be divided; be fragmented; be torn. → ¶반대 당을 분열시키다 split the opposition party.

●**분열상** a mitotic phase. **분열 생식** [생] reproduction by fission[through division]; schizogenesis.

분열식(分列式) a march-past; [비행기의 공중 분열식] a flyby; (영) a flypast. ¶병사들은 대통령 앞에서 ~을 했다 The soldiers marched past the President's stand.

분열하다(分列-) file off.

분외(分外) ¶~의 [분수에 넘치는] inordinate / excessive / immoderate / not within proper limits / [당치 않은] undue / undeserved / unmerited / [특별한] special // ~의 영광으로 생각합니다 I am afraid I do not deserve this great honor. / It is an honor I hardly deserve.

분원(分院) a branch (of an institute); (병원의) a branch hospital; a local clinic.

분위기(雰圍氣) [대기] the atmosphere; the air; [환경] an environment; [느낌] an atmosphere. ¶가정적인 ~ a family[homely] atmosphere // 딱딱한[어색한] ~ an uncomfortable atmosphere // 예술가적인 ~를 지닌 사람 a person with an artistic air about him // ~가 감도는 여인 a woman with an air about her / a woman with a certain air // ~를 자아내다 create[produce] an atmosphere // ~를 깨뜨리다 [망치다] destroy[mar] an atmosphere // ~가 마음에 들지 않는다 The atmosphere is not to my liking. // 그는 학문적 [종교적] ~ 속에서 자랐다 He was brought up in a scholarly[religious] atmosphere [environment]. // 방에는 우울한 ~가 감돌고 있었다 A gloomy atmosphere hung over the room. // 그녀는 자유로운 ~ 속에서 소녀 시절을 보냈다 She spent her girlhood in a free and open atmosphere. // 이 식당은 이국적인 ~가 있다 This restaurant has an exotic atmosphere.

분유(粉乳) powdered[dry / dried] milk. ¶탈지 ~ nonfat dry milk.

분자(分子) 1 [수] a numerator; [물][화] a molecule. ¶그램 ~ [화] a gram molecule / a mole. 2 [구성원] an element; a faction. ¶바람직하지 않은 ~들 undesirable elements / 당내의 불평[반동] ~를 일소해야 한다 We must cleanse[purge] the party of its discontented[reactionary] elements.
● **분자 구조** molecular structure. **분자량** molecular weight. **분자식** a molecular formula (pl. -las, -lae).

분잡(紛雜) crowdedness; confusion. ¶~을 타서 in the confusion. **분잡하다** crowded; confused.

분장(扮裝) (배우의) makeup; getup; impersonation(배역의); [변장] disguise. ¶햄릿의 ~ the impersonation of Hamlet. **분장하다** [차려입다] dress (up) (as); garb oneself (in); assume the costume (of); make up; put on a makeup; [변장하다] disguise (oneself) (as); [배우가] play the part of; appear in the character of; impersonate; dress (for one's role). ¶분장한 채로 in stage costume[makeup] // 왕자로 ~ dress (up) as a prince // 그녀는 남자의 모습으로 분장하고 있었다 She disguised herself[was disguised] as a man. // 나는 오셀로로 분장했다 I played the part of[acted as] Othello.
● **분장실** a dressing room; the greenroom; the backstage.

분재(盆栽) growing (a plant) in a pot; a potted plant; a dwarf tree. ¶~ 소나무 a dwarf pine tree. **분재하다** plant[grow] (a tree) in a pot; pot (up) (a plant).

분쟁(分爭) factional rivalry[conflict / dissensions / feud] / party strife[struggle]. ¶~을 일삼다 be given up to party squabbles // ~에 끼어들지 않다 stand aloof from[keep away] party strife. **분쟁하다** be pitted against one another; have a factional fight[dispute].

분쟁(紛爭) a dispute; (a) complication; trouble; [다툼] a quarrel. ¶국제적인 ~ an international dispute // 학원 ~ campus disturbances // 학생 riot // 노사 ~ conflicts between labor and management // ~을 중재하다 mediate a dispute // 고용주와 종업원 사이에 ~이 일어났다 There was trouble [Trouble arose] between the employer and the workers. // 아버지의 유산은 형제간의 ~의 씨가 되었다 The property our father left behind caused trouble[led to dissension] among us brothers. // 나는 ~을 피하려고 대폭 양보했다 In order to avoid complications, I made substantial concessions. **분쟁하다** have[get into] trouble (with); have a dispute[quarrel] (with).
● **분쟁 지역** troubled parts[areas]; a volatile part.

분전(奮戰) a (hard) struggle. ⇨*분투

분절(分節) [가름]. **분절하다** break something down into (its constituent) parts.

분점(分店) a branch (store); a branch (office [firm]). ¶그녀는 마포에 ~을 냈다 She opened a branch shop at Mapo.

분주하다(奔走−) busy. ¶분주한 사람 a busy person // 분주한 일정 one's tight[heavy] schedule // 일 때문에 몹시 ~ I am very busy with my work. // 나는 항상 ~ I am always kept busy. // 그는 정치 운동으로 ~ He busies himself with political movements. / He is busily engaged in a political movement. // 지금은 급한 일로 몹시 ~ Right now I have my hands full with rush jobs[I am very busy with rush work]. **분주히** busily; in a hurry[hurried manner]. ¶~ 돌아다니다 bustle about // 일자리를 찾기 위해 ~ 뛰어다니다 make every effort to find a job // 기자들은 ~ 건물을 드나들고 있다 Reporters are hurrying busily in and out of the building.

분지(盆地) [지] a basin; a (round) valley; a hollow. ¶이 지역은 ~를 이루고 있다 This area forms a (natural) basin.

분지르다 break (off). ⇨*부러뜨리다

분책(分冊) [제본] binding[printing] in fascicles; [여러 권으로 나눠 묶은 책] a fascicle; a separate volume. ¶이 백과사전은 ~을 해서 팝니까 Do you sell volumes of this encyclopedia separately[singly]? // 그 소설은 ~으로 출판되었다 The story was published in parts [several volumes]. **분책하다** issue[bind / print] in fascicles.

분첩(粉貼) (화장용) a (powder) puff; (습자용) a writing slate.

분초(分秒) [분과 초] a minute and a second; [짧은 시간] a moment; a second; a short space of time. ¶이 문제는 ~를 다툰다 This matter must be dealt with immediately. / We can't afford to waste a moment in settling this problem. / This is a matter of urgency.

분출(噴出) gushing; spouting; gust; spurt; jet; ejection; effusion; effusiveness; (화산의) eruption; belch; (용암의) extrusion; ebullition; extravasation. **분출하다** spout; gush (out); well out(▶ spout는 작은 분출구에서, gush는 다량으로 세차게 흘러나오는 모양, well out은 솟아 나오는 모양); jet; spurt; effuse; (온천 등이) boil out; (불길·연기 등이) spout; belch out; [뿜어내다] vomit; emit; eject. ¶화산이 용암을 분출했다 The volcano erupted. / (문어) The volcano spewed forth lava. // 땅에서 가스가 분출했다 Gas jetted [shot] out of the ground. // 화산이 화염과 연기를 분출하고 있었다 The volcano was belching out flames and smoke.
● **분출구** a jet; an exhaust nozzle.

분침(分針) [시계의 분을 가리키는 바늘] the minute[long] hand.

분탄(粉炭) coal dust; powdered[pulverized] coal; slack.

분통(憤痛) resentment; vexation; spite; indignation; fury. ¶~이 터지다 resent (at) / get furious / be greatly vexed // 생각하면 ~ 터져 견딜 수 없다 The thought of it makes my blood boil. // 참으로 ~이 터지는구나 How vexing!

분투(奮鬪) a (hard) struggle; hard fighting; a plucky[desperate] fight; a tight[close] fight; strenuous effort(s). ¶그의 오늘의 영광은 ~ 노력의 덕분이다 He owes this victory to his strenuous efforts. **분투하다** fight; struggle; strive (for); exert oneself; make a strenuous efforts. ¶선전 ~ put up a good fight // 끝까지

분파 ~ fight to the finish [to the bitter end] / fight it out // 끝까지 분투하다가 죽다 die in the last ditch / die game // 우리는 분투했으나 패배를 감수해야 했다 We had to endure defeat in spite of having put up a good fight. // 그들은 최후까지 분투했다 They fought it out to the very end. // 그는 성공하기 위해 밤낮으로 분투하고 있다 He is struggling for success day and night.

분파(分派) a branch; a subbranch; an offshoot; (종교의) a sect; a denomination (sect 보다 큰 분파); (정당 등의) a faction; a fraction; a splinter party. ¶이것은 기독교의 한 ~다 This is a Christian denomination. // 그들은 당의 새로운 ~를 조직하려 하고 있다 They are trying to organize a new party faction. **분파하다** branch; divide; form a new sect.

분패(憤敗) a defeat by a narrow margin.

분포(分布) (a) distribution. ¶동식물의 ~ the geographical distribution of plants and animals // 수직 [수평] ~ vertical [horizontal] distribution // 인구 ~ the spread of population. **분포하다** be distributed; range (from one place to another). ¶전 세계에 분포하고 있다 have a worldwide distribution // 이 식물은 아시아에 분포하고 있다 This plant grows [is distributed] throughout Asia.

●**분포 곡선** [수] a distribution curve. **분포도** a distribution chart [map].

분풀이(憤-) revenge; retaliation; giving vent to one's indignation. ¶~로 by way of revenge [retaliation] / to vent one's anger // 그것으로 다소 ~가 됐다 That was some consolation to me. **분풀이하다** revenge oneself (on a person for something); give vent to one's indignation; vent one's anger [spite] (on).

분필(粉筆) chalk. ¶색 ~ colored chalk // ~ 한 자루 a piece of chalk // ~로 쓰다 write with [in] chalk / chalk (down).

분하다(扮-) dress (up) (as); disguise (oneself) (as). ⇨ 분장하다(⇨분장).

분하다(憤-) 1 [원통하다] vexatious; mortifying; vexing; [화가 나다] (구어) be mad at oneself. ¶분한 마음 vexation / chagrin / mortification // 분한 나머지 from [out of] spite / in one's mortification [vexation] / spurred by chagrin // 분하게도 to one's chagrin // 분하게 여기다 [분해하다] be [feel] mortified [vexed / chagrined] (at / on) / be frustrated / be angry with oneself // 분해서 울다 cry in vexation // 사람들 앞에서 매도를 당하다니 ~ It is mortifying to be called names in public. // 그에게 감쪽같이 속은 것이 분하기 짝이 없다 I'm mad at myself for being so neatly [cleverly] taken in by him. // 우리는 경기에 져서 분했다 It chagrined us to lose the game. // 그는 발을 구르며 분해했다 He stamped the ground in vexation [frustration]. // 나는 그 손실 때문에 ~ I am chagrined by the loss. / (문어) I rue the loss.

2 [섭섭하다] regrettable; regretful; sorry. ¶그녀를 볼 기회를 놓쳐서 ~ I am sorry I missed the opportunity of seeing her. // 좀 더 조심했더라면 하고 생각하니 ~ I deeply regret that I was not more careful. / How I wish I had been more careful!

분할(分割) [나누어 쪼갬] division; partition; dismemberment. ¶토지 [국토]의 ~ the partition of land [a country] // 황금 ~ the golden section [mean]. **분할하다** divide (up); cut [carve] up; split; partition; lot out; parcel off [into lots]; dismember; separate. ¶분할할 수 없는 indivisible / inseparable / impartible // 농장을 택지로 ~ divide [split] a farm into building lots // 땅을 분할하여 팔다 sell one's land in lots // 하나의 블록을 10개로 분할했다 We subdivided each block into ten sections [parts]. ➔그 토지는 세 아들에게 분할되었다 The estate was divided among the three sons.

●**분할 매입** [영] buying on the hire-purchase plan; (미) buying on the installment [easy-payment] plan. **분할불** payment in a lump installments; an installment [a partial payment] plan; (미) an easy-payment [(영) a hire-purchase] plan. **분할 상속** divided succession; division of succession. **분할 인도** installment delivery.

분할(分轄) [나누어 관할함] separate control [administration]. **분할하다** control separately; exercise separate control.

분해(分解) 1 [해체] disjointing; disintegration; disassembly; dismantling; [논] partition. ¶~식의 take-down. **분해하다** disjoint; dismantle; disassemble; disintegrate; break down; take (a machine) apart [down]. ¶그 소년은 시계를 분해했다 The boy took the clock apart. // 이 총은 분해하기 쉽다 This gun takes to pieces easily.

2 [화] decomposition; resolution; dissolution; disassembly; degradation; [생] disassimilation; disintegration. ¶화학 ~ chemical decomposition // 전기 ~ electrolysis. **분해하다** resolve (itself) (into); dissolve (into); diffract; decompose; be decomposed; be reduced to (its) components [elements]. ¶분해할 수 없는 irresoluble / indecomposable / indissoluble / simple / [화] stable // 분해할 수 있는 resoluble / decomposable / dissoluble // 화합물을 원소로 ~ resolve [reduce / break down] a chemical compound into its constituent elements // 일광을 스펙트럼으로 ~ resolve [break down] sunlight into the spectral colors.

●**분해능** [광] resolution; [물] resolving power. **분해도** [건] a deal drawing.

분향(焚香) ¶~ 헌화하다 burn incense and offer flowers / make an offering of incense and flowers. **분향하다** burn [offer] incense. ¶고인을 위하여 분향했다 I burned incense for the soul(s) of the deceased.

분홍(색)(粉紅色) pink.

분화(分化) specialization; differentiation. **분화하다** specialize; differentiate; be specialized [differentiated]. ¶이 기관은 적으로부터 몸을 지키기 위해 분화한 것이다 This organ became specialized for defense against enemies. ➔¶분화되지 않은 unspecialized / undifferentiated / [생] indifferent (세포 등이) // 의학은 여러 부문으로 분화되어 있다 Medicine is divided into various specialties.

분화(噴火) an eruption; volcanic activity(화산). **분화** ~ a volcanic eruption // ~중인 화산 a volcano in action / an active volcano. **분화하다** erupt; burst into eruption; emit [belch] fire; become active. ¶분화하고 있다 be in eruption // 그 화산은 아직도 분화하고

있다 The volcano is still active. // 한라산은 분화하지 않는 화산이다 Hallasan(Mt. Halla) is a dormant volcano.
● 분화구 a crater. ⇨ "화구3.

분회(分會) a branch (organization); a (local) chapter.

붇다 **1** [물에 젖어 커지다] swell up; grow [become] sodden; sodden; macerate. ¶더운 물에 불어 버린 손 a hand sodden[swollen] with hot water // 물에 담가 불려 두다 keep (a thing) steeped[soaked] in water // 국수가 퉁퉁 불어 터졌다 The Chinese noodles have gone soft. // 하룻밤 물에 담가 두었더니 콩이 불었다 Soaked in water overnight, the beans swelled up.
2 [늘다] increase; multiply; grow bulky(부피가); mount[run/go] up (to a large sum) (비용·지출이); accumulate(쌓이다); (물이) rise (high); swell; go up. ¶물이 불은 강 swollen river / a river in flood / 양이[수가] increase[grow] in volume[numbers] // 젖이 불어 있다 The breast is swollen. // 호우로 인해 강물이 불었다 The heavy rain swelled the waters (of the river). // 체중이 2킬로 불었다 I have gained two kilograms. // 참가자가 500명으로 불었다 The participants swelled to 500 people.

불 **1** (a) fire; [화염] flame; blaze. ¶~ 같은 fiery / blazing / burning // ~이 붙기 쉬운 inflammable // ~이 붙다 catch on fire / be ignited / the fire catches // ~에 타다 burn / be burnt / be destroyed [consumed] by fire // ~에 태우다 burn / put[throw] (a thing) into a fire / commit to the flames // ~을 때다 make a fire / burn coal[wood] / fire up(아궁이 등에) / stoke(보일러 등에) // ~을 일으키다[피우다] make[kindle / build] a fire / get a fire going // ~을 붙이다 burn / set (a piece of paper) alight / (속어) fire up(파이프 등에) / ignite / light[kindle] a fire // ~을 켜다 strike fire[a spark] (부싯돌로) / strike a light(성냥으로) // ~을 끄다 put out a fire // ~을 부치다 fan the flame // 아궁이에 ~을 지피다 make a fire in the fireplace // ~을 쬐다 (사람이) warm oneself at the fire / have a heat[warm] at the fire / (사물을) put (a thing) over a fire // ~을 쬐십시오 Please warm yourself by the fire. // 여기 와서 ~을 쬐어라 Come here and warm yourself at[by] the fire. // 그는 손에 ~을 쬐었다 He warmed his hands over the fire. // 이 나무는 ~이 잘 붙는다[붙지 않는다] This wood kindles [doesn't kindle] easily. // 그는 헛간에 ~을 붙였다 He set fire to the barn. / He set the barn on fire. // 그녀의 스커트에 ~이 붙었다 Her skirt caught fire. // 좀 빌려 주시겠습니까 May I have a light? / Could you give me a light? // 그는 벽난로의 ~을 들쑤셔 일으켰다 He stirred[poked up] the fire in the fireplace. // 가스의 ~을 줄이시오 Please turn the gas down.
2 a fire. ⇨ "화재(火災) ¶큰 ~ a big[large] fire / (문어) a conflagration / ~을 지르다 set fire (to a house) / set (a house) a fire [on fire] / fire (a house) // ~을 잡다 [진화하다] put out[extinguish] a fire / get a fire under control / subdue flames // 자기 집에 ~ 지를 사람 있을까 Who would set fire to his own house? // 마을 한구석에서 ~이 났다 A fire broke out in one corner of the town. // ~은 도시의 3분의 1을 휩쓸었다 The flames swept one third of the town. // ~ 조심 (게시) Beware of Fire. / Use Caution in Handling Fire. // ~이야 Fire!
3 [어둠을 밝히는 것] a light; a lamp. ¶전깃 ~ electric light // 반딧 ~ the glow[glimmer] of a firefly / glowfly light // ~이 안 켜진 방 an unlighted room // ~이 켜지다[들어오다] be lighted / be lit / (the light) come[go] on // ~이 나가다 the (electric) light is out[cut off] / ~~을 켜다 light a lamp[light] / light up (a room) / make a light / (전등의) turn[put] on the light // ~을 끄다 put out[extinguish] the light[lamp] / (전등의) turn[switch] off the light // 양초[램프]에 ~을 켜다 light a candle [lamp] // ~을 켜 놓은 채 잠들다 fall into sleep with the light on // ~이 켜져 있다 The light is on. / The lamp is burning[alight]. // ~이 너무 어둡다 The light is too dim. // ~이 꺼졌다 The light is[has gone] out.
4 [격렬한 정열·감정] burning passion; flame; fire. ¶정열의 ~ flame[fire] of passion // 눈에서 번쩍 ~이 나다 see stars / see a flash of red // 두 나라의 영토 문제로 ~이 붙어 전쟁이 시작되었다 The territorial dispute between the two countries ignited into a war.

불에 놀란 놈이 부지깽이만 보아도 놀란다(속담) Once bitten, twice shy.; A burnt child dreads the fire.

불을 뿜다 (총이) fire; (야구의 타봉이) strike fire.

불(弗) a dollar. ⇨ "달러

불(佛) [불타] Buddha; Gautama[Gotama] Buddha.

불-(不) not; non-; un-; im-; ir-; il-; dis-. ¶~합리 irrationality / illogicality / unreasonableness.

불가(不可) [옳지 않음] wrong; unfairness; unrighteousness; impropriety. **가**(可) / ~ right or wrong / good or bad // 표결의 결과 가가 18명 ~가 3명이었다 The voting resulted in 18 ayes and 3 nays. // 그것은 가도 아니고 ~도 아니다 It is neither good nor bad. **불가하다** wrong; bad; improper. ¶그것은 불가하다고 생각한다 I don't think that's right.

불가(佛家) **1** [불교 신도] a Buddhist. **2** a (Buddhist) temple. ⇨ "절

불가결(不可缺) indispensability; absolute necessity; essential. **불가결하다** indispensable (to); absolutely necessary; requisite (to). ¶성공에 불가결한 조건 conditions absolutely necessary[indispensable to / essential to] success // 그는 우리에게 불가결한 사람이다 He is indispensable to us. / We can't get along without him. // 물은 인간 생활에 ~ Water is indispensable for[to] human life.

불가능(不可能) impossibility. ¶~을 가능하게 하다 turn an impossibility into a possibility / make the impossible possible. **불가능하다** impossible; unattainable; impracticable; unfeasible; inexecutable; beyond the range of possibilities. ¶불가능한 일을 기도하다 attempt the impossible // 해외여행이란 내게는 실현 불가능한 일이다 A trip[tour] abroad is an impossibility for me. / It is impossible for me to travel abroad. // 그것은 불가능한 제안이다 It's an impossible proposition.

불가분(不可分) indivisibility; impartibility. ¶

불가불 ~의 [나눌 수 없는] indivisible / [뗄 수 없는] undetachable / inseparable // ~의 관계 an inseparable relation / an undetachable connection // 명예심과 자기애는 ~의 관계가 있다 Self-love is inseparable from the desire for fame.

불가불(不可不) unavoidably. ⇨ 부득불

불가사리 1 [쇠를 먹는다는 상상의 동물] a mythical creature said to eat metal, to expel nightmares. 2 [동] a starfish (pl. ~, ~es); an asteroid; a fingerfish.

불가사의(不可思議) a mystery; a wonder; a miracle; a riddle. ¶세계의 7대 ~ the Seven Wonders of the World. **불가사의하다** [이상하다] wonderful; [불가해하다] incomprehensible; [기묘하다] strange; [신비하다] mysterious; [기적적이다] miraculous; [기이하다] odd. ¶불가사의하게도 strangely enough / strange to say // 그의 불가사의한 실종 his mysterious disappearance // 불가사의한 사건이 잇달아서 일어났다 Strange things happened one after another.

불가시광선(不可視光線) [물] → 비가시광선

불가지(不可知) unknowableness; inscrutability; inconceivability. ¶~의 unknowable / inscrutable / inconceivable.
● **불가지론** [철] agnosticism.

불가침(不可侵) nonaggression; inviolability; sacredness(신성 불가침). ¶~의 inviolable / sacred // 양국은 ~ 서약을 교환했다 The two countries exchanged pledges of nonaggression. // 이 지역을 ~ 구역화하기로 결정했다 It has been decided to make this region an inviolable sanctuary.
● **불가침 조약** a nonaggression pact[treaty].

불가피하다(不可避-) unescapable; inevitable; unavoidable; ineluctable. ¶불가피하게 unavoidably / inevitably / out of (sheer) necessity // 불가피한 사정으로 owing to circumstances beyond one's control / owing to [through] unavoidable circumstances / under unavoidable situations // 그런 결과에 이른 것은 불가피하였다 It is inevitable that it should have turned out that way. // 어느 정도의 손실은 불가피하였다 Some losses could not be helped[avoided]. // 교섭의 결렬은 ~ A rupture in the negotiations is unavoidable [inevitable]. / The negotiations will inevitably break down.

불가항력(不可抗力) inevitability; (an) irresistible force; [법] an act[Act] of God. ¶~의 uncontrollable / beyond control / inevitable / unavoidable / irresistible // ~의 사고 an inevitable accident / an accident beyond (human) control // 그 사고는 ~이었다 The accident was unavoidable.

불가해(不可解) mysteriousness; mystery; mysticism; incomprehensibility; inscrutability. **불가해하다** mysterious; incomprehensible; inscrutable. ¶불가해한 일 a mystery / a mysterious affair // 불가해한 인물 a mystery man / an enigma // 그의 동기는 ~ His motives are inscrutable.

불간섭(不干涉) nonintervention; noninterference. **불간섭하다** do not meddle[interfere] (in / with).
● **불간섭주의** a nonintervention policy; a policy of noninterference; (특히 상공업에 대한) (a policy of) laissez-faire.

불감증(不感症) 1 [성적인] frigidity; sexual insensitivity; [의] sexual anesthesia[anaesthesia]. ¶~의 frigid. 2 [감각이 둔함]. ¶최근에는 거리의 소음에 ~이 되었다 Recently I have become insensitive[immune] to street noise. (▶ insensitive는 「느끼지 않는」, immune은 「면역이 생긴」)

불개미 [동] a red ant.

불개입(不介入) noninvolvement; nonintervention; neutrality; holding[keeping] the ring.

불거지다 project; protrude; jut out; bulge out; swell out.

불걱거리다 (질긴 것을) chew away; (빨래를) scrub; rub briskly.

불걱불걱 chewing away (on); scrubbing away (at). **불걱불걱하다** chew away. ⇨ 불걱거리다

불건전하다(不健全-) [건전하지 않다] unsound; unwholesome; [건강하지 않다] unhealthy; [병적이다] morbid. ¶불건전한 놀이 an unwholesome game // [오락] unhealthy amusements // 그의 생각은 ~ His ideas are not healthy[are morbid]. / He has some unhealthy[sick] ideas.

불결하다(不潔-) unclean; dirty; filthy. (▶ dirty나 unclean은 더러워져 있는 경우. filthy는 더러움의 정도가 심하고, 더러운 것 또는 사람에 대한 혐오의 기분을 내포함) ¶불결한 음식물 bad[tainted] food // 불결한 물 dirty [tainted / impure] water // 불결한 거리 dirty streets // 공중변소는 지독히 불결했다 The public lavatory was absolutely filthy. **불결히** dirtily; uncleanly.

불경(不敬) disrespect; (신에 대한) impiety; want of respect; irreverence; [모독] blasphemy. **불경하다** [예의를 결하다] disrespectful; irreverent; [신을 숭배하지 않다] impious; blasphemous. ¶그런 곳에 불상을 안치하는 것은 불경한 일이다 It is a sacrilege to put a Buddhist image in such a place.
● **불경죄** [법] lese majesty.

불경(佛經) the Buddhist scriptures; Buddhist classics; the sutra. ¶~을 외다 chant[recite] a sutra / intone the service.

불경기(不景氣) bad[hard] times; [불황] a depression; [경기 후퇴] a recession; [침체] dullness; a slump. ¶~의 inactive / dull / depressed / slack / stagnant // 심각한 ~ a serious depression // ~가 되다 grow dull [flat] / slacken / (점포 등이) fall on hard times // ~는 모르自는 be always prosperous // 우리 회사로서는 ~의 한 해였다 It was a lean [bad] year for our firm. // 지금은 최악의 ~다 The depression is at its worst now. // 작년에는 ~여서 실업자가 급증했다 Business was so slow[slack] last year that unemployment increased rapidly. // 최근에 콜레라 환자가 발생하여 수산 시장은 ~ Owing to the recent outbreak of cholera, the fish market is inactive[quiet].

불계승(不計勝) [바둑] a victory by a wide margin; a one-sided game. ¶~으로 이기다 [지다] win[lose] (a game) by a wide margin. **불계승하다** win (a game) by a wide margin.

불고기 bulgogi; grilled[broiled] (slices of) meat.

불고하다(不顧-) disregard; neglect; be indifferent (about); pay no attention to; be impudent[shameless / brazen-faced]. ¶체면 ~ have no regard to appearance // 염치 불고하고 그에게 일을 부탁했다 I stooped to ask

him for it.
불공(佛供) a Buddhist mass[prayer / service]. **불공하다** offer a Buddhist mass.
불공대천(不共戴天)〔같이 살 수 없을 정도의 큰 원한〕. ¶~의 원수 a mortal[an irreconcilable] enemy / a sworn[dearest / deadly] foe∥둘은 ~의 사이다 There is a deadly feud between them.
불공정(不公正) unfairness; inequity; injustice. **불공정하다** unfair; inequitable; unjust. ¶불공정하게 unfairly / unjustly / partially / 불공정한 경쟁[거래] unfair rivalry[trade].
불공평하다(不公平−) unfair; partial; unjust; inequitable; biased; discriminating. ¶불공평한 처사 an unfair dealing / 불공평하게 사람을 다루다 treat a person unfairly∥그는 법관으로서 ~ He is unfair[unjust] as a judge. / He is not a fair judge.∥법률은 어느 누구에게도 불공평해서는 안 된다 Laws must not be discriminatory[be unfair to anyone].
불과(不過) only; merely; no more than; nothing but. ¶~ 일 주일 전에 but[only] a week ago / ~ 3년 동안에 in three short years / in a mere three years. **불과하다** be nothing but[no more than / only]. ¶청중은 10명에 불과했다 The audience consisted of only ten people. / There were no more than ten people in the audience.∥그것은 억측에 ~ It's a mere guess.∥그저 해야 할 일을 한 것에 ~ I only have done what I ought to (do).
불교(佛敎) Buddhism. ¶~의 Buddhist / Buddhistic∥~를 믿다 believe in Buddhism∥장례식은 ~식으로 행해졌다 The funeral was held according to Buddhist rites.
●**불교도** / **불교 신자** a Buddhist; a believer in Buddhism. **불교문화** Buddhist culture [civilization].
불구(不具)〔신체 일부의 기능 마비나 기형 상태〕 deformity; malformation; abnormity; disablement. ¶~의 deformed / malformed / maimed / crippled / lame /〔자유롭지 못한〕 disabled / (얼굴이) disfigured∥~가 되어 be deformed[crippled / disabled / maimed]∥~가 되다 be deformed[crippled / disabled / maimed]∥그는 ~로 태어났다 He was born deformed.∥그는 자동차 사고로 ~가 되었다 He was disabled[crippled] in a car accident.(▶ disabled는 일상의 활동을 할 수 없게 된 경우, crippled는 수족이 부자유하게 된 경우에 씀)
●**불구자** a disabled person; a deformed [maimed] person; a cripple;〔집합적〕 the disabled; the (physically) handicapped.
불구대천(不俱戴天) ⇨ **불공대천**
불구하고(不拘−)〔얽매여 거리끼지 않고〕 though; although; in spite of; despite (of); disregarding; in disregard of; notwithstanding; no matter (how / what); for all; with all. ¶그럼에도 ~ nevertheless / none the less / for all that∥반대에도 ~ in the teeth[face] of opposition∥충고에도 ~ in disregard of [after all]∥그는 가난함에도 ~ 행복해 보인다 He is poor, but nevertheless[nonetheless] he looks happy.∥그녀는 친절한 마음씨를 가졌음에도 ~ 사람들에 대해 심한 비평을 한다 She is kindhearted, but for all that her criticism of people can be scathing.∥온갖 어려움에도 ~ 계획은 실행되었다 The plan was put into practice in spite of[in the face of /(문어) despite] all difficulties.∥나는 노력을 했음에도 ~ 실패했다 I failed in spite of all my efforts.∥그녀는 비가 오는데도 ~ 나갔다 She went out in spite of[(문어) despite] the rain.∥그는 재능이 있는데도 ~ 불우했다 With all his ability, he lived in obscurity.∥그들은 최선을 다했으나, 그럼에도 ~ 전원을 구출할 수 없었다 Although [Though] they did their best, they could not save all of them.∥그는 몸이 좋지 않은데도 ~ 회의에 출석했다 He attended the meeting in spite of his illness. / Though he was ill, he attended the meeting.∥그는 돈이 많은데도 ~ 검소한 생활을 하고 있다 For [With] all his wealth, he leads a frugal life.
불굴(不屈) indomitability; fortitude. ¶~의 indomitable / inflexible / unyielding / invincible / indefatigable∥~의 정신 an indomitable[an unyielding / a dauntless] spirit / ~의 용기 stubborn[sturdy] courage∥~의 정신으로 with an indomitable[unconquerable] spirit∥그는 악덕 정치가의 진상 폭로를 위해 ~의 노력을 계속했다 He continued his dogged attempt to expose the corrupt politician.
불귀객(不歸客) a dead[deceased] person. ¶~이 되다 die / pass away / join the majority.
불규칙(不規則) irregularity; lack of system. **불규칙하다** irregular; anomalous; unmethodical; unsystematic. ¶불규칙하게 irregularly / unsystematically / fitfully∥불규칙한 생활을 하다 keep irregular [inordinate] hours / lead an irregular life∥저런 불규칙한 방법으로는 연구를 성공시키지 못할 것이다 With such unsystematic methods he will not succeed in his research.
●**불규칙 동사**〔언〕 an irregular verb. **불규칙 활용** / **불규칙 변화**〔언〕 irregular conjugation.
불균형(不均衡) imbalance; unbalance; disproportion; inequality; disparity. ¶과세액의 ~ inequalities in tax assessments / 남녀간의 사회적 지위의 ~ the inequality between men's and women's social positions∥몫은 서로 ~이 없기로 하자 Let's equalize our shares. / 연령의 ~이 그 부부의 불화의 원인 중 하나였다 Difference[Disproportion] in age was one of the reasons for the couple's incompatibility.∥수출과 수입이 ~이 되었다 Imports and exports became unbalanced. **불균형하다** out of balance; ill-balanced; unbalanced; out of proportion (to); disproportionate; disproportional; unequal; lopsided. ¶불균형한 예산 an unbalanced budget∥그의 머리는 몸에 비하여 불균형하게 크다 His head is disproportionately big for his body.
불그레하다 reddish; tinged with red.
불그스름하다 reddish; tinged with red.
불긋불긋하다 splashed[dotted] with red.
불기(−氣) the heat of a fire. ⇨**불기운**
불기(佛紀) Buddhist Era(약어 B.E.). ¶~ 2천 5백 46년 2546 B.E..
불기둥 a pillar[column] of fire[flames]. ¶폭탄이 떨어진 자리에서 ~이 솟았다 A column of fire rose (at the spot) where the bomb fell.
불기소(不起訴) non-prosecution; nonindictment. ¶~로 하다 drop (a case) / do not prosecute (a person)∥돈을 훔친 소년은 ~가 되었다 The boy who stole the money was not

불기운 the heat of a fire; [화세(火勢)] the force[spread] of the fire. ¶~을 낮추다 turn the fire low / (가스의) lower the flame∥~이 세어졌다[떨어졌다] The fire gained force[went down].

불길 the flames; the fire; blazes. ¶분노의 ~ the heat of anger∥~이 확 치솟다 burst into flame(s) / flame[blaze] up∥~이 거세다 The fire is raging.∥~이 꺾였다 The fire has abated[died down].∥집들은 차례로 ~을 뿜으며 탔다 One after another the houses burst into flame.∥빨간 ~은 성의 망루를 한꺼번에 삼켜 버렸다 The keep of the castle fell an easy prey to the roaring flames.∥그녀는 사랑의 ~에 사로잡혔다 She was consumed with the fire of passion.∥그는 질투의 ~에 사로잡혀 있다 He is burning with jealousy.∥~이 무섭게 번졌다 The spread of the flames was alarmingly fast.

불길하다(不吉-) unlucky; ominous; sinister; inauspicious; unpropitious; malign; malignant. ¶불길한 [흉조를 나타내는] ill-omened / ominous / [불행한] unlucky∥불길한 새 an unlucky bird / an ill-omened bird / (문어) a bird of ill-omen∥불길한 예감 an ominous presentiment∥불길한 전조[징조 / 조짐] an unlucky[evil / ill] omen∥불길한 별 아래 태어나다 be born under an unlucky[(문어) inauspicious] star∥내 꿈은 불길한 전조로밖에 생각되지 않는다 I cannot help regarding my dream as ominous[an ill-omen / (문어) auguring ill].∥그가 곧 죽는 것이나 아닐까 하는 불길한 예감이 든다 I have a premonition[an uneasy feeling] that he will die before long.

불까다 castrate; emasculate; (주로 동물을) geld. ¶불깐 소[말] a bullock[gelding]∥말을 ~ geld a horse∥그는 그의 개를 불깠다 He had his dog neutered.

불꽃 [화염] a flame; a blaze; [불똥] a spark; (놀이의) fireworks; a sparkler; a firecracker. ¶~을 올리다 display[set off / shoot] fireworks∥~을 튀기다 spark / emit[give off] sparks∥~이 오르다 flame[flare] up / blaze (up)∥진홍빛 ~이 건물에서 솟아올랐다 Brighted flames rose from the building.

불꽃(이) 튀다 1 [불꽃이] 사방으로 튀어 흩어지다 sparkle; spark. ¶(전차의) 집전기에서 불꽃이 튀었다 The pantograph sparked[gave off sparks].∥기둥에 부딪혔을 때 눈에서 불꽃이 튀었다 I saw stars when I ran into the pillar. 2 [겨루는 모양이] 치열하다. ¶그 법안을 둘러싸고 불꽃 튀는 토론이 벌어졌다 They had a heated[hot] argument about the bill.∥후보자 세 사람이 지사 자리를 놓고 불꽃 튀는 경쟁을 벌이고 있다 The three candidates are producing a lot of sparks in their fight for the governorship.

●**불꽃놀이** a display[an exhibition] of fireworks; a fireworks display. ¶~를 하다 display fireworks / do a fireworks display. **불꽃반응** [화] a flame reaction.

불끈 1 (갑자기 성내는 모양). ¶그는 ~ 성을 내며 일어섰다 He stood up in a rage. **불끈하다** fly into a rage[passion]; be stirred into passionate anger; flare up (in anger); flame out; (구어) see red. ¶불끈하여 in a fit of passion / in a (fit of) rage∥그는 불끈하는 성미다 He is hot[quick-]tempered. / He is a man with an explosive temper. 2 [단단히]. ¶주먹을 ~ 쥐다 clench one's fists.

불나다 a fire breaks out[starts / occurs]. ¶불난 집 a house on fire∥어디에 불났어 Where is the fire?∥우리 집에 불났다 Our house is on fire.

불난 집에 부채질한다(속담) add[put] oil to the fire[flame]; pour oil on the flame; add fuel to (the disturbance).

불나방 [동] a garden tiger moth.

불놀이 1 [불꽃놀이] a fireworks display; a display of fireworks. ¶오늘 밤에 ~가 있다 There will be a display of fireworks this evening. **불놀이하다** display[set off] fireworks. 2 →불장난

불능(不能) impossibility. ⇨불가능 ¶지불 ~ [법] insolvency∥회수 ~의 대부 bad debts∥폭우로 인해 도로가 통행 ~이 되었다 The road was impassable because of the heavy rain.∥파업 때문에 공항은 발착 ~이 되었다 The airport could not be used because of the strike.

불다¹ (바람이) blow. ¶산과 들을 뚫고 불어 대는 바람 a wind blowing through the mountains and fields∥바람이 세차게 불고 있다 It[The wind] is blowing hard.∥솔솔바람이 불고 있다 A gentle breeze is blowing.∥바람이 그녀의 얼굴에 연기를 불어 댔다 The wind blew the smoke into her face.∥미닫이문 사이의 좁은 틈새에서 차가운 외풍이 불어 들어 왔다 A cold draft[(영) draught] blew in through the narrow opening between the sliding doors.∥바람이 불기 시작하여 파도가 높아졌다 It began to blow, and the waves ran high.

불다² 1 (입으로) blow on (a fire, one's hands, etc.); breathe out(입김을). ¶뜨거운 차를 훌훌 불어 식히다 blow on hot tea to cool it∥비눗방울을 ~ blow bubbles∥휘파람을 ~ whistle / give a whistle∥촛불을 ~ blow at the candle∥안경에 입김을 불어 닦았다 I breathed on my glasses and wiped them. 2 (관악기를) blow[play] (a trumpet); play (on) (a flute). ¶피리를 불기 시작하다 begin to play a flute∥호각을 불거든 일을 중지하시오 Stop work when the whistle blows[when I blow the whistle].∥아침 6시면 기상나팔을 분다 Reveille blows at six o'clock every morning. 3 (사실을 털어놓다) confess; own up; come clean; make a clean breast (of). ¶사실을 ~ confess the facts as they are∥죄상을 ~ confess to a crime.

불단(佛壇) a Buddhist altar; a family Buddhist altar[shrine].

불당(佛堂) a Buddhist temple[shrine / sanctum].

불덩이 a mass[ball] of flames[fire]; a fireball. ¶온몸이 ~가 되다 [고열이 나다] have [get] high fever.

불도(佛徒) a Buddhist. ⇨불교도(⇨불교)

불도(佛道) [부처의 가르침] the teaching of Buddha; buddhist doctrines; Buddhism.

불도그 a bulldog.

불도저 a bulldozer. ¶~로 고르다[밀다] bulldoze out (a tennis court, a mound, etc.).

불똥 1 (심지의) the snuff (of a candlewick). 2

[불타고 있는 물체에서 튀어나오는 작은 불덩이] flying sparks. ¶화재 발생의 원인은 모닥불에서 튀어나온 ~에 있었다 Sparks from a bonfire were responsible for the fire.

불똥(이) 튀다 come to involve (another). ¶그 수뢰 사건의 실마리는 정계로 불똥이 튀었다 The trail of the corruption case led to political circles. / The corruption case had repercussions in political circles.

불뚝 [갑작스레 무뚝뚝하게 화를 내는 모양] in a fit of passion; in (a fit of) rage; with a flare of temper. ¶~ 화를 내다 fly into a (great) rage / burst into a fit of rage / explode with anger / flare up in anger.

불뚝불뚝 with repeated rude bursts of anger; flaring up again and again.

불란서(佛蘭西) 〈음역〉 France. ⇨프랑스

불량(不良) **1** [질의 열등] badness; inferiority. ¶영양 ~ malnutrition // 소화 ~ indigestion // 발육 ~ poor development // 정비 ~ poor maintenance. **불량하다** bad; poor; inferior; faulty; deleterious; unwholesome. ¶발육이 불량한 어린이 an underdeveloped child // 그녀는 시험 성적이 불량했다 She got poor [bad] marks on the exam. **2** [품성이 나쁨] delinquency. **불량하다** wicked; delinquent; depraved. ¶불량한 짓을 하다 indulge in delinquent behavior // 불량해지다 go to the bad / become delinquent.
● **불량 도체** [전] a nonconductor; a bad conductor. **불량배** a gang of hoodlums [hooligans]; the depraved. **불량 식품** adulterated food. **불량품** inferior goods; condemned goods.

불러내다 [불러서 나오게 하다] call (a person) (out); call (a person) to (the office); (전화통에) call[ring] (a person) to (on the phone); call (a person) to the telephone; [꾀어내다] decoy; lure; (마술로) invoke [conjure up] (evil spirits). ¶문간으로 ~ call (a person) to the door // 밤늦게 불러내어 미안합니다 I am very sorry to have troubled you to come[for calling you] so late at night.(▶ calling은 전화로).

불러들이다 [불러서 들어오게 하다] call[hail] (a person) in[into]; have (a person) in; [소환하여] (문어) summon. ¶방으로 ~ call (a person) into a room // 아버지는 아이들을 병상으로 불러들였다 My father called us children to his sickbed. // 재판관은 두 사람의 증인을 불러들였다 The judge summoned two witnesses.

불러오다 [불러서 오게 하다] call (a person) to come; [소환하다] summon; (사람을 시켜) send for. ¶사람을 보내 ~ send for (a person) // 의사를 ~ send for[call in] a doctor // 그는 부하를 불러와서 야단쳤다 He summoned his subordinate and scolded him.

불러일으키다 rouse[gather] up; arouse; stir up; excite; call forth. ¶센세이션을 ~ create a sensation // 기억을 ~ recall something to one's mind // 그것이 그의 의심을 불러일으켰다 It raised doubts in his mind. // 그 산들은 그녀에게 그리운 옛 추억을 불러일으켰다 Those mountains brought back precious memories to her. // 그의 보고는 나의 흥미를 불러일으켰다 His report excited[aroused] my curiosity[interest]. // 장관의 발언은 논쟁을 불러일으켰다 The Minister's speech aroused much public discussion. // 그것이 재난을 불러일으켰다 That brought about the disaster. // 그의 행위는 선생님의 분노를 불러일으켰다 His actions incurred the teacher's anger. // His behavior made the teacher mad.

불로 소득(不勞所得) (이자·배당 등에 의한) an unearned[investment] income; (우연한) windfall income[profits].

불로장생(不老長生) perpetual youth and longevity[long life]; eternal[perennial / ageless] youth. ¶~의 비결 the secret of eternal youth and longevity. **불로장생하다** live ever-young; enjoy eternal youth; be ageless.

불로초(不老草) a herb of eternal youth.

불룩거리다 swell and subside; palpitate; quiver; vibrate. ¶좋아서 코를 ~ be puffed up with pride.

불룩하다 swollen; baggy; bulging; fat; inflated; protuberant; bulky. ¶불룩한 가방 a bulky[bulging] bag // 여성의 불룩한 젖가슴 the rich[well-fleshed] breast of a woman // 불룩한 지갑 a fat[an overstuffed] pocketbook // 타이어가 불룩해졌다 The tire filled out.

불륜(不倫) [인륜에서 벗어남] immorality; obliquity; [비인륜적 행위] immoral conduct; a liaison(이성 간의). ¶~의 사랑 illicit love.

불리다¹ [(배를) 부르게 하다] fill one's stomach / stuff out the belly / [비유] enrich oneself / feather one's (own) nest // 공직을 이용하여 자기 배를 ~ seek personal ends taking advantage of one's office // 그는 공금으로 자기 배를 불렸다 He enriched himself with public fund.

불리다² **1** (쇠를) temper (metal); harden; anneal. ¶쇠를 ~ temper iron. **2** (곡식을) winnow; fan. ¶곡식[밀]을 ~ winnow grain [wheat].

불리다³ **1** [부름을 받다] be called; [소환되다] be summoned (to); [초대받다] be invited (to). ¶그는 선생님에게 불려 갔다 He was called before a teacher. // 나는 법원에 증인으로 불려 갔다 I was summoned to appear as a witness in court. **2** [이라고] be called; be named. ¶그는 어렸을 때 신동이라고 불렸다 As a child he was called an infant prodigy.

불리다⁴ (바람에) be blown; blow. ¶바람에 불린 먼지가 문틈으로 들어왔다 Dust blew through every crack. // 바람에 불려 촛불이 깜박거렸다 Fanned by the wind, the candle flame flickered.

불리다⁵ **1** (액체에) steep; soak; sodden; macerate. ¶쌀을 물에 ~ soak rice in water // 물에 불려 두다 keep (a thing) steeped [soaked] in water. **2** [재물을 붙게 하다] add to; increase (one's fortune). ¶재산을 ~ increase[add to] one's fortune. **3** [과장하다] exaggerate; magnify; stretch (the fact); [분량을 늘리다] pad; (자본 등을 과대평가하여) water. ¶불려서 말하다 exaggerate (a story) / talk big // 그는 필요 경비를 불려서 지출한 탓으로 파면당했다 He was fired for padding his expense account.

불리다⁶ **1** (관악기를) make (a person) blow. ¶나는 그에게 나팔을 불렸다 I had him blow a trumpet. **2** (노래를) make (a person) sing. **3** [자백시키다] make (a person) admit himself guilty; (미국 속어) smoke (a person) out. ¶그 형사는 내게 죄상을 강제로 불렸다 The detective forced[compelled] a confes-

불리하다

sion from me. / The detective forced me into confession.

불리하다(不利─) disadvantageous; unfavorable; bad; adverse; impolitic. ¶나는 불리한 입장에 있다 I am at a disadvantage. / I am in a disadvantageous position. // 시합의 형세는 우리에게 불리했다 The game went against us. // 우리가 불리한 점은 자금 부족이다 Our disadvantage[handicap] is lack of funds. // 그는 피고에게 불리한 증언을 했다 He gave evidence against[unfavorable to] the defendant. // 선거는 우리 당에 불리한 결과가 되었다 The election went against[badly for] our party. // 전황은 우리에게 불리하게 되었다 The tide of war turned against us. // 형편은 그에게 불리하였다 The situation was unfavorable for him. // 그 상황은 그에게는 disadvantage. // 프랑스 어를 말할 줄 모른다는 것은 그에게 불리했다 His inability to speak French put him at a disadvantage. // 이것은 너에게 ~ This is against[detrimental to] your interests.

불림 tempering metal(쇠의).

불만(不滿) dissatisfaction; discontent; [불평] a complaint; (특히 부당한 취급에 대한) a grievance. ¶~을 말하다 complain (of / about) / make a complaint (of / about / against) / [불평하다] grumble (at / about / over) / 아무런 ~이 없다 have no complaints (about) // 지금 처지에 아무런 ~도 없습니다 I am quite satisfied with my present surroundings. // 나는 이 결정에 대해 아무런 ~도 없다 I am perfectly satisfied with these arrangements. // 나의 어떤 점이 ~인지 말해 주게 Tell me what in me displeases you. / Tell me what you don't like about me. // 시민들은 시장의 결정에 ~을 나타냈다 The citizens expressed their disapproval of the mayor's decision. // 기숙사 생활에 ~은 없습니까 Do you have any complaints about life in the dormitory? // 무슨 ~은 없습니까 Do you have any complaint[grievances]? // 나는 이 호텔의 서비스에 ~이다 I am dissatisfied with the service at this hotel. // 급료에는 전혀 ~이 없다 I am perfectly satisfied with my salary. **불만하다** dissatisfied (with); discontented (with).

불만스럽다(不滿─) dissatisfied (with); discontented (with); unsatisfactory. ¶불만스러운 결과 unsatisfactory results // 이 책은 30대의 독자에게는 불만스러울 것이다 This book won't satisfy readers in their thirties.

불만족(不滿足) dissatisfaction. ⇨ 불만

불매 동맹(不買同盟) a boycott (movement); boycotting; a buying strike; a consumers' strike. ¶소비자 ~ a consumers' boycott / a buyers' strike / ~을 맺다 stage a boycott / boycott[taboo] (goods).

불면증(不眠症) insomnia; sleeplessness; [병] vigilance. ¶~에 걸리다 suffer from[be troubled with] insomnia.

불멸(不滅) (정신적) immortality; (물질적) athanasia; indestructibility; imperishability. ¶영혼의 ~ immortality of the soul // 물질 ~의 법칙 the law of the indestructibility of matter // ~의 사랑 undying love // 그는 ~의 위업을 성취하였다 He has accomplished a monumental work. **불멸하다** do not die [perish]; be immortal[indestructible / undying / imperishable]. ¶그녀의 이름은 영원히 불멸할 것이다 Her name will live forever. // 인간의 영혼은 불멸할지도 모른다 The human soul may be immortal.

불명(不明) 1 [분명하지 않음] indistinctness; obscurity; [애매함] ambiguity; [불가해] incomprehensibility. ¶원인 ~의 사고 an accident of unknown origin // 국적 ~의 군함 a warship of unidentified nationality. **불명하다** indistinct; obscure; unclear; vague; ambiguous; incomprehensible. ¶불명한 태도 an indefinite[a dubious / a noncommittal] attitude // 그 전문의 뜻은 ~ The meaning of the telegram is not clear. 2 [사리에 어두움] lack of sagacity[foresight]; [무지] ignorance. **불명하다** unwise; injudicious; ignorant.

불명료하다(不明瞭─) indistinct. ⇨ 불분명하다

불명예(不名譽) dishonor; disgrace; discredit; ignominy; infamy; shame. ¶이것은 학교의 ~다 This will disgrace the school[bring disgrace on (the good name of) the school]. **불명예하다** [명예롭지 못하다] dishonorable; disgraceful; [창피하다] shameful.

불명예스럽다(不名譽─) dishonorable; shameful. ⇨ 불명예하다(⇨ 불명예) ¶불명예스러운 해고 [죽음] an ignominious dismissal [death] // 불명예스러운 행위[패배] a shameful conduct[defeat].

불모(不毛) 1 [작물이 되지 않음] sterility; barrenness. ¶~의 sterile / barren / [황무지의] waste / [생산이 없는] unproductive / [~의 땅] barren[waste] land / sterile soil. 2 [노력해도 성과가 없음] ¶~의 1년 a barren year / a wasted year / a year of futile effort.

●**불모지** barren[arid] land; a hungry soil; [황무지] wasteland; a desert.

불문(不問) taking no notice; regardlessness. **불문하다** take no notice of; do not ask [question]; do not care whether ... or ...; ignore; disregard. ¶다소를 불문하고 regardless of quantity // 대소를 불문하고 large or small // 날씨를 불문하고 regardless of the weather / rain or shine // 남녀노소를 불문하고 irrespective[regardless] of age or sex // 때와 장소를 불문하고 in all times[ages] and places // 비용의 다과를 불문하고 사들이겠다 I will buy it regardless of (the) expense. // 유능한 사람이라면 남녀[연령]를 불문하고 채용하겠다 We will employ a person who is able irrespective of sex[age]. // 그의 찬성, 불찬성을 불문하고 나는 가겠다 I will go whether he approves or not.

불문에 부치다 ignore; overlook; let go; lay aside (a question); wink at; connive at; overlook (a person's faults); leave (a matter) out of consideration; take no notice of; shut one's eyes to. ¶이 문제를 불문에 부칠 수는 없다 I cannot pass over[by] this question in silence.

불문(佛文) 1 [프랑스 어로 된 글] a French sentence. ¶그 편지는 ~으로 씌어 있었다 The letter was written in French. 2 French literature. ⇨ 불문학(⇨ 불문)

●**불문과** the Department of French literature. **불문학** French literature.

불문(佛門) Buddhism; priesthood. ¶~에 들어가다 become a (Buddhist) priest / enter the Buddhist priesthood.

불문가지(不問可知) ¶~의 일이다 You can

easily understand it (without asking). / It goes without saying.

불문곡직(不問曲直) ¶~하고 (whether) right or wrong / without inquiring into the rights and wrong (of the case).

불문법(不文法) an unwritten law[rule]; a consuetudinary law; common law(영미의).

불문율(不文律) an unwritten law. ⇨ 불문법

불미스럽다(不美-) bad; unfavorable; unsavory; nasty; unworthy; scandalous; disgraceful; ugly; shameful. ¶불미스러운 일[것] a shameful thing / a shame // 신사로서 불미스러운 행동 an act unworthy of a gentleman / an ungentlemanly act // 불미스러운 사건 a scandalous[an ugly] case / a scandal // 그 사람은 불미스러운 소문이 나 있다 There are unsavory rumors about that man.

불바다 〔넓은 지역에 걸쳐 사납게 타오르는 불〕 a sea of flames. ¶~가 되다 become a sheet of fire // 방 안은 ~였다 The room was in flames. / The room was a sea of flame. / The room was ablaze. // 번화가는 ~가 되었다 The shopping district turned into a blazing inferno.

불발(不發) 1 (폭약의) misfire. ¶폭탄은 ~이었다 The bomb did not go off[explode]. **불발하다** miss fire; misfire; snap(권총이). 2 〔계획했던 일을 못하게 되는 것〕. ¶그 계획은 ~로 끝났다 The scheme misfired[ended in failure].
●**불발탄** a blind shell; a dud.

불법(不法) 〔위법〕 unlawfulness; illegality; illegitimacy; 〔무법·무리함〕 lawlessness; outrage; 〔도리에 어긋남〕 wrong(fulness); injustice; iniquity. ¶~으로 illegally / unlawfully / wrongfully. **불법하다** unlawful; illegal; unjust; illegitimate; iniquitous; injurious; malfeasant; wrong(ful); outrageous; unwarrantable; unwarranted; unjustifiable; unjustified. ¶불법한 짓을 하다 act unlawfully [outrageously] / do (a person) wrong[an injustice] // 미성년자의 흡연은 불법한 행위다 For minors, smoking is an illegal[unlawful] act.
●**불법 감금** illegal confinement[detention]. **불법 입국** illegal entry[immigration]. **불법 출국** illegal exit. **불법 행위** an unlawful[illegal] act; wrongful conduct; 〔법〕 tort.

불법(佛法) 〔불〕 Buddhism; 〔부처의 교법〕 the law[teaching] of Buddha; a Buddhist canon.

불벼락 〔번갯불〕 lightning; a bolt[streak / flash] of lightning; a thunderbolt; 〔불같이 사나운 명령·책망〕 a tyrannical decree[order / instruction]; thundering cries. ¶~을 맞다 be struck by lightning // ~을 내리다 issue a severe[terrible] order[tyrannical decree].

불변(不變) unchangeability; immutability; constancy; permanence. ¶질량[물질] ~ [물] conservation of mass[matter] // ~의 unchangeable / invariable / inalterable / immutable / incommutable / indissoluble / constant / permanent // ~ 불멸의 진리 unchanging and everlasting truths // ~의 법칙 invariable [unchangeable / immutable] laws. **불변하다** do not change; be unchangeable[invariable / inalterable / immutable / constant].
●**불변색** a permanent [fast / fixed / grain] color. **불변 자본** a constant[an invariable] capital.

불볕 the burning[scorching / blazing] sun. ¶오늘은 사뭇 ~이다 It is scorching[broiling / smoking] hot today. // ~이 난다 The sun comes out blazing.
●**불볕더위** the sweltering[scorching] heat.

불복(不服) 1 insubordination (to). ⇨ 불복종 2 〔복죄 아니함〕 a disapproval; a denial (of one's guilt); a protest; an objection; a dissatisfaction. ¶그는 일심 판결에 ~ 항소했다 He appealed against the finding of the court of the first instance. **불복하다** deny one's guilt; plead not guilty; be dissatisfied; protest against; object to.
●**불복 신청** 〔법〕 an appeal[institution] of dissatisfaction.

불복종(不服從) insubordination (to); disobedience (to an order). **불복종하다** disobey; be disobedient; be insubordinate; be rebellious. ¶상관의 지시에 ~ do not respond to the instructions given by one's senior (officer).

불분명하다(不分明-) indistinct; obscure; be not clear; ambiguous. ¶불분명한 태도 an ambiguous[a dubious] attitude // 불분명한 대답 a vague answer // 불분명하게 indistinctly / obscurely // 그는 발음이 ~ His pronunciation is not clear[articulate / distinct]. // 양자 간의 경계선이 ~ The line of demarcation between the two is not well-defined.

불붙다 catch (on)[take] fire; light up; kindle; ignite. ¶불붙기 쉽다 kindle [catch fire] easily / be easy[quick] to catch fire / be combustible / be inflammable // 그 집에 불붙었다 The house caught fire. // 이 장작은 좀체로 불붙지 않는다 This wood is slow to kindle [catch fire]. / This wood will not kindle. // 10일간에 걸친 선거전이 불붙기 시작했다 The ten-day election campaign has gotten underway.

불붙는 데 키질하기(속담) casting oil in the fire; making matters worse.

불붙이다 set (a piece of paper) alight; set (kindling) on fire; light (up); kindle; ignite; apply (a fire / a flame) to(도화선 등에); 〔비유〕 touch off (a quarrel). ¶나무에 ~ kindle wood / light the firewood // 양초에 ~ light a candle // 성냥으로 나무에 ~ kindle a wood with a match // 담배에 ~ light (up) a cigarette // 확대경으로 종이에 불붙일 수 있습니까 Can you ignite paper[set paper on fire] with a magnifying glass?

불비(不備) deficiency; imperfection; defectiveness; inadequacy; 〔부족〕 lack. ¶위생 설비의 ~ lack of proper sanitation // 교통 기관의 ~ lack of means of conveyance / imperfect [defective] means of transportation // 하수도의 ~ lack of an adequate sewage system. **불비하다** defective; faulty; deficient; imperfect; incomplete. ¶불비한 점 a defect / an imperfection / a loophole(법률 등의) / an omission // 불비한 점을 시정하다 correct[remedy] a defect / bring (a matter) to perfection // 서류가 ~ The documents are not in order. / These documents are not properly made out.

불빛 light from fire; firelight; light; rays of light. ¶(전등의) ~이 약하다 (the bulb) give a dim[poor] light // ~이 밝다[밝다] The light is dim[bright]. // 어른거리는 모닥불의 속에서 그는 행복스럽게 보였다 In the flickering light of the bonfire, he looked happy. // 그

불사 는 밤의 어둠 속에서 ~이 다가오는 것을 보았다 He saw a light approaching in the darkness of the night.

불사(不死) [불멸] immortality; [영생] eternal life. ¶~의 deathless / undying / immortal / imperishable // ~불멸 (enjoy) immortality [indestructibility / imperishability / athanasia]. **불사하다** never die; be immortal; enjoy immortality.

불사르다 burn (up); set (a thing) on fire; destroy (a thing) by fire. ¶쓰레기를 ~ make a bonfire of rubbish / burn garbage // 시체를 ~ cremate / burn the body to ashes // 헌 신문을 ~ burn old newspapers.

불사신(不死身) 1 [고통·상해에도 견디어 내는 굳센 몸] an invulnerable body; invulnerability; [고통을 느끼지 않음] insensibility to pain; [죽지 않음] immortality. ¶~의 [죽지 않는] immortal / [상처 나지 않는] invulnerable // 신은 ~이다 God is immortal. / He lives forever. // 그는 ~이다 He has nine lives! / He has a charmed life. 2 [굳센 성격을 가진 사람] a man of indefatigable industry. ¶~이다 be a man of a dauntless spirit.

불사조(不死鳥) the phoenix; the secular [undying] bird.

불사하다(不辭-) fail to decline; do not decline; act in an unreserved way. ¶…하기를 ~ be ready[willing] to do // 경우에 따라서 죽음도 불사하겠다 I am ready to die in case of need. // 그가 끝까지 양보하지 않는다면 우리는 재판에 회부하는 것도 불사하겠다 If he is adamant in refusing to make concessions, we are ready to take the case to court.

불상(佛像) a Buddhist image[statue]; an image of Buddha.

불상사(不祥事) a disgraceful [deplorable] affair; a scandal; an unhappy[ill] event. ¶시험 문제가 누설되는 ~ the scandal of the examination questions being leaked.

불서(佛書) [불] the Buddhist scriptures; Buddhist literature.

불성실하다(不誠實-) insincere; dishonest; unfaithful; faithless; untruthful; untrustworthy; perfidious; false. ¶불성실한 친구 a faithless[false] friend // 불성실한 여자 an untrustworthy woman // 불성실한 대답 insincere answers // 불성실한 행위 a faithless deed // 학습 태도가 ~ You take your studies too lightly. / You are not studying seriously. // 당신은 ~ You should be more serious.

불세출(不世出) ¶~의 extraordinary / unparalleled / unequaled / peerless // ~의 음악가 an unparalleled musician // ~의 대정치가 a great statesman of unequaled ability // ~의 천재 an extraordinary genius / a prodigy.

불소(弗素) [화] fluorine. ⇨플루오르 ¶~의 fluoric // 물의 ~ 처리 water fluoridation // 수돗물에 ~를 넣다 add fluorine to the public water supply.

불손하다(不遜-) haughty; arrogant; insolent; presumptuous; assuming; overbearing. ¶불손한 태도를 취하다 assume an arrogant [a haughty] attitude / have an insolent air // 불손하게 굴다 behave haughtily[arrogantly].

불수(不隨) paralysis (pl. -ses). ¶반신[전신] ~ partial[total] paralysis // 반신~의 partially paralyzed / paralyzed on one side // 그는 하반신 ~이다 He is paralyzed from the waist down.

불수의(不隨意) ¶~의 involuntary.
● **불수의근** [생] an involuntary muscle.

불순(不純) impurity. **불순하다** impure; foul; mixed. ¶불순한 마음 an impure mind[heart] // 불순한 동기 a mixed[dishonest / selfish] motive / an interested[ulterior] motive // 그는 불순한 동기에서 그것을 제안했다 He proposed it out of impure motives.
● **불순물** impurities; [의] foreign matter. ¶~이 섞이지 않은[섞인] 금 pure[impure] gold // ~이 없다 be free from impurities[heterogeneous elements] // 이 휘발유에 뭔가 ~이 섞여 있다 This gasoline[[영] petrol] has some impurities in it. / This gasoline is not pure.
불순분자 an impure element. ¶당내의 ~ rebellious elements of a party.

불순종(不順從) disobedience; indocility; recalcitrance; insubordination. **불순종하다** disobey; be disobedient; refuse to obey. ¶불순종하는 disobedient / indocile / wayward / recalcitrant / insubordinate (to one's superiors) // (사람이) 불순종하게 되다 kick over the traces.

불순하다(不順-) 1 [온순하지 못하다] disobedient; rude; rebellious. 2 [순조롭지 못하다] unseasonable; [변덕스럽다] changeable; [불규칙하다] irregular. ¶날씨가 불순하여 on account of the unseasonable weather // 날씨가 불순한 이때에 부디 몸조심하십시오 As the weather is changeable nowadays[At this time when the weather is so unreasonable], please take good care of yourself. // 그녀는 생리가 불순하여 고민하고 있다 She has trouble with irregular menstruation.

불승인(不承認) disapproval; [거부] veto; nonrecognition. **불승인하다** disapprove; veto; reject.

불시(不時) ¶~의 [제철이 아닌] untimely / out of season[time] / [뜻하지 아니한] unexpected / [예측할 수 있는] unforeseen / [비상의] emergency / [돌발적인] accidental / incidental / contingent // ~의 손님 an unexpected guest // ~의 검사 a surprise inspection[examination] / (미) a snap quiz // ~의 습격 a surprise (attack) // ~의 죽음 an untimely[a sudden] death // 그는 ~의 재난을 당해 오른손을 잃었다 He had[met with] an accident and lost his right hand.

불시에(不時-) unexpectedly; untimely; contingently; abruptly; without (previous) notice[warning]. ¶~ 공격하다 surprise (a person) / make a surprise[sudden] attack on / take (a person) unawares / attack [take] (the enemy) by surprise / take (a person) off (his) guard[at a disadvantage] / catch[take] (a person) napping.

불시착(不時着) a forced[an emergency] landing; a crash landing. **불시착하다** make [attempt] a forced[an emergency] landing (at); crashland; be ditched(해상의). ¶짙은 안개 때문에 그 비행기는 불시착했다 The airplane was forced down by a dense fog. // 그 비행기는 앞바다에 불시착했다 The plane was ditched off the shore.

불식하다(拂拭-) wipe out[away]; sweep off; eradicate; overcome. ¶지난날의 기억을 마음 속에서 불식해 버리다 wipe the memory of the past from one's heart // 의혹을 ~ overcome one's distrust. →¶우울한 생각이 불식되었다 My gloomy feelings were wiped away.

불신(不信) mistrust; distrust; disbelief; discredit; lack[want] of confidence (in). ¶~을 사다 lose one's credit / bring discredit on oneself / incur the distrust (of) // 정부에 대한 ~이 증대하고 있다 Mistrust of the government is growing. // 그의 행위는 사람들의 ~을 산다 His action incurs people's distrust [causes everyone to distrust him]. **불신하다** distrust; discredit; disbelieve.
● **불신감** (a) distrust; (a) suspicion. ¶~을 품다 be distrustful of / have a distrust of. **불신 풍조** a trend of mutual distrust.

불신임(不信任) nonconfidence; want[lack] of confidence. ¶~내각 want of confidence in the Cabinet // 교수진은 학장에 대한 ~동의를 냈다 The staff[The professors] moved a vote of nonconfidence in the President. **불신임하다** distrust; have no confidence (in).
● **불신임 결의** a nonconfidence resolution; a vote of censure. **불신임안** nonconfidence motion. **불신임 투표** a vote of nonconfidence [no-confidence]; a nonconfidence [no-confidence] vote.

불심(佛心) [불] [부처의 마음] the mercy [merciful heart] of Buddha; [해탈] deliverance (from worldly cares).

불심 검문(不審檢問) ¶~을 받지 않고[에 걸리지 않고] 지나가다 go through unquestioned // 나는 형사의 제지를 받고 ~을 당했다 I was stopped and questioned by a police detective.

불쌍하다 [가엾다] poor; pitiful; [애처롭다] sad; pitiable; piteous; [비참하다] miserable; wretched; [불행하다] unfortunate; [동정이 가다] pathetic; touching; [가슴 아프다] regrettable. ¶어미 없는 불쌍한 망아지 a poor [pitiful] motherless colt // 불쌍한 고아 a poor orphan // 어머니를 여읜 저 아이가 몹시 ~ I feel terribly sorry for that child who lost her mother. // 그는 불쌍한 사람이다 He is to be pitied. // 불쌍하기도 해라 Poor thing! / What a pity! / Poor man[girl, etc.]! / Poor soul [creature]! / Alas! the pity of it. / God help him! / I am so sorry. (▶ 직접 본인을 보고 말할 때 "You are poor[pitiful]."이라고는 하지 않음) // 불쌍한 그 아이는 맨발이었다 The poor child had no shoes on. // 불쌍한 것은 그 어린 자매들이었다 It was the little sisters who aroused our compassion. // 그는 강아지가 불쌍해서 집으로 데려갔다 He took pity on the puppy and took it home. // 그 불쌍한 노인은 추위에 떨고 있었다 The poor old man was shivering with cold. // 저렇게 젊은 나이에 죽다니 참 ~ What a pity[It is a pity] that he should have died so young. // 그는 불쌍해서 그 여자를 고용했다 He hired her out of pity [sympathy]. **불쌍히** with a pity; piteously; pitiably; pitifully; miserably. ¶~ 여기다 [동정하다] pity / have[take] pity (on) / feel pity (for) / sympathize [feel sympathy (for)] (with) (▶ pity에는 불행한 사람, 손아랫사람을 가엾이 여긴다는 뜻이 있음. sympathize는 동정, 동감한다는 뜻으로 가엾다의 의미는 없음) / [가슴 아파서] regret / be sorry (for) // 그는 집 없는 아이를 ~ 여겨 집으로 데리고 갔다 He pitied[took pity on] the homeless child and took him into his home. // 그들은 내 처지를 ~ 여겨 재정적인 원조를 제의했다 Out of pity for my circumstances, they offered to help me financially. // 그를 ~ 여겨 용서해 주어라 Be compassionate [understanding] and forgive him.

불쏘시개 a (fire) lighter; kindling wood; a kindler; (미) kindling(s); a spill. ¶나뭇조각을 ~로 쓰다 use pieces of wood as kindling [to light a fire].

불쑥 1 [갑자기 쑥 내미는 모양] suddenly; unexpectedly; abruptly; unusually; (별안간·뜻밖에) all of a sudden; unexpectedly; (예고 없이) without (previous) notice[warning]; unawares. ¶창밖으로 머리를 ~ 내밀다 pop one's head out of the window // 주먹을 ~ 내밀다 thrust out one's fist // 물속에서 그의 머리가 ~ 나왔다 His head popped up from the water. // 이렇게 ~ 찾아와서 미안합니다 I hate to barge in on you like this. // 그는 어디서 ~ 나왔는지 나타났다 He appeared suddenly from out of nowhere. // 오늘 아침 그가 사무실에 ~ 나타났다 He popped in at my office this morning. // 검은 복장의 사나이들이 숲 속에서 ~ 튀어나왔다 Men in black rushed[came rushing] out of the woods. **2** [앞뒤 생각 없이] carelessly; bluntly. ¶~ 튀어나온 말 a remark spoken out carelessly / an unguarded remark // ~ 말하다 blurt out a remark / talk abruptly // 그는 나에게 ~ 질문을 던졌다 He popped a question at me.

불쑥거리다 1 [자꾸 내밀다] keep putting [sticking] out abruptly. ¶주먹을 ~ keep thrusting one's fist out. **2** [앞뒤 생각 없이 말하다] blurt out a remark; talk bluntly.

불쑥불쑥 (pop out / bulge out / come out) one after another; here and there. **불쑥불쑥하다** bulge out here and there; be full of projections, large or small; have pieces sticking up.

불쑥하다 projecting; protruding; sticking up [out]; bulgy; swelling.

불씨 1 [불을 이어 가는 부덩이] a live coal[live charcoal] to build a fire with (▶ charcoal은 숯불, a는 붙이지 않음). ¶화로에 ~가 하나도 남지 않았다 There is no live charcoal left in the brazier to build[make] a fire with. **2** [사건의 실마리] a cause; a source; the origin; the apple. ¶분쟁의 ~ an apple of discord / the cause of a quarrel // 영토 문제가 ~가 되어 전쟁이 발발하였었다 The territorial dispute led to the war.

불안(不安) **1** [걱정] uneasiness; anxiety; worry; apprehension; misgivings; suspense; fear. ¶끊임없이 ~에 떨다[시달리다] be[sit / stand / walk] on thorns // 건강에 ~을 느끼다 have[feel] misgivings about one's health // 그는 늘 지진에 대한 ~에 떨고 있다 He is in constant fear of earthquakes. // 갑자기 알 수 없는 ~이 그를 엄습했다 Suddenly he was attacked by an inexplicable disquiet. **불안하다** uneasy; ill at ease; restless; anxious. ¶불안해지다 feel uneasy // 나는 불안한 하룻밤을 보냈다 I passed an anxious[uneasy] night. / I passed the night in anxiety. // 불안한 생각으로 집에서 편지가 오기를 기다렸다 I awaited the letter from home with anxiety [uneasily]. // 아버지의 안부를 알 수 없어 ~ I am worried about my father's safety. // 그는 거짓말이 탄로 날까 봐 불안해했다 He feared [was afraid] that his lie might be discovered. // 그 아이가 혼자서 여행한다고 하니 매우 ~ I feel very uneasy[anxious] about the child traveling all by himself.

불안정

2 [불안정] insecurity; [사회적 동요] unrest. ¶현 정계의 ~을 일소하다 put an end to the current political unrest and instability // 정계[사회]의 ~이 주가의 대폭락을 가져왔다 Political [Social] unrest caused a drastic fall in stock prices. **불안하다** insecure; precarious; uncertain. ¶불안한 정계 the unsettled political world // 불안한 날씨 disturbing weather // 불안한 걸음걸이로 with unsteady [uncertain / faltering / tottering] steps // 불안한 자리[지위]에 있다 be in an insecure position // 그는 아주 불안한 생활을 하고 있다 He ekes out a precarious living.

● **불안감** a sense of unease; a feeling of uneasiness[anxiety]. ¶~이 내내 사라지지 않았다 My feeling of anxiety did not subside.

불안정(不安定) lack of stability; instability; insecurity. ¶통화의 ~ currency instability // 정서적 ~ emotional instability. **불안정하다** unstable; unsettled; shaky; crank(y); changeable; insecure; precarious(위험을 안은). ¶불안정한 사회 정세 unstable social conditions // 불안정한 입장 uncertain ground / a precarious position // 불안정한 정부 an unsettled government / an unstable [a wobbly] government // 불안정한 시세 a fluctuating market / an unsettled market // 불안정한 걸음걸이로 with faltering [tottering] steps / on shaky legs // 수입이 ~ earn a precarious livelihood // 그는 곧 도산할 것 같은 회사에서 불안정한 위치에 있다 He is in a precarious position in a struggling company. // 이 의자는 ~ This chair is rickety [unstable]. / This chair wobbles. // 금일 주식 시장은 불안정한 상태로 개장했다 The stock market opened in an unsettled[uncertain] mood today.

불알 the testicles; the testes (*sing.* -tis); the stones; (속어) the balls; (미국 속어) family jewels. ¶~을 까다 castrate / geld(동물의).

불알을 긁어 주다(속담) curry favor with (one's superior).

불야성(不夜城) [밤에도 밝은 도시] a nightless city; [환락가] all night entertainment areas; nightless[gay] quarters. ¶밤마다 그 건물은 ~을 이루었다 Every night the building was brilliantly illuminated.

불어(佛語) **1** French. ⇨ 프랑스 어(⇨프랑스) **2** [불] Buddhistic terms(불교 용어).

불어나다 increase; grow; accumulate; run [go / mount] up; pile [roll] up; rise. ¶강물이 ~ the river rises // 빚이 ~ get deeper in debt / one's debt gets heavy // 그의 재산이 점점 불어나고 있었다 His wealth was gradually accumulating. / His fortune was gradually increasing. // 소년 범죄가 계속 불어나고 있다 Juvenile delinquency goes on increasing. // 비용은 불어날 것이다 The expenses will run [pile] up. // 호우로 강물이 불어났다 The heavy rain swelled the waters (of the river). // 이 도시의 인구는 10년 동안에 세 배로 불어났다 Population of this town has tripled in the past ten years.

불어넣다 (사상·의식을) inspire; infuse; indoctrinate; inoculate; imbue; inform. ¶반공 사상을 ~ inspire a person with anticommunist sentiments // engraft anticommunist sentiments in a person's mind // 청년들에게 열렬한 애국 사상을 ~ inoculate the young with patriotic fervor // 학생들에게 새로운 열의를 ~ inform one's students with new zeal // 시장 거래[시세 / 주가]에 활기를 ~ activate the market / drive up the price of stocks // 나는 그에게 골프 열을 불어넣었다 I infused him with an enthusiasm for golf.

불여우 [동] a red fox. ¶~ 같다 be foxy.

불여의하다(不如意-) (서술적) go contrary to one's wishes; go wrong[amiss]. ¶만사가 ~ Everything goes wrong (with me).

불연성(不燃性) non(in)flammability; incombustibility. ¶~의 non(in)flammable / incombustible / noncombustible / uninflammable.

● **불연성 물질** incombustibles; nonflammables.

불연속(不連續) discontinuity. ¶~의 discontinuous.

● **불연속면** [기상] a surface of discontinuity; frontal surface. **불연속선** [기상] a line [front] of discontinuity; a gap in the isobaric line.

불온(不穩) **1** [평온하지 아니함] unrest; disquiet. **불온하다** disquieting; alarming; turbulent; restless; unsettled; disorderly; [심상치 않다] threatening. ¶불온한 정세 a threatening situation / an unsettled condition // 불온한 소문 a disquieting[an alarming] rumor // 불온한 분위기 a charged atmosphere // 나는 불온한 공기를 느꼈다 I had a feeling that trouble was brewing. // 형세가 ~ The situation looks ugly [threatening].

2 [사상 등이 온당치 않음] impropriety; inappropriateness. **불온하다** improper; inappropriate; [부당하다] unjust; unfair; unreasonable; unwarrantable; [과격하다] immoderate; violent; riotous. ¶불온한 처사 an unfair action[dealing] / an unjust measure // 불온한 행동으로 나오다 stir up trouble / behave in a riotous[a disorderly / a quarrelsome / an improper] manner // 불온한 언사를 쓰다 use improper [immoderate] words / use [indulge in] strong[violent] language.

● **불온 문서** seditious [subversive] documents [literature]. **불온 분자** a disturbing element; riotous[turbulent] people. **불온사상** a disturbing idea; a disquieting thought.

불완전(不完全) incompleteness; imperfection; defectiveness; faultiness. **불완전하다** [부족한 부분이 있다] incomplete; [완벽하지 않다] imperfect; [결함이 있다] defective; faulty. ¶불완전한 지식 imperfect[incomplete] knowledge // 이 계기들은 조립이 ~ These meters have been defectively assembled. // 사람은 누구나 ~ Every man has his faults.

● **불완전 고용** underemployment. **불완전 연소** [물] incomplete combustion. **불완전 자동사** [타동사] [언] an incomplete transitive [intransitive] verb.

불요불굴(不撓不屈) inflexibility; tenacity; gameness; dauntlessness; indomitableness. ¶~의 정신으로 with an indomitable [unconquerable] // ~의 젊은이 an unyielding [indomitable] youth // ~의 의지 indefatigable purpose. **불요불굴하다** inflexible; tenacious; dauntless; indomitable; unyielding; unflinching; resolute; indefatigable; unflagging.

불요불급하다(不要不急-) nonessential; nonurgent; unnecessary; not pressing. ¶불요불급한 지출을 억제하다 cut down unnecessary expenses.

불용(不用) [쓰지 아니함] disuse; desuetude. [소용 없음] inutility; uselessness. **불용하다** do not use; disuse; discard; junk.

불용성(不溶性) [화] indissolubility; insolubility; insolubleness; infusibility. ¶~**염류** insoluble salts.

불우하다(不遇-) ill-fated; ill-starred; unfortunate; unfavored; adverse; hapless; obscure. ¶그의 불우한 시절은 오래가지 않았다 His days of misfortune did not last long. / His days of [unfavored] days did not last long.∥그는 일생을 불우하게 살았다 He lived in obscurity all his life.∥그는 가정적으로 불우하였다 His home life was not a happy one.

불운(不運) (a) misfortune; bad luck(▶ 보통 misfortune 쪽이 중대한 것에 쓰임. bad luck 은 우연성이 강함); ills; adverse fortune [circumstances]; ill[cross] luck[fortune]; a tough luck; (문어) a hapless fate; an evil [untoward / adverse] fate; a bad break; ill chance; (a) mischance; (구어) hoodoo. ¶~의 일생을 살다 have an ill-fated life / be hapless to the end of one's life∥~을 겪다 have bad luck / (문어) suffer adverse fortune∥~으로 여기고 체념하다 accept [resign oneself to] one's fate∥갖가지 ~이 우리에게 닥친 것 같다 We seem to be jinxed. / Every possible misfortune has befallen us. **불운하다** unfortunate; unlucky; luckless; (숙명처럼) ill-fated; (문어) hapless; evil-[ill-] starred; infelicitous.

불원간(不遠間) [오래지 않아] at an early date [day]; in the near future; before long; soon; at no distant date[day]. ¶그는 ~ 자신이 잘못했다는 것을 깨닫게 될 것입니다 In (the course of) time he will discover for himself that he was wrong.∥~ 한번 찾아뵙겠습니다 I will call on you one of these days.

불원하다(不遠-) 1 [거리가 멀지 않다] not far (from); not so distant; not a long way. ¶당신 집에서 불원한 곳에 not far from your house. 2 (시일이) (서술적) be not far in the future.

불유쾌하다(不愉快-) disagreeable; unpleasant; uncomfortable; unhappy. ¶불유쾌한 녀석 an unpleasant guy∥그는 우리에게 불유쾌할 정도로 정중히 절을 했다 He bowed to us in an obsequious manner.

불응(不應) noncompliance; noncompliance; declination; disobedience; [거부] refusal; rejection. **불응하다** do not accept[grant / meet / comply with / consent to]; decline; do not answer[respond to]; disobey; refuse; reject; turn down; turn a deaf ear to. ¶호출에 ~ disobey a summons∥질문에 ~ do not answer[respond to] a question∥규칙에 ~ do not comply with a regulations.

불의(不意) suddenness; unexpectedness. ~의 [돌연히] sudden / abrupt / [우연의] incidental / casual / [예상 밖의] unexpected / unlooked-for / unforeseen / [긴급의] emergent / contingent∥~의 방문객 an unexpected visitor∥~의 재난 a [an unexpected] disaster / an unforeseen calamity∥~의 죽음 a sudden[violent] death∥~의 사건 a contingent occurrence / an unexpected event / an unforeseen occurrence∥~의 사고를 당하다 have[meet with] an accident∥그녀는 ~의 자동차 사고로 죽었다 She was killed in a car accident.

불의(不義) 1 [부도덕] immorality; impropriety; [부정] injustice; iniquity; unrighteousness. 2 [도의에 벗어난 남녀 관계] illicit intercourse; criminal[improper] connection; misconduct; liaison; intrigue; adultery. ¶~의 씨 a child born in a sin / a bastard / adulterate offspring / a child born out of wedlock∥~의 관계를 맺다 have improper connection (with) / make [commit] misconduct / misconduct oneself (with) / make an intrigue (with) / live in sin (with)∥그에게는 ~의 씨가 있다 He has an illegitimate child.

불이익(不利益) disadvantage; a handicap; a loss; a drawback; inadvisability; inexpediency. ¶그는 형에게 ~을 주었다 He inflicted a loss on his brother. **불이익하다** disadvantageous; unprofitable; unremunerative; against one's interests; inadvisable; inexpedient; unfavo(u)rable.

불이행(不履行) default; nonfulfillment; nonperformance; breach; nonobservance; failure. ¶계약 ~ nonfulfillment of a contract∥채무 ~ failure to pay one's financial debt / [법] default∥의무 ~ failure in duty / a breach of duty / nonperformance of an obligation / [법] nonfeasance∥조약 ~ nonobservance of a treaty∥약속 ~ failure to keep (one's) promise / (a) breach of promise∥물품 인도 ~ 시는 in default of delivery∥나는 계약 ~으로 위약금을 내야 했다 I had to pay a penalty for not fulfilling the terms of the contract. **불이행하다** fail to fulfill[perform / observe / carry out]; break.

불인가(不認可) disapprobation; disapproval; disallowance; [각하] rejection; refusal. **불인가하다** disapprove; reject; refuse; turn down.

불일간(不日間) shortly; soon. ⇨ ²**불일내**

불일내(不日內) [오래지 않아] shortly; soon; before long; in a short time; in a few days; one of these days.

불일치(不一致) disagreement; [불화] discord; discordance; [일관성이 없음] inconsistency; [통일성이 없음] lack of unity; dissonance; incongruity; inconformity; dissidence. ¶언행의 ~ discordance between one's words and one's actions∥의견의 ~ diversity of opinion∥성격의 ~가 이혼의 원인이었습니다 Incompatibility of temperament was behind our divorce.∥부부간의 의견 ~는 어린이에게 악영향을 끼친다 Parental discord has a bad effect on children. **불일치하다** disagree; discordant; dissonant; inharmonious; (서술적) be in discord (with).

불임(不妊) sterility. ¶~의 sterile / barren. ●**불임 수술** sterilization. ¶나는 ~을 받았다 I underwent a sterilization operation. / I had myself sterilized. **불임증** sterility; infertility; infecundity. ¶~에 걸리다 [~이 되다] become sterile / lose one's reproductive power.

불입(拂入) (a) payment. ¶분할 ~ payment by installments∥일부 ~ partial payment / payment on account∥일시 ~ payment in lump sum∥전액 ~ payment in full. **불입하다** pay in; transfer (money) to (a person's account). →¶나의 예금 계좌에는 5만 원이 불입되어 있다 Fifty thousand won has been paid into my account.∥나의 급료는 은행에 자동 불입되고 있다 My salary is paid automatically into the bank.

불자동차(-自動車) a fire engine. ⇨ ²**소방차** (⇨)

불장(佛葬) a Buddhistic funeral. ¶~으로 하다 bury (a person) according to Buddhist rites.

불장난 1 [아이들이 불을 가지고 노는 장난]. **불장난하다** play with fire[matches]. **2** [위험한 행위의 비유]. ¶대통령은 상대국을 도발하는 언사로 위험한 ~을 하고 있다 The President is playing with fire by using provocative language to the other nation. **불장난하다** play with fire. **3** [남녀간의 무분별한 사귐]. **불장난하다** play with love[fire]; have an idle love affair; flirt (with). ¶남자와 ~ flirt with a man.

불전(佛典) the Buddhist scriptures. ⇨ '불경(佛經)

불전(佛前) [부처의 앞]. ¶~에 바치다 place (something) before the Buddhist altar.

불전(佛殿) a Buddhist temple. ⇨ 불당(佛堂)

불제자(佛弟子) a Buddhist; a believer in Buddhism.

불조심(-操心) precautions against fire. **불조심하다** be careful with fire; take precautions against fire; take care not to start a fire; look out for fire.

불좌(佛座) the seat of a Buddhist idol.

불집 a (fire) hazard. ¶~을 건드리다 cause a troublesome situation / stir up[put one's hand in] a hornet's nest / bring[raise / arouse] a hornet's nest about one's ears / overturn an anthill.

불착(不着) [도착하지 않음] nonarrival; nondelivery. **불착하다** do not arrive.

불찬성(不贊成) [불승인] disapproval; disapprobation; disfavor; [의견 차이] disagreement; dissent; dissension; [반대] (an) objection. ¶그는 찬성인지 ~인지 말하여라 Say whether you are for it or against it. // 그는 ~이라는 답을 보내왔다 He sent me a negative answer. // 그는 그 계획에 ~이다 He is against[objects to / disapproves of] the plan. // 그의 아버지께서는 그의 결혼에 ~이시다 His father objects to his marriage. // 그의 양친은 그의 대학 진학에 ~이다 His parents do not want him to go[not approve of his going] to college. **불찬성하다** disapprove (of); express one's disapproval (of); disagree (with / to); dissent (from); object (to); take[make an] objection (to). ¶그런 제안에는 불찬성한다 I do not approve of such a proposal. // 네 의견에는 불찬성한다 I disagree [do not agree] with you.

불찰(不察) [부주의] carelessness; negligence; lack of attention; thoughtlessness; imprudence; [실수] a fault; a mistake; a blunder; [미숙] inexperience; [무능] incompetence. ¶손님의 출발 시간을 적어 두지 않았던 것은 나의 ~이었다 It was very careless of me not to write down the time[hour] of the guest's departure. // 그것을 그에게 맡긴 것은 당신의 ~이었다 It was imprudent of you to have trusted him with it. // 아픈 사람에게 그런 말을 한 것은 당신 ~이오 It's was thoughtless of you to say such a thing to a sick person. // 모두가 제 ~로 생긴 일입니다 Everything is the result of my incompetence.

불참(不參) absence; nonattendance; a failure in attendance; default; nonappearance. **불참하다** be absent (from); absent oneself (from); fail to attend[appear (in)]; stay away (from); do not participate (in). ¶우리는 처음부터 그 회의에 불참한다는 뜻을 전했다 We have said from the beginning that we would not attend the conference. // 그는 마라톤에 불참했다 He did not participate in the marathon.
●**불참자** an absentee; a person not attending. ¶그 모임에는 ~가 많았다 The meeting was badly[poorly] attended.

불철저하다(不徹底-) inconclusive; not thorough (going); [논지 등이] inconsistent; weak; unconvincing; indefinite; halfway; lukewarm. ¶불철저한 조사 an inexhaustive investigation // 불철저한 논의 an inconsistent [inconclusive] argument // 불철저한 조치 a half(way) measure.

불철주야(不撤晝夜) day and night; by day and (by) night; around[round] the clock. ¶~로 일하다 work night and day[day and night] / work double shifts[tides] / work around[round] the clock.

불청객(不請客) a self-invited[an uninvited / an unbidden] guest; (미) a gate-crasher. (미) a crasher.

불체포 특권(不逮捕特權) privilege of exemption from apprehension; nonapprehension privilege.

불초(不肖) [못나고 어리석음]. ¶~자식 an unworthy son / a son unworthy of his father. **불초하다** unworthy; (서술적) be not worth.

불출(不出) [어리석고 못난 사람] a stupid [dullheaded] person; a good-for-nothing; a failure.

불충(不忠) [충성을 다하지 아니함] disloyalty; infidelity; perfidy; failure in one's duty; [반역] treachery; treason. **불충하다** disloyal; unfaithful; undutiful; perfidious; treacherous; false. ¶불충한 신하 a disloyal vassal.

불충분(不充分) insufficiency; imperfection; inadequacy. ¶그는 증거 ~으로 불기소되었다 He was acquitted for lack[want] of evidence [because of insufficient evidence]. **불충분하다** insufficient; not enough; deficient; scanty; imperfect; incomplete. ¶불충분한 설명 a sketchy explanation // 자금이 ~ be short of [do not have enough] funds (to do) // 준비[장비]가 ~ be ill prepared[equipped] // 너의 설명은 ~ Your explanation is incomplete. / You have not made yourself perfectly clear.

불충실하다(不充實-) unfaithful; disloyal; faithless. ¶주인에게 ~ be disloyal[faithless] to one's master // 그는 직무에 ~ He is unfaithful to his duty.

불치(不治) [병이 낫지 않거나 고칠 수 없음] incurability; malignity. ¶~의 incurable / irremediable / fatal / malignant / immedicable / irrecoverable // ~의 환자 a hopeless case / an incurable[a confirmed] invalid / an invalid for life // 그는 ~의 병을 앓고 있다 His disease is incurable. / He will never get better.
●**불치병** an incurable[a remediless / a fatal] disease. ¶그는 ~에 걸렸다 He contracted an incurable disease.

불친절(不親切) unkindness; unfriendliness; inhospitality. **불친절하다** unkind; unfriendly; disobliging; inhospitable. ¶당신은 아주 불친절하군 That's very unkind of you.

불침번(不寢番) (행위) night watch; sleepless [all night] vigil; (사람) a night watchman [watcher / watch]. ¶~을 서다 keep vigil [a night watch] / be on duty as night watchman.

불쾌지수(不快指數) a temperature-humidity index(약어 THI); a discomfort index(약어 DI).

불쾌하다(不快-) 1 [싫다] unpleasant; displeasing; [마음에 들지 않다] disagreeable; offensive [거북하다] uncomfortable; [기분이 좋지 않다] displeased; ill humored; [부아가 나다] provoking; [짜증이 나다] irritating; [분하다] exasperating. ¶불쾌한 사람 a disagreeable person // 불쾌한 태도 unpleasant manners / provoking [exasperating] behavior // 불쾌한 냄새 a bad [disagreeable] smell / an unpleasant [offensive] smell // 불쾌하게 하다 make a person unhappy // 그는 상당히 불쾌했다 He was very much displeased. // 그는 불쾌한 얼굴로 잠자코 있었다 With a look of displeasure on his face he remained silent. / He frowned and said nothing. // 불쾌하게 해서 미안합니다 I am sorry I hurt your feelings [offended you / displeased you / made you uncomfortable]. // 그는 불쾌한 표정을 지었다 [얼굴을 했다] He looked displeased [offended]. // 그녀는 그의 뻔뻔스러움에 심히 불쾌했다 His impudence annoyed her greatly. **불쾌히** displeasedly; unpleasantly; disagreeably. ¶~ 생각하다 [느끼다] feel displeased [uneasy / uncomfortable] / feel hurt / take offense (at).
2 [몸이 찌뿌드드하다] (서술적) be not well; be [feel] unwell; be indisposed; be out of condition [form / sorts]. ¶그는 약간 불쾌해서 자리에 누워 있다 He feels slightly under the weather [isn't feeling well], and is staying in bed.

불타(佛陀) Buddha. ⇨부처

불타다 1 [불이 붙어 타다] burn; blaze; be in flames. ¶빨갛게 불타고 있는 난로 a red-glowing stove // 지는 해로 불타는 듯한 서쪽 하늘 the western sky aglow with the setting sun // 활활 ~ burn briskly [vigorously / furiously] // 불타기 쉽다 be easy to burn / catch fire easily / be inflammable [inflammable / flammable] // 불탄 자리에서 시체를 찾다 search in the debris for bodies // 배가 불타고 있다 The ship is on fire. // 집이 불타고 있다 The house is burning [on fire] // 집이 불타 버렸다 The house burned down [was reduced to ashes]. // 목조 가옥은 불타기 쉽다 Wooden houses burn [catch fire] easily.
2 [정열·의욕 등이 끓어오르다] burn; glow; be aflame. ¶불타는 fervent / burning // 불타는 사랑 a burning [passionate] love / an ardent love / flaming love // 불타는 정열 a burning [consuming fiery] passion // 불타는 욕망 burning desire // 맹렬한 투지에 ~ burn with intense fighting spirit // 질투심에 ~ burn with jealousy // 그는 복수심에 불타고 있었다 He was boiling [burning] with the desire for revenge. // 그는 권력욕에 불타고 있다 He is burning with a thirst for power. // 그들은 애국심에 불타고 있다 Their hearts burn [glow] with patriotism. // 그의 눈은 분노에 불탔다 His eyes flashed with anger. // 그들은 희망 [향학열]에 불타고 있다 They are full of hope [a love of learning].

불탄일(佛誕日) Buddha's birthday; the Day of Buddha's coming. ¶~ 축제 (the) Buddha's birthday festival.

불탑(佛塔) a pagoda.

불통(不通) 1 (교통·통신의) impassability; suspension; interruption (of telephone service); stoppage; tie-up. ¶열차 [전신]의 ~ the interruption of train service [telegraphic communication] // ~이 된 곳 a break (on the line) // 통신 ~이 된 지방 an isolated district // 호남선은 ~이 되었다 Service on the Honam [Daejeon-Mokpo] Line has been suspended [interrupted]. / The Honam [Daejeon-Mokpo] Line is not running. // 대지진 때문에 전신 전화는 ~이다 Telegraph and telephone service has been interrupted [broken off] as a result of the big earthquake. **불통하다** be suspended; be stopped; be blocked; be interrupted; be cut off; be tied up.
2 (이해·사정의) no understanding; unfamiliarity; ignorance. ¶세상 일에 ~이다 be ignorant of the world / know little of the world // 그는 사리를 말해도 ~이다 He is dead to reason. **불통하다** have no understanding; be not familiar [well acquainted] (with); be ill informed (of); be ignorant (of). ¶의사가 서로 ~ do not understand each other.
3 (교제·연락 등의) no association; no communication; lack of contact. ¶소식 ~이다 hear nothing from (a person). **불통하다** have no association [intercourse] (with); be not communicated; lack contact.

불퇴전(不退轉) determination; a firm resolve; firm belief in Buddha. ¶~의 결의로 with an indomitable resolve // ~의 노력을 하다 make unremitting exertions [efforts].

불투명(不透明) opacity. **불투명하다** opaque; turbid; thick; milky. ¶불투명한 태도 a vague [an ambiguous] attitude / an uncertain [a noncommittal] attitude // 어떻게 될 ~ It is difficult to say how things will turn out.
● **불투명체** an opaque body [material].

불투수층(不透水層) an impermeable layer.

불퉁거리다 talk bluntly [shortly]; speak stiffly.

불퉁불퉁 1 (물체의 겉면이) with lots of knots [bumps]. **불퉁불퉁하다** rough (surface); rugged (features); jagged [ragged] (rocks); bumpy (road); knagged [knaggy] (timber); knotty (hand); gnarled (tree). ¶불퉁불퉁한 길 a rough [bumpy] road. 2 (말 등이) bluntly; surlily. **불퉁불퉁하다** talk bluntly. ⇨불퉁거리다

불퉁스럽다 (언동이) curt; rough; brusque; rude; gruff; [동정심이 없다] blunt. ¶불퉁스러운 남자 a gruffish [rude] man // 그는 불퉁스럽게 대답했다 He gave a curt [blunt] reply. // 그는 불퉁스럽게 말한다 He is blunt in his speech.

불퉁하다 [툭 비어져 있다] bulgy; protuberant.

불특정(不特定) unspecificness. ¶~의 unspecific / unspecified // 이 부사는 ~의 때를 나타낸다 This adverb denotes indefinite time.
● **불특정 다수** an unspecified number of the general public. ¶~의 구매층 a general run of buyers.

불티 sparks; embers; fire-flakes. ¶~가 튀다 spark / sparkle / throw sparks.

불티나다 (서술적) (상품이) command [have /

불패(不敗) invincibility. ¶~의 [쓰러뜨릴 수 없는] invincible / unbeatable / [진 적이 없는] unbeaten.∥그 팀은 10년 동안 ~의 기록을 자랑하고 있다 The team boasts on undefeated record over the past ten years.

불펜〔야구〕 the bull pen.

불편(不便) **1**〔편리하지 못함〕 (an) inconvenience; inexpediency; incommodiousness; unhandiness. ¶남에게 ~을 끼치다 put a person to inconvenience / inconvenience a person∥~을 참다 put up with inconveniences∥이런 벽지에 사는 ~을 생각해 보십시오 Think of the inconvenience of living in such an out-of-the-way place.∥식모가 집에 돌아가 버려서 손님들에게 많은 ~을 끼쳤다 Our maid having gone home, we put our guest to a great deal of inconvenience [our guest had to suffer much inconvenience].

불편하다 inconvenient; incommodious; unhandy; unwieldy. ¶쇼핑을 하기에 불편한 곳 a place inconvenient for shopping∥쓰기에 불편한 방 an inconvenient room∥그 시간은 그에게 ~ It is an inconvenient time for him.∥불편하신 건 없으세요 Is everything all right?∥여행 일정에 불편한 점은 없습니까 Is the itinerary quite all right with you?∥집이 불편한 곳에 있다 The house is inconveniently situated [located].∥이 근처는 교통이 ~ Public transportation in this area is poor.∥이 라디오 카세트는 가지고 다니기에 ~ This radio-cassette tape recorder is not easy [handy] to carry around.∥이 부엌의 구조는 ~ This kitchen is badly planned.
2〔몸·마음 등이 편하지 못함〕 (an) indisposition; (a) discomfort; a disorder; a bad condition; an ailment; malaise. **불편하다**〔서술적〕 be not well; be [feel] unwell [ill]; be indisposed; be [feel] out of sorts [form / condition]. ¶몸이 불편해서 그를 만날 수가 없다 I do not feel equal to receiving him.∥여기 있으면 마음이 불편합니다 I feel out of place here. / I feel rather awkward staying here.

불편부당하다(不偏不黨-) impartial; nonpartisan; neutral; fair; unbias(s)ed; unprejudiced; disinterested; independent. ¶불편부당한 신문 an independent newspaper / a newspaper free from party affiliation∥불편부당한 태도를 취하다 adopt a neutral attitude.

불평(不平) 〔불만〕 discontent; dissatisfaction; displeasure; (정치상의) disaffection; 〔불평의 말〕 a grievance; a murmur; an idle complaint; (속어) a grouse; (미국 속어) a beef. ¶~이 많은 grumbling / grumbly / querulous (about)∥~을 토로하다 complain / 〔투덜거리다〕 grumble∥주민들 사이에는 ~의 소리가 높다 Loud cries of discontent are being voiced among the people. / The residents are voicing their discontent loudly.∥이 결정에 대해 ~이 있습니까 Are you dissatisfied with the arrangement?∥그는 교장에게 여러 가지 ~을 늘어놓았다 He made various complaints to the principal. / He reeled off a list of various complaints to the principal.∥자네는 지금 하고 있는 일에 대해 전혀 ~을 하지 않는군 You never grumble [(구어) gripe / (구어) grouse] about your present job, do you?∥아내는 ~ 한마디 없이 어머니를 돌보아 주었다 My wife took care of my mother without a single complaint. **불평하다** grumble at [about / over] (one's food); complain of; make a complaint; murmur at [against]; grunt; (미국 속어) gripe; beef. ¶남의 일하는 방식에 대해 ~ complain to [grumble at] a person about his work∥그녀는 옷에 대해서 불평했다 She complained about her clothes.
● **불평가** / **불평꾼** a grumbler; (미국 속어) a grouser; a malcontent.

불평등(不平等) inequality. ¶부(富)의 분배의 ~ inequality in the distribution of wealth.
불평등하다 unequal; (불공평하다) unfair. ¶불평등한 대우 a discriminatory [an unfair] treatment / unfair discrimination∥그 아이들을 불평등하게 대해서는 안 된다 You must treat the children impartially [be fair to all the children].
● **불평등 조약** an unequal treaty.

불포화(不飽和) unsaturation. **불포화하다** be unsaturated.
● **불포화 화합물**〔화〕 an unsaturated compound.

불필요하다(不必要-)〔필요하지 않다〕 unnecessary; needless; 〔쓸모없다〕 useless; 〔남아돌다〕 superfluous; 〔청하지도 않다〕 uncalled-for; 〔사용하지 않다〕 disused. ¶대학 입시에 불필요한 과목 subjects which are not required for university entrance examinations∥불필요한 걱정을 하다 worry needlessly∥불필요한 말을 하다 make an unnecessary remark∥그건 ~ That's no use.∥그것은 내게 불필요합니다 I don't need it. / I can do without it.∥입장권은 불필요합니다 Admission tickets are unnecessary.

불하(拂下) (a) disposal; (a) sale (of government property); (a) transfer (of state property to private ownership). **불하하다** sell; dispose of; transfer. ¶정부는 국유림의 일부를 불하하였다 The government disposed of [sold off] parts of the national forest. ➔¶이 공유지는 내년에 불하된다 This public land will be disposed of [put up for sale] next year.
● **불하품** articles disposed of by the government; articles sold by the government.

불학무식(不學無識) (utter) ignorance; illiteracy. **불학무식하다** (utterly) ignorant; (densely) illiterate; unlettered.

불한당(不汗黨) **1**〔강도〕 (a gang of) burglars [robbers / bandits / brigands]; a gang. **2**〔깡패〕 (a gang of) hooligans; (street) gangsters; hoodlums (and racketeers).

불합격(不合格) 〔낙제〕 failure; 〔실격〕 disqualification; rejection. ¶그 카메라는 수출 ~이 되었다 Those cameras were rejected for export. **불합격되다** be disqualified [rejected / eliminated]; come [fall] short of the mark [standard]; be found ineligible [unfit]; (시험에) fail (in) (an examination); (시험에) flunk (an examination). ➔¶그는 폐가 약해서 징병 검사에 불합격되었다 His weak lungs disqualified him for military service. / He didn't pass his military physical test because of weak lungs.
● **불합격자** a disqualified [rejected] person; an unsuccessful applicant [candidate]; a failure. ¶~는 모두 50명이었다 In all, fifty applicants were rejected. / All together [told] there were fifty unsuccessful applicants. 불

합격품 rejected goods; a throw-out.

불합리(不合理) irrationality; absurdity; illogicality; unreasonableness; unreason; inconsistency. **불합리하다** [이성을 결하다] irrational; [논리에 맞지 않다] illogical; [도리에 맞지 않다] unreasonable; [터무니없다] preposterous; [모순되다] inconsistent. ¶불합리한 가격 a ridiculous[preposterous] price // 불합리하기 짝이 없는 out of all reason // 네가 하는 말은 ~ What you are saying is illogical [unreasonable].

불행(不幸) [행복하지 않음] unhappiness; infelicity; misery; [불운] misfortune; ill fortune[luck]; adversity; [재난] a disaster; a calamity; an accident; a mishap; woe. ¶~을 당하다 meet a misfortune / suffer misfortune / have[meet with] a misfortune // ~을 면하다 escape misfortune // ~이 잇따르다 have a run of ill luck // 어떠한 ~을 겪을지라도 no matter what misfortune one may experience // 이보다 더한 ~은 있을 수 없다 There could be no worse misfortune. **불행하다** unhappy; miserable; wretched; infelicitous; unfortunate; unlucky; luckless; hapless; ill-starred[-fated]. ¶불행한 결혼 an unhappy[infelicitous] marriage // 이대로 가다가는 둘 다 불행해진다 If we go on like this, both of us will come to grief. // 그는 불행하게도 졸업 직전에 병에 걸렸다 He had the misfortune[was so unfortunate as] to be taken ill just before graduation. **불행히** unfortunately; unluckily; by misfortune[ill fortune]. ¶~ 그때 그의 아버지가 죽었다 Unfortunately, his father died then. // 그는 ~ 실명을 했다 Unfortunately he went blind. / He had the misfortune to lose his eyesight.

불행 중 다행 one consolation in sadness; a stroke of good luck in the midst of misfortune. ¶중상자가 없다는 것이 ~이다 It is consoling to know that none was injured seriously. // 내가 사고를 당했는데 골절만으로 끝난 것은 ~이었다 I was fortunate to come out of the accident with only a fractured bone.

불허(不許) disapproval; nonpermission; disapprobation; disallowance. **불허하다** disapprove; do not permit[allow / grant / admit]; disallow; reject; turn down. ¶복제를 불허함 All rights reserved. / Reproduction prohibited. // 현 정세는 낙관을 불허한다 The situation does not warrant optimism. // 그녀의 작품은 타의 추종을 불허한다 Her productions elude all attempts at imitation. // 사태는 일각의 지체도 불허한다 The situation does not admit of a moment's delay.

불현듯(이) suddenly; on[all of] a sudden; unexpectedly. ¶…하려는 생각이 ~ 일어나다 have a sudden desire to (do) / be seized with a desire to (do) / suddenly feel like (doing) // ~ 집 생각이 나다 be overcome with sudden homesickness / suddenly feel homesick.

불협화음(不協和音) **1** [음] a dissonance. ⇨안 어울림음 **2** [일치하지 않는 관계]. ~의 dissonant / inconsonant // 최근 양국 간에 ~이 생기고 있다 There has been discord between the two nations recently.

불호령(-號令) [급하고 무서운 명령] an impetuous order; a fiery command; [미난] thunder; a roaring scolding. **불호령하다** issue an impetuous[a fiery] order; give a strict command; storm (at a person).

불혹(不惑) [마흔 살]. ¶~의 나이 the age of forty (when one should be free from vacillation).

불화(不和) [사이가 좋지 않음] discord; [분쟁] trouble; [의견의 차이] differences. ¶가정 내의 ~ family trouble[discord] // 양국의 ~ the differences between the two countries // 집안과 집안의 ~ [장기간에 걸친 반목] a family feud // 내각과 당이 ~를 빚고 있다 There is discord[disagreement] between the cabinet and the party. // 그녀는 남편과 ~ 상태에 빠졌다 She fell out[quarreled] with her husband. // 이젠 ~를 씻어 버릴 때다 It's high time you buried your differences. // 부모의 ~는 어린이에게 나쁜 영향을 준다 Parental discord has a bad effect on children. **불화하다** (서술적) be at strife[issue / enmity / feud / war] (with); be in discord (with); [미] be at outs (with).

불화(弗化) [화] fluoration. ⇨플루오르화(⇨플루오르)

불화(弗貨) dollar; the U.S. dollar.

불확실성(不確實性) uncertainty.

불확실하다(不確實-) [확실하지 않다] uncertain; [불안정하다] insecure; unsteady; [위태롭다] precarious; [미덥지 않다] unreliable; [의심스럽다] doubtful. ¶불확실한 대답 an indefinite[uncertain] answer // 불확실한 보도 an unreliable[unauthentic] report // 불확실한 정보 unreliable information // 성공이 불확실한 작전 a strategy of uncertain[doubtful] success // 불확실한 수입 [불안정한 수입] an insecure[irregular] income / [기대할 수 없는 수입] an unreliable income // 나는 예정이 ~ I am uncertain about my plans. // 내 불확실한 기억으로는 90세가 넘었다 According to my hazy recollection he is past ninety. // 그의 성공은 ~ There is little hope of his success. // 예정은 아주 불확실합니다 Our plans are quite uncertain. // 남편의 수입은 불확실했다 The husband's income was insecure[precarious]. // 불확실한 일은 말하는 것이 아니다 You must not state anything you do not know for certain[sure].

불확정 기한(不確定期限) [법] a time uncertain.

불확정하다(不確定-) [확실하지 않다] uncertain; [결정되지 않다] indefinite; do not decide upon[settle / confirm]. ¶방침은 아직 ~ The course to be taken is not yet decided upon. // 기한은 ~ The term is indefinite.

불환 지폐(不換紙幣) [경] nonconvertible [inconvertible] notes; [미] fiat money.

불활성 기체(不活性氣體) [화] an inert gas. ⇨비활성 기체

불황(不況) [일시적인] (a) recession; bad business; a weak market; [심각한] a depression. ¶~의 dull / slack / depressed // 무역[경제]의 ~ a trade[an economic] depression // 주식 시장의 세계적 ~ (a) worldwide depression on stock markets // 예견되는 ~에 능동적으로 대처하기 위해 만반의 준비를 갖추다 be fully prepared to cope actively with the expected economic depression // ~은 차차 회복되고 있다 Business is looking up.

불효(不孝) [부모를 공경하지 않음] want of filial piety; unfilial behavior[[영] behaviour]; [부모에게 순종하지 않음] disobedience to one's parents. ¶부모님보다 먼저 이

세상을 하직하는 ~의 죄를 용서하십시오 Dear parents, please pardon me for preceding you in death. **불효하다** undutiful; unfilial; impious; disobedient; (자동사) treat one's parents disrespectfully.
● **불효자** an unfilial child; a disobedient child; an ungrateful child.

불후(不朽) immortality; imperishability. ¶~의 immortal / undying / undecaying / imperishable / fadeless / incorruptible / everlasting / eternal // ~의 명성 immortal [everlasting] fame // ~의 명작 an immortal work // ~의 이름을 남기다 win eternal fame [an imperishable memory] / perpetuate [immortalize] one's name // 만유인력의 법칙은 뉴턴의 이름을 ~의 것으로 만들었다 The theory of universal gravitation immortalized Newton [Newton's name]. **불후하다** never die [decay]; endure; last [live] forever.

붉다 red; ruddy; (심홍색의) crimson; (진홍색의) scarlet; rubicund (face); (병적으로) hectic; (사상이) communistic. ¶붉은 뺨 red [rosy] cheeks // 붉게 물들이다 dye red // 서쪽 하늘이 저녁노을로 붉게 물들었다 The western sky was aglow with the setting sun.

붉디붉다 deep red; crimson.

붉어지다 [붉게 되다] turn [grow] red; redden; (얼굴이) blush. ¶흥분하여 얼굴이 ~ flush with excitement // 저녁노을에 산이 붉어졌다 The mountain is glowing in the setting sun. // 그녀는 부끄러운지 뺨이 붉어졌다 Her cheeks reddened [She blushed], perhaps because she was embarrassed. // 그는 화가 나서 얼굴이 붉어졌다 He was flushed [red] with anger. // 그는 술을 마셔 얼굴이 붉어졌다 He is flushed with alcohol.

붉으락푸르락하다 (서술적) turn alternately pale and red. ¶화가 나서 얼굴이 ~ turn purple [(구어) boil] with rage.

붉히다 blush; color up; change color. ¶(부끄러워) 얼굴을 ~ blush (for [with] shame) / turn red with embarrassment // 볼을 붉히고 with a blush on one's cheeks // 그는 자기의 어리석음을 부끄럽게 생각하여 낯을 붉혔다 He blushed at his own stupidity. // 그는 화가 나서 얼굴을 붉혔다 He is flushed with anger. // 그녀는 부끄러워 얼굴을 붉혔다 She blushed [flushed / turned red] with shame. // 그의 말에 나는 얼굴을 붉혔다 His words made me blush. / I blushed at his words.

붐 a boom; [일시적 유행] a fad. ¶~이 일다 boom // ~을 타다 ride the crest of the (building) boom // ~을 일으키다 touch off a boom // 관광 ~이 일고 있다 A sightseeing boom is on. // 골프 ~은 진정될 것 같지 않다 The golfing boom is not likely to subside.

붐비다 (서술적) be crowded [thronged] (with people); be bustling; bustle; be packed [congested / jammed / jam-packed]; [만원이다] be full up. ¶붐비는 거리 a busy [crowded] street // 붐비는 버스 a crowded bus // 붐비는 시간 (at / during) the rush hour(s) [period] // 지독하게 붐비는군 What a throng [crush]! // 전차는 몹시 붐볐다 The train was jammed with people. / (미) The train was packed to capacity. // 바야흐로 붐비는 시간이다 It's just the rush hour now. // 이 근방은 주말이 되면 사람들로 붐빈다 This neighborhood is alive with people on [(영) at] weekends. // 이 상가는 늘 사람들로 붐빈다 The shopping area is bustling with activity all the time. // 광장은 늘 사람들로 붐비고 있다 The square is always bustling. / The square is always thronged [crowded] with people. // 공원은 밤늦게까지 많은 사람들이 붐비고 있었다 The park was bustling [thronged] with people until late at night. // 가게는 손님들로 붐비고 있었다 The shop was crowded [busy / filled] with customers. // 거리는 인파로 붐비고 있었다 People are surging through [thronging] the streets.

붓 [모필] a writing brush; [화필] a paint brush; [펜] a pen. ¶~을 놀리다 write [make a stroke] with brush // ~을 들다 write / take up one's pen.

붓을 꺾다 [던지다] [작가 생활을 그만두다] give up literary activity.

붓을 놓다 1 [그만 쓰다] stop writing; lay [put] down one's brush [pen]; (편지의) close. 2 give up literary activity. ⇨ 붓을 꺾다 (⇨붓)

붓꽃 [식] a blue flag; an iris (pl. ~es, irides).

붓끝 [붓의 위세] the power [force] of the pen.

붓다¹ 1 [살가죽이 부풀어 오르다] swell (up / out); bloat (out); become swollen [dropsical] (▶ dropsical은 수종으로 부었을 때를 말함). ¶부은 swollen / bloated / tumid // 부은 얼굴로 with a swollen face // 임파선이 ~ develop swollen lymphatic glands // 울어서 눈이 ~ have one's eyes swollen with crying / cry one's eyes out // 다친 팔목이 몹시 부었다 The injured wrist swelled up badly. // 그는 각기병으로 다리가 부어 있었다 His legs were swollen [dropsical] with beriberi.
2 [성이 나다] get angry (at); become sullen; get sulky [cross / peevish]; sulk; fret; (구어) get sore (at / on / over). ¶부은 angry / cross / sulky / sullen / sour // 부은 얼굴 a sulky look [face] // 무엇 때문에 부어 있느냐 What makes you (so) sulky? // 그녀는 걸핏하면 붓는다 She gets sulky [She gets put out / She pouts] at the least little thing.

붓다² 1 [액체를] pour (in / into); fill (a cup) with (coffee); put (water in a bowl); feed (a lamp with oil). ¶부어라 마셔라 하며 큰 소란을 피우다 have a wild party / raise the roof at a party / carouse // 콘크리트를 틀에 ~ pour concrete into a form // 끓고 있는 주전자에 물을 ~ add some water to a boiling kettle // 나는 병에 든 우유를 유리컵에 부었다 I poured milk from the bottle into the glasses. // 그는 한 잔 더 부으라고 잔을 내밀었다 He held out his cup for a refill. // 이 동상은 청동을 부어 만든 것이다 This statue is cast in bronze.
2 [배게 뿌리다] sow (seed) thickly. ¶모판에 씨앗을 ~ sow seeds in a seedbed.
3 [불입금·곗돈 등을 치르다] pay in [by] instal(l)ments. ¶월 5만 원씩 ~ pay a monthly instal(l)ment of 50,000 won // 그는 가진 돈을 몽땅 새로운 사업에 부어 넣었다 He invested all his money in [He sank all his money into] the new enterprise.

붓대 a brush handle; the shaft of a writing brush.

붓두껍 a brush cap; a metal cap for a brush tip.

붓질 drawing; painting; a stroke [touch] with a brush. **붓질하다** draw; paint; stroke; make strokes [touches] with a brush.

붕 1 [방귀 소리]. ¶방귀를 ~ 뀌다 break wind / (비어) let a fart / fart / (비어) poop. **2** (벌 등의) humming; buzzing; droning; (비행기 등의) whirring; buzzing. **3** (엔진 등의) whirring; humming. **4** [어떤 것을 허망하게 잃거나 날린 모양] in vain; in smoke; fleetingly. ¶(계획 등이) ~ 뜨다 end[go up] in smoke.

붕괴(崩壞) [허물어짐] a fall; a breakdown; (a) collapse; (건물·광산 등의) a cave-in. ¶제방의 ~ the breaking of an embankment // 그 내각은 ~ 직전에 있었다 The cabinet was on the verge of collapse. **붕괴하다** fall down; break down; collapse. ¶그 집은 지진으로 붕괴했다 The house collapsed[fell down / (구어) caved in] in the earthquake. // 지진으로 수많은 가옥이 붕괴했다 The houses collapsed [were destroyed] in the earthquake. // 홍수로 둑이 붕괴됐다 The flood destroyed the embankment(s).

붕긋하다 1 (언덕 등이) swollen; (배 등이) bulging; bulgy. **2** (배접한 것이) loose; blistered.

붕당(朋黨) a faction; a clique; a coterie. ¶~을 이루다 form a coterie / clique together.

붕대(繃帶) a bandage. ¶두루마리 ~ a roller (bandage) / (고무가 든) an elastic bandage // 압박 ~ a compression bandage // ~를 감다 apply a bandage to (a person's) / bandage (a person's arm) / dress (a wound) // ~를 풀다 unbandage / remove a bandage // ~를 갈다 [바꾸다] change a bandage / renew a dressing // 그녀는 팔꿈치에 ~를 감았다 (다른 사람을 시켜서) She had her elbow bandaged.

붕붕 [비행기·곤충 등이 날 때 나는 소리] buzzing; [자동차·배 등의 경적 소리] honking. ¶비행기의 ~ 소리 the roar[drone] of a plane // 모터가 ~ 돌아가고 있다 The motor is purring. // 벌이 내 귓전에서 ~ 날고 있다 A bee is buzzing around my ears.

붕사(硼沙) borax. ¶천연 ~ native borax / tincal // ~를 함유한 boric / boracic.

붕산(硼酸) [화] bor(ac)ic acid.

붕소(硼素) [화] boron(기호 B).

붕어 [동] a crucian carp; a Prussian carp; a roach; a gible.

붕우(朋友) a friend; a companion.
●**붕우유신**(-有信) Faith should reign over the relation between friends.

붕장어(-長魚) [동] a sea eel; a conger (eel).

붙다¹ 1 [부착하다] stick (to); cling (to); cleave (to). ¶전단이 벽에 붙어 있었다 A bill was pasted up[stuck] on the wall. // 나는 땀이 나서 셔츠가 등에 착 붙었다 I was so wet with perspiration that my shirt clung to my back. // 모든 우리 상품에는 분명히 가격표가 붙어 있습니다 All our goods are clearly priced.
2 [소속되다] belong to; be attached to; join; [좇아 따르다] follow; accompany; (편들다) take sides[a side] with; take the side of; side with. ¶반대당에 ~ join the opposite party // 공산당에 ~ join the communist party // 그는 늘 이기는 쪽에 붙는다 He always takes the winning side. // 그 사람에게 붙어 있으면 넌 손해는 없다 Under him you will have nothing to lose.
3 [바싹 가까이하다] keep[stand] close (to). ¶벽에 꼭 붙어서 서다 stand close to the wall / (미국 속어) hug the wall // 그렇게 꼭 붙어서 걷지 마라 Don't walk so close to me! // 두 집

은 서로 붙어 있다 The two houses stand close to each other. // 나는 어머니가 물건을 사는 동안에 꼭 붙어 다녔다 I followed my mother around[stuck to my mother] as she did the shopping.
4 [귀신이] be possessed (by / with); be obsessed (by); by haunted (by). ¶귀신이 붙은 possessed / bewitched / devil-possessed // 그는 귀신이 붙은 사람 같았다 He was like a man possessed of devils.
5 (불이) catch (fire); be ignited. ¶담뱃불이 아직도 붙어 있었다 The cigarette was still aglow.
6 (시험에) pass (an examination). ¶학교에 ~ be admitted into a school / obtain[get] admission to a school.
7 [생기다]. ¶버릇이 ~ get[fall] into a habit (of) / get in the way of (doing) // 취미가 ~ acquire a taste (for) / have a fondness [liking] (for) / take an interest (in) // 입맛이 ~ one's appetite improves[increases] / get a keen appetite // 그녀는 영어 실력이 붙기 시작했다 She is getting much better in English. // 이 정기 예금에는 6%의 이자가 붙는다 This fixed deposit bears 6 percent interest.
8 [딸리다] be joined (with); be connected (with); be coupled (with); be attached (to). ¶이 열차에는 식당차가 붙어 있다 There is a dining car attached to this train.
9 [수발들다] attend[wait] on; [동반하다] accompany; go along with; follow. ¶간호사가 환자에게 붙어 있었다 A nurse tended the patient. // 그 중환자에게는 의사가 쭉 붙어 있었다 The doctor was in constant attendance on the dangerous patient. // 그에겐 두 명의 비서가 붙어 있다 He has two secretaries.
10 [오래 머무르다] stay long; do not leave one's post; attend on (a person) constantly. ¶그 집에는 가정부가 오래 붙어 있지 않는다 Maids won't stay long (in service) in that family.
11 [싸움 등이 시작되다] be started. ¶싸움이 ~ start a quarrel.
12 (일 등이). ¶일이 손에 안 ~ cannot bring oneself (to do) / have no mind (to do) / be in no mood (to do / for doing).

붙다² [교미하다] link[lock] in copulation; copulate; couple; mate; pair.

붙들다 1 [꽉 쥐다] catch; (갑자기, 힘껏) seize; take[get / catch / lay] hold of; 움켜잡다] grasp[grip / grab]. ¶팔을 ~ seize (a person) by the arm // 머리채를 붙들고 끌어당기다 drag (a woman) by the hair // 붙들고 놓지 않다 keep one's hold on // 말을 ~ stop [curb] a horse // 개를 ~ hold a dog down // 사다리를 꼭 붙들어라 Hold[steady] the ladder. // 나는 바람에 날리지 않게 문을 꼭 붙들고 있었다 I held the door firmly against the wind. // 그 사람은 내 옷소매를 꽉 붙들고 놓아주지 않았다 The man grabbed my sleeve [seized me by the sleeve / held fast to my sleeve] and would not let me go. // 우리는 그가 움직이지 못하도록 손발을 꼭 붙들고 있었다 We held his arms and legs down firmly so that he couldn't move. // 그는 나의 어깨를 붙들었다 He grabbed[seized] me by the shoulder. // 날뛰는 말을 꽉 붙들었다 I overpowered the wild horse. // 밧줄을 꽉 붙들고 있어라 Keep tight hold of[a good hold on]

붙들리다
the rope. / (구어) Hang on tight to the rope. // 이 쇠사슬을 붙드시오 Take[catch] hold of this chain. // 그는 그것을 붙들고 꽉 쥐었다 He seized it and held it tightly. // 배가 흔들리자 그녀는 당황하여 난간을 붙들었다 As the ship rolled, she hurriedly gripped the rail.
2 [붙잡다] catch; arrest; capture; apprehend; nab. ¶도둑을 ~ arrest[catch / capture / nab] a thief.
3 [만류하다] keep[hold] (a person); detain; buttonhole (a person). ¶나는 통행인을 붙들고 길을 물었다 Stopping a passerby, I asked the way. // 떠나려 했으나 그는 자꾸만 붙들었다 I wanted to go but he would buttonhole me. // 외로운 그 노인은 손님을 붙들고 놓아주지 않았다 The lonely old man wouldn't let the guest go[leave / go home]. // 그는 만나기만 하면 나를 붙들고 긴 이야기를 늘어놓는다 He buttonholes me every time I met him. // 그는 붙들면 놓지 않는 사람이다 he is as close as a vice.
붙들리다 be caught; be detained; be arrested [apprehended]; be made to stay. ¶도둑이 현장에서 붙들렸다 The thief was caught in the act. // 그 친구한테 붙들리면 도망갈 수 없다 You can not get out of his clutches. // 그 사람에게 붙들리기 싫으니까 다른 길로 가겠다 I will take another way so that I won't get caught by him.

붙박이 a fixture; a fixed[built-in] article; a fitting. ¶~로 as a fixture / immovably / constantly // 그것은 ~에서 떼어 낼 수가 없다 It is fixed[built] in, and cannot be taken down. // 이 책상은 마루에 ~로 되어 있다 The desk is fixed to the floor.
● **붙박이 가구** fittings. **붙박이장** a built-in wardrobe.
붙박이다 be fixed; be fastened firmly [immovably]. ¶집에 ~ confine oneself to[in] one's house / be confined in one's house / keep the house / stick at home // 집에 붙박혀 있지만 말고 밖에 나가거라 You shouldn't shut yourself up in the house ― go outdoors.
붙어살다 live with (a person at his expense); be a parasite (to); be a dependent (on). ¶친척 집에 ~ live[sponge / hang] on one's relations.
-붙이 **1** [가까운 사람의 겨레] the same blood. ¶살~ kith and kin / lineage // 일가~ (family) relations / relatives / kinsfolk. **2** [같은 종류] things of the same kind [class / group]. ¶쇠~ metals [ironware].
붙이다 **1** stick; (풀로) paste. ¶천 조각을 이어 ~ patch pieces of cloth // 전단을 스카치테이프로 문에 ~ stick a notice to the door with Scotch tape // 판자에 종이를 ~ paste paper to the board // 트렁크에 꼬리표를 ~ fix [fasten] a tag to a trunk // 이력서에 사진을 ~ attach a photograph to one's personal history // 편지에 우표를 붙였습니까 Did you put[stick] a stamp on the letter? // 우리는 포스터를 벽에 붙였다 We put up posters on the walls. // 이 판자는 몇 장의 종이를 붙여 만든 것이다 This board is made of several sheets of paper put together. // 그는 고약을 어깨에 붙였다 He applied plasters to his shoulders.
2 [서로 닿게 하다]. ¶양 무릎을 바짝 붙이고 서다 stand with one's knees close together // 책장을 벽에 붙여 놓아 주시오 Put the bookcase up against the wall, please.
3 [말을 걸다] speak[talk] to[address (oneself to)] (a person).
4 [의견·설명 등을 첨가하다] add (to); attach (to); affix (to); annex (to); append (to). ¶의견을 ~ make an additional comment [opinion] / give [offer / deliver] one's opinion (in a debate) // 그들은 경품을 붙여 상품을 팔았다 They sold the article(s) with a premium [free gift / (구어) giveaway (attached)]. // 그가 술 배를 끊는다는 조건을 붙여 그녀는 그와 약혼했다 She promised to marry him on condition that he [If he would] stop smoking. // 그들의 데모에는 두 가지 조건이 붙여졌다 Their demonstration was permitted on two conditions.
5 [때리다] spank; slap. ¶한 대 올려 ~ give (a person) a slap / slap (a person).
6 [사이에 들어 어울리게 하다] bring two parties for (doing something); get two parties to (do); arrange. ¶싸움을 ~ make (persons) quarrel / kindle a quarrel / set (dogs) fighting (each other) // 흥정을 ~ get two parties to arrange [strike] a bargain.
7 [내기에 돈을 걸다] bet [stake / wager / put] (a thousand won).
8 [마음에 들게 하다] take; have; acquire. ¶재미를 ~ take (an) interest (in) / find pleasure (in) // 취미를 ~ have [cultivate] a taste (for music).
9 [딸리게 하다] let (a person) be attended [waited upon]; have (a person) in attendance. ¶환자에게 간호사를 ~ have a nurse in attendance upon a patient / have a patient attended by a nurse // 피고에게 변호사를 ~ provide the defendant with a lawyer [counsel].
10 [교미시키다] mate; copulate; pair. ¶개를 ~ mate a dog // 암소를 황소에게 ~ put a cow to a bull.
11 [이름·제목 등을 달다] give (a name to). ¶이름을 ~ name / give a name (to) // 제목을 ~ give a title (to a composition) // 그들은 그 기린에게 톰이라는 이름을 붙였다 They named [called] the giraffe Tom. / They gave the giraffe the name of Tom.
12 [불이 붙게 하다] light; kindle; ignite. ¶담뱃불을 ~ light a cigarette [pipe].
13 [가입시키다] admit (a person to membership); let [allow / take] in; let (a person) join (in something). ¶저 애는 붙여 주지 말자 Let's not let him in.
붙임성 (―性) sociability; affability; amiability; companionableness; friendliness. ¶~ 없는 unsociable / unaffable / repulsive // ~ 있는 [없는] 사람 a sociable [an unsociable] person / a person easy [hard] to get acquainted with / (미국 구어) a good [bad] mixer // ~ 있는 태도 an affable [a sociable] manner // ~ 이 있다 be sociable [affable / amiable / suave] / love company / be easy to approach // 그 소년은 아주 ~이 있는 아이였다 The boy was very friendly [affable].
붙잡다 **1** [잡다] catch; take [get / catch] hold of (a thing); hold; clasp; clutch; [쥐다] grab; grasp. ¶소매를 ~ catch [seize] (a person) by the sleeve // 기회를 ~ seize [catch / take] an opportunity / take the (one's) chance (of) // 그녀는 내 팔을 붙잡았다 She seized my arm [caught me by the

arm].// 경찰관이 강도의 팔을 붙잡았다 The policeman caught the robber by the arm.// 나는 매달린 밧줄을 붙잡았다 I caught hold of the dangling rope.// 그 사람이 내 소매를 붙잡고 놓아주지 않았다 The man grabbed my sleeve[seized me by the sleeve / held fast to my sleeve] // 밧줄을 단단히 붙잡으시오 Keep tight hold of[a good hold on] the rope. / (구어) Hang on tight to the rope.
2 [체포하다] arrest; capture; collar; (구어) nab. ¶도둑을 ～ arrest[seize / catch / capture] a thief // 현장에서 ～ arrest (a person) in the act // 경찰이 납치범을 붙잡았다 The police arrested[caught / captured] the kidnapper.
3 [못 가게 말리다] detain; hold (a person). ¶사람을 붙잡고 긴 이야기를 늘어놓다 buttonhole (a person) // 손님을 오래 붙잡아 두다 detain[keep] a guest long // 오래 붙잡지는 않겠다 I won't keep you long.
4 [일자리를 얻다] secure[obtain / get] a job; find employment.
5 [돕다] help; aid; give[lend] a hand; give [lend] (a person) a helping hand. ¶버스를 타도록 붙잡아 주다 help (a person) into a bus // 일어나도록 붙잡아 주다 help (a person) to his feet // 나를 좀 붙잡아 주시오 Please lend me a hand.

붙잡히다 〔잡히다〕 be taken hold of[be grasped; 〔체포되다〕 be caught; be arrested; 〔남의 수중에 빠지다〕 fall into (a person's) hands[clutches]; 〔만류당하다〕 be detained. ¶붙잡히지 않도록 하다 keep out of (a person's) clutches // 범인은 아직도 붙잡히지 않고 있다 The culprit is still loose[at large]. // 두 소년이 가게 물건을 훔쳐 붙잡혔다 Two boys were arrested for shoplifting. // 그는 추적자들에게 붙잡혔다 He was caught by his pursuers. // 달아난 사자는 아직도 붙잡히지 않고 있다 The escaped lion is still loose[at large]. // 척후병이 적에게 붙잡힌 것 같다 The scout seems to have fallen into enemy hands.

뷔페 a buffet; a refreshment[snack] bar.
뷰렛 [화] a buret(te).
브라만 Brahman; a Brahmin; (여자) a Brahmani; a Brahmanee.
●**브라만교**(-敎) Brahmanism; Brahminism.
브라보 bravo. ¶～를 외치다 bravo.
브라스 밴드 a brass band.
브라우저 a browser.
브라운관(-管) [TV] a cathode-ray tube; a picture tube; a Braun tube.
브래지어 a brassière; (속어) a bra. ¶～를 하고 있다 wear a brassière.
브랜드 a brand.
브랜디 brandy. ¶소다수[물]를 탄 ～ brandy and soda[water] // ～를 한 잔 마시다 have a brandy.
브러시 a brush.
브레이크[1] a brake. ¶비상 ～ an emergency brake // ～ 수동[공기] a hand[an air] brake // ～를 걸다 apply[put on / throw on] the brakes // ～를 걸고[걸지 않고] with the brakes on[off] // ～를 꽉 밟다 step on the brake hard // ～를 늦추다 take off the brake // ～를 밟아 세우다 brake (a car) to a stop // ～가 듣지 않는다 The brakes refuse to work [are out of order]. // ～가 듣지 않았다 The brakes didn't work. // 그는 ～를 걸어 차를 멈추었다 He braked his car to a halt. // 우리는 그의 두목 행세에 ～를 걸어야 한다 We must put a stop to his bossiness. // 그것이 물가 상승을 억제하는 ～가 되었다 It acted as a brake on rising prices.
브레이크[2] [권투] a break.
브레인스토밍 brainstorming; a brainstorming session.
브로마이드 bromide.
브로치 a brooch; (미) a breastpin. ¶옷에 ～를 달다 wear a brooch on one's dress.
브로커 a broker; a middleman. ¶부동산 ～ a real estate agent[broker] // ～ 노릇을 하다 act as a broker[middleman].
브롬(⑥Brom) [화] bromine.
브리지 1 [의] [가공 의치] a (dental) bridge. ¶이에 ～를 하다 fix a bridge (between natural teeth) / bridge (a tooth). **2** [카드놀이] bridge. ¶～를 하다 play bridge. **3** [레슬링] a bridge.
브리핑 (a) briefing. ¶～을 하다 give (the reporters) a briefing (on) / brief.
브이티아르 a VTR(▶ videotape recorder의 약어). ⇨비디오테이프리코더
블라우스 a blouse; (미) a shirtwaist. ¶꽃무늬의 ～ a blouse with a flower[floral] pattern // 긴[반]소매의 ～ a long-sleeved[short-sleeved] blouse // 빨간 ～를 입은 소녀 a girl in a red blouse.
블라인드 (영) a (window) blind; (미) a shade. ¶～를 내리다[올리다] pull down [draw up] a blind // 나는 창문의 ～를 내렸다 I pulled down the blinds[the shades] over the windows. / I lowered the Venetian blinds.
블랙 black. ¶커피를 ～으로 마시다 [drink] coffee black // 나는 커피는 ～이 좋다 I like my coffee black.
●**블랙커피** black coffee.
블랙리스트 a blacklist; a black book. ¶～에 올라 있는 사람 a man on the blacklist // ～에 오르다 be blacklisted / be (put) on the blacklist // ～에 올리다 blacklist (a person) / put (a person) on the blacklist.
블랙홀 a black hole.
블랭크 a blank; a gap. ¶～를 메우다 fill in the blanks (of a notebook) / fill the blank (caused by ...).
블로킹 [체] blocking.
블록[1] [동맹] a bloc. ¶경제 ～ an economic bloc.
●**블록 경제** bloc economy.
블록[2] **1** [시가의 구획] a block. ¶그 은행은 저쪽으로 두 ～ 지나서 있다 The bank is two blocks up that way. **2** [건] a concrete [cement] block.
블록버스터 [큰 성공을 거둔 대작 영화] a blockbuster.
블론드 blond(e). ¶～의 (여자) blonde / (남자) blond.(▶ blond를 공용으로 쓰는 경향이 있음)
블루머 bloomers.
블루스 1 [음] blues. ¶～조(調)의 blue // ～를 부르다 sing blues. **2** [남녀가 느리게 추는 춤] a slow dance.
블루진 (blue) jeans. ¶～을 입은 (a young man) in blue jeans / jeaned (teenagers).
비[1] (내리는) rain; (한 번의 강우) a rain; a rain-

비

fall; a shower(소나기). ¶부슬~ a sprinkling of rain∥이슬~ a misty[fine] rain∥큰~ a heavy rain∥억수 같은 ~ a torrential [pouring / driving] rain / a downpour∥조용히 내리는 ~ a soft rain∥계속 내리는 ~ a constant[continuous] rain∥오락가락하는 ~ an intermittent rain∥지나가는 ~ a passing rain / a shower∥~ 오는 날[밤] a rainy[wet] day[evening]∥~ 오듯 흐르는 땀 a profuse perspiration∥~ 오듯 날아오는 탄환 a shower[hail] of bullets∥~가 많이 오는 rainy / pluvial∥~가 그친[멈춘] 사이에 in the intervals between rains / between rains / during a lull[break] in the rain∥~가 갠 뒤의 좋은 날씨 fine weather just after a rainfall∥~가 그치기를 기다리다 wait for the rain to leave off∥~가 오든 안 오든 rain or shine∥~에 젖다 get wet with rain∥~를 만나다 be caught in a rain[shower]∥~를 피하다 take shelter[refuge / cover] from the rain / shelter oneself from (the) rain∥~를 맞고 be exposed to rain / ~를 맞으며 (걷다) (walk) in the rain∥~를 맞히다 expose (a thing) to rain∥~가 내린다 It rains.∥~가 내리기 시작했다 It began[started] to rain. / It started raining. / Rain began to fall.∥~가 방 안으로 들이쳤다 It rained into the room.∥~가 올 것 같다 It threatens to rain. / It looks like rain.∥~가 억수로 퍼부었다 It rained hard[heavily / in torrents]. / It rained cats and dogs.∥~가 오락가락한다 It is raining on and off.∥~가 계속 내렸다 It went on raining. / It rained continuously.∥올해는 ~가 많이 왔다 We had a lot of[a great deal of] rain this year.∥올해는 ~가 조금밖에 오지 않았다 There was[We had] little rain this year.∥지붕에서 ~가 몹시 샌다 The roof leaks badly.∥오랫동안 ~가 왔다 We have had a long spell of rain[rainy weather].∥오랫동안 ~가 오지 않았다 We have had a long spell of dry weather.∥나무 밑에서 ~를 피했다 I took shelter[sheltered myself] from the rain under a tree.∥~ 때문에 1주일 동안 집에 갇혀 있었다 I was kept indoors by the rain for a week.∥나는 ~를 피해 집 안에 있었다 I stayed indoors to keep out of[to take shelter from] the rain.∥그 시합은 ~ 때문에 중지되었다 (미) The game was rained[washed] out.∥얼굴에서 땀이 ~ 오듯이 흘러내렸다 Sweat poured down his face.∥눈물이 ~ 오듯이 흘러내렸다 Her eyes rained tears.∥소이탄이 ~ 오듯 머리 위에 떨어졌다 Tons of fire bombs rained down on our heads.∥~를 피하려고 추녀 밑으로 뛰어들어갔다 I ran under the eaves to avoid[get out of] the rain.∥추녀 밑에서 ~가 그치기를 기다렸다 I waited under the eaves for the rain to stop.

비가 온 뒤에 땅이 굳어진다(속담) After a storm comes a calm.; A storm will clear the air.

비² (쓰는) a broom; a besom(마당비). ¶~로 마당을 쓸다 sweep a garden with a broom.

비(比) (수) (a) ratio (pl. ~s). ¶8대 3의 ~ a ratio of 8 to 3 / an eight-to-three ratio / the ratio 8:3∥남녀의 ~는 3대 2였다 The ratio of men to women[the male-female ratio] was three to two.

비(妃) [왕의 아내] a queen (consort); a princess; [황태자의 아내] a crown princess.

비(非) [그름·잘못] (an) injustice; (a) wrong; a mistake; an error

비(碑) [묘비] a tombstone; a gravestone; [기념비] a monument. ¶…을 위한 ~를 세우다 raise[erect] a tombstone[monument] to the memory of …∥문호를 위한 ~를 세우다 erect a monument to the memory of a great writer.

비-(非) non-; un-; anti-. ¶~공식 unofficialness∥~과학적 unscientific∥~애국적 unpatriotic∥~인도적 inhuman∥~사교적 unsociable∥~사회주의자 an antisocialist∥~전투원 a noncombatant.

-비(費) expenses; costs. ¶여행~ traveling expenses∥영업~ business expenses∥생활[생산]~ living[production] costs.

비가(悲歌) an elegy; a song of sorrow; a dirge; a threnody.

비가시광선(非可視光線) [물] invisible [dark] rays.

비각(碑閣) a pavilion for a monument.

비감(悲感) sad feeling; sorrow; grief. **비감하다** sad; sorrowful; grievous.

비강(鼻腔) the nasal[rhinal] cavity.

비걱거리다 creak. ⇨ "삐걱거리다

비겁하다(卑怯-) 1 [겁이 많다] cowardly; (문어) craven; dastardly; sneaking. ¶비겁한 행위 cowardly act∥이제 와서 물러난다는 것은 비겁한 짓이다 It is cowardly of you to pull out now. / You're a coward if you back out now.∥비겁하게도 그는 도망쳤다 He was timid enough to run away. 2 [야비하다] mean; [남자답지 못하다] unmanly; [부정(不正)하다] foul; unfair. ¶비겁한 짓[체] a foul play∥비겁한 짓을 하다 play a mean trick (upon a person) / (승부에서) play foul / hit (a person) below the belt∥그는 내게 비겁한 짓을 했다 He played a mean[dirty] trick on me.

비견하다(比肩-) take rank (with); rank [range] (with); equal; bear[stand] comparison (with); compare favorably (with); be comparable (with). ¶이 점에서는 그녀와 비견할 사람이 없다 No one can compare with her in this respect. / She has no rival[She is unrivaled] in this respect.∥그는 기술에 있어서는 나와 비견한다 He equals[is equal to] me in skill.∥그는 스승에 비견하는 실력을 갖추고 있다 He ranks with his teacher in ability.

비결(祕訣) a secret (of); the mysteries (of); a key (to). ¶건강[성공]의 ~ the secret of[the key to] good health[success]∥장사의 ~ the tricks of a trade∥얼룩을 빼는 ~ a tip for extracting stains∥태권도의 ~을 가르치다 initiate (a person) into the mysteries of *taegwondo*∥그녀는 사람을 끄는 ~을 알고 있다 She has the knack of attracting people.∥성공의 ~은 근면과 정직이다 The secret of[A key to] success is hard work and honesty.

비경(祕境) [남이 모르는 장소] unexplored regions (of the world); secluded regions; [신비스러운 곳] a land of mystery.

비계¹ [건] a scaffold; scaffolding; (미) staging; a falsework(파괴 공사의). ¶~용 기둥 a scaffolding pole∥~ 위에 서다 stand on a scaffold∥~를 설치하다 set up[put up / erect] a scaffold / scaffold (a house).

비계² [짐승의 가죽 바로 안쪽에 붙은 기름 조각] lard(돼지의); fat.

비계(祕計) a secret plan; a deep plot; a secret [underhand] scheme; the best card; one's trump (card). ¶~를 쓰다 play one's best [trump] card.

비고(備考) a[an explanatory] note; remarks (for reference).
● 비고란 a remarks[reference] column; (표제로서) Remarks; Notes. ¶~에 기입하다 write in[fill up] a remarks column.

비곡(悲曲) a plaintive melody; a doleful air.

비공개(非公開) ¶~의 private / secret / not open to the public / closed-door (session) / ~의 편지 a personal letter // 재판은 ~가 될 것이다 The trial will be held in camera. // 재판은 ~로 열렸다 The trial was held behind closed doors. // 이 궁전은 일반에게는 ~로 되어 있다 This palace is not open to the public.
● 비공개 입찰 a closed tender. 비공개 회의 a closed(-door) meeting[conference]; a conclave.

비공식(非公式) informality; unofficialness. ¶~의 (공적이 아닌) unofficial / [약식의] informal / [사적인] private // ~으로 informally / unofficially // ~ 모임이오니 허심탄회하게 말씀해 주십시오 As this is an informal meeting, please speak freely.

비과세(非課稅) tax exemption. ¶~의 tax-free / tax-exempt // 이 예금 이자는 ~이다 The interest on this deposit is not taxable[is tax-exempt].
● 비과세 물품 a tax free article. 비과세 소득 (a) tax-free income.

비과학적(非科學的) [과학적이 아닌] unscientific; [과학과 관계없는] nonscientific. ¶~으로 unscientifically / nonscientifically // 문제의 ~ 연구 an unscientific approach to a problem.

비관(悲觀) pessimism; [낙심] disappointment. 비관하다 be pessimistic (about / of); take a pessimistic [dark] view (of); look on the gloomy side (of); despond (of the future); [낙심하다] be disappointed; lose heart. ¶인생을 ~ take a gloomy view of life / lose interest in one's life / lose all hopes of life / be tired of life // 앞날을 ~ take a gloomy view of the future / be despondent over the future // 극도로 ~ be in the depths of despair // 세상을 비관하여 자살하다 kill oneself[commit suicide] in despair[out of sheer pessimism] // 그는 인생을 비관하고 있다 He has a pessimistic view of life. / He looks on the dark side of life. // 그는 앞날을 비관했다 He was discouraged about the [his] future. // 그렇게 비관할 필요 없다 You don't need to be so pessimistic (about it).
● 비관론 a pessimistic view; pessimism. 비관론자 a pessimist; (미국 속어) a crape-hanger[crepehanger].

비관적(悲觀的) pessimistic; dark. ¶~으로 보다 take a pessimistic [dark] view (of) / look on the gloomy side (of).

비교(比較) (a) comparison; a parallel. ¶~가 안 되다 cannot bear[stand] comparison (with) / cannot compare[be compared] (with) / be more than a match (for) / be no match (for) / there is no comparison (with / between) // ~도 안 될 만큼 beyond[past] comparison[compare] / (훨씬) far and away (the best) // 그는 형과 ~가 안 된다 He cannot compare with his older brother. // 이 둘은 ~가 안 된다 There is no comparison between the two. // 이것은 그것과 ~가 안 된다 This cannot bear comparison[is not to be compared] with that. / This is not comparable to that. // 메리와 엘리스는 도저히 ~가 안 된다 There can be no comparison between Mary and Alice. // 그의 그림은 르누아르의 그림과 ~도 안 된다 His paintings cannot compare [be compared] with Renoir's. / His paintings do not rank with Renoir's. // 나는 골프에서는 그와 ~가 안 된다 I am no match for him in golf. // 그 그림은 ~가 안 될 정도로 아름답다 The picture is beautiful beyond comparison. // 이것은 ~가 안 될 만큼 좋다 This one is better beyond comparison. / This one is incomparably better. / This one is by far the better. // 그는 나와는 ~가 안 되게 연설을 잘한다 As a public speaker, he is in a completely different class from me. **비교하다** compare (the two / A with [to] B); make a comparison (between A and B); draw a comparison (between); [대비하다] set (one thing) against (another); contrast (A with B). ¶비교할 수 있는 comparable // …과 비교하여[비교하면] (as) compared with[to] ... / compared (with) ... / in contrast to ... // …과 비교하여 낫다[못하다] be better[inferior] as compared with ... // 비교할 것이 없다 (문어) be without [beyond / past] compare / be unparalleled / stand unrival(l)ed / be unique // 이 필적을 그 것과 비교해 보세요 Compare this handwriting with his. // 어느 쪽이 나은지 잘 비교해 보아라 Make a careful comparison of them and see which is the better. // 존과 비교할 때 데이비드는 아직 멀었다 Compared [As compared] with John, David is still inferior. / David is not yet comparable to John. // 그의 노력은 너와는 비교할 수 없을 정도로 부족하다 His efforts are nothing to yours. / His efforts cannot stand comparison with yours. // 지난번 작품에 비교하면 이번 작품은 빈약하다 Compared with his previous work, this one is very poor. / This work is very poor in comparison with the previous one. // 엘리스와 그 여동생을 비교해 보면 성격의 차이를 쉽게 알 수 있다 If you contrast Alice and her sister, you will find a remarkable difference between them in character.
● 비교급 [언] the comparative degree. 비교 문법 comparative grammar. 비교 문학 comparative literature. 비교 심리학 comparative psychology. 비교 연구 a comparative study.

비교적(比較的) comparative; relative. ¶~으로 comparatively / relatively / in[by] comparison / rather // 이곳은 ~ 서늘하다 It is comparatively[relatively] cool here. // 너희 회사는 봉급이 ~ 좋구나 Your company pays relatively good salaries. // 이 모자는 ~ 싸다 This hat is rather cheap.

비구(比丘) [불] a bhikku; a Buddhist priest [monk].
● 비구니(-尼) [불] a bhikkuni; a Buddhist priestess[nun]. 비구승 [불] a bhikku. ⇨ 비구

비구(飛球) [야구] a fly ball.

비구름 [기상] nimbostratus. ⇨ 난층운

비굴하다(卑屈-) mean-spirited; mean; servile; obsequious; subservient; sneaking.

비극

¶비굴한 사나이 a sneak / a sneaker / an unmanly fellow(남자답지 않은 남자)∥비굴한 근성 a servile spirit∥그는 비굴하게 헤헤 웃었다 He laughed[gave] a servile[an obsequious] laugh.∥너의 비굴한 근성을 단단히 고쳐 놓겠다 I'll teach you to show a little more backbone. / I'm going to knock some pride into you.

비극(悲劇) (a) tragedy; a tragic drama. ¶가정의 ~ a domestic tragedy∥~으로 끝나다 end in a tragedy / end tragically∥~을 상연하다 enact a tragedy∥~이 일어났다 A tragedy has taken place.∥폭력이 가정의 ~을 낳았다 Violence led to[caused] a domestic tragedy.∥두 사람의 결혼은 ~으로 끝났다 Their marriage ended tragically[in tragedy].∥그것은 정말로 ~이었다 That certainly was a tragedy.

비극적(悲劇的) tragic; tragical. ¶~ 사건 a tragic affair / a tragedy∥~ 장면 a tragic scene∥전쟁이 남긴 ~인 상처 a tragic legacy left behind by the war.

비근하다(卑近-) familiar; common; homely; plain; simple. ¶비근한 예를 들다 give[use / cite] a familiar example.

비금속(非金屬) [화] a nonmetal. ¶~의 nonmetallic.
●비금속 광물 a nonmetallic mineral. 비금속 원소 a nonmetallic element.

비금속(卑金屬) [화] a base[an imperfect] metal.

비기다¹ 1 [승부를 가리지 못하다] tie[draw] (with); end in a tie[draw]; be drawn; come out even. ¶비긴 경기 a tie / a drawn game∥그 경기는 비겼다 The game[match] was drawn[a tie]. / The game[match] ended in a tie[draw].∥2대 2로 비겼다 We tied at 2 [two-two / two-to-two]. / We tied at 2 points[runs] a piece[each] (▶ runs는 야구에서).∥우리는 연세대에 이기고 고려대와 비겼다 We beat Yonsei and drew with Korea.∥이 시합은 비긴 것으로 하자 Let's stop without deciding the winner. / Let's call this game a draw.∥이것으로 비긴 것으로 하자 Let's call it quits[even].
2 [상쇄하다] offset[cancel] each other; set off; countervail; counterbalance.

비기다² 1 [비교하다] compare (one thing) with (another). 2 compare (to). ⇨비유하다(에 비유). ¶잠을 죽음에 ~ compare sleep to death∥눈송이를 꽃잎에 ~ liken[compare] snowflakes to flower petals∥우리는 흔히 인생을 여행에 비긴다 We often compare[liken] life to a journey.

비길 데 없다 there is nothing like[comparable to]; (문어) be beyond[past] compare; be beyond comparison[description]; [상대가 없다] matchless; peerless; unrivaled; [비교할 데가 없다] incomparable; [도전할 사람이 없다] unchallenged. ¶비길 데 없는 미인 a woman of matchless beauty∥그의 비길 데 없는 통찰력 his unparalleled[unequaled / matchless] insight∥그 경치는 비길 데 없이 아름답다 The scenery is beautiful beyond all description.∥그것의 웅대함은 비길 데가 없었다 The magnificence of it was incomparable [beyond comparison / (문어) beyond compare].

비김수(-手) [장기 등에서 비기게 되는 수] a tying[drawing] move[run / point]; a draw.

비꼬다 1 (실·끈 등을) twist (up); entwist. ¶실을 비꼬아 노끈을 만들다 twist threads into a string. 2 (말을) make sarcastic remarks (on); give a sarcastic[cynical] twist to one's words. ¶비꼬는 sarcastic (remark) / ironic(al) / cynical / sardonic / sneering∥비꼬는 말 cynical words / a sarcastic remark∥비꼬아 말하다 make sarcastic[cynical] remarks (on) / speak [talk] ironically[cynically]∥그렇게 비꼬지 마라 Don't be so cynical [ironical].∥그녀의 말에는 비꼬는 데가 있다 There is a touch of irony in what she says.∥그는 (매사에) 비꼬는 태도를 취한다 He poses as a cynic.

비꼬이다 1 (실·끈 등이) get[be] twisted; (사건·문제 등이) get[become] entangled[tangled]; become complicated. 2 (마음이) get peevish; become crooked[distorted]; be perverse. ¶비꼬인 성질 a crooked disposition∥그는 성질이 비꼬여 있다 He has a crook in his character. / He has a perverse mind.

비꼬러매다 tie (up); fasten (together); bind. ¶말을 ~ tie a horse (to a post).

비끼다 slant; be oblique; be bent; lie aslant [at an angle]. ¶(빛이) 비껴 비치다 shine at an angle.

비난(非難) (an adverse) criticism; blame; (a) reproach; reprobation; (a) censure; denunciation(공공연한); [공격] (an) attack. ¶~의 여지가 없다 be impeccable / be irreproachable / be above[beyond] reproach∥~의 대상이 되다 become the focus[target] of criticism∥~을 면치 못하다 be open to censure [criticism]∥~을 초래하다 incur a censure / lay oneself open to censure∥~조로 말하다 speak in reproachful tone[vein]∥그녀는 그 추문으로 신문에서 호되게 ~을 받았다 She was attacked[criticized] severely in the newspapers for causing such a scandal.∥그의 발언은 ~을 초래했다 His statement laid him open to criticism[censure]. / He came under fire for his statement.∥그는 그런 어리석은 짓을 해서 세상의 ~을 초래했다 By doing such a stupid thing, he incurred public censure[brought public criticism upon himself].∥정부가 취한 조치는 ~의 대상이 되었다 The step taken by the government became a target of criticism.∥그가 문제를 처리한 방법은 ~의 여지가 없었다 His handling of the matter was impeccable [irreproachable].∥그의 처사는 불공평하다는 ~을 면치 못한다 The step he has taken is open to the charge of favoritism.∥시장에 대한 ~이 심하다 The mayor is being severely criticized[under intense pressure of criticism].∥나 혼자서만 모든 ~을 받고 있다 I am getting all the blame[(구어) flack].∥시장은 교육 예산을 삭감했다는 이유로 ~을 받았다 The mayor came under attack[The mayor was attacked] for cutting the education budget.∥법무 장관은 경솔한 발언을 하여 야당 의원들의 호된 ~을 받았다 Members of the opposition parties jumped on the Minister for Justice when he made a careless comment.∥몇몇 텔레비전 프로는 청소년 범죄를 유발한다는 ~을 받고 있다 Some TV programs are blamed[criticized] for inciting juvenile crime.∥그는 ~을 받고 사임했다 He resigned under criticism.∥그 조치에 대해서는 ~의 소리가 높다 The measure is loudly censured. 비난하다 criticize unfavorably [adversely]; censure; blame; reproach; denounce; condemn; attack; blast; cry out on[upon]; make a charge against; charge [accuse] (a person) with (a fault). ¶비난할 만한 blamable / censurable / blameworthy / reproachable // 그들은 노동조합을 비난했다 They put the blame on the labor union. // 국민들은 부패한 정치가들을 비난했다 The people denounced [cried out against] the corrupt politicians. // 그들은 그를 무능하다고 비난했다 They criticized him for being incompetent. // 시의회는 시장의 불법 행위를 비난했다 The city Assembly condemned [denounced] the mayor's irregularities. // 신문은 정부의 새 정책을 신랄하게 비난했다 The press laced into [slammed] the government's new policy. / The press severely criticized [attacked] the government's new policy. // 그는 비난하는 표정으로 나를 바라보았다 He looked at me reproachfully [with reproach]. / He gave [shot] me a critical look. ➔ ¶그는 자기의 잘못을 비난받아 마땅하다 He deserves censure for his mistake.

비너스 [로마 신화] Venus.
비녀 a binyeo; a rod-like hairpin; an ornamental hairpin. ¶~를 꽂다 wear a binyeo.
비논리적(非論理的) illogical; irrational.
비뇨기(泌尿器) the urinary organs.
● **비뇨기과** urology.
비누 soap. ¶가루 ~ soap powder // 물 ~ liquid soap // 세탁 [빨랫] ~ (a bar of) washing [laundry] soap // 약용 ~ medicated soap // 역성 (逆性) [양성 (陽性)] ~ invert [cation-active] soap // 종이 ~ soap paper / a soap leaf // 칼리 ~ soft soap // 화장 [세숫] ~ toilet soap // ~ 한 개 a cake of soap // ~로 손을 씻다 wash one's hands with soap and water // ~를 많이 칠하다 rub plenty of soap (into a shirt collar / onto one's hands) // 얼굴에 ~칠을 하다 lather one's face.
● **비누 거품** soap bubbles [froth]; soapsuds; suds; lather. **비누질** soaping. ¶손에 ~을 하다 soap one's hands. **비눗갑** a soap case [dish]. **비눗물** soapy water; [거품이 인] soapsuds; suds. **비눗방울** a soap bubble. ¶~이 떨어지다 blow (soap) bubbles.
비늘 a scale; a shard; a squama (pl. -mae). ¶~ 모양의 scalelike / squamose / squamous // ~이 있는 scaled // ~이 없는 scaleless / nude // ~로 덮여 있는 be covered with scales / be scaly // 생선의 ~을 벗기다 remove the scales from a fish / scale a fish // ~이 떨어지다 [물고기가] scale off.
비늘구름 [기상] a cirrocumulus. ⇨ 권적운
비능률적(非能率的) inefficient. ¶일을 ~으로 하다 work inefficiently.
비닐 vinyl; plastic (▶vinyl은 화학 전문 용어로 「비닐 수지」를 뜻하며, 일상생활에서는 plastic을 사용함). ¶염화 ~ [화] vinyl chloride / chloro-ethylene.
● **비닐봉지** a plastic bag. **비닐 수지** vinyl resin. **비닐하우스** (*vinyl house) a plastic greenhouse.
비닐론 vinylon.
비다 (속이) empty (cupboard); vacant (space); hollow (tree trunk); unoccupied (room); free (of engagements). ¶빈 병 [깡통] an empty bottle [can] / 빈 상자 an empty box [case] // 빈방 [집] (가구 없는) an empty room [house] / (쓰지 않는) a vacant [an unoccupied] room [house] / (세놓을) a room [house] for rent [(영) to let] // 빈자리 a vacant [an unoccupied] seat / [결원] a vacant post / a vacancy // 빈 차 an empty car / (택시의 게시) For hire. / Vacant. // 빈손 empty hands // 머리가 빈 사람 a rattlebrain // 빈 곳을 채우다 fill (in) a blank // 머리가 비어 있다 be empty-headed // 배 속이 ~ have an empty stomach / feel empty // 속이 텅 비어 있다 have no substance (실질이 없다) // 손이 비어 있다 have one's hands free / be unoccupied [disengaged] / be free // 주머니가 이 자리가 비었습니까 Has this seat been taken? // 이 자리는 비어 있습니다 The seat is unoccupied. // 언제 집이 비게 됩니까 When will the house be vacated? // 비어 있는 방이 있습니까 Do you have a vacant room? // 가방을 열었더니 속이 비어 있었다 I opened the bag and found it empty. // 그 나무는 속이 비어 있었다 I found the tree trunk hollow. // 열차는 비어 있었다 The train was not crowded. / There were few passengers in the train. // 좌석은 많이 비어 있었다 There were plenty of vacant [empty] seats. // 그 집은 살인 사건이 있은 이래 비어 있다 The house has been vacant [No one will live in the house] since the murder. // 지금 판매 주임 자리가 비어 있다 [공석이다] The post of sales manager is vacant [open] at present. // 위원장이 사임해서 그 자리가 비어 있다 The post of committee chairman opened up when he resigned. // 이번 주에는 손이 비지 않는다 I have my hands full (of work) this week. // 다음 주에는 손이 비게 됩니다 I'll be free next week.

비단 (非但) merely; merely; only. ¶~ ... 뿐 아니라 ... not only [merely] ... but also ... // 그것은 ~ 건강에 해로울 뿐만 아니라 비경제적이다 It is not only unhealthy but also wasteful.
비단 (緋緞) silk fabrics; silk goods [stuff]; silk(s); satin (공단). ¶~의 silk / made of silk / [비단 같은] silken / silky / sericeous.
● **비단결** the texture of silk; a velvety texture. ¶~ 같다 be as soft as velvet // 마음이 ~ 같은 soft-hearted / tender-hearted / sweet-tempered // 그녀의 피부는 ~ 같다 Her skin is a velvety texture. **비단옷** silk dress [clothes].
비대(증) (肥大症) fleshness; corpulence; plumpness; [의] hypertrophy. ¶심장 ~ enlargement [[의] hypertrophy] of the heart / an athlete's heart (과도한 운동에 의한) // 편도선 ~이 있다 have enlarged tonsils.
비대칭(非對稱) [수] asymmetry; dissymmetry. ¶~의 asymmetric(al) / dissymmetric(al).
비대하다 (肥大 —) fat(ty); fleshy; corpulent; plump; [의] hypertrophied; hypertrophic. ¶당신의 심장은 비대해 있습니다 Your heart is enlarged.
비도덕적(非道德的) immoral.
비동맹국(非同盟國) a nonaligned nation.
비둘기 a dove (들비둘기); a pigeon (집비둘기). ¶군용 ~ a military [an army] carrier pigeon // 통신용 ~ a carrier [homing] pigeon // ~ 편으로 보내다 be carried by a carrier pigeon // ~를 날리다 toss [fly / let loose] pigeons (into the air).
● **비둘기자리** [천] the Dove; Columba. **비둘기장** a dovecot(e); a dovehouse; a pigeon

비듬 house. **비둘기파**(-派) the doves; a softliner. ¶매파와 ~ the hawks and the doves.

비듬 dandruff; scurf. ¶투성이의 머리 scurfy hair / hair full of dandruff // ~이 생기다 become dandruffy // ~을 없애다 remove dandruff.

비등(沸騰) 1 [끓어오름] boiling; seething; ebullition; [거품 읾] effervescence; bubbling. **비등하다** boil; seethe; effervesce(탄산수 등이); bubble. 2 [소란·격동] fermentation; commotion; excitement; agitation; tumult. **비등하다** become[be] agitated[excited / heated]; be roused; be in a ferment. ¶여론이 비등하고 있다 Public opinion is agitated[aroused / in a ferment].

● **비등점**(-點) [물][화] the boiling point. ⇨ "끓는점

비등하다(比等-) about equal; much[about / nearly] the same; (be) on a par (with). ¶비등한 조건으로 on nearly even[equal] terms // 그는 친구와 학교 성적이 ~ He does as well as his friend at school. / His schoolwork is on a par with that of his friend. // 그들은 나이가 모두 ~ They are all much the same age.

비디오 1 video. 2 videotape. ⇨ "비디오테이프 (⇨). 3 a videorecorder. ⇨ "비디오테이프리코더(⇨비디오)

● **비디오 아트** video art. **비디오테이프** videotape. ¶프로를 ~에 녹화하다 videotape a program / record a program on (a) videotape. **비디오테이프리코더** a videotape recorder(약어 VTR).

비딱하다 slanting; sloping. ⇨ "삐딱하다

비뚜로 aslant; slantwise; askew; obliquely; at an angle. ¶그는 모자를 ~ 썼다 He cocked his hat at an angle.

비뚜름하다 somewhat slanting[oblique / askew]; (서술적) be at an angle. **비뚜름히** somewhat aslant[slantwise / askew]; on a little slant. ¶그는 모자를 ~ 썼다 His hat is on somewhat askew. // 그림이 ~ 걸려 있다 The picture hung askew.

비뚤다 crooked; awry; wry; skew; tilted; slanting; (서술적) be out of the straight. ¶비뚤게 하다 crook / tilt / slant // 코가 ~ have a crooked nose // 길이 ~ The road is crooked. // 그림이 ~ The picture is crooked.

비뚤비뚤 [흔들흔들] wobblingly; totteringly; shakingly; ricketily; [구불구불] windingly; crookedly; meanderingly; in zigzags. ¶~한 길 a winding road // ~ 놓인 책상들 desks in a zigzag line.

비뚤어지다 1 [한쪽으로 기울어지거나 쏠리다] get crooked; become awry[wry]; slant; incline (to); be tilted; get out of the straight. ¶비뚤어진 코 a crooked nose // ~ 나무 a gnarled[crooked] tree // 넥타이가 비뚤어졌어요 Your tie is crooked[awry]. // 모자가 비뚤어졌어요 Your hat is crooked. // 벽의 그림이 약간 비뚤어져 있다 The picture on the wall is tilted[slanting] a little to one side. // 책상의 위치가 비뚤어져 있다 The desk is not in the right place.
2 [마음·성격 등이 비비 꼬이다] get[become] crooked[perverse / cross-grained / distorted / warped / sour]. ¶성질이 비뚤어진 소녀 a little girl with a warped character // 비뚤어진 마음 a warped[perverse] mind // 마음이 비뚤어진 사람 a man with a twisted[perverse] mind / a perverse man // 비뚤어진 성격 a warped disposition[nature] / a jaundiced spirit // 비뚤어진 견해 a distorted[warped] view / [편견] prejudice // 비뚤어진 학생 an erring student / a student gone wrong // 비뚤어진 눈으로 세상을 보다 look upon the world with a jaundiced eye // 그는 마음이 비뚤어져 있다 He has a perverse[warped / twisted] mind. // 그녀는 성격이 비뚤어져 있다 She has a crook in the character. // 그는 매사를 비뚤어지게 본다 He takes a distorted[warped] view of everything. // 그는 젊어서 고생을 해서 성격이 비뚤어졌다 Hardships in his youth warped his personality.

비래하다(飛來-) [날아오다] come flying; (비행기로) come by air[plane].

비럭질 begging; mendicancy. **비럭질하다** go (about) begging.

비렁뱅이 〈속〉 a beggar. ⇨ 거지

비련(悲戀) tragic love; blighted [disappointed] love. ¶~의 이야기 a tale of tragic love // ~을 울다 be lovelorn and weep.

비례(比例) [비교] (a) proportion; (a) ratio(비율). ¶단[복]~ simple[compound] proportion // 정[반 / 역]~ direct[inverse / reciprocal] proportion. **비례하다** be proportioned[proportionate / proportional] (to); be in proportion (to). ¶…에 비례하여 in proportion to // A는 B에 비례한다 A is proportional to B. // 물가는 비례해서 오른다 Prices go up proportionately. // 습도의 상승에 비례하여 불쾌지수가 높아진다 The discomfort index rises in proportion to a rise in humidity. // 보수는 작업량에 비례하여 지급한다 The payment will be proportionate to the work done.

● **비례 대표** proportional representation. **비례 대표제** the system of proportional representation. **비례식** a proportional expression.

비로소 for the first time; not … until[till] …. ¶나는 그때 ~ 부모님의 은혜를 알았다 I realized then for the first time how much I owe my parents. // 사람이란 건강을 잃고서야 ~ 그 고마움을 안다 People do not know the blessing[value] of health until they lose it. // 가난해진 후에야 ~ 나는 돈의 소중함을 알았다 I did not know the value of money until I became poor. // 며칠 지나서 ~ 그 사실을 알았다 It was not until a few days later that I learned the truth. // 나는 졸업하고 나서야 ~ 학교생활이 좋다는 것을 알았다 I learned to appreciate school life only after my graduation.

비록 if; even if; (even) though; although; admitting[granting / supposing] that. ¶~ 농담으로라도 even in joke // ~ 그렇다 할지라도 admitting[granting] that it is so / even if it were so / even so // ~ 부자일지라도 however[no matter how] rich one may be // ~ 그는 나이는 젊지만 though he is young // ~ 무슨 일이 일어날지라도 나는 가겠다 I will go, whatever[no matter what] may happen. // 그는 ~ 가난하지만 매우 낙천적이다 Poor as he is [Though he is poor], he is very optimistic[cheerful].

비록(祕錄) a confidential document[notes]; a (secret) memoir. ¶최근의 대통령 선거 운동 ~ the confidential notes on the recent presidential election campaign.

비롯하다 [처음 시작하다] begin; start; com-

mence; [기원하다] originate (in); have (its) origin [rise] (in); arise (from). ¶…을 비롯하여 including … / … and / as well as … / beginning with … / headed by … //국무총리를 비롯한 전 국무 위원 the Cabinet Members, including the Prime Minister // 선장을 비롯해서 승무원 전원이 사망했다 The whole crew, including the captain, died. // 그 소문은 어디서 비롯했는가 Where did the rumor start? / 이 운동은 전쟁에 대한 깊은 분노에서 비롯한 것이다 The movement grew out of [arose from] deep anger at the thought of war.

비료(肥料) (자연의) manure; (인조의) (a) fertilizer. ¶배합 ~ mixed fertilizer // 인조[합성] ~ artificial [synthesized] fertilizer // 질소[인산 / 칼리] ~ nitrogenous [phosphatic / potash] manure // 합성 ~ synthesized fertilizer // 화학 ~ chemical manure [fertilizer] // 땅에 ~를 주다 fertilize [manure] land / spread fertilizer on land.

비루(의) (가축의 피부병) mange.

비루먹다 catch [get / suffer from / be affected by] mange.

비루스 →바이러스

비루하다(鄙陋-) mean; base; low; abject; contemptible. ¶비루한 근성 a base [mean] spirit.

비름 [식] an amaranthus; pigweed.

비리(非理) irrationality; unreasonableness; absurdity. ¶~의 unreasonable / irrational / absurd ~ 공무원[국회의원] a government official [Representative] who is suspected of corruption [who is under a cloud] // ~를 추방하다 drive out absurdities and evil customs.

비리다 1 (생선이) fishy; smelling of fish; (피가) bloody; smelling of blood. ¶우유의 비린 맛 a "cowy" taste in milk. 2 [인색하다] stingy; niggardly; miserly; [초라하다] poor; shabby. ¶비린 사람 a niggard / a skinflint / (미국 속어) a penny pincher / (미국 속어) a cheap skate. 3 [아니꼽다] disgusting; odious; nasty; nauseous; revolting; loathsome. ¶비린 짓을 하다 do a disgusting thing / behave offensively.

비린내 a fish-like [fishy] smell; a bloody smell.

비린내(가) 나다 [유치하다] be babyish; [미숙하다] be green.

비릿비릿하다 (냄새가) fishy; smelling of fish [blood]; [아니꼽다] disgusting; sickening; nauseating. ¶그의 행동이 ~ I am nauseated [disgusted] by his conduct.

비릿하다 somewhat fishy [bloody]; (서술적) smell a little bloody [fishy].

비만(肥滿) corpulence; fatness; obesity; portliness. **비만하다** [보기흉하게 살찌다] [문어] obese; corpulent; [비계살이 찌다] fat; [체격이 크다] stout(▶ 완곡한 말씨); [통통하게 살찌다] plump; (아이가) chubby. ¶키가 작고 비만한 사람 a pyknic / a pycnic // 비만해지다 grow corpulent / grow fat [stout].

● **비만아** an obese [an overweight] child. **비만증** [의] obesity. **비만형**(-型) a pyknic [pycnic] type.

비말(飛沫) a spray (of water); a splash. ¶바닷물의 ~ sea spray // 폭포의 ~ the spray of a waterfall // ~을 튀기다 splash water about.

비망록(備忘錄) a notebook; a datebook; a note; a memorandum (pl. ~s, -da); (구어) a memo (pl. ~s). ¶다른 국장들에게 ~을 송부하다 send a memorandum to the other department heads // 일에 관해서 배운 것을 ~으로 만들어 두는 것이 좋을 것이다 You'd better make some notes of what you have learned about your job.

비매품(非賣品) an article not for sale; (게시) "Not For Sale"; "Not to be sold"; "Privately Printed [Distributed]."

비명(非命) [제 목숨대로 다 살지 못함]. ¶~에 죽다 die an unnatural [untimely] death // 그는 ~에 죽었다 He died an unnatural death. / He met (with) a violent death.

● **비명횡사** an unnatural [untimely / accidental] death; death by violence.

비명(悲鳴) [놀라서 지르는 소리] a scream; a shrill [piercing] cry; [새된 소리] a shriek. ¶~을 지르다 scream / give [let out] a scream / shriek / give a shriek // 나는 상자 속에 뱀이 있었기 때문에 깜짝 놀라 ~을 질렀다 I screamed in alarm because there was a snake in the box.

비명(碑銘) an epitaph; an inscription (on a monument).

비목(費目) items of expense. ¶경비를 ~별로 나누다 itemize the expenses / list the expenses by item.

비몽사몽(非夢似夢) ¶~간에 between asleep and awake [sleeping and waking] / dreamily // 나는 하루 종일 ~간에 지냈다 I was half asleep and half awake all day. // 나는 ~간에 그의 목소리를 들었다 Only half awake [Half dreaming], I heard his voice.

비무장(非武裝) demilitarization. ¶~의 unarmed / demilitarized.

● **비무장 도시** an open city. **비무장 지대** a demilitarized zone(약어 DMZ).

비문(碑文) an epitaph; an epigraph; an inscription; a monumental inscription. ¶기념비의 ~ an epitaph on a monument // 그의 업적을 찬양하는 ~이 돌에 새겨졌다 A eulogy of his achievements was inscribed on the stone.

비문화적(非文化的) uncultured; uncivilized; unenlightened.

비민주적(非民主的) undemocratic; nondemocratic (policy).

비밀(祕密) secrecy; confidentiality; [비밀인 일] a secret; a confidence; a mystery. ¶~의 secret / confidential(▶ confidentiality, a confidence, confidential 은 당사자 사이의 은밀한 일을 말함) // 공공연한 ~ an open secret // 신서(信書)의 ~ the privacy of (personal) correspondence // ~을 누설하다 leak [let out] a secret / (무심코) let a secret slip / let the cat out of the bag // ~의 열쇠를 쥐다 hold a key to the mystery // ~을 캐다 pry into a secret // ~을 폭로하다 reveal [disclose / (lay) bare] a secret // ~을 털어놓다 [밝히다] confide [reveal / disclose] a secret to (a person) / let (a person) into a secret / take (a person) into one's confidence / (미국 속어) spill the beans // 우리들 사이에는 아무런 ~도 없다 We have no secrets between us. // 이것은 ~입니다. 누구에게도 말하지 마세요 This is strictly confidential. Don't tell anybody. // ~이 샜다 The secret leaked [got] out. // 그는 그들에게 ~을 털어놓았다 He let them in on the secret. / [믿고 털어놓다] He confided the secret to them. // 그녀가 ~의 열

쇠를 쥐고 있다 She holds the key to the mystery.// 그는 내 ~을 알고 있다 He knows my secret.// 계약은 ~리에 체결되었다 The contract was concluded in secret[secretly].// 연구는 엄중한 ~ 속에 진행되었다 The research was conducted in strict secrecy.// 넌 내게 무슨 ~이 있는 모양이구나 You seem to be keeping something (secret) from me.// 그 문제는 나만의 ~로 해 두기로 했다 I decided to keep the matter to myself.// 심문은 ~리에 행해졌다 The interrogation was held behind closed doors. **비밀히** secretly; confidentially.
● **비밀 결사** a secret[an underground] organization[society]. **비밀경찰** the secret police; the security police; (구소련의) the KGB; the Committee of State Security; (옛 이태리의) the Gestapo. **비밀 단체** a secret organization; a sub-rosa group. **비밀번호** (통장·신용카드의) a PIN(Personal identification number 의 약어); a PIN number; (컴퓨터의) a password. **비밀 외교** secret diplomacy. **비밀 투표** secret ballot. **비밀 회담** a closed-door talk.

비바람 rain and wind; a rainy wind; (바람을 동반한 비) wind-driven[windswept / wind-blown] rain; [폭풍우] a (rain) storm; a tempest. ¶~을 맞은 묘비 a weather-beaten tombstone// ~을 맞다 be exposed to the weather// ~을 피하다 protect oneself from the weather// 우리는 모진 ~을 맞았다 We had [There was] a heavy rainstorm.// 그는 ~을 무릅쓰고 출발했다 He set out in spite of the storm.

비바리 [바다에서 해산물을 채취하는 처녀] a girl diver.

비바체 [음] vivace.

비방(祕方) [처방전] a secret recipe[formula]; a secret medical prescription; [비법] a secret method[process]. ¶~을 쓰다 play one's trump card// 이것이 나의 최후의 ~책이다 This is my last resort. / Here's my last trump card.

비방(誹謗) slander; slanderous statements; calumny; vilification; abuse; reprobation. **비방하다** slander; abuse(▶ slander는 명예를 손상케 하는 일, abuse는 비난, 욕설을 하는 뜻); calumniate; malign; reprobate; defame; speak ill of. ¶그의 정적들은 시장이 업자로부터 돈을 받았다고 비방했다 His political opponents slandered the mayor by saying that he had received money from the business concerned.// 그는 나를 마구 비방했다 He greeted me with a stream of abuse. / He showered abuse on me.

비버 [동] a beaver.

비번(非番) off duty; (경계의) off guard. ¶~의 순경 a policeman off duty// ~의 야경꾼 an off-duty night watchman// ~이다 be off duty // 나는 목요일마다 ~이다 I'm off duty on Thursdays.
● **비번일** a day off; an off day.

비범하다(非凡-) extraordinary; uncommon; unique; unusual; remarkable; prodigious. ¶비범한 사람 a man of unusual ability / (천재) a genius// 비범한 솜씨 rare[unusual] ability[skill]// 비범한 재능 an unusual gift [talent]// 그녀는 그림에 비범한 재능을 갖고 있다 She has a genius[an extraordinary talent] for painting.

비법(祕法) a secret method[process]; a mystique; a mystery; (악의) a secret recipe [formula]. ¶~을 전수하다 initiate (a person) into the mysteries[secrets] (of)// ~을 터득하다 master the mysteries (of)// ~을 전수받다 be initiated in the secrets (of)// 건강의 ~이라도 있습니까 What is the secret of your good health? / Do you have some secret formula for good health?

비보(悲報) [슬픈 소식] sad news. ¶~에 접하다 receive[hear] sad news// ~를 전하는 그의 말소리는 떨리고 있었다 His voice was trembling as he broke the sad news.

비분(悲憤) [슬프고 분한 것] indignation; resentment. ¶~의 눈물을 흘리다 shed tears of indignation. **비분하다** resent; be indignant; be resentful.

비분강개하다(悲憤慷慨-) deplore; be indignant (at / over); resent. ¶관리들의 부패에 대해 ~ deplore[be indignant over] the corruption among government officials.

비브라토 [음] a vibrato (pl. ~s).

비브라폰 a vibraphone.

비브리오 [장염을 일으키는 세균] a vibrio (pl. ~s).

비비 [여러 번 꼬이거나 뒤틀린 모양] windingly; twistingly. ¶~ 꼬다 twist[entwist / twine] many times[over and over again]/ [빈정대다] take ironically / give an indirect cut// ~ 꼬이다 be[get] twisted[entwisted / twined / thrown] many times// ~ 틀다 twist [wrench / screw] (a person's arm) hard// ~ 틀리다 get twisted[wrenched] hard// 몸을 ~ 꼬다 twist the body about / writhe// 실을 ~ 꼬다 twist thread// 넥타이가 ~ 꼬여 있다 have one's tie (all) twisted up.

비비(狒狒) [동] a (dog-faced) baboon; a dog ape.

비비다 1 [문지르다] rub; scrub(박박); grate; [비벼서 떼대다] scrape. ¶비벼 틀다 rub off// 양손을 ~ rub one's hands together// 구두의 진흙을 비벼 털다 scrape mud off one's shoes // 아무리 비벼도 이 자국은 지워지지 않는다 This mark won't rub off.// 개가 내 다리에 몸[머리]을 비벼 댔다 The dog rubbed itself[its head] against my legs. 2 [아부하다] flatter; curry favor (with). 3 (둥글게) (make a) roll. 4 [버무리다] mix (food). ¶밥을 ~ mix boiled rice with subsidiary articles of diet / make (a) hash (with rice).

비비대다 [자꾸 대고 비비다] rub repeatedly.

비비적거리다 rub and rub; chafe against; rub against.

비빔국수 noodles with assorted mixtures.

비빔밥 bibimbap; boiled rice with assorted mixtures.

비사(祕史) hidden history; historical secrets; unknown historical facts.

비사교적(非社交的) unsociable; solitude-loving; retiring. ¶~인 사람 an unsociable person / (미) a bad mixer.

비산하다(飛散-) scatter; disperse; fly. ¶바람에 날려 재가 비산했다 The wind scattered the ashes all around.

비상(非常) a contingency; an emergency; an unlooked-for event. ¶~에 대비하다 prepare for the worst// ~이 걸리다 be put on emergency[special] alertness / be under the emergency duty orders.
● **비상경계** (be on) special guard. **비상경보** an alarm (signal / bell); an emergency

비상warning[alarm]. **비상계단** an emergency staircase; a fire escape. **비상 관제** emergency control. **비상구** an emergency exit [door]; a fire exit. **비상금** an emergency fund; a nest egg. **비상등** an emergency light(선박 등의). **비상사태** a state of emergency. ¶**국가 ~ 선언** declaration of a state of national emergency / a state-of-national-emergency declaration // ~를 **선언하다** declare a state of emergency // ~에 **있다** be in a state of emergency. **비상선**(-線) (경찰의) a police cordon; (화재의) a fire line. ¶~을 **치다** set up [establish] a cordon / ~을 **돌파하다** break[escape] through a cordon // 그 일대에 ~이 쳐졌다 The area was cordoned off. // 그는 ~을 뚫고 도망쳤다 He broke through the cordon [police lines] and made his escape. **비상소집** an emergency summons [call]; an extraordinary summons to the colors. **비상수단** an emergency measure. ¶~을 **쓰다** take drastic measures // 그는 ~을 강구했다 He took [resorted to] emergency [unusual / exceptional] measures. **비상시**(-時) an emergency; a crisis. ¶~에 in case of emergency / in an emergency // ~에 **대비하다** be prepared for an emergency // 그는 ~에 침착하게 행동했다 He acted calmly in the emergency. **비상시국** an emergency situation. **비상식량** emergency rations. **비상용** for emergency; (개시) For emergency use only.

비상(飛翔) a flight; flying; soaring. **비상하다** fly; take a flight; soar (up). ¶비상하는 매 a hawk in flight.

비상(砒霜) [약] arsenic poison.

비상근(非常勤) (a) part-time service. ¶~의 part-time // ~으로 **일하다** work part-time.
●**비상근직** a part-time position.

비상장주(非上場株) an unlisted stock [share].

비상하다(非常-) extraordinary; out of the ordinary; unusual; uncommon; remarkable; exceptional; excessive; extreme; immense. ¶비상한 솜씨 remarkable [exceptional] ability / unusual [uncommon / great] skill // 비상한 관심을 보이다 show[display] an extreme interest (in) // 고양이는 그것에 대해 비상한 관심을 나타내었다 The cat showed a great interest in it. // 그는 비상한 재능의 조각가이다 He is a sculptor of no mean ability.

비생산적(非生產的) nonproductive; unfruitful; unproductive. ¶~ **사업** an unproductive business / ~ **자본** dead capital.

비서(祕書) 1 [요직자 밑에서 기밀문서 등의 용무를 맡은 사람] a (private) secretary. ¶**개인 ~** a private secretary / a man Friday / (경멸) a flunky // **수석 ~** a chief secretary // **대통령 공보 담당 ~관** the Press Secretary to the President // 그녀는 사장의 ~로 일하고 있다 She is [acts as] secretary to the president. 2 [소중히 간직한 책] a treasured [a secret] book [document].
●**비서실** a secretary's office; a secretariat. ¶**장관 ~** the Minister's Secretariat. **비서실장** a chief secretary.

비석(碑石) a stone monument; a monumental stone.

비소(砒素) [화] arsenic(기호 As).

비소(誹笑) a sardonic smile. ⇨ 비웃음

비속(卑俗) vulgarity; vulgarism. **비속하다** vulgar; coarse; broad; low. ¶비속한 취미[말] vulgar taste [language] // 비속한 텔레비전 프로 a low-level TV program.

비속(卑屬) [법] (직계의) a lineal descendant; (방계의) a collateral descendant.

비수(匕首) a dagger; a dirk; a knife. ¶~로 **찌르다** stab (a person) with a dagger.

비술(祕術) a secret (art); the mysteries (of an art); stratagem; occult arts. ¶나는 그에게 태권도의 ~을 전수하였다 I initiated him into the secrets [mysteries] of taegwondo. / I taught him the secrets of taegwondo.

비스듬하다 slant(ing); sloping; skew; oblique; diagonal. ¶비스듬한 선 a slant line // 비스듬한 아치 a skew arch // 탑이 한쪽으로 ~ A tower leans on one side. **비스듬히** aslant; askew; obliquely; askance; diagonally. ¶줄을 ~ 긋다 draw an oblique [diagonal] line / draw a line diagonally // 그는 모자를 ~ 쓰고 있었다 He wore his hat at a slant. // 길은 철도를 ~ 가로지른다 The road crosses the track obliquely [at an oblique angle].

비슷하다 somewhat similar; rather alike. ¶비슷한 데가 있다 there is some resemblance (between) // 그들은 성격이 ~ They are somewhat alike in character.

비스무트 [화] bismuth(기호 Bi).

비스코스 viscose.

비스킷 (미) (짠맛의) a cracker; (단맛의) a cookie; (영) a biscuit. (▶ (미)에서 biscuit은 베이킹파우더 등을 넣고 구운 작은 빵을 말함. (영)에서는 cookie와 cracker의 총칭).

비슷비슷하다 much the same; of a piece; of a [the same] sort. ¶**생김새가 ~** (the two) look alike // 그들은 나이가 ~ They are about the same age. // 그들은 키가 ~ They are all much the same in height. // 두 사람은 솜씨가 ~ There is little difference [little to choose] between the two in workmanship.

비슷하다¹ slant(ing); sloping. ⇨ 비스듬하다

비슷하다² [거의 같다] similar; (a)like; resembling. ¶비슷한 사건 a similar incident // 이것과 비슷한 물건 an article similar to this // 그와 비슷한 이야기 a story like that / a similar tale // …과 비슷한 데가 있다 there is something that resembles … // 비슷하지 않다 bear no resemblance [similarity] to / look different // 이 두 잎은 ~ These two leaves look alike. // 그들은 예술적 재능이 ~ They are almost equal [about the same] in artistic talent. // 초상화가 점점 대상과 비슷하게 되어 갔다 The portrait became [grew] more and more like its subject. // 비슷한 사건이 몇 년 전에도 일어났다 A similar case occurred several years ago. // 그의 경력은 내 경력과 비슷한 데가 있다 His career bears some parallels to mine.

비시지 BCG (vaccine)(▶ Bacillus Calmette-Guérin의 약어). ¶~를 **접종하다** inoculate a person with BCG (vaccine)(▶ 미국에서는 일반에게는 시행되고 있지 않으므로 a tuberculosis vaccine [a vaccine against tuberculosis] called BCG 등으로 말하여야 함).
●**비시지 접종** inoculation by BCG.

비신사적(非紳士的) ungentlemanlike; ungentlemanly. ¶~**인 행위** a conduct unbecoming to a gentleman.

비실거리다 totter; reel; stagger; dodder; falter; move unsteadily. ¶**무거운 짐을 지고 ~** stagger under a heavy load // **한 대 얻어맞고 ~** reel under a heavy blow // 비실거리며 거리를 걸어가다 totter feebly along the street

비실비실 //그는 발길에 채어 비실거렸다 He received a staggering kick.

비실비실 totteringly; staggeringly; reelingly; falteringly. ¶~ 걸어가다 dodder along / walk with faltering steps//주정뱅이는 ~ 길에 쓰러졌다 The drunk collapsed in a heap on the road.//한 노파가 ~ 길을 건너갔다 An old woman tottered across the street. / An old woman walked across the street unsteadily. **비실비실하다** totter; reel. ⇨비실거리다

비싸다 1 [상품의 값이 너무 많다] dear; expensive; costly; high in price; high-priced. ¶비싼 값 a high price//비싼 값으로 팔다 sell a thing at a high price//가장 비싼 값을 매기다 make the highest bid (for)//생선 값이 ~ Fish is expensive. / Fish is high in price.//그것은 너무 ~ That's too expensive[steep]. / It costs too much. / It costs a fortune. / It costs an arm and a leg.//이 코트가 30만 원이라면 좀 비싼 것 같다 Three hundred thousand won seems to be a rather high[(구어) stiff] price for this coat.//그는 집을 비싸게 팔았다[샀다] He sold[bought] a house at a high price.//그는 이런 하찮은 물건을 비싸게 불렀다 He asked an unreasonable price[charged too much] for this little article.//이런 종류의 우표는 아무리 비싸도 팔린다 Stamps of this kind sell at any price.//겨울 옷을 가을에 사면 비싸게 먹힌다 If you buy winter clothes in autumn you have to pay more.//그렇게 비싼 모피 코트는 도저히 살 수 없다 I couldn't possibly buy such an expensive fur coat. / Such an expensive fur coat is out of my reach.

2 [도도하다] arrogant; proud; haughty. ¶비싸게 굴다 behave oneself haughtily.

비아냥거리다 make cynical remarks; be sarcastic (about). ¶그는 내게 비아냥거렸다 He made insinuations against[insinuating remarks about] me.

비애(悲哀) [슬픔] sorrow; grief; sadness; misery; pathos. ¶인생의 ~ the sorrows of life//그녀는 여자의 ~를 절실히 느꼈다 She felt keenly the grief of being a woman.

비약(飛躍) 1 [뛰어오름] a jump; a leap. **비약하다** jump; leap. 2 [활약] activity. **비약하다** be active; play an active part. 3 [빠른 진보·향상] rapid progress. ¶이제 우리는 일대 ~을 할 때이다 Now is the time for us to take a great leap forward.//그의 사업은 ~적으로 발전하였다 His business moved ahead grew by leaps and bounds. **비약하다** make rapid progress. 4 [논리 등의] a jump. ¶당신의 말에는 논리의 ~이 있다 There's a gap in your reasoning. / There's an illogical jump in what you say. **비약하다** fly; jump. ¶화제는 개에서 골프로 비약했다 The conversation jumped from dogs to golf.

비약(祕藥) a secret medicine[remedy]; a nostrum(엉터리 같은).

비어홀 (미) a beer hall; (영) a beerhouse; an alehouse.

비어(卑語·鄙語) [천한 말] vulgar language; a vulgar word[expression]; a vulgarism; a slang(속어); [낮춤말] a depreciatory term.

비어지다 1 [튀어나오다] stick out; protrude; work its way out. ¶어린이의 발이 담요 밑으로 비어져 나와 있었다 The child's legs were sticking out from under the blanket.//틈새로 속이 비어져 나와 있었다 The padding was bulging out of the tear. 2 [탄로 나다] be revealed; come to light; be laid there.

비엔날레 the Biennale. ¶~전(展) a biennial exhibition.

비엘 [선하 증권] a B/L(▶ bill of lading의 약어).

비역 [남색] sodomy; buggery; p(a)ederasty; male homosexuality. **비역하다** commit[practice] sodomy.

비열(比熱) [물] specific heat.

비열하다(卑劣-) sordid; nasty; sneaking; cowardly; contemptible; dastard(ly); mean-spirited; dirty; (구어) low-down; [천하다] base; mean; ignoble; [뻔뻔스럽다] shameless; [경멸스럽다] despicable. ¶비열한 사람 a despicable[base] man//비열한 말 ignoble[shameless] words//비열한 남자 a cad / a despicable fellow//나는 아무리 가난해도 그렇게까지 비열해지고 싶지는 않다 I may be poor, but I wouldn't stoop that low.//얼마나 비열한 짓이냐 What a mean[dirty / low-down] trick!/나를 중상하다니 정말 ~ That's really dirty (of you) to spread lies about me.//그는 비열한 놈이다 He is a despicable person.

비염(鼻炎) (a) nasal inflammation; nasal catarrh; [의] rhinitis.

비영리(非營利) ¶~적인 nonprofit.
● **비영리 단체** a nonprofit institution; a nonprofit organization. **비영리사업** nonprofit business.

비오리 [동] a common merganser; a goosander.

비옥하다(肥沃-) fertile; rich; productive; fruitful. ¶비옥한 땅[토양] fertile land[soil]//비옥해지다 grow fertile[rich]//이곳의 토양은 ~ The soil here is fertile.

비올라 a viola.

비옷 a raincoat; a mac(k)intosh(고무를 입힌). ¶~을 입다 put on[wear] a raincoat.

비용(費用) [지출] an expense; [특정한 사물에 출비하는 금액] expenses; [특정한 값에 대하여 지불된 돈] a cost; [경비] costs. ¶여행 ~ traveling expenses//가변 ~ variable cost//제(諸) ~ (sundry [miscellaneous]) expenses //소송 ~ legal expenses//~을 절감하다 cut down[back] on expenses//~을 탕진하다 go to a lot of expense for nothing//불필요한 ~을 줄이다 cut down on unnecessary expenses//~은 적어도 20만 원 정도 될 것이다 The expense[cost] will amount[come] to at least 200,000 won.//그것은 ~이 많이 든다 It will cost a great deal.//~이 많이 들어도 나는 개의치 않는다 I don't care how much it costs.//나는 10만 원의 ~으로 여행했다 I took a trip at a cost of 100,000 won.//그 trip cost 100,000 won.//그는 아주 적은 ~으로 방 한 칸을 증축했다 He added on an extra room for almost nothing.//그는 아주 적은 ~으로 가게를 냈다 He opened his store on a shoestring.

비우다 1 [비게 하다] empty (a box, a glass, etc.); exhaust (the water in a vessel); clear out the contents of. ¶상자를 ~ empty a box//유리잔의 물을 냄비에 부어 ~ empty the water out of a glass into a pan//병을 ~ empty a bottle//그 상자를 비웠다 The box was emptied. / The contents of the box have been removed.//어제는 우리 둘이서 10병의

맥주를 비웠다 Yesterday we drank up ten bottles of beer between the two of us.∥음악회가 끝나자 홀은 곧 비워졌다 The hall emptied as soon as the concert was over.
2 (점유지·건물을) vacate; evacuate; (외출하여) leave (one's house) empty; [쓰지 않고 빈 채로 두다] leave (a house) vacant; leave (a place) clear; hold (a position) open (for a person). ¶집을 ~ [명도하다] evacuate a house / clear out of a house / move out / (외출하여) leave one's house empty∥종이의 한 쪽 면을 비워 두다 leave a margin on one side of the paper∥집을 비워 주고 되거하다 vacate a house∥숙박 손님들은 오전 10시까지 방을 비워 주십시오 Guests are requested to vacate their rooms before 10:00 a.m.∥우리는 1주일 동안 집을 비웁니다 We'll be away for a week.∥1인용 방을 하나 비워 두시오 Reserve a single room for me.∥내주 금요일과 토요일을 비워 두겠습니다 I will keep next Friday and Saturday open.∥사고는 어머니가 잠시 방을 비운 틈에 일어났다 The accident occurred when mother left the room for a moment.∥잠시 자리를 비워도 되겠습니까 May I be excused (for) a moment?

비운(悲運) misfortune; ill[hard] luck. ¶~을 만나다 have bad luck / (문어) suffer a misfortune∥그는 ~에 빠졌다 He fell on evil days[hard times].∥그녀는 자신의 ~을 한탄했다 She complained of her misfortunes [bad luck / ill luck].

비웃다 sneer (at); be cynical (about); [조롱하다] jeer (at); [짓궂게 놀리다] ridicule; [업신여겨 조소하다] mock; [빈정거리다] be sarcastic (about). ¶세상을 ~ mock[satirize] the world∥당신이 한 말을 비웃을 생각은 조금도 없습니다 I don't mean to mock what you said.∥동급생들이 나를 겁쟁이라고 비웃었다 My classmates jeered at me and called me a coward.∥그는 여러 사람 앞에서 나를 비웃었다 He ridiculed[mocked] me in public.∥범인은 경찰을 비웃듯이 도망치고 있었다 The criminal is evading the police as if he were ridiculing[deriding] them.∥그는 나의 제안을 비웃었다 He laughed mockingly at my proposal.

비웃음 a sardonic[cynical / scornful] smile [laugh]; a mocking laughter; a sneer; ridicule. ¶~을 사다 incur[excite] ridicule; bring[draw] ridicule upon oneself∥나의 제안은 ~만 사고 일축되었다 My proposal was dismissed with scorn.∥그의 실수는 사람들의 ~을 샀다 His blunder incurred ridicule [provoked people's derision].∥그는 전교의 ~거리가 되었다 He made himself the laughingstock of the whole school.

비원(悲願) **1** [비장한 소원] one's earnest [pathetic] prayer[wish]. ¶~을 이루다 attain [achieve] one's earnest wish answered [fulfilled]. **2** [불] a merciful prayer (to save mankind).

비위(脾胃) **1** [지라와 위] the spleen and the stomach.
2 [기호] taste; liking; palate; choice. ¶~에 맞는 음식 a favorable food∥~에 맞다 suit one's taste / be to one's taste[liking]∥그 음식은 내 ~에 맞지 않는다 The food goes against my stomach.
3 [기분] humor; temper; mood. ¶~를 맞추기 힘든 사람 a person hard to please∥남의 ~를 맞추는 사람 a flatterer / (구어) a yes-man∥~를 **맞추다** humor (a person) / let a person have his way / (마음에 들도록 하다) curry favor with a person / (문어) ingratiate oneself with a person / (구어) get on the good side of a person[on a persons good side] / (구어) butter a person up / [아부하다] fawn on[flatter] a person∥자기 상사의 ~를 맞추려고 하다 try to see what one's superior wants / (문어) consult one's superior's pleasure∥그는 사장의 ~를 잘 맞추어서 전무가 되었다 He became a managing director by currying favor with the president.∥나는 그의 ~를 맞추기 위해 포도주 한 병을 보내 주었다 I sent him a bottle of wine to please him[to keep him sweet / to get on the right side of him].

비위(를) 거스르다 offend; rub (a person) the wrong way; get under one's skin.
비위(를) 건드리다 give offence to; hurt (a person's) feeling; incur the displeasure (of). ¶그의 거만한 태도가 내 비위를 건드린다 His arrogant attitude is galling[galls me / (구어) makes me sick].∥그는 상사의 비위를 건드렸다 He incurred his superior's displeasure.
비위(가) 상하다 be displeased (with / at / by); feel disgusted (at / by / with); feel hurt.
비위(가) 약하다 have a weak stomach.
비위에 거슬리다 be offensive; be displeasing; be disagreeable to (a person's) feeling.
비위(가) 틀리다 be displeased; get out of humor; be in (an) ugly mood.

비위생적(非衛生的) [더러움·병균 등으로 지저분한] insanitary; unsanitary; unhygienic; [전반적으로 건강에 나쁜] unwholesome. ¶~인 음식 food prepared under insanitary [unhygienic] conditions∥~인 식당 a dirty [an insanitary] restaurant∥~인 생활 상태 unhygienic[insanitary] living conditions∥그의 생활은 아주 ~이다 He pays little attention to personal hygiene.

비유(比喩·譬喩) a figure of speech; a simile(직유); a metaphor(은유); [우화] an allegory; a parable. ¶~를 쓰다 use a metaphor∥그는 여러 가지 ~를 써서 이야기를 했다 He used various similes and metaphors in telling his story. **비유하다** compare (to); liken (to); use a simile[metaphor]; speak figuratively[metaphorically]. ¶비유해서 말하면 figuratively[metaphorically] speaking / to use a simile[metaphor]∥단풍나무의 붉은 잎들은, 비유해서 말하면 온 산을 불꽃으로 뒤덮은 것 같았다 The crimson leaves of the maples, figuratively speaking[so to speak], covered the whole mountain with flames.

비유적(比喩的) metaphorical; figurative. ¶~인 표현[의미] a figurative expression[sense]∥~으로 말하자면 너는 쓰레기 더미 위에 있는 학이야 Figuratively speaking, you are a crane on a rubbish heap.∥「꽃이 웃는다」는 봄의 기쁨을 ~으로 표현한 것이다 "Flowers smile" is a metaphorical statement of the joy of spring[a metaphorical way of expressing the joy of spring].

비육(肥育) fatting[fattening] (up). **비육하다** fat[fatten] up (cattle); raise (cattle). ➔¶비육된 소 fattened cattle.
●**비육우** beeves[(미) beefs]; (집합적) beef cattle.

비율(比率) (a) ratio; (a) percentage; rate; proportion. ¶구성 ~ distribution ratio // 남녀 ~ the proportion of males to females // 큰 ~ a large percentage // 3, 3, 5의 ~ 3:3:5 ratio / a ratio of 3:3:5 (▶ three to three to five로 읽음) // 그것은 5대 3의 ~을 이루고 있다 They appear in a ratio of five to three. / 출생과 사망의 ~이 역전되었다 The ratio of births to deaths[The birth-death ratio] has reversed itself.

비음(鼻音) [언] a nasal sound; a nasal.
비인간적(非人間的) inhuman; impersonal. ¶(자연력·운명 등의) ~인 힘 impersonal forces.
비인도적(非人道的) inhumane. ¶~인 범죄 a crime against humanity.
비일비재하다(非一非再) frequent; repeated; (서술적) occur often. ¶비일비재한 사례 a frequent case // 그런 일은 ~ It is just one of those common things. / It is of frequent occurrence.
비자 a visa; visé. ¶이민 ~ an immigrant visa // 입국[출국] ~ an entry[exit] visa // 여권에 ~를 받다 have one's passport visaed[visa'd / viséed / visé'd].
비장(祕藏) storing in secrecy; treasuring; hoarding. ¶~의 treasured / prized / (사랑하고 아끼는) favo(u)rite // ~의 보물 a (precious) treasure // ~의 상자 a treasured casket. **비장하다** store in secrecy; treasure (up); prize; cherish; keep (a thing) under lock and key[with great care]. ¶나는 돌아가신 어머니의 손거울을 비장하고 있다 I treasure the hand mirror that my (late) mother left me.
비장의 무기[카드] an ace up one's sleeve; (미) an ace in the hole.
● **비장품** a treasure; a treasured article; a hoard.
비장(脾臟) [생] the spleen. ⇨ 지라
비장하다(悲壯) pathetic; touching; tragic. ¶비장한 각오 a tragic but brave resolution / a tragic decision in one's mind / a heroic resolve // 그는 비장한 최후를 마쳤다 He died a hero's[heroic] death.
비적비적 [여기저기서 비어져 나옴] protruding[coming out] here and there.
비전 (a) vision; foresight. ¶~이 있는 사람 a foresighted person // 그 시대에는 ~을 가진 정치가들이 더러 있었다 Some statesmen in the era had vision.
비전(祕傳) a secret; a recipe; the mysteries (of). ¶~의 묘약 a proprietary medicine // ~을 전수하다 initiate a person into the mysteries (of) / hand down a secret to a person.
비전문가(非專門家) a layman. ¶~를 위한 책 books for laymen // ~의 생각 a layman's view[way of looking at something] // ~의 안목 nonprofessional eye // ~의 눈에는 그 다이아몬드는 진짜로 보인다 The diamond looks real to inexpert eyes.
비전투원(非戰鬪員) a noncombatant; a civilian(민간인). ¶~을 소개(疏開)시키다 evacuate noncombatants (from).
비전해질(非電解質) [화] a nonelectrolyte.
비접 a change of place (for a sick person); a change of air[climate]. ¶~을 나가다 move to another place (for one's health) / go to (a place) for a change of (air).
비정규(非正規) ¶~의 irregular.
● **비정규군** irregulars; irregular troops.

비정상(非正常) anything unusual; abnormality; irregularity. ¶~의 abnormal / unusual / exceptional / singular // 생후 2개월의 갓난 아이가 이가 나는 것은 ~이다 It is abnormal for a baby to have teeth at the age of two months.
● **비정상아** an abnormal child. **비정상인** [심] a deviate.
비정하다(非情) 1 [인정이 없다] unfeeling; heartless; cold-hearted. ¶비정한 사람 a cold-hearted person // 그런 비정한 일은 할 수 없다 I cannot do such an unfeeling[a cruel] thing. 2 [감정이 없다] insentient; senseless.
비정형(非定型) ¶~의 atypical.
비조(鼻祖) the founder. ⇨ 시조(始祖)
비좁다 narrow; confined; cramped; incommodious. ¶비좁은 집 a narrow[cramped] house // 비좁아서 갑갑하다 be too narrow for one's comfort // 되게 비좁군 There's no room to swing a cat here. // 모두 들어가기는 했지만 몹시 비좁았다 We all got in, but it was really a tight squeeze.
비주룩하다 projecting[protruding] a bit. ¶담장 밖으로 비주룩한 나무 a tree jutting a bit beyond the walls.
비주류(非主流) non(-)mainstreamers; the non(-)mainstream faction[group].
비죽 poutingly; protrudingly; projectingly. ¶입을 ~ 내밀다 pout one's lips // 얼굴만 ~ 내밀고 가다 show one's nose of a moment and disappear // 칼끝이 그의 호주머니 밖으로 ~ 나왔다 The point of his knife stuck out of his pocket.
비죽거리다 pout[twist] one's lips[mouth]; make a pout; screw up one's mouth. ¶울려고 ~ pout[sulk] almost in tears // 소년은 입을 비죽거리며 항의했다 The boy protested with a pout[with his lips protruding].
비준(批准) ratification. ¶이 조약은 ~을 필요로 한다 This treaty is subject to ratification. **비준하다** ratify (a treaty); sanction.
● **비준서** an instrument of ratification; a ratification instrument. ~의 기탁[교환] the deposit[exchange] of ratification.
비중(比重) 1 [물] specific gravity. ¶~을 재다 measure[find out] the specific gravity (of). 2 [중요성의 정도] relative importance. ¶시험 결과보다 출석에 ~을 두다 place more weight on students' attendance than no examination results // 가계비 중에서 식비가 큰 ~을 차지하고 있다 We spend a large part of our family budget on food.
● **비중계** a specific gravity balance; a (standard) hydrometer; a gravimeter; a areometer(액체의).
비즈니스 [사업·영업] business.
● **비즈니스맨** [실업가] a businessman.
비지 [두부를 만들고 남은 찌꺼기] bean-curd dregs.
비지 먹은 배는 연약과도 싫다 한다(속담) A full stomach is not interested in delicacies.; Provide enough bread and no one will ask for cake.
● **비지땀** beads of sweat; heavy sweat. ¶~을 흘리다 sweat heavily / perspire profusely / get into a profuse[heavy] perspiration / sweat one's guts out // ~을 흘리다 all in [of] a sweat / dripping (wet) with sweat // 그것 때문에 ~을 뺐다 It was really a horrid sweat.
비지떡 a bean-dregs cake.

비질하다 sweep with a broom.
비집다 1 〔틈 내다〕 split open; 〔벌리다〕 pull [force] open; spread apart. ¶비집고 들어가 wedge (oneself) in[into] / thrust[squeeze] oneself in[into] // 만원 버스에 비집고 들어가다 squeeze oneself into a crowded bus // 나는 드라이버를 문과 기둥 사이에 비집어 넣어 자물통을 열었다 I opened the lock by forcing [pushing] a screwdriver between the door and the doorpost. 2 〔눈을 비벼 뜨다〕 rub one's eyes open.
비쭉 poutingly. ⇨ 비죽
비쭉거리다 pout one's lips. ⇨ 비죽거리다
비참하다 (悲慘-) 〔몹시도 불행하다〕 miserable (surroundings); wretched; 〔가엾게 보이다〕 pitiable; 〔가련하다〕 pathetic (stories); 〔비극적이다〕 tragic (events / death). ¶비참한 광경 a pathetic[horrible] sight / 그해의 가장 비참한 사건 the most tragic event of the year // 비참한 생활을 하다 lead a miserable [wretched] life // 비참한 처지에 있다 be in sad circumstances // 그는 비참한 최후를 마쳤다 He met with[had] a tragic end. / He died a miserable death. // 그는 비참한 생애를 보냈다 He lived his life (out) in misery. // 그는 비참한 목소리로 우리에게 사죄했다 He begged our pardon in a pitiable[wretched] voice. // 그런 비참한 소리는 하지 마라 Never say die! / Never give up! // 그 광경은 참으로 비참했다 It was a really pitiable sight to see. **비참히** miserably; cheerlessly; wretchedly. ¶~ 죽다 die in misery.
비창하다 (悲愴-) sad; pathetic; sorrowful; plaintive.
비책 (祕策) a secret plan[scheme / measure]; a subtle stratagem. ¶그는 그녀에게 ~을 털어놓았다 He confided the secret plans to her. // 그들은 ~을 궁리했다 They devised [worked out] a secret stratagem.
비척거리다 totter; stagger. ⇨ 비틀거리다
비척비척 totteringly; staggeringly. ⇨ 비틀비틀
비천하다 (卑賤-) low; lowly; obscure; humble. ¶비천한 몸[사람] a person of humble [lowly] origin[birth / of low birth] / a nonentity // 비천한 태생이다 be of humble birth.
비철 (非-) off season; out of season.
비철 금속 (非鐵金屬) nonferrous metals.
비추다 1 〔빛을 보내다·빛을 받게 하다〕 shine on; shed[throw] (a) light on; flash (on); light (up). ¶불빛을 ~ flash a beam (on a thing) / light up (the dark corner) // 남의 얼굴을 ~ throw a light on another's face // 커다란 장식 전등이 거실을 환하게 비추었다 A large chandelier lighted up the living room. // 태양은 부자에게나 가난한 사람에게나 똑같이 비춘다 The sun shines on the rich and the poor alike. // 탐조등이 해상을 비추었다 The searchlight flashed over the sea.
2 〔빛이 통하게 하다〕 hold (up) (a thing) to [before / against] the light. ¶나는 지폐를 불빛에 비추어 보았다 I looked at the bill[note] through the light. // 종이를 태양에 비추어 보니 비침무늬가 똑똑히 보였다 When I held up the paper against the sun I could see the watermark distinctly.
3 〔반사체에 다른 물체의 모양이 나타나게 하다〕 reflect; mirror; project; cast. ¶그녀는 거울에 얼굴을 비쳐 보았다 She looked at her reflection[face] in the mirror. // 자식은 부모를 비추는 거울이다 Children mirror[reflect] their parents. / Children are a mirror reflecting their parents.
4 〔비교하다〕 compare (with); refer (to); judge by[from]. ¶전례에 비추어 보아 in the light of[judging from] past precedents // 오늘날의 세계 정세에 비추어 in the context of the world situation today // 그 건은 전례에 비추어서 결정되었다 The case was decided by consulting precedent. // 이러한 사실에 비추어 보면 그의 설이 옳다는 것이 분명하다 In the light of these facts, it is clear that his theory is correct.
비추이다 be shone; be lighted (up); be reflected[mirrored]; have light shed (on a thing); get reflected[mirrored].
비축 (備蓄) saving for[against] emergency; storing; a stock (of goods). ¶그들은 식량의 ~이 충분치 않다 They do not have a sufficient stock[store] of food[provisions]. **비축하다** store; stockpile; save for emergency. ¶등유를 ~ lay in a supply of kerosene // 겨울 연료를 ~ store up fuel for the winter // 비축한 노트가 떨어졌다 Our reserve stock of notebooks has run out. // 뒷방에 세제를 비축해 놓은 것이 있다 We have a stock of detergent in the back room. // 그녀는 1년치의 비누를 비축했다 She has hoarded[stocked] enough soap for a year. // 그들은 석유를 대량 비축해 두었다 They had a large quantity of oil stored away[in store].
비취 (翡翠) 〔보석〕 green jadeite; jade.
● **비취색** jade green.
비치 (備置) equipment; provision; fitting. ¶교무실의 ~ 도서 books kept in the teacher's room. **비치하다** 〔설비하다〕 furnish; provide (with); equip (a factory with machinery); fit; install (a telephone); 〔준비해 놓다〕 keep [have] (a thing) ready. →¶비치되어 있는 신문 newspapers kept on file // 구급함에 비치된 의약품 medicine kept in the first-aid kit // 거의 모든 기선에는 무선 전신기가 비치되어 있다 Almost all steamers are fitted with wireless apparatus.
비치다 1 〔빛이〕 shine (in / into / upon). ¶쨍쨍 ~ blaze away / 희미하게 ~ shimmer / glimmer // 〔햇빛이〕 구름 사이로 ~ break through the cloud // 해가 밝게 비치고 있다 The sun is shining brightly. // 이 방은 오후에는 햇빛이 세게 비친다 The afternoon sun shines into this room hard. // 햇빛이 그의 얼굴에 비치고 있었다 The sun was in his face.
2 〔투영되다〕 be reflected; be imaged; be mirrored; be projected; fall[be thrown] upon. ¶텔레비전에 비친 그의 얼굴 his face (projected) on the television // 장지문에 누군가의 그림자가 비쳤다 Someone's shadow fell on the sliding paper door. // 등나무 꽃이 물에 비치고 있다 The wisteria flowers are reflected in the water. // 그녀는 거울에 비친 자신의 모습을 보고 웃었다 She smiled at herself in the mirror.
3 〔인상을 주다〕 impress; […으로 보이다] appear (to). ¶좋게 ~ impress (another) favorably[in one's favor] / leave a favorable impression on (a person's mind) / give (another) a favorable impression // 외국인의 눈에 비친 한국 Korea as she appears to foreign eyes / Korea through a foreigner's

eye // 눈에 비치는 것은 모두 아름다웠다 Everything I saw was beautiful. // 그의 눈에는 그녀가 천사처럼 비쳤다 In his eyes, she was an angel. / She looked like an angel to him.
4 [투시되다] show through; be seen through; be transparent; clear / (문어) limpid. ¶살이 비치는 옷 a see-through dress // 이 종이는 비친다 This paper is transparent. // 인쇄가 뒷면에 비친다 The printing shows through on the other side. // 레이스 커튼을 통해서 실내가 비쳐 보인다 The inside of the room is visible through the lace curtain.
5 [암시하다] hint (at / that); suggest; imply; give [drop] a hint (to a person). ¶불만을 ~ betray one's feeling of discontent // 그는 승낙할 뜻을 비치고 있다 He gives us to understand that he will consent. // 나는 그 일에 관해 말을 비쳐 봤다 I sounded him on the subject. / I felt him out on the matter. // 나는 넌지시 내 생각을 비쳐 봤다 I dropped hints of [hinted at] my intention. // 며칠 전에 그는 내게 사임할 뜻을 비쳤다 The other day he intimated to me his intention to resign.
6 [나타나다] appear; show [turn] up; show oneself; drop in (at). ¶그는 하루 종일 회사에 얼굴도 비치지 않았다 He didn't put in an appearance at the office all day. // 스크린에 그녀의 얼굴이 비쳤다 She appeared on the screen.

비치파라솔 (*beach parasol) a beach umbrella.

비칭(卑稱) a humble name [title / term].

비커 [화] a beaker.

비켜나다 step [move] aside (from); sidestep; step back; get out of the way (of); (자리를) retire; withdraw.

비켜서다 stand [move] aside; step back [aside]. ¶얼른 ~ dodge quickly // 그들은 그 [그의 차] 가 지나가도록 비켜섰다 They made way for him [his car].

비키니 a bikini.

비키다 1 (옆으로) step [move] aside (from); sidestep; move off; (뒤로) step back; [피하다] dodge; make a dodge; turn aside. ¶요리조리 ~ dodge about // 조금 비켜 주시겠어요 Won't you step aside?
2 (물건을) move (a thing) aside. ¶의자를 조금만 비켜 주시겠습니까 Will you please move your chair a little aside?
3 (자리를) retire; withdraw. ¶자리를 좀 비켜 주시겠습니까 Would you kindly leave me [us] alone? // 나는 둘이 이야기하고 있는 동안 자리를 비켜 주었다 I stayed out while they talked with each other.
4 (길을) move out of the way; make room [way] (for); get out of the way (of). ¶길을 비켜라 Get out of my way!

비타민 vitamins (▶ 보통 복수형). ¶종합 ~ multivitamin // 음식물의 ~을 파괴하다 destroy the vitamins in food / deprive the food of vitamins // 당근은 ~ A가 풍부하다 Carrots are rich in [contain a lot of] vitamin A. / ~ C는 감귤류에 들어 있다 Vitamin C occurs in oranges.
● **비타민 결핍증** a vitaminosis; a vitamin deficiency disease. **비타민제** (조제약) a vitamin compound [preparation]; (정제) a vitamin tablet; (환약) a vitamin pill. ¶종합 ~ a multivitamin pill.

비타협적(非妥協的) unyielding; uncompromising; intransigent. ¶~인 태도 intransigence / intransigency.

비탄(悲歎) grief (over / about / for); deep sorrow (for / over); anguish; lamentation. ¶~에 잠기다 be crushed with grief / be heartbroken / abandon oneself to grief / be overcome [overwhelmed] with grief [sorrow] (over a person's death) // 그녀는 ~으로 거의 미칠 지경이었다 She was driven almost insane by grief. / She went nearly mad with grief. **비탄하다** grieve; mourn; sorrow (over / on); lament; deplore. ¶너무 비탄한 나머지 in the excess of one's grief // 비탄하심은 당연하오나 I sympathize with you in your grief, but ....

비탈 (오르막·내리막의) a slope; an incline; a hill; (오르막) an upward slope; an ascent; an acclivity; (내리막) a downward slope; a descent; a declivity. ¶완만한 [가파른] ~ a gentle [steep] slope [incline] // 오르막 [내리막] ~ an uphill [a downhill] slope / an up [a down] grade [(영) gradient] // ~을 오르다 go uphill / go up a hill // ~을 내려가다 go downhill / go down a hill // 그 교회는 ~ 위에 [밑에] 있었다 The church stood at the top [bottom] of a slope [hill]. // 그 정원은 ~져 강가에 이르고 있다 The garden slopes down to the river.
● **비탈길** a sloping road; a slope.

비통하다(悲痛―) sad; grievous; sorrowful; bitter; touching; affecting; pathetic. ¶비통한 마음을 안고 with bitter grief in one's heart // 비통한 생각에 잠기다 be filled with deep sadness // 그는 비통한 표정이었다 He looked extremely sad. / He had a pained look on his face.

비트[1] **1** [음] a beat. ¶~가 강한 음악 music with a strong [powerful] beat // 에이트 ~ eight-beat time. **2** [수영에서의 물장구] the flutter kick.
● **비트족**(-族) a beatnik; a beat; (집합적) the beat generation.

비트[2] [컴퓨터에서 데이터를 나타내는 최소 단위] a bit.

비틀거리다 [이리저리 쓰러질 듯이 걷다] totter; (균형을 잃고) stagger; (현기증 등으로) reel; (발이 물건에 걸려) stumble; trip (against / over / on). ¶돌부리에 걸려 비틀거리며 넘어지다 stumble [trip] over a stone and fall // 비틀거리며 걷다 stumble along // 그는 헛발을 디뎌 앞으로 비틀거렸다 He stumbled and lurched forward off balance. // 그는 열 걸음쯤 비틀거리며 걸어가다가 쓰러졌다 He staggered along for ten steps and then fell down. // 노인은 비틀거리며 일어섰다 The old man stood up unsteadily [staggered to his feet]. // 그는 피로에 지쳐서 비틀거리고 있다 He was staggering with exhaustion. // 그는 비틀거리며 방으로 들어왔다 He staggered [stumbled] into the room. // 할머니는 버스 속에서 비틀거리며 서 있었다 The old woman stood, tottering and swaying, in the bus. // 노인은 비틀거리며 걸어갔다 The old man tottered along. / The old man walked along with tottering [unsteady / faltering] steps. // 그는 머리를 얻어맞고 비틀거리며 뒤로 물러섰다 The blow on the head sent him reeling [staggering] backward.

비틀걸음 faltering[tottering/unsteady] steps; a tottering gait. ¶~으로 걷다 walk staggeringly[with tottering steps] / reel along.

비틀다 1 (손으로) twist; give (a rope) a twist; wrench; screw; wring; wrest; distort; warp. ¶사과 꼭지를 가지에서 비틀어 따다 wrench an apple off a branch // 닭 모가지를 ~ wring a chicken's neck // 나는 그의 팔을 비틀었다 I gave his arm a twist. / I wrenched his arm. // 그가 손잡이를 세게 비틀었더니 떨어져 나갔다 He wrenched the handle off. // 장난꾸러기 아이가 인형의 팔을 비틀어 잡아뗐다 The naughty boy tore[yanked] off the doll's arm. 2 (몸을 틀다) twist; bend. ¶허리를 ~ twist one's body at the waist // 그 선수는 몸을 1회전 반 비튼 다음에 착지했다 The athlete landed after doing one and a half twists.

3 [일을 어그러지게 하다] thwart; counteract.

비틀리다 get[be] twisted[wrenched / thwarted].

비틀비틀 totteringly; staggeringly; reelingly; falteringly; waddlingly. ¶~ 걷다 stagger [shamble / dodder] along / walk with tottering steps // ~ 일어서다 stagger[totter] to one's feet / get shakily to one's feet. **비틀비틀하다** totter; stagger. ⇨˚비틀거리다

비틀어지다 1 (꼬이다) get twisted[distorted]; grow warped. ¶날씨가 가물어서 비틀어진 판자 a board warped by dry weather // 문에 부딪혀서 안경테가 비틀어졌다 I bent the frame of my glasses when I ran into the door. 2 (마음이) become perverse; get crooked. 3 (일이) go wrong[amiss]; be spoilt; be ruined.

비파(琵琶) a *bipa*; a Korean mandolin[lute].

비판(批判) (a) criticism; (a) comment; (a) critique; (a) forum (*pl.* ~s, fora). ¶자기 ~ self-criticism // 칸트의 순수[실천] 이성 Kant's Critique of Pure[Practical] Reason // 신랄한 ~ a harsh[bitter] criticism // 불공정 세제에 대한 국민의 ~ public criticism of unfair taxation. **비판하다** [비평하다] criticize (for); [논평하다] comment (on)(▶ 비평 criticism, criticize는 종종 「혹평」의 뜻으로 씀); pass judgment (upon). ¶논문을 ~ criticize [comment on] a paper // 그는 나를 부주의하다고 비판했다 He criticized me for my carelessness[being careless].

● **비판력** critical power[ability]. ¶~이 있는 독자 a critical reader. **비판 철학** critical philosophy.

비판적(批判的) critical. ¶그 문제에 대해서는 그는 ~인 입장이다 On that matter, he has taken a critical stance[position]. // 그는 내가 하는 일에 ~이다 He is critical of what I do.

비평(批評) [비판] (a) criticism; (a) critique; [논평] (a) comment; [신문·잡지 등에 실리는 단평] a notice(▶ mixed notices, rave notices처럼 복수형으로 쓰는 일이 많음). ¶문예 ~ a literary criticism // 본문[해석] ~ textual [interpretative] criticism // 그는 이 책의 ~을 내게 부탁했다 (의견을) He asked my opinion of this book. / (서평을) I was asked to review [write a review of] this book. // 이 소설은 너무 어둡다는 ~을 받았다 This novel was criticized as being too gloomy[for its gloominess]. **비평하다** [비판하다] criticize[(영) criticise] (for)(▶ that절은 쓰지 않음); [논평하다] comment (on); [서평을 쓰다] review; [감상을] remark (that / on). ¶이 작품은 비평할 가치가 없다 This work is beneath criticism[is no worth commenting on]. // 그들은 모두 이러쿵저러쿵 내 모자를 비평했다 They all commented variously on [about] my hat.

● **비평가** a critic. ⇨˚평론가(⇨˚평론) **비평안**(-眼) a critical eye. ¶~이 있다 have a critical [discerning] eye.

비폭력주의(非暴力主義) (the doctrine of) ahimsa; nonviolence. ¶~의 nonviolent (resistance).

비품(備品) 〔집합적〕 equipment; 〔부착된 것〕 fixtures; 〔비치하는 가구〕 furnishings. ¶부엌의 ~ kitchen fixtures // 사무용 ~ office equipment[appointments] // 실험실의 ~ laboratory[(구어) lab] equipment // 어학 실습실의 ~을 갖추다 equip a language laboratory.

비프스테이크 (a) steak; (영) (a) beefsteak.

비하(卑下) 〔자신을 낮춤〕 abasement; self-humbling; 〔땅이 낮음〕 low level of ground; 〔지위가 낮음〕 low standing[position]; humbleness. **비하하다** disparage oneself. ¶비하하여 humbly / modestly.

비하다(比一) compare (one thing) with[to] (another). ¶비할 수 없을 만큼 beyond (all) comparison // 나이에 비하여 for[considering] one's age[years] // 그는 비할 데 없이 건강하다 No one surpasses him in robust health. // 내 그림은 색채의 아름다움에 있어서 나의 언니의 그림에 비할 바가 못 된다 My painting cannot compete with my sister's in beauty of color. // 그의 근면에 비하여 동생은 게을러빠져서 한심스럽다 In contrast to his diligence, his younger brother is deplorably lazy. / He is diligent, while his younger brother is deplorably lazy. // 그의 이번 작품은 지난번 작품에 비해서 빈약하다 Compared with his previous work, this one is very poor.

비합리적(非合理的) irrational; unreasonable. ¶~인 사고방식 an irrational way of thinking // ~인 정책 an unreasonable policy.

비합리주의(非合理主義) irrationalism.

비합법적(非合法的) illegal; unlawful; out of order. ¶~ 행위 an illegal[unlawful] act.

비핵무장 지대(非核武裝地帶) nuclear-free zones.

비핵화(非核化) denuclearization. **비핵화하다** denuclearize (a nation / an area).

비행(非行) 〔못된 행위〕 misconduct; (문어) misdeed; misdemeanor; an evil deed; an irregularity; a malpractice; wrongdoing. ¶청소년의 ~ juvenile delinquency // ~을 저지르다 commit an irregularity / misconduct oneself // ~을 폭로하다 bring[put] (a person's) crime to light / unmask a hypocrite // 그의 ~이 우연히 드러났다 His past misdoings happened to come to light. // 그는 ~을 저질러서 해고당했다 He was dismissed for wrongdoing[misconduct].

● **비행 소년** a juvenile delinquent.

비행(飛行) a flight; flying; 〔항공〕 a plane flight; aviation; aerial navigation; air voyage. ¶고공[저공] ~ a high[low] flight // 곡예 [고등] ~ stunt (flying) / aerial acrobatics // 무사고 ~ accident-free flying / flying without an accident // 무착륙 ~ a nonstop flight // 선회 ~ a circuitous flight // 세계 일주 ~ a round-the-world flight // 시험 ~ a test[trial]

비행기

flight // 야간 ~ a night flight // 연습 ~ a training[an exercise] flight // 정기 ~ a regular air service // 정찰 ~ a scouting flight // 정체불명의 ~ 물체 an unidentified flying object / a UFO (*pl.* UFO's, ~s) // 시계가 나빠서 조종사는 계기 ~을 해야만 했다 Visibility was so bad that the pilot had to fly blind. // 이런 악천후에는 ~이 불가능하다 We cannot fly in this bad weather. **비행하다** fly (in the air); make a flight; take the air; travel by air; aviate. ¶비행하기에 적합한 비행기 airworthy craft // 우리는 1만 미터 높이로 비행할 것이다 We will be flying at an altitude of 10,000 meters.
● **비행 거리** (한 번의) a flight. **비행복** a flying dress[suit / jacket / clothes]; flying gear; a flight uniform[suit]; an aviation garment. **비행사** an aviator; a flier; a flyer; an airman; a pilot; a flying man; an aeronaut. (속어) a birdman. ¶**여류** ~ an aviatress / a woman [lady] aviator // **민간** ~ a civilian aviator // ~ **가 되다** take to the air. **비행선** an airship; a dirigible. ¶**경식**[연식] ~ a rigid[nonrigid / flexible] dirigible // **반경식** ~ a semi-rigid dirigible. **비행 속도** (an) air speed; (a) flying speed. **비행장** an airfield[airport / airstrip]; (미) an airdrome. ¶**해상** ~ a floating aerodrome.

비행기 (飛行機) [항공기] an airplane; a plane; (영) an aeroplane; (집합적) aircraft. ¶**군용** [민간] ~ a military[commercial] plane // **단엽** [복엽 / 삼엽 / 다엽] ~ a monoplane [biplane / triplane / multiplane] // **무인** ~ a pilotless plane // **수륙 양용** ~ an amphibian (plane) // **수상** ~ a seaplane / a hydroplane // **수송** ~ a transport plane // **여객** ~ a passenger[cabin] plane // **연습** ~ a training plane // **정기** ~ an airliner / (미) a clipper // **정찰용** ~ a scout plane / a reconnaissance machine // **종이** ~ a paper airplane / an airplane // **화물** ~ a goods[cargo] plane / a freighter // ~ **로 가다** go by air[by plane / in an airplane] / fly // ~ **를 타다** have a ride[go up] in an airplane / take an airplane / (오르다) get into[get aboard] an airplane / emplane / enplane // 서울에서 부산까지 ~로 갔다 I flew[took a plane] from Seoul to Busan.

비행기(를) 태우다 flatter; soft-soap; tickle (another's) vanity; say nice things (to); praise (a person) to the skies. ¶너무 비행기 태우지 마라 Spare my blushes.

비현실성 (非現實性) unreality.

비현실적 (非現實的) [실제적이 아닌] impractical; [계획 등이 실행 불가능한] impracticable; [실제하지 않는] unreal; [공상적인] fantastic. ¶~**인 사람** an impractical person // ~**인 계획** an impracticable[infeasible] plan // ~**인 생각** a fantastic idea.

비협조적 (非協調的) uncooperative.

비호 (庇護) protection; (후원) patronage; aegis; egis. ¶**부자의** ~ **아래** under the protection[patronage / egis] of a rich man / under the wing of a rich man // **아이들은 부모의** ~**를 받고 자란다** Children grow up under the protection[care] of their parents. **비호하다** [보호하다] protect; [은닉하다] shelter; shield; take (a person) under one's wings; (죄인 등을) cover; harbor.
● **비호자** a guardian; a protector.

비호같다 (飛虎—) be as quick as lightning. ¶비호같이 달리다 run like a streak (of lightning).

비화 (飛火) 1 [튀어 박히는 불똥] flying sparks (of a fire); a leap of the flames. **비화하다** flames[sparks] leap (to another place). 2 [의외의 곳으로의 영향] an effect felt in unexpected quarters. **비화하다** spread repercussions. ¶**사건이 진전됨에 따라 의외의 방면으로 비화했다** As the affair developed, its effect was felt in unexpected quarters.

비화 (秘話) a secret story[history]; a behind-the-scenes story; an untold[a suppressed] story.

비화 (悲話) a sad story; a tragic story.

비활성 기체 (非活性氣體) [화] an inert gas.

비효용 (非效用) [경] disutility.

빅뱅 the big bang; the Big Bang.

빅수 (—手) a tying move. ⇨비김수

빈객 (賓客) [점잖은 손님] a guest (of honor); an honored guest.

빈곤 (貧困) [가난] indigence; poverty; pauperism; [궁핍] need; want; destitution; [결여] lack; dearth; shortage. ¶**사상의** ~ poverty of ideas // **정치의** ~ a lack of proper government[political ingenuity] // ~**을 벗어나다** emerge from poverty // ~**에 빠지다** sink into poverty // ~**에 허덕이다** suffer extreme poverty. **빈곤하다** indigent; poor; penurious; destitute; needy. ¶**빈곤한 사람들** the poor (and needy) // **빈곤한 가정** a poor[needy] family // **빈곤해지다** be reduced to poverty // **빈곤한 가운데 자라다** be brought up in poverty.

빈국 (貧國) a poor[needy / have-not] country.

빈궁 (貧窮) indigence. ⇨빈곤

빈궁 (嬪宮) [왕세자의 아내] the wife of the crown prince; the crown princess.

빈농 (貧農) a poor peasant[farmer]; a needy peasant.

빈뇨증 (頻尿症) [의] pollakiuria.

빈대 [동] (미) a bedbug; (영) a (house-)bug. ¶~**를 잡으려고 초가삼간을 태우다** burn the barn down to get rid of the mice.

빈대떡 *bindaetteok*; a mung-bean pancake. ¶~**을 부치다** make *bindaetteok*.

빈도 (頻度) frequency. ¶**이 말은 사용** ~**가 높다** This word is very frequently used. // **이 지방에서는 지진의** ~**가 어느 정도입니까** How often[frequently] do earthquakes occur in this district?
● **빈도수** the frequency (number). ¶~**가 높은 말** a word of high frequency / a word which appears frequently.

빈둥거리다 loaf[idle / laze / dawdle / snooze] one's time away; loaf; idle; loiter; lounge; be on the loaf; lead an idle life. ¶**빈둥거리고 있을 때가 아니다** This is no time for idling. // **너를 하루 종일 빈둥거리게 놓아두지는 않겠다** I won't have you doing nothing[lying about] all day. // **나는 하루 종일 빈둥거리고 있었다** I just loafed around all day[idled away the day].

빈둥빈둥 [빈둥거리는 모양] idly; lazily; dawdlingly; doing nothing; (구어) on the bum. ¶~ **놀다** idle one's time away / lie about idly / just lie around // **그는** ~ **지내고 있다** He is idling his [time] away. **빈둥빈둥하다** loaf one's time away. ⇨빈둥거리다

빈들거리다 loaf one's time away. ⇨빈둥거리

다
빈들빈들 idly; lazily. ⇨"빈둥빈둥
빈말 〔실속이 없는 말〕 (an) idle[empty] talk; an empty promise; empty prattle; empty [hollow/vain] words; lip service. ¶~로 하는 칭찬 empty words of praise / empty [hollow/idle/mere] compliments / flummery // ~뿐인 사람 a man of words and no action / someone who is all talk. **빈말하다** talk idly; make empty promises. ¶빈말하는 사람 a windy speaker / an idle talker.
빈민(貧民) poor people; the poor; paupers; the needy; the indigent; poverty-stricken people. ¶~을 구제하다 relieve[give aid to] the poor[needy].
● **빈민가** a slum. **빈민 구제** the relief of the poor (and needy); poor relief. **빈민굴** a slum; 〔집합적〕 the slum[poor] quarters; the slums. ¶~의 사람들 inhabitants of the slum quarters / slummers // ~을 없애다 clear [wipe out] slums.
빈발(頻發) frequent occurrence; frequency. ¶~지진 an earthquake swarm // 비행기 사고의 ~ the (high) frequency of aviation accidents / frequent airplane accidents. **빈발하다** occur frequently; be frequent; often happen. ¶교통사고가 빈발한다 Traffic accidents occur very often. // 이 지방에서는 지진이 빈발한다 A cluster[series] of earthquakes are frequent [occur frequently] in this region.
빈방(-房) 〔비어 있는〕 a vacancy; a vacant room; 〔사람이 없는〕 an empty room; 〔셋방〕 a room for rent[〔영〕 to let]. ¶~ 없음 (호텔 입구에 붙는 게시) No vacancies. //~이 있습니까 Do you have an empty room?
빈번하다(頻繁-) frequent; incessant. ¶교통이 빈번한 거리 a busy[bustling] street / a street with heavy traffic // 빈번한 출현 frequent appearance // 요즈음 시내 각처에서 교통사고가 ~ These days traffic accidents are frequently reported from various parts of the city. **빈번히** frequently; at frequent[short] intervals; very often; incessantly. ¶~ 일어나는 일 a matter of frequent occurrence //~ 사용하다 use frequently / put (a thing) to frequent use // 최근에 사고가 ~ 일어나고 있다 There have been frequent[(구어) a good many] accidents recently. // 이 무렵에는 화재가 ~ 일어난다 Fires are frequent at this time of (the) year.
빈 볼 〔야구〕 (throw) a bean ball. ¶~을 먹이다 bean (a batter).
빈부(貧富) 〔가난과 부유〕 wealth and poverty. ¶~의 차별 없이 rich and poor alike / whether they are rich or poor // ~의 격차를 좁히다 narrow the distinction in wealth between the wealthy and the poor // ~의 차가 심하다 There is a tremendous gap between the rich and the poor.
빈사(瀕死) a dying condition; (being on) the brink of death. ¶~ 상태의 환자 a dying [moribund] patient / a patient on the verge of death[on the deathbed] // ~ 상태에 있다 be dying / be in dying condition / be at the point of death / be on the verge of death / lie at death's door // 우리 회사는 지금 ~ 상태에 있다 Our company is facing a crisis that threatens its survival. / Our company is on the brink of bankruptcy.
빈상(貧相) a countenance that bespeaks poverty; 〔궁상맞은 모습〕 a meager[haggard] look[face]. ¶~인 poor-looking / seedy / unprepossessing // 그는 얼굴이 ~이다 He looks seedy.
빈소(殯所) a mortuary; a room where a coffin is placed until the funeral day.
빈속 an empty stomach. ¶~에 술을 마시다 have a drink on an empty stomach // 나는 ~으로는 일할 수 없다 I cannot work on an empty stomach.
빈손 empty hands. ¶~으로 with empty hands / without taking any present (with one) // 탐색에서 ~으로 돌아오다 return from a quest empty-handed // 그는 ~으로 나갔다 He went out empty-handed. / He wasn't carrying anything when he went out. // 그의 집을 ~으로 찾아갈 수는 없다 I can't call on him without taking a present. // 그는 물건을 사러 갔다가 ~으로 돌아왔다 He went shopping but came home empty-handed.
빈약하다(貧弱-) poor; scanty; meager; limited. ¶빈약한 체격 a poor physique / a feeble body // 빈약한 남자 an insignificant-looking man // 내용이 빈약한 책 a book poor in substance // 그는 차림새는 빈약했으나 품위가 있었다 He looked dignified despite his shabby clothes. // 그의 연설 내용은 빈약했다 His speech was poor[meager] in content. // 그의 상상력은 아주 빈약했다 He had little [a poor] imagination. // 나의 빈약한 지식으로는 이 현상을 해석할 수 없다 I cannot explain this phenomenon with my meager[poor / scanty] knowledge.
빈자(貧者) a poor man; the poor; needy [indigent] people; a pauper. ¶구호를 기다리는 ~ needy people waiting for relief.
빈자리 1 〔빈 좌석〕 a vacant[an unoccupied] seat; 〔여지〕 room. ¶~가 눈에 띄었다 There were a conspicuous number of vacant seats. // 아직도 ~가 남아 있습니까 Are there still seats available? // ~가 전혀 없다 All the seats are taken. / There are no vacant seats. // 지금은 ~가 더러 있다 There are some empty[unoccupied] seats now. / Some seats are available now.
2 〔공석〕 a vacancy; an opening; a vacant post. ¶~가 나다 cause a vacancy / a vacancy occurs // 너의 회사에 ~가 있느냐 Is there an opening[vacancy] in your firm? // 그가 떠난 ~를 매우지 않으면 일이 진척되지 않는다 The work won't make any headway unless the vacancy[vacant post] he left is filled.
빈정거리다 〔놀리다〕 poke fun at; make fun [sport] of; tease; banter; ridicule; gibe; 〔비꼬다〕 speak ironically; make cynical[caustic / sarcastic] remarks; be cynical[sarcastic] (about); insinuate; 〔구어〕 take a dig (at). ¶그는 빈정거리며 그렇게 말했다 He said it sarcastically. // 그의 빈정거리는 말투가 비위에 거슬린다 His sarcastic remarks jarred on my nerves. // 그는 충고하는 체하면서 나를 빈정거렸다 He took a few digs at me under the pretext of giving advice. // 이것은 현대의 세상을 빈정거리는 희극이다 This is a comedy satirizing the state of the present-day world.
빈주먹 an empty[bare] hand; naked fists. ¶~으로 empty-handed[barehanded] / without funds / with one's bare[naked] hands[fists] // ~으로 장사를 시작하다 start a

business without means / go into business with almost nothing // 그는 ~으로 시작해서 엄청난 재산을 모았다 Having nothing to start with, he has made a colossal fortune. / He has made an enormous fortune starting with nothing.

빈집 [비어 있는 집] a vacant [an empty] house; [사람이 살지 않는 집] an unoccupied [an uninhabited / untenanted] house. ¶~인 채로 있다 be left vacant / remain empty // 이 집은 ~이다 No one is living in this house now. / This house is at present vacant. // 그 집은 얼마 전부터 ~으로 있다 The house has been standing empty for some time.

빈촌(貧村) a poor village.

빈축(嚬蹙·顰蹙) a frown; a scowl; a grimace. ¶그의 무례한 태도는 출석자의 ~을 샀다 His rude manner was frowned at [on] by those present. // 그 법관의 행위는 세상 사람들의 ~을 샀다 The judge's conduct disgusted people. / People were scandalized by the judge's conduct. **빈축하다** frown [scowl] at [on]; look on (something) with scorn [disdain]; be scandalized (at). ¶빈축할 만한 scandalous / despicable / disdainful / objectionable.

빈칸 a blank column; a blank (space). ¶~을 메우다 fill in a blank / fill up a space / fill a vacancy // ~을 남겨 두다 leave a blank [space / margin] // 모르는 단어는 모두 ~으로 남겨 두다 leave blanks for all the words one does not know // 다음 문장의 ~을 메우시오 Fill in the blanks in the following sentence.

빈탕 1 (과실의) an empty nut. ¶그 호두는 ~이었다 The walnut was empty in the shell. **2** [텅 빔] emptiness; vacancy. ¶그 상자는 ~이다 The box contains nothing. // 지갑을 보니 ~이었다 I found my purse empty. / There was not a farthing in my purse.

빈털터리 a penniless person; a fellow without a penny; a person destitute of money. ¶~가 되다 go [be] clean broke / become quite penniless // ~에서 다시 시작하다 (구어) start afresh from scratch // 저 녀석은 언제나 ~이다 That fellow is always penniless [(구어) flat broke / (구어) dead broke]. // 나는 오늘 은 ~이다 I am broke today. / I haven't got a penny today. // 그는 사업에 실패하여 ~가 되었다 He lost [was stripped of] all his property when his business failed.

빈틈 1 [비어 있는 사이] a gap; an opening; a crack; a chink; an aperture; [여백] a space; a blank; [여지] room; space. ¶~을 메우다 fill [stop] a gap / fill in a blank / fill up a space // 여기에 ~을 지금 더 남겨 놓는 것이 좋다 There should be a little more space left (open) here. **2** [허술하거나 부족한 점] unpreparedness; a blind side; an unguarded moment [point]; an opening (for attack); [부주의] inattention; carelessness; imprudence; unwatchfulness; incautiousness; [방심] a slip; an oversight; inadvertence. ¶무슨 일이건 ~이 없다 know what one is about / 돈벌이에 ~이 없다 be keen on gain / be alert to moneymaking // 장사에 ~이 없다 have a keen eye to one's business / be shrewd in business // ~을 보이다 lay oneself open to attack / stand at open guard // ~을 노리다 watch for an unguarded moment / try to catch (a person) off his guard // 그는 매사에 ~이 없다 He is smart in all things. / He does everything neatly. // 그는 ~을 보이지 않으려고 잔뜩 긴장하고 있다 He is straining every nerve to stay on the alert.

빈틈없다 1 [비어 있는 사이가 없다] close; compact; leave no space (between them). **빈틈없이** closely; compactly; leaving no space (between them). ¶~ 채워 넣다 pack [crowd] to the full / fill to the utmost (capacity) // ~ 들어차 있다 be packed to the full / be chockfull / be crammed (with) / (승객 등이) be packed [jammed] like sardines. **2** [허술한 부분이 없다] shrewd; smart; sharp; clever; knowing; alert; canny; cunning; keen; tactful; [꼼꼼하다] attentive (to details); careful; cautious; wide-awake; [사려 깊다] thoughtful; considerate; circumspect; [신중하다] scrupulous; prudent; [철저하다] throughout. ¶빈틈없는 사람 a shrewd [sharp] fellow / a knowing man // 빈틈없는 방비 an airtight defense // 빈틈없는 서류 a watertight document // 그는 빈틈없는 사람이다 He is a man of scrupulous care. / He is attentive [careful] even to the (minutest) details. **빈틈없이** shrewdly; cannily; smartly; carefully; cautiously; cleverly; scrupulously. ¶~ 경계[감시]하다 keep a sharp watch [lookout] // ~ 간호하다 nurse (a person) with the best of care.

빈한하다(貧寒—) destitute; poverty-stricken; indigent; needy; penurious. ¶빈한한 살림 narrow [straitened / needy] circumstance // 빈한하게 살다 live in poverty / lead an indigent life / be badly off // 빈한한 집에 태어나다 be born poor [in a poor family].

빈혈(貧血) poverty of blood; [의] an(a)emia. 뇌~ cerebral anemia // 악성 ~ pernicious anemia // ~이 되다 become anemic / be impoverished [drained] of blood // ~을 일으키다 have an attack of anemia.

빌다 1 [구걸하다] beg; ask; [간청하다] solicit; plead (for); appeal (for). ¶밥을 ~ beg one's bread / beg food // 목숨을 살려 달라고 ~ beg [plead / appeal] for one's life / beg one's life // 그는 도와 달라고 두 손 모아 빌었다 He put his hands together in supplication and begged me for help. **2** [기원하다] pray (to God); invoke; supplicate; wish; entreat. ¶두 손 모아 ~ pray with folded [joined] hands // (병의) 쾌유를 ~ pray (to God) for (a person's) recovery // 남편이 무사하기를 ~ pray to God for the safety of one's husband // 행운[성공]을 빌니다 I wish you good luck [success]. // 부디 그의 병이 낫기를 빈다 May he recover from his illness! // 그 소식이 진실이 아니기를 빈다 I wish the news may not prove true. // 그는 하느님의 은총을 열심히 빌었다 He prayed fervently for a divine favor. **3** [사과하다] ask [beg] (a person's) pardon; apologize (a person) for; make [beg] an apology (to a person). ¶용서를 ~ beg [implore] forgiveness / ask [seek] (for) forgiveness // 손이 닳도록 ~ humbly beg (a person's) pardon / be profuse in one's apologies // 무릎 꿇고 ~ beg (a person's) pardon on one's knees // 그는 아버지한테 무릎 꿇고 자기의 잘못을 빌었다 He got down on his knees and apologized to his father for his misbehavior.

빌딩 a building; an office building.

빌레몬서(-書) [성] (The Epistle of St. Paul to) Philemon(약어 Philem).

빌리다 1 borrow; (미) rent; (영) hire; lease; charter.(▶ borrow가 주로 무료로 돈·책·펜·자동차 등을 빌리는 것인 데 반해, rent / hire 는 자동차·집·방 등을, lease는 땅·빌딩 등을, charter는 버스·비행기·배 등을 유료로 빌리는 것을 가리킴) ¶빌려 주는 사람 a lender // 월 10만 원에 집을 빌려 주다 rent[let] a house at[for] 100,000 won a month // 토지를 빌려 주다 lease[rent] land // 보트를 빌려 줄 수 있습니까 (미) Will you rent me a boat? / (영) Can I hire a boat? // 그녀는 학생에게 방을 빌려 주어 생계를 유지하고 있다 She makes a living by leasing[renting] rooms to students. // 나는 자전거를 시간제로[1시간 2,000원에] 빌렸다 I rented[(영) hired] a bicycle by the hour[for two thousand won an hour]. // 나는 그에게서 돈을 빌렸다 I borrowed some money from him. // 나는 도서관에 책을 빌리러 갔다 I went to the library to borrow[(미) check out] a book. // 은행은 이자를 받고 돈을 빌려 준다 A bank lends money at interest. // 담뱃불 좀 빌려 주시오 May I have a light, please? / Please give me a light. // 5만 원을 빌려 줄 수 있는지 그에게 부탁해 보겠다 I will ask him for a loan of[to lend me] fifty thousand won.
2 [남의 도움을 받다] have[get] (a person's) help[aid]; enlist the help of; employ (a person's) assistance. ¶다수의 힘을 빌려서 on the strength of majority // 그의 말을 빌리면 그것은 어린애 장난과 같은 것이다 In[To use] his words, it is no more than child's play. // 그는 술의 힘을 빌려서 그녀에게 프로포즈했다 Finding courage in what he had drunk, he proposed to her. // 그의 이름을 발기인의 한 사람으로 빌리고 싶다 I'd like to use his name on the list of promoters.

빌립보서(-書) [성] The Epistle of St. Paul (the Apostle) to the Philippians; Philippians(약어 Phil.).

빌미 [불행이나 탈이 생기는 원인] a curse; the cause of evil[trouble]. ¶~가 붙다 inflict a calamity[an evil] on / haunt.

빌미잡다 [빌미로 삼다] attribute (a calamity) to; blame (for calamity).

빌붙다 [들러붙어서 아첨하고 알랑거리다] flatter (a person); fawn upon (a person); play up to (a person); curry favor with (men of influence); grovel; ingratiate oneself with. ¶당대의 권력자에게 ~ curry favor [ingratiate oneself] with those in authority [power] of the day.

빌어먹다 beg (one's bread); go begging; live as a beggar; (미국 구어) panhandle. ¶빌어먹는 신세 beggary / mendicancy // 빌어먹고 다니다 beg from door to door // 빌어먹는 한이 있더라도 even if one would be reduced [brought] to beggary[begging].

빌어먹는 놈이 콩밥을 마다할까(속담) Beggars must[should] be no choosers.

빌어먹을 Damn ……!; Damn[Hang / Darn / Confound] it!; (미) Gosh! ¶이 ~ 놈아 Confound[Damn] you! // ~ 비가 오네 Damn the rain! // 저 ~ 놈이 그랬어 He has done it, bad luck to him. // ~ 시험 To hell with exams!

빔 a beam.

빗 a comb. ¶휴대용 ~ a pocket comb // 얼레 [참]~ a wide-tooth[fine-tooth] comb // ~으로 빗다 comb (down) (one's hair); pull [run] a comb through (one's hair).

빗- [잘못] mis-; mistaken; wrong; [비뚤어진] crooked; [비스듬히] sidewise; aslant.

빗각(-角) [수] an oblique angle.

빗금 an oblique (line). ⇨ˮ사선

빗기다 1 [빗어 주다] comb (a person's hair). ¶동생의 머리를 ~ comb one's (younger) sister's hair. 2 [빗게 하다] get someone to comb (a person's hair). ¶하녀에게 개털을 ~ have the maid comb the dog.

빗나가다 (총알 등이) miss; go wide[astray]; miss the mark; dart aside; (계획 등이) go wrong[amiss]; miscarry; fail; (이야기 등이) deviate[diverge] (from); wander (from). ¶계획이 ~ be baffled in one's design // 과녁에서 ~ miss the target / go wide of the mark // 예상이 ~ (사물이) fall short of one's expectations / (사람이) be disappointed of one's expectations // 이야기가 ~ wander [digress] from the subject // 화살이 빗나갔다 The arrow missed the mark. // 일기 예보가 빗나갔다 The weather forecast proved wrong. // 우리의 코스가 북쪽으로 빗나간 것 같다 We seem to have swerved north from our course. // 네 말은 좀 빗나간 것 같다 What you say seems to be a little off[rather beside] the point. // 그의 추측은 빗나갔다 His guess was wide of[missed] the mark.

빗다 comb (a person's hair); pull[run] a comb through (a person's hair); (양털·삼 등을) card. ¶잘 빗은 머리 well-combed hair // 빗지 않은 머리 unkempt[uncombed] hair // 그는 흰머리를 아주 조심스럽게 빗었다 He combed his white hair very carefully. // 그녀는 흐트러진 머리를 빗어 올렸다 She combed up her loose[stray] hair.

빗대다 1 [빙 둘러서 말하다] have a sly dig (at); make an insinuating remark (at); hint (obliquely) at; give an indirect cut; insinuate; satirize; (영) satirise. ¶그의 말은 실은 나를 빗대어 하는 말이다 He is really talking at me. / His remark is intended for me [a cut at me / directed at me]. // 그가 누구를 빗대어 말하고 있었는지를 나중에 알았다 I finally realized to whom he was alluding. // 그는 자네가 파렴치하다고 빗대어 말하고 있다 He insinuates that you have no sense of shame. 2 [틀리게 대다] misstate; make a false statement; perjure. ¶사실[이름]을 ~ give a false fact[name].

빗돌(碑-) a stone monument; a monumental stone.

빗맞다 1 [목표와 다른 곳에 맞다] miss the mark; go wide of the mark; glance off. ¶어뢰가 빗맞았다 The torpedo missed its mark [went wild]. // 그는 연방 쏘았으나 모두 빗맞았다 He fired by volley, but all the shots missed. 2 [뜻한 일이 잘못되다] go wrong [awry / amiss]; miscarry; backfire; misfire; be baffled.

빗면(-面) [수] an inclined[oblique] plane.

빗물 rainwater. ¶흐르는 ~ runoff // ~이 괸 곳 a rainpool.

빗발 streaks of rain; lines traced by rain as it falls. ¶~이 날리기 시작했다 It began to rain.

빗발치다

/ It started raining. // ~이 차차 빨라졌다 The beat of the rain gradually quickened. // ~이 굵어졌다 It's raining hard now. // ~이 가늘어졌다 The rain has eased off[let up]. / It is raining less hard.

빗발치다 rain; hail; shower like hail; come thick and fast; shower (arrows) upon. ¶빗발치듯 thick and fast (like streaks of rain) / in (great) streaks / in rain [torrents / showers] / like rain (and hail) // 빗발치는 질문 a volley[barrage] of questions // 빗발치는 화살 a rain [hail / shower] of arrows // 빗발치는 비난을 받다 be subjected to clamorous censure [a storm of criticism].

빗방울 a raindrop. ¶~이 듣는다[떨어진다] Raindrops fall.

빗변(-邊) [수] an oblique side; (직각 삼각형의) a hypotenuse; (삼각형의) a leg.

빗살 the teeth of a comb. ¶~이 한 개 빠져 있다 One tooth of the comb is gone.

빗소리 the sound of rain; rain.

빗속 (in) the midst of rain. ¶~을 산책하다 take a walk in the rain // 우리는 ~을 계속 걸어갔다 We walked on in the rain.

빗자루 a broom. ⇨ "비²"

빗장 a bolt; a crossbar; a bar. ¶~을 지른 문 a bolted gate // 문에 ~을 지르다 bar the gate // 문의 ~을 벗기다 unbar the gate.

빗장뼈 [생] the collarbone; the clavicle.

빗줄기 great streaks[sheets] of rain. ¶~가 세차다 It pours down. / It rains cats and dogs.

빗질 combing (one's hair). **빗질하다** comb (one's hair). ¶엉킨 머리카락을 빗질하여 풀다 comb[brush] the knots[tangles] out of one's hair.

빙¹ [한 바퀴 도는 모양] round; (미) around. ¶목을 ~ 돌리는 운동 a neck rotation exercise // 섬을 한 바퀴 ~ 돌다 go round the island / make a tour of the island // 한쪽 뒤꿈치로 ~ 돌다 spin on one's heel // 공원을 ~ 돌다 take a turn in the park // 먼 길로 ~ 둘러 가다 go by a roundabout way // 그는 사방을 ~ 둘러보았다 He looked all about him. / He looked around in every direction.

2[둘러싼 모양] (all) round; in a circle. ¶~ 둘러싸다 surround (a person / a thing) / encircle / shut in on all sides // 둘러앉다 sit in a circle // 구경꾼에게 ~ 둘러싸이다 be surrounded[crowded round] by spectators.

3[아찔해지는 모양]. ¶머리가 ~ 돌다 get dizzy [giddy] / one's head swims [spins] / be stunned(얻어맞고) // 그는 턱을 얻어맞고 잠시 정신이 ~ 돌았다 The blow to his jaw stunned him for a moment.

4[글썽해지는 모양]. ¶눈물이 ~ 돌다 be suddenly moved to tears.

빙고 [숫자가 적힌 공이나 카드로 하는 놀이] bingo; beano.

빙고(氷庫) an icehouse; a storehouse for ice.

빙과(氷菓) ices. ⇨ "얼음과자(⇨얼음)"

빙그레 with a smile; smilingly; beamingly; with a beaming face. ¶~ 웃다 smile / beam (upon a person) / beam with[break into] a smile.

빙그르르 (turn / skate / glide) around smoothly. ¶빙판을 한 바퀴 ~ 돌다 take a smooth turn around the ice // 뒤꿈치로 ~ 돌다 spin on one's heel // 비행기는 ~ 맴돌면서 추락했다 The plane went into a spin[tailspin] and crashed. // 나뭇잎이 가을 바람에 ~ 돌며 떨어졌다 The leaves came whirling down in the autumn wind.

빙글거리다 smile (at a person); beam (upon a person).

빙글빙글¹ [도는 모양] round and round smoothly. ¶~ 돌다[돌리다] turn round and round / spin / twirl // 접시를 ~ 돌리다 spin a plate // 팔을 ~ 돌리다 wave one's arm around // 풍차가 ~ 돌기 시작했다 The windmill began to revolve [turn]. // 천장이 ~ 도는 것 같았다 I felt the room spin(ning). / I felt as if the whole room were whirling round and round. // 모자가 강풍에 ~ 날아올랐다 My hat whirled up in the strong wind.

빙글빙글² [웃는 모양] smilingly; beamingly; with a smile. ¶~ 웃는 얼굴 a beaming [smiling] face / a radiant look // ~ 웃다 smile (at) / beam (at) / be all smiles. **빙글빙글하다** smile (at a person). ⇨ "빙글거리다"

빙긋거리다 smile (at a person). ⇨ "빙글거리다"

빙긋(이) with a smile. ⇨ "빙그레"

빙모(聘母) one's wife's mother. ⇨ "장모"

빙벽(氷壁) (산의) an ice ridge; an ice wall [cliff]; a wall of ice.

빙부(聘父) one's wife's father. ⇨ "장인(丈人)"

빙빙 round and round; repeatedly. ¶~ 돌다 go [turn] round and round / circle (round) / turn and turn about / whirl / wheel // 한순간 눈앞에서 물건이 ~ 도는 것 같았다 For a moment things swam before [in front of] my eyes. // 자리에서 일어서자 나는 머리가 ~ 돌았다 My head swam [I felt dizzy] when I stood up.

빙산(氷山) an iceberg; an ice floe; a floating mass of ice. ¶~의 일각에 지나지 않다 be but the visible peak on an iceberg / be only the (visible) tip of an [a submerged] iceberg / be nothing but the small part of the iceberg that shows above the surface // 이번의 밀수 사건은 ~의 일각에 지나지 않는다 This smuggling case is just the tip of the iceberg.

빙상(氷上) ¶~의[에서] on the ice.
● **빙상 경기** ice sports.

빙설(氷雪) ice and snow. ¶지난주 일요일부터 마을은 ~에 갇혀 있다 The village has been shut [cut] off from the outside world by ice and snow since last Sunday.

빙수(氷水) **1** iced water. ⇨ "얼음물(⇨얼음)" **2** [잘게 부순 얼음에 설탕과 감미료를 섞은 음료] shaved ice with syrup. ¶~ 한 그릇 a bowl of shaved ice with sugar syrup.

빙어 [동] a smelt; a pond smelt; a sparling.

빙원(氷原) an ice field; (해상의) a floe; an ice floe.

빙자(憑藉) **1** [의지] dependence; reliance; leaning (on). **빙자하다** depend [rely] (on); lean (on); be dependent (upon); rely (on one's connection); hide behind the authority of. ¶법률을 빙자하여 on the strength [authority] of law // 아버지의 세도를 빙자하여 거드럭거리다 give oneself airs under the shelter of one's father's influence.

2 [핑계] a pretext; a pretence; an excuse; a cloak; a plea; a feint. **빙자하다** make a pretence [pretext] of; make an excuse of; make a plea of; plead; find an excuse in. ¶…을 빙자하여 under cover [the cloak / the mask]

(of) / on[under] the pretext[plea / pretence] (of)//취직 알선을 빙자하여 사기하다 swindle (a person) out of money under the pretext of finding employment/결혼을 빙자하여 과부의 돈을 뜯다 swindle money out of a widow under promise of marriage.
빙장(聘丈) one's wife's father. ⇨°장인(丈人)
빙점(氷點) [물] the freezing point. ⇨°어는점 ¶~하(下)의 subzero (winter) / below-zero (temperature) / below the freezing point//온도계는 ~하 10도였다 The mercury stood at 10° below (the) freezing point.//온도는 ~하 3도로 내려갔다 The temperature dropped [sank] to −3℃.(▶ minus three degree centigrade로 읽음)
빙초산(氷醋酸) [화] glacial acetic acid.
빙충맞다 clumsy; dull-witted; heavy; stupid and timid; thickheaded; lumbering.
빙충이 a thick-witted[dull-headed] person; a dolt; a lubber; a stupid and bashful person; a clumsy fellow; (구어) a saphead; (미국 구어) a gawk; a milksop.
빙탄(氷炭) [부조화] incompatibility; discord; contradiction.
빙탄불상용(-不相容) be as irreconcilable as oil and water; agree like cats and dogs; be contradictory [antagonistic] and water; agree like cats and dogs; be contradictory [antagonistic] to each other.
빙판(氷板) an icy road[place]; a frozen road; (the) ice.
빙하(氷河) 1 [얼어붙은 강] an icebound river. 2 [지] a glacier. ¶~의 glacial// ~ 전기의 preglacial// ~ 후기의 postglacial.
● **빙하기** a glacial epoch; the ice age. **빙하 시대** the ice age; the glacial age[period]. **빙하 작용** glaciation; glacial action.
빙해(氷海) a frozen sea; icy waters.
빚 1 [남에게 갚아야 할 돈] a debt; a loan; liabilities; what one owes. ¶엄청난 ~ a heap of debts / a mammoth debt//이자 없는 ~ a passive debt//회수 가망 없는 ~ a bad debt // 노름 ~ a gambling debt / a debt of honor // ~이 있다 be in debt (to / with) / have a debt to pay / owe (a person) money // ~이 없다 be out of debt / be free from[of] debt(s) // ~을 부탁하다 ask (a person) for loan // ~을 갚다 pay[repay / discharge] one's debts // ~을 청산하다 clear (up) one's debts / clear [pay] off one's debts / free [clear] oneself from debts // ~을 떼어먹고 달아나다 run away from one's debts / bilk[jump] (a creditor / one's debt) // ~으로 꼼짝 못하다 be deeply[over head and ears / up to the ears] in debt / be immersed [sunk deeply] in debt // ~으로 살아가다 live on borrowed money // 나는 그에게 ~이 있다 I am in debt to him // 나는 숙부에게 100만 원의 ~이 있다 I owe my uncle a million won.//그는 ~을 떼어먹었다 He refused to pay his debts. / He welshed on his debts.
2 [남에게 입은 은혜]. ¶당신에게는 많은 ~을 지고 있습니다 I am much indebted to you.// 그 일로 그 사람에게 큰 ~을 지게 되었다 I put myself under a great obligation to him because of that matter.//은인에게 ~을 갚지 않으면 안 된다 I must repay my benefactor for his kindness.
빚 주고 뺨 맞기(속담) having good repayed with evil; lending money and getting slapped.
빚(을) 놓다 lend (out) money; (미) loan (a person) money. ¶고리로 ~ lend money at a high rate of interest / practice usury.
빚(을) 주다 lend out money; make loans; run a moneylending business.
● **빚 독촉** a dun; a demand for (the) payment of a debt.
빚내다 borrow money (from); get[float] a loan; obtain a loan (from). ¶집을 담보로 ~ raise[borrow] money on one's house//그는 친구에게서 200만 원을 빚냈다 He borrowed 2,000,000 won from a friend of his.
빚다 1 (술을) brew; ferment; distil. ¶술을 ~ brew rice wine//라이보리로 위스키를 빚는다 Some whiskey is made from rye. 2 (송편 등을) shape dough for (*songpyeon*); roll into balls (as dumplings). ¶떡을 ~ shape dough for *tteok*//만두를[송편을] ~ make dumplings[*songpyeon*]. 3 (어떤 부정적인 사태를) bring about[on]; give rise to; cause; breed; engender. ¶분쟁을 ~ give rise to a dispute//물의를 ~ evoke much criticism / raise a scandal.
빚돈 a loan; a debt; borrowed money. ¶~을 내다 make a loan//나는 한 푼의 ~도 없다 I owe nothing to any one. / I owe no one.
빚쟁이 [채권자] a creditor; [수금원] a (bill) collector; [채귀(債鬼)] a dun; [고리대금업자] a usurer; a money lender; (미국 속어) a loan shark. ¶~에게 시달리다 be hounded by one's creditors / be dunned (for payment of a debt) / be tormented[pressed / (구어) hounded] by creditors.
빚지다 fall[run / get] into debt; contract [incur] a debt[loan]; owe. ¶많이 ~ make a lot of debts//빚지고 달아나다 run away leaving one's debt unpaid / bilk one's debt [bill]//그는 여러 사람에게 빚지고 있다 He owes money to many people.

빛 1 [광명] (a) light; [광선] a ray; a beam; [섬광] a flash; a gleam(어둠 속의); [광휘] a luster; radiance; twinkle(별의); a sparkle(보석 등); a glitter; (희미한) a glimmer. ¶달 ~ the light of the moon / moonlight//석양~ the glow of the sunset//별 ~ the twinkle of a star / starlight//햇 ~ the light of the sun / sunshine / sunlight//개똥벌레의 ~ the glow of a firefly//밝은 ~ bright light//희미한 ~ dim[feeble / faint] light / glimmer//진주의 ~ the luster of a pearl//다이아몬드의 ~ the brilliance of a diamond//칼의 차가운 ~ the cold glitter of a sword// ~의 굴절[간섭 / 반사 / 분산 / 산란 / 투과 / 흡수] refraction [interference / reflection / dispersion / scattering / transmission / absorption] of light// ~의 속도 the speed of light// ~의 전자설 the electromagnetic theory of light// ~이 잘 드는 방 a sunny room// ~이 들어오게 하다 let in light / admit light// ~을 발하다 emit [give out] light / send out rays of light / radiate // ~을 발하는 물체 a luminous body//수면에서는 ~이 번쩍번쩍 반사하고 있었다 There was a dazzling reflection coming from the water.
2 [물질·물체가 나타내는 색] a color; a hue; a tint; a shade; a tinge. ¶가을~ autumnal tints//밝은[어두운] ~ a delicate[soft] color //푸른 기가 도는 붉은~ red of[with] a blue tint//짙은[옅은] ~ a deep[light] color// ~의 배합 a color scheme// ~의 조화 color

빛깔

harmony∥…한 ~을 띠다 be tinted[tinged] with (crimson)∥~이 바래다 fade / discolor ∥~이 변하다 change color / discolor∥이 천은 ~이 바래지 않는다 This cloth holds dye well.

3 [안색·태도] complexion; color; a look; an expression; an air; a sign; a mark; an indication. ¶실망의 ~ a look of disappointment ∥우려의 ~ the imprint of anxiety on one's face∥싫어하는 ~ 도 없이 without (any appearance of) reluctance∥무서워하는 ~ 없이 without (showing) any (outward) sign of fear∥피로한 ~ 을 보이지 않다 show no trace of fatigue∥그의 얼굴에 당황하고 있는 ~ 이 보였다 I observed marks of confusion in his face.∥그녀의 얼굴에 실망의 ~이 떠올랐다 Signs of disappointment appeared on her face.

4 [희망] hope; a bright future[prospect]. ¶희망의 ~ a ray[gleam] of hope∥세상의 ~ [그리스도] the Light of the World∥어둠 속에서 ~을 발견하다 see the silver lining in the dark cloud∥~은 동방에서 Light from the East.∥그 발견은 그 문제의 해명에 ~을 던질 것이다 This discovery may throw[shed] some light on the problem.

5 [공인·실현]. ¶~을 못 보고 있는 작가 an obscure[unacknowledged] writer∥(계획 등이) ~을 보게 되다 be realized / materialized∥[실현되다] see the light of day∥세상에서 ~을 못 보다 be obscure / be little known in the world.

빛 좋은 개살구 a gimcrack; a trumpery; window dressing.

빛깔 a color; a hue; a shade; a tint; a tinge(색조). ¶머리 ~ hair color∥동물의 털 ~ fur color∥~을 가장 좋아하는 one's favorite color∥서로 잘 어울리는 ~ harmonizing colors∥여러 가지 ~로[의] in various colors∥~을 넣은[넣이] in color(s)∥~을 칠하다 color / paint∥~을 입히다 color / tint / tinge∥밝은 ~로 그리다 paint in bright[glowing] colors∥~이 잘 나왔다 The color has come out well.

빛나다 1 [비치다·번쩍이다] shine; be bright[brilliant]; be radiant; be luminous; glitter(금은 등이); glimmer(희미하게); gleam(번쩍); glisten(반사하여); glint; beam; twinkle(별이); sparkle(보석 등이); [번득이다] flash; [윤이 나다] be lustrous[glossy]. ¶하늘에 빛나는 별 twinkling stars in the sky / stars sparkling in the heavens∥기쁨에 빛나는 눈 eyes sparkling with joy[delight]∥반짝반짝 ~ glitter / dazzle∥달이 밝게 빛나고 있었다 The moon was shining brightly.∥번개가 하늘을 가로질러 빛났다 Lightening flashed across the sky.∥그녀의 다이아몬드가 밝은 빛을 받아 빛났다 Her diamonds sparkled in the bright light.∥빛나는 것이라고 다 금은 아니다 All is not gold that glitters.

2 [영광이 드러나다] be glorious[splendid]; shine brilliantly. ¶빛나는 장래 promising future / bright prospects∥빛나는 ~ 명성 a shining[brilliant] reputation∥청사에 길이 ~ remain long[immortal] in history / go down[shine forth] in history∥그는 영예에 빛나는 업적을 이루었다 His was glorious[splendid] achievement.∥그는 마라톤으로 빛나는 기록을 세웠다 He set a brilliant record in the marathon.

3 [돋보이다] look better[to advantage]; shine (among / amid); be prominent; be outstanding; be distinguished; cut a figure (among / with). ¶교사로서 ~ shine as a teacher∥그녀는 신인 중에서 빛나는 존재이다 She shines[stands out] among the newcomers[new faces / beginners].

빛내다 [빛나게 하다] light up; make (a thing) shine; brighten; [광을 내다] luster; give luster (to); gloss; glaze; polish up; burnish; [영광스럽게 하다] bring glory[fame / distinction] to; glorify. ¶국위를 ~ enhance (the) national prestige / bring glory to one's country∥이름을 ~ make the name illustrious / win (international) fame / immortalize one's name.

빛살 rays of light.

빠각 creaking; squeaking. ⇨ 바각

빠개다 1 [조각을 내다] split; cleave; rip; chop. ¶장작을 ~ chop[split] firewood∥나무 토막을 ~ cleave a block of wood into two. **2** [일을 틀어지게 하다] spoil; destroy. ¶거의 다 된 일을 빠개 놓다 spoil a plan which is almost accomplished.

빠개지다 1 [갈라지다] split; cleave; break; be broken. ¶머리가 빠개질 듯한 두통 a splitting headache / a headache of a skull-bursting kind∥어떤 나무는 잘 빠개진다 Some kinds of wood split easily.∥머리가 빠개질 듯이 아프다 I have a splitting[racking] headache. / My head is splitting. **2** [일이 틀어지게 되다] be[get] spoilt; be ruined; come to nothing[naught]. ¶내 모든 계획이 빠개지고 말았다 All my plans came to naught.

빠그르르 (boil) simmering; bubbling. ⇨ 바그르르

빠글빠글 boiling (briskly); bubbling; in swarms. ⇨ 바글바글

빠꾸 1 → 후진3 **2** → 퇴짜

빠끔빠끔[1] with puffs. ⇨ 빠끔빠끔[1]

빠끔빠끔[2] with cracks here and there. ⇨ 빠끔빠끔[2]

빠끔하다 split; cracked. ⇨ 빠끔하다

빠닥빠닥하다 hard. ⇨ 빼덕빼덕하다

빠드득 with a grinding sound. ⇨ 바드득

빠듯하다 1 [꼭 맞다] tight; close. ¶와이셔츠의 목이 ~ I feel the white shirt tight about the neck. **빠듯이** tightly; closely. ¶~ 들어가는 모자 a tight cap. **2** [겨우 미치다] barely enough; bare; narrow; marginal. ¶빠듯한 생활 marginal subsistence∥빠듯한 예산 a tight budget∥빠듯한 일정 a hard schedule∥기차 시간에 빠듯하게 대다 be just in time for the train∥살기가 ~ eke out a living / be on the margin of (bare) subsistence. **빠듯이** barely; hardly; narrowly; with difficulty. ¶~ 살아가다 live up to one's means / live barely within one's income.

빠뜨리다 1 [물·허방 등에 빠지게 하다] let (a person / a thing) fall into; drop (something) in[into]; sink; drown; [계략 등으로 위험·곤란에 몰아넣다] entrap; ensnare; plunge; (유혹에) tempt; allure; entice. ¶상자를 물속에 ~ let a box fall into the water∥함정에 ~ lure[entice] a person into a trap / entrap∥함정에 빠뜨려 파멸시키다 entrap a person to destruction∥유혹에 ~ lead a person into temptation∥그들은 그 남자를 곤경에 빠뜨렸다 They plunged the man into a difficult situation.∥그는 기회 있을 때마다 나를 함정에

빠뜨리려고 했다 He never lost an opportunity to set a trap for me.
2 [빼놓다] omit; leave out; miss out; pass [skip / look] over. ¶한 단어를 빠뜨리고 읽다 skip a word // 어려운 구절을 빠뜨리고 읽다 skip over difficult passages / look over [miss] difficult passages (in reading) // 세부 사항을 ~ miss out [pass over / omit] a detail // 빠뜨리지 않고 with nothing omitted // 소년은 한 주도 빠뜨리지 않고 수업을 받았다 The boy didn't miss one of his weekly lessons. / The boy attended his weekly lessons without fail. // 이것은 일상생활에서 빠뜨릴 수 없는 것이다 This is (something) essential for everyday life. // 말할 것을 빠뜨리게 있다 There is something I forgot to say. // 나는 보고서에서 중요한 사항을 빠뜨리고 말았다 I've left out[omitted] an important item in my report. // 나는 그의 편지를 소리 내어 읽다가 한 줄을 빠뜨리고 말았다 I left out a line when I read his letter aloud. // 당신의 보고서에는 빠뜨린 데가 많이 있었다 There was a great omission in your report. // 그 서류에는 무엇인가 빠뜨린 게 있다 Something is missing in[from] the papers. // 이 교정자는 오식(誤植)을 못 보고 많이 빠뜨린다 The proofreader misses[fails to notice] printer's errors very often. / A lot of misprints get past this proofreader. // 나는 그가 미성년자란 말을 빠뜨렸다 I forgot[(영) omitted] to mention that he was a minor. // 그가 빠뜨린 말이 가장 중요한 것이었다 What he left unsaid was the most important thing. // 하나라도 빠뜨리지 않도록 하시오 Be careful not to leave anything out. // 나는 깜박 신입 회원의 이름을 빠뜨리고 말았다 I carelessly omitted the new member's name. // 그는 사소한 부분까지도 빠뜨리지 않고 샅샅이 조사했다 He made a thorough investigation down to the minutest detail. // 한 놈도 빠뜨리지 말고 체포하라 Arrest every one of them. / Arrest them to a man. / Arrest all of them without exception.
3 [잃어버리다] lose; drop; [두고 가다] leave. ¶전차 안에 우산을 ~ leave one's umbrella in the train.
빠르다 1 [민첩하다] quick; (계속되는 움직임이) fast; [급속하다] rapid; (고속도로) speedy; (대답 등이) prompt. ¶빠른 기차 a fast train // 빠른 말 a speedy horse // 발이 ~ be swift of foot / (결음이) be a good walker // 그녀는 반응이 빨랐다 She was quick to respond. // 그는 학습 속도가 ~ He is quick at learning. / He is a fast learner. // 비행기는 기차보다 ~ An airplane is faster than a train. // 그는 너무 빠르게 말해 무슨 말인지 알아들을 수 없었다 He spoke so fast that I couldn't catch his words. // 그의 대답은 빨랐다 He made a prompt reply. / He replied promptly. // 그 나라는 공업화가 빨랐다 The country industrialized rapidly. // 그녀는 회복이 빨랐다 She made a speedy recovery. // 세월은 정말 ~ Time really[certainly] flies. // 발이 빨라졌다 My pace quickened[grew quicker]. // 차의 속도가 빨라졌다 The car speeded up. // 택시를 잡으면 더 빨리 갈 수 있다 You can make better time if you take a taxi.
2 [이르다] early; too soon; premature (시기상조). ¶그 사건에서 손을 떼는 것은 너무 ~ It may be premature to abandon the case. // 그는 빨라도 내주 월요일에나 돌아온다 He won't be back before next Monday at the earliest. // 이 시계는 3분 ~ This watch is three minutes fast. // 이 시계는 1주일에 1분가량 ~ This watch gains a minute or so a week. // 출발 시간이 2시간 빨라졌다 The time for departure was advanced[moved forward / moved up] (by) two hours.
3 [손쉽다] easy; simple; (속의의) quick; rapid; (첩경의) shortcut. ¶빠른 길 a shorter way / a near[nearer] way / a royal road // 빠른 방법 shortcut methods // 편지를 쓰는 것보다 만나는 것이 ~ It is easier to see him than to write to him.
빠른우편 (—郵便) (미) special delivery mail; (영) express delivery post.
빠이빠이 〈소아〉 bye-bye!; bye, bye!; ta-ta!
빠지다[1] **1** [떨어져 들어가다] fall[get] into; run into; be led into; lapse into; be drowned[sunk into] (물에). ¶물에 ~ fall[plunge] into water / drown // (차가) 도랑에 ~ be mired in a ditch // 함정에 ~ fall into[be caught in] a trap // 혼수상태에 ~ lapse[fall] into (a state of) coma[delirium / stupor] // 위험에 ~ run into danger / be endangered // 내 구두 뒤축이 진흙에 빠졌다 My heels sank into the mud. // 나는 개골창에 빠졌다 I fell into a ditch. // 그는 몹시 곤란한 처지에 빠져 있다 He is in great trouble[in utter distress]. // 그는 물에 빠져 죽게 된 사람을 건졌다 He save a drowning man.(▶ a drowning man은 물에 빠져 죽은 사람)
2 [마음을 빼앗기다] be steeped[immersed / bogged down] in; indulge (oneself) in (gambling); abandon[surrender] oneself to; give oneself (up[over]) to; be given to[in / on]; be absorbed[engrossed] in; be crazy[wild] with[about]. ¶사랑에 ~ be lost[fall] in love (with) / be deeply[gone] in love (with) // 주색에 ~ give oneself up to women and wine // 도박에 ~ be addicted to gambling // 그 녀석은 유행에 넋이 빠져 있다 He is a slave to[of] fashion. // 삼촌이 우표를 몇 장 준 후 그는 우표 수집에 빠져들었다 After his uncle gave him some stamps he got hooked on stamp collecting. // 그는 잠자는 것도 잊고 독서삼매경에 빠졌다 He was so completely lost[absorbed / engrossed] in the novel that he forgot even to go to bed.
3 [박힌 것이 그 자리에서 나오다] come[fall] out[off]; be taken[broken] off; get removed. ¶머리털이 ~ one's hair falls out[off] / one's hair thins (out) // 이가 ~ a tooth comes out / (그릇 등의) (a cup) chip (off) / be chipped // 못이 빠져 있다 A nail is missing. // 이 새는 깃털이 빠지기 시작한다 This bird is starting to lose its feathers[to molt]. // 그의 자동차가 빠졌다 A wheel came off[flew off] his car.(▶ fly off는 세차게) // 이 접시는 이가 빠졌다 This plate is chipped.
4 [누락되다] be left out; be omitted; [없다] be missing; [제외되다] be excluded (from); be not included. ¶두 페이지가 빠져 있다 There are two pages missing. // 필요한 것 중에서 빠진 것은 하나도 없다 We want for[lack] nothing. // 그의 이름이 명단에서 빠져 있다 His name is missing[has been omitted] from the list. / His name was left off the list. // 중요한 구절이 빠져 있다 The important passage is left out. // 빠진 것이 없나 잘 살펴

빠지다

봐 See that nothing is omitted. / See that things are all as they should be.

5 [흘러 나가다] drain; flow off; run out; [새어 나가다] (물 등이 줄다] subside; abate; fall; go down; sink. ¶싱크대의 물이 잘 빠지게 하다 improve the drainage of a sink // 그 땅은 물이 잘 빠진다[안 빠진다] The ground drains well [badly]. // (홍수의) 물이 빠진다 The water sinks [goes down / subsides]. // 이 타이어는 바람이 빠졌다 This tire is flat [has gone flat].

6 [힘·김·냄새 등이 없어지다] be gone; be got rid of; be free from; be got over; grow weak; be exhausted; get flat; become stale; fail; vanish; disperse; give out. ¶맥주가 김이 빠졌다 The beer drinks flat. // 그는 기운이 다 빠져 있다 He's in very low spirits. / He's very depressed. / All his strength is gone.

7 [여위다] get [become] lean [thin / peaked]; grow gaunt [slim]; lose (one's) weight; lose flesh(병으로). ¶살 빠지는 약 a fat-reducer / a flesh-reducer / an antifat remedy [cure] // 너는 살이 빠진 것 같다 You appear to have lost weight [flesh].

8 [제거되다] be removed; be taken out(얼룩 등이); wash off [out] (때 등이); run(염색이); fade [discolor](빛깔이 바래다). ¶얼룩이 잘 빠지지 않는다 The stains will not come off. // 이 비누는 때가 잘 빠진다 This soap washes out dirt [stains] well. / This soap really gets things clean.

9 [탈퇴하다·관계를 끊다] leave; quit; withdraw (from); drop out; break off the connections (with); secede from. ¶자리에서 빠져나오다 leave one's seat / slip out of the room // 네가 가입하지 않는다면 나도 빠지겠다 If you not join, I will cry off. // 그가 경쟁에서 빠져서 우리는 수월해졌다 Things become easy for us thanks to his withdrawal from competition.

10 [통과하다] go by [through]; pass [cut / get / run] through; lead (to / into); [돌파하다] break [smash] through; [탈출하다] escape; slip [steal] out; get away; [피하다] evade; avoid; dodge; excuse oneself from. ¶빠져나갈 수 없는 골목 a blind [dead] alley [lane] / an impasse // 3루를 빠지는 안타 a single past third / 위험한 곳에서 빠져나오다 escape danger / find one's way out of danger // 법망을 빠져나가다 evade [get round] the law / dodge [ward off] the law / slip from the grip of the law // 감시의 눈을 빠져나가다 elude the vigilance of the guard // 군중 틈을 빠져나가다 get [push] through a crowd / (쫓기는 몸이) dodge one's way through the crowd // 수업을 빼먹고 학교를 빠져나오다 (미국 속어) cut a lesson and beat it // 배가 다리 밑을 빠져나갔다 A boat passed under the bridge. // 여기서 빠져나가자 Let's cut through [across] here. // 여기서 빠져나갈 수가 없다 I can't get out of here. // 그는 나를 피하듯이 골목길로 빠져 버렸다 He struck into an alley as if to avoid me. // 사원 문으로 빠지자 본당이 눈앞에 있었다 After I passed through the temple gate I saw the main building right in front of me. // 소매치기가 사람들 틈을 빠져 도망쳤다 The pickpocket slipped through the crowd and ran away. // 좁은 길에서 나의 차는 간신히 트럭 옆을 빠져나갔다 My car barely managed to get [edge] past the truck [(영) lorry] on the narrow road.

11 [뒤떨어지다] be inferior to; be worse than; be below; fall [lag] behind; yield to; compare unfavorably with. ¶그녀의 옷이 그 중 빠졌다 Her dress was the least attractive one there.

12 [모자라다] lack; want; be short of. ¶한 달에서 3일 빠진다 It is three days short of a month.

빠지다² [심하게 되다] become [get / be] very [quite / utterly / thoroughly] ...; exhaustively; all-out; through and through; to the core [marrow]. ¶낡아 빠진 사상 a moss-grown [threadbare] idea // 썩어 ~ be rotten to the core // 시어 ~ turn all sour // 게을러 ~ be very lazy [indolent / sluggish] // 그는 마음이 썩어 빠졌다 He is corrupt [corrupted] at heart.

빠짐없이 without omission [exception]; in full; one and all; wholly; thoroughly; exhaustively. ¶~ 조사하다 make a thorough [an exhaustive] investigation // (긴) 연극을 ~ 상연하다 stage a (long) play without any omissions // 빈칸을 ~ 메우시오 Please fill in all the blanks (without omission). // 전원이 ~ 끝까지 달렸다 Everyone of the entrants completed the race. / The entrants all finished the race.

빡빡¹ (grate / rasp / scrape) hard; ripping up; close. ⇨ '박박¹

빡빡² (pockmarked) all over (the face). ⇨ '박박²

빡빡³ (puff) hard; with puffs. ¶담배를 ~ 빨다 (피우다) puff hard at one's pipe / puff away / puff a cigarette [cigar].

빡빡하다 1 [물기가 적다] thick; dry and hard; soupy. ¶빡빡한 국 a thick soup // 먹기에 ~ 하다 be hard to eat // 빡빡해지다 thicken / become thick // 삶은 달걀이 먹기에 너무 ~ The boiled egg is too hard to eat.

2 [꽉 차다] closely packed; chock-full; crammed (with); [꼭 끼다] pinched; cramped; tight; stiff. ¶빡빡한 예정 a crammed schedule // 빡빡하게 차 있다 be packed to the full / be chock-full (of) / be crammed (with) // 구두가 ~ My shoes are hard on my feet. / My shoes pinch (my feet).

3 [기계 등의 작동이 매끄럽지 않다] stiff; lack smoothness; hard; tight; be not greasy. ¶빡빡한 피스톤 a stiff piston // 이 장지문은 빡빡해서 잘 여닫히지 않는다 These paper sliding doors do not open and shut smoothly.

4 [고지식하다] unadaptable; hidebound; strait-laced; (미국 구어) stuffed. ¶빡빡한 선생 an inexorable teacher // 그렇게 빡빡하게 굴지 말고 요구를 들어주어라 Don't be so obstinate, but accept the claim.

빤드르르 smoothly. ⇨ '반드르르

빤들거리다 shine; be shrewd; idle. ⇨ '반들거리다

빤들빤들 smoothly; shrewdly; idly. ⇨ '반들반들

빤빤하다 shameless; impudent. ⇨ '뻔뻔하다

빤지르르 glossily; deceptively. ⇨ '반지르르

빤질거리다 be slippery; be idle. ⇨ '반질거리다

빤질빤질 sleekly; idly. ⇨ '반질반질

빤짝 with a flash; suddenly; lightly. ⇨ '반짝

빤하다 1 [환하다] light; bright. ¶동쪽이 빤하게 트이었다 The east grows faintly luminous. / The first faint streaks of down show

in the east. 빤히 bright(ly). ¶날이 다시 ~ 들었다 The sky is bright and clear again.
2 [분명하다] plain; obvious; evident; manifest; self-evident. ¶빤한 거짓말 a transparent lie / 빤한 말을 하다 talk platitudes / adjust one's style to fit the occasion∥그의 장래란 ~ We cannot expect much from his future.∥우리 팀이 진다는 것은 빤한 일이었다 That our team would lose was a foregone conclusion.∥빤한 일을 묻지 말게 Don't ask obvious questions. 빤히 [분명히] plainly; obviously; evidently; palpably; patently; (시선 등이) fixedly; steadily; intently. ¶~ 알면서 though one knows well [is well aware (of)] / having a good [clear] knowledge (of)∥속이 ~ 들여다보이는 수를 쓰다 resort to a shallow trick / make a hollow imposture∥~ 쳐다보다 gaze [stare fully] at (a person) / look hard at (a person) / stare fixedly at (a person) / stare (a person) in the face∥너의 속이 ~ 들여다보인다 I can see your true intentions. / Your true intention is obvious. ∥그는 ~ 들여다보이는 거짓말을 한다 He tells the kind of lies that can easily be seen through [that are soon found out].∥나는 몸에 나쁘다는 것을 ~ 알면서도 담배를 못 끊는다 I can not give up smoking, knowing well as I do that it is bad for the health.
3 [잠깐 틈이 있다] free; unoccupied; disengaged; (be) at leisure. ¶빤한 틈 spare moments.
4 [병세가 조금 낫다] 〔서술적〕 get a bit [a little] better; improve slightly.
빨가벗기다 strip (a person) bare [to the skin]. ➪ 발가벗기다
빨가벗다 strip oneself of all one's clothes. ➪ 발가벗다
빨강 〔적색〕 red (color); 〔진홍색〕 crimson; 〔주색〕 vermil(l)ion; 〔주홍색〕 scarlet.
빨갛다 〔붉은〕 red; 〔진홍색의〕 crimson; 〔주색의〕 vermil(l)ion; 〔주홍색의〕 scarlet. ¶빨간 코 a red nose / (숱꾼의) a copper nose∥빨갛게 물든 하늘 a crimson [flaming red / (문어) ruddy] sky∥뺨이 ~ have red cheek∥숯이 빨갛게 타고 있었다 The charcoal was burning (a) bright red.∥불길이 하늘을 빨갛게 물들였다 The fire reddened the sky.
빨개지다 turn red [scarlet / crimson]; redden; color; blush(부끄러워서); flush (up) (흥분하여). ¶부끄러워서 귀밑까지 ~ blush to the roots of one's ears [up to the ears]∥나뭇잎이 빨개졌다 The leaves turned red.∥그녀의 얼굴은 부끄러움으로 빨개졌다 Her face went red [She blushed] with embarrassment.∥그는 술만 마시면 금세 얼굴이 빨개진다 His face gets red as soon as he drinks alcohol.
빨갱이 〔공산당원〕 a Communist; 〔구어〕 a commie(▶ 흔히 경멸을 나타냄); (집합적) the Reds.
빨그스름하다 reddish. ➪ 발그스름하다
빨다[1] 〔입으로〕 suck (up); suck at; sip; draw at; take a drag at; inhale; 〔흡수하다〕 suck up [in]; absorb. ¶오렌지의 즙을 ~ suck the juice from an orange∥젖을 ~ suck the [one's mother's] breast∥아기가 엄마의 젖을 빨고 있다 The baby is sucking on [at] its mother's breast.∥그는 조용히 앉아서 파이프를 뻐끔뻐끔 빨고 있었다 He sat quietly sucking away at his pipe.
빨다[2] 〔세탁하다〕 wash; clean; launder; scour. ¶빨아도 줄지 않다 do not shrink in the wash / be shrink-proof∥이것은 빨면 준다 This shrinks in washing [in the wash].∥"이 옷감은 빨아도 됩니까?" "빨면 상합니다." "Will this material wash? [Is this material washable?]" "It doesn't wash [launder] well."
빨다[3] 〔뾰족하다〕 tapering; pointed. ¶끝이 빤 pointed / sharp-pointed / tapering (finger) ∥턱이 ~ have a pointed [tapering] jaw.
빨대 (suck through) a straw; a sipper(종이로 만든). ¶~로 우유를 마시다 drink milk through a straw.
빨딱 suddenly; on one's back. ➪ 발딱
빨랑빨랑 hurriedly; in a hurry; in haste; quickly. ¶책의 페이지를 ~ 넘기다 leaf through [turn over the pages of] a book quickly∥~ 해라 (미) Hurry up! / Be quick!
빨래 1 〔세탁〕 wash; washing; laundering; laundry; cleaning. ¶이 천은 ~가 잘 된다 [안 된다] This cloth launders well [badly]. **빨래하다** wash; do (the) washing; do a wash. ¶하루에 두 번 ~ do two washings a day. **2** 〔세탁물〕 wash(ing); laundry. ¶~ 말리는 곳 a drying place / a place for drying clothing∥~를 햇볕에 말리다 dry (the) washing in the sun∥~를 걷어 들이다 take [bring] in the washing [wash]∥~가 산더미 같다 I have mountains [a heap] of washing to do.∥그녀는 ~를 널었다 She hung the washing [laundry] out to dry.
● **빨래집게** a clothespin; (영) a clothespeg. **빨래판** a wash board. **빨랫비누** laundry [washing] soap. **빨랫줄** a clothesline; a wash-line.
빨리 1 〔신속히〕 quickly; fast; swiftly; rapidly; hastily; in haste; 〔기민하게〕 quickly; promptly. ¶~ 해라 (Be) quick! / Hurry up! / Make haste!∥~ 대답을 해라 Answer promptly. / Give me a prompt answer.∥좀 ~ 걸어 주세요 Please walk quickly.∥~ 일을 해치우자 Let's finish our job quickly.∥그렇게 ~ 말하지 마라 Don't speak so fast [rapidly].∥이런 환자는 ~ 손을 써야 한다 Such a case requires prompt attention.∥~ 내 생일이 왔으면 좋겠다 I wish my birthday would hurry up and come.∥~ 해. 아주 급하단 말이야 Don't be long about it, as I'm in a hurry.∥하나 더 가져와. ~ Get me another one. On the double.
2 〔일찍〕 early; 〔곧〕 soon; immediately; instantly; at once; without delay. ¶될 수 있는 대로 ~ as soon as one can / as soon as possible∥(예정 시간보다) 5분 ~ 닿다 arrive at (a place) five minutes ahead of time∥우리는 너무 ~ 왔다 We arrived too early.∥시험 결과를 ~ 알고 싶다 I am anxious to know the result of the examination.∥될 수 있는 대로 ~ 대답해 주십시오 Please give me your answer as soon as possible. / (특히 편지에서) Please answer at your earliest convenience.
빨리다[1] 〔빪을 당하다〕 be sucked; 〔착취당하다〕 be squeezed [extorted] (out of). ¶돈을 ~ be squeezed out of one's money.
빨리다[2] 〔빨게 하다〕 give suck to (a baby); let (a baby) suck at the breast; suckle (a baby); nurse (a baby). ¶아기에게 젖을 ~ give the breast to a baby / give a child the breast / suckle a baby.
빨병(-甁) 〔수통〕 a canteen; a flask; (영) a

빨부리 a mouthpiece. ⇨ 물부리
빨빨 profusely; bustlingly. ⇨ 뻘뻘
빨아내다 suck[draw] out; [의] aspirate. ¶종기의 고름을 ~ draw the pus from a boil // 스펀지로 ~ dry[soak up] (water) with sponge // 압지로 ~ dry (ink) with blotting paper // 그는 뱀에 물린 상처에서 독을 빨아냈다 He sucked the poison from the snake bite wound.
빨아들이다 (액체를) suck in[up]; imbibe; (기체를) breathe[draw / take] in; imbibe; (흡수하다) absorb; soak in[up]. ¶담배 연기를 ~ inhale[draw in] the smoke // 편지의 잉크를 (압지로) ~ blot a letter with blotting paper // 해면은 물을 빨아들인다 A sponge sucks up water. // 이 스펀지는 물을 잘 빨아들인다 This sponge absorbs water well. // 무명은 견직물보다 땀을 잘 빨아들인다 Cotton absorbs perspiration better than silk.
빨아먹다 squeeze[extort] (money from a person); suck; sponge; exploit; sweat (workers); siphon over (a person's wealth). ¶가난한 유럽의 피를 ~ suck the blood of the poor // 유럽은 아프리카의 부를 빨아먹었다는 비난을 받고 있다 Europe is criticized for siphoning off[exploiting] African resources.
빨아올리다 suck[draw] up; (펌프로) pump up. ¶펌프로 우물물을 ~ pump water from a well // 식물은 땅에서 수분을 빨아올린다 Plants suck up moisture[water] from the earth.
빨치산 a partizan; a partisan. ¶~식 전법 guerilla warfare.
빨판 [동] a sucker; a sucking disk; (파리 등의) a cupule; (거머리 등의) an acetabulum (pl. -s, -la); (낙지 등의) parapodium (pl. -dia).
빳빳하다 1 [단단하고 곧다] rigid; straight; stark; [꼿꼿하다] stiff; [풀기로] starchy. ¶빳빳한 머리카락 wiry hair // 빳빳한 콧수염 a bristly m(o)ustache // 빳빳한 털 coarse hair / a bristle // 빳빳한 새 지폐 a crisp bank note // 목이 ~ have a stiff neck // 고양이가 죽어서 빳빳해져 있었다 The cat lay stiff in death. // 시트가 풀을 먹어 ~ The sheet is stiff with starch. **빳빳이** straight(ly); stiffly. ¶~ 서다 stand straight // 와이셔츠에 풀을 너무 ~ 먹였다 They have put too much starch in my shirts.
2 [완강하다] strong; firm; shout. ¶빳빳한 태도 a firm attitude (toward). **빳빳이** head-strong; firm. ¶~ 버티다 be unyielding / stand firm.
빵¹ bread. ¶롤~ a roll (of bread) // 옥수수 corn pone // 크림~ a cream bun // 프랑스~ a French roll // 흑~ brown bread // 버터[잼] 바른 ~ bread and butter[jam] // ~에 잼[버터]을 바르다 spread jam[butter] on (the slice of) bread // ~을 굽다 bake bread / (토스트) toast bread // 사람은 ~만으로 살 수 없다 Man shall not live by bread alone.
빵² 1 [터지는 소리] with a bang[pop]; bang; pop. ¶~ 하고 경적을 올리다 beep[honk] a horn // 샴페인을 ~ 터뜨리다 pop open a champagne bottle. 2 [구멍 난 모양] gaping; with a hole (in a thing). ¶~ 뚫리다 break open / gape.

빵가루 (dry) bread crumb; crumbs (of bread).
빵구 ⇨ 펑크
빵빵 1 [총소리] bang! bang!; [자동차 등의 경적 소리] a honk; [터지는 소리] popping and popping. ¶총을 ~ 쏘다 fire a gun in rapid succession // 샴페인을 ~ 터뜨리다 pop open champagne bottles / uncork champagne bottles one after another // 폭죽이 ~ 터졌다 The firecrackers popped in bunches. / "Bang! Bang!" went off the firecrackers. // 자동차가 교차점에서 ~ 경적을 올리고 있다 A car is honking its horn at the intersection. 2 [구멍 난 모양] with (several) holes (in a thing).
빵집 a bakery; a bakehouse; (미) a bakeshop.
빻다 pound[crush] up; grind down[up]; pulverize; (보리 등을) crush; (약 등을) bray; (광석 등을) stamp. ¶밀가루를 ~ grind wheat into flour // 분쇄기로 ~ crush in a mortar.
빼각거리다 creak. ⇨ 삐걱거리다
빼기 [수] subtraction.
빼내다 1 [박힌 것·속의 것을 뽑다] extract; pull[draw / pluck / take] out; pull up; root up (a tree); (든 것을) take out; let (at thing) out of; [없애다] take away[off]. ¶상처에서 탄알을 ~ extract a bullet from the wound // 손가락의 가시를 ~ pick a thorn out of a finger.
2 [골라내다] select (out of many); pick[single] out; sort out; choose; [추출하다] extract (from); make an extract (from); make an abstract (of). ¶식물에서 독물질을 ~ extract poison from a plant.
3 [훔쳐 내다] pilfer (from); steal; filch; [완곡] abstract. ¶정보를 ~ coax forth information / get a tip out of (a person) / fish for information / derive information from (a chat).
4 [꾀어 내다] hire (a star player) away (from); pick out; entice (a movie star) from (another studio). ¶(운동선수 등의) 빼내기 작전 a battle of enticing star players from another team // 고용인을 ~ hire an employee away.
5 [얽매인 몸을] liberate; set (a person) at liberty; set (a person) free (from restraint); let (a person) go; help (a person) get out of (adversities). ¶교도소에서 ~ bail[get] (a person) out of jail / spring (a person).
빼놓다 1 [제쳐 놓다] exclude; except (from); omit; leave (a person) out (in the cold); put (a person) on one side; treat (a person) as an outsider. ¶일이 있는 경우를 빼놓고는 except on business // 친구 사이에서 ~ exclude[omit] (a person) from one's company // 나는 빼놓아 주게 Count me out. 2 [생략하다·거르다] omit; leave[cut / miss] out; skip (over) (a passage). ¶(책의) 어려운 부분은 빼놓고 넘어가다 skip[jump] (over) difficult passage. 3 [골라 놓다] pick[single / sort] out; select.
빼다 1 [속의 것·박힌 것을] take[put] out; get out; draw[pull / pluck] out; extract; (물을) draw off[pump out] (water); drain off [away]. ¶서랍을 ~ pull[draw] out a drawer // 이를 ~ extract[draw / pull out] a tooth / (남의 손을 빌려) have a tooth out // 타이어의 공기를 ~ let the air out of a tire // 목욕탕의 물을 ~ drain the water from the bathtub / let the water run out of the tub // 반지를

take a ring off one's finger // 권총을 ~ draw a revolver // 칼을 번개같이 ~ whip out a sword // (구경하려고) 목을 길게 ~ crane one's neck.
2 〔감하다〕 subtract (from); 〔공제하다〕 deduct[subtract] (from); take away[off]. ¶급료에서 1할을 ~ deduct 10% from the salary / 급료에서 세금을 뺀 금액 the amount (left) after taxes are deducted from one's salary // 5에서 3을 ~ subtract 3 from 5 / 10에서 4를 빼면 6이 남는다 4 from 10 leaves 6. / Ten minus four equals[is equal to] six.
3 〔없애다〕 take out; eliminate; remove; (때를) wash off; 〔제외하다〕 exclude; except; get out (of the program); 〔생략하다〕 leave [cut] out; omit; skip; pass over. ¶얼룩을 ~ remove a stain (from) / 관계없는 항목 등을 ~ leave out[exclude] irrelevant items // 서론은 빼고 본론에 들어가자 Let's leave out [omit] the preliminaries and go straight to the point. // 식대는 팁을 빼고 만 원이었다 The restaurant bill was ten thousand won without[excluding] the tip. // 처음의 100페이지는 빼도 좋다 You may omit the first 100 pages. // 그의 답안은 한 문제를 빼고 모두 맞았다[정확했다] His paper was correct except for one answer. // 그를 빼면 우리 팀의 인원이 모자란다 If we exclude[don't include] him, we won't have enough members for a team.
4 (힘·살 등을) cause to lose (force / weight). ¶힘을 ~ weaken / enfeeble / 김을 ~ stale / make stale[flat / vapid].
5 〔짐짓 꾸미다〕 make an affected pose; assume airs[an air of importance]; give oneself airs[frills / (구어) the dog / (미국 속어) lugs]. ¶점잔을 ~ be prudish[genteel] / do the genteel.
6 〔회피하다〕 evade; shirk (one's duty); give an evasive answer; excuse oneself; dodge; shuffle out of (one's responsibility); 〔손을 떼다〕 draw back; resile (from). ¶발을 ~ shirk [evade] one's responsibility / shuffle off [out of] one's responsibility / be freed from one's responsibility / 그만 좀 빼. 우리 네가 노래 잘 부르는 거 다 알아 Stop hiding your light under a bushel. We all know you're a good singer.
7 〔내빼다〕 run [scamper / (속어) scoot] away; make[take] off. ¶몰래 ~ sneak[slip] away[off].
8 〔차려입다〕 dress[smarten] oneself up; adorn[preen] oneself; (속어) doll (oneself) up. ¶오늘은 쭉 빼셨군요 You are quite dressed up today, aren't you? / 그는 쭉 빼고 있었다 He was dandified all over.

빼도 박도 못하다 be on the horns of a dilemma. ¶빚이 쌓여서 빼도 박도 못하게 되었다 He got mired down with accumulated debts. / He got stuck in the mire [bog] of accumulated debt.

빼돌리다 (물건을) hoard secretly; keep secret; conceal; hide; (사람을) shelter; hide (a person) away. ¶빼돌려 둔 돈 pin money / a secret hoard / 아나운서를 ~ entice[steal] an announcer from his present company / poach an announcer.

빼먹다 1 〔빠뜨리다〕 omit; leave out; miss out; look over. ¶몇 자 ~ leave[miss] out a few words (in writing) // 어미의 음을 ~ clip (off) one's (final) g's // 그는 호명할 때 내 이름을 빼먹었다 He skipped my name in calling the roll. **2** (수업을) miss one's lessons; (미) cut a class; (학교를) play truant from school; (강의를) cut a lecture. ¶수업을 2시간 ~ cut two lessons[classes] // 나는 수업을 빼먹었다 [수업 중에 도망치다] I cut school[a class]. / 〔중·고교에서 꾀를 부려 학교를 쉬다〕 (구어) I played hooky. **3** 〔남의 물건을 돌려내서 가지다〕 pilfer (from); steal; filch. ¶짐을 ~ pilfer from a load.

빼박다 → 빼쏘다

빼빼 〔몹시 여윈 모양〕 gaunt; haggard; skinny; emaciated. ¶~ 마른 사람 a man of skin and bones / a living skeleton / a mere shadow / ~ 마르다 be reduced to a (mere) skeleton[bag of bones] / be worn to a shadow.

빼쏘다 be as like as two peas[eggs]; be exactly alike; be a replica[copy] (of). ¶저 소녀는 자기 어머니를 빼쏘았다 That girl is the very image[a carbon copy] of her mother. // 젊은이는 25세 무렵의 그의 아버지를 빼쏘았다 The young man looks exactly as his father did at about twenty-five.

빼앗기다 1 〔탈취하다〕 be deprived [snatched] of (something); be dispossessed; have (a thing) taken[snatched] away; 〔강탈당하다〕 be robbed of (a thing); have (something) stolen. ¶자유[권리]를 ~ be deprived of one's liberty[right] // 목숨을 ~ be deprived of one's life / 돈을 ~ have one's money taken[stolen] / be robbed of one's money // (속아서) be cheated out of one's estate // 그 비행기 추락으로 50명이 목숨을 빼앗겼다 The plane crash killed[took the lives of] fifty people. // 그녀는 어름어름하다가 제 몫을 빼앗기고 말았다 She had her share snatched away when least prepared for a misfortune. // 그녀는 불량소년에게 돈을 빼앗겼다 Some juvenile delinquents took away her money[frightened her into giving them money]. // 그는 재산을 빼앗겼다 He was robbed of his property.
2 〔사로잡히다〕 be absorbed[engrossed] (in one's work); 〔매료당하다〕 be fascinated [charmed / captivated] by. ¶여자에게 마음을 ~ be fascinated by a woman / lose one's heart to a woman // 음악에 정신을 ~ be enraptured[carried away] by music // 그는 손자가 하는 짓에 주의를 빼앗기고 있었다 He was absorbed[engrossed] in his grandson's movements. / His attention was [was riveted] on his grandson's actions. // 관객들은 그녀의 훌륭한 연기에 정신을 빼앗겼다 The spectators were enchanted by her remarkable performance. // 그는 그 소녀의 아름다움에 정신을 빼앗겼다 He was captivated[fascinated] by the young girl's beauty.
3 〔짓밟히다〕 be seduced[dishonored] (정조를); be infringed(인권을).

빼앗다 1 〔억지로 제것으로 만들다〕 take (a thing) by force; snatch (something) from (a person); rob[deprive] (a person) of (a thing); dispossess (a person) of (his property); 〔탈취하다〕 take away; rob[fleece] (a person) of (his money); 〔강탈하다〕 plunder (▶ 특히 전쟁이나 동란 때에); pillage; (지위를) usurp (a rank); divest (a person) of (his office). ¶목숨을 ~ take a person's

빼어나다

life / kill a person // 돈을 ~ (강요·공갈해서) extort money from a person / (속여서) cheat a person of his money / swindle money out of a person / (감언이설로) wheedle money out of a person // 상대 팀의 피처로부터 히트 15개를 ~ (야구에서) collect fifteen hits off the opposing pitcher // 저 녀석의 서류는 어떤 방법으로 빼앗을까 How shall I get the papers away from him? // 내 단골손님을 빼앗아 가지 마라 Don't steal my customers[clients]. // 우리는 적의 탱크를 빼앗았다 We captured on enemy tank. // 그는 어린 동생의 사탕을 빼앗았다 He took[(미국 구어) swiped] his little brother's candy. // 친구의 애인을 빼앗다니 너는 비겁하다 It was mean of you to steal your friend's girlfriend (away from him). // 그에게서 그 여자를 빼앗아 버리겠다 I will take the woman away from him. // 그는 그녀의 핸드백을 빼앗고 달아났다 He robbed her of[stole / took] her handbag and ran away.
2 [생각·마음을 사로잡다] absorb; engross; [매료하다] fascinate; charm; [사람의 눈을 현혹하다] dazzle. ¶관객의 넋을 ~ enthrall the audience // 넋을 ~ captivate (a person).
3 [짓밟다] seduce[violate / dishonor](정조를); infringe(인권을). ¶정조를 ~ violate [seduce / dishonor] a woman.

빼어나다 [뛰어나다] (서술적) tower (high) above the rest; be outstanding; be prominent; distinguish oneself; cut a prominent figure (in / among). ¶여럿 중에서 가장 ~ rise above the common level // 빼어난 정치가 an eminent[a preeminent] statesman // 저 아이는 수학에서 ~ That child is head and shoulders above the rest in mathematics. // 그는 그 점에서 ~ He is superior to (the) others in that respect.

빽 [갑자기 지르는 소리] whistling; crying. ¶~ 하고 나발을 불다 blow a bugle / give a blast on a bugle // 기적이 ~ 울다 The steam whistle blows // ~ 소리 지르다 cry at the top of one's voice.

빽빽 [새소리 등] peep, peep; [신호 소리] bleep, bleep. ¶~ 울다 cheep / peep / chirp / pipe(어린애가).

빽빽하다 1 [촘촘하다] dense; thick; close-packed; jam-packed; compact; crammed. ¶사람들이 빽빽하게 들어찬 열차[기차] a packed[jammed / jam-packed] train // 열차는 사람이 빽빽하게 차 있었다 The train was jammed full[jam-packed]. // 나는 옷을 가방에 빽빽하게 쑤셔 넣었다 I squeezed my clothes into a trunk. 빽빽이 close(ly); tight(ly); compactly; thickly; densely. ¶글자가 ~ 적힌 편지 a closely written letter // ~ 들어차 있다 be closely packed (with) / be jam-packed (with people) // 홀에는 사람들이 ~ 들어차 있었다 The hall was filled[packed / crammed] to capacity with people. // 그렇게 빽빽이 쓰면 읽기 어려워요 It is hard to read if you write so closely.
2 [구멍이 막히다] be stopped up; be blocked [clogged / choked]; stuffy[close / cramped] (갑갑하다). ¶코가 ~ My nose is clogged [stuffy]. // 담뱃대가 ~ The pipe is clogged.
3 [속이 좁다] illiberal; ungenerous; narrow-minded. ¶그는 빽빽한 사람이다 He is a narrow-minded person.

뺀들뺀들 idly; lazily. ⇨뺀들뺀들
뺄셈 subtraction. **뺄셈하다** subtract; take away (2 from 5).
● **뺄셈표** [수] the sign of subtraction; a negative[minus] sign.
뺑 round; in a circle. ⇨뺑
뺑소니 abscondence; flight; decampment; bolt; fleeing; running away.
● **뺑소니차** a hit-and-run car.
뺑소니치다 abscond (from); run[whip] away (from); take (to) flight; (구어) make a bolt for it; (자동차가 사람을 치고) (미) (make a) hit and run; drive away after hitting a person with one's car. ¶돈을 가지고 ~ run away[make off] with money / abscond[bolt] with money // 그는 빚을 떼어먹고 뺑소니쳤다 He has given his creditors the slip.

뺨 1 [관자놀이에서 턱 위까지의 부분] a cheek. ¶불그레한 ~ red[rosy] cheeks // 홀쭉한 ~ sunken[hollow] cheeks // 복스러운 ~ plump [chubby] cheeks // ~이 홀쭉하다 have hollow[sunken] cheeks // be hollow-cheeked // ~을 때리다 slap (a person) in the cheek / give (a person) a slap in the cheek // ~을 맞다 get slapped in the cheek // ~을 불룩하게 하다 puff out one's cheeks / be sulky(불만이 있어) // 종로에서 ~ 맞고 한강에서 눈 흘긴다 A coward vents his anger on a third person.
2 [좁고 기름한 물건의 폭] breadth; width.
뺨따귀 〈속〉 a cheek. ⇨뺨1
뺨치다 [능가하다] outdo; outshine; be superior to; outrival. ¶저 아이는 어른도 뺨칠 정도이다 The child puts adults to shame. // 그는 전문가도 뺨칠 정도의 연기를 했다 He outshone the professionals with his excellent performance.

뼈개다 split; spoil. ⇨빠개다
뼈개지다 split; be spoilt. ⇨빠개지다
뼈걱 creaking; squeaking. ⇨버걱
뼈그러뜨리다 split; upset. ⇨버그러뜨리다
뼈그러지다 split apart; be upset. ⇨버그러지다
뼈그르르 (boil) simmering; bubbling. ⇨버그르르

뼈근하다 1 [움직임이 거북하다] (서술적) feel heavy[stiff]; grow stiff; have a dull pain. ¶가슴이 ~ feel heavy in the chest // 어깨가 ~ feel stiff in the shoulders / have a stiff shoulder / one's shoulders grow stiff // 뼈근한 어깨를 주물러서 풀다 relieve the stiffness in the shoulders by massage // 그것을 보고 있었더니 목이 뼈근해졌다 I got a stiff neck from looking at it. **2** [일이 힘에 벅차다] hard; tiring; exhausting; back-breaking; hard to handle. ¶뼈근한 일 a heavy[hard / laborious / backbreaking] task / a tough[an extracting / an arduous] job.

뼈기다 [잘난 체하다] put on airs; give oneself airs; [도도하게 굴다] be proud (of); be haughty; be pompous; swagger; wear a high hat; make one's importance felt; [호언하다] boast; talk big[high / tall]. ¶뼈기는 사람 an arrogant[a haughty / an overbearing] person / a man swollen with pride // 뼈기는 어조 authoritative tones // 뼈기며 haughtily / overbearingly // 뼈기며 걷다 swagger / strut (about / along) / stalk (about) / walk tall // 뼘시 ~ throw one's weight around // 부하들에게 ~ domineer over one's inferiors // 그렇게 뼈기지 마라 Don't be puffed up.

뼈꾸기 [동] a cuckoo. ¶~시계 a cuckoo clock.

뽀뽀 〈소아〉 a kiss. ¶(아기에게) ~ Kiss-kiss! / Give us a kiss!
뽀얗다 milk-white; hazy. ⇨ 보얗다
뽐내다 be proud (of/that); be arrogant; be haughty; be puffed up; be uppish; hold one's head high; 〔젠체하다〕 put on airs; give oneself airs; 〔속어〕 be high-hatted; 〔자랑하다〕 take pride in; pride oneself on; boast (of); brag (of/about). ¶뽐냄 affectation / posturing∥뽐내는 사람 an arrogant [a haughty] person / a man swollen with pride ∥뽐내며 걷다 strut (about/along); swagger / walk tall∥처녀들은 나들이옷을 입고 뽐내고 있었다 The girls were behaving affectedly in their best clothes. / The girls were giving themselves airs in their best clothes. ∥그는 뽐내는 걸음걸이로 단상에 올라갔다 He walked onto the platform with an affected gait.(▶ 여성의 경우는 a mincing gait라고도 함)∥이겼다고 너무 뽐내지 마라 Don't crow too much after a victory.∥그는 열등감에서 뽐내는 것이다 His inferiority complex leads him to put on airs.∥뽐내며 걸어 다니는 저들을 좀 보라구요 Look how they strut and swagger about!∥(네가) 좋은 가문 출신이라고 해서 뽐낼 것은 못 된다 Good birth is nothing (for you) to boast about.∥그녀는 상을 여러 개 탔지만 조금도 뽐내지 않는다 She has won several prizes, but she is not at all puffed up (with) pride.∥제일 먼저 도착했다고 너무 뽐내지 마라 Don't act so triumphant about being the first to arrive.∥그는 부하들에게 지위를 뽐내고 있었다 He throws his weight about among his subordinates. / He lords it over his men.∥그는 아들이 성공했다고 뽐내고 있다 He boasts [brags] about his son's success.(▶ boast는 과장되게 자랑하다, brag는 허풍을 떨다)∥그는 "언젠가 본때를 보여 주겠다."라고 뽐내 보였다 He put on a bold front and said, "Someday I'll get you."

뽑다 1 〔잡아 빼다〕 pull [draw / pluck / take] out; root up (a tree); extract. ¶가시를 ~ pull out a splinter∥이를 ~ have a tooth pulled (out) [extracted]∥잡초를 ~ dig up weeds∥제비를 ~ draw [cast] lots∥카드 한 장 ~ pull out a card (from a pack [〔미〕 from a deck])∥칼을 ~ draw a sword∥포도주의 병마개를 ~ uncork [open] a bottle of wine∥풀을 ~ weed a garden∥그는 내 손가락에 박힌 가시를 용케 뽑아냈다 He skillfully pulled out [extracted] the splinter from my finger.
2 〔선발하다〕 pick [single] out; select; choose; 〔선거하다〕 elect; (국회의원으로) return. ¶응모자 5만 명 중에서 ~ single out of 50,000 applicants∥의장으로 ~ elect (a person) (to be) chairman∥가는 책장에서 책을 한 권 뽑았다 I picked out [selected] a book from the ones on the shelf.
3 〔모집하다〕 enlist; enroll; raise; recruit. ¶사무직원을 ~ invite applications for the position of clerk∥학생을 ~ enroll [admit] students.
4 〔본전 등을 도로 찾아내다〕 return; recover. ¶본전을 ~ return [recover] one's investment.

뽑히다 1 〔빠지다〕 be taken [pulled] out; come off. ¶아무리 해도 병마개가 뽑히지 않는다 I cannot get the cork out. 2 〔선발되다〕 be singled out; be chosen [elected / selected]; be allowed to enlist. ¶야구 선수로 ~ be singled out as a baseball player∥그는 의장으로 뽑혔다 He was elected chairman.

뽕¹ 1 a mulberry (tree). ⇨ 뽕나무 2 mulberry leaves. ⇨ 뽕잎
뽕² 〔breaking wind / farting〕 with a boo [poop].
뽕나무 a mulberry (tree).
뽕빠지다 〔결판나다〕 sustain [suffer] a heavy loss; go [become] bankrupt; be brought to ruin; be broke. ¶혼인 잔치 치르기에 뽕빠졌다 I am broke after giving the wedding reception.
뽕잎 mulberry leaves. ¶~을 따다 pick mulberry leaves∥누에에게 ~을 주다 feed mulberry leaves to silkworms.

뾰로통하다 sulky; pouty; sullen. ¶뾰로통한 얼굴 a sulky [sullen] look∥뾰로통해지다 get sulky (at) / become sullen / take offense (at)∥그 소녀는 뾰로통해서 가 버렸다 The girl sulked herself to go.
뾰루지 an [a skin] eruption; a pimple; a tumor; a boil; a brash; a rash. ¶얼굴에 ~가 나다 have [break out with] pimples∥그는 온몸에 ~가 났다 He has rashes all over the body. / The eruptions have broken out all over him.
뾰족구두 high-heeled shoes; shoes with pointed toes.
뾰족뾰족하다 all pointed; equally pointed.
뾰족탑(-塔) 〔꼭대기가 뾰족한 탑〕 a pinnacle; a steeple; a spire.
뾰족하다 1 〔물체의 끝이 날카롭다〕 pointed; sharp; peaked; spicular; tapering. ¶뾰족한 구두 pointed shoes∥뾰족한 연필 a pencil with a sharp point∥뾰족하게 하다 make sharp / sharpen / point∥끝이 ~ be pointed at the end / have a sharp point∥입을 뾰족하게 내밀다 pout one's lips / make a pout [lip]∥나는 연필을 뾰족하게 깎았다 I sharpened my pencil. 2 〔신통하다〕 wonderful; miraculous; marvelous; extraordinary.
뽀드득 with a grinding sound. ⇨ 부드득
뿌듯하다 1 〔꼭 끼다〕 tight; close. ¶뿌듯하게 맞다 fit tightly / suit to a T. **뿌듯이** tightly; closely. 2 〔벅차다〕 full to the brim; brimful. ¶가슴아 ~ (사람이) feel a lump in one's throat / (일이) give (a person) a lump in (his) throat∥자랑스런 감정으로 가슴이 ~ fill one's heart with pride∥나는 가슴이 뿌듯해 아무 말도 못 했다 I could say nothing because there was a lump blocking my throat. / My heart was too full for words. **뿌듯이** brimfully.
뿌루퉁하다 swollen; sullen. ⇨ 부루퉁하다
뿌리 1 〔식물의〕 a root. ¶생강 ~ a root of ginger / a race (접목의) 접본이 되는 ~ a rootstock∥~가 깊다 take [spread] deep root / root deep∥~를 내리다 [박다] take [strike / make] root / root∥~를 **뽑다** root up / uproot / pull [pluck] up (a tree) by the roots / tear up (weeds) by the roots∥잡초를 ~째 뽑다 pull up [out] weeds by the roots∥폭풍에 나무는 ~째 뽑혔다 The tree was uprooted by the storm.∥꺾꽂이한 나무는 ~가 내렸다 The cuttings have taken root.∥나무는 땅속 깊이 ~를 뻗었다 The tree had its roots fastened deep into the soil.∥버들가지는 쉽게 ~를 박는다 A willow branch easily strikes [takes] root.∥산나무의 묘목이 ~를

뿌리내리다

박았다[내렸다] Cedar saplings have taken root.
2 [밑동]. ¶머리카락의 ~ the root of a hair / 귀의 ~ the base of an ear // 종기의 ~ the core of a boil.
3 [근원] the origin; the cause; the source; the foundation. ¶두 문제는 같은 ~이다 The two problems have the same source [are rooted in the same soil].

뿌리(가) 깊다 [사물이 연유하는 바가 오래다].
¶뿌리 깊은 편견 deep-rooted [inveterate / ingrained] prejudice // 정부에 대한 국민의 뿌리 깊은 불신감 the people's deep-seated [deep-rooted] distrust of the government / 이 문제는 ~ This problem has [results from] a deep cause. / (간단하게 해결되지 않음) This problem cannot be solved so easily. // 의외로 사건의 뿌리가 깊었다 The roots of the trouble went deeper than had been thought. // 나는 그에 대한 뿌리 깊은 증오를 억누를 수 없다 I cannot overcome my deep-rooted hatred of him.

뿌리(를) 뽑다 [근본을 없애 버리다] root out [up]; eradicate; exterminate (a thing) root and all. ¶병[악]의 ~ eradicate [root out] the causes of disease [evil].

● **뿌리등걸** a stump; a grub; (미) a grub. **뿌리줄기** [식] a rootstock; a rhizome; a rhizoma (pl. ~ta); a subterranean stem. **뿌리털** [식] a root hair; a fibril. **뿌리혹** a (root) tubercle.

뿌리내리다 take root; take firm hold. ¶합리주의가 그들의 사고에 깊이 뿌리내리고 있다 Rationalism is deep-rooted in their thinking. // 반정부 감정이 국민 사이에 뿌리내리기 시작했다 Antigovernment feelings began to take firm root among the people. // 그날 그의 행동으로 그녀의 마음속에 깊은 불신감이 뿌리내렸다 After what he did that day, a strong distrust of him was rooted [fixed] in her heart. // 민주주의가 이 나라에 뿌리내리기는 용이했다 Democracy took root easily in this country. // 야생 조류 보호 운동도 우리나라 전체에 뿌리내린 것 같다 The drive to protect wild birds seems to have become established [established itself / taken root] in Korea.

뿌리다 1 [눈·비 등이 날리어 떨어지다] sprinkle; rain in sprinkles. ¶비가 뿌리고 있다 The rain is sprinkling. // 비가 뿌리기 시작했다 It has begun to sprinkle.
2 (가루·씨·물 등을) sprinkle (on / with); scatter; strew; spread; spray. ¶설탕을 뿌린 쿠키 a cookie sprinkled with sugar // 천에 물을 ~ spray water on cloth // 채소에 소금을 ~ sprinkle salt on the vegetables // 콩을 ~ scatter beans // 고기에 후추를 ~ sprinkle [shake] pepper on meat // 빙판에 모래를 ~ scatter sand on an icy road // 화단[잔디밭]에 물을 ~ water a flower bed [the lawn] // 몸에 향수를 ~ spray perfume / wear perfume // 전단을 ~ distribute handbills // 초지(草地)에 클로버를 ~ sow a pasture with clover // 꽃을 ~ strew flowers // 불타고 있는 차에 물을 ~ spray water on the burning car // 그들은 폭도를 향하여 호스로 물을 뿌렸다 They turned water hoses on the mob. // 우리는 새들을 위해 눈 위에 씨앗을 뿌렸다 We scattered seed for the birds on the snow. // 아이들은 서로 물[모래]을 뿌리고 있다 The children are splashing water [are flinging sand] over one another. // 그들은 사방에 선전 전단을 뿌렸다 They distributed the leaflets everywhere. // 그는 취한의 얼굴에 물을 뿌렸다 He poured water on the drunk's face. // 우리는 정원에 씨를 뿌렸다 We planted seeds in the garden. // 그들은 밭에 옥수수 씨를 뿌렸다 They seeded the field with corn. // 뿌린 대로 거둔다 One must sow before one can reap. / No pains, no gains.
3 [낭비하다] squander (on); spend wastefully (in / on); lavish. ¶돈을 ~ squander money // 그는 유명해지기 위해 폐 많은 돈을 뿌린 듯하다 He seems to have thrown a lot of money around to get himself known. // 그는 가는 곳마다 돈을 뿌리고 다녔다 He spent his money lavishly wherever he went.

뿌리박다 take root; take firm hold. ⇨ **뿌리내리다**

뿌리치다 1 [붙잡은 것을 놓치게 하거나 못 붙잡게 하다] break loose (from); shake oneself loose [free] from (a person's grasp); shake off. ¶남의 손을 ~ shake off a person's hand / shake oneself free [loose] from a person's grasp // 누군가가 나의 옷소매를 잡았으나 나는 뿌리치고 도망쳤다 Someone grabbed hold of my sleeve, but I shook myself free and escaped. // 나는 매달리는 어린것을 뿌리치고 집을 나왔다 I left home, tearing myself away from my clinging child. // 감기 따위는 한잔 마시고 뿌리쳐 버려라 Shake off your cold with a drink.
2 [퇴짜 놓다] reject; refuse; turn down; [버리다] stave [ward] off; keep away from. ¶강매를 ~ turn away [get rid of] an aggressive door-to-door salesman // 그는 그녀의 신청을 뿌리쳤다 He shoved [brushed] aside her proposal [suggestion]. // 그는 그녀가 말리는 것을 뿌리쳤다 He rejected her pleas to stay. // 그는 아내를 뿌리치고 다른 여자 곁으로 가 버렸다 He deserted [abandoned] his wife and went to live with another woman. // 그의 반대는 가볍게 뿌리칠[무시할] 수 없다 His objection can't be shrugged off [passed over] lightly.

뿌옇다 milk-white; hazy; blurred. ⇨ **부옇다**
뿌예지다 get misty; become hazy. ⇨ **부예지다**
뿌유스름하다 somewhat pearly. ⇨ **부유스름하다**

뿍 with a scratching sound. ⇨ **북⁴**

뿐 1 [다만 어떠하거나 어찌할 따름] only; just; simply; merely; nothing but. ¶한 번 말해 봤을 ~이다 I only said it (but did not mean it). // 그것은 억측일 ~이다 It is merely a guess [a mere guess]. // 오고 싶어서 왔을 ~이다 I came just [simply] because I wanted to (come). // 나는 확인하고 싶었을 ~이다 I wished merely [I just wished] to make sure. / All I wanted (to do) was to make sure. // 그는 똑같은 일을 되풀이할 ~이었다 He merely repeated the same thing. // 그는 신문을 통해서 그것을 알았을 ~이다 I just read it in the newspaper. // 그는 성미가 급할 ~만 아니라 의심이 많다 He is not only hot-tempered but also suspicious of people. // 그녀는 미인일 ~만 아니라 재능도 있다 Besides being beautiful, she is talented. // 그는 영어를 말할 수 있을 ~ 아니라 프랑스 어도 말한다 He speaks not only English, but also French.
2 [단지·다만] only; alone (▶ 한정하는 말 뒤에

붙임); merely(▶ 보통 한정하는 어구 앞에 둠); solely; all; nothing but; […뿐만 아니라] not only ... but (also); as well as. ¶이유는 그것~이다 That is the only reason.//정확한 답을 한 것은 그 사람 한 사람~이었다 Only he gave the right answer. / He alone answered correctly.//내가 가지고 있는 것은 그것~이다 That is all I have with me.//나를 도와준 사람은 손 씨~이었다 Mr. Son was the only one who helped me.//돌아온 사람은 나~이었다 I alone returned.//생존자는 그 사람~이었다 He was the sole survivor.//내가 서울에 있는 것도 오늘~이다 This is my last day in Seoul.//이 나라의 민주주의는 이름~이다 Democracy is a mere name in this country. //나는 자네가 하라고 해서 한 것~이다 You told me to do it and so I did. That's all there is to it.//그녀는 남성~만 아니라 여성에게도 인기가 있다 She is popular among women as well as men[among both men and women].//내가 말하고 싶었던 것은 그것~이다 That's all I wanted to talk about.//그것~만 아니라 그녀는 내게서 돈까지 빌려 갔다 And that's not all. She even borrowed some money from me.

뿐더러 not only[merely] ... but (also); as well as.

뿔 1 (소·양·염소 등의) a horn; (사슴의) an antler(▶ 보통 복수형). ¶~ 모양의 horn-shaped / corniform // ~ 비슷한 hornlike / keratoid / ceratoid // ~이 있는[없는] 염소 a horned[hornless] goat // ~로 만든 단추 a horn button // ~로 받다 horn / toss up // ~로 찌르다 gore // ~을 떼어[잘라] 내다 dehorn // 송아지에 ~이 돋치기 시작했다 The calf has begun to grow horns.//사슴이 ~을 갈았다 The deer shed its antlers.//그는 황소 ~에 떠받혀 죽었다 He was gored to death by a bull. 2 [물건의 머리 부분이나 표면에 불쑥 나온 부분] a projection; a pointed tip (of); a horn; (모가 진 돌기) a cornu (pl. -a).

뿔나다 be angered; be enraged. ¶그가 늦게 돌아와 보니 아내는 뿔나서 문간에 서 있었다 Coming home late, he found his wife standing at the door looking furious.

뿔내다 get angry.

뿔뿔이 [흩어져] scatteringly; dispersedly; [따로따로] separately; severally; independently; singly. ¶~ 흩어진 scattered / dispersed in all directions // ~ 헤어지다[흩어지다] get separated[scattered] / break up // 군중은 ~ 흩어졌다 The crowd broke up[scattered / dispersed].

뿔싸움 horning each other(황소 등).

뿔테 a horn rim.
● **뿔테 안경** horn-rimmed glasses.

뿔피리 a bugle; a bugle horn; a (huntsman's) horn.

뿜다 (물·피 등을) spout (out); spurt (out / up); gush out; (연기·불 등을) blow off[up]; emit (smoke / fire); belch forth (fire); send out; (물보라를) spray[sprinkle] (water) on [over]. ¶(화산이) 용암을 ~ spout lava // 피를 뿜고 쓰러지다 fall in a spray of blood // 판자에 방부제를 ~ spray a board with preservative // 고래가 물을 뿜었다 A whale blew [spouted].//엔진이 갑자기 불꽃을 뿜었다 The engine suddenly burst into flames.//나는 고래가 바닷물을 뿜는 것을 보았다 I saw a whale blow[spout].//굴뚝에 연기를 뿜고 있다 The chimney is giving off smoke.

쀼루퉁하다 sulky. ⇨ 뾰로통하다

삐걱 with a creak; with a creaking sound. **삐걱하다** creak. ⇨ 삐거덕 ¶문이 삐걱하고 열렸다 The door opened with a creak.

삐걱거리다 creak; squeak; grate. ¶삐걱거리는 소리 a creaking[squeaking] sound // 삐걱거리는 계단 a creaking stairway // 노를 삐걱거리며 배를 젓다 row a boat with a creak of the oars // 경첩이 녹슬어서 문이 삐걱거린다 The door grates on its rusty hinges.//걸으면 마루가 삐걱거린다 The floor creaks under my feet.//철문이 삐걱거리며 열렸다 The iron door opened with a grating sound.//낡은 요람이 흔들릴 때마다 삐걱거린다 The old cradle creaked whenever anyone gave it a push.//짐차는 삐걱거리며 나아갔다 The wagon creaked along.//저 삐걱거리는 차를 운전하는 것은 위험하다 It's dangerous to drive that rickety car.

삐걱삐걱 with a creak; creaking; with[in] a squeak. ¶~ 소리 a creak / a squeak / a grating sound // (마루 등이) 걸으면 ~ 소리 나다 creak beneath one's feet. **삐걱삐걱하다** creak. ⇨ =삐걱거리다

삐다¹ [괸 물이 빠져서 줄다] subside; go down; sink; drain. ¶(홍수의) 물이 삐고 있다 The water is sinking[going down / subsiding].

삐다² (손목·발목 등을) dislocate; sprain [strain / twist / wrench] (one's ankles). ¶손목을 ~ strain one's wrist // 다리를 ~ have a strain[sprain] in a[one's] leg // 목을 ~ wrick one's neck // 허리를 ~ throw one's back out / one's back goes out // 그는 스키를 타다가 발목을 삐었다 He sprained[twisted] his ankle while skiing.

삐딱거리다 sway; shake; swing; wobble; be shaky[rickety].

삐딱삐딱 in a shaking[shaky / rickety / wobbly] manner.

삐딱하다 slanting; sloping; leaning; inclined; oblique; skew. ¶모자를 일부러 삐딱하게 쓰다 wear a hat deliberately tilted[slanted] / wear a hat at a rakish angle(▶ 멋으로).

삐뚜로 aslant; slantwise. ⇨ 비뚜로

삐뚤다 crooked; awry. ⇨ 비뚤다

삐뚤삐뚤 wobblingly; windingly. ⇨ 비뚤비뚤

삐라 → 전단(傳單)

삐삐 gaunt; haggard.

삐악 (병아리 울음소리). ¶~~ 울다 peep-peep / cheep-cheep.

삐죽 poutingly. ⇨ 비죽

삐치다¹ (글자의 획을) draw a downward left-hand stroke.

삐치다² [토라지다] become[turn] sulky; be cross. ¶뼈쳐서 말도 않다 sullenly refuse to speak / maintain a sulky silence // 어린애가 삐쳤다 The child has the sulks. 2 [기운이 빠지다] become languid[tired / weary].

삑 whistling. ⇨ 삐

삥 round; (all) round. ⇨ 빙

삥그르르 turn around smoothly. ⇨ 빙그르르

삥글삥글¹ round and round smoothly. ⇨ 빙글빙글¹

삥글삥글² smilingly; beamingly. ⇨ 빙글빙글²

삥땅 (미국 속어) knocking down; pocketing; pilfering (of the proceeds). ¶~을 떼다 knock down (some of the collected fares).

삥삥 round and round. ⇨ 빙빙

사¹ [단춧구멍 등을 실로 감치기] a buttonhole stitch; buttonholing; hemstitching.
사² [음] sol; G. ¶올림[내림] ~ G sharp[flat].
사(死) [죽음] death. ¶생과 ~ life and death.
사(私) (공(公)에 대한) privateness; privacy; [자기] self; [사리] self-interest; [비밀] secrecy; [정실] favoritism; partiality. ¶~를 버리다 sink[efface] self / rise above oneself.
사(邪) [악] evil; vice; wrong; [부정] injustice; unrighteousness; crookedness; [이단] heterodoxy.
사(社) [회사를 뜻하는 말] a company; (미) a corporation; a firm; [사무소] an office. ¶신문~ a newspaper publishing company / a newspaper office.
사(紗) (silk) gauze; thin silk; gossamer(얇은 것).
사(四) four. ¶제 ~ the fourth // ~ 배 four times // ~ 분의 1 a[one-]fourth / a quarter // ~차원 the fourth dimension.
-사(史) [역사] history; (편년사) annals(▶ 복수형으로 쓰임); a chronicle. ¶영국~ English history / the[a] history of England(▶ "a"가 붙은 것은 역사책 등을 가리킴) / 한국~ Korean history / the history of Korea.
-사(寺) a temple. ¶보문~ the Bomun Temple.
-사(辭) [말] an address; a speech; a message. ¶취임~ an inauguration speech / 환영~ an address of welcome / 고별~ a farewell address (to the deceased at a funeral) / 그가 개회[폐회]~를 했다 He gave the opening[closing] address at the meeting.
사가(史家) a historian. ⇨역사가(⇨역사(歷史))
사가(私家) [개인의 살림집] a private house[residence]; one's home.
사각(四角) a rectangular; a quadrilateral. ¶~의 square / four-cornered.
●**사각기둥** a square pillar. **사각모자** (학생의) a (square) college cap; (외국의 대학에서 의식 때 쓰는) a mortarboard; (일반적으로) a square-shaped cap. **사각뿔** a quadrangular pyramid. **사각형** a quadrangle; [사변형] a quadrilateral; a tetragon. ¶정~ a regular tetragon.
사각(死角) 1 [보이지 않는 범위] a blind spot; [총알이 미치지 못하는 범위] dead ground. 2 [가까이 있어도 보이지 않는 곳]. ¶시 전체를 밝게 하여 범죄의 ~지대를 없앨 작정이다 We are going to light up the town and leave no dark corners where crime can occur.
사각(射角) an angle of fire; an elevation.
사각(斜角) ➡빗각
사각거리다 crunch; crisp; be crisp; eat crisp[brittle / short]. ¶사과 씹는 소리처럼 ~ be as crisp as the munch of an apple.
사각사각 with a crunch[crunching sound]; crisply. ¶~ 먹다 crunch / munch / eat with a crunch. **사각사각하다** crunch. ⇨°사각거리다

사갈시하다 (蛇蝎視-) abominate (a person) like a serpent[viper]; hate (a person) like poison; abhor; detest; execrate; regard (a person) with great aversion.
사감(私憾) a spite; a grudge; a bitter[an ill] feeling; ill will; malice; rancor. ¶…에게 ~이 있어서 through ill feeling against ... / out of spite for ... / ~을 품다 bear[cherish / nurse / owe] (a person) a grudge[an ill will] / have it in for (a person) // 네겐 아무 ~도 없다 I have no resentment against you. / I don't bear any malice towards you.
사감(舍監) a dormitory superintendent; (여자) the matron of a dormitory; a dormitory mother. ¶그녀는 그 기숙사의 ~이었다 She was the resident housemother of the dormitory.
사개 1 (상자 등의) the tongues and grooves of dovetail joints; (그 요철의 하나) a dovetail. ¶~를 물리다 dovetail. 2 [건] (기둥의) pillar tenons.
사거(死去) death; decease; demise; passing. **사거하다** die; decease; pass away.
사거리(四-) a crossroads. ⇨네거리
사거리(射距離) (a) shooting range. ¶유효~ (within / out of) the effective range (of a gun).
사건(事件) 1 [주목을 끌 만한 일] (큰) an event; (우발적인) a happening; (작은) an incident; (문제가 되는) a matter; an affair; (살인·도난 등의) a case; [사고] an accident; [음모] a plot; [말썽] complications; a trouble; a difficulty; [추문] a scandal. ¶간통 ~ an adultery scandal // 괴~ a mystery / a strange occurrence // 사기~ a fraud case / 살인~ a murder case // 수회(收賄)~ a graft[bribery] case // 연애~ a love affair // 중대~ a matter of grave concern / a serious affair // 역사적~ a historical event / an event in history // 일상적인~ daily happenings // 뜻밖의 ~ an unforeseen accident // ~을 일으키다 start some trouble // ~에 관계하다 be involved[have a hand] in the affair // 잊을 수 없는 ~이 생겼다 An unforgettable event occurred[happened]. / 그 ~에 관계하다 be involved[have a hand] in the affair. // 그의 신상에 중대한 ~이 일어났다 He is now in serious trouble. // 경찰은 그 ~을 아직도 수사 중이다 The police are still working on the case. / The police haven't solved the case yet. // 그날은 별다른 ~은 일어나지 않았다 Nothing remarkable[unusual] happened that day.
2 a suit. ⇨소송 사건(⇨소송)
3 [수] an event.
사격(射擊) [표적을 향해 총을 쏨] target[rifle] practice; shooting; firing; fire; gunshot. ¶실탄~ firing with live ammunition // 그 명수는 an expert in marksmanship / a crack shot / 각개[일제]~ independent[volley] firing // 간접~ indirect fire // 공격 준비~ [군] preparation / preparatory fire // 유효~ effective

fire∥트랩 ~ trap[lay pigeon] shooting∥그는 ~이 능숙[노련]하다 He is an expert marksman[a good shot].∥그는 내게 ~ 방법을 가르쳐 주었다 He taught me how to fire [use] a gun. **사격하다** shoot; fire at (a person); fire upon[on] (a fortress). ¶그는 매를 사격했다 He shot (at) the hawk.(▶ shot at은 그곳을 향해 쏘는 일, shot은 쏘아서 탄환이 명중했음을 뜻함)∥아군은 적을 사격했다 Our army fired at[on] the enemy.
● **사격 개시** Fire!; Begin firing! **사격술** marksmanship. **사격장** a rifle[pistol] range; a shooting gallery(유희장). **사격 중지** Cease fire!

사견(私見) one's personal opinion[views]; one's point of view. ¶내 ~으로는 그 사람은 훌륭한 사람이다 In my opinion, he is a fine man.∥그 사건에 대하여 그는 ~을 제시했다 He presented his personal view of the affair.

사경(死境) 〔죽을 지경〕 a deadly situation; the brink of death; a dying condition; 〔궁경〕 miserable conditions; a sad plight; hard lines; a deadly pass. ¶~에 **처하다** be at the point [brink] of death / (궁경에) be placed in a sad plight / fall into great straits / ~을 벗어나다 be saved from the jaws of death / (궁경을) get out of a sad plight∥그는 ~을 헤매고 있다 He hovers[hangs] between life and death. / His life hangs by a thread.∥그는 추위와 굶주림으로 ~에 처해 있었다 He was on the point of dying from cold and hunger.

사경제(私經濟) 〔경〕 private[individual] economy.

사계(四季) 1 the four seasons (of the year). ⇨사철(四~)1 2 〔사계삭〕 the last month of each season.

사계(射界) a field[zone] of fire.

사계(斯界) this circle; this world[field]. ¶~의 권위자 an expert[authority] in the field.

사계절(四季節) the four seasons. ¶한국은 ~이 뚜렷하다 Korea has four distinct seasons.

사고(社告) an announcement by a company.

사고(事故) 1 〔나쁜 사건〕 an accident; 〔비교적 작은 불행한 사건〕 a mishap; 〔진행 등의 정지 않은 지장〕 a hitch; an incident; an untoward event; a crack-up; trouble. ¶교통~ a traffic accident∥~를 **일으키다** cause an accident∥비행기 ~를 당하다 be in an airplane accident∥~를 **방지하다** prevent accidents∥그는 철도 (자동차) ~로 죽었다 He was killed in a railroad (or railway) [automobile] accident.∥~가 일어났다 There has been an accident.∥아무런 ~도 없이 끝났다 It ended without mishap. / (지장 없이) It ended off without a hitch.
2 〔사정·까닭〕 circumstances; reasons. ¶~로 **퇴학[결석]하다** leave[be absent from] school owing to circumstances beyond one's control∥무슨 ~로 오지 못했습니까 What kept you from coming?
● **사고뭉치** a trouble maker. **사고 빈발 지점** (게시) Accident Danger Zone.; (영) Accident Black Spot! **사고사** (an) accidental death.

사고(思考) thought; thinking; consideration. **사고하다** think; consider; conceive; intellectualize.
● **사고력** thinking power[faculty]; the power of thought. ¶어린이의 ~을 계발하다 develop children's ability to think. **사고방식** one's way of thinking. ¶구태의연한 ~ obsolete way of thinking.

사고무친하다(四顧無親-) 《서술적》 have no one to turn[look] to; be thrown upon the world. ¶사고무친한 떠돌이 a wanderer as helpless as a boat drifting alone in the sea.

사골(四骨) the bones of the four legs of a cow [bull]; the shank of beef; a soupbone.

사공(沙工) a boatman. ⇨뱃사공
사공이 많으면 배가 산으로 간다(속담) Too many cooks spoil the broth.

사과(沙果) 〔사과나무의 열매〕 an apple. ¶풋~ a green apple∥새빨간[신] ~ a red-cheeked [sour] apple∥~ **껍질** the peel[skin] of an apple∥~ 같은 뺨 rosy cheeks∥~ 껍질을 벗기다 pare an apple.
● **사과나무** an apple tree.

사과(謝過) an apology (for). ¶서면 ~ a written apology / ~(의) 말 an apology (for) / words of apology. **사과하다** apologize; make an apology [excuse] (for); beg [ask] pardon (of a person); offer (a person) an apology; beg (a person's) forgiveness (for); express regret (for). ¶진심으로 ~ offer one's sincere apology (a person) / tender a heartfelt apology (for) / make a humble apology (for) / 남에게 자기의 잘못을 ~ apologize to a person for one's fault / beg another's pardon for one's fault / 자기 아들의 잘못을 ~ make an excuse for one's son∥죽음으로 잘못을 ~ atone for one's fault with one's life / 자네에게 사과해야겠다 I owe you an apology.∥별로 사과할 일이 없다 There is no apology needed.∥몇 번이고 사과합니다 I ask you a thousand pardons[apologies].∥사과할 길이 없습니다 I do not know what excuse to offer. / I have no words to apologize to you.∥사과할 사람은 자네가 아니라 날세 It is not you but I that have to apologize.
● **사과 편지** a letter of apology.

사관(士官) an[a commissioned] officer. ¶육군 [해군] ~ a military [naval] officer.
● **사관생도** a military cadet(육군); a midshipman(해군); an aviation cadet(공군). **사관학교** the Military Academy; (간부 후보생의) an officers training school(약어 O.T.S.).

사관(史觀) a historical view. ⇨역사관(⇨역사(歷史)) ¶유물 ~ the materialist(ic) view of history.

사관(史官) a historiographer; a chronicler.

사광(沙鑛) a placer; an alluvial gold mine.

사교(邪敎) a heretical religion; heresy; (기독교도·유대교도·이슬람교도가 본) heathenism. ¶~의 heretical / heathen / ~의 신들 heathen gods / ~에 **빠지다** fall into [be guilty of] heresy.
● **사교도** a heretic; a pagan; a heathen; an infidel.

사교(社交) social contact; society; social intercourse; social life; the social round. ¶~상의 예의 social etiquette∥~를 **좋아하다** be fond of society[mixing with people]∥그녀는 ~를 싫어한다 She doesn't like social gatherings. / She shuns society.∥그것은 ~상 어쩔 수 없는 일이다 That's unavoidable in social life.∥그 사람과는 ~상의 교제가 있을 뿐이다 I have contact with him only at social gatherings.
● **사교가** a sociable person; (미국 구어) a good mixer; a society man[lady]. **사교계** the

사교적 fashionable world; (polite) society; society circles. ¶~의 social // ~의 명사 a socialite / (집합적) the smart set / ~의 사람들 society people / (미) club people / ~의 여왕 a society beauty / a belle[queen] of society / ~의 꽃 women prominent in society // ~에 나오다 make one's debut in society. **사교성** sociability; sociality; a social nature. ¶~ 좋은[나쁜] 사람 a sociable[an unsociable] person / (구어) a good[bad] mixer // ~이 있 다[없다] be sociable[unsociable] / be outgoing[too shy]. **사교술** the art of social intercourse.

사교적(社交的) social; sociable; (be) sociably inclined. ¶~인 모임 a social function // ~인 사람 a sociable person / (미국 구어) a good mixer / 남 앞에서 ~으로 행동하다 behave socially in public.

사구(四球) [야구] a base on balls. ⇨포볼

사구(死球) [야구] a pitch which hits the batter. ⇨데드 볼

사구(沙丘) [지] a dune; a sandhill; a sand pile; a down.

사군자(四君子) [미] a *sagunja*; the Four Gracious Plants(▶ plum, orchid, chrysanthemum and bamboo를 가리킴); the four gentlemanly plants.

사권(私權) a private[personal] right.

사귀다 [친하게 되다] make friends (with); become[get] acquainted (with); strike up a friendship / an acquaintance (with); [교제하 다] keep company with; associate with; hold intercourse with. ¶남자[여자]를 ~ become involved with a man[woman] / have[take] a lover[mistress] / 그는 사귀기 좋은 사람이다 He is easy to get along with. / (상냥하다) 그는 사귀기 좋은 사람이다 He is an affable man. / 그는 친구를 빨리 사귄다 He is quick to make friends. / 그들과 사귀고 나서 좋은 일이라곤 하나도 없었다 Everything has gone wrong since I began to associate with them. / 그와 사귀는 것은 즐겁다 I enjoy his company. // 그는 그녀와 사귀는 것을 그만 두었다 He broke off his friendship with her. // 아버지는 나에게 그와 사귀지 말라고 말씀을 하셨다 My father advised me not to associate with her. / My father warned me not to see him anymore. / 싫은[나쁜] 사람들과 사귀 지 마시오 Don't associate[keep company] with undesirable people. / Keep away from bad company. // 그녀는 수상한 남자와 사귀고 있는 것 같다 She seems to be going about [around] with a questionable man. // 그는 사 귀기 까다로운 사람이다 He is hard to get along with. // 그녀는 낯선 사람들과 사귀는 일 에는 어려움을 느꼈다 She found it difficult to mix with strangers.

사귐성(-性) sociability; sociableness; sociality; affinity; companionableness. ¶~이 있는 [없는] 사람 a sociable[an unsociable] person / (미국 구어) a good[bad] mixer // ~ 이 있다[없다] be sociable[unsociable].

사규(社規) the company regulations.

사그라뜨리다 resolve; collapse; make (a thing) subside; let (a thing) wither; make (a thing) rust away.

사그라지다 go down; subside; recede; wither; (썩어서) rot away; decompose; (녹슬어서) rust away; (녹아서) melt away; (종기 등이) resolve; be resolved. ¶불이 ~ burn low / sink // 기운이 ~ lose one's spirit / a damp-

ness falls upon one's spirit / get down in the dumps // 이 숯은 빨리 사그라진다 This charcoal burns out fast.

사극(史劇) a historical play[drama]. ⇨역사 극(⇨역사(歷史))

사근사근하다 1 (성품이) affable; amiable; agreeable; pleasant; pleasing; engaging; companionable; compliant; sweet and gentle. ¶사근사근한 사람 an affable person // 사근사근한 여자 a selfless[docile] woman / a woman of compliant disposition. **사근사근히** amiably; affably; with affability; winningly; pleasantly. ¶~ 대하다 make oneself agreeable to (one's guest). 2 (입에) crisp. ¶이 사 과는 ~ This apple eats[munches] crisp. **사 근사근히** crisply.

사글세(-貰) monthly rent[rental].

사금(沙金) gold dust; alluvial[placer] gold. ¶ ~을 채취하다 (모래를 일어서) wash for gold / (냄비로 선광하여) pan (for) gold.
● 사금 채취 alluvial[placer] mining.

사금융(私金融) private loaning[financing / banking]; private money lending.

사금파리 a potsherd; a crock; a fragment[a broken piece] of earthenware.

사기(士氣) morale; fighting spirit. ¶~가 왕성 하다 have high morale / be full of fighting spirit / ~를 꺾다 depress the morale / demoralize / ~가 꺾이다 become demoralized // ~를 진작하다[북돋우다] raise[lift / stiffen] the morale (of the men) / (사물이) have an inspiring effect of the morale / give a stimulus to the fighting spirit (of the men) // 군대의 ~를 높이다 raise[heighten] the morale of the troops // 군의 ~가 높다[낮다] The morale of the troops is high[low]. // 그들 은 첫 경기에 이겨 ~가 충천했다 After winning the first game, their spirits soared.

사기(史記) a history (book); annals; a chronicle.

사기(沙器·砂器) porcelain. ⇨사기그릇(⇨사 기)
● 사기그릇 porcelain; chinaware. **사기전**(-廛) a china store[shop]. **사기 접시** a porcelain[china] dish.

사기(邪氣) 1 [병을 일으키는 나쁜 기운] malarial[poisonous] air; pestilential[noxious] vapor; a miasma (*pl.* -mata); poison. ¶~를 없애다 purge[clear away] noxious vapor. 2 [요정의 기운] malice; wickedness. ¶~가 있는 wicked / malicious / evil / sinister / ~가 없는 innocent / harmless / guileless.

사기(社旗) the flag of a company; (배의) a house flag.

사기(詐欺) trickery; a swindle; a trick; [신용 거래에서의 협잡] a confidence trick[(미) game]; (a) fraud; swindling; a swindle; a hoax; (문어) (an) imposture; (승부에서의) foul play. ¶~결혼 a marriage fraud // ~를 치다 play a trick (on a person) / swindle / practice deception (on a person) / [부정을 하다] do something crooked (승부에서) / play foul[dirty] / cheat // 나는 ~를 당해 돈을 빼앗겼다 I was swindled out of my money. // 그는 ~를 쳐서 큰돈을 우려냈다 He obtained a large sum of money by fraud. / He swindled a great amount of money. // 그 것은 사실상 ~나 다름없다 That's virtually the same as fraud! / That comes to nothing

more than fraud! / That's nothing but (a polite name for) fraud! **사기하다** practice [perpetrate] a deception (on a person); swindle; commit a fraud (on); defraud; shark. ¶그는 나한테서 백만 원을 사기해 갔다 He swindled one million won out of me.
● **사기꾼** a swindler; a cheat; (성명·신분을 사칭한) an impostor; (신용 거래 등에서의) a confidence[(구어) con] man; a humbug; a fraud; a crook; (구어) a sharper. ¶신사로 가장한 ~ a wolf in sheep's clothing // 그는 대단한 ~ 이다 He is a terrible impostor [humbug]. **사기죄** [법] fraud; false pretenses.
사기업 (私企業) [경] (집합적) private enterprise; (개개의) a privately owned company.
사나이 [남자] a man; the male (sterner) sex. ¶~ 마음 a man's heart // ~ 중의 ~ a man among men / a courageous man // ~다운 manly / masculine // ~답게 굴어라 Be a man. / Behave like a man. // ~는 배짱이 있어야 한다 A man must have guts.
사날 [삼사 일] three or four days; three days or so; several [a few] days.
사납다 fierce (animal); rough [heavy] (sea); rude; wild (waves); harsh; violent; outrageous; ferocious; savage; truculent; (운수가) unlucky. ¶사나운 사람 a person of violent temper / a violent-tempered person // 사나운 짐승 a wild animal / a fierce beast // 사납게 생긴 불도그 a ferocious-looking bulldog // 사나운 말 an unbroken horse / a restive [vicious] horse / a spirited horse // 사나운 여자 a shrew / a termagant / a virago // 사나운 바다 stormy seas / rough seas / a troubled sea / a heavy [high] sea // 사납게 fiercely / roughly / violently / harshly / outrageously / (구어) like craze [mad] // 사납게 보이다 (생기다) look fierce // (바람이) 사납게 불다 blow furiously [smartly] // 사납게 덤벼들다 fly out (at / against) // 사나워지다 become furious / be raging / rage [rave] in all (its) fury // 성질이 ~ have a violent temper // 말투가 ~ use harsh language / be rough in speech // 운수가 ~ be unlucky / have bad [ill] luck // 인심이 ~ be ungenerous [unkind] / be tightfisted [stingy] / be harsh [bitter] // 산에는 태풍이 사납게 불어닥치고 있다 A storm is raging in the mountains.
사낭 (沙囊) [동] a gizzard. ⇨ 모래주머니 (⇨ 모래).
사내 1 a male. ⇨ 사나이 ¶~ **대장부** a man / a great man. 2 〈속〉 a husband. ⇨ 남편.
● **사내아이** a boy; a male child; a boy baby. **사내종** a servant; a slave.
사내 (社內) ¶~의[에] in the firm [company] // ~의 사람들 the staff of a company // 그는 ~에서 으뜸가는 능력가이다 He is the ablest man in his company [office].
● **사내 연수** in-house training. **사내 유보** internal reserves.
사냥 [수렵] hunting; a hunt; [총사냥] shooting. ¶토끼 [사슴 / 여우] ~을 가다 go hare [deer / fox] hunting // 새 ~을 하다 shoot game birds // ~이 해금되었다 The hunting [The shooting] season has opened. // 들꿩 ~은 금지되어 있다 It is forbidden to shoot ptarmigans. **사냥하다** hunt; have a hunt; shoot. ¶맹수를 ~ hunt big game // 그들은 숲으로 사냥하러 갔다 They went hunting [shooting] in the woods.
● **사냥감** [사냥의 대상이 되는 짐승·새] game (▶ 집합적으로 씀); [1회의 사냥으로 잡은 포획량] a take; a bag (▶ a bag은 주로 작은 새·짐승의 경우); quarry; the spoils of a chase. ¶~을 잡다 bag game // 오늘은 ~이 많았다 [적었다] We had a good [bad] bag [take] today. **사냥개** a hound; a hunting [sporting] dog; a gundog; a hunter. ¶~를 풀어놓다 slip [unleash / cast off / let loose] a hound. **사냥꾼** [사냥하는 사람] (미) a hunter; (영) a huntsman (영국에서 hunter는 사냥용 말을 가리킴); a huntress (여자); a sportsman. **사냥터** a hunting ground [field]; a (game) reserve; (영) a chase (개인 소유의).
사념 (邪念) [나쁜 생각] a wicked [an evil] thought; [목적에서 벗어난 생각] an irrelevant thought; a vicious mind; an evil intention. ¶~이 없다 have no depraved thoughts // 아무리 ~을 떨쳐 버리려 해도 할 수 없었다 No matter how hard I tried, I just could not shake off those awful thoughts.
사념 (思念) thought.
사농공상 (士農工商) the scholarly, agricultural, industrial, and mercantile classes; the traditional four classes of society (in order of esteem) — scholars, farmers, artisans and tradesmen.
사다 1 [구입하다] buy; purchase (▶ 격식 차린 말). ¶귤을 1개 100원에 ~ buy oranges at one hundred won a piece // 스웨터를 30,000원에 샀다 I bought [got] a sweater for thirty thousand won. // 이것을 얼마에 샀느냐 How much did you pay for this? // 잉크 좀 사다 주오 Get me a bottle of ink. // 나는 저 가게에서 꽃을 싸게 샀다 I bought flowers cheaply at that store. // 나는 조카딸에게 인형을 사 주었다 I bought [got] a doll for my niece. // 어제 나는 명동에 물건 사러 갔었다 I went shopping in the Myeongdong. // 사랑을 돈으로 살 수 없다 Money cannot buy love. / Love cannot be bought with money. // 그녀는 바겐세일 때 필요 없는 물건도 샀다 At the bargain sale she bought even things she didn't need. // 지금은 명예도 돈으로 살 수 있는 세상이다 Even honor may be bought today. // 술은 어느 가게에서 늘 사느냐 At which shop do you usually buy liquor? // 이 넥타이를 사겠습니다 I will take this tie.
2 [초래하다] incur; invite; evoke; bring [draw] upon oneself. ¶무심코 한 말이 그의 역정을 샀다 My chance remark incurred [aroused] his displeasure. // 그는 그녀의 환심을 사기 위해서는 무슨 짓이라도 했을 것이다 He would have done anything to win her favor. // 그는 상사의 노여움을 샀다 He incurred his superior's displeasure. / He fell into disfavor with his superior. // 그의 마음을 살 짓을 했느냐 Have you done anything to incur his displeasure? // 그는 상사의 미움을 사고 있다 He is in disfavor [(구어) the doghouse] with the boss.
3 [공연히 하다]. ¶싸움을 사서 하다 accept [take up] a person's challenge.
4 [인정하다] set [put] (much / a high) value on [upon]; put (a person's services) at high valuation; appreciate. ¶비평가들은 그의 작품을 높이 사고 있다 Critics think highly [have a high opinion] of his works.
5 [고용하다] engage; employ; take on. ¶사람

사다리 을 ~ engage[hire] a person.
6 [곡식을 팔아 돈으로 바꾸다] sell (grain) in exchange for money.
사다리 a ladder. ¶신축 ~ (소방용) an extension ladder // 공중 ~ (소방용) an aerial ladder // 줄 ~ a rope ladder // 비상 ~ an emergency ladder / (화재용) a fire ladder / (곡예의) ~ 타기 ladder-top stunts / acrobatic performances on a ladder.
● **사다리꼴** [수] (미) a trapezoid; (영) a trapezium (pl. -zia, ~s). ¶~ 대형 [군] an echelon formation. **사다리차** (소방용) a (hook and) ladder truck; an aerial ladder truck.
사다새 [동] a pelican.
사닥다리 a ladder. ⇨사다리
사단(事端) 1 [사건의 단서] the origin[cause] of an affair; the beginning; the inception. 2 →사달
사단(社團) a corporation; an association.
● **사단 법인** a corporation; an incorporated body; [법] a corporate juridical person.
사단(師團) an army division; a division. // ~을 편성하다 organize a division.
● **사단 사령부** the division(al) headquarters(약어 D.H.Q.). **사단장** a division(al) commander.
사달 [사고·탈] an occurrence; an event; a happening; an incident; an accident; a trouble.
사담(私談) a private conversation; a confidential[private] talk; a whispering. **사담하다** talk privately[in private] (with); have a private[confidential] talk (with); talk in whispers (with).
사당(私黨) a private party; a faction; (음모의) a cabal; (비밀 결사의) a junto (pl. ~s).
사당(祠堂) (집안의) a sadang; an ancestral shrine[tablet hall]; a household shrine; (일반적인) a shrine; a sanctuary. ¶~에 제사드리다 offer worship at the sadang.
사대(事大) submission[subserviency] to the stronger; worship of the powerful. **사대하다** submit to the stronger; worship[serve] the powerful; become a toady[flunk(e)y].
● **사대주의** worship of the powerful; flunkeyism; toadyism; a trimming policy. **사대주의자** a truckler; a trimmer; a timeserver; a toady; a toadeater; a flunk(e)y.
사대부(士大夫) [고관] a high (government) official; a (high-)ranking official; a dignitary; [명문가] a man of high birth[distinguished lineage]; a person of good ancestry; a man of noble family.
사도(私道) a private road[path].
사도(邪道) [그릇된 길] an evil way; an evil course; a wrong course; vice. ¶~에 빠지다 be led astray / go astray[wrong] / stray from the right path[the path of virtue] / deviate from virtue / err[wander] from the path of virtue / be led into the wrong course // 그것은 ~다 You are doing it in the wrong way. / You are not doing it in the proper way.
사도(使徒) an apostle. ¶십이 ~ the Twelve Apostles.
● **사도 신경** the Apostles' Creed. **사도행전** [성] the Acts (of the Apostles).
사도(師道) the duty of a teacher; teacher's code.
사돈(查頓) a member of the family of one's daughter-[son-]in-law; a relative[relation] by marriage; (미국 구어) in-laws. ¶~ 간이 되다 get related by marriage (to).
사돈 남 말 하네 Look who's talking!; You can't tell.
사돈의 팔촌 [아주 먼 친척] a distant cousin [relative].
● **사돈댁** [사돈의 아내] the wife of in-laws; [사돈집] the family related by one's son's [daughter's] marriage.
사동(使童) an errand [office] boy; a page (boy); a messenger (boy).
사동사(使動詞) [언] a causative verb.
사두마차(四頭馬車) a carriage[coach] and four; a carriage-[coach-]and-four; a four-horse coach[carriage].
사들이다 buy (in); purchase; lay in(▶ purchase는 격식을 차린 말. lay in은 사서 쌓아 두기); (공사채 등을) subscribe. ¶통조림을 많이 ~ lay in a large stock of canned food // 식품을 사들이기 위해 슈퍼마켓에 가다 go to the supermarket to buy food // 야채를 사들이기 위해 생산지에 가다 go to a producing district to lay in vegetables // 헌 피아노를 싸게 사들였다 I bought an old piano cheap. // 가게 주인은 봄볕 옷을 많이 사들였다 The storekeeper has bought[laid in] a large stock of spring wear.
사디스트 a sadist.
사디즘 sadism.
사또 a lord; (2인칭으로) my lord. ¶이제 와서 계획을 세워 봐야 ~ 떠난 뒤에 나팔 부는 격이다 It is too late to work out a plan now.
사라사(@saraça) printed cotton; chintz; (미) calico; (영) print.
사라지다 disappear; go away; vanish; fade (away); die away[out / off]; go out of sight; go(물건·아픔·희망·구름 등이); fall(빛·소리·냄새 등이); be gone. ¶사라지지 않는 인상 a lasting[(문어) an indelible] impression // 그의 모습이 안개 속으로 사라졌다 He [His figure] disappeared into the fog. // 금고 속의 보석이 사라졌다 The jewels had vanished [were missing] from the safe. // 발소리가 사라졌다 The footsteps died away. // 노여움이 차츰 사라졌다 My anger gradually faded away. // 통증이 사라졌다 The pain is gone [has left me]. / I am relieved of the pain. / The pain went away[subsided]. // 그는 곧 마을에서 사라졌다 He soon disappeared from the village. // 전쟁의 기억이 차츰 사라지기 시작한다 The memory of our wartime experiences is beginning to fade. // 전후에 오랜 전통이 사라졌다 After the war old traditions were lost. // 그의 죽음과 더불어 그 가문은 사라졌다 With his death the family died out. // 그는 군중 속에서 사라졌다 He disappeared [was lost] in the crowd. // 열차는 금세 내 시야에서 사라졌다 The train soon disappeared from view[vanished from my sight]. // 기적 소리가 멀리 사라져 갔다 The whistle faded [died] away in(to) the distance. // 그녀는 한때는 그렇게 아름답더니 그 매력이 사라져 버렸다 Even though she was once such a beauty, her charm has faded away. // 그들은 사라져 버렸다 They have vanished[disappeared] into thin air. // 100만 원이 사라져 버렸다 A million won went for nothing[took to itself wings]. // 그녀는 연기처럼 사라졌다 She disappeared from our sight like a puff of smoke. / She vanished like vapor. // 그 소식

을 듣자마자 나의 모든 걱정은 사라졌다 All my anxiety vanished immediately at the news.∥그녀의 웃음을 보자 나의 슬픔은 사라졌다 When I saw her smile, my sorrow vanished.∥그 소식으로 우리의 마지막 희망마저 사라졌다 The news blasted[destroyed] our last hope.∥희망은 완전히 사라지고 사람들은 절망에 빠졌다 Hope was completely gone[all hope evaporated], and despair seized the people. / The people lost all hope and fell into despair.

사람 1 [인류] man; mankind. ¶~은 물이 없으면 살지 못한다 Man cannot live without water.∥~은 누구나 죽게 마련이다 Man is mortal.
2 [개개의 사람] a person; (남자) a man; (여자) a woman. ¶젊은 ~ a young person/부유한 ~들 rich people / the rich/다른 ~의 주선으로 through (the good office of) another∥~을 중간에 넣어서 타협을 제의하는 offer a compromise through an intermediary ∥민이라는 ~이 찾아왔습니다 A Mr. Min[A man named Min] is here to see you.∥반대하는 ~도 있는 것 같다 There seem to be some objections.∥희망하는 ~에게는 팸플릿을 보내 드립니다 Pamphlets will be sent to those who ask for them.∥거리에는 ~이라고는 보이지 않았다 Not a soul was to be seen on [in] the street.∥그는 읍내의 모든 ~들이 싫어하는 ~이다 He is disliked by everybody in (the) town.∥통행증이 없는 ~은 들어오지 못함 (게시) No Admittance Without A Pass.∥그 ~의 이름은 네게 말해 줄 수 없다 I cannot tell you his[her] name.∥그래 그 ~들은 어찌 되었습니까 And what become of them.∥~은 죽어도 이름은 남는다 A men dies, but his name remains.∥~은 외양으로 판단할 것이 아니다 A man is not to be judged by his appearance.
3 [세상 사람] people; men; [남들] another; others; other people. ¶~들 앞에서 in company / in public / before others / in the presence of others∥~들이 뭐라고 할까 What will people say?∥~들이 뭐라고 하든 나는 개의치 않는다 I am indifferent to what (other) people say about me. / I don't care about what others say. / I am indifferent to public criticism.∥그녀는 ~들 앞에 나서기를 좋아하지 않는다 She does not like to be in company much. / She does not enjoy being among company. / She dislikes company.
4 [됨됨이·성질] personality; character; nature; disposition. ¶~을 만들다 build a fine character / bring up a useful citizen∥그녀는 ~ 볼 줄 안다[모른다] She is a good[poor / no] judge of character. / She is able [unable] to judge people's character.∥그는 ~이 너무 좋다 He is too good-natured [-humored]. / He is kind-hearted.∥그는 어떤 ~입니까 What is he like? / What sort of person[(a) man] is he?∥그는 요즘 ~이 달라졌다 He is not what he used to be. / He is quite another man these days.
5 [일정한 지역에 사는 구성원] people; a native; an inhabitant. ¶미국 ~ an American / Americans∥서울 ~ a Seoulite / a native[an inhabitant] of Seoul / (집합적) the people of Seoul∥그는 수원 ~입니다 He is[comes] from Suwon. / He is a Suwon man.
6 [인재] an able man; a man of talent; a capable[competent / fine] man; [집합적] talent; [책임자] the right man. ¶그를 위원장으로 선출하다니 ~도 없는 게로군 They must lack able men if they have to elect him chairman.∥그녀는 교육계에서는 찾기 힘든 ~이다 It is hard to find anyone else of her ability in educational world[circles].
7 [손님] a visitor; a guest; a caller; [심부름꾼] a messenger. ¶우리 집에는 좀처럼 ~이 찾아오지 않는다 We seldom have visitors.∥최 씨 댁에서 ~을 보내왔습니다 A messenger came from the Choe's.∥의사를 부르러 ~을 보내시오 Please send someone for the doctor.
8 [자기] I. ¶~ 무시하지 말게 Don't look down on me. / Do not hold me down.∥~ 살려 Help me!
9 (수로 세어서) one; a person; (복수) persons; those. ¶~씩[한 ~ 한 ~] one by one / one at a time / one after another / in turn(차례로) / 친척 가운데 한 ~ one of one's relatives/내 친구 중의 한 ~ a friend of mine∥두 ~ two persons / a pair / a couple∥대여섯 ~ several people[persons] ∥우리는 모두 합해서 스무 ~이다 We are twenty in all.∥이 가게는 우리 두 ~이 경영하고 있다 The two of us run this shop together.∥우리 두 ~만의 이야기로 해 두자 Let's keep this to ourselves.∥그들은 두 ~ 모두 학생입니다 They are both students.∥두 ~ 다 성공할 것 같지 않다 Neither of them is likely to succeed.∥이 동네에서 영어를 할 줄 아는 ~은 몇 안 된다 There are not many people who[Only a very few people] can speak English in this town. ∥한 ~씩 와 주세요 Please come one by one [one at a time].∥한 ~도 남지 않고 죽었다 They were killed to a man. / They were all killed.∥오늘은 선생이 한 ~도 여기 오지 않았다 None of the teachers is[are] here today.∥합격자는 10명, 나도 그중의 한 ~다 Ten passed the examination, myself among the number.∥정답을 낸 ~은 그이 한 ~밖에 없었다 Only he[He alone] answered correctly.∥"거기서 옛 친구를 몇이나 만났느냐?" "한 ~도 만나지 못했다." "How many old friends did you see there?" "None at all[Not one]."

사람 위에 사람 없고 사람 밑에 사람 없다(속 담) All men are equal under the sun.

●**사람됨** [성미] one's nature; one's disposition; [성격] one's character; [인품] one's personality. ¶그러한 행위는 그녀의 ~을 나타내고 있다 Such conduct is characteristic [typical] of her. / Such conduct shows what she is (like).

사랑 love; (지속적이고 잔잔한) affection; [애착] attachment; tender passion[sentiment]; [연인] one's love; a sweetheart. ¶어머니의 자식에 대한 ~ a mother's love[affection] for her child / maternal love∥딸에 대한 어머니의 헌신적인 ~ a mother's devotion to her daughter∥부부간의 ~ the love of a husband and wife / conjugal love∥이웃 간의 neighborly love∥부모 [형제] 간의 parental [fraternal] love∥친구의 friendly affection∥하느님의 ~ divine love∥자연 [학문]에 대한 ~ love of nature [learning]∥~이

사랑

담긴 편지 an affectionate letter // ~의 정표[표시] a love-token / a token of affection [love] / a gage of love // ~이 없는 가정 a loveless family // ~의 신 the god of love / [그리스 신화] Eros / [로마 신화] Cupid // 이루지 못한 ~ hopeless [forlorn] love / unrequited [unreturned] love // ~에 빠진 여자 a woman in love // ~에 빠지다 fall in love (with) / ~의 보금자리를 꾸미다 build a love nest / make a lovers' sweet home / make a happy home // 아름다운 소녀에게서 ~을 받다 win the heart of a beautiful girl / be loved[liked] by a beautiful girl / receive a beautiful girl's love // ~을 속삭이다 whisper sweet nothings (in a girl's ear) // ~에 보답하다 reciprocate [return / requite] (a person's) affection / return (a person's) love / love (a person) back // 그녀는 자식들에 대한 ~에 빠졌다 She doted on her children. / 나는 그녀에게 ~을 고백했다 I confessed[declared] my love to her. // 그녀는 ~에 번민하고 있다 She is lovesick[lovelorn]. // 그녀는 ~에 멍들었다[실패했다] She was disappointed [crossed / betrayed / thwarted] in love. / 버림받다 She was deserted[abandoned] by the man she loved[by her love(r)]. // 그녀는 ~에 눈이 멀었다 She is blind[blinded] with love. / 그녀의 그에 대한 ~이 식었다 Her affection for him waned[cooled]. / She has fallen out of love with him. / She no longer loves him. / 그녀는 그의 ~을 얻었다 She won his love [affection]. / She gained his heart. / She earned his love. // 그녀는 그의 ~을 받아들였다 She accepted his love. / 그녀는 그의 ~을 잃었다 She lost[forfeited] his love. // 그 아이는 우리 ~의 결실이다 The child is the fruit of our love. // 내 ~이여 My love[darling / sweetheart / (구어) sweetie]! **사랑하다** love; [친애하는 감정을 가지다] have an affection for; be fond of; [애착을 느끼다] be attached to; set one's affection on; have a tender feeling (toward). ¶사랑하는 자식 one's dear [(문어) beloved] child / 자연을 사랑하는 사람들 those who love nature // 그들은 사랑하는 사이다 They are in love with each other. / They are lovers. / (구어) They are thick with each other. // 그는 그녀를 사랑하고 있다 He loves her. / He is[has fallen] in love with her. // 그들은 사랑하는 사이가 되었다 They fell in love with each other. / Love grew up between the two. // 그녀는 그를 죽자 사자[몹시] 사랑하고 있다 She is burning with love for him. / She is madly in love with him.
● **사랑니** a wisdom tooth. ¶그녀는 지난해에 ~가 처음으로 났다 She cut her first wisdom tooth last year. **사랑싸움** a lovers' quarrel; a love[matrimonial] quarrel.

사랑(舍廊) a detached reception room used as master's quarters.
● **사랑채** the men's part of a house; a detached building used for a reception room.

사랑스럽다 lovable; lovely; affable; amiable; charming; attractive. ¶사랑스러운 소녀 a lovable girl.

사략(史略) a concise[brief / short / shortened / succinct] history; a historical sketch; a sketch history.

사레들리다 swallow the wrong way; get something caught in one's windpipe; be choked[stifled / smothered] (by / with). ¶그는 커피를 마시다가 사레들렸다 He chocked on[over] his coffee. / His coffee choked him. / The coffee went down in the wrong way.

사려(思慮) [주의 깊은 생각] thought; [고려] consideration; prudence; discretion; (good) sense. ¶~ 깊은 [주의를 기울이는·남의 사정을 헤아리는] thoughtful / considerate / [신중한] prudent / discreet / [분별 있는] sensible / judicious / well-advised // ~ 없는 thoughtless / imprudent / indiscreet / injudicious / ill-advised // ~ 깊은 사람 a man of discretion[good sense] / a prudent man // ~ 깊은 조처에 대해 감사합니다 Thank you for your considerate[thoughtful] treatment. **사려하다** consider; think over; deliberate.

사력(死力) ¶~을 다하여 desperately / to the best[utmost] of one's power[ability] // 그는 ~을 다했다 He made desperate[frantic] efforts. // 나는 ~을 다해 그를 도와주었다 I moved heaven and earth to help him. // 그들은 ~을 다하여 적으로부터 조국을 지켰다 They fought desperately[a desperate fight / to the death] in defending their country against the enemy.

사련(邪戀) illicit love; immoral[wild] love; (a) forbidden passion (for). ¶~에 빠지다 be infatuated (with a forbidden woman[man]).

사령(司令) [군] 1 [지휘·감독] command; control; a position[post] of command. 2 [(일직·주번의) 책임 장교] officer. ¶일직 ~ an orderly[a duty] officer.
● **사령관** a commandant; a commander; an officer in command; a commanding officer(약이 C.O.). ¶총~ commander in chief. **사령부** the headquarters(약이 HQ, H.Q.). ¶총~ the General Headquarters(약이 GHQ, G.H.Q.). **사령탑** (군함의) a conning tower.

사령(辭令) 1 [응대하는 말] wording; diction. ¶외교~ diplomatic language / honeyed words // 그는 외교~에 능하다 He is skilled in the way he phrases[puts / expresses] things. 2 [관직의 발령] a government order; an official announcement of appointment; a commission. ¶임명[해임] ~을 내리다 issue a government order // ~을 받다 receive an official announcement[a notification] of appointment.
● **사령장** a letter[warrant / writ] of appointment (to the office of ... as an officer); an official written notification (of appointment).

사례(事例) [실례] an example; an instance; a case; [전례] a precedent. ¶~별로 case by case.
● **사례 연구** [심] a case study.

사례(謝禮) [감사] thanks; gratitude; acknowledgment; appreciation; [보수] a reward; (문어) (a) remuneration; (의사·변호사 등의) a fee; (강연 등 지적 봉사에 대한) an honorarium (pl. ~s, -ria); a recompense; a consideration; a recognition. ¶~의 표시로 as a[in] token of one's thanks[gratitude] (for) / 그녀에게 지난번의 환대에 대한 ~의 편지를 보냈다 I sent her a letter of thanks[a thank-you letter / a thank-you note] for her recent hospitality. // ~로 얼마를 주시겠습니까 How much can you offer me by way of remunera-

tion? // 그토록 애썼는데도 ~는 아주 적었다 I got very little reward for my pains. / I was paid very little for all that hard work. **사례하다** reward; remunerate; recompense; give a reward; pay a fee to; fee. ¶후히 ~ reward (a person) generously [handsomely] // 개를 찾아 주시는 분에게는 사례하겠습니다 I will remunerate [give a reward to] the finder of the dog.
● **사례금** a reward; a fee; a recompense; an honorarium (*pl.* -ria, ~s); a remuneration.

사로잡다 1 [생포하다] catch [take / capture] (animal) alive; capture (a person); take (a person) prisoner [captive]. ¶토끼를 ~ catch [capture] a hare alive // 경찰은 간첩을 사로잡았다 The police captured a spy. 2 [생각·마음을 한쪽으로 쏠리게 하다] captivate; enslave; seize; win; enthrall; hold in thrall. ¶여자의 마음을 ~ win a woman's heart [hand] // 절망이 그를 사로잡았다 Despair seized him. // 그의 말이 내 마음을 사로잡았다 I was deeply impressed [moved] by his speech. // 그는 청중을 사로잡는 데 능하다 He knows how to captivate [take / win] his audience.

사로잡히다 1 [붙잡히다] be caught [seized / taken] alive; be captured; be taken [led] prisoner [captive]. ¶적군에게 ~ be captured (alive) by the enemy.
2 [생각·마음이 매혹되다] be fascinated [captivated] by; be a captive to; be enslaved by; be a slave to; [얽매이다] be a slave to; stick [adhere] to; be shackled by; be prepossessed by [with]; (격한 감정 등에) be seized [stricken] with; be carried away by. ¶공포에 ~ be seized with panic / be struck with terror [horror] / be horror-stricken // 망상에 ~ be obsessed [possessed] by delusions // 그녀는 사랑에 사로잡혀 있다 She is a slave to love. / She is pining away for love. // 감정에 사로잡혀 사물을 판단해서는 안 된다 You shouldn't let your emotions run away with you when judging things. / Don't let sentiment interfere with judgment. // 눈앞의 이익에 사로잡혀서는 안 된다 Don't let the desire for [thought of] a quick profit get the better of you. / Don't be swayed by the needs of the moment. // 그는 그 여자의 미모에 완전히 사로잡혔다 He became a captive to [was enslaved by] her beauty. / He was captivated by [fell a victim to] her charm. / Her beauty captivated him. // 그는 죽음의 공포에 사로잡혀 있다 Fear of death obsessed him. / He is under an obsession of the fear of death. / He is [has fallen] a prey to the fear of death.

사료(史料) historical records [document / materials]. ¶제2차 세계 대전의 ~를 편찬하다 compile materials on the history of World War Ⅱ.
사료(思料) thought; consideration; considered judgment. **사료하다** think; consider; regard; deem; judge.
사료(飼料) (일반적인) feed; provender; (마소의 여물) fodder; (목장의 목초) forage. ¶배합 ~ assorted [mixed] feed / a mixture of feeds // 말에게 ~를 주다 fodder [give fodder to] a horse / feed a horse // 말에게 건초는 ~로 주다 give a horse a feed of hay / fodder a horse with hay // 우리는 돼지에게 배합 ~를 준다 We feed the pigs on a mixture of feeds. / We give the pigs mixed feed.
사륙 배판(四六倍判) a large [royal] octavo.
사륙판(四六判) twelvemo; duodecimo(약어 12mo; 12°). ¶~의 책 a duodecimo / a twelvemo.
사륜차(四輪車) a four-wheel(ed) vehicle; a four-wheeler.
사르다 1 [태워 없애다] burn (up / away); destroy (a thing) by fire; throw into (the) fire; commit (old documents) to the flames. ¶묵은 편지를 불에 ~ throw old letters into the fire. 2 [불붙이다] light [make / kindle] a fire; fix [build (up)] a fire; make a fire burn. ¶아궁이에 불을 ~ make a fire in the fireplace.
사르르 lightly; easily. ⇨<스르르
사리 [국수·새끼 등의 감은 뭉치] a coil; a small pile (of noodles). ¶한 ~의 새끼 a coil of rope // 국수 한 ~ a coil of noodles.
사리(私利) self-interest; one's own interests; personal profit [gain]. ¶~를 취하다 feather one's own nest // 그는 ~에 눈이 어두워 나를 배반했다 Blinded by self-interest, he betrayed me.
● **사리사욕** self-interest and selfish desire. ¶~을 채우다 satisfy [gratify] one's selfish interests and desires / feather one's own nest.
사리(事理) reason; facts; propriety. ¶~를 (분별할 줄) 아는 사람 a man of (good) sense / a sensible man / an enlightened person / a fair-minded person // ~에 맞지 않는 unreasonable / unjustifiable / without reason / absurd // ~에 닿다 [맞다] stand to reason [sense] / accord [be consistent] with reason / be reasonable // ~에 닿지 [맞지] 않다 do not stand to reason / be against [contrary to] reason / be inconsistent with reason // ~에 밝다 be reasonable [sensible] / have common sense [good sense] / see reason / listen to reason // ~에 어둡다 be unreasonable / be impervious [inaccessible] to reason.
사리(舍利·舍利) [불] 1 [불타·성자의 유골] a (fragment of a) bone of the Buddha [a Buddhist saint]; relics of Buddha [a Buddhist saint]; (범) sarira. 2 [불타의 유적인 경전] Buddhist scriptures; the Sutras.
● **사리탑** a sarira stupa; a Buddhist reliquary (shaped like a stupa).
사리다 1 (국수·새끼 등을) coil; [해] fake (down) (a rope, a cable, etc.). ¶국수를 ~ wind noodles into a ball // 새끼줄을 ~ coil up a rope. 2 (뱀 등이) coil itself (up). ¶큰 뱀이 몸뚱이를 사리고 있다 A big snake has coiled itself up [is coiled up]. / A big snake is lying in a coil. 3 (몸을) spare oneself; be sparing of oneself; shrink from danger. 4 (박아서 나온 못을) clinch; clench; hammer back (the point of protruding nail).
사립 a gate made of branches and twigs. ⇨'사립문(⇨사립)
● **사립문** a gate made of branches and twigs; a brushwood gate; a twig gate.
사립(私立) ¶~의 private / nongovernmental // 우리 학교는 ~이다 The school we go to is private. / Our school is private institution. / Our school is under private management.
● **사립대학** a private university [college]. 사

립학교 a private school; a nongovernmental school.

사마귀[1] [피부 위의 군살] a wart; [의] a verruca (*pl.* -cae). ¶내 목에 ~가 났다 I have a wart on my neck. / A wart has grown [formed] on my neck.

사마귀[2] [동] a (praying) mantis (*pl.* ~es, mantes).

사막(沙漠·砂漠) a desert. ¶사하라 ~ the Sahara Desert // 끝없는 ~ a limitless desert.

사망(死亡) death; decease; demise; passing (away). ¶심장 발작에 의한 ~ death from a heart attack. **사망하다** die; pass away. ¶그는 버스 사고로 사망했다 He died[was killed] in a bus accident.
● **사망률** mortality; a death rate; percentage of mortality; a mortality [fatality] rate. ¶영아 ~ infant mortality // ~이 높은 병 a very murderous disease / a decimating illness / a disease with a high fatality rate. **사망 신고** a death notice; an announcement of a person's death. **사망자** a dead person; (집합적) the dead; [특정 고인] the deceased(▶ 단수·복수 취급); (사고 등에 의한) persons killed; deaths. ¶항공기 사고 ~ (수) airline fatalities // 그 사고에서 ~는 없었다 No one was killed in the accident. // 지진으로 많은 ~가 발생하였다 The earthquake caused many deaths. / Many lives were lost in the earthquake. / The earthquake took a heavy toll of lives. **사망 진단서** a certificate of death; a death certificate.

사면(四面) 1 [전후 좌우의 둘레] all sides. ¶~이 바다로 둘러싸인 나라 a seagirt country / a country encircled[surrounded / girdled] by the seas / a country within the girdle of the sea // ~팔방으로 on all sides / on every side / in every direction / far and wide / every which way. 2 [네 면] the four sides.
● **사면체** a tetrahedron. ¶정~ a regular tetrahedron.

사면(赦免) a pardon; a remission; amnesty; [가] indulgence; [가] absolution. ¶일반 ~ a general pardon // 특별 ~ a particular [special] pardon. **사면하다** pardon; remit; let (a person) off (a penalty); absolve; grant clemency to (a prisoner) for; [석방하다] discharge; liberate; set (a person) free. → ¶그는 3·1절에 사면되었다 He was pardoned on the Anniversary of the *samil* Independence Movement (of Korea).
● **사면장** a letter of pardon; a pardon.

사면(斜面) 1 [경사진 면] a slope; a slant; a sloping[slanting] surface. ¶지붕의 ~ the slope of a roof // 급~ a steep slope / an escarpment // 완만한 ~ a slight[an easy] slope. 2 → 빗면
● **사면도** an oblique section.

사면발이 1 [동] a crab [public] louse (*pl.* lice). 2 [여러 곳으로 다니며 아첨을 잘하는 사람] a flatterer; a toady; a sycophant; a groveler.

사면초가(四面楚歌) ¶그들은 ~였다 They had the whole world against them. / They were surrounded by enemies[foes] on all sides. / They were forsaken by everybody. // 나는 ~였다 I found myself deserted by everybody.

사멸(死滅) extinction; annihilation; destruction; death. **사멸하다** perish; die out; become extinct; be annihilated; extirpated.

사명(社命) an order of the company.

사명(使命) [맡겨진 임무] an appointed task; [천직] a calling; a vocation; [사자(使者)로서 받은 명령] a mission. ¶~을 **다하다** accomplish [execute / perform / fulfill / discharge] one's mission // 그는 ~을 완수했다 He carried out his mission successfully. // 그는 외교적 ~을 띠고 아프리카로 갔다 He went to Africa on a diplomatic mission. // 그는 정치적 ~을 띠고 중동으로 날아갔다 He flew to the Middle East on a political mission.
● **사명감** a sense of duty.

사모(思慕) 1 [그리워함] longing (for); yearning (for); deep attachment. **사모하다** long [pine] for; love; yearn after; have a deep attachment (to). ¶그는 내 누이를 사모하고 있다 He is very much attached to my sister. // 그녀는 그를 애타게 사모했다 She was pining for his love[affection]. / She was desperately[madly] in love with him. / She was burning with yearning for him. / She was mad about him. 2 [경모] love and respect; admiration; adoration. **사모하다** love and respect; admire; adore; hold (a person) in esteem and reverence. ¶스승의 덕을 ~ adore one's teacher for his virtue.

사모님(師母-) [남의 부인에 대한 경칭] madam; your (good) lady; Mrs. -; your ladyship; milady.

사무(事務) [주로 책상에서 처리하는 일] clerical work; desk work [job]; office work [jobs / labor]; [실무] business; [업무] affairs. ¶~상의 절차 business[office] routine // ~를 보다 do office work / be engaged in business / attend to the duties of an office [to one's business] / be[sit] at the [one's] desk / transact [manage / conduct / execute] business // ~에 바쁘다 be full occupied with office work // ~를 인계하다 transfer [hand over] business[one's affairs] // ~를 인수하다 take over business [the charge of an office] (from another) // 그는 ~에 밝다[능숙하다] He is experienced in (handling) business. / He is familiar with the routine of the office. / He has wide experience in office work. // 그는 ~에 바빠서 여행을 취소했다 He canceled his trip on account of[by] the pressure [press / whirl] of business. // 그는 ~에는 적임자이다 He is fit for office [clerical] work. / He is made for deskwork. // 그 대학에서는 컴퓨터를 사용하여 ~를 처리하고 있다 The university conducts [transacts / manages / executes] its affairs[business] by using computers. // 그녀는 다년간 ~ 경험을 가지고 있다 She has years of experience in office work. / She has long clerical experiences. // 일요일에는 ~는 보지 않습니다 On sundays no business is transacted.
● **사무관** a secretary. **사무국** a secretariat; an executive office. ¶유엔[국제 연합] ~ secretariat of the United Nations. **사무소** / **사무실** an office. ¶법률 (변호사) ~ a lawyer's office / a law office[firm]. **사무 용품** office supplies; stationery. **사무원** a clerk; an office worker [girl]. **사무 자동화** office automation(약어 OA). **사무장** an office manager; a head officer; (상선·비행기의) purser. **사무총장** a secretary-general (*pl.* secretaries-~).

사무엘 전서(-前書) [성] The First Book of

Samuel; I Samuel(약어 I Sam.).
사무엘 후서(-後書) [성] The Second Book of Samuel; II Samuel(약어 II Sam.).
사무적(事務的) businesslike; practical. ¶~으로 in a businesslike manner[way] / in a matter-of-fact way / matter-of-factly / in a perfunctory manner / perfunctorily // 그는 도무지 ~인 데가 없다 He is most unbusinesslike.
사무치다 pierce; penetrate; come[go] home to (one); be brought home to (one); strike (one) home. ¶가슴에 ~ pierce[come home to] one's heart / go to one's heart / cut one to the heart / sting one to the quick / sink deep in one's mind // 나는 그에 대한 원한이 뼈에 사무친다 I bear him a deep[an inveterate] grudge. / I have deep-rooted rancor against him. // 아버지의 꾸지람이 가슴에 사무쳤다 My father's reproof came home to me [struck me home]. // 그는 아버지의 교훈이 마음에 사무쳤다 His father's instructions sank deep into his mind. // 나는 고향이 얼마나 좋은가를 마음에 사무치게 느꼈다 I felt keenly that my old hometown was a very nice place.
사문(死文) (a law that has become) a dead letter. ¶~화된 규칙 a rule that is no longer enforced // ~화하다 end as[become] a mere scrap of paper.
사문(査問) inquiry; inquisition; hearing. **사문하다** interrogate; examine; inquire (into a matter). ¶위원회는 그 문제를 정식으로 사문했다 The committee made an official inquiry into the matter.
● **사문위원회** an inquiry[a rogatory] commission. ¶~를 열다 hold an inquiry (into a matter) / hold an inquest (on / over).
사문서(私文書) a private document.
● **사문서 위조** forgery of a private document.
사문석(蛇紋石) [광] serpentine; ophiolite(뱀무늬 대리석).
사물(死物) a dead[lifeless] thing; an inanimate object.
사물(私物) one's (private) property; one's personal effects. ¶이것은 내 ~입니다 This is my personal belongings[private property / personal effects].
사물(事物) things; affairs; a matter.
사물놀이(四物-) a *samullori*; the (Korean) traditional percussion quartet; a folk music accompanied by four percussion instruments.
사뭇 1 [거리낌 없이 마구] as one pleases [likes / wishes]; willfully; foolhardily. ¶술을 마시면 ~ 시부렁거리게 된다 Wine loosens people's tongues. 2 [줄곧] without break; all through. ¶한 달 내내 ~ 바빴다 I was busy all through the month. 3 [매우] wholly; utterly; very (much); quite. ¶생각했던 것과는 ~ 다르다 It is quite different from what I thought.
사바나 [열대 초원] a savanna(h).
사바(세계)(娑婆世界) this world; here below. ¶~의 earthly / worldly / mundane // ~가 싫어졌다 I am sick of this world.
사박거리다 crunch softly.
사박사박 with a soft crunch. ¶모래사장을 ~ 걷다 walk across the sand with a soft crunch // 사과를 ~ 씹다 munch an apple. **사박사박하다** crunch softly. ⇨사박거리다

사반세기(四半世紀) a quarter of a century.
사발(沙鉢) a (china) bowl. ¶밥~ a rice bowl // 밥 한 ~ a bowl of rice.
● **사발시계** a bowl-shaped (table) clock. **사발통문**(-通文) a round robin.
사방(四方) 1 [네 방위] four sides; [여러 곳] all directions. ¶~의 산들 mountains on all sides // ~에 [으로] on all sides / on every side / in every direction / in all directions / all around // ~에서 from all quarters / from every quarter[direction] // ~을 찾다 seek every corner for (something) // 이것은 ~ 5미터다 It is[measures] five meters square. // ~이 고요하다 Everything is quiet. // 소문은 ~으로 퍼졌다 The rumor spread far and wide [in every direction]. // ~에서 불길이 치솟았다 Flames rose from all directions[quarters] // 나는 ~을 둘러보았다 I looked all around. // 나는 ~이 높은 산으로 둘러싸인 마을에서 태어났다 I was born in a village surrounded by high mountains on every side [all sides]. // ~에서 사람들이 모여들었다 People gathered from all quarters.
2 a square (shape). ⇨네모
● **사방팔방** [모든 방면] every direction; all directions; all sides; everywhere. ¶~에서 from all quarters / from every quarter [direction] // 불은 ~으로 퍼졌다 The fire spread on all sides. // ~이 온통 눈이었다 There was snow everywhere.
사방(沙防) erosion control; sand arrestation; sandbank fixing.
● **사방 공사** erosion control work; sand guard; anti-erosion work; sand arrestation work. **사방림**(-林) an erosion control forest.
사방형(斜方形) ➡ 평행 사변형(⇨평행)
사범(事犯) an act[deed] subject to punishment[penalty]; an illegal act; an offense; a crime. ¶정치 ~ a political offense // 경제 ~ an economic offense // 선거 ~ election illegalities[irregularities] / an election law violation // 폭력 ~ (a) violent crime.
사범(師範) 1 [무술·기예 등을 가르치는 사람] a teacher; a master; a preceptor; an instructor; a coach. ¶검도 ~ a fencing master / a sword instructor // 태권도[유도] ~ a *taegwondo*[judo] teacher[master]. 2 [모범] a model[an example] (to others).
● **사범 대학** a college of education.
사법(司法) [재판·법무의 운용] the administration of justice; judicature. ¶~의 judicial / judiciary // ~적 해결 a judicial settlement // 근대 국가에서는 행정·입법·~의 삼권은 독립되어 있다 In modern nations the three powers of administration, legislation and jurisdiction are independent of each other.
● **사법 경찰** the judicial police. **사법권** judicial[judicatory] power; powers of jurisdiction. ¶~의 독립 independence of the judicature // ~의 행사[남용] exercise[abuse] of judicial power // ~을 발동하다 invoke[exercise] judicial power / exercise jurisdiction. **사법 시험** a state law examination. **사법 연수생** a judicial apprentice. **사법 제도** the judicial system.
사법(死法) a dead law.
사법(私法) [법] private law[statute].
사법인(私法人) a private corporation; a private incorporated body.
사변(四邊) 1 [사방의 변두리] the frontiers (of

a country). **2** [주위·근처] the neighborhood. **3** [수] the four sides; all sides.
- **사변형** a quadrangle. ⇨ *사각형* ⇨ *사각(四角)*

사변(斜邊) ➡ 빗변

사변(事變) 1 [변고] an accident; a mishap; an untoward event[accident]; a disaster [calamity](재해). **2** [변란] an incident; a trouble; a disturbance; an upheaval; an uprising; [급변] an emergency; an exigency. ¶만주 ~ the Manchurian Incident.

사변(思辨) 1 [철] speculation. ¶~적 speculative/ ~적 방법 a speculative method. **2** [변별·판별] discrimination; distinction.
- **사변 철학** speculative philosophy.

사별(死別) separation by death; bereavement. **사별하다** be bereaved (of one's husband); be separated from (one's parents) by death. ¶남편과 ~ lose one's husband through death / be parted from one's husband by death // 양친과 ~ lose one's parents / be bereaved of one's parents / be left an orphan // 그녀는 서른 살에 남편과 사별했다 She lost her husband when she was thirty.

사병(士兵) a private (soldier); (미) a enlisted man; [집합적] the rank and file. ¶일개 ~에서 대장까지 오르다 rise from the ranks to be a general.

사보타주(㊏sabotage) going slow; a slowdown (strike); [영] a work-to-rule [go-slow] strike. **사보타주하다** go slow; stage [go on] a go-slow strike; [영] work to rule.

사보텐 [식] a cactus (pl. ~es, -ti).

사복(私服) [관복·제복이 아닌 보통 옷] plain [ordinary] clothes; private [civilian] clothes; [미국 구어] civvies; [약식] mufti(군인 등의). ¶~로 in plain clothes / in civilian attire / out of uniform. **사복하다** wear plain clothes.
- **사복 경찰관** a plainclothes policeman; a policeman in civilian clothes. **사복형사** a plainclothesman.

사복(私腹) ¶~을 채우다 stuff [fill / line] one's (own) pocket [purse] / feather one's (own) nest / enrich oneself / (공인(公人)이) graft / practice jobbery // 그는 공금을 횡령하여 ~을 채웠다 He lined his own pockets by misappropriating public funds.

사본(寫本) a copy; a transcript(등사물); a duplicate(부본); [필사본] a (book in) manuscript(약어 MS); a written copy. ¶증서의 ~ a copy [duplicate] of bond // 영수증 ~ the duplicate copy of a receipt // ~을 뜨다 copy / make a copy [duplicate] of / duplicate (a letter).

사부(四部) [네 부분] four parts.
- **사부작** a tetralogy; a four-part book. **사부합창** a (vocal) quartet(te). ¶~곡 a four-part song.

사부(師父) [아버지처럼 우러러 받드는 스승] a fatherly master; an esteemed teacher; one's teacher.

사부(師傅) 1 a teacher. ⇨ *스승* **2** [태사·태부] a tutor to king's sons [grandsons]; prince's fosterer and tutor.

사북 1 (부채 등의) the pivot; a pivot pin (on a fan). **2** [가장 긴요한 부분] a main [vital] point; the point; a pivot; the key (to).

사분(四分) quartering; dividing in four. ¶~의 1 one [a] quarter / one fourth // ~의 3 three fourths / three quarters. **사분하다** divide in four; separate [divide] into four parts; quarter.
- **사분기(一期)** a quarter; one forth; a forth part. ¶1~ the first quarter of the year. **사분면** [수] a quadrant. **사분쉼표** [음] a quarter rest. **사분음표** [음] (미) a quarter note; (영) a crotchet.

사분거리다 1 [우스운 소리를 하며 조르다] tease (a person) humorously. **2** [가만가만 지껄이다] whisper; talk in a low voice.

사분사분 softly; quietly; lightly. **사분사분하다¹** tease (a person) humorously; whisper. ⇨ *사분거리다*

사분사분하다² (성품·마음이) affable; amiable; good-natured.

사분오열(四分五裂) disruption; utter disunion [division / break-up]. **사분오열하다** go to pieces; be utterly disrupted.

사뿟사뿟 softly; lightly. ⇨ *사뿐사뿐*

사비(私費) one's own expense; private expense. ¶~로 at one's own expense // ~를 쓰다 spend one's money (on).

사비(社費) the company's expenses; the upkeep of a company(경비); the outlay(s) of a company(지출). ¶그들은 ~로 연회를 열었다 They had a feast at the expense of the company.

사뿐 softly; lightly; with a soft step. ¶땅으로 ~ 내려서다 jump [leap / hop] down to the ground with a soft [muffled] thud.

사뿐사뿐 softly; lightly; with soft steps. ¶~ 걷다 walk lightly / walk with soft steps / walk with a light tread.

사사건건(事事件件) each and every case [matter / affair / event]. ¶~ 반대하다 oppose (a person) in every way.

사사기(士師記) [성] (The Book of) Judges(약어 Judg.).

사사롭다(私私ー) personal; private; informal. ¶사사로운 감정[일] personal feeling [affairs] // 사사로운 정에 이끌리다 be swayed [influenced] by personal feelings // 사사로운 일이므로 남에게는 알리지 않았습니다 As it was a private matter, we kept it to ourselves. **사사로이** personally; privately; in private; informally.

사사오입(四捨五入) ➡ 반올림

사사하다(師事ー) study under (a person); look up to (a person) as one's teacher; apprentice oneself to; become (a person's) pupil; receive instruction (at a person's feet); be a disciple of (a person). ¶고명한 스승에게 ~ study under a renowned scholar / have an instruction from one of the prominent professors // 나는 다년간 그분에게 사사했다 I sat at his feet for many years.

사산(死産) (a) stillbirth. **사산하다** have a stillbirth; have a baby born dead. ¶나는 아기를 사산했다 My baby was born dead [stillborn].
- **사산아** a stillborn baby; a stillbirth.

사살하다(射殺ー) kill by shooting; shoot (a person) dead [to death]. ¶우리는 탈주하는 자는 사살하라는 명령을 받고 있었다 Our orders were that, if we saw anyone who tried to escape, we should shoot to kill.

사삿일(私私ー) personal affairs; private matters [concerns]. ¶남의 ~에 참견하다 interfere in a person's private concerns / go [pry / poke one's nose] into a person's private affairs.

사상(史上) in history. ¶~ 최대의 … the greatest … in history∥~ 초유의 거사 an epoch-making event∥~ 최고의 기록 the highest record in history / (미국 구어) (hit) the historical high∥~ 최초의 우주 비행 the first space flight in history / ~ 유례가 없는 사건 an incident unprecedented[without precedent] in history.

사상(死相) 1 [죽을 상] a countenance presaging death; the shadow of death on (a person's) face. ¶환자의 얼굴은 이미 ~이었다 The patient already looked like a dead man. / (문어) The shadow of death was already on the sick man's face. 2 [죽은 사람의 얼굴] a dead person's face.

사상(死傷) [죽음과 부상] death and injury.
● **사상병**(一兵) the killed and injured soldiers; troop casualties. **사상자** casualties; the killed and the injured[wounded]; losses. ¶승객 중 30명의 ~가 났다 Thirty passengers were either killed or injured.∥지진으로 많은 ~가 났다 The earthquake caused many[heavy] casualties. / The earthquake killed and injured great numbers of people.

사상(事象) a phenomenon (pl. -na); a matter; an event; an aspect; a phase. ¶사회적 ~ a social phenomenon.

사상(思想) thought; an idea; [이데올로기] an ideology. ¶신 ~ a new idea∥정치 ~ political thought∥근대 ~ modern thought∥동양[서양] ~ Eastern[Western] thought[ideas]∥사대~ flunk(e)yism / toadyism∥공산주의 ~ Communist idea∥자유 ~ liberal thought∥중심 ~ the central idea∥진보 ~ a progressive idea∥건전한 ~ healthy[sound] thought∥신구 ~의 충돌 a conflict between new and old ideas∥한국 ~의 주류 the main current of Korean thought∥~이 건전한 sound-thinking (people)∥~을 전달하다 communicate one's thought (to) / convey one's ideas across (to)∥~을 말로 표현하다 express one's thought by means of words∥~을 엄격히 통제하다 maintain strict thought control / exert strict control[censorship] over ideas∥~을 탄압하다 suppress ideas∥위험한 ~을 불어넣다 inoculate (a person) with dangerous ideas∥그는 ~이 건전하다 He has sound ideas. / His thinking is quite sound.
● **사상가** a (profound) thinker; a man of thought. **사상계** the world of thought; the thinking world; the realm of ideas. **사상범**(~犯) a thought offense; (사람) a political offender. **사상전** ideological warfare; an ideological battle.

사상(絲狀) [실처럼 가늘고 긴 모양]. ¶~의 filiform / thready.
● **사상균**(~菌) a filamentous fungus; a mold. **사상충**(~蟲) a heartworm; a filaria (pl. -ae).

사상(寫像) [물] representation; [수] mapping; [심] an image.
● **사상주의** imagism.

사상누각(沙上樓閣) a house of cards; (build) a castle in Spain[the air].

사색(四色) 1 [네 가지 색] four colors. 2 [역] the Factions (of the Joseon Dynasty).
● **사색당쟁** (party) strife[intrigue] among the Four Factions. **사색판**(~인) four-color printing.

사색(死色) deadly[ghastly] pale look; blanching complexion; deathly paleness. ¶~이 되다 turn deadly pale (with horror)∥그 소식을 듣자 그녀의 얼굴은 ~이 되었다 Her face went ashy pale to hear the news.

사색(思索) speculation; thinking; cogitation; contemplation; meditation. ¶~적인 speculative / meditative∥~적인 생활 a life of meditation∥~에 잠기다 be given to contemplation[speculation] / be lost[absorbed] in thought[meditation]∥그는 ~에 잠겨 근처를 서성거렸다 He wandered about deep in contemplation[lost in thought]. **사색하다** think; muse[speculate / meditate] on; contemplate (on); cogitate; ponder.
● **사색가** a (philosophical / speculative) thinker; a thinking person.

사생(死生) life and death. ¶~을 함께하다 share one's fate (with).
● **사생결단** desperation; risking one's life. ¶~하다 risk one's life / be desperate / do (something) at the risk of one's life∥~하고 at the risk[peril] of one's life / in desperation∥~하고 싸우다 fight to the death / fight it out at the risk of one's life / fight desperately.

사생(寫生) sketching; drawing[painting] from nature. **사생하다** sketch; paint[draw / sketch] from nature; draw[paint] from [after] life; make a sketch of (a view). ¶사생하러 가다 go sketching.
● **사생화** a picture drawn from life[nature]; a sketch.

사생아(私生兒) an illegitimate child; a natural[love] child; a bastard; a child of shame; a child born out of wedlock. ¶~로 태어나다 be born on the wrong side of the blanket∥그녀는 ~를 낳았다 She was delivered of a love child.

사생활(私生活) one's private life. ¶~에 간여하다 dig[nose] into (a person's) private life∥남의 ~에 간여하지 마시오 You should not interfere in other's private concerns.

사서(史書) a history (book).
사서(司書) a librarian.
사서(四書) the Four Books (of Ancient China)(=the Analects of Confucius(논어), the Works of Mencius(맹자), the Doctrine of the Mean(중용), and the Great Learning(대학)).
● **사서삼경** the Four Books and Three Classics.

사서(辭書) a dictionary. ⇨ 사전(辭典).
사서함(私書函) a post-office box(약어 P.O.B. / POB); (미) a call box. ¶중앙 우체국 ~ 67호 C.P.O. Box No. 67∥국제 우체국 ~ 108호 I.P.O. Box No. 108 / ~ 235호로 회답 바랍니다 Please direct your answer to P.O.B. No. 235.

사석(私席) an informal[an unofficial / a private] occasion. ¶~에서 informally / unofficially∥~에서 남의 욕을 하지 마라 Don't speak ill of others at the unofficial occasion.

사선(死線) [감옥·포로수용소 주위에 친 가상선] a deadline; [생사에 관계된 위기] a life-or-death crisis. ¶~을 넘어 across the deadline∥~을 넘다 cross the deadline / brave death / survive a life-or-death crisis∥그는 전쟁터에서 여러 번 ~을 넘었다 He was often face to face with death on the battlefield.

사선(斜線) an oblique (line); a slant (line); (and / or 경우의) a slanting stroke; a slash (mark); a virgule. ¶~을 그은 부분 the shaded portion.

사설(私設) [관형어적] private. ¶그 철도는 ~이다 The railway is under private management. **사설하다** establish privately.
● **사설 시장** a private market. **사설 학원** a private[(미)] proprietary] school[institute].

사설(社說) a leader (on economics); a leading article; (미) an editorial (article). ¶격렬한 ~ a highly explosive editorial // 강경한 ~ a strong editorial // ~에서 논하다 discuss (a matter) in an editorial / comment editorially (on) / editorialize (on) // 경제 문제에 관한 ~이 실렸다 There was an editorial on the economic subject in the paper.
● **사설란** the editorial column.

사설(辭說) 1 [언사] words; speech; [기술한 글] (a) description; an account; [노래·연극 사이의] narration; description. 2 [잔소리] tattering; babbling; prattling; [불평] grumbling; nagging.
● **사설시조** a form of *sijo* with unlimited length in the middle verse.

사성(四聖) the four greatest sages of the world(=Confucius, Buddha, Jesus, and Socrates).

사성(四聲) the four tones (of Chinese characters).

사세(事勢) the situation; the state of things [affairs]; the aspect of affairs; the way things are. ¶지금의 ~로서는 in the present state of things / judging by the current situation // ~가 불리하다 The situation is unavoidable for me.

사세부득이(事勢不得已) unavoidably; inevitably; out of sheer necessity; driven by[owing to / through] unavoidable circumstances. ¶~한 경우에는 when circumstances compel [require] / in an unavoidable case.

사소설(私小說) an "I" story; a first-person novel; a novel dealing with[based on] the author's own life; an autobiographical tale [story].

사소하다(些少-) trifling; trivial (matter); small; minor (fault); petty (sum); meager; scanty; slight (difference); insignificant. ¶사소한 일 a trifle / a trifling[trivial] matter // 사소한 잘못 a trifling[minor] error / a light[an insignificant] mistake // 그녀는 언제나 사소한 일로 화를 낸다 She always gets angry at trifles. / She always takes offense on the slightest provocation. // 그는 사소한 일로 법석을 떨었다 He made a fuss about trifles. // 그것은 사소한 일이다 It is nothing to speak of.

사수(死守) a desperate [stubborn] defense [(영) defence]. **사수하다** defend to the last [to the death]; defend desperately[stubbornly]. ¶진지를 ~ defend a position to the last.

사수(射手) a marksman; a shooter; a gunner; a rifleman; (활의) an archer; a bowman. ¶기관 ~ a machine gunner // 명 ~ a master [crack / dead] shot.

사숙하다(私淑-) adore (a person) (in one's heart); look up to (a person) as one's model; be strongly influenced (by). ¶그는 송 박사를 사숙했다 He was strongly influenced by[He modeled himself on] Dr. Song, though he was not his direct pupil.

사순절(四旬節) (기독교의) Lent. ¶~의 Lenten // ~의 금식 예배 the Lenten fast services.

사술(邪術) black magic; the black art; sorcery; witchcraft.

사슬 a chain; (개를 매는) a tether. ¶~에 매인 개 a dog on a chain / ~에 매인 포로 a captive fastened (to a pole) with chains / a war prisoner (shackled) in chains // ~로 매다 enchain / chain up / put (men) in chains // ~을 풀다 unchain / undo the chain / put (a dog) out of chain // ~에서 벗어나다 [비유] free oneself from restraint / throw[cast / shake / fling] off the fetters[shackles] (of) / break away from the yoke (of) // 개는 ~에 매여 있다 The dog is on a chain.
● **사슬고리** a link.

사슴 a deer (단수·복수 동형); a stag(수컷); a doe(암컷); a hind(암컷). ¶~의 cervine // 새끼 ~ a fawn / a spitter // 한 떼의 ~이 풀을 뜯고 있다 A herd of deer are feeding grass.
● **사슴 가죽** deerskin; buckskin. **사슴뿔** an antler.

사시(四時) 1 [사철] the four seasons. 2 at[in] all seasons (of the year). ⇨ 사시사철(⇨사시)
● **사시사철** at[in] all seasons (of the year); all the year round.

사시(史詩) an epic; a historical poem.

사시(斜視) 1 a squint; [의] strabismus. ¶내 ~ convergent[cross-eyed] strabismus // 외 ~ divergent[wall-eyed] strabismus // ~의 squint / squinting / squint-eyed / cross-eyed / strabismal / (영국 구어) boss-eyed // ~이다 have a squint / have a cast in the eye. 2 [흘겨봄] looking askance.
● **사시안** a squint (eye); a cockeye.

사시나무 [식] an aspen, a (white) poplar; an abele; a quaking[trembling] aspen.

사시나무 떨듯 quake[tremble] like an aspen leaf.

사식(私食) private food sent into a prisoner.

사식(寫植) phototypesetting. ⇨ 사진 식자(⇨사진)

사신(私信) a private message[letter]; a private communication.

사신(使臣) an envoy; an ambassador(대사); a minister(공사). ¶각국의 ~ envoys from each nation // ~을 파견하다 dispatch [send] an envoy (to).

사실(史實) a historical fact; a matter of history; historical evidence. ¶이 드라마는 ~에 충실하다 This drama is faithful to history.

사실(事實) 1 [실제의 일] a fact; an actual fact; a reality; actuality(현실); [법] a factum (pl. -ta); [진실] the truth; the case. ¶뚜렷한 [기정] ~ an obvious[established] fact // 적나라한[꾸밈없는] ~ the naked[plain] truth // ~을 말하자면 to tell the truth / honestly (speaking) / to be quite honest (about it) / as a matter of fact // ~이 되다 [예상했던 대로 되다] come[(문어) prove] true / [실현되다] materialize // ~을 밝히다 reveal the truth // ~은 나도 적잖이 놀랐다 To tell the truth, I was not a little surprised myself. // ~대로 말하자면 그것은 잘못이었다 To tell the truth [To be frank with you] / Frankly speaking] that was a mistake. // 그 소문은 ~과 다르다 The rumor is contrary to the fact. // 이 한 가지 ~만 보아도 그가 선량하다는 것을 알 수

있다 This one instance is enough to show his goodness.// 제가 늦은 것은 ~입니다 It is true that I was late.// ~은 그에게 그만한 돈이 없다 The fact is that he does not have that much money.// ~은 소설보다 기묘하다 Truth is stranger than fiction.// 이 이야기는 ~에 근거하고 있다 This story is based on fact.
2 [실제로] actually; really; [사실인즉] in fact; [실은] as a matter of fact. ¶그는 괴짜라는 평이 있는데 ~ 그렇다 He is said to be eccentric and he really is.// 그는 겁쟁이로 보이지만 ~ 꽤 용감한 사람이다 He looks timid, but actually he is quite courageous.// 그는 ~ 백만장자다 He is in fact a millionaire.

사실(寫實) representing things as they really are; exact, objective description; realism.
● **사실 소설** a realistic novel. **사실주의** realism; literalism. ¶~의 대가 a master of realism. **사실주의자** a realist; a realistic writer; a literalist.

사실적(寫實的) realistic; true to life[nature]; objective; graphic. ¶~으로 realistically / graphically // ~으로 묘사하다 describe [depict] realistically / give a graphic description (of).

사심(邪心) a wicked heart; an evil[a vicious] mind; a malicious intention; an evil design.

사심(私心) selfishness; a selfish motive; self-interest. ¶~이 없는 unselfish / disinterested // ~을 갖고 행동하다 act from a selfish motive// 그는 절대로 ~을 개입시키지 않는다 He never acts from ulterior motives.

사십(四十) forty; [제40] the fortieth. ¶~ 대의 사람 a person in his forties // ~ 정도의 (연령·수량의) fortyish // ~ 전의 under[on the sunny side of] forty // ~을 넘은 over forty / on the wrong[other] side of forty.

사악하다(邪惡-) [도덕에 어긋나다] wicked; evil; [악의가] malicious; vicious. ¶사악한 사람 a malicious person / a villain / a godless person.

사안(私案) one's private plan[program / scheme / idea / design].

사안(事案) a case.

사암(沙巖) [광] sandstone.

사약(賜藥) (the King's) bestowal of poison. ¶~을 내리다 bestow poison (for an official to kill himself with).

사양(斜陽) **1** [저녁 햇볕] the setting[declining / slanting / sinking] sun; the evening sun(light). **2** [점점 쇠퇴하여 감]. ¶~의 석탄 산업 the declining coal industry.
● **사양 산업** a fading[an eclipsed / a declining] industry; an industry on the decline.

사양(辭讓) [양보] declining in favor of another; concession; [사절] courteous refusal[(미) declination / denial]; refusal with appreciation; [삼감] reserve; restraint; deference; modesty; holding back. **사양하다** [양보하다] decline (something) in favor of another; give way to (another); make room for (another); concede; make a concession; [사절] refuse courteously; decline with thanks[regrets]; excuse oneself (from); ask to be excused; [삼가다] be reserved [modest]; stand on[upon] ceremony; refrain [abstain / keep] from; hold back. ¶초대를 ~ decline an invitation// 사양하지 않고 unreservedly / without reserve[ceremony / formality] / freely / without hesitation// 사양할 것 없다 You need not hesitate (to do it).

사어(死語) a dead language(언어); an obsolete word(낱말). ¶고대 그리스 어는 ~다 Ancient Greek is a dead language.

사업(事業) **1** [기업] an enterprise; [실업] an industry; a business. ¶관영[국영 / 민간] ~ a government[national / private] enterprise // 전기 ~ [집합적] the electric(al) industry // 위험 부담이 많은 ~ a risky business // 공공 ~ a public utility enterprise / public works / (public) utilities // 방송 ~ the broadcasting industry // ~을 시작하다 start a business // ~을 경영하다 run a business // ~을 하다 carry on business // 견실하지 못한 ~에 손을 대다 embark on a risky business[venture] // ~에 실패하다 fail in business // 그는 ~에 열심이다 He is a serious businessman.// 무슨 ~을 하십니까 What line of business are you in?// ~ 은 잘되고 있습니까 How's your business doing?
2 [일] work; [인계받은 또는 꾸민 일] an undertaking; [계획적인 일] a project. ¶사회 ~ social work // 교육[자선] ~ educational [charitable] work.
● **사업가** [사업주] an entrepreneur; [실업가] a businessman. **사업부** an operation division; an enterprise department. **사업비** business expenses. **사업소** / **사업장** a place of business; an establishment. **사업 소득** a business income; an income from an enterprise. **사업 자금** business funds; funds for equipment.

사에이치 클럽(四—) a Four-H[4-H] club(▶ 4-H는 the head, heart, hand, health).

사역(使役) employment; [군] a fatigue. **사역하다** employ; use; work; set (a person) to work. →¶그들은 매일 건설 공사에 사역되었다 They were employed in construction work every day.
● **사역 동사** [언] a causative verb. ⇨ 사동사

사연(事緣) [사정] circumstances; considerations; the state of things[matters / affairs]; [연유] the matter; the case; the story. ¶말 못할 ~이 있어서 for some secret[inexpressible] reasons // 거기에는 복잡한 ~이 있다 There are wheels within wheels.

사연(辭緣) [내용] content(s); [취지] the import; the gist; the point. ¶편지 ~은 무엇이냐 What is the letter about?

사열(査閱) (an) inspection; an inspection [a review] of troops. ¶~을 받다 be inspected (by) / undergo inspection. **사열하다** inspect [review] (troops).
● **사열대** a reviewing stand. **사열식** a review; an inspection parade.

사염화(四鹽化) [화] tetrachloride.
● **사염화탄소** carbon tetrachloride.

사영(私營) private management[operation]. ¶~의 privately operated[run].

사영(射影) [수] projection. ¶~의 projective // 정 ~ orthogonal projection. **사영하다** project.
● **사영 기하학** projective geometry.

사옥(社屋) the office building of a company.

사욕(沙浴·砂浴) (사람의) a sand bath; (동물의) a dust bath; dust bathing; dusting. **사욕하다** have[take] a sand bath; bathe in dust.

사욕(私慾) [이기심] self-interest; [자기 욕심] (a) selfish desire. ¶~이 있는[없는] 사람 a

사용 selfish [an unselfish] man // ~을 채우다 satisfy one's selfish desires // 그는 ~에 눈이 멀었다 He was blinded by self-interest.

사용(私用) 1 [사사로이 씀] private use; (공용물의) (an) appropriation; (a) misappropriation. ¶그것을 ~으로 써서는 안 된다 Don't use it for private purposes. **사용하다** put [turn] (a thing) to private use; use (a thing) for private [one's own] purposes; misappropriate; appropriate (to oneself); embezzle. ¶공로에 주차하는 것은 공로를 사용하는 것이나 마찬가지다 By parking your car on a public road, you are making private [personal] use of it. 2 [사적 용무] private business.

사용(使用) use; employment; application(응용); consumption(소비); appropriation(충당). ¶~을 금하다 forbid [ban] the use (of) // 중 (방·화장실 등의) (게시) Occupied. // ~ 금지 (게시) Not in use. // 화장실이 ~ 중이다 The toilet is occupied. // 볼펜 ~은 허락되지 않는다 The use of a ball-point pen is not allowed. **사용하다** use; make use of; put (a thing) to use; (도구·수단 등을) (문어) employ; apply; consume; appropriate; devote. ¶사용한 우표 a used stamp // 사용하지 않는 방 an unused room // 사용할 수 있는 usable / practicable / fit for use // 될 수 있는 대로 [효과적으로] ~ make the best (possible) use of // 자유로이 ~ have the free use (of) / be at liberty to use (a thing) // 그는 더러운 수단을 사용했다 He used dirty means. // 여기에 있는 것은 마음대로 사용해도 좋습니다 These things are at your disposal.

● **사용권** the right to use a thing; [법] a usufructuary right. **사용량** the amount (of something) used; the quantity (of something) consumed. **사용료** a rental fee; the rental; the rent; the hire. ¶기술 ~ technological [license] fees // 스키의 ~ the ski rental charge / the charge for renting skis // 항만 ~ port dues // 부두 ~ wharfage. **사용법** how to use [handle / treat]; usage; directions (for use) (약 등의). ¶나는 이 다목적 공구의 ~을 모른다 I don't know how to use this multipurpose tool. // 이 어구의 ~은 틀렸다 The usage of this phrase is wrong. **사용자** [이용자] a user; [소비자] a consumer; [고용주] an employer.

사우(社友) 1 [회사의 동료] a colleague in a company. 2 [회사와 관계가 깊은 사람] a friend of a company [firm].

사우나 [증기 목욕] a sauna.

사우스포 [야구·권투] a southpaw.

사운(社運) ¶이 제품에 ~이 걸려 있다 The fortunes of our company are riding on this product.

사운드 [음향] a sound.

● **사운드 카드** a sound card. **사운드트랙** (필름의) a sound track.

사원(寺院) a (Buddhist) temple; (기독교의) a temple; a church; a monastery(수도원); (회교의) a mosque.

사원(社員) an employee; a member of the staff (of a company); a partner(조합원); (집합적) the staff. ¶신입 ~ a new [an incoming] employee // 정 ~ a full-fledged [regular] employee of a company // 퇴직 ~ an outgoing partner [employee] // 노무 출자 [업무 담당] ~ a working [managing] partner // 준 ~ a junior member // 그는 그 회사의 ~이다 He is on the staff of the company.

● **사원 명부** the roster (of a company).

사원(私怨) [사사로운 원한] personal [private] grudge [spite / grievance / resentment]. ¶~으로 out of [from] personal spite // ~을 풀다 work off a personal grudge.

사월(四月) April(약어 Apr.).

사위 a son-in-law (pl. sons-in-law). ¶큰 [맏] ~ the oldest son-in-law // 작은 ~ a younger son-in-law // 그는 돈 많은 주류 도매상의 ~가 되었다 He married the daughter of a well-to-do liquor dealer. // 그는 친구의 아들을 ~로 삼았다 His friend's son entered the family as his son-in-law.

● **사윗감** a suitable match for one's daughter; a likely son-in-law. ¶~으로 훌륭하다 [사윗감이다] be a good [poor] match for one's daughter // ~을 구하고 계신다지요 I hear you are looking for a man to marry your daughter.

사위다 [불이 다 타서 재가 되다] burn (itself) out; burn up.

사유(私有) [관형어적] private; privately owned. ¶이 전답은 ~이다 These fields are private property. **사유하다** possess oneself of.

● **사유권** the right of private property; private ownership [rights]. **사유물** one's private possessions. **사유 재산** private property. **사유지** private land; privately-owned land.

사유(事由) [이유] a reason; a cause; a ground; conditions. ¶…한 ~로 for the reason that ….

사유(思惟) [생각함] thinking; speculation. **사유하다** think [speculate] (about).

사육(飼育) breeding [raising] (of cattle); rearing. ¶마소의 ~ the breeding of horses and cattle. **사육하다** breed; raise.

● **사육자** a raiser; a breeder; a rearer; a (bird) fancier. **사육장** a breeding farm; (말의) a stud farm.

사육제(謝肉祭) the carnival.

사은(謝恩) [받은 은혜에 사례함] an expression of gratitude; appreciation (of [for] a person's help). **사은하다** repay (another's) kindness; express (one's) gratitude; appreciate (a person's) favors.

● **사은 세일** a thank-you sales. **사은회** a dinner [party] given (by the students) in honor [(영) honour] of (their teachers); a thank-you party for the teachers.

사음자리표(一音一標) a treble clef. ⇨ 높은음자리표

사의(謝意) 1 [감사하는 마음] gratitude; thanks(▶ 복수형으로 씀). ¶여러분이 베풀어 주신 친절에 대하여 깊은 ~를 표합니다 I wish to thank you [express my gratitude to you] for all your kindness. // 그녀는 머리를 숙여 정중하게 ~를 표하였다 She bowed to him her most profuse thanks. 2 [사죄하는 마음] an apology; apologetic feelings.

사의(辭意) [사임할 의사] one's resolution [intention] to resign. ¶~를 비추다 [표명하다] intimate [announce] one's intention of resigning (from one's office) // 그는 ~를 재고한 것 같다 He seems to have reconsidered his resignation. // 그의 ~는 굳다 He is bent on resigning. / He is firmly resolved to quit.

사이 1 [공간] an interval; a space; [틈] a gap; an opening; [둘 사이] between; [여럿 사이] among(st); [한가운데] amid(st); [중앙] halfway; midway; [도중] on the way. ¶~에 든 사람[중개자] a go-between / a middleman / [조정자] a mediator // 학생들 ~에 인기가 있는 선생 a teacher who is popular with the students // 벽을 하나 ~에 두고 on the other side of the wall // 일정한 ~를 두고 at regular intervals // ~를 떼다 [벌리다] leave a space / space out // 나는 그와 탁자를 ~에 두고 앉았다 I sat across the table from him. // 그 부부 ~에는 자식이 없다 That couple have no children.
2 [시간적인 겨를] an interval; time; while; a space; a period; a span; a spell; a pause; a break; a gap; [여가] leisure; spare time; time to spare; odd moments; [음] (a) rest. ¶잠깐 ~에 in a minute[moment] / in no time / in an instant // 집을 비운 ~에 when [while] one is out / in one's absence // 쉴 ~도 없다 I have no time to rest. // 너는 만 원쯤은 눈 깜짝할 ~에 써 버리고 만다 You spend ten thousand won in no time.
3 [서로 맺은 관계] a relationship; a relation (relationship이 보다 현대적임); [사귀는 정분] terms. ¶부모 자식 ~ the relation[ties] between parent and child / the parent-child relationship // 당신들은 어떤 ~입니까 What is your relationship? // 그와는 친한 ~이다 They are very close to[intimate with] each other. (▶ intimate는 완곡하게 성적 관계를 의미하는 경우가 많음) // 그들은 서로 육체 관계가 있는 ~인 것 같다 They seem to be on intimate terms with each other. // 그들은 사랑하는 ~인 것 같다 They seem to be in love with each other. // 둘은 서로 사랑하는 ~가 되었다 The two fell in love with each other. // 그들은 ~가 좋다[나쁘다] They are on good [bad] terms. // 그와는 서로 방문하는[농담하는] ~다 I am on visiting[joking] terms with him. // 두 소년은 아주 친한 ~다 The two boys are close friends. // 그는 그 부부 ~를 이간할 계획을 꾸미고 있다 He is scheming to separate the couple [estrange the man from his wife]. // 아무도 우리 ~에 끼어들 수 없다 No one can come between us. // 그녀는 시어머니와 ~가 좋다 She is getting on well with her mother-in-law. // 그들은 사랑하는 ~다 They are in love with each other. / They love each other. / [육체 관계가 있다] They are lovers. // 너희들은 친구 ~가 아니냐 You're pals, aren't you? // 그는 동생하고 ~가 나쁘다 He is on bad terms[has had a falling-out] with his brother. // 그는 아내와의 ~가 좋지 않다 He and his wife don't get along very well together any more.

사이다 (*cider) [음료] pop; (영) aerated water; [미] soda (pop); (상표명) Sprite.(▶ cider는 미국에서는 「사과즙」, 영국에서는 「사과주」)

사이드라인 a sideline.

사이드 미러 an outside mirror; a rearview mirror; a side mirror.

사이드 스텝 [권투] a side step. ¶그는 ~으로 펀치를 피했다 He slipped a punch by side-stepping.

사이드 아웃 [배구·배드민턴]. ¶~이 되다 call a side out.

사이드카 (오토바이의) a sidecar; [사이드카가 달린 오토바이] a motorcycle combination.

사이렌 a siren; a whistle. ¶정오의 ~ a noon siren // ~을 울리다 sound a siren // ~이 울리고 있다 A siren is blowing. // 공습을 알리는 ~이 울려 퍼졌다 An air-raid siren wailed [went off].

사이버 공간 (-空間) cyberspace.

사이버네틱스 [생물의 제어 기구와 기계의 제어 기구의 공통 원리를 규명하는 학문] cybernetics.

사이버섹스 cybersex.

사이보그 [기계 등으로 개조된 인간] a cyborg.

사이비 (似而非) [관형어격] false; would-be; sham; pretended; mock; spurious; pseud(o)-; quasi-; (프) soi-disant.
● **사이비 기자** a quasi-reporter. **사이비 종교** a pseudo-religion.

사이사이 [사이와 사이] intervals; spaces; gaps. ¶줄 ~를 메모로 채우다 fill (in) interlinear spaces with memos. 2 [틈틈이] intervals (of / in / between). ¶일하는 ~에 in the intervals of business / in spare moments from one's work.

사이좋다 intimate; close; friendly. ¶사이좋게 on good[friendly / cordial] terms (with) / in peace[harmony / concord] (with) // 사이좋게 지내다 get on[along] well (with) / keep intimate relations (with) / make friends with / be on good terms with // 사이좋게 살다 live together happily / live in peace [amity] (with) // 서로 사이좋게 지냅시다 Let us be good neighbors.

사이즈 size; (여성 신체의) vital statistics; [옷 등의 치수] a size. ¶~를 재다 measure the size (of) // 이 구두의 ~는 내게 맞지 않습니다 These shoes are not my size. // ~가 얼마입니까 What size do you wear? // 여러 가지 빛깔과 ~가 있습니다 We have them in all colors and sizes.

사이참 a recess (between working hours); a snack eaten between regular meals.

사이클 1 [주파수] a cycle. ¶매초 120~로 진동하다 vibrate at 120 cycles a second. 2 [기계 등의 회전]. ¶4~ 엔진 a four-stroke engine. 3 [주기]. ¶경기(景氣)에는 ~이 있다 Prosperity and hard times move in a cycle. 4 [자전거] a cycle; a bicycle; (구어) a bike.
● **사이클 선수** a bicycle racer. **사이클 히트** (*cycle hit) [야구] the cycle; a hat trick. ¶~를 치다 hit for the cycle.

사이클로이드 [수] a cycloid. ¶내(內)~ a hypocycloid.

사이클로트론 [물] a cyclotron.

사이클링 [자전거를 타고 멀리 나가는 일] cycling; bicycling; bicycle riding. ¶~을 하러 가다 go cycling / go for a bicycle ride.

사이트 a (web) site.

사이펀 [물] a siphon; a syphon.

사인¹ 1 [서명] a signature(▶ 서명의 뜻의 명사로 sign을 쓰는 것은 잘못임); [유명인의 자필 서명] an autograph. ¶저자의 ~이 있는 시집 an autographed volume of poems // 졸업장에는 총장의 ~이 있다 The diploma has the president's signature on it. / The president's signature is on the diploma. **사인하다** sign (a letter); sign one's name (to / on). ¶이 서류에 사인해 주십시오 Sign these papers. 2 [신호] a sign; a signal. ¶그는 1루수에게 ~을 보냈다 He flashed a signal to the first baseman. **사인하다** make a sign (to

사인

a person to do).
● **사인 공세** storming for autographs. ¶~를 받다 be besieged [plagued] by autograph hunters. **사인펜**(*sign pen) a felt-tip (pen). **사인회** an autograph session.

사인² [수] a sine(약어 sin).

사인(死因) the cause of a person's death. ¶~불명으로 die from some unknown cause // ~을 조사하다 inquire into the cause of (a person's) death // …의 ~이 되다 be the death of // 그의 ~은 암이었다 He died of cancer. / Cancer brought about [was the cause of] his death. // 그의 ~은 연탄가스 중독으로 보인다 The cause of his death is believed to be briquette gas poisoning.

사인(私人) a private citizen [individual]; an individual. ¶~의 자격으로 in one's private [individual] capacity.

사인(私印) a private seal.
● **사인 위조** forging [forgery] of a private seal.

사인교(四人轎) a sedan chair borne by four men.

사일로 [겨울철 사료 저장고] a silo (*pl.* ~s).

사임(辭任) resignation; retirement from office; stepping out [down]; going out of office. ¶그 사고에 책임을 지고 그는 ~ 의사를 표명했다 Holding himself [Feeling] responsible for the accident, he indicated his desire to resign. **사임하다** resign (from) (one's place); step out; go out of office. ¶관직을 ~ resign a government office // 만약 이 계획이 실패하면 나는 사임해야 할 것이다 I will have to resign if this plan fails. / I'll stake my post [job / career] on this plan.

사자(死者) a dead person; the deceased; (집합적) the dead. ¶~는 말이 없다 Dead men tell no tales.

사자(使者) a messenger; [사절] an envoy; [밀사] an emissary. ¶평화의 ~ an ambassador of peace // ~를 보내다 send a messenger // 그가 ~가 되어 평화 협상을 했다 He was an envoy to the peace-negotiations.

사자(嗣子) [대를 이을 아들] an heir.

사자(獅子) a lion cub. (암컷) a lioness; (별명) the king of beasts.
● **사자 새끼** a lion cub. **사자자리** [천] the Lion; Leo. **사자코** a pug nose; a snub nose; an upturned nose. **사자후**(—吼) (부처님의) the (great) sermon [preaching] of Buddha; [열변] a thunderous [an impassioned] speech; a harangue. ¶~를 토하다 make an impassioned speech / harangue / declaim with unction.

사자(寫字) copying; transcription.
● **사자생** [필사생] a copyist; a scribe; an amanuensis (*pl.* -enses).

사장(死藏) hoarding; dead storage. **사장하다** hoard (up); keep (something) idle. →**사장된 자금** money lying unused // 그 집에는 귀중한 책이 사장되어 있다 There are valuable books shut up [locked up / stored away] in that house.
● **사장품** hoarded goods.

사장(沙場) the sands; a sandbank; a shoal; a sandy beach.

사장(社長) the president of a company; the head (of a firm). ¶부~ a vice-president // ~이 되다 become president of a company / assume the presidency of a corporation.

● **사장실** the president's office.

사장(查丈) [항렬이 높은 사돈] seniors-in-law; senior relatives by marriage.

사장(寫場) a photo studio. ⇨사진관(⇨사진)

사장조(—長調) [음] G major.

사재(私財) private property [funds / means / assets / fortune]. ¶~를 털어서 out of one's own purse [pocket] / at one's own expense // 그는 ~를 몽땅 털어서 도서관을 세웠다 He gave all the money he had [his whole fortune] to build the library.

사저(私邸) one's private residence [mansion / house].

사적(史的) historic. ⇨역사적
● **사적 고증** historical researches.

사적(史跡) a place [spot] of historical interest; a historical site; historical relics [remains / landmarks]. ¶~을 찾아가다 visit a historical spot // ~을 보존하다 preserve sites of historical value // ~이 많다 be rich in historic remains.

사적(私的) private; personal; individual; unofficial. ¶~으로 privately / individually / unofficially // ~인 일에 대한 질문이 되겠습니다만 I'm afraid this is a personal question, but ... // 저는 당신의 ~인 일에 관여하고 싶지는 않습니다 I don't want to meddle in your (private) affairs. // ~으로 말씀드릴 것이 있습니다 I'd like to have a private talk with you.

사적(事績) [일의 실적·공적] an achievement; a deed; an exploit; services; merits. ¶선인들의 ~ the achievements of our predecessors // 위인의 ~ the deeds of great man.

사적(事跡·事蹟) [사업의 남은 자취] evidence; a vestige; a trace.

사전(事前) ¶~의 beforehand / before the fact / advance // ~에 방지하다 prevent an affair from arising // ~에 통고하다 [알리다] notify [inform] (a person) in advance // ~에 경고하다 give warning // ~에 준비하다 prepare in advance / have (a thing) ready beforehand // 그런 일은 자네가 ~에 말해 주었어야 했다 You should have notified us of that beforehand [ahead of time].
● **사전 검열** prepublication censorship; pre-censorship. **사전 동의** a prior consent; a consent before the fact. **사전 승인** prior approval.

사전(事典) a cyclop(a)edia.

사전(辭典) a dictionary; a wordbook; a lexicon; (용어 해설) a glossary; (전문어·학술어의) a nomenclature; (보전(寶典)) a thesaurus. ¶살아 있는 ~ a walking [living] dictionary // ~과 씨름하다 struggle with [make constant use of] a dictionary // ~을 찾다 (모르는 단어를 알기 위해) consult [refer to] a dictionary (for the meaning of a word) / (미) look up (a word) in a dictionary // ~을 찾다 (어디에 두었는지 몰라) find a dictionary / look for a dictionary.
● **사전 편집자** a compiler of a dictionary; a lexicographer. **사전학** lexicography.

사절(使節) [나라를 대표하여 외국에 파견되는 사람] an envoy; [회의 대한 대표] a delegate; (그 일행) a delegation; [특별 사명을 띤 사절] a mission. ¶친선 ~ (한 사람) a good-will ambassador // 무역 ~ (단) a trade mission // 교육 [문화] ~ (단)을 미국에 파견하다 dispatch an educational [a cultural] mission to the States.

사절(謝絕) (a) refusal; (a) rejection; [거절] declining. ¶면회 ~ (구두로) I'm sorry, but we cannot accept visitors. / (게시) No visitors. // 입장 ~ (게시) No Admittance. // 외상 판매 [수표 / 크레디트 카드] ~ No credit [checks / credit cards] allowed[accepted]. / Payment in cash only. **사절하다** refuse(단호하게); decline(정중하게); deny. ¶팁을 ~ decline (to accept) tips // 면회를 ~ refuse to see visitors / decline visitors // 나의 초대를 정중히 ~ decline a person's invitation // 모처럼의 제의였으나 정중히 사절했다 I did appreciate his offer, but I declined. // 우리는 다섯 사람으로부터 초대를 사절한다는 편지를 받았다 We received five letters declining our invitation. // 그 요구는 사절할 수밖에 없다 I must refuse[turn down] that request.

사정(私情) [사사로운 정] personal feelings [regard / consideration / sentiment]; bias. ¶~에 좌우되다 be swayed by one's personal feelings / ~을 개입시키다 interject one's own feelings (into a matter) / ~을 버리다 set aside one's personal feelings.

사정(事情) 1 [일의 형편·처지·까닭] circumstances; conditions; reasons; the situation; the state of things[matters / affairs]. ¶~에 따라서는 according to the situation / depending on[upon] the circumstances // 이와 같은 ~으로 under these circumstances // 어쩔 수 없는 ~으로 owing to circumstances [for reasons] beyond one's control // 가정 ~으로 for family reasons // 이런 ~입니다 This is how it happened. // 이런 ~이어서 갈 수 없습니다 And so [(문어) Such being the case] I cannot go. / I cannot go for the reasons I have just mentioned. // ~에 따라서는 내가 직접 가지 않으면 안 된다 Depending on how the situation develops, I may have to go myself. // 그쪽 ~은 내가 잘 모른다 I don't know too much about the situation. // 그는 ~이야 어떻든 계속 항의의 목청을 높였다 He kept on protesting loudly without thinking of the circumstances [consequences]. // 일신상의 ~으로 그는 사직했다 He resigned for personal reasons. // 그들이 어떻게 해서 결혼하게 되었는지 그간의 ~을 나는 정확히는 모른다 I have no exact knowledge of the circumstances leading to their marriage. // 그는 ~이 있어 조부모 밑에서 자랐다 For a certain reason, he was brought up by his grandparents. // 그녀는 ~이 있는 듯한 얼굴로 어머니가 집에 없다고 말했다 She said with a significant [meaningful] look that her mother was not at home. // 신입생들은 학교의 ~을 잘 몰라서 어리둥절했다 The new pupils were at a loss, because they did not know much about their school yet. // 그는 ~을 자세히 설명해 주었다 He explained the circumstances to me in full. // 그는 중동의 ~에 밝다 He is well informed about conditions [the state of affairs] in the Middle East. // 주택 ~이 완전히 변했다 The housing situation has changed completely. // 여기서는 ~이 전혀 다르다 Here things [matters] are quite different.

2 [간청] entreaty; solicitation; supplication; an earnest appeal. **사정하다** beg (a person's) consideration(s) [leniency / indulgence]; entreat [implore / solicit] (a person for); plead (for help); make an earnest appeal (to a person for something). ¶도와 달라고 ~ implore (a person) to give help / implore aid (from a person) / solicit (a person) for his help [aid] // 이제 남은 길은 당신에게 도와 달라고 사정하는 것뿐입니다 My only hope is to entreat you for help.

사정(査定) assessment (a taxes); revision (of the budget); (자격의) screening. **사정하다** assess (taxes); make an assessment of; value; revise (a budget). ¶세액을 ~ assess taxes / 예산을 ~ decide on a budget. →¶손해 배상금은 20만 원으로 사정되었다 Damages were assessed at two hundred thousand won.

●**사정 가격** an assessed value [price]. **사정기관** an assessing agency.

사정(射程) (a) (shooting) range. ⇨사정거리 (⇨사정) ¶원 [근] 거리 ~ a long [short] range.

●**사정거리** (a) (shooting) range. ¶이 권총의 ~는 얼마나 됩니까 How far does this pistol range? // 적함은 5마일의 ~에 있었다 The enemy warship lay at a range of five miles. // 이 대포는 ~가 15킬로미터 이상이다 This gun [cannon] has a range of over fifteen kilometers.

사정(射精) ejaculation; discharge [emission] of semen; seminal emission. **사정하다** ejaculate; emit [discharge] semen.

사정사정(事情事情) pleadingly; imploringly. **사정사정하다** beg (a person's) consideration(s) [leniency / indulgence]; plead (for); earnestly request [ask for]; implore; solicit; entreat.

사정없다(事情—) merciless; heartless; relentless; ruthless; unsparing; severe; inexorable. **사정없이** mercilessly; heartlessly; ruthlessly. ¶한여름의 태양이 ~ 내리쬐었다 The midsummer sun blazed [beat] down mercilessly. // 그는 ~ 아이를 때렸다 He beat the boy without mercy [pity]. // 그는 비서를 ~ 꾸짖고 변명할 기회도 주지 않았다 He scolded his secretary unmercifully [mercilessly] and didn't even give her a chance to explain.

사제(司祭) a Catholic priest; (미사 등의) a celebrant.

●**사제관**(—館) a parsonage.

사제(私製) private [illicit] manufacture. ¶~의 privately made / private.

●**사제품** privately made [manufactured] goods [articles]; goods [articles] of private manufacture.

사제(師弟) master and pupil; teacher and student.

●**사제간 / 사제 관계** the relation of [between] teacher and student.

사조(思潮) the trend [current] of thought; the drift of public opinion. ¶근대 ~ modernism // 문예 ~ the trend of literature // 시대 ~ the spirit of the times // 현대 ~ contemporary thought.

사족(四足) 1 [네 발] four feet. 2 〈속〉 the limbs. ⇨사지(四肢)

사족(을) 못 쓰다 be awfully fond of; have a weakness [passion] (for); be spellbound; be a sucker (for); be crazy (about). ¶그는 과일이라면 사족을 못 쓴다 He is exceedingly fond of fruit. / He has a weakness for fruit.

●**사족수**(—獸) a quadruped; a four-footed animal.

사족(蛇足) a superfluity; something redundant; a redundancy. ¶~의 superfluous / redundant // ~을 달다 make an unnecessary addition (to) / add (out) (a speech / writing) / paint the lily // 그것은 ~이다 That's superfluous. / That is (like putting) a fifth wheel to the coach.

사죄(死罪) a capital crime; [가] a mortal [deadly] sin.

사죄(赦罪) (a) pardon; (a) remission; absolution; (an) amnesty(대사(大赦)); [가] absolution. **사죄하다** pardon; remit (a punishment); absolve (a person from[of]).

사죄(謝罪) an apology (pl. -gies). ¶그들은 나에게 ~를 요구했다 They demanded an apology from me. **사죄하다** apologize; beg a person's pardon [forgiveness]; make an apology. ¶그는 무릎을 꿇고 아버지에게 자신의 비행을 사죄했다 He got down on his knees and apologized to his father for his misbehavior. // 뭐라고 사죄해야 할지 모르겠습니다 I don't know how to apologize to you. / I am very sorry. / I beg your pardon. // 혹시 당신에게 무슨 일이 일어난다면 당신 아버님께 사죄할 길이 없게 됩니다 If anything should happen to you, I wouldn't know how to apologize to your father.

사주(四柱) [민] *saju*; the horoscopic data (of a bride[bridegroom]); the "four pillars"

사주(를) 보다 have one's fortune told; consult a fortuneteller.

●**사주쟁이** a fortuneteller; a diviner. **사주팔자** the Four Pillars and the Eight Characters (for the year, month, the day and hour of one's birth); [운수] fate; destiny; fortune; one's lot. ¶~가 좋다[나쁘다] be born under a lucky[an unlucky] star.

사주(社主) the head of a company; the proprietor[owner] of a firm.

사주(使嗾) instigation; incitement. ¶그들은 누군가의 ~를 받아 그런 소동을 일으켰음에 틀림없다 Someone must have put them up to making such a row. **사주하다** instigate; incite; abet; stir up; entice; egg (a person) on. ¶사주하여 …시키다 incite[instigate] (a person) to (do) / 사주하여 죄를 범하게 하다 incite[instigate] (a person) to (commit) a crime / abet (a person) in a crime / 노동자들에게 파업을 ~ instigate workers to down tools / instigate a strike.

●**사주자** an instigator; an incendiary.

사주(沙洲) a sandbar; a sandbank; a reef.

사중(四重) [네 겹] quadruple; fourfold. ¶~의 quadruplex / fourfold // ~으로 quadruply.

●**사중주** [음] a quartet(te). ¶현악 ~ a string quartet(te).

사증(査證) a visé; a visa. ¶입국[출국] ~ an entry[exit] visa // ~이 있는 visé'd / visaed / visa'd // 나는 내 여권에 ~을 받았다 I had a visa stamped in my passport.

사지(四肢) the limbs; the legs and arms; the members. ¶~가 멀쩡하다 have no physical defects // 그는 침대에 누워 지친 ~를 뻗다 Exhausted, he stretched out on the bed. / He tumbled onto the bed and stretched out his tired limbs.

사지(死地) the jaws of death; a fatal position [situation]; deadly circumstances. ¶~에 빠지다 fall into the jaws of death / be at death's doorstep / be on the brink of death // ~를 벗어나다 escape from the jaws of death / come out of a fatal position // ~로 들어가다 go to certain destruction / go[throw oneself] into the jaws of death.

사지(沙紙) emery cloth. ⇨사포

사직(司直) administration of justice; (집합적) the judicial authorities; the court; the bench. ¶~ 당국이 그 사건에 손을 댔다 The judicial authorities have taken action on that case. / The arm of law has reached the affair.

사직(社稷) [토지와 곡식의 신] the gods of soil and grain; the guardian deities of the State; [나라] the State; [조정] the (Royal) Court.

사직(辭職) (a) resignation. ¶총~ a resignation en masse[in a body] / a mass resignation // ~을 권고하다[강요하다] advise[urge] a person to resign // ~을 만류하다 dissuade (a person) from resigning. **사직하다** resign (one's office[post]); (미국 구어) check out (of office); give[throw] up one's office; quit [go out of] office; step out[down]. ¶회사를 ~ leave (the service of) the company / 신병을 이유로 ~ resign on the ground of illness [for reasons of health].

●**사직원** one's resignation; a letter of resignation. ¶~을 내다 submit [hand in / (문어) tender] one's resignation // ~을 수리하다 accept (a person's) resignation.

사진(寫眞) a photograph; a photo (pl. ~s); a picture; [스냅 사진] a snap(shot). ¶컬러 ~ a color picture // 즉석 ~ a fast photo // 항공 ~ an aerial photo // 광택 ~ a glazed photograph // 연속 ~ a picture sequence // 전신[반신] ~ a full-length[half-length] photograph // 합성[확대 / 수험용] ~ a composite [an enlarged / an exam] photograph // 현미경 ~ a microphotograph // 흑백 ~ a black and white photograph // 잘된[잘 안 된 / 실물 이상의] ~ a good [bad / flattering] photograph // ~이 찍히는 거리 내에(서) within camera range // ~을 찍다 take a picture [photograph] (of) // ~을 현상하다 develop (a roll of) film // ~을 인화[확대]하다 print [enlarge] a photograph // ~발이 좋다 be photogenic / photograph well / come out well in a photograph (영화에서) screen well // ~발이 좋지 않다 photograph badly // ~ 찍기를 싫어하다 be shy of camera / be camera-shy // 기록용 ~을 찍다 make a photographic record // 나는 ~을 (부탁하여) 찍었다 I had my photograph taken. // 죄송하지만 ~ 좀 찍어 주시겠어요 Excuse me. Could you take a picture for us[me], please? // 나는 ~이 잘 안 나온다 I don't take very good pictures. (▶ 사진을 잘 못 찍는다는 뜻도 됨) / I don't photograph very well. / I am not very photogenic.

●**사진가** a photographer; a cameraman (pl. -men). **사진관** a photo studio (pl. ~s). **사진기** a camera. **사진 기자** a (newspaper) cameraman. **사진사** a photographer. **사진술** photography. **사진 식자** phototypesetting; photocomposition; filmsetting. **사진 전송** phototelegraphy; facsimile transmission. **사진첩** a photo(graph) album. **사진틀** a picture [photo] frame. **사진판** a photo plate; a photostat; a phototype(철판); a photogravure(요판).

사차 방정식(四次方程式) a biquadratic [quartic] (equation).

사차원(四次元) [제4차원] the fourth dimension; [4개의 차원] four dimension. ¶~ fourth-dimensional / four-dimensional (world).

사찰(寺刹) a (Buddhist) temple. ⇨절

사찰(査察) investigation; inspection. ¶공중 ~ an aerial inspection // 세무 ~ tax investigation. 사찰하다 inspect; make[do] an inspection of; investigate.

사창(私娼) a streetwalker; an unlicensed prostitute; a woman of the streets; a girl of the town. ¶~ 생활을 하다 practice clandestine prostitution / be on the street // ~을 단속하다 repress[suppress] clandestine prostitution.
● **사창가**(-街) an unlicensed gay [prostitute] quarters. **사창굴** a [an unlicensed] brothel; a house of ill fame; a bawdy house.

사채(私債) a private loan[debt]; a personal liability. ¶~를 쓰다 obtain a private loan / use private loans.
● **사채놀이** private loan business; moneylending (business). **사채 동결** loan freeze. **사채 시장** the private money market; the non-institution financial market; a curb loan market. ¶고금리 ~ an usurious private money market. **사채업자** a private[curb] moneylender; a curb loan dealer; a loan shark.

사채(社債) a corporate[company] bond; (특히 무담보의) a debenture. ¶장기[단기] ~ a long-term[short-term] corporate bond // 기명 [무기명] ~ a registered [bearer] bond [debenture] // 저당권[담보]부(付) ~ a mortgage[secured] bond [debenture] // 무담보 ~ a naked [an unsecured] debenture // 공 ~ public and corporate bonds // ~를 발행하다 issue a corporate bond.
● **사채권**(-券) a debenture bond. ¶~ 양도 [신탁] debenture transfer[trust]. **사채 발행** flotation of debentures; debenture issue [flotation]. **사채 상환** debenture redemption. **사채 이자** debenture interests.

사천(왕)(四天王) [불] the Four Devas.

사철(四) 1 [사시절] the four seasons (of the year). 2 [항상] in[through] all seasons; all the year round; throughout the year; always; perpetually.

사철(沙鐵) iron[magnetic] sand.

사철나무(四-) [식] a spindle tree.

사체(死體) a corpse. ⇨시체(屍體)
● **사체 검안 / 사체 부검** an autopsy; a postmortem (examination).

사체(斜體) (letters in) italics; (필기의) an oblique hand. ¶~의 italicized.

사초(莎草) 1 [식] a sedge. ¶~의 sedgy. 2 [잔디] turf; sod. 3 [무덤에 떼를 입힘]. **사초하다** sod[turf] a grave.

사촌(四寸) a cousin; a first[full] cousin. ¶외~ a cousin on the mother's side // 이웃~ A good neighbor is better than a brother far off.
● **사촌 간** cousinship; cousinhood. ¶그와 나는 ~이다 He is cousin to me. **사촌 형제[자매]** a cousin brother [sister].

사춘기(思春期) [청년기] adolescence; [성적으로 성숙한 시기] puberty. ¶~의 adolescent / pubescent // ~의 소년[소녀] an adolescent boy[girl] // ~에 달하다 reach puberty / arrive at [attain] the age of puberty.

사출(射出) 1 [탄환 등을 쏘아서 내보냄]. **사출하다** [탄환을 발사하다] fire; [방출하다] eject. ➔이 버튼을 누르면 조종사는 비행기에서 사출된다 This button will eject the pilot from the airplane. 2 [액체의 분출] spouting. **사출하다** spout. 3 [부채꼴로 뻗어 나감] radiation. **사출하다** radiate.
● **사출기** a catapult.

사취(詐取) fraud; a swindle. **사취하다** obtain [get] (money) by fraud; swindle (money from a person); defraud (a person of a thing); cheat (a person out of a thing). ¶돈을 ~ get[obtain] money by fraud / defraud a person of his money // 그는 그의 형의 재산을 사취했다 He cheated[swindled] his brother out of his property.

사치(奢侈) [필요 이상으로 돈이 듦] (a) luxury; [분에 넘침] (an) extravagance; extravagancy. ¶~성 소비재 luxurious consumer goods // 우리는 그런 ~를 할 여유가 없다 We cannot afford such luxury. // 별장은 내게는 분에 넘치는 ~다 I can't afford the extravagance of a summer cottage. // "내게 다이아몬드 브로치라고? 존, 그것은 분에 넘치는 ~야." "A diamond brooch for me? John, how extravagant!" // 이 이상 바라는 것은 ~다 We cannot reasonably wish[ask] for more. // 그의 새 저택은 ~를 극한 건물이다 His new residence is a most luxurious house. / His new house is one equipped [provided] with every luxury imaginable. **사치하다** be extravagant; indulge in luxury; live[roll] in luxury. ¶옷에 ~ indulge in luxurious clothing.
● **사치세** taxes on luxuries; a luxury tax. **사치품** luxuries; a luxurious article; luxury goods. **사치 풍조** sumptuous moods; luxurious trends; the extravagance tendency.

사치스럽다(奢侈-) (사물이) luxurious; extravagant; expensive; sumptuous; fine; (사람이) extravagant; indulge in luxury. ¶사치스러운 사람 an extravagant person / a man of extravagant habits / a high liver // 사치스럽게 살다 live in luxury // 그들은 사치스런 생활을 하고 있었다 They led a luxurious life[a life of luxury]. / They lived in luxury. / (구어) They lived high on the hog. // 그녀는 사치스럽게 자랐다 She was brought up in (the lap of) luxury. // 그는 사치스러운 생활을 하는 경향이 있었다 His life-style tended to the luxurious. / He was inclined to wallow in the lap of luxury.

사칙(四則) [수] the four fundamental rules of arithmetics.

사칙(社則) the company regulations.

사친회(師親會) a parent-teacher association (약어 P.T.A., PTA); (모임) a parent-teacher meeting.

사칭(詐稱) misrepresentation; a false statement. ¶신분 ~ misrepresentation of one's identity[position] // 학력 ~ a false statement about one's academic [educational] background // 연령 ~ lying about [misrepresentation of] one's age. **사칭하다** pretend (to be); (문어) feign; assume another's[a false] name. ¶이름을 ~ [남의 이름을 도용하다] assume another's name / [거짓 이름을 사용하다] take[use] an assumed [a false] name // 나의 아버지의 이름을 사칭한 사기꾼 a

사카린

swindler who assumed[used] my father's name / 그는 남편의 절친한 친구라고 사칭하고 내게서 10만 원을 빌려 갔다 Under the pretext of being my husband's best friend, he borrowed 100,000 won from me.

사카린 [化] saccharin(e).
사타구니 the crotch. ⇨ ¹살
사탄 [악마] satan.
사탑(斜塔) a leaning tower. ¶피사의 ~ the Leaning Tower of Pisa.
사탕(沙糖) **1** sugar. ⇨ 설탕 **2** [과자] (미) candy[candies]; (영)sweets; sweetmeats; confection. ¶얼음 ~ crystal sugar / (미) rock candy / (영) sugar candy.
● **사탕무** a (sugar) beet. **사탕발림** sugar-coated[honeyed / sweet] words; cajolery; flattery; blarney; soft soap; a mere show; deceptive appearance; (속어) oil. ¶~에 녹다 be coaxed by honeyed words // ~으로 유혹하다 entice[allure] (a person) with fair words // ~을 하다 use honeyed[sugar-coated / sweet] words / sweet-talk / sugar (one's words) / sugar up / butter up. **사탕수수** sugarcane.
사태 the shank of beef.
사태(沙汰) **1** [무너짐] (산비탈 등의) a landslide; (흙의) a landslip; (눈의) a snowslide; (눈·얼음의) an avalanche. ¶눈 ~ a snowslide // ~가 나다 slide down // 큰비 때문에 벼랑에 ~가 났다 Owing to the heavy rain there was a landslide[(영) landslip].
2 [범람] a rush; a flood; a deluge; an avalanche; [많음] lots (of); a multitude (of). ¶사람 ~ an avalanche of people / a surging crowd of people / a tide of humanity // 주문 ~가 나다 have a rush[flood] of orders // 신청 ~가 나다 be flooded[deluged] with applications[offers] // 불경기로 감원 ~가 났다 Depression caused[brought about] a drastic cut in the staff.
사태(事態) the situation; the state[position] of affairs[things]; the aspect[look] of affairs. ¶심상치 않은 ~ a serious situation / the gravity of the situation // ~를 관망하다 watch[wait and see] (the development of) the situation / see how the matter develops // ~를 개선하다 mend matters[the matter] / improve the situation // ~를 깨닫다 realize the situation / ascertain the position of affairs // ~를 완화[악화]시키다 relieve[aggravate] the situation // 국가 비상 ~를 선포하다 declare a state of national emergency // ~는 악화됐다 Things have grown more serious. / The situation has worsened. // 당신이 이 ~를 수습할 수 있겠습니까 Do you think you can manage[cope with] the present situation? // 긴급 ~가 발생했다 An emergency situation[A crisis] arisen[developed]. / An emergency has arisen. // 우리는 ~를 잘 수습하고 있다 We have the situation well in hand.
사택(社宅) a company house (for employees); [집합적] company housing.
사토장이(莎土~) a gravedigger; a sexton.
사통(私通) **1** [편지로 사사로이 연락함] private correspondence (about public affairs); [사통하는 편지] a private letter[note / message]. **사통하다** correspond[keep a correspondence] (with a person) (about public affairs). **2** [밀통] illicit intercourse; an illicit liaison

[amour / love affair]; intimacy(미혼자와의); fornication(미혼자와의); adultery(기혼자와의). **사통하다** have an amour[affair] (with); have improper relations (with); establish illicit liaisons (with); become intimate (with).
사통팔달(四通八達) running[stretching] in all directions. **사통팔달하다** run[stretch] in all directions. ¶사통팔달한 곳 a place accessible from all directions / the focus of the arteries of traffic / a center of traffic // 이 지방은 철도가 사통팔달해 있다 There is a network of railway in this district.
사퇴(辭退) **1** [사절하여 물리침] declining; declinature; nonacceptance (of an invitation). **사퇴하다** decline; turn down; refuse to accept. ¶경제 원조의 제의를 ~ decline[turn down] an offer of financial help. **2** [사직] resignation. ¶자진 ~ voluntary resignation. **사퇴하다** resign (one's post[office]). ¶공직에서 ~ resign[abdicate] one's office / resign from public life / leave[retire from] one's office.
사투(死鬪) a desperate struggle; a mortal combat. **사투하다** fight desperately; engage in a life-and-death[life-or-death] struggle (with); (뒤얽혀서) grapple[scuffle / close] (with a person) in mortal combat.
사투리 an[a provincial] accent; a dialect; a patois; a provincialism. ¶시골 ~로 말하다 speak in a country[local] dialect // 그는 지독한 지방 ~로 말한다 He speaks with a heavy [broad] provincial accent. // 그녀는 조금도 ~가 없다 She speaks without a provincial accent. // 강한 런던[경상도] ~ a strong[(영) broad] cockney[Gyeongsangdo] accent // 그의 말에서는 시골 ~가 조금 풍긴다 There is a trace of some local accent in his speech.
사파리 a safari. ¶~ 재킷 a safari jacket / ~ 파크 a wild animal park / (영) a safari park.
사파이어 [광] a sapphire; [사파이어 빛] sapphire.
사팔눈 a squint (eye); cockeye. ¶~의 squint-eyed // 그녀의 오른쪽 눈은 약간 ~이다 Her right eye has a slight squint.
사팔뜨기 a squint-eyed[cross-eyed] person; a squint-eye; a squinter. ¶~의 squint-eyed // 그는 ~다 He has a bad squint.
사포(沙布) emery cloth[paper]; sandpaper.
사표(死票) a dead vote.
사표(師表) a model; a pattern; a paragon. ¶이 세상의 ~ the salt of the earth / the light of the world // ~가 되다 become a paragon of virtue for the public // 일세의 ~로 숭앙되다 be honored as a model man / be looked to (by one's contemporaries) for light and leadership.
사표(辭表) a (written) resignation; a letter of resignation. ¶일괄 ~ (tender) resignation enmasse // ~를 내다 send[hand] in one's resignation(▶ hand in은 직접 건네주다) // ~를 철회하다 withdraw one's resignation // ~를 수리[반려] accept[turn down / reject] a person's resignation // 그는 ~를 철회했다 He withdrew his resignation. // 그는 즉석에서 ~를 제출했다 He tendered his resignation on the spot. // 시장은 시의회에 ~를 제출했다 The mayor sent[handed] in his resignation.
사풍(社風) the ways of a company; a company's custom[tradition].

사풍(沙風) a sandstorm.
사프란 [식] a saffron.
사필귀정(事必歸正) [당연한 결과] a corollary; a natural result. ¶~이다 Right will prevail in the end. / Truth wins out in the long run. / Wrong cannot last long. / Nothing goes uncorrected for long. / Justice has long arms.
사하다(赦-) [용서하다] forgive; pardon; excuse; absolve (a person) of (sin); remit.
사학(史學) history; historical studies [science]. ⇨ 역사학(⇨역사)
● **사학가** a historian.
사학(私學) [개인이 세운 학교] a private school [college / university].
사항(事項) [일] matters; [사실] facts; data; [항목] articles; particulars; items. ¶관련 relevant particulars // 주요 ~ the essential [main / major / principal / key] particulars // 일체의 ~에 대하여 on all matters // 우리는 그 에 대하여 이의 ~ 은 없다 We find nothing in that to complain about. // 특기 ~ 없음 Nothing of particular note. / Nothing noteworthy.
사해(四海) 1 [사방의 바다] the seven seas. 2 [세계] the whole world. ¶~가 조용하다 [평화롭다] The world is at peace.
● **사해동포 / 사해형제** universal brotherhood [fraternity].
사행(射倖) speculation. ¶~적 speculative.
● **사행심** a speculative spirit; the temptation to try for a quick and easy profit. ¶~을 돋우다 stir up [arouse] a person's gambling spirit.
사향(麝香) musk. ¶~이 든 musk-scented // ~내가 나다 be musky / be scented with musk / smell like musk.
● **사향노루** [동] a musk deer; a musk. **사향뒤쥐** [동] a muskrat; a musk shrew. **사향수** musk water [scent].
사혈(瀉血) phlebotomy; bloodletting; venesection. **사혈하다** phlebotomize; let blood (from a patient); venesect.
사형(死刑) capital punishment; death on the scaffold; (a) death penalty; the punishment of death. ¶~에 처하다 put (a person) to death / punish (a person) with [by] death // ~에 처해지다 go to [mount] the scaffold // ~을 폐지하다 abolish the death penalty // ~을 면하다 escape the chair // ~을 집행하다 execute a death sentence / execute (a criminal) / electrocute (전기의자로) // ~을 선고하다 pass a sentence of death (on) / condemn [sentence] (a person) to death // ~을 선고받다 receive a death sentence // 그는 ~에 처해졌다 He was put to death. **사형하다** condemn (a person) to death; put (a person) to death.
● **사형 선고** a capital [death] sentence; a sentence of death. **사형수** a condemned criminal; a criminal under sentence of death. **사형장** an execution ground; (가스의) a gas chamber; the place of execution. **사형집행인** an executioner; (교수형의) a hangman.
사형(私刑) [법] lynching; lynch (law); a private action. **사형하다** lynch; take the law into one's (own) hands.
사화(士禍) [역] a purge [massacre] of Confucian scholars [literati].

사화(史話) a(n) historical story [tale].
사화(私和) 1 [송사(訟事)를 화해함] settlement out of court; an out-of-court settlement; (a) private settlement. **사화하다** settle (a matter) privately [out of court]; bring (a matter) to an amicable settlement between the parties concerned. 2 [일반적인 화해] (a) reconciliation; reconcilement; peace-making; the restoration of friendship. **사화하다** become [beget] reconciled (with); make (it) up (with).
사화산(死火山) [지] an extinct [a dead] volcano (pl. ~es, ~s).
사환(使喚) an attendant; a runner; a page. ¶~ 아이 an errand boy / an office boy [girl] / a boy.
사활(死活) life and [or] death. ¶~의 투쟁 (engage in) a life-and-death struggle / a struggle for life or death // 그것은 내게 있어 ~의 문제다 It is a matter of life and death to me. // 내각의 ~은 그 문제의 해결에 달려 있다 The fate of the Cabinet depends on how the matter is settled.
사회(司會) 1 [회의 등을 진행함] direction of [directing] a meeting [ceremony]; chairmanship; chairing (a meeting). ¶한 씨의 ~로 with Mr. Han in the chair / under the chairmanship of Mr. Han // 송 씨가 모임의 ~를 보았다 Mr. Song presided at [over] the meeting. / Mr. Song chaired the meeting. **사회하다** preside at [over] (a meeting); take the chair; conduct; (목사 등이) officiate (at a ceremony); (방송 등의) act as master [mistress] of ceremonies (for); (미국 구어) emcee (a show). 2 a master of ceremonies. ⇨ 사회자(⇨사회)
● **사회봉**(-棒) a gavel. **사회자** (파티 등의) a master of ceremonies(약어 M.C.); an emcee; (회의의) a chairman; a chairwoman; a chairperson; (토론회 등의) (미) the moderator; (의식의) the officiant; (토크 쇼의) a talk show host(남자); a talk show hostess(여자); (퀴즈의) a quiz master. ¶텔레비전 퀴즈의 ~ a master of ceremonies on TV quiz shows.
사회(社會) [공동생활의 집단] (a) society; [지역 사회] (a) community; [세상] the world; (군대·감옥 등에서 본) the outer world; the public. ¶국제 ~ the world community of nations // 문명 ~ a civilized community // 상류 [중류 / 하류] ~ the higher [middle / lower] classes [stratum of society] // 원시 [봉건] ~ primitive [feudal] society // 시민 ~ civic society // 혈연 ~ blood society // 예술가의 ~ the world of artists // ~의 social / [공공의] public / communal // ~의 제재 social sanctions // ~의 일원 a member of society // ~의 적 a public enemy / an enemy of society // 인류 ~의 진화 the evolution of human society // ~를 위하여 for the good of the public [society] / for the welfare of society // ~에 나가다 go out into [set out in] the world // ~에 내보내다 give (a person) a start in life // ~에 해독을 끼치다 do harm [be harmful] to society / exert an evil influence on the public mind // ~에서 은퇴하다 retire from society [active life] // ~에 공헌하다 contribute to social [public] welfare // ~로 복귀하다 (군인이) return to civilian life / (죄수가) get out of prison / ~로 진출하다 become a working member of society // ~를 개량 [개선] 하다

사회적

reform[ameliorate] society // ~를 알다 know the world / ~를 위해 진력하다 labor[work / exert oneself] for the public good.
● 사회 경제 social economy. 사회 계약설 the theory of social contract. 사회 과학 social science. 사회 교육 (a) social education; adult education(성인 교육); (a) lifelong [continuing] education(평생 교육). 사회 구조 the framework of society; the social framework. 사회면 (신문의) the general news page(s); the social page; the local news page [section]. 사회 문제 a social problem. ¶~가 되다 constitute a public[social] problem. 사회 보장 social security. ¶~을 받다 enjoy the benefits of the social security services. 사회 보장 제도 the social security system. 사회 복지 social welfare. ¶~에 크게 공헌하다 contribute tremendously to the (general) public welfare[to the welfare of society] // ~를 도모하다 take a measure with a view to[aimed at] social welfare. 사회봉사 social[public] service. 사회 불안 social unrest. ¶~을 낳다 [일으키다] breed[cause] social unrest // ~을 조성하다 ferment social unrest // ~을 제거하다 dispel[remove] social unrest. 사회사업 social work[service]; public welfare service. ¶~을 하다 engage in public welfare service / work for (the) public good. 사회 사업가 a social worker. 사회상 a social aspect; phases [aspects] of life. 사회생활 life in society; social life. ¶~을 (영위)하다 live socially. 사회성 sociality; a social nature. ¶~이 있는 사람 (사회에 관심이 있는) a person who has keen interest in social problems. 사회악 a social evil; social abuses[ills]. 사회 운동 a social movement; a public campaign; (사회주의의) a socialist movement. 사회인 a full-fledged [working] member of society. ¶~이 되다 join adult society / become a working member of society / take one's place in[as a member of] society. 사회장(—葬) a public funeral. 사회 정의 social justice. 사회주의 socialism. ¶~의 socialist / socialistic // 국가 [공상적] ~ state [Utopian] socialism // 수정 ~ revised-socialism. 사회주의자 a socialist. 사회 질서 public[social] order. 사회층 a social stratum (pl. social strata). 사회학 sociology; social science. 사회학자 a sociologist. 사회 현상 a social phenomenon (pl. -na). 사회화 socialization. ¶~하다 socialize (industry). 사회 환경 social environment.

사회적(社會的) social; societary; societal. ¶반~ antisocial // ~으로 보아 from a social point of view / socially speaking // ~으로 매장되다 be ruined socially / lose one's social standing // ~으로 인정받다 win public recognition // ~으로 보면 그는 상당한 사람이다 He is a somebody in society. // 인간은 ~인 동물이다 Human beings are social creatures.

사후(死後) ¶~에 after one's death / posthumously // ~의 after death / posthumous / postmortem // ~의 세계 the world after death / the world to come // ~ 출판된 작품 a posthumous work / a work published posthumously // ~의 일을 생각하다 look beyond the grave // ~의 일을 걱정하다 worry about things after one's death // ~의 일을 부탁하다 give (another) the charge of the affairs after one's death.

사후 약방문(속담) Prescription after death; After death comes a doctor.
● **사후 경직** [의] cadaveric rigidity; rigor mortis.

사후(事後) ¶~의[에] after the fact / (라) expost facto // 그들은 ~ 처리를 잘못했다 They made a mistake in dealing with what had happened.
● **사후 검열** post censorship. **사후 관리** post management. **사후 보고** an ex post facto report.

사훈(社訓) the motto of a company.

사흗날 the third day of a month. ¶유월 ~ the third of June.

사흘 1 [3일] three days. ¶~마다 every three days / ~ 걸러 every fourth day / with three intervening days. 2 the third day of a month. ⇨초사흗날

사흘 굶어 도둑질 아니 할 놈 없다(속담) Necessity knows no law.

사흘이 멀다 하고 very often; almost every other day.

삭감(削減) a cut; (a) curtailment; (a) reduction; a cutback. ¶대 ~ a drastic reduction [cut] // 생산 [주문] ~ a cutback in production[orders]. **삭감하다** (비용 등을) cut (down); curtail; reduce; (구어) slash; [남아도는 것을 깎다] trim; [서서히 줄이다] pare down; (생산·인원 등을) cut back. ¶경비를 ~ reduce overhead / slash costs / cut expenditure(s) // 군사비를 ~ curtail military spending // 정부는 복지 예산을 삭감했다 The government cut down on the welfare budget.

삭과(蒴果) [식] a capsule.

삭다 1 (옷 등이) wear thin[threadbare]; get rotten; decay; crumble into decay. ¶(옷이) 삭아서 너덜너덜해지다 be worn to rags.
2 (죽 등이) become sloppy[watery]; turn bad.
3 (먹은 음식이) be digested; digest. ¶이 음식은 잘 삭는다 This food is easily digested. // 먹는 것이 삭지 않고 그대로 내려간다 The food does not stay in my stomach.
4 (분(憤) 등이) be alleviated[appeased / mitigated]. ¶~에 대한 분이 ~ relent toward (a person).
5 (김치 등이) acquire[pick up / absorb / develop] flavor; (술이) ferment.

삭도(索道) an aerial cableway. ⇨가공 삭도(架空)¶광석을 ~로 운반하다 haul [transport] ore by cableway.
● **삭도차** a cable car.

삭막하다(索莫 - 索漠 -) [황량하다] dreary; bleak; desolate; [생각이 잘 나지 않다] dim [vague] (in one's memory). ¶삭막한 풍경 a dreary[bleak] scene.

삭망(朔望) 1 [음력 초하루 및 보름] the first and fifteenth days of the lunar month. 2 [그때 지내는 제사] memorial services held on the first and the fifteenth days of the lunar month.

삭발(削髮) haircutting; (a) tonsure; [짧은] close cutting; short cropping. **삭발하다** tonsure; shave the head of; have one's hair cut. ¶그는 삭발하고 중이 되었다 He took the tonsure and became a bonze.

삭신 the sinews and joints. ¶~이 쑤시다 have an acute pain all over / feel sharp[tingling] pains in the sinews and joints.

삭월세(朔月貰) →사글세

삭이다 1 [소화시키다] digest (food). ¶삭이기

쉽다[어렵다] be easy[hard] to digest // 잘 먹고 잘 ~ eat well and digest well. **2** [가라앉다] mitigate; alleviate; appease; calm down. ¶노여움을 ~ mitigate[swallow / appease] one's anger.

삭정이 a withered[dead] branch.

삭제(削除) [깎아[지워] 없앰] deletion; elimination; erasure; cancellation; striking out. ¶두 자 ~ two words crossed out. **삭제하다** delete; remove; cancel; strike out[off]; cross out; erase; [인] kill. ¶삭제한 곳 a deletion / 명단에서 이름을 ~ strike a person's name off a list / 2, 3행 ~ cross out [cancel / delete] a few lines (▶ cross out는 선을 그어 지움) // 법안 중의 1항을 ~ delete [strike out] a section in a bill / 제5조 1항을 삭제함 Art. V, Clause Ⅰ is rescinded.

삭탈관직하다(削奪官職−) deprive (a person) of office; remove (a person) from office.

삭풍(朔風) a north wind of winter; a piercing wind; (시어) Boreas.

삭히다 [발효시키다] ferment (a thing); [익히다] make (a thing) ripe.

삯 1 [품삯] wages; pay; hire; [보수] remuneration; a reward. ¶하루 5만 원의 ~을 받고 일하다 work at a wage[the wages] of 50,000 won a day. **2** [물건 등을 이용한 대가] a rent(집[땅]세); a fare(찻삯); freight(짐삯); carriage(운반비); a charge(사용료); a fee(수수료). ¶기차 ~ a railway fare / 인천까지 찻~이 얼마입니까 What is the fare to Incheon?

삯바느질 needlework for pay.

삯일 job work, a job (of work); wage labor; (작업량에 따라 삯을 주는) piecework; work done by the piece; (시간제로 삯을 주는) timework. **삯일하다** do job work[piece work]; do odd jobs; do work at piece rates. ¶삯일하는 사람 a pieceworker / a timeworker / a jobber.

산(山) **1** [산악] a mountain; a mount; (봉우리) a peak; a hill(구릉); a knoll(둥근 언덕); a height(고지); a down(모래 언덕). ¶설악~ Seoraksan(Mt. Seorak) / 민둥~ a bare [deforested] mountain // 낮은 ~ a low mountain // 꼭대기 the summit[top] of a mountain // 기슭 (at) the foot[base] of a mountain // 등성이 the ridge of a mountain // 중턱 a hillside / the side of a mountain // ~ 너머 ~ mountain upon mountain // 너머에 across[beyond] the mountain // ~ 너머에서 (come) from beyond the mountain // ~과 들[골짜기] hills and fields [(문어) dales] // ~이 많은 mountainous (country) / hilly (districts) // ~에 오르다 climb (up) a mountain / go up a mountain[hill] / make an ascent of a mountain / scale a mountain(기어오르다) // ~을 내려가다 climb down a mountain / (문어) descend a mountain // ~을 넘다 go over[cross] a mountain // ~에 가다 go to the mountains // 우리는 ~을 오르내리며 환상의 버섯을 찾아 헤맸다 We went looking for the fabled mushrooms up hill and down dale. // 나는 여름휴가를 ~에서 지낼 작정이다 I am going to spend my summer vacation in the mountains. // 나는 스키하러 ~에 갔다 I went skiing in the mountains.
2 a grave. ⇨ 산소(山所).
¶산에 가야 범을 잡지 (속담) Nothing venture, nothing have[win].

산(酸) [화] an acid. ¶~의 acid.

●**산 과다증** [의] hyperacidity.

-**산**(産) [산물] a product; manufacture (of). ¶외국~ [국~] 담배 foreign[home-grown] tobacco / 아라비아~ 말 a horse bred in Arabia / 북미~ 오리의 일종 a kind of North American duck.

산간(山間) [산과 산 사이] a place between hills[mountains]; [산협] a ravine. ¶~ 마을 a mountain village / a hamlet[village] among[in] the mountains / a village nestling in the mountains[among the mountains] // ~을 흐르는 급류 a rapid stream in a mountain valley // 버스 한 대가 ~을 달리고 있는 것이 보였다 A bus could be seen running between the hills.

●**산간벽지** a secluded [an out-of-the-way] place in [among] the mountains.

산개(散開) [군] [병사의 배치] loose order; deployment; extension; development. **산개하다** spread out; extend in open order; deploy; extend; form in open order. ¶병사들은 산개하여 횡대를 지었다 The soldiers spread out to form a line.

●**산개 대형** open[extended] order.

산계(山系) a mountain system [range / chain]. ¶알프스 ~ the Alpine mountain range.

산고(産苦) [출산의 고통] birth[parturient] pangs; travail. ¶~를 **견디다** endure birth pains[pangs].

산고(産故) childbirth; delivery.

산골(山−) a mountain[mountainous] district; a secluded place. ¶~ 사람 mountain folks[people] / a mountaineer / (미) a hillbilly // ~에서 살다 live deep in the mountains.

산골짜기(山−) hills and valleys; a ravine; a gorge; a glen.

산과(産科) [학문] obstetrics; (병원의) the obstetrical department. ¶~의 obstetrical.

●**산과 의사** an obstetrician.

산광(散光) [물] scattered[diffused] light.

산굴 a mountain cave.

산굽이(山−) a mountain bend.

산기(産氣) labor pains; travail; [진통] pangs [pains] of childbirth. ¶~가 있다 labor starts / (사람이) begin to labor / have[feel] labor pains / suffer the pains of childbirth / 그녀는 갑자기 ~를 느꼈다 All of a sudden she went into labor[started to have labor pains]. / Her labor pains started suddenly.

산기(産期) the expected time of delivery [parturition]; period[term] of delivery; one's time. ¶~가 되다 come to one's time (of parturition).

산기슭(山−) (at) the foot[base] of a mountain. ¶~의 호수 a lake at the base[foot] of a mountain.

산길(山−) [산의 좁고 험한 길] a mountain path[trail]; (a mountain) pass; (자동차길 등을 포함하여) a mountain road. ¶~을 걷다 follow[walk along] a mountain path.

산꼭대기(山−) the summit[top] of a mountain[hill]; the mountaintop; a peak; a crest. ¶그 ~에는 사철 눈이 있다 The mountain is crowned with snow all the year round.

산나물(山−) wild edible greens. ¶~을 캐다 pick wild greens.

산달(産−) the month of giving birth.

산대놀음(山臺−) a masked drama.

산더미 (山-) a heap; a pile; a great mass; a huge amount; a mountain (of); an accumulation. ¶~ 같은 a mountain of (debts) / lots of / a world of / like a mountain / mountain-like / mountainous / mountain-high // ~ 같은 숙제 a ton[pile] of homework // ~ 같은 파도 mountainous waves // ~처럼 쌓인 장작 a big pile of firewood // ~처럼 쌓다 heap (a desk with books) / pile (a cart) high (with straw) / make a tall pile (of) // 책을 ~처럼 쌓다 pile books in heaps // 낙엽을 ~처럼 쌓아 올리다 pile up dead leaves // ~ 같은 빛 mountainous load of debts // 짐을 ~처럼 실은 차 a high-laden cart // 할 일이 ~처럼 쌓여 있다 I have lots of things to do. // 마루에는 잡동사니가 ~처럼 쌓여 있었다 The floor was piled high with rubbish [junk]. // 숙제가 ~만큼 쌓여 있다 I have lots of [a mountain of] homework to do.

산도 (産道) [의] the parturient[obstetric / birth] canal.

산도 (酸度) [화] acidity.
●**산도 측정** acidimetry.

산돼지 (山-) [동] a wild boar[hog].

산들거리다 (the wind) blow cool and gentle; sigh.

산들바람 [시원하고 가볍게 부는 바람] a soft wind; a gentle[light] breeze. ¶나뭇잎을 스치는 ~ a breeze passing through the leaves // ~이 불고 있다 A gentle breeze is blowing.

산들산들 [바람이 잇달아 부드럽게 부는 모양] gently; softly; in cool ripples. ¶봄바람이 ~ 불고 있다 A spring breeze is blowing softly. / There is a gentle spring breeze.

산등성이 (山-) a (mountain) ridge; the ridge[back / spine] of a mountain. ¶~를 따라서 가다 ~를 타다] go along the ridge(s).

산딸기 (山-) mountain[wild] berries.

산뜻하다 1 [깨끗하다] clean; neat and tidy; [빛깔·모양 등이] 선명하다] vivid; bright [fresh] (color); [보기 좋다] splendid; beautiful; smart; clear-cut. ¶산뜻한 빨간 빛깔 bright [brilliant] red // 나무들의 산뜻한 초록빛 the fresh green [(문어) verdure] of trees // 산뜻한 옷차림을 하고 있다 be neatly dressed // 그 작가는 정경을 산뜻하게 묘사했다 The writer described the scene vividly.
2 (성격이) frank; open-hearted; (음식 맛이) plain; simple; light (meal); racy. ¶산뜻한 음식 light [plain] food // 산뜻한 맛이 없다 lack freshness.
3 [상쾌하다] cool; fresh; crisp (weather). ¶산뜻해지다 feel refreshed / 기분이 좋아지다 feel relieved.

산란 (産卵) laying eggs; egg-laying; (어패류의) spawning; (곤충의) oviposition. **산란하다** (새 등이) lay eggs; (어패류 등이) spawn; (곤충이 과일 등에). blow.
●**산란관** (곤충의) an ovipositor. **산란기** the breeding [spawning] season.

산란하다 (散亂-) dispersed; scattered about; littered (with scraps of paper). ¶산란한 마음을 가라앉히다 calm down the restless mind // 나는 그녀의 아리따운 모습을 보고 마음이 산란해졌다 Her lovely figure made me lose all my self-possession. // 그녀의 마음은 온갖 생각으로 산란해졌다 Her heart was torn by various contradicting sentiments. // 마지막 희망이 사라지자 그의 마음은 산란해졌다 He went to pieces when his last hope was gone. // 그녀는 그 소식을 듣고 마음이 산란해졌다 She was upset by the news.

산록 (山麓) (at) the foot of a mountain. ⇨ⁿ산기슭
●**산록대** a piedmont district; a piedmont.

산류 (酸類) [화] (the) acids.

산림 (山林) 1 [산중의 숲] a forest in the mountains. 2 [산과 숲] mountains and forests. ¶~의 조성[벌채] afforestation [deforestation] // ~을 보호하다 conserve forests.
●**산림 보호** forest conservancy. **산림청** the Forestry Administration. **산림학** forestry; [수목학] dendrology.

산마루 (山-) the ridge[top] of a mountain.
●**산마루터기** the top of a ridge; the ridgetop.

산막 (山幕) a mountain hut (for climbers); a cottage; a shanty (for hikers).

산만하다 (散漫-) vague (notion); loose (thinking / style); vagrant (thought); distracted (attention); discursive (mind); desultory (reading). ¶산만한 문체 a loose [diffuse] style // 생각이 산만한 사람 a careless [haphazard / sloppy / woolly] thinker // 그의 주의력이 산만해졌다 His attention wandered. // 바깥 소음에 정신이 산만해져서 공부가 되지 않는다 The noise outside distracts me from my study. / I cannot keep my mind on study because of the noise outside. // 여러 가지 일로 정신이 산만해져서 한 가지에도 집중할 수가 없었다 I was attracted by so many things that I was unable to concentrate [fix my attention] on any one of them. // 저 아이는 항상 주의가 ~ That boy's attention always wanders.

산매 (散賣) retail(ing). ⇨ⁿ소매(小賣)

산맥 (山脈) a mountain range [chain]. ¶로키 ~ the Rocky Mountains // 알프스 ~ the Alps / the Alpine range // 태백 ~ the Taebaek Mountains.

산모 (産母) a woman delivered of a child; a woman in childbed[in her confinement / in the state of maternity].

산모퉁이 (山-) the spur of a hill[mountain]; the corner of a mountain foot.

산목숨 one's life. ¶~을 겨우 이어 가다 eke out one's living.

산문 (散文) prose. ¶운문을 ~으로 바꾸다 turn a verse into prose // ~으로 쓰다 write in prose.
●**산문시** a prose poem; a poem in prose. **산문체** prose style; prosaism; (in) prose.

산물 (産物) 1 [산출물] a product; a production; [집합적] produce. ¶주요 ~ staple products[produce] // 그 지방의 ~로는 이렇다 할 것이 없다 The district produces nothing worth mentioning. 2 [어떤 결과로 얻어지는 것] a result; a fruit; an outgrowth; a product; an outcome. ¶노력의 ~ the fruit [harvest / product] of sheer labor [hard work] // 시대의 ~ creature of the times [day].

산미 (酸味) acidity; sourness; a sour taste. ¶~가 있는 sour / acid // ~를 띠다 have an acid[a sour] taste / taste sour.

산바람 (山-) a mountain wind [blast]; a breeze from the mountain.

산발 (散發) sporadic occurrence. **산발하다** occur sporadically [now and then]; happen occasionally; (야구에서 안타를) scatter. ¶최

근에 이 지역에서 날치기 사건이 산발하고 있다 There have been several [scattered] cases of bag-snatching in this area recently.
산발(散髮) dishevel(l)ed [unkempt] hair. **산발하다** make [wear] one's hair disheveled [unkempt]. ¶산발한 여자 a woman with disheveled hair.
산발적(散發的) sporadic(al). ¶~으로 sporadically / ~ 안타 scattered hits // ~인 총격이 밤새도록 계속되었다 Sporadic shooting continued through the night.
산법(算法) arithmetic.
산병(散兵) 〔흩어진 병졸〕 scattered soldiers; skirmishers; 〔군대를 풀어 병사를 흩음〕 scattering [dispersing] soldiers; 〔산개 대형〕 loose [extended / open] order.
산보(散步) a walk. ⇨ⁿ산책
산봉우리(山-) a (mountain) peak; the summit [top] of a mountain.
산부인과(産婦人科) obstetrics and gynecology.
●**산부인과 의사** 〔산과〕 an obstetrician; 〔부인과〕 a gynecologist.
산불(山-) a forest fire on a mountain; (미) a wood fire. ¶~ 조심 (게시) Prevent forest fires.
산비둘기(山-) a ringdove; a collared dove.
산비탈(山-) a steep mountain slope.
산사(山寺) a temple in a mountain; a mountain temple.
산사나무(山査-) 〔식〕 a hawthorn.
산사람(山-) 〔산에 사는 사람〕 a woodsman; a hillman; (미) a hillbilly; 〔산에서 일하는 남자〕 a mountain laborer; 〔등산가〕 a mountaineer; 〔집합적〕 mountain folks [people].
산사태(山沙汰) a landslide; (영) 〔규모가 작은 것〕 a landslip; a landfall. ¶~가 나기 쉬운 landslide-prone [ledge] / ~에 마을에 ~ 덮혔다 The village was hit by a landslide [(영) landslip]. // ~로 도로가 막혔다 A landslide [landslip] has blocked the road. // 비가 와서 ~가 났다 The rain caused a landslide.
산산이(散散-) 〔조각조각으로〕 to [in] pieces [fragments]; to atoms [smithereens]; 〔흩어져서〕 scatteringly; scatteredly; sporadically; 〔따로따로〕 separately; severally. ¶~ 부서지다 break [be broken] to fragments [splinters] / be smashed to atoms // 그 집안은 ~ 흩어졌다 The family was broken up [torn asunder]. // 비행기가 산에 부딪혀 ~ 부서졌다 A plane was crushed to fragments against the mountain.
산산조각(散散-) broken pieces; bits and pieces; atoms; fragments; smithereens. ¶~이 나다 come to pieces / (무너져서) crumble into dust // ~으로 부수다 break [smash] a thing into pieces [fragments] / shatter / be shattered / be smashed to pieces [(구어) to smithereens] // 대리석 조상(彫像)은 ~이 났다 The marble figure was broken [smashed] into pieces.
산삼(山蔘) 〔식〕 (a) wild ginseng.
산상(山上) ¶~의 [에] at [on] the top [summit] of a mountain.
●**산상 수훈**(-垂訓) (성서의) the Sermon on the Mount.
산새(山-) 〔산에 사는 새〕 a mountain bird [fowl].
산성(山城) a mountain fortress wall; a hill-fort; walls on a hill.

산성(酸性) 〔화〕 acidity. ¶~의 acid / 〔산미 많은〕 acidic / (땅이) sour // ~이 되다 become acid / acidify.
●**산성도** acidity. **산성 반응** an acid reaction. **산성비** acid rain. **산성 비료** acid fertilizer. **산성 식품** acid [acidic] foods. **산성 토양** acid soil.
산세(山勢) the physical aspect [geographical features] of a mountain.
산소(山所) a grave; a tomb.
산소(酸素) 〔화〕 oxygen (기호 O). ¶~ 결핍 an oxygen shortage / 〔의〕 hypoxia / (특히 혈액의) anoxemia / (특히 조직의) anoxia // 액체 ~ liquid oxygen / lox // 공기 중의 ~ 농도 the oxygen content of the air // 생물학적 ~ 요구 the biological oxygen demand.
●**산소마스크** an oxygen mask. **산소 요법** oxygen treatment; oxypathy. **산소 화합물** an oxygen compound; an oxide. **산소 흡입기** an oxygen inhaler.
산속(山-) the heart [recesses] of a mountain. ¶깊은 ~에 deep in the mountains / far up (in) the mountain / in the recesses [depths / heart / bosom] of a mountain // ~의 외딴집 a solitary cottage among the mountains [in a mountain recess].
산송장 a living corpse; the living dead. ¶~이나 다름없다 be as good as dead / be more dead than alive // 그녀는 ~에 지나지 않았다 She is nothing more than a living skeleton.
산수(山水) 1 〔산과 물〕 hills and rivers [lakes]; 〔경치〕 a landscape. ¶~의 아름다움 natural [scenic] beauty // 부여는 ~가 아름다운 곳이다 Buyeo is noted for its scenic beauty. 2 〔산에서 흐르는 물〕 (water from) a mountain spring.
●**산수화** (화법) landscape painting; (그림) a landscape. **산수화가** a landscape painter; a landscapist.
산수(算數) 1 arithmetic. 2 ➡수학(數學)
산수소(酸水素) 〔화〕 oxyhydrogen.
●**산수소 불꽃** oxyhydrogen flame.
산술(算術) arithmetic; the science of numbers. ¶~의 arithmetical // ~을 하다 do sums / cipher // ~을 잘 [못] 하다 be good [poor] at sums / have a good [poor] head for figures.
●**산술급수** arithmetic progression [series]. **산술 평균** an arithmetic [numerical] mean.
산스크리트 어(-語) Sanskrit (약어 Skr., Skt., Sans.). ¶~의 Sanskrit.
산신령(山神靈) the guardian spirit of a mountain; the god of mountains.
산실(産室) 〔해산하는 방〕 a maternity room (in a hospital); a delivery room; a lying-in room.
산아(産兒) 〔해산〕 childbirth; 〔아이〕 a newborn baby. **산아하다** give birth to a baby.
●**산아 제한** birth control; birth [family] limitation. ¶~의 필요성 the need for birth control // ~을 하다 practice birth control / control conception / limit one's family [offspring].
산악(山岳·山嶽) mountains. ¶~의 [에서 자라는 / 에서 사는] 〔생〕 montane (flora).
●**산악병** 〔고산병〕 mountain sickness. **산악부 / 산악회** a mountaineering [an alpine] club. **산악전** mountain warfare. **산악 지대** a mountainous area.

산야(山野) fields and mountains; hills and fields; moor and hill. ¶~의 초목 wild plants.

산양(山羊) **1** a goat. ⇨*영소* **2** an antelope. ⇨*영양(羚羊)*
● **산양자리** [천] the Goat; Capricornus.

산언덕(山−) a hillock; a hill; a mound.

산업(産業) industry. ¶국내 ~ the domestic industry // 방위[자동차] ~ the defense[automobile] industry // 수출 ~ the export industry // 정보 ~ the communication[information] industry // 주요[기초] ~ the chief [basic] industries // 기간~ the key industries // 철강 ~ the iron and steel industry // 평화 ~ peace industries // 1차[2차 / 3차] ~ (a) primary[secondary / tertiary] industry.
● **산업가 / 산업인** an industrialist. **산업 개발** industrial development[exploitation]. **산업계** industrial circles; the industrial world. **산업 공해** industrial pollution. **산업 구조** industrial structure. **산업 단지** an industrial complex. **산업 도로** an industrial road. **산업 박람회** an industrial exhibition. **산업 스파이** an industrial spy. **산업예비군** an industrial reserve force. **산업 자본** industrial capital. **산업 자원부** the Ministry of Commerce, Industry and Energy. **산업 재해** industrial disaster. ¶~자 an industrial disaster victim. **산업 폐기물** industrial wastes. **산업 혁명** the Industrial Revolution. **산업화** industrialization. ¶~하다 industrialize. **산업 훈장** the Order of Industrial Service Merit.

산역(山役) tomb work; making a grave; construction of a tomb. **산역하다** make a grave.
● **산역꾼** a grave maker; a graveyard worker.

산욕(産褥) confinement; childbed; puerperium. ¶~에 눕다 be confined.
● **산욕기** a confinement; puerperium (*pl.* -ria). **산욕열** childbed[puerperal] fever.

산울림(山−) an echo (*pl.* ~es); the rumbling of a mountain. ¶아침부터 ~이 울렸다 The mountain has been rumbling since morning.

산울타리 a (quick) hedge; (영) a quickset (hedge); a live[quick] fence. ¶~를 두르다 enclose (a house) with a hedge / surround (a house) with a hedge / hedge (a garden) // ~를 만들다 plant[lay] a hedge // 부지는 ~로 둘러싸여 있다 The grounds are surrounded with a hedge.

산원(産院) a maternity; a lying-in hospital.

산월(産月) the month of parturition.

산유국(産油國) an oil producing country.

산입(算入) inclusion; calculating. **산입하다** include in; count[reckon in]; add in; take into account. ¶청구서에 교통비도 산입해 주십시요 Please include traveling expenses in the bill.

산자수명(山紫水明) beautiful scenery; scenic beauty; purple hills and crystal streams. **산자수명하다** scenically beautiful. ¶산자수명한 곳 a place of outstanding natural beauty.

산장(山莊) a mountain villa; a hillside cottage.

산재(山災) industrial disaster. ⇨*산업 재해* (産災)

산재하다(散在−) (사물이) lie[be] scattered; lie sporadically; straggle; be found here and there; (장소가) be dotted with 《something》. ¶산재한 scattered / sporadic // 집들이 산재하는 마을 village consisting of a few scattered houses // 회원은 전국에 산재해 있다 Members are scattered[are spread out] all over the country. // 후미에는 작은 섬들이 산재해 있다 The inlet is studded with small islands.

산적(山賊) a bandit (*pl.* ~s, -ti); (특히 옛날의) a highwayman. ¶~의 떼 a gang of bandits // ~의 소굴 a bandits' den / a robber's roost // ~을 만나다 fall among bandits // ~이 되다 become a bandit / take to the road[bush].

산적(散炙) shish kebab; meat and vegetables broiled on a skewer; [사슬산적] unskewered shish kebab.

산적하다(山積−) pile up; accumulate; form a (huge) pile; lie in a heap; lie in piles. ¶산적한 쓰레기 a heap[mountain] of rubbish / a huge amount of rubbish // 일이 산적해 있어서 만날 수가 없다 I am too busy[too much engaged] to see you. // 정리되지 않은 서류가 책상 위에 산적해 있다 Unsorted documents are accumulating[piling up] on the desk. // 역에는 도착 화물이 산적해 있다 There lie piles of goods undelivered[awaiting delivery] at the station.

산전(産前) ¶~에 before childbirth[delivery] // ~ 산후 before and after childbirth // ~ 후의 휴가 (a) maternity leave.

산전수전(山戰水戰) fighting all sorts of hardships. ¶~을 다 겪은 사람 a man of the world / an old hand / (여자) a knowing jade // 인생의 ~을 다 겪다 go through the ups and downs of life / have a checkered career // 그녀는 ~을 다 겪었다 She suffered unspeakable hardships.

산정(山頂) the summit[top] of a mountain. ⇨*산꼭대기* ¶백두산 ~의 분화구 the crater on the summit of Baekdusan(Mt. Baekdu) // ~에 at the summit[on (the) top] of a mountain / on the mountaintop // ~에 도달하다 attain[reach] the summit[peak].

산정(算定) [계산하여 정함] (a) calculation; computation; [어림잡음] an estimate; (an) estimation; [평가] assessment. ¶소득세의 ~ calculation of income tax // 상환액의 ~ assessment of the amount of redemption // ~을 잘못하다 make a mistake in calculation / miscalculate. **산정하다** calculate; compute; [어림잡다] estimate; [평가하다] assess. ¶판매 가격을 ~ compute a selling price // 건축비를 5천만 원으로 ~ estimate the building costs at fifty million won.
● **산정 가격** estimated price[value]; appraisal.

산줄기(山−) [뻗어 나간 산의 줄기] a mountain range; a chain[line] of mountains. ¶태백산 ~ the Taebaek range.

산중(山中) [산속] a mountain recess; the bosom of hills. ¶~의[에서] in[among] the mountains // ~의 오솔길 a narrow mountain path.

산증(疝症) [한] scrotal hernia.

산지(山地) a mountain[mountain] district[region]; a hilly district; an intermountain area.

산지(産地) (물건의) a production center; a producing area; (동식물 등의) the home; the habitat; a breeding center(말 등의); a growing district(식물의); a locality; (사람의) a birthplace; a home. ¶버섯의 ~ a production center for mushrooms / a mushroom-producing[-growing] area // 작송의 사과 apples fresh from the district where they were grown[from the orchard] // 이 동물의 ~는 남미이다 This animal comes from South America. // 제주도는 귤의 ~로 유명하다 Jejudo is famous for its[for producing] tangerines.

산지기(山−) (산의) a (forest) ranger; (묘의) a grave keeper.

산짐승(山−) a mountain animal.

산채(山菜) wild edible greens. ⇨산나물
● **산채 요리** a dish prepared from wild plants.

산채(山寨·山砦) 〔산속의 요새〕 a mountain stronghold[fort]; 〔산적의 소굴〕 a den of mountain bandits; a mountain hangout.

산책(散策) a walk; a stroll; a lounge; an airing; a promenade; (구어) a constitutional(건강을 위한). ¶아침 ~ a morning walk // 한 시간 동안의 ~ an hour's walk // ~을 가다 go for a walk // ~에 나서다 go out for a walk // 아버지는 ~ 가셨습니다 My father is out for a walk. **산책하다** stroll; promenade; saunter; ramble[lounge] about; take the air; take a walk[stroll]. ¶산책하는 사람 a stroller / 거리를 ~ stroll through a street / 교외를 ~ take a walk in the suburbs / 멀리 산책하러 가다 take[go for] a long walk.
● **산책로** a promenade; a walk; (해안·호숫가 등의) an esplanade. ¶자연 ~를 걷다 follow a natural trail.

산천(山川) mountains and streams.
● **산천초목** 〔자연〕 nature; natural scenery; landscape.

산촌(山村) a mountain village.

산출(産出) production; output; yield; 〔제조〕 manufacturing. ¶석유 ~국 a petroleum-producing country. **산출하다** produce; yield; bring forth; manufacture; turn out. ¶이 광산은 석탄을 산출한다 This mine produces coal. // 이 학교는 유능한 인재를 많이 산출했다 This school has turned out[produced] many able men.
● **산출물** a product; a production. **산출액 / 산출고** the (amount of) production; the output; the yield. **산출지** a producing center; a place of production[origin].

산출(算出) calculation; computation; reckoning. **산출하다** calculate; compute; reckon. → ¶산출된 세액 a calculated tax amount / 건축비 총액은 약 5천만 원으로 산출되었다 The total cost of construction was calculated at approximately fifty million won.

산타클로스 Santa Claus; (영) Father Christmas.

산탄(霰彈) a shot (pl. ~(s)); a case shot; (집합적) shot; buckshot; slugs. ¶~ 1발 a charge of shot.
● **산탄총** a shotgun.

산턱(山−) a shoulder (of a hill[mountain]); the ledge of a mountainslope.

산토끼(山−) a hare; a wild rabbit; a jackrabbit(북미의).

산통(算筒) a case for bamboo fortune slips [counting-sticks].

산통(을) **깨다** spoil; ruin; make a mess [muddle] of.

¶**산통이 깨지다** be spoiled[ruined]; turn to dust and ashes.

산파(産婆) a midwife (pl. -wives); a maternity nurse.
● **산파술** midwifery; obstetrics; 〔철〕 the maieutic method. **산파역** the job of a midwife; 〔비유〕 a sponsor; the originator. ¶~을 하다 act as (a) midwife / (비유) assist (in the formation of an organization).

산판(山坂) 〔멧갓〕 a forest reserve.

산패(酸敗) 〔화〕 acidification. **산패하다** acidify; turn sour.
● **산패액** 〔식물〕 water brash. **산패유** sour milk.

산포(散布) distribution; scattering; sprinkling; spraying; spreading; dispersion; diffusion. **산포하다** distribute; scatter; sprinkle; spray; spread; diffuse.
● **산포도** 〔수〕 (measure of) dispersion.

산포도(山葡萄) **1** wild grapes. ⇨머루 **2** 〔식〕 an ivy. ⇨담쟁이덩굴

산표(散票) 〔흩어진 표〕 scattered votes. ¶그는 ~를 획득했을[긁어모았을] 뿐이다 He secured [raked up] only scattered votes.

산하(山河) mountains and rivers. ¶고향의 ~ the natural surroundings of one's native place.

산하(傘下) ~의 subsidiary / affiliated / under the influence[protection] (of) / 삼성 ~의 회사 subsidiary companies of Samsung / companies affiliated with Samsung // 대한 노조 ~의 노조 a labor[trade] union under the control of the Federation of Korean Trade Unions // 미국의 ~에 있다 be under the umbrella of the United States.

산학 협동(産學協同) industrial-educational cooperation; industry-university cooperation.

산해(山海) mountains and seas; land and sea.
● **산해진미** all sorts of delicacies; a sumptuous feast; dainties of all lands and seas. ¶~로 대접하다 entertain (a person) with all sorts of delicacies // 상은 ~로 꽉 차 있다 The table groans with dainties of many kinds. / The table has all sorts of delicacies.

산허리(山−) a hillside; a mountainside; the side of a mountain. ¶~에 있는 오두막 a hut on a hillside / ~에 있다 The temple lies halfway up the hill.

산협(山峽) 〔골짜기〕 a gorge; a ravine; 〔두메〕 a remote and isolated place in the mountains.

산호(珊瑚) **1** coral. **2** 〔산호충〕 a coral insect; a polyp. ¶돌~ stony coral // ~(빛/제)의 coral 모양의 coralliform // ~를 채집하다 fish for coral.
● **산호도 / 산호섬** a coral island. **산호초** a coral reef; 〔환초〕 an atoll. **산호충** a coral insect; a polyp.

산화(散花) **1** 〔장렬한 전사〕 a heroic death in battle[action]. **산화하다** fall as flowers do; die a glorious[heroic] death. ¶전쟁에서 산화한 병사들 the soldiers who died in the war. **2** 〔불〕 〔꽃을 뿌리는 일〕 a Buddhist rite of scattering[strewing] flowers.

산화(酸化) 〔화〕 oxidation; oxidization; oxygenation; combustion. ¶일[이]~탄소 carbon monoxide [이]~ **산화하다** oxidize; oxidate; be oxidized. ¶산화하기 쉬운 금속 an easily oxidizable metal.

●**산화마그네슘** magnesium oxide; magnesia. **산화물** an oxidized substance. ¶금속 ~ a metallic oxide∥양성 ~ an amphoteric oxide∥중성 ~ a neutral oxide. **산화 방지제** an antioxidant. **산화수소** oxide of hydrogen. **산화철** iron oxide. **산화칼슘** calcium oxide. **산화 환원 반응** an oxidation-reduction reaction.

산회(散會) adjournment; rising. ¶~를 제의합니다 I move that we adjourn. **산회하다** adjourn; rise; break up; disperse. ¶모임은 5시 반에 산회했다 The meeting broke up [adjourned] at five thirty.

산후(産後) ¶~의[에] postpartum / after childbirth[parturition] / after one's confinement∥~의 몸조리 postpartum care∥회복 상태가 좋다[나쁘다] The mother's convalescence after giving birth is going well [badly].

살¹ 1 (뼈를 둘러싼) flesh. ¶~이 fleshy / sarcous∥~이 찐[많은] fleshy / fat / meaty∥~이 알맞게 찐 중키의 신사 a gentleman of medium height and build∥~을 에는 듯한 추위 biting[cutting / penetrating] cold∥~이 되는 음식 nutritious[nourishing] food / substantial food / substantials∥~이 되다 be nutritious / be nourishing∥그는 ~이 쪘다 He's fat.∥바람은 ~을 에는 듯이 찼다 The wind was so cold it seemed to cut[bite] right through me.

2 (식용의 고기) meat(짐승의); fish(생선의); game(사냥감의). ¶질긴[연한] ~ tough[tender] meat.

3 (호두·조개·게 등의 껍질 속의) meat; (과육의) flesh; pulp. ¶게의 ~ crab meat∥새우의 ~ the meat of a lobster∥견과(堅果)의 ~ the meat of a nut∥~이 많은 과일 pulpy fruit.

4 (살갗) the skin. ¶맨~ bare[naked] skin∥~빛 the color of (human) flesh∥~이 검은 남자 a man of dark complexion∥그녀는 ~이 곱다 She has clear[spotless] skin. / She has a smooth[beautiful] complexion.

살(이) 내리다[빠지다] lose flesh; become leaner[thinner]; get thin; flesh falls off. ¶그녀는 요즘 살이 내렸다[빠졌다] She has lost weight recently.∥살 내리게 하려면 규정식을 들어야 한다 If you want to reduce, you must go on a diet.

살(이) 붙다[오르다 / 찌다] put on[gain / get / gather] flesh; grow fleshy; flesh up[out]. ¶그녀는 요즘 살이 붙었다[올랐다 / 쪘다] Lately she has put on[gained] weight.∥나는 요즘 허리에 살이 붙기 시작했다 Recently I've put on weight around the waist. / (구어) Recently I've been developing a spare tire.∥음식이 좋아지자 아이들은 곧 살이 붙기[오르기 / 찌기] 시작했다 On a better diet the children soon began to flesh up.

살(을) 붙이다 (소설의 인물 등에) give body and substance (to); (이론 등에) round off; (조각에) model. ¶작중 인물에 ~ round out one's characters.

살(을) 섞다 live a married life; share bed and board (with); cohabit.

살² 1 (뼈대가 되는 부분) a rib; a stretcher; a spoke; a support; a stay; a stick; [살로 된 뼈대] a framework (composed of strips); lattice. ¶부챗~ the ribs[stretchers] of a fan∥창~ (세로의) a stile / a bar / a mullion / (가로의) a (window) rail / (격자창의) a lattice strip / a lattice / latticework∥우산~ the frame[spokes / ribs] of an umbrella∥자전거 바퀴의 ~이 하나 부러졌다 One of the spokes in my bicycle is broken.

2 (빗의) a tooth. ¶빗~ teeth of a comb∥~이 가는 빗 a fine-toothed comb.

3 (벌의 꽁무니에 있는 침) a sting. ¶말벌의 ~ a wasp's sting∥~에 쏘이다 get stung.

4 (어살) a fishing weir.

5 (화살) an arrow; a shaft; a dart. ¶~같이 빠르다 be as swift as an arrow∥~을 쏘다 shoot[send / discharge] an arrow (at)∥~은 과녁 복판에 맞았다 The arrow hit the target right in the center.

6 (빛의) a ray; a beam; (흐름의) a flow; a current. ¶햇~ a sunbeam∥빠른[센] 물~ a rapid[swift] stream[current].

7 (떡살로 찍은 무늬) a pattern (pressed on a cake).

8 (구김살) creases; rumples; folds; wrinkles.

살³ (나이) age; years (of age). ¶다섯 ~ 난 사내아이 a five-year-old boy / a boy of five (years) / a boy five years old∥50~에 죽다 die at the age of) fifty / die at age 50∥몇 ~입니까 How old are you?∥열여덟 ~입니다 I am eighteen (years / years old / years of age).∥그녀는 20~이 채 안 되었을 것이다 She is yet on the right[this] side of twenty, I think.

살(煞) 1 (악령) an evil spirit; baleful[evil] influence; plague; damnation; the devil; the devil's work; an ill-fated[unlucky] touch; a black hand. ¶~이 붙은 possessed / bewitched / devil-possessed∥~이 낀 날 a fateful[all ill-starred] day / a day of doom∥~을 풀다 exorcise evil spirits (from a person [place]) / exorcise (a person[place]) of evil spirits / drive out[away] evil spirits∥그녀는 ~이 있다[세다] She is plagued (with the devil). / She is an ill-starred woman. / She is a femme fatale.

2 (나쁜 따앗) bad blood; poor relations [animosity] with in a family. ¶그 집 형제들은 ~이 세다 The brothers of that family are bitterly on the outs[are at daggers drawn with one another].

살갑다 [마음이 너르다] broad-minded; liberal; generous; openhanded; [다정하다] kind; warm(-hearted); genial.

살갗 the skin. ⇨피부

살결 (skin) texture; complexion. ¶고운 ~ smooth[fine / delicate] skin / a smooth complexion∥거친 ~ a coarse[rough] skin∥~이 검은 사람 a person of dark complexion∥~이 흰 fair / fair-[light-]complexioned / fair-skinned∥~이 곱다 have a spotless [clear] skin / have a smooth complexion∥그녀는 ~이 비단 같다 Her skin is (of) a silk-velvety texture.

살구 [식] an apricot.

●**살구꽃** apricot blossoms. **살구나무** an apricot tree.

살균(殺菌) sterilization; pasteurization; disinfection; pasteurize; disinfect. **살균하다** sterilize; pasteurize; disinfect.

●**살균기** a sterilizer. **살균력** sterilizing [germicidal] power. **살균제** a disinfectant; a germicide; a bactericide; a sterilizer; a fungicide; a germicidal agent; a microbicide; a sanitizer(식품 가공용의).

살그머니 stealthily; secretly; furtively; by stealth; in secret; on the sly; quietly. ¶~ 들어오다[나가다] sneak in[out] // ~ 다가오다 steal near / sneak (up / on) / sneak (stalk) (up to) // ~ 보다 cast stealthy [furtive] glances (on) / steal a look [glance] (at) // 돈을 ~ 손에 쥐어 주다 slip a coin into a person's hand // ~ 사슴에게 다가갔다 He approached the deer stealthily.

살금살금 stealthily; secretly; furtively; sneakingly; by stealth; in secret; quietly; on the sly[quiet]. ¶~ 걷다 pussyfoot / walk noiselessly [stealthily] / walk on tiptoe // ~ 돌아다니다 skulk [slink / sneak] about // ~ 나가다 [들어오다] steal [sneak / slip] out [in] // ~ 뒤를 밟다 shadow (a person) stealthily / (미국 속어) gumshoe // ~ 다가가다 make a stealthy approach (to) / approach (a person) stealthily [with a cautious tread] / near (a person) on tiptoe // 그는 ~ 밖으로 나갔다 He stole [slipped / sneaked] out. // ~ 도망치는 자가 있었다 Someone sneaked away.

살기(殺氣) [독살스러운 기운] a thirst for blood; blood thirstiness; [긴장된 분위기] a stormy atmosphere. ¶~를 띠다 fall into a truculent mood / grow excited / become thirsty for blood // 해산 명령이 떨어지자 장내는 ~를 띠었다 A stormy atmosphere fell on the hall as the meeting was ordered to break up. // 실내에 ~가 가득했다 An air of imminent violence pervaded the room.

살기등등하다(殺氣騰騰-) be bloodthirsty; one's blood is up; be roused to violence; seethe with anger. ¶살기등등해 있었다 There was a wide-spread thirst for blood. / Death was in the air. / 살기등등한 군중이 입구에 몰려왔다 The crowd made a mad rush [dash] for the door. / The frenzied crowd shoved toward(s) the entrance.

살길 a means to live; a livelihood. ¶~을 찾다 seek a way to make a living // ~을 잃다 lose one's livelihood // ~을 마련해 주다 procure a means of living for (a person).

살날 the rest of one's life; (the remainder [remnant / rest] of) one's days; one's remaining days. ¶그가 ~도 얼마 남지 않았다 His days are numbered. / He has only a short time to live. / His days are drawing to their close.

살다¹ 1 [생존하다] live; subsist; exist; [소생하다] revive. ¶산 물고기 a live fish // 사는 기쁨 the joy of living // 사느냐 죽느냐의 문제 a matter of life and death // 살아 있는 한 so long as one lives / as long as one has a drop of blood in one // 살아 있는 사람에게 말하듯이 말하다 speak as if to the living // 한 사람이 사느냐 죽느냐의 갈림길에 서 있을 때 when a person's life is at stake // 그는 100세까지 살았다 He lived to be a hundred. / 무엇 때문에 우리는 사는가 What do we live for? // 사는 보람이 없다 I have nothing to live for. // 그는 5일 동안 물만 마시고 살았다 He lived on only [lived on a diet of / had nothing but] water for five days. // 사람은 빵만으로 사는 것이 아니다 [성] Man shall not live by bread alone. // 그는 아직 살아 [living]. // 포격이 계속되는 동안은 살아 있다기보다는 죽은 느낌이 들었다 During the bombardment I felt more dead than alive. // 이 병에 걸리면 사는 사람은 거의 없다 Few survive this kind of disease. // 살아서 창피를 당하느니 죽는 편이 차라리 낫겠다 I would rather die than live in disgrace.

2 [생활을 영위하다] live; get on [along / by]; lead [live] a life. ¶혼자 사는 노인 an old man living alone // 고난 속에 살아온 10년 ten years spent in hardship // 잘[못] ~ be well [badly] off // 편안히 ~ live comfortably [in comfort] // 가난하게 ~ live in poverty // 검소하게 ~ live in a small way [on a cramped scale] // 사치스럽게 ~ live in luxury / lead a luxurious life // 바쁘게 ~ live a busy life // 과거의 영광에 대한 회상 속에 ~ live in the recollection of one's past glories // 그는 오직 학문만을 위해 살았다 He lived solely for learning. // 그녀는 행복하게 살고 있다 She is living happily [leading a happy life].

3 [거주하다] live (in / on / at); reside (in) (▶ 격식차린 말); [서식하다] inhabit(▶ 진행형으로 쓸 수 없음). ¶살기에 적합한 inhabitable / good [fit] to live in // 살기에 적합하지 않은 uninhabitable / unfit to live in // 숲에 사는 새 birds living in a wood // 사람이 살지 않는 집 an unoccupied [a vacant] house / a deserted house // 그는 종로에 산다 He lives in Jongno. // 피난민은 살 곳이 없다 The refugees have no place to live [are homeless]. // 그 지역에는 아직도 많은 인디언들이 살고 있다 The area is still inhabited by a large Indian population. // 많은 인디언들이 그 지역에 살고 있다 Many Indians live in the area even today. // 이 집은 오랫동안 사람이 살고 있지 않다 This house has been vacant [has not been lived in] for a long time. // 그녀가 그 주소에 정말 살고 있는지 확인해 볼 필요가 있다 It is necessary to ascertain whether she is really domiciled at the address. // 저 나라는 살기 어려운 나라다 That country is difficult to live in. // 이 세상은 썩 살기 좋은 곳은 아니다 This world of ours is not very agreeable place to live in. // 대도시는 편리하지만 살기 좋은 데는 아니다 Large cities are convenient but not very pleasant to live in. // 나는 태어나서부터 줄곧 이곳에서 살아왔다 I have lived here since I was born. // 우리는 오래 살던 집을 판다는 것이 시골펐다 We were very sad to sell our dear old home.

4 [소용·효력이 있다] be effective; be useful; be valid; be of use. ¶이 법률은 살아 있다 This law is still valid.

5 [생동하다] be enlivened; have life given to (it). ¶살아 있는 듯한 초상화 a lifelike portrait // 이 그림은 배경의 강 때문에 살아 있다 The river in the background sets off the picture to advantage. // 이 낱말 하나로 문장이 살게 되었다 This one word has put life into the sentence [has made the sentence come to life].

6 (바둑 등에서) get permanently secure; get permanently free from danger; be freed from check.

7 [야구] be safe.

살다² (벼슬·징역을) serve (one's term). ¶5년간 징역을 ~ serve a sentence of five years' penal servitude / do a five-year prison stretch // 그는 벼슬을 살고 있다 He is in the government service. / He holds an office under the government.

살담배 cut [pipe] tobacco; shred(ded) tobacco.

살덩어리 a piece [lump] of flesh.
살뜰하다 [알뜰하다] thrifty; frugal; saving; provident (of); (애정이) affectionate (toward); attached (to); fond (of).¶살뜰한 주부 a frugal housewife∥그녀는 외아들에게 살뜰했다 She dearly loved her only son.∥그녀는 ~ She is prudent [frugal] with (her) money. **살뜰히** [알뜰하게] frugally; economically; with frugality; [애정 깊게] affectionately; lovingly; fondly; dearly.

살랑거리다 1 (바람이) blow gently [softly]. ¶가을바람이 살랑거린다 An autumn breeze blows softly. 2 (걸음걸이가) walk gracefully; walk with a mincing gait.¶살랑거리며 걷다 walk like a fashion.

살랑살랑 (바람이) with a rustle [whisper]; gently; softly; with a rustling noise; (걸음 모양이) with a mincing gait; briskly. ¶~ 소리 내다[나다] rustle / whistle / murmur∥그녀가 방 안을 왔다 갔다 하자 옷이 스치는 소리가 났다 Her dress gave out a continual rustle as she swept about the room. **살랑살랑하다** blow gently; walk gracefully. ⇨살랑거리다

살래살래 shaking. ⇨설레설레

살롱 (웅접실·상류 사회의 모임) a salon; [배 등의 담화실·바] a saloon; (파리에서 열리는 미술전] the Salon.
●**살롱 음악** salon music.

살리다 1 [소생시키다] revive; resuscitate; bring (a person) back to life; bring round [to]. ¶잃어버린 풍습을 ~ revive lost customs.
2 [산 채로 두다] spare a person's life; let (a person) live; keep (an animal / a fish) alive. ¶낚은 물고기를 활어조에 살려 두다 keep one's catch alive by putting it in a fish crawl∥우리는 그를 살려 둘 수 없다 We can't let him live.
3 [잘 이용하다] make (the best) use of. ¶폐물을 ~ utilize [make use of] refuse materials∥자신의 재능을 충분히 ~ use one's talent to the full / make full use of one's talent∥그는 에스파냐 어의 지식을 살려서 라틴 아메리카 국가들과 장사를 시작했다 Putting his knowledge of Spanish to (practical) use, he started doing business with Latin American countries.
4 [생기가 있게 하다] give life [vividness] (to); vivify; put vigor [life] (into). ¶그림을 ~ put life into a painting.
5 [인] (지운 곳을) stet (약어 st.). ¶지운 곳을 ~ restore a deleted passage.

살려 주다 save; rescue; spare (a person's) life; help (a friend) in need. ¶물에 빠진 사람을 ~ rescue [save] a person from drowning∥"살려 줘요!"라고 외쳤다 cry, "Help, help!"∥목숨만 살려 주십시오 Spare me! / Have mercy on me.

살리실산 (-酸) [화] salicylic acid.
살림 [생계] (a) living; (a) livelihood; [생활] life; subsistence; existence; [살림 형편] circumstances; [살림살이] housekeeping (establishment); housekeeping. ¶홀아비 ~ (미혼자의) a bachelor's household / (상처자의) a widower's household∥가난한 ~ a needy domestic establishment / small housekeeping∥~을 잘하는[못하는] 여자 a good [bad] housewife∥~이 풍족하다 make a good living / be well [comfortably] off / be well-to-do (미) be well fixed∥~이 어렵다 make a poor living / be badly off / (미) be poorly fixed∥~을 잘하다[못하다] be a good [poor] housekeeper [housewife] / be good [bad] at housekeeping∥~을 꾸려 가다 live / make a [one's] living / earn one's livelihood [bread] / make the pot boil / 집안의 ~을 도맡아 하다 support [maintain] one's family∥~을 나다 be set up in a separate family∥~을 내다 keep a separate house∥~을 줄이다 cut down one's living expenses∥그는 ~이 전보다 못해졌다 He is worse off than before.∥그의 아들은 드디어 ~을 차린다 His son is at last setting out to be a family man. **살림하다** keep house; manage a household; housekeep. ¶그녀는 살림할 줄을 몰랐다 She did not know how to manage her household.∥아무리 세심하게 살림한다 하더라도 5인 가족에 월 50만 원으로는 무리다 Five hundred thousand won a month is hardly enough for a family of five, no matter how carefully you may manage your household.

살림(을) 맡다 take charge of the household; keep house.
●**살림꾼** [살림을 맡은 사람] a housekeeper; the mistress of a house; [알뜰한 사람] a good housewife [manager]. ¶그녀는 ~이다 She is a good housewife [housekeeper]. **살림도구** household goods (necessaries). **살림살이** [살림을 차려 삶] housekeeping; [household; [세간] household goods. ¶가난한 ~ meager living / a needy household∥물가고로 인해 ~가 어렵다 be badly off owing to the high cost of living. **살림집** a private home.

살맛¹ 1 [남의 살의 감각] the touch (of another's skin); the feel. 2 [성적 경험]. ¶~을 알다 have a sexual experience / know a woman∥~을 모르다 have no carnal knowledge of woman.

살맛² ¶~이 있다[없다] have something [nothing] to live for∥~을 느끼다 find one's life worth living∥~이 없어지다 grow weary [get sick] of life / lose interest in life.

살며시 1 [살그머니] stealthily; furtively; secretly; in private. ¶~가 버리다 go away stealthily / slip away∥~ 집을 나가다 steal out of the house∥~ 다가오다 steal near / sneak (up on) / steal [sneak / stalk] (up to)∥~ 웃다 laugh in one's sleeves. 2 [가만히] quietly; gently; lightly; softly; cautiously. ¶~ 자리를 뜨다 leave one's seat quietly∥~ 걷다 walk with soft steps [tread]∥아기를 ~ 안다 pick up a baby cautiously.

살모넬라균 (-菌) [의] (a) salmonella (pl. -lae).
살무사 [동] a (kind of) pit viper. ¶(성질이) ~ 같은 viperine / viperish / viperous.
살문 (-門) [건] a lattice door [window]; a lattice.
살바람 1 [틈으로 새어 드는 찬 바람] (미) a draft; (영) a draught. 2 [봄철의 찬 바람] a chill spring wind. ¶초봄의 ~ a chill wind in early spring.

살벌하다 (殺伐-) bloody; [살기를 띠다] bloodthirsty; [잔인하다] savage; [사납다] fierce; sanguinary; brutal; violent; warlike (people). ¶살벌한 분위기 a warlike atmosphere∥계엄령이 선포되자 시가는 살벌한 기운이 감돌았다 As the martial law was proclaimed, the city was in a tense and violent

살보시(-布施) sexual relations with a Buddhist priest. **살보시하다** have illicit sexual relations with a priest.

살붙이 1 [가까운 혈육] one's kith and kin; a relative; kinsfolk. ¶~라고는 딸 하나밖에 없다 My daughter is my only relative alive. 2 [짐승의 살고기] meats.

살빛 [피부색] the color of the skin; flesh color; complexion; cast; hue; the color of (human) flesh. ¶~ 스타킹 natural-colored stockings // ~이 희다 have a fair skin [complexion] / be fair // ~이 검다 have dark skin / be dark-complexioned.

살살¹ stealthily; slowly; softly; (melt) well; tactfully; gradually. ⇨슬슬

살살² gently; with a brisk crawl; with a gentle shake of the head. ⇨설설

살살³ [배가 약간 아픈 모양]. ¶배가 ~ 아프다 have a slight pain in the stomach.

살살이 a wily[tricky] person; a schemer; a back-scratcher; a shirk(er); a slacker; (미국구어) a goldbrick(er).

살상하다(殺傷-) kill and wound; shed blood.

살생(殺生) destruction of life; butchery; shooting and fishing(새·물고기의). ¶~을 금하다 prohibit killing animals // 무익한 ~을 자행하다 kill animals needlessly[without any reason]. **살생하다** destroy[take] life; kill animals.

살수기(撒水器) a sprinkler.

살수차(撒水車) a sprinkler (truck); a water cart.

살수하다(撒水-) water; (세차게) spray water; (여기저기) sprinkle water (on). ¶뜰에 ~ water a garden / sprinkle a garden with water // 장미에 ~ water the roses.

살신성인하다(殺身成仁-) sacrifice oneself to preserve one's integrity; become a martyr to humanity.

살아가다 1 [생명을 이어 가다] lead a life; live; get along; sustain[maintain] life; keep on living. ¶간신히 ~ keep body and soul together // 그럭저럭 ~ rub[scrape] through life / manage to get on[along] // 세상을 정직하게 ~ go straight / pursue an honest career // 인생은 살아갈 가치가 있을까 Is life worth living? 2 [살림을 영위하다] live; make a[one's] living; earn one's livelihood[bread]. ¶분수에 맞게 ~ live within one's means / 얼마 안 되는 월급으로 ~ live on a small salary // 우리는 그런 적은 급료로는 살아갈 수 없다 We can't live[get along] on such a small salary.

살아나다 1 [소생하다] revive; recover consciousness; come to oneself[to one's senses]; be brought round; return to life. ¶살아나게 하다 bring (a person) round (to) / recall[restore] (a person) to life / revive / resuscitate // 인공호흡으로 ~ be resuscitated by artificial respiration // 우리는 그가 살아나지 못할 것으로 단념했다 We gave him up for dead. // 비가 오자 시든 초목이 다시 살아났다 After a rain the drooping grass and plants have come to life again.
2 [구조되다] be saved[rescued / relieved]; be spared; survive (a disaster); (모면하다) escape (death); live. ¶간신히 ~ have a narrow[bare] escape / escape by a hair's breath // 기적적으로 ~ have a miraculous escape // 구사일생으로 ~ have a narrow [hairbreadth] escape / have a close shave / escape by the skin of one's teeth // 인제 살아 났구나 What a blessed relief!
3 (불 등이) burn[flame up] again. ¶숯불이 다시 살아난다 The charcoal fire grows again.
4 (형태가) be restored to (the original form); resume.

살아남다 survive; live through; outlive. ¶살아남는 surviving (people) // 살아남는 사람들 the survivors // 전 중대에서 살아남은 사람은 단 5명뿐이었다 Only five survived out of the whole company. // 그 비행기 사고에서 살아남은 사람은 아무도 없었다 No one survived the plane crash. // 적의 포격으로 파괴된 그 고장에 살아남은 사람은 소수에 불과했다 Only a few people were left alive in the town after it was destroyed by the enemy bombing.

살아생전(-生前) one's lifetime. ¶~에 in [during] one's lifetime / while alive [in life] / before one's death // 너의 출세를 보고 싶구나 I hope I may live long enough to see you rise in the world.

살얼음 a thin coat[sheet] of ice; thin ice; cat [cat's] ice. ¶~을 밟다 risk great danger / walk a tightrope // 연못에 ~이 얼었다 The pond was thinly coated with ice.
● **살얼음판** a tricky [delicate / touchy] situation.

살육(殺戮) killing; slaughter; massacre; butchery; carnage(전쟁에 의한). ¶대량 ~ mass murder / a great massacre / a blood bath / genocide(국민·민족 등에 대한) // ~을 자행하다 kill recklessly / massacre [butcher] brutally[cruelly]. **살육하다** massacre; slaughter; butcher.

살의(殺意) murderous intent; intent to murder[kill]; [법] malice aforethought [prepense]. ¶~를 품고 with murderous intent / with intent to kill (a person) // ~를 품다 have[conceive] a murderous design / intend to kill (a person) / seek (a person's) life // 처음부터 ~가 있었던 것은 아니었다 It was not his original intention to kill the man.

-살이 living; life. ¶더부~ parasitism / dependence // 머슴~ working as a farmhand // 시집 ~ living with one's husband's parents // 징역 ~ serving one's term of imprisonment // 처가 ~ living with the family into which a man has married.

살인(殺人) murder; manslaughter; homicide.(▶ 법률 용어에서 murder는 모살, manslaughter는 살해 의도 없는 살인, 우발적 살인, homicide는 위 둘을 포함한 일반적인 말) ¶대량 ~ mass[multiple] murder // 무차별 ~ a massacre // 정부 ~ murder by contract // 그런 일에 군대를 출동시키는 것은 바로 ~ 행위이다 To send troops on such an errand is sheer murder. **살인하다** commit murder [homicide]; kill[murder] (a person); do murder.
● **살인마** / **살인귀** a devilish homicide; a cutthroat; a bloodthirsty felon; a ghoul. **살인미수** an attempted[a frustrated] murder; a murder attempt. **살인범** / **살인자** a homicide; a murderer; a murderess(여자); a killer; a slayer. **살인 사건** a case of murder; a murder case. **살인 용의자** a murder suspect. **살인죄** homicide; (모살) murder; (우발적)

살인적(殺人的) deadly (heat); hectic (confusion); cutthroat (competition). ¶이~ 더위 deadly [(구어) awful] heat.

살점(-點) a piece of meat; a chop; a cut.

살지다 1 [살이 많다] fleshy; fat; stout; plump. ¶살진 돼지 a plump pig // 살진 암탉 a fat hen. 2 [땅이 기름지다] fertile; rich.

살집 fleshiness. ¶~이 좋은 [건강한] strapping [여자가 통통하고 젖가슴이 불룩한] buxom // ~이 좋은 여자 a woman with a well-filled-out frame // ~이 좋다 be fleshy [plump / stout].

살짝 1 [남이 모르게] furtively; by stealth; stealthily; quietly; secretly; on the quiet [sly]. ¶~ 만나다 have a clandestine meeting // ~ 보다 cast a stealthy [furtive] glance (on) / steal a look [glance] (at) / spy on (a person's movement) // 그녀는 얼굴을 붉혔다 She blushed faintly. // 그녀는 ~ 눈을 떴다 She opened her eyes slightly [partway]. 2 [힘들이지 않고 가볍게] lightly; slightly; softly. ¶~ 등을 두드리다 tap (a person) on the back // ~ 만지다 give a light touch.

살짝곰보 a slightly pockmarked face [person].

살쩍 the hair under the temple; the sidelocks; (미) sideburns. ¶그는 ~에 흰 털이 섞여 있다 He is gray [His hair is graying] at the temples.

살찌다 [살이 많아지다] grow stout [fat] (▶ fat은 일반적으로 쓰이는 말, stout은 주로 단단하게 살찐 것을 말함. 또 살찐 여자에 대해서는 fat을 피하고 stout을 씀); gain weight; fatten; put [take] on flesh; gather [gain / get] flesh. ¶살찌는 것을 막다 keep down weight / wear off the fat // 돼지를 살찌게 하다 fatten a pig // 나는 요즘 퍽 살쪘다 Recently I have gained [put on] a lot of weight. // 너무 살찌는 것은 건강에 좋지 않다 Obesity is not good for the health.

살찌우다 make (a pig) fat; fatten; fat [feed] up; batten. ¶시장에 내려고 돼지를 ~ fatten (up) pigs for market.

살창(-窓) a lattice window.

살촉(-鏃) an arrowhead. ⇨화살촉(⇨화살)

살충제(殺蟲劑) an insecticide; a vermicide; a pesticide; an insect powder(가루); a larvicide(유충의); an adulticide(성충의). ¶정원수에 ~를 뿌리다 spray an insecticide on garden trees / spray garden trees with insecticide.

살충하다(殺蟲-) kill [destroy] insects; destroy worms; vermifuge.

살코기 lean [red] meat.

살쾡이 a wildcat; a leopard cat.

살판나다 become rich; be lucky; have a stroke of luck; strike it rich; come into a fortune; one's ship comes in. ¶그는 부잣집에 장가들어 살판났다 His ship came in when he married into a wealthy family.

살펴보다 [잘 보다] observe [watch] carefully; [확인하다] make sure (of); look around [about]; watch for; look into; examine. ¶무슨 문제가 생기지나 않을까 하고 ~ keep an eye out for potential problem // 사방을 ~ look all around // 그는 뒷문을 살펴보고 있다 He is keeping watch on the back gate.

살포기(撒布器) a sprinkler; a sprayer.

살포시 softly; gently; quietly; lightly; [살며시] stealthily; by stealth; on the sly. ¶나뭇잎이 ~ 땅바닥에 떨어졌다 A leaf dropped softly [fell gently] to the ground.

살포제(撒布劑) (피부용 파우더) dusting powder; (액체) a spray.

살포하다(撒布-) [분말·액체 등을 뿌리다] sprinkle; (분무기 등으로) spray; (가루를) dust. ¶비행기에서 분말 농약을 ~ crop-dust // 살충제를 정원수에 ~ spray [dust] garden plants with an insecticide / spray [dust] an insecticide on garden plants // 먼지를 재우기 위해 물을 ~ sprinkle water to lay the dust // 비행기가 전단을 살포했다 The plane dropped leaflets from the air.

살풀이(煞-) [민] salpuri; exorcism; exorcising an evil spirit. **살풀이하다** exorcise; have an exorcism.

살품 the space between clothes and the chest; the bosom; the breast. ¶어린아이가 어머니의 ~에 손을 넣었다 The child thrust the hand into its mother's bosom.

살풍경하다(殺風景-) 1 [황량하다] desolate; bleak; dreary; [단조하다] drab. ¶살풍경한 정원 a bleak garden // 살풍경한 해변 desolate beach // 가구가 거의 없는 살풍경한 방 a drab [bleak] room almost bare of furnishings. 2 [정취가 없다] prosaic; matter-of-fact; unimaginative. ¶과밀 도시의 살풍경한 생활 a prosaic [humdrum] life in an overcrowded city.

살피다 1 [관찰하다] observe; make observation (of); [조사하다] examine; take a good look at; inspect; study. ¶눈치를 ~ read (a person's) feelings / 사방을 ~ look around / glance about // 형세를 ~ wait and see how the wind blows [lies] / see how things stand [go on].
2 [주의하다] pay [give] attention (to); keep close watch (on); [경계하다] look out (for); beware of. ¶교통 신호를 ~ look [pay attention] to traffic signals // 아이들이 다치지 않도록 잘 살펴라 See [Take care] that the children do not get hurt. // 살펴 가시오 Take care of yourself. / Good-bye.
3 [판단하다] judge; gather; [양찰하다] consider; take into consideration; sympathize with; enter into (a person's) feelings. ¶그의 말하는 품으로 살피건대 as I gather from his words // 그는 남의 기분을 살피지 못한다 He lacks consideration for the feeling of others. // 사정이 이러하오니 부디 살펴 주시기 바랍니다 Such being the case, I hope you will kindly excuse me [sympathize with my situation].

살해(殺害) killing; [살인] a murder (case); homicide. ¶부친 [모친] ~ patricide [matricide] // 유아 ~ infanticide // ~를 기도하다 make an attempt on (a person's) life / attempt (a person's) life. **살해하다** [생명을 빼앗다] kill; (불법으로) murder; (문어) slay; (대량으로 죽이다·도살하다) slaughter. ➔노파는 그녀의 돈 때문에 살해되었다 The old woman was killed [murdered] for her money. // 많은 죄 없는 사람들이 살해되었다 A great number of innocent people were slaughtered. // 두목은 가장 믿었던 자에게 살해되었다 The boss was done in by the man he trusted most.

●**살해자** a slayer; a murderer; a murderess (여자); an assassin(암살자).
삵괭이 →살쾡이
삶 living; subsistence; existence; [생활] life. ¶~의 쓰라림 bitterness of life∥~을 위한 투쟁 struggle for life∥~에 지치다 get tired of living∥어렵게 ~을 이어 가다 scrape a living / earn meager living.
삶다 1 [끓이다] boil; seethe; cook; (뭉근한 불로) simmer. 삶은 달걀 boiled eggs∥삶아지다 be boiled[cooked] / boil / seethe∥고기를 푹 ~ do meat well[thoroughly]∥빨래를 ~ boil clothes / (영국 방언) buck (a dirty linen)∥너무 ~ overboil / overdo∥호물호물 하도록 ~ boil (something) to (a) pulp∥감자를 ~ boil potatoes∥야채를 뭉근한 불로 ~ let vegetables boil gently[simmer] / stew vegetables.
2 [구슬리다] cajole; coax; wheedle; win (a person) over; [매수하다] buy (a person) over; bribe. ¶형사를 ~ bribe[buy / fix] a detective∥아무튼 삶아서 …시키다 wheedle a person into (doing …)∥그를 삶아서 그것을 하게 할 수 있는지 알아보아라 See if we can buy him over to do it.
3 [흙을 부드럽게 만들다] harrow; till; rake the soil smooth.
삼[1] [식] flax; a flax plant(아마); a hemp (plant)(대마); ramie(모시풀); jute(황마); [그 섬유] flax; hemp; jute.
삼[2] (태아의) the amnion and the placenta. 삼(을) 가르다 cut the umbilical cord.
삼[3] [의] a leucoma; a white speck; (get) a phlyctenula (pl. -e). ¶(눈에) ~이 생기다[서다] get a leucoma / have a white speck in one's eye.
삼(三·參) three. ¶제 ~ the third∥~ 회 three times / thrice.
삼(參) 1 [산삼과 인삼] the wild ginseng and the ginseng. 2 ginseng. ⇨인삼
삼가 respectfully; reverently; humbly; courteously. ¶~ 말씀드립니다 I beg to inform you. ∥~ 용서를 빕니다 I humbly beg your pardon.∥~ 감사의 말씀을 드립니다 I respectfully express my thanks to you.∥자당의 서거에 ~ 조의를 표합니다 Please accept my deepest sympathy on your mother's death.∥~ 애도의 뜻을 표합니다 I respectfully express my condolence.
삼가다 1 [억제하다] restrain oneself; abstain [refrain / keep] from; be restrained [moderate / temperate] (in). 나는 술[담배] 을 삼가고 있다 I'm refraining[abstaining] from drinking[smoking]. ∥폭음 폭식을 삼가 시오 Don't drink or eat too much. / You should eat and drink in moderation. / You must be more moderate in your eating and drinking habits.∥제 의견을 말하는 일은 삼가겠습니다 I will refrain from expressing an opinion.∥남의 소문 이야기는 삼가는 게 좋다 It would be better to stop your indulgence.∥그는 어떠한 비평도 삼가기로 결심했다 He decided to refrain from making any criticism.∥당신은 술을 삼가는 것이 좋습니다 You had better moderate your drinking.∥상중이기 때문에 그 모임에 참석하는 것은 삼가 겠습니다 I will stay home from[refrain from attending] that party as I am in mourning. ∥여기서는 흡연을 삼가 주시기 바랍니다 You are requested to refrain from smoking here.

2 [조심하다] be prudent[careful]; be cautious; caution oneself (against); be discreet; be circumspect; reserve. ¶삼가는 [조심스럽고 마음을 터놓지 않는] reserved / [절도 있는] restrained∥언행을 ~ be discreet in word and deed∥말을 삼가시오 Weigh your words (carefully). / Be discreet.

삼각(三角) a triangle. ⇨ 삼각형(⇨삼각). ¶~의 triangular∥~으로 triangularly / in a triangular form∥~으로 하다 triangulate.
●**삼각건**(-巾) a triangle (bandage); a cravat. **삼각관계** the eternal triangle; a triangular[triple] love affair; a three-cornered romance; a love triangle. ¶~의 한 사람 a principal in a three-cornered romance[a love triangle]∥그들의 관계는 ~가 되었다 Their relations developed into a love triangle. **삼각기둥** / **삼각주**(-柱) a trigonal[triangular] prism. **삼각 무역** trilateral trade. **삼각법** [수] trigonometry; triangulation. ¶평면 [구면] ~ plane [spherical] trigonometry∥~의[에 의한] trigonometric(al). **삼각뿔** / **삼각추** a trigonal[triangular] pyramid. **삼각자** a set square; a triangle. **삼각주**(-洲) a delta. **삼각함수** [수] trigonometrical function. **삼각형** a triangle; a trilateral. ¶정~ an equilateral triangle∥직각 ~ a right(-angled) triangle∥이등변 ~ an isosceles triangle∥예각 [둔각] ~ an acute-[obtuse-]angled triangle∥구면 ~ a spherical triangle∥~의 triangle / triangular∥~으로 된 땅 a triangular plot of land / a triangular plot of land∥~으로 자르다 cut (a thing) into a triangular form.

삼각(三脚) a tripod. ⇨삼각가(⇨삼각). ¶~의 three-legged / tripodal∥2인 ~ 경기 a three-legged race.
●**삼각가** a tripod. **삼각의자** a three-legged stool.
삼강(三綱) the three basic[fundamental] principles in human relations; the three bonds.
●**삼강오륜**(-五倫) the three bonds and the five moral disciplines in human relations.
삼거리(三-) a crossing with three corners; a concourse of three streets; a forked road.
삼경(三更) midnight; the dead of night.
삼경(三經) the Three Classics (of Ancient China)(▶ the Book of Odes, the Cannon of History and the Book of Changes를 가리킴). ¶사서~ the Four Books and Three Classics (of ancient China) / the Seven Chinese Classics.
삼계탕(蔘鷄湯) *samgyetang*; chicken broth with *insam*(ginseng) (and other ingredients).
삼관왕(三冠王) [체] a triple crown. ¶~이 되다 get[win] a triple crown.
삼교(三校) [인] the third proof.
삼국(三國) three countries[states]. ¶제~ the third power[state / country]∥제~인 a third national.
●**삼국 동맹** a triple alliance. **삼국 협상** a triple entente[negotiation / talk].
삼군(三軍) [전군] the whole army; [육해공군] three armed services; the three services(▶ the army, the navy and the air force를 가리킴). ¶육해공의 ~ the three services — land, sea and air∥~을 지휘하다 command the armed forces∥~을 호령하다 command a great army.

삼권 분립(三權分立) [법] the separation of the three branches [of the administrative, legislative, and judicial branches] of government.

삼극(三極) ¶~의 tripolar.
● 삼극 진공관 a triode.

삼나무(杉-) [식] a Japan[Japanese] cedar; a crypromeria.

삼년상(三年喪) mourning of three years; a three year memorial service (for ancestors).

삼노(끈) a hemp rope [cord].

삼다¹ […으로 정하다] make; make (a thing) of; have [use / regard] (a thing / a person) as. ¶소일 삼아 just to kill time // 장난삼아 half in fun // 재미 삼아 partly out of sport / partly for fun / by way of amusement // 양자로 ~ adopt (an orphan) // 사위 ~ make (a person) one's son-in-law // …을 구실 삼아 on the pretext[plea] of / making (it) an excuse to … // …을 벗 ~ make a friend [companion] of / make friends with // 그는 그 고아를 양자로 삼았다 He adopted the orphan. // 그 점은 문제 삼지 않아도 된다 That point may be left out of consideration.

삼다² (신 등을) make (a sandal); (삼 등을) spin. ¶짚신을 ~ make straw sandals // 삼을 ~ spin hemp.

삼단 a bunch of hemp.

삼단 같은 머리 locks of long, flowing hair; tresses; luxuriant hair.

삼단 논법(三段論法) [논] a syllogism. ¶생략 ~ an enthymeme // 정언적 [가언적 / 선언적] ~ a categorical [hypothetical / disjunctive] syllogism.

삼대(三代) [아버지·아들·손자의 세 대] three generations. ¶우리는 ~가 함께 사는 대가족이다 Three generations of the family live together in our house.
● 삼대독자 the third generation of only sons; the third generation only son.

삼동(三冬) 1 [겨울의 석 달] the three winter months. 2 [세 해의 겨울] the winters of three years.

삼두근(三頭筋) [생] the triceps (*pl.* ~(es)).

삼두 정치(三頭政治) triumvirate; triarchy.

삼등(三等) [셋째 등급] the third class [rate]. ¶~으로 여행하다 travel (by) third class / travel (in the) steerage(배의).
● 삼등객 a third-class passenger(기차 등의); a steerage passenger(배의). **삼등국** a third-rate power [nation]; a minor country.

삼등분(三等分) trisection. **삼등분하다** trisect; cut [divide] (a thing) into three equal parts; divide (a thing) equally among the three.

삼라만상(森羅萬象) all [the whole of] creation; all nature; the universe; (문어) Nature.

삼루(三壘) [야구] the third base. ¶~ 쪽의 응원석 the rooters' seats behind third base / the third-base rooting [cheering] section // ~에 나아가다 go [advance] to third / take third.
● **삼루수** a third baseman. **삼루타** [야구] a three-base hit; (속어) a three-bagger; a triple. ¶~를 날리다 swat [slam / power] a triple / triple.

삼류(三流) the third rate [grade]. ¶~의 third-rate [-class / -grade] / of the third order // ~의 인물 a third-rater.
● 삼류 극장 a lower-class theater.

삼륜차(三輪車) (ride) a tricycle; (구어) a three-wheeler; (유아용) a velocipede; (엔진 달린) an autotricycle; a motor tricycle.

삼림(森林) a wood; woods; a forest.(▶ a forest가 woods보다 큼) ¶~을 도벌하다 fell a forest tree in secret.
● **삼림대**(一帶) a forest belt [zone]. **삼림 보호** forest conservation; protection of forests. **삼림욕** a forest bath. **삼림학** forestry; dendrology.

삼매(三昧) absorption; ecstasy; concentration; devotion. ¶~경에 들어가다 enter into the perfect state of spiritual concentration // 독서~에 빠지다 be absorbed in reading / be immersed in one's book.

삼면(三面) [세 방면] three sides [faces]. ¶~에 on three sides // ~이 산으로 둘러싸이다 be surrounded by hills on three sides.
● **삼면경**(一鏡) a dresser [vanity] with three mirrors; a dressing table surmounted by three mirrors.

삼모작(三毛作) planting [raising / growing] three crops a year; triple-cropping.

삼목(杉木) [식] a Japan [Japanese] cedar. ⇨ 삼나무

삼 민 주 의(三民主義) (쑨원(孫文)의) Sun Yatsenism; the Three Principles of the People.

삼바 [음] (a) samba.

삼박자(三拍子) [음] three-part time; triple time [measure]. ¶~의 곡 a piece [number] in triple time.

삼반규관(三半規管) [생] semicircular canals. ⇨ 반고리관

삼발이 a trivet; a tripod; a spider; a footman.

삼 베 sambe; hemp cloth; flax; linen; cambric(흰). ¶굵은 ~ crash // ~옷 a linen robe.

삼복(三伏) (the three 10-day periods of) the dog days; the hottest period of summer (from mid-July to mid-August); midsummer.
● **삼복더위** the midsummer heat; the heat of the dog days.

삼부(三部) [세 부분] three parts [sections]; (부처의) three departments; (서적의) three volumes. ¶~로 tripartite.
● **삼부작** a trilogy. **삼부 합창**[합주] [음] a chorus [an ensemble] of three parts; a trio.

삼분(三分) dividing into three (parts); trisection. ¶~의 1 one(-)third / a third // ~의 2 two(-)thirds. **삼분하다** divide (a thing) into three (parts); trisect; [수] divide by three. ¶천하을 ~ divide the country into three independent parts.

삼사분기(三四分期) the third quarter of the year.

삼산화물(三酸化物) [화] a trioxide.

삼산화비소(三酸化砒素) [화] arsenic trioxide; arsenious acid.

삼산화황(三酸化黃) [화] sulfur trioxide.

삼삼오오(三三五五) by twos and threes; in groups (of twos and threes). ¶~ 떼를 지어 오다 come by twos and threes // ~ 이야기를 하며 가다 go in small conversing groups // 소녀들은 ~ 짝을 지어 교회에 도착했다 The girls arrived at the church by twos and threes.

삼삼하다 1 [기억에 생생하다] fresh; vivid. ¶그것은 지금도 내 기억에 ~ It is still vivid [fresh] in my memory.∥돌아가신 어머님의 모습이 내 머릿속에 삼삼하게 보인다 I see by my bedside a vivid image of my dead mother. **2** [싱거우면서 맛있다] not salty enough but dainty[nice].

삼색(三色) **1** [세 가지 빛깔] three colors. ¶~의 three-color / tricolored. **2** the three primary colors. ⇨삼원색
● **삼색기** a tricolor (flag).

삼선(三選) election for the third term. ¶상대 후보의 ~를 저지하다 prevent the reelection of the other candidate to a third (successive) term. **삼선하다** be (re)elected for the third (consecutive) term. ➔대통령에 삼선되다 be elected president for the third term.

삼세번(三—番) exactly three times; just thrice. ¶턱걸이를 ~만 해라 Chin yourself just three times.

삼승(三乘) ➔세제곱

삼시(三時) [세 끼니] three daily meals; [세 때] morning, noon, evening.

삼신(三神) [세 신령] the three gods governing childbirth.

삼십(三十) thirty. ¶제 ~ the thirtieth∥~대의 사람 a person in the thirties∥~을 갓 넘은 in one's early thirties / just out of one's twenties∥~에 [~ 대에] 죽다 die at thirty [in one's thirties].

삼십육계(三十六計) [뺑소니] abscondence; flight; running away. ¶~를 놓다 beat a retreat / take to flight.

삼십육계 줄행랑이 제일(속담) The wisest thing to do in this case is to run away.; Discretion is the better part of valor.

삼엄하다(森嚴—) solemn; grave; awe-inspiring. ¶그 근처는 삼엄한 분위기였다 An awe-inspiring atmosphere pervaded the place.∥그는 경찰의 삼엄한 경계망을 뚫고 도망쳤다 He ran away [disappeared himself] through tightly-guarded police.

삼오야(三五夜) [음력 보름날 밤] a full moon night; the 15th night of a lunar month. ¶~밝은 달 the bright full moon (on the fifteenth night).

삼원색(三原色) the three primary colors.

삼월(三月) March(약어 Mar.).

삼위일체(三位一體) [가][기] the Trinity. ¶~가 되어 forming a trinity.
● **삼위일체론** Trinitarianism.

삼인조(三人組) a trio; a threesome; a triad. ¶~ 강도 a trio of robbers / a gang of three robbers.

삼인칭(三人稱) [언] the third person.
● **삼인칭 단수**[복수] the third person singular [plural].

삼일(三日) (출산·결혼 후의) the third day after childbirth [marriage].

삼일 예배(三日禮拜) [기] Wednesday evening church service.

삼일 운동(三一運動) the *Samil* [1919] Independence Movement (of Korea).

삼일장(三日葬) burial on the third day after death.

삼일절(三一節) Anniversary of the *Samil* Independence Movement.

삼일천하(三日天下) a very brief reign; a short-lived rule [reign]. ¶그 내각은 ~로 끝났다 The cabinet was in power only for a very short period.

삼자(三者) **1** [세 사람] three persons; the three parties. ¶~ 간의 tripartite (discussion) / triple (alliance). **2** (당사자 이외의) the third party; [국외자] an outsider.
● **삼자 범퇴** [야구] All the three batters retired [went out] in quick order; Three batters were easily put out.

삼재(三災) **1** [민] [불길한 운성(運星)의 하나] one of the baleful stars. **2** [불] the three disasters; flood, fire and wind; war, pestilence and famine.

삼족(三族) (one's) whole family [clan]. ¶~을 멸하다 exterminate the whole clans of (a person).

삼중(三重) triple. ¶~의 threefold / treble / triple / triplicate∥~으로 trebly∥~으로 하다 treble / triple / triplicate∥상자를 ~으로 포개다 pile the boxes three deep∥아군은 ~으로 포위당했다 Our troops were surrounded trebly by the enemy.
● **삼중 결합** triple bond. **삼중고**(—苦) a triple handicap (of being blind, deaf, and dumb); triple distress. **삼중주**(단) [음] an ensemble of the three instruments; a trio (*pl.* ~s). **삼중창** [음] a trio (*pl.* ~s).

삼지창(三枝槍) **1** [세 갈래로 갈라진 창] a three-pronged spear; a trident. **2** 〈속〉 a fork. ⇨포크

삼진(三振) [야구] a strikeout. ¶~을 시키다 strike (a person) out / (속어) fan [whiff] (a batter)∥(투수가) 세 타자를 ~으로 물리치다 fan [strike out] three batters in a row∥~을 당하다 be [get] struck out / strike out / (속어) be fanned / (속어) fan∥그는 상대 팀으로부터 ~ 12개를 빼앗았다 He struck out [(구어) fanned] twelve opposing batters.

삼짇날 the third day of the third lunar month.

삼차(三次) [수] cubic; the third power.
● **삼차 방정식** a cubic (equation); an equation of the third degree.

삼차원(三次元) three dimensions. ¶~의 three-dimensional (space) / 3-D∥~의 세계 the three-dimensional world / the world of three dimensions.

삼창(三唱) (만세의) three cheers; (노래 등의) reciting [singing] three times. **삼창하다** (만세를) give three cheers (for); (노래를) sing (the national anthem) three times.

삼척동자(三尺童子) a mere child. ¶그것은 ~도 안다 Even a child knows it.

삼천리(三千里) the whole (land) of Korea; all our country. ¶~강산에 all over Korea / throughout Korea∥~ 방방곡곡에 at every corner of the land of Korea.

삼촌(三寸) an uncle; one's dad's younger brother.

삼총사(三銃士) a triumvirate; a trio.

삼추(三秋) **1** [가을의 석 달] the three autumn months(=early autumn, mid-autumn, and late autumn). **2** [삼 년 세월] three years. **3** [긴 세월]. ¶하루가 ~ 같다 feel a moment as if it were three years / be dying to see (one's lover) / miss (one's sweetheart) for a single day as if it were three years.

삼출(滲出) exudation; percolation; [의] effusion; exosmosis. **삼출하다** exude; percolate; ooze (out).
● **삼출액** / **삼출물** an exudate; a percolate.

삼층집(三層—) a three-story house; a three-

storied[-storeyed] house; a house of three stories[storeys].
삼치 [동] a Spanish mackerel.
삼키다 1 [목구멍으로 넘기다] swallow; gulp down; choke down; take[get] down; down; drink in. ¶단숨에〔꿀꺽〕~ gulp down (water) / swallow (the pills) at one gulp // 통째로 ~ swallow whole // 군침을 ~ swallow one's saliva / catch[hold] one's breath(긴장 등으로) // 음식을 너무 급히 ~ swallow one's food too quickly // 고기 한 조각을 ~ swallow a piece of meat // 뱀이 개구리를 삼켰다 The snake swallowed a frog. // 소년은 그 덩어리를 통째로 삼켰다 The boy swallowed[bolted] the lump whole[without chewing it]. // 파도가 아이를 단숨에 삼켜 버렸다 The waves swallowed up the child. // 어둠이 모든 것을 삼켜 버렸다 Everything was swallowed up by the darkness.
2 [억지로 참다] bear; suppress. ¶눈물을 ~ keep back one's tears / gulp[choke] down one's sobs // 하품을 ~ suppress[smother / gulp down] a yawn.
3 [횡령하다] misappropriate; appropriate (for[to] oneself); pocket; embezzle; peculate; take to[for] oneself. ¶공금을 ~ divert public money into one's own pocket // 남의 것을 ~ take the belongings of another for oneself.
삼태(三胎) (giving birth to) triplets.
삼태기 a straw basket (for carrying earth).
삼투(滲透) [물][생] osmosis. **삼투하다** osmose; pass by osmosis.
●**삼투압** osmotic pressure.
삼파전(三巴戰) a three-cornered[-sided/-way] battle[fight]; a triangular fight [struggle]. ¶치열한 ~ a heated triangular fight[struggle] // ~을 벌이다 break out[engage in] a three-sided struggle // 연세, 고려, 중앙의 ~이다 It's a three-sided[-way/-cornered] fight between Yonsei, Korea, and Jungang. // It's a triangular struggle between Yonsei, Korea, and Jungang.
삼판양승(三―兩勝) the rubber.
삼팔선(三八線) the 38th latitude.
삼포(蔘圃) [인삼을 재배하는 밭] a ginseng field; a field of ginseng.
삼한(三韓) [역] (마한·변한·진한) the Three Han states; the Three Hans.
삼한 사온(三寒四溫) [기상] a cycle of three cold days and four warm days.
삼항식(三項式) [수] a trinomial (expression).
삽 a shovel; a spade; (소형의) a scoop. ¶모래 한 ~ a shovelful of sand // ~으로 땅을 파다 spade (up) the soil / dig the earth with a shovel // ~으로 모래[석탄]를 푸다 shovel up sand[coal] // 도로의 눈을 ~으로 긁어내다 shovel snow off the road // ~으로 눈 위에 길을 내다 shovel a path[way] through the snow.
삽사리 a shaggy dog. ⇨삽살개
삽살개 a shaggy dog.
삽상하다(颯爽―) (cool and) crisp; fresh; refreshing. ¶삽상한 가을바람 a crisp autumn breeze.
삽시간(霎時間) a moment; an instant; a second; a flash. ¶~에 in an instant / in a moment[flash / trice] // 그것은 ~에 벌어진 일이었다 All that happened in a moment. // 그녀의 기쁨은 ~에 사라졌다 Her joy was but short-lived.
삽입(挿入) insertion; interposition; interpolation. **삽입하다** insert; put in[between]; interpose; interpolate. ¶(신문에) 삽입한 광고지 an insert / an inserted bill // 계약서에 한 마디를 ~ insert a sentence in the contract.
●**삽입구** a parenthesis (pl. -ses); an inserted comment. **삽입법** an insertion; an interpolation; an interposition. **삽입부** [음] an episode. **삽입 장면** [영] an insert.
삽지(揷紙) [인] (hand) feeding. **삽지하다** feed paper.
●**삽지공** a feeder.
삽질 shoveling; spading; spadework; scooping. **삽질하다** shovel; scoop; spade.
삽화(挿話) an episode; a little story.
삽화(挿畵) an illustration[a cut-in]; a cut. ¶색채도 인쇄의 ~ a three-color illustration // ~가 들어 있는[있지 않은] 잡지 an illustrated[unillustrated] magazine // ~를 넣다 illustrate (a book) / insert[put in] an illustration // 책의 ~를 그리다 draw[do] illustrations for a book // 이 잡지에는 ~가 많이 들어 있다 This magazine is profusely[copiously] illustrated.
●**삽화가** an illustrator (to[for] a book).
삿갓 a satgat; a conical bamboo rain-hat.
삿대 (boat man's) pole; a punt pole. ¶~로 밀다 (배를) pole off / push by means of a pole // ~로 배를 밀고 나아가다 pole[punt] a boat / propel a boat with a pole.
●**삿대질** (배의) poling; punting; (상대에게) shaking one's fist[finger]. ¶~을 하다 (배의) pole (a boat) / (상대에게) propel (a boat) with a pole / (상대에게) punt (a boat) / (상대에게) shake one's fist[finger] (at).
삿자리 a reed mat. ¶~를 깔다 spread a reed mat.
상(上) 1 a king. ⇨¹임금 2 [위·상부] upper. ¶~반신 the upper half[part] of the body. 3 [윗길이 되는 등급] the first (class / grade); the best; the superior; the top (class). ¶~의 the very best / extra fine / superfine // 그의 학교 성적은 ~에 속한다 His schoolwork [school record] is rather good. 4 [책의 상권] the first book[volume]; Book [Volume] One.
상(床) a (dining) table; a small table (for one person); a desk. ¶~을 차리다 set[lay] a meal before (a person) / lay the table (for dinner) / set a dinner table // ~을 치우다 [물리다] clear the table / remove [take away] the cloth // ~에 올려놓다 serve (fish / meat) at (a person's) table // 그들은 ~을 차렸다 They have prepared a meal. / They have set [laid] the table. // ~을 치우자 Let's clear the table. // ~을 차려 놓았습니다 The table is ready. / Dinner is on the table.
상(相) 1 [인상(人相)] physiognomy; lineaments; [용모] countenance; features; [표정] a look; a face. ¶울~ a face ready to cry / a sad face // ~이 천한 ~ a low cast of countenance // ~을 찌푸리고 with a grimace / with a wry face // 그는 장수할 ~이다 He has the seal [signature] of longevity on his face. 2 [상태] an aspect; a phase; a facet. ¶사회 ~ an aspect of society / a phase of social life // 현대의 모든 생활~ all phases of current life. 3 [물] (a) phase. ¶액체~ liquid phase. 4 [언] (verbal) aspect.
상(을) **보다** tell (a person's) fortune by

physiognomy.

상(喪) mourning. ¶~중 in mourning // ~을 입다[당하다] go into[take to] mourning for (one's father) / observe mourning // ~을 벗다 leave off[go out of] mourning // ~을 알리다 announce[notice] (a person's) death // 나제 ~을 벗었습니다 We went out of[left off] mourning. / The period of mourning is over [expired].

상(像) 1 [사람·사물의 형체를 본떠 만든 것] an image; a figure; a statue; [그림] a picture; a portrait. ¶사자의 ~ a figure of lion // 성모 마리아의 대리석 ~ a marble image of the Virgin Mary // 자유의 여신 ~ the Statue of Liberty // ~을 만들다 make an image (of) // ~을 세우다 erect[set up] a statue to (a person) // 병사의 ~이 벽에 새겨져 있었다 There were figures of soldiers carved on[in] the wall. 2 [물] an image. ¶실[허](虛)~ a real[virtual] image.

상(賞) a prize; an award; a reward(보수). ¶우등~ an honor prize // 노벨 평화~ the Nobel prize for peace // 퓰리처 ~ the Pulitzer Prize // …의 ~으로 as a prize for ... / in reward for ... / in appreciation[recognition] of ... // ~을 타다 win[gain / get / obtain] a prize / receive[be awarded] a prize / bear[carry] away a prize // ~을 받다 receive[be awarded] a prize // ~을 주다 award[give / present] a prize (to) / bestow a prize (on) / ~을 걸다 offer a prize // 너는 ~을 탈 만하다 You deserve a reward. // 나는 추첨에서 큰 ~을 타다 I won a big prize in the lottery. // 나는 국제 관계에 관한 논문으로 ~을 탔다 I won a prize for an article on international relations. // 그는 이 소설로 2001년도의 동인 문학~을 받았다 He received[was awarded] the Dongin prize for 2001 for this novel.

-상(上) […이라는 점에서 보아] from the viewpoint[standpoint] of (morality); viewed in the light of (discipline); as a matter of (fact). ¶교육~ from the educational point of view[standpoint / viewpoint] // 역사~ historically / from the historical point of view // 편의~ for convenience's sake // 도의~ in the cause of morality / in honor // 역사~의 인물 historical characters.

-상(狀) [모양·상태] -shaped; -form; in the form[shape] of. ¶액체~의 ~ in the form of liquid // 얼음은 고체~의 물이다 Ice is water in a solid state.

-상(商) [장수] a merchant; a dealer; a tradesman; [장사] business; commerce; trade. ¶도매~ (상인) a wholesale merchant [dealer] / (상사) wholesale business[trade] / 귀금속~ (상인) a jeweler / a dealer in jewelry / (가게) a jewelry store // 그는 서적~을 하고 있다 He keeps a bookstore.

상가(商街) a business section[quarter / center]; a commercial quarter; a shopping district[center]; a downtown.
● **상가아파트** an apartment house with stores on the ground floor.

상가(喪家) a house of mourning; a family [household] in mourning. ¶~에 문상 가다 go to offer one's condolences to the family in mourning.

상갓집 개(속담) a thin[an emaciated] low-spirited man.

상각(償却) (a) repayment; (a) refundment; redemption(공사채의); amortization(연부(年賦)에 의한). ¶감가~ depreciation // 미(未)~의 unrepaid / unredeemed / unamortized. **상각하다** repay; refund; pay[clear] off; extinguish[wipe out] (a debt); redeem; amortize; sink (a loan); write off(고정 자산 등을). ¶부채를 ~ pay off[repay] a loan.

상감(上監) a king. ⇨ 임금

상감(象嵌) inlaying; damascening; damaskeening; [입] inlay; mortising. ¶은 ~을 한 담뱃갑 a cigarette case inlaid with silver. **상감하다** inlay (a thing with gold); damascene (metal).
● **상감 세공** inlaid work.

상갑판(上甲板) [해] an upper[a spar] deck; (앞 돛대보다 앞의) the forecastle.

상거래(商去來) a commercial transaction; a business transaction[deal]; commercial dealings. ¶~가 활발하다 Business transactions are briskly carried on there. // 우리는 그 상사와 ~가 있다 We deal[have dealings] with that firm.

상거지(上-) the most wretched[miserable] of beggars.

상견(相見) meeting; interview. **상견하다** meet [see] each other; interview; face each other.
● **상견례**(-禮) [신랑·신부의 맞절] the bride-bridegroom formal bow.

상경하다(上京-) come[go] up to the capital; leave for Seoul. ¶그는 상경하여 그림 공부를 하고 있다 He is in Seoul, studying painting.

상계(商界) the world of commerce. ⇨ 상업계 (⇨ 상업).

상고(上古) ancient times; remote ages; (remote) antiquity. ¶~의 ancient / in[of] remote ages[ancient times] // ~로부터 from ancient times / from time immemorial.
● **상고사** an[the] ancient history.

상고(上告) [법] a final appeal; an appeal to a higher court. ¶~를 기각[취하]하다 dismiss [reject / withdraw] a (final) appeal. **상고하다** appeal (to a higher court); bring a final appeal (in a court); enter[file / lodge / make] an appeal. ¶그는 대법원에 상고했다 He appealed to the supreme court.
● **상고 법원** a court of final appeal; a court of last resort; a final appellate court. **상고심** a hearing of final appeal.

상고(尙古) worship of ancient culture. **상고하다** worship ancient culture; make much of things ancient.
● **상고주의** classicism.

상고머리 (머리 모양) a square-cut hair; a crew cut; (미국 구어) a flattop; (머리) a square cropped[crew-cut] head. ¶~로 깎다 dress[cut] one's hair square / get crew cut [a flattop] / have one's hair cut in a flattop.

상공(上空) [하늘] the sky; the skies; [하늘의 높은 곳] the upper air[regions]. ¶서울의 ~에서 in the skies of Seoul / over Seoul // 높은 ~에서 far[high] up in the sky[air] / (구어) way up in the sky / high above // 5천 미터 ~에서 at an altitude[a height] of 5,000 meters / at 5,000 meters (high) in midair // ~으로 날아오르다 fly up into the air // 헬리콥터는 도시의 ~을 날았다 The helicopter flew over the city.

상공(商工) commerce and industry. ⇨ 상공업 (⇨ 상공).
● **상공업** commerce and industry. ¶~의

상과 commercial and industrial∥~에 중점을 두다 lay[place/put] (great) emphasis on [upon] commerce and industry. **상공 회의소** The Chamber of Commerce and Industry.

상과(商科) a commercial course[department]; a department of business administration.
● **상과 대학** a college of commerce; a commercial college; a business college.

상관(上官) a senior officer[official]; a higher [superior] officer[official]; a senior; a chief; an officer of superior rank. ¶~을 모욕하다 insult one's senior (in rank)∥~의 명령을 어기다 disobey one's senior[superior]∥~의 명령에 복종하다 obey one's chief's order[the orders of one's superior]∥~의 명령에 반항하다 mutiny against one's senior∥그는 나의 ~이다 He is my superior.

상관(相關) 1 [상호 관계] (a) correlation; (an) interrelation; a mutual relationship. ¶~적인 [적으로] correlative(ly). **상관하다** be related to; bear on; have an interrelation(ship) (with).
2 [관련] relation; connection; [관여] participation; involvement; [간섭] interference; meddling; [관심] concern; care. **상관하다** [관련 있다] have something to do (with); have relations[connections] with; [관계하다] be concerned in[with]; [관여하다] take part in (a plot); participate; [말려들다] be involved[implicated] in; get mixed up (in); [간섭하다] interfere; meddle (in); put[poke / thrust] one's nose (into); [개의하다] concern[trouble] oneself (about); care (about); mind; have a regard for. ¶…에 상관하지 않고 regardless of / without regard to / irrespective of∥내 일에 상관하지 마라 Leave me[Let me be] alone!∥네가 상관할 일이 아니다 That's none of your business.∥그는 아들이 무엇을 하든 상관하지 않는다 He does not interfere in what his sons do.
3 [성교] connection; (sexual) relations [intercourse]; misconduct; liaison(밀통). **상관하다** have connection[relations] (with); have sexual intercourse (with). ¶젊은 과부와 ~ 하다 form a liaison with a young widow.
● **상관 계수** [수] a coefficient of correlation; a correlation coefficient. **상관관계** correlation; interrelation; mutual relation. ¶이들 두 요소에는 ~가 있다 These two factors are correlated[mutually related]. **상관성** interrelationship; correlationship.

상관습(商慣習) a commercial practice; business usage[custom]; the custom of trade.

상관없다(相關—) 1 [관계없다] irrelative; irrelevant; impertinent; unrelated; unconnected; (서술적) be irrespective (of); have nothing to do (with); bear no relation (to); have no reference (to); have no dealings (with); be not concerned (about); have no concern; [말려들지 않다] be not involved[mixed up] (in); [무방하다] (사람이) be allowed to (do); be justified in (doing); (사물이) be justifiable; be all rightive. ¶…에 상관없이 independent(ly) of / irrespective(ly) of / regardless of∥그 건과는 이제 전혀 생관없습니다 I have nothing more to do with it. / I've washed my hands of it.∥그것은 나이에 상관없이 누구나 할 수 있는 운동이다 It is a sport anyone can play regardless[irrespective] of age.∥술 담배는 조금쯤은 해도 ~ A little liquor or tobacco will do you no harm.
2 [염려할 것 없다] do not care[mind]; be indifferent (to); [중요하지 않다] do not matter. ¶…에 상관없이 regardless of / without regard to / irrespective of∥무슨 일이 생기든 나는 ~ I don't care[It doesn't matter] what happens.∥비용이 들어도 ~ I don't care about the expense. / I don't mind if it's expensive. The cost doesn't matter.∥깨끗하기만 하면 어떤 손수건이라도 ~ Any handkerchief will do, as long as it's clean.∥그녀가 예쁘고 안 예쁘고는 ~ It doesn't matter whether she is beautiful or not.∥그건 아무래도 상관없지 않은가 What does it matter?

상궁(尙宮) a court lady.

상권(上卷) [두 권 이상으로 가른 책의 첫째 권] the first volume[book] (of two or three); volume one; book one.

상권(商權) [법] commercial rights; [상업상의 권력] commercial power[supremacy]. ¶~을 장악하다 acquire commercial supremacy / dominate the market∥그는 동생에게 ~을 빼앗겼다 His brother deprived him of his trade.

상궤(常軌) a common[normal proper] course (of action); a proper bounds; a beaten track; a right way; normality. ¶~를 벗어난 abnormal / (성격·행위 등이) eccentric∥~를 벗어난 이론 a crackpot theory∥~를 벗어나다 break bounds / go off the rails / get off the beaten track / go out of the common road∥~를 벗어나지 않다 keep within bounds.

상규(常規) [늘 변하지 않는 규칙] established [conventional] rules; established usage; [일반적인 규정·규칙] a common standard.

상극(相剋) (a) conflict; incompatibility; natural repugnance (to); (an) antipathy to each other; (an) antagonism (between A and B). ¶~이다 be incompatible with / be discordant with / be naturally repugnant (to) / be antagonistic (to)∥물과 기름은 ~다 Oil and water have an antipathy to each other[do not mix / are mutually exclusive].

상근(常勤) full-time[whole-time] employment. ¶~의 full-time. **상근하다** work full-time.
● **상근자** a regular[full-time] employee; a full-time member of the staff.

상금(賞金) [현상금] prize money; a prize; an award; [보상금] a reward; a premium. ¶삼백만 원의 ~ a prize of three million won∥논문에 ~을 걸다 offer a prize for an essay∥~을 타다 win[get] a prize / (경기 등에서) win a purse∥범인 체포에 ~을 걸다 set (up) a prize on the arrest of the offender∥그는 퀴즈의 정답을 맞혀 백만 원의 ~을 탔다 He won a prize of a million won for his correct answer to the quiz.∥최우수 논문에는 100만 원의 ~이 주어진다 A prize of 1,000,000 won is awarded for the best essay.

상급(上級) [위의 등급] an upper[a higher] grade; (학교의) an upper[a higher] class; (과목) an advanced course. ¶~의 upper(-class) / higher(-grade / -rank) / superior / (정도가) advanced∥프랑스 어의 ~ 코스 an advanced course in French∥~ 학년에 재학 중이다 be in a higher grade of school∥이것은 ~ 과정의 학생들을 위한 책이다 This book is for more advanced students. ●**상급 법원** a higher[superior] tribunal[court]. **상급생** an upper-class student; a senior student[boy/girl]; an advanced student; (미) an upper-classman(대학·고등학교의). **상급 학교** a school of higher grade; an advanced school; (대학) a college[university].

상급(賞給) 〔상으로 줌〕 prizegiving; 〔상〕 a prize; an award; a reward. **상급하다** award[present] a prize (to); bestow a prize (on). ¶돈을 ~ reward (a person) with money.

상기(上記) the above statement. ¶~와 같이 as above-mentioned[-stated] / as stated above.

상기(上氣) a rush of blood to the head; dizziness; (얼굴의) flushing; a glow; 〔한〕 congestion of the head. **상기하다** have a rush of blood to the head; get[feel] dizzy; (얼굴이) flush (up); blush; 〔흥분하다〕 get[be] excited. ¶그녀는 상기하여 얼굴이 새빨개졌다 She flushed crimson. →¶상기된 뺨 flushed cheeks∥운동한 뒤라 소녀들의 얼굴은 상기되어 있었다 The girls had bright red cheeks after their exercise.

상기(想起) recollection; remembrance. **상기하다** recollect; remember; recall; call[bring] to mind. ¶그것은 내 어린 시절을 상기하게 한다 It reminds me of my childhood. →¶상기시키다 remind (a person) of / put (a person) in mind (of) / recall[call] (something) to memory∥상기되다 come back into one's mind / come to mind[one's recollection]∥그 일은 아직도 가끔 상기된다 The thing still comes up in my memory now and then.

상길(上−) the best quality; the highest[finest] quality; top-grade[first-class / first-rate] article[goods]. ¶~의 of the highest[finest] quality / of superior grade / first-class / first-rate / ~의 담배 the best quality cigarettes∥~의 종이 paper of the finest quality.

상납(上納) tax payment to the government[authorities]; (뇌물을) offering a bribe (to one's superior). **상납하다** pay to the government[authorities]; (뇌물로) offer a (regular) bribe (to). ¶돈[물건]으로 ~ pay (to the authorities) in money[kind]. →¶매월 백만원씩 상납받다 take[accept / receive] one million won monthly as a bribe (from subordinates).

●**상납금** money paid as tax; money offered to one's superior.

상냥하다 〔부드럽다〕 gentle; tender; soft; suave; 〔다정하다〕 sweet; affectionate; kind(hearted); 〔붙임성이 있다〕 amiable; affable. ¶상냥한 사람 a gentle-mannered[tender-hearted] person / a person of affable disposition∥그녀는 상냥한 목소리로 말한다 She speaks in a gentle[soft] voice.∥그는 누구에게나 ~ He is nice to everyone. / He makes himself agreeable to everybody. **상냥히** gently; kindly; nicely; tenderly; sweetly; affectionately; soothingly; good-naturedly. ¶…에게 ~ 대하다 be kind[good / nice / sweet / tender / affectionate / gentle] to (a person) / treat (a person) kindly[nicely] ∥나는 그녀가 ~ 웃는 얼굴을 잊을 수가 없다 I cannot forget her amiable[genial] smile.∥그녀는 우리를 ~ 맞아 주었다 She greeted us pleasantly[agreeably].

상년(常−) **1** 〔신분이 낮은 여자〕 a low[vulgar] woman; a woman of low birth. **2** 〔본데없이 막된 여자〕 a mean woman; a bitch; a lewd woman; a slut.

상념(想念) a thought; a notion; a conception; an idea.

상놈(常−) **1** 〔신분이 낮은 남자〕 a low man[fellow]; a man of low birth; a clod; a lower class person; (집합적) rabble; the lower orders. **2** 〔본데없이 막된 남자〕 an ill-bred fellow; a vulgar [mean] fellow; a churl; a hangdog; a cad; a cur. ¶그런 ~은 혼을 내 주어야 해 Such a bastard deserves a lesson.

상다리(床−) table legs. ¶~가 휘어지게 음식을 차리다 serve all sorts of delicacies on the table∥~가 부러질 것 같았다 The table literally groaned with food.

상단(上段) an upper portion[division / paragraph].

상단(上端) the top; the upper end; the tip. ¶안테나의 ~ the top end of an antenna.

상달(上達) a report (to superior [higher official]). **상달하다** report[state] (to a superior official); submit a report (to one's chief).

상담(相談) (a) consultation; counsel; (a) conference; advice; a talk; (구어) a confab. ¶~에 응하다 give counsel[advice] (to) / ~ 중이다 We are in consultation. **상담하다** consult (a person / with a person about a matter); (문어) confer (with a person about a thing); have a talk (with); talk over (a matter with a person); seek[ask] (a person's); advice; take counsel (with[of] a person). ¶상담한 후에 after consultation with (a person) / by agreement∥상담하러 가다[오다] go[come] to (a person) for advice∥일신상 문제를 ~ consult (a person)[seek (a person's) advice] about one's personal affairs∥모여서 ~ consult together / lay their heads together∥나는 그 일에 관하여 친구와 상담했다 I consulted with a friend of mine about the matter.

●**상담소** an information bureau; a consultation office. ¶결혼~ (a) marriage counsellor's (office) / (영) a marriage guidance bureau / a matrimonial advice office∥민원 ~ the Civil Service Consultation Center∥무료 ~ a free-advice office∥법률 ~ a legal advice office∥직업 ~ an employment agency [bureau] / a vocational clinic. **상담역** (회사 등의) a counselor; a consultant(전문적인); (개인의) an adviser; a consultant; (집합적) an advisory board[body]; **상담원** a counselor[(영) counseller]; an adviser[advisor].

상담(商談) 〔상업상의 대화〕 a business talk; a business discussion[meeting]; bargaining; 〔상업상의 교섭〕 a deal; (business) negotiations. ¶~에 응하다 〔들어가다〕 enter into negotiations (with)∥~을 중단하다[집어치우다] drop[break off] negotiations (with)∥~을 진행하다 go ahead with a business talk ∥~이 진행 중이다 Negotiations are in progress[under way]. **상담하다** have a business talk (with); talk business (with). ¶우리 사장은 지금 A 씨와 상담하고 있다 The head of our firm is talking with Mr. A for business.

상당(相當) 〔알맞음〕 suitableness; properness; befittingness. ¶~의 〔알맞은〕 suitable

상당하다

/ becoming / befitting / [엇비슷한] equivalent / corresponding // ~수의 as many as / a good many // 봉급 2개월분 ~의 보너스 a bonus equivalent to two months' pay.

상당하다(相當-) **1** [적당·합당하다] suitable; proper; fit; due; appropriate; adequate; [어울리다] becoming; befitting; [결맞다] be proportionate to. ¶상당한 보수 a worthy [due] reward // 능력에 상당하는 급료 a salary proportionate to one's ability // 지위에 상당하는 수입 an income befitting a person's rank.

2 [보통 수준을 넘어선 상태에 있다] considerable; pretty; fair; good; tolerable; passable; [훌륭하다] decent; respectable. ¶상당한 교육 a good education // 상당한 재능 fair ability // 상당한 사례 a good round fee // 상당한 성공 considerable success // 상당한 화가 a full-fledged painter // 상당한 인물 a person of (some) consequence / (a) somebody // 상당한 금액의 돈 a large [considerable / sizable] amount of money / a good [round] sum of money (▶ round는 천, 만 등 자리의 한계가 있다는 뉘앙스) // 상당한 수량의 주문 a sizable [large] order // 상당한 수량의 책 a good number of books // 상당한 집안 a decent [respectable] family // 상당한 도움이 되다 be of real [some] service (to) // 여기서 상당한 거리이다 It is a good distance from here. // 그녀는 상당한 미인이었던 것 같다 She seems to have been a very beautiful woman. // 그것은 상당한 돈이다 That's quite a bit of money. / That's a pretty good sum. // 그것은 상당한 금액이다 It is a considerable [substantial] sum of money. // 그는 상당한 음악가다 He is something of a musician. / He is a rather famous musician. // 그는 이 분야에서 상당한 인물이 될 것이다 I'm sure he will be somebody in this field. **상당히** fairly; quite; pretty; rather; considerably; decently; tolerably; passably; moderately; to no small degree [extent]. ¶~ 먼 rather far // ~ 비싼 값 a pretty high price // ~ 잘살다 be pretty well off / make a decent living // 그는 책을 ~ 많이 갖고 있다 He has a good many books. // 그녀는 영어를 ~ 잘한다 She speaks fairly good English.

3 [해당하다·맞먹다] corresponding; equal to; equivalent to; (서술적) be worthy of; correspond [answer] to. ¶그 말에 상당하는 영어는 없다 There is no English equivalent for the word. / There is no corresponding expression [for it] in English. // 미화 1달러는 한화 1,200원에 상당된다 One dollar is equivalent to 1,200 won. / One thousand two hundred won goes to a dollar.

상대(相對) **1** [대면] facing [confronting] each other; being opposite to each other; [만나봄] an interview. **상대하다** face [confront / see] each other; be [stand] over against each other; be opposite to each other.

2 [친구] a companion; a mate; a fellow; (미) a date (남녀 교제의); [짝] a partner; a pal (단짝); [대상] an object. ¶놀이 ~ a playmate // 술 ~ a boon companion // 이야기 [말] ~ a (talking) companion / a companion [someone] to talk to / one's crony // 의논 ~ a person to consult with // 댄스의 ~ a dancing partner // 유쾌한 [싱거운] ~ an agreeable [a poor] companion // ···을 로 with ... as a companion [partner] / in the companionship of ... // ···을 ~로 장사를 하다 do business with ... as customers // 그녀는 노부인의 ~를 해 주었다 She kept the old lady's company. // 나는 말 ~가 없어 외롭다 I am lonesome because I have no one to talk to. // 그는 ~를 가리지 않고 말을 걸었다 He talked to anybody and everybody. // 그것은 ~가 누구냐에 달려 있다 It depends on what kind of person you're dealing with. **상대하다** keep company (with); make a companion of; keep [bear] (a person) company; deal with; be a companion to; entertain (손님을); give (a person) one's company; go [run] with. ¶상대할 사람이 없어서 for lack of company // 상대하지 않다 refuse to deal [do anything] (with) / have nothing to do (with) / take no notice (of) / do not care (for) / ignore // 그녀를 상대하는 것은 즐겁다 I enjoy her company. // 누가 손님 좀 상대해 드려요 Will somebody entertain the visitors? / 아무도 그를 상대해 주지 않는다 Nobody takes him seriously. / Nobody will have anything to do with him. // 돈이 없다면 상대할 가치도 없는 여자다 She is nothing without her money.

3 [적수] an opponent; a rival; a competitor; an antagonist; an adversary; [호적수] a match; an equal; [상대방] the other man [person]; the other [opposite] party. ¶···을 ~로 하여 in opposition to / in rivalry with ... // 나는 ~를 쉽게 이겼다 I beat my opponent hands down. // 그 점에서는 나는 그의 ~가 될 수 없다 I am no match for him in that respect. // 이 두 권투 선수는 서로 알맞은 ~다 These boxers are a well-matched pair. // 그는 나의 ~로서 부족이 없다 He's an opponent worth my while. / He'll be a good match for me. // 우리는 그들의 ~가 될 수 없었다 Our opponents were too good for us. / We were no match for our opponents. // 그는 회사를 ~로 손해 배상 소송을 제기했다 He sued [filed a suit against] the company for damages. // 노련한 (바둑의) 기사조차도 이 신동에게는 ~가 되지 못했다 Even veteran *baduk* (go) players were no match for this child prodigy. **상대하다** deal with; contend (with); play (against) (a person); take (a person) up on a challenge. ¶아무나 나와, 내가 상대해 주겠다 Let any one come, I am his man. // 그에게는 상대할 적수가 없다 There is no one anywhere who is a match for him. // 그런 대국을 상대한다는 것은 미친 짓이다 It is madness for us to take on [fight against] such a big power.

4 [철] relativity; reciprocity; [이원성] [수] duality.

● **상대 개념** [오차] a relative concept [error]. **상대방 / 상대편** the other party; the other man [person]; (경쟁의) the opposite party; one's opponent party; the opposing team; an adversary; a rival; an opponent; a competitor; an antagonist. ¶~의 주장 [말] what the other side [party] has to say. **상대성** relativity; [이원성] [수] duality. **상대성 이론** [물] the theory of relativity; Einstein's theory. **상대역** (연극·영화의) the player of an opposite role; (춤의) a partner; [동등한 상대] a counterpart. ¶~을 하다 play a part opposite (to) (an actor). **상대자** [상대방] the other

상대(商大) a college of commerce. ⇨`상과 대학`(⇨)`상과`

상대적(相對的) relative; correlative. ¶~으로 relatively / correlatively // ~ 진리 a relative truth.

상도(常道) 1 [평상시의 방식] a common way [path]; an ordinary way; a beaten track; the normal[proper / regular] course; a universal rule[practice]. ¶학문의 ~ a regular course of learning // ~로 복귀하다 restore to (its) normal course // ~를 걷다 trace[follow] the beaten track. 2 [지켜야 할 도리] proper behavior[conduct]. ¶그는 ~에서 벗어났다 He deviated from accepted standards of behavior.

상도덕(商道德) business[trade] morality. ¶~ 이 땅에 떨어졌다 The ethics of business has degenerated. / Business is morally corrupt.

상동(相同) 1 the same[similar] relation. 2 [생] homology. ¶~의 homologous / homogenous // ~이다 be homologous (with) / homologize (with).
● **상동 기관** a homologous organ; a homologue.

상등(上等) superiority; excellence. ¶~의 first-class[-rate] / very good[nice] / of superior grade / excellent / fine / superior / up to grade // 최~의 of the highest[finest] quality / of prime[top] quality / of extra superior quality / the best / superfine / A1 // ~의 위스키 whisky of superior quality / choice whisky.
● **상등품** first-class[rate] articles; the best (articles); superior[choice] articles; an article of excellent[superior] quality.

상등병(上等兵) [군] a private 1st class. ⇨`상병`

상등하다(相等-) [서술적] be equal to one another; be similar (in shape); be as good as.

상량(上樑) [기둥의 보 위에 마룻대를 올리는 일] putting up the ridge beam; raising the framework (of a house); [미] house-raising; [마룻대] a ridge beam[pole]. **상량하다** raise[set up / put up] the framework (of a house).
● **상량식** a framework-raising ceremony; the ceremony of putting up the ridge-beam [-pole]; a roof-raising ceremony.

상례(常例) a (common) usage; a [an established] custom; one's usual practice; convention; conventional form. ¶~의 customary / usual / conventional / common / ordinary // ~에 따라 in accordance with the custom[usage] // ~대로 as is customary with (a person) / as usual // ~에 따르다 follow[observe] the conventional practice / follow the (common) usage[custom] // ~를 무시하다 be contrary to[defy] customary practice // ~에 어긋나다 be against the custom // 회의가 끝난 뒤 회식을 하는 것이 그들의 ~이다 It is customary for[the custom with] them to have dinner together after the conference.

상례(喪禮) funeral rites; the ceremonies of mourning; mourning decorums.

상록(常綠) ¶~의 evergreen / indeciduous.
● **상록수** an evergreen[indeciduous] tree; (집합적) evergreens.

상론(詳論) a detailed explanation; a full discussion[treatment]. **상론하다** treat (a subject) in detail; dwell[expatiate / enlarge] upon; deal with (a subject) in detail; enter into details.

상류(上流) 1 [강의] the upper stream; the upper reaches[waters] of a river. ¶~의[에 / 로] upstream / upriver // ~로 거슬러 올라가다 row upstream / sail up a river // ~ 로 저어 가다 row upstream[up a river] // 그 강의 ~ 3마일 지점에 작은 마을이 있다 There is a small village three miles up the river. // 배는 모두 ~로 향하고 있었다 The boats were all headed upstream[up the river]. // 2킬로미터 ~에 댐이 있다 There is a dam two kilometers upstream[up the river]. 2 [지위·생활 정도 등이 높음] the upper [higher] classes; polite [fashionable] society; high society. ¶그는 ~ 가정 출신이다 He comes of an upper-class family.
● **상류 사회** high[polite / refined / fashionable] society; the upper reaches of society; fashionable circles; the higher[upper] classes. **상류 생활** high[fashionable] life.

상륙(上陸) landing; disembarkation; going ashore. ¶~을 허가하다 grant (a sailor) shore leave // ~을 금지하다 (선원에게) withhold shore leave / (선객에게) forbid disembarkation. **상륙하다** land (in a country / at a port); make a landing; get to land; (군대가) disembark; (선원이) go[come] on shore; (태풍이) strike. ¶상륙해 있다 be ashore / be on shore // 적전에 ~ effect a landing in the face of the enemy // 무사히 ~ come safe to land // 선객은 모두 상륙했다 All the passengers have gone ashore. // 우리는 부산에 상륙했다 We landed at Busan. // 오늘 아침에 태풍이 제주도에 상륙했다 The typhoons struck[hit] Jejudo this morning. ➔ **상륙시키다** put (a person) on shore[ashore].
● **상륙 거점** a beachhead. **상륙 작전** landing operations.

상말(常-) a vulgar word[expression]; a vulgarism; vulgar[foul] language; a foul-letter word; indecent talk; abusive language; a slang expression. ¶~을 쓰다 use vulgarisms [vulgar language] // 그런 ~은 하지 마라 Stop using such vulgar[coarse] language.

상머리(床-) the table side. ¶~에 앉다 sit down to table / sit (down) at table (식사하려고) / sit at the table side.

상면(相面) a (face-to-face) meeting; an interview; [첫대면] the first meeting. **상면하다** see; meet (face-to-face); have an interview; meet for the first time.

상무(尙武) militarism; warlike spirit. ¶~의 기상 militaristic[martial] spirit / martial ardor. **상무하다** encourage[exalt] militarism; pursue the policy of militarism.

상무(常務) 1 [일상의 업무] regular business; routine work[duties]. 2 a member of a standing committee. ⇨`상무위원`(⇨)`상무`) 3 an executive[managing] director. ⇨`상무이사`(⇨)`상무`
● **상무위원** a member of a standing committee. **상무이사** an executive[managing] director.

상무(商務) commercial[business] affairs; business operations.

●**상무관** a commercial attache[agent].

상미(上米) first-class rice; best quality of rice; grade-A rice; rice of fine quality.

상민(常民) a commoner; (집합적) the common people; the lower classes; (속어) pleb. ¶~으로 태어난 lowborn / of humble birth [origin].

상박(上膊) the brachium (pl. -chia); the upper arm. ¶~의 brachial.
●**상박골** a humerus (pl. -ri). **상박근** a brachial muscle.

상반(相反) being contrary to each other; conflicting with each other; mutual contradiction; reciprocity. **상반하다** be contrary to (each other); run counter to (each other); disagree with (each other); conflict with (each other); be mutually contradictory. ¶두 국가 간의 상반하는 이해관계 the conflicting interests of the two countries/그들의 의견은 상반한다 Their opinions are opposed./Their opinions clash. ➔¶두 개의 상반된 의견(반대의) two contrary opinions[views] / (모순되는) two contradictory [contradicting] opinions [views] // 그의 진술은 사실과 상반된다 His statement disagrees with[runs counter to] the fact.//돈벌이는 그의 예술적 양심과 상반된다 Making money is incompatible with his artistic conscience.//그들의 이익은 우리의 이익과 상반되었다 Their interests ran [were] counter to ours.

상반기(上半期) the first half (of the year); the first half year. ¶~ 결산 보고 the balance sheet for the first half year.

상반신(上半身) the upper half[part] of the body; the bust. ¶~의 half-length/~을 내밀다 lean oneself] forward.

상방(上方) the upper part. ¶3마일 ~ three miles upward // ~의 upper//~에 above upward(s).

상배(喪配) the death of one's wife. ⇨"상처(喪妻)

상배(賞杯) a prize cup; a trophy.

상벌(賞罰) reward and punishment; prizes and penalties; praise and blame; justice. ¶~을 주다 mete out justice / adjudicate praise and blame // 공정한 ~을 주다 allot (a person's) praise and blame impartially / decide rewards and punishments with fairness//공과(功過)에 준하여 ~을 상.... reward or punish according to[after] (a person's) desert // ~ 없음(이력서에서) No reward and no punishment. / I have no criminal record(▶ 영·미에서는 이력서에 이 항이 없음).

상법(商法) (법률) commercial[mercantile] law; (법전) the commercial code.

상병(上兵) a private 1st class(육군); a seaman(해군); a lance corporal(해병); an airman 1st class(공군).

상병(傷病) the sick and wounded.
●**상병병**(-兵) a sick[wounded] soldier; sick and wounded soldiers; (집합적) the sick and wounded; invalids. **상병자** a sick [wounded] person.

상보(床褓) a tablecloth; a table cover; a meal cloth; a cloth-covering for a meal. ¶~를 덮다 put a cloth over a meal.

상보(詳報) a detailed[full] report (of / on); detailing; particulars; full [detailed] information; (경기의) a play-by-play account. ¶사건의 ~ a full account of the affairs / details of the affairs // 후에 ~를 알려 드리겠습니다 I will make a detailed report on it later. **상보하다** report in full[detail]; make a full report (on / of); give a full account (of); detail.

상복(喪服) a mourning dress; funeral garments; (시어) sables; widow's weeds(미망인의). ¶~을 입은 여인 a woman in black / a woman wearing mourning//~을 입고 있다 wear [be in] mourning[a mourning dress] / wear black / be in (mourning) black.

상봉하다(相逢-) meet[see] (each other). ¶부자(父子)는 20년 만에 상봉했다 Father and son met after twenty years' separation.

상부(上部) 1 [윗부분] the upper part; the top [head] (of); [위쪽] the upside. ¶~의 upside//상(像)의 ~ the upper part of a statue//꽃병의 ~에 균열이 있다 There is a crack at the top of the vase. 2 [상급 기관] superior offices [authorities]; the ruling [directing] office; [상급 직위] a senior post. ¶~의 명령 an order from above // ~의 지시에 따르다 follow the ruling office's directions // ~의 지시가 있을 때까지 기다리다 wait for further instructions from the superior authority.
●**상부 구조** a superstructure.

상부상조(相扶相助) interdependence; mutual dependence; mutual help[aid]. ¶~는 사회생활에서 가장 중요하다 Mutual help is the essence of social life. **상부상조하다** help[aid] each other; be interdependent. ¶친구 간에는 상부상조해야 한다 Friends should stand by each other.

상부하다(喪夫-) lose [be bereaved of] one's husband; become a widow; be widowed (by the war).

상비(常備) ¶~의 standing / permanent / regular / [예비의] reserve. **상비하다** [예비하다] reserve (something) for (a sudden need); [준비해 두다] have (something) always ready[on hand]; [감추어 두다] be provided with (something). ¶이 건물은 층마다 소화기를 상비하고 있다 This building is provided with fire extinguishers on every floor.
●**상비군** a standing[stand-by / regular] army [squadron]; ready troops. **상비금** a reserve fund. **상비약** a household medicine.

상사(上士) a master sergeant(육군·해병대); a senior chief petty officer(해군); a senior master sergeant(공군).

상사(上司) (기관) superior authorities; (사람) one's superior; one's boss; (집합적) the company higher-ups; one's chief. ¶~의 명령에 의해 by order[under the authority] of a superior officer//~의 허가를 얻어 on the approval of superior authorities.

상사(相似) (a) resemblance; (a) similarity; (a) similitude; [생] (an) analogy. **상사하다** similar (to); analogous (to); like.
●**상사 기관** [생] an analogous organ; an analogue. **상사물** an analogue; an analogy.

상사(相思) mutual love; reciprocal affection; pining [longing] for each other. **상사하다** be in love with each other; be strongly attached to each other.
●**상사병** lovesickness. ¶~에 걸린 lovesick / lovelorn / love-smitten // ~을 앓다 pine with love / languish for love / be lovesick [lovelorn] // ~으로 죽다 die of love (for a

상사(商社) a commercial company. ⇨상사회사(⇨상사(商事)). ¶외국인 ~ a foreign firm // 종합 ~ a general [an overall] trading company.

상사(商事) business affairs; commercial matters.
● 상사 계약 a commercial contract [agreement]. 상사 회사 a commercial company [firm]; a business concern; 〔무역 회사〕 a trading company.

상사(常事) an ordinary affair; a matter of common [everyday] occurrence.

상사(喪事) an occasion for mourning; a mournful occasion; mourning. ¶~가 나다 have mourning [a mournful occasion].

상상(想像) imagination; (a) fancy; 〔가정〕 (a) supposition; 〔추측〕 (a) guess; (a) conjecture. ~의 imaginary / fanciful / fancy / fancied / 〔가정적인〕 supposed // 단지 ~에 의 거하여 be based on mere supposition // ~으로 그리다 see in imagination [with one's mind's eye] / picture [figure] to oneself // 나머지는 ~에 맡긴다 You may imagine [can guess] what followed. / I leave the rest to your imagination. // 나머지는 독자의 ~에 맡긴다 What followed must be left to the imagination of the reader. // 손해는 ~도 하지 못할 만큼 컸었다 The degree of damage staggered the imagination. / The damage was incredibly heavy. **상상하다** imagine; fancy; conceive (in imagination); picture [figure] to oneself; 〔가정하다〕 suppose; 〔추측하다〕 conjecture. ¶상상할 수 있는 imaginable / conceivable / thinkable // 상상할 수 없는 unimaginable / inconceivable / unthinkable // 아무리 상상해 보아도 by any stretch of (the) imagination // 마음껏 ~ give full scope [play] to one's imagination // 상상하기에 어렵지 않은 easy to imagine / easily conceivable // 그녀가 배우가 되다니는 상상하지도 못할 일이다 I can't see her as an actress. // 그녀는 상상하지도 못할 만큼 순진했다 She was the most innocent woman imaginable. / She was unbelievably pure-hearted. // 나는 100년 뒤의 미래는 상상할 수 없다 I cannot image what the future is going to be like in one hundred year's time. / 자네가 런던에 있다고 상상해 보게 Imagine yourself (to be) in London.
● **상상력** imaginative power [faculty]; (power of) imagination. ¶~이 있는 imaginative / ~을 발휘하다 exercise one's imagination // ~이 풍부하다 [부족하다] be imaginative [unimaginative] / have a vigorous [little] imagination // ~을 불러일으키다 (사물이) fire [kindle / stir / stimulate] (a person's) imagination. **상상 임신** imaginary [false] pregnancy.

상상봉(上上峯) the highest peak (of Hallasan).

상서롭다(祥瑞-) be of good omen; be auspicious [felicitous / lucky / propitious]. ¶상서로운 일 an auspicious [a happy] event.

상석(上席) 〔윗자리〕 an upper [a higher] seat; the top seat; 〔주빈석〕 the seat [place] of honor. ¶~을 take a front [the best] seat / 〔식탁에서〕 sit at the head of the table // …에게 ~을 양보하다 give the place of honor to.

상석(床石) the stone table [altar] in front of a tomb.

상선(商船) a merchantman; a merchant ship [vessel]; (집합적으로 한 나라의) the merchant [commercial / mercantile] marine. ¶~의 선원 a merchant seaman.

상설(常設) permanent establishment. ¶~의 〔항구적〕 permanent / 〔상시 설치의〕 standing. **상설하다** establish permanently. ¶위원회를 ~ appoint a committee permanently.
● **상설 위원회** a standing committee.

상세도(詳細圖) a detailed drawing [plan].

상세하다(詳細-) minute; detailed; full; circumstantial. ¶상세한 보고 a detailed [minute] report // 상세한 것은 제가 다음 편지에서 알려 드리겠습니다 I will go into detail [inform you of the details] in my next letter. // 그의 설명은 매우 상세했다 He explained the matter down to the minutest details. // 상세한 것은 송 씨에게 물어보십시오 Apply to Mr. Song for further particulars [information]. **상세히** in detail; minutely; at length; at large; in full; fully; circumstantially; in every particular. ¶이유를 ~ 말하다 tell [state] the reasons in detail [minutely / at length] // 그것을 ~ 설명하시오 Give a detailed [minute] explanation of it. // ~ 쓰지 않아도 된다 You needn't write in detail [go into detail]. // 그는 계획을 ~ 설명했다 He explained the plan in minute detail.

상소(上疏) a memorial to the Throne. **상소하다** send up a memorial to the Throne; memorialize the King.

상소(上訴) an appeal; a recourse. ¶~를 취하하다 withdraw an appeal. **상소하다** appeal to a higher court.
● **상소권** the right of appeal. **상소심** an appellate trial.

상소리(常-) a vulgar word [expression]. ⇨상말.

상속(相續) succession; inheritance. ¶공동 ~ joint inheritance [succession] // 재산 ~ succession to (a person) property // 호주 ~ succession to (the headship of) a house // 그 토지는 ~에 의해 그의 것이 되었다 The land came to him by inheritance. **상속하다** succeed [fall heir] to (the estate of a person); inherit. ¶아버지의 재산을 ~ inherit [succeed to] one's father's estate // 그녀는 막대한 재산을 상속하였다 She came into a large fortune.
● **상속권** (the right of) inheritance; heirship. **상속세** an inheritance [a succession] tax. **상속인** a successor; an inheritor; an heir(남자); an heiress(여자). ¶공동 ~ a joint heir / a coheir / a coinheritor // 법정 ~ a legal heir / an heir-at-law (pl. heirs-) // 추정 ~ an heir presumptive (pl. heirs presumptive) // 호주 ~ the successor to a house / the heir / (여자) the heiress // ~을 정하다 settle upon (a person) as one's successor. **상속 재산** an inheritance; a hereditament; a heritage; inherited property.

상쇄(相殺) an offset; a setoff. **상쇄하다** offset [cancel] each other; set off (a merit against a fault); countervail; counterbalance (each other). ➜손익이 상쇄되었다 The profit and loss are on a par.
● **상쇄 계정** an offset account. **상쇄 관세** a countervailing duty.

상쇠 [민] (농악의) a leading gong-player (in a folk band).

상수 (上手) (사람) a better hand (at something); an expert; (솜씨) (veteran) skill; dexterity. ¶…보다 ~다 be superior (to) / be more skillful (than) / (바둑·장기에서) occupy the superior side of the board // 그는 너보다 ~다 He is a cut [stroke] above you.

상수 (上水) 1 waterworks. ⇨상수도(⇨상수) 2 [수돗물] city [tap / service] water.
● **상수도** waterworks; water service [supply].

상수 (常數) 1 [수] a constant; an invariable (number). ¶마찰 ~ a constant of friction / 절대 ~ an absolute constant. 2 [정해진 운명] the natural course of things; fatality; destiny; fate.

상수리 [식] an acorn.
● **상수리나무** an oak (tree).

상순 (上旬) the first ten days (of a month). ¶3월 ~에 at the beginning of [early in / in early] March // 내달 ~에 early [toward(s) the beginning of / in the first part of] next month.

상술 (商術) [장사 요령] a trick [knack] of the trade; [상재(商才)] business ability [talent / acumen]; [상혼] commercialism. ¶~에 능하다 have a good sense [head] for business / have a shrewd business acumen.

상술 (詳述) expatiation; a detailed explanation; a full account. **상술하다** explain in full [detail]; make a detailed explanation (of); give a full account (of); enlarge [expatiate] (of); detail (a matter). ¶상술하면 to be more particular.

상술하다 (上述-) say [mention / state] above. ¶상술한 the above-mentioned [-stated] / the aforesaid / the aforementioned / the said // 상술한 바와 같이 세 사람의 의원은 그 의안에 반대 투표를 했다 As stated [mentioned] above, the three (National) Assemblymen voted against the bill.

상스럽다 (常-) vulgar; low; indecent; gross; mean; sordid; contemptible; boorish. ¶상스러운 사람 a vulgar [mean] person // 상스러운 말 ribald language / a vulgar expression / indecent language // 상스러운 [외설적] 이야기를 늘어놓다 tell a vulgar story // 상스러운 짓을 하다 behave shamefully / be coarse [unrefined] in manners // 상스러우리만큼 품위가 없는 crude to a point of indecency // 상스러운 말을 마시오 Stop using such vulgar [coarse] language. // 나는 그녀의 상스러운 행동에 놀랐다 I was surprised at her disgraceful behavior.

상습 (常習) (세상의) a convention; a usage; a regular [an established] custom; a common practice; (개인의) a habit; an inveterate habit.
● **상습범** (범인) a habitual [a confirmed / an inveterate] criminal; a chronic [an old] offender; a jailbird; (범죄) a habitual crime. ¶소매치기 ~ a confirmed pickpocket. **상습자** a habitual offender. ¶도박 ~ a confirmed gambler // 마약 ~ a drug addict / a dope fiend // 음주 ~ a habitual drunkard.

상습적 (常習的) habitual; confirmed; regular. ¶~으로 habitually // ~으로 …하다 be in the habit of (doing) // 그는 ~으로 도둑질을 한다 He has thieving ways. / His fingers are light [lime-twigs].

상승 (上昇) a rise (in temperature); the ascent (of a balloon); ascension; [상승 경향] upward tendency; a rising trend; an upturn. ¶급~ a sudden rise (of prices) // 가격의 대폭 ~ a big jump in price // 물가의 ~ a rise [an advance] in price // 내 수입은 물가 ~을 따라 잡지 못한다 My income cannot keep up with the rise in prices. **상승하다** rise; go up; ascend; climb. ¶계속 ~ continue to rise / rise steadily // 상승하고 있다 be on the rise / 주가가 상승했다 Stock [(영) Share] prices rose [went up].
● **상승 곡선** a rising [mounting] curve. **상승 기류** a rising current of air; an ascending (atmospheric) current. ¶~를 타다 rise with the ascending current. **상승세** an upward tendency; (증권) a bull (market). ¶물가는 ~이다 Prices are going up [are on the rise]. **상승 식물** a climber.

상승 (相乘) [수] multiplication. **상승하다** multiply; involve.
● **상승비** (-比) a geometrical ratio. **상승 작용** [생] synergism (of penicillin and streptomycin).

상승 (常勝) ¶~의 ever-victorious / (무적의) invincible.
● **상승군** an ever-victorious army [force].

상시 (常時) ordinary [normal] times; (at) all times. ¶~의 usual / ordinary / everyday / habitual // ~에(는) ordinarily / normally / usually / always (항상).
● **상시 고용인** a regular employee.

상식 (常食) daily [usual] food; staple; a diet. **상식하다** live [diet / subsist] on (rice). ¶중국인들은 대부분 쌀을 상식한다 Many Chinese exist on a diet of rice.

상식 (常識) [판단력] common sense; [지식] common knowledge. ¶법률 ~ common sense in law / ~이 있는 사람 a man of common sense // ~을 벗어난 (사람·성격 등이) eccentric / (사고방식 등이) absurd / preposterous // ~이 있다 have common sense / be sensible // ~이 없다 have no [be wanting in] common sense // ~에 어긋나다 [벗어나다] be against common sense / be eccentric // 그것은 ~이다 Everybody knows that. // 그것이 이 업계에서는 ~이 되어 있다 That's common practice in this trade. // 그 제의는 거절하는 것이 ~이라고 생각된다 You would be sensible to decline the offer. // 그는 ~이 있기 때문에 그런 일은 하지 않는다 He has more sense than to do that. // 그런 일을 맞대놓고 묻는다면 그것은 전혀 ~이 없는 사람이다 Anyone who would ask a person such a thing to his face is lacking in common decency. // 암을 고칠 수 있다는 건 오늘날 ~이 되었다 It is common knowledge nowdays that cancer can be cured.
● **상식 철학** common-sense philosophy.

상식적 (常識的) common-sense; sensible; wise; matter-of-fact; practical; (보통의) ordinary; normal. ¶~ 견해 a common-sense view / ~ 문제 a matter of common sense / a sensible question // 그것이 거짓이라는 것은 ~으로 판단이 된다 Common sense will tell [teach] you [us] it not true.

상신 (上申) a report (to a superior [higher] official). **상신하다** report to one's superiors (on a matter); submit a report (to one's superior).

●**상신서**(-書) (submit) a written report. **상신자** a reporter.
상실(喪失) loss; forfeiture. ¶권리의 ~ the forfeiture [loss / lapse (소멸에 의한)] of one's right // **기억** ~ loss of memory // **자격** ~ disqualification / incapacitation. **상실하다** lose; be deprived (of sight); forfeit; divest oneself (of). ¶자격을 ~ be disqualified (from / for) // 지금은 대개의 사람들이 도덕 감각을 상실해 버렸다 Nowadays most people have lost their sense of morality.
상심(傷心) a broken heart; heartbreak; grief; distress; sorrow. ¶나는 ~을 달래기 위해 여행을 떠났다 I started on a trip to heal my grief [to forget my sorrow]. **상심하다** grieve; be grieved (at heart); be heartbroken; sorrow; be sorrow-stricken; be distressed. ¶상심한 heartbroken // 남편을 잃고 ~에 be grieved over the loss of one's husband // 그녀는 상심한 나머지 자살했다 She killed herself in grief. / Overcome with grief, she committed suicide.
상아(象牙) ivory. ¶상앗빛의 ivory-white [-colored] (skin) // **인조** ~ artificial ivory // **식물** ~ vegetable ivory.
●**상아 제품** ivory manufactures; (~ 속에) ivories. **상아질**(-質) (이의) dentin(e). **상아탑** a tower of ivory; an ivory tower. ¶~에 들어 **박히다** live in [keep to] an ivory tower / remain behind cloistered walls / lead a scholastic life detached from the world.
상악(上顎) [생] the upper jaw. ⇨위턱
●**상악골**(-骨) the upper jawbone. ⇨위턱뼈 (⇨위턱)
상앗대 a boat (man's) pole. ⇨삿대
●**상앗대질** poling; shaking one's fist. ⇨=삿대질(⇨삿대)
상어 [동] a (giant) shark. ¶~ 지느러미 요리 shark's fin with chop suey // ~ 밥이 되다 become food for a shark.
●**상어 가죽** sharkskin; shagreen; fishskin; sea leather. **상어 기름** shark oil.
상업(商業) [산업] commerce; trade; [장사·거래] business. ¶~의 commercial / business / mercantile // ~상 commercially / from the commercial point of view // ~의 중심지 the center of commerce / a commercial [business] center // **이 침체하다** commerce stagnates // **~을 영위하다** carry on commerce [trade / business] / conduct a business.
●**상업계** the world of commerce; the business world; commercial circles. **상업 고등학교** a commercial high school. **상업 광고** a commercial. **상업 구역 / 상업 지역** a business [commercial] section [district / center / quarter]. **상업 디자인** commercial design. **상업 미술** commercial art. **상업 방송** commercial broadcasting; (1회의) a commercial [sponsored] broadcast [telecast]; [프로그램] a commercial radio [TV] program. ¶~을 개시하다 begin broadcasting [telecasting] on a commercial basis. **상업 부기** commercial bookkeeping. **상업영어** business [commercial] English. **상업주의** commercialism. **상업 통신**(문) commercial [business] correspondence.
상여(喪輿) a "death carriage"; a hearse; a bier; a catafalque. ¶꽃 ~ a colorfully decorated bier // ~를 메다 bear [take / carry] a bier on the shoulders / shoulder a bier.
●**상여꾼** a bier-carrier. **상엿소리** a bier-carriers' song.
상여금(賞與金) [보너스] a bonus; [상금] prize money; a prize; a reward. ¶**연말** ~ a year-end bonus // **특별** ~ a special bonus // 봉급 3개월분의 ~ a bonus equivalent to three months' pay // **~을 주다** give (a person) a bonus // ~은 1년에 두 번 지급된다 We are given a bonus [Bonuses are paid] twice a year. // 노동조합은 봉급 4개월분의 ~을 요구했다 The union demanded a bonus equivalent to four months' pay.
상연(上演) dramatic presentation; presentation [staging] (of a play); performance. ¶무단 ~ 금지 All rights reserved. / No performance may be given without written permission. // 그 연극은 ~ 금지를 당했다 The play has been interdicted. / A stage ban is placed on the play. **상연하다** perform; present (▶ perform은 주로 배우의 입장에서, present는 흥행주의 입장에서 말할 때 씀); put (a drama) on the stage; stage. ¶우리는 가을에 햄릿을 상연한다 We will present Hamlet in the fall. → 그 뮤지컬은 1년 이상 장기 상연되었다 That musical had a long run of over a year. // 춘향전이 내일부터 국립극장에서 상연된다 *Chunhyangjeon* will be staged at the National Theater beginning tomorrow.
●**상연권** performing [acting] rights.
상영(上映) screening; showing. ¶**동시** ~ a double feature / a two picture program // 계속 ~ a continued run (of a film) // 지금 ~ 중인 영화 a picture now showing [on show / running]. **상영하다** screen; put on the screen; show; exhibit; run off; play. ¶영화를 ~ show a movie // 저 극장에서는 '바람과 함께 사라지다'를 상영하고 있다 "Gone with the wind" is showing [is on] now at that theater. → 이 영화는 앞으로 3주간 더 상영된다 This film [movie] will be shown for three weeks more. / They will continue to show this film for another three weeks.
●**상영 시간** the running time (of a movie).
상오(上午) the forenoon; the morning; a.m.; A.M.
상온(常溫) 1 [보통 온도] normal temperature. ¶이 약은 ~에서 보존하시오 Store this medicine at room temperature. 2 [일정 온도] constant temperature. ¶방을 ~으로 유지하다 keep a room at a fixed [uniform] temperature. 3 [평균 온도] average temperature.
상용(常用) 1 [일상적으로 사용함] common [constant / ordinary] use; daily [everyday] use. **상용하다** use commonly. → 상용되는 표현 an expression in common use / a commonly used expression // 이 도구들은 아직도 원주민 사이에서 상용되고 있다 These implements are still in common use among the natives. 2 [상습적으로 사용함] habitual [regular] use. **상용하다** use habitually [regularly]; make regular use of (a medicine). ¶그는 수면제를 상용하고 있다 He takes sleeping pills regularly [habitually]. // 이 약은 상용하면 부작용이 생긴다 Habitual use of this medicine may cause harmful side effects.
●**상용로그** [수] common logarithms. **상용어** common words; words in everyday use. **상용자** a constant user; (마약 등의) an addict. ¶

마약 ~ a drug addict. **상용한자** the Chinese characters in common use.

상용(商用) (commercial) business. ¶~으로 방문하다 make a business call (on a person / at an office).
● **상용문** commercial correspondence; a business letter. **상용어** commercial [business] term.

상원(上院) the Upper House; (미) the Senate; (영) the House of Lords.
● **상원 의원** a member of the Upper House; (미) a Senator; (영) a member of the House of Lords.

상위(上位) a higher [an upper] rank; a high position; precedence. ¶~의 레슬링 선수 a high-ranking wrestler // ~를 차지하다 rank high / hold a high rank / take [have] (the) precedence (over [of] others) // …의 ~에 놓이다 be placed above (another) // 반에서 헬렌은 존보다 ~에 있다 Helen ranks higher in her class than John. // 지금은 여성 ~ 시대다 Women are placed above men today.

상위(相違) (a) difference; disagreement; (a) disparity; (a) discrepancy; a gap. ¶위와 같이 ~ 없음 I affirm the above to be true (and correct) in every particular [respect]. **상위하다** differ (from); be different (from); disagree (with); vary (from); be contrary to (the fact); be at variance (with).

상응(相應) 1 [대응] correspondence. **상응하다** correspond (to); answer (to). 2 [적합] fitness; suitability. **상응하다** be suitable (for / to); suit; be suited; [어울리다] befit; become; be due (to); be proper (for). ¶그는 그의 역량에 상응하는 급료를 받고 있다 He gets the salary proportionate to his ability.

상의(上衣) a coat; a jacket; an upper garment; a blouse; (미) a shirtwaist; a tunic(군복의). ¶~를 입다 [벗다] put on [take off] one's coat // ~를 벗고 일을 하다 work in one's shirt-sleeves.

상의(上意) the will [wish / intention] of the sovereign [one's superior]. ¶~를 하달하다 communicate [convey] the wishes [will / orders] of the ruler [leader] to those under him / (구어) pass the word down.

상의(相議) (a) consultation(▶ 복수로 쓸 경우가 많음); (a) conference; a talk; (속어) a confab. ¶~ 중이다 be in consultation [negotiation]. **상의하다** consult (a person / with a person about a matter); have a talk (with); talk (with a person over a matter); discuss (a matter with a person). ¶이마를 맞대고 ~ lay [put] their [our] heads together [about a matter] // 우리는 그녀의 변호사와 상의했다 We held consultations [consulted / had a talk] with her lawyer. // 우리는 상의의 결과 이혼에 합의했다 After talking it over, we agreed to get a divorce. // 내일 충분히 상의해 봅시다 Let's have a long talk about it [talk it over carefully] tomorrow.

상이군인(傷痍軍人) a disabled ex-serviceman [(미) veteran] (▶ disabled는 그 상처가 영구히 남는 것을 의미함); [부상병] a wounded soldier; (집합적) the war disabled.

상인(商人) a merchant; a tradesman; a dealer (in rice); [소매 상인] a storekeeper; a shopkeeper; (집합적) tradespeople. ¶노점 ~ a street trader // 대~ a big merchant // 도매 [소매] ~ a wholesale [retail] merchant / a wholesaler [retailer] // 소~ a small tradesman // 악덕 ~ a wicked trader.

상인방(上引枋) [건] the upper lintel.

상일(常一) physical labor; manual labor; rough work. ¶~을 하다 labor / do manual labor.
● **상일꾼** a manual laborer.

상임(常任) a permanent post. ¶~의 [항구적인] permanent / [정규의] regular / standing.
● **상임 위원** a member of a standing [permanent] committee. **상임 위원회** a standing [permanent] committee. **상임 이사** an executive director. **상임 이사국** a permanent member of the UN Security Council. **상임 지휘자** the regular conductor (of an orchestra).

상자(箱子) a box; a case; a packing case; a bin(큰); a casket(작은). ¶과자 ~ a box [package] of cake / a carton of biscuit [candy] // 나무 ~ a crate // 보석 ~ a jewel box // 유리 ~ a glassed case // 음악 ~ a music [(영) musical] box // 한 ~ 가득 boxful // ~에 넣다 put [pack] (a thing) in a box [case] / encase // ~로 사다 buy (a thing) by the box // ~를 열다 unpack a case.
● **상자 뚜껑** the lid of a box; a boxtop.

상잔(相殘) [동족 ~ 골육 ~] an internal strife [feud] / a dog-eat-dog fight. **상잔하다** struggle [fight] with each other.

상장(喪章) (가슴에) a mourning ribbon; (팔의) a mourning band; a black armband. ¶~을 달다 (가슴에) wear a mourning ribbon on one's chest / (팔에) wear a band of mourning [a crape] on one's sleeve.

상장(賞狀) a certificate of merit; (honor with) a testimonial. ¶우등~ a diploma of honors / an honors diploma // 그는 개근~을 받았다 He was awarded a certificate for perfect attendance.

상장주(上場株) listed stocks. ¶비~ unlisted [outside] stocks [shares].

상장하다(上場-) list (stocks). ➔증권 거래소 2부에 우리 회사 주식이 상장되었다 Our company is listed on the Second Market.

상장 회사(上場會社) a listed company; an enterprise [a firm] listed on the Korea Stock Exchange; listed firms.

상재(商才) business ability [acumen / capacity]; a knack for business.

상재(霜災) frost damage. ¶~를 입다 suffer from frost.

상쟁(相爭) a strife [struggle / conflict] with each other; a dispute. **상쟁하다** struggle [quarrel / wrangle] with each other; have a dispute.

상전(上典) [주인] one's master; [고용주] the employer; [상관] one's higher [superior] officer. ¶~을 깍듯이 섬기다 serve one's master faithfully // ~의 명령에 복종하다 obey the orders of one's master [superior].

상전벽해(桑田碧海) violent changes in nature; convulsions of nature; the changeableness of things.

상점(商店) (미) a store; (영) a shop. ¶~을 내다 open [set up / start] a store // ~을 열다 [닫다] open [close] the store.
● **상점가** a shopping district; (교외의) a shopping center.

상접(相接) contact. **상접하다** come in contact

상정(上程) laying before the House; presentation (of a bill). **상정하다** (일정에) introduce [present] (a bill) on the agenda; (의회에) lay (a bill) before the House; (토의에) bring up (a bill) for discussion. ¶의안을 국회에 ~ introduce a bill in the National Assembly / present [place] a bill before the National Assembly. →¶예산안이 상정되었다 [일정에 올려졌다] The budget bill was placed [put] on the agenda of the day. / [심의에 부쳐졌다] The budget bill was brought up for discussion.

상정(常情) (ordinary) human nature [feeling]; the way of the world. ¶인지~ human nature.

상정(想定) a hypothesis (*pl.* -ses); (an) assumption; (a) supposition. **상정하다** assume; suppose; imagine; [어림하다] estimate.

상제(上帝) God. ⇨하느님

상제(喪制) 1 (사람) a person in mourning; a mourner. ¶맏~ the chief mourner // ~가 되다 be bereft of one's parents. 2 (제도) the mourning custom [practice]; the ritual of mourning.

상조(相助) mutual aid [help / assistance]; interdependence. **상조하다** aid [help / assist] each other; cooperate.

상존하다(尙存-) be still in existence [being]; there is [are] still; still exist; [잔존하다] remain.

상종(相從) association; intercourse; company; society; friendship; acquaintanceship. **상종하다** associate (with); hold intercourse (with); keep company with; mix (with). ¶상종하지 못할 놈 a despicable [contemptible] fellow // 상종하지 않다 refuse to deal with / break off friendship with / sever acquaintance with.

상종가(上終價) [증권] (hit) the daily permissible ceiling.

상좌(上座) [상석] the top [upper] seat; (주빈의) the seat [place] of honor; the head. ¶~에 앉다 take a front [the best] seat / sit at the head of the table.

상주(上奏) a report [an address] to the Throne. **상주하다** report to the Throne; submit (a matter) to the Throne. ¶수상은 이 조례(條例)에 대해 왕에게 상주했다 The Prime Minister reported to the King about the regulation.
●**상주문** / **상주서** a memorial to the Throne.

상주(喪主) the chief [principal] mourner.

상주인구(常住人口) a settled population.

상주하다(常住-) reside (habitually) (in / at). ¶한국에 상주하는 외국인 the foreign residents in Korea.

상주하다(常駐-) be permanently stationed (at). ¶외국군이 그 나라에 상주하고 있다 A foreign army is stationed in the country.

상중(喪中) the period of mourning; in mourning. ¶~에 있다 be in mourning // 나는 어머니의 ~이다 I am in mourning for my mother. // 그는 지금 부친의 ~이다 He is now in mourning for his father.

상중하(上中下) [3단계] the first, the second, and the third grades [classes]; (품질·능력 등의) good, better, and the best; the three grades of quality [ability] — good, fair, and poor. ¶~ 3권 a set of three volumes / (소설) a three-decker.

상지상(上之上) the best (of the best); the very best; the top.

상징(象徵) a symbol (of); an emblem; [모양으로 나타내기] symbolic representation. ¶~적(인) symbolic(al) ¶백합은 순결의 ~이다 A lily is symbolic of purity. **상징하다** symbolize; emblematize; be symbolic (of); stand as a symbol (for). ¶이 시의 빨간 장미는 사랑을 상징한다 The red rose symbolizes [is a symbol of] love in this poem.
●**상징극** a symbolic play [drama]. **상징시** (집합적) symbolical poetry; (한 편) a symbolical poem. **상징주의** symbolism. ¶~자 a symbolist.

상책(上策) the best plan; a good [capital] plan [idea]; the best policy; the wisest thing (to do). ¶도망치는 것이 ~이다 It is best to run away. // 먼저 그에게 상의하는 것이 ~일 것입니다 It would be best to consult him first. // 말하지 않는 것이 ~이다 Better leave it unsaid.

상처(喪妻) the death [loss] of one's wife; bereavement of one's wife. **상처하다** lose one's wife by death; be bereaved of one's wife; meet the death of one's wife.

상처(傷處) 1 [부상] an injury (사고 등에 의한 상처); a wound (전상(戰傷)·총·칼 등에 고의로 입혀진 상처); a hurt; a cut (벤 상처); a bruise; a scratch (타박상). ¶가벼운 ~ a slight wound // 칼에 의한 ~ a sword cut // ~를 입은 wounded / injured // ~를 **입다** get [be] hurt [injured / wounded] / get a wound (in the face) // 가벼운 ~를 입다 be slightly wounded // (문어) sustain a slight wound // ~를 **치료하다** treat a wound / (조심하여 치료하다) nurse a wound // ~를 꿰매다 stitch [sew up] a wound // ~에 붕대를 감다 dress [bind up] a wound // ~가 매우 아프다 The wound hurts badly. // 그의 볼에 ~ 자국이 있다 There is a scar on his cheek. // ~가 곪았다 The wound became infected [septic]. // ~가 아물었다 The wound has closed.
2 [피해를 입은 자리] ~ 받은 마음 a wounded heart // 전쟁의 ~ 자국 scars left by war / the scars of war // ~ 받기 쉬운 나이 a vulnerable [sensitive] age // 그의 말에 그녀의 마음이 깊은 ~를 받은 것 같다 She seemed deeply hurt by his words. // 그녀의 마음의 ~는 치유될 수 없을 것이다 The emotional wound she received will never heal. / She will never recover from the trauma. // 그의 묵은 ~를 들추지 않는 것이 좋다 You had better not expose his past faults. // 그 사건은 소년의 마음속에 ~를 남겼다 The affair left a scar in the boy's heart.

상체(上體) the upper (part of the) body. ¶~를 앞으로 굽히다 bend down // ~를 뒤로 젖히다 bend over backwards.

상추 [식] (a) lettuce.
●**상추쌈** cooked rice wrapped in lettuce.

상춘(賞春) enjoying spring; admiring spring scenery.
●**상춘객** springtime merrymakers [picnickers].

상충(相衝) contradiction; conflict. **상충하다** contradict; conflict (with).

상층(上層) **1** the upper floor. ⇨위층 **2** (사회의) the upper classes; a higher stratum of society[life]. ¶정부[사회]의 ~부 the upper levels[strata] of government[society].
● **상층 기류** a high altitude air current. **상층운** the upper clouds.

상치(相馳) a conflict; a collision; a clash; discord. **상치하다** conflict [with]; be in conflict[discord] (with); collide[clash] (with); be contrary (to); run counter (to); be incompatible (with). ¶자기의 원칙과 이해가 상치하는 때도 있다 Sometimes one's principles run counter to one's interests.

상쾌하다(爽快─) refreshing; exhilarating (drink); bracing; invigorating; crisp (breeze). ¶상쾌한 가을 공기 the bracing [refreshing] air of autumn(▶ bracing은 몸이 죄는 듯한)//상쾌한 기분이 되다 feel refreshed / (큰 짐을 덜어) feel relieved//더운 날씨에는 찬 음료가 ~ Cold drinks really hit the spot[are refreshing] on a hot day.//집 밖으로 나가면 기분이 ~ The open air cheers me up.//우리는 마음도 상쾌하게 소풍을 떠났다 We set off on the excursion cheerfully[in high spirits].//겨울에 해변을 걸으면 기분이 상쾌해진다 It is invigorating[bracing] to walk by the seaside in winter.//목욕을 하면 기분이 상쾌해질 것입니다 A bath will freshen you up.//숙제를 끝내고 나니 기분이 ~ I feel relieved now that I have finished my homework.

상큼상큼 with light steps; light-footedly; briskly; lightly. ¶~ 걷다 walk briskly.

상큼하다 slender-legged; long-legged; lanky.

상태(狀態) a state(▶ 보통 단수형); a condition; [상황] conditions(▶ 보통 복수형); [국면] a situation; [광경] a sight; [양상] an aspect. ¶건강 ~ one's state of health//경제 ~ the economic condition[situation]//생활 ~ living conditions//위험 ~ a critical [dangerous] condition / a crisis//재정 ~ a financial condition//혼수~ (fall into) a comatose[lethargic] condition[state]//그 나라의 현재 ~ the present state of the country//건강 ~가 좋다[나쁘다] be[feel] well[unwell / ill] / be in good[poor] health// 한심한 ~이다 be in (a) wretched condition// 건강 ~는 어떠하십니까 How do you feel? / How are you feeling now?//기상 ~가 좋지 않다 Weather conditions are unfavorable.// 위장 ~가 좀 이상하다 Something seems to be the matter with my stomach.//지금 ~로는 실업 문제가 점점 더 심각해질 것이다 Under the present circumstances, the unemployment problem will probably get worse[more serious].//지금 ~로는 그는 좀 처럼 일자리를 구할 수 없을 것이다 As things are with him now, he will never be able to find a job.//그는 태풍의 피해 ~를 얘기했다 He described the havoc wreaked by the typhoon. / He gave an account of the damage done by the typhoon.//이 이는 ~가 패 안 좋다 This tooth is in pretty bad shape.

상통(相通) **1** [마음과 뜻이 통하는 것] mutual understanding; coincidence; accordance. **상통하다** understand each other; coincide (with); be in accord (with); together. ¶너는 그녀와 마음이 상통할 것이다 You'd get on very well with her. **2** [공통] commonness; community. **상통하다** have something in common (with). ¶그들은 상통하는 점이 없다 They have nothing in common with each other. **3** [길이 트임] communication. **상통하다** communicate (with).

상투 a sangtu; a topknot (of hair). ¶~를 틀다 wear one's hair in a knot.
● **상투쟁이** a person with a topknot.

상투(常套) conventionality; commonplaceness; platitude; triteness; staleness.
● **상투 수단** a well-worn device; an old trick; stereotyped[worn-out] measures; one's usual[hackneyed] practice; familiar steps [ways]. ¶~을 쓰다 use one's old [favorite] trick. **상투어** a conventional [set / stock] phrase[expression]; [진부한 표현] a trite [hackneyed / stereotyped] phrase[expression]; a household word; a platitude; a cliché.

상투적(常套的) [틀에 박힌] conventional; [혼해 빠진] commonplace; hackneyed. ¶~ 문구[말] a favorite[hackneyed / stereotyped] phrase / a set phrase//그것은 그의 ~ 수단이다 That is an old [a favorite] trick of his. / That's a favorite ploy[gimmick] of his.

상판대기(相─) {속} a face. ⇨얼굴

상팔자(上八字) [좋은 팔자] good fortune; a happy lot; a lucky star. ¶~다[로 지내다] live in (ease and) comfort / live in easy circumstances / live in clover / live comfortably.

상패(賞牌) a medal; a medallion. ¶~를 수여하다 award a medal.

상편(上篇) the first volume (of a book in two or three volumes).

상표(商標) a trademark; a brand; a label. ¶등록 ~ a registered trademark//외국 ~ a foreign trademark//유명 ~ a renowned brand[trademark]//올빼미 ~가 붙은 볼펜 ball-point pens with an owl trademark//~를 도용하다 pirate[infringe on] a trademark//~를 등록하다 trademark / register a trademark//~를 붙이다 put[affix] a trademark (on) / trademark / brand.
● **상표권** trademark rights. ¶~을 침해하다 infringe upon a trademark. **상표 도용** trademark piracy.

상품(上品) **1** [일등품] a first-class [choice] article; a superior article. **2** [불] the Highest Paradise.

상품(商品) a commodity; an article of commerce[trade]; (집합적) merchandise; goods; wares; commodities. ¶가정용 ~ 코너 the household goods corner//~화 계획 a plan to commercialize (a product)//주요 ~ a staple [major] goods//특매 ~ a loss leader//~이 많다[적다] (종류가) keep a rich [limited] assortment of goods / (수량이) have a large [small] stock of goods / (점포에서) ~을 들여 놓다 lay in a stock (of goods)//~을 처분하다 dispose of goods//2백만 원어치의 ~의 재고가 있다 carry a two million won stock//이 가게에서는 많은 종류의 ~을 취급하고 있다 They deal in many kinds of merchandise at this store.//이것은 ~이 아닙니다 These items are not for sale.
● **상품 견본** a (trade) sample; (옷감의) a pattern; Samples(우편물의 표시). ~ **시장** a trade fair. **상품 관리** merchandise management[control]. **상품권** a gift certificate; a merchandise bond[coupon]; a credit slip;

an exchange ticket[check]. **상품 목록** a catalog(ue); (재고의) an inventory. **상품 진열장** a showcase. **상품진열창** show window. **상품학** the study of merchandise.

상품(賞品) a prize; a trophy; a pot. ¶~을 내주다 hand out a prize (to) / ~을 받다 receive[get] a prize.

상피(上皮) [생] the epithelium (pl. ~s, -lia); [표피] the epidermis. ¶~의 epithelial / epidermal.
● **상피 세포** an epithelial cell.

상피(相避) incest.

상피병(象皮病) [의] elephantiasis.

상하(上下) 1 [위와 아래] top and bottom; the upper and lower sides[parts]. ¶~의 up-and-down / vertical // ~로 up and down / vertically / upward and downward / (높게 낮게) high and low / ~로 움직이다 move[go] up and down / rise and fall / seesaw / (배 등이) heave and set / pitch. 2 (신분·지위 등의) the upper and lower classes; high and low; superiors and inferiors. ¶~ 구별 없이 irrespective of social standing / without distinction of social standing / both high and low / ~가 단결하여 all classes being unanimous // 우리 클럽은 ~ 관계가 엄격하다 Our club has a strict pecking order.

상하권(上下卷) the first and second volumes.

상하다(傷-) 1 [물건 등이] damage; be damaged; hurt; be hurt; injure; be injured; [상처 나다] flaw[crack be bruised]; [헐다] wear [be worn] out; become deteriorated; (우유 등 음식이) go bad; turn sour; be spoiled; become addled; be stale(생선 등이). ¶상한 (상하지 않은) 배 a bruised[sound] pear / 상한 토마토 a rotten tomato / 상하기 쉬운 물건 [깨지기 쉬운 물건] a fragile article / a delicate thing / [썩기 쉬운 물건] perishable goods / perishables / 상하기 쉬운 음식 food that goes bad[spoil] quickly // 이 옷감[옷]은 세탁기로 빨면 상할 게다 This material [dress] will be damaged if you wash it in the washing machine. / This material [dress] is not machine-washable. // 홈통이 많이 상했다 The gutter is in need of repair. // 이런 종류의 계기류는 습기에 의해 상하기 쉽다 Instruments of this kind are easily affected by moisture. // 복숭아는 빨리 먹지 않으면 상할 게다 The peaches will spoil unless they are eaten soon. // 상한 냄새가 난다 It smells as if it has gone bad. // 이 케이크는 1주일 동안은 상하지 않을 게다 This cake will keep for a week. // 날음식은 상하기 쉽다 Uncooked food goes bad[spoils] easily. / Uncooked food doesn't keep.
2 (몸을[이]) grow haggard; become thin; be emaciated; (건강이) be broken (in health); injure (one's health). ¶얼굴이 ~ have a face all pinched and drawn // 건강을 ~ impair[injure] one's health / lose[ruin] one's health.
3 (마음·기분 등을[이]) hurt; get[be] hurt; injure; be injured; impair; harm; worry; be worried about; grieve; be grieved (at). ¶기분이 ~ take offense (at) / get out of humor // 속이 ~ be worried[troubled] (about) / be grieved at heart / trouble one's mind / worry[trouble] oneself (about) / feel bad // 남의 감정을 상하게 하다 hurt[injure] (a person's) feelings /

hurt[offended] (a person) // 그는 기분이 상한 것 같았다 He looked offended.

상하수도(上下水道) water and sewage; (영) water and drainage services.

상학(商學) business administration; commercial science; (과목) business courses.

상한(上限) [수] the supremum; the least upper bound.
● **상한선** the upper limit; (최대한) the maximum. ¶미곡가에 ~을 설정하다 set [place] an upper limit on the price of rice.

상한(象限) ➡사분면(⇨사분)

상항(商港) a mercantile[trading] port; a commercial harbor.

상해(傷害) (an) injury; bodily harm. ¶…에게 ~를 가하다 inflict bodily injury on a person // ~죄로 체포되다 be arrested on a[the] charge of inflicting (bodily) injury upon (a person). **상해하다** injure; do (a person) an injury; inflict an injury upon (a person).
● **상해 보험** accident insurance. **상해 치사 (죄)** (a) bodily injury resulting in death.

상해(詳解) a detailed[minute] explanation (of); a full commentary (on). **상해하다** explain in detail; give a minute explanation (of the Iliad); explain minutely; make a detailed explanation (of); provide copious annotations.

상해(霜害) frost damage. ⇨"서리 피해(⇨서리)

상행(上行) ¶~의 up // 경부 고속도로는 현재 ~이 순조롭게 진행되고 있다 At present, traffic bound for Seoul on the Gyeongbu [Seoul-Busan] expressway is flowing smoothly. **상행하다** go up; go toward Seoul.
● **상행선** an up line; an upswing. **상행 열차** an up train. ¶다음 ~는 몇 시입니까 What time is the next up train?

상행위(商行爲) a commercial [business] transaction. ¶역구내에서 ~를 금함 (게시) No Commercial Transaction Allowed on Station Premises.

상향(上向) 1 [위쪽을 향함]. ~의 upward. 2 [(시세의) 오르는 기세] an upward tendency; an upturn; an upswing. **상향하다** look up; tend toward. ¶경기는 상향하고 있다 Business is looking up[turning up]. // 시황은 상향하고 있다 Market activity is on the upswing. ➔¶(시세가) 상향하되 have [show] a rising[an upward] tendency / tend upward / look up.

상현(上弦) [천] the first quarter; the dichotomy.
● **상현달** a waxing crescent moon; the moon in its first quarter.

상형 문자(象形文字) a hieroglyph; a hieroglyphic (character). ¶~의 hieroglyphic // ~로 쓴 것 hieroglyphics(▶ 보통 복수형).

상호(相互) reciprocity; mutuality. ¶~ 간(間)의 mutual / reciprocal // ~ 간의 이익을 위하여 (work) for the mutual benefit (of) // ~ 간에 mutually / reciprocally / each other / one another // ~ 협조하다 help[aid / offer aid to] each other // 회원 ~ 간의 친목을 도모함을 목적으로 한다 It is our aim to promote friendship among the members.
● **상호 관계** mutual[reciprocal] relation; interrelationship. **상호 방위 조약** a mutual defense treaty[pact]. ¶한국은 미국과 ~을 맺고 있다 Korea has a mutual defense treaty with the United States. **상호 신용 금고** a

상호 mutual financing [loan] company; a deposit premium company. 상호유도 / 상호감응 [전] mutual induction. 상호 의존 interdependence; mutual dependence. 상호 작용 reciprocal action; (an) interaction; (an) interplay. 상호 협력 mutual cooperation.

상호(商號) a firm [trade] name; a shop name.

상혼(商魂) a commercial [mercantile] spirit; salesmanship.

상환(相換) exchange; change; conversion(태환). 상환하다 exchange; convert.

상환(償還) (a) repayment; (a) refund; (a) reimbursement; (공사채의) redemption; (연부의) amortization. ¶국채 ～액 the amount of the national loan redeemed // 만기 전 ～ prior redemption // 10년 후 ～의 채권 a bond redeemable in ten years. 상환하다 repay; refund; redeem; reimburse. ¶국채를 ～ redeem a government bond // 부채를 ～ pay back [repay] a loan.

● 상환금 redemption money; money repaid; a repayment. 상환 기금 a fund for redemption; a redemption fund. 상환 기한 the term of redemption; (만기일) the date of maturity. ¶이 채권은 ～이 5년이다 This bond is redeemable in five years.

상황(狀況) the state of affairs [things]; conditions; a situation; circumstances(▶ circumstances는 자기의 주위 상황을 말함). ¶부대 ～ attendant condition // 유리한[불리한] ～ favorable [unfavorable] conditions // 해외 commercial conditions abroad // ～을 조사하다 inquire into the state of things // ～을 파악하다 grasp the situation / see how matters stand // 거절할 수 없는 ～이었다 Circumstances forced me to consent. / Under the circumstances I could not refuse. / 우리는 어떤 ～에서도 사람을 죽여서는 안 된다 We must not kill human beings under any circumstances.

● 상황 분석 circumstantial analysis. 상황 판단 circumstantial judgment. ¶～을 잘못하다 misjudge the situation.

상황(商況) the market (situation); business trends; trade [business / market / commercial] conditions. ¶～이 활발 [부진] 하다 Trade [The market] is brisk [sluggish]. // ～이 회복 [악화] 하기 시작했다 Business has begun to improve [decline / get worse].

● 상황 보고 a market report [bulletin]. 상황 부진 a dull [a slack / an inactive] market; depression (in trade). 상황 시찰 a market survey.

상회(商會) a firm; a (trading) company; a commercial firm [concern]. ¶스미스 ～ Smith & Co.

상회하다(上廻—) top; be more than; exceed; surpass. ¶원가를 상회하는 이익 the gain over the cost (of ...).

상훈(賞勳) [포상] citing for (a person's) merits.

상흔(傷痕) a scar. ¶～이 남아 있다 A scar still remains. // 이 도시에는 곳곳에 전쟁의 ～이 남아 있다 Scars left by the war are visible everywhere in this town.

샅 [서혜부] the crotch; the crutch; the groin.

샅바 (씨름의) a *satba*; a wrestler's thigh band; (죄수의) a rope for binding up a prisoner by the legs.

● 샅바 씨름 wrestling with a thigh band.

샅바지르다 bind the legs of.

샅샅이 all over; in every nook and corner; throughout; all through; thoroughly; everywhere. ¶～ 뒤지다 look in every nook and corner / leave no corner unsearched / search every corner [cranny] / hunt [search] high and low / scour [comb] (a place for something) // 집 안을 ～ 뒤지다 ransack the house (for) / search the whole house // 책상 속을 ～ 뒤지다 rummage all through a desk // 이탈자를 찾아 그 일대를 ～ 뒤지다 comb the area for the deserter // 무기를 찾으려고 집집마다 ～ 뒤지다 go from door to door in search of weapons.

새¹ [조류] a bird; a feathered creature; a fowl; (참새) a sparrow. ¶～ 가게 a bird shop // ～에게 모이를 주다 feed a bird (on) // ～를 기르다 keep a bird // ～를 쫓다 shoo birds away // ～를 잡다 catch a bird // ～가 울고 있다 Birds are singing.

새 까먹은 소리(속담) a groundless rumor; a canard.

새 발의 피(속담) a mere smidgen [particle]; (be) practically nothing.

새² an interval; time; a relationship. ⇨ 사이

새³ [새로운] new; [신기한] novel; [신선한] fresh; [최근의] recent; latest; hot; [현대적] up-to-date; modern. ¶～ 사상 an up-to-date idea // 빳빳한 ～ 지폐 뭉치 a wad of brand-new [crisp] bills // ～ 유행 a new vogue / the latest fashion // ～ 소식 fresh [hot] news.

새- [빛깔이 짙고 산뜻함] deep; dark; intense. ¶～빨갛다 deep red // ～까맣다 deep black // ～하얗다 snow [pure] white.

새가슴 a chicken [pigeon] breast. ¶～의 chicken- [pigeon-] breasted.

새것 a new one [brand]. ¶～처럼 보이다 look like new // ～이나 다름없다 look brand-new / be [look] as good as new // 사무실의 헌 타자기가 ～으로 바뀌었다 The old typewriter in our office was replaced by a new one.

새겨듣다 (주의해서) listen attentively [intently / carefully] to (a person); [알아듣다] catch [get] the meaning of what (a person) says. ¶내 말을 새겨들어라 Note what I say. / Now understand me!

새경 the annual salary given to a farm servant.

새그물 a fowler's [fowling] net; a sparrow net(참새용).

새근거리다¹ 1 (숨을) breathe hard [roughly]; puff; pant. ¶새근거리며 panting(ly) / out of breath // 새근거리며 말하다 pant [puff] out. 2 (어린아이가) breathe calmly [peacefully].

새근거리다² feel an arthritic pain. ⇨ 시근거리다

새근새근¹ 1 (숨을) panting(ly); out [short] of breath. 2 (sleep) calmly; quietly; peacefully.

새근새근² with an arthritic pain. ⇨ 시근시근

새근하다 feel [have / suffer] a dull pain (in a joint); be slightly painful (in an elbow joint).

새기다¹ 1 [조각하다] carve (in / on / out of); [표면에 파다] engrave; sculpt; sculpture; cut; (끌로) chisel; inscribe; [칼자국을 내다] nick; notch. ¶～ 불상을 ～ carve a Buddhist figure out of [from / in] stone // 그의 묘비에는 그의 시 한 줄이 새겨져 있다 On his gravestone is carved [inscribed / engraved] a line

from one of his poems.∥그들은 아이의 성장을 기록하기 위해 기둥에 눈금을 새겼다 They nicked[notched / cut nicks on] the pillar to mark the growth of their child.∥나는 나무줄기에 그의 머리글자를 새겼다 I cut[carved] his initials in a tree trunk.∥그는 대리석으로 조상(彫像)을 새겼다 He carved[sculptured] a statue out of marble.∥He carved marble into a statue.∥그 묘비에는 그의 이름만이 새겨져 있었다 Only name was engraved on the tombstone / The only inscription on the tombstone was his name.
2 [명심하다] impress (deeply); stamp; engrave; inscribe. ¶가슴(마음속) 깊이 ~ (사람을) be deeply impressed (with / by) / grave (the words) in the heart / (사물이) be brought home to (one) / be deeply impressed on[engraved in] one's mind / 그 광경은 그의 마음속 깊이 새겨졌다 The scene was deeply etched in[chiseled or engraved on] his mind.∥나는 선생님의 충고를 마음에 새겼다 I took my teacher's warning to heart.

새기다² **1** [풀이하다] interpret; construe; explain; paraphrase; elucidate; expound. ¶올바로[잘못] ~ interpret rightly[falsely] / give[put] a correct[wrong] interpretation (upon). **2** [번역하다] translate (into).

새기다³ [반추하다] chew the cud; ruminate. ¶소가 먹은 것을 새기고 있다 The cow is chewing its cud.

새김 **1** [풀이] paraphrase; interpretation; translation(번역); [한자의 뜻] the Korean rendering of a Chinese character. **2** [조각] carving; engraving; sculpture; cutting.
●**새김칼** a graver; a burin; a chisel.

새김질 〔반추〕 rumination; 〔조각〕 carving; engraving; sculpture.

새까맣다 deep[coal]-black; jet(-black). ¶새까만 머리 raven(-black) hair / (윤기가 있는) jet-black hair / 새까맣게 탄 사체 a charred body∥새까매지다(별에 타서) be[get] thoroughly tanned / be charred / be burned black∥그녀는 생선을 새까맣게 태웠다 She burned the fish black.

새끼¹ 〔줄〕 a straw rope. ¶~ 한 사리 a fold of rope∥~를 꼬다 make[twist / strand] a rope∥~를 치다 stretch a rope (around a place) / rope off[out] (a place).

새끼² **1** [동물의 어린것] 〔집합적〕 the young; (가금류의) a chick; a newly-hatched bird; (갓 날기 시작한) a fledg(e)ling; (한 마리) a young; a youngling; (여우·곰·사자의) a cub; (개·여우·이리 등의) a puppy; a pup; (고양이의) a kitten; a kitty; (소의) a calf 〔*pl.* calves, calfs〕; (말·사슴의) a colt; (양의) a lamb; (치어·개구리의) a fry; (염소의) a kid; (조류의) a young bird; a nestling. ¶한배 ~ a litter (of puppies) ∥코끼리 ~ a baby elephant / an elephant calf∥~를 까다 hatch baby birds∥~를 배다 be with young / be in pup(개가) ∥~를 낳다 bring forth (its) young / litter / cub / calf(소가) / kitten(고양이가) / pup(개가) ∥나는 이 오리들을 ~ 때부터 길렀다 I raised these ducks from ducklings.
2 [자식] one's son[daughter]; [욕하는 말] a fellow; a guy; a chap. ¶그 ~ that fellow[swine / brute] / 이 ~ 야 (이놈) You little punk! / You little creep! / (비어) You little bastard! / (소년에게) You little brat! / (노인을 청년에게) (미) You young whippersnapper! / You young upstart!
새끼(를) 치다 bear[yield] interest (at 7%).
●**새끼발가락** a little toe. **새끼벌레** 〔동〕 a larva. ⇨⁰애벌레 **새끼손가락** a little[small] finger. **새끼집** the womb (of an animal).

새나다 leak out; get[slip] out; be disclosed. ¶세상(밖)으로 ~ leak out to the world.

새날 [새로 밝아 오는 날] a new day; [새로운 시대] a new era[stage / epoch].

새다¹ [날이 밝다] dawn; break. ¶날이 새기 전에 before dawn[daybreak] / before daylight∥날이 새자 곧 일행이 도착했다 The party arrived a little after daybreak.∥마침 날이 새고 있었다 The day was just dawning.

새다² **1** (액체·기체 등이) leak; escape; get [find] vent; run out. ¶물이 새지 않는 천 waterproof cloth / 공기[가스]가 새지 않는 파이프 an airtight[a gastight] tube∥파이프에서 가스가 새고 있다 Gas is leaking[escaping] from the pipe.∥수도꼭지에서 물이 졸졸 새어 나온다 Water is trickling from the faucet.∥지붕에 비가 샌다 There is a leak in the roof. / The roof has a leak.∥우리 집 지붕은 비가 몹시 샌다 The roof of our house leaks badly.
2 (불빛 등이) come[shine / break] through; (말소리가) be heard outside. ¶나무 사이로 새어 들어오는 햇빛 sunlight shining through the trees∥커튼 틈으로 새어 나오는 불빛이 보인다 Light can be seen through the small opening between the curtains.∥이 커튼은 빛이 바깥으로 새지 않는다 This curtain does not let the light out.∥봄의 햇살이 나뭇가지 사이로 새어 들었다 The spring sunshine streamed through the branches of the trees.
3 (말·감정 등이) get[find] vent; find expression. ¶그의 입에서 (자기도 모르게) 욕이 새어 나왔다 A curse escaped his lips.∥그녀의 입술에서 흐느낌 소리가 새어 나왔다 Faint sobs escaped her lips.
4 (비밀이) get[slip] out; leak (out); transpire; be disclosed. ¶비밀이 샜다 The secret was out[has leaked out].
5 [슬쩍 빠져나가다] sneak away; slip off[out / away]. ¶일행 속에서 슬쩍 ~ sneak away from company.
6 [줄거리에서 빠져나가다]. ¶그의 이야기는 자주 줄거리에서 벗어나 옆길로 샌다 When he speaks, he often digresses[gets off the subject].

새달 next month; the coming month. ¶~ 초하루 the first of next month.

새댁(─宅) a bride. ⇨¹새색시

새되다 high-pitched (tone); shrill; sharp. ¶새된 목소리 a shrill voice / a shriek∥새된 목소리로 말하다 speak in a high-pitched voice∥공포에 질려 새된 목소리를 지르다 scream[shriek] in terror.

새둥주리 a bird's nest; a cage.

새뜻하다 fresh and bright. ¶새뜻한 빛깔 bright color∥새뜻한 옷을 입고 있다 be neatly dressed.

새로(이) new(ly); anew; afresh. ¶~ 지은 집 a newly-built house∥~ 페인트칠을 한 집 a freshly-painted house∥~ 온 선생님 a new teacher∥~ (들어)온 사람 a newcomer / a new arrival / a freshman∥~ 일을 시작하다 start a new job∥~ 시작하다 begin afresh∥~ 출발하다 make a fresh[new] start∥결의를 ~ 하다 make a fresh determination∥그

는 각오를 ~ 하여 일에 몰두했다 He changed his attitude and threw himself into his work.

새록새록 in succession; with one (new) thing popping up after another. ¶여러 가지 사건이 ~ 일어났다 Things happened in succession. / One thing happened after another.

새롭다 [지금까지 있은 적이 없다] new; [생생하다] fresh; [최신이다] latest; [현대적·진보적이다] up-to-date; modern; [신기하다] novel; [독창적이다] original; [절실하다] essential; [아쉽다] be in need[want] of. ¶새로운 방법 a new method[way] (of) // 새로운 유행 the latest fashion // 새로운 뉴스 fresh [hot] news // 일자리가 ~ I am in want of a job. // 그 사건은 아직도 기억에 ~ The event is still fresh in my memory. // 그 노인은 사고 방식이 ~ The old man is modern [up-to-date] in his thinking. // 설비가 죄다 새로워졌다 All the equipment was modernized. // 이 광고는 전혀 새로운 것이다 This advertisement[commercial] is quite an innovation. / This is quite a new type of advertisement [commercial]. // 그에게는 눈에 보이는 것이 모두 새로웠다 Everything he saw was new [fresh] to him. // 그의 생각은 조금도 새로운 것이 없었다 There was nothing new in his idea. / His idea lacked originality. // 새로운 긴장이 필요하다 A renewed sense of urgency is necessary. // 가게가 새롭게 단장되어 문을 열었다 The shop opened after having been remodeled and redecorated.

새마을 운동(-運動) the *Saemaeul*[New Community] Movement. ¶농촌[도시] ~ the rural[urban] new community movement.

새마을 정신(-精神) *Saemaeul*[New Community] Spirit.

새매 [동] the Asiatic sparrow hawk.

새물 1 (과일·생선 등의) the first product of the season; the first supply (of tomatoes). ¶ ~ 사과 early apples. 2 (옷의) clothes fresh from washing; newly washed clothes.

새벽¹ [날이 밝을 무렵·먼동이 트기 전·여명] dawn; daybreak; the break of day; the peep of day; (미) the crack of dawn. ¶~부터 해거름까지 from dawn till dark // ~에 early in the morning / at dawn[daybreak] / at break of day / before daybreak // ~ 하늘 the sky at dawn / the dawning sky // ~같이 early in the morning / before sunrise.
● **새벽녘** the peep of dawn[day]; the prime. **새벽달** the waning moon[crescent] (at dawn). **새벽일** early-morning chores. **새벽잠** a sound[deep / fast] sleep at dawn. ¶~이 들다 fall fast asleep at dawn.

새벽² [건] fine loamy earth; loam(모래·짚 등을 섞은). ¶에 ~을 바르다 plaster a wall.
● **새벽질** plastering. ¶~을 하다 do plastering / plaster.

새봄 [닥쳐오는 봄] coming spring; the new [fresh] spring; [이른 봄] early spring.

새빨갛다 [짙게 빨갛고 새뜻하다] deep red; crimson(짙은 다홍빛); scarlet(주홍빛). ¶새빨갛게 단 쇠 red-hot iron.
새빨간 거짓말 a downright lie; an outright lie. ¶그것은 ~이었다 It was a perfect fake.

새빨개지다 turn[become] red[crimson]; (상기하여) flush deeply; (부끄러워서) blush scarlet[crimson] (for shame); color deeply. ¶머리끝까지 ~ blush[redden] to the roots of one's hair / 그는 화가 나서 얼굴이 새빨개졌다 He turned red[crimson] with rage. // 나는 술을 조금만 마셔도 얼굴이 새빨개진다 A little drink makes me deeply flushed.

새사람 1 [갱생자] a new man; a reborn [reformed] person. ¶그는 ~이 되었다 He became a new man. 2 [신부] a bride.

새살 granulation tissue; proud flesh. ¶~이 돋다 granulate // 상처가 나을 때 ~이 돋아난다 Wounds granulate in healing.

새살거리다 carry on[behave] flippantly; chatter merrily.

새살궂다 very light and talkative; dreadfully flippant[frivolous].

새살림 a new home.

새살스럽다 flippant; frivolous; shallow. ¶새살스런 여자 a shallow woman.

새삼 [식] dodder; love vine.

새삼스럽다 abrupt; new; fresh. ¶새삼스러운 말 a remark unnecessary to say anew [again] // 새삼스럽게 anew / afresh / again / specially(특히) / formally(형식적으로) / now(이제 와서) // 나는 새삼스럽게 그의 친절에 감동되었다 I was all the more deeply moved by his kindness. / I realized his kindness afresh[anew]. // 나는 새삼스럽게 노여움을 느꼈다 I felt myself getting angry all over again. // 새삼스럽게 말할 것도 없지만 열심히 공부해라 Needless to say, you must study hard. / There's no point in repeating it [saying it over again], but you must study hard. // 새삼스럽게 할 말은 아무것도 없다 I have nothing more[in particular] to say now. // 새삼스럽게 말할 필요도 없이만 울릉도에는 눈이 많이 내린다 It is hardly necessary to say[nothing new to say] that it snows a lot in Ulleungdo. // 늦었는데 새삼스럽게 사과한들 무슨 소용이냐 What is the use of apologizing now when it's too late?

새색시 a bride; a newly married[wedded] woman. ¶~를 얻다 take[get] a wife / get married.

새서방(-書房) 〈속〉 a bridegroom. ⇨신랑

새소리 a birdcall; a note[song] of a bird; a bird's note; a woodnote.

새시 [금속제 창틀] a sash. ¶창문 ~ a window sash // 알루미늄 ~ an aluminium sash.

새싹 [새로 돋은 싹] a sprout; a shoot; [어린 잎·꽃눈] a bud. ¶장미의 ~ a new[young] shoot of a rose // ~이 트다 sprout / put forth leaves[buds] // 장미의 ~이 났다 The roses has begun to put forth new shoots. // 나는 실수하여 ~을 부러뜨렸다 I carelessly broke off a sprout[shoot]. // 뿌린 씨에서 아직 ~이 나지 않았다 The seeds I sowed have not germinated[come up] yet.

새아기 one's new daughter-in-law.

새알 an egg of a sparrow; a bird's egg. ¶~ 꼽재기만 하다 be a mere particle / be small or worthless.
● **새알심**(-心) a small dumpling in red-bean gruel.

새암 =샘¹.

새앙 a ginger. ⇨²생강

새옹지마(塞翁之馬) blessing in disguise. ¶인간 만사 ~ Inscrutable are the ways of heaven[providence]. / It is impossible to know[tell] man's destiny beforehand.

새우 [동] a lobster(큰 새우); a spring lob-

ster(닭새우); a prawn(보리새우); a shrimp(작은 새우). ¶~로 잉어를 낚다 throw a sprat to catch a mackerel[a herring / a whale] / give an egg to gain an ox.
●**새우등** a bent[rounded] back; round[stooped] shoulders; a stoop. ¶~의 노인 an old man bent almost double with age. **새우 잠** ¶~을 자다 sleep[lie] curled up / curl oneself (in bed). **새우젓** tiny salted shrimps; pickled shrimps.
새우다 〔철야하다〕 sit[stay] up all night; sit the night out. ¶이야기로 밤을 ~ talk the night away / talk all (through) the night // 하룻밤을 울며 ~ pass a whole night in tears // 공부하며 밤을 ~ study all night long // 밤을 새워 간호하다 sit up with (an invalid) all night / keep an all night vigil (over) // 밤을 새워 가며 회의하는 것 봤나 have an all-night conference.
새장(-欌) a birdcage; a cage for birds. ¶~에 넣다 cage (a bird) / put (a bird) in a cage // 그녀는 ~에 갇힌 새 같은 비참한 생활을 하고 있었다 She was leading as wretched a life as a caged bird.
새조개 〔동〕 an edible cockle; an egg cockle.
새중간(-中間) right in the middle[midst] (of); the very middle.
새집¹ 〔신축한 집〕 a newly built house; 〔새로 이사 온 집〕 one's new house; 〔새로 맺은 사돈집〕 the house of a new relative by marriage. ¶~ 살림을 시작하다 take up residence in a new house // ~으로 이사하다 move to a new house.
새집² 〔들새를 위한 인공 상자〕 a birdhouse; 〔드물게〕 a bird box; 〔새의 집〕 a bird's nest; 〔참새 집〕 a sparrow's nest.
새참 1 〔일을 하다가 잠시 쉬는 동안〕 a recess (between working hours); a break; (a) rest; a respite; time off; a time-out. 2 〔잠시 쉬는 동안에 먹는 간식〕 a snack eaten between regular meals; between-meals refreshments. ¶~을 먹다 eat (a snack) between meals / have a snack // ~으로 고구마를 먹다 eat sweet potato between meals / eat sweet potato for one's snack.
새총(-銃) 1 〔공기총〕 an air rifle; 〔엽총〕 a fowling piece. 2 〔고무줄 새총〕 (미) a slingshot; (영) a catapult. ¶소년은 ~으로 돌을 쏘아 창문을 맞혔다 The boy hit the window with a stone from his slingshot.
새치 a gray[white] hair in youth. ¶~를 뽑다 pull out a white hair // 그는 ~가 많다 Though young, he has gray streaks of hair.
새치기하다 break into the queue; cut in; 〔영국 구어〕 jump the queue; snatch (another's portion). ¶새치기하지 마시오 In order, please. // 저 여자 새치기하는 것 봤나 Did you see that woman cut in the line?
새치름하다 standoffish. ⇨ 새침하다 ¶새치름해져서 뎨연하게 놀람을 받자 그녀는 갑자기 새치름해졌다 Being chaffed at, she straightened her face suddenly.
새침데기 〔얌전한 체하는 사람〕 a person who pretends innocence; 〔태도가 새침한 사람〕 a prude; a prim-looking person.
새침하다 standoffish; prim; 《서술적》 look prim; assume a prim air. ¶새침한 소녀 a prim girl / 남자 아이가 다가오면 그녀는 새침했다 When the boys came by, she assumed a prim air.

새카맣다 deep-black. ⇨ 까맣다
새콤하다 sourish; tartish; vinegarish.
새큼하다 sourish. ⇨ 시큼하다
새털 〔깃털〕 a feather; a plume; plumage 〔집합적〕; 〔솜털〕 down.
●**새털구름** 〔기상〕 a cirrus. ⇨ 권운
새파랗다 1 〔짙푸르다〕 deep blue (sky); indigo(-blue). ¶새파란 바다 the deep blue sea. 2 〔몹시 질려 있다〕 deadly [ghastly] pale; as white as a sheet. ¶새파랗게 질린 얼굴 a pallid[wan / cadaverous] face // 무서워서 새파랗게 질리다 turn deadly pale with fright / be scared blue[green] // 그녀는 무서워서 [화가 나서] 새파랗다 She turned white with fear[rage]. // 그는 집에 질려 얼굴이 새파래졌다 [새파래져 있었다] He turned pale[was white]. 3 〔썩 젊다〕 young; green. ¶새파란 젊은이 a green youth.
새하얗다 pure-white; snow(y)-white; (as) white as snow; immaculately white. ¶새하얀 셔츠 an immaculate shirt.
새해 the New Year; a new year. ¶~에 at the beginning of the year / 〔정월 초하루에〕 on New Year's Day // ~ 복 많이 받으십시오 I wish you a happy New Year! / Happy New Year! // ~에 찾아뵙겠습니다 I will call on you early in New Year.
●**새해 문안 / 새해 인사** a New Year's greeting. ¶그는 친척들에게 ~을 하러 다녔다 He made New Year calls on his relatives.
새호리기 〔동〕 a hobby.
색 〔자루〕 a sack; 〔피임용 콘돔〕 a condom(▶ 영어의 sack은 석탄·곡물 기타 식료품 등 무거운 물건을 넣는 자루).
색(色) 1 〔색채〕 a color; 〔색조〕 a hue; a tint; a tinge; a tincture; 〔농담〕 a shade; 〔그림물감의〕 a color. ¶~의 다른 셔츠 a shirt of a different color // 짙은[엷은] ~ a deep[light] color // 조화되는 ~ harmonizing colors // ~의 배합 a color scheme // ~이 바랜 washed-out // ~을 칠하다 color / paint // ~같은 스웨터로 이 다른 것이 있습니까 Do you have the same kind of sweaters in other colors? // 이 ~은 세탁을 해도 바래지 않는다 This color will not come off in the wash. / This color will stand the wash.
2 〔같은 부류〕 the same sort.
3 〔색욕·여색〕 lust; carnal desire; sexual passion; sensual pleasure. ¶~을 좋아하다 be amorous / be lustful / be given to lust / be lewd / be licentious / be lecherous / be sensual // ~을 쫓다 dangle after women / go in for amorous adventures // ~에 빠지다 indulge in sensual pleasures.
색(을) 쓰다 〔성교하다〕 have sex[sexual relations]; copulate; 〔교태 부리다〕 sex up; play the coquette.
색각(色覺) the color sense; color vision; color sensation. ¶이 화가는 ~이 예리하다 This painter has a keen sense of color.
색감(色感) 1 〔색에 대한 감각〕 a sense of color 〔영〕 colour. ¶~이 예민하다 have a keen sense of color. 2 〔색에서 받는 느낌〕 the impression of a color.
색골(色骨) a lecherous[lewd] person; a lecher; a satyr.
색광(色狂) a sex-crazed person; a sex maniac; a sex fiend; an erotomaniac(남자); a nymphomaniac(여자).
●**색광증** sex(ual) mania[craze]; erotoma-

nia; (남자의) satyriasis; (여자의) nymphomania.

색깔(色-) a color. ⇨"빛깔

색다르다(色-) extraordinary; unusual; uncommon; out of the way [ordinary]; offbeat; unconventional; (신기한) novel; (기묘한) strange; curious; peculiar; singular (personality); odd; queer. ¶색다른 생각[계획] an original idea[plan] // 색다른 학생 a different type of student / an unconventional student // 색다른 쇼윈도 장식 a peculiar window dressing [display] // 색다른 예술 작품 an unconventional [(구어) offbeat] work of art // 색다른 발상 a novel idea // 색다른 것 something that is out of ordinary // 색다른 것을 좋아하다 be fond of novelty / care for anything new // 그는 색다른 인물이다 He's one of a kind. // 그는 교사로서 He is an unusual sort of teacher. // 무슨 색다른 일은 없습니까 Is there any news? / Is there anything new?

색도(色度) chromaticity; [조명] chroma; color.

색동(色-) (cloth with) stripes of many colors.
● **색동옷** a rainbow-striped garment for children. **색동저고리** a girl's jacket with sleeves of multicolored stripes.

색등(色燈) a colored lantern [light].

색떡(色-) a colored rice-cake.

색마(色魔) a sex-crazed person. ⇨"색광

색맹(色盲) color [(영) colour] blindness. ¶녹~ green-blindness // 적록~ red-green blindness / Daltonism (선천성) // 전(全) ~ total color blindness / achromatopsia / achromatic vision // ~이다 be color-blind.
● **색맹 검사** a color-blindness test.

색상(色相) [색의 3요소의 하나] the hue; the tone of color; a color tone.

색색(호흡하는 소리) with a hissing sound; hissingly. ¶아기가 ~ 숨소리를 내며 잠들어 있었다 The baby was asleep, breathing quietly.

색색거리다 breathe lightly [softly].

색색이(色色-) in [with] various [diverse] colors.

색소(色素) [생] (a) pigment; coloring matter. ¶식용 ~ food colors // 멜라닌 ~ melanin.
● **색소 결핍증** [의] albinism. **색소액** a staining solution. **색소체** a chromatophore; chromatogen; a plastid. **색소 형성** [생] pigmentation.

색소폰 a saxophone; (구어) a sax.
● **색소폰 주자** a saxophonist; a saxophone player.

색 수차(色收差) [물] chromatic aberration; chromatism.

색시 1 [처녀] a maiden; a girl. ¶촌~ a country girl. 2 [접대부] a waitress; a barmaid. 3 [신부] a bride. ⇨"새색시
● **색싯감** a likely [prospective] bride. **색싯집** [처가] one's wife's home [family]; [갈보 집] a brothel.

색실(色-) colored [(영) coloured] thread.

색안경(色眼鏡) 1 [빛깔 있는 안경] (a pair of) colored [(영) coloured] glasses; dark glasses [sunglasses]. ¶~을 건 여자 a woman in dark glasses. 2 [편협한 관찰] unfairly prejudiced view. ¶사물을 ~을 쓰고 보다 see [look at] (a thing) through darkly tinted spectacles / look at things from a biased viewpoint.

색약(色弱) color [(영) colour] amblyopia.

색연필(色鉛筆) a colored [(영) coloured] pencil.

색욕(色慾) lust; sexual desire; sexual [carnal] appetite; a craving for sex. ¶~에 빠지다 indulge in [give oneself over to] carnal desires [pleasures].

색유리(色琉璃) colored [(영) coloured] glass; [스테인드글라스] stained glass.

색인(索引) an index (pl. ~es, -dices) (to a book). ¶자구(字句) ~ an index verborum // 지명 ~ an index locorum // 책에 ~을 붙이다 index a book.
● **색인 카드** an index card.

색정(色情) lust; sexual desire. ⇨"색욕 ¶~이 일어나다 be roused sexually / be seized with sexual desire // ~을 자극하다 excite one's sexual desires.
● **색정광** a sex-crazed person. ⇨"색광 **색정 도착증** erotopathy; sexual perversion.

색정적(色情的) seductive; (구어) sexy; (여자가) alluring. ¶~인 눈길 an amorous look.

색조(色調) a tone [shade] of color [(영) colour]; a hue; a tone; [미] tonality. ¶옷의 ~ the coloring of a dress // 부드러운[강렬한] ~의 방 a room in a soft [garish] color.

색종이(色-) colored [(영) coloured] paper; a square sheet of thick paper (for writing poems, or painting pictures on).

색주가(色酒家) [작부] a whorish barmaid [waitress]; [술집] a shady bar; a barwhorehouse.

색채(色彩) 1 [빛깔] a color; (영) a colour; coloring; coloration; [색조] a hue; a tint. ¶강렬한 ~ loud colors // ~가 풍부하다 be colorful / be full of color // ~가 빈약하다 be colorless. 2 [기미] a color; (영) a colour; coloring; a tinge. ¶지방적 ~ local color // 종교적 ~ a religious tinge // 정치적 ~를 띤 단체 a politically-colored group.
● **색채 감각** the color sense. ⇨"색각 **색채 조절** color control. **색채학** chromatics; chromatology. **색채 효과** a color effect.

색출(索出) ¶부정 공무원의 ~ exposure of corrupt officials. **색출하다** [뒤져서 찾아내다] find (out). ¶색출하기 시작하다 begin to search [look] (for) // 진범(인)을 ~ find [hunt down] the true criminal // 경찰은 범인을 색출해 냈다 The police ferreted out the criminal.

색칠(色漆) 1 [칠] colored lacquer. 2 [칠하기] coloring; painting. **색칠하다** paint; color; apply colored lacquer. ¶지도에 ~ color a map.

색탐(色貪) lust; lewd [lecherous] desire. **색탐하다** lust (for sex); have lecherous desires.

샌님 1 [생원님] a gentleman scholar; a gentleman. 2 [얌전한 사람] a meek person; a milksop; [보수적인 사람] a conformist.

샌드백 a sandbag.

샌드위치 a sandwich. ¶치즈[계란] ~ a cheese [an egg] sandwich // 햄 ~ ham sandwiches.
● **샌드위치맨** a sandwich man. ¶~의 광고판 a sandwich board.

샌드페이퍼 sandpaper. ¶~로 닦다 [문지르다] sandpaper / polish with sandpaper.

샌들 (a pair of) sandals. ¶~을 신은 어린이 a child in sandals.

샐러드 salad. ¶햄 ~ a ham salad // 야채 ~ a

●샐러드드레싱 salad dressing. 샐러드유 / 샐러드 오일 salad oil.

샐러리맨 (*salary man) an office worker; a white-worker; a salaried worker[man].

샐룩 with a twitch. ⇨실룩

샐비어 〔식〕 a scarlet sage; a salvia; (약용의) a sage.

샐쭉하다 distort; be distorted; be displeased. ⇨실쭉하다

샘¹ a spring; a fountain. ¶물이 콸콸 솟는 ~ a gushing[live] spring // 희망의 ~ the spring of hope // ~을 파다 tap a spring / ~이 말랐다 The spring has run dry.

샘² jealousy; (green) envy; the green-eyed monster. ¶그가 성공했다는 소식을 듣고 나는 ~이 났다 The news of his success aroused [(문어) excited] my envy. **샘하다** be[feel] jealous[envious] (of); envy. ¶몹시 ~ be green with jealousy / feel intense jealousy (toward) // 그는 곧잘 샘한다 He is apt to be jealous (of others).

샘구멍 a fountainhead; a headspring; a source.

샘나다 feel jealous (of); feel envy (of / at). ¶샘나서 from [out of] jealousy / through [out of] envy // 샘나는 [부러운] enviable / [사람이 탐을 내는] envious // 나는 그의 인기에 샘났다 I was envious[jealous] of his popularity. / I envied his popularity. // 그의 행운에 난 정말 샘난다 I am really envious of his good luck.

샘물 spring water. ¶~ 줄기 a stream of spring water.

샘솟다 gush[spring] out[forth]; spout; spurt; well up[out / forth]. ¶콸콸 ~ gush out with a rush[in a steady flow].

샘터 1 a fountain place[site]. 2 washing place watered by a spring. ¶~에서 빨래하다 do the laundry at a fountain.

샘플 a sample. ¶~을 하나 보여 주시오 Show me a sample.

샘플링 sampling.

샛- 〔빛깔이 짙고 산뜻함〕 deep; dark; intense. ¶~말갛다 be limpid.

샛강(-江) a by-channel of a river enclosing a low island; a bayou.

샛길 〔큰길에서 갈린 작은 길〕 a branch road; a byroad; a bystreet; a byway; a side road; a by-passage. ¶우리는 ~로 빠져서 숲 속으로 들어갔다 We took a branch road and entered a forest.

샛노랗다 vivid[bright / golden] yellow.

샛문(-門) a side gate[door].

샛바람 〔동풍〕 an east[easterly] wind.

샛밥 →곁두리

샛별 1 〔금성〕 the morning star; venus. ¶초저녁의 ~ the evening star // 새벽의 ~ the morning star. 2 〔장래에 큰 발전을 이룩할 사람〕 a star. ¶오페라의 ~ a star of the operatic world / an opera(tic) star.

샛서방(-書房) a paramour; an adulterer; a secret lover.

생 a ginger. ⇨°생강

생(生) living; subsistence. ⇨°삶

생-(生) 1 〔조리하지 않은〕 raw (fish); uncooked; 〔덜 조리된〕 underdone; half-boiled; rare; 〔날것의〕 unripe; green; 〔가공하지 않은〕 crude; raw; natural; unprocessed; wild. ¶~쌀 uncooked[raw] rice // ~우유 raw milk // ~나무가 그을며 타고 있다 The green wood on the fire is smoldering.

2 〔방송 등이 녹화[녹음]가 아님〕 live. ¶~방송 〔연주〕 a live broadcast[performance] // ~음악 live music // 개회식 상황이 ~방송되었다 The opening ceremony was broadcast live.

3 〔살아 있는〕 live; living; green. ¶~백신 live vaccine / live-virus vaccine // ~가지 a live (tree) branch.

4 〔엉뚱한·공연한〕 unreasonable; irrational; arbitrary; forced. ¶~트집 a false charge [accusation] // ~사람 잡다 inflict injury upon an innocent person.

-생(生) 1 〔생년의〕 born in (a year)[on (a date)]. ¶저는 5월~입니다 I was born in May. // 당신은 몇 년~입니까 In what year were you born? 2 〔식물의〕 living (but one year[more than two years]). ¶다년~ perennial (plant). 3 〔학생〕 a student of .... ¶법학 〔의학〕~ a law[medical] student.

생가(生家) the house where one was born; the house of one's birth; one's parent's [paternal] home.

생가죽(生-) (a) rawhide; (a) green hide; (a) raw pelt; (an) undressed skin.

생가지(生-) a live (tree) branch.

생각 1 〔사고(思考)〕 thinking; 〔사상〕 (a) thought; ideas. ¶진보적인 ~을 가진 사람 a man with progressive ideas / a progressive thinker // 마음속 깊이 간직한 ~ one's intimate thoughts // ~이 좁은 사람 a narrow-minded person // ~이 깊은 deep-thoughted // 그 일에 대해서는 ~을 정리할 때까지 좀 기다려 주십시오 Please give me some time to collect my thoughts on the matter. // 그는 일방적인 ~을 우리에게 강요하려고 했다 He tried to force his own ideas[one-sided judgment] on us. **생각하다** think (of / on / about / that ...); 〔속어〕 have a think (about); consider; give (a) thought to. ¶생각해야 할 일 something to think about // 어떤 일을 ~ think about something // 우리 집 형편으로는 해외여행은 생각할 수 없는 일이다 As for my family, going abroad is unthinkable[out of the question]. // 당신의 말이 옳다고 생각합니다 I think you are right. // 그 일을 생각하면 가슴이 두근거렸다 It was exciting to think of it. / I was restless at the thought of it. // 사제도 그는 자신이 가수라고 생각하고 있다 Even so, he thinks he's a singer. // 졸음이 와서 생각할 수도 없었다 I was too sleepy to think. / 생각해 보겠습니다 I'll think about it.(▶ 완곡하게 거절할 때 등) // 처자를 생각하면 그런 부정한 짓을 할 수 없었다 The thought of his wife and children kept him from doing such a dishonest thing. // 생각한 바를 실행하면 된다 You may act on your belief. // 친구가 늦을 것으로 생각하고 나는 천천히 점심 식사를 했다 Assuming that my friend would be late, I ate a leisurely lunch. // 좀 더 홀가분하게 [진지하게] 생각하라 Take it easy[more seriously]. // 그것은 생각은 나름이다 That depends on how you look at it. // 그는 오랫동안 골똘히 생각하고 있었다 He was lost in thought for a long time. // 너무 심각하게 생각하지는 마라 Don't brood over it. / Don't take it so seriously. // 다시 생각해 보겠다 I'll consider it [think it over] once more. / I'll reconsider it.

2 〔관념·착상〕 an idea; a notion; a conception; a thought; 〔취향〕 a plan; 〔창의〕 initiative. ¶좋은[멋진] ~ a capital[bright / happy

/ good] idea.// 잘못된 ~ a mistaken [wrong] idea.// **~이 떠오르다** (사람이) think of / hit on [upon] / (사물이) occur to one.// 좋은 ~이 떠올랐다 I've just thought of [hit upon] a good idea. / A good idea occurred to me [flashed into my mind].// 무슨 좋은 ~이 없습니까 Can't you think of [Haven't you got] some good idea?// 좋은 ~이 있으면 말해 주시오 Please give me a suggestion. / Suggest a good idea.// 그건 좋은 ~이 아니다 I don't think that's a very good idea.// 그것은 잘못된 ~이다 That is a mistaken idea.// 내 ~에 잘못이 없다면 그는 적어도 60세는 되었을 것이다 If I am not mistaken, he must be (at least) sixty years old.// 사악한 ~을 버려라 Discard your evil thoughts. **생각하다** conceive.

3 〔의견〕 an opinion; a view; 〔신념〕 a belief; one's persuasion; 〔인상〕 an impression; 〔제안〕 a suggestion.¶이 점에서 너와 나는 ~이 다르다 I don't agree with you on this point.// 그들이 사직해야 한다는 것이 그의 ~이었다 It was his opinion [He was of (the) opinion] that they should resign.// 내 ~으로는 당장 하는 것이 좋겠다 In my opinion, we had better begin at once.// 당신의 ~으로는 이것이 진짜입니까 In your opinion, is this genuine?// 나는 어린애였지만 그가 안됐다는 ~이 들었다 Though I was but a child, I felt sorry for him. **생각하다** view (a thing); take a view (of a thing); be of (the) opinion (that). ¶사물을 피상적으로[깊이] ~ have a superficial [deep] view of things.// 당신은 요즈음의 세태를 어떻게 생각합니까 What is your view of present social conditions?// 그 문제는 여러 가지로 생각할 수 있다 The subject may be viewed in different ways.

4 〔의도〕 an intention; a design; a view; an aim; an idea; a purpose; 〔동기〕 a motive. ¶나쁜 ~ an evil design.// 그는 새 사업을 시작할 ~으로 이 땅에 찾아왔다 He came to this area with the intention of [with a view to] starting a new business.// 그의 부친은 그를 목사로 만들 ~이었다 His father intended [meant] him to be a clergyman.// 그것은 그의 ~에 달려 있다 It depends on what he decides [intends] to do.// 무엇을 할 ~인가 What do you intend to do? / (구어) What are you up to?// 나는 그를 만날 ~은 없다 I have no intention of seeing him. **생각하다** intend to (do); mean to (do); think of (doing); plan to (do); contemplate (doing). ¶그는 노부인을 속여 돈을 빼앗으려고 생각했다 He thought of cheating the old woman out of her money.// 나는 상사와 그것을 결말 지으려고 생각하고 있다 I intend [mean] to arrange [settle] it with my boss.// 나는 곧장 집으로 돌아가려고 생각했다 I intended to [thought I would] go home directly.// 다음 달에 런던으로 가려고 생각하고 있다 I am thinking of going to London next month.// 그 녀는 법정에서 진실을 털어놓으려고 생각했다 She made up her mind to tell the truth in court.

5 〔사려·분별〕 discretion; prudence; sense; 〔판단〕 judgment. ¶~이 있는 prudent / discreet / thoughtful.// 내가 정말 ~ 없는 짓을 했구나 How thoughtless [imprudent] I was! // 당신에게 그런 말을 하다니 그는 아주 ~ 없는 사람이군요 It was very indiscreet [inconsiderate] of him to say such a thing to you, wasn't it? (▶ indiscreet는 생각이 얕은, inconsiderate는 인정이 없다는 뜻).// 그녀는 앞뒤 ~도 없이 가출하고 말았다 She ran away from home without giving it much thought.// 당신의 ~은 옳다[옳지 않다] You are right [wrong].// 그의 ~에 맡기자 Let's leave the matter to his discretion. **생각하다** judge; conclude; 〔오인하다〕 take for; mistake for.¶처음에 나는 그를 독일인이라고 생각했다 At first I took [mistook] him for a German.

6 〔고려〕 consideration; account; 〔배려〕 thought; regard; 〔참작〕 allowance. ¶~ 깊은 considerate / thoughtful / …에 대해 ~을 하지 않다 leave (something) out of consideration [account] / take no account of (something).// 부모님 ~을 하니 그런 일은 도저히 할 수 없었다 When I thought of my parents, I found that I simply could not do it.// 거기까지는 ~이 미치지 못했다 I hadn't thought of that. / That did not occur to me. **생각하다** 〔고려하다〕 consider; consult (one's own interests / convenience); take (a matter) into consideration [account]; 〔걱정하다〕 concern oneself about; worry (oneself) about; 〔참작하다〕 make allowance for; 〔간주하다〕 regard (a person as); look (up) on (a person as). ¶그는 늘 고향의 부모를 생각하고 있었다 He was always concerned about his parents at home.// 나는 부모님의 마음을 생각해서 가업에 종사하기로 했다 Considering my parents' feelings, I decided to go into the family business.// 내 건강을 생각해 주어 고맙다 Thank you for your concern about my health.// 나는 더위 따위는 아무렇지도 않게 생각한다 I don't mind the heat.➔그는 믿을 수 있는 친구라고 생각되었다 He was considered [regarded as / looked on as] a reliable friend.// 그가 큰 인물로 생각되었다 He has impressed me as a great man.// 그는 당의 장래의 지도자로 생각되고 있다 He is regarded [looked upon] as a future leader of the party.

7 〔숙고〕 deliberation; consideration; 〔사색〕 (a) thought; 〔심사〕 meditation; 〔반성〕 reconsideration; reflection. ¶(깊은) ~에 잠기다 be lost in thought [meditation] / 그 소식을 듣고 그는 ~에 잠겼다 The news set him thinking.// 그는 잠시 ~에 잠겼다 He was lost in thought for a while.// 나는 어떤 ~에 골몰하고 있었으므로 그가 언제 들어왔는지 알아채지 못했다 As I was lost in thought [preoccupied], I did not notice when he came in.// 나는 책상 앞에 앉아 ~에 잠겼다 I sat at my desk, lost [buried] in thought [reflection]. **생각하다** consider; 〔think 〔ponder〕 over; deliberate [muse / dwell] on; turn (a matter) over (in one's mind); weigh; meditate. ¶그는 앉아서 그 일을 골똘히 생각하고 있었다 He sat meditation on [pondering] it.// 잘 생각해 보고 나서 대답하겠다 I will give you an answer after thinking it over.// 이 문제는 좀 더 생각해 볼 필요가 있다 We have to give this problem more careful consideration.// 하룻밤 자면서 잘 생각해 보겠다 I'll sleep on it.// 나는 이 위기를 어떻게 넘길 것인가 하고 깊이 생각했다 I pondered [I thought hard] hunting for a way to get through the crisis.// 이것은 깊이 생각

해야 할 점이다 This calls for careful consideration. / We've got to think this over carefully.
8 [각오] a resolution; [결심] decision. ¶~을 **정하다** decide (to do) / make up one's mind (to do / to an act). **생각하다** [각오·준비하다] be ready (for / to do); be prepared for; provide against. ¶만일의 경우를 생각해 두어라 You had better be prepared for the worst. // 나는 회사가 도산할 때를 생각해서 새 일자리를 찾고 있다 I am looking for a new job in case our company should go bankrupt. // 그는 장래를 생각해서 돈을 저축하고 있다 He is saving money for the future.
9 [기대] expectation(s); hope; [소망] wish; desire; [그리움] longing. ¶~ 밖의 unexpected / unlooked-for / unforeseen / unanticipated // 그가 도와주리라 ~은 빗나갔다 We were disappointed in our hope that he would help. // 무릇 일이란 ~대로 되지 않는 법이다 Things don't always go as we would wish. **생각하다** [예기하다] expect; hope; [바라다] wish; desire; want. ¶10년만 더 젊었더라면 하고 생각한다 I wish I were ten years younger! // 생각한 대로 되지 않는다고 해서 히스테리를 일으킬 것까지는 없다 You needn't become hysterical just because you can't have your way. // 의장에 선출되리라고는 꿈에도 생각지 못했다 I never thought [dreamed] I would be elected chairman. // 내가 생각한 대로 일이 진행되었다 Things went just as I had expected. // 그의 실각은 생각지 못할 일은 아니었다 His downfall was not completely unforeseen. // 그가 그런 무명 선수에게 지리라고는 생각할 수 없다 It's unthinkable that he will lose to such an unknown player. // 내일 그가 오리라고 생각하지 않는다 I doubt if he will come tomorrow. // 나는 아버지는 이제 오래 사시지 못할 것으로 생각한다 I am afraid my father won't live long. // 만나 뵐 수 있으리라 생각하고 댁으로 찾아갔습니다 I went to your house in (the) hope [in hopes] of finding you.
10 [상상] imagination; supposition; fancy; (a) guess(추측). ¶처음에는 피해가 얼마나 되는지 ~이 미치지 못했다 At first, we had no idea of the extent of the damage. // ~보다는 잘하는군 You do well, considering. // 그녀에게 새 애인이 생겼다고 생각한 것은 나의 지나친 ~이었다 I thought she'd found someone new, but it turned out to be a groundless fear. // 그것은 너의 지나친 ~이다. 그것은 단순한 우연이었다 It was only coincidence! You're making too much of it. // ~만 해도 눈물이 나온다 The thought brings tears into my eyes. **생각하다** [상상하다] imagine; figure; [추측하다] suppose; fancy; (미) guess. ¶여름휴가를 생각하기만 해도 마음이 들뜬다 The mere thought of the summer vacation fills me with joy. // 그녀는 생각했던 만큼 아름답지는 않았다 She was not quite as beautiful as I had imagined. // 그는 자신을 위대한 정치가라고 생각하고 있다 He fancies himself to be a great statesman. // 이런 일이 일어나리라고는 꿈에도 생각하지 못했다 I never dreamed such a thing would happen.
11 [추억·회상] retrospection; recollection; remembrance. ¶어렸을 때의 ~ a childhood memory // 옛 ~에 잠기다 indulge in reminiscence // 그를 전에 본 ~이 난다 I remember seeing him once. // 나중에 ~이 나도록 표를 해 두겠다 I will put a mark to jog my memory in the future. **생각하다** recall; remember; recollect; look back upon (the past); think of; call to mind. ¶우리는 전쟁 희생자를 생각한다 We think of [remember] those who died in (the) war. // 네가 한 짓을 잘 생각해 보아라 Reflect upon [Think about] what you have done. // 잘 생각해 보니 역시 제가 잘못했습니다 On reflection, I must admit I was wrong. // 당시를 생각하니 감개무량하다 Looking back on [upon] those days, I am overwhelmed with emotion. // 3년 전에 죽은 아내를 생각하면 가슴이 메어지는 것만 같다 It wrings my heart to recall my wife who died three years ago. // 생각해 보니 그것은 18살 때 일이었다 I think it was I was eighteen. // 그때를 돌이켜 생각하면 격세지감이 있다 Looking back, it seems as if ages had passed since then.
12 [기분] a feeling. ¶…하고 싶은 ~이 나다 feel inclined (to) // 그를 용서할 ~이 도무지 나지 않는다 I simply cannot bring myself to forgive him. // 지금은 가고 싶은 ~이 없다 I don't feel like going now. / I'm not in the mood to go now. // 휴일은 평일보다 짧은 것 같은 ~이 든다 I feel that a holiday is shorter than a weekday. // 그 남자와는 결혼할 ~이 나지 않는다 I cannot bring myself to marry him. // 어째서 아프리카에 갈 ~이 났으니까 What induced you to go to Africa? **생각하다** feel.
생각건대 in my opinion; to my mind [thinking]; I think that …; it seems to me that …; methinks; meseems. ¶~ 인생이란 꿈과 같은 것이다 When we think of it, life is nothing but a dream.
생각다 못하여 at the end of one's tether; at one's wit's [wits] end. ¶그는 ~ 숙부에게 사실을 털어놓았다 He told his uncle the truth because he was quite at a loss what to do [he was at this wit's end].
생각해 내다 1 [상기하다] recall; call to mind; recollect; remember; be reminded of. ¶그의 이름을 ~ recall his name. **2** [안출하다] devise; work out; (구어) come up with; [풀다] puzzle out; solve. ¶그 방식은 누가 생각해 낸 것인가 Who devised [worked out] that method? // 그는 옛날이야기를 녹음해 둘 것을 생각해 냈다 He thought up the idea of tape recording old stories. // 그는 재미있는 장치를 생각해 내기를 잘 했다 He was good at contriving [thinking up] interesting gadgets. // 참 그럴듯한 평계를 생각해 내는구나 What a plausible excuse you have come up with!
생각나다 (사물이) come to mind [one's recollection]; occur to one [one's mind]; flash on one [one's mind]; strike one; (사람이) think of; remember; recall; call [bring] to mind; recollect; hit upon. ¶생각나게 하다 remind (a person) of (a thing) / suggest (an idea) to (a person) / recall [call] (something) to (a person's) mind / bring (something) to memory / be suggestive of // 그러고 보니 [그 말을 듣고 보니] 생각난다 That reminds me. // 그녀의 이름이 생각나지 않는다 I can't remember [recall] her name. // 갓난아이의 좋은 이름이 생각났다 I thought of a good name for the baby. // 볼일이 생각나서 돌아갑니다 (구어) I've just remembered something I

생강 have to do, so I'll be going now.∥그를 보면 죽은 그의 아버지가 생각난다 He reminds me of his late father. / Every time I see him, I am reminded of his late father.∥그 일이 생각나면 지금도 오싹해진다 Even now I can't think of it without a shudder.∥나는 생각나는 대로 써 내려갔다 I wrote down whatever came into my mind.

생강(生薑) a ginger; [생강의 뿌리] a race[root] of ginger; ginger root.
● 생강차 ginger tea.

생것(生-) raw stuff; uncooked food.
생견(生絹) raw silk.
생경하다(生硬-) crude; raw; immature; unrefined; stiff. ¶그의 문장은 ~ His writing is unpolished[crude]. / His writing lacks style.

생계(生計) a living(▶ 단수형으로만 쓰임); (a) livelihood. ¶~가 어렵다[넉넉하다] be badly[well] off∥간신히 ~를 유지하다 eke out a living / scrape a bare living∥그 액수의 돈으로 ~를 꾸려 갈 수 있습니까 Can you live on that (much)? / Can you make both ends meet on that much?∥그녀는 가정부로 일하며 ~를 유지하고 있다 She earns a living by serving as a domestic help.∥그는 거리에서 물건을 팔아 ~를 이어 가고 있다 He earns his living by selling things on[(미) in] the street.
● 생계비 living expenses; the cost of living.
생계 수단 a means of making a living. ¶그는 ~을 잃었다 He has lost his (means of) livelihood.

생고무(生-) raw[crude] rubber.
생과부(生寡婦) a separated[neglected / divorced] wife; a grass widow.
생과실(生果實) unripe[green] fruits.
생과자(生菓子) (a) cake.
생굴(生-) a raw[fresh] oyster.
생글거리다 smile gently. ⇨ 싱글거리다
생글생글 grinningly. ⇨ 싱글싱글
생금(生金) unrefined gold; native[rude] gold. ¶~덩이 a nugget (of gold).
생긋 ¶~ 웃다 smile sweetly.
생기(生氣) life; vitality; vigor[(영) vigour]; animation; spirit. ¶~ 있는 lively∥~ 없는 lifeless∥~ 있는 안색 a fresh complexion∥~가 넘치는 거리 a bustling street∥~를 잃다 turn[go] pale[white] / lose color∥그는 ~가 넘치는 자이다 He is full of vigor[life].∥그는 ~가 부족하다 He lacks vitality.∥시장은 ~를 되찾았다 The market has come to life[brightened up / became active] again.∥밤이 되면 그는 ~가 난다 When night falls, he comes to life.∥아이들이 떠나고 나니 집 안에서 ~가 없어진 것 같다 Since the children left, life seems to have gone out of the house.

생기다 1 [없던 것이 새로 있게 되다] come into being[existence]; form. ¶새 정당이 생겼다 A new political party was formed[organized / born].∥곧 새 제도가 생길 것이다 A new system will be set up before long.∥이 회사는 생긴 지 50년이 된다 It has been fifty years since this company was founded.∥학교에 새로운 위원회가 생겼다 The school established a new committee.∥정부의 노인 연금 제도가 새로 생겼다 The government's old age pension system came into being.
2 [얻다] obtain; get; come by. ¶직업이 ~ get[find] a job∥돈이 좀 ~ get some money / come into some money.
3 [발생하다] happen; occur; take place; come about[up]; come of[from]; arise (from); break out(전쟁·분쟁이). ¶자본에서 생기는 이자 interest occurring on capital∥겨우 한 건 해결되었다 싶었더니 뒤미처 다른 어려운 문제가 생겼다 Just when the case was at last settled, another difficult problem arose[reared its head].∥급한 일이 생겨 그는 집으로 갔다 Something urgent came up, and he went home.∥뜻밖의 결과가 생겼다 It brought about[had] unexpected results.∥그들의 불화는 왜 생겼습니까 What gave rise to [caused / led to] the trouble between them? ∥폭력은 공포에서 생긴다 Violence is born of fear. / (문어) Fear engenders violence.∥의혹이 생겼다 Doubt(s) arose.∥위궤양이 생긴 것 같다 An ulcer seems to have formed in my stomach. / I seem to have a stomach ulcer.
4 [아기가] be born; have (a baby); (친구가) make (a friend); (애인이) have (a girl friend). ¶그들에게 딸이 생겼다 A girl baby was born to them.∥내년에 아이가 또 하나 생깁니다 I will have another child next year.∥그녀는 애인이 생긴 것 같다 She seems to have found a lover.
5 (모양·얼굴이) look (like); have looks [appearance]. ¶예쁘게 생긴 소녀 a good-looking[an attractive] girl∥못생긴 여자 a plain(-looking)[(미) homely] woman∥잘생긴 젊은이 a handsome youth∥그녀는 잘생겼다 She has good looks.
6 (용기·관습 등이) spring (from); grow; form. ¶한번 생긴 버릇은 고치기 어렵다 Once formed, habits are difficult to change.

생김새 [형상] (a) form; (a) shape; [외관] (an) appearance; [용모] features; looks; a countenance. ¶~가 사내답다 look manly / bear a manly semblance∥그녀는 ~가 그저 그렇다 She has passably good looks.

생나무(生-) [살아 있는 나무] a live tree; [벤 채로 마르지 않은 나무] unseasoned wood [timber]; green wood(갓 베어 낸 땔나무). ¶~를 찍어 넘어뜨리다 cut down a live tree.

생년(生年) the year of one's birth.
● 생년월일 the date of one's birth. ¶~을 쓰다 put down the date of one's birth.

생니(生-) a healthy[good] tooth.
생담배(生-) a cigarette[tobacco] burning of itself.
생도(生徒) ¶사관~ a cadet / (해군의) a midshipman.
생돈(生-) money spent to no purpose. ¶~을 쓰다[없애다] waste[throw away / fritter away] one's money (on).
생동(生動) a lively motion; vividness. **생동하다** move lively; be full of life; be vibrant with life; be vivid[lifelike / graphic / true to life]. ¶봄에는 만물이 생동한다 In spring everything is fresh and vivid.∥이 그림은 생동하고 있다 This picture looks so lifelike.
● 생동감 (the feeling of) movement. ¶~에 찬 그림 a painting full of movement.

생득(生得) ¶~의 (문어) innate / inborn.
● 생득 관념 [철] innate ideas. **생득권** one's birthright.

생때같다(生-) healthy; robust; sound; fine and dandy.
생떼(生-) unreasonable persistence[adher-

ence]; perverse[insistent] asking; an unreasonable[impossible] demand. ¶~를 쓰다 stubbornly persist (in) / stick to (it) doggedly / make an unreasonable demand of (a person).

생략(省略) [뺌] (an) omission; [연] (an) ellipsis (*pl.* ellipsies); [줄임] (an) abbreviation; (an) abridgment. ¶이하 ~ The rest is omitted. **생략하다** [빼다] omit; leave out; [줄이다] abbreviate; abridge; shorten. ¶제5장은 생략하기로 한다 We shall omit Chapter Five.//지면 관계로 그것은 생략해야만 했다 We had to omit it[leave it out] for want of space.//설명은 생략하도록 하겠습니다 Please allow me to leave out the explanation.//우리는 이 항목을 표에서 생략했다 We omitted this item from the list.//상세한 것은 생략하겠습니다 I will omit the details.//이 관계 대명사는 생략할 수 있다 We can leave out this relative pronoun.//격식은 생략합시다 Let's do without[dispense with] formalities [ceremony].//그는 노래의 2절과 3절을 생략하고 노래했다 He skipped[omitted] the second and third stanzas of the song.//주소를 생략하지 말고 써 주십시오 Please write your address in full.//이력서는 생략하지 말고 써 주십시오 Write your personal history in full. ➔¶그 부분은 영화에서 생략되어 있었다 That part was left out in the movie.
● **생략문** an elliptical sentence. **생략법** [문] (an) ellipsis (*pl.* -ses). **생략 부호** an apostrophe(기호 ').

생령(生靈) [생민] people; [영혼] lives; souls.

생리(生理) 1 [생물이 생활하는 원리] physiology. 2 menstruation. ⇨월경(月經) ¶전 지금 ~ 중이에요 I'm having my period now.
● **생리대** a hygienic band; a sanitary napkin [towel / belt]. **생리 작용** a physiological function. **생리통**(-痛) menstrual pain. **생리학** physiology. **생리 휴가** a menstrual leave; a special monthly leave for women.

생리적(生理的) physiological. ¶~인 결함 a physiological defect // ~ 현상 a physiological phenomenon // 동물은 ~으로 불에 대하여 공포감을 갖고 있다 Animals have an instinctive fear of fire.

생매장하다(生埋葬-) bury (a person) alive.
➔¶산사태로 세 사람이 생매장되었다 Three people were buried alive in a landslide.

생맥주(生麥酒) draft[(영) draught] beer; beer on draft[(영) draught]; beer on tap. ¶~를 한 잔 마시다 have a glass of draft[(영) beer].

생면부지(生面不知) a total[perfect] stranger; a man one has never seen before.

생멸(生滅) [불] birth and death; appearance and disappearance.

생명(生命) 1 [목숨] life. ¶~이 없는 것 lifeless things // ~을 (내)걸고 at the risk[hazard] of one's life // ~을 걸다 risk[hazard] one's life / risk one's neck // ~을 걸고 맹세하다 swear on[upon] one's life // ~을 구하다 save a person's life // ~을 위태롭게 하다 (사물이) endanger[imperil] one's life // 그의 ~에는 별 지장이 없다 His life is not in danger. / There is no danger of his life. // 그분은 저의 ~의 은인입니다 I owe him my life. / He is the preserver[savior] of my life. / He saved my life. // 어린아이는 유괴되어 ~이 위태롭다 The child has been kidnapped and his life is in danger.//그들은 조국을 위해 ~을 내던졌다 They threw away[laid down] their lives for their country. / They gave[offered / sacrificed] their lives for their country.//열 사람이 ~을 잃었다 Ten lives were lost.//그의 정치 ~은 끝났다 His political life[career] is finished[at the end].//한국의 작가들은 대체로 작가로서의 ~이 짧다 Korean writers are, as a rule, short-lived as such.//그림에 좀 더 ~감을 불어넣어라 Put more life into your painting.
2 [가장 중요한 점] the life; the soul. ¶그의 소설의 ~은 그 해학성이다 The soul of his novel lies in its humor.//카메라는 렌즈가 ~이다 The lens is what determines the worth of[the most important part of] a camera.
● **생명 과학** life science. **생명력** one's life force; one's will to live. **생명 보험** [경] (영) life assurance; (미) life insurance. ¶간이 ~ post-office life insurance / postal (life) insurance // 보통 ~ ordinary insurance // ~에 들다 insure one's life / have one's life insured [(영) assured] // ~에 들어 있다 have a policy in a life insurance company / one is insured against death / one's life is insured. // 그는 1억 원의 ~에 들어 있다 He carries a hundred million won insurance on his life. **생명선**(-線) [삶과 죽음의 경계선] one's lifeline; (손금의) the line of life; the lifeline. ¶지중해는 ~이라고 일컬어진다 The Mediterranean is said to constitute Britain's lifeline. **생명수**(-水) life-giving[lifesaving / life-restoring] water. **생명수**(-樹) a lifespring; a source of life.

생모(生母) one's own[real / natural] mother.

생목(生-) unbleached cambric.

생목(生-) regurgitated food. ¶~이 오르다 regurgitate / (undigested food) come back.

생목숨(生-) 1 [살아 있는 목숨] life; body and soul; living and breathing. ¶~을 이어가다 barely keep one's life / barely sustain one's living. 2 [억울하거나 공연한 목숨] an innocent[a blame-less] life. ¶~을 앗아 가다 take the life of an innocent person / deprive an innocent person of his life / kill (a person) without provocation.

생몰(生沒) birth and death.
● **생몰년** the years of (one's) birth and death.

생무지(生-) a novice; a green[an untrained] hand; a greenhorn; a neophyte; (미국 속어) a tenderfoot; a rank amateur; an outsider. ¶장사에는 ~올시다 I am a greenhorn in the business.

생물(生物) a living[an animate] thing; a [living] creature; an organism; (집합적) life. ¶숲 속의 ~(체) creatures of the forest // 이 지구 상의 ~ life on this planet // 온갖 ~ many[various] forms of life // ~을 죽이다 destroy life / kill an animal // 달에는 (살고) 있는 흔적이 전혀 없었다 There was no sign of life on the moon.
● **생물계** the biological world; the animate nature. **생물 공학** biotechnology; bioengineering; bionics. **생물 생태학** bioecology. **생물학** biology. **생물학자** a biologist.

생방송(生放送) live broadcasting; live (TV) coverage; a live broadcast; a live telecast; a live program. ¶현장으로부터의 ~ live broadcasting[a live broadcast] from the scene(▶

a live broadcast는 방송 프로그램을 가리킴). 생방송하다 cover[carry] (an event) live (by radio / television); broadcast [televise / channel] (an event) live. ¶야간 경기를 ~ broadcast a night game live // 쇼를 ~ telecast a show live. ➡ ¶개회식의 실황이 생방송 되었다 The opening ceremony was broadcast live. // 이 쇼는 MBC 홀에서 생방송되고 있다 This show is being broadcasted [televised] live from MBC Hall.

생배앓다(生-) be sick with envy; be[feel] jealous (of / over).

생벼락(生-) an unreasonable reproof; an unexpected disaster. ⇨날벼락

생부(生父) one's real[true] father.

생부모(生父母) one's real[true] parents; one's parents by blood.

생불(生佛) a living Buddha; an incarnation of Buddha; a saintly man; a merciful person.

생사(生死) life and [or] death; (안부) safety; (운명) face. ¶~ 불명의 사람들 persons whose fate is unknown / missing persons // ~가 걸린 문제 a matter of life and [or] death / a vital question // 그녀는 그와 ~를 같이하기로 결심했다 She made up her mind to share his fate. / She was resolved to throw [cast] in his lot. // 그는 지금 ~지경을 헤매고 있다 He is now hovering between life and death. / He is now lingering on the brink [verge] of death.

생사(生絲) raw silk. ¶고치에서 ~를 뽑다 reel off raw silk from cocoons.

생사람(生-) 1 [아무 잘못 없는 사람] an innocent person[party]. 2 [관계없는 사람] an unrelated[unconnected] person; an outsider; the third party; a disinterested person. 3 [생때같은 사람] a man of strong health.

생사람(을) 잡다 lay a fault to an innocent person's charge; get the wrong person; bark up the wrong tree. ¶생사람 잠시 마세요 You've got the wrong man.

생산(生産) 1 production. ¶국내 ~ domestic production // 국민 총~ the gross national product(약어 GNP) // 대규모 ~ large-scale production // 대량 ~ mass production / high-volume production // ~의 감소 a fall in production // ~을 늘리다 increase[build up / step up / boost] the production (of) // ~을 줄이다[감축하다] curtail[cut back] production. **생산하다** produce; make; turn out; (기계를 사용하여 대규모로 제조하다) manufacture. ¶오토바이를 ~ manufacture motorcycles // 이 회사에서는 월 2천 대의 자동차를 생산하고 있다 Two thousand cars are produced by this company a month. ➡ ¶이 도시에서는 철강이 생산되고 있다 This town produces steel.
2 (아이의) (child)birth; (a) delivery. **생산하다** give birth to a baby; be delivered of a child.
● **생산 가격** price of production. **생산고** an output; a turnout; an outturn; production; a yield; a crop. **생산 관리** production control. **생산력** productive capacity; producing [manufacturing] power; productivity. ¶한계 ~ marginal productivity. **생산물** a product; (집합적) produce. ¶농업 ~ farm products [produce]. **생산비** the cost of production; production cost. ¶평균[한계] ~ the average [marginal] cost of production // ~를 절감하다 curtail[cut down] the cost of production. **생산 설비** production[productive] facilities; plants and equipment. **생산성** productivity. ¶노동 ~ productivity of labor // 아시아 ~ 기구 Asia Productivity Organization(약어 APO) // ~ 향상 a productivity increase // ~을 높이다 increase[raise] the productivity (of). **생산자** a producer; a maker. **생산재** producer's [producer / production / productive] goods. **생산지** a producing center[district]. ¶사탕수수의 ~ a sugar cane-producing center.

생산적(生産的) productive. ¶~ 노동 [사고] productive labor [[심] thinking].

생살(生-) [성한 살] raw[healthy] flesh; [새 살] proud flesh.

생색(生色) a demonstration of benevolence; patronage; a credit.

생색나다(生色-) get credit; reflect credit [honor] on (oneself); (구어) do (a person) credit. ¶생색나는 선물 an impressive gift // 그 것으로 그는 크게 생색났다 It reflected great credit on him.

생색내다(生色-) take credit to oneself (for); (구어) do oneself proud[credit]; emphasize the favor done to (a person); demonstrate benevolence. ¶이 정도 선물 가지고 생색내는 구먼 You are doing yourself proud by giving this small present, aren't you? // 저 사람은 당신에게 뭣 좀 해 주고는 금방 생색낸다 Whenever he does anything for you, he expects you to be terribly grateful.

생생하다 fresh; lively; vivid; green; lifelike; vivacious; graphic; full of life. ¶생생한 뉴스 hot news // 생생한 기억 a fresh [green] memory[recollection] // 아직도 기억에 생생하게 남아 있는 a memory still fresh in one's mind // 생생한 사건 묘사 a vivid [graphic / lively] description of an incident // 그 사건은 아직도 내 기억에 ~ The remembrance of the event is still present to me. / The incident is still vivid[fresh] in my memory. // 이 기사는 그의 생생한 체험에 근거를 둔 것이다 This article is based on his own firsthand experiences. // 그 엄하셨던 선생님의 얼굴이 ~ I can recall the face of the strict teacher vividly. / I have a vivid [clear] recollection of that strict teacher. **생생히** lively; vividly; sprightly; animatedly; with flesh and blood; true to life. ¶그녀의 편지에는 그 시가의 모습이 ~ 그려져 있다 She depicts street scenes vividly in her letters. / Her letters give a vivid description of the town. // 그는 수필에서 이 위대한 화가를 ~ 그리고 있다 In his essay he gives a vivid description[a graphic account] of this great artist.

생석회(生石灰) quicklime; lime; calcium oxide.

생선(生鮮) fresh[raw] fish; fish (*pl*. ~(es)). ¶~을 굽다 broil fish // ~을 요리[손질]하다 dress fish // 저 요리집에서는 좋은 ~을 쓴다 They use good fish at that restaurant.
● **생선 가게** a fish shop. **생선구이** roast [broiled] fish. **생선묵** fish paste. **생선회** (fresh) slices of raw fish; sliced raw fish; [요리] a dish of sliced raw fish (and vegetables seasoned in vinegar). ¶~를 치다 slice raw fish / prepare sliced raw fish.

생성(生成) creation; formation; generation; [철] becoming. ¶화산의 ~ the formation of a

volcano. **생성하다**〈생겨나다〉be created; be formed; come into being [existence]; become; 〔생기게 하다〕create; form; generate; make.
● **생성 문법**〔언〕generative grammar. **생성물**〔화〕a product.

생소하다(生疏-) 1〔낯설다〕unfamiliar (with); be a stranger (to); new (to/at); unaccustomed (to); unacquainted [unconversant] (with); uninformed [ignorant] (of). ¶생소한 사람 a stranger / an unacquainted person // 그곳 지리에 ~ be unfamiliar with [be new to / be raw to] the locality [neighborhood] // 이 고장은 아주 생소한 곳이다 I am a complete [an utter] stranger in this town. / I'm quite new to this town. // 시골 생활은 그녀에게 ~ She is unaccustomed to country life. 2〔익숙하지 못하여 서투르다〕inexperienced; inexpert; unskillful; unpracticed; unaccustomed.

생수(生水) spring water; unboiled water.

생시(生時) 1〔난 시간〕the hour [time] of one's birth; 〔생존시〕one's lifetime. 2〔깨어 있을 때〕one's waking hours; 〔현실〕reality. ¶그것이 꿈이냐 ~냐, 아니면 환상이냐 Is it a dream, reality, or a vision! // 꿈에나 ~에나 그는 그 여자를 잊을 수 없었다 Awake or asleep he could never get her image out of his mind.

생식(生殖) reproduction; procreation; generation. 유성[무성] ~ sexual [asexual] reproduction. **생식하다** reproduce; procreate; generate.
● **생식기**(-期) a period of reproduction; a reproductive period. **생식기**(-器) the organs of generation [reproduction]; the genital [reproductive / generative / sexual] organs; genitals; genitalia. **생식 기능** the generative [reproductive] function. **생식력** reproductive [procreative / generative] power; (남성의) virility; (여성의) fecundity. **생식 불능**〔의〕impotence. **생식샘** a genital [sex / sexual] gland; a gonad. **생식 세포** a reproductive [generative / germ] cell.

생식하다(生食-) eat raw; eat uncooked food; live on raw grains and vegetables.

생신(生辰) one's birthday. ⇨생일

생쌀(生-) uncooked [raw] rice.

생애(生涯) a life; one's lifetime; a career. ¶화려한〔brilliant〕career // 교육자로서의 ~ a career in an educator // 의사로서 ~를 보내다 follow a career as a doctor // 암 연구에 ~를 바치다 devote one's life to cancer research.

생약(生藥) a herb medicine; a crude drug; a natural medicine.

생억지(生-) irrational insistence; perversity; arbitrariness; stubbornness. ¶~를 쓰다 demand one's own way exorbitantly [stubbornly] / stick to one's unreasonable insistence / insist stubbornly on unreasonable things / make an unreasonable demand (of a person).

생업(生業) an occupation; a profession; a calling; a business; a trade; a vocation. ¶농사를 ~으로 삼다 make a living by farming / be a farmer by trade / make a livelihood out of farming [as a farmer].

생우유(生牛乳) raw milk.

생울타리(生-) →산울타리

생원(生員)(옛날의) a person who passed the minor civil examination; (존칭) mister(약어 Mr.); esquire(약어 Esq.)

생육(生育) birth and breeding; 〔발육〕growth; development. **생육하다**〔키우다〕grow; raise; 〔자라다〕grow (up); be born and bred [brought up].
● **생육기**〔식〕a growing [vegetative] period.

생으로(生-) 1〔날로〕raw; fresh; uncooked. ¶생선을 ~ 먹다 eat fish raw [fresh] // 당근을 ~ 먹다 eat a carrot uncooked. 2〔무리하게〕by force; forcibly; compulsorily; willy-nilly; against one's will; 〔부당하게〕unreasonably; irrationally; unjustly; causelessly; without any cause [reason]; arbitrarily; wrongfully. ¶~ 사람을 치다 hit a person no provocation / knock a person without any reason [cause].

생이별(生離別) a lifelong separation [parting]. **생이별하다** part (from a person) never to meet again; part (from a person) for life [forever]. ¶그 부부는 전쟁으로 생이별했다 The couple were separated by the war.

생인손 a whitlow [felon] in a finger; (a) paronychia.

생일(生日) one's birthday; one's natal day. ¶~을 축하하다 celebrate (a person's) birthday // 50회의 ~을 맞이하다 mark [attain] one's 50th birthday // ~을 축하합니다 Happy birthday to you! / I wish you many happy returns of the day.
● **생일 선물** a birthday gift [present]. **생일잔치** (give) a birthday party [feast].

생자(生者) living things; animate nature [beings]; (사람) a living person; (집합적) the living.

생자필멸 All living things must [are bound to] die.; All that lives must die.

생장(生長) growth. ¶~을 돕다 foster [help] (the) growth.

생전(生前) 1〔살아 있는 동안〕one's lifetime. ¶그가 ~에 이룩한 업적 his achievements reached before his death [while alive / in life / during [in] his lifetime // ~의 공로를 치하하여 in recognition of the services done [rendered] by the departed in his lifetime // ~에) 처음으로 for the first time in one's life // 한국에는 이번이 ~ 처음이다 This is my first visit to Korea. // 그는 ~에 불교 신자였다 He was a Buddhist in his life. // ~에 그가 애독하던 책 몇 권을 관 속에 함께 넣었다 Several books that he had loved while alive were put into his coffin. // ~에는 그의 공로가 인정되지 않았다 His services were unrecognized during his lifetime.
2〔아무리 애써 보아도〕for all one's efforts; by no means; on no account; in no way. ¶~ 해 봐라 되는가 However hard you may try, you will not be able to do it. // ~ 내가 그 집을 사나 봐라 I wouldn't buy that house on any account.
3〔전혀〕entirely; wholly; quite; completely; totally; altogether; never. ¶~ 모르는 사람 a total [complete] stranger // 나는 거기에는 ~가 본 적이 없다 I have never been there.

생존(生存) existence; being; life; subsistence; 〔살아남음〕survival. 적자~ the survival of the fittest. **생존하다** exist; live; 〔살아남다〕survive. ¶생존해 있는 전우 one's fellows in arms (who are) alive // 생존해 있다 be alive

생죽음 [living] / be in existence // 양친께서는 생존해 계십니까 Are your parents alive?
●생존 경쟁 the struggle for existence. 생존권 the right to live. 생존자 a survivor. ¶난선의 ~들 the survivors of [from] a shipwreck // 그 사고에서 ~는 한 사람도 없었다 No one survived the accident.

생죽음(生-) death by violence; a violent [an unnatural / an untimely] death. 생죽음하다 die [meet] a violent [an unnatural / an accidental] death; die by violence.

생쥐 [동] a (house) mouse (*pl.* mice). ¶물에 빠진 ~처럼 되다 be [get] wet [drenched / soaked] to the skin / get [be] wet through / be dripping wet / be like [as wet as] a drowned mouse.
생쥐 볼가심할 것도 없다 (속담) haven't a crumb; be as poor as a church mouse; be in dire poverty.

생지옥(生地獄) a hell on earth.
생질(甥姪) a nephew; one's sister's son.
생질녀(甥姪女) a niece; one's sister's daughter.
생질부(甥姪婦) one's sister's daughter-in-law; the wife of one's nephew.

생짜(生-) something raw [fresh]; uncooked food; unripe [green] fruit; raw fish [meat, etc.]; undried [unseasoned / green] timber [firewood, etc.].

생채(生菜) a green vegetable dish, a vegetable salad; a salad. ¶무~ a radish salad.

생채기 a scratch. ¶남의 얼굴에 ~를 내다 scratch a person's face // 다리에 ~가 나다 get [receive] a scratch on the leg.

생철(-鐵) tinned iron. ⇨양철(洋鐵)
생체(生體) a living body; an organism.
●생체 공학 bionics; bioengineering. 생체 실험(perform) an experiment on a living creature. 생체 해부 vivisection.

생태(生態) [생] [생물의 생활 상태] the habits of living things; ecology. ¶곰팡이의 ~ the ecology of molds // 원숭이의 ~ the ecology of monkey.
●생태계 an ecosystem. 생태 변화 ecological adaptation. 생태학 ecology; biology; bionomics; ethology. ¶각개 ~ autecology // 군집 ~ synecology // 식물 ~ ecological botany.

생트집(生-) faultfinding; a false accusation [charge]. ¶그는 걸핏하면 ~을 잡는다 He is ready to find fault with others. 생트집잡다 find [pick] fault (with); make a false charge [accusation] (a person); accuse (a person) falsely; (구어) crab.

생판(生-) 1 [전혀 모름] utter [complete] ignorance. ¶그녀는 집안 살림에 대해서는 ~이다 She is completely ignorant of housekeeping. 2 [아주 (생소하게)] wholly [totally / utterly / entirely / quite / completely] {ignorant of); [터무니없이 (무리하게)] groundlessly; unreasonably; unfoundedly; unjustly; forcibly. ¶~ 모르는 사람 a perfect [a total / an utter] stranger (to) // 그들은 성격이 ~ 다르다 They are quite [entirely] different from each other in character.

생포(生捕) capturing [catching] alive. 생포하다 catch [take / capture] (an animal) alive; take (a person) captive [prisoner]. ¶곰을 ~ catch [capture] a bear alive.

생피(生-) blood just shed [let]; blood of a living man [animal]; vital blood; lifeblood.

생핀잔(生-) an arbitrary rebuke; undeserved reproaches. ¶~을 주다 rebuke [reprove] (a person) without any cause [reason].

생화(生花) a natural flower.
생화학(生化學) biochemistry; chemicobiology.
●생화학자 a biochemist.

생환(生還) 1 [살아서 돌아옴] returning alive. 생환하다 come back alive [safe]; return alive. 2 [야구] reaching the home plate. 생환하다 cross [reach] the home plate; score home. →¶(타자가 주자를) 생환시키다 drive [bring] (the runner) home / score (the runner) // 그는 2루타로 두 주자를 생환시켰다 He drove [knocked / brought] in two runs with a double. / He brought home two runners with a double.
●생환자 a survivor.

생활(生活) [살아 나감] life; existence; [생계] livelihood; living; subsistence. ¶도시 ~ city [urban] life // 문화 ~ a cultural [cultured / modern] life // 전원 ~ rural [country] life / living in the country // 사회 ~ social life // 일상 [결혼 / 독신] ~ everyday [married / single] life // 최저 ~ a minimum standard of living [life] // 원시 ~ a primitive (form of) life / primeval life // 이중 ~ a dual [double] life // 군대 ~ army [military] life // 은둔 ~을 하다 live one's life in seclusion // 분수에 맞는 ~을 하다 live within one's means / cut one's means / cut one's coat according to one's cloth // 분수에 넘치는 ~을 하다 live above [beyond] one's means // 방탕한 ~을 하다 live fast / live it up // ~이 어렵다 find it difficult to make both ends meet [to keep body and soul together] / be unable to make a living / be badly off / be in needy circumstances // ~이 넉넉하다 be well [comfortably] off / make a good living / be in easy circumstances // ~을 윤택하게 하다 enrich one's life. 생활하다 live; exist; [생계를 세우다] make a living; subsist. ¶월급으로 ~ live on one's salary // 그 노부인은 바느질품으로 생활하고 있다 The old lady lives by taking in [doing] sewing.
●생활고 hardships of life. 생활공간 life space. 생활권(-圈) a zone of life. 생활력 vitality; vital energies; one's capacity for living [life]; one's earning power. ¶~이 강하다 be full of vitality / have high earning power // 그는 ~이 없다 He doesn't have the ability to earn much of a living. / He is unable to earn his own living. 생활 보호 livelihood protection [assistance]; [빈민 구제] relief of the poor (and the needy). ¶~ 세대 a household receiving welfare benefits / a family on welfare // a welfare family // 정부의 ~를 받다 (미) be on welfare / (미) be on social security (▶ (미)에서 social security 는 퇴직자와 그 배우자에 대한 사회 보장을 가리킴) / (실업으로) receive unemployment insurance [영] benefit] / (구어) be on the dole. 생활비 living expenses; cost of living. ¶서울은 ~가 많이 든다 Seoul is an expensive place to live in. // 시골은 도시보다 ~가 덜 든다 Living in the country is less expensive [costs less] than in the city. 생활수준 a standard of living; a level of life; a living standard. ¶~의 향상 [저하] a rise [decline] in the standard [scale] of living // ~이 높다 [낮다] have a high [low] standard of living

[life] // ~을 높이다 [낮추다] raise [lower] the standard of living. 생활양식 a mode [manner] of living; a way of life; a life-style; (라) a modus vivendi (pl. modi vivendi). ~을 바꾸다 change one's mode [style] of living. 생활 통지표 a report card [book]; (영) a school-report. 생활필수품 the necessaries [necessities] of life; essentials [essential goods] of life; daily [living] necessaries. 생활 환경 one's living environment.

생후(生後) after [since] one's birth. ¶~ 1주일 만에 죽다 die a week after its birth // 그 아기는 ~ 2개월 만에 처음으로 웃었다 The baby first smiled at two months after birth. // 그녀에게는 ~ 6개월 된 아기가 있다 She has a six-month-old baby.

생흙(生-) fresh soil.
샤머니즘 shamanism.
샤쓰 a shirt. ⇨°셔츠
샤워 a shower (bath). ¶~를 하다 have [take] a shower (bath) / shower.
샤프 1 a propelling pencil. ⇨°샤프펜슬(⇨)샤프 2 [제] a sharp. ⇨°올림표
●**샤프펜슬**(°sharp pencil) a mechanical [an automatic / (영) a propelling] pencil.
샤프하다 [날카롭다] sharp; shrewd. ¶머리가 샤프한 사람 a sharp [shrewd] person.
샴페인 champagne; (영국 구어) fizz. ¶~으로 건배하다 drink champagne in celebration [honor] (of) // 그는 ~의 마개를 펑 하고 땄다 He opened the champagne bottle with a pop. / He popped open the champagne bottle.
●**샴페인 글라스** a champagne glass.
샴푸 (a) shampoo. ¶~로 (머리를) 감다 shampoo (one's hair) / have a shampoo.
샷 1 [제] a shot. 2 →숏
샹들리에 a chandelier; a pendant; (전등의) [an electric] chandelier; an electrolier.
샹송 (프) a chanson. ¶~ 가수 a chanteur(남자) / a chanteuse(여자) / (특히 카바레에 출연하는) a chansonnier(남자) / a chansonniere(여자).
섀미 [염소 등의 무두질한 가죽] chamois (leather); shammy, shamoy.
서[1] [음] a reed.
서[2] three. ¶~ 말 three mal.
서[3] at; from. ⇨°에서1·2 ¶그는 부산~ 왔다 He is from Busan.
-서 너무 지쳐~ 공부할 수가 없군요 I am too tired to study. // 숙제를 다 하고~ 잠자리에 들었다 After having done my homework, I went to bed.
서(西) the west. ⇨°서쪽
서(序) [서문] a foreword; a preface.
서(署) an office; a station; [경찰서] a police station.
서가(書架) a bookshelf (pl. -shelves); (도서관의) a bookstack; the stacks. ¶~에 책을 나란히 꽂다 arrange books on a bookshelf.
서간(書簡) a letter; a communication. ⇨°편지
●**서간문** letter writing. ⇨°서한문(⇨)서한) **서간체** (write in) an epistolary style. ¶~ 소설 an epistolary novel.
서거(逝去) death; decease. ⇨¹사거(死去)
서걱거리다 crunch; crisp. ⇨°사각거리다
서경(西經) (the) west longitude. ¶~ 25도 Long. 25° west(▶ longitude twenty-five degrees west라 읽음).
서고(書庫) a library; (도서관의) a stack room.

서곡(序曲) [음] a prelude; an overture; (특히 가극의) a prologue. ¶~을 연주하다 play an overture [a prologue] / prelude.
서관(書館) a bookseller's. ⇨°서점
서광(曙光) the first streak of daylight; (the first light of) dawn. ¶문명의 ~ the dawn of civilization // 사태 해결의 ~ the first ray of hope for the solution of the matter // 희망의 ~이 나타났다 A ray of hope appeared. // 평화의 ~은 아직 보이지 않는다 There is as yet no prospect of the return of peace.
서구(西歐) [서양] Europe; the West; the Occident; [서구라파] West(ern) Europe.
●**서구 문명** Western civilization [culture]. **서구화** Europeanization; Westernization; Occidentalization.
서글서글하다 [너그럽다] generous; liberal; magnanimous; open-minded; broad-[large-] minded; [부드럽다] soft; tender; gentle; suave; [상냥하다] amiable; affable; sociable. ¶서글서글한 눈 gentle eyes / bright [clear] eyes.
서글프다 sad; sorrowful; plaintive; melancholy; lonesome; lonely; forlorn; [언짢다] cheerless; dreary; inconsolable. ¶서글픈 노래 a touching [plaintive] song // 서글프게 말하다 tell [talk] in a lonesome [plaintive] manner // 서글퍼지다 feel somewhat [little / rather] sad // 어쩐지 ~ I am so sad, I know not why.
서기(西紀) the year of grace [Christ / our Lord]; the dominical year; the Christian Era; Anno Domini(약어 A.D.). ¶~ 1998년 (the year) 1998 A.D. // ~ 2002년에 in A.D. 2002 / in the year of our Lord 2002 / (미) in 2002 A.D.
서기(書記) 1 (관직) a clerk; a secretary. ¶법원 ~ a clerk of a law court. 2 (기록하는) a copyist; a scribe.
●**서기관** a fourth grade official; a section-chief-grade official; a secretary. ¶일등 ~ a first secretary. **서기장** a chief secretary; (정당의) a secretary-general (pl. secretaries-general).
서기(瑞氣) an auspicious sign; a good omen.
서까래 [건] a (common) rafter.
서남(西南) the southwest. ¶~의 southwestern / southwesterly // ~에 in the southwest (of) (서남부) / to the southwest (of) (서남방) / on the southwest (of) (서남쪽) // ~으로 southwestward.
●**서남풍** a southwester; a southwesterly wind. **서남향** facing southwest; (having) a southwest aspect.
서낭당(-堂) a seonangdang; the shrine for a tutelary deity.
서낭신(-神) a tutelary deity; a local deity [god]; (라) a genius loci.
서너 three or four; a few; several. ¶백묵 ~ 개 a few pieces of chalk // ~ 차례 three or four times / several times.
서넛 three or four; a few; several.
서녘(西-) the west; the western direction.
서늘하다 1 [선선하다] cool; refreshing. ¶서늘한 날 [바람] a cool day [breeze] // 서늘한 나무그늘에서 in the cool shade of a tree // 서늘해지다 get [become] cool // 여기는 서늘해서 기분 좋다 It is pleasantly cool here. // 서늘한 바람이 불어온다 A refreshing breeze has sprang up. // 서늘한 곳에 두시오 (포장 표기)

서다

"Keep cool." **2** (마음이) (서술적) be [feel] chilled; feel a chill; [오싹해지다] shudder (at); be horrified; be frightened; have a thrill of horror. ¶놀라서 가슴이 서늘했다 I was chilled with fright.

서다 **1** (사람이) stand; take a stand (at). ¶똑바로 ~ stand erect∥줄을 ~ form a line [row / file] / line up∥일렬로 ~ stand in a line / (차례를 기다리며) queue [line] up∥줄지어 (늘이)~ stand in a row / line (a street) ∥서 있다 be standing / (착석에 대하여) be on one's feet / be standing up∥종일 서 있다 keep standing all day long∥연극을 서서 보다 see a play standing∥그녀는 창 옆에 서 있었다 She was standing beside the window. ∥나는 버스 안이 혼잡해서 죽 서 있었다 The bus was so crowded that I had to stand [keep standing] all the way. ∥그의 옆에 서 주시오 Stand next to him. / Stand by his side. / Stand side by side with him.
2 (물건이) stand erect; (높은 것이) rise; tower; soar. ¶게시판이 서 있다 There is a bulletin board put up there. ∥그 소나무는 여러 개의 버팀목에 간신히 서 있다 The pine is barely kept from falling by a number of supports. ∥도시의 고층 건물들은 북적대는 사람들 위에 우뚝 서 있다 The city's skyscrapers tower above its bustling humanity.
3 [(사람이) 일어서다] stand up; rise; get on [rise to] one's feet; draw oneself up. ¶자리에서 (일어)서다 rise from one's seat∥서! Stand up! / Up with you! / Get to your feet! / On your feet!
4 [정지하다] stop; halt; come to a stop [stand / halt]; make a stop [halt]; roll to a stop (차륜); draw [pull] up (말 차 등이); (배가) fetch up; heave to; (동력이) run down. ¶시계가 ~ a watch stops [runs down]∥팽이가 ~ a top sleeps∥딱 ~ stop dead / come to a standstill [dead stop / full stop]∥갑자기 ~ stop short [dead / suddenly] / make [come to] a sudden stop [halt] ∥서 있다 be at a stop / be at a standstill / stand still∥(기차 등이 도중의 역 등에) 서지 않고 가다 run without stopping [a stop] / run past (a stop) ∥이 기차는 수원에 선다 This train will stop at Suwon.∥손목시계가 섰다 My watch has run down. ∥서! (지르는 소리) Stop! / Hold on! / Pull up! / [구령] Halt!
5 (건물이) stand; [건립되다] be built; be erected; be set up; rise; go up; [설립되다] be established; be founded. ¶(건물이) 설 곳 [부지] the site (for) / (고인이) 그의 동상이 섰다 A bronze statue was erected [set up] to his memory. ∥새 정부[회사]가 섰다 A new government [company] was established. ∥우리집 주변에 주택들이 자꾸 (들어)선다 Houses are springing up all over my neighborhood.
6 […의 위치에 서다] stand. ¶증인으로 ~ stand [be] witness / be on [take] the witness stand∥보증 ~ stand security (for) / stand surety [guarantee] (for) / (give) guarantee∥중매를 ~ arrange a marriage (between) / act [serve] as middleman [go-between] (for) ∥들러리를 ~ attend the bride [bridegroom] ∥보초를 ~ stand [go on] sentry∥교단에 ~ stand on the platform / teach a class / be a teacher∥우위에 ~ stand [be] at advantage (over) / hold priority (to) / gain predominance (over)∥인간 평등의 입장에 ~ take a stand for the equality∥교단에 선 지 10년이 된다 I have been teaching for ten years.
7 (날이) be sharpened; be edged; (핏발이) become bloodshot. ¶핏발이 선 눈 bloodshot eyes∥날이 ~ have a keen [sharp] edge∥(눈 등에) 핏발이 ~ be bloodshot∥그의 오른쪽 관자놀이에 핏줄이 섰다 Veins stood out at his right temple.
8 (조리 등이) hold good; hold water; be made good; (이유가) pass; be admissible [justifiable / excusable]; (계획 등이) be formed; be laid; be established; be worked out. ¶조리가 ~ stand to reason / be reasonable∥조리가 서지 않는 말을 하다 talk incoherently / make disjointed remarks∥그것은 전혀 조리가 서지 않는다 That's against all reason.∥외교 정책이 새로 섰다 A new foreign policy has been formulated [worked out].
9 (위신·체면 등이) save (one's face [honor]). ¶그렇게 되면 내 체면이 선다 That will save my face [honor]. ∥그렇게 되면 내 체면이 서지 않는다 That will put me out of countenance. ∥당신의 체면이 설 수 있도록 이번에는 그 조건을 수락하겠습니다 We will accept the terms this time to save your face.
10 (질서가) be orderly; be in good order; (명령이) be obeyed; be followed; be carried out. ¶질서가 서 있다 be orderly / be in good [perfect] order∥명령이 섰다 Orders were thoroughly obeyed [followed / carried out]. / Orders had [carried] authority.∥군대에서는 규율이 엄격히 서 있다 Discipline is strictly enforced in the army.∥규율이 서 있지 않다 Discipline is lax [loose / slack].
11 (결심이). ¶결심이 ~ be determined / be resolved / make up one's mind / make a resolve [resolution] / decide (to do) ∥결심이 서 있지 않다 be hesitating / be in two minds (about / as to / whether) ∥나는 좀처럼 결심이 서지 않는다 I'm having a hard time making [I find it difficult to make] up my mind.
12 (장이) open; be opened [held]. ¶장이 서는 날 [마을] a market day [village] ∥여기서 매일 아침 장이 선다 A morning fair is held here every day.∥오늘은 장이 서는 날이다 This is the day for the fair. / It is market day today.
13 (아이가) conceive; become pregnant. ¶아이가 선 지 4개월이다 be four months gone with child∥그녀에게 첫아이가 섰다 She was pregnant with her first child.
14 (무지개가) (a rainbow) span [hang in] the sky. ¶넓은 들판에 무지개가 섰다 A rainbow stood bestriding the wide field.

서당(書堂) a *seodang*; a village school [schoolhouse]; a private school for the study of Chinese classics.
서당 개 삼 년에 풍월을 한다(속담) A saint's maid quotes Latin.; The sparrows near a school sing the primer.

서도(西道) the northwestern districts [provinces] of Korea.

서도(書道) calligraphy; penmanship.

서두(序頭) the beginning; the inception; the opening (sentence); (연극 등의) a prolog(ue); a prolusion; (말 등의) a preliminary statement. ¶이야기의 ~ the opening sentence [paragraph] of a story∥~를 떼다 make introductory [prefatory] remarks∥그는 ~에

서두 농담을 한 차례 하고 나서 연설을 시작했다 He prefaced his speech with a joke. // 그는 이야기의 ~에서 셰익스피어를 인용했다 He quoted from Shakespeare at the beginning of his talk[lecture]. / He opened his talk [lecture] by quoting from Shakespeare. // 그는 ~의 인사에서 청중의 반감을 샀다 His opening remarks[words of greeting] antagonized the audience.

서두(書頭) 〔序論〕 an introduction (to a book); an introductory part (of a book).

서두르다 〔빨리 하다〕 hasten; hurry (up); nip; make haste; (미) make time; (구어) step on it; (미국 속어) get a move on; 〔빨리 걷다〕 walk fast[quickly]. ¶서둘러서 hurriedly / in haste[a hurry] // 서두른 나머지 in one's hurry // 서두르고 있다 be in haste[a hurry] / be pressed for time // 몹시 서두르고 있다 be in a great[big / deadly] hurry / be in a big rush // 될 수 있는 대로 ~ make the best of one's way / hurry as much as one can / make as much haste as possible // 일을 ~ speed (up) one's business / rush one's job / make haste with one's work // 그는 몹시 서두르고 있었다 He was in a great hurry. // 나는 서둘러 역으로 갔다 I hurried[rushed] to the station. // 나는 서둘러 식사를 했다 I rushed my meal. // 나는 몹시 서둘러 그것을 하고 있는 중이다 I'm doing it in a great hurry[as quickly as I can]. / I'm hurrying it. // 그는 현장으로 서둘러 갔다 He hastened [hurried] to the scene. // 환자는 서둘러 병원으로 옮겨졌다 The patient was rushed to the hospital. // 상사의 기분이 안 좋았기 때문에 나는 서둘러 물러났다 I beat a hasty retreat because the boss was in a bad mood. // 서둘러라 Hurry up! / Make haste! / Be quick! / (속어) Jump to it! / Get a move on! // 일을 서둘러 Speed up your work. // 서둘러 결론을 내리지 마라 Don't jump to conclusions. // 왜 그렇게 서두르냐 Why are you in such a hurry? / What's the rush[hurry]? / Why all this haste? // 그렇게 서두르지 마라 Don't be in such a hurry. / Don't be so impatient. // 서두를 필요 없다 There's no hurry. // 서두를 것 없다. 시간은 많으니까 You don't need to hurry. We have plenty of time. // 서두르면 서두를수록 더디다 More haste, less speed. // 나는 일을 서둘러서 해야 했다 I was made to hurry the work. // 우리는 늦지 않도록 서둘렀다 We hurried so as not to be late. // 늦지 않으려면 서둘러서 가야 한다 If you don't want to be late, you had better hasten there at once. // 서두르지 않으면 기차를 놓칠 것이다 Hurry up, or you will miss the train. // 급히 서두르는 바람에 지갑을 집에 놓고 왔다 In my hurry I left home without my wallet. // 마감날은 모레니까 너무 서두르지 마라 Take it easy[Don't panic] — the deadline isn't until the day after tomorrow. // 너무 서두르면 일을 그르친다 Haste makes waste.

서랍 a drawer. ¶위에서 두 번째 ~ the second drawer from the top // ~에 가득한 편지 a drawerful of letters // ~ 깊숙이 in the back of a drawer // ~을 열다〔닫다〕 open[shut] a drawer // ~을 빼다 pull[draw] out a drawer // 나는 책상 ~에 일기장을 넣어 둔다 I keep my diary in a drawer in my desk.

서러움 sadness; sorrow. ⇨*설움

서러워하다 grieve (at the news / over a friend's death); be grieved (at / over); be sad (at); feel sad (about); be sorrowful; feel sorrow (for); have a heavy[broken] heart; 〔통탄하다〕 deplore; lament; mourn (for / over); regret. ¶서러워하여 in sorrow / sorrowfully // 어머니의 죽음을 ~ mourn[lament] one's mother's death / grieve[sorrow] over one's mother's death // 남의 불행을 ~ feel sorry for another's misfortune // 지금은 그저 서러워하고만 있을 때가 아니다 This is no time to give way simply to sorrow.

서럽다 sad; sorrowful; mournful; doleful; plaintive; lamentable; deplorable; grievous. ¶서러운 표정 a sad look[countenance / face] // 서러운 추억 a sad memory // 서러운 나머지 in one's sorrow[grief] // 그 말을 들으니 ~ His remarks made me sad. // 나의 일생은 서러운 일뿐이었다 My life has been a series of sorrows.

서력(西曆) the year of grace[christ / our Lord]. ⇨*서기(西紀)

서로 mutually; reciprocally; with each other(주로 두 사람); with one another(주로 세 사람 이상). ¶~의 mutual / reciprocal / each other's / one another's // ~의 이익[이해] mutual interest[understanding] // ~의 이익을 도모하다 consult mutual interests // ~ 돕다[믿다] help[trust] each other [one another] // ~ 사랑하다 love each other / love and be loved // ~ 욕하다 call each other names // 헐뜯다 find fault with each other // ~ 싸우다 fight with each other // ~ 얼굴을 마주 보다 look at each other / look at each other's faces // 그들은 ~ (깊이) 사랑하고 있다 They are (deeply) in love with each other. / They love each other (deeply). // 그들은 ~ 사랑에 빠졌다 They fell in love with each other. // 아이들은 ~ 물을 튀겼다 The children splashed water on each other. // 그들은 ~ 죄를 전가하려 했다 Each tried to put the blame on the other. // 그들은 말없이 ~를 노려보았다 They glared at each other without saying a word.(▶ each other는 두 사람의 경우, one another는 세 사람 이상의 경우에 쓰인다고 하나, 세 사람 이상의 경우에도 each other를 쓸 때가 있음)

서론(序論·緒論) an introduction; introductory [prefatory] remarks; a proem. ¶~으로서 by way of introduction / as an introduction (to one's story) // ~으로서 사건의 개요를 말하겠습니다 By way of introduction, I will give a brief explanation of the incident.

서류(書類) 〔(공)문서〕 a document; 〔일반 서류〕 a paper. ¶관계 ~ relative [related] documents / papers relating to (an affair) // 비밀 ~ confidential [(미) classified] paper / secret documents // 법률 ~ legal documents // 선적 ~ shipping documents // 일건(一件) ~ a dossier (concerning an affair) // 중요 ~ important documents // 증거 ~ documentary evidence / papers [documents] which prove (a fact) // ~를 작성하다 draw up [write out] a document // ~를 제출하다 submit [send in / present] papers // ~를 정리하다 set the papers in order / file the papers // ~를 훑어 보다 run one's eyes through [look over] papers.

●**서류 가방** a briefcase; an attaché case. **서류 양식** the form of papers[documents]. **서류 전형** selection[screening] of candidates

서른 by examining their report cards [personal histories] (for further examination). **서류철** a file; a folder (판지를 둘로 접어서 만든). **서류함** a filing [file] cabinet.

서른 thirty. ¶~ 살 thirty years old [of age] // ~ 번째 the thirtieth // ~이 넘다 be over [older than] thirty.

서리[1] (가루 얼음) frost; hoar [hoary / white / rime] frost. ¶된~ a heavy [hard / severe / strong / sharp] frost // 무[첫]~ the first frost of the year [season] // ~가 내린 아침 a frosty morning // ~가 내리다 it frosts / frost falls [forms] // ~가 몹시 내리다 have a heavy frost // ~를 맞다 be frosted // ~를 맞다 be nipped [shriveled / touched] by frost (식물이) // ~로 피해를 입다 be damaged [nipped] by frost / suffer from frost // ~를 제거하다 defrost (a window / a refrigerator) // 풀에 ~가 내렸다 There is frost on the grass. // 오늘 아침에 첫~가 내렸다 We had the first frost of the season this morning. // 갑작스러운 추위로 잎이 모두 ~를 맞아 떨어졌다 All the leaves were frosted off by the cold snap. **서리(를) 맞다** be (hard) hit; suffer a blow; be socked; be frustrated; receive a setback. ¶그로 인해서 면업계는 되게 서리를 맞았다 The cotton industry was hard hit by it. ● **서리 피해** frost damage; damage by frost. ¶~를 입다 suffer from frost // 야채가 ~를 입었다 The vegetables were damaged by frost. **서릿바람** a frosty [chilly / cold] wind; a cold wind on a frosty morning.

서리[2] (훔치기) stealing ((water)melons, chickens, etc.) for fun; a mischievous raid (on another's farm products, etc.); a naughty poaching. ¶닭~ a mischievous raid on (another's) chickens // ~를 맞다 be raided by rogues. **서리하다** steal (a person's chickens) for fun; raid (a person's orchard).

서리(署理) [대리하는 사람] a deputy (official); a proxy; an acting director; [대리하는 일] administering as a deputy [an acting director]; procuration; attorneyship; subrogation; proxy. ¶국무총리 ~ an acting premier // 의장 ~ a deputy chairman. **서리하다** act for; act in place [behalf] of; stand [be] proxy for; administer as an acting director.

서리다[1] 1 (김·안개 등이) rise; gather; be clouded (up) (with); steam [fog / cloud] up; (그을음이) be covered (with soot); (냄새가) fill the air; float [hang] in the air. ¶김이 ~ 스팀 (up) / get steamed // 안경에 김이 서렸다 My glasses steamed up. // 유리창에 김이 서려 있다 The windowpanes are clouded up with steam. **2** (줄 등이) be tangled [entangled]. ¶천장에는 거미줄이 서려 있었다 The ceiling was covered with cobwebs. **3** (생각이) be kept deep in one's heart [mind]. ¶마음속에 서린 추억 memories enshrined in one's heart // 한이 ~ harbor enmity (toward) / bear [cherish] (a person) a grudge. **4** [어려 있다] be filled [fraught] (with). ¶애정이 서린 눈 eyes fraught with affection.

서리다[2] coil; coil itself (up). ⇨ 사리다·2

서리서리 in a coil; coil after coil; round and round; in a circle. ¶줄을 ~ 감다 wind a rope round (a thing).

서림 (書林) a bookseller's. ⇨ ☞서점

서릿발 1 (서리의) ice columns [needles]; frost columns [pillars]. **2** [엄함] rigor; severity; sternness; relentlessness.

서릿발 같다 be rigorous [severe / stern / relentless]. ¶서릿발 같은 논고 (make) a most relentless argument (against) // 서릿발 같은 명령 a stern [relentless] order.

서막 (序幕) **1** (연극의) the opening [first] act [scene]; a curtain raiser (단막극의). **2** (일의 시초) a prelude (to an entertainment); a beginning; an inception. ¶그것이 혁명의 ~이었다 It was the prelude [prologue] to the revolution.

서머스쿨 a summer school. ⇨ ☞여름학교(⇨여름)

서머 타임 daylight saving (time) (약어 DST); (영) summer time (약어 S.T.). ¶~을 실시하다 put daylight saving time into effect // ~이 되다 go on summer time.

서먹(서먹)하다 [낯이 설다] unfamiliar; estranged; alienated; (무감하지 않다) reserved; formal; [어색하다] awkward; (서술적) feel awkward [nervous / out of place]; feel small [cheap / embarrassed] (in company); feel ill at ease; be not at home. ¶서먹서먹한 침묵을 지키다 keep awkward silence // 서먹서먹하게 대하다 treat (a person) like a stranger // 두 사람 사이가 서먹서먹해졌다 The two became estranged. / They don't get on so well as before. / Some coldness has come between the two.

서면 (書面) [편지] a letter; [문서] a document; [내용] contents. ¶~으로 by letter / in writing / in written statement // ~ 또는 구두로 in writing or orally // 본인이 직접 또는 ~으로 personally or through the mail / in person or in writing // ~화하다 put (something) in writing / commit (something) to writing // ~으로 신청 [탄원]하다 submit [send in] a written application [petition] (to) // ~으로 알리다 let (a person) know by letter. ● **서면 결의** a documentary resolution [decision]. **서면 심리** (법원의) (a) documentary examination.

서명 (書名) the title of a book. ¶「새 생명」이라는 ~의 책 a book entitled "New Life."

서명 (署名) a signature; an autograph (자기의 사진·저서 등에 하는); [서명하기] signing; autographing. ¶~이 있는 signed [by the author] / autographed [photo] / carrying [bearing] (a person's) signature // ~이 없는 편지 an anonymous [unsigned] letter // 저자의 ~이 있는 책 a book signed [autographed] by the author // …의 ~이 있다 carry the signature of … // ~ 날인하다 set one's hand and seal (to an instrument) / add one's signature and seal (to a document) / sign and seal (a bond) // 서류에 ~ 날인하다 sign and seal a document. **서명하다** sign [write (down)] one's name; sign (a treaty); autograph; affix [attach / put] one's signature (to a document); subscribe one's name (to a document). ¶조약에 ~ sign a treaty // 협약에 ~ put an agreement under one's signature // 방명록에 ~ sign [enter] one's name in the visitors' register // 여기에 서명해 주십시오 Please write [sign] your name here. / Sign here, please. / Your John Hancock here, please.

●**서명 운동** a signature-collecting campaign. ¶~을 하다 conduct a campaign to collect signatures (for a petition). **서명자** a signer; [법] the undersigned(개인·단체에 모두 쓰임).

서모(庶母) one's father's concubine; a stepmother.

서목(書目) 1 [적요] a summary[an epitome] (attached to a report). 2 [도서 목록] a list [catalog(ue)] of books.

서무(庶務) general affairs.
●**서무과** the general affairs section.

서문(序文) a preface. ⇨˚머리말(⊝)머리

서민(庶民) the (common / ordinary) people; the populace; the commonality; the masses; (한 사람) a commoner. ¶~적(인) popular / common / democratic // ~적인 오락 popular amusements[entertainment] // 이런 음식은 우리 같은 ~의 입에는 맞지 않는다 We common[ordinary] people don't enjoy food like this.
●**서민 계급** the mass of (the) people; the populace[masses]; the working classes. **서민 금융** petty loans for the people; small-loan finance. **서민 아파트** an apartment (building) for the low income bracket.

서반구(西半球) the western hemisphere.

서방(西方) [서쪽] the west; [서쪽 지방] western districts; [나라] western countries; [서유럽의 자유주의 국가] the West. ¶~ 측[편] a pro-Western / a pro-Westerner // ~ 측 진영 the Western camp[bloc] // 동방에서 ~으로의 망명 flight from the East to the West.
●**서방 정토**(불) [극락] the Buddhist Elysium; the Western Paradise.

서방(書房) 1 [남편] one's husband[man]; (구어) a hubby. 2 [호칭] Mr.; (흔히 하인에게) Old .... ¶최 ~ Mr. Choe // 정 ~ Old Jeong. **서방**(을) **맞다** take[get] a husband; get married (to a man).
●**서방질** adultery (of a married woman); cuckolding. ¶~을 하다 cuckold [deceive] one's husband / commit adultery.

서벅거리다 crunch softly. ⇨ᐧ사박거리다

서벅서벅 with a soft crunch. ⇨²사박사박

서법(書法) penmanship; calligraphy.

서법(敍法) [언] the mood.

서부(西部) the western part(s); the west. ¶~의 western // 나의 집은 서울의 ~에 있다 My house is in the western part of Seoul.
●**서부극** a horse opera; a western (film); a cowboy picture; an oater. **서부 전선** the Western Front.

서북(西北) 1 [서쪽과 북쪽] west and north; [방위] the north-west(약어 NW). ¶~으로 northwestern / northwesterly // ~쪽 (to the) northwest (of) // ~으로 northwestward // ~으로 2킬로를 가다 go two kilometers northwest // 학교는 마을의 ~쪽 모퉁이에 있다 Our school is in the northwestern corner of our town. 2 [서도와 북관] the northwestern districts of Korea.
●**서북풍** a northwester; a northwestern [northwesterly] wind. **서북향** facing the northwest; a northwestern exposure [aspect].

서브 [체] a service; a serve. ¶~를 넣다 serve (a ball) // ~를 받다 receive the service / receive the served ball // ~를 넘기다 return a serve // ~가 훌륭하다[서투르다] be a good [poor] server // ~는 어느 쪽이냐 Whose serve[service] (is it)? **서브하다** serve a ball. ¶이번에는 네가 서브할 차례다 It's your serve. / It's your turn to serve.
●**서브권** (one's) serve. ¶~을 얻다 get the serve // ~을 되찾다 get back the serve.

서브타이틀 a subtitle. ¶~을 붙이다 subtitle (a book).

서비스 1 [봉사] service(▶ 영어 service에는 「덤」, 「공짜」의 뜻이 전혀 없음). ¶~가 좋다 [나쁘다] They give good[poor] service (in that hotel). // 그 식당은 ~가 좋다[나쁘다] The service at that restaurant is good[bad]. / You get good[poor] service at that restaurant. // 그 가게는 ~가 만점이다 The service there is perfect. // 이건 ~입니다 (상점에서 경품을 얹어 주며) This is a free gift. / This is on the house. / We'll throw this in. / This is a little something extra. / I'll throw this in for free. // 호텔에서 아침 식사를 ~로 제공했다 The hotel gave us a complimentary breakfast. 2 [채] a service. ⇨˚서브
●**서비스 라인** the service line. **서비스료** a service charge; (요청 등의) the cover charge. ¶1할의 ~ a ten-percent service charge // ~ 포함 (호텔 등에서) Service charge included. **서비스업** a service industry.

서사(敍事) [문] narration; description. ¶~적인[체의] epic / descriptive / narrative // ~체로 쓰다 write (a composition) in a narrative style. **서사하다** narrate; describe.
●**서사문** a description; a narrative. **서사시** an epic (poem); (집합적) epos; epic poetry. ¶영웅 ~ a heroic epic // ~적[의] epic.

서산(西山) the western hill[mountain].

서생(庶生) [첩의 소생] a child by a concubine.

서서히(徐徐─) slowly; without haste. ⇨˚천천히

서설(序說) a preface. ⇨˚머리말

서성거리다 walk up and down restlessly; hover (about); hang about[around] (a house). ¶그는 어찌할 바를 몰라서 집 주위를 서성거렸다 He hovered around the house, uncertain what to do. // 이 근처에서 서성거리지 말게 I don't want to see you around here.

서수(序數) [수] an ordinal (number).

서술(敍述) description; depiction; delineation; narration; [논] predication. ¶~ 형식 the form[manner] of description[narration] // ~을 잘하다 be good at describing. **서술하다** describe; depict; delineate; narrate. ¶자세히 ~ describe minutely[in minute / detail].
●**서술부 / 서술어** the predicate (of a sentence).

서스펜션 [화] suspension; a suspension (of silt) in (water).

서스펜스 suspense. ¶~가 넘치는 suspenseful // 스릴과 ~가 넘치는 이야기 a story full of thrills and suspense.
●**서스펜스물** a thriller; (미) a mystery story; (미국 속어) whodunit.

서슬 1 (날붙이의) a sharp [keen-edged] part (of a blade); a burnished blade. ¶~이 시퍼런 칼 a gleaming[shining] sword[blade]. 2 [날카로운 기세] the brunt (of an attack / argument); sharpness; acuteness; impetuosity.

서슬이 푸르다[시퍼렇다] (권세 등이) be

서슴다

mighty [powerful]; (공격 등이) be violent; (태도가) be dreadful [threatening / menacing / fierce]; (노하여) be in a rage; be in hot blood. ¶서슬이 푸른 표정[태도] a threatening [menacing] look [attitude] // 서슬이 푸른 얼굴로 노려보다 glare fiercely at (a person) with rage.

서슴다 hesitate; scruple; waver; hang [hold] back; be shy (of doing); vacillate; falter; shilly-shally; be irresolute [hesitant]. ¶서슴지 않고 without hesitation [flinching] / unhesitatingly / without scruple [wavering] / [격의 없이] unreservedly / without reserve // …을 서슴지 않다 do not hesitate about [in] doing [to do] … / feel free to do … // 죽기도 서슴지 않다 do not hesitate even to die // 그는 살인도 서슴지 않을 사람이다 He will not stick at murder. // 저 상인[정치가]은 무슨 짓이든 서슴지 않고 할 사람이다 That merchant [politician] would stop at nothing. // 그는 어떤 극단적인 짓도 서슴지 않고 할 것이다 He will go to any extreme. // 그는 서슴지 않고 그 제안에 덤벼들었다 He jumped at the offer (without a moment's hesitation). // 건강이 나쁘면 언제라도 서슴지 말고 병가를 얻으세요 Don't hesitate to take sick leave whenever you are ill.

서슴없다 unhesitating; (서술적) be not hesitant; have no scruples about; make no scruple of; do not stick at. **서슴없이** without hesitation [flinching]; unhesitatingly; without scruple [wavering]; [격의 없이] unreservedly; without reserve; [노골적으로] boldly. ¶~ 말하다 speak without hesitation // 좋고 싫은 것을 ~ 말하다 express one's likes and dislikes in no measured terms // 그는 무엇이든 ~ 할 사람이다 He would stop [stick] at nothing. / He will go to any extreme. // 원하는 것이 있으면 ~ 말하시오 Don't scruple to ask for anything you want. // 그녀는 ~ 자기 의견을 충분히 말했다 She went right ahead and said clearly what she thought. / She spoke up boldly and stated her opinion.

서식(書式) a (due [prescribed]) form. ¶제5호 ~ form No. 5 // ~대로 in due [proper] form / in accordance with [according to] the form prescribed // ~에 기입하다 fill out [(영) in] a form [(미) blank] // ~대로 쓰다 write in the proper [due] form // 정해진 ~이 있습니까? "예. 이 ~에 기입해 주십시오." "Is there any fixed form?" "Yes. Please fill out this form." // 이 서류는 ~이 다릅니다 This paper does not follow the correct form.

서식(棲息) inhabitation. ¶~에 적합한 inhabitable. **서식하다** 장소를 목적어로 하여 타동사로만 씀); live (in the river). ¶물속에 ~ live in the water // 숲 속에 ~ inhabit a forest // 이 늪에 서식하는 동물 the creatures living in [inhabiting] this marsh.
● **서식지** a habitat; a haunt; a home.

서신(書信) [편지 왕래] correspondence; communication; [편지] a letter; an epistle; a note; a missive. ¶~으로 사귀는 친구 one's pen pal / one's pen-friend // …과 ~ 왕래를 하고 있다 be in correspondence with … / keep in touch with each other by letter // …과 ~ 왕래를 계속하다[끊다] maintain [stop / quit] correspondence with … // …에게 ~을 보내다 write a letter to (a person) // …과 왕래가 끊이지 않다 be in constant correspondence with … // 그녀와는 꾸준히 ~ 왕래를 하고 있습니다 Are you in constant [regular] correspondence [communication] with her?

서안(西岸) the west coast.

서약(誓約) an oath (▶ 성서 등에 걸고 하는 선서); a vow; a pledge (▶ 굳게 약속함); [법] a recognizance. ¶~대로 faithful [true] to one's vow / in conformity with one's pledge / according to one's promise // ~을 실행하다 put one's pledge into effect // ~을 이행하다 discharge [fulfill] one's vow // ~을 지키다 keep one's pledge [vow] // ~을 어기다 break one's oath [vow] / violate one's pledge. **서약하다** swear; vow; pledge; make [take / swear] an oath (that); give one's pledge [word] (that); make a vow (to do / that); pledge [bind / commit] oneself (to do); make a covenant (to do / that). ¶비밀을 지킬 것을 ~ take an oath [a vow] of secrecy / pledge oneself to secrecy // 그는 비밀을 지키겠다고 서약했다 He pledged himself to secrecy.
● **서약서** a written oath [pledge / promise / pact]; a covenant. ¶~를 쓰다 make a written pledge. **서약자** a party to a covenant; a recognizor.

서양(西洋) the West; the Occident; Europe; Europe and America; [서양 여러 나라] Western countries. ¶~의 Occidental / Western / European.
● **서양 문명** [사상] Western civilization [ideas]. **서양사** Occidental [European] history. **서양식** a European [Western] style [fashion]; Western ways [habits]. ¶~의 European / Occidental / Western // ~으로 after [in] European fashion / in Western style // ~ 사고방식 the Western way of thinking [mode of thought] // ~으로 하다 Europeanize. **서양인** [구미 사람] a Westerner; an Occidental; [유럽 인] a European. **서양화**(~化) westernization; Europeanization. ~하다 become westernized / westernize / Europeanize. **서양화**(~畵) (a) Western [European] painting; (an) oil painting (유화).

서언(序言·緒言) a preface; a prefatory [an introductory] note [remark]; an introduction; a foreword.

서역(西域) the countries to the west of China.

서열(序列) rank; ranking; grade; order. ¶~에 따라 in order of importance // 정확한 ~대로 손님을 앉히다 seat the guests in correct order according to rank // ~이 A의 다음이다 stand next to A in line // 당 ~ 제3위를 차지하다 rank No. 3 in the party hierarchy.

서예(書藝) seoye; calligraphy; penmanship. ¶~의 대가 a master [great] calligrapher.
● **서예가** a calligrapher.

서운(瑞雲) auspicious clouds; clouds of good omen. ¶그곳에는 ~이 서려 있다 Auspicious clouds hang over the place.

서운하다 (마음이) sorry; regrettable; unsatisfied; (하는 짓이) unsatisfactory; heartless; indifferent; unkind; unfair; displeasing. ¶이별로 ~ be sorry [sad] to part from (a person) // 아들이 없어 ~ miss one's son // 서운해하다 be [feel] sorry [regrettable / unsatisfied] / miss (something / a person) / con-

sider (a person / something) heartless [unkind / unfair] / be displeased at / feel mistreated[hurt] // 처사를 서운해하다 consider the treatment unfair // 서운하게 대하다 treat (a person) in a displeasing way[with unkindness] / behave unfairly toward (a person) // 네가 거기에 오지 않아서 퍽 서운했다 I missed you very much there. // 당신을 두고 가니 몹시 마음이 ~ I am very sorry[I hate] to leave you here.

서울 [수도] a capital; a metropolis. ¶영국의 ~ 런던 London, the capital of England.

서원(書院) *seowon*; a private academy [school].

서원(署員) ('서(署)' 자가 붙은 관서에 근무하는 사람) a member of an office; an official; (집합적) the staff (of an office). ¶세무서 ~ a tax office clerk[agent] / a tax official.

서원(誓願) a vow; an oath; a pledge. **서원하다** swear; vow; pledge; take[make] a vow; pronounce a vow (to God); pledge oneself (to do). ¶수녀들은 평생 독신을 지킬 것을 서원한다 Nuns are under a vow of lifelong celibacy.

서유럽(西-) West(ern) Europe; the West.

서임(敍任) [임명] appointment; [취임] installation; investiture. **서임하다** appoint; install; invest (a person with a position).

서자(庶子) [첩의] a son by a concubine; (사생아) a son born out of wedlock.

서장(署長) [일반적] the head[chief / superintendent] (of); a (town / fire) marshal(경찰서·소방서의). ¶경찰서 ~ the head[chief] of a police station / (미) a police chief / (영) a chief constable // 소방서 ~ (미) the head of the fire department / (미) a fire marshal / (영) the head of the fire brigade.

서재(書齋) a study; a library. ¶~에 틀어박히다 be confined in one's study.

서적(書籍) a book; a volume. ⇨ ˚책(冊)

  ● **서적상** (사람) a bookseller; (가게) a bookstore; (영) a bookshop.

서전(緖戰) the beginning[an early stage] of war; (경기의) the first match[game]. ¶~을 승리로 장식하다 (전쟁에서) win a victory at the beginning of the war / (경기에서) win one's first match.

서점(書店) a bookseller's; (미) a bookstore; (영) a bookshop. ¶그는 ~을 경영하고 있다 He keeps a bookstore. // 나는 이 책을 신촌에 있는 ~에서 샀다 I bought this book at a bookstore in Sinchon.

서정(抒情·敍情) delineation [description] of feeling[passions]; lyricism. ¶~적인 lyric(al) // ~적으로 lyrically // 이 작가는 서경(敍景)보다 ~에 뛰어나다 This writer is a skillful delineator of passions rather than of scenery.

  ● **서정시** a lyric (poem); an ode; (집합적) lyric poetry; lyrical verse. **서정시인** a lyric poet; a lyricist.

서정(庶政) civil services.

  ● **서정쇄신** purification[renovation] of officialdom; (strict) enforcement of official discipline.

서주(序奏) [음] an introduction.

서지(書誌) a bibliography.

  ● **서지학** bibliography. **서지학자** a bibliographer.

서진(書鎭) a paperweight; a weight.

서쪽(西-) the west(약어 W). ¶~의 west / western / westerly // ~에 [서쪽 방향으로 떨어진 곳에] to the west (of) / [서부에] in the west part (of) / (경계를 접하여) on the west side (of the house) // 서울의 ~ to the west of Seoul // ~으로 west / westward / toward(s) [to] the west / in westerly direction // ~으로 가다 go west[westward] / (해는) ~으로 진다 The sun sets in the west. // 대상은 ~으로 향했다 The caravan headed westward [(to the) west]. // 도서관은 공원에서 50미터 ~에 있다 The library is 50 meters to the west of the park. // 그의 집은 우리 집 ~에 있다 (서쪽 방향에) His house stands to the west of mine.

서창(西窓) a west(-side) window; a window facing west; a window open to the west.

서책(書冊) a book; a volume. ⇨ ˚책(冊)

서천(西天) the western sky.

서첩(書帖) an album of excellent calligraphic works; a collection of calligraphic specimen of notables.

서체(書體) [글씨체] a style of handwriting; (활자의) a style of type. ¶~는 고딕체로 해 주십시오 Please set this in Gothic type.

서출(庶出) an offspring of a concubine; ¶~의 born of a concubine / born out of wedlock / illegitimate.

서치라이트 a searchlight. ¶~가 그 국적 불명의 배를 비추었다 A searchlight was turned on[upon] the unidentified ship.

서캐 [이의 알] a nit.

서캐 훑듯 한다(속담) comb[scour] (a place for concealed weapons); look in every nook and corner (of a house for something).

서커스 a circus.

  ● **서커스단** a circus troupe.

서클(˚circle) [동아리] a club. ¶테니스 ~에 들어가다 join a tennis club.

  ● **서클 활동** club activities.

서투르다 unskillful; inexpert; poor; awkward; clumsy; unhandy; bungling; [익숙하지 않다] unfamiliar (with); unaccustomed [unused] (to); ignorant (of); strange; new (to / at). ¶ 서투른 목수 an incompetent[unskilled] carpenter // 서투른 변명 a poor excuse // 서투른 솜씨의 수 embroidery of poor workmanship // 나의 서투른 이야기 my inept remarks // 참으로 서투른 번역 a very poor translation // 서투른 영어를 말하다 speak broken English // 그녀는 글씨가 ~ She writes a poor hand. / She has bad handwriting. // 나는 영어가 ~ I am weak in English. // 그는 노래가 ~ He is a poor singer. / (구어) His singing is awful. // 저 목수는 ~ That carpenter is clumsy. // 나는 바느질[재봉]이 ~ I'm poor [not much good] at sewing. // 그녀는 요리가 아주 ~ She is a terrible [very poor] cook. // 그는 젓가락질을 서투르게 한다 He handles chopsticks awkwardly [in an awkward manner]. // 솜씨는 매우 서투르지만 나는 그림 그리기를 좋아합니다 I like to paint pictures, though I'm not very good at it. // 나는 서투른 영어로 식사를 주문했다 I ordered a meal in my awkward English. // 표현은 서투르지만 그의 이야기는 내 가슴에 와 닿는 것이 있었다 I was touched by his story, though he was clumsy[awkward] in presenting it. // 그 일기는 서투른 문장으로 쓰여 있었다 The diary was written in a poor[clumsy] style.

서투른 무당이 장구만 나무란다(속담) A bad workman quarrels with his tools.
서평(書評) a book review. ¶~을 하다 review a book.
● 서평가 a book reviewer. 서평란 the book review columns.

서표(書標) a bookmark(er). ¶~를 책갈피에 끼우다 put a bookmark between the pages of a book.

서푼 ¶그 서류는 ~의 값어치도 없다 The document is not worth a penny[farthing / fig / straw].

서품(敍品) [가] ordination.

서풍(西風) a west[westerly] wind; (시어) Zephyr(의인화하여). ¶~이 분다 There is a west wind. / The wind is from the west.

서핑 1 surfing; surfboarding. ¶~을 하는 사람 a surfer // ~을 하다 surf / ride the surf. **2** (web) surfing.

서학(西學) western learning.

서한(書翰) a letter; a communication. ⇨편지
● 서한문 letter writing. 서한체 (write in) an epistolary style. ⇨서간체⇨서간

서해(西海) the western sea; [황해] the Yellow Sea.

서행(徐行) ¶~ (게시) Go Slow. / Drive Slowly. / Slow Down. / 최고 ~ (게시) Slow Down To Limit. / Dead Slow. 서행하다 [천천히 나아가다] go slow(ly); go at a slow speed; [속력을 떨어뜨리다] slow down. ¶서행하고 있는 차 a slow-moving car // 이 길은 위험하니 서행하는 것이 좋다 You'd better slow down because this road is dangerous. // 버스는 건널목에 이르러 서행했다 The bus slowed down for the railroad crossing.

서향(西向) a western exposure; a western [west] aspect.
● 서향집 a house facing west[exposed to the west]; a house looking to[toward] the west; a house with a western exposure.

서혜(鼠蹊) the crotch. ⇨살
● 서혜부 the groin; the inguinal region.

서화(書畵) paintings[pictures] and calligraphic works; works of pictorial art and calligraphy.
● 서화 전시회 an exhibition of paintings and calligraphic works.

서훈(敍勳) conferment of a decoration. 서훈하다 decorate (a person for service); confer a decoration (on a person).

석 three. ¶~ 달 three months // ~ 자 three feet.

석(石) a *seom*. ⇨섬²

-석(席) a seat; a place; a gallery. ¶일반~ a general admission seat.

석가모니(釋迦牟尼) (the) Buddha; S(h)akyamuni.

석각(石刻) [돌에 새김] stone carving; [새긴 돌] a carved stone. 석각하다 carve stone (for a statue into a shape); carve (a statue) out of stone.

석간(夕刊) [석간지] an evening paper; (조간에 대하여) an evening edition.
● 석간신문 an evening paper.

석경(石鏡) a mirror; a (looking) glass.

석고(石膏) (천연의) gypsum; (분말의) plaster. ¶설화 ~ alabaster // 소(燒)~ plaster of Paris.
● 석고 붕대 plaster bandage. 석고상 a plaster figure; (흉상) a plaster bust. 석고 세공 a plasterer.

석공(石工) **1** a (stone) mason. ⇨석수(石手) **2** [석공업] masonry.

석관(石棺) a sarcophagus (*pl.* -gi, ~es); a stone coffin.

석교(石橋) a stone bridge. ⇨돌다리

석굴(石窟) a stone cave[cavern].
● 석굴암 the Seokguram.

석권하다(席卷─) [휩쓸다] carry everything before one; sweep (over / across); pour over (a land); [정복하다] conquer; make a conquest of. ¶적의 영역을 ~ sweep over enemy territory // 외국 자본이 국내 시장을 석권했다 Foreign capital overwhelmed our market(s).

석기(石器) stoneware; stonework; [고] a stone implement[tool].
● 석기 시대 [고] the stone Age. ¶신[구]~ the Neolithic[Pal(a)eolithic] era / the New [Old] Stone Age.

석녀(石女) a barren[sterile] woman.

석다 (눈이) thaw; melt; (술 등이) ferment.

석단(石壇) a stone platform[stage].

석도(石刀) a stone blade.

석등(石燈籠) a stone lantern.

석류(石榴) [식] a pomegranate.
● 석류나무 a pomegranate tree.

석류석(石榴石) [광] garnet.

석면(石綿) [광] asbestos; asbestos; amiantus(질이 좋은).

석명(釋明) (an) explanation; elucidation; explication; an apology(사과); (a) vindication(변명). 석명하다 explain; elucidate; explicate; apologize (for); vindicate (oneself); clear up.

석문(石門) a stone gate.

석물(石物) stonework set before a tomb.

석방(釋放) (a) release; discharge; liberation; (an) acquittal. ¶가~ (a) parole // 조건부 ~ conditional release // 비행기 납치범들은 교도소에 수감되어 있는 동지들의 ~을 요구했다 The hijackers demanded the release of their imprisoned comrades. 석방하다 release (a person); set (a person) free; let off; turn loose; liberate; acquit. ¶형기를 마친 복역수을 ~ release a convict who has completed his sentences[has served his time]. ➔전쟁 포로 중에서 5명이 석방되었다 Five of the prisoners of war were released[set free]. // 그는 100만 원의 보석금을 내고 석방되었다 He was released[set free] on bail of one million won.

석벽(石壁) [돌로 쌓은 벽] a stone wall; [절벽] rockwall.

석별(惜別) unwillingness to part (from); reluctance to leave; parting with regrets. ¶~의 눈물 tears at parting // ~의 정 unwillingness to part / reluctance to leave // ~의 정을 나누다 express one's sorrow at[on] parting. 석별하다 grudge [regret] parting [to part] (from a person); be unwilling [sorry / loath] to part (from one's friend); be reluctant to leave (a place).
● 석별연 a farewell [going-away] party; a send-off dinner.

석부(石斧) a stone ax(e). ⇨돌도끼

석불(石佛) a stone Buddhist image.

석비(石碑) (기념의) a (stone) monument; (묘석) a tombstone; a gravestone.

석사(碩士) **1** [선비] a scholar (holding no office); (칭호) Mr. **2** [학위] Master. ¶문학[이

학 / 공학] ~ a master of arts [science / engineering] (약어 M.A., M.Sc., M.Eng.).
● **석사 과정** a master's course (in law). ¶나는 시카고 대학에서 ~을 마쳤다 I got [received] my master's [degree] at Chicago University. **석사 논문** a master's thesis (in anthropology). **석사 학위** a master's degree (in economics). ¶나는 예일 대학의 이학사 를 갖고 있다 I have an M.Sc. from Yale University.
석산(石山) a stony [rocky / rugged] mountain.
석상(石像) a stone statue [figure]. ¶그는 ~처럼 꼼짝 않고 앉아 있었다 He sat as still as a statue.
석상(席上) ¶~에서 [회합에서] at the meeting [assembly] / [사람들 속에서] in company [public] / [그때] on the occasion // ~에서 on a public occasion.
석쇠 a gridiron; a grill; a toasting net. ¶~로 쇠고기를 굽다 grill beef on a gridiron.
석수(石手) a (stone) mason; a stonecutter.
● **석수질** masonry (work).
석순(石筍) [광] stalagmite.
석실(石室) a stone chamber [hut].
석양(夕陽) the setting sun; the evening sun; the declining [westering] sun. ¶~의 희미한 빛 the lingering glow of the sunset // 여름의 ~ the afternoon sun in summer // ~은 산 너머로 졌다 The sun set behind the mountain. // 그는 ~을 향해 걸었다 He walked into the setting sun.
● **석양 녘** toward sunset.
석연하다(釋然-) (사람이) satisfied (with the explanation); relieved from doubt; feeling free from doubt; (사물이) satisfactory; comprehensible; understandable. ¶석연치 않은 인물 a doubtful character // 석연치 않다 (사물이) unconvincing [unsatisfactory / incomprehensible / ununderstandable / unaccounted-for] / (기분이) be (still) in doubt (of / about) / be not quite satisfied (with the explanation) // 뭔가 석연하지 않은 데가 있다 There is something inexplicable in the matter. / There is something to be clarified.
석연히 with sudden illumination. ¶그에 대한 의심은 ~ 가시지 않고 있다 My suspicions about him have not really been cleared up [(문어) been dispelled].
석영(石英) [광] quartz. ¶녹(綠)~ prase // 유(乳)~ milky quartz.
● **석영 유리** quartz glass.
석유(石油) oil; petroleum; (등유) kerosene. ¶~의 petrolic // ~를 함유한 oil-bearing // 해저 ~의 채굴 offshore oil drilling.
● **석유갱** a petroleum [an oil] well. **석유 공업** the petroleum [oil] industry. **석유난로** an oil stove; an oil burner; a kerosene heater. **석유 매장량** (an estimated amount of) oil deposits. **석유 수출국 기구** Organization of Petroleum Exporting Countries (약어 OPEC). **석유 자원** petroleum resources; oil riches. ¶~이 없는 oil-poor // ~을 개발하다 develop [exploit] petroleum resources. **석유 정제** oil refining. ¶~ 공장 an oil refinery. **석유 제품** petroleum [oil] products. **석유 탱크** an oil tank. **석유 화학** petrochemistry.
석이(버섯)(石耳-) [식] a manna lichen.
석인(石人) a stone image of a person (set before a tomb).

석자 a ladle with meshes.
석재(石材) (building) stone.
● **석재상** (사람) a stone dealer [merchant]; a dealer in stone; (가게) a stone dealer's (shop).
석전(石田) a stony field.
석전놀이(石戰-) a mock fight with stone missiles.
석전(釋奠) the festival in honor of Confucius.
석조(石造) stone construction. ¶~의 stone / made of stone.
● **석조 건물** a stone building.
석존(釋尊) [석가세존] [불] Sakyamuni; the Buddha.
● **석존제** Buddha's birthday festival.
석주(石柱) a stone pillar.
석죽(石竹) [식] a pink. ⇨"패랭이꽃(⇨패랭이)
석차(席次) 1 [자리의 차례] the seating order; [의식 등에서의 서열] precedence. 2 [성적의 순위] (academic) standing (in one's class); ranking. ¶졸업 ~ one's graduation standing // 그의 ~가 10등 올랐다 [떨어졌다] His standing [rank] in the class has risen [fallen] ten places. / He has gone up [come down] ten places in his class. // 학급에서 그의 ~는 5등 이내이다 He ranks among the top five in his class.
석창포(石菖蒲) [식] a sweet flag; a sweet rush.
석촉(石鏃) [고고] a flint arrowhead.
석총(石塚) a cairn.
석탄(石炭) coal; [무연탄] hard coal. ¶~을 불에 넣다 feed coal to the fire // ~을 때다 burn coal // ~을 채굴하다 mine coal / dig out coal // ~을 연료로 하다 use coal for fuel // ~을 지피다 put coal(s) on (the fire) / feed (a stove) with coal // ~을 적재하다 bunker [take (in)] coal / ship coal // ~을 삽으로 퍼 넣다 shovel coal(s) (into).
● **석탄 가스** coal gas. **석탄 광산** a coal mine [pit]. **석탄 갱부** a (coal) miner; a pitman. **석탄 건류** coal carbonization. **석탄광** [광] a coal mine. ⇨"탄광 **석탄 산지** a producing center of coal; a coalfield. **석탄층** a coal seam [bed].
석탑(石塔) a stone pagoda [tower].
석판(石板) a slate.
석판(石版) [그림을 그리는 인쇄판] a lithograph; [석판 인쇄술] lithography.
● **석판 인쇄공** a lithographer.
석패(惜敗) a defeat by a narrow margin; a regrettable defeat. **석패하다** be defeated [lose a game] by a narrow margin; lose a close game. ¶배구에서 한국 팀은 중국 팀에 석패했다 In the volleyball match the Korean team was defeated by a narrow margin by the Chinese team.
석필(石筆) a slate pencil.
석학(碩學) [학문이 깊은 사람] an erudite scholar; a man of great [profound] learning.
석호(潟湖) [해안의 호소(湖沼)·늪] a lagoon; [개펄] a tideland; [만] a bay.
석화(石火) [불꽃] flint fire; a flint spark; [몹시 빠름] a flash. ¶전광~같이 like (a flash of) lightning.
석화(石花) [동] an oyster. ⇨"굴
석회(石灰) lime. ¶생~ quicklime / unslaked lime // 소(消)~ slaked [slack / dead] lime // 탄산[인산] ~ calcium carbonate [phosphate] // ~분이 많은 식품 food rich in lime // ~를 함

섞갈리다

유하지 않은 limeless.
● **석회 가루** lime powder. **석회수** limewater. **석회암/석회석** limestone. **석회질** compounds of calcium.

섞갈리다 get [become] confused; get complicated [entangled / tangled / mixed]; be mixed up; become involved(사건 등이). ¶계산이 ~ get confused in calculation // 그 문제는 많은 다른 문제들과 섞갈려 있다 The question is entangled with many others.

섞다 [한데 합치다] mix (A and B / A with B); (분리할 수 없을 정도로) blend (A and B / A with B); admix; compound; mingle. ¶여러 가지 종류를 섞은 캔디 assorted candy / an assortment of candies // 설탕과 버터를 ~ mix sugar and butter // 몇 가지 커피를 ~ blend several kinds of coffee // 두 가지 약을 ~ compound two kinds of medicine // 농담을 섞어 가면서 이야기하다 talk throwing in an occasional joke [a joke from time to time] // 패를 잘 섞으시오 Please shuffle the cards carefully.

섞바꾸다 alternate (with each other); interchange regularly [repeatedly] with (something).

섞이다 be mixed; be blended. (▶ be mixed는 섞은 것이 식별되는 경우나 식별되지 않는 경우에도 쓰지만, be blended는 잘 섞여서 식별할 수 없을 때 씀) ¶마가 섞인 면직물 cotton fabric blended with [containing] some linen // 노랑과 파랑이 섞이면 녹색이 된다 Yellow and blue blend into green. // 큰 조각과 작은 조각이 함께 섞여 있다 Large pieces and small ones are mixed in together. // 저 소녀는 한국인과 미국인의 피가 섞여 있다 The girl is of mixed Korean and American parentage. // 이 언어에는 여러 가지 요소가 섞여 있다 Diverse elements are blended in this language. // 그의 마음에는 슬픔과 동경과 희망이 섞여 있었다 Sorrow, longing, and hope were intermingled in his mind. // 그들은 현지인들과 섞여서 살았다 They lived mixing themselves among the aborigines. // 그의 머리에는 흰 머리털이 섞여 있었다 His hair was sprinkled with gray.

섟 [노여움] a fit of anger [temper / passion / rage / the spleen]; a flare of temper; [의심] a sudden feeling of doubt [suspicion]; a passing [quick] doubt; a flash of suspicion.
섟(이) 삭다 (노여움이) be allayed; (사람이) relent (toward a person); (의심이) be resolved [dispelled / removed / cleared].

선 an interview [a meeting] with a view to marriage; a marriage meeting. ¶~을 보다 see each other with a view to marriage / have an interview with [get a look at] a prospective bride [bridegroom] // 두 사람은 ~도 보지 않고 결혼했다 They were married without even going through the formality of a preliminary interview [without even a previous chance of seeing each other].

선- [서투르고 덜됨] inexperienced; unskilled; untrained; poor; clumsy; green; immature; raw. ¶~머슴 a naughty [wild / mischievous] boy // ~무당 an inexperienced [a new / a green] shaman // ~잠 a light sleep / a catnap / a dognap.

선(先) [바둑] placing the first stone; the first move; [장기] moving first; the first move; (트럼프 등에서) (the) lead; (구기에서) serve; delivery. ¶~을 하다 [두다] make [have] the first move (in a game of *baduk*) // 누가 ~이냐 Whose deal [lead] is it?

선(善) the good; goodness; virtue; [선행] a good deed. ¶최고~ the highest good // ~과 악을 확실히 구별하다 make a clear distinction between right and wrong [good and evil] // ~을 행하다 do (what is) good / practice virtue // ~은 악을 이긴다 Virtue triumphs over vice.

선(腺) [생] a gland. ¶갑상~ the thyroid gland // 내분비~ a ductless gland / an endocrine (gland) // 림프~ a lymphatic gland.

선(線) **1** [길고 가는 줄] a line. ¶~을 긋다 draw a line / (밑줄을) underline (a word). **2** [기준이 되는 한도] a level. ¶최후의 ~을 넘다 exceed [go beyond / overstep] the limit // 동정과 연민 사이에 명확한 ~을 긋다 draw a clear [neat] line between sympathy and pity // 한국의 공업은 중진국의 ~을 넘었다 Korean industry has surpassed the level of developing countries. **3** [정해진 코스·방침] a line. ¶이번 계획은 그 ~에서 시행합시다 Let's proceed along those lines with our present project. **4** [전선] a wire; a line. ¶집에 (전등)~을 끌다 wire a house for electricity [electric light]. **5** [맺고 있는 관계] connection; relations. ¶~이 닿다 have relation (to) / be related (to) // ~을 끊다 sever [break off / cut] the connections with.

선(縇) an edge; an edging; a hem; a selvage; a selvedge; a frill; a border; a rim; a fringe. ¶~을 두르다 [치다] put a border on (a skirt) / hem (a handkerchief) / sew on a frill [border].

선(選) selection; choice; (편집의) compilation; editing; composition. ¶명작~ a selection of masterpieces [famous literary works].

선(禪) Zen. ¶~을 실천하다 practice Zen.

선-(先) [죽은] deceased; [먼저의] pre-; fore-. ¶~보름 the early half of a month.

-선(船) a ship; a vessel. ¶여객~ a passenger ship // 운송~ transport ship.

-선(線) [노선·전선] a line; a wire. ¶상행 [하행] ~ (고속도로 등의) the inbound [outbound] lane (of traffic) // 전화~ a telephone wire // 3번~에서 발차하다 depart from Platform 3 [(미) Track No. 3].

선가(禪家) [선종] the Zen sect; [참선하는 집] a Zen temple; [참선하는 사람] a Zen priest.

선각(先覺) **1** [앞서서 깨달음] foresight; seeing [perceiving] in advance. **선각하다** foresee; foreknow; have prescience of. **2** a pioneer (leader). ⇨ **선각자**(⇨선각)
● **선각자** a pioneer (leader); a leading spirit; a forerunner; a farsighted leader; a pathfinder; a prophet. ¶여성 교육의 ~ a pioneer in the education of women // 그는 시대의 ~였다 He was ahead of his times.

선개교(旋開橋) a swing [swivel / turn] bridge.

선객(船客) a passenger. ¶1등 [2등] ~ a first-class [second-class] passenger.
● **선객 명부** a passenger list [manifest].

선거(船渠) a dock. ¶건(乾)~ a dry dock // 습(濕)~ a wet dock.
● **선거 사용료** dockage; dock charge [dues].

선거(選擧) (an) election. ¶공명~ a fair [clean] election // 국회의원~ the election of the Assemblymen // 대통령~ a presidential election // 무효 ~ an invalid election // 보궐 ~ a by-election / (미) a special election // 중간 ~ an interim election / (미) an off-year election // 총~ a general election // ~의 전망 electoral prospects // ~의 예상 an election prediction // ~에 입후보하다 run in [(영) stand for] an election // ~의 회장 ~에 입후보하다 run [(영) stand] for president // ~를 행하다 hold [have / conduct] an election // ~를 참관하다 be witness at polling [the polls] // 우리 당은 ~에서 승리했다 [졌다] Our party won [was defeated in] the election. 선거하다 elect; vote (for); return.

● 선거 관리 위원회 the Election Administration Committee. 선거구 an election [an electoral / a voting] district; an electorate; a constituency; (미) a precinct. ¶대 [중] ~제 the major [medium] constituency [electorate] system // 소 ~제 a small constituency system / [1인구제(一人區制)] the single-(representative) constituency system. 선거권 the (voting / elective) franchise; the suffrage; the right to vote; voting rights. ¶~을 주다 enfranchise / give the franchise (to) // ~을 박탈하다 deprive (a person) of the right of casting the ballot / disfranchise / disenfranchise // ~을 행사하다 exercise one's franchise / exercise the ballot. 선거법 election [electoral] law. 선거 사무소 an electioneering [a campaign] office. 선거 사범 election crimes. 선거 소송 an election case [lawsuit]. 선거 연설 a campaign speech; an election address (정견 발표의); a vote-getting speech (응원의). 선거 합동 ~ (make) a campaign speech in a joint meeting of candidates. 선거 운동 an election campaign; canvassing; electioneering; the hustings. ¶사전 ~ (take legal measures against) premature election campaigning. 선거 유세 a canvassing [an electioneering / a speaking] tour; (미) a stumping tour; a campaign tour [trip]. ¶~를 하다 go canvassing [campaigning] / make an electioneering tour / (미) take [go on] the stump / stump (it). 선거인 an elector; a voter; a constituent; (집합적) the electorate; the constituency. 선거일 the day of election; the election [polling] day. 선거 입회인 a witness. 선거전 (-戰) an electoral campaign [race]. ¶대통령 ~ a presidential race / a race for presidency // 10일간의 ~에 들어가다 start a ten-day electoral campaign. 선거 제도 an election system.

선견지명 (先見之明) foresight; farseeing intelligence [wisdom]. ¶~이 있는 farseeing / foresighted / farsighted / longsighted / prescient // ~이 있는 사람 a man of foresight / a foreseer // ~이 없는 lacking foresight / short-sighted // ~이 없는 사람 a bad prophet // ~이 있다 possess the gift of foresight / have a long head (on) / have farseeing wisdom / be wise and farsighted // ~이 없다 lack the gift of foresight / be unable to see afar [far ahead] / be short-sighted.

선결 (先決) a previous decision; prior settlement. 선결하다 decide [settle] beforehand; decide [come] first.

● 선결문제 the first consideration; a previous [prior] question; a matter calling for prior settlement. ¶돈이 ~이다 Money is the first question [consideration]. / The question of money comes first.

선경 (仙境) [신선이 산다는 곳] an abode [a land] of wizards; a fairyland; an elf land; (속세를 떠난) an enchanted land [garden].

선고 (宣告) 1 [결정 사항 등의 통고] (a) pronouncement; announcement; (특히 판결의) a sentence; a verdict; adjudication. ¶파산 ~ a decree of bankruptcy // 사형 ~를 내리다 sentence (a person) to death / pass [pronounce] a death sentence (upon a person). 선고하다 [공표하다] announce; pronounce; (판결을) sentence; pass sentence of; (문어) adjudge (▶ 법률 용어로도 쓰임). ¶피고의 유죄를 ~ adjudge a defendant (to be) guilty of the crime // …에게 살인죄를 ~ find a person guilty of murder // 재판장은 도둑에게 5년 징역을 선고했다 The judge sentenced the thief to five years in prison. / The judge pronounced a sentence of five years penal servitude on the thief. ➔ 그는 사형을 선고받았다 He was sentenced to death. / (문어) They pronounced a sentence of death on him. // 그는 유죄 [무죄]를 선고받았다 He was convicted [was acquitted of the charge]. 2 [경기에서의 심판의 판정] a call. ¶심판은 그를 아웃으로 ~했다 The umpire called him out.

● 선고문 a written sentence. 선고 유예 probation.

선곡 (選曲) selection of music. ¶그의 ~은 아주 적절했다 The pieces of music he selected were just right [(문어) most appropriate]. 선곡하다 select (a piece of) music.

선공 (先攻) batting first (in baseball). ¶상대팀의 ~으로 경기가 시작되었다 The game began with our opponents batting first. 선공하다 attack first; (야구에서) bat first; go to bat first.

선과 (善果) good fruit [result / outcome].

선광 (選鑛) dressing [selecting out] ore; ore dressing. ¶비중 [부유 / 자력] ~ ore dressing by gravity separation [floatation / magnetic separation]. 선광하다 dress (ore).

● 선광기 an ore separator.

선교 (宣教) propagation; (특히 기독교의) missionary work. ¶그는 기독교의 ~에 몸을 바쳤다 He devoted himself to missionary work [the propagation of Christianity]. 선교하다 propagate; preach the gospel; evangelize.

● 선교사 (宣教師) a propagator; a missionary (worker).

선교 (船橋) 1 [배다리] a pontoon [floating / bateau] bridge. 2 [배의 브리지] a bridge.

선구 (先驅) a pioneer. ⇨선구자(⇨선구) ¶학생 운동의 ~가 되다 lead [be at the forefront of] the student movement // 사회 개혁의 ~가 되다 take the initiative in social reform / initiate social reform.

● 선구자 a pioneer; a herald; a forerunner; an outrunner; a precursor; a pathfinder; a man of light and leading. ¶~가 되다 be ahead of one's times / take the lead // 그녀는 우리나라 여성 참정권 운동의 ~었다 She was the pioneer of the women's suffrage movement in this country.

선구 (船具) (집합적) a ship's fittings; [삭구] rigging; gearing; [조정 도구] tackle.

● 선구상 a ship chandler; a tackle store.

선구 (選球) [야구] ¶그는 신중하게 ~했다 He watched [waited] carefully for a good pitch

선국 to hit.
● **선구안**(-眼) [야구] the batting eye.
선국(選局) tuning. **선국하다** tune. ¶MBC를 ~ tune in to MBC.
선글라스 (a pair of) sunglasses; (wear) dark glasses.
선금(先金) a deposit; earnest money; a prepayment. ¶~을 주다[치르다] pay in advance / make an advance / prepay // ~을 받다 take [receive] money in advance // 6만 원의 ~을 지불하다 deposit [make a deposit of / put down] 60,000 won (on) // 그는 그 집을 사기 위해 약간의 ~을 지불했다 He put down some earnest money to buy the house [for the purchase of the house].
선급(船級) (ship's) classification [class].
선남선녀(善男善女) good [virtuous] men and women; [불] pious people [men and women]; the faithful; Buddhists.
선납(先納) prepayment; payment in advance. ¶회신료 ~ 전보 a collect [reply-paid] telegram. **선납하다** pay in advance; prepay. ¶회비를 ~ pay the membership fee in advance.
선녀(仙女) a fairy; a celestial maiden; a dryad; a nymph (▶ 강이나 산 등에 사는 요정). ¶~의 춤 an angel's dance.
선다형(選多型) a multiple choice method.
● **선다형 문제** [시험] a multiple-choice question [test].
선단(船團) a fleet (of vessels); [호위되고 있는 선대] a convoy. ¶포경[화물 수송] ~ a fleet of whalers [cargo ships] // 수송 ~ a convoy of transport ships // 출어 ~ a fishing fleet.
선대(先代) [선조] a predecessor; a forebear; [앞시대] the previous age; [앞 세대] the previous [last] generation. ¶저 가게는 ~ 때 번창했었다 The shop used to be prosperous in the day of the present owner's predecessor.
선도(先渡) [경] forward [future] delivery.
선도(先導) guidance; leadership. ¶안내인의 ~로 우리는 산에 올랐다 We climbed the mountain under the leadership of [following] the guide. // 순찰자의 ~ 아래 행렬은 광장으로 나아갔다 Led by a patrol car, the parade proceeded toward the square. // 그들은 소비자 동맹을 설립하는 데 있어서 ~적 역할을 했다 They took the initiative in setting up a consumers' union. **선도하다** lead (the way); guide; go ahead of; conduct; precede. ¶경찰관이 그의 차를 선도했다 A police outrider went ahead of his car.
● **선도자** a leader; a guide.
선도(善導) [올바른 길로 인도함] proper guidance. ¶사상의 ~ proper guidance of public thought / thought guidance / edification. **선도하다** lead [guide] properly; guide aright; instruct; lead (people) to the path of virtue; lead (people) into the right path; edify. ¶아이들을 ~ guide children properly [in the right direction].
● **선도책** measures for proper [judicious] guidance.
선도(鮮度) [싱싱함] freshness. ¶~가 높은 very fresh // ~가 낮은 not very fresh // ~가 떨어지다 become less fresh / lose (some of) (its) freshness.
선돌 [역] a menhir.
선동(煽動) instigation; abetment; (an) incitement; demagogy; demagogism; (미) demagoguery; (an) agitation (▶ 정치적·사회적인 일 등으로). ¶민중 ~가 a rabble-rouser // ~적 (인) incendiary / inflammatory / seditious / agitative / demagogic // 파업은 극좌분자의 ~으로 일어났다 The strike was instigated [incited] by left-wing extremists. **선동하다** agitate; instigate; abet; [부추기다] incite; stir up; set [egg] (a person) on (to (do) something); fan. ¶선동할 목적으로 for agitative purposes // 민중을 선동하여 난동을 부리게 하다 instigate [incite / excite] people to violence // 개혁 [반체제]을 ~ agitate for reform [against the regime] // 임금 인상을 ~ agitate for higher wages // 그는 노동자를 선동하여 파업을 하게 했다 He instigated [incited] the workers to strike. // 그는 군중을 선동하여 폭동을 일으키게 했다 He stirred up [incited] the crowd to riot. →¶학생들은 외부 사람들에 선동되어 수업을 거부했다 The students were stirred up by outsiders and boycotted their classes.
● **선동자** an agitator; an instigator; a setter-on; a firebrand; [법] an abettor. **선동죄** sedition; abetment.
선두(先頭) [행렬 등 이어진 것의 맨 앞] the head; the front; the top; the lead; the van; the first. ¶~에 세우고 with (a person) in the lead / led [spearheaded] by (a band) // ~가 되다 get ahead of (others in a race) / get [have] the lead (in a race) // ~에 서다 be at the head (of) / be in the forefront [van] (of a parade) / take [gain] the lead (in) / take [lead] the van / head / top // ~에 서서 …하다 take the lead in (doing) // 그는 사람들의 ~에 서서 걷기 시작했다 He began to walk ahead of the others [rest]. // [열거의] ~가 누구지 Who's at the head [front] of the line? // ~의 다섯 사람은 앉아도 좋다 The first five persons may sit down. // 그는 경주에서 ~에 섰다 He took the lead in the race. // 행렬의 ~가 흐트러졌다 The beginning [front] of the procession fell into confusion [disorder]. // 그는 학생 운동의 ~에 섰다 He was in the van [was at the head] of the student movement. // ~에 서는 사람은 책임감이 있어야 한다 A leader must have a sense of responsibility.
● **선두 주자** a front-running man; (선거에서) a front runner. ¶개발도상국의 ~로 부상하다 emerge as a forerunner among the developing countries. **선두 타자** [야구] (멤버 중의) a lead-off man; (그 회(回)의) the first batter.
선두(船頭) the bow(s); the prow; the head; the head (of a boat); the eyes.
선둥이(先-) the firstborn of twins.
선득 (추위서) chilly; (놀라서) shudderingly. **선득하다** feel chilly; shudder (at). ⇨ 선득거리다 ¶나는 가슴이 선득했다 My blood ran cold [chill]. / A cold shiver ran through me.
선득거리다 (추위서) feel chilly; feel a chill; (놀라서) shudder (at); be horrified; have a thrill of horror.
선들거리다 (the wind) blow cool and gentle. ⇨ 산들거리다
선들바람 a soft wind. ⇨ 산들바람
선뜻 [빨리] quickly; nimbly [쾌히] readily; willingly; [서슴없이] without hesitation; [즉석에서] instantly; at once; offhand; (미) right away; [가볍게] lightly; lightheartedly. ¶~ 승낙하다 [응하다] readily [willingly]

consent (to it) / comply willingly [with a good grace] / give a ready consent∥ 돈을 ~ 빌려 주다 lend money with a good grace∥ 그는 나의 부탁을 ~ 들어주었다 He was ready and willing to comply with my request.

선뜻하다 clean; frank; cool. ⇨ 산뜻하다

선량(選良) 〔엘리트〕 an elite; the nation's choice; a representative of the people; 〔국회의원〕 a member of the National Assembly. ¶ 그것은 ~으로서 부끄러운 행위다 Such conduct is unworthy of a member of the National Assembly.

선량하다(善良-) good; virtuous; right; good-natured. ¶ 선량한 시민 good citizens / law-abiding citizens.

선령(船齡) a ship's age; the age of a vessel. ¶~ 15년 이상의 배 ships over 15 years old.

선례(先例) **1** a precedent. ⇨ 전례(前例) **2** 〔법〕 prejudication.

선로(船路) a ship's route [course]; a sea route; a seaway.

선로(線路) a (railroad / (영) railway) track [line]. ¶~를 부설하다 lay a line [track] ∥~를 따라 걷다 walk along [follow] the track ∥~에 들어가지 마시오 (게시) Keep off the track.
●**선로 공사** 〔선로 부설〕 tracklaying; (보강·수리 등) track maintenance (work).

선루프 a sunroof.

선린(善隣) (being) good neighbors; neighborly friendship; a good-neighbor relationship.
●**선린 관계** good neighborly relations. **선린 정책** a good neighbor policy.

선망(羨望) envy. ¶ 그녀는 눈초리로 보다 enviously (at) / 그녀의 아름다움은 ~의 대상이었다 Her beauty was the object of envy. / Everybody envied [was envious of] her beauty. **선망하다** envy; be envious (of); feel envy (at); regard (a person) with envy; look enviously (at).

선매(先賣) an advance sale; selling ahead. ¶ 입도(立稻) ~ the sale of a standing rice crop. **선매하다** buy [purchase] in advance; sell in advance; sell ahead [beforehand].

선매권(先買權) (the right of) preemption. ¶~을 얻다 preempt.

선머리(先-) the head; the lead; the van. ¶ 행렬의 ~ the van of procession [parade].

선머슴 a mischievous boy; a naughty rogue; a little monkey; a little demon of a child; an imp; an urchin.

선명(宣明) proclamation; announcement; declaration; promulgation; enunciation. **선명하다** announce; proclaim; declare.

선명도(鮮明度) definition; visibility; (사진의) resolution; (텔레비전의) distinction.

선명하다(鮮明-) clear; clear-[sharp-] cut; distinct; sharp; plain; 〔생생하다〕 vivid. ¶ 선명한 색깔 vivid colors / 선명한 인상 a vivid impression / 선명한 영상 a clear [distinct] image ∥ 인쇄가 선명하지 않다 The print is not clear. / 인상이 선명할 때 그려야겠다 I will finish painting it while it is still vividly impressed on my mind. **선명하게** clearly; distinctly; vividly. ¶~ 기억하다 have a distinct memory (of an incident) / 네온등이 밤하늘에 ~ 떠올랐다 The neon light stood out clearly against the night sky.

선모충(旋毛蟲) a trichina (pl. -nae). ¶~병 trichinosis.

선묘(線描) line drawing. **선묘하다** draw in lines.

선무당 a new [novice] shaman.

선무당이 사람 잡는다(속담) A little knowledge is a dangerous thing.

선무당이 장구 탓한다(속담) A bad [An ill] workman quarrels with his tools.

선물(先物) 〔경〕 futures. ¶~을 매입하다 〔주식의 선물을 사다〕 buy [deal in] futures / 〔시세가 오를 것을 예상하고 사다〕 speculate ∥ ~로 팔다 sell for futures delivery / sell forward.
●**선물 거래** futures trading. ¶~를 하다 deal in futures. **선물 시장** the forward [future] market.

선물(膳物) 〔선사품〕 a present; a gift; 〔바치는 것〕 a tribute; 〔기념품〕 a souvenir. ¶ 생일 [크리스마스] ~ a birthday [Christmas] present / 마음에 드는 ~ an acceptable present [gift] ∥ ~을 보내다 send a person a present ∥ ~을 주다 [받다] give a person a present [receive a present] / 이것을 ~로 받았지요 I received this as a gift. / This was given me as a present. ∥ 나는 그녀에게 손수건을 ~로 보냈다 I sent her some handkerchiefs as a gift [present]. ∥ 이 종합 초콜릿은 ~용입니다 This assortment of chocolates is intended to be a gift. ∥ 이 포도주 병을 ~용으로 포장해 주세요 Please gift-wrap this bottle of wine. ∥ 이 소식이 부모님께 드리는 무엇보다 좋은 ~이 될 것입니다 This news will be the best possible present I can take home to my parents. **선물하다** give (a person) a present. ¶ 반지를 ~ make (a person) a present of a ring.
●**선물 가게** a gift shop; a souvenir store. **선물 세트** a gift set.

선미(船尾) the stern; the buttock(s); the poop. ¶~에 in the stern (of a boat) / astern / aft / abaft ∥ ~를 (이쪽으로) 돌리고 stern on ∥ ~부터 가라앉다 sink by (the) stern.
●**선미 갑판** a quarter-deck.

선민(選民) the chosen people; (기독교에서) the elect.
●**선민사상** elitism.

선박(船舶) a vessel; a ship; a bottom; 〔집합적〕 shipping; seacraft. ¶~의 출입 the movements of shipping ∥ 항내 ~ vessels in port.
●**선박 등기부** the shipping register. **선박 소유자** a shipowner. **선박업** the shipping industry. **선박업자** a shipping man; 〔집합적〕 the shipping interests. **선박 중개인** a ship broker. **선박 회사** a shipping company.

선반 a shelf (pl. shelves); (그물·격자 모양의) a rack. ¶~을 달다 put up a shelf / fix a shelf (to the wall) ∥ ~ 위에 두다 [얹다] put [place] (a thing) on a shelf / shelve.

선반(旋盤) 〔공〕 a lathe; an engine lathe. ¶ 자동 ~ an automatic lathe ∥ ~에 걸다 lathe.
●**선반공** a lathe worker; a turner. **선반 공장** a turnery.

선발(先發) going ahead; starting first. ¶ 누가 ~이지 Who starts first? **선발하다** start in advance (of another); go ahead (of); start first; precede (another to).
●**선발대** an advance party [force / element / contingent]. **선발 투수** 〔야구〕 a starting pitcher.

선발(選拔) selection; choice; picking out. ¶ 그는 팀의 ~에서 누락되었다 He wasn't picked for [He didn't make] the team. **선발하다**

선방

선 select; pick out; choose; mark out (for); single out; draft. ¶그들은 우수한 선수를 선발했다 They picked [singled] out players. // They selected [chose] best players. → 선발된 picked / selected // 선발된 선수들 the very best players // 그는 200명의 지원자 가운데서 선발되었다 He was selected [picked] from among two hundred applicants.
- **선발 시험** a selective examination. **선발팀** an all-star team.

선방(善防) a good defense [(영) defence]. **선방하다** put up a good defense; defend well.

선배(先輩) a senior; a superior; an elder; a predecessor; (미국 구어) an old timer.(▶ senior는 단순히 연장자를 뜻할 뿐, 우리말의 「선배」가 가지는 서열 의식을 전혀 나타내고 있지 않음. 영어에는 따르고 대접해야 할 대상으로서의 「선배」에 해당하는 말이 없음) ¶대~ a big senior // ~ 티를 내다 pose [give oneself airs] as a senior / assume [put on] an air of seniority // 그는 나보다 5년 ~이다 He has five years more experience [seniority] than I do. / (회사에서) He has been in the company five years longer than I have. / (학교에서) He was five years ahead of me in school. // 제 2년 ~이시군요 You are two years my senior. / You are my senior by two years. // 그녀는 동문회의 대~이다 She is one of the oldest members of the alumnae association.

선별(選別) sorting; selection; (광석의) concentration; dressing. **선별하다** sort; [좋은 것을 가리다] select; concentrate; dress. ¶홈는 물건을 ~ sort out defective articles. → ¶사과는 크기에 따라 선별되었다 The apples were sorted according to size. // 광석은 모래나 그 밖의 불순물로부터 선별된다 Ore is concentrated [dressed] from sand and other impurities.
- **선별기** a sorter; a selector; a sorting machine; (광석의) a concentrating [dressing] machine. ¶우편물 ~ a mail [postal] sorter.

선복(船腹) 1 [배의 허리 부분] the side(s) of a ship. 2 [적재 능력] tonnage. 3 [배의 화물실] the hold.

선봉(先鋒) the van; the vanguard; the spearhead; [전초선] the scouting line. ¶~에 서서 in the van (of the attack on ...) // ~이 되다 lead the van / spearhead (an operation) / become the spearhead of an advance [attack] // ~ 다툼을 하다 vie with one another to reach the enemy camp first // 그의 회사는 한국의 소프트웨어 업계의 ~이었다 His company was in the van of [led] the Korean software industry. // 그는 사회 개혁 운동의 ~이다 He is in the vanguard [van] of the social reform movement.

선분(線分) [수] a segment.

선불 a stray bullet.

선불 맞은 호랑이 뛰듯(속담) hopping mad; furious.

선불(을) 걸다[놓다] aim a clumsy blow [move] at; get hoist with his own petard.

선불(先拂) advance payment; payment in advance; payment; cash before delivery (약어 C.B.D). ¶송료 ~로 [부치는 사람 지불로] freight [(영) carriage] paid // 우편료 ~ postage prepaid // 운임 ~ freight prepaid [included] / carriage prepaid // ~의 조건으로 on condition of advance payment // 요금 ~ 전보 a collect telegram // 운임 ~로 짐을 부치다 send goods freight prepaid // 인지세의 3할은 ~이다 Thirty percent of your royalties will be paid in advance. **선불하다** pay [disburse] in advance; advance (money); make an advance; prepay (of wages). ¶방세를 3개월치 ~ pay three months' room rent in advance // 그는 회사에서 월급을 한 달분 선불받았다 He got his company to advance him a month's salary.
- **선불금** prepayment; an advance payment.

선비 [학자] a *seonbi*; a (classical) scholar; a learned man; [덕이 있는 사람] a man of virtue.

선사(膳賜) [위로·존경·친근·애정 등의 뜻으로 선물을 줌] presentation. **선사하다** give [make / send] (a person) a present; make a gift (to a person); present (a person with a thing). ¶시계를 ~ present (a person) with a watch / present a watch to (a person). → ¶선사받다 receive a present.
- **선사품** a present; a gift.

선사(先史) [관형어적] prehistoric.
- **선사 시대** the prehistoric age. ¶~의 생물 prehistoric life // ~ 유적 prehistoric remains.

선사(禪師) a Zen priest [master]; an esteemed priest; the Rev ....

선산(先山) one's family graveyard. ⇨ 선영

선상(船上) ¶~에(서) on board (a ship) / aboard // 그 증기선 ~에서 일어난 사고 the accident on board the steamship.
- **선상 난민** (월남의) boat people. **선상 생활** life on board [shipboard].

선상(線上) [어떠한 상태]. ¶그들은 기아~에 있었다 They were on the point of starvation. / They were on the verge of starvation.

선상지(扇狀地) [지] a fan; an alluvial fan.

선생(先生) 1 (일반적으로) a teacher; a master; an instructor. ¶고등학교의 ~ a high school teacher // 꽃꽂이 ~ a master [teacher] of flower arrangement // 그는 화학 ~이다 He teaches chemistry. / He is a teacher of chemistry [chemistry teacher].
2 [남을 존대하는 경칭]. ¶(교사인 경우) 최 ~ Mr. [Mrs. / Miss] Choe(▶ 일반적으로 Mr. [Mrs. / Miss]를 붙여 성을 부르는 것이 보통. 대학 선생인 경우는 교수·조교수의 구별 없이 professor Choe로 부르는 경우도 있음. 상대방이 박사인 경우에는 Doctor [Dr.] Choe 라고도 할 수 있음) / (의사인 경우) Doctor [Dr. / Mr. / Mrs. / Miss] Choe / (변호사·작가·지도하는 사람, 그 밖의 일반적인 경칭으로서) Mr. [Mrs. / Miss] Choe.

선서(宣誓) an oath; parole. ¶법정에서의 ~ a judicial oath // 취임 ~를 하다 take the oath of office // ~를 하고 증언하다 give evidence under oath. **선서하다** swear; take [make / swear] an oath; pledge one's word of honor; lift (up) the hand. ¶그는 성서에 손을 얹고 진실을 말할 것을 선서했다 With his hand on the Bible he swore to tell nothing but the truth. → ¶선서시키다 administer an oath to (a person) / attest / swear / put (a person) on (his) oath.
- **선서문** a deposition; an affidavit; a written oath. **선서식** the administering of an oath.

선선하다 1 [시원하다] cool; refreshing. ¶선선한 바람 cool [refreshing] breeze // 여기는 아주 ~ It is nice and cool here. 2 (성격이) frank; candid; open-hearted; unreserved; (동작이) brisk; spirited; active; quick. ¶말하는 것이

~ be outspoken. **선선히** [기꺼이] readily; willingly; with (a) good grace; [솔직히] candidly; frankly; openly. ¶부탁을 ~ 들어주다 comply with (another's) request with good grace // ~ 승낙하다 readily [willingly] consent (to) / give a ready consent (to) / readily accept (an invitation)/~ 대답하다 answer frankly/자기 잘못을 ~ 인정하다 acknowledge one's fault candidly.

선셈(先-) prepayment; settling accounts in advance. **선셈하다** prepay; settle accounts in advance.

선소리 foolish [silly] talk; rubbish; an absurd remark. **선소리하다** talk nonsense; make an absurd remark.

선손(先-) forestalling. ⇨⁼선수(先手)1

선수(先手) 1 [기선을 제압하기] forestalling; the initiative; anticipation. ¶~를 빼앗기다 [앞질리다] be forestalled / [주도권을 빼앗기다] / [후진에서 활약하다] lose the initiative / [후진에서 활약하다] act as rearguard // 우리들의 대책은 항상 ~를 빼앗겼다 Our countermeasures were always one step behind [too late]. 2 [바둑·장기 등에서 먼저 두는 일] the first move; [선수로 두는 사람] the first mover. ¶~로 바둑을 두다 make the first move in a *baduk*(go) game.

선수(를) **쓰다**[치다] steal a march on (a person); (미국 구어) beat (a person) to it [the punch]; take [obtain] the initiative (from a person in something); forestall; anticipate; get a jump on (a person). ¶선수를 친 것은 내가 아니고 그였다 It was he, not I, that took the initiative. // 총장은 그날 학생 소요로 선수를 쳐서 휴교토록 했다 The president forestalled the student riot by having the university closed for the day.

선수(船首) the bow. ⇨⁼이물

선수(選手) a player; an athlete (▶ player는 야구·축구 등 게임의 선수). ¶후보 ~ a substitute / (야구의) a bench polisher / 테니스 [야구] ~ a tennis [baseball] player / 수영 ~ a swimmer // 그는 배구 ~이다 He is a volleyball player. / He is on the volleyball team.

● **선수권** a championship; a title. ¶세계 ~ the world championship // 전국 ~ a national championship // ~을 차지하다 [잃다] win [lose] the championship // ~을 보유하다 hold [retain] the championship // (권투에서) ~을 방어하다 defend the title // ~을 빼앗다 wrest the championship (from). **선수단** a team; a squad. **선수촌** an athletes' village. ¶태능 ~ the Taeneung Training Center.

선술집 a tavern; a (stand-up) bar; (미) a saloon; a groggery; (영) a public house; (영국 구어) a pub.

선승(禪僧) [불] a Zen Priest [monk].

선승하다(先勝-) win the first game; score the first point. ¶데이비스컵 경기에서 미국 팀이 선승했다 In the Davis Cup tournament the American team won the first match.

선실(船室) a cabin; (특실) a stateroom; (집합적) the passenger's quarters. ¶1등 ~ a first-class cabin / a stateroom // 2등 ~ a second-class cabin // 3등 ~ the steerage // 호놀룰루행의 ~을 예약하다 book passage for Honolulu.

선심(善心) 1 [선량한 마음] virtuous mind; virtue; conscience; moral sense. 2 [자비로운 마음] a merciful heart; mercy; benevolence; kindness; [너그러운 마음] generosity; liberality. ¶~ 공세 pork-barreling / the use of patronage for political advantage.

선심(을) **쓰다** have mercy on (a person). ¶그들이 선심을 써 주는 바람에 사장을 만날 수가 있었다 They were kind [good] enough to let me see the president.

선심(線審) (정구·축구 등의) a linesman.

선악(善惡) good and evil [bad]; [정사(正邪)] right and wrong; virtue and vice. ¶~을 구별하다 discriminate the good from the bad [between right and wrong] / 그 나이쯤이면 ~을 판별할 줄 알아야 한다 At your age, you ought to be able to tell right from wrong [good from bad].

● **선악과**(-果) [성] the fruit of the Tree of Knowledge (of Good and Evil).

선약(先約) a previous engagement. ¶~이 없다 have no previous engagement / be disengaged / be free // ~이 있어서 참석할 수 없다 I'm afraid a previous engagement will prevent me from attending. // 저는 ~이 있습니다 I have a previous engagement.

선약(仙藥) an elixir; (a) medicine with magical (healing) power.

선양(宣揚) enhancement; increase. **선양하다** enhance; raise; increase; exalt; heighten. ¶국위를 ~ enhance national prestige / promote the national glory.

선언(宣言) [규약·규정에 따른 통고] (a) declaration; (a) proclamation; [정식 발표] (an) announcement. ¶공산당 ~ the Communist Manifesto // 미합중국의 독립 ~ the Declaration of Independence // 세계 인권 ~ the Declaration of Human Rights // 포츠담 ~ the Potsdam Declaration // 폭탄~을 하다 drop [throw] a bombshell / make a bombshell announcement. **선언하다** declare; make a declaration (of); proclaim; announce. ¶의장은 개회 [폐회]를 선언했다 The chairman announced the opening [closing] of the meeting. / The chairman declared the meeting in session. / (미) The meeting was called to order. // 그 섬들은 독립을 선언했다 The islands proclaimed their independence. // 시장은 긴급 사태를 선언했다 The mayor proclaimed an emergency.

● **선언서** a (written) declaration; a manifesto (*pl.* ~(e)s); a statement. ¶~를 기초 [발표]하다 draw up [issue] a declaration.

선열(先烈) our worthy predecessors; previous martyrs. ¶순국~ previous martyrs for our country.

선영(先塋) [조상의 무덤] one's family graveyard; one's ancestral burial ground.

선왕(先王) the late [preceding] king.

선외(選外) ¶~의 left out of selection [choice].

● **선외가작** a good but unaccepted work.

선용하다(善用-) [알맞게 잘 쓰다] make good use of (one's knowledge); turn (spare time) to good account; employ (time) well [wisely / profitably]. ¶여가를 ~ make good use of one's spare time. 2 [좋은 일에 쓰다] put (money) to good use. ¶저축한 돈을 ~ use the money one has saved for a good purpose.

선웃음 a forced [a feigned / an affected] laugh [smile]; a smirk; a (conscious) simper. ¶~을 치다 force [affect / feign] a laugh [smile] / simper / smirk.

선원(船員) a sailor; a seaman; a crewman;

a mariner; (집합적) the crew; a ship's company; officers and crew. ¶고급 ~ an [a ship's] officer / (집합적) the quarterdeck // 보통 ~ ratings / 하급 ~ (집합적) the forecastle / [개인] a sailor / (구어) a jack tar / (속어) a jacky / [화부] a stoker // ~이 되다 go to sea / become a sailor.
● **선원 보험** seamen's insurance. **선원수첩** a seaman's pocket ledger. **선원실** the crew's quarters; the crew space.

선위 (禪位) abdication (of the throne). **선위하다** abdicate; vacate the throne. ¶고대 중국에서는 황제가 덕 있는 인물에게 선위하고 퇴위하는 예가 있었다 In ancient China, there were some cases in which an Emperor abdicated in favor of a virtuous man.

선율 (旋律) a melody; a tune. ¶대(對)~ a countermelody / a counterpoint // 아름다운 ~의 작곡가 a fine melodist.
● **선율학** melodics.

선의 (善意) [좋은 뜻] a favorable sense; [좋은 의도] good will; good intentions; [법] good faith. ¶~의 well-meaning (people) / wellintentioned / well-meant // ~로 in good faith / with good intent [intentions] // ~로 한 일 a well-meaning [well-intentioned] attempt // 그것은 그녀가 정말 ~에서 한 일입니다 She did it out of simple good will. // ~로 해석하자면, 그는 너무 열중한 나머지 불쑥 말해 버린 것 같다 To give him the benefit of the doubt, I suppose he (must have) blurted it out in an excess of enthusiasm.

선인 (仙人) **1** a legendary hermit with miraculous powers. ⇨ 신선(神仙) **2** [도를 닦는 사람] a wizardlike unworldly man; a hermit.

선인 (先人) **1** my deceased [late] father. **2** [전대의 사람] one's predecessors; [선구자] a forerunner; a pioneer. ¶~ 미답의 땅 a previously untrodden [unexplored] area // ~의 발자취를 더듬다 follow in the footsteps of one's predecessors // 그는 ~들의 과학상의 업적을 한 걸음 진보시켰다 He carried the scientific achievements of his predecessors [those who had gone before him] a step further.

선인 (善人) a good man; a good-natured man; a virtuous person. ¶~과 악인 the good people and the bad / the sheep and the goats / the goodies and the baddies // ~은 흥하고 악인은 망한다 Virtue triumphs over vice.

선인선과 (善因善果) the results [fruits] of good deeds; the rewards of virtue; Good deeds bear good fruit.

선인장 (仙人掌) [식] a cactus (pl. ~es, -ti); an opuntia.

선일 a job which requires one to stand; a stand-up task; working on one's feet.

선임 (先任) [전임] seniority; [전임자] a predecessor. ¶~의 senior / elder // 내가 입사했을 때 ~ 사원이 10명 있었다 When I joined the firm, there were already ten employees.
● **선임권** the seniority right. **선임자** a senior member.

선임 (選任) [선출] (an) election; [임명] (an) appointment; (an) assignment. ¶변호인의 ~ designation (by the Government) of counsels. **선임하다** elect; appoint; assign. ¶사장은 신설된 지점장에 그를 선임했다 The president appointed him manager of the new branch [to manage the new branch]. ➔ ¶그는 사회당 위원장으로 선임되었다 He was elected chairman of the Socialist Party.

선입관 (先入觀) a preconception; a preoccupation; a prepossession; a prejudice; a bias; a preconceived idea [notion]. ¶~을 가지다 have a preconceived idea [opinion] / ~을 버리시오 Get rid of your prejudices [preconceived notions]. // 그는 상류 사회에 대해 어처구니없는 ~을 가지고 있었다 He had foolish preconceptions about high society.

선잠 a nap; a doze; a snooze; a dogsleep; a light [short] sleep; slumber(s). ¶~을 자다 take a nap / doze / snooze / slumber / have a light [short] sleep // ~에서 깨다 awake from one's light sleep [one's slumber].

선장 (船長) the captain of a ship; a (ship's / sea) captain; the master (of a ship); a master mariner; a commander; a skipper (소형 상선·어선의); a ferry master (연락선의).
● **선장실** a captain's cabin [room].

선재 (船材) (ship-building) timber [lumber].

선저 (船底) the bottom of a ship.

선적 (積) [적하] loading (a ship); lading; [발송] shipment (약어 shipt, shpt); shipping. ¶부분 ~ part [partial] shipment // 분할 ~ split shipment / shipment by installments // 지급 ~ 요망함 Request prompt shipment. **선적하다** load (a ship); lade (a ship with cargo); ship (a cargo); make a shipment. ¶우리는 홍수 피해국에 보낼 의약품을 선적했다 We loaded the boat with medical supplies for shipment to the flood-stricken county.
● **선적 서류** shipping documents. **선적 송장** a shipping invoice. **선적 화물** cargo; shipping goods.

선적 (船籍) the nationality of a ship; a ship's flag. ¶미국 ~의 배 a ship of American nationality [registry] // 불명의 배 a vessel [ship] of unknown nationality // ~을 등록하다 register a ship // 이 배는 한국 ~이다 This ship flies the Korean flag. / This ship is of Korean nationality. / This ship sails under the Korean flag.
● **선적 증서** a certificate of nationality.

선전 (宣傳) propaganda (정부 등이 유리한 정보를 흘림); publicity (정보를 일반에게 알림); propagation; propagandism; [광고] advertisement; an advertising campaign; (미국 구어) buildup. ¶가두 ~원 a town-crier / an advertisement man // 자기 ~ self-advertising // 흑색 ~ a malicious [false] propaganda // ~의 무기 a propaganda weapon // ~에 말려가다 swallow the propaganda // 지금은 ~의 시대다 This is the age of advertising. // 그 새 부티크는 사전 ~으로 많은 손님을 끌어 모았다 The new boutique attracted many customers with its advance advertising. **선전하다** propagate; publicize; propagandize; give publicity (to); conduct [make] propaganda; disseminate; spread abroad; [광고하다] advertise; (미국 구어) give a buildup (to). ¶대대적으로 ~ carry on propaganda on a large scale / (미국 구어) give a big buildup (to) / 요란하게 ~ make much propaganda / propagandize [advertise] extensively / carry on [out] an active [a vigorous] propaganda // 자신을 선전하는 일도 때로는 필요하다 It is necessary to advertise yourself

sometimes.∥우리 가게를 친구분들에게 선전해 주십시오 Please recommend this store to your friends. / Tell your friends about this store.∥신문은 그의 작품을 대대적으로 선전하는 기사를 썼다 The newspaper gave his work a big buildup.∥그의 연주회는 사전에 선전한 만큼은 좋지 않았다 His concert was not so good as the advance publicity had made out.∥그들은 군비 강화의 필요성을 선전해 왔다 They have been spreading a lot of propaganda about the need for a military buildup. ➔유럽 영화제에서 상을 받자 그 영화는 크게 선전되었다 That movie got a lot of free publicity when it won a prize in a European film festival.
● **선전 공세** propaganda offensive; a propaganda attack; a propaganda[an advertising] onslaught. **선전 기사** a publicity article. **선전대**(-隊) a propaganda squad. **선전 문구** (상품의) a sales message; [광고 문안] copy. **선전전**(-戰) a propaganda war(fare). **선전 효과** the impact[effectiveness] of advertising [propaganda].

선전 포고(宣戰布告) a declaration[proclamation] of war. ¶~나 다름없는 중대한 도발 행위 a grave and serious provocation tantamount to a declaration of war (against).

선전하다(善戰-) fight well [magnificently / admirably]; fight a good fight[battle]; make [put up] a good fight. ¶그들은 선전했음에도 불구하고 패했다 Although they fought very well[hard], they were defeated.∥상대방 후보자가 예상외로 선전했다 The rival candidate put up a better fight than we had expected.∥그의 부대는 최후까지 선전했다 His platoon fought gamely to the end.

선점(先占) prior occupation. **선점하다** preoccupy.
● **선점(권)자** an occupant. **선점 취득** acquisition by occupancy.

선정(善政) good[wise] government[administration]; just rule. ¶그는 ~을 베푼 황제로 알려져 있다 He is known as an emperor who governed well[wisely].

선정(選定) (a) selection; (a) choice. ¶~ 중이다 be in the course of selection. **선정하다** select; choose; make a selection[choice] (of)(▶ select가 격식을 차린 말). ¶역사상의 중요 사건을 ~ pick out important event in history.
● **선정 기준** a basis of selection; criteria for selection.

선정적(煽情的) suggestive; inflammatory; voluptuous; lascivious; sultry; sensational. ¶~인 신문 a sensational newspaper(세상을 시끄럽게 하는) // ~인 포스터 a suggestive poster(정욕을 불러일으키는).

선제(先制) a head start. ¶~ 2점을 올리다 score the first two runs // ~ 홈런을 치다 start the scoring by hitting a homer[home run].
● **선제공격** a containment offensive; a leadoff attack(권투 등의); a preemptive nuclear attack(핵전쟁의). ¶~을 가하다 strike (the enemy) first[before he goes into] action / carry out a preemptive strike against (the enemy's nuclear installations) // 그는 상대방에게 ~을 가했다 He seized the offensive first. / He went on the offensive first.

선조(先祖) an ancestor; a forefather; a progenitor; a predecessor; [법] a stirps (*pl*. stirpes). ¶8대 ~ one's ancestors in the eighth generation.

선종(禪宗) [불] Zen Buddhism; the Zen sect. ¶~의 승려 a Zen priest[monk].

선주(船主) a shipowner.

선지 blood from a slaughtered animal.
● **선지피** fresh blood. ¶코에서 ~가 흐르다 blood gushed from the nose.

선지자(先知者) a prophet; a prophetess(여자); a predictor; a prognosticator.

선진(先陣) the van (of an army); the advance guard; the vanguard; a scouting line(전초선). ¶~을 맡다 lead the van.

선진(先進) [앞섬] being advanced; [배해] a senior; a superior; an elder; a predecessor; a progenitor; [선구자] a pioneer; a precursor; a farsighted leader. ¶~의 advanced / developed.
● **선진국** an advanced[a developed] country [nation]; a forefront nation. ¶**공업** ~ an industrially advanced nation // ~ 대열에 끼다 join the ranks[columns] of advanced countries. **선진 기술** advanced technology. ¶~의 도입 the inducement of advanced technology.

선집(選集) a selection; an anthology; selected works. ¶**영시** ~ an anthology[a selection] of English poems // **키츠** ~ a selection of Keats' poetry / selected poems of Keats.

선착(先着) [먼저 도착함] the first arrival. ¶~ 200명까지 특별석으로 모십니다 The first two hundred persons can have special seats.∥호텔 예약은 ~순으로 접수합니다 Room will be reserved on a first-come-first-served basis.∥~순으로 줄을 서 주세요 Please line up in the order of arrival. **선착하다** arrive [come] first.
● **선착자** the first (person) to arrive; the first comer.

선착장(船着場) [부두] a wharf; [상륙지] a landing place.

선창(先唱) (노래 등의) the lead (in singing); [주창] advocacy; initiation; promotion; instance. **선창하다** lead the song[chorus / singing]; [주창하다] play first violin; advance[introduce] (a new doctrine); advocate; initiate; promote. ¶만세 삼창을 ~ lead (a group of people) in giving three cheers // 데이 씨가 건배를 선창하겠습니다 Mr. Day will propose a toast.∥당신이 선창하시면 모두 따르겠습니다 You lead[call the tune] and we'll follow.
● **선창자** (노래의) a chorus leader; (건배의) a toastmaster; [주창자] a leader; an advocate; a ring leader(파업 등의).

선창(船窓) a porthole.

선창(船艙) a (landing) pier; a jetty; [부두] a wharf (*pl*. ~s, -ves); a quay. ¶**부양식** ~ a floating pier // **여객선용** ~ a landing pier // 배를 ~에 대다 bring a boat alongside a pier.

선처(善處) amicable[adequate] management; proper dealing. **선처하다** make the best of (a bad bargain); tide over (difficulties); act with prudence; use discretion (in); deal adequately[wisely] with (a difficult situation); deal with (something) as one thinks fit; adjust oneself (to). ¶다시는 그런 일이 일어나지 않도록 ~ take proper measure [appropriate steps] to prevent such a thing from recurring // 우리는 이 문제에 대해 총리가 선처해 주기를 바란다 We would like the prime minister to deal prudently with this matter. // 아무쪼록 선처해 주시기 바랍니다 Please arrange things as well as possible.

선천성(先天性) apriority; innateness; inbornness; inherence. ¶~ 백혈병 congenital leukemia // ~ 이상 a birth defect / congenital anomaly // ~ 질환 a congenital disease.

선천적(先天的) native; inborn; innate; congenital. (유전적인) inherited; hereditary. ¶~인 재능 (a) natural [(an) inborn / (an) innate] talent // ~인 불구 a congenital deformity // 그는 ~으로 낙천가이다 He is optimistic by nature.

선철(先哲) an ancient sage; a wise [learned] man of the past. ¶~의 가르침 the teaching of an ancient sage.

선철(銑鐵) cast iron. ⇨ 주철

선체(船體) a hull; the body of a ship. ¶~는 두 조각이 났다 The hull [body of the ship] broke in two.

선출(選出) election; [법] choice. ¶전국구 의원 a councilor elected from the national constituency. **선출하다** elect; (영) return. ➔ ¶그녀는 학급 대표로 선출되었다 She was elected class representative. // 홍 씨는 서울에서 국회의원으로 선출되었다 Mr. Hong was elected to a member of the National Assembly from Seoul.

선취(先取) taking first; preoccupation; preoccupancy. **선취하다** take first; preoccupy; preempt. ¶우리는 1점을 선취했다 We scored the first point of the game.
●**선취권 / 선취 특권** a preferential [prior / priority] right; (the right of) priority; priority of claim; a lien. ¶~이 있다 have the prior right (to) / have a priority right (over) / have a prior lien (on). **선취점** the point(s) scored first; (야구에서) the run(s) scored first. ¶~을 올리다 score first / get on the score first.

선측(船側) the side of a ship; a ship's side.
●**선측 인도** [적화] free alongside (ship)(약어 F.A.S.); [양륙] ex ship.

선친(先親) my deceased [late] father.

선탄(選炭) coal dressing [washing]; concentration of coal.

선태(蘚苔) [식] moss(es); a bryophyte.
●**선태류** bryophyte. **선태학** bryology.

선택(選擇) (a) choice; (a) selection; option; selectivity. ¶~의 자유 the liberty of choice // 다른 ~의 여지가 없다 I have no other choice [option]. // ~은 네 자유이다 The choice is mine. / It's up to me. / I can choose freely. // 회의 날짜의 ~은 당신에게 맡기겠습니다 We will leave the selection of a date for the meeting up to you. **선택하다** select; choose; pick up; make a [one's] choice. ¶잘 ~ make a good choice // 잘못 ~ make a bad [the wrong] choice / choose the wrong thing // 읽을거리를 ~ select in one's reading.
●**선택 과목** (영) an optional (subject); (미) an elective (subject). **선택권** an option; (right of) choice. ¶~이 있다 have the right of choice / have the [one's] pick (of).

선팅 [창유리에 색깔 있는 얇은 필름 막을 붙이는 일] (window) tinting.

선팽창(線膨脹) [물] linear expansion.

●**선팽창 계수** a coefficient of linear expansion.

선편(船便) shipping service. ⇨ 배편 ¶그 섬에는 ~이 하루에 한 번 있다 There is steamer [ferry] service to the island once a day. / A boat stops at the island once a day. // 그 소포는 ~으로 부치겠다 I will send this parcel by sea [by surface mail].

선포(宣布) proclamation; promulgation; announcement. **선포하다** proclaim; make public; promulgate; announce; publicize; make promulgation of; issue a proclamation. ¶전쟁을 ~ declare war // 계엄령을 ~ proclaim martial law.

선폭(船幅) the beam. ¶~이 30미터인 배 a ship thirty meters in the beam.

선풍(旋風) a whirlwind; a cyclone; a tornado (pl.-(e)s). ¶검거 ~ a wholesale [mass] arrest / a sweeping roundup // 역 ~ an anticyclone // ~에 휘말리다 be caught up in a cyclone // 그의 그림은 미술 평론가들 사이에 ~을 일으켰다 His paintings created a sensation among art critics.

선풍기(扇風機) an electric fan; a motor fan. ¶천장 ~ a ceiling [an overhead] fan // ~의 바람 the draft [breeze] from an electric fan // ~를 틀다 set an electric fan in motion / start [turn on / switch on] an electric fan // ~를 끄다 turn [switch] off an electric fan // ~ 바람을 쐬다 get [enjoy] the breeze from an electric fan.

선하(船荷) cargo; freight; lading; freightage. ¶미착 ~ cargo [load] afloat.
●**선하주** the shipper. **선하 증권** a bill of lading(약어 B/L). **선적** ~ a shipped B/L // 지시식 ~ an order B/L.

선하다 vivid [fresh] (before one's eyes); graphic; feel as if one actually saw. ¶눈에 ~ be fresh in one's memory / live vividly in one's memory // 그 광경이 아직도 ~ The scene is still lingering in my eyes. / I have a vivid recollection of it. // 그녀의 모습이 여전히 눈에 ~ The memory of her visage still haunts me. **선히** vividly; freshly; graphically. ¶~ 떠오르는 그녀의 모습 the memory of her visage recalled with the vividness of real life // 그들의 무시무시한 얼굴이 아직도 눈에 ~ 떠오른다 Their ghastly looks still haunt my eyes.

선하다(善—) good(-natured). ⇨ 착하다

선하품 a slight yawn; a forced yawn. ¶~을 삼키다 suppress [stifle] a yawn.

선행(先行) precedence; antecedence; preceding; going first; walking ahead (of). **선행하다** precede; be [go / walk] ahead (of). ¶이 명사에 선행하는 형용사 the adjective preceding this noun // 그의 사상은 시대에 선행하고 있었다 His ideas were ahead of the times.
●**선행 조건** a condition precedent; an essential prerequisite.

선행(善行) good conduct; a good deed. ¶~을 쌓다 accumulate [keep on doing] good deeds // ~을 표창하다 reward (a person) in recognition of (his) good conduct // 죄수들은 ~에 의해 형기가 단축되는 일이 있다 Prisoners may be released early [(영) gain remission of sentence] for good conduct.
●**선행상** a prize for good conduct.

선향(線香) a stick of incense; a joss stick; an incense stick.

선험론(先驗論) 〔철〕 transcendentalism.
선험적(先驗的) transcendental. ¶~ 인식 transcendental cognition.
선헤엄 treading water; standing stroke. ¶~을 치다 tread water.
선현(先賢) an ancient sage. ⇨선철(先哲)
선혈(鮮血) fresh blood; life blood. ¶소년은 ~이 낭자했다 The boy was dripping with blood. / The body was covered with blood.
선형(扇形) 1 a fan shape. 2 ➡부채꼴(⇨부채)
선형(船形) the type of a ship[vessel]; (모형) a model of a ship.
선호(選好) preference. ¶남아 ~ 사상 a notion of preferring a son to a daughter∥유동성 ~ 〔경〕 liquidity. **선호하다** prefer (to).
선홍색(鮮紅色) scarlet.
선화(線畫) (그림) a line drawing.
선회(旋回) revolution; turning; rotation; circling; gyration; gyre; evolution(댄스·스케이트 등의). ¶수직 ~ 〔항〕 a vertical turn∥비행기의 꼬리 ~ a spin / a tailspin. **선회하다** revolve; turn; rotate; circle round; gyrate; whirl [swing] round; wheel. ¶대머리수리가 우리 머리 위를 선회하였다 The condor circled over our heads.∥비행기가 왼쪽으로 선회하였다 The plane took a turn to the left.
● **선회 비행** circuitous flying; (a) circular flight. **선회 운동** a turning[rotating / gyrating] movement.
선후(先後) front and rear; beginning and end; (순서) order; sequence. ¶~가 뒤바뀌었다 The order is inverted[reversed].∥일의 ~가 뒤죽박죽이 되어 구별이 안 되었다 The matter was so mixed up that nothing could be made out of it.
선후(지)**책**(善後之策) a remedial[relief] measure; a countermeasure; remedies. ¶~을 강구하다 take corrective measures / devise[work out] remedial measures / resort [have recourse] to an expedient / consider the best course[how best] to deal with the situation.
섣달 the twelfth month of the lunar calendar; December(약어 Dec.). ¶~그믐 the last day of the year / New Year's Eve.
섣부르다 〔어설프다〕 awkward; clumsy; unskillful; tactless; 〔부주의하다〕 careless; heedless; thoughtless; inadvertent; 〔경솔하다〕 rash; hasty; (미) brash. ¶섣부른 짓을 하다(어설픈) make sad work[a bad job] of it / 〔경솔한〕 commit[do] a rash act / act rashly[foolishly / unwisely]. **섣불리** 〔어설프게〕 awkwardly; clumsily; tactlessly; 〔부주의하게〕 carelessly; thoughtlessly; heedlessly; inadvertently. ¶남의 말을 ~ 믿다 believe too easily what one hears[what they say]∥~ 기밀을 누설하다 reveal a secret carelessly∥이것은 ~ 손댈 수 없는 일이다 This is certainly a matter not to be lightly handled. / The matter requires careful handling.
설 〔음력 1월 1일〕 *seol*; the lunar New Year's Day; the New Year's Day by the lunar calendar. ¶~ **연휴** the New Year's holidays by the lunar calendar∥~을 **쇠다** observe[celebrate] *seol*.
설- insufficient; not; imperfect; half-done. ¶~익은 (음식) half-cooked [-done / -boiled] / underdone / (과일) unripe / half-ripe / ~익히다 parboil.
설(說) 1 〔의견·주장〕 an opinion; a view; (종교 상의) (속어) a doxy. ¶자기의 ~을 굽히다[고집하다] change[stick to] one's opinion[view]∥…이라는 ~을 주장하는 사람도 있다 Some say[are of (the) opinion] that …∥그 기원에 대해서는 여러 ~이 있다 There are a variety of views about its origin.
2 〔학설·신조〕 a theory; a doctrine. ¶새로운 ~을 주장하다 advance[propose / put forward] a new theory∥맬서스의 ~ the Malthusian theory[doctrine]∥플라톤의 ~을 신봉하다 follow Plato.
3 〔풍설〕 a rumor[(영) rumour]; a report. ¶그러한 ~이 항간에 떠돌고 있다 Rumors to that effect are in the air.∥그가 제주도로 귀양 갔다는 ~이 있다 One version says[has it] that he was banished to the Jejudo.
설거지 〔그릇을 씻어 치움〕 dish-washing; (영) washing-up. **설거지하다** do the dishes [washing-up]; wash the dishes; wash up. ¶그녀는 어머니를 도와 설거지했다 She helped her mother with the washing-up.
● **설거지통** a dishwater bucket. ⇨개수통
설겅거리다 be half-cooked and eat hard; be not thoroughly cooked; be half-done; taste lumpy; chew hard. ¶콩이 설겅거린다 The beans are half-done and eat hard[tough].∥이 감자는 잘 삶지 않아 아직 설겅거린다 This potato isn't cooked enough — it's still hard.
설겅설겅 eating hard; hard-chewing; lumpy-tasting. **설겅설겅하다** be half-cooked and eat hard. ⇨설겅거리다
설경(雪景) a snow scene[view]; a snowy landscape; a snowscape; a landscape of snow. ¶정원의 ~은 아름다웠다 The snow-covered garden was beautiful. / The garden looked beautiful in the snow.
설계(設計) (건물 등의) a plan; (형체·구조·외관 등의) a design. ¶도시 ~ city planning∥생활 ~ life planning∥컴퓨터 지원 ~ computer-aided design(약어 CAD)∥자동차의 ~ the design of a car∥~가 잘된[잘못된] 집 a well-planned[an ill-planned] house∥…의 ~로 짓다 build (a house) upon[from] the design of … / build (a house) after the plans of …. **설계하다** plan; design; project; make a plan; work out a design (for); 〔도면을 그리다〕 lay out; draw up a plan. ¶교회를 ~ plan[make a plan for] a church∥정원을 ~ design[lay out] a garden∥나는 보통 설날에 한 해를 설계한다 On New Year's Day I usually lay plans for the year. ➔¶이 철도 역은 잘못 설계되었다 This station is not well planned.
● **설계도** a plan; a blueprint; a design drawing. **설계서** specifications. **설계자** a designer; a planner; a drafter; a projector.
설교(說敎) 1 〔교리를 가르침〕 a sermon; preaching; a preachment; a religious discourse. ¶~를 듣다 hear[listen to] a sermon. **설교하다** preach (a sermon); deliver[give] (a person) a sermon; occupy the pulpit. ¶열변을 토하며 설교하는 사람 a pulpit orator∥가두에서 ~ preach on the streets∥장황하게 ~ deliver a long sermon.
2 〔훈계〕 a moralizing discourse[lecture]; 〔잔소리〕 scolding; remonstrance; admonition; preaching; a lecture; a lesson. ¶~를 듣다 be given[get / receive] a scolding / be lectured [scolded]∥나는 아버지한테서 단단히 ~를 들었다 I had a long lecture from my father.∥

내게 ~는 그만두게 Stop preaching at me! // 또 ~인가 Oh, not another sermon! **설교하다** lecture (a person); admonish (a person for something); give (a person) a scolding; read (a person) a lesson[lecture].
● **설교단** a pulpit. **설교자** a preacher; (경멸) a pulpiteer. ¶~**처럼 말하다** talk like a preacher.

설근 (舌根) [생] the root of the tongue.

설날 seollal; New Year's Day; the first of the year. ¶~ **아침 일찍에** early on the morning of seollal.

설늙은이 a person prematurely aged; a man old for his years; a person who is decrepit with premature old age.

설다¹ 1 [덜 익다] be half-boiled[half-cooked / half-done]; be undercooked[underdone]; (과일 등이) be unripe. ¶**선 밥** half-boiled [undercooked] rice / **선 과일** unripe fruits. 2 (술 등이) be not thoroughly fermented; (김치 등이) be not fully pickled. 3 (잠이) be insufficient; want; lack; be short of. ¶**잠이 설어서 기분이 개운치 않다** I feel sick from want of sleep.

설다² [생소하다] unfamiliar; strange; [서투르다] inexperienced; green. ¶**이곳은 낯이 ~ 다** I am a stranger here. // **그녀의 얼굴은 내게 ~** Her face is unfamiliar to me.

설다루다 botch a job; handle carelessly; do a poor job (of it). ¶**개를 설다루면 물린다** If you don't handle the dog carefully you will get bitten.

설득 (說得) persuasion. ¶**우리의 ~은 모두 허사였다** All our efforts at persuasion were fruitless. / **나는 그의 ~에 져서 그 일을 떠맡았다** I yielded to his persuasion and agreed to do the work. **설득하다** persuade; (문어) prevail on; (문어) solicit (assistance); talk (a person) into compliance; talk (a person) over[round]; urge[induce] (a person to do); reason with (a person)(▶ persuade는 설득하여 그것이 성공했음을 뜻함). ¶~**을 설득하여 …시키다** persuade[prevail upon / induce] a person to (do) / reason[talk / argue] a person into (doing) / **…을 설득하여 …하지 못하게 하다** dissuade a person from (doing) / reason[argue / talk] a person out of (doing) / **나는 그것을 단념하도록 그를 설득했다** I urged[tried to persuade] him to give it up. // **아무리 설득해도 그는 귀향하려 하지 않았다** Nothing would induce him to go home. // **나는 그녀에게 대학에 진학하도록 설득했다** I persuaded her to enter a university. / I talked her into entering a university.(▶ 이 두 문장은 그 결과 입학했음을 뜻함) / I urged her to enter a university.(▶ 권고했으나 그 결과는 모름) / **나는 딸에게 이혼하지 말도록 설득했다** I talked my daughter out of getting a divorce. / I dissuaded my daughter from getting a divorce. // **우리는 협력하도록 그를 설득했다** We solicited his cooperation.
● **설득력** persuasiveness; persuasive[reasoning] power. ¶~ **있는 persuasive / 그의 문장은 굉장히 [참으로] ~이 있다** His writing has tremendous persuasive power[is very convincing].

설렁거리다 blow gently; walk gracefully. ⇨ ²**살랑거리다**

설렁설렁 with a rustle; with a mincing gait. ⇨ ²**살랑살랑**

설렁탕 (-湯) seolleongtang; cow bone and internals soup with rice.

설렁하다 chilly; rather cold. ⇨ "**썰렁하다**

설레다 1 [마음이 들떠서 두근거리다] throb (audibly / violently); beat high (with the hope of); palpitate; flutter. ¶**설레는 가슴** a loudly throbbing heart // **가슴을 설레며** with a leap of one's heart / **가슴을 설레게 한다** make one's heart beat[leap] // **설레는 가슴을 달래다** calm one's agitated mind // **어머니를 다시 뵌다는 생각만으로도 기뻐서 가슴이 설렌다** Just the thought of seeing my mother again gives me a thrill of joy. // **요트로 달리는 것은 정말 가슴 설레는 일이었다** It was really thrilling[exciting] to sail in a yacht. // **산꼭대기에 올라선 기분은 정말 가슴 설레는 것이었다** It was indeed a stirring feeling to reach the top of the mountain. // **그녀는 그 광경에 가슴이 설레었다** Her heart leaped[leapt / began to pound] at the sight.
2 [이리저리 움직이다] be restless; move about uneasily; fidgety. ¶**설레지 말고 자리에 앉아 있어라** Don't be so restless. — Keep your seat.

설레설레 (머리를) waving; shaking; (꼬리를) swishing(소가); wagging(개가). ¶**고개를 ~ 젓다** shake[wag] one's head // **그는 내 질문에 고개를 ~ 흔들었다** He shook his head in answer to my question.

설령 (設令) even if[though]; though; although; granting[supposing] that …. ¶~ **그렇다 치더라도** granting[admitting] that it is so / even if it were so // **네가 옳다 치더라도** even if you are in the right // **어떠한 일이 생기더라도** come what may / whatever [no matter what] may happen // ~ **그것이 사실이라 하더라도 네가 한 일은 용서받을 수 없다** Even if it's true, what you did is still impermissible. / Even so, that doesn't justify what you did.

설립 (設立) establishment; foundation; setting up; institution; (회사 등의) promotion; incorporation; flotation; organization. ¶**회사 ~ 자금** fund for the establishment of company. **설립하다** establish; found; set up; institute; promote; incorporate; organize. ¶**우리 회사는 자본금 5,000만 원으로 설립되었다** Our company was originally established[started] with a capital of 50 million won. // **그 회사는 설립된 지 80년이 된다** The company has been in existence for eighty years.
● **설립 등기** registration of incorporation. **설립자** a founder; an organizer.

설마 surely (not); (not) possibly[by any possibility]; it is not[least] likely (that …); by no means; on no account; never. ¶~ **Indeed! / Impossible! / The idea! / You don't say so! /** (미국 구어) You're telling me! / (미국 구어) **What do you know? / Well, I never! / Well, I declare!** / "~ **자네는 아니겠지?**" "**물론 아니네**." "Surely it wasn't you?" "Never!" // ~ **자네가 한 짓은 아니겠지** Surely you didn't do it, did you? / Don't tell me you did it? / ~ **지금 그것을 하고 싶다는 것은 아니겠지** Surely you don't want to do that now! // "**저 사람이 대통령의 아들이야**." "~?" "That's the president's son." "Indeed?" / ~ **1등이 될 줄은 몰랐다** I had never dreamed that I might win (the) first prize. // "**내가 때렸습니**

다." "~ 그럴 리가." "I gave him a beating[I hit him]." "You can't mean it[You didn't]!"〃~ 나를 잊지는 않았겠지 You have never forgotten me!〃~ 일이 그렇게 될 줄은 몰랐다 I little suspected that things would turn out that way. / I had least expected that things would come to such a pass.〃~ 오늘은 비가 안 오겠지 It is hardly going to rain today.〃~ 더 이상 나를 사랑하지 않는다는 건 아니겠지 Don't tell me you don't love me anymore.

설맞다 receive a flesh wound; graze(스치다); be nicked by (an arrow / a bullet). ¶총알이 설맞았다 A bullet missed the vital parts.〃너 매를 아직 설맞았구나, 좀 더 맞아야겠다 You have just had a taste of the beating you deserve, you need a little more.

설맞이 welcoming the New Year.

설맹(雪盲) snow blindness; 〔의〕 niphablepsia. ¶~의 snow-blind / affected with snow blindness〃~이 되다 become[go] snow-blind.

설명(說明) explanation; account; exposition; interpretation; elucidation; illustration(도해); presentation; enucleation; description; a legend(도표 등의); a caption(사진 등의). ¶~적인 explanative / explanatory / illustrative / expositive / elucidative / elucidatory〃~조로 in a recitative tone〃…의 ~으로서 in explanation[illustration] of ...〃그의 ~은 아주 분명하여 모두가 이해할 수 있었다 His explanation [exposition] was so clear that everybody could understand.〃~은 150페이지를 보시오 For description[explanation] see page 150.〃그것은 ~이 필요 없다 It needs no explanation. / It is self-evident.〃나는 사건의 자세한 ~을 듣고 싶다 I'd like (to have) a full account of the incident. **설명하다** explain; give an explanation (of) ; account (for); give an account (of); interpret; make clear; elucidate; describe; expound; illustrate. ¶설명할 수 있는 explainable / explicable〃설명할 수 없는 unexplainable / inexplicable〃슬라이드로 ~ illustrate with [by] slides〃대충 ~ explain briefly [roughly] / give a brief explanation〃자세히 ~ explain in details[at large / at length]〃왜 그런 행동을 했는지 설명해 보시오 Please account for your conduct.〃그 교수는 우주의 본질을 설명했다 The professor elucidated the nature of the universe.〃선생님은 그 점을 자세히 설명하셨다 The teacher explained [dealt with] the point at length.〃인생에는 설명에는 없는 것이 많이 있다 There are many inexplicable things in life.
●**설명문** an explanatory note; an explanation. **설명서** an explanatory pamphlet; a manual; a description(제품의). **설명회** a briefing session; an explanatory meeting.

설문(設問) a question. ¶다음 ~에 답하라 Answer the following questions. / Answer the questions given below. **설문하다** pose [make up] a question.

설법(說法) 〔불〕 a Buddhist sermon; preaching. **설법하다** preach; preach [deliver] a sermon.

설보다 see[look / read] carelessly; take an inattentive look (at); see wrongly [unclearly].

설복(說伏) persuasion. ⇨설득

설봉(舌鋒) the tongue. ¶날카로운 ~으로 with an incisive [a bitter] tongue / (criticise) sharply〃~이 날카롭다 have an incisive[a trenchant] tongue.

설비(設備) equipment; provision; installation; arrangements; appointments; conveniences; facilities (for) (시설); accommodations(숙박·수용 설비). ¶가정용 난방 ~ home heating equipment〃과잉 ~ excessive facilities〃근대적 ~ modern conveniences〃생산 ~ plant〃위생 ~ sanitary arrangements [facilities]〃취사 ~ arrangement for cooking〃하수 ~ drainage arrangements〃~가 빈약한 poorly-equipped / poorly-appointed〃~가 잘 된 well-equipped / well-appointed / well-furnished〃이 지역은 하수 ~가 갖추어져 있다 This area has a sewer system. / (영) Main drainage has been provided [laid on] in this neighborhood.〃그 병원에는 1,000명의 환자를 수용할 수 있는 ~가 있다 The hospital has accommodation(s) for 1,000 patients.〃그 공장은 자가 발전 ~를 갖추고 있다 The factory has its own lighting plant. **설비하다** equip [fit / provide / furnish] (with); install (electric lights); accommodate; arrange; appoint; organize. ¶물 끓이는 기구를 ~ have a water heater installed. ➔호화롭게 설비된 방 a gorgeously furnished room〃…이 설비되어 있다 be equipped [provided / furnished / installed] with ...〃방에는 책상과 의자 및 선반이 설비되어 있었다 A desk, a chair and a set of shelves were provided in the room.
●**설비 자금** funds for equipment. **설비 투자** equipment [facility] investment; investment in plant and equipment.

설빔 the New Year's garb; a fine dress worn on the New Year's Day. **설빔하다** dress up for New Year's Day.

설사(泄瀉) 〔의〕 diarrh(o)ea; laxity [looseness] (of the bowels); loose bowels. ¶물 같은 ~ explosive [watery] diarrhea〃심한 ~ violent purging〃~를 멎게 하다 bind the bowels〃어젯밤 먹은 생선 튀김 때문에 ~가 났다 The fried fish I ate last night gave me [brought on] diarrhea. **설사하다** have diarrhea; have loose bowels(▶ 전자가 많이 쓰임). ¶나는 요 며칠 사이 설사하고 있다 My stomach has been upset [I've had diarrhea] these few days.
●**설사약** a binding medicine; a diarrhea remedy; a paregoric(소아용).

설사(設使) even if. ⇨설령

설산(雪山) snow-covered mountains; snowy mountains; a mountain covered with snow.

설상(舌狀) ¶~의 tongue-shaped / lingulate / linguiform.

설상가상(雪上加霜) misfortune on top of misfortune. ¶~으로 to make matters worse / to add to one's misery / on top of all other misfortunes / as if to rub salt in [into] the wound〃~으로 비가지 내리기 시작했다 To make us more miserable, it began to rain.〃불경기인데다가 ~으로 전염병까지 퍼져서 사람들을 괴롭혔다 In addition to the general business depression, an epidemic raged and afflicted the people.

설설 1 〔끓는 모양〕 gently; warmly. ¶물이 ~ 끓다 water simmers〃방바닥이 ~ 끓었다 The floor of a room was comfortably hot. **2** 〔기는 모양〕 with a brisk crawl [creep];

creeping; crawling; at a lively pace. **3** [머리를 내젓는 모양] with a gentle shake of the head. ¶그는 머리를 ~ 흔들었다 He shook his head gently.

설설 기다 be timid; be nervous; cower; falter; cringe; be awe-stricken; be struck with awe. ¶아내 앞에서 설설 기는 남편 a henpecked husband // 어머니 앞에서 ~ keep one's head low[be awe-struck] before one's mother / cringe before one's mother.

설신경(舌神經) a lingual [gustatory] nerve.

설암(舌癌) [의] cancer of the tongue.

설야(雪夜) a snowy night.

설왕설래하다(說往說來-) argue back and forth; bandy [cross] words (with); wrangle.

설욕(雪辱) **1** (치욕 등의) vindication of one's hono(u)r. **설욕하다** wipe out a shame; vindicate one's honor; clear oneself of a disgrace. **2** (패배의) revenge. **설욕하다** take revenge (for); get revenge for one's defeat; settle [square] accounts (with); (경기에서) settle the account; get even (with); redeem oneself. ¶그녀는 그의 모욕에 대해 마침내 설욕했다 She finally avenged herself on him. [(구어)] She finally got even with him] for his insult. // 우리는 작년 시합에서의 패배를 설욕했다 We avenged our loss to them in last year's game [match].
●**설욕전** a return match[game]; a fight for vindication; a campaign to recover one's honor [credit].

설움 sadness; sorrow; grief; woe; mourning; lamentation; distress. ¶북받치는 ~ the sorrow welling up within one // ~에 겨워 in (the excess of) one's grief[sorrow] // ~을 겪다[당하다] come to grief[misery] / be treated with contempt (for) / be looked down (up) on (for) / be held in contempt // ~을 못 이기다 be overwhelmed with grief.

설원(雪原) a snowfield.

설원(雪冤) clear oneself (of a false charge); exonerate oneself (from guilt); prove one's innocence.

설유하다(說諭-) admonish; reprove; exhort; caution.

설음(舌音) [언] a lingual (sound).

설익다 1 (음식이 덜 익다). ¶설익은 half-done [-boiled / -cooked] // 설익은 밥 half-cooked rice / rice with a hard center // 이 돼지고기는 설익었다 This pork is underdone [only half-done]. **2** (과일이) be unripe [underripe / partly ripe]. ¶설익은 과일 unripe [green] fruits.

설잡다 hold (a thing) loosely; drop (a thing) from one's grasp.

설전(舌戰) a (verbal) quarrel. ⇨"말다툼 ¶~을 벌이다 wage wordy warfare (with) / exchange verbal attacks with each other // 그들은 격렬한 ~을 벌이고 있다 They are engaged in a heated war of words.

설정(設定) establishment; creation; fixing; setting up; institution. ¶저당권 ~ settlement of mortgage. **설정하다** establish; set up; create; fix; institute. ¶규칙을 ~ fix a rule / 문제를 ~ pose a problem // 상황을 ~ establish[set up] a theory about the circumstances / postulate the circumstances // 새로운 운영법을 ~ institute a new system of management.

설죽다 be half-alive; be nearly killed.

설중(雪中) ¶~의[에] through the (midst of) snow / in the snow.

설측음(舌側音) [언] a lateral (sound). ⇨"혀옆소리

설치(設置) [설비] equipment; (기구 등의) installation; (가구 등의) furnishing; institution; (기관 등의) establishment; (학교 등의) foundation. ¶에어컨의 ~ 공사가 끝났다 The installation of the air conditioner was finished. // 이 난방 장치는 ~가 간단하다 This heater can be installed very easily. **설치하다** equip (with); fit up (with); install; found; institute; establish; found. ¶모금 위원회를 ~ set up[organize] a fund-raising committee // 우리는 사무실에 중앙난방을 설치했다 We had central heating installed in our office. // 우리는 각 칸에 소형 텔레비전을 설치하기로 결정했다 We decided to equip each booth with a small television set. →¶창틀이 잘못 설치되어 있다 The window sash is not well fitted [built] in.

설치다 1 [중도에서 그치다] leave (a thing) half-done; stop (work) halfway; (잠을) fail to get to sleep (enough); sleep badly; be sleepless. ¶그는 잠을 설친 모양이다 Sleep seemed to have deserted his pillow. **2** [몹시 날뛰다] run wild[amuck / riot]; rave [ramp / rage] about; be rampant; overrun; infest; be unruly. ¶데모대가 거리를 설치고 다녔다 The demonstrators stormed through the street.

설치류(齧齒類) [동] rodents. ¶~의 rodential.

설탕(雪糖) sugar. ¶각~ cube [cut / lump / block] sugar // 백~ refined sugar // 흑~ raw [unrefined] sugar / muscovado // ~을 넣은 sugared / sweetened with sugar // ~으로 조린 candied (fruits) // ~을 입히다 ice [frost / coat] with sugar // ~에 절이다 preserve in sugar // 홍차에 ~을 넣다 take [have / put] sugar in one's tea
●**설탕물** sugared water.

설태(舌苔) [의] fur (on the tongue); a coated tongue. ¶~가 낀 혀 a coated [furred] tongue // 혀에 ~가 끼었다 The tongue is coated.

설파(說破) [밝혀 말함] clear statement; exposure; elucidation; [논박] confutation; refutation. **설파하다** [밝혀 말하다] express [point out] clearly; state plainly; elucidate; [논파하다] confute (one's opponent); refute; (an argument); disprove.

설파제(-劑) [약] a sulfa drug; sulfas.

설핏하다 rather loose-woven; gauze-like; somewhat coarse.

설해(雪害) snow damage; damage from [by] snow. ¶농작물이 ~를 입었다 The crops were damaged by (the) snow.

설형(楔形) [쐐기꼴]. ¶~의 wedge-shaped / cuneiform / sphenoid(al).
●**설형 문자** a cuneiform (character); sphenogram.

설혹(設或) even if. ⇨"설령(設令)

설화(舌禍) an unfortunate [a disastrous] slip of the tongue; trouble brought on by a slip of the tongue. ¶~ 사건 a trouble caused by one's incriminating utterance (in public) // ~를 입다 take the blame for a slip of the tongue // 법무부 장관이 최근에 ~를 일으켰다 The Minister of Justice is being severely criticized for what he said recently.

설화(雪花·雪華) 1 a flake (of snow). ⇨ˮ눈송이 2 [나뭇가지에 꽃처럼 붙은 눈발] snow on the branches.

설화(說話) [옛이야기] a tale; a story; [우화] a fable. ¶~적인 narrative.
● **설화 문학** narrative [legendary] literature. **설화체** a narrative style. ¶~의 시 a poem in narrative form.

섬¹ 1 [멱서리] a straw sack. ¶쌀 ~ a straw rice bag. 2 [곡식의 용량 단위] a *seom*(▶ equivalent to 5.12 U.S. bushels). ¶쌀 두 ~ two bags of rice.

섬² [도서] an island; [작은 섬] an islet; (시어(詩語)) an isle. ¶외딴 ~ a solitary [a detached / an isolated] island // ~의 insular.

섬광(閃光) a flash (of light); a glint [sudden gleam] of light; [천] scintillation. ¶그것은 ~을 발하고 사라졌다 It flashed and (then) disappeared.
● **섬광 사진** flash light photography. **섬광 전구** a flash bulb [lamp]; a photoflash lamp.

섬기다 serve (one's master); be in (a person's) service; render service to (one's country); work under (another); [모시다] attend on; wait on. ¶부모를 ~ take care of one's parents / be devoted to [dutiful toward] one's parents // 한 남자를 충실히 ~ be true [constant] to one man.

섬나라 an island [a seagirt / an insular] country; an island empire [kingdom].

섬돌 a stepping-stone; a flight of steps; stone steps.

섬뜩하다 frightened; horrified; (서술적) have a fright [scare]; be taken aback. ¶섬뜩하여 in a fright // 섬뜩하게 하다 take (a person's) breath away / (속어) make one's hair stand on end / startle // 저 소설에는 섬뜩한 데가 있다 There's something gruesome [dreadful] about that novel. // (구어) That novel really blows your mind. // 그의 목소리는 ~ He has a frightening voice.

섬망(譫妄) [의] delirium; allophasis. ¶~에 빠지다 lapse into delirium.

섬멸(殲滅) extermination; annihilation. **섬멸하다** exterminate; annihilate; wipe out; destroy totally.
● **섬멸전** an exterminatory war.

섬모(纖毛) [세포 표면의 짧은 털 모양의 것] a cilium (*pl.* cilia, ~s); [집합적] ciliation. ¶ ~의 ciliary // ~가 있는 ciliate(d) / cillolate. 2 [가는 털] thin hair.
● **섬모 운동** ciliary movement. **섬모충** a ciliate.

섬사람 an islander; a native [an inhabitant] of an island.

섬섬옥수(纖纖玉手) slender [soft / delicate] hands.

섬세하다(纖細-) delicate; fine; nice; exquisite; subtle. ¶섬세한 감수성 (a) delicate [fine] sensibility // 섬세한 관심 delicate attentions / 섬세하게 만들어진 delicately constructed / 음악에 대한 감각이 ~ have a delicate [exquisite] ear for music.

섬약하다(纖弱-) frail; delicate; weak; feeble. ¶그의 체격은 섬약했다 He was delicately built [(문어) of a weak constitution].

섬유(纖維) (a) fiber [(영) (a) fibre]; a strand; textiles. ¶경질 [인피 (靭皮)] ~ a hard [cordage] fiber // 단 ~ filament // 동물성 [식물성] ~ an animal [a vegetable] fiber // 목 [면] ~ a wood [cotton] fiber // 인조 ~ (a) man-made fiber [textile] // 합성 [화학] ~ a synthetic [chemical] fiber // 천연 ~ a natural fiber // ~가 거친 [고운] 천 cloth of coarse [fine] texture.
● **섬유 공업** the textile [fiber] industry. **섬유소**(-素) (음식물의) fibrous cell; [동] fibrin; [식] [화] cellulose. ¶천연 ~ natural cellulose. **섬유 제품** a textile goods; textiles. **섬유 조직** [식] fibrous tissue. **섬유질** fibroid material.

섬화(閃火) a flash; a spark.

섭렵(涉獵) extensive reading. **섭렵하다** (책을) read extensively; range over; scour. ¶널리 문헌을 ~ range extensively [dig deeply into] the literature (connecting something).

섭리(攝理) 1 [하느님의 뜻] providence; dispensation; [신] economy. ¶신의 ~ divine providence [disposal] / the Providence of God // 자연의 오묘한 ~ a happy dispensation of Nature // 신의 ~에 맡기다 trust in Providence // 나는 자연의 ~에 감탄했다 I marbled at the operations of Nature. 2 [몸조리] taking care of one's ill health. **섭리하다** take care of one's ill health; recuperate oneself.

섭생(攝生) care of health. ⇨양생1 ¶~을 게을리 하다 take little care of one's health / disregard rules of health.
● **섭생법** rules for maintaining good health; a regimen.

섭섭하다 1 [헤어지기가 어렵다] sad; sorry; regretful; (서술적) be reluctant (to do). ¶헤어지기가 섭섭한 듯이 reluctantly / lingeringly / wistfully / with a regretful glance // 헤어지기가 ~ be sad [sorry] to part from (a person) / be reluctant [feel loath] to leave (a place) // 그녀는 헤어지기가 섭섭한 듯이 떠나갔다 She went her way with lingering steps. **섭섭히** sadly; regretfully.
2 [유감스럽다] sorry; regrettable; [서운하다] miss. ¶…은 참으로 ~ it is really [highly] regrettable that ... // 지금 그것을 포기한다는 것은 섭섭한 일이다 I am reluctant [(구어) hate] to give it up now. // 그가 의장을 그만둔 것은 섭섭한 일이었다 His resignation as chairman was regrettable. // 우리는 네가 없어서 아주 섭섭했다 We missed you badly. **섭섭히** regrettably; regretfully.
3 [원망스럽다] reproachful; rueful; [불만스럽다] disappointed. ¶섭섭한 듯한 모습으로 with a reproachful look / with a wistful regret // 네가 우리를 구하러 오지 않아 매우 섭섭했다 I thought it cruelly unkind of you not to have come to my rescue. **섭섭히** reproachfully; ruefully; disappointedly.

섭씨(攝氏) [온도계의 눈금 명칭] centigrade (약어 C., C, Cent.); Celsius(약어 C., C, Cels). ¶~ 10도 2분 ten point two degrees centigrade / 10.2℃ // ~ 5도의 물 water at 5℃.
● **섭씨온도계** a centigrade thermometer.

섭외(涉外) [대외 관계] public relations(약어 P.R.); [조직 간의 연락] liaison (work).

섭정(攝政) [임금 대신 다스림] regency; [그 사람] a regent. ¶~을 두다 set up regency / appoint a regent. **섭정하다** attend to the affairs of the state as a regent.
● **섭정 황후** the Queen [Empress] Regent.

섭조개 [동] a blue mussel.

섭취(攝取) 1 (음식·영양분의) intake; ingestion; intussusception. ¶단백질의 ~ the intake of protein // 칼로리 ~량 caloric intake // 2000 칼로리의 ~ a 2,000-calorie intake / an intake of 2,000 calories. **섭취하다** take: ingest; incept; take in; swallow. ¶영양을 ~ take nutrition. 2 (지식·문화 등의) adoption; assimilation; absorption. **섭취하다** adopt; [동화하다] assimilation; [흡수하다] absorb. ¶외국 문화를 ~ assimilate[absorb / take in] foreign culture.
● **섭취물** ingesta.

성 [노여운 감정] anger; rage; indignation; wrath; displeasure; offense. ¶~이 나게 하다 make (a person) angry [[미국 속어] mad] / stir to anger / anger / outrage / [벌컥] rouse (a person) to anger / set (a person's) blood on fire // ~을 가라앉히다 calm [appease] (a person's) anger / quell [appease] one's anger // ~을 잘 내다 be liable to fits of temper / be quick to take offense / be inflammable // 벌컥 ~을 내다 be roused to anger / fly into a (great) rage.

성(姓) a surname; a family name; (미) a last name. ¶~도 이름도 없는 사람 a man of obscure origin // ~과 이름을 대다 give one's full name // 그가 날 이기면 내 ~을 갈겠다 I'll eat my hat if he beats me.

성(性) 1 (남녀의) (a) sex. ¶~ 관계 sexual relations // ~ 문제 a sex problem // ~ 본능 the sex instinct // ~ 억제 sex control // ~ 호르몬 sex hormone // ~의 자각 the sexual awakening // ~의 구별 없이 regardless [irrespective] of sex // ~을 의식하고 있다 have a sexual awareness. 2 [본성] nature. 3 [언] gender. ¶남 [여 / 중] ~ the masculine [feminine / neuter] gender.

성(省) 1 (내각의) a ministry; an office; (미국의) a department. ¶국방~ (미) the Department of Defense / (영) the Ministry of Defense // 내무~ (미) the Department of the Interior / (영) the Home Office // 재무~ the Finance Ministry / (미) the Department of the Treasury / (영) the Exchequer // ~의 ministerial / department(al) / official. 2 (중국의 행정 구역) a province. ¶산동 ~ Shantung Province.

성(城) a castle; a fortress; a citadel; [성벽] a wall; (castle) walls. ¶~을 빼앗다 take [capture] a castle // ~을 쌓다 build a castle // ~을 적에게 넘겨주다 surrender a castle to the enemy // ~을 포위하다 besiege [lay siege to] a castle.

성(聖) [성인] a saint; a sage. ¶~ 베드로 St. [Saint] Peter.

성가(聖歌) a sacred song; a hymn. ¶그레고리오 ~ the Gregorian chants.
● **성가대** a choir. ¶~원 a chanter / (특히 소년) a chorister. **성가집** a hymnal; a hymnbook.

성가(聲價) (a) reputation; repute; [명성] fame; (인기) popularity. ¶~가 높아지다 rise in public [popular] estimation // ~가 떨어지다 fall in public [popular] estimation / lose one's reputation [credit / popularity] // ~를 높이다 enhance one's reputation // ~를 얻다 win a reputation / gain popularity // 그 사건으로 그의 ~는 높아졌다 [떨어졌다 / 훼손되었다] The affair enhanced [lowered / hurt] his reputation. // 그는 대담한 담력으로 남자로서의 ~를 인정받았다 He has built up a reputation for his courage.

성가시다 [귀찮다] bothersome; troublesome; harassing; annoying; burdensome; vexatious; irksome; [주체스럽다] cumbrous; [끈덕지다] pertinacious; (자꾸 캐물어서) inquisitive; [졸라 대어서] importunate. ¶성가신 아이 a troublesome child // 성가신 사람 a nuisance // 성가신 듯이 with an annoyed air [look] // 성가시게 tiresomely / annoyingly / importunately / persistently // 성가시게 굴다 give (a person) trouble / bother / trouble // 성가시게 조르다 ask importunately for (money) / importune (a person) for [to give one] (a thing) // 성가시게 여기다 find [consider] (a person) troublesome / regard [look upon] (a thing) as a nuisance // 성가시게 굴지 마라 Don't bother me! // 일이 성가시게 되었다 Here's a (pretty) go. / Things have come to a nice [pretty] pass. // 그가 자주 찾아와서 ~ I am annoyed by his frequent visits.

성감(性感) sexual feeling. ¶~을 높이다 (사물이) promote [work up] one's sexual feeling.
● **성감대**(-帶) an erogenous zone.

성게 [동] a sea urchin [chestnut]; an echinoid.

성격(性格) character; personality. ¶~상의 결점 a flaw [defect] in one's character // ~의 차이 disparity [dissimilarity] in character // ~이 좋은 사람 a good-natured person / an agreeable character // ~에 맞다 suit one's nature / be congenial to (one) // ~에 맞지 않다 do not suit one's nature / be uncongenial to (one) / be not in one's line // ~이 맞다 [맞지 않다] be similar [dissimilar] in character / be agreeable [disagreeable] to each other // ~을 만들다 (환경 등이) shape (a person's) character // ~ 차이가 우리 이혼의 원인이었다 Incompatibility of temperament was behind our divorce. // 그녀의 ~은 나와 정반대다 Her character is diametrically opposed to mine.
● **성격 묘사** character portrayal [delineation / drawing]. **성격 배우** a character actor [actress].

성결(性-) (a) nature; (a) temper; (a) disposition; personality. ¶~이 곱다 be of gentle disposition / have a sweet temper // ~이 사납다 have a nasty disposition.

성결교(聖潔敎) the Holiness Church.
성결하다(聖潔-) holy and pure.

성경(聖經) the (Holy) Bible; a holy book; the Scriptures; the Holy Writ. ¶개역 ~ the Revised Version (of the Bible) // 신약 [구약] ~ the New [Old] Testament // 흠정 영역 ~ the Authorized [(미) the King James] Version (of) ~ // ~의 Biblical / Scriptural.
● **성경 구절** a Biblical expression; a scriptural phrase. **성경 이야기** a Bible story.

성공(成功) 1 [뜻을 이룸] (a) success; [히트] a hit; a coup; [일의 성취] achievement. ¶~을 거두다 achieve [gain / win] success / make [pull off] a coup // 사업의 ~을 위해 축배하다 toast the success of the enterprise // ~적으로 달성하다 bring (a scheme) to a successful issue // ~적으로 끝나다 result [end] in success / be crowned with success // 공연은 대~이었다 The performance was a great hit [went off very well / was a great success]. // 그 시도는 대~ [실패] 이었다 The

attempt was[proved] a great success[a failure]. / The attempt was very successful [was unsuccessful].∥수술은 대〜이었다 The operation was a success[successful].∥당신의 〜은 거의 가망이 없다 There is a slim chance of your success.∥요트에 의한 세계 일주는 획기적인 〜을 거두었다 His cruise around the world by yacht was crowned with epoch-making success.∥기자 회견은 매우 〜적이었다 The interview went very well. / The interview was a great success. **성공하다** (사람이) succeed (in); be successful (in); win[achieve] success; (사물이) succeed; be [prove] successful. ¶사업에 〜 succeed in one's undertaking∥성공할 가망이 충분히 있다 stand[have] a good chance of success∥그는 그 계획에 성공[실패]했다 He succeeded [failed] in the attempt.∥그는 몇 번이고 해 보았지만 성공하지 못했다 He tried again and again to no purpose.∥최종 시험에는 쉽게 성공했다 I easily passed[(구어) made it in] the final exam.
2 [출세를 함] success in life[the world]. **성공하다** succeed[rise] in the world; get on in life. ¶그는 학자로서 성공했다 He was a success[succeeded] as a scholar.
● **성공담** a success story. **성공 비결** the secret of[key to] success.
성공회 (聖公會) (미) the Protestant Episcopal Church; (영) the Anglican Church. ¶한국 〜 the Episcopal Church of Korea.
성과 (成果) a result; a fruit; a product; an outcome. ¶노력의 〜 the result of one's efforts / the fruit[product] of one's labor∥〜를 올리다[거두다] (사물이) be crowned with great success / obtain[get] good results / be rewarded with good fruits∥좋은 〜를 얻다 have[produce] good results∥소기의 〜를 거두지 못하다 fail to realize the anticipated result / the result falls short of one's expectation∥그의 오랜 동안의 연구가 〜를 거두었다 His long years of research bore fruitful results.∥우리들의 노력은 결국 〜를 거두지 못했다 After all, our efforts did not bear fruit [were not rewarded].
● **성과급** 이 일은 〜으로 임금이 지불된다 This work is paid for by the piece.∥그는 〜으로 일하고 있다 He is working by the piece [on a piece(-rate) basis].
성곽 (城郭) [성] a castle; [성채] a fortress; a stronghold; [성벽] castle walls. ¶〜을 쌓다 build a castle.
● **성곽 도시** a walled city.
성교 (性交) (sexual) intercourse[connection / union]; [의] coitus; [법] (부부의) access. **성교하다** have sexual intercourse (with); have sex[intercourse] (with); have coitus(▶ 의학적 표현); (구어) make love (to / with).
● **성교불능** impotence; impotency. ¶〜자 an impotent person.
성교육 (性教育) sex education; sex information.
성구 (成句) an idiomatic phrase[expression]; a set phrase.
● **성구어** an idiom.
성군 (聖君) a good and wise king.
성극 (聖劇) a Biblical drama; a scriptural play.
성금 (誠金) a gift of money; a donation; a contribution; a subscription. ¶방위 〜 a contribution to the national defense fund∥원호 〜 a donation for the needy∥〜을 내다 donate / contribute / subscribe to (a fund).
성급하다 (性急-) hasty; impatient; impetuous; rash; quick-[short- / hot-]tempered. ¶성급한 기질 a hasty temper / impetuous disposition∥성급한 노인 a short-[quick- / hot-]tempered old man∥성급한 행동 rash action[behavior]∥그녀는 원래 〜 She is impatient by nature.∥그가 성급한 짓을 하지 않는다면 좋으련만 I only hope he won't take any rash action[he won't do anything rash].∥성급하면 손해 본다 Out of temper, out of money.∥벌써 준비를 시작하다니 정말 성급한 사람이군 You really are impatient to start getting ready so soon.∥성급한 그는 벌써 퇴근 채비를 하고 있었다 Being impatient by nature, he was already getting ready to leave.∥그는 성급해서 실수를 잘 한다 He tends to make mistakes by acting too hastily. **성급히** hastily; impatiently; impetuously; rashly. ¶〜 결정하다 decide too hastily∥〜 굴어서는 안 된다 Don't be too hasty. / (구어) Don't jump the gun.∥그는 〜 땅을 팔고 말았다 He rashly sold his land.
성기 (性器) sexual organs.
성기다 1 [거리·간격이 뜨다] loose; sparse; coarse; rough; thin; open. ¶성긴 수염 a thin moustache∥성긴 옷감 loose fabric∥성긴 체 a (wire) sieve of large meshes∥성기게 난 풀 a thin growth of herbage∥머리털이 〜 be thinly haired[covered with hair]∥굵은 털실로 성기게 짜다 knit loosely with heavy wool∥나무를 성기게 심다 put in plants at considerable distance from each other∥이 주변의 나무는 꽤 성기게 나 있다 There is a lot of open space between these branches. 2 [서먹하다] not on good terms (with); estranged; alienated.
성깃성깃 here and there; sparsely; thinly; scatteringly. **성깃성깃하다** loose. ⇨ *성기다*
성깃하다 loose; thin; (서술어) be rather sparsely spaced; be somewhat far apart; be a bit separated. ¶성깃하게 뜨다 knit with large stitches.
성깔 (性-) a sharp temper; a fierce[crabby] temperament; (미국 구어) a conniption (fit). ¶〜 있는 사람 a short-[hot- / quick-]tempered person / a man of violent temper.
성나다 1 [화나다] get[become / grow] angry (with a person / at something); feel angry (with[(미)] at] a person); be furious; be angered[offended / enraged] (by); (미) get mad; fly into a fury[passion]; be in a fume [huff]. ¶성나서 in one's anger / in a fit of anger / angrily∥몹시 〜 fret[fuss] and fume / get hopping mad / blow one's top / (불처럼) be hot with anger[rage] / boil with rage∥성나 있다 be angry (with / at) / be in a bad temper / (미) be mad / be in fury∥그는 몹시 성나서 돌아왔다 He came home in a towering rage.
2 [흥분되어 거칠어지다] get[become] rough; rough (up); rage. ¶성난 파도 a rough[high / heavy] sea / raging waters / wild waves.
3 [덧나다] get worse; (곪다) fester. ¶종기가 성났다 A boil got worse.
성내 (城內) ¶〜에 within[inside] the castle (walls) / within the city.
성내다 get angry (about a thing / with[at] a

person). ⇨ ²화내다 ¶발끈 성내어 in a fit of anger.
성내어 바위를 치니 발부리만 아프다(속담) Quarreling does not pay.; Cut off your nose to spite your face.

성냥 a match. ¶안전 ~ a safety match // 종이 ~ a matchfolder / a matchbook / a book of matches // ~ 한 갑 a box [pack(et)] of matches // ~을 긋다 strike [scratch] a match // ~을 켜다 light a match / strike a light / scrape a match into flames.
●**성냥갑** a matchbox. ¶~ 같은 집 a house like a matchbox / a matchbox of a house. **성냥개비** a match(stick). ¶~의 대 the stem of a matchstick. **성냥불** the light of a match.

성녀(聖女) [가] a saintess; a holy [saintly] woman; a female saint.

성년(成年) adult [full / lawful] age; man's [woman's] estate; (문어) majority. ¶~에 달하다 come of age / reach [attain] one's majority / reach full age / arrive at manhood [womanhood] // 그는 아직 ~이 되지 않았다 He is still under age [a minor]. / He hasn't come of age yet.
●**성년식** a coming-of-age celebration. **성년의 날** Coming-of-Age Day. **성년자** an adult; a person of legal age.

성능(性能) efficiency; capacity; power; (기계의) performance; property(특징). ¶고~ 엔진 a high-performance engine // 기계의 ~ the efficiency [performance] of a machine // ~이 좋은 (a car) of good [high] performance / high-power // ~이 좋은 퍼스널 컴퓨터 an efficient personal computer // 카메라의 ~을 개량하다 improve (the performance of) a camera // 이 기계는 겨우 5년 썼는데 ~이 떨어져다 The performance of this machine has fallen off in just five years.
●**성능 시험 / 성능 검사** a performance [an efficiency] test.

성단(星團) a group [cluster] of stars; a star cluster. ¶산개 ~ an open star cluster // 플레이아데스 ~ the Pleiades.

성단(聖壇) [제단] an altar; a shrine; [강단] a pulpit.

성담곡(聖譚曲) [음] an oratorio. ⇨ 오라토리오

성당(聖堂) 1 (천주교의) a (Catholic) church. 2 (공자의) a shrine of Confucius.

성대(聲帶) the vocal cords [bands]. ¶가~ a false vocal cords // 사람의 목소리는 ~의 진동으로 난다 The human voice is produced by the vibration of the vocal cords.
●**성대모사** imitation of a person's voice; vocal mimicry. ¶~를 하다 (사람의) imitate a person's voice [way of singing / way of speaking] / (동물 등의) imitate an animal's cry [a bird's singing].

성대하다(盛大-) grand; magnificent; splendid; pompous; flourishing; prosperous. ¶성대한 결혼식 a grand [magnificent] wedding ceremony // 그는 성대한 환영을 받았다 He was received with great enthusiasms. / He received a lavish welcome. **성대히** grandly; magnificently; splendidly; with pomp; with splendor; on a large scale; in grand style; pompously. ¶개회식은 ~ 치러졌다 The opening ceremony was a grand event [was held on a grand scale]. // 취임식은 ~ 거행되었다 The inauguration was held in grand style.

성덕(盛德) flourishing [illustrious] virtue(s).

성덕(聖德) (성인의) saints' [saintly] virtues; (왕의) royal virtues; royal favor.

성도(聖徒) a Christian. ⇨ ¹기독교 신자(⇨기독교)

성도(聖都) the Holy City; Jerusalem.

성도덕(性道德) sexual morality.

성도착(性倒錯) sexual perversion; abnormal sexuality.

성량(聲量) the volume of (one's) voice. ¶~이 풍부한 목소리 a voice of great volume / a powerful voice // 그녀는 ~이 빈약하다 Her voice is weak [doesn't have much volume].

성령(聖靈) the Holy Spirit [Ghost].
●**성령 강림절** Whitsuntide; the season of Pentecost.

성례(成禮) a marriage [wedding] ceremony. **성례하다** hold [solemnize] a wedding.

성루(城壘) a fort; a fortress; ramparts. ¶~를 지키다 take one's stand in a fortress / guard the ramparts.

성리학(性理學) Sung Confucianism; the doctrines [teachings] of Chu-tzū.

성립(成立) 1 [생겨남] coming into existence [being]; [실현] realization; materialization. **성립하다** come [be brought] into existence [being]; be materialized [realized]; materialize. ➔¶**성립시키다** bring [call] into existence [being] / (실현시키다) bring about / materialize / effect(uate) // 그 계획은 성립되지 않았다 The project fell through. / The plan failed to materialize. / The plan wasn't realized. // 그런 이론은 성립되지 않는다 Such a theory is not valid [does not hold water]. // 그 회의 [그의 계획]는 성립되지 못하고 말았다 The meeting [His plans] fell through [failed / ended in failure]. // 의안은 성립되지 않았다 The bill failed to pass [was voted] down. (▶ vote down은 투표로)
2 [조직됨] formation; organization. ¶새 위원회의 ~은 그의 열의에 힘입은 바가 크다 The formation of the new committee owes a great deal to his zeal. **성립되다** be formed [organized]; [···으로 이루어지다] consist of; be made [composed] of. ➔¶**성립시키다** form / organize // 연립 내각이 성립되었다 A coalition cabinet was formed.
3 [체결] conclusion; completion. **성립하다** be concluded [completed]. ➔¶우리는 그들과의 거래를 성립시켰다 We have concluded a deal with them.

성마르다(性-) short- [quick-] tempered; narrow-minded and hot-tempered; impetuous; impatient; hasty. ¶성마른 사람 an irritable [a touchy] person // 성마른 a hotspur.

성명(姓名) (a) (full) name; one's family name and given name. ¶~부지의 사람 an unidentified person / a man whose name is unknown // ~이 없다 nameless / unknown / unrecognized // ~을 대다 give one's name / identify oneself // ~을 감추다 conceal [veil] one's identity // ~을 속이다 give a false name.

성명(聲明) a declaration; a proclamation; a statement; an announcement; a manifesto. ¶공동 ~ a joint communiqué [statement] // ~을 내다 issue [deliver] an official statement // 파업에 찬성 [반대] ~을 내다 announce one's approval of [opposition to] the strike. **성명하다** announce; declare;

proclaim(▶ announce는 공식으로 발표함, declare는 명확히 발표함, proclaim은 일반인에게 중대한 사항을 권위를 가지고 선언함); make[issue] a statement (on). ¶전쟁에 찬성[반대]임을 ~ declare oneself for[against] war∥수상은 자신은 이 문제와는 전혀 관련이 없다고 성명했다 The Prime Minister declared that he had nothing to do with the matter.
●**성명서** a statement; a public[an official] statement; (주권자·정부·단체 등이 내는) a manifesto (pl. ~(e)s); communiqué. ¶~를 **발표하다[내다]** issue[give out] a statement / issue a manifesto.

성모 (마리아)(聖母-) [가][기] the Virgin Mary; the Blessed Mary; the Holy Mother; Our Lady; the Virgin Mary.

성묘(省墓) a seongmyo; a visit to one's ancestral grave. **성묘하다** pay a visit[one's homage] to one's ancestor's grave; visit one's ancestor's grave; worship at one's ancestor's grave.

성문(城門) a castle gate; the gate of castle.

성문(聲門) [생] the glottis (pl. ~es, -tides); the vocal chink.
●**성문 폐쇄음** [언] a glottal stop.

성문법(成文法) [법] a statute (law); a written law; statutory law; (라) a lex scripta; a jus scriptum.

성문화(成文化) codification. **성문화하다** codify; put in statutory form; reduce into writing. ¶규칙을 ~ codify regulations / put regulations in statutory form.

성미(性味) [성질] nature; disposition; [기질] temperament; temper; spirit; [성격] character; [성정과 취미] bent. ¶~가 고약한 ill-natured / ill-disposed / evil-minded / wicked / vicious / malicious∥~가 좋은 사람 a good-natured person / a man of good disposition / a jolly good fellow / (미국 속어) a regular guy∥~가 까다로운 사람 a man hard to please / a man of moods∥차분한 ~ a calm temper∥급한 ~ a quick[a hot / short] temper∥~에 맞는 일 congenial work ∥~가 급하다 be short-[quick- / hot-]tempered / have a quick[hot / short] temper / have a temper / have little patience∥그와 나는 ~가 맞는다 He and I hit it off well together. / I hit it off with him. / I get along well with him. / (문어) He and I are similarly disposed. / I agree with him.∥이 일은 내 ~에 맞지 않는다 This job is not in my line. / This job isn't my cup of tea.∥그것을 그렇게 하는 것은 내 ~에 안 맞는다 It is not in my nature to do it that way. / It goes against the grain[hair] for me to do it that way. / I am not so constituted as to[that I can] do it that way. ∥영국 기후는 그녀의 ~에 맞지 않았다 The climate of England did not agree with her.∥나는 쉽게 발끈하는 ~이다 I lose my temper easily.∥그녀는 흥분하기 쉬운 ~다 She has an excitable temperament.

성범죄(性犯罪) a sex[sexual] offense[crime].
●**성범죄자** a sexual criminal.

성벽(性癖) one's natural disposition; an inclination; a natural tendency; (문어) a propensity (to / for / to do); a proclivity; a mental habit; a bent; a bias.

성벽(城壁) a castle wall; a rampart; a circumvallation; (도시의) the town walls. ¶~을 쌓다 build a rampart / wall (a castle).

성별(性別) the distinction of sex. ¶등록 카드에 ~을 기입해 주십시오 Please enter your sex on the registration card.∥~, 연령에 관계없이 응모할 수 있음 Anyone may apply regardless[(문어) irrespective] of sex or age.

성병(性病) a venereal disease(약어 V.D., VD); a sexual disease; (미) a social disease. ¶~의 예방 prevention of venereal disease.
●**성병 감염** venereal infection. **성병 환자** a person venereally infected.

성부(成否) success or failure. ⇨=성불성

성부(聖父) [신] the Father; Our Father.

성분(成分) 1 [혼합물의 요소] an ingredient; [한 물체의 구성 요소] a component; a constituent; an element. ¶주~ (one of) the main[principal / chief] ingredients∥부(副)~ an accessory ingredient / **약효** ~ medically effective ingredients∥빵의 ~ the constituent parts of bread∥물의 ~ the constituents[the constituent parts] of water∥나일론의 중요 ~ an important element of nylon. 2 [언] constituent.
●**성분 표시** an ingredients label.

성불(成佛) 1 [불] [불과(佛果)를 얻음]. **성불하다** become a Buddha; enter Nirvana; attain Buddhahood. 2 [사람이 죽음] death. **성불하다** die; pass away; depart (from the life) in peace.

성불성(成不成) success or failure; [결과] the result; the issue. ¶~ 간에 whether successful or not / whatever the result may be / regardless of the issue.

성사(成事) accomplishment; achievement; attainment; fulfil(l)ment; realization; success. ¶모사는 재인(在人)이요, ~는 재천(在天)이라 Man proposes, God disposes. / Do your best and leave the rest to Providence. **성사하다** accomplish; achieve; attain; fulfil(l); realize; be settled; be arranged; succeed. ➔양가(兩家) 사이에 혼담이 성사되었다 A marriage has been arranged linking two families.

성사(聖事) 1 [성스러운 일] divine service. 2 [가] a sacrament. ¶칠(七)~ the seven sacraments∥혼배 ~ the sacrament of matrimony / the marriage sacrament.

성상(星霜) years; time. ¶5백 ~이 흘렀다 Five centuries have passed[elapsed].∥나는 열두 ~이 지나서 그녀와 다시 만났다 I met her again after twelve years had passed.

성상(聖上) (His Majesty) the King.

성상(聖像) a sacred image[portrait]; [가][기] an icon[eikon / ikon].
●**성상 예배 / 성상 숭배** iconolatry.

성상학(性相學) physiognomy.
●**성상학자** a physiognomist.

성생활(性生活) sex(ual) life.

성서(聖書) the (Holy) Bible; the Scriptures; the Holy Writ. ¶~의 biblical / Biblical∥**구약**[신약] ~ the Old[New] Testament∥**개역** ~ the Revised Version (of the Bible)(약어 R.V.) ∥**흠정역** ~ the Authorized[(미) King James] Version (of the Bible)(약어 A.V.)∥~의 구절 a Biblical expression / a scriptural phrase∥~에 나오는 이름 a Biblical name∥~에서 인용한 구절 a Biblical quotation.
●**성서 문학** Biblical literature.

성선(性腺) a genital gland. ⇨=생식샘 ⇨생식(生殖)

성선설(性善說) [윤] the ethical doctrine that human nature is fundamentally [essentially] good; the theory that man's inborn nature is good.

성성하다(星星-) hoar(y); gray-haired; gray [white-]headed. ¶백발이 성성한 gray-white[-flecked] hair / grizzled[frosty] hair / graying hair / hair streaked with gray.

성세(聖世) a glorious reign [era].

성쇠(盛衰) ups and downs; rise and fall; prosperity [rise] and decline; vicissitudes. ¶국운의 ~ the ebb and flow of a nation's fortunes // 로마 제국의 ~ the ups and downs [the ebb and flow / the vicissitudes] of life.

성수(聖水) [가] holy water.

성수기(盛需期) a high-demand season. ¶그 상품은 ~를 맞고 있다 The articles are now in great demand.

성숙(成熟) 1 [잘 익음] ripeness; maturity. ¶과일의 ~ the maturity of fruit. **성숙하다** ripen; be[get] ripe; mature.
2 [어른스럽게 됨] full[complete] growth; maturity. **성숙하다** reach[come to] maturity; attain[reach] full growth; mature; ripen; grow into adulthood. ¶성숙하여 여자답게 되다 ripen into womanhood // 요즘 아이들은 빨리 성숙한다 Recently children have begun to mature earlier.(▶ 나이가 어린 가운데 성숙하다) / Young people today mature rapidly.(▶ 성장의 속도가 빠르다) // 군대 경험이 나를 성숙하게 만들었다 My army experience matured me.
3 [때·기회가 무르익음] maturity; ripeness. **성숙하다** mature; ripen; attain[come to] maturity. ¶과감한 개혁에 착수할 시기가 바야흐로 성숙했다 The time is ripe for[to initiate] a drastic reform.

● **성숙기** (the period of) maturity; [사춘기] puberty; adolescence; the age of puberty [adolescence]. ¶~에 이르다 arrive at puberty / become adolescent / attain (to) maturity.

성스럽다(聖-) [신성하다] holy; sacred; divine; heavenly; [장엄하다] solemn; sublime. ¶성스러운 장소 a spot of sanctity / a holy[sacred] place.

성시(成市) opening a fair[market]. ¶문전을 이루다 have a constant stream of visitors / be thronged with callers / (a shop) have a crowd of customers. **성시하다** open a fair; keep a fair.

성신(聖神) the Holy Spirit. ⇨성령

성신(星辰) stars; heavenly bodies.

● **성신 숭배** [종] astrolatry.

성실(誠實) sincerity; honesty; integrity; faithfulness; fidelity; devotion; earnestness; seriousness. **성실하다** sincere; honest; faithful; truthful; devoted; earnest; serious. ¶성실한 사람 an honest[a reliable] person / a man of sincerity / a man of integrity / 성실한 하인 a loyal[faithful] servant / a man Friday / 성실하지 않은 insincere / dishonest / untruthful / false / faithless // 성실하지 못한 말 insincere[hypocritical] words // 성실하지 못한 친구 a false friend // 성실한 학생 an earnest student // 그는 성실한 사람이다 He is sincere [honest]. / He is a man of integrity [sincerity]. **성실히** sincerely; faithfully; honestly; earnestly; in (sober / good / real / dead) earnest; with (all) sincerity; in good faith. ¶~ 일하다 work earnestly [conscientiously] / do one's work with sincerity / work faithfully // ~ 말하다 speak in all sincerity[with sincerity] // ~ 행동하다 act in good faith // 앞으로 ~ 살겠습니다 I will live an honest life hereafter. / I will live [go] straight hereafter. // ~ 그 문제와 씨름해 보기 바라네 I hope you will tackle the problem earnestly.

● **성실성** sincerity; honesty; faithfulness; good faith; fidelity; truth. ¶~이 없다 lack[be wanting] in sincerity.

성심(誠心) sincerity; a true[single] heart; devotion.

성심껏(誠心-) sincerely; wholeheartedly; devotedly; with one's whole heart; with a single heart; heart and soul; with devotion. ¶그는 ~ 친구에게 충고했다 He advised his friend in all sincerity. // 그는 그 일을 ~ 처리했다 He dealt with the matter wholeheartedly [in all sincerity]. / He gave the matter his undivided attention. / He went heart and soul into the matter.

성싶다 look; seem; appear; be likely (to do). ¶비가 올 ~ It looks like rain. / It is [seems] likely to rain. / It threatens to rain. / It looks as if it's going to rain. // 그가 있을 성싶은 곳은 모조리 찾아보았다 I looked for him in every likely place. // 어느 팀이 이길 성싶은가 Which team looks like winning? // 그가 올 성싶지 않다 It is not likely that he will come. / He is not likely to come.

성씨(姓氏) a family name; a surname; (미) one's last name; a patronymic.

성악(聲樂) vocal music. ¶~ 연습 training of one's voice / voice culture // ~ 레슨을 받다 take lessons in singing / take singing lessons / take vocal lessons.

● **성악가** a vocalist; a singer.

성악설(性惡說) [윤] the ethical view that human nature is fundamentally [essentially] evil.

성안(成案) a definite plan[scheme]; a concrete program. **성안하다** form a definite plan; map out a concrete program.

성애(性愛) sexual love.

성어(成魚) an adult fish; a mature fish; a fully-grown fish.

성어(成語) a (set) phrase; an idiom; an idiomatic phrase.

성업(盛業) a thriving business. ¶~ 중이다(장사가) drive a thriving[prosperous / roaring / booming] trade / (병원 등이) have[enjoy] a large practice // 그 가게는 ~ 중이야 The store is thriving[doing very well]. // ~을 축하드립니다 I congratulate you on[upon] your success in business.

성업(成業) [학업을 이룸] the completion of one's studies[a school course]; [사업을 이룸] the completion of one's work. **성업하다** complete one's work[study].

성에 (a layer of) frost; frostwork; frost flowers [ferns]. ¶유리창에 생긴 ~ the frost which has formed on the windowpane // (냉장고의) ~ 제거 장치 a defroster / a defrosting device // ~가 앉은 유리창 a frosted windowpane // 냉장고의 ~를 제거하다 defrost a refrigerator // 유리창에는 온통 ~가 끼어 있었다 The windowpanes were covered with frost[frostwork].

성역(聖域) sacred[holy] precincts; a consecrated ground. ¶침입자들은 원주민의 ~을 침범하였다 The invaders trespassed on the holy ground of the aborigines.∥그 절은 가출한 여자들의 ~이었다 The temple was a sanctuary for runaway women.

성역(聲域) a range of voice; [음] a register.

성욕(性慾) sexual[carnal] desire[appetite]; lust; sexuality; (완곡) untidy passion. ¶변태 ~ abnormal sexuality∥~이 강한 strongly [highly-]sexed∥~을 자극하다 arouse[stimulate / excite] one's sexual desire∥~을 만족시키다 satisfy[satiate] one's sexual desire / gratify one's carnal appetite[lust].

성우(聲優) (TV·영화의) an actor[actress] specializing in dubbing films; (라디오 방송의) a radio actor[actress].

성운(星雲) [천] a nebula (pl. -lae, ~s); a nebulosity. ¶암흑 ~ a dark nebula∥와상(渦狀) ~ a spiral nebula∥가스 ~ a gaseous nebula∥환상(環狀) ~ an annular nebula / a ring nebula.

성원(成員) 1 [단체의 조직원] a member. ¶우리 회의 ~은 20명이다 The membership of our society numbers 20. 2 [회의 성립에 필요 인원] a quorum; a constituent (member). ¶~이 되다 [make / constitute] a quorum / (영국 하원에서) make a House.
● **성원 미달** lack of a quorum.

성원(聲援) 1 [격려] (a shout of) encouragement; (경기의) cheering; (미국 속어) rooting. ¶열렬한 ~을 보내다 give enthusiastic encouragement (to) / (경기에서) (미국 속어) root wildly (for a team) / give (a person) a big yell. **성원하다** encourage; shout encouragement (for / to); cheer (a team on to victory); (미국 속어) root (for a team). 2 [도와 줌] support; patronage. **성원하다** support; give one's support (to); patronize. ¶앞으로도 계속해서 저희를 성원해 주시기 바랍니다 We hope you will favor us with your continued patronage.

성유(聖油) [가] holy[consecrated] oil; chrism.

성은(聖恩) 1 [임금의 은혜] the benevolence [graciousness] of the king; Royal favor [grace / benevolence]. 2 [가][기] the goodness of Heaven; heavenly blessings.

성의(誠意) sincerity; good faith; a true heart; devotion. ¶~가 없는 insincere / false / fickle / faithless / hollow-hearted / heartless / empty∥~가 없다 lack [be lacking in] sincerity∥~ 없는 행동을 하다 act in bad faith∥~를 보이다 show one's good faith∥~를 다하다 be faithful [devoted] (to) / devote oneself (to) / act sincerely (toward)∥그의 말에는 ~가 없다 You can't put any faith in what he says. / He's not at all serious about what he says.

성인(成人) an adult; a grown-up (person). ¶~(용) 영화 adult movies∥~이 된 아들 a grown-up son∥~이 되다 grow up to be a man[woman] / grow into a man / attain [arrive at] manhood[womanhood] / become an adult / come of age / become a man [woman] / reach adulthood / grow up∥이것은 ~ (취향의) 영화이다 This film is for adults.∥입장료는 ~이 3,000원입니다 Admission to the garden is three thousand won for adults.∥그 아이도 마침내 ~으로 일할 수 있게 되었다 At last the boy is old enough to do a man's work.
● **성인 교육** adult education. **성인병** [의] disease of adult people; geriatric diseases. **성인식** a coming-of-age ceremony.

성인(聖人) a sage; a saint; a holy man. ¶옛 ~ a sage of old∥~ 같은 saintly / saintlike.

성자(聖子) [성] the Son.

성자(聖者) a sage; a saint. ⇨성인(聖人)

성장(成長) growth. ¶경제 ~ economic growth / growth in economy∥고도 ~ rapid growth / a high growth rate∥경제의 안정 ~ stable growth∥그녀는 손자들의 ~이 최대의 즐거움이었다 She found her greatest joy in the growth of her grandchildren.∥그의 소년기의 지적 ~은 참으로 놀랄 만하였다 His mental development in his boyhood was truly remarkable. **성장하다** grow (up); be brought up. ¶늦게 ~ grow slowly / be of tardy growth∥금붕어가 성장하는 과정을 관찰하다 observe (how) goldfish grow[develop]∥아이들은 빨리 성장한다 Children grow (up) very quickly [rapidly]. / Children run up rapidly.∥그는 훌륭한 의사로 성장하였다 He grew up to be fine doctor. / He grew into a fine doctor.∥그녀는 옷이 작아서 안 맞을 정도로 성장했다 She has grown out of[outgrown] her clothes.
● **성장기** a period of growth; a growth period; a growth phase. **성장률** a rate of growth; a growth rate. ¶경제 ~ a rate of economic growth. **성장 산업** [경] the growth industry. **성장주** [증권] a growth stock.

성장(盛裝) gala dress; beautiful attire. **성장하다** be in gala[full] dress; be dressed up; be decked out; attire oneself in rich clothes; be finely [richly] dressed; be dressed in one's (Sunday) best; (구어) dress up in full rig; (미국 속어) be dolled up. ¶성장하고 온 [full] array / in full[gala] dress / (구어) in full rig[fig].

성적(成績) 1 [일 등의 성과] performance; a result; a showing; a record; (개인의) merit. ¶영업 ~ (a firm's) business performance / business showing∥좋은 ~을 올리다 (일이) obtain[bring about] gratifying [satisfactory] results / (사람이) make a good record / obtain [gain / attain] good [excellent] results / do an excellent job / make a good [fine] show[record] / (구어) give a good account of oneself / bear substantial fruit / do well∥그는 작업 ~이 좋았다 He has made a good showing in his work.
2 [교] [학업의 기록] a (school) record; [시험 등의 결과] results; [성적의 평가] grades; (영) a mark. ¶시험 ~ the result of an examination∥학교 ~ one's school record[performance / achievements] / one's scholastic marks∥나는 화학에서 좋은 ~을 얻었다 I got a good grade[good marks] in chemistry. / I made a good record in chemistry. / In chemistry I did well.∥그의 학교 ~이 올라가고[떨어지고] 있다 His grades are improving [getting worse / falling / dropping].∥그는 학교 ~이 좋다[나쁘다] He is doing well [poorly] at school. / He gets[makes] good [poor] grades in his studies.∥그는 학급에서 ~이 제일 우수하다 He is at the top of his class. / He ranks highest in his class.∥그의 학교 ~은 어떻습니까 How are his grades [(미) marks] at school? / How is he getting

성적

along in school? / How are his records at school? // 그의 ~은 그저 그렇다 He has fair grades.
- **성적순** the order of merit. ¶~으로 앉다 sit in the order of merit [the achieved performance records]. **성적표** (학교의) a list of students records; a report card [(영) a term report] (통지표); (경기의) a scorecard.

성적(性的) sexual. ¶~ 관계 sexual relation // ~ 욕구[충동] a sexual desire[impulse] // 그녀는 ~으로 조숙했다[늦되었다] She was sexually precocious[backward].
- **성적 매력** sex appeal; sexual attractiveness; (미국 속어) "it". ¶~이 있는 여자 a woman with (strong) sex appeal / (구어) a glamor[sexy] girl // ~이 있다 have sex appeal / be sexy / be sexually attractive. **성적 욕망** sexual appetite[drive].

성전(聖殿) a sacred shrine; a sanctuary.

성전(聖戰) a holy war; a crusade; a war undertaken for a sacred cause.

성전환(性轉換) the change of sex; a sex change.
- **성전환 수술** a sex change operation. **성전환자** a transsexual.

성정(性情) one's nature [disposition / character / temper].

성조(聲調) 1 [목소리의 가락] a tone of voice. 2 [소리 높이의 변동] variations in voice pitch [in the pitch of one's voice]. 3 (중국어 등의) a tone.

성조기(星條旗) (정식 호칭) the Star-Spangled Banner; (속칭) the Stars and Stripes(▶ 단수 취급).

성좌(星座) [천] a constellation. ⇨ **별자리**
- **성좌도** a star chart; a planisphere.

성주(城主) the lord of a castle; a castellan; [봉건 시대의 한 지방의 영주] a feudal lord.

성주간(聖週間) [가] Holy Week.

성지(聖地) a sacred place; holy ground; (팔레스타인의) the Holy Land.
- **성지 순례** a pilgrimage to the Holy Land; a pilgrimage to sacred places. ¶~를 하다 make[go on] a pilgrimage to the Holy Land / visit the Holy Land.

성직(聖職) [가][기] the clergy; the ministry (▶ 영국에서는 주로 성공회 이외의); a religious vocation; (holy) orders.
- **성직자** a churchman; a clergyman.

성질(性質) 1 [마음의 바탕] one's nature; one's disposition; one's temperament; one's temper. ¶~이 좋다[나쁘다] good-natured [ill-natured] / ~이 급하다 be short-[quick-] tempered / have a [short / hot / quick] temper // 타고난 ~은 어쩔 수 없다 One cannot help[alter] one's nature. / The leopard cannot change his spots. 2 [사물·현상의 고유의 특성] a property; a nature; a quality; character. ¶어떤 종류의 풀에는 병을 낫게 하는 ~이 있다 Some herbs have healing properties. // 문제의 ~상 신중히 다뤄야 한다 Because of its nature, this problem requires careful handling.

성질내다(性질─) get[become / grow] angry (with / at); take offense (at); (미) get mad; get into a rage[passion]; get out of temper; show temper; fire up; lose one's temper. ¶나는 그녀가 성질내는 것을 본 적이 없다 I never saw her out of temper with anyone.

성징(性徵) a sex [sexual] characteristics. ¶1

차 [2차] ~ a primary[secondary] sexual characteristic.

성찬(盛饌) a capital [grand / an elaborate] dinner; a splendid meal; a feast; a banquet; a lavish meal; sumptuous fare; good [dainty] dishes. ¶~을 베풀다 give a capital dinner / set a good table / feast / serve a banquet // 그것은 진수~이었다 It was a real banquet[feast].

성찬(聖餐) [가] Holy Communion; the Lord's Supper; the Eucharist; the Sacrament. ¶~용 포도주 [빵] the Sacramental wine [wafer / bread].
- **성찬식** the Communion [Lord's supper] service.

성찰(省察) reflection; introspection; self-examination. **성찰하다** reflect; introspect; examine oneself.

성채(城砦) a stronghold; a fort; a fortress; fortifications; a fastness; a bulwark. ¶~를 쌓다 build a fort / fortify (a town).

성체(成體) [생] an adult organism.

성체(聖體) 1 [임금의 몸] the person of a king; the Royal person. 2 [가][기] the body of Christ; the holy bread; the (blessed / holy) Sacrament [sacrament]; the Host; the Eucharist; the bread and wine taken at Holy Communion. ¶영(領) ~ (Holy) Communion // ~를 영(領)하다 [영~하다] receive [take] Communion / commune.
- **성체 성사** (the sacrament of) the Eucharist.

성충(成蟲) [동] an imago (pl. ~es, imagines). ¶애벌레가 ~이 되다 develop from larvae into imagoes.

성취(成就) accomplishment; fulfil(l)ment; achievement; attainment; completion; consummation; realization. **성취하다** accomplish; fulfill; achieve; attain; complete; consummate; realize; effect. ¶우리는 목적을 성취했다 We attained [achieved] our goal. / We accomplished [realized / effected] our purpose. / We gained our end. →¶내 소원이 성취되었다 My prayers were answered. / I have my desire fulfilled. / I have my wish realized.

성층(成層) [지] bedding; stratification.
- **성층권** the stratosphere.

성큼 with a long step. ¶좁은 개울을 ~ 건너다 stride over a narrow creek // ~ 걷다 stride (along) / take [walk with] long [big / large / great] steps [strides].

성탄(聖誕) 1 [성인·임금의 탄생] the birth of a saint[king]. 2 [가][기] Christmas (Day). ⇨ **성탄절**(⇨**성탄**)
- **성탄절** [가][기] Christmas (Day).

성터(城─) the site of a castle; the ruins of a castle.

성토(聲討) censure; arraignment; impeachment; denunciation. **성토하다** censure; arraign; impeach; denounce.
- **성토 대회** an indignation meeting; a rally.

성패(成敗) success or failure; [결과] the result. ¶~에 관계없이 whether successful or not / whatever the result may be // ~ 여부는 알 수 없다 I am not sure of succeeding [that I will be successful]. // 이 계획의 ~은 날씨에 달려 있다 Whether this plan succeeds or not depends on the weather.

성폭행(性暴行) sexual violence [abuse]; (a)

rape. 성폭행하다 attack[assault] (a woman); rape; do sexual violence to.

성품(性品) [성질] nature; disposition; [기질] temper; temperament. ¶~이 좋은 사람 a good-natured man / a man of good character / a man of the right kidney.

성하(盛夏) the middle[height] of summer; midsummer; high[deep] summer.

성하다 1 [온전하다] intact; undamaged; whole; sound; flawless; faultless; spotless. ¶깨지지 않고 성한 접시라고는 하나도 없다 Not a plate is left whole. / There isn't a whole plate left. 2 [병이나 탈이 없다] healthy; (safe and) sound; (alive and) well; fit; robust. ¶성한 몸 a healthy[sound] body. 성히 safely; in safety; safe and sound; in good health. ¶~ 지내다 be quite well / be fine / be in[live in / enjoy] good health / get along well[all right] / (노인이) be hale and hearty.

성하다(盛-) 1 (기운·세력이) prosperous; flourishing; thriving; active; energetic; lively. ¶기력이 ~ energetic / vigorous / full of vitality // 그곳은 예술이 ~ The arts flourish there. // 그 도시는 주로 관광이 ~ The town thrives primarily on tourism. / Tourism flourishes remarkably in the town. ¶불길이 ~ The flames are intense. / The fire gains force. 2 (초목이) thick; luxuriant; dense (forest); exuberant (foliage); leafy (woods); rampant[rank] (weeds).

성함(姓銜) (a) (full) name. ⇨ '성명(姓名) ¶~이 어떻게 되십니까 May I have your name, please? // ~은 익히 들어 알고 있습니다 I have often heard your name[of you].

성행(盛行) prevalence; vogue; a fad; a rage. **성행하다** prevail; be prevalent; have a great vogue; be much in fashion[vogue]; be in the height of fashion; be very popular; rage; be rife; be rampant. ¶투기가 성행하고 있다 Speculation is widely prevalent. // 한국제 물건이 크게 성행하고 있다 There is quite a vogue for Korean-made things.

성행위(性行爲) a sex[sexual] act. ¶~를 하다 perform a sexual act / have sex (with).

성향(性向) an inclination; a disposition; a propensity; a tendency. ¶소비 ~ the propensity to consume // 청년들의 ~이 흔히 그렇듯이 그는 자신만만하다 He is too sure of himself, as is the tendency with young men.

성현(聖賢) sages. ¶~의 가르침 the teaching of the sages / the words of the wise.

성형(成形) [의] correction of deformities; [얼굴의] face-lifting. **성형하다** correct[put right] a deformity; face lift. 2 [공] forming; shaping; molding. **성형하다** mold; cast. ¶찰흙[금속]을 성형하여 소상(塑像)을 만들다 cast a statue in clay[metal] / cast clay[metal] into a clay. ●**성형 수술** a plastic operation. **성형외과** plastic surgery; (특히 미용을 위한) cosmetic surgery; (그 기술) reconstructive[restorative] surgery; (병원의 과(科)) the plastic surgery department.

성호르몬(性-) [생] (a) sex hormone.

성홍열(猩紅熱) [의] scarlet fever; scarlatina.

성화(成火) annoyance; vexation; irritation; worry; heartburnings; (a) bother; (a) trouble. ¶~가 나다 be vexed / be irritated / fret / become impatient[nervous] // 그들은 우리에게 책값을 내라고 계속 ~를 대었다 They kept after us to pay for the book.

성화(星火) 1 [천] a shooting star. ⇨ 유성(流星) 2 [별똥 빛] the light of a meteor[a shooting star]. 3 [몹시 급한 일] an urgent matter; an emergency. 4 [불티] a spark (of charcoal fire).

성화(聖火) the sacred fire[flame]; a sacred torch. ¶올림픽의 ~ (경기장의) the Olympic Flame / (릴레이의) the Olympic Torch.
●**성화대** a flame-holder. **성화 주자** a flame-bearer. ¶올림픽의 최종 ~ the anchor[last runner] of the Olympic sacred-fire relay.

성화(聖畵) a religious[holy] picture.

성화같다(星火-) urgent; pressing; importunate. ¶빚 독촉이 ~ press (a person) hard for the payment of his debt / make an importunate demand upon (a person) for the payment of his debt.

성황(盛況) prosperity; a boom; a success. ¶~을 이루다 be prosperous / be thriving / be flourishing / enjoy prosperity / (상점 등이) be doing a flourishing business / do thriving business / (모임 등이) be a success / be well attended // 그 모임은 ~리에 끝났다 The meeting ended successfully.

성황당(城隍堂) the shrine for a tutelary deity. ⇨ 서낭당

성희롱(性戲弄) sexual harassment; (완곡) inappropriate behavior. **성희롱하다** harass sexually.

섶[1] [버티기 위한 막대기] a prop; a stay; a support; a crotch. ¶~으로 버티다 support (a plant) with a stick / prop (up).

섶[2] a gusset. ⇨ 옷섶

섶[3] brushwood; firewood.

세 [셋] three. ¶~ 번 three times / thrice // ~ 남자 three men.

세 살 적 버릇이 여든까지 간다(속담) Custom [Habit] is a second nature.; What is learned in cradle is be carried to the tomb.

-세 [동료나 아랫사람에게 함께하자는 뜻] let us; let's; let (me / him). ¶가~ Let's go. // 내일 보~ See you tomorrow. // 그들에게 한번 시켜 보~ Let them just try it.

세(世) 1 [지] an epoch. ¶홍적 ~ the diluvial epoch. 2 [대(代)] an age; a generation. ¶제임스 2~ James Ⅱ [the second].

세(貰) [임대·임차] lease; tenancy; location(부동산의); hire; hiring(물건의); charter(배의); [임대료] (a) rent; hire; charterage(선박의). ¶집[방] ~ a house[room] rent // 비싼[싼] (집) ~ a high[low] rent // 밀린 ~ back rent / rent in arrears // ~ 놓는 사람 a lessor // ~를 든[낸] 사람 a hirer / a lessee / a tenant / a leaseholder(부동산의) // ~를 놓다[주다] rent [lease (out)] (a house) / put out (land) to lease / let (a house) / let (bicycles) out on hire // ~를 들다[대다] (부동산의) lease (land) / take[hold] (land / a house) by[on] lease / (집) rent (a house) / hire.

세(稅) [조세] a tax; a duty; an imposition; dues; rates(지방세 등); [과세] taxation. ¶개인[법인] ~ an individual[a corporate] income tax // 국~ a national taxy // 상속 ~ a death[a succession / an inheritance] tax // 영업[물품 / 소비 / 증여] ~ a business[commodity / consumption / gift] tax // 입항[통행] ~ harbor[canal] dues // 지방 ~ (미) a local tax / (영) the rates // 주민[재산] ~ a municipal[property] tax // 수입 ~ import

세 duties∥유흥~ an amusement tax∥주(酒)~ liquor tax∥직접[간접]~ a direct[an indirect] tax∥누진~ a progressive[graduated] tax∥부가 가치~ a value-added tax(약어 VAT).

세(勢) influence; force. ⇨¹세력1·2

세(歲) age; years. ¶80~ 노인 an old man of eighty∥10~의 소녀 a ten year-old girl∥30~이다 be thirty years old.

세가(世家) a distinguished[noble] family.

세가(勢家) 1〔권세 있는 집안〕a powerful family. 2 a man of influence. ⇨세력가(⇨세력)

세간〔살림에 쓰는 온갖 물건〕household furniture[utensils / goods / stuff / things / effects]; furniture and kitchen utensils necessary for housekeeping. ¶부엌~ kitchen utensils[appliances] / kitchenware / (집합적) kitchen equipment∥~이 별로 없는 방 a scanty furnished room.

세간(을) 나다 establish[set up] a branch [separate] family; create a new family; establish oneself in a new[branch] family; set up a house. ¶그는 장가들어 세간을 났다 He got married and made a new home.

세간(을) 내다 set up separate home[household] (of). ¶아들을 ~ set up a separate home for one's son.

세간(世間) 1〔온 사람이 살고 있는 사회〕the world; society; life. 2〔불〕the mundane world.

세계(世界) 1〔온 세상〕the world; 〔지구〕the earth; the globe. ¶전 ~ the whole world / the world at large∥~의 international / world∥~의 끝까지 to the end of the world∥~가 넓다 하여도 in all the wide world∥~에서 in the world / all over the world / on earth∥~를 일주하다 go[trip] (a)round the world / travel (all over) the world∥내일의 ~를 건설하다 build tomorrow's world∥~를 움직이다[동요시키다] move[shake] the world. 2〔사물 현상의 일정 범위·분야〕a world; a society; circles; a realm; sphere. ¶꿈의 ~ the realm of dreams / dreamland∥이상의 ~ an ideal world∥공상의 ~ the realm of fancy∥정치의 ~ the political world∥그와 나는 사는 ~가 다르다 He and I live in two different worlds.∥시작(詩作)은 나의 활동 밖의 ~이다 Writing poetry lies outside the sphere of my activities.

● **세계 각지** all parts of the world; the four corners of the world. **세계관** an outlook on the world; a view of the world; a world view [outlook]. **세계 기록** a world record. ¶~을 세우다 establish[make / set (up)] a world record (in). **세계 대전** the World War. ¶제1 [2]차 ~ the First[Second] World War / World War Ⅰ[Ⅱ]. **세계 무역 기구** the World Trade Organization(약어 WTO). **세계 보건 기구** the World Health Organization(약어 WHO). **세계사** world history; the history of the world. **세계상**(-像) a picture of the world; a world picture. **세계어** a world[a universal / an international] language. **세계 인권 선언** the Universal Declaration of Human Rights. **세계정세** the situation of the world; the drift of affairs in the world. **세계주의** cosmopolitanism; internationalism. **세계 지도** a map of the world. **세계 평화** world peace; the peace of the world.

세계적(世界的) world; world-wide; international; global; universal. ¶~ 문제 an international problem / a universal[global] issue∥~ 불경기 a world-wide depression∥~ 인물 a world figure∥~으로 유명한 world-famous [-renowned / -famed] (person)∥~ 의미로 보아 in a world-wide sense∥그는 ~으로 유명하다 He is world-famous.

세공(細工)〔잔손질이 많이 가는 수공〕work; workmanship; craftsmanship. ¶금속 ~ metalwork∥조가비 ~ shellwork∥정교한[공들인] ~ delicate[elaborate] workmanship∥~ 솜씨가 좋다[어설프다] be of good[bad] workmanship. **세공하다** work (in / on); craft. ¶대나무에 ~ work on bamboo∥보석에 ~ work on a precious stone∥은으로 ~ work in silver. →¶정교하게 세공되어 있다 be cunningly wrought.

● **세공인** a worker; a craftsman; an artisan. ¶금속 ~ a metal worker / a smith. **세공품**·**세공물** a (piece of) work; (a) handiwork; a ware. ¶미술 ~ an art object / ornamental ware∥(프) an objet d'art∥죽 ~ a bamboo work / (집합적) bamboo ware.

세관(稅關)〔미〕a customhouse;〔영〕a customs house; the customs(▶〔영〕에서는 복수 취급, 〔미〕에서는 단수 취급이 보통임). ¶인천 ~ the Incheon Customhouse∥~의 검사 (a) customs inspection[examination]∥~을 통과하다 go through (the) customs∥~에서 소지품을 신고하다 declare something∥~에서 관세를 지불하다 clear goods∥나는 ~에서 짐에 대한 엄격한 조사를 받았다 I had my baggage closely inspected at (the) customs.∥우리 일행은 ~의 조사가 면제되었다 Our party was exempted from the customs examination.

● **세관 수속** customs formalities[procedure]. **세관 신고서** a customs declaration. **세관원**·**세관공무원** a customs officer; a customs officer [inspector]; a customs agent.

세광(洗鑛) 〔광〕ore washing. **세광하다** wash (ore); scrub (ore).

● **세광반**(-盤) a frame.

세교(世交) a long-standing[traditional] friendship between families; generations of family friendship.

세균(細菌) a bacillus (pl. bacilli); a bacterium (pl. bacteria); a germ; a microbe. ¶~의 bacterial / bacillar / bacillary∥~이 없는 우유 bacteria-free milk∥~을 죽이다 destroy [kill] germ / sterilize∥상처는 ~에 감염되기 쉽다 Wounds are apt to become infected.

● **세균 검사** a bacteriological examination; bacilloscopy. **세균 배양** germ culture; cultivation of bacteria; germiculture; bacilliculture. **세균전** bacteriological[germ / biological] warfare. **세균학** bacteriology; microbiology.

세금(稅金) a tax; dues; 〔영〕the rates(지방세); a duty (on) (물품세); a toll(통행세). ¶부당한 ~ an irrational[unreasonable] tax∥미납 ~ unpaid taxes∥체납된 ~ taxes in arrears / delinquent[back] taxes∥~의 부담 a tax burden[load]∥~의 징수[납부] the collection[payment] of a tax∥~이 붙는 dutiable / taxable∥~이 붙지 않는 tax-free / tax-exempt (bond) / free of duty∥~으로 내는 돈 a tax payment∥~을 부과하다 impose

a duty (on an article) / levy a tax (on a person) / charge a tax (on an income) // ~을 징수하다 collect taxes (from) / draw a tax (from) // ~을 지불[납부]하다 pay a tax [duty] (on) // ~을 속이다 defraud a tax // ~을 포탈하다 evade a tax // ~을 환불하다 refund a tax // ~을 경감하다 lighten taxes // ~이 체납되어 있다 be in arrears[be behind] with taxes // 임금 생활자의 ~ 부담을 줄이다 lighten the tax burden of wage earners // 무거운 ~에 시달리다 groan under heavy taxation // 나는 ~을 물납(物納)했다 I paid my tax in kind. // 그는 ~을 면제받고 있다 He is exempt from taxation.
● 세금 공제 the personal tax deduction. 세금 혜택 a tax favor. ¶ ~을 주다 give a tax favor (to).

세기(世紀) a century. ¶금~ this[the present] century // 20~ the twentieth [20th] century // 전~ (the) last century // ~의 위업 (one of) the greatest achievement of the century // ~의 대사건 the salient event of the century // ~의 영웅 the hero of the century // ~의 전환기 the turn of the century // 18~ 초[중 / 후] 엽에 in the early [mid / late] eighteenth century // 여러 ~에 걸쳐서 through[over] many centuries / for centuries // 21~가 막이 열렸다 The 21st century opened.
● 세기말 the end [turn] of a century; (프) fin de siècle. ¶~의 불안 fin de siècle [decadent] mood [unrest].

세끼 three (regular) meals (a day); daily meals.

세나다 [잘 팔리다] sell[be selling] well; be in great demand[request]; have[enjoy] a good demand; command a large[good] sale; be a good seller; be rare [precious / hard to come by]. ¶세나는 물건 a good[quick] sell(er).

세내다(貰-) hire (a boat, a horse, etc.); engage (a carriage); rent (a house, land, etc.); take (a house, a room, etc.); lease (land); (배를) charter (a vessel). ¶세낸 사람 a lodger / (미) a roomer // 건물을 ~ take a lease of a building.

세놓다(貰-) hire[let] out (a boat); (집을) let [rent] (a house to a person); rent out (a mansion); [법] locate; (토지를) lease. ¶방을 ~ rent [(영) let] a room [rooms] / take in lodgers // 자전거를 ~ let bicycles out on hire.

세뇌(洗腦) brainwashing; indoctrination. ¶전쟁 포로의 ~ the brainwash of war prisoners. 세뇌하다 brainwash (a person); indoctrinate. ➔그는 세뇌당하여 비밀을 털어놓고 말았다 He was brainwashed into revealing the secret.
● 세뇌 공작 brainwashing. 세뇌 교육 (undergo) indoctrination education.

세다[1] [머리털이 희어지다] turn white[gray]; become grizzled[grizzly]; (얼굴이 혈색이 없어지다) turn pale[white] (with fear). ¶센 머리 gray[white / hoary] hair // 머리가 ~ one's hair turns gray / get gray-haired // 걱정으로 그녀의 머리가 하얗게 세었다 Anxiety has turned her hair all gray.

세다[2] (수를) count; reckon; calculate; number; numerate; enumerate; take count of (votes). ¶다시 ~ recount / count (all over) again / count over // 잘못 ~ count wrong / miscalculate / miscount // 정확히 ~ count accurately / reckon [number] correctly // 1에서 1,000까지 ~ reckon [count] from one to a thousand / reckon to a thousand // 10에서 1까지 거꾸로 ~ count backwards from ten to one / count down from ten // 손꼽아 ~ count on one's fingers // 대충 세어 ~이 되다 be roughly estimated at ... // 나는 그것이 언제 일어났는지 날짜를 세어 보았다 I counted the days to see when it had happened.

세다[3] **1** (힘이) [많다] strong; powerful; mighty; vigorous; muscular; robust (강건하다). ¶힘이 센 사람 a strong[powerful] man / a brawny man // 힘이 세어 보이는 strong-looking // 기운[힘]이 무척 ~ be as strong as a horse / have the strength of a lion // 힘이 세어지다 become [grow] powerful[strong / stout] // 지금은 힘이 센 자가 이기는 세상이다 In this world the strong are sure to win.
2 (기세가) [강하다] tough; firm; stubborn. ¶고집이 ~ be stubborn[obstinate] // 배짱이 ~ have pluck[mettle] / have iron nerves.
3 (바람·불길 등이) [거세다] violent; strong; hard; severe; fierce; intense; heavy; rough; forcible; keen. ¶센 바람 a strong[heavy / violent] wind // 센 물살 a swift [strong] current / rapids // 센 빛 a strong [an intense] light // 바람이 ~ it is blowing hard / (장소가) be windy // (바람이) blow hard (against) // 화력이 ~ have strong caloric force // 물결이 ~ The sea is rough.
4 [능력·수준이 정도 이상이다] good (at); strong (in). ¶그는 바둑이 ~ He is a good baduk(go) player. / He is good at baduk. // 그는 술이 ~ be a heavy drinker. / He drinks quite a lot. / He can hold his liquor.
5 [궂은일이 자주 생겨 좋지 않다] ill-omened; unlucky; ill-fated; evil-[ill-]starred. ¶팔자가 ~ be ill-fated / have a hard fate[lot] // 터가 ~ (집이) have an unlucky aspect / The site is unlucky[ill-omened].
6 (물이) hard; (풀이) stiff. ¶센물 hard water // (먹인) 풀기가 너무 ~ be starched too stiff.

세단(자동차) a sedan; (영) a saloon.

세단뛰기(-段-) [체] the hop, step and jump; the triple jump.

세대(世代) a generation. ¶유성[부성] ~ [생] the sexual[asexual] generation // 다음 ~ the next generation // 새로운 ~ the new generation // 젊은 ~ the rising[younger] generation // 한[몇] ~ 전 one generation [a few generations] ago // ~ 간의 차[단절] a generation gap // 다음 ~를 이끌어 갈 운명에 있다 be destined to lead the next generation // 그 집에는 모두 3~가 살고 있다 Three generations live together in that house. // 우리는 모두 전후 ~이다 We all belong to the postwar generation. // 그와 이야기할 때 나는 ~ 차이를 느꼈다 As I talked with him, I became aware of a generation gap between us.
● 세대 교번 [생] alternation of generations. 세대교체 a shift in generation. ¶~를 부르짖다 call for a shift in generation.

세대(世帶) a household; a family. ⇨가구(家口)

세도(勢道) power; authority; influence; (holding) the reigns of government. ¶~를 부리다 exert[exercise / wield] one's authority [power] // 군인이 ~를 부리는 나라 a country where the military makes its influence felt // 그는 이 근방에서는 ~를 부린다 He is influ-

ential in this neighborhood. 세도하다 have one's own way about state affairs; seize political power; assume the reins of the government.
● 세도가 / 세도꾼 a man of power[influence]; a person in power; an influential person.

세레나데 [음] a serenade.

세력(勢力) **1** [지배력] influence; power; strength; might; sway. ¶안정 ~ a stabilizing force[factor] // ~ 있는 influential / powerful / mighty // ~ 없는 uninfluential / powerless // ~이 있다 exercise[have] influence (over / with) / carry weight (with / among) // ~이 증대하다 increase in power / gain in influence // ~이 백중하다 be almost equal in power / ~을 꺾다 break (a person's) power / destroy[undermine] (a person's) influence // ~을 떨치다 wield power[influence] / hold[bear] sway / dominate // ~을 늘리다 promote[increase] one's influence // ~을 얻다 acquire[gain] influence / become powerful[influential] // ~을 잃다 lose one's power / forfeit one's influence // ~을 펴다 establish [fix] one's influence // ~을 확대하다 extend [broaden] one's power[influence] // 그 파벌의 ~은 기울어지고 있다 The influence of the faction is declining. / The faction is losing its influence[(구어) clout]. // 나폴레옹은 한때 거의 전 유럽을 그의 ~ 아래 두었다 At one time Napoleon had almost all Europe under his thumb.
2 [물리적 힘] force; energy. ¶(바람 등이) 차차 ~ 을 더하다 gather strength / 태풍의 ~이 약해졌다 The typhoon weakened[lost strength].
3 [특정 집단] a group; a party. ¶혁신 ~ the progressive political group.
● 세력가 a man of influence[weight]; an influential man; a powerful man; a power(사업계에서). 세력권 a sphere [scope] of influence[power]; (깡패 등의) one's range [domain]; one's territory. ¶깡패의 ~ 다툼 a fight for spheres of influence[a territorial dispute] between gangsters // ~을 넓히다 widen[enlarge / expand] one's sphere of influence / extend one's territory // ~ 내에 있다 be within one's territory[orbit / sphere of influence]. 세력 균형 the balance of power; the power balance. 세력 다툼 a struggle[contest / grab / scramble] for power; a power struggle.

세련되다(洗練-) polished; refined; finished; elegant. ¶세련된 신사 a polished[refined] gentleman // 세련된 문장 a polished style // 세련된 태도[말씨] refined[polished] manners [speech] // 태도가 ~ have polished manners // 말을 세련되게 하다 refine (on[upon]) one's language // 그녀는 세련된 영어로 대답했다 She responded in polished[refined] English. // 그의 재능은 아직 세련되지 못했다 He has undeveloped[raw] talent. / He is a rough diamond. // 그녀의 연기는 원숙하여 더욱 세련되어졌다 Maturity added to the refinement[polish] of her performances. // 너는 세련된 옷차림을 하고 있다 She is stylishly dressed.

세례(洗禮) baptism; palingenesis; christening(유아의). ¶유아 ~ pedobaptism // 재 rebaptism // ~를 받다 accept[receive] baptism / be baptized / be christened // ~를 베풀다 baptize a person / administer baptism (to) // 포화의 ~를 받다 receive[undergo] one's baptism of fire / be under fire / be exposed to fire // 주먹~를 퍼붓다 hail blows upon (a person) // ~를 받고 신자가 되다 be baptized into the Christian faith.
● 세례명 a baptismal[Christian] name. 세례식 baptism; a baptismal ceremony; baptismal service.

세로 [가로에 대하여] length; [높이] height; [수직으로] perpendicularly; vertically; lengthwise; longitudinally; endwise. ¶~ 3피트 가로 5피트 three feet by five / three feet long and five feet wide // ~가 5미터다 be five meters long / measure five meters in length // ~로 째다 cut lengthwise / sliver // ~로 쓰다 write vertically // ~로 줄을 긋다 draw a vertical line // 나는 카드를 ~로 놓았다 I lined the cards up lengthwise. / I placed the cards end to end. // 이 판자는 ~가 2미터 폭이 50센티다 This board is two meters long and fifty centimeters wide.
● 세로줄 a perpendicular[vertical] line; a (longitudinal) stripe; a file(장기판 등의). 세로축 [수] the axis of ordinates.

세로쓰기 vertical writing. 세로쓰기하다 write vertically; write in vertical lines.

세류(細柳) a weeping willow. ⇨=세버들

세륨 [화] cerium(기호 Ce).

세리(稅吏) a tax collector; a revenue officer.

세면(洗面) washing up (one's face). 세면하다 wash one's face; have a wash.
● 세면기 (미) a washbowl; (영) a washbasin; a (washhand) basin. 세면대 a washstand; a washing stand; (영) a washhand stand.

세모 triangularity.
● 세모꼴 a triangle. ⇨=삼각형(⇨삼각(三角)) 세모뿔 a trigonal pyramid. ⇨=삼각뿔(⇨삼각(三角))

세모(歲暮) the year-end. ⇨=세밑

세모나다 have three corners; be three-cornered. ¶세모난 모자 a three-cornered[tri-cornered] hat.

세모시(細-) ramie cloth of fine texture.

세모지다 have three corners. ⇨=세모나다

세목(細目) details; particulars; (specified) items; specifications. ¶교수~ a detailed plan for instruction / a (teaching) syllabus // ~으로 나누다 itemize / specify // 지출을 ~별로 나누다 break down (the) expenditure.

세목(稅目) items[headings] of a tariff; items of taxation; tax items.

세무 →새미

세무(稅務) taxation business; tax affairs.
● 세무사 a licensed tax accountant. 세무서 a tax[taxation] office; a revenue office. 세무 조사 a tax investigation[surveillance]; a tax probe. ¶정밀 ~ an intensive tax investigation. 세무 회계 tax accounting; accounting for taxation.

세물(貰物) an object for hire[(미) rent].

세미나 a seminar (on public finance). ¶한국사 ~ a seminar in Korean history.

세미콜론 [쌍반점] a semicolon. ¶~을 찍다 put a semicolon (to).

세밀하다(細密-) minute; detailed; fine; close; elaborate. ¶세밀한 관찰 close observation // 세밀한 주의 close attention / meticulous care / detailed instructions(지시) // 세밀한 서술 a detailed description. **세밀히** minutely; in detail; closely; elaborately. ¶~조사하다 inquire minutely into (a matter) / examine closely [minutely] // 실험 결과를 ~ 분석하다 analyze the results of an experiment closely [minutely] / make a close [minute] analysis of the results of an experiment // 그는 그 정경을 ~ 묘사했다 He described the scene minutely [in great detail].

세밀(歲-) the year-end; the end [close] of the year. ¶~의 거리 풍경 a year-end scene of the street.

세발(洗髮) (a) shampoo; washing of the hair; hair wash(ing). ¶~료 1,000원 (게시) Shampoo 1,000 won / 1,000 won For A Shampoo. **세발하다** wash the hair. ¶(이발소 등에서) ~ have one's hair shampooed.

세발자전거(-自轉車) a tricycle.

세배(歲拜) [정초에 하는 인사·절] a sebae; the New Year's greetings [call / visit]; a formal bow of respect to one's elders on New Year's Day. **세배하다** perform [make] a New Year's bow; exchange the New Year's greetings. ¶세배하러 가다 pay one's respects (to) at the New Year / pay a New Year's call [visit] (to).

●**세뱃돈** the New Year's gift of money given to one's juniors; a handsel. ¶~을 주다 give (a child) a handsel.

세버들(細-) a weeping willow.

세법(稅法) [법률] the tax law.

세부(細部) [상세] particulars; the fine parts; the minutiae. ¶~를 조사하다 go into details [particulars].

세부득이(勢不得已) by force of circumstances; by an unavoidable circumstance. **세부득이하다** unavoidable. ¶세부득이한 경우에는 in situations [cases] that demand [compel] it / when unavoidable.

세분(細分) subdivision; fractionation; a breakdown. **세분하다** subdivide; fractionate; fractionalize; fractionize; break down [into parts]; itemize. ¶네 종류로 ~ subdivide into four sets / itemize (things) into four.

세비(歲費) [지출] annual expenditure; [매년 보수·수당] yearly pay; an annual allowance [salary].

세사(世事) worldly affairs. ⇨=세상사(⇨세상). ¶~에 능한 사람 a worldly-wise man / a man of the world // ~에 밝다 be a man of the world / have seen much of life / know the world // ~에 어둡다 know little of the world [the ways of the world] / be ignorant [have little knowledge] of the world / be impractical in worldly affairs.

세사(細沙) fine sand.

세상(世上) 1 [세계] the world; (a) society(사회); the public(사람들); [인생·생애] life; existence; one's life time. ¶이 ~ this world [life] // 저~ the next world / the world beyond // ~의 관습 the way(s) of the world // 덧없는 이 ~ this transitory world / this fleeting life // ~에 알려진 well-known / widely known / famous / notorious(악명이) // ~에 알려지지 않은 obscure / unknown / nameless / little known (in the world) // ~과의 인연을 끊다 shut oneself up from the world / renounce the world // ~의 화제가 되다 become the talk of the town / make a noise in the world // ~의 쓴맛 단맛을 다 맛보다 taste the sweets and bitters of life // ~의 덧없음을 느끼다 feel the vanity of this life // ~의 거센 물결을 헤쳐 나가다 manage to ride out the troubled waves of life // ~의 물의를 일으키다 give birth to public controversy / bring on the censure of the public // ~의 웃음거리가 되다 be made a laughingstock of the public / be held up to public ridicule // ~의 주목을 끌게 되다 come into the limelight // ~에 나오다 [태어나다] be born into the world / see the light (of day) / [사회로 나오다] go out into the world [in life] // ~에 내보내다(자식 등을) send out to the world / place out in life / (사물을) give (a book) to the public [world] // ~에 알려져 있다 be known to the world / be famous in the world // (나쁜 짓이) ~에 드러나다 get abroad / come to light / become public // ~에 호소하다 appeal to the public // ~에 적응하다 adapt oneself to the times / 풍파에 부대끼다 be exposed to the ways of the world // ~에서 잊혀지다 be buried in oblivion / be forgotten by the world // ~에서 버림받다 be rejected [forsaken] by the world / be shut [cast] out of society // ~이 싫어지다 be [get] sick (and tired) of the world / become [be] weary of life [the world] // ~을 살아가다 live / get along in the world / make one's way [get / go] through the world / pass through life // ~을 알고 있다 know the world / have seen much of life // ~을 놀라게 하다 create [make] a stir / astonish the world / (깜짝) take the world by surprise // ~을 피하다 shun public notice / avoid the eyes of the world // ~을 시끄럽게 하다 create a sensation / make a noise in the world // ~이란 그런 거야 That is the way of the world. // 그는 ~을 잘 알고 있다 He knows much of the world. / He is a man of the world. // 나는 ~이 싫어졌다 I am thoroughly tired of life. // 너는 ~을 도무지 모르는구나 You know nothing of the world. // 그건 ~이 다 아는 사실이다 All the [The whole] world knows it. / It is a matter of common [universal] knowledge. // 그의 이름은 ~에서 잊혀지고 있다 His name has been forgotten (by the world). // 그는 ~ 경험을 많이 했다 He's been around. / He has seen a lot of life. // 그의 연애 사건은 ~을 시끄럽게 했다 His love affair created a sensation. // ~은 말이 많은 법이니 이건 비밀로 해야 해 People will talk, so we must keep this a secret. // 그는 그것이 ~에 알려지지 않게 했다 He kept it from the public. // 그녀는 ~에 시달러 매우 약다[아직도 숫되다] She is terribly wise to [knows nothing of] the ways of the world. / She's terribly hardened to the ways of the world [She's still completely naive].

2 [시대] the age; the era; the period; the times. ¶~의 변천 the change of the times / the march of times // ~에 둘도 없는 악당 the greatest scoundrel alive // 요새 같은 ~에 with things as [the way] they are now // ~에 뒤지다 fall [lag / get] behind the times / get out of the touch with the world // ~에 뒤지지 않도록 하다 keep up with the times / keep abreast of [with] the times // ~에 역행하다 swim against the current (of the times) // ~이 변했다 Times have changed. // ~은 바야흐

세상모르다

로 컴퓨터 시대다 This is truly the age of the computer.// 돈이면 안 되는 일 없는 ~이다 Money is everything nowadays. / We live in an age in which money is everything.
3 [독무대]. ¶(…의) **~이다** (사람이) be one's own master[boss] / have one's own way / be in power[the saddle] / (사람이) be in one's hands// 그가 없어졌으니 우리 ~이다 Now that he is gone, we are our own masters.// 여기는 내 ~이다 Here I am absolutely my own boss[master].

세상(을) 떠나다[뜨다] die; pass away; depart this life; leave[go out of] the world; end[close] one's days.

세상(을) 버리다 forsake the world; hide oneself from the world; 〔자살하다〕 kill oneself; commit suicide; end one's own life. ¶그녀는 괴로운 세상을 버리고 여승이 되었다 She abandoned[renounced] this weary world and became a nun.

세상을 등지다 turn one's back on the world; 〔은둔하다〕 retire from public life; 〔출가하다〕 renounce the world (and become a monk).

●**세상맛** the sweets and bitters of life. ¶**~을 다 본 사람** a man of the world / a worldly-wise man// **~을 알다** know what the world is like. **세상 물정** (the condition of) the world; the ways of the world; worldly matters; 〔인간의 속성〕 human nature; humanity. ¶**~에 밝은 사람** a man of the world / a sensible man// **~을 알게 되다** get used to the ways of the world / become worldly-wise// 그는 ~을 모른다 He knows nothing of the world. / He has seen but little of the world. / He is wet under the ears. **세상사 / 세상일** worldly affairs; mundane affairs; the ways of life; the business of the world. **세상살이** the way of living; the mode of life; living.

세상모르다(世上-) be ignorant of the world; have seen (but) little of the world. ¶나는 너무 지쳐서 세상모르고 갔다 I was so tired that I slept like a log.// 그는 세상모른다 He knows nothing of the world[real life]. / He's naive.

세상없어도(世上-) 〔무슨 일이 있더라도 꼭〕 for all the world; at any cost; at all costs [risks]; by all means; under[in] any circumstances; on no account; for the life of one; by hook or by crook; whatever may happen. ¶~ 그따위 것은 못 하겠다 I wouldn't do that on any account.// ~ 이 일은 해야 한다 Nothing shall hinder me from accomplishing my purpose.// 나는 ~ 목적을 달성해야겠다 I will move heaven and earth to attain my end.

세상없이(世上-) 〔이 세상에 다시없이〕 ever so; beyond words; beyond comparison; utterly.

세상에(世上-) (how / what / why) on earth [in the world / in the name of God]. ¶~ 이게 무슨 일이냐 What in the world is it?// ~ 별일 다 보겠다 Of all things! / Well, now I've seen everything!// ~ 어쩌자고 이런 짓을 하는 거지 What the devil[in the nation] do you mean by doing that?

세세하다(細細-) **1** [미세하다] small; fine; minute. ¶세세한 물건 small things// 그녀는 세세한 것에 마음을 쓴다 She worries about little things.

2 〔상세하다〕 detailed; minute; circumstantial; 〔정밀하다〕 close. ¶극히 세세한 점에 이르기까지 to the remotest particulars [minutest details]// 세세한 데까지 미치다 (주의가) be attentive in details / be very careful / (배려가) be thoughtful / be considerate. **세세히** minutely; circumstantially; with particulars; in detail; to the smallest detail. ¶~ 기록하다 write down the full particulars// 어머니는 나에게 ~ 주의를 하셨다 My mother gave me detailed advice[directions]. / 〔잔소리를 하다〕 My mother scolded me about every little thing.// 일의 경과가 ~ 기록되어 있었다 The full particulars of what had happened were recorded.

세속(世俗) 〔풍습〕 common[popular / vulgar] customs; 〔세상〕 the (mundane / secular) world; the common people. ¶~의 common / worldly / mundane / vulgar / secular / temporal / (속어) lowbrow// ~에서 말하는 in common[vulgar] parlance / as is commonly said// ~에 영합하다 cater to the masses / curry favor with the hoi polloi// ~을 초월하다 stand aloof from[rise above] worldly things / be free from the trammels of ordinary life / be unworldly.
●**세속주의** secularism. **세속화** secularization. ¶~하다 secularize / vulgarize.

세속적(世俗的) worldly; earthly; social. ¶~ 명성[욕망] worldly fame[desire]// ~인 사람 a worldly person// ~ 지위 one's social standing[position]// ~인 지식이 없다 have no knowledge of the world / know nothing of the world / be ignorant of the world.

세수(洗手) face[hand] washing. **세수하다** wash one's face and hands; have a wash; wash oneself. ¶식사 전에 ~ wash up before a meal.
●**세수수건** a (face) towel. **세숫대야** a wash basin. **세숫물** water for washing up.

세수(입)(稅收入) 〔조세로 얻은 수입〕 tax revenues; tax yields. ¶~의 증가[감소] an increase[a drop] in revenue.

세슘 (화) cesium; caesium.

세습(世襲) transmission by heredity; descent. ¶~의 hereditary / patrimonial. **세습하다** transmit from generation to generation.
●**세습 군주** a hereditary monarch. **세습 재산** hereditary property[estate]; freehold; patrimony; heritage.

세습(世習) 〔세상의 풍습〕 the way[customs] of the world.

세시(歲時) **1** 〔새해 첫머리〕 the New Year; the beginning of the year. **2** 〔절기〕 times and seasons.

세심하다(細心-) very careful; prudent; scrupulous; circumspect; elaborate; deliberate; attentive. ¶세심한 주의 scrupulous care / careful attention// 세심한 주의를 하다 pay the closest attention (to)// 그는 다른 사람에 대해 세심한 사람이다 He is a conscientious man.// 그녀는 다른 사람에 대해 세심한 배려를 한다 She shows much delicacy of feeling for others. **세심히** with the greatest circumspection[care]; with scrupulous [meticulous] care; most carefully; prudently; scrupulously.

세쌍둥이(-雙-) triplets. ¶~를 낳다 have three at a birth.

세안(洗眼) eyewashing. **세안하다** wash one's

eyes; have one's eyes washed.
세안(洗顔) face[hand] washing. ⇨**세수**(洗手)
세액(稅額) 〔조세의 액수〕 the amount of a tax; the tax amount; the tax liability; an assessment. ¶결정 ~ the settled tax amount // ~을 정하다 assess.
● **세액 산정** the assessment of a tax.
세우다 **1** 〔서게 하다〕 stand (a candle); make (a thing) stand; erect; raise; set up; put up (a notice board); set (a book) on edge [end]; stand (a long thing) on end; hoist (a flag); plant (a car). ¶간판을 ~ put up a sign (board) // 달걀을 바로 ~ stand an egg on end // 책을 세로로 ~ set a book on its edge [on end] // 기둥을 ~ plant [set up] a post // 사람을 세로[가로] 두 줄로 ~ arrange [stand] people in two lines [rows] // 그는 코트의 깃을 세워 입고 있었다 He wore his coat with the collar turned up. // 그 소리에 개는 귀를 쫑긋 세웠다 The dog pricked up its ears at the sound. // 학교 정문 앞에 시위자들의 많은 플래카드가 세워져 있었다 A lot of demonstrator's signs had been set up in front of the school gate.
2 〔멈추게 하다〕 stop; put a stop to; bring to a stop [halt / standstill]; hold up [on]. ¶차를 ~ bring a car to a halt [to rest] / (불러서) call a halt / 〔주차시키다〕 park a car // 택시를 ~ (손을 들어) stop [hold up] a cab // 차를 대문 앞에 세워 주시오 Pull the car up at the gate. // 차를 세울 데가 없다 There is no room to park my car.
3 〔날카롭게 하다〕 sharpen; put [forge] an edge (on); give an edge (to); edge; hone; set (a razor). ¶칼날을 날카롭게 ~ put a sharp edge on a knife // 톱날을 ~ set (the teeth of) a saw.
4 〔뜻을〕 have (an object) in view; establish in one's mind; set (an object before one); be determined to (do); be inspired by ambition; have (a fixed purpose) (in life). ¶정치가가 되고자 뜻을 ~ aspire to be a politician.
5 〔건조하다〕 build; construct; erect (a statue / monument); set [put] up; raise (an edifice); rear. ¶동상을 ~ erect [put up] a bronze statue // 새로 집을 ~ have a new house built / build oneself a new house // 광장에 가설 흥행장이 세워졌다 A show tent was set up in the square. // 역전에 기념비가 세워졌다 The monument was erected in front of the station. // 황제는 여기에 웅장한 궁전을 세웠다 The Emperor had a magnificent palace built here [on this site]. // 이전에 논이었던 곳에 거대한 공장이 세워졌다 A huge plant has been built in what was once a rice field.
6 〔설립하다〕 establish (a school / firm); found; set up; organize (a union); institute. ¶학교[회사]를 세우다 start [establish / found] a school [company] // 조합[협회]을 세우다 organize [(영) organise / form] a union [a society / an association] // 그는 새 회사를 세웠다 He established [set up / founded] a new firm.
7 (제도·조직 등을) institute (a system); lay down (rules); establish (regulations); enact (a law). ¶규칙을 ~ lay down rules / establish regulations.
8 (계획을) form [make / lay] (a plan); shape; lay (down) (one's course); map out (a program). ¶예산[예정]을 ~ make [draw up] a budget [a plan] // 목표를 ~ set up [establish] a goal // 인생의 목표를 ~ set an aim [a goal] in life.
9 (학설·이론 등을) advance; set up; frame; set forth; put forward (an argument); lay down (a proposition); make out one's case; develop; formulate (a theory). ¶원칙을 ~ formulate [lay down] a principle // 새 학설을 ~ advance [set up / formulate] a new theory // 나는 새 이론을 세웠다 I formulated [developed] a new theory.
10 (사람을 어느 위치에) put up; appoint; nominate (a person for governor). ¶후보자로 ~ put up a candidate / have (a person) stand for (the Assembly) // 보증인을 ~ find [give] surety [security] for / give a reference (신원 보증인) // 두목으로 ~ acknowledge (a person) as a boss / place (a person) at the head.
11 (공로·업적 등을) render (distinguished services); perform (meritorious deeds). ¶공을 ~ perform a feat / do a meritorious deed // 업적을 ~ produce achievements // 100미터 경주에서 신기록을 ~ set [establish] a new record in the 100-meter dash.
12 (체면을) keep up; save one's face [honor]. ¶체면을 ~ save [keep up] appearances / save one's situation / save (a person's) honor [face].
13 〔기대 놓다〕 put [rest / lean] (a thing) against. ¶우산을 벽에 ~ stand an umbrella against the wall // 사다리가 벽에 세워져 있었다 A ladder was leaning against the wall.
14 (주장·고집을). ¶고집을 ~ be obstinate [stubborn] / have one's own way.
세워총(-銃) 〔군〕 〔구령〕 Order arms!
세월(歲月) **1** 〔시간〕 time (and tide). ¶긴[짧은] ~ a long [short] period [space] of time // ~이 감에 따라서 with the lapse of time / as time passes by / as days [the years] go by // 오랜 ~이 지난 후에 after long years / after (a lapse of) many years // ~을 보내다 spend one's time [days] (in doing) // ~을 허송하다 pass time idly / idle [dawdle] one's time away / live to no purpose // 청춘 시절에 나는 연극에 미쳐 ~을 보냈다 In my youth, I spent all of my time on drama [I was completely absorbed in the theater]. // 나는 무용 레슨으로 ~을 보내고 있다 All my time is taken up with dancing lessons. // ~이 지남에 따라 그 사건은 잊혀져 갔다 As years went by, the event was forgotten. // 내 자신이 사업을 할 수 있을 때까지는 상당한 ~이 필요한 것이다 It will be many years before I can go into business for myself. // ~이 유수와 같다 Time flies. // 참 빠르군 How time flies! // ~이 지남에 따라 그녀는 더욱더 아름다워졌다 She became more and more beautiful as the years went by [as time passed]. // 그 문서는 ~이 흘러 누렇게 되어 있었다 The document was yellow with age.
2 〔시세·경기〕 times; things; business; conditions. ¶~이 좋다[없다] The times are good [bad / hard]. / Business [The market] is brisk [dull / quiet]. // ~이 별로 없습니다 Business is kind of slow. / Business [The market] is dull. / Trade is bad. // ~이 차차 좋아진다 Things are going better with us. / There is (a) good time coming.

세월없이

세월은 사람을 기다려 주지 않는다(속담) Time and tide wait for no man.

세월 가는 줄 모르다 be absorbed (in doing).

세월없이(歲月－) long; for a long time. ¶나는 ～ 기다리고 있었다 I was kept waiting for a long time.

세율(稅率) the tax [taxation] rate; the rate of taxation; (관세의) a tariff. ¶협정[특혜] conventional [preferential] tariff // ～을 올리다[내리다] raise [lower] the tax rates [the tariff(관세의)] // ～을 정하다 tariff (goods).

● **세율표** a table of tax rates; tax rate scales; a tariff.

세이레 [삼칠일] the twenty-first day after a baby's birth.

세이프 [야구] safe. ¶3루에서 간신히 ～가 되다 be narrowly safe on the third base // ～를 **선언하다** declare safe // 주자, 일루 ～ The runner is safe at first [base].

세인(世人) people; the world; the public. ¶～의 이목을 피하다 avert people's eyes / avoid public notice.

세일 a sale. ¶바겐～ a bargain sale // 재고 정리 ～ a clearance (sale) // 저 가게에서는 의류의 연말 ～을 하고 있다 That store is having a year-end sale on clothing. // 이 옷은 백화점의 ～에서 샀다 I bought this dress on sale [at a bargain sale] at a department store.

세일즈맨 a salesman; (지방으로 도는) a traveling salesman; a commercial traveler; (호별 방문하는) a house-to-house salesman. ¶책의 ～ a salesman in books // 자동차의 ～ an automobile [a car] salesman.

세입(稅入) the yield [income] of taxes; tax revenues [yields]. ¶～의 증가[감소] an increase [a drop] in revenue.

세입(歲入) (국가의) an annual revenue; (개인의) an annual income. ¶금년도의 국가 ～은 대폭으로 증가되었다 The nation's revenue for this year has greatly increased.

세입자(貰入者) a tenant; a lessee.

세자(世子) the Crown Prince; the princely heir. ¶그는 ～로 책봉되었다 He was formally installed as Crown Prince.

● **세자빈**(－嬪) the Crown Princess.

세전하다(世傳－) hand down from generation to generation.

세정(洗淨) washing; rinsing; cleaning. **세정하다** wash; rinse (a bottle); clean.

세정(世情) the ways of the world; worldly matters; (the condition of) the world; [인정] human nature; humanity. ¶～에 어두운 소년 an unsophisticated boy / a callow youth / a greenhorn // ～에 밝은 사람 a man of the world // ～에 어둡다 know little of the world // 그 소년은 제법 ～에 밝은 것처럼 처신했다 The boy behaved as if he knew much of the world [(구어) had been around]. // 그는 ～에 밝은 사람이다 He is a man of [is wise in the ways of] the world. / He is well versed in worldly matters.

세정(稅政) tax administration.

세제(洗劑) a detergent; (a) cleanser; a cleansing agent; a detersive. ¶합성 [중성] ～ a synthetic [neutral] detergent.

세제(稅制) the taxation system; a system of taxation.

● **세제 개혁** (a) tax reform [revision].

세제곱 [수] cubing; cube. ¶x의 ～ x cubed / x to the third power // ～의 cubic // 그 상자의 부피는 30~센티미터이다 The box is a thirty-centimeter cube. / The box is 30 cubic centimeters in volume. // 2의 ～은 8이다 The cube of 2 is 8. **세제곱하다** cube; multiply (a number) by its square.

● **세제곱근** a cube root. ¶～ 풀이 extraction of the cubic root // 27의 ～은 3이다 The cubic root of 27 is 3. **세제곱미터** a cubic meter [(영) metre] (기호 m³). ¶2～의 상자 a box each side of which is two meters.

세존(世尊) Buddha; Sakyamuni.

세주다(貰－) hire [let] out (carriages and horses by the day); (가옥·토지 등을) let (one's house for the winter); rent (a house to a person); rent out (a mansion); [법] locate; (토지를) lease; let out (land) on lease; grant a lease. ¶방을 ～ take in lodgers [roomers] / (미) rent a room / (영) let a room [lodging] // 여기서 배를 세줍니까 Are there any boats on hire here?

세차(洗車) car washing; car wash. **세차하다** wash a car [an automobile].

● **세차장** a car wash.

세차다 violent; strong; vehement; fierce; furious. ¶세찬 바람 a strong [severe / violent / sharp] wind // 비바람이 창문에 세차게 몰아치고 있다 The wind and rain are blowing hard against the window. // 두 사람은 세차게 맞붙었다 They laid hold of each other with a smack.

세찬(歲饌) [새해 선물] a New Year's gift [present]; a handsel; [세배객에게 대접하는 음식] food for serving New Year's guests.

세척(洗滌) washing; cleansing; cleaning; rinsing; lavation; [의] irrigation; lavage(물을 내쏘아서 하는); toilet(수술 후의). **세척하다** [씻다] wash; [깨끗이 하다] clean; (상처 등을) irrigate. ¶위를 ～ carry out a gastric lavage.

● **세척기** a syringe; a washer; a washing [cleansing] device. **세척제** a washing lotion; a wash; an abstergent; a detergent.

세출(歲出) annual expenditures [(영) expenditure]. ¶～을 세입 이하로 억제하다 keep expenditures in line with revenue.

세칙(細則) detailed rules [regulations]; by-laws. ¶시행 ～ rules for operation / regulations relative to the application of the law // ～은 따로 정한다 Detailed regulations are given separately.

세칭(世稱) what is called [known as]; what people call; so they say; so-called. ¶～ 일류고교 a so-called prestige high school.

세컨드 1 [권투] a second. 2 [첩] one's secondary wife; a (kept) mistress.

세쿼이아 [식] a (giant) redwood; a sequoia.

세탁(洗濯) wash; washing. ⇨ 빨래. ¶～이 잘 되는 옷감 washable cloth // 이 옷감은 ～이 잘 된다 This material is washable. // 이 천은 ～을 해도 줄어들지 않는다 This material is shrink-proof [sanforized].

● **세탁기** a washing machine; a washer. ¶전기 ～ an electric washing machine / an automatic washer. **세탁물** wash; washing; (집합적) laundry. ¶～이 산더미처럼 쌓여 있다 I have mountains [a heap] of washing to do. **세탁비누** laundry [washing] soap. **세탁소** a laundry(▶ 빨래방이나 아파트·호텔·병원 등의 공동 세탁실을 주로 가리킴); the cleaner's; a dry cleaner('s)(▶ 드라이클리닝을 전문으로 하

는 가게를 가리킴).¶드레스를 ~에 보내다 send a dress to the laundry.

세태(世態) [세상의 형편] the prevailing state of society; the order [condition / current] of the world; [사회 정세] social conditions; [생활의 양상] a phase [an aspect] of life. ¶어지러운 ~를 반영한 사건 an event which reflects the disturbed [unsettled] social conditions // 그들의 행동에서 ~의 한 단면을 엿볼 수 있다 We can see one aspect of society [life] in their behavior.

세터 1 [개] a setter. 2 [배구] the person who sets up the ball.

세톱(細─) a fine-tooth saw.

세트 1 [기구 등의 한 벌] a set (of); (가구의) a suite (of). ¶홍차 a tea set // 다섯 개 한 ~ a five-piece set // 응접실 ~ a drawing-room suite. 2 [극·영화의 장치] a set. ¶~에 들어가다 [들어가 있다] go [be] on the set. 3 [경기의] a set. ¶5~의 시합 a five-set match // 테니스를 3~ 하다 play three sets of tennis. 4 [머리털의 손질]. ¶머리를 ~ 해 주시오 I want to have my hair set.

세파(世波) the storm [rough-and-tumble] of life ¶그는 험한 ~에 시달렸다 He was tossed about by the angry waves of life. // 그는 험한 ~와 싸웠다 He struggled with the hardships of life.

세평(世評) [세상의 평판] (a) reputation; public opinion; popular judgment [verdict]; (인기) popularity; (소문) rumo(u)r; hearsay. ¶~에 의하면 according to public opinion / People [They] say that .... / It is said [reported] that .... // ~이 좋다 have [enjoy] a good reputation // ~이 좋지 않다 have a poor reputation // ~에 오르다 be talked about // ~을 무시하다 be indifferent to praise or censure [to public opinion] / do not care about what people say.

세포(細胞) 1 [생] a cell. ¶~의 cellular // 생식 ~ a generative cell // 원생 ~ bioplasm // 다의 multicellular. 2 [활동의 소단위] a cell. ¶공산당의 ~ a communist cell [fraction] // 지하 ~ an underground cell.
●**세포막** [생] the cell [cytoplasmic] membrane. **세포 분열** cell division; meiosis. **세포 조직** cellular tissue. **세포질** [생] cytoplasm.

세필(細筆) 1 [가는 붓] a slender-writing brush; a hair pencil(수채화용). 2 [잔글씨를 씀]. **세필하다** write in a fine hand.

섹스 sex. ¶~의 sexual. **섹스하다** have sex [sexual intercourse] (with); (구어) sleep (with).
●**섹스어필** sex appeal. ¶그녀는 ~하다 She is sexually attractive. / She is sexy? / She has sex appeal.

섹시하다 sexy; sexually attractive [appealing]; having sex appeal; glamorous. ¶섹시한 여자 a sexy [glamour] girl / (속어) a sex pot / a sex bomb.

센말 [언] an intensive [emphatic] variant of a word.

센머리 gray hair; white [hoary] hair.

센물 [경수(硬水)] hard water.

센서 [감지기] a sensor.

센서스 a census.

센세이셔널하다 sensational. ¶그 신문은 센세이셔널한 기사가 전문이다 The paper specializes in sensational [scandalous] news.

센세이션 a sensation. ¶그의 최근의 소설은 ~을 불러일으켰다 His latest novel caused [created] a sensation.

센스 a sense. ¶이건 ~ 있는 선물이군 This is a tasteful present.

센터 1 [야구] center field; [중견수] a center fielder. 2 [종합적 시설]. ¶서비스 ~ a service center // 의료 ~ a medical center // 쇼핑 ~ a shopping center [district].

센터링 [공] centering; [축구] centering. ¶~을 하다 center / (영) centre.

센트 a cent(약어 c.; 기호 ¢). ¶25~ twenty-five cents / a quarter / (미국 속어) two bits.

센티멘털리즘 [감상주의] sentimentalism.

센티멘털하다 sentimental; (속어) gooey; heart-tugging. ¶센티멘털한 이야기 a sticky tale.

센티미터 a centimeter [(영) a centimetre](약어 cm).

셀러리 [식] celery.

셀로판 cellophane.
●**셀로판지**(─紙) cellophane paper.

셀룰로오스 [화] cellulose.

셀룰로이드 celluloid. ¶~ 제품 celluloid ware.

셀프서비스 self-service. ¶~ 레스토랑 a self-service restaurant / a cafeteria // 이 가게는 ~입니다 This store is run on a self-service basis. // 이 사무실에서는 차는 ~입니다 We make our [You have to make your] own tea at this office.

셀프타이머 a self-timer.

셈 1 [계산] count; counting; reckoning; calculation; computation. ¶~에 빠르다 [느리다] be quick [slow] at figures [accounts] // ~이 틀리다 make a mistake in calculation / miscalculate / calculate wrongly // ~에 넣다 take (a thing) into account [consideration] // ~에 넣지 않다 leave (a thing) out of account.
2 [지불] settlement of accounts; payment of bills. ¶~이 남아 있다 one's bill remains unpaid / one's account stands unsettled // ~을 치르다 pay a bill / settle one's accounts / settle [square] accounts (with a person).
3 [분별] discretion; prudence; good sense; judgment.
4 [작정·속셈] an intention; a design; a purpose. ¶…할 ~으로 with the intention [object / aim / idea] of doing / with a view to do // 그럴 ~이다 have a mind to [mean to] do so / have the intention of [think of] doing so // 그는 어쩔 ~일까 What is he going to do? / What does he intend to do?
5 [형편·셈판] the situation; circumstances; the matter; the case; reason; cause. ¶어찌 된 ~이냐 Tell me why. / What's the story? / I think I deserve an explanation. // 혹 떼러 갔다가 혹 붙인 ~이었다 It was an instance of the biter bit.
6 […라고 가정함] suppose; assume; grant (that ...). ¶그것은 잃어버린 ~ 치자 Let us suppose that we lost it. // 죽을 ~ 치고 해 보자 Let us do or die. // 그것을 사실이라 치더라도 역시 네가 틀렸어 Granting that it is so, you are still in the wrong. // 죽을 ~ 치고 한다면 못 할 일이 없다 Nothing is impossible to one who does not fear death.

셈(을) 치다 [계산하다] count; reckon; calculate. ¶셈 쳐 주다 pay [square (up)] the bill / pay the check.

셈나다 know better; grow sensible; acquire good sense; attain one's years of discretion; cut one's wisdom teeth; begin to understand what is going on around one; become possessed of discretion. ¶인제 셈났구나 You are a man[young lady] now.

셈속 [일의 속 내막] the inside details[story]; the real state of things. ¶그 사건의 ~ the inside of the event. 2 [속셈의 실상] hidden intention; an ulterior motive; a personal interest; one's intention[bosom]. ¶뭔가 ~이 있어서 for some hidden object.

셈여림표(-標) [음] dynamic marks; dynamics.

셈판 [까닭] (a) reason; (a) cause; ground; [형편] the situation; circumstances; the matter. ¶어찌 된 ~이오 What's the story? / 무슨 ~인지 모르겠다 I don't know how the matter stands. / I can not make head or tail of it. / 그가 오지 않으니 무슨 ~일까 What's the matter with him that he doesn't come? / 나보다 네가 먼저 알고 있으니 어찌 된 ~이냐 How come I should have known it before me.

셈하다 1 [계산을] count; reckon; calculate; do [work] a sum[sums]. ¶수판으로 ~ reckon on the abacus / 이자를 ~ compute interest. 2 [차를] pay[make out] a bill; settle one's account; settle[square] accounts (with a person).

셋 three; Ⅲ(로마 숫자).

셋돈(貰-) rent. ¶~을 내다 pay one's rent.

셋방(貰房) [미] a room for rent; [영] a room [an apartment] to let; (관광객을 위한) a tourist apartment; [세든 방] a rented room. ¶~에 살다 live in a rented room // ~ 있음 (광고) Rooms for rent[to let [영]]. / Vacancy. // ~ 구함 (광고) Room wanted.
● **셋방살이** a living in a rented room. ¶~를 하다 live in a rented room / live in lodgings.

셋집(貰-) [미] a house for rent; [영] a house to let; a rental [rented] house; (빈민가의) a tenement (house). ¶~ 주인 an owner of rental houses // ~ 있음 (게시) [미] For Rent. / [영] To Let. // 그는 ~에 살고 있다 He lives in a rented house(▶ 이 경우는 [영]에서도 rented를 씀). // ~을 찾고 있다 I'm looking for a house for rent[[영] to let].

셋째 the third.

셋톱 박스 [디지털 TV 수신 장비] a settop box.

셔벗 [미] (a) sherbet; [영] (a) sorbet.

셔츠 [와이셔츠·스포츠 셔츠] a shirt; [내복] [미] an undershirt; [영] a vest. ¶티 ~ a T-shirt / 긴[반] 소매 ~ a long-sleeved[short-sleeved] undershirt[[영] vest].
● **셔츠블라우스** a shirt-blouse.

셔터 1 [문의] a shutter. ¶가게는 이미 ~가 내려져 있었다 The shop had already closed its shutters. // 가게의 겉문은 자동 ~식으로 되어 있다 The shop front is fitted with automatic shutters. 2 [카메라의] a shutter; a shutter (release) button. ¶카메라의 ~를 찰칵 누르다 click[press] the shutter button of a camera.

셔틀콕 [배드민턴의] a shuttlecock; a shuttle; (구어) a birdie.

셧아웃 1 [공장 폐쇄] [미] a shutout. 2 [야구] a shutout.

셰르파 a Sherpa (pl. ~(s)).

셰어 [시장 점유율] a (market) share. ¶~ 20%의 시장을 점유하고 있다 have a 20% market share (in agricultural machines).

셰이커 a (cocktail) shaker.

셰퍼드 an Alsatian (wolf dog[wolf hound]); a German sheep dog; a German shepherd (dog); a German police dog.

소¹ [암소] a cow; [수소] a bull; [노역용의 거세한 수소] an ox (pl. oxen); [새끼 낳기 전의 젊은 암소] a heifer; [송아지] a calf (pl. calves); [집합적] cattle. ¶20마리의 ~ twenty cows / 수입 ~ imported cattle // ~를 기르다 raise cattle // 남을 ~ 말처럼 부려 먹다 use a person like a beast of burden // ~걸음으로 걷다 walk at a snail's[turtle's] pace // 우리 ~는 곧 새끼를 낳을 것이다 Our cow will calve soon.
소 닭 보듯 닭 소 보듯(속담) look absent-mindedly (about); moon (over).
소 잃고 외양간 고친다(속담) That's like locking the barn door after the horse is stolen!; After death, the doctor.
소같이 먹다 eat like a horse.

소² [만두·떡 등의] stuffing; filling; dressing. ¶팥 ~ adzuki bean jam // ~를 넣은 stuffed // 만두에 ~를 넣다 stuff a dumpling.

소(小) a small thing. ¶~를 죽이고 대를 살리다 sacrifice small things to save great ones // 대는 ~를 겸한다 A large thing serves the purpose of a small one as well.

소(沼) a swamp; a marsh; a bog; a pond.

소-(小) small; little; minor; lesser; miniature. ¶~아시아 Asia Minor / ~위원회 a subcommittee // ~극장 a small theater(▶ 독립된 소극장·대극장 안의 소극장은 the little theater 또는 the Little Theater라고 함).

소가족(小家族) a small family.
● **소가족 제도** the small-family system.

소가지 〈속〉 mind; nature. ⇨심성 ¶~가 나쁘다 be ill-natured / be wicked.

소각(燒却) destruction by fire; incineration; cremation. **소각하다** destroy (a thing) by fire; incinerate(먼지·쓰레기 등을); cremate; burn up; commit (a thing) to the flames; throw into fire; reduce to ashes. ¶쓰레기를 ~ burn up the rubbish / make a bonfire of the refuse.
● **소각로 / 소각기** an incinerator; a trash burner.

소갈머리 [지각] discretion; prudence; sense. ¶~ 없는 indiscreet / imprudent / thoughtless / senseless / ill-advised / reckless / rash // ~ 없는 사람 a thoughtless[inconsiderate] person / an insensible man.

소갈증(消渴症) [한] a disease symptomized by thirst.

소감(所感) one's impressions[thoughts]. ¶~을 말하다[묻다] give one's[ask for a person's] impressions (of) // 당신의 계획에 대해서 한마디 ~을 말씀드리고 싶습니다 I'd like to say a few words about your plans.

소강(小康) a (temporary) lull; a (brief) respite; a letup; an easing; a breathing spell (of peace). ¶아버지의 병은 ~상태이다 My father's illness is in a state of remission. / My father's condition is stable [somewhat better]. // 날씨는 당분간 ~상태가 계속될 것 같다 There will be a lull[letup] in the weather for some time. // 양국 간의 관계는 현재 ~상태에 있다 The two countries are on relaxed terms with each other for the present.

소개(紹介) **1** [인사시킴] (an) introduction; presentation. ¶자기 ~ (a) self-introduction∥나는 한 교수의 ~로 홍 선생을 알게 되었다 I got to know Mr. Hong through the kind introduction of Professor Han.∥저 입후보 예정자는 자기~[선전]를 하러 돌아다니고 있다 The candidate-to-be is going around trying to make himself known [advertise himself] to the people. **소개하다** introduce; (정식으로) present. ¶나는 친구를 아저씨에게 소개했다 I introduced my friend to my uncle.∥윤 선생을 소개하겠습니다 May I introduce [present] Mr. Yun to you?
2 [추천·알선] good[kind] offices; a service; recommendation. ¶…의 ~로 through the good offices of … / at the recommendation of …∥방 씨의 ~로 나는 도서관 출입을 허가 받았다 I was admitted to the library through the introduction [(문어) good offices] of Mr. Bang. **소개하다** use [exercise] one's good offices; do (a person) a service; (중개하다) mediate (between); intercede (with A for B). ¶일자리를 ~ get [find] (a person) a job.
3 [어떤 사실이나 내용에 대한 설명]. **소개하다** ¶한국을 호의적으로 소개하는 기사 an article presenting Korea favorably∥나는 2, 3권의 신간 서적을 잡지에 소개하였다 I reviewed a few new books in the magazine. ➔¶그 사건은 신문에 소개되었다 The incident was reported in the papers.
● **소개업** brokerage; commission agency; go-between business. **소개장** a letter of introduction. ¶~을 써 주다 write a letter of introduction

소개(疏開) [산개] dispersal; deployment (군대의); [철거] removal; [퇴거] (an) evacuation. ¶강제 ~ compulsory evacuation. **소개하다** [분산시키다] disperse; [철거하다] remove; [퇴거하다] evacuate (Seoul); move [flee] (to a place) for safety.

소거(消去) **1** [말소] erasure; [제거] elimination. **소거하다** erase; eliminate. **2** [수] elimination. **소거하다** eliminate.
● **소거법** [수] elimination.

소견(所見) one's view(s); one's opinion; one's impression. ¶어떤 것에 대해서 ~을 말하다 give one's view(s) on a matter∥그는 ~이 좁다 He is narrow-minded.∥진료 차트에는 의사의 진단 ~이 기입되어 있었다 The doctor's observations and diagnosis were entered on the medical chart.

소경 1 [맹인] a blind [sightless] person; (집합적) the blind. ¶~의 blind∥~이 되다 go [become] blind / lose one's sight. **2** [문맹자] an ignoramus; an unlettered person; an illiterate (person). ¶남을 ~으로 아는군 He apparently thinks I know nothing at all.∥그것을 모르다니 너는 눈 뜬 ~이로구나 You are a blind fool not to recognize it.
소경 매질하듯(속담) at random; recklessly.
소경 잠자나 마나(속담) That's quite a vain [useless] effort.

소계(小計) a subtotal. ¶10일분 식비의 ~를 내다 add up [subtotal] the food expenses for the ten days∥2만 5천 원이 되다 The subtotal is [comes to] 25,000 won.

소고(小鼓) a *sogo*; a tabor; a small drum.

소곡(小曲) a short piece (of music).

소곤거리다 talk in a whisper [subdued tone]; whisper; murmur; speak under one's breath. ¶소곤거리는 소리 a whispering [suppressed] voice / a whisper∥소곤거리며 in a whisper / in whispers / in a subdued tone∥서로 ~ exchange whispers / whisper to each other.

소곤소곤 in a suppressed [low] voice; in an undertone; in whispers; secretly; softly. ¶그들은 강의 중에 ~ 이야기를 했다 They talked in whispers during the lecture.∥그는 ~ 말을 하기 시작했다 He began to talk in a subdued voice.

소관(所管) jurisdiction; competency; control. ¶…의 ~이다 be under the jurisdiction (of) / fall within the jurisdiction (of)∥~ 밖이다 be beyond the jurisdiction (of).
● **소관 관청** the competent [proper] authorities; the authorities concerned.

소관(所關) what is concerned; matters concerned. ¶그녀는 아들이 일찍 죽은 것도 팔자 ~이라고 생각했다 She believed that Fortune had predetermined her son's early death.
● **소관사** one's business; one's concern; one's affairs. ¶그것은 네 ~가 아니다 It is no affair [concern] of yours.

소괄호(小括弧) [인] parentheses; round brackets

소국(小國) a small country [nation]; [약소국] a minor power.

소굴(巢窟) a den; a haunt; a nest; a lair; (범죄의) a breeding place; a hotbed; (미국 속어) a hangout. ¶악의 ~ a den [nest] of vice∥도둑의 ~ a den of robbers [thieves] / a robber's hideout∥거지의 ~ a haunt for beggars∥범죄의 ~ a hotbed of crime.

소권(訴權) [법] the right to bring an action in a court (against a person for a matter).

소규모(小規模) a small scale. ¶~ 가족 a peanut-size family∥~의 small-scale / on a small scale∥~로 on a small scale / in a small way∥그는 ~로 사업을 시작했다 He started doing business in a small way [on a small scale].

소극(消極) the negative pole; the negative; the cathode; (작용) depolarization.
● **소극성** passivity; passiveness.

소극(笑劇) a farce.

소극장(小劇場) a little theater.

소극적(消極的) negative; passive; half-hearted(▶ negative는 부정적, passive는 수동적, half-hearted는 마음이 내키지 않음을 뜻함); conservative. ¶성질이 ~인 사람 (삼가는) a man of retiring disposition∥~ 정책 a negative policy∥그녀의 태도는 매우 ~이었다 Her attitude was very passive [half-hearted].∥그렇게 ~으로 나간다면 아무것도 못 팔 것이다 If you continue to be so unenterprising, you'll never sell anything!

소금 salt. ¶식탁용 ~ table salt∥~으로 음식의 간을 맞추다 season food with salt / salt food∥~에 절이다 preserve in salt / (채소를) pickle with [in] salt∥~을 뿌리다 sprinkle [shake] salt (on)∥~을 쳐서[찍어] 먹다 eat with salt.
● **소금기** a salty [briny] taste; saltiness. ¶~ 있는 물 brackish water∥~가 좀 모자란다 This wants a touch of salt. **소금물** salt water; brine(▶ 절임 등을 할 때 쓰임). ¶~에 담그다 soak [steep] in brine∥~로 양치질하다 rinse (out) one's mouth with salt water.

소금쟁이 [동] a pond skater; a water strider

소급 [skipper].

소급(遡及) retroaction; retroactivity. **소급하다** be retroactive (to); retroact (to); go back (to the past); retrospect (to). ¶소급하여 retroactively / retrospectively // 소급하여 지불되는 급료 retroactive[back] pay // 이 규칙은 4월에 소급하여 적용된다 This rule applies retroactively from April. / This rule is retroactive to April. // 그들은 6개월 전으로 소급한 봉급 인상을 따냈다 They won a retroactive wage increase of six months.
● **소급법** a retroactive law[statute].

소기(所期) one's expectation; anticipation. ¶~의 expected / anticipated / desired / hoped-for // ~와 같이 as one expected [hoped for] / as was expected / as might have been expected // ~의 성과를 얻다[거두다] achieve the expected results // 우리는 ~의 목적을 달성하지 못했다 The results fell short of our expectations. / We were unable to obtain the desired[expected] results.

소꿉 toy flatware[kitchenware]; toy goods used in playing house.
● **소꿉놀이** / **소꿉장난** playing house. ⇨소꿉질(⇨소꿉) **소꿉동무** a childhood friend; a friend [playmate] of one's childhood; a friend from one's childhood. ¶우리 두 사람은 ~였다 We have known each other since we were boys[children]. **소꿉질** playing house; playing at housekeeping. ¶~을 하다 play (at) house / play at housekeeping[keeping house] / play ladies.

소나기 a (sudden) shower; a passing rain; a squall(남양의). ¶~가 지나가기를 기다리다 wait for the shower to pass[stop] // 나는 ~를 만났다 I was caught in a sudden shower. // ~가 올 것 같다 It looks like rain [There's going to be a shower]. // ~가 그쳤다 The shower has passed[is over]. // ~가 쏟아지기 시작했다 It began to rain suddenly.
● **소나기구름** a shower cloud; a thundercloud.

소나무 [식] a pine (tree).
소나타 [음] a sonata. ¶베토벤의 ~ a sonata by Beethoven / a Beethoven sonata.
● **소나타 형식** sonata form.
소네트 a sonnet.

소녀(少女) a young[little] girl; a maiden. ¶10대 ~ a teenage(d) girl / a girl in her teens // 다운 girlish / maidenly / maidenlike.
● **소녀 시절** (young) girlhood. ¶~에 as a girl / in one's girlhood (days).

소년(少年) a boy; a lad; a youth. ¶불량~ a bad [delinquent] boy // 비행 ~ a juvenile delinquent.
● **소년단** the Boy Scouts. **소년 범죄** juvenile delinquency. **소년 소녀** (young) boys and girls; (집합적) young people. **소년 시절** one's boyhood. ¶~에 in one's boyhood [childhood] / when[as] a boy // ~부터의 친구 a childhood friend. **소년원** (미) a reformatory; a reform school; (영) a community home(▶ 16세 이하); a borstal(▶ 16~21세의).

소농(小農) a small[petty] farmer; a peasant; (집합적) peasantry.
소뇌(小腦) [생] the cerebellum (pl. -bella). ¶~의 cerebellar.
소다 soda. ¶세탁 ~ washing soda.
● **소다수** (탄산수) soda water; (미) club soda; (감미료·향료 등을 가한) a soft drink (▶ 간혹 탄산을 함유시키지 않는 경우도 있음); (구어) (soda) pop.

소달구지 an oxcart; an ox-wagon.
소담(笑談) a funny[humorous] story. **소담하다** tell a funny story.
소담스럽다 delicious-looking; juicy-[tasty-] looking; (서술적) look nice and ripe.
소담하다 pleasantly plump; buxom; big and beautiful; full; juicy; tasty; nice and ripe. ¶소담한 복숭아 a fat juicy peach // 소담한 꽃송이 a full-petaled flower // 상에는 좋은 음식이 소담하게 차려져 있었다 The table was well covered with good things.

소대(小隊) (보병·공병 등의) a platoon.
● **소대장** a platoon leader [commander].
소뚜껑 the lid [cover] of a kettle [key]; a pot lid.
● **소댕꼭지** the handle of a kettle cover.
소도(小島) an islet; a small island; a cay.
소도구(小道具) [연극] stage property; (구어) props.
소도둑놈 1 [소도둑] a cattle thief; a cattle rustler. 2 [능글맞은 욕심쟁이] an avaricious [a grasping] man; a grabber; a greedy and bad-tempered person.
소도리 a small hammer.
소도시(小都市) a small [smaller] town.

소독(消毒) disinfection; (끓이기 등에 의한) sterilization; (우유 등의) pasteurization; (훈증) fumigation; (정화) decontamination. ¶일광 ~ disinfection by sunlight // 유황[증기] ~ sulfur [steam] disinfection // 열탕 ~을 하다 scald (an instrument) // ~이 잘되어 있다 be properly disinfected. **소독하다** kill the germs; disinfect; sterilize; pasteurize; fumigate; decontaminate. ¶소독한 disinfected / sterilized / 상처를 알코올로 ~ disinfect a wound with alcohol // 증기로 ~ sterilize by steam // 끓는 물로 ~ sterilize in boiling water // 일광으로 ~ disinfect by the sun's rays.
● **소독기** a sterilizer; a disinfector. **소독약** a disinfectant; an antiseptic. **소독저** sanitary [sterilized] chopsticks.

소동(騷動) [법석] (a) disturbance; (an) uproar; an upheaval; (옥신각신) a strife; a dispute; a trouble; (싸움) a quarrel; a brawl; (혼란) confusion; disorder; a row; a tumult; (동란) a commotion; (폭동) a riot; an uprising; (사건) an affair. ¶이혼 ~ the fuss about a divorce // 공연히 (을 일으키다) (raise) a great fuss about nothing // ~을 일으키다 cause a disturbance[commotion] / make a fuss // ~을 가라앉히다 suppress [put down] a disturbance // 그 소식은 집안에 큰 ~을 일으켰다 The news caused great excitement in the family. // 회장에는 큰 ~이 벌어졌다 The hall was thrown into a tremendous roar.

소동맥(小動脈) [생] an arteriole; a small arterial branch. ¶~의 arteriolar.
소두(小斗) a smaller [half] *mal* measure.
소득(所得) [수입] income; [수익] earnings; profits. ¶개인 [법인] ~ individual [corporate] income // 국민 ~ national income // 근로[불로] ~ earned [unearned] income // 명목 ~ nominal income // 순[총] ~ net [gross] income // 실질 ~ real income // 연간 ~ annual income / yearly income // 현물 ~ income in kind // 가정의 ~ a family's income

~ 범위 내에서 생활하다 live within one's income∥그는 ~이 아주 많다 He has an enormous [a very large] income.∥그 사람은 부동산업으로 상당한 ~을 얻고 있다 The man draws a considerable income from the real estate business.
●소득 공제 deductions from income. 소득세 an income tax. ¶개인 ~ the individual income tax∥종합 ~ the consolidated [composite] income tax. 소득 수준 an income level. 소득액 (the amount of) one's income. ¶~을 신고하다 make[file] income tax returns.

소등(消燈) blackout. ¶~을 명하다 order lights out∥~나팔을 불다 sound taps / sound "lights out". 소등하다 put out[turn off] lights.
●소등 시간 lights-out; the time for putting out lights. ¶~은 12시다 All lights have to be put out at twelve.

소라 [동] a turban[wreath] shell; a top shell; a turbo (*pl.* turbines, ~s).
●소라딱지 the shell of a turbo.

소라게 [동] a hermit crab; a pagurian.

소란(騷亂) [소동] a disturbance; a commotion; a riot; fuss; ado; bustle; stir; [시끄럼] (a) noise; (an) uproar; a hubbub; a clamor; a din; a tumult; (구어) a row. ¶~을 일으키다 make a row / kick up a shindy[racket] / [어떤 일이] create a commotion / cause a stir∥주민들이 철거를 반대하여 ~을 피우고 있다 The inhabitants are clamoring against eviction.∥이 ~은 어찌 된 일이냐 What's all this noise?∥~ 피우지 마라 (미) Don't make a scene. 소란하다 disturbing; noisy; boisterous; uproarious; clamorous; vociferous; tumultuous (crowd). ¶소란한 교실 a noisy classroom∥이웃을 소란하게 하다 disturb (the peace of) the neighborhood.

소량(少量) a small quantity[amount / portion / dose]; a little; a modicum; a touch; a dash; a hint; a suspicion; a morsel (of). ¶~의 위스키 a little whisky∥~ 거래 transactions in small lots∥~ 주문 a petty order∥~의 모르핀 a small dose of morphine.

소련(蘇聯) the Soviet Union; Soviet Russia; (공식명) the Union of Soviet Socialist Republics(약어 U.S.S.R.); Russia.(▶ 1991년 붕괴되어 11개국으로 이뤄진 독립 국가 연합이 결성됨)

소령(少領) (육군) a major; (해군) a lieutenant commander; (공군) (미) a major; (영) a squadron leader.

소로(小路) a (narrow) path; a lane; an alley.

소론(小論) an article; a small article.

소르르 1 [풀어지는 모양] smoothly; easily; readily. ¶(허리띠가) ~ 풀리다 slip off. 2 [바람이 부는 모양] softly; gently. ¶바람이 ~ 분다 There is a gentle breeze. / The wind blows gently. 3 [눈이 오는 모양] drowsily. ¶잠이 ~ 오다 sleep steals upon one∥~ 조는 사이에 잠이 들어 버렸다 Doziness[A drowsy feeling] coming over me, I soon fell asleep.

소름 gooseflesh; goose pimples[bumps]; horripilation. ¶~이 끼치다 get (the) gooseflesh / be gooseflesh[goose pimples] all over / feel a chill creep over one / feel a shudder∥~ 끼치는 이야기 a bloodcurdling [hair-raising] story∥~이 끼치는 bloodcurdling / hair-raising / horrifying∥그것은 듣기만 해도 ~이 끼친다 I shudder at the mere mention of it.∥그의 유령 이야기를 듣고 우리 모두는 ~이 끼쳤다 His ghost story sent a chill through us all[made our blood run cold].∥그 광경은 우리를 ~ 끼치게 했다 The sight (of it) struck us with horror. / We were horrified by the sight.∥너무 무서워서 ~이 끼쳤다 I was so scared I had goose bumps. / Fear gave me gooseflesh.

소리 1 [음향] (a) sound; [소음] a noise; a report(총포 등의); a din(왁자지껄하는); a roar(꽝). ¶방울 ~ the sound of a bell∥큰[작은] ~ a loud[low] sound∥폭포의 ~ the sound of a waterfall∥시끄러운[요란한] ~ a loud[an alarming] noise∥시계 ~ the ticking of a clock∥천둥~ a roll[peal] of thunder∥울부짖는 바람 ~ the roar of the wind∥나뭇가지를 스치는 ~ the whispering of the wind in the trees∥유리잔이 닿는 ~ the clink of glasses∥파도가 부딪치는 ~ the splash of waves (against the shore) / (멀리서의) the booming of the breakers∥~의 높이[높낮이] pitch∥~의 강도[강약] loudness∥~도 없이 noiselessly / quietly∥~를 내다 make a sound∥그때 엔진이 이상한 ~를 냈다 Just then, the engine made a strange [peculiar] noise.∥텔레비전의 ~를 작게[크게] 해 주세요 Please turn the T.V. down [up].∥라디오 ~가 좋지 않다 We're not getting good reception on the radio. / The radio has bad sound quality. / The reception is bad on this radio.∥이 바이올린은 ~가 좋다 This violin produces a good tone.∥지붕에서 이상한 ~가 난다[들린다] I hear a strange noise on the roof.∥귀에 거슬리는 ~다 The sound grates upon my ears.

2 [목소리] a voice; a tone (of voice); [외침 소리] a cry; an outcry; (새·벌레의) notes; call; chirp; a song. ¶벌레가 우는 ~ the chirping of insects∥큰[작은] ~가 / 낭랑한 / 목쉰 / 맑은 ~ a loud[deep / thin / sonorous / husky / clear] voice∥(꺼질 듯한) 작은 ~ (in) a feeble[thin] voice∥고함 ~ a cry∥큰 ~로 읽다[웃다 / 울다] read[laugh / weep] aloud∥종달새의 명랑하게 지저귀는 ~ the merry note of a lark∥~를 지르다 yell / shout / cry (in a loud voice) / speak loudly / raise[lift (up) / put forth] one's voice∥화가 나서 ~를 지르다 roar with anger∥그렇게 ~ 지르지 마라 Don't yell[shout] like that.∥정부의 물가 통제에 대해서 반대의 ~를 높이다 raise a cry of protest against state control of prices∥나는 무서워서 ~도 내지 못했다 I was so frightened that my voice failed me.∥~를 지르면 죽이겠다 Don't say a word, or you're a dead man.

3 [판소리 등 노래] a folk song; a ballad. ¶~를 잘하다 sing (a tune) well. 소리하다 sing a folk song.

4 [말] a talk; a word; a statement; a remark. ¶이상한 ~ 같지만 it may sound strange, but ...∥듣기 좋은 ~를 하다 say a pleasant thing∥그게 무슨 ~냐 What do you mean?

5 [항간의 소문] a rumor; a report; news; an account. ¶그 ~는 금방 퍼졌다 The rumor spread fast.

소리 소문도 없이 without telling a soul. ¶그는 ~ 마을을 떠났다 He left the village without telling a soul.

●**소리굽쇠** [물] a tuning fork. **소리글자** a phonogram. ⇨표음 문자(㊀표음)
소리〈小利〉 a small profit; little gain. ¶목전의 ~에 눈이 어두워지다 be blinded by a small immediate profit.
소리소리 in[with] a loud voice; yelling; hollering. ¶~ 지르다 yell / roar.
소리치다 cry; yell; shout; holler; bawl; give [utter] a cry. ¶"도둑이야!" 하고 ~ cry "Thief!" // 불나라 하고 ~ give a fire alarm / 사람 살리라고 ~ cry[scream] for help / 귀미거리가 아니니 소리칠 것 없다 I'm not deaf, you needn't shout. // 누군가가 "브라보" 하고 소리쳤다 Somebody called "Bravo!".
소립자〈素粒子〉 [물] an elementary particle.
●**소립자론** the theory of elementary particles.
소망〈所望〉 (a) desire; a wish; a hope; a request; an expectation. ¶~에 따라 at[in compliance with] (a person's) request / by request from (a person) // ~이라면 if one wishes[desires] // 간절한 ~ an ardent desire / an earnest wish // 오랜 ~ a long-cherished desire // ~을 이루다 realize one's desire[wishes] / attain one's object / have one's wishes fulfilled // 남의 ~을 이루어 주다 grant a person's wish // 의사가 되고 싶다는 것이 그의 ~이었다 It was his earnest [dearest] wish to become a doctor. // 그녀는 부자와 결혼하고 싶다는 ~을 갖고[품고] 있다 She wanted[(문어) cherished a desire] to marry a rich man. // 그들의 ~에 따라 그는 또 한 곡 연주했다 At their request he played one more piece. // 모든 일이 그의 ~대로 되었다 Everything turned out as he wished [desired]. // 너의 ~은 이루어질 것이다 You will have your wish. / Your desire will be satisfied[realized]. **소망하다** desire; wish for; hope (for).
소매 a sleeve; (양복의) an arm. ¶~가 없는 블라우스 sleeveless blouse // 소매가 긴[짧은] 셔츠 a long-sleeved[short-sleeved] shirt // 래글런 ~ raglan sleeves // 긴~ long sleeves / 반~ short sleeves // ~를 잡아 남을 붙들다 hold a person by the sleeve // 남의 ~를 끌다 [잡아당기다] pull a person by the sleeve / pull at a person's sleeve // ~를 걷어 올리다 roll[turn] up one's sleeve // ~을 달다 attach a sleeve (to the body of a shirt) // ~를 끌다 [잡아당겨] pull[tag] (at / on) a person's sleeve / (주의를 주다) give a person's sleeve a warning tug.
●**소매통** the width of a sleeve. ¶~이 좁다 A sleeve is rather tight. **소맷부리** (옷의) the edge[lower part] of a sleeve; (서츠의) a cuff; a wristband.
소매〈小賣〉 retail(ing); retail sale. ¶~로 at retail (price) // 이 물건은 ~로 6,000원이다 This article retails for six thousand won. // ~로는 도맷값의 거의 배가 된다 The retail price is nearly double[twice] the wholesale price. // 우리는 도매상이므로 ~를 하지 않습니다 We're wholesalers, so we don't sell retail. // 그는 도매로 가져와서 ~로 판다 He buys wholesale and sells at retail. **소매하다** retail; sell (at) retail; (영) sell by retail.
●**소매가격** a retail price. **소매상** retail trade. **소매 시장** a retail market. **소매점** a retail store[shop].
소매치기 (사람) a pickpocket; a cutpurse; (미

국 속어) a dip(per); (행위) pocketpicking; (미국 속어) dipping. ¶~를 당하다 have one's pocket picked // 주의 (게시) Beware of [Look out for] pickpockets. // 현금을 찾아가는 때는 ~, 날치기를 조심해라 When you draw cash, beware of pickpockets and muggers. **소매치기하다** pick (a person's) pocket (of a purse); (미국 속어) dip (a watch from another's pocket); commit pocket-picking.
소맥〈小麥〉 wheat; (영) corn.
●**소맥분** (wheat) flour.
소멸〈消滅〉 [전멸] extinction; extinguishment; [소실] disappearance; [실효] nullification; termination. ¶권리의 ~ the lapse of a right / 죄의 ~ expiation of one's sins // 자연 ~ natural extinction[death] // 계약의 ~ the discharge of contract. **소멸하다** [전멸하다] become extinct; cease to exist; disappear; vanish; lapse; become null[void]; be nullified; be extinguished; terminate; be expiated(죄가). ¶그 종족은 자연 소멸하였다 That species has died out.
●**소멸 시효** extinctive[negative] prescription.
소멸〈燒滅〉 [불타서 없어지는 것] destruction by fire. **소멸하다** destroy by fire; reduce [be reduced] to ashes.
소멸〈掃滅〉 [싹 쓸어서 없애는 것] a (clean) sweep; extermination. **소멸하다** sweep away [off]; drive off; clear away[off]; make a clean sweep of; [근절] make an end of; stamp[root] out; exterminate; eradicate.
소명〈召命〉 [임금이 신하를 부르는 명령] a royal summons. ¶~을 내리다 call / summon / ~을 받들어 in response to a royal summons.
소모〈消耗〉 consumption; [완전히 써 버림] exhaustion; dissipation; waste; wear and tear; (체력의) emaciation. **소모하다** consume; exhaust; dissipate; waste; use up. ¶정력을 ~ dissipate[waste] one's energy / 전력[연료]을 ~ consume electric power[fuel] // 나는 그 일로 체력을 소모했다 I was worn out by the work. / The work wore me out. → ¶우리의 자원은 완전히 소모되었다 Our resources have been exhausted[used up].
●**소모비** wear and tear expenses. **소모열** hectic fever. **소모율** the attrition rate. **소모전** a war of attrition. **소모품** articles of consumption; expendable supplies; (특히 군수품 등) expendables. ¶사무용 ~ office supplies.
소모사〈梳毛絲〉 worsted; combed yarn.
소목장이〈小木-〉 a joiner; a cabinetmaker.
소몰이 [소를 모는 일] cattle droving; [소를 모는 사람] a cattle drover.
소묘〈素描〉 a (rough) sketch; a dessin.
소문〈所聞〉 a rumor; a report; hearsay; gossip; common talk; (미국 속어) scuttlebutt. ¶~에 의하면 according to the rumor // 근거 없는 ~ a groundless rumor / an unfounded report / 헛~ an idle rumor // ~을 퍼뜨리는 사람 a gossipmonger // **~으로 듣다** hear of / know by hearsay // 그 ~은 온 고을 전체에 퍼졌다 The rumor has spread all over town. // 아버지에 대한 불쾌한 ~을 들었다 I heard unpleasant stories about my father. // ~에 의하면 그는 이번에 입후보할 것 같다 Rumor has it[It is said] that he will run in the next election. // 그가 살아 있다는 ~이 나돌고 있다 There's a rumor[It is rumored]

that he is alive.// 누가 그런 ~을 퍼뜨렸느냐 Who started such rumor?// 그녀는 ~에 듣던 대로 미인이었다 She was the beauty we had heard so much of.// 세상 ~은 며칠 안 간다 It will be a nine days' wonder.// 그가 여배우 와 결혼한다는 ~이 있다 Rumor has it [It is rumored] that he is going to marry an actress.

소문나다(所聞-) be talked [gossiped] about; become the talk (of); be in everybody's mouth; be in the air. ¶소문난 악당 a notorious villain [scoundrel] / an infamous scoundrel// 소문난 거짓말쟁이 a notorious liar// 그는 거짓말 잘하기로 소문나 있다 He is notorious for lying. / He is a notorious liar. // 그의 요리 솜씨는 소문나 있다 He is universally acknowledged to be a good cook.

소문난 잔치에 먹을 것 없다(속담) Much noise and no substance.; Great cry and little wool.

소문내다(所聞-) spread [start / circulate / give currency to] a rumor; set a rumor a float.

소문자(小文字) a small letter; minuscule; a lowercase letter. ¶~로 쓰다 write in tiny lettering [small handwriting].

소박(疏薄) maltreatment; ill treatment; mistreatment; abuse; desertion (of one's wife).
소박하다 maltreat [ill-treat] 《one's wife》; desert; abandon. ¶아내를 ~ abuse [desert] one's wife.
●**소박데기** a mistreated [an abused] wife; a deserted [an abandoned] wife.

소박맞다(疏薄-) be mistreated [abused]; get deserted.

소박이(오이의) stuffed cucumber *gimchi* (kimchi); [소를 넣은 음식] stuffed food.

소박하다(素朴-) simple (and honest); unsophisticated; ingenuous; artless; naive. ¶소박한 생각 an unsophisticated [a naive] idea// 그녀의 소박함이 매력적이다 Her naiveté [simplicity] is appealing.// 나는 그의 소박한 말투가 좋다 I like his unsophisticated way of talking.// 그의 생각은 지나치게 ~ His ideas are too naive.

소반(小盤) [상] a small dining table; [쟁반] a tray.

소방(消防) fire fighting; fire service; the prevention and extinction of fires. **소방하다** put out and prevent fires; fight a fire; arrest the spread of a fire; get a fire under control; extinguish a fire.
●**소방관** a fire fighter; a fire officer; a fireman. **소방 기구** fire-fighting equipments [apparatus]. **소방대** a fire brigade; a fire company; a fire-fighting team [unit] (공장이나 군대의). **소방서**(消-brigade) station; a fire department; (미) a firehouse. **소방차** a fire engine [truck].

소변(小便) water; pee. ⇨⁼오줌 ¶~의 uric; urinary// ~을 누다 [보다] urinate / pass [discharge / void] urine / make [pass] water / answer a call of nature / (비어) pass / (구어) (소아어) pee// 검사를 하기 위해 환자의 ~을 받다 take a patient's urine for examination// 한데서 [길가에서] ~을 보다 urinate outdoors [by the roadside]// ~을 참 다 contain one's urine / retain one's water / ~을 싸다 be incontinent / lose control of one's bodily functions// ~이 마렵다 Nature calls (me).
●**소변 검사** urine examination. **소변 금지** (게시) Decency forbids.; No nuisance here.; (영) Commit no nuisance.; No Urinating.

소복(素服) [흰옷] white clothes; [상복] (white) mourning clothes [garments]. **소복하다** wear white clothes.

소복하다 heaped up; swollen. ⇨⁼수북하다

소비(消費) [소모] consumption; [지출] expenditure; spending. ¶~자가 ~ self-consumption// 일인당 쌀의 ~량 the per capita consumption of rice// 나는 지난달의 전기 ~량이 많은 데 놀랐다 (개인의) I was surprised at how much electricity we used last month. / (국가나 지방의) We were surprised by the high consumption of electricity last month. **소비하다** consume; use (up); (시간·정력 등을) expend. ¶시간을 ~ spend [waste] time / (구어) put in time / 돈을 ~ spend money / 쌀을 ~ consume rice // 시시한 일에 시간 [정력]을 소비하지 마라 Don't spend your time [energy] on trifling matters.
●**소비 경제** consumer economy. **소비 도시** a consuming [consumer] city. **소비 성향** the propensity to consume. **소비세** a consumption tax [duty]. **소비액** the amount of consumption. **소비자** a consumer. ¶~ 가격 a consumer [consumers'] price (of rice)// ~ 단체 a consumer organization// ~ 물가 지수 the consumer [consumers'] price index (약어 CPI, c.p.i.). **소비재** consumption goods; consumer [consumers'] goods [items]. ¶내구 ~ consumer durables / durable consumer goods. **소비조합** a consumers' cooperative (society); (구어) a co-op.

소사(小使) an errand boy; a servant; a janitor; a messenger; an office boy; a caretaker.

소사(小辭) [논] a minor term.

소사(掃射) machine-gunning; strafe; volley (of small arms). **소사하다** machine-gun (a house); sweep (the enemy's position) with fire; mow (the enemy); (비행기에서) strafe.

소사(燒死) death by fire. **소사하다** burn [be burned] to death; perish in a fire [in flames]. ¶그 화재로 세 사람이 소사했다 Three people died [lost their lives] in the fire.

소산(所産) a product; fruit(s); an outcome; an outgrowth; a result. ¶노력의 ~ the fruit of one's efforts// 노동의 ~ the products of labor// 이 그림은 그의 상상력의 ~이다 This picture is the product of his imagination.
●**소산물** products; produce (농산물).

소상(小祥) the first anniversary of the death of a person.

소상(塑像) a plastic image; a clay figure [image / statue].

소상인(小商人) a small trader [tradesman / businessman]; a small-scale merchant; a retail dealer [merchant]; a retailer.

소상하다(昭詳-) full; detailed; minute; circumstantial. ¶소상한 보고 a minute report // 소상히 보고를 하다 give a detailed report. **소상히** minutely; circumstantially; in detail; at length. ¶사건을 ~ 조사하다 investigate the case closely [in detail]// 언쟁의 이유를 ~ 밝히다 make clear the reasons for a dispute / clarify the causes of a dispute.

소생(小生) I; me; myself.

소생(所生) one's children [offspring]; progeny. ¶첩의 ~ a child by a concubine / an issue of half-blood // ─이 없다 be childless / be without issue.

소생(蘇生) revival; resuscitation; reanimation. **소생하다** come back to life again; be brought back to life; revive; resuscitate (from death); be resuscitated; be restored [recalled / brought back] to life; rise from the dead; come to (oneself [one's senses]); recover [regain] consciousness. ¶그는 죽어가고 있었으나 인공호흡으로 소생했다 He was nearly dead but they resuscitated [revived] him with artificial respiration. **소생시키다** bring (a person) back to life / restore (a person) to consciousness / (가사 상태에서) resuscitate / revive / reanimate / (문어) resurrect.

-소서 please do; I beg you to do ...; pray. ¶만수무강하~ Long may you live! / Long live the king! (왕에게) ~ 용서하~ I beg you to forgive me. // 주여 우리를 불쌍히 여기~ May God have mercy on us!

소서(小暑) *soseo*; one of the 24 seasonal divisions (c. 7 July).

소석고(燒石膏) plaster of Paris; burnt [oxidized] plaster.

소석회(消石灰) calcium hydroxide. ⇨ "수산화칼슘(⇨수산화)

소선거구(小選擧區) a small electoral district; (1구 1인의) a single-member constituency.
● **소선거구제** the single-member electorate [constituency] system.

소설(小說) a novel; a (fictional) story; a romance; a tale; (집합적) fiction. ¶교양 ~ an educational novel // 단편 ~ a short story / a novelette / a storiette // 모험 ~ a story of adventures / an adventurous story // 문제 ~ a problem novel // 반~ (프) anti-roman // 사실 ~ a realistic novel // 신문 ~ a newspaper novel // 심리 ~ a psychological novel // 역사 ~ a historical novel // 연애 ~ a love story // 장편 ~ a (full-length) novel // 추리 ~ a detective story / a mystery story / (구어) a whodunit // 통속 ~ a light [lowbrow] novel / popular literature // 대하~ a saga / a roman-fleuve // 과학 ~ science fiction (약어 S.F.) // ~ 같은 이야기 a romantic [fictionlike] story // 사건을 ~화하다 turn an affair [incident] into a novel // ~을 쓰다 write a novel // 그는 신문에 ~을 연재하고 있다 He is writing a novel which is appearing serially in a newspaper.
● **소설가** a novelist; a fiction [story] writer; a fictionist. **소설책** a story book; a novel; a book of fiction.

소설(小雪) (24절기의 하나) *soseol*; one of the 24 seasonal divisions (c. 22 Nov.).

소성(塑性) [물] plasticity. ¶~이 있다 be plastic.

소소하다(小小─) trivial; trifling; insignificant; small.

소속(所屬) one's position [post / place]. ¶회사 ~의 실험실 a laboratory belonging to a company / a laboratory under the control of a company // 민주당 ~ 의원 a Democratic Congressman // ~ 미정의 unassigned / unattached. **소속하다** belong (to); be attached (to); affiliate oneself (with); be under the command [control] (of). ¶나는 회사의 출판부에 소속하고 있다 I'm with the publishing arm of the company. ➔ **소속시키다** attach / assign / put under the command [control] of.
● **소속 부대** one's unit.

소송(訴訟) a lawsuit; a suit; an action (at law); litigation; legal proceedings [steps]; (고소) a complaint. ¶민사 [형사] ~ a civil [criminal] suit // 손해 배상 ~ the action for damages // 이혼 ~ a suit [an action] for divorce / 행정 ~ administrative litigation // 나는 ~을 취하했다 I dropped the suit. // 나는 그에게 이혼 ~을 제기했다 I filed [brought] (a) suit against him for divorce. // 우리는 ~에 이겼다 [졌다] We won [lost] the suit. // 우리는 ~의 변호를 그에게 의뢰했다 We asked him to defend us in the suit. // 그녀는 그 주간지에 대해 명예 훼손죄로 ~을 제기했다 She brought [filed] a lawsuit [an action] against the weekly magazine for libel. / She sued the weekly magazine for libel. // 법원은 피해자의 ~에 따라 그 사건의 조사를 명했다 The court ordered the incident to be investigated when the injured party lodged a complaint. **소송하다** sue (a person for damages); bring an action [a suit] (against a person for a matter); go to suit; go to law (with [against] a person over a matter); take [institute] legal proceedings (against). ¶그 사건을 소송하지 않고 해결하는 길은 없을까 Is there no way to settle the matter out of court? // 우리는 소송해서라도 싸울 작정이다 We're ready to fight, even if we have to take it to court.
● **소송 대리인** a counsel; an attorney. **소송법** the code of legal procedure. ¶민사 [형사] ~ the code of civil [criminal] procedure. **소송 비용** the costs of a lawsuit. **소송 사건** a suit; a (legal) case; a court case; a case in litigation; a law case; a lawsuit. ¶(변호사가) ~을 맡다 take a brief. **소송 의뢰인** a client; (집합적) clientele. **소송 절차** legal proceedings [procedure].

소수(小數) [수] a decimal (fraction). ¶유한 [무한] ~ a finite [an infinite] decimal / a terminate [an interminate] decimal // 대(帶)~ a mixed decimal.
● **소수점** [수] a decimal point. ¶~ 이하를 잘라 버리다 omit decimals // ~ 이하를 반올림하다 raise decimals to the next whole number // ~ 이하 다섯째 자리까지 계산하다 calculate to the fifth decimal place.

소수(少數) a small number; a minority. ¶~로 in small numbers // ~의 사람소 a small number of people / a few persons / a handful of persons // ~의 회원 a few members // ~ [선택된] ~의 사람들 the gifted [chosen] few // 회원은 ~이다 The membership is small. // 그 나라는 ~의 군인이 장악하고 있었다 The country was under the control of a handful of military men.
● **소수당** the minority; a minor (political) party. **소수 민족** a minority race; a minority. **소수 의견** the opinion of the minority; a minority opinion. **소수정예주의** elitism; the principle of the able minority. **소수파** a minority group [faction]; the minority.

소수(素數) [수] a prime (number).

소스 1 [일종의 서양 조미료] sauce; Worcester(shire) sauce(▶ 우리가 흔히 말하는 소스

에 가장 가까운 것). ¶**화이트** ~ white sauce // ~**를 치다** put sauce (on) / pour sauce (over) / sauce (meat). **2** 〔출처〕 a source. ¶ 확실한 ~ a reliable source.

소스라치다 take fright [alarm]; be taken aback; be frightened; be startled; be stunned. ¶비명 소리에 ~ be startled at a shriek/소스라치게 놀라다 be frightened out of one's wits.

소슬하다 (蕭瑟−) 〔으스스하고 쓸쓸하다〕 bleak; dreary; chilly; lonely and desolate. ¶소슬한 가을바람 a bleak autumnal wind [blast].

소승 (小乘) 〔불〕 Hinayana; Theravada; the Lesser Vehicle. ¶~적 견지 a narrow-minded [short-sighted] view.
● **소승 불교** Hinayana[Theravada] Buddhism.

소시민 (小市民) a petty[petit] bourgeois (*pl.* petty[petits] bourgeois). ¶~적 petty[petit] bourgeois.

소시지 (a) sausage. ¶비엔나~ Vienna sausage // 프랑크푸르트 ~ frankfurt sausage / a frankfurter / a frankforter // 볼로냐~ Bologna sausage / bologna // 햄 ~ ham sausage.

소식 (小食) light eating. **소식하다** have a small appetite; eat like a bird; do not eat much; eat lightly.
● **소식가** a light eater. ¶그녀는 ~다 She is a light eater. / She eats very little.

소식 (消息) **1** 〔전갈〕 word; 〔뉴스〕 news; 〔문어〕 tidings; 〔보고〕 a report; 〔통지〕 a notice; 〔편지〕 a letter. ¶오늘의 ~ today's news // 그 후 아무 ~이 없다 I have had no news [haven't had one letter] from him since. / I haven't heard from him at all since. // 가끔 ~이나 전해 주십시오 Please write to me [drop me a line] once in a while. // …이라는 ~을 받았다 We received word that …. // ~이 늦어졌다 Word[The news] was delayed. / The news came in late. // 그의 사망 ~을 듣지 못했다 We were not notified of his death. **2** 〔상황·동정을 알리는 보도〕 information. ¶그는 정계의 ~에 정통하다 〔밝다〕 He is well-informed[knowledgeable / in the know] about political affairs. // 그는 내게 재계의 ~을 늘 전해 준다 He keeps me posted on developments in the financial world.
● **소식통** (−筋) (well-)informed circles [quarters / sources]; a source; a channel; (사람) a well-informed person; an insider; a person in the know. ¶정계의 ~ a man conversant with political affairs / a political wiseacre // 믿을 만한 ~ a reliable source // ~에 의하면 according to well-informed sources.

소신 (所信) 〔신념〕 one's belief[conviction]; 〔의견〕 one's opinion[view]. ¶~을 굽히지 않다 be firm[unshaken] in one's convictions / stick[hold fast] to one's view[belief] // ~에 따라 행동하다 act according to one's convictions // 어떤 문제에 대하여 ~을 피력하다 express one's opinions[views] on a question.

소실 (小室) 〔첩〕 a (kept) mistress; a concubine. ¶~의 자식 a child by a concubine // ~을 두다 keep a mistress.

소실 (消失) disappearance; vanishing; vanishment. **소실하다** disappear; vanish; die away.

소실 (燒失) destruction by fire. **소실하다** lose (a thing) in the fire; be destroyed by fire; be burned down; be razed to the ground; be reduced to ashes. ➔3,000 평방미터의 지역이 ~ 소실되었다 An area of 3,000 square meters was destroyed[ravaged] by the fire.
● **소실 가옥** houses burned down; houses destroyed by fire.

소심하다 (小心−) **1** 〔겁이 많다〕 timid; cowardly(▶ timid는 늘 겁먹은 듯한, cowardly는 위험에 직면하여 패기가 없는); faint-hearted; chicken-hearted; timorous; weak; 〔도량이 좁다〕 narrow-minded; of small mind. ¶소심한 사람 a timid person / a coward // 결정적인 순간에 달아나다니 그는 참 소심한 사람이다 What a coward to take to his heels at the critical moment! **소심히** timidly; cowardly. ¶그는 형세가 어떻게 돌아가는지 ~ 눈치만 살피고 있다 He is timidly trying to see which way the wind is blowing.
2 〔지나치게 조심스럽다〕 extremely cautious; meticulous; prudent; scrupulous; circumspect. **소심히** prudently; cautiously.

소시적 (少時−) (the time of) one's boyhood [youth]. ¶~에 in one's youth / in one's early days / when young.

소아 (小我) one's smaller self; 〔자아〕 the ego.

소아 (小兒) an infant; a small child; a young [little] child. ¶~ 시절에 as a small child / in one's infancy [early childhood].
● **소아과** pediatrics; pediatry. **소아과 병원** a children's hospital. **소아과 의사** a children's doctor; a child specialist; a pediatrist [pediatrician]. **소아마비** infantile paralysis; (acute anterior) poliomyelitis; 〔구어〕 polio. ¶뇌성 ~ cerebral palsy. **소아병** a children's [an infantile] disease; 〔비유〕 infantilism.

소아병적 (小兒病的) infantilistic.

소아시아 (小−) Asia Minor.

소액 (少額) a small[petty / limited] sum [amount] (of money). ¶~의 기부 a small contribution.
● **소액 거래** small business transactions. **소액 지폐** a bill [(영) note] of small [low] denomination. **소액환** (−換) a postal order (약어 P.O. / p.o.); (미) a postal note.

소야곡 (小夜曲) 〔음〕 a serenade. ⇨세레나데

소양 (素養) a grounding (in); knowledge (of); 〔조예〕 acquirements; attainments; accomplishments. ¶~이 있다 have a grounding (in) / have some knowledge (of) // 음악에 ~이 있다 〔지식이 있다〕 be well versed in music / 〔취미가 있다〕 have a taste for music // 그는 어학에 ~이 있다 He is well-grounded in language. / He has a good foundation in language. // 그는 서양 철학에 대한 ~이 있다 He has a (good) grounding[a fundamental knowledge] in Western philosophy.

소양증 (搔癢症) 〔의〕 pruritus; itching.

소연 (小宴) (적은 인원의) (hold) a small party; (약식의) an informal dinner.

소연하다 (騷然−) noisy; clamorous; confused; agitated; tumultuous; uproarious. ¶회장은 매우 소연했다 The hall was in a great uproar. **소연히** tumultuously; noisily; clamorously; confusedly.

소염제 (消炎劑) an antiphlogistic (agent); an anti-inflammatory.

소엽 (小葉) **1** 〔동〕 a lobule; a lobelet. **2** 〔식〕 a foliole; a leaflet.

소옥(小屋) a small house; a hut; a cottage.
소외(疏外) (an) estrangement; alienation; neglect. **소외하다** estrange; alienate; neglect; slight; avoid[shun] (a person's) company; keep (a person) at a distance. → ¶친구들에게 소외하다 be treated distantly by one's friends // 그는 친구들에게 소외당하게 되었다 His friends began to avoid[keep away from] him.
● **소외감** a sense of alienation. ¶~을 느끼다 feel alienated[left out in the cold].

소요(所要) what is needed[required]; the need; requirement. ¶~되다 be necessary [required / needed].
● **소요 시간** the time required.

소요(逍遙) a ramble; a saunter; a walk. **소요하다** walk leisurely; stroll[ramble / saunter] about; take a stroll. ¶숲 속을 ~ ramble in the woods.

소요(騷擾) a disturbance; an agitation; a commotion; a riot; a sedition. ¶~를 일으키다 create a disturbance / start a riot.
● **소요죄** a crime of sedition; sedition.

소용(所用) [쓸데] a use; service; [쓰임] [유용성] usefulness; the use; [필요] necessaries; expenses. ¶그런 훈련이 언젠가는 ~이 있을 것이다 Such training will help you someday. // 이 헌 자전거가 무슨 ~이 있을까 Can you find any use for this old bicycle?

소용돌이 (강이나 바다의) a whirlpool; an eddy(▶ eddy는 whirlpool 보다 작은 느낌이며, 연기·바람·모래바람 등에도 씀); a whirl; a swirl; a vortex; a convolution; (크고 요란한) a maelstrom; [나선] a spiral; (고등 등의) a gyration. ¶~ 모양의 volute / spiral // ~에 휘말리다 be drawn into a whirlpool[vortex] / [비유] be drawn into the maelstrom[vortex] (of war) / be involved[entangled / embroiled] in (a quarrel) // 그들은 혁명의 ~에 휩쓸렸다 They were drawn into the vortex of revolution. // 그의 작품은 찬반의 ~를 일으켰다 His works aroused a whirlpool[storm] of praise and criticism.

소용돌이치다 eddy; swirl; (연기가) curl. ¶소용돌이치는 탁류 a swirling muddy stream // 조류는 소용돌이치고 있었다 The tide was swirling[swirling around / eddying]. // 그의 마음속에는 질투가 소용돌이치고 있었다 His heart was in a whirl of jealousy. / His heart was reeling with jealousy. / 연기가 소용돌이치며 올라갔다 The smoke curled up.

소용없다(所用─) useless; of no use. ¶소용없는 노력 wasted labor // 아무 ~ It is of no use. // 아무리 후회해도 ~ No amount of regret will mend[help] matters. // 그는 아무 짝에도 ~ He is no good at anything. / He can't do anything right. // 아무리 노력해도 소용없었다 All my efforts were useless[came to nothing]. // 그에게 친절하게 해 주어 봤자 ~ All kindness is wasted upon that man. // 운명에 거역해 보아야 소용없는 일이다 It is no use[good] struggling against fate. // 그에게 충고는 해야 소용없었다 My advice to him was wasted[futile]. // 우리들이 모처럼 베풀어 준 호의도 그에게는 소용없었다 All our thoughtful consideration was lost on him.

소우주(小宇宙) a microcosm(os); a miniature universe.

소원(所願) [소망] a desire; a wish; (a) hope; one's prayer(신에 대한). ¶이루지 못한 ~ an unfulfilled desire // ~대로 as one wishes / according to one's desire // 제발 ~이니 for God's sake / for mercy's sake // ~을 들어주다 grant a person's wish / (문어) comply with a person's request // 오랜 ~을 이루다 attain one's long-cherished hope[desire] // 그의 ~이 이루어졌다 He has had his desire[wish] fulfilled. / He has had his wish. // 나는 내 ~대로 의과 대학에 입학하였다 I entered the medical college as I had wished. // 그는 부모의 간절한 ~을 무시하였다 He disregarded his parents' earnest entreaties. // 하느님이시여 제 ~을 들어주시옵소서 May God answer [hear] my prayers! **소원하다** desire; wish [hope] for.

소원(訴願) a petition; an appeal. **소원하다** petition; appeal (to); lodge[file / submit / hand in / send in] a petition (to). // 감형을 ~ petition[send a petition to] (a person) for a commutation of a sentence.

소원하다(疏遠─·踈遠─) estranged; alienated; distant. ¶소원해지다 be[become] estranged [alienated] (from) // 나는 친척들과 소원해진 것이 슬프다 It makes me sad to be estranged from my relatives. // 웬일인지 그와는 소원해졌다 Somehow he and I drifted apart. // 지난 10년 동안 그들과는 소원해져다 I have not seen them[heard from them] once in the last ten years. // 한번 소원해진 사이는 좀처럼 다시 진해지기 어렵다 People once estranged do not easily become friends again. // 두 사람 사이는 점차로 소원해졌다 The two have gradually drifted apart.

소위(少尉) (육군) a second lieutenant; (해군) (미) an ensign; (영) a second sublieutenant; (공군) (미) a second lieutenant; (영) a pilot officer.

소위(所爲) one's conduct; an act; a deed; one's doing[work]; what one does.

소위(所謂) what is called; what you[we / they] call; (경멸) so-called. ¶그는 ~ 음악의 천재이다 He is what we call a musical genius. // 그들은 ~ 폭주족이다 They are so-called hot rodders.

소위원회(小委員會) a subcommittee.

소유(所有) possession; ownership. ¶개인[공동] ~ individual[joint] ownership // 이 집은 누구의 ~입니까 Who owns this house? // 그 책상은 내 ~다 The desk belongs to me. **소유하다** have; own; possess; hold; be in possession of; hold possession of; be possessed of; have (a thing) in possession. ¶그는 호텔 세 개를 소유하고 있다 He owns[has] three hotels. // 이 훌륭한 수집품은 누가 소유하고 있습니까 Who possesses[owns] this marvelous collection?
● **소유격** [언] the possessive[genitive] case.

소유권 [법] (the right of) ownership[proprietorship]; proprietary[proprietorial] rights; a right[title] (to a thing); proprietary; property; possessive rights; (토지의) dominium; dominion. ¶그는 그 땅에 대한 ~을 주장했다 He claimed title to the land. **소유물** one's possessions; [재산] one's property; one's belongings[goods]. ¶이것은 K 씨의 ~이다 This belong to [is owned by] Mr. K. // 그 집은 아버지가 돌아가신 후 내 ~이 되었다 This house came into my possession[fell into my hands] after my father's death. **소유욕** a

소유 desire to possess; possessiveness. ¶~한 possessive / grasping / acquisitive / covetous. **소유자** [소유주] an owner; a possessor; [경영자] a proprietor. ¶~ 불명의 토지 land of uncertain ownership // ~가 바뀌다 (물건이) change hands / pass into the possession of another person / shift [change] its owner [proprietor] // 이 농장의 ~는 누구입니까 Who owns this farm? // 그녀는 친절한 마음씨의 ~이다 She has a kind heart. / She is a kindhearted woman. **소유지** land owned by [belonging to] one; one's land; one's landed property; one's estate.

소음(騷音) noise; a racket; (지속적인) (a) din(▶ racket이나 din이나 혼란스런 소음. 이 뜻으로는 복수형이 되지 않음); (특히 외침 소리의) (an) uproar. ¶~의 noisy / clamorous // 대도시의 ~ the din and bustle of a great city // 경적의 ~ the din of horns // 거리의 street noise // ~을 내다 make a noise [a din] // 나는 자동차 ~ 때문에 잠을 잘 수 없었다 I couldn't sleep because of the traffic noise. // 이 거리는 ~이 심하다 This street is very noisy. // 나는 지금 도시의 ~에서 떠나서 살고 있다 I am living far from the noise [din] of the city. // 회의장의 ~ 때문에 그의 목소리는 들리지 않았다 The uproar in the hall drowned out his voice.
● **소음 공해** noise pollution. **소음 방지** prevention of noise; noise prevention.
소음기(消音器) (자동차 등의) a muffler; a silencer; (피아노의) a damper pedal.
소읍(小邑) a small town.
소이(所以) [까닭] a reason; (the reason) why …. ¶이것이 그 이름이 생긴 ~이다 Hence (comes) its name. / This is why it is so named.
소이탄(燒夷彈) an incendiary; an incendiary bomb [shell]; a fire.
소인(小人) [어린이] a child; a minor; 〈구어〉 a little one; [난쟁이] a little man; a pigmy; a dwarf; [겸칭] I; me; myself; [소인물] a small-minded person; a mean man.
● **소인국** a land of pygmies; Lilliput (걸리버 여행기의). **소인배** 〈구어〉 a (group of) small-minded person.
소인(素因) **1** [원인] a (causative) factor; a primary cause; a principle. ¶두 파의 대립의 ~ the basic factor behind [the basic reason for] the antagonism between the two parties // 그것이 장래의 발전의 ~이 될지도 모른다 It may prove to be a prime factor in future development. **2** [의] a (pre)disposition 《to tuberculosis》; a diathesis.
소인(消印) a postmark; a (postal) canceling [cancellation] mark. ¶편지에 ~을 찍다 postmark a letter // 5월 1일자 서울의 ~이 찍힌 편지 a letter postmarked from Seoul on May 1 // 신청은 6월 30일자 ~까지 유효합니다 Applications should be postmarked not later than June 30. // 이 엽서에는 ~이 찍혀 있지 않다 This card doesn't have a postmark. **소인하다** postmark; cancel (with a stamp).
소인수(素因數) [수] a prime factor.
소일거리(消日-) a time killer; a pastime; a diversion.
소일하다(消日-) pass [spend] one's time; kill [while away] time; idle [dawdle] one's time away. ¶독서로 ~ spend one's time (in) reading.

소임(所任) [임무] duties; a task; [공직] an office; [지위] a post; [사명] a mission. ¶~을 맡다 take up one's duties [post] / take office / 〈미〉 fill one's office [position] // ~을 다하다 fulfill one's duties / perform one's office / carry out one's mission.
소자(小子) (부모에게) I; me; myself.
소자(小字) a small letter [character].
소자(素子) (트랜지스터 · 콘덴서 등의) a device; microelectronics devices; (텔레비전 · FM 안테나의) a circuit element.
소작(小作) tenancy; tenant farming; 〈미〉 sharecropping. **소작하다** tenant (a farm); engage in tenant farming; [수확물의 일부를 소작료로 내다] 〈미〉 sharecrop.
● **소작농** tenant farming; tenancy. **소작료** farm rent; rent for tenancy; a share rent; rent paid by a tenant farmer. **소작인** a tenant (farmer); a cottage farmer; 〈미〉 a sharecropper; [집합적] tenantry; the peasantry. **소작 제도** the tenant(-farming) system. **소작지** a tenant (farm) land; 〈미〉 sharecropped land.
소장(小腸) [생] the small intestine; chitterlings (돼지 등의).
소장(少壯) vigorous youth; the young.
● **소장파** the young group [faction].
소장(少將) (육군) a major general; (해군) a rear admiral; (공군) 〈미〉 a major general; 〈영〉 a vice-marshal.
소장(所長) a head [chief / manager] (of an office / a factory). ¶영어 교육 연구소 ~ the director of the English Language Education Institute.
소장(所藏) one's possession. ¶홍 씨 ~의 책 a book in Mr. Hong's possession / a book owned by Mr. Hong // A 집안의 ~ property of the A family. **소장하다** possess; own; have. ¶이 그림은 한 씨가 소장하고 있는 것이다 This picture belongs to [is the property of] Mr. Han. / This picture is in Mr. Han's collection. // 이 도서관은 약 100만 권의 도서를 소장하고 있다 This library owns [houses] about a million volumes.
● **소장 골동품** one's collection of curios; curios in one's possession.
소장(訴狀) a petition; a (written) complaint; a bill (of complaint). ¶~을 제출하다 present [submit] a petition (to) / lodge [file] a complaint 《with》 // 우리는 ~을 당국에 제출하였다 We presented a petition to the authorities.
소재(所在) (사람의) one's whereabouts; (the place) where a person is; (물건의) (the place) where a thing is (kept); (건물 등의) the location; the site; [위치] the position; the situation. ¶~를 알 수 없다 one's whereabouts is unknown / be missing // ~을 **알아내다** discover [find out] (a person's) whereabouts / locate (the enemy's camp) // 책임의 ~를 분명히 하다 clarify where the responsibility lies / find out who is responsible (for).
● **소재지** the location; the site; the seat. **도청 ~** the seat of a provincial government.
소재(素材) a material; [제재(題材)] subject matter; (신문 기사 등의) copy. ¶소설의 ~ material for a novel.
소전(小傳) a brief account of 《a person's》 life; a biographical sketch (of a person); a short biography; a sketch of one's life.
소전제(小前提) [논] a minor premise [prem-

소절(小節) 1 [대수롭지 않은 예절] a minor principle. 2 [음] a bar; a measure. ¶제1∼ the first measure / measure I.

소정(所定) ¶∼의 fixed(정해진) / appointed(지정된) / prescribed(규정된) / stated / designated / established / set // ∼의 절차를 밟다 go through the prescribed formalities // ∼의 과정을 수료하다 complete a required course // ∼의 금액을 초과하다 go over[exceed] the allotted sum[budget] // 신청은 ∼의 양식을 사용할 것 An application must be made in a [the] prescribed form.

소제(小題) a subtitle; a subhead.

소제(掃除) cleaning; dusting. ⇨청소

소주(燒酒) *soju*; [증류주] a white distilled liquor; hard liquor; [희석주] diluted liquor; [화주] ardent spirits. ¶막∼ crude[low-grade] spirits.

소죽(-粥) boiled cattle feed. ⇨쇠죽

소중하다(所重-) [중요하다] important; weighty; momentous; significant; [귀중하다] valuable; valued; dear; precious. ¶소중한 물건 a valuable[treasured] article / a treasure / (집합적) valuables / 아주 소중한 것 the apple of the[one's] eye / 목숨보다도 ∼ hold (something) more valuable than one's life // 그는 소중한 친구를 잃었다 He lost a valuable [his dearest] friend. **소중히** carefully; with (much) care; with caution. ¶이 컵은 깨지기 쉬우므로 ∼ 다루어 주십시오 Please handle these glasses carefully, because they are fragile. // 몸을 ∼ 하십시오 Take care of yourself. // 그는 모든 사람들로부터 ∼ 여겨지고 있다 He is always made much of. // 내가 ∼ 여기던 반지가 없어졌다 A ring which I treasure is missing. // 그는 물건을 ∼ 다루고 오래 쓴다 He uses his things carefully and keeps them for a long time.

소지(所持) possession. **소지하다** [소유하다] possess; own; [휴대하다] have (money) about[with / on] one; have (a revolver) on one's person; bear; carry (with one). ¶그렇게 많은 현금을 소지하고 있으면 위험하다 It's not safe to carry so much cash around (with you). // 신분 증명서를 소지하고 있습니까 Do you have an identification[(영) Have you an identity] card on[with] you?
●**소지인** / **소지자** a possessor; a holder; a bearer. ¶면허증 ∼ a license holder. **소지품** one's things[belongings]; one's (personal) effects. ¶∼ 전부에 자기 이름을 붙이다 put one's name on all one's belongings // 이 펜은 누구의 ∼입니까 Whose pen is this? / Who does this pen belong to? / 호주머니에 있는 ∼을 여기 꺼내 놓아라 Take out what you have in your pockets and put it here. // ∼ 조심 (게시) Beware of pickpockets.

소지(素地) [소질] the makings; [바탕] groundwork; foundation. ¶그는 음악가가 될 ∼가 있다 He has the makings of a musician. // 그녀에게는 정치가의 ∼가 있었다 She had an aptitude for politics. / She had (in her) the makings of a fine politician.

소진(消盡) vanishing completely; total disappearance; exhaustion. **소진하다** vanish; disappear altogether; exhaust.

소진하다(燒盡−) [건물이] be burnt down; be destroyed[consumed] by fire; be reduced to ashes; be razed to the ground; [연료가] be burnt out; be exhausted. ¶교가가 화염으로 순식간에 소진했다 The flames licked up [devoured / consumed] the church in no time. // 그 마을은 맹화로 소진했다 The raging fire burned up the town.

소질(素質) [자질] the makings; temperament; character; nature; fiber; [재능] talent; [체질] constitution; make-up; [경향] a tendency. ¶문학적 ∼이 있는 사람 a person of a literary turn (of mind) // 그는 붓글씨에 ∼이 있는 것 같다 He seems to have an aptitude [a talent] for calligraphy. // 미선이는 피아니스트가 될 ∼을 가지고 있다 Miseon has the makings of a pianist. // 그녀는 화가의 ∼이 없다 She is not endowed with any artistic talent.

소집(召集) (사람·회의 등의) a call; (명령에 의한) a summons (*pl.* ∼es); (회의 등의) convocation; (군대의) a call-up; conscription; a muster; a levy; (미) a draft. ¶국회의 ∼ the convocation of the National Assembly // ∼에 응하다 respond to the call. **소집하다** (회의를) call; convene; convoke; summon; (군대를) levy; muster; call up[out]; (군대의) call (a person) into the army; (미) draft (a person) (for service). ¶임시 국회를 ∼ convene [summon] a special session of the National Assembly // 비번의 경찰관을 ∼ call out police reserves // 위원회를 소집하겠습니다 I will call[convene] a meeting of the committee.
●**소집령** (issue) a draft call. **소집 영장** a call-up paper; a draft notice; a summons to the colors. **소집일** the date of induction.

소쩍새 [동] a scops owl.

소차(小差) a small[slight / little] difference; a narrow[slim] margin.

소찬(素饌) a plain[homely] dish; a plain dinner; a vegetarian dish; a skimpy [chintzy] meal.

소책자(小冊子) (종이 표지의) a booklet; (가철(假綴)의) a pamphlet; a brochure; a tract. ¶∼로 내다 issue[publish] in pamphlet form.

소철(蘇鐵) [식] a cycad; a sago[fern] palm.

소청(所請) a request; an entreaty. ¶∼에 의하여 at the request (of a person) / at (a person's) request // ∼이 있다 have a favor to ask (of a person) / ∼을 들어주다 grant [comply with] a request // ∼을 물리치다 turn down[refuse] (a person's) request.

소총(小銃) a rifle; (집합적) small arms. ¶엠십육 ∼ an M-16 (rifle) / 카빈 ∼ a carbine.

소추(訴追) (형사상의) prosecution; indictment; accusation. ¶파면의 ∼ removal proceedings (against a judge). **소추하다** prosecute[indict] (a person for a crime); accuse (a person of a crime). ➔¶법관은 수회죄로 소추되었다 The judge was impeached for taking bribes.
●**소추자** a prosecutor.

소출(所出) the yield; the crop. ¶벼의 ∼ the rice harvest[crop] // 밀의 ∼ wheat yields / a crop of wheat // ∼이 많은 heavily[highly] productive [land].

소치(所致) what is brought[caused] by; the result. ¶젊은 열정의 ∼로 on account of[in excess of] one's youthful ardor // 이것은 그의 무능의 ∼다 This is due to his incompetence. // 이것은 모두 저의 부덕의 ∼입니다 I am solely to blame for it. / It's all my fault. // 이

것은 모두 저의 불찰의 ~입니다 My carelessness has brought all this about.
소켓 a socket. ¶쌍[세 갈래] ~ a two-[three-]way socket∥~ 을 달다 fix a socket∥전구를 ~에 끼우다 screw a light bulb into a socket.
소쿠리 a bamboo[wicker] basket.
소탈하다(疏脫-·疎脫-) informal; free and easy; unceremonious; unconstrained; bohemian; freely-thinking and freely-acting. ¶그는 어딘지 소탈한 데가 있는 사람이다 He has something free and easy about him.
소탐대실(小貪大失) incurring a great loss by pursuing a small profit. **소탐대실하다** suffer a big loss in going after a small gain.
소탕(掃蕩) sweeping; clearing; a sweep; (잔적(殘敵) 등의) mopping up; a mop-up; a cleanup. **소탕하다** sweep; clear; scour; stamp[wipe] out; get rid of; (잔적 등을) mop up; clean up; clear out. ¶적을 ~ clear [sweep / rid] (the sea) of the enemy∥잔적을 ~ mop up the remnants of the enemy / clean up enemy remnants.
●**소탕 작전** a sweep; a mopping-up operation; a cleanup operation.
소태(식] [소태나무] a picramnia wood; a kind of sumac; [소태껍질] sumac bark. **소태 같다** be as bitter as gall.
소택(沼澤) a marsh; a bog.
●**소택지** marshland; bogland.
소통(疏通) (의사의) mutual understanding; communication; (물 등의) drainage. ¶두 사람은 의사~이 부족했다 There was a lack of understanding[communication] between the two of them.∥우리는 다른 회원과의 의사 ~을 도모했다 We tried to develop better communication with the other members. **소통하다** (의사가) come to understand each other; come to a mutual (good) understanding; be understood (by); have[enjoy] mutual understanding; (물 등이) drain off.
소파 a sofa; a couch. ¶그녀는 ~에 기대고 있었다 She was lounging on the sofa.
소파(搔爬) [의] curettage; curettement. ¶~ 수술을 하다 undergo curettage. **소파하다** curet(te); scrape[remove] (a growth from a cavity) with a curette.
소포(小包) (미) a package; (영) a parcel. ¶국내[국제] ~ domestic[international] parcels∥~ 찾는 곳 2층 후문 (게시) To pick up parcels, use rear entrance on the second floor.
●**소포 우편** (제도) parcel(s) post; [우편물] a (postal) parcel; a (postal) package. ¶~으로 보내다 send (a thing) by parcel post / (미) mail (a thing) (to). **소포 우편료** parcel post postage[charge / rates].
소폭(小幅) (폭의) single breadth; (범위의) narrow range; narrow limits. ¶~의 증자(增資)를 하다 make a small capital increase / increase capitalization by a small margin∥주가는 ~의 움직임을 보였다 Share prices moved within narrow limits.
●**소폭 등락** fluctuations of a narrow range.
소품(小品) **1** (문학의) a short piece[work]; a (literary) sketch; (음악의) a short (musical) composition; (회화의) a small work of art; a small painting; (조각의) a small sculpture. **2** [자그마한 도구] small tools; (무대의) (stage) properties; (구어) props.
●**소품 담당자** a prop(erty) man[master]. **소품실** a property room.
소풍(逍風) [바람 쐬기] taking the air; airing oneself; [산책·피크닉] an excursion; a holiday expedition; a walking tour; an outing; a hike; a tramp; [들놀이] a picnic. ¶학교의 ~ a school excursion∥~ 가기에 좋은 날씨 ideal weather for an outing[for holiday-walking]∥~ 기분으로 in a holiday mood∥~을 가다 go on an excursion[a picnic / a hike] / go on an outing∥안양으로 ~ 가다 go on a trip as far as Anyang. **소풍하다** [바람 쐬다] take the air; get some fresh air; [산책·들놀이하다] go on an excursion[a hike]; take a long walk.
●**소풍객** an excursionist; (미) a vacationer; (영) a holiday maker.
소프라노 (음) soprano; (가수) a soprano (pl. ~s, -ni); a soprano singer. ¶메조~ a mezzo-soprano.
소프트드링크 [비알코올성 음료] a soft drink.
소프트볼 (놀이) (play) softball; (볼) a softball.
소프트웨어 [컴] software.
소피(小避) urination; relieving oneself. **소피하다** do one's needs. ⇨**소피보다**
소피보다(小避-) do one's needs; ease nature; pass[make] water; urinate.
소피스트 (고대 그리스의) a sophist.
소한(小寒) [24절기의 하나] sohan; one of the 24 seasonal divisions; the period of the severest cold.
소해(掃海) sea clearing; mine sweeping [dragging]. **소해하다** sweep for mines; sweep up mines; drag the sea for mines; clear the sea.
●**소해정**(-艇) a mine sweeper.
소행(所行) an act; a deed; one's doing[work]; what one does. ¶악마의 ~ the work of the Devil∥~이 사납다 ill-behaved∥이건 그의 ~임에 틀림없다 It must be his doing.
소행(素行) conduct; behavior; one's natural character. ¶~이 나쁜 남자 a man of dubious morality[character] / a degenerate∥~이 나쁘다 lead a fast[dissolute] life / be a loose fish.
소행성(小行星) an asteroid.
소형(小型) a small size; a pocket size. ¶~의 small / small-sized (cups).
●**소형 권총** a pocket pistol. **소형 자동차** a minicar; a compact car. **소형 카메라** a miniature camera; a minicam.
소호 SOHO(▶ small office; home office의 약어).
소호(沼湖) marshes and lakes.
소홀하다(疏忽-) negligent; neglectful; remiss; careless; [경솔하다] rash; slipshod; sloppy. ¶이 연구소에서는 약품 관리가 ~ They are very careless about the way they keep chemicals in this laboratory.∥딴생각을 하느라고 하던 일을 소홀하게 했다 Thinking of something else I forgot what I was doing. **소홀히** indifferently; rudely; roughly; negligently; carelessly; inattentively. ¶~ 하다 neglect / disregard / be negligent[neglectful] (of) / pay no attention (to)∥물품을 ~ 다루다 handle an article roughly∥일을 ~ 하다 neglect one's work / be negligent in one's work∥이 문제는 ~ 다룰 수 없다 This problem can't be treated[passed over] lightly.∥검사를 ~ 했던 모양이다 The in-

소화

spection seems to have been carelessly done.// 요즈음 아이들은 물건을 ~ 한다 Children nowadays make light of things. / Nowadays children don't take good care of things [handle things carelessly].

소화(消火) fire extinguishing; fire fighting. ¶~용의[으로] for fire-extinguishing [fire fighting] purposes// ~에 힘쓰다 fight a fire/ 마을 사람들 모두가 ~에 나섰다 All the villagers fought the fire. **소화하다** put out [extinguish] a fire.
● **소화기** a fire extinguisher. **소화전**(-栓) a (fire) hydrant; a fireplug.

소화(消化) **1** (음식의) digestion. ¶~가 잘되는 음식 digestible [light] food// ~가 잘 안 되는 음식 indigestible food / food that is hard to digest // ~를 돕다 promote [aid] (the / one's) digestion // ~를 방해하다 disturb [upset] one's digestion. **소화하다** digest. ¶위는 음식물을 소화한다 The stomach digests what has been eaten. ➔ ¶반숙한 달걀은 잘 소화된다 A soft-boiled egg is easy to digest [easily digested].
2 (지식·기술 등의) digestion; [흡수] assimilation. **소화하다** digest; assimilate; understand; take in. ¶나는 이 책을 소화할 수 없다 This book is too difficult [(구어) tough] for me.// 이 책은 그들이 소화하기에는 너무 어렵다 This book is too difficult for them to digest. // 그는 샤일록 역을 매우 훌륭하게 소화하고 있다 He performs Shylock's part quite well. // 그녀는 그리스 어의 원전도 소화할 수 있다 She is capable of digesting [understanding] the book in the original Greek.
3 [소비] consumption. **소화하다** [소비하다] consume; (시장이 상품 등을) absorb. ¶국민이 소화할 수 없을 만큼 제품을 생산하는 것은 헛된 일이다 It is no good manufacturing more products than the nation can consume. // 시장이 그 많은 전기 기구를 다 소화할 수 있을까 Can the market absorb so many electric appliances? // 우리는 컴퓨터 덕택에 일을 빨리 소화할 수 있다 We can take care of business rapidly, thanks to computers.
● **소화기 / 소화기관** the digestive organs. ¶~계통 the digestive system // ~계통의 병 an alimentary disease / a gastrointestinal disease // ~ 장애 (a) digestive trouble. **소화불량** indigestion; dyspepsia. ¶~을 일으키다 have indigestion. **소화제** a digestive; a digester; a peptic.

소화물(小貨物) a parcel(▶ (영)에서는 특히 우편 소화물); a packet; (미) a package. ¶~을 보내다 send [forward] a packet / (미) express a package // 나는 나의 의류 ~을 철도편으로 보냈다 I sent a package containing my clothes by rail.

소환(召喚) a summons (pl. ~es); a call; (a) monition; (a) citation; a subp(o)ena. ¶~을 받고 있다 be under subp(o)ena // ~에 응하다 answer [obey] a summons // 그는 위원회의 ~에 불응했다 He did not respond to the summons of the committee. **소환하다** summon; call; cite; subp(o)ena. ¶관계자를 ~ summon the parties concerned / serve summonses on the parties concerned. ➔ ¶그는 증인으로서 법정에 소환되었다 He was summoned to appear in court as a witness.
● **소환장** (issue) a (writ of) summons [subp(o)ena]; a citation. ¶증인에 대한 ~ a subpo(e)na to testify // ~을 발부하다 issue a summons (against a person) / serve (a person) with a summons.

소환(召還) (a) recall. **소환하다** recall; call [order] back. ➔ ¶주미 대사가 소환되었다 The ambassador to the U.S. was recalled.

속 1 [안] the inside; the interior; the inner part; the innermost [inmost] recess; the heart. ¶동굴 ~ 깊숙한 곳에 in the inner part of [at the back of] a cave // 우리는 정글 ~ 깊숙이 전진했다 We advanced deep into the jungle. // 이 상자 ~에는 무엇이 들어 있습니까 What's in this box? // 그녀는 스웨터 ~에 블라우스를 입었다 She wore a blouse under [underneath] a sweater. // 그는 열광의 박수 ~에서 퇴장했다 He left the hall amid a storm of applause. // 그는 고뇌 ~에 생애를 마쳤다 He died in great mental anguish. / He died with his mental sufferings unrelieved. // 택시 요금은 여비 ~에 포함되지 않는다 Taxi fares are not counted as a travel expense.
2 [마음·이면] the depth; the bottom; the heart. ¶~이 깊지 않은 사람 a shallow personality // ~을 알 수 없는 사람 a mysterious character // 그는 절망 ~에 빠져 있다 He is in the depths of despair. // 나는 마음 ~으로는 그 계획에 반대였다 I was opposed to the plan at bottom. // 그들은 ~으로 그의 경솔을 비웃고 있었다 They were secretly [inwardly] laughing at his rashness. // 누구나가 ~으로는 같은 감정을 가지고 있었다 Everyone had the same feeling in (the depths of) his heart.
3 [내용물] content(s); [실질] substance; (박제품·요리 등의) stuffing; a filling; (의자 등의) pad; padding; (이불 등의) wad; wadding; a filler. ¶매트리스에 ~을 넣다 stuff the mattress // 박 ~을 파내다 hollow out [excavate] a gourd // 그릇의 ~을 비우다 drain a vessel of its contents.
4 (배 속) (구어) insides; stomach. ¶빈 ~ empty stomach // ~이 비다 get hungry / feel empty // ~이 쓰리다 have a burning feeling in the stomach // ~이 좋지 않다 have something wrong with one's inside(s).
5 (중심·핵) the center; the heart; (과일의) the core; (초목의) a pith; (뼛속) the marrow. ¶사과의 ~을 도려내다 core an apple // 이 기둥은 ~이 썩어 있다 The heart [center / core] of this pillar is rotten. // 그는 ~까지 썩어 있다 He is rotten to the core. // 어찌나 추운지 추위가 뼛~까지 스머드는 것 같았다 It was bitterly cold, and I was chilled to my very bones [frozen to the marrow].

속(을) 긁다 offend; hurt (a person's) feeling; put (a person) in a bad humor.

속(이) 달다 be anxious [eager] (for / to do); be impatient (for / to do); be nervous (about); fret (oneself) (about); be in a stew (about / over). ¶결과를 알지 못해 ~ be anxious to know the result // 그렇게 속 달아 할 것 없네 Don't jitter [fret yourself] like that.

속(이) 보이다 be transparent; be easily seen through. ¶속 보이는 짓을 하다 resort to a shallow trick.

속(을) 주다 take (a person) into one's confidence; let (a person) know one's mind; unbosom oneself (to a person); open one's heart (to a person); lay bare one's heart.

속(이) 타다 be distressed (about / by); be vexed[irritated] (at); be worried (about / that); be nervous; be harassed[annoyed]; be fretful. ¶속이 타는 마음 an aching[a troubled] heart // 근심 걱정으로 ~ be distressed[tormented] with cares and anxieties // 속이 타는 일 the source[matter] of worry / worries / troubles / cares // 아들의 장래를 생각하니 속이 탄다 I am terribly anxious about my son's future.

속(을) 태우다 1 (스스로) worry (oneself) (about); bother (oneself) (about); trouble oneself (with); be anxious[nervous] (about); be troubled[distressed / worried]; be annoyed[bothered / vexed]. ¶하찮은 일에 ~ worry over trifles // 그런 일로 속 태우지 마라 Don't worry yourself about such a thing. / Don't let that worry you. // 무엇 때문에 속을 태우는가 What are you so nervous about? / What's your worry[trouble]? / What is eating (on) you? **2** (남을) vex; annoy; worry; cause worry[anxiety]; bother; distress; trouble; make nervous. ¶친구를 ~ cause anxiety to friends // 그 일로 그녀를 ~ bother her with the matter // 아이들은 종종 부모님을 속 태운다 Children often bother their parents.

속(屬) [생] a genus (pl. -nera, ~es).

속(束) [묶음·다발] a bundle (of fag(g)ot).

속(續) a second series; a sequel. ¶「~근대 문명론」(저서명) Later Thoughts on Modern Civilization.

속가(俗歌) a popular[folk] song; a ditty; a ballad.

속가량(-假量) a rough estimate (based on one's feelings).

속간(續刊) continuation of publication. ¶이 총서는 현재 ~ 중이다 The publication of the subsequent volumes in this series is now moving forward[in progress]. **속간하다** continue to publish (a series of works).

속개(續開) resumption; continuation. **속개하다** 또 resume; continue. ➔¶위원회는 오늘 오후에 속개된다 The committee will resume its session this afternoon.

속격(屬格) [언] the genitive case.

속결(速決) a prompt decision. ⇨"즉결(卽決)

속계(俗界) the [this] world; earthly [secular] world. ¶그는 ~의 일에 전혀 관심이 없다 He is completely indifferent to matters of the world [mundane matters / the humdrum affairs of everyday life].

속고갱이 the (very) heart[core]. ¶양배추의 ~ the heart of a cabbage.

속곳 a slip; a petticoat; underwear. ¶~ 바람으로 with nothing on but a slip.

속공(速攻) a swift attack. ¶(경기에서) 다양한 ~을 펼치다 charge (the American team) with varied types of quick attacks. **속공하다** launch a swift attack on[against] (the enemy).

속구(速球) [야구] (throw) a fastball; a speed ball; (구어) a fireball. ¶~를 던지다 throw hard / (구어) burn it in / (구어) put smoke on the ball.

속국(屬國) a dependency; a subject[vassal] state[country]; [공물을 바치는 나라] a tributary (state). ¶대국의 ~ a dependency [tributary] to a big power // …의 ~이 되다 come[pass] under the sway[rule / yoke] of (another state) / become (a) tributary to (some power) / be subject to (another country) // 이 나라는 어느 강대국의 ~도 된 일이 없다 This country has never been subject to [been colonized by] any power.

속귀 [생] the internal[inner] ear; the labyrinth.

속기(速記) **1** [속필] rapid[fast] writing. **속기하다** write[note down] fast[rapidly]; take rapid notes (of). **2** shorthand; stenography. **속기하다** write[take] down in shorthand; take stenographic notes (of); stenograph. ¶그는 강연을 속기했다 He took down the speech in shorthand.

●**속기록** a stenographic record; shorthand [stenographic] notes. ¶의회의 ~ parliamentary records. **속기사 / 속기자** a shorthand writer [reporter]; a stenographer; a stenographist; [타자로 속기하는 사람] a stenotypist. **속기술** shorthand; stenography.

속기(俗氣) vulgarity; worldliness; worldly ambition. ¶~가 있다 be vulgar / be worldly // ~가 없다 be above the world.

속껍질 an inner skin [coat].

속내 the real state (of affairs); the internal conditions; the inside (facts); concealed [undisclosed] circumstances; the inside story; [장사의] inner workings. ¶~를 들여다보다 see behind the scenes // ~를 알고 있다 have an inside knowledge (of) / have the low-down (on) / be in the know.

속눈썹 eyelashes; lashes; (구어) winkers. ¶긴 ~ long eyelashes // 인조 ~ false eyelashes.

속다 be[get] deceived[cheated / deluded / hoaxed / defrauded / fooled]; be imposed (up)on; be taken in; be caught in a trap. ¶잘 속는 사람 a dupe / a sucker / a credulous person // 속아서 돈을 빼앗기다 be cheated [fooled] out of one's money / be stung (for a fiver) // 물건을 속아 사다 get gypped in buying an article / buy a lemon // 가짜를 속아 사다 be fobbed[palmed] off with a counterfeit // 또 속았다! Sold again! // 나는 그의 달콤한 말에 완전히 속았다 I was completely taken in[deceived] by his honeyed words. // 주부들은 화장품 광고에 속았다 The housewives were fooled by that cosmetics advertisement. // 그는 쉬 속아 그녀에게 돈을 주었다 He was easily deceived [neatly taken in] and gave her some money. / He fell neatly for her trick and gave her some money. // 우리 딸은 그 녀석에게 속아 함께 가출해 버렸다 Our daughter fell for his line [his sweet talk] and ran away with him.

속아 넘어가다 be deceived[cheated / fooled / taken in]. ¶감쪽같이 ~ be nicely[neatly / fairly] taken in / fall an easy victim to (another's) trick // 나는 그의 달콤한 말에 감쪽같이[고스란히] 속아 넘어갔다 I was completely taken in by his honeyed words.

속닥거리다 whisper secrets; whisper slyly to (a person); exchange subdued remarks; talk in whispers; talk in whispers; talk in a subdued tone.

속단(速斷) **1** [너무 이른 단정] a hasty conclusion. ¶그것은 당신의 ~이겠지요 That's just what you are rashly assuming. **속단하다** conclude hastily; form[come to / leap to] a hasty conclusion; make[draw] a hasty con-

속달

clusion; jump to [at] a conclusion; decide hastily. ¶이것으로 성공은 틀림없다고 속단해서는 안 된다 You must not jump to the conclusion that this will ensure your success. // 그는 갈 필요가 없다고 속단해 버렸다 He rather hastily concluded that it wasn't necessary to go.
2 [빠른 판단] an immediate judgment [decision]; a prompt decision; a speedy decision. ¶~을 내릴 수 없었다 He could not make an immediate decision [make up his mind on the spot]. 속단하다 pass [form] an immediate judgment (on); be prompt in deciding (that ...).

속달 (速達) (미) special delivery; (영) express delivery. ¶나는 ~로 편지를 보냈다 I sent a letter by express. / I mailed a letter by special delivery.
● **속달료** a special [an express] delivery charge; a special delivery fee. **속달 우편** ➡ 빠른우편

속담 (俗談) a proverb; a (common) saying; an adage. ¶~에서 말하듯이 as the proverb says [goes] / ~에 말하기를 A proverb has it [says] (that) .... // ~에서 말하듯이 세월은 쏜살 같다 As the proverb says [saying goes], time flies like an arrow.

속답 (速答) an immediate answer; a prompt reply. 속답하다 give an immediate answer; make a prompt reply.

속대 (푸성귀의) the heart of greenstuff. ¶배추의 ~ the heart of a cabbage.

속도 (速度) 1 (a) speed; (a) velocity (▶ speed와 velocity는 거의 같은 뜻으로 쓰이나, 과학 용어로서는 후자를 쓰는 것이 보통임); a pace; (a) rate. ¶초 [종] ~ initial [final] velocity // 최고 ~ maximum speed // ~를 줄이시오 (게시) Slow Down. / Reduce Speed. // 빛 [소리] 의 ~ the speed of light [sound] // 제한 ~를 지키다 keep within [observe] the speed limit // 우리는 ~가 느린 차를 추월했다 We passed a slow car. // 그는 읽는 ~가 빠르다 He reads rapidly. / He is a rapid reader. // 그는 마시는 ~가 빠르다 He drinks at a rapid pace. // 지금 비행기는 어느 정도의 ~로 날고 있는 것일까 How fast is the plane flying (now)? // 이 배는 ~가 빠르다 This steamer is very fast. // 그는 연설의 ~를 유효 적절하게 조절한다 He varies the pace of his speeches very effectively. // 이 ~로는 9시까지 거기에 도착하지 못하겠다 At this rate we won't get there by nine o'clock. // 교통 체증에서 빠져나오자 차는 ~를 높였다 Getting out of the traffic jam, the car picked up speed [speeded up].
2 [음] (a) tempo.
● **속도계** a speedometer; a speed indicator. **속도위반** speeding; going over [exceeding] the speed limit; violation [infringement] of the speed regulations. ¶~자 a speeder / a violator of the speed regulations // 단속 경찰관 a speed cop // ~을 하다 break [violate] the speed regulations // 그는 ~으로 붙잡혔다 He was caught for speeding. **속도 제한** a speed limit. ¶~ 표지 a speed-limit sign / ~을 어기다 break [go over] the speed limit.

속독 (速讀) rapid [speed] reading (▶ speed reading는 특수한 기술로 대단히 빨리 읽는 일). 속독하다 read (a book) fast [rapidly].

속돌 [광] a pumice stone. ⇨부석

속되다 (俗-) [세속적이다] secular; earthly;

worldly; mundane; [통속적이다] common; popular; [천하다] vulgar; low; coarse. ¶속된 말로 in common parlance // 속된 사람 a worldly (-minded) person // 속된 욕망 worldly desires [ambitions] // 속된 말을 쓰다 use vulgar language // 그는 속된 인간이다 He is a low sort (of person). // 그녀는 속된 취미를 가지고 있다 She has cheap taste(s). // 속된 말로 그것은 삼각관계였다 It was what people call a love triangle.

속등 (續騰) a continued advance [rise] (in stock prices); a further rise [appreciation]. 속등하다 continue to advance [rise].

속뜻 1 [참뜻] the inner [true] meaning [sense / significance]. 2 [본심] one's real intention; one's true motive. ¶그의 ~을 알 수 없다 I can't see what he really means. / I can't make out what he is driving at.

속락 (續落) a continued fall [drop]; a continuous drop; sagging; a further decline; sliding. ¶화폐 가치의 ~ a continued fall of the value in money. 속락하다 continue to fall [drop]; keep declining [sagging / sliding]. ¶주가는 속락하는 경향이다 Stock prices continue to follow a downward path. / Stock prices tend continually downward(s) [tend to sag].

속량 (贖良) 1 [몸값을 받고 종의 신분을 풀어줌] emancipation of slaves; redemption (of a slave). 속량하다 redeem (a slave); ransom (a captive). 2 [신] satisfaction. ⇨ 속죄2

속력 (速力) (a) speed; (a) velocity; (a) rate. ¶ 경제 ~ an economic speed // 최대 ~ the greatest [maximum] speed // 제한 ~ a regulation speed // ~을 올리다 increase [pick up] speed / gather speed / speed up / accelerate // ~을 늦추다 reduce [decrease / slacken] one's speed / slow down // ~을 더 내 Speed [Pick] it up! / Step on it! / Faster! // 로켓은 중력권을 탈출할 만한 충분한 ~을 내지 못했다 The rocket failed to attain [gather] enough velocity to escape the sphere of gravity.

속령 (屬領) [부속 영토] a territory; a possession; [속국] a dependent domain; a dependency; a subject province. ¶강대국들의 과거의 ~ former dependencies [territories] of the great powers.

속례 (俗例) a popular custom; a common usage; a common way; convention.

속류 (俗流) the common (run of) people; the vulgar masses.

속마음 one's inmost heart [thought(s)]; one's real intention; the bottom of one's heart. ¶~으로는 at bottom / at heart // ~을 아는 친구 an old and trusted friend / (신뢰할 수 있는) a reliable friend // ~을 알 수 없는 사람 someone who is not a close friend // ~을 터놓다 open up to (a person) // ~을 모두 털어놓으십시오 Please tell me everything you have in mind. // 그녀와 나는 서로 ~을 아는 사이이다 She and I know each other well [(구어) inside out]. // 그 말은 그의 진정한 ~을 드러낸 것이었다 The remark revealed his true intentions. // 당신의 ~을 내게 털어놓지 않겠소 Won't you tell me what you're really thinking?

속말 a confidential [private] talk; a confidence. **속말하다** have a private [confidential] talk (with); speak out of one's heart; make

속명(俗名) **1** [속칭] a popular [familiar] name; (학명에 대하여) a common [vernacular] name. **2** [불] (계명에 대하여) a secular name; one's name as a layman.
속명(屬名) [생] a generic name.
속물(俗物) **1** [속사에만 마음이 이끌리는 사람] a worldly-minded person; a completely materialistic person; a person who values money, position, and fame. **2** [속된 물건] mean [vulgar] stuff.
● **속물근성** snobbery; philistinism.
속바지 underpants; drawers.
속박(束縛) binding; [억제] restraint; [제한] restriction; [구속물] fetters; shackles; trammels; a yoke. ¶~을 받다 be placed under restraint / be fettered (by) // ~을 벗어나다 free ourself from restraint / break away from the yoke (of) // 남의 ~을 풀어 주다 release a person / set a person free // 마침내 나는 ~에 해방되었다 I finally gained my freedom [shook off my fetters]. **속박하다** restrain; restrict; trammel; shackle; enchain; fetter; bind; lay [place] under restraint. ¶사람을 ~ restrain a person / 언론의 자유를 ~ restrict freedom of speech. →¶시간에 속박되어 여행 같은 건 할 수 없다 There are restrictions on my time and I can't go on pleasure trips.
속발(續發) successive [frequent] occurrence; a succession [series] (of events). **속발하다** happen [occur] in succession; come out [crop up] one after another. ¶속발하는 사건 a rash [close sequence] of events // 최근 화재가 속발한다 Fires are frequent these days.
속배포(-排布) one's real intention; one's undisclosed plans [schemes]; one's innermost thought(s); one's ulterior motive. ¶~가 있는 사람 a man of intrigue / a schemer // ~가 다르다 have something in the back of one's mind / have an ax(e) to grind.
속병(-病) an internal [intestinal] disease.
속보(速步) a quick pace; quick steps; [군] a quick march; [마술(馬術)] trotting; a trot. ¶~로 걷다 (말이) trot / (빠른 걸음의) walk with quick steps / walk fast.
속보(速報) a prompt [quick] report [announcement]; a (news) flash. ¶개표 ~ prompt [up-to-the-minute / hour-by-hour] reports of the election returns. **속보하다** report promptly; announce quickly; make a quick report (on). →¶사고의 뉴스는 텔레비전으로 속보되었다 The news of the accident was flashed onto the television screen immediately.
● **속보판** a bulletin board; (영) a newsboard.
속보(續報) a continued [subsequent / follow-up] report; a follow-up; further news; additional [further] particulars. ¶사건의 ~가 속속 들어왔다 Follow-up reports (of the incident) arrived in quick succession. // ~를 기다리고 있는 중이다 We are waiting for further news [reports / information / details].
속사(俗事) earthly [worldly / mundane] affairs; petty affairs of life [this world]; commonplace [everyday] business [affairs]; routine work; daily routine [chores].
속사(速射) quick firing [fire]; firing in rapid succession. ¶~의 명수 (미) a snap shooter / (영) a snapshotter. **속사하다** fire quickly; fire in rapid succession.
● **속사포**(-砲) a rapid-firing [rapid-fire] gun; a quick-firing [quick-fire] gun [cannon]; a quick firer. ¶질문을 ~처럼 잇따라 퍼붓다 fire off questions one after another in rapid succession.
속사(速寫) quick copying; [사진] snapshooting; snapshotting. **속사하다** copy rapidly [quickly]; [사진] snapshot; take a snapshot (of).
● **속사 사진** a snap; a snapshot.
속사정(-事情) the inside story; the real state of affairs. ¶그의 집안의 ~은 매우 복잡하다 His domestic circumstances are very complicated.
속삭이다 whisper; murmur; talk in whispers; speak under one's breath. ¶사랑의 속삭임 sweet whispers of love / soft nothings // 시냇물의 속삭임 murmurs [murmuring] of a brook // 귀에 대고 ~ whisper in (another's) ear // 서로 ~ whisper to each other / exchange whispers // 그녀는 언니 귀에 대고 한두 마디 속삭였다 She whispered a word or two into her sister's ear.
속산(速算) a rapid calculation. **속산하다** do [make] a rapid calculation.
속살 1 (옷 속의) the part of the body usually covered by clothing. ¶~의 내비치는 블라우스 a see-through blouse // 그녀의 ~은 백설같이 희다 Her skin under clothes is as white as snow. **2** [옹골찬 살] the inside flesh. **3** [소의 입 안에 붙은 고기] the meat from the inside of a cow's mouth.
속살(이) 찌다 1 [살찌다] be plumper than (he) looks; be solidly fleshy. **2** [실속 있다] substantial; solid; rich; plump.
속상하다(-傷-) [마음이 좋지 않다] feel sore (about); feel depressed [distressed]; be troubled [unhappy]; [짜증스럽다] be irritated [fretful]; [분하다] be [feel] vexed (at one's failure); be annoyed; be exasperated (at); [걱정스럽다] be worried; feel anxious; be troublesome; be distressing; be worrisome. ¶속상한 일투성이다 be full of cares and vexations // 속상해하다 feel sore (about) // 속상하게 하다 hurt (a person's) feeling / cause (a person) distress // 아이 속상해 How vexatious [disappointing]! // 무엇이 그리 속상하니 What's the worry [trouble]? / What are you sore [mad] at? // 아들의 성적이 좋지 않아서 어머니는 몹시 속상해했다 The boy's low grades caused his mother great distress. // 그는 기차를 놓쳐서 속상했다 He felt chagrined at having missed the train. / He was vexed when he missed the train.
속새 [식] a scouring [Dutch] rush; a shave grass.
속설(俗說) a common [popular] saying; a popular version (of an incident); [전설] folklore; (a) tradition; a legend. ¶~에 의하면 33세가 여자의 액년이라고 한다 It is commonly [popularly] believed [said] that 33 is an unlucky age for women.
속성(俗姓) [불] one's secular surname.
속성(速成) [단기 양성] an intensive training (in); [빨리 완성시킴] rapid completion. ¶나는 프랑스 어를 3개월 ~으로 배웠다 I acquire French by three months' intensive study. // 우리는 그들에게 교원 ~ 교육을 시켰다 We gave them intensive training in

속성

속성 teaching. / We trained them quickly as teachers. **속성하다** train quickly; complete rapidly.
● **속성과** a short [an intensive] course. **속성재배** forcing culture. ¶~를 하다 force.

속성(屬性) [논] an attribute; a property; [생] a generic character.

속세 (-世) the [this] world; (secular) society; mundane life; earthly existence. ¶~를 떠나서 away from the tainting influence of the world // ~를 버리다 renounce [retire from] the world / go to live in seclusion // ~를 둥지다 turn one's back upon the world // ~를 버리고 은둔자가 되다 [출가하다] renounce this world and become a hermit [enter the priesthood].

속셈 1 [마음속으로 하는 궁리] inner calculation [thought(s)]; an ulterior motive [purpose]; one's secret [real] intention; a deep design. ¶…할 ~으로 with the secret intention of … / with the inward view of … // …할 ~이다 intend (to do / doing) / mean to (do) / have the intention of (doing) // ~이 있다 have a plot in mind / have a secret design / have something up one's sleeve // 그들은 ~이 있어 나를 초대했던 것이다 They had some ulterior motive in inviting me. // 그의 ~을 모르겠다 I don't understand what he has in mind. / I cannot quite see his motive [idea / design]. // 그의 ~은 뻔하다 His intentions are obvious. / I can see through his intentions. // 그는 나의 ~을 알아차렸다 He saw through my intentions. // 그는 나를 사람들 앞에서 놀림감으로 만들 ~인 것이다 He intends to make a fool of me in public. // 그들은 무슨 ~일까 What are they plotting?
2 mental arithmetic. ⇨"암산

속속(續續) successively; in (rapid [close / quick]) succession; one after another; one upon the heels of another. ¶~ 들어오는 청구서 [편지 / 신청서] a crop of bills [letters / applications] // ~ 밀려오다 rush on (a place) // ~ 탈랑하다 leave the party one after another // 주문이 ~ 들어온다 Orders pour in. / We are flooded with orders.

속속들이 thoroughly; thoroughgoingly; inside out; to the core [bottom]. ¶~ 썩다 be rotten to the core // ~ 알다 know (something) through and through / have a thorough [full] knowledge (of) / be quite at home (on / in) // ~ 캐묻다 inquire of (a person) about every detail of (a matter) // 비밀을 ~ 캐내다 root out a secret // 그 장사는 내가 ~ 알고 있다 I know the business inside out. // 그들은 우리 전략을 ~ 간파했다 They saw through to the very bottom of our strategy.

속수무책(束手無策) helplessness; resourcelessness. ¶~이다 be at one's wits' [wit's] end / be at the end of one's resources / be quite at a loss (what to do) / do not know what (else) to do // ~이구나 Nothing doing. / Nothing can be done. / What (else) could be done? / 나는 ~이었다 I was at a loss what to do. // 나로서는 ~이다 It's all up with me. / There's nothing more I can do.

속씨식물(-植物) an angiosperm.
속악하다(俗惡-) vulgar; low [brow]; coarse; inelegant.
속어(俗語) (집합적) colloquial language; (속어) slanguage; (낱말의) a colloquial expression [word]; a colloquialism; a vulgarism; [비어(卑語)] slang; a slang [slangy] word [expression]. ¶~를 쓰다 use slang [vulgar speech].

속어림 one's guess; one's conjecture. ¶~으로 in one's estimation [estimate] / by guess [guesswork] / in one's thought.

속없다 [줏대가 없다] spineless; (back) boneless; poor-spirited; (서술적) (be) without settled convictions; (악의 없다) innocent; harmless. ¶그들의 속없는 행동에 화가 난다 We are angry at them for their irresponsible behavior.

속연(續演) the continuation of a show. ¶60일간의 ~ 60 days' run. **속연하다** continue to stage [put on] (a play); run (a movie) consecutively (for two months).

속옷 underwear; an undergarment; an undershirt; underlinen; underclothes; underclothing; (여성의) lingerie; (구어) undies. ¶~을 갈아입다 change one's underlinen.

속요(俗謠) a popular [folk] song; a ballad; a ditty.

속이다 1 [기만하다] deceive; cheat; swindle; trick; hoax; gull; dupe; fool; take in; impose [play] upon; hoodwink; play (a person) a trick. (▶ 보통 cheat는 부정한 수단, 사기 등으로, trick은 교묘한 책략으로, deceive는 거짓말 등으로 남을 속임) ¶속이기 쉬운 gullible / credulous // 속이기 쉬운 사람 a dupe / a gull / (미) a sucker // 남의눈을 ~ hoodwink a person / pull [draw] the wool over a person's eyes / cast [throw] a mist before a person's eyes // 저울을 ~ give short weight / shortweigh // 자신을 ~ deceive oneself // 노름을 ~ cheat in gambling // 계산서를 ~ cook up a bill / 숫자를 ~ juggle with figures // 속여서 빼앗다 defraud [hoax] (a person) of (something) / cheat [bilk] (a person) (out) of (something) / swindle [trick / do] (a person) out of (something) // 감언이설로 속여서 빼앗다 cajole [wheedle] (a person) out of (something) / cajole (something) out of (a person) // 남을 속여 돈을 빼앗다 cheat [swindle] a person out of money // 속여서 하게 하다 trick [deceive / cheat] (a person) into (doing) // 속여서 결혼시키다 cheat (a person) into marrying // 물건을 속여 팔다 sell a thing fraudulently.
2 [거짓말을 하다] lie; tell a lie; fake; falsify; misrepresent. ¶사실을 ~ misrepresent a fact // 나이를 ~ misrepresent [lie about] one's age // 그는 경력을 속였다 He misrepresented the facts of his career. / He gave a false account of [lied about] his career.
3 [가장하다] feign; pretend; dissemble. ¶이름을 ~ assume [give] a false name // 대학생이라 ~ feign [pretend to be] a university student / pass [palm] oneself off as a university student // 그는 할아버지가 돌아가셨다고 속이고 직장을 쉬었다 He stayed home from work on the false pretext that his grandfather had died.

속인(俗人) 1 (성직자에 대하여) a layman; a man of the world; (집합적) the laity. 2 (세속인·속물) a common person; a worldling; an earthling; a vulgar [materialistic] person.

속인주의(屬人主義) [법] the personal [nation-

속임수(-數) trickery; swindle; imposture; humbug; juggling; a fake; a trick; fraud; deception; a hoax. ¶~를 쓰다 cheat / deceive / swindle / take [let] (a person) in / play (a person) a (deceitful) trick / play a trick (upon) / practice an imposture (on) // ~에 넘어가다 be imposed upon / be cheated / be taken in / become a victim of a deception // ~를 …하게 하다 trick (a person) into (doing) // ~로 돈을 빼앗다 obtain money by fraud // 나는 그의 ~에 넘어가 돈을 잃었다 I fell an easy prey to his wiles and lost my money. // 이 일은 순전한 ~ 다 This work is all humbug. // 그에게는 ~가 통하지 않는다 Deception won't work on him. // 그런 ~는 내겐 안 통해 None of your tricks!

속잎 inner leaves (of a vegetable).

속자(俗字) the popular (simplified) form of a Chinese character.

속장(-張) (책의) the inside pages.

속적삼 an undershirt.

속전속결(速戰速決) blitz warfare; an intensive [all-out] surprise offensive [attack]; (독) a blitzkrieg.

● 속전속결 전법 blitz tactics.

속절없다 [가망 없다·소용없다] hopeless; futile; vain; unavailing; [불가피하다] unavoidable; inevitable; (서술적) cannot help (giving up); (it) cannot be helped. // 속절없는 세상 the vain [futile] world. 속절없이 hopelessly; helplessly; futilely; unavoidably; inevitably; [단념하여] resignedly; with resignation. ¶~ 굶다 starve helplessly // ~ 붙잡히다 be arrested [held] with no way out // 숙박할 곳이 없어 나는 ~ 노숙을 하기로 했다 Finding no lodging, I resigned myself to passing the night under the stars.

속죄(贖罪) 1 [죄를 씻음] atonement for [expiation of] one's sin(s). 속죄하다 atone [make amends] for one's sin; expiate one's sin; make amends for one's offenses [crime]. ¶과거를 ~ make amends for the past // 죽음으로써 ~ expiate a crime with death // 그는 자기가 저지른 죄에 대해 이미 충분히 속죄했다 He has made atonement in full for the wrong he did. → 그는 속죄되리라고 믿고 있었다 He believed he would be redeemed from sin. 2 [성] satisfaction; redemption. ¶그리스도의 [에 의한] ~ the (Vicarious) Atonement / the Redemption. 속죄하다 redeem; satisfy.

● 속죄론 the doctrine of atonement.

속지주의(屬地主義) the territorial principle; the principle of territorial privilege for jurisdiction.

속진(俗塵) [세상의 티끌] the world; earthly [mundane] affairs. ¶~을 피하다 [멀리하다] be free [isolated] from the hustle and bustle of ordinary [everyday] life / live secluded from the world / get away from all earthly affairs [the din and bustle of secular life] / (문어) avoid [keep aloof from] the madding crowd.

속짐작(-斟酌) a guess; a conjecture; a surmise; (in) one's estimation.

속창 an inner sole; an insole. ¶~을 깔다 lay an inner sole in one's shoes.

속출(續出) successive [frequent] occurrence. 속출하다 appear [occur] in succession [one after another]; crop up. ¶말썽거리가 속출했다 We had a crop of troubles. // 1만 미터 경주에서, 낙오자가 속출했다 In the ten-thousand meter race, runners dropped out one after another [in rapid succession]. // 지독한 더위로 병자가 속출했다 Because of the excessive heat, people fell ill one after another.

속취(俗臭) [세속의 더러운 냄새] low [vulgar] taste; vulgarity; earthiness; [범속한 기풍] worldly-mindedness.

속치레 [속을 잘 꾸민 치레] interior decoration. 속치레하다 decorate the interior.

속치마 an underskirt; a petticoat; a slip.

속칭(俗稱) a popular [familiar] name; (학명과 대조적으로) a common [vernacular] name. ¶~을 …이라 하다 be commonly called … / be popularly known as … // 그는 ~ 꼬마 존으로 알려져 있었다 He was popularly [commonly] known as Little John. 속칭하다 call (something) commonly [in common parlance]; be popularly known as ….

속탈(-頉) a stomach trouble [disorder / upset]. ¶~이 나다 get one's bowels out of order / disarrange [injure] the stomach.

속태(俗態) a vulgar [low / unrefined] appearance.

속편(續篇) a sequel (of / to); a continuation (of); (미) a follow-up; a supplementary [second] volume [film]. ¶이 소설의 ~ a sequel to [continuation of] this story.

속표지(-表紙) the title page; the front page; the title leaf.

속필(速筆) [글씨를 빨리 씀] quick writing; writing with a facile pen. ¶그 소설가는 ~이다 That novelist writes quickly.

속하다(屬-) [관계되어 딸리다] belong (to / in / among / with); appertain [pertain] (to); be among [one of] (the great cities in Korea); (분류) come [fall] under [within] (a head); (나라를) be subject to (another nation); be under the rule [sway] of (a greater nation). ¶호랑이는 고양잇과에 속한다 The tiger belongs [Tigers belong] to the cat family. // 이 꽃은 장미과에 속한다 This flower belongs to the rose family. // 고래는 물고기가 아니고 포유류에 속한다 Whales are not fish but mammals [but belong to the mammal family]. // 너는 어느 팀에 속해 있었느냐 Which team did you belong to [were you a member of]? // 그는 민주당에 속해 있다 He is affiliated with the Democratic Party. // 우리 그룹은 국제 단체에 속해 있다 Our group is affiliated with an international organization. // 이 섬은 바로 얼마 전까지 프랑스에 속해 있었다 This island was under French rule until quite recently.

속하다(速-) quick; fast; swift; speedy; rapid; prompt (민활하다). 속히 quickly; fast; swiftly; rapidly; hastily; in haste (서둘러); [기민하게] quickly; promptly. ¶~ 대답하다 answer promptly / make a prompt reply / give (a person) a prompt answer // ~ 해 (Be) Quick! / Hurry up! / (미) Make it snappy! // ~ 대답해 Answer promptly.

속히 더운 방 쉬 식는다(속담) Soon hot soon cold.

속행(速行) [빨리 감] going [walking] fast; [빨

속행 리 행함] prompt action. **속행하다** go[walk] fast[quickly]; take prompt[quick] action; carry out speedily.

속행(續行) [계속하여 행함] continuation; continuance. **속행하다** proceed (with); continue (to do / with the work); go[carry] on (with); keep on (doing); pursue; [재개하다] resume. ¶토의[회의]를 ~ continue[proceed with] debates[its session] // 경기를 ~ proceed with the game. ➔¶이 문제의 심의는 내주에 속행된다 Discussion of the question will be continued[resumed] next week.

속화(俗化) vulgarization; popularization; secularization. **속화하다** vulgarize; popularize; secularize; spoil; [속되게 변하다] be vulgarized[popularized]; become vulgar.

속회(續會) resumption (of a meeting). **속회하다** resume (a meeting).

속효(速效) an immediate effect; an instant results. ¶~가 있다 have[produce] an immediate effect (on) / give quick[immediate] relief(통증 등에).
● **속효성 비료** [농] a quick-acting fertilizer.
속효 약 a quick remedy; a quick-acting medicine.

솎다 thin[cull] (out) (plants). ¶시금치를 ~ thin out (the) spinach seedlings.

솎음 [농] thinning (out). **솎음하다** thin[cull] out.

손[1] 1 the hand. ¶오른[왼] ~ the right[left] hand // ~으로 만든 물건 a handmade article // 바로 ~이 닿는 곳에 within ready reach (of a person) / where one can reach (it) handily // 호주머니에 ~을 넣고 with one's hands in one's pockets // ~이 닿지 않는 곳에 있다 be beyond one's reach / be out of one's grasp // ~이 닿는 곳에 있다 be within one's reach[grasp] / be within one's[the reach of one's] hands // ~에 잡다[들다] take (a thing) in one's hands / ~ 건네주다 give (a thing) into another's hand / hand over (a thing to a person) / place (a thing) in (a person's) hands // ~을 잡고 걷다 walk hand in hand // 책을 ~에 들고 산책하다 take a walk, book in hand[with a book in one's hand] // ~으로 만들다 make by hand // ~으로 입을 가리다 cup one's hand to one's mouth // ~을 들고 with one's hands up / (stand) with upraised hand // ~을 모으다 fold[clasp] one's hands / ~을 모아 빌다 pray with one's hands pressed together // ~을 뻗치다 stretch (out) one's hand / reach out (to) // ~을 흔들다 wave one's hand / ~을 잡고 잡아당기다 pull (a person) by the hand // ~이 곱다 (one's hands[fingers] are) numb [stiff / benumbed] (with cold) / (서술적) have numb hands[fingers] // 추워서 ~이 곱았다 The cold benumbed our fingers. // ~이 곱아 펜을 쥘 수가 없다 My fingers are so contracted by cold that I cannot hold a pen. / 불에 ~을 쬐다 spread one's hands before the fire / warm one's hands over the fire // 그는 그녀의 ~을 잡았다 He took her hands into his. // 그녀가 ~에 갖고 있는 것은 금메달이다 What she has in her hand is a gold medal. / 아이들은 ~을 잡고 서 있었다 The children stood with their hands joined. // 그는 책을 집으려고 ~을 뻗었다 He stretched out his hand to pick up the book. / He reached for the book. // 교황은 군중을 향하여 ~을 흔들었다 The pope waved to the crowd. // 그녀는 아이의 ~을 잡고 계단을 내려가게 했다 She took the child's hand and led him down the stairs.

2 [일손·도움] a hand; a help. ¶같은 사람의 ~으로 그린 두 장의 그림 two pictures by the same hand / …의 ~을 거쳐 through (a person's) hands / through the hands of // …의 ~을 거치다 pass through (a person's) hands // 많은 사람의 ~을 거치다 pass through many hands // 세 사람의 ~이 더 필요하다 We need[want] three more hands [helpers / workers] // 이 일은 여러 사람의 ~이 필요하다 This work requires[calls for] many hands. // 이 일은 사람의 ~에 의존할 수밖에 없다 This work must be done by human hands.

3 [영향력·권한의 범위] possession; hands. ¶~에 들어오다 come into one's possession / come to[fall into] one's hands / 남의 ~에 넘어가다 fall into another's hands / pass into another's possession / 남의 ~에 넘기다 hand over (a thing) into another's hands // 서울은 적군의 ~에 넘어갔다 Seoul fell into the enemy's hands. // 격렬한 전투 끝에 도시는 그들의 ~에 넘어갔다 The city fell into their hands after a fierce struggle. // 그 그림은 마침내 그의 ~에 넘어갔다 In the end the painting passed into his possession. // 그녀의 운명은 내 ~에 달려 있다 Her fate lies in my hands. / Her life is at my disposal.

4 [수고] trouble; [돌봄] care; charge. ¶~을 덜 수 있다 (일이) save trouble / 그것으로 크게 ~을 덜 수 있다 That saves much trouble.

5 [수완·꾀] a trick; an artifice; a trap; a snare; an art. ¶…의 ~에 걸려 죽다 die[fall] by (a person's) hand(s) / meet one's death at the hands of … // ~에 암살자의 ~에 죽다 He died at the hands of[He was killed by] an assassin.

손(이) 가다 take (much) trouble; require (much) work; take (a lot of) care; be troublesome. ¶손이 많이 가는 일 laborious [troublesome] work / a piece of work requiring great care // 이 일은 손이 많이 간다 This is painstaking work.

손(이) 거칠다 light-fingered; sticky-fingered [-handed]; thievish; (서술적) have light [sticky] fingers. ¶손이 거친 사람 a kleptomaniac / a thievish person // 그 아이는 ~ The boy has sticky fingers[thievish habits / taking ways / straying hands].

손(을) 끊다 sever (one's) connection with; cease to deal with; break with; break away from; cut oneself free of. ¶그 사람과 일절 손을 끊어 버렸다 I have broken off all relations with him. // 그는 그 여자와 손을 끊었다 He cut (off) all ties with the woman. / He broke with the woman. // 그는 의견이 맞지 않아 동료와 손을 끊었다 He broke with his partner because they had differing opinions [because they didn't agree]. // 그는 그 일과는 완전히 손을 끊었다 He washed his hands of the whole business. // 나는 그 일에서 손을 끊었습니다 I don't have anything to do with that job any more. / I'm no longer connected with that job. // 그런 일에서는 오래전에 손을 끊었다 I got out of that sort of thing long

ago.∥그의 파트너는 이 거래에서 손을 끊고 싶어 한다 His partner wants to back out of [withdraw from] the deal.
손(을) 넘기다 1 [잘못 세다] skip [omit] numbers in counting; miscount; miscalculate; count wrong. 2 [때를 놓치다] miss [lose] an opportunity; let a chance slip [go].
손(이) 달리다 [모자라다 / 부족하다] be short-handed; be short of hands; be undermanned. ¶손이 모자라서 [달려서 / 부족해서] 어려움을 겪고 있다 We are having a hard time because we are short-handed.
손(을) 떼다 [관계를 끊다] get (something) off one's hands; wash one's hands of; sever connection with; withdraw oneself (from …); break with (a person); break away from; back out; [끝내다] finish; bring to a close [an end]; get [be] through (with); put an end (to). ¶이제 와서 손 뗄 수는 없다 It is too late now to get out of it.∥손을 뗀 지 오래지만 장기라면 누구에게도 지지 않는다 Though I'm long out of practice, I don't think anyone can beat me at *janggi*[chess].∥손을 뗀 지가 오래지만 어디 한번 해보자 I'm out of practice, but I will try (to do it).
손(이) 맑다 1 [생기는 것이 없다] poor; (서술적) be inept at moneymaking. 2 [인색하다] stingy; miserly.
손(을) 붙이다 begin; start; set one's hand (to); set about (to).
손(을) 비다 have no work on hand; be disengaged; be free; be at leisure. ¶지금, 손이 비어 있다 I have no work [I have nothing to do / I'm not busy] right now.∥나는 그가 손이 빌 때까지 기다리기로 했다 I decided to wait till he was free [he finished his work].∥나는 지금 손이 비지 않는다 I'm busy just now. / (미) My hands are full.
손(을) 빌리다 ask for help; call in the aid of. ¶손을 빌리지 않고 without another's help / unaided / single-handed∥우리는 너무 바빠서 누구든지 간에 손을 빌려야겠다 We are so busy we'll take any help we can get.∥그는 경찰청에 있는 유력 인사의 손을 빌려 이 사건을 뭉개 버리려고 했다 He tried to hush up the case by asking for the help of some influential man at police headquarters.
손(을) 뻗치다 concern oneself in [with] (a matter). ¶그 회사는 유럽 쪽에 손을 뻗치려고 한다 The firm is going to extend its relations in Europe.∥그는 식당 경영에까지 손을 뻗치고 있다 He has branched out even to the point of operating a restaurant.
손(이) 서투르다 unskillful; clumsy; bungling; (서술적) be a poor hand (at); be clumsy with one's hands; be all thumbs; have two left hands.
손에 걸리다 fall into (another's) hand; fall into a trap [snare] of.
손에 넣다 get; obtain; come by; get [come] at; secure; win; take [get / gain] possession of. ¶새로운 정보를 손에 넣었다 I am in possession of new information.∥그는 염원하던 캐딜락을 마침내 손에 넣었다 He finally got a Cadillac after wanting one for a long time.
손에 땀을 쥐다 ¶손에 땀을 쥐고 with suppressed excitement / in breathless suspense / with breathless interest∥손에 땀을 쥐게 하는 경주 a breath-taking [very exciting] race∥손에 땀을 쥐고 곡예를 지켜보았다 We watched the acrobatic feats breathlessly.
손에 잡히다 ¶일이 손에 잡히지 않다 cannot go about [settle to] one's work / be in no mood for work∥나는 아버지 일이 걱정되어 일이 손에 잡히지 않는다 I am so worried about my father that I cannot get (down) to work.∥나는 너무 기뻐서 일이 손에 잡히지 않는다 I am too happy to settle down to [concentrate on] my work.
손을 놓다 loose [let go] one's hold (on / of); release one's hands (together).
손을 늦추다 relax one's hands [grasp].
손(에) 익다 be [get] accustomed to; be familiar with; be skilled [skilled] (in); be (quite) at home (on / in); be a good [skilled / practiced] hand (at). ¶손에 익은 일 an accustomed work.
손(이) 잠기다 have one's hands full; have one's time fully engaged; be pressed with business; be busy; be engaged. ¶일에 손이 잠겨서 나갈 수 없다 I have my hands too full to go out.
손(이) 크다 1 [씀씀이가 후하고 크다] freehanded; open-handed; generous; liberal; unsparing. ¶손이 큰 사람 an open-handed [a generous] person / a liberal [bountiful / generous] giver. 2 [수단이 좋다] resourceful.
손(을) 타다 [도둑맞다] have (one's rice) stolen little by little.
손[2] a caller; a guest; a customer. ⇨**손님**
손(을) 치르다 entertain one's guests; give a party; play host (to).
손[3] [돌아다니면서 사람의 활동을 방해하는 귀신] a wandering evil spirit.
손[4] [양보]. ¶~ 치더라도 if / even if [though] / though / although / granting [supposing] that / no matter (how / when / which / what / where)∥그는 그 돈을 전부는 아니었다~ 치더라도 반 이상이나 써 버렸다 He has spent more than half the money, if not all.
손(孫) a descendant. ⇨**후손**(後孫)
손가락 a finger. ¶엄지~ the thumb∥집게 [둘째] ~ the forefinger / the index [first] finger∥가운뎃~ the middle [long / second] finger∥넷째 [약] ~ the third [medical] finger∥새끼~ the little finger∥다섯 ~ the five fingers / the thumb and fingers∥~ 자국 a (dirty) finger mark [print] / a thumb mark∥~에 끼다 place [put] (a ring) on a finger∥~으로 세다 count (off) … on one's fingers∥~으로 집어먹다 eat with the fingers∥~을 딱딱 꺾다 crack one's finger joints [knuckles]∥(아이가) ~을 입에 물다 take [put] a finger in one's mouth∥…을 ~을 꼽으며 세다 count [number] … on one's fingers∥열 ~으로도 모자라다 be less than ten∥다섯 ~으로 셀 정도밖에 안 되다 be less than five∥소년이 ~을 입에 물고 있었다 The boy had a finger in his mouth.∥그녀는 다섯 ~을 능숙하게 사용하여 베를 짰다 She wove a piece of cloth using her thumb and fingers [her five fingers] deftly.∥그런 사람은 열 ~으로 셀 수 있을 정도다 Such men may be counted on the fingers.∥그는 금년도 최고 납세자로서 다섯 ~ 안에 들었다 He was listed among the top five taxpayers this year.
손가락 하나 까딱 않다 do not lift a finger; be laziness itself. ¶그는 게을러빠져서 손가락 하나 까딱하지 않는다 He is too lazy to do any-

손가락질하다

thing. / He will not exert himself in any way. / He is the sort of person who never lifts a finger to help.
- **손가락 마디** a finger joint; knuckle. **손가락 사이즈** ring size. ¶~가 어떻게 됩니까 What's the ring size? **손가락표**(-標) an index (mark); [인] a fist.

손가락질하다 1 [가리키다] point (to/at); point (with) the finger (to/at); indicate (the door). ¶손가락질하는 것은 실례이다 It is impolite to point. 2 [흉보다] point at (a person); talk about (a person) with scorn [in contempt]. →¶손가락질받다 be scorned by (persons) / be pointed at [talked about] with scorn / be talked of in contempt / be an object of social contempt // 나는 남에게 손가락질받을 만한 일은 절대로 하지 않겠다 I will never do anything which will bring contempt upon me.

손가방 a portfolio (pl. ~s); a briefcase; a brief bag; a valise; (여자용) a handbag; a vanity case[bag].

손거스러미 an agnail; a hangnail. ¶~가 생기다 have a hangnail.

손거울 a hand glass[mirror]. ¶그녀는 ~에 자신을 비춰 보았다 She looked at herself in a hand mirror.

손결 the texture[skin] of the[one's] hand. ¶비단같이 고운 ~ a hand's skin of velvety texture / 그녀는 ~이 곱다 Her hands are of fine[delicate] texture.

손궤(-櫃) a (portable) case[box]; a casket.

손금 the lines of the palm. ¶~이 좋다[나쁘다] have lucky[unlucky / ominous] lines in one's hand.
  손금(을) 보다 read (in) (a person's) palm [hand]; tell fortune by the lines of the hand. ¶내 손금 좀 봐 주시오 Read my palm, please.
- **손금쟁이** a palm reader; a palmist.

손금(損金) a loss of money; a pecuniary loss; (the amount of) one's financial loss.

손길 1 [내밀어 뻗는 손] one's reach; arm('s) reach. ¶~이 닿는 곳에 within one's reach [hands]. 2 [보살펴 매만지는 손] a (healing) hand. ¶따뜻한 구호의 ~을 뻗다 extend a warm helping hand (to a person).

손꼽다 [손가락을 꼽아 수를 세다] count (the days) on one's fingers; [두드러지게 뛰어나다] stand[tower] high above the others; distinguish oneself; come out on top (of). ¶손꼽는 leading / principal / prominent / outstanding // 손꼽는 학자 a leading[a distinguished / an eminent] scholar // …을 손꼽아 기다리다 look forward to … / wait eagerly for … // 그런 사람은 손꼽을 정도밖에 없다 Such people can be counted on your fingers. // 그녀는 생일을 손꼽아 기다리고 있었다 She was eagerly waiting for her birthday. // 아버지가 돌아오시는 날을 손꼽아 기다렸다 We waited for our father's return counting the days (on our fingers).

손끝 1 [손가락 끝] the tip of a finger; fingertip(s); a finger end. ¶~을 다치다 be injured in the fingertip / have one's fingertip wounded // ~이 닳도록 일하다 work oneself [one's fingers] to the bone / toil and moil // 나는 ~을 다쳤다 I was hurt on the fingertip. 2 [일솜씨] manual dexterity. ¶나는 천성적으로 ~이 무디다 I was born clumsy. 3 finger-

print. ⇨ 손때

손끝(이) 맵다 1 [손질한 결과가 좋지 않다] have an evil-working[a contaminating] touch; have an evil hand; foul up (everything) one touches; spoil (everything) one comes in touch with. ¶그는 모든 일에 ~ He fouls up everything he touches. / He spoils everything he comes in touch with. 2 [야무지다] be dexterous[deft].

손끝(을) 맺다 remain idle; look on with folded arms[with one's hands in one's pockets]; stand by one's arms folded. ¶지금은 손끝을 맺고 있을 때가 아니다 This is no time for us to remain idle.

손끝(이) 여물다 be deft-fingered; be clever at handicraft; be dexterous[deft]. ¶그는 ~ He is dexterous[nimble-fingered / skillful with his fingers].

손녀(딸)(孫女-) a granddaughter.

손님 1 [방문객] a caller; a visitor; (구어) company (단수·복수 동형). ¶~을 맞다[만나다] receive[see] a visitor[caller] / receive company // ~이 있다 have a caller[visitor] // 고향에서 ~이 오다 have a visitor from one's home // ~을 반갑이 맞다 welcome a visitor / 지금 ~이 와 계십니다. 좀 기다려 주시겠습니까 We have a visitor[company] just now. Would you mind waiting for a while? // 오늘 저녁 식사에 ~이 오신다 There's company for dinner tonight.
2 [초대되어 온 사람] a guest; [체류객] a sojourner; (호텔의) a guest; (하숙의) a boarder; (아파트의) a lodger. ¶~을 초대하다 invite a guest // 다과회에 ~을 초대하다 invite company to tea // ~을 대접하다 entertain a guest // 점심에 ~이 다섯 분 오실 예정이다 We expect to have five guests for lunch. // 당신이나 부인이나 ~ 접대가 기막히군요 You and your wife are very good hosts[entertain guests very well].
3 [고객] a customer; a patron; (집합적) custom; (집합적) trade. ¶극장의 ~ (집합적) an audience // 처음 온 ~ a first-time buyer // 구경만 하고 사지 않는 ~ a window-shopper / a customer who comes in just to look[browse] (▶ browse는 주로 책방, 레코드 가게 등에서 보고 사지 않음) // ~에게 시중들다 wait[attend] on a customer // ~을 끌다 attract customers / draw custom / (유객꾼이) tout / solicit (customers) // ~이 많다 have a large custom / ~이 적다 have but small custom / attract few customers // ~이 없다 have no custom // ~이 줄다 lose customers / be less patronized than before // ~ 접대가 좋다[나쁘다] be hospitable[inhospitable] / (가게 등에서) give good[bad] service // 저 가게는 ~이 많다 That store has many customers. / The shop enjoys a large patronage. // 저 레스토랑은 ~이 많다[적다] That restaurant is well[poorly] patronized. // 그 가게에서는 경품을 주어 ~을 끌려고 한다 That shop is trying to attract customers by giving out presents. // 그 가게는 마침내 단골 ~이 생기기 시작했다 The shop finally began to acquire regular customers. // 오늘은 ~이 적다 (극장에서) There is only a small audience today. / (가게 등에서) There are only a few customers today. // ~!(여자에게) Madam! / (남자에게) Sir!

손대다 1 [건드리다] touch. ¶절대로 손대지 못하게 하다 keep a thing absolutely intact.// 이 돈에는 손대고 싶지 않다 I want to leave this money untouched[to keep this money intact].// 손대지 마시오 (게시) Hands Off. / Please Don't Touch.
2 〔착수하다〕 turn[put / set] one's hand to (a task); set about (work); set to (work); get started (on a literary work); 〔…에 관계하다〕 concern oneself with; have a finger[a hand / an oar] in; 〔여성과 관계하다〕 become intimate with (a girl); have carnal connection with. ¶사업에 ~ start[embark in] a business[an enterprise]// 정치에 ~ meddle in politics// 투기에 ~ take to[dabble in] speculation// 그는 협회의 개혁에 손댔다 He started out to reform the society.// 그는 증권에 손댔다가 파산했다 He dabbled in stocks and went bankrupt.// 그가 첫 작품에 손댄 것은 23세 때였다 He started to write his first book at the age of 23.// 그녀는 그림에 싫증이 나서 도예에 손댔다 As she was tired of painting, she took up ceramics.
3 〔때리다〕 beat; strike; knock; hit; give[deal / deliver] (a person) a blow. ¶어떤 일이 있어도 아이들에게 손대서는 안 된다 You must not strike[raise your hand against] your children in any circumstances.
4 〔착복하다〕 pocket; embezzle. ¶공금에 ~ embezzle public funds// 그녀는 가게의 돈에 손댔다가 해고되었다 She pocketed the store's money and was fired.
5 〔수정하다〕 correct.
6 〔처리하다〕. ¶손댈 수 없다 〔할 바를 모르겠다〕 be at a loss what to do with / 〔손쓸 수가 없다〕 be in a deadlock / be uncontrollable // 이 일은 어디서부터 손대야 좋을지 모르겠다 I am at a loss where to start on this work.

손대중 measuring[weighing] by hand; hefting. ¶~으로 by hand measure// ~으로 재다 measure by hand / heft (something). 손대중하다 measure[weigh] by hand. ¶그는 정확히 손대중했다 He measured by hand fairly accurately.

손도끼 a hand ax(e); a hatchet; an adz(e).

손도장 (-圖章) a thumbmark. ⇨ *지장(指章)

손독 (毒) a hand-borne infection; hand poisoning. ¶~이 오르다 be infected by touching with one's hands// 상처를 만지지 마라, 그러면 손독이 오른다 Don't touch the wound, or it will be infected.

손동작 (-動作) hand movement(s); manual activity.

손들다 1 〔손을 들다〕 raise[lift] a[one's] hand; hold up one's hands; (때리려고) lift one's hand against (a person); (찬성하여) show one's hand. ¶손들어 (항복 또는 찬성의 표시로) Hands up! / (강도가) Stick'em [Hold'em] up!// 답을 아는 사람 손들어 Raise your hand if you know the answer.
2 〔지다〕 be defeated; throw up one's hands (in despair); 〔포기하다〕 give up. ¶완전히 ~ be beaten hollow// 심한 중노동에 그는 손들고 말았다 The work was so hard that he gave up[had to give up].// 네게는 손들었다 I give in. / You win!// 손들었다고 말하기 전에는 놓아주지 않겠다 〔구어〕 I won't let go (of you) until you say surrender[say uncle]!(▶ say uncle은 (미))// 이 문제에는 손들었다 This problem is too much for me. I give up. / This question is beyond me. / 〔구어〕 This is a hard nut to crack.// 나는 저 아이의 장난에 손들었다 I've had enough of that boy's tricks [pranks]!

손등 the back of the hand.

손때 fingerprint; finger marks; dirt from the hands. ¶~가 묻은 책 a book soiled by handling[use] / ~가 묻다 be well-thumbed // 흰 옷에 손때를 묻히다 soil a white dress[make a white dress dirty] by touching it// 피아노에 ~를 묻히지 마라 Don't get any fingerprints on the piano.

손료 (損料) hire; (a) rent. ¶~를 물다 pay for the hire (of)/ ~를 받고 빌려 주다 let out (a thing) on hire / rent[hire] out / take rent for.

손목 a wrist; 〔의〕 a carpus (pl. -pi). ¶그는 그녀의 ~을 잡았다 He seized her by the wrist.
● **손목시계** a wristwatch.

손바느질 needlework; sewing by hand. **손바느질하다** do needlework; sew by hand.

손바닥 the palm[flat] of the hand; the palm; the hollow of the hand. ¶~만 한 땅 a tiny plot / a tiny of land// 그녀는 ~으로 그의 뺨을 때렸다 She slapped his face[slapped him on the face].// 아버지는 아이의 엉덩이를 ~으로 때렸다 The father gave his child a spanking. / The father smacked his child on the bottom. / 그녀는 꽃잎을 ~에 올려놓았다 She laid a petal on the palm of her hand.

손바닥(을) 뒤집듯 하다 change like a weather-cock. ¶그의 태도는 손바닥 뒤집듯 했다 His attitude changed quite abruptly.

손발 〔손과 발〕 hands and feet; hand and foot; limbs. ¶그는 ~이 부자유스럽다 He has trouble using his limbs[hands and feet]. / 〔전혀 못 쓴다〕 He has lost the use of his limbs. // 나는 도둑에게 ~이 묶였다 I was bound hand and foot by the robber.

손발(이) 맞다 ¶파업자들은 손발이 맞지 않았다 There was lack of unity among the strikers.

손버릇 〔손에 익은 버릇〕 any habitual action of the hands; 〔도벽〕 a habit of stealing. ¶그는 ~이 나쁘다 He is light-fingered. / He is a compulsive thief.

손보기 1 repair(s); care; correction. ⇨ 손질 2 〔매음〕 prostitution; harlotry.

손보다 1 〔돌보다〕 care for; take care of; 〔수리하다〕 repair (a house); service (a car); mend; (원고 등) correct; touch up. ¶집을 좀 손봐야겠다 My house wants[needs] repairing. 2 〔혼내 주다〕 treat (a person) cruelly; give (a person) a hard time. ¶그 녀석 좀 손봐야겠다 I'll give him a hard time.

손부 (孫婦) the wife of one's grandson.

손부끄럽다 troubled; embarrassed. ¶돈을 꾸어 주지 않아서 손부끄러웠다 I am embarrassed by his refusal of my request for a loan.

손뼉 the flat of the hand. ¶~을 쳐서 하녀를 부르다 clap hands for a maid// 구경꾼들은 ~을 쳤다 The spectators clapped their hands.

손상 (損傷) damage; (an) injury. ¶신체 내부의 ~ an internal injury// 전쟁으로 그의 신경이 심한 ~을 입었다 His nerves were left in shreds[were shattered] by the war. // 이 나무는 차량의 배기가스로 ~을 입고 있다 This tree has been harmed by car exhaust fumes. / This tree is suffering from the effects of car exhaust fumes. **손상하다**

damage; injure; impair; hurt; [법] damnify. ¶나라의 명예를 손상시키다 stain [besmirch] national honor // 그는 가명(家名)을 손상시켰다 He brought disgrace on his family (name). // 그러한 행위는 그룹의 조화 정신을 손상시킨다 Such conduct will mar the spirit of harmony of the group. // 그의 명예가 손상되었다 His honor was stained [besmirched]. // 절은 폭풍우에 손상되어 옛 모습을 찾아볼 수 없었다 The temple was heavily damaged by the storm.

손색(遜色) inferiority. ¶이것은 전문가의 작품으로서 ~이 없다 This work would do credit to a professional. // 이것은 타사 제품에 비해 조금도 ~이 없다 These can easily stand comparison with [are in no way inferior to] the products of other companies. // 학력에 있어서 나는 그에 ~이 없다 I can hold my own with him academically.

손수 with [by] one's (own) hand(s); [몸소] in person; personally; (do it) oneself. ¶~ 만든 of one's own making / homemade // 황태자가 ~ 나무를 심었다 The crown prince planted the tree with his own hands. // 공주는 그에게 ~ 선물을 건네주었다 The princess handed him the present in person.

손수건(-手巾) a handkerchief (pl. ~s).

손수레 a handcart; (영) a handbarrow; [일륜차] a wheelbarrow. ¶~로 나르다 convey [carry] (something) in a handcart / wheelbarrow.

손쉽다 easy; simple; light. ¶손쉬운 방법 the easy way // 돈을 손쉽게 벌다 make an easy gain // 손쉽게 이기다 win easily / win hands down // 그런 것은 손쉽게 할 수 있다 I can do it quite easily [without any difficulty]. // 이것은 손쉬운 일이다 This is an easy job. // 그것은 손쉬운 일이다 That's quite easy [no trouble at all / nothing].

손실(損失) a loss. ¶인명 ~ casualties // 금전의 ~ a financial loss // 화재 [전쟁]로 인한 ~ fire [war] loss(es) / losses due to fire [war] // 크나큰 ~ a great [heavy / serious / severe] loss // ~을 거듭하다 incur loss upon [after] loss // 그의 죽음은 국가적으로 돌이킬 수 없는 ~이었다 His death meant an irreparable loss to the nation. / The nation suffered an irreparable loss in his death.

손심부름 a petty errand.

손쓰다 take measures; adopt [resort to] a measure; take a course; take action. ¶미리 ~ take preventive measures (against) // 달리 ~ try some other means // (어떻게) 손써 볼 수가 없다 be in a deadlock / be at one's wit's [wits] end // 위험을 피하려면 뭔가 손써야 한다 We must do something to avert the danger.

손아귀 the space between the thumb and the fingers; the (power of one's) grip; [수중] (in) the hands. ¶그들은 우두머리의 ~에 쥐어 있었다 They were under the thumb of their boss. // 나는 그 수위를 완전히 ~에 넣었다 I got that porter under my thumb.

손아래 juniority. ¶~의 younger / junior / subordinate // 다섯 살 ~인 동생 a brother five years one's junior.

● **손아랫사람** [지위가 낮은 사람] one's inferior(s); one's subordinate(s); [나이가 아래인 사람] one's junior(s).

손어림 measuring [weighing] (roughly) by (the) hand; hand measure. **손어림하다** measure [weigh] roughly by (the) hand; make a rough [rude] estimate by (the) hand.

손위 seniority. ¶~의 elder / elder(ly) / senior / superior // 그는 나보다 다섯 살 ~다 He is my senior [older than I] by five years.

● **손윗사람** one's elder; one's senior; one's superiors.

손익(損益) profit and loss; loss and gain; [이익과 불이익] advantages and disadvantages; pluses and minuses. ¶~ 없음 The profit and loss are on a par.

● **손익 계산서** a statement of profits and losses.

손일 handwork; handicraft; manual labor [work].

손자(孫子) a grandson.

손잡다 1 [손을 붙잡다] take (a person) by the hand; grasp another's hand; [악수하다] shake hands; clasp hands (with). ¶손잡고 걸어가다 walk hand in hand.
2 [화해하다] make peace (with); [제휴·합작하다] join [clasp] hands (with); cooperate (with); join together; tie up (with); go hand in hand (with); [동맹하다] combine (with); join forces (with). ¶그들은 선거 운동에서 손잡았다 They joined forces in the election campaign. // 두 나라는 서로 손잡았다 The two countries made peace with each other. // 우리는 그들과 손잡고 이 난국에 대처할 필요가 있다 We must cooperate with them to get through this difficult situation.

손잡이 a handle; a grip; [문 등의] a doorknob; [찻잔 등의] a ear. ¶~가 한쪽에만 있는 냄비 a pan with a handle / (깊은 것) a saucepan / a pot with a handle // 국자의 ~가 부러졌다 [떨어졌다] The handle of the ladle has broken [come off].

손장난하다 finger (a button); fumble [fiddle / fidget] with (a key); [가지고 놀다] play [toy] with (fire); trifle with (papers). ¶만년필을 가지고 ~ toy with a fountain pen.

손장단 beating time with the hand. ¶~을 치다 beat time with the hand / keep time (to the music) with hand-clapping.

손재간(-才幹) hand skill. ⇨ *손재주

손재주 hand skill; dexterity [deftness] of hand; manual dexterity [adroitness]. ¶~가 좋은 handy // ~가 있다 be smart [clever] with one's hand // 그는 ~가 좋아서 의자 같은 것은 재깍 만들어 낸다 He's good with his hands and can make chairs and things like that in a jiffy. // 그녀는 ~가 있다 She is a dexterous person. / She is quick and clever [skillful] with her fingers.

손전등(-電燈) an electric torch; (미) a flashlight; a flashlamp.

손주 → 손자(孫子)

손질 1 [수리·수선] repair(s); mending; remodeling. **손질하다** repair (a house); make repairs; mend (shoes); remodel. ¶손질하고 있다 be under repairs // 이 집은 들어가 살기 전에 손질할 필요가 있다 The house needs to be repaired before it can be lived in.
2 [매만짐·보살핌] care; pruning; trimming. (나무·뜰·머리 등) ¶~이 잘된 정원 (구석구석까지 손질이 미친) a well-kept garden / a garden that is well cared for / (공들여 설계한) an elaborately laid-out garden.

손질하다 care for; take care of; tend; trim (a tree); groom (a horse). ¶막 정원수를 손질하였다 The trees in the garden have just been trimmed. ➜¶집이 참 살 손질되어 있군요 Your house is really well taken care of.
3 [정정] correction; retouch. 손질하다 correct; touch up. ¶선생님이 손질한 작문은 composition improved by a teacher // 이들 규정은 현상에 맞도록 손질할 필요가 있다 These regulations need to be revamped to cope with the (changed) conditions of today. // 현행 세제는 손질할 필요가 있다 The current taxation system needs to be rectified [corrected]. // 편집자는 이 회상록을 많이 손질했다 The editor has made many changes in these memoirs. // 내가 쓴 글을 손질하는 데 온 하루가 걸렸다 I spent a whole day trying to improve what I had written. // 이 그림은 누군가 다른 사람이 손질한 것 같다 This picture seems to have been retouched by somebody else. ➜¶그 번역은 여러 번 손질되었다 That translation was reworked a number of times. // 이 보도는 당국에 의해 손질되었다 This report has been doctored by the authorities.
4 a blow. ⇨~손찌검.
손짓 a gesture; (문어) (a) gesticulation; signs; a hand signal. ¶~으로 이야기하다 talk by signs[gestures] / talk in sign language // 그는 ~으로 자기가 말하고 싶은 바를 이해시켰다 He made himself understood by gestures. // 그들과 ~으로 간신히 의사가 통했다 I managed to communicate with them by gesture. **손짓하다** gesture; gesticulate; make gestures; motion (for a person to do); give a hand signal. ¶남을 손짓하여 부르다 beckon to a person // 남을 손짓해 불러들이다 beckon a person in // 그는 나에게 뒤를 따르라고 손짓했다 He beckoned (to) me to follow him.
손찌검 a blow; beating; striking; hitting. **손찌검하다** beat; strike; knock; hit; slap; give [deal / deliver] (a person) a blow.
손톱 a nail; a fingernail. ¶엄지~ a thumbnail // ~을 기르다 let one's nails grow long // ~은 깎아야겠다 Your nails need cutting [trimming / clipping]. // ~에 때가 끼었습니다 You have dirt under your fingernails. / You have dirty nails. // 나는 미장원에서 ~을 손질했다 I got a manicure at the beauty parlor. // 그녀는 친절한 마음이라고는 ~만큼도 없다 She doesn't have even a scrap of kindness in her. // 나는 네가 아버지의 미덕을 ~만큼이라도 본받기를 바란다 You should try to be like [문어] emulate) your father. / I wish you had even a thousandth of your father's virtues. ●**손톱깎이** nail clippers; (a pair of) nail scissors. **손톱자국** a nail mark. ¶~을 내다 mark with one's nails.
손틀 [손기계] a hand[-operated / -worked] machine; [손재봉틀] a hand sewing machine.
손풍금 (-風琴) an accordion.
손해 (損害) [손상] damage; (an) injury; harm; [손실] a loss. ¶~와 이득 losses and gains // 물적 ~ property damage // ~ 보는 거래 a bad bargain // 폭격[홍수]에 의한 ~ damage from [caused by] bombing [a flood] // 2천만 원의 ~ twenty million won worth of damage // ~를 보다 lose / suffer a loss // 큰 ~를 보다 suffer heavy [serious / extensive] damage / be heavily [seriously] damaged // ~를 입히다 damage / cause damage (to property) // 1만 원 ~ 보다 suffer a loss [deficit] of ten thousand won // 1만 원 ~ 보고 팔다 sell at a loss of ten thousand won // ~를 변상하다 make good the damage / cover (up) a loss // 그로 인해 약 5,000만 원의 ~가 났다 It caused damage to the extent of[amounting to] some fifty million won. // 태풍으로 벼농사에 큰 ~가 났다 The typhoon devastated the rice crop. // 우리는 이번 태풍으로 큰 ~를 보았다 We suffered great damage because of this typhoon. // 「싫다」는 말을 못하는 사람은 결국 ~ 보기 쉬운 성격이다 People who can't say no tend to come out on the losing end. // 그것 때문에 ~ 보는 일은 없을 것이다 You won't be the loser by it. / You will lose nothing by it. / You won't come out any the worse for it.
●**손해 배상** (a) compensation for damages [a loss]; reparation for injury; indemnity (for damage done). ¶~을 요구하다 claim damages // ~은 꼭 하겠습니다 I will be sure [promise] to compensate you for the loss.
손해 보험 insurance against loss; indemnity [nonlife] insurance; (재산 손해 보험) property insurance. ¶~에 들다 insure one's property against damage.
솔¹ [식] a pine (tree). ⇨소나무.
솔² [브러시] a brush. ¶옷[구둣] ~ a clothes [shoe] brush // ~로 털다 brush (a hat) / brush away [off] (dust).
솔³ a seam. ⇨솔기.
솔⁴ [음] (음계의) sol; so; G.
솔가리 fallen pine needles; pine straw. ¶~를 긁다 rake up fallen pine needles.
솔가지 pine twigs (for fuel).
솔개 [동] a (black) kite.
솔기 a seam; a stitch. ¶바지의 ~가 터졌다 The seam of your trousers has come undone [come apart].
솔깃하다 welcome; encouraging; inviting; (서술적) be interested (in); be enthusiastic (about). ¶귀가 솔깃해지는 조건 a tempting offer / inviting terms // 그의 이야기에 나는 귀가 솔깃해졌다 I was drawn into his story.
솔나방 [동] an egger; an eggar.
솔다¹ [긁으면 아프고 그냥 두면 가렵다] itchy and sore; irritating; [공간이 좁다] narrow; cramped; small; tight; skimpy. ¶이 옷은 품이 ~ This coat is tight under the arm.
솔다² [귀가 아프다] get[be] sick of hearing; hear more than enough of; have sore ears. ¶마누라의 바가지가 귀에 솔았다 My ears have stayed sore from hearing my wife's nagging complaints. 2 [단단히 굳다] dry up; tighten up[contract] with dryness. 3 [물결이] foam; surge.
솔로 a solo (pl. ~s, -li). ¶바이올린 ~ a violin solo // 피아노 ~ a piano solo // ~로 노래하다 sing (a) solo / give a vocal solo.
솔방울 a pine cone; a cone.
솔밭 a pine grove; a pinery.
솔부엉이 [동] a brown hawk-owl.
솔선수범하다 (率先垂範-) take the initiative and set an example (for others). ¶네가 솔선 수범해야 한다 You should first [take the initiative and] set an example for [(영) to] the others.

솔선하다(率先-) take the lead[initiative]; take up the running. ¶솔선해서 on one's own initiative∥솔선해서 …하다 be the first to (do) / take the lead[initiative] in (doing) / set an example (of abstinence to others) / act as a pioneer in (doing)∥그는 무엇이든지 솔선하여 한다 He takes the initiative in everything.∥그는 솔선해서 규칙을 지켰다 He took the lead in observing the rule. / He was the first to follow the rule.

솔솔 soft-flowing; lightly; fluently. ⇨술술

솔숲 a pine wood; a pinery.

솔잎 a pine needle.

솔직하다(率直-) straightforward; frank; candid; plain; honest; straight; open; outspoken.(▶ frank는 기탄없는, candid는 정직하게 있는 그대로의, open은 숨김이 없는, straightforward는 에두르거나 모호함이 없음을 뜻함) ¶솔직한 사람 a frank[a straight forward / an honest] person∥독자의 솔직한 소리를 듣고 싶다 I want to hear the readers' candid opinions.∥그는 태도가 솔직한 사람이다 His manner is frank and open. / He is straightforward in manner.∥내 솔직한 기분을 알고 싶다 I'd like to know your true feelings.∥솔직한 비평을 해 주시기 바랍니다 Please let me hear your frank criticism. **솔직히** straightforwardly; frankly; candidly; plainly; honestly; open-heartedly. ¶~ 말하면 frankly speaking / to be frank[plain] with you / to be perfectly honest∥~ 말해 주십시오 Please speak out freely[without reserve]. / Please state your views candidly. / Give me your candid opinion.∥~ 말하면 그것은 대단한 문제는 아니다 Frankly speaking, it doesn't matter much.∥~ 말해서 더 이상 그것을 하고 싶지 않다 To tell the truth, I don't want to do it any more.∥~ 말해서 그 때는 쥐구멍을 찾고 싶었다 I confess that [Honestly] at that time I felt like crawling under the rug.∥~ 말하면 네가 나빠 To be frank (with you)[Frankly speaking], you are wrong.∥~ 말하면 네 주장은 전혀 설득력이 없다 To put it bluntly[Frankly speaking], your argument is not at all convincing.∥~ 말하자면 네가 먼저 그에게 사과해야 한다고 생각해 I'll be quite candid with you. I think you should first of all apologize to him.∥~ 이야기합시다 Let's talk frankly. / Let's be honest with each other.∥그는 ~ 자기 잘못을 인정했다 He frankly admitted his mistake.∥그는 내 논문을 ~ 비평했다 He was outspoken in his criticism of my thesis.

솔질 brushing. **솔질하다** brush (a hat); give a brush (to a hat). ¶옷을 ~ give one's clothes a brushing.

솔트 SALT(▶ Strategic Arms Limitation Talk의 약어).

솜 cotton (wool). ¶이불[옷]에 넣는 ~ cotton wool / batting / wadding / padding∥탄 ~ whipped cotton (wool)∥귀를 ~으로 틀어막다 stop one's ears with cotton / plug one's ears with wads of cotton∥~을 타다 whip [willow] cotton∥이불에 ~을 두다 pad bedclothes with cotton.

솜뭉치 a wad of cotton.

솜버선 cotton-padded socks.

솜사탕(-砂糖) spun sugar; candy fluff [floss]; cotton candy.

솜씨 a way of moving[using] one's hands; [교묘함] skill; dexterity; deftness; knack; [만듦새] performance; make; hand; workmanship; [수완] ability; capacity; (교제의) tact. ¶훌륭한 ~ (기술 면에서) excellent skill / (만듦새 면에서) fine workmanship / (경기에서) (a) fine[good / nice] play∥~ 있는[좋은] skillful[(영) skilful] / fine∥훌륭한 ~로 만든 찻잔 a teacup of good[excellent] workmanship∥훌륭한 ~로 만든 화초대(臺) a flower stand of fine workmanship∥골퍼의 ~ 있는 플레이 the golfer's brilliant[fine] shot∥익숙한 ~로 with a practiced hand∥~를 보이다 show[display] one's skill∥~를 자랑하다 one's skill with (a person)∥~를 자랑하다 plume oneself on one's skill (at)∥훌륭한 ~를 보여 주다 (기술적으로) exhibit one's skill / (만듦새에서) exhibit fine workmanship / (경기에서) show[(구어) pull off] a fine[an excellent] play / (연기에서) give a fine performance∥회사 경영에 ~를 발휘하다 show one's ability[talent] to work in the management of a company∥요리 ~를 발휘하다 show[demonstrate] one's cooking skills∥그녀의 ~ 있는 처리에 우리 모두가 탄복했다 We admired her efficient[adept] handling of the matter.∥경관들은 군중들을 ~ 있게 통제했다 The policemen controlled the crowd quite adeptly.∥그녀는 날랜 ~로 감자 껍질을 벗겼다 She peeled the potatoes with dexterous hands[skillfully / dexterously].∥그는 ~ 있게 회의를 주재하였다 He chaired the meeting skillfully[brilliantly].∥이 가구는 만든 ~가 좋지 않다 This furniture is poorly made.∥그의 운전 ~는 대단하다 He's a very good[skillful] driver. / (구어) He's awfully good at driving a car.∥그는 ~를 충분히 발휘하지 않고 있다 He is not working up to his ability.∥그의 ~로는 이 일은 무리다 This work is beyond him[his ability].∥피아노 ~ 좀 들어 봅시다 Let us hear how well you can play the piano.∥그는 카드놀이에서 멋진 ~를 보여 주었다 He showed[displayed] marvelous skill at cards.∥그는 ~가 대단한 목수이다 He is quite a skillful carpenter.∥내 요리 ~가 좋아졌다[못해졌다] My cooking has gotten[(영) got] better[worse]. / My skill in cooking has improved[deteriorated].∥그들은 서로 ~를 겨루었다 They pit their skills against each other.∥그 사람의 ~는 대단하다 What an able man he is! / He's really good at it.

솜옷 wadded[padded] clothes.

솜저고리 a wadded jacket.

솜털 (새의) down; fluff; downy[fine soft] hair (on a boy's face). ¶민들레의 ~ dandelion fluff∥~ 방석 a downy cushion∥~이 난[로 덮인] downy / fluffy.

솜틀 a willow(er); a willowing machine; a cotton gin.

솜화약(-火藥) cotton powder; guncotton.

솟구다 raise; make a rise. ¶몸을 ~ spring [leap / jump] up.

솟구치다 rise quickly; (불길이) blaze up; burn [go] up (in a flame).

솟다 1 (샘 등이) gush out[forth]; spring. ¶상처에서 피가 솟았다 Blood gushed out of the wound.∥그의 이마에 비지땀이 솟았다 A greasy sweat broke out on his forehead.

2 [우뚝 서다] rise; tower; soar. ¶하늘 높이 솟아 있는 산 a mountain soaring high into

[one's doors] (to foreigners); exclude foreigners from the country.
● **쇄국주의 / 쇄국 정책** isolationism; a closed-door policy; seclusionism. **쇄국주의자** a seclusionist.
쇄도(殺到) a rush; a flood; a stampede. **쇄도하다** rush (in / to); come with a rush; rush [pour] in; [밀어닥치다] rush [throng] to (a place); storm (a place); swoop down on (the enemy). ¶신청이 ~ (사람·단체)가 되 flooded [deluged] with applications [offers] // 그 책의 주문이 쇄도했다 There was a rush of orders for the book. // 그 유명한 배우를 보려고 사람들이 쇄도했다 People thronged [flocked] to see the famous actor. // 봄에는 관광객이 진해에 쇄도한다 Tourists pour into [flood] Jinhae during the spring months. // 항의 편지가 쇄도했다 Letters of protest poured in. // 사고 직후 항공 회사에는 문의가 쇄도했다 The airlines office was swamped with inquiries immediately after the accident.
쇄빙(碎氷) breaking the ice. **쇄빙하다** break ice; smash [crush] ice.
● **쇄빙선** an icebreaker.
쇄신(刷新) (a) complete reform; (a) renovation; (an) innovation; a cleanup. ¶생활양식의 ~ a reform of the mode of living / 정계의 ~ a political reform [cleanup] // 교육 제도의 ~을 도모하다 plan a complete reform of the educational system / 일대 ~ 하다 carry out radical reforms / make drastic changes. **쇄신하다** reform completely; introduce [make] a reform; renovate; innovate; clean up. ¶공직 사회의 기강을 ~ renovate the discipline in bureaucracy.
쇠 1 iron. ⇨ˉ철(鐵)
2 [쇠붙이] metal.
3 a key. ⇨ˉ열쇠1
4 a lock. ⇨자물쇠
5〈속〉money. ⇨돈
6〈속〉a magnet. ⇨자석
쇠- [소의] of cattle; ox-; cow-. ¶~고기 beef.
쇠가죽 leather; [생가죽] cowhide; [무두질한] cowskin; [송아지의] calfskin. ¶~ 핸드백 a leather handbag.
쇠갈고리 a (cargo) hook; [소방용] a fire hook.
쇠고기 beef. ¶**수입** ~ the imported beef / ~의[같은] beefy // ~ 토막 (a) (beef) steak.
쇠고랑 〈속〉handcuffs. ⇨수갑 ¶~을 찬 (a person) in shackles / ~을 차다 be arrested (for) / be in irons / ~을 채우다 handcuff (a person) / put [place] handcuffs (a person).
쇠고리 an iron ring; a metal hoop; a metal band; a clasp. ¶~를 걸다 clasp // ~를 끄르다 unclasp.
쇠귀 cow's ears; ox-ear.
쇠귀에 경 읽기(속담) It is like preaching to the wind [deaf ears].
쇠귀신(-鬼神) 1 [죽은 소의] the ghost of a cow. 2 [완고한 사람] a stubborn person.
쇠기름 (beef) tallow.
쇠꼬리 (소의) a cow's tail; oxtail.
쇠꼬챙이 a skewer; an iron skewer; a spit.
쇠다[1] 1 [채소가 억세다] become tough (and stringy). ¶배추가 쇠었다 Cabbage has lost its tenderness and become tough and stringy. 2 [병이 심해지다] get [grow] worse; grow chronic. ¶그의 위병이 ~ His stomach trouble becomes worse.
쇠다[2] (명절을) observe; keep (one's birthday); celebrate. ¶명절을 ~ observe [celebrate] a festival day.
쇠도리깨 an iron flail; a flail.
쇠딱지 dirt on children's heads.
쇠똥[1] [쇠 부스러기] iron slag; dross; scoria.
쇠똥[2] (소의) cattle dung.
쇠뜨기 [식] a field horsetail.
쇠망(衰亡) [멸망] fall; ruin; [쇠퇴] decline; decay. ¶로마 제국 ~사 The Decline and Fall of the Roman Empire. **쇠망하다** [멸망하다] fall; be ruined; go to ruin; go down; [쇠퇴하다] decline; decay; fall into decay.
쇠망치 a [an iron] hammer.
쇠먹이 cattle feed; fodder.
쇠멸하다(衰滅-) (나라 등이) decline and fall; (생물 등이) become extinct.
쇠못 a [an iron] nail.
쇠몽둥이 an iron bar; an iron club.
쇠문(-門) an iron gate [door].
쇠뭉치 a mass of iron; a pig; pig iron.
쇠버짐 a ringworm. ⇨백선(白癬)
쇠붙이 metal things; ironware; hardware.
쇠비름 [식] a purslane.
쇠뼈 cow [bullock] bones; ox-bone.
쇠뿔 a bull's [cow's] horn. ¶~이 나다 grow horns // ~에 받히다 be gored by a bull.
쇠뿔도 단김에 빼랬다(속담) He who hesitates is lost.; Strike while the iron is hot.; Make hay while the sunshines.; There's no time like the present.
쇠사슬 a chain; an iron chain. ¶~에 묶인 죄수 a criminal in chains // ~에 줄줄이 묶인 죄수들 a chain gang // ~에 개를 매어 두다 chain a dog // 개를 ~로 개집에 묶어 두다 chain a dog to its kennel // 개의 ~을 풀어 주다 unchain a dog // 죄수를 ~로 묶다 put [place] a prisoner in chains.
쇠스랑 [농] a rake; a forked rake; a scraper.
쇠심 beef [ox] tendon.
쇠약하다(衰弱-) weak; enfeebled; [노령으로] infirm; emaciated (야윈). ¶쇠약해지다 become [grow] weak / weaken / decline / sink / be debilitated / be enervated / be worn out / be emaciated // 그녀는 오랫동안 병을 앓아 쇠약해졌다 She has become [grown] weak [feeble] from long illness. // 어머니는 몹시 쇠약해서 야위셨다 Mother was emaciated. // 그가 쇠약한 원인은 영양실조이다 His weakness [feebleness] is due to malnutrition. // 그의 건강이 눈에 띄게 쇠약해졌다 His health has declined [failed] noticeably. // 그는 기력이 쇠약해졌다 He has lost heart.
쇠운(衰運) declining fortunes; one's waning star. ¶~에 접어들다 begin to decline [wane] / be on the decline [wane].
쇠잔하다(衰殘-) decline; fail; emaciate; decay; wear off [out]. ¶쇠잔한 몸 a wreck of one's former self // 몸이 쇠잔해지다 decline in health.
쇠족(-足) ox-hoof.
쇠죽(-粥) boiled cattle feed.
쇠줄 (iron) wire; a cable; a chain.
쇠진(衰盡) decay; exhaustion. **쇠진하다** decay; become exhausted.
쇠창살(-窓-) an iron window bar; a grate; a grill(e); a grating.
쇠코뚜레 a cow's [bull's] nose ring; a cattle leader.
쇠톱 a hacksaw.
쇠퇴(衰退) a decline; decay. ¶체력 [건강]의 ~

쇠파리 [동] a warble fly; a gadfly.

쇠푼 a small[petty] sum of money; some money.

쇠하다 (衰-) [쇠약해지다] become weaker; decline; lose vigor; be enfeebled; be weakened; be enervated; waste away; be languish; be run down; flag; atrophy; [쇠퇴하다] fall off[away]; fail; dwindle; go downhill; ebb (away); decline; decay; go[fall] into decay; (기운 등이) sink; wane; collapse; slacken. ¶건강이 ~ decline[be broken] in health / fall in one's health // 기억력이 쇠하여 가다 one's memory is failing // 나의 몸은 나날이 쇠하여 가고 있다 I am wasting away[in body] day after day.

쇤네 I; me; your humble servant.

쇳가루 iron filings.

쇳내 a metallic taste; a taste of iron. ¶이 물에서는 ~가 난다 This water tastes of iron. // 우물물에서 ~를 없애다 remove the metallic taste from well water.

쇳덩이 a lump of metal.

쇳독 (-毒) metallic poison(ing).

쇳물 1 [녹물] a rust stain. ¶내 셔츠에 ~이 묻었다 I have a rust stain on my shirt. 2 [녹인 쇠] melted[fused] iron.

쇳소리 a metallic sound[clang]; [날카로운 목소리] a piercing[shrill] voice. ¶~가 나다 sound like something metallic.

쇳조각 a piece[scrap] of iron; bits of iron.

쇼 a show. ¶패션 ~ a fashion show // 자동차 ~ (미) an auto show // 뉴스 ~ a news show[program] // 원맨 ~ a one-man show // 플로어 ~ a floor show.

쇼걸 a show girl.

쇼맨십 showmanship.

쇼윈도 a show window. ¶~에 진열되어 있다 be displayed in a show window // 그냥 ~를 들여다보며 다녔을 뿐이다 I was just window-shopping.

쇼크 a shock. ¶~를 **주다** give (a person) a shock / ~를 **받다** be shocked (at) / receive a shock // 나는 그 광경을 보고 심한 ~를 받았다 I was terribly[deeply] shocked at the sight. // 그는 페니실린 ~로 죽었다 He died of penicillin shock. // 아들의 죽음은 그에게 심한 ~였다 His son's death was a great shock to him.

● **쇼크사** (-死) death shock. **쇼크 요법** shock treatment.

쇼킹하다 shocking. ¶쇼킹한 뉴스 shocking news.

쇼트 [전] a short circuit; (구어) a short.

● **쇼트커트** a short cut.

쇼핑 [사기] shopping. ¶명동에 ~ 가다 go shopping in Myeongdong. **쇼핑하다** shop; do one's[the] shopping[marketing]; make a purchase. ¶쇼핑할 것이 조금 있다 I have some shopping to do[purchases to make]. // 차는 쇼핑한 것으로 가득 찼다 The car was filled with his purchases.

● **쇼핑몰** a shopping mall. **쇼핑백** a shopping bag. **쇼핑센터** a shopping center[(영) centre].

숄 [여성의 어깨걸이] (wear) a shawl. ¶~을 걸치다 [걸치고 있다] put on[wear] one's shawl.

숄더백 [어깨에 메는 가방] a shoulder bag.

숏 [영] a shot.

수 1 [도리·수단] (단수·복수 동형); a way; a resource; help. ¶나는 웃지 않을 ~ 없다 I can't help laughing. // 나는 눈물을 금할 ~ 없었다 I was unable to hold back[repress] my tears. // 우리가 꾸물거리고 있을 ~는 없다 We have no time to lose. / There is no time[not a moment] to be lost. // 그는 모든 ~를 써서 그 책임을 모면하려고 했다 He tried every conceivable means to avoid the blame. / (구어) He tried every trick in the book to duck responsibility. // 그들은 모든 ~를 동원하여 잃은 돈을 찾으려고 했다 They left no stone unturned to find the missing money. // 그것은 어떻게 해 볼 ~가 없다 It cannot be helped. / There is nothing I can do about it. // 이 시계는 고칠 ~가 없다 This watch cannot be repaired. // 이 정보만으로는 검토할 ~가 없다 We can't consider it without more information. // 손을 쓸 ~가 없었다 There was nothing to be done about it. // 나는 하는 ~ 없이 부모님의 말씀대로 했다 I was obliged[forced] to do as my parents told me. // 나는 그의 애원을 차마 거절할 ~ 없었다 I couldn't bring myself[I couldn't find it in my heart / I didn't have the heart] to refuse his entreaty. // 사장의 명령이니까 하는 ~ 없다 As an order from the president, so there's nothing you can do about it. // 이제 와서 불평을 해 보았자 별~ 없다 It's no use[There is no use (in)] complaining now. // 그는 하는 ~ 없이 떠났다 He was compelled[forced / obliged] to leave. / He left against his will. // 우리는 그 비행기를 타는 ~밖에 없었다 We had no choice but to take the plane.

2 [가능성·능력] possibility; likelihood; ability; capability. ¶영어를 말할 ~ 있는 사람 a person who speaks[can speak] English // 할 ~ 있는 데까지 as much[far] as one can / as much[far] as possible[practicable] // 할 ~ 만 있다면 if possible[practicable] / if one can // 그것은 상상할 ~도 없다 That's unimaginable[incredible]. // 그는 내가 상상할 ~도 없는 것을 생각하고 있다 What he is thinking is beyond the bounds of my imagination. // 나는 그렇게 하면 된다는 것을 생각할 ~도 없었다 I never realized that it was possible if we did it that way. // 그는 참을 ~ 없는 녀석이다 He is unsufferable. // 이제 그것을 더 이상 참을 ~ 없다 I can't stand it anymore. // 내가 할 ~ 있는 일은 다 하겠다 I will do anything in my power[everything I can]. // 내가 할 ~ 있는 일은 다 했다 I did my best. / I did all[that] I could. // 어떻게 그

런 일이 있을 ~ 있겠는가 How can it be?

수- [수컷의 동식물] a male; [조류와 새우·게·연어 등의] a cock; (오리·집오리의) a drake; (어린 가금의) a cockerel; (사슴·토끼·쥐 등의) a buck; (거세하지 않은 돼지의) a boar; (코끼리·고래·거세하지 않은 소 등의) a bull; (거세한 소의) an ox; (고양이의) a tom[cat]. ¶ ~꽃 a male flower // ~나사 a male screw // ~벌 a drone // ~소 a bull / [거세한 소] an ox // ~숫양 a ram // ~여우 a male fox // ~숫염소 a he-goat / a billy goat // ~참새 a male sparrow.

수(手) [바둑·장기의] a move; [수단] a means [단수·복수 동형]; [계략] a trick; an artifice. ¶그는 체스에서 묘한 [나쁜] ~를 썼다 He made a clever[poor] move in chess. // 그는 브리지에서 묘한 [나쁜] ~를 썼다 He made a clever[poor] play[maneuver] in bridge(▶ 카드놀이에는 move를 쓰지 않음). // 체스는 그가 나보다 한 ~ 위이다 He is better than I am at chess. / He is a better chess player than I am. / He is superior to me in chess. // 뻔뻔함에 있어서는 네가 나보다 한 ~ 위이다 You are a cut above me when it comes to impudence. // 그가 매사에 나보다 한 ~ 위였다 He was a cut above me in everything. / He was better than I was in everything. // 이 ~밖에는 없다 This is the best of all moves. / No better move! // 또 그 ~로군 You are up to your old trick, aren't you? / The same old game!

수(秀) (학업 성적의) Excellent; (미) A. ¶전 과목 ~ straight A's // ~를 받다 get an "Excellent" (in one's composition) // 전 과목 ~로 졸업하다 graduate (from a school) with an all A mark[with straight A's].

수(壽) [연령] age; one's natural life(천수); [장수] a long life; (a) longevity. ¶백 세의 ~를 누리다 live to be a hundred (years old) / be blessed with a longevity of a hundred years / be a centenarian.

수(數) 1 [수효] a number; a figure. ¶많은[적은] ~ a large[small] number // 상당한 ~의 군대 a good-sized army // 너의 반은 학생 ~가 몇 명이냐 How many students are there in your class? / What is the number of students in your class? // 그 도시에는 학교 ~가 많다[적다] There are many[only a few] schools in the town. // 이 아이는 벌써 ~를 셀 줄 안다 He[She] can already count. // 이 식은 n이 어떤 ~라도 성립된다 This equation holds for any number n. // 응모자의 ~는 5,000명에 달했다 The total number of applicants amounted to five thousand. // 그 문제를 푼 학생의 ~는 적었다 Only a small number of[Only a few] students solved that problem. // 우리는 ~에 당할 수 없다 We are outnumbered. / We are inferior in number. // 그들은 ~의 힘으로 이겼다 They won by force of numbers. // 교통 사고의 ~는 해마다 증가하고 있다 Traffic accidents are increasing year by year. 2 one's star; luck. ⇨운수(運數) ¶~가 좋다[나쁘다] have good[bad] fortune.

수(를) 때우다 ward off evil with a prior, lesser ordeal.

수(-) embroidery; crewelwork(소모사의); facings(군복의 깃·소매에 놓은). ¶~를 놓다 embroider (a figure on a table cover / a handkerchief with one's initials) / do[make] embroidery (on).

수(首) 1 [시나 노래를 세는 단위] a poem; a piece (of poetry). ¶한 ~ 읊다 compose [recite] a poem (on). 2 [마리]. ¶닭 20 ~ twenty chickens.

수-(數) [몇몇의] several; a few; [많은] a number of. ¶~차 several times // ~백 명의 사람 several hundred people.

-수(囚) ¶미결~ an unconvicted [under trial] prisoner / a prisoner under trial // 사형~ a condemned criminal / (구어) a gallows bird.

수가(酬價) a medical charge[fee]; a doctor's bill[fee]; medical treatment charges.

수간(獸姦) bestiality; zooerastia.

수간호사(首看護師) a head nurse.

수감(收監) confinement; imprisonment; commitment. **수감하다** imprison (a person); put (a person) in prison. ➡수감되다 be put away / be thrown in jail / be locked up / (미국 속어) be sent up / (영국 속어) go down // 그는 수감되어 있다 He is (confined) in prison.
● **수감자** a prisoner; a prison inmate.

수갑(手匣) handcuffs; (문어) manacles(▶ 족쇄 뜻함); (구어) cuffs. ¶~을 찬 범인 a criminal in handcuffs // …에게 ~을 채우다 put[place] handcuffs on a person / handcuff a person / slip[snap] handcuffs on a person(▶ slip은 가만히, snap은 덥석).

수강(受講) taking lectures. **수강하다** take lectures; attend a lecture class; become a trainee; join a seminar. ¶하계 강습을 ~ attend summer school[a summer course].
● **수강료** tuition; a tuition fee. **수강생** a trainee; a student attending a lecture [class]; a person present at a lecture class; a participant(참가자).

수개월(數個月) few[several] months. ¶지난 ~ 동안 for months past / for the last[past] few months.

수거하다(收去-) take away; remove.

수건(手巾) a (hand) towel; [세수수건] a facecloth; (미) a washcloth; (영) a (face) flannel. ¶세수~ a face towel // 손~ a (pocket-)handkerchief // ~으로 닦다 wipe [rub] with a towel / dry (one's hand) on a towel // ~으로 몸을 닦다[문지르다] towel oneself // ~을 짜다 wring a towel [out / dry] // 나는 ~으로 몸을 닦았다 I dried myself with a towel.

수검자(受檢者) an examinee; a subject of inspection.

수검하다(受檢-) undergo[go through] an examination; be inspected; be subjected to inspection.

수결(手決) a signature; a written seal; a hand. ¶~을 두다 sign / put[affix] one's signature to.

수경(법)(水耕法) hydroponics; aquiculture. ⇨물재배.
● **수경 농장** a hydroponic farm.

수경성(水硬性) [화] hydraulicity; hydraulic property.

수계(水系) ¶아마존 ~ the Amazon basin [river] system.

수고 trouble; labor; (문어) toil; pains(▶ 이 의미로는 복수형); efforts; [헛수고] wasted effort / a complete[sheer] waste of effort // ~를 끼치다 give (a person) trouble / put (a person) to trouble // ~를 아끼다 be sparing of oneself

수고롭다

/ be stingy of labor / spare on pains[efforts / trouble] to (do) / do not spare oneself.∥~를 끼쳐서 미안합니다 I am sorry to have put you to so much trouble[given you such trouble].∥그녀는 아이들을 돌보는 데 ~를 아끼지 않았다 She spared no pains in taking care of the children.∥계산기를 쓰면 많은 ~를 덜 수 있다 It saves a lot of trouble if you use a calculator.∥당신은 내가 날마다 시장 보러 가는 ~를 덜어 주고 있습니다 You save me the trouble of going shopping every day.∥~ 좀 해 주시겠습니까 Could I ask you to do something for me? **수고하다** take pains [trouble] (about); take the trouble (to do); make efforts; labor (hard). ¶수고했습니다 Thank you very much! / Thank you for your trouble. / (간단한 표현) Thanks a lot!∥저를 위해 여러 가지로 수고해 주셔서 감사합니다 Thank you very much for all the trouble you have taken for me.∥나는 수고한 보람도 없이 일을 끝내지 못했다 For all my pains[the trouble I went to], I could not finish the work.

수고롭다 troublesome. ⇨ 수고스럽다

수고스럽다 troublesome; toilsome; laborious; bothersome; painstaking. ¶수고스러운 일 laborious[painstaking] work∥수고스럽기만 하고 보람 없는 일 laborious but fruitless work∥수고스럽지만 이 편지 좀 부쳐 줘요 May I trouble you to post this letter?

수고양이 a tomcat; a he-cat; a male cat.

수공(手工) manual arts[work]; handicraft; handwork; handiwork. ¶~이 들다 take much trouble / involve much labor / be laborious.
● **수공업** manual industry; handicraft manufacturing; handicraft industry. **수공품** a piece of handiwork; a product of one's fingers; (집합적) handicraft.

수공예(手工藝) crafts; handicrafts; manual arts and crafts.

수관(水管) a water pipe[tube]; [동] a siphon.

수관(樹冠) [식] a crown.

수교(手交) handing; delivery by hand; delivery in person. **수교하다** deliver; hand over (to); hand over (a thing) into another's own hands; hand (a thing) to (a person); place (something) in (a person's) hand. ¶각서를 ~ hand a memorandum / deliver a note.

수교(修交) amity; friendship; friendly relations. **수교하다** form a friendly relationship (with).
● **수교 조약** a treaty of amity[friendship]. **수교 훈장** the Distinguished Order of Diplomatic Service.

수구(水球) [체] water polo.

수구(守舊) conservatism; conservativeness; adherence to traditional customs. ¶~의 conservative. **수구하다** be conservative; adhere to traditional customs.
● **수구 세력** conservative force. **수구파** the conservatives.

수국(水菊) [식] a hydrangea.

수군(水軍) the naval forces.

수군거리다 talk in a whisper. ⇨ 소곤거리다

수권(授權) authorization; delegation of legal power.
● **수권 자본** authorized capital.

수그러지다 1 [머리가 숙이다] hang down; become low; lower; sink; droop; drop. ¶그의 고개가 푹 수그러지고 눈이 감겼다 His chin sank on his chest and his eyes shut.∥그녀의 희생정신에는 머리가 수그러진다 I take off my hat to her self-sacrificing spirit.
2 [태도·기세가 누그러지다] soften; become calm; calm down; be pacified; flag; (병세가) be relieved; be suppressed; be subdued; (바람 등이) go[die / calm] down; subside; sink; abate. ¶맹렬한 불길이 수그러진 것 같다 The fury of the flames seems to be dying down [slackening off].∥그의 살기등등한 기세가 수그러졌다 His murderous spirit has flagged.∥몸의 열이 수그러졌다 The fever abated.∥해가 지자 더위가 수그러졌다 The heat diminished as the sun went down.

수그리다 bend oneself (forward). ⇨ 숙이다

수금(收金) collection (of money); bill collection[collecting]. **수금하다** collect money [bills]. ¶지대(地代)를 ~ collect (rent) from a tenant∥그는 가스 요금을 수금하러 다닌다 He is making his round collecting gas bills.
● **수금원** a bill[money] collector.

수급(需給) supply and demand(▶ 영어의 어순은 우리말과 반대인 점에 유의할 것). ¶~을 조정하다 keep the balance of supply and demand.
● **수급 조정** adjustment of demand and supply.

수긍(首肯) assent; consent; a nod. ¶이렇게 설명하면 충분히 ~이 가리라 생각한다 I think this explanation is sufficiently convincing.∥그녀의 설명에는 ~이 가지 않는 데가 있다 Her explanation fails to convince us in some particulars. **수긍하다** nod; assent (to); consent (to); nod one's assent (to); agree (to something / with a person); [납득하다] be convinced (of / that); be persuaded (of / that). ¶수긍할 수 있는[없는] convincing [unconvincing]∥수긍하게 하다 win (a person's) consent / bring the truth to (a person's) heart / convince[persuade] (a person) of something / that ...)∥그의 의견은 수긍하기 어려웠다 I could not agree with him[his view]. / I could not accept his views. / (구어) I couldn't go along with his ideas.

수기(手記) a note; [각서] a memorandum (pl. -da, ~s); [회상록] memoirs. ¶~를 쓰다 note[take / put] down / take notes (of) / make memoranda (of).

수기(手旗) a handflag; a semaphore flag.
● **수기 신호** flag signaling[(영) signalling]. ¶보이 스카우트들이 ~를 하고 있다 The Boy Scouts are signaling with flags.

수꽃 [식] a male[sterile / staminate] flower.

수꿩 a male pheasant; a cock-pheasant.

수나사(-螺絲) a male[positive] screw.

수난(水難) [익사] drowning; being[getting] drowned; [해난] a disaster at sea; a shipwreck; [수해] a flood (disaster); an inundation. ¶~을 당하다 [익사] drown / be drowned / [수해를 당하다] suffer damage from a flood / [난파하다] be shipwrecked.

수난(受難) sufferings; [혹독한 시련] ordeals; severe trial. ¶그리스도의 ~ the Passion / the Crucifixion∥~을 당하다 suffer / undergo hardships[trials].
● **수난일** Good Friday.

수납(收納) 1 [금전 등의] receipt. ¶국고 ~금 money taken into the (National) Treasury.

수납하다 receive (payment). 2 [안에 넣음]. ¶양곡 ~ collection[purchase] of food grains. **수납하다** put (a thing) away[up]; put (a thing) away (in a box).
● **수납계(원)** a receiver; a receiving clerk; (은행의) a receiving teller. **수납액** the amount received.

수납 (受納) receipt; acceptance. **수납하다** accept; receive.

수녀 (修女) a nun; [가] a sister. ¶~가 되다 enter a nunnery / enter [go into] a convent / take the vows of a nun.
● **수녀원** a nunnery; a convent.

수년 (數年) several [some / a few] years; a number of years. ¶나는 ~ 전에 외국 여행을 했었다 I traveled abroad several years ago. // ~ 동안 따뜻한 겨울이 계속되고 있다 For several years we have had unusually mild winters. // ~ 후에 그의 아내는 죽었다 A few years later [afterwards] his wife died. // ~ 내에 우리도 우리 집을 갖게 될 것이다 In a few years we will be able to buy a house of our own.

수놈 a male (animal). ⇨⁼수컷

수놓다 (繡-) embroider (a pattern on a handkerchief with figures). ¶비단에 꽃을 ~ embroider flowers on silk // 금실로 새를 ~ embroider figures of birds in gold thread (on).

수뇌 (首腦) a head; a leader; a chief. ¶군의 ~ the brains of the armed forces // 정당의 ~ the soul of a party // ~가 되다 head (a group) / take the lead / play the leading part (in).
● **수뇌부** the chief [top-level] executives (of a company). **수뇌 회담** a top-level [summit] meeting [conference].

수뇨관 (輸尿管) [생] the ureter.

수다 [말이 많음] talkativeness; [재잘거리기] prattle; (문어) loquacity; chattering. ¶~를 떨다 talk / chat / have a chat (with) / gossip (about) / chatter / babble like a brook // 시시한 ~를 그만 떨면 좋겠다 I wish you'd stop your chatter (▶ chatter는 시시한 이야기를 말함). // 그녀는 혼자 ~를 떨어 우리를 침묵시켰다 She talked us into silence.
● **수다쟁이** a prattler; a prater; a rumormonger; a gossip (monger); a talkative [garrulous / loquacious] person.

수다스럽다 talkative; garrulous; (문어) loquacious. ¶술을 마시면 그는 수다스러워진다 Alcohol makes him talkative.

수다하다 (數多-) numerous; many; innumerable. ¶수다한 학생 가운데서 among so many students.

수단 (手段) a means (단수·복수 동형); a measure; a way; a step; [고안] a device; [편법] an expedient; a shift; a resource; [도구] an instrument. ¶부정 ~ a foul means / an unjust step // 과감한 [단호한] ~ a drastic [decisive] step [measure] // ~이 대단한 사람 a man of unlimited resource // …한 ~으로 by way of …ing // 최후의 ~으로서 as a [in the] last resort / as the last measure [resource] // ~을 가리지 않고 by any means / fair or foul / by hook or by crook // 부정 ~으로 돈을 벌다 make money by foul means // ~을 강구하다 devise [find] a means (to) // 그렇게 할 수밖에 다른 ~이 없다 I can find no other alternative [way] but to do so. // 그는 목적을 위해서는 ~을 가리지 않는다 He makes no scruples of doing anything [sticks at nothing] to attain his object. / He goes all lengths to attain his goal. // 어떤 ~을 써서라도 그놈을 찾고야 말겠다 I will leave no stone unturned until I find him. // 우리의 제의가 받아들여지지 않는다면 최후의 ~에 호소하겠다 We will turn to our last resort if our proposal is refused.

수달 (水獺) [동] an otter.
● **수달피** an otter fur.

수당 (手當) [봉급 외에 지급되는 돈] extra benefits; an allowance. ¶가족 [주택] ~ a family [housing] allowance // 근무지 ~ a regional allowance // 시간 외 ~ an overtime allowance // 실업 ~ unemployment benefits // 전시 ~ a war(-time) allowance / [군] a field allowance // 제 ~ various allowances / sundry allowance // 초과 근무 ~ an over-time allowance / overtime pay // 퇴직 ~ a retirement allowance / (회사 사정으로 실직한 사람을 위한) severance pay // 특별 ~ a special [an extra] allowance / ~을 주다 give an allowance / recompense (a person) for // ~을 타다 draw an allowance // 여기는 ~이 후하다 I am well paid here.

수더분하다 good-natured [-tempered]; tenderhearted; kindhearted; (서술적) have a sweet temper; be of gentle [good] disposition. ¶수더분한 사람 a good-natured person / a man of good nature / a regular guy.

수도 (水道) [상수도 시설] a water supply; [수돗물] tap water. ¶~를 끌다 [놓다] have water pipes laid / have water supplied / lay on water // ~를 틀다 [잠그다] turn on [off] the tap // 이 마을에는 ~ 설비가 없다 There is no water service in this village. // 그 새집에는 아직 ~가 들어와 있지 않다 The new house doesn't have (running) water yet. / The new house hasn't been connected to the water mains yet. / Water pipes haven't been laid to the new house yet. // 여기 ~는 잘 나온다 [나오지 않는다] The tap water runs [doesn't run] well here.
● **수도관** a water [service] pipe; a water main (본관). **수도꼭지** a tap; a hydrant. ¶~를 틀었다 잠갔다 하다 turn the tap [spigot / (미) faucet] on and off // ~를 틀어 놓다 leave the faucets [taps] running // 나는 그녀에게 ~를 잠가 [틀어] 달라고 말했다 I asked her to turn off [on] the faucet [tap]. **수도료** water rates [charges]. **수돗물** tap [city / running / piped] water.

수도 (首都) a capital; a metropolis. ¶~의 metropolitan // 주(州)의 ~ a state capital // 파리는 프랑스의 ~이다 Paris is the capital of France.
● **수도권** the National Capital region; the Metropolitan [Capital] area. ¶~ 방위 the defense of the Metropolitan area // ~ 인구 분산책 a measure of decentralizing the Capital area population // ~ 전철화 electrification of Metropolitan railroads // ~ 재개발 redevelopment of the Metropolitan area.

수도 (修道) spiritual exercise; asceticism; ascetic practices; religious austerities; [종] discipline. **수도하다** lead an ascetic life; practice asceticism [religious austerities].
● **수도사** a monk. ⇨⁼수사(修士) **수도승** Buddhist monk. **수도원** a religious house;

수동 (남자의) a monastery; an abbey; (여자의) a nunnery; a convent; [수사가 사는 건물] priest's[monks'] quarters[cells]. ¶~ 생활 a monastic[cloistered] life. **수도회** a religious [monastic] order; an order. ¶프란체스코 ~ the Franciscan order.

수동 (手動) ~의 hand-operated[worked] / manual∥이 펌프는 ~이다 This pump is worked by hand.
● **수동 펌프** a hand pump.

수동 (受動) passivity; passiveness. ¶~성의 passive.
● **수동태** [형][언] the passive voice[form].

수동적 (受動的) passive. ¶~으로 passively / ~이 되다 be acted upon / lose the initiative / [수세에 서다] be[stand] on the defensive ∥그는 매사에 너무 ~이다 He is too passive in everything.

수두 (水痘) [의] varicella; chicken pox.
● **수두 백신** a chicken pox vaccine.

수두룩하다 (다량) much; a good[great] deal of; a lot[wealth] of; plenty[lots] of; plentiful; (서술적) abound in[with]; (다수) many; a good[great] many; a large number of; numerous; [흔하다] common; stock (examples). ¶할 일이 ~ have much[a lot / many things] to do∥그런 일은 ~ It is no uncommon occurrence.∥그런 사람들이 ~ There are lots[plenty] of people like that. **수두룩이** plentifully; abundantly; commonly.

수라 (水剌) [임금에게 올리는 진지] the King's meal[food].
● **수라상** the king's dinner table.

수라장 (修羅場) a scene of carnage[bloodshed / utter confusion]; a shambles; a pandemonium. ¶한길은 ~이 되었다 The main street turned into a scene of carnage[bloodshed]. ∥화재 현장은 ~을 이루고 있었다 The scene of the fire was one of great[utter] confusion.

수락 (受諾) acceptance. ¶~을 거절하다 refuse [reject] to accept / decline acceptance. **수락하다** accept (an offer); agree to (the conditions). ¶선뜻 ~ give ready consent (to) / 두말 않고 ~ accept (a proposal) without question∥취임을 ~ accept the post (of chairman)∥귀하의 제의를 기꺼이 수락하겠습니다 We will gladly accept your offer. → ¶**수락시키다** make (a person) accept (something)∥설득해 수락시키다 talk[reason] (a person) into compliance / persuade (a person) to accept (an offer).

수란 (水卵) a poached egg.

수란 뜨다 poach an egg.

수란관 (輸卵管) [생] the trumpet; the oviduct. ⇨나팔관

수량 (水量) the quantity[volume] of water. ¶ ~이 풍부하다 be in a great volume of water ∥저수지의 ~이 1미터 증가[감소]하였다 The water level in the reservoir rose[fell] by a meter.
● **수량계** a water gauge[meter].

수량 (數量) (an) amount; (a) quantity. ¶~으로 quantitatively∥~이 늘다[줄다] increase[decrease] in quantity∥가격은 ~에 따라 다릅니다 The price depends on the quantity.

수렁 a quagmire; a mire; a morass; a bog; a slough. ¶~에 빠지다 fall in the mire / sink in a bog / [비유] be bogged[mired] down / get stuck in a bog / mire oneself (in)∥~에 서 빠져나오다 pull oneself out of the mire / find a way out of the swamp∥점점 더 깊은 ~에 빠지다 get bogged deeper in the mud.

수레 a wagon; a cart; a handcart(손수레); a carriage(마차); an oxcart(소가 끄는). ¶~로 운반하다 cart[dray] (it) away / carry (goods) in a cart∥~를 끌다 draw[pull] a cart.
● **수레바퀴** a (wagon) wheel.

수려하다 graceful; beautiful; handsome; fine. ¶미목(眉目)이 수려한 청년 a handsome youngman.

수력 (水力) waterpower; hydraulic power. ¶~으로 움직이는 water-powered / hydraulic∥~을 이용하다 make use of waterpower∥~으로 발전하다 generate electricity by hydraulic power.
● **수력 발전** water-power[hydroelectric power] generation. **수력 발전소** a hydroelectric power[hydropower] plant[station].

수련 (修鍊·修練) training; practice; culture; discipline; drill. ¶주야로 ~을 쌓다 practice [rehearse] day and night∥자네는 ~이 부족해 You need more training. **수련하다** train; practice[(영) practise]; cultivate; discipline.
● **수련의** (-醫) an apprentice doctor; an intern(e).

수련 (睡蓮) [식] a water[pond] lily. ¶~의 잎 lily pad.

수렴 (收斂) **1** [거두어들임] extortion[exaction] of taxes; laying[imposing] crushing taxes (on). **수렴하다** extort[exact] heavy taxes (from); tax heavily; impose heavy unjust taxes (on). **2** [오그라들게 함] [의] astriction; [물][수] convergence. **수렴하다** be astringent; be astrictive; converge. **3** [여론 등을 한데 모으는 것] collecting; (a) reflection. **수렴하다** collect.
● **수렴 렌즈** a converging lens (pl. ~es).

수렴청정 (垂簾聽政) regency by the queen mother (from behind the veil).

수렵 (狩獵) hunting. ⇨사냥
● **수렵기** the hunting season; the open season (on deer).

수령 (守令) [지방관] a chief magistrate[administrator]; a local governor.

수령 (受領) receipt; acceptance. ¶시립 도서관은 도서의 ~을 일시 정지했다 The city library temporarily suspended the accession of books. **수령하다** receive; accept. ¶연금을 ~ receive a pension∥100만 원을 정히 수령함 I hereby acknowledge receipt of a million won.∥틀림없이 수령하였음 Received with thanks.
● **수령인** a receipt stamp. **수령자** a receiver; a recipient; (어음 등의) a payee. ¶연금 ~ a pensioner / a recipient of a pension. **수령증** a receipt.

수령 (首領) a chief; a leader; (모반자의) a ring-leader. ¶도둑들의 ~ the leader of a band of robbers∥~이 되다 become a leader / lead (others in something).

수령 (樹齡) the age of a tree. ¶이 나무는 ~이 400년이 넘는다 This tree is over four hundred years old.

수로 (水路) **1** a watercourse; (항행할 수 있는) a waterway; [강·바다·호수 등의 뱃길] a channel; [운하] a canal. ¶관개 ~ an irrigation canal∥~로 [해로로] by sea / [배로] by ship[boat] / [운하로] by (a) canal∥두 도시

사이에 ~를 개설하다 cut [dig] a canal between the two cities. **2** (수영장의) a course. ¶장~ the long distance course.
- **수로** an aqueduct (bridge). **수로 안내** pilotage. ⇨도선(導船) **수로 표지** a beacon.

수록하다(收錄-) [모으다] gather; collect; [기재하다] record; write down; mention; [자기테이프에 녹음하다] tape. ¶그날의 행사를 테이프[비디오테이프]에 수록했다 We taped [videotaped] the events of the day. ➔¶이 책에 수록되어 있는 논문은 20편이다 Twenty theses are printed in this book.

수뢰(水雷) [어뢰] a torpedo (*pl.* ~es); [기뢰] a mine.
- **수뢰정** a torpedo boat.

수뢰(受賂) bribery; (미국 구어) graft. **수뢰하다** take a bribe; take graft. ¶그는 1억 원을 수뢰했다 He accepted [took] a bribe of a hundred million won.

수료(修了) completion. **수료하다** complete; finish. ¶나는 고등학교 과정을 수료했다 I have finished [completed] my high school course.
- **수료증** a diploma; a certificate of the completion of one's studies.

수류(水流) a (water) current; a stream (of water).

수류탄(手榴彈) [군] a (hand) grenade; (군사 속어) a pineapple. ¶~을 던지다 throw a hand grenade (at).

수륙(水陸) land and water. ¶~ 양면으로 물자를 수송하다 send supplies by both land and sea.
- **수륙 공동 작전** amphibious operations. **수륙 양서 동물** an amphibious animal; an amphibian. **수륙 양용기** an amphibious plane; an amphibian. **수륙 양용 전차** an amphibious tank; an amphibian.

수리 [동] an eagle. ¶~ 새끼 an eaglet.

수리(水利) **1** [수상 운송상의 편리] navigability. **2** [물의 이용] utilization of water; (급수) water supply; (관개) irrigation.
- **수리 사업** irrigation works [projects]. **수리 시설** irrigation facilities. ¶~이 잘되어 있는[되어 있지 않은] 지역 a well-[poorly] watered area∥이 땅은 ~이 잘되어 있다 The land is well watered [irrigated].

수리(受理) acceptance. **수리하다** accept; receive; take up. ¶사표를 ~ accept 《a person's》 resignation∥청원서를 ~ accept a petition.

수리(修理) repair(s); mending. ¶이 낡은 자동차는 ~가 잘되어 있다[있지 않다] This old car is in good [a bad state of] repair.∥지붕은 ~ 중이다 The roof is under repair.∥~ **중**(게시) Under Repair.∥내부 ~ 중 휴업 (게시) Closed for alterations. **수리하다** repair; mend; (미) fix; (▶ repair는 비교적 복잡한 물건의 수리, mend는 간단한 수리에 각각 쓰임. (미) fix는 어느 쪽으로도 쓸 수 있음) ¶우리 집의 낡은 뻐꾸기시계는 이젠 수리할 수가 없을 정도이다 Our old cuckoo clock is beyond [past] repair.∥나는 시계를 수리했다 I had my watch repaired.∥이 사다리를 수리할 수 있습니까 Can you fix this ladder?∥이 집은 수리해야겠다 This house needs repairs. / This house needs to be done up [over].
- **수리공** a (car) repairman (*pl.* -men). ¶텔레비전 ~ a TV repairman. **수리비** repairing charges; the cost of repairing.

수리(數理) **1** [수학의 이론·이치] a mathematics; a mathematical principle. ¶~적(인) mathematical. **2** [계산의 이치] arithmetic; accounts; figures. ¶그는 ~에 밝다 He is good at figures [strong in arithmetic]. / He is well grounded in the mathematical principle. / He is clever at mathematics.
- **수리 경제학** mathematical economics.

수리학(水理學) hydraulics.

수림(樹林) a forest; a wood; a grove.

수립(樹立) establishment; founding; setting-up. ¶새 정부의 ~ the establishment of a new government. **수립하다** establish; found; set up. ¶외교 관계를 ~ 하다 set up diplomatic relations [ties] 《with》∥그들은 그곳에 새 국가를 수립하였다 There they established a new state [founded a new nation].➔¶새 정부가 수립되었다 A new government has been formed [has been established].

수마(水魔) [수해] a disastrous flood. ¶이 지역은 해마다 ~가 휩쓸고 지나간다 This area suffers from disastrous floods every year.

수마(睡魔) [졸음] drowsiness; sleepiness; (전설·동화 등의) the sandman; the dustman; [그리스 신화] Morpheus. ¶~가 엄습해 오고 있다 The dustman [sandman] is coming.∥나는 ~와 싸우면서 리포트를 썼다 I wrote my paper fighting off sleep [drowsiness]. / I wrote my paper trying not to fall asleep.∥나는 그의 강연 중에 ~에 사로잡혔다 I became sleepy [drowsy] during his lecture.

수만(數萬) tens [scores] of thousands. ¶1년 동안에 ~ 명의 인구가 증가했다 The population increased by tens of thousands in a (single) year.

수많다(數-) a good [great] many; numerous; numbers of; a (great) numbers of; a lot of; a host [hosts] of. ¶수많은 사람들 a great number of [a great many] people / numbers [scores / crowds] of people.

수말 a stallion; a (male) horse.

수매(收買) buying; a purchase; (정부의) procurement. ¶정부의 미곡 ~ 가격 the government purchasing [purchase] price of rice. **수매하다** purchase; buy (out).

수맥(水脈) **1** [뱃길] a water route; a waterway; a channel; [항로] a sea route; a seaway. **2** [지하수의 줄기] a water vein. ¶~을 찾아 내다 strike [hit] (a vein of) water∥~을 찾아서 파다 dig [drill] for water.

수면(水面) the surface of the water. ¶~에서 2미터 위[아래] two meters above [below] the surface (of the water)∥~**에 뜨다** float on the surface (of the water)∥~에서 공중으로 뛰어오르다 leap clear of the water∥잠수함이 ~에 떠올랐다 The submarine surfaced.∥커다란 물고기가 ~에 떠올랐다 A big fish broke [rose to / came up to] the surface.

수면(睡眠) sleep; slumber. ¶~을 제대로 취하다 sleep regular hours∥~**을 방해하다** disturb [interrupt] one's sleep [slumber]∥충분한 ~을 취하다 take [have / enjoy] a good sleep / get enough [sufficient] sleep∥4시간으로는 ~이 모자란다 Four hours sleep [a four-hour sleep / a sleep of four hours] is not enough. **수면하다** sleep; slumber; have a sleep [slumber].
- **수면 부족** want [lack] of sleep; insufficient sleep. ¶그는 ~으로 신경이 예민해져 있다 His nerves are on edge from want of sleep

수명 [from curtailed sleep / owing to insufficient sleep]. // 너의 두통은 ~ 때문이다 Your headache is due to lack of sleep. ¶수면 시간 sleeping hours; hours of sleep. ¶그는 공부하기 위해 ~을 줄였다 He cut down (on) [curtailed] his sleeping hours[hours of sleep / sleep] to study. **수면제** [의] sleeping drug[dose / potion / powder / pill / tablet / draught]; a soporific (drug); a somniferous drug; [마취제] a narcotic; an anesthetic.

수명 (壽命) 1 [목숨] life; man's[the human] life span; the span of life; one's lifetime; the length of one's days. ¶인간의 평균 ~ the average span [longevity] of human life [human beings] / [보험] the (average) life expectancy // ~이 길다[짧다] be long-lived [short-lived] / have[enjoy] a long[only a short] life // ~이 연장되다 prolong one's life / take[win] a new[fresh] lease of life(병의 완쾌 등으로) / ~을 줄이다 [단축시키다] shorten one's (span of) life / drive[put] a nail in[into] one's coffin / add a nail to one's coffin / bring one to an early grave // ~을 늘이다 lengthen one's (span of) life // 이 나라 여성의 평균 ~은 80세이다 The average life expectancy of women in this country is 80 years. // 그의 ~은 얼마 남지 않았다 His days are numbered. // 한국인의 ~이 길어졌다 The life expectancy of the Koreans has lengthened. / The span of life of the Koreans has been extended.
2 (물건의) wear; durability; life. ¶기계의 ~ a machine's life // 자동차의 ~ the expected life span of motorcars // 이 전지의 ~은 불과 100시간이다 The battery has a life of only 100 hours. // 이 책은 ~이 긴 베스트셀러이다 This is a longstanding bestseller. // 이 차는 이제 ~이 다 됐다 This car has had it.

수모 (受侮) contempt; scorn; disdain; insult; affront; indignity. ¶~를 참다 bear an affront / eat the leek / brook[pocket / swallow (down)] an insult / (미국 속어) eat crow [dirt] / (영국 속어) eat humble pie. **수모하다** be held in contempt; suffer an insult [indignity / affront]; be insulted[slighted / despised]; be subjected to indignity.

수목 (樹木) 1 [살아 있는 나무] trees. ¶~이 울창한 woody / wooded // ~이 우거진 지역 a (thickly) wooded area // ~이 울창한[없는] 고지 a wooded[treeless] plateau. 2 [식] [목본] an arbor (*pl.* ~es).
● **수목원** a tree garden; an arboretum (*pl.* -ta, ~s).

수몰 (水沒) submergence. **수몰하다** be submerged[submersed]; go under water; sink out of sight; be flooded[inundated]. ➔ ¶홍수로 마을이 수몰되었다 The flood submerged the village. / The flood covered the village with water.
● **수몰 지역** submerged districts; a flooded area; an area (to be) under water.

수묵 (水墨) [빛이 옅은 먹물] India(n) ink.
● **수묵화** a drawing[painting] in India(n) ink; an Indian ink painting; a black-and-white drawing.

수문 (水門) [갑] a sluice (gate); a water gate; (방조[防潮]용) a floodgate; (운하의) a lock (gate). ¶~을 열다[닫다] open[shut] a floodgate[sluice] // ~ 있는 수로 a sluiceway // (배가) ~을 통과하다 pass through a lock.

● **수문지기 / 수문 관리인** a lockkeeper; a lockman.

수문장 (守門將) [역] a chief of gatekeepers; the commander of guards.

수미 (愁眉) [근심에 잠긴 눈썹] knitted (eye) brows; a cloud on one's brow; a worried look.

수밀도 (水蜜桃) a (white) peach.

수박 a watermelon.

수박 겉 핥기 (속담) superficiality; shallowness. ¶~의 superficial / shallow / half-read // ~식 지식 a smattering / a superficial [half] knowledge // 그는 그리스 어를 ~로 알고 있다 He has a smattering[knows a bit] of Greek.

수반 (水盤) a basin; (꽃꽂이용의) a flower bowl [basin]; a shallow container for displaying flower arrangements.

수반 (首班) the head. ¶내각 ~ the head of a cabinet / the prime minister / the premier // 현 내각은 존슨 씨를 ~으로 하고 있다 The present cabinet is headed by Mr. Johnson.

수반 (隨伴) 1 [수행] accompaniment; (문어) attendance (on a journey). **수반하다** accompany; attend (a person on a journey); be attendant on[upon]; follow. 2 [어떤 일과 함께 생김] accompaniment; concomitance. **수반하다** accompany; be attendant on[upon]; follow; attend; carry. ¶행정 개혁에 수반하는 여러 문제 the problems accompanying[(문어) concomitant with] administrative reforms // 전쟁과 이에 수반하는 여러 가지 고난 hardships attendant on war / war and its attendant hardships // 위험이 수반하는 직업 a hazardous job.

수방 (水防) [홍수의 예방] prevention of floods; [댐·수로 등에 의한 수해 조절] flood control.
● **수방 대책** (take) measures to prevent floods.

수배 (手配) 1 [갈라 맡아서 하게 함] arrangements; preparations (to). **수배하다** arrange; prepare (for). ➔ ¶차량은 수배되어 있습니까 (출영할 분의 차의 준비 연락)// (언제라도 탈 수 있는 상태로) Is the car ready?
2 [범인 체포를 위한 조치] (a) search. ¶~ 중인 강도범 a man wanted[sought] for robbery // 현상 ~범 an outlaw with a price upon his head // 지명 ~ arrangements for the search of an identified criminal. **수배하다** institute[begin] a search for; cast a dragnet for; issue[put out] an order to search for (and arrest) (a criminal); put a person on a wanted list. ➔ ¶그는 살인 혐의로 전국에 지명 수배되었다 He was put on the wanted list throughout the country for murder.
● **수배자** a person wanted by the police; a wanted criminal. ¶지명 ~ a most wanted criminal // ~의 사진 a wanted person's photo / a photograph of a wanted criminal / (미국 속어) a mug shot / (미국 속어) an art.

수백 (數百) hundreds. ¶~ 명의 사람 hundreds of people // ~의 사상자가 생겼다 There were several hundred casualties.

수백만 (數百萬) millions. ¶~ 명 several million men / [몇 백만] millions of men.

수법 (手法) 1 [수단·방법] a way (of doing a thing); a method; (간교한) a trick[game]; (범죄자의) (라) a modus operandi (*pl.* modi operandi)(약어 M.O.). ¶**범죄** ~ a method employed in a crime / ~을 **바꾸다** play another trick upon / resort to other means / try some other means // 온갖 ~을 다 쓰다 use[try] all conceivable means / pull every wire possible // 똑같은 ~으로 나를 속이려 들다 It's no good trying the same old trick on me. // 이것이 그가 즐겨 쓰는 ~이다 This is his usual trick [way of doing things]. // 세 사람이 똑같은 ~에 걸려 돈을 사기당했다 Three persons fell for the same trick and were swindled out of their money. 2 [작품의 표현 방법] a technique; technical skill. ¶그는 유화의 ~을 체득했다 He learned the technique of oil painting. // ~에 있어 그는 스승을 능가했다 In technical skill he surpassed his master.

수병(水兵) a seaman (*pl.* -men); a sailor; a bluejacket; 《집합적》《영》 naval ratings.

수복(收復) recovery [reclamation] (of a lost territory). **수복하다** recover; reclaim; 《구어》 win back.
● **수복민** repatriated people. **수복 지구** a reclaimed area.

수복(壽福) longevity and happiness. ¶~강녕 하다 enjoy [be blessed with] longevity, good health and happiness.

수부(水夫) a sailor; a seaman; a mariner; 《구어》 a jack-tar; 《집합적》 the forecastle; the fo'c'sle.

수북수북 in heaps. **수북수북하다** be heaped up (with).

수북하다 1 [쌓여 있다] heaped up; heaping. ¶수북한 오렌지 a heap of oranges. **수북이** in a heap; full(y). ¶사과를 ~ 담은 쟁반 a tray with a heap of apples on it // 어머니는 내 접시에 샐러드를 ~ 담아 주셨다 My mother heaped salad on [onto] my plate. / My mother heaped my plate with salad. // 소년은 사발에 ~ 담은 밥을 순식간에 깨끗이 먹어 치웠다 The boy polished off a heaping bowlful of rice in no time. // 눈이 도로에 ~ 쌓였다 The snow piled up on the highway. 2 [살이 부어 있다] swollen. ¶수북한 눈 a swollen eye.

수분(水分) water; [습기] moisture; humidity; [액즙] juice; [수액] sap. ¶~을 **세스하다** dehydrate / remove water [moisture] (from) / dehumidify / anhydrate(특히 식품 가공 때) / [탈수 건조시키다] desiccate [dry (up)] // ~을 많이 섭취하다 drink a lot of liquids [water] // 이 과일에는 ~이 많다 This fruit is juicy. // 이 주변의 대기에는 ~이 많이 함유되어 있다 The air is humid [moist] around here.(▶ humid는 습기가 차서 불쾌한 느낌)

수분(受粉) [식] pollination. **수분하다** be pollinated. ¶바람[곤충]에 의해 수분하는 꽃도 있다 Some flowers are pollinated by the wind [by insects].

수비(守備) 1 defense; 《영》 defence; garrisoning. ¶~를 **강화하다** reinforce [strengthen] one's defense // 전원 ~에 들어갔다 All the men took up defensive positions. // 그들은 성문의 ~을 맡고 있다 They are guarding the castle gate. **수비하다** defend; guard; garrison. ¶요새를 ~ defend a fort. 2 [야구] fielding. ¶~를 **잘하다**[~**가 허술하다**] be good [poor] at fielding / be a good [poor] fielder // 9회 말의 ~에 들어가다 take the field for the bottom of the ninth. **수비하다** field.

● **수비대** a garrison; guards. **수비병** a garrison; guards. **수비율** [야구] field average.

수사(修士) a monk; (탁발의) a friar.

수사(修辭) a figure of speech. ¶~에 뛰어난 사람 a rhetorician.
● **수사법 / 수사학** rhetoric. **수사학자** a rhetorician.

수사(搜査) (a) criminal investigation; [수색] a search; (미) a manhunt(범인의). ¶**과학** ~ scientific crime detection / criminalistics // **범죄** ~ criminal investigation // ~ 선상에 나타나다 [떠오르다] appear on the network of police search // 가택 ~를 하다 search [make a search of] a house (for). **수사하다** investigate; make [conduct] an investigation (into / of); [수색하다] search (for); make a search (for).
● **수사과** the criminal investigation section [division]. **수사관** a criminal investigator; a police detective. **수사망** the police dragnet. ¶~에 걸리다 be caught in the police dragnet // 경찰의 ~에 걸려있었다 The dragnet of the police caught him up. // 경찰은 산속 작은 마을에까지 ~을 폈다 The police had cast [spread / dropped] a dragnet that reached even the smallest village in the mountains. **수사반** a crime [criminal investigation] squad. **수사본부** the investigation headquarters.

수사(數詞) [언] a numeral. ¶**서**(序)[**기**(基)]~ an ordinal [a cardinal] numeral.

수사납다(數-) unlucky; unfortunate; luckless; [서술적] be out of luck; be down on one's luck.

수산(水産) [수산물] marine [aquatic] products.
● **수산 가공품** processed marine products. **수산업** the marine products industry; fisheries. **수산업 협동조합** the fisheries cooperative union.

수산(蓚酸) [화] oxalic acid. ⇨ ˚**옥살산**
● **수산염** an oxalate.

수산화(水酸化) [화] hydration.
● **수산화나트륨** sodium hydroxide. **수산화물** a hydroxide. **수산화칼슘** calcium hydroxide.

수삼(水蔘) undried [green] ginseng.

수상(水上) [수면] water surface; [상류] the upper reaches of a river. ¶~**의** aquatic / water-surface // 축제는 ~에서 벌어졌다 The festival was held on the water. // 잠수함이 ~에 모습을 드러냈다 The submarine surfaced.
● **수상 경기** water [aquatic] sports. ¶~ **대회** an aquatic competition / a swim(ming) meet. **수상생활** aquatic life; life on the water. ¶~**자** a man who lives [makes a living] on the water. **수상 스키** (도구) water skis; (경기) water-skiing. ¶그들은 ~를 타고 있다 They are water-skiing.

수상(手相) the lines of the palm.

수상(受賞) winning a prize. **수상하다** win [receive] a prize; be awarded a prize.
● **수상자** a prize winner [awardee]. ¶**노벨상** ~ a winner of the Nobel Prize / a Nobel-prize winner / a Nobel laureate // ~ **명단** a (prize) winners' list. **수상 작품** a prize winner; (소설) a prize-winning novel.

수상(首相) the prime minister; the Prime Minister; the premier; the Premier; the chancellor(독일의). ¶**전**(前) ~ an ex-premier / a former prime minister // ~**이 되다** hold

수상

(the) premiership / head a Cabinet.
- **수상 관저** the prime minister's official residence.

수상(授賞) prize-giving. **수상하다** award [give] a prize (to a person); recognize.

수상(隨想) random [desultory / occasional / stray] thoughts.
- **수상록** essays; memoirs; stray notes; jottings. ¶몽테뉴 ~ The Essays of Montaigne.

수상기(受像機) a television receiver [set]; a TV set; (컬러텔레비전의) a color set.

수상스럽다(殊常-) strange; mysterious. ⇨= 수상하다 ¶수상스러운 이야기 a questionable [fishy] story // 점원이 나를 수상스러운 듯이 바라보았다 The store clerks stared at me suspiciously [with suspicious eyes]. // 수상스러운 남자가 집 주위에서 서성거리고 있다 A suspicious-looking man is hanging around the house.

수상하다(殊常-) strange; mysterious; questionable; dubious; doubtful; unreliable; suspicious; suspicious-looking; shady; (구어) fishy; queer. ¶수상한 사람 a suspicious (-looking) person / a dubious [suspicious] character / a questionable [shady] character // 수상한 소문 disturbing rumors / a scandal // 수상한 장사를 하는 가게 a shop with a shady reputation // 그 남자가 ~ I suspect that he is guilty. / I suspect [am suspicious of] him. / There is something suspicious [fishy] about him. / He looks very suspicious. // 그는 수상한 사람이다 He is a man of questionable [dubious / doubtful] character. // 그의 말은 ~ What he says is unreliable [questionable / dubious]. // 그녀의 순진한 태도가 ~ Her air of naivety isn't to be trusted [is just a put-on]. // 수상한 사람은 가까이 하지 않는 것이 좋다 You'd better keep away from questionable [suspicious] characters. // 네가 오지 않으면 사람들이 수상하게 여긴다 People will be suspicious [It will look strange] if you don't come. (▶ suspicious는 의심한다, look strange는 이상하게 여겨지다) // 두 사람의 진술(陳述)이 일치하지 않는 점이 ~ The discrepancy between the two men's statements arouses our suspicion. // 날씨가 아주 ~ The weather looks very doubtful. // 두 사람 사이가 ~ I suspect there is [may be] something going on between the two. / 나는 어둠 속에서 수상한 그림자를 보았다 I saw a mysterious figure in the dark. **수상히** strangely; mysteriously; dubiously; doubtfully; suspiciously; queerly.

수색(搜索) (a) quest; a search; (미) a manhunt (범인의); [수사] (an) investigation. ¶행방불명의 어부의 ~ a search for a missing fisherman // 철저한 [대대적인] ~을 펴다 institute a thorough [massive] search (for) / mount an all-out hunt (for) // ~원을 내다 ask the police to search (for) / apply to the police for a person's search. **수색하다** search [look / hunt] (for); make [prosecute] a search (for); rummage; drag. ¶샅샅이 [철저히] ~ search thoroughly (for) / comb // 몸을 ~ frisk (a person) / conduct a body search / rub down (a person) // 경찰은 용의자의 방을 수색했다 The suspect's room was searched by the police.
- **수색대** a search party. **수색 영장** a search warrant. ¶가택 ~ a warrant to search the house.

수색(愁色) a worried [a sorrowful / an anxious] look; a melancholy [gloomy] air; the traces of sorrow (in one's face). ¶(얼굴에) ~을 띠다 wear a worried look / look sad [concerned / anxious / gloomy].

수생(水生) ¶~의 aquatic / living [growing] in the water.
- **수생 생물** (집합적) aquatic life.

수서(水棲) ¶~의 aquatic / living in the water.
- **수서 동물** an aquatic (animal).

수석(首席) [맨 윗자리] the top seat [place]; [우두머리가 되는 사람] the head; the chief. ¶외교단의 ~ the doyen of the diplomatic corps // ~으로 졸업하다 graduate first (on the list) // ~반에서 ~을 차지하다 stand first in one's class / lead one's class / be at the head [top] of the class / be before others in class // ~을 다투다 contend for the top seat [place] / compete to be first in (the class).
- **수석대표** the chief representative [delegate]; the head of the delegation.

수선 noise; fuss; ado; bustle. ¶~을 떨다 [부리다 / 피우다] make [raise] a fuss / fuss (about) / bustle (about) // (구어) make a production // 손님을 맞느라고 ~을 피우다 make much ado to receive a guest. **수선하다** noisy; clamorous; vociferous; bustling.
- **수선쟁이** a bustling fellow; a fusspot; a rattler; a chatterbox.

수선(垂線) [수] a perpendicular (line). ¶밑변으로 향해서 ~을 긋다 draw a perpendicular line toward the base.

수선(修繕) repair(s); mending. ¶~ 중이다 be undergoing repairs / be under repair // ~ 전문 (게시) Mending work only. **수선하다** repair; make repairs (on); mend; fix (up); do up; recondition. ¶수선해야 하다 need repairing [mending] / be in want of repairs // 수선할 수 없다 be beyond [past] repair // 내 구두는 수선하러 보냈다 My shoes are sent to the shoemaker for mending. / I have taken my shoes to be repaired. // 우산 수선할 것 있어요 Do you have any umbrellas that need mending? // 그는 구두를 수선했다 (남을 시켜서) He had his shoes repaired.
- **수선공** a mender; a repairer; a repairman. ¶구두 ~ a shoe repairman / (영) a shoe repairer / (영) a cobbler. **수선비** the cost of repairs; repairing expenses.

수선스럽다 noisy; clamorous. ⇨= 수선하다 (⇨ 수선) ¶수선스러운 분위기 a rowdy [rough] atmosphere / a noisy atmosphere // 수선스러운 남자 a rough [an unpolished] man.

수선화(水仙花) [식] a narcissus (pl. ~es, -cissi).

수성(水性) ¶~의 aqueous.
- **수성 가스** water gas. **수성 도료** water paint; water-based paint; (영) distemper. **수성 사인펜** a felt-tip pen.

수성(水星) [천] Mercury. ¶~의 Mercurian.

수성(獸性) brutality; the beast in man; beastliness; bestiality; animality. ¶그는 ~을 드러냈다 He revealed his animal nature [the beast in him]. / He exposed brutality.

수세(水勢) the force of water [a current].

수세(守勢) a defensive attitude [position]; the defensive. ¶~를 취하다 assume [take] the

defensive / stand[be / act] on the defensive // ~로 몰아넣다 put[throw] (the union) on the defensive // 강경한 반대에 부딪쳐 그는 도리어 ~에 몰렸다 Strong opposition placed [put] him rather on the defensive.

수세미 a scrubbing brush; a pot cleaner; a luffa; a loofah; a vegetable sponge.

수세식(水洗式) ¶변소를 ~으로 개조하다 convert the lavatory into a flush toilet.
●**수세식 변소** a flush toilet.

수소 (거세하지 않은) a bull; (거세한) an ox (pl. oxen); [2~4세의 수송아지] a steer.

수소(水素) [화] hydrogen(기호 H). ¶중~ heavy hydrogen / [이중 수소] deuterium / [삼중 수소] tritium // ~와 화합시키다 hydrogenate / hydrogenize / combine with hydrogen // ~를 첨가하다 hydrogenate / hydrogenize.
●**수소 가스** hydrogen gas. **수소 폭탄** an H-bomb; a hydrogen [fusion / thermonuclear] bomb.

수소문하다(搜所聞-) ask around; inquire here and there.

수속(手續) (a) procedure; formalities; (a) process; proceedings; steps. ¶입국 ~ formalities for entry // 입학 ~은 이달 안으로 마쳐야 한다 The entrance procedures must be completed by the end of this month. // 해외여행에는 어떠한 ~이 필요한지 알려 주십시오 Please tell me what steps I must take (in order) to go abroad. // 이 물건을 수입하기 위해서는 복잡한 ~이 필요하다 You have to go through complicated formalities to import the article.

수송(輸送) transport; transportation; transit; (문어) conveyance; traffic; carriage; deportation. ¶화물 ~ the transport of goods / freightage // 국내[국외 / 장거리] ~ inland [overseas / long-distance] transport [transportation] // 육상[해상 / 철도 / 항공] ~ land [sea / rail / air] transport / transport [carriage] by land [sea / rail / air] // 요즈음은 신선한 채소의 ~에도 항공기가 사용된다 Nowadays airplanes are used for the transport of fresh vegetables. // 그 화물은 ~중에 파손되었다 The goods were damaged in transit. **수송하다** transport; (문어) convey; deport; carry. ¶항공기는 승객뿐만 아니라 우편과 화물도 수송한다 Planes transport [carry] not only passengers but also mail and freight.
●**수송기** a transport (plane). ¶군용 ~ a troop transport plane / a troop carrier // 화물 ~ a freighter / a cargo craft / a skyfreighter. **수송 기관** a means of transportation[conveyance]. **수송량** (volume of) traffic; transport volume; quantity of goods transported; (화물의) carloadings. **수송선** a transport (ship). **수송 열차** a transport train.

수수 [식] an African [Indian] millet; durra; a kaoliang(고량); a sorghum.
●**수수경단** a millet dumpling. **수수깡** a millet stalk.

수수께끼 a riddle; a conundrum; a puzzle; an enigma; a mystery. ¶스핑크스의 ~ the riddle of the sphinx // ~의 사나이 a mystery man / a man of mystery / a sphinx (pl. ~es, sphinges) // 우주의 ~를 푸는 열쇠 a clue [key] to the mystery [riddles] of the universe // ~를 내다 give (a person) a puzzle [conundrum] to guess[make out] / ask [set] (a person) a riddle to guess[make out] / ask[put / pose / propose / propound] a riddle to (a person) // ~를 풀다 unriddle / solve [interpret / guess / undo / find out] a riddle / answer [solve / work out / make out] a puzzle / solve [untangle] a mystery // ~를 놀이하다 play at riddles / ask riddles // 네게 ~를 하나 내겠다 I will give you a riddle to guess. / Here's a riddle for you. // 그는 ~ 같은 죽음을 당했다 He died a mysterious death. // 그녀는 입가에 ~ 같은 미소를 띠었다 An enigmatic smile played about her lips. // 그 사건은 아직도 ~다 The affair is still cloaked [shrouded] in mystery. / The affair remains an unsolved mystery. // 너는 ~ 같은 소리를 하는구나 You talk in riddles.

수수료(手數料) [구전] a commission; brokerage(거간의); [요금] a fee; a charge. ¶등록 ~ the registration fee // 매입[판매] ~ a buying [selling] commission // 매상고에 대한 10퍼센트의 ~로 at[for] a commission of 10% on sales // 적정 ~를 내다 give (a person) a fair commission / ~는 1,000원 받다 charge (a person) a 1,000 won commission / take a 1,000 won commission // ~를 징수하다 levy a charge (for trouble) // ~를 받지 않다 make no charge // 그는 차를 한 대 팔 때마다 10퍼센트의 ~를 받고 있다 He receives a commission of 10 percent on the sale of each car.

수수방관하다(袖手傍觀-) merely watch; stand by idly and watch; look on (a scene) with folded arms; sit back and watch; be [remain] an idle onlooker. ¶그들은 수수방관할 뿐이었다 They just looked on without doing anything. / They just remained spectators. // 수수방관하여서는 아무 일도 해결할 수 없다 You can't solve anything by merely watching with your arms folded. // 그들의 곤경을 수수방관할 수 없다 We cannot stand idly by[be idle onlookers] when they are in distress.

수수하다 (맵시가) ordinary-looking; plain; simple; quiet; (질이) moderate; average; (빛깔이) sober; [점잖다] unpretentious; restrained; undemonstrative; uninteresting. ¶수수하게 unaffectedly / plainly / simply / quietly / soberly // 수수한 빛깔의 블라우스 a blouse of a quiet [subdued] color // 수수한 옷차림을 하고 있다 be soberly [quietly] dressed[attired] // 그녀는 수수한 머리 모양을 하고 있었다 She does up her hair simply. // 그녀는 옷차림이 ~ She is unobtrusively dressed.

수수하다(授受-) give and receive; deliver; transfer.

수술 [식] a stamen (pl. ~s, stamina); an androecium (pl. -cia).

수술(手術) a surgical operation; an operation. ¶대[소] ~ a major [minor] operation // 복부 ~ an operation on the abdomen (of a patient) // ~ 전[후]의 preoperative [postoperative] // ~을 받다 have [undergo / go through] an operation (for gastric ulcer) / be operated on (for appendicitis) / go [be] under the knife // 무릎 ~을 받다 have one's knee operated on // ~을 두려워하다 be afraid [have a horror] of the knife [operation] // ~중에 죽다 die under the knife // ~은 아주 잘

되었다 The operation was a great success.∥나는 맹장염으로 ~을 받았다 I had an operation for appendicitis. **수술하다** operate; perform[conduct] an operation. ¶맹장을 ~ perform an appendectomy∥수술하기에는 너무 늦었다 It is too late to perform an operation on him.
● **수술대** an operating table. **수술비** charges for operation; operation charges. **수술실** an operating room[(영) theatre]; a surgery. **수술의** a surgeon; an operating surgeon.

수습(收拾) control; settlement. ¶~ 방안을 논의하다 discuss measures to save the situation∥사태 ~에 힘쓰다 make an effort to put the situation under control∥사태는 ~이 어렵게 되었다 The situation got out of control[hand]. **수습하다** control; get under control; save. ¶수습하기 어려운 difficult[hard] to deal with / hard to manage[control / settle]∥민심을 ~ gain public opinion / win the hearts of the people∥사건을 ~ settle a matter / put[give] an end to a matter∥원만히 ~ reach a peaceful settlement∥사태는 수습할 수 없게 되었다 The situation got out of control[hand].∥마침내 우리는 사태를 수습했다 We finally settled the matter. / We have the situation under control[in hand] now.∥나는 어떻게 수습해야 좋을지 몰라 난감했다 I was utterly at a loss how to smooth things over. ➔¶말썽이 원만히 수습되었다 The trouble was settled amicably.

수습(修習) apprenticeship; probation. ¶~ 중이다 be on probation / be in training. **수습하다** practice oneself (in a trade); receive training (in); learn (by observation). ¶사무를 ~ learn the business routine of an office.
● **수습공** an apprentice. **수습 기간** a probationary[probation] period; (게시의) a period of apprenticeship[probation]. **수습기자** a cub reporter; a junior reporter. **수습사원** a probationary employee. **수습생** an apprentice student; a trainee; a probationer.

수시로(隨時-) [언제든지] at any time; at all times; [필요에 따라] (문어) as occasion demands; on[upon] occasion; [때때로] from time to time. ¶누구든지 ~ 신청할 수 있습니다 Anyone can apply at any time.∥우리는 점원을 ~ 고용하고 있다 We employ a clerk whenever necessary[as occasion demands].∥버스는 정원이 차면 ~ 발차한다 The bus will start as soon as[when] it has enough passengers.∥이 학교에서는 학생의 입학을 ~ 허용하고 있다 Students are admitted at any time into this school.

수식(水蝕) [지] erosion (by the action of water).

수식(數式) a numerical formula (pl. ~s, -lae); a numerical expression.

수식(修飾) 1 [장식] (a) decoration; ornamentation; embroidery; (an) adornment; (an) embellishment; [음] (a) figuration; (문장 등의) a rhetorical flourish. ¶그는 ~이 많은 문장을 쓴다 He writes in ornate[florid] style. **수식하다** decorate; adorn; ornament; [음] figure; [윤색하다] embellish; embroider; garnish. [문장을 미사여구로 ~ ornament one's writing with flowery words. ➔¶그의 이야기는 상당히 수식되어 있다 His stories are highly embellished. 2 [언] modification;

qualification. **수식하다** modify; qualify. ¶이 부사는 어떤 말을 수식하는가 What does this adverb modify?
● **수식어** a modifier; a qualifier.

수신(受信) reception; the receipt of a message. ¶라디오 ~ radio reception∥단파 ~ short-wave reception. **수신하다** receive; receive a message[letter]. ¶라디오로 수신한 음악 a music received by radio∥그는 뉴욕으로부터의 텔렉스를 수신하였다 He received a telex message from New York.
● **수신국 / 수신소** a receiving station[office]; an office of receipt. **수신기** a receiver. **수신인** an addressee; a recipient. ¶~ 불명의 편지 a blind letter.∥그 편지는 ~ 불명으로 반송되었다 The letter was returned marked "addressee unknown."

수신(修身) moral culture[training]. **수신하다** cultivate oneself; practice moral culture; lead a virtuous life.
● **수신제가** moral culture and home management. ¶~하다 cultivate one's moral culture and manage one's family[household].

수실(繡-) embroidery thread.

수심(水深) the depth of water. ¶~이 깊은 항구 a deep-water harbor∥~ 약 10미터인 곳에(서) at a depth of about ten meters∥~를 재다 sound[measure] the depth of the water / take soundings∥그 호수의 가장 깊은 곳은 ~이 30미터나 된다 The lake is thirty meters deep[in depth] at its deepest point. ¶"이 연못의 ~은 얼마나 됩니까?" "3미터입니다." "How deep is this pond?" "It is three meters deep[in depth]."
● **수심 측량** sounding; plumbing.

수심(垂心) [수] an orthocenter.

수심(愁心) anxiety; worry; sorrow; grief; apprehension(s); gloominess; melancholy. ¶~에 잠기다 be sorrow-stricken[disconsolate] / be oppressed with sorrow / be sunk[plunged] in grief∥~을 띠다 wear a worried look / look concerned[gloomy / sad]∥비보에 접하여 온 도시가 ~에 잠겼다 The whole town was overshadowed by the sad news.

수심(獸心) a brutal heart; a bestial mind. ¶인면 ~ man in face, brute in mind / a beast with a human face.

수십(數十) scores; dozens; several tens. ¶~만 원 hundreds of thousands of won∥~ 년 간 for (several) decades / for dozens of years∥사망자는 ~ 명에 이르렀다 Dozens[Scores] of people died[were killed].∥지난 ~ 년 동안에 여러 가지 변화가 생겼다 Many changes have taken places during the last[past] several decades.

수압(水壓) water pressure; hydraulic pressure. ¶~이 높다[낮다] The water pressure is high[low].∥~이 갑자기 올라갔다[내려갔다] The hydraulic pressure suddenly rose [dropped].
● **수압계** a water-pressure gauge; a piezometer.

수액(樹液) sap; milk. ¶~이 많은 sapful / sappy∥~을 채워하다 sap[tap] (a tree)(▶ tap은 칼자국을 내어)∥~이 흐른다 The sap runs (in a tree).

수양(收養) [관용어적] adopted; adoptive; foster.
● **수양부모** adoptive[foster] parents. **수양아**

들[딸] a foster[an adopted] son[daughter].
수양아버지[어머니] a foster father[mother].
수양(修養) cultivation (of the mind); moral [mental] culture; (mental) training; character-building. ¶정신 ~ spiritual [moral] culture // ~을 쌓다 cultivate one's mind / build up one's character // 그는 ~이 부족하다 He lacks self-discipline. // 요가는 육체의 ~뿐만 아니라 정신의 ~도 된다 Yoga is good training for the mind[good for training the mind] as well as the body. **수양하다** improve oneself; cultivate one's mind; train.
수양버들(垂楊-) [식] a weeping willow.
수업(修業) pursuit of knowledge; study. **수업하다** pursue knowledge; study; get one's education[training] (from). ¶의학을 ~ study medical science.
● **수업 연한** years required for graduation. ¶우리 학교의 ~은 4년이다 The course of study in our school extends over four years.
수업(授業) teaching; instruction; (학교 전체의) school; (학급의) a class; [과업] (school) lessons. ¶과외 ~ a special class / an extra lesson // 야간 ~ night classes // ~ 중에 during a class / in the middle of a class // ~이 끝난 뒤에 after school (is over) // ~을 끝내다 dismiss a class // ~을 빼먹다 dodge [skip / cut] a lesson // ~에 들어가다 (교사가) go to one's class / teach (a school / class) / meet the class / (학생이) attend school // 학생들은 ~ 중입니다 The boys are now at school [in class]. // 우리는 하루 다섯 시간씩 1주 5일 간의 ~을 6개월간 받는다 We have six months' lessons, of five hours a day and of five days a week. // 내일은 ~이 없다 We have no school[classes] tomorrow. // ~은 9월 10일 시작된다 School [Classes] will begin on September 10. // 선생님의 ~ (담당 시간)는 몇 시간입니까 How many classes do you teach? // ~은 몇 시에 시작됩니까 What time does school begin? // ~ 중에 잡담 금지 No talking in class. // 나는 송 교수의 ~을 받았다 I took lessons from Prof. Song. **수업하다** teach; instruct; give lessons[classes]. ¶완전히 영어로 ~ conduct a class entirely in English.
● **수업료** tuition (fees); school[college] fees. ¶~가 없는 학교 a free school // ~ 없이[한 월 5만 원으로] 가르치다 teach a person without charging anything[for fifty thousand won a month]; **수업 시간** school hours; [교사가 가르치는 시간] one's teaching hours [load]. **수업 일수** the number of school days.
수없다(數-) [셀 수 없이 많다] numberless; countless; innumerable; incalculable; uncounted. ¶하늘에는 수없는 별이 반짝이고 있었다 Countless stars were twinkling in the sky. **수없이** countlessly; innumerably; without[out of] number; in large numbers; beyond[out of] count. ¶~ 되풀이하다 repeat a hundred times.
수여(授與) (증서 등의) conferment; presentation; (상품의) awarding. ¶졸업 증서 ~ the presentation of diplomas. **수여하다** give; grant; confer (a degree on a person); award (a medal to a winner); present (a thing to a person / a person with a thing); decorate (a person with an order). // 면허증[졸업 증서]를 ~ grant a person a license[diploma] // 학위

[훈장]를 ~ confer a degree[decoration] on a person // 대학은 그에게 박사 학위를 수여했다 The university conferred a doctor's degree on him. ➔¶그는 그 대학으로부터 박사 학위를 수여받았다 He was given a doctor's degree by[received a doctor's degree from] that university.
● **수여식** a conferment ceremony.
수역(水域) an area (of the sea); waters. ¶경제 ~ an economic zone (off the coast) // 공동 규제 ~ a jointly controlled waters[fishing zone] // 국제 ~ international waters // 전관 ~ an exclusive zone // 강의 위험 ~ a dangerous area of the river.
수연(壽宴) a birthday feast for old man (to celebrate his long life).
수열(數列) [수] a series; (a) (numerical) progression; a sequence (of numbers). ¶등비 ~ (a) geometric progression[sequence] // 등차 ~ (an) arithmetical progression [sequence] // 유한[무한] ~ a finite [an infinite] sequence of numbers.
수염(鬚髯) 1 [콧수염] a mustache; (영) a moustache; [구레나룻] whiskers; [턱수염] a beard; [염소수염] a goatee. (▶ 영어에서는 우리말 "수염"과 같은 총칭어가 없고, 수염이 나는 부위에 따른 beard, mustache, whiskers 등의 단어만 있을 뿐임) ¶가짜 ~ a false mustache [beard] // 빽빽한 ~ a bristly mustache [beard] // 숱이 많은 ~ a heavy mustache // 끝이 치켜 올라간 ~ a turned-up mustache // ~이 있는 mustached / bearded / whiskered / ~이 없는 beardless / (면도를 해서) clean-[smooth-]shaven // ~을 기르다 grow[raise] a mustache[beard] // ~을 기르고 있다 wear[have] a mustache[beard] // ~을 깎다 (자신이) shave (oneself) / (이발소에서) have[get / take] a shave / get shaved // ~을 쓰다듬다 stroke one's beard // 나는 ~이 빨리 자란다 My beard grows quickly.
2 (고양이·쥐 등의) whiskers; (물고기 등의) a barbel.
3 (보리의) barley beard; (옥수수의) corn silk; corn tassel. ¶(옥수수의) ~을 뽑다 pluck the tassel off (a corn).
수염이 대 자라도 먹어야 양반이다(속담) Food comes before the maintenance of dignity; Life comes before pride.
수영(水泳) swimming; bathing; a swim; (영) a bathe. ¶~의 명수 an expert swimmer // ~을 배우다 take lessons in swimming / learn how to swim // ~을 연습하다 practice swimming // ~을 잘하다[잘 못하다] be a good [poor] swimmer / be good [no good / poor] at swimming. **수영하다** swim; (영) bathe (in the sea); have a swim; (영) have a bathe. ¶수영하러 가다 go swimming[for a swim] / (영) go bathing[for a bathe] // 풀장에 수영하러 가자 Let's go swimming in the pool.
● **수영 경기** a swimming race; (the sport of) swimming. **수영복** a swimming [bathing] suit; a swimsuit; [남자용 팬츠] (a pair of) swimming trunks. **수영 선수** a swimmer; (남자) (미) a merman; (미) mermaid. **수영장** a swimming [bathing] place; a swimming pool [tank].
수예(手藝) handicraft; manual arts.
● **수예품** a fancy work [article]; (집합적) handiwork; handicraft.
수온(水溫) the temperature of the water;

water temperature. ¶연못의 ~ the temperature of the water in the pond.

수완(手腕) ability; capability; capacity; skill; (미국 구어) faculty. ¶외교 ~ diplomatic ability // ~이 있는 able / capable / competent / talented // ~이 없는 incapable / incompetent / inefficient // ~을 발휘한다 exercise one's ability[skill] / display[exhibit / show] one's ability[skill] // 네 ~이 놀랍다 I admire your ability. ¶그는 그 교섭을 (성공적으로) 타결지을 ~이 있다[없다] He is capable[incapable] of bringing the talks to a (successful) conclusion. / He has[does not have] the ability to arrange a negotiated settlement.
● **수완가** an able[a capable] man; a man of ability; (미국 구어) a go-getter; (약빠른 사람) a shrewd person. ¶그는 상당한 ~다 He is full of resources. / He is a man of action. / (미국 구어) He is a real go-getter.

수요(需要) demand; request. ¶가 ~ false needs[demand] / fictitious demand / speculative demand(투기적인) // 계절적인 ~ seasonal demand // 꾸준한 ~ steady demand // 소비자[개인] ~ consumer demand // 실 ~ actual demand // 유효 ~ effective demand // 일시적 ~ temporary demand // 잠재 ~ latent demand // 총 ~ aggregate[gross / total] demand // ~의 탄력성 elasticity of demand // ~를 충족시키다 meet[supply] the demand // 이 종류의 물품은 ~가 많다[적다] Articles of this kind are in great[little / poor] demand. // ~가 공급을 상회한다 The demand exceeds the supply. / Supply cannot catch up with demand. // ~가 둔화되고 있다 The demand is lagging[diminishing].
● **수요 가격** the demand price. **수요 공급** supply and demand(▶ 어순이 한국어와 반대임). **수요 공급의 법칙** the law of supply and demand. **수요자** a consumer (소비자); a prospective customer[buyer].

수요일(水曜日) Wednesday(약어 Wed.). ¶그는 지난주 ~에 여기에 왔다 He came here last Wednesday[on Wednesday last].

수욕(獸慾) [음란한 욕망] carnal[animal] desires; bestiality; sexual[beastly] appetite(s)[instinct]. ¶~을 채우다 satisfy[gratify] one's carnal desires.

수용(收用) expropriation. ¶강제 ~ compulsory expropriation // 토지 ~ land expropriation // 토지 ~법 Compulsory Purchase of Land Act / law of expropriation of land / the land expropriation act. **수용하다** expropriate (a person's estate). ➔¶고속도로 건설로 그의 토지는 강제 수용당했다 His land was expropriated to build an expressway.

수용(收容) accommodation; reception; admission; seating; housing; (난파 선원 등의) picking up; a picking. **수용하다** accommodate; admit; seat; receive; intern; house; pick up. ¶그 호텔은 1,000명까지 수용할 수 있다 The hotel can accommodate up to a thousand people. / The hotel has accommodations[(영) accommodation] for a thousand people. // 강당은 5,000명을 수용할 수 있다 The auditorium seats five thousand people. ➔¶그 다섯 소년은 소년원에 수용되었다 The five boys were sent to a reformatory. // 범인은 교도소에 수용되어 있다 The criminal is locked up in jail. // 부상자는 근처의 병원에 수용되었다 The wounded persons were taken to a neighboring hospital.
● **수용 능력** capacity; (호텔 등의) sleeping accommodation(s); (극장 등의) a seating capacity. ¶공회당의 ~은 3,000명이다 The public hall has a seating capacity of 3,000. **수용소** a concentration camp(적국인의); a repatriate reception center(귀환자의). ¶포로 ~ a prisoner of war camp(약어 a POW camp). **수용자** inmates(양로원 등의); inpatients(병원의); prisoners(교도소의).

수용(受容) acceptance; reception. ¶~적인 receptive / recipient // ~ 계획 an immigration induction[reception] program. **수용하다** accept; receive. ¶이 나라가 수용하는 이민 수는 연간 2천 명으로 규정되어 있다 The quota of immigrants to be received[accepted] into this country is set at 2,000 per year.
● **수용성** receptiveness; receptivity; recipience; receptive capacity.

수용(需用) consumption. ¶전력[가스]의 ~ consumption[use] of electric power[gas]. **수용하다** consume.
● **수용가** a consumer; a user; a customer. ¶전력 ~ a consumer[user] of electricity.

수용성(水溶性) ¶~의 water-soluble.
● **수용성 비타민** water-soluble vitamin.

수용액(水溶液) an aqueous[a water] solution.

수운(水運) water transportation; water traffic; transportation by water. ¶~의 편의가 좋다 have good facilities for water transport[transportation] (▶ transport는 주로 화물의, transportation은 주로 사람의 수송).

수원(水源) the source[head]; the fountainhead; a riverhead; a headspring; the headwaters; (수도의) the source of water supply; the water source; a reservoir(저수지). ¶그 강의 ~은 알프스 산맥이다 The river flows from the Alps. // 서울시의 상수도의 ~은 한강이다 Seoul depends on the Hangang(Han River) for its water supply.
● **수원지** the catchment area[basin]; a gathering ground.

수월찮다 (일이) not easy; troublesome; hard; difficult; (수량이) not a few[little]; no small; some; many; much; considerable. ¶수월찮은 수입 a good[handsome / tidy] income // 빈곤한 사람이 여러 자식을 키우기란 ~ It is a hard job for a poor man to bring up a lot of children. **수월찮이** fairly; pretty; considerably; rather. ¶~ 돈이 든다 cost fairly much of money.

수월하다 easy; simple. ¶수월한 일 an easy[a light] task / a soft job (미국 속어) a cinch / a pushover // 하기가 ~ be easy[no trouble] to do / have no difficulty in doing. **수월히** easily; readily; handily; with ease; without difficulty[trouble / effort]. ¶~ 이기다 win easily / win an easy victory (over) // ~ 할 수가 있다 be easy to do / be easily done // ~ 돈을 벌다 make an easy gain // 문제가 아주 ~ 풀렸다 I was able to solve the problem quite easily.

수위(水位) water level. ¶위험 ~ the dangerous water level // ~가 낮다[높다] The water level is low[high]. // ~가 내려갔다 The water level dropped[fell]. // 저수지의 ~가 1미터 올

라갔다[내려갔다] The water level in the reservoir rose[fell] by a meter.∥해빙으로 강의 ~가 2미터 올라갔다 The (water level of the) river rose by two meters with the thaw.
● 수위계 a water gauge; a hydrograph. 수위표 a watermark.
수위(守衛) 〔지키는 일〕 guard; 〔경비원〕 a guard; a security guard; 〔문지기〕 a doorman; a doorkeeper; a gatekeeper; a janitor; a porter. **수위하다** guard.
● 수위실 a gatehouse; a guard office; a porter's lodge.
수위(首位) the first [top / premier] place; the foremost [leading] position. ¶~를 다투다 fight for first place / ~를 차지하다 occupy [win] (the) first place / rank [stand] first (in) / be at the head [top] (of)∥그는 항상 학급에서 ~를 차지하고 있다 He is always at the top of his class.
● 수위 타자 the leading hitter.
수유(授乳) nursing; breast-feeding; lactation. **수유하다** nurse; feed; suckle; give suck [the breast] to; lactate. ¶젖먹이에게 ~ nurse a baby / breast-feed a baby.
● 수유기 period of lactation; the lactation.
수육 〔삶아 익힌 쇠고기〕 cooked [boiled] beef.
수육(獸肉) flesh of animals; (식용의) meat. ¶갓 잡은 ~ green meat.
수은(水銀) mercury; quicksilver; hydrargyrum(기호 Hg). ¶염화[염화 제1/염화 제2] ~ mercury [mercurous / mercuric] chloride∥유기 ~ (화합물) an organic mercury compound∥~의 mercurial / mercuric(수은 2가(價)를 함유하는) / mercurous(수은 1가를 함유하는) / ~으로 처리하다 treat with mercury.
● 수은등 a mercury lamp; 〔증기등〕 a mercury vapor lamp; 〔아크등〕 a mercury arc lamp. 수은 온도계 a mercury thermometer. 수은주 a column of mercury; a mercurial column. ¶~가 34도까지 올라갔다 The mercury went up to thirty-four degrees. 수은 중독 mercury poisoning; mercurialism.
수음(手淫) masturbation; self-abuse; onanism. **수음하다** masturbate; indulge in masturbation; practice masturbation [onanism]; commit self-abuse.
수의(壽衣) a shroud; a winding sheet; cerements; grave clothes.
수의(隨意) voluntariness; option; pleasure. ¶~ free / (임의 선택의) optional / (자발적인) voluntary∥~로 voluntarily / freely / at will / as one pleases / at one's pleasure [option]∥~로 처분하다 deal with (a matter) as one thinks fit [at one's discretion].
● 수의 계약 a private [free] contract. 수의근 〔생〕 a voluntary muscle.
수의(사)(獸醫師) 〔의〕 a veterinary surgeon; (미) a veterinarian; (구어) a vet.
● 수의학 veterinary science [medicine].
수익(收益) profit; earnings; gainings(이익); income(소득·수입); a return (on the investment)(▶ 노동·투자·장사 등의 이익으로, 흔히 복수형); proceeds(판매 등의 이익). ¶세금 포함 [공제] ~ pretax [after-tax] yield∥주식의 배당 ~ dividend yield / 순[총] ~ net [gross] earnings∥가옥[토지] 임대 ~ income from rented houses [land]∥자선 바자회의 ~ proceeds of [from] a charity sale∥~이 있는 profitable / lucrative∥~이 좋다 [나쁘다] yield [bear] a good [bad] return∥~을 올리다 realize [make / turn out] profit / make [fetch] (a million won)∥매출의 ~은 500만 원이었다 The returns from the sale were five million won.
● 수익금 earnings; gains; 〔매상금〕 proceeds; profits. ¶자선 공연의 ~ the proceeds from [raised by] a charity performance. 수익률 an earning rate; (주가의) price-earnings ratio; (토지 생산력의) a rate of yield.
수익자(受益者) a beneficiary; a person who stands to benefit(▶ a beneficiary는 주로 유산·배상금 등을 받는 사람). ¶도로의 포장은 ~ 부담이다 Those who will benefit have to bear the cost of paving the road.
수인(囚人) a prisoner. ⇨~죄수
● 수인 호송차 a prison van.
수인성 전염병(水因性傳染病) waterborne infection.
수일(數日) a few days; several days. ¶~ 내에 in a matter of days / in several [a few] days.
수임(受任) acceptance of an appointment. **수임하다** be nominated; accept an appointment [office]; take office (a person).
● 수임자 a nominee; an appointee; 〔법〕 a mandatory; a mandatary.
수입(收入) 〔소득〕 an income; earnings; 〔세입〕 a revenue; 〔매상금〕 receipts; 〔수익〕 proceeds; takings. ¶고정 ~ a fixed [regular / periodical] income∥국가 ~ national revenues∥실 ~ a net income / an actual income / net earnings∥임시 ~ perquisite∥잡 ~ miscellaneous earnings / sundry receipts∥총 ~ a total [gross] income / gross earnings∥~과 지출 incomings and outgoings / income and outgo / receipts and expenses / 〔세입과 세출〕 revenue and expenditure∥상점의 ~ the takings of a shop∥바자회의 ~ the proceeds from the bazaar∥보통 ~의 가정 a family of average income∥~이 좋은 직업 a gainful [profitable] occupation [profession]∥…의 ~이 있다 have [enjoy / earn / gain / draw] an income (of)∥~이 많다 [적다] have [earn] a large [small] income(수입이)∥ ~ draw a large [small] income(월급이)∥~을 얻다 earn [gain / obtain] an income (of) / derive [draw] one's income (from)∥그것은 ~이 있는[되지 않는] 일이다 It is remunerative [unremunerative] work.∥~과 지출을 맞추기가 힘듭니다 I have difficulty making both ends meet.∥그들은 ~에 맞는 [이상의] 생활을 하고 있다 They live within [beyond] their means.
● 수입원 the source of one's income. 수입 인지 a revenue stamp; a fiscal stamp.
수입(輸入) (산물의) import; importation; (제도·사상 등의) introduction. ¶무환(無換) ~ no-draft import∥밀 ~ smuggling∥자유 ~ free import∥직 ~ direct [indirect] import∥~을 허가하다 permit the import∥~을 금지하다 ban [prohibit] the import∥~을 제한하다 limit [restrict] the import∥~ 장벽을 높이다 step up import barriers (against)∥~의 문호를 좀 더 개방하다 open one's import market more widely∥그 나라에서는 쇠고기의 ~이 규제되어 있다 In that country the import of beef is restricted.∥조깅이라는 말은 최근의 ~ 외래어이다 The word "jogging" is a foreign word of recent introduction [is a recently introduced foreign word]. **수입하다** import;

수자원

수입할 수 있는 importable // 우리나라는 브라질에서 커피를 수입하고 있다 Our country imports coffee from Brazil.
● 수입 가격 an import price. 수입 관세 import duties. 수입국 an importing country. 수입 면장 an import license. 수입상 / 수입업자 an importer; an import trader [merchant]. 수입 신용장 an import (letter of) credit. 수입액 the amount of imports. 수입 의존도 the rate of dependence on imports. 수입 자유화 liberalization of imports. 수입 제한 import restriction [controls]. ¶~ 품목표 a negative list. 수입 초과 an excess of imports. 수입품 imported goods[articles]. 수입 할당 제도 the import quota system. 수입항 an import port.

수자원(水資源) water resources.
● 수자원 개발 the development of water resources.

수작(秀作) an excellent [outstanding] work (of art).

수작(酬酌) 1 [술잔을 주고받음] an exchange of cups of wine. 수작하다 exchange cups of wine. 2 [말을 주고받음] exchanging words; [그 말] words exchanged; a talk. ¶허튼~하다 talk nonsense / say silly things // (이성에게)~을 걸다 court / woo / pay court [one's addresses] (to). 수작하다 exchange remarks [words]; talk back and forth.

수장(水葬) 1 [물속에 장사 지냄] burial at sea [in the sea]; water burial. 수장하다 bury at sea [in the sea]. ➔¶세 선원의 시체는 수장되었다 The bodies of the three sailors were buried at sea. 2 [물속에 가라앉힘] ¶~되다 be sent to the ocean's bottom / be swallowed by the sea.

수장(收藏) garnering; storage. 수장하다 garner (up) (곡물 창고 등에); store up; keep [put] (something) in storage.

수장(袖章) a sleeve badge; sleeve stripes; (갈매기 모양의) a chevron. ¶~을 달다 put on a chevron.

수재(水災) flood damage. ➪수해(水害)
● 수재민 flood sufferers [victims]; sufferers from a flood.

수재(秀才) [뛰어난 재주] great ability [talent]; genius; [그런 재주를 지닌 사람] a brilliant person; a genius; a prodigy; a talented person. ¶그 학교는 많은 ~를 배출했다 The school has produced many brilliant men.

수저 1 a spoon. ➪숟가락 2 [숟가락과 젓가락] spoon and chopsticks. ¶은~ 한 벌 a set of silver spoon and chopsticks.
● 수저통 a spoon stand.

수적(數的) numerical. ¶~으로(는) numerically / in number // ~으로 우세하다 exceed (the enemy) in number / be numerically superior (to) / be stronger (than us) (in number) / outnumber (us).

수전(水田) a paddy field; a (rice) paddy; a wet field.

수전노(守錢奴) a stingy man; a miser; a niggard; a skinflint; a screw; (미국 속어) a tightwad; (구어) a penny-pincher.

수전증(手顫症) [한] tremor of the hand; palsy in the arm.

수절하다(守節-) [절개를 지키다] keep one's integrity unsullied; keep[remain faithful to] one's principles; hold[stick / live up] to one's principles; (정조를) defend one's chastity; retain one's virtue; (과부가) do not remarry.

수정(水晶) (a) (rock) crystal; crystallized quartz. ¶~의 crystal / crystalline // 자~ amethyst // 연~ smoky quartz // ~같이 맑은 물 crystal-clear water.
● 수정 시계 a quartz [crystal] watch [clock]. 수정체 (눈의) the crystalline lens [humor]; the eye lens.

수정(受精) [생] fertilization; fecundation; [식] pollination. ¶인공 ~ artificial insemination // 자가 ~ self-fertilization // 체내 ~ internal fertilization // 체외 ~ external fertilization. 수정하다 be fertilized [fecundated]; be pollinated. ➔¶수정시키다 fecundate / fertilize / pollinate.
● 수정 능력 fertility; fertilizing power. 수정란 a fertilized egg. 미(未)~ an unfertilized egg.

수정(修正) an amendment(▶ 법안이나 헌법에 쓰이는 경우가 많음); a revision; (a) modification; (an) alteration; (잘못의) (a) correction; (a) rectification. ¶예산의 대~ a drastic revision of the budget // 궤도 ~ an orbit correction // 헌법 ~ 제1조 (미) the First Amendment (to the Constitution) // 원고에 ~을 가하다 revise a draft / make some revisions in a manuscript. 수정하다 amend; revise; modify; correct; rectify. ¶의안을 ~ amend a bill / 자구를 ~ amend some words (in a contract) / revise wording (of one's letter).
● 수정안 (원안의) a draft amendment; a proposed revision; [수정된 안] an amendment; a revised [amended] bill. ¶~을 제출하다 propose [put forward] an amendment (to a bill). 수정자 an amender. 수정 자본주의 modified [revised] capitalism. 수정주의 revisionism.

수정(修整) adjustment; regulation; [사진] retouching; a retouch. 수정하다 adjust; regulate; [사진] retouch (a negative). ¶사진을 ~ retouch[touch up] a photograph.

수정과(水正果) sujeonggwa; a fruit punch.

수정관(輸精管) [생] a spermatic duct; a spermaduct; a seminal duct.

수제(手製) ¶~의 [손으로 만든] handmade / handwrought / made by hand / [자가 제작의] homemade(식품이) / made by oneself.
● 수제품 a handmade article.

수제비 sujebi; clear soup with dough flakes.
수제비(를) 뜨다 [맑은장국에 반죽한 밀가루를 조금씩 떼어 넣다] put flakes of dough into clear soup; [물수제비뜨다] skip stones.

수제자(首弟子) one's best pupil [disciple] (of). ¶그는 신 선생의 ~였다 He was (at) the top among Mr. Sin's pupils. / He was the most brilliant of Mr. Sin's students.

수조(水槽) a water tank; a cistern. ¶양어[실험]용 ~ a fish [test] tank.
● 수조차 a tank car [truck].

수조(水藻) an aquatic plant.

수족(手足) hands and feet; ➪손발 ¶~을 못 쓰게 되다 lose the use of one's limbs // 남의 ~처럼 일하다 serve a person like a tool / move [act] at another's beck and call.

수족관(水族館) an aquarium (pl. ~s, aquaria). ¶해양 ~ an oceanarium (pl. ~s, -ria).

수주(受注) acceptance [receiving] an order;

booking. ¶~가 감소하고 있다 Orders are falling off. / The number of orders received is decreasing. **수주하다** receive[accept] an order.
● **수주액** the amount of orders received.
수준(水準) **1** [수평면] water level.
2 [표준] a standard; [정도] a level. ¶최고 ~ the highest level / the peak / the high-water mark (of English poetry) // 문화 ~ a cultural level // 생활~ a standard of living / a living standard // ~에 이르다 reach a certain level / come up to the standard // ~에 미치지 못하다 [~ 이하이다] be below[fall short of] the standard / (구어) be below par // 그의 연기는 아직 아마추어의 ~을 벗어나지 못했다 His playing is no better than that of an amateur. / His playing is still at the level of an amateur[is still amateurish]. // 그는 일반 대중이 받아들일 수 있도록 ~을 낮추어서 글을 썼다 He lowered the level of his writing to appeal to the general public. // 그의 학력은 ~ 이상[이하]이다 His academic ability is above[below] average. // 우리의 수학 ~은 그들보다 높다[과 같다] In mathematics we are on a higher level than[on the same level as] they are.
● **수준기** a (water) level.
수줍다 shy; bashful; diffident; timid; (소녀가) coy. ¶수줍은 남자 a shy[timid] man // 수줍은 표정[미소] a shy look[smile] // 수줍은 소녀 a modest[shy / bashful] girl // 아이는 수줍게 웃었다 The child smiled shyly. // 그녀는 수줍어서 얼굴을 들지 못했다 She was too shy [bashful] to look up.
수줍어하다 be[feel] shy; be coy; be bashful; be abashed. ¶수줍어하는 사람 a bashful [shy] person.
수줍음 shyness; coyness; self-consciousness; timidity. ¶남 앞에서 ~을 타다 be shy and timid in another's presence.
수중(水中) underwater. ¶~의 underwater / subaqueous / aquatic // ~에 in[under] the water // ~에 나는 식물 plants growing in water // 수구는 ~에서 하는 경기이다 Water polo is an aquatic sport. // 그것은 ~에 가라앉았다 It sank into[below the surface of] the water. // 그것은 ~에 잠겨 있었다 It was under water. / It was submerged[immersed] in the water.
● **수중 발레** synchronized swimming. **수중안경** (관측용의) a hydroscope; (상자형의) a water glass; (수영용의) water[swimming] goggles. **수중 전파 탐지기** (미) a sonar; (영) an asdic.
수중(手中) (in) the hands. ¶~의 (a thing) in one's hands // ~의 현금 ready money / cash on hand // ~에 넣다 secure / capture / take[gain] possession of / get (something) in one's pocket // 그는 ~에 한 푼도 없었다 He had no money with him. / He had no cash on hand.
수증기(水蒸氣) (aqueous / water) vapor [(영) vapour]; steam. ¶대기 속의 ~ the water [aqueous] vapor of the air[in the atmosphere] // ~를 내다 emit vapor.
수지(收支) income and expenditure; earnings and expenses; incomings and outgoings. ¶국제 ~ the balance of international payments / the international balance of payments // 국제 ~의 적자[흑자] a balance of payments deficit[surplus] // ~를 맞추다 balance the budget // ~가 맞습니까 Do the accounts balance? // 그러면 ~가 맞지 않는다 It won't pay. // 이 사업은 ~가 맞는다[맞지 않는다] This business pays[does not pay]. // 그렇게 해서[그 방안을 실행해서] ~가 맞는지 안 맞는지가 문제다 The question is whether the plan can be carried out on a paying basis.
● **수지 계산** calculation; reckoning; accounts; balancing. ¶~만 따지다 be given to calculation / be bent on gain / be calculative / be commercial(ly)-minded // 3,000부가 팔리면 겨우 ~이 맞는다 If we sell three thousand copies, we will just about break even. **수지 균형** the balance[equilibrium] between incomings and outgoings.
수지(樹脂) resin(끈끈한); rosin(단단한). ¶고무 ~ gum resin // 합성 ~ plastics // ~의[가 많은] resinous.
● **수지 광택** resinous luster.
수지(獸脂) animal fat; grease; tallow.
수지맞다(收支-) have a balanced income and outgo; (장사가) be on a paying basis; pay (well); pay off; be profitable; be in the black; (사람이) find one's account in (it); find (it) pay. ¶수지맞는 (직업 등이) remunerative / paying / (거래 등이) profitable / (자리 등이) advantageous // 수지맞는 장사 a paying business / a good bargain(거래) // 그 투자로 톡톡히 수지맞았다 The investment paid off handsomely.
수직(垂直) perpendicularity; verticality. ¶~의 perpendicular / vertical(▶ perpendicular는 어떤 것에 대해서 직각, vertical은 수평선에 대해서 직각) / plumb // ~으로 perpendicularly / vertically / plumb / sheer / at right angles (to) // 두 선은 ~으로 교차한다 The two lines cross perpendicularly. / The two lines meet [cross] at right angles. // 장대가 땅에 ~으로 서 있었다 A pole stood vertical[perpendicular / at right angles] to the ground. / The pole stood straight up in the ground.
● **수직 강하** [항] a vertical descent; a nose-dive. **수직선** [면] a perpendicular [vertical] line[plane]. **수직 이착륙기** a vertical takeoff and landing aircraft; a VTOL plane.
수직기(手織機) a handloom.
수질(水質) the quality[(degree of) purity] of water; the water quality. ¶음료로 적합한 ~ water (of a quality) fit to drink.
● **수질 검사** (an) examination of water; an analysis of water quality. **수질 오염** water pollution.
수집(收集) collection; gathering; ingathering. ¶쓰레기 ~은 1주일에 3일 실시된다 They gather garbage three days a week. **수집하다** gather; collect. ¶정보를 ~ collect information / get information // 그 사건에 관한 자료는 도서관이 수집했다 The library has gathered[amassed] materials on the incident.
수집(蒐集) gathering; collecting; (an) accumulation; [모은 것] a collection. ¶우표 ~ stamp collecting / philately. **수집하다** collect; gather; accumulate (data); make a collection of (stamps). ¶그는 외국 우표를 수집하고 있다 He collects foreign stamps. // 그는 초판본을 꽤 수집했다 He has quite a collection of first editions.
● **수집가** a collector (of). ¶미술품 ~ an art

수차 collector // 우표 ~ a stamp collector / a philatelist. **수집벽**(-癖) a mania for collecting things; a collecting mania.

수차(水車) 1 a waterwheel. ⇨물레방아 2 a water pump. ⇨무자위

수차(數次) several times. ¶그들은 ~ 조사했다 They investigated several times.

수채 a sewer; a sink; a ditch. ¶~를 쳐내다 clean[scour] a drain[sewer] // ~가 막혔다 The drain is obstructed[stopped up / clogged up].
● **수채통** a drain[sewer] pipe. **수챗구멍** an outfall; a sinkhole.

수채화(水彩畫) a watercolor (painting); a picture[painting] in watercolors. ¶~를 그리다 paint with watercolors.
● **수채화가** a watercolor painter; a watercolorist.

수척하다(瘦瘠-) emaciated; gaunt; haggard; worn; wasted. ¶수척한 얼굴 a haggard face // 수척해지다 lose a lot of weight / become emaciated / grow very thin / waste away // 너는 남자 친구가 죽은 후에 수척해졌다 She pined away after the death of her boyfriend. // 그녀는 걱정으로 수척해졌다 She became haggard[gaunt] from care[anxiety]. // 어머님은 오랜 병환으로 수척해지셨다 My mother has lost a lot of weight[is very emaciated] because of her long illness.

수천(數千) (several) thousands. ¶~ 명의 군중 a crowd of several thousand people.

수첩(手帖) a (pocket) notebook; a reminder [memorandum] book; a pocket book; a (pocket) diary. ¶학생 ~ a students handbook // ~에 적어 두다 put[jot] (something) down in one's notebook.

수청(守廳) bed service.
수청(을) **들다** give (a person) bed service; attend[wait] on (a man) at night as (his) mistress.

수초(水草) [물속이나 물가에 자라는 풀] a water[an aquatic] plant; a water grass; a waterweed.

수축(收縮) contraction(근육 등의); shrinking, shrinkage(열 등으로 오그라듦); constriction. **수축하다** shrink; contract; be constricted; deflate(배기하여). ➔¶뜨거운 물은 모직물을 수축시킨다 Hot water shrinks woolen cloth.
● **수축성** contractibility; contractility.

수축(修築) repair. **수축하다** make repairs (on a house).

수출(輸出) export; exportation. ¶기아 ~ hunger export // 설비 ~ plant export // 재 ~ re-export // ~을 늘리다 raise exports / increase the amount of export (of) // 농산물의 ~을 금하다[허가하다] prohibit[permit] the export of agricultural products // 정부는 금 ~을 금지했다 The government put an embargo on the export(ation) of gold. // 이 나라는 ~과 수입의 균형이 잡혀 있다 In this country exports and imports are well-balanced. / This country has a good balance of trade. // 근년에 텔레비전의 ~이 신장했다 There has been an increase in the number of TV sets exported in recent years. / TV exports have grown in recent years. **수출하다** export; ship abroad. ¶우리나라는 아시아의 여러 나라에 카메라를 수출하고 있다 Our country exports cameras to Asian countries.
● **수출 가격** an export price. **수출 경쟁력**

competitiveness in exports. **수출 공업 단지** the export industrial complex[estate]. **수출 관세** an export duty; export duties. **수출국** an exporting country; an exporter (country). **수출 금지** an (export) embargo; an export ban. ¶금[무기] ~ an embargo on the export of) gold[arms] / a gold[an arms] embargo // ~를 해제하다 lift[remove / take off] the embargo (on). **수출 면장** / **수출 허가서** an export permit. **수출 산업** the export industry. **수출업자** an exporter; an export merchant[trader]. **수출 송장** an export invoice. **수출 시장** the export market. ¶~ 다변화 a diversification of export markets. **수출 신용장** an export letter of credit. **수출 실적** the actual exports. ¶~ …달러를 기록하다 establish[make] the actual export record of $ …. **수출액** the amount of export (in terms of money). **수출 총~** the total export. **수출 어음** an export bill. **수출업** export trade; the export business. **수출업자** an exporter; an export trader. **수출입** exportation and importation; import and export. ¶~의 차액 the balance of trade // ~의 불균형 an imbalance between imports and exports / a trade imbalance. **수출 장려금** an export subsidy; an export bounty. **수출 초과** an excess of exports; a favorable balance of trade. **수출품** an export(▶ 종종 복수형); an article for export; exported goods. ¶중요 ~ important [principal / staple] exports. **수출항** an export port; an outport.

수취(受取) receiving; receipt; (어음 등의) an acknowledgment. **수취하다** receive; bear; accept.
● **수취인** a recipient; a receiver; a taker; a payee(어음의); a remittee(환 등의).

수치(羞恥) shyness; shame; dishonor; reproach; ignominy; [명예를 더럽히는 일] (a) disgrace. ¶~를 씻다 wipe away a reproach[disgrace] / clear one's name // 그녀는 남자들 앞에서 ~를 느끼지 않는다 She is not shy[bashful] before men. // 그는 ~를 모르는 사람이다 He has no sense of shame [honor]. / ~를 알아라 For shame! / You ought to be ashamed. // 게으름쟁이는 집안의 ~다 A lazy man is a dishonor to his family.
● **수치심** a sense of shame. ¶그는 ~이 없다 He is quite without shame. / He has no sense of shame.

수치(數値) 1 [수] numerical value. 2 [계산·측정하여 얻은 값] the result. ¶현재의 대기 오염 정도를 ~로 나타내다 explain the present state of air pollution numerically[in numbers].

수치스럽다(羞恥-) shameful; disgraceful; dishonorable; infamous; ignoble. ¶수치스러운 일 a shameful thing / a shame // 그런 짓을 하는 것은 ~ It would be shameful[a disgrace / disgraceful] for you to do a thing like that.

수칙(守則) rules; regulations; [지시] directions; instructions. ¶근무 ~ office regulations // 학생 ~ rules for students // 그는 아이들에게 수영 ~을 말해 주었다 He gave the children some pointers about[on] swimming.

수캐 a he-dog; a male dog.

수컷 a male (animal); a cock(새의); a bull(코끼리·고래·물소 등의); (구어) a he. ¶당신의

개는 ~인가요, 암컷인가요 Is your dog a he or a she?

수키와 a convex (roofing) tile. ¶~와 암키와 convex and concave (roofing) tiles.

수탁(受託) trust; (상품 판매의) consignment. **수탁하다** be given in trust; be entrusted with (a thing); take charge of (a thing).
● **수탁금** money placed in trust[charge]. **수탁물** a thing placed one's custody; a thing entrusted with. **수탁자** a trustee; (판매의) a consignee; (권리 등의) an assignee; a fiduciary.

수탈(收奪) plundering; exploitation. **수탈하다** plunder; exploit.

수탉 a cock; a rooster.

수태(受胎) conception; impregnation; (생) fecundation; fertilization. ¶인공 ~ artificial conception [fertilization]. **수태하다** (문어) conceive (a child); be impregnated [fecundated]; become pregnant. ➡¶**수태시키다** fecundate / impregnate / fertilize.
● **수태 고지(-告知)** [기] the Annunciation. **수태 능력** fertility; conceiving power. **수태 조절** conception control.

수톨쩌귀 the pintle of a hinge.

수통(水桶) a water bottle; (군인용·여행용) a canteen; a flask; [보온병] a thermos bottle.

수통(水筒) [수관(水管)] a water pipe[tube]; a conduit; [수도전] a hydrant; a tap.

수퇘지 a boar; a male pig.

수틀(繡-) an embroidery frame[hoop]; a tabo(u)ret; a tambour(원형의). ¶**형겊을** ~에 끼우다 stretch a piece of cloth over a tambour.

수판(數板) an abacus; a counting board; (a set of) counting beads. ¶~으로 계산하다 count[reckon] on the abacus // ~을 놓다 use[work] an abacus / count[figure / reckon] on the abacus // ~을 잘 놓다 be clever with one's abacus.
● **수판알** a counter; a bead. ¶그는 ~을 튕기고 있다 [이해득실을 계산하고 있다] He is guided solely by self-interest.

수평(水平) horizontality. ¶~의 level / horizontal(▶ level은 보통 면에 대해, horizontal은 수직에 대응하는 말로서 흔히 선에 대해 말함) // ~으로 horizontally / at a level (with) // ~으로 하다 [유지하다] make[keep] a bar level[even] with the ground // 이 지방은 ~이 아니다 This sill is not level[horizontal]. // 그녀는 기울어져 있는 액자를 ~으로 바로잡았다 She set the tilted frame at level. / She made the tilted frame level.
● **수평 거리** a horizontal distance. **수평면** a horizontal plane; a level surface. **수평 비행** (a) level flight. **수평 사고** lateral thinking. **수평선** the horizon; [수평한 선] a horizontal line. ¶~ 위[아래]에 above[below] the horizon // ~ 아래로 지다 sink beneath the horizon // 멀리 ~까지 뻗어 있다 stretch as far as the horizon // ~에 배가 한 척 나타났다 A boat appeared on the horizon.

수평아리 a male chick.

수포(水泡) bubbles; transience. ⇨ 물거품 ¶그의 모든 노력은 ~로 돌아갔다 All his efforts have come to nothing. / All his efforts ended in vain. / (구어) All his efforts went down the drain[(영) went up the spout]. / All his hard work went for nothing. // 나의 모든 노력은 이것 때문에 ~로 돌아갔다 All my efforts have come to nothing because of this. / This has wiped out all my hard work. // 그의 계획은 ~로 돌아갔다 His plans fell through. / His plans came to naught.

수포(水疱) [의] a (water) blister; a vesicle(작은); a bulla (pl. bullae).
● **수포진(-疹)** [의] vesicular exanthema.

수폭(水爆) an H-bomb. ⇨ 수소 폭탄(⇨ 수소(水素))

수표(手票) (미) a check; (영) a cheque. ¶횡선[지급 보증] ~ a crossed[certified] check // 10만 원짜리 ~ a check for 100,000 won // 부도 ~ a bad check // 여행자 ~ a travelers' check // 분실[위조 / 변조] ~ a lost [forged / raised] check // 무기명 ~ a check to bearer / a bearer check // 보통 ~ an open check // ~로 지불하다 pay by check // ~를 끊다 make out[write] a check // ~를 발행하다 issue[draw] a check // ~를 현금으로 바꾸다 cash a check // 그의 ~가 부도가 났다 His check bounced.
● **수표 발행인** the issuer of a check; a check drawer[(영) writer]. **수표장 / 수표책** (영) a chequebook; (미) a checkbook.

수풀 a wood. ⇨ 숲

수프 soup. ¶야채 ~ vegetable soup // 콩소메[포타주] ~ consommé[potage] // 진한[묽은] ~ thick[thin] soup // ~를 마시다 have[eat] soup // ~를 마실 때는 소리를 내면 안 된다 Don't make noise when you eat soup.
● **수프 접시** a soup plate; (공기처럼 운두가 높은 것) a soup bowl.

수피(樹皮) (the coat of) bark; cortex.

수피(獸皮) a hide; an animal skin; a fell; [모피] a fur.

수필(隨筆) an essay; stray[random] notes; an occasional essay; miscellaneous[occasional] writings; a miscellany.
● **수필가** an[a light] essayist; a miscellaneous writer; a miscellanist. **수필집** a collection of essays; the collected essays (of).

수하(手下) [손아래] one's junior; one's subordinate; [부하] a follower; a subordinate; an underling; (집합적) a following; men under one's orders; a staff.

수하(誰何) 1 [누구] who; anyone; anybody. ¶이 법률을 어긴 자는 ~를 막론하고 처벌된다 Whoever breaks this law shall be punished. 2 [검문] a challenge. ¶보초에게 ~를 받다 be challenged by a sentry. **수하하다** challenge (an unknown person).

수하다(壽-) live long; enjoy longevity; live to a great age.

수학(修學) pursuit of knowledge; study; learning; education. **수학하다** pursue knowledge; study; learn; get an education.
● **수학여행** (go on) an observation tour [trip]; a tour[trip] for study[information]; a school excursion[trip]. ¶아이들은 경주로 ~을 갔다 My children are[went] on a school excursion to Gyeongju.

수학(數學) mathematics; (미국 구어) math; (영국 구어) maths. ¶~적인[으로] mathematical(ly) // 고등 ~ higher mathematics // 응용 ~ applied mathematics // ~은 내가 잘 하는[못하는] 과목이다 Math(ematics) is my strong(est)[weak(est)] subject.
● **수학 문제** a mathematical problem; a problem of mathematics. **수학자** a mathematician.

수해(水害) [홍수 피해] flood damage; [참화] flood disaster; [홍수] a flood; an inundation. ¶～를 입다 (사람이) suffer from a flood / (물건이) be damaged by a flood(▶ 지역인 경우는 양쪽 표현을 다 쓸 수 있음)∥이 지역은 빈번히 ～를 당한다 This area frequently suffer from[is frequently damaged by] floods.∥태풍으로 인해 발생한 ～는 전(全) 도에 미쳤다 The damage wrought by the rain and flooding caused by the typhoon extended over the whole province.
● **수해 대책** (구제를 위한) a flood-relief measure; (방지를 위한) a flood-control measure. **수해 이재민** flood victims[sufferers]; sufferers from flood. **수해 지역** a flooded district; a flood(ed) area.

수해(樹海) a sea of trees; a broad expanse of dense woodland; a wavy sea of emerald leaves.

수행(修行) self-discipline; self-improvement [-cultivation]; practice; [수련] training; [불] ascetic practices. ¶～을 쌓다 get a thorough training / be well trained∥그는 아직 ～이 부족하다 He has not undergone enough training yet. **수행하다** discipline[train] oneself; work (at self-improvement); [불] practice asceticism.
● **수행자** a trainee; an ascetic; a disciplinant.

수행(遂行) accomplishment; execution; performance; achievement; prosecution (of a war). ¶전쟁의 ～ the conduct of the war∥그는 임무 ～ 중에 사고를 당했다 He met with an accident in the line of duty. **수행하다** [이룩하다] accomplish; perform; [실행하다] execute; carry out(▶ execute는 좀 딱딱한 말). ¶임무를 ～ perform[execute / carry out] one's duties∥그는 일을 수행함에 있어 수완을 발휘했다 He showed his ability in carrying out[the way he carried out] his work.

수행(隨行) attendance[accompaniment] (on a journey). **수행하다** accompany[(문어) attend] (an important person on a journey); go along with; tag along with (a person on a tour); follow. ¶…을 수행하여 in attendance upon (a person) / in the suite of (a person)∥그는 총리를 수행하여 오스트레일리아를 방문했다 He visited Australia as a member of the prime minister's party.∥그는 무역 사절단을 수행하여 프랑스에 갔다 He accompanied the trade mission to France.
● **수행원** a member of person's party; an attendant; [수행단] a party; (문어) an entourage; a suite; a retinue; a train of attendants. ¶～를 데리고 가다 be accompanied by attendants∥～을 안 데리고 가다 go unattended∥대통령과 그 ～은 특별기로 도착했다 The President and his suite arrived by (a) special plane.

수험(受驗) undergoing[going through] an examination. ¶～ 준비를 하다 prepare (oneself) for an examination∥～ 준비를 지도하다 coach[tutor] (a student) for an examination∥～ 자격이 있다 be qualified for examination. **수험하다** take a test; take [undergo / go through] an examination; sit [go in] for an examination.
● **수험 과목** subjects of examination. **수험료** the examination fee; the expense for the examination. **수험 번호** an examinee's (seat) number. **수험생** an examinee; a candidate for an examination; a testee. **수험표** a certificate for examination; an admission ticket to an examination.

수혈(輸血) (a) blood transfusion. ¶나는 ～을 받았다 I had[was given] a blood transfusion.∥내 목숨을 살리기 위해 형이 ～을 신청했다 My brother offered to give blood to save my life. **수혈하다** give a blood transfusion (to a person); transfuse (a person's) blood (into another); transfuse (a patient). ¶의사는 내 피를 그에게 수혈했다 The surgeon transfused my blood into him.

수협(水協) the fisheries cooperative union. ⇨수산업 협동조합(⇨수산(水産))

수형(受刑) being under sentence. **수형하다** serve one's sentence[time] (for murder).
● **수형자** a convict; a convicted person; a prisoner under sentence.

수호(守護) protection; guard; safeguard; defense. ¶수도 ～의 임무를 맡다 undertake to safeguard the capital city. **수호하다** protect; guard; keep guard (over / around); keep (a place) safe (from); defend. ¶나라를 ～ guard[protect] the nation.
● **수호신** a guardian[tutelar(y)] deity[god / spirit]. **수호자** a protector; a guardian.

수호(修好) (문어) amity; friendship; friendly relations. **수호하다** form a friendly relationship; get along amicably.
● **수호 조약** a treaty of amity[friendship]. ¶～을 맺다 conclude a treaty of amity[friendship] (with).

수화(水化) [화] hydration. **수화하다** hydrate.
● **수화물** a hydrate.

수화(手話) [손짓으로 말함] talking with the hands[fingers]; [그 말] sign[finger] language. ¶～로 말하다 use[talk using] finger language.

수화기(受話器) a (telephone) receiver; an earpiece; a headpiece; (무전의) radio earphones; a receiving set. ¶～를 들다 pick up [lift] the receiver∥～를 놓다 hang up (the receiver)∥～를 귀에 대다 put the receiver to one's ear∥～가 제대로 놓여 있지 않다 The receiver[phone] is off the hook.

수화물(手貨物) [휴대하는 짐] (personal) luggage; (미) (hand) baggage(▶ 영국에서 baggage는 선박 또는 항공기 여행에 쓰나 미국에서는 육로 여행에도 쓰임. 집합 명사로서 항상 단수 취급을 함); [소지품] personal effects; (속어) traps. ¶중량 초과 ～ excess [overweight] baggage∥휴대 ～ hand luggage / (미) hand baggage∥한 개 a piece of baggage∥～을 맡기다 have one's baggage[(영) luggage] checked / check one's baggage∥～을 역에 맡기다 register [book] one's baggage to a station∥～을 포터에게 맡기다 leave one's baggage with a redcap[porter]∥～이 세관에서 통과되었습니까 Has your baggage cleared customs?
● **수화물 취급소** a luggage office; (미) a baggage room[office].

수화상극(水火相剋) mutual aversion; incompatibility.

수확(收穫) 1 [곡식을 거두어들임] harvesting; [수확물] a harvest; a crop; a yield. ¶～ 중인 밭 a harvest field∥올해의 보리[쌀] ～ this year's barley[rice] harvest∥작년에는 ～이 많았다[적었다] There was a good[poor]

harvest[crop] last year.// 벼의 ~은 어떻습니까 How is the rice crop?// 올해는 귤 ~이 좋다 This has been a good year for oranges.// 농부들은 감자 ~으로 분주하다 The farmers are busy harvesting potatoes[getting in the potato crop]. **수확하다** gather (in) a harvest; harvest; reap; gather[take] in. ¶사람들은 벼를 수확하기에 바쁘다 People are busy harvesting[gathering in] the rice.
2 [성과] the fruit (of labor); a (spiritual) harvest. ¶~이 있는 토의 a fruitful[productive] discussion // 대학 4년 동안의 ~은 헤아릴 수 없이 많다 There's no way I can measure all that I got out of[gained from] my four years in college. /(문어) The harvest that I have reaped during my four years of college is immeasurable.// 그와 장시간 얘기를 나누었지만 이렇다 할 ~은 없었다 I had a long talk with him, but it yielded nothing special[I didn't gain anything in particular from it].
● **수확고** the yield; the crop. ¶예상 ~ a crop [harvest] estimate // 올해는 벼의 ~가 많다 We had a good rice crop this year. **수확기**(-期) the harvesting season; the harvest (time).

수회(收賄) acceptance of a bribe; corruption; bribery; (미국 구어) graft. **수회하다** take [accept] a bribe; (미국 속어) take graft; boodle. ¶그는 2억 원을 수회했다 He accepted[took] a bribe of two hundred million won.
● **수회 사건** a bribery case [affair]; (미) a graft scandal. **수회죄** bribery.

수회(數回) a number of times; several times. ¶~에 걸쳐 several times / on several occasions.

수효(數爻) a number; a figure; an amount. ¶사람의 ~ the number of people // ~가 많다 [적다] be many[few] / be large[small] in number // ~가 늘다 grow[increase] in number // ~를 세다 (count the) number / count / take count of // ~를 늘리다[줄이다] increase[decrease] the number (of) // ~를 채우다 make up the number // ~를 틀리다 count wrong / miscount // ~에 넣다 count in [among] the number (of) / include in the number / take into account // ~에 넣지 않다 be not counted (among) / be not included / be excluded.

수훈(垂訓) teachings (of Christ); a precept. ¶산상 ~ [성] the Sermon on the Mount.

수훈(殊勳) distinguished[conspicuous] services; meritorious deeds. ¶최고의 선수 [야구] the most valuable player(약어 MVP) // ~을 세우다 render distinguished services / distinguish oneself (in a battle) / fight[play] with distinction.
● **수훈상** (운동 경기 등의) the outstanding performance award.

숙고(熟考) (mature / due) consideration; deliberation; meditation; mature reflection. **숙고하다** think over (a matter); ponder on [over] (a problem); consider (carefully); deliberate (over / on / about); meditate; reflect upon (a problem); chew the cud. ¶숙고한 끝에 after due [careful / mature] consideration / after mature reflection / on second thought(s) // 그녀는 그가 한 말에 대해 숙고했다 She thought [pondered / reflected] on what he had said.// 그것에 대해서 숙고해 보겠다 I will think it over carefully.

숙군(肅軍) a purge in the army; restoration of military discipline. **숙군하다** purge disloyal elements from the army; execute [effect / institute] a purge in the army.

숙녀(淑女) a lady; a gentlewoman (pl. -women). ¶~다운 ladylike / becoming (to) a lady // 전혀 ~답지 않은 utterly unbecoming (to) a lady of gentle birth.

숙다 **1** [앞으로 기울어지다] droop; bow; be bent; be heavy. ¶벼 이삭이 ~ The rice stalks are (bent) heavy with grain. **2** [기운이 줄다] go[die] down; subside.

숙달(熟達) proficiency; mastery; skill. ¶영어 ~법 how to master English. **숙달하다** attain proficiency (in English); become proficient [skillful / skilled / adept] (in teaching); gain in [acquire] skill; master (English). ¶외국어에 ~ master [become proficient in] a foreign language / acquire [get] a mastery of a foreign language // …에 숙달해 있다 be proficient in (flower arrangement) / be a master [have mastery] of (the piano) / be versed [well up] in (French) / be (fairly) conversant with (English) / be skilled [adept] in (drawing) // 그는 영어에 점점 [빨리] 숙달하고 있다 He is making gradual [rapid] progress in his English.

숙당(肅黨) a purge in the party. **숙당하다** purge [eliminate / institute purge of] disloyal elements from the party.

숙덕거리다 whisper secrets; whisper slyly to (a person); exchange subdued remarks; talk in whispers; talk in a subdued tone.

숙독(熟讀) careful reading; perusal. **숙독하다** read thoroughly [carefully / with care / through and through]; peruse.

숙련(熟練) (veteran) skill; dexterity; adroitness; expertness; facility; mastery; [연습] practice. ¶미~의 unskilled / inexperienced // ~을 요하는 delicate (job) / ticklish (affair). **숙련하다** become skillful [dexterous] (in [at] the trade); get skilled (in riding). ➔ **숙련된** skilled / skillful / trained / experienced / practiced / expert // 그가 새로운 기술에 숙련되기까지에는 오랜 시일이 걸렸다 It took him a long time to master the new technique.// 그는 교수법에 숙련되어 있다 He is practiced in teaching.
● **숙련공** a skilled worker [workman / hand / laborer / craftsman]; a master mechanic; (집합적) skilled [trained] labor. ¶미~ an unskilled laborer. **숙련자 / 숙련가** a man of experience; an expert (at / in); a practiced [skilled] hand; a past master.

숙맥(菽麥) [어리석은 사람] a foolish [stupid] person.

숙면(熟眠) a sound [profound / heavy] sleep. **숙면하다** sleep well [soundly / heavily]; have a good sleep; fall [sink] into a deep sleep; sleep like a top [log]. ¶그는 숙면하고 있다 He is fast [sound] asleep.// 나는 숙면할 수 없다 I am a bad [light] sleeper.

숙명(宿命) fate; destiny; fatality; karma. ¶~이라고 체념하다 accept [resign oneself to] one's fate // …할 ~ be fated [destined] (to do) / be predestined (for a diplomat) // 이렇게 되는 것이 내 ~이다 This is my destiny. / I'm destined to come to this pass.

숙명적

●**숙명론** fatalism; necessitarianism. ¶～적(인) fatalistic. **숙명론자** a fatalist.

숙명적(宿命的) fateful. ¶～으로 fatally // ～인 사건 a fateful event.

숙모(叔母) an aunt; the wife of one's father's younger brother.

숙박(宿泊) (a) lodging; (군대의) billeting; quartering. ¶호텔에 ～을 예약하다 make reservation at a hotel. **숙박하다** lodge (in / at); stay (at / with); stop (in / at); put up (at); take up one's lodging; be registered (at a hotel); (미) check in (at a hotel); (군대가) be billeted; be quartered. ¶여관에 ～ stay [put up] at an inn // 분산 ～ be billeted separately (at different hotels) // 민가에 ～ be billeted in private homes (of a town) // 친구 집에서 ～ stay with a friend / stop at a friend's house. → 학생 두어 사람을 숙박시켜 줄 수 있겠습니까 Can you put up a few students?

●**숙박객** (호텔·여관의) a hotel guest; (가정의) a house guest. **숙박료** hotel charges [expenses]; a hotel bill; accommodation [lodging] charges. ¶～를 지불하다 [매기다] pay [jump] a hotel charges // ～는 1박에 3만원입니다 The charge at the hotel [inn] is thirty thousand won for a night [per night]. / The charge for a room is ten thousand won a night. **숙박부** a hotel [an inn] register [book]; a visitors' book (of a hotel). ¶～에 적다 enter [register] one's name (and address) in a hotel book [register] // (여관에서) ～ 좀 써서 주십시오 Please put down here your name and address. **숙박 시설** accommodations.

숙변(宿便) [장 속에 오래 머물러 있던 대변] feces contained long in the intestines.

숙부(叔父) an uncle; one's father's [dad's] younger brother; (문어) a younger paternal uncle.

숙성(熟成) [전][화] ag(e)ing; [화] ripening; maturing; maturation; [사진] digestion.

숙성하다(夙成一) precocious; (서술적) be wise above one's age; be big for one's age(몸집이). ¶숙성한 아이 a precocious child // 그 아이는 나이에 비해 ～ He is precocious. / He is too grown-up [smart] for his age. / The child has an old head on young shoulders.

숙소(宿所) one's address; one's place of abode; one's lodgings [quarters]; [여관] an inn; a hotel. ¶～을 정하다 [잡다] take up one's lodgings [quarters] (in a house) / [숙박하다] put up at (an inn) / stay (at a person's house / with a person) // ～를 옮기다 change one's lodgings (to) // 나는 그의 ～를 알고 있다 I know where he stays. / I have his address.

숙수(熟手) [음식을 잘 만드는 사람] a fancy cook; [음식을 마련하는 사람] a caterer.

숙식(宿食) board and lodging; bed and board. **숙식하다** board and lodge.

●**숙식비** the charge for board and lodging.

숙어(熟語) [관용구] an idiom; an idiomatic phrase [expression]; [성구] a set [fixed] phrase; [한자의 복합어] a (Chinese) compound word.

●**숙어집** a phrase book; a dictionary of phrases.

숙연하다(肅然一) [조용하다] silent; quiet; hushed; [엄숙하다] solemn; austere; [경건하다] reverential. **숙연히** silently; quietly; solemnly. ¶～ 옷깃을 여미다 be struck with reverence.

숙영(宿營) billeting; quartering. **숙영하다** set up (camp); camp; be billeted; billet (in a house); be quartered (in). ¶대원은 민가에 숙영하였다 The troops were quartered with [billeted on] the villagers.

●**숙영지** a billet; a billeting area [place].

숙원(宿怨) an old grudge [score / rancor]; deep-rooted enmity; an old feud; a long-harbored resentment [enmity]. ¶～을 품다 have an old grudge against (a person) / be rancorous against (a person).

숙원(宿願) a long-cherished [-fostered] desire [hope / ambition]; one's heart's desire. ¶～을 이루다 attain one's long-cherished ambition // 파리 구경이 나의 ～이었다 I had always wanted to see Paris. // 나의 ～이 이루어졌다 My long-cherished desire [dream] has been realized.

숙의(熟議) (due) deliberation; careful [mature] consultation; exhaustive discussion. **숙의하다** deliberate on [over] (a matter); discuss (a matter) fully; talk (a matter) over; consult carefully. ¶숙의한 끝에 after careful consideration // 문제에 대해서 거듭 ～ fully discuss [deliberate on] the question / mull the matter over // 나는 그녀와 문제를 숙의했다 I went over the matter thoroughly with her.

숙이다 (몸을) bend oneself (forward); stoop; (머리를) hang down (one's head); bow [droop / bend / drop / incline / sink] (one's head). ¶고개를 ～ bow one's head / [풀이 죽어 창피해서] hang one's head // 고개를 숙이고 몸을 낮추다 bow to the ground // 고개를 숙인 채 대답하다 answer with downcast eyes // 소녀는 부끄러운 듯이 고개를 숙였다 The girl bashfully dropped her eyes [cast her eyes downward]. // 사나이는 고개를 숙이고 걸어갔다 The man walked away with his head (hung) down [with his head drooping]. // 그는 슬픈 듯이 고개를 숙이고 그곳에 서 있었다 He stood there, his head drooping sadly. // 그는 엄연한 사실 앞에 고개를 숙였다 He hung [bowed] his head before the solemn fact. // 그녀는 부끄러워 고개를 숙이고 있었다 She hung her head in shame.

숙적(宿敵) an old enemy [foe]; an enemy [a rival] of long standing.

숙정(肅正) [단속] regulation; enforcement; [정화] purification; [숙청] a purge; a cleanup. ¶관기 ～ purification of official discipline. **숙정하다** regulate; enforce; purify; clean (up). ¶공무원들을 ～ enforce discipline among government officials.

●**숙정 작업** a cleanup campaign (against corruption).

숙제(宿題) 1 (학교의) homework; a home task; (미) an assignment; home lessons. ¶방학 ～ a holiday task // ～가 많다 have lots of homework to do // ～를 내다 set (pupils) a home task / give (pupils) homework // ～를 하다 do one's homework // ～를 도와주다 help (a boy) with his homework // 여름 방학에는 ～를 내지 않겠다 I am not giving [(미) assigning] any homework for the summer. 2 [검토 중인 문제] a pending question; [미결 문제] an open question. ¶～를 해결하다 settle a pending question // ～로 남겨 두다

leave (a matter) open [in abeyance] // 이것은 다음 회의까지 ~로 남겨 두자 Let's leave the question open until our next meeting. // 그 문제는 아직 ~로 남아 있다 The question is still pending. // 그 문제는 언제까지나 ~로 남겨 둘 수 없다 We can't leave the matter unsettled forever.

숙주(宿主) 〔생물이 기생하는 동식물〕 the host. ¶중간 ~ an intermediary host.
● 숙주 식물 the host plant.

숙주나물 green bean sprouts.

숙지(熟知) full knowledge; familiarity. **숙지하다** know well [fully / thoroughly]; be well aware [informed] of (a fact); be [become] familiar [well acquainted] with (a matter); have thorough [full / an intimate] knowledge of (a matter). ¶그것을 숙지하고 있다 I am fully aware of it. // 이것은 여러분이 숙지하고 있는 사실이다 It is a fact (that is) familiar to you all.

숙직(宿直) night duty; night watch. ¶어젯밤 ~은 누구였나요 Who was on duty last night? // 그는 오늘 밤 ~이다 He is on duty tonight. **숙직하다** be on night duty; keep night watch.
● 숙직 교사 a night-duty teacher. 숙직실 a night watchman's room.

숙질(叔姪) an uncle and his nephew [niece].

숙청(肅淸) a cleanup; a purge; liquidation; housecleaning. ¶~ 공작을 시작하다 begin a housecleaning // 혁명 후에 일련의 ~이 행해졌다 A series of (political) purges followed the revolution. **숙청하다** purge; clean up; houseclean; liquidate. ¶당내의 유해 분자들이 숙청되었다 The party was purged of its undesirable elements [members].

숙체(宿滯) 〔오래 묵은 체증〕 chronic indigestion [dyspepsia].

숙취(宿醉) a hangover; the aftereffects of the night's drink; (구어) the morning after; a morning head. ¶너무 마시면 내일 ~로 고생할 것이다 Beware of drinking too much, or you will have a "head" tomorrow morning. **숙취하다** have a head; suffer from the aftereffects of (the previous night's) drink.

숙환(宿患) 〔오래 묵은 병〕 a chronic [an inveterate] disease; a deep-rooted [confirmed / persistent] disease. ¶~이 도져 자리에 누워 있다 be confined to bed by an attack of a chronic disease // ~으로 쓰러지다 fall a prey to one's chronic disease.

순(旬) 〔10일간〕 a period of ten days; a third of a month. ¶상〔중 / 하〕 ~ the first [middle / last] part of a month.

순(筍) a sprout; a shoot; a bud. ¶죽~ a bamboo shoot // 이 나다 bud (out) / sprout // ~을 치다 cut [nip] off extra sprouts / trim off sprouts.

순(純) 〔순수한〕 pure; genuine; 〔순전한〕 sheet; utter; out-and-out; 〔금・은 등의〕 pure; fine; sterling; solid(도금 등에 대하여); 〔진짜의〕 genuine, unalloyed; unmixed; 〔이익 등의〕 net; clear. ¶~ 거짓말 a pure fabrication [prevarication] / ~ 한국식 purely Korean style / orthodox Korean fashion // ~ 수입 net income // ~이익 net profit // ~ 한국제 [국산] 기계 a machine of entirely Korean make [manufacture] // ~ 우리 식이다 It is purely Korean [our style].

-순(旬) 〔해당 수에 10을 곱한 나이〕 a decade. ¶칠~ 노인 a person of seventy years old / 칠~이 넘다 be over seventy years old / be over seven decades old.

-순(順) 〔순서〕 order; 〔차례〕 turn. ¶성적~(in) the order of merits [the scholastic rank of a student] // 날짜~으로 in sequence of date / 크기~으로 according to size // ABC [번호 / 연대]~으로 in alphabetical [numerical / chronological] order // 키 [나이]~으로 in order of height [age] // 선착 [접수]~으로 by order of receipt / 신청~으로 in the order of application // 가나다~으로 배열하다 arrange (a list) alphabetically [in alphabetical order] // 진열품은 연대~으로 배열되어 있다 The exhibits are arranged in chronological order.

순간(旬刊) ¶~의 (a magazine) published [issued] every ten days.

순간(瞬間) a moment; a second; an instant. ¶~의 [적인] momentary / instantaneous // ~적으로 instantaneously / in a moment / in an instant / in a flash (of lightning) // 한~ (for) an instant // 그 ~에 at that moment [instant] / 구심적인 ~ a dramatic moment / 그것은 ~에 일어난 일이었다 It happened in an instant [a flash]. // 방에 들어간 ~에 남자가 창으로 달아나는 것을 보았다 Just as [the moment] I entered the room I saw a man escape from the window. // 한눈을 판 ~에 내 차가 나무에 부딪혔다 My car ran into a tree the instant I took my eyes off the road. // 과자를 먹으려고 입을 벌린 ~에 과자가 손가락에서 미끄러져 나갔다 The moment I opened my mouth to eat the cake, it slipped out of my fingers. // 나는 비틀거리는 ~에 머리를 벽에 부딪혔다 I bumped my head against the wall as I staggered. // 도둑은 수위와 마주친 ~ 그에게 덤벼들었다 The thief grappled with the guard the instant [moment] they came across each other. // 그녀는 그를 본 ~ 노발대발했다 As soon as she saw him, she flew into a rage. // 우리는 결코 한~도 그에게서 눈을 뗄 수 없다 We simply can't take our eyes off him for even a moment. // 나는 넘어지는 ~ 지갑을 떨어뜨렸다 I dropped my wallet when I fell down. // 나는 차를 비키려고 하는 ~ 전신주에 부딪혔다 In trying to dodge a car, I ran into a telephone pole. // 그녀의 ~적인 기지로 우리는 살아났다 We were saved by her quick wits. // 나는 자전거를 피하려는 ~에 넘어졌다 I fell in the act of dodging a bicycle. // 마지막 ~에 와서 달아나다니 그는 비겁하다 He is cowardly to run away at the last moment.
● 순간 최대 풍속 the maximum instantaneous [momentary] wind velocity.

순결(純潔) 〔결백〕 purity; integrity; 〔티 없음〕 innocence; immaculacy; 〔동정〕 chastity; virginal purity; maid(en)hood. ¶~을 더럽히다 sully [stain] the purity (of a woman) / deflower (a maiden) // ~을 잃다 lose one's chastity [innocence] (▶ innocence는 마음의 순결을 가리키는 수도 있음) // ~을 빼앗기다 be deprived of one's virginity. **순결하다** pure; clean; immaculate; unspotted; 〔성적으로〕 chaste; vestal. ¶순결한 사랑 platonic [pure] love // 마음이 순결한 사람 a purehearted person / a person pure in heart.
● 순결 교육 education in sexual morality; purity [wholesome sex] education.

순경(巡警) [순찰] patrol(ling); [경관] a policeman; an officer(▶ 부를 때는 officer!라고 함); a police officer; a (police) constable; (미) a patrolman; (미국 속어) a cop(per); (집합적) the police. ¶교통~ a traffic policeman∥기마~ a mounted policeman∥사복~ a policeman in plain clothes∥송~ Officer Song!∥~을 부르다 call[summon] police.

순경(順境) [모든 일이 뜻대로 이루어진 경우] a favorable condition; favorable [propitious] circumstances. ¶~에서나 역경에서나 in prosperity as well as in adversity / in good times and in bad.

순계(純系) [생] a pure line.

순교(殉教) religious martyrdom; baptism of blood. **순교하다** become a martyr; die a martyr for one's faith; martyrize oneself; be martyred; die for one's belief[faith]; suffer martyrdom. ¶그는 기독교 박해의 희생이 되어 순교했다 He died a martyr to the persecution of Christians.
● **순교자** a martyr.

순국(殉國) dying for one's country. **순국하다** die for one's country.
● **순국선열** a (patriotic) martyr.

순금(純金) pure[solid / true / virgin] gold. ¶~의 all-gold / pure-gold∥~ 반지 a solid gold ring∥~의 촛대 a solid gold candlestick∥~으로 된 불상 an image of (the) Buddha in pure gold.

순대 sundae; (a) sausage made of beef and bean curd stuffed in pig intestine.
● **순댓국** pork soup mixed with sliced sundae sausage.

순도(純度) degree of purity. ¶금의~ gold purity / fineness of gold∥~가 높은[낮은] 금 gold of a high [low] degree of purity.

순두부(-豆腐) [눌러서 굳히지 않은 두부] uncurdled bean curd.

순력(巡歷) [각처로 돌아다니는 것] a tour; an inspection tour (in former days). **순력하다** tour; make a tour of; travel (through / about).

순례(巡禮) a pilgrimage. **순례하다** make [go on] a pilgrimage.
● **순례자** a pilgrim; a palmer. **순례지** a place of pilgrimage; a pilgrimage resort.

순록(馴鹿) [동] a reindeer (pl. ~s, (집합적) reindeer).

순리(純理) pure reason[logic]; [학리(學理)] scientific principles.

순리(順理) submission to reason; reasonableness; rationality. ¶~적 reasonable / rational / right / proper∥~적으로 reasonably / rationally / in a rational manner∥그렇게 되는 것이 ~다 It is natural that it should be so.

순면(純綿) pure[all] cotton; 100% cotton; all-cotton stuff. ¶~의 all-cotton∥~의 셔츠 an all-cotton shirt

순모(純毛) pure[all] wool. ¶~의 all-wool.
● **순모 제품** all-wool goods[fabrics].

순무 [식] a turnip.

순문학(純文學) serious literature; pure[polite / imaginative] literature[letters]; (프) belles-lettres.

순박하다(淳朴-・醇朴-) (성질이) simple; naive; simple and honest; unsophisticated; simple-hearted; simple-minded; (풍속이) homely; simple-mannered (people). ¶순박한 시골 노인 an old country man, simple and honest by nature∥순박한 사람 a native[an unsophisticated] person∥그는 말씨가~ He speaks in an unaffected way. / His way of speaking is quite simple.

순방(巡訪) a round of calls[visits]. **순방하다** make a round of calls; visit one after another. ¶각국을~ make a tour of various countries.

순배(巡杯) passing the wine cup around. ¶한~ a round of drinks∥~이 몇~ 돈 다음에 after the cup has circulated a few times / after wine has gone round several times. **순배하다** pass (a winecup) round.

순백(純白) a pure[snowy] white; sheer [virginal] white. ¶~의 pure-[snow-]white / white as snow / immaculate∥~의 식탁보 a snow-white[pure-white] tablecloth∥~의 옷 an immaculate white dress / a pure-white dress.

순백하다(純白-) snow-white; immaculate.

순번(順番) [순서] order; [차례] turn. ¶~을 틀리게 하다 mix up[confuse] the order∥~을 기다리다 wait for one's turn∥카드는~이 잘못되어 있다 The cards are out of order.∥드디어 내~이 왔다 At last my turn came.

순보(旬報) [열흘에 한 번씩 발행하는 신문] a ten-day report; a bulletin [report / periodical] issued [published] every ten days.

순사(殉死) 1 [나라를 위해 목숨을 바침] suicide committed for one's country. **순사하다** die for one's country. 2 [임금・남편의 뒤를 따라 자살하여 죽는 것] self-immolation (of an attendant on the death of his lord); suttee(과부의). **순사하다** immolate [kill] oneself on the death of one's lord[master]; die a martyr's death; follow one's lord to the grave.

순산(順産) an easy delivery[labor / birth]. **순산하다** give an easy birth to; have an easy labor[delivery]. ¶어젯밤 그녀는 아들을 순산했다 She gave an easy birth to[was safely delivered of] a boy last night.∥아내가 여자 아이를 순산했다 My wife was safely delivered of a baby girl.

순색(純色) [순수한 빛깔] unmixed color; solid color; (of) one color.

순서(順序) [차례] (sequent) order; sequence; [방법] a system; a method; [절차] procedure; course; formalities. ¶~대로 in good [regular] order∥~를 밟다 go through the proper procedure[the required formalities]∥일정한~를 밟다 follow a set method∥~가 틀리다 be out of order∥~ 있게 이야기하다 speak in an orderly fashion∥먼저 교장에게 이야기하는 것이~일 것이다 The proper procedure is to speak to the principal first.∥어떤~로 시작합니까 In what order shall we begin?∥어떤 일에나~가 있다 There is a correct[proper] order in doing anything.

순소득(純所得) net income. ¶월 60만 원의~이 있다 have a monthly net income of ₩600,000.

순수(純粋) purity; pureness; genuineness. **순수하다** pure; genuine (Celtic people); real; incorrupt; (잠것이 섞이지 않은) unalloyed; unmixed (blessing); unadulterated (friendship); undiluted. ¶순수한 마음 a pure heart / a heart pure of any taint∥순수한 영국인 a

pure[trueborn] Englishman / an Englishman born and bred // 순수한 한국식 가옥 an authentic[genuine] Korean house / a house in pure Korean style // 음악에 대한 순수한 정열 genuine enthusiasm for music // 순수하지 않은 impure / mixed(섞음질한) // 순수한 동기에서 한 일이다 I did it from unmixed motives.
●**순수 문학** pure literature. **순수 소설** pure fiction. **순수 시** pure poetry. **순수 예술** pure art. **순수 이성 비판** (칸트의) the Critique of Pure Reason.

순순하다(順順−) obedient; gentle; meek; docile; unresisting; submissive. **순순히** meekly; gently; tamely; obediently; submissively; without resistance; quietly. ¶~ 자백하다 own up / confess without concealment [with a good grace] // ~ 물러서다 withdraw without making a fuss // ~ 명령에 따르다 obey[submit to] an order meekly // ~ 오랏줄을 받다 surrender tamely / suffer oneself to be bound / be arrested without resistance // 남의 충고를 ~ 받아들이다 accept other's advice without objecting[protesting] // 그는 나를 ~ 따라왔다 He followed me meekly without any resistance].

순순하다(諄諄−) kind and gentle (in admonishing). **순순히** gently; kindly. ¶~ 타이르다 admonish gently / talk[advise] patiently / explain [reason with a person] patiently // 그는 ~ 타일러서 그녀의 잘못을 깨우쳐 주려고 했다 He tried patiently to convince her of her error. / He tried to talk her out of her silly ideas.

순시(巡視) a tour[round] of inspection; an inspection; a round of visits. ¶연두 ~ the new year inspection tour. **순시하다** make a tour[go a round] of inspection; inspect; (담당 구역을) patrol; walk one's beat. ¶공장을 ~ inspect[go over] a factory // 피난민 수용소를 ~ make a tour of refugee camps // 장교는 영내를 순시했다 The officer made an inspection of the camp. / The officer went around the camp on an inspection tour.
●**순시선** a patrol boat.

순식간(瞬息間) a brief instant; a moment; a second. ¶~에 in a moment / in an instant / in[like] a flash / in a twinkling / in the twinkling of an eye / in a wink / instantly / in almost no time / (as) quick as a flash[wink] // ~에 먹어 치우다 eat[devour] in an instant / make short work of (it) // 차는 ~에 지나가 버렸다 Cars flashed[rushed] by in an instant[in the twinkling of an eye]. // 그것을 보자 그는 ~에 마음이 달라졌다 He changed his mind the moment he saw it. // 그의 성공의 꿈은 ~에 사라져 버렸다 His dreams of success vanished in an instant. // 그의 운명은 ~에 역전되었다 He suffered an instantaneous reversal of his fortunes. // 그녀의 기분은 ~에 변해 버린다 Her mood changes in the twinkling of an eye. // 그것은 ~에 일어난 일이었다 It all happened in an instant. / It was now over before I realized what was happening. // 5년이란 세월이 ~에 흘러가 버렸다 Five years flew by in a flash.

순양(巡洋) a cruise; cruising. **순양하다** cruise; sail about.
●**순양함** a cruiser. ¶경~ a light cruiser // 중~ a heavy cruiser.

순연(順延) postponement; deferment. ¶우천 ~ In case[In the event of] rain, to be postponed[be put off] till the next fine day[till the first fine day following]. **순연하다** postpone; defer; put off. →경기는 다음 주로 순연되었다 The game was postponed[put off] until next week. // 회의는 2일간 순연되었다 The meeting was postponed for two days.

순열(順列) [수] (a) permutation; (a) linear arrangement. ¶~과 조합 permutations and combinations.

순위(順位) order; ranking; standing; placing; precedence. ¶~를 **다투다** contend for precedence / ~를 **결정하다** decide ranking.
●**순위 결정전** (동점자 간의) a play-off; (도약의) a jump-off; (사격의) a shoot-off; (펜싱의) a fence-off. **순위표** a graded[ranking] list.

순은(純銀) pure [solid / fine / refined] silver. ¶~의 of pure [solid] silver / all-silver // ~ 수저 [주발] a spoon[bowl] of sterling silver.

순음(脣音) a labial (sound). ⇨˝입술소리(⇨)입술).
●**순음화** labialization.

순응(順應) adaptation; accommodation; adjustment; sympathy. **순응하다** adapt [adjust / accommodate / (미) acclimate] oneself (to new circumstances). ¶…에 순응하여 in sympathy with (the national policy) // 환경의 변화에 ~ adapt oneself to the change in one's surroundings // 시대[시류]에 ~ go [swim] with the tide [stream / current / times] / 대세에 ~ follow the general trend of the times // 그는 시대에 순응한다 He goes [swims] with the current of the times.
●**순응성** adaptability; adaptableness; flexibility.

순이익(純利益) a net [neat / clean / pure] profit [gain]; net proceeds. ¶3만 원의 ~이 있다 have a net gain of 30,000 won // 5백 달러의 ~을 얻다 net [gross / clear / realize] a profit of 500 dollars // 1년에 3천 파운드[2할 5푼]의 ~을 올리다 net three thousand pounds [25 percent] a year // 나는 그 거래에서 20만 원의 ~을 올렸다 I netted 200,000 won from the deal.

순익(純益) a net profit. ⇨˝순이익

순잎(筍−) a sprouted leaf.

순전하다(純全−) [순수하다] pure (and simple); sheer; genuine; [진정하다] true; real; [완전하다] absolute; utter; perfect; downright; entire; total; complete; 100-proof; out-and-out; thorough. ¶순전한 사기 [거짓말] a downright swindle [lie] // 순전한 사삿일 a purely personal matter // 순전한 오해 a sheer misunderstanding // 순전한 낭비 a sheer waste (of money) // 순전한 문외한 a rank outsider // 그것은 순전한 거짓말은 아니었다 It was not an absolute lie. **순전히** wholly; purely; completely; utterly; perfectly. ¶~ 돈만을 위하여 solely for money.

순절(殉節) self-immolation for one's loyalty [chastity]. **순절하다** sacrifice [immolate] oneself for one's loyalty [chastity]; die for one's chastity.

순정(純情) a pure (and simple) heart [mind]; pure-minded feeling (for a person); (프) naïveté; naivety; (헌신) self-sacrificing devotion.
●**순정 소설** a boy-meets-girl story; (구어) a puppy [calf] love story(풋사랑 이야기).

순정적(純情的) naive; pure in heart; unsophisticated. ¶~인 소녀 a simple-hearted girl∥그녀는 ~이다 She has a pure heart. / She is pure in heart.

순조롭다(順調-) favorable; fair; satisfactory; smooth; normal; (날씨가) seasonable. ¶순조로운 날씨 seasonable [favorable] weather∥모든 것이 순조로우면 if everything goes [comes out] well∥만사가 순조로웠다[순조롭지 못했다] Everything went smoothly [wrong].∥만사가 순조로워 다행이다 I am glad things have gone well.∥요즘은 날씨가 ~ The weather has been favorable.∥환자가 수술 후 경과가 ~ The patient has been making satisfactory progress since the operation. **순조로이** favorably; satisfactorily; well; smoothly; swimmingly; normally; without a hitch. ¶~ 진행되다 progress satisfactorily / proceed favorably / go smoothly [well] / go on swimmingly∥~되다 take a favorable turn / improve∥~ 되지 않다 go wrong[amiss] / be unsatisfactory∥~ 팔리다 enjoy a steady sale∥일은 ~ 되어 가고 있다 Things are going well [smoothly] with me.∥회의는 ~ 진행되었다 The meeting progressed smoothly [without a hitch].∥나의 일은 ~ 진척되어 가고 있다 I am making steady progress in my work.∥교섭은 ~ 진행되었다 The negotiations went smoothly.∥일이 ~ 진척되지 못했다 Things did not go smoothly.∥사업은 ~ 시작되었다 The enterprise got off to a good start.

순종(純種) a full[pure] blood; a thoroughbred. ¶~의 full-[pure-]blooded / thoroughbred / purebred (dog) / (a dog) of unmixed [genuine] breed∥~의 말 a blood [pedigreed] horse / a thoroughbred horse∥~의 포인터 a pointer of pure stock / a pedigree(d) pointer∥이 개는 ~의 진돗개이다 This is a pure-blooded [purebred] *Jindotgae.*

순종(順從) (meek) obedience; (tame) submission. **순종하다** follow (a person) obediently; obey (a person) meekly; submit to (a person) tamely. ¶그 아이는 부모에게 잘 순종한다 The child is obedient to his parents.∥그녀는 평생을 남편에게 순종하였다 She served her husband submissively [obediently] all her life.

순직(殉職) death at one's post (of duty); death in the line of duty; death in harness. **순직하다** die at one's post (of duty); die in the line of duty; be killed at work [in the pursuit of one's duties]; die in harness. ¶그는 순직했다 He died in the course [line] of duty.
● **순직자** victim to his post (of duty); a martyr to duty.

순직하다(純直-) naive and honest; simple (-minded) and upright.

순진하다(純眞-) naive; pure; genuine; sincere; ingenuous; innocent; unsophisticated. ¶순진한 웃음 an innocent smile∥순진한 처녀 a maiden pure in[of] heart / an innocent girl∥순진한 어린이 an innocent child∥순진한 마음 a pure and simple heart / a heart of gold∥순진한 사랑 [platonic] love∥순진한 생각 a simple [an unsophisticated] idea∥그는 순진한 사람이다 He is pure in [of] heart. / He has a pure heart. / He is a simple soul.∥너는 정말 순진하구나 You are as innocent as a newborn babe. / You don't know anything, do you!∥나는 그런 일을 믿을 만큼 순진하지는 않다 I am not so simple as to believe something like that.

순차(順次) order; turn. ¶~로[적으로] in (serial / consecutive) order / successively / in regular succession [sequence / series].

순찰(巡察) a round of inspection; a patrol. ¶~ 중인 경찰관 a policeman on patrol∥~을 나가다 set out on a round of inspection [official calls]∥그 경관은 ~ 중이다 The policeman is now on patrol (duty) [on his beat]. **순찰하다** make [do] one's rounds; make [go] a round of inspection; patrol. ¶경찰관은 순찰하러 나갔다 The policeman went out on patrol.∥야경꾼은 빌딩 안을 순찰하였다 The night watchman went around the building.∥저 경찰관은 매일 이 지역을 순찰한다 That policeman patrols [makes his rounds of inspection] this district everyday.
● **순찰대** a patrol party. **순찰차** a (police) patrol car; a squad car.

순치음(脣齒音) (언) a labiodental [dentilabial] sound.

순탄하다(順坦-) (길이) even; level; smooth; (일 등이) favorable; fair; smooth. ¶순탄한 길 a (broad-)level road / a royal road∥순탄한 생활 an uneventful life / an even tenor of life. **순탄히** smoothly; favorably; well. ¶~ 자라다 be bred in favorable circumstances∥~ 진행되다 go smoothly / go well / be well along / proceed favorably∥경기는 8회까지 ~ 진행되었다 Up to the eighth inning the game proceeded uneventfully.

순풍(順風) a fair [favorable / free / tail / following] wind. ¶~에 돛을 달고 가다 sail before [with] the wind / sail with a fair wind / be under easy sail∥인생은 ~에 돛 단 듯이 되지는 않는다 Life is by no means smooth [plain] sailing.

순하다(順-) 1 [온순하다] gentle; mild; meek; [고분고분하다] obedient; submissive; tame; docile. ¶순한 성질 a gentle nature / a meek disposition∥순한 아이 meek [an obedient] child∥그는 천성이 순하고 정직하다 He is a docile [an obedient] child. / The child listens to what you tell him. 2 [맛이 독하지 않다] mild (tobacco); light (wine); bland. ¶순한 맛의 맥주 mild beer∥이 술은 ~ This wine is light.∥이 담배는 ~ This cigarette is mild. 3 [일이 쉽고도 잘되다] smooth; easy. ¶일이 순하게 진척되고 있다 The works are well forward [under way].

순항(巡航) a cruise; cruising. ¶~ 중이다 be on a cruise∥그 여객선은 태평양을 ~ 중이다 The liner is cruising in the Pacific. **순항하다** cruise [make a cruise] (on the Atlantic).
● **순항 미사일** a cruise missile. **순항선** a cruiser; a cruise boat. **순항 속도** (at full) cruising speed. ¶시속 20마일의 ~로 at a cruising speed of twenty miles an hour.

순행(巡行) a patrol; a round; a tour. **순행하다** go round; go the round of (the district); (담당 구역을) go [make] one's rounds; go on patrol; make a tour of (the village).

순혈(純血) pure [full] blood.

순화(純化) purification. **순화하다** purify; refine.

순화(醇化) refinement; sublimation. ¶국어 ~

운동 (launch) a campaign to refine[purify] the Korean language. **순화하다** refine; purify; sublimate.

순환(循環) 1 [변화의 과정을 되풀이함] circulation; rotation; cycle. ¶계절의 ~ the cycle [round] of the seasons∥경기 ~ a business [(영) trade] cycle∥악 ~ a vicious circle. **순환하다** circulate (through); rotate; cycle; recur; repeat; move in a cycle; go in cycles [circles]. ¶주기적으로 ~ move in a cycle / 계절은 순환한다 The seasons rotate [revolve].∥경기와 불경기는 순환한다 Prosperity and depression move in a cycle. 2 (혈액의) circulation of blood. ¶혈액 ~을 잘 되게 하다 improve the circulation of blood / 혈액 ~이 잘 된다[되지 않는다] I have a good[bad / poor] circulation (of blood).
● **순환 계통** (특히 혈액의) the circulatory system; the system of circulation. ¶~의 병 a disease in circulatory system / a circulatory disease. **순환기**(-期) a cycle. **순환기**(-器) a circulatory organ. **순환 도로** a circular road. ¶남산 ~ the Namsan(Mt. Nam) Circular Road. **순환선** a belt[loop] line; a circular railway. ¶교외 ~ the suburbs loop line.

순회(巡廻) (의사 등의) a round; (경찰·정찰대 등의) a patrol; a tour. ¶지방 ~ a provincial tour (of a theatrical company)∥(극단 등이) ~ 중이는 on a tour∥(미) be on the road. **순회하다** go round; go[make] one's[the] rounds; walk one's round(s); go the circuit; make[go / walk] the round (of a district); patrol; make[go on] a tour (of inspection); (미국 구어) circulate. ¶담당 구역을 ~ (미) make the round of one's assigned block [beat]∥명승지를 ~ make a tour of noted places.
● **순회 강연** a lecturing[lecture] tour; barnstorming. **순회공연** a provincial[local] performance; a show on tour; a road[touring] show. ¶그 극단은 지방을 ~ 중이다 The theatrical company is on the road[touring the provinces]. **순회 대사** a roving ambassador. **순회도서관** an itinerant[an itinerating / a traveling] library; a library on wheels; (미) a bookmobile. **순회 재판** assizes.

숟가락 a spoon. ¶찻 ~ a teaspoon∥밥[설탕] 한 ~ a spoonful of rice[sugar]∥두 ~ two spoonfuls∥~으로 뜨다 spoon out[up]∥~으로 젓다 stir with a spoon∥~으로 밀가루를 조금 냄비에 떠 넣다 spoon a little flour into a pot.

술[1] [취하는 음료] liquor; alcoholic drink; an intoxicant; wine; spirits. ¶독한[약한] ~ a strong[weak] wine / a hard[light] liquor∥오래 묵은 ~ old wine / aged wine / old vintage∥단[쓴] ~ sweet[dry] wine∥물을 타지 않은 ~ undiluted[unadulterated] liquor∥한 잔 의 ~ a cup of liquor / a glass of wine∥~의 힘을 빌려서 under the influence of wine / on the courage of liquor / emboldened by liquor∥~이 들어가면 when one drinks / when in wine∥~ 취하면 우는 사람 a maudlin drinker∥~이 싫어지는 약 Antabus(상표명)∥~ 상대를 하다 keep company in drinking∥~ 생각이 나다 get thirsty for drink∥~이 세다 be a heavy drinker∥~이 약하다 be a light[poor] drinker∥~이 늘다 gain in one's alcoholic capacity∥~에 취하다 get drunk / become intoxicated∥~에 취해[빠져] 이성을 잃다 drown one's reason in the bottle∥~에 빠지다 indulge in wine / give oneself up to drinking / be addicted to drinking∥~에 젖다 be steeped in liquor / be soaked in drink / keep oneself saturated with wine∥~에 물을 타다 water wine∥~로 슬픔을 달래다 drown one's grief in drink / 괴로움을 ~로 풀다 drink sorrow down∥~을 마셔 몸을 따뜻하게 하다 keep warm on liquor∥~로 밤을 지새우다 drink all night long / drink the night away∥~로 재산을 날리다 drink [guzzle] away one's fortune[property]∥~을 마시다 drink / take liquor / have a drink∥~을 마시며 이야기하다 talk over a bottle [glass]∥~을 마시다가 잠들다 drink oneself asleep[to sleep]∥한 방울도 ~을 마시지 않다 do not touch wine / be a total abstainer∥~을 빚다 brew (rice) wine∥~을 데우다 warm [heat] rice wine∥~을 데워서[데우지 않고] 마시다 drink rice wine warm[cold]∥~을 벌컥벌컥 마시다 guzzle / drink like a fish∥~을 가까이하다 take to drinking[the bottle]∥~을 끊다 give up[quit] drinking / become a teetotaler / total abstainer / cut out wine∥~을 삼가다 refrain[abstain] from drinking [liquor]∥~을 따르다 serve wine / serve (a person) with liquor / help (a person) to liquor / pour out wine (for a person) / fill (a glass) with wine∥~을 권하다 offer (a person) (a glass of) wine∥~을 억지로 권하다 press[force] wine upon (a person) / press (a person) to drink∥그는 ~이 세다 [약하다] He can drink quite a lot[can't drink much].∥그는 ~에 취했다 He is drunk.∥나는 ~을 전혀 마시지 못한다 I can't drink at all.∥나는 ~을 줄였다가 지금은 아주 끊어 버렸다 I had cut down on drinking, but now I have given it up entirely.∥그는 ~이 들어가면 딴사람이 된다 He looks quite another man when the wine is in.∥그는 ~을 곱게 마신다 He is merry in his cups. / He is a good drunk.∥그는 ~을 마셔도 끄떡없다 He carries his liquor well.∥그는 매일 ~만 마시고 있다 He is soaked in drink every day.∥~은 마셔도 제정신을 잃어서는 안 된다 You must not let liquor get the upper hand. / You must keep control of your drinking.∥그는 ~이라면 사족을 못 쓴다 He is simply mad so far as wine is concerned.∥그는 원래 ~을 못한다 He is a teetotaler by nature.
술은 백약의 장(속담) Wine is the best of all medicines.; Good wine engenders good blood.

술 먹은 개 When wine is in, wit[truth] is out.

술[2] [한 숟가락의 분량] a spoonful; a small quantity[amount].

술[3] (장식용의) a tassel; a tuft; a fringe. ¶~이 있는[달린] tassel(l)ed / tufted / fringed∥~ 달린 모자 a cap with a tassel (on it)∥~ 달린 기 a tassel(l)ed flag∥~ 달린 커튼 a fringed[tassel(l)ed] curtain∥~을 달다 tassel.

술값 [음주 대금] (a) drink charge; [술 마실 돈] money for drinking[a drink]; beer-money; drink money. ¶~을 내지 않고 도망치다 bilk a bar / make[run] away without paying for one's drink∥그가 버는 돈은 모두 ~으로 나간다 All the money he earns goes

술고래

for drink. ∥ 그는 가진 돈을 모두 ~으로 써 버 렸다 He spent all his money on drink [liquor].

술고래 a strong[heavy / hard] drinker; a tippler; a boozer; a soaker. ¶그는 ~다 He drinks like a fish. / He is a regular sponge.

술구더기 rice grains floating in rice wine.

술국 drinker's soup.

술기(-氣) the smell of liquor. ⇨ 술기운

술기운 [주기] the smell[odor] of liquor; an alcoholic smell; [취기] intoxication; tipsiness. ¶~이 돌다 grow[become / get] tipsy [drunk] / feel intoxication coming on / feel the effect of drink ∥ 그는 ~이 돌기 시작했다 The liquor has started to affect him.

술김 the influence of liquor. ¶~에 under the influence of liquor[alcohol] ∥ ~에 의한 by liquor / ~에 하는 싸움 a drunken brawl ∥ ~에 부리는 객기 Dutch courage ∥ ~에 싸우다 quarrel[brawl] under the influence of liquor ∥ 그는 ~에 허풍을 떨었다 Made bold [Emboldened] by alcohol, he talked big. ∥ 그것은 ~에 한 짓이었다 It was done under the influence of liquor.

술꾼 a (heavy) drinker; a tippler; (구어) a boozer; [애주가] a thirsty soul. ¶그는 틀림없이 ~일 게다 I am sure he drinks.

술내 the smell[odor] of liquor; an alcoholic smell. ¶~가 나다 smell of liquor / reek of wine / have an alcoholic breath ∥ ~를 풍기며 쳐들어왔다 He came barging in reeking of alcohol. ∥ 그의 입김에서는 ~가 난다 His breath reeks[smells] of liquor.

술독 [항아리] a liquor jug; [술고래] a sot; a tippler; a heavy drinker.

술독(-毒) alcohol poisoning; alcoholism. ¶~이 오르다 have a blotchy face (due to alcohol).

술래 a tagger; it. ¶네가 ~다 You're it. ∥ ~는 누구냐 Who is the tagger? / Who is it?
● **술래잡기** tag; tig; touch; touch-last; (a game of) hide-and-(go-)seek; hy spy; I spy. ¶~를 하다 play tag[tig] / play hide-and-seek.

술렁거리다 be disturbed[perturbed]; be stirred[agitated]; be unsettled; be restless [uneasy]; be in (a) commotion. ¶온 나라가 승리로 술렁거리고 있었다 The whole nation was astir[alive] with the excitement of victory. ∥ 청중은 한순간 술렁거렸다 There was a momentary stir in the audience. ∥ 너가 입장하자 청중이 술렁거렸다 There was a general stir as she entered.

술렁술렁 astir; disturbed; perturbed; agitatedly; in a commotion. **술렁술렁하다** be disturbed. ⇨ 술렁거리다

술밥 [지에밥] steamed rice for brewing rice wine; [주반(酒飯)] rice boiled with wine, soysauce, and sugar.

술버릇 ¶~이 나쁘다 be quarrelsome in one's cups / be a bad drunk / ~이 아주 나쁘다 be a terrible[vicious] drunk / ~이 좋다 be a good drunk / ~는 ~이 좋다 He can hold his liquor. / He can take his drink. / He doesn't get nasty when he drinks.

술법(-法) [복술] divination; fortunetelling; [요술] magical tricks; conjury; magic; mysteries. ¶~을 쓰다 use magic / practice sorcery[divination] / lay a spell.

술병(-病) sickness caused by drinking; an alcoholic disorder. ¶~이 나다 drink oneself sick[ill] / be sick from drink.

술병(-甁) a (liquor) bottle. ¶~에 채우다 bottle.

술상(-床) a drinking table. ¶~을 차리다 prepare dishes for drink / set a drinking table.

술수(術數) 1 divination; magical tricks. ⇨ 술법 2 an artifice. ⇨ 술책 ¶~를 쓰다 use tactics[diplomacy] / resort to wiles[trickery / machination].

술술 1 [거침없이] soft-flowing(물 등이); smoothly; swimmingly; without a hitch; without let or hindrance; [막힘없이] fluently; facilely; [쉽게] easily; with ease; readily. ¶목을 ~ 넘어가다 go smoothly down the throat / 어려운 문제를 ~ 풀다 solve a hard question easily[without (any) effort] / 주전자에서 물이 ~ 샌다 The kettle leaks badly. / Water is leaking from the kettle in a steady stream. / 얽힌 실이 ~ 풀렸다 The tangled thread straightened out nicely.
2 [가만히] lightly; gently; softly. ¶비가 ~ 온다 It drizzles. ∥ 바람이 ~ 분다 The wind blows gently. / There is a gentle breeze.
3 [유창하게] fluently; glibly; smoothly; [솔직히] frankly; unreservedly. ¶~ 말하다 speak fluently[with fluency / off the reel / without hesitation] ∥ ~ 자백하다 confess frankly [with a good grace] ∥ 그녀는 영어를 ~ 지껄인다 She speaks English fluently. / She speaks fluent English. ∥ 그는 그 시를 ~ 암송했다 He recited the poem without any trouble[without stumbling] at all.

술안주(-按酒) a relish (taken with wine); a (side) dish; appetizers[(프) hors d'oeuvres served with drinks; an accompaniment of wine. ¶~로 as a side dish for wine ∥ 이것은 ~로 좋습니다 This goes very well with wine. ∥ ~가 아무것도 없습니다 I have nothing to take with wine.

술어(述語) the predicate (of a sentence). ⇨ 서술어(⇨서술)
● **술어 동사** a predicate verb.

술어(術語) a technical term; [집합적] technics; professional language; (scientific) terminology; nomenclature. ¶전문 ~ the jargon of one's science.

술자리 a drinking party; a banquet; a feast. ¶~를 마련하다 hold a party.

술잔(-盞) a winecup; a wineglass; a goblet(굽이 높은). ¶이별의 ~ a parting cup ∥ ~을 주다[받다] offer[accept] a cup ∥ ~을 주고받다 exchange cups of wine (with) / help one another to wine ∥ ~을 (가득) 채우다 fill the cup[glass] (to the brim) ∥ ~을 비우다 drain[drink off] the cup / drink the cup dry / empty the cup to the last drop ∥ ~을 부딪치다 touch (their) cups ∥ ~을 나누며 이야기하다 have a chat (with another) over winecups.

술잔치 a feast; a drinking bout[party]; a carousal; a carouse; a banquet. ¶~를 벌이다 hold a banquet / have[go on] a drinking bout / have a carousal / have[give] a feast / carouse

술장사 [주류 판매] liquor(-selling) business [trade].

술집 [유흥 주점] a drinking house; (미) a bar; (미) a barroom; (미국 구어) a saloon; a

tavern; (영) a public house; (영국 구어) a pub. ¶~을 돌아다니며 마시다 loaf around saloons / barhop / go barhopping / (영) do a pub crawl.
●술집 여자 a barmaid; (미국 속어) a B-girl.
술집 주인 a barkeeper; (영) a public-house keeper; (영국 구어) a publican; (미) a saloon keeper.

술책(術策) an artifice; a stratagem; a trick; an intrigue; tactics; wiles; a policy. ¶~에 뛰어난[능한] artful[resourceful] (man) / (a man) of resources / fertile in[full of] resources / wily / ~을 부리다 resort to tricks //…의 ~에 빠지다 walk into[fall into / fall for / be caught in] a trap set by (a person) / play into the hands of (someone) / be entrapped[taken in] by (a person).

술추렴 [술값 각출] pooling the expenses for a drinking bout[party]; [돌아가며 내는 술] a drinking party that everyone gives by turns.
술추렴하다 pool[club] the expenses for a drinking bout; have everyone chip in [(미국 속어) kick in] for a drinking bout; (everyone) serve (up) drinks[give a drinking party] by turns.

술친구(-親舊) [술벗] a drinking companion; a boon[convivial / bottle / pot] companion; a companion in one's revels; a fellow toper.

술타령 [술만 마심] indulgence in wine; [술만 찾음] asking for[suggesting] nothing but liquor; [술 생각만 함] thinking only of a liquor. ¶그는 ~만 한다 He has nothing but drinking on his mind.//그는 아침부터 계속 ~이다 He has been drinking since morning.//그는 실직한 뒤에 매일 ~만 해 왔다 He has been drunk every day since he lost his job. **술타령하다** indulge in wine; ask for [suggest] nothing but liquor; think only of liquor; be always thirsty.

술통(-桶) a wine cask[barrel / keg].
술파다이아진 [약] sulfadiazine; diazine.
술판 (the scene[place] of) a drinking bout [party]. ¶~을 벌이다 hold[give / have] a drinking bout.

술회(述懷) [생각을 말함] an effusion of one's thoughts (and feelings). **술회하다** relate [express] one's thoughts. ¶자기의 생각을 ~ relate one's thoughts.

숨 1 [호흡] a breath; breathing; respiration. ¶단~에 at a breath / in one breath / at[on] a stretch / in a single spell //~을 헐떡이며 out of breath / panting / breathless(ly) / gaspingly //~이 가쁘게 out of breath / panting / breathless(ly) / gaspingly //내가 ~을 쉬고 있는 한[내 생명이 붙어 있는 한] while I still breathe / as long as I live / while there is life in me //~을 쉬다 breathe / respire / take breath / draw (one's) breath //~을 내쉬다 breathe out[forth] / give out breath / exhale //~을 들이쉬다 breathe in / take in breath / inhale //~을 깊이 들이쉬다 와 천천히 내쉬다 breathe in deeply[take a deep breath] and breathe out slowly //~을 헐떡이다 get out [short] of breath / gasp[pant] (for breath) //~이 가쁘다 breathe hard / be out[short] of breath / be panting[puffing / gasping] for breath //~이 답답하다 be choky[stuffy] //~이 끊어지다 die / gasp one's life away / breathe one's last(breath) //코로 ~을 쉬다 breathe through the[one's] nose //~ 쉴 겨를도 없다 have scarcely time to breathe / have hardly a breathing spell //그는 ~이 가쁜 듯했다 He looked as if he was having difficulty in breathing.//그들은 곧 ~이 가빠졌다 They were soon short of breath.//그는 심장이 좋지 않아 몹시 ~이 가쁘다 He is extremely short of breath because of his bad heart.//그녀는 ~이 가빠서 말을 잇지 못했다 She stopped talking for lack of breath.//나는 너무 허둥대어 ~이 가빴다 I hurried so much that I got out of breath.//그는 ~이 칠어[빨라]졌다 His breathing became short [quickened]. / He began to breathe hard [fast]. /환자는 금방 ~이 끊어질 것 같다 The patient is gasping for breath[breathing feebly / dying].//그는 ~을 쉴 때마다 그르렁거렸다 His throat made a wheezing sound at each breath.
2 (야채 등의) freshness; crispness (of fresh vegetables).

숨(을) 거두다 breathe one's last (breath); gasp one's life away; expire; die; give up one's breath. ¶할아버지는 오늘 아침에 숨을 거두셨다 My grandfather died[breathed his last] this morning.

숨(을) 돌리다 take[gather] breath; catch [recover] one's breath; pause for breath; [쉬다] take a pause. ¶숨 돌릴 겨를도 주지 않고 giving (a person) not a moment's respite // 2, 3일 숨 돌릴 겨를이 있다면 if I can have a few days' breathing space / 숨도 돌리지 않고 without taking breath / [단숨에] (all) in a breath // 숨 돌릴 겨를도 없다 I have no time to rest[take a rest]. //나는 숨 돌릴 겨를도 없이 바빴다 I was so busy that I had no time to relax[catch my breath].//이제 좀 숨을 돌리겠다 Now I feel relieved.//그는 한 문장이 끝날 때마다 숨을 돌렸다 He took a breath at the end of each sentence.//그는 잠깐 숨을 돌리고는 다시 이야기를 시작했다 He paused a moment for breath, but soon began to talk.//50만 원만 더 있으면 숨을 돌리겠는데 If I had five hundred thousand won more, I could tide over the difficulty.

숨(이) 막히다 be choked; be suffocated; be stifled. ¶숨 막히는[숨이 막힐 듯한] breathtaking / thrilling / [질식할 듯한] choking / stifling / suffocating / oppressing // 숨 막히는 침묵 an oppressive[a breathless] silence // 숨 막히는 방 a stuffy[close] room // 숨 막히는 더위 suffocating heat // 숨 막히는 열전 a breathtaking game / a game that keeps the spectators on the edge of their seats // 연기 때문에 ~ be suffocated by smoke //그 좁은 방은 후텁지근하여 숨이 막힐 것 같았다 It was sultry in the small room and I felt suffocated.//방 안은 담배 연기가 자욱해서 숨이 막힐 지경이었다 The room was so thick with cigarette smoke that I almost choked[suffocated].//이 방은 환기가 잘 되지 않아 숨이 막힐 것 같다 This room is so poorly ventilated that it's almost stifling[suffocating]. / This room is stuffy because it's poorly ventilated.//숨 막힐 듯한 침묵이 몇 분 동안 이어졌다 The oppressive silence lasted several minutes.

숨(이) 죽다 [야채가 소금에 절여져 싱싱한 기운을 잃다]. lose the crispness; wilt; languish. ¶배추가 숨이 죽었다 The cabbage has lost its crispness.

숨결 breathing; respiration. ¶봄의 ~ a breath of spring // ~이 거칠다 breathe hard [short / heavily] / be gasping.

숨구멍 [숨통] the windpipe; the trachea (*pl.* ~s, -cheae); (식물의) a pore; a stoma (*pl.* -mata); (곤충의) a stigma (*pl.* ~s, -mata).

숨기다 1 (모습·물건 등을) hide (oneself); conceal (one's money); ensconce (oneself); secrete (stolen goods); bury (one's mistakes); [덮어 가리다] cover (a fact); veil (one's displeasure); draw [throw] a veil over (a fact); cloak (one's ignorance); dissemble (a fact); [막아 가리다] screen; obstruct. ¶몸을 ~ hide (oneself) (behind / under / in) / shelter oneself (under / beneath / behind) // 보이지 않는 곳에 ~ conceal (a thing) from view // 범죄를 숨기기 위해 방화하다 set a fire to cover up crime // 그는 품에 단도를 숨기고 있었다 He had a knife concealed under his shirt. // 그는 중요한 물건을 다락방에 숨겼다 He hid the valuable article in the attic. // 그는 재빨리 문[나무들] 뒤로 몸을 숨겼다 He quickly hid himself behind the door [among the trees]. // 이것은 그녀의 숨겨진 성격의 일면을 나타내는 것이다 This shows a hidden part of her character.

2 [비밀로 하다] keep (a matter) secret [back] (from); keep (a matter) dark; [숨겨 주다] harbor; shelter (a criminal); give refuge [shelter / harbor] to (a runaway). ¶숨기지 않고 말하면 to be frank with you / to tell the truth // 나이를 ~ conceal [make a secret of] one's age // 사실을 ~ repress [cover up / wrap up / disguise] a fact // 진실을 ~ conceal the truth // 신원을 ~ conceal one's identity // 숨기지 않다 make no secret of (an affair) / have no secret of (a matter from a person) / have nothing (secret) (from) / be frank [open / candid] // 그는 자기 빚을 아버지에게 숨기고 있었다 He kept [hid] his debt from his father. // 우리는 당신에게 숨기는 것이 아무것도 없소 We have no secrets from you. / We aren't hiding anything from you. // 이것은 숨길 수 없는 사실이다 The fact is not to be disguised. / This is a patent [an undeniable / an obvious] fact. // 대부분의 가정에는 남에게 숨기고 싶은 사정이 있기 마련이다 Most families have a skeleton in the cupboard [closet]. // 숨기지 말고 말해라 Speak it out. / (속어) Spit it out. // 나에게는 아무것도 숨기지 말아 주시오 Please don't hide things [anything] from me. (▶ hide things는 무엇인가를 숨기고 있다고 의심할 때, hide anything은 지금은 숨기고 있다고 생각하지 않으나 숨기지 말라고 다짐할 때 쓰임)

숨김없다 open-hearted; unreserved; straightforward; (서술적) (be) frank. **숨김없이** without reserve; without concealment; unservedly; frankly; openly; straightforward; straight out. ¶~ 말한다면 to be frank with you / frankly speaking // ~ 말하다 speak (straight) out / be open [frank / straightforward] with (a person) // ~ 털어놓다 make a clean breast of (a secret) / lay bare one's heart // 그는 그 진상을 ~ 내게 털어놓았다 He told me the whole truth. / He made a clean breast of it to me. // 그 문제에 대하여 자네의 의견을 ~ 말해 주게 Tell me your ideas on the subject without any reserve. / I want your candid opinion about the matter.

숨넘어가다 breathe one's last; gasp one's life away [out]; expire; die. ¶숨넘어가는 소리로 말하다 gasp [pant] out // 그 죽어 가는 사람은 숨넘어가는 소리로 자기 외아들을 돌보아 줄 것을 내게 부탁했다 The dying man gasped out a request for me to look after his only son.

숨다 1 [몸을 감추다] hide (behind the door / among the trees); hide [conceal] oneself; take cover; be [lie] in hiding; lie hidden; [피난하다] take [seek] refuge [shelter] (in / under / behind / with); [보이지 않게 되다] disappear (from sight); be hidden [lost] from sight. ¶숨은 hidden / concealed // 숨어서 out of sight / [몰래] in secret / secretly / by stealth / under cover // 나무 뒤에 ~ conceal oneself [lie concealed] behind a tree // 이웃집에 ~ seek refuge [(미국 속어) hole up] with a neighbor // 벽장 속에 ~ hide oneself in a closet // 산속에 ~ lurk in the mountain // 숨어 있다 lie hid(den) [concealed] / be in hiding / keep out of sight / be behind (a screen) // (숨바꼭질에서) 꼭꼭 숨어라 Hide fox and all after. // 도둑은 수풀 속에 숨어 있었다 The thief was in hiding in the bushes. // 위험을 느끼고 그는 지하에 숨었다 Sensing danger, he went underground. // 달이 구름 뒤에 숨었다 The moon went [disappeared / vanished] behind the clouds. // 그는 당황하여 나무 뒤에 숨었다 In a sudden panic, he hid himself behind a tree.

2 [은둔하다] live in seclusion; retire from the world. ¶그는 숨어 살고 있다 He is living an obscure life. / He remains [has remained] quiet.

3 [알려져 있지 않다] be unknown; be anonymous. ¶숨은 hidden (genius / meaning) / latent (defects) / unknown (inventor) / anonymous (philanthropist) / unrecognized (scholar) // 숨은 의미 a hidden [an inner] meaning // 숨은 인재 a person with unrecognized [hidden] talent // 너에게 그런 숨은 재주가 있는 줄 몰랐다 I didn't know you had such a hidden talent.

숨바꼭질 (a game of) hide-and-(go-)seek; I spy; hy spy. **숨바꼭질하다** play hide-and-seek.

숨소리 the sound of breathing. ¶~를 죽이고 holding one's breath / with bated breath // ~를 죽이다 hold [catch] one's breath.

숨어들다 get in by stealth; pass in secretly; steal in [into]; sneak in [into]. ¶방 안에 ~ steal [sneak] into a room // 지하에 ~ go underground.

숨은열 (-熱) [물] latent heat.

숨죽이다 1 [(잠시) 숨을 멈추다] hold [catch / keep / taut] one's breath; stop [shut out] one's breath. ¶숨죽이고 지켜보다 watch with breathless attention // 그들은 숨죽이고 그 광경을 지켜보았다 They watched the scene with breathless interest. // 다섯 살 먹은 아들이 지붕 위에 서 있는 것을 보고 나는 숨죽였다 I caught my breath on seeing my five-year-old son standing on the roof. 2 [조용히 하다] keep quiet [still]; be silent. ¶숨죽이고 이야기하다 speak in a calm tone // 숨죽여 이야기하자 Now, let's not get excited but talk it over calmly.

숨지다 breathe one's last; gasp one's life away [out]; expire; die. ¶교통사고로 ~ die

숨차다 (서술적) be out of breath; be short of breath[wind]; be breathless; be short-winded[-breathed]. ¶숨찬 목소리로 말하다 gasp[puff / pant] out[forth / away] // 나는 숨차서 더 이상 달릴 수가 없다 I am out of breath and can't run any further. // 가파르지도 않은 비탈을 오르는 데도 숨찬다 I pant for breath even when going up a gentle slope.

숨통(-筒) [생] the windpipe. ⇨기관(氣管) ¶~을 끊다 put an end to (a person's) life / give (a person) his quietus.

숫- pure; virgin; spotless; immaculate; undefiled; innocent. ¶~처녀 a virgin / an innocent girl / an immaculate virgin.

숫구멍 (젖먹이 머리의) the fontanel(le).

숫기(-氣) manly openness; boldness. ¶~가 없다 be shy[bashful / diffident] / be coy(특히 소녀가) // 그 애는 ~가 없어서 말도 잘 못한다 That boy is coy of speech. / That boy is too shy to speak.
‖ **숫기(가) 좋다** be unabashed[bold / confident / outgoing]. ¶숫기 좋게 말하다 speak out unabashed[unreservedly].

숫돌 a whetstone; a rubstone; a grindstone (둥근); a grinder; (면도의) a hone. ¶~에 갈다 sharpen (a knife) on a whetstone / whet[grind] (a knife) / hone (a razor).

숫되다 innocent; ingenuous; simple; artless; naive; unsophisticated; unspoiled; unaffected. ¶숫된 처녀 an innocent[ingenuous] girl // 숫된 새색시 a bride in her naivety.

숫자(數字) a figure; a number(▶ 일반적인 말); a numeral(▶ number보다 딱딱한 말). ¶두 자리 ~ a two-digit number[figure] / two-figure number // 아라비아[로마] ~ an Arabic [a Roman] numeral // 유효 ~ significant figures // 천문학적 ~ astronomical figures // 정확한 ~ exact[precise] figures // ~상 numerically / in figures // ~상의 numerical // ~상의 잘못 numerical errors // ~로 나타내다 state[express] in figures // ~를 들다 give [cite] figures // 굉장한 ~에 달하다 reach [attain / amount to / mount up to] big figures // 그는 ~에 밝다[약하다] He is good [no good] at figures. // 자동차 번호판은 문자와 ~로 되어 있다 A license plate[(영) numberplate] bears both letters and numbers.

숫제 1 [차라리] rather (than); sooner (than); better (than); preferably. ¶창피를 당할 바에야 ~ 죽어 버리겠다 I would rather[sooner] die than suffer disgrace. // ~ 서 있는 편이 낫다 I prefer standing (to sitting). / I prefer to stand (rather than sit). // 그렇게 할 바에야 ~ 죽어 버리겠다 I would sooner die than do it.
2 [전적으로] (not) at all; [처음부터] from the first[beginning]. ¶장사가 ~ 안 됩니다 My business is no good at all. // 너는 ~ 가지 않는 것이 좋다 You had better not go at all. // 나는 그녀가 오리라고는 ~ 기대하지 않았다 I did not at all expect that he would come. // 나는 ~ 그 책을 펴 보지도 않았다 I never even opened the book. // 이것은 ~ 모르겠는데요 I can't head or tail of this.
3 [진심으로] sincerely; heartily; wholeheartedly. ¶~ 마음을 바치다 devote oneself (to one's husband) wholeheartedly.

숫처녀(-處女) a pure[an undefiled] virgin; an innocent[immaculate] virgin.

숫총각(-總角) a (male) virgin; an innocent bachelor.

숭고하다(崇高-) lofty; sublime; grand; noble. ¶숭고한 이상 a lofty ideal // 그는 숭고한 정신의 소유자이다 He is high-minded [noble-minded]. // 그들은 숭고한 이상을 실현했다 They realized their lofty ideals. // 그의 숭고한 행위를 누구나가 칭송했다 Everyone praised[commended] his noble deed.

숭굴숭굴하다 1 (생김새가) comely; personable; good-looking; plump (and buxom); chubby. ¶숭굴숭굴하게 생긴 아이 a plump and well-looking child // 그녀의 얼굴은 숭굴숭굴하게 생겼다 She has a cherubic face. **2** (성질이) good-natured; good-humored; amiable; smooth; pleasant; pleasing; easy to get along with. ¶숭굴숭굴한 사람 an amiable [a good-natured] person.

숭늉 sungnyung; water boiled with burned rice.

숭덩숭덩 with hasty whacks. ⇨송당송당

숭배(崇拜) worship; adoration; admiration; cult. ¶개인~ the cult of personality // 우상 ~ idol worship / idolatry // 자연 ~ the cult of nature / nature worship / naturism // 조상 [영웅] ~ ancestor[hero] worship // ~의 대상 an object of veneration. **숭배하다** worship; venerate; adore; admire; idolize; make an idol of. ¶…을 맹목적으로 ~ make a fetish of (a person) / be a blind adorer [devotee] of (a person) // 그는 칸트를 숭배하고 있다 He admires Kant. / He is an admirer of Kant. // 나는 베토벤을 진심으로 숭배하고 있다 I am an ardent admirer of Beethoven.
● **숭배자** a worshiper; an adorer; an admirer; an idolater; a votary.

숭상(崇尙) respect; veneration. **숭상하다** respect; venerate; esteem; revere. ¶무(武)를 ~ pursue the policy of militarism.

숭숭 (chop) into small pieces; full of small holes. ⇨송송

숭어 [동] a gray mullet.

숯 [목탄] charcoal. ¶~을 굽다 process [make] charcoal // ~이 되다 be charred // 불에 ~을 넣다 add charcoal to the fire / replenish the fire with charcoal.

숯이 검정 나무란다(속담) The kettle calls the pot black.

숯가마 a charcoal kiln. ¶~에 숯을 굽다 burn [make] charcoal in a charcoal kiln.

숯검정 charcoal soot.

숯내 the fumes of charcoal. ¶~가 나다 smell charcoal burning // ~를 맡다 get poisoned by the fumes of charcoal / be charcoaled.

숯불 a charcoal fire. ¶~을 피우다 make [build] a fire with charcoal // ~로 뱀장어를 굽다 grill eels over charcoal (a charcoal fire).

숱 (머리털 등의) thickness; density; richness; (분량) quantity. ¶~이 많은 검은 머리 thick [abundant] black hair // 머리~을 치다 thin one's hair out // 머리~이 많다 have thick [heavy] hair // ~이 적다 have thin[spare] hair.

숱하다 [많다] plentiful; abundant; copious; rich; [흔하다] very many; numerous. ¶숱한 불평[잘못] numerous complaints[errors] // 숱하게 많다 be abundant (in) / be rich (in / with) / be plentiful // 배에 쥐가 숱하게 많다 The ship abounds in[with] rats.

숲 (마을 부근에 있고 forest 보다 작은) a wood;

숲길 a path[trail] through a forest[wood]; a woodland path.

쉬(이) shoo! ¶~ 참새를 쫓다 shoo (the sparrow) away.

쉬¹ [파리의 알] eggs of a fly; flyblows. ¶파리가 ~를 슬다 a fly lays eggs (upon meat) / a fly blows (meat).

쉬² 〈소아〉 piddling; piddle; wee-wee; wee; (속어) pee. **쉬하다** piddle; (속어) pee; go[have a / (영) do] wee-wee; wee-wee; tinkle. ¶바지에 ~ wet one's pants // 엄마, 쉬할래 Mommy, I gotta go wee-wee.

쉬³ easily; soon. ⇨ 쉬이

쉬 더운 방이 쉬 식는다 (속담) Soon hot, soon cold.

쉬⁴ [조용히] hush!; sh!; mum!; [쫓는 소리] scat!; shoo! ¶~ 조용히 해 Hush! / Be quiet! / Silence!

쉬다¹ (음식이) go bad; turn sour; spoil. ¶쉰내 a sourish[stale] smell // 쉰밥 spoiled rice.

쉬다² (목소리가) get[become / grow] hoarse[husky / harsh]; hoarsen. ¶쉰 목소리로 말하다 speak in a husky[hoarse] voice // 목이 ~ become husky[hoarse] // 목이 쉬도록 응원하다 cheer oneself hoarse // 목이 쉬었군요 You sound hoarse. // 그는 큰 소리를 너무 질러 목이 쉬었다 He shouted himself hoarse.

쉬다³ **1** [휴식하다] rest (up); take[have] a rest (from); repose[rest] (oneself); stop (from work). ¶5분간 쉬고 나서 after five minutes rest // 충분히 쉬었습니까 Did you have a good rest? // 누워서 쉬는 게 좋다 You'd better lie down and rest. // 잠깐 공부를 쉬자 Let's take a break[rest] from our study. // 저 다방에서 좀 쉬는 것이 어때 How about stopping at that coffee shop for a rest? // 그녀는 바느질을 멈추고 10분간 쉬었다 She stopped sewing and took a ten minutes rest. / She took a rest[rested] from her needlework for ten minutes. // 새가 한 마리 가지에 앉아서 날개를 쉬고 있다 A bird is sitting on a branch and resting its wings. // 쉬어 가며 하자꾸나 Let's relax[take things easy]. // 소파에서 편히 쉬십시오 Sit on the sofa and relax[make yourself at home / make yourself comfortable], please. // 그는 편히 쉬면서 파이프 담배를 피우고 있다 He is relaxing with pipe. // 나는 그런 호화로운 방에서는 편히 쉴 수가 없었다 I could not feel at home[feel at ease / relax] in such a luxurious room. // 너는 좀 쉴 필요가 있다 You need some relaxation. // 나는 좀 쉬려고 여행했다 I took a trip to give myself some rest[a break].

2 (일·활동을) knock off[drop] (work); take a rest from (one's work); give oneself rest. ¶휴일에 일한 대신 ~ take a day off to make up for having worked on a holiday // 오늘은 학교가 쉰다 We have no school today. // 은행은 일요일은 쉰다 Banks are closed on Sundays. // 그는 오늘 하루 쉬고 있다 He has a day off today. // 당신은 한 달간 쉬어야 합니다 You need a month off. // 일요일에 운동회가 있기 때문에 대신 학교는 월요일에 쉰다 As we are going to hold an athletic meet on Sunday, school will be closed on Monday to make up for it. // 그는 결코 일을 쉬지 않는다 He never misses work.

3 [중단하다] suspend; pause; discontinue. ¶우리 공장은 일을 쉬고 있다 Work is suspended at our factory. / Our factory has suspended operation.

4 [결석·결근하다] be absent[absent oneself] (from school / from one's office); stay[keep] away (from school / work); do not attend (school). ¶나는 어제 학교를[직장을] 쉬었다 I was absent from school[the office] yesterday. // 상사는 어제 그를 하루 쉬게 했다 The boss gave him the day off yesterday. // 나는 아들이 감기에 걸려서 학교를 쉬게 했다 As he had a cold, I kept my son home from school.

5 [자다·취침하다] go to bed; retire; [잠자다] sleep. ¶푹 ~ sleep well[soundly] / have a good night.

쉴 새 없이 incessantly; continuously; continually; unceasingly; ceaselessly; without (a) letup; without a break. ¶~ 지껄이다 talk without ceasing [a pause] / chatter ceaselessly // ~ 일하다 work without rest[stopping] // ~ 전화가 걸려 왔다 I had calls one after another. // ~ 비가 오고 있다 It has been raining without intermission [raining steadily].

쉬다⁴ (숨을) breathe; respire; draw (one's) breath; (한숨을) sigh; heave [draw / fetch] a sigh. ¶깊이 숨을 ~ draw[take] a deep[full] breath // 안도의 숨을 ~ give[heave] a sigh of relief / breathe relief // 긴 한숨을 ~ draw a long breath // 깊이[길게] 한숨을 쉬고 with a deep[long] sigh // 깊이 숨을 쉬어라. 그러고 나서 내뱉어라 Breathe in[Take in breath / Inhale] deeply, and then exhale [breathe out].

쉬르레알리슴 (ⓔsurréalisme) [초현실주의] surrealism. ¶~의 surrealistic.

쉬쉬하다 hush[cover / smother] up (a scandal); (속어) hush-hush. ¶쉬쉬하며 말하다 talk hush-hush // 당국은 부정 사건을 쉬쉬해 버리려고 하고 있다 The authorities are trying to hush up[put a lid on] the scandal.

쉬슬다 [파리가 알을 여기저기 낳다] (a fly) lay eggs (upon meat); (a fly) blow (meat). ¶쉬슨 고기 blown[flyblown] meat.

쉬어 [구령] (미) At ease!; (영) Stand at ease!

쉬엄쉬엄 with frequent rests; by easy[short] stages; off and on; on and off; in an off-and-on way; intermittently. ¶~ 가다 go resting at frequent intervals / travel by easy stages // ~ 일하다 work taking frequent breaks / do a job by easy stages // 환자는 ~ 걸어갔다 The invalid took a rest[stopped to catch his breath] every few steps.

쉬이 **1** [쉽게] easily; readily; with ease; without difficulty. ¶~ 풀 수 있는 문제 a problem easy to solve. **2** [곧] soon; before long; presently; shortly. ¶눈은 ~ 녹아 버릴 것이다 The snow will melt away soon[before long].

쉰 fifty. ¶~ 살 fifty years of age // 나이 ~을 바라보다 be close upon fifty / be getting on

쉰내 a sour[sourish smell]; a stale smell.

쉼표(-標) [음] a rest; a pause. ¶온[2분/4분/8분]~ a whole[a half / a quarter / an eighth] rest / (영) a semibreve [minim / crotchet / quarter] rest.

쉽다 1 [용이하다] easy; [간단하다] simple; [평이하다] plain. ¶쉽게 easily / with ease [facility] / without difficulty [great effort] / plainly / simply / [바로] readily // 쉬운 질문 an easy question // 쉬운 일[문제] an easy job [question] // (표현을) 쉽게 하다 simplify (English) / paraphrase in plain language // 우리는 쉽게 이겼다 We won easily [with ease]. // 그는 큰 돌을 쉽게 들어 올렸다 He lifted the big stone without difficulty. // 그녀는 쉽게 사기꾼에게 당했다 She fell easy prey to the swindler. // 나는 위원장 직을 너무 쉽게 수락한 것을 후회하고 있다 I regret having agreed so readily to serve as chairman. // 나이를 먹으면 쉽게 피로해진다 One tires quickly with age. / You tire easily when you get old. // 남을 비판하기는 쉬운 일이다 It is easy to criticize other people. // 남의 흠을 잡기는 ~ It is easy for us to find fault with others. // 그는 쉬운 영어로 썼다 He wrote in plain [simple] English. // 생각했던 만큼 쉽지 않다 It is more difficult than I thought. // 쉬운 문제부터 시작하자 Let's start with the easier questions. // 해답을 찾기란 쉬운 일이 아니다 It's no simple matter to find a solution (for it). // 그 다리를 건설하는 것은 쉬운 일이 아니다 It will be no easy task to build that bridge. // 그 기계의 구조를 이해하기는 아주 쉬웠다 I had no difficulty (in) understanding the mechanism of the machine. / The mechanism of the machine was easy [not difficult] to understand. // 나는 쉬운 말로 설명했다 I explained in plain words [in a simple way]. // 이것은 다른 어느 사전보다도 이용하기가 ~ This is easier to use than any other dictionary. // 쉬운 말로 하면 그는 실각한 거야 In short, he fell from power.
2 [경향이 있다] be susceptible to; be liable to; be apt to; be prone to. ¶깨지기 쉬운 자기 fragile china // 이런 일은 자칫 잊어버리기 ~ We are apt to forget this kind of thing. // 그것은 소녀들이 빠지기 쉬운 감상에 지나지 않는다 That is the kind of sentimentality to which most girls are subject. // 그런 사고는 흔히 일어나기 ~ Accidents like that do happen. // 그는 지나치게 열중하기 쉽다 He is apt to be too enthusiastic. // 사람은 이기적이기 ~ People are liable [apt] to be selfish. // 그런 사람들은 미신에 빠지기 ~ Such people are prone to superstition. // 젊은이들은 게을러지기 ~ The young men are inclined to be lazy. // 그는 남의 아첨에 넘어가기 ~ He is susceptible to flattery. / He is easily flattered. // 나는 쉽게 배[차]멀미를 한다 I tend to get seasick [carsick].

쉽사리 (very) easily; readily; with ease [facility]; without trouble [difficulty]; without effort; with no effort; hands down. ¶~ 접근할 수 없다 be difficult of access // ~ 대답할 수 없다 cannot give an offhand answer // 이 문은 ~ 열리지 않는다 This door will not open. // 그의 병은 ~ 낫지 않았다 It was long before he got well. // 그가 ~ 승낙할 것 같지 않다 I am afraid he will not consent readily.

슈크림 (*㉢chou+cream) a cream puff.

슈트 [야구] shoot.

슈퍼(마켓) a supermarket. ¶~에 쇼핑하러 가는 길이다 I'm going to shopping at a supermarket. // 저 ~는 물건 값이 싸다 Prices are reasonable at that supermarket.

슈퍼맨 a superman.

슛 (축구·농구 등에서) a shot. ¶~을 **성공시키다** (농구에서) sink a shot / make a basket / (축구에서) shoot a goal. **슛하다** shoot (the ball). ¶골에 ~ shoot for a goal.

스낵 a snack; junk food. (▶ 우리말 「스낵」은 주로 바삭바삭하게 튀긴 과자류를 가리키나, 영어 "snack"은 간식거리를 총칭하는 말이며, "junk food"는 맛은 있으나 건강에는 도움이 안 되는 음식을 얕잡는 듯으로 이르는 말임)
● **스낵바** a snack bar [counter / stand] (▶ a snack bar는 간이식당이며 술 종류는 거의 팔지 않음)

스냅 1 [야구] [손목 힘을 쓰기] a snap. ¶야구공에 ~을 주다 (미) throw a ball with a snap of the wrist / put some snap on a ball / (영) whip a ball. 2 a snapshot. ⇨→스냅 사진(㉢스냅) 3 a snap fastener. ⇨→똑딱단추
● **스냅 사진** [사진] a snapshot; a snap. ¶~을 찍다 take a snapshot (of) / snap (shot) (the scenery).

스노클링 snorkeling.

스노타이어 a snow tire [(영) tyre].

스님 1 [사승(師僧)] one's teacher [master] in Buddhist faith; (호칭) (the) Rev. (=Reverend). 2 a Buddhist priest. ⇨→승려

스라소니 [동] a lynx (*pl.* ~ (-es)).

-스럽다 (서술적) be (like); look (like); seem. ¶영광~ be glorious // 예~ look old / be archaic // 바보~ be foolish.

스르르 lightly; easily; gently; softly; [저절로] of itself. ¶눈을 ~ 감다 softly close one's eyes // 입에서 ~ 녹다 melt away in the mouth // 배가 호수 위를 ~ 미끄러지듯 나아간다 A boat glides along the lake. // 매듭이 ~ 풀렸다 The knot came untied of itself.

-스름하다 1 (빛깔이) tinged with ~; somewhat; -ish. ¶불그~ be tinged with red / be reddish [somewhat red]. 2 (형상이) somewhat; -ish. ¶동그~ be roundish.

스릴 [전율] a thrill. ¶~을 **느끼다** have a kick [thrill] (from) / be thrilled (by).

스마트하다 [맵시 있고 말쑥하다] stylish; smart; spruce. ¶그녀는 옷을 스마트하게 입고 있다 She is stylishly [smartly] dressed. // 그녀는 태도가 ~ She is stylish in manner. / She carries herself with grace.

스매시 (탁구 등에서) a smash. ¶멋진 ~로 점수를 올렸다 I gained points with my marvelous smashes. **스매시하다** smash (a ball).

스멀거리다 [근질거리다] itch; feel itchy [creepy / crawly]; be creepy-crawly. ¶등이 ~ feel itchy in one's back / one's back itches // 온 몸이 스멀거린다 I feel itchy all over.

스멀스멀 itchy; creepy; crawly.

스며들다 1 (액체·기체 등이) soak in [into / through]; sink in [into]; infiltrate (into / through); filter into; permeate (the soil); penetrate; pierce. ¶물은 마른땅에 천천히 스며들었다 The water was slowly permeated (through) the dry soil. // 빗물은 금방 마른땅에 스며들었다 The rain sank into the dry

스모그 smog. ¶~가 낀 대기 중에 in the smoggy air // ~가 심한 smoggy / smog-laden (city).

스무 twenty. ¶~ 날 the 20th day / twenty days // ~ 살의 청년 a young man twenty years old / a young man of twenty // ~째 the twentieth // ~ 배 ~ 개 twenty pears / a score of pears.

스무고개 (the game of) twenty questions.

스무드하다 smooth. ¶모든 일이 스무드하게 진행되었다 Everything went smoothly [(구어) went off without a hitch]. // 그 문제는 스무드하게 수습되었다 The problem has been smoothed over [settled amicably].

스물 twenty; a score; [스무 살] twenty years of age; one's twentieth year. ¶~ 하나 twenty-one // 그는 아직 ~이 안 되었다 He is still in his teens.

스미다 1 (액체·기체 등이) soak in [into / through]; sink in [into]; infiltrate (into / through); filter into; permeate (the soil); penetrate; pierce. ¶스며 나오다 ooze out / exude / percolate / filter through / seep / transude / soak out // 수액이 줄기에서 스며 나오고 있었다 Sap was oozing out of the (tree) trunk. // 벽에서는 물이 스며 나온다 Water oozes [seeps] from the walls. 2 (감정·사상 등이) sink into; be impressed (on one's mind); filter into [through]; be imbued. ¶(교훈 등이) 가슴에 ~ sink into one's mind / come home to one's heart.

스스럼없다 unreserved; unconstrained; free (from constraint); unshy. ¶스스럼없는 친구 a friend you can feel free with // 스스럼없는 태도로 말하다 talk in a free and easy manner. 스스럼없이 unreservedly; without reserve [ceremony / restraint]; freely. ¶좀 더 ~ 말하는 것이 어떻습니까 Hadn't you better speak a little more informally?

스스럽다 reserved; constrained; backward; modest; diffident; shy; coy. ¶여기서는 조금도 스스러워하지 않아도 됩니다 You can make yourself at home here.

스스로 1 [혼자 힘으로] for oneself; by oneself; unaided. ¶~ 결정하다 decide (a matter) for oneself. 2 [몸소] oneself; in person; personally; [자진하여] of one's own accord. ¶그는 사고의 책임을 ~ 졌다 He took the responsibility for the accident on himself. // ~ 가는 것이 좋다 Go yourself. / You had better go in person. 3 [저절로] naturally; spontaneously; of its own accord; of itself. ¶문이 ~ 열렸다 The door opened all by itself. 4 [자기 자신] oneself. ¶~의 one's own / personal / ~ 목숨을 끊다 kill oneself / end one's own life // ~ 를 돌이켜보다 reflect on oneself [one's own conduct].

스승 a teacher; a master (▶ master는 예술의 거장 등에 씀); a mentor; a preceptor; an instructor. ¶옛 ~ one's former teacher // ~과 제자 master and disciple / teacher and pupil [student] // 그는 송 선생님을 ~으로 모시고 공부했다 He studied under Mr. Song. / He had Mr. Song for his instructor. // 그는 ~의 은혜에 감동했다 He was struck by how much he owed his teacher.

스웨터 (미) a sweater; (영) a jersey; [풀오버] a pull-over (sweater); (앞이 트인 것) a cardigan. ¶~ 차림의 소녀 a sweatered girl // ~를 뜨다 knit a sweater.

스위치 a switch. ¶전등의 ~ a light switch // 전등의 ~를 켜다 [끄다] switch [turn] on [off] an electric light // 텔레비전의 ~를 켜다 [switch] on the TV // 라디오의 ~를 끄다 switch [turn] off the radio.
●스위치히터 [야구] a switch-hitter.

스윙 1 [야구·권투] a swing. ¶큰 ~ a big swing // ~ 아웃을 당하다 strike out [go down] swinging // 그의 ~은 날카롭지 못하다 His swing isn't sharp enough. / He swings his bat sluggishly. 2 [음] swing (music).

스쳐보다 [곁눈질로 보다] look askance (at a person); look with a sidelong glance (at); cast a side(long) glance [look] (at); squint [leer] (at); [대강 보다] run one's eyes through (a book); skim [run] through (a book). ¶사람을 ~ steal a glance at a person // 일람표를 ~ take a cursory glance at a list.

스치다 graze; barely touch; go past by (a person); brush past (a person); rub [scrape] (against / past); (수면 등을) skim along; scud; (생각 등이) flit. ¶두 열차는 전속력으로 스쳐 지나갔다 The two trains passed each other at full speed. // 방금 스쳐 지나간 사람을 아느냐 Do you know the man who just went by? // 공은 내 머리 위를 스칠 듯이 날아갔다 The ball almost grazed my head [whistled past my ear]. // 차는 담을 스칠 듯이 지나갔다 The car passed within a hair-breadth of the wall. // 차는 전봇대를 스쳐서 지나갔다 The car brushed past the telephone pole. // 탄환이 귀를 스쳤다 The bullet grazed my ear. // 그녀의 스카프 끝이 바람에 날려 내 뺨을 가볍게 스쳤다 The tip of her muffler, blown by the wind, brushed gently against my cheek. // 바람이 불어 나무와 나무가 서로 스쳤다 The trees rubbed against one another in the wind. // 손님들의 어깨가 서로 스칠 정도로 가게는 혼잡했다 The store was so crowded that people kept bumping into one another. // 그는 나와 스쳐 지나가면서 가볍게 인사했다 He bowed slightly to me as we passed each other. // 잠자리가 수면을 스치면서 날고 있다 Dragonflies are flitting just above the surface of the water. // 태풍은 제주도의 서부를 스쳐 갔다 The typhoon brushed [grazed] the western part of Jejudo. // 버스는 전봇대를 스치고 지나갔다 The bus scraped against the telegraph pole. // 꿈과 같은 생각이 언뜻 마음을 스쳤다 A fanciful idea flitted through my mind.

스카우트 a scout. ¶각 팀마다 신인 ~에 혈안이 되어 있다 Every team is searching frantically for new talent. 스카우트하다 scout (for young talent); recruit (new members). ¶딴 팀에서 인기 선수를 ~ entice popular players away from other teams // 우리는 KBS에서 아나운서를 스카우트했다 We hired an announcer away from KBS. ➔¶그는 배우를

스카우트되었다 He was spotted and recruited as a potential actor.

스카이다이빙 sky diving. ¶~을 하다 skydive.

스카이라인 〔산이나 건물이 하늘과 구획하는 윤곽〕 a skyline; 〔지평선〕 the horizon. ¶도시의 ~ the skyline of a city.

스카이웨이 〔고가 도로〕 a skyway; 〔산의 유람 코스〕 a (scenic) mountain highway. ¶북악 ~ the Bugak Mountain Highway.

스카치위스키 Scotch whisky.

스카치테이프 Scotch Tape(상표명). ¶~로 붙이다 scotch-tape.

스카프 a scarf (pl. ~s, (영) scarves). ¶~를 매다 wear a scarf.

스캔들 a scandal. ¶그의 ~ the scandal he caused / scandal about him(▶ 우리말의 스캔들은 그 행위를 가리키지만, 영어의 scandal은 행위에 대한 사람들의 반응을 가리킴)//~을 은폐하다 cover up a scandal//그 ~이 세상에 알려졌다 The scandal was disclosed to the public.//그는 그 ~에 말려들었다 He got involved in the scandal.

스커트 a skirt. ¶롱~ a long skirt//플레어[개더]~ a flared[gathered] skirt//타이트~ a tight skirt//미니~ a miniskirt//~를 입다[벗다] put on[take off] a skirt.

스컹크 〔동〕 a skunk.

스케이트 〔운동 기구의 하나〕 (a pair of) skates. ¶스피드 ~ speed skates//피겨 ~ figure skates//롤러 ~ roller skates//~를 타다 skate//~를 잘[잘 못] 타다 be good[no good / poor] at skating / be a good[poor] skater//그는 ~를 잘 탄다 He is an excellent skater.
● **스케이트장** a skating rink; an ice rink.

스케이팅 〔스케이트로 얼음을 지치는 일〕 skating. ¶스피드 ~ speed skating//피겨 ~ figure skating//롤러 ~ roller skating//스피드 ~ 선수권 대회 a speed skating championship. **스케이팅하다** skate.

스케일 a scale. ¶~이 큰 사업 a large-scale undertaking//~이 큰 인물 a man of high [remarkable] caliber.

스케일링 〔치석을 제거하는 일〕 scaling. **스케일링하다** scale; scale tartar from the teeth.

스케줄 a schedule (for); a program. ¶꽉 짜인 ~ a crammed[crowded / heavy / tight] schedule//~에 따라 as scheduled / according to schedule / on schedule//~을 다시 짜다 reschedule//기획의 ~을 짜다 make out the schedule for a project//우리의 공연 ~은 꽉 짜여 있다 The schedule of our performances is very tight.//마지막 초읽기가 ~대로 행해졌다 The final countdown took place on schedule.

스케치 1 〔사생(화)〕 sketching; a sketch. **스케치하다** sketch; make[do] a sketch (of). ¶꽃을 ~ sketch a flower / make a sketch of a flower//스케치하러 가다 go sketching. 2 〔음〕 〔묘사적인 짧은 곡〕 a sketch.
● **스케치북** a sketchbook.

스코어 〔체〕 〔득점〕 a score. ¶민수가 ~를 기록했다 Minsu kept score.//배구 결승전의 ~는 3대 2였다 The score in the volleyball finals was 3 to 2.//5대 4의 ~로 우리 팀이 이겼다 Our team won by a score of 5 to 4.//1대 1로 타이가 되었다 The score was tied at 1 to 1.
● **스코어보드** a scoreboard.

스코어링 포지션 〔야구〕 〔득점이 가능한 위치〕 scoring position.

스콜 〔소나기〕 a squall.

스콜라 철학 〔-哲學〕 Scholasticism.

스쿠버 〔수중 호흡 장치〕 scuba(▶ self-contained underwater breathing apparatus의 약어).
● **스쿠버 다이빙** scuba diving.

스쿠터 a (motor) scooter. ¶~를 타다 ride on a scooter.

스쿠프 a scoop. **스쿠프하다** scoop; get a scoop on(▶ 목적어는 상대방 회사). ¶그가 그 수회 사건을 스쿠프했다 He scooped the bribery case.

스쿨버스 a school bus.

스쿼시 1 〔과즙 음료〕 squash. ¶레몬 ~ (미) fizzy lemonade / (영) lemon squash. 2 〔체〕 squash tennis[rackets(▶ 단수 취급)].

스퀴즈 번트 〔야구〕 a squeeze bunt.

스퀴즈 플레이 〔야구〕 a squeeze play.

스크랩 scraps; (미) a clipping; (영) a cutting (from a magazine). **스크랩하다** make a clipping[cutting] of an article; cut out an article.

스크럼 1 〔럭비〕 a scrum(mage). ¶~을 짜다 scrummage / form[line up for] a scrum. 2 〔여럿이 팔을 끼고 늘어서는 일〕. ¶데모대는 ~을 짜고 행진했다 The demonstrators marched down the street arm in arm.

스크롤바 〔컴〕 〔화면을 전후 또는 상하로 이동시키는 막대〕 a scroll bar.

스크루 a screw; (배의) a screw (propeller).
● **스크루 볼** 〔야구〕 a screwball.

스크린 〔영사막·화면〕 a screen. ¶대형 ~ a wide screen.

스크립터 〔대본 작가〕 a scriptwriter; (구어) a scripter.

스크립트 〔대본〕 a script.

스키 〔기구〕 (a pair of) skis; (운동) skiing. ¶노르딕 ~ nordic skiing//알파인 ~ alpine skiing//~를 타러 가다 go skiing//나는 ~를 타고 비탈을 활강했다 I skied down the slope.
● **스키 대회** a ski meet. **스키복** skiwear; a ski suit[outfit]. **스키어** a skier. **스키장** a skiing ground; a ski slope. **스키화** (a pair of) ski boots.

스킨 다이빙 skin diving.

스킨십 (*skinship) 〔피부 접촉〕 close physical contact.

스타 1 〔인기 연예인·운동선수 등〕 a star. ¶영화 a movie[film] star//그녀는 ~의 자리에 올랐다 She has achieved stardom. 2 generals. ⇨장성(將星)
● **스타덤** stardom. ¶~에 오르다 rise to stardom[fame]. **스타플레이어** a star player.

스타디움 a stadium (pl. ~s, -dia). ¶올림픽 ~ the Olympic Stadium.

스타일 〔문체·양식·화풍〕 style. ¶그의 문장은 독특한 ~로 유명하다 His writings are noted for his peculiar style.//그의 편지나 일기나 모두 독특한 그의 ~로 쓰여 있다 Both his letters and his diary are written in his own characteristic style[in a style all his own]. 2 (옷의) a style. ¶최신 유행의 ~ the latest style//파리는 세계 유행의 ~을 결정한다고 했다 Paris was said to set the style in fashion for the world. 3 〔풍채〕 one's form; one's figure. ¶~이 좋다 [나쁘다] have a good [poor] figure//그녀는 호리호리하면서도 ~이 좋다 She is slender and has a good figure on top of that.

스타카토 [음] staccato. ¶이 부분은 ~로 쳐라 Play this part staccato.

스타킹 (a pair of) stockings[nylons]. ¶나일론 ~ nylon stockings // 망사 ~ fishnet stockings // 올이 나간 ~ a run [(영) laddered] stockings // ~을 신다[벗다] pull on [off] one's stockings.

스타트 a start; (경마·자동차의) (구어) a getaway. ¶남보다 ~가 빠르다 have a good start of others // 그는 ~가 좋았다[나빴다] He started well [badly]. / He got off to a good [poor] start. // 그가 ~를 끊었다 He made a start.
● **스타트 라인**(*start line) a starting line; a balkline. ¶러너들이 ~에 늘어섰다 The runners lined up at the starting line.

스타팅 멤버 a starting member[lineup].

스태그플레이션 [경] stagflation.

스태미나 stamina; staying power. ¶~를 기르다 develop stamina [staying power] // 그는 ~가 좋다[없다] He has a lot of [no] stamina. // 그는 ~를 기르기 위해 매일 아침 조깅을 한다 He goes jogging every morning to build himself up.

스태프 [집합적] the staff; (한 사람) a member of the staff; an employee. ¶~ 일동을 대표하여 on behalf of all the member of the staff // ~가 잘 짜여진 well-staffed (laboratories) // ~를 바꾸다 restaff.

스탠드 1 [관중석] the stands; (지붕이 없는) (미) the bleachers. ¶~에서 우레 같은 박수가 터졌다 A storm of applause rose from the stands. // 공은 좌익수 뒤쪽의 ~에 떨어졌다 The ball went into the stands behind the left fielder. 2 [대(臺)] a stand. ¶잉크 ~ an inkstand. 3 [전기스탠드] (탁상용) a desk[table] lamp; (바닥에 놓는) (미) a floor lamp; (영) a standard lamp.
● **스탠드바**(*stand bar) a bar with only a counter.

스탠바이 [대기·준비] a standby. ¶~ 중이다 at the standby.

스탠스 [야구·골프] a stance. ¶오픈[클로스] ~ an open[a close] stance // 그는 ~를 넓게 잡았다 He took a wide stance.

스탬프 [도장] a stamp; [소인] a postmark. ¶기념 ~ a commemorative stamp // 이 카드에 ~를 찍어 주세요. Please stamp this card. // 나는 그림엽서에 기념 ~를 찍었다 I stamped a picture postcard with a commemorative (rubber) stamp.

스턴트맨 [영화의 대역] a stunt man.

스테레오 [음향 장치] a stereo (*pl.* ~s); a stereo set; [입체 음향 재생 방식] the stereophonic sound (reproduction) system. ¶브루노 월터 지휘에 의한 브람스의 ~판 Brahms in stereo (conducted) by Bruno Walter // ~로 듣다 listen to (a recording of a symphony) on stereo // ~로 녹음하다 make a stereo (phonic) recording of (Strauss's Salome) / record (music) in stereo // 나는 그 교향곡을 ~로 들었다 I listened to the symphony on my stereo.
● **스테레오 방송** stereophonic broadcasting.

스테이지 a stage. ¶~를 밟다[떠나다] go on [off] the stage.

스테이크 1 a steak. 2 (a) beefsteak. ➪비프스테이크 ¶설로인 ~ a sirloin steak // ~ 하우스 a steakhouse // "~를 어떻게 해 드릴까요?" "살짝[중간 정도로 / 완전히] 익혀서 주세요." "How would you like your steak?" "Rare [Medium / Well-done], please."

스테이플러 a stapler.

스테인리스강(-鋼) stainless steel. ¶~의 싱크대 a stainless steel sink // ~제(製)의 (a gas range) of stainless steel.

스텐실 a stencil.
● **스텐실 페이퍼** stencil paper.

스텝 (춤 등의) a step. ¶왈츠의 ~을 밟다 practice a waltz step.

스토리 [이야기 줄거리] a story.

스토브 [난로] a stove; a heater. ¶가스[석유 / 전기] ~ a gas [an oil / an electric] heater // ~를 피우다 light a heater [stove] / make a fire in the stove // ~를 끄다[켜다] turn off[on] the gas stove.

스토아학파(-學派) the stoic school; the stoics. ¶~의 철학 Stoicism // ~의 철학자 a Stoic.

스토커 [따라다니며 귀찮게 하는 사람] a stalker.

스토킹 [따라다니며 귀찮게 하는 일] stalking.

스톡 옵션 [자사 주식 매입권] a stock option.

스톱 [정지] stop. **스톱하다** stop. ➔스톱시키다 put a stop (to) / call a halt (to).
● **스톱 위치** a stopwatch. ¶나는 ~로 경주 시간을 쟀다 I timed the race with a stopwatch.

스튜 (a) stew. ¶비프 ~ beef stew / stewed beef.

스튜디오 a studio (*pl.* ~s). ¶KBS ~ a KBS studio // 텔레비전 ~ a TV studio // 영화 ~ a film studio / (미) a movie lot.

스튜어디스 [항공기의 여자 서비스원] a stewardess; an air hostess.

스트라이크 1 [동맹 파업[휴교] a strike; a walkout. ¶~ 중이다 be on (a) strike // ~를 하다 [~에 들어가다] go [come out] on (a) strike / walk out // ~를 중지하다 halt [call off] a strike. 2 [야구] a strike. ¶~ 아웃 a strikeout / ~ 아웃이 되다 strike out / get [be] struck out // 제3구는 ~였다 The third pitch was a strike. // 카운트는 투 ~ 스리 볼이다 The count (on the batter) is three (balls) and two (strikes). 3 [볼링] a strike.

스트레스 [생체가 나타내는 방어 반응] stress. ¶~를 풀다 get rid of[relieve] one's stress / let off steam // 나는 도시 생활에 ~를 느끼기 시작했다 I'm beginning to feel the stress [pressures] of urban life. // 자네는 2~3일 쉬어 ~를 해소하는 편이 좋겠다 You'd better take a few days off and relax. // 그녀는 ~가 쌓이면 화를 잘 낸다 She becomes irritable when stress builds up.

스트레이트 1 [연속적임]. ¶나는[우리는] ~로 이겼다 (테니스, 배구 등에서) I[We] won in straight sets. / I won without dropping a set [game]. // 나[우리]는 ~로 졌다 I[We] lost in straight sets. / I lost without winning a single set [game]. 2 [야구] a straight ball [pitch]. 3 [권투] (give) a straight punch (on). ¶강력한 오른손 ~ a hard right straight. 4 [음주] (양주를 물을 타지 않고 그대로 마시기). ¶위스키를 ~로 마시다 drink whisk(e)y straight.

스트렙토마이신 [약] streptomycin.

스트로 [빨대] a (drinking) straw.

스트로크 [테니스·골프·수영·조정에서의 한 번의 동작] a stroke. ¶한 ~ 차로 우리 대학 팀이 이겼다 Our university team won by a

stroke.

스트론튬 [화] strontium(기호 Sr). ¶~ 90 strontium 90.

스트리퍼 (스트립쇼의) a stripper; a striptease dancer; a stripteaser.

스트립쇼 (a) striptease; a strip show.

스티커 1 [붙임 딱지] a sticker; an adhesive label. ¶이 ~가 좀처럼 벗겨지지 않는다 This sticker won't come off. 2 [교통 위반 딱지] a (citation) ticket. ¶경찰이 그에게 ~를 발부했다 The policeman gave him a ticket.

스틱 1 [지팡이] a (walking) stick; cane. 2 [인] (식자공의) a (composing) stick.

스틸[1] [야구] a steal. ⇨도루 ¶홈 ~ a home steal.

스틸[2] [강철] steel.

스틸[3] [사진] a still (picture).

스팀 [증기] steam. ¶~ **난방** steam heat / central heating // ~으로 방을 덥게 하다 heat a room by steam // **~이 들어오다** be steam-heated (in a room) // ~으로 난방하다 be heated by steam // 그 교사에는 ~이 들어온다 The school is heated with steam[steam-heated].

스파게티 [국수 모양의 이탈리아 음식] spaghetti. ¶~는 너무 끓이면 퍼져서 맛이 없다 Spaghetti is no good of it's overcooked because it loses its consistency[gets too soft].

스파르타 Sparta. ¶~식의 Spartan.
●**스파르타 교육**[훈련] Spartan education [training].

스파링 [권투의 연습 경기] sparring.
●**스파링 파트너** a sparring partner.

스파이 [간첩] a spy; a secret agent; (행위) espionage. ¶산업 ~ a industrial spy // 영화 a cloak-and-dagger film / a spy movie // 이중 ~ a double agent // ~ 활동 espionage (action) // ~ 노릇을 하다 (act as) spy // 미국을 위해 ~ 활동을 하다 spy for the U.S. // 그는 ~ 혐의로 체포되었다 He was arrested on suspicion of espionage[on a spying charge].

스파이크 1 [배구에서 내리치기] spike. ¶~로 1점을 얻다 spike the ball in for a point / pick up a point on a spike. **스파이크하다** spike. 2 track shoes. ⇨스파이크 슈즈(⇨스파이크)
●**스파이크 슈즈** [트랙 경기용의 스파이크] track shoes; (영) running spikes; (야구용) spikes.

스파크 [전기 불꽃] a spark.

스패너 [볼트·너트 돌리개] a spanner; (미) a wrench. ¶멍키[자재] ~ a monkey wrench [spanner] / a screw wrench / a universal spanner.

스팸 메일 [컴] [원치 않는 광고성 이메일] spam; junk mail.

스퍼트 [스포츠에서 일시적인 역주·분발] a spurt. ¶라스트 ~ the last spurt. **스퍼트하다** spurt; make[put on] a spurt. ¶주자들은 골이 가까워지자 스퍼트했다 The runners put on bursts of speed as they neared the finish line. // 그는 우승하기 위해 막판에 스퍼트했다 In an effort to win, he put on a spurt at the end.

스펀지 [해면] (a) sponge. ¶~ **고무** sponge rubber // ~ 볼 a sponge ball // ~케이크 (a) sponge cake // ~로 더럽을 닦아 내다 sponge off the dirt.

스페어 [여분] a spare; spare parts. ¶~ **단추** a spare button // ~ **잉크** a spare cartridge of ink // ~**타이어** a spare tire [(영) tyre].

스펙터클 영화 (-映畵) a spectacular film.

스펙터클하다 spectacular.

스펙트럼 [물] the spectrum.
●**스펙트럼 분석** spectrum analysis.

스펠링 spelling. ¶~ **미스** (a) misspelling / a spelling mistake / a misspelled word // 틀린 ~ a misspelling / a spelling mistake // ~ 미스를 하다 misspell // 단어의 ~을 잘못 쓰다 misspell a word // 자기 이름의 ~을 생략하지 않고 완전히 쓰다 write one's name out in full // 이 단어의 ~을 아십니까 Can you[Do you know how to] spell this word? // 그 낱말의 ~이 틀렸습니다 You have misspelled the word.

스포이트 (⑭spuit) [액체 주입기] a syringe; a fountain pen filler.

스포츠 sports; (개개의) a sport. ¶~의 sport / sports // ~를 **즐기다** enjoy sports / take part in sports // 나는 ~를 좋아한다 I like sports. / I am a sports fan. // 아버지가 좋아하시는 ~는 테니스다 My father's favorite sport is tennis.
●**스포츠계** sports circles; the world of sport(s); (미) sportsdom. **스포츠 뉴스** sports news. **스포츠맨** [운동선수] a sportsman. ¶~다운 sportsmanlike. **스포츠맨십** (sports 정신) sportsmanship. ¶~을 발휘하여 정정당당히 싸우다 play in a sportsmanlike way. **스포츠 신문** a sporting newspaper[journal]. **스포츠 용품** sports equipment; sporting goods. **스포츠웨어** sportswear.

스포트라이트 [연] a spotlight. ¶~를 **비추다** spotlight // ~를 **받다** be spotlighted.

스포트라이트를 받다 [주목을 받다] be in the spotlight[limelight]; be at the center of attention. ¶정계에 뛰어들어 끊임없이 스포트라이트를 받고 있다 Now that he's entered politics he is constantly in the spotlight.

스포티하다 sporty. ¶스포티한 차림으로 그녀가 나타났다 She appeared in sporty clothes[in sportswear] (▶ sporty clothes는 경쾌하고 화려한 복장, sportswear는 운동복).

스폰서 1 [광고주] a sponsor. ¶공동 ~ a cosponsor // 텔레비전 프로의 ~ the sponsor of a TV program // (프로의) ~를 **얻다** get [find] a sponsor (for a program) // ~를 그만두다 discontinue sponsorship (for a program) // 이 프로의 ~는 비엠 회사다 This program is sponsored by BM Company. 2 [기부금·자금을 내는 사람] a sponsor; a patron; a financial supporter.

스폿 광고 (-廣告) spot advertising; a spot (commercial).

스폿 뉴스 spot news.

스푼 1 a spoon. ¶설탕 두 ~ two spoonfuls of sugar // ~으로 뜨다 scoop up with a spoon / spoon up // 우리는 ~으로 수프를 먹는다 We eat soup with a spoon. 2 [골프에서 클럽의 3번 우드] a spoon.

스프레이 [분무] a spray; [분무기] an atomizer; a sprayer. ¶헤어~를 뿌리다 use[apply] hair spray.

스프린터 [100·200·400m의 단거리 육상 선수] a sprinter.

스프링 (용수철) a spring.
●**스프링보드** a springboard; a diving board.

스프링 캠프 a spring training camp.

스프링클러 [빌딩 천장 등의 자동 살수 장치

스피드 또는 관개용 살수 기구 a sprinkler. ¶~ 장치 a sprinkler system // ~를 설치하다 install sprinklers.

스피드 [속력·속도] speed. ¶~ 출세를 하다 be promoted rapidly / get ahead rapidly / rise rapidly in the world.
● **스피드광**(-狂) a speed demon; a speed maniac. **스피드 시대** the age of speed.

스피디하다 speedy; quick. ¶이재민 구호는 스피디하게 실시되었다 Relief was promptly sent to the victims. // 그녀는 집안일을 스피디하게 해치운다 She is very quick about her housework.

스피츠 [개의 한 품종] a spitz.

스피치 [연설] a speech. ¶테이블 ~ a dinner speech // 대통령은 훌륭한 ~를 했다 The President gave an excellent speech. **스피치하다** make [deliver] a speech.

스피커 [라디오·텔레비전 등의 확성기] a (loud) speaker; [확성장치] the PA(▶ the public-address (system)의 약어). ¶고음용 ~ a tweeter // 저음용 ~ a woofer // ~ 폰 a loud-speaker telephone // ~로 사람을 부르다 [출발 비행편을 알리다] call a person [announce flight departures] over the public-address [P.A.] system.

스핀 [스케이트·댄스·테니스·볼링·자동차 등에서의 회전·선회, 비행기의 회전 급강하] (a) spin. ¶공에 ~을 넣다 put spin on a ball.

스핑크스 [고대 오리엔트 및 그리스 신화에 나오는 괴물] a sphinx (pl. ~es, sphinges).

슬개골(膝蓋骨) [생] the kneepan; the knee-cap; the patella (pl. -knae).

슬관절(膝關節) a knee joint.

슬그머니 stealthily; secretly. ⇨살그머니

슬금슬금 stealthily; secretly. ⇨살금살금

슬기 wisdom; [지력] intelligence; [꾀] wit(s); [지각] sense. ¶그것을 말하지 않을 만한 ~가 그에게는 있었다 He had the wisdom to leave it unsaid.

슬기롭다 intelligent; sagacious; wise; bright; prudent; sensible; witty. ¶슬기로운 사람 a man of wisdom / a wise man // 슬기롭지 못한 방법 a stupid [an unwise] way of doing a thing // 자네의 슬기로운 판단에 맡기네 I submit the matter to your sound judgment.

슬다[1] 1 [채소가 시들어 가다] wither; wilt. 2 [자국이 없어지다] disappear; be gone; vanish.

슬다[2] 1 [곤충 등이 알을 깔겨 놓다] lay; deposit; [물고기가] spawn. ¶매미는 흙 속에 알을 슨다 Cicadas deposit [lay] their eggs in the ground. // 파리가 쉬를 슬었다 A fly blew eggs. 2 [녹이 생기다] gather [form] rust; get [become] rusty; (곰팡이가) gather mold; become [get] musty [moldy]; mildew. ¶녹슨 칼 a rusty sword [knife] // 곰팡이가 스는 것을 막다 keep (a thing) from getting musty [moldy].

슬라이더 [야구] a slider.

슬라이드 [환등] a (lantern) slide; (현미경의) a slide; [계산자] a slide rule.

슬라이딩 [야구] sliding. **슬라이딩하다** slide into (second base).

슬랙스 slacks. ¶~를 입은 (girls) in slacks.

슬랭 a slang word [expression]; a word of slang; (집합적) slang.

슬러거 [야구] a slugger; a hard hitter.

슬럼 a slum.
● **슬럼가**(-街) the slum quarters [areas]; the slums.

슬럼프 a slump. ¶~에 빠지다 hit [be in] a slump // ~에서 헤어나다 come out of a slump.

슬레이트 [석판] a slate; (집합적) slating. ¶~ 지붕의 집 a slate-roofed house // 지붕을 ~로 이다 slate a roof / roof (a house) with slates.

슬로건 a slogan; a motto (pl. ~es, ~s). ¶~라는 ~을 내걸고 under the slogan of ... // ~을 내세우다 publish a slogan.

슬로 모션 slow motion. ¶~으로 (shoot the motions of a swimmer) in slow motion.

슬로 볼 [야구] a slow ball.

슬롯머신 [도박기] (미) a slot machine; (영) a fruit machine.

슬리퍼 (a pair of) slippers; (뒤축이 없는) backless slippers; scuffs. ¶~로 갈아 신다 change one's shoes for slippers.

슬립 [여자의 속옷] a slip; an underslip.

슬며시 [드러나지 않게] stealthily; furtively; [가만히] gently; softly; quietly; lightly; tenderly. ¶~ 자리를 뜨다 leave one's seat quietly [stealthily] // 아기를 ~ 안다 pick up a baby cautiously.

슬슬 1 [남이 모르게] stealthily; secretly; by stealth; in secret.
2 [천천히] slowly. ¶~ 걷다 walk slowly // ~ 떠나기로 [가 보기로] 하자 Let's be going. / Shall we be going? // ~ 시작할 시간인걸 It's about time we started [for us to begin].
3 [가볍게] softly; gently; lightly. ¶~ 문지르다 rub lightly / give (something) a light rub.
4 [녹는 모양] (melt) well; imperceptibly. ¶이 과자는 입 안에서 ~ 녹는다 This cake melts in the mouth. // 날씨가 따뜻해지자 눈은 ~ 녹아 버렸다 The snow soon melted away when the warm weather came.
5 [꾀거나 달래는 모양] tactfully; adroitly; cunningly. ¶아이를 ~ 달래다 comfort [persuade] a child gently // ~ 꾀어 빼앗다 cajole [wheedle] (a person) out of (something).
6 [점차] gradually; little by little; by degrees. ¶안개가 ~ 걷힌다 The fog melts away. // 이제 ~ 모기가 나올 철이다 We shall soon have mosquitoes.

슬쩍 furtively; lightly. ⇨살짝

슬퍼하다 feel sad [be sorrowful] (at); grieve (at / over); have a heavy [broken] heart; [통탄하여] deplore; lament; mourn (over / for); be distressed (over); regret. ¶남의 불행을 ~ feel sorry for another's misfortune // 남의 죽음을 ~ mourn [lament] another's death / grieve [wail] over another's death // 모두가 그 영웅의 죽음을 슬퍼했다 Everybody grieved over [lamented] the death of the hero. // 그저 슬퍼하고만 있을 때가 아니다 This is no time to give way simply to sorrow.

슬프다 1 (마음이) sad; (문어) sorrowful; unhappy; doleful; mournful; miserable. ¶슬픈 목소리 a plaintive [sorrowful] voice // 슬픈 표정 [모습] a sad look [countenance / face] // 슬픈 나머지 (in the excess of) one's sorrow [grief] // 슬픈 생각이 들다 [슬퍼지다] feel sad [sorrowful] / be saddened / feel miserable [unhappy] // 그녀는 언제나 슬퍼 보인다 She always looks sad. // 시험에 떨어져서 ~ I feel miserable because I failed the examination. // 슬프게도 그의 아버지는 고기를 잡으러 나갔다가 영영 돌아오지 않았다 To his sorrow

[Sad to say], his father went fishing never to return. **슬피** sadly; sorrowfully; dolefully; mournfully. ¶~ 울다 cry sorrowfully [in a mournful manner].

2 (일이) sad; sorrowful; pathetic; touching; doleful; plaintive; [통탄스럽다] lamentable; deplorable; grievous. ¶자식을 잃은 어머니의 슬픈 노래 a lament of a mother who lost her child // 슬픈 이야기 a sad [tragic / pathetic] story // 슬픈 사건 [추억] a sad event [memory] / 기쁠 때나 슬플 때나 in joy and in sorrow / 선악을 구별하지도 못하는 사람이 있다니 정말 슬픈 일이다 It's a pity [What a pity] that there should be persons who cannot tell right from wrong. // 전후 청년들의 도덕 관념이 희박한 것은 슬픈 일이다 It is a matter for regret that the postwar youths are weak in moral sense. **슬피** sadly; sorrowfully; dolefully; plaintively.

슬픔 (a) sorrow; sadness; [비통] (a) grief; [비탄] lamentation; [애도] mourning; [괴로움] distress. ¶인생의 기쁨과 ~ the joys and sorrows of life // ~에 찬 얼굴 a sad [sorrow-stricken] face / a sorrowful face // 남 모르는 ~ a hidden sorrow // ~에 잠기다 be in deep grief [sorrow] / be buried in grief / yield to sorrow // 기쁨과 ~이 엇갈리다 have a mingled feeling of joy and sorrow // 세월이 흐르면 ~도 가라앉는다 Time blunts the edge of sorrow. // 그녀는 매일 ~에 잠겨 있었다 She passed every day lost in her grief. // 그의 ~이 절실히 느껴진다 I can really feel his grief. // ~을 못 이겨 그녀는 몸져누웠다 In sorrow [grief], she fell ill. // ~으로 가슴이 찢어지는 것만 같았다 My heart was almost broken with sorrow. // 자식을 잃은 어머니는 여생을 ~ 속에서 살았다 The bereaved mother lived the rest of her life in sorrow.

슬하(膝下) (under) one's paternal roof [care]; the care of one's parents. ¶부모 ~를 떠나다 leave one's paternal roof [home] // 그는 부모 ~에서 17세 때까지 자랐다 He grew up under his parents' care until he was seventeen. // 나는 15세 때 부모의 ~를 떠나 서울에 있는 학교에 들어갔다 When I was fifteen, I left home and entered a school in Seoul.

습격(襲擊) a surprise attack; a sudden assault(▶ attack보다 격렬함); a raid(급습). ¶우리는 적의 ~에 대비하였다 We prepared for an enemy attack [assault]. **습격하다** raid; attack; assault. ¶적을 ~ attack [make an attack on] the enemy // 적진을 습격하여 탈취했다 The enemy camp was taken in a surprise attack.

습곡(褶曲) [지] folding.

습관(習慣) [버릇・습성] a habit; [관례] a custom; a practice.(▶ a custom은 그 사회의 구성원의 공통적인, a habit은 개인적인 장기간의 습관, a practice는 양쪽 모두에 쓰임) ¶~의 habitual / customary // ~이 된 음주 habitual drinking // **~이 붙다** get [fall] into the habit (of doing) / form [acquire] the habit (of doing) // **~을 버리다** break (off) [shake off] a habit / give up [discard] a habit / 나쁜 ~을 고치다 (자신의) cure oneself of [get over] a bad habit / (타인의) cure [break] a person of a bad habit // 그는 일찍 일어나는 ~이 있다 He is in the habit of getting up early. // 아침 식사 전에 조깅을 하는 것이 그의 ~이다 It is his practice to go jogging before breakfast. // 취침 전에 목욕을 하는 것이 그의 ~으로 되어 있었다 As a rule [Usually] he took a bath before he went to bed. // 그는 호주머니에 손을 집어넣고 걷는 ~이 있다 He is in the habit of walking with his hands in his pockets.
습관은 제2의 천성 Habit [Custom] is (a) second nature.
●**습관성** tendency; habituation. ¶~이 있는 habit-forming // ~ 의약품의 판매를 금지하다 ban sales of habit-forming medicines.

습기(濕氣) moisture; humidity; damp(ness); wet(ness). ¶~가 차다 get damp / (쿠키 등이) get soggy / (엿) go soft // ~가 차므로 깡통을 연 뒤에는 냉장고에 보관할 것 As it absorbs moisture easily, keep it in the refrigerator after opening the can.

-습니까 are (you / they) ...? ➾-ㅂ니까 ¶바깥 날씨가 춥~ Is it cold outdoors? / 그는 어디에 있~ Where is he? / 어디서 오셨~ Where have you come from? / 돈 좀 갖고 있~ Do you have any money with you?

-습니다 be; do. ➾-ㅂ니다 ¶오늘은 날씨가 덥 [춥]~ It is hot [cold] today. / 언제라도 좋~ Anytime will do. // 이제 가 봐야겠~ I must be going now.

습도(濕度) humidity. ¶~를 재다 measure the humidity (of the atmosphere) // ~가 높다 show a high percentage of humidity.
●**습도계** a hygrometer. ¶자기(自記) ~ a hygrograph.

습득(習得) learning; acquirement. ¶기술의 ~ acquirement of technics. **습득하다** [배우다] learn; [배워서 몸에 익히다] acquire (a skill); [숙달하다] master. ¶완전히 ~ achieve a complete mastery (of) // 그 기술은 간단히 습득할 수 있다 The skill is easily acquired [mastered].

습득물(拾得物) a found article. ¶열차 내의 ~ articles found in the train.

습득하다(拾得-) [발견하다] find; [줍다] pick up. ¶보도에 떨어져 있는 지갑을 습득했다 I found [picked up] a coin purse lying on the sidewalk.

-습디까 did you hear that ...? ➾-ㅂ디까 ¶이 사건에 대해 무슨 말이 있~ Have you heard anything about this incident?

-습디다 they say. ➾-ㅂ디다

습성(習性) a habit; behavior [(영) behaviour]; a peculiarity; a habitude. ¶그는 고릴라의 ~을 연구하고 있다 He is studying the behavior [habits] of gorillas. // 양은 집단으로 행동하는 ~이 있다 Sheep by nature move in flocks.

습성(濕性) wetness.

습속(習俗) manners and customs; usage; [사] folkways; [한 집단의 도덕적 기준이 되는 것] mores(▶ 보통 복수형). ¶그 고장의 ~을 보고 익히다 follow local manners and customs // 고대의 ~을 연구하다 study the folkways [usages] of ancient times.

습자(習字) (펜의) penmanship; (붓의) calligraphy.
●**습자지** writing paper.

습작(習作) a study; (프) an étude. **습작하다** study.

습전지(濕電池) a wet cell.

습지(濕地) a marshy [swampy] place; damp [boggy] ground.

습지대(濕地帶) a damp area [region].

습진(濕疹) [의] eczema; humid[moist] tetter.
습포(濕布) a wet compress[pack / pad cloth]; [의] a poultice; a cataplasm. ¶냉~ a cold compress[pad] // 온~ a stupe / a hot compress. **습포하다** apply a poultice (to); put a wet compress (on). ¶발목에 냉[온]~ put [apply] a cold[hot] compress on one's ankle.
● **습포제** poultice (medicine).
습하다(濕−) damp; moist; wet; dampish; humid; [축축하다] soppy; soggy. ¶습한 공기 damp[dampish / humid] air // 습한 날씨 soft weather // 습한[wet / muggy] day.
승(乘) [수] multiplication. **승하다** multiply.
승(僧) a monk.
승(勝) a victory; a win. ¶3~ 1패(로) (with) three victories[wins] and [against] one defeat // 이 팀은 3~ 2패 1무승부였다 This team had three wins, two losses and one draw.
승강(昇降) [오르내림] going up and down; ascent and descent; [상하] rise and fall. **승강하다** go[come] up and down; ascend and descend; rise and fall.
● **승강구** an entrance; (선실로의) a hatch. **승강기** an elevator; [영] a lift.
승강(乘降) getting on and off (a car); boarding and alighting.
● **승강구** the place where one gets on and off (a train). **승강장** a (station) platform.
승강이(昇降−) a quarrel; a wordy conflict; wrangling; disputing. ¶서로 ~를 벌이다 wrangle against each other. **승강이하다** quarrel with a person (about / for / over); wrangle (with); dispute; altercate; have (angry / high / hot / sharp) words (with).
승객(乘客) a passenger; a fare(택시 등의). ¶그 비행기의 ~은 180명이었다 The plane was carrying 180 passengers. / There were 180 passengers on (board) the plane.
● **승객 명부** a register[list] of passengers; a passenger list; a waybill.
승격(昇格) the raising of status; promotion in status. **승격하다** be promoted[raised] to a higher status; be elevated to (the rank of). ¶나는 과장으로 승격했다 I was promoted to (the position of) section head. →¶그는 언제 교수[과장]로 승격되었습니까 When was he promoted to professor[section chief]? // 그 영사관은 대사관으로 승격되었다 The consulate was raised to the status of an embassy.
승계(承繼) succession. ➪ 계승(繼承)
승급(昇級) promotion to a higher grade; advancement; preferment. ¶~이 빠르다 win [get] speedy[rapid / quick] promotion. **승급하다** be promoted[advanced / elevated] (to a higher grade); obtain[get / win] promotion; rise in rank. ¶과장에서 국장으로 ~ 은 be promoted from the section chief to the bureau director. →¶승급시키다 promote / prefer / advance (a person).
승급(昇給) a raise[(영) rise] in salary; a pay hike; a raise. **승급하다** have one's salary raised; get a raise; (남의 급료를) raise a person's salary. ¶시간급 고용인의 급료를 시간당 1200원 ~ raise part-timers' wages 1200 won an hour. →¶우리 회사에서는 해마다 5퍼센트씩 승급시켜 준다 In our company we get a five percent raise in salary every year.

승기(勝機) a chance of victory; a chance to win. ¶~를 놓치다 miss a chance to win / let a chance to win slip through one's fingers // ~를 잡다 seize a chance of victory.
승낙(承諾) consent; (an) agreement; acceptance; (문어) assent. ¶구두[서면] ~ a verbal[written] acceptance // 사전 ~ a previous consent // 조건부 ~ a qualified consent // 그의 승낙 없이[얻지 않고] with [without] his consent // 나는 그의 ~을 얻는 일을 단념했다 I gave up trying to win his consent[win him over]. // 그는 유럽 여행에 대해 아버지의 ~을 얻었다 He got[obtained] his father's consent[approval] for his trip to Europe. // 그들은 학교 당국의 ~ 없이 클럽을 만들었다 They organized a club without the approval of the school authorities. // 이번에는 ~을 받아 낼 테다 This time I will make him say yes[give his consent]. **승낙하다** consent; agree (to); give one's consent[assent] (to); (문어) assent. (▶ consent는 윗자리에 있는 사람이 허가를 할 때, 또는 신청이나 제안을 받아들일 때 쓰임. agree는 논의나 설득의 결과로 동의하기) ¶상사는 그의 제의를 승낙했다 His boss consented[assented / agreed] to his proposal. // 이 안을 승낙하시겠습니까 Will you consent to this plan? // 이 제안을 승낙하실 것으로 기대합니다 I hope you will give your approval to this suggestion. // 그녀는 그와 결혼할 것을 승낙했다 She agreed[consented] to marry him.
● **승낙서** (취임 · 일의 인수 등의) written consent; (수용 · 채용 등의) a letter of acceptance.
승냥이 [동] a Korean wolf; (미) a coyote.
승단(昇段) promotion. **승단하다** be promoted to a higher rank.
승려(僧侶) a Buddhist priest; a bonze; a monk.
승률(勝率) the percentage of victories (to the total number of matches[games]); a winning average.
승리(勝利) a victory; a triumph(▶ 승리감이 따르는). ¶대~ a great[sweeping] victory // 악에 대한 선의 ~ a triumph of good over evil // ~에 도취하다 be triumphant / triumph // 뜻밖의 ~를 거두다 pick up an unexpected win / achieve[pull off] a surprise victory / pull a game out of the fire // 우리 팀이 ~를 거두었다 Our team won. / The match ended in a victory[triumph] for our team. // 시합은 그의 ~로 끝났다 The match ended in victory for him. // 그는 ~감에 도취하여 손을 흔들었다 He waved his hands triumphantly [in triumph]. // 마지막 ~를 거둘 자는 누구인가 Who will come out best in the end? **승리하다** win a victory; score a triumph; come out[emerge] victorious.
● **승리자** a victor; a winner. **승리 투수** the winning pitcher.
승마(乘馬) horseback riding; riding; horsemanship; riding horse(말). **승마하다** ride a horse; get on[mount] a horse. ¶승마하러 가다 go for a ride.
● **승마복** riding clothes; (여성용) a riding habit.
승무(僧舞) a seungmu; music and dancing performed in Buddhist attire; a Buddhist dance.

승무원(乘務員) 〔집합적〕 the crew; (한 사람) a crew member; a member of the crew; 〔열차의〕 (미) a train man; 〔집합적〕 a train crew; 〔전차 등의〕 a carman; 〔비행기의〕 a crewman; 〔집합적〕 a flight crew. ¶**여자** ~ (여객기의) a stewardess / an air hostess / ~은 전원 무사히 구조되었다 The crew members were all rescued. // 이 배의 ~은 40명이다 This ship has a crew of 40.

승병(僧兵) a monk soldier; a fighting monk.

승복(承服) **1** 〔동의〕 consent; 〔수락〕 acceptance; 〔복종〕 submission; obedience. **승복하다** 〔동의하다〕 consent[assent] (to); 〔받아들이다〕 accept; 〔복종하다〕 submit to (authority); yield to (power); obey (an order). ¶승복할 수 없는 조건 unacceptable terms // 그 조건은 승복할 수 없다 I cannot accept that condition. **2** 〔죄의 고백〕 confession[admission] of one's crime. **승복하다** plead[own oneself] guilty; confess[acknowledge] one's guilt.

승복(僧服) a priest's[monk's] robe.

승부(勝負) 〔승패〕 victory or defeat; the outcome; the issue; 〔시합〕 a contest; a game; a match; a bout. ¶무~ a drawn game / a draw / (경주에서) a dead heat // ~를 내다 try conclusions (with) / fight to the finish / fight it out / play off(동점자끼리) // ~를 다투다 contend for victory / compete / vie (in / with) // ~가 났다 The game is over[finished]. / The contest has been decided. // 좀처럼 ~가 나지 않았다 It was a close game[contest].
● **승부차기** 〔축구〕 a penalty shoot-out; spot kicks after a tie.

승산(勝算) prospects of success[victory]; one's chances (of winning). ¶~ 없는 싸움 a hopeless battle[struggle] // 그는 ~이 없다 The chances[odds] are against him. // 지금으로서는 상대방 팀 쪽에 ~이 있다 At present the other team[side] is ahead of[has the edge on] us. // 우리는 ~이 있다 Our chances are good. / The chances[odds] are in our favor.

승선(乘船) (an) embarkation. **승선하다** get on; board; go on board; embark. ¶미국행 배에 ~ board a ship for America // 승무원은 8시까지 승선해야 했다 The crew was required to be on board by eight o'clock. // 그는 이 배에 승선하고 있다 He is one of the passengers on[is aboard] this ship.
● **승선권** a passage[boat] ticket. **승선료** passage money[fare].

승소하다(勝訴-) (사람이) win[gain] the case [one's suit]; (사건이) in favor of one. ¶피고가 승소하였다 The case was decided in favor of the defendant. / The defendant won the suit [case].

승수(乘數) 〔수〕 a multiplier. ¶피~ a multiplicand.

승승장구하다(乘勝長驅-) make a long march flushed with victories; follow up a [one's] victory; win victory after victory. ¶아군은 승승장구하여 진격했다 Our army marched on carrying everything before them.

승압기(昇壓器) a step-up transformer; a booster.

승압하다(昇壓-) 〔전압 등을〕 boost [raise] the voltage (of).

승용차(乘用車) a (passenger) car; a (motor) car; (미) an automobile.

승원(僧院) 〔절〕 a temple; 〔수도원〕 a monastery; a cloister.

승인(承認) 〔공인〕 recognition; acknowledgment; admission; 〔동의〕 consent; agreement; 〔인가〕 approval; 〔문어〕 approbation. ¶부모의 ~ 없이 without one's parents' consent // 그것은 (주)지사의 ~을 요한다 That requires the approval of the governor. **승인하다** recognize; acknowledge; approve; admit; consent (to); hold with. ¶국가의 독립을 ~ recognize the independence of a nation // 증서를 ~ acknowledge the validity of) a deed // 선생님은 학생들의 요청을 승인했다 The teacher consented to the students' request. // 그는 그녀의 제의를 승인하여 고개를 끄덕였다 He nodded his approval of her proposal. // 그의 생각의 어떤 점까지는 승인할 수 있다 His idea is admissible up to a point.
● **승인서** a written acknowledgment.

승인(勝因) the cause of victory.

승자(勝者) a victor; (게임 등의) a winner. ¶예선의 ~ the survivors of the preliminaries.

승적(僧籍) the holy orders. ¶~에 들어가다 enter[be ordained to] the priesthood / become a priest[monk] / take (holy) orders.

승전(勝戰) a successful battle[war]; a triumph. **승전하다** win a war[battle]; gain[win] a victory.
● **승전고**(-鼓) the drum of victory.

승제(乘除) 〔수〕 multiplication and division.

승직(僧職) priesthood; the clerical profession.

승진(昇進) promotion; advancement; preferment; a rise in rank. ¶그는 ~이 빨랐다 He has won quick promotion. // 나는 ~의 가망이 거의 없다 I have little hope of promotion. **승진하다** obtain[win / get] promotion; be promoted[advanced] (to); rise (in rank); move up (to). ¶과장으로 ~ work one's way up[be promoted] to the position of section head // 그는 평사원에서 계장으로 승진했다 He was promoted from clerk to assistant section chief. // 그는 실력으로 승진했다 He was promoted on his own merits. // 그는 나를 앞질러 승진하였다 He was promoted over me. // 공적에 의해 그는 1계급 승진했다 On account of his distinguished service, he was promoted one grade in rank.

승차(乘車) taking a train[car / taxi]; entrainment(군대의). **승차하다** take a train[car / taxi]; get on a train; (미) board a train; get in (a car); (군대 등의) entrain. ¶택시에 ~ get in(to) [take] a taxi // 서울역에서 인천행 열차에 ~ get on[take] a train for Incheon at Seoul station // 모두 승차하십시오 All aboard!
● **승차구** the entrance to the platform; a (bus / train) door; (게시) Way In. **승차권** a (railway / streetcar) ticket; a passenger ticket. ¶무임 ~ a free pass / 우대 ~ a complimentary pass / 정기 ~ a season ticket / a commutation ticket // 좌석[입석] ~ 발매 중 (게시) Tickets for seat [standing] available. **승차권 매표소** a ticket window[office]. **승차요금** the (railway / bus) fare; the carfare; the transit fare. **승차장** 〔정류장〕 a car[bus] stop; a (bus) depot; a platform.

승차(勝差) 〔야구〕 the difference in the number of games won. ¶자이언츠는 라이온스에게 3~ 뒤졌다[앞섰다] The Giants have won three fewer[more] games than the Lions.//그들은 2위와의 ~를 넓혔다 They pulled away from the second place team.

승천(昇天) (예수의) the Ascension; (성모 마리아의) the Assumption; [죽음] death. **승천하다** ascend to[into] heaven; [죽다] go to heaven[glory]; die; pass away.
● 승천일 Ascension Day.

승패(勝敗) victory or defeat; the issue[outcome] (of a battle). ¶~를 겨루다 contend for victory // ~가 결판날 때까지 싸우다 fight it out (till one side wins) // 그 스매시가 ~를 결정지었다 The smash decided (the outcome of) the game. // 그 시합은 ~가 나지 않았다 The game ended in a draw. // ~는 운이다 Victory[The outcome of a contest] is (partly) a matter of chance.

승하(昇遐) (왕의) (문어) demise; death; passing (away). **승하하다** die; pass away; demise. ¶임금님이 승하하셨다 The king has passed away.

승합(乘合) riding together; sharing a vehicle.
● 승합자동차 an omnibus; an autobus.

승홍(昇汞) [화] corrosive sublimate; mercuric chloride.
● 승홍수 a solution of corrosive sublimate.

승화(昇華) [화][심] sublimation. ¶나프탈렌은 ~성이 있다 Naphthaline can be sublimed. **승화하다** sublimate; sublime. →¶성 충동을 예술로 승화시키다 sublimate a sexual impulse in art.
● 승화열 heat of sublimation.

시¹ [못마땅할 때 내뱉는 말] bah!; fie!; bow-wow!; pshaw!; huh!; hmph!

시² [음] si; ti; H.

시- deep; dark. ⇨ 새- ¶~꺼멓다 be deep-black / be jet-[coal-]black // ~퍼렇다 be deep[dark] blue.

시(市) [도시] a city; a town; [행정 구역] a si; a municipality. ¶~의 city; municipal / urban // 의정부~ the City of Uijeongbu / (드물게) Uijeongbu City // ~ 당국 the municipal authorities // ~로 승격되다 be raised to the status of a city.

시(是) (what is) right; righteousness; justice.

시(時) [시간] an hour; [시각] o'clock; time. ¶여덟 ~ eight o'clock / the hour of eight // 8~반의 기차로 by[(미) on] the 8:30 train // 오전[오후] 네 ~에 at four (o'clock) in the morning[afternoon] / at 4 a.m.[p.m.] // 지금 몇 ~ 입니까 What time is it? / What's the time? / What time do you have? / Do you have the time? / What does your watch say? // 3~ 15분입니다 It is a quarter past three (o'clock). / It is three fifteen. // 몇 ~에 오시겠습니까 When[What time] shall I expect you? **시도 때도 없이** irrespective of time or place.

시(詩) [집합적] poetry; (한 편) a poem; lines; [운문] verse. ¶산문~ a prose poetry[poem] // 서사[서정]~ epic[lyric] poetry // ~를 짓다 [감상하다] write[enjoy] a poem // ~로 묘사하다 describe[depict] (a sense) in poetry // ~를 이해하다 have a poetic sense // 그 경치는 ~로 노래할 만하다 That scenery deserves to [should] have a poem written about it.

시-(媤) of the husband; (an aunt) on the husband's side; (a woman's father)-in-law. ¶~누이 a sister of one's husband.

시가 cigar.

시가(市街) [거리] the streets; [시] a city; a town. ¶신[구]~ a new[the old] section of a city.
● 시가전 street(-to-street) fighting. **시가지** a city area; an urban district. ¶~ 개발 urban development. **시가행진** a demonstration. ¶~을 하다 stage a demonstration (parade) / demonstrate.

시가(市價) the market price[value]. ¶~의 변동 market fluctuations // ~ 50,000원의 서류가방 a briefcase which sells for 50,000 won // ~가 올랐다[내렸다] The market advanced [declined]. // ~는 변동하고 있다 The market is fluctuating. // 나는 이 침대를 ~에서 3할 할인된 가격으로 샀다 I got this bed at (a discount of) 30 percent off the market price.

시가(時價) the current price (of strawberries). ¶~로 어림하여 estimated at current prices // ~ 30만 원의 찻잔 a tea bowl worth three hundred thousand won in today's money.
● 시가 발행 (주식의) public offering of new shares at market price.

시가(媤家) one's husband's home. ⇨ 시집(媤-).

시가(詩歌) [집합적] poetry; poems.

시각(時刻) time; the hour. ¶약속의 ~ the appointed time // ~이 ~에 at this time[hour] (of day) // ~이 지나다 past[beyond] the time / behind time / overdue // ~이 늦다 The hour is late. // 이제 돌아갈 ~이다 It is time to go home.
● 시각표 a schedule; a timetable. ¶열차의 ~ a train schedule.

시각(視角) 1 [물] the optic angle; one's angle of vision. ¶~을 바꾸어 보다 look at a thing from a different angle. 2 [사물을 생각하는 입장] one's viewpoint; a point of view; a way of looking (at). ¶~의 차이 a difference of viewpoint // 문제를 보는 ~이 다르다 take a wrong view of a matter // 그 문제는 다른[새로운] ~에서 보아야 한다 You had better look at the matter from another angle [from a different point of view / in a new light].

시각(視覺) (the sense of) sight[vision]; visual sensation; eyesight; seeing. ¶~적(으로) visual(ly) // ~화하다 visualize // ~을 잃다 lose one's eyesight.
● 시각 교육 visual instruction[education]. **시각 언어** (a) visual language. **시각 예술** visual arts. **시각 장애인** a visually challenged[handicapped / impaired] person (▶ handicapped보다 impaired나 challenged가 완곡하고 부드러운 말임).

시간(時間) 1 [시간을 세는 단위] an hour. ¶한 ~ 이내에 within an hour // 두세 ~에 in two or three hours // 몇 ~ 동안 for (many) hours // 세 ~ 반 걸린다 It takes three and a half hours[three hours and a half]. // 한 ~에 한 대의 버스편이 있다 There is an hourly bus service[one bus an hour]. // 나는 한 ~에 5,000원으로 아르바이트를 하고 있다 I'm being paid five thousand won per hour for this part-time work. // 여기서 학교까지는 ~이나 걸립니까 How long does it take from here to the school? // 1주일에 몇 ~이나 일합니까 How many hours a week do you work? 2 [때] time. ¶~과 공간 time and space // 소요 ~ the time required // ~을 절약하다 save time // ~을 내다 make time (for) // ~에 매이다 be tied to a schedule / have little time of one's own // ~을 때우다 kill time // ~을 벌다 buy time // 심심풀이로 ~을 보내다 kill time // 충분히 ~을 들이다 take as much time as one likes // 그것은 ~의 낭비다 It is a waste of time. // 오늘 저녁 ~이 있나요 Do you have time tonight? / Are you available tonight? // 잠깐 ~ 좀 내주시겠어요 Could you spare (me) a minute? // 참 되게 안 가는군 How time drags! // 그는 ~을 벌기 위해 계속 지껄였다 He kept on talking in order to buy time. / He played for time by talking on. // 나는 ~을 주체할 수 없었다 Time hung heavy on my hands. // 그것을 할 ~이 있습니까 Have you got the time to do it? // 이제 ~이 없다 We're running out of time. / We don't have much time left. // 우리는 ~ 여유가 있다 We have plenty of time. // 우리는 ~의 여유가 없다 We don't have any time to spare. // 나는 편지를 쓸 ~이 없다 I have no time to write letters. // ~은 오래 걸리지 않습니다 I won't keep you long. // 이걸 고치는데 ~이 너무 많이 걸리지는 않을 것이다 It won't take much of your time. // ~이 있으면 이것을 고쳐 주십시오 When you can find the time [get a chance], would you correct this, please? // 신문을 볼 ~이 있으면 접시를 씻어라 If you have enough time to read the newspaper, wash the dishes. // 연사가 오는 것이 늦어져서 사회자는 어떻게든 ~을 메우려고 애를 썼다 The speaker had been delayed, so the emcee tried this and that to fill in the time. // 메리의 집을 찾는 데 꽤 ~이 걸렸다 It took me a long time to find Mary's house. // 무엇 때문에 그리 ~이 걸렸느냐 What kept [took] you so long? // ~이 다 되어서 나는 작품을 완성할 수가 없었다 Time ran out before I finished writing my composition. / I failed to finish my composition within the time limit. // 그를 납득시키는 데는 ~이 걸릴 것이다 It will take you time to convince him. // ~이 흘러감에 따라 그의 기억은 사라졌다 As time passed [went by] my memories of him faded. // ~은 돈이다 Time is money. // 그들은 질문을 연발해서 ~을 벌었다 They gained [played for] time by asking one question after another. // 즐거운 ~을 보내시기 바랍니다 I hope you will have a good time. / I hope you will enjoy it. // 한가할 ~이 많아서 이번 주에는 소설을 다섯 권이나 읽었다 With so much time at my disposal, I read five novels this week. // 이 기계는 많은 ~(과 수고)을 덜어 주었다 This machine saved us a lot of time (and labor). // 그녀는 ~과 수고를 요리에 들이는 것을 개의치 않는다 She does not mind devoting a lot of time and effort [energy] to cooking. / She doesn't mind going to a lot of trouble over cooking.

3 〔시각〕 time. ¶정확한 ~ the correct time // 한국 〔현지〕 ~으로 오후 3시에 at 3 p.m. Korea [local] time // (시계의) ~을 빠르게 하다 [늦추다] set the clock forward [back] // ~이 다 되었습니다 Time's up. // 그는 ~에 맞추어 [~ 전에] 도착했다 He arrived on [ahead of] time. // 버스는 제~에 왔다 The bus came on schedule [time]. // 회사에 가야 할 ~이다 It's about time I left [for me to start] for work [the office]. // 그는 ~을 잘못 알고 왔다 He came at the wrong time. // 알고 보니 이미 ~이 지났었다 It was already past the time when I noticed it. // 모임의 ~이 변경되었다 The hour of the meeting has been changed. // 그는 언제나 ~을 지킨다 He is always punctual. // ~을 라디오의 시보에 맞추어라 Set your watch by the radio. // ~ 좀 지켜라 Be punctual [prompt], please. // 그는 ~을 어기지 않고 왔다 He came on time [punctually]. // 괘종시계가 ~을 알렸다 The clock struck the hour.

4 〔수업·근무·휴식 등의〕 hours; 〔수업 시간〕 school hours. ¶영업~ business [office] hours // 근무 ~ working hours // 쉬는 ~에 at break / (미국의 초등학교에서는) at recess / (회사·회의의) during a break / (연극 등의) during intermission // 영어 ~에 during the English lesson. // 첫 ~은 역사다 I have history in the first period. // 수학 ~에 소설을 읽고 있었다 I was reading a novel during the math class.

●시간관념 an idea of time. 시간대 (표준시의) a time zone; (일련의 예정 속에서의) a time slot. ¶아침 8시에서 9시까지는 전철이 붐비는 ~이다 Trains are crowded between eight and nine in the morning. // 이 프로그램은 심야의 ~에 편성되었다 This program was given a late-night slot. 시간문제 a question [matter] of time. ¶내가 교향악단에 들어가는 건 ~예요 It's just a matter of time before I'm playing for the philharmonics. 시간 엄수 punctuality. 시간 외 근무 working overtime; overtime work. ¶~를 하다 work overtime [extra hours / after usual hours]. 시간 외 수당 overtime allowance [pay]. 시간제 ¶~로 일하다 work by the hour. 시간표 a timetable; (미) a (class) schedule. ¶기차 ~ a train timetable / a railroad schedule // 학교 ~ a teaching schedule // ~대로 on schedule.

시건방지다 saucy; 〔구어〕 cheeky; pert; impudent. ¶그는 시건방진 데가 있다 There is something saucy [cheeky] about him. // 시건방진 소리하지 마라 None of your impudence [〔구어〕 cheek]!

시경 (市警) 〔시 경찰청〕 the Metropolitan Police.

시경 (詩經) the Book of Odes [Poetry].

시계 (時計) 〔탁상시계〕 a (table) clock; 〔벽시계〕 a (wall) clock; 〔회중·손목시계〕 a watch; a wrist watch (손목시계); (자명종) an alarm clock; 〔집합적〕 a timepiece; a timekeeper. ¶디지털 ~ a digital clock [watch] (시각이 표기되는) // 뻐꾸기 ~ a cuckoo clock // 아날로그 ~ an analogue clock [watch] // 야광 ~ a glow [luminous] watch / a self-winding watch / a self-winder // 전기 ~ an electric clock // 전자 ~ an electronic watch // 진자 [추] ~ a pendulum clock // 탁상 ~ a table [desk / mantel] clock // 탑 ~ a tower clock // 정확한 [부정확한] ~ a good [bad / poor] timekeeper // ~의 속뚜껑 a cap // ~의 장침[단침 / 초침] an hour [a minute / a second] hand // ~처럼 like a clock / like clockwork // ~ 방향의[으로] right-handed / clockwise // ~ 방향과 반대의[로] counterclockwise / (영) anti-clockwise // ~ 방향으로 돌다 turn clockwise // ~태엽을 감다 wind (up) a clock [watch] // ~를 보다 look at [consult / refer to] one's watch // ~를 고치다 mend [repair] a watch / put a watch [clock] in order // ~를 빨리 가게 하다 put [set] a watch fast [on] (ten minutes) / advance [set ahead] a clock // ~를 늦게 가게 하다 put [set] a watch slow [back] / turn back a clock // ~를 10분 빨리[늦게] 가게 하

시계

다 put a watch ten minutes forward[back] // ~를 맞추다 put one's watch right // ~를 분해 청소하다 have one's watch cleaned // ~를 …에 맞추다 set a watch by (the radio) / set [synchronize] a watch with (the radio time signal) // ~로 주자의 시간을 재다 time a runner with a watch // ~가 가고 있다 The watch is going. // 자네 ~는 몇 시인가 What time is it by your watch? // 이 ~는 10분 빠르다 [늦다] This clock is ten minutes fast [slow]. // 자네 ~는 정확한가 Does your watch keep good[perfect] time? // 내 ~는 정확하다 My watch keeps good time. // 내 ~는 좀 빠르다[늦다] My watch gains[loses] a little. // 내 ~는 3분 빠르다[늦다] My watch is three minutes fast[slow]. // ~가 섰다 My watch has stopped[run down].

● **시계탑** a clock tower. **시계포** a jeweler's; a jewelry store; a watchmaker's. **시곗바늘** the hands of a clock[watch]. **시곗줄** a watch chain[guard]; a fob (chain).

시계(視界) a field of vision. ⇨ "시야" ¶~에서 사라지다 go out of sight // ~가 갑자기 열렸다 My field of vision suddenly opened up. // ~ 제로[양호] Zero[good] visibility. // 비 때문에 ~가 나빠 비행기는 공항에 착륙할 수 없었다 Visibility was so bad because of the rain that the airplane could not land at the airport.

시고모(媤姑母) an aunt (who is a sister of one's husband's father).

● **시고모부** the husband of an aunt on one's husband's side.

시골 (도시에 대하여) the country; the countryside; (전원) rural districts; (지방) local areas; (구어) the sticks(▶ 경멸적으로 씀); (고향) one's home; one's native place; one's birthplace. ¶~의 rural / country / (소박한) rustic / (지방 특유의 또는 편협한) provincial // ~에서 자란 country-bred // ~에서 갓 올라온 fresh from the country // ~풍의 사고방식 a provincial way of thinking // ~ 태생의 country-born / born in the country // ~ 출신의 (a maidservant) from the country // ~에서 살다 live in the country[sticks] // ~에 가다 go into[down to] the country // ~에서 자라다 be brought up in the country // ~로 내려가다 go home / go back to one's native place // ~로 은둔하다 retire into the country.

● **시골 길** a country road[path(▶ 작은 길)]. **시골내기** a country person; a farmer; a rustic; rural folk. **시골뜨기** a countryman; a provincial; (집합적) country folk; (경멸적) a boor; a hick; a yokel; a bumpkin. **시골말** (사투리) a regional dialect; (방언의 어구) a regional word[expression]. **시골 사람** a country person; (집합적) rural people; country folk. **시골집** a farmhouse(농가); a country cottage(보통 1층짜리, 소형의 집). **시골티** the rural[rustic / country] air. ¶~가 나는 countrified / rustic / rural / (문어) bucolic(▶ rustic과 rural은 거의 같은 뜻으로 쓰이나 rustic은 촌스럽다는 뜻이 포함됨) // ~가 나는 모습 rustic[countrified] appearance.

시공(施工) construction; execution; operation. ¶신관의 ~이 시작되었다 Construction of the new building has begun. **시공하다** construct; carry out (a construction project); undertake construction. → 서울 건축 회사에 의해 시공된 빌딩 a building constructed[put up] by the Seoul Construction Company.

● **시공자** a builder; an operator.

시공(時空) (물) space-time. ¶~의 spatiotemporal.

시구(始球) opening of a baseball game. ¶지사의 ~로 시합이 시작되었다 The game was opened[started] with the first ball tossed by the governor.

● **시구식** the opening ceremony of a baseball game in which an honorary guest throws (out) the first ball. ¶~을 하다 throw[pitch] the first ball / throw out the first ball (from the grandstand).

시구(詩句) (시의 한 구) a phrase in a poem; (시의 한 행) a line of a poem; (시의 절) a verse; a stanza.

시국(時局) the situation; the (current) state of affairs[things]. ¶비상 ~ an emergency / a crisis (pl. -ses)(위기) / wartime(전시) // ~의 추이 changes in the situation // ~에 관한 의견 one's view on the situation // ~을 고려하여 in view of the situation[current state of affairs] // ~에 대처하다 meet the situation / deal[cope] with a situation // ~을 악화시키다 [수습하다] aggravate[save] the situation.

● **시국 강연회**[간담회] a consultation [lecture] meeting on the current situation.

시굴(試掘) prospecting; trial digging[boring]; appraisal drilling. **시굴하다** prospect (a mine); bore for (oil / coal); launch an appraisal drilling; (미) wildcat. ¶금을 ~ prospect for gold // 석유를 ~ drill for oil.

● **시굴갱** a test [trial] pit. **시굴권** a prospecting right. **시굴자** a prospector; a wildcatter.

시궁창 (도랑) a ditch; (하수도) a gutter; a (street) drain; a sewer; (물이 고인 곳) a cesspool. ¶~에 빠지다 fall into a ditch // ~을 치다 clear (out) a ditch / scour a drain // ~이 메었다 The drains are choked.

시그널 a signal. ¶~을 빈번히 보내다 send signals frequently.

시극(詩劇) a drama in verse; a poetical [poetic] drama; a dramatic poem.

시근거리다 (관절이) feel an arthritic pain. ¶뼈마디가 시근거린다 I am aching in my joints.

시근벌떡거리다 gasp and gulp; pant.

시근시근 (관절이) with an arthritic pain.

시금(試金) assaying; an assay. **시금하다** assay; make an assay of.

시금떨떨하다 sour and puckery; sourish and astringent.

시금석(試金石) 1 (순도 판정용의 돌) a touchstone; a Lydian stone. 2 (사물의 가치를 판단하는 표준) a test; a touch; a test case. ¶이 기획은 그의 솜씨를 시험하는 ~이 될 것이다 This project will serve as a test of his ability. / This project will put his ability to the test.

시금치 (식) spinach; spinage.

시금털털하다 sour and puckery. ⇨ '시금떨떨하다'

시급하다(時急—) urgent; pressing; emergent; immediate; imminent. ¶시급한 문제 a pressing question. **시급히** at once; as soon as possible; urgently; immediately. ¶이것은 ~ 해결해야 할 문제이다 The matter must be settled without delay.

시기(時期) 1 (정한 때) time; the times. ¶중대 [적당]한 ~ a crucial[an appropriate] time // 사람을 방문하기에는 ~가 나쁘다 I do not think this is a good time to pay a visit.∥이 사업을 위해서는 ~가 좋다 The timing is right for this enterprise. **2** [계절] season; the time of (the) year. ¶해마다 이 ~에는 벚꽃이 핀다 Cherry blossoms come out at this time of the year.

시기(時期) an opportunity; a chance; the time; season; [알맞은 때] the (proper) moment. ¶~에 알맞은[적절한] opportune / timely / appropriate / well-timed / seasonable∥~에 맞지 않는 inopportune / inappropriate / untimely / out of season∥~를 **기다리다** wait for a favorable time[a ripe opportunity]∥~를 **타다** take advantage of an opportunity∥~를 **잡다**[포착하다] seize [take] the opportunity∥~를 놓치지 않고 …하다 lose no time in (beginning work)∥~를 보아 …하다 take occasion to (do)∥~는 왔다 The time has come. / Now is the moment. ∥그것은 ~에 알맞은 발언이었다 That was a timely remark.∥은행주는 지금이 팔 ~이다 This is the best time[Now is the time] to sell bank stocks.∥나는 ~를 놓쳤다 I missed an opportunity[my chance].∥~를 보아 그에게 진실을 말하겠다 I will wait for[choose] an appropriate moment and tell him the truth.
●**시기상조** being too early to (do). ¶결정을 내리는 것은 ~이다 It is too early yet to decide.∥그것을 지금 결정하는 것은 ~다 It would be premature to decide that now.∥투자하기에는 ~다 The time is not yet ripe for investment.

시기(猜忌) jealousy; green envy. **시기하다** be jealous (toward). ¶그는 너의 명성을 시기하고 있다 He is jealous of your good name.∥그는 친구의 승진을 시기하고 있다 He is jealous of his friend for being promoted.
●**시기심** jealousy.

시꺼멓다 1 (색깔이) deep-black; jet-[coal-]black; inky(-black); sooty. ¶시꺼멓게 타다 be scorched black. **2** (마음이) blackhearted; evilhearted; malicious; wicked. ¶그는 뱃속이 ~ He is wicked at heart[blackhearted].

시끄럽다 1 [소란하다] noisy; loud; boisterous; uproarious; clamorous; tumultuous; (미국 속어) rip-roaring. ¶시끄러운 라디오 소리 the noisy sound of a radio∥시끄럽게 noisily / clamorously / boisterously / uproariously∥시끄럽게 하다 make noise∥그는 시끄러운 사람이다 He is a noisy person. / He is a noisemaker.∥시끄러워서 그의 목소리가 들리지 않았다 His voice was drowned out by the noise. / We could not hear him because of the noise.∥내 방 밖이 시끄러워졌다 It got noisy outside my room.∥이웃 사람들이 너무 시끄럽게 떠들어서 나는 잠을 잘 잘 수가 없었다 My neighbors were making such a racket that I couldn't sleep well.
2 (의론·여론이) much-talked-of; much-discussed; vexed. ¶시끄러운 문제 a controversial[much-discussed / burning] question∥세상이 ~ [어지럽다] The times are out of joint. / [사회적으로 불안하다] There is social unrest everywhere.∥우리는 시끄러운 세상에 대응할 수 있는 마음가짐이 필요하다 We have to be ready to face the turbulent times. / We must face up to these difficult times. / 나라 안이 ~ The whole country is in turmoil.
3 [귀찮다·곤란하다] troublesome; vexing; annoying. ¶시끄러운 문제[아이] a trouble-some problem[child]∥시끄러워 Be quiet! / Silence!

시끌벅적하다 noisy; tumultuous; noisy and crowded; wild and noisy. ¶시끌벅적한 술집 a bar which is very noisy and crowded.

시나리오 a scenario (pl. ~s); a screenplay.
●**시나리오 작가** a scenarist; a screenwriter; a scenario writer.

시나브로 [모르는 사이에 조금씩 조금씩] by imperceptible degrees; little by little; bit by bit.

시내 a stream; a brook(개울); (미) a creek; a brooklet; a rivulet; a streamlet.
●**시냇가** the bank of a stream. **시냇물** the water of a brook[stream].

시내(市內) the city; the area within the city limits. ¶~에 있는 학교 the schools in the city∥~에 **있다**[없다] be in[out of] town∥~에 **살다** live in the city∥~를 **구경하다** go sightseeing the city / see[do] the city.
●**시내 관광** sightseeing in the city. **시내버스** an urban bus. **시내 통화** a city call; a local call.

시네마스코프 [영] (상품명) CinemaScope.

시녀(侍女) a waiting woman[maid]; a lady-in-waiting; a lady attendant; a lady's maid; an abigail.

시누(이) (媤－) one's husband's sister; a sister-in-law. ¶나는 ~와는 사이좋게 지내고 있다 I get along very well with my husband's sister.

시늉 [흉내] mimicry; imitation; apery; aping; (속어) a take-off; [체하기] (false) show; (a) pretense; make-believe; sham; simulation. ¶우는 ~을 하다 pretend to cry∥귀머거리 ~을 하다 assume to be deaf∥죽은 ~을 하다 feign[sham / simulate] death∥미친 ~을 하다 pretend to be mad / feign oneself to be mad∥그저 먹는 ~만 하다 merely make a pretense of eating∥앓는 ~을 하다 feign oneself to be sick.

시니컬하다 [냉소적이다] cynical.

시다 1 (맛이) sour; acid; tart; vinegary. ¶신 포도 sour grapes∥나는 신 사과는 싫다 I don't like tart apples. **2** (뼈마디가) stinging; painful. ¶발목이 ~ feel a dull pain in one's ankle. **3** (눈이) dazzling; glaring; blinding. ¶눈이 시어서 뜰 수가 없다 The light is so bright that I cannot keep my eyes open.

시달(示達) (문서에 의한) written instructions [directions]; a directive; (공문에 의한) a public[government] notification[notice]; an official notice; an order(명령). ¶엄중한 ~ strict orders[instructions]. **시달하다** instruct; direct; notify. ¶엄중히 ~ strict instructions.

시달리다 be troubled (with); be worried (with); be annoyed (by / with / at); be harassed[molested / vexed]; suffer (from) (병에); be jostled (in a crowd) (세파 속에); be tried; see[experience] hardships. ¶가난에 시달리는 가족 a poverty-stricken family∥병에 ~ suffer from a disease∥빚에 ~ be struggling with debts∥나는 일에 시달리고 있다 I'm up to my neck in work.∥그는 빚에 시달리고 있다 He is burdened with debt.∥그들은 근처 공장의 소음에 시달리고 있다 They are disturbed[bothered / vexed] by the noise from the nearby factory.∥회사는 자금 부족으로 시달리고 있다 The company is suf-

시달다 fering from a lack of capital.//그는 신경통에 시달리고 있다 He is suffering from[is tormented by / is afflicted with] neuralgia.//나는 시끄러운 아이들에게 시달렸다 I was bothered by the noisy children.//나는 밤새 모기에 시달렸다 I was pestered by mosquitoes all night long.

시답잖다 (서술적) be unsatisfied; (사물이) be not quite[entirely] satisfactory; be unsatisfactory; go against the grain; be not to (a person's) liking. ¶시답잖은 소리를 하다 say something offensive.

시대(時代) **1** [지금 있는 그 시기] the times. ¶～의 흐름 the current of the times//～의 총아 the most popular figure of the times / (문어) the lion of the day//～의 유행 the fashion of the day//～에 뒤떨어진 outdated / old-fashioned//～에 뒤떨어진 사람 a person behind the times / a person who cannot keep up with the times / (구어) a fuddy-duddy//**～에 역행하다** go against the times//그의 생각은 ～에 앞서[뒤져] 있다 His ideas are ahead of[behind] the times.//～가 바뀌었다 Times have changed.//그는 ～에 적응하는 감각이 빠르다 He is quick to adapt to the trend of the times.
2 [역사상의 구분된 일정 기간] an era; an age. ¶조선 ～ the Joseon Period//석기 ～ the Stone Age//원자력 ～ the atomic age//기계 ～ a machine age//신화 ～ mythological times//삼국 ～ the era of the Three Kingdoms//우주 ～ the space age//자동차 ～ the motor age[era]//새 ～가 개막되다 bring in a new age / mark the beginning of a new era.
●**시대감각** the sense of the times. **시대상**(－相) the phases[indications] of the times [age]. **시대정신** the spirit of the age [the times]; (독) Zeitgeist. **시대착오** (an) anachronism.

시댁(媤宅) one's husband's home. ⇨¹시집(媤－).

시도(試圖) a trial; a try; (미) an attempt; a venture(모험적인); an experiment. ¶새로운 ～ a new trial[attempt] / (사업 등의) a new departure[venture] / 그들이 그를 함정에 빠뜨리려는 ～에 성공[실패]했다 They succeeded[failed] in an attempt to trap him.//영국 해협을 헤엄쳐 건너려는 그의 ～가 성공했다 He succeeded in his attempt to swim across the English Channel. **시도하다** make plans[take steps] to carry out; implement; try to realize [to put into effect]; try out; test; (make an) attempt (at / to do). ¶그는 다시 한 번 시험을 치르기를 시도했다 He made another attempt to pass [(구어) took another stab at / had another go at] the examination.//그는 내년에 에베레스트 등반을 시도한다 He will attempt to climb Mt. Everest next year.//처음에 실패해도 또 다시 시도해 보아라 If at first you don't succeed, (try,) try again.

시동(始動) starting. ¶～을 **걸다** switch on the ignition / start (a machine)//엔진의 ～이 걸렸다 The engine started.//우리는 엔진의 ～이 잘 걸리지 않아서 애를 먹었다 We had difficulty starting (up) the engine.
●**시동 장치** a starting device[gear / system].

시동생(媤同生) one's husband's younger brother; a brother-in-law.

시들다 **1** (초목이) wither (away / up); wilt(▶ wither는 한창때를 지나, 또는 수분 부족이나 기후 때문에 생기를 잃음. wilt는 주로 수분 부족으로); shrivel(쭈그러들다); droop (away); languish. ¶시든 잎[꽃] dead leaves [flowers] / 꽃이 시들었다 The flower has withered [faded].//이 소나무는 시들었다 This pine tree is dead.//화분의 식물이 모두 시들어 버렸다 All my potted plants withered up and died.//이 시금치는 시들었다 This spinach is wilted[limp].//꽃병의 꽃이 시들었다 The flowers in the vase wilted.
2 (기운이) weaken; lose strength; wane; (매력·청춘이) wither; go[run] to seed. ¶인기가 ～ lose[fall in] popularity.

시들시들하다 slightly wilted.

시들하다 [마음에 차지 않다] unsatisfactory; dissatisfied; [내키지 않다] halfhearted; lukewarm; reluctant; unwilling; uninterested; [흥미가 없다] unattractive; uninteresting; [대수롭지 않다] trivial; of no account [value]. ¶시들한 이야기 a dull [an uninteresting] story / 시들한 일 unattractive work / a poor job / 인생이 시들해지다 lose interest in life / grow weary [get sick] of life//대화가 시들해졌다 The conversation began to flag[brag].//그가 돌아간 후 모임은 시들해졌다 After he left, the party became dull [lifeless].//그는 시들한 어조로 그렇게 말했다 He said so in a dismal [deflated] tone. **시들히** unconcernedly; halfheartedly; lightly; belittlingly. ¶～ **여기다**[보다] take lightly / make light of / think little of / hold (a thing) in low esteem / slight / neglect / disdain / disfavor // ～ **대답하다** give a dry answer / answer in a halfhearted manner.

시디 CD(▶ compact disc의 약어).
●**시디롬** a CD-ROM; a CD/ROM(▶ compact disc read-only memory의 약어).

시래기 dried radish leaves.

시럽 sirup; (영) syrup. ¶**과즙** ～ fruit syrup.

시렁 a (wall) shelf; a ledge; a rack; a trellis(등나무·포도나무 등의). ¶포도(덩굴) ～ a vine trellis//～**에 얹다** put[place] (a thing) on a shelf / shelve.

시력(視力) sight; eyesight; vision; visual power[acuity]. ¶～**을 잃다** lose one's eyesight / go blind//～**을 회복하다** regain one's eyesight//그는 ～이 좋다[나쁘다] He has good[bad / poor] sight[eyesight].//최근 몇 년 동안에 내 ～이 점점 약해졌다 During the past few years my eyesight has been failing little by little.//네 ～이 얼마니 What's your eyesight?//내 오른쪽 눈의 ～은 1.0이다 My eyesight in my right eye is 1.0.(▶ 영·미에서는 I have 20/20 [twenty-twenty] vision이라고 함. 이것은 20피트 거리에서 지표 20의 글자가 보이는 것을 말하며, 우리의 1.0에 해당함)
●**시력 검사** an eye[eyesight] test; a test of one's vision. ¶나는 ～를 받았다 I had my eyesight[vision] tested. **시력 검사표** an eye test chart.

시련(試鍊·試練) a trial(고난); an ordeal(특히, 가혹한 시련); a test; [신] a probation / 신의 ～ (시험) a divine test / (벌) an infliction from God//～**을 겪다** go through [undergo] an ordeal / 인생의 ～을 견디다 endure [stand] the trials of life//그는 세상의 모진 ～에 견디어 왔다 He has stood the severe trials of life.//그는 모진 ～을 견디어 냈다 He endured a severe ordeal. **시련하다** try; make a trial; give an ordeal.

시론(時論) 1 [시사에 관한 논의] discussion on current topics[events]. 2 [당시의 세론] a current view; a contemporary opinion; public opinion[sentiment] (of the day). ¶~에 눈을 감다[~를 무시하다] ignore the public opinion of the day.

시론(試論) [평론] an essay on poetry; [이론] a theory on[of] poetry; [시학] poetics.

시료(試料) [광석의] a sample ore.

시루 a rice steamer.

시루에 물 퍼 붓기(속담) pouring water into a sieve; waste of labor.

●**시루떡** steamed rice cake.

시류(時流) [그 시대의 흐름·풍조] the current of the times; the trend of the world; the general drift of affairs; [유행] the fashion of the day. ¶~를 따르다 follow the fashions of the day // ~에 **영합하다** curry favor with the public // ~를 **거스르다**[역행하다] go[swim] against the stream[tide / current of the times] // ~에 물들지[영향을 받지] 않다 be independent of[be not affected by] the trends of the times // 그와 같은 생각은 ~에 맞지 않는다 Such a way of thinking is out of step with the times.

시름 anxiety; apprehension(s); worry; care; trouble; grief; sorrow; heaviness of mind. ¶~겨운 안색 a worried[an anxious] look // 하루하루의 ~을 잊다 forget the cares[worries] of everyday life // 술로 실연의 ~을 달래다 drown the anguish of a broken heart in alcohol / drink away the sadness[sorrows] of unrequited love // 그들의 얼굴은 ~에 잠겨 있었다 They wore a worried look[wore an anxious look / looked anxious].

시름을 놓다[덜다] be relieved of one's anxiety; feel relieved; set[have] one's mind [heart] at rest[ease]; unload one's mind.

시름시름 lingeringly. ¶~ 앓는 병 a lingering illness // 그는 ~ 앓았다 He was long in recovering from his illness.

시름없다 1 [근심·걱정으로 맥이 없다] worried; depressed; dispirited; disheartened. **시름없이** worriedly; depressedly; dispiritedly; dishearatedly. 2 [명하다] absent-minded; blank; vacant. **시름없이** absent-mindedly; blankly; vacantly. ¶~ 먼 산을 쳐다보다 look vacantly at mountains far away.

시리다 (achingly / painfully) cold; chilled. ¶귀가 시려서 떨어져 나갈 것 같다 My ears tingle with the cold. // 나는 발이 시려서 잠들 수가 없다 I cannot sleep with my feet getting chilly.

시리즈 [문고·총서·연속 영화나 경기] a series. ¶월드 ~ [야구] the World Series // 그 이야기는 ~로 출판되고 있다 The story is being published serially[in a series].

시립(市立) ¶~의 municipal / city // 이 학교는 ~이다 The school is under municipal management.

●**시립 도서관** a city library. **시립 병원** a municipal hospital.

시말(始末) the beginning and the end; [사정] the fact of the matter; the state of things; the circumstances; the particulars.

●**시말서**(-書) a written apology[explanation]. ¶나는 ~를 제출해야만 되었다 I had to submit a written apology.

시멘트 cement. ¶벽에 ~를 바르다 cement a wall.

●**시멘트 공사** cement work. **시멘트 공장** a cement factory[plant].

시무(始務) the opening of government offices for the year; reopening of office business after the New Year holidays.

●**시무식** the opening ceremony (for the year).

시무룩하다 sullen; grim(기분이 언짢다); taciturn(말이 없다); peevish; sour; glum; grumpy; ill-humored. ¶시무룩한 얼굴 a sulky look[face] // 시무룩하여 with a displeased look / with a sulky silence // 시무룩한 얼굴을 하다 look displeased[glum / sullen] // 그는 늘 저렇게 ~ He is always moody [sullen] like that.

시문(詩文) [시와 산문] poetry and prose; [문학 작품] literary works.

시뮬레이션 액션 [심판의 눈을 속이는 동작] simulation (action).

시민(市民) [개인] a citizen; [집합적] the citizens; the townsmen; the townspeople; the townsfolk; the citizenry. ¶서울 ~ a citizen [the citizens] of Seoul // 뉴욕 ~ a citizen of New York / a New Yorker // 그는 미국 ~이다 He's a citizen of the United States. // ~의 과반수가 현 시장에게 투표했다 The majority of the citizens voted for the present mayor.

●**시민 계급** (프) bourgeoisie. **시민권** citizenship; civic [civil / citizens'] rights. ¶미국 ~을 얻다[잃다] acquire[lose] American citizenship // ~을 부여하다 grant citizenship to (a person) / (미) citizenize. **시민 사회** civil society. **시민 혁명** a people's[popular] revolution.

시발(始發) the first departure (of a train [car]). ¶~은 오전 4시 30분이다 The first train[car] starts at 4:30 a.m. **시발하다** start; depart the terminal. ¶용산에서 시발하는 열차 a train starting from Yongsan.

●**시발역** the starting station; the station of origin. ¶서울역은 경부선의 ~이다 The Gyeongbu[Seoul-Busan] Line starts from Seoul Station. **시발점** a starting point.

시방서(示方書) specifications. ¶설계 ~ building specifications // ~를 **변경하다** change specifications.

시범(示範) showing[setting] an example; a model for others. ¶~적으로 by way of showing an example / as a model. **시범하다** show[set / give / offer] an example (to others).

●**시범 경기** (play) an exhibition game; (give) an exhibition (of fencing).

시보(時報) 1 [보도] (current) news; a report; a gazette; a bulletin; [평론] a review. 2 [시간을 알리기] a time signal[siren]; (라디오의) an announcement of (the) time; (correct) time casting[broadcasting]; (미국 속어) a timecast. ¶시계를 라디오의 ~에 맞추다 set one's watch by the radio (time signal) // 나는 정오의 ~를 들었다 I heard the noon whistle.

시보(試補) [수습] probationary; [수습자] a probationer. ¶사법관 ~ a probationary judicial officer / a judicial officer on probation.

시부렁거리다 prattle; chatter; jabber; talk nonsense; talk useless things.

시부모(媤父母) one's parents-in-law; the

시비 parents of one's husband.

시비(市費) municipal [city] expense; municipal expenditure(경비). ¶~로 at municipal [city] expense / at the expense of the city.

시비(是非) 1 [잘잘못] right and [or] wrong; [적부] the propriety (of). ¶~의 판단 discrimination of right and wrong // 당시는 너무 어려서 ~를 가릴 줄 몰랐다 I was then too young to know [tell] right from wrong. / 이 이론에 대한 ~는 쉽사리 가려지지 않는다 We cannot decide readily whether the theory is right or wrong. 시비하다 comment (on); criticize.
2 [말다툼] a dispute; a quarrel; a wrangle; an altercation; an argument. ¶~가 벌어지다 get into an altercation (over) [arguments (with)] // ~를 걸다 pick up a quarrel with (a person) / provoke (a person) to a quarrel / egg (a person) on to a quarrel // 그들은 ~ 끝에 치고받고 했다 They proceeded from words to blows. / The quarrel came to hard blows. 시비하다 quarrel (with); have a quarrel [dispute] (with); dispute [argue] (with a person about something).
● 시비조 a quarreling [fighting / defiant] attitude; an aggressive attitude. ¶~로 말하다 say something aggressive // 그는 항상 ~다 He is always looking for fight.

시비(施肥) fertilization; manuring. 시비하다 fertilize; manure (▶ 주로 유기질 비료를); apply [give] manure (to a field).

시비(詩碑) a monument inscribed with a poem. ¶소월(素月)의 ~ a monument in memory of Sowol inscribed with one of his poems.

시뻘겋다 deep red. ⇨새빨갛다

시사(示唆) [제언] (a) suggestion; [암시] a hint. 시사하다 suggest; give [offer] (a person) suggestions (as to); hint (at). ¶시사하는 바가 많은 [자극이 되는] stimulating / [생각케 하는] thought-provoking // 그의 논문은 문화 인류학의 새로운 방법을 시사하고 있다 His essay suggests a new direction for anthropology. // 그의 연설은 여당과의 협조 가능성을 시사했다 His speech hinted at the possibility of cooperation with the ruling party.

시사(時事) current [present] events [affairs / questions]; the events [news] of the day. ¶~에 밝다 be well-informed of current events [affairs] / be in touch with the times // ~에 어둡다 be out of touch with the times // ~를 논하다 discuss current events / argue on topics of the day.
● 시사 문제 a current question; issues of the day; questions of the day [times]; current topics. 시사 주간지 a newsweekly. 시사평론 comments on contemporary [current] topics; a contemporary [current] topics; a contemporary. 시사 해설 news commentary; comments on current topics.

시사(試射) (a) test-firing; trial firing. 시사하다 test-fire (a gun).

시사(試寫) a preview; a private showing; a trade première [show] (영화 관계자만의). 시사하다 preview a film; give [hold] a preview of a film.
● 시사회 a cinema [movie] preview; a trade show. ¶영화의 ~를 하다 give a preview of a film / preview a film.

시산(試算) 1 [어림잡기 위한 계산] a test calculation. 시산하다 calculate as a test. ¶총비용을 ~ make a trial calculation of the total cost. 2 [검산] checking. 시산하다 check one's figures; prove (a calculation).
● 시산표 a trial balance (sheet).

시삼촌(媤三寸) an uncle of one's husband.

시상(時相) [언] a tense.

시상(詩想) [시적 감정] poetic(al) sentiment; poetic sensibility; [시적인 상념] poetical imagination; [시인의 착상] an inspiration. ¶~이 가득한 작품 a work full of poetical imagination // ~이 떠올랐다 Poetic sentiment [A poetic urge] has begun to stir in me.

시상식(施賞式) a ceremony of awarding a prize.

시상하다(施賞─) award (a person) a prize; bestow a prize (on).

시새우다 be [feel] jealous (of); be green with envy (of). ¶네가 시새울 정도로 나는 부자가 아니다 I don't have so much money that you need to be jealous. // 그들은 서로 시새운다 They are jealous of each other.

시생대(始生代) [지] the Arch(a)eozoic era.

시선(視線) one's eyes; one's gaze. ¶(…로) ~을 돌리다 turn one's gaze [eyes] on / look at // ~을 딴 데로 돌리다 look [glance] away (from) / turn [put [문어]) avert] one's gaze [eyes] (from / off) // ~을 피하다 avoid (a person's) eyes [gaze] // 자기 등 뒤에 누군가의 ~을 느끼다 feel someone's eyes on one's back // 나는 그녀에게서 ~을 뗄 수가 없었다 I could not take my eyes off her. // 그들의 ~이 마주쳤다 Their eyes met. // 손님들의 ~이 모두 그에게 집중되었다 The eyes of all the guests were focus(s)ed on [turned upon] him.

시선(詩仙) a great poet; a poetic genius; a master poet.

시선(詩選) selected poems; a selection of poems; an anthology. ¶현대 영~ (저서명) Selections from [An Anthology of] Modern British Poetry.

시설(施設) [건물] an institution; an establishment; [설비] facilities; equipment; [수용소] a home (for the aged). ¶공공 ~ a public institution / a public service // 교육 ~ educational facilities [institution] // 오락 ~ recreation(al) [amusement] facilities // 군사 ~ a military installation [facility] / military facilities // 후생 ~ public health [healthcare] facilities / recreational facilities // 항만 ~ port [harbor] facilities // 산업 ~ industrial facilities // 호텔 ~ hotel facilities [accommodation / appointments] // 방화 ~ fire prevention equipment [devices] / fire protection // 위생 ~ sanitary [health] facilities [arrangements] // 취사 [조리] ~ arrangements for cooking // 하수 ~ sewerage [drainage] arrangements / a sewer system // 최신 ~을 갖춘 호텔 a hotel with modern conveniences // ~이 좋은 [나쁜] well- [poorly-] equipped / well- [poorly-] appointed / well- [poorly-] furnished // 그 호텔은 ~이 잘 되어 있다 The hotel is well accommodated. 시설하다 equip [provide / furnish] (with); install; establish.
● 시설비 installation expense; the cost of equipment; expenditure for facilities and

시성(詩聖) a great [master] poet; a poetic genius; the sage of the poets.

시세(市勢) 1 [시의 종합적인 상태] the demographic, social and economic conditions in a city. 2 [경] market conditions; the market (position); the tone [condition/movements] of the market.

시세(時勢) 1 [세상의 형편] the tendency [drift/trend] of the times; the signs of the times; the spirit of the age [the times]; the conditions of life; the times; the day. ¶~에 뒤지다 be behind the times / be out of touch with the times / be out-of-date ∥ ~에 따르다 keep pace (up) with the times / swim with the current / keep abreast with [of] the times / go [float] with the stream ∥ ~는 변했다 Times have changed. ∥ 그는 ~을 역행하고 있다 He is going against [running counter to the spirit of] the times. / He is fighting [rowing / going / swimming] against the current [stream] of the times. / He is contending against the drift of the times. ∥ 그는 ~의 흐름에는 당할 수가 없었다 He had to submit to the tide [current] of the times. 2 the current price (of strawberries). ⇨ ＝시가(時價) ¶주식 ~ stock quotations [prices] ∥ 암~ a black-market quotation ∥ 공정 [명목] ~ an official [a nominal] quotation ∥ 소매 [도매] ~ the retail [wholesale] price ∥ 최고 ~ the ceiling price / the (price) ceiling ∥ 최저 ~ the bottom price ∥ 환~ the (foreign) exchange rate ∥ ~의 변동 fluctuations in the market price ∥ ~가 오르다 rise [go up] in price / quotations [prices] advance [rise] / ∥ ~가 내리다 fall [go down] in price / quotations [prices] decline [fall] ∥ ~를 조종 [조작] 하다 rig [manipulate] the market ∥ 석유는 보통 ~로 팔리고 있다 Oil is selling [being sold] at the market price [(구어) the going price]. / ∥ ~는 상향이다 The market is advancing. / Prices are [The market is] rising. / ∥ ~는 하향이다 The market is [Prices are] falling. ∥ 밀 ~는 현재 안정되어 있다 The wheat market is stable at present. ∥ 금 ~가 급등했다 The price of gold has suddenly jumped. ∥ ~가 안정세를 보였다 The market has grown tight [turned firm]. ∥ 요즘 ~가 없다 Business is dull [off] these days.

시세(가) 닿다 be reasonable [proper] in price; get one's price; come up with a fair price; reach a good price. ¶시세가 닿아서 땅을 팔았다 When I got my price, I sold the land.

●**시세 폭** a price range; price changes [fluctuations]. ¶큰 [작은] ~ a wide [narrow] range of prices.

시소 a seesaw; a teeter(-totter). ¶~를 타다 (play on a) seesaw.

●**시소게임** a seesaw [close] game. ¶연ㆍ고전은 ~이었다 Yonsei and Korea had a seesaw [close] game.

시속(時俗) the manners and ways of the age.

시속(時速) speed per hour. ¶그 열차는 ~ 200킬로미터이다 That train goes (at) 200 kilometers per [an] hour [at a speed of 200 k.p.h.]. ∥ 제한 ~ 40킬로미터 (게시) Speed Limit: 40 KPH [km/h].

시솝 [컴] [게시판 운영자] a sysop; a system operator.

시숙(媤叔) one's husband's brother; a brother-in-law.

시술(施術) the administration of medicine. **시술하다** administer medicine (to a person); give medical treatment; perform an operation (on a person).

시스템 a system. ¶이 회사는 어떤 ~으로 되어 있습니까 How is this company organized? / On what sort of system is this company run? ∥ 이 도시는 쓰레기 수거 ~이 잘되어 있다 This city has a good system of collecting garbage.

●**시스템 공학** a systems engineering.

시승(試乘) a test [trial] ride [trip]. **시승하다** take a test ride; test (a car); have a trial ride; try out; make a trial trip. ¶우리는 부산까지의 여행으로 내 새 차를 시승하였다 We tried out my new car by taking a trip to Busan.

시시각각(時時刻刻) [명사] every moment [hour / minute]; [부사] momently; hourly; momentarily; from hour to hour; from moment to moment; moment by moment. ¶~ 변하는 날씨 ever-changing weather ∥ 산의 정상에서는 날씨가 ~으로 변한다 At the top of the mountain the weather varies from hour to hour. ∥ 위험은 ~ 다가오고 있었다 Danger was coming closer (moment by moment). / Danger was imminent. / Danger was creeping nearer. ∥ 마감 시간이 ~ 다가오고 있다 The deadline is drawing nearer and nearer. ∥ 피해 소식이 ~ 들어오고 있다 News about the damage is coming in every minute. ∥ 흙탕물이 ~ 불어났다 The muddy water rose higher moment by moment [every moment]. ∥ 우리는 죽음이 ~ 다가오고 있다는 것을 알았다 We knew that death was imminent [we were faced with imminent death].

시시덕거리다 chat and giggle; make mirth; flirt; laugh and talk.

시시때때로(時時-) sometimes; once in a while. ⇨ ＝때때로

시시비비(是是非非) 1 [잘잘못] right and [or] wrong. ¶~를 가리다 distinguish between right and wrong / tell right from wrong. 2 [옳고 그름을 판단함]. **시시비비하다** call a spade a spade; call what is right right, and wrong wrong; render an impartial [unbiased] decisions; pass fair judgement; judge fairly.

시시콜콜(히) inquisitively. ¶~ 따져 묻다 inquire of (a person) about every detail of (a matter) / catechize (a person) to the last details about (a matter) ∥ ~ 따지지 마라 Don't nit-pick. / Stop fussing [complaining] about nothing [minor details / inconsequential details].

시시하다 [사소하다] trifling; trivial; petty; inconsiderable; insignificant; of little importance; of no consequence [account]; [쓸데없다] useless; of no use; [가치 없다] worthless; valueless; unworthy; [평범하다] common; monotonous; flat; prosaic; [어리석다] stupid; foolish; silly; despicable. ¶시시한 소설 a cheap novel / (미) a dime novel / (영) a penny dreadful / (영국 구어) a shocker ∥ 시시한 책 a worthless [stupid / boring] book / a book of no value ∥ 시시한 경기 a dull [slow / joyless] game ∥ 시시한 일 a

시식하다 matter of no importance [weight / consequence / account] / a trifling thing / a trifle / a trivial [trifling] matter [affair] *∥* 시시한 너석 a nobody / a worthless [an insignificant / a good-for-nothing] fellow / a man of no [small] account / a person of no importance / a bore / (구어) a no-good / (미국 구어) a snip / (속어) a half-pint / (미국 속어) a punk *∥* 시시한 소리 좀 그만 해 Don't be absurd! / Don't keep talking nonsense! / Nonsense! / Stuff! / Humbug! / Don't talk rot [rubbish]! / Don't say silly things! *∥* 그들은 시시한 일로 다투고 있다 They are quarreling over a trifling matter. *∥* 시시한 일로 고민하지 마라 Don't worry about little things [trifles]. *∥* 이 잡지는 정말 ~ This magazine is absolute rubbish [absolutely worthless]. *∥* 그의 강의는 정말 시시했다 His lecture was quite tedious [(구어) a real bore]. *∥* 정말 시시하군 What nonsense! *∥* 시시한 공연이었어 It was a backwater performance. / It wasn't very impressive performance. / 그는 학생 시절에는 시시했어 He was a nothing in his school days. / 그가 하는 말은 시시한 것들뿐이다 There is nothing important in what he says. / What he says is all rubbish. / His conversation runs on the most trivial topics. *∥* 그는 시시한 물건만 산다 He buys nothing but junk. *∥* 그녀는 시시한 녀석과 결혼을 했다 She has married a nobody [an insignificant fellow]. *∥* 시시한 일에 공연히 시간을 허비하지 마라 Don't waste your time on trifles.

시식하다 (試食-) sample; try; taste; have a foretaste (of). ¶인도네시아 요리를 ~ 하다 [sample / have a taste of] Indonesian dish.

시식회 (試食會) a tasting party; a sampling party.

시신 (屍身) a corpse; a (dead) body.

시신경 (視神經) [생] the optic [ophthalmic / visual] nerve.

시심 (詩心) poetic sentiment [disposition / feeling / spirit]; a poetic turn of mind; poetry; taste for poetry.

시아버지 (媤-) a father-in-law; one's husband's father.

시아주버니 (媤-) elder [older] brothers of one's husband.

시안 (試案) a tentative plan [draft / proposal]; a draft (plan); a tentative. ¶~을 작성하다 draw up [make out] a tentative plan *∥* 행정 개혁의 ~을 내다 propose a tentative plan for administrative reform.

시앗 a concubine [mistress] of one's husband. ¶~을 보다 (one's husband) keep [set up] a concubine [mistress].

시야 (視野) 1 [시력의 범위] a field [range] of vision; a visual field; a view; (a field of) view; sight. ¶~에 들어오다 come in sight / come into view / come within the range [sweep] (of a telescope) *∥* ~를 가리다 obstruct (a person's) field of vision *∥* ~를 벗어나다 [에서 사라지다] go [get / pass] out of sight / vanish from sight *∥* 위로 올라감에 따라 ~가 점점 넓어졌다 As we climbed up, our field of vision [our view] broadened.
2 [식견·사려의 범위] one's mental [intellectual] horizon; outlook. ¶~가 좁은 [넓은] having a narrow [wide] mental horizon *∥* ~가 넓은 사람 a person with a broad outlook on life *∥* ~가 좁은 사람 a person with a narrow outlook on life / a person who takes a narrow view of things / a person whose mental vision [horizon] is narrow *∥* ~를 넓히다 broaden one's outlook (on) / widen one's mental [intellectual] horizon *∥* 그들은 정치적 ~가 좁다 They are narrow in their political outlook.

시약 (試藥) [화] a (chemical) reagent. ¶네슬러 ~ Nessler's reagent.

시어 (詩語) a poetic word; (집합적) poetical language [diction].

시어머니 (媤-) a mother-in-law; one's husband's mother.

시업 (始業) commencement of work; opening; inauguration. **시업하다** commence [begin / start] work; open.
● **시업식** the opening ceremony (of the school year [term]); an inauguration (ceremony).

시에프 모델 (*CF model) a commercial actor [actress]; an ad actor [actress].

시엠 (*CM) [방송용 광고] a commercial (▶ CM은 한국식 약어로, 영미에서는 쓰이지 않음).
● **시엠송** (*CM song) a commercial jingle.

시연 (試演) a demonstration; a trial performance; a preview. ¶공개 ~ a public demonstration / a public rehearsal. **시연하다** (시험적으로) give a trial performance (of a play); [연습하다] rehearse (a play).

시영 (市營) municipal management [operation / ownership / enterprise / undertaking]. ¶~의 municipal / municipally owned and operated / city / city-run / city-operated.
● **시영 버스** (노선) a municipal [city] bus (line). **시영 주택** a municipal dwelling house.

시오니즘 Zionism.

시외 (市外) the outskirts of a city; outside the city limits; the suburbs. ¶우리 학교는 서울 ~에 위치하고 있다 (시의 바깥에) Our school is situated on the outskirts of (the city of) Seoul. / (교외에) Our school is in the suburbs of Seoul.
● **시외 거주자** an out-of-towner. **시외버스** a cross-country bus. **시외 전화** (선) a toll line; (영) a trunk line; (통화) a toll [a long-distance / an out-of-town] call; (영) a trunk call. ¶~를 걸다 make an out-of-town call.

시용 (試用) trial. ¶신약품의 ~ trying out a new medicine. **시용하다** try (out); make a trial (of a medicine).

시운 (時運) the tide of the times. ¶~이 그에게 유리해졌다 The tide turned in his favor. *∥* ~이 나쁘다 The condition is unfavorable to us. / The times are against us.

시운전 (試運轉) a trial [test] run; (배의) a trial cruise; (기계의) test working; a test. ¶엔진의 ~ a test run of an engine. **시운전하다** make a trial [test] run (of); run a trial.

시원섭섭하다 (서술적) feel relief and sorrow at the same time; feel mixed emotions of joy and sorrow. ¶막내딸을 시집보내고 나니 ~ I feel relieved but sad at having married off my youngest daughter.

시원스럽다 frank; clear; bright. ⇨ 시원시원하다 *∥* 눈매가 시원스러운 아이 a boy with clear and bright [large and bright] eyes *∥* 성격이 시원스러운 사람 a person of frank disposition.

시원시원하다 (성격이) frank; unreserved; open-hearted; (말이) clear; outspoken; straightforward; (행동이) bright; brisk; active; lively; prompt; quick; (구어) snappy; crisp. ¶말씨가 시원시원한 사람 a man with a crisp manner of speaking∥∼하는 것이 ∼ work with alacrity[in a crisp manner] / be a brisk[lively / prompt / snappy] worker∥∼한 성격이 ∼ He has an open[an outgoing / a frank] personality. **시원시원히** frankly; unreservedly; briskly; clearly; actively; fluently; without reserve; promptly. ¶그는 ∼ 대답했다 He answered frankly[candidly]. / He gave a frank[an unreserved] answer.

시원찮다 〔좋지 않다〕 not good; poor; humble; 〔만족스럽지 않다〕 unsatisfactory; unsatisfying; 〔보잘것없다〕 worthless; of little value[importance]; little; small. ¶시원찮은 음식 poor food∥시원찮은 대답 an unsatisfactory answer∥결과가 별로 ∼ I am not quite satisfied with the result. / The result is not much to my mind[has turned out unsatisfactory].∥사업이 처음에는 시원찮았다 The business was hard-pressed[hard going / not doing well] at first.

시원하다 1〔서늘하다〕 cool. ¶시원한 바람 a cool breeze∥아침나절의 시원한 때에 in the cool of the morning∥시원한 나무 그늘에서 in the cool shade of tree∥시원한 데에 두다 keep (a thing) in the cool[a cool place]∥여기는 시원해서 좋다 It is pleasantly cool[nice and cool] here.
2〔상쾌하다〕 refreshing; reviving; bracing; invigorating; 〔후련하다〕 (feel) refreshed [relieved]; 〔기쁜하다〕 (feel) good; 〔만족스럽다〕 satisfactory; (be) satisfied[appeased / gratified]. ¶시원해 보이는 옷 a cool(-looking) dress∥시험이 끝나서 ∼ Now that the examination is over, I feel revived.∥박하 사탕을 먹으면 입 안이 시원해진다 Eating mint candy makes the (inside of the) mouth feel cool and refreshed.∥할 말을 다 하고 나니 속이 ∼ Now that I have said my say, I feel better[relieved].
3 frank; clear; bright. ⇨시원시원하다 ¶말하는 것이 ∼ speak frankly[without reserve] / be outspoken / get right down to the point / give a satisfactory account / make a bright [brisk] statement.

시월(十月) October(약어 Oct.).
시위 a bowstring. ⇨활시위 ¶∼를 매우다 string a bow.
시위(示威) show of force; demonstration; display. ¶가두 〔연좌〕 ∼ a street[sit-in] demonstration∥전쟁 반대 ∼ an anti-war demonstration∥불만을 품은 노동자들이 ∼를 벌였다 A demonstration was staged[carried out / held] by dissatisfied[disaffected] workers. **시위하다** show force; demonstrate; display.
●**시위행진** a (demonstration) parade.
시유(市有) municipal[city] ownership. ¶∼의 municipal / city-owned / owned by[belonging to] the city / municipally-owned / city.
●**시유 재산** municipal property. **시유지** city land.
시음하다(試飲−) sample; taste; try.
시음회(試飲會) a sampling party. ¶와인 ∼ a wine-tasting party.
시의(時宜) opportuneness; timeliness. ¶∼에 맞는 발언 a timely remark∥∼에 맞다 be opportune / be timely / be pertinent[proper] to the occasion∥그 조치는 ∼에 맞았다 [맞지 않았다] The action was well-timed[ill-timed]. / The action was taken at a most opportune[inopportune] moment.∥그는 언제나 ∼에 맞는 발언을 한다 He always says the right thing at the right moment[time].

시의(猜疑) 〔시기〕 jealousy; 〔의심〕 suspicion. ¶∼의 눈으로 보다 look at[(문어) upon] (a person) with suspicious eyes / regard (a person) with suspicion / suspect (a person of lying). **시의하다** be suspicious of; be jealous of; suspect. ¶그녀는 시의하는 눈으로 남편의 행동을 감시하기 시작했다 She began to watch her husband's behavior suspiciously[with suspicion].

시의회(市議會) the municipal[city] assembly; the city council.
●**시의회 의원** a member of the municipal assembly[a city council]; a municipal assemblyman; (미) a (city) councilman; (영) a city councillor. ¶∼ 선거 a municipal election.

시인(是認) admission; acknowledgement; approval; (문어) approbation. **시인하다** admit; acknowledge; approve of; approbate; endorse. ¶그는 자기의 잘못임을 시인했다 He acknowledged his mistake. / He admitted [(미) conceded] that he was wrong. / He admitted himself (to have been) in the wrong.∥그는 어머니의 꽃병을 깨뜨렸음을 시인했다 He admitted breaking his mother's vase.

시인(詩人) a poet(남자); a poetress(여자).
시일(時日) 1〔때와 날〕 the date; the day. ¶회의의 ∼을 정하다 set a date for the meeting ∥∼과 장소를 정하다 fix time and place∥∼을 정하다 fix the date / appoint[choose] the day. 2〔기일·기한〕 time; days. ¶∼의 경과 the passage[lapse / progress] of time∥∼이 경과함에 따라 as time passes[goes by] / as the days go by / with the passing of time∥그것은 오랜 ∼이 걸리는 일이다 It will take a long time.

시작(始作) 1〔개시·착수〕 the beginning; the start; the opening; the commencement; the outset. ¶회의의 ∼은 자네가 맡아 주게 You open the meeting.∥저 봐 또 ∼이군 (어느 때의 버릇이) There he goes again! / Up to the same old thing again! / He is at it again. / (평소의 수작이) There! He is at his old tricks again.∥이것은 ∼에 지나지 않는다 This is a mere beginning. / This is only the beginning. ∥그것을 ∼으로 그는 많은 것을 발명했다 With that as a beginning[starter], he invented many things.∥그것을 ∼으로 해서 전국에 폭동이 일어났다 With that as a start, riots broke out throughout the country.∥그의 제안을 ∼으로 열띤 토의가 벌어졌다 His proposal was the start of[led to / brought on] as enthusiastic discussion.∥더위는 이제 ∼에 불과하다 This is only the beginning of the hot weather. / It has only just started to get hot.∥∼이 좋으면 끝도 좋다 A good beginning makes a good ending. **시작하다** begin; start; open; commence; make a start [beginning]; initiate; set about; take to; enter into[upon]; take up; fall to (doing); embark in[(up)on]. ¶웃기 ∼ begin to laugh

/ burst out laughing // 음악[골프]을 ~ take up music[golf] // 처음부터 다시 ~ begin again // 비가 내리기 시작했다 It started raining. / It began[started] to rain. // 소설에 일단 손을 대기 시작하니까 술술 쓰여졌다 Once I got started on the novel, it wrote itself. // 그는 부친의 도움으로 사업을 시작했다 His father assisted him[got him started] in business. // 선생님은 수업을 시작하셨다 The teacher began his lesson. // 제1권부터 시작하자 Let's begin with the first volume. // 꽃이 피기 시작한다 The flowers are coming out [beginning to bloom]. // 그가 먼저 싸움을 시작했다 He was the one who started the fight. / He started it. // 나는 이제 막 일을 시작했다 I have just begun[set about] my work. / I have just gone[fallen / set] to work. // 아직 시작하지 마라 Don't start yet. // 점차 날씨가 따뜻해지기 시작한다 It is getting warmer day by day. // 학교는 3월 8일에 시작한다 School begins on March 8. // 나는 요즘 살이 찌기 시작했다 Recently I have put on weight. // 그는 점점 일에 싫증이 나기 시작했다 He got more and more tired of his job. // 모임은 몇 시에 시작합니까 When does the meeting? ➔ 그 계획은 막 시작되었다 The project has just been started[gotten under way / got afoot / got off the ground]. // 쇼는 마술 프로로 시작되었다 The show opened with a juggling act. // 사업이 순조롭게 시작되어 꽤 안심이 된다 I am so relieved (that) the business has started off well[gotten off to a good start]. // 전시회가 내주 월요일에 시작된다 The exhibition opens[will be opened] next Monday. // 장마는 6월 중순경에 시작된다 The rainy season sets in[starts] about the middle of June. // 전시회는 언제 시작됩니까 when does the exhibition open[start]?
2 [처음] origin; beginning. ¶서기의 ~ the beginning of the Christian Era. **시작하다** originate (in); have (its) origin[rise] (in); arise (from); begin. ➔¶이 의식은 고려 시대에 시작되었다 This ceremony originated[was begun] in the Goryeo Period. // 그 관습은 중국인에게서 시작되었다 The practice has originated with the Chinese. // 그 관습은 14세기에[청교도가 정착한 무렵부터] 시작된 것이다 The custom dates back to the 14th century [dates from the Puritan settlement]. // 인더스 강은 히말라야 산맥에서 시작된다 The Indus River has its source in[flows from] the Himalaya Mountains.

시작이 반이다(속담) Well begun is half done.; A good start is half the battle.
시작(詩作) [시를 지음] verse writing; versification; poeti(ci)zing. **시작하다** write[compose] a poem; write poetry; versify.
시작(試作) **1** [제작] trial manufacture [production]. **시작하다** manufacture[produce] by way of trial[experiment]; make (a machine) on an experimental basis. ¶그는 신식 제초기를 시작했다 He produced experimentally a new type of mowing machine. **2** (미술 작품 등의) a study; (프) an étude. **시작하다** write[compose / sculpture] as an experiment.
● **시작품** a trial product; an article [equipment] made on an experimental basis.
시장 hunger. **시장하다** hungry; (구어) starving; (속어) famishing. ¶몹시 ~ I'm hungry.

/ I am good and hungry. / I am (as) hungry as a hunter. / I haven't had anything to eat. / I am dying with hunger. / I have a wolf in my stomach. / I'm starving. / I'm famished.
시장이 반찬(속담) Hunger is the best sauce.; A good appetite is a good sauce.
● **시장기**(-氣) hunger. ¶~를 느끼다 feel hungry / feel hunger / hunger // ~를 덜다 appease[alleviate / allay] one's hunger.
시장(市長) a mayor; (스코틀랜드의) a provost. ¶런던 ~ the Lord Mayor of London // 서울 ~ the Mayor of Seoul // ~ 임기 중에 during one's mayoralty // ~ 관사 a mayor's mansion // ~ 부인 a mayoress.
● **시장 선거** a mayoral(ty) election. **시장 직** mayoralty; mayorship.
시장(市場) a market; a mart; a market place; [거래소] an exchange. ¶공개 ~ an open market // 구매자 ~ a buyer's market // 국내 ~ a domestic [home] market // (노천의) 고물 ~ a flea market // 금융 ~ the financial [money] market / the investment market // 노동 ~ the labor market // 도매[소매] ~ a wholesale [retailing / retail] market // 암 ~ a black market [mart] // 어~ a fish market // 외국[해외] ~ an oversea(s) [a foreign] market // 자본 ~ the capital market // 주식 ~ the stock market [exchange] // 청과(물) ~ a vegetable and fruit market // 투기 ~ the speculative market // 투자 ~ the investment market // 현물 ~ a spot market // 판매자 ~ a seller's market // ~에 내다 put [place] (goods) on the market / bring [take] (goods) to market / market (a product) // 농작물을 ~에 내놓다 take [bring] crops to market // ~에 나오다 come onto the market / come into [on] the market / be put [placed] on the market / hit the market / be offered for sale / be up for sale / go on sale // 신상품의 ~을 개척하다 cultivate [open up / develop] a market for a new product // ~을 확장하다 extend [expand] a market (for goods) // ~을 독점하다 engross [swipe] the market // 해외 ~을 개척하다 develop an overseas market // ~ 개방을 요구하다 demand the opening of a market // ~은 부진 상태에[약세에] The market is flat [dull / slack / weak / stagnant] // 그 신형 차들은 지금 ~에 나와 있다 Those new model cars are on the market now.
시장(을) 보다 go to market; do some shopping [make purchases] at a market.
● **시장 가격** market prices; a market rate. **시장 경제** the market economy. **시장성** marketability. ¶이런 냉장고는 ~이 있다[없다] This kind of refrigerator is marketable [unmarketable]. **시장 점유율** a (market) share. **시장 조사** a market survey; a market research (시장 자체에 대한); a marketing research (시장 활동 전반에 걸친).
시재(時在) **1** [당장 가지고 있는 돈·곡식] the amount on hand; goods [grain] on hand; goods [grain] in stock. **2** now; presently. ⇨ 현재1
시적(詩的) poetic; poetical. ¶~ 감흥이 일다 feel [have] a poetic inspiration [urge].
시적거리다 do [speak] reluctantly [unwillingly / grudgingly]; do [speak] slowly [tardily / sluggishly / listlessly].
시절(時節) **1** a season. ⇨ 계절 ¶꽃피는

the flower season // ~에 맞는 seasonable // ~에 맞지 않는 out of season / unseasonable. **2** [일정한 시기] the time; an occasion; days. ¶젊은[청년] ~ one's early[youthful / young] days / the time of one's youth // 고난의 ~ one's dark days / one's hard times // 지난 ~ the good old days // 소년의 한순간의 사랑 a fleeting love of one's boyhood. // 저 거지도 한때는 좋은 ~이 있었다 The beggar has seen better days.

시점(時點) a point in[of] time. ¶현~에서 at present / at this time[stage] // 현~의 상황 the present situation // 현~에 이르기까지 사태는 개선되지 않았다 To date the situation has not improved. // 현~에서 우리가 제공할 수 있는 정보는 그것뿐이다 As of now, that is all the information we can give you. // 그~에서는 그 사실을 인정할 수밖에 없었다 At that point there was nothing for it but to admit the truth. // 우리는 2월 10일(오후 5시)의 ~에서 수색을 중단했다 We stopped the search as of February 10 (at five p.m.). // 이 ~에서는 그것이 최선의 길일지도 모른다 That may be the best we can do at this stage [point / juncture].

시접 [옷 솔기 속으로 접혀 들어간 부분] a margin to sew up[to seam].

시정(市井) **1** [인가가 모인 곳] a town; a street; streets. ¶~의 소문 common gossip // ~의 사람 the man in the street // 그는 ~의 사람으로 일생을 보냈다 He passed his life as an ordinary citizen. **2** [시정아치] a market dealer[trader / tradesman / merchant].

시정(市政) municipal[city] administration [government]. ¶~의 개혁[쇄신] (make) a civic[municipal] reform // ~에 참여하다 participate in municipal government.

시정(是正) correction. **시정하다** correct; put right; rectify; set (something) to rights. ¶사회의 폐습을 ~ put right[(문어) redress] social abuses. ➔잘못은 즉시 시정되지 않으면 안 된다 A mistake must be corrected promptly.

시정(施政) administration; government. **시정하다** administer; govern.
●**시정 방침** an administrative policy; (정당의) a party line. **시정 연설** an administrative policy speech; a speech on one's administrative policies[program].

시정(詩情) poetic(al) sentiment. ¶~이 풍부한 사람 a man full of poetic sentiment.

시제(時制) [언] a tense. ¶현재[미래 / 완료] ~ the present[future / perfect] tense // 과거 ~ the past tense / the preterit(e) (tense).

시제(時祭) ancestor-memorial services performed in each season of the year.

시제(詩題) a subject[theme] for a poem.

시조(始祖) the founder; the originator; the father; the progenitor. ¶한국 천주학의 ~ the originator of Catholic studies in Korea // 영시의 ~ the father of English poetry // 조선의 ~ the founder of Joseon.

시조(時調) a sijo; a three-verse[-stanza] Korean ode[poem]. ¶~를 읊다 recite a sijo.

시조새(始祖—) [동] an archaeopteryx (pl. -es); an archaeornis.

시종(始終) **1** [처음과 끝] the beginning and the end. **2** [처음부터 끝까지] from start [beginning] to finish[end]; from first to last; all the time[while]; all[right] along; all the way; all through; throughout. ¶~일관 consistently // ~여일하다 be consistent / be all the same from beginning to end // 그녀는 ~ 침묵을 지키고 있었다 She kept[remained] silent throughout[the whole time]. // 그는 ~ 의견을 바꾸지 않았다 He did not change his opinion from beginning to end. // 그 모임에서 그는 ~ 미소를 짓고 있었다 He had a smile on his face the whole time he was at the party.

시종(侍從) a chamberlain; a lord[gentleman] in waiting.

시주(施主) [불] (사람) a donor; an offerer; a benefactor; (행위) donation; offering; oblation. **시주하다** offer; make an offering (to a temple); donate.

시중 attendance; attending; waiting on; serving; (식탁에서의) service (at table). **시중하다** attend (on); wait on[upon]; serve (a person); do (a person) a service; take care of. ¶환자를 ~ attend[care for] an invalid // 부모를 ~ take care of[wait upon] one's parents.

시중(市中) (in) the city[town / streets]. ¶~에(서) in the city[town] / on[in] the streets // ~의 경기는 어떻습니까 How does trade go in the town?
●**시중 금리** the open market (interest) rate; the commercial (interest) rate. **시중 은행** a city[commercial] bank.

시중들다 attend (on); wait on[upon]; serve (a person); do (a person) a service; take care of. ¶남편을 ~ take care of[wait upon] one's husband. // 그 내외는 병든 부모를 정성껏 시중들었다 The couple took good care of their sick parents.

시즌 a season. ¶야구[수영] ~ the baseball [bathing] season.

시진(視診) an ocular inspection. ¶~만으로 …이라고 진단하다 make an ocular inspection of (a patient) and diagnose his illness as (neurosis). **시진하다** make an ocular inspection; visually examine.

시집(媤—) one's husband's home[family]; the family a woman marries into; (구어) a woman's in-laws. ¶~ 식구들 a woman's in-laws // ~에서 쫓겨나다 be compelled to leave her husband's home.
●**시집살이** a woman's married life[housekeeping] (in the home of her husband's parents). ¶~에 고생하다 lead a hard married life (in one's parents-in-law's home).

시집(詩集) a collection of poems; collected poems; an anthology(명시선). ¶「키츠 ~」 (저서명) The Poetic Works[The Collected Poems] of Keats.

시집가다(媤—) marry (a man / into a family); be[get] married to (a doctor / lawyer); take a husband. ¶좋은 데로 ~ marry[be married] well / get well married / make a good marriage // 시집간 여자 a married woman // 시집갈 준비를 하다 prepare for marriage // 그녀는 상인한테 시집갔다 She married a merchant. // 그녀는 홍씨 집안으로 시집갔다 She married into the Hong family. // 딸 셋이 다 시집갔다 Our three daughters have been married off. // 그녀는 시집갈 나이가 지났다 She is past marriageable age. // 그녀도 이젠 시집갈 나이다 She is old enough

시집보내다 to be [get] married. / She has reached a marriageable age.

시집보내다 (媤-) give (one's daughter) (away) in marriage; marry (one's daughter to a man [into another's family]); marry (one's daughter) off. ¶작년에 큰딸을 시집보냈다 I gave my oldest daughter in marriage last year.

시차 (時差) 1 [지방시의 차] a [the] difference in time; a time difference. ¶서울과 런던과는 9시간의 ~가 있다 There is nine-hour [There is nine hours'] difference between Seoul and London time. / There is a nine-hour difference in time between Seoul and London. 2 [천] the equation of time.

●**시차제** staggering work-hour system. ¶~ 출근 differentiation of office attendance hours / (adopt) staggered office [commuting] hours // 도로가 붐비지 않도록 출근 시간을 ~로 하다 stagger office hours so that roads will not be crowded.

시차 (視差) [천] parallax.

시찰 (視察) (an) inspection; observation. **시찰하다** inspect; make an inspection of (a school); visit. ¶현장을 ~ make an on-the-spot inspection / take a view of the scene // 현지를 ~ make an on-site inspection (of) / have an on-the-spot look (at Vietnam) // 여러 학교를 ~ inspect [make an inspection of] various schools // 공장을 ~ inspect a factory // 그는 암 연구 시설을 시찰하기 위해 도미했다 He went to the United Sates to inspect [visit] cancer research facilities.

●**시찰단** an inspection team [party]. **시찰 여행** an inspection [observation] tour; a tour of inspection; a trip to observe (dam construction methods); a study tour.

시채 (市債) a municipal [city] loan [debt]; a municipal bond. (채권)

시책 (施策) (정책) a measure; a policy; (시행) enforcement of a policy. ¶~을 잘못하다 take a wrong measure [step] // 오염 방지 ~을 시행하다 put an antipollution policy into effect. **시책하다** enforce [execute] a policy.

시청 (市廳) a municipal [city] office; (청사) a city [municipal] hall; the City Administration Building. ¶~ 직원 a city [municipal] official // 그는 ~에 근무하고 있다 He's a local government official. / He works at City Hall.

시청 (視聽) looking and listening; [주의] attention. ¶텔레비전 ~료 a TV subscription fee. **시청하다** look and listen; see and hear. ¶TV를 ~ teleview / watch television.

●**시청률** [TV] a program [an audience] rating; (popularity) rating. ¶~이 높은 프로 a popular program / ~이 가장 높은 텔레비전 프로 the top-rated TV program // 그 프로의 ~은 30%이다 That program has an audience rating of thirty percent. **시청자** [TV] a (TV) viewer; a televiewer; 《집합적》 the TV audience.

시청각 (視聽覺) (the senses of) sight and hearing; the visual and auditory senses.

●**시청각 교실** an audio-visual classroom; a language laboratory. **시청각 교육** audio-visual education. **시청각 교재** audio-visual materials [aids].

시체 (屍體) a corpse; a (dead) body; (동물의) carcass. ¶~ 더미 heaps of corpses // 타살 ~ the body of a murdered person // ~로 발견되다 be found dead // ~를 발견하다 find [recover] a body // ~를 안치하다 lay the remains in state // ~를 인도하다 hand (a person's) body over (to) // ~를 인수하겠다고 하다 claim the body. // 그 ~의 신원은 알아낼 수 없었다 It was impossible to identify the body.

●**시체 검안** a post-mortem (examination). **시체 부검** an autopsy. **시체 유기** abandonment of a dead body. **시체 해부** dissection of a dead body; necrotomy; (검시를 위한) an autopsy; a post-mortem examination; (구어) a post-mortem; necroscopy.

시초 (始初) the beginning: the inception; the start; the outset; [기원] the origin; the source; the genesis; (원인) the cause. ¶만물의 ~ the genesis of things // 싸움의 ~ the original cause [ground] of the quarrel.

시추 (試錐) drilling; boring. ¶석유 ~ oil(-well) drilling.

●**시추기** (-機) a drill; a drilling machine. **시추선** an oil drilling ship [rig].

시치다 tack; baste.

시치미 feigned [assumed] innocence [ignorance]; false pretense; dissimulation.

시치미(를) 떼다 feign [affect] ignorance [innocence]; play [do] (the) innocent; pretend to be ignorant (of); pretend not to know; assume an air of innocence; keep a straight face; wear [put on] an innocent look; keep a straight face; put on a blank [poker] face. ¶시치미를 떼고 with an air of innocence / affecting innocence [ignorance] / pretending not to know / as if nothing had happened / with a nonchalant look // 나는 시치미를 떼고 물어보았다 I asked him about it as if I did not know. // 그는 시치미를 떼고 있다 He is putting an air of innocence. // 그녀는 끝끝내 시치미를 떼려고 했다 She tried to brazen it out. // 나는 그것에 대해서 시치미를 떼었다 I feigned ignorance about it. / I pretended ignorance [to know nothing] about it. // 경찰관의 심문에 대해 그녀는 아들의 거처를 모른다고 시치미를 뗐다 In answer to the policeman's questions, she pretended to have no knowledge of her son's whereabouts.

시침 (時針) (시계의) the hour [short] hand.

시침질 tacking; basting. **시침질하다** tack; baste.

시커멓다 deep-black; blackhearted. ⇨ 시꺼멓다

시큰둥하다 [건방지다] impertinent; saucy; pert; forward; cheeky; impudent; smart aleck; (미국 구어) fresh. ¶시큰둥한 대답 a pert answer / a saucy reply // 시큰둥하게 말하다 talk impudently (to) / give (a person) cheek.

시큰시큰 with an arthritic pain. ⇨ 시근시근

시큼하다 sourish; somewhat sour; vinegarish.

시키다 (강제) make (a person do); cause (a person to do); force [compel] (a person to do); induce (a person to do); (허락·방임) let (a person do); allow (a person to do); (부탁·의뢰) get (a person to do); have (a person do); (일러서) tell (a person to do); bid (a person do); (주문) order (something from a person / a person to do); call for (an ice

cream). ¶일을 ～ make (a person) work / put (a person) to work // 노래를 ～ have (a person) sing a song / ask (a person) to sing // 극장 구경을 ～ treat (a person) to a show / 서울 구경을 ～ show (a person) round[over] Seoul // 아들에게 대학 공부를 ～ give one's son a university education / let one's son go to college // 불고기[국수]를 ～ order *bulgogi* [noodles] // 식사 준비를 ～ have (the waiter) prepare the table // 의사를 부르도록 ～ send (a person) (out) for a doctor // 시키는 대로 하다 do as one is told (to do) // 그 일은 제게 시켜 주십시오 Let me do it, please. // 그는 시키는 대로 그곳에 갔다 He went there as ordered. // 그는 논문을 남을 시켜서 타자로 찍게 했다 He had someone [got someone to] type his essay. / He had [got] his essay typed. // 가까운 가게에서 불고기를 시켜 먹자 I'll order *bulgogi* to be delivered from a nearby shop. // 나는 식당에서 카레라이스를 시켰다 I ordered curry and rice at the restaurant. // 저 녀석이 시키는 대로 행동하지 마라 Don't let him make you dance to his tune. // 그는 저 정치가가 시키는 대로 하고 있다 He is at the beck and call[a cat's-paw] of that politician.
-**시키다** ¶구두를 수선～ have one's shoes mended // 연구를 ～ make (a person) study [research (into)] // 조사～ have (a person) investigate[inquire (into)] // 우리는 그를 자백시키지 못했다 We failed to produce confession from him. // 그놈이 내 딸을 임신시켰다 The guy got my daughter with child.
시트¹ [자리] a seat. ¶그 자동차의 뒤쪽 ～는 세 사람이 앉을 만큼 충분히 넓다 The back seat of the car is wide enough for three people.
시트² (침대의) a (bed) sheet; sheeting. ¶(침대의) ～를 갈다[깔다] change[spread] a sheet.
시트르산(-酸) [화] citric acid.
시판(市販) marketing; sale at a market. ¶공동 ～ joint marketing. **시판하다** market; put [place] (goods) on the market; place on sale; sell at a market. ➜시판되고 있는 공책 a notebook sold[obtainable] at a store // 시판되다 come into the market // 이 물건은 이미 시판되고 있다 This article is already on the market.
시퍼렇다 1 deep blue; (안색이) deadly [ghastly] pale; pallid. ¶시퍼런 바다 the deep blue sea // 시퍼런 호수 a sapphire lake / emerald waters of the lake // 시퍼렇게 멍 들도록 때리다[꼬집다] beat[pinch] (a person) black and blue 2 (당당하다) powerful; influential; stately. ¶권세가 ～ be very powerful [influential] // 서슬이 ～ have a threatening [menacing] look[attitude].
시퍼렇게 살아 있다 be in the land of the living; remain on two legs.
시편(詩篇) 1 [책 속의 시 부분] the poetry section (of a book). 2 [시를 편찬한 책] a book of poems; a volume of poetry. 3 [성] the Book of Psalms; the Psalms(약어 Ps., Psa.).
시평(時評) comments[criticism] on current events[topics]; (신문 지상의) leaderettes; (미) editorial comments[notes]. ¶문예 ～ comments on current literature.
● **시평란** a column on current events.
시풍(詩風) a style of poetry; a poetical style.
시하(侍下) [부모나 조부모를 모시고 있는 사람] a person supporting his parents[grandparents].
시하(時下) [이때] now; at present; at this time of (the) year. ¶～ 춘난지제(春暖之際)에 in this season of warm spring.
시학(詩學) study of poetry; poetics(시론); prosody(운율법).
시한(時限) a time limit; a deadline; [폐문 시간] closing time; lockup. ¶법적 ～ the legal deadline.
● **시한폭탄** a time bomb; a delayed action bomb.
시할머니(媤-) one's husband's grandmother.
시할아버지(媤-) one's husband's grandfather.
시합(試合) (주로 오락으로서) a game; (테니스·크리켓 등의) a match; a contest; an event; a bout; a meet; a tilt; (권투의) a fight; (미국 속어) an encounter; (일련의) a tournament; (연속적인) a series; [시합하기] play; playing. ¶첫 ～ the first game / (야구에서, 더블헤더의) the opener // 연습[야간] ～ a practice [night] game // 야구 ～ a baseball game // 테니스 ～ a tennis match // 열띤 ～ a heated game[match] // ～에 나가다 take part in a game // ～에 이기다[지다] win[lose] a match [game / bout / tournament] // ～의 막(幕)을 열다 open[start] a game / play ball // ～을 제의하다 challenge (a team) to a match [game] // ～을 포기하다 give up (hope of winning) a game // 농구 ～을 하다 have a basketball game (with) // 일방적인 ～이 되다 end in a one-sided affair // 내일 야구 ～이 있다 [자기가 참가함] We (are going to) have a baseball game tomorrow. / [자기가 선수로서 참가하지 않음] There is a baseball game tomorrow. // 그는 어제 테니스 ～에 출전했다 He took part in a tennis tournament yesterday. // 그녀는 그에게 탁구 ～을 제의했다 She challenged him to a game of ping-pong [table tennis].
시행(施行) enforcement; operation. **시행하다** (법률을) enforce; put in force; put into operation; give effect (to); carry into effect; execute; [실제로 행하다] carry out; conduct. ➜시행되다 be enforced / be put in force / come into force [operation] / become operative [effective] / take [go into] effect / (미) become effective // 시행되고 있다 be in force [operation] // 그 법률은 아직 시행되지 않고 있다 The law is not yet in force [being forced] (▶ be in force는 법률이 유효하다, be enforced는 정해진 법률을 지키게 하고 있음을 뜻함).
● **시행 규칙** enforcement regulations; regulations relative to the application [enforcement] of a law. **시행령** an Enforcement Ordinance.
시행착오(試行錯誤) trial and error. ¶그는 많은 ～ 끝에 그 발명에 성공했다 He succeeded in the invention after many trials and errors. // 나는 ～ 끝에 그것을 완성했다 I completed it after repeated trial and error.
시향(時享) (가묘에의) seasonal ancestral rites; (산소에의) an annual ancestral feast.
시험(試驗) 1 […에 대한 평가] (문어) an examination; (구어) an exam; a test; (교실에서 간단히 행하는) (미) a quiz (*pl.* quizzes); an interview(면접). ¶수학[영어] ～ an exami-

nation in mathematics [English] // 경쟁 [구두] ~ a competitive [an oral] examination // 국가 ~ a state examination // 기말 ~ a term examination // 모의 ~ a sham examination // 본 [예비] ~ a final [preliminary] examination // 자격 ~ a qualifying examination // 중간 ~ a midterm examination / (구어) the midterm // 채용 [선발] ~ an examination for service [selection] // 최종 [졸업] ~ the final examination / (구어) the finals // 진급 ~ an exam(ination) for promotion // 추가 ~ a supplementary exam(ination) // 취직 ~ an examination for employment / employment examination // 필기 ~ a written examination / an examination on paper // 학과 ~ examinations on academic subjects // 학기말 [학년말 / 임시] ~ a term [an annual / a special] examination // 어려운 ~ a stiff examination // ~ 성적 통지서 a report of one's score on a test // 무~으로 without examination // ~을 치다 [치르다 / 보다] go [come] up for an examination / take [(문어) sit for] an examination / undergo an examination / go in for an exam // 영어 ~을 보다 have an examination in English / examine (a class) in English // ~에 합격하다 [붙다] pass an examination [a test] / succeed [be successful] in an examination // ~에 떨어지다 [낙제하다] fail in an examination [a test] / fail an examination / (미국 구어) flunk a quiz // ~을 감독하다 proctor an examination / (영) invigilate // ~에 나오다 (문제가) be asked [given] in an examination // 대리 ~을 치게 하다 get (another) to sit for the examination for [in place of] one // ~ 중이다 The examination is going on now. // 오늘은 역사 ~이 있다 We have an examination [exam] in history today. / We have a history test today. / 그는 ~에 합격 [낙제] 했다 He passed [failed] the examination [test]. / 이 학교에 입학하려면 ~을 치러야 한다 Entrance to this school is through examination. // 그 문제가 ~에 나왔다 The question is asked in the examination. // 나는 ~ 채점에 바쁘다 I am busy looking over the examination papers. // ~ 잘 쳤나 How have you fared in your exam? 시험하다 conduct [hold / give / set] an examination; give [make] a test; test; examine (pupils) in (English). ¶시험한 후에 on [through / after] examination.

2 (실험) an experiment; a test; a trial; a try. ¶강도 [내구성] ~ a strength [durability] test // 성능 ~ an efficiency test // ~ 삼아 by way of experiment [trial] / experimentally / on [for] trial / tentatively / as a test [an experiment] // ~ 삼아 해 보다 try / have a try (at) / make an attempt (at) / give (a thing) a trial / do (something) on [as a] trial / try one's hand (at) / take chances (with) // ~ 삼아 고용하다 employ (a person) by way of experiment [on a trial basis] / engage (a person) on trial [probation] / hire (a person) tentatively // 한 달 동안 ~ 삼아 써 보다 give (a person) a month's trial // ~ 삼아 써 보다 give a thing a trial / try using a thing to see how it works // ~ 삼아 먹어 [마셔] 보다 try / taste / sample // ~ 삼아 해 보라 Just try it. / (구어) Give it a try. / Have a try (at it). / Take a chance (망하든 흥하든). // 성능 ~을 하다 conduct [run] an efficiency test (on a new model) // 마이크 ~ 중입니다 Testing, testing, testing. One, two, three testing. // 이 신식 가스노로는 ~ 중이다 This new gas heater is being tested. // 이 신약은 아직 ~ 단계에 있다 This new medicine is still in the experimental stage. // 새 차는 ~이 끝났다 The new car has successfully passed the test it was subjected to. // ~ 결과는 우수하였다 It proved excellent on trial. // ~필 (게시) Tried. // ~ 삼아 이 약을 먹어 보겠다 I will try this medicine. 시험하다 experiment (a substance); make an experiment (on / with / in); test; put (a thing) to trial [the test]; give (a thing) a trial; try (out); have a try at; make a trial (with / of). ¶기계를 ~ test a machine // 인물을 ~ put a person's character to the test / measure a person's character // 시험한 후에 on [upon] trial.

●시험 과목 the subjects for examination; an examination subject. 시험관 (~官) an examiner; an examinant. 시험관 (~管) a test tube. 시험관 아기 a test-tube baby; a tube-baby. 시험 문제 questions (for an examination); a test [an examination] question. 시험 발사 a test fire; test-firing. 시험 비행 a test [a trial / an experimental] flight; a flying test. ¶~을 하다 test-fly (an airplane) // ~은 성공했다 The trial flight was successful. 시험장 (학교의) an examination hall [room]; [시험소] a laboratory; a [an experimental] station. ¶농업 ~ an agricultural experiment station. 시험지 an examination paper; [화] a test [litmus] paper.

시현 (示現) revelation; manifestation. 시현하다 reveal; manifest.

시형 (詩形) a form of verse; a verse [poetic] form.

시혜 (施惠) favoring; a favor. 시혜하다 favor; do (a person) a favor; bestow a favor on (a person).

시호 (諡號) a posthumous name [title]. ¶~를 내리다 give a posthumous name (to).

시화 (詩畵) [시와 그림] a poem and a picture; [그림을 곁들인 시] an illustrated [a pictorial] poem.

●시화전 an exhibition of illustrated poems (by).

시화법 (視話法) visible speech.

시황 (市況) market conditions; the tone [condition / position / movements] of the market; the market (position). ¶불안정한 ~ an unsteady market // 활발한 ~ an active [a brisk / a free] market // ~은 침체 상태에 있다 The market is dull [idle].

시효 (時效) [법] prescription; [화] ag(e)ing. ¶취득 [소멸] ~ acquisitive [extinctive] prescription / positive [negative] prescription // ~에 걸리다 be barred [extinguished] by prescription / prescribe / lapse // ~에 걸리지 않다 be unprescribed // ~에 의하여 권리를 주장하다 prescribe (for / to) // 경찰은 ~가 지났기 때문에 범인을 체포할 수 없었다 The police couldn't arrest the criminal because the statute of limitations had run out.

●시효 기간 the period of prescription. 시효 중단 / 시효 정지 interruption [suspension] of prescription.

시흥 (詩興) poetic inspiration. ¶~이 일다 feel poetically inspired / be inspired to verse // 달을 보고 있으니 ~이 일었다 The moon

inspired me to compose a poem.
식(式) 1 [의식] a ceremony; rituals; rites(종교상의); 《집합적》 rituals; a (ceremonial) functions; a celebration; an observance; 〔미〕 (inauguration) exercises. ¶ ~을 거행하다 [올리다] hold [have / perform] a ceremony / celebrate (a wedding) // ~을 사회하다 preside at a ceremony // ~의 날짜를 정하다 fix a day for a ceremony.
2 [방식] a method; [논] a system; [양식] a style; a form; a type; a fashion; a mode; a way; a manner; [건] [기둥 양식] an order. ¶ 가르치는 ~ a method of teaching / a teaching method // 이런[저런] ~으로 in this[that] way[manner] / like this[that] / after this [that] fashion // ~을 따르다 conform to forms // ~을 갖추어 딸을 결혼시키다 marry one's daughter in proper style // 하는 ~을 터득하다 get the hang (of) / catch [acquire] the knack (of) // 이런 ~으로 써라 Write in this way[manner]. / Write like this. // 어떤 ~의 집을 원하십니까 What style of house do you want? // 편지의 겉봉은 이런 ~으로 쓰는 거야 This is the way to write an address on an envelope. / This is how to address an envelope. // 나는 내 ~으로 일한다 I have my own way of doing things. // 그런 ~으로 해서는 안 된다 Don't do it that way[like that].
3 [수] an expression; [화] a formula (*pl.* ~s, -lae); [방정식] an equation. ¶ 구조~ a structural[constitutional] formula // 대수~ an algebraic expression // 2항~ a binomial expression [formula] / a binominal // 분자~ a molecular formula // 화학~ a chemical formula // ~으로 나타내다 formularize / formulate.

-식(式) 1 [의식] a ceremony; rituals; rites(종교상의); 《집합적》 rituals; a (ceremonial) functions; a celebration; an observance; 〔미〕 (inauguration) exercises. ¶ 개회[폐회]~ opening[closing] exercises // 세례~ rites of baptism // 장례~ a funeral (service) / funeral rites.
2 [방식] a method; a system; [양식] a style; a form; a type; a fashion; a mode; a way; a manner. ¶ 미국~ 교육 the American method of education // 존스~ 발음 기호 the Jones's system of phonetic notation // 고딕~ 건축 Gothic architecture // 순 한국~ 가옥 a house in pure Korean style // 미국~ 호텔 an American-style hotel // 영국~ 악센트 a British accent // 피카소~ 그림 a picture in Picasso's style [the style of Picasso] // 한국~ 사고방식 a Korean mode[way] of thinking // 한국~으로 인사하다 greet a person in the Korean fashion // 두 사람은 서양~으로 악수했다 They shook hands in Western fashion.
식각(蝕刻) [인] etching. ⇨ ˚부각(腐刻)
식간(食間) ¶ ~에 (eat) between meals // ~에 복약하다 take medicine between meals // 이 약은 ~에 복용해야 한다 This medicine is to be taken between meals.
식객(食客) a hanger-on (*pl.* hangers-on); a dependent; a parasite; a sponger. ¶ ~ 노릇을 하다 be a dependent [parasite] on (a person) / feed [live / sponge] on (a person) // ~이 되다 become a dependent (on) / eat (a person's) salt // 그는 우리 집의 ~ 노릇을 하고 있다 He lives off me.
식견(識見) knowledge; judgment; insight; discernment; vision; intelligence; [견해] one's view; opinions; ideas. ¶ ~이 높은 사람 a man of exalted ideas / a man of great insight.
식곤증(食困症) languor[languidness / drowsiness] after a meal.
식구(食口) mouths to feed; one's dependents; members of a family; one's family. ¶ ~ 수 the number of mouths to feed / the number of dependents // ~를 부양하다 support one's family // ~ 수를 줄이다 reduce the number of mouths to feed // ~가 많다[적다] have many [few] mouths to feed / have a large [small] family to support // ~가 많은 집 a large [big] family // ~가 늘다[줄다] have new [less] mouths to feed // 우리는 네 ~다 We are [Ours is] a family of four. / My family members are four. // 우리 집 ~들은 모두 남자다 The members of our household [family] are all men. // 그는 ~가 많아 생계가 어렵다 Having a large family to feed, he finds it hard to make both ends meet. // 그의 ~들은 모두 개를 좋아한다 Everyone in his family likes dogs. / Members of his family like dogs. // 그들은 ~ 수를 줄이기 위해 아들을 양자로 보냈다 In order to cut down [reduce] the number of mouths they had to feed, they had their son adopted by another family. // 그는 나를 한 ~처럼 대해 준다 He treats me like [as] one of the family.
식권(食券) a meal [food] ticket [coupon].
식기(食器) tableware; a table service; (정찬용) a dinner set; flatware(접시·나이프·포크·스푼 등); 〔영〕 (a piece of) plate(금·은제의). ¶ 40개로 된 ~ 한 벌 a table service of 40 pieces.
식다 1 [차게 되다] cool (down [off]); get cold. ¶ 다 식은 커피 stone-cold coffee // 식지 않도록 해 두다 keep (something) hot // 커피[수프]가 식어 버렸다 The coffee [soup] has got(ten) cool. // 식기 전에 수프를 드십시오 Help yourself to the soup before it cools [while it's hot]. // 차가 조금 식을 때까지 기다려라 Wait till the tea cools a little.
2 [줄거나 가라앉다] abate; subside; lapse back [away]; (열성 등이) flag; be dampened; cool down [off]. ¶ 열의가 ~ lose interest (in) / grow less enthusiastic // 열이 식었다 The fever has broken [dropped]. // 그 계획에 대한 나의 열의는 식어 버렸다 My enthusiasm for the project has cooled. // 그의 경마 열도 좀 식은 것 같다 His craze for horse racing seems to have cooled off a bit. // 오랫동안 헤어져 있는 사이에 그들의 애정은 식었다 During their long separation their love had cooled.
식은 죽 먹기(속담) an easy task[job]; 《구어》 a piece of cake.
식단(食單) a menu; a (menu) card; a bill of fare. ¶ ~을 짜다 make out a menu // ~을 보다 consult a menu.
식당(食堂) a dining room [hall]; (군대·공장 등의) a mess hall; (역·열차 내의) a refreshment room; (대학·수도원 등의) a refectory; [음식점] a restaurant; (삼류 식당) an eating house. ¶ 간이~ a lunchroom / 〔미〕 a lunch counter // ~ 바 a snack bar / a cafeteria (셀프서비스의) // 학생 ~ a students' dining hall // ~ 겸 부엌 a dining kitchen // ~은 부엌 옆에 있습니다 The dining room is

식대

next to the kitchen. // 점심은 대개 학교 ~에서 먹습니다 I usually eat my lunch in the lunchroom.
● **식당차** (미) a dining car; (영) a dining coach; (영) a restaurant car; a diner; (서서 먹는) a buffet[refreshment] car. ¶~를 **연결하다** attach a dining car to (a train) // 이 열차에는 ~가 연결되어 있습니다 This train has a dining car attached to it.

식대(食代) (식당의) the charge for food; (하숙의) (the charge for) board; (가정의) table expenses.

식도(食刀) a kitchen knife. ⇨ 식칼

식도(食道) 〔생〕 the gullet; the alimentary canal; the esophagus (pl. ~es, -gi).
● **식도암** cancer of the esophagus.

식도락(食道樂) epicurism; epicureanism; gourmandism; addiction to the pleasures of the table. ¶~의 epicurean.
● **식도락가** an epicure; a gourmet; a gourmand. ¶그는 ~다 He is given to luxury in eating[addicted to the pleasures of the table]. / He is (quite) an epicure.

식량(食量) one's eating capacity.

식량(食糧) provisions; food. ⇨ ˚양식(糧食)1 ¶ **비상** ~ emergency rations // **예비** ~ a reserve of provisions // 3일분의 ~ food [provisions] for three days // ~**을 비축하다** stock[lay in] provisions // ~**을 공급하다** provide[supply] (a person) with food / provide food (for a person) / provision (a district) // ~**을 확보하다** secure foodstuffs // ~**이 떨어졌다** The provisions have run out. / We have run out of provisions. // ~**이 모자란다** The provisions have fallen[run] short. / We have run short of provisions. // ~**은 충분하다** We have enough food. / We have plenty of food. // 우리는 여행 갈 때 일 주일분의 ~을 갖고 갔다 We took a week's provisions on our journey.
● **식량난** the difficulty of obtaining food. **식량 문제** the food problem. ¶아프리카의 ~는 심각하다 The food problem in Africa is serious. **식량 위기** a food crisis[shortage].

식료(食料) food; foodstuffs; fare; victuals. ¶~**가 되다** be edible / be good to eat.
● **식료품** 〔음식의 재료가 되는 채소 등의 물품〕 an article of food; foodstuffs; 〔집합적〕 foodstuffs; provisions; groceries; eatables; victuals. **식료품점** a food store; (미) a grocery (store); (영) a grocer's (shop).

식모(食母) a kitchen maid; a maidservant; a maid; a housemaid; a (home) help; a domestic; (미) a domestic help. ¶~**를 두다** keep a kitchen maid // ~ **구함** 〔광고〕 Domestic servant[kitchen maid] wanted. / Help wanted. / Wanted a maid.
● **식모살이** domestic service. ¶~**를 하다** be in domestic service.

식목(植木) tree planting. **식목하다** plant trees; do planting.
● **식목일** a tree-planting day; (미) Arbor Day.

식물(植物) a plant; 〔집합적〕 vegetation; plant life; 〔한 지역·한 시대의 식물의 총칭〕 a flora (pl. ~s, -rae); the botany (of Korea). ¶**고산** 〔열대〕 ~ an alpine[a tropical] plant // **기생** ~ a parasitic plant / a phytoparasite // **다년생** ~ a perennial (plant) // **양성** ~ a sun plant // **음성**〔음지〕 ~ a shade plant // **현화**(顯花)〔**은화**(隱花)〕 ~ a flowering[flowerless] plant / a phanerogam[cryptogam] // **한국** ~ **도감** a pictorial[an illustrated] book of the Korean flora // ~**의 분포** a geographical distribution of plants // ~**을 채집하다** collect plants / botanize.
● **식물계** the vegetable[plant] kingdom. **식물상**(一相) a flora. **식물성** vegetability; vegetable property[nature]. ¶~**의** vegetable. **식물원** botanical gardens. **식물인간** a (human) vegetable. ¶~**으로 살아가다** (구어) live as a cabbage[vegetable] / keep alive at a vegetable level. **식물 채집** plant collecting; botanization; herborization. ¶~**을 하러 가다** go botanizing[herborizing / plant collecting] (in / at). **식물학** botany; phytology.

식민(植民) colonization; settlement; (사람) a colonist; a settler; a colonial. **식민하다** colonize (in) (a land); settle (in) (a region); plant (a country) with colonists.
● **식민 정책** a colonial[colonization] policy; colonialism. **식민주의** colonialism. **식민지** a colony; a settlement; 〔영〕 a plantation. ¶**해외** ~ an overseas colony // ~**를 건설하다** found [establish / settle] a colony / plant a settlement[colony]. **식민지화** colonialization. ¶~**하다** colonialize / bring (another nation) into subjection by colonialism.

식별(識別) discrimination; identification; discernment. ¶**색각**[**색깔**] ~ color vision. **식별하다** discriminate[distinguish] (A from B / between A and B); discern; tell[separate] (A) from (B). ¶**식별할 수 없을 정도로** indistinguishably / beyond[out of] recognition / **진위를** ~ winnow the false from the true / winnow truth from falsehood // 어둠 속에서 사람들의 얼굴을 ~ distinguish people's faces in the darkness.
● **식별력** discriminating power; judgment.

식복(食福) one's luck[blessing] of having things to eat. ¶~**이 있다** be blessed with things to eat.

식비(食費) food expenses; (the charge for) board(하숙의); table expenses(가정의). ¶**매월 10만 원의** ~**를 내다** pay 100,000 won for one's board every month // ~**를 줄이다**〔**절약하다**〕 cut down on one's food expenses[what one pays for food] // ~**는 얼마나 내고 있느냐** How much do you pay for your board? // **방값과** ~**로 한 달에 30만 원을 내고 있다** I pay 300,000 won a month for room and board. // ~**로 매달 10만 원씩 받고 있다** I receive a monthly food allowance of 100,000 won.

식빵(食—) (a loaf[slice] of) bread; sandwich bread.(▶ 얇게 썬 것은 sliced bread, 썰지 않은 것은 loaf of bread라고 함)

식사(式辭) an address; a message; an oration(격식을 차린 것). ¶**졸업식** ~ (미) a commencement address / (영) a graduation address(▶ 대학의) / (영) a speech at the final assembly(▶ 대학 이하의) // ~**를 하다**〔**낭독하다**〕 give[read] an address.

식사(食事) a meal; dinner; fare; a diet(특히 규정된); board(기숙의). ¶**간단한**〔**간소한**〕 ~ simple[frugal] meal / a homely fare // **야채만의** ~ a vegetable diet // **가벼운** ~ a light meal // **충분한**〔**실속 있는**〕 ~ a good[substantial / square] meal // **호사스런** ~ sumptuous dinner // **형편없는** ~ (구어) a shocking dinner // **일정한**〔**제한된**〕 ~ a restricted meal

한국인의 ~ 습관 the eating[dietary] habits of the Koreans // ~ 중에 during a meal / at table // 전[후]에 before[after] meal / ~ 제공 월 30만 원의 방 a room with board [meals] at three hundred thousand won a month // ~ 중이다 be at table // ~ 준비를 하다 (요리의) prepare [(미) fix] a meal / (식탁의) set the table / lay the cloth / get a meal ready // ~ 대접을 하다 treat (a person) to a meal / serve (a person) with a meal / dine (a person) // ~에 초대받다 be asked[invited] to dinner // (남을) ~에 초대하다 invite[ask] a person to dinner // ~를 제한하다 (환자의) put (a patient) on a (restricted) diet / diet (a person) // ~를 함께하다 dine[have a meal] with (a person) // 우리는 하루에 세 번 ~를 한다 We have[eat] three meals a day. // 그는 지금 ~ 중이다 He is eating[in the middle of his meal] now. // 나의 아침 ~는 보통 빵과 우유다 My morning meal usually consists of bread and milk. // ~ 준비가 아직 안 되었나 Isn't breakfast[lunch / supper] ready yet? // ~ 준비가 다 되었으니까 드십시오 Dinner is served [ready / set]. // 오늘 저녁에는 밖에서 ~를 하자 Let's eat[(문어) dine] out tonight. // 의사는 내 ~를 제한했다 The doctor put me on a (restricted) diet. // 나는 ~를 제한하여 체중이 10파운드 줄었다 I lost ten pounds by dieting. // 하숙인들의 ~는 그녀가 차린다 She prepares meals for the roomers. // 20명분의 ~가 준비되어 있습니다 Dinner[A table] has been laid[set] for twenty persons. // ~ 중에 말을 많이 하지 마라 Don't talk too much at meal. // 그는 세 끼 ~보다 영화 보기를 더 좋아한다 He'd rather see movies than eat. **식사하다** have [take] a meal; dine; eat. ¶급히 ~ eat a hurried meal / 제때에 ~ have regular mealtimes // 밖에서 ~ have one's meal [dinner] out / dine[eat] out // 식사하면서 이야기하다 talk at table // 식사하러 나감 (게시) Out to lunch.
● **식사법** table manners. **식사 시간** a mealtime; a dinnertime. ¶~**이다** It is time for dinner.

식상 (食傷) [배탈] a stomach trouble; indigestion; [물림] surfeit; glut. **식상하다** have a stomach trouble; suffer from indigestion; [물리다] be surfeited[cloyed / sated / satiated] (with); be fed up (with); glut oneself (with). ¶나는 인도에서 카레에 식상했다 I had so much curry in India that I got sick and tired of it. // 나는 그의 낙관론에는 식상하고 있다 I'm fed up with his optimistic talk. // 그런 얘기에는 이제 식상했다 I'm fed up with such talk. / I've had more than enough of such stories. // 이제 그런 경기라면 식상했다 I am fed up with that sort of game.

식생활 (食生活) (식사 전반에 관한) eating habits; (식사의 질·양) diet. ¶~의 변화 a change of diet / a change in one's eating [dietary] habits / 한국인의 ~ the eating [dietary] habits of the Koreans // ~을 보다 즐겁게 하다 add interest[variety] to what one eats[one's diet] / enhance the pleasure of the table // 체력을 증강하기 위해서는 ~을 개선해야 한다 You have to improve your diet [eating habits] to increase your (physical) strength.

식성 (食性) taste; preference; palate. ¶~에 맞는 음식 agreeable[favorite] food // ~에 맞다 suit[please] one's taste[palate] // ~이 까다롭다 be fastidious about food / have a delicate palate.

식수 (植樹) tree planting. ⇨식목

식수 (食水) drinking water; potable water.

식순 (式順) the program of a ceremony.

식식거리다 gasp (for breath); pant. ⇨씩씩거리다

식언하다 (食言-) [약속한 말을 안 지키다] go back on one's word; eat one's words; retract [break] one's words[promises].

식염 (食鹽) (table) salt; (common) salt.
● **식염수** a solution of salt; a saline solution.

식욕 (食慾) appetite; desire to eat. ¶~을 돋우는 냄새 an appetizing smell // 나는 오늘 ~이 좋다[없다] I have a good[a poor / no] appetite. // 젊은 사람들은 ~이 왕성하다 Young people have good[hearty] appetites. // 저 식당의 비프스테이크는 정말 ~을 돋운다 The steak at that restaurant really makes my mouth water[is really appetizing]. // 그는 ~이 왕성하다 He has a big[keen] appetite. // 나는 요즈음 ~이 증진[감퇴]됐다 Recently my appetite has increased[fallen off]. // 그 소식을 들으니 ~이 완전히 없어졌다 The news spoiled my appetite. / I lost my appetite when I heard the news.
● **식욕 감퇴** a decrease[falling-off] of appetite; a poor[dull / feeble] appetite; loss of appetite. **식욕 부진** lack[loss] of appetite; inappetence; anorexia.

식용 (食用) edibility; table use. ¶~의 edible / eatable // ~에 적합하다 be edible / be good [suitable] to eat // 깻잎을 ~으로 하다 use the leaves of sesame for food // ~으로 쓰이다 be used for food / be eaten as food. **식용하다** use (a thing) for food.
● **식용 개구리** an edible frog; a bullfrog. **식용 색소** food coloring. **식용유** cooking oil.

식육 (食肉) 1 [식용육] meat. 2 [육식] eating flesh. ¶~의 carnivorous. **식육하다** eat meat; be carnivorous.
● **식육 가공업자** a meat processor.

식은땀 (a) cold sweat (▶ cold perspiration이라고는 하지 않음). ¶~을 흘리다[흘리고 있다] break into[be in] a cold sweat // 그것은 지금 생각해도 ~이 날 지경이다 Even now I break into a cold sweat when I remember it. // 그는 이마에 구슬 같은 ~이 솟아났다 A cold sweat stood in beads upon his forehead.

식음 (食飮) eating and drinking. ¶~을 전폐하다 give up eating and drinking / fast. **식음하다** eat and drink.

식이 (食餌) a diet; [의] alima.
● **식이 요법** alimentotherapy; a diet[dietary] cure; a dietetic treatment. ¶나는 (체중을 줄이기 위해) ~을 하고 있다 I'm on a diet (to lose weight). / I am on a restricted diet. // 의사는 그에게 ~을 시켰다 The doctor put him on a diet.

식인 (食人) man-eating; cannibalism. ¶~의 man-eating / cannibal / cannibalistic.
● **식인종** cannibals; a cannibalistic tribe; a cannibal race; man-eaters.

식자 (植字) typesetting; composing; composition. ¶사진 ~ photo-letter composition / photographic lettering **식자하다** compose [set (up)] type.
● **식자공** a typesetter; a typo (pl. ~s); a compositor. **식자기** a typesetting[compos-

식자 ing] machine; a typesetter; a linotype. ¶사진 ~ a photocomposer // 자동 ~ a composing machine.

식자(識者) men of intelligence; intelligent [informed / intellectual] people; the wise; thinking people; persons of good sense; (집합적) intellectuals; the intelligentzia.

식자우환(識字憂患) Where ignorance is bliss, 'tis folly to be wise.; A little learning is dangerous thing.

식장(式場) the hall [place] of ceremony; the place where a ceremony is held; a ceremonial hall. ¶~은 어딥니까 Where is the ceremony (going) to be held?

식전(食前) ¶~에 [밥 먹기 전에] before a meal / [아침밥 먹기 전에] before breakfast / [아침 일찍이] early in the morning. // ~ 기도를 드리다 say grace. // ~에 한 알씩 드세요 Take a tablet before each meal.

식전(式典) a ceremony; a service. ⇨의식(儀式)

식중독(食中毒) [음식 중독] food poisoning. ¶~에 걸리다 get [suffer from] food poisoning / (음식이) disagree with one // 그는 ~에 걸린 것 같다 Something he ate seems to have disagreed with him. // 메스껍다. 뭔가 먹은 것이 ~을 일으킨 게 틀림없다 I feel sick. Something I ate must have disagreed with me. // 그는 상한 굴을 먹고 ~에 걸렸다 He got food poisoning by eating an oyster which had gone bad.

식체(食滯) indigestion; dyspepsia.

식초(食醋) vinegar. ¶~에 담그다 pickle in vinegar // 드레싱에 ~를 치다 add vinegar to salad dressing.

식충(食蟲) 1 insect-eating. 2 a glutton; a gourmand. ⇨식충이(⇨식충)
● **식충 식물** an insectivorous plant; a carnivore. **식충이** (탐식자) a glutton; a gourmand; a gorger; a belly-slave; [하는 일 없이 지내는 사람] a good-for-nothing.

식칼(食-) a kitchen knife; a cleaver; a butcher knife. ¶~ 가는 사람 a knife-sharpener // ~로 고기를 썰다 cut meat with a kitchen knife.

식탁(食卓) a (dining) table; the board; a mess table(합선의). ¶~ 예절 table manners // ~용의 for table use // ~에 앉다 sit down [take one's seat] at the table // ~을 준비하다 [치우다] set [clear] the table // ~에 둘러앉다 sit around the table // ~에 앉아 주십시오 Please take your seat at the table. // ~에서는 즐거운 화제를 고르도록 해야 한다 You must try to choose pleasant topics (of conversation) at (the) table(▶ (미)에서는 흔히 the를 붙임).
● **식탁보** a cloth; a tablecloth. **식탐. 식탐하다** be greedy; be gluttonous; be voracious.

식품(食品) an article of food; foodstuffs; groceries. ¶저칼로리 ~ low-calorie food // 불량 ~ inferior [unwholesome / unsanitary] foodstuff / substandard [illegal] food // 인스턴트 ~ precooked food / convenience [jiffy cooking] food / (속어) instant.
● **식품 관리** food control. **식품 위생** food sanitation [hygiene]. **식품점** (영) a grocer's (shop); (미) a grocery (store). **식품 첨가물** food additives.

식피술(植皮術) [의] a skin grafting operation.

식혜(食醯) sikhye; a sweet drink made from fermented rice.

식후(食後) ¶~에 after dinner [a meal] // ~의 휴식 (take) a short recess [brief rest] after a meal // ~의 휴게 시간 (학교·회의 등의) a recess after a meal // ~ 30분에 복용할 것 (지시문) To be taken half an hour after meals.

식히다 1 [차게 하다] cool; let (a thing) cool; (얼음으로) ice. ¶수프를 ~ cool soup // 입김을 불어 차를 ~ blow on the tea to cool it // 더운 물을 ~ cool hot water / let hot water cool / blow hot water to cool it(불어서) // 열을 ~ reduce a fever // 그 약은 열을 식힌다 The medicine reduces [brings down] the fever. // 환자의 머리를 얼음으로 식혔다 I cooled the patient's head with cracked ice. // 찬 맥주 한 잔이 더위를 식혀 준다 Drinking a cold beer makes me forget about the heat [drives the heat away / dispels the heat]. **2** [열의를] dampen (one's eagerness); cast a damper on (one's enthusiasm); pall; spoil.

신¹ footgear; footwear; shoes. ¶갖 ~ Korean leather shoes // 고무 ~ rubber shoes // 나막 ~ wooden clogs // 에나멜 ~ patent-leather shoes // 짚 ~ straw sandals // ~을 신다 put on one's shoes / wear shoes // ~을 벗다 take off one's shoes // ~을 닦다 polish [clean / (미) shine] one's [another's] shoes // ~을 벗고 들어가시오 (게시) Do not enter with shoes on.
● **신 뒤축** a shoe heel. ¶~이 높은 [낮은] 신 high-heeled [low-heeled] shoes // ~이 높다 [낮다] have high [low] heels / be high- [low-] heeled // ~이 다 닳았다 The shoes are down at heels [(the) heel]. / The heels of my boots are worn out. **신 바닥** the sole [tread] of a shoe; a boot sole.

신² [신명] joy; delight; amusement; enthusiasm; excitement; spirits; dash; elation; warmth; fervor. ¶~ 나는 이야기 a highly amusing story / a very interesting [entertaining] talk // ~이 나다 be spirited / cheer up / be animated / be elated (by / with) / warm (up) (to) / become enthusiastic / get excited (at / by) // 혼자 ~이 나서 낄낄거리다 chuckle with delight to oneself // ~이 나서 혼자 멋대로 지껄이다 give reins to one's tongue // 그는 장래의 계획을 ~ 나게 들려주었다 He told me about his future plans enthusiastically [in an excited tone]. // 더 ~ 나게 노래해라 Sing with more gusto! // 오늘 밤은 ~ 나게 놀아 보자 Let's have a good time [live it up] tonight. // 정치 이야기를 할 때면 그는 ~이 난다 He gets excited [spirited] when talking politics. // 관중들은 아주 ~이 났다 The audience was [were] frantic with joy.

신³ a scene. ¶라스트 ~ the last scene // 러브 ~ a love scene // 극적인 ~ a dramatic scene // ~이 바뀌었다 The scene shifted [changed]. / There was a change of scene.

신(神) (일신교의) God; the Almighty; Providence; the Supreme Being; the Lord; the Creator; the Divinity; (회교의) Allah; (다신교의) a god; a goddess(여신); a deity; a divinity; a spirit(신령); a demo(악신). ¶전지전능한 ~ the Almighty God / God Almighty // 이교의 ~ a heathen god [deity] // ~의 조화 an act of God / divine work / (기적) a miracle // ~의 가호 divine protection / providence //

~의 뜻 the divine will // ~의 심판 divine judgment // 호국의 ~이 되다 die for the country and become its guardian spirit / ~을 믿다 believe in God // ~을 찬양하다 glorify God // ~에게 기도하다 pray to God (for) / ~에게 맹세하다 swear before Heaven // ~을 공경하다 revere God / be pious.
신(이) 내리다 (a medium) fall into trance; be possessed by a spirit.
신-(新) new; [현대적] modern; latest; novel; [신식] up-to-date. ¶~여성 the modern woman // ~무기 a new weapon // ~발명 a new invention // ~고전주의 neoclassicism // ~유행 the latest fashion.
신간(新刊) [신간서] a new book; a new publication; a newly-published book; a recent release. ¶~의 newly-published[-issued] / new // ~을 소개하다 a review (new) books. 신간하다 publish (a new book).
●**신간 목록** a list of new publications. **신간 비평** a book review. **신간 서적** a new book (publication).
신격(神格) divinity; godhead.
●**신격화** deification; apotheosis. ¶~하다 deify / apotheosize.
신경(信經) [종] a creed. ¶아타나시오 ~ the Athanasian Creed // 사도 ~ the Apostles' Creed.
신경(神經) 1 [생] a nerve. ¶~의 nerval / neural / nervine // ~성의 nervous (fever) / neural (paralysis) // 구심성 ~ an afferent nerve / an excitor // 시(視) ~ optic nerves // ~이 없는 nerveless // ~을 죽이다 [마비시키다] 뽑다] kill [deaden / extract] a nerve.
2 [감각] sensitivity; [감수성] sensibility; [개의(介意)] care; concern; consideration. ¶~에 거슬리는 소음 a nerve-racking noise // ~의 피로 [과로] nerve strain // ~이 예민한 nervous / sensitive / sensible / susceptible / jumpy / touchy / edgy / thin-skinned // ~의 발작적 흥분 a fit [an attack] of nerves // ~이 날카로워지다 one's nerves become edgy / (사람이) become excited [jittery / touchy] / (영) be nervy // ~에 거슬리다 jar [get / grate / work] on one's nerves / irritate one's nerves // ~에 부담을 주다 be a (great) strain on one's nerves / be trying to nerves // ~을 초조하게 하다 [건드리다] irritate [jar on] one's nerves / set [put] one's nerves on edge / make (a person) jittery // ~을 가라앉히다 [안정시키다] soothe [quiet / tranquilize] one's nerves // 저 금속음은 ~에 거슬린다 That metallic noise gets on my nerves. // 그녀의 말하는 투가 그의 ~을 건드렸다 Her way of speaking irritated him. // 내 말이 그의 ~을 건드린 듯하다 My remarks seem to have jarred [grated] on his nerves. / My remarks seem to have irritated him. // 그는 ~이 과민한 사람이다 He is all nerves. / He is a bundle of nerves. // 장남의 수험 준비 때문에 온 집안이 ~을 곤두세우고 있다 Everyone in the family is on edge because the eldest son is preparing for entrance examination.
신경(을) 쓰다 mind; care (about); be careful; be thoughtful of (one's reputation); be sensitive (about one's appearance). ¶신경을 쓰지 않다 do not care [mind] / care nothing for / be indifferent to / pay [have] no regard (to) // 그는 작은 일에는 신경을 쓰지 않는다 He does not care about [pays no attention

to] minor points. // 저에게 신경 쓰지 마십시오 Don't bother [mind] about me. // 세상의 소문 따위에는 신경 쓰지 마라 Don't mind what the world says (about you).
●**신경계** [생] the nervous system. ¶**중추**[자율 / 말초] ~ the central [autonomic / peripheral] nervous system. **신경과민** nervousness; oversensitiveness; morbid sensitiveness. ¶~의 highly nervous / oversensitive / morbidly sensitive / high-strung / overstrung / (구어) jumpy / touchy / (영국 구어) nervy // ~이 되다 have a fit of nerves / get nervous / suffer from nerves / become hypersensitive / (구어) get [be] jumpy. **신경과 (전문) 의사** a neurologist. **신경 세포** a nerve cell; a neuron(e). **감각 [운동]** ~ a sensory [motor] neuron. **신경 쇠약** [의] nervous prostration [debility / depression / exhaustion]; a nervous breakdown; neurasthenia. ¶~에 걸리다 suffer from nervous prostration [a nervous breakdown] // ~에 걸려 있다 have a nervous breakdown. **신경염** [의] neuritis. ¶**다발성**(多發性) ~ multiple neuritis. **신경 중추** the nerve center [(영) centre]. **신경증** an illness brought on by mental strain; [정신 신경증] (a) neurosis. ¶~ **환자** a neurotic. **신경질** a nervous temperament [constitution]; nervousness; nervosity. ¶~의 nervous / high-strung / jittery / thin-skinned // (영국 구어) nervy / (구어) jumpy // ~을 부리다 get nervous [fretful / peevish] / ~이 나게 하다 make (a person) nervous [fretful / peevish] // ~이 나다 get irritated / (초조해지다) become impatient // 그가 일하는 것을 보고자니 ~이 난다 I get impatient [irritated] at his way of doing things. // 그녀는 너무 ~적이다 She is too nervous [all nerves]. **신경통** neuralgia. ¶~을 앓다 have [suffer from] neuralgia.
신경지(新境地) a new phase [field / vista]. ¶~를 개척하다 break new ground / open up a new ground (in the sphere of art).
신경향(新傾向) a new tendency [trend].
신고(申告) a report (보고); a return; a declaration (세관에서); (▶ report, return은 주로 수입(收入)에 대해 쓰는네 declaration은 관세품과 수입에도 쓸 수 있음); a notice; a statement; a notification; filing. ¶**녹색** ~ a green return / a greenpaper report (on business income) // **사망** ~ a notice of death // **세관** ~ a customs declaration // **소득세** ~ an income tax return // **전입 [전출]** ~ a moving-in [-out] notification // **출생** ~ a register [notification] of birth // **확정** ~ a final return [declaration] // ...라는 ~가 있었다 A report came in to the police [authorities] that .... / The police [authorities] were notified that .... **신고하다** report; make [send in] a report; declare; state; give [submit] notice; notify (the authorities); file (a return); register. ¶**습득물을 경찰에** ~ hand over [turn in] a find to the police // **경찰에 피해를** ~ report the damage to the police / notify the police of the damage // **소득세를** ~ make a declaration of one's earnings [income] (at the tax office) / make [file / fill out] an income tax return (with the tax office) // **세관에** ~ make a declaration at the custom house // **세관에 카메라를** ~ declare a camera at customs // **도난을 경찰에** ~ report a theft to the police

신고 //장기 결석을 할 경우에는 그 사유를 학교에 신고해야 한다 In case of a long absence you have to inform the school of the reason.// 나는 주운 돈을 갖고 파출소에 가서 신고했다 I took the money I had picked up to the police box.// 수배된 인물을 발견하면 경찰에 신고해 주십시오 If you see the wanted man, please notify [report to] the police.
● **신고서** a (written) report; a notice; a declaration; a statement; a (tax) return(세금의). ¶소득세 ~ an income tax return// 수출[수입] ~ an export [import] declaration. **신고자** a reporter; (세금의) a filer; a declarer. **신고제** the return system.

신고(辛苦) 〔고난〕 hardship(s); 〔시련〕 trials; 〔노고〕 pains; labor; trouble; toil. ¶~를 겪다 go through [suffer] hardships / (구어) have a hard time. **신고하다** struggle; toil; labor; go through [suffer] hardships; take pains.

신고스럽다(辛苦-) laborious; toilsome; painful.

신곡(神曲) (단테의) the Divine Comedy; (이) Divina Commedia.

신곡(新曲) a new musical composition; a new tune [piece].

신관(信管) a fuse (of an explosive charge). ¶시한 ~ a time fuse// ~을 자르다 [장치하다] cut [set] a fuse// ~이 바지지하며 타고 있다 The fuse is sputtering.

신관(新官) a newly-appointed official; a new appointee. ¶~ 사또 the newly-appointed governor [administrator].

신관(新館) a new building; 〔별관·증축 건물〕 an annex; (미) an extension.

신교(新教) Protestantism; the Reformed Faith.
● **신교도** a Protestant.

신구(新舊) the old and the new(▶ 신과 구의 어순이 반대임에 주의). ¶~ 서적 old and new books// ~의 old and new// ~ 장관 the incoming and outgoing ministers// ~ 사상의 충돌 a collision between old and new idea// 지금이 바로 ~ 교체의 시기다 It is time for the old to give way to the new.// 어제 ~ 위원들의 첫 상면이 있었다 Yesterday the new committee members were introduced to the old.// ~ 회장이 각각 5분 동안 인사를 했다 The outgoing and incoming presidents each made an address of five minutes.

신국면(新局面) a new phase [aspect].

신권(神權) divine right. ¶제왕 ~ 설 (the theory of) the divine right of kings.
● **신권 정치** (a) theocracy(▶ 국가의 뜻일 경우는 가산 명사).

신규(新規) a new regulation; a new project. ¶~의 new / fresh// ~로 anew / afresh / newly// ~로 채용하다 hire [employ] a new hand// ~로 은행 계좌를 트다 [개설하다] open an account at a bank.
● **신규 사업** a new enterprise [undertaking / business / project]. **신규 예금** new deposits. **신규 채용** new hiring.

신극(新劇) a new play [drama]; the new school of drama; a style of modern Korean drama which developed under the influence of Occidental drama.

신기(神技) consummate [divine / superhuman] skill; a superhuman feat. ¶~에 가깝다 That is beyond human power.// 그 묘기는 ~였다 I couldn't imagine that such a feat was humanly possible./ It was beyond human power.

신기다 put (shoes) on (a person); get (a person) to put on (shoes). ¶아이에게 양말[신]을 ~ put socks [shoes] on a child / have a child put on his [her] socks [shoes] / make a child have his [her] socks [shoes] on.

신기록(新記錄) a new record [mark]; (미국 구어) a new high. ¶(세계) ~을 수립하다 establish [set] a new (world) record// 이달 들어 교통사고가 ~을 세웠다 The number of traffic accidents has reached a new [an all-time] high this month.// 물가 앙등이 ~을 이루고 있다 The prices are on all-time high.

신기루(蜃氣樓) a mirage. ¶~가 나타났다 A mirage appeared.

신기원(新紀元) a new era [epoch]. ¶~을 긋는 발견 an epoch-making discovery// ~을 이루는 사건 an epoch-making [epochal] event// ~을 긋다 mark a new epoch (in physics)// 컴퓨터가 로켓의 발달에 ~을 이룩했다 Computers inaugurated a new epoch in the development of rockets.

신기축(新機軸) (an) innovation; a new departure [device]; a novel contrivance; a novelty; a dodge; (구어) a wrinkle. ¶~을 이루다 make a new departure / strike out a new line [a line for oneself]// 관례를 탈피하여 ~을 이룩하다 make a new departure from convention// 편집에 ~을 이루다 strike out a new direction in editing / take a new line in editing / introduce innovations in editing.

신기하다(神奇-) marvelous; wonderful; mysterious; miraculous; magic(al); supernatural. ¶신기한 일 [것 / 사람] a marvel / a wonder // 신기하게 marvelously / wonderfully / mysteriously / like magic// 신기하게 여기다 marvel / wonder / be surprised (at)// 약이 신기하게 잘 듣는다 The medicine works like magic. / The medicine has a marvelous efficacy [curative power].// 그가 빠져나갔다니 ~ His escape is little short of a miracle.

신기하다(新奇-) novel; new; original. ¶신기한 방법 (in) a novel way// 신기한 고안품 a novel [an original] device// 신기한 듯이 curiously / with curiosity [curious eyes]// 신기한 것을 좋아하다 be fond of novelty [the unusual]// 당시엔 그것이 아주 신기했다 It was then a great novelty.// 그것은 이제 신기하지 않다 It has lost [outgrown] its novelty.

신년(新年) the New Year. ⇨새해 ¶~ 초에 early in the New Year / at the beginning of the New Year// ~을 맞이하다 [축하하다] greet [celebrate] the New Year// ~을 축하합니다 I wish you a happy New Year! / Happy New Year!

신념(信念) (a) belief; (a) faith(▶ 굳은 신념. 반드시 이성에 결부되는 것은 아님. 이런 뜻으로 복수형을 취하는 경우는 없음); (a) conviction(확신). ¶~에 따라 in accordance with one's beliefs// ~을 관철하다 carry through [stick to] one's convictions// 그는 자기의 ~을 끝까지 지켰다 He held [stuck] to his principles.// 그는 마침내 ~을 굽혔다 He finally compromised [gave up] his principles.// 그는 교육에 굳은 ~을 갖고 있다 He has a firm [strong] faith [belief] in education.// 그의 설교를 듣고 오히려 내 ~이 흔들렸다 Ironically, his sermon shook my faith.

신다 (동작) put on; get on; (상태) wear (shoes); have (shoes) on. ¶구두를 갈아 ~ change one's shoes // 신을 실수로 바꾸어 ~ put on another's shoes by mistake // 오른쪽 구두를 왼발에 잘못 ~ have the right shoe on the left foot // 그는 장화를 신고 왔다 He came in long boots[with long boots on]. / 구두를 신은 채로 있어도 된다 You may keep your shoes on. // 이 구두는 더 이상 신을 수 없다 These shoes will not stand further wear. / The shoes are worn out.

신당(新黨) a new political party. ¶~을 결성하다 organize a new political party.

신대륙(新大陸) the New Continent; [아메리카 대륙] the New World; Americas.

신데렐라 [하루 아침에 명사가 된 사람] a Cinderella.

신도(信徒) a believer; a devotee; [지지자] an adherent (of scientism); a follower; (집합적) the faithful; (기독교의) the flock. ¶기독교 ~ a Christian // 불교 ~ a Buddhist.

신동(神童) a (child)[an infant] prodigy; a wonder boy[child]; a boy wonder. ¶그 아이는 ~이다 The child is a marvel.

신들리다(神−) ¶무대에 선 나의 신들린 듯한 모습이 모든 사람의 시선을 끌었다 My bewitching stage presence drew everyone's attention. // 그는 신들린 듯한 묘기를 보였다 He gave[put on] an inspired performance.

신디케이트 [경] a syndicate. ¶~를 조직하다 form a syndicate.

신랄하다(辛辣−) [날카롭다] sharp; [통렬하다] bitter; [엄하다] severe; [귀에 따갑다] harsh; [찌르는 듯하다] biting. ¶신랄한 말을 biting[caustic] remark // 신랄하게 비평하다 criticize (a thesis) severely[scathingly] // 신랄한 비평을 받게 되다 be exposed to severe criticism // 그의 말에는 다분히 신랄한 데가 있다 There is plenty of vitriol in his words. // 그는 신랄한 비평으로 유명하다 He is well-known for his sharp[harsh / severe] criticism.

신랑(新郞) a bridegroom; a groom; a newly-wed husband. ¶~은 아주 잘생긴 남자였어요 The bridegroom was a very good-looking man.

●**신랑감** a suitable[likely] bridegroom. ¶그는 네 ~으로 잘 어울릴 거야 I think he would be a good match for you. **신랑 신부** the bride and (the) (bride)groom. ¶~를 위해 건배했다 We toasted the bride and bridegroom.

신력(新曆) 1 the new calendar. 2 the solar calendar. ⇨⁼태양력(⇨태양)

신령(神靈) [신] a god; a deity; a spirit; [망령] a soul. ¶~의 가호 divine protection // 산~ the god of a mountain / the guardian spirit of a mountain.

신록(新綠) (문어) fresh verdure; tender [spring] green; new foliage. ¶~의 계절 the season of fresh green / the season of new green leaves // ~의 산들 mountains covered with fresh verdure // ~으로 덮이다 be mantled[robed] in fresh verdure.

신뢰(信賴) confidence (in); trust (in); reliance (on); dependence (on). ¶세인의 ~를 받다 win public confidence // ~에 보답하다 prove worthy of (a person's) trust / live up to (a person's) expectation // ~를 저버리다 betray (a person's) trust[confidence] (in one) // 그는 부모의 ~를 저버렸다 He fell short of his parents' expectations. **신뢰하다** [신용하다] trust; put confidence (in); [의지하다] rely (on); depend (on). **신뢰할 수 있는** trustworthy / reliable / dependable / worthy of one's trust // 신뢰할 수 없는 사람 an unreliable person // 그는 신뢰할 수 없다 He is not to be trusted. // 너는 그의 말을 지나치게 신뢰하고 있다 You put too much confidence in what he says. // 아이들은 어머니를 완전히 신뢰하고 있다 Children have complete trust in their mothers. // 이 통계표는 신뢰할 수 있을까 Can we depend[rely] on these statistics? / Are these statistics reliable[trustworthy]?

신망(信望) confidence and popularity; prestige. ¶~을 떨어뜨리다 lose one's good reputation // ~을 되찾다 restore one's former reputation // 세인의 ~을 얻다 win public confidence // 그것을 함으로써 그는 크게 ~을 얻었다 He gained[added greatly to his] credit [prestige] by doing it. // 용감한 행위가 그의 ~을 높였다 His brave act won him credit [raised him in the estimation of the people]. // 그는 학생들에게 ~이 있다 He is popular with his pupils. / He enjoys the confidence of his pupils. // 그는 의사로서 ~을 얻었다 He gained prestige as a doctor. // 거듭되는 실패로 그는 ~을 잃어버렸다 His repeated failures cost him his reputation.

신명(−) ¶~이 나다 get[become] lighthearted [cheerful / gay(-spirited) / enthusiastic] / be exhilarated / get excited // ~이 나서 in the excess of mirth / in a merry mood / enthusiastically.

신명(身命) one's life. ¶~을 걸고 at the risk of one's life // ~을 바치다 sacrifice [give / lay down] one's life (for) // 그는 나라를 위해 ~을 바쳐 싸웠다 He went to fight and laid down his life for his country.

신명(神明) a deity; a divinity; God. ¶천지~에 맹세하다 swear by God[before Heaven].

신묘하다(神妙−) mysterious; marvelous; wondrous.

신문(訊問) questioning; (cross-)examination (of a witness); a query; an inquest; inquiry; an interrogation. ¶유도 ~ a leading question // 반대 ~ a cross-examination // 그는 엄중한 ~을 받았다 He underwent a severe cross-examination. **신문하다** question; (증인·피고 등을) examine; interrogate; cross-examine. ¶피의자를 ~ examine a suspected person.

●**신문 조서** an interrogatory; a protocol of examination. ¶~를 받다 take a deposition.

신문(新聞) a (news)paper; a paper; a journal; (집합적) the press. ¶일[주]간 ~ a daily [weekly] paper // 영자 ~ an English-language paper // 학급[학교] ~ a class[school] paper // 오늘 ~ today's paper // ~의 삽입 광고지 an inserted bill / an insert // 조간 [석간] ~ a morning[an evening / an afternoon] paper // ~을 접다 fold a newspaper // ~을 펴다 spread (out) a newspaper // ~에 나다 appear in the paper // ~에 보도되다 be reported in the papers[press] // ~을 배달하다 deliver newspapers // ~에서 호평을 받다 be favorably noticed by the press // ~에 공격하다 open a newspaper campaign (against) // ~에서 얻어맞다 be attacked

신물

[pounded] in the press // 너는 무슨 ~을 보느냐 What paper do you take? // ~에 그렇게 나 있다 The paper says so. // 그것을 나는 ~에서 읽었다 I read it in the newspaper. // ~들이 그 독직 사건을 대서특필했다 The papers played up the bribery case. // 우리는 3가지 ~을 구독한다 We take[subscribe to] three papers.

● **신문 광고** newspaper advertising; a newspaper advertisement. **신문 구독료** the subscription rate for a newspaper. ¶1개월의 ~는 얼마요 What is your charge[What do you charge] for the newspaper? **신문 구독자** a subscriber to a newspaper; a newspaper reader[subscriber]. **신문 기사** a newspaper account[article]; (짧은 것) a news item. **신문 기자** a newspaper reporter; a newsman; a newspaperman; a journalist; (영) a (newspaper) pressman. **신문 배달원** a newsman; a newsboy; a newspaper delivery man; a (news)paper boy. **신문 보급소** a newspaper agency. **신문사** a newspaper publishing company; a newspaper office. ¶~에 근무하다 be on (the staff of) a newspaper. **신문지** a newspaper; the newspaper itself. ¶헌 ~ an old newspaper // ~ 크기의 사진 a photograph of the size of a newspaper page.

신물 bile vomited up; [진저리 남] repugnance; disgust.

신물(이) 나다 [지긋지긋하다] be disgusted (with a person); loathe; get sick and tired (of). ¶저놈의 목소리만 들어도 신물이 난다 It makes me sick at my stomach just to hear his voice.

신바람 excitement; enthusiasm. ⇨°어깻바람 (⇨)어깨) ¶~이 나서 나가다 go out cheerfully [lightheartedly] // 그들은 ~이 나서 파티장으로 함께 갔다 They went off happily to the party together.

신발 footgear; shoes. ⇨°신¹ ¶문밖에서 ~ 소리가 그쳤다 The footsteps stopped outside my door.

● **신발 가게** (미) a shoe store; (영) a shoe [boot] shop. **신발장** a shoe chest. ⇨°신장(-欌)

신발명(新發明) a new[recent] invention. ¶~의 newly-invented / of recent invention. **신발명하다** make a new invention.

신방(新房) a bridal room. ¶~에 들다 consummate a marriage / get into the bridal bed.

신변(身邊) one's person; oneself. ¶~에 near oneself / close (to) // ~ 소지품 paraphernalia / a set[kit] of tools // …의 ~을 돌보아 주다 look after a person's personal needs // ~의 위험을 무릅쓰고 at the risk of one's personal safety // ~을 경호하다 guard a person // ~에 어떤 일이 다가오는 것을 느끼다 feel a thing close to one // 그의 ~이 위태롭다 His life is in danger.

● **신변 소설** a personal novel; a novel depicting the author's private life. **신변잡기** personal episodes.

신병(身柄) one's person. ¶~을 맡다 have a person under one's charge // ~을 구속하다 take a person into custody // ~을 송치하다 commit a person for trial / 그는 동생의 ~을 인수하러 경찰서에 갔다 He went to the police station to claim his brother.

신병(身病) (bodily) illness; a disease. ¶~으로 because of [owing to / on account of] illness // ~으로 드러눕다 be ill[sick] in bed / be laid up (with illness) // ~으로 사직하다 resign on account of ill health.

신병(新兵) a (raw) recruit; [징집병] a new conscript. ¶~이 배편으로 계속 도착했다 Fresh groups of soldiers arrived one after another by boat.

● **신병 훈련** recruit[boot] training.

신복(臣僕) a (liege) subject; a retainer; a vassal; (집합적) the lieges.

신봉(信奉) belief; faith. **신봉하다** [믿다] believe (in); [굳게 믿다] have faith (in); [따르다] follow (the teachings of Christ). ¶그는 마르크스주의를 신봉했다 He believed in [(문어) espoused] Marxism.

● **신봉자** [신자] a believer (in); [열성가] a devotee (to); [추종자] a follower (of); [열성적 지지자] an adherent (of).

신부(神父) [가] a father; the Reverend(약어 the Rev.). ¶브라운 ~ Father Brown / (the) Reverend[Rev.] Brown(▶ the를 붙이는 것이 보통이다)

신부(新婦) a bride.

● **신부 들러리** a bridesmaid; (미) a matron of honor(기혼 부인). **신붓감** a prospective bride.

신부전(腎不全) [의] renal insufficiency [failure].

신분(身分) 1 [지위] (a) social standing [status]; (one's) rank. ¶~이 높은 사람 a man of rank // ~의 차이 difference in social standing[status] // ~에 맞게[맞지 않게] according to[beyond] one's means // 학생 ~에 벤츠 자동차는 너무 사치스럽다 A Bentz is too luxurious for a student like you. 2 [가문] origin; birth. ¶~이 높은[낮은] 사람 a person of high[low] birth. 3 [신원] identity. ¶~을 밝히다 disclose one's identity // ~을 증명할 만한 것을 가지고 있습니까 Do you have anything to prove your identity?

● **신분증명서** an identification[ID] card.

신불(神佛) the gods and Buddha. ¶~의 가호를 기원하다 pray to the gods and Buddha / invoke divine protection.

신비(神秘) (a) mystery. ¶~적 mystic / [수수께끼 같은] mysterious // 우주의 ~를 모두 해명하다 solve all the mysteries of the universe // 그의 출생은 ~에 싸여 있다 His birth is veiled[shrouded] in mystery. **신비하다** mysterious; mystic(al); miraculous; occult. ¶신비한 분위기 a mystique / a mystic atmosphere.

● **신비주의** mysticism.

신비스럽다(神秘-) mysterious; mystic(al). ⇨°신비하다(⇨신비) ¶그녀는 신비스러운 미소를 띠었다 She smiled a mysterious smile.

신빙(信憑) trust; reliance; credence. **신빙하다** trust; rely on. ¶신빙할 만하다 be reliable / be trustworthy.

● **신빙성** [신용도] reliability; [확실성] authenticity. ¶~이 있는[없는] 정보 reliable [unreliable] information // 이 증거는 ~이 없다[없다] This evidence is credible[lacks credibility].

신사(紳士) a gentleman (pl. -men); (집합적) gentry. ¶~적인 gentlemanly / gentlemanlike // ~인 체하다 pose as a gentleman / play the gentleman // 그런 일은 ~의 체면을 손상시킨

다 That would be beneath your dignity as a gentleman. // 그는 전형적인 ~이다 He is a typical gentleman.

●**신사도** the code[ideals] of a gentleman. **신사복** men's clothing; menswear; (미) a business suit; (영) a lounge suit. ¶조끼 달린 ~ a (man's) three-piece suit // ~의 윗옷 a jacket / a suit coat.

신산(辛酸) hardships; privations. ¶~을 겪다 go through[suffer] many hardships[trials and tribulations]. **신산하다** tough; laborious; arduous.

신상(身上) 1 [처지] one's station in life; (one's) circumstances. ¶나는 그녀의 ~을 걱정했다 I felt concerned about her welfare. 2 [인생] one's history[life]. 3 [몸] one's person; one's body.

●**신상 문제** one's personal affairs. ¶~를 의논하다 consult (a person)[seek (another's) advice] about one's personal affairs.

신상(神像) an image[idol] of a deity[god].

신상필벌(信賞必罰) ¶그 새로운 지배자[통치자]는 ~을 행하였다 The new ruler never failed to reward good conduct nor to punish evildoing.

신생(新生) 1 [새로 태어남] (a) new birth; [거듭남] (a) rebirth. 2 [새로운 생활] a new life.

●**신생국** a newly emerging nation[force]; a new[nascent] nation[country]. **신생대** [지] the Cenozoic[Cainozoic] era[period]. **신생아** a newborn infant. ¶~의 사망 (a) neonatal death.

신서(信書) a letter; (집합적) correspondence. ¶~의 비밀을 침범해서는 안 된다 You mustn't read other people's personal correspondence.

신서(新書) [신간 서적] a new book; a newly-published book.

신석기(新石器) [역] a neolith; a neolithic stone implement.

●**신석기 시대** the Neolithic era[age]; the New stone Age.

신선(神仙) a legendary hermit with miraculous powers; an immortal; a benevolent wizard living in the mountains.

신선도(新鮮度) (the degree of) freshness. ¶~가 높은 very fresh / lively / ~가 낮은 not very fresh / deficient in freshness // ~가 높은 [낮은] 생선 a sound[an unsound] fish // ~가 떨어지다 lose (some of) (its) freshness.

신선로(神仙爐) Sinseollo; a cooking brazier.

신선미(新鮮味) freshness. ¶~ 있는 기획 a fresh[a novel / an original] plan // 작품에 ~를 내다 strike a fresh note[show originality] in one's work // 최근 그의 기예에는 ~를 잃었다 Recently his art has lost its freshness.

신선하다(新鮮-) fresh (vegetables, fish, etc.); new. ¶신선한 달걀 fresh eggs // 신선한 공기 fresh air // 창문을 열고 신선한 공기를 방안에 넣어라 Open the window and let in fresh air. // 그 생각의 어디가 신선한가 What's new about that idea?

신설(新設) establishment; organization; founding. ¶~의 newly-organized / newly-established. **신설하다** establish; organize; found. ¶학교를 ~ found a school // 부국(部局)을 ~ establish[set up / organize] a department.

●**신설 회사** a newly-established[-organized] company; a new company.

신성(神性) divine nature; divinity.

신성(神聖) holiness; sacredness; sanctity. ¶~불가침의 sacred and inviolable / sacrosanct // ~을 더럽히다 desecrate / profane // 인도에서는 소가 ~시되고 있다 In India the cow is regarded as a sacred animal. **신성하다** holy; sacred; divine.(▶ sacred는 「신에 관한 것, 숭배할 가치가 있는」을 말하며, 또한 「세속적인」 (secular)과 대조적으로 쓰임. divine은 sacred에 가까우며 「신의, 신에 의한」의 뜻이 더욱 강함. holy는 대개 올바른 것, 신적인 것을 말함) ¶신성하게 하다 consecrate / make holy / sanctify // 결혼은 신성한 것이다 Marriage is sacred[a holy thing].

●**신성 로마 제국** the Holy Roman Empire.

신성(新星) 1 [천] a nova (pl. ~s, -vae). 2 [연예계의 새로운 스타] a new star.

신세(身世) 1 [일신상의 처지와 형편] one's lot [condition / circumstances]; one's personal affairs. ¶불쌍한 ~ sad[pitiful] circumstances / a sad lot // 딱한 ~ adverse circumstances // 외로운 ~ lonely[lonesome / solitary] circumstances // 거지 ~가 되다 be reduced to beggary. 2 [은혜] a favor; an obligation; (a) moral obligation; a debt of gratitude; [도움·돌봄] help; care; support; [친절] kindness; goodness; [의지] dependence; [폐] (a) trouble; a burden. ¶~는 언제까지나 잊지 않겠습니다 I will[(영)] shall] never forget your kindness[what you have done for me].

신세(를) 지다 be indebted[obliged] to (a person); owe (a person) a debt of gratitude; be under indebtedness to (a person); [도움을 받다] receive assistance; be under the care of; [짐이 되다] be a burden to; live at (a person's) expense; live with[on] (a person). ¶신세 지는 사람 a sponger / a dependent // 부모의 ~ sponge off one's parents // 나는 아직도 부모님 신세를 지고 있다 I am still dependent on my parents. // 그에게 크게 신세를 진 일을 지금도 잊지 않고 있다 I still feel deeply indebted to him. / I still feel I owe him a lot. // 고맙습니다, 큰 신세를 졌습니다 Thank you, I'm deeply indebted to you.

●**신세타령** a hard-luck story; a tale of woe. ¶~을 하다 grieve about one's hard[ill] luck / bewail one's ill fortune.

신세계(新世界) 1 [새로운 세계] a new world. 2 the New Continent. ⇨=**신대륙**.

신세대(新世代) the new generation.

신소리 [재치 있게 받아 넘기는 말] a wisecrack; a jibe; (속어) lip. ¶~ 작작 해 Less of your lip!

신소설(新小說) (집합적) the new-style fiction; a new-style novel[story].

신속하다(迅速-) [민첩한] quick; [날쌘] swift; [급속한] rapid; [고속도의] speedy; [즉석의] prompt. ¶그들의 행동이 ~ They are swift in action. // 사태의 신속한 개선을 기대할 수 없을 것 같다 I'm afraid we cannot expect a rapid[speedy] improvement in the situation. // 신속한 조처가 필요하다 Prompt[Quick] action is needed[called for]. **신속히** quickly; rapidly; swiftly; promptly; with speed[promptitude]; like fury. ¶~ 배달해 드리겠습니다 We will deliver it promptly. // ~ 가옥을 건축해 주면 좋겠다 I want you to build the house with all possible speed. // 정

신수 부는 ~ 시찰단을 파견했다 The government promptly sent an inspection party[team].

신수(身手) 〔안색〕 (a) complexion; color; a countenance; 〔용모·풍채〕 looks; (one's personal) appearance; air; mien. ¶~가 훤하다 have a fine appearance[presence] / have a good[refined] bearing / cut a fine figure.

신수(身數) 〔운명〕 one's fortune; one's luck; one's future. ¶~가 피다 be in luck's way / one's fortune changes for the better / fortune turns in one's favor // ~를 말하다[보아 주다] tell (a person's) fortune / forecast the future of (a person's) life // ~를 보다 have one's fortune told / have one's future looked into // 금년은 ~가 좋다[나쁘다] This is a lucky[an unlucky] year for me. / My star is ascendant[descendant] this year. // 그녀는 올해 ~가 좋다[나쁘다] Her star is in a favorable[unfavorable] position this year. / Her star is visiting (falling) this year. // 나는 점쟁이한테 가서 ~를 보았다 I had my fortune told by a fortuneteller. / I had a fortuneteller tell my fortune.

신승하다(辛勝—) win (a game) by a narrow [small] margin; carry[win] the day after a hard struggle[fight]. ¶접전 끝에 우리가 신승했다 We won by a narrow margin after a close game.

신시(新詩) 1 〔새로 지은 시〕 a new poem. 2 the new-style poetry. ⇨ 신체시

신식(新式) 〔새 유행·신형〕 the present fashion; (모양) a new style[type]; (방법) a new method. ¶~의 〔현대적인〕 modern / 〔최신식의〕 up-to-date // ~으로 in the present (-day) fashion // 그 오래된 주택에는 ~ 가구가 어울리지 않는다 Modern furniture looks out of place in that old house.

●**신식 무기** a new-type weapon.

신신당부(申申當付) (an) entreaty; solicitation; supplication; imploration; an earnest [a repeated] appeal[request]. **신신당부하다** ask[appeal / request] repeatedly[earnestly / over and over again]; entreat; solicit; supplicate; implore.

신신부탁(申申付託) (an) entreaty; solicitation. ⇨ 신신당부

신실하다(信實—) steady and honest; sincere; faithful; truthful. ¶신실한 사람 an honest and trustworthy man / a steady[solid] character. **신실히** sincerely; faithfully; truthfully.

신심(信心) faith; belief; piety; devotion; reverence for God. ¶~이 깊은 (deeply) religious / devout / pious / godly / faithful.

신안(新案) 〔새로운 고안·제안〕 a new idea; a new device; 〔새로운 의장〕 a new design. ¶실용~ a utility model.

●**신안 특허** a patent on a practical new device[design]; a utility model patent. ¶~ 출원 중 patent applied for / patent pending // ~를 얻다 obtain a patent on a new device.

신앙(信仰) 〔종교적 믿음〕 faith; 〔일반적으로 신념·믿음〕 belief. ¶~이 없는 unbelieving / impious / faithless / godless // ~이 두터운 pious / religious / devout / (문어) godly // ~의 자유 freedom of belief[religion] // ~을 버리다 give up[forsake] one's faith // 그는 ~(심)이 독실한 가정에서 자랐다 He comes of a God-fearing family. **신앙하다** believe[have faith] in (God / Christianity).

●**신앙 고백** a confession of faith; profession.

신앙생활 a religious life; a life of faith. **신앙인** a believer; a devotee.

신약(神藥) a wonder[miracle] drug; a wonder-working remedy.

신약(新約) 1 〔새 약속〕 a new promise. 2 〔기〕 the new Covenant. 3 〔성〕 the New Testament(약어 NT, N.T.).

신약(新藥) a new medicine.

신어(新語) a new word; a neologism; 〔신조어〕 a newly-coined word. ¶~를 만들어 내다 coin a new word.

신여성(新女性) a modern woman[girl]; the new woman.

신역(新譯) a new translation[version]. **신역하다** translate anew; make a new translation.

신열(身熱) (a) fever; fever heat; pyrexia; (구어) a temperature. ¶~이 있다 have (a) fever / be feverish / ~이 높다 have a high fever [temperature] // ~이 나다 become feverish / run a fever[temperature] / develop a fever / come to have fever // ~이 내리다 one's fever breaks[subsides / abates] / one's temperature falls[goes down].

신예(新銳) ¶~의 new and powerful.

●**신예기**(—機) a newly produced airplane; an up-to-date aircraft.

신용(信用) 1 〔신뢰〕 confidence; trust; faith; reliance.(▶ confidence는 경험이나 증거에 입각한 신용에, trust는 존경 등 주관에 입각한 신용에 쓰이는 일이 많음, 또 faith는 이성을 초월한 강한 신용, reliance는 의지하여 신뢰하는 일) ¶~을 얻다 win[gain] the confidence (of) // ~을 잃다 lose the confidence (of) // ~을 회복하다 regain the confidence (of) // ~을 손상하다 sully one's reputation / stain one's good name // ~을 유지하다 maintain one's reputation // ~이 있다 have[enjoy] the confidence (of) / be trusted (by) // ~이 없다 have no confidence (of) / lack (a person's) trust // 나는 그녀에게 ~이 있다 I think I am fully trusted by her. / She trusts (in) me. // 그의 ~이 문제가 되고 있다 His sincerity is in question. / He is distrusted. **신용하다** believe; trust; have[put] trust (in); place confidence (in). ¶신용할 수 있는 reliable / trusty / trustworthy // 나는 그녀를 전적으로 신용하고 있다 I have perfect trust in her. // 그런 일을 계속한다면 아무도 그를 신용하지 않을 것이다 If he goes on doing such things, everyone will lose faith in him. // 그녀는 신용할 수 있다 She is trustworthy[reliable]. // 그 남자는 신용할 수 없다 That man is not to be trusted [relied upon].

2 〔평판〕 reputation; 〔거래 상대의 신용도〕 credit. ¶무담보 ~ clean credit // 상업 ~ commercial[trade] credit // 우리 가게에 ~을 떨어뜨리는[에 관계되는] 일은 하고 싶지 않다 I do not want to do anything to injure [affect] the credit[reputation] of our store. // 당신은 ~ 있는 상사와 교섭해 보는 것이 좋을 겁니다 You had better negotiate with a reputable firm. // 나는 ~으로 돈을 좀 빌렸다 I have borrowed some money on credit. // 그것은 우리 가게의 ~에 관계되는 문제다 It affects the reputation of our shop. // 저 상점은 ~이 있다 That store has a high reputation. **신용하다** ¶그는 얼마나 신용할 수 있는지 그 회사의 재정 상태를 조사하고 싶어 했다 He wanted to investigate the financial standing of the firm to determine what

credit should be extended.
●**신용 거래** (증권에서) a margin transaction; margin trading; (상업에서) credit transactions; sale on credit. ¶~를 하다 sell[buy] on credit[tick / strap] / do[carry on] credit transactions (with). **신용 대출** a credit[fiduciary] loan; a loan on credit. ¶~로 on credit ∥ 장기[단기] ~ a long[short] credit / ~ 기간을 경과하다 run beyond one's term of credit. **신용도** credit rating. ¶그의 ~는 높다[낮다] He is a good[poor / bad] credit risk. **신용 상태** a credit standing; one's financial status[standing]. ¶회사의 ~ the credit status of a firm / ~를 조사하다 inquire into [make sure of] a person's financial status. **신용장** a letter of credit(약어 L/C) a bill of credit; a credit. ¶내국 ~ a local L/C / 수출[수입] ~ an export[import] L/C / 은행 인수 ~ a bank acceptance L/C / ~의 발행[양도 / 분할 / 갱신] issuance[transfer / division / renewal] of a credit ∥ ~을 개설하다 open[establish] an L/C (with a bank / by cable / for a sum / against an order) / ~을 발행[확인]하다 issue[confirm] an L/C. **신용 조회** a credit[confidential] inquiry. **신용 카드** a credit[plastic] card; plastic. ¶~ 받습니다 (게시) Credit cards (are) accepted here.

신우(腎盂) [생] the pelvis of the kidney.
신우염 [의] pyelitis.
신원(身元) [일신에 관계되는 자료] one's birth and parentage; (정체) one's identity. ¶~을 조사하다 (가문을) inquire into a person's birth and parentage / (출생과 전력을) inquire into a person's birth and antecedents / look into[check up on] a person's background / ~ 불명의 피해자 an unidentified victim / ~이 확실한 사람 a person with good references / a person who comes well recommended / ~을 증명하다 prove one's identity / ~을 감추다[밝히다] conceal[reveal / disclose] one's identity / ~을 조회하다 refer to (a company) for (a person's) character / reference / 시체의 ~을 확인하다 establish the identity of the corpse. ∥ ~ 미상의 사람이 두세 사람 있었다 There were a few unidentified men.
●**신원 보증** (personal) reference; a certificate of good character. **신원 보증인** a surety; a guarantor; a guarantee (for fidelity). ¶~를 세우다 furnish[give] a security. **신원 증명서** an identification card; identity papers.
신음(呻吟) a groan; a moan(▶ groan이 소리가 더 낮음). ¶나는 아파서 나도 모르게 ~ 소리를 냈다 I uttered a moan of pain in spite of myself. / I couldn't help moaning in pain. ∥ 부상자는 의사가 상처를 건드리자 ~ 소리를 냈다 The injured man groaned when the doctor felt his wound. ∥ 아들의 사망 소식을 접하고 노인은 ~ 소리를 냈다 At the news of his son's death, the old man uttered a groan. **신음하다** [앓는 소리를 내다] moan; groan; [괴로움·고통으로 고생하다] suffer severely. ¶부상의 아픔 때문에 신음하고 있다 The pain of their wounds is making them groan[moan]. ∥ 병사는 고통으로 신음했다 The soldier groaned in[with] pain.
신의(信義) faith; fidelity; truthfulness; loyalty. ¶~를 중히 여기는 사람 a man of honor / ~를 지키다[저버리다] keep[break] faith (with a person) / be faithful[unfaithful] ∥ ~를 가지고 이 약속을 합니다 I make this promise in good faith. ∥ 그것은 회사의 ~에 관계되는 일이다 That affects the honor[reputation] of the company.
신의(神意) divine[God's] will; Providence.
신인(神人) **1** [신과 사람] man and god. ¶~이 공노했다 Gods and men were angry alike. **2** [신처럼 거룩한 사람] a godlike person; [신과 같은 힘을 지닌 사람] a person with godlike powers.
신인(新人) [새로 나타난 사람] a new figure; (연예계 등의) a new face[star]; (스포츠의) a rookie. ¶미국 팀은 ~ 선수를 투입했다 The American team sent in a new player.
●**신인 가수** a new singer. **신인왕** the rookie king.
신임(信任) confidence; trust. ¶~을 얻다[잃다] win[gain] the confidence (of) ∥ ~을 잃다 lose the confidence (of) ∥ 그는 사장의 두터운 ~을 받고 있다 He is trusted by the president. / He has[(문어) enjoys] the full confidence of the president. ∥ 그는 사장의 ~을 얻어 유럽 출장을 갔다 He won the president's confidence and was sent to Europe on business. **신임하다** trust; have[(문어) enjoys] the full confidence (in). ¶내각을 ~ (의회에서) vote confidence in the government / give the Government a vote of confidence.
●**신임안** a confidence motion. **신임장** credentials; a letter of credence. ¶~을 제출하다 present one's credentials (to). **신임 투표** a vote of confidence; a confidence vote.
신임(新任) a new appointment. ¶~의 newly-appointed ∥ ~ 인삿말을 하다 make an inaugural address. **신임하다** newly appoint to office.
신입(新入) ¶~의 new / incoming / entering.
●**신입 사원** a new employee; a new member of the staff. **신입생** a new pupil; a new student; (대학·고교의) (미) a freshman; (영국 속어) a fresher.
신자(信者) [믿는 사람] a believer; an adherent (of scientism). ¶불교 ~ a believer in Buddhism / a Buddhist ∥ 그녀는 기독교 ~다 She is a believer in Christianity.
신작(新作) [새로 만든 작품] a new work; [새로 만든 작곡] a new composition. ¶~의 무용 a new[newly-choreographed] dance ∥ ~을 발표하다 (소설 등) publish a new work / (음악의 초연) give the first performance of a new piece of music / perform a new work.
신작로(新作路) a newly constructed road; a highway.
신장(-欌) a shoe chest; a boot cupboard.
신장(身長) height; (문어) stature. ¶한국인 남자의 평균 ~ the average height of Korean men / ~이 크다[작다] be tall[short] / ~을 재다 measure a person's height / see how tall a person is / 그는 ~이 170센티다 He is 170 centimeters tall[in height].
신장(伸張) extension; expansion. ¶사업의 ~ the expansion of a business. **신장하다** extend; expand; elongate. ¶세력을 ~ extend one's influence. ∥ 국위를 해외에 ~ extend the national prestige overseas.
●**신장성** expansibility; elongation.
신장(新裝) [새로 장식함] redecoration; [개장] refurbishing. ¶12월 4일 ~ 개업 (광고 등에서) Completely remodeled[redecorated] Dec. 4. / Reopening Dec. 4. **신장하다** give a new

신장 look (to); refurbish; redecorate; (장비의) refurnish; reequip; [개조하다] remodel. ¶쇼윈도를 ~ give a face-lift[a new look] to a showpindow.

신장(腎臟) [생] a kidney. ¶나는 ~이 좋지 않다 I have kidney trouble.
● **신장 결석** a kidney stones; a renal calculus (*pl.* -li). **신장병** kidney disease[trouble]. **신장염** nephritis; inflammation of a kidney [the kidneys].

신전(神殿) a shrine; a sanctuary; a tabernacle; a temple(큰); a fane. ¶아폴로 ~ the Temple of Apollo.

신접살림(新接-) a life in a new home. **신접살림하다** make a new home.

신접살이(新接-) a life in a new home. ⇨신접살림

신정(神政) theocracy; thearchy; government [political rule] of a state by priests[clergy] (as representatives of God).

신정(新正) [양력 1월 1일] the New Year's Day.

신제도(新制度) a new system.

신제품(新製品) a new product; an article newly manufactured[produced] (by).

신조(信條) 1 [신앙의 조목] a creed; an article of faith. 2 [신념] a belief; [주의] a principle. ¶나의 ~ my belief / what I believe // 생활~ one's principles in life / one's philosophy of life // ~를 지키다 stick to one's principles.

신조(新造) new construction. ¶~의 new / newly-made[-built] / (어구가) new / newly-coined. **신조하다** construct[build] (anew); (말 등을) mint; coin.
● **신조어** a new[newly-coined] word; a neologism.

신종(新種) a new kind; (동식물의) a variety (of orange). ¶~의 튤립 a new variety of tulip.
● **신종 사기** a new type of swindling.

신주(神主) [죽은 사람의 위패] a *sinju*; a spirit tablet. ¶조상의 ~ an ancestor tablet.

신주(新株) new stocks; [영] new shares. ¶~를 공모하다 collect new stocks publicly // ~를 무상 배당하다 allot new stocks free of charge.

신중(愼重) prudence; discretion; circumspection; caution; care. ¶말의 선택에 특별히 ~을 기하라 pay special attention to one's choice of words / ~을 기하는 것보다 좋은 것이 없다 You will never lose by being careful. / (구어) There's nothing like [Nothing beats] being careful. // 나는 ~을 기하여 의사의 진찰을 받았다 I consulted a doctor just as a precaution. // 우리는 ~을 기하여 보결 요원 3명을 남겼다 We kept three alternates [(영) reserves], just to be on the safe side [play it safe]. // 심사는 ~을 기해야 한다 The investigation requires circumspection. **신중하다** [사려 깊은] prudent; [조심성 있는] cautious; [행동·말 등에 신중한] discreet; [주의 깊은] careful. ¶신중한 사람 a cautious man // 결혼에 관해서는 그는 매우 ~ As far as marriage is concerned, he is very cautious. // 감독은 신중한 작전을 하기로 결심하고 타자에게 번트를 지시했다 The manager decided to play it safe, and ordered the better to bunt. **신중히** prudently; cautiously; discreetly; carefully. ¶~ 협의한 결과 after careful consideration[discussion] // 그들은 ~ 계획을 세웠다 They worked out their plan very carefully [with careful deliberation]. // 나는 자네가 좀 더 ~ 행동해 주기를 바란다 I wish you'd act more prudently[discreetly]. // ~ 생각해 보겠다 Let me consider the matter carefully. // 찬반양론은 ~ 검토하지 않고는 결정할 수 없다 We cannot decide until we have made a thorough study of the pros and the cons.

신진(新進) ¶~의 rising / coming // ~기의 비평가 a young and spirited critic.
● **신진 작가** a rising writer.

신진대사(新陳代謝) 1 [생] metabolism. ⇨물질대사(⇨물질) ¶생물체에서는 ~가 끊임없이 이루어지고 있다 Metabolism is taking place continuously in living things. 2 [새것·묵은 것의 교체] renewal; replacement of the old with the new. ¶저 회사는 사원의 ~가 필요하다 That company needs some new blood. / The staff of that company needs an infusion of fresh blood [to be rejuvenated].

신짝 1 [신의 한 짝] an odd shoe (of a pair). 2 footgear; shoes. ⇨신[1]

신착(新着) new arrival. ¶~의 newly-arrived / newly-received. **신착하다** newly arrive; be a new arrival.
● **신착품** new arrivals; newly arrived [imported / received] goods.

신참(新參) (고참에 대하여) a newcomer; [영] a freshman; [미숙한 사람] a new [green] hand. ¶~ 사원 a new employee // 이 일에 저는 아직 ~입니다 I am new at this job.
● **신참 선수** a rookie.

신창 a shoe sole. ¶~을 갈다 resole shoes.

신천옹(信天翁) [동] an albatross.

신천지(新天地) [새세계] a new world; [새로운 활동을 할 장소] a new field of activity. ¶~를 개척하다 open up a new field[sphere] of activity.

신청(申請) 1 [제의·제안] a proposal; an offer (of marriage); an overture (of peace); [도전] a challenge (to a duel); [요청·의뢰] a request (for an interview); (재심 등의) [법] (a) motion. ¶결혼 ~을 하다 make a marriage proposal [a proposal of marriage] // 피고는 정당방위의 ~을 했다 The defendant pleaded self-defense. / The defendant entered a plea of self-defense. // 그 가옥은 채권자의 ~에 의해 압류되었다 The house was attached at the instance of creditors. // 소녀 가수에게 텔레비전 출연 ~이 있었다 The young girl was invited to appear on a TV program. // ~이 있는 대로 그것을 우송해 드립니다 We will mail it to you on [upon] request. // 우리는 그 합병 ~을 거절했다 [수락했다] We rejected [accepted] the offer of a merger. **신청하다** propose; offer (mediation); make an overture (of peace); lodge [file] (a protest with a person against a matter); enter (oneself) for (a contest); challenge (a person); request (a loan); ask for (an interview); [법] move (for a rehearing). ¶증인의 소환을 ~ move that a witness be summoned // 그는 영사관에 비자 발급을 신청했다 He applied to the consulate for a visa. // 그는 그 제안에 이의를 신청했다 He raised an objection to the proposal. // 그는 3개월의 휴가를 신청했다 He asked [applied] for a three months' leave of absence. // 그는 자기의 요구사항을 철회한다고 신청했다 He proposed to

withdraw his demands.∥그는 메리에게 결혼을 신청했다 He proposed (marriage) to Mary.∥그들은 사장에게 면회를 신청했다 They requested an interview with the president.
2 [출원·지원·응모] application (for employment); [출자·기부의 약속] subscription (for stocks). ¶~은 본인이 본사로 하십시오 Apply to the head office personally[in person].∥여자 마라톤 대회에 1000명의 참가 ~이 있었다 There were a thousand entries for the women's marathon.∥~이 쏟아져 들어왔다 Applications came pouring in. / We were flooded with applications. **신청하다** apply [make an application] (for a position); file an application (with a film); put in (for a work transfer); subscribe (for bonds / shares); send a subscription (to a newspaper); reserve. ¶본인이 직접 또는 서신으로 신청해도 된다 You may apply in person or by letter.∥나는 그 잡지의 정기 구독을 신청했다 I took out a subscription to the magazine.∥나는 그 호텔에서 가장 좋은 방을 신청했다 I reserved the best room in the hotel.∥사무실에 신청하십시오 Ask at the office.
● **신청 기한 / 신청 마감** a time limit [deadline] for applying; the application deadline. **신청서** a written application; an application (in writing); (용지) an application (form); an application blank. ¶~를 내다 send in an application / apply. **신청인 / 신청자** an applicant; a petitioner; a claimant(배상의); a proposer; a subscriber(구독자).

신체(身體) the body. ¶~의 physical / bodily / personal∥~ 건전한 젊은이들 young people sound in body / healthy young people∥~가 건강하다 be sound in body / be physically strong / have[be of] a robust constitution∥~를 단련하다 build up a healthy body.
신체의 자유 [법] personal liberty.
● **신체검사** a physical[medical] examination; (구어) a medical checkup; (미) a physical checkup; (미국 구어) a physical. ¶~를 받다 undergo[get] a physical examination / check up[examine] one's health. **신체장애** a physical disability. **신체장애인** a physically challenged[handicapped] person(▶ handicapped보다 challenged가 완곡하고 부드러운 말임).

신체시(新體詩) the new-style poetry; a new-style poem.
신체제(新體制) a new system[structure / order].
신축(伸縮) expansion and contraction; elasticity. **신축하다** expand and contract; be elastic; be stretchy.
● **신축 관세** (미) a flexible tariff. **신축성** elasticity. ¶~이 없다 lack elasticity. **신축자재** elasticity.
신축(新築) new construction. ¶우리 집은 ~ 중이다 Our house is being built[under construction]. **신축하다** build (a house); construct. ¶신축한 집 a new[newly-built] house∥신축한 건물 a new building.
신춘(新春) the new spring. ⇨ *새봄
● **신춘문예** a literary contest in spring. ¶~ 소설 부문 당선작 a prize winning entry in the department of novels of a spring literary contest (sponsored by K newspaper).

신출귀몰(神出鬼沒) elusiveness; preternatural swiftness; sudden appearance and disappearance. **신출귀몰하다** appear in unexpected places and at unexpected moments; suddenly appear and suddenly disappear. ¶나는 그가 신출귀몰하므로 잡을 수가 없다 As he appears at unexpected times and places and disappears quickly, I can't catch him.∥신출귀몰하는 도둑 때문에 경찰은 어찌할 바를 몰랐다 The police didn't know what tactic to use, because when the thief struck he seemed to be everywhere at once.

신출내기(新出–) a greenhorn; a novice; a fledgling; (구어) a tenderfoot; (속어) a rookie. ¶그는 출판계에서는 ~에 불과하다 He is just a beginner in the publishing business.
● **신출내기 기자** a cub reporter. **신출내기 작가** a sucking[cub] writer.

신탁(信託) trust. ¶금전[대부] ~ a money [loan] trust∥공익 ~ a charitable trust∥법인[개인] ~ a corporate[personal] trust∥보험 ~ an insurance trust∥투자 ~ investment trust. **신탁하다** trust (a person) with (a thing); leave (a thing) in trust with (a person). ¶재산을 남에게 ~ entrust one's property to a person / leave one's property in trust with a person.
● **신탁 기금** a trust fund. **신탁 예금** a trust deposit. **신탁 증서** a trust certificate [deed]. **신탁 통치** trusteeship. **신탁 통치령** a trust territory (under Great Britain).

신탁(神託) an oracle; a divine message[revelation]. ¶~을 전하다[받다] deliver[receive] an oracle∥~대로 되었다 The oracle was fulfilled.

신통력(神通力) an occult[a supernatural] power; a divine power; magic powers; the supernatural. ¶~이 있다 have supernatural [occult] powers.

신통하다(神通–) [신기하게 통달하다] wonderful; miraculous; marvelous; divine; admirable; extraordinary; [만족할 만하다] satisfactory; desirable; good; favorable. ¶신통한 아이 a wonder child / an extraordinary child∥신통한 효험이 있는 약 a medicine of marvelous efficacy / a drug of great virtue∥신통하지 않은 학업 성적 unsatisfactory schoolwork∥(약 등이) 신통하게 잘 듣다 do [work / perform] wonders∥그가 그런 일을 해 내다니 신통하군 It is marvelous that he should have done such a thing. / I marvel that he managed it.∥실험 결과는 신통하지 않았다 The results of the experiment were not encouraging.∥아버지의 건강은 신통하지 않다 My father does not seem to be getting any better. / My father is in an unfavorable condition. / The condition of my father is unfavorable[not reassuring].∥불경기로 신통한 직장을 구할 수 없다 Suitable[desirable] jobs are hard to find now because of the recession. **신통히** wonderfully; miraculously; marvelously; admirably; favorably.

신트림 the eructation of an acid fluid; acrid eructation. **신트림하다** belch[eruct(ate)] an acid[sour] fluid.

신파(新派) **1** [새 유파] a new school. **2** a new-school drama. ⇨ *신파극(⇨)신파)
● **신파극** a new-school drama[play].

신판(新版) [신간] a new publication; [개정판] a new[revised] edition. ¶~을 내다 publish a new edition.

신품(新品) a new[brand-new] article. ¶이 피아노는 ~이나 다름없다 This piano is as good as new. / This piano is nearly-new. / This piano looks brand-new.

신하(臣下) a (liege) subject; a retainer; a vassal; (집합적) the lieges; vassalage.

신학(神學) theology; divinity. ¶목회 ~ pastoral theology // 사변 / 계시 (啓示) ~ speculative [natural / revealed] theology.
● **신학교** (성직자 양성의) a seminary; an ecclesiastical seminary; (신학 교육의) a theological [divinity] college [school / seminary].
신학자 a theologian; a theologist; a divine.

신학기(新學期) a new school term.

신학문(新學問) the new learning; modern sciences.

신형(新型) a new [the latest] style [model / fashion / design]. ¶최~ 모자 hats of the latest style[fashion].
● **신형 자동차** a new-model car; a motorcar of the latest model.

신호(信號) a signal; (몸짓 등의) a sign; (무대에서의) a cue. ¶경계 ~ a warning [cautionary / caution] signal // 교통 ~ a traffic signal // 기상 ~ a weather signal // 무선 ~ a wireless signal // 발화 ~ flashlight signal // 수기(手旗) ~ a flag signal / (군대의) semaphore // 안개 ~ a fog signal // 위험 ~ a danger signal / (교통의) a red light / (철도의) a red lamp // 음향 ~ an acoustic [an audible / a phonic] signal // 자동 ~ (철도의) an automatic signal // 자동 폐색 ~ (철도의) an automatic block signal // 적 ~ a red signal // 청 ~ a green (traffic) signal // 정지 ~ a signal of "stop" / a stop-light / a red light // 주의 ~ a precaution signal / a signal of "Caution" // 조난 ~ an SOS / a distress signal / a signal of distress // 진행 ~ a clear signal / a signal of "Proceed" // 철도 ~ a railroad signal [semaphore] // 출발 ~ a signal for starting / a starting signal // 통화 ~ a busy signal / (영) an engaged signal // 코치의 ~로 at a sign from the coach // 호각 소리를 ~로 at the[a] whistle // ~을 보내다 signal / make [give] a signal // 회전등으로 ~를 보내다 send a signal by flashlight // 구조선을 부르는 ~을 보내다 signal for a rescue boat // ~를 주고받다 exchange signals // (길에서) ~를 기다리다 wait for a signal [(traffic) light] // ~를 무시하다 disregard a signal // ~를 무시하고 길을 건너다 (미) jaywalk // ~를 잘못 보다 [읽다] mistake [misread] a signal **신호하다** signal; give [make] a signal; (손짓 등으로) make a sign; (몸짓으로) motion (a person to do). ¶순찰 중이던 경찰관이 나에게 자전거를 세우라고 신호했다 A patrolling policeman signaled (to) me to stop my bicycle. // 그는 그들에게 입 다물라고 신호했다 He motioned them to stop talking.
● **신호기**(-旗) a signal flag; (선박의) a code flag. **신호 등** a signal lamp [light]; a blinker(명멸 방향 지시등 등의). **신호수** / **신호원** a signalman; a signaler; a flagman; [군] (속의) a buzzer.

신혼(新婚) a new marriage. **신혼하다** be newly married; become a newlywed.
● **신혼부부** a new(ly)-married couple; a newly-wed couple [pair]; (구어) newlyweds. **신혼 생활** newly married life. **신혼여행** a honeymoon; a wedding trip [tour / journey]; a bridal journey. ¶~을 떠나다 go (off) on a honeymoon / go on a bridal tour // ~을 하다 honeymoon (in / at) / make a wedding trip // ~은 어디로 갑니까 Where are you going away for the [your] honeymoon?

신화(神化) deification; apotheosis. **신화하다** deify; apotheosize.

신화(神話) a myth; (집합적) mythology. ¶~의 [~적인] mythical / mythological // 건국 ~ the birth myth of a nation / a state-founding myth // 그리스 [로마] ~ Greek [Roman] myths [mythology] // 단군 ~에 의하면 according to Dangun myth / (문어) Dangun myth has it that ….
● **신화학** mythology.

신흥(新興) ¶~의 rising / burgeoning / new / newly-rising [-risen / -arisen]. **신흥하다** newly rise.
● **신흥 계급** a newly-rise [-rising] class; a newly-awakened class. **신흥 도시** a new town; (급속히 발전한) a boom [mushroom] town. **신흥 종교** a new [newly-risen] religion.

싣다 1 (운반할 목적으로) load (up) (a truck) with (goods); carry; freight; put on board; have [take] on board; take in (미) on; (배에) ship (a cargo); (말에) pack. ¶여행자의 짐을 실은 자동차 a car loaded with the baggage of the travelers // 짐을 실은 배 a laden vessel // 건초를 실은 수레 a cart laden [loaded] with hay // 차를 트레일러에 ~ load a car on [onto] a trailer // 배에 석탄을 ~ load a ship with coal / lade [stow] a ship with coal // 말에 장작을 많이 ~ burden a horse with firewood // 트럭에 짐을 ~ load a truck [(영) lorry] with goods // 우리는 배에 화물을 실었다 We loaded the cargo on board the ship. // 이 화물은 깨지기 쉬우므로 맨 위에 실을 것 This is to be packed [loaded] on top, as it is breakable. // 그 배는 200톤의 화물을 싣고 있었다 The ship was carrying a cargo of 200 tons. // 그들은 스키를 자동차의 지붕에 싣고 출발했다 They set out with their skis on the roof of their car.

2 [기사 등을 게재하다] publish (an article) in (a newspaper); carry; record; put (an event) on record; put [place]; enter; print; insert; mention. ¶대통령 교서를 전파에 내보내다 broadcast the President's message // 소설을 신문에 ~ publish [print] a novel in a newspaper // 일 주일간 광고를 ~ run an advertisement for a week // 오늘 신문에는 재미있는 기사가 실려 있다 Today's paper carries an interesting story. / There is an interesting story in today's paper. // 신문은 일기 예보를 싣고 있다 Newspapers carry weather reports. // 그 신문은 일부러 그 사건을 싣지 않았다 The paper deliberately left the affair unreported.

3 [물을 괴게 하다] impound [collect / store] (water in a paddy [reservoir]).

실 (재봉용) thread; (직물·편물용의) yarn. ¶무명 [비단] ~ cotton [silk] thread // ~뭉치 a ball of thread // ~을 감다 reel thread / quill // ~을 잣다 spin yarn / spin thread (out of cotton) // 바늘에 ~을 꿰다 thread a needle // 고치에서 ~을 뽑다 reel silk off cocoons // 엉킨 ~을 풀다 unravel [unloose] tangled thread // 구슬

에 ~을 꿰다 thread beads on a string // ~이 끊어졌다 The thread broke. // 환자는 수술 일 주일 만에 ~을 뽑았다 The patient had the stitches taken out a week after the operation.

-실(室) 〔방〕 a room. ¶연구~ a study room // 건조~ a drying room // 탈의~ a changing room // 102호~ room number[NO.] 102(▶ one oh two로 읽음).

실가(實價) 1 〔실제의 값〕 the actual[real] price. 2 〔에누리없는 값〕 the cost price.

실각(失脚) 1 〔발을 헛디딤〕 a slip of the foot; losing one's footing. **실각하다** slip; lose one's footing. 2 〔자리·지위를 잃음〕 loss of position; a[one's] downfall; a fall. **실각하다** lose one's position [social standing]; fall from power[grace]; be toppled from power; be overthrown. ¶실각한 정치가 a fallen[an ousted / a knocked-out] politician // 그는 수회죄로 실각했다 He lost his position because [on account] of a bribery case. / His involvement in a bribery case caused [brought about] his downfall. / He fell, being implicated in a scandal.

실감(實感) actual feeling[sensation]; solid sense; realization. ¶~ 나는 realistic / true to nature / lifelike / graphic // ~ 나게 노래하다 sing with feeling and expression // 이 그림은 온천장이 ~ 있게 그려져 있다 The picture gives you the feel[atmosphere] of hot spring resort. // 나는 아직 대학생이라는 ~이 나지 않는다 I don't yet really feel that I am a college student.

실감개 a spool; a bobbin; a reel; (베틀의) a beam. ¶~에 감다 spool / reel / wind (thread) on a spool[bobbin] / quill.

실개천 a streamlet; a brooklet; a small brook; a rivulet; 〔시학〕 a rill; a rillet.

실격(失格) disqualification; elimination. ¶그녀는 어머니로서는 ~이다 She is far from what a mother should be. / She has no right to be called a mother. **실격하다** 〔자격을 잃다〕 be disqualified (from / for); 〔제외되다〕 be eliminated (from); (경주에서) be put out of the race. ¶그는 코스에서 벗어나서 실격했다 He strayed from the course and was put out of the race. ➔ 그는 준결승전에서 실격되었다 He stayed from the course and was put out of the race.
●**실격자** a disqualified person.

실고추 shredded red pepper.

실과(實科) a practical course; a practicum.

실국수 thin[threadlike] noodles.

실권(失權) loss[forfeiture] of one's right(s); disfranchisement; loss of power. **실권하다** forfeit[lose] one's rights[power].

실권(實權) real power[control]. ¶~이 없는 사장 a president in name only // ~을 잡다[쥐다] hold real power[control] // 이 사업의 ~은 그가 쥐고 있다 He (actually) controls the business.

실그러뜨리다 〔기울어지게 하다〕 tilt; lean; slant; tip; 〔비뚤어지게 하다〕 distort.

실그러지다 get out of shape[balance]. ⇨ "씰그러지다

실금 a fine crack; a threadlike fissure. ¶~이 가다 get a fine crack (in it) // 찻잔에 ~이 갔다 The tea cup got a fine crack in it.

실기(實技) actual technique[technics]; practical[actual] skill[talent]; (체육의) practical [physical] training.
●**실기 시험** practical (talent) examination; driving test. ¶체육[음악] ~ a test of one's practical skills[ability] in sports[music] // 미술 ~ fine arts talent test.

실기하다(失期-) be[get] too late; be a day after the fair; be past cure[treatment]; be past[beyond] remedy.

실기하다(失機-) miss[lose / fail to catch) an opportunity[a chance]; let slip[go] a chance.

실꾸리 a ball[skein] of thread[yarn].

실낱 a strand; a ply; a (single) thread. ¶~같은 목숨 a life hanging by a thread // ~같은 희망을 갖고 with faint hope.

실내(室內) indoors; the interior of a room. ¶~에(서) indoors / in[inside] a room // ~의 indoor // ~를 장식하다 upholster a room // 비가 오는 통에 온종일 ~에 갇혀 있었다 We were kept indoors all day by the rain. // ~가 너무 건조하다 The air in the room is too dry.
●**실내경기** indoor sports. **실내악** chamber music. ¶~ 연주회 chamber concert. **실내 운동** indoor exercise. **실내 장식** interior design; interior[house] decoration; upholstery. ¶~가 an interior decorator // ~을 하다 upholster a room. **실내화** slippers; scuffles; babouches; house shoes.

실눈 narrow eyes. ¶~을 하다 narrow one's eyes // ~을 뜨고 바라보다 look through half-closed eyes / look at (a thing) with one's eyes half-shut[half-shut / slightly open].

실뜨기 cat's-cradle. **실뜨기하다** play cat's-cradle.

실랑이(질)하다 〔남을 못살게 굴다〕 bother [pester] (a person); nag; 〔승강이하다〕 quarrel; wrangle; have an altercation.

실력(實力) 1 〔실제의 역량〕 one's (real) ability [power]; efficiency; merit; capacity; competence; competency; 〔학력〕 attainments; acquirements; 〔지식〕 knowledge. ¶어학 ~ one's linguistic ability // ~으로 through ability / by (sheer) talent // ~이 있는 able / capable / talented / efficient // ~ 있는 의사 a skilled[skillful] doctor // ~ 있는[없는] 교사 an able[an incompetent] teacher // ~ 있는 사람 a man of ability[merit / real worth] / an able[capable] man // 영어 ~이 있다 have a good command of English / be proficient in English // ~을 기르다 develop[cultivate] one's ability / improve oneself (in) / make oneself proficient (in) / foster real ability // ~을 발휘하다 show one's ability (to the full) / do oneself (full) justice (in a contest) // 영어 ~을 기르다 improve one's ability in English // 그는 ~이 있다 He is a man of ability. / He is an able man. // 그는 물리학 ~이 너무 없다 He is not good enough at physics. / He is too weak[poor] in physics. // 그는 ~을 인정받아 과장으로 승진했다 He was promoted to section chief on account of his efficiency. // 당사는 ~ 위주로 사람을 채용한다 "Ability first" is our motto in employing men.
2 〔무력·완력〕 force; arms. ¶~을 행사하다 use force / appeal to arms / employ force / (노동조합이) go on a strike.
●**실력 사회** meritocracy. **실력자** an influential person; a man of influence. ¶정계의 ~ a powerful man[figure] in politics / an influ-

실례 ential leader of a political party / a strong man [one of the prominent figures] in politics. **실력 테스트** a proficiency test; a test of one's ability. **실력 행사** use of force; appeal [recourse] to arms; (파업 등의) a strike. ¶(노동 쟁의에서) ~에 들어가다 go on a strike.

실례(失禮) impoliteness; rudeness; bad manners [form]; discourtesy; a breach of etiquette. ¶그렇게 하는 것은 ~다 It is impolite [(문어) a breach of etiquette] to do such a thing.∥~ 아닙니까 Isn't that rude? / How rude!∥~를 무릅쓰고 충고하겠습니다 Please let me take the liberty of advising [make bold to advise] you.∥이런 말씀을 드리는 것은 ~일지 모르지만 Perhaps I shouldn't say so, but …. / If I may say it without disrespect [who shouldn't], ….∥~지만 잠깐 드릴 말씀이 있어요 Excuse me, but may I speak to you for a few minutes?∥~이오나 서면으로 보고를 드립니다 Please allow me to inform you by letter.∥~지만 무슨 일로 오셨습니까 May I ask what your business is?∥식사 중에 담배를 피우는 것은 ~다 It is against etiquette to smoke at table. **실례하다** be impolite; act impolitely; commit a discourtesy; be rude. ¶실례합니다 (남의 집을 찾아갔을 때) Hello! / (방에 들어갈 때) May I come in? / (잠시 자리를 뜰 때) Excuse me (for) a moment. / (남의 앞을 지나갈 때) Excuse me (for passing before you).∥그럼 (먼저) 실례하겠습니다 (물러날 때) Well, I must be going [leaving] now. / I'm afraid I must say good-by now. / Excuse my going first [ahead].∥그럼 실례하고 눈 좀 붙여야겠습니다 If it's all right with you [if you please], I think I'll take a little nap.∥아이고, 실례했습니다 I beg your pardon. / I apologize for my rudeness. / Excuse my rudeness. / I am sorry. / Sorry! →¶**실례되는** impolite / rude / impudent (▶ impolite, rude는 예의범절을 지키지 않는, impudent는 뻔뻔스러운) / discourteous∥**실례되는 행동을 하다** act rudely / be rude to (a person) / behave discourteously (to) / commit a breach of etiquette.

실례(實例) an example; an instance; a concrete case; a case in point; an illustration. ¶~를 들다 cite [give] an instance / set [give] a concrete example [illustration]∥그 이론은 ~를 들어 설명하라 Illustrate the theory by giving [citing] examples.∥정규 교육을 받지 않아도 성공한 ~는 얼마든지 있다 There are many instances of people succeeding in spite of their lack of formal education.

실로(實-) really; truly; in truth; surely; to be sure; in fact; very much; (ever) so; indeed; very; (구어) tremendously; (구어) awfully. ¶~ 동감입니다 I (do) indeed agree with you.∥~ 아름다운 경치다 How beautiful the scenery is!

실로폰 a xylophone.

실록(實錄) a true [an authentic / a faithful] record [history]. ¶조선왕조~ a true record of the Joseon dynasty.

실루엣 a silhouette.

실룩 with a twitch [wink / quiver / jerk / spasm]. **실룩하다** twitch; quiver; wink. ¶그는 뺨을 실룩했다 His cheek twitched.

실룩거리다 twitch (and twitch); wink (repeatedly); quiver.

실룩실룩 with (repeated) twitches [jerks] twitchingly. **실룩실룩하다** twitch (and twitch). ⇨실룩거리다 ¶그가 얼굴을 실룩실룩하는 것을 보았다 I saw his face twitching [working].

실리(實利) utility; (an actual) benefit [profit]; material interests [gain]. ¶~적(인) utilitarian / practical.

●**실리주의** utilitarianism. **실리주의자** a utilitarian.

실리다 1 [기재·기록되다] be reported; be recorded; be mentioned; be printed; be given; be put on (a book). ¶신문에 ~ appear [be printed / be reported] in a newspaper / be carried [published] in a daily∥신문에 광고를 ~ insert [run] an ad(vertisement)∥오늘 신문에 재미있는 기사가 실려 있다 Today's paper carries an interesting story. / There is an interesting story in today's paper.∥이 사전에는 용례가 많이 실려 있다 This dictionary gives a lot of examples showing the actual use of words.∥그 신문에는 대지진에 관한 기사가 실려 있었다 The newspaper ran [carried] the story of a severe earthquake.∥그의 단편이 잡지에 실렸다 One of his short stories has been printed in a magazine.∥김치라는 단어가 영어 사전에도 실려 있다 The word *gimchi*(kimchi) is [is given / is mentioned / is found] in English dictionaries, too.∥그의 이름은 승객 명부에 실려 있었다 His name was on the passenger list.

2 [실음을 당하다] (a car / goods) be loaded (up); be put on board; (a ship) be freighted. ¶실려 가다 be carried [taken] away / be carted away∥맛있는 냄새가 부엌에서 미풍에 실려 왔다 The breeze wafted an appetizing aroma from the kitchen.∥부상자 세 사람이 병원으로 실려 왔다 The three injured persons were carried into the hospital.∥화물은 모두 트럭에 실렸다 All the packages were piled up [loaded] on the truck [(영) lorry].

3 [싣게 하다] get (goods) loaded; have (a person) load (up) (a car / goods); let (a cargo) be put on board [be stowed aboard].

실리콘 [화] silicone. ¶~ 처리를 한 siliconized.

실린더 a cylinder.

실링 a shilling (약어 s.).

실마리 1 [실의 첫머리] the end of a thread.
2 [일의 단서] a clue; a key; a lead. ¶이것을 ~로 하여 with this clue to go upon∥경찰은 그의 주소록에서 사건 해결에 중요한 몇 가지 ~를 얻었다 His address book provided the police with several valuable leads to help solve the case.∥그의 소재지를 알아낼 ~는 하나도 없다 We don't have a single clue to his whereabouts.∥마침내 우리는 문제 해결의 ~를 찾아냈다 At last we found a clue to the solution of our problem.∥그것이 ~가 되어 사건은 해결되었다 It served as the clue that led to the solution of the case.∥그의 행방에 대한 단 하나의 ~는 그의 편지의 소인이었다 The only clue [lead] to his whereabouts was the postmark on his letter.∥우리는 이 난문제를 해결할 ~가 전혀 없다 We have no key to the solution [We have no approach likely to lead to a solution] of this difficult problem.∥그 강도는 그의 신원을 알아낼 만

한 ~는 하나도 남겨 놓지 않았다 The robber has left no clues to his identity at all.

실망(失望) disappointment; despair; (구어) letdown. ¶그의 새 소설은 ~이었다 His new novel was a disappointment. **실망하다** be discouraged; be dejected; be let down; be disappointed (at / in / of / with); despair (of); lose one's hope[heart]; be thrown into despair. ¶나중에 실망하지 않도록 to save disappointment // 비싼 생선회를 준비했는데 아무도 먹지 않아 실망했어 It was disappointing that[I was disappointed because] nobody ate the expensive raw fish I had served. // 그녀는 몹시 실망하여 음식을 전혀 먹지 못했다 She was so dejected[disappointed] that she could not eat a bite. // 실망하지 마라 Don't lose heart. / (기운을 내라) Cheer up! // 그 말에 저는 실망했습니다 My heart sank when I heard it. / I felt really let down when I heard it. // 그가 안 와서 실망했어 To my disappointment, he did not come. // 어떤 사태에도 그는 결코 실망하지 않았다 He never lost hope, no matter what the circumstances. // 그 영화에 실망했어 The film disappointed me. / The film was disappointing. // 저는 당신에게 실망했어요 I'm throughly disappointed in you! // 그녀가 사진만큼 예쁘지 않아 난 실망했어 To my disappointment she was not as beautiful as her picture. // 그는 일의 결과가 기대에 어긋나서 실망하고 있다 He is let down because things didn't work out as he expected. // 그는 실망하여 그 고장을 떠났다 He left the place in disappointment[despair]. / He lost[gave up] hope and moved out of that area. ➔ **실망시키다** let down / disappoint / dash[crush] a person's hope. // 나를 실망시키지 마라 Don't let me down.

실명(失明) loss of one's eyesight; blindness. **실명하다** lose one's eyesight[sight]; become sightless; become[go] blind. ¶한 눈을 ~ lose the sight of one eye / become blind of one eye // 그는 자동차 사고로 실명했다 He was blinded in a car accident. / He lost his eyesight[went blind] as the result of a car accident.

실명(實名) (in) one's own[real] name.

실무(實務) practical business affairs. ¶~에 밝다 be familiar with office routine / be versed[experienced] in business // ~에 종사하다 go into[engage in] business // ~를 배우다 study the practice of business / receive a training[train oneself] in practical // ~ 경험이 있다 have business experiences // 그는 ~ 능력이 있다 He has practical business ability. / He has a talent for handling business affairs. / He is possessed of business ability.

● **실무자** the person[clerk / official] in charge (of the business). **~(급) 회담** a working (level) conference[meeting].

실물(實物) 1 [실제의 물건] the real thing; the actual object; (진짜) a genuine article; (그림에 대하여) real life; (사진에 대하여) the original. ¶~과 똑같은 초상화 a lifelike [true-to-life] portrait // 그녀의 사진은 ~과 다르다 (실물이 나은 경우) The photo does not do her justice. / (사진이 나은 경우) She looks better in the photo. // 이 사진보다는 ~이 낫다 This picture does not flatter you. / This picture doesn't do justice to you. // 이 사진은 ~보다 잘 나왔네 This picture flatters you. 2 the (actual) thing. ⇨ 현물

● **실물 거래** (a) spot transaction. **실물 경제** object economy. **실물대**(-大) actual [life] size; the size of the original. ¶~의 as large as life / life- [full-] size(d) / of natural [actual] size // ~의 사진 a life-size [full-size] photo.

실바람 a slight air; a light breeze.

실밥 1 (옷·수술한 곳을 꿰맨 실의) a seam; a stitch. ¶~이 풀어지다 a seam starts / ~을 뽑다 undo [rip up] a seam / cut a seam open // 그 환자는 수술 후 1주일 만에 ~을 뽑았다 The patient had the stitches taken out a week after the operation. 2 (옷 솔기에서 뜯어낸 실의) drawn thread; waste (pieces of) thread [yarn]; ravelings; thrums.

실뱀 [동] a small stringy snake.

실버들 a slender weeping willow.

실보무라지 [실의 부스러기] waste (pieces of) thread [yarn]; raveling; a little piece of thread.

실비(實費) 1 [실제로 드는 비용] actual expense(s). ¶생산 ~ the cost [expense] of production. 2 [원가] cost; the cost price; the prime cost. ¶~로 제공하다 offer (an article) at cost // 이것은 ~로 팔고 있습니다 We are selling these articles at cost [at cost price].

● **실비 제공** a cost sale.

실사(實寫) a picture [photograph] of an actual event; a film shot on the spot; a photograph [picture / film] taken from life [taken on the spot]. **실사하다** take a photograph [picture] on the spot; (영) film [make a film of] (an event).

실사(實辭) [언] a substantive.

실사회(實社會) the real [workaday / everyday] world; the actual [sober] world; realities of life; a practical life. ¶~에 나가다 go [launch out] into the world / get a start in life [the world] / take one's place in society.

실상(實狀) the fact; the truth; the real [true] facts [circumstances]; the real [true] condition state of affairs. ¶~은 in fact / really / in reality // ~은 알 수가 없다 We cannot get at the truth.

실상(實相) real facts [aspects]; the real [true] state of affairs; reality. ¶북한의 ~ the real state of affairs in North Korea // 그 조직의 ~ 은 외부 사람으로서는 알 수가 없었다 The true nature of the organization was impenetrable to outsiders. // 오랫동안 영국에 살았어도 영국인의 생활의 ~은 파악하지 못했다 Though I lived for years in England, I never saw [understood] the real life of the English.

실상(實像) [광] the real image.

실색하다(失色-) turn pale; lose color; change countenance. ¶그는 소식을 듣자 실색했다 Color left his face when he heard the news.

실생활(實生活) real [actual / practical] life; (the realities of) life. ¶~에서 취재한 이야기 a tale taken from real life // ~에 소용이 안 되다 be useless in life // 학교에서 배우는 것은 ~에 그다지 도움이 되지 않는다 The greater part of school learning is not of much use in actual life.

실성(失性) mental derangement; distraction; insanity; madness; (a) frenzy. **실성하다** become mentally deranged [unbalanced]; go

실세 mad; become insane; lose one's head; go out of one's mind. ¶절망한 나머지 실성하여 in a frenzy of despair // 그는 실연하여 실성했다 Disappointed in love, he has lost his head. / Disappointment in love has driven him to distraction.

실세(實勢) [실제의 세력] actual influence [power].

실소(失笑) sudden uncontrollable[irrepressible] laughter. **실소하다** laugh in spite of oneself. ¶그녀의 엉뚱한 대답에 모두들 실소했다 Everybody burst out laughing at her funny answer.

실속(實-) substance; matter; substantiality; real worth; solidity. ¶~ 있는 substantial / solid / meaty / voluminous / instructive // ~ 이 있는 장사 a solid business // 허울을 버리고 ~을 차리다 discard the shadow for the substance.

실수(失手) [실책] a blunder; a mistake; a bungle; a mess; (구어) a mess-up; [실패] a failure; [부주의] carelessness; [못 보고 빠뜨림] an oversight; [잘못] an error; a fault; a slip; [무례] impoliteness. ¶~를 저지르다 do a careless thing / make a blunder[stupid mistake] / blunder / (구어) make a mess // 그(가 하는 일에)는 ~가 없다 He makes no mistakes (in what he does). // 그녀는 ~ 없이 자기 일을 잘 처리한다 She always does her work well. / It's hard to find fault with the way she handles her job. // 회사의 ~가 파산을 초래했다 Bad management[Mismanagement] led to the failure of the firm. // 그의 사소한 ~로 계획은 실패로 돌아갔다 Owing to his small mistake, the whole project fell through. // 그는 또 ~를 저질렀다 He blundered[(구어) goofed / (속어) blew it] again. // ~가 없도록 각자가 조심하기를 바란다 I want each one of you to be careful so that there are no slipups[mistakes / slips]. // 그 사업에 손을 댄 것은 나의 ~였다 I made a blunder[mistake] in taking a hand in that business. // ~가 없도록 아주 조심해 주십시오 Do be very careful. // ~로 인한 결함이 있어서는 안 되므로 내가 다시 한 번 점검해 보겠다 I'll check it again to make sure there has been no oversight. / (구어) We can't afford any slipups, so I'll check it once more. // 그것은 내 판단 ~였다 I was wrong in my estimation[judgment]. // 그를 신용한 것은 ~였다 It was a mistake to trust him. / Trusting him was a big mistake. // 그녀는 자신의 ~를 정중하게 사과했다 She apologized to me politely for her blunder[carelessness]. // 뜻밖의 ~를 해서 미안합니다 I'm sorry to have been so careless[impolite]. // 내가 그만 ~를 저질렀습니다 Do forgive me for my blunder. // 손님에게 ~가 없도록 해라 (가정이나 호텔에서) You must be courteous to our guests. / (가게에서) See that our customers are well attended to[taken care of]. // 그것은 그의 ~였다 It was his fault. // 그것은 네 ~다 You are to blame for it. / It is your fault. // 그것은 그의 ~이지 내 ~가 아니다 The fault lies with him, not me. **실수하다** make a mistake [slip]; commit an error[a fault]; err; blunder; bungle; make[commit] a blunder; botch; (속어) goof. ¶경찰이 실수하여 범인을 놓쳤다 The police made a bad job of it and let the culprit get away. // 그는 이제까지 한번도 실수한 일이 없다 He has never slipped up.

실수(實收) [실제의 수입] net income; real income; [급료의] take-home pay[wages]; [실제의 수확] the actual yield. ¶그의 월급은 세금을 제하고 ~ 90만 원이다 His monthly salary[income] is 900,000 won after taxes.

실수(實數) 1 [실제의 수] the real[actual] number. ¶5만 명이 온 것으로 되어 있지만 ~는 3만 명에 불과했다 Fifty thousand people were reported to have turned out, but the actual number was only thirty thousand. 2 [수] a real number[quantity]; a multiplicand.

실수요(實需要) actual demand.

● **실수요자** an end user.

실수입(實收入) actual[net / real] income.

실습(實習) practice; (practical) exercise; [연습] drill; training; probation. ¶공장 ~ on-the-job training // 교육 ~ teaching practice // 우리는 3주일간의 교생 ~을 했다 we had three weeks of practice[student] teaching. **실습하다** practice; have (practical) training. ¶요리를 ~ practice cooking.

● **실습생** a trainee; a student apprentice; an apprentice; (병원의) an intern(e); student assistant; (교육 실습의) a student teacher.

실시(實施) enforcement; operation; execution; implementation; practical application; [법] effectuation. ¶조약의 ~ the enforcement of a treaty // ~를 명하다 order (a program) into effect. **실시하다** put into effect; put (a law) into force; enforce[give effect to] (a law); carry (a program) into effect; execute; implement; effectuate. ¶신체검사는 내일 실시합니다 The medical examination will be carried out tomorrow. ➔ ¶실시되다 be enforced / go[come] into effect[operation] / become operative / take effect // 그 법률은 내년 1월부터 실시된다 The law will take effect [goes into effect / comes into force] next January. // 우리는 그 계획이 가능한 한 빨리 실시되기를 바라고 있다 We hope to put the plan into practice as soon as possible.

실시간(實時間) real time.

실신(失神) a swoon; a faint; a coma; a fainting fit; a blackout. **실신하다** swoon; faint (away); fall into a swoon; fall unconscious; lose consciousness[one's senses]; black out. ¶실신한 사람처럼 like a man in a trance // 실신해 있다 be in a swoon[faint] // 그녀는 실신한 것 같다 She looks faint.

실실 with a silly snicker[snigger]. ¶~ 웃다 cackle / giggle / laugh like an idiot.

실액(實額) actual amount of money.

실어증(失語症) aphasia.

● **실어증 환자** an aphasi(a)c.

실언(失言) a slip of the tongue; a verbal lapse; an impropriety in speech. ¶~을 취소하다 retract[take back] one's improper remark // ~을 사과하다 apologize for one's improper language. **실언하다** make a slip of the tongue; use improper language[words]; drop one's buckets; commit an impropriety in speech; one's tongue slips (in one's statement); (미국 구어) put[stick] one's foot in the[one's] mouth.

실업(失業) unemployment; loss of employment; joblessness. ¶계절적[주기적] ~ seasonal[cyclical] unemployment // 구조적 ~

structural unemployment // 만성적 ~ **chronic unemployment** // 잠재적 ~ **latent unemployment / potential [disguised] unemployment**. **실업하다** lose one's employment [work / job]; fall [be thrown] out of employment [work]. ¶이 때문에 몇 천 명의 근로자가 실업했다 It created [caused] unemployment for thousands of workers.
● **실업 대책** an unemployment policy; measures to combat unemployment. ¶~ 사업 relief work for the unemployed. **실업률** an unemployment rate. **실업 문제** the unemployment problem. ¶~가 심각해졌다 The employment problem has come to assume a grave aspect. / Unemployment has become an urgent question. **실업 수당** an unemployment allowance [dole / benefit]. ¶~을 지급하다 grant (a person) an unemployment allowance / put (a person) on the dole / ~을 받다 go on [draw] the dole. **실업자** a person who is out of work; an unemployed person; a jobless person; (집합적) the unemployed; the jobless. ¶거리를 헤매는 ~들 out-of-work men mooching about the streets // ~를 구제하다 relieve unemployed people // ~가 늘었다 Unemployment was on the increase.

실업(實業) 〔생산업〕 industry; 〔상업·실무〕 business.
● **실업가** a businessman; a businesswoman; 〔기업가〕 an industrialist. **실업계** the industrial [business] world; business circles. ¶~에 투신하다 enter the business world / enter business life / go into business.

실없다(實−) 〔성실하지 못하다〕 insincere; faithless; untrustworthy; unreliable; hollow-hearted; 〔무의미하다〕 foolish; absurd; idle. ¶실없는 소리 absurd remarks / silly talk / nonsense // 실없는 사람 an untrustworthy person / a senseless [silly] person // 실없는 소리 마라 Don't talk rubbish [rot]! **실없이** nonsensically; senselessly; frivolously; rubbishly; uselessly; flippantly. ¶~ 말하다 make idle [flippant] remarks.

실연(失戀) disappointed [unrequited / unreturned] love; a disappointment in love; a broken heart. **실연하다** be disappointed [crossed] in (a person's) love. ¶실연한 사람 a brokenhearted person // 그는 실연했다 He has been disappointed [unlucky] in love. / He is suffering from a broken heart.

실연(實演) **1** 〔실제로 해 보이기〕 a demonstration. ¶요리의 ~을 하다 give a demonstration of cooking. **2** 〔무대에서 연기하기〕 a stage show [performance]; a performance on the stage. **실연하다** act [perform / sing] on the stage; present on the stage.

실오리 a piece of thread [string]. ¶~ 같은 희망 a shadow [ray / flash] of hope // 몸에 ~ 하나 걸치지 않은 [않고] without a stitch [shred / strip] of clothing (on).

실온(室溫) the temperature of a room; room temperature. ¶~을 섭씨 27도로 유지하다 keep the room temperature at 27℃.

실외(室外) outdoors. ¶~의 outdoor // ~에(서) outside (of) a room / outdoors / out of doors // ~에 내놓다 put (a thing) out of the room.

실용(實用) practical use; utility. ¶~ 본위의 가구[의복] utility furniture [clothes]. **실용하다** put [turn] (a thing) to practical use.

● **실용성** practicality; utility. ¶~이 있다[없다] have a [no] practical use. **실용신안** a practical new device [design]; a new design for practical use. **실용주의** practicalism; 〔철〕 pragmatism. **실용주의자** a pragmatist. **실용품** an article for practical use; a practical [useful] article; daily necessities (일용품); domestic articles (가정용품). **실용화** ¶~하다 put [turn] (a thing) to practical use // 그의 발명이 ~되었다 His invention has been put to practical use.

실용적(實用的) (intended) for practical [actual] use; practical. ¶~인 물건 an article for practical use / a practical [useful] article // ~이다 be of practical use // 그것은 ~이 못 된다 It is of no practical use.

실은(實−) really; in reality [fact]; in point of fact; 〔사실을 말하자면〕 the fact [truth] is ...; to tell [speak / confess] the truth; to speak honestly; truth to say; to be frank [candid] with you. ¶~ 이렇다 I'll tell you what. / The truth is this. // ~ 그는 오늘 오지 않는다 To tell the truth, he is not coming today.

실의(失意) disappointment; despair; dejection. ¶~에 빠진 사람 a disappointed [broken] man / 〔실연한 사람〕 a man with a broken heart // 그는 ~의 바다를 헤매면서도 희망을 잃지 않았다 He never lost hope even in adversity. // 거듭되는 실패에 그는 완전히 ~에 빠져 있다 He is terribly depressed [utterly dejected] by his repeated failures. // 외아들이 죽어 그녀는 ~에 빠져 있다 The death of her only son has caused her to lose heart completely. // 한 씨 부부는 ~에 찬 그를 도왔다 Mr. and Mrs. Han stood by him when he was in despair. **실의하다** be disappointed; be disheartened; be thrown into despair.

실익(實益) 〔실수익〕 an actual [a net] profit; 〔실리〕 usefulness; practical use; material gain; utility; benefit. ¶~이 없는 계획 an impractical scheme // ~이 있다 be profitable / be of practical use / be useful.

실인(實印) a registered seal; a legal seal. ¶계약서에 ~을 찍다 set [fix] one's registered seal to a contract.

실장(室長) the head of an office; (연구실의) the head of a laboratory; (부·국의) a section chief; (기숙사 등의) a senior roommate.

실재(實在) real [actual] existence; actual being; actuality; reality; 〔철〕 essence; entity. **실재하다** exist (really); be in existence; have a real existence. ¶실재하지 않는 도시 an imaginary [a fictitious] town // 그런 동물은 실재하지 않는다 No such animals really exist.
● **실재론** 〔철〕 realism; externalism.

실적(實績) (actual) results; one's record of performance; solid results; positive achievements. ¶수출 ~ actual exports / the actual export record // 금년도의 영업 ~ the business performance [showing] for this year // ~을 올리다 get results / give [attain] actual [satisfactory] results / bear fruit / bring results.

실전(實戰) actual fighting [fight / warfare]; a battle; an action; active service; (스포츠에서) a real game [match / fight]. ¶~ 경험이 많은 노병 a veteran of considerable combat experience // 그는 ~ 경험이 있다 He has seen action. / He has combat experience.

실점(失點) (경기 등에서) points given up; runs given up(야구); points lost(테니스); points[runs] one allows one's opponent in a game. ¶나는 요즈음 ~을 거듭하고 있다 I am in the middle of a losing streak. / I have lost many matches in a row. / (실수의 연속) I have made one mistake after another. 실점하다 lose a point; be beaten; be defeated.

실정(失政) misgovernment; misrule; maladministration. 실정하다 misgovern; misrule.

실정(實情) the actual condition [circumstances]; the real state of affairs[things]; the real condition; the facts (of a case); the real situation; (속어) the lowdown. ¶~을 알다 know the actual circumstances / know how the matter (really) stands // ~에 밝다 be in the swim // ~에 어둡다 be out of the swim / be out of touch with things as they are / 그것이 대체적인 ~이다 That's about the size of it.

실정법(實定法) [법] the positive law.

실제(實際) [사실] the (exact) truth; a fact; [실정] an actual state; the actual condition of things; [실지] practice; [현실] reality; actuality. ¶~의 practical / actual / real / (사실상의) virtual / [구체적] concrete / (미국 속어) down-to-earth // ~이론과 ~ theory and practice // ~의 가치 real[actual] value // ~에 응용하다 put (a theory) into practice / apply (a rule) in practice // 나는 ~ 그렇게 생각한다 I do think so. // 상상과 ~는 딴판이었다 I found the reality quite different from what I had imagined. // 이 두 가지는 ~ 동일한 것이다 The two are practically [virtually] the same.

● 실제 경험 practical[actual] experience; practical knowledge. 실제 소득 a real income.

실제로(實際-) actually; really; as a matter of fact; in fact; practically; in practice; virtually; in effect; to tell the truth. ¶그는 햄릿을 ~ 흉내 내려고 한다 He is trying to imitate Hamlet in real life. // 그것은 ~ 있었던 일이다 It was an actual occurrence. / It actually happened. // 그는 기인이라는 소문이 있는데 ~ 그렇다 He is said to be eccentric and he really is. // 내가 본 일이다 I actually saw it. / I saw it with my own eyes. // ~ 그렇다 It's a fact.

실제적(實際的) practical; matter-of-fact; businesslike. ¶~인[이 아닌] 사람 a practical[an impractical] man // ~인 의견 a practical view // ~으로 in a practical manner / in a matter-of-fact style.

실조(失調) (a) malfunction; disharmony. ¶영양~ malnutrition / undernourishment / unbalanced nutrition.

실족(失足) [잘못 디딤] a false step; a misstep; (행동상의) a misdeed; a failure. 실족하다 miss one's foot[step]; lose one's footing; make[take] a false step; slip; [행동을 잘못하다] do an unwise act; fail (in something). ¶계단에서 ~ miss one's footing on the stairs // 실족하여 추락사하다 lose one's footing and fall to death // 그는 계단에서 실족하여 떨어졌다 He missed (lost) his footing on the stairs and fell.

실존(實存) existence. ¶~의 existent. 실존하다 exist. ¶용은 실존하는 동물이 아니다 Dragons never really existed.

● 실존주의 existentialism. 실존주의자 an existentialist. 실존 철학 existential philosophy.

실종(失踪) disappearance; missing; absconding. ¶~ 상태에 있다 be missing // 우리는 그의 ~을 신고했다 We reported him missing [his disappearance]. 실종하다 disappear; abscond; drop from sight; [행방불명되다] be missing.

● 실종 신고 a report of (a person's) disappearance. 실종자 a missing person; [가출인] a runaway.

실주(實株) a real stock; a spot share.

실증(實證) a proof; an actual proof; corroborative evidence. ¶~적(으로) positive(ly) / demonstrative(ly) // ~을 잡다 have[be in possession of] actual proof // ~을 가지고 있다 hold the actual proofs of // ~을 들다 give an actual proof (of a thing) // ~에 의해 확신을 얻다 corroborate one's belief. 실증하다 prove; demonstrate; corroborate (a proof); establish (a fact)(이론이나 실례에 의해서); bear out; verify[justify] (one's reputation); substantiate. ➔ ¶사건의 보고서는 목격자에 의해 실증되었다 The report of the accident was verified by eyewitnesses.

● 실증주의 [철] positivism. 실증주의자 a positivist. 실증 철학 positive philosophy; positivism; Comtism(Comte의).

실지(失地) [잃은 영역·땅] lost territory.

● 실지 회복 recovery of lost territory. ¶지난 번 선거에서 패한 전 지사는 ~을 노리고 있다 The former governor, who was defeated in the last election, is aiming at recovering his lost position.

실지(實地) (actual) practice; the practical side; [실제] actuality; reality. ¶~의 practical / actual // 이론과 ~ theory and (actual) practice.

● 실지 경험 practical [actual] experience; practical knowledge. ¶~이 있는 사람 a man of (journalistic / teaching) experience // ~을 하다 have practical experience (in) // 그는 장사의 ~이 부족하다 He lacks practical experience in business. 실지 훈련 on-the-job training.

실지렁이 [동] a tubificid; a tubifex.

실지로(實地-) actually; really. ⇨ *실제로 ¶~ 소용되는 영어 practical English // ~ 행하다 carry[put] (a theory) in practice / practice (a theory) // 그는 중국의 상태를 ~ 배우기 위해 중국에 갔다 He went to China to study conditions there first-hand.

실직(失職) unemployment; loss of employment. 실직하다 lose one's employment[work / job]; fall[be thrown] out of employment [work]. ¶실직한 unemployed / jobless // 실직한 상태이다 be out of work [employment / job].

● 실직자 an unemployed person; a person who is out of work; (집합적) the unemployed.

실질(實質) [실체] substance; [본질] essence; [소질] quality; [재료] matter; material; [내용] contents. ¶~이 있는 substantial / tangible // ~이 없는 unsubstantial / impalpable / hollow // 겉보기보다 ~을 택하라 Prefer substance to appearance[shadow].

● 실질 소득 real income. 실질 임금 real wages; (속어) take-home pay[wages].

실질적(實質的) substantial; essential; material; solid. ¶~ 원조 substantial aid // ~ 진보 substantial progress // ~인 동의 substantial agreement // ~으로 [본질적으로] in essence / essentially / [실제로] practically // 그것은 ~인 가격 인상이다 That amounts to an increase in prices.

실쭉거리다 distort; move at a bad angle [in a misshapen way]; sulk.

실쭉하다 1 (얼굴 등을) distort; contort; pout; (얼굴 등이) be distorted; be misshapen. ¶입을 ~ screw up one's mouth / make a wry mouth. **2** [고깝게 여기다] be displeased; be discontented; look glum [sullen]. ¶실쭉해서 입술을 삐쭉 내밀다 pout / thrust [push] out the lips in displeasure [sullenness].

실책(失策) a blunder; a slip; a bungle; an error; a mistake; a misstep. ¶대~ a gross [huge] blunder [error] // ~을 저지르다 do (a matter) amiss / commit an error [a blunder] / bungle / fall into an error // 그의 부인에 대해서 운운한 것은 ~이었다 It was a mistake to mention his wife. / 그 발언은 대통령의 ~이었다 That statement proved disadvantageous to the President. / The President lost favor with the public because of that statement. // 그는 ~을 거듭했다 He made repeated errors.

실천(實踐) practice. ¶~적 practical. **실천하다** practice; put (a theory) in practice; execute. ¶자기의 신념을 ~ live up to one's beliefs [principles] // 아침 일찍 일어나기를 ~ practice [(영)practise] getting up early.
● **실천가** a man of deeds [action]; a person of practical mind. **실천력** power of execution; executive faculty [ability]; action; initiative. ¶~이 있는 사람 a person [man] of action // 그는 계획은 잔뜩 있으나 ~이 없다 He has a full of schemes, but lacks the power of execution.

실체(實體) substance; subject; (phenomenon 에 대한) noumenon; entity; [본성] the true nature (of). ¶~가 있는 substantial / solid // ~가 없는 unsubstantial / incorporeal / insubstantial / impalpable (forms and figures) // 사물의 ~를 파악하다 grasp the facts of a case / get at the heart of things // 교육의 ~는 단지 학과를 배우는 것이 아니라, 생활에서 효과를 내게 하는 데 있다 The substance of (an) education is its effect on one's life, not just the subjects one learns. // 그것의 ~를 모르겠다 I do not know what it really is.
● **실체론** ontology. ⇨존재론(⑤존재). **실체법** a substantial law; the substantive law. **실체화** substantiation. ¶~하다 substantiate.

실추(失墜) loss; fall. ¶권력의 ~ one's fall from power. **실추하다** [잃다] lose; forfeit; [떨어지다] fall; sink. ¶권력을 ~ fall from power. ➔위신이 실추되다 lose (one's) prestige // 그는 스캔들이 탄로 나서 민중의 신망이 실추되었다 When the scandal concerning him came to light, he lost credit with the people [he fell in the public estimation].

실측(實測) (actual) measurement; (a) survey. **실측하다** measure; survey; make a survey of (a forest).
● **실측도** a survey map; (영) an ordnance map; a survey. ¶25만분의 1 ~ a 250,000 scale [1/250,000th] map / a map (drawn) on a scale of 1/250,000 [1 to 250,000].

실컷 to one's heart's content; to one's satisfaction; heartily; as much as one likes [wishes]; to the full; to the fullest measure; to the utmost; to the hilt; without reserve; unreservedly(거리낌 없이). ¶나는 ~ 꾸중을 들었다 I got a good scolding [(구어) telling-off]. / I was severely scolded. // 나는 그 녀석을 ~ 때려 주었다 I hit him all I wanted [to my heart's content]. // 나는 대학원에 들어가 ~ 공부하고 싶다 I want to enter graduate school and study as hard as I can. // 나는 ~ 먹었다 I ate my fill. // 나는 ~ 울었다 I cried my heart out. // ~ 먹어라 Eat as much as you like. / Eat your fill. / (속어) Eat up. / 오늘은 ~ 쉬십시오 Please stay as long as you like today. // 자, 나를 ~ 때려라 Go on and hit me until you're satisfied. / 나는 ~ 마셨다 I have drunk my fill. // ~ 즐기자 Let's enjoy ourselves to our hearts' content.

실켜다 (누에고치에서) reel off silk threads.

실크 [생사·견직물] silk. ¶~의 silk.

실탄(實彈) (소총의) a live cartridge; a solid (bullet); (대포의) a loaded [live] shell; a solid [round] shot; (집합적) live ammunition. ¶ ~을 쓰지 않는 dry (firing) // ~을 발사하다 fire ball cartridges.
● **실탄 사격** (소총의) live shooting; (대포의) target practice with live shells.

실태(實態) the actual condition [state]; the realities. ¶실업자의 ~를 조사하다 investigate the actual conditions of [among] the unemployed.
● **실태 조사** research on (an investigation into) the actual condition; a fact-finding survey.

실토(實吐) a true confession; telling the whole truth; speaking with sincerity. **실토하다** confess (to); disclose one's real intention; spit out the truth; tell the whole truth; reveal one's real motive. ¶실토하게 하다 get the truth out of (a person) // 그는 모든 것을 실토했다 He made a clean breast of everything. // 실토해라 Own up! / (미) Come clean!

실톱 (U 자형의) a coping saw; (곡선으로 자르는) a jig saw; (장식 도형을 오려 내는) a fretsaw; (전동의) a saber saw.

실투(失投) [야구] a careless pitch [throw]; the careless delivery of a ball by a pitcher. ¶그의 단 한 번의 ~였는데, 그것으로 승부가 결정되어 버렸다 He made a mistake with only one pitch, but it was enough to cost him the game. // 훌륭한 타자는 ~를 놓치지 않는다 A good batter never lets an easy pitch go by. **실투하다** make a careless pitch.

실파 (가느다란 파) a small green onion.

실팍하다 solid; firm; strong; stout; strongly [sturdily] built. ¶실팍한 사나이 a man of solid [sturdy] build // 이 책상은 ~ This desk is strongly built.

실패 a spool; a reel; a bobbin; a beam. ¶~에 실을 감다 wind thread on a spool.

실패(失敗) (a) failure; ill success; blunder; (구어) a flop; (속어) a washout; (속어) a goof. ¶대~ a glaring [a complete / an utter] failure / a fiasco // ~(e)s // ~로 끝나다 end in failure / go amiss // 모든 노력이 ~로 돌아갔다 All our efforts ended in [(문어) met with] failure. / All our efforts were in vain [went wrong]. // ~는 성공의 어머니다

실하다

Failure is a stepping stone to success. / Failure teaches success.∥그 연극은 완전한 ~였다 That play was a complete flop [failure].∥그 시도는 ~로 끝났다 The project fell through. **실패하다** (사람이) fail; be unsuccessful (in); be frustrated [foiled/balked] (in an attempt); (구어) draw a blank; [영락하다] sink[come down] in the world; (일이) fail; miscarry; prove[turn out] a failure; end[result] in (a) failure; meet with failure; go wrong [amiss]; come to naught. ¶그는 입학시험에 실패했다 He failed [was unsuccessful] in the entrance examination.∥그의 연극은 실패했다 His play was a failure[(구어) flop].∥그 계획은 실패했다 The plan fell through.∥그는 사업에 실패하여 몰락했다 He failed in business and was ruined. / He lost everything as a result of his failure in business.
●**실패자** a failure; a social failure(낙오자). **실패작** a failure; a flop(책·연극 등); an article of poor workmanship.

실하다(實-) 1 [튼튼하다] strong; solid; firm; substantial; sturdy; strongly built. ¶몸이 실한 남자 a man of solid[sturdy] build∥실한 제본 durable binding. 2 [재산이 있다] well-to-do; wealthy; solid; sound. ¶장사 밑천이 ~ have enough[sufficient] business funds. 3 [믿을 만하다] reliable (man); trustworthy; solid; substantial. 4 [내용이] full; substantial; solid; rich in content. ¶내용이 실한 저작 a substantial work∥6마일이 ~ be full six miles.

실학(實學) practical science; realism.
●**실학파** a realistic[positive] school.

실행(實行) [실천] practice; action; deed; [수행] execution; performance; prosecution; [이행] fulfilment; [실시] enforcement; implementation; [실현] realization. ¶~상 practically / in practice∥~상의 practical / executive∥~ (불가능한) (im)practicable / (in)feasible∥우리의 생각을 ~에 옮기다 put our idea into practice[action]. **실행하다** practice; put (something) in[into] practice; execute; implement; carry out (a plan); carry (a plan) into execution[effect]; enforce. ¶실행할 수 없는 impracticable / infeasible / unworkable∥계획을 ~ put a plan into action. →¶그런 비현실적인 계획은 아마 실행되지 않을 것이다 Such an impractical project can't possibly[will never] be carried out.
●**실행력** power of execution; executive ability[faculty]. ¶~**이 있다** have executive talent.

실험(實驗) (과학의) experimentation; (실험실에서의) laboratory work; (한 번의) (an) experiment; [시험] a test. ¶동물 ~ experiments with[using] animals∥핵 ~ a nuclear experiment[test]∥화학 ~ a chemical experiment / an experiment in chemistry∥~적인 experimental / (학술상의) empirical / ~적으로 experimentally / on an experimental basis∥과학 ~을 하다 do[make] a scientific experiment∥~으로 가르치다 demonstrate / teach by the help of experiments∥그것은 현재 ~ 중이다 It is in[at] the help of experiments. **실험하다** experiment (on / in); make[conduct] an experiment[a test] (on / in / with); put (a thing) to the test[proof]; experimentalize.
●**실험 과학** empirical science. **실험대** a laboratory table; a testing bench; an experiment stand. **실험실** a laboratory / (속어) a lab. ¶화학 ~ a chemical laboratory. **실험장** a proving[test] ground; a test center.

실현(實現) realization (of one's hopes); materialization; attainment; actualization; fruition. ¶~ (불)가능한 (un)realizable. **실현하다** realize; actualize; materialize; fulfill; effectuate; bring to fruition[realization]; (꿈·희망이) come true. ¶실현할 수 있는 realizable / possible of realization∥실현할 수 없는 unrealizable / impossible of realization / infeasible. →¶실현되다 be materialized / be realized / come to pass / become a reality∥그녀의 꿈은 실현되었다 Her dream has come true.∥그의 위대한 꿈이 마침내 실현되었다 His grand plan has materialized[been realized] at last.

실형(實刑) a prison sentence; imprisonment; (기간) the real term of imprisonment. ¶그는 3년 징역의 ~을 선고받았다 He was sentenced to three years imprisonment [in prison].

실화(失火) an accidental fire. ¶그 화재는 ~였다 The fire was of accidental origin. **실화하다** have a fire started (in a house) by accident.

실화(實話) a true story; a story (taken) from real life; an authentic account. ¶범죄 ~ a factual account of crime.

실황(實況) [실정] the real[actual] condition; the actual state of things; [광경] the actual scene; [실시 상황] actual operation. ¶~을 조사하다 inspect actual conditions / make an on-the-spot inspection.
●**실황 방송** [TV] an on-the-spot telecast; [라디오] minute-to-minute [on-the-spot] broadcasting; a running commentary; (스포츠의) play-by-play broadcasting; outside broadcasting; a mike-side account of (a special event). ¶스포츠 ~ 아나운서 a sportscaster / a play-by-play announcer∥~을 하다 broadcast live[from the spot] / (스포츠의) keep up a running commentary (on a game).

실효(失效) a lapse; invalidation; losing; losing effect; becoming null and void; abatement. ¶내 면허장은 갱신하지 않아서 ~가 되었다 My license expired[ran out] because I didn't renew it. / The license lost its validity because it had not been renewed. **실효하다** [유효성을 잃다] lapse; [법] lose validity; [기한이 다 되다] expire; (구어) run out. →¶그 계약은 예전에 실효되어 있었다 The contract had lapsed many years before.

실효(實效) [효과] a practical effect; efficacy; practical results; [능률] efficiency. ¶~ 있는 [없는] effective [ineffective] ∥~를 거두다 give satisfactory results / do good work / work.
●**실효성** effectiveness.

싫다 [불쾌하다] disagreeable; unpleasant; distasteful; disgusting; odious; offensive; nasty; nauseous; [달갑지 않다] undesirable; unwelcome; [지긋지긋하다] hateful; loathsome; abominable; (서술적) dislike; hate; detest(▶ 이 순서로 뜻이 강해짐); be unwilling[reluctant] (to do). ¶싫은 여자 a disgusting[nasty] woman // 싫은 표정[눈매] a disagreeable look // 싫건 좋건 whether one will[like it] or not / whether willing or not / willy-nilly // 그녀는 주위 사람들에게 언제나 싫은 소리를 한다 She keeps saying disagreeable things to those around her. // 그는 내가 늦게 왔다고 싫은 표정을 지었다 He looked displeased because I was late. // 나는 담배 연기가 ~ I hate cigarette smoke. // 그는 꼬치꼬치 내 일을 캐물으므로 나는 ~ He annoys me by digging into my affairs too much. // 때로 파티에 참석하는 것도 나는 싫지 않습니다 I don't mind[(문어) am not averse to] going to parties occasionally. // 싫다면 싫은 줄 알아 If I say no, I mean no! / If I say I won't, then I won't! // "함께 가지 않겠냐?" "싫어!" "Won't you go with me?" "No thank you!"(▶ 강한 어조로 말함) // 정말 ~ [지겹다] Oh, no! / Ooh, how awful! // 그는 좋고 싫음을 얼굴에 나타낸다 He lets his likes and dislikes show on his face. // 그녀의 짙은 화장은 정말 보기 ~ Her thick makeup is disgusting.

싫어지다 come to dislike (something); become disgusted (with); lose taste (for); [물리다] become sick[tired / weary] (of); lose interest (in); [식상하다] be fed up (with). ¶세상이 ~ lose interest in life / become [grow] sick[weary] of life[the world] // 좋았던 여자가 ~ fall out of love with one's girl // 나는 세상이 싫어졌다 I am tired of my life. // 나는 그가 싫어졌다 I come to dislike him. / I took a dislike to him. // 넌 (퍼스널) 컴퓨터가 싫어졌니 Have you lost in your (personal) computer? // 나 자신이 싫어졌다 I am disgusted with myself. // 단조로운 이 일이 나는 싫어졌다 I am fed up with[sick (and tired) of] this monotonous work.

싫어하다 dislike; have a dislike to[for]; grudge (doing); be unwilling[reluctant] (to do). ¶몹시 ~ hate / loathe / detest / have a distaste for / have an aversion[antipathy] to / have a hatred for / be prejudiced against / feel repugnance for / abhor / be averse to // 싫어하는 abominable / detestable / loathsome // 싫어하는 것 what one does not like / an abomination // 남들이 싫어하는 사람 / a pest / an abominable [odious] person // 내가 아주 싫어하는 스타일의 남자 the type[sort] of man I hate[detest] // 영어를 ~ dislike English // 담배 냄새를 ~ abhor the smell of tobacco // 돈을 내놓기를 ~ grudge money // 그는 생선을 싫어한다 He hates[doesn't like] fish. // 그는 공부를 싫어한다 He detests study. // 나는 여자를 싫어한다 I hate woman. / (문어) I am a misogynist. // 그 아이는 우유를 싫어해서 먹으려고 하지 않았다 The child had a dislike for milk and would not drink it. // 그 여자는 누구나가 싫어했다 She was disliked[hated] by everybody. // 나는 그를 단지 싫어하는 것이 아니라 혐오한다 I don't simply dislike him — I detest[loathe] him. // 그는 마을 사람들이 싫어했다 He was an object of hatred in the village. / He was shunned by the villagers. // 그들은 싫어하는 것 같았다 They seemed unwilling. // 제 딸이 싫어하므로 우리는 여행을 그만두겠습니다 My daughter is unwilling[doesn't want / is reluctant] to do and so we will give up our trip. // 그녀는 남이 하기 싫어하는 일을 자진해서 떠맡는다 She volunteers to do the jobs other people hate (to do).

실증(-症) an aversion; dislike; disgust; a repugnance (to / for); weariness. ¶~이 나다 feel a repugnance to[for] / be[get / grow] tired of / get sick of / be[become] disgusted with / become weary of / be bored (with) / lose interest in // ~이 나지 않는 일 [무늬] work[a pattern] which one doesn't get tired of // 공부에는 이제 ~이 났다 I'm tired of studying. // 나는 이따금 일에 ~이 난다 I sometimes get tired of my job. // 그는 그녀에게 ~이 났다 He has fallen out of love with his girl. // 그는 자기 일에 ~을 느껴 그만두었다 He got tired of[(구어) fed up with] his job and quit. // 그의 장황한 이야기에 우리는 ~이 났다 We were bored by his long-winded talk. // 그들의 말다툼엔 이제 ~이 났다 I've had enough of their quarrels. / I'm fed up with their quarrels. // 그의 이야기는 두서가 없어 ~이 난다 His rambling conversation is a bore. // 그는 매사에 곧 ~을 낸다 He soon gets tired of[loses interest in] things. / He gets tired of[bored with] things very quickly. / He never remains interested in anything for very long. // 그녀는 곧 ~을 내서 남자 친구를 언제든지 바꾼다 She gets tired of people right away[soon tires of people] and is always switching boyfriends.

심(心) **1** [중심부] the center; (과실의) the core; (목재의) the heart. ¶~까지 썩다 be rotten to the core // 이 공은 ~이 납이다 The core of this ball is lead. **2** [옷 등의 속에 넣는 것] interlining; foundation; padding; a pad; a wad; (양초의) a wick; (연필의) lead. ¶~을 넣다 pad (a sash) / interline (a coat) // 양초의 ~을 자르다 snuff a candle. **3** [줄기] a string; a fiber[fibre]; a vein. ¶무의 ~이 있다 A turnip is stringy. **4** [새알심] small dumplings in adzuki bean porridge.

-심(心) a heart; a mind; a spirit; a sense. ¶경쟁~ a competitive spirit // 애국~ patriotism // 충성~ sense of loyalty.

심각하다(深刻–) serious; grave; keen; acute; poignant. ¶심각한 인구 문제 a serious population problem // 심각한 표정으로 with a serious[grave] look // 심각한 얼굴을 하다 look serious[grave] / assume [put on] a serious[grave / sober] look // 지나치게 심각하게 생각하다 take (a matter) too seriously // 심각하게 되다[심각해지다] become intensified[aggravated] / worsen / (문제·형세가) assume an acute phase[a serious aspect] / become more acute [critical / urgent / strained] // 날로 심각해지는 교통 문제의 해결을 위한 방안을 마련하다 work out a plan to solve the ever-serious traffic problems // 사태는 더욱 심각해졌다 The situation became more serious[critical]. / The situation grew worse. // 생활난이 더욱 심각해졌다 The difficulty of living is felt more and more keenly. // 그녀는 갑자기 심각해졌다 She suddenly fell grave. // 너무 심각하게 생각하지 마십시오 Please don't take it so seriously.

심경(心境) a frame[state] of mind; a mental attitude[state]. ¶현재의 ~ one's present state of mind // 평온한 ~ a tranquil[serene] mind // ~의 변화 a change of mind / a change in one's mental attitude // ~을 토로하다 express one's feelings / speak one's mind / unbosom oneself[one's soul] (to) /

open one's heart (to) / talk about one's opinions (of) // ~의 변화를 가져오다 undergo a change of mind / change one's mind // 그녀의 그러한 ~에는 동정이 간다 I sympathize with her in her mental attitude. // 나는 그 책을 읽고 ~의 변화를 일으켰다 Reading that book brought about a change in my state of mind. // 당신의 지금 ~은 어떻습니까 What are your feelings at the present? // 그것이 현재의 나의 ~이다 That is how I feel now.

심근(心筋) [생] the myocardium (pl. -dia); a cardiac[heart] muscle.
● **심근 경색증** myocardial[cardiac] infarction.

심금(心琴) heartstrings.
심금(을) 울리다 touch[pull at] (a person's) heartstrings; touch a cord[string] in (a person's) heart; touch the lutestrings of (a person's) heart. ¶독자의 ~ awake a responsive cord / strike a chord of feeling in the hearts of the readers // 그의 이야기는 청중의 심금을 울렸다 His story struck a responsive chord in the hearts of the audience.

심기(心氣) (a) humor; a temper; a mood; feelings. ¶~가 편하다 be in a good humor[mood] / be cheerful // ~가 불편하다 be in an ill[bad] humor[mood] / be out of humor[temper] / be in a bad temper / be displeased.

심기다 [심어지다] get planted; be planted.

심기일전하다(心機一轉-) one's mind takes a new turn; (사람이) change one's mind; turn over a new leaf; become a new man. ¶그는 심기일전하여 담배를 끊었다 He turned over a new leaf and stopped smoking. // 그는 심기일전하여 열심히 일함으로써 가업을 다시 일으켰다 He turned over a new leaf and rescued the family business through hard work.

심난하다(甚難-) extremely[very] difficult[hard].

심낭(心囊) [생] a pericardium (pl. -dia); the pericardial[heart] sac.

심다 1 (식물을) plant; set (out); transplant(옮겨 심다). ¶정원에 나무를 ~ plant trees in a garden / plant a garden with trees // 정원에 잔디를 ~ [떼를 입히다] sod a garden (with grass[turf]) / put down a lawn in a garden / (씨를 뿌리다) sow grass seed in a garden // 감자를 ~ dibble in potatoes // 그는 밭에 토마토 모종을 심었다 He planted tomato seedlings in the field. // 공원에는 많은 은행나무가 심어져 있다 The park is planted with a number of ginkgo trees.
2 (사상 등을) implant; plant; fix; inculcate; impregnate; imbue. ¶국민에게 자신감과 희망을 심어 주다 implant self-confidence and hope in the people // 그날의 그의 행동이 그녀의 마음에 강한 불신감을 심어 놓았다 His conduct that day planted[implanted / instilled] a strong distrust in her heart. // 이들 사상이 그들 마음속에 확고히 심어져 있다 These ideas are firmly rooted[implanted / fixed] in their minds. // 나는 건강이 무엇보다도 소중하다는 것을 그녀의 머릿속에 단단히 심어 주었다 I have got it firmly into her head that health is more important than anything else.

심대하다(甚大-) very great[large]; immense; enormous; tremendous; serious; heavy. ¶심대한 영향 a profound influence // 심대한 손해 serious damage / a heavy loss // 그는 정계에서 심대한 영향력이 있다 He has great[enormous] influence in the political world.

심덕(心德) virtue; uprightness of heart.

심도(深度) depth; fathom. ¶~를 재다 measure[plumb] the depth (of a lake) / sound (the sea / (the distance to) the bottom).
● **심도계** a sea gauge; a depth gauge.

심드렁하다 1 [탐탁지 않다] rather unwilling (to); uninterested (in); indisposed (to do).
2 [병이 그만저만하다] lingering; dragging.

심란하다(心亂-) (서술적) be disturbed[confused] in mind; be upset[agitated]. ¶그녀는 그 소식을 듣고 심란해졌다 She lost her presence of mind at[She was upset by] the news.

심려(心慮) uneasiness of heart; anxiety; worry; concern; apprehensions. ¶~를 끼치다 give[cause] (a person) occasion to feel anxiety / cause anxiety to (a person) / give (a person) trouble // 여러 가지로 ~를 끼쳐 죄송합니다 I am sorry to have occasioned you (so) much anxiety. **심려하다** worry about[over]; worry oneself about; be anxious[concerned] (about); apprehend.

심력(心力) [마음의 작용] (a) faculty; [마음이 미치는 힘] mental power.

심령(心靈) spirit.
● **심령술** [강신술] spiritualism. **심령술사** a spiritualist. **심령학** psychics. **심령학자** a psychicist; a student of the occult[psychic phenomenon].

심로(心勞) [심려] cares; anxiety; worries; [마음의 피로] mental fatigue; worry; boredom.
심로하다 be worried; be mentally tired[fatigued]; suffer from mental[nervous] strain.

심리(心理) a state of mind; a mental state; mentality; psychology. ¶군중 ~ mass[mob] psychology // 미묘한 ~ delicate shades of psychology // 범죄자의 ~ the psychology of criminals // 어린이의 ~ children's psychology[mentalities] // 그는 여성의 섬세한 ~를 모른다 He doesn't understand the delicate psychology of women. // 그의 ~를 알 수가 없다 I have no idea of his real state of mind. / I cannot understand his psychology. // 이것은 일반적인 미국인의 ~를 잘 말해 주는 것이다 This speaks eloquently of the mentality of an average American.
● **심리극** [심] (a) psychodrama. **심리 묘사** (a) psychological description. **심리 상태** a state of mind; a mental state; psychology. ¶그때의 그의 ~는 비정상적이었다 He was in an abnormal state of mind at the time. **심리전 / 심리 전쟁** psychological warfare; (구어) a psywar. **심리학** psychology; the science of mind; mental psychology. ¶동물 ~ animal psychology // 인종[발달] ~ ethnical[development] psychology // 형태[심층 / 위상 / 행동] ~ Gestalt[depth / topological / behavioristic] psychology // 군중 ~ mass[mob] psychology // 실험[임상 / 응용] ~ experimental[clinical / applied] psychology // 이상[범죄 / 산업 / 사회 / 교육 / 민속 / 아동 / 일반] ~ abnormal[criminal / industrial / social / educational / folk / child / general] psychology // 비교[문화] ~ comparative[cultural]

psychology. 심리학자 a psychologist.

심리(審理) (a) trial; (an) examination; (an) inquiry; (형사 사건의) (a) hearing. ¶재~ (a) retrial / (a) rehearing / (a) reexamination / [법] a review // ~를 **받다** be tried (in the court for theft) // ~ 중이다 be under [on] trial // 그 사건은 ~ 중이다 That case is before the court [is being tried now / is being heard now]. // ~ 중인 사건에 대한 신문 논평은 바람직하지 않다 Newspaper comments on cases subjudice [under trial] are undesirable. **심리하다** try [examine / hear] (a case); conduct the trial of (a person for murder); inquire into (a case).

심리적(心理的) mental; psychological. ¶~으로 psychologically / mentally // ~으로 나쁜 영향을 주다 be bad [harmful] in its psychological effect on (a child) / have a bad effect on the mind of (a child).

심마니 a ginseng digger.

심문(審問) a trial; an inquiring; a hearing; an inquest; an examination; a formal interrogation. ¶증인 ~ examination of a witness // ~을 **받다** be given a hearing / be tried / be examined [questioned] (at the police station) // 수회 사건의 ~이 7일에 열린다 The hearing of the bribery case will be held on the seventh. **심문하다** try; inquire; hear (a case); give a hearing (to a case); put (a person) to trial; examine [into] (a case); interrogate (a witness); question closely (a witness). ¶그들은 나를 엄하게 심문했다 They quizzed me relentlessly. / I had to undergo a severe and persistent cross-examination. / (구어) They grilled me.

심미(審美) (a)esthetic appreciation; appreciation of the beautiful. ¶~적 (a)esthetic(al).
● **심미안** an eye for the beautiful; an (a)esthetic sense; a sense of the (a)esthetic; an (a)esthetic appreciation. ¶아버지는 ~이 있으시다 My father has an eye for the beautiful.

심박동(心搏動) [의] a heart beat.
● **심박동수** (an increase in) heart rate.

심방(心房) [생] an atrium (of the heart) (pl. -ria); an auricle.

심방(尋訪) a visit; a call. **심방하다** call (on a person at a house); come to see; visit; pay a visit to.

심벌 a symbol; an emblem. ¶청춘의 ~ a symbol of youth.
● **심벌마크**(*symbol mark) an emblem.

심벌즈 [악기] cymbals. ¶~를 **치다** sound [crash] cymbals.
● **심벌즈 주자** a cymbalist.

심병(心病) [근심] anxiety; sickness at heart; worry; [졸도] [의] syncope; a fainting fit.

심보(心−) nature; disposition; spirit; mind; temper. ¶~가 나쁜 evil-minded / perverse / crooked // ~가 고약한 사람 an ill-natured man // ~가 **고약하다** be evil-minded / be ill-disposed / be a malicious person at bottom.

심복(心腹) **1** [가슴과 배] the heart and the stomach. **2** [긴요한 것] the [things] indispensable; necessaries; (라) sine qua non. **3** [믿을 수 있는 부하] one's confidant; one's confidante(여자); one's confident; one's right-hand man. ¶~인 부하 [하인] a devoted retainer [servant] / a confidential follower [servant] // ~이 **되다** act as a most useful second // 자기의 ~으로 삼다 admit [take] (a person) into one's confidence // 그는 10년 간 사장의 ~ 노릇을 했다 He served as the president's right-hand man [assisted the president faithfully] for ten years.

심부름 an errand; a message; a mission; running errands. ¶~을 **보내다** send (a person) (out) on an errand // ~을 **가다** go [run] on an errand [a mission] / do [run] an errand // 딸아이는 ~을 갔습니다 My daughter went on an errand. // 그는 가게에 ~ 갔다 He has gone on an errand to the store. // 그는 시내에 ~ 갈 일이 있다 He has an errand to do in town. // 아이들이 ~을 해 준다 My children run errands for me. // 누구를 ~ 보낼까 Who shall I send on the errand? // 잠깐 ~을 가 주겠니 Will you run an errand [some errands] for me? **심부름하다** do [run] an errand; run errands. ¶심부름할 일이 있다 I have an errand to do.
● **심부름꾼** an errand boy; a messenger; the bearer(편지 등의); an emissary(특히 밀사로 서의); an office boy(사무실의). ¶~ 편에 편지를 보내다 send a letter (to the office) by messenger [hand].

심부전(心不全) [의] cardiac insufficiency; insufficiency of the heart; heart failure.

심사(心事) the thoughts of the heart; cares; concerns.

심사(心思) ill will; malicious intention; malice; malevolence. ¶~가 **나다** get cross [sour] / bear malice // ~를 **부리다** do (a person) something mean / say something spiteful(말로) / [방해하다] thwart / disturb / get in the way / put a spoke in (a person's) wheel // ~가 나서 남을 비방하다 disparage a person out of spite // 놈이 ~를 부려서 계획이 못쓰게 되었다 Our plan was spoiled by him and his ways.

심사가 사납다[나쁘다] be malicious; be ill-natured; be evil-minded; be spiteful; be malevolent.

심사(深謝) [감사] hearty [sincere] thanks; deep [heartfelt] gratitude; [사죄] a sincere apology. **심사하다** [감사하다] thank (a person) heartily; express [extend] one's hearty [cordial] thanks; tender [express] one's sincere gratitude; [사죄하다] make [tender / offer] a sincere apology.

심사(審査) [검사] (an) examination; (an) inspection; [조사] (an) investigation; [감정] judgment; [선별] screening. ¶최종 ~ final screening // 재~ (a) reexamination / [법] a review // ~에 **합격하다** pass the examination / be accepted / be found eligible // ~을 받다 be under examination // ~ 결과를 보고하다 report one's findings // 출입국법의 ~에 통과하다 pass inspection under the Immigration Law // 그의 그림은 ~에 합격했다 His painting was accepted (for the exhibition). **심사하다** examine; inspect; investigate (into); judge; (미) screen.
● **심사관 / 심사원 / 심사 위원** a judge; an examiner; a juror; (집합적) a panel of judges; a board of examiners; a judging [screening] committee; a jury. **심사 위원회** a judging committee; a screening [an examining] committee. **심사 제도** the screening

심사숙고

심사숙고(深思熟考) meditation; mature[due] consideration; deliberation; rumination; deep thought. **심사숙고하다** meditate (on); contemplate; ruminate (on / over); muse (on / upon); consider (a matter) carefully; give deep thought; be deep in meditation. ¶심사숙고한 끝에 after careful[due / mature] consideration / after much[serious] thought // 심사숙고하는 deep-thinking / thoughtful / prudent // 그 결론은 심사숙고한 끝에 도달한 건가 Did you come to that conclusion after careful (and thorough) consideration?

심산(心算) inner calculation[thought(s)]. ⇨ 속셈1 ¶어떻게 할 ~이냐 What do you intend to do? // 그렇게 할 ~이다 I intend to do so. // 무슨 ~인지 모르겠다 I cannot quite see [understand] his motive[idea]. // 무슨 ~으로 자네 그렇게 말했나 In[With] what spirit did you say so? // 그 이야기로 너를 불안하게 만들 ~이었다 The story was calculated to keep you in suspense.

심산(深山) a deep[remote] mountain; the heart of a mountain; mountain recesses.
● **심산유곡** steep[deep] mountains and deep [dark] valleys; a remote mountainous region. ¶~에 deep in the mountains // ~에 들어가다 go deep into the mountains.

심상(心象·心像) [심] an image; a mental picture[image]. ¶내 마음속의 히말라야 ~ the picture of the Himalayas I have in my mind / my image of the Himalayas.

심상하다(尋常-) ordinary; common; usual; average; [평범하다] commonplace; [범용하다] mediocre; [이상 없다] normal. ¶심상치 않은 unusual / extraordinary / uncommon / serious / alarming / important // 심상치 않은 사태 a grave[critical / serious] situation // 심상치 않은 소리 an alarming sound // 심상치 않은 일 something unusual[serious] // (일이) 심상치 않게 되다 become[grow] serious [grave] / (affairs) take a serious turn // 일이 심상치가 않다 It is no common case[trivial matter]. / Something unusual must have happened. // 그녀의 병세가 심상치 않다 Her illness has taken a serious turn (for the worse). // 사태는 심상치 않을 것 같다 The situation threatens to grow worse[is getting more ugly]. // 이대로 두면 심상치 않은 사태가 벌어질 것이다 If left to take its own course, this will lead to alarming results.

심성(心性) [마음씨] mind; mentality; [타고난 성질] nature; disposition; temperament.

심술(心術) a cross temper; ill nature; perverseness; perversity; cantankerousness; crabbedness. ¶~을 내다 give vent to one's cross[bad] temper / get[become / grow] cross[perverse] / behave perversely // 그는 늙을수록 점점 ~이 더해 갔다 He grew more and more cantankerous as he got older.
● **심술꾸러기 / 심술쟁이 / 심술통이** an ill-natured person; a cross-grained [-tempered] person; a perverse[cantankerous / crabbed] person; a dog in the manger; a crosspatch; (구어) a crank.

심술궂다(心術-) perverse; cross(-minded); cross-grained[-tempered]; ill-natured; evil-minded[-disposed]; crabbed; cantankerous; churlish; wicked; malicious. ¶심술궂은 웃음 a mischievous laugh // 그녀는 심술궂은 얼굴을 하고 있다 She has a crabby look on her face. // 집주인은 심술궂게 생긴 여자다 The landlady looks cross-tempered. // 그는 심술궂게 내게 개물었다 He grilled me maliciously.

심술부리다(心術-) do (a person) something mean; be unkind to (a person); treat (a person) unfairly; act surly[cross]; behave perversely; persist in. ¶심술부리지 말고 길을 비켜라 Don't be so cross, but get out of the way.

심술스럽다(心術-) screwy; somewhat ill-natured.

심신(心身) mind and body; body and mind [soul]. ¶~의 피로 mental and physical exhaustion // ~을 단련하다 cultivate[train] one's mind and body // ~이 모두 건전하다 be sound in mind and body / be mentally and physically sound // 이 샤쾌해지다 feel refreshed in mind and body // 그는 ~이 모두 지쳐 있었다 He was exhausted both in mind and body. / He was mentally and physically exhausted.
● **심신 장애** a mental and physical disorder. **심신 장애인** a mentally and physically handicapped[disabled] person.

심실(心室) [생] the ventricle(s) of the heart; the cardiac ventricle(s). ¶우[좌]~ the right [left] ventricle (of the heart).

심심풀이 killing time; beguiling tedious hours; a pastime; (a) diversion. ¶~로 by way of killing time / to kill (one's) time / to beguile an idle hour / to pass the tedious hours / as a pastime // ~가 되는 것 a kill-time / a time killer // ~가 되다 serve to kill time // ~로 꽃을 가꾸다 grow flowers as a hobby // ~로 책을 읽다 read a book to pass the time // ~로 바둑을 두다 play *baduk*(go) to kill time[by way of killing time] // ~로 뜨개질을 하다 take up knitting as a pastime // ~로 잡지를 훑어보았다 I leafed through a magazine to kill time[pass the time]. // ~로 그림이라도 그리는 것이 어떠냐 How about painting pictures to relieve your ennui[for a change]? // 낚시질은 좋은 ~다 Fishing is a good time-killer. **심심풀이하다** kill one's time; beguile [while away / relieve] the tedium[weariness]; drive away[be relieved from] ennui.

심심하다[1] [무료하다] be bored; feel ennui; find (the evening) very dull; feel weary. ¶심심해서 because one has nothing to do / to relieve the ennui // 심심해 보이다 look bored / wear a bored look // 심심해서 독서를 하다 relieve oneself from ennui by reading // 할 일이 없어 ~ be weary of having nothing to do // 심심해 죽겠다 I'm bored to death. / I'm suffering from ennui. / I've time on my hands. // 그녀는 심심해 죽을 지경이었다 She was overcome with ennui[tedium]. / (구어) She was bored to death.

심심하다[2] [조금 싱겁다] rather unsaline [unsalty].

심심하다(甚深-) deep and profound. ¶심심한 감사 profound gratitude / cordial[heartfelt] thanks // 심심한 사의를 표하다 (감사의 뜻) express [extend] one's deepest gratitude [thanks] (to) / thank very sincerely [cordially] / (사과의 뜻) offer one's sinceresst [deepest] apologies / apologize most humbly // 심심한 감사의 뜻을 표하고자 합니다 I would like to express my deep gratitude to you.

심안(心眼) [마음눈] one's mind's eye; inward eyes; mental vision. ¶~으로 보다 see with one's mind's eye.

심야(深夜) the dead of night; the middle of the night; midnight. ¶~에 at [in the] dead of night / at midnight // ~까지 till late at night / far [deep] into the night / until midnight(한밤중까지).
● 심야 방송 midnight broadcasting; a midnight [nightcap / late-night] broadcast [(radio / TV) program]. ¶나는 전에 라디오의 ~을 자주 들었었다 I used to listen to midnight broadcasting [radio programs]. 심야 영업 late-night operation. 심야 프로 a midnight broadcast; a late-night (radio / TV) program.

심약하다(心弱-) feeble- [weak-] minded; fainthearted. ¶나이를 먹은 탓인지 나는 심약해졌다 Perhaps because of my age, I've grown less willing to take chances [to try new things]. /(구어) I'm losing my gumption. I guess I'm getting old.

심연(深淵) an abyss; a gulf; a ravine; an abysmal chasm. ¶절망의 ~ an abyss of despair // 슬픔의 ~에 빠지다 sink into the abyss [depths] of sorrow.

심오하다(深奧-) deep; profound; abstruse; esoteric. ¶심오한 원리[교리] an esoteric principle[doctrine] // 심오한 연구 recondite researches[studies] // 심오한 학문 profound [deep] learning // 심오한 뜻 a deep [profound] meaning.

심원(心願) one's heart's desire; one's heartfelt wish; one's dearest wish.

심원(深怨) a deep grudge[resentment]; a legacy of ill will[hatred] (대대손손의). **심원하다** bear [have] a deep grudge (against).

심원하다(深遠-) profound (theory); deep (meaning); abstruse (idea); recondite (doctrine); unfathomable; esoteric.

심의(審議) [심사하고 토의함] deliberation; consideration; careful discussion; review; (미국 구어) [철저한] a going-over. ¶~를 거듭한 끝에 after much deliberation / after due consideration // ~ 중이다 be under consideration [discussion / deliberation] / be on the carpet [tapis] // ~에 부치다 refer (a matter) to discussion / bring (a matter) upon the tapis // ~에 부치다 come on the tapis / be taken into deliberation // ~를 보류하다 shelve [pigeonhole] (a bill) // 문제를 위원회의 ~에 회부하다 refer a matter to a committee // 그 문제는 아직 ~ 중이다 The question is still under deliberation [consideration]. / They are still deliberating (upon / about) the question. **심의하다** deliberate (on) (a matter / subject); consider; discuss; go through. ¶법안을 계속 ~ carry the deliberation on a bill over (in)to the next session of the Assembly // 축조 ~ discuss (a bill) article by article / review (a document) clause by clause / go through (a proposal) item by item.
● 심의 기관 an organ of consultation. 심의회 a (deliberative) council; an inquiry commission. ¶교육[경제] ~ an educational [economic] council.

심인(心因) [의] ¶~성의 psychogenic.
● 심인성 반응 psychogenic reaction.

심장(心臟) 1 [생] the heart. ¶~의 cardiac // ~의 고동 the beating [throbbing / thumping / palpitation] of the heart / a heartbeat // ~의 기능 the function of the heart // ~**이 강하다**[튼튼하다] have a strong[stout] heart // ~이 몹시 펀다[고동친다] My heart is beating violently [fast]. // ~이 두근두근했다 My heart went pit-a-pat. // 그는 ~이 나쁘다[약하다] He has heart trouble [a weak heart]. // 그의 ~(의 고동)이 멈추었다 His heart stopped beating. // 그 소식을 듣고 나는 ~의 고동이 멈추는 것 같았다 My heart almost stopped beating when I heard the news.
2 [뱃심] nerve; cheek. ¶~이 약한 사내 a nerveless fellow // ~**이 강하다** have much [a lot of] nerve / be impudent [cheeky / brazen / brazen-faced] // 넌 ~이 너무 약해 You want more nerve. // 정말 어지간한 ~이구나 (반어적) I like your nerve! // 그녀에게 그런 말을 하다니 자네 ~도 어지간하군 The nerve of you to say such a thing to her!
● 심장 마비 heart failure; a heart attack; paralysis of the heart; cardiac paralysis. ¶~로 죽다 die of heart failure [a heart attack] // ~를 일으키다 have a heart attack. 심장병 a disease of the heart; a heart disease; heart trouble; heart [cardiac] disease; cardiopathy. 심장부 [생] the region of the heart; [비유] the heart // 도시의 ~ the heart of a city. 심장 이식 (수술) a heart transplant [graft] (operation). ¶~을 하다 perform a heart transplant (operation) (on a person). 심장 질환 a cardiac disorder. 심장 판막증 valvular disease of the heart.

심장하다(深長-) profound; deep; abstruse. ¶표현은 간략하되 의미는 ~ Simple in expression, deep in meaning. / The words are simple, but of profound significance.

심적(心的) mental; psychological.
● 심적 상태 a mental state; a state of mind; mentality. ¶그녀는 심문을 견디어 낼 만한 ~에 있지 않았다 She was in no state of mind to endure cross-examination. 심적 작용[결함] a mental action [defect].

심전도(心電圖) [의] an electrocardiogram(약어 ECG, E.C.G.).

심정(心情) one's heart; one's feelings. ¶~을 알아주다 enter into (a person's) feelings [sentiment] / (동정하다) feel for (a person) / sympathize with another // 너의 ~은 잘 알겠다 Of course I understand your feelings. / I can enter into your feelings. // 울고 싶은 ~이다 I feel like crying. // 그녀의 가련한 표정으로 그 ~을 짐작할 수 있었다 We could imagine her innermost feelings from her pitiful expression. // 그의 ~을 생각하니 말이 안 나왔다 I felt so sorry for him that I could say nothing.

심줄 a tendon; a vein; a fiber. ⇨=힘줄

심중(心中) the heart; the mind; one's inmost thoughts; one's real intention; the bottom of one's heart; one's true motive; the heart's core; the depths of one's bosom. ¶~에 품다 keep (a secret) in one's bosom / cherish (a hope) in one's heart // ~을 헤아리다 enter into[share] (a person's) feelings / sympathize with (a person) // ~을 꿰뚫어 보다 see through (a person's) heart (to the core) /

심증(心證) 1 [법] [법관이 마음에 얻게 된 확신] a strong[firm] belief; (a) conviction. ¶~을 갖다 have a strong belief (that) // ~을 얻다 gain a confident belief // …이라는 ~을 굳히다 be confirmed in one's belief that …. 2 [마음에 받는 인상] an impression.

심지(心-) a (lamp) wick. ¶~를 자르다 (양초의) snuff a candle / (램프의) crick[trim] a wick[lamp] // 램프의 ~를 올리다 turn up the wick / screw up a lamp // (램프의) ~를 줄이다 lower[turn down] a wick.

심지(心地) nature; temper; disposition; character. ¶~가 고운 사람 a tender-hearted person // ~가 사납다 be perverse / be crooked / be ill-natured // 그 녀석은 ~가 사나운 놈이다 He has a crooked disposition. / He is warped by nature.

심지(心志) (a) will; volition; (an) intention; [속뜻] an aim; purpose.

심지어(甚至於) what is worse; worst of all; the extreme case is …; not so much as; on top of all this. ¶그는 ~ 자기 이름조차 쓸 모른다 He cannot even his own name. // 그녀는 ~ 결혼반지까지 팔아 버렸다 She went so far as to sell her wedding ring. // ~ 하인들까지도 그를 업신여긴다 Even his servants despise him. // 그녀는 ~ 그가 거짓말쟁이라고까지 했다 She went so far as to say that he was a liar. // 그는 ~ 자기 먹을 것까지도 주어 버렸다 He even gave away his own food.

심취(心醉) [어떤 일에 깊이 빠져서 도취함] admiration; adoration; idolization; [몰두] devotion. **심취하다** be fascinated (with); be devoted (to); adore; idolize. ¶예술에 심취한 사람 a devotee of an art // 서양 문명에 심취하고 있다 be wholly devoted to western civilization // 그는 소월에 심취해 있다 He is an ardent admirer of Sowol. / He adores Sowol.

심층(深層) the depths (of one's consciousness). ¶의식의 ~을 탐색하다 fathom the depths of one's consciousness.
- **심층 구조** [언] deep structure. **심층 심리학** depth psychology.

심통(心-) ill nature; a cross temper. ¶~이 사납다 be perverse[crooked / cantankerous / crabbed] person // ~이 나다 get cranky / become perverse // ~ 부리지 말고 비켜라 Don't be so cross, but get out of the way.

심판(審判) 1 [판정·판결] judgment; adjudgment. ¶최후의 ~ the Last Judgment // 최후의 ~의 날 the doomsday / the Judgment Day / the Day of Judgment // 공평[불공평]한 ~ a fair[an unfair] judgment // ~의 판정 an umpire's decision // L 씨의 ~으로 with Mr. L as umpire / Mr. L acting as umpire // ~을 보다 (경기의) referee (a game) / act as umpire[referee] / umpire // 권투 시합의 ~을 보다 referee a boxing match // ~에 항의하다 object to[kick at] an umpire's decision // ~을 받다 be judged / be tried / face one's trial. **심판하다** referee (a game); umpire; act as (an) umpire; judge; adjudge. ¶사건을 공평하게 ~ pass a fair judgment[verdict] on a case / judge[decide] a case fairly[impartially].
2 [판정하는 사람] a judge (경기·게임의);

an umpire (야구·테니스 등의); a referee (권투·축구·농구·배구·럭비 등의).
- **심판원** a judge. ⇨**심판**

심포니 [교향곡] a symphony.
- **심포니 오케스트라** symphony orchestra.

심포지엄 a symposium (pl ~s, -sia). ¶현대미술 ~을 갖다[열다] hold a symposium on modern art.

심하다(甚-) 1 [지나치다] extreme; excessive; heavy (damage); [격렬하다] severe; violent; intense; hard. ¶심한 감기 a bad[nasty] cold // 심한 통증 an acute[a severe / a violent] pain // 심한 바람 a violent[strong] wind // 심한 비바람 a severe[heavy / violent] storm // 심한 더위[추위] intense[bitter / severe] heat[cold] // 심한 손해 a heavy[stupendous] loss // 심한 경쟁 (a) keen[hot / fierce / vehement / cutthroat] competition // 심한 상처 a serious wound / a deep gash // 기침이 ~ I have a bad cough. // 그 사업은 경쟁이 ~ There is keen competition in that business. // 그의 횡포는 점점 더 심해지고 있다 His unruly conduct is getting worse and worse. // 농담이 너무 ~ You carry your joke too far. **심히** extremely; exceedingly; excessively; severely; violently; intensively; heavily; badly. ¶이런 사고가 빈발하는 것은 ~ 유감스러운 일이다 It is a matter of sincere regret that such accidents should happen so frequently.
2 [가혹하다] cruel; harsh; rough; merciless; heartless; hard; [난폭하다] outrageous; atrocious. ¶심한 처사 cruel treatment / (a) cruelty / harsh usage // 심한 처벌 undeserved punishment // 심한 짓을 하다 do a cruel thing / commit cruelties / do (a person) an injustice // 그건 너무 ~ Don't be so hard on me. // 그는 심한 말을 했다 He used abusive[bad / strong] language. **심히** cruelly; harshly; hard; outrageously.

심해(深海) the deep sea; the depths of the sea; an abyss. ¶~의 abyssal / abysmal.
- **심해어** a deep-sea[an abyssal] fish. **심해어업** deep-sea fishing; fishing[fishery] for abyssal fish.

심혈(心血) the heart's blood; [비유] heart and soul; one's whole energy. ¶~을 기울여 heart and soul / with one's heart's blood // ~을 기울인 작품 a work embodying the author's whole mental energy / one's most laborious work // 일에 ~을 기울이다 put one's heart and soul into one's work / devote oneself to one's work // 그는 연구에 ~을 기울였다 He put his heart and soul into his research.

심호흡(深呼吸) deep breathing[respiration]; a deep breath. **심호흡하다** breathe deeply; do deep breathing; take a deep breath; draw a deep[full] breath; take deep breathing exercises.

심혼(心魂) one's heart[soul]. ¶그는 연구에 ~을 기울였다 He put his heart and soul into his research.

심홍색(深紅色) deep red; crimson; ruby (red).

심화(心火) fire of anger[jealousy]; heart-burning. ¶~를 태우다[가 나다] burn with wrath[jealousy].

심화(深化) deepening. **심화하다** deepen.

십(十) ten; [로마 숫자] X. ¶제 ~ the tenth // ~분의 1 one-tenth / a tenth // ~ 년 ten years / a decade // ~ 일(for) ten days / (날짜) the tenth (day) // ~ 주년 기념일 a tenth anniversary / (미) a decennial // 수~ 개씩 by the dozen(s) // 수~ 번 dozens[scores] of times // ~ 대(代) (연령의) one's teens // ~ 대의 소녀 a teenager / a girl in her teens.

십년공부 도로 아미타불[나무아미타불] (속담) One hour's cold will spoil seven years warming.

십 년이면 산천[강산]도 변한다(속담) Ten years is an epoch.

십각형(十角形) [수] a decagon. ¶~의 decagonal.

십계명(十誡命) [성] the Ten Commandments; the Decalogue. ¶모세의 ~ Moses' Ten Commandments.

십년감수하다(十年減壽-) have one's life shortened by ten years; cut ten years from one's life; [혼나다] have a hard[bad] time (of it).

십년지계(十年之計) a far-sighted policy.

십년지기(十年知己) an old acquaintance; a friend of long standing.

십만(十萬) a hundred thousand. ¶수~ hundreds of thousands (of people) // 수~의 희생자 hundreds of thousands of victims.

십분(十分) [충분히] enough; sufficiently; fully; thoroughly; in full; to the full; to perfection; [풍부히] amply; copiously; plentifully; in plenty; [만족스럽게] satisfactorily; to one's satisfaction; to one's heart's content. ¶~ 이용하다 make full use of / make the best use of // 실력을 ~ 발휘하다 show one's ability to the full // 그 가치를 ~ 인정하다 come to a full appreciation of its value.

십상 1 [제격] the right thing (for); the very thing wanted; just the thing (for). ¶~인 ideal / suitable (for) / fit (for) / the very / right / just // 하이킹하기에 ~인 날씨 ideal weather for hiking // 그거 ~이군 That is made to order for me. / That's just the thing I wanted. 2 [썩 알맞게] just (well); right; exactly; fairly; perfectly. ¶낚시하기에 ~ 좋은 날씨다 It is an ideal weather for angling. // 재떨이로 쓰기 ~ 좋다 It makes an admirable ashtray.

십시일반(十匙一飯) Every little helps.; Many a little makes a mickle[muckle].

십억(十億) (미) a billion; (영) a thousand million(s); a milliard.

십이궁(十二宮) the twelve mundane houses; the (twelve) signs of the zodiac.
●**십이궁도** the horoscope.

십이월(十二月) December (약어 Dec.).

십이지장(十二指腸) [생] the duodenum (pl. ~s, -na). ¶~의 duodenal.
●**십이지장 궤양** a duodenal ulcer. **십이지장충** [동] an ancylostome; a hookworm.

십인십색(十人十色) So many men, so many minds.; Several men, several minds.; Tastes differ.

십일월(十一月) November (약어 Nov.).

십일조(十一租) (영) tithes. ¶~를 부과[납부]하다 tithe.

십자(十字) a cross. ¶~로 crosswise // ~를 긋다 cross oneself / cross one's heart / make the sign of the cross on one's breast.
●**십자가** a cross; [기] the Holy Rood. ¶~에 못 박다 crucify // ~에 못 박히다 be nailed to a cross / be crucified // ~를 지다 bear one's cross. **십자군** [역] the Crusade; a crusade; the crusaders. **십자로** a crossroads; crossing[intersecting] streets.

십자매(十姉妹) [동] a society finch; a Bengalee; a Bengalese.

십장(什長) a foreman (of navvies); an overman; a boss; (영) a gaffer; a gangmaster; (영) a ganger.

십종 경기(十種競技) decathlon; ten events.

십중팔구(十中八九) [부사] in nine cases out of ten; ten to one; nine times out of ten; most likely; in all probability; in all (human) likelihood; (미국 속어) nine-tenths; [거의] almost; nearly. ¶그는 ~ 성공할 것이다 Ten to one he'll succeed. // ~ 그 사람이 틀림없다 Ten to one[Most probably / Most likely] it's him. // ~ 그는 살아나기 어렵다 His case is almost hopeless.

십진법(十進法) the decimal system[scale]; the denary scale[notation]. ¶~으로 decimally // ~으로 하다 decimalize.

십팔번(十八番) [장기(長技)] one's forte[speciality]; one's favorite part[performance]. ¶저것은 그녀의 ~이다 That is her forte. / (노래 등) That's her favorite song. // 「망향」이 그의 ~이다 Manghyang is his speciality.

싯- deep; dark. ⇨샛-

싯누렇다 vividly[deep] yellow.

싱겁다 1 [짜지 않다] insufficiently[slightly] salted; not salty enough; not well salted; [별 맛이 없다] flat; tasteless; insipid; (술·담배 등이) weak[mild] (cigarette); watery[light / thin] (liquor). ¶싱거운 술 weak[washy] liquor / sloppy drink // 싱거운 커피 weak coffee // 맛이 ~ taste flat / be flat to the taste / be insipid // 이 국은 ~ This soup needs a bit of salt. // 이 김치는 ~ These gimchi(kimchi) are not sufficiently salted.
2 [언행이 멋적다] dull; pointless; tedious; boring; irksome; wearisome; flat. ¶싱거운 사람 a boring person / a wishy-washy person // 싱거운 이야기 a dull story // 싱거운 승리 a too easy victory / an easily-won victory // 그의 농담은 싱거웠다 His jokes fell flat upon our ears. // 싱거운 시합이었어, 안 그래 That was a dull game, wasn't it?

싱글 1 [테니스] (a match of) singles. ¶남자 ~ 준결승전 a man's singles semifinal match // ~에서 그는 송에게 졌다 He lost to Song in the tennis singles. 2 [야구] a base hit. ⇨싱글 히트(⇨싱글) 3 (양복의) a single-breasted coat. 4 [독신자] singles.
●**싱글베드** a single bed. **싱글 히트**(*single hit) [야구] a single; a base hit; an one-bagger.

싱글거리다 smile gently[sweetly / affably]; smile an affable smile; beam with a gentle smile. ¶싱글거리면서 with a smile on one's face.

싱글벙글 with a broad smile; with a smiling face; smilingly; beamingly. **싱글벙글하다** smile gently. ⇨싱글거리다

싱글싱글 grinningly; with a smile on one's face. **싱글싱글하다** smile gently. ⇨싱글거리다

싱숭생숭하다 (서술적) feel restless[fidgety / nervous / uneasy]; be in a fidget; be ill at ease. ¶봄이면 그녀는 마음이 싱숭생숭해지곤 했다 Her mind used to wander during the

싱싱하다 springtime.

싱싱하다 young and fresh; fresh as paint; fresh (and juicy); fresh-looking; juicy; green. ¶싱싱한 생선 a fresh fish / a fish fresh from the water / freshly caught fish∥싱싱한 야채 fresh vegetables∥갓 따온 싱싱한 과일 fresh (and juicy) fruit just plucked from a tree / juicy fruit from the tree∥비에 젖어 잎이 싱싱해 보인다 The leaves look fresh in the rain.

싱커 [야구] a sinker.

싱크로나이즈드 스위밍 [수중 발레] synchronized swimming.

싶다[1] […일 것 같다] (서술적) look; seem; appear; be likely (to do). ¶비가 올 듯~ It looks like rain.∥그녀가 올 성싶지 않다 It is not likely that she will come. / She is not likely to come.∥그 아이는 크게 될 성~ The boy gives promise of a great future.

싶다[2] 1 […할 의향이] (서술적) want (to do); wish (to do); should[would] like to see [hear]. ¶꼭[몹시] …하고 ~ be anxious [eager / impatient / dying] to (do)∥…했으면 ~ feel like (doing) / feel inclined to (do)∥하고 싶은 대로 하다 do as one likes [pleases] / act at will / have everything one's own way∥하고 싶지 않다 hate (doing / to do) / be unwilling[reluctant / loath] (to do)∥울고 싶은 기분이다 feel like crying∥말하고 싶은 대로 말하다 speak without reserve / say what one likes∥빨리 가고 ~ I am impatient to go.∥가고 싶지 않다 I don't want to go. / I don't feel like going.∥영국에 유학하고 ~ I want to study in England.∥올 여름에는 유럽 여행을 하고 ~ I want[would like / (영) should like] to go to Europe this summer.(▶ would[should] like to (do)라고 하는 것이 완곡한 표현임)∥일 주일에 한 번 수영을 하고 ~ I am hoping to swim once a week.∥넓은 땅이 있는 집을 갖고 ~ (구어) I have a hankering for a large house with acres of land.∥나는 술이 마시고 싶었다 I felt like drinking wine.∥그 책을 읽어 보고 싶은 가 Would you like[care] to read the book?∥감기 때문에 아무것도 하고 싶지 않다 Because of my cold, I don't feel like doing anything at all.∥나는 아이를 만나고 싶어 견딜 수 없었다 I longed[was dying] to see my child.∥아이는 밖에 나가 놀고 싶어 안절부절 못했다 The child was impatient to go out to play.∥나는 프랑스 어가 배우고 싶어 죽겠다 (구어) I am itching[dying] to learn French.∥지금도 영화 보러 가고 싶은 생각이 없지 않다 I have a full wish to go to the movies even now.∥그는 부모님을 기쁘게 해 드리고 싶어 열심히 공부했다 He studied hard out of a desire to please his parents.∥그는 부와 명성을 얻고 싶어 안달이다 He has an itch for wealth and fame.∥아이가 젖을 먹고 싶어 울고 있다 The baby is crying for milk.∥어머니는 무엇이든 하고 싶은 대로 하신다 My mother does everything her own way.

2 [희망을 가정적으로 나타냄]. ¶내일은 날씨가 좋았으면 ~ I hope it will be fine tomorrow.∥나는 아버지가 하다못해 1년만 더 사셨더라면 ~ I wish my father had lived at least one more year.

싶어 하다 want to; desire to; be desirous of; be eager to; be anxious to. ¶몹시 …하고 ~ be eager[anxious / impatient] to (do)∥교제하고 ~ long for (a person's) companionship∥외제차를 갖고 ~ (구어) hanker for a foreign car∥그는 가고 싶어 한다 He wants to go.∥그는 첼로를 몹시 갖고 싶어 한다 He badly wants a cello.∥그는 항상 새로운 일을 하고 싶어 한다 He is always eager to try new things.∥그는 고향 소식을 듣고 싶어 했다 He was anxious for[to hear] new from home.∥그는 몹시 술을 마시고 싶어 했다 He was longing[(구어) dying] for a drink.

싸개 [포장용 종이·헝겊] a wrapper; wrapping paper[cloth]; cover material; a (slip) cover.

싸고돌다 1 [에워싸다] crowd round; cluster [throng] around (a person); form a small clique[an inside group / an intimate circle] around (a person). ¶그들은 사장을 싸고도는 사람들이다 They are the ones who are close to the head of the firm. 2 [두둔하다] protect (the weak); cover (a guilty person); shield [screen / shelter] (a person from); take (a person) under one's wings. ¶아버지가 화를 내면 어머니가 딸을 싸고돌았다 The mother screened her daughter from her father's anger.

싸구려 a cheap[low-priced] article; cheap junk. ¶~ 핸드백 a cheap handbag∥~ 보석 flashy jewelry∥~ 물건은 척 보면 알 수 있다 I can tell cheap articles at a glance.∥그녀는 몸에 ~만 걸치고 있다 She is cheaply dressed from head to foot.∥~ 물건을 샀더니 결국 싼 것이 비지떡이었다 It was after all a waste of money to buy cheap goods.

싸늘하다 1 [한랭하다] cold; chilly; cool; frigid; icy; [황폐하여 쓸쓸하다] wintry; dreary. ¶싸늘한 바람 a cold wind∥싸늘한 날씨 wintry weather. 2 [냉담하다] cold; icy; frigid; distant; indifferent; cold-hearted; cold-blooded. ¶싸늘한 태도 a cool[cold] attitude / a distant air∥싸늘한 웃음 a frosty smile.

싸다[1] (대·소변을) excrete (urine or feces); void; discharge. ¶오줌을 ~ pee / wet one's pants / (잠자리에서) wet the bed / make [pass] water∥똥을 ~ defecate / have a movement of the bowels / (속어) get a real raw deal.

싸다[2] 1 [물건을 포장하다] wrap (in); do up (a parcel); pack (up) (goods); bundle (clothes). ¶보자기에 ~ tie[do / wrap] up (things) in a cloth wrapper∥짐을 종이에 ~ do[wrap] up the package in paper / wrap paper round a thing∥과자를 예쁜 포장지로 ~ package the candy in colorful wrappers∥싸 드릴까요 Shall I wrap it up?∥이것을 종이에 싸 주세요 Please wrap this up in paper.∥나는 그 꽃병을 선물용 포장지로 싸도록 했다 I had the vase gift-wrapped. 2 (도시락을) (미) fix a lunch; prepare a luncheon; put up a lunch; pack a lunch basket[box].

싸다[3] 1 [입이 가볍다] glib(-tongued); tale-bearing; tattling; talkative; loquacious; prattling; gabby. ¶입이 싼 사람 a talkative person / a blabber / a tattler / a chatterbox(여자·아이 등). 2 [속도가 빠르다] fast; swift; quick. ¶걸음이 싼 사람 a quick walker / a light-footed person∥걸음이 ~ be quick [swift / (문어) fleet] of foot / have a quick step / be quick on one's feet[legs / pins]∥싸게 걷다 walk at a brisk[quick / rapid] pace / walk at a quick step / walk with a rapid

싸다⁴ 1 [(물건 값이)] cheap; inexpensive; low-priced; of low price; moderate; moderately-priced(▶ cheap는 「싸구려」의 느낌을 나타낼 때가 있음). ¶싼 집세 a low rent // 싼 카메라 a low-priced camera // 값이 싸고 질이 나쁜 구두 shoes of low price and poor quality / (영) cheap and nasty shoes // 값은 싸나 좋은 옷 an inexpensive but good dress // 싸게 산 물건 a good[a great] bargain // 싸게 치이다 cost little / come cheap / prove economical // 싸게 팔다 sell cheap[at low prices / at a small profit / at a bargain] // 싼 물건을 찾아다니다 look[hunt] for a bargain // 아주[터무니없이] ~ be cheap as dirt / be dirt-[dog-] cheap / be ridiculously cheap // 굉장히 싸게 사셨네요 It was a steal. / It's a real good buy[bargain]. // 나는 싼 임대료로 차를 빌렸다 I rented[(영) hired] a car at low rates. // 지방이 대도시보다 물가가 ~ Prices in the country are lower than in big cities. // 시계를 싸게 샀다 I bought a watch cheap[at a low price]. // 그 값이면[5,000원이면] ~ It's a bargain at that price[at 5,000 won]. // 좀 더 싼 것은 없읍니까 Haven't you anything less expensive? // 좀 더 싸게 할 수 없을까요 Couldn't you come down a little more[cut the price down a bit more]? / Can't you make it a little cheaper? / Can't you reduce the price a little? // 수입 오렌지가 싸졌다 Imported oranges have gone down (in price) [have become cheaper]. // 설탕은 저 슈퍼마켓이 더 ~ Sugar is cheaper at that supermarket. / They are selling sugar cheap[at low prices] at that supermarket. // 저게 잘 샀군(미국 구어) It's a buy. // 냉장고를 20% 싸게 샀다 I bought a refrigerator at a twenty percent discount on the fixed price. / I got a refrigerator for twenty percent off the list price.
2 [(죄에 대한 벌이) 마땅하다] (서술적) be well deserved; be none too little. ¶욕먹어도 ~ deserve censure / need to be scolded // 그 놈, 죽어 싸지 He deserves death. / He needs to be killed. // (내 말을 듣지 않더니) 그 꼴을 당해도 ~ It serve(s) you right! / You richly deserve it! / (구어) Serves[And serve] you right! / (미) You had it coming!
싼 것이 비지떡 (속담) Low price means low quality.; Buy cheap and waste your money.; You get what you pay for.

싸다니다 hang around[about]; gad[wander / traipse] about; loiter; roam; (미국 속어) bum around. ¶시내를 ~ wander through the town // 그녀는 싸다니기를 좋아한다 She is a great gadabout. / She doesn't like to stay at home.

싸라기 1 [쌀의 부스러기] broken rice; crushed[waste] rice. 2 snow grains. ⇨싸라기눈(⇨싸라기)
● **싸라기눈** snow grains; snow pellets; soft hail.

싸락눈 snow grains. ⇨싸라기눈(⇨싸라기)

싸리(나무) [식] bush clover.

싸매다 wrap and tie up. ¶머리와 볼을 ~ cover[wrap] one's head and cheeks (with a towel) // 머리를 싸매고 누워 있다 be[lie] in bed with a towel worn[tied] round one's head // 그는 머리를 싸매고 어려운 문제를 풀고 있다 He is cudgeling[racking] his brains trying to solve a difficult problem. / He is solving a difficult problem with all his might [as hard as he can].

싸우다 1 [다투다] fight; [논쟁하다] dispute; argue; have a dispute[an argument]; [말다툼하다] quarrel; wrangle; exchange [have] words; [사이가 틀어지다] disagree (with one's wife); fall out (with). ¶옆방에서 싸우는 소리가 들렸다 I heard the voices of people quarrelling in the next room. / I heard raised voices coming from the next room. // 뒤뜰에서 두 남자가 싸우고 있는 것이 보였다 Two men were seen fighting in the backyard. // 그는 걸핏하면 싸우려 든다 He is a quarrelsome man. / He's always looking for a fight. // 그는 여자 친구와 싸우고 헤어졌다 He split with his girl friend after a quarrel. / He quarreled with his girl friend and they broke up. // 하이에나들이 먹이를 놓고 서로 싸우고 있었다 The hyenas were fighting over their prey.
2 [전쟁을 하다] make war (on / against); [전투를 하다] fight; do battle (with / against). ¶우세한 대군[적군]과 ~ fight against overwhelming odds[with an enemy] // 적이지만 그들은 훌륭히 싸웠다 Enemy though they were, I must admit that they put up a good fight. // 그때 한국은 일본과 싸우고 있었다 Korea was at war with Japan then.
3 [경쟁하다] contend (with). ¶송 군과 최 군은 우승을 놓고 싸웠다 Song and Choe fought for the championship. / Song fought [contended / strove] with Choe for the championship. // 정정당당히 싸우자 Let's play fair. // 잘 싸워서 이기자[잘 싸우자] Let's go in and win.
4 [투쟁하다] struggle; fight (against / with). ¶운명과 ~ fight[struggle] against fate // 평화를 위해 ~ strive for peace // 유혹과 ~ resist temptation // 졸음과 ~ fight off sleep // 근로자들은 임금 인상을 위해서 싸웠다 The workers fought for an increase in wages. // 배의 승무원들은 파도와 필사적으로 싸웠다 The crew of the boat fought desperately with the high waves.

싸움 1 [말다툼] a quarrel; a fight; [시끄러운 말다툼] a row; (사소한 일로 인한) a squabble; [논쟁] a dispute; (시끄러운) a brawl; [격투] a scuffle; (가족·씨족 등의 반목) a feud; [불화] (a) discord; strife. ¶눈 ~ a snowball fight // 연 ~ a kite battle // 칼 ~ a sword fight // 형제간의 ~ a quarrel between brothers // 부부 ~ a quarrel between husband and wife / a domestic quarrel // ~의 원인 the cause of a quarrel / the subject of a dispute // ~을 걸다 pick[provoke] a fight (with a person) / provoke (a person) to a quarrel // 이 문제를 둘러싼 학자끼리의 ~ a controversy[an argument] among scholars on this subject // 스미스가(家)와 잭슨가 사이에는 수세대에 걸친 가문 ~이 있었다 There was discord[a family feud] between the Smiths and the Jacksons for many generations. // 두 집안은 물~을 하고 있었다 The two families were at loggerheads over water rights. // 이 점에 관해서 법정 ~이 계속되고 있다 A judicial dispute is going on concerning this point. // 나는 직업 문제로 아버지와 대판 ~을 했다 I had a terri-

ble quarrel with my father about my job.∥그들은 여자 문제로 늘 ~을 벌이고 있다 They are always quarrelling over women.∥거리에서 깡패들끼리 ~이 벌어졌었다 There was a fight among hooligans in the street. **싸움하다** fight; quarrel. ⇨゠싸우다1
2 [전쟁] (a) war; warfare; [전투] a fight; a battle; an encounter; an engagement; an action; a campaign; (1대 1의) a combat; (소규모의) a scuffle; a skirmish. ¶목숨을 건 ~ battle for life∥~에 대비하다 prepare for war∥~에 이기다 gain[win] a victory / gain[win / carry] the day / come out victorious (in a battle)∥~에 지다 lose the day[a battle] / be defeated (in a battle) / be beaten in a battle. **싸움하다** make war (on / against). ⇨゠싸우다2
3 [시합·경쟁] a contest; a contention; a competition; (a) rivalry. ¶~에 이기다[지다] win[lose] a game. **싸움하다** contend (with). ⇨゠싸우다3
4 [투쟁] a struggle; a strife; a conflict. ¶이성과 욕망의 ~ a conflict[struggle] between reason and desire∥시간과의 ~ one's fight against time∥노사간의 ~ a struggle between capital and labor / a war of capital versus[against] labor∥병과의 ~ the war against disease. **싸움하다** struggle. ⇨゠싸우다4
● **싸움꾼** a quarrelsome[contentious] person; a fire-eater; (속어) a scrapper. **싸움터** a battlefield; a field of battle; a battle front [ground / site]; a field of death; the theater [seat] of war; a war theater; the front. ¶옛 ~ an old battlefield∥~에서 on the battlefield∥~에 나가다 go to the front / take the field / go (off) to war∥그 도시는 ~로 변했다 The town turned into a battlefield. **싸움판** a scene of a quarrel[fight]. ¶~이 벌어졌다 A fight took place. / A quarrel broke out. **싸움패** (a gang of) hooligans; hoodlums; (미국 속어) hoods; rowdies; roughs; roughnecks.
싸이다 get[be] wrapped[covered]. ¶수수께끼에 ~ be wrapped up in (a) mystery∥어둠에 ~ be wrapped in darkness∥화염에 ~ be enveloped in flames.
싸잡다 put[lump] together; sum up; cover up; round up; include. ¶물건을 싸잡아 팔다 sell things in large amounts[in quantity / in a lump / (미) in the gross]∥모두 싸잡아서 얼마입니까 How much is it all together[for the lot]?∥그들을 싸잡아 비방해서는 안 된다 You must not denounce them indiscriminately[wholesale]. / You must not make a sweeping denunciation of them.
싸전 (-廛) [곡물 가게] a rice store.
싸하다 (박하 맛처럼) minty; pepperminty; mentholated; cool; (아릿듯이) piquant; pungent; spicy; sharp; (샴페인처럼) fizzy.
싹[1] **1** a bud; (나무의) a leaf bud; (햇가지의) a sprout; a shoot; (씨에서 돋아난) a seedling. ¶~이 트다 sprout / bud / put forth buds [shoots] / shoot out buds / (나무가) burgeon / come[burst] into leaf∥~이 트는 버드나무 a germinant[germinating / sprouting] willow∥초목이 ~이 틀 무렵 when plants bud in the spring∥날씨가 따뜻하여 밀이 일찍 ~이 텄다 The warm weather has caused the wheat to sprout early.∥내가 뿌린 씨는 아직 ~이 트지 않았다 The seeds I sowed have not germinated yet.∥나무들이 ~이 트기 시작했다 The trees are budding. / The trees have begun to put forth[send out] buds. / 뿌린 씨에서 아직 ~이 돌아나지 않는다 The seeds I sowed have not germinated [come up] yet.
2 a good omen; hope(s). ⇨゠싹수
싹[2] **1** [완전히] quite; entirely; completely; thoroughly. ¶다음 날 아침 나는 그 일을 ~ 잊고 있었다 (중요한 일을) By the next morning it had completely slipped my mind. / (싫은 일을) By the next morning I had forgotten all about it.∥그 사건 이후 그는 ~ 달라졌다 He has completely changed since that event. **2** [베는 소리·모양] with a (single) snip[swish]; with a swishing sound [motion]. ¶종이를 ~ 베다 cut paper with a snip∥나는 식칼 끝으로 감자의 싹을 ~ 잘라 냈다 I trimmed[cut] out the eyes of the potatoes using[with] the heel of the kitchen knife.
싹둑거리다 slice; mince; chop; snip.
싹둑싹둑 snip-snap. ¶종이를 ~ 자르다 cut paper up snip-snap. **싹둑싹둑하다** slice; mince. ⇨゠싹둑거리다
싹수 a good omen; hope(s); promise; possibility; probability; (a) chance; likelihood. ¶~가 있다 be promising / be hopeful / (사업 등이) have a bright prospect / (사람이) have a bright future before one∥그 녀석은 ~가 틀렸다 His chance is up. / (구어) He's a goner.
싹수(가) 노랗다 be hopeless; be a lost cause; show no promise of success; have no prospect (of); (구어) There is not a dog's [cat's] chance.; (미국 속어) There's a fat chance.
싹수없다 be hopeless. ⇨゠싹수(가) 노랗다(⇨싹수)
싹싹 1 [완전히] completely; clean(ly); [힘들여] roughly. ¶~ 쓸어 내다 sweep (the dirt) out[away] thoroughly∥~ 빨다 wash roughly∥수건으로 몸을 ~ 문지르다 scrub oneself with a towel∥그녀는 테이블 위를 ~ 치웠다 She cleared the table quickly. **2** [베는 모양·소리] with a snip[swish]; with a swishing motion[sound]. **3** [비는 모양] imploringly; entreatingly; humbly. ¶눈물을 흘리며 ~ 빌다 beg for forgiveness with tears in one's eyes∥살려 달라고 ~ 빌다 beg for one's life wringing one's hands.
싹싹하다 affable; amiable; suave; openhearted; good-humored; sociable; jolly. ¶싹싹한 사람 (속어) a soft-soaper∥그는 아주 싹싹한 사람이다 He is well matured[well rounded off] in experience. / He is quite a hail-fellow-well-met sort of a person.
싹쓸이하다 sweep (the board). ¶그 수영 선수는 전 종목을 싹쓸이했다 The swimmer swept all the events.
싹트다 [일이 일어나다] arise; [자라기 시작하다] begin to grow. ¶그들 사이에는 사랑이 싹텄다 Love budded between them.∥그녀의 가슴속에 질투심이 싹텄다 Jealousy sprang up in her heart.∥젊은이들 사이에 새로운 사상이 싹트고 있다 A new way of thinking is appearing among young people.
싼값 a low[cheap] price. ¶(…보다) ~을 매기다 underquote[underbid] (a person)∥(남보다) ~으로 팔다 undersell (one's competitors)∥터무니없는 ~으로 팔다 sell at a sacrifice

쌀 1 [벼 껍질을 벗긴 알맹이] (raw / un-cooked) rice. ¶볶은 ~ parched [popped] rice // 묵은 ~ old rice / rice stored from a previous year's harvest // 그날그날 먹을 ~이 없다 be in want of even the day's supply of rice / want the bare necessaries of life // ~을 씻다 wash rice // ~을 안치다 prepare rice for boiling // ~을 찧다 hull [husk] rice / refine rice by pounding. **2** nonglutinous rice. ⇨˚멥쌀 **3** [포아풀과의 곡식 껍질을 벗긴 알] any hulled grain.

쌀가게 a rice store [shop].

쌀값 the price of rice; the rice price. ¶~이 오른다 [내린다] Rice rises [falls] in price. // ~을 동결하다 leave the price of rice at its current level / freeze the price of rice (at the previous year's level).

쌀겨 rice bran.

쌀뜨물 water from washing rice; the washing water of rice.

쌀밥 boiled [cooked] rice.

쌀보리 [식] rye.

쌀쌀 ⇨˚살살.

쌀쌀맞다 distant; cold-hearted. ⇨˚쌀쌀하다2 ¶쌀쌀맞은 사람 a cold fish // 쌀쌀맞게 거절하다 give a flat [point-blank] refusal / spurn (a demand) point-blank [bluntly].

쌀쌀하다 1 [날씨가] [차다] chilly; rather cold; cool; [음산하다] dreary; dismal; melancholy; gloomy. ¶쌀쌀한 날씨 gloomy [chilly] weather // 쌀쌀한 공기 sharp air // 날로 쌀쌀해집니다 It is getting cooler day by day. // 오늘 아침은 공기가 몹시 ~ There is a nip in the air this morning.
2 [사람이] distant; cold-hearted; chilly; indifferent; cool; unkind; frigid. ¶쌀쌀한 인사 a curt [brusque] greeting // 쌀쌀한 태도 (put on) a distant [cool] air // 수년이 지난 후에 다시 만났을 때 그는 매우 쌀쌀해 보였다 When I saw him again after many years, he was indeed cold and distant. // 그녀는 딱딱하고 쌀쌀한 만큼 그의 요청을 거절하였다 With formal and cold words, she snubbed him. // 그 여자는 쌀쌀한 눈으로 나를 보았다 The woman looked at me coolly [distantly]. **쌀쌀히** coldly; coolly; icily; cold-heartedly. ¶~ 대하다 give a person the cold shoulder / [딱딱하게 대하다] act standoffish / stand on ceremony with a person // 그녀는 ~ 대답했다 She gave a curt answer. / She answered curtly. // 그녀는 그에게 ~ 대했다 She gave him the cold shoulder.

쌀알 [쌀의 알] a grain of rice.

쌈 [상추 등에 밥과 반찬을 싼 음식] ssam; cooked rice wrapped in lettuce [laver]. ¶상추 [김] ~ lettuce- [seaweed-] wrapped rice.

쌈[2] **1** [바늘의 포장 단위] a pack (of 24 needles). **2** [금 백 냥쭝] 100 taels of gold. **3** [피륙 뭉치] a bundle (of cloth).

쌈[3] a quarrel; (a) war; a contest; a struggle. ⇨˚싸움.

쌈지 a tobacco pouch.

쌀싸래하다 slightly bitter.

쌉쌀하다 slightly bitter; (taste) bitterish; of a bitterish taste.

쌍(雙) [짝] a pair; twins; [암수] a couple; a brace (단수·복수 동형). ¶꿩 한 ~ a brace of pheasants // 두 ~ two pairs // 한 ~의 젊은 부부 a young (married) couple // ~이 되다 make [form] a pair // 이 인형은 한 ~으로 되어 있다 These two dolls make [form] a pair.

쌍가마[1] (머리의) a double whirl of hair on the head; a pair of hair whirls.

쌍가마[2] (雙-) [탈것의] a sedan-chair carried by two horses, one fore and the other aft.

쌍갈랫길(雙-) a forked road.

쌍갈지다(雙-) divide [fork] into two branches; bifurcate; [길·강이] fork; branch off in two directions. ¶쌍갈진 가지 twin branches // 우리는 길이 쌍갈진 곳에 당도했다 We reached the parting of the roads. / We came to the fork of the road.

쌍견(雙肩) one's [both] shoulders.

쌍겹눈(雙-) a double eyelid eye.

쌍곡선(雙曲線) [수] a hyperbola (pl. ~s, -lae); a hyperbolic curve. ¶~의 hyperbolic // ~을 그리다 describe a hyperbolic curve.

쌍꺼풀(雙-) a double(-edged) eyelid. ¶~이지다 have a double-edged eyelid.

쌍날(雙-)칼 a double-edged blade; a double edge.

쌍날칼 a double-edged sword.

쌍년 〈비〉 a mean woman. ⇨상년2

쌍놈 〈비〉 an ill-bred fellow. ⇨상놈2

쌍동이(雙童-) ⇨쌍둥이

쌍두(雙頭) a pair of (animals); two head(s). ¶ ~의 뱀 a double-headed snake.

●쌍두마차 a carriage and pair.

쌍둥이(雙-) twins; twin children; twin sons [daughters]; twin brothers [sisters]; (그중의 한 사람) a twin. ¶남자 [여자] ~ boy [girl] twins / twin brothers [sisters] // 일란성 ~ identical [one-egg] twins (▶ 한 사람은 identical twin) // 이란성 ~ fraternal [two-egg / biovular / dizygotic] twins // 남녀 (의) ~ mixed twins / a pigeon pair / twin boy and girl // 그의 ~ 형 [아우] his twin brother [sister] // 세 ~ triplets / 네 ~ quadruplets / (구어) quads / ~를 낳다 give birth to twins / ~로 태어나다 be born twins / be twinborn // 두 사람은 ~처럼 닮았다 Those two are exactly alike. / Those two are as like as two peas (in a pod).

●쌍둥이자리 [천] the Twins; Gemini.

쌍떡잎(雙-) [식] a double seed-leaf [-cotyledon].

●쌍떡잎식물 [식] a dicotyledon; a dicotyledonous plant.

쌍무(雙務) ¶~적인 bilateral / reciprocal.

●쌍무 계약 a bilateral [reciprocal] contract.

쌍무지개(雙-) a double rainbow.

쌍반점(雙半點) a semicolon.

쌍발(雙發) (엔진의) (having) twin engines [motors]; (총의) (having) double-barrels. ¶ ~의 [항] bimotor(ed) / twin-engine(d) [-motor(ed)] / (총의) double-barreled [-chambered].

●쌍발기 a twin-motor(ed) [-engine(d)] plane; a bimotored airplane.

쌍방(雙方) both; both parties. ⇨˚양방(兩方) ¶ ~의 both / mutual // ~의 이익 [의무] mutual interest [obligation] // ~의 행위 bilateral action // ~의 합의에 의하여 by mutual consent [agreement] // 노사 ~의 양보에 의해 through concessions by both management and labor // ~의 오해를 풀다 clear up the misunderstanding between the two parties

쌍벽(雙璧) 〖우열을 가릴 수 없이 뛰어난 둘〗 the two greatest authorities; the matchless twin stars. ¶현대 한국 화단의 ~ the twin master painters of contemporary Korea.

//그것은 ~을 모두 만족시킬 것이다 That will satisfy both parties.//~의 말을 듣지 않고는 판단을 내릴 수가 없다 I must hear both sides (of the story) before I judge.//나는 ~을 다 안다 I know both of them. / I know them both.

쌍봉낙타(雙峯駱駝) 〖동〗 a Bactrian [two-humped] camel.

쌍분(雙墳) twin graves.

쌍생아(雙生兒) twins; twin children. ⇨˝쌍둥이

쌍수(雙手) both hands. ¶~를 들어 찬성하다 second [support] (a proposal) with all one's heart / give one's hearty support (to) / give unqualified approval (to a proposal)//나는 그 안에 ~를 들어 찬성합니다 I support the proposal wholeheartedly.//우리와 함께 일해 주신다면 ~를 들고 환영하겠습니다 We will give you a wholehearted welcome [We will be delighted] if you decide to work with us.

쌍심지(雙心-) a double wick. ¶눈에 ~를 켜고 with glaring eyes / with one's eyes wide open//~나다 [서다 / 오르다] burn [be furious] with anger / have eyes glaring with anger / flare up.

쌍십절(雙十節) 〖대만의 국경일〗 the Double Tenth (Anniversary).

쌍쌍이(雙雙-) two and [by] two; in pairs; in couples; by twos. ¶~ 떠나다 [짝 짓다] pair off//그들은 ~ 나갔다 They went out in pairs.

쌍안(雙眼) two eyes; both eyes; a pair of eyes; binocular.

쌍안경(雙眼鏡) a binocular (telescope); (a pair of) binoculars; (육상용) field glasses; (해군용) marine glasses; (극장용) opera glasses. ¶~으로 보다 look through a field glass.

쌍알(雙-) a double-yolked egg.

쌍자엽식물(雙子葉植物) 〖식〗 a dicotyledon. ⇨˝쌍떡잎식물(⇨쌍떡잎)

쌍장부(雙-) 〖건〗 twin tenons. ¶~끌 a kind of double-bladed chisel.

쌍점(雙點) a colon.

쌍지팡이(雙-) 〖두 개의 지팡이〗 (a pair of) crutches. ¶그녀는 남의 일에 ~ 짚고 나서기를 잘한다 [참견을 잘한다] She is always nosing into what doesn't concern her.

쌍창(雙窓) a window consisting of two panes.

쌍칼(雙-) two swords.
● **쌍칼잡이** a two-sword fencer; a two-sworded man.

쌍태(雙胎) twin embryos [fetuses].

쌓다 1 〖포개어 올리다〗 pile (up); (난잡하게) heap (up); (건초·짚 등을 정연하게) stack (up); lay; make a pile; pile one above [on] another. ¶흙 [모래]를 쌓아 올리다 heap up earth [sand]//건초를 높이 ~ stack hay high//나는 선반 위에 책을 많이 쌓았다 I piled [heaped] up many books on the shelf.//그들은 콘크리트 블록을 쌓아(올려) 담을 쌓았다 They built a wall by piling up concrete blocks.

2 〖구축하다〗 build; erect; raise; construct. ¶성을 ~ build a castle/돌담 [둑]을 ~ construct a stone wall [an embankment]//탑을 ~ erect a tower.

3 〖축적하다〗 accumulate; acquire; store up; amass. ¶부(富)와 명성을 ~ build up a reputation and a fortune / amass a fortune and make a name for oneself//경험을 ~ gain [acquire / enrich] experience//너는 더 훈련을 쌓아야 된다 You should practice harder.//그는 막대한 부를 쌓았다 He accumulated [amassed] a huge amount of money.//그는 회사를 위해 확고한 기초를 쌓았다 He laid [built up] a firm foundation for the company.//그는 도제에서 시작하여 현재의 지위를 쌓아 올렸다 He built up his present position after starting as an apprentice.//젊었을 때 지식을 쌓아라 Accumulate knowledge while you are young.//그의 이 논문은 오랜 세월의 연구를 쌓아 올려 된 것이다 This paper is the culmination of his long years of research.//이 일은 오랜 세월 동안 경험을 쌓아야 비로소 할 수 있게 된다 You become able to do this work only after accumulating years of experience.

쌓이다 1 〖퇴적되다〗 be piled up; lie (on). ¶책이 높이 쌓였다 The books were piled up high.//나는 쌓인 낙엽을 쓸었다 I raked up the heaps of fallen leaves.//눈이 내려 쌓여 있다 The snow lay thick on the ground.//테이블에는 먼지가 쌓여 있었다 The table was covered with dust. / Thick dust lay on the table.//화산의 재가 5센티나 쌓여 있다 Volcanic ash lay five centimeters deep on the ground.//텔레비전 스크린에 먼지가 쌓여 있다 Dust collected on the TV screen.//도랑에 쓰레기가 쌓여 있었다 The shelf was covered with (a layer of) dust.//트럭에 목재가 산더미같이 쌓여 있었다 The truck [(영) lorry] was piled high with timber.//이 지방에서는 눈이 1미터쯤 쌓이는 것은 드문 일이 아니다 It is not unusual in this district for a meter of snow to accumulate on the ground.

2 〖일이 밀리다〗 stagnate; be stagnant; be left undone. ¶일이 잔뜩 쌓여 있다 There is a good deal of work undone.//할 일이 잔뜩 쌓여 있다 I have stacks of work to do.

3 〖원한 등이〗 be pent up; be congested; (빚 등이) accumulate; get accumulated. ¶쌓이고 쌓인 원한 suppressed [pent-up] hatred//그녀는 쌓인 원한을 털어놓았다 She gave full vent to her pent up resentment.

쌔근쌔근 panting(ly); (sleep) calmly. ⇨˝새근새근¹

쌔다 1 get [be] wrapped [covered]. ⇨˝싸이다 2 be piled up; stagnate; be pent up. ⇨˝쌓이다 ¶쌔고 쎈 superabundant / superfluous.

쌔비다 〈속〉 steal (a thing from a person). ⇨ 훔치다

쌕쌕거리다 breathe lightly. ⇨˝색색거리다

쌕쌕이 〈속〉 a jet (plane). ⇨제트기(⇨제트)

쌩 whistling; whizzing. ⇨˝생

써내다 write and submit [present / hand in / turn in / give in]; submit.

써넣다 write in; fill in; enter (in a register); make an entry (in); inscribe (in); make [write] notes; interline(행간에). ¶용지에 ~ (영) fill in a blank [form] / (미) fill out a form/설문지에 ~ fill in [out] a questionnaire/카드에 이름을 ~ fill in one's name in a card/숙박부에 이름과 주소를 ~ enter one's name and address in a hotel register//페이지의 난외에 주석을 ~ write notes [comments] in the margin of a page//약속을

써늘하다 cold; chilly; icy. ⇨싸늘하다

써다 [조수가 밀려 나가다] ebb; flow back; recede; [양이 줄다] subside; sink; go down.

써레 [농] a harrow; a rake. ¶~질하다 harrow (the field) / rake (the ground).
● **써렛발** the prongs[pegs / spikes / tines / teeth] of a harrow.

써리다 [농] harrow (a field); rake (the soil smooth).

써먹다 use; make use of; utilize. ¶써먹을 만하다 be useful[usable] / be of use // 써먹을 데가 없다 be useless[of no use] / be good for nothing / be no good.

썩[1] 1 [대단히] very; very much; exceedingly; greatly; so. ¶~ 좋은 생각 a very good idea // 그녀는 노래를 ~ 잘 부른다 She sings very well. / She is a very good singer. 2 [어서 빨리] at once; immediately; directly; instantly; (미) straightway; (영) straightaway [straight away]. ¶~ 나가지 못할까 Get out of here right this minute. / Be off with you at once.

썩[2] quite; entirely; with a (single) snip. ⇨싹

썩다 1 [부패하다] rot; go bad[rotten]; decompose; spoil; decay; corrupt; (우유 등이) turn sour; (고기 등이) putrefy; (생선이) become stale; (물이) become foul; (쇠가) corrode. ¶썩은 생선 rotten fish // 썩은 달걀 an addled[a bad / a rotten] egg // 썩은 버터 rancid butter // 썩은 귤 a rotten orange // 썩은 나무 decayed wood // 썩은 이 a decayed[bad] tooth // 쥐의 시체가 썩기 시작했다 The body of the dead rat has begun to decompose. // 낡은 나무다리가 완전히 썩어 버렸다 The old wooden bridge completely rotted away.
2 [재능·사물이 활용되지 않다] gather dust; become[get] rusty; be left to rust; rust away. ¶도서관에서 책이 썩고 있다 The books are gathering dust on the library shelves. // 결국 그의 재능은 썩고 말았다 There was after all no chance to turn his talent to account.
3 [타락하다] be corrupted; become depraved; be morally tainted. ¶그의 정신은 완전히 썩어 있었다 He was utterly corrupt.
4 [걱정 등으로 마음이 상하다] feel depressed [gloomy]; become heavy; be disheartened. ¶방탕한 아들 때문에 그녀의 속이 썩었다 She was sick at heart because of her prodigal son.

썩어도 준치(속담) An old eagle is better than a young crow.

썩어 빠지다 rot[decay] completely; rot away; fall into[go to] decay; be utterly rotten. ¶정신이 썩어 빠진 사람 a morally bankrupt man // 그는 정신이 썩어 빠진 사람이다 He is rotten to the core. / He is a hopeless degenerate.

썩썩 completely; with a snip; imploringly. ⇨싹싹

썩이다 (마음을) worry (oneself) [be worried] (about / over); be anxious (about); bother (oneself) (about); make one's heart break. ¶방탕한 아들의 일로 속을 ~ eat one's heart out with the matter of one's prodigal son // 딸이 아버지의 속을 ~ a daughter breaks her father's heart // 그는 집안일로 속을 썩이고 있다 House troubles weigh heavy on him [are preying on his mind]. // 그런 문제로 속을 썩인들 아무 소용없는 일일세 What is the use of jittering about such an affair?

썩정이 1 [썩은 물건] something rotten [spoiled / decayed]. 2 →삭정이

썩히다 1 [부패시키다] rot; putrefy; corrupt; let (a thing) rot[spoil]. ¶낙엽을 썩혀서 거름을 만들다 let dead leaves decay to make compost // 달걀을 썩혀 버렸다 I let the eggs go bad. 2 [안 쓰다] keep (something) idle; let (something) go to waste. ¶그 때문에 그는 아까운 재능을 썩히고 말았다 That destroyed his rare talent. / He was not able to develop his rare talent because of it. // 이렇게 훌륭한 물건을 썩힌다는 것은 부끄러운 일이다 It is a shame to leave such a fine article to rust.

썰다 cut; chop (up); hack (to pieces); hash (meat); slice; shave(얇게); mince(가늘게); dice; cube; cut in dice[cubes / chunks].(▶chunks는 꽤 큰 것을 두껍게 토막 친 것, cubes는 가지런한 것, dice는 작고 가지런한 것을 말함. cubes와 dice는 야채에, chunks는 살코기나 큰 생선, 일부의 야채에 씀) ¶깍두기 꼴로 썬 야채 diced[cubed] vegetables // 두껍게 썬 쇠고기 chunks of beef // ~ (something) into[in] slices[thin pieces] // 두껍게 ~ cut (something) into thick pieces // 길쭉하게 ~ cut in long strips // 길게 ~ cut lengthwise // 둥글게 ~ cut in[into] round slices[rounds] // 당근을 네모나게 ~ cut a carrot into small cubes[square pieces] // 오이를 잘게 ~ cut a cucumber into a small pieces.

썰렁하다 chilly; rather cold; somewhat [slightly] cold.

썰매 a sled; (영) a sledge; (주로 말이 끄는) a sleigh; (미국·캐나다의) a toboggan. ¶~를 타다 sled / sledge / sleigh / ride on a sled [in a sledge / in a sleigh] // ~를 몰다 steer a sledge // 그곳은 ~를 타고 여기서 1시간 걸린다 It's an hour's sleigh-ride from here.
● **썰매타기** sleigh-riding; sleighing; sledding.

썰물 an ebb[an ebbing / a falling] tide. ¶~ 때에 at low tide[water] // ~이 되다 ebb / be on the ebb // 3시에 ~이 되다 The tide goes out[ebbs] at three. // ~이 되기 시작했다 The tide is on the ebb[is beginning to go out].

쏘가리 [동] a mandarin fish.

쏘다 1 [화살·총 등을 나가게 하다] shoot (an arrow / a birds); fire (a gun); discharge. ¶총을 ~ fire[shoot] a gun // 새를 ~ shoot a bird // 화살을 ~ shoot an arrow // 대포를 ~ fire a cannon // 쏘아 죽이다 shoot (a person) dead[to death] // 고사포로 적기를 쏘아 떨어뜨리다 shoot[bring] down an enemy plane with anti-aircraft guns // 나는 세 발을 쏘아 1발을 맞혔다 I fired three times and made one hit. // 오늘 밤 남산에서 꽃불을 쏘아 올린다 Fireworks are going to be displayed[be shot of] over the Namsan(Mt. Nam) this evening.
2 [벌 등이 침으로 찌르다] sting.
3 [날카롭게 말하다] make cutting remarks; make a sharp[cutting] retort; say spiteful things; deliver (a person) pinpricks.
4 [혀·코 등을 자극하다] taste hot; be pungent; bite. ¶톡 쏘는 맛이 나는 biting to the

쏘다니다 taste// 겨자는 톡 쏘는 맛이 난다 Mustard has a hot[sharp / burning] taste.

쏘다니다 gad[wander] about; run[bustle] about; loiter; (미국 속어) bum around. ¶잘 쏘다니는 사람 a regular gadabout // 쏘다니기를 좋아하다 have a roving foot // 나는 하루 종일 사방을 쏘다녔다 I have spent the whole day in visiting one place after another.

쏘삭거리다 ransack; instigate. ⇨<쑤석거리다

쏘시개 a (fire) lighter. ⇨불쏘시개

쏘아보다 scowl at(눈살을 찌푸리고); glare at(화난 표정으로); look fiercely[menacingly] (at); look sharply in the face; look daggers (at). ¶그는 나를 매섭게 쏘아보았다 He gave me a fierce look. // 그 사람이 날카로운 눈으로 그들을 쏘아보았다 The man glared hard at them.

쏘아붙이다 make cutting remarks. ⇨=쏘다3

쏘이다 (벌레에) be stung. ¶벌에 ~ get stung by a bee // 팔을 ~ be stung on the arm // 나는 벌에 쏘였다 I was stung by a bee. // 나는 모기에 쏘였다 I was bitten by a mosquito. // 벌레에 쏘인 자리가 부었다 The sting of an insect has swollen up.

쏙 (protruded) way out; with a jerk. ⇨<쑥3

쏙닥거리다 whisper secrets; whisper slyly to (a person). ⇨′속닥거리다 ¶그들은 뭔가를 쏙닥거리고 있었다 They were whispering about something.

쏙독새 [동] a (Korean) goatsucker.

쏜살같다 (서술적) be swift as an arrow. **쏜살같이** as swift as an arrow; like an arrow[a shot]; in a shot[flash]; with lightning speed (swiftness). ¶~ 달리다 run at full speed // 그는 골을 향해 ~ 달렸다 He dashed full tilt for the goal. // 소녀는 ~ 언덕을 달려 내려갔다 The girl made a headlong dash down the hill.

쏟다 1 [붓다] pour (in / into / out); spill; empty. ¶잉크를 ~ spill ink // 눈물을 ~ shed profuse tears // 물통의 물을 ~ pour the water out of the bucket // 물을 양동이에 ~ pour water into a bucket.
2 [집중하다] concentrate (one's efforts on something); pay[direct] (one's attention to a thing); give (one's mind to something); devote (to). ¶애정을 ~ devote[fix] one's affection on (a person) / be strongly attached to (a person) // 우리는 일에 전력을 쏟았다 We concentrated[focused] our energies on the job. // 그들은 그 운동에 온 정력을 쏟았다 They threw all their energy into the movement.
3 [심중을 털어놓다] pour out; give vent (to one's anger); lay open[bare] (one's thought). ¶울분을 ~ vent[work off] one's (pent-up) anger (on).
4 [피·눈물 등을 흘리다] shed (tears); drop (blood).

쏟아지다 pour on[out / down]; (물 등이) gush out[forth]; spurt; spurt; get[be] spilt. ¶쏟아지는 비 (a) pouring rain // 햇빛이 뜰에 쏟아지고 있었다 The sunshine poured into the garden. // 참았던 말이 한꺼번에 그녀의 입에서 쏟아졌다 The suppressed words gushed[poured] from her lips. // 상처에서 피가 쏟아져 나왔다 Blood gushed[spurted] from the wound. // 우유가 식탁 위에 쏟아졌다 Some milk spilled on the table. // 눈물이 볼을 타고 쏟아졌다 Tears rolled[ran] down her cheeks. // 물이 바닥에 쏟아져 있다 Someone has spilled water on the floor.

쓸다 gnaw; nibble. ¶줄을 쏠아서 끊다 gnaw through a rope // 벽을 쏠아 구멍을 내다 gnaw a hole through a wall.

쏠리다 1 [기울다] lean (to / toward); incline (to). 2 [경향을 띠다] incline (to); tend (to); lean[trend] (toward). ¶자연주의로 ~ lean to naturalism. 3 [시선·마음 등이 집중되다] focus (on / at); center (on / in / at); converge (on). ¶예쁜 처녀에게 시선이 ~ have one's eye on a pretty girl // 그녀는 자기 딸을 그 부자와 결혼시키는 일에 마음이 쏠려 있었다 She was eager[anxious] to marry her daughter to the rich man.

쏠쏠하다 tolerable; passable. ⇨<쑬쑬하다

쏴 with a cool gust. ⇨′솨

쐐기 (V 자형의) a wedge; (바퀴나 통의) a chock; (차 바퀴의) linchpin. ¶~ 모양의 wedge-shaped / cuneiform // 적진을 ~ 대형으로 공격하다 drive a wedge into[between] the enemy's defenses.

쐐기(를) 박다 make sure; confirm; make (a person) pledge. ¶그가 약속을 지키도록 쐐기를 박아 둘 필요가 있다 We must take steps to make sure that he will keep his promise.

쐐기풀 [식] a nettle.

쐬다[1] expose (to the wind); air; bare. ¶바람을 ~ (물건을) expose (thing) to the air / (사람이) expose oneself to the wind / air oneself(바깥 공기를) // 옷에 바람을 ~ give clothes airing // 저녁 바람을 ~ enjoy the cool of the evening // 햇볕을 ~ bask[bathe] in the sun // 필름을 햇빛에 쐬면 안 된다 Don't expose the film to the sun. // 나는 화분의 화초를 햇볕에 쐬었다 I put the potted plants in the sunshine.

쐬다[2] be stung. ⇨쏘이다

쑤다 boil; make; prepare. ¶죽을 ~ boil rice into gruel / cook gruel / simmer porridge.

쑤석거리다 1 [뒤지다] ransack; rummage; stir up; (막대기 등으로) poke[stir] about (with a stick); rake[poke up] (the fire). ¶(찾느라고) 서랍 속을 ~ ransack[rummage (in)] a drawer (for something) // 꺼져 가는 불을 쑤석거려 일으키다 revive[stir (up)] a dying[dwindling] fire. 2 [꼬드기다] instigate; incite; prod; needle; set[spur / egg] (a person) on.

쑤시다[1] 1 (구멍 등을) pick; poke. ¶이를 ~ pick one's teeth // 흙벽을 쑤시어 구멍을 내다 poke a hole in a mud wall // 그는 성냥개비로 충치 구멍을 쑤셨다 He picked a troublesome cavity in a tooth with the point of a match. 2 (불을) poke[stir up] (the fire); rake (the fire); give (the fire) a stir. ¶그는 난로의 불을 쑤셔서 타오르게 했다 He poked up a blaze in the stove.

쑤시다[2] [아프다] ache; smart(손가락 등이); tingle; throb with pain(종기 등이); jump; fester; rankle(염증을 일으켜); be sore; twine; prick; prickle. ¶귀가 ~ have a sore ear // 머리[골치]가 ~ have a splitting headache // 옆구리가 ~ have a smart pain in the side // 온몸이 쑤신다 I feel sharp pains all over my body. // 마디마디가 쑤신다 I am aching in the joints. // 충치가 몹시 쑤신다 A decayed tooth aches[pains me] awfully. // I have a terrible toothache. // 상처가 쑤셔서 밤새 잠을 못 잤다 The smart of[pain from] my wound kept me

쑥¹ [식] a mugwort; a wormwood; (말려 비빈 것) moxa. ¶~을 태우다 burn moxa (on the skin).

쑥² [못난이] a dupe; a fool; an ass; a donkey; a simpleton. ¶그런 말에 속아 넘어가다니 너도 어지간한 ~이구나 You must be very simple to be taken in by such a story.

쑥³ 1 [내밀거나 들어간 모양] (protruded) way out; (sunken) way in. ¶~ 나온 턱 a prominent jaw // 들어간 눈 deep-set[hollow/sunken] eyes // ~ 들어가다 cave in / give in // 나는 드럼통을 방망이로 쳐서 ~ 들어가게 했다 I hit drum can with a bat and put a dent in it. // 그의 볼은 ~ 들어가 있다 He has hollow cheeks. / He is hollow-cheeked.
2 [밀어 넣거나 뽑는 모양] with a jerk; with a vigorous pull. ¶이불 속으로 ~ 들어가다 slide[slip] between sheets // 인형의 손이 ~ 빠졌다 A hand came clean off the doll. // 마개가 ~ 빠졌다 The stopper came out easily [with a light pop]. // 문의 손잡이를 잡아당겼더니 ~ 빠져 버렸다 When I pulled on the doorknob, it came right off in my hand. // 공은 그의 미트 속으로 ~ 들어갔다 The ball plunked[plonked] right into the middle of his mitt.

쑥갓 [식] a crown daisy.

쑥대강이 disheveled[unkempt] hair. ¶네 머리는 ~구나 Your hair is a mess.

쑥대머리 disheveled hair. ⇨ 쑥대강이

쑥대밭 [쑥이 우거진 땅] a mugwort field; an area overgrown with mugwort; [황무지] wasteland; a wilderness; [폐허] the ruins. ¶~을 만들다 lay waste / devastate (land) / ruin / turn (a place) into ruins / lay (a city) flat // ~이 되다 be ruined / be devastated / go to ruin / fall into ruins / run waste.

쑥덕거리다 whisper secrets; whisper slyly to (a person). ⇨ 숙덕거리다

쑥덕공론 (-公論) a secret conference; secret talks; a talk in whispers. ¶~으로 계획을 세우다 plan (a thing) through secret talks. **쑥덕공론하다** discuss things under one's breath; hold a secret conference[discussion]; exchange subdued remarks. ¶머리를 맞대고 ~ lay heads together in secret consultation.

쑥떡 ssuktteok; a rice-flour cake flavored with mugwort.

쑥밭 a mugwort field. ⇨ 쑥대밭

쑥스럽다 1 [걸맞지 않다] unbecoming; improper; unseemly; indecent. ¶쑥스럽게 굴다 behave unseemly / cut a ridiculous figure // 내 입으로 말하기는 쑥스럽지만 우리 아이는 천재요 My son is a genius, though I say it who should not.
2 [겸연쩍다] awkward. ¶쑥스러워하다 feel awkward[nervous] (before an audience) / feel small[cheap/embarrassed] (in company) / be[feel] abashed / be self-conscious // 사람들 앞에서 노래하는 것이 나는 쑥스러웠다 I was embarrassed to sing in front of people. / I felt very self-conscious about singing in people. // 그는 쑥스러운 듯이 머리를 숙였다 He bowed self-consciously.

쑥쑥 1 [들어가거나 내민 모양] all (protruded) way out; all (sunken) way in. ¶~ 내밀다 protrude all way out // ~ 들어가다 sink all way in. 2 [뽑는 모양] pulling[jerking/yanking] out repeatedly. ¶무를 ~ 뽑다 uproot radishes. 3 [쑤시는 모양] (hurt) sharply from time to time. ¶~ 쑤시다 shoot / prick / prickle // ~ 쑤신다 My tooth stings. // 머리가 이따금 ~ 쑤신다 My head aches on and off. // 팔이 ~ 쑤셨다 Pain shot up my arm. 4 [솟는 모양] quickly; rapidly. ¶~ 자라는 나뭇가지 a branch growing out straight // ~ 자라다 grow taller and taller.

쑬쑬하다 tolerable; passable; fairly good; so-so. ¶생김생김이 ~ be fairly good-looking / (미국 구어) be fair to middling. **쑬쑬히** so-so; passably; tolerably; moderately.

쑤개 headgear; (여자의) headdress; hat.

쓰다¹ (글씨를) write (a letter); (글을) compose (an essay / a poem); write (a story); make (a composition); [적다] put (down) (one's opinion) in writing; put [lay / jot / set] down; [기술하다] describe. ¶새로 쓴 소설[희곡] a newly written novel[play] // 편지 쓰는 법 how to write a letter // 글씨를 잘[못] ~ write well[badly] // 펜으로 ~ write with a pen // 잉크로 ~ write in ink // 시를 ~ compose a poem // 잡지에 소설을 ~ write a novel for a magazine // 부모에게 편지를 ~ write (a letter) to one's parents // 수필을 단숨에 ~ write off an essay at a stretch[at one sitting] // 행(行) 속에 한 낱말을 덧붙여 ~ insert a word into a line // 단어의 철자를 잘못 ~ misspell a word // 무심코 잘못 ~ make a slip of the pen // 그 단어[이름]는 어떻게 씁니까 How do you spell the word[name]? // 나는 지금 새 희곡을 쓰고 있다 I am working on a new drama. // 신문[게시/편지]에 그렇게 씌어 있다 This newspaper [notice / letter] says so. // 이 소설을 쓰는 데 그는 5년이 걸렸다 He spent five years working on this novel. // 그는 필요조건을 조목조목 들어 썼다 He enumerated the necessary conditions. // 벽에는 온통 알아볼 수 없는 말들을 갈겨써 놓았었다 The wall was scribbled all over. / Some illegible marks were scribbled all over the wall. // 그는 노트에 숫자를 갈겨썼다 He scrawled some figures in his notebook. // 그는 잡지에 싸구려 소설을 마구 써 주고 있다 He dashes off cheap stories for magazines. // 그는 그 주제에 대해 아직 다 쓰지 못했다 He still hasn't exhausted the subject. // 그는 편지에 추신을 덧붙여 썼다 He added a postscript to his letter. // 그는 나의 결점을 하나하나 써 놓았다 He enumerated my faults in writing. // 나는 잘못 써서 5장이나 버렸다 I wasted five sheets of paper because of mistakes. // 그녀는 머지않아 다시 편지를 쓰겠다고 추신에 곁들여 썼다 She wrote[added] in the postscript that she would write again soon. // 그는 소품을 술술 써 내려갔다 He wrote the short piece with great facility[with a facile pen]. // 이 한자는 쓰기 어렵다 This Chinese character is difficult to write. // 이 펜은 잘 써지지 않는다 This pen does not write well. // 나는 글을 쓰기에 바쁘다 I am busy with my writing. // 나는 보고서에 중요한 것을 빠뜨리고 썼다 I left out[forgot to mention] an important matter in my report. // 좀 더 간략하게 써 보십시오 Try to put it into simpler words.

쓰다² 1 [착용하다] put on; wear(▶ put on은 동작, wear는 상태를 나타냄); cover. ¶안경을 쓴 남자 a man wearing glasses / a man with

쓰다

쓰다¹ glasses on // 베레모를 쓴 남자 a man in a beret // 가면을 ~ wear a mask / mask one's face / dissemble(감정 등) / [변장하다] disguise oneself (as) / (위선적으로) play the hypocrite // 그는 안경을 쓰고 있다 (습관적으로) He wears glasses. // 그는 오늘은 선글라스를 쓰고 있다 He is wearing sunglasses today. / He has sunglasses on today. // 그녀는 마스크를 쓰고 있다 She is wearing a mask. // 어린이는 모자를 쓰고 있었다 The child had a cap on. // 그는 급히 모자를 썼다 He hastily put on his hat.

2 (우산을) hold [put] up (an umbrella) over one's head. ¶우산을 쓰고 under an umbrella.

3 [푹 덮다] pour (water) on (oneself); be covered with (dust); pull [draw] (the bedspread) over (one's head). ¶담요를 쓰고 자다 sleep with the blanket pulled over one's head.

4 (누명 등을) be falsely [wrongly] charged (with murder); be falsely [unjustly] accused (of stealing).

쓰다³ 1 (물건을) use; make use of; put to use; employ; [취급하다] work [operate] (a machine); handle a tool; manipulate (an instrument). ¶아직 쓸 수 있는 중고차 a serviceable secondhand car // 어떤 포지션에도 쓸 수 있는 선수 a player who can play (in) any position / (야구의 만능 보결 선수) a utility man // 발을 ~ kick // 오래 쓸 수 있다 stand long use / give a long service // 쓰지 않게 되다 pass from use / fall into disuse / be [get / go / fall] out of use // 그 기계는 널리 쓰이고 있다 The machine is widely used. / The machine is in wide [general] use. // 저 타자기는 지금은 쓰지 않고 있다 That typewriter is not in use. // 그는 오른손을 잘 쓰지 못한다 He can't use his right hand very well. // 이 탁자는 아직도 쓸 수 있다 This table is still usable. // 이 도구는 두 가지로 쓸 수 있다 This tool can be used in two ways. // 이 표는 이달 말까지 쓸 수 있다 This ticket is valid till the end of this month. // 이 유리컵은 꽃병으로 쓸 수 있다 This glass can serve as a vase. // 어느 방이나 마음대로 쓰십시오 Please make free use of any room you like. // 그 방법은 오래전부터 쓰지 않고 있다 That method has long been out of use. // 그 원고는 쓸 만합니까 Is the manuscript (of) any good? // 그런 책을 읽어서 어디에 쓸 것인가 What's the good [use] of reading such a book?

2 (사람을) employ; hire; take (a person) into one's service; [고용하고 있다] keep [have] (a person) in one's employ [service / pay]; keep (a servant); [잘 다루다] handle; manage. ¶시험 삼아 써 보다 take (a person) on trial / give (a person) a trial // 그 공장은 6백 명의 직공을 쓰고 있다 The plant gives employment to 600 hands. // 그는 나이는 젊지만 그 일에 쓸 만하다 He is young, but quite useful at the job. // 저를 이 가게에 써 주시겠습니까 Will you employ me [give me a job] at this store?

3 [채택하다] adopt; follow; take; apply(적용하다). ¶뇌물을 ~ give a bribe // 별별 수단을 다 ~ use [try] every conceivable means // 계략을 ~ adopt [use] a stratagem // 그는 모든 수단을 다 써서 빚을 얻어 냈다 Using every possible means, he managed to borrow money.

4 [소비하다] spend (돈을); consume; use(소모품을). ¶시간을 유효적절하게 ~ make good use of one's time // 돈을 헛된 일에 ~ waste one's money on silly things // 돈을 물 쓰듯 ~ squander money / spend money like water // 다 써 버리다 use up / spend all (one's money) / go [run] through (money) / run [give] out of / consume / exhaust / squander // 내 돈의 대부분은 나는 책 사는 데 쓴다 I spend most of my money on books. // 이 돈을 결혼 비용의 일부로 써 주십시오 Please use this money to cover part of your wedding expenses.

5 [말하다] speak. ¶독일어를 ~ speak German // 문자를 ~ talk like a book // 고운 말을 ~ use beautiful [courteous] words // 브라질에서는 무슨 말을 씁니까 What language is spoken [do they speak] in Brazil?

6 (마음·머리 등을) exert; exercise; give play [scope] to; call [bring] into play. ¶머리를 ~ use one's head [brains] / think // 너무 마음을 쓰지 마라 Don't worry too much about it. / Take it easy. // 이 작업은 상당히 신경이 쓰인다 This work is hard on the nerves. / This is nerve-racking work. // 그녀는 시어머니에게 매우 신경을 쓰고 있다 She is very careful of her mother-in-law's feelings.

7 (술법 등을) practice; do; play; resort to. ¶최면술을 ~ practice mesmerism // 요술을 ~ juggle / do conjuring tricks // 계략을 ~ resort to tricks // 폭력을 쓰면 안 된다 Don't use [resort to] force.

8 (약을) administer (a medicine); dose (a patient); use; apply (an ointment to). ¶하제를 ~ take a laxative.

9 (빚을) borrow money; raise a loan of money.

10 [음식을 대접하다]. ¶한턱 ~ stand treat for (one's friend) / give (a person) a treat / (구어) stand (a person) dinner.

11 (장기 등에서). ¶말을 ~ move a piece / make a move.

12 [합당하다] be suitable [proper / fit]; be all right. ¶그에게 그런 말을 하면 쓰나 You ought not to say such a thing to him.

쓰다⁴ (뫼를). ¶뫼를 ~ bury in [at] // 선산에 뫼를 ~ bury (a person's remains) in the family graveyard.

쓰다⁵ (맛이) bitter; [쓰라리다] hard; trying. ¶~ 달다 말없이 without saying yes or no [this or that] / without response // 쓴 약 bitter medicine // 입맛이 ~ (미각) taste bitter / (기분) feel unpleasant / be disgusted (with / at).

쓰다듬다 1 [손으로 쓸어 어루만지다] stroke; pass one's hand over [across] (one's face); smooth; caress; (가볍게 두드리듯) pat. ¶턱[턱수염]을 ~ stroke one's chin [beard] // 아이의 머리를 ~ pat a child on the head // 개는 배를 쓰다듬어 주면 좋아한다 Dogs like to be rubbed [stroked] on the stomach. // 어린 아이를 ~ caress a child. **2** [달래다] soothe; allay; pacify; calm (down); stroke; caress. ¶우는 아이를 ~ soothe [still] a crying child.

쓰디쓰다 very bitter; bitter as bitter can be; as bitter as gall. ¶쓰디쓴 웃음 (smile) a bitter [grim] smile.

쓰라리다 1 (상처가) smart; sore; tingling;

burning. ¶가슴이 ~ have heartburn // 상처가 아직도 ~ The wound still smarts. 2 [괴롭다] painful; sore; bitter; trying; hard (to bear). // 쓰라린 생활[세상] a hard life[world] // 쓰라린 운명 a hard[heavy] lot[fate] // 쓰라린 고생 a sore affliction // 나는 여러 번 쓰라린 경험을 했다 I have had several trying [bitter] experiences.

쓰라림 (상처의) soreness; smartness; [괴로움] pain; painfulness; bitterness; sorrow. ¶가난의 ~ the bitterness of want // 이별의 ~ the sorrow[wrench] of parting.

쓰러뜨리다 1 (서 있는 것을) bring down; throw down; level (a house to the ground); blow down (바람이 집을); lodge; lay (벼 등을); fell (베어 넘어뜨리다); (사람을) throw (a person) to the ground; floor (a person); knock down; trip up (발을 걸어); topple [bring down] (a person). ¶집을 ~ (지진 등이) demolish[destroy] a house / [헐다] pull down a house // 나는 부주의로 꽃병을 쓰러뜨렸다 I carelessly knocked the vase over. // 간밤의 폭풍이 나무를 많이 쓰러뜨렸다 Last night's storm blew down many trees.
2 [지우다] defeat; beat; [멸망시키다] overthrow; ruin; [죽이다] kill. ¶그는 강적을 쓰러뜨렸다 He defeated a powerful opponent. // 그는 현 정부를 쓰러뜨려야 한다고 주장했다 He claimed that the present government should be overthrown.

쓰러지다 1 (서 있는 물건이) fall; come[go] down; (흔들려서) topple (over); collapse; (사람·동물이) fall; fall over[down]; drop; go [roll] over; be off one's feet; sink to the ground. ¶금방 쓰러질 것 같은 집 a tumble-down house // 나는 뒤로[앞으로] 쓰러졌다 I fell flat on my back[face]. // 그녀는 그 자리에서 쓰러졌다 She collapsed on the spot. / She crumpled[slumped] to the ground on the spot. // 탑이 태풍으로 쓰러졌다 The tower was blown over by the typhoon. // 그 불상은 지진으로 쓰러졌다 The statue of Buddha was toppled by the earthquake. // 담은 불도저에 밀려 쓰러졌다 The wall was knocked down by a bulldozer. // 그녀는 슬픔에 못 이겨 그 자리에 쓰러졌다 So great was her sorrow [grief] that she collapsed on the spot.
2 (과로 등으로) break down; have a breakdown; crack up; succumb[give way] to (a disease); [졸도하다] fall senseless; fall in a faint. ¶일사병으로 ~ be laid low by sunstroke // 지쳐서 ~ break[sink] down from exhaustion // 짐은 과로로 쓰러졌다 Jim collapsed from exhaustion. // 나는 졸업 직전에 병으로 쓰러졌다 I fell ill just before my graduation. // 나는 크리스마스 때 독감으로 쓰러졌다 I came down with the flu at Christmas.
3 [죽다] fall down dead; fall a victim [prey] to; succumb to (the wound); die. ¶…의 손에 ~ fall[meet one's end] at the hand of ... // 콜레라로 ~ be carried off[cut down] by cholera // 총탄에 ~ be shot to death / die of a bullet // 쓰러질 때까지 싸우다 fight to the death / die fighting // 쓰러질 때까지 하겠다는 각오가 필요하다 Determination to do or die is essential. / This is a case of do or die.
4 [망하다] be ruined; go to ruin; [와해·붕괴하다] collapse; fall; be overthrown; [도산하다] go[become] bankrupt; (미국 구어) go broke. ¶쓰러져 가고 있다 be on the point of falling / (은행·회사 등이) be on the verge [brink / eve] of bankruptcy // 현 내각은 쉽게 쓰러지지 않을 것이다 The present Cabinet will not fall easily.

쓰레기 (일반적 또는 주방의) garbage; [폐물] (미) trash; (영) rubbish; (구어) junk; [먼지] dust; refuse; sweepings; waste. ¶~투성이의 복도 dusty passage / passage covered with dust // 야채 ~ scraps of vegetables / 부엌 ~ kitchen refuse / (미) garbage // 인간 ~ the dregs of mankind / the scum of society // ~ 버리는 곳 a garbage dump // ~를 버리다 throw out the garbage[trash] // 바닥의 ~를 청소하라 sweep the dust off the floor // ~를 버리지 말 것 (게시) No dumping. // 유원지에는 행락객들이 버린 ~가 산더미처럼 쌓여 있었다 The pleasure resort was covered with heaps of rubbish[trash] left by the picnickers. // 그는 ~ 같은 인간이다 He is a good-for-nothing. // 이 근방에는 ~ 버릴 곳이 없다 There's no place to dump rubbish around here.

● **쓰레기장** a dumping ground. **쓰레기차** a garbage wagon; a disposal truck; (영) a dust cart. **쓰레기통** [휴지통] a wastepaper basket; (미) a waste basket; (공공장소의) (미) a trash basket; (미) a litter basket; (영) a litterbin; (가정의) (미) a garbage can; (미) a trash can; (영) a dustbin; a circular file (특히 사무실의). ¶~에 넣다 put (refuse) into a wastebasket.

쓰레받기 a dustpan. ¶~에 쓸어 담다 sweep into a dustpan.

쓰레질 sweeping (and) cleaning. **쓰레질하다** sweep (and clean).

쓰르라미 [동] a clear-toned[green-colored] cicada (pl. ~s, -dae).

쓰리다 1 [아프다] smart; sore; tingling; burning. ¶속이 ~ have a burning feeling in one's stomach / have a sour stomach. 2 (마음이) sore; bitter; heartrending; heartaching.

쓰이다[1] 1 [써지다] be written (with); write. ¶글씨가 잘 쓰이는 종이 a paper on which a pen writes well // 편지에 이렇게 쓰여 있다 the letter says[reads] that ... // 이 일에 대해서 신문에는 뭐라고 쓰여 있나 What do the papers say about it? 2 [쓰게 하다] get (a person) to write (a letter); have (a letter) written.

쓰이다[2] 1 [사용되다] be used; be made use of; be utilized; be employed; serve. ¶일상생활에 쓰이는 물건 articles in daily use // 널리 [일반적으로] ~ be widely[generally] used // 쓰이게 되다 come into use / come to be used // 쓰이지 않게 되다 get[go / fall] out of use // 그 단어는 지금은 쓰이지 않는다 The word is out of use[is obsolete]. // 이 방은 내 서재로 쓰이고 있다 This room now serves as my study. // 이것은 무엇에 쓰이는가 What is this (used [intended]) for? 2 [소용되다] be spent; be consumed; be used; require; need. ¶겨울철에는 등유가 많이 쓰인다 A great deal of kerosene is consumed during the winter.

쓰적거리다 1 [비벼지다] rub[chafe] against; be rubbed (against). 2 [대강 쓸다] sweep [broom] hastily[roughly].

쓱 [슬쩍] (slip away) quickly and quietly; [척] (bolt) abruptly; [빨리] (pass by) rapidly; [슬슬] (rub) deftly[lightly]. ¶방문을 ~ 열다 open the door quietly // 방에서 ~

쓱싹하다
나가다 slip [steal] out of the room // 서류를 ~ 훑어보다 take a glance [read hastily through] the document // 이마의 땀을 ~ 문지르다 mop one's brow // 그는 방을 ~ 둘러보았다 His glance swept about the room.

쓱싹하다 1 [착복하다] pocket; take (something) to oneself; divert (public money) into one's own pocket. 2 [비밀히 처리하다] settle (a matter) secretly; cover [hush] up. 3 [셈을 맞비겨 버리다] balance [square] the accounts.

쓱쓱 [비비는 모양] rubbing; scrubbing; (일 등을) easily; with ease; without (any) trouble [difficulty]. ¶~ 손을 ~ 비비다 rub one's hands (together) // 머리를 ~ 쓰다듬다 smooth (down) (a person's) hair // 일을 ~ 해치우다 do a work with ease.

쓴맛 a sharp [bitter] taste. ¶~ 단맛 the bitters and the sweets (of life) / sorrows and joys / prosperity and adversity // 세상의 ~ 단맛을 본 그 사람 a man whose troubles have taught him understanding // ~**이 나다** taste bitter / be bitter // 인생의 ~ 단맛을 다 보다 taste the bitters and sweets [joys and sorrows] of life // 이 주스는 ~이 난다 This juice tastes bitter. // 우리 아버지는 세상의 ~ 단맛을 다 본 분이시다 My father has known both the bitter and the sweet of life. // 나는 이 세상의 ~ 단맛을 다 맛보았다 I have tasted the bitter and the sweet of life.

쓴웃음 (smile) a bitter [wry] smile (▶ bitter smile은 속이 상했을 때의 몹시 언짢은 기분, wry smile은 종종 자기를 비웃는 기분을 나타냄). ¶그는 큰 실수를 저지르고 ~을 지었다 He smiled wryly [an embarrassed smile] at his own blunder. // 그가 아무것도 몰라서 나는 ~이 나왔다 I could not suppress a wry [bitter] smile at his ignorance.

쓸개 [생] the gall bladder; the gall. ¶~ 빠진 관리들 weak-kneed [spineless] government officials.
●**쓸개즙** [생] bile; gall.

쓸다¹ (비로) sweep (with a broom). ¶마루를 ~ sweep the floor // 정원을 ~ sweep the garden // 먼지를 쓸어 (밖에) 버리다 sweep the dirt away [out] // 낙엽을 쓸어 모으다 sweep up the fallen leaves / sweep fallen leaves together [into a heap].
2 [유행병이 널리 퍼지다] spread; sweep; prevail; be prevalent [widespread]; (홍수 등이) sweep; (황폐시키다) devastate. ¶전염병이 전국을 쓸었다 An infectious disease was prevalent throughout the country. / An epidemic swept all over the country.
3 [일소하다] sweep away [off]; clear off [away]; clean out; wipe; banish; make a clean sweep (of); [근절하다] make an end of; stamp [root] out.
4 (판돈을) sweep the (gambling) board; (경기 에서) make a clear sweep [score].

쓸다² [줄로 닦게 하다] file; rasp (off / away). ¶줄로 쓸어서 반드럽게 하다 file (a thing) smooth / file away roughness.

쓸데없다 [소용없다] useless; unserviceable; of no use [avail / good]; [필요없다] needless; unnecessary; [군더더기이다] superfluous; redundant; [청한 바 없다] unwanted; uninvited; uncalled-for. ¶쓸데없는 것 a useless object // 쓸데없는 걱정을 끼치다 cause a person unnecessary worry [trouble] // 쓸데없

는 말을 하다 say unnecessary things / make an uncalled-for remark // 쓸데없는 논의는 삼가 주시오 There's no need for discussion! 쓸데없이 uselessly; futilely; idly; without avail; wastefully; superfluously. ¶~ 시간을 허비하다 waste time / squander one's time // ~ 허세를 부리다 be vainly pretentious.

쓸리다¹ [쓸게 하다] let [make] (a person) sweep; [쓸어지다] be swept; get swept. ¶백 마리의 말이 홍수에 쓸려 갔다 A hundred horses were swept away in the flood.

쓸리다² (줄에) get rasped [filed].

쓸리다³ (살갗이) be grazed [chafed].

쓸모 use; usefulness; utility; help; convenience; worth; (a) merit; value. ¶~**가 있다** be useful / be of use // 무엇이든지 ~가 있는 법이다 Everything has its use. // 지금 이것을 공부해 두면 언젠가는 ~가 있을 것이다 Studying this now will prove of use someday. // 이 책을 읽어 두면 ~가 있다 Reading this book will be useful. // 그의 영어는 그런대로 ~가 있다 He has a working [functional] knowledge of English. / His English is passable [good enough to get by on]. // 자동차도 가솔린이 없다면 아무 ~가 없다 A car is useless without gasoline [(영) petrol]. // 이 작은 탁자는 ~가 많다 This little table can be used for various purpose [in many ways]. // 이 계획은 도무지 ~가 없다 The plan is absolutely good for nothing. // 이 낡은 자전거가 어디 ~가 있을까 Can you find any use for this old bicycle? // 저 젊은이는 여러 가지로 ~가 많다 That young man is helpful in many ways.

쓸모없다 be useless. ¶쓸모없는 사람 a good-for-nothing (person) // 쓸모없게 된 것을 버리다 throw away [discard / get rid of] things which are no longer useful // 내 딸애는 아무 쪽에도 쓸모없는 남자에게 속았다 My daughter was taken in by a good-for-nothing [worthless] man. // 그는 전혀 ~ He is absolutely worthless [good-for-nothing]. // 우리 집 푸들은 집 지키는 개로서는 쓸모없지만 아주 귀엽다 Our poodle is useless as a watchdog, but he's perfectly cute.

쓸쓸하다 1 [적적하다] lonely; lonesome; cheerless; [황량하다] desolate; deserted; [외롭다] solitary. ¶쓸쓸한 고독 a bleak loneliness // 쓸쓸한 곳 a lonely place // 쓸쓸한 웃음 a wan [melancholy / sad] smile // 나는 혼자 남아 쓸쓸했다 Left by myself, I felt lonely. // 네가 가 버리면 나는 쓸쓸해질 거야 I'm going to miss you when you're gone. / When you go away, I'm going to be very lonely. // 젊은이들이 대도시로 가 버려서 마을은 쓸쓸해 보였다 The village looked deserted after the young people had gone to the big cities. // 나무에 잎이 떨어지고 없으면 정원은 쓸쓸해 보인다 The garden looks bare without any leaves on the trees [with the leaves all gone].
쓸쓸히 lonesomely; cheerlessly; [처량하게] desolately; desertedly; [외롭게] all by oneself; solitarily. ¶~ 지내다 [살다] lead [live] a lonely life // 그는 ~ 웃었다 He smiled sadly [a sad smile].
2 chilly; dreary. ⇨ **쌀쌀하다**1

쓸어버리다 sweep out [away]; brush up.
쓿바귀 [식] a lettuce.
씀씀이 expenditure; expense. ¶~가 헤픈 사람 a spendthrift / an extravagant person // 그는

~가 헤프다 He is wasteful of[with] money. / He throws away his money.

씁쓰레하다 slightly bitter. ⇨ 쌉싸래하다
씁쓸하다 slightly bitter. ⇨ 쌉쌀하다
씌다 1 [귀신에 접하다] be possessed (by [with]) a spirit); be obsessed (by). ¶악마가 씌어 있다 be possessed by[of] a demon[an evil spirit] // 그는 마치 귀신이 쐰 사람 같았다 He was like a man possessed of devils. / 그는 무엇에 씐 사람처럼 공부를 했다 He studied like mad. / He studied like one [as if] possessed. 2 be written (with); get (a person) to write (a letter). ⇨ 쓰이다¹ 3 be used; be spent. ⇨ 쓰이다²
씌우다 1 [덮다] cover (a thing) with; put (a thing) on; [도금하다] plate (a thing) with. ¶아이에게 모자를 ~ put a cap on a child // 냄비에 뚜껑을 ~ put the lid on the pan // 이에 금을 ~ cap[crown] a tooth with gold // 나는 소파를 벨벳으로 갈아 씌웠다 I had the sofa reupholstered in[with] velvet. // 나는 의자에 가죽을 씌우게 했다 I have had the chairs upholstered[covered] with leather. 2 (죄 등을) charge[fix] (a guilt on a person); fasten[pin] (a crime on a person); put (the murder upon others); impute (a crime to a person); lay (the guilt upon / a blame at another's door); [오명을] fasten (a stigma upon a person). ¶남에게 죄를 덮어 ~ charge a person with a crime / lay the blame for a crime on a person / fasten a crime on[upon] a person // 그는 오명이 씌워졌다 He had his reputation stained. / His name was blackened.
씨¹ 1 [종자] a seed (pl. ~(s)); [과실의 핵] a stone; (사과 등의) a pip. ¶사과 ~ pips of an apple // 복숭아~ the stone of a peach // 호박 ~ a pumpkin seed // ~ 없는 포도 seedless grapes // 밭에 곡식의 ~를 뿌리다 seed[sow] a field with grain // 포도 ~를 빼다 seed grapes // ~를 받다 gather (the) seeds // ~가 생기다 seed / go[run] to seed // 우리는 정원에 ~를 심었다 We planted seeds in the garden. 2 [가축의 품종] a breed; a strain; a stock. ¶~가 좋다 be of[bred from] a good[fine] stock / be of a fine breed // ~를 받다 breed from (a stock) / ~를 받기 위하여 기르다 keep for breeding (purposes).
3 [사물이 발생한 근원] a cause; a source. ¶불화의 ~ the cause of strife / an apple of discord / a bone of contention // 그는 언제나 불화의 ~를 뿌리고 다닌다 He is always planting the seeds of trouble. // 자기가 뿌린 ~는 자기가 거두어야 한다 You must reap what you have sown.
4 [사람의 혈통] paternal blood. ¶불의의 ~ a child born in sin / a child born out of wedlock // 다른 형제[자매] a half brother [sister] // 아무의 ~를 배다 be (big) with child by a person / conceive a child of a person // 그들은 ~는 같지만 배가 다르다 They are of the same father but of different mothers.
씨² (피륙 등의) the woof; the weft; threads which run crosswise. ¶~와 날 woof and warp.
씨(氏) 1 (남자에게 붙여서) Mr. (pl. Messrs.); (여자에게 붙여서) Mrs. (pl. Mmes.); Miss; Ms.(▶ Ms.는 Mrs.나 Miss의 구별을 싫어하는 여자에게 붙임. (영)에서는 마침표를 생략하는 경향이 있음). ¶한·홍 양 ~ Messrs. Han and Hong // 모~ Mr. So-and-so. 2 (특정인을 가리켜) the gentleman; he. ¶~에 의하면 according to him / in his opinion / he says that ... // ~는 목포 출신입니다 He comes[is] from Mokpo.

-씨(氏) [씨족] a family; a clan. ¶송~(네) the Song family[clan] / the Songs.
씨감자 a seed potato.
씨근거리다 breathe hard[roughly]; puff; pant.
씨눈 [생] an embryo. ⇨ =배(胚)
씨닭 a breeding cock.
씨돼지 (수컷) a boar; (암컷) a breed[brood] sow.
씨름 1 (운동) ssireum; wrestling; a wrestling match. ¶발~ ankle[shin / leg] wrestling // 팔~ arm[Indian] wrestling // ~에 이기다 [지다] win[lose] a wrestling bout // ~을 한 판 벌이다 have a wrestling bout[match] (with). **씨름하다** wrestle (with). 2 [노력] a (hard) struggle; strenuous effort(s). **씨름하다** exert oneself; make a strenuous efforts; come to grips (with). ¶나는 사전과 씨름하면서 그것을 번역했다 I translated it with the constant help of[by referring constantly to] a dictionary. // 그는 산더미 같은 숙제와 씨름하고 있다 He is grappling with a heap of assignments.
씨말 a studhorse; a stud; a breeding horse; a (breeding) stallion; a sire; a brood mare(암말).
씨방(一房) [식] an ovary.
씨뿌리기 sowing; seeding.
씨실 the woof; the weft.
씨알 1 [종란] an egg for breeding. 2 [광] a grain[particle] of mineral. 3 [종자로서의 낟알] a grain of seed cereal; seed.
씨알머리 ¶~ 없는 녀석 an ill-bred fellow / a hangdog / a churl // ~ 없다 be ill-bred / be nasty.
씨암탉 a brood hen; a breeder.
씨앗 seeds (of grain / vegetables). ¶~을 뿌리다 seed (a garden) / sow[plant] seed(s) / sow[plant] (the field).
씨젖 [식] an albumen. ⇨ =배젖
씨족(氏族) (공동 조상을 가진) a clan; [일가] a family; (고대 로마의) a gens (pl. gentes). ●**씨족 사회** a clan society. **씨족 제도** the family[clan] system.
씨주머니 [식] an ascus. ⇨ =자낭(子囊)
씨줄 [지] a parallel (of latitude). ⇨ =위선(緯線)
씨 [싱겁게 웃는 모양] with a quick smile. ¶~ 웃다 grin.
-씩 [같은 수효로 나눔]. ¶조금~ little by little / bit by bit / inch by inch / piecemeal / (서서히) gradually / by degrees // 하나~ one by one / one after another // 두 사람~ two by two / two at a time / by twos // 세 사람에 하나 ~ one to every three persons // 하나에 백 원 ~ a hundred won apiece // 하루에 세 번~ three times a day // 1주일에 두 번~ twice a week // 아이들에게 천 원~ 주다 give the children 1000 won each // 소년들은 각각 오천 원 ~ 받았다 Each of the boys received five thousand won. / The boys received five thousand won each. // 우리는 견본을 네 사람에 하나~ 나눠 주었다 We distributed one sample to every four persons. // 우리는 다섯 사람~ 한 조가 되었다 We formed teams of

씩씩거리다 five people each. / We grouped into teams of five. // 동조자가 두세 사람~ 늘어났다 Sympathizers increased by twos and threes.

씩씩거리다 gasp (for breath); pant; breathe hard[heavily]; (천식 등으로) wheeze. ¶화가 나서 ~ huff and puff / fume (with rage) // 씩씩거리며 말하다 gasp[pant / puff] out.

씩씩하다 manly; virile; valiant; vigorous; brave; strong; energetic. ¶씩씩하게 bravely / valiantly / gallantly / vigorously // 씩씩한 남자 a fine strapping fellow / a dashing fellow // 씩씩한 기상 a dashing[brave / valiant] spirit // 씩씩하게 걷다 step lively / walk briskly // 씩씩하게 싸우다 fight bravely [gamely / gallantly] / fight a valiant battle // 이윽고 인기 선수들이 씩씩한 모습으로 나타났다 Before long the smart figure of the star player appeared.

씰그러뜨리다 misshape; distort.

씰그러지다 get out of shape[balance]; get distorted; be pushed out of shape; wobble; lean; slant.

씰룩거리다 twitch (and twitch). ⇨ 실룩거리다

씹 1 a pussy. ⇨ 보지 2 (sexual) intercourse. ⇨ =성교

씹다 1 chew; masticate. ¶씹는 담배 chewing tobacco // 껌을 ~ chew a gum // 음식을 잘[꼭꼭] ~ chew (one's food) well [thoroughly] // 하품을 씹어 삼키다 suppress [stifle / smother (up)] a yawn // 그것을 꼭꼭 씹으면 단맛이 난다 Chew it well, and it will taste sweet. 2 (비난하다) chew (a person) out. ¶내가 늦은 거 나도 아니까 씹을 거 없어 I know I'm late, you don't have to chew me out!

씹히다 [씹어지다] be chewed; be masticated; [씹게 하다] let (a person) chew[masticate] (on). ¶밥에 돌이 ~ bite on a grit in boiled rice // 잘 ~ be chewed well [easily] // 잘 씹히지 않다 be hard to masticate / be tough(질기다) // 어린아이에게 밤을 ~ give a child a chestnut to chew on.

씻가시다 wash out; rinse (out). ¶병을 ~ rinse[wash] out a bottle.

씻기다 1 [씻음을 당하다] be washed[wiped]. ¶잘 ~ be washed easily[well] // 씻겨 내려가다 be washed[carried] away (by a flood) / wash away // 그릇이 잘 씻기지 않는다 A dish does not wash well. // 소나기에 길이 깨끗이 씻겼다 The road was washed clean with a (rain) shower. 2 [씻게 하다] let[have] (a person) wash (a thing). ¶딸에게 그릇을 ~ have one's daughter wash dishes // 때를 ~ have[let] (a person) wash[scrape / rub] off the dirt.

씻다 1 (물 등으로) wash (one's face); cleanse (a wound); rinse (a bottle); bathe (one's eyes in warm water). ¶물로 ~ wash in water // 잘 ~ wash (a thing) well / give (a thing) a good wash // 손[몸]을 ~ wash one's hands[oneself] // 접시를 ~ do[wash] the dishes // 쌀을 ~ wash rice // 씻어 내리다 wash away[down] / clean down(벽 등을) / flush (a toilet / sewer pipes / streets) // 씻어 버리다 [내다] wash away[off / out] / clean away // 찬물로 얼굴을 ~ wash one's face in cold water // 벽의 얼룩을 씻어 내다 wash a stain off the wall // 옷에 묻은 얼룩을 씻어 내다 wash out dirty stains from a clothes // 수세식 변기를 물로 씻어 내리다 flush the toilet // 목욕을 해서 땀을 씻어 내라 Take a bath and wash away your perspiration. // 이 얼룩은 물로 씻기만 해도 빠진다 This stain will come out with just (plain) water.

2 [닦다] wipe (away); mop (up); swab(걸레 등으로). ¶이마의 땀을 ~ wipe the sweat off one's brow // 입을 ~ wipe one's mouth (with a handkerchief) // 눈물을 ~ wipe tears from one's eyes / dry one's eyes / wipe away the tears // 그는 손으로 이마를 씻었다 He wiped his hand across his forehead.

3 (오명·치욕 등을) clean [clear] oneself of the stain; wipe; mop (up). ¶씻을 수 없는 치욕 an indelible disgrace / an ineffaceable humiliation // 오명을 ~ clear oneself of the stain / remove[wipe off] the disgrace / cleanse one's dishonor // 누명을 ~ clear oneself of a false charge // 그는 마침내 불명예를 씻었다 He finally cleared his name [vindicated his honor]. / 그 사건은 가명(家名)에 씻을 수 없는 오점을 남겼다 The incident left an indelible [ineradicable] stain on the family name.

4 (원한 등을) pay[work] off (a grudge).

씻은 듯이 clean(ly); completely; thoroughly; entirely. ¶종기가 ~ 나았다 A boil is all healed up. // 약을 먹었더니 두통이 ~ 가셨다 The headache has clean gone by virtue of the remedy. // 하늘이 ~ 맑다 The sky is as clear as can be.

씽 whistling; whizzing; with a whistle [whiz(z)]; ping; zing; zip. ¶~ 소리 a whistling sound / a whistle / a whiz(z)(화살·총알 등의) / a sough(바람의) // 바람이 ~ 불고 있었다 The wind was whistling[hissing / piping]. // 총알이 ~ 머리를 스쳐 갔다 A bullet whistled[whizzed] past my head.

ㅇ

아¹ **1** [감동·놀람 등을 나타내는 소리] Ah!; Oh!(▶ ah는 얼마 전부터 느낀 기분을 나타내며, oh보다 더 깊이가 깊음) ¶~ 기쁘다 Oh, I'm so glad! // ~ 당신이었군 Oh, Qit's you. // ~ 오늘 밤은 네가 정말 아름답구나 Ah, how lovely you look tonight!
2 [슬픔·실망 등을 나타내는 소리] Ah!; Alas! ¶~ 슬프다 Alas! / Woe is me! / ~ 나도 이제 늙었구나 Ah, I'm getting old. // ~ 이제는 늦었구나 (문어) Alas! It's too late. // ~ 슬프다, 그는 이제 가고 없구나 Alas, he is dead and gone!
3 [깨우침·응답·동조 등을 나타내는 소리] Oh; O; O yes; Ah; Well. ¶~ 이제 알겠다 Aha! Now I get it! // ~ 그래요 Oh, is that so? / Really? // ~ 그렇군요 Oh, I see.
4 [말을 걸 때의 소리] Oh; O; Well; I say; Listen. ¶~ 여보세요 Hello! / I say! / Hey! // ~ 이 사람아 Say [I say], you! / Hey, you!
아² [부르는 말]. ¶미순~, 이리 오너라 Come here! Misun! / 사내답게 굴어라, 아들~ Be a man, my son!
아-(亞) [버금가는] sub-; near-. ¶~열대 the subtropical zones // ~황산 sulfurous acid.
아가 My Dear!; My pretty!; (미) say; Look (hear).
아가리 1 〈속〉 a mouth. ⇨ 입¹ ¶~ 닥쳐 Shut up! / Hold your tongue! / Stop [Hold] your jaw! / Hush (your mouth)! **2** (그릇 등의) a mouth. ¶~가 넓은 병 a wide-mouthed bottle // 병의 ~를 열다 [막다] open [close] a bottle / take the lid off [put the lid back on] a bottle.
아가미 [동] the gill(s) (of a fish); the branchiae (sing. branchia). ¶~가 있는 gilled / branchiate.
아가씨 a young lady; (부르는 말) Miss; young lady. ¶촌 [도시] ~ a country [town] girl // 어여쁜 ~ a lovely [charming] little girl // 응석둥이 ~ a spoiled [(영) spoilt] young lady // 그 ~는 누구지요 Who is the young lady?
아가위 the fruit of the hawthorn; a haw.
아가페 [신의 사랑] agape.
아강(亞綱) [생] a subclass.
아교(阿膠) glue (made from oxhide). ⇨ 갖풀
아구창(鵝口瘡) [한] aphtha; thrush.
아군(我軍) our forces [troops / army]; [우군(友軍)] friendly troops [army].
아궁이 a fuel [fire] hole; the opening of a firebox.
아귀¹ **1** [갈라진 곳] an angle; a corner; a junction. ¶손~ the junction of the thumb and fingers. **2** (두루마기 등의) a side slit (in a raincoat); a placket (in a skirt). ¶두루마기에 ~를 트다 provide a Korean overcoat with side slits. **3** [씨의 싹이 나오는 곳] the commissure of a seed (through which the plumule comes up). ¶(씨가) ~ 트다 sprout (out) / bud (out) / pullulate. **4** (활의) the curved-in part of an archer's bow.
아귀(를) 맞추다 complete [make up] the number. ¶그녀는 식기 세트를 아귀 맞추기 위해 컵과 받침 접시들을 샀다 She bought the cups and saucers to complete her set of dishes.
아귀² [동] an angler(fish); a frogfish; a sea toad.
아귀(餓鬼) **1** [불] a starving ghost; a famished devil [demon]. **2** [염치없이 먹을 것을 탐하는 사람] a greedy person; a person of voracious appetite. ¶~ 같은 greedy / gluttonous // 마치 ~들 같군 You are like so many hungry kids.
아귀다툼 a quarrel; a bickering; a dispute.
아귀세다 1 [마음이 굳세다] obstinate; obdurate; unyielding; stubborn; mulish. ¶아귀센 사람 a stubborn [an obstinate / a stiff-necked] fellow. **2** [악력이 세다] 〈서술적〉 have a strong grip [grasping power].
아그레망 an agrément; approval; acceptance. ¶~을 주다 give an agrément (to) // 미국 정부는 새 대사 임명에 대한 한국 정부의 ~을 요청해 왔다 The United States asked the Korean Government for an agrément on the appointment of the new ambassador.
아기 1 a baby; an infant. ⇨ ＝어린아이 ¶~가 서다 conceive (a baby) / become pregnant // ~가 사내입니까 여자 아이입니까 Is it [your baby] a boy or a girl [a he or a she]? **2** (나이 어린 딸이나 며느리의 애칭) one's dear daughter; one's dear [darling].
아기자기하다 1 [잘 어울려 보여서 예쁘다] harmonious in appearance; visually charming; picturesque. ¶아기자기한 방 a(n) harmonious room. **2** [잔재미가 있다] (이야기 등이) juicy; colorful; interesting; amusing; jolly; (분위기 등이) harmonious; on intimate [friendly] terms. ¶아기자기하게 harmoniously / happily / affectionately // 아기자기하게 지내다 live happily together / be happy with (one's wife) // 둘 사이가 아주 ~ (친구끼리) The two are on very friendly terms. / (부부간에) There is completely conjugal harmony between them.
아기집 [생] the womb. ⇨ ＝자궁
아까 a short while ago; a short time ago. ¶~부터 for some time / since a while ago // 그 일에 대해서는 ~ 들었습니다 I('ve) just heard about it. // ~부터 정전이다 The electricity has been off since a little while ago.
아깝다 1 [소중하다] precious; dear; valuable; worthy; ill-spared. ¶아까워하다 value / set [put] much [a high] value on [upon] / make much of // 나는 목숨이 ~ Life is dear [precious] to me. // 정말 아까운 사내가 죽었다 His death is a great loss (to us). // 목숨이 아깝거든 꼼짝 마라 Do not, for your life, stir from the spot. / Stay where you are, if you want to stay alive.
2 [아쉽다] wasteful; too good (for); worthy of a better cause. ¶아까운 듯이 grudgingly / with an air of reluctance / reluctantly // 그가 비서로 있기에는 아까운 사람이다 It's a waste for him to remain a secretary. // 버리기에는 아직은 ~ It is still too good to throw [be

아끼다

thrown] away.∥네게 주는 것은 아깝지 않다 I don't begrudge giving it to you.∥이삼천 원 내는 것은 아깝지 않다 I don't grudge [mind giving] a few thousand won.∥그는 그 돈 내기를 아까워했다 He was unwilling to pay the money.∥그는 시시한 회의에 그렇게 많은 시간을 허비하기가 아까웠다 He grudged having to spend so much time at pointless meetings.∥그렇게 마구 흐르게 하면 물이 ~ How wasteful[What a waste] to let the water run like that.∥그는 그 경주에서 아깝게 졌다 He lost the race by a narrow margin.

3 〔유감이다〕 regrettable; pitiful; disappointing. ¶그가 이 경험에서 배운 바가 없었다니 참 아까운 일이다 It is a pity that he should not have learned from this experience.∥아깝게도 그를 만나지 못했다 I'm so sorry that I couldn't meet him.∥아깝게 승부였다 / Unfortunately I missed a chance to see him.∥참 아까운 승부였다 It's a shame we lost when we were so close to victory.∥거 참 — That's a pity! / That's too bad. / It is a matter for regret. / It is a thing (much) to be regretted.

아끼다 1 〔소중히 여기다〕 prize; value; set great value on; esteem (highly); think [make] much of; hold (a thing) dear. ¶어머니가 가장 아끼는 찻잔 세트 my mother's best tea set∥가장 아끼는 손녀[모자] one's favorite granddaughter[hat]∥나는 촌음을 아껴서 공부했다 I studied without taking time off[(미) out] for anything.∥그는 부장이 가장 아끼는 사람이다 He is the section chief's favorite[(구어) blue-eyed boy].∥여러분, 다시 오지 않는 청춘을 헛되이 보내지 말고 아끼세요 Listen, all of you. Youth comes only once, so don't waste it.∥그는 경기에서 아픈 다리를 아끼느라고 제대로 뛰지 못했다 As he was favoring[being careful of] his injured leg, he could not do his best in the game.∥그는 손재주가 있어 모든 사람이 그를 아낀다 As he is clever with his hands, he proves useful to everyone.

2 〔함부로 쓰지 않다〕 spare; economize; be frugal (of); 〔내놓기 싫어하다〕 grudge; be stingy; be stint. ¶비용을 아끼지 않고 regardless of expense∥몸을 아끼지 않고 일하다 work without sparing oneself∥내 아들의 안전을 위해서라면 나는 아무것도 아끼지 않겠다 I would give anything to guarantee my son's safety.∥그런 일이라면 협력을 아끼지 않겠다 If so, I am willing[ready] to cooperate with them. / If so, I will not hesitate to give [I will not grudge] them my cooperation.∥그는 팁을 아꼈다 He was stingy with his tips.∥그는 종이를 아끼느라고 달력의 뒷면에다 글을 썼다 He scrimped on paper and used the back of pages from an calendar for writing on.∥나는 용돈을 아껴 쓰고 있다 I use my pocket money sparingly.∥후일 필요한 때에 대비하여 정력을 아껴야겠다 I will save my energy just in case (I need it later).∥종이를 아껴라 You must economize on paper.

아낌없다 unsparing; unstinting; ungrudging; lavish; generous. ¶청중은 그에게 아낌없는 박수를 보냈다 The audience was unstinting in its applause. / The audience gave him a generous ovation. / 모두가 그의 행동에 아낌없는 칭찬을 보냈다 All of them showered unstinting praise on him for his conduct. **아낌없이** 〔미련 없이〕 without regret; ungrudg-

ingly; 〔후함으로〕 freely; generously. ¶~ 돈을 쓰다 spend money freely[generously / lavishly](▶ generously는 보통 남을 위해 씀)∥그는 전 재산을 ~ 장학 기금에 기부했다 He generously donated his entire fortune to a fellowship fund.

아나운서 an announcer; 〔뉴스 보도자〕 a newscaster. ¶여자 ~ a woman[lady] announcer.

아나크로니즘 (an) anachronism.

아나키스트 an anarchist.

아낙 1 〔내간〕 a lady's private sitting room; the ladies' quarters; a boudoir. **2** a woman. ⇨아낙네(⇨아낙)

● **아낙네** a woman. ¶~들 the womenfolk∥~ 같은 womanish / feminine / effeminate.

아날로그 〔전〕 analog(ue).

아내 a wife (*pl*. wives); 〔배우자〕 a spouse. ¶연상의 ~ a wife older than her husband∥남편을 하늘처럼 받드는 ~ a wife who takes care of her husband devotedly∥~가 있는 남자 a married man∥~를 맞아들이다 marry / (고) take a wife∥미국 여자를 ~로 맞다 marry an American woman∥좋은 ~가 되다 make a good wife∥좋은 ~는 집안의 보배다 A good wife is a household treasure.

아네모네 〔식〕 an anemone; a windflower; a snowdrop.

아녀자(兒女子) **1** 〔어린이와 여자〕 children and women. **2** a woman; a lady. ⇨여자1

아늑하다 snug; cozy; neat; compact; trim. ¶아늑한 방 a cozy room / a snug room.

아니¹ 〔부정·반대〕 not; never; no. ¶~ 가다[오다] do not go[come]∥~ 좋아하거나 ~ 좋아하거나를 불문하고 whether one likes it or not∥금세기 최대의, ~ 유사 이래 최대의 화산 폭발 the greatest eruption of this century — no, in recorded history.

아니 땐 굴뚝에 연기 날까(속담) There is no smoke[No smoke] without fire.

아니² 1〔대답이 부정일 때〕 no; nay; 〔대답이 긍정일 때〕 yes; 〔주저하여〕 well. ¶"자넨 그것을 보았나?" "~, 보지 못했어." "Did you see it?" "No, I didn't."∥"자넨 보지 못했나?" "~, 보았어." "Didn't you see it?" "Yes, I did."∥난 자네의 「~」라는 대답은 용납하지 않겠다 I won't let you say no. / I won't take no for an answer.∥이 아이는 열까지 셀 수 있다, — 열 다섯까지다 This child can count up to ten — no, to fifteen.

2 〔놀람·의아〕 dear me; why; what; good heavens; well. ¶~ 〔이런!〕 고맙소 Why, thank you! / Oh, how nice of you!∥~, 더운물이 없다구요 What, no hot water?∥~, 이게 웬일이야 Why, what happened?

아니꼽다 1 〔속이 메스껍다〕 sick; nauseated; 〔서술적〕 be sick at the stomach; feel sick [nausea / queasy].

2 〔불쾌하다〕 saucy; sickening; revolting; offensive; repulsive. ¶아니꼬운 사람 an affected person / 〔신앙하는 속물〕 a snob.∥아니꼬운 태도 an irritating attitude∥그 녀석은 정말 아니꼬운 녀석이다 (속어) He's a real pain in the neck[(비어) ass].∥그 말이 아니꼬워 화가 났다 I was offended[irritated] by his remark.∥그는 정말로 — He really gets on my nerves[(구어) gets my goat].∥그의 자만심은 정말 ~ I am quite disgusted with his self-conceit. / (구어) His self-conceit makes me sick.

아니다 not; no. ¶…도 아니고 …도 ~ neither ... nor.// 그것은 그런 것이 ~ It is not so.// 그가 실패했다는 것이 ~ It's not that he failed.// 이것은 네 펜이 아니냐 Isn't this your pen?// 이제 어린애도 아닌데 바보같이 굴어서는 안 돼 Don't be so foolish, you are no longer a child.// 꼭 와야만 된다는 것은 ~ You need not necessarily come.// 바보가 아닌 이상 그런 짓은 하지 않을 것이다 None but a fool would do such a thing.// 일이 싫은 것이 아니라 그 일을 감당 못하겠다 Not that I dislike the task, but I am unequal to it.// 그는 거짓말할 사람이 ~ He is above telling a lie.// "이것 네 것이냐?" "~." "Is this yours?" "No."// 그는 그것이 자기 것이 아니라고 주지 않았다 He wouldn't give it to me saying that it was not his (own).

아닌 밤중에 홍두깨(속담) a bolt from[out of] the blue; a thunderbolt from a clear sky.

아니나 다를까 as one expected; as (was) expected; as feared; sure enough. ¶~ 그는 거기 있었다 Sure enough, I found him there.// ~ 그는 나타나지 않았다 As might have been expected, he failed to turn up.

아니면 either ... or; [그렇지 않으면] or; (or) else. ¶맥주로 할까 ~ 위스키로 할까 Which will you have, beer or whisky?// 자유가 ~ 죽음을 달라 Give me liberty, or give me death!

아닌 게 아니라 just as one thought; as (was / may be / had been) expected; sure enough; indeed; truly; certainly. ¶~ 자네 말이 옳아 To be sure, what you say is right.// ~ 그녀는 미인이다 Sure enough she is a beauty.// ~ 그는 한 박사의 수제자란 말도 들을 만하다 He fully justifies[lives up to] his fame as one of the best disciples of Dr. Han.

아닌 밤중에 [뜻하지 않은 밤중에] at midnight; at dead of night; in the dead [depth] of the night; [느닷없이] abruptly; suddenly; all of a sudden.

아니요 (대답이 부정일 때) no; (대답이 긍정일 때) yes. ¶"홍 박사의 강연을 들었습니까?" "~." "Did you attend Dr. Hong's lecture?" "No, I didn't."// "이거 실례했습니다." "~, 별 말씀을." "Excuse me." "Not at all[Don't mention it]."

아니참 Well!; Oh!; Uh!; I just happen to recall it. ¶~ 오늘이 금요일이지 Oh, it's Friday, isn't it?

아니하다¹ do not. ⇨ 않다²
아니하다² not. ⇨ 않다³
아닐린 [화] anilin(e).
-아다가 ⇨ -어다가
아다지오 [음] adagio. ¶~ 곡 an adagio.
아담하다(雅淡-) [단아하다] elegant; refined; graceful; [조촐하다] nice; neat; trim; tidy; [아늑하다] snug; cozy. ¶아담한 집 a trim house / a cozy[snug] house // 제법 아담한 가게가 있어 There's a rather elegant shop.
아데노이드 [의] adenoids. ¶~의 adenoidal.
-아도 even if; although. ⇨ -어도 ¶아무리 돈이 많~ 죽음을 면할 수는 없다 No matter how wealthy he may be, a man cannot escape death.// 아무리 그가 영리해도 이것은 알아차리지 못할 것이다 However[No matter how] clever he may be, he will not notice this.
아동(兒童) a child; a juvenile; [학동] a pupil; [집합적] children; boys and girls. ¶~의 juvenile // 취학 전의 ~ preschool children // 초등학교 ~ elementary school children // 학령 ~ children of school age // ~용의 juvenile / (book) for children.
● **아동 교육** juvenile education; the education of children. **아동 문학** juvenile literature. **아동복** children's clothing[garments / wears]. **아동 복지** child welfare. **아동 상담소** a child consultation center; child-guidance clinics. **아동 심리학** juvenile[child] psychology.

아둔패기 a dull[stupid] person; a dullard; a dunce. ¶그는 형편없는 ~이다 He is a hopeless dullard.

아둔하다 stupid; dull; dull-witted; slow; muddle-headed; unintelligent; [서술적] be thick in head. ¶그는 아둔해서 잘 속는다 He is so stupid that he is easily taken in.

아드님 your[his] esteemed son.
아드레날린 [화] adrenalin.
아득하다 1 (거리가) far; faraway; far-off; distant; remote; [서술적] be a long way off. ¶갈 길이 ~ have a long way to go. **아득히** far; at a great distance; distantly; remotely. ¶~ 먼 곳 a faraway place // ~ 바라보이다 be seen from a great distance[a long way off] / be seen from far away.
2 (시간이) remote; far-off. ¶아득한 옛날을 생각하다 think of the days long past / think of far-off times // 그 전통이 사라질 날은 ~ The tradition is a long way from being defunct. **아득히** long.
3 (정신이) vague; dim; hazy; obscure; indistinct; fuzzy. ¶아득한 기억을 더듬다 trace back a vague memory // 정신이 ~ have a dim consciousness. **아득히** vaguely; dimly.

아들 a son; a boy. ¶대를 이을 ~ my son and heir // 방탕한 ~ a profligate son // 좋은[나쁜] ~을 가지다 be blessed with a good son [cursed with a bad son].
● **아들놈 / 아들아이 / 아들자식** my son[boy]. **아들딸** son(s) and daughter(s).

아들자 a vernier (scale).
아딧줄 a brace.
아따 [몹시 심하거나 못마땅할 때 내는 소리] Gosh!; (Oh) Boy!; My!; My goodness!; Gee!; Whiz!; Good lord! ¶~ 이 사람 급하기도 하지 Oh! What are you in such a hurry?// ~ 걱정도 많다 Dammit, don't worry so much.

아뜩하다 suddenly dizzy; giddy; dazed; stunned; vertiginous. ¶나쁜 소식을 들어 정신이 ~ I'm stunned at the bad news.

-아라 Do!; How ...! ⇨ -어라
아라베스크 [미][음] an arabesque.
아라비아 숫자 (-數字) Arabic numerals [figures].
아라비안나이트 [문] the Arabian Nights' Entertainments; the Tales of One Thousand and One Nights.
아람 (밤·상수리 등의) fully ripened nuts. ¶밤 ~ ripe chestnuts.
아랑곳 [관여] concern; interest; [유의] heed; attention; notice; regard; [간섭] meddling; interference. **아랑곳하다** be concerned about; concern oneself about; take (an) interest in; take notice of; meddle[interfere] in[with]; [상대하다] have to do with. ¶그는 남이 뭐라고 하든 아랑곳하지 않았다 He was indifferent to what others said about him.// 그는 남의 기분 따위는 아랑곳하지 않았다 He paid no attention[gave no thought] to other people's feelings. / He was unmindful of

아랑곳없다

other people's feeling.// 그는 추위도 아랑곳하지 않고 얇은 옷차림으로 산책에 나섰다 Making nothing of[Taking no notice of] the cold, he went for a walk in thin clothes.// 모두가 야단법석을 떨고 있는데도 그는 아랑곳하지 않았다 Even though everyone else was making a big fuss, he remained indifferent [unconcerned].

아랑곳없다 (서술적) have no concern with; have nothing to do with; have no interest in. ¶그것은 나에게는 아랑곳없는 일이다 I have nothing to do with the matter./ It's no concern of mine. **아랑곳없이** unconcernedly; with an air of perfect nonchalance; as if nothing had happened. ¶그는 혹평에도 ~ 계속 글을 썼다 He calmly continued writing in spite of harsh criticism.

아래 1 [하부·아래쪽] the lower part; the bottom; the foot; the base. ¶~의 under / lower / downstair(s) // ~에(서) under / below / beneath / underneath(바로 아래) / downstairs // ~(쪽으)로 down / downward(s) // 나무 ~에서 under a tree // 다리 ~에 under [beneath] a bridge // 눈 ~에 below one's eyes // 층계[언덕 / 산] ~에서 at the foot of stairs[a slope / a mountain] // ~에서 다섯째 줄 the fifth line from the bottom // 저 ~ 사람들 the people down there // ~로 떨어지다 fall down / fall to the ground // ~를 보다 look down // 총부리를 ~로 향하다 lower the barrel of a gun // 눈을 ~로 내리깔다 lower one's eyes // ~에서 받치다 support (a thing) from below // 이 강을 100킬로미터 ~로 내려가자 Let's go a hundred kilometers down this river.

2 [하위]. ¶맨 ~ 아이 the youngest child // ~의 lower / subordinate / inferior // ~에 below / under / beneath // 평균보다 ~ below the average // 그는 나보다 3살 ~입니다 He is three years younger than I[than me / than I am]. // 10살 ~ 아이들은 오면 안 된다 Children under ten cannot come. // 나는 그보다 한 학년 ~였다 I was one year below [behind] him at school. // 성적은 내가 그보다 ~이다 My grades aren't as good as his. // 천원 ~로 팔면 우리가 밑진다 If we sell it for less than 1,000 won, we'll lose money on it.

3 [영향 등이 미치는 범위]. ¶~에서 […을 받아] under / […에 의거하여] on / under / [(선생) 밑에서] under // ~의 지휘[지도 / 감독] ~ under the command[direction / supervision] of ... / under ... // …의 지원 ~ with the support[help] of ... / under the auspices of ... // …이라는 협정 ~ on the understanding that ... // …이라는 조건 ~ under the condition of[that] ... // …의 압제 ~ 신음하다 groan under the tyranny of ... // 그는 한 교수의 지도 ~ 프랑스 문학을 연구하고 있다 He is studying French literature under[with] professor Han.

● **아래옷** lower garment; a pair of trousers(양복바지); breeches. **아래위** top and bottom; the upper and lower sides[parts]. ¶~로 up and down / upward and downward / above and below / high and low // ~로 움직이다 go[move] up and down / rise and fall // 남의 ~ 훑어보다 look a person up and down / survey a person from head to foot. **아래윗벌** a suit (of clothes); upper and lower garment. **아래쪽** [아래 방향] a downward direction. ¶~ 방향으로 downward / in a downward direction // ~으로 나아가다 move downward // ~을 보다 look down (ward) // ~에 마을이 보인다 A town can be seen down below. **아래채** an outhouse[outbuilding] (near the gate). **아래층** the lower floor [story]; the downstairs. ¶~에[의/으로] downstairs // ~의 방 a room downstairs / a downstair(s) room // ~에 사는 이웃 one's neighbors downstairs // ~으로 가다 go downstairs. **아래턱** the lower jaw; the underjaw; the inferior maxilla. ¶~을 쓰다듬다 rub [stroke] one's chin. **아래턱뼈** the lower jawbone; the mandible. **아랫것** [지체가 낮은 하인] servants; employees; [손아랫사람] one's inferiors. ¶~들을 불쌍히 여기다 be considerate of[sympathetic with] one's inferiors. **아랫길** [아래쪽의 길] the lower road; the way below; [다른 것에 비하여 훨씬 못한 품질] lower grade; inferior quality. **아랫녘** [남부 지방] the southern part (of Korea). **아랫니** the lower[under] teeth. **아랫도리** [하체] the lower part of the body; [하의] lower garment. **아랫목** the warmer[lower] part of an ondol floor. **아랫물** the water of the lower stream[reaches / course] (of a river); the lower waters (of a river). **아랫방** a detached (spare) room. **아랫배** the lower abdomen; the belly(▶ 위 등을 포함하는 일도 있음); (완곡) the stomach; [장] the intestines; the bowels. ¶갑자기 ~가 몹시 아팠다 I felt a sudden sharp pain in my stomach. / I suddenly got a bad bellyache. // 그는 ~에 힘을 주고 소리쳤다 Tensing his abdominal muscles, he gave a shout. **아랫사람** [손아랫사람] one's junior; [부하] a subordinate; an underling; a minion; [집합적] a following; one's men; men under one's orders; a staff. ¶~이 되어 일하다 work under (a person) // 그는 ~에게 친절하다 He is kind to his subordinates. **아랫수염** a (chin-)beard; a goatee. **아랫입술** the lower[under] lip. ¶~이 나와 있다 have a protruding lower lip. **아랫집** the house just below.

아랫자리 1 [하위] a subordinate position; [아랫사람들의 자리] seats for one's juniors [subordinates]. 2 [낮은 곳의 자리] a seat on a lower place; the seats below. 3 [수] one place down; the next decimal place.

아량(雅量) tolerance; magnanimity; generosity.(▶ tolerance는 남의 의견 등을 받아들일 수 있음. magnanimity는 남의 무례·허물 등을 용서할 수 있을 정도로 도량이 넓음) ¶~이 있는 tolerant / magnanimous / broad-minded // ~이 없는 intolerant / narrow-minded // ~을 보이다 show oneself to be magnanimous.

아련하다 dim; faint; vague; indistinct; obscure; hazy; misty. ¶아련한 달빛 a dim moonlight // 기억이 ~ have a dim memory (of). **아련히** dimly; vaguely; faintly. ¶~ 보이다 be seen dimly[at a dim distance].

아령(啞鈴) a dumbbell. ¶한 쌍의 ~ a pair of dumbbells // ~으로 운동하다 do exercises with dumbbells.

아로새기다 engrave[carve] delicately; make an elaborate bas-relief. ¶그는 반지에 꽃무늬 장식을 아로새겼다 He engraved the ring in a floral pattern. // 그 광경이 내 마음에 아로새겨졌다 The scene was burned into[branded on] my memory.

아롱거리다 spot; dapple.

아롱다롱하다 spotted; mottled; dappled; speckled; streaked. ¶아롱다롱한 무늬의 옷감 cloth with a mottled pattern.

아롱아롱하다 mottled; variegated.

아롱지다 1 [아롱아롱한 무늬가 있다] spotted; mottled; dappled; speckled; motley. 2 [아롱아롱한 무늬가 생기다] spot; dapple.

아뢰다 tell; inform; say; mention; state. ¶전날 아뢴 바와 같이 as I told you the other day.

아류(亞流) 1 [둘째가는 사람·사물] a secondary; a second-rater. 2 [모방하는 사람] an imitator; [形容詞] imitative. ¶그는 마르크스주의자로 자칭하고 있으나 (사실은) ~이다 He declares himself a Marxist, but he is only a poor mockery of one. // 그는 피카소의 ~이다 He is just an imitator of Picasso.

아르 [면적의 단위] an are(기호 a). ¶2~의 대지 a plot of 200 square meters[two ares].

아르곤 [화] argon.

아르바이트 (⑤Arbeit) a part-time job; a side job. ¶그녀는 ~를 하면서 대학을 나왔다 She worked her way through college[(영) university]. // 나는 학생들에게 ~로 영어를 가르치고 있다 I teaches students English on the side. **아르바이트하다** work at a part-time job; do a side job; (자기 직업 이외에) go into other work.

아르키메데스의 원리(-原理) Archimedes' [the Archimedean] principle.

아른거리다 flicker; blink. ⇨어른거리다

아름 an armful. ¶~의 장미 an armful of roses // 그는 책을 한 ~ 가지고 들어왔다 He came in with an armful of books. // 그 나무줄기는 한 ~이나 되었다 The tree trunk was so big a person could just get his arms around it.

아름다움 beauty; splendor; (영) splendour. ¶미녀들이 서로 ~을 겨루고 있었다 The women were vying in beauty. // 나는 그 화원의 ~에 도취되었다 I was entranced by the beauty of the flower garden. // 그들은 그녀의 마음[목소리]의 ~에 감동하였다 They were moved by the purity of her heart[the beauty of her voice].

아름답다 1 [예쁘다] beautiful; pretty(▶ pretty는 beautiful보다 사랑스러운 느낌을 나타냄); lovely(▶ 칭찬이나 애정을 불러일으킴); fine; eye-filling; handsome; good-looking; fair; charming. ¶아름다운 여인 a beautiful lady / a beauty // 아름다운 얼굴 (여자의) a beautiful face / (남자의) a handsome face / 아름다운 옷 beautiful[fine] clothes / 아름다운 목소리 a sweet voice / 이곳에서의 전망은 매우 ~ 하다 The view from here is truly beautiful. // 메리는 아름답게 차려입고 있었다 Mary was dressed up beautifully. // 거리를 아름답게 하자 Let's beautify the streets. // 집 뒤에 아름다운 정원이 있다 There is a lovely garden behind the house. // 참 언제나 아름다우시군요 How lovely you always look!
2 [훌륭하다 특기하다]. ¶그 소녀는 아름다운 마음의 소유자였다 The girl was pure in[of] heart. / The girl had a pure heart. / She was a good-hearted girl. // 얼마나 아름다운 이야기냐 What a beautiful[moving] story it is! // 그녀의 아름다운 마음에 사람들은 감동했다 They were moved by the purity of her heart.

아름드리 ¶~나무 a tree measuring more than one stretch[span] of one's arms.

아리다 1 (맛이) hot; pungent; acrid; biting; burning; (서술적) taste hot; have a biting[burning] taste. 2 (상처·살갗 등이) smart; tingling; burning; biting; prickling. ¶연기 때문에 눈이 ~ The smoke make my eyes sting. / My eyes smart from the smoke. // 불에 덴 데가 ~ The burn smarts. // 이 물약을 벤 상처에 바르면 ~ This lotion smarts when it is put on a cut.

아리땁다 pretty; lovely; beautiful; comely; charming.

아리송하다 [분간이 안 되다] indistinguishable; [희미하다] dim; indistinct; vague; faint; obscure; hazy. ¶아리송한 답변[설명] an equivocal[evasive] answer[explanation] // 아리송하게 대답하다 give an equivocal[a vague] answer / give a noncommittal answer.

아리아 [음] an aria (pl. ~s, arie). ¶오페라의 ~ an operatic aria.

아릿하다 acrid; pungent; (서술적) taste acrid; sting[bite] the tongue; be biting to the taste.

아마 probably; perhaps; possibly; (미) maybe(▶ probably가 가능성이 가장 크며, possibly는 확실성이 적음. maybe는 가능성이 반반 정도이며, perhaps는 maybe보다는 확률이 조금 많음); likely; in all likelihood[probability]; (as) likely as not; [십중팔구] in nine cases out of ten; ten to one; by all odds; [염려하여] I am afraid; I fear; [의심이 날 때] I suspect. ¶그는 ~ 시험에 합격할 것이다 He will probably pass the examination. // "내일 비가 올까?" "~ 올 거야." "Will it rain tomorrow?" "Probably[I'm afraid so]." // 그는 ~도 날짜를 잊어버렸을 거야 Maybe[Perhaps] he has forgotten the date. // 그는 ~도 그것 때문에 주저하고 있을 것이다 That is possibly the reason for his hesitation. // 그것은 ~ 일어나지 않을 것이다 That is not likely[is unlikely] to happen. / It is not likely that it will happen. // 그는 ~ 올 것이다 Maybe he'll come. / It is possible that he may come. // 그건 찾지 못할 것이다 I am afraid[Probably] it will not be found. / It is not likely to be found. // 그는 ~ 기차를 놓쳤을 것이다 Probably he missed the train. // ~ 그럴 거야 Perhaps[Maybe] it is so. / It may be true. / Maybe so. / I suppose so. // ~도 모든 일이 잘될 걸세 I am fairly[almost] sure everything will go well.

아마(亞麻) flax. ¶~색의 머리 flaxen hair.
● **아마사**(-絲) a flax yarn[line]. **아마인유** linseed oil. **아마포** linen.

아마추어 an amateur. ¶~다운 의견 an amateurish opinion / ~ 수준을 넘어서다 (일이) be free from amateurishness / be far from amateurish / be as good as professional / (사람이) have more than amateur's skill.
● **아마추어 규정** requirements for amateurship. **아마추어 정신** amateurism.

아말감 [화] amalgam.

아메리칸 인디언 American Indians; the Red Indians.

아메리칸 풋볼 [미식축구] American football. ¶~ 선수 an American footballer / (미국구어) a gridder.

아메바 an amoeba (pl. ~s, -bae).
● **아메바 운동** amoeboid movement.

아멘 Amen! ¶~이라고 하다 say amen.
아명(兒名) one's milk name; one's baby [childhood] name.
아모스서(-書) [성] The Book of Amos(약어 Amos).
아목(亞目) [생] a suborder.
아몬드 [식] an almond (tree). ⇨ "편도(扁桃)
아무¹ **1** (사람) anyone; anybody; any person; (부정) no one; nobody; none. ¶~나 붙들고 의논하다 consult anyone one can find // 그 집안 사람들은 ~도 모릅니다 I don't know anyone in that family. // 여기에는 ~도 없읍니다 No one is here. // 그런 문제는 ~나 풀 수 있다 Anyone could solve such a problem. // ~도 그 문제를 풀지 못했다 Nobody was able to solve the problem. // ~도 완전하지 못하다 No one is perfect. / Everyone has faults. / There is no one but has some faults. // ~나 좋아하는 사람을 고르시오 Choose who(m)ever [anyone] you like. // 그때 그 방에는 ~ 없었다 No one [Nobody] was in the room at the time. // ~에게도 말해서는 안 된다 You must not tell anybody.
2 a certain person; Mr. So-and-so. ¶문 ~ a (certain) Mr. Mun.
아무² [어떠한·아무런] any; (부정) no; not at all. ¶그는 ~ 이유도 없이 사직했네 He resigned from his post without any reason. // 나는 그 사건과는 ~ 관련이 없다 I have no connection whatever [have nothing to do] with the matter. // 그것에 관해서는 ~ 의심할 여지가 없다 There is nothing questionable about it. // 나는 아무리 열심히 연습해도 ~ 진전이 없다 No matter how hard I practice, I make no progress at all. // 그에게 충고해도 ~ 소용이 없었다 It was [did] no good advising him. // 그는 ~ 쓸모도 없는 사람이야 He is good for nothing [no good]. / He is useless. // 그녀는 나와 ~ (친척) 관계도 없다 She is no relative of mine. / She has no connection [relation] with me. / She is not in any way related with me.
● **아무 데** any place; anywhere; (부정) nowhere. ¶그는 ~서나 드러눕는다[침을 뱉는다] He sprawls out[spits] anywhere [no matter where he is]. // ~나 앉고 싶은 데에 앉아라 Sit wherever you like. // ~도 안 가겠다 I am not going anywhere. / I am going nowhere. **아무 때** (at) any time [moment]; anytime; any day; always; all the time. ¶~라도 오고 싶을 때 오시오 Please come (at) any time [whenever] you like [please]. / You are welcome at any time. // 우리는 ~고 출발할 수 있다 We are ready to start at a moment's notice. // ~나 좋습니다 Any time will do. **아무 말** any word; a (single) word. ¶~ 않다 say nothing / keep silent [quiet] // 그는 ~ 없이 나가 버렸다 He has gone out without saying anything [a word]. / He has gone out without a single word. / [허가 없이] He has gone out without leave [permission].
아무 일 something; anything; (부정) nothing. ¶그 모임은 ~ 없이 산회됐다 The meeting adjourned quietly [without incident]. // 그날 밤은 ~ 없이 지나갔다 The night passed quietly [peacefully]. // ~도 없었다는 듯이 자리에 앉았다 He sat down as if nothing had happened.
아무개 a certain person; Mr. X; Mr.[Mrs. / Miss] So-and-so; (Mr.) what's-his-name; (Mrs. [Miss]) what's-her-name; Mr. ―. ¶한 ~ a man called Han or something / a (certain) Han // 그 ~ 말이야, 그 사람은 어떻게 됐지 What has become of him ― that Mr. what's-his-name? // 그의 이름은 송 ~ 지 아마 His name is Song something, isn't it?

아무것 anything; something; (부정) nothing; (영) none. ¶"무슨 일이야?" "아니, ~도 아니야." "What's the matter?" "Nothing." // 그런 일은 ~도 아니다 It's nothing. / I don't care at all. // 도둑놈은 ~도 안 가지고 도망쳤다 The thief took to his heels without taking a single article. // 그는 1킬로 헤엄치는 것쯤은 ~도 아니다 It's nothing to [It's quite easy for] him to swim one kilometer. // 이 편지를 타이핑하는 건 ~도 아니야 It will be no trouble to type this letter. // 그는 육류는 ~도 안 먹는다 He does not eat (any) meat. // 걱정할 일은 ~도 없다 There is nothing to worry about. // 이런 더위 정도는 ~도 아니다 This heat is nothing. / This heat doesn't bother me. / Heat like this is no big deal [no great shakes].

아무래도 1 [어떻든] in any way; anyhow; [반드시] surely; inevitably; must; [싫건 좋건] whether willing or not; willingly or unwillingly; willy-nilly; [결국] in the end; after all; [어느 면으로 보나] in all respects; in every respect; all things considered; (미) to all appearances; (영) to all appearance. ¶~ 가 봐야겠다 I must go no matter what. // 결과는 ~ 좋다 The result does not matter. / The result makes no difference [odds] to me. // 그의 의도 따위는 ~ 좋다 I don't care what he is after. // 성적은 ~ I'm not interested in my grades. // "내일 피크닉 갈까, 가지 말까?" "나는 ~ 좋아." "Shall we go on a picnic tomorrow, or not?" "Whichever you like." // 이기든 지든 ~ 좋지 않니 What difference does it make whether we win or lose? // 사람이란 ~ 남의 일보다는 자기 일을 우선 생각하기 쉽다 One can't help thinking of himself before others. // ~ 비가 올 것 같다 It sure looks like rain. / I am afraid it is going to rain. // ~ 길을 잘못 든 것 같다 It looks as though we have taken the wrong road. // ~ 그는 약속을 잊어버린 것 같다 He seems to have forgotten his promise. // ~ 그의 승리로 끝날 것 같다 It is likely that he will come out victorious. // 그 귀중한 필름을 잃어버린 것이 ~ 원통하다 It is really awful that I should have lost that precious film. // ~ 그렇게 될 것 같다 There is every likelihood that it will come to that. // ~ 이젠 떠나야겠다 I have no choice but to leave now. / I have to leave whether I like it or not. // ~ 물가가 다시 오르겠어 Prices are sure to go still higher. // 그녀는 ~ 부활절에 쓸 새 모자가 있어야겠다고 말했다 She said she must have a new hat for Easter.
2 [아무리 하여도] by any means; on any account; possibly; by any possibility; at all; for anything; for all the world; (영국 속어) for nuts. ¶~ 그 사람의 이름이 생각나지 않는다 I just can't remember his name. I can't, for the life of me, remember his name. // ~ 그를 도와줄 수가 없다 There is no way to help him. // ~ 가망이 없다 There is no hope at all [in the world]. / There is no possible

hope in the wide world.
아무러면 whatever it is; no matter what [how] it is; whatever anybody may do; whoever does [says] it. ¶그거야 ~ 어떤가 What does it matter? / Let that go. / What of that?//옷이야 ~ 어떠냐 Don't mind what you wear. / Don't bother to dress up. / It doesn't matter how your clothes look.
아무런 [아무러한] any; (부정) no; not at all. ¶~ 생각 없이 unconsciously / unintentionally / unwittingly // ~ 예고도 없이 with no notice whatever // 두 형제는 ~ 문제도 없이 여러 해를 살았다 Both brothers lived many years without any problems of any kind.//그녀의 말에는 ~ 악의도 없다 She means no harm.//나는 그 사건과는 ~ 관계가 없다 I have no connection whatever [have nothing to do] with the matter.
아무렇게나 [되는 대로] at random; at [by] haphazard; haphazardly; by guesswork; [건성으로] carelessly; half-heartedly; indifferently; in a slovenly way. ¶~ 하는 대답[말] a random [casual] answer [remark] // ~ 다루다 handle carelessly [roughly] // 저고리를 ~ 걸치다 throw one's jacket carelessly over one's shoulder // 그녀는 일을 ~ 한다 She does things sloppily [in a slipshod manner]. / She does thing carelessly. / (미국 구어) She does her work any which way. / (미국 구어) She does her work any old how. / She scamp [fudge / slur over / huddle over] her work [duty]. // ~ 마음대로 생각하게 Take it any way you like. // 나는 ~ 대답해 주었다 I made a haphazard answer. / I gave the first answer that came into my head. // 쏜 총알이 과녁에 ~ 맞았다 The bullet I had carelessly fired [I had blindly fired / I had shot without aim] hit the mark. // 그는 ~ 몇 사람의 이름을 말했다 He mentioned several names at random. // 그는 ~ 나오는 대로 말해 버리는 버릇이 있다 He has the habit of saying whatever comes into his head. // 일을 그렇게 ~ 하면 소용없다 It's no use doing your work all anyhow like that.
아무렇다 [아무러하다].
아무렇든지 at any rate; in any case [event]; anyway; anyhow; at all events; whatever; however. ¶~ 출발 전에 알려 주겠다 In any event, I will let you know before I start.
아무렇지(도) 않다 [태연하다] indifferent; unconcerned; [무사하다] safe; sound; all right. ¶아무렇지도 않은 듯이 with an unconcerned air / in an indifferent [a light-hearted / an unconcerned / a nonchalant / a casual] manner [way] / lightly / casually // 그는 약속 어기는 일을 아무렇지 않게 여긴다 He doesn't give [care] a damn about breaking his promise. // 욕을 먹어도 나는 ~ I don't care if people speak ill of me. // 몸은 ~ Nothing is the matter with me physically. / I am quite healthy.
아무러니 [설마] Impossible!; You don't say so.; You are telling me! ¶~ 내가 문을 닫지 않았을까 (You) Don't tell me I forgot to shut the door. // ~ 그가 그런 짓을 했을까 I can't believe he had done such a thing. / Why, he is the last person in the world who would have done such a thing.
아무렴 Of course!; Certainly!; Naturally!; (미국 구어) Sure! ¶~, 그렇고말고 It is just as you say. / You are right. / Oh yes, to be sure. / Yes, indeed. / Of course, it is. / (미국 구어) Sure.
아무리 **1** [어떻게 하여도] however; whatever. ¶~ 노력해도 할 수 있는 일에는 한계가 있다 However [No matter how] hard we (may) try, there is a limit to what we can do. // ~ 생각해도 그럴 수는 없어 That simply cannot be. // 그녀는 ~ 보아도 30세는 넘었다 She is thirty (years old), if a day. // 대문이 잠겨 있어서 ~ 해도 구내에 들어갈 수 없었다 The gate was shut, so we could not get into the premises anyhow. // ~ 생각해도 받은 기억이 없다 I am fairly certain [(구어) pretty sure] I never received it. // ~ 급히 간다 해도 이젠 늦었다 You won't make it, no matter how you hurry. // 일이 ~ 힘들어도 최선을 다하겠다 However hard the work may be, I will do my best. // ~ 기다려도 답장은 안 올 거야 However long you (may) wait, no answer will come. // 네가 ~ 노력해도 그를 설득시키지 못한다 You cannot persuade him no matter how hard you try. // ~ 해도 거기까지 시간 안에 도착할 수 없다 We can't get there in time no matter what we do. // ~ 부자라도 영원한 젊음은 살 수 없다 The [Even the] richest man cannot buy eternal youth. // ~ 적어도 50킬로의 수확은 있을 것으로 예상된다 It is estimated that we will have a yield of fifty kilograms at the worst [of at least fifty kilograms]. // ~ 늦어도 8시에는 그가 도착할 것입니다 He will arrive by eight at the latest. // ~ 경험이 많은 그일지라도 이 어려운 일을 감당하지는 못할 것이다 With [In spite of] all his experience, he will not be equal to this difficult task. // ~ 잘되어도 수지 타산은 본전 치기다 At best we can barely make both ends meet. // ~ 그래도 그것은 너무하다 That's going too far, to say the least. // ~ 그래도 이것은 터무니없이 비싸다 No matter how you look at it [what you say], this is unreasonably expensive.
2 Impossible! ⇨ =아무러니
아무아무 such-and-such persons.
아무짝 ¶~에도 쓸모가 없는 사람 a good-for-nothing (fellow) / a ne'er-do-well / a worthless fellow / a useless mouth / a waster / (미) a no-good / (영국 속어) a rotter // 그것은 ~에도 쓸모가 없다 It is good for nothing. / It is utterly useless. / It is no use [good] whatever.
아무쪼록 [될 수 있는 대로] as much [far] as one can; as much [far] as possible [practicable]; [꼭] by all means; [부디] kindly; (if you) please; [힘껏] to the best of one's ability. ¶~ 확답을 주시기 바랍니다 We ask that you kindly give us a definite answer. / Would you please give us a definite answer? / Please let us have your definite answer. // ~ 열심히 공부해라 Study as hard as you. // ~ 몸조심하십시오 Do take good care of yourself. / I hope you will take good care of yourself. // ~ 그녀가 무사히 돌아오기를 May she return in safety! // ~ 그렇게 해 보겠다 I'll try my best to do so.
아무튼 anyway; anyhow; at any rate; in any case [event]; at all events; somehow or other. ¶~ 내일 거기에 가겠다 In any case, I'll go there tomorrow. // 비가 올지 모르지만 ~ 외출하겠다 It may rain, but anyhow I am

아물거리다 1 [어른거리다] glimmer; shimmer; [깜박이다] flicker; [희미하다] be dim; be hazy; (눈 앞이) be dizzy. ¶눈이 아물거린다 My eyes are dazzled.// 불빛이 희미하게 아물거렸다 A faint light flickered[glimmered]. **2** [말·행동이 꼬물거리다] talk[act] ambiguously.

아물다 heal[close] (up); be healed. ¶상처가 아물었다 The wound has closed.// 상처가 완전히 아물 때까지 가만히 누워 있어야 한다 You must lie still until the wound has healed completely.

아물리다 1 (상처를) heal; make[help] (a wound) heal; treat (a wound). **2** (일 등을) finish; complete; bring (one's work) to completion; wind up.

아물아물 [아물거리는 모양] glimmeringly; shimmeringly; flickeringly; dimly; vaguely; dazzlingly. **아물아물하다** glimmer; talk ambiguously. ⇨아물거리다 ¶등불이 아물아물하게 보였다 I saw a flickering light in the distance.

아미(蛾眉) [미인의 눈썹] the eyebrows of a beauty; fine[delicate] eyebrows.

아미노산(－酸) an amino acid. ¶필수 ~ the (eight) essential amino acids.

아미타불(阿彌陀佛) [불] Amitabha; Amida.

아바타 [채팅·게임 등에 쓰이는 애니메이션 캐릭터] an avatar.

아버지 1 a [one's] father; (미국 중·남부) one's pappy; (구어) one's old man; dad; (영국 구어) one's pater; (영국 속어) one's governor [guv'nor / guvnor]; (낡) papa; (미국 구어) pop; (소아어) daddy. ¶~의 사랑 fatherly [paternal] affection// ~의 유산 patrimony// ~ 없는 아이 a fatherless child / [사생아] an illegitimate [a love] child// ~ 쪽의 (친척) (a relative) on the father's[paternal] side (남의 아이에게) ~ 노릇을 하다 father (a child) / act as a father (to a child)// ~를 여의다 lose one's father / be left fatherless// 어린이는 어른의 ~ The child is father of[to] the man.
2 [어떤 일을 처음 완성한 사람] the father. ¶영소설의 ~ the father of the English novel. **3** [가][기] Father.

아범 1 [아버지] your father; his father. **2** [자기 남편] my husband. **3** [늙은 남자 하인] an old[aged] manservant.

아베 마리아 Ave Maria; Hail Mary

아베크족(⊕avec族) a pair of young lovers; boys and girls on a date. ¶커피숍에는 ~이 많이 온다 A lot of couples[young men and women] come to the coffee shop.

아부(阿附) flattery; sycophancy; adulation; toadyism. ¶~를 잘하다 have a well-oiled tongue// 저 친구는 ~로 출세했다 That fellow got his present position by flattery[apple-polishing].// 그에게는 ~가 통하지 않는다 He is proof against flattery. **아부하다** flatter; curry favor[(영) favour] (with); (구어) butter (a person) upon; (구어) soft-soap (a person); toady to (a person); play up to (a person); (구어) apple-polish; court (a person's) favor; cringe to (a person); fawn on[upon] (a person). ¶아부하는 사람 a flatterer / an apple-polisher / a toady / a toad-eater// 아부하는 웃음 a servile[an insinuating / an oily] smile// 아부하는 언동 obsequious[servile / subservient] behavior.

아비규환(阿鼻叫喚) (비유) shrieking in agony; agonizing cries; appalling confusion; pandemonium. ¶사고 현장은 그야말로 ~이었다 The scene of the accident was simply hell.

아비산(亞砒酸) [화] arsenic trioxide. ⇨삼산화비소

아빠 〈소아〉 papa; pa; (구어) pop(s); (구어) dad; daddy. ⇨아버지1

아뿔싸 [뉘우칠 때 내는 소리] Oops!; Hang it!; Dash it!; Confound it!; Deuce take it!; Gosh! ¶~ 우산을 안 가져왔군 Gosh! I forgot to bring an umbrella with me.

아사(餓死) [굶어 죽는 것] death from hunger; (death by) starvation. ¶~지경에서 헤매다 be on the verge of starvation. **아사하다** starve to death; die of hunger[starvation]; be starved[famished] to death; perish by [with] famine. ➔¶아사시키다 starve (a person) to death / starve out (a person).

아삭거리다 be crunchy[crisp]; crunch. ¶아삭거리며 당근을 먹다 eat a carrot with a crunching sound / crunch a carrot.

아삭아삭 crunching; crisping. **아삭아삭하다** be crunchy[crisp]. ⇨아삭거리다

-아서 (and) so; and then; to. ⇨-어서

아성(牙城) the inner citadel; the keep; a stronghold; the bastion; an impenetrable fortress. ¶보수당의 ~에 육박할 수 있느냐가 문제다 The question is whether we can make inroads on[march on / press on to] conservative strongholds.

아성(亞聖) [성인에 버금감] a sage of second order.

아성층권(亞成層圈) the substratosphere. ¶~의 substratospheric.

아 세안 ASEAN (▶ the Association of Southeast Asian Nations의 약어).

아세테이트 acetate.

아세톤 acetone. ¶~의 acetonic.

아세트산(－酸) [화] acetic acid.

아세틸렌 [화] acetylene.

아셈 ASEM (▶ the Asia Europe Meeting의 약어).

아수라(阿修羅) ¶병사들은 ~같이 싸웠다 The soldiers fought in an absolute frenzy[like a demon / like Kilkenny cats].
●**아수라장** a scene of carnage[utter confusion].

아쉬워하다 (없어서) miss; feel the loss[want / miss] of; feel regret at[feel keenly] the absence of; [서운해하다] be unwilling; be reluctant. ¶이별을 ~ be reluctant[sorry / unwilling / loath] to leave [part from] a person// 나는 그녀와 헤어지기가 아쉬워서 잠시 더 머물렀다 I stayed a while longer, unable to part from her.// 오락이 없으면 그들이 아쉬워할 것이다 They won't be satisfied without entertainment.

아쉽다 (서술적) want for; miss; feel inconvenienced by the lack of; be unsatisfied [discontented] with the lack[miss] of; be [stand] in need[want] of. ¶아쉬운 소리를 하다 make a request (of a person) / ask a favor of (a person)// 아쉬운 것 없이 지내다 live in comfort / be comfortably off / be above want / be well off / live in plenty [luxury]// 돈이 ~ want for[need] money//

아옹다옹하다

일행 중에 그가 없어서 못내 아쉬웠다 Without him in the group, I felt something was missing[wanting]. // 전체적으로 통일성이 결여된 점이 ~ It's too bad that it lacks unity as a whole. // 아쉽게도 그때 그는 그의 능력을 십분 발휘하지 못했다 Unfortunately, at that time he wasn't able to show what he really could do.

아쉬운 대로 lacking anything better; inconvenient though it is; such as it is; as a temporary makeshift; anyway; making do with what one has. ¶~ 이만큼 있으면 할 수 있다 We can do with this amount for the time being. // 이걸 쓰시지요 Use this as a makeshift. // 칼을 잊어버리고 와서 안됐지만 ~ 으로 쓰자 It's too bad we forgot to bring a knife with us, but let's make do with this as best we can.

아스라하다 [아득하다] faraway; far-off; remote; [희미하다] dim; faint; vague; indistinct; hazy. **아스라이** far; far off[away]; in the distance; a long way off; faintly; dimly; vaguely. ¶~ 들리는 소리 a faint sound // 새는 ~ 날아갔다 The bird has flown away in the sky[has flown away in the distance].

아스러지다 1 [조각 나다] be crushed to pieces; be smashed into atoms[fragments]; crumble; shatter. ¶뼈가 ~ have a bone shatter. 2 [살이 벗겨지다] be grazed; be abraded; be chafed.

아스파라거스 [식] asparagus. ¶~ 통조림 canned[(영) tinned] asparagus.

아스팍 ASPAC(▶ the Asian and Pacific Council의 약어).

아스팔트 asphalt; (미) blacktop(▶ blacktop은 아스팔트 포장도로의 뜻으로만 쓰임). ¶~로 포장하다 pave[lay] (a road) with asphalt / asphalt (a road).

아스피린 [약] aspirin. ¶~을 세 알 먹다 take three aspirin tablets / take three aspirins.

아슬아슬하다 [위태롭다] risky; dangerous; perilous; thrilling; critical; [차이가 근소하다] close; narrow; near; hairbreadth; touch-and-go. ¶아슬아슬한 경기 a close game[match / contest] / a tight game[match] / (미국 구어) a nip and tuck[neck and neck] game // 아슬아슬한 재주의 연기 a breathtaking gymnastic performance // 아슬아슬한 짓을 하다 take a big chance / run a risk / attempt a chancy maneuver / play a risky[touchy] game / sail near[close to / close against] the wind(법 등에 저촉될 듯 말 듯하게) // 아슬아슬하게 시간에 대다 make it just in the nick of time[by the skin of one's teeth] // 아슬아슬하게 이기다 win by a narrow margin / win an eleventh-hour[a paper-thin] victory / gain a victory by a slim margin / win by a neck(경마에서) // 그는 시험에 아슬아슬하게 통과했다 He barely squeezed through the exam. // 우리는 아슬아슬하게 도망쳤다 We had a narrow[hairbreadth] escape. // 이 영화에는 아슬아슬한 장면이 많다 There are a lot of thrilling scenes in this film. // 그는 아슬아슬하게 죽음을 모면했다 He had a narrow[hairbreadth] escape from death[a close brush with death]. // 그는 escaped death narrowly[by a hairbreadth]. // 총알이 아슬아슬하게 그의 머리를 빗나갔다 The bullet missed his head by a hairbreadth.

아시아 Asia. ¶~의 Asian / Asiatic // 동남~ Southeast Asia // 동북~ Northeast Asia // 소~ Asia Minor // 중앙~ Central Asia.
● **아시아 경기 대회** the Asian Games. **아시아인 / 아시아 사람** an Asian; an Asiatic; (집합적) Asians; the people of Asia.

아씨 (경칭) madam; (호칭) your (good) lady; Mrs. –; your ladyship; mistress; madam[ma'am].

아악 (雅樂) aak; court music. ¶~을 연주하다 give performances of aak.

아야 Ouch!; How it hurts!; That hurts!

-아야 should[ought to] (do); however much one may[might] (do). ⇨-어야

-아야지 would; be going to. ⇨-어야지

아양 coquetry; flirtation. ¶~을 떨다[부리다 / 피우다] play the coquette / behave in a coquettish manner / act coquettishly[seductively] / speak in coquettish tone / put on coquettish airs / play[make] up to / make eyes at (a man) / flirt / purr at / coquet(te) / coo (at) / play the baby (to) // ~ 떠는 목소리로 in a wheedling[an insinuating] voice // 그 여자는 남자 친구에게 반지를 사 달라고 ~을 부렸다 She purred to her boyfriend and asked him to buy her a ring.

아역 (兒役) [어린이 역] a child's part[role] (in a play); [어린이 역을 맡은 배우] a child[juvenile] actor[actress].

아연 (亞鉛) [화학(기호 zn)]. ¶산화~ zinc oxide // 황화~ zinc sulfide // 황산~ zinc sulfate // 염화~ zinc chloride.
● **아연 도금** zinc galvanizing; galvanization; zincification. **아연판** [인쇄판·인쇄물] a zincograph; a zincotype.

아연 (俄然) (all) of a sudden; all at once; suddenly; abruptly. ¶~ 긴장하다 become tense suddenly / be strained all of a sudden. **아연하다** sudden; abrupt.

아연실색하다 (啞然失色-) turn pale with surprise[fright]. ¶그 소식을 듣고 그는 아연실색 했다 At the news he changed color.

아연하다 (啞然-) be agape; be aghast; be stunned; be dum(b)founded; be tongue-tied; be struck dumb[speechless] with astonishment; be taken aback. ¶그는 그만 아연하여 할 말을 잊었다 He was struck speechless[dumb] with astonishment. // 나는 아연하여 그의 얼굴을 바라보았다 I watched his face in dumb[blank] surprise. // 그는 아연하여 그 자리에 그냥 서 있었다 He just stood there (with his mouth open) in utter amazement. // 그는 그 광경에 아연한 따름이었다 He stood aghast at the spectacle. // 그 소식을 듣고 나는 한동안 아연했다 I was struck dumb by the news for a while. **아연히** agape (with wonder); aghast; in utter amazement.

아열대 (亞熱帶) the subtropical zones[regions]; the subtropics. ¶~의 subtropic(al) / near-tropical.
● **아열대 기후** a subtropical climate. **아열대 식물[동물]** a subtropical plant[animal].

아예 [애초부터] from the outset[beginning / start]. 2 [절대로] (not) at all; altogether; entirely; never. ¶거짓말은 ~ 하지 마라 Never tell a lie. // 어제는 그는 외출하지도 않았다 I didn't go out at all yesterday.

아옹다옹하다 [하찮은 일에 서로 자꾸 다투다] quarrel (with); dispute; argue; altercate; bicker; wrangle; squabble; engage in wordy warfare; bandy words (with).

아우 a man's younger[little / kid] brother; a woman's younger[little / small] sister.
아우(를) 보다 have[get] a younger sister [brother].
아우(를) 타다 suffer a younger sibling; get thin from premature weaning as a result of the mother's new pregnancy.

아우성(一聲) a shout; an outcry; a clamor; a hubbub; a bawl; a howl; a squawk.

아우성치다(一聲-) clamor; bawl (out); bawl and squall; set up a clamor[shout]; (응원 등에서) yell; give a yell (to); (불만으로) let out a squawk.

아우트라인 an outline.

아욱 [식] a mallow (특히 당아욱).

아울러 1 [동시에 함께] (joining) together. ¶그는 장점과 단점을 ~ 갖고 있다 He has[is endowed with] both strengths and weaknesses. ¶사람은 누구나 선악 양면을 ~ 갖고 있다 There is a good and bad side to everyone. **2** [곁들여서] in addition; besides; at the same time. ¶인사차 찾아뵙고 ~ 한 가지 부탁드리려고 합니다 I intend to pay a visit and beg a favor of you in person.

아웃 1 [야구] an out; a put-out(약어 PO); (판정) Out! ¶~을 시키다 pick (a runner) off (base) / throw (a runner) out // ~이 되다 be put out // 나는 스리 스트라이크로 ~이 되었다 I struck out. / I was out[went down] on strikes. // 그는 센터 플라이로 ~이 되었다 He was out on a fly to the center fielder. // 9회 말 투 ~입니다 There are two outs in the bottom of the ninth (inning). // 투 ~ 만루더 The bases were loaded with two men out. **2** [골프] the outgoing course.
●**아웃사이더** an outsider. **아웃소싱** outsourcing. **아웃코너** [야구] the outside corner (of the plate). ¶공은 ~를 벗어났다 The pitch missed the outside corner of the plate.

아이 [자식·후사(後嗣)] a child (pl. children); [법] [문어] one's issue; one's offspring; [미국 구어] a kid; [아들] a son; [딸] a daughter; (집합적) [문어] offspring (▶ 단수·복수 동형으로 동사는 어린이가 둘 이상이면 복수형). ¶5살의 사내 [여자] ~ a five-year boy [girl] // 우리 집 ~ my son[daughter] // 전처의 ~ a child by one's first wife // 배 속의 ~ an expected[a coming] child // ~ 같은 childish / (장난꾸러기의) mischievous // ~같이 굴다 behave childishly // ~ 적에 in one's boyhood [childhood / infancy] // when [as] a child[boy] // ~를 낳다 give birth to a child / (문어) bear a child / ~를 보다 take care of [look after] a baby / (부모가 외출 중에) baby-sit // ~가 서다 get with child / become pregnant // ~가 없다 be childless / (문어) [법] have no issue / (불임) be sterile // 그는 여자에게 ~를 배게 했다 He made a woman pregnant. // 그는 화가의 ~이다 He was born in[into] a painter's family. / His father is a painter. / 나는 누구의 ~인지 오랫동안 몰랐다 I did not know who my parents were for a long time. // 착한 ~지 There's[That's] a good boy[girl]. // 나는 ~가 둘 있다 I have two children. // 그들에게 ~가 생겼다 A baby [child] was born to them.

아이도 낳기 전에 포대기 장만한다(속담) To count one's chickens before they are hatched.

아이고(머니) 1 [반갑거나 좋을 때 내는 소리] Ah!; Oh! ¶~, 고맙기도 해라 Thank you very much. // ~, 좋아라 What a delight! / Hallelujah!
2 [놀라거나 기막힐 때 내는 소리] Oh!; Oh dear!; Dear me!(▶ 여성 용어); Gee whiz!; Good(ness) gracious!; Good heaven(s)!; Good Lord!; Good bless me!; My eye!; Why!; [아프거나 힘들 때 내는 소리] Ouch! ¶~, 돈을 가져오는 걸 잊었구나 Oh dear! I forgot to bring money. // ~, 민 선생이다 Why, it's Mr. Min. // ~, 아파 Ouch! // ~, 내가 망쳐 놓았구나 Oh, no, I've made a mess of it. // ~, 돈을 놓고 왔구나 Oh, dear! I have forgotten my money(▶ Damn은 남녀 모두 쓸 수 있으나, 공식 석상에서는 쓰지 않음. 종교적 이유로 이 말을 꺼리는 사람도 있음). // ~, 너였구나 Why, was it you? / Oh, it was (only) you. // ~, 또 오믈렛인가 Oh, no, another omelet! / What? Omelets again? // ~, 그 사람 또 우산을 놓고 갔어 Oh dear, he's left his umbrella behind again!

아이디어 an idea. ¶좋은 ~ a good[bright] idea // 멋진 ~가 떠올랐다 I hit upon a great [capital] idea. // 그 ~는 누가 냈나 Who put that idea into your head? / Who gave you that idea?

아이러니 (an) irony.

아이러니컬하다 ironical. ¶아이러니컬하게도 through the irony of chance / by the irony of fate / ironically (enough).

아이비아르디 [국제 부흥 개발 은행] IBRD (▶ the International Bank for Reconstruction and Development의 약어).

아이섀도 eye shadow. ¶~를 바르다[바르고 다] put on[wear] eye shadow.

아이쇼핑 (*eye shopping) window shopping.

아이스 댄싱 ice dancing.

아이스 링크 an ice rink.

아이스박스 a cooler; an icebox.

아이스커피 iced coffee; ice coffee.

아이스케이크 (*ice cake) (미국 속어) a popsicle.

아이스크림 (an) ice cream; (영) an ice.

아이스티 iced tea; ice tea.

아이스하키 ice hockey. ¶~ 선수 an ice hockey player / a puckster.

아이엘오 ILO(▶ the International Labor Organization의 약어).

아이엠에프 IMF (▶ the International Monetary Fund의 약어). ¶~ 8조국 an IMF Article 8 nation.

아이오시 IOC(▶ the International Olympic Committee의 약어).

아이젠 (⑤Eisen) (등산용) climbing irons; climbing spikes; crampons.

아이코 Oops!; Whew!; Gee whiz!; Wow!

아이콘 [컴퓨터에 명령을 내릴 수 있는 도형 표시] an icon.

아이큐 [지능 지수] an IQ[I.Q.]; an intelligence quotient. ¶그 소년의 ~는 109다 That boy has an IQ of 109.

아이템 an item.

아이피 주소 (一住所) [숫자로 나타낸 인터넷 사이트 주소] an IP address.

아작거리다 munch; crunch; eat with a munching sound.

아작아작 with a munching sound. ¶~ 먹다 crunch / munch (crackers). **아작아작하다** munch; crunch. ⇨°아작거리다

아장거리다 1 (아기가) toddle; totter; shamble. ¶아장거리는 아기 a toddler. 2 [한가로운 태도로 거닐다] hang[loiter / hover / linger] about [around]; muddle about; (속어) pad it[the hoof].

아장걸음 toddling step[gait]; mincing steps.

아장아장 toddlingly; with toddling steps. ¶~ 걷는 아기 a toddler / a toddling baby // ~ 걷다 (어린아이가) toddle (about) // 아기가 ~ 걷기 시작했다 The baby began to toddle.

아쟁(牙箏) [음] a *ajaeng*; a bowed seven-stringed instrument.

아저씨 1 [삼촌] an uncle. 2 [부모 또래] a man; [호칭] Mister; Sir; Pop; Uncle. ¶낯선 ~ a strange gentleman.

아전(衙前) [서리] a petty official (of former times, whose job was permanent and hereditary and usually unsalaried).

아전인수(我田引水) drawing water to one's own mill; turning everything to one's own advantage; seeking[promoting] one's own interests; arguing from a self-centered angle; interested consideration. ¶~인 selfish / self-seeking / self-centered[(영)-centred] // ~ 격인 견해 a selfish view.

아주¹ 1 [대단히] very (much); exceedingly; excessively; extremely; remarkably; greatly. ¶그녀는 ~ 친절한 선생님이셨다 She was a very kind teacher. // 어제는 ~ 더운 날이었다 It was extremely hot yesterday. // 일이 ~ 순조롭게 진행되었다 It went perfectly [quite] well. // 그녀는 ~ 늙어 버렸다 She has really aged. / She has grown quite old. // 나는 ~ 즐거웠다 I was really pleased. // 이번 회에 점 넣은 것은 ~ 값진 것이다 The run we scored in this inning has great weight[is very important]. // 그는 ~ 성가신 녀석이다 He is such a nuisance. // ~ 시끄러워서 잠이 안 온다 It is so noisy that I can't sleep. // ~ 오래전에 당신을 만난 적이 있소 I remember meeting you once long ago[a long time ago]. 2 [전혀·완전히] quite; utterly; entirely; completely; perfectly; altogether. ¶~ 모르는 사람 an utter stranger // 난 지금은 ~ 기분이 좋아졌소 I feel quite well now. / I have completely recovered. / I feel fine again. // 그는 ~ 가 버렸다 He has gone for good.

아주² [감탄사] ¶~, 모르는 체하긴 As if you didn't know! // ~, 너에게 질까 봐 Damn it! ─ See who is the stronger!

아주(亞洲) the continent of Asia.

아주까리 [식] a castor-oil plant. ⇨ˉ피마자
  ● **아주까리기름** castor oil. ⇨ˉ피마자유(⇨피마자)

아주머니 1 [숙모] an aunt; an older[a younger] sister of one's father[mother] (▶영어에서는 특히 백모와 숙모를 구별하지 않음). ¶헬렌 ~ Aunt Helen. 2 [한 항렬의 남의 아내] an auntie[aunty]. 3 [부인] a lady.

아주버니 one's husband's older brother.

아줌마 a lady. ⇨ˉ아주머니3

아지랑이 heat haze; waves of heat; heat waves; (a veil of) heat shimmer; shimmering of heated air. ¶~가 일고 있다 The air is shimmering. / The air is waving with heat. / The heat is waving the air.

아지작 with a crunch; with a crunchy sound.
  아지작하다 crunch; munch. ⇨ˉ아지작거리다

아지작거리다 crunch; munch; champ. ¶사과를 ~ munch an apple.

아지트(⒭agitpunkt) [은신처] a hiding place; a safe house (for underground activists); (미) a hideout; [비밀 본부] a secret headquarters (of a leftist movement).

아직 [어떤 일이 이루어질 때가 채 못 되어] (not) yet; still; as yet; with no change; even now; so far; [계속해서] still more. ¶~ 봄이 오지 않은 산들 mountains not yet touched by spring // 그는 ~ 자고 있다 He is still sleeping. // 그는 ~ 돌아오지 않았다 He has not come back yet. // ~ 백부님은 뵌 적이 없다 I have never met my uncle. // 그것은 네가 ~ 태어나지 않았을 때의 일이다 It was before you were born. // 나는 ~ 건강하다 Up till now[so far] I have been in good shape. // 그때부터 ~ 1주일밖에 되지 않았다 It has been only a week since then. // 이 나라의 공업화는 ~ 앞날이 멀다 The industrialization of this country still has a long way to go. // 정상까지는 ~ 멀다 It is still a long way to the summit. // 그의 기술은 전문가로서는 ~ 멀었다 His skill is still far from that of an expert.

아직껏 [아직까지] so[thus] far; up to[until] now[the present]; till now; hitherto; as yet. ¶나는 ~ 이렇게 큰 고무풍선을 본 적이 없다 I have never seen such a big balloon. // 그는 ~ 내게 소식을 보내지 않았다 He still hasn't written (to) me. / He has not written (to) me yet. / I have heard nothing from him yet.

아질산(亞窒酸) [화] nitrous acid.
  ● **아질산염** nitrite.

아집(我執) [자기만을 내세움] egocentricity; self-centeredness[(영) self-centredness]; egoistic attachment; egotism; tenacity; obstinacy. ¶~을 버리다 get rid of one's self-centeredness // 그는 ~이 강한 사나이다 He is an egocentric man.

아찔하다 dizzy; giddy; faint. ¶나는 정신이 아찔해졌다 I began to feel faint[woozy].

아차 [잘못된 것을 갑자기 깨닫고 내는 소리] Heavens!; Hang it!; Damn it!; Oh my! (여성어); Darn it!; Dear me!; Deuce take it!; Gosh!; Confound it! ¶~ 할 사이도 없이 in an instant / in the twinkling of an eye / in no time at all // ~ 하는 순간에 그는 브레이크를 밟았다 He slammed on the break at once. // ~, 지갑을 잊고 안 가져왔군 Oh dear! I have forgotten my money(여성의 표현). / Damn! I have forgotten my wallet[money].

아첨(阿諂) flattery; adulation; sycophancy; toadyism; a compliment; sugary[sweet] words. ¶~에 넘어가지 않다 be above being flattered / be insusceptible[impervious] to flattery // 마음에도 없는 ~을 하다 offer a person an insincere compliment. **아첨하다** flatter; adulate; toady; curry favor (with one's superior); fawn upon (a person); butter up (to); apple-polish; pay (a person) a compliment. ¶남에게 ~ (구어) soft-soap a person / (구어) butter a person up / flatter[compliment] a person (on / about) / pay a compliment to a person // 사장에게 ~ flatter the boss // 권력자에게 ~ fawn upon [curry favor with] men of influence // 그녀는 언제나 상사에게 아첨한다 She is always flattering[trying to curry favor with] his superiors. / (구어) He's always sucking up to his superiors. / He is always buttering up[(구어) apple-polishing] his superiors. // 너무

아취
아첨하지 마라 Don't lay it on so thick.
●아첨꾼 a flatterer; a toady; a bootlicker; a yesman; (미국 구어) an apple-polisher; a fawning sort of (a person).

아취(雅趣) [아담한 정취 또는 그러한 취미] elegance; tastefulness; artistry. ¶~가 있는 tasteful / elegant / graceful / refined // ~ 없는 tasteless / commonplace / flat // ~ 있는 생활을 하다 lead a tasteful life.

아치 an arch. ¶~ 모양의 arch-shaped / bow-shaped // 장미의 ~ an arch of roses // ~문 an arched gateway / an archway // ~ 모양의 창문 an arched window.
●아치교(-橋) an arch bridge.

아치(雅致) [아담한 풍치] good taste; elegance; grace; artistic effect; gusto. ¶~ 있는 elegant / graceful / refined / tasteful / artistic // ~ 있는 별장 a tasteful cottage // 그 정원은 매우 ~ 있게 꾸며져 있다 The garden is very tastefully laid out.

아침 1 (때) morning; (시어) morn. ¶~마다 every morning // ~ 해 the morning sun // 떠오르는 ~ 해 the rising sun // ~ 예배 a morning service // 이른 ~ early morning // 오늘 ~ this morning // ~부터 밤까지 from morning till night / all day long // 3일 ~에 on the morning of the third / in the morning on the third // ~ 일찍이 early in the morning / at an early hour // 토요일 ~에 on Saturday morning (▶ 특정한 날의 아침에는 on을 씀) // 내일 ~까지 by tomorrow morning // ~에는 무엇보다도 먼저 그것을 해야겠다 I'll do it first thing in the morning. // 그녀는 ~에 일찍 일어난다 She gets up early in the morning. / She is an early riser. // 어제 ~에 약한 지진이 있었다 There was a minor earth tremor (early) yesterday morning. // 내일 ~까지는 비가 계속될 것 같다 It is likely to be still raining tomorrow morning. // 그는 오늘 ~ 일찍 도착했다 He arrived early this morning. // ~부터 사고가 나다니 재수 없다 It is unlucky to have an accident so early in the morning. // 나는 일요일 ~ 일찍이 출발한다 I'm leaving early Sunday morning.
2 breakfast. ⇨아침밥(⇨아침)
●아침결 the forenoon. 아침 기도 a morning prayer; matins(교회의). 아침나절 the forenoon; the first half of the day between breakfast and lunch. 아침밥 breakfast; the morning meal. ¶~ 겸 점심밥 a late breakfast / (미국 구어) brunch // ~을 먹다 eat [take] (one's) breakfast / breakfast // ~을 마치다 finish one's breakfast. 아침저녁 [아침과 저녁] morning and evening. ¶~으로 in the morning and evening / day and night / [늘] day in day out / always // ~으로 서늘하다 We have cooler mornings and evenings now.

아카데미 an academy.
●아카데미상(-賞) an Academy Award; [수여되는 황금빛 상] an Oscar. ¶이 영화는 세 부분에서 ~을 탔다 This film has won three Oscars.

아카시아 [식] an acacia; a locust tree.
아 카펠라 [음] a cappella.
아케이드 an arcade. ¶~가 있는 거리 an arcaded street.
아코디언 [음] an accordion.
●아코디언 연주자 an accordionist.
아크등(-燈) an arc lamp [light].
아크릴 [화] acryloyl; acrylyl; acryl.

●아크릴 섬유 acrylic fiber [(영) fibre]. 아크릴 수지 acrylic acid resin.

아킬레스건(-腱) [생] the Achilles' tendon; [비유] one's Achilles' heel; a vulnerable point; a chink in one's armor; a glass jaw.

아톰 [원자] an atom.
아틀라스 [그리스 신화] Atlas.
아틀리에 an atelier; a studio (pl. ~s); a workshop.

아파트 [개별 가구의 아파트] (미) an apartment; a condominium (▶ apartment는 주로 기업이 소유하는 임대 아파트를 가리키고, condominium은 개인 소유의 아파트를 가리킴); (영) a flat; [건물 전체] (미) an apartment house [building]; a condominium; (영) a block of flats. ¶고층 ~ a high-rise apartment (building) // 서민 ~ an apartment building for the low incomers [income bracket] // 임대[분양] ~ a rental [lot-sold] apartment / condominium // 호화 ~ a luxury apartment [condominium].
●아파트 단지 an apartment complex.

아파하다 feel a pain; feel sore; hurt; complain of pain. ¶아파하는 pained (look) // 아파하고 있다 be in pain.

아편(阿片) opium. ¶~을 피우다 smoke opium // 그는 ~을 상용했다 He was addicted to (the use of) opium. / He was an opium user.
●아편굴 an opium den [joint]. 아편 전쟁 the Opium War. 아편 중독 opiumism; (suffer from) opium poisoning. 아편 중독자 an opium addict; a dope; a hop head; an opium fiend; [흡음자] an opium smoker [eater].

아포스트로피 an apostrophe(기호 ').
아폴로 1 [그리스·로마 신화] Apollo. 2 [미국의 우주선] Apollo.
●아폴로 계획 the Apollo program.

아프다 1 (육체적으로) painful; sore(염증 등으로); (서술적) hurt; [욱신거리다] prickle; feel prickly; smart; ache. ¶아픈 상처 a painful wound // 가슴이 ~ I have a pain in my chest. / [죄는 듯하다] I feel something pressing [as if something is pressing] on my chest. // 나는 목구멍이 아파서 오래 이야기할 수 없다 I have a sore throat and cannot talk long. // 그는 배가 쿡쿡 쑤시고 아팠다 He had the gripes. // 상처가 몹시 쑤시고 ~ My wound smarts terribly [awfully]. / I feel a sharp, stinging pain in the wound. // 머리가 빠개질 듯이 ~ My head is throbbing terribly. / I have a racking [splitting] headache. // 무릎이 ~ My knee hurts [pains me]. // 발[목]이 ~ I have sore feet [a sore throat]. // 이가 몹시 ~ I have an awful toothache. // 아이고, 아파 Ouch! That hurts! // 아프니까 Do you feel [have] any pain? / Does it hurt (you)? // 조금도 아프지 않습니다 I feel no pain. / It doesn't hurt at all. // 어제 화상을 입은 곳이 ~ It smarts [stings] where I burned [(영) burnt] myself yesterday. // 유행성 감기로 온몸이 ~ My whole body aches with (the) flu. // 손가락의 벤 상처가 ~ The cut on my finger is painful [hurts]. // 겨울이 되면 나는 다리와 허리가 ~ In winter I have pains in my hips and legs. // 발뒤꿈치의 물집이 따끔따끔 ~ The blisters on my heels sting [smart]. // 뼈의 마디마디가 ~ I ache in the joints. / My joints ache. // 간밤에는 이가 몹시 아파 잠을 못 잤다 A bad toothache kept me awake last night. // 어디가 아프니까 Where

아프다 2 (정신적으로) painful; trying; (서술적) be grieved; ache; have a pang; be hard to bear. ¶그녀는 언제나 나의 아픈 곳을 건드린다 She always touches me on a sore[tender] spot. / She always touches me on a raw nerve.// 네 말은 그의 아픈 곳을 찔렀다 Your remark stung[cut] him to the quick.// 그것은 골치 아픈 문제다 That's a vexing question. / That problem gives me a headache.// 그녀는 그 이야기를 듣고 가슴이 아팠다 She was grieved to hear the story.// 그 일을 생각하면 가슴이 ~ I am pained[feel very sad] when I think of it.// 그것은 가슴 아픈 이야기다 That's a pitiful[pathetic] story.

아프로디테 [그리스 신화] Aphrodite.

아프트식 철도 (一式鐵道) an Abt-system railroad; a cog[rack] railway.

아플리케 [오려 대기] appliqué. ¶~ 달린 에이프런 an appliqué apron.

아픔 [통증] a pain; an ache; a sore; (마음의) (mental) pain; [슬픔] grief; sorrow; (쑤시는) a smart. ¶가슴[위]의 ~ a pain in the breast [stomach]// 심한 ~ a severe[a sharp / an acute] pain// 상처의 ~ the smart of a wound// 정신적[육체적] ~ mental[physical] pain// 이별의 ~ the pain of parting.// ~을 느끼다 feel pain// ~을 가라앉히다 allay[alleviate / mitigate / ease / relieve / lighten / soothe] the pain// ~을 없애다 remove[banish / kill] (the) pain// ~이 가셨다 The pain has left me[has gone]. / I no longer feel any pain.

아하 Dear me!; My goodness!; Well!; What-do-you-know! ¶~, 그것을 깜박 잊었구나 Oh my goodness! It slipped right out of my mind!

아하하 [거리낌 없이 큰 소리로 웃는 소리] Ha-ha!; Hmmph!; Well look at that will you! ¶~ 웃다 laugh aloud[loudly] / (일부러) force[feign] a laugh.

아한대 (亞寒帶) [온대와 한대의 중간의 기후대] (북반구의) the subarctic zone; (남반구의) the subantarctic zone.

아호 (雅號) a pen name; a pseudonym; a literary name; (프) a nom de plume. ¶~를 붙이다 name / call// 그는 늘 소월이라는 ~로 작품을 발표했다 He always published his works under the pen name of Sowol.// 할아버지의 ~는 범우라고 했다 My grandfather called himself[used the name] Beom-u.

아홉 nine. ¶아버지는 내가 ~ 살 때 돌아가셨다 My father died when I was nine (year old) [nine years of age].

아홉수 (~數) years of age ending in 9, considered climacteric.

아홉째 the ninth.

아황산 (亞黃酸) [화] sulfurous[(영) sulphurous] acid.

● 아황산가스 sulfur dioxide. ⇒ 이산화황

아흐레 1 [아홉 날] nine days. 2 the ninth day (of a month). ⇒ 초아흐렛날

● 아흐렛날 the ninth day.

아흔 ninety.

악¹ [남을 놀라게 할 때 지르는 소리] Bo!; Boh!; Boo!; [놀랐을 때 지르는 소리] Ugh!; Oh!; Wow!; Ooh!

악² [모질게 쓰는 기운] desperate effort; franticness; desperation; [노한 감정] desperation; anger; exploding[pent-up] feelings. ¶~이 오르다 get mad.

악에 받치다 become[grow] desperate; be [become] excited. ¶악에 받쳐 desperately / in desperation / frantically / excitedly / [미친 듯이] like mad.

악 (惡) badness; (an) evil; wickedness; crimes; [악덕] (a) vice. ¶사회 ~ social ills [evils] // ~의 소굴 criminal quarters / the underworld // ~에 물들다 (문어) be steeped in vice // ~에 빠지다 fall into[be given to] evil ways // 탐욕은 ~이다 Avarice is a vice.// 돈은 모든 ~의 근원이다 Money is the root of all evil.// 그는 ~의 화신이다 He is the incarnation of evil[wickedness].

악감정 (惡感情) [나쁜 감정] ill feeling; an ill will; animosity; an unfavorable impression; [반감] antipathy. ¶국제간의 ~ international animosities // ~을 사다 make an unfavorable impression (on another's mind) / impress (a person) unfavorably / offend // ~을 품다 have ill feeling (toward(s)) / feel antipathy (toward(s) / against / for) // 그 두 사람 사이에는 ~이 있다 There is a lot of bad blood between them.

악곡 (樂曲) a musical piece[composition]; a piece of music.

악골 (顎骨) [생] a jawbone. ⇒ 턱뼈

악공 (樂工) [역] a court musician.

악귀 (惡鬼) an evil spirit; a demon; a devil; the Evil One. ¶~가 들리다 be possessed by [with] an evil spirit // 집안의 ~를 쫓아내다 exorcise a house.

악극 (樂劇) a musical (drama / play); an operetta.

● 악극단 an operetta troupe[company]; a musical troupe.

악기 (樂器) a musical instrument. ¶현[관 / 타] ~ a stringed[wind / percussion] instrument // 건반 ~ a keyboard instrument // ~에 맞도록 편곡하다 arrange (music) for instruments / instrument.

● 악기점 a music shop; a musical instrument store.

악녀 (惡女) an evil[a wicked] woman.

악다구니 [소리를 지르면서 서로 다투는 것] (exchange of) high[sharp] words; a name-calling quarrel; a brawl; an altercation. **악다구니하다** have high words[a row] (with); brawl; altercate.

악단 (樂團) 1 [음악 연주를 위해 조직된 단체] a (musical) band; an orchestra. 2 an operetta troupe. ⇒ 악극단(⇒악극)

악단 (樂壇) the musical world; musical circles.

악담 (惡談) 1 [저주하는 말] a curse; a malediction; [욕] abusive[bad] language; abuse. ¶~을 퍼붓다 abuse (a person) soundly / curse and swear // 갖은 ~을 늘어놓다 let out a stream of curses / reel off[let loose with] a stream of abuse. **악담하다** swear; curse; abuse; revile; call (a person) (ill) names. 2 [비방] slander; backbiting. **악담하다** backbite (a person); speak ill of (a person); badmouth.

악당 (惡黨) a rascal; a villain; [깡패] a hooligan; (미국 구어) a hoodlum. ¶(이) ~ 같으니 (You) Devil! / (You) Bastard! / (You) Son of a bitch! (▶ 이러한 표현은 쓰지 않는 것이 바람직함)

악대 (樂隊) a (musical) band; (취주악의) a

악덕(惡德) (a) vice; corruption; immorality; evil conduct. **악덕하다** vicious; vice-ridden; corrupt; immoral; depraved.
● 악덕 기업주 a vicious entrepreneur. 악덕 상인 / 악덕 업자 a dishonest [wicked / tricky] trader [dealer]; a jockey.

brass band. ¶육군[해군·공군] 군~ a military[a naval / an air force] band // ~의 연주회 a band concert // ~를 선두로 with a brass band at the head.

악독하다(惡毒−) most wicked; infernal; atrocious; brutal; devilish; villainous. ¶악독한 짓 an atrocious[infernal] act / an atrocity.

악동(惡童) a brat; a bad boy[girl]; a naughty child.

악랄하다(惡辣−) vicious; wicked; [파렴치하다] unscrupulous; [비열하다] mean; (구어) dirty; [교활하다] crafty; wily. ¶악랄한 상슬 crooked dealing // 악랄한 방법 a vicious way to do things // 악랄한 짓을 하다 play a mean [(구어) dirty] trick / play foul // 그는 악랄한 방법으로 큰돈을 벌었다 He made a big profit by unscrupulous means.

악력(握力) a grip; grasping power. ¶~이 세다 [약하다] have a strong[weak] grip.

악령(惡靈) an evil spirit; a black angel.

악마(惡魔) the Devil; Satan; a fiend; a demon; Old Serpent; [악령] an evil spirit. ¶~의[적인] satanic[Satanic] (influence) / demonic (power) // ~ 같은 devilish / satanic / fiendish / diabolical // ~를 쫓다 exorcise [drive out / drive away] evil spirits (from a person) // ~가 들리다 be possessed by evil spirits[a devil].

악명(惡名) [나쁜 평판] a bad reputation; ill repute[fame]; a bad name; notoriety; infamy. ¶높은 큰 도둑[강도] a notorious burglar // 그는 수전노라는 ~이 붙었다 He has acquired a bad reputation as a miser [penny-pincher].

악몽(惡夢) [나쁜 꿈] a bad dream; [무서운 꿈] a nightmare; [불길한 꿈] an ominous dream. ¶~을 꾸다[~에 시달리다] have[be troubled by] a nightmare[bad dream] // ~에서 깨어나다 start up from a nightmare / [제정신이 들다] come to one's senses // 그는 매일 밤 ~에 시달렸다 Night after night he was oppressed by a nightmare.

악물다 clench[clamp / set] (one's teeth). ¶이를 악물고 고통을 견디다 endure the pain by clenching one's teeth.

악바리 1 [영악한 사람] a hard shrewd person. 2 [모진 사람] a (harsh) tough fellow.

악법(惡法) a bad[an evil] law.

악보(樂譜) [집합적] music; (한 장의) a sheet of music; a score(총보); a music book(악보집). ¶관현악용 ~ an orchestral[a full] score // 피아노 ~ a piano score // ~ 없이 연주하다 play without music[by ear / from memory] // ~를 읽다 read music // ~에 가사를 붙이다 set the words to music // ~를 보지 않고 노래하다 sing without (looking at) the music.
● 악보집 a music book.

악사(樂士) a band(s)man; a musician. ¶거리의[떠돌이] ~ a street[strolling] musician / (영국 구어) a busker.

악서(惡書) an evil[a bad / a harmful] book.

악선전(惡宣傳) vile[pernicious] propaganda; false propaganda; a sinister rumor. **악선전하다** launch false propaganda (about); spread a bad rumor (about).

악성(惡性) malignancy; malignity. ¶~의 malignant (influenza) / virulent (disease) / vicious // ~의 불황 a deep[persistent] recession // 그는 ~ 루머에 의해 매장되었다 He was ruined by vicious rumors.
● 악성 종양 a malignant[vicious] tumor.

악성(樂聖) a celebrated[master / famous] musician; a great musical artist. ¶~ 베토벤 Beethoven, the great musician.

악센트 1 [고저·강약의 변화] an accent; [강세] a stress. ¶~가 있는[없는] (un)accented / (un)stressed // 둘째 음절에 ~를 붙이다 stress[put the accent on] the second syllable // 이 단어는 둘째 음절에 ~가 있다 This word is stressed on the second syllable. 2 [어조·음조] a tone; an accent. ¶그의 말에는 남부 ~가 있다 He speaks with a Southern accent. 3 [강조점] emphasis; stress. ¶이 블라우스는 칼라의 자수가 ~다 The embroidery on the collar accents[sets off] the blouse. // 대통령의 연설은 실업 문제에 ~를 두고 있다 The President laid stress on[emphasized] the unemployment problem in his speech.

악셀 → 액셀러레이터

악송구(惡送球) [야구] a wild ball. **악송구하다** throw a wild ball.

악수(握手) a handshake; handshaking. ¶남에게 ~를 청하다 offer one's hand to a person // 여배우는 팬들의 ~ 공세를 받았다 The actress was surrounded by a crowd of fans who wanted to shake hands with her. **악수하다** shake hands (with). ¶두 사람은 악수했다 They shook hands with each other [clasped each other's hands].

악수(惡手) (바둑·장기 등의) (make) a bad move; a wrong move. ¶나는 엄청난 ~를 두었다 I made a disastrous move.

악순환(惡循環) a vicious circle; a vicious spiral. ¶빈곤의 ~ the vicious circle of poverty // 고임금과 고물가의 ~ a vicious circle[spiral] of rising wages and rising prices[wage and price hikes] // ~에 빠지다 be caught[locked] in a vicious circle.

악습(惡習) [나쁜 버릇] a bad habit; [나쁜 풍습] a bad custom; [나쁜 관행] a corrupt practice. ¶뇌물의 ~ the corrupt practice [(영) practise] of bribery // ~이 붙다 fall into[form] a bad habit // (사회의) ~을 일소하다 extirpate evil practices // 나는 이 ~을 버려야겠다 I will get rid[break myself] of the bad habits.

악심(惡心) an evil mind[intention]; a malicious intent; an evil thought[impulse]; a sinister motive. ¶~을 일으키다 be tempted (to do) / yield to temptation // 그는 문득 ~을 일으켜서 도둑질을 하였다 In a moment of temptation he committed theft.

악쓰다 1 [소리치다] shout[bawl] out; yell out (in anger)[protest]. ¶부하 직원[남편]에게 ~ bawl at one's subordinate [husband] // 악쓰면서 울다 shout[yell] in tears // 악써서 목이 쉬다 roar oneself hoarse. 2 [기를 쓰다] try hard; struggle; (미국 구어) go all out. ¶악쓰고 덤비다 tackle with all one's strength.

악어(鰐魚) [동] a crocodile(아프리카산); a gavial(인도산); an alligator(북미산); a cayman(남미산).

악어의 눈물 [위선적인 거짓 눈물] crocodile

tears.
- 악어가죽 crocodile skin[hide]; alligator skin[leather].

악업(惡業) 1 [나쁜 짓] an evil deed; a sin. 2 [불] evil deeds[sins] committed in a former existence; karma. ¶전세의 ~은 피할 수 없다 There is no escape from the karma.

악역(惡役) the role of a villain; a villain's role [part]. ¶상대를 돋보이게 하는 ~을 맡다 serve[act] as a foil (for)//그녀는 ~을 잘한다 She is good at playing the part of social outcasts.//그는 ~을 전문으로 하는 배우다 He specializes in playing villains' roles. / (구어) He always plays the bad guy.
- 악역 배우 a villain[ruffian] actor; the (heavy) villain.

악연(惡緣) [좋지 못한 인연] a bad[an undesirable] relationship; [불행한 결혼] a bad[poor] match; an unsuccessful[unhappy] marriage.

악연실색하다(愕然失色-) turn pale with consternation; be terror-stricken.

악연하다(愕然-) aghast; appalled; amazed; shocked; startled. ¶악연하여 어찌할 바를 모르다 be frightened out of one's wits. **악연히** in surprise[terror / amazement]; amazedly.

악영향(惡影響) a bad[harmful] influence; infection; an adverse [a baleful] effect. ¶~을 미치다 have[(문어) exert / exercise] a bad [baleful] influence (on / upon)//흡연은 주변 사람들의 건강에 ~을 미친다 Smoking affects the health of those around the smoker.

악용(惡用) abuse [əbjúːs]; misuse; an improper use. [신용-[권위]의 ~] an abuse of trust[authority]. **악용하다** abuse [əbjúːz]; make bad use (of); misuse; turn (a thing) to evil account. ¶보험 제도를 ~ abuse the insurance system//경찰 수첩을 ~ make bad use of one's policeman's identification card / use one's policeman's identification card for a bad purpose.

악운(惡運) 1 [악인의 행운]. ¶그는 ~이 센 사람이다 He has the devil's own luck.//그는 ~이 다하여 경찰에 체포되었다 Having come to the end of his luck, he was arrested by the police. 2 [운이 나쁨] bad[ill] luck. ¶요즘 나는 ~의 연속이다 I have had a spell of bad luck these days.//그에게는 ~이 따른다 An evil fate pursues him.

악의(惡意) 1 [나쁜 마음] ill will; [적의] malice. ¶~ 있는 ill-intentioned / malicious //~에 찬 말 malicious words//~가 없는 사람 a man free of malice[ill will]//~를 품다 bear ill will[malice] (toward(s))//그는 반은 ~로 말한 것이다 He said it half in malice.// ~가 있어서 그렇게 말한 것은 아니다 I meant no offense[(영) offence].//그는 ~라곤 조금도 없는 사람이다 He has no (trace of) malice in him. 2 [나쁜 뜻] a bad meaning. ¶그녀는 내 말을 ~로 해석했다 She took what I said amiss.

악의악식(惡衣惡食) poor[coarse] clothing and meager[poor] food. **악의악식하다** be poorly clad and eat meager food; be ill-clad and poorly fed.

악인(惡人) a bad[wicked] man; a villain; an evildoer; a scoundrel; a hoodlum(불량배). ¶ ~은 망하고 선인은 흥한다 The wicked are punished, the good come into their own.

악장(樂長) a bandmaster; a conductor; a music master; a musical director; an orchestra leader.

악장(樂章) [음] a movement (of music); a chapter. ¶제1[제2] ~ the first[second] movement.

악전고투(惡戰苦鬪) a desperate struggle; a tough fight; a hard battle; a close game(경기); a tight match; a close contest(경쟁). ¶우리는 ~ 끝에 겨우 이겼다 We finally won the game after a tough fight. **악전고투하다** fight desperately (against heavy odds); fight with one's back to the wall. ¶선거에서 ~ have a bitter contest in the election against powerful candidates.

악절(樂節) [음] a passage.

악정(惡政) misgovernment; (국왕의) misrule; [실정] maladministration. ¶~에 시달리다 suffer from bad government[misgovernment]//~에 신음하다 groan (and suffer) under misgovernment.

악조건(惡條件) adverse[unfavorable] conditions[factors / circumstances]; bad conditions; a handicap.

악종(惡種) [흉악한 동물·사람] a bad seed; a hoodlum; a villain; a scoundrel; a wicked fellow; a rascal.

악질(惡疾) a malignant[bad / foul / virulent] disease. ¶~에 걸리다 be seized with a malignant disease.

악질(惡質) bad[inferior] quality; evil nature; malignancy; wickedness. ¶~의 vicious / (문어) wicked / bad / coarse / [열등한] inferior / (병의) malignant//~적인 외판원 an unprincipled[unscrupulous] salesman//~의 사기 a vicious[(문어) an unconscionable] fraud//그는 ~의 소문으로 매장되었다 He was ruined by vicious rumors.//적의 ~의 선전 활동을 하고 있다 Our enemies are spreading pernicious[vile] propaganda.
- 악질분자 bad[undesirable] elements; undesirables.

악착같다(齷齪-) be unyielding[stouthearted]; be tough[stubborn]. ¶그녀는 악착같은 여자다 [끈덕지다] She is persistent. / [양보하지 않다] She is unyielding. / [부지런하다] She is a hard-worker. **악착같이** [끈질기게] perseveringly; persistently; [악을 쓰고] desperately; (구어) like hell. ¶그는 ~ 일했다 He worked very hard. / He worked furiously. //그렇게 ~ 공부를 안 해도 될 텐데 You needn't study so madly.

악착스럽다(齷齪-) be unyielding. ⇨악착같다

악처(惡妻) a bad wife; a Xanthippe.

악천후(惡天候) [몹시 나쁜 날씨] foul[bad / poor / unfavorable] weather; [사나운 날씨] rough[stormy / inclement] weather. ¶~를 무릅쓰고 in spite of bad[nasty] weather//~로 인하여 because of bad weather//우리는 ~로 인해서 출발하지 못했다 The inclemency of the weather prevented us from setting out.

악취(惡臭) a bad[foul / nasty] smell; an offensive odor[(영) odour]; a stench; a stink; a malodor. ¶지독한 ~ powerful stink //~ 나는 bad-smelling / stinking//~가 나다 smell bad / give-off a bad smell[a stench] / stink//~를 제거하다 remove a bad smell / drown[destroy] an offensive odor / deodorize//~가 코를 찔렀다 An offensive smell greeted my nose.//그 거리에서는 쓰레기의 ~

악취미
가 났다 The street stank of garbage.// 지독한 ~다 It stinks.// 지하실에서 지독한 ~가 난다 The basement gives off a terrible[an offensive] smell. / The stench from the basement is awful.
악취미(惡趣味) bad[vulgar / cheap] taste; loud taste(복장 등의).
악평(惡評) 〔나쁜 평판〕 a bad reputation; (문어) ill fame; 〔헐뜯는 비평〕 unfavorable[(영) unfavourable] criticism. ¶~이 나 있는 사람 a person with a bad reputation / (문어) a person of ill repute // ~이 자자한 notorious // (신문 등에서) ~을 받다 be criticized unfavorably / be attacked // 그에 대해서는 ~이 끊이지 않는다 He is a constant subject of scandal. **악평하다** speak ill (of); make malicious remarks (about); comment unfavorably (on); talk scandal (about); (신문 등에서) criticize unfavorably[severely]; cut[cry / write] down.
악폐(惡弊) a corrupt[vicious / wrong] practice; an evil; a vice; an abuse. ¶정계의 ~를 제거하다 clean up[out] the corruption in the political world // 우리는 사회의 ~를 일소해야 한다 We must sweep away social abuses.// 그들은 사회의 ~를 바로잡으려고 했다 They tried to reform social abuses.
악풍(惡風) a bad habit[custom]; vicious manners; evil ways[practices]; a vice. ¶~에 물들다 fall into evil ways / pick up bad habits // 도시의 ~에 물들다 be tainted with the vices of the city // 소년들은 사회의 ~에 물들기 쉽다 Boys are easily infected with the evil ways of the world.
악필(惡筆) bad[poor] handwriting; (write) a bad[poor] hand; (알아볼 수 없는) illegible handwriting. ¶그는 ~이다 His handwriting is very poor. / He writes a bad[poor] hand. // 그녀는 정말 ~이다 Her handwriting is terribly awkward. / Her writing is a wretched scrawl.
악하다(惡-) bad; evil; wrong; immoral; sinful; wicked; malicious; villainous; roguish. ¶악한 사람 a wicked man // 악한 짓을 하다 do wrong[evil] / commit a sin[crime] // 그는 착하지도 악하지도 않다 He is quite a mediocrity.
악한(惡漢) a villain; a rascal; a scoundrel; a knave; (구어) a bad guy(▶ 작품 중의 악한인 한 사람인 경우에는 the를 붙임). ¶나도 모르는 사이에 내가 ~이 되어 있었다 Before I knew it, I was being made out to be the villain.
악행(惡行) evildoing; (개개의) an evil deed; a wicked act; a misdeed; a sinful deed. ¶그들은 ~에 ~을 거듭하였다 They retaliated with violence.
악형(惡刑) a cruel[severe] punishment; torture. ¶~을 과하다 punish cruelly[severely] / inflict a severe punishment (on).
악화(惡化) (형세·상태의) a change[turn] for the worse; aggravation; getting worse[more serious]; (품질 등의) deterioration; debasement; [의] ingravescence; (풍속 등의) degeneration; corruption. ¶전황(戰況)의 ~ the aggravation of the war situation // 우리나라의 경제는 ~ 일로를 걷고 있다 Our economy is going steadily downhill.// 병세는 ~의 양상을 나타내고 있다 The condition of the patient threatens to become worse[become more serious / take a turn for the worse]. **악화하다** become[grow] worse; worsen; go from bad to worse; aggravate; deteriorate; be deteriorated; (병이) take a bad[serious] turn; take a turn for the worse; (사태가) grow more serious. ¶감기가 악화하여 폐렴이 되었다 The cold worsened and turned into pneumonia. // 이 증상이 악화하면 암이 될지도 모른다 There is a possibility that this condition may develop into cancer.// 그 병약자의 병세는 다시 악화하여 위독한 상태가 되었다 The invalid took another turn for the worse and went into critical condition again. // 저 점포는 경제적 사정이 상당히 악화하고 있다 The store is not doing as well as it used to. / The store is going downhill.// 사태는 점점 악화하였다 The matter was aggravated. / Matters got worse and worse.// 그들의 부친이 개입해서 사태는 더욱 악화하였다 Because of their father's intervention, the situation was further aggravated.// 그들의 관계가 악화하였다 Their relationship became strained. →¶악화시키나 (상황 등을) make worse / aggravate / (품질 등을) deteriorate // 병을 악화시키다 aggravate an illness // 그는 암이 상당히 악화되어 있었다 His cancer had reached an advanced stage.// 그의 부주의한 발언이 사태를 더욱 악화시켰다 His careless remark made the situation more difficult.// 각자가 제멋대로 하는 바람에 사태를 악화시키고 말았다 Each of them did what he wanted and only succeeded in complicating the situation. / Everyone did as they pleased and the whole thing turned into a mess.
악화(惡貨) bad money; a bad coin.
악화는 양화를 구축한다 Bad money drives out good.
안[1] 〔내부〕 the interior; the inside. ¶~에 [내로] within / inside / inward // 기차 ~의 사람들 the passengers in[on] the train // 배 ~의 사람들 the passengers aboard (ship) // ~방 the inside of the room // 그는 집 ~에서도 들릴 만큼 큰 소리로 불렀다 He called in a voice loud enough to be heard inside the house. // ~에서 기다리자 Let's wait inside [indoors]. // ~으로 들어가도 좋습니까 May I come in? // 우리는 이 방 ~에서 나갈 수 없다 We cannot get out of[leave] this room. // 그들은 모두 역 ~으로 들어갔다 They all went into the station. // 그는 손님을 ~으로[거실로] 맞이였다 He showed the visitor in[into the living room]. // 비가 와서 우리는 ~으로 들어갔다 It began to rain, and so we went inside [indoors]. / 그 문은 ~에서 열리지 않는다 The door doesn't open from the inside.
2 〔때·동안〕. ¶… ~에 〔이내에〕 within / 〔…중에〕 in (the course of) / 〔…까지에〕 before / not later than // 일 주일 ~에 within[in less than / inside of (미)] a week // 수일 ~에 within a few days / in the course of a few days / inside of a few days // 3일 ~에 대답해 주면 좋겠다 I'd like to have your answer within three days.
3 〔한정된 범위 내〕. ¶교통비는 예산 ~에 포함되어 있다[있지 않다] Transportation costs are included in[excluded from] the budget.
4 〔안감〕 a lining. ¶~을 댐 lining / backing(▶ backing은 빈틈없이, lining은 필요한 부분만) // 그 드레스는 ~을 대지 않았다 The dress is not lined[is unlined].

5 [내실] the women's quarters of the house; the main (living) room; a boudoir. ¶어머니는 ~에 계십니다 Mother is in the main room. **6** [아내] a wife (*pl.* wives).

안² not; never; no. ⇨ "아니¹"

안(案) 1 [제안] a proposal; a proposition; a suggestion. ¶~을 내다 make a proposal / advance a suggestion // 송 씨가 그 제도를 폐지하는 게 어떻겠느냐는 ~을 냈다 Mr. Song made a proposal [made a suggestion / proposed / suggested] that the system (should) be abolished. // 조합의 총회에서 한 씨의 ~이 채택되었다 Mr. Han's proposal was adopted at the general meeting of the union.
2 [고안] an idea; a device; a design. ¶~을 짜다 work over [on] one's idea / polish an idea // 어떤 좋은 ~이 있습니까 Have you got a good idea? / Does anyone have a good idea?
3 [계획] a plan; a program; a project; a scheme. ¶~을 세우다 make [draft] a plan / map out a plan / work out a program / plan (for).
4 [의안] a bill. ¶예산~ a budget bill // 정부~ a Government bill // …법 개정~ a bill for amending the ... Act // ~을 제출하다 [통과시키다] submit [pass] a bill.

안간힘 ¶~을 쓰다 hold back an urge / restrain (one's indignation) / strain / struggle / make great [strenuous] efforts // 분을 참느라고 ~을 쓰다 try hard to restrain one's indignation // 사업에 성공하려고 ~을 쓰다 struggle to succeed in business.

안감 lining (material); a cloth for lining. ¶모피 ~이 달린 외투 a fur-lined overcoat // 스커트에 나일론 ~을 대다 line a skirt with nylon // 이 코트에는 실크 ~이 대어져 있다 This coat has a silk lining. / This coat is lined with silk.

안갚음 requital [repayment] of parental love. **안갚음하다** repay [return / requite] one's parents' love; feed one's parents in return.

안개 (a) mist; (짙은) (a) fog; (a) haze. ¶~ 낀 아침 a misty [foggy] morning // 짙은 ~ a dense [thick] fog // ~가 끼다 be hazy [misty] / mist over // 산에는 ~가 끼어 있었다 A haze hung [lay] over the hills. // ~가 끼었다 A fog has set in. // ~가 짙어졌다 The fog has thickened. // ~가 갰다 The mist has cleared (up / off). / The fog has lifted. // 그 도시는 하얀 ~에 덮여 있었다 A white mist lay (thick) over the city.
●**안개비** (a) drizzle; (a) mizzle. ⇨ "가랑비"

안거(安居) a quiet [peaceful / tranquil] life. **안거하다** live quietly; lead a peaceful life.

안건(案件) a matter; a case; an item; [의안] a bill. ¶중요 ~ an important matter / a matter of importance [significance] // 회의의 중요 ~ the important items on the agenda // 교수 회의에 ~을 상정하다 submit a matter to the faculty meeting for consideration.

안경(眼鏡) (a pair of) glasses; (격식) spectacles; (구어) specs; [강풍·먼지·광선을 막는 보호 안경] goggles. ¶코~ nose glasses // 근시 [원시] ~ (미) glasses for a nearsighted [farsighted] person / (영) glasses for a shortsighted [longsighted] person // 금테 ~ gold-rimmed spectacles // 볼록 렌즈 bull's-eye glasses // 외알 ~ an eyeglass / a monocle // 색 ~ sunglasses // 테 없는 ~ rimless glasses [spectacles] // 도수가 센 [약한] ~ strong [weak] glasses // ~을 쓴 남자 a man in glasses [spectacles] // ~ 너머로 over [from above] one's spectacles / over the edges [rims / tops] of one's spectacles // ~을 쓰고 있다 wear glasses // ~의 도수가 내 눈에 맞지 않는다 The lenses of these glasses are not of the right strength for my eyes. // 그는 ~ 너머로 나를 보았다 He looked at me over the top of his glasses.
●**안경다리** (미) the bows [temples] of a pair of spectacles; (영) the sides of a pair of spectacles. **안경알** a spectacle lens. **안경점** an optician's (shop). **안경집** a spectacle case. **안경테** the rim [frame] of a pair of spectacles.

안계(眼界) the range [field / radius] of vision; sight; view; the visual field; prospect; the sweep [reach] of the eye. ¶~에 들어오다 come in (one's) sight / appear [come] in sight / break [burst] upon one's view / (경치가) spread before one // ~ 내[외]에 있다 be within [beyond] the field of vision // ~가 넓다 [좁다] have a wide [narrow] field of view / have a wide [narrow] mental horizon // ~에서 사라지다 vanish (out of sight) / get [go / pass] out of sight / disappear (from view).

안고나다 take (a person's fault / responsibility) upon oneself; be charged with (a duty). ¶네가 손해보면 내가 안고나겠다 I'll answer for your possible losses. // 내각에 대한 비난을 그가 전부 안고났다 He took upon himself the criticism levelled at the cabinet.

안공(眼孔) an eyehole. ⇨ "눈구멍"

안과(眼科) [의] ophthalmology; (병원의) the department of ophthalmology.
●**안과 병원** ophthalmic hospital; the eye doctor's; an ophthalmological clinic. **안과 의사** an ophthalmologist; an oculist; an eye doctor [specialist].

안광(眼光) [눈의 정기] the glitter of one's eyes; [통찰력] penetration; discernment; insight; power of observation. ¶~이 형형하여 with one's eyes glaring // ~이 날카롭다 be sharp-eyed / have piercing [penetrating] eyes.

안구(眼球) an eyeball. = 눈알
●**안구 건조증** xerophthalmia. **안구은행** an eye bank.

안구(鞍具) saddlery; saddle gear; horse gear; harness.

안기다¹ [안음을 당하다] go [move] into (a person's) arms; throw oneself in (a person's) arms; be embraced; be in (a person's) arms. ¶엄마 품에 안겨 있는 어린애 an infant nestling in its mother's bosom // 자연의 품에 ~ be (nestled) in the bosom of nature // 아기는 엄마 품에 안겨 자고 있었다 The baby is sleeping in its mother's arms. // 소녀는 아버지에게 안겼다 The girl threw herself into her father's arms. / The girl clung to her father.

안기다² **1** [안게 하다] make (a person) hold [take / carry] (someone) in his arms; make (a person) embrace [hug]. ¶어머니에게 아기를 ~ put the baby in its mother's breast [bosom].
2 [책임 등을] charge (a person with responsibility); lay (a duty on a person); put (the

안내
responsibility for something) on (a person); entrust (a person with a task). ¶친구에게 책임을 ~ give a friend the responsibility // 빚을 ~ hold (a person) liable for the debt.
3 [상품을 떠맡기다] force[press] (a person) to buy (the wares); force (a sale) on; intrude on; tout; (가짜를) pass[palm] off (a thing upon a person); foist[impose] (a thing upon a person). ¶나쁜 물건을 ~ palm [impose] a bad article upon (a person).
4 [알을 품게 하다] make (a hen) sit on (eggs); set (a hen) on (eggs). ¶닭에게 알을 ~ set the hen (on the eggs).
5 [치다] lodge a blow; give[deal / deliver] (a person) a blow. ¶주먹을 한 대 ~ give (a person) a punch[clout] (on the head).
6 [기타]. ¶선물을 ~ press gifts on (a person) / 물벼락을 ~ pour[throw] water upon [over] (a person).

안내(案內) [인도] guidance; conduct; lead; [청해 들임] showing in; [통지] notice; [초대] invitation. ¶~가 있는[없는] 여행 a conducted[an unconducted] tour / **개점** ~ an announcement of the opening of a store // 남의 ~로 under the guidance of a person / accompanied by a person // 손님들은 점원의 ~로 불타는 백화점을 탈출했다 The shoppers escaped from the burning department store under the guidance of[conducted by / led by] the clerks. // 내가 그의 ~를 맡았다 I acted as his guide. / I showed [guided] him around. // 나는 입구에서 ~를 청했다 I requested[asked for] admittance at the entrance. / I announced myself at the entrance. **안내하다** [관광객 등의 길 안내를 하다] guide; [선도하다] lead; (방 등에) show; (좌석 등에) usher; [초대하다] invite; ask; [통지하다] notify[inform] (a person of / that ...). ¶관광객을 안내하여 읍을 돌다 guide tourists around town // 역까지 안내하겠다 I will show you the way to the station. / I will take you to the station. // 그는 우리를 내전으로 안내하였다 He conducted[guided] us to the inner palace. // 그는 서울 시내를 두루 안내해 주었다 He took me around Seoul. // 손님을 101호실로 안내해라 Show the gentleman to Room 101. // 좌석으로 안내해 주십시오 (극장 등에서) Please usher me to my seat. ➔나는 내실로 안내되었다 I was ushered[shown] into a back room. // 우리는 응접실로 안내되었다 We were shown[ushered] into the parlor.
● **안내서** a guidebook; a roadbook; a handbook; a guide. **안내소** an inquiry office; an information bureau. ¶**여행** ~ a tourist bureau. **안내원** a guide; (호텔 등의) a clerk at the information desk; a desk clerk; (극장 등의) an usher(ette); a theater attendant [guide]. **안내자 / 안내인** (관광객의) a guide; a tour conductor; (영) a courier; (극장 등의) an usher; a cicerone(관광 명소의). **안내장** a letter[note] of invitation; an invitation (card / note); [경] an advice; an advice note.

안녕(安寧) **1** [안전하고 태평함] (public) peace; tranquility; [복지] welfare; well-being. ¶사회의 ~을 지키다 maintain peace and order in a society / maintain social stability // 사회의 ~을 어지럽히다 disturb the tranquility[stability] of a society. **2** [작별 인사] good-by(e); (I'll) see you again[later];

(구어) by(e) (now); (구어) so long; (특히 어린애가) bye-bye; (문어) farewell. ¶「~!」이라고 인사하다 say good-bye (to) / bid a person good-bye // **여러분** ~ Good-bye, boys and girls. // 내주까지 ~ Good-bye till next week. / See you next week. // 한국이여, ~ Farewell to Korea.

안녕하다(安寧-) **1** [평안하다] peaceful; calm; uneventful; [건강하다] healthy; in good health; hale and hearty(노인 등이); (서술적) be (quite) well; be doing well. ¶"어머님께서는 안녕하시냐?" "예, 안녕하십니다." "How is your mother?" "Thank you, she is fine." **안녕히** well; nicely; in peace. ¶~ 지내다 live in peace.
2 [인사]. ¶안녕하세요 How are you? / How's is going? / How're you doing? / How's everything going? / Hi! / (오전 중에) Good morning! / (오후에) Good afternoon! / (친한 사이에, 오전·오후 관계없이) Hello! / 안녕하셨습니까 How have you been? **안녕히** ~ 가십시오 (헤어질 때) Goodby(e). / Look after yourself. / Take care! / Good luck! / (뱃길을 떠나는 사람에게) Bon voyage! / (퇴근할 때 동료에게) Good night. / See you tomorrow.

안노인(-老人) the old mistress of a household[family].

안다 1 [껴안다] hold[take / carry] (a person) in one's arms; [포옹하다] embrace; hug; give (a person) a hug; cuddle. ¶아기를 품에 ~ embrace a baby / hug a child // 안아 일으키다 lift up (a person) / help (a person) get to his feet / (자고 있는 사람을) help (a person) sit up in bed // 아기를 안고 자다 sleep[lie] with a baby in one's arms // 끌어~ draw (a person) closer to one's breast / clasp (a person) in one's arms // 두 팔로 ~ hold a thing in one's arms // 그녀는 인형을 안고 있었다 She was holding[had] a doll in her arms. // 안아 줘요 Give me a hug [squeeze].
2 [맞받다] meet; confront. ¶바람을 안고 서다 stand breasting the wind.
3 [입다] suffer; sustain; incur; receive. ¶손해를 ~ suffer[receive] damage / suffer [sustain] a loss.
4 [떠맡다] undertake (another's responsibility); bear[assume / shoulder] (the responsibility for[of]); hold oneself responsible for; answer for. ¶빚을 ~ hold oneself liable for a debt / shoulder another's debt(남의 빚을).
5 [알을 품다] sit[brood] (on eggs); set. ¶암탉이 알을 안았다 A hen set on her eggs.
6 [마음에 품다] hold; have; bear. ¶희망을 ~ cherish[entertain] a hope.

안단테 [음] andante.

안달 fret; fuss; impatience; (구어) stew. ¶~이 나서 impatiently // ~**이 나다** grow impatient // ~ 나게 하다 irritate / make (a person) feel impatient / keep (a person) on tenterhooks // 아이들을 ~ 나게 만들다 tease children // 나는 그새 줄곤 ~이 났었다 I fretted the whole time. // 나는 빨리 보고 싶어서 ~이 났다 I am impatient to see it. / I can hardly wait to see it. // 그는 ~이 나서 견딜 수가 없었다 He was very nervous. / He couldn't sit still. **안달하다** be impatient (to do / for); be nervous (about); fret (about); worry (oneself) (about); be overanxious; be in the fidgets[a fidget]; (구어) stew (over /

안벽

about); be in a stew (about). ¶그는 하찮은 일에 안달한다 He fusses over trifles [about little things]. // 안달하지 말고 가만히 앉아 있어요 Sit still, and don't fidget. // 그녀는 고향에 가고 싶어 안달하고 있었다 She was dying to go home.

안대(眼帶) an eye bandage; a patch over the eye. ¶~를 하다 have a bandage [patch] over one's eye.

안도(安堵) relief; reassurance. ¶~의 한숨을 쉬다 heave a sigh of relief / feel greatly relieved / breathe again freely // ~의 가슴을 쓸어내리다 heave a sigh of relief. **안도하다** feel relieved [reassured]; feel at ease; set one's mind at rest; breathe again. ¶우리는 그의 약속에 안도했다 We were relieved by his promise. / His promise reassured us. // 살인범이 잡혔다는 소식을 듣고 나는 크게 안도했다 I felt greatly relieved when I heard that the murderer had been arrested.
● **안도감** (a sense of) security; a relieved feeling; a feeling of relief. ¶네가 옆에 있어 주면 ~이 생긴다 I feel secure in your presence.

안되다 1 [유감이다] regrettable; sympathize (with); be [feel] sorry (for / to hear that …); be a pity; have [take] pity (on); feel pity (for). ¶안된 이야기지만 to my regret / I regret to say that … // 안됐다는 듯이 sympathetically // 바깥양반께서 많이 편찮으시다니 정말 안됐습니다 I am so sorry to hear that your husband is so ill. // 참 안됐습니다 I'm so sorry.(▶ 본인을 보고 You are pitiful.이라고는 하지 않음) // 그가 불행을 당해서 참 안됐다 I feel sorry for his misfortune. // 참 안됐지만 그 수에는 안 넘어갈 거야 (구어) Too bad [(미)] Tough luck! I won't fall for that! // 정말 안됐습니다 I deeply sympathize with you [your feelings]. // 그 프로를 못 보게 되다니 안됐구나 It's a pity you can't watch the program.
2 [일 등이 좋게 이루어지지 않다] 〔서술적〕 be a failure; be unsuccessful; fail. ¶일이 ~ one's work is not done / fail in one's attempt // 그는 손대는 일마다 안된다 Everything he puts his hand to proves a failure.

안되면 조상 탓(속담) A fool blames others if something goes wrong for him.

안뜰 a courtyard; a[an inner] court; an inner garden; (사각형의) a quadrangle; 《구어》 a quad.

안락사(安樂死) (artificial) euthanasia; mercy-killing; an easy death.

안락의자(安樂椅子) an easy chair; a club chair; an armchair; a grandfather('s) chair.

안락하다(安樂-) comfortable; easy; cozy. ¶안락한 생활을 easy [a carefree] life / a comfortable living // 안락하게 comfortably / in (ease and) comfort // 안락하게 살다 live in (ease and) comfort // 안락한 생활을 / live in easy circumstances(부유하게) / live comfortably / make a comfortable living / live at one's ease / live on a bed of down [roses / flowers] // 그는 안락한 생활을 하였다 He lived in ease and comfort.

안력(眼力) insight; penetration; power of observation; [시력] eyesight.

안료(顔料) 1 [화장품] cosmetics; a face paint.
2 [도료] a color; a paint; [색소] a pigment.

안마(按摩) massage; shampoo(ing). **안마하다**

(남을) massage; give a massage (to); (남을 시켜서) have a massage; have oneself massaged. ¶어깨를 안마하게 하다 have one's shoulders massaged.
● **안마기** a kneader. **안마사** a massager; a masseur(남자); a masseuse(여자); a rubber.

안마(鞍馬) [기계 체조의 도구] 〔영〕 a side horse; 〔영〕 a pommel horse; [남자 체조 경기 종목] the side horse; the pommel horse.

안마당 a courtyard. ⇨ ˚안뜰

안면(安眠) [편안히 잠을 자는 것] a sound [good / quiet / restful] sleep; a peaceful slumber; a comfortable sleep. ¶~을 방해하다 disturb a person's (quiet) sleep. **안면하다** sleep soundly [well / quietly]; have a quiet [sound / good] sleep; have a good night's rest; sleep in peace.
● **안면방해** disturbance of sleep; nuisance at night. ¶~가 되니 라디오를 꺼 다오 Turn off the radio. It disturbs our sleep.

안면(顔面) 1 a face. ⇨ ˚얼굴¹ 2 [친분] acquaintance. ¶~이 있는 사람 an acquaintance / a person one knows by sight // ~이 있다 be (personally) acquainted (with) / know (a person) by sight // ~이 없다 have no personal acquaintance (with) / do not know (a person) by sight / be a stranger // ~ 박대하다 slight (an acquaintance) / treat meanly // 그와는 ~이 있다 I am acquainted with him. // 나는 그와는 ~은 있으나 아직 이야기는 못해 봤다 I know him by sight, but I have never spoken to him. // 그와는 전혀 ~이 없다 He is a complete [total] stranger to me.
● **안면 경련** facial tics [spasm]. **안면부지**(-不知) [얼굴을 모름 또는 그 사람]. ¶~의 인물 an utter [a total / a perfect] stranger / a man whom one has never met. **안면 신경 마비** [의] facial paralysis.

안목(眼目) an appreciative eye; a discerning [critical] eye; discernment; (a sense of) discrimination; judgment; penetration; insight. ¶전문가의 ~ an expert('s) eye / a professional eye // ~이 있다 have an eye [a discerning eye] (for old works of art) // 사물을 보는 ~이 있다 have the seeing eye // 골동품에 대한 ~이 있다 have an eye [be connoisseur] for curios / be a judge of old art objects // ~이 높다 have a critical [an expert] eye / be a good judge (of) / be sharp-eyed // 예술에 대한 ~을 기르다 train [develop] artistic judgment [discrimination] // 긴 ~으로 보다 take a long (range) view (of) // 그는 조각에 대해서 전문가의 ~이 있다 He has an expert's eye for sculpture.

안무(按舞) the arrangement of a dance; dance composition; choreography. **안무하다** design the postures; arrange a dance; choreograph; undertake [compose] the choreography (of).
● **안무가** a choreographer; a dance director [composer].

안문(-門) an inner door [window].

안방(-房) an anbang; the main room.

안배(按排·按配) [배치] arrangement; disposition; [배분] distribution; assignment. **안배하다** arrange; distribute; assign. ¶역할을 ~ distribute parts (to / among) / assign duties (to).

안벽(-壁) [건] the inside of the wall.

안벽(岸壁) **1** (항만·운하의) a quay (wall); a wharf(부두); a jetty(방파제). ¶배를 ~에 대다 bring[moor] (a steamer) alongside the quay. **2** [물가의 벼랑] a bluff; palisades.

안보(安保) security. ¶집단[총력] ~ collective [all-out] security // 국가의 ~ 문제 national security problems // 물샐틈없는 ~ 태세 water-tight security posture.
● **안보 외교** diplomacy for national security.

안부(安否) [무사 여부] safety; [지내는 형편] how (a person) is; (a person's) welfare; [문안] an inquiry; [문안 인사] regards; wishes. ¶~를 묻다 inquire[ask] after a person[a person's health] // (조난 시에) ~ 를 염려하다 be concerned about a person's safety // ~를 알리다 let (a person) know how one is // 그들은 행방불명자의 ~를 염려했다 They are concerned about the safety of the people who are missing. / They are worried about what has happened to the people who are missing. // 나는 그에게 ~를 묻는 전보를 쳤다 I sent him a telegram inquiring after his safety. // 아들에게 편지로 ~를 물었다 I wrote (to) my son to ask how he was doing[ask if he was all right]. // 우선 부모님께 ~를 알리시오 You had better first let your parents know that you are safe. // 그녀에게 ~ 전해 주십시오 Please give her my best regards. // 자당님께 ~ 전해 주십시오 Please send your mother my best wishes. / Kindly remember me to your mother. // 아드님에게 부디 ~ 전해 주시오 Please say hello to your son for me. / Please give my best regards to your son. // 댁의 여러분에게 ~ 전해 주십시오 Please remember me to all your family. / (편지의 끝맺는 말) With kind regards to all. **안부하다** inquire after (a person's) welfare; pay one's respects to (a person).

안분(按分) proportional division. **안분하다** divide[distribute] proportionally (among).

안빈낙도(安貧樂道) contentment with poverty and delight in the (Taoist) Way. **안빈낙도하다** be content with poverty and delight in the (Taoist) Way.

안사돈(─査頓) a son's[daughter's] mother-in-law; a son-[daughter-]in-law's mother.

안사람 my wife.

안살림(─살이) household[home] management; housekeeping.

안색(顔色) complexion; colo(u)r. ⇨얼굴빛(⇨얼굴)

안성맞춤(安城─) ¶~의 suitable (for) / adapted (for / to) / fit (for) / ideal / the very / right / just / ~의 날씨 ideal weather (for) // ~의 것[사람] the very thing[man] wanted / the right thing[man] (for) / just the thing [man] (for) / 캠핑에 ~인 장소 an ideal place for camping // 이것은 ~이다 This is the thing I wanted[wished for]. / This is exactly what I have been wanting[need]. / This will suit my needs[me] to a T. // 그 자리는 그에게 ~이다 The post is most suitable[just right] for him. / He is the very person to fill the post. / The post was made for him. // 테니스 하기에는 ~의 날씨다 It is ideal[perfect] weather for tennis. // 그는 이 중요한 역에 ~이다 He is just the right man for this important role. // 이곳은 ~의 은신처이다 This is just the place for hiding. // 이것은 네게 ~인 일이다 This is the perfect[very] job for you. / (구어) This job fits you to a tee. // 그 빈 터는 아이들이 놀기에 ~이었다 The empty lot was an ideal place for the children to play. // 그곳은 천막을 치기에 ~인 곳이었다 It was an ideal[excellent] place to pitch a tent.

안섶 [두루마기나 저고리의 안으로 들어간 섶] the turned-in collar of a Korean jacket.

안손님 a woman caller; a lady visitor; a guest of one's wife.

안수(按手) [기] the imposition of hands; the laying on of hands. **안수하다** impose[lay] hands on (a person); confirm (a person).

안쓰럽다 →안쓰리다

안식(安息) rest; repose. **안식하다** rest; repose.
● **안식교** the Seventh-Day Adventist Church. **안식일** the Sabbath; a Sabbath day; the Lord's day; Sunday. **안식처** a place to find peace; a place to rest; a resting place; a refuge; a shelter; an asylum; a (safe) haven.

안식(眼識) [안목과 식견] discernment; insight; penetration; a critical [discerning] eye; discrimination. ¶전문가의 ~ an expert's eye // ~이 있는 사람 a discerning [keen-eyed] person / a man of insight // ~이 있다 have a discerning eye // 그것은 시인의 ~이 필요하다 It needs a poet's eye.

안식구(─食口) **1** [여자 식구] the female member of a family. **2** my wife. ⇨안사람

안식향(安息香) **1** [식] a benzoin. **2** [화] benzoin; gum benjamin [benjoin].

안심 [소의 갈비 안쪽 고기] lean beef ribs.

안심(安心) [근심이 없음] peace of mind; freedom from care [anxiety]; [안도감] (a sense of) relief; [안전] (a sense of) security; safety; assurance; reassurance. ¶~이 되다 feel relief / be reassured // ~이 안 되다 feel uneasy (about) / be anxious (about) / fear // 환자는 이제 ~입니다 The patient is out of danger. // 그가 그렇게 말하니까 ~이 된다 I am reassured by his saying so. // 그 사람이라면 무슨 일을 맡겨도 ~이다 He can be trusted to do anything. // 일이 이만큼 진행되었으니 이제 ~이다 Now that such progress is made on the work, we can take things easy. // 이만치 도망쳤으니 이제 ~이다 We've fled this far, so we should be safe now. // 그가 혼자 강에 가서 ~이 안 된다 I am a little worried about his having gone to the river all alone. **안심하다** feel easy (about); feel at rest [ease]; [마음을 놓다] feel [be] relieved (about); relax; [안전하다고 여기다] feel reassured; be [rest] assured; be confident (of). ¶안심하고 [근심 없이] feeling at rest / without anxiety / free from fear [care / anxiety] / [안도하여] with a sense of relief / [안전하다고 느끼고] with a sense of security // 안심할 수 없는 병세 a serious [dangerous / critical] condition // 안심할 수 있는[없는] 사람 a reliable [an unreliable] person // 그 말을 듣고 안심했다 I am relieved to hear that. // 춘부장께서 건강하시다는 말씀을 듣고 안심했습니다 I was relieved to learn that your father is well. // 그 점은 안심하십시오 Put [Set] your mind at rest [ease] about that [on that score]. // 안심하고 그자를 믿을 수는 없다 We cannot safely unbend with him. // 사건이 해결되어 모두 크게 안심했다 The matter has been settled to the great relief of everybody. // 고비를 넘겼으니 안심해라 I can assure you that the worst is over. // 안심하고 시험을 치러

라 You may take your examination with confidence. →¶**안심시키다** set (a person) at ease / ease (a person's) mind / relieve (a person) of his anxiety.

안심부름 [집안 부녀자의 심부름] errands around the house; household chores; a woman's errand.

안심찮다(安心-) **1** [안심이 안 되다] unsafe; uneasy; uncertain; apprehensive; not sure; [믿을 수 없다] unreliable; precarious; insecure. ¶안심찮은 친구 a not very reliable friend // 안심찮은 듯이 anxiously / apprehensively // 안심찮아 보이다 look anxious // 안심찮게 여기다 feel uneasy / be anxious (about) / be uncertain (over) / have misgivings (about) / be in suspense. **2** [꺼림하다] be sorry.

안쓰럽다 (서술적) be sorry for troubling someone who is worse off than oneself.

안아맡다 [남의 일을 맡아 책임지다] bear [assume / accept / shoulder / undertake (another's responsibility); take upon oneself; take (a matter) in one's hand; take charge of; answer [hold oneself responsible] for. ¶남의 빚을 ~ shoulder another's debt.

안약(眼藥) eyewash; (an) eye lotion; eyewater; medicine for the eyes; an eye salve; eye drops. ¶~을 넣다 apply eye lotion / drop some eye lotion into one's eyes.

안어울림음(-音) [음] a dissonance; a discord. ¶~의 dissonant.

안염(眼炎) [의] ophthalmia; ophthalmitis; inflammation of the eyes.

안온하다(安穩-) peaceful and quiet; tranquil; calm. ¶안온한 생활 a placid life // 안온한 세상 peaceful[tranquil] times. **안온히** peacefully; in peace; quietly; tranquilly. ¶~ 살다 live in peace // 집에서 ~ 살다 remain quietly at home.

안울림소리 [언] a voiceless[an unvoiced] sound.

안위(安危) safety (or danger); fate; destiny; welfare. ¶국가의 ~ a national crisis // 국가의 ~에 관한 중대 문제 a matter of vital importance to the destiny of the nation // 이 정책은 국가의 ~에 관계된다 This policy concerns [is vital to] the destiny of our nation.

안이하다(安易-) easy; easygoing. ¶안이한 생활 an easy life // 안이한 생각 an easygoing[a happy-go-lucky] way of thinking // 안이한 생활을 하다 live an easygoing life // 안이하게 easily / [태평하게] at ease / at one's ease // 안이하게 생각하다 take things easy // 그렇게 안이하게 생각해서는 안 된다 You must take it more seriously.

안일 housework; women's work.

안일(安逸) (idle) ease; idleness; indolence; sloth. ¶무사 ~주의 a peace-at-any-price // ~에 빠지다 live in idleness / lead an idle life / pass one's days in indolence / idle away one's time / eat the bread of idleness. **안일하다** idle; indolent. ¶안일한 생활 a life of (idle) ease // 안일하게 살아가다 lead an idle life / live in idleness.

안장(安葬) [편안하게 장사 지내는 것] burial; interment. **안장하다** bury; inter; lay (a person's body) to rest; entomb; commit to the earth [ground / grave]. →¶**안장되어 있다** be buried (at) / lie beneath a grave.
●**안장지** a burial[burying] ground.

안장(鞍裝) a saddle. ¶~을 얹다[내리다] saddle (up) [unsaddle] (a horse) / put a saddle on [take a saddle off] (a horse) // 말을 ~을 얹지 않고 타다 ride bareback.

안전(安全) safety; security; freedom from danger. ¶~을 위해 for safety's sake // 생명과 재산의 ~ security of life and property // 작업의 ~ safety in work operations // 일신의 ~을 도모하다 look to one's own safety // ~을 위협하다 threaten the security (of) // ~을 유지하다 maintain the safety // 교통의 ~을 위협하다 endanger safe traffic // 집안의 ~을 빌다 offer prayers for peace and prosperity to the family // ~을 위하여 그것을 은행에 맡겨라 For the sake of safety, deposit it in the bank. // 보행자의 ~을 우선으로 해야 한다 We must give priority to the safety of pedestrians. **안전하다** safe; secure; free from danger. ¶안전한 장소 a place[zone] of safety // 안전한 투자 a sound investment // 안전한 은신처 a secure hiding place // 안전한 장사 a safe [sound] trade // 안전한 장소에 두다 keep (a thing) out of harm's way // 안전한 곳에 아이들을 피난시키다 shelter children in a safe place // 이젠 [여기는] ~ We are safe [free from danger] now[here]. // 모양은 안 좋지만 안전한 차다 It may not look smart, but it is a very reliable car. // 이만큼 떼어 놓았으니 이제 ~ We have a safe lead now. // 이 집은 지진에도 안전합니다 This house is safe from earthquakes [is earthquake-proof]. // 서류는 화재가 나도 안전한 곳에 보관되어 있다 We keep the documents in a place safe from fire. **안전히** safely; in safety; securely. ¶~ 하다 [모험을 하지 않다] play it safe.
●**안전 관리** safety supervision. **안전교육** safety education. **안전등**(-燈) (광산용의) a safety lamp; (항공기의) a blaze orange. **안전벨트 / 안전띠** a safety belt; a safety band; (좌석의) a seat belt. ¶~를 매어 주십시오 Please fasten your seat belt. / Please wear your seat belt. / Buckle up, please. **안전 보장** security. ¶집단 ~ collective security // 국가 ~ 회의 (미국의) the National Security Council. **안전 보장 이사회** (유엔의) the Security Council. **안전장치** a safety device [appliance]; a safety gear; (총·엘리베이터 등의) a safety; a safety catch; safety lock. ¶~를 한 총 a gun with the safety catch on // (총의) ~를 풀다 slip [release] the safety catch // 기계에 ~를 달다 install a safety device on a machine / provide a machine with a safety device. **안전 제일** safety first. **안전지대** a safety zone [island]; (도로의) a safety island [isle]; a street [traffic / pedestrian] island; an island. **안전핀** a safety pin.

안전(眼前) ⇨눈앞.

안절부절못하다 be [grow] restless; be fidgety; be nervous; be impatient; get [have] the fidgets; jitter; be on pins and needles. ¶안절부절못하는 사람 a restless person / a fidgety person / a fidget // 안절부절못하여 restlessly / uneasily / impatiently / nervously / in a restless manner / in a fidget // 안절부절못하게 하다 fidget / give (a person) the fidgets / make (a person) nervous / give (a person) the jitters // 그녀는 안절부절못하고 있었다 She was in a fidget. // 그는 아침부터 안절부절못하고 있다 He's been restless [fidgety] since this morning. // 하루 종일 나는 안절부절못하

머 지냈다 I spent the whole day in a state of nervous excitement. // 그녀는 아들의 도착이 기다려져서 안절부절못하고 있다 She is so impatient for her son's arrival that she can't sit still. // 오늘 그 결과를 알게 된다고 생각하니 안절부절못하겠다 I can't help being on tenterhooks when I think that I'll find out the results today.

안정 (安定) stability; stabilization; steadiness; [균형] equilibrium; balance; [침체] settlement; composure. ¶물가[경제/통화]의 ~ price [economic / currency] stabilization // 생활의 ~ the stabilization [stability] of livelihood // ~ 속에 발전을 바라는 대다수의 국민 the majority of the people in wish of progress amid stability // ~을 잃다 lose equilibrium [balance / stability] // 생활의 ~을 얻다 secure one's livelihood / find a sure means of living // 우선 생활의 ~을 꾀하지 않으면 안 되겠다 First of all I must secure a steady income. // 현 정부하에서는 민심의 ~을 기대할 수 없다 Under the present government the people can have no peace of mind. **안정하다** be stabilized; become stable; balance; settle; be settled. →¶안정된 사회 a stable society // 안정된 마음 a well-balanced mind // 안정되어 있다 be stable / be steady / be in equilibrium / be well-balanced / be settled / be at rest // 안정되지 않다 be unstable [unsettled] / lack stability // 안정시키다 stabilize / equilibrate / balance / put at rest / settle // 민심을 안정시키다 put the people's mind at rest // 정국은 안정되어 있다 The political situation is stable. // 소비자 물가가 지금은 안정되어 있다 Consumer prices are now holding steady.
● **안정감** a sense of security. ¶~이 있는 stable / secure / well-balanced / ~이 없는 unstable / insecure / shaky / unsettled. **안정도** stability. **안정 성장** [경] a stabilized [stable] growth. **안정 세력** a stabilizing force; a steadying influence.

안정 (安靜) rest; quiet; repose. ¶절대 ~ absolute [complete / thorough] rest [quiet] // 의사는 절대 ~을 명했다 The doctor ordered complete bed rest. **안정하다** tranquil; quiet; peaceful. ¶안정하고 있다 lie [rest] quietly in bed / keep quiet. →¶안정시키다 set at ease / quiet / relieve.

안정 (眼睛) the pupil (of the eye). ⇨눈동자

안존하다 (安存―) [얌전하고 조용하다] quiet and gentle; genial; docile; [편안히 있다] be at peace.

안주 (安住) living in peace; peaceful living; a serene life; a comfortable life. **안주하다** live in peace; lead a comfortable life [peaceful living]. ¶안주할 땅 a place where one can live in peace // 안주할 땅을 찾다 seek a place for peaceful living // 현상(現狀)에 ~ be content with the status quo // 그는 불교에서 안주할 곳을 찾았다 He sought peace in Buddhism. // 그는 사장 자리에 안주하고 있다 He is enjoying the comfort of the company president's chair. / He has settled down comfortably into the post of company president.

안주 (按酒) a relish (taken with wine). ⇨술 안주 ¶술과 ~ wine and some eatables // ~는 무엇이 있습니까 What eatables do you have with your wine? / What are the cocktail dishes? / What is the appetizer? // ~는 별로 없지만 많이 드십시오 I'm sorry I don't have much to go with it, but please drink heartily.
● **안줏감** hors d'oeuvres makings.

안주머니 an inside (breast) pocket (of the coat); an inner pocket. ¶~에 넣어 두다 keep (a thing) in one of one's inside pockets // 나는 ~에 그의 명함을 넣었다 I put his card in my inner pocket.

안주인 (―主人) [주부] a mistress; the lady of the house; (여관·하숙의) a landlady; a hostess; (가게의) a proprietress.

안중 (眼中) ¶~에 in one's eyes // ~에 없다 leave (a person / a thing) out of account [consideration] / not pay (a person / a thing) any mind / take no account [notice] (of) / think nothing (of) / disregard / ignore / set (a person / a thing) at naught // 자기 이외에는 ~에 없다 think of none but oneself // 남들이 어떻게 생각하는가는 그의 ~에 없었다 He paid no attention to [totally ignored / disregarded] what other people would think. // 그는 마치 ~에 아무도 없다는 태도다 He behaves as if he thinks of nobody but himself [he is the only one that counts]. // 그런 녀석은 ~에 없다 He is beneath my notice. // 저런 여드름투성이 아이는 ~에도 없어 I couldn't careless about a pimply boy like that.

안질 (眼疾) an eye disease. ⇨눈병

안집 [안채] the inner building; the main building (of a house).

안짝 [나이나 거리가 일정한 기준에 미치지 못한 범위] within; inside a limit; less [not more] than; not exceeding. ¶천 원 ~의 금액 a sum not exceeding a thousand won // 팔십만 원 ~의 수입 an income short of eight hundred thousand won // 1마일 ~ a short mile / a distance short of a mile // 그녀는 나이가 기껏해야 20세 ~이다 She is twenty at the most. // 우리 학교는 역에서 50미터 ~에 있다 Our school is situated within fifty meters of the station.

안짱다리 [두 발끝이 안쪽으로 향한 다리] varus; [그런 다리를 가진 사람] a pigeon-toed [knock-kneed] person. ¶~의 knock-kneed / pigeon-toed // ~로 걷다 walk pigeon-toed [in toed] / pigeon-toe // 그녀는 ~로 걷는 버릇이 있다 She has way of walking pigeon-toed [with her toes pointed inward].

안쪽 the inside; the interior; the inner part; the back. ¶~의 inside / inner / interior // ~에 (on the) inside / within / inward // ~에서 from within / on the inside // ~에서 열다 open (a door) from within // ~에서 잠그다 lock [fasten] (a door) from [on] the inside / lock (a door) from within // 트랙의 ~ 코스를 달리다 have the inside track // 병의 ~을 깨끗이 해라 Clean the inside of the bottle. // 문은 ~으로 열립니다 The door opens inward(s) [to the inside]. // 문은 ~에서 잠겨 있었다 The gate was locked from the inside.

안차다 [겁이 없고 깜찍하다] fearless; dauntless; intrepid; daring. ¶안찬 사람 a bold person.

안착 (安着) safe arrival; (물품의) safe receipt. ¶~을 알리다 inform (a person) of one's safe arrival. **안착하다** (사람이) arrive safe [safely / in safety]; reach (London) safe and sound;

안장 a shoe liner; an inner sole. ¶~을 갈다 put liners in shoes.
안채 an *anchae*; the main building (of a house); the inner house.
안출(案出) 〔생각하여 내는 것〕 contrivance; invention. **안출하다** 〔문어〕 contrive; devise; originate; invent; design; 〔구어〕 think[work / strike / hammer] out; study out. ¶일책(一策)을 ~ think[work] out a plan.
● **안출자** a contriver; an originator.
안치(安置) **1** 〔모셔 둠〕 installation; enshrinement. **안치하다** install; enshrine; (관 등을) lay in state. ¶절의 본당에 불상을 ~ enshrine[install] a Buddhist image in the main hall of a temple. ➔ 유해는 일단 강당에 안치되었다 The corpse was temporarily laid in state in the lecture hall (of the temple). **2** 〔귀양 간 죄인을 가두어 두는 것〕. **안치하다** enclose[confine] (a banished offender) in.
안치다 〔어떤 물건을 솥에 넣다〕 get (rice) ready to cook; prepare (rice) for cooking [boiling]. ¶저녁을 안쳐 두다 leave the supper to cook (on the stove).
안타(安打) 〔야구〕 (a safe) hit; a safety; a base hit; (미) a crash. ¶내야 ~ an infield hit // 산발 ~ scattered hits // 중전 ~ a hit to center // 우전[좌전] ~ a hit to the right[left] // 적시 ~ a timely hit // 집중 ~ bunched hits [fireworks / a swat parade [streak] // 무 ~ 시합 a no-hit game / 〔구어〕 a no-hitter // 멋진[깨끗한] ~ a clean hit // 3루를 뚫는 ~ a hit through third // 투수의 머리 위로 빠지는 ~ a hit over the pitcher's head // ~를 치다 hit (safely) / get a hit / make a (safe) hit // 연속 ~가 나오다 unleash a barrage // (투수가) 상대 팀을 무~로 봉쇄하다 keep the opposing team hitless // (투수가) 상대 팀을 3~로 누르다 hold the other team to three hits // 5 ~를 치다 make five hits.
안타까워하다 1 〔애태우다〕 be impatient; fret [be in a fret] (about / at / over); be fretful; be restless; have the jitters; be[feel] irritated; be tantalized[vexed] at; be nervous [agitated] about; 〔개탄하다〕 deplore (a fact); regret. ¶정치의 부패를 ~ deplore the corruption of politics // 자식이 없는 것을 ~ regret one is childless // 몹시 ~ fret oneself to death // 그들은 결과 발표가 늦어져서 안타까워했다 They became impatient at the delay of the announcement of the results. // 너무 안타까워 마라. 내일이면 결과를 알게 될 테니 Don't be so impatient, we will know the result tomorrow.
2 〔딱하게 여기다〕 feel pity (for); pity (a person); be distressed[anguished] (at); grieve (at / over); 〔남의 불행을〕 ~ feel sorry for another's misfortune.
안타깝다 1 (사람이) impatient; irritated; nervous; vexed; (사물이) irritating; tantalizing; vexatious; 〔개탄스럽다〕 deplorable; regrettable; lamentable. ¶보기만 하고 만지지 못하니 안타까운 일이다 It is tantalizing to see it but not to touch it. // 시간 가는 것이 안타까웠다 Times hung heavy on my hands. // 그것은 안타깝기 짝이 없다 It is really a matter for regret. // 그녀가 시험에 떨어졌다니 참 안타까운 일이다 It is sad that she failed (in) her examination. // 공중도덕이 문란하다는 것은 정말 ~ It is deplorable[a matter for regret] that the public morals should be so corrupt. // 안타깝게도 돈이 없다 The trouble is[It is a pity] that I have no money. // 참 ~ How vexing[provoking]! / You try my patience. / I am losing my patience with you.
2 〔딱하다〕 poor; pitiable; pitiful (sight); pathetic; touching. ¶안타까운 처지 a miserable[pitiable] condition / a sad plight // 안타깝게 여기다 feel pity for (a person) / pity (a person) // 어린애가 저렇게 우는 것을 보니 ~ It makes my heart hurt to see the baby crying like that. // 안타깝게도 그녀는 전쟁으로 남편을 잃었다 The poor thing lost her husband in the war.
안테나 an antenna (*pl.* ~s); (영) an aerial. ¶래빗 ~ a rabbit-eared aerial // 수신 ~ a receiving antenna // 실내 ~ an indoor antenna // 자동차용 ~ an auto antenna // 지향성 〔송신 / 수직〕 ~ a directive[sending / vertical] antenna // 텔레비전 ~ a T.V. antenna // ~를 달다 set up an antenna.
안티몬 〔화〕 antimony; stibium(기호 sb).
안팎 1 〔안과 밖〕 the interior and exterior; the inside and the outside; 〔안쪽과 겉쪽〕 obverse and reverse; the ins and outs. ¶~의 internal and external // ~으로 within and without / inside and outside (a house) / in and out // 회사 ~의 복잡한 사정 the complicated internal and external circumstances of the company // 나는 집의 ~을 페인트칠을 시켰다 I had my house painted inside and out. // 건물의 ~에 삼엄한 경계망이 쳐졌다 The building were heavily guarded inside and out.
2 〔언동의 표리〕 duplicity. ¶~이 다른 사람 a double-dealer / a hypocrite / a double-faced person // ~이 다른 행동을 하다 play on [with] both hands // 사람은 ~이 달라서는 못 쓴다 You must not be one thing in a person's presence and another behind his back.
3 〔내외〕 about; around; some. ¶5만 원 ~ fifty thousand won or so / around[about / some] fifty thousand won // 1주일 ~ a week or thereabouts // 그들의 나이는 30 ~이었다 Their ages, I should say, were round about thirty. // 그의 월수입은 100만 원 ~이다 His monthly income is around 1,000,000 won [1,000,000 won or so].
4 〔부부〕 husband and wife; a couple.
안하무인(眼下無人) haughtiness; arrogance. ¶~의 high-handed / overbearing / arrogant / haughty // ~으로 haughtily / highhandedly // ~으로 굴다 act[behave] highhandedly [overbearingly] / behave in a very highhanded manner // 그녀는 ~이다 She disdains everybody. / She doesn't care a fig about other people's feelings.
앉다 1 (자리에) sit [squat] down; take[have] a seat; seat oneself; 〔앉아 있다〕 sit; be seated. ¶의자에 ~ sit down on [in] a chair // 책상 ~ sit at one's desk // 벤치에 ~ sit on a bench // 편히 ~ sit at one's ease / make oneself comfortable[at home] // 털썩 ~ plump[plunk] oneself down // 무릎을 꿇고 ~ sit with one's legs under one // 이 소파에 세

사람이 앉기는 무리다 Three people can't sit on this sofa. / This sofa can't seat three people.∥노인은 마루에 앉아 있었다 The old man sat (with his legs under him) on the floor.∥어린이는 피아노 앞에 앉았다 The child sat down at the piano.∥단정히 앉아라 Sit up straight.∥앉은 채로 계십시오 Please keep your seats. / Please don't stand up. / You may remain seated.∥아버지는 의자에 털썩 앉으셨다 My father dropped[flopped] into a chair.∥지금 가면 앉을 수는 없을 것이다 You won't be able to sit down[find a seat] if you go now. / You'll have to stand if you go now.∥한 의자에 두 사람이 앉아 주십시오 Please sit two in a seat.∥자 앉으십시오 Please sit down[be seated / have a seat]. / (자리가 정해져 있을 때) Please take your seats.∥"여기 앉아도 괜찮겠습니까?" "아무렴 되고말고요." "May I sit here?" "Please[By all means] do!"∥지금은 텔레비전 덕택으로 안락의자에 앉은 채로 세계의 정세를 알 수 있다 Today, thanks to television, we can be informed of what's going on in the world without moving from our armchairs.
2 (새 등이) perch〔alight / light / sit / settle〕 on; roost〔홰에); (비행기 등이) land; make a landing.¶새가 홰에 앉아 있다 A bird is on the perch.∥비둘기는 전화선에 앉아 있었다 The pigeon perched on a telephone wire.∥나무에 몇 마리의 참새가 앉아 있다 There are some sparrows in the tree.∥네 머리에 파리가 앉아 있다 There is a fly on your head.
3 (건물 등이) be located〔situated〕 (in / on); face (on).¶이 집은 잘못 앉아 있다 This house has a bad[poor] aspect.∥너의 집은 잘 앉았다 Your house is nicely situated 〔located〕.
4 (지위에) take one's post; take〔assume〕 office (as).¶권좌에 앉아 있는 사람들 men in the saddle / those in (position of) power∥학장 자리에 ~ take one's place as president∥좋은 자리에 앉아 있다 hold a good position∥높은 자리에 앉아 있다 hold a high rank (among) / stand high (among)∥그는 회장 자리에 앉았다 He took office as president. / He took[(문어) assumed] the office of presidency.
5 (먼지 등이) lie (on); collect; gather; form a mass; (딱지 등이) be covered (with a scab); scab; (종두가) take.¶시설(柹雪)이 앉은 곶감 a dried persimmon with sugary white deposits on its skin∥테이블에는 먼지가 앉아 있었다 The table was covered with dust. / Thick dust lay on the table.

앉은뱅이 a cripple.¶그는 ~이다 He is crippled (with rheumatism).
●**앉은뱅이저울** a platform scale.
앉은일 sedentary work; a sedentary job 〔pursuit / occupation〕.¶~을 하는 사람 a man engaged in sedentary work / a sedentary.
앉은자리 〔즉석〕.¶~에서 on the spot / extempore / extemporaneously / impromptu / offhandedly∥~에서 만들다 improvise (a poem) / extemporize (a song) / make (a thing) on the spot∥~에서 일을 해치우다 finish one's work straight out / finish a job at a[one] sitting∥~에서 맥주 세 병을 마셔 버리다 finish up three bottles of beer at a stretch[sitting]∥~에서 승낙하다 give a ready consent (to) / accept (an invitation) on the spot.
앉은장사 sedentary business〔trade / commerce〕.¶~를 하다 keep a shop / run a store.
앉은키 one's height when sitting; one's sitting height.¶~가 작은 short-bodied∥그녀는 ~가 크다〔작다〕 She is long-waisted[short-waisted].
앉을자리 a place to sit; (물건의) a place to put (something) on; a site〔an emplacement〕(건물의).¶건물의 ~ a building site 〔lot〕.
앉음새 a sitting posture〔position〕; the way one sits; one's seated posture.¶~를 바로잡다 sit up straight / sit upright / draw oneself up / straighten oneself.
앉히다 1 (좌석에) seat〔sit〕 (a person); have (a person) sit down.¶안락의자에 ~ seat 〔have〕 (a person) in an armchair∥손님을 식탁 상좌[윗자리]에 ~ seat a guest at the head of the table.
2 (지위에) make (a person) take〔assume〕 office (as); place〔install〕 (a person in a position).¶왕위에 ~ set (a person) on the throne / make (a person) king∥지사[회장] 자리에 ~ establish (a person) as governor 〔president〕∥그는 아들을 그의 후계자로 앉혔다 He made his son his successor.
3 〔버릇을 가르치다〕 teach (a person) manners; give (a person) lessons in manners; discipline.
4 〔문서에 기록하다〕 set down〔enter〕 as an item.

않다[1] do not.¶조금도 … ~ not ... at all / not ... in the least.

않다[2] do not.¶~가지〔먹기〕 ~ do not go〔eat〕∥…도 않고 …도 ~ neither ... nor ...∥그는 오늘 오지 않을 것이오 I don't think he'll come today.(▶ 영어에서는 think를 부정하는 것이 보통)∥이번 주에는 물건을 별로 사지 않았다 I have bought few things this week.

않다[3] not.¶예쁘지〔쉽지〕 ~ be not pretty 〔easy〕∥…이 없지도 ~ not without ...∥…도 않고 …도 ~ neither ... nor ...∥나는 가고 싶지 ~ I don't want to go.∥그는 가고 싶은 생각이 없지도 ~ He is not entirely unwilling 〔reluctant〕 to go.∥성공할 가망이 없지도 ~ There is some hope of success.∥덥지도 않고 춥지도 ~ It is neither hot nor cold.∥가난하지 않다면 해외여행을 할 텐데 I would go abroad if I were not poor.∥"이번의 새 계획은 어떻습니까?" "좋지 않아." "How do you like the new plan?" "It's no good."

알 1 (새·벌레 등의) an egg; (물고기·개구리 등의 알 덩어리) spawn; (식용의 물고기 알) roe; spat(조개·주로 굴의); seed(굴의).¶오리 ~ a duck egg∥한 번에 품는 ~ a laying / clutch of eggs∥갓 낳은 ~ a new-laid egg∥~을 낳다 (새 등이) lay an egg / (물고기·개구리 등이) spawn∥닭에게 ~을 품기 하다 set a hen on eggs∥~을 까다 hatch an egg∥~을 깨다 break〔open〕 an egg∥~을 슬다 (물고기가) spawn / shoot〔deposit〕 spawn / (곤충이) oviposit / lay〔deposit〕 eggs / (파리가) blow∥1년 내내 ~스는 곤충도 있다 Some insects keep on laying eggs the year round.∥~을 까는 데 3주일 걸렸다 It took three weeks for those eggs to hatch.
2 〔작고 둥근 것〕 a ball; a bulb; a bead;

sphere; a globe. ¶눈~ an eyeball // 유리~ a glass bead // 안경~ a lens / a glass / an eyepiece // 탄~ a ball / a bullet(소총탄) / a shot(산탄) / a shell(포탄) // ~이 고른 진주 matched pearls / pearls of even size // 콩~만하다 be no bigger than a bean.

3 [작은 열매·낟알] a nut; a berry; a grain. ¶한 ~의 쌀 a grain of rice // ~이 작은 오렌지 a small-sized orange // ~**이 들다** go [run] to seed // ~약을 두 ~ 먹었다 I took two pills.

4 (배추의) a bulb; a head. ¶~이 잘 밴 양배추 a cabbage with a good head.

알갱이 [낱알] a grain (of rice); a kernel; [미립자] a granule. ¶한 ~의 보리 a grain of barley.

알거지 a penniless person; a beggar; a person with no property but his own body.

알겨먹다 defraud [hoax / mulct] (a weaker person) of (something); cheat (a person) (out) of (something); swindle [(문어) cozen / wheedle / trick / bamboozle] (a person) out of (something).

알곡 (-穀) [낱알 곡식] grain; (영) corn; [알곡식] clean grain; [깍지 벗긴 곡식] husked grain.

알궁둥이 the naked buttocks; the bare bottom.

알다 1 (일반적으로) know; be aware of; learn; be acquainted with. ¶아시는 바와 같이 as you know [are aware] // 내가 아는 바로는 as far as I know // 아는 체하는 사람 a wiseacre / (구어) a know-it-all // 자기 자신을 ~ know oneself // 아는 체하다 talk knowingly // 우리가 모이는 곳이 어딘지 아십니까 Do you know where we are meeting? // 그 사건은 즉시 세상 사람들이 알게 되었다 People learned about the incident in no time. // 그녀는 러시아 어를 조금 알고 있다 She has some knowledge of [knows a little] Russian. // 나는 그 회사의 내막을 잘 알고 있다 I have a lot of inside knowledge about that company. // 난 그 요령을 안다 I have the knack of it. // 당신은 부산을 잘 압니까 Are you familiar with Busan? // 자금이 점점 달린다는 것은 알고 있다 I realize that our funds are running short. / I am well aware that we are running out of money. // 심사원을 알아 두는 것이 어느 모로나 유리하다 It would be to your advantage to get to know the members of the screening committee. // 그녀는 그 지방의 전통에 대해서는 알지 못한다 She is ignorant of the traditions of the district. // 나는 수판을 놓을 줄 안다 I know how to use [reckon on] the abacus. // 아시는 바와 같이 모임은 10시에 시작됩니다 The meeting will begin at ten, as you (may) know. // 알고 있습니다 I know. // 한 박사를 아십니까 Do you know Dr. Han? // 그것이라면 잘 알고 있지요 I understand that very well. / I am fully aware of it.

2 [이해하다] understand; appreciate; know; comprehend; make sense (of); see; make out. ¶나는 건강의 중요성을 알게 되었다 I have come to understand [(문어) appreciate] the importance of health. // 그는 하나를 듣고 열을 아는 사람이다 He is so quick that one word is enough to tell him everything. // 나는 그것을 내 의무로 알고 있소 I understand that to be my duty. // 나는 그렇게 알고 있소 So I understand. / So I am told. // 그는 이 문제에 대해서는 잘 알지 못했다 He didn't see clearly in this specific case. // 내가 아는 그것은 대단한 문제가 아니다 So far as I am concerned, it doesn't matter much. // 그가 사양한 이유를 알 수 있있다 I was able to see [tell / guess] why he declined it. // 나로서는 도저히 알 수가 없다 It is above [beyond / past] my comprehension [head / intelligence]. / It is beyond me [my reach / my depth]. / It is out of my depth. / It defeats [beats] me. // 내 말 알겠나 Do you understand me? / Do you go with me? / Do you take me? // 이제야 알겠다 Now I understand. / Now I've got it. / I see it all now.

3 [낯이 익다] be acquainted (with); know. ¶아는 사람 an acquaintance // 나는 그 여자의 얼굴 [이름]은 알고 있다 I know her by sight [name]. // 어떻게 그분을 알게 되었습니까 How did you come to know him? // 나는 최 씨를 잘 안다 I know Mr. Choe very [quite] well. / I am quite well acquainted with Mr. Choe. // 우리는 런던에서 서로 알게 되었다 We got to know [got acquainted with] each other in London. // 저 사람을 아십니까 Do you know that man? / (격식 차려) Are you acquainted with him? // 선생께서도 아시는 송 선생도 오실 것입니다 Mr. Song — whom you know — will come, too. // 그와 알게 된 것은 다행이었다 I was fortunate to make his acquaintance. // 그와는 어릴 때부터 잘 아는 사이다 I have known him very well since we were boys. // 그녀와는 조금 아는 사이다 I am only slightly acquainted with her.

4 [인지·인정하다] recognize; realize; be awake [alive] to. ¶중요성을 ~ recognize [be awake to] the importance (of) // 필요성을 ~ recognize (something) as necessary // 자기의 잘못을 ~ be convinced of one's (own) error // 정직한 사람으로 ~ give (a person) credit for being an honest man.

5 [깨닫다] find; see; notice; perceive; realize; sense; become [be] conscious [cognizant] (of); [발견하다] find out; detect. ¶나는 길을 잘못 잡았다는 것을 알았다 I found that I had taken the wrong road. // 그는 자기의 구혼을 상대방이 달가워하지 않는 것을 알았다 He sensed [realized] that his proposal was unwelcome. // 나는 그것이 속임수라는 것을 알고 있었다 I was aware that it was a trick. // 나는 낌새를 알고 있었다 I had an inkling of it. // (남을 혼내 주고 나서) 이제 알겠지 Now you've learned a lesson, haven't you? // (새로운 발견을 하고) 알았다 I have got [found] it! / Eureka!

6 [느끼다] feel; be conscious of; be sensible of [to]; be alive to. ¶은혜를 ~ feel gratitude / be grateful // 부끄러움을 ~ have a sense of honor / be sensible to shame.

7 [기억하고 있다] remember; have [bear / keep] in mind. ¶똑똑히 알고 있다 have a clear recollection of / remember clearly [distinctly] // 어렴풋이 알고 있다 have a dim remembrance [recollection] of / remember vaguely // 내가 누군지 알겠습니까 Do you remember me?

8 [분별하다] recognize. ¶걸음걸이로 …임을 ~ recognize [know] (a person) by his manner of walking [by the way he walks] // 옳고 그른 것을 ~ know right from wrong / know the difference between right and wrong // 사람은 그가 사귀는 친구로 알 수 있

알딸딸하다

다 A man is known by the company he keeps.
9 [미루어 헤아리다] infer; guess; gather (from a person's talk). ¶남의 의중을 ~ enter into (a person's) feelings // 그 결과는 미루어 알 수 있다 The result may easily be inferred [imagined]. // 그의 말씨로 그가 배운 사람임을 알 수 있다 His speech suggests that he is a man of education.
10 [아랑곳하다] be concerned with; have to do with. ¶그것은 내가 알 바가 아니다 I have nothing to do with it. / It's no concern of mine. / It has nothing to do with me. / It's none of my business.(▶ 맨 끝 표현이 가장 무뚝뚝함) // 나중에 어떻게 되든 내가 알 바가 아니다 I don't give a damn what happens afterward(s). // 내 게 뭐야 Who cares? // 그것은 내가 알 바가 아니다 It is none of your business.
11 [소양이 있다] have accomplishments; have some knowledge (of); [감상 능력이 있다] appreciate. ¶요리법을 대충 ~ have some[a general] knowledge of cooking // 그녀는 음악을 잘 안다 She is pretty well up in music. / She has a great appreciation for music.
12 [경험이 있다] have experience (of); taste (the fear of poverty). ¶남자[여자]를 ~ have carnal knowledge of man[woman] // 그녀는 가난을 알고 있다 She is no stranger to poverty. // 그는 술맛을 알게 되었다 He has learned the taste of wine. // 넌 배고프다는 것이 정말 어떤 것인지 아느냐 Do you know what it is like to be really hungry? / Have you ever been really hungry?
13 [동의·승낙하다] consent to; agree to. ¶알았습니다 (승낙) All right. / Very well. / Certainly, sir. // "내 자리 하나 잡아 주겠니?" "알았어." "Will you save a seat for me?" "OK [All right]." // 알았습니다. 내가 하지요 Very well. I'll do it. // 부탁해, 알았지 I want you to take care of it — understand?
14 [간주하다] take (for); look upon (as); regard (as). ¶잘못 ~ mistake [take] (A for B) // 나를 누구로 알고 있지 Who do you think I am? / Who do you take me for? // 당신을 스승으로 알아 모시고 있소 I regard you as my teacher. // 처음에 나는 그가 미국인인 줄 알았다 At first I took[mistook] him for an American.

아는 것이 힘이다(속담) Knowledge is power.
아는 길도 물어 가랬다(속담) Look before [ere] you leap.
알딸딸하다 mellow; tipsy.
알뜰살뜰 thriftily; with frugality. **알뜰살뜰하다** extremely frugal[thrifty]; prudently saving. ¶아무리 알뜰살뜰해도 한 달에 30만 원 가지고는 못 산다 I cannot keep body and soul together on less than 300,000 won a month, even if I practice severe economy.
알뜰하다 1 [헤프지 않고 아끼다] thrifty; frugal; saving; provident (of). ¶성품이 알뜰한 of a frugal mind // 알뜰하게 살아가다 live [lead] a frugal life // 그녀는 결혼하더니 알뜰해졌다 She has become thrifty since her marriage. // 그녀는 매사에 ~ She is economical in every way. 2 [빈틈없고 정성스럽다] careful and earnest; conscientious; scrupulous. ¶알뜰히 만들다 make with patient [the utmost] care. 3 [정이 두텁고 자상하다]

warm; tender; close; thick; deep. ¶알뜰한 사랑 warm affection / tender feeling.
알라 [이슬람교의 절대·유일신] Allah.
알랑거리다 flatter; toady; curry favor (with one's superior); cringe [truckle] to (a person); fawn upon (a person). ¶윗사람에게 ~ fawn upon a superior // …의 총애를 얻으려고 ~ curry favor with a person // 알랑거리며 비위를 맞추다 tickle [titillate] (a person) by flattery // 그녀에게는 아무리 알랑거려야 소용없다 She is proof against flattery. // 그는 늘 상사에게 알랑거리고 있다 He is always flattering [trying to curry favor with] his superiors.
알랑쇠 a flatterer; an apple-polisher; a toad-eater; a toady.
알랑알랑 flatteringly; fawningly; with flattery; in a flattering manner. ¶~ 여자를 꾀다 seduce a girl with flattery.
알량하다 [보잘것없다] trifling; trivial; twopenny(-halfpenny); [무가치하다] worthless; rubbish; (구어) rubbishing; drossy. ¶알량한 선물 a trifling gift // 알량한 녀석 a worthless [good-for-nothing] fellow // 그런 알량한 일에 돈을 버리지 마라 Don't waste money on such a worthless thing.
알레고리 an allegory.
알레그레토 (이) (음) allegretto.
알레그로 (이) (음) allegro.
알레르기 1 [과민 반응] an allergy. ¶~ (체질)의 allergic // 달걀에 대해 ~가 있다 be allergic to eggs // 우유 ~가 되다 develop an allergy to milk. 2 [거부 반응]. ¶유럽 사람들은 핵무기에 대한 ~가 심하다 The European people have an antipathy [(구어) allergy] to nuclear weapons.

● **알레르기성 반응** an allergic reaction. **알레르기성 비염** allergic coryza. **알레르기성 질환** an allergic disease.

알려지다 1 [남이 알게 되다] become known (to); come to (a person's) knowledge. ¶세상에 널리 ~ become generally known / be known to the general public / become public [common] knowledge / (소문이) get abroad [out] / spread widely // 알려지지 않도록 하다 keep (a matter) (secret) from (a person) / keep (a person) in the dark (about a matter) // 그 사건은 세상에 널리 알려져 있다 The matter is widely known. / It is a matter of common knowledge. // 그 사건은 즉각 세상에 알려졌다 People learned about the incident in no time. // 그것은 절대로 알려져서는 안 된다 The matter must be kept absolutely secret. // 어떻게 된 건지 이 일이 경찰에 알려지고 말았다 This somehow came to the knowledge of the police. // 그의 비밀이 모두에게 [근방에] 알려졌다 His secret became known to everybody [in the neighborhood]. // 그들이 브라질로 간다는 소문이 널리 알려져 있다 A rumor has spread that they will go to Brazil. // 장관과 배우와의 관계가 널리 알려져 있었다 The relationship between the Minister and the actress was noised about [abroad].
2 [판명되다] be found; be revealed; be disclosed; come to light; turn out (to be); prove (to be); be identified (신원 등). ¶사인은 아직 알려지지 않고 있다 The cause of his death still remains a mystery [unknown]. // 소문은 거짓이라는 것이 알려졌다 The rumor turned

out false.∥거짓말을 해도 곧 알려지고 말걸 Your lie will soon be found out.
3 [유명해지다] become famous[well known]; earn[win] fame; come[rise] to fame. ¶전 세계에 알려진 학자 a scholar known to the world / a world-famous scholar∥맛을 아는 사람들에게 잘 알려진 포도주 a wine well-known to those who appreciate its taste∥알려지지 않은 unknown / obscure / nameless∥그는 의사로서보다도 문인으로서 더 잘 알려져 있다 He is better known as a man of letters than (as) a physician.

알력(軋轢) [불화] (a) discord; [장기간의 반목] a feud (between / among); friction; jar; dissension; clash. ¶이 문제로 두 사람 사이에 ~이 생겼다 Discord arose between them over this matter. / They clashed over the matter.∥두 나라 사이에는 오랫동안 ~이 있어 왔다 The two countries have long been at odds. / There has long been friction between the two countries.∥조합원 사이에 ~이 생긴 것 같다 It seems that discord has arisen among the union members.

알로까다 very shrewd[sharp]; wide-awake; knowing. ¶알로깐 놈 shrewd[smart / knowing] fellow.

알로에 [식] aloe.

알로하셔츠 an aloha shirt.

알루미늄 [화] aluminum; (영) aluminium(기호 Al). ¶~을 입히다 aluminize.
● **알루미늄 새시** an aluminum sash. **알루미늄 제품** aluminum ware.

알리다 [알게 하다] let (a person) know; [전하다] tell (a person about [that]); [문어] inform (a person of a matter); [통보하다] notify; report; [예고하다] give notice; [공표하다] announce. ¶이미 알려 드린 바와 같이 (보도 등에서) as previously [already] announced [reported]∥사고를 사람에게 ~ inform[notify] a person of an accident∥어떤 일을 남에게 알리지 않다 keep a matter (secret) from a person∥어느 장소에 가는 길을 ~ tell (a person) how to get to a place / direct (a person) [show (a person) the way] to a place∥위험이 있음을 ~ warn (a person) of danger∥경찰에 ~ communicate with the police / report (a fact) to the police∥될 수 있는 대로 빨리 알려 드리겠습니다 I will let you know as soon as possible.∥나는 그것을 아직 그에게 알리지 않았다 I have not told him about it yet.∥나에게 한 달 전에 알려 달라 Give me a month's notice.∥물품 도착 즉시 알려 드리겠습니다 As soon as the article arrives, I will let you know.∥화재 발생을 늦게 알려 대참사가 일어났다 The delay in reporting the outbreak of the fire caused a great tragedy.∥그 여자는 이름을 알리지 않고 가 버렸다 The woman went away without giving[telling] her name.∥나는 그에게 사임할 뜻을 알렸다 I informed him of my intention to resign.∥매미의 울음소리가 여름의 끝을 알리고 있다 The chirping of cicadas signals the end of summer.∥닭이 울어서 새벽을 알린다 A cock crows to tell the coming of dawn.

알리바이 an alibi. ¶확실한 ~ a solid [an airtight] alibi∥~를 세우다 prove [set up / establish] an alibi / [make / fix] an alibi∥~를 **조작하다** concoct [frame / create] an alibi∥그는 ~가 있다 He has an alibi.∥그는 그녀의 ~를 입증했다 He fixed (up) [built up] an alibi for her.∥그는 자신의 ~를 증명했다 [날조했다] He established [faked] an alibi.

알맞다 [적당하다] suitable; proper; right; [다루기 쉽다, 편리하다] handy; [도를 지나치지 않다] moderate; [타당하다] proper; reasonable. ¶야영하기에 알맞은 장소 a place suitable for camping∥알맞은 운동 moderate exercise∥알맞은 값 a reasonable [moderate] price∥선물하기에 꼭 알맞은 물건 an article just right for a present∥혼자 살기에 알맞은 집 a house suitable for living alone∥때에 알맞은 조언 timely advice∥알맞은 크기의 널빤지 a board of suitable size∥평상복에 알맞은 블라우스 a blouse suitable for everyday wear∥휴대하기에 알맞은 사전 a dictionary handy to carry around∥알맞은 시간에 at a proper time / at the right moment∥알맞은 방법으로 in a proper way∥알맞게 moderately / within bounds∥이 드레스는 파티용으로 ~ This dress is suitable for the party. / This dress is just right for the party.∥그의 지시는 그 경우에 알맞은 것이 아니었다 His instructions were not suitable for [suited to] the occasion.∥이 입문서는 초보자에게 알맞은 것이다 This primer is suited [just right] for beginners.∥그 일은 내게는 알맞지 않다 The job does not suit me.∥이곳은 조용한 생활을 하기에는 알맞은 곳이 아니다 This is not a good place to live a quiet life.∥여기 기후는 나에게 꼭 ~ The climate here agrees with me.∥그는 그런 역할에 알맞은 사람이다 He is fit [suited] for such a role.∥이 책은 다섯 살 난 아이들에게 꼭 알맞은 책이다 This book is just right for five year-old children.∥이 레스토랑은 값이 ~ Prices at this restaurant are moderate.∥우리는 200명의 아동을 수용하기에 알맞은 건물을 발견했다 We found just the right building [a house of just the right size] to accommodate two hundred children.∥칠면조는 알맞게 구워졌다 The turkey is done to a turn.∥이 수프는 맛이 ~ The soup is just right. / The soup is perfectly seasoned.∥그는 자기 형편에 알맞게 [벗어나지 않게] 생활을 하고 있다 He lives within [beyond] his means.∥그것은 그 물건에 알맞은 값이다 It is a reasonable price for the article.∥그녀는 자기 신분에 알맞게 차려입고 있다 She dresses appropriately [suitably] for a person of her position.∥각자 자기가 한 일에 알맞은 보수를 받았다 Each one received payment proportional [proportionate] to the work he had done.∥이것은 네게 알맞은 일이다 This is a job that suits you. / You are the right man for the job.∥식장에 가시려면 알맞은 복장을 하고 가셔야 합니다 If you are going to attend the ceremony, you should wear suitable [appropriate] clothes.

알맹이 [껍데기 속에 든 것] a kernel; [실질] substance; matter; [내용] contents. ¶호두 ~ the kernel of a walnut∥~ 있는 substantial / solid / meaty∥~ 없는 unsubstantial / contentless / empty (talk)∥~ 없는 토의 a futile discussion∥~ 없는 책 a book poor [meager] in contents [substance]∥~ 없는 말 an inane remark / a vacuous platitude∥그것은 ~가 별로 없는 이야기였다 There was little substance in the speech.

알몸 1 [아무것도 입지 않음] nakedness; nudity; a naked [nude] body. ¶~의 stark-

알밤

[mother-] naked / completely nude / naked / bare / nude // ~으로 with nothing on / stark-naked / in the altogether / (구어) (all) in the buff / in one's birthday suit // ~인 아기 a baby with nothing on // ~의 모델 a model in the nude // ~이 되다 take off (all) one's clothes / undress / strip oneself bare [stark-naked] / strip oneself of (all) one's clothes / (남에 의해서) be stripped of one's clothes [to the skin / (구어) to the buff] // ~으로 걸어 다니다 go about stark-naked [with nothing on / in the nude] // ~으로 헤엄치다 swim in the nude [(구어) in the raw] // 그녀는 실오라기 하나 걸치지 않은 ~으로 거기 누워 있었다 She lay there without a shred of clothing on.
2 [가진 것이 없음] pennilessness. ¶~뿐인 사람 a man with no property but his own body / a penniless man // ~으로 with an empty pocket // ~이 되다 be reduced to one's naked personal merit / be stripped of all one's possessions / (속어) go (clean) broke // 나는 ~뿐이다 I haven't a cent[penny] to my name. / I have no money at all. / I am clean[flat] broke. // 그는 ~으로 장사를 시작했다 He started his business from nothing [from scratch].

알밤 [밤톨] a (shelled) chestnut.

알배기 1 [배가 부른 생선] a (full-)roed fish. **2** [겉보다 속이 야무진 상태] an object rich in contents; a substantial thing.

알부민 [화] albumin; albumen.

알비노 an albino (pl. ~s).

알뿌리 [식] a bulb.

알선(斡旋) **1** [주선] good[kind] offices; service; recommendation. ¶직업 ~ 소 an employment agency / (미) an employment office / (영) a (servants') registry office / (영) a registry // 친구의 ~으로 through the influence[help] of a friend / (문어) through [by] the good offices of a friend // ~을 부탁하다 ask for (a person's) good offices / seek the good offices (of a person) / request (a person's) services // 나는 숙부의 ~으로 일자리를 얻었다 I got a job through the good offices of my uncle. // 나는 그의 ~으로 이 회사에 들어왔다 I got a job with this company on the strength of his recommendation. **알선하다** offer[led / exercise / use] one's good offices; do[render] a service; use one's influence; extend facilities. ¶일자리[직업]를 알선해 주시겠습니까 Will you help me (to) find a job?
2 [법] mediation; intercession; (노동 쟁의의) conciliation. ¶화해의 ~ mediation for a settlement // ~을 의뢰하다 ask for (a person's) mediation. **알선하다** mediate (between); intercede (with a person for another); conciliate; go between (two parties); act as a medium (for). ¶제가 알선해 드릴까요 Shall I serve as your mediator?
● **알선자** a mediator; an intermediary; an intercessor; (노동 쟁의의) a conciliator.

알심 1 [동정하는 마음] hidden sympathy [compassion / consideration]. **2** [보기보다 야무진 힘] hidden[veiled] strength. **3** →고갱이

알싸하다 sharp; acrid; pungent; piquant; biting (to the taste); pricking; hot. ¶겨자를 먹으면 혀가 ~ Mustard burns the tongue.

알쏭달쏭하다 1 (줄·무늬가) variegated; diversified; motley; mottled; jumbled; intermingled; intricated. ¶알쏭달쏭한 무늬 a jumbled [motley / intermixed] pattern / a bewildering[puzzling] design. **2** [분간이 안 되다] inscrutable; incomprehensible; vague; ambiguous; obscure; equivocal; evasive; elusive; dubious; shady; indefinite; dim; hazy. ¶알쏭달쏭한 말을 하다 equivocate / prevaricate / talk ambiguously / evade the point // 그가 뜻하는 바가 뭔지 알쏭달쏭했다 I couldn't understand what he meant. / His meaning was incomprehensible.

알아내다 get (information) out of (a person); find out (the truth); discover; detect; worm[pump] (a secret) out of (a person); (의미 등을) make out; grasp; understand. ¶소재를 ~ locate / (정확히) pinpoint / [군] spot(지도로 적군의 소재를) // 음모를 ~ discover a plot // 남의 비밀을 ~ dig a person's secret out / sniff out a person's secret // 인용문의 출처를 ~ run down a quotation / dig up the source of a quotation / trace a quotation to it's original source // 경쟁 회사에서 일하는 친구에게서 정보를 ~ try to get[(구어) pump / (구어) worm] some information out of a friend who works for a rival company // 그 사람한테서 아무것도 알아낼 수 없었다 I could get nothing [(구어) no change] out of him. / I could extract no information from him.

알아듣다 [남의 말뜻을 알다] catch; get; follow; understand; comprehend; [납득하다] hear[listen to] reason; be reasonable; [분간하다] recognize; tell (a difference) by hearing. ¶알아듣기 어려운 단어 a difficult word to hear[catch] // 영어를 알아듣는 실력 the ability to understand spoken English // 남의 이야기를 ~ follow[catch] what a person says[a person's words] // 잘 알아듣도록 설명하다 explain in terms that anyone could understand / explain convincingly [understandably] / give a careful, easily understandable explanation // 부모님의 말씀을 ~ listen to what one's parents say // 그의 말은 너무 빨라서 알아들을 수가 없다 He speaks so quickly that I can't follow him. // 귀하의 생각은 잘 알아들었습니다 I understand your viewpoint[opinion]. // 나는 ~ 당신이 말씀하시는 뜻을 I understand what you mean. // 그것은 통 알아듣지 못하겠다 It's beyond me[my comprehension]. // 그는 내가 비꼬아서 한 말을 칭찬으로 알아들고 He took my irony for praise. // 그의 말은 도무지 알아들을 수 없었다 I could hardly follow him. / I could hardly catch what he said.

알아맞히다 guess right; make a good guess; hit the mark. ¶수수께끼를 ~ guess a riddle right / find out a riddle // 못 ~ guess wrong / miss one's guess / make a wrong guess // 답을 ~ guess at the answers(▶ guess at 쪽이 guess보다 일반적으로「단순한 어림짐작」이라는 느낌이 강함) // 그녀가 몇 살인지 ~ make a guess at her age / make a guess as to how old she is // 알아맞혀 봐 Make a guess! / Guess! // 어때, 내가 바로 알아맞혔지 I've guessed right, haven't I? // 그는 딱 알아맞혔어 He guessed[hit] it. / He guessed (it) right. / (구어) He hit the nail on the head. //

내 손에 무엇이 있는지 세 번 안에 알아맞춰 봐 I'll give you three guesses what's in my hand.

알아보다 1 [조사하다] examine (into); investigate; check (up on); look into [over]; [살펴보다] search; feel out; [확인하다] ascertain; [문의하다] inquire; refer (to). ¶원인을 ~ look [inquire] into the cause // 남의 의향을 ~ sound a person's inclination // 취직 자리를 ~ look (out) for a job [place / situation] // 기상대에 날씨를 ~ inquire weather conditions of the weather bureau // 교통사고의 원인을 ~ investigate [search into] the causes of a traffic accident // 동료들의 생각을 알아봐야 한다 I must find out what my colleagues think. // 송 씨가 안 되면 황 씨를 알아봐 If Mr. Song cannot [won't] do it, try Mr. Hwang. // 상황이 어떤지 알아보겠다 I'll check the lay of the land. / I'll sound out the situation. // 그가 당신에게 알아보라고 했습니다 He referred me to you for information. // 상세한 것은 사무실에 알아보십시오 For all particulars apply [address inquiries] to the office. / Please inquire at the office for all particulars. // 알아보니 그 보도는 허위였다 On [Upon] inquiry, the report turned out to be false. 2 [분간하다] recognize; make out; [판단하다] judge (of). ¶예술품을 알아보는 눈이 있다 have an eye for works of art / be a good judge of objects of art // 그의 키가 너무 자라서 알아보지 못했다 He'd grown so tall that I didn't recognize him. // 그 도시는 알아볼 수 없을 정도로 변해 버렸다 The town has changed beyond [past / out of] recognition. // 그들이 내 얼굴을 알아볼 테니 자네 대신 가 주게 Please go instead of me, for they will recognize me. // 그 아기는 벌써 엄마 얼굴을 알아본다 The baby already knows its mother's face.

알아주다 1 [인정해 주다] recognize; appreciate; acknowledge. ¶그 남자의 능력을 ~ appreciate the man's ability // 당신 실력은 알아줘야겠군 I've got to hand it to you! 2 [이해해 주다] understand; feel for [with]; sympathize (with). ¶너는 내 마음을 조금도 알아주지 않는 것 같다 It seems that you never understand my feelings. // 아내는 내가 말하고 행하는 모든 것을 알아준다 My wife understands everything I say and do.

알아차리다 1 [깨닫다] realize; discover; notice, become aware (of); (문어) perceive; find; take notice (of); be awakened to. ¶그는 누군가가 뒤에 따라오는 것을 알아차렸다 He noticed [became aware] that someone was following him. // 지갑이 없어진 것을 알아차렸다 I noticed that my wallet was missing. / I discovered [realized] that I had lost my watch. // 나는 그의 상태가 심상치 않은 것을 알아챘다 I did not suspect [was unaware of] the seriousness of his case. // 그것이 사실이 아니라는 것을 곧 알아차렸다 I realized [(문어) perceived] at once that it was not true. // 나는 그를 처음 보았을 때 정직한 사람임을 알아차렸다 When I first met him, I perceived him (to be) that he was an honest man. // 그가 미국 사람이라는 것을 곧 알아차렸다 I spotted him at once for [as] an American. 2 sense; perceive. ⇨알아채다

알아채다 sense; perceive; detect; suspect; become aware (of / that); be conscious (of); scent; get wind [scent] of; guess; infer; gather; surmise; smell; have an inkling of. ¶나는 그가 거짓말을 하고 있다는 것을 알아챘다 I sensed that he was lying. // 나는 그가 실망하고 있음을 알아챘다 I was aware of [I sensed] his disappointment. // 그들의 표정에서 어떤 중대한 일이 일어났음을 알아챘다 It could be gathered [It could be inferred / I could guess] from their looks that something important had happened. // 그가 그것을 어떻게 알아챘을까 How did he get the wind of [get on to] it? // 그녀는 위험이 다가옴을 알아챘다 She sensed [was aware of] the approaching danger. // 그는 그녀의 목소리에 불안감이 있는 것을 알아챘다 He detected in her voice a note of apprehension. // 나는 그가 알아채지 못하도록 조심스럽게 그를 미행했다 I shadowed him carefully so that I wouldn't be noticed. // 그의 태도로 내가 남아 있지 않아도 되겠다는 것을 알아챘다 I gathered from his attitude that I did not have to stay.

알알이 grain by grain; berry after berry.

알알하다 (매워서) pungent; piquant; (서술적) taste hot; have burning taste; (상처 등이) smart; (서술적) have a tingling pain. ¶먹어 보니 혀가 알알했다 It stung my tongue. // 맞은 빰이 ~ My cheeks tingle from slap. // 긁힌 데가 아직도 ~ The scratch still smarts.

알약 (-藥) a tablet; a tabloid; a pill.

알은척하다 poke one's nose into; recognize. ⇨알은체하다

알은체하다 1 (어떤 일에 대해) poke [thrust] one's nose into; butt [break / cut] in; show concern [interest]; [간섭하다] interfere [meddle] in. ¶남의 일에 알은체하지 마라 Mind your own business. / That's none of your business. / That's my own business. / Do not interfere in [butt in on] what is not your business. // 그는 아무 일에나 알은체한다 He pokes [thrusts / puts] his nose into everything. 2 (사람을) recognize; notice. ¶그는 길에서 나를 보고도 알은척하지 않았다 He cut me (dead) [gave me the go-by] on the street. / He pretended not to recognize me.

알음 1 [사람끼리 서로 아는 일] acquaintance (-ship). ¶~이 있다 have acquaintance with // 그와는 전혀 ~이 없다 I have no (personal) acquaintance with him. / He is a total stranger to me. 2 [알고 있는 것] knowing; knowledge.

알음알음 1 [아는 관계] mutual acquaintance. 2 [친분] shared intimacy; friendship.

알젓 pickled roe; salted spawn.

알짜 the essence; the quintessence; the pith (and marrow); the cream; the pick; the choice; the best. ¶~만 가려 내다 get the cream (of) / choose [select] the best (from among many) / extract the essence.

알짱거리다 1 [알랑거리며 속이다] cajole; coax. 2 [자꾸 돌아다니다] loaf around idly; hang around [about]; ramble about.

알츠하이머병 (-病) Alzheimer's disease.

알칼로이드 [화] an alkaloid. ¶~의 alkaloidal.

알칼리 [화] alkali. ¶~의 alkaline / alkali.
● **알칼리성** alkalinity. ¶~의 alkaline / alkali.

알코올 alcohol; spirits. ¶공업용 ~ industrial alcohol // 무수 ~ absolute alcohol // ~ (성)의

알토 alcoholic∥~에 담근 표본 a specimen (preserved) in spirits[alcohol]∥~에 담그다 preserve in alcohol[spirits] / alcoholize∥그는 ~은 전혀 입에 대지 않는다 He does not touch[abstains from all] alcohol (drinks).
●알코올램프 a spirit lamp; (미) an alcohol lamp. 알코올음료 alcoholic drinks; liquor. 알코올 의존자 an alcoholic. 알코올 의존증 [의] alcoholism; alcoholic poisoning. ~에 걸리다 suffer from alcoholism. 알코올 중독 ➡ 알코올 의존증(⇨알코올)

알토 [음] alto; (가수) an alto (singer).
알통 the biceps (pl. ~, ~es). ¶그가 팔을 구부리면 위팔에 ~이 나온다 When he bends his arm, the flexor muscle stands out on his upper arm. / When he flexes his arm, his biceps stand out(▶ 이 경우는 복수형).
알파 [어떤 미지수] (그) alpha. ¶천 원 플러스 ~ 1,000 won plus something∥2만 원 플러스 ~의 승급(昇給)으로 타협했다 We agreed on a raise of 20,000 won plus (a little) something extra.
알파와 오메가 alpha and omega.
●알파선 [물] α-rays; alpha rays. 알파 입자 [물] α[alpha] particles.
알파벳 the alphabet. ¶~의 alphabet(al)∥~순으로 (배열)하다 arrange alphabetically[in alphabetical order] / alphabetize∥~순으로 목록을 작성하시오 List them alphabetically. / Make a list of them in a alphabetical order.
알파카 [동] an alpaca. ¶~의 털 alpaca (wool).
알현(謁見) a royal audience; an audience. ¶~을 허락하다 receive (a person) in audience / grant[give] an audience to (a person). 알현하다 be received in audience; have[be granted] an audience with; be presented to. ¶그는 황제를 알현했다 He was granted an audience by the Emperor.
●알현실 an audience[a presence] chamber.
앎 knowledge; learning; information; wisdom.
앓다 1 (병을) suffer from; be ill (with); be sick; be afflicted[troubled] (with). ¶중병을 ~ be very[seriously / dangerously / critically] ill / get[fall / be taken] seriously ill / suffer from a serious[severe / grave] illness [disease]∥앓아 누워 있다 be laid up with illness / be ill in bed / be confined to bed (by illness)∥그는 폐병을 앓고 있었다 He was suffering from a lung disease. / He had chest trouble.

2 (비유) be worried (about); be troubled [distressed / afflicted] (with). ¶사랑을 앓고 있는 젊은이 a lovesick youth∥골머리를 ~ bother one's brain (about)∥앓는 소리를 하다 groan / give[heave] a groan / moan / make complaints∥앓는 소리 좀 작작 하라 Never say die! / Don't cry uncle!
앓던 이 빠진 것 같다(속담) I feel quite relieved.
암 Of course! ⇨아무렴
암- [생물의 자성(雌性)] a female. ¶~고양이 she-cat / ~사자 a lioness / ~캐 a bitch / a she-dog / ~나귀 a jenny ass / ~곰 a female bear / ~염소 a nanny goat.
암(癌) 1 [의] cancer. ¶~의 cancerous∥위~ cancer of the stomach / gastric cancer∥식도~ cancer of the esophagus∥유방~ mammary cancer / breast cancer∥직장~ cancer of the rectum∥폐~ cancer of the lung / lung cancer∥피부~ skin cancer∥~의 조기 발견 early detection of cancer∥~ 검진을 받다 undergo an examination[a test] for cancer∥나는 ~에 걸려 있다 I have (a) cancer. 2 [화근·폐단] a cancer; a curse; a gangrenous evil; a stumbling block. ¶그것이 우리나라 정치의 ~이다 It is a cancer on our government.
암갈색(暗褐色) dark brown (color); umber (color); dun.
암거래(暗去來) black-market[underground] dealings[activities]; underhand[undercover] transactions; black-marketeering; under-the-table transactions. ¶~를 단속하다 crack down on the market / police the black market / put a stop to black-market dealings[activities]∥이것은 ~로 입수한 것이다 I got this in an undercover transaction. / I got this on the black market[through an illegal channel]. 암거래하다 black-marketeer; black-market; sell[buy] (goods) in the black market; handle[engage in] a black-market business. ➔다이아몬드가 암거래되고 있다 Diamonds are traded illegally[under the table].
●암거래상 a black marketeer; a black-market operator.
암굴(巖窟) a stone cave. ⇨석굴
암기(暗記) learning by heart; memorizing; memory work. ¶영어 단어 ~법 how to learn [memorize] English words∥~를 잘하다 excel in memory work∥그는 ~ 과목을 잘한다 He is good at memory work[subjects which require memorization]. 암기하다 learn by heart[by rote]; get (off) by heart; commit to memory; memorize; con. ¶영어 단어를 ~ memorize English words.
●암기력 (one's powers of) memory; retentive power. ¶~이 좋다[나쁘다] have a good [bad / poor] memory / be strong[weak] in memory.
암꽃 [식] a female (pistillate) flower.
암나사(-螺絲) a female screw; a negative[an interior] screw.
암내¹ [발정 냄새] the odor of a female animal in heat[estrus]. ¶~가 나다[~를 내다] go in heat / get[come] on heat / come into heat [season] / become[be] ready to accept the male / ~가 난 소 A cow is in rut[heat].
암내² (겨드랑이의) body odor[(영) odour]; [의] tragomaschalia; the offensive smell of the armpit; axillary[underarm] odor; (구어) B.O. ¶그는 ~가 심하게 난다 He has a strong body odor. / (구어) He has B.O.
암녹색(暗綠色) dark green.
암달러(暗-) a black-market dollar.
●암달러상 an illegal currency dealer.
암담하다(暗澹-) dark; gloomy; dismal; depressing; hopeless. ¶암담한 앞길[전망] a gloomy[dismal] outlook / black [gloomy] prospects∥암담한 표정으로 with a gloomy look on one's face[(문어) countenance]∥암담한 기분이다 I am most depressed[absolutely without hope]. / 나는 친구의 죽음에 암담해졌다 I was overcome with grief at the news of[when I heard of] my friend's death. ∥우리 앞에는 암담한 미래만이 남아 있다 For us there remains only a miserable future.
암띠다 1 [비밀스러운 것을 좋아하다] secre-

tive; closed. 2〔부끄러움을 잘 타는 성질이 있다〕shy; retiring (in disposition). ¶그녀는 암 띠어서 남 앞에서 말도 잘 못한다 She is too shy[bashful] to speak in public.

암류(暗流) 1〔물 바닥의 흐름〕an undercurrent. 2〔겉으로 드러나지 않은 움직임〕a hidden drift[tendency]; an undercurrent. ¶그의 말에는 원한의 ~가 흐르고 있었다 There was an undercurrent of resentment beneath his words.

암만〔밝힐 필요가 없는 수효나 분량〕a certain amount; a certain sum (of money).

암만해도 by all means; in every respect[way]; to all appearance; at any cost; at all costs. ¶~ 가망이 없다 There is no hope at all.

암말 a mare.

암매(暗買) black-marketing; black-marketeering; a black-market purchase; unauthorized[illegal] purchase. 암매하다 buy in the black market.

암매(暗賣) a black-market sale; black-marketeering. 암매하다 sell on[in] the black market; black-marketeer.

●**암매상**(－商) a black-marketeer; a dealer in the black market; a black-market trader [operator / agent];〔영국 속어〕a spiv;〔미국 속어〕(주류의) a bootlegger.

암매장(暗埋葬) secret burial. 암매장하다 bury (a body) secretly[in secret].

암맥(巖脈)〔지〕a dike.

암모늄〔화〕ammonium. ¶염화~ ammonium chloride / sal ammoniac /〔황산[질산 / 탄산]〕~ ammonium sulfate[nitrate / carbonate] // 수산화~ ammonium hydroxide.

암모니아〔화〕ammonia. ¶고형 ~ rock ammonia // 액체 ~ liquid ammonia.

암묵(暗默) silence; taciturness; unspokenness. ¶~의 tacit // ~의 양해 a tacit understanding / an unspoken agreement // ~의 동의 tacit consent / ~리에 tacitly / by a tacit consent[understanding] / by implication /〔agree〕in silence // ~리에 허락하다 give a tacit[an implicit] permission.

암반(巖盤) bedrock; base rock; a rock bed. ¶이 도시는 ~ 위에 세워져 있다 This city is built on solid rock.

암벌 a female bee; a queen (bee).

암범 a tigress.

암벽(巖壁) a rockwall; a wall of rock; a rock face.

●**암벽 등반** rock-climbing.

암산(巖山) a rocky mountain; a craggy mountain.

암산(暗算) mental arithmetic; mental calculation. ¶~으로 in mental arithmetic. 암산하다 do sums in one's head; calculate mentally; do sums mentally; work mental sums; do mental arithmetic. ¶216 곱하기 29를 ~ multiply 216 by 29 mentally.

암살(暗殺) (an) assassination. ¶~을 꾀하다 make an attempt on (a person's) life / attempt (a person's) life / plot the death of (a person) / plot for (a person's) assassination // 수상에 대한 ~ 기도는 미수에 그쳤다 The attempt on the prime Minister's life failed. 암살하다 assassinate. ➜¶암살당하다 be assassinated / fall a victim to an assassin // 수상은 암살되었다 The prime Minister was assassinated.

●**암살자** an assassin.

암상〔잔망스런 심술〕jealousy; (green) envy. ¶~을 부리다 show jealousy / burn with jealousy. 암상하다 jealous; cantankerous (out of green envy).

●**암상꾸러기** a jealous person.

암석(巖石) (a) rock; a crag(울퉁불퉁한). ¶~이 많은 rocky / craggy (hill / coast).

●**암석학** petrology; lithology; lithological science.

암세포(癌細胞) cancer cells.

암소 a cow; (새끼를 낳지 않은 3세 미만의) a heifer.

암송(暗誦) recitation; recital. ¶시의 ~ a recitation of a poem // 영어의 ~ a recitation in English. 암송하다 recite; repeat from memory; say[recite] by rote; say by heart. ¶시를 ~ recite a poem // 영어를 ~ give an English recitation // 그는 라틴 어 시를 암송했다 He recited a Latin poem by heart[by rote / from memory].

암수 male and female; both sexes.

암수(暗數) trickery; swindle. ⇨ㄷ속임수

암술〔식〕a pistil.

●**암술대**〔식〕a style.

암시(暗示) a hint; a suggestion; an intimation; an allusion. ¶자기 ~ an autosuggestion // ~를 받다 receive a hint[suggestion] (from) // 그녀는 자신의 신원에 대해 전혀 ~를 주지 않았다 She gave no hint of her own background. // 나는 그의 소설에서 ~를 얻어 이 그림을 그렸다 His novel gave me the idea for this painting. // 그가 무심결 흘린 한마디에서 ~를 얻어 우리는 그 문제를 해결할 수 있었다 What he let slip out provided the hint that helped us solve the case. 암시하다 hint; suggest; give[drop] a hint; allude (to); intimate. ¶요전날 그는 내게 사의를 암시했다 The other day he intimated to me his intention to resign.

●**암시 요법** suggestive therapy.

암시세(暗時勢) a black-market price; off-the-books quotations. ¶~로 입장권을 팔다 sell admission tickets at a black-market price /〔미〕scalp[〔영〕tout] admission tickets.

암시장(暗市場) a black market. ¶나는 이것[이 물건]을 ~에서 구했소 I got this[this article] on the black market[through illegal channels]. // 그것은 ~에서는 값이 두 배다 It is twice as expensive on the black market. // 그는 배급쌀을 ~으로 흘려 보내곤 했다 He used to divert rice for rationing onto the black market.

암실(暗室) a (photo) darkroom.

암암리(暗暗裏) tacitness; implicitness. ¶~에 tacitly / implicitly / by implication /〔몰래〕secretly / covertly / unknown to others // ~에 승낙하다 give tacit consent // ~에 계획을 추진하다 carry forward a scheme in secret.

암야(暗夜) a dark[moonless] night. ¶~를 틈타서 under (the) cover of night[darkness].

암약(暗躍) secret maneuvers. 암약하다 be active behind the scenes; engage in secret maneuvers[machinations]. ¶선거 공작을 하기 위해 ~ engage in electoral manipulations[covert election-rigging] / be active in behind-the-scenes election maneuvering.

암염(巖鹽)〔광〕rock salt; halite.

암영(暗影)〔어두운 그림자〕a dark shadow;〔불안〕a gloom;〔장애·어려움〕an obstruc-

암운(暗雲) dark [murky / sullen] clouds. ¶~이 드리워지고 있다 Dark clouds are hanging low.∥이번 내각의 전도에는 벌써부터 ~이 드리워져 있다 Ominous clouds are already threatening the prospects of this Cabinet.

암자(庵子) [작은 절] a small (Buddhist) temple; [승려의 거처] a hermitage; a (hermit's) cell [cottage]. ¶그는 산중의 ~에 들어 박혔다 He secluded himself in a mountain hermitage.

암자색(暗紫色) dark purple.

암장(暗葬) secret burial. ⇨암매장

암적색(暗赤色) dark red; garnet. ¶~의 dark-red / garnet.

암죽(-粥) thin gruel (for a baby).

암중모색(暗中摸索) groping in the dark. **암중모색하다** grope (blindly) in the dark. ¶그 사건에 대해 경찰은 그저 암중모색하고 있을 뿐이다 When it comes to that case, the police are just groping in the dark right now.

암중비약(暗中飛躍) secret maneuvers. ⇨암약

암초(暗礁) a (sunken) rock; an unknown reef; [비유] a deadlock; a rock. ¶~에 부딪히다[걸리다] strike a rock / go [run / founder] on a rock / reach [come to] a deadlock∥(배가) ~를 피해 가다 steer clear of a rock∥배가 ~에 부딪혀 난파했다 The ship was wrecked on a rock. / The ship grounded and was wrecked.

암치질(-痔疾) [의] internal hemorrhoids.

암캐 a she-dog; a bitch.

암컷 a female (animal / bird / insect); a she; a doe(사슴·토끼·양·염소 등의). ¶그것은 ~이냐 수컷이냐 Is it a she[female] or a he[male]? / What is its sex?∥~인지 수컷인지 모르겠다 I can't tell its sex.

암키와 [건] a concave tile.

암탉 a hen; a pullet(1년 미만의 어린). ¶알을 품고 있는 ~ a sitting hen.
암탉이 울면 집안이 망한다(속담) It goes ill in the house where the hen sings and the cock is silent.
암탉이 울다 henpeck; dominate (one's) husband.

암톨쩌귀 the knuckle (of a hinge); a gudgeon; a pan.

암퇘지 a female hog; a sow.

암투(暗鬪) a secret [smoldering] strife [feud]; veiled enmity. ¶그들은 오랫동안 ~를 계속하고 있다 They have long been at odds [loggerheads] behind the scenes. **암투하다** be at a secret feud (with); feud silently (with); struggle under cover.

암팡스럽다 short but tough [plucky / spunky / aggressive / dauntless]. ¶암팡스러운 얼굴 a dauntless look∥암팡스럽게 싸우다 fight dauntlessly [ferociously]∥암팡스럽게 말대꾸하다 answer back aggressively.

암페어 [물] an ampere. (기호 A). ¶10~의 전류 a current of 10 amperes.

암평아리 a pullet; a she-chick[-chicken].

암표(暗票) a scalper's ticket; an illegal ticket. ¶~를 팔다 scalp (theater tickets).
● **암표상**(-商) (행위) ticket-scalping; (사람) a (ticket) scalper; an illegal ticket-broker.

암행(暗行) traveling incognito. **암행하다** travel incognito [in secret / in disguise].
● **암행어사** a secret Royal inspector.

암호(暗號) a secret language; a cryptogram; a cryptogram; (전신의) a cipher; a (secret) code; (군호) a password; a watchword; a countersign. ¶문자 ~ a letter code∥숫자 ~ a figure code∥전신 ~ a telegraphic code / a cable code∥~로 in cipher∥~를 해독하다 decode [decipher] (a message)∥~로 쓰다 write in cipher / cipher / encipher / encode∥~를 대다[말하다] give a password∥~로 전보를 치다 send a telegram in code [cipher]∥~로 wire cryptographically∥~를 대지 않으면 통과하지 못한다 Give the password, or you shall not pass.
● **암호문** a cryptogram; a cryptograph. **암호해독** code-breaking; cryptanalysis; cryptography.

암흑(暗黑) darkness; blackness. ¶~의 dark / black / gloomy∥불이 다 나가서 우리는 ~속에 있었다 All the lights went out and we were left in the dark.
● **암흑가** the underworld; a gang land. **암흑시대** a dark age; the Dark Ages(중세 유럽의 5세기 ~ 11세기 초).

압권(壓卷) 1 [다른 것보다 뛰어난 것] the best; a masterpiece. ¶현대 소설 중의 ~ the best modern novel / the greatest work of modern fiction. 2 [가장 훌륭한 부분] the best part (of a book); the highlight (of the evening). ¶그의 연설은 대회의 ~이었다 His speech was the best part of the convention. ∥이 아리아는 오늘 밤 오페라의 ~이다 This aria is the highlight of tonight's opera.

압도(壓倒) overwhelming; overcoming; surpassing. **압도하다** overwhelm; overpower; overcome; overrule; crush; weigh down; [능가하다] surpass; excel; exceed; outrival. ¶야당[반대당]을 ~ snow under the opposition∥(외제품이) 국산품을 ~ outrival [outsell] domestic products / drive Korean goods out of market∥품질에서 다른 물건을 단연 ~ be far superior to others in quality∥이 책은 자료의 풍부함에 있어서 다른 책들을 압도하고 있다 This book excels[outshines] other books in richness of data. ➜나는 그의 큰 도량에 압도당했다 I was overwhelmed by his generosity. ∥우리는 상대에게 압도되어[기가 꺾여] 져 버렸다 We were defeated because we were cowed[overwhelmed] by our opponents(▶ cow는 위협하여, overwhelm은 압도적인 세력으로).

압도적(壓倒的) overwhelming. ¶~으로 overwhelmingly∥~ 승리 an overwhelming [a sweeping] victory / (선거에서의) a landslide (victory)∥~ 승리를 거두다 win an overwhelming[a sweeping] victory (over) / (미) score a landslide (victory)(선거에서)∥~ 다수로 선출되다 be elected by an overwhelming majority∥대통령 선거는 그의 ~ 승리로 끝났다 The presidential election ended in a landslide [sweeping] victory for him. ∥우리 팀은 ~ 승리를 거두었다 Our team won a one-sided [lopsided] victory.

압력(壓力) 1 [물] pressure; (gravitational) stress. ¶대기 ~ atmospheric pressure∥총[최대 / 절대] ~ total [maximum / absolute] pressure∥타이어의 ~이 정상인지 살펴보다 see that the tire pressure is right∥~이 높다

[낮다] The pressure is high[low].// 이 타이어에는 1인치당 20파운드의 ~이 가해져 있다 There is a pressure of 20 pounds to the inch on this tire. **2** [비유] pressure. ¶경제적 ~ economic pressure (on consumers) // 외부 ~ external pressure // ~을 가하다[넣다] apply pressure to / put pressure on[upon] (a person / a movement) / exert pressure on // ~을 넣어 …하게 하다[못하게 하다] pressure (a person) into[out of] (an act / doing something) // ~에 굴하다 bow[bend] to (another's) pressure // ~를 받다 be put under pressure (to do) / be pressured (to do / into doing) // 물가 상승을 억제하도록 정부에 ~을 가하다 pressure the government to suppress price hikes.
● 압력계 a manometer; a pressure gauge. 압력 단체 a pressure group. ¶그는 ~의 조종을 받고 있다 He is manipulated by a pressure group. 압력솥 a pressure cooker.
압류(押留) [법] attachment; seizure; distraint; distress. ¶가~ provisional attachment[seizure] / sequestration // 부동산[동산] ~ real[personal] distress // 저당물 ~ foreclosure of a mortgage // ~ 딱지를 붙이다 paste distraint paper (on goods) // ~ 중에 있다 be under attachment[distraint] // ~를 당하다 have one's property attached // ~를 해제하다 release[relieve] (a person's property) from attachment. 압류하다 attach; seize; distrain; place (a person's property) under distraint. ¶재산을 ~ attach[levy (distress) on] (a person's) property // 물품을 ~ seize [distrain] (a person's) goods. → ¶그는 재산을 압류당했다 His property was attached [placed under distraint].
● 압류 명령 an order of attachment. 압류장 a warrant[writ] of attachment; a seizure note; a distress warrant. 압류 재산 property under distraint; attached[seized] property.
압박(壓迫) pressure; oppression; compulsion; coercion. ¶생활의 ~ the stress[pressure] of life // 정신적 ~ moral pressure // 피~ 민족 an oppressed people // ~을 받다 be pressed / be pressurized / be subjected to [come under] pressure // ~을 가하다 put [exert] pressure upon / put[apply] the screw(s) on // ~을 강화하다 intensify the pressure on // 학교 당국의 ~으로 계획은 중단되었다 The plan was given up under[because of] the pressure of the school authorities. 압박하다 [누르다] press; oppress; [탄압하다] oppress; be oppressive to; suppress (freedom); use pressure; clamp down on. ¶가난하고 약한 사람을 ~ oppress the poor and the weak // 언론의 자유를 ~ place[put] a gag upon the freedom of speech.
● 압박감 a sense of oppression; an oppressive sensation. ¶나는 무엇인가를 해야 한다는 ~을 느꼈다 I felt pressed to do something. 압박 붕대 a compress. 압박자 an oppressor.
압사(壓死) death from pressure. 압사하다 be crushed[pressed / squeezed] to death. ¶축대가 무너져 ~ be crushed to death by the collapse of the wall // 그는 불행히도 대들보에 깔려 압사했다 He had the misfortune of being crushed to death under a fallen beam.
압살(壓殺) killing by pressing[squeezing]. 압살하다 crush[press / squeeze] to death.

압송(押送) sending (a criminal) in custody. 압송하다 send (a criminal) under escort; transfer a convict[prisoner] to (a different) prison.
압수(押收) [법] (a) seizure; (a) confiscation; attachment. 압수하다 seize; take over; attach; confiscate; (증권·서류 등을) impound; take legal possession of (a person's property). ¶서류를 ~ capture[retain] papers // ~ seize evidence // 밀수품을 ~ confiscate smuggled goods. → ¶재산을 압수당하다 have one's property confiscated // 그는 재산을 압수당했다 His property was confiscated.
● 압수물 a seized article; seized property. 압수 영장 a warrant for seizure.
압승(壓勝) an overwhelming[a sweeping] victory; (선거에서의) a landslide (victory). ¶대통령 선거는 그의 ~으로 끝났다 The presidential election ended in a landslide [sweeping] victory for him. 압승하다 win an overwhelming victory (over); defeat decisively[overwhelmingly]; overwhelm; swamp. ¶챔피언은 도전자에게 압승했다 The champion won an overwhelming[a sweeping] victory over the challenger. // 그는 선거에서 압승했다 He won a landslide victory in the election.
압연(壓延) rolling. ¶냉간[열간] ~ cold[hot] roll(ing). 압연하다 roll.
● 압연기 a rolling machine[mill].
압운(押韻) rhyme; rhyming. 압운하다 rhyme; (미) rime.
압정(押釘) (미) a thumbtack; a tack; a pushpin; (영) a drawing pin. ¶~으로 고정시키다 tack down (a carpet) / tack / thumbtack // 벽보를 ~으로 벽에 고정시켰다 I tacked up a poster on the wall.
압정(壓政) despotism; tyranny. ¶~에 신음하다 groan[crouch] under tyranny[oppression] / suffer from tyranny.
압제(壓制) oppression; tyranny; despotism. ¶~적(인) oppressive / repressive / high-handed / despotic / tyrannical // ~적으로 in an oppressive manner / oppressively / tyrannically / with a high hand // ~에서 벗어나다 be freed from oppression[tyranny] // ~에 신음하다 groan[crouch] under tyranny[oppression] / suffer from tyranny. 압제하다 oppress; tyrannize (over); rule with an iron hand; rule with a rod of iron.
● 압제자 an oppressor; a despot; a tyrant. 압제 정치 despotism.
압지(壓紙·押紙) blotting paper; a blotter. ¶~로 잉크를 빨아들이다 blot (up) ink with blotting paper.
압착(壓搾) pressure; compression; pressing. 압착하다 press; compress.
● 압착기 a compressor; a press.
압축(壓縮) **1** [줄임·좁힘] compression; constriction; condensation. 압축하다 compress; compact; constrict; condense. ¶압축할 수 있는 compressible / condensable // 공기[가스]를 ~ compress air[gas]. **2** [요약] condensation; summarization; epitomization. 압축하다 condense; summarize; epitomize. ¶다섯 권의 저서를 한 권으로 ~ condense a five-volume book into one.
● 압축가스 compressed gas. 압축계 a piezometer. 압축 공기 compressed air. 압축기 a compressor.

압출(壓出) pressing[squeezing] out. **압출하다** press out; extrude (plastics).

앗 1 [다급하거나 놀랐을 때 내는 소리] oh!; o dear!; Dear me!; Good(ness) gracious!(Good) heavens!; By Jove!; God bless me!; Why; [아프거나 뜨거울 때 내는 소리] Ouch! ¶~ 큰일났다 Good Heavens! / Dear me! // ~ 지갑이 없어졌다 Oh! My wallet is gone! // ~ 모자를 잊었군 Dear me! I've left my hat behind.

앗다 1 [빼앗다] take (a thing) by force; snatch (something) from (a person); deprive (a person) of (something); (마음 등을) 빼앗다] fascinate; charm; captivate. 2 [씨를 빼다] remove the seeds from; gin (cotton). 3 [일을 해 주고 일로 갚게 하다] pay for labor in kind[with labor]. ¶품을 ~ exchange labors.

-았자 [⋯을 인정하더라도] even if[though] ...; granting[supposing] that .... ¶당신이 지금 가 보~ 그를 만나지는 못한다 Even if you start now, you will not be able to see him. // 푸념을 늘어놓~ 소용없다 It is no use complaining.

앙 1 [어린아이의 울음소리]. ¶~ 하고 울다 cry loudly; burst out crying. 2 [남을 놀라게 하려고 지르는 소리] bo!; boh!; boo!

앙가슴 the middle of the chest.

앙감질 hopping (on one leg). **앙감질하다** hop (on one leg).

앙갚음 tit for tat; an eye for an eye; revenge; retaliation; requital. ¶~으로 in revenge [retaliation] (for); by way of retaliation / out of vengeance[revenge / spite] // ~으로 남을 죽이다 kill (a person) for revenge[out of spite] // 그녀는 부모에 대한 ~으로 죽음을 택했다 She chose death as a way to get back at her parents. // 그의 몰인정에 대한 ~으로 나는 그의 비밀을 폭로했다 I exposed his secret out of revenge[to get back at him] for his unkindness. // 그에게 이렇게 모욕을 당했으니 ~을 해 주고 싶다 I want to revenge myself on him for this insult. // 이 ~은 꼭 할 테다 I will pay you out for this. **앙갚음하다** give[pay] tit for tat; revenge (one's wrongs); revenge oneself[be revenged / have one's revenge] (on a person for something); get even[square] with (a person); retaliate on [against] (a person); pay back; (속어) get back at[on] (a person). ¶(상대방과) 같은 수법으로 ~ pay (a person) in (his) own coin / serve (a person) with the same sauce // 불공평한 처사[모욕]에 대하여 ~ revenge an injustice [insult].

앙그러지다 1 [먹음직스럽다] delicious-looking; appetizing. 2 [하는 짓이 어울리다] smart. 3 [모양이 보기 좋다] nice; smart; stylish.

앙금 [침전물] sediment; settlings; deposit; (술 등의) dregs; lees; (커피 등의) grounds. ¶~을 휘젓다 disturb[stir up] the sediment // ~이 앉았다 Dregs settled. / Dregs are deposited at the bottom.

앙등(昂騰) a rise (in prices). ⇨**등귀**(騰貴)

앙망하다(仰望−) [바라다] wish; hope (for); be solicitous for; look forward to(기대하다); [부탁하다] beg; ask (for); solicit; entreat. ¶조속한 답장을 앙망하나이다 Kindly favor me with an early answer. / I am looking forward to your early reply[hearing from you soon]. // 만찬회에 참석해 주시기를 앙망하나이다 We request the pleasure[honor] of your company at dinner.

앙모하다(仰慕−) look up to; respect; adore; admire. ¶스승으로 ~ look up to (a person) as one's teacher. ➔대정치가로서 앙모받다 be looked up to as a great statesman.

앙바틈하다 thickset; short and thick; fat and short; stocky; stodgy; chunky; stumpy. **앙바틈히** stockily; stodgily; stumpily.

앙상블 (프) an ensemble. ¶스포티한 ~ (여성복의) a sports ensemble.

앙상하다 loose; sparse; lean. ⇨<**엉성하다**

앙숙(怏宿) [앙심을 품고 미워함]. ¶~**이다** lead a cat-and-dog life / be at enmity (with) / be at loggerheads (with) / be on bad terms (with) // 그들은 서로 ~이다 They are cat and dog. / There is no love lost between them. / They are at daggers drawn with each other. / They can't stand the sight of each other. / There is bitter enmity between them.

앙심(怏心) spite; grudge; ill will; rancor. ¶~ 깊은 여자 a revengeful[vindictive] woman / ~을 품다[먹다] bear (a person) (an) ill will / have[harbor] a grudge against (a person) // 그는 나에게 ~을 품고 있다 He has a grudge against me. // 그녀는 아직도 그 일로 내게 ~을 품고 있다 She still bears me ill will over that matter.

앙알거리다 grumble (at / over); mutter (about); complain (of).

앙앙 ¶~ 울다 cry[weep] bitterly.

앙양(昻揚) exaltation; enhancement; elevation; (spiritual) uplift. ¶애국심의 ~ an upsurge of patriotic sentiment. **앙양하다** exalt; enhance; uplift; promote; raise; uphold. ¶국위를 ~ heighten[raise / enhance] national prestige // 자유 민권 사상을 ~ promote the ideal of civil liberties // 사회 도의를 ~ promote social morality.

앙증맞다 disproportionately small[little]; [아주 작은] tiny; miniature (tube). ¶앙증맞은 손 little pretty hands // 앙증맞은 아이 a mere dot of a child.

앙천대소하다(仰天大笑−) laugh heartily [loudly]; have[laugh] a hearty laugh; burst out laughing; roar with laughter. ¶그 일로 모두들 앙천대소했다 We all had a good laugh over it.

앙칼지다 (일에) unyielding; unbending; (태도가) vehement; furious; fierce; sharp; keen; aggressive. ¶앙칼진 여자 an aggressive woman / a woman of violent temper // 앙칼지게 쏴붙이다 snarl[snap] at (a person) / make a retort with a sharp remark // 앙칼지게 공격하다 make a fierce[furious] attack on.

앙케트(ⓔenquête) a questionnaire; an opinionnaire. ¶~에 대한 회답 replies submitted to a questionnaire // 어린이의 독서 경향에 관한 ~ a questionnaire on children's reading habits // ~를 내다 send out a questionnaire / obtain information through a questionnaire // 전화로 ~ 조사를 하다 address a telephone questionnaire (to a person on a matter).

앙코르 an encore. ¶~를 받다 receive[get] an encore.

앙큼하다 wily; insidious. ⇨**엉큼하다**

앙탈하다 [앙탈 부리다] scheme to disobey;

try to evade[shirk]; grumble angrily; whine; nag; fuss; do against. ¶공연히 ~ make a big fuss over nothing / grumble at nothing / 버릇없는 아이처럼 ~ whine like a spoiled child // 무슨 이유로 앙탈하느냐 What are the grounds of your complaint? // 그녀는 그 일을 하지 않으려고 앙탈했다 She tried frantically to get out of the work.

앞[1] **1** [전면] the front; the fore part; [전방] ahead; beyond; off; away. ¶~의 차량 the front cars[carriages] // 집 ~의 한길 the street in front of the house // ~에서 다섯 번째 자리 the fifth seat from the front // ~으로 **나아가다** proceed / go forward // ~으로 (전진) (행진을 계속할 때) March on! // ~을 주의해서 보시오 Look carefully in front of you. // 행렬이 천천히 ~으로 나아갔다 The procession slowly moved ahead[forward]. // 약 100미터 ~에 트럭이 달리고 있다 A truck[(영) lorry] is running about a hundred meters ahead (of us). // 자동차의 바로 ~이나 뒤로 횡단하는 것은 위험하다 It is dangerous to cross the street immediately in front of or behind a car. // 나는 이순신 장군의 동상 바로 ~에 섰다 I stood right in front of the bronze statue of Yi Sunshin. // 우체국 바로 ~에서 왼쪽으로 도시오 You turn left just before you come to the post office. // 그는 나의 세 걸음 ~에서 멈춰 섰다 He stopped three steps (away) from me. // ~을 똑바로 보시오 Look straight before[ahead of] you.
2 [행렬·순서의 먼저] the head; the foremost; the first(맨 앞). ¶~의 절반 the first half // 페이지에 on the previous page // ~에 서서 가다 walk[go] ahead of (others) / lead the way // ~ 다투어 하다 try to get ahead of others in doing / struggle to do // 두 사람은 서로 ~을 다투는 접전을 벌였다 The two had a close race with first one ahead and then the other. // 그의 이름이 맨 ~에 나와 있다 His name leads the list. // ~의 예가 뒤의 예보다 낫다 The former example is better than the latter.
3 [면전·대중 앞] the public; company; the presence of (a person). ¶남들 ~에서 in public[company] / in the presence of others / before[around] people // 남의 ~도 가리지 않고 without any regard to decency // 아이들 ~에서는 만사가 순조로운 체했다 I pretended that everything was going well in the presence of my children. // 나는 사람들 ~에서 창피를 당했다 I was disgraced in front of people[in public]. // ▶ in public(공중의 면전에서) // 아이들 ~에서 그런 말을 해서는 안 돼 Don't talk about things like that in front of the children. // 법 ~에서는 만인이 평등하다 All men are equal before the law.
4 [미래] the future. ¶~을 내다보지 못하는 사람들 people who are so short-sighted // ~으로 2, 3일 for some days to come / for the next few days / for a few days ahead // ~으로 4년 (동안) for the next[coming] four years / for the four years to come // ~을 내다보는 long-sighted / farsighted // ~을 **내다보다** look into the future / look ahead[to the future] // ~으로는 내가 해 보겠습니다 I will try to do it by myself in (the) future[after this]. // ~으로 더욱 조심하겠습니다 I will be more careful in the future[after this]. // 나는 ~으로의 일에 대해서는 생각하지 않고 있다 I am not think-ing about[planning for] the future. // ~으로 언제까지 계속할 것인가 How much longer is it going to continue? // ~으로 무엇을 할 작정인가 What are you going to do from now on[after this]? // ~으로 어떤 일이 일어날지 모른다 We don't know what is in store for us. // 나는 ~이 캄캄하다 I have lost all hope[have no hope] for the future. // ~으로 1년 동안 우리 집은 경제적으로 쪼들리게 될 거다 This coming year will be a hard one for us financially.
5 [몫] a share; a portion; a quota. ¶학생 한 사람 ~에 볼펜 두 자루씩 주었다 I gave the pupils two ball-point pens each[apiece]. / I gave two ball-point pens to each pupil. // 겨우 이만큼이 내 ~으로 떨어졌다 This much has fallen to my lot. // 그의 재산의 대부분이 손자 ~으로 갔다 Most of his estate went to the grandson. // 그녀는 제 ~만 차린다 She is out for her own interest only. / She is out to feather her own nest. // 한 사람 ~에 봉지 2개씩을 마련했다 We prepared two bags per person[per head / apiece].
6 [먼저 부분] the preceding[foregoing] part. ¶~에서 말한 바와 같이 as previously stated / (문장에서) as stated above // 이 문제에 관해서는 ~에서 간단히 언급했다 I have touched on this subject briefly above.
7 [국부] the private[privy / secret] parts; the privates. ¶~을 **가리다** cover one's privy parts.
앞(을) 못 보다 be blind. ¶아버지는 앞을 못 보신다 My father is blind.

앞[2] **1** (편지 등의) addressed to (a person). ¶장씨 ~으로 된 편지[소포] a letter[parcel] addressed[directed] to Mr. Jang // 회사 ~으로 그에게 편지를 보냈다 I wrote to him care of his company. **2** (어음 등의) drawn in one's favo(u)r. ¶C 은행 ~으로의 수표 a check drawn upon C Bank // 한 씨 ~으로 어음을 발행하다 draw a bill for[in favor of] Mr. Han.

앞가림하다 have just enough education to get by.
앞가슴 the breast; the chest (of the body / of a garment).
앞길 1 [앞에 난 길] the road ahead; [가야 할 길] the way yet to go; the distance yet to cover; the journey before one. ¶~**이 멀다** have a long[far] way to go // 횃불로 ~을 비추다 light one's way with a torch // 이제 너의 ~을 가로막는 것은 아무것도 없다 Nothing stands in your way now. // ~은 매우 험난하다 The road ahead of us is very rough.
2 [전도] one's future; prospects; (an) outlook. ¶~이 창창한 젊은이 a young man with a bright future // ~**을 망치다** spoil[blight] one's future // 나의 ~은 암담하다 My prospects are gloomy. // 그의 ~은 창창하다 He has the world before him. / He has his whole life in front of him. // 우리의 ~에는 많은 어려움이 기다리고 있을 것이다 A lot of problems lie ahead of[are waiting for] us.
앞날 the days ahead[to come]; one's future; [여생] the remaining years[days] (of one's life). ¶**밝은** ~ a bright[rosy] future // 어두운 ~ a dark future / gloomy prospects // ~을 **염려하다** feel anxious about one's future // ~을 **생각하다** think ahead[of the future] / look ahead[to the future] // 우리는 신혼부부

앞니
의 ~을 축복하여 건배했다 We drank to a happy future for the newly married couple. // 그녀의 ~이 멀지 않다 She is not long for this world / Her days are numbered. // 아버지의 ~이 그리 길지 못하다 My father has only a short time to live.

앞니 a front tooth; a foretooth; an incisor. ¶세 개가 부러지다 have three of one's front teeth broken // 아기가 ~가 났다 The baby cut his front teeth.

앞다리 (네발짐승의) a foreleg; a front leg; a forelimb; (바다 짐승의) a flapper; a flipper. ¶올챙이의 ~가 나오기 시작했다 The tadpoles have begun to grow forelegs.

앞당기다 move up; advance (a date); make (anything) earlier. ¶여행 예정을 ~ curtail one's itinerary // 출발 날짜가 3일 앞당겨졌다 The date of departure was moved up [advanced] by three days. // 퇴근 시간이 6시에서 5시로 앞당겨졌다 Quitting time was moved up from six o'clock to five. // 그들은 경기를 화요일에서 월요일로 앞당겼다 They put the game forward from Tuesday to Monday. // 회의의 일정이 앞당겨졌다 The conference schedule has been moved up. // 파티 날짜가 사흘 앞당겨졌다 The date of the party was advanced by [moved up] three days.

앞두다 have (a period / distance) ahead; have (an examination) near [close] at hand. ¶졸업을 앞둔 학생 a student about to graduate // 시험을 앞두고 with the examination just before on [near at hand] // 선거일을 2주일 앞두고 with the election day two weeks off [ahead] // 닷새를 ~ have five days to go [run] // 20마일을 ~ have twenty miles ahead (to cover).

앞뒤 1 (위치의) front and rear. ¶~의[에] before and behind // ~로 backward(s) and forward(s) / back and forth / front and rear // ~로 흔들리다 swing back and forth // ~를 둘러보다 look before and behind / look around [about] one // 적의 ~를 공격하다 attack the enemy front and rear // ~를 주의해서 살피시오 Look carefully to the front and the rear. // 내 차 ~에 대형 트럭이 달리고 있었다 Large trucks [(영) lorries] were running in front of and behind my car.
2 [순서] order. ¶~를 뒤바꾸다 reverse [(구어) mess up] the order.
3 [주위 사정] circumstances; consequence. ¶~를 가리지 않고 recklessly / rashly / without considering the consequences // 그는 ~ 가리지 않고 즉시 사표를 제출했다 He at once sent in his resignation without thinking of the consequences.
4 [일관성] coherence; consistency; [조리] logical sequence. ¶~가 닿지 않는 변명 [의론] a lame excuse [argument] // ~가 맞다 [안 맞다] (일치 여부) consistent [inconsistent] / (사리에 맞는지 여부) logical [illogical] // 그의 말은 ~가 맞지 않다 He contradicts himself. / What he says is (self-)contradictory. / (구어) His story doesn't hang together.
5 [문맥] the context. ¶~를 보고 문장의 뜻을 새기다 interpret a sentence by the context.

앞뒷집 two houses, one in front and the other in (the) rear; two neighbor houses. ¶~에 살다 live in the vicinity / be next-door neighbors.

앞뜰 a front yard [court / garden].

앞머리 1 [정수리 앞쪽 부분의 머리] the forehead; [의] the sinciput; [앞쪽의 머리칼] a forelock; (단발머리의) a bang. ¶그녀는 ~를 이마까지 잘라 단발머리를 하고 있다 Her hair is cut squarely across the forehead. / (미) She wears her hair in bangs. **2** [물건의 앞부분] the front end; the head. **3** [선두] the forefront; the head; the van; the vanguard.

앞문(-「門) the front gate; the front door; the front entrance.

앞바다 the offing; the open sea. ¶인천 ~ off Incheon // 1킬로미터 ~에 표류물이 있다 There is some flotsam [driftage] a kilometer offshore.

앞바람 1 the south wind. ⇨마파람 **2** a head wind. ⇨역풍

앞바퀴 a front [fore] wheel. ¶~가 빠졌다 The front wheel came off.

앞발 (네발짐승·곤충 등의) a forefoot (pl. -feet); (발톱이 있는 짐승의) a (front) paw; (발굽이 있는 짐승의) a front hoof (pl. hooves). ¶(개를 보고) ~ 들어! Beg!
● **앞발질** kicking with the forefeet; pawing.

앞산(-「山) a mountain (standing) in front.

앞서 1 [이전에] previously; before; earlier. ¶~부터 for some days [time] past // ~ 결정한 대로 행동해 주기 바란다 You are requested to proceed in accordance with the previous arrangements. // 개회에 ~ 대의원의 등록이 실시되었다 Registration of the delegates preceded the meeting.
2 [다른 사람·다른 일보다 먼저] before; earlier (than); prior to; ahead (of); in advance (of). ¶~ 가다 go ahead of / go before // ~ 가며 계획을 추진하다 take the initiative in pushing on with a plan // 시류에 ~ 가다 be ahead of the times // 내 아들이 나를 두고 ~ 갔다 My son has died leaving me behind. / I have outlived my son. / My son has died (before me). // 그는 나보다 ~ 산꼭대기에 올라가 있었다 He beat me to the top of the hill. // ~ 간 3사람은 곧 되돌아왔다 Soon afterward the three who had gone ahead came back. // 그가 결승선에 왔을 때는 다음 주자를 2미터 ~ 있었다 When he reached the finishing line, he was two meters ahead of the next runner.

앞서다 run ahead (of); outdistance(월등히); go in advance of; go ahead (of); precede; be antecedent (to); head; lead (others); take precedence. ¶시대에 ~ go ahead of the times [one's age] // 행렬에서 ~ lead the procession // 그녀는 2등보다 3미터 앞서서 골인했다 She reached the goal three meters ahead of the second runner. // 수학에서는 미숙이가 금순이를 완전히 앞섰다 Misuk has completely outdistanced Geumsun in math. // 우리는 2위 팀을 크게 앞섰다 We have increased our lead over the team in second place. // 우리 팀이 2점 앞섰다 Our team got off to a two-point [two-run] lead. (▶ two-run은 야구의 경우) // 그들의 생각은 그 시대 사람들보다 훨씬 앞서 있었다 Their views were far ahead of the times.

앞서거니 뒤서거니 ¶~ 하다 alternate for [in] lead / run neck and neck / be nip and tuck.

앞세우다 1 [앞서게 하다] make (a person) go ahead; let (a person) lead [precede]; set (a person) at the head. ¶국기를 앞세우고

with the national flag at the head (of a procession)∥그 행렬은 대학생을 앞세우고 행진했다 The procession was led by college[university] students.∥경제 문제보다 정치 문제를 앞세워야 한다 We must give priority to political problems over economic ones. **2** [손아래 식구를 먼저 여의다] survive[outlive] (one's son).

앞수표(-手票) [실제 발행일보다 뒷날을 발행일로 정하는 수표] a postdated check[bill].

앞앞이 [각 사람의 앞에] before[in front of] each person; [몫몫이] to[for] each person; each; respectively. ¶~ 하나씩 one for each person / one piece each / one apiece∥~ 방이 있다 Each one of us has a room to himself. / We each have our own room.

앞어금니 [생] [소구치] a premolar; a bicuspid.

앞에총(-銃) [구령] Port arms! ¶~ 자세 the port ~을 하다 port.

앞으로가 [구령] Forward!; March!

앞일 things to come; the future; future development. ¶~에 대비하다 provide[prepare] for the future∥~을 생각하다 think of[take thought for] the future (of)∥~을 걱정하다 worry about one's future∥~을 예언하다 predict[forecast] the future (of)∥멀리 ~을 내다보다 see far ahead into the future∥~에 대해서 희망에 가득 차 있다 be full of hope for the future.∥~은 알 수 없다 There is no knowing what the future may bring forth.∥네가 게을러서 ~이 걱정된다 Your idleness makes me worry about your future.∥이 아이의 ~이 걱정된다 I am worried about this child's future.

앞자락 the front hem[skirt] (of a garment).

앞잡이 1 [안내자] a guide; a cicerone(관광객의); a leader. ¶~가 되다 lead (a party) / act as a guide. **2** [끄나풀 노릇을 하는 사람] an agent; a tool; a cat's-paw; a pawn; (문어) a minion. ¶경찰의 ~ a stool pigeon / a police spy[agent] ∥ ~가 되다 act as an agent (for) / make oneself a cat's-paw of (a person) / 정부 권력의 ~로 일하다 work as a tool of the government authorities.

앞장서다 lead; head; be at the head; be the first (to do); take the lead[initiative]. ¶앞장서서 at the head of∥앞장서서 계획을 추진하다 take the initiative in pushing on with a plan∥유행에 ~ lead[set] the fashion∥그는 (무슨 일에나) 늘 앞장선다 He always takes the lead.

앞줄 the front row. ¶그는 교실에서 항상 ~에 자리를 잡는다 He always takes a seat in the front row[a front-row seat] in the classroom.∥홍순도 씨는 ~ 왼쪽에서 다섯째입니다 Mr. Hong Sundo is the fifth from the left in the front row.

앞지르다 outrun; pass (another in the race); outstrip; steal a march upon; be beforehand with; outpace; pass (another car) ahead; outsail(배가); get ahead of (another); [능가하다] outdo; surpass. ¶남을 ~ forestall a person∥(신문사가) 특종으로 다른 신문을 ~ scoop a rival paper∥남의 말을 앞질러 미리 결론을 말해 버리다 anticipate the conclusion of a person's story∥그는 경쟁 상대를 앞질러 그 백화점과 계약을 맺었다 He got the jump[stole a march] on his rivals by signing a contract with the department store.∥자전거가 나를 앞질러 갔다 A bicycle passed me.∥다른 사람들이 나를 앞질렀다 The others got ahead of me. / The others passed me by.∥그는 경쟁자에게 앞지름을 당했다 He was outstripped by his rival.∥그녀는 늦게 시작했지만 곧 다른 사람들을 앞질렀다 Though she started later, she was soon ahead of[she soon surpassed] the others.∥그는 나를 앞질러 갔다 He passed me.∥결코 그가 나를 앞지르지 못하게 하겠다 I won't let him get ahead of me.∥한 달도 못 되어 그는 동료들을 앞질러 뛰어난 성적을 올리게 되었다 Before a month had passed, he began to outdo his colleagues and produce excellent results.

앞집 [앞으로 이웃한 집] the house in front; [길 건너의] the opposite house.

앞쪽 [앞 방면] the front; [앞부분] the fore (part). ¶행렬의 ~에 서다 stand near the head of a line∥~을 주의해서 보아라 Look carefully in front of you.∥우리 ~의 언덕은 모두 포도밭이다 The whole hill before[in front of / ahead of] us is a vineyard.∥그 가게는 여기서 약 50미터 ~에 있습니다 You will find the store about fifty meters ahead.∥아버지는 나보다 20미터 ~를 달리고 있었다 My father was running twenty meters ahead of me.∥그 빵집은 바로 ~입니다 The bakery is right up there.

앞차(-車) [앞서 떠난 차] the last bus[train]; [앞에 가는 차] a preceding vehicle; the car (that goes) ahead. ¶~와의 거리를 충분히 두고 운전하시오 Don't drive too close to the car in front (of you).∥그는 ~에 충돌했다 He ran into the car ahead of him.

앞창(-窓) the front window.

앞치마 an apron. ¶~를 두르고 일하다 work in an apron.

애¹ 1 [초조·걱정] anxiety; worry; trouble. ¶이 아이는 ~를 많이 먹인다[먹이지 않는다] This child gives us a lot of trouble[no trouble].∥넌 참 ~를 먹이는구나 You cause[put people to] quite a bit of trouble, don't you? **2** [수고로움] pains; trouble; effort(s); labor(s). ¶타이어가 펑크 나서 ~를 먹고 있다 I'm in a fix because I have a flat tire.∥그는 그것을 조사하느라 ~를 썼다 He went to great pains investigating it.

애² a child; a kid. ⇨아이

애가(哀歌) [비가] a song of sorrow; a lament; [만가] a dirge; an elegy. ¶애절한 ~ a heartrending song of sorrow∥예레미야 ~ the Lamentations (of Jeremiah).

애개(개) [아뿔싸] My!; O dear!; Why!; Gosh!; Golly!; [대단치 않은 것을 업신여겨 내는 소리] How puny[skimpy / little / paltry]! ¶~, 이것뿐이냐 My, is that all?∥~, 저 조그만 차 좀 봐 Look, what a tiny car it is!

애걸(哀乞) begging; pleading; imploring; supplication; entreaty; an appeal. **애걸하다** beg [plead] for; implore; cry (a person) mercy; ask for mercy. ¶그는 그녀에게 가지 말라고 애걸했다 He implored her not to go.

애걸복걸하다(哀乞伏乞-) beg earnestly; implore; supplicate.

애견(愛犬) one's pet dog.
  ●**애견가** a lover of dogs; a dog lover.

애고(머니) Ah!; Oh!; Oh dear! ⇨아이고(머니)

애교(愛嬌) charms; winsomeness; attractiveness; courtesy(상인 등의). ¶~ 있는 웃음 a

애교심

winning[an engaging] smile // ~ 없는 여자 a sour-looking[an unattractive] woman // 그녀는 손님들에게 ~를 부리고 있었다 She was making herself agreeable to all her guests. // 그의 실수는 언제나 ~가 있어 미움을 사지 않는다 His mistakes are always so humorous as to be totally disarming.

애교심 (愛校心) love of[for] one's school; attachment to one's alma mater.

애국 (愛國) patriotism; love [devotion] of[for] one's country. ¶~적인 patriotic.
● **애국가** Aegukga; the Korean national anthem. ¶~를 부르다 sing our[the Korean] national anthem. **애국 단체** a patriotic society[organization]. **애국선열** deceased patriots. **애국심** patriotic sentiment[feeling / spirit]; patriotism; nationalism. ¶~을 고취하다 infuse[instil] patriotism into the heart of (people) // 그는 ~이 강하다 He is very patriotic. / He loves his country deeply. **애국자** a patriot.

애기 →아기

애꾸 1 blindness of[in] one eye. ⇨ 애꾸눈(⇨ 애꾸) 2 a one-eyed person. ⇨ 애꾸눈이(⇨ 애꾸) ¶~인 남자 a one-eyed man / a man who has lost one eye // ~가 되다 lose one eye / become blind in one eye / lose the sight of one eye // 그는 ~이다 He is blind in one eye.
● **애꾸눈** blindness of[in] one eye. **애꾸눈이** a one-eyed person.

애꿎다 innocent; blameless; guiltless; undeserved. ¶애꿎은 사람 an innocent[a blameless] person // 애꿎은 개에게 화풀이하다 vent one's anger on one's innocent dog.

애끊다 feel one's heart rent[torn to pieces]; feel as if one's heart were breaking; feel as if one's heart would break; one's heart bleeds. ¶그 말을 들으니 애끊는 듯했다 I felt my heart would break to hear that. / My heart was fit to break when I heard it.

애끓다 be anxious[worried] (about); worry (oneself) (about); be all roiled up; (구어) be in a fidget[a stew] (about).

애늙은이 a stuffy youngster; a person who looks[acts] older than his years.

애니메이션 a cartoon film; an animated cartoon.

애달다 be anxious (to / about); be impatient (at); worry; fret (about / over). ¶그는 너를 만나고 싶어 애달아 했다 He was anxious to meet you.

애달프다 heartbreaking; aching; sorrowful; pathetic; painful; distressing; anguishing. ¶애달픈 소식 heartbreaking news // 애달픈 마음을 털어놓다 confess a heartrending sorrow // 그가 죽었다니 정말 애달픈 일이다 It is really heartbreaking to hear of his death.

애도 (哀悼) condolence; sympathy; mourning; grief; sorrow; lamentation; regret. ¶~의 편지 a letter of condolence // ~의 말 a funeral oration // ~의 뜻을 표하여 with one's deepest sympathy // 상처한 친구에게 ~의 뜻을 표하다 express one's sympathy to a friend who has lost his wife / offer condolences to a friend on his wife's death // 우리는 자당님의 서거에 대해 ~의 말씀을 드립니다 We offer our condolences to you on your mother's death. // 진심으로 ~의 말씀을 드립니다 Please accept my deep sympathy. / Allow me to offer my sincere condolences. / (친한 사람에게) I'm so sorry (about your father). **애도하다** lament; be grieved (at); grieve; mourn (over); sorrow (over a person's death). ¶죽은 사람을 ~ mourn for the dead // 친구들은 모두 그의 죽음을 애도했다 All of his friends mourned for him[mourned (over) his death].
● **애도사** a funeral oration.

애독 (愛讀) love of reading; reading (for pleasure). **애독하다** read (a book) with pleasure; be fond of reading (a book); read (a magazine) regularly. ¶나는 그의 소설을 애독했다 I loved reading[to read] his novels. / His novels were my favorites. // 그는 헤밍웨이를 애독하고 있다 Hemingway is his favorite author. // 이것은 대학생들이 애독하는 책이다 This book is popular among[with] college students.
● **애독서** (one of) a person's favorite (영) favourite books. **애독자** a devoted reader; (정기적인) a regular reader; (잡지·신문의) a subscriber. ¶동아 일보의 ~ a subscriber to the Dong-A // 이 잡지는 ~가 많다 This magazine has a large readership.

애드리브 [즉흥적인 연설[연주]] an ad lib. ¶~로 개그를 집어넣다 ad-lib some jokes / throw in some jokes that aren't in the script.

애드벌룬 an advertising balloon.

애련 (哀憐) pity; compassion. ¶~의 정을 금치 못하다 be overwhelmed with pity (for). **애련하다** piteous; pitiable; pitiful; poor; touching. ¶애련한 노래 a plaintive song.

애로 (隘路) 1 [좁고 험한 길] a narrow path; a defile(산속의). 2 [장애] a bottleneck. ¶그 계획을 진행시키는 데는 ~가 많았다 There were a series of bottlenecks in the way of the program. // 자금 부족이 생산의 ~이 되고 있다 Lack of capital is a bottleneck to production.

애마 (愛馬) one's favorite[pet] horse.

애매(모호)하다 (曖昧模糊─) [불확실하다] uncertain; indefinite; [불명료하다] unclear; [모호하다] vague; ambiguous; equivocal.(▶ambiguous는 고의로 속이려는 의도가 있다고는 할 수 없으나, equivocal은 고의로 발뺌하려는 의도가 수반됨) ¶애매한 설명 an unclear explanation // 애매한 의미 an ambiguous meaning // 애매한 태도 a noncommittal attitude // 그는 언제나 애매한 말만 한다 He never commits himself to anything definite. // 그는 애매한 태도를 취하고 있었다 He didn't take a definite position. / He maintained a noncommittal attitude. // 그는 애매한 대답을 했다 He gave an evasive[a vague / an ambiguous] answer. // 그 문장은 뜻이 ~ The meaning of that sentence is ambiguous[obscure].

애매하다 [아무 잘못이 없는데 책망을 받아서 억울하다] be falsely charged (with); be unjustly[falsely / wrongly] accused (of); be under a false charge; be unjustly suspected of a guilt; get an unwarranted scolding. ¶애매한 사람을 죽이다 kill an innocent man // 애매하게 의심받다 be suspected unjustly / be the object of groundless suspicion // 애매하게 꾸중을 듣다 get an unwarranted scolding.

애먹다 have bitter experience; have a hard time of it; be greatly embarrassed; have trouble; suffer[go through] hardships; be hard put to it; be at[be driven to] one's wit's end; find (a person / a thing) unmanageable. ¶설득에 ~ have a great tug to persuade // 나는 수학 문제를 푸는 데 애먹었다 I tried hard to solve[racked my brains over] a mathematical problem. // 우리는 엔진의 시동이 잘 걸리지 않아 애먹었다 We had difficulty starting (up) the engine. // 나는 그 아이를 다루는 데 애먹고 있다 I have a lot of trouble managing the boy. // 그가 매우 고집이 세서 나는 애먹고 있다 I have a hard time of it because he is so willful.

애먹이다 put (a person) out; put (a person) at[drive (a person) to] his wit's end; give (a person) much trouble. ¶이 아이는 애먹이지 않는다 The child is no trouble at all.

애먼 1 [엉뚱한] wrong; irrelevant; absurd; farfetched; unlikely. 2 [죄 없는] innocent; uninvolved; wrongly accused. ¶~ 사람 죄인 만들지 마라 Don't get the wrong man for your culprit.

애모(愛慕) love; yearning; affection (for / toward); attachment (to / for). ¶~의 정 a feeling of affection // ~를 받다 be (dearly) beloved by[of] // 학생들에게 ~를 받다 be the idol of one's pupils. **애모하다** love; be attached to; yearn after [for].

애무(愛撫) caress; caressing; a pet stroke; petting; endearment. **애무하다** caress; fondle; (동물을) pet.

애물(-物) 1 [애태우는 것] a cause[source] of worry[anxiety]; a thorn in the[one's] flesh [side]. 2 [어린 나이로 부모보다 먼저 죽은 자식] a son who preceded his parents to the grave.

애벌 [초벌] the first[preliminary] stage (in the procession of work). ¶~ 빨다 do a first and rough washing[laundering].

● **애벌갈이** [농] the first[preliminary] plowing[(영) ploughing / tilling]. **애벌빨래** a rough washing[laundering]. **애벌칠**(-漆) (페인트 등의) undercoating; an undercoat; the first[ground] coat. ¶~을 하다 put[lay] the undercoat (on) / give the first[ground] coat (to).

애벌레 [동] a larva (pl. -vae); a green caterpillar; a grub. ¶나비의 ~ a caterpillar.

애사(哀史) [개인이나 국가의 슬픈 역사] a tragic[sad / pathetic] history.

애사심(愛社心) (the spirit of) loyalty (to one's company). ¶그는 ~이 강하다 He is truly devoted to his company.

애상(哀傷) sorrow; grief; (시어) dolor. **애상하다** sorrow; grieve; mourn; lament.

애서가(愛書家) a lover of books; a book lover; a bibliophile; a bibliophilist; a philobiblist.

애석하다(哀惜-) feel[be] sorry (for / that); repent (for) sad; sorrowful; mournful; doleful; plaintive; repentant; pitiful; regrettable; disappointing. ¶애석히 하다 grieve [sorrow] (over) / lament [mourn (over) / regret / repent (of) // 그런 천재가 세상에서 인정받지 못하는 것은 애석한 일이다 It is a pity that such a genius as he should not be appreciated. // 이번 사건은 그에게는 애석한 일이었다 The recent affair was a lamentable [deplorable] business for him. // 그녀는 애석하게도 낙선했다 To our regret [disappointment], she was defeated in the election. 애석히 sadly; sorrowfully; pitifully; regrettably. ¶친구의 죽음을 ~ 여기다 lament over one's friend's death.

애소(哀訴) [슬프게 호소하는 것] an appeal (to a person / for a thing); (문어) (an) entreaty; (문어) (a) supplication (for). **애소하다** appeal (to a person / for a thing); (문어) entreat (a person (to do) / for a thing); (문어) supplicate (a person (to do) / for a thing).

애송이 a very young[a new] person; a greenhorn; a novice. ¶~인 주제에 시건방진 소리 좀 하지 마라 Don't talk so impudently, you greenhorn.

애송하다(愛誦-) love to recite[read] (a poem); read[recite] with pleasure. ¶그는 워즈워스의 시(詩)를 애송한다 He loves to recite Wordsworth[Wordsworth's poem].

애수(哀愁) an indefinable sadness; (문학 작품 등의) (문어) pathos. ¶~에 잠긴 얼굴 a sorrowful face / a grief-stricken face // ~를 자아내는 노래 a song that makes a person feel sad / a song that moves a person to tears / a song of sorrow // ~를 느끼다 feel sorrow / feel sorrowful[sad] / be grief-stricken // ~에 잠기다 be merged in a sentiment of sadness // ~를 자아내다 make (a person) feel sad / excite (a person's) grief / induce sadness in (a person) // 나는 그 시에서 일말의 ~를 느꼈다 I felt a touch of pathos in the poem.

애쓰다 [힘쓰다] make efforts; take pains; work hard; take trouble; exert oneself; endeavor; strive; struggle; labor; try hard; (남을 위해) render service[assistance] (to); render[do] (a person) a service. ¶애써 번 돈 hard-earned money // 나라를 위해 ~ render services to one's country / place oneself in the service of one's country / serve one's country // 부자가 되려고 ~ endeavor after wealth // 문제를 풀려고 ~ endeavor[set oneself] to solve a problem // 울지 않으려고 ~ struggle not to cry // 학교 교육의 개선을 위해 ~ exert oneself to improve [for the improvement of] public education // 애써 자신을 억제하려고 하다 struggle for self-control // 애써 변명하지 말게 Don't trouble to explain. // 그는 애쓴 보람이 없었다 All his efforts came to nothing[were of no avail]. / His labors were fruitless [unavailing]. / All his labors were lost[wasted]. / All his trouble went for nothing. / He has labored in vain[for nothing]. / He has gotten nothing for his pains. / He has exerted himself to no purpose. / He has made fruitless[vain] efforts. / He has ended in a (mere) waste of labor. // 그는 내 취직을 위해 애써 주었다 He went to a great deal of trouble to help me find employment. / He used his influence to find me a job. // 그런 사람을 위해서는 애쓸 필요가 없다 You don't need to put yourself out trying to help such a fellow.

애연가(愛煙家) a habitual[regular] smoker. ¶그는 대단한 ~다 He is a heavy[habitual] smoker. / He is addicted to smoking.

애오라지 [마음에 부족하나 겨우] only; solely. ¶~ 독서가 유일한 위안이다 Reading is my sole[only] consolation.

애완(愛玩) ¶~용 a pet // ~용 고양이 a pet cat // 나는 ~용으로 개를 기르고 있다 I keep a

애욕

dog as a pet. **애완하다** pet; make a pet of (a cat); prize; treasure; care for fondly. ¶그가 애완하는 골동품 his favorite [cherished / prized] curios.
● **애완견** a pet dog; a lap dog. **애완동물** a pet. ¶나는 ~을 기르고 있다 I keep a pet.

애욕(愛慾) love and lust; (sexual) passion; sexual desire.

애용하다(愛用-) use regularly [habitually]; make habitual use of; patronize. ¶애용하는 가방 one's favorite bag // 애용하는 호텔 a hotel one patronizes // 애용하는 카메라 a camera for one's personal use // 국산품을 ~ buy [stick to] home products / use [buy] homemade articles (in preference to foreign-made ones).

애원(哀願) 〔문어〕 (an) entreaty; an appeal; 〔문어〕 supplication. **애원하다** entreat [implore] (a person for a thing [to do] / a thing from a person); plead (with a person for a thing [to do]); appeal (to a person for mercy); petition (a person for pardon). ¶나는 그에게 도와 달라고 애원했다 I entreated [implored / pleaded with] him to help me.

애인(愛人) a lover(▶ 단수일 때는 보통 남성[정부(情夫)]을 가리킴; 서로 사랑하는 짝은 lovers; 현재는 시·가사·옛 문학을 제외하고는 모두 깊은 관계가 있는 경우에 씀; (남성에 대하여) one's lover; boyfriend; (여성에 대하여) one's love; a ladylove; one's (best) girl; (남녀 모두) (미) one's steady; a sweetheart. ▶ lover는 섹스 파트너의 의미가 강하므로 남에게 자기 애인을 소개하거나 남의 애인을 언급할 때 boyfriend나 girlfriend라는 말을 쓰는 것이 일반적임) ¶~**이 생기다** have a (secret) lover / get a girlfriend [boyfriend] // 자네 ~은 잘 있나 How is your girl [girlfriend]?

애자(碍子·碍子) 〔전〕 an insulator.

애잔하다 1 [매우 약하다] weak; delicate; feeble; fragile; frail. 2 [애처롭다] touching; pathetic; affecting; plaintive.

애장하다(愛藏-) treasure; cherish. ¶애장하는 초판본 one's cherished [treasured] collection of first editions.

애절하다(哀切-) pathetic; plaintive; mournful; sorrowful; sad. ¶애절하기 그지없는 이야기 a most pathetic story // 그녀는 애절하게 울었다 She cried in a piteous way. // 그녀의 애절한 이별가를 듣고 청중은 모두 감동하여 눈물을 흘렸다 She sang the farewell song with such feeling that the audience was moved to tears.

애정(愛情) love; affection; attachment; devotion; a tender feeling [sentiment / emotion]. ¶자식에 대한 부모의 ~ parent's love of their children // ~ 깊은 어머니 a loving [tender] mother // ~ 없는 결혼 a loveless marriage [match] // ~이 담긴 편지 an affectionate letter / a letter of affection // ~이라고는 조금도 없는 사람 a stony-hearted [hard-hearted] person / a person without a spark of affection // ~에 굶주린 아이들 love-starved children // …에게 ~을 나타내다 show affection for [toward] a person // ~ 없는 [있는] 결혼을 하다 marry without [from] affection // 노인은 그 소년에게 ~을 갖고 있다 The old man has affection for [toward(s)] the boy. // 그 자매는 서로 깊은 애정을 갖고 있다 The sisters are deeply attached to each other. / The sisters are deeply affectionate to [toward] each other. // 그들 사이에는 ~이라고는 털끝만큼도 없다 They don't care about each other at all. / They have no affection for each other. // 그는 ~을 얻기를 원했다 He wanted to win her heart [affection / love].

애제자(愛弟子) one's favorite pupil [disciple].

애조(哀調) 〔슬픈 가락〕 a mournful [plaintive / sad / sorrowful] tone; 〔슬픈 곡조〕 a sad [mournful] melody; 〔음〕 a minor key. ¶~를 띤 곡 a plaintive [sad] piece // ~ 띤 노래 a sad [doleful / plaintive] song / an elegy / a dirge / a lament // ~ 띤 목소리로 노래하다 sing in a plaintive [mournful] tone.

애족(愛族) love of one's people [nation]. ¶애국 ~ love of one's country and people.

애주(愛酒) love of wine. **애주하다** drink [take] habitually; be fond of drinking.
● **애주가** a habitual drinker.

애증(愛憎) love and hatred [hate]. ¶그는 아버지에 대해 ~이 뒤섞인 감정을 갖고 있었다 He had mixed feelings of love and hatred toward(s) his father.

애지중지하다(愛之重之-) treasure; prize; cherish; set great value on; love blindly; value highly; set store by; dote on [upon]; 〔구어〕 wrap in cotton wool. ¶아이를 애지중지하는 부모 doting parents // 그녀는 그 아이를 애지중지한다 Her child is the apple of her eye. / She dotes upon her child.

애착(愛着) attachment; love; affection; devotion. ¶친구에 대한 ~ attachment to one's friend // 그는 고향 마을에 강한 ~을 갖고 있다 He feels a strong attachment for his native village. / He is strongly attached to his native village. // 그녀의 국악에 대한 ~이 깊어 갔다 Her love for Korean music deepened. **애착하다** attach oneself (to).

애창곡(愛唱曲) one's favorite [(영) favourite] song.

애창하다(愛唱-) love to sing (a song). ¶그는 그 노래를 애창했다 He was very fond of singing that song.

애처(愛妻) one's (beloved) wife; one's dear wife.
● **애처가** a devoted husband; a doting [uxorious] husband. ¶그는 ~다 He is devoted to his wife. / He thinks of his wife before himself.

애처롭다 plaintive; piteous; pitiable; pitiful; touching; sorrowful; sad-looking. ¶애처로운 목소리로 in a plaintive voice // 갑자기 부모를 잃고 세상에 홀로 남게 된 아이들의 처지가 참 ~ The plight of the children, left alone in the world by their parents' sudden death, is heartening [enough to bring tears to the eyes]. // 병으로 여윈 그녀를 보니 애처로웠다 Emaciated by her illness, she was a pitiful sight. / She was so emaciated by her illness that it broke my heart to look at her. // 그 어린아이가 어머니의 죽음 앞에서도 애써 꿋꿋하려는 모습은 보기에도 애처로웠다 It was almost more than I could take to see the little child trying to bear up under his mother's death. // 그 소녀가 어린 여동생을 돌보는 모습이 애처로웠다 It was a touching sight [I was touched] to see the girl taking care of her little sister. // 그 광경은 너무 애처로워 끝까지 보고 있을 수 없었다 It was too pitiful [distressing] a scene [sight] for me to watch to the end. **애처로이** plaintively;

piteously; touchingly. ¶그는 도와 달라고 ~ 호소했다 He begged me in a piteous way to help him [to do something for him].

애첩(愛妾) one's (favorite) concubine; a mistress a man is very fond of.

애초(-初) the very first; the beginning; the outset [start]; the commencement. ¶~의 first / primary / initial / original // ~의 계획 the original plan [intention] // ~의 목적 primary object // 그는 ~부터 나를 무시했다 He ignored me from the beginning [start]. // 마이크가 고장이 나서 ~부터 그의 연설은 망쳐 버렸다 The start of his speech was spoiled by a faulty microphone. // ~에는 그것이 무엇인지 몰랐었다 At first I didn't know what it was. // ~부터 우리는 불공평하게 대우받았다 Right from the beginning [From the very beginning] we've been unfairly treated.

애칭(愛稱) a term of endearment; a pet [a affectionate] name; a nickname. ¶~이 「야옹이」이다 be called by the pet name of "kitty" // 빌은 윌리엄의 ~이다 Bill is a nickname for William. // 부모님은 「하니」와 같은 ~은 좀처럼 쓰지 않으셨다 My parents rarely used term of endearment such as "honey".

애타(愛他) altruism. ¶~적(인) altruistic.
●**애타심** altruism; an altruistic spirit.

애타다 be nervous (about); be anxious [worried] (about / for); be in suspense; be jittery; be on tenterhooks; be in a stew; be impatient. ¶애타게 그리워하다 burn with love (for) // 애타서 죽을 지경이다 be worried to death // 애타게 기다리다 wait impatiently (for) / wait in anxious suspense (for).

애태우다 (남을) worry; bother; fidget; fret (a person's) heart; keep [hold] (a person) in suspense; put [throw] (a person) into a flutter; (자기 자신에 대하여) be [feel] anxious (about); worry (oneself) (about); bother (oneself) (about); trouble oneself (with); fidget (about); (미) jitter (about); be impatient. ¶그는 항상 부모를 애태운다 He is a constant source of anxiety [a bother] to his parents. // 그들은 새 정보를 입수하려고 애태우고 있다 They are impatient to obtain [anxious for / eager for] new information. // 그는 정말 나를 애태우는군 He tries my impatience. // 그는 그 이유를 알고 싶어 애태우고 있다 He is anxious [impatient] to know the reason. // 병이 낫지 않아서 그는 애태우고 있다 He is fretting because he does not get better.

애통하다(哀痛-) sad and painful; (서술적) grieve [be grieved] (at / over); deplore; lament; be distressed (over); mourn (for / over). ¶아들을 잃은 어머니는 얼마나 애통할까 How sad [distressed] the mother who lost her son must be! // 온통 애통한 마음뿐이었다 I was filled with heartrending sorrow.

애틋하다 1 [애타다] worried; anxious. 2 [아깝고 서운하다] regrettable; pitiful. 3 [정을 느끼게 하는 티가 있다] lovable; affectionate. ¶애틋한 정 tender [deep] affection.

애티 childishness; childlike look [behavior]; puerility; juvenilities. ¶~가 흐르다 be childlike / look childish // 그 아이는 ~를 벗었다 The boy in him has died.

애프터서비스(*after service) after-sale(s) service; warranty; (수리) (repair) service. ¶저 가게는 ~가 좋다 That shop provides good service (on the articles they sell). // 이 히터의 ~를 해 주시겠습니까 Will you do repair service on this heater?

애해 Well!; Ha(h)!; Eh!; Pshaw!; Oh yeah!

애헴 ahem; hem.

애향심(愛鄕心) love for one's hometown [native place]. ¶~이 있다 love one's hometown.

애호(愛好) love (for / of); a liking (for). ¶우리는 평화 ~ 국민이다 We are a peace-loving nation. **애호하다** love; be fond of; have a liking for; care for (movies). ¶그는 커피를 애호한다 He loves [is fond of] coffee.
●**애호가** (음악·문학 등의) a lover [devotee] (of music / literature); a dilettante (pl. ~s, -ti); an amateur; (동물 등의) a (bird) fancier; a (sports / football / movie) fan; a maniac; an enthusiast; an aficionado (pl. ~s); a votary. ¶문학 ~ a literary enthusiast // 사이클링 ~ a cycling enthusiast // 미술 ~ a devotee of the fine arts // 컴퓨터 ~ a computer buff // 연극 ~ a theater lover / a theatergoer / a playgoer // 영화 ~ a movie fan // 그는 커피 ~이다 He is a coffee-lover.

애호(愛護) protection; kind(ly) treatment; tender [loving] care. ¶동물 ~ 주간 Be kind To Animals Week. // (영국의) 동물 ~ 협회 the Society for the Prevention of Cruelty to Animals (약어 S.P.C.A.). **애호하다** protect; treat (an animal) kindly [with tender care]; be kind to (an animal). ¶동물을 ~ protect animals from harm / be kind to animals.

애호박 a young pumpkin.

애환(哀歡) joys and sorrows.

액(厄) [모질고 사나운 운수] a calamity; a misfortune; a disaster; an evil; ill luck. ¶~을 막다 ward off evil fortune / protect (a person) against [from] evils // ~을 쫓아내다 exorcise / drive out [get rid of] an evil.

액(液) (과즙) juice; (액체) a liquid; (유동체) a fluid; (수액) sap; (용액) a solution; (분비액) secretion.

-액(額) (분량) a quantity; an amount; a volume; (수효) a number; (액수) a sum; an amount of money. ¶생산~ the volume of manufacture / the amount of production // 소비~ the amount consumed // 예정~ the budget sum [figure] / the estimate // 매출~은 얼마 되지 않았다 The sales didn't amount to anything.

액년(厄年) an unlucky [a bad / an evil] year; (연령의) a climacteric [critical] age (in one's life); a climacteric.

액때우다(厄-) forestall an impending misfortune by undergoing one of lesser degree; take the edge off [the sting out of] a calamity by having one of lesser degree.

액땜(厄-) an escape from a calamity. ¶~으로 여기다 bear (a misfortune) as the price for the escape from a misfortune of greater degree. **액땜하다** forestall a disaster with a lesser sacrifice.

액막이하다(厄-) ward off [prevent / take steps against] evil [misfortune]; exorcise evil spirits (from [out of] a person [place]); exorcise (a person [place]) of evil spirits.

액면(額面) 1 face [par] value. ⇨ **액면 가격**(⇨ 액면) ¶~ 이상으로 [이하로] above [below] par / at a premium [discount] // ~대로 at par // 주식은 ~ 이상으로 팔리고 있다 The shares

액상 (液狀) a liquid state. ¶~의 liquefied // 수은은 ~의 금속이다 Mercury is a metal in liquid form. // 물은 보통 영하의 온도에서는 ~을 유지할 수 없다 Ordinarily, water at temperatures below zero does not remain [keep] liquid [liquefied]. // 천연가스를 ~으로 하면 운반할 수 있다 Natural gas can be transported if liquefied.

액세서리 accessories. ¶그녀는 좀체 ~를 달지 않는다 She seldom wears accessories.

액셀러레이터 an accelerator. ¶~를 밟다 step [press] on the accelerator [gas pedal] / push [shove] one's foot down on the accelerator [gas pedal] / push down the gas / tread on the gas / press on the gas // ~를 계속 밟다 keep one's foot on the accelerator // ~에서 발을 떼다 take one's foot off the accelerator.

액션 an action.

액수 (額數) a sum; an amount (of money). ¶많은[적은] ~ a large[small] amount // 상당한 ~의 돈 a good sum of money / a sizable amount of money / (미) a considerable sum of money // ~가 많은 청구서 a stiff bill // 청구서의 ~는 2,000달러에 이른다 The bill amounts to $2,000. // (물건 사는 데) 예정된 ~를 초과해서 돈을 썼다 I spent more than I had intended (on my purchases).

액와 (腋窩) the armpit. ⇨겨드랑이1

액운 (厄運) (a) misfortune; ills; adverse [bad] fortune; an evil [untoward / adverse] fate; a bad luck.

액일 (厄日) a bad[an unlucky] day. ¶발을 삐고, 돈도 잃고, 오늘은 정말 ~이다 What with spraining my ankle and losing my money, it has been a very unlucky day for me.

액자 (額子) a (picture) frame. ¶~에 끼운 결혼 사진 a framed wedding picture // 그림을 ~에 끼우다 frame a picture / put[set] a picture in a frame // ~를 벽에 걸다 hang a framed picture on the wall.

액정 (液晶) [화] a liquid crystal.

액체 (液體) liquid; fluid.
● **액체 연료** liquid fuel. ¶~식 로켓 a liquid fuel rocket.

액취 (腋臭) body odor; axillary[underarm] odor.

액포 (液胞) [생] a vacuole.

액화 (液化) liquefaction. **액화하다** (물건을) liquefy; (물건이) be liquefied; liquefy.
● **액화 가스** liquefied gas. **액화 석유 가스** liquefied petroleum gas. **액화 천연가스** liquefied natural gas.

앨범 an album. ¶붙이는 ~ a paste-in album // 끼워 넣는 ~ a slip-in album.

앰프 (증폭기) (구어) an amp; an amplifier. ¶~를 단 기타 an amplified guitar.

앳되다 (서술적) look young for[younger than] one's age.

앵¹ [벌레가 나는 소리] humming; buzzing; with a buzz[a bum].

앵² [불쾌할 때 내는 소리] Tut!; Shucks!; Phew!; Pshaw!; Fie!; Hang it all!

앵글 an angle. ¶카메라 ~ a camera angle // 낮은 ~에서 찍은 사진 a picture taken from a low angle.

앵글로·색슨 Anglo-Saxon. ¶~ 민족 the Anglo-Saxon race / the Anglo-Saxons.

앵돌아지다 become[get] sulky[cross / peevish]; sulk; pout; pet; take the pet; (미국 구어) grouch. ¶앵돌아진 sullen / sulky / sour.

앵두 a cherry. ¶~ 같은 입술 cherry[rosy / red] lips / lips as red as a cherry.

앵두(를) 따다 shed[drop] tears; weep.

앵무새 (鸚鵡—) [동] a (gray) parrot; a parakeet. ¶~처럼 흉내 내다 repeat like a parrot / repeat[echo / mimic] another's words / poll-parrot another's words / speak[parrot] (a thing) back.

앵앵 humming; buzzing; with a buzz[a bum]. **앵앵하다** buzz; hum. ⇨앵앵거리다

앵앵거리다 buzz; hum; make a humming sound.

앵커 1 an anchorman. ⇨앵커맨(⇨앵커) 2 [체] the anchor (man) (on a team). ¶~를 맡다 be the anchor / anchor (the race) / run [swim] anchor position[the anchor leg] (on a relay team).
● **앵커맨** an anchorman; an anchor person. **앵커우먼** an anchorwoman.

야¹ 1 [놀랍거나 반가울 때의 소리] Oh!; Oh my!; Dear me!; Wow!; Good Gracious!; Good [Great] Heavens!; By Jove!; Gosh; Gee! Oh!; Ah! ¶~, 이건 너무했다 By Heavens, this is really too much. // ~, 이거 손 군 아닌가 Well, well, well, if it is not Mr. Son. // ~, 놀랐다 Oh, what a surprise! // ~ 좋다 Oh[Ooh], how nice! 2 [허물없이 부를 때의 소리] hello; hullo; hallo; hey; hi; I say; come; hey there; there; here. ¶~, 일어나 Hey, wake up, you! // ~, 거기 누구냐 Hey there! Who are you? // ~ 한 군, 오래간만이군 Hi, Mr. Han! I haven't seen you for ages.

야² 1 [강조]. ¶결과~ 어찌 되건 내가 알 바 아니다 I don't care for what may come of it. / I don't care for[I can't help] the consequence. // 그는 이번에~ 합격하겠지 He is sure to succeed in examination this time. // 다음 날에~ 나는 그 사실을 알았다 It was not till the next day that I knew the facts. // 이렇게 늦어서~ 어떻게 떠나나 How can we start when it's so late now? // 어른이 되어서~ 건강의 고마움을 깨달았다 I did not know the blessing of health till I grew up. 2 [호칭] hullo; hello; hallo; (미) hi. ¶철수~ my dear Cheolsu!

야 (野) [야당] a party out of power; a non-government party; the outs; the Opposition (party). ¶~에 있다 (반대 당에) be in opposition.

야간 (夜間) night; nighttime. ¶~용 벨 night bell // ~용 망원경 night glasses // ~에(는) at night / in the night / during the night / in the nighttime / between dusk and dawn / (주간에 대하여) by night // 그들은 ~에 일하고 주간에는 쉰다 They work by night and rest by day. / They work at night and sleep during the day.
● **야간 개장** opening at night. **야간 경기** / **야간 시합** a night game[match]. **야간열차** a night train. **야간 영업** (게시) Open Evenings. **야간작업** night work. **야간 통행금지** a curfew. **야간 학교** a night school.

야경(夜景) a night[nocturnal] view[scene]. ¶명동의 ~ the night view of Myeongdong.
야경(夜警) night watch. ¶~을 돌다 make the round (of a district) at night / go on one's rounds at night∥~을 서다 be[keep / stand] on night watch∥여기서는 우리가 교대로 ~을 한다 Here we take turns keeping the night watch. **야경하다** keep night watch; keep watch at[during the] night; be[stand] on night watch.
● **야경꾼** a night watchman[watch]; a night watcher. ¶밤이 깊으면 ~이 돈다 Night watchmen go on their beat late at night.
야고보서(-書) (The General Epistle of St.) James (약어 Jam.).
야광(夜光) noctilucence. ¶~의 noctilucent / noctilucous.
● **야광 도료** a luminous paint. **야광 시계** a watch with a luminous[an illuminated] dial. **야광충** a noctiluca (pl. -cae).
야구(野球) baseball. ¶빈 터에서 하는) **어린이** ~ sandlot baseball∥**프로** ~ professional baseball∥~를 하다 play baseball.
● **야구공** a baseball. **야구광 / 야구 팬** a baseball fan. **야구 방망이** a bat. **야구 선수** a baseball player; a baseballer. **야구장** a baseball ground[field]; a ballpark.
야근(夜勤) [야간 근무] night duty; night work; (주야 교대의) a night shift. ¶~이 막 끝났다 I've just come off night duty[the night shift].∥이번 주에는 우리가 ~이다 We are on the night shift this week. **야근하다** be on night work[shift]; take night duty.
● **야근 수당** a night-work allowance. **야근 시간** night shift; nightwork hours.
야금(冶金) metallurgy. ¶~의 metallurgical.
● **야금학 / 야금술** metallurgy.
야금(野禽) a wild fowl[bird].
야금거리다 nibble (at); gnaw; bite (a thing) by nips.
야금야금 little by little; bit by bit; by nips; gradually; by degrees; piecemeal. ¶~ 먹다 eat (a cake) bit by bit[little by little] ∥ ~ 먹어 들어가다[잠식하다] encroach upon[make an inroad into] gradually. **야금야금하다** nibble (at). ⇨**야금거리다**
야기(夜氣) [밤의 공기] night air; [냉기] the cool of the night. ¶차가운 ~가 방으로 들어왔다 The cool of the night crept into the room.
야기하다(惹起-) bring about; provoke; induce; create; cause. ¶문제를 ~ cause trouble / raise a problem∥물의를 ~ lead to controversy∥전쟁을 ~ provoke a war∥그것이 중대한 문제를 야기할지도 모른다 It may give rise to a serious trouble.∥압제가 국민의 반란을 야기했다 Oppression provoked the people to rebellion. ➜¶그의 부주의로 심각한 분규가 야기되었다 His carelessness gave rise to[brought about / led to] serious trouble.
야뇨증(夜尿症) bed-wetting; [의] night[nocturnal] enuresis.
야누스 [로마 신화] Janus.
야단(惹端) 1 [소란] an uproar; a hubbub; a tumult; a din; a racket; [소동] a commotion; a stir. ¶웬일로 이 ~이냐 What's all this noise? ∥ 왜 ~들이냐 What's the racket? **야단이다** raise [make] an uproar; fuss about; kick up a row; raise[make / kick up] a racket. ¶입장시키라고 ~ clamor for admission∥시시한 일을 가지고 ~ make a great fuss about trifles / raise the wind over trifles.
2 [꾸짖음] (a) scolding; a chiding; a rebuke; a lecture; a nagging. **야단하다** scold; chide; rebuke; take[call / bring] (a person) to task (for); give (a person) a scolding; have[call] (a person) on the carpet; haul[call] (a person) over the coals. ¶마구 ~ storm at / thunder against / fulminate.
3 [곤란] a trouble; a difficulty; a perplexity; [곤경] a predicament; a quandary; a plight. ¶그렇게 되면 ~인데 If things should come to that pass, we shall be in trouble.∥비가 쉬 오지 않으면 ~인데 If it doesn't rain soon, we'll be in a hell of a fix.
● **야단법석** wild[boisterous] merrymaking; a spree; a racket. ¶~을 떨다 go on a spree [binge] / (속어) paint the town red / whoop it up∥하찮은 일로 ~을 떨다 (구어) make a big fuss[get all upset] over nothing∥파티에서 ~을 떨었다 We really raised the roof at the party.∥그녀는 (울고불고) 한바탕 ~을 떨었다 She made a scene.∥대통령이 온다고 온 마을이 준비에 ~을 떨고 있었다 The whole town was in a bustle preparing for the President's visit.∥그들은 사윗감을 찾느라고 ~을 떨고 있다 They are making a great fuss over searching for a husband for their daughter.∥사람들은 클린턴 대통령이 내한한다고 ~이다 People are agog with excitement over the expected visit of President Clinton.
야단나다(惹端-) [소란·소동이 벌어지다] a commotion breaks out; a stir is created; get serious; [곤란하다] come[reach] to a nice [pretty] pass; get into trouble; get[be] in a fix[quandary / pickle]; be at a loss; be out on a limb. ¶이거 야단났군 Here's[what] a go. / Here's a pretty go! / what a business (it is)!∥정말 야단났군 I'm really at a loss what to do[at my wit's end].
야단맞다(惹端-) [꾸지람을 듣다] be scolded [rebuked] (by); (미국 구어) catch[get] it hot (from dad); catch[have / get] a scolding; catch[get] hell (from). ¶그것 때문에 나는 단단히 야단맞았다 I got a good scolding [dressing down] for it.∥그런 짓을 하면 넌 야단맞는다 (구어) If you do that, you'll catch it.∥조지는 조심성이 없다고 상사에 야단맞았다 George got a good dressing-down [telling-off] from the boss for his carelessness.∥나는 남의 험담을 하여 야단맞았다 I was scolded[(문어) chided] for speaking ill of others.
야단스럽다(惹端-) uproarious; noisy; clamorous; tumultuous (crowd); vociferous. ¶원 야단스럽긴! 그까짓 할퀸 자국을 가지고 What a fuss about such a scratch!
야단치다(惹端-) [꾸짖다] scold; chide; rebuke. ¶선생님은 그 소년을 늘 야단치신다 The teacher is always scolding that boy.∥그는 덮어놓고 아이를 야단쳤다 He gave his child a real tongue-lashing without hearing his side of the story.∥사장은 나를 지독하게 야단쳤다 The president gave me a real scolding[(구어) talking-to]. / (구어) I really got hauled over the coals by the president.∥선생님은 숙제를 하지 않은 학생들을 크게 야단치셨다 The teacher gave the boys a good scolding for having forgotten their homework.

야담(野談) an unofficial version of historical tale.
  ● **야담가** a (professional) historical storyteller.
야당(野黨) the party out of office; (양당제의) the Opposition (party). ¶그 당은 아직도 ~이다 The party is still in opposition.//여당 ~을 막론하고 그 법안은 만장일치로 가결되었다 The bill received bilateral support and was passed unanimously. / Both the ruling party and the Opposition supported the bill, and it was passed unanimously.
  ● **야당 공세** an offensive (move) taken by the outs against the government. **야당 당수** an Opposition leader. **야당석** the Opposition benches. **야당 의원** a member of the Opposition.
야드 a yard(=3 feet, 0.9144 meters).
야들야들하다 smooth[soft] and shiny; tender; velvet(y); silky. ¶야들야들한 피부 silky-smooth skin//야들야들한 가죽 limp leather//감촉이 ~ feel soft / be soft to the touch//야들야들하게 하다 make (a thing) soft (and shiny) / make silky[satiny / velvet(y)].
야로 an ulterior design. ⇨흑막2
야릇하다 odd; queer; strange; peculiar; curious; mysterious. ¶야릇한 꿈 a strange dream//야릇한 세상 this treacherous life//야릇한 감정이 들다 feel strange / have a strange sensation//야릇한 얼굴을 하다 make a queer face / look puzzled//운명이란 참으로 ~ Fate plays strange tricks.
야만(野蠻) savageness; barbarism; barbarity. ¶~의 [미개한] barbarian / [미개하고 무교양한] barbarous / savage(▶ 두 말 모두 잔인하다는 뜻을 내포하는 경우가 많음).
  ● **야만인** a barbarian; a savage; savage people. **야만족** a savage tribe.
야만스럽다(野蠻—) savage (tribe); barbarous (nation / custom); unrefined (person). ¶일본을 야만스러운 나라로 생각하는 외국인이 아직도 많다 Many foreigners still regard Japan as a barbarian[a primitive / a backward / an uncivilized] country.//이 따위 야만스러운 풍습은 조속히 폐지해야 한다 We must abolish such barbarism at once.
야만적(野蠻的) barbarous; savage; uncivilized. ¶~인 풍습 uncivilized[barbarous] manners//~인 행위 barbarism / barbarity / savagery//전쟁은 아무리 좋게 보아도 ~인 행위이다 War at best is a barbarism.
야말로 the very; just; indeed; precisely; exactly; really. ¶그~ indeed / quite//나~ 편지를 했어야 했다 It is I, not you, that who should have written to you.//이것이~ 내가 오랫동안 찾고 있던 것이다 This is the very thing[just the thing] that I have been looking for.//이번에~ 그 녀석을 놓치지 않겠다 He shall not escape me this time.//이번에~ 꼭 성공해야 한다 I must succeed this time or never.
야망(野望) (an) ambition; (an) aspiration; a great desire. ¶~이 있는 ambitious / aspiring//~을 품다 be full of ambitions / have [cherish / harbor] an ambition / aim high / aspire after greatness//천하를 정복하였다는 그의 ~은 이루어졌다 [깨졌다] His ambition to conquer the whole country was realized [frustrated].

야맹증(夜盲症) night blindness; [의] nyctalopia. ¶나는 ~이 있다 I am night-blind.
야멸스럽다 heartless; cold; hard; harsh; hard-hearted; pitiless; cruel; merciless; flinty. ¶야멸스런 처사 cold treatment//야멸스럽게 heartlessly / cold-heartedly / pitilessly / coldly / harshly / cruelly//야멸스런 말을 하다 speak cruelly / say a harsh[mean] thing//야멸스럽게 거절하다 give a point-blank[flat] refusal//그들은 야멸스러운 사람들이다 They are people without feelings.
야멸차다 →야멸치다
야멸치다 heartless; cold; hard. ⇨야멸스럽다
야무지다 hard; strong; tough; firm; solid. ¶야무진 목소리 a firm voice//야무진 사람 a man of firm[strong] character//솜씨가 ~ be dexterous / be deft-handed / be clever with one's hands//그는 무슨 일이든 야무지게 못한다 He does everything in a slovenly way.
야물다¹ fill with the corn. ⇨여물다
야물다² tight. ⇨여물다
야바위 trickery; swindle; imposture; fraud; deception; a hoax; (구어) flimflam. ¶~에 걸려 만 원을 빼앗기다 be swindled out of 10,000 won//그건 순전한 ~다 [영국 속어] It's all a do.
야바위(를) 치다 cheat; deceive; swindle; take [let] (a person) in; play off a fraud (upon); play a trick (upon). ¶야바위를 쳐서 …시키다 trick[(속어) hornswoggle] (a person) into (doing).
  ● **야바위꾼** an impostor; a swindler; (구어) a sharper; a cheat; a trickster; a mountebank; (구어) a slicker.
야박하다(野薄—) unfeeling; heartless; cold-hearted; stonehearted. ¶야박한 말 cruel [unkind] words / heartless speech//야박한 세상 a hard world (to live in) / hard times//세상은 참 야박하기도 하다 What a hard world we are (living) in! / These are hard times.//그는 야박하게도 곤경에 빠진 친구를 저버렸다 He was coldhearted enough to let down a friend in trouble. **야박히** heartlessly; cruelly; pitilessly.
야반(夜半) (in) the middle of the night. ⇨밤중
  ● **야반도주** flight by night; (영국 속어) moonlight flitting. ¶~를 하다 skip out by night (without paying his rent) / run away under cover of night / flee by night//그는 ~나 다름없이 서울을 떠났다 His departure from Seoul was the same as running away under cover of darkness.//그 가족은 집세도 물지 않고 ~를 했다 The family did a midnight disappearing act[(영국 구어) did a moonlight flit], leaving the rent unpaid. **야반도주자** (미국 속어) a fly-by-night(er).
야밤중(夜—中) midnight. ⇨한밤중
야비하다(野卑—·野鄙—) [속되고 천하다] vulgar; crude; [거칠고 막되다] coarse; [거칠고 사납다] rude; [천하고 비루하다] base; (문어) mean; [무례하다] ill-mannered. ¶태도가 야비한 사람 a rude[an ill-mannered] person//야비한 농담 a broad[coarse / vulgar / crude] joke / a dirty joke(천한)//야비한 이야기 low talk / an improper[a dirty] story(천한)//야비한 취미 vulgar[poor] taste//그런 야비한 말은 그만 해 Stop using such vulgar[coarse] language.//그는 죽은 병사의 금품을 훔친 야비한 인간이다 He is a

base [mean / repulsive] fellow who steals money and valuables from dead soldiers.
야사(野史) an unofficial history [chronicle].
야산(野山) a hillock; a hill.
야상곡(夜想曲) [음] a nocturne.
야생(野生) wildness. ¶~의 wild / ferine / feral / savage / undomesticated // ~의 사슴 a wild deer / ~의 동백 a wild camellia. **야생하다** (식물이) grow wild; (동물이) live in the wild state. ¶벚나무는 야생한다 These cherry trees grow wild [naturally].
● **야생 동물** wild [feral] animals. **야생 식물** a wild plant; a wilding.
야성(野性) wild [savage / unpolished] nature; rusticity; uncouthness. ¶~의 wild // ~을 잃은 원숭이 a monkey which has lost its wild nature // ~으로 돌아간 개 a feral dog / a dog which has reverted to its wild state // 개는 갑자기 ~을 드러내어 어린아이에게 덤벼들었다 The dog suddenly went wild and jumped at the child.
● **야성미** unpolished beauty.
야성적(野性的) wild. ¶그 사람은 어딘지 ~인 데가 있다 There is something unrefined [rough] about him(▶ unrefined는 세련되지 않은, rough는 거친의 뜻). // 나는 그의 ~인 매력에 끌린다 His toughness [ruggedness] appeals to me.
야속하다(野俗-) unkind; unfeeling; heartless; coldhearted; inhospitable; unfriendly; unsympathetic; pitiless. ¶그는 야속하게도 나의 청을 들어주지 않았다 He was so unkind as to refuse my request. **야속히** unkindly; unfeelingly; heartlessly; pitilessly. ¶~ 굴다 be hard on (a person) / behave coldly [heartlessly] (towards) // ~ 여기다 feel bitter (against a person).
야수(野手) [야구] a fielder. ¶내~ an infielder // 외~ an outfielder.
● **야수 선택** a fielder's choice. ¶~으로 1점을 얻었다 One run scored on a fielder's choice.
야수(野獸) a wild [savage] animal [beast]; beasts of the field. ¶~적인 brutal / beastly / bestial // 저 녀석은 ~ 같은 사나이다 He is a beast [brute].
● **야수성** brutality; bestiality; brutal [bestial] nature. ¶~을 나타내다 show one's brutality [bestiality]. **야수파** (미) the Fauvists(사람); Fauvism(주의).
야습(夜襲) a night attack [raid / assault]. **야습하다** make [attempt] a night attack [raid] (on the enemy); raid [attack] (the enemy) at night; make an attack (on a person) at night.
야시장(夜市場) a night market; a night fair.
야식(夜食) a midnight [late-night] meal [snack]. ¶~으로 라면을 먹다 have instant noodles for a midnight snack. **야식하다** take [have] a midnight snack [meal].
야심(野心) 1 [야망] (an) ambition. ¶~적인 ambitious // ~적인 지도자 an ambitious [aspiring] leader // 그는 정치가가 되겠다는 ~을 불태우고 있었다 He had a burning ambition [He was burning with ambition] to be a politician. // 나는 부자가 되겠다는 ~은 없습니다 I have no desire to be wealthy [for wealth]. / 그의 오랫동안의 ~이 실현되었다 [깨어졌다] His long-cherished ambition was realized [frustrated]. // 그는 신진 작가로서 ~ 만만하다 He is a rising [promising] novelist who is full of ambition. // 그는 ~적인 계획을 갖고 있다 He has an ambitious plan. / His plan is ambitious. // 그는 정치에는 전혀 ~이 없다 He has no political ambitions whatsoever.
2 [나쁜 계획] (문어) an ill design. ¶그는 친구를 곤궁에 빠뜨리려는 ~은 없었다 He lacked any malicious intention to entrap his friend.
● **야심가** an ambitious [aspiring] person; a highflier. **야심작** an ambitious work.
야심하다(夜深-) late at night. ¶야심하도록 책을 읽다 read (a book) till midnight / sit up reading far into the night // 야심할 때까지 일하다 work far into the night / work till late at night.
야영(野營) encampment; camping-out; bivouac. **야영하다** encamp; pitch (a) camp; make camp; camp out; (군인이) bivouac. ¶우리는 숲 속에서 야영했다 We pitched camp in the forest.
● **야영지** a camp; a camping ground [site]. ¶~에서 철수하다 strike [break up] camp.
야옹 [고양이의 울음소리] me(o)w. ¶고양이는 나를 보고 ~ 울었다 The cat saw me and let out a long meow. // 고양이가 ~~ 울고 있다 A cat is mewing [meowing].
야외(野外) [들] the fields; [옥외] the open air; the outdoors; [교외] the outskirts (of a town); the suburbs (of a city). ¶~에 [에] outdoors / out of doors / in the open air // ~에서 스포츠를 즐기다 enjoy outdoor sports // ~에서 점심을 먹다 have lunch out of doors [outdoors / outside / in the open air] // 이 의자는 ~용으로 고안되었다 This chair is designed to be used outdoors [for outdoor use].
● **야외 경기** field games. **야외극장** an open-air theater [(영) theatre]. **야외 연주회** an open-air concert. **야외 운동** an outdoor [a field] sports; outdoor exercises. **야외 작업** fieldwork; field study. **야외 촬영** location. ¶~ 중이다 be on location.
야위다 become [grow / get] thin [lean / spare]; lose (one's) weight; (병으로) lose flesh; (근심으로) pine away. ¶근심 걱정으로 몸이 ~ become thin from worries // 그는 많이 야위었다 He has become much thinner. / He has lost a lot of weight. // 아버님이 병으로 아주 야위셨다 My father has wasted away [grown thin and worn out] because of his illness. / My father has become emaciated as a result of his illness.
야유(揶揄) [남을 빈정거려 놀림] ridicule; jeering; heckling; raillery; banter; hooting; catcalling. ¶~가 너무 심해서 그의 연설은 아무도 듣지 못했다 There was so much hooting and jeering that no one could hear his speech. // 그들은 연사에게 ~를 보냈다 They jeered at [heckled] the speaker. // 국회에서 격한 ~의 응수가 있었다 There was a bout of vehement heckling in the Parliament. **야유하다** jeer; (불만·경멸을 나타내이) hoot; (부 소리 내어) boo; (쉬 소리 내어) hiss; [웃음거리로 만들다] make fun of; [비웃다] ridicule; deride. ¶청중은 연설자를 야유했다 The audience heaped ridicule on the speaker. / The audience jeered the speaker.
➔¶배우는 야유당하고 무대에서 물러났다 The actor was hissed [hooted] off the stage.

야유회 (野遊會) a picnic. ¶~를 가다 go on a picnic / go picnicking.

야음 (夜陰) the darkness of night. ¶그는 ~을 틈타 담장을 넘었다 He got over the fence under cover of darkness[night]. / He took advantage of the darkness to climb over the fence.

야인 (野人) 1 [시골 사람] a person from the country; a rustic. 2 [교양 없고 거친 사람] an unrefined[uncouth] person. 3 [재야의 사람] a person out of office[power]; a member of the opposition; [민간인] a person unconnected with the government; a civilian. ¶~으로 있다 be in private life / remain out of public office / be out of office[power] // 그는 5년이나 ~ 생활을 하고 있다 He has been five years out of government service.

야자 (椰子) 1 a palm(tree). ⇨야자나무(⇨야자) 2 [야자나무의 열매] a coconut.
● **야자나무** a palm(tree); a palmetto (pl. (e)s). **야자유** coconut oil.

야적 (野積) open-air storage (of freight [goods]). **야적하다** ⇨¶석탄이 야적되어 있었다 Coal was piled up out in the open.
● **야적장** an open-air yard.

야전 (夜戰) a night battle[operation].

야전 (野戰) a field battle; open[field] warfare; an open battle.
● **야전군** a field army. **야전 병원** a field hospital; an ambulance. **야전잠바** a field jacket.

야조 (野鳥) a wild bird; [집합적] wildfowl. ¶~를 관찰 연구하다 bird watch.

야찬 (夜餐) a nighttime meal. ⇨"밤참

야채 (野菜) vegetables. ⇨"채소
● **야채샐러드**[수프] vegetable salad[soup]. **야채 요리** a vegetable[vegetarian] dish.

야크 [동] a yak (pl. ~s, 집합적 ~).

야트막하다 somewhat shallow; shallowish.

야포 (野砲) a field gun; [집합적] field artillery.
● **야포대** a field artillery corps; (중대) a field battery.

야하다 (冶-) [남의눈에 띄다] showy; [저속·화려하다] gaudy; [값싸다] tawdry; [색깔 등이 강하다] garish; loud. ¶야한 장식품을 gaudy decorations // 야한 간판 a garish signboard // 야한 광고판 gaudy-colored billboards[(영) hoardings] // 화장이 야한 여자 a woman wearing heavy makeup // 그녀는 야하게 치장하고 있다 She is gaudily[showily] dressed. // 방이 야하게 꾸며져 있었다 The room was ostentatiously decorated. // 그 실내 장식은 너무 야하여 내 취향에 맞지 않았다 The interior was too gaudy[tawdry] for my taste.

야학 (夜學) a night school; an evening school. ¶그는 낮에는 일하고 밤에는 ~에 다니고 있다 He works during the day and goes to school in the evening.
● **야학생** an evening[a night] school student.

야합 (野合) 1 [부부 아닌 남녀가 서로 정을 통함] an illicit union[intercourse / connection]. **야합하다** have an illicit liaison (with a person). ¶야합하여 in collusion[conspiracy / league] (with). 2 [공모] conspiracy; collusion. **야합하다** conspire[plot / collude] (with a person). ¶두 당은 야합했음에 틀림없다 There must be some collusive agreement between the two parties.

야행 (夜行) traveling by night; night[nocturnal] traveling. ¶~ 열차로 갑시다 Let's take a night[an overnight] train. / Let's go by night train. **야행하다** go[travel] by night.
● **야행성** the nocturnal habits (of an animal). ¶~ 동물[새] a nocturnal animal [bird].

야호 [등산객이 서로 부르는 소리] Yoo-hoo! ¶~ 하고 소리 지르다 yoo-hoo.

야화 (野話) [항간에 떠도는 이야기] a folk tale [story].

야회복 (夜會服) (남성·여성의) an evening dress[suit]; (여성의) an evening gown; a dress suit; (남성의) a dinner jacket[(미) a tuxedo]; (구어) white tie and tails.

약 (葯) an anther. ⇨"꽃밥

약 (藥) 1 [약품] (a) medicine; a drug; a remedy; (가루약) a powder; (환약) a pill; (정제) a tablet; (캡슐) a capsule.(▶ medicine은 일반적인 단어, drug는 medicine과 같은 뜻으로 쓰이지만 치료용이 아닌 약물, 특히 마약의 뜻으로도 쓰이므로 주의할 것. remedy는 잘 듣는다는 것을 전제로 한 단어) ¶먹는 ~ an internal medicine // 바르는 ~ [연고] an ointment // [타박상 등에 바르는 물약] (a) liniment // 덴 데 바르는 ~ a remedy for burns // 배 아픈 데 먹는 ~ a medicine for stomachache // 처방전 없이도 살 수 있는 ~ an over-the-counter drug / a nonprescription drug // 처방전이 있어야 살 수 있는 ~ a prescription drug // ~ 한 첩 a dose of medicine // 엉터리 ~ a quack medicine[remedy] // ~을 조제[처방]하다 compound[prescribe] a medicine (for a person) // ~을 먹다 take medicine(▶ eat medicine이라고는 하지 않음) // 상처에 ~을 바르다 apply medicine[an ointment] to a wound // 환자에게 ~을 먹이다 administer medicine to a patient // 이 ~는 잘 듣는다 This medicine works well. // 이 ~은 감기에 잘 듣습니까 Is this medicine good for a cold? // ~ 받는 곳 (게시) Pick up medication here.
2 [유약] (an) enamel; (a) glaze. ¶도자기에 ~을 바르다 glaze[enamel] pottery[earthenware].
3 [화학 약품] chemicals; chemical preparations.
4 [몸이나 마음에 유익한 것] benefit; good; remedy. ¶모르는 게 ~이다 Ignorance is bliss. // 실연에 듣는 ~은 없다 There is nor real remedy for a broken heart. // 실패는 그 아이에게는 ~이 될 것이다 The failure will do him good. / The failure will be a good lesson for him. // 좋은 ~은 입에 쓰나 몸에 이롭다 A good medicine is bitter to the mouth but of value for the body. // 그에게는 동정심 따위는 ~에 쓰려도 없다 He has not an ounce[not a particle] of sympathy in him.
5 〈속〉 a bribe; palm oil. ⇨뇌물 ¶~을 쓰다 grease (a person) / grease the hand[palm] (a person).

약 (約) about; some; nearly; approximately (100); (100) in round numbers[figures]. ¶~ 3시간 about three hours // ~ 2만 명의 사람들 some twenty thousand people // 손해는 ~ 1억 원으로 추산되고 있다 The loss is estimated roughly at one hundred million won. // 우리는 ~ 2마일쯤 도보로 나아갔다 We proceeded on foot for two miles or so. // 값은 ~ 5백만 원쯤 들 것입니다 It will cost something like five million won. // 물가는 ~ 10퍼센트 올랐다 Prices have risen by about

약가심(藥-) chasing[killing] the bitter taste of medicine. **약가심하다** kill[take off] the aftertaste of the medicine.

약간(若干) a number (of); an undetermined number (of); a few; a bit; somewhat; a little; any(▶ 의문문·조건절에서). ¶~의 설탕 a little [some] sugar // 나는 ~ 기분이 좋아졌습니다 I feel a little better. // 나는 에스파냐 어를 ~ 알고 있다 I have some knowledge of Spanish. // 기분이 ~ 좋아졌습니까 Do you feel any better?

약값(藥-) a medical fee[charge]. ¶~을 치르다 pay the charge for[price of] medicine / pay a pharmacist's bill.

약골(弱骨) **1** [몸이 약한 사람] a weakling; a weak[feeble] fellow; (미국 속어) a jellyfish. **2** [약한 골격] a weak[feeble / delicate] build [constitution].

약과(藥果) **1** [유밀과] a fried honey cake. **2** [쉬운 일] an easy task[job]; (구어) a piece of cake. ¶그까짓 건 ~다 That's nothing. / Nothing is easier. / (미국 속어) That's (as) easy as pie. / (미국 속어) That's a cinch. / 그런 일하기는 ~다 It is quite easy to do such a thing.

약관(約款) [조약·계약 등에서 정해진 조항] a stipulation; a provision; an article; a clause. ¶이 계약의 ~에 따라 according to the provisions of this contract // 지불 방법은 ~에 명기되어 있음 The method of payment is stipulated in the contract.

약관(弱冠) [남자 나이 20세] twenty years of age. ¶~에 at the age of twenty / in one's twentieth year.

약국(藥局) a pharmacy; (미) a drugstore; (영) a chemist's (shop).(▶ pharmacy는 전용 약국을 가리키거나 병원 안의 약국이나 drugstore·슈퍼마켓 안의 약 파는 코너를 가리키고, 미국의 drugstore는 약 이외에도 일용 잡화와 간단한 음식을 파는 곳을 가리키며, 영국의 chemist's (shop)은 미국의 drugstore와 거의 같은 곳을 가리킴)

약기(略記) jotting; a brief note; a brief[short / rough] sketch; a sketch; an outline. **약기하다** give a rough sketch (of); make[take] a brief note (of / on); sketch; outline. ¶이름은 약기하지 말 것 The name should be written in full. / Write your name in full.

약다 shrewd; clever; smart; smartish; sharp; cunning; keen; wide-awake; [재치 있다] tactful. ¶약게 smartly / agilely / cleverly // 약은 꾀 shrewd tricks[wiles] // 약은 녀석 a shrewd man / an old fox / a smart guy / a cute chap // 약은 수작 a shrewd way (of handling business) // 약게 굴다 act smartly [cleverly] / be tactful // 그 사람은 약아서 자기가 다칠 일은 하지 않는다 He is too clever [smart] to do anything that might hurt him. // 그는 돈벌이에는 약은 사람이다 He is smart [quick-witted] when it comes to making money. // 장사에서 그보다 약은 자는 없다 In business transactions nobody is as clever [shrewd] as he. // 그는 처세에서 ~ He gets along cleverly in the world.

약대 [동] a camel. ⇨낙타

약대(藥大) a pharmaceutical college. ⇨약학 대학(⇨약학)

약도(略圖) a (rough) sketch; (지도의) a rough [route / sketch] map (of); (설계 등의) a rough plan (of). ¶…의 ~를 그리다 take a rough sketch of / draw a route map (from ... to ...) // 나는 역에서 우리 집까지의 ~를 그렸다 I've drawn [made] a rough map showing how to get from the station to my house.

약동(躍動) a lively motion; a stir; a throb; a palpitation; a movement. ¶자연에서 생명의 ~을 느낀다 I can feel the throbbing pulse of life in nature. **약동하다** move lively; be quick with life; stir; throb. ¶생기가 약동하는 청년 an energetic young man. →¶이것은 청소년의 피를 약동시키는 드라마이다 This is a drama that stirs the blood of young people.

약력(略歷) a brief summary of a person's career; a brief history; a brief personal record; a sketch of one's life; (죽은 사람의) a memoir.

약리 작용(藥理作用) medicinal action.

약리학(藥理學) pharmacology.

약리학자 a pharmacologist.

약물(藥-) **1** medicine[mineral] water. ⇨=약수(藥水) **2** [약을 우린 물] an infusion; [약을 달인 물] a (medical) decoction; [약을 탄 물] a solution of a drug. **3** [탕약을 달일 물] water for decoction.

약물(藥物) drugstuffs; drugs; medicines; medicinal substances; (라) materia medica. ¶그가 마신 콜라에서 ~이 검출되었다 A drug was detected in the cola he had drunk. ●**약물 검사** examination by medicine. **약물 요법** medication; treatment with drugs; medicinal therapy; [의] pharmacotherapy. **약물 중독** medicinal poisoning.

약밥(藥-) *yakbap*; a sweet rice dish; flavored glutinous rice.

약방(藥房) **1** a pharmacy. ⇨=약국 **2** an apothecary. ⇨=약종상(⇨약종)
약방에 감초(속담) [필수적인 사물] an indispensable thing (to); indispensable; [불가결의 인물] an indispensable man; a keyman; [참견꾼] a person active in all sorts of affairs; a man who is in on everything.

약방문(藥方文) a (medical) prescription. ¶~을 쓰다 write (out)[give] a prescription / prescribe.

약병(藥甁) a medicine bottle; a vial; a phial.

약봉지(藥封紙) a paper packet of medicine.

약분(約分) [수] abbreviation; reduction (of a fraction) to its lowest[lower] terms(▶ lowest는 기약 분수로 하기). **약분하다** reduce a fraction to its lowest[lower] terms; abbreviate; cancel. ¶약분할 수 있는 reducible // 약분할 수 없는 irreducible // 3/9을 약분하면 1/3이 된다 If the fraction 3/9 is reduced to its lowest terms, we get 1/3.(▶ 3/9은 three ninths로 읽음) // 이 분수는 약분할 수 있다[없다] This fraction is reducible [irreducible].

약빠르다 shrewd; sharp; smart; tactful; cunning; quick-[ready-]witted; (서술적) have quick wits. ¶약빠르게 shrewdly / smartly / tactfully / cleverly / cunningly / quickly / nimbly // 약빠른 사업가 a shrewd businessman // 약빠르게 굴다 act tactfully / move smartly // 저 늙은이는 상당히 ~ That old fellow is quite shrewd. // 그는 약빠르게도 그 기회를 놓치지 않았다 It was very smart of him not to miss the chance.

약빠리 [약빠른 사람] a shrewd[sharp / cunning / smart] one; a quick-witted person; a smart guy.

약사(略史) an abridged[a shortened] history; a historical sketch; an outline history. ¶한국의 ~ an outline[a shortened] history of Korea/한국 자동차 산업 ~ an outline history of the automobile industry in Korea.

약사(藥師) a pharmaceutist; a pharmacist; a dispenser; (영) a (pharmaceutical[dispensing]) chemist; (미·스코) a druggist.

약사발(藥沙鉢) [독약을 담은 사발] a cup of poison offered by the king as an honorable execution. ¶~을 받다 be given a hemlock cup/~을 내리다 offer (a person) a hemlock cup.

약삭빠르다 [실제적 일에 기민하다] shrewd; [판단력 등이 날카롭다] astute; [꾀가 많다] smart. ¶약삭빠른 사업가 a shrewd[smart] businessman//그는 ~ (구어) He doesn't miss a trick.//그는 약삭빠르게 거래를 한다는 정평이 나 있다 He is well known for shrewdness in his dealings[for his sharp dealings].//그는 자기의 이익이 되는 일에는 약삭빠른 사람이다 He is alert to anything which will profit him.//그는 약삭빠르게 핑계를 미리 만들어 놓고 있었다 He is astute enough to have prepared an excuse in advance.//그는 아주 약삭빠른 사람이다 He is very clever [smart / intelligent].

약산(弱酸) [화] a weak acid.

약석(藥石) [온갖 치료] every medical treatment. ¶~의 효험 없이 죽다 die in spite of careful medical treatment.

약설(略說) [간략한 설명] a brief explanation; summarization. **약설하다** summarize; abridge; sum up; give an outline of; outline. ¶1년간의 계획을 약설하겠다 I will outline [give an outline of] the project for the year.

약성(藥性) the nature[properties] of a drug [medicine].

약세(弱勢) [증권] bearishness; bearish sentiment (due to bad news); a slack. ¶~ bearish / weak / bear / easy//~가 되다 slacken//원자재 가격으로 국제 시장에서 ~를 유지하고 있다 Raw material prices remains in a bearish trend in the international market.//주가는 ~이다 Stock prices are bearish.

● **약세 시장** a bear market; a weak market.

약소(弱小) [관형어적]. **약소하다** puny; small and weak.

● **약소국(가)** a lesser[minor] power; a small and weak nation. **약소민족** the people of a small and weak power; [소수 민족] a minority race; [피압박 민족] an oppressed race.

약소하다(略少-) [적다] few; little; scanty; [보잘것없다] trifling; slight; trivial; meager. ¶약소한 돈 a petty sum of money.

약속(約束) 1 [서약(하기)] a promise; [협약] an agreement; [서약한 말] one's word. ¶군은 ~ a solemn promise / a pledge//말뿐인 ~ an insincere promise//구두 ~ a verbal agreement//그는 ~을 잘 지키는 사람이다 He is a man of his word.//~을 이행했습니까 Did you carry out your promise? / Did you do as you promised?//그는 ~을 어기지 않았다 He did not break his promise.//He kept his word[promise].//그들은 회사와의 ~을 깼다[취소했다] They broke[canceled / broke off] their agreement with the company.//그는 ~대로 2시에 도착했다 True to his word, he arrived at two.//우정의 굳은 ~으로 이것을 간직해 주시오 Keep this as a pledged [word]. **약속하다** promise; give one's word. ¶남과 새끼손가락을 걸고 ~ take a pledge by linking little fingers with a person//나는 아들에게 동물원에 데리고 가겠다고 약속했다 I promised my son to take[that I would take] him to the zoo.//그는 내게 생일 선물로 카메라를 주겠다고 약속했다 He promised (to give) me a camera as a birthday present.//다른 사람에게 발설하지 않겠다고 약속한다면 비밀을 말해 주겠다 I will tell you the secret on condition that you[if you promise to] keep it to yourself.//그녀는 의사와 결혼을 약속했다 She is engaged to a doctor.//우리는 누구에게도 그것을 절대로 말하지 않기로 약속했다 We pledged[promised] that we'd never tell anyone else about it. / (구어) We shook hands on it that we'd never tell anyone else about it.

2 [만남] an appointment; an engagement; (특히 이성과의) a date. ¶나는 그와 만나기로 ~이 되어 있다 I have an appointment to see him.//나는 의사와 3시에 만나기로 ~을 했다 I made an appointment with my doctor for three o'clock.//오늘은 여러 가지 ~으로 시간이 꽉 차 있다 Today all my time is taken up with various engagements. **약속하다** make an appointment[an engagement] (with). ¶나는 약속한 날[시간]에 그의 사무실로 갔다 I went to his office on the appointed day[at the appointed time].

3 (거래의) a bargain; an agreement. ¶~을 지키다 abide by an agreement.

4 [규칙·관례] rule; convention. ¶무대의 ~ stage conventions//우리의 모임에는 지켜야 할 ~이 있다 Our association has some rules which must be observed.

5 [운명·예정]. ¶그에게는 유망한 장래[교수 자리]가 ~되어 있다 A great future[A professor's chair] is waiting for[assured] him.

● **약속 어음** a promissory note; (영) a contract note; a note of hand; a bill of debt. ¶~을 발행하다 issue[write] a promissory note//그는 은행에 200만 달러의 ~을 발행했다 He drew a promissory note on a bank for two million dollars.

약손(藥-) 1 the third finger. ⇨**약손가락** 2 [어루만져 낫게 하는 손] a medicinal hand; a soothing touch of the hand.

약손가락(藥-) [약지] the third finger; (특히 왼손의) the ring finger.

약솜(藥-) [탈지면] absorbent[sanitary] cotton; (영) cotton wool.

약수(約數) [수] a measure; a divisor. ¶공~ a common measure[divisor]//최대 공~ the largest common divisor.

약수(藥水) medicine[mineral] water.

● **약수터** a mineral spring; a spa.

약술(藥-) medicinal wine[spirits].

약술(略述) a brief account; an outline; a summary; a brief[short / rough] sketch. **약술하다** summarize; give a rough sketch (of); make a short sketch (of); sketch; outline; give an outline (of). ¶십자군에 대하여 약술하라 Give an outline of the Crusades.

약시(弱視) [의] weak eyesight; weakness of sight; amblyopia. ¶~의 weak-eyed [-sighted].

약시중하다(藥-) administer medicine; serve

약식(略式) informality. ¶~의 informal / unceremonious / summary // ~으로 informally / without formality / in an informal way // 우리는 ~으로 결혼식을 올렸다 We had an informal wedding (ceremony).
● **약식 기소(장)** information. **약식 재판** a summary trial; summary proceedings. **약식 절차** informal proceedings; [법] summary procedure.
약식(藥食) yaksik; a sweet rice dish. ⇨=약밥
약실(藥室) 1 a pharmacist's office. ⇨=약제실 (⇨약제) 2 [총의 탄약을 장전하는 부분] a powder [cartridge] chamber.
약어(略語) an abbreviation; a shortened word.
약 오르다 1 [화나다] be [feel] sore [angry] (at / about); feel irritated [injured]; feel vexed [annoyed] (with a person / at a thing); be chagrined (at); be nettled [exasperated]. ¶나는 그의 말에 약이 올랐다 I was offended [irritated] by his remark. // 뭐가 그렇게 약이 오르냐 What are you sore [mad] at? / What hurt your feeling? // 참 약이 오른다 How vexatious! // 그가 성공하다니 약이 오른다 His success is a sore point with me. // 그에게 지다니 약이 오른다 I can stand being beaten by a man like that. 2 [고추·담배 등이 성숙하여 자극성 성분이 생기다] ripen to its full flavor.
약 올리다 provoke; irritate; vex; grate on (a person's) nerves; sting [cut] (a person) to the quick; try (a person's) patience. ¶어린애를 ~ tease children // 그녀는 그를 놀리면서 약을 올렸다 She provoked him by her teasing. // 약을 올리지 말고 어서 보여 다오 Please hurry up and show it to me. You are playing with my expectations. // 자식 약을 올리네 How he irritates me!
약용(藥用) medicinal use. ¶이 식물의 뿌리는 ~이 된다 The root of this plant can be used for medicinal purposes. **약용하다** use (a thing) for medicinal purposes.
● **약용 비누[크림]** medicated soap [cream]. **약용 식물** a medicinal plant [herb].
약육강식(弱肉强食) the survival of the fittest; the law of the jungle; the right of the strongest. ¶우리는 ~의 세계에서 살고 있다 We live in a world where the stronger prey upon the weaker.
약음기(弱音器) a mute; (관현악기의) a sordine; a sordino; (피아노·취주 악기의) a damper. ¶현(弦)에 ~를 달고 with muted strings.
약자(弱者) a person of feeble strength; a weak person; (집합적) the weak. ¶~를 괴롭히다 bully [tyrannize over] the weak // ~ 편에 서다 stand by the weak // 강자를 꺾고 ~를 돕다 side with the weak against the strong // ~를 괴롭히지 마라 Don't bully the weak [weaker person].
약자(略字) (한자의) an abbreviated [a simplified / a simpler] form (of a Chinese character).
약장(略章) a miniature medal [decoration]; a service ribbon.
약장(藥欌) a medicine-chest.
약재(藥材) medicines; drugs. ⇨=약재료
약재료(藥材料) medicines; drugs; drugstuffs; pharmaceuticals; medica.
약전(弱電) a weak electric current.
약전(略傳) a brief account of (a person's) life. ⇨=소전(小傳)
약전(藥典) a pharmacop(o)eia. ¶대한(大韓) ~ the Korean Pharmacop(o)eia // ~에 의한 처방전 an official prescription.
약점(弱點) [약处] a weak point [spot / side]; a weakness; a vulnerable point; [결점] a shortcoming; a defect; a flaw; [불리한 점] a disadvantage; one's blind side; [아픈 곳] a sore spot [place]. ¶~을 이용하다 take advantage of another's weak point [Achilles' heel] // 남의 ~을 건드리다 hit a person where it hurts // ~을 찔리다 be struck at one's most vulnerable point // ~을 드러내다 betray at one's weak point / show the white feather // 적에게 ~을 잡히다 give a handle to the enemy // 사람은 누구나 ~이 있게 마련이다 Every man has his weak point. // 나는 내 ~을 극복하려고 노력하고 있다 I am trying to conquer my shortcomings. // 그녀는 언제나 태연한 태도로 절대로 ~을 보이지 않는다 She always puts on a bold front and never betrays [reveals] her vulnerability. // 나는 그에게 ~을 잡히고 있어 그가 하라는 대로 할 수밖에 없다 He has something on me, so I have to do what he wants. // 그의 ~을 이용하면 수월하게 이길 수 있다 You can win easily if you take advantage of his weak point.
약정(約定) [약속] a promise; an engagement; [계약] a contract; a compact; a bargain(매매); [협정] an agreement; an understanding; an arrangement; a convention; [계약 조항] a stipulation. ¶가 ~ a provisional contract [agreement] / a conditional contract // 구두 ~ a verbal promise / a spoken agreement // ~에 따라 그렇게 결정된 것이다 It has been arranged that way by agreement. / It has already been agreed upon. // 대부분의 클럽은 입회금을 반환하지 않는다는 ~ 아래 회원을 모집하고 있다 Most clubs accept members under the agreement that the admission fee will not be paid back. // 우리는 그의 회사와 거래 ~을 맺었다 We entered into a contract with his firm. **약정하다** promise; agree; engage; contract; bargain for (something); stipulate for (something); make a contract; enter into an agreement.
● **약정 기간** the stipulated time. **약정서** an agreement; a (written) contract; a deed of contract; a bond; a pact. **약정 이율** the rate of interest agreed upon; the agreed rate of interest.
약제(藥劑) a medicine; a drug; a chemical(화학 약품).
● **약제사** a pharmacist; a druggist; (영) a chemist. **약제실** a pharmacist's office; a pharmacy; a druggist's; a drugstore; a doctor's medicine room.
약조(約條) [언약] a promise; a pledge; [규정] rule; an agreement; a condition. ¶~를 지키다 keep one's pledge [engagement] / keep faith with a person. **약조하다** promise; pledge. ¶약조한 바에 따라 according to the agreement.
약졸(弱卒) [약한 군졸] a cowardly [weak] soldier; a poltroon.
약종(藥種) medicines; drugs. ⇨=약재료
● **약종상** an apothecary; (미) a druggist; (영) a chemist.

약주(藥酒) 1 medicinal wine. ⇨약술(藥-) 2 refined rice wine. ⇨맑은술 3 liquor; alcoholic drink. ⇨술¹

약지(藥指) the third finger. ⇨약손가락

약진(弱震) a minor earthquake [tremor]; a mild quake. ¶~이 있었다 A slight earthquake was felt.

약진(躍進) a rush; a dash; a charge; an onrush; an onslaught; rapid progress [advance]. ¶한국의 경제적 ~ the rapid [remarkable] economic advance of Korea // ~에 ~을 거듭하다 advance by leaps and bounds // 일대 ~을 하다 make a great advance / make rapid strides // 한국의 산업은 근년에 눈부신 ~을 이룩했다 Korean industry has made remarkable progress[has developed remarkably] in recent years. **약진하다** [돌진하다] rush (for / at); dash (for / at); make a rush[dash] (for / at); make an onslaught; [진보하다] make rapid progress [advance]; advance rapidly[by leaps and bounds]; take[make] great[rapid] strides. ¶내년에는 사업이 크게 약진할 것으로 기대하고 있다 We hope our business will make a great advance[make rapid strides] next year. // 그 회사는 급속히 성장하여 일류 기업으로 약진했다 The company grew by leaps and bounds into a first-rate enterprise.

약질(弱質) a weakling. ⇨약골¹

약체(弱體) 1 [약한 몸] a weak body. ¶~이 weak // ~화하다 weaken / become weak [effete]. 2 [약한 조직체] a weak system. ¶현정부는 다소 ~다 The present Government is making rather a poor show.
● **약체 내각** an effete [a frail] Cabinet.

약초(藥草) a medicinal herb; a medical plant.
● **약초상** a herbalist. **약초 채집가** a herbalist.

약칭(略稱) an abbreviated designation. ¶FBI는 연방 수사국의 ~이다 FBI is short for the Federal Bureau of Investigation.

약탈(掠奪) plunder; pillage; loot; spoilage; spoliation; despoliation; despoilment. **약탈하다** plunder; pillage; despoil; loot; sack; strip (a person of something); ravage (a land). ¶그들은 궁전에서 보물을 약탈했다 They plundered the palace of its treasures. // 폭도는 그 지역의 모든 상점을 약탈하였다 The rioters looted every shop in that district. ➔온 마을이 적병에 의해 약탈당했다 The whole village was sacked[plundered] by enemy soldiers. // 큰 거리의 가게들은 군중에게 약탈당했다 The stores along the main street were looted by the mob. // 박물관이 약탈당했다 The museum was vandalized.
● **약탈자** a plunderer; a looter. **약탈품** loot; plunder; spoils(▶ 보통 복수형, 수사는 쓰지 않음).

약탕관(藥湯罐) a pipkin for preparing decoctions. ⇨약탕기

약탕기(藥湯器) a pipkin for preparing decoctions; a clay pot preparing medicines.

약포(藥圃) [약초를 심는 밭] a herb garden.

약품(藥品) [의약품] (a) medicine; (미) a drug; [화학 약품] a chemical.(▶ medicine은 질병을 치료하는 것, drug는 치료하는 것, 흥분한 것, 잠이 오게 하는 것 등 그 효능이 가지가지임) ¶불량 ~ illegal [fraudulent] medicines [drugs].
● **약품명** drug names. **약품 회사** a pharmaceutical company.

약하다(弱-) weak; feeble; [부서지기 쉽다] frail; fragile; [허약하다] weakly; infirm; [미약하다] faint; feeble; [섬약하다] delicate; (술 등이) light; mild; [서투르다] unskilled; poor. ¶약한 토대 a weak foundation // 약하게 만든 의자 a flimsy chair // 약한 천[종이] cloth [paper] that tears easily // 약한 바람 a gentle breeze // 약한 술 weak liquor / mild wine // 약한 나라[팀] a weak nation [team] // 설득력이 약한 논의 a weak[an unconvincing] argument // 학력이 약한 학생들 pupils who are poor at school subjects // 사람의 약한 마음 the fragility of the human heart // 의지가 ~ be weak-willed // 성격이 ~ have a weak character // 약해지다 abate / grow[get] weak // 약하게 하다 weaken // 민족주의자의 힘을 약하게 하다 decrease[weaken] the influence of the nationalists // 과로는 몸을 약하게 한다 Too much work is bad for [(문어) injurious to] your health. // 수면 부족은 그의 건강을 약하게 했다 Lack of sleep impaired his health. // 가스의 불을 약하게 하지 않으면 고기가 탄다 Turn down [Lower the flame of] the gas, or the meat will burn. // 이 산은 물을 타서 약하게 했다 This acid is diluted. // 바람이 약해졌다 The wind dropped [died down] (▶ died down은 서서히). // 폭풍우가 약해졌다 The storm is abating. // 그의 맥박이 점점 약해졌다 His pulse became feebler and feebler. // 나는 요즘 시력이 약해졌다 These days my eyesight is beginning to fail [getting weaker]. // 나이가 들어 기억력[시력]이 약해졌다 My memory [eyesight] is failing with age. // 그녀는 몸이 ~ She is physically weak[in delicate health]. / She has a frail constitution. // 나는 위가 ~ I have poor digestion. // 약한 자를 골리지 마라 Don't bully the weak. // 이 기계는 아주 약한 진동도 기록한다 This instrument records even the slightest tremor [shock]. // 이 필름은 약한 광선에도 감광한다 This film is sensitive even to very faint [feeble] light. // 그의 주장은 근거가 ~ His assertion does not rest on a firm [solid] base. / He has little basis for his claim. // 나는 약한 입장에 있다 [불리한] I am in a disadvantageous position. // [큰코칠 수 없는] I have to maintain a low profile now. // 그는 수학이 ~ Mathematics is his weak point. / He is weak in [poor at] mathematics. // 그는 바둑이 ~ He is a poor hand at baduk(go). / He is a poor baduk player. // 그는 여자에게 ~ [좋아한다] He has a weakness for women. / [잘 속는다] He is a sucker for women. / [다룰 줄 모른다] He does not know how to deal with women. // 그는 술이 ~ He gets drunk very easily. // 이 천은 마찰에 ~ This material cannot stand much friction. // 「약한 자여, 그대 이름은 여자이니라」 "Frailty, thy name is woman!"

약하다(略-) omit; leave out. ⇨생략하다(⇨생략)

약학(藥學) [약제학] pharmacy; [약리학] pharmacology.
● **약학과** the pharmaceutical department. **약학 대학** a pharmaceutical college; a college of pharmacy. **약학사** a Bachelor of Pharmacy [Pharmacology] (약어 Phar. B.).

약호(略號) [전신] a code [cable] address; a code; [간략화한 부호] a mark; a symbol. ¶

신 ~ a telegraphic address(약어 TA) / a cable address∥전신 ~ 문자 a code word∥「빼다」「살리다」 등의 교정상의 ~. proofreaders' marks such as "dele" and "stet".

약혼(約婚) an engagement; a promise to marry; a betrothal. ¶존과 베스의 ~ the engagement of John to Beth∥그는 그녀와의 ~을 파기했다 He broke (off) their engagement. **약혼하다** be engaged (to); promise to marry; make an engagement; engage oneself (to a person / to marry a person); betroth oneself (to a person); be engaged [betrothed] (to). ¶그녀는 학자와 약혼했다 She got engaged to a scholar.∥두 사람은 약혼했다 The two became engaged.
● **약혼반지** an engagement ring. **약혼 선물** a betrothal present[gift]. **약혼식** an engagement[a betrothal] ceremony. **약혼자** a fiancé(남자); a fiancée(여자). ¶이 사람이 제 ~입니다 This is my fiancé.

약화(弱化) weakening; enfeeblement. ¶지도력의 ~ the decline in one's leadership ability∥그 기구의 ~가 우리의 목표이다 We are trying to weaken [emasculate] that organization. **약화하다** become weak [weaker]; weaken. ➔¶약화시키다 make weak[weaker] / weaken / enfeeble / debilitate ∥과로로 시력이 약화되었다 Overwork weakened my eyesight.

약화(略畵) a sketch.

약효(藥效) the efficacy [virtue / power / effect] of a medicine [drug]; remedial result. ¶~가 있을지 없을지 확실치 않다 Whether the medicine will work or not is uncertain.∥서서히 ~가 나타났다 The medicine took effect gradually.∥~의 보람도 없이 그는 죽었다 He died in spite of the medical care he was given.

얄궂다 〔얄릇하고 짓궂다〕 perverse; treacherous; nasty; provoking; aggravating; quaint; queer; odd; curious; 〔얄망궂다〕 eccentric; erratic. ¶얄궂게 ironically / in irony / sarcastically∥얄궂은 운명 a curious [strange] irony of fate∥암의 명의가 암으로 죽다니 얄궂은 운명이다 It is an irony (of fate) that a great cancer doctor should die of cancer himself.

얄따랗다 rather[somewhat] thin.

얄망궂다 erratic; frivolous; uncompliant; imprudent. ¶얄망궂게 굴다 behave erratically.

얄밉다 hateful; detestable; disgusting; spiteful; provoking; mean (and nasty); 〔뻔뻔스럽다〕 saucy; cheeky. ¶얄미운 말 nasty [ugly] words∥얄미운 짓 hateful behavior∥얄밉게 hatefully / detestably / provokingly∥얄미운 소년 a hateful [horrid] boy∥얄밉게 굴다 behave detestably [provokingly]∥그는 종종 얄미운 소리를 한다 He often uses aggressively provoking[disagreeable] language.∥그녀는 얄미울 정도로 침착했다 She was disgustingly[provokingly] cool.∥그녀가 추파를 던져도 그는 얄미울 정도로 무관심했다 He was provokingly [exasperatingly] indifferent to her seductive glances.∥그는 그녀가 얄미워졌다 She was becoming repugnant [odious] to him.

얄타 회담(-會談) the Yalta Conference.

얄팍하다 〔얇다〕 thin; small (volume); sleazy (blanket); 〔천박하다〕 shallow (argument); shallow-minded; superficial (knowledge). ¶얄팍한 생각 shallow [superficial] thinking∥얄팍한 교양 a thin veneer of education [culture]∥얄팍한 짓[말] frivolous behavior [remarks].

얇다 thin. ¶얇은 널빤지 thin board∥얇은 옷 a flimsy dress∥얇게 썬 빵 a thin slice of bread∥입술이 ~ have thin lips / be thin-lipped∥빵을 얇게 썰다 cut the bread thin [into thin slices]∥그 소녀는 얇은 야회복을 입고 덜덜 떨고 있었다 The girl was shivering in her flimsy party dress.

얌전 떨다 be prudish; behave nicely. ¶그는 웬일인지 오늘은 별나게 얌전 떨고 있다 For some reason, he is strangely well-behave [docile] today.

얌전하다 1 〔겸손하다〕 modest; 〔온화하다〕 meek; 〔조용하다〕 quiet; gentle; 〔예절 바르다〕 well-behaved; 〔착하다〕 good; 〔고분고분하다〕 obedient; submissive; docile; 〔실이 좋다〕 well-behaved; as good as gold(어린아이가); well-[mild-]mannered. ¶얌전한 아가씨 a gentle [well-behaved] young lady∥그녀는 얌전한 데가 없다 She has nothing sweet about her.∥저 개구장이도 선생님에게 호된 꾸지람을 듣고 오늘은 ~ The little rascal is on his best behavior today since he got a round scolding from the teacher.∥그가 평소와는 달리 얌전한 얼굴을 하고 있다 He looks unusually serious.∥참 얌전한[얌전하지 못한] (계집)애로군 What a well-behaved [a badly-behaved / an ill-mannered] child she is! / That child has such good [bad] manners. **얌전히** 〔온순히〕 gently; meekly; 〔고분고분히〕 obediently; docilely; 〔조용히〕 quietly; like a lamb[sheep]. ¶~ 있어라 Be good! / Be a good boy[girl]!∥~ 않으면 야단칠 거야 I'll teach you to disobey me! / You'll get a (good) scolding if you don't behave yourself.∥신부는 남편 옆에 서 있었다 The bride was standing modestly beside her husband.∥소녀들은 선생님 말씀을 ~ 듣고 있었다 The girls were listening to their teacher respectfully.∥~ 앉아요 Sit properly.∥~ 굴어라 Behave yourself.
2 〔꼼꼼하고 정성 있다〕 nice; neat; good. ¶얌전한 솜씨 good workmanship. **얌전히** nicely; neatly. ¶글을 ~ 쓰다 write neatly∥일을 ~ 하다 do a nice job.

얌체 a selfish [shameless] person.

양 1 〔가장〕. ¶…인 ~하다 set up for (a scholar) / pose as (a poet) / affect / pretend to. **2** 〔작정〕. ¶…할 ~으로 with a view to [of] (doing) / with the intention [hope] of (doing) / for the purpose of (doing) / on purpose to (do) / with intent to (do)∥…할 ~이면 if one is going to (do) / if one has the intention of (doing)∥비밀을 훔쳐낼 ~으로 with intent to steal the secret.

양(羊) a sheep (단수·복수 동형); 〔수양〕 a ram; 〔암양〕 a ewe; 〔새끼 양〕 a lamb. ¶~의 울음소리 bleating(새끼 양의)∥길 잃은 ~ a stray sheep / a lost sheep∥~같이 순한 as gentle as a lamb.
양의 탈[가죽]을 쓴 늑대 a wolf in sheep's clothing. ¶저 녀석은 ~다 He is a wolf in sheep's clothing.
● **양 떼** a flock of sheep.

양(良) 〔성적을 매기는 기준의 하나〕 C. ¶영어에서 ~을 받다 get a C in English.

양(胖) (소의) ox-stomach; the cud pouch; tripe(처녑).

양(陽) 1 (기운·성질) the positive; [철] Yang. ¶음과 ~ the positive and the negative / the male and the female. **2** [수] plus; positive. ¶~수 a positive number // ~의 정수 a positive integer. **3** [전] the anode; the positive pole. ⇨양극(陽極) ¶~전기 positive electricity // ~이온 a positive ion / a cation.

양(量) 1 [수량] quantity; [총량] amount; [용량] volume; [수] magnitude. ¶~보다 질 quality before[rather than] quantity // 상당한 ~의 일 a fair amount of work // 하루에 할 수 있는 일의 ~은 제한되어 있다 There is a limit to the volume[amount / quantity] of work I can handle in a day. // ~이 많다 [적다] There is a large[small] amount [quantity]. **2** [먹을 수 있는 한도] one's eating capacity.

양(兩) ¶~ 끝(에) (at) both ends // ~ 끝을 자르다 cut (a stick) at both ends.

양(孃) Miss. ¶최 ~ Miss Choe // K ~ 자매 the Ms Ks.

양-(洋) Western; European; foreign. ¶~담배 imported tobacco / American cigarettes // ~요리 Western food[dishes].

양가(良家) a good[respectable] family. ¶~의 자녀들 sons and daughters of[boys and girls from] good families // 그녀는 ~의 출신이다 She is[comes] of a good family.

양가(兩家) two[both] houses[families].

양가(養家) an adoptive family(▶ 정식 결연이 아닌 경우는 a foster family). ¶~의 아버지 one's adoptive father.

양가죽(羊-) sheepskin.

양각(陽刻) [미] relief; embossed carving; relievo. **양각하다** emboss; carve [sculpture] in relief. ¶그는 아버지의 옆 얼굴을 양각하였다 He carved a relief of his father's profile.
● **양각 세공** relief work; embossment.

양갈보(洋-) a foreigners' whore[prostitute]; a prostitute who caters to foreigners.

양감(量感) ¶~이 있는 voluminous / massive.

양계(養鷄) poultry farming[keeping]; chicken raising; egg-raising. ¶그는 ~를 하고 있다 He raises poultry[keeps chickens]. // 이 마을은 ~을 성하다 Poultry keeping thrives in this village. **양계하다** raise poultry.
● **양계업** poultry raising[farming]; the poultry industry. **양계장** a poultry farm [yard]; a chicken farm [run]; a chickyard.

양고기(羊-) mutton.

양곡(糧穀) (영) corn; (미) grain; cereals; provisions. ¶정부 ~의 방출 가격 the selling prices of staple grains held by the government // ~을 운반하다 haul grain / carry corn.
● **양곡 도매상** a corn-factor; (미) a grain broker. **양곡상** a grain[corn] merchant. **양곡 창고** a granary; a corn reserve; (미) a grain elevator.

양공주(洋公主) a foreigners' whore[prostitute]. ⇨양갈보

양과자(洋菓子) Western-style cakes[confections].

양국(兩國) the two countries. ¶~ 간의 유대 (friendly) ties between the two countries // 나는 한미 ~의 친선을 위해 최선을 다하겠다 I will do my best to promote friendly relations between Korea and the United States. // ~의 수상이 회담하였다 The prime ministers of the two nations talked together.

양군(兩軍) both[two] armies; both[two] teams(양편 팀). ¶~에 사상자가 많이 났다 There were heavy casualties on both sides.

양궁(洋弓) [활] a small Western bow; [양궁 경기] a game of (Western) archery.

양귀비(楊貴妃) [식] a poppy. ¶~의 씨 a poppy seed.

양극(兩極) [양 끝] both extremities; [남북 양극] the two[north and south] poles; [양극과 음극] the positive and negative poles. ¶~은 bipolar.
● **양극 지방** the polar circles[areas].

양극(陽極) [전] the anode; the positive pole; the zincode(전지의).
● **양극선** anode rays.

양극단(兩極端) both extremes. ¶~이 일치하다 (two) extremes meet // 그들의 의견은 ~으로 갈라져 있었다 They were poles apart in their opinions. / Their opinions were diametrically opposed. // 그 제안에 대하여 그의 생각은 찬성과 반대의 ~ 사이에서 오락가락하였다 His thinking swayed between the extremes of agreement and opposition to the proposal.

양기(陽氣) 1 [햇볕의 기운] sunshine; sunlight. **2** [양의 기운] vitality; vital power; vigor. **3** [남자의 정기] energy; virility; vigor; vitality. ¶~ 좋은 사람 a man of energy / an energetic man // ~가 넘치다 be full of energy / have great vigor [energy] // ~를 보하다 tone up one's energy.

양껏(量-) to one's fill; to one's heart's content. ¶~ 먹다 eat[drink] one's fill.

양난(兩難) a dilemma. ¶(진퇴)~이다 be in a dilemma [fix] / be on the horns of a dilemma.

양날(兩-) ¶~의 double-edged.
● **양날톱** a double-edged saw.

양녀(養女) an adopted[a foster] daughter. ¶~가 되다 be adopted as daughter (by a person) / become (a person's) foster daughter // ~로서 기르다 foster (a girl) as one's daughter // 그는 조카딸을 ~로 삼아 키웠다 He brought up his niece as his daughter.

양념 [향신료] spice(s); condiment(s); (집합적) spicery; [조미료] a seasoning; a flavoring. ¶~을 한 spicy // ~을 많이 한 highly spiced [seasoned] // ~을 치다[넣다] spice (a dish) with spice. **양념하다** season; flavor; spice; give flavor to.

양다리(兩-) both[two] legs.
양다리(를) 걸치다 try to have[play] it both ways; play (a) double (game); try to have one's cake and eat it too. ¶양다리를 걸치는 사람 a double-dealer / a timeserver / an opportunist // 나는 그녀가 애인으로서 그와 나에게 양다리를 걸치고 있는 줄을 몰랐다 I did not know she had shared her love between him and me.

양단(兩端) both ends; either end.
양단(兩斷) bisection. **양단하다** bisect; break [split] in two; cut (a thing) in two. ¶일도~ cut a thing in two with a single stroke of a sword. → ¶선체는 양단되어 버렸다 The ship has broke in half[twain].

양단(洋緞) brocade.

양단간(兩端間) [둘 가운데] between the two; one or the other; this or that; [좌우간] at any rate; in any case [event]; at all events; somehow or other; anyway; anyhow. ¶~에 결정하다 decide between this and that // ~에 단안을 내리다 decide between two choices // ~ 해 보거나 하자 At any rate, let's try. // ~에 해야 할 일이다 I must do it anyhow. / It must be done somehow or other. // ~에 손해는 없다 We shall not be a loser whichever way the matter ends.

양달(陽-) a sunny place [spot]. ¶~에 내놓아 keep (a thing) in the sun // 옷을 ~에 (서) 말리다 dry one's clothes in the sun // ~에 빨래를 널다 hang the wash out in a sunny spot.
● **양달 쪽** the sunny side (of the street); a sunny place. ¶~에 in the sun.

양담배(洋-) a foreign [an American] cigarette; American tobacco.

양당(兩黨) two parties. ¶~의 bipartisan / bipartizan / two-party.
● **양당 정치** [제도] the two-party politics [system].

양도(讓渡) a transfer; conveyance; [법] alienation; (어음의) negotiation; assignment; (영토의) cession. ¶재산 ~ alienation of property. **양도하다** hand [make] over (one's property) to (one's son); transfer (property to one's son); alienate (land to a person); negotiate (securities); convey (by deed) (미) deed; assign. ¶양도할 수 있는 transferable / alienable / assignable / (어음의) negotiable / 양도할 수 없는 inalienable (rights of life) / untransferable / unassignable / (어음의) nonnegotiable // 재산을 ~ transfer property to (a person) // 소유권을 ~ yield [transfer] ownership (of something to a person) // 권리를 ~ transfer one's right to (another) // 아버지는 재산을 아들에게 양도했다 The father transferred [made over] his property to his son.
● **양도 가격** a transfer price. **양도 담보** a mortgage; (양도된 재산) mortgaged property. **양도성 예금** a negotiable (certificate of) deposit. **양도 소득** capital gains; income from transfer. **양도 소득세** a transfer income tax; a capital gains tax. ¶부동산 ~ a realty-transfer tax // ~를 부과하다 impose a transfer income tax. **양도인** (a transferrer; a releasor; an assignor; an alien(at)or. ¶피 ~ a transferee / an assignee. **양도 자산** transfer property; property (to be) transferred. **양도 증서** (a deed of) transfer; a conveyance; an assignment; a grant; (재산의) a common assurance; an assurance; (부동산의) a (deed of) conveyance.

양도체(良導體) [물] a good conductor (of heat). ¶이 물질은 열의 ~이다 This substance is a good thermal conductor [a good conductor of heat].

양돈(養豚) hog [pig] raising; pig keeping [breeding / farming]. **양돈하다** breed hogs; raise pigs; hog-farm.
● **양돈가** a pig breeder [farmer]; a hog raiser [grower]; a hog-farmer. **양돈업** the hog raising industry. **양돈장** a swinery; a piggery; a hoggery; a pig [hog] farm; a hog yard.

양동이(洋-) a (metal) pail; a bucket. ¶~로 물을 긷다 draw water with a pail.

양동 작전(陽動作戰) a feint operation; diversionary activities. ¶~을 펴다 make a feint / feint.

양두구육(羊頭狗肉) advertising [crying] wine, and selling vinegar; using a better name to sell inferior goods; making an extravagant advertisement. ¶~의 광고 a deceptive advertisement.

양두 정치(兩頭政治) diarchy; dyarchy.

양딸(養-) a foster daughter. ⇨ =수양딸(⇨수양(收養))

양딸기(洋-) [식] a (Chilean) strawberry.

양떼구름(羊-) [기상] an altocumulus. ⇨ =고적운.

양력(陽曆) the solar calendar. ⇨ =태양력(⇨태양).

양력(揚力) [물] (dynamic) lift.

양로(養老) [노후의 대비] provision for old age; [봉양] taking good care of the aged; [노후의 안락] living at ease in one's old age.
● **양로 시설** an institution for the aged. **양로원** an asylum [a home] for the aged; an old people's home.

양론(兩論) both arguments; both sides of the argument. ¶찬반~에 귀를 기울이다 listen to the pros and cons (of a matter) / listen to the arguments for and against (a matter) // 의견은 찬반~으로 갈라졌다 Opinion was divided between those in favor and those against [between the pros and the cons].

양륙(揚陸) unloading; discharging; landing; disembarkation. ¶뱃짐의 ~ the discharge [unloading] of cargo // 뱃짐의 ~이 끝났다 The ship finished unloading [discharging its cargo]. / They finished unloading the ship. **양륙하다** unload (a ship); disembark; (배가) discharge (her cargo); (육지에) land (goods / cargo).
● **양륙비** landing charges. **양륙장**(-場) a landing; a landing place [platform / pier]; a wharf.

양립(兩立) coexistence; compatibility. **양립하다** be compatible (with); be consistent (with); coexist (with); stand together. ¶양립할 수 없다 be incompatible (with) / be inconsistent (with) / cannot exist together // 자본주의와 사회주의는 양립할 수 없다 Capitalism is incompatible with socialism. // 이 사상은 우리나라의 전통과 양립할 수 없다 This idea is inconsistent with the tradition of this country. ➔일과 취미를 양립시키다 reconcile [unite] duty and pleasure.

양막(羊膜) [생] the amnion (pl. ~s, -nia).

양말(洋襪) (짧은) socks; (여성용의 긴) stockings; (a pair of) hose(주로 상용어); (집합적) hosiery(▶ (영)에서는 주로 신사용 양말·내의류를 말함). ¶나일론 ~ nylon stockings [socks] / (여성용) (a pair of) nylons // 순모 ~ all-wool socks // 신사용 ~ socks for gentlemen / men's socks // 무릎까지 오는 knee socks // ~을 신고 있지 않은 stockingless // ~을 신다 pull [put / have] on stockings / wear socks // ~을 벗다 pull [take / peel] off one's stockings [socks] // 네 ~의 올이 풀렸다 [네 스타킹이 나갔다] There's [You've got] a run [(영) ladder] in your stockings.
● **양말 대님** (미) garters; (영) suspenders. ¶~을 매다 fasten (stockings) with garters / garter (stockings) // ~으로 고정시킨 양말 stockings fastened with garters / gartered stockings.

양면(兩面) both faces[sides]. ¶~의 double-faced / both-sided // 레코드의 ~ both sides of a record // 인생의 ~ both bright and seamy sides of life // 용지의 ~에 쓰다 write on both sides of the paper // 모든 사물에는 ~이 있다 There are two sides to everything.
● **양면 인쇄** printing on both sides of the paper. **양면 작전** double-sided operations.

양명(揚名) fame; distinction; renown; celebrity. **양명하다** make a[one's] name[mark]; win[make] a name for oneself; win[get] oneself a name; make oneself famous[celebrated]; rise to fame.

양모(羊毛) wool. ¶~의 wool / woolen (cloth) // ~ 같은 woollike / woolly (nylon) // ~로 만든 woolen // ~를 깎다 shear[fleece] sheep.
● **양모 제품** woolen goods. **양모직** woolen fabric[textiles].

양모(養母) an adoptive mother. ⇨양어머니

양모제(養毛劑) a hair tonic.

양미간(兩眉間) the space between the eyebrows; the brow. ¶~이 넓다 [좁다] have wide-set[close-set] eyebrows[eyes].

양민(良民) law-abiding[good] citizens[people]; (집합적) good citizenry.
● **양민 학살** massacre[slaughter] of innocent people.

양반(兩班) **1** [역] (the) yangban; the nobility; the aristocratic[yangban] class; (한 사람) a yangban. ¶~ 태생이다 be of noble birth. **2** [점잖고 착한 사람] a gentleman; [남자] a man; [자기 남편] my husband. ¶우리 집 ~ my old man / my hub [hubby] / 주인 ~ the master (of a house) / 정거장 가는 길은 저 ~한테 물어보시오 Ask the man the way to the station.

양방(兩方) both; both parties[sides]; the two; (부정) neither (of them).

양배추(洋-) (a) cabbage.

양버들(洋-) [식] a Lombardy poplar.

양변(兩邊) both sides; either side. ¶길[강] ~에 on either side[both sides] of the street [river] / 길 ~엔 많은 사람들이 늘어서 있었다 There were crowds of people on either side of the street. / The street was lined with people on either side.

양병(養兵) building up[maintaining / training] an army. **양병하다** build up[maintain / train] an army.

양보(讓步) concession; conciliation; compromise. **양보하다** concede; make a concession; compromise; be conciliatory; give way to (a person); give in; back down; yield (to); meet (a person) halfway. ¶자리를 ~ make room (for a person) / offer one's seat (to a lady) // 요구에 대해 ~ make a concession to a demand // 서로 ~ make mutual concessions / meet each other halfway / compromise / concede // 일보 ~ yield a step / concede a point // 마지못해 ~ reluctantly grant[make] a concession // 조금도 양보하지 않다 make no concession(s) / do not yield a single point / do not recede[yield] an inch // 최대한으로 ~ make the maximum concessions (to a person) // 요구를 한 걸음도 양보하지 않다 do not bate a jot of one's demands / do not budge an inch / make no concessions // 양보하여 조건에 동의하다 yield to the conditions // 어느 쪽도 양보하지 않으려고 한다 Neither would give in. // 이 점은 양보할 수 없다 We cannot concede this point. // 경영자 측은 그들의 요구에 대해 양보했다 The management gave in[conceded] to their demands. // 적대 관계에 있는 두 파벌은 서로 양보했다 The two rival factions met each other halfway [agreed on a middle course]. // 쌍방이 양보하여 분쟁은 해결되었다 The dispute was settled through mutual concessions. // 노동 조합 측은 한 치도 양보하지 않았다 The union did not yield an inch. // 그들은 문간에서 서로 길을 양보했다 They said "After you" to each other at the door. // 두 대의 차는 서로 길을 양보하려 했다 The two cars tried to make way for each other. // 그는 자신의 공을 남에게 양보한다 He disclaims his own merit in favor of others. // 그 사건은 노사가 서로 양보하여 해결되었다 The case was settled by mutual concessions[a compromise] between workers and management. // 그는 한 치도 양보하지 않았다 He held his ground. / He didn't compromise at all[(구어) budge an inch]. // 그가 양보할 때까지 우리는 몇 번이고 설득했다 We urged him repeatedly until he gave in.

양복(洋服) [서양식 의복] (a suit of) clothes; a suit; a dress; (한복에 대하여) Western [European] clothes. ¶~을 입다[벗다] put on[take off] one's dress // ~을 한 벌 맞추다 have[get] a suit of clothes made.
● **양복감 / 양복지** suiting; cloth; stuff. **양복장** a wardrobe; (미) a bureau; (영) a chest of drawers. **양복장이** [양복을 만드는 사람] a tailor; a slopseller(기성복 등의). **양복점** a tailor's (shop); (미) a tailor shop; (값싼 기성복점) a slopshop.

양봉(養蜂) beekeeping; bee raising; (대규모의) apiculture. ¶~의 apiarian // ~에 종사하다 engage in apiculture / keep bees. **양봉하다** keep[culture] bees.
● **양봉가** a beekeeper; an apiarist; an apiarian; an apiculturist. **양봉업** bee farming.

양부(良否) [좋음과 나쁨] whether (a thing) is good or bad; (질) quality. ¶물건의 ~를 조사하다 examine the quality of an article / examine an article to see whether it is good or bad // 물건의 ~를 조사한 후에 확답을 드리겠습니다 We will give a definite answer after examining the quality of the goods.

양부(養父) an adoptive father. ⇨양아버지

양부모(養父母) foster[adoptive] parents.

양분(兩分) bisection. **양분하다** cut in two; bisect; divide (a thing) into two parts; cut [break] (a thing) into halves; halve.

양분(養分) nourishment; nutriment; nutrient; nutritious substance[matter]; sustenance. ¶~이 있다 be nourishing / be nutritious / contain nourishment // ~을 섭취하다 take nourishment (from) // ~을 주다 nourish // 흙은 식물에 ~을 준다 The soil nourishes plants. // 기생 식물은 숙주로부터 ~을 흡수한다 Parasitic plants take nourishment from their hosts.

양산(陽傘) a sunshade; a parasol. ¶~을 쓴 여자 a woman under a parasol // ~을 쓰다 put up[raise] a parasol // ~을 펴다 open [spread / unfold] a parasol // ~을 접다 close [shut / fold] a parasol.

양산(量産) mass production; production on a large scale. ¶~의 mass-produced. **양산하다** mass-produce; make (a thing) in large

양상(樣相) an aspect; a phase; a condition; appearance; looks; outlook; [논] modality. ¶…의 ~을 나타내다 assume an aspect of … // 심상치 않은 ~을 나타내다 look unusual / assume a serious [an extraordinary] aspect // ~을 **일변시키다** change the whole situation [climate] / 새로운 ~을 띠게 되다 enter on [upon] a new phase // 사태는 비극적인 ~을 띠기 시작했다 Things began to take on a tragic aspect. / Things began to look tragic. // 전쟁은 역사의 한 ~이다 War is one aspect of history. // ~을 일변시키는 사건이 일어났다 An incident took place which changed the whole outlook [situation].

양상군자(梁上君子) [도둑] a thief; a housebreaker; a burglar.

양생(養生) 1 [건강관리를 잘함] care of health; preservation of one's health; (병후의) recuperation. ¶적당한 ~으로 이 병은 반드시 치유될 것이다 With proper care, you are sure to recover from this illness. // 우리는 건강을 유지하기 위해 ~에 힘써야 한다 We must be careful about [(문어) of] our health to keep (our bodies) fit. **양생하다** take care [be careful] of one's health; improve [promote] (one's) health; (병후에) recuperate oneself. 2 (콘크리트 등의). ¶콘크리트를 ~하다 cure the concrete surface.
● **양생법** a regimen; rules for one's health; rules for maintaining good health.

양서(良書) a good book; a valuable work. ¶~를 구하다 [고르다] seek [choose] good books.

양서(洋書) a foreign book; a book published in a Western country.

양서류(兩棲類) [동] the amphibia. ¶~의 amphibian / batrachian / ~의 동물 a batrachian.

양성(良性) ¶~의 [의] benign [benignant] (disease).
● **양성 종양** benign tumor [(영) tumour].

양성(兩性) both [the two] sexes. ¶~의 bisexual.
● **양성 생식** amphigony; gamogenesis. **양성화** a bisexual [an androgynous] flower.

양성(陽性) 1 [의] positivity. ¶~의 positive / [식] plus // 그는 투베르쿨린 반응이 ~이었다 His reaction to the tuberculin test proved positive. 2 [적극적이고 활동적인 성질] a positive [an active / an extrovert / a sunny / a cheerful] disposition. ¶성격이 ~인 사람 a man of positive [sunny] disposition / an extrovert.
● **양성 반응** (a) positive reaction. **양성자** [물] a proton. **양성화**(-化) legalization. ¶무허가 건물의 ~ legalization of unauthorized buildings // 정치 자금을 ~하다 bring (out) the sources of political funds to light [into the open] / legalize political funds.

양성(養成) training (of teachers); education; nurture; cultivation. **양성하다** train; educate; bring up; rear; cultivate; nurse. ¶인재를 ~ cultivate men of talent [ability] // 후진을 ~ train the younger [next] generation // 올림픽 선수를 ~ train athletes for the Olympics // 간호사를 ~ train women [girls] as nurses // 교원을 ~ train teachers // 기술자를 ~ train technicians // 외교관으로 ~ train (a person) for the diplomatic service // 법률가로 ~ bring up (a boy) to the legal profession.
● **양성 기간** a training period; the period of apprenticeship. **양성소** a training school [center / institute]. ¶교원 ~ a training school for teachers // 배우 ~ an academy of drama / a theater school / an acting school // 그 대학은 사실상 관리의 ~였다 The University was in practice the nursery of government officials.

양속(良俗) a good [fine] custom. ¶미풍~ a good and beautiful custom / good morals and manners // 공서(公序) ~에 반하다 offend [(문어) be prejudicial to] public order and morals.

양손(兩-) both [two] hands. ¶~에 [으로] in [with] both hands // ~으로 들다 hold (a thing) with both hands // ~에 쥐다 hold (a thing) in both hands // ~을 벌리다 open both hands.

양손녀(養孫女) an adopted [a foster] granddaughter.

양손(자)(養孫子) an adopted [a foster] grandson.

양송이(洋松栮) a mushroom; a champignon.
● **양송이 재배**[수출] mushroom cultivation [export].

양수(羊水) amniotic fluid; [의] liquor amnii; waters. ¶(출산 전에) ~가 나왔다 The waters broke.

양수(兩手) both [two] hands. ⇨=양손
● **양수걸이** (일 등의) having [playing] it both ways; playing (a) double (game); (장기 등의) scoring a double point with a single move. **양수겸장**(-兼將) a double check; (서양 장기의) a fork. **양수잡이** (사람) an ambidexter; an ambidextrous person; (장기 등의) scoring a double point with a single move.

양수(揚水) raising water; pumping (up) water. **양수하다** raise water; pump (up) water.
● **양수기** a water pump. ⇨=무자위

양수(陽數) [수] a positive number.

양순음(兩脣音) [언] a labial (sound). ⇨=입술소리(⇨입술)

양순하다(良順-) good; gentle; meek; obedient; docile. ¶양순한 아이 a docile [a meek] child // 양순한 백성 law-abiding [obedient] people. **양순히** gently; meekly; docilely. ¶~ 말을 듣다 do as told without objection.

양식(良識) good sense. ¶~ 있는 사람 a sensible [sound-thinking] person / a person of good sense / a person of sound judgment // ~이 결여되어 있다 [없다] lack [be lacking in] good sense // 당신의 ~을 의심하지 않을 수 없다 I must say you acted foolishly. / It makes me doubt your good sense. // 당신의 ~ 있는 행동을 기대한다 We expect you to act sensibly.

양식(洋式) Western [European / American] style. ¶~ 방 a room furnished in Western style // 그의 집은 모두 ~으로 지어졌다 His whole house was built in Western style.

양식(洋食) Western [European] food [dishes]; Western cooking [cookery]. ¶~ 먹는 법 Western [European] table manners.
● **양식 요리(법)** Western cooking. **양식집** / **양식점** a restaurant (serving European dishes); a European-style restaurant.

양식(樣式) 1 [독특한 방식·형] a mode; a

양식 manner; [논] modality; [건] (a) style; an order. ¶생활~ a style[mode] of living / a way of life / one's life-style[way of living] // 건축 ~ a style of building // 행동 ~ patterns of behavior // 고딕 ~의 대성당 a Gothic cathedral // ~화된 연기 a stylized performance // ~화하다 stylize / conventionalize. 2 [일정한 형식] a (fixed) form. ¶법률 문서의 ~ the form of legal documents // 이 서류는 정말 복잡한 ~으로 되어 있다 This document is written in a very complicated form.

양식(養殖) raising; culture; cultivation; breeding; rearing. ¶굴 ~ oyster farming // 진주 ~ culture of pearl / pearl culture. 양식하다 rear; raise; breed; cultivate. ¶방어를 ~ raise young yellowtails.
● 양식업 cultivating[breeding] industry; fish-raising industry. 양식장 a nursery; a farm; a breeding ground. ¶송어 ~ a trout farm[hatchery / nursery]. 양식 진주 a culture(d)[cultivated] pearl.

양식(糧食) 1 [먹을거리] provisions; food; (food) supplies; victuals; (할당된) rations. ¶~ 부족 a shortage of food // ~이 떨어지다 provisions give out / (사람이) run out of provisions // ~이 부족해지다 provisions fall[run] short / (사람이) run short of provisions // ~은 충분히 있다 have an ample supply of food / be well provisioned // 나날의[일용할] ~을 벌다 earn one's daily bread // ~을 사들이다 [비축하다] lay in[up] provisions // 3일분의 ~을 휴대하다 take a three-day supply of food // ~이 떨어졌다 We have run short of food. // 그 배에는 한 달분의 ~이 준비되어 있다 The ship is provisioned for a month. 2 [지식 등의 원천이 되는 것] food. ¶마음의 ~ mental[spiritual] food / mental pabulum / mental[intellectual] nourishment // 생명의 ~ [성] the bread of life // 빵은 생명의 ~이다 Bread is the staff of life.

양심(良心) conscience; the inner voice; the still small voice. ¶한 조각의 ~ a scrap of conscience // ~상 for conscience(') sake / for the sake of one's conscience // ~의 소리 the voice of conscience // 학자적 ~ academic[scientific] honesty / a scholarly conscience // ~이 있는 conscientious // ~이 없는 conscienceless // ~이 있는 사람 a person of conscience // ~이 없는 사람 a person without conscience // ~에 따라 according to (the dictates of) one's conscience // ~에 반하여 against one's conscience // ~에 비추어 in conscience // ~에 거리끼지 않는 행동 a conscientious action[deed] // ~에 부끄러운 행위 shameful conduct // ~의 가책을 받다[느끼다] be conscience-stricken / be stung by conscience / suffer from a guilty conscience / have[suffer] the qualms of conscience // ~이 없다 have no conscience / be without conscience // ~에 걸리다 have (something) on one's conscience / lie heavy on one's conscience // ~에 거리낌 없다[떳떳하다] have a clear[good] conscience // ~에 거리끼다[부끄럽다] have a guilty[bad] conscience // ~에 맡기다 leave (a person) to (his) conscience // ~에 걸려서 그런 일은 도저히 할 수 없다 I cannot, in all conscience, do such a thing. // 자네 ~에 맡기겠네 I leave (it) to your conscience. // 자네 ~에 물어보게 Listen to what the still small voice bids you.

양심적(良心的) conscientious. ¶~인 상인 an honest merchant // ~인 가게 an honest shop / ~으로 conscientiously // 비~인 unconscientious // ~인 가책 the pangs [qualms / pricks] of conscience / a sting of conscience.

양아들(養-) an adopted child. ➪=양자(養子)
양아버지(養-) an adoptive father; a foster father.

양아치 [넝마주이] a ragpicker; a ragman.
양악(洋樂) Western[European] music.
양안(兩岸) both sides[banks]; either bank. ¶강의 ~에 벚나무가 심어져 있었다 Cherry trees were planted on both banks[either bank] of the river.

양안(兩眼) both eyes. ¶그는 ~을 실명하였다 He lost sight[went blind] in both eyes.

양약(良藥) a good medicine; an efficacious medicine[remedy]. ¶~은 입에 쓰다 Good medicine tastes bitter. / The best advice is hardest to take.

양양하다(洋洋-) 1 [바다가 광대하다] wide; broad; vast; boundless. ¶양양한 대해 a broad[vast / boundless] expanse of ocean. 2 [장래가 희망적이다] bright (future); rosy (prospects); promising. ¶전도가 양양한 청년 a young man with a bright future / a promising young man // 여러분의 전도는 ~ You have a bright future before you.

양양하다(揚揚-) elated; triumphant.
양어(養魚) fish breeding[culture / farming]; pisciculture.
● 양어장 a fish farm; a hatchery.
양어깨(兩-) both[one's] shoulders.
양어머니(養-) an adoptive mother.
양여(讓與) concession (of a privilege / of a right); (영토의) cession; [양도] transfer; surrender; assignment. 양여하다 concede (a privilege to a person); yield possession of (something); transfer[assign] (property to one's son); make[hand] over; cede (a territory).

양옥(洋屋) a Western-[European-]style house; a house in Western[European] style.
양요리(洋料理) Western[European] food [dishes]; (요리법) Western[European] cooking[cuisine].
양용(兩用) (for) double use. ¶수륙 ~ 전차 [비행기] an amphibious tank[plane].
양원(兩院) the two Houses. ¶상하 ~ the Houses of Representatives and Councilors / the Lower House and the Upper House // ~ 일치의 의결 a concurrent vote of both Houses.
● 양원제 a bicameral system.
양위(讓位) abdication (of the Throne); demise of the Crown. 양위하다 abdicate the Throne (in favor of 《the Crown Prince》); demise the Throne.
양육(羊肉) mutton; (새끼의) lamb.
양육(養育) breeding. 양육하다 bring up; rear; foster; nurse; raise. ➔¶그녀는 할머니에 의해 양육되었다 She was brought up by her grandmother.
● 양육비 the expense of bringing up children; fostering expenses. 양육원 a workhouse; a poorhouse; (고아의) a home for orphans; an orphanage; (기아의) a foundling hospital[home]. 양육자 a fosterer; a rearer; a breeder.

양은(洋銀) nickel silver; German silver.
● **양은그릇** nickel silver ware.
양의(洋醫) a Western (medical) doctor; a Western physician.
양이온(陽-) [물] a positive ion; a cation.
양익(兩翼) both wings; (대형의) both flanks.
양인(兩人) two persons. ⇨ 양자(兩者)
양일(兩日) two days; a couple of days. ¶~간 during[for] two days // ~간에 in[within] two days.
양자(兩者) two persons; both; both sides [parties]; a couple[pair]. ¶~ 합의하에 by mutual consent[agreement] // 이 연구는 ~의 협력으로 완성되었다 The cooperation of the two brought this research to completion [fruition].
● **양자택일** a choice between two things; selecting one alternative. ¶~을 하다 choose between the two / select one alternative // 우리는 항복이냐 죽음이냐의 ~에 몰렸다 We were given the choice of submission of death. / We were forced the choose either submission or death.
양자(陽子) [물] a proton. ⇨ 양성자(⇨ 양성(陽性))
양자(量子) [물] a quantum (pl. -ta).
● **양자론** the quantum theory. **양자 물리학** quantum physics. **양자 역학** quantum mechanics.
양자(養子) an adopted child; one's son by adoption. ¶~로 삼다 adopt (a child) (as one's son) / make an adopted child of // 그는 조카를 ~로 삼기로 결정했다 He decided to adopt his nephew. // 나는 윤 씨 집에 ~로 갔다 I was adopted into the Yun family.
양잠(養蠶) sericulture; silkworm raising; silk culture[raising]. **양잠하다** raise[rear / breed] silkworms.
● **양잠가** a sericulturist. **양잠 농가** a silk-raising farmer. **양잠업** the sericultural industry.
양장(洋裝) 1 [여성의 서양식 옷] women's Western[European] clothes; women's Western-style dress. ¶~미인 a beautiful woman in Western clothing // 그 노부인은 ~ 차림이었다 The old lady was dressed in Western style. **양장하다** be dressed in Western[European] style; wear Western(-style) dress[clothes]. 2 [서양식 장정] binding a book in Western style.
● **양장본** a book bound in Western style. **양장점** a dressmaking shop; a couture house.
양재(良材) 1 [좋은 재료] good material; [재목] good timber. 2 [우수한 인재] a man of ability[talent].
양재(洋裁) (Western-style) dressmaking. ¶~를 배우다 learn[take lessons in] dressmaking.
● **양재사** a dressmaker.
양재기(洋-) enamelware; an enameled iron bowl[pot].
양잿물(洋-) caustic soda; lye; alkaline solution.
양적(量的) quantitative. ¶~으로 quantitatively / in terms of quantity.
● **양적 증가** an increase in quantity.
양전기(陽電氣) [물] positive[plus] electricity. ¶~의 electropositive.
양전자(陽電子) [물] a positron.
양전하(陽電荷) positive charge.

양젖(羊-) goat('s) milk.
양조(醸造) brewing; brewage. **양조하다** (맥주를) brew; (증류하여 위스키를) distill[[영] distil]. ¶맥주를 ~ brew beer // 약주는 쌀로 양조한다 *Yakju* is brewed[made] from rice.
● **양조업** the brewing industry; the brewery business. **양조자** a brewer; a distiller. **양조장** (맥주의) a brewery; (위스키의) a distillery.
양주(洋酒) whisk(e)y and wine; alcoholic beverages introduced to Korea from the West.
양지(陽地) a sunny place[spot]; a sunshine; the sun.
양지가 음지 되고 음지가 양지 된다(속담) Sunny spots get darkened and dark spots get sunny.; Life has many ups and downs.
● **양지쪽** the sunny side (of the street); a sunny place. ¶~에 in the sun // ~에다 말리다 dry in the sun.
양지(諒知) [이해] understanding; [승인] acknowledgment. **양지하다** understand; acknowledge; approve. ¶양지하시기 바랍니다 This is to give notice (that). // 이 건은 낙착된 것으로 양지하여 주십시오 Please understand that this matter has been settled.
양지머리 the brisket of beef.
양지바르다(陽地-) sunny; full of sunshine; (서술적) admit ample sunshine. ¶양지바른 방 a sunny room // 양지바른 곳 a sunny place // 양지바른 집 a house with a sunny aspect // 우리 집은 남향이어서 ~ Facing the south, my house admits[gets] plenty of sunshine.
양질(良質) good quality. ¶~의 버터 high-quality butter.
양쪽(兩-) both; both sides[parties]; either side; the two sides; each of the two; (부정) neither. ¶~의 both / either // ~ 다 both / the two // 길의 ~ on either side[both sides] of the street // ~ 다 좋다 Both are good[acceptable]. // ~ 다 나쁘다 They are both to blame. // ~ 모두 잘못이 있다 Both are to blame. // ~ 다 모른다 I don't know either of them. / I know neither of them. // ~ 다 일리가 있다 There's something to both arguments. // 그렇게 하면 ~ 다 만족할 것이다 That will satisfy both parties. // ~이 팽팽히 맞서고 있다 They are evenly matched.
양처(良妻) a good wife. ¶현모~ a good wife and wise mother.
양철(洋鐵) tinned iron; a tin plate.
● **양철공** a tinner; a tinman; a tinsmith. **양철 지붕** a tin roof. **양철통** (미) a can; (영) a tin. **양철판** galvanized sheet iron; a tin plate.
양초(洋-) a (wax) candle; a taper(가는 것). ¶~를 켜다 burn[light] a candle // (불이) 끄다 put[blow] out a candle // ~가 다 닳아져 간다 The candle is burning low.
● **양초 동강** a candle ends. **양초 심지** a candlewick; the wick (of a candle).
양춘가절(陽春佳節) the pleasant springtime.
양측(兩側) both sides[parties]; either side. ¶길 ~에 훌륭한 저택들이 줄지어 있었다 The street was lined with fine homes on both sides.
양치기(羊-) [양을 치는 일] sheep-raising; [양을 치는 사람] a shepherd.
양치류(羊齒類) [식] a fern; (집합적) fernery.
양치(질) [이를 닦기] brushing one's teeth; [입 안을 가심] rinsing the mouth; gargling. **양치(질)하다** brush one's teeth; rinse (out)

양친 the mouth; gargle (the throat). ¶소금물로 ~ rinse out one's mouth with salt and water.
● **양칫물** gargling water.
양친(兩親) (one's) father and mother; one's parents. ¶~의 parental.
양코(洋-) a Westerner's nose; a large protruding nose.
● **양코배기** a Westerner; Yankee(미국 사람).
양키 a Yankee; a Yank.
양탄자(洋--) a carpet; a rug. ⇨°융단 ¶두꺼운 ~가 깔린 a thick-carpeted floor // ~를 깔다 spread a carpet / carpet (a floor) // 들에는 꽃들이 만발하여 ~를 깔아 놓은 것 같았다 The fields were carpeted with wild flowers in full glory.
양태(樣態) a mode.
양털(羊-) wool. ¶~을 깎다 shear a sheep.
양파(洋-) an onion; (음식물로서의) onion.
양팔(兩-) two [both] arms. ¶~ 가득히 책을 안다 hold an armful of books / have one's arms full of books // ~을 펴다 hold out both arms // ~로 끌어안다 embrace (a child).
양편(兩便) both; both sides. ⇨°양쪽
양푼 a (large) brass bowl [basin].
양품(洋品) Western-style apparel and accessories; haberdashery; fancy goods.
● **양품점** a shop dealing in Western-style apparel and accessories.
양풍(良風) a good [laudable] custom.
양피(羊皮) sheepskin; a roan(제본용).
● **양피 구두** sheepskin [goatskin] shoes. **양피지** parchment; sheepskin; membrane.
양학(洋學) Western [European] learning [scholarship]. ¶~의 도입 the introduction of Western learning.
양해(諒解) (an) understanding; consent; agreement. ¶그의 ~를 얻어서 with his consent // 그의 ~를 얻다 [구하다] obtain [ask for] his consent // 나는 가지 않겠으니 자네가 대신 적당히 ~를 구해 주게 I'm not going, but make some feasible excuse for me, will you? **양해하다** understand; consent (to); agree (to / with / in / upon). ¶그는 그 제안을 양해하였다 He agreed [consented] to the proposal.
● **양해 사항** items of agreement; [법] stipulation.
양호(養護) [관형어적] protective. **양호하다** care; nurse; protect.
● **양호 교사** a school nurse; a nursing teacher. **양호 시설** a protective institution; a home for dependent, neglected and abused children.
양호하다(良好-) good; fine; excellent; favorable; satisfactory. ¶환자의 수술 후 경과는 ~ The patient is progressing satisfactorily after the operation. // 마이크의 감도는 ~ The microphone picks up sounds well.
양화(良貨) good money. ¶악화는 ~를 구축한다 Bad money drives out good.
양화(洋靴) (a pair of) shoes; high shoes. ⇨°구두
● **양화점** (미) a shoe store; a shoemaker's.
양화(陽畵) [사진] a positive (picture); a positive photograph [print].
양회(洋灰) cement. ⇨°시멘트
얕다 1 (깊이가) shallow. ¶얕은 접시 a shallow dish // 물이 얕은 곳 a shoal / a shallow // 얕은 물에서 수영하다 swim in shallow water // 시냇물을 얕은 곳에서 건너자 Let's cross the stream where it is shallow.
2 (생각·지식이) shallow; superficial. ¶생각이 얕은 사람 a shallow-brained [-headed] person // 얕은 지식 [소견] a superficial knowledge [view] // 얕은 경험이 ~ be green in experience // 컴퓨터에 관한 내 지식은 아직은 ~ My knowledge of computers is still shallow. // 너의 역사에 대한 견해는 ~ Your view of history is superficial. // 그런 짓을 하다니 자네는 생각이 ~ It is thoughtless of you to do such a thing.
3 (정도가) slight; (높이가) low; humble; lowly; (키가) short. ¶얕은 잠 (a) light sleep // 천장이 얕은 방 a room with a low ceiling // 얕은 잠을 자므로 나는 밤중에 자주 깬다 Being a light sleeper, I wake up very often during the night.
얕은 내도 깊게 건너라 (속담) One cannot use too much caution.; Much caution does no harm.
얕보다 look down upon [on] (a person); make light [little] of; slight; belittle; disparage; depreciate; hold (a person) in contempt; disdain. ¶사람을 얕보는 a superior [condescending] air // 남의 솜씨를 ~ underrate a person's skill // 나를 얕보지 마라 Don't underestimate me [my power]. // 이것은 상당히 어려운 일이다. 얕보지 말다 This is quite a tough job. Don't make light of it.
얕은꾀 shallow resources [cunning]; superficial craftiness.
얕잡다 make a low estimate of; underrate; hold (a person) cheap; belittle; make light of; look down upon. ¶나는 그를 얕잡아 보고 있었다 I underestimated him. / (구어) It was a mistake to think him a soft touch. // 그는 처음부터 상대방을 얕잡아 보고 있었다 He made light of his opponent from the start.
얕추 [얕게] in a shallow fashion; shallowly.
얘 1 [이 애] this child [boy / girl]; he; she; it. ¶~가 왜 이래 What's the matter [What's wrong] with this child? **2** (아들을 부를 때) Sonny; My boy; (남을 부를 때) You; Hey; Buster; Here; There. ¶~, 잠깐 기다려 Hey, just a minute! // ~야 Hey, you! // ~ 너 이리 오너라 Hey, you, come here! // ~, 네 선생님이 오신다 Look, there is your teacher on his way here now.
얘기 a talk; a tale; a rumor; consultation; the facts. ⇨°이야기
● **얘깃거리** a topic (of conversation). ⇨°이야깃거리(⇨이야기)
어 (놀람 등을 나타내는 소리) Oh!; Why!; Well!; (손아랫사람에게 대답하는 소리) Yes; Yea. ¶~, 한 선생 Ah [Oh], Mr Han! // ~, 지금 가네 Yes, I'm coming. // ~, 내 가방이 없네 Well, What happened to my bag?
-어(語) (단어) a word; (전문어) a term; (국어) language. ¶법률~ legal terms // 외국~ a foreign language // 전문~ technical terms / a nomenclature // 비속~ a slang / a vulgarism.
어간(語幹) [언] a stem.
어감(語感) (말의 뉘앙스) the nuance of a word; (말에 대한 감각) (have) a keen sense of language. ¶좋은 ~ euphony // ~이 좋다 sound well / be euphonic.
어거지 →억지
어구(語句) words and phrases.
어구(漁具) fishing implements; (집합적)

fishing gear[tackle].
어구(漁區) a fishing ground[area]; a fishery.
어군(魚群) a school[shoal] of fish.
● **어군 탐지기** a fish finder; a fish detector.
어군(語群) [언] a word group.
어귀 an entrance; (미) an entry (to a river); the mouth (of a harbor); an approach (to a tunnel). ¶강~ the mouth of a river / a river mouth / an outfall / an estuary // 마을 ~ the verge[end] of a village / an approach to a village.
어그러지다 1 [빗나가다] be out of joint [order]; be twisted[dislocated]; swerve [deviate] from. ¶책상 다리 하나가 어그러졌다 One of the legs of the table slipped out of joint.
2 [생각과는 맞지 않다] be[act] against [contrary to] (the rule); go against; go back on; run counter to; depart[deviate] from; transgress; violate. ¶기대에 ~ be contrary to one's expectation // 긴급회의 때문에 나의 여행 계획이 어그러졌다 My plans for a trip were ruined[wrecked] by an emergency meeting. // 내가 하는 일은 모조리 어그러지기만 한다 Things are contrary[go wrong] with me. / Things go badly with me.
3 [사이가 나쁘게 되다] break[fall out] (with); become estranged[alienated] (from); get into discord (with). ¶친구와 사이가 ~ be estranged from one's friend // 오해가 생겨 둘 사이가 어그러졌다 Mutual misunderstanding led to their estrangement [to bad feelings between them].
어근(語根) the root[stem / base / radical] of a word; [언] a radix (*pl.* ~es, -dices).
어금니 a molar (tooth); a grinding tooth; a grinder; a back[check] tooth.
어금지금하다 nearly alike; much the same; about[nearly] the same; quite even. ¶두 사람의 성적은 ~ It is difficult to say which of the two has the better grades[record]. // 어금지금한 승부였다 They had a close game. / It was an evenly-balanced match.
어긋나기 [식] growing in alternation. ¶~의 alternate.
● **어긋나기잎** alternate leaves (on a plant).
어긋나다 1 [엇갈리다] go crisscross (with); [일정한 기준에서 벗어나다] run counter (to); be contrary (to); go against; go amiss [away]; go wrong; deviate from. ¶길이 ~ cross[pass] each other (on the way) / leave just before another arrives // 가르침에 ~ deviate from (a person's) teaching // 생각[의견]이 서로 ~ hold contrary[different / divergent] opinions // 도의에 어긋나는 행동을 하다 act contrary to morality // 이것은 내 기대에 어긋난다 This is not what I wanted. // 신 선생의 최신작은 그의 명성에 어긋나지 않는 작품이다 Sin's latest work lives up to [is worthy of / justifies] his reputation. // 그 정책은 인도주의 원칙에 어긋나는 것이었다 The policy was out of line with humanitarian principles. // 낭비는 나의 신조에 어긋난다 Wastefulness is contrary to[against] my principles. // 그것은 규칙에 어긋난다 This is against rules. // 그의 행동은 예의범절에 어긋난다 His behavior is a violation[breach] of etiquette.
2 [꼭 맞지 않다] be out of joint[order]; be dislocated. ¶어깨뼈가 ~ have[get] one's shoulder dislocated // 무릎뼈가 어긋났다 My knee popped[came] out of joint.
3 [상호 간의 마음에 틈이 벌어지다] become estranged[alienated] (from); break[fall out] (with); have a break (in); have a disagreement (with).
어긋놓다 place[set / lay] (thing) crisscross.
어긋물리다 engage[join] crisscross; fit together crisscross.
어기다 [위반하다] violate; infringe; break; transgress; [상반하다] go[act] against; be contrary to; run counter; go back on; [따르지 않다] disobey; disregard; act against. ¶약속을 ~ break[go back on] one's promise[word] // 명령을 ~ disobey[disregard / ignore] an order // 규칙을 ~ break [violate / infringe] the rule // 시간을 1분도 어기지 않고 be punctual[(미) be on time] to the minute // 그는 결코 약속을 어기지 않습니다 He always keeps[fulfills] his promises. / He is true to[never breaks] his word. // 그는 내 경고를 어기고 강으로 헤엄치러 갔다 He went swimming in the river in spite of my warning.
어기대다 oppose; put[set] oneself against; defy; disobey; be insubordinate (to); (구어) give cheek to.
어기야디야 Yo-ho!; Yo-heave-ho!
어기여차 Yo-ho!; Yo-heave-ho!
어기적거리다 waddle[wallop] (along); walk in an awkward way; walk with a toddling gait.
어기적어기적 (walk) in an awkward way [like a duck]. **어기적어기적하다** waddle (along). ⇨°어기적거리다
어기차다 resolute; determined; firm; headstrong; obstinate; willful; unflinching; dauntless.
어김없다 unerring; infallible; never failing [missing]. ¶그는 어김없는 사람이다 He is quite a reliable person. **어김없이** without fail; surely; certainly; for sure[certain]. ¶9시까지는 ~ 이리 와 주십시오 Don't fail[Be sure] to come here by nine. // 두 사람은 만나면 ~ 다툰다 The two never meet without quarrelling.
어깨 1 (신체의) the shoulder. ¶[척(축)] 벌어진 [처진] ~ square[sloping] shoulders // ~가 처진[민틋한] 여자 a woman with sloping shoulders // ~가 넓다[좁다] be broad-shouldered[narrow-shouldered] / have broad [narrow] shoulders // ~를 펴다 open [square] one's shoulders // ~를 으쓱하다 raise[perk up] one's shoulders // ~를 움츠리다 shrug one's shoulders / give a shrug of the shoulders // ~로 밀어제치다 shoulder (a person) out of the way // ~에 메다 shoulder (one's bag) / bear[carry] on one's shoulder // ~가 뻐근하다 I have stiff shoulders. / My shoulders are stiff.
2 [옷의 소매와 깃의 사이] the shoulders (of a coat). ¶~에 패드를 넣은 상의 a jacket with padded shoulders // ~에 패드를 넣다 pad the shoulder (of a coat).
3 [불량배] a rowdy; a rough; a rascal; rogue; a ruffian; a scoundrel; a (street) gangster; (속어) a hooligan; (미국 속어) a hoodlum; (미국 속어) a roughneck.
어깨가 가볍다 be relieved of one's burden [responsibility]; the burden[responsibility]

어깨 is off one's shoulders; feel the load off one's shoulders; feel relieved. ¶그것으로 나는 어깨가 가벼워졌다 That's a load off my shoulders.

어깨가 무겁다 shoulder[assume / take / bear] heavy[high] responsibility; shoulder an important[irksome] burden; be burdensome; be a burden to one; be too much for one.

어깨가 처지다 one's shoulders drop. ¶그는 그 말을 듣자 어깨가 처졌다 His shoulders dropped[His face fell] when he heard it.

어깨를 겨누다[겨루다] rank with (another); rank beside (another); take rank with; can compare with (another); stand abreast with (a person); equal (another in something). ¶이론 물리학에서는 그와 어깨를 겨룰 사람이 없다 He has no equal[match / rival] in (the field of) the theoretical physics.

어깨를 나란히 하다 1 [나란히 서다] stand shoulder to shoulder[side by side]. ¶우리들은 어깨를 나란히 하고 앉아 있었다 We sat shoulder to shoulder. 2 rank with (another). ⇨ˇ어깨를 겨누다(⇨ˇ어깨)

어깨를 으쓱거리다 square one's shoulders. ¶어깨를 으쓱거리며 걷다 walk with one's shoulders squared // 그 남자는 어깨를 으쓱거리며 살고 있지만, 실은 쉽게 외로워하는 사람이다 He pretends to be strong and independent[He puts on a bold front], but actually he gets lonely very easily.

● **어깨번호** a superior[superscript] number.

어깨뼈 [생] a shoulder blade; a bladebone; a scapular; a scapula (*pl.* -lae, ~s). ¶~가 부러지다 get one's bladebone broken. **어깨춤** a shoulder dance. ¶~을 추다 (기뻐서) dance for[with] joy / (어깨를 으쓱거리며) dance with one's shoulder moving up and down. **어깻바람** [어깻짓] swinging[swaying / wiggling] one's shoulders with delight; [신바람] excitement; enthusiasm; vigor; [뽐냄] swaggering; being puffed up. ¶~이 나서 in high spirits / with great fervor // 장교는 ~을 내며 돌아다녔다 The officer swaggered[strutted] about. **어깻죽지** the shoulder. ¶~가 시리다 I feel cool around the shoulder.

어깨너머로 learn something by watching[without being taught] // 그는 ~ 장사의 요령을 배웠다 He picked up the knack of doing business just by watching.

어깨동무하다 put arms around each other's shoulders; take[hold] each other round the shoulders.

어깨총 (-銃) [구령] Slope[Carry] arms!; Shoulder arms!

어눌하다 (語訥-) stammer; falter; stutter; (서술적) have an impediment in (one's) speech; be awkward[clumsy] in speech; [말이 느리다] be slow of speech. ¶그는 어눌한 사람이다 He falters in speaking. / He stammers[stutters]. / He does not have a glib tongue.

어느 1 [어떤] which; what. ¶~ 가게에서 샀느냐 At which store did you buy it? // 그는 ~ 대학을 나왔느냐 What university did he graduate from? // 문 선생님이 ~ 분입니까 Which is Mr. Mun? // 그는 ~ 쪽으로 갔습니까 Which way[In what direction] did he go? // ~ 쪽이 이겼습니까 Which side won? // ~ 것이 가장 좋은 계획일까 I wonder which is the best plan?

2 [그중의 어느] whichever; any. ¶~ 모로 보나 from every point of view / in every respect [way] / in all respects / in whatever way you may look at it / (미) to all respects / (영) to all appearance / every bit[inch] // 그는 ~ 모로 보나 시인이다 He is every inch a poet. / He is a poet, every inch of him. // 그녀는 ~ 모로 보아도 아름답다 She's beautiful from any angle. // ~ 것이든 마음에 드는 것을 택하게 Choose anything[whichever] you like (better). // 이 중에 ~ 것도 마음에 안 든다 I don't care for any of these. / None[Neither] of them pleases me (neither 는 둘 중, none 은 셋 이상). // ~ 쪽이라고 말하지 못하겠다 I can't say which. / I can't give a definite answer. // 그 병이라면 ~ 것이든 된다 Either [Any] of those bottles will do(▶ either 는 2개의 경우, any 는 3개 이상의 경우).

3 [막연한 어떤] a; one; a certain; some. ¶~ 날 아침 one morning // 그들은 ~ 정도 목적을 달성했다 They achieved their purpose to some degree[to a certain extent]. // 그것은 ~ 의미에서는 옳다 That is correct in a certain sense.

어느 겨를에 when with so little time to spare; before one knows[is aware]; while one was not aware of it; before one is conscious; unawares; unnoticed; unobserved; without one's knowing[realizing] it; in no time (at all); so soon. ¶~ 부엌에 개가 들어와 있었다 A dog stole into the kitchen unnoticed[without my knowledge].

어느 누구 anyone; anybody; whoever. ¶링컨이 아니고서는 ~도 할 수 없었을 것이다 None but Lincoln could have done it. // 도대체 어느 누가 그런 소리를 했느냐 Whoever told you such a thing?

어느 때고 (at) any time; anytime; at a moment's notice; [어느 날이나] any (old) day; [계절을 가리지 않고] in season and out of season; [늘] always; all the time; at all times[hours]; [언젠가는] some day; (at) some time or other. ¶~ 좋습니다 Anytime will do. / Any time you say. // ~ 후회할 날이 있을 거다 You will be sorry for it sooner or later. // ~ 찾아 주십시오 Please call on me anytime. / You may come any day.

어느 세월에 when on earth; how many years hence; by what time; when. ¶~에 다리가 놓일는지 It will be a long time before the bridge is built.

어느 천년에 when on earth. ⇨ˇ어느 세월에(⇨ˇ어느)

어느 틈에 when with so little time to spare. ⇨ˇ어느 겨를에(⇨ˇ어느) ¶~ 벌써 갔다 왔니 How did you get back so soon?

어느덧 before one knows[is aware]; without one's knowledge; without one's knowing [realizing] it; unawares; unnoticed; while one was not aware of it; so soon. ¶~ 봄이 지나갔다 Spring slipped away[past / by] before I realized[I was aware of it]. // ~ 가을이 되었다 Autumn has stolen over[on] us.

어느새 before one knows[is aware]. ⇨ˇ어느덧 ¶~ 비가 내리고 있었다 It had started raining before I was aware of it[I realized it]. // 봄 방학도 ~ 지나가 버렸다 The spring vacation [(영) holidays] passed all too soon. // 그는 ~ 없어졌다 He had slipped away.

어는점(-點) [물] the freezing point; the ice point. ¶~ 이하로 내려가다 fall below (the) freezing point // ~ 이상으로 올라가다 rise above (the) freezing point.

-어다가 ¶꽃을 꺾어 꽃병에 꽂다 pluck a flower and put it in a vase.

-어도 [양보] even if; although; in spite of; notwithstanding; despite; no matter (what, how, who, etc). ¶우리는 어떤 일이 있~ 항복하지 않는다 Whatever may come [Come what may], we shall never surrender. // 그는 피로하였~ 열심히 일했다 Though (he was) tired, he worked hard. // 적~ 세 번은 내가 그에게 전화를 했다 I phoned him at least three times. // 아무리 길~ 10일 이상은 걸리지 않을 것이다 It won't take more than ten days at the most. // 아무리 싫~ 해야 한다 Even if you don't like it, you must do it. / You have to do it, whether you like it or not.

어두(語頭) the beginning of a word. ¶~에 anti-를 붙이다 prefix a word with anti- / place anti- at the beginning of a word.

어두컴컴하다 dark; dusky. ¶어두컴컴한 밤 a dark night // 어두컴컴한 데서 부딪치다 run into (a person) in the dark / collide against (a post) in the dark.

어둑어둑하다 dusky; dim; gloomy. ¶어둑어둑한 겨울 저녁 a dusky winter evening // 나는 아직 어둑어둑할 때 집을 나섰다 I left home in the gray [dark] of dawn [in the morning twilight]. // 날이 어둑어둑해서 그가 왔다 He came at dark [in the dusk of the evening].

어둑하다 gloomy; dusky; dim.

어둠 darkness; the dark. ¶~ 속에서 in the dark / in (the) darkness // ~을 무서워하다 be afraid of [get scared of] the dark // 캄캄한 ~ 속에서 in pitch [dead] darkness // 열차는 밤의 ~ 속으로 사라졌다 The train vanished into the dark night. // 그는 ~을 틈타 집에서 몰래 빠져나왔다 He stole out of the house under (the) cover of darkness [night]. // 갈수록 ~이 짙어져 갔다 It became darker and darker.
● **어둠길** a dark road [passage / path]. **어둠 상자** a camera obscura; [주름상자] bellows.

어둠침침하다 gloomy; somber; dusky; dim; dimly-lit; dark and dismal. ¶어둠침침한 방 a dimly-lit [ill-lighted] room // 긴 복도는 어둠침침했다 The long corridor was only dimly lit.

어둡다 1 [빛이 없다] dark; dim; dusky; murky; gloomy. (▶ dark는 일반적으로 쓰이는 말로 빛이라고는 전혀 또는 거의 없는 상태, dim은 빛이 충분하지 않고 물건이 또렷이 보이지 않는 상태, dusky는 새벽이나 저녁 같은 때의 박명 상태, murky는 짙은 안개처럼 무거운 느낌을 주는 어둠, gloomy는 구름 낀 음산한 어둠) ¶어두운 밤 a (pitch-)dark night / a moonless night // 어두운 방 an ill-lit room // 어두운 빨강 dark red // 어둡게 하다 darken / make dim / dim // 방을 어둡게 하다 darken [shade] a room // 전등을 어둡게 하다 dim [lower] the light // 불빛이 어두워서 책을 못 읽겠다 The light is so dim that I can't read (the book). // 어둡기 전에 오너라 Come home before (it gets) dark. // 무대가 어두워졌다 The stage was darkened.
2 [시력·청력이 약하다], ¶눈이 ~ be weak-sighted / be weak in sight / have bad [weak] sight // 귀가 ~ be hard [dull] of hearing / have a bad [poor] ear / have difficulty [be weak] in hearing // [비유] 그는 돈에 눈이 어두워졌다 He was blinded by money.
3 [잘 알지 못하다] ignorant (of); not familiar (with); not well acquainted (with); (서술적) be ill informed (of); be a stranger (to). ¶그는 이곳의 지리에 ~ He is a stranger in this town. / He is new to this part of the town. // 그 사람은 세상 일에 ~ He knows very little of the world. / He is ignorant of [inexperienced in] the ways of the world. // 그 사람은 정세에 ~ He knows nothing about the situation. // 나는 계산에 ~ I am slow at figures.
4 [표정·분위기가 무겁고 침울하다] gloomy; dismal; somber; dark; shadowy. ¶어두운 음악 melancholy music // 어두운 면을 보다 look on the dark side of things // 어두운 인생을 보내다 live a drab [dreary / dismal] life // 어두운 표정을 짓다 pull a long face // 그녀의 얼굴에 어두운 그림자가 비쳤다 A shadow [cloud] passed over her face. // 우리의 전망은 ~ Our prospects are gloomy. / We have a dark future before us. // 그녀는 어두운 과거가 있는 듯하다 She seems to have a shadowy [an unfortunate] past.

어드밴티지 [체] advantage; (구어) ad.
● **어드밴티지 룰** an advantage rule. **어드밴티지 리시버** an advantage receiver. **어드밴티지 서버** an advantage server.

어디[1] [어느 곳] what place; where; whereabouts; [어떤 곳] somewhere; anywhere (의문문에서). ¶~ (에서)든지 anywhere / (미국구어) anyplace / everywhere (도처에) // ~고 (모두) every part (of) / everywhere // ~나 할 것 없이 all over (the place) / everywhere / throughout (Korea) // ~로 보나 seen from anywhere // ~ 가든지 wherever (you may) go // 옛날의 영광 지금은 ~로 Where are the glories of bygone days? // 그는 ~라 정처도 없이 떠났다 He left for an unknown destination. / (구어) He is gone nobody knows where. // ~서 일하고 있습니까 Where do you work? // ~서 오셨습니까 Where do you come from? / Where are you from? // 그가 ~서 온 누구인지 알고 싶은데요 I wish I knew who he was and where he came from. // 그것은 전 세계 ~서나 마찬가지이다 It is the same all over the world. // 행락지는 ~나 사람들로 초만원을 이루었다 All the pleasure resorts were [Every pleasure resort was] packed with people. // 여기가 어딜까 Where are we now? // 그런 것은 ~서나 볼 수 있다 You will find things like that everywhere [wherever you go]. // ~든지 차로 모셔다 드리지요 I'll drive you anywhere you like. // ~까지 가면 호텔이 있습니까 How far do we have to go to find a hotel? // 서울의 ~에 살고 계십니까 In what part of Seoul do you live? // 열차는 ~까지 갔을까 How far has the train gone? // 지난번에 내가 ~까지 읽었지 Where did I stop reading last time? // 어딘가 다른 데를 찾아보자 Let's look for some other place. // 그는 어딘가에서 장사를 하고 있는 것 같다 He seems to have gone into business somewhere or other.
2 [어떤 점] in some respects; in some way. ¶어딘가 다르다 There certainly is some difference, though indescribable (between the two). // 그에게는 어딘지 모르게 서먹서먹한 데가 있다 There is something unfriendly about him. // 그녀는 어딘가 어머니를 닮았다 She

resembles her mother in some[an indefinable] way.∥그는 어딘가 외로워 보였다 He looked somewhat lonely. / Somehow he looked lonesome.∥산의 푸르름이 어딘지 깊어진 것 같다 The mountain seems (to have turned) a shade[a bit] greener. / (It may be just my imagination, but) The green of the mountain seems to have slightly deepened.∥그녀에게는 어딘가 괴상한 점이 있다 There is something odd about her.∥그 사람이 어디가 좋으냐 What good do you see in him?∥~가 좋아서 그 여자와 결혼했을까 I wonder what he saw in her to induce him to marry her.

어디까지나 1 [어디에든지] anywhere; to the end of the world[earth]. ¶너하고 함께라면 ~ 가겠다 I would go to the world's end with you. 2 [어떤 일이 있어도] through thick and thin; [최후까지] to the end. ¶나는 ~ 너의 편이다 I'm with you all the way. 3 [어느 모로 보나] in all respects; in every point; [철저히] thoroughly. ¶~ 공평하게 with rigid impartiality∥어린아이는 ~ 어린아이다 Boys will be boys.

어디² well; well now; just; let me see. ¶~ 두고 보자 You will have to pay for this.∥누가 왔는지 ~ 가 보자 I will just go and see who it is.∥~ 입어 보아라 Just try it on.∥~ 영어 한번 해 보아라 Well now, let me hear you speak some English.

어따 Gosh!; (Oh) Boy! ⇨ ~아따

어때 [어떠해] ¶장사는 ~ How about your business?∥산책 가면 ~ How about going for a walk?∥내 말대로지, ~ See? I told you so / See? What did I tell you?∥꾸지람을 들으면 ~ What if I am scolded?(▶ am에 악센트를 두고 문미를 내림) / I don't mind if I'm scolded.

어떠하다 how; what. ⇨어떻다

어떤 1 [무슨] what (book); what kind[sort] of (book); what ... like. ¶~ 학교입니까 What kind of school is it?∥~ 방법으로 달아났느냐 How did you (manage to) get away?∥권 씨는 ~ 사람입니까 What sort of man is Mr. Gwon?∥~ 이유로 그 사람을 만나러 갔느냐 Why did you go to see him?∥~ 이유인지는 모르지만 그는 거절했다 He refused for some reason or other. / I don't know why, but he refused.
2 [여하한]. ¶~ 상황 아래에서도 거짓말을 해서는 안 된다 You must not tell a lie under any circumstances.∥~ 일이 생길지라도 나는 그것에 대한 각오[준비]가 되어 있다 Whatever happens, I am prepared for it.∥~ 희생을 치르더라도 그것을 해내고야 말겠다 I will accomplish it at any cost[at all costs].∥~ 일이 있어도 나는 반대한다 I am dead set against it.∥~ 일이 있어도 그녀와는 헤어지지 않겠다 I won't part with her for all the world.
3 [어느] a certain; one; some.(▶ one은 부정의 경우, some은 미지의 사람이나 사물에, a certain은 알고는 있으나 분명히 하고 싶지 않을 때 씀) ¶~ 곳에 at a certain place∥~ 날 one day∥~ 때에 once∥~ 경우에는 in some cases∥~ 사람 a certain person / somebody∥이것은 ~ 책에서 읽은 적이 있다 I read about it in a certain book.∥~ 사람은 그렇게 말할지도 모른다 Some may say so.∥나는 그렇게 생각하나 ~ 사람은 그렇지 않다 I think so but some people don't.∥사람들은 바다로, ~ 사람들은 산으로 갔다 Some people went to the sea and others to the mountains.

어떻게 1 [어찌] how; in what way[manner]; by what means. ¶~ 지내십니까 How are you?∥그 영화를 ~ 생각하십니까 How did you like that movie?∥~ 감사를 드려야 할지 모르겠습니다 I don't know how to express my gratitude.∥~ 생각하세요 What do you think? / What do you say?∥저 문제를 ~ 생각하느냐 What do you think about that affair?∥그의 완고함은 ~ 할 도리가 없다 I felt completely helpless in the face of his obstinacy.
2 [몹시] how (much); what; so; to what extent. ¶당신을 만나 ~ 기쁜지 모르겠다 I'm so glad to see you!∥그는 ~나 고통이 심한지 잠도 못 잔다 He suffers to such a degree that he can't sleep.
3 [어떻게든] anyway; anyhow. ¶이 소란을 ~ 좀 해 주시오 Do something about this racket.

어떻게 되다 1 (사람·일이). ¶당신 부인이 집을 나간다면 어떻게 될까 What if your wife should leave home?∥도대체 어떻게 된 거냐[무슨 일이라도 있었느냐] What on earth happened (to you)? / (좀 이상한 경우) What is the matter with you? / (속어) What's eating you?∥일은 어떻게 되어 가고 있는가 How are you coming along with your work?
2 (그럭저럭) turn out somehow (or other); [변통되다] be managed. ¶어떻게 되었지 Somehow it will come out all right.∥걱정 마라, 어떻게 될 터이니 Take it easy, I think I can manage it somehow.∥그 정도의 돈이라면 어떻게 되겠지 If that is all the money required, I think I can manage (to raise) it for you.

어떻게든 anyway; anyhow; somehow (or other); by some means (or other); by any means. ¶~ 그 그림을 보고 싶다 I simply must see that picture somehow or other.∥~ 그 조각을 손에 넣고 싶다 I want that sculpture no matter what I have to do to get it!∥~ 그 법안의 통과를 저지하지 않으면 안 된다 We must block the passage of the bill by some means or other.∥나는 ~ 그것을 갖고 싶다 I want to get it somehow or other [one way or another].

어떻게 하다 do[manage] by some means or other; do somehow; manage somehow; manage to do. ¶동생을 어떻게 하면 좋을지 모르겠다 I wonder what I ought to do with my brother.∥어떻게 해서든 좀 더 빨리 오실 수 없겠습니까 Couldn't you manage [contrive] to get here a little earlier?∥어떻게 해서든 이 책을 완성하지 않으면 안 된다 I must finish writing this book by all means [somehow or other].∥나는 어떻게 해서든 시간을 내어 그를 만났다 I managed to find [make] time to see him.

어떻다 1 [의향·상태] how; what. ¶그 일을 지금 그녀에게 이야기해 주는 것은 좀 어떨까 생각한다 I'm afraid it's not advisable to tell her about it now.∥그것에 대해 당신의 의견은 어떻습니까 What is your opinion about[of] it? / What do you think of it?∥요새는 어떻습니까 How are things with you?
2 (권하면서). ¶차 한 잔 더 어떻습니까 Won't you[Wouldn't you like to] have another cup

of tea? // 내년 봄 제주도 여행은 어떻습니까 What [How] about a trip to Jejudo next spring? // 거기에 가는 것은 어떻습니까 What do you say to our going there?
3 〔지정해 말함〕. ¶어떻다고 말하기 힘든 이상한 음악 a weird and indescribable music // 어떻다고 말할 수 없다 Nothing definite can be said on it.

어떻든지 anyway; anyhow; in anyway; in any case; at any rate; either way; one way or the other. ¶그것은 ~ no matter what it may be / however it may be // 비용은 ~ to say nothing of expenses / apart from the question of expense.

-어라 1 〔명령〕 Do!; you had better (do). ¶힘껏 밀~ Push with all your might. // 도장을 찍~ Put your seal (to the bond). **2** 〔감탄〕 How …!; What …! ¶아이고 가엾~ What a pity! // 부모의 사랑은 가없~ How boundless the parental love is!

어란(魚卵) spawn; roe; fish eggs.

어레미 a coarse sieve; a riddle.

어려움 〔곤란〕 hardship; difficulty; 〔곤경〕 distress; misery; adversity; 〔수고〕 trouble; 〔곤궁〕 privation; 〔고뇌〕 affliction; suffering(s); 〔시련〕 a trial; an ordeal. ¶많은 ~을 참다 bear [endure] many hardships // ~을 극복하다 overcome [surmount] a difficulty [difficulties / hardships] // 그는 나를 ~에서 구해 주었다 He rescued me from the trouble I was in. // 나는 갖가지 ~을 겪어 왔소 I have gone through various ordeals [hardships].

어려워하다 feel constraint (in a person's presence); be afraid of giving trouble; have a regard for (a person's) feelings; have scruples (about doing); keep (a person) at a (respectable) distance. ¶어려워하는 기색 a constrained manner [air] / an air of constraint // 어려워하지 않고 without reserve [scruple] // 어려워할 것 없어 You needn't trouble yourself about me. // 그는 조금도 어려워하지 않는 태도였다 His manner was altogether free from constraint.

어련하다 certain; natural; infallible; reliable; trustworthy; believable. ¶그의 말이니 어련하겠나 We have every reason to believe in his words. // "나는 이 일 때문에 무척 애를 썼지." "어련하시겠습니까." "I took much pain to do this." "I can easily imagine." **어련히** naturally; surely; certainly; undoubtedly; infallibly; as a natural consequence; in the natural course of events. ¶내버려 둬, ~ 알아서 하려고 Let him alone, he will take care of himself. // 저녁때가 되면 ~ 돌아오려고 Depend upon it, he will be here by evening.

어렴성 a sign [an indication] of feeling constraint (in a person's presence); regardfulness for (a person's) feelings. ¶~ 없는 unreserved / unconstrained / free from constraint // ~ 없이 without showing constraint / without a polite reserve / at (one's) ease // 그들은 생각한 바를 ~ 없이 말했다 They unreservedly said just what they thought about it.

어렴풋하다 〔희미하다〕 faint; 〔확실하지 않다〕 dim; 〔막연하다〕 vague; indistinct; obscure; dreamy. ¶어렴풋한 옛 추억 a vague memory of the past // 나무들 사이로 어렴풋한 불빛이 보였다 A dim light came into view through the woods. **어렴풋이** 〔조금〕 slightly; 〔희미하게〕 vaguely; dimly; faintly; indistinctly; obscurely. ¶나는 그것을 ~ 알고 있었다 I had some inkling of it. // 그는 그것을 ~ 짐작하고 있는 것 같다 He seems to be dimly [vaguely] aware of it. // 나는 ~ 생각날 뿐이다 I have only a vague [hazy] memory of it. // 두 사람 사이에는 애정이 ~ 싹트고 있는 듯하다 There seems to be a faint feeling of attachment growing between the two. // 나는 그 도시에 갔던 일을 ~ 기억하고 있다 I vaguely remember visiting that town. // 종소리가 ~ 들린다 The sound of a bell is faintly heard.

어렵(漁獵) **1** 〔고기잡이와 사냥〕 fishing and hunting. **2** 〔고기잡이〕 fishery.

어렵다 1 〔힘들다〕 hard; difficult; laborious; 〔의심스럽다〕 doubtful. ¶어려운 일 a difficult task / a hard [tough] job / laborious work // 입수하기 [얻기] 어려운 hard [difficult] to get [obtain] // 저항하기 어려운 세력 a force difficult to oppose [resist] // 어려운 구절 a difficult passage // 고치기 어려운 병 a serious case [illness] // 어렵지 않게 easily / with ease // 일을 어렵지 않게 해치우다 do [accomplish] something without difficulty // 존은 얻기 어려운 친구이다 A friend like John is hard to come by. // 러시아 말은 초심자에게는 ~ Russian is difficult for beginners. // 선악을 판단하기는 ~ It's difficult to judge whether it is right or wrong. // 이 추위는 견디기 ~ This cold weather is very hard [really tells] on me. // 나는 그의 논점을 이해하기가 ~ I am at a loss [find it very difficult] to see his point. // 우승하기는 어렵겠다 It will be hard (for me) to win the championship.
2 〔까다롭다〕 troublesome; 〔미묘하다〕 delicate. ¶어려운 정세 a delicate [ticklish / loaded] situation // 거기가 어려운 대목이다 That is a trickish [delicate] point.
3 〔거북하다〕 (서술적) feel awkward [constraint]; be [feel] ill at ease; have scruples about (doing). ¶그는 우리의 요구를 어렵지 않게 받아 주었다 He readily consented to our request. // 저 선생님은 참 ~ Somehow I feel awkward [uncomfortable] in the presence of that teacher.
4 〔가난하다〕 poor; indigent; needy; penurious; destitute. ¶어려울 때의 친구가 참된 친구다 A friend in need is a friend indeed.

어로(漁撈) fishing; fishery.
● **어로 금지 구역** a restrictive fisheries zone. **어로선** a fishing boat. ⇨ 어선 **어로장** a fishing ground. **어로 협정** a fisheries agreement.

어록(語錄) analects; a collection [book] of sayings [aphorisms]. ¶처칠 ~ Quotations from Winston Churchill.

어뢰(魚雷) a torpedo (pl. ~es). ¶공중 ~ an aerial torpedo // ~를 발사하다 discharge [fire] a torpedo // ~를 맞다 take a torpedo hit.
● **어뢰 발사관** a torpedo tube; a launching tube. **어뢰정** a torpedo boat; (미) a PT boat(▶ PT는 patrol torpedo의 약어).

어루러기 〔의〕 pityriasis [tinea] versicolor; chromophytosis.

어루만지다 1 〔쓰다듬다〕 stroke (one's beard); pat (a child on the head); pass one's hand over [across] (one's face); smooth down (one's hair); 〔애무하다〕

어룽거리다 caress (a boy) with the hand. ¶남의 등을 ~ stroke[(구어) paw] a person's back over // 손으로 머리를 ~ stroke[smooth] down one's hair with one's hand. 2 [마음을 달래다] soothe; calm (down); pacify; mollify; appease. ¶화난 아내를 잘 어루만져 주다 appease one's angry wife.

어룽거리다 spot; dapple.

어룽더룽하다 spotted; mottled. ⇨아롱다롱하다

어류(魚類) fishes; the finny tribe; the Pisces. ¶~의 piscine / ichthyic.
● **어류학** ichthyology. ¶~의 ichthyological. **어류학자** an ichthyologist.

어르다 (앉거나 무릎 위에 놓고 흔들어) dandle; play with (a baby); (잠을 재우기 위해) lull; 〔물건 등을 주어 비위를 맞추다〕humor; flatter; pacify; 〔꾀어서 하게 하다〕entice; coax (into doing / to do). ¶어머니는 아이를 얼러서 약을 마시게 했다 The mother coaxed her child into taking the medicine.// 겁을 주다가 어르다가 해서 그를 가게 했다 By alternating threats with flattery, we got him go. // 어머니는 아기를 얼러 잠재웠다 The mother lulled her baby to sleep. // 고양이가 쥐를 어르고 있다 The cat is toying with a mouse.

어르신(네) 1 〔남의 아버지에 대한 존칭〕your [his] esteemed[honored] father. ¶~께서는 안녕하신가 Has your esteemed father been well? / How is your father? 2 〔노인·연장자〕 an elder; sir. ¶~께서는 그 사람을 어떻게 생각하십니까 Sir, what do you think of the man?

어른 1 〔성인〕 a man; a woman; an adult; a grown-up (person); a full-grown man. ¶~과 같은 like a (grown-up) man / full-fledged // ~답지 않은 〔어린애 같은〕 childish / puerile / 〔어른 값을 못하는〕 unbecoming for a grown-up person / unworthy of a man (of discretion) / 〔옹졸한〕 mean // ~이 되다 grow up (to be a man[woman]) / become a man [woman] / enter[grow to] adulthood / grow into a man[woman] // ~처럼 행동하다 act [behave] like a grown-up.// 저 아이는 ~ 같은 말을 한다 That child talks like a grown-up.
2 〔윗사람·노인〕 a superior; a senior; an elder; an older[elderly] person; 〔고참〕 an old-timer. ¶마을의 ~들 village seniors [elders] / elders of the village // 집안의 ~ the head of a family // ~ 앞에서 그런 말을 하면 못쓴다 You shouldn't talk like that in the presence of your elders.
3 your[his] esteemed[honored] father. ⇨어르신(네)1

어른거리다 (눈·마음에) flicker; glimmer; shimmer; quiver; (빛이) blink. ¶어른거리는 등불 a blink of light // 죽은 아이의 모습이 눈앞에 ~ be haunted by the image[memories] of the dead child // 그녀 모습이 눈앞에 어른거린다 Her image keeps flitting around my mind. / Her image keeps coming back to haunt me.

어른스럽다 (look) like a grown-up (person); 〔조숙하다〕 precocious. ¶그녀는 나이에 비해 ~ She looks quite mature for her age. // 저 아이는 어른스럽게 말을 한다 The boy talks like a grown-up.

어른어른 flickering(ly); glimmering(ly); shimmering(ly); quivering(ly). **어른어른하다** flicker; glimmer. ⇨어른거리다

어름 1 〔맞닿는 곳〕 a junction; a commissure. 2 〔한가운데〕 the very middle; the center.

어름거리다 1 〔언행을〕 act[talk] ambiguously; equivocate; prevaricate; shuffle. ¶대답을 ~ equivocate in replying / give a vague[a non-committal / an equivocal] answer // 말을 ~ speak ambiguously / equivocate / prevaricate / palter (with). 2 〔일을〕 shuffle[rub] along[through]; muddle (with one's work).

어름어름 〔불분명하게〕 ambiguously; vaguely; equivocally; 〔눈속임으로〕 carelessly and hastily; sloppily. ¶~ 말하다 talk ambiguously. **어름어름하다** act[talk] ambiguously; shuffle[rub] along[through]. ⇨어름거리다

어리 (병아리의) a hencoop; a chicken coop.

어리광 a child's winning ways; playing the baby. ¶~만 부리는 아이 a spoilt[pampered] child // ~을 부리다〔떨다 / 피우다〕 play the baby (to) / behave like a spoilt child.

어리굴젓 salted and spiced oysters.

어리다¹ 1 〔눈물이 괴다〕 (one's eyes) swim [dim / moisten / glisten] with tears. ¶눈에 눈물이 ~ one's eyes swim[dim / moisten / glisten] with tears / tears stand [there are tears] in one's eyes / tears come to [gather in] one's eyes / be moved to tears / be going to shed tears // 어린 눈 liquid eyes // 그녀는 눈물 어린 눈으로 미소를 지었다 She smiled in a mist of tears.
2 〔눈에 삼삼하다〕 haunt; be haunted. ¶죽은 자식의 모습이 눈에 ~ be haunted by the image[memories] of the dead child.
3 〔깃들어 있다〕 be filled[fraught] (with). ¶애정 어린 편지 an affectionate letter (to one's son) // 그의 한마디 한마디에는 성의가 어리어 있었다 Every word he uttered breathed[was fraught with] sincerity.
4 〔엉기다〕 congeal; coagulate; clot(피가); curdle(우유가).

어리다² 1 〔나이가 적다〕 infant; (very) young; juvenile; of tender age[years]. ¶어릴 때에 as a mere child / in one's infancy[childhood / early life] / at an early age / when (one was) very young / when (one was) a child / 어릴 때부터 from one's childhood[infancy] / from an infant[a child / an early age] / since one's tender age // 나이는 어리지만 young as one is // 그를 어릴 때부터 알고 있다 We have known him since he was a child. // 나는 어린 마음에도 죽음이 무엇인지 알 수 있을 것 같았다 Child though I was, I felt I knew what death meant. // 어릴 때 기억이 되살아났다 Memories of my childhood days came back to me.// 내게도 너와 같은 어린 시절이 있었다 I was once a child[boy / girl] like you. // 그는 나보다 다섯 살 ~ He is five years younger than I.
2 〔유치하다〕 childish; infantile; puerile; immature; 〔미숙하다〕 green; crude; raw; inexperienced. ¶어린 생각 a childish idea // 그는 생각하는 것이 ~ His ideas are green.

어리대다 hang[dawdle / loiter / hover / linger] about[around] (a place); putter about[(미) around]. ¶수상한 사나이가 집 근처에서 어리대고 있었다 A suspicious-looking man was hanging around the house.

어리둥절하다 stupefied; stunned; dazed; bewildered; perturbed; embarrassed; perplexed; puzzled; confused; flurried. ¶어리둥

어리 절한 표정으로 with a perplexed[puzzled] look // 어리둥절해 있다 look puzzled / look blank / wear a stupid look of amazement.

어리벙벙하다 dumbfounded; bewildered; dazed; confounded; disconcerted. ¶그는 그 소식을 듣고 한동안 어리벙벙했다 The news struck him speechless[dumb] for a while. / Hearing the news he was not himself for some time. // 새 일을 맡고 보니 모든 것이 ~ I feel out of myself in this new line of business. **어리벙벙히** bewilderedly; dazedly; confoundedly; disconcertedly.

어리보기 a half-wit; a dimwit; a dullard; a sluggard.

어리석다 〔명청하다〕 foolish; stupid; silly (foolish는 일반적, silly는 foolish보다 약간 구어적이고 경멸적으로 쓰이며, 요령이 없다는 등의 뜻을 포함함. stupid는 지능이 낮음을 강조함); 〔조소를 받을 만하다〕 ridiculous; 〔도리에 맞지 않다〕 absurd. ¶어리석은 사람 a fool / a foolish person / an idiot // 어리석은 행위 a nonsensical[stupid] act // 어리석은 짓을 하다 blunder / make a blunder / bungle (something) / 〔구어〕 goof / do a foolish[stupid] thing / make an ass of oneself // 그런 말을 하다니 너는 참말로 어리석었구나 What a fool [How foolish] you were to say such a thing! / It was stupid of you to say such a thing. // 그런 짓을 하는 것은 어리석기 짝이 없다 It would be the height of folly to do such a thing. // 이런 시시한 물건을 많은 돈을 주고 샀다니 어리석은 일이다 It's absurd[ridiculous] that you should have paid so much for such rubbish.

어리숙하다 →어수룩하다

어리어리하다 (정신이) dim; hazy; vague; indistinct; (눈이) dazzled; dazed. ¶내 눈이 ~ My eyes are dazzled. / The light dazzles my eyes.

어린것 a little one[child]; one's child[kid]. ¶우리 집 ~ my little child.

어린아이 a child; 〔속어〕 a kid; a boy(남자); a girl(여자); 〔연소자〕 a juvenile; 〔젖먹이〕 a baby; an infant(유아); 〔집합적〕 little ones [fellows]. ¶~다운 〔천진난만한〕 innocent / childlike / 〔유치한〕 childish (behavior / remarks) // ~ 같은 childish / immature / 〔문어〕 puerile // ~ 시절 one's boyhood / one's girlhood / 〔어렸을 때〕 one's infancy // 남을 ~ 취급하다 treat a person like a child / baby a person // ~를 업다 carry a child on one's back // ~를 어르다 dandle a baby // 그는 ~ 시절부터의 친구이다 He and I have been friends since we were children. / He is a childhood friend. // 화를 내다니 ~ 같군 It is childish of you to get angry. // ~ 같은 짓을 그만둬라 Don't behave so childishly.

어린이 a child; a kid. ⇨어린아이 ¶~의 juvenile / ~의 읽을거리 juvenile reading.

●**어린이날** Children's Day. **어린이 헌장** the Children's Charter.

어림 a rough[gross] estimate; an approximation; a (rough) guess. **어림하다** estimate [calculate] roughly; make a rough estimate (of); guess.

●**어림셈** a rough estimate[computation / calculation]. **어림수** round number[figures]; an approximate figure.

어림없다 wide of the mark; off the point; far (from); 〔당찮다〕 nonsensical; preposterous; absurd; ridiculous; fabulous; unreasonable. ¶어림없는 수작 a damned[darn] silly remark // 어림없는 요구 a preposterous demand // 나를 속이려고? Do you mean to take me in? I am no gull, I tell you. // 영어 실력으로는 나는 그에게 ~ He is far beyond me in English. // 그가 학자라니 어림없는 소리 마라 He a scholar? Don't be silly! [That's ridiculous!]. // 어림없는 소리 마라 What a thing to say! / Absurd! / Impossible! / Far from it!

어림잡다 estimate[calculate] roughly; make a rough estimate (of); guess. ¶아무리 적게 어림잡아도 at the lowest estimate // 우리는 그것을 천만 원으로 어림잡고 있다 We estimate it at ten million won. // 어림잡아 약 100달러 든다 According to rough estimates, it will cost approximately 100 dollars.

어림짐작(-斟酌) a rough[random / wild] guess; guesswork. ¶~으로 by[at a] guess / by guesswork / at haphazard[random] / as a shot / ~으로 알아맞히다 make a good shot (at) / guess right. **어림짐작하다** guess (at); make a shot (at); make a random guess.

어림치다 estimate[calculate] roughly. ⇨어림잡다

어릿거리다 act sluggishly[lazily]; be spiritless[dull]; be inactive. ¶어릿거리지 마라 Make it snappy! / Get a move on you!

어릿광대 1 〔광대〕 a clown; a buffoon; a comedian. 2 〔남을 잘 웃기는 사람〕 a jester; a joker.

어마어마하다 1 〔엄청나다〕 tremendous; immense; enormous; colossal; 〔많다〕 innumerous; stupendous; countless. ¶어마어마한 돈 an ocean of money / a hell of a lot of money // 어마어마한 부자 a man of great [colossal] wealth // 어마어마한 액수[수] a huge sum[number] // 어마어마한 비용 an enormous expense / a huge cost // 어마어마한 인파 a tremendous turnout of people / a mammoth crowd // 그는 키가 어마어마하게 크다 He is terribly tall.

2 〔과장적이다〕 high-sounding; ostentatious; pretentious; showy. ¶사소한 일을 어마어마하게 떠들어 대다 make much ado[a great fuss] about nothing.

3 〔장엄하다〕 grand; stately; imposing; magnificent; majestic; awe-inspiring. ¶어마어마한 고층 건물 an imposing skyscraper // 그녀는 어마어마한 저택에서 살고 있다 She lives in a palatial mansion.

어망(漁網·魚網) a fishing net.

어머(나) Oh!; Why!; Dear me!; My!; O my!; Oh, my goodness!; Heavens!; Good gracious! ¶~, 그래요 Really? / Indeed! / (Is) That so? [!] // ~, 당신이었군요 Oh, it's you! // ~, 물론이에요 Why, of course! // ~, 그 사람이 왔어요 Look, here he comes! // ~, 오랜만이에요 My goodness! I haven't seen you for ages! // ~, 또 실수했네 Oh no! I've done it again!

어머니 1 〔모친〕 a mother; 〔소아어〕 mamma; mama; mam; mom; mum; mummy; mommy. ¶~의 one's real mother // ~의[같은 / 다운] motherly / maternal // ~의 사랑 maternal affection[love] / a mother's love // ~쪽의 친척 a relative on the mother's side // ~가 없는 motherless (child) // ~가 되다 have a baby / give birth to a child / become a mother // ~를 여의다 lose one's mother /

어머님

be left motherless // 남을 ~처럼 돌보다 mother a person // 그 여자는 이제 두 아이의 ~다 She is now the mother of two children. // ~, 지금 돌아왔습니다 Mom, I'm home! // 그 형제는 ~가 다르다 They are brothers by different mother.
2 [사물의 근원] (the) cause; a motive; the mother (of). ¶필요는 발명의 ~ Necessity is the mother of invention.

어머님 (my) dear mother.

어멈 1 [하녀] a woman servant; a housemaid; an amah. **2** a mother. ⇨ˇ어머니₁

어명(御命) a Royal [King's] command [mandate]. ¶~을 내리다 issue a Royal command // ~을 거행하다 execute the Royal command.

어묵(魚-) boiled fish paste [sausage].

어물(魚物) [생선] fishes; [말린 생선] dried fishes; stockfish.
● 어물전 a fish shop; a dried-fish store.

어물거리다 [주저하다] waver; hesitate; be irresolute; be hesitant; shilly-shally; dillydally; [모호하게 하다] be ambiguous; be noncommittal. ¶대답을 못 하고 ~ give a vague answer / evade any definite answer // 말을 못 하고 ~ hesitate to say // 결단을 못 내리고 ~ waver in one's determination // 어물거리다가 기회를 놓치다 dally away one's opportunity // 어물거리지 말고 네 생각을 말해 보아라 Out with it! Never stand shilly-shallying.

어물어물 [머뭇거리며] hesitatingly; waveringly; shilly-shally; [모호하게] indefinitely; vaguely; ambiguously; noncommittally. ¶문제점을 ~ 넘기다 hedge upon a point // ~ 넘길 게 아니야. 우리는 확답을 바라고 있어 Don't use such evasive words. We want a definite answer. 어물어물하다 waver; hesitate. ⇨ˇ어물거리다

어물쩍 equivocally; quibblingly; evasively. ¶질문을 ~ 넘기다 turn a question off / parry [evade / dodge] a question. 어물쩍하다 equivocate; prevaricate. ⇨ˇ어물쩍거리다 ¶어물쩍하지 말고 똑똑히 대답해 Don't shuffle; give a clear answer. // 그는 화제를 바꾸어 교묘하게 어물쩍해 버렸다 He changed the topic and skillfully evaded the point.

어물쩍거리다 equivocate; prevaricate; quibble; pass off; shuffle.

어미 1 a mother; mamma. ⇨ˇ어머니₁ **2** [새끼를 낳은 동물의 암컷] a dam; a mother animal. ¶~ 새 [개/고양이] a mother bird [dog/cat].

어미(語尾) [언] the end(ing) [termination] of a word. ¶~가 -sh로 끝나는 말 words ending in -sh // ~가 자음으로 끝나다 end in a consonant // ~에 -s를 붙이다 add [attach] -s to the end of a word / suffix -s to a word.
● 어미변화 conjugation; inflection. ⇨ˇ활용₂ ¶라틴 어는 ~가 많다 Latin is a highly inflected language.

어민(漁民) fishermen; fisherfolk; fishing people.

어버이 parents. ¶~의[다운] parental // ~를 섬기다 [공경하다] be dutiful [respectful] toward one's parents // ~를 잃다 lose one's parents / be deprived of one's parents // ~를 따르다 obey [be obedient to] one's parents // ~에게 효도하다 serve one's parents devotedly // ~에게 불효하다 be unkind to one's parents / ill-treat one's parents // 자식은 ~를 본받는다 As the old birds sing, so the young ones twitter.
● 어버이날 Parent's Day.

어벌쩡하다 cajoling; wheedling; deceitful; cunning; tricky. ¶어벌쩡한 거짓말 a plausible lie.

어법(語法) (a mode of) expression; usage (of language); wording; phraseology; grammar; diction. ¶~상의 잘못 a wrong expression / a mistake in wording // 미국식 영어의 ~ American usage (in English) / an Americanism // ~에 어긋나다 be solecistic.

어부(漁夫·漁父) a fisherman; a fisher.
● 어부지리(-之利) ¶~를 얻다 fish in troubled waters / make profit out of two contestants / gain the third party's profit // 우리가 싸우면 저놈이 ~를 얻는다 If we should quarrel, he would be the one to profit from it.

어분(魚粉) fish meal; fish protein concentrate.

어불성설(語不成說) unreasonable talk; lack of logic; illogicality. ¶~이다 be illogical [unreasonable] / do not stand to reason / do not hold any water / lack logic.

어사(御史) [역] **1** [왕명으로 파견되던 임시 관리] a Royal emissary. **2** a secret Royal inspector. ⇨ˇ암행어사(⇨ˇ암행)

어사리(漁-) fishing with a net; netting. 어사리하다 fish with a net; net.

어살(魚-) a (fish) weir; a kiddle; a fish trap; a fishpound.

어색하다(語塞-) **1** [열없다·거북하다] awkward; self-conscious; [서술적] feel awkward [embarrassed / (con)strained / nervous]; feel ill at ease; feel diffident; find it hard to .... ¶어색한 침묵을 지키다 keep awkward [uneasy / strained] silence // 여기 있기는 좀 ~ I feel out of place here. // 그 사람 앞에서는 어색해서 말이 잘 안 나온다 I feel too awkward [ill at ease] to speak well in his presence. // 두 사람 사이가 어색해졌다 The relationship between the two grew strained [grew awkward / soured]. / They don't get on so well as before.
2 [서투르다·부자연스럽다] awkward; clumsy; unnatural; artificial. ¶어색한 걸음(걸이) an awkward style [manner] of walking / an ungainly gait // 어색한 태도 an awkward [a stiff] manner // 어색한 문장 an awkward [a stiff] style // 어색한 웃음을 웃다 smile an artificial [a forced] smile // 어색하게 춤추다 dance in an ungainly way // 그녀는 어색한 옷차림을 하고 있다 She is wearing an ill-fitting [poorly designed] dress. / She is awkwardly dressed. // 그가 없으면 아무래도 어색해지겠다 It will be an awkward party without him.
3 [말이 막히다] [서술적] be at a loss for a word; be stuck for words; stumble at one's words; falter.

어서 1 [빨리] quick(ly); fast; promptly; rapidly; without delay [hesitation]. ¶~ 오너라 Come quick. // ~ 말하시오 Tell me without hesitation. // ~ 대답해라 Answer promptly. / Give me a prompt answer. **2** [부디] please; kindly; [환영의 뜻으로] right; with pleasure; welcome. ¶~ 들어오십시오 Come right in, please. // ~ 오십시오 Welcome! / You are welcome. / (점포에서)

Good afternoon[evening / morning], sir. What can I do for you[I show you]?

-어서 (and) so; and then; to; for; from; as; so as to; so ... that ...; because (of); on account of. ¶너무 적~ 나누기가 어렵다 be too little to divide∥이렇게 늦~ 미안합니다 I'm sorry to be so late.

어석거리다 crunch; crush with one's teeth; chew with a crushing[crunching] sound.

어선(漁船) a fishing boat[vessel / craft]; a fisherboat; (미) a smack(활어조(活魚槽)를 갖춘). ¶소형 ~ a cog.

어설프다 1 (성기다) coarse; rough; loose. ¶어설프게 뜬 그물 a net with large meshes. **어설피** coarsely; roughly; loosely.
2 [어색하고 엉성하다] poor; awkward; clumsy; sloppy; slovenly; careless; [데알다] imperfect; incomplete; smattering; superficial. ¶어설픈 지식 a smattering / a superficial[half] knowledge∥일하는 게 ~ be a sloppy worker / do a slovenly job∥그의 영어는 매우 ~ His English is very uncertain [rather poor].∥그는 어설픈 솜씨로 사과를 깎고 있었다 He was peeling an apple clumsily[with clumsy hands / with awkward hands]. **어설피** poorly; clumsily; imperfectly; in a clumsy[slovenly] way.

어세(語勢) a tone (of voice); emphasis; stress. ¶강한 ~로 말하다 speak emphatically[with emphasis].

어수룩하다 [숫되다] unsophisticated; naive; simple; simple-minded; [어리석다] half-witted; somewhat stupid. ¶어수룩한 사람 a simple soul / a simple-minded person∥어수룩한 생각 a simple[an unsophisticated] idea∥어수룩하게 보다 (사물을) take (things) simple and easy / (사람을) hold (a person) cheap / think (a person) an easy man to deal with∥내가 그것을 믿을 만큼 어수룩해 보이는가 Do you think I am so naive as to believe it?

어수선하다 1 (사물이) disordered; disarranged; confused; (서술적) be in disorder [disarray / confusion]; be out of order; be in a mess[muddle]; (세상이) troublous; tumultuous. ¶어수선한 세상 troublous [troubled / unsettled] time / wild[stormy] times∥어수선한 머리 unkempt[disheveled] hair∥어수선하게 disorderly / in disorder [confusion] / in a jumble∥어수선해지다 get confused / go out of order / fall into disorder [confusion]∥그 방은 어수선했다 The room was untidy[messy / in disorder].∥선반 위에는 병들이 어수선하게 놓여 있었다 Bottles were lined up on the shelf in a disorderly fashion.∥이사하느라고 어수선한 틈에 책을 몇 권 잃어버렸다 I lost several books in the confusion of moving.
2 (마음이) agitated[confused]; flurried; distracted; disturbed; upset. ¶어수선한 마음을 가라앉히다 collect[gather] one's scattered wits / compose oneself∥그 소식을 듣고 마음이 어수선해졌다 My mind was disturbed at the news.

어순(語順) word order. ¶~을 틀리다 make an error in the arrangement of words.

어스 (전) (미) grounding; (영) earthing.

어스러지다 1 (말·행동이) become abnormal [eccentric / erratic]; go off the rails[track]; go contrary (to). ¶어스러진 행동은 일절 없도록 해라 You must avoid all deviations from the normal (course of action). **2** (솔기가) turn; become unstraight.

어스럭송아지 a grown calf.

어스레하다 dusky; gloomy; dim. ¶어스레한 빛 dim[feeble / faint] light∥아직 어스레한 새벽 5시였다 It was five in the morning, still gray.

어스름 dusk; [미광] dim[feeble / faint] light.

어스름하다 dusky; gloomy. ⇨ 어스레하다

어슬렁거리다 [천천히 걸어 다니다] stroll [ramble] about; saunter [loiter] along; gad about; prowl; [배회하다] hang[loiter / hover / linger] about[around] (a place). ¶바닷가를 ~ take a stroll on the beach∥밤에 유흥가를 ~ hang around[loiter about] the amusement quarters at night.

어슬렁어슬렁 sluggishly; lazily; slowly; idly. ¶~ 걷다 walk sluggishly[lazily / slowly / idly] / lounge (about) / walk at a leisurely pace∥노인은 ~ 걸었다 The old man strolled along at a leisurely pace. **어슬렁어슬렁하다** stroll[ramble] about. ⇨ 어슬렁거리다

어슴푸레 dimly; faintly; hazily. ¶~ 밝아 오는 하늘 the dawning sky∥~ 알고 있다 be slightly acquainted with (a matter) / have an inkling of (a fact)∥~ 기억하고 있다 have a hazy recollection (of) / dimly remember∥날이 ~ 밝기 시작했다 Day was beginning to break[dawn]. **어슴푸레하다** dim; faint; hazy; misty; indistinct; vague.

어슷비슷하다 (서술적) be much[nearly] the same; be much of a muchness; be almost similar; be six of one and half-a-dozen of the other; be about and about. ¶어느 것이나 ~ They are both of a hair[sort]. / It is six of one and half-a-dozen of the other.∥두 사람의 처지는 ~ There is little[not much] to choose[There is little difference] between the two persons in their circumstances.

어슷하다 slant; oblique; inclined; diagonal; (서술적) be on the tilt[slant]. ¶어슷하게 aslant / askant / obliquely / slopewise / on the[a] slant∥어슷하게 자르다 cut diagonally.

어시장(魚市場) a fish market.

어안 렌즈(魚眼-) a fisheye lens.

어안석(魚眼石) a fisheye stone.

어안이 벙벙하다 be astonished; be amazed; be dazed; be taken aback; be dum(b)-founded; be at a loss for words. ¶어안이 벙벙하여 in blank[mute] amazement / in open-mouthed astonishment / dum(b)-founded / in speechless wonder∥그 소식을 듣고 그녀는 잠시 어안이 벙벙했다 The news struck her speechless[dumb] for a while.∥뜻밖의 결과에 모두가 어안이 벙벙했다 Everyone was dum(b)founded by the unexpected results.

-어야 1 [당연·의무·필요·유감] should [ought to] (do); must[have to] (do); should[ought to] (have done). ¶아이들은 부모님의 말씀을 들~ 한다 Children should obey their parents.∥천 원이 들~ 들어갈 수 있다 You have to pay one thousand won to get in.∥너는 일찍 일어났~ 했다 You ought to have got up earlier.∥제가 미리 말씀드렸~ 했는데요 I should have told you beforehand.
2 [아무리 …하여도] however much one may [might] (do); to whatever extent. ¶핑계를 대~ 소용없다 It is no use[good] trying to

-어야지 excuse yourself. // 늦~ 9시까지는 올 것이다 I will be here by 9 at the latest. // 네가 먹~ 얼마나 먹겠니 You can't possibly eat very much.

-어야지 1 [가벼운 의지] would; be going to. ¶그녀에게 빌린 책을 돌려주~ I am going to return her a borrowed book. 2 [아쉬움·실망]. ¶네 제안을 받아들이고 싶지만 형편이 되~ I'd like to accept your proposal, but, unfortunately, I'm in no position to do so.

어어 (Good) Gracious!; Gracious Heaven [me]!; My Gracious!; (My) God!; Why! ¶~ 벌써 11시다 Why! It is eleven.

어언간 (於焉間) before one know [is aware]; while one was not aware of it; without one's knowing [realizing] it; (all) too soon. ¶~ 세월이 흘렀다 Years came and went on. // ~ 3년이 지났다 So three years glided away.

어업 (漁業) fishery; the fishing industry. ¶근해 ~ coast [offshore] fishery // 연안 ~ inshore [coastal] fishery // 원양 ~ pelagic [deep-sea / ocean] fishery // 한일 ~ 회담 the Korean-Japanese fishery talks.
●**어업권** a fishery [fishing] right. ¶공동 ~ common of fishery [piscary]. **어업 전관 수역** (exclusive) fishing waters [fishery zone]. **어업 허가증** a fishing license. **어업 협동조합** a fishermen's cooperative association. **어업 협정** a fisheries agreement.

어여차 [힘을 합할 때 내는 소리] yo-(ho-)ho; yo-heave-ho. ¶~ 들어 올리다 lift (a thing) with an effort / heave (a thing).

어엿하다 respectable; decent; good; honorable; stately; imposing; unblamable. ¶어엿한 신사 a decent [an honorable] gentleman // 어엿한 아내 a legitimate [respectable] wife // 어엿한 작가 a full-fledged writer // 그는 이제 어엿한 가장이다 Now he is a respectable master of his own house.

어용 (御用) king's [royal] use; government use [service].
●**어용 신문** a kept press; a government organ (기관지); a mouthpiece organ. **어용 학자** a government-patronized scholar; a scholar under the government's thumb.

어우러지다 get joined [be put] together (in good harmony); well-matched (with); harmonized united. ¶기름과 물은 어우러지지 않는다 Oil and water do not combine [will not mix]. // 가을이 되면 적색, 갈색, 황색이 어우러져 숲을 수놓는다 In autumn the woods are a symphony in red, brown, and yellow.

어우르다 [하나로 합치다] put [join] together; unite; combine; [협력하다] go hand in hand (with). ¶여러 파를 어울러서 하나의 정당을 만들다 combine several factions into a party.

어울리다 1 [어우르게 되다] associate (with); join (with); mix [mingle] (with); keep company (with). ¶한데 ~ join in a group / get together // 외국 사람과 ~ mix with foreigners // 좋은 [나쁜] 친구와 ~ keep good [bad] company // 남과 어울리지 않다 keep to oneself // 그는 남과 어울리는 것을 싫어한다 He dislikes company. / He shuns society. // 대체로 예술가는 예술가끼리 어울린다 Artists usually associate [consort] with artists. // 그런 패들과는 어울리지 마라 Don't mix in such company. / Keep away from such company.
2 [조화되다] become; match; suit; fit; befit; go (well) (with); be becoming (to); harmonize (with); be suitable (to / for); be in keeping (with). ¶어울리는 부부 a well-matched [-mated] couple // 어울리지 않는 부부 an ill-matched [-mated] couple // 어울리지 않는 결혼 an ill-assorted marriage / (신분상으로) a misalliance // 그 경우에 어울리는 연설 a speech appropriate to the occasion // 신사에게 안 어울리는 행위 ungentlemanly [ungentlemanlike] conduct / conduct unbecoming to [unworthy of] a gentleman // 어울리지 않다 do not suit [match / go well with] / be unbecoming (to / in) / be unsuitable (for) / be inappropriate (for / to) / be out of place // 신분에 어울리지 않는 생활을 하다 live above oneself / live beyond one's social standing // 그 옷은 네게 잘 어울린다 That dress becomes you well. / You look nice [well] in the suit. // 그 넥타이와 셔츠는 잘 어울린다 The tie and the shirt match [go well together]. / The tie matches [goes with] the shirt well. // 그 머리 모양이 네게 어울린다 You look nice with that hairdo. // 그 드레스가 당신에게 아주 잘 어울립니다 You look best in that dress. // 당신은 피부가 희기 때문에 무슨 색이나 잘 어울립니다 Any color will suit [go well with / look nice with] your fair complexion. // 그것은 그에게 썩 어울리는 일이다 It is the kind of job that suits him perfectly. // 그는 나이에 어울리게 침착한 태도로 대답했다 He answered with a composure becoming his age. // 그런 일은 내게 어울리지 않는다 I am not fit for such work. / Such work is not in my line. // 선생 노릇은 너한테 어울리지 않는 듯 하다 Your being a teacher doesn't seem right to me somehow. // 이 벽지는 이 방에 어울리지 않는다 This wallpaper is out of harmony with the room. // 네 복장은 오늘 모임에는 전혀 어울리지 않는다 Your clothes are totally out of place at this gathering.

어울림 (-音) [음] a consonance; a concord. ¶~의 consonant.

어울림 음정 (-音程) [음] a consonant interval.

어원 (語源·語原) [언] the origin [derivation] of a word; etymology. ¶~ (학)상의 etymological // ~상으로 etymologically // ~을 조사하다 trace a word to its origin / study the etymology (of) // 이 말들은 ~이 같다 These words have the same pedigree [origin].
●**어원학** etymology. **어원학자** an etymologist.

어유 (魚油) fish oil.

어육 (魚肉) 1 [생선의 고기] fish (meat). 2 [생선과 짐승의 고기] fish and meat.

어음 [경] a bill; a draft; a note. ¶개인 ~ a private bill / 기일 경과 [만기] ~ an overdue [a matured] bill / 기한부 ~ a term bill / usance (bill) // 단기 [장기] ~ a short [long] (-dated) bill // 백지 ~ a blank bill [note] // 부도 ~ a dishonored [bad] bill [draft] // 사고 ~ a foul bill // 상업 ~ a commercial [mercantile] paper [bill] // 신종 기업 ~ a commercial paper (which a short-term financial firm has underwritten) (약어 cp) // 약속 ~ a promissory note / a note of hand // 융통 ~ an accommodation bill // 은 (행) ~ a bank draft [bill] / an addressed bill // 일람불 ~ a note at sight / a sight [presentation] bill / a demand draft // 일람 후 정기불 ~ bills

payable (so many) months [days] after sight // 정기불 ~ bills payable on fixed date / a time bill // 즉시불 ~ a prompt note / 지급 ~ a bill payable // 지시식 ~ a bill to order / 추심 ~ a bill for collection // 할인 ~ a discount bill // 환 ~ a bill of exchange (in B/E) / a draft // 100만 원짜리 ~ a draft [bill] for 1,000,000 won // 3개월 지급 ~ a bill due in three months // ~으로 **지급하다** pay by draft // ~을 **인수**[거절] **하다** accept [dishonor / repudiate] a bill // ~을 **발행하다** draw a bill (for a sum on a person) / give a promissory note // ~을 **매매하다** negotiate a bill // ~을 **할인하다** discount a bill // ~을 **결제하다** honor a bill // ~이 **만기가 되었다** The bill falls due. // 나는 런던 지점 지급 500파운드짜리 ~을 발행했다 I drew a draft for 500 pounds on the London branch. // 이 ~은 내일까지는 현찰로 바꿀 수 없습니다 You cannot cash this draft until tomorrow. // 은행은 이 ~의 지급을 거절했다 The bank did not accept [honor] this draft. / The bank dishonored this draft. // 그 ~은 지급 기한이 지났다 The draft is overdue.
●**어음 교환** bill clearing (of bills); (bill) clearance. **어음 교환소** a clearing house. **어음 발행** drawing a bill. **어음 발행인** the drawer of a bill [draft]; (약속 어음) the maker of a bill. **어음 수취인** the payee of bill. **어음 인수** acceptance of a bill. **어음 인수인** the acceptor of a bill. **어음 할인** discounting a bill; a discount (on a bill).

어의(御醫) a court physician; a physician in ordinary (to a king).

어의(語義) the meaning of a word. ¶~를 분명히 하다 define [clarify the meaning of] a word.

어이¹ why; how. ⇨²어찌 ¶~ 하여 그녀는 자살을 했을까 Why did she kill herself? / 당신이 모르는데 내가 ~ 알겠소 How should I know if you do not?

어이² [부르는 소리] hull; hulloa; halloa; hello; hey; (미) say; (영) I say; (look) here; there. ¶~, 뭘 하고 있나 Hey, old boy! What's that you're doing there? // ~, 잠깐 기다려 Hey, just a minute!

어이구(머니) Ah!; Oh! ⇨아이고(머니)

어이없다 amazing; surprising; shocking; absurd; ridiculous; (서술적) be amazed (at); be appalled (at); be dum(b)founded; be stunned (by); be taken aback; be [stand] aghast (at); be flabbergasted (by); (구어) be shocked [scandalized] (at / by); be astounded (by); be disgusted (at / with). ¶어이없는 가격 a ridiculous price / an extravagant [exorbitant / absurd / unreasonable / impossible] price / a staggering [dazzling] price // 어이없는 거짓말 a damned [whopping] lie / a whopper // 그 남자가 학자라니 ~ It is quite astonishing that he should be called a scholar. // 그의 어리석음이 하도 어이없어 말이 안 나온다 I'm too shocked by his stupidity to say a word. // 그가 거절하여 어이없었다 I was dumbfounded [stunned] by his refusal.

어이쿠 Oops!; Whew! ⇨아이코

어장(漁場) a fishing ground [place]; fishing banks; a fishery. ¶근해 [원양] ~ inshore [deep-sea] fisheries.

어적거리다 munch; eat with a munching sound; champ.

어적어적 with a munching sound. ⇨²아작아작

어전(御前) the presence of the King; the King's presence. ¶~에 부름을 받다 be summoned into the presence of the King // ~에서 물러나다 leave [withdraw from] the King's presence.

어정거리다 toddle; hang about. ⇨²아장거리다
어정어정 toddlingly. ⇨아장아장
어정쩡하다 1 [마음에 꺼림하고 의심이 가다] uneasy [ill at ease] (about); uncertain (over); dubious. ¶어째 좀 ~ feel [have] some misgivings (about) / be under some uneasiness (at) / entertain some apprehensions (about). 2 [애매하다] noncommittal; ambiguous; borderline; equivocal; vague. ¶어정쩡한 대답 a noncommittal [a vague / an equivocal] answer // 어정쩡한 태도를 취하다 take a noncommittal attitude / do not commit oneself / sit on the fence. 3 [난처하다] perplexed; embarrassed; awkward. ¶어정쩡한 듯이 with a perplexed air / in a puzzled way.

어제 [오늘의 바로 전날] yesterday. ¶~ 아침 yesterday morning // ~ 신문 yesterday's newspaper // 그때 일이 ~의 일처럼 생각난다 I remember it as well if it had happened yesterday. 2 [과거] the past; the yesterdays. ¶그는 ~의 그가 아니다 He is not what he was [used to be].
●**어제오늘** [아주 최근] the latest; the most recent. ¶그건 ~의 일이 아니다 It's nothing new. / It is not something that has only just started. / It is not of recent occurrence. // ~은 환자의 상태가 그리 좋지 않았다 The patient hasn't been very well the last few days. **어젯밤** last night; yesterday evening. ¶~의 텔레비전 프로그램 a TV program that was on last night // ~엔 잘 주무셨습니까 Did you sleep well (last night)? // 그가 ~ 늦게 찾아왔다 He came to see me late last night.

어조(語調) a tone (of voice); an accent; a note; a strain. ¶연설하는 [격렬한] ~로 in an oratorical [a sharp] tone // 흥분한 ~로 in an excited tone // 단호한 [신랄한] ~로 in a resolute [an acid / a cutting] tone of voice // 단조로운 ~로 in a monotone / monotonously // 딱딱한 ~로 in formal [bookish / pedantic] way (of expression) // ~를 부드럽게 하다 soften one's voice // ~를 **높이다** raise one's voice // 그는 화난 ~로 그것을 부인했다 He denied it in an angry tone.

어조사(語助辭) [언] [한문의 토] a particle (in classical Chinese).

어족(語族) a family of languages; a linguistic family. ¶인도·유럽 ~ the Indo-European family of languages.

어줍다 1 [말·행동이) 조심스러워 자유롭지 못하다] constrained; dull; stiff. 2 [서투르다] unskilled; clumsy; awkward; unhandy. ¶젓가락을 어줍게 쓰다 be awkward at handling chopsticks // 바느질 솜씨가 ~ be clumsy with one's sewing.

어중간하다 (於中間-) halfway; noncommittal. ¶어중간한 액수 an odd sum of money // 어중간한 입장 a betwixt and between status // 어중간한 시간에는 뜨개질을 한다 I knit at odd moments. // 지금 출발하기에는 시간이 ~ If we start now, we shall arrive there at an awkward hour. / It will be too early[late] if we go now.

어중되다 〔於中-〕 either too small[little / short] or too big[much / long]; unsuitable [insufficient] either way; not perfectly fit.

어중이떠중이 all the world and his wife; (every) Tom, Dick and Harry; the butcher, the baker, the candlestick-maker; (anybody and) everybody; the rabble; the ruck; the riffraff; all sorts and conditions of men. ¶요즘은 ~가 모두 해외여행에 나선다 Everybody and his brother[Every Tom / Dick and Harry] travels abroad these days.

어지간하다 〔적당하다〕 moderate; reasonable; proper; suitable; 〔보통이다〕 average; ordinary; common. ¶그곳 더위가 ~ It is hot enough there.∥그건 어지간한 사람이면 누구나 할 수 있다 Any man of ordinary[average] talents can do it. **어지간히** moderately; reasonably; properly; suitably; ordinarily. ¶장난도 ~ 해 두게 Stop your mischief. / No more of your pranks.

어지러뜨리다 scatter (thing) (about); put out of order; put[throw] into disorder [confusion]; disarray; disarrange. ¶방을 어지러뜨려 놓다 leave a room untidy[in disorder / out of order].

어지럼증 〔-症〕 giddiness; dizziness. ⇨ˆ현기증 ¶~을 타다 be liable to feel dizzy.

어지럽다 1 〔정신이 얼떨떨하다〕 dizzy; giddy; dazing; vertiginous. ¶어지러운 춤 a giddy dance∥술 냄새만 맡아도 ~ Just the smell of alcohol makes me dizzy[makes my head swim / makes my brain reel]. **어지러이** dizzily; dazedly; giddily. ¶~ 돌아가는 세상 the dizzy[dazing] bustle of life / the dizzy whirl of life / the bustling[busy] world.
2 〔혼란하고 수선하다〕 confused; disorderly; untidy; cluttered; disordered; in disorder [disarray]; disturbed; agitated; troubled; chaotic. ¶어지러운 시대 troubled[turbulent / stormy] times∥조용한 세상을 어지럽게 하다 disturb the peaceful world∥방 안이 몹시 ~ The room is in great disorder[confusion]. **어지러이** in disorder[confusion]; promiscuously; in a jumble; wildly; pell-mell. ¶정세는 ~ 바뀌고 있다 The situation is changing with dizzy rapidity.∥휴지 조각이 방 안에 ~ 널려 있다 Waste paper is scattered all over the room.∥그의 주위에는 책들이 ~ 쌓여 있었다 Books were piled pell-mell around him.

어지럽히다 disturb; upset; confuse; disarrange; throw (one's mind) into commotion; distract (one's mind). ¶나라를 ~ put [throw] a country into confusion[disorder / a chaotic state].

어지르다 scatter (about); put in[throw into] disorder[confusion]; make untidy[disordered]; disarrange; clutter (up); litter (up); make a better; 〔구어〕 mess up. ¶엉망으로 어질러진 방 a messy[disordered] room∥물건들을 어질러 놓다 leave things scattered about[lying around]∥정돈해 놓은 책을 ~ mess up neatly arranged books∥어질러져 있다 〔물건이〕 be[lie] scattered around / 〔구어〕 be all over the place / 〔장소가〕 be in disorder / be in a mess∥그녀는 늘 방을 엉망으로 어질러 놓는다 She leaves the room in awful disorder.

어질다 〔인자하다〕 benign; benevolent; merciful; gracious; 〔덕행이 높다〕 virtuous. ¶어진 임금 a benignant sovereign∥어진 사람 a good-natured person / a person of (a) mild disposition / a man of virtue.

어질어질하다 dizzy; faint; feel dizzy[giddy / faint]. ¶머리가 ~ My head is reeling [spinning / swimming]. / My head is going around and around. / I feel dizzy.∥그는 타박상으로 인해 정신이 어질어질했다 He was faint with the bruises.

어째서 why; for what reason[purpose]; 〔구어〕 what ... for; 〔구어〕 how come; on what ground. ¶그런 일이 일어났는가 How come it happened?∥그렇게 생각합니까 What makes you think so? / Why do you think so?

어쨌든 anyhow; anyway; at any rate; in any case; somehow or other; setting aside [apart]; aside[apart from]; not to speak of; not to mention; whatever; however; whether ... or not. ¶정말인지 아닌지는 몰라도 ~ 그런 소문이 떠돌고 있다 Whether it's true or not, there are rumors to that effect.∥얼굴이야 ~ 마음씨는 아주 고운 여자다 Leaving her looks out of it[Looks apart], she is very good-natured.∥~ 우선 당신 원고를 보기나 합시다 Anyway, first let me see your manuscript.∥이유야 ~ 그는 무단결석은 하지 말았어야 했다 Whatever the reason, he shouldn't have been absent without notifying us.

어쩌고저쩌고 this and[or] that; one thing or another; something or other.

어쩌다(가) 1 〔우연히〕 accidentally; casually; unexpectedly; by (some) chance; by accident. ¶~ 알게 된 사람 a casual[chance] acquaintance / 〔미〕 a pickup∥내가 의장이 되어 버렸다 I became chairman by chance.∥우리는 ~ 같은 열차에 탔다 It chanced[happened] that we rode in the same train. 2 〔이따금〕 occasionally; once in a while; from time to time; now and then; at times; between times[whiles]; at long[rare] intervals. ¶~ 있는 일 a rare occurrence / a thing of infrequent occurrence∥~ 오는 손님 a casual visitor / a stray customer.

어쩌면 1 〔어찌하면〕 how; what. ¶~ 좋을지 모르겠다 I am at a loss what to do.∥~ 그 사람을 만날 수 있을까 What shall I do in order to meet him? 2 〔아마〕 possibly; probably; maybe; perhaps. ¶~ 그는 거짓말을 하고 있는지 모른다 He may possibly be lying.∥~ 그가 옳을지도 모른다 Possibly he is right. / He may be right.∥~ 사태가 악화될지도 모른다 I'm afraid the situation may possibly take a turn for the worse. 3 〔도대체 어떻게 해서〕 what; how. ¶~ 그가 그렇게 무정한 말을 할 수 있을까 I wonder how he can say such heartless things.∥~ 머리칼이 그렇게 아름다울까 What wonderful hair you have!

어쩐지 1 〔어찌된 까닭인지〕 somehow; in some way; for some reason or other; without knowing why. ¶~ 슬프다 I feel somewhat sad.∥~ 불안하다 I don't know why, but I have an uneasy feeling about it. / I feel uneasy without knowing why.∥그는 ~ 그 집이 싫었다 Somehow[For some reason or other], he disliked the house.∥~ 그가 올 것 같다 I have a hunch he will come. / I have an idea somehow that he will come.

2 [그런 연유로] so that is why; (it is) no wonder. ¶~ 그가 투덜거리고 있더라 No wonder that he makes complaints. // 외투를 입고 올 것을 깜빡했구나. ~ 춥더라니 I forget to put on my overcoat so that's why I feel cold.

어쭙잖다 1 [분수를 벗어난 데가 있다] beyond the bounds; out of one's place; self-conceited. ¶어쭙잖게 네가 충고하겠다니 You to offer advice to me? How ridiculous! **2** [대수롭지 않다] of little importance; of no account. ¶어쭙잖은 일 a matter of no importance / a trivial [trifle] affair.

어찌 1 [어떠한 이유로] why; for what reason; how; (구어) what ... for; (구어) how come. ¶~ 그렇게 말할 수 있단 말이냐 How come you (to) say so? / How can you say a thing? // ~ 여기에 와 있는가 How is it that you are here? / What has brought you here? **2** [어떠한 방법으로] how; in what way. ¶먼 길을 ~ 갈꼬 How can I make a long journey? // 내가 ~ 알겠는가 How do [should] I know? **3** how; what; too. ⇨ =어찌나

어찌나 how; what; too; too much; very; quite; so. ¶~ 추웠던지 It was quite [so] cold. // ~ 재미있는 분들이냐 What interesting people they are! // ~ 반가운지 I'm so glad to see you!

어찌하다 ¶그는 어찌하든 일류 회사에 들어가고 싶어 한다 He wants to find a position in a first-rate company somehow or other. // 그것은 어찌할 도리가 없다 It can't be helped. / It is unavoidable.

어찌할 바를 모르다 be at a loss; be at one's wit's [wits'] end; be bewildered; be puzzled [perplexed] what to do; do not know what to do. ¶나는 그에게 거절을 당해 어찌할 바를 몰랐다 I was at a loss [at my wit's end] when he turned me down.

어찌할 수 없다 1 [불가피하다] unavoidable; inevitable; [긴급하다] urgent; pressing. ¶어찌할 수 없는 사정으로 under [owing to / on account of] unavoidable circumstances / driven by circumstances // 나는 어찌할 수 없이 사직했다 I was forced to resign my post. // 그것은 ~ It can't be helped. / It is unavoidable. **2** [다룰 수 없다] incontestable; indisputable; undeniable. ¶어찌할 수 없는 사실 an undeniable [indisputable] fact / a fact beyond dispute // 나이는 ~ Age will tell. / There is no contending against age. / Age brings its unmistakable signs with it. // 아이들은 ~ Children are children.

어찔하다 dizzy; giddy. ⇨ 아찔하다

어차피(於此彼) anyhow; anyway; one way or the other; in any [either] case; after all; at all. ¶~ 그것은 끝내야 한다 Anyway, I must finish it. // ~ 그것은 쓸모가 없다 It won't help you one way or the other. // ~ 그것 때문에 우리가 곤란을 겪게 된다 We are going to suffer for it in any case. // ~ 갈 바에는 일찍 떠나는 게 낫다 If we have to go, we'd better leave early. // ~ 낫지 않을 병이다 After all, he is not going to recover. // ~ 그럴 테지요 If you say so (▶ 점잖게 말하면 순순히 인정한 꼴이 되므로 내뱉듯이 말함)

어처구니없다 amazing; surprising. ⇨ 어이없다 ¶어처구니없는 거짓말 an egregious lie // 어처구니없는 생각 a fabulous idea // 어처구니없는 계획이로군 It is really a wild [fantastic / crazy] plan. // 그는 틀림없이 무엇인가 어처구니없는 일을 저질렀을 게야 He must have done something crazy [terrible / monstrous].

어촌(漁村) a fishing village [hamlet]; a sea village.

-어치 worth. ¶그는 과자를 2천 원~ 샀다 He bought two thousand won('s) worth of sweets.

어투(語套) one's way [manner] of talking [speaking]. ⇨ =말투

어퍼컷 [권투] an uppercut. ¶~을 먹이다 deal [land] (a person) an uppercut / deliver an uppercut (to the jaw) // ~을 맞다 take [get hit with] an uppercut // 그는 턱에 ~을 먹었다 An uppercut landed on his jaw.

어폐(語弊) a misleading [faulty] expression. ¶~가 있다 be misleading / be liable to be misunderstood // 이렇게 말하면 ~가 있을지 모르지만… I'm afraid this expression may be misleading, but …. / This may be the wrong word, but …. / I doubt the propriety of the word, but ….

어포(魚脯) [생선을 얇게 저며서 갖은 양념을 하여 말린 포] dried slices of fish seasoned with spices.

어프로치 1 [접근] an approach (to). **2** [골프] an approach shot. ¶그는 피치 샷으로 ~를 했다 He pitched onto the green.

어필 appeal. 어필하다 appeal (to).

어학(語學) language study; (언어학) linguistics. ¶~의 linguistic // ~의 천재 a born linguist / a genius in language [for languages] // ~의 재능이 있다 have linguistic talent // 그는 ~ 실력이 상당하다 He is proficient [strong] in languages. / He is a good [clever] linguist.

● **어학 교육** linguistic education; language instruction. **어학자** a linguist.

어항(魚缸) a fish basin; (유리제) a fish bowl; (둥근 것) a fish globe; (큰 것) an aquarium.

어항(漁港) a fishing port.

어허 Dear me!; My goodness! ⇨ 아하

어험 Hem!; Ahem!; Hum hum!

어형(語形) a form of a word; a word form.

● **어형 변화** (언) (an) inflection; (영) (an) inflexion. ~의 inflective / inflectional.

어획(漁獲) fishery; fishing. ¶~이 많다 get [make] a good catch / the catches are large // 이 구역에서는 대구의 ~이 많다 Cod are caught in large quantities in this area.

● **어획량 / 어획고** a haul [catch] (of fish); a fish catch; taking.

어휘(語彙) a vocabulary; a glossary. ¶풍부한 ~ an abundant [an extensive / a copious] vocabulary // ~를 풍부히 하다 enrich [enlarge / increase] one's vocabulary // 그녀는 프랑스 어의 ~가 풍부하다 She has an extensive French vocabulary. // 그는 영어의 ~가 부족하다 He has a meager [small / poor] vocabulary of English.

억(億) a [one] hundred million. ¶2~ 5천만 two hundred and fifty million // 10~ (미) a billion / (영) a thousand million / (영) a milliard.

억겁(億劫) [불] eternity; perpetuity.

억누르다 [내리누르다] press [put / hold] down; force down; [진압하다] suppress; put down; repress; subdue; get under; control; bring [keep] under control; oppress; [억제하다] restrain; control; check; master; sub-

억누르다 due; contain; resist; keep under; stifle. ¶억누를 수 없는 슬픔 uncontrollable grief // 격정을 ~ restrain one's passion / hold one's passion in check // 분노를 ~ control[contain / repress] one's anger // 나는 화를 억누를 수가 없었다 I could not swallow[gulp down] my anger. / I could not hold[rein] in my temper. / I could not master my wrath. // 나는 감정을 억누를 수 없었다 My emotions overpowered me. // 나는 하고 싶은 말을 억눌렀다 I swallowed my words. / I gulped back my words.

억눌리다 get pressed down; be repressed [suppressed].

억류(抑留) detention; detainment; internment; seizure. **억류하다** detain; intern; hold in custody; seize; apprehend; (배를) arrest. ➔아버지는 시베리아에 억류되어 있었다 My father was interned in Siberia.
● **억류선** an interned ship. **억류자** a detained person; a detainee; an internee.

억만(億萬) 1 a[one] hundred million. ⇨ **억** ¶~ 년 전 millions of years ago. 2 [아주 많은 수효] countless numbers; myriads.
● **억만장자** a billionaire; a multimillionaire.

억새 [식] a eulalia.

억설(臆說) a hypothesis (*pl.* -theses); conjecture; a surmise; (a) speculation; an assumption; a supposition. ¶이 문제에 대해서는 여러 가지 ~이 분분했다 Various conjectures about the matter were flying about.

억세다 1 [굳고 세차다] strong; tough; firm; stout; tenacious; persistent; pushy; unyielding; resolute; (근육이) brawny; sinewy. ¶억센 팔 a sinewy[brawny / muscular] arm // 억센 다리 sturdy legs // 억센 손 a muscular hand // 그는 나이를 먹었지만 꽤 ~ He's elderly but quite tough. 2 [뻣뻣하다] tough; hard; stiff. ¶억센 수염 a tough beard // 이 양배추는 ~ This is a tough cabbage.

억수 a downpour (of rain); a pouring[heavy / torrential / drenching] rain; (미) cloudburst. ¶~ 같은 비 a heavy rainfall / a downpour // 비가 ~같이 쏟아졌다 It rained cats and dogs. / It rained in buckets. / The rain came down in torrents.
● **억수장마** a long spell of heavy rain. ¶~가 들다 a steady heavy rain sets in.

억압(抑壓) [억제·활동 금지] suppression; [압박] oppression; [활동 제한] (a) restraint. ¶노동 운동의 ~ the suppression of labor movements // 그 조직은 정부의 ~을 받았다 The organization was kept down by the government. **억압하다** suppress (information); oppress (the people); restrain; check. ¶여론을 ~ suppress public opinion // 그는 반대의 견을 억압했다 He repressed opposing voices. ➔그 시대에는 신앙의 자유가 억압되어 있었다 Freedom of religion was suppressed in those days.

억양(抑揚) intonation; modulation; accent; swell; infection. ¶좀 더 ~을 붙여서 읽어 보아라 Read it with a more pronounced intonation. // 그의 ~이 없는 말소리를 듣고 있자니 졸음이 온다 His singsong voice[monotonous way of talking] makes me drowsy.

억울하다(抑鬱-) mortified (by); regrettable; feel pent-up[chagrined / mortified / mistreated]; suffer unfairness; (허위) false; untrue; groundless. ¶억울한 ~에 under a false accusation / on a false charge // 억울한 조처 unfair treatment // 억울한 누명을 씌우다 accuse (a person of theft) unjustly / charge (a person) unjustly (with bribery) // 억울해 죽겠다 I am mortified at being mistreated.

억장이 무너지다(億丈-) be heartbroken; feel like the end of the world. ¶그는 죽은 아들을 생각하면 억장이 무너지는 것 같다 It is heartbreaking for him to think of his dead son.

억제(抑制) control; restraint; suppression; repression; holdback; constraint; check; curb; [심] inhibition. ¶인플레 ~ an inflation curb. **억제하다** restrain; control; check; repress(▶ repress는 주로 무엇인가를 하고 싶은 기분이나 감정 등을 참는 일); suppress; inhibit (one's desire); hold[keep] in check. ¶인플레이션을 ~ control[check] inflation // 감정을 억제하지 못하다 give way to emotion [passion] / give way to one's feelings // 인구 증가를 ~ control population growth / check an increase in population. ➔억제된 감정 repressed emotions.
● **억제력** restraint; control.

억조(億兆) one hundred million and a trillion [(영) a billion]; [썩 많은 수] billions.
● **억조창생**(一蒼生) myriads of people; the (common) people; the multitude; the masses; the million(s).

억지 (a) push; willfulness; headstrongness; stubbornness; obstinacy; unreasonableness; perversity. ¶~를 부리는 pushy / [끈질긴] persistent / [뻔뻔스러운] audacious / [공격적인] aggressive // ~를 **부리다** insist on having one's own way / persist stubbornly / insist doggedly // ~ 부리지 마라 Be reasonable. / Don't be obstinate, you know.

억지 춘향(이) something narrowly done by force; doing against one's will; compelling; compulsion; coercion; forcing. ¶~으로 by force / against one's will / under compulsion / under forced pressure.
● **억지웃음** a forced[feigned / strained / set] smile. ¶그녀는 ~을 웃었다 She forced a smile.

억지(抑止) (a) restraint; deterrence. **억지하다** restrain; deter (from). ¶핵전쟁을 ~ prevent nuclear war.

억지로 [무리하게] by force; forcibly; against one's will; willy-nilly; compulsorily; under compulsion. ¶~ ···하게 하다 force[compel / coerce] (a person) to[into] (do[doing]) // ~ 밀어 넣다 force into / thrust into / push into / (몸을) force oneself into // 내가 싫다고 하는데도 그는 ~ 돈을 얼마간 내 주머니에 밀어 넣었다 In spite of my refusal he pushed [thrust] some money into my pocket.

억지스럽다 [고집스럽다] willful; obstinate; stubborn; headstrong; [불합리하다] unreasonable; [부당하다] unjustifiable; [부자연스럽다] unnatural; [강제적이다] compulsory; forcible.

억척 being unyielding[unwieldy]; toughness; stiffness; stubbornness. ¶~을 **떨다**[**부리다**] act[behave] unyieldingly[toughly / persistently] / show toughness[stubbornness].
● **억척꾸러기** a tough[hard-headed] person; an unrelenting[an indefatigable / a dauntless] person.

억척같다 unyielding[unrelenting / tough /

strong-minded / dogged]. **억척같이** unyieldingly; toughly; persistently. ¶~ 공부하다 go at one's studies hammer and tongs.

억척스럽다 unyielding [unrelentive / tough / strong-minded / dogged].

억측(臆測) a (random) guess; a conjecture; guesswork; a supposition; a speculation; a surmise; an inference. ¶당치 않은 ~ a wild [wrong] guess // 네가 말하고 있는 것은 ~에 지나지 않는다 What you are saying is only guesswork [mere conjecture]. **억측하다** make a guess; surmise; conjecture; speculate (about / upon); (대중없이) try a shot in the dark; (문어) hazard a conjecture [guess]. ¶멋대로 ~ indulge in speculation / give flight to one's fancy.

억하심정(抑何心情) ¶무슨 ~으로 Why [How] on earth [in the world] ...? // 무슨 ~으로 그런 말을 했을까 I wonder why he said such a thing.

언감생심(焉敢生心) [감히 그런 마음을 품을 수도 없음] How dare ...? ¶~ 어찌 네가 나에게 그런 말을 할 수 있느냐 How dare you say such a thing to me?

언급(言及) reference; mention; comment; allusion. **언급하다** refer (to); mention; make reference to; make mention of; (간접적으로) (문어) allude (to). ¶앞서 언급한 abovementioned / above alluded to / as stated above // 연사는 종종 그 점에 대해서 언급했다 The speaker often referred to [mentioned / touched upon] that point. // 여기서는 그 문제에 대하여 언급하지 않기로 한다 We will not take up the subject here.

언니 one's older [elder] sister; (구어) one's big sister (▶ 종종 어린이가 말하는 경우). (▶ 영어에서는 특별한 경우를 제외하고는 자매끼리 손위·손아래를 구별하지 않고 그냥 sister라고 함. 그것을 굳이 구별할 때에는「언니」는 older sister, 「동생」은 younger sister라고 함. 한편, sister는 우리말「언니」와는 달리 호칭어로 쓰이지 않으며, 언니를 부를 때는 이름을 사용함)

언더라인 an underline; underlining. ¶중요한 말에 ~을 긋다 underline important words.

언더스로 [야구] an underhand throw. ⇨**언더핸드 스로**. ¶~로 던지다 throw a ball underhand.

언더웨어 underwear; underclothing.

언더 파 [골프] under par. ¶그는 1~ 71로 돌았다 He finished the round one stroke under par at 71.

언더핸드 스로 [야구] an underhand throw; underhand pitching.

언덕 a hill; a hillock (▶ hill보다 작음); a knoll; a height; a rise; [둔덕] a mound. ¶가파른 ~ a steep hill // ~을 오르다 [내려가다] go up [down] a hill.
● **언덕길** a slope; a sloping road; a hill. ¶~을 달려 내려오다 run down the hill [slope] // 가파른 ~을 오르다 climb a steep hill. **언덕배기** [가파른 곳] a steep [sharp] hillside / [꼭대기] a hilltop; the top of a hill.

언도(言渡) (a) pronouncement; a sentence. ⇨**선고**(宣告)1. ¶무죄 ~ a pronouncement of "not guilty" // 사형 ~ a sentence of death.

언동(言動) words and actions; speech and behavio(u)r. ¶~을 삼가다 be careful in one's speech and behavior [mind one's p's and q's / conduct].

언뜻 [얼른] in an instant; in a flash; [문득] suddenly; unexpectedly. ¶호수가 ~ 보였다 We had [caught] a glimpse of the lake. / The lake appeared for an instant. // 불안감이 내 마음을 ~ 스쳤다 A feeling of uneasiness flashed across my mind.

언론(言論) speech (and writing); discussion; views. ¶~의 힘 power of speech // ~의 탄압 pressure on discussion [public opinion] / a gag upon freedom of speech [the press].
언론의 자유 (통제) (controls on) freedom of speech [the press] (▶ freedom of the press는 출판·신문의 자유).
● **언론계** the press. **언론 기관** an organ of public opinion [expression].

언명(言明) (a) declaration; (an) assertion; a positive statement; affirmation. **언명하다** declare; assert; make a positive statement; affirm; proclaim; voice. ¶정부가 최근에 앞서 언명한 바와 같이 as was recently declared by the Government.

언문(諺文) the Korean script; the Korean letters.

언문(言文) the written and spoken styles of a language; the colloquial and the literary.
● **언문일치** the unification [identity] of the written and spoken styles of a language; unity of speech and writing. ¶~체로 쓰다 write in (a) colloquial style.

언밸런스 unbalance. ¶~의 unbalanced.

언변(言辯) oratorical talent [skill]; [말씨] speech; [웅변] eloquence. ¶~이 좋다 be eloquent [fluent] / have a fluent [ready / glib] tongue // ~이 없다 be slow of speech / be awkward in speaking / be a poor speaker.

언사(言辭) [화자의 말씨] words; speech; language; an expression. ¶온당치 못한 ~를 쓰다 use intemperate language.

언성(言聲) a voice; a tone (of voice). ¶화난 ~ an angry voice // 굵은 ~ a deep voice // 가냘픈 ~ a faint voice // ~을 높여 loudly / aloud / in a rough [hard] voice / in a harsh tone // ~을 높이다 raise [lift] (one's) voice.

언약(言約) a verbal [an oral] promise; one's word; a vow; a pledge. ¶~을 지키다 [어기다] keep [break] one's word [promise]. **언약하다** give [make] a verbal promise; promise orally; give one's word (▶ give one's word는 책임 있는 약속을 한다는 뜻). ¶사랑을 ~ exchange vows of love / pledge oneself to each other / (문어) plight one's troth // 두 사람은 사랑을 굳게 언약한 사이다 They are plighted lovers.

언어(言語) (a) language; speech (▶ language는 한 나라, 한 민족의 말처럼 일반적으로 말에 의한 전달 수단을 나타내고, speech는 현재 사용되고 있는 말을 나타냄); words. ¶~(상)의 linguistic // ~의 섬 [언] speech island // ~에 의한 묘사 a verbal picture (of a scene) // ~가 통한다 A language is used [understood].
● **언어 감각** a linguistic sense. **언어도단** ¶~의 [말로 나타낼 수 없는] unspeakable / [터무니없는] outrageous / (문어) abominable / shocking / [불합리한] preposterous / absurd / [용서할 수 없는] inexcusable // ~의 행위 a scandalous conduct. **언어 심리학** linguistic psychology. **언어 장애** a speech disorder; a speech impediment; [의] aphasia. ¶~자 a person who has difficulty in speaking / [실어증 환자] an aphasic // ~ 교정학 logopedics. **언어 중추** the speech center; the speech-

control centers of the brain. **언어학** linguistics; philology. ¶~상의 linguistic / philological // 구조[비교] ~ structural[comparative] linguistics // 심리 ~ psycholinguistics. **언어학자(言語學者)** a linguist; a philologist.

언외(言外) ¶~의 implied / unspoken // ~의 의미를 파악하다 (이야기의) catch the implied meaning / (문장의) read between the lines.

언월도(偃月刀) a scimitar; a falchion.

언쟁(言爭) a (verbal) quarrel; an argument. ⇨말다툼 ¶~이 주먹다짐으로 번졌다 They proceeded from words to blows. / The quarrel came to hard blows.

언저리 the edge; the brim; the rim; bounds; limits. ¶입 ~ parts around the mouth // 접시 ~ the brim of a dish // 눈~가 검다 have dark rings around one's eyes.

언제 1 [의문] when; (at) what time; how soon; what date [day]; whenever. ¶~부터 from what time / since when / how long // 어느 때(에) (at) any moment[time] / every moment // ~쯤 about what time / when / how soon // 이 법률은 ~부터 시행됩니까 When will this law take effect? // ~부터 기다리고 있는가 How long have you been waiting? // ~쯤 찾아뵐까요 About what time shall I come? // ~ 내 양복이 다 되겠습니까 How soon will my dress be ready? // ~까지 미국에 체재합니까 How long will you stay in the United States? // ~까지 회사에 있습니까 Till when [What time] will you be in your office? **2** [미래] some day; some time; some other day[time]; in the near future; one of these days; [조만간] sooner or later; sometime or other. ¶~ 한번 다시 뵙고 싶습니다 I would [should] like to see more of you some time. // ~ 한번 놀러 와라 Come and see me one of these days. // 그것에 대해 ~ 한번 상의해 보자 We'll talk about it some other time. **3** [과거] once; the other day. ¶~인지도 모를 시대부터 from time unknown // ~ 한번 그를 만난 기억이 난다 I remember seeing him once. **4** [항상] always; all the time; [언제고] any time; some time (or other); some day; someday; in (due course of) time. ¶그녀는 ~ 보아도 아름답다 She is always beautiful. // ~고 그 원수는 꼭 갚고야 말겠다 I shall get even with him in time.

언제든지 [어느 때라도] (at) any time; [항상] always; all the time; whenever. ¶~ 좋다 Any time will do. // ~ 형편 닿는 대로 오십시오 Please come at any time that suits you. // ~ 출발할 준비가 되어 있다 We are ready to start at a moment's notice.

언제나 [항상] always; all the time; at any time; ever; never(부정); [평소] usually; [습관적으로] habitually; […할 때마다] every time; whenever; [변함없이] invariably; [끊임없이] constantly. ¶~ 지각하는 사람 a habitual latecomer // 경찰관이 ~ 지키고 있다 Policemen are always on guard. // 내가 ~ 열차를 놓치는 것은 아니다 I don't miss the train every time. // 밖에 나가면 ~ 차를 조심해요 Be sure to watch out for cars whenever you go out.

언젠가 1 (과거의) the other day; some time ago; once; on one occasion; at one time. ¶~ 당신을 만난 적이 있습니다 I have met you before. // 이것이 ~ 말씀드렸던 책입니다 This is the book I told you about the other day. **2** (미래의) sometime; [영] some time; someday; [영] some day; one day; one of these days; before long. ¶~ 가까운 장래에 나는 아프리카 여행을 할 작정이다 I intend to go on a tour of Africa sometime in the near future. // 그도 ~는 깨닫게 될 것이다 Someday he'll wake up. // ~ 꼭 찾아뵙겠습니다 I'll come and see you one of these days without fail. // ~ 전화를 드리겠습니다 I'll call you some other time. // 이번의 손해는 ~ 벌충이 될 것이다 This loss will be made up in the long run.

언죽번죽 brazen-faced; unabashed; shamelessly; brazenly; audaciously; cheekily; impudently; unblushingly. **언죽번죽하다** brazen-faced; brazen; shameless; audacious; impudent.

언중유골(言中有骨) the implied meaning [veiled intention] in a remark. ¶~이다 He speaks up with implicit bitterness.

언중유언(言中有言) implications in [behind] a direct statement. ¶~이다 The word implies some other meaning. / What he says is very suggestive.

언질(言質) a pledge; a promise; a commitment. ¶~을 주다 give a pledge[one's word] (to do / that ...) / make a promise / commit oneself (on a matter / to do) // 확실한 ~을 주지 않다 make no (firm) commitment (for) // ~을 잡히지 않도록 조심하다 be careful not to commit oneself.

언질(을) 잡다 obtain[(문어) extract] a person's pledge[word]; (구어) nail a person down (on).

언짢다 1 [불쾌하다] unpleasant; disagreeable; offensive; ill-humored; (서술적) feel bad. ¶기분이 ~ feel vexed / be cross // 언짢은 얼굴을 하다 look displeased / make a sour face // 그는 하루 종일 기분이 언짢았다 He felt out of sorts[was on edge] all day. // 그는 기분이 ~ He is in foul temper. / He is in a bad humor[mood]. **2** [불길하다] ill; ill-omened; bad; unlucky; sinister; [꺼림칙하다] hateful; loathsome; abominable; [마뜩잖다] undesirable; unwelcome; repulsive. ¶언짢은 꿈 a bad[an ominous] dream // 언짢은 소식 sad[ill / unwelcome] news.

언청이 a harelip; a split lip; (사람) a person with a harelip. ¶~의 harelipped.

언치 (마소의) a pad; a saddlecloth.

언턱 a raised part; a ridge. ¶문 ~ a doorsill / a threshold.

언필칭(言必稱) [말할 때마다 반드시] as one always [habitually / invariably] says; never fail to (say); every time one opens one's mouth (it is invariably to say ...); in one's favo(u)rite phrase. ¶그는 ~ 그 말을 한다 He never opens his mouth without saying it.

언해(諺解) Korean annotation[translation] of Chinese classics. **언해하다** annotate[translate] (a Chinese classic) in Korean.

언행(言行) speech and behavior [(영) behaviour]; words and deeds; sayings and doings. ¶~이 일치하다 live[act] up to one's words [what one says] / one's words correspond with one's actions // ~을 일치시키다 suit one's actions to one's words / practice what one preaches // 그는 ~이 일치하지 않는다 He

says one thing and does another.
- **언행일치** consistency of speech and action; acting up to one's words.

얹다 put on; place [lay / set] (a thing) on; load(짐을). ¶얹어 주다 [덤으로 주다] give an extra / throw in (something) extra // 돈을 조금 얹어 주다 pay a little extra (to a person) // 그는 아들의 어깨에 손을 얹었다 He put [laid] his hand on his son's shoulder.

얹혀살다 be a dependent on (a person); depend upon (a person) for support; feed [live / hang / sponge] on (a person); live at the expense of (one's friend). ¶얹혀사는 사람 a dependent [dependant] / a hanger-on (*pl*. hangers-on) / sponge.

얹히다 1 [놓이다] be place [put] on (a table). ¶그릇이 선반 위에 얹혀 있다 The dishes are put on the shelf. 2 [체하다] oppress the stomach; sit [lie] heavy on the stomach; do not sit well on the stomach; remain undigested in the stomach. ¶이 음식은 잘 얹힌다 This food sits [lies] heavy on the stomach. / This is not easily digested. 3 be a dependent on (a person). ⇨⁼얹혀살다

얻다 1 [획득하다] get; have; obtain; acquire; secure; procure; derive (from); (일하여) earn; (승리 등을) win; (받다) receive; be given; [채취하다] produce (gas from coal); [추출하다] extract. ¶콜타르에서 얻은 약품 medicines made [produced] from coaltar // 그녀의 사랑을 ~ win her love [heart] / win (the heart of) her // 남의 호의를 ~ get a person's favor // 자식 하나를 ~ have a child / (어머니가 낳다) give birth to [(문어) bear] a child // 양자를 ~ adopt a child // 지위 [부]를 ~ get [obtain] a position [wealth] // 신용을 ~ win (a person's) confidence / gain [enjoy] credit (with a person) // 명성을 ~ make a name / win [get] fame // 권력을 ~ gain [(문어) attain to] power // 승리를 ~ win [achieve / score] a victory (over) // 자격을 ~ obtain a qualification (for) // 인가를 ~ obtain [secure / get] sanction [authorization] (from) / obtain a license [permit] (from) // 허가를 ~ get [obtain] permission // 인기를 ~ become popular (among / with) / get into public favor [with / among] // 이익을 ~ make [realize] profits // 자격증을 ~ obtain [take] a certificate // 3일간의 휴가를 ~ take three day's vacation [holiday] // 크게 얻는 바가 있다 gain [get] much (from / by) / get [derive] much benefit (from) / be much benefited (by) / learn a great deal (from) // 그의 동의를 얻었다 I got his agreement. // 그는 그 사업에서 막대한 이익을 얻었다 He made an enormous profit on that undertaking [project].
2 [아내 등을 맞다] marry (a woman); take (a woman) in marriage; take (a woman) to wife; take a wife. ¶부잣집 딸을 ~ marry a fortune / marry money.
3 [앓게 되다] catch (flu); contract (a disease); get (cancer); be attacked [affected] by (a disease). ¶어디선가 눈병을 얻었다 I have picked up [contracted] pinkeye somewhere.

얻어듣다 hear of; be informed [told] (about); hear [learn] from others; learn [know] by hearsay; happen to hear (of / about); get wind of. ¶내가 얻어들은 이야기 something which casually came to my knowledge / a piece of information acquired at second hand // 얻어들은 영어 English that one has picked up.

얻어맞다 1 (매 등을) get [receive] a blow; be beaten [struck / knocked / hit / thrashed / punched]; (구어) be licked. ¶머리를 ~ be struck [hit] on the head // 그런 짓을 하면 얻어맞는다 If you do such a thing, you will got licked. // 그는 턱을 한 대 얻어맞고 넘어졌다 He was knocked down by a blow on the chin. // 또 얻어맞고 싶으냐 Do you want another thrashing? 2 [공격받다] be criticized; take a beating; get a rap. ¶신문에서 ~ be attacked in [by] the newspaper // 여론에 ~ be flayed by public opinion.

얻어먹다 1 (밥 등을) beg one's bread; beg food(빌어먹다); get treated to(대접받다); rely [depend] on (a person) for one's food; live on [off] (a person). ¶밥을 ~ beg one's food // 냉면을 ~ be entertained with *naengmyeon* // 친구에게 술을 얻어먹었다 I got treated to drinks by a friend of mine. 2 [욕을 듣다] get called (names); suffer (harsh words); be abused; be slandered; be spoken ill of.

얼¹ [겉의 흠] a scratch (on). ¶~이 가다 get scratched.

얼² [정신] spirit; mind; [혼] soul. ¶한국의 ~ the spirit of Korea // 순국 지사의 ~ the spirits of those who laid down their lives for the country.

- **얼(을) 빼다** drive (a person) out of (his) mind; make (a person) senseless; daze; stun; stupefy; bewilder; infatuate; fascinate(매혹시키다). ¶고함을 쳐서 ~ stupefy (a person) [drive (a person) out of his mind] with one's shouting.

얼간 salting slightly [lightly].
- **얼간 고등어** lightly-salted mackerel.

얼간이 a dull [stupid] fellow; a fool; a simpleton; a half-wit; a fathead. ¶~ 같은 놈 You stupid donkey [blockhead]!

얼갈이 1 [논밭의] winter plowing [(영) ploughing]. 2 [겨울에 푸성귀를 심는 일] growing vegetables in the wintertime; [그 푸성귀] winter-grown vegetables; early vegetables of the year which were grown in the wintertime; winter-sown greens.

얼개 structure; (a) construction. ⇨⁼구조(構造)

얼결에 in the confusion of the moment. ⇨⁼얼떨결에

얼굴 1 [낯] a face; a visage; [안색] a complexion; [이목구비] features. ¶옆~ a side face // 예쁜 ~ a pretty face // 못생긴 ~ an ugly face // 둥근 ~ a round [plump] face // 갸름한 ~ an oval face // 복스러운 ~ a plump and well-looking face // 달덩이 같은 ~ a moonface // 햇볕에 탄 ~ a sunburnt [-tanned] face // 주름 진 ~ a wrinkled face // 윤곽이 뚜렷한 ~ a face with clear-cut features // ~이 잘생긴 handsome / good-looking // ~을 두 손으로 가리고 with one's face buried in one's hands // ~이 잘생긴 사람 a good-looking person / (구어) a good-looker // 예쁜 [~의 여인 a woman with a pretty [an attractive] face // ~이 예쁜 [못생긴] 소녀 a good-looking [(미) homely / (영) plain] girl // ~에 미소를 띠고 with a smile on one's face / with

얼근하다

a beaming face∥~을 맞대고 (sit) face to face (with) / (sit) tête-à-tête (with) / facing each other∥~을 들다 raise [lift] one's face / look up (from the paper)∥남의 ~을 똑바로 보다 look (a person) in the face∥~을 마주 **보다** look at each other / exchange glances [looks]∥~을 씻다 wash oneself / have a wash∥~을 찌푸리다 make grimaces / grimace / mop and mow / make a (wry) mouth (at)∥~을 기억하고 있다 remember (a person / who a person is) / recognize (one's acquaintance)∥~을 돌리다 turn [look] aside / look away [the other way] (from) / turn one's face away∥두 손에 ~을 묻다 drop one's face on one's hands∥그녀는 어머니와 ~이 닮았다 She has mother's looks. / Her features resemble [Her face resembles] her mother's.∥그 여자의 ~을 알고 있다 I know her by sight.∥그는 화가 나서 ~이 빨개졌다 He was red with anger.
2 [표정] a face; a look; a countenance; an expression. ¶웃는 ~ a laughing countenance∥밝은 ~ a sunny face∥슬픈 ~ a sad face [look / countenance]∥성난 ~ an angry countenance [look]∥놀란 ~ a look of surprise∥실망한 ~ a look of disappointment / a disappointed look∥진지한 ~ a serious look [countenance]∥풀이 죽은 ~ a downcast look∥생글생글 웃는 ~ a beaming face∥무서운 ~ a grim face∥찌든 ~ a care-worn face∥감정을 ~에 나타내다 betray one's emotions∥행복한 [슬픈 / 실망한] ~을 하고 있다 look happy [sad / disappointed]∥우울한 ~을 하다 look gloomy / wear [pull] a long face∥심각한 ~을 하고 있다 look grave∥흉악한 ~을 하고 있다 bear an evil look∥그는 뭔가 미심쩍은 ~을 하고 있었다 He put on [wore] a questioning look.∥그녀는 마음의 동요를 ~에 나타내지 않았다 She disguised [did not show] her uneasiness.∥거짓말을 하고 있다는 것이 네 ~에 빤히 나타나 있다 It shows [is written] on your face that you are lying.
3 [체면] honor; prestige. ¶자네 ~을 봐서 잔만 더 마시겠네 I'll drink just one beer on your account.
4 [비유] acquaintance; appearance. ¶~이 널리 알려진 사람 a man with many contact∥~이 잘 알려져 있다 be widely known / have a wide acquaintance∥사람들 앞에 ~을 못 들 짓은 하나도 안 했다 I have done nothing that makes me unable [ashamed] to look people in the face.∥동창회에는 같은 ~만 모였다 There were only the same old faces at the alumni reunion.∥이 쇼의 출연진에는 새로운 ~이 없다 There are no new faces in the cast of this show.∥요즘은 통 그녀의 ~을 못 보겠다 I have seen nothing of her lately.∥가끔 ~이나 봅시다 I hope to see something of you.

얼굴(을) 붉히다 become red in the face; color up; (부끄러워서) blush (for [with] shame).

얼굴에 똥칠 [먹칠]을 하다 cause (a person) to lose face; disgrace [shame] (a person). ¶아버지의 얼굴에 똥칠 [먹칠]을 하는 짓은 하지 마 Don't stain your father's reputation [good name]. / You mustn't be a disgrace to your father's reputation [good name].

얼굴에 씌어 있다 be written all over (a person's). ¶네가 무슨 생각을 하는지 얼굴에 다 씌어 있어 It is written on your face what you are thinking.

얼굴을 깎다 ¶그런 소문을 퍼뜨려서 내 얼굴을 깎을 생각이냐 Do you mean to disgrace me [bring shame on me] by spreading such a rumor? / Do you want to make me lose face by spreading a rumor like that?

얼굴을 내밀다 [비치다] show one's face; show oneself; turn [show] up; put in an appearance; attend (출석하다).

얼굴이 두껍다 [얼굴에 철판을 깔다] be thick-skinned. ¶이 일을 하려면 얼굴이 두꺼워야 해 You have to be thick-skinned to do this job.

● **얼굴 마사지** a facial. ¶~를 하시겠습니까 Would you get a facial? **얼굴빛** complexion; colo(u)r; countenance; looks. ¶~이 나쁘다 look pale [be colorless∥~이 좋다 look well [fresh] / have rosy cheeks / have a high color∥~이 희다 [검다] have fair [dark] complexion∥~을 살피다 read (a person's) face [countenance] / study the pleasure of (a person) / hang on (a person's) smiles∥~이 변하다 a change comes over (one's face)∥그는 아무리 심한 말을 들어도 ~이 변하지 않았다 However severely he was criticized, he remained calm.∥~으로 그가 성난 것을 알았다 I read [saw] anger in his countenance.∥그는 그 소식을 듣고 ~이 달라졌다 He changed color at the news.

얼근하다 **1** (맛이) rather hot [hot-tasting]; somewhat peppery [pungent]; heavily seasoned. ¶음식이 ~ The food tastes rather hot. **2** (술이) mellow; tipsy. ¶얼근하게 취해 있다 be rather intoxicated / be tipsy.

얼금뱅이 [곰보] a pockmarked [pocky] person; a person with a pitted [pocked] face.

얼기설기 in a disorderly way; confusingly; complicatedly; in a disorderly heap. ¶~ 얽힌 confusedly interlaced [intertwined] / complicated∥~ 얽히다 be tangled confusedly∥일이 ~ 얽혔다 The matter has become quite complicated.

얼김에 on the spur [impulse] of moment; under the impulse (of); in spite of oneself. ¶~ 말해 버리다 say on the spur of the moment∥나는 ~ 귀중한 반지를 주겠다고 그녀에게 약속했다 I promised to give her my precious ring on the spur of the moment.∥그것은 내가 ~ 한 일이다 I did it without knowing what I was doing.

얼다 **1** [결빙하다] freeze; be frozen; [응결하다] congeal. ¶꽁꽁 ~ be frozen up∥추워서 꽁꽁 ~ be benumbed with cold∥얼어 죽다 be frozen [freeze] to death / be frozen dead∥추워서 손이 얼었다 My hands were benumbed with cold.∥추위로 몸이 얼었다 I am almost frozen with cold. **2** [기가 죽다] be cowed [intimidated]; be scared stiff; feel timid [small]; be nervous. ¶시험에서 ~ get nervous at an examination∥나는 첫 무대에서 얼어 버렸다 It was my first stage, and I was scared stiff [had a terrible attack of stage fright].

얼떨결에 in the confusion of the moment; in a moment of bewilderment. ¶~ 그렇게 말해 버렸다 I said so in my bewilderment.∥~ 그 것을 깜빡 잊었다 I clean forgot about it in my confusion.∥~ 기차를 잘못 탔다 In my hurry I took a wrong train.

얼떨떨하다 [정신을 못 차리다] confounded; confused; flurried; perturbed; bewildered; upset; perplexed; puzzled. ¶얼떨떨한 표정[기색] a puzzled look[expression] // 얼떨떨한 얼굴로 with a perplexed[puzzled] air[look] // 얼떨떨하여 in a puzzle / perplexedly / in a perplexity / in a flurry // 느닷없는 질문에 나는 잠시 얼떨떨했다 I felt dazed for a moment at the sudden question. // 시험 문제를 보고 나는 얼떨떨했다 I was bewildered when I saw the examination questions.

얼뜨기 [정신이 얼뜬 사람] a half-wit; a dim-wit; an idiot; a ninny; a dunce; a blockhead. ¶이 ─야 You idiot! /《속어》 What an ass you are!

얼뜨다 [어리석다] slow-witted; dim-witted; stupid; foolish; silly; [얼빠진] absent-minded; abstracted; [겁이 많다] cowardly; timid; chickenhearted. ¶이 얼뜬 녀석아 You stupid donkey! / Blockhead! // 그는 좀 ~ He is a bit soft (in the head). / He has a soft place in his head.

얼러맞추다 humor (one's husband); please (a person's) humor[whim]; play up to; fawn upon; flatter; (남의 마음에 들려고) curry favor with (a person). ¶칭찬하며 ~ soothe a person with praise // 남편을 ~ contrive to get to the soft side of (her) husband // 얼러맞추기 힘들다 be hard to please.

얼러붙다 grapple with; wrestle with; come to a fist fight. ¶얼러붙어 싸우다 fight hand to hand / fight a close fight / grapple with (a person).

얼러치다 1 [한꺼번에 때리다] strike[hit / knock] (two or more objects) at one time. 2 [값을 함께 셈하다] lump[put] together; sum up. ¶얼러쳐서 all put together / in total / (all) in all / in the lump // 얼러쳐서 모두 얼마요 How much (is it) all together?

얼렁뚱땅 trickily; cunningly; flatteringly; playing false. ¶일을 ~ 해치우다 scamp[muddle with] one's work / do a slapdash work. **얼렁뚱땅하다** juggle; play a trick on; hoodwink; (말을) palter (with a person); prevaricate; (일을) scamp. ¶얼렁뚱땅하여 돈을 빼앗다 juggle (a person) out of his money // 얼렁뚱땅하지 말고 똑똑히 대답해 Don't shuffle, give a clear answer. // 나한테는 얼렁뚱땅해 봐야 소용없다 It is no use trying to juggle with me. // 얼렁뚱땅하지 말고 정신 차려 일해라 Don't be so sloppy, pay more attention to your work.

얼레 a reel; a spool. ¶~에 실을 감다 spool / reel / wind thread on a reel[spool] // ~에서 실을 풀다 unwind thread from a reel.

얼레빗 a coarse-tooth comb.

얼루기 1 [점] spots; mottles. 2 [얼룩덜룩한 동물] a spotted [dappled / dotted] animal; a piebald; (얼룩덜룩한 고양이) a tabby.

얼룩 1 [반점] spots; mottles; dapples; speckles. ¶~이 있는 spotted / mottled / dapple(d) / speckled (작은 반점의) varicolored / motley / (새·짐승 등이) pied / spotted / brindle(d) (호랑이) // 다갈색 ~이 있는 흰 개 a white dog with brown spots.
2 [자국] a stain; a blot; a smudge; a spot; a blob; a smut; a smear; a blotch. ¶잉크의 ~ a spot of ink / an ink stain[spot] // 비가 샌 ~ a patch of damp // 지워지지 않는 ~ an indelible stain // ~ 빼는 약 a spot remover // ~이 있는 stained / smeared / blotted / spotted // ~이 없는 stainless / spotless / blotless / clean / immaculate // **~이 생기다** become stained[blotted / smudged] // **~을 빼다** take[get] out a stain[blot] / remove stains[blotches] (from) // 그 ~은 아무리 해도[빨아도] 지워지지 않는다 The stain will not come[wash] out.
● **얼룩말** a zebra; a piebald horse. **얼룩소** a brindled ox[cow].

얼룩덜룩하다 spotted; mottled; dapple(d); speckled (잔무늬가); variegated; varicolored; parti-colored; motley; (새·짐승 등이) pied; brindle(d)(호랑이) 무늬처럼. ¶얼룩덜룩한 옷감 varicolored cloth // 얼룩덜룩한 옷을 입은 wearing pied clothing.

얼룩얼룩하다 spotted; mottled. ⇨ *얼룩덜룩하다

얼룩지다 become stained[smudged]; stain; take a stain. ¶얼룩진 stained / spotted / blotted / smeared // 얼룩지게 하다 stain / blot / smear / smudge // 이 옷감은 얼룩지기 쉽다 This material spots easily. // 그녀의 얼굴은 눈물로 얼룩져 있었다 Her face was smudged with tears.

얼른 [빨리] quickly; speedily; rapidly; fast; in a hurry; hastily; [즉시] at once; immediately; promptly; in a moment; (미국 구어) straight[right] away. ¶~ 가거라 Go right away. / Go quickly. // ~ 해라 (be) quick! / Hurry up! // ~ 대답해라 Answer promptly. / Give me a prompt answer. // 그녀의 이름이 ~ 떠오르지 않았다 I couldn't think of her name [instantly]. // 그 정도의 일은 ~ 해치울 수 있다 I can do that in no time.

얼리다 [얼게 하다] freeze; refrigerate. ¶생선을 ~ refrigerate[freeze] fish // 물을 ~ freeze water / turn water into ice.

얼마 1 [값] what price; some[a certain] price; [금액] what sum[amount] (of money); some amount. ¶~쯤 깎아 줄 수 있습니까 Can you make any discount? / Can you come down a little? // 이것은 ~입니까 How much is this? / What is the price[charge / fare / fee]? // 그것을 ~에 샀습니까 What [How much] did you pay for it? // 이 사과는 ~요. How do you sell these apples? / How much do you sell your apple for? // 이 핸드백은 ~지요 What price is this handbag? // 모두 ~요. How much is it all (together)? / What do they come up to altogether? / What does the bill amount to? // 그것은 1파운드에 ~입니까 How much is it a pound? // ~에 팔겠습니까 What do you ask for it?
2 [기간] a while; some length of time. ¶~ 전 some time ago // ~ 안 되어 soon / presently / shortly / before (very) long / in a short time / in no time // 있다가 some time after / after a (little) while / later on // 여기 ~ 동안 있겠느냐 How long will you be here? // ~ 후에는 따뜻해지겠지요 It will get warmer after a while. // 그들은 결혼한 지 ~ 되지 않는다 They have not been married long. / They have only recently[just] been married. // 학교가 설립된 지는 ~ 안 된다 It is not (very) long[It is only a short time] since our school was founded.
3 [수량] what number[amount]; a certain number[amount / quantity] (of); some; so much (what); [정도] some degree (of). ¶~

얼마간

안 되는 수입 a meager[slim] income // ~ 되는 학식 a beggarly amount of learning // 내게 돈이 ~ 있다 I have some money with me. // 재고는 ~ 없다 There are not many left. // ~만큼의 돈이 필요한가 How much money do you need? // 이 탱크에는 물이 ~만큼 들어갑니까 How much water does this tank hold? // 지갑 속에는 돈이 ~ 남아 있지 않았다 I did not have much money left in my billfold.
4 (무게·높이 등) what weigh[measure]; some weight[measure]. ¶몸무게가 ~냐 What is your weight? // 그의 키는 ~입니까 How tall is he?
5 [거리] what distance; some distance. ¶여기서 학교까지는 ~ 안 된다 It is but a step from here to the school. // ~ 안 가면 정거장이 있다 The station is not far off.
6 [비율] by. ¶한 시간당[1인당] ~로 at so much an hour[a head] // 이 상품은 한 다스당 ~로 팔린다 These articles are sold by the dozen. // 나는 가이드를 일당 ~로 고용했다 I hired a guide by the day.
7 [일부분] (a) part (of); a portion (of); some (of); something. ¶수입에서 ~를 저축하다 save something from one's income.

얼마든지 as many[much] as one likes; [한없이] without limit; ever so many[much]; [부정문] (not) many[much]. ¶~ 있다 be available as many[much] as one wishes // ~ 가져도 좋다 You may take as much[many] as you like. // 돈은 원하는 대로 ~ 주겠다 I will give you as much money as you want. // 돈이라면 ~ 있다 As for money, we have enough and to spare. // 값은 ~ 좋으니 꼭 구해 주시오 Get it for me, whatever it costs. // 시간은 ~ 있다 I have tons of time.

얼마간(-間) **1** [다소] some; somewhat; a little; more or less; to some extent; in some degree; [일부분] partly; in part. ¶~의 돈 a certain sum of money / some money // 그는 내 생각을 ~ 이해하고 있다 He understands my thinking to some extent. // 오늘은 기분이 ~ 낫다 I feel a little better today. **2** [얼마 동안] for some time (to come); some time; for a while[time]. ¶~만 더 기다려 주십시오 Kindly wait a little longer. // 그는 친구 집에서 ~ 묵을 생각으로 찾아갔다 He visited his friend for some stay.

얼마나 1 [값] how much; what; [수량] how many[much]. ¶그 양복은 ~ 주었습니까 How much[What] did the coat cost you? / What did you give for your coat? // 돈 가진 게 ~ 되지 How[How much] money have you got with you? // 하루에 담배를 ~ 피우십니까 How many cigarettes do you smoke a day? // 이 도서관에 책이 ~ 있는지 모르겠다 I don't know how many books this library has.
2 [정도·동안] how (large, deep, high, wide, thick, far, long, old, etc.); how much. ¶당신의 체중은 ~ 됩니까 How much do you weigh? / What is your weight? // 에베레스트산의 높이는 ~ 됩니까 How high is Mt. Everest? / What is the height of Mt. Everest? // 그 호수의 깊이는 ~ 됩니까 How deep is the lake? // 이 상자의 무게는 ~ 됩니까 How heavy is the box? / What is the weight of the box? // ~ 기다리셨습니까 How long have you waited? // 그는 나이가 ~ 되었을까 How old might he be? // 한국에 오신 지 ~ 됩니까 How long have you been in Korea? // 정거장에서 버스로 ~ 갑니까 How far is it by bus from the station?
3 [감탄] how; how much; to what extent; what. ¶그녀의 노래가 ~ 감미로운지 너는 모를 게다 You have no idea (as to) how sweetly she sings. // 우리가 ~ 걱정했는지 너는 모른다 You don't know how much we worried[how worried we were] about you. // 나는 영숙 씨에게 내가 그녀를 ~ 사랑하는지를 고백했다 I told Yeongsuk how deeply I loved her. // ~ 슬펐겠는가 How sad he must have been!

얼마(만)큼 [어느 정도] to some[a certain] degree[extent]; up to a certain point; how; to what extent[amount]. ¶너도 그 일에는 ~ 책임이 있다 You are also more or less responsible for the matter. // 그를 ~ 신용할 수 있을지 나로서는 모르겠다 I hardly know to what extent he can be trusted.

얼버무리다 1 (말을) speak ambiguously; say something ambiguous; equivocate; prevaricate; shuffle; quibble; palter; dodge; do not commit oneself; gloss over[cover up] (one's fault). ¶대답을 ~ equivocate in replying / give an evasive[a vague / a noncommittal] answer // 농담으로 ~ turn (a matter) off with a joke // 그는 논쟁의 요점을 얼버무렸다 He dodged[evaded] the main point of the argument. **2** (음식을) swallow without chewing well; bolt (one's food). **3** [대충 버무리다] roughly mix.

얼보다 have a vague[an incorrect] view (of); see dimly[incorrectly].

얼보이다 [흐릿하게 보이다] be seen dimly [vaguely / indistinctly]; be blurred; [바로 보이지 않다] be seen incorrectly[distortedly]. ¶얼굴이 얼보이는 거울 a mirror which distorts one's features.

얼부풀다 [얼어서 부풀어 오르다] swell with cold.

얼빠지다 be abstracted[stupefied] (with fear); be dazed[stunned] (by the news); be absent-minded; be absent in one's mind; look blank. ¶얼빠진 abstracted / absent-minded / blank / [바보스러운] stupid / silly / foolish / fatuous / softheaded // 얼빠진 사람 a dunce / a lackwit / a bonehead / (미국 속어) a moony face // 얼빠진 짓 a foolish act / foolery // 얼빠진 듯이 바라보다 look with an abstracted gaze // 슬픔으로 ~ be stupefied with grief // 그런 짓을 하다니 너도 얼빠졌군 How stupid of you to do such a thing!

얼싸 [흥겨워 내는 소리] Yippee!; Whoopee!; Goody-goody!; Oh boy!; Hurray! ¶~ 좋구나 Yippee-hurray!

얼싸안다 embrace; hug; give (a person) a hug; hold[take] (a person) in one's arms; clasp to one's bosom[breast]. ¶서로 ~ embrace[hug] each other / go into each other's arms // 목을 ~ throw[lock / fold] one's arms around[about] another's neck // 그들은 얼싸안고 울었다 The two threw themselves into each other's arms and wept.

얼씨구 Whoopee!; Yippee!; Hurrah!; Hurray!; Oh boy!; Goody-goody! ¶~ 잘한다 Well done! / Capital! / Good for you!

얼씬거리다 make frequent appearances; frequent; haunt; hang[hover] around. ¶왜

근처에서 얼씬거리느냐 What are you hanging around here for anyway?//그는 이제 우리 집에 얼씬거리지도 않는다 He no longer calls on us at all.
얼씬 못 하다 dare not come round[show up]; cannot appear before (a person's) eyes at all. ¶집에 얼씬 못 하게 하다 forbid (a person's) access to the house / turn (a person) from one's doors//그는 감히 다시는 내 집에 얼씬 못 할 것이다 He will never dare to enter my house again.
얼씬얼씬 loiteringly; loafing[hanging] around. **얼씬얼씬하다** make frequent appearances. ⇨ ゚얼씬거리다
얼씬하다 appear briefly; make one's appearance; put in an appearance; show oneself; show[turn] up. ¶얼씬하지 않다 do not appear at all//그는 요새 얼씬하지도 않는다 I have seen nothing of him lately.
얼어붙다 freeze (on) to (something); be frozen fast[hard] (to). ¶얼어붙은 길[파이프] a frozen road[pipe] // 얼어붙은 호수 an ice-covered[a frozen] lake//꽁꽁[온통] 얼어붙은 연못[강] a pond[river] frozen hard[all over] //강이 얼어붙었다 The river is frozen over.// 수도꼭지가 얼어붙었다 The faucet froze.//배가 호상에 얼어붙어 있었다 The boat was frozen fast to the ice on (the surface of) the lake.
얼얼하다 1 (매워서) hot; burning; pungent; piquant; biting; stinging. ¶혀가 ~ My tongue smarts[stings / burns] // 매워서 입안이 ~ It makes my mouth burn.//고추를 먹었더니 입 안이 ~ My mouth is burning from the red pepper. 2 (상처가) smart; tingling; prickly. ¶얼얼하게 아프다 have a tingling pain / smart with pain//햇볕에 타서 등이 ~ My sunburnt back smarts[tingles].
얼음 ice. ¶~ 같은[~같이 찬] icelike / icy / ice-[icy-]cold // ~을 넣은 위스키 whisky on the rocks // ~이 얼다 be frozen (over) // ~이 되다 turn[be frozen] into ice // ~에 채우다 ice / put (beer) on (the) ice / cool (a thing) with ice // 맥주를 ~에 채우다 ice beer / cool beer with[on] ice // 생선을 ~에 pack fish in ice // ~을 지치다 skate on the ice / skate // ~을 깨다 crush ice / break[crack] ice // (배 등이) ~에 갇히다 be locked by ice / be icebound // ~으로 뒤덮이다 be covered with ice / be ice[frozen] over // ~이 갈라졌다 [금이 갔다] The ice broke[cracked]. // ~이 녹는다 The ice melts (away)[thaws]. // 맥주는 ~에 채워 두었습니다 The beer is on the ice.
얼음(이) 박이다 [동상에 걸리다] (사람이) be [get] frostbitten; get[have] chilblains (on one's hand); (국부가) be affected with chilblains; become frostbitten. ¶얼음 박인 발가락 frostbitten toes//귀에 ~ get one's ears frostbitten.
●**얼음과자** ices; (영) icelolly; (미) popsicle; [아이스 캔디] a bar of sherbet (on a stick). **얼음덩이** a block[lump] of ice(큰 덩이). ¶잘게 깬 ~ cracked[chipped] ice / chips of ice. **얼음물** [냉수] iced water; (미) ice water. **얼음장** a layer [coat] of ice; a block[piece/sheet] of ice. ¶ ~ 같다 be (as) cold as ice // 방바닥이 ~ 같다 The floor is as cold as ice. **얼음판** an icy [iced] ground; the ice. ¶~에서 미끄러지다 slip and fall on the ice.

얼쩍지근하다 1 [살이 얼얼하게 아프다] tingling; burning; smarting; pricking; prickling. ¶따귀를 맞아서 빰이 얼쩍지근했다 My cheek smarted from the slap. 2 [맵다] somewhat hot[pungent / biting / stinging]; a bit spicy.
얼쩡거리다 cajole; loaf around idly. ⇨ ゚알짱거리다
얼추 [거의] nearly; almost; practically; wellnigh; [대충] for the most part. ¶일이 ~ 끝났다 The work is practically finished.//그 편지를 ~ 훑어봤다 I glanced (my eyes) over the letter. / I ran my eyes over the letter.//그 수는 ~ 보아 40~50을 넘지 않았다 The number did not exceed, roughly speaking, 40 or 50.
얼추잡다 estimate roughly; make a rough estimate (of); (계획 등을) make a draft; lay an outline; sketch up. ¶비용을 ~ make a rough estimate of the expense (for)//방문객 수는 얼추잡아 1,000명가량이다 The number of visitors is roughly estimated at 1,000.
얼치기 something half-and-half an in-between. ¶~로 일을 하다 do (something) by halves / leave (something) half-done.
얼크러지다 get[become] entangled[involved / complicated / messed up]. ¶얼크러진 실을 풀다 untie entangled knots / unravel a (tangled) thread // 실이 얼크러졌다 The thread has got entangled. / The thread was raveled.
얼큰하다 rather hot; mellow. ⇨ ゚얼근하다
얼키설키 in a disorderly way. ⇨ ゚얼기설기
얼토당토아니하다 [당찮다] unreasonable; absurd; preposterous; nonsensical; [관계없다] irrelative; irrelevant; wide of the mark [purpose]. ¶얼토당토아니한 질문 questions irrelative to the subject // 얼토당토아니한 요구 an unreasonable[a preposterous] demand // 얼토당토아니한 이야기 Nothing could be farther from the truth.//얼토당토아니한 이유로 해고당했다 I was dismissed for reasons not grounded on fact.
얼핏 ¶~ 보고 at a cursory glance // ~ 보다 glance at (a thing) / take a quick glance [look] at (a thing)//~ 보이다 get[catch] a glimpse.
읽다[1] 1 (얼굴이) be pitted (with the smallpox); be[get] pockmarked. ¶읽은 자리 smallpox marks / pockmarks / pocks//얼굴이 읽은 남자 a pockmarked man / a man with a pitted face. 2 (물건의 표면이) be uneven[rugged / jagged / ragged].
읽다[2] 1 [묶다] tie[fasten] up; bind. ¶새끼로 ~ bind (a thing) with a rope//짐을 ~ tie [fasten] up a parcel. 2 [없는 일을 꾸미다] fabricate; frame[make] up.
읽매다 tie up; bind. ⇨ ゚얽어매다 ¶꽁꽁 ~ tie fast[hard] // 규칙으로 ~ restrict (a person) by rule.
읽매이다 [묶이다] be bound; [속박 받다] be restricted[restrained / tied down / bound]; [분주하다] be busy with; be occupied with; be engrossed in. ¶관습에 얽매이지 않는 사람 a man unbound to custom//아이들 일에 ~ be taken up with the care of children // 가사에 ~ be occupied with household duties // 규칙에 ~ be bound by a rule / be screwed down to a rule // 인습에 ~ be tied to[bound by] tradition / be fettered by convention / be a slave to convention // 시간에 ~ be restrict-

얽어매다 ed by time.

얽어매다 tie up; bind; fasten; truss. ¶한데 ~ tie (things) into a bundle// 두 발을 ~ tie (a person's) feet together.

얽히다 1 [감기다] get twisted (a)round; coil around; [뒤얽히다] get entangled. ¶덩굴이 얽힌 나무 a tree entwined with vines// 얽히게 하다 intertwine / interlace / entangle / enwind / interlock (with)// 그 문제가 아주 복잡하게 얽혀 버렸다 The matter has become quite complicated. 2 [연루되다] be involved in; [관련되다] be related (to). ¶그것에 얽힌 전설 the legend that has grown up [been woven] around it// 그의 실종에 얽힌 수수께끼 the mystery surrounding his disappearance.

엄격하다(嚴格-) strict; stern; severe; rigorous; austere.(▶ strict는 규율이나 의무 수행을 요구함. stern은 표정이나 태도에도 타협하지 않는 기분이 나타나 있음을 뜻함. severe는 가혹하리만큼 엄함) ¶엄격한 아버지 a stern [strict] father// 엄격한 훈육 strict [rigid] discipline// 엄격한 규칙 a strict rule// 엄격한 검사 a close inspection// 그는 아이들에 대하여 ~ He is strict with his children. // 그녀는 엄격한 가정에서 자랐다 She was brought up in a stern family. **엄격히** strictly; sternly; rigorously; severely. ¶~ 말하면 strictly speaking.

엄금(嚴禁) strict prohibition; a ban; an interdict. ¶흡연 ~ No smoking. // 무용자 출입 ~ No admission except on business. // 소변 ~ Commit no nuisance. // 화기 ~ Inflammable. / Use of fire strictly prohibited. **엄금하다** prohibit [forbid] strictly; interdict; place (a thing) under a ban; taboo. ¶외출을 ~ strictly [rigidly] forbid (a person) to go out// 총장은 학교 구내에서의 학생의 음주를 엄금했다 The president strictly prohibited the students from drinking on the school grounds.

엄니 a tusk(코끼리·멧돼지 등의); a fang(개 등의). ¶~를 드러내다 bare [show] one's fangs.

엄단하다(嚴斷-) take stern legal action (against).

엄달하다(嚴達-) give [issue] strict orders [instructions].

엄동(嚴冬) a rigorous [severe / hard] winter; the depth of winter.
● **엄동설한** (in) a hard snowy winter.

엄두 the very thought (of doing something); daring. ¶~를 못 내다 cannot even conceive the idea of (doing) / be hardly thinkable // 그와 이야기한다는 것은 아무도 ~를 못 냈다 No one dared to speak with him. // 저항 따위는 ~도 못 낼 일이다 Resistance is inconceivable [out of the question].

엄마 〈소아〉 ma(m)ma; (미) mommy; mom; (영) mummy; mum. ⇨어머니1

엄명(嚴命) a strict order [command]; stringent directions; rigid instructions. ¶사령관의 ~에 따라 under strict orders from a commander. **엄명하다** give a strict order [command] (that ...); strictly order (to do).

엄밀하다(嚴密-) strict; precise; close; rigid; strictly confidential. ¶엄밀한 의미에서 in the strict sense of the word// 엄밀한 조사 [검사] 를 하다 make a close [rigid] investigation [examination] / investigate (a matter) closely. **엄밀히** strictly; exactly; closely;

rigidly. ¶~ 말하자면 strictly speaking // ~ 구별하다 make a clear-cut distinction (between).

엄벌(嚴罰) a severe [heavy] punishment. ¶~에 처하다 punish (a person) severely / inflict a severe [harsh] punishment on (a person) // 그는 ~을 받아 마땅하다 He deserves a severe punishment. **엄벌하다** punish (a person) severely; deal severely with (a person).

엄벙덤벙 at random; sloppily; rashly; recklessly; carelessly; frivolously; blindly; thoughtlessly. **엄벙덤벙하다** act thoughtlessly [rashly]; go at it half-heartedly; be frivolous.

엄벙하다 1 [떠벌리다] inflated; [애매하다] ambiguous; evasive. ¶엄벙하게 말하다 speak ambiguously [evasively] / quibble. 2 [일을 어름어름하다] sloppy; slipshod; slack (in one's work). ¶일을 엄벙하게 하다 do a doubtful job of it.

엄부(嚴父) (엄격한) a stern [strict] father.

엄살 exaggeration [pretension] of pain [hardship]; a big fuss; feigned [overdone] dismay. ¶~을 부리다 exaggerate [pretend] pain [hardship] / make a (great) fuss (about trifles) // 무섭다고 ~ 부리다 simulate fear // 그만한 상처를 가지고 ~을 부리다니 What a fuss about such a scratch! **엄살하다** be a fusspot; be a crybaby.
● **엄살꾸러기** a fussy person; a fusser; a crybaby.

엄선(嚴選) careful selection. **엄선하다** select carefully. ¶엄선한 결과 미스 서울로 신경숙양이 뽑혔다 After careful screening, (miss) Sin Gyeongsuk was chosen as Miss Seoul.// 그는 그 임무를 위해 제 손으로 5명을 엄선했다 He handpicked five men for the mission.

엄수(嚴守) strict observance [observation]; rigid adherence (to rules). **엄수하다** observe [keep] strictly; rigidly adhere to. ¶규칙을 ~ observe a regulation strictly / adhere rigidly to the rules // 그는 항상 시간을 엄수한다 He is always punctual (to the minute).

엄수하다(嚴修-) conduct [hold] (a funeral service, etc.) solemnly; duly perform (a funeral service, etc.).

엄숙하다(嚴肅-) solemn; serious; grave. ¶엄숙한 표정 a stern [grave] look // 그는 엄숙한 표정을 지었다 He put on a solemn [grave] look. **엄숙히** gravely; with a dignified [majestic] air; in a dignified manner; [엄하게] sternly. ¶식은 ~ 거행되었다 The ceremony was performed solemnly.

엄습(掩襲) a surprise [sudden] attack; a surprise. ¶폭풍우의 ~을 받다 be visited by a storm / be caught in a storm. **엄습하다** make a sudden [surprise] attack; take (the enemy) by surprise; (감정이 사람을) come over; take (possession of); (재난 등이) visit; strike (down); sweep; hit. ¶공포감이 ~ be seized with fear // 갑자기 추위가 엄습해 왔다 The cold weather took the people by surprise.
➔ ¶**엄습당하다** be attacked unawares / be taken by surprise.

엄연하다(儼然-) solemn; grave; real; actual; undeniable. ¶엄연한 태도를 취하다 assume a grave air [attitude] // 그것은 엄연한 사실이다 It is an undeniable [a real / a hard] fact.

엄연히 solemnly; gravely; actually. ¶영혼은 ~ 존재한다고 믿는다 I believe that souls actually exist.// 이 도덕률은 지금도 ~ 존재한다 This moral law is still in full force.

엄정하다(嚴正-) exact; strict; fair; impartial; unprejudiced. ¶엄정한 법률 a rigid law. **엄정히** strictly; rigorously; fairly; impartially. ¶~ 다루다 deal with (an affair) in strict fairness.

엄존(嚴存) real existence. **엄존하다** (사실이) (really) exist; (법률이) be in full force. ¶엄존하는 사실 a stern reality // 그 법률은 아직도 엄존한다 The law is still in full force.

엄중하다(嚴重-) strict; stringent; severe; stern; rigorous; rigid; close. ¶엄중한 검사 a severe [close] inspection // 엄중한 경계(ا) strict [close] watch. **엄중히** strictly; severely; sternly; rigorously; rigidly; closely. ¶남을 ~ 감시하다 keep (a person) under close guard [watch] // 그와 같은 자는 ~ 처벌해야 한다 Such a person should be punished severely.

엄지 [엄지가락] the thumb; the big finger [toe]; the first digit.
● **엄지발가락** the big [great] toe. **엄지손가락** the thumb; the big finger.

엄징(嚴懲) severe punishment. **엄징하다** chastise [punish] (a person) severely; inflict a severe punishment (on a person).

엄책(嚴責) a severe [stern] reprimand; a bitter [harsh] criticism. **엄책하다** reprimand [rebuke / reprove] severely [harshly]; give (a person) a sharp punishment.

엄처시하(嚴妻侍下) petticoat government; a henpecked husband. ¶~의 남편 a henpecked [submissive] husband / a man tied to his wife's apron strings // ~이다 be tied to one's wife's apron strings / be a henpecked husband.

엄청나다 exorbitant; preposterous; extraordinary; extravagant; excessive; absurd. ¶엄청나게 awfully / terribly / absurdly / exorbitantly / excessively / extravagantly / extraordinarily // 엄청난 인파 a tremendous crowd of people // 엄청난 소동이 일어났다 There was an incredible [unbelievable] fuss. // 엄청나게 비싸군 How shockingly expensive! // 그가 살인과 같은 엄청난 짓을 할 리가 없다 He cannot have committed such a monstrous [dreadful] crime as murder. // 엄청난 실수를 하고 말았다 I made a big [an awful] blunder.

엄친(嚴親) a stern [strict] father; (자기의) one's own father.

엄폐(掩蔽) hiding; concealment; cover; [천] occultation. **엄폐하다** cover up; screen; mask; conceal(꾀를); suppress(사실을); cover [keep] (a fact) dark. ¶범죄의 흔적을 ~ cover up the traces of a crime.
● **엄폐물** a cover; a shelter. **엄폐호**(-壕) a covered trench; an entrenchment; a dugout; a bunker; a shelter.

엄포 (a) bluff; bluffing; (a) treat; intimidation; a menace. ¶~에 지나지 않다 be nothing but a bluff // 그의 ~에 속을 내가 아니다 I won't be taken in by his bluff and bluster.

엄포(를) 놓다 utter (cold) empty threats (against); use empty menaces [threats] (to); bluster (out / forth). ¶엄포를 놓아도 우리에게는 소용없다 It's no use trying to frighten us with big words.

엄하다(嚴-) severe; strict; stern; rigid; austere; rigorous; (가혹하다) hard; harsh; stringent. ¶엄한 규칙 a strict rule // 엄한 훈련 rigorous training // 엄한 단속 tough controls // 엄한 벌 a severe [harsh] punishment // 엄한 표정을 짓다 look stern // 그의 부모는 매우 ~ His parents are quite strict. **엄히** severely; strictly; rigorously; rigidly; sternly. ¶~ 꾸짖다 scold a person severely // (구어) ~하다 tighten one's control over.

엄한(嚴寒) intense [severe] cold; the rigor of winter.

엄형(嚴刑) severe [heavy / harsh] punishment. ¶~에 처해지다 be sentenced to severe punishment.

엄호(掩護) cover(ing); protection. ¶~하에 under cover (of) / backed up (by) // 포병의 ~ 아래 under artillery cover. **엄호하다** cover; protect; shelter; screen. ¶전진할 테니 엄호해 주게 We're going to advance, so give us cover [cover us].
● **엄호 사격** a covering fire; curtain fire.

업(業) 1 an occupation; a calling. ⇨ ⁼직업 2 (법) karma.

업계(業界) business circles [quarters / world]; [특정 산업] the industry; the trade. ¶영화 ~ the movie world // 섬유 ~ the textile industry // ~의 거물 a bigwig [big shot] in the world of business // 존스 씨는 ~의 거물이다 Mr. Jones is a leading figure in the business.
● **업계지**(-紙) a trade paper.

업고(業苦) [불] karmic suffering; the wages of sin.

업그레이드 an upgrade.

업다 1 (등에) carry (a person, a pack, etc.) on the back. ¶아기를 (등에) ~ carry a baby on one's back. 2 [끌고 들어가다] implicate; involve in. ¶그는 죄를 혼자 지지 않고 친구들을 업고 들어갔다 Refusing to take the guilt upon himself alone, he dragged his friends into it too. 3 [연을 빼앗다] grab another person's kite by entangling the two kitestrings. 4 [교미하다] copulate.

업데이트 [데이터 갱신] an update.

업둥이 a foundling foster child.

업로드 an upload.

업무(業務) business (affairs); service; operation; (임무로서의) duties. ¶철도 수송 ~ railroad transportation service // ~용의 for business use [purposes] // ~상의 전화 business calls // ~상의 비밀 trade secrets // ~를 게을리 하다 neglect one's duties // ~에 힘쓰다 attend diligently to one's duties // ~를 방해하다 interfere with a person's work // 나는 ~ 관계로 부산에 갑니다 I'm going to Busan on business.
● **업무 관리** business management [control]. **업무 보고** a report on operation(s); a business [an operational] report. **업무부** the Operation Department; the Business Department. **업무 시간** office [business] hours.

업보(業報) [불] retribution for the deeds of a former life [a previous incarnation]; karma effects.

업신여기다 despise; ignore; slight; make light of; set a naught; look down on [upon]; hold (a person) in contempt. ¶업신여기는 듯한 태도 a contemptuous attitude [air] // 남을 ~

업신여김 treat a person with contempt / hold a person cheap // 그는 언제나 사람을 업신여긴다 He is always looking down on people. // 너는 자신을 하찮은 인간이라고 업신여겨서는 안된다 You shouldn't call yourself worthless and run yourself down.

업신여김 contempt; disdain; slight; scorn; disregard. ¶ ~ 을 당하다[받다] be slighted / be taken lightly / be held in contempt.

업어 치기 [유도] a back[shoulder] throw; throwing over one's shoulder.

업자(業者) [장사꾼] a trader; (집합적) the trader. ¶관계 ~ traders[businessmen / dealers] concerned // (제조업자) makers [manufactures] concerned // 악덕 ~ a crooked dealer // 수출 ~ an exporter // 해운[은행] ~ shipping[banking] interests // ~ 간의 매매[거래] trade sales // 관계 ~ 들을 소집하다 call in traders concerned.

업적(業績) (개인의) work; achievements; results; contributions; (회사 등의) business results. ¶금년도의 ~ (보고서) the results [business report] for this year // 그의 언어학상의 ~ his achievements in linguistics // ~ 을 올리다 produce achievements / achieve results // 금년도의 우리 회사 ~ 은 부진하다 Our business showing this year has been poor.

업종(業種) a category of business; a type of industry.
● **업종별** industrial classification; classification by industry. ¶ ~ 로 according to the type of business // ~ 전화번호부 a telephone directory classified by the type of business.

업체(業體) a (business) enterprise. ¶민간[개인] ~ a private enterprise // 영세 ~ a "hole-in-the-wall" enterprise // 생산[수출] ~ a production[an export] enterprise.

업태(業態) business conditions[status]. ¶금년도 ~ (회사의) the results for this year.
● **업태 보고** (회사의) a business report. **업태 조사** a business conditions survey.

업히다 1 [등에] ride[be carried] on a person's back. ¶어머니에게 업혀 on one's mother's back. **2** [···위에] lie upon another; be piled on another.

없다 1 [존재하지 않다] there is no ...; do not exist. ¶내가 없는 동안에 during my absence / while I am away // 없는 거나 다름없다 be next to nothing // 유령 따위는 ~ Ghost do not exist. / There are no such beings as ghosts. // 대답하는 사람이 없었다 No one answered. // 그래도 없는 것보다는 낫다 It's better than nothing. // 지난 일은 없었던 것으로 하자 Let bygones be bygones. // 그런 약속은 없었던 것으로 해 달라 Forget that there was any such agreement. // 그가 친절하다는 것은 부정할 수 ~ There is no denying that he is kind. // 그 후 그의 모습을 본 사람은 아무도 ~ Nobody has seen him since. // 그가 없으면 우리는 이 계획을 실행할 수 ~ We cannot carry out this plan without him.
2 [갖고 있지 않다] have no ...; be without; [보이지 않다] be missing; cannot be found. ¶돈이 ~ have no money // 할 일이 ~ have nothing to do // 나는 아이[친척]가 ~ I have no children[relatives / kith and kin]. // 나는 흥미가 ~ I'm not interested. // 더 이상 말할 것이 ~ I have nothing more to say. // 내 책이 ~ My book is gone[missing]. // 내 시계가 아무 데도 없었다 I couldn't find my watch anywhere. // 나는 현금이 ~ I don't have any cash. / I've run out of cash. // 시간이 거의 없었다 I had little time.
3 [결어되다] want; lack; be wanting[lacking]. ¶예의가 ~ lack good manners // 용기가 ~ lack[be wanting in] courage // 의리가 ~ fail to carry out one's duty[obligations].
4 [오지 않다]. ¶그로부터는 아직도 전화가 ~ I haven't had a (telephone) call from him yet.(▶ a telephone call은 (영))
5 [다 떨어지다] be exhausted[used up / consumed]; be out of. ¶우물에 물이 ~ The well has run dry. // 나는 용돈이 ~ I have run short of pocket money.
6 (결점 등이) be free[clear] from. ¶결점[잘못]이 ~ be free from faults[mistakes] // 혐의가 ~ be clear from suspicion.
7 [죽고 없다] be deceased[defunct]. ¶아버지가 ~ have no father / one's father is deceased // 그는 이제 가고 ~ Alas! He is no more!
8 [가난하다] poor; needy. ¶없는 사람들 poor // 없는 집에 태어나다 be born poor[in a poor family].
9 [기타]. ¶그가 그렇게 기뻐하는 것을 본 적이 ~ I had never seen him so happy. // 나는 웃을 수밖에 없었다 I could not help laughing. // 어찌할 수 ~ I can't help it.

없애다 1 [제거하다] take off; take away; remove(▶ remove보다 take away 쪽이 보다 (구어)); eliminate; eradicate; get rid of; [삭제하다] leave out; omit; (냄새를) drown[mash] (a smell); (산성·독 등을) counteract (the effects of a medicine); neutralize. ¶장애물을 ~ get rid of hindrances / remove obstacles // 잔디밭의 잡초를 ~ weed the lawn // 불순물을 ~ remove impurities // 공포심을 ~ overcome[get rid of] one's fear // 잡념을 ~ put idle thoughts out of one's mind // 명부에서 이름을 ~ strike (a person's) name off a list // 이 편지를 읽고 나면 없애 버리시오 After you have read this letter, please destroy it. // 주민의 불안을 없애는 일이 가장 중요합니다 The most important thing is to remove[dispel] the anxiety of the inhabitants.
2 [폐지하다] abolish; do away with; cancel; discontinue; put out of existence. ¶나쁜 습을 ~ do away with evil practices.
3 [다 써 버리다] use up; exhaust; run out of; [낭비하다] throw away; spend (wastefully); waste. ¶재산을 ~ run through one's fortune / squander one's fortune // 시간을 ~ waste[spend] time / kill time away.
4 [죽이다] kill; (불법으로) murder; [숙청하다] liquidate; 《미국 속어》 blot (out); erase; put out; make[do] away with; dispatch. ¶없애 버려라 Down with him! / Finish him! // 그는 방해자를 없애 버릴 작정이었다 He was determined to kill[(구어) liquidate] those (who were) in his way.

없어지다 1 [분실되다] be[get] lost; be missing; be gone. ¶금고에서 그 보석이 없어졌다 The jewel is missing[has disappeared] from the safe. // 그는 없어진 책을 찾고 있다 He is looking for his missing[lost] book.
2 [떨어지다] run short[out] (of); run low; give out; be gone; be out; be used up; be exhausted. ¶돈은 곧 없어졌다 The money went quickly. // 9시 반이 지나면 버스가 없어

진다 There is no bus service after nine thirty.
3 [사라지다] disappear; vanish; be gone. ¶나도 모르는 사이에 열이 없어졌다 My fever was gone before I knew it.∥이 약을 먹으니 통증이 없어졌다 This medicine gave me relief. / This medicine took the pain away.∥아픔은 이제 없어졌습니까 Is your pain gone?∥더 이상 기다릴 생각이 없어졌다 I don't feel like waiting any longer.∥이제 우리에게 모든 가능한 수단이 없어졌다 We had exhausted every available means. / We could not think of anything else to try.∥버릇은 한번 들면 좀처럼 없어지지 않는다 A habit is very difficult to get rid of[shake off] once it is formed.

없이 without; sans; minus. ¶휴일도 ~ without holidays∥예외 ~ without exceptions∥할 수 ~ unavoidably / out of sheer necessity∥~ 살다 live in poverty / make a poor living / be badly[poorly] off∥한 푼 되다 become penniless∥생물은 물 ~ 는 살아갈 수 없다 Without water, nothing can live.

엇- [비뚜로·어긋나게·조금] crooked; curved; diagonal; (a)slant; deviate; wrong; crosswise; mutual; almost; not quite.

엇가다 go astray; go contrary to reason; deviate; be perverse. ¶말이 ~ make perverse remarks.

엇각(-角) [수] alternate interior angles.

엇갈리다 (길이) pass[cross] each other; miss each other on the way; (의견 등이) differ (from); disagree (with); [번갈아들다] alternate; take turns. ¶그들은 의견이 서로 엇갈려 있다 They have different[conflicting] opinions[views] (on the matter). / There is a discrepancy in their opinions[views].∥나는 역으로 그를 마중 나갔으나, 우리는 서로 엇갈려 혼자 돌아왔다 I went to the station to meet him, but we crossed each other somewhere and I came home alone.∥내 마음에 희비가 엇갈렸다 Joy and sorrow mingled in my heart.

엇걸다 cross[intersect / cut] (each other); join (things) crosswise. ¶총을 ~ stack [pile] rifles∥국기를 ~ cross[intertwine / entwine] national flags.

엇걸리다 be crossed; lie across; cut[cross] each other; be intersected; intersect.

엇구수하다 (음식이) rather tasty; [이야기가 이치에 그럴듯하다] palatable (to); plausible.

엇깎다 shave [sharpen] aslant[obliquely].

엇나가다 1 (줄 등이) stray (from); deviate [swerve] (from a course); (일이) go crisscross; go awry[wrong]. ¶오늘은 만사가 엇나가는 날인 모양이다 Everything appears to go wrong[amiss] today. **2** (행동이) deviate[go away] from the right path; go astray[wild]; get on the loose. ¶그들은 대도시의 화려한 생활에 현혹되어 엇나갔다 They were led astray by the big city and bright lights.

엇대다 **1** [어긋나게 대다] put[fix / join / place] crosswise[askew / cockeyed]. ¶반창고를 ~ apply a sticking plaster (to the wound) crosswise. **2** [비꼬아 빈정거리다] make an insinuating remark (at); give an indirect cut; make an oblique[a sly] hint (at).

엇뜨다 squint (at); leer (at).

엇먹다 **1** [비꼬다] have a sly dig (at); give an indirect cut; make an oblique[a sly] hint (at). **2** [톱날이 어슷하게 먹다] (a blade) cut at an angle; cut crooked.

엇메다 sling (a wallet, a rifle, etc.) over the shoulder and across the breast; carry (a bag) at the side by a shoulder belt.

엇바꾸다 exchange (one thing) for (another); exchange[interchange / swap] (hats).

엇베다 cut (off) aslant[obliquely]; bevel; make an oblique cut. ¶천을 ~ cut cloth (on the) bias.

엇보(-保) [서로 서는 빚보증] (stand) mutual guarantee[security / suretyship].

엇비뚜름하다 crooked a bit on one side; askew a bit.

엇비슷하다 similar; like; kindred; akin (to); analogous; (서술적) be much[nearly] the same; be about and about. ¶두 사람의 실력은 ~ They are even in ability. / Their abilities are about the same.∥엇비슷하게 알아맞혔다 That isn't far off the mark. / (알아맞히기에서) You're (getting) warm.∥그와 나는 키가 ~ He is about as tall as I am.

엇섞다 mix[blend / mingle] in alternation.

엇셈 striking; a balance; an offset; a setoff. **엇셈하다** strike a balance; balance; cancel debts to each other; offset.

엇송아지 a young ox; a calf.

-었자 even if[though] .... ⇨-았자

엉거주춤하다 **1** [몸을 반쯤 굽히고 있다] half-sit; half-rise. ¶엉거주춤한 자세로 in a half-sitting posture / half-sitting [-rising]∥그런 엉거주춤한 자세로 때리면 공이 날아가지를 않아요 (야구·골프 등에서) The ball won't fly far if you hit it with your rear stuck out like that. **2** [망설이다] hesitate (to do); waver. ¶엉거주춤하는 사람 a man on the fence∥그 시장은 엉거주춤한 태도로 답변했다 The mayor answered irresolutely [without confidence].

엉겁결에 in the confusion of the moment; in a moment of bewilderment.

엉겅퀴 [식] a thistle.

엉금엉금 (아기가) crawling; creeping; sprawling. ¶~ 기어가다 creep [crawl] about / go on all fours / crawl about on hands and knees.

엉기다 **1** [응결하다] coagulate (피 등이); curdle(우유 등이); congeal; solidify; condense; clot. ¶엉긴 피 a clot of blood / coagulated [clotted / curdled] blood / grume / gore. **2** [일을 뭉개다] be slow at one's work; busy oneself ineffectively; putter. **3** [얽히다] be all tangled up.

엉기정기 in disorder; pell-mell; higgledy-piggledy; promiscuously.

엉덩방아 a fall on one's backside[behind / buttocks]; (미국 구어) a prat(t)fall. ¶~를 찧다 fall on one's buttocks / land on one's rear end∥의자에 앉다가 잘못하여 ~를 찧었다 I missed the chair and sat right down on the floor.

엉덩이 [불기] the buttocks; (구어) the bottom; (구어) the butt; the rear; (속어) the ass; (구어) the behind; [골반 좌우로 내민 부분] the hips(▶ a hip은 한쪽을 가리킴); (동물의) the rump. ¶~가 가볍다 do not stay long (in a place) / frequently change (one's business) / be a rolling stone∥~를 흔들다 swing [wag] one's hips[behind]∥그녀의 ~는 크다 She is big in the hips. / She has broad hips

엉덩춤
[is broad-hipped].
엉덩이가 무겁다 〔게으르다〕 be lazy; be indolent; 〔오래 있다〕 stay too long; outstay one's welcome.
●**엉덩잇짓** swinging one's hips; hip-swinging; (꿀벌의) a tail-wagging dance. ¶~을 하다 swing one's hips.
엉덩춤 hip dancing; a hip dance.
엉뚱하다 〔건방지다〕 pert; saucy; impertinent; impudent; forward; 〔다르다〕 different; wrong (direction); 〔뜻밖이다〕 unexpected; strange; 〔무관하다〕 irrelevant; irrelative; 〔사리에 안 맞다〕 inconsistent; incoherent; absurd; 〔무모하다〕 wild; extravagant. ¶엉뚱한 질문을 하다 ask[(구어) pop] an unexpected question∥그 이야기는 아주 엉뚱하므로 믿어지지 않는다 The story is too wild [fantastic] to believe.∥그 아이는 엉뚱한 짓을 잘한다 That child does wild[strange / startling / unexpected] things.∥그들은 서로 엉뚱한 주장을 계속하고 있었다 They kept arguing at cross-purposes.∥그는 엉뚱한 대답을 했다 His answer was far off the mark.
엉망 a mess; (in) bad shape; a ruin; a wreck. ¶~을 만들다 make a mess of it∥큰비가 와서 길이 ~이다 The road is very bad after a heavy rain.∥방이 ~입니다 My room is in a mess[in disorder].∥그는 시험을 ~으로 치렀다 He did very poorly[badly] in[(미) on] the examination. / He did miserably on the examination.∥그의 갑작스런 죽음으로 모든 것이 ~이 되었다 His sudden death threw everything into confusion.∥폭발 사고 현장은 ~이었다 The scene of the explosion (accident) was in turmoil.∥그의 부주의 탓으로 계획이 ~이 되었다 His carelessness messed up[made a mess of] the plan.
엉성하다 1 〔꼭 짜이지 못하다〕 loose; careless; slipshod; slovenly; imperfect; faulty. ¶엉성한 번역[문체] a loose translation[style]∥이 사전은 편집이 ~ This dictionary is carelessly compiled. **엉성히** loosely. ¶이 계획은 ~ 짜여져 있다 This plan is not precise enough[faulty].
2 〔성기다〕 loose; sparse; large (mesh). ¶엉성한 그물 a net of large meshes. **엉성히** loosely; sparsely
3 〔마르다〕 lean; haggard; scraggy; angular; gaunt; starveling. ¶엉성한 사람 a skinny [lean] person / a (living) skeleton / a bag of bones / a man of skin and bones∥가지만 엉성한 나무 a bare[leafless] tree. **엉성히** leanly; haggardly; gauntly.
엉엉 ¶~ 울다 cry[weep] bitterly / cry one's heart out.
엉클다 tangle; entangle. ⇨형클다 ¶실뭉치를 ~ make a tangle of a ball of yarn / tangle a ball of twine.
엉클어지다 tangle; get[become] tangled. ⇨형클어지다
엉큼성큼 with long[big / large / great] steps [strides]. ¶~ 걸어가다 stride (along) / take large steps[strides].
엉큼하다 wily; insidious; treacherous; deep; subtle; sly. ¶엉큼한 사람 an insidious man / (속어) a deep one∥엉큼한 생각[속셈] a wily scheme∥엉큼한 눈짓[미소] a treacherous glance[smile].
엉키다 tangle; get[become] tangled. ⇨형클어지다

엉터리 1 〔미덥지 못한 사람〕 a fake; a quack; a sham; a gyp; 〔허울만 좋은 물건〕 a gimcrack; a gewgaw; a trumpery. ¶~ 의사 a quack∥~ 회사 a bogus company∥~ 영수증 a counterfeit[forged] receipt∥그것은 틀림없이 ~다 I'm sure it's a fake.∥그것은 전부 ~였다 It was all nonsense. / There wasn't an ounce of truth in it. 2 〔대강의 윤곽〕 an outline; a sketch. ¶일의 ~를 잡다[알다] grasp the general idea[outline] of a job.
엉터리없다 contrary to reason. ¶엉터리없는 사람 an irresponsible man∥엉터리없는 말을 하다 talk nonsense / talk irresponsibly.
엊그제 〔며칠 전〕 a few days ago.
엊그제 a few days ago. ⇨엊그저께
엊저녁 last night; yesterday[last] evening.
엎다 turn over; turn down; lay (a thing) face down; lay (a thing) upside down; overthrow; undermine; subvert. ¶컵을 엎어 놓다 set a glass bottom up[upside down]∥현 정부를 ~ overthrow[subvert] the present government.
엎드러지다 fall on one's breast[nose]; fall down. ¶돌에 걸려 ~ fall[tumble] over a stone.
엎드려쏴 〔군〕 Firing from a prone[lying-down] position.; Prone fire.
엎드리다 lie on one's face; lie (with one's) face down[downward]; lie[be] prone[face on]; throw oneself flat (on one's stomach). ¶엎드려 팔 굽혀 펴기 push-up∥그녀는 엎드려 자고 있었다 She was sleeping on her stomach[in a prone position].∥그녀는 내 발 아래 엎드려 용서를 빌었다 She throw herself at my feet and begged my pardon.
엎어누르다 press down; keep[hold / pin] (a person) down.
엎어지다 1 〔앞으로 넘어지다〕 fall on one's breast[nose / face]; fall down. ¶마루바닥에 ~ fall down on the floor. 2 〔위아래가 뒤집히다〕 be turned over[be turned upside down]; (배 등이) keel[heel] over; turn turtle; capsize. ¶꽃병이 엎어졌다 The vase has been upset.∥배가 엎어져서 세 사람이 익사했다 The boat capsized and three men were drowned.
엎어지면 코 닿을 데 a spitting distance; a stone's throw[cast]. ¶우리 집에서 ~ 우체국이 있었다 There was a post office close to[at a stone's throw from] my house.
엎지르다 spill; slop. ¶마루에 물을 ~ spill water on the floor.
엎지른 물 Spilt water cannot be gathered again.; What is done cannot be undone.; It is no use crying over spilt milk.
엎치다 turn over; turn down. ⇨=엎다
엎친 데 덮치다 Misfortunes never come singly.; Throwing good money after bad.; Out of the frying pan and into the fire. ¶이건 마치 엎친 데 덮친 격이다 This is like being kicked when I'm already down. / It is like having salt rubbed into a wound.∥엎친 데 덮치듯이 불행한 일이 그에게 닥쳤다 Misfortune afflicted[(문어) befell] him one after another.
엎치락뒤치락하다 1 〔전전반측하다〕 toss [roll / thrash] about (in bed); (의)jactitate. ¶그는 머리가 아파서 엎치락뒤치락하고 있었다 He lay turning from side to side, his head aching. 2 〔일진일퇴하다〕 seesaw. ¶엎치락뒤

치락하는 경주[게임] a seesaw[dingdong] race[game / match]∥엎치락뒤치락한 끝에 우리 팀이 승리를 거두었다 Our team won the day after the lead had changed hands time and time again.

에[1] **1** [못마땅할 때 내는 소리] oh; fie; what a .... ¶~ 보기 싫어 Fie, for shame!∥~ 귀찮아 What a nuisance! / Oh, bother it! **2** [뒷말이 나오지 않아 뜸을 들일 때 내는 소리] well; let me see; er-; er-hum-er.

에[2] **1** [처소] at; in. ¶문~ 서 있다 stand at the door / stand in the doorway∥창가~ 서 있다 stand by the window∥다방~만 드나들다 do nothing but frequent tea houses∥왼손~만 장갑을 끼고 있다 have a glove only on the left hand∥군~ 가 있다 be in the army∥나는 지금 백부님 집~ 머물고 있다 I am staying at my uncle's[with my uncle].∥누님은 부산~ 산다 My sister lives in Busan.∥종이~ 이름을 쓰시오 Write your name on the paper.∥그는 벽~ 몸을 기대었다 He leaned against the wall.
2 [방향] [목적지] to; for. ¶싸움터~ 나가다 go to the front∥내일 부산~ 간다 Tomorrow I am going to Busan.∥그는 제주도~ 갔다 He left for Jejudo.∥언제 당신은 집~ 도착할 것인가요 When will you get home?
3 [때] at; on; in(▶ 일반적으로 시각은 at, 날은 on, 달·해·시대는 in을 씀). ¶1시~ at one (o'clock) / 정오[새벽]~ at noon[dawn] / 오전 중[아침]~ in the morning / 한밤중~ in the middle of the night∥3월~ in March∥2002년~ in (the year) 2002∥7월 2일 아침~ on the morning of[in the morning on] the second of July∥일요일~ on Sunday∥만년~ in one's later[last] years∥고대[현대]~ in ancient[modern] times∥그는 3년 후~ 돌아올 예정이다 He is due to return home in three years[in three years' time].∥그는 10세~ 소나타를 작곡했다 He composed a sonata at (the age of) ten.∥그는 10대[30대]~ 장사를 시작했다 He set up a business in his teens[thirties].
4 [단위·비율] at; to; in; for; per; by. ¶한 벌의 양복을 8만 원~ 팔다 sell a suit at[for] eighty thousand won∥싼값~ at a low price / (buy an article) cheap∥비싼 값~ at a high price / (buy an article) dear∥스웨터를 5,000원~ 샀다 I bought a sweater for five thousand won.∥이 잡지는 1년~ 4번 발행된다 This magazine is issued four times a [per] year.∥사과는 5개~ 2,000원이었다 I paid two thousand won for five apples.∥이 고기는 600그램~ 9,000원이었다 The meat cost nine thousand won per[for] six hundred grams.∥한 사람~ 한 다스씩 연필을 가지고 있었다 We each had a dozen pencils.
5 [비교·관계] for; to; in; with; of; on. ¶건강~ 좋다 be good for (the[one's]) health / be beneficial to health∥질문~ 대답하다 answer[reply to] a question∥그는 형~ 비하면 키가 작다 Compared with his brother, he is rather short.∥그는 그 사건~ 관련되어 있다 He is connected[has something to do] with that incident.
6 [이유·원인] for; with; of; from; in; because of. ¶더위~ 시달리다 suffer from heat∥그들은 추위~ 떨었다 They shivered with cold.∥그녀는 수치심 때문~ 얼굴을 붉혔다 She blushed for shame.
7 [첨가] to; in; at; on. ¶10~ 3을 더하다 add three to ten∥홍차~ 설탕을 더 넣어라 Put more sugar in the tea.
8 [수단] with; on; in; to. ¶물~ 담그다 soak [put / immerse] in water∥젖은 셔츠를 불~ 말렸다 I dried my wet shirt by[over / in front of] the fire.
9 [표준] by; to; at; [기준] on. ¶시계를 시보~ 맞추다 set[time / synchronize] a watch by the timecast∥값은 크기~ 따라 다르다 The price varies with the size.
10 [작용의 원인] by; with; under; in. ¶바늘~ 찔리다 be pricked with a needle∥돌~ 맞다 be struck by a stone∥비~ 젖다 get wet with rain∥눈~ 덮이다 be covered with snow∥총(알)~ 맞다 be hit by a bullet / get [receive] a bullet (in one's arm).
11 [대조] on; against; with; and; in contrast (with). ¶청색 바탕~ 금빛 글자 gold characters on a blue ground.
12 [열거] and (the like). ¶술~ 고기~ 잘 먹었다 I have had enough drinks, meat and the like.

에게 to; for; with; by(피동); from. ¶미국인~ 영어를 배우다 learn English from an American∥나는 아들~ 책을 주었다 I gave my son a book. / I gave a book to my son.∥나는 여동생~ 핸드백을 사 주었다 I bought my sister a handbag. / I bought a handbag for my sister.∥그~ 의지하지 마라 Don't depend[rely] on him.∥그것은 나~ 큰 도움이 된다 It is of great help to me. / It is very helpful[useful] to me.∥나는 그~ 속았다 I was fooled by him.∥그것을 누구~ 들었습니까 From whom did you hear that? / Who told you about it?

에게로 to; toward; at. ¶책임을 그~ 돌리다 lay the fault to his charge / lay the blame at his door.

에게서 from; of; through; with. ¶멀리 있는 친구~ 온 편지 a letter from a friend far away [from a distant friend]∥네가 온다는 말은 그~ 들었다 He told me that you were coming.∥그녀는 그~ 피아노를 배웠다 She took piano lessons from him.

에고 (the) self; (the) ego. ⇨ =자아(自我)
에고이스트 an egoist. ⇨ =이기주의자(⇨이기주의)
에고이즘 egoism. ⇨ =이기주의
에구구 Oh oh!; O dear! ¶~, 가엾기도 해라 O dear, what a pity it is!
에나멜 enamel. ¶~을 입히다 enamel.
● 에나멜가죽 patent leather. 에나멜선 enameled wire.
에너지 1 [물] energy. ¶결합 ~ binding energy∥열~ heat energy∥운동~ kinetic[actual / motive] energy / energy of motion∥위치 [정지] ~ potential[static] energy∥전기~ electrical energy∥태양 ~ solar energy∥핵 ~ nuclear energy∥화학 ~ chemical energy∥~를 비축하다 conserve energy. **2** [정력·기운]. ¶그는 ~가 있다 He is energetic.
● 에너지 보존 법칙 the principle of the conservation[indestructibility] of energy. 에너지 효율[준위(準位) / 양자(量子)] an energy efficiency[level / quantum].
에누리 1 [값을 더 부름] an overcharge; a fancy[fictitious] price; two prices. ¶~ 없는 무게 net weight. 에누리하다 overcharge; ask

에다
a fancy price[two prices].
2 [값을 깎음] (a) reduction in price; (a) discount. ¶~는 일절 없습니다 We never make a reduction. / We never ask two prices. / (게시) No reduction allowed. 에누리하다 reduce [abate / lower] the price; make[give / allow] a reduction[discount]; discount; mark [beat] down. ¶조금 에누리해 드리겠습니다 We will make it a little cheaper. / A small reduction may be allowed.
3 [말을 과장함] (an) exaggeration; (an) overstatement. ¶~ 없이 말해서 frankly speaking / to be frank[plain] with you / to be candid // ~ 없이 말하다 state the fact as it is / give one's honest opinion. 에누리하다 exaggerate; overstate; overdraw.

에다[1] cut[scoop / scrape] out; gouge (out). ¶살을 에는 바람 a piercing wind // 살을 에는 듯한 아픔 an acute[a sharp] pain // 살을 에는 듯한 추위다 It's bitterly cold. / This cold pierces[cuts] to the bone. // 굶주린 고아들을 보고 가슴을 에는 듯한 아픔을 느꼈다 It was harrowing to see the crowd of starving orphans.

에다[2] to; in; on. ⇨ 에다가

에다가 to; in; on; at; for; and. ¶소금~ 매실을 절이다 preserve plums in salt / salt plums // 벽~ 연필로 낙서를 해 놓았다 There are pencil scribblings on the wall.

에덴 Eden. ¶~동산 the Garden of Eden.

에델바이스 [식] an edelweiss.

에돌다 [주위를 돌다] go by[take] a roundabout way[route]; make a detour.

에두르다 1 [둘러막다] enclose (with / in); surround (with / by); encircle; gird. ¶울타리를 에두른 집 a house surrounded[enclosed] by a fence // 성벽으로 에둘러져 있는 도시 a walled town. 2 [둘러말하다] talk[speak] in a roundabout way; beat around[about]; euphemize; mince matters. ¶그는 에둘러 말하는 버릇이 있다 He has a tendency to talk in a roundabout way[to beat around the bush]. // 그는 에둘러 그 제의를 거절했다 He indirectly declined the offer.

에라 1 [체념의 소리] well; all right. ¶~ 모르겠다 Well, I don't care (if I fail). // ~ 술이나 마시자 Well, let's drink, anyway. 2 [비키라는 소리] Move[Step] aside!; Get out of the way! 3 [말리는 소리] Don't!; Stop! ¶~ 그러지 마라 Don't! None of that!

에러 an error; a bungle; a fumble(야구의). ¶~를 범하다 make an error / bungle / fumble.

에로 eroticism. ¶~의 erotic / sexy / sensual / obscene.
● **에로 문학** erotic literature; pornography; erotica. **에로 영화** a pornographic[an erotic] film; a sex film; (미국 속어) a purple film.

에로스 [그리스 신화] Eros.

에로틱하다 erotic; lewd; sensual.

에메랄드 an emerald. ¶~의[빛의] emerald // ~ 목걸이 an emerald necklace.

에보나이트 ebonite; hard rubber.

에비 Boo! ¶~, 만지지 마라 Boo! Don't touch it!

에서 1 [장소] at; in(▶ 장소를 지점으로 볼 때는 at를 씀); on. ¶슈퍼마켓~ 산 쇠고기 the beef I bought at a supermarket // 안양~ 버스를 내리다 get off a bus in Anyang // 강~ 해엄을 치다 swim in a river // 해안~ 놀다 play on the beach // 서울~만 팔리다 sell only in Seoul // 한국~도 산출되다 be produced also in Korea // 농장~ 일하다 work on a farm // 2층~ 자다 sleep upstairs // 거리~ 우연히 그를 만났다 I happened to meet him on[((영)) in] the street.
2 [시발점] from; out of; off; through; down; over. ¶서울~ 부산까지 from Seoul to Busan // 기차~ 내리다 get off a train // 15페이지~ 시작하다 begin at page 15 // 그는 방~ 나갔다 He went out of the room. // 벽의 틈새~ 햇빛이 들어오고 있다 Light is coming in through a crevice in the wall. // 해는 동쪽~ 뜬다 The sun rises in the east.
3 [범위] from. ¶15세~25세까지의 젊은 여성들 young women from 15 to 25 // 1시~3시 사이에 와 주십시오 Please come between one and three. // 그는 10명의 응모자 중~ 뽑혔다 He was chosen out of[from / among] ten applicants. // 이 영화는 아이~ 어른까지 즐길 수 있다 Both children and adults can enjoy this film.
4 [동기] from; out of; in; through. ¶친절한 마음 ~ out of kindness // 욕심~ for profit [money] // 그는 호기심~ 방 안을 들여다보았다 He looked into the room out of curiosity.
5 [근거·관점·표준] by; from; on; according to. ¶그 점~ in that respect // 교육적 견지~ from the[an] educational point of view // 이것은 셰익스피어의 작품~ 인용한 것입니다 This is a quotation from Shakespeare.
6 [비교] than. ¶이~ 더한 불행[사랑]은 없다 There can be no greater misfortune[love] than this.
7 [앞말이 주어가 됨]. ¶나라~ 정한 축제일 a national holiday // 이 비용은 회사~ 부담한다 The firm bears the whole expense of this.

에세이 an essay.

에세이스트 an essayist.

에스겔서 (一書) [성] (The Book of) Ezekiel(약어 Ezek.).

에스더서 (一書) [성] (The Book of) Esther(약어 Esth.).

에스에프 [공상 과학 소설] SF(▶ a science fiction의 약어). ¶~ 영화 a science-fiction[a sci-fi / a scifi / an SF] film.

에스오에스 an SOS; a signal of distress. ¶그들은 ~를 발신했다 They radioed an SOS.

에스카르고 (프) an escargot(▶ 식용 달팽이).

에스캅 ESCAP(▶ Economic and Social Commission for Asia and the Pacific의 약어).

에스컬레이터 an escalator.

에스코트 an escort.

에스키모 an Eskimo (pl. ~s); an In(n)uit (pl. ~s, ~)(▶ In(n)uit는 캐나다에서의 공식 호칭). ¶~인 Inuit / Eskimo.

에스테르 [화] ester.

에스페란토 Esperanto. ¶~ 사용자 an Esperantist.

에스프리 [정신·기지] (프) esprit.

에야디야 Yo-ho!; Yo-heave-ho! ⇨ 어기야디야

에어 [공기] air.
● **에어 브레이크** an air[a pneumatic] brake. **에어컨** an air conditioner.

에어로빅댄스 an aerobic dance; aerobics.

에어로졸 (an) aerosol.

에우다 1 [둘러싸다] encircle; surround. 2 [다른 길로 돌리다] go round; go by a roundabout way. 3 [지우다] cross[strike] out[off]; blot out; erase; write off.

에움길 a roundabout way[route]; a detour; (영) a diversion.

에워가다 go round; go by a roundabout way; take a detour[circuitous route]; make a detour.

에워싸다 surround; (사람이) crowd round; cluster[close / throng] around; (담 등으로) enclose; encircle; hem[edge] in[round]; [포위하다] besiege; lay siege to. ¶적을 ~ surround the enemy∥울타리로 정원을 ~ enclose a garden with a fence∥많은 사람들이 그 여배우를 에워쌌다 A crowd gathered around the actress.

에이비시 [초보] the basics; the first step. ¶외교의 ~를 배우다 learn the basics of diplomacy.

에이스 1 (트럼프·주사위 등의) an ace. ¶하트의 ~ the ace of hearts. **2** [테니스] an ace; a (service) ace. **3** [야구] an ace pitcher [hurler].

에이아르에스 [컴] ARS(▶ audio response system의 약어).

에이엠 [진폭 변조] AM; A.M.(▶ Amplitude Modulation의 약어); [오전] a.m.; A.M.(▶ ante meridiem의 약어).

에이즈 [후천성 면역 결핍증] AIDS(▶ Acquired Immnue Deficiency Syndrome의 약어).

에이커 an acre.

에이펙 [아시아 태평양 경제 협력체] APEC(▶ Asia-Pacific Economic Cooperation의 약어).

에이프런 an apron. ¶~을 두르고 일하다 work in an apron.

에인절피시 [동] an angelfish (*pl.* ~(-es)).

에잇 [마음이 불쾌할 때 내는 소리] Darn (it / me / you)!; Damn!

에취 [재채기 소리] ahchoo; achoo.

에칭 [부식 동판 기법] etching; [부식 동판 작품] an etching.

에탄올 [화] ethanol.

에테르 [물][화] ether; aether. ¶~로 마취시키다 etherize.

에튀드 [음] an étude; a study.

에티켓 etiquette. ¶손님을 대하는 ~ etiquette toward(s) a guest∥~을 지키다 observe the rules of etiquette∥그의 태도는 ~에 어긋난다 His attitude is against[contrary to] etiquette.

에틸 [화] ethyl. ¶~의 ethylic.
●**에틸알코올** ethyl[grain] alcohol.

에틸렌 [화] ethylene.

에페 (프) [펜싱] an épée.

에프엠 FM; F.M.(▶ Frequency Modulation의 약어); fm; f-m; f.m.
●**에프엠 방송** (개개의) an FM broadcast; [방송 사업] FM broadcasting. ¶이 라디오는 ~도 들을 수 있다 This radio picks up FM stations, too.

에피소드 [일화] an anecdote; a memorable event; a reminiscence; story. ¶한미 경제 교섭에 얽힌 ~ an interesting story concerning the U.S.-Korea economic negotiations.

에필로그 an epilogue.

에헤 Well!; Ha(h)! ⇨*애헤

에헴 ahem; hem. ¶그는 말을 꺼내기 전에 두번 ~ 기침했다 He cleared his throat twice before starting his talk.

엑기스 →진액2

엑스 1 [수학에서 미지수를 나타내는 기호] an X. **2** a cross; an x. ⇨*가새표

엑스선 (-線) [물] X-rays; Roentgen[Röntgen] rays. ¶~을 비추다 X-ray / roentgenize∥~을 쪼이다 X-radiate.
●**엑스선 사진** an X ray; an X-ray [a Roentgen] picture[photograph]. ¶~을 찍다 take an X ray / X-ray.

엑스트라 [영] an extra (hand). ¶~ 역을 하다 play an extra part (in a movie).

엔간하다 [적당하다] moderate; reasonable; proper; suitable; [보통이다] average; ordinary; common. ¶그런 말을 하다니 자네도 참 엔간하군 It is too cruel[heartless / inconsiderate] of you to say such a thing. **엔간히** moderately; reasonably; properly; suitably; ordinary. ¶~ 마셔라 Don't drink too much. ∥~ 좀 해라 That's enough. Stop it!

엔들 [반어의 뜻을 나타냄]. ¶날씨가 좋다면 어느 곳~ 못 가랴 I would go anywhere I like, if[so far as] the weather permits.

엔지 [영] N.G.(▶ no good의 약어). ¶~를 내다 spoil[ruin] a sequence.

엔지니어 an engineer.

엔진 an engine. ¶선박용 ~ a marine engine∥항공기용 ~ an aeroengine∥디젤[로터리] ~ a diesel[rotary] engine∥~을 멈추다 stop an engine∥~을 걸다 start an engine / set an engine going[at work]∥~이 꺼졌다 The engine stopped[ran down / came to a standstill].
●**엔진 고장** stalling (of a motor[an engine]); an engine breakdown[failure]; (제트 엔진의) a flameout. ¶이런 차는 ~이 잦다 The engines of this model of car often stalls [breaks down].

엔트로피 [물] entropy.

엔트리 an entry.

엘니뇨 [페루 해류에 이상 난류가 흐르드는 현상] El Niño.

엘레지 an elegy.

엘렉트라 콤플렉스 [심] the Electra complex.

엘리베이터 an elevator; (영) a lift. ¶소형 화물 ~ a dumbwaiter∥~가 없는 건물[아파트] a walk-up / a walk-up building[apartment house]∥~의 올라가는[내려가는] 단추를 누르다 press the up[down] button∥~로 올라가다[내려가다] go up[down] in an elevator∥~를 타다 take an elevator / ride in an elevator.

엘리트 the elite; (프) élite.
●**엘리트 사원** an elite employee; an employee whose future is assured. **엘리트 의식** elitism.

엘엔지 LNG(▶ liquefied natural gas의 약어).

엘피 가스 LP gas.

엘피반 (-盤) an LP (record album) (*pl.* LPs, LP's)(▶ LP는 long-playing의 약어).

엘피지 LPG(▶ liquefied petroleum gas의 약어); LP gas.

엠시 [연회 사회자] an MC[emcee]; [TV 토크 쇼 진행자] a talk show host(남자); a talk show hostess(여자); [퀴즈 진행자] a quiz master.

엠아르아이 MRI(▶ magnetic resonance imaging[imager]의 약어).

엠앤드에이 M&A(▶ merger and aquisition의 약어).

엠티 (*MT) membership training(▶ 영어에서는 MT와 같은 약어는 사용하지 않음). ¶우리는 ~ 갈 계획을 세웠다 We planned to go on a retreat for membership training.

엠피 [군] an MP; an M.P.(▶ the Military

엥겔 계수

Police의 약어).
엥겔 계수(-係數) [경] Engel's coefficient.
엥겔 법칙(-法則) [경] Engel's Law.
여(輿) ins. ¶~야 ins and outs.
-여(餘) above; over; more (than); beyond; ... and over [more]. ¶20~ 년간 for twenty odd years / for over twenty years.
여가(餘暇) leisure; spare time [moments]; free time; leisure time [hours]; time to spare; time when one is unoccupied [has nothing to do]. ¶~가 없다 have no time to spare // 당신은 ~에 무엇을 합니까 [~를 어떻게 지내십니까] What do you do in your spare time [leisure hours]? / How do you enjoy [spend / fill] your leisure [spare time]? // 그는 ~를 내서 [이용해서] 정원 손질을 한다 He makes [finds] time for gardening.
여각(餘角) [수] a complementary angle; a complement.
여간(如干) ordinarily; normally; commonly. ¶ 아이를 기른다는 게 ~ 어려운 일이 아니구나 It is very [awfully / exceedingly] hard to bring up a child. / It is no easy thing [task] to foster a child. // 그가 집을 팔았다는 말을 듣고 ~ 놀라지 않았다 I was much [not a little] surprised (to hear) that he had sold his house. // 그녀는 너의 축하 편지를 받고 ~ 기뻐하지 않았답니다 She was greatly [highly / exceedingly] delighted at receiving [to receive] your letter of congratulation. **여간하다** ordinary; normal; common. ¶그는 여간해서는 승낙하지 않을 것이다 He won't consent easily.
여간(이) 아니다 uncommon; unusual; extraordinary; great; out of (the) common [ordinary]. ¶그 일을 하느라고 고생이 여간 아니었다 I have taken a great deal of trouble over the work. // 더위가 ~ It is terribly [very] hot.
● **여간내기** an ordinary [common] person; a mediocrity. ¶그는 ~가 아니다 He is no common [ordinary] man.
여객(旅客) [여행자] a traveler; [승객] a passenger.
● **여객기** a passenger airplane; (정기의) an airliner. **여객선** a passenger ship [boat]; (대양 항로의 정기선) a passenger liner. **여객 열차** a passenger train. **여객 운임** passengers' fares [tariffs].
여건(與件) 1 [주어진 조건] a given condition [circumstance]. ¶~이 허락한다면 if the circumstances permit. 2 [논] a datum (pl. data).
여걸(女傑) a heroine; a heroic woman; an Amazon.
여겨듣다 listen carefully [attentively / intently] (to); listen with all one's mind.
여겨보다 watch carefully; see closely; take [have / get] a close [good] look (at); take a hard look (at).
여격(與格) [언] the dative (case).
● **여격 동사** a dative verb.
여경(女警) a policewoman (pl. -women); (구어) a woman cop.
여계(女系) the female line; the maternal [distaff] side (of a family).
여고(女高) a girls' (senior) high school. ⇨ 여자 고등학교(⇨여자)
● **여고생** a student at a girls' high school; a high-school girl.

1284

여공(女工) a factory girl; a female operative [mill hand]; a woman worker (pl. women workers); a workwoman; a workgirl.
여과(濾過) filtration; filtering; percolation. ¶흡인 ~ sucking filtration. **여과하다** filter; filtrate; pass (a liquid) through a filter; percolate. ¶~를 ~ filter water // 오수를 여과하여 불순물을 제거하다 filter (out) impurities from unclean water.
● **여과기** a filter; a percolater; [액체 여과기] a strainer. **여과성** filterability. **여과지**(-紙) a filter paper. ⇨ 거름종이
여관(旅館) an inn; a hotel. ¶~의 손님 a hotel guest; a guest (staying) at a hotel [an inn] / a paying guest // ~에 묵다 stay [put up] at a hotel // ~에 들다 register at an inn [a hotel] / (미) check in.
● **여관방** a hotel room. **여관비** hotel charges [expenses]; a hotel bill. **여관 주인** an innkeeper; a hotel keeper; (영) a landlord; a hotel proprietor; a host; (여자) a landlady; a hotel proprietress; a hostess.
여광(餘光) [해 진 뒤의 남은 빛] an afterglow; remaining [lingering] light.
여교사(女敎師) a schoolmistress; a lady [female / woman] teacher; a schoolmarm.
여군(女軍) a woman soldier; the Women's Army Corps.
여권(女權) women's rights; [여성 참정권] woman suffrage.
● **여권 신장** extension of women's rights. ¶ ~ 운동 a feminist [women's rights] movement. **여권주의자** a feminist; [여성 참정권 획득 운동가] a woman suffragist; a suffragette.
여권(旅券) a passport. ¶관용 ~ an official passport // ~을 취득하다 procure [obtain] a passport // ~을 발급받다 have a passport issued / obtain [get] a passport.
● **여권 사증** a passport visa.
여급(女給) a waitress; a waiting maid; a girl waiter; (바의) a barmaid.
여기 1 [이곳] here; [이 단계 [점]] this point [place]. ¶~ 사람들 (이곳의) the people of this district / (이 지방의) the people of this district // ~까지 up to here // ~에는 아무도 없다 There is nobody here. // ~서 나가라 Get out of here [this]. // ~는 덥다 It's hot in here. // ~에 책이 있다 Here is a book. // ~가 어디죠 (길을 잃었을 때) Where am I? // 그 여자 아이는 ~서 납치되었다 The girl was away from this spot. / The girl was kidnapped at this spot. // ~가 내가 태어난 곳이오 This is where I was born. // 그녀는 ~까지 걸어왔다 She walked this far [to this point]. // ~까지는 순조로운 항해였다 So [(문어) Thus] far we have enjoyed a smooth voyage. // ~까지는 만사가 순조로웠다 Things have gone well so far. // 오늘은 ~까지 합시다 Let's stop (our work) here for today. / This is all for today. / So much for today. / We shall [Let us] leave off here.
2 [이곳에] here; in this place; at this point. ¶자, ~ 있습니다 (찾고 있는 것, 원하는 것을 줄 때) Here you are! / (우리가 찾고[원하고] 있는 것이) Here we are! / (물건을 건넬 때) There you are!
여기(餘技) a hobby. ¶~로 그림을 그리다 paint (pictures) as a hobby [pastime].
여기다 think; consider (as); deem (as); treat

(as); take (for); hold; (의아·의심스럽게) wonder; doubt; suspect. ¶불쌍히 ~ feel pity (for) / have a pity (on) // 대수롭지 않게 ~ think nothing [little] of / have a low opinion of // 나를 바보로 여기느냐 Do you take me for a fool? / Do you consider me (to be) a fool? / Do you regard [look upon] me as a fool? // 그녀는 그의 위협을 농담으로 여겼다 She treated his threat as a joke. // 그녀는 그 남자를 수상히 여겼다 She suspected the man. / She held [thought] the man suspect.

여기자 (女記者) a woman [female] reporter; a newspaperwoman.

여기저기 here and there; in places; [모든 곳] (in) every direction; (in) all direction; (on) all sides. ¶~(로) hither and thither / to and fro / back and forth / up and down // 들판 ~에 제비꽃이 피어 있다 Violets are blooming here and there in the field. / Violets are dotted over the field. / The field is dotted with violets. // ~서 사람들이 모여들었다 People assembled from all over. / People flocked from far and near. / People came from all [different / various] quarters. // 비슷한 사건이 ~서 일어났다 Similar cases occurred in many [various] places. // ~에서 편지가 왔다 I received letters from various quarters. // 그들은 ~를 헤매다녔다 They wandered from place to place. // 그들은 ~로 그를 찾아다녔다 They looked for him everywhere [high and low / far and near / far and wide / (구어) all over the place].

여뀌 [식] a smartweed; a water pepper.

여남은 ten odd; more than [somewhat over] ten. ¶~ 사람 a dozen men / a little over ten men // ~ 해 ten-odd years.

여념 (餘念) different [other] intention; other thoughts; divided attention. ¶~이 없다 be devoted to / give undivided [absorbing] attention to / be absorbed [engrossed / buried] in / be bent [intent] on / be solely occupied with / busy oneself in / think of nothing but // 그는 연구에 ~이 없다 He devotes himself completely [body and soul] to his research. / He is buried in his research work. // 그는 돈벌이에 ~이 없었다 He thought of nothing but [was keen on] money-making.

여느 [그 밖의 다른] other; [다른 보통의] ordinary; usual; common. ¶~ 때와는 달리 unusually / unwontedly / contrary to one's habit [wont] // ~ 때처럼 as usual / in one's usual way / as is usually the case with (one) / as is one's wont [habit] // ~ 사람과 다르다 be unusual [extraordinary] / be out of the common run // 나는 ~ 때 다니던 길로 귀가했다 I took the usual road home. // 남편은 ~ 날처럼 7시에 나갔습니다 My husband left home as usual at seven. // ~ 때보다 빨리 학교에 도착했다 I arrived at school earlier than usual. // 그녀는 ~ 때처럼 오후의 쇼핑을 했다 She did her regular afternoon shopping.

여단 (旅團) a brigade.
● **여단장** a brigade commander; (영) a brigadier (general).

여닫다 open and close [shut] (a door).

여닫이 a hinged door [window].

여담 (餘談) a digression; a by-talk. ¶~이지만 In this connection I may add that …. / Incidentally [In passing] I may [let me] say that …. // ~은 그만두고… So much for digressions …. // 그의 이야기는 ~으로 흘렀다 He digressed [wandered (away) / went aside] from the main subject [issue] in his talk. // 이건 ~입니다 This is by the way.

여당 (與黨) the Government party; the party in power; the ruling party; the party in office; (미) the Administration party; (영) the Ministerial party.

여대 (女大) a women's college [university].
● **여대생** a girl [woman / female] college student; a college woman; (미국 구어) a co-ed (남녀 공학의).

여덟 eight. ¶~ 번 eight times.

여덟째 the eighth.

여독 (旅毒) sickness from the fatigue of travel. ¶~을 풀다 banish the fatigue of travel / take a rest after the fatigue of one's journey.

여독 (餘毒) the remaining effect of (a) poison; the aftereffect of a sickness.

여드레 1 [8일] eight days. 2 the eighth day (of a month). ⇨초여드렛날
● **여드렛날** the eighth day.

여드름 a pimple; a blackhead; (집합적) acne (▶ 여드름이 있는 상태, 복수로 쓰지 않음). ¶~ 자국 an acne spot [pit] // ~투성이의 청년 a pimple-faced [pimply] youth // ~을 짜다 pop a pimple / squeeze a blackhead // ~이 곪아서 터졌다 Pimples has popped. // 그의 얼굴에 ~이 났다 Pimples came out on his face. / His face broke out in pimples. // 그는 ~이 심하다 He has a bad case of acne. / His face is covered with acne spots.

여든 eighty. ¶~ 살의 노인 an old man [woman] of eighty / an 80-year-old man [woman] / an octogenarian.

여러 [수효가 많은] many; plenty of; [몇 개의] several; [여러 가지] various; a variety of; diverse. ¶~ 번 several times / many times / many a time / (very) often / frequently / [되풀이해서] repeatedly / over and over (again) // ~ 날 동안 for (many) days / for many a day / for a number of days / for days and days // ~ 해 동안 for (several [many]) years / for years and years // 나는 ~ 번 해 보았지만 성공하진 못했다 I tried again and again [over and over (again)], but couldn't succeed. / I tried and tried, but did not succeed. // 그는 자신에게는 ~ 잘못이 없다고 ~ 번 말했다 He repeated that he was not wrong.

여러 가지 different kinds [sorts]; various kinds. ¶~의 various / varied / diverse / several / many [all] kinds [sorts] of / a variety of // ~로 variously / diversely / in many [various / different] ways / in every way / manifoldly // ~ 용도 a variety of uses // ~ 크기의 상자 boxes of various sizes // ~ 이유로 그것을 인수할 수 없었다 I cannot undertake it for various reasons. // ~로 애써 보았으나 되지 않았다 I tried all sorts of things [every means (possible)], but nothing worked. / I tried to do in various ways, but nothing worked. // ~로 고맙습니다 Thank you for your many kindness. / Thank you very much for all you have done for me. // 컵, 칫솔, 그 밖에 ~를 사 왔소 I bought a cup, a toothbrush, and whatnot [and all that / and all the like].

여러모로 in various[many] ways; one way or other; in more ways than one; in everything. ¶소개장이 있으면 ~ 편리하다 A letter of recommendation will be useful in more ways than one[in many ways]. // 그것은 ~ 쓸모 있다 It is useful for one thing or another.

여러분 you; all of you; ladies and gentlemen; everybody; everyone. ¶신사 숙녀 ~ Ladies and gentlemen! // ~ 잘 들으시오 Listen to me, all of you. // ~ 안녕하세요 Good morning, everybody. / (학생들에게) Good morning, boys and girls. // 이 문제에 관하여 ~의 의견을 듣고 싶습니다 We'd like to hear comments about this problem from all of you.

여러해살이 [식] perennation.
● **여러해살이식물** a perennial (plant). **여러해살이풀** [식] a perennial herb.

여럿 (사람) many; a large number. ¶~이 왔었나 Did many come? // 그 도시를 찾는 관광객이 ~ 된다 A good many of tourists visit the city.

여력 (餘力) remaining power[strength]; surplus[reserve] energy[strength / power]; (돈의) money to spare. ¶~이 충분히 있다 have[keep] much energy[strength] in reserve / have energy[money] enough to spare for (some other work) // 그에게는 아직 ~이 있는 것 같다 He seems still to have plenty of energy left (in him). // 보석을 살 ~은 없다 I have no money to spare[don't have enough money] for jewelry.

여로 (旅路) a journey. ¶~에 오르다 start on a journey // [사흘 동안의] ~에서 돌아오다 return from a long journey[three day's journey].

여론 (輿論) public opinion; public sentiment; popular voice. ¶~에 귀를 기울이다 (미) have[keep] one's ears to the ground / pay careful attention to the trends of public opinion // ~에 호소하다 appeal to public sentiment[opinion] // ~을 무시하다 defy public opinion // ~에 따르다[~을 좇다] obey the dictates of public opinion / act in accordance with public opinion.
● **여론 조사** a survey of public opinion; a public opinion census[poll]; an opinion poll; (지상(紙上)의) a straw poll. ¶~를 하다 take a public opinion poll (on a matter) / poll people on their opinion (about a matter) // 물가에 대한 ~를 하다 make a survey of public opinion on prices.

여류 (女流) [관형어적] woman; female; lady.
● **여류 시인** a poetess. **여류 작가** a female [fair] writer; a woman writer[novelist]; a fair author; an authoress. **여류 화가** a lady [woman] painter.

여름 summer; summertime; the summer season. ¶올 ~ this summer // 초 ~에 in (the) early summer / early in summer // 한 ~에 in the middle[height] of (the) summer / in midsummer / in high summer // 늦 ~에 in late summer / in the last of the summer / late in summer.

여름(을) 타다 be vulnerable to[succumb to / suffer from] the summer heat; have a low tolerance of hot weather; fall away in summer; take hot weather hard. ¶그는 여름을 타지 않는다 The hot weather never bothers him.

● **여름날** a summer day. ¶어느 ~ 아침에 on a summer morning. **여름 방학** the summer vacation; (영) the summer holidays. ¶~ 동안에 during[through] summer vacation // ~ 숙제 homework for the summer vacation // ~은 다음 주에 시작이다 Summer vacation at school begins[Schools break up for the summer] next week. **여름옷** summer wear [clothes]; a summersuit. **여름철** summertime; the summer season. **여름학교** a summer school.

여름내 through(out) the summer.

여리다 1 [연하다] tender; soft; [약하다] weak; fragile; frail; feeble; flimsy. ¶여린 피부 a tender skin // 여린 싹 a tender shoot // 여린 꽃 fragile flowers // 마음이 ~ be easily moved / be tender-hearted / be sentimental. 2 [부족하다] insufficient; short; lacking; (서술적) be not enough.

여망 (餘望) the remaining hope; the hope for the future.

여망 (輿望) popularity; esteem; reputation; credit; trust. ¶국민의 ~을 짊어지다 enjoy the trust[confidence] of the whole nation.

여명 (餘命) the remainder[rest / remnant] of one's life; one's remaining days. ¶그녀의 ~이 얼마 남지 않았다 Her days are numbered. / She has only a short time to live. / Her end is drawing near. / She has but few days left[to live]. / The sands of her life[Her sands] are remaining out.

여명 (黎明) daybreak; dawn; the gray of morning; morning twilight. ¶~에 at dawn / in the gray of the morning / at daybreak // 문명의 ~기 the dawn of civilization.

여물 [마소의 먹이] fodder; forage. ¶소에 ~을 먹이다 give a cow fodder / feed a cow (with fodder).
● **여물통** a manger; a crib.

여물다¹ [곡식·과일 등이] fill with the corn [seed]; corn; grow[get / become] ripe; ripen; mature; come to maturity. ¶벼가 ~ rice corns

여물다² [살림 등을 알뜰히 하다] tight; firm frugal. ¶그녀는 ~ She manages her household frugally. / She is of an economical turn of mind.

여미다 adjust; arrange; fix (up). ¶옷깃을 ~ adjust the neckband[collar] of one's clothes / adjust oneself[one's dress].

여반장 (如反掌) an easy task[job]; (구어) a piece of cake. ¶그런 것쯤이야 ~이다 That's nothing. / Nothing is easier. / That's as simple as turning one's hand. / (미국 속어) That's (as) easy as pie. / (미국 속어) That's a cinch.

여배우 (女俳優) an actress. ¶최우수 ~상 the Best Actress award // 주연 ~ the leading actress.

여백 (餘白) (공백) a blank; (a) (blank) space; (난외) a margin. ¶~이 많은 페이지 a short page // ~이 있으면 if space permits // ~을 남겨 두다 leave a blank[space / margin].

여벌 (餘-) remainings; remnants; surplus; spare; a spare one. ¶~ 옷 a change[spare suit] (of clothes) // ~이 있다 There is an extra.

여보 1 excuse me; hallo(a). ⇨여보세요.1 **2** (부부 사이에) (my) darling; honey; sweetheart.

여보게 old thing[chap / buddy / man]; my

여보세요 1 excuse me; hallo(a); hullo; (미) say; (미) see here; (영) I say; hey; listen; look here; please; if you please. ¶~ 이것은 당신 손수건이 아닌가요 Excuse me, but isn't this your handkerchief? 2 (전화에서) Hello. ¶~, 윤 선생이십니까 Hello! Is this[(영) that] Mr. Yun?

여보시게 old thing[cheap / buddy / man]. ⇨ ¹여보게

여보시오 excuse me; hallo(a). ⇨ ¹여보세요1

여봐라 I say; Hullo.

여봐란듯이 in an ostentatious way; ostentatiously; demonstratively; for[out of] show; showily; for[out of] display[parade]; to show off. ¶그녀는 ~ 반지 낀 왼손을 흔들었다 She waved her left hand about to show off her ring.

여부(與否) yes or no; whether or not; if. ¶성공 ~ success or failure // 승낙 ~를 알려 주십시오 Please let us know whether you accept it or not. // 우리는 이 행사에의 참가 ~를 둘러싸고 토론했다 We discussed whether or not we ought to take part in this event.

여부없다(與否-) sure; certain; unquestionable; be beyond[out of] doubt. ¶"그 기차를 탈 수 있을까?" "~!" "Can we catch the train?" "Of course! [Certainly! / There is no question about it.]"

여북 how; how much; very; indeed. ¶~하면 그가 울겠니 What miserable circumstances he must be in to make him cry! // ~ 원통하랴 I may well imagine how grieved he is.

여분(餘分) the remainder; the remnant. ⇨ ¹나머지1

여비(旅費) travel[traveling] expenses; travel cost; mileage(공무원의). ¶~를 지급하다 allow [pay] (a person) traveling expenses // ~를 절약하다 save travel expenses // 대구까지의 ~는 왕복 얼마입니까 What will it cost for a journey to Daegu and back? / How much does it cost to travel to Daegu and back? // ~는 각자 부담입니다 You must pay your own traveling expenses.

여사(女史) Mrs.; (기혼자) Mrs.; (미혼자) Miss(▶ Ms.는 미혼·기혼을 구별하지 않을 때 쓰지만, 본인이 원할 때만 쓰는 것이 무난함). ¶최 ~ Mrs. [Miss / Ms.] Choe.

여사무원(女事務員) a woman office worker; a female clerk.

여상(女相) a man's face having feminine features.

여색(女色) 1 [여성과의 성교] sexual intercourse with a woman; coition; [색욕] lust; carnal desire. ¶~에 빠지다 go in for[lose oneself in] love affairs. 2 [미색] a woman's beauty; feminine charms; [미인] a beautiful woman. ¶~에 매혹되다 fall a victim to a woman's charms / be infatuated with a woman.

여생(餘生) the rest[remainder] of one's life; one's remaining years[days]; one's afterlife. ¶그는 ~을 서예를 즐기며 조용히 보냈다 He spent the rest of life quietly enjoying calligraphy. // 나는 ~을 저술에 바칠 생각이다 I intend to devote my remaining years to writing.

여섯 six.

여섯째 the sixth.

여성(女性) 1 [여자] a woman (pl. women); [집합적] women; womankind(▶ womankind는 멋부린 표현). ¶~의 feminine // ~의 권리 women's rights // ~적인 남자 an effeminate [a womanish] fellow[man] / (구어) a sissy // ~화하다 feminize. 2 [언] the feminine gender.

● **여성관** a view of women. ¶그의 ~을 알고 싶다 I'd like to know how he regards women. **여성 문제** feminist issues; women's questions. **여성복** a woman's dress. **여성 운동** the women's movement; a movement for the emancipation of women. **여성 차별 discrimination against women. 여성 해방론** feminism(▶ 주로 19, 20세기의 여권 신장론). **여성 호르몬** a female hormone.

여성(女聲) a woman's[female] voice.

● **여성 합창** a female[women's] chorus.

여세(餘勢) surplus power[energy]; reserve energy; momentum (pl. -ta, ~s); [물] impetus; inertia. ¶그는 10km를 달린 ~를 몰아 1km를 더 달렸다 Driven on by the speed and vigor with which he had run 10 kilometers, he did another kilometer.

여송연(呂宋煙) a cigar. ⇨ 엽궐련

여수(旅愁) loneliness on a journey. ⇨ ²객수 (客愁) ¶~를 달래다 relieve one's loneliness on a journey / amuse[console] the weary heart of a traveler.

여수(餘數) remainder; surplus; excess.

여승(女僧) a Buddhist nun. ¶~이 되다 become a Buddhist nun / enter a nunnery.

여식(女息) my daughter.

여신(女神) a goddess; a female deity. ¶봄의 ~ the Goddess of Spring // 자유의 ~ the Goddess of Liberty.

여신(與信) credit; financing; lending; a loan.

● **여신 업무** a loan business. **여신 한도(액)** a credit line [limit]; a line of credit.

여신(餘燼) the remaining ashes; embers; cinders.

여실하다(如實-) real; realistic; true (to life); vivid. **여실히** truly; realistically; true to life; as things really are; vividly; graphically. ¶~ 나타내다 represent (something) to the life.

여심(女心) (win) a woman's heart.

여아(女兒) 1 [딸] my daughter. 2 [계집아이] a girl; a lass.

여압(與壓) pressurization.

여액(餘額) the balance; the remainder.

여야(與野) the Government party and the Opposition party; the ins and the outs; the in party and the out party.

여열(餘熱) [남은 열] remaining[residual] heat; lingering fever.

여염(餘炎) 1 [타ође 남은 불꽃] lingering flames; burning cinders. 2 [남은 더위] lingering summer heat.

여염(閭閻) residential districts; a middle class community.

● **여염집** a middle-class home; a commoner's home[family].

여왕(女王) 1 [왕·왕후] a queen; a queen regnant(군주). ¶엘리자베스 ~ 2세 Queen Elizabeth Ⅱ // ~ 폐하께서 그 의식에 임석하시다 Her Majesty will be present at the ceremony(▶ 여왕을 2인칭으로 부를 때에는 Your Majesty를 씀). 2 [비유] a belle; a queen; a mistress. ¶사교계의 ~ a society queen.

●여왕벌[개미] a queen bee[ant].
여우 a fox; a vixen(암컷); a cub(새끼). ¶~ 같은 foxlike / foxy / vulpine // ~ 같은 놈 an old fox[bird] / a foxy fellow / a sly[cunning] man // ~에 홀리다 be put under a spell by fox / 그는 ~에 홀린 듯한 얼굴을 하고 있었다 He looked bewildered[puzzled].
●여우볕 a brief spell of sunshine on a rainy day; intermittent[fitful] sunshine. ¶~이 났다 The sun came out for a few minutes on this rainy day. 여우비 a sudden rainfall[a shower] in the sunshine; a light rain while the sunshines; a sun-shower. 여우 사냥 fox hunting; a fox hunt. 여우자리 [천] the Little Fox; Vulpecula. 여우털 목도리 a fox-fur muffler.
여우(女優) an actress. ⇨여배우
여우원숭이 a lemur; a macaco (*pl.* ~s); a galago (*pl.* ~s).
여운(餘韻) 1 [여음] a lingering sound[tone]; a resonance; (종 등의) reverberations; echoes. ¶길게 ~을 남기는 퉁소 소리 the lingering[trailing] notes of a *tungso*. 2 [뒤에 남는 운치] an aftertaste; an aftereffect; (글 등의) suggestiveness. ¶그의 시가 지니는 ~을 아는 사람은 드물다 Few can appreciate the lingering imagery[subtle overtones] of his poems.
여울 rapids; a shoot; a swift[strong] current. ¶~을 건너다 ford rapids.
●여울목 the neck of the rapids.
여위다 lose (one's) weight; become lean [thin]; grow[become] gaunt; get emaciated; lose flesh(병으로); fall away (in flesh); pine away(근심으로). ¶여윈 lean / thin / skinny / haggard / emaciated / gaunt // 여윈 몸 a thin [an emaciated] body / 여윈 사람[개] a lean [thin] man[dog] // 그녀는 병이 난 후 많이 여위었다 She lost a lot of weight after becoming ill.
여원잠 a light[bad / poor] sleep. ¶~을 자다 pass[have] a poor[bad] night / sleep badly.
여유(餘裕) 1 [장소의] room; space; (시간의) time (to spare); (경비 등의) a margin; allowance; [넉넉함] something extra; [기계 등의 운동 여지·놀] play. ¶교통 체증에 의한 지연을 예상하고 약 30분의 ~를 두다 allow about thirty minutes for delays caused by traffic jams // ~ 있는 생활을 하다 live in affluent circumstances[comfortably] // 시간의 ~가 없다 I don't have any time to spare. // 자동차에 우리 아이를 태워 줄 ~가 있습니까 Do you room for my child in your car? / 날짜를 정할 때에는 ~를 두는 것이 좋을 거다 In deciding the date, we'd better allow[leave ourselves] some[a little] leeway[latitude]. // 그들에게는 남아둘 만큼 돈의 ~가 있었다 They had money enough and to spare. // 지면에 ~가 있으면 이 기사도 실어 주게 If there is space, please put in this story.
2 [침착성] composure; placidity; one's presence of mind; calmness. ¶~ 있는 태도를 잃어서는 안 된다 Do not lose your presence of mind. ¶그는 자기 문제에 열중하여, 다른 사람에 대해서 생각할 ~가 없다 He is so absorbed in his own affairs that he cannot afford to pay any attention to other people.
여유작작하다(餘裕綽綽-) calm and composed; (서술적) have enough and to spare(금전 등의). ¶그는 시험 전날인데도 여유작작했다 He was very calm and looked as if he had had plenty of confidence even on the day before his examination.
여의다 1 [사별하다] have (one's father) die; be bereaved[bereft / deprived] of; lose. ¶자식을 ~ survive[lose] one's child / 남편을 ~ be bereaved of one's husband / lose one's husband / be left a widow / be widowed. 2 [멀리 떠나 보내다] send (a person) far away. 3 [시집보내다] marry off (one's daughter). ¶딸을 ~ marry off one's daughter (to a person).
여의사(女醫師) a woman[lady / female] doctor.
여의주(如意珠) a magic stone that bestows omnipotence on him who acquires it.
여의하다(如意-) (서술적) be to one's desire; turn out as one wishes. ¶매사가 여의치 않다 Everything goes wrong with me[goes contrary to my wishes / falls short of my expectations].
여인(女人) a woman (*pl.* women). ¶~의 마음 a woman's heart.
●여인국 a land of women; a manless land.
여인 금제(-禁制) (게시) Off Limits to women.; No admittance to women.; Closed to women.
여인숙(旅人宿) a lodging house; an inn; (싼) a cheap inn; (미국 속어) a flophouse; (영국 속어) a doss house. ¶~에 들다 put up at an inn.
여자(女子) 1 [여성] a woman (*pl.* women); [부인] a lady; [미혼의 젊은 여성] a girl; [집합적] women(▶ 관사를 붙이지 않음). ¶~의 female / feminine(▶ feminine에는 「여자다움」의 뜻이 포함됨) // ~다운 womanly / ladylike / womanish / effeminate // ~답지 않은 unwomanly / unfeminine / unworthy of a lady // ~용의 (intended[suitable]) for women // 거리의 ~ (매춘부) a prostitute / a streetwalker // 저 회사에서는 아직도 ~는 남자와 차별되고 있다 That company still discriminates between the sexes[against women]. // 그 녀석은 ~ 같은 남자다 He's a sissy. // 우리 반에는 남자가 30명, ~가 20명 있다 There are 30 boys and 20 girls in our class. // 그는 아직 ~를 모른다 He still hasn't had a woman. / He's still a virgin. // 그 아이는 요새 점점 ~다운 데가 나타나고 있다 Recently she has become more womanly.
2 [애인] a woman; a girlfriend; one's mistress. ¶그에게는 ~가 있는 것 같다 It looks as if he's got a woman[he is having an affair with a woman].
여자 셋이 모이면 새 접시를 뒤집어 놓는다(속담) Three women (and a goose) make a market.; Where there are women and geese, there wants no noise.
●여자 고등학교 a girls' (senior) high school; a girls' upper secondary school. 여자 대학교 a women's college[university]. 여자 중학교 a girls' junior high school; a girls' middle school.
여장(女裝) (분장) woman's disguise; (복장) female clothing[attire / costume]. ¶살인범은 ~을 하고 도망쳤다 The murderer made his escape disguised as a woman. 여장하다 dress up like[disguise oneself as] a woman; put on women's clothing. ¶여장한 남자 a man in woman's disguise / a man in skirts.

여장(旅裝) a traveling outfit[suit / attire / kit]; a traveler's equipment. ¶~을 갖추다 make preparations[prepare / equip oneself] for a journey // ~을 풀다 take off one's traveling attire / [숙박하다] stop[put up] at an inn.

여장부(女丈夫) a heroine; an Amazon; an unusually capable woman.

여전하다(如前-) 《서술적》 remain unchanged; be as usual[before]; be as (it) used to be; be just as it was. ¶아버지의 병세는 여전하시다 My father's condition remains the same. **여전히** [전과 같이] as before; [여느 때와 마찬가지로] as ever; as usual; as [like] always. ¶그녀는 ~ 그에게 호의를 가지고 있었다 She was as fond of him as before. / She still liked him. // 그는 ~ 뚱한 얼굴을 하고 있었다 He looked as sullen as ever. // 휴일인데도 아버지는 ~ 바쁘시다 Even though it's a holiday, my father is (as) busy as usual.

여점원(女店員) a saleslady; a saleswoman; salesgirl; a shopgirl; (미) a female sales clerk; (영) a female shop assistant.

여정(旅程) (거리) a distance (to be covered); (일정) (make) the plan[schedule] of[for] one's trip; an itinerary. ¶하루의 ~ a day's journey.

여정(旅情) the weary heart[thoughts] of a traveler; the tedium of a journey. ¶~을 풀다 [달래다] beguile[relieve] the tedium [monotony / ennui] of a journey / amuse [console] the weary heart of a traveler.

여제(女弟) one's (younger) sister. ⇨ 누이동생
여제(女帝) [여자 황제] an empress (regnant).
여종(女-) a female[woman] slave[servant].
여죄(餘罪) other[further] crimes[charges]; additional charges. ¶철도에 체포된 남자는 ~를 추궁받고 있다 The man arrested for theft is being questioned about other crimes.

여주인(女主人) (주부) a mistress; (여관 등의) a landlady; (요정 등의) a hostess; (가게의) a proprietress.

여주인공(女主人公) a heroine.
여중(女中) a girls' junior high school. ⇨ 여자중학교(⇨여자)
●**여중생** a middle-school girl.
여중호걸(女中豪傑) a heroic woman; a heroine; an Amazon.
여증(餘症) the remaining symptom(s) of a disease.

여지(餘地) room; space; a margin; a scope; a place; a blank(여백); leeway. ¶~를 남기다 leave some room for (later discussion) // 이 점에 대해서는 검토할 ~가 있다 The point in question is open to further discussion. // 우리 집 대지에는 집을 한 채 더 지을 ~가 있다 There is just enough space on our land to build one more house. // 이 기획에는 내가 활동할 ~가 충분히 있다 This project provides ample room[scope] for me to play an active role. // 강연회장은 입추의 ~가 없었다 The lecture hall was packed to overflowing. // 그의 행동이 범죄임은 증거에 의해 의심할 ~가 없다 The evidence leaves no room for[(문어)] admits of no doubt about] the criminal nature of his activities. // 변명할 ~가 전혀 없습니다 There is no excuse whatever.

여지껏 →여태껏

여진(餘震) [지] an aftershock; a secondary shock; an after tremor[quake]. ¶도합 여덟 번의 ~이 있었다 There were[We had / We felt] eight aftershocks altogether.

여질(女姪) a niece. ⇨ 조카딸(⇨조카)
여쭈다 1 [아뢰다] tell (to a superior); inform; say; mention; state. ¶인사를 ~ greet (a superior). 2 [문의하다] ask (a person about something); inquire (of a person about something). ¶또 한 가지 여쭈어 볼 일이 있습니다 I have one more question to ask you.

여쭙다 tell (to a superior); ask (a person about something). ⇨ 여쭈다 ¶좀 여쭙겠는데요. Excuse me, but ....

여차여차하다(如此如此-) such and such. ¶여차여차한 이름의 사람 a man called Mr. So and So // 여차여차한 경우에 on such occasions // 이유는 ~ The reason is such and such.

여차하면(如此-) in case[time / the hour] of need; in case of emergency; if need be.

여창(女唱) a male's singing in a female voice; (노래) the song sung by a male in a female voice.

여체(女體) the body of (a) woman.
여축(餘蓄) a store; a stock; savings; supplies; a reserve(예비). ¶한 푼의 ~도 없다 have not a penny saved[laid by] // 그들은 식량의 ~이 충분하지 않다 They do not have a sufficient stock[store] of food[provision]. **여축하다** save; put by; put[lay] aside; reserve; store.

여치 [동] a grasshopper; (미) a katydid.
여타(餘他) the other(s)(▶ one에 대한 나머지가 하나이면 the other, 둘 이상이면 the others); [나머지] the rest; the remainder. ¶하나는 컸으나 ~의 것은 작았다 One was big and the other was[the others were] small.

여탈(與奪) giving and depriving. ¶생살~권 the power of life and death.
여탕(女湯) the women's section (of a public bathhouse).
여태 till[by] now; until[up to] now[the present]; up[down] to date; hitherto; so [thus] far; till[to] by this time; yet. ¶~ 없었던 사건 an unprecedented event // ~ 사람에게 알려지지 않은 비밀 a secret hitherto unknown to people // ~ 그녀에게서 소식[편지]이 없었다 I haven't heard from her yet. // ~ 이렇게 어려운 고비를 당한 적이 없다 I have never had such a trying time in my life.

여태껏 till[by] now. ⇨ 여태
여트막하다 somewhat shallow. ⇨ 야트막하다
여파(餘波) an aftermath; an aftereffect; a secondary effect; a side issue; a sequel; a consequence; an influence; (the) backwash (of a war); (폭풍 등의) a trail. ¶태풍의 ~ the aftereffects of a typhoon // 전쟁의 ~로 in the aftermath of the war // 유럽의 경제 불황의 ~가 우리나라에까지 미치기 시작했다 The effects of the recession in Europe began to be felt in our country.

여편네(女便-) 1 [자기 아내] my wife. 2 [결혼한 여자] a married woman.
여필종부(女必從夫) A wife should follow her husband.; Wives should be submissive (to their husbands).
여하(如何) [어떠함] how; what. ¶이 계획의 성공 여부는 주민의 협력 ~에 달려 있다 Whether this attempt succeeds or not de-

여하간(如何間) anyhow; anyway. ⇨ *하여간

여하튼(如何-) anyway; anyhow. ⇨ *아무튼 ¶~ 떠나자 Let's start anyway.// 우리가 경기에 졌다 After all we lost the game.

여학교(女學校) a girls' (high) school.

여학생(女學生) a girl[female / lady] student; a schoolgirl; (미) a coed(남녀 공학의).

여한(餘恨) a smouldering[lingering / surviving] grudge[regret].

여한(餘寒) the lingering cold; the after-winter cold. ¶~이 아직 가시지 않는다 The cold still lingers.

여행(旅行) a trip; travel(s); a journey; (시찰·관광의) a tour; (항공·해상의) a voyage; 〔유람〕 an excursion. ¶기차 ~ railway traveling /(미) a train journey[trip] / 무전~ a penniless journey/세계 일주 ~ a round-the-world trip/수학~ a school excursion[trip] /신혼~ a honeymoon / a wedding trip / 우주~ space travel/해외 ~ a trip abroad / traveling abroad / overseas travel// ~ 기간 duration of ~ // ~ 중에 during one's trip [journey] / on one's travels / while (one is) traveling[on a journey]//세계 일주 ~을 하다 go on a round-the-world trip//그는 3개월의 ~을 떠났다 He set out[started] on a three months' journey.//그는 ~을 떠나고 없다 He is away on a trip.//그는 ~을 떠났다 He has gone on a journey.//나는 어젯밤에 ~에서 돌아왔다 I returned home from my trip last night. **여행하다** travel; tour; journey; make a journey[trip / tour]; make a voyage; make an excursion; 〔여행가다〕 go[start / set out] on a journey[tour / trip]. ¶그들은 제주도로 여행했다 They took a trip to Jejudo.// 그는 유럽을 널리 여행하였다 He traveled extensively[widely] in Europe.

●**여행가** a (great) traveler. **여행 가방** a traveling[traveler's] bag; a suitcase; (대형의) a trunk; (단기용) an overnight bag. **여행기**(-記) a book of travel; a travel book; a record [an account] of one's travels; a travel sketch; an itinerary. ¶미국 ~ a record of one's travels America. **여행담** an account[a story] of one's travels; a travelog(ue). ¶~을 말하다 talk about[give an account of] one's experiences on one's travels. **여행사** a tourist bureau; a travel bureau. **여행자** a travel(l)er; a tourist. **여행자 수표** a travel(l)er's check[(영) cheque](약어 TC).

여행(勵行) strict enforcement[observance]; rigorous execution. **여행하다** observe[carry out] strictly; enforce rigidly; execute rigorously.

여향(餘香) a lingering odor; a remaining fragrance.

여호수아서(-書) 〔성〕 The Book of Joshua; Joshua(약어 Josh.).

여호와 〔성〕 Jehovah.

여흥(餘興) **1** 〔아직 남은 흥〕 unexhausted merriment[fun]. ¶파티는 끝났으나 ~은 가시지 않았다 The party is over, but the fun is not. **2** 〔연예·오락〕 an entertainment; a side show. ¶~으로 by way of entertainment / as a side show / for an amusement//그가 ~으로 피아노를 연주했다 He entertained us by playing the piano.

여히(如一) 〔같이〕 like; as. ¶하기와 ~ as follows / as in the following/상기와 ~ as stated[mentioned] above / as in the preceding.

역(役) 〔영화 등에서 배우가 맡은 소임〕 a part; a role. ¶어린이 ~ a child role / the role of a child / a juvenile part//알맞은 ~ a fit role [part] / a part well-suited to (a person)//…의 ~을 맡아 하다 play[take / act / perform / enact] the part[role] of / play[do / personate](Caesar)//어머니와 딸의 1인 2~을 하다 perform the double role of mother and daughter// ~을 배정하다 assign[cast] the part[role] (of Cleopatra) to (a person) / cast (an actor) for[in] the part[role] (of Cleopatra) / cast (an actor) as (a widow)// 그녀에게는 카르멘의 ~이 맡겨졌다 She was cast as[in the role of] Carmen.

역(逆) 〔반대〕 the contrary; the opposite; reverse; 〔거꾸로임〕 the inverse; 〔논〕〔수〕 converse. ¶~의 contrary / reverse / opposite / inverse//~으로 conversely / inversely / the other way around[around] / contrariwise / on the contrary//~의 경우도 얼마든지 있다 There are many cases to the contrary.//~이 반드시 참은 아니다 The opposite is not always true.

역(譯) (a) translation. ⇨ *번역 ¶축어[직]~ a literal[verbatim / word-for-word] translation //신약 성서의 한국어 ~ a Korean rendering [version / translation] of the New Testament.

역(驛) a railroad[(영) railway] station; (미) a (railroad) depot; a stop. ¶서울~ Seoul Station/ 출발[도착] ~ a departure[an arrival] station/(미) a terminal station /(영) a terminus (pl. -mini, -es)// ~전 광장 a station square[plaza]// ~에서 사람을 전송[마중]하다 see off[meet] a person at the station.

역결(逆-) 〔거꾸로 된 나뭇결〕 a reverse grain; a grain (of wood, etc.) running counter to the others.

역겹다(逆-) disgusting; revolting; sickening; nauseating; nauseous; fulsome; detestable; offensive; (서술적) feel sick; be nauseated [disgusted] (at / by / with); be sick at the stomach (from). ¶역겨운 광경 a sickening [nauseating] sight/역겨운 아첨 fulsome flattery//그는 ~ He nauseates me.

역경(易經) the Book of Changes. ⇨ *주역(周易)

역경(逆境) adversity; adverse fortune[situation]; a reverse of fortune; adverse[unfavorable] circumstances. ¶~에도 굴하지 않고 without being discouraged by adversity// ~에 처하다 be in adversity / be down on [upon] one's luck / be in[under] adverse circumstances// ~과 싸우다 struggle [wrestle] with adversity[adverse circumstances]// ~을 극복하다 tide over a difficult situation// ~에 빠지다 fall into adversity / fall on bad days// ~에 잘 대처하다 make the best of one's ill fortune//그는 ~ 속에서도 희망을 버리지 않았다 Though things seemed [went] against him, he did not give up hope.

역광(선)(逆光線) backlight; (조명 방법) backlighting. ¶~으로 사진을 찍다 take a picture

against the light [into the sun].
● **역광(선) 사진** a backlighted shot.

역군 (役軍) a navvy; a laborer; a coolie(중국 등지의); [유능한 일꾼] an able worker[man]. ¶사회의 ~ a pillar of society // 개혁 운동의 ~ an active worker for a reform.

역기 (力器) [체] a barbell; the weight. ¶~를 들다 lift weights / exercise a barbell.

역내 (域內) ¶~의[에서] within the area.
● **역내 무역** regional trade; intra-trade(▶ EEC 등, 공동 무역 지역 내에서의 거래).

역년 (曆年) a calendar [civil] year.

역단층 (逆斷層) [지] an overthrust.

역대 (歷代) [여러 대] successive generations; [대대의 왕] successive kings. ¶~ 왕 successive kings / a chronological list of sovereigns(연대표로 한) // 내각 successive cabinets.
● **역대기 상[하]** [성] The First[Second] Book of the Chronicles; Ⅰ[Ⅱ] Chronicles.

역도 (力道) [체] weight lifting. ¶~를 하다 lift weights / do weight lifting.
● **역도 선수** a weight lifter.

역도 (逆徒) (a group of) rebels; insurgents; traitors.

역량 (力量) [능력] ability; (a) capacity; capability; caliber; (영) calibre. ¶~이 있는 사람 a man of ability [talent] / a talented [an able] man / a man of high caliber // ~ 있는 정치가 an able [a capable / competent] statesman // ~을 보이다[발휘하다] display one's ability / show one's paces // ~을 시험하다 test [try] (a person's) ability / put (a person) through (his) paces // …할 만한 ~이 있다 be equal to [competent for] the work / have the ability to do the work // …할 만한 ~이 없다 have no capacity to (do) [of (doing)] / be not equal to (the task) // 그는 장관으로서의 ~이 있다 He has the ability [capacity] to be a minister of state. // 그는 정치가로서의 ~을 발휘했다 He showed his competence as statesman.

역력하다 (歷歷-) clear; plain; obvious; manifest; unmistakable; vivid. ¶역력한 사실 an obvious [a glaring] truth // 교살당한 흔적이 ~ There is unmistakable evidence of his having been strangled. **역력히** clearly; plainly; evidently; obviously; manifestly; unmistakably. ¶그것은 그의 얼굴에 ~ 나타나 있다 It can be plainly seen on his face. // 우리는 그가 기뻐하고 있다는 것을 알 수 있었다 We saw clearly that he was glad.

역류 (逆流) a counter current; an adverse [inverse] current; a counterflow; a back flow; a backward flow; (조수의) an adverse tide; [역류하기] flowing backward; (체액·음식의) reflux; regurgitation. **역류하다** flow backward [upstream]. ¶물이 역류하고 있다 The water is flowing backward(s).

역리 (疫痢) [의] children's dysentery; infant diarrhea.

역리 (逆理) unreasonableness. ⇨배리(背理)

역마 (驛馬) a post horse. ⇨역말₁

역마을 (驛-) a post town [village].

역마차 (驛馬車) a stagecoach; a stage.

역말 (驛-) **1** [역참의 말] a post horse; a relay horse. ¶~을 갈아타다 take another relay (horse). **2** a post town. ⇨역마을

역모 (逆謀) a treasonable conspiracy; a plot of treason. **역모하다** plot treason (against); conspire (against); conspire to rise in revolt [mutiny].

역무 (役務) labor; service; utility and constructional services.
● **역무배상** reparation in services; a service indemnity.

역무원 (驛務員) a station employee [attendant]; (집합적) the station staff.

역문 (譯文) a translation; a version; a rendering.

역반응 (逆反應) [화] an reverse reaction.

역방 (歷訪) (make) a round of calls [visits] (to).

역법 (曆法) the calendar.

역병 (疫病) an epidemic; a pestilence; a plague; (가축의) an epizootic; an epizooty. ¶~이 발생했다 An epidemic broke out. // ~이 돌고 있다 An epidemic is raging [prevalent].

역부족 (力不足) want of ability. **역부족이다** (서술적) (사물이) be beyond one's capacities [reach]; be above one's ability; be not in [out of] one's power; be more than one can do; (사람이) be unequal [not equal] (to the task); be incompetent (to do / for doing); bite off more than one can chew.

역불급하다 (力不及-) (서술적) be beyond one's power; be above one's ability.

역비 (逆比) [수] an inverse ratio. ⇨반비(反比)

역비례 (逆比例) [수] an inverse proportion. ⇨반비례

역사 (力士) a man of great strength. ⇨장사(壯士)

역사 (役事) construction; construction works; work of construction; engineering [public] works. **역사하다** do construction [engineering] works.

역사 (歷史) **1** [인류의 흥망·변천 과정] history; (책) a history; annals; a chronicle. ¶한국 ~ Korean history / the history of Korea // 서양 ~ Occidental [European] history // 동양 ~ Oriental history // ~ 이전의 prehistoric // ~ 이전에 in prehistoric times / before the dawn of history // ~가 시작된 후로 since the beginning [dawn] of history // ~를 만든 사람들 people who made history // ~에 남다 go down [be recorded / find a place / stay put] in history // 길이 ~에 남다 remain long [be recorded / live] in history // ~에 이름을 남기다 leave one's mark on history // 세계 ~에 유례가 없다 be unparalleled in the annals of world history // ~를 장식하다 adorn the history (of) // ~를 더듬다 trace the history (of) // ~를 거슬러 올라가다 go back in history // ~는 되풀이한다 History repeats itself. / History runs its cycle. // 그 사건은 ~에 실려 있지 않다 The event is not mentioned in history. // ~에 의하면 그것은 사실이 아닌 것 같다 History shows [tells] that it was not true.

2 [내력·유래] history; [전통] tradition. ¶~가 오랜 대학 an old [ancient] university // 우리 은행은 50년의 ~를 지니고 있다 Our bank has (had) a history of fifty years. // 우리 대학은 장구하고 빛나는 ~를 자랑하고 있다 Our university can boast a long and glorious history.
● **역사가** a historian. **역사관**(-觀) a historical view; a [one's] view of history. **역사극** a historical play [drama]. **역사 소설** a historical novel. **역사의식** historical consciousness.

역사학 history; historical studies [science].

역사(驛舍) (철도의) a station building.

역사적(歷史的) historic. ¶~ 사실[인물] a historical fact [person(age)] // ~으로 (보아) historically / from a historical point of view // 이 건물은 ~으로 중요하다 This building is of historical importance.

역산(逆算) inverse [reverse] operation. **역산하다** count [reckon / calculate] backward(s); calculate back (to).

역서(曆書) an almanac. ⇨ *책력

역서(譯書) a (Korean) translation [version] (of).

역선전(逆宣傳) counterpropaganda; a forestalling move. **역선전하다** carry out counterpropaganda.

역설(力說) emphasis; stress; assertion. **역설하다** emphasize; stress; put [lay] stress [emphasis] (upon); assert emphatically [with emphasis]; insist (upon). ¶그녀는 그러한 설비의 필요성을 역설했다 She was very emphatic about the need for such facilities. / She urged [pressed] upon them the need for such institution. // 그는 그 사건에 관계가 없다고 역설했다 He insisted that he had nothing to do with the affair.

역설(逆說) a paradox.
● **역설가** a paradoxist.

역설적(逆說的) paradoxical. ¶~으로 말하면 paradoxically speaking // ~으로 들릴지 모르지만 It may sound [seem] paradoxical, but ....

역성 (undue) favoritism; partiality; nepotism (친척에 대한). **역성하다** be partial (to); show favoritism [partiality] (toward); take part [sides] (with). ¶그는 학생 누구에게도 역성하지 않는다 He does not show any preference for any one of his pupils. / He treats all the pupils fairly. / He doesn't have any pets.

역성들다 be partial (to). ⇨ *역성하다(⇨ *역성)

역수(逆數) [수] a reciprocal (number); an inverse number. ¶3의 ~는 1/3이다 The reciprocal of 3 is 1/3.

역수입(逆輸入) reimportation; reimport. **역수입하다** reimport.

역수출(逆輸出) reexportation; reexport. **역수출하다** reexport.

역술(譯述) translation; rendering. **역술하다** translate; render (into Korean).
● **역술자** a translator.

역습(逆襲) a counterattack; a sortie; a counteroffensive; (말로써의) a retort; a repartee. **역습하다** counterattack; make [launch] a counterattack (on / against); [반론하다] retort (on); give a retort (on); turn the tables (on a person). ¶야당이 여당을 역습했다 The opposition made a counterattack on the ruling party. // 그녀는 그의 비난에 대해 날카롭게 역습했다 She retorted sharply to his reproach. → **역습당하다** meet with a reverse / have the tables turned upon (one).

역시(亦是) **1** [또한·마찬가지로] too; also; (not) either; as well; likewise; like the rest; as is usual (with). ¶나 ~ 그렇소 So am I. / (구어) Me too. // 그 계획에 나 ~ 반대입니다 I am against the plan, too. // 수현이도 예뻤지만 미영이 ~ 예뻤다 Suhyeon was beautiful, and so was Miyeong [but Miyeong was beautiful too]. // 아버지도 ~ 당근을 싫어하신다 My father doesn't like carrots, either. // 나 ~ 그런 짓은 하기 싫다 Neither do I wish to do such a thing. **2** [여전히] still; all [just] the same. ¶그녀는 지금도 ~ 아름답다 She is as beautiful as ever. **3** [결국] after all (is said and done). ¶어린이는 ~ 어린이다 Boys will be boys. **4** [그래도] but then; notwithstanding; nevertheless; though; however; in spite of; with all (one's wealth); none the less; for all (one's faults). ¶그녀는 결점이 많지만 나는 ~ 그녀를 좋아한다 I do not love her the less for all her faults. / She has many faults, but I love her none the less. // 아무리 돈이 많아도 죽음은 ~ 면할 수 없다 No matter how wealthy he may be, a man cannot escape death. **5** [생각했던 대로] as (was) expected; true to one's expectations; as one expected. ¶~ 그는 실패했다 He failed as I feared. // 그 소문은 ~ 헛소문이었다 The rumor turned out to be false just as I (had) expected [suspected]. // 내가 말한 대로지 Didn't I tell you so?

역시(譯詩) a translated poem; a poem in translation. ¶하이네의 ~를 읽다 read Heine's poems in translation.

역신(疫神) **1** [천연두를 앓게 하는 귀신] the (evil) spirit of smallpox. **2** smallpox. ⇨ *천연두

역암(礫巖) [지] conglomerate; pudding stone.

역어(譯語) words [terms] used in a translation; an (English) equivalent (for); an equivalent term in translation. ¶~를 고르다 choose apt [appropriate] terms for translation // 이 번역에는 타당하지 않은 ~가 아주 많다 This translation contains a large number of terms which are not quite appropriate. // 이 낱말에는 적절한 우리말 ~가 없다 There is no proper [appropriate / adequate] Korean equivalent for this word. // 영어 「스프링」의 ~는 「봄」이다 The Korean (equivalent) for the English word "spring" is "bom".

역연하다(歷然—) clear; manifest; obvious; evident; plain; unmistakable. ¶역연한 사실 a glaring [an obvious / an undeniable] fact.

역외(域外) ¶~에서 out of the area.

역용(逆用) a reverse use. **역용하다** make a reverse use (of); turn (the enemy's propaganda) to one's own advantage; take advantage of (a person's kindness).

역원(驛員) a station employee. ⇨ *역무원

역일(曆日) a calendar [civil] day.

역임(歷任) successive [consecutive] service in various posts. **역임하다** successively fill [hold] various (Government) posts. ¶그는 여러 유럽 국가의 대사 직을 역임했다 He was ambassador to various European countries, one after another.

역자(譯者) a translator (of Hamlet).

역작(力作) a labored [laborious / great] work; a (literary) work bearing marks of labor and effort; a masterpiece; (프) a tour de force (pl. tours de force). ¶문학[예술]상의 ~ a fine literary [artistic] effort / a masterpiece. **역작하다** make [produce] a masterpiece; work laboriously [strenuously] (on).

역작용(逆作用) a reaction; an adverse effect. ¶~을 일으키다 cause a reaction (against) / produce a backlash.

역장(驛長) a stationmaster (at Seoul); (미) a station agent(작은 역의).

역저(力著) [힘써서 지은 책] a literary effort; a fine literary work.

역적(逆賊) a rebel; a traitor; an insurgent. ¶~모의를 하다 plot treason (against) / conspire rebel[traitor].
● **역적질** (a) rebellion; (high) treason.

역전(力戰) hard fighting; a hard[good / desperate] fight. **역전하다** fight hard[well / desperately]; put up a good[hard] fight. ¶그들은 역전하였으나 지고 말았다 They fought with all their strength, but in vain. / They put up a good fight but lost.

역전(逆轉) a reversal; a reversion; a turnabout; a turn around; [항] a loop; [기상] (기온의) (an) inversion. ¶기온의 ~ a temperature[thermal] inversion. **역전하다** reverse (itself); be reversed; go into reverse; (기온이) be inverted; invert; (비행기가) loop the loop; [해] work aback. ¶형세가 역전하여 우리에게 유리해졌다 The situation reversed (itself) in our favor. / The situation changed[The tide turned] to our advantage.
● **역전승** a come-from-behind victory. ¶~을 하다 win (a game) after defeat seems certain / (미국 구어) win[gain] a come-from-behind victory (over) // 옥스퍼드가 ~했다 Oxford came from behind[turned the tables] and won the game[beat (the opposing team)]. **역전패** suffering a come-from-behind defeat. ¶~를 하다 suffer a (5-4) come-from-behind defeat (to) // 우리는 ~했다 We lost the game after our victory seemed certain. // 나는 마지막 순간에 가서 그에게 ~했다 He turned the tables on me at the last moment.

역전(歷戰) [많은 싸움을 겪는 것] long record of active service. ¶~의 용사 a (combat) veteran (soldier) / an experienced [a seasoned] soldier / battle-tried warrior / (영) an old soldier.

역전(驛前) a station front. ¶~의 거리 a station road / (미) a depot street // ~에서 at [in front of] a station.
● **역전 광장** a station square[plaza].

역전 경주(驛傳競走) a long-distance relay (road) race.

역점(力點) [중심이 되는 점] emphasis; stress. ¶~을 두다 lay[put / place] emphasis [stress] on (a matter) / emphasize / accent / accentuate / attach importance (to) // 우리는 어학에 ~을 두고 있다 We emphasize the study of languages. **2** [물] the point (of a lever) where (the) force is applied.

역정(逆情) anger. ¶~이 나다[~을 내다] become [get / grow] angry (at) / be angered by [at].

역조(逆潮) [풍향과 반대의 조류] a weather tide; [배의 진로와 반대로 흐르는 조류] a counter tide; a head tide; an adverse current; [배의 진로를 가로지르는 조류] a cross tide.

역조(逆調) an unfavorable[adverse] condition. ¶무역 ~ an unfavorable balance of trade / an adverse trade balance / import excess.

역조(歷朝) [역대의 왕조] successive reigns [dynasties]; [역대의 임금] successive kings [emperors].

역주(譯註) translation and annotation; translation with notes.

역주(力走) sprinting. **역주하다** run as fast [hard] as one can; run for all one is worth; (경주에서) make[put on] a spurt; spurt; sprint.

역진(力盡) [힘이 다하는 것] exhaustion (of strength). **역진하다** (사람이) be exhausted; be spent up; be wrung out.

역진세(逆進稅) degressive tax.

역청(瀝青) [광] (mineral) pitch; bitumen; asphalt. ¶~질의 bituminous.
● **역청탄** bituminous[pitch / soft] coal.

역코스(逆—) the reverse course. ¶~를 가다 follow the reverse[opposite] course / go in the opposite direction.

역투(力投) [야구] all-out pitching. **역투하다** pitch[hurl] with might and main[all one's strength]; pitch hard; put everything one has into one's pitching.

역투(力鬪) hard fighting. ⇨**역전**(力戰)

역풍(逆風) a head wind; an adverse [an unfavorable / a contrary / a foul] wind. ¶~을 무릅쓰고 in the teeth of foul wind // 주자는 ~을 받으며 달렸다 The runner ran against an unfavorable [a head] wind.

역하다(逆—) [비위에 거슬리다] sickening; nauseating; repulsive; repellent; revolting; disgusting; offensive; rank. ¶역한 냄새 a repulsive smell / a disgusting odor // 그녀에 대한 생각만 하여도 나는 역했다 I was repelled by the very thought of her.

역학(力學) dynamics; mechanics. ¶동(動)~ kinetics // 정(靜)~ statics // 응용 ~ applied mechanics // ~상의 [적인] dynamic // ~상 [적] 으로 dynamically.

역학(易學) the science of divination.

역할(役割) (a) duty; an office. ⇨**구실** ¶~을 정하다 allot [assign] a part[role] (to a person) // 중요한 ~을 하다 play an important[a key / a large / a major] part[role] (in a matter) // 빛은 식물의 성장상 중요한 ~을 한다 Light plays an important part in the growth of plants. // 그는 교장으로서의 ~을 그다지 잘 수행하지 못했다 He could not perform his duties as principal very well.

역행(力行) endeavor(s); (strenuous) effort(s). **역행하다** endeavor; make (strenuous) efforts; exert oneself; strive; try hard to do.

역행(逆行) **1** reverse[backward]; retrogression; retrogradation; countermarch. ¶~적 retrogressive. **역행하다** go back; move[go] backward(s); retrogress; retrograde; recede; reverse; [거스르다] run counter (to); be contrary (to). ¶시대[시류]에 ~ go against [run counter to] (the trend of) the times / row[swim] against the stream / [비유] put back the clock // 민주주의에 ~ run counter to democracy. **2** [역행 운동] [천] the retrograde motion (of a planet).

역혼(逆婚) marriage in reverse order. **역혼하다** marry in reverse order.

역효과(逆效果) an opposite effect; a contrary [reverse / boomerang] effect; a contrary [counter] result; an adverse reaction. ¶~를 내다[가져오다 / 초래하다] have the opposite [reverse / adverse] effect[result] to what was intended / bring about a contrary [boomerang] effect / produce a contrary result / defeat its own end[purpose] // 엄격한

엮다

제한이 ~를 냈다 The effect of the strict controls was contrary to what was expected.

엮다 1 [읽어 만들다] weave; plait; entwine (a garland); [묶다] tie (with a rope). ¶야자 잎을 엮어 만든 오두막집 a hut made of woven [plaited] palm fronds∥골풀로 돗자리를 ~ weave mats (out) of[from] rushes. **2** [편찬하다] weave (in / into); compile; edit. ¶이야기를 ~ weave a tale[story]∥역사 연표를 ~ compile[edit] a history chart∥세 가지 이야기를 엮어서 하나의 소설을 만들다 weave three stories together into a novel.

엮음 1 [엮는 일] weaving; plaiting; [엮은 것] a woven thing[item]. **2** [편찬] compiling; editing; a compilation(편집물). ¶P씨 ~ compiled by Mr. P.

연(年) a year. ¶~ 수입 an annual[a yearly] income∥~ 평균 the yearly mean∥~ 1회 once a year / annually∥~ 1회의 yearly / annual∥~ 2[4]회의 지불 semiannual [quarterly] payment∥~ 9퍼센트의 이자 interest of nine percent a year[per annum] / annual interest of nine percent∥~ 2회 상여금을 받는다 The bonus is given twice a year.∥이 지방의 ~ 강우량은 약 500밀리이다 The annual[yearly] precipitation in this district is [amounts to] about 500mm.

연(鉛) lead. ⇨ᵇ납

연(鳶) a kite. ¶~을 날리다 fly a kite∥바람에 ~을 올리다 let up a kite with the wind∥~을 당기다 pull at the string of a kite∥~을 내리다 draw[reel] in a kite / bring down a kite.

연(蓮) [식] a lotus. ⇨ᵇ연꽃1

연-(連) continuous(ly); continual(ly); consecutive(ly); in succession; successive(ly); without a break. ¶~ 사흘 (for) three consecutive days / (for) three days in succession[in a row] / for three days running[on end].

연-(延) [통틀어] the total; the aggregate. ¶~ 근로 시간 the total number of working hours / the total man-hours∥~면적[평수] the total[gross] floor area[space] (in *pyeong*)∥~ 일수 the total number of (working) days / the total man-days∥~톤수 total tonnage.

연가(戀歌) a love song[poem]; a song[poem] of love; an amatory poem.

연간(年刊) [일 년에 한 번씩만 간행을 하는 간행물] a yearly. ¶~의 published once a year / yearly (magazines) / annual (bulletins).

연간(年間) ¶~의 yearly / annual∥~ 50억 달러에 달하다 amount to 5 billion dollars a year∥자동차는 ~ 몇 대가 생산됩니까 How many cars are produced a year?

● **연간 계획** a program for the year. **연간 소득** an annual income.

연감(年鑑) a yearbook; an almanac. ¶경제[통계] ~ an economic[a statistical] yearbook∥세계 ~ (저서명) The World Almanac.

연강(軟鋼) mild [soft] steel.

연거푸(連-) successively; in succession; consecutively; on end. ¶~ 묻다 fire questions in rapid succession∥~ 다섯 번을 이기다 win five consecutive victories / win five victories consecutively∥~ 때리다 strike without stopping / give repeated blows∥사고가 ~ 발생했다 Accidents occurred in (rapid) succession[one after another].∥기침이 ~ 났다 I had a fit of coughing.∥그는 담배를 ~ 피운다 He is a chain smoker. / He chain-smokes.∥총소리가 세 번 ~ 났다 There were three gun shots in quick succession.

연건평(延建坪) the total floor space. ¶이 건물은 ~이 2,000제곱미터이다 This building has a floor space of 2,000 square meters [has 2,000 square meters of floor space] (in total).

연결(連結) coupling; connection; interconnection; linking; (인공위성·우주선의) docking. ¶5량 ~의 열차 a five-car[-carriage/-coach] train. **연결하다** couple; attach; connect; interconnect; join; interlink. ¶파이프를 3개 ~ connect three pipes∥기관차[식당차]를 ~ couple[attach] a locomotive to [dining car] (a train)∥이 버스 노선은 두 도시를 연결한다 This bus route connects the two cities. ➜¶이 열차에 침대차가 연결되어 있습니까 Are there sleeping cars attached [coupled on] to this train?∥이 길은 100미터 앞에서 고속도로와 연결되어 있다 This road connects with [is connected to] the superhighway 100 meters ahead.

● **연결기(-器)** a coupler; a connector; a connecter.

연계(連繫) connection; linking; liaison; contact; touch. ¶긴밀한 ~가 있다 keep in close touch[contact] (with) / be closely connected (with).

연고(軟膏) (an) ointment; (a) salve; (an) unguent; (an) inunction. ¶수은[붕산] ~ mercurial[boric] ointment∥상처에 ~를 바르다 apply ointment[salve] to a wound.

연고(緣故) 1 a reason; a cause. ⇨ᵇ사유(事由) **2** [관계·연분] relation; (a) connection; affinity; a tie-in; (속어) (a) pull. ¶모차르트의 ~가 있는 곳 a place noted [remembered] for its connection with Mozart∥~가 없다 have no connection (with) / have nothing to do (with)∥깊은 ~가 있다 be closely [intimately] connected (with) / be in close connection (with).

● **연고권** preemptive rights. ¶~을 인정하다 give (a person) preemptive rights. **연고자** a relative; a relation.

연골(軟骨) 1 [생] (a) cartilage; (요리에) gristle. ¶~성의 cartilaginous∥~질의 gristly∥~뼈 a cartilage bone∥갑상 ~ the thyroid cartilage. **2** [어린 사람] a young person; a man of tender age.

● **연골어류** cartilaginous fish. **연골 조직** cartilage [cartilaginous] tissue. **연골한(-漢)** a weak-willed man; a spineless [backboneless] fellow.

연공(年功) 1 [다년간 근무한 공로] long service. ¶~으로 승급시키다 raise a person's salary as a reward for long service∥~에 따라 승진하게 된다 You will be promoted according to the length of your service [the seniority system]. **2** [다년간의 경험] long experience. ¶~을 쌓다 gain experience (in)∥그는 변호사로서 ~을 쌓은 사람이다 He has a great deal of experience as a lawyer.∥그는 판매원으로서 ~을 쌓았다 He has many years of experience in selling [as a salesman].

● **연공서열 제도** the seniority system.

연관(煙管) 1 a pipe. ⇨ᵇ담뱃대(⇨담배) **2** [연기가 통하는 관] a smoke pipe[tube]; a breeching.

연관(鉛管) a lead pipe[tube]; plumbing.

●연관공 a plumber. 연관 공사 plumbing.
연관(聯關) **1** connection; relation. ⇨관련 **2** [생] linkage. ¶~군 a linkage group.
연구(研究) (a) study; research(es); [조사] (an) investigation; (an) inquiry.(▶ study는 연구·공부 등의 뜻으로 일반적으로 쓰이는 데 대하여 research는 무엇인가 새로운 발견을 목표로 하는 연구로, 단수의 의미로서 복수가 되는 경우는 있어도 수사(數詞)를 쓰는 일은 없음. 셀 때는 a piece of research 등이라 함. investigation은 정성을 들인 조사 등에 쓰임) ¶나의 개구리에 대한 ~ my research [researches] on toads // ~ 결과를 발표하다 (출판물로) publish the results of one's research work (in a bulletin) / (구두로) read one's paper // ~를 **계속하다** continue one's study / ~를 끝내다 complete [conclude] one's study / 그 문제에 대해서는 지금 ~ 중이다 The problem is now under study. **연구하다** study; make a study (of); do research (in); investigate; inquire (into). ¶그는 사회학을 연구하고 있다 He is doing research in sociology. / 무엇을 연구하고 있습니까 What kind of study are you engaged in?
●**연구 개발** research and development(약어 R&D). **연구 논문** a treatise; a research paper; a thesis (pl. -ses); a dissertation(학위 논문); a monograph(전공 논문). **연구 단체** a research organization[body]. **연구 발표** the presentation of the results of one's study [research]. ¶~를 하다 (출판물로) publish the results of one's research (work) (in a bulletin) / (구두로) read one's paper (at a meeting). **연구비** research funds[expenses].
연구생(員) a research student[worker]. **연구소** a research institute; a (research) laboratory; (구어) a lab. **연구실** a study room; (화학 등의) a laboratory; (대학의 세미나용의) a seminar room; (대학교수 개인의) an office. **연구회** (단체) a society for the research [study] (of); (집회) a study meeting.
연구(軟球) a softball; a rubber ball.
연구(聯句) a linked verse; a couplet.
연구개(軟口蓋) [생] the soft palate; the velum (pl. -la).
●**연구개음** a velar (sound).
연극(演劇) **1** [극] (집합적) drama; (개개의 작품) a play; a drama. ¶~적인[상의] dramatic / theatrical // ~의 장기 공연 a long run of a play // 소설을 ~으로 꾸미다 dramatize a novel // 사건을 ~으로 꾸미다 make a play of an incident // ~을 **하다** present[give] a play / perform a play on the stage / (극장·극단이) put on a play // ~을 보러 가다 go to (see) plays[a play / the theater] // 주간 공연의 ~을 보러 가다 go to a matinee. **2** [거짓을 사실처럼 꾸미는 일] acting; playacting; a fake; (구어) a put-up job. ¶~을 하다[부리다] act (as if) / playact / pretend / fake / feign / use a trick // 그녀는 ~을 하고 있어 She is just putting on an act. / She is only acting a part. // 그녀는 어디까지가 ~인지 알 수 없다 I can't tell how much is an act and how much is her true self. // 그 나라의 친소 정책은 단순한 ~이다 The pro-Soviet policy of the country is only an act[a gesture].
●**연극계** the theatrical[dramatic] world. **연극 애호가** a playgoer; a theatergoer. **연극인** a man of the theater.

연근(蓮根) [식] a lotus root[rhizome].
연금(年金) a pension; an annuity.(▶ pension은 특히 국가·회사에서 나오는 연금) ¶**종신**[**질병·노령**] ~ a life[a disability / an old-age] pension // **유족** ~ an annuity for a bereaved [fatherless] family // **복지** ~ a welfare pension // ~**을 받다** receive a pension / draw one's pension // **국민** ~에 들어 있다 I am covered by the national pension plan. // 그는 ~으로 생활하고 있다 He lives on a pension.
●**연금 수령자** a pensioner; an annuitant. **연금 제도** a pension plan.
연금(軟禁) lenient[informal] confinement; house arrest. **연금하다** confine (a person) leniently. →¶그는 자택에 연금되어 있다 He is confined informally in his own house. / He is under house arrest.
연금술(鍊金術) alchemy.
●**연금술사** an alchemist.
연기(延期) [기한을 뒤로 물림] postponement; deferment; adjournment(회의의); respite(집행·징수 등의); [유예] grace; reprieve. ¶3일간의 ~ an extension[additional run] of three days // 지불의 ~ delayed[deferred] pay. **연기하다** postpone; put off; [휴회하다] adjourn. ¶나는 편지의 답장을 쓰는 것을 며칠 연기했다 I put off answering the letter for several days. →¶연기되다 be put off / be postponed / be deferred // 소풍은 비로 인해 하루 연기되었다 The excursion was postponed until the following day because of rain. // 형 집행이 연기되었다 The condemned man was given a respite[stay]. // 회의는 모레까지 연기되었다 The meeting was adjourned until the day after tomorrow. / The meeting will be resumed the day after tomorrow. // 그들은 지불 기일을 연기시키려고 했다 They tried to have the due date of payment postponed.
연기(煙氣) smoke; fumes(특히 악취가 나거나 해로운). ¶**한 줄기의** ~ a streak of smoke // **뭉게뭉게 피는** ~ billows of smoke // ~를 **내뿜고 있는 화산** a volcano emitting[giving out] smoke // ~를 **내다** send up[out] smoke // ~**가 나다** smoke / smolder[(영) smoulder] // ~**에 숨이 막히다** be choked by smoke // ~**에 질식하여 죽다** be suffocated [choked] to death by smoke / die of smoke inhalation // ~**처럼 사라지다** vanish[melt] into thin air / (희망 등이) go up in smoke // 기관차가 ~를 내뿜었다 The locomotive puffed (out) smoke. // 담배 ~가 눈에 매웠다 The cigarette smoke irritated my eyes.
연기(演技) (연극 등의) acting; performance(▶ 체조나 피겨 스케이팅의 경우에도 쓸 수 있음). ¶그는 훌륭한 ~를 보여 주었다 He gave a wonderful performance. // 그는 ~를 잘한다 [~가 서투르다] He is a good[poor] actor. / He performs well[poorly]. // 그의 서투른 ~가 연극을 망쳐 놓았다 His poor acting spoiled the whole play. **연기하다** perform; (어떤 장면을) enact; put on. ¶그는 햄릿 역을 연기했다 He played[performed] the part of Hamlet.
●**연기자** a performer.
연기 투표(連記投票) cumulative voting; a vote[ballot] with plural entry. ¶**무기명** ~ a secret[vote] with plural[multiple] entry.
연기하다(連記-) list (the names); make a list (of); write[put] down (the names). ¶(투표에서) 2명 ~ write down two names on a ballot.

연꽃(蓮-) [식] **1** [수련과의 여러해살이 물풀] a lotus; an Indian lotus. **2** [그 꽃] a lotus flower.

연날리기(鳶-) kite-flying. ¶~ 대회 a kite-flying contest [meet].

연내(年內) ¶~에 within the year / before the end of the year / before the year is out.

연년(年年) every year; yearly. ⇨매년
● **연년생** a child born within a year of another; children born in (two) successive years. ¶그 형제는 ~이다 The brothers were born in consecutive years [within a year of each other].

연년(連年) consecutive [successive] years; (for) years running [on end].

연놈 man and woman; male and female beings; a chap and a bitch.

연단(演壇) a platform; a rostrum (pl. ~s, -tra). ¶~에 서다 take [stand on] the platform [rostrum] // ~을 떠나다 leave the platform // 나는 아직 ~에 서 본 일이 없다 I have never appeared before the audience. / I have never made a speech in public.

연달다(連-) continue; keep. ⇨잇달다 ¶연달은 흉악 범죄 a succession of atrocious crimes // 연달은 3안타 three back-to-back [consecutive] hits // 변호사의 연달은 질문에 증인은 당황했다 Faced with successive questions from the lawyer, the witness lost his presence of mind. // 그는 연달아 책을 다섯 권 출판했다 He published five books in (rapid) succession. // 기자들은 총리에게 연달아 질문을 퍼부어 댔다 The reporters showered [rained] questions on the Prime Minister. // 나는 연달아 기침이 나왔다 I had a fit of coughing. // 연달아 사고가 발생했다 Accidents occurred in (rapid) succession [one after another].

연대(年代) **1** [시대] an age; an epoch; a period. ¶1990년대에 in the nineteen-nineties / in the 1990's // 세종 ~에 in the Sejong Era [Period] // 화석의 ~를 추정하다 estimate the age of a fossil. **2** [사건이 일어난 때] a (historical) date (of a battle). ¶~를 알 수 없는 dateless // 나는 역사 ~를 암기하는 것이 서투르다 I'm bad at memorizing dates.
● **연대기**(-記) a chronicle; annals. **연대순** chronological order; order of date. ¶~의 chronological // ~으로 chronologically / in chronological order / in order of date // 다음 사건들을 ~으로 배열하여라 Put the following events in chronological order. **연대표** a chronological table.

연대(連帶) solidarity. ¶~의 joint // ~로 jointly // ~로 돈을 차용하다 borrow money on joint and several responsibility. **연대되다** be collectively responsible (to); be jointly and severally liable (to).
● **연대감** a sense [feeling] of solidarity [common bonds]. **연대 보증** joint liability on guarantee. ¶~을 서다 stand [go] joint and several surety (for the loan of one million won which A receives from B) / hold joint and several liability / be jointly and severally liable (for the debt of one million won that A owes to B). **연대 보증인** a joint surety. **연대 책임** joint liability; collective responsibility. ¶~을 지다 be collectively responsible (to a person for a thing) // 사고에 대한 ~을 지다 take joint [collective] responsibility for the accident.

연대(聯隊) [군] a regiment. ¶~의 regimental // 보병 ~ a foot [an infantry] regiment // 기병 ~ a cavalry regiment.
● **연대 본부** the regimental headquarters. **연대장** a regimental commander; the colonel of the regiment.

연도(年度) the year. ¶사업 [영업] ~ the business year // 회계 ~ (미) the fiscal year / (영) the financial year // 미곡 ~ the rice (crop) year // ~ 초 [말기]에 at the beginning [end] of the fiscal year // ~본 ~의 사업 계획 the business plan for the current year // 2002년도의 예산 the budget for fiscal 2002 // 내년도의 교육 과정 the curriculum for the next academic [school] year.

연도(沿道) a route; a roadside (길가). ¶~의 [에] along the route [road / way] / by the roadside // ~에는 환영하는 군중이 줄지어 있었다 The route was lined with welcoming crowds. // ~ 양측에는 구경꾼들이 꽉 차 있었다 Both sides of the street were crowded with spectators.

연도(煙道) a (fire) flue; a chimney flue; a smoke duct.

연도(連禱) [가] litany; rogations.

연동(聯動·連動) working [operating] together; [공] gearing; linkage.
● **연동기** a clutch. **연동 장치** an interlocker; an interlocking device; a gear (of a machine); gearing.

연동 운동(蠕動運動) [생] peristalsis; a peristaltic motion [movement]. ¶~을 하다 move peristaltically.

연두(年頭) (at) the beginning of a year. ¶~ 인사 New Year('s) greetings.
● **연두 교서** (the President's annual) State of the Union Message to Congress (미국의); the State of the National Message (한국의). **연두사** the New Year's address [message].

연두(색)(軟豆色) yellowish [light] green.
● **연둣빛** yellowish [light] green. ⇨연두

연락(連絡·聯絡) **1** [관계] (a) connection; junction; [접촉] (a) contact; touch; [연계] liaison; concert; [군] communication(s). ¶긴밀한 [끊임없는] ~ a close [constant] contact [touch] (with) // ~과 ~이 있다 have connection with ... / be connected [linked] with ... // 무선으로 ~을 유지하다 maintain radio contact (with an astronaut) // 그와는 ~이 잘 되지 않는다 I'm having trouble getting in touch with him. // 기지와의 ~이 끊어졌다 We've been cut off from the base. / We have lost contact with the base. **연락하다** contact; make contact (with); connect (with); get in touch (with); communicate (with). ¶경찰과 ~ contact the police.
2 [통신] communication; correspondence. ¶외부와의 ~이 끊기어 있다 be held incommunicado // ...으로부터 ~을 받다 receive a communication from // 그녀로부터 ~이 있었다 I have heard [had word] from her. // 그들과 정기적으로 ~을 취하고 있다 We correspond with them regularly. / We keep up a regular correspondence with them. // 그 비행기는 이륙한 지 한 시간 후에 ~이 끊기었다 The airplane went out of communication an hour after its take-off. **연락하다** communicate (a person that...); let (a person) know. ¶전화로 ~ speak to (a person) over

the telephone / contact (a person) by phone // 편지로 ~ write (to a person).
3 [교통편의 접속] connection; communication. ¶이 열차는 다음 역에서 버스와 ~이 된다 This train connects to [with] a bus at the next station. / There is a bus connection at the next station. **연락하다** connect with; communicate with; join; meet. →¶본선과 연락되다 join the main line (at).
● **연락부절** ceaseless traffic. **연락선**(-船) a ferryboat; a ferry steamer. ¶**부관**(釜關) ~ a Busan-Shimonoseki ferryboat. **연락소** a liaison office. **연락 장교** a liaison officer. **연락처** where to make contact.

연래(年來) (some) years (past); these several [many] years. ¶~의 of long standing // ~의 현안 a long-pending question // 그는 마침내 ~의 소망을 이루었다 He has finally accomplished his long-cherished desire.

연령(年齡) age; years. ⇨나이 ¶**평균** ~ the average age // **결혼** ~ the age at which a person marries // **정신** ~ one's mental age // 잭과 존은 같은 ~이다 Jack and John are (of) the same age. // 그는 ~에 비해 젊게 보인다 He looks young for his age. // ~과는 상관없이 참가할 수 있다 People can participate irrespective of age. / There is no age limit for participation.
● **연령 제한** the age limit(s). **연령층** an age group [bracket]. ¶이 영화는 2, 30세의 ~에 인기가 있다 This film is popular with the age group between 20 and 30.

연례(年例) [관용어적] yearly; annual. ¶~적인 여름 축제가 시작되었다 The annual summer festival has begun.
● **연례 보고** an annual report. **연례행사** an annual function [event].

연로하다(年老-) aged; old; senile. ¶연로한 사람들 the aged [old] / old people / people far advanced in life // 연로한 부모를 모시고 있다 have one's old parents to support.

연료(燃料) fuel. ¶**액체** [고체 / 기체] ~ liquid [solid / gaseous] fuel // **핵** ~ nuclear fuel // **배** [비행기] 에 ~를 보급하다 refuel a ship [an airplane].
● **연료 보급** refueling. **연료비** the cost of fuel; fuel expenses.

연루(連累) implication; involvement; complicity. **연루하다** be implicated in (a crime); be involved in (an affair); be entangled in (a plot). →¶이 사건에는 아무래도 그가 연루되어 있는 것 같다 He seems to be involved in this case. // 그는 그 수회 사건에 연루되어 있다 He is caught up in the bribery case.
● **연루자** an accomplice; a confederate; a partner; a person concerned [involved].

연륜(年輪) 1 [식] an annual ring. ⇨나이테 2 [여러 해 쌓은 경력]. ¶그에게서는 인생의 ~이 느껴진다 I can see the effect of the years on him. / I can see that he has gone through a lot (in the course of his life).

연리(年利) annual interest. ¶~ 8푼으로 돈을 빌렸다 [빌려 주었다] I borrowed money [gave (him) a loan] at an annual [a yearly] interest of 8 percent. / I borrowed money [gave (him) a loan] at (the rate of) 8 percent a year.

연립(聯立) coalition; alliance; fusion. **연립하다** ally oneself (with); coalesce (with a party); combine (with); unite (with); consociate (with).
● **연립 내각** a coalition cabinet; a fusion administration. **연립 방정식** [수] simultaneous equations. **연립 정부** a coalition government. **연립 주택** a tenement house; row houses.

연마(研磨·練磨·鍊磨) 1 [공] grinding; abrasion; polishing. **연마하다** grind; polish; whet. 2 [학문·정신 등을 갈고 닦음] training; drilling; practice; cultivation; improvement. **연마하다** study hard; apply oneself to the study (of English); train; drill; practice; cultivate; improve. ¶승마술을 ~ practice the art of riding // 젊은이의 심신을 ~ train the mind and bodies of young people.
● **연마기** a grinder; an abrader; a polisher (렌즈 등의). **연마분** polishing powder.

연막(煙幕) 1 [군] a smoke screen. ¶~을 치다 lay [spread] a smoke screen // 적군은 ~을 잔뜩 쳤다 The enemy troops threw up an extensive smoke screen. 2 [비유]. ¶그녀는 자기가 좋아하는 사람이 누군지 알지 못하게 ~을 피우고 있다 She is putting up a smoke screen to prevent others from finding out who she likes.
● **연막전술** smoke-screen tactics. **연막탄** a smoke shell.

연말(年末) the year-end; the end [close] of the year. ¶~에 [까지] at [by] the end of the year.
● **연말 대매출** a year-end (bargain) sale. **연말 정산** a year-end tax adjustment.

연맹(聯盟) a league; a federation; a union; a confederation; an alliance. ¶**국제** ~ the League of Nations // **육상 경기** ~ the Federation of Athletic Associations // **학생** ~ the students' league // 우리나라와 ~을 맺은 국가들 the nations allied with us // ~에 **가입하다** join [take part in] a league.
● **연맹국** allied countries.

연면하다(連綿-) consecutive; continuous; uninterrupted; unbroken. **연면히** continuously; consecutively; uninterruptedly; in an unbroken line [succession]; without a break. ¶~ 이어져 내려오는 전통 an old tradition handed down from generation to generation.

연명(延命) maintenance of a scanty existence; [생명의 연장] the prolongation of life. ¶정부는 ~책을 강구하고 있다 The government is trying to come up with some way to prolong its life. **연명하다** eke out a scanty existence [livelihood]; keep body and soul together; live on the edge of subsistence. ¶간신히 ~ barely live alive / keep body and soul together.

연명(連名·聯名) a joint signature. ¶~으로 in our [their] joint names / under the joint signatures of … // ~으로 초대장을 내다 send an invitation under joint signature. **연명하다** sign jointly; join one's name (to a circular).
● **연명 상소** a joint petition to the ruler.

연모 [도구] an instrument; an appliance; an implement; a utensil; [공구] a tool; [재료] (a) material; stuff.

연모(軟毛) [부드러운 털] soft [downy] hairs; down; pubescence.

연모(戀慕) love (for); (an) attachment (to); (a) tender feeling (for). **연모하다** love; be

연목구어 [fall] in love (with); be [become] attached (to); be enamored (of). ¶그녀는 남몰래 그를 연모했다 She secretly pined for his affections.

연목구어(緣木求魚) "seeking a fish in a tree"; attempting the impossible; flogging a dead horse; It is very hard to shave an egg.

연못(蓮-) a lotus pond; a pond.

연무(煙霧·烟霧) 1 [연기와 안개] smoke and fog; [안개 같은 안개] thick [dense] fog; [기상] (dry) haze. 2 [스모그] smog.

연무(演武) military exercises; practice of military [martial] arts. **연무하다** practice military arts; engage in military exercises.
- **연무장** a military exercise hall; a drill hall.

연무(鍊武) (a) military drill [training]. **연무하다** practice a military drill; train oneself in military arts; receive military training.

연미복(燕尾服) a tailcoat; (구어) tails.

연민(憐憫) compassion; pity; mercy; commiseration. ¶~의 정을 일으키다 [느끼다] have [take] pity (on) / feel pity (for) / be moved to pity (by the sight of ...) / pity / feel compassion (for / toward) / be touched with compassion (for) // 나는 ~의 정에 사로잡혔다 I was overcome with compassion.

연발(延發) [늦게 떠남] delayed departure. **연발하다** start late; start behind time. ¶열차는 15분 연발했다 The train started five minutes behind schedule.

연발(連發) running fire; a volley. ¶6~ 권총 a six-shot [six-chamber(ed)] revolver / a six-shooter / a six-gun // 2~ 총 a double-barreled gun / double-chambered rifle // ~식의 quick-firing (guns) / (자동식의) automatic // 하품의 ~ a succession of yawns // 사고의 ~ a series of accidents // 폭언의 ~ a (running) stream of abuse // 질문의 ~ a running fire of questions. **연발하다** fire in rapid succession [in volleys]; fire shots (at a person) in succession. ¶질문을 ~ ask [assail a person with] one question after another / put questions (to a person) in rapid succession / fire questions (at a person).
- **연발총** a magazine rifle [gun / pistol]; a repeating firearm [rifle]; a repeater.

연방 continuously; incessantly; ceaselessly; successively; without interruption [a break]. ¶전화가 ~ 걸려오다 have (telephone) calls without a break [one after another] // 자동차들이 거리를 ~ 지나간다 There is a constant stream of motorcars along the street.

연방(聯邦) a federation (of states); a federal state; a confederation; a union (of nations); a commonwealth. ¶영~ the British commonwealth of Nation // ~의 federal / confederate.
- **연방 수사국** (미) the Federal Bureau of Investigation(약어 FBI). **연방 정부** the federal government. **연방 제도** a federal system; federalism.

연배(年輩) [비슷한 나이] (similar) age; [비슷한 연령의 사람] a person of one's age; (one's) contemporary. ¶자네 ~의 남자 a man of your age // 메리는 나와 같은 ~이다 Mary is about my (own) age. / Mary is about as old as I am. / Mary is about the same age as me [I am].

연백(鉛白) [화] white lead; lead foil.

연변(年邊) annual interest. ⇨연리(年利)

연변(沿邊) the area along a road [river / railway / border]. ¶도로 ~의 찻집 a teahouse by [along] the roadside [wayside].

연병(練兵) (a) (military) drill [training]. **연병하다** drill; have a drill.
- **연병장** a drill ground [field].

연보(年報) an annual report [bulletin].

연보(年譜) a chronological list of the main events (of a person's life); a chronological record (of a person's career); a chronological history (of a company / of an association).

연보(捐補) contribution; subscription; donation; offering. **연보하다** contribute [donate] (money) to (a fund); subscribe; offer.

연보라(軟-) light [pale] purple; lavender; lilac; orchid.

연봉(年俸) [일 년 동안에 지급하는 봉급] an annual salary; a yearly stipend. ¶그는 ~이 3,000만 원이다 He draws [gets] an annual salary of thirty million won. / He earns thirty million won a year. // 그는 ~으로 급료를 받고 있다 He is paid by the year [so much a year].

연봉(連峯) [죽 이어져 있는 산봉우리] a mountain range; a chain [range] of mountains. ¶히말라야의 ~ the peaks of the Himalayas.

연부(年賦) a yearly [an annual] installment. ¶~로 사다 buy (a thing) by [in] yearly installments // 차입금은 10년 ~로 상환하기로 되어 있다 I have to repay the debt in year [annual] installments over a period of ten years.

연분(緣分) [하늘이 베푼 인연] fate; destiny; predestination; [관계] a relation; a connection; affinity. ¶천생 ~ predestined [Heaven-ordained] relation // ~이 있으면 if fate so ordains // ~을 맺다 form a connection (with) // 부부의 ~을 맺다 contract a marriage / tie the nuptial [marriage] knot / get married // 부부의 ~을 끊다 break off conjugal relations / divorce one's husband [wife] / get a divorce // 그는 우리와는 아무런 ~도 없다 He is a complete [perfect] stranger to us.

연분홍(軟粉紅) light [soft] pink.

연불(延拂) deferred payment.
- **연불 방식** a deferred payment basis.

연비(連比) [수] a continued ratio.

연비(燃比) mileage; fuel efficiency. ¶이 차는 ~가 높다 This car gets good mileage.

연뿌리(蓮-) [식] a lotus root. ⇨연근

연사(演士) a (public) speaker; an orator; a lecturer.

연사(練絲) scoured thread [yarn].

연삭(硏削) [공] grinding. ⇨연마(研磨)1
- **연삭기** a grinder; a grinding machine.

연산(年産) [일 년 동안의 생산고] a yearly [an annual] output [production]. ¶쌀의 ~을 감축하다 reduce the amount of rice produced annually // 이 공장의 카메라 ~은 50만 대이다 This plant produces 500,000 cameras a year.

연산(演算) [수] operation; calculation; working. ¶역~ an inverse operation. **연산하다** operate; calculate; cipher; figure out; do [work] sums(▶ 한 문제를 할 때는 do [work] a sum).
- **연산자**(-子) an operator.

연상(年上) seniority (in age). ¶~의 older /

elder / senior / major // ~의 아내 a wife older than oneself[her husband] // **3년 ~이다** be three years older than a person / be a person's senior by three years / be three years a person's senior // **누가 ~이냐** Which is older[elder]? // **네 누님은 너보다 몇 살 ~이시지** How much older is your sister than you? // **그는 나보다 3살 ~이다** He is three years older than I (am). / He is my senior by three years.

연상(聯想) association (of ideas). ¶**유사[대비 / 근접] ~** association by similarity[contrast / contiguity]. **연상하다** be reminded of; associate (A with B). ¶**나는 홍수라 하면 노아의 방주를 연상한다** I associate Noah's Ark with floods. → ¶**…을 연상시키다** remind (a person) of ... / put (a person) in mind of (something) / suggest (something) to (a person's) mind / bring up the image of ... / **이것을 보면 무엇이 연상되느냐** What does this remind you of? / **이 음악은 봄을 연상시켜 준다** This music produces[gives one] an impression of spring.

연서(連署) a joint signature; countersignature(부서(副署)). ¶**보증인 ~로** under the joint signature of the sureties. **연서하다** sign (a petition) jointly [with]; affix one's signature (to a deed) jointly (with).
●**연서인** a cosignatory; a joint signer.

연서(戀書) a love letter. ⇨"연애편지(⇨연애)

연석(宴席) (one's seat in) a banqueting hall. ¶**~에 참석하다** attend a banquet[feast / dinner] // **~을 베풀다** hold a banquet / give a dinner (party) // **~에서 연설하다** speak at a banquet[dinner].

연석(連席) sitting together[in a row]; (참석) attendance; presence. ¶**~하에 with ... in attendance. 연석하다** sit[be seated] in a row (at); attend; be present (at). ¶**회의에 ~ sit** (as a member) at a meeting.
●**연석회의** a joint meeting[conference]. ¶**정부·여당 ~** a government-ruling party joint conference // **상하원 ~** a joint session [convention] of the two Houses.

연석(緣石) a curb; (영) a kerb; (한 개) a curbstone; (영) a kerbstone.

연설(演說·장중한) an address; (공식의) an oration; (연설하기) (public) speaking. ¶**5분 ~** a five-minute speech // **기조 ~** a keynote address[speech] // **시정 ~** an administrative policy speech // **영어 ~** an English speech / a speech in English // **~ 원고 작성자** a speech writer // **~을 부탁받다** be called on to make a speech // **일장 ~을 하다** make a speech // **~조로 말하다** speak in a declamatory[an oratorical] tone // **그렇게 서툰 ~은 들어 본 적이 없다** That was the worst(-delivered) speech I have ever heard. // **그녀는 ~을 잘한다[못한다]** She is a good [poor] speaker. **연설하다** make[deliver / give] a speech[an address]; speak (to[before]) an audience on a subject); address (an audience); orate. ¶**금주에 관해서 ~ speak on temperance // 대중 앞에서 ~ speak at a large gathering[audience] // 라디오·텔레비전을 통해 국민에게 ~ address the nation over radio and TV // 의사당에서 ~** (미) take the floor.
●**연설자** a (public) speaker; an orator. **연설회** an oratorical meeting; a speech (meeting).

연성(延性) [물] ductility. ¶**~의** ductile.

연성(軟性) softness; mildness. ¶**~의** soft / elastic.
●**연성 세제** a soft detergent.

연세(年歲) age; years. ⇨나이 ¶**~가 많다** be advanced[well up] in years[age] / be old // **~가 80이다** be at the great age of eighty / be eighty years old [of age].

연소(延燒) the spread of a fire. ¶**~를 막다** check the spread of a fire. **연소하다** (불이) spread (to); (건물이) catch fire; burn down by the spreading fire. → **집을 연소당하다** have one's house burnt by a spreading fire.

연소(燃燒) burning; combustion. ¶**완전[불완전] ~** perfect[imperfect] combustion // **완전 ~ 장치** a smoke consumer // **자연 ~** spontaneous combustion. **연소하다** burn. ¶**연소하기 쉬운** combustible / flammable.
●**연소물** combustibles. **연소실** a combustor; a combustion chamber; (제트 엔진의) a burner.

연소자(年少者) a youth; a young person [one]; young people; juveniles; juniors; [미] 성년자) a minor; underage people. ¶**반[셋 중]의 최~** the youngest in the class[of the three] // **~ 입장 금지** (게시) No admittance children. / No minors. / Adults only.

연소하다(年少-) [나이가 어리다] young (in years); juvenile. ¶**연소한 사람들** young people // **연소하다는 이유로** on account of [in consideration of] one's minority[one's being too young] // **그는 나보다 세 살 ~** He is three years younger than I am.

연속(連續) continuity; continuation; continuance; succession; a sequence; a series; a chain. ¶**~적** successive / continuous / consecutive // **24시간 ~의** round-the-clock // **3안타 ~** three back-to-back[consecutive] hits // **~ 3주간** for three weeks running / for three consecutive weeks. **연속하다** continue; be continuous; go on; last. ¶**연속해서** in succession / consecutively / continuously / one after another // **그 영화는 3개월간 연속해서 상영이 되었다** The movie had a run of three months[a three months' run]. // **그는 2개월간 연속해서 결석했다** He absented himself from school for two months on end.
●**연속극 / 연속 드라마** a soap opera; a serial drama[play]. ¶**일일[주간] ~** a daily [weekly] serial drama. **연속 상영** consecutive [continuative] showing of a film. **연속성** continuity. **연속 함수** a continuous function.

연쇄(連鎖) a chain; links; a series; [관계] connection; (유전자의) linkage. ¶**~ 살인 사건** consecutive murder incidents.
●**연쇄 구균** [의] a streptococcus (pl. -cocci). **연쇄 반응** (a) chain reaction. ¶**~을 일으키다** cause[trigger / touch off / set up] a chain reaction. **연쇄 사건** a chain of events. **연쇄점** (미) a chain store; (영) a multiple shop.

연수(年收) an annual[a yearly] income. ¶**그~는 1,500만 원이다** He earns[get / makes] fifteen won a year. / His yearly [annual] income is fifteen million won.

연수(年數) the number of years. ⇨햇수 ¶**~가 지난** old / aged // **사업의 완성에 소요된 ~** the number of years required for completing an undertaking // **이 소재는 내구 ~가 길다** This material lasts for many years.

연수(延髓) [생] the hindbrain; the afterbrain; (라) medulla oblongata (*pl.* medulla oblongatas, medullae oblongatae); the bulb (of the spinal cord). ¶~의 bulbar.

연수(研修) research study; study and training; (신입 사원 등의) an induction course. ¶신입 사원들에게 컴퓨터 ~를 시켰다 The new employees were given training in operating computers. **연수하다** study (science); take [go through] a training (in); pursue the study (of history).
● **연수생** a trainee. **연수원** a[an in-service] training institute. ¶사법 ~ the Judicial Training Institute // 외무 공무원 ~ the Foreign Service Training Institute. **연수 제도** the training system.

연수(軟水) soft water. ⇨단물4 ¶경수(硬水)를 ~로 만들다 soften hard water.

연수정(煙水晶) smoky quartz; morion(흑(黑) 수정).

연습(演習) 1 (계속적·규칙적인) practice; (영) practise; (반복적인) exercises; (a) drill. ¶사격 ~ rifle practice // 영문 해석 ~ exercises in English-Korean translation // 예행 ~ a rehearsal. **연습하다** practice; carry out exercises. 2 (군대에서의) maneuvers; (영) manoeuvre. ¶방공 ~ anti-air-raid maneuvers. **연습하다** hold [carry out] maneuvers.
● **연습장**(-場) (육상 경기 등의) a practice [training] field [ground / track]; (권투 등의) a gym(nasium); (연극·음악 등의) a rehearsal hall [room]; a practice room.

연습(練習) practice; training; (a) drill; (an) exercise; (경기 직전의) a warm(ing)-up; (연극 등의) a rehearsal. ¶무대 ~ a stage rehearsal // (연극 등의) 총~ a run-through // 사전 ~으로 as a preliminary test / as a warm-up // ~이 부족하다 lack training [practice] / be half-trained [not sufficiently trained] / be out of practice // ~을 시작하다 go into training // 듣는 ~을 하다 train one's ears / practice hearing // 승마 ~을 하다 practice riding // ~을 시키다 give (a person) training // 속셈 ~을 시키다 drill (students) in mental arithmetic // ~을 해야 완벽해진다 Practice makes perfect. // 내가 자네의 ~ 상대를 해 주겠다 I'll give you a chance to practice on me. // 젊은 선수들이 그를 ~ 상대로 하여 연마했다 The young players practiced by pitting their skills against him. // 그는 ~ 부족으로 대사를 실수했다 He muffed his line because he hadn't practiced [rehearsed] enough. **연습하다** practice; train; drill; rehearse; exercise (oneself) (in). ¶나는 매일 규칙적으로 피아노를 연습한다 I practice (on [at]) the piano regularly every day. // 그들은 시합에 대비하여 맹렬히 연습하고 있다 They are having smart practice [are in hard training] for the game. →학생들에게 영어 발음을 연습시키다 drill [practice] students in English pronunciation.
● **연습 경기** a practice game [match]; a workout. **연습곡** [음] an étude. ⇨에튀드 **연습 문제** (one's) exercises (in grammar). ¶~를 하다[풀다] do exercise (in algebra). **연습생** a student; a trainee. **연습장**(-帳) an exercise [a drill] book; a workbook.

연승(連勝) straight [consecutive / successive] victories; a series of victories. **연승하다** gain [win] consecutive [successive] victory; win victory after victory. ¶5회 ~ win five straight [consecutive / successive] victories (over) / win five games consecutively [straight / in a row] // 그들은 연승했다 They did not lose a single game. / They won every game they played.

연시(年始) the New Year (season).

연시(軟枾) a ripe and soft persimmon; a mellow persimmon.

연식(軟式) nonrigid [soft] type.
● **연식 야구** (미) softball; rubber-ball baseball. **연식 정구** softball tennis.

연실(鳶-) [연줄로 쓰는 실] a kite string. ¶~을 감다[풀다] reel in [pay out] the string of a kite.

연안(沿岸) the coast; the shore. ¶~의[에] on [along] the shore [coast] / 대서양 ~ the Atlantic coast // 태평양 ~의 도시들 cities on [along] the Pacific // ~을 항해하다 sail along the coast.
● **연안 경비대** the coast guard. **연안 무역** coastal [coasting / coastwise] trade. **연안 어업** coastal [inshore / longshore] fishery. **연안 항로** coastal [coastwise / coasting] route [service].

연애(戀愛) love; amour; tender passion [emotion / sentiment]; affections; love making. ¶동성 ~ homosexual [unisexual] love / homosexuality / (남자 간의) sodomy / (여자 간의) lesbian love / lesbianism // 삼각 ~ a triangular love affair / a love triangle // 자유 ~ free love // 순결한[정신적인] ~ pure [platonic / spiritual] love // ~에 빠지다 fall in love (with) // ~ 관계에 있다 be in love with each other / have an affair (with). **연애하다** love; fall [be] in love (with).
● **연애결혼** a love marriage [match]. ¶그는 그녀와 ~을 했다 He married for love. **연애 사건** a love affair; an amour; a romance. **연애 소설** a love story. **연애시** a love poem. **연애편지** a love letter [note]; (프) a billet-doux (*pl.* billets-doux).

연액(年額) [한 해 동안의 금액] an annual sum; a yearly amount. ¶~ 천만 원의 이익 an annual profit of ten million won / a profit amounting to ten million won a year [per annum] // ~ 100만 원씩을 상환하다 return one million won every year / pay back the money in yearly installments of one million won.

연야(連夜) [며칠 밤을 계속하여] every night; night after night. ¶~의 nightly // 사흘 동안 ~ 작업하다 work for three consecutive nights.

연약하다(軟弱-) tender; mild; weak; feeble; frail; delicate; weak-kneed. ¶연약한 아녀자 helpless women and children // 몸이 연약한 소년 a boy with a weak [delicate] constitution.

연어(連語) (a) collocation; (복합어) a compound word; (구) a phrase.

연어(鰱魚) [동] a salmon (*pl.* ~ (s)). ¶소금에 절인[훈제한] ~ salted [smoked] salmon.

연역(演繹) deduction; deductive reasoning. **연역하다** deduce (particular details from general principles and known facts).
● **연역법** the deductive method; deduction; apriorism; syllogism.

연역적(演繹的) deductive. ¶~으로 deductively // ~(인) 추리 deductive reasoning [inference // ~ 토론 an a priori argument // ~ 허위 a deductive fallacy.

연연하다(戀戀-) **1** [미련을 가지다] (서술적) cling to (one's position). ¶지위에 ~ return a lingering desire for the position / be reluctant to give up one's position / cling to one's post. **2** [그립다] lingering; tender; longed-for; (서술적) be ardently [fondly] attached to (a girl); be (very) fond of (a girl); pine [long / yearn] (for). ¶연연한 마음 a lingering love [affection] (for).

연예(演藝) (dramatic / musical) entertainments; (흥행장의) a variety show; (미) vaudeville; performance(연기). **연예하다** perform; entertain; put on entertainment; act.

● **연예계** the entertainment world [business]. **연예인** a performer; an entertainer; an artiste. ¶인기 ~ a star [principal] performer [artiste] / (미) a headliner. **연예장** an entertainment hall; a variety theater; (미) a vaudeville house [theater]; a music hall.

연옥(軟玉) [광] nephrite; kidney stone; greenstone.

연옥(煉獄) [가] Purgatory. ¶~의 purgatorial (sufferings / fires) // ~의 고통을 겪다 go through the purgatory.

연옥색(軟玉色) light bluish green.

연와(煉瓦) a (piece of) brick. ➪ 벽돌

연원(淵源) the origin; the source; the beginning; the rise; the inception; the fountainhead. ¶…의 ~을 찾다 trace the origin of … / trace (something) to its source.

연월일(年月日) the date. ¶본사 설립의 ~ the date of the founding of our company / the date on which our company was founded // 영수증에 ~을 적다 date a receipt / enter the date on a receipt // ~순으로 철하다 file in chronological order.

연유(煉乳) condensed milk.

연유(緣由) the origin; the root; the rise; the source; the derivation; [사유] (a) reason; (a) cause; ground(s). ¶이 관습의 ~를 아느냐 Do you know how this custom came about? **연유하다** originate (in); have (its) origin [rise] (in); arise (from); be derived (from); date (from); date back (to); be caused (by).

연음(延音) a prolonged [held / lengthened] sound; a long vowel [syllable].

● **연음 기호** [음] a fermata. ➪ 늘임표

연이율(年利率) an annual interest rate [rate of interest].

연인(戀人) (남녀의) one's love; one's sweetheart; (남자) boyfriend; one's boy; one's lover(▶ lover는 「정부(情夫)」라는 뉘앙스가 강함); (여자) one's girlfriend; one's girl. ¶한 쌍의 ~ a pair of lovers.

연인원(延人員) the total number of persons [workers]; the total man-days. ¶그 작업에는 ~ 3,000명이 필요했다 The total number of man-days required for the work was 3,000. / The work required 3,000 man-days in all.

연일(連日) every day; day after [by] day; day in and day out; for days on end; several days in succession. ¶~ 계속되는 악천후로 말미암아 because of the continued [a long spell of] bad weather // 그 극장은 ~ 대만원이다 The theater is drawing a full house every day.

● **연일연야**(-連夜) day(s) and night(s).

연임(連任) reappointment. **연임하다** be reappointed (to the office); resume the office.

연이다(連-) **1** [연속하다] continue; follow one after another; occur in succession. ¶연이어 continuously / consecutively / successively / in succession / uninterruptedly / without intermission [a break] / at a stretch / one after another // 3일간 연이어 for three consecutive [successive] days / for three days running [on end] // 우리 팀은 다섯 게임을 연이어 이겼다 We won five games in a row [in succession]. / We won five successive games. // 어제 나는 8시간을 연이어 일했다 Yesterday I worked for eight hours straight [at a stretch / without pause / without a break]. // 9일간 연이어 비가 내렸다 It rained continually [continuously] for nine days.(▶ continually는 단속적(斷續的)으로 이어짐, continuously는 끊임없이 이어짐을 말함)
2 [연결하다] join (some pieces of paper) together; connect [link] together; piece up [together]; patch (bits of cloth) together; glue (two things) together(아교로). ¶천 조각 등을 연이어서 쿠션을 만들다 sew pieces of cloth together and make a cushion.

연잎(蓮-) a lotus leaf.

연자매(研子-) a millstone worked by a horse or ox.

● **연자맷간** a beastworked mill.

연자방아(研子-) a millstone worked by a horse or ox. ➪ 연자매

연작(連作) **1** (농작물의) repeated cultivation. **연작하다** plant (a field) with the same crop every year. **2** a work produced in collaboration. ➪ 연작(聯作)

연작(聯作) a work produced in collaboration. **연작하다** produce a work [novel] in collaboration.

연장 a tool; an instrument; a utensil. ¶목수 ~ a carpenter's tools [kit / outfit] // 농사용 ~ a farming tool // ~ 한 벌 a kit / an outfit.

● **연장궤** a toolbox; a tool chest; a workbox; a kit.

연장(年長) seniority. ¶~의 senior / older / elder // 그분은 나보다 5년 ~이다 He is five years older than I am.

● **연장자** a senior; an elder; a superior (in age). ¶집안의 최 ~ the oldest man in a family.

연장(延長) **1** (길이의) (an) extension. **연장하다** [어느 점 이상으로 늘이다] extend; [길게 하다] lengthen. ¶도로를 ~ extend a road // 지하철을 분당까지 ~ extend the subway [(영) underground (railway)] to Bundang // (기하에서) 선을 어느 한 점까지 ~ extend [produce] a line to a point. ➪ ¶그것은 3미터 연장되었다 It was made three meters longer.
2 (기간의) (an) extension; (a) prolongation. **연장하다** (기간을) extend; (오래 끌게 하다) prolong. ¶기한을 [영업시간을] ~ extend the deadline [one's business hours] // 한국 체류를 1주일 ~ extend [prolong] one's stay in Korea for a week // 회기를 ~ prolong [extend] a session // 회의를 ~ prolong [draw out] a meeting // 우리는 계약 기간을 연장하였다 We renewed our contract. // 호평을 받아 공연을 1주일간 연장합니다 The performance will be continued another week because it has been so well received.

3 [전장] length. ¶이 강의 ~은 300km에 이른다 The length of this river is three hundred kilometers. / The river extends for three hundred kilometers.
4 [내용적 연계]. ¶대학은 고교의 단순한 ~이 아니다 A university is not a mere extension [continuation] of a high school.
● **연장선** (기하의) a product; (철도 등의) an extension (line). ¶그것은 이 생각의 ~상에 있다 It is an extension of this idea. **연장전**(-戰) an extended game; [야구] an extra-inning game[contest]. ¶~ 끝에 지다 lose in overtime (to the Tigers) // (야구에서) 시합은 ~으로 접어들었다 The match went into extra innings.

연재(連載) serialization; serial publication. ¶동아일보에 ~ 중인 소설 a novel (which is now) appearing serially[regularly] in the Dong-A-Ilbo. **연재하다** publish (a novel) serially[in serial form]; serialize. ¶소설을 잡지에 ~ publish a novel in installments in a magazine. →¶연재되다 be published[appear] serially (in a magazine) / be serialized (in).
● **연재만화** serial comic strips; serial comics. **연재물** a serial (story). ¶신문의 ~ a serial story in a newspaper. **연재소설** a serial novel.

연적(硯滴) a container for inkstone[ink slab] water.
연적(戀敵) a rival[corrival] in love; a rival lover[suitor].
연전(年前) ¶~에 some [a few / a couple of] years ago.
연전(連戰) a series of battles; successive battles; battle after battle; every battle. **연전하다** fight a series of battles; participate in successive battles.
● **연전연승** a succession[series] of victories. ¶~을 하다 win[gain] consecutive [a series of] victories / win every battle one fights / win battle after battle // 3일간 ~한 레슬링 선수 a wrestler who won his bouts for three consecutive days. **연전연패** a succession [series] of defeats. ¶~를 하다 lose [be defeated in] every battle / lose one battle after another [battle after battle].

연접(連接) connection; junction; combination. **연접하다** connect; combine; interlock(열차 등을); switch(전화를).
연정(戀情) love (for); tender passion[feeling] (for / to); attachment (for / to). ¶불타는 ~ a burning passion // ~을 품다 cherish[have] attachment (for) / have a tender passion (to).
연제(演題) the subject [theme] of a lecture [an address / a speech]. ¶그는 「여성 교육」 이라는 ~로 연설했다 He spoke on "Women's Education." // 브라운 박사는 「민주주의와 자유」란 ~로 강연했다 Dr. Brown lectured [spoke] on (the subject of) "Democracy and Freedom."
연좌(連坐) [연루] implication; involvement; complicity; [잇대어 앉음] sitting down in a row. ¶~의 sit-in / sit-down. **연좌하다** be implicated[involved] (in a scandal case); sit down in a row.
● **연좌데모** (go on) a sit-in[-down] demonstration. **연좌제** the guilt-by-association system; the involvement system.

연주(演奏) a (musical) performance; (독주) a recital; (자기 해석에 의한) a rendering. **연주하다** perform; give a performance[recital]; play (a sonata); render; (즉흥적으로) ad-lib. ¶실내악 (피아노)을 ~ play chamber music [the piano] // 연주하기 시작하다 begin to play[perform] / strike up (an air).
● **연주 곡목** a (musical) program; (그중의 한 곡) a piece [number] on the program; a repertory [repertoire]. **연주법** execution; interpretation. **연주자** a performer; a player. **연주회** a concert; a recital(독주회). ¶피아노 ~ a piano recital / 합동 ~ a joint recital // ~에 가다 go to [attend] a concert // ~를 개최하다 give a concert [recital].

연주창(連珠瘡) [한] scrofula; scrofulosis (pl. -loses); the king's evil.
연줄(鳶-) a kite string; twine [(a) string] for a kite.
연줄(緣-) connections; (a) pull; influence; (have) an in (with / to); contacts. ¶~ 채용 hiring through personal connections / …의 ~로 through the influence [good offices] of // ~이 있다 have a (good) connections / have a (good) pull // 그는 재계에 강력한 ~을 갖고 있다 He has an influential supporter in the financial world. // 나는 그 회사에 이렇다 할 ~이 없다 I have no particular pull in [connection with] the firm. // 나는 ~로 채용되었다 I got a [my] job through (a) pull [personal contacts]. // 그는 유력한 ~이 있어 그 회사에 취직했다 He had influential connections and got a job in the firm. / He had a friend who used his influence to get him a job in the firm. // 그는 ~로 관계에 들어갔다 He entered government service through the influence of an acquaintance [with the help of an influential man].
연줄연줄(緣-緣-) through one's connections; through one connection after another.
연중(年中) (all) the year round; throughout the year; the whole year; every day of the year; all times of the year; always(항상). ¶그는 ~ 내내 바쁘다 He is perpetually busy. / He is busy all the year round [throughout the year].
● **연중무휴** ¶이 상점은 ~입니다 This store is open all the year round [throughout the year / in all seasons (of the year) / at any season]. // 그는 ~로 일하고 있다 He works without any days off at all. // ~ (게시) Open Throughout The Year. **연중행사** an annual [yearly] function [event / affair / feature] (of). ¶철도 운임의 인상은 이를테면 ~가 되었다 The raising of railroad fares has become an annual event, so to speak. // 체육 대회는 학교의 ~ 중 하나이다 An athletic meeting is a part of the annual school calendar [routine]. // 그 축제는 마을에서 가장 성대한 ~였다 The festival was the biggest event [occasion] of the year in the village.

연지(臙脂) **1** [화장용의 붉은 빛깔의 염료] rouge; [입술 연지] (a) lipstick. ¶볼~ cheek rouge // ~를 바른 볼 rouged cheeks / cheeks touched with rouge // ~를 바른 입술 lipsticked lips // ~를 바르다 (입술에) put rouge on one's lips / put on lipstick / apply rouge [lipstick] to one's lips / rouge one's lips / touch one's lips with rouge / (볼에) rouge one's cheeks / put rouge on one's cheeks. **2**

[자색과 적색의 혼합 물감] deep red; crimson.

연직(鉛直) perpendicularity; verticality; plumb. ¶~의 perpendicular / vertical / plumb.

연질(軟質) ¶~의 soft.
● **연질 고무** soft rubber. **연질 유리** soft glass.

연차(年次) ¶~의 annual / yearly.
● **연차 계획** a yearly plan[program]. **연차(유급) 휴가** an annual paid holiday[vacation].

연착(延着) (a) late[delayed] arrival; (발송품의) (a) delay (in delivery). **연착하다** arrive late; be delayed (in arrival[delivery / transmission]); (기차 등이) be overdue. ¶열차가 한 시간 연착하였다 The train arrived one hour late[behind schedule]. / The train was an hour behind time[overdue].

연착륙(軟着陸) (a) soft landing. **연착륙하다** make a soft landing (on the moon); softland (on).

연천하다(年淺-) 1 [나이가 적다] young; juvenile. 2 [햇수가 얼마 안 되다] short; not long.

연철(軟鐵) [광] soft iron.
연철(鍊鐵·練鐵) [광] wrought iron.

연체(延滯) (a) delay; procrastination; (채무·납세 등의) arrears. **연체하다** be delayed; be in arrear(s); become remiss in one's payment(s). ¶그는 회비가 2년이나 연체되어 있다 He is two years behind in[in arrears with] his dues. // 집세가 3개월 연체되어 있다 The rent is three months overdue.
● **연체금 / 연체료** (an) arrearage charge. ¶하루 3,000원의 ~를 물다 be charged at the rate of three thousand won per day for the delay in payment. **연체 이자** overdue[default] interest; interest for[on] delay[arrears].

연체동물(軟體動物) a mollusk; a mollusc; [연체동물류] the mollusks.

연초(年初) the beginning of the year. ¶~에 at the beginning of the year / in the fresh of the year / early (in the) next year.

연초(煙草) [식] a tobacco. ⇨ 담배

연출(演出) direction; production. ¶송 씨의 연극 a play directed by Mr. Song. **연출하다** direct; produce.
● **연출가** a (program) director; (영) a producer.

연타하다(連打-) hit[beat / strike] (a person) repeatedly; deliver a barrage of blows (at / against); give blow after blow; give repeated blows; rain[shower] blows (on); (종 등을) ring[clang] (a bell) repeatedly.

연탄(煉炭) a briquet(te). ¶~을 갈다 change a briquet.
● **연탄가스 (중독)** briquet gas (poisoning). ¶연탄가스 중독으로 죽다 die from briquet gas (poisoning). **연탄난로** a briquet stove. **연탄불** briquet fire.

연통(煙筒) a chimney; (공장·기선 등의) a smokestack; (공장·기선 등의) a funnel; (난로의) a stovepipe. ¶~의 갓 a chimney cap // ~을 소제하다 sweep a chimney.

연투하다(連投-) [야구] go on[take] the pitcher's mound in (two) consecutive games.

연판(連判) a joint signature[seal]. ¶~으로 under joint signature. **연판하다** sign[seal] jointly.
● **연판자** a cosignatory.

연판(鉛版) a stereotype; a stereo (*pl.* ~s). ¶~을 뜨다 make a stereotype (of) / stereotype.
● **연판공** a stereotyper. **연판 인쇄** stereotypography.

연패(連敗) successive defeats; a succession[series] of reverses. ¶3~ [야구] a three-game losing streak[string]. **연패하다** suffer[meet with] successive[straight] defeats. ¶5~ lose five games straight[in a row / in succession] / suffer five successive[consecutive] defeats.

연평수(延坪數) the total[gross] floor space. ¶이 집의 ~는 35평이다 The total floor space of this house is 35 *pyeong*.

연표(年表) a chronological table. ⇨ 연대표(⇨ 연대(年代)) ¶한국사 ~ a chronological table of Korean history.

연풍(軟風) a (gentle) breeze; a light[soft] wind; (시어) a zephyr.

연필(鉛筆) a (lead) pencil. ¶빨간(색) ~ a red (colored) pencil // 제도 ~ a drawing pencil // 색 ~ a color pencil // HB ~ an HB pencil // 몽당 ~ stubby pencil / a (pencil) stump / a stub // 끝이 뾰족한 ~ a pencil with a sharp point // 끝이 둥근 ~ a pencil with a dull point / a blunt pencil // ~로 쓰다[그리다] write[draw] with a pencil / write[draw] in pencil / pencil (down) // ~을 깎다 sharpen a pencil.
● **연필깎이** a pencil sharpener. **연필심** the lead (of a pencil); (a) pencil lead. **연필통** a pencil case.

연하(年下) juniority. ¶~의 younger / junior // 그는 나보다 여섯 살 ~이다 He is my junior by six years. / He is six years my junior. / He is six years younger than I (am)[than me].

연하(年賀) New Year(s) greetings.
● **연하우편** New Year's mail. **연하장** a New Year's card. ¶~을 보내다 send (a person) a New Year's card[the New Year's greetings].

연하다(連-) adjoin; be adjacent[contiguous] to; be connected (to); [계속되다] continue. ¶거실은 식당과 연해 있다 The living room adjoins the dining room.

연하다(軟-) 1 [무르고 부드럽다] soft; tender; supple. ¶연한 고기 tender meat // 연하게 삶은 콩 beans cooked (until they are) tender. 2 [빛이 옅고 산뜻하다] light (color); mild (shade); mellow (light); weak[watery] (tea). ¶연한 청색 light[pale] blue(▶ pale이 더 연함) // 연한 차 weak tea // 연한 빛깔의 스커트 a light-colored skirt // 빛깔이 ~ be light in color / be of a light color[shade] // 빛깔을 연하게 하다 make the color light[mild / soft] / lighten the color // 그림에 연한 색을 칠하다 paint a picture in pale colors.

-**연하다**(然-) […인 체하다] pretend to; act as if; pose as; set up for; affect[act / play] (the hero). ¶그녀는 자못 숙녀연하고 있다 She behaves like a true lady. // 그는 예술가연하고 있다 He has[assumes] the air of a true artist about him. // 그는 학자연하고 있다 That he is a scholar is written all over him. / He pretends to learning[scholarship]. / He sets up for a scholar.

연한(年限) a term; a period. ¶수업[복무] ~ a term of study[service] // 근무 ~ a term of service[office] // 4년의 의무 ~이 끝났다[찼다] The obligatory[compulsory] term of four years has expired[is up] . ¶그는 복역 ~을 채우고 있다 He is serving a his prison sentence.

연합(聯合) 1 [결합] combination; union; association; consociation; league; confederacy; coalition(정당의); a combine(기업); (an) alliance(동맹); 《 국제 ~ the United Nations(약어 UN) // 기업 ~ a cartel / a combination of companies. 연합하다 combine; unite; confederate; league; ally oneself; consociate; coalesce. ¶강대국과 연합하고 있는 국가들 nations in alliance[league] with a big power // 세 파가 연합하여 당을 결성했다 The three factions combined to form a faction. // 두 식민지가 연합하여 새 국가가 이루었다 The two colonies were united into a new state.

2 association (of ideas). ⇨ 연상(聯想)
● 연합국 (1, 2차 대전 때의) the Allied Powers[Nations]; the Allies; (1차 대전 때의) the Allied and Associated Powers. 연합군 the Allied Forces; the Allies; the combined forces.

연해(沿海) [육지에 가까운 바다] the sea along the coast; the coastal waters; the inshore; [바다 가까운 육지] the coast. ¶~의 coastal / inshore / longshore / littoral.
● 연해 어업 coastal[inshore / longshore] fisheries.

연해연방(連-) successively; continuously; one after another; without intermission[a break]; in succession. ¶~ 불행이 생기다 have a run of ill luck / one misfortune follows another // 이 도로는 자동차가 ~ 지나간다 There is a constant stream of vehicles on this road.

연행하다(連行-) take[walk] (a suspect to a police station); haul[bring] (a person) before (the police authorities). ➔ 그 남자는 살인 혐의로 경찰서에 연행되었다 The man was taken[hauled / marched] to the police station on suspicion of murder.

연혁(沿革) (a) history; changes(변천); the (origin and) development(발달). ¶우리 회사의 ~ the history of our company.

연호(年號) the name[designation] of an era; an era name.

연화(軟化) softening; mollification. ¶뇌 ~증 softening of the brain / encephalomalacia. 연화하다 become[get] soft; soften; tone down; (사람이) be mollified; relent; become less aggressive; become conciliatory.
● 연화제 (경수를 연수로 바꾸는) a softener; a softening agent.

연화(軟貨) soft money[currency]; [지폐] a banknote.

연화(蓮花) a lotus flower. ⇨ 연꽃2

연회(年會) an annual convention; a yearly meeting.

연회(宴會) a party; a dinner (party); a feast; a banquet; a junket; an entertainment. ¶~를 벌이다[베풀다] give[hold / tender] banquet / give[have] a (dinner) party // ~에 참석하다[나가다] attend[join] a party / attend a banquet[dinner (party)] / (구어) party.
● 연회장 a banquet[banqueting] hall.

연후(然後) ¶~에 after that / afterward(s) / (and) then.

연휴(連休) consecutive holidays; holidays in a row. ¶하루 거른 ~ holidays that would be consecutive but for an intervening workday / sandwiched holidays // 3일간의 ~가 있다 have three consecutive holidays / have three day's holiday running.

열 [10] ten; half a score. ¶하나에서 ~까지 그의 말에 순종할 순 없다 I cannot obey him in every particular. // 그는 하나를 들으면 ~을 안다 He is quick to understand[quick to grasp things / quick at learning].

열 길 물속은 알아도 한 길 사람의 속은 모른다(속담) It is hard to fathom the real minds and intentions of men.

열 번 찍어 아니 넘어가는 나무 없다(속담) Little strokes fell great oaks.

열 손가락 깨물어 안 아픈 손가락이 없다(속담) Every child is dear to his parents.

열에 아홉 ten to one; in nine cases[times] out of ten; most likely; (most) probably; in all probability; in all (human) likelihood; the greater[best / most] part; mostly. ¶참석자들은 ~은 대학생이었다 Those present were mostly college students.

열(列) a row; a line; (층을 이룬) a tier; (세로의) a file; a column; (가로의) a rank; a row; (차례를 기다리는) (미) a line; a queue. ¶2~ two rows // 2~ 횡대[종대] a double line[file] // ~을 짓다 form a line[row / file / queue] / line[queue] up // ~을 정돈하다 dress to ranks // ~을 지어 나아가다 advance in ranks[files] / parade in columns // ~에 끼어들다 step[break] into a line / join the queue // ~에서 이탈하다 fall[drop] out of the lines[ranks] / leave the ranks // 2~로 서다 form two rows / (세로로) form a double file / (가로로) form a double line // 2~로 나아가다 march (in a) double file / march two abreast // 경관이 연도에 2~로 서 있다 Policemen stood two deep along the road. // 사람들이 가게 앞에 ~을 지었다 People had lined [queued] up in front of the shop. // 군인들이 4~ 종대로 행진하였다 The soldiers marched in columns of four[in four columns].

열(熱) 1 [뜨거운 기운] heat. ¶복사 ~ radiant heat // ~을 가하다 apply heat (to) / heat (up) // ~을 발산[복사 / 흡수]하다 give off [radiate / absorb] heat // ~을 내다[발생하다] generate[produce] heat // 마찰하니까 ~이 났다 The friction produced heat. // 이 유리는 ~에 강하다 This glass is heat-resistant.

2 [신열] (a) temperature; (병으로 인한) (a) fever. ¶좀처럼 내리지 않는 ~ a lingering fever // ~이 있다 have a temperature / have (a) fever // ~이 높다 have a high fever[temperature] // ~을 재다 take one's[a person's] temperature // ~을 내리게 하다 lower[send down] the fever // ~이 오른다 My temperature[fever] rises[mounts / heightens / goes up]. // ~이 내린다[가라앉는다] My temperature falls[goes down]. / My fever breaks[subsides / abates]. // ~이 좀 있다 You have a slight[a little] fever. / You are slightly[a little] feverish. // ~은 몇 도입니까 What is your[my] temperature? // 환자의 ~은 39도 8분입니다 The temperature of the patient is 39.8[thirty-nine point eight] degrees. // 이제 ~은 없습니다 Your fever is

gone. / The fever (has) left you. // ~이 정상으로 돌아왔다 My temperature returned to normal. // 푹 잤더니 ~이 없어졌다 The fever left me [disappeared] while I was having a good sleep. // 그는 ~이 나서 의식이 혼미해져 있다 He is delirious with fever.
3 [화·격분] anger; rage; passion; wrath; indignation. ¶~에 받쳐 때리다 strike (a person) in (the heat of) passion [spurred by anger].
4 [흥분] heat; ardor; zeal; excitement. ¶경기는 점점 ~을 더해 갔다 The game heated up. // 그는 점점 이야기에 ~을 올리기 시작했다 He was waxing warm [gradually warmed up] to his subject.
5 [열성·열의·유행] a mania; a craze; a rage; (a) fever; enthusiasm; fever(일시적). ¶야구~ enthusiasm for baseball / a baseball fever [mania] // 우표 수집~ a stamp-collecting craze / a rage for stamp collecting // 스포츠~이 대단하다 There is a lot of enthusiasm for sports. // 요즈음 스키~이 대단하다 Skiing is the latest craze [rage]. / Skiing has become all the rage.

열(을) 받다 **1** get hot by heat. **2** [흥분하다] get upset over (a thing); be steamed about (a thing). ¶그 문제에 대해 너무 열 받지 마라 Don't get so steamed about the issue.

열을 올리다 become enthusiastic (about / over / for); (미국 구어) enthuse (about / over); be mad (about / after / over); have a crush (on a girl); lose one's head (over a woman). ¶그들은 외국 자본 유치에 열을 올리고 있다 They are working hard to attract foreign investment(s).

열이 식다 one's passion [enthusiasm, etc.] becomes calm; calm down; cool (down). ¶그의 태도에 우리는 열이 식어 버렸다 His attitude was enough to cool down our ardor (for it). // 그는 연극에 대한 열이 식었다 His passion for drama cooled down [left him / was dampened].

열가소성(熱可塑性) [화] thermoplasticity. ¶~의 thermoplastic.
열각(劣角) [수] a minor angle.
열강(列强) the Great Powers (of the world); the World Powers.
열거(列擧) enumeration. **열거하다** enumerate; list; mention; name one by one; go [run] through the list [catalogue] (of). ¶증거를 ~ produce one piece of evidence after another / line up evidence // 그는 그 계획의 결점을 열거했다 He enumerated the disadvantages of the plan. / He listed the drawbacks to the plan. // 이러한 과오를 열거하자면 끝이 없다 There is really no end to the list of such errors. / It is virtually impossible to exhaust the list of such errors. / These errors are too numerous to mention.
열 관리(熱管理) [공] control of heat; heat control.
열광(熱狂) (wild) enthusiasm; frenzy; fanaticism; mania; craze; furor[(영) furore]; fever heat; extreme excitement. **열광하다** be [get] wildly [extremely] excited (at / about / over / by); go [get / be] wild (with / about); be enthusiastic (over / about); (미국 구어) enthuse (over / about); be [go] crazy (over / for / about); be fanatic(al) (about); run mad (after). ¶전 국민이 그의 연설에 열광하였다 The whole nation was extremely excited by his speech. // 팬들은 승리에 열광했다 The fans were mad with joy at the victory. // 그 젊은 가수에게 열광하는 소녀들이 많다 Many girls are crazy about the young singer. →¶열광시키다 arouse [excite / stir up] (a person's) enthusiasm // 그의 연설은 청중을 열광시켰다 His speech made the audience wild with excitement.

열광적(熱狂的) extremely excited; enthusiastic; ardent; wild; mad; crazy; frantic; fanatical(광신적). ¶그는 클래식 음악을 ~으로 좋아한다 He is crazy about classical music. // 그들은 손수건을 ~으로 흔들었다 They waved their handkerchiefs frantically. // 그녀는 ~인 환영을 받았다 She was given an enthusiastic welcome. / She was received [greeted] with wild [immense] enthusiasm. // 이렇게 ~인 환영은 받아 본 적이 없습니다 This is the most enthusiastic welcome I have ever been given.

열국(列國) all countries; the nations (of the world); the (world) powers(열강). ¶유럽 ~ the European countries [powers] / ~ 회의 an international conference / a conference of the powers.
열기(熱氣) **1** [뜨거운 공기] heat; hotness; hot air. ¶낮 동안의 ~가 아직도 벽에 남아 있었다 The day's heat still clung to the walls.
2 [흥분한 기운] heat; enthusiasm; fever; eagerness; excitement; zeal. ¶~를 띠다 get [become / grow] heated / become excited / (영) hot up // 그의 어조는 ~를 더해 갔다 His tone became more and more fervent. // 회장은 ~가 가득했다 The hall was filled with enthusiasm [excitement]. // 그 마을에는 아직도 선거의 ~가 남아 있었다 The excitement of the election campaign still lingered in the village.
3 [높은 신열] a high fever; feverishness. ¶몸에 ~가 있다 I feel like I have some temperature. / I feel feverish. / I have a slight fever.
●**열기 소독** hot-air disinfection; heat sterilization; (우유의) pasteurization.
열기관(熱機關) [공] a thermomotor; a heat engine.
열기구(熱氣球) a hot-air balloon.
열김(熱−) **1** [가슴속의 열의 운김] passion; emotion; enthusiasm. ¶~에 under the influence [impulse] of (strong) passion / driven [impelled / prompted / swayed / urged] by one's emotion / carried away by one's feelings. **2** [홧김] (a fit of) anger; an angry mood; fume; fury; indignation. ¶~에 in a fit of anger [temper / rage] / in a moment [tumult] of anger / in the heat of passion.
열나다(熱−) **1** [신열이 나다] become feverish; run a fever [temperature]; develop a fever; come to have fever; have an attack of fever.
2 [열성이 나다] become enthusiastic (in / about / over / for); (미국 구어) enthuse (about / over); be mad [crazy] (about / over); be keen [intent / bent] (on). ¶그녀는 열나게 공부하고 있다 She is studying feverishly [ardently]. / She is immersed [absorbed] in her studies.
3 [화나다] get [become / grow] angry; be offended [enraged] (by); (미) get mad (at /

열녀

about); become indignant (at / with); be heated (with passion); get into a passion [huff]; fly into a fury. ¶그는 잔뜩 열나서 나를 때렸다 He struck at me in a fury. / 사람 열나게 하지 마라 Do not rub me the wrong way. / Don't put me out [ruffle my temper].

열녀(烈女) a chaste (and strong-minded) woman; a virtuous [constant] woman; a faithful wife.

열다¹ [(열매를) 맺다] bear fruit; fructify; fruit; (열매가) grow (on a tree). ¶열매가 많이 여는 나무 a fruitful tree / a good bearer // 많이 ~ bear much [abundant] fruit / bear well // 이 지방에서는 오렌지가 열지를 않는다 Orange trees won't bear fruit in this area. // 이 사과나무는 언제 열매가 열지요 When does this apple tree bear fruit?

열다² 1 (닫힌 것 등을) open. ¶문을 ~ open a door / (열쇠로) unlock a door // 뚜껑을 ~ lift [take off / undo] the lid [cover] // 창문을 ~ open a window // 서랍을 ~ open a drawer / (잠아당겨서) draw [pull] out a drawer // 입을 ~ open one's mouth [lips] // 그는 문을 억지로 열었다 He forced [burst] the door open. / He opened the door by force. // 문을 비틀어 열었다 I wrenched the door open.
2 [개최하다] hold (a meeting); open (a conference); give (a party). ¶파티를 ~ hold [give] a party / (미) throw a party // 무도회를 ~ give [hold] a dance // 토론회를 ~ hold a discussion meeting // 전람회를 ~ open [hold] an exhibition.
3 [운영하기 시작하다] open (a shop); set up [start] (a store); commence; establish; found. ¶화랑을 ~ open [start / set up] a gallery / 꽃 가게를 ~ set up as a florist // 그는 거기에 병원을 열었다 He founded a hospital there. // 그는 종로에서 가게를 열고 있다 He keeps [runs] a store in Jongno. // 그 가게는 10시에 연다 The store opens at ten.
4 [(새 기틀을) 마련하다] open (up); clear; break; make. ¶후진을 위해 길을 열어 주다 open [pave] the way for younger men / give younger men [fellows] a chance // 출셋길을 열어 주다 open a path [way] for (a person's) promotion [advancement].

열대(熱帶) the tropics; the torrid zone; the tropical zone.
● **열대 기후** a tropical climate. **열대병** (의) a tropical disease. **열대 식물** [식] a tropical plant; (집합적) tropical flora. **열대어** [동] a tropical fish. **열대 저기압** a tropical cyclone. **열대 지방** the tropics; tropical regions.

열도(列島) an archipelago (*pl.* ~(e)s); a chain [group] of islands. ¶일본 ~ the Japanese Islands [Isles / Archipelago].

열등(劣等) inferiority; a low grade [class]. **열등하다** inferior; low-grade; low-class; low; base; of poor [lower] quality. ¶이것은 품질이 ~ This article is of inferior quality.
● **열등감** a sense [feeling] of inferiority; (an) inferiority complex. ¶~을 가지다 have a sense of inferiority / have [be possessed by] inferiority complex // 돈 많은 친구 앞에서는 어쩐지 ~이 느껴진다 I feel somehow small [cheap] in the presence of a rich friend. // 영어에 있어서는 같은 반 친구들에게 ~을 갖고 있다 I feel inferior to my classmates in English. **열등생** a backward [very poor] pupil [student].

열띠다(熱−) 《서술적》 get [become / grow / passionate] heated [excited / enthusiastic]. ¶열띤 환영 an enthusiastic [an ardent / a warm / a hearty / a cordial] welcome // 그들은 열띤 논쟁을 벌였다 They had a heated argument with each other. // 그는 열띤 어조로 핵무기 금지를 호소했다 He appealed passionately [fervently] for the prohibition of nuclear weapons.

열락(悅樂) pleasure; joy; delight; mirth; ecstasy. **열락하다** take [find] pleasure [delight] (in); delight (in); rejoice (at / in / over); be in ecstasies (over).

열람(閱覽) reading; (문어) perusal; inspection. ¶~ 환영 [사절] (게시) Admission Free [Closed To The Public]. / Inspection free [declined]. **열람하다** read; peruse. ¶신문을 ~ read [(문어) peruse] a newspaper / look through newspapers. ➔ 고서를 일반에게 열람시키다 offer an old book for public inspection [perusal].
● **열람실** a reading room. **열람표** a call slip.

열량(熱量) heat capacity [value]; quantity [amount] of heat; [발열량] calorific value; [단위] calorie. ¶~이 많은 [적은] 음식 a high-caloried [low-caloried] food / a food high [low] in calorie [calorific value / calorific content] // 그 음식은 1,500 칼로리의 ~이 있다 The diet represents a heat value of 1,500 calories.
● **열량계** a calorimeter.

열렬하다(熱烈−) ardent; fervent; passionate; impassioned; enthusiastic; vehement. ¶열렬한 사랑 passionate [fervent / ardent] love / 열렬한 개혁주의자 an ardent [a fervent] reformer // 열렬한 기독교 신자 a devoted [fanatic] Christian // 그는 열렬한 음악 애호가다 He is a great fan of music. / He is an ardent lover of music. / He is passionately fond of music. // 그는 그 시인의 열렬한 숭배자다 He is an enthusiastic admirer of the poet. **열렬히** ardently; fervently; passionately; enthusiastically; with ardor [fervor]. ¶~ 환영하다 greet [welcome] (a person) most warmly [with immense enthusiasm] / receive (a person) with wild [great] enthusiasm // 저 두 사람은 ~ 사랑하는 사이다 Those two are madly [deeply] in love with each other. / Those two love each other passionately [with all their soul].

열리다¹ (나무가) bear (fruit); fruit; be in fruit; (열매가) grow (on a tree). ¶이 나무는 열매가 열립니까 Does this tree bear [produce / bring forth] fruit? // 오렌지가 주렁주렁 열려 있었다 Oranges were growing in clusters (on the tree). / The tree was covered [(문어) laden] with oranges. / The tree was full of oranges. // 올해는 밤이 잘 [많이] 열렸다 Chestnut trees bore [fruited] well this year.

열리다² 1 (닫힌 것 등이) open; be opened. ¶열린 문 [창문] an open door [window] // 문이 잘 열리지 않는다 The door will not open. // 서랍이 잘 열리지 않았다 The drawer was tight. // 미닫이문이 10센티미터 정도 열려 있었다 The sliding door was ten centimeters or so ajar.
2 [개최되다] be held [given]; take place. ¶전시회는 내일 열린다 The exhibition will open [be opened] tomorrow. // 이사회는 매월 열린다 The board of directors meets every month. // 그의 수상 축하 파티가 열렸다 A

party was held to celebrate his receiving the prize.
3 [트이다] open; be open(ed). ¶승진의 길이 ~ be given a chance to rise (in rank) / the way[door] to promotion is opened∥읽을 능력이 생기자 그에게 새로운 세계가 열렸다 The ability to read opened up a new world for him.

열망(熱望) an ardent desire[wish]; a fervent desire[hope / aspiration]; an eager desire; (구어) a yen; a longing. **열망하다** be eager [anxious] (for / to do); desire ardently [eagerly / earnestly] (to do / that); long (for / to do); thirst[hunger] for[after]; crave (for); have an eager[desire] (for / to do). ¶우리는 평화를 열망하고 있다 We long[are longing] for peace.∥We have intense aspirations toward peace.∥이 제도의 개선을 열망합니다 We fervently hope that this system will be improved.∥그는 아들의 소식을 듣기를 열망하고 있었다 He was hungry for[He craved] news of his son.

열매 (a) fruit; a nut(견과); a berry(장과). ¶~가 잘 열리는 나무 a fruitful tree / a good bearer∥~가 열리지 않는 fruitless / unfruitful / barren∥~**가 열(리)다** bear[produce / give] fruit∥~**가 잘 열다** fruit well / bear well[bountifully]∥~**가 익다** the fruit grows ripe[ripens]∥~**를 맺다** bear[produce / bring forth] fruit / [비유] bear fruit / produce a result / come[be brought] to fruition / fructify∥이 나무는 ~가 많이[잘] 열린다 This tree produces a lot of fruit[is a good bearer].∥그들의 연구는 ~를 맺었다 Their research bore fruit[was remunerated]. / Their research was fruitful.∥그들의 꿈이 ~를 맺었다 Their dreams were realized [came true].

열무 a young radish.
●**열무김치** young radish *gimchi*(kimchi).

열반(涅槃) [불] **1** [해탈의 경지] Nirvana; nirvana. **2** [입적] (석가의) the death of (the) Buddha; (승려의) death of a Buddhist priest.

열변(熱辯) an impassioned[a fervent / a vehement] speech; passionate[fiery] eloquence. ¶~**을 토하다** make[deliver] an impassioned[a fiery] speech / speak with fervor / harangue[declaim] (against / for)∥변호인은 피고의 결백에 대해 ~을 토했다 The lawyer made[delivered] an impassioned speech arguing the innocence of the accused.

열병(閱兵) a review; inspection of troops. **열병하다** inspect troops; review (troops); pass troops in review; inspect soldiers at a parade.
●**열병식** a review (of troops).

열병(熱病) a fever; a febrile disease; pyrexia. ¶~**에 걸리다** contract[catch / suffer from] a fever.

열복사(熱輻射) [물] heat[thermal] radiation.
열분해(熱分解) [화] pyrolysis.
열사(烈士) a patriot; a hero. ¶순국~ a martyr.
열사(熱沙) burning[hot / scorching] sand.
●**열사욕**(−浴) a (hot) sand bath; [의] (요법) arenation; ammotherapy.
열사병(熱射病) [의] heatstroke; heat prostration[exhaustion]. ¶~**에 걸리다** suffer from [be affected by] heatstroke.

열상(裂傷) a laceration; a lacerated wound. ¶등에 ~을 입다 have one's back lacerated / receive lacerations on one's back / one's back is lacerated.

열석(列席) attendance; presence. **열석하다** attend; be present at; be in attendance at.

열선(熱線) **1** [물] infrared rays. ⇨적외선 **2** [가열 도선] a hot wire.

열성(劣性) inferiority. ¶~**의** (유전) recessive / (병) dysgenic.
●**열성 형질** a recessive (character[trait]).

열성(列聖) (대대의 여러 임금) successive kings; (여러 성인) a number of saints.

열성(熱誠) earnestness; warmth; enthusiasm; ardor; zeal; devotion(헌신); sincerity(성실). ¶~ 어린 충고 earnest advice∥~**적인** earnest / enthusiastic / devoted / hearty / ardent / warm / zealous∥~**적으로**[~을 다하여] with eagerness[zeal / devotion] / warmly / earnestly / enthusiastically / devotedly / heart and soul∥~**이 넘치다** be overflowing with enthusiasm∥그의 한 마디 한 마디에는 ~이 서려 있었다 Every word of his speech reflected his earnestness. / Every word breathed his ardor.
●**열성가** an enthusiast; a zealot(열광자); a devotee. **열성분자** earnest[enthusiastic / devoted] elements (of a party).

열세(劣勢) inferiority in strength[numbers]; numerical inferiority. ¶~**의** 만회하다 rally from an inferior position / make a comeback. **열세하다** (서술적) be inferior in numbers[strength]; be outnumbered (by).

열쇠 1 (자물쇠를 여는 쇠붙이) a key. ¶현관(금고)의 ~ a key to the front door[to the safe] ∥~**를 꽂다** insert[put] a key in a lock / fit a key to a lock∥~**를 돌리다** turn a key (in a lock)∥~**로** 자물쇠를 열다 open a lock with a key / unlock (a door). **2** (단서) a key; a clue. ¶암호의 ~ the key word / **세로**[가로] ~ (크로스워드의) the down[across] clues∥해결의 ~를 쥐다 hold the key to the solution (of) / 문제 해결의 ~를 발견할 수 없다 I can't find any key to the solution of[any clue to help solve] the problem.
●**열쇠고리** a key ring. **열쇠 구멍** a keyhole. ¶~**으로 들여다보다** look[peep / spy] through a keyhole.

열심(熱心) eagerness; enthusiasm; zeal; fervor; ardor; earnestness; keenness; warmth. ¶~**인** eager (for / about / to do) / enthusiastic (about / in / over) / zealous (in / for) / keen (on / about) / devoted (to)∥~에 ~인 사람 a person full of zeal for (music) / an enthusiast for (sports)∥그는 일에 ~이다 He is devoted[He devotes himself] to his work. / He is enthusiastic in his work.∥그는 우표 수집에 ~이다 He is keen on collection stamps.

열심히(熱心-) eagerly; enthusiastically; zealously; ardently; fervently; earnestly; warmly; passionately; keenly; devotedly; in (good) earnest; with fervor[ardor / zeal]; hard; diligently; wholeheartedly. ¶~ 공부하다 work [study] hard∥일을 ~ 하다 work hard [assiduously]∥도서관에 ~ 다니다 make frequent trips to a library / (문어) frequent a library∥아이들은 ~ 듣고 있었다 The children listened to him attentively.∥넌 이 일을

정말 ~ 하고 있니 Are you doing this work seriously? // 나는 ~ 공부했다 I studied as hard as I could. // 그녀는 시어머니의 마음에 들도록 ~ 노력했다 She was eager [did her best] to please her mother-in-law. // 좀 더 ~해라 Do it with more enthusiasm [zeal]. / You must work more earnestly / Put more heart into your work. // 소녀는 ~ 그림을 그리고 있었다 The little girl was absorbed in drawing a picture.

열십자(一十字) a cross. ¶~(꼴)의 cross-shaped // ~로 crosswise / crisscross // 소포에 ~로 리본을 매다 tie a ribbon crosswise around a package.

열씨(列氏) Réaumur(약어 R, R.). ¶~ 55도 이상의 온도 a temperature of more than 55° R.
● 열씨온도계 a Réaumur thermometer.

열악하다(劣惡－) inferior; poor; coarse; of poor quality; (설비가) inadequate. ¶열악한 환경 속에 살다 live in poor surroundings.

열애(熱愛) passionate[ardent] love; a strong attachment; devotion. **열애하다** love fervently [passionately / ardently]; be madly [passionately] in love (with a person); be devoted (to a woman); have passionate love (for); be an ardent lover (of); (구어) be everything (to); be head over heels (in love with).

열어젖히다 open (a door) wide; swing[fling / throw] (a door) open; push (a door) open(밀어서); force[burst] (a door) open(억지로). ¶나는 덧문을 열어젖혔다 I opened up the shutters.

열어제치다 →열어젖히다

열없다 1 [겸연쩍고 부끄럽다] awkward; shy; ill at ease. ¶열없어 하다 be abashed[embarrassed] / feel small[cheap] / feel awkward [nervous] (before an audience) / be self-conscious. **열없이** abashedly; shyly; self-consciously. ¶그는 회의에 늦어 ~ 들어왔다 He was late for the meeting and entered the room with an embarrassed[a sheepish] look on his face. 2 [소심하다] timid; fainthearted; chicken-hearted; weak-kneed; cowardly. ¶열없는 사람[아이] a timid person[child] / a coward. **열없이** faintheartedly; timidly; cowardly; weak-kneedly. ¶~ 웃다 give a timid smile.

열에너지(熱－) thermal energy.

열역학(熱力學) [물] thermodynamics.

열연(熱演) an enthusiastic[impassioned] performance. **열연하다** perform[play] enthusiastically [with much nerve]; give an impassioned performance; put much [a lot of] spirit into one's performance. ¶그들은 모두 열연했다 They all played their parts with enthusiasm.

열왕기(列王記) [성] the (books of) Kings. ¶~상[하] The First[Second] Book of Kings.

열용량(熱容量) [물] thermal[heat] capacity.

열원(熱源) a heat source[reservoir].

열의(熱意) enthusiasm (for / about); zeal (for); ardor (for); eagerness (for / after / about). ¶~ 있는 enthusiastic / zealous // ~ 없는 unenthusiastic / [내키지 않는] half-hearted / [무관심한] indifferent // ~를 보이다 show[manifest] zeal (for) / display great[a great deal of] enthusiasm (for) // 그는 공부에 ~가 있다 He is devoted to [enthusiastic about] his studies. // 그들은 그 사업에 ~가 없었다 They were not enthusiastic about [They showed little enthusiasm for] the enterprise. // 야구에 대한 그의 ~는 차차 식어 갔다 His enthusiasm for baseball gradually cooled down.

열적다 →열없다

열전(列傳) a series of biographies. ¶노벨상 수상자 ~ the lives of Nobel prizewinner.

열전(熱戰) a furious [hot] battle; a hard [fierce] fight; (경기) a heated [hot] contest; a close[tough] game; a hot war(냉전에 대하여). ¶~을 벌이다 put up a hard fight (with) / run a neck-and-neck race (with) / fight fiercely[hotly] // 두 사람은 ~을 전개했다 A close game developed between the two. // 두 팀 사이에는 ~이 벌어질 것이다 We are expecting an exciting game between the two teams.

열전기(熱電氣) [물] thermoelectricity. ¶~의 thermoelectric.
● 열전기쌍(－雙) a thermocouple; a thermo-electric couple.

열전도(熱傳導) heat[thermal] conduction.
● 열전도율 heat[thermal] conductivity.

열전류(熱電流) a thermoelectric current; a thermocurrent.

열전자(熱電子) [전] a thermion; [물] a thermoelectron. ¶~의 thermionic / thermoelectronic.
● 열전자관 a thermionic tube.

열정(熱情) ardor; passion; fervor; warmth; [열렬한 애정] ardent[passionate] love. ¶개혁에 대한 ~을 북돋우다 stir up zeal for reform / add fuel to flames of reform // 그는 젊은이다운 ~에 불타고 있었다 He was burning with youthful passion.

열정적(熱情的) passionate; ardent; fervent. ¶~인 시 an impassioned poem.

열중(熱中) enthusiasm; absorption; zeal; (a) craze. **열중하다** become[be] enthusiastic (in / about / over); get[be] engrossed[absorbed / immersed] (in); have a mania [craze / rage] (for); be mad[crazy / wild] (about / over); be devoted[dedicated] (to); devote [dedicate] oneself (to); be keen (on); be intent[bent] (on); give oneself up[over] (to); abandon oneself (to); go[put one's] heart and soul (into); (구어) enthuse (over / about). ¶사진[꽃꽂이]에 ~ be absorbed [engrossed] in photography[flower arrangement] // 신흥 종교에 ~ be a fanatic follower of a new religion // 저 학생은 정치 운동에 열중하고 있다 (구어) That student has really thrown himself[plunged] into political activities. // 그들은 이야기에 열중하고 있었다 They were deep in conversation. // 그녀는 프랑스어 공부에 열중하고 있다 She's immersed in her study of French. // 그는 연구에 열중하고 있다 He is enthusiastic about his research. // 그는 요즈음 우표 수집에 열중하지 않게 되었다 He has lost his enthusiasm for collecting stamps recently. // 그는 로큰롤에 열중하고 있다 He's really into rock. // 그는 도박에 열중하여 가정을 돌보지 않았다 He was too intent on gambling to think of his family. // 그들은 춤에 열중하고 있다 They are wild [mad / crazy] about dancing. // 그는 투기에 열중해 있다 The speculation bug has bitten him badly.

열증(熱症) [의] a fever; a febrile disease; pyrexia.
열진(烈震) a tremor of the 6th degree on the seismic scale.
열째 the tenth.
열쩍다 →열없다
열차(列車) a train; a railroad[(영)railway] train;(영) a railway carriage. ¶급행~ an express[a fast] train∥보통[완행]~ a slow [a local / an accommodation /(미)a way] train∥상행[하행]~ an up[a down] train∥야간~ a night train∥여객~ a passenger train∥임시~ a special[an extra] train∥직행~ a through train∥특급~ a limited express (train) /(미국 구어) a cannonball / (초특급) a superexpress (train)∥화물(미)~ a freight (train) /(영) a goods train∥~ 편으로 by train∥오전 8시 반 출발 서울행 급행~ the 8:30[eight-thirty] a.m. express (train) (bound) for Seoul∥오후 7시 도착 대구발 특급~ the limited express (train) from Daegu due (to arrive) at 7 p.m.∥~에 타다 take a train /(미) board a train∥~의 전복을 꾀하다 attempt to wreck a train∥~을 운행[운전]하다 run[operate] a train∥마지막~를 놓치다 miss the last train∥역이 가까워지자 ~가 속도를 늦추었다 The train slowed down as it approached the station.∥폭설 때문에 ~들이 여러 시간 늦어지고 있다 Trains have been delayed many hours because of [due to] heavy snowfall.
● **열차 사고** a train[railroad] accident. **열차 시간표** a (train) timetable;(미) a railroad [train] schedule.
열창(-窓) [건] a window that opens; an openable window; a casement (window).
열처리(熱處理) heat treatment. **열처리하다** treat with heat; heat-treat (a metal).
● **열처리 장치** a heat treatment equipment.
열탕(熱湯) boiling water; hot water. ¶~으로 소독을 하다 scald (an instrument) / disinfect (dishes) in boiling water.
열파(熱波) [물] a heat[hot] wave; (핵융합의) a thermal wave.
열패(劣敗) (a) defeat through one's inferiority. ¶우승~ the survival of the fittest / the weakest goes to the wall. **열패하다** be defeated through one's inferiority; be bested; be outdone; be worsted.
열팽창(熱膨脹) thermal expansion.
● **열팽창률 / 열팽창 계수** a coefficient of thermal expansion; thermal expansivity.
열풍(烈風) a heavy[strong / severe / violent] wind; a gale.
열풍(熱風) a hot wind[blast]; (a blast of) hot air; (북아프리카 사막의) a sirocco (pl. ~s); a simoom[a simoon](모래 폭풍); (용광로의) a hot blast.
열학(熱學) [물] thermotics; calorifics.
열핵(熱核) ¶~의 thermonuclear.
● **열핵 무기** a thermonuclear weapon; (구어) a thermonuke. **열핵 반응** (a) thermonuclear reaction. **열핵 실험** a thermonuclear test.
열혈(熱血) [더운 피] hot[warm] blood; [열정] enthusiasm; fiery zeal; ardor.
● **열혈한 / 열혈남아** a hot-blooded[-headed] man; an arduous[a fervent] soul. ¶그는 ~이다 He is a hot-blooded man. / He has a passionate nature.

열호(劣弧) [수] a minor[conjugate] arc.
열화(烈火) [맹렬히 타는 불] a blazing[raging] fire; furious[devastating] flames. ¶~같이 노하다 fire[flare] up / flame[burn] with anger[wrath] / blaze[flush] with anger [fury] / be enraged[infuriated].
열화(熱火) 1 [뜨거운 불길] furious flames; a blazing fire. ¶~ 같은 더위 fiery heat∥~ 같은 연설 a fiery speech. 2 [매우 급한 화증] a hot[quick / short] temper; (a) passion.
열화학(熱化學) thermochemistry. ¶~의 thermochemical.
열 확산(熱擴散) thermal diffusion; thermodiffusion.
열효율(熱效率) thermal efficiency.
열흘 1 [10일간] ten days. ¶~도 못 되어 in less than ten days. 2 the tenth day (of a month). ⇨초열흘날
● **열흘날** the tenth (day) of the month. ¶매월(초)~에 봉급을 타다 get paid on the tenth of every month.
엷다 1 [두께가 적다] thin. ¶엷은 판자[소책자] a thin board[pamphlet]∥뜰에는 눈이 엷게 쌓여 있었다 The garden was covered with a thin coat[layer] of snow.∥소녀는 엷게 화장을 하고 있었다 The girl was lightly made up. 2 [색 농도가 연하다] light (in color); pale. ¶엷은 청색 light[pale] blue∥엷은 빛깔의 스커트 a light-colored skirt∥그림을 엷은 색으로 칠하다 paint a picture in pale colors. 3 [언행이 얄팍하다] shallow; frivolous; superficial; short-witted; short-sighted. ¶속이 엷은 사람 a shallow[frivolous] fellow. 4 [농도·밀도가 얕다] thin; (액체 등의 성분이 약하다) weak. ¶엷은 안개 a thin mist.
염(炎) [의] (an) inflammation. ⇨~염증(炎症) ¶늑막~ pleurisy / pleuritis.
염(殮) shrouding. ⇨염습
염(鹽) salt. ⇨소금 ¶재제(再製)~ refined salt.
염가(廉價) a low[cheap] price. ⇨싼값 ¶~의 cheap / inexpensive / low-priced(▶ cheap는 문맥에 따라 싸구려의 뜻으로 해석됨)∥~로 cheap(ly) / at a low price / at a bargain∥~로 팔다 sell cheap[at a reduced price / at a bargain price] / clear off(재고품 정리로) / undersell(경쟁자보다).
● **염가 판매** a bargain sale; a sacrifice(투매). ¶중고차 ~ [광고] Secondhand[Used] cars sold cheap. / Bargain-priced used cars.∥저 가게는 월요일마다 ~를 한다 They have a (bargain) sale at that store on Mondays. **염가품** popular-priced[low-priced] goods.
염기(厭忌) [싫어하고 꺼리는 것] hatred; dislike; repugnance; abhorrence. **염기하다** hate; dislike; loathe; detest; abhor; abominate.
염기(鹽基) [화] a base. ¶유기~ an organic base∥~성의 basic / positive / electropositive.
● **염기도**(-度) basicity. **염기류** the bases; the base group. **염기성 산화물** a basic oxide.
염두(念頭) mind. ¶그는 그 가르침을 늘 ~에 두고 있었다 He always kept[bore] that teaching in his mind.∥네 자신의 입장을 ~에 둔다면 그런 일은 할 수 없을 것이다 If you consider[think of] your position, you will see that you cannot do such a thing.∥그녀의 추억이 늘 ~에서 떠나지 않았다 The

염라국(閻羅國) Hades; Hell; the Underworld; the Nether World.

염라대왕(閻羅大王) the King[Ruler / Judge] of Hell; the Lord[Prince] of Hades; [일본] Yama; [그리스 신화] Pluto; [그리스·로마 신화] Dis; Orcus; the Great King Yama.

염량(炎涼) 1 [한서] heat and cold. 2 [사리를 분별하는 슬기] discernment; discretion; good sense; prudence. 3 [세력의 성쇠] rise and fall[decline]; ups and downs; vicissitudes.

염려(念慮) worry; anxiety; care; concern; fear; apprehension; uneasiness; solicitude; misgivings. ¶~스런 표정으로 with a worried [an anxious] look∥그의 석방이 연기될 ~가 있다 There is some fear[danger] that his release may be postponed.∥나는 가족에 대한 ~ 없이 여행을 떠났다 I started on my trip free of worry about my family.∥나는 아들의 장래에 대해 ~를 한다 I worry (myself) about my son's future. / I am worried [concerned] about my son's future.∥~를 끼쳐 드려서 죄송합니다 I am sorry to have troubled you so much. **염려하다** feel anxiety; be anxious[apprehensive / concerned / worried]; worry (about); concern oneself (about); be solicitous (about); have[feel] misgivings (about); be[feel] uneasy (about); care; fear; apprehend (danger). ¶그녀는 아이가 감기에 걸리지 않을까 염려하고 있었다 She was afraid her child might catch cold.∥염려할 필요가 없다 There is no need of apprehension.∥염려해 주셔서 감사합니다 I appreciate your thoughtfulness.∥그 일은 너무 깊이 염려하지 마라 Don't worry about the matter so much.∥비용에 관해서는 염려하지 마십시오 Never mind (about) the expenses.

염료(染料) (a) dye; (a) dyestuff(▶ 종종 복수형으로 쓰임). ¶염기성 ~ a basic dye∥인조[천연] ~ an artificial[natural] dye∥직접 ~ a direct dye∥합성 ~ a synthetic dye.
● **염료 공업** the dye industry.

염류(鹽類) salts. ¶~의 saline.
● **염류천** a salt[saline] spring; a mineral salt spring.

염매(廉賣) a bargain[reduction / cheap] sale; selling at small profits; dumping. **염매하다** sell cheap; sell at a bargain[discount]; sell at low prices.

염문(艷聞) gossip[(a) rumor] about a person's love affair(s); one's episode of love; a romance. ¶~이 있다 be associated with a love affair / have a romance∥그는 ~이 끊이지 않는다 His love affairs provide constant fuel[food] for the gossip mills.

염병(染病) 1 typhoid (fever). ⇨˚장티푸스 2 a contagious disease. ⇨˚전염병(⇨˚전염)

염병할(染病-) Go to hell! / Curse (on) you! / ~ 자식 Devil take you! / Plague take him!

염복(艷福) good fortune in love; many romances; successes in love.

염분(鹽分) salt; salinity. ¶~이 있는 salty∥~을 많이 함유하다 contain much[a lot of] salt∥식사의 ~을 줄이다 cut down on the salt in one's diet∥나는 혈압이 높아서 ~이 적은 식사가 필요하다 I need a low salt diet because I have high blood pressure.

염불(念佛) a prayer[an invocation] to (the) Buddha; a Buddhist invocation[prayer]; the repetition of the sacred name of Amitabha. **염불하다** pray to Amitabha; chant[say] a prayer to; tell[say / recite] the[one's] beads.

염산(鹽酸) [화] hydrochloric acid; (상품명) muriatic acid.
● **염산가스** hydrogen chloride. ⇨˚염화수소(⇨˚염화)

염색(染色) dyeing. ¶머리 ~약 a hairdye∥이 명주천은 ~이 잘된다[안 된다] This silk material dyes well[poorly]. **염색하다** dye. ¶머리를 ~ dye one's hair / have one's hair dyed∥검게 ~ dye (a thing) (in) black / get (a thing) dyed black.
● **염색공** a dyer. **염색법** a process of dyeing; how to dye; (현미경용·) staining techniques [procedures]. **염색사**(-絲) [생] a chromonema (pl. -mata); a genonema. **염색체** [생] a chromosome. ¶X[Y] ~ an X[a Y] chromosome∥성 ~ a sex chromosome∥~의 chromosomal (defect).

염생 식물(鹽生植物) a salt plant; a halophyte.

염서(炎暑) extreme heat (of summer days). ⇨˚염열

염서(艷書) a love letter; (프) a billet-doux (pl. billets-doux).

염세(厭世) pessimism; weariness of life[the world].
● **염세주의 / 염세관** pessimism; a pessimistic view of life[the world]; pessimism. **염세주의자** a pessimist.

염세적(厭世的) pessimistic; world-weary. ¶~사상 a pessimistic idea∥그녀는 요즈음 ~이다 She has become pessimistic[has lost interest in life] lately. / She has wearied of life recently.

염소 a goat. ¶숫~ a he-goat / a billy (goat)∥암~ a she-goat / a female goat / a nanny (goat)∥새끼 ~ a kid / a kidling / a goatling / a young goat∥~가 울고 있다 The goat is bleating.
● **염소 가죽** goatskin; (새끼 염소의) kid. **염소자리** [천] the Goat; Capricorn; Capricornus.

염소(鹽素) [화] chlorine(기호 Cl). ¶~의 chlorine / chlorous(염소와 합친) / chloric(염소를 함유하는)∥액체 ~ liquid chlorine.
● **염소 가스** chlorine gas. **염소산** chloric acid. **염소 소독 / 염소 살균** chlorination; chlorine disinfection.

염수(鹽水) brine; salt[saline] water.

염습(殮襲) shrouding. **염습하다** wash and shroud (a person's) dead body; prepare [dress] the body for burial.

염열(炎熱) extreme[intense] heat (of summer days); blazing[scorching / withering] heat; sultriness; broiling weather.
● **염열 지옥** a blazing inferno; the flames of Hell.

염원(念願) one's heart's desire; one's (dearest [heartiest]) wish. ¶오랜 ~ something that one has wanted[wished] to do for a long time / one's long-cherished desire∥그것은 내 20년 동안의 ~이었다 It has been my heart's desire[my dearest wish] for twenty

염보다

years.∥나의 ~이 드디어 이루어졌다 My dream has come true at last. / My wishes have been fulfilled at last. 염원하다 desire; wish (for); pray (for). ¶세계 평화가 언제까지나 계속되기를 염원한다 I pray with all my heart for lasting world peace.∥젊은 시절에는 미술가가 되기를 염원했다 When I was young, I longed to become an artist.∥그녀는 남편이 무사하기를 항상 염원하고 있었다 She prayed constantly for her husband's safety.

염장이(殮-) a (corpse) shrouder; [장의사] an undertaker; a mortician.

염하다(鹽藏-) preserve with salt [in brine]; salt; souse; corn.

염전(鹽田) a saltpan; a salt farm [field]; a saltern; a salina.

염주(念珠) 1 (a string of) beads; a (Buddhist) rosary. ¶~를 굴리다[세다] tell [say / recite / count] the [one's] beads. 2 [식] Job's tears; tear grass.
● 염주 알 (알 하나) a bead; (전체) the beads (of a rosary); [식] Job's tears.

염증(炎症) [의] (an) inflammation. ¶~(성)의 inflammatory ∥ 그는 감기로 목에 ~이 생겼다 The cold caused an inflammation in his throat. / His throat is inflamed due to the cold.

염증(厭症) an aversion; dislike. ⇨ 싫증 ¶~이 나다 become disgusted (with) / tire [get tired] (of) / get sick (of) / get fed up (with).

염천(炎天) 1 [몹시 더운 날씨] hot [broiling] weather; the summer heat (여름의); [땡볕] the blazing [burning / scorching] sun. ¶~(하)에 under [in] the blazing sun. 2 [남쪽 하늘] the southern sky.

염천(鹽泉) a brine [saline] spring.

염출하다(捻出-) 1 [어렵게 생각해 내다] devise; work [think] out; contrive. 2 [어렵게 돈을 짜내다] contrive to raise; manage to make. ¶용돈에서 2만 원을 염출했다 I squeezed out 20,000 won from my pocket money. ∥ 우리는 어렵게 자금을 염출했다 We raised the funds with difficulty.

염치(廉恥) a sense of shame [honor]. ¶~있는 사람 a person of honor ∥ ~가 있다 [~를 알다] have a sense of honor / be sensible to shame / be (keenly) alive to shame [to the feeling of honor] ∥ ~ 불구하고 …하다 bear shame to (do) / stoop to (do) ∥ 그는 ~라고는 없다 He is dead to all sense of shame. / He is quite shameless [brazen-faced]. ∥ ~를 알아야지 [~가 있어야지] For shame! / Shame (on you)! You ought to be ashamed.

염치없다(廉恥-) have no sense of honor; be lost to [dead to / past] shame. ¶염치없는 사람 a shameless [brazen-faced] person.

염탐꾼(廉探-) a spy; a secret agent; a scout.

염탐하다(廉探-) spy (upon / on); spy into (a secret); feel (out); pry about [into]. ¶적정(敵情)을 ~ feel [spy on] the enemy's movements ∥ 형세를 ~ feel out the situation ∥ 회사의 내부 사정을 ~ investigate the inside affairs of a company.

염통 [생] the heart. ⇨ 심장1

염하다(殮-) wash and shroud (a person's) dead body. ⇨ 염습하다(⇨염습).

염화(鹽化) [화] chloridation; salification. 염화하다 chloridate; chloridize; salify.
● 염화나트륨 sodium chloride. 염화물 a chloride. 염화 비닐 vinyl chloride; chloroeth-ylene. 염화수소 hydrogen chloride. 염화은 silver [argentic] chloride. 염화칼륨 potassium chloride. 염화칼슘 calcium chloride.

엽견(獵犬) a hound; a hunting dog. ⇨ 사냥개(⇨사냥)

엽궐련(葉-) [여송연] a cigar. ¶~을 물고 with a cigar in one's mouth [between one's teeth] ∥ ~을 피우다 smoke a cigar / puff at one's cigar ∥ ~을 물다 hold [have] a cigar in one's mouth.

엽기(獵奇) bizarrerie hunting. 엽기하다 seek [hunt] the bizarre.
● 엽기 소설 a bizarre story.

엽기(獵期) an open season; a hunting [shooting] season.

엽기적(獵奇的) bizarre; bizarrerie- [curiosity-] seeking [hunting]. ¶~인 살인 사건 a grotesque murder case.

엽록소(葉綠素) [식] chlorophyl(l). ¶~의 [~가 든] chlorophyllous.

엽록체(葉綠體) [식] a chloroplast.

엽맥(葉脈) [식] the veins (of a leaf). ⇨ 잎맥

엽상(葉狀) ¶~의 leaflike / foliated / [식] foliaceous / foliar / phylloid.
● 엽상 식물 a thallophyte.

엽색(獵色) debauchery; lechery. 엽색하다 philander.
● 엽색꾼 a woman chaser; a womanizer; a wolf; a philanderer; a debauchee; a lecher.

엽서(葉書) (미) a postal card (관제); (미국 구어) a postal; a postcard (사제); (영) a postcard (관제·사제). ¶그림 ~ a picture postcard / (미) a postcard ∥ 반신용 ~ a reply (postal) card ∥ 봉함 ~ a letter card ∥ 왕복 ~ a reply-paid [prepaid] postcard / a reply (postal) card / a double postal card (with a reply card attached) ∥ ~로 by postcard / (send one's regrets) on a postcard ∥ ~를 내다 send [drop] a postcard (to) ∥ ~로 답하다 answer [reply] by postcard.

엽전(葉錢) a brass coin (with a square hole in the middle).

엽조(獵鳥) a game bird; (집합적) (winged) game.

엽차(葉茶) coarse (green) tea; (green) tea of inferior quality.

엽채류(葉菜類) leafy vegetables; green vegetables; edible herbs.

엽초(葉草) leaf tobacco. ⇨ 잎담배

엽총(獵銃) a sporting [hunting] gun [rifle]; a shotgun (산탄총); [조총] a fowling [birding] piece.

엿¹ yeot; taffy; (영) toffee.

엿² [여섯] six. ¶~ 말 six mal.

엿가래 a stick of taffy [(영) toffee].

엿기름 malt; germ barley [wheat]; dried barley [wheat] sprouts. ¶~을 만들다 malt.
● 엿기름가루 powdered malt.

엿당(-糖) maltose.

엿듣다 eavesdrop (on) (a conversation); overhear; listen secretly; (전화 등으로) listen in (on); (도청기를 사용하여) tap (wires); wiretap; bug (a telephone). ¶엿듣는 사람 an eavesdropper / a wiretapper ∥ 남의 이야기를 ~ eavesdrop on the conversation / overhear another's talk ∥ 전화를 ~ tap wires / listen in on (a person's) telephone conversation ∥ 엿보거나 엿듣거나 해서는 안 된다 You must not peep or overhear.

엿보다 1 [훔쳐보다] steal a glance (at); look

엿새 furtively (at); watch (a person) with a furtive eye; [들여다보다] peep into [through]. ¶나는 장지문의 좁은 틈새로 방 안을 엿보았다 I peeped into the room through the narrow opening between the paper sliding doors.∥그는 방 안을 엿보다가 그녀에게 들켰다 He was caught by her while stealing a glance into her room.
2.[기회를 노리다] watch[wait] for (a chance). ¶원수를 갚을 기회를 ~ watch for [await] one's opportunity to take revenge on (a person)∥그는 반격할 기회를 엿보고 있었다 He was looking for a chance to counterattack.
3 [살피다] spy on. ¶형세를 ~ wait and see how the wind blows[lies].
4 [헤아려 알다] guess; infer; gather; surmise. ¶그의 얼굴에는 굳은 결의가 엿보였다 His firm resolution was revealed in his countenance.∥좋은 가문에서 자랐음이 그녀의 말씨에서 엿보인다 Her manner of speaking shows[indicates] that she is well-bred.

엿새 1 [여섯 날] six days. 2 the sixth day (of a month). ⇨ ̄초엿샛날
● **엿샛날** the sixth (day) (of a month).
엿장수 a taffy seller[vendor].
엿치기 *yeotchigi*; a taffy-breaking game. **엿치기하다** play a taffy-breaking game.
영 entirely; not at all. ⇨ ̄전혀
영(令) 1 [명령] an order; a command. 2 a law; an ordinance. ⇨ ̄법령
영(零) zero; a cipher; naught; nought; nothing. ¶~의 zero∥3대 ~으로 이기다 win (a game) by a score of three to nothing∥4에 ~을 곱하여도 그 답은 ~이다 Multiply four by nothing, and the result is nothing.∥5대 ~으로 우리가 이겼다 We defeated our opponents five to nothing[(영) five (goals to) nil].
영(嶺) a (mountain) pass; a ridge; a high hill.
영(靈) 1 the soul. ⇨ 영혼 ¶~과 육 the spirit and the flesh∥~의 세계 a world of spirit. 2 a god; a deity. ⇨ 신령
영가(靈歌) a spiritual. ¶흑인 ~ a black [Negro] spiritual.
영감(令監) 1 [존칭] lord; sir. 2 [늙은 남자] an old man; an elderly man. 3 [나이 든 남편] one's husband. ¶**여보** ~ Dear. / My Dear. / Darling. / My darling. / (미) Honey. / My honey.
영감(靈感) (an) inspiration; (영국 구어) a brain wave; (미국 구어) a brainstorm; [심] extrasensory perception(약어 ESP). ¶~의 번득임 a flash of inspiration∥(갑자기) ~이 떠오르다 have an[a sudden] inspiration∥~을 받다 be inspired (by) / get[receive / draw] inspiration (from) / (구어) have a brain wave∥그때 그는 ~을 얻었다 At that time an inspiration seized him.∥그에게 갑자기 ~이 떠올랐다 An inspiration burst upon him.∥그는 달을 보고 ~을 받아 시를 한 수 지었다 Inspired by the moon, he composed a poem.
영걸(英傑) [영웅과 호걸] a great man; a hero; a mastermind; [영특하고 기상이 뛰어남] heroic qualities[character].
영검 divine response[answer] to one's prayer; a miracle; miraculous virtue. **영검하다** wonder-working; magical[miraculous] in its effect; wonderfully efficacious. ¶그 불상은 영검하다고 한다 The Buddhist image is believed to be highly responsive to prayers.
영검스럽다 wonder-working; magical in its effect. ¶영검하다(⇨영검) ¶영검스런 약 a miraculous medicine / a miracle[wonder] drug.
영겁(永劫) [불] eternity; perpetuity. ¶~ 불변의 eternal / everlasting / permanent. ¶~
영결(永訣) the last[final] parting[farewell]; separation by death. **영결하다** bid one's farewell to the dead; pay one's last respects to the deceased.
● **영결식** a funeral ceremony[service]; funeral rites.
영계 a (spring) chicken.
● **영계백숙** a boiled chicken.
영계(靈界) 1 [정신계] the spiritual[psychic(al)] world[sphere]; [영혼의 세계] the world of the spirit[soul]; the land of departed souls. ¶~와 교통하다 communicate with the world of the spirit.
영고(성쇠)(榮枯盛衰) prosperity and decline; rise and fall; ups and downs of life; the vicissitudes of fortune[life].
영공(領空) territorial sky[air]; (sovereign) airspace. ¶캐나다의 ~을 침범하다 invade [violate] (the) Canadian airspace[the territorial sky of Canada]∥터키의 ~을 비행하다 fly over Turkish territory.
● **영공권** aerial domain.
영관(領官) (육군에서) a field(-grade) officer (집합적); a colonel(대령); a lieutenant colonel(중령); a major(소령); (해군에서) a captain(대령); a commander(중령); a lieutenant commander(소령); (미 공군에서) colonel(대령); lieutenant colonel(중령); major(소령); (영 공군에서) a group captain(대령); a wing commander(중령); a squadron leader(소령).
● **영관급** the field grade.
영광(榮光) an honor; a glory; a privilege(특전). ¶신의 ~ the glory of God∥~에 빛나다 be covered in glory / be crowned with glory∥~으로 알다 feel honored∥…하는 ~을 갖다[누리다] have the honor of (doing) / have the pleasure[honor] to (do)∥분에 넘치는 ~을 얻다 receive undeserved honor∥하나님 [천주]께 ~ 있으라 Glory be to God!∥~입니다 I am[feel] honored. / You do me proud.∥뵙게 되어 큰 ~입니다 I'm very honored[It is a great honor] to meet you.∥이 성대한 모임에서 여러분께 말씀드리게 된 것을 큰 ~으로 생각하는 바입니다 I esteem[deem] it a great honor[favor] (for me) to address you at this grand meeting.∥그녀와 말을 나누는 것만으로도 ~이다 To converse with her is itself a privilege.∥왕림해 주신 것을 큰 ~으로 생각합니다 I take your visit as a great honor.∥이 모임에 참석하게 된 것을 큰 ~으로 생각합니다 I feel highly honored to be present at this meeting.
영광스럽다(榮光-) glorious; honorable; honored. ¶영광스러운 역사 a glorious history∥영광스러운 고립 a glorious[splendid] isolation∥영광스럽게도 …하다 have the honor of doing … / have the pleasure [honor] to do ….
영구(永久) [관형어적] permanent; lasting; eternal. ¶반~적인 semipermanent∥~적인 정책을 세우다 form a permanent policy∥~

불변하다 remain unchanged forever. **영구하다** eternal; everlasting; permanent; perpetual. **영구히** forever; eternally; permanently; perpetually; for good (and all). ¶한국을 ~ 떠나다 leave Korea for good.

영구(靈柩) a coffin; (미) a casket(장식이 있음).

●**영구차** a (motor) hearse; a funeral car [coach].

영국(英國) Britain; England; Great Britain(영국 본토, 즉 England / Wales / Scotland); the United Kingdom; (공식명) the United Kingdom (of Great Britain and Northern Ireland)(약어 U.K.); the British Empire; Greater Britain(식민지를 포함한「대영 제국」); the British Commonwealth of Nations(영연방). ¶~의 English / British / Britannic / Anglican / ~제의 English-made / of English make / made in England.

●**영국 국교회** the church of England; the Anglican Church. **영국 국기** the British flag; the Union Jack. **영국 연방** the Commonwealth of Nations; (구칭) the British Commonwealth (of Nations). **영국인** an Englishman; an Englishwoman(여자); a Britisher(대브리튼 사람; 미국인이 본국인이라는 의미로 사용하는 경우가 많음); a Briton(대브리튼 사람); John Bull(별명); (집합적) the British; the English. **영국 해협** the (English) Channel.

영남(嶺南) [경상남북도 지방] the Yeongnam district[area]; the Gyeongsang-do provinces; the southeastern part[section] of Korea.

영내(領內) the domains; the territory. ¶한국의 ~에서 within Korean territory.

영내(營內) inside barracks. ¶~에 살다 live in barracks.

●**영내 거주** living in barracks.

영농(營農) farming; agriculture. ¶과학적 ~ scientific farming // 복합 ~ combined agriculture // 전천후 ~ all-weather agriculture // ~의 기계화 agricultural mechanization / mechanization of farming. **영농하다** farm; be engaged in agriculture.

●**영농가** an agriculturist; a farmer. **영농 자금** a farming fund. ¶~을 방출하다 release (the 700 billion won of) farming loans.

영단(英斷) a wise decision; a decisive judgment; [뛰어난 조치] a decisive [resolute] step; a drastic measure. ¶~을 내리다 make a decision / take a decisive step[a drastic measure] // 이 사건은 총리의 ~을 필요로 한다 This matter calls for a (final) decision [judgment] by the Prime Minister. // 정부의 ~이 기다려진다 We look eagerly to the government for a wise decision.

영달(榮達) distinction; [출세] advancement (in life); rise (in the world). ¶~을 구하다 [바라다] seek distinction / hanker after (worldly) fame.

영도(零度) zero (degree); the freezing point. ¶절대 ~ absolute zero // ~ 이하의 온도 a sub-zero temperature // ~ 이하의 기후 a sub-zero climate // ~ 이상으로 오르다 rise above zero // 기온이 ~로 떨어졌다 The thermometer dropped to zero. // 오늘 아침에는 ~ 이하로 내려갔다 It[The temperature] fell below zero[the freezing point] this morning.

영도(領導) leading; lead; leadership; guidance; direction. ¶…의 ~하에 under the leadership[guidance / direction] of … // 그는 정계에서 ~적 역할을 하고 있다 He plays a leading role in the political world. **영도하다** lead; take the lead; give a lead (to); head; guide; direct. ¶연립 정부를 ~ head the coalition government.

●**영도력** one's leadership (over); (have) qualities[the capacity] as a leader. **영도자** a leader; the mentor of a group.

영동(嶺東) [강원도 대관령 동쪽의 땅] the Yeongdong district[area]; the Gangwon-do province; the middle-eastern part[section] of Korea.

영락(零落) ruin; downfall; reduced circumstances; (구어) comedown. **영락하다** be ruined; go[come] to ruin; sink[go / come] down in the world; sink in one's fortunes; be in reduced circumstances; be reduced to want[poverty]; be in distress; go broke; (미국 속어) be busted. ¶영락한 생활 a wretched life // 영락한 집안 a family in reduced circumstances / a family which has fallen on hard times // 거지로 ~ be reduced to beggary.

영락없다(零落−) absolutely correct[exact]; invariably right; quite free from mistakes [errors]; sure[certain] enough; unfailing; infallible. ¶영락없는 서울내기 a Seoulite to the core[born and bred] // 네 꼬락서니는 영락없는 거지다 You look like a beggar, every inch of you. // 그가 영락없는 범인이라고 짐작했다 I felt dead sure that he was the (very) man who committed the crime. **영락없이** without fail[any slip]; infallibly; surely; for sure; certainly. ¶화살이 과녁 복판을 ~ 맞혔다 The arrow hit the target right in the center. // 그는 내 생각을 ~ 알아맞혔다 He guessed exactly what I was thinking.

영랑(令郞) your son. ⇨~영식(令息)

영령(英靈) the spirit of revered memory; (전사자의) the souls[spirits] of the war dead [heroic dead / fallen heroes]; (애국지사의) the spirits of the fallen patriots. ¶~이시여 고이 잠드소서 May your noble soul rest in peace!

영롱하다(玲瓏−) brilliant; clear and bright; bright and translucent; clear; lucid; serene. ¶영롱한 구슬 a bright germ // 영롱한 가을 달 a serene autumn moon // 옥같이 영롱한 문체 a crystal-clear[lucid] style. **영롱히** brilliantly; clearly; lucidly; serenely.

영리(營利) profit(-making); gain; moneymaking. ¶~적인[의] profit-making / moneymaking // 비~적인[의] nonprofit(-making) / noncommercial // ~를 도외시하고 without any thought of gain[profit] // ~를 목적으로 on a commercial basis / for profit // ~에 급급하다 be engrossed in moneymaking / be bent [intent] on gain // 이 단체는 ~ 목적이 아니다 This is a non-profit organization.

●**영리 단체** a profit-making organization. ¶비(非)~ a nonprofit(-making) organization. **영리 사업** a profit-making enterprise; an undertaking for profit; a commercial enterprise. **영리주의** commercialism.

영리하다(怜悧−·伶俐−) [현명하다] clever; bright; wise; intelligent; brainy; sensible; sharp; [빈틈없다] shrewd; smart. ¶영리한 아이 a bright child / a clever[an intelligent]

영림 boy [girl] // 영리한 사람 a clever person / a bright man / (빈틈없는) a shrewd [smart] fellow // 영리해 보이는 intelligent-looking / bright-looking // 영리해 보이는 look brainy [intelligent / smart] // 그는 영리한 사람이다 He has lots of brains. / He is a sensible man. // 개는 영리한 동물이다 The dog is an intelligent [a smart / a clever] animal. // 그걸 알아채다니 과연 영리하구나 How clever of you to notice that!

영림(營林) forest management [administration]; forestry; [식림] afforestation; reforestation.
● **영림 사업** a forestry enterprise.

영마루(嶺─) the top of a (mountain) pass.

영망(令望) good repute; (high) reputation; fame; renown.

영매(令妹) your [his, etc.] younger sister.

영매(靈媒) a (spiritualistic) medium (*pl.* ~s). ¶~인 mediumistic.

영면(永眠) eternal sleep [rest]; death; passing (away); quietus. ¶파리가 그 화백의 ~의 땅이 되었다 Paris became the final resting place of the great painter. **영면하다** die; pass away; sleep one's final sleep; go to one's final rest.

영명(令名) a fair name; good repute; (a) (high) reputation; fame. ¶~이 높다 be noted [famous / famed / well-known / renowned / celebrated / illustrious] / be highly renowned / enjoy an excellent reputation // ~을 얻다 become famous / gain a reputation / win fame // ~을 더럽히다 tarnish [compromise] one's fair name // 그는 정치가로서 ~이 높다 He is distinguished [well known] as a statesman.

영명하다(英明─) clever; bright; brilliant; clear-sighted; intelligent; sagacious.

영몽(靈夢) an inspired [a prophetic] dream; a divine revelation in a dream. ¶~을 꾸다 have [dream] an inspired dream.

영묘(靈廟) a mausoleum (*pl.* ~s, -lea); a shrine.

영묘하다(靈妙─) miraculous; mysterious; supernatural; exquisite; heavenly; wonderful. ¶영묘한 피리 소리 a marvelous note from a flute. **영묘히** miraculously; mysteriously; exquisitely; wonderfully.

영문 1 [형편·사정] circumstances; the situation; the state of things [affairs / matters]. ¶~을 캐묻다 inquire into the circumstances // 무슨 ~인지 모르다 cannot make out what it is all about / do not know what's what. 2 [까닭] (a) reason; (a) cause; ground(s); the matter. ¶~ 모를 살인 a wanton murder // 무슨 ~인지 모르지만 for some unknown reason / for no reason that could be discovered // 모임이 왜 취소되었는지 ~을 모르겠다 I don't know (the reason) why the meeting was canceled. // 어떻게 된 셈인지 ~을 모르겠다 There is neither rhyme nor reason about it.

영문(英文) English(영어); an English sentence [composition]; English writing. ¶~으로 쓰다 write (a letter) in English // ~으로 읽다 read (a story) in English // ~을 (잘) 쓰다 write English (well) / be a (good) writer of English // ~을 한역하다 translate English into Korean // 다음 문장을 ~으로 옮겨라 Put [Translate] the following sentences into English.
● **영문 소설** an English novel; a novel [story] in English. **영문 편지** an English letter; a letter (written) in English.

영문(營門) a barrack [camp] gate.

영문법(英文法) English grammar. ¶~ 책 an English grammar book.

영문학(英文學) English literature. ¶~을 전공하다 specialize in English literature / (대학에서) (미) major in English literature course / (영) read English.
● **영문학과** the English Literature course(전공과목); the department of English (literature)(학부).

영물(靈物) a spiritual being; [영리한 동물] a very intelligent animal.

영미(英美) England and America; Britain and the United States. ¶~의 English [British] and American / Anglo-American.
● **영미인** the British and Americans.

영민하다(英敏─) bright; intelligent; clever. ¶영민한 두뇌 a clear head / keen intellect. **영민히** brightly; cleverly; intelligently.

영법(泳法) [수영 방법] a swimming form [style / stroke].

영봉(靈峯) a sacred mountain.

영부인(令夫人) your [his] wife. ¶K 씨 ~ Mrs. K // P 씨와 (그) ~ Mr. and Mrs. P.

영빈관(迎賓館) a reception hall; a guesthouse.

영사(映寫) projection. **영사하다** project [throw / show] (a picture) on a screen; screen (a film).
● **영사기** a projector. **영사 기사** an operator; (미) a projectionist. **영사막** a (projection) screen. **영사실** a projection room [booth].

영사(領事) a consul; a consular representative. ¶~대리 an acting consul // 명예 ~ an honorary consul // 부~ a vice-consul // 카이로 주재 한국 ~ the Korean consul at Cairo // 주한 미국 ~ an American consul (stationed) in Korea.
● **영사관** a consulate. **영사관원** a consular official [attaché]; (집합적) the staff of a consulate; the consular staff. **영사 송장**(─送狀) [경] a consular invoice.

영사(營舍) (a) barracks; a cantonment.

영상(映像) (거울·수면에 비친) a reflection; a reflex; (렌즈 등에 의한) an image; (TV의) a picture; an image; the field(영상면); (레이더의) a blip. ¶거울의 ~ a reflection in a mirror // 텔레비전의 ~이 흐리다 The picture on the TV screen is blurred [out of focus].

영상(零上) ¶~ 10도 ten degrees above zero.

영상(領相) the prime minister. ⇨영의정

영생(永生) eternal life; immortality. **영생하다** live eternally; enjoy immortality; be immortal.

영선(營繕) building and repairs; repairs (work). **영선하다** build and repair.
● **영선과** a building and repairs section.

영성(靈性) divine nature; divinity; spirituality.

영성체(領聖體) [가] (Holy) Communion. **영성체하다** take [receive] (Holy) Communion; commune. ¶영성체하는 사람 a communicant.

영세(永世) all ages; all generations; eternity; permanence. ¶~의 everlasting / perpetual / permanent / eternal // ~토록 forever [(영)

forever] / through all ages[eternity] / eternally / permanently.
● **영세불망** everlasting remembrance; eternal gratitude. ¶~하다 remember[bear in mind] forever. **영세 중립** permanent neutrality. ¶~국 a permanently neutral country [state].

영세(零細) being petty[small / poor]. **영세하다** trifling; petty; small. ¶영세한 이익 (a) trifling[small] profit // 영세한 소매업자 a petty retail merchant.
● **영세 기업** a small business. **영세농** / **영세농민** a petty[an ultra-small] farmer; a poor landed peasant. **영세민** a needy[destitute] person; a poverty-stricken[-ridden] person; (집합적) the destitute[indigent]; the poor [needy]. ¶도시 ~ the low-income citizens // ~을 돕다 relieve the destitute / give aid to the poor (and needy). **영세업자** a small-scale businessman.

영세(領洗) [가] baptism. ¶~를 주다 baptize / administer baptism (to) // ~를 받다 accept [receive] baptism / be baptized.
● **영세명** a baptismal name; a Christian name. **영세자** a baptist.

영속(永續) permanence; permanency; perpetuity; perpetuation; (long) continuance; [불멸] imperishableness. ¶~적인 lasting / everlasting / enduring / permanent / perpetual / [불멸의] imperishable / immortal. **영속하다** last long[for a long time / forever]; remain permanently; continue[stand] forever; endure long. ¶영속하지 않다 be shortlived / be of short duration. →¶영속시키다 perpetuate // 양국의 우호 관계는 영속되지 않았다 The friendly ties between the two nations were short-lived[did not last long].
● **영속성** perpetuity; permanence; permanency. ¶~이 있는 lasting / permanent / of long standing // ~이 없는 not lasting / transient / of short duration // 이 장사는 ~이 없다 This business will not last[prosper] long.

영솔하다(領率-) lead (a party); head (a group); be at the head (of); command (an army); be in command of (an army).

영송(迎送) meeting and farewell. **영송하다** welcome[meet] and see[send] off.

영수(領收·領受) receipt. ¶계산서에 ~필이라 표시하다 receipt a bill / stamp a bill "paid" (도장을 찍다) // ~필(畢) Received. / Paid. **영수하다** receive. ¶일금 백만 원을 틀림 없이 영수하였습니다 I certainly received[I acknowledge receipt of] (the sum of) one million won. // (증서에) Received (from[of] Mr. A) the sum of ₩1,000,000.
● **영수인** a receiver; a recipient. **영수증** a receipt (for); a voucher (for); an acknowledgment (for). ¶~ 주고받기 운동 a receipt-giving-and-taking drive // ~을 쓰다 write a receipt (for) / issue a receipt // ~을 써 주다 make (a person) out a receipt / give (a person) a receipt (for) // ~을 받다 get a receipt (made out).

영수(領袖) a leader; a chief; a head; a boss. ¶정당의 ~ the leader of a political party / a political[party] leader / a boss.

영시(英詩) [영어로 쓰여진 시] English poetry [verse]; [그 한 편] an English poem; a poem in English.

영시(零時) [자정] (twelve o'clock) midnight. ¶~ 30분 half past[after] twelve / twelve thirty.

영식(令息) [남의 아들] your[his, her, etc.] son.

영아(嬰兒) a nursing baby; a suckling; an infant.
● **영아 살해** infanticide.

영악하다 clever; bright; shrewd; smart; sharp. ¶영악한 아이 a smart[bright] child / a clever boy[girl].

영악하다(獰惡-) (extremely) vicious; fierce; ferocious; savage. ¶영악한 놈 a rough / a savage.

영안실(靈安室) a mortuary (of a hospital). ¶~에 안치하다 place a dead body in a mortuary of a hospital.

영애(令愛) [남의 딸] your[his, her, etc.] daughter.

영약(靈藥) a wonder drug; a miracle drug; a miraculous medicine; a marvelous[sovereign] remedy; a royal elixir.

영양(令孃) your daughter. ⇨ *영애

영양(羚羊) [동] an antelope; a goral(아시아 남동부산의).

영양(營養) nutrition; nourishment; nutriment; alimentation. ¶~이 많은[있는] nourishing / nutritious / nutritive // ~이 없는 unnourishing / innutritious // ~이 좋은 아이 a well-fed[well-nourished] child // ~면에서 균형이 잡힌 식사 a nutritionally balanced diet // ~이 모자라다 (사람이) be underfed / be undernourished / (음식이) be low in nutritional value // ~을 섭취하다 take[get] nourishment // 이런 식사로는 ~이 모자란다 You cannot get enough nutrition from food [a meal] like this.
● **영양가** nutritive[nutritional] value; (be low in) food value. ¶~ 높은 of high nutritive value / highly nutritious // 나는 ~ 높은 음식을 잔뜩 먹었다 I took plenty of nourishment. **영양 부족** undernourishment; malnutrition; insufficient[want of] nutrition. ¶~의 ill-fed / poorly fed / undernourished // ~으로 (인한) through lack of nourishment // 그는 ~으로 병이 났다 He became ill from insufficient nourishment. **영양분** nutritive substance[elements]; a nutriment. **영양사** a dietitian; a dietician; a nutrition technician; a nutritionist. **영양 상태** nutritive conditions. **영양소** nutritive substance; a nutriment; a nutrient. **영양실조** malnutrition; unbalanced nutrition; dystrophy; dystrophia. ¶~의 underfed / dystrophic // ~에 걸리다 suffer from malnutrition. **영양제** a medicine for promoting nutrition; a nutrient (substance); a tonic. **영양학** dietetics; (the science of) nutrition; nutritional science.

영어(英語) English; the English language. ¶구어체 ~ colloquial[spoken] English // 근대 [중세 / 고대] ~ modern [middle / old] English // 미국[영국] ~ American[British] English // 상업 ~ business[commercial] English // 시사 ~ current English // 실용 [살아있는] English // 일상 ~ everyday English // 표준 ~ standard English / (영)the Queen's[King's] English // 현대 ~ current [present-day] English // 회화체 ~ conversational (form of) English // 세련된 ~ polished[refined] English // 어법에 맞는 ~ idiomatic English // ~가 늘다 improve

영어

[make progress] in one's English // ~로 번역하다[옮기다] translate into English // ~를 유창하게 말하다 speak English fluently[fluent English] // 그는 ~을 잘한다[~가 서툴다] He is good[poor] at English. / He is a good [poor] speaker of English. / He speaks good [poor] English. / He has a good [poor] knowledge of English. // 나는 ~로 의사소통을 할 수 있다 I can make myself understood in English. // "종이"를 ~로 무엇이라 합니까 What is the English for *jong-i*?(▶ 정관사가 따름) // ~는 이제 세계어가 되어 있다 English is now a world[an international] language. // 그의 ~는 완벽하다 His English is perfect. / He has a perfect knowledge[command] of English. // 그는 ~ 신문을 읽을 수 있다 He can read English-language newspaper.
● **영어 교사 / 영어 선생** a teacher of English; an English teacher. **영어 교육** the teaching of English; English-language teaching. **영어권** the English-speaking world. **영어 회화** English conversation. ¶~를 시작하다 enter[get] into conversation (with) // ~를 연습하다 practice speaking English (on a person) // 그는 ~를 잘한다 He is a good speaker of English. / He speaks good English.

영어(營漁) fishing; fishery.

영업(營業) business; trade; [영업 활동] business activities; [업무의 운영] operation(s). ¶개인 ~의 가게 a store under private management // 풍속~ the entertainment and amusement business(es) // ~상의 비밀 a trade secret // ~을 시작하다 open for business // 남의 ~을 방해하다 obstruct a person's business // ~을 쉬다 suspend business / close one's shop // ~을 허가하다 authorize (a person) to carry on the business // ~ 중 (게시) Open. // 저 사람은 무슨 ~을 하고 나요. What line of business is he in? // 이것이 저희 회사의 ~ 개요입니다 This[Here] is an outline of our business activities. **영업하다** do [conduct / carry on / en-gage in] business; trade[deal] in (cotton); run[operate] business; make a business of (photography). ¶그 가게는 영업하고 있느냐 Is the shop open? // 일요일을 제외하고는 매일 영업합니다 Business goes on daily except on Sunday.
● **영업 감찰** a business[trade] license. **영업권** trade rights; goodwill. ¶~을 팔다 sell out [dispose of] one's business / sell the goodwill (of a shop) // 오래된 가게의 ~을 양도하다 transfer the goodwill of an old shop. **영업 금지** prohibition of business; a shutdown. **영업 방침** a (company's) business policy. **영업부** a business[sales] department. **영업부장** a business[sales] manager. **영업소** an office; a business[sales] office; a place of business. **영업시간** business[office] hours. ¶~: 10시부터 4시까지 Open from ten (a.m.) to four (p.m.) / Business hours: 10 a.m.–4 p.m. **영업 실적** business performance; business turnover. **영업용** ¶~ 자동차 cars kept for business (purposes). **영업 정지** suspension of a business license. ¶~를 당하다 be ordered to suspend business / be (temporarily) close down // 그 레스토랑은 ~를 당했다 The restaurant had its operating license suspended. **영업주** a business proprietor. **영업 허가** a business license. ¶~를 받다 secure a license to operate.

영역(英譯) (a) translation into English; (an) English translation[version]. ¶국문 ~ translating Korean into English / Korean-English translation // 나는 그 책을 ~으로 읽었다 I read the book in an English translation. // 그 소설의 ~은 두 가지가 있다 There are two English versions[translations] of that novel. **영역하다** translate[render / turn / put] into English. ¶다음 글을 영역하여라 Translate the following passage into English.

영역(領域) 1 [영유 구역] a territory; a domain. ¶~을 침범하다 invade[encroach upon] (another's) territory // 이 국경 저쪽은 캐나다의 ~이다 The land beyond this boundary is Canadian territory[belongs to Canada].
2 [분야] a domain; a field; an area; a province; a sphere. ¶화학은 나의 ~이 아니다 Chemistry is not in my line[sphere]. // 그의 연설은 여러 교육 ~에 걸쳐 있었다 His speech touched on various fields[areas] of education. // 그것은 과학의 ~을 넘어서 있다 It is beyond the limits of science. // 그녀는 아동 문학의 ~에서는 유명하다 She is well-known in the realm of children's literature.

영역(靈域) sacred[holy] grounds[precincts]; a holy place.

영영(永永) forever; for good (and all); eternally; permanently. ¶한국을 ~ 떠나다 leave Korea for good // 그에게서는 ~ 소식이 없다 I have heard nothing from him.

영예(榮譽) honor; glory; distinction; [명성] fame; renown. ¶그 노벨상 수상자는 그 나라의 ~였다 The Nobel laureate was an honor to the country. // 이 모임에서 연설을 하게 되니 저의 크나큰 ~입니다 It's a great honor [privilege] for me to speak at this meeting.

영예롭다(榮譽-) honorable; glorious.

영예스럽다(榮譽-) honorable. ⇨영예롭다

영외(營外) outside barracks. ¶~에 거주하다 live[take one's lodgings] outside [out of] barracks.

영욕(榮辱) honor and disgrace.

영웅(英雄) a hero (*pl.* ~es); a great man. ¶~의 국민적 ~ a national hero.
● **영웅담** an epic. **영웅주의** heroism. **영웅호색** All great men are also great lovers [womanizers].; Heroes enjoy the pleasures of flesh.

영웅적(英雄的) heroic. ¶~인 행위 a heroic deed[action] / (an act of) heroism.

영원(永遠) eternity; permanence; [불멸] immortality. ¶~의 [시간을 초월한] eternal / [언제까지나 계속되는] everlasting / [불멸의] permanent / [불멸의] immortal // 영혼의 ~성 the immortality of the soul. **영원하다** eternal; permanent; everlasting; immortal; perpetual. ¶영원한 사랑 everlasting love // 영원한 평화 everlasting[permanent] peace // 영원한 잠 eternal sleep / everlasting rest // 영원한 생명 immortal life / 영원한 충성을 맹세하다 swear eternal loyalty // 그들은 영원한 사랑을 맹세했다 They pledged their eternal love. // 예술은 ~ Art is eternal. // 평화야말로 인류가 추구하는 영원한 염원이다 Peace is mankind's eternal wish. // 이것이 우리의 영원한 이별이 될지도 모른다 This may be our last meeting. **영원히** forever; (영) for ever;

eternally; permanently; for good. ¶이처럼 행복한 시간이 ~ 계속되면 좋으련만 I wish these happy hours could last forever. // 지나간 청춘은 ~ 돌아오지 않는다 One's lost youth never returns. // 넬슨의 이름을 ~ 기리기 위해 이 기념비가 세워졌다 This monument was erected to immortalize Nelson's name. // 그의 발견은 ~ 기억될 것이다 His discovery will be remembered forever.

영위(營爲) 〔관리〕 management; administration; 〔운영〕 operation; running; conduct. **영위하다** manage; run; operate; carry on; conduct; keep; engage in. ¶정직한 삶을 ~ lead an honest life.

영유(領有) possession. ¶…의 ~로 돌아가다 fall into a person's heads / be annexed to (a state). **영유하다** possess; get[gain / take] possession of; be in possession of.
● **영유권** dominium. **영유지 / 영유물** a possession.

영육(靈肉) body and soul[mind / spirit].

영의정(領議政) the prime minister; the premier.

영인(影印) a facsimile (of a manuscript); a photographic reproduction. **영인하다** photoprint; print[reproduce] by phototypography.
● **영인본** a facsimile edition.

영일(寧日) a peaceful[quiet] day; rest. ¶~이 없다 Not a single day passes quietly.

영자(英字) an English letter.
● **영자 신문** an English (language) (news) paper; a newspaper in English.

영작(문)(英作文) (an) English composition. ¶~을 쓰다 write an English composition / make a composition in English / 〔국문을 영역하다〕 translate Korean into English.

영장(令狀) a warrant; a writ; a written order. ¶소집 ~ a call-up paper[card] // 소환 ~ a writ of summon // 수색 ~ a search warrant // 체포〔구속〕 ~ a warrant of arrest / an arrest warrant // ~에 의한〔에 의하지 않은〕 체포 an arrest with[without] a warrant // ~에 의해 체포되다 be arrested on a warrant // ~에 의해 수색되다 be searched under a warrant // ~을 발부하다〔청구하다〕 issue [request] a warrant (for a person's arrest) // ~을 집행하다 execute a (search) warrant / serve a writ on (a person) // ~ 없이는 가택 수색을 못합니다 You can't search my house without a warrant.

영장(靈長) ¶인간은 만물의 ~이다 Man is the lord of (all) creation.
● **영장목** 〔동〕 Primates.

영재(英才) 〔탁월한 재주〕 talent; genius; unusual talent; 〔탁월한 재주를 가진 사람〕 a man of great talent; a gifted person; a man of ability; a genius.
● **영재 교육** an educational program for the special education for the precocious.

영적(靈的) spiritual; incorporeal.
● **영적 교감** spiritual communion. **영적 교류** spiritual sympathy.

영전(榮典) 1 〔위계·훈장 등〕 honors; marks of honor. 2 〔경사스러운 의식〕 a ceremony; a function.

영전(榮轉) promotion; preferment; transference on promotion. ¶그의 전임은 ~이 아니다 His transfer is not a change for the better. **영전하다** be promoted[transferred] to a higher post. ¶그는 뉴욕 지점장으로 영전했다 He was promoted to the head of the New York office.

영전(靈前) ¶~에 before the spirit of the departed[deceased] // ~에 꽃을 바치다 offer flowers to the spirit of a dead person.

영점(零點) 1 〔무득점〕 (a) zero (pl. ~(e)s); nothing; no marks; no point. ¶~을 받다 get (a) zero (in English) / get nought (in physics) / receive a zero marking[mark] / (경기에서) get a duck / (미국 속어) get skunked // 답안지에 ~을 매기다 put (a) zero on a paper // 그의 팀은 ~이었다 His team didn't score. 2 〔무능·무성과〕 nothing; nought; a failure. ¶그녀는 어머니로서는 ~이다 She is a failure as a mother. 3 〔물〕 the freezing[ice] point.

영접(迎接) reception; meeting. ¶총리는 공항에서 대통령의 ~을 받았다 The prime minister was greeted by the president at the airport. **영접하다** go[come] (out) to meet (a person) on arrival; receive; greet; meet.

영정(影幀) a (scroll of) portrait.

영조(營造) building; construction. **영조하다** build; construct; erect; set[put] up.
● **영조물** 〔건축물〕 a building; 〔공공 건조물〕 public works.

영주(領主) a (feudal) lord; the proprietor of a manor.

영주(永住) permanent residence. ¶그들은 보스턴을 ~의 땅으로 정했다 They made Boston their permanent home. **영주하다** settle down (in); reside[live] permanently (in); put down permanent roots (in). ¶그는 그곳에 영주하기로 결심했다 He decided to settle[reside] there permanently.
● **영주권** the right of permanent residence; denizenship. ¶~을 얻다 be denizened / obtain the right of permanent residence. **영주권 카드** a green card. **영주자** a permanent resident; a settler; a denizen. **영주지** one's (permanent) home; a permanent domicile.

영지(領地) 1 (a) territory. ⇨ = 영토 2 a feudal estate. ⇨ 봉토1

영지(靈地) a holy[hallowed] ground[land]; a sacred place.

영차 Yo-ho!; Yo-heave-ho!

영창(詠唱) 〔독창·咏唱〕 〔음〕 an aria. ⇨ 아리아

영창(營倉) 〔건물〕 a guardhouse; (미) a stockade; (영국 속어) the glasshouse; (형(刑)) detention in the guardhouse. ¶그는 ~에 갇혔다 He was confined in the guardhouse.

영천(靈泉) 〔신기한 약효가 있는 샘〕 a wonderworking[magical / miraculous] fountain.

영치(領置) 〔법〕 provisional holding; keeping in custody. **영치하다** detain; place in the custody (of the prison officer).
● **영치금** money and personal belongings deposited by inmates.

영탄(詠歎) 1 〔읊음〕 emotional recitation; recital with deep emotion. **영탄하다** recite (a poem) emotionally; chant[sing] with deep emotion. 2 〔감탄〕 exclamation; admiration. **영탄하다** exclaim; admire; be (deeply) moved [touched].

영토(領土) (a) territory; (a) dominion; (a) domain; (a) possession; soil. ¶~의 territorial // 한국 ~ 에서 on Korean soil / in[within] Korean territory // ~를 확장하다 expand one's domain[territory] // ~를 획득〔병합〕하다 acquire[annex] a territory // 다른 나라의

~를 침략하다 encroach upon the territory of another country.
● **영토권** territorial rights. **영토 문제** the territorial problems. ¶~가 해결되지 않으면 양국 간의 평화 조약은 결코 체결되지 않을 것이다 Without solving the territorial issue the peace treaty between the two countries will never be concluded. **영토 분쟁** a territorial dispute. **영토 확장** expansion of territory; territorial expansion [aggrandizement].

영특하다 (英特−) sagacious; intelligent; exceptional; extraordinary; great.

영판 →아주¹

영패 (零敗) a whitewash; a shutout; (구어) a skunk. **겨우 ~를 면하다** barely miss being shut out. **영패하다** fail to score; be whitewashed; be shut out; (구어) be skunked. ➔ ¶상대방 팀을 영패시키다 shut out the opposing team / hold the opposing team scoreless.

영하 (零下) ¶~의 기온 a sub-zero temperature // 온도가 ~로 내려갔다[떨어졌다] The temperature fell [dropped / went down] (to 16 degrees) below zero [below the freezing point / (영) of frost]. // 20도였다 It was 20 degrees below zero [(영) 20 degrees of frost]. / The temperature was minus twenty degrees.

영한 (英韓) English-Korean; Anglo-Korean.
● **영한 대역** an English-Korean translation. **영한사전** an English-Korean dictionary.

영합 (迎合) flattery; adulation; ingratiation. **영합하다** [아첨하여 좇다] flatter; curry favor with; fawn upon; […의 뜻을 받들다] cater to [anticipate] a person's wishes [feelings]; adjust one's opinions and behavior to please a person. ¶여론에 ~ accommodate oneself to public opinion // 시류에 ~ swim with the tide // 그는 쉽사리 다른 사람들의 주의에 영합한다 He goes along easily with other people's principles. // 저 신문은 대중적 취향에 영합한다 That newspaper caters to popular tastes.

영해 (領海) (the) territorial waters; [국제법] a closed sea. ¶한국의 ~에서 within Korean territorial waters // ~ 12해리 안[밖]에서 within [outside] the twelve-mile limit of territorial waters // 한국 ~를 침범하다 violate the territorial waters of Korea.

영향 (影響) [다른 것에 작용하는 힘] (an) influence; [효과] (an) effect; [충격력] (an) impact. ¶~이 있는 influential // 원폭의 ~ the effects of the atomic bomb // …의 ~으로 under the influence (of) // ~을 주다[미치다] influence / have [exert] an influence (on) / have [produce] an effect (on) / affect(▶ influence, affect는 다른 것에 변화를 일으킨다는 뜻이고 have an effect는 어떤 효과를 초래한다는 뜻) // ~을 받다 be affected [influenced] (by) // 그는 재즈의 ~을 받아 이 곡을 만들었다 He composed this piece under the influence of jazz. // 사람은 책의 ~을 크게 받는다 Men are greatly influenced by books. / Books have (a) great influence on men. // 그 회사는 인플레이션의 ~을 받지 않았다 The firm wasn't affected by inflation. // 근대 과학에 미친 아인슈타인의 ~은 매우 크다 Einstein had a tremendous impact on modern science. // 이 업종은 불황의 ~을 별로 받지 않는다고 한다 It is said that this type of business is not much effected by recessions. // 경제계는 불경기의 ~을 받고 있다 The business world is being hit by the effects of the recession. // 과음이 그의 건강에 나쁜 ~을 주었다 Excessive drinking told on him. // 물가 상승의 ~이 가계부에 나타나 있다 The rise in prices is making itself felt [is having an effect] on our family budget.
● **영향력** (an) influence; the power of influence. ¶~이 있다 be influential (with them) / (one's words) tell (with a person) // 그는 자기의 ~을 행사하여 부하들을 요직에 앉혔다 He used his influence to assign important positions to his subordinates. // 그는 출판계에서 ~이 있다[없다] He is powerful (or influential) [powerless / not influential] in the publishing world. // 그는 사장의 ~으로 입사했다 He entered the company through the influence of the president.

영험 (靈驗) divine response [answer] to one's prayer. ⇨°영검

영혼 (靈魂) the soul; the spirit. ¶~의 불멸을 믿다 believe in the immortality of the soul // 그의 ~이 평안하기를 비는 바입니다 I pray that his soul may rest in peace.
● **영혼 불멸(설)** (the doctrine of) the immortality of the soul.

영화 (映畵) a film; a moving picture; (영) a movie; (집합적) the movies; (영) the cinema. ¶개봉 ~ a first-run film / a newly released film // 공상 과학 ~ a science-fiction [an SF] film // 교육 ~ an educational film // 뉴스 ~ a newsreel / a news film // 단편 ~ a short motion picture / a shorty / a briefy / a short // 무성 ~ a silent film [picture] // 극~ feature film // 문화 [기록 / 만화] ~ a cultural [documentary / cartoon] film // 발성 ~ a sound film [picture] / a talkie / a talking picture [film] // 입체 ~ a three-dimensional motion picture // 전쟁 ~ a war picture // 천연색 [흑백] ~ a (Techni)color [black and white] film // 1회에 두[세] 편 상영하는 ~ a double [triple] feature // 재미있는 ~을 보러 가다 see an interesting film // ~를 보러 가다 go to the movies [pictures / (영) cinema] / go to a movie // ~를 개봉하다 release a film // ~를 상영하다 show a film // ~를 검열하다 censor a film // ~를 제작하다 produce a film // ~를 촬영하다 shoot a movie // ~에 나오다 appear on the screen / appear in a movie / be in the movies // 그 ~는 상영 금지가 되었다 That film was banned. // 「햄릿」을 ~로 보았다 I saw Hamlet as a movie.
● **영화 각본** a scenario. ⇨°시나리오 **영화감독** a film [(미) movie] director; (영) a producer. **영화 검열** film censorship. **영화계** (미) the motion-picture [movie] world; the movies; (영) the film world; the cinema. **영화관** a movie theater; (영) a cinema; a picture hall. **영화배우** a film [movie / screen] actor (actress). ¶~ 지망자 an aspirant to a screen career // ~가 되다 appear on the screen. **영화 산업** the film [movie / motion-picture] industry. **영화 음악** film music. **영화제** a film festival. **영화 제작** film production. **영화 제작자** a film producer; a moviemaker. **영화 촬영소** a movie [film] studio. **영화 팬** a movie [cinema / film] fan; a moviegoer. **영화 평론가** a film [movie] critic. **영화화** cinematization; filming; (영) picturi-

ization. ¶~하다 make a movie (version) of / make (a novel) into a movie [film] / cinematize / film (a novel)// 소설을 ~하다 make a film of a novel // 이 대본은 ~하기 쉽다 This script will film easily. // 그녀의 자서전이 ~되었다 Her autobiography was made into a movie.

영화(榮華) 〔번영〕 prosperity; opulence(부유); (호사) splendor; luxury; (영예) glory. ¶~를 극도로 누리다 be at the height [zenith] of one's prosperity / go to extremes of luxury // 그는 ~를 맘껏 누렸다 He commanded both power and fortune.

옅다 1 shallow; superficial; slight. ⇨얕다 2 (빛깔이) light (color); pale; faint. ¶옅은 초록색 light [pale] green // 옅은 색 옷 a pastel dress.

옆 (측면) the side; the flank; (근처) neighborhood; vicinity. ¶~의 (측면의) side / lateral / flanking / (이웃하는) neighboring / adjacent / nearly / next (to) / ~에 beside / by [at] the side of // 집 ~을 지나가다 pass by a house // ~을 향하게 하다 turn (a thing / a person) sideways // 나는 괴로워하고 있는데 그는 ~에 서서 보고만 있었다 He just stood by and watched while I suffered. // 나는 전신주 ~의 한 사나이를 보았다 I saw a man beside the telephone pole. // 아무도 그의 ~에 가지 않았다 No one approached [went near] him. // 그녀 ~에 앉아 있는 사람은 누구지요 Who is that sitting beside [next to] her? / 나는 우연히 그의 ~에 앉았다 I happened to sit side by side with him. // 그녀는 눈물을 감추기 위해 얼굴을 ~으로 돌렸다 She turned her face away [turned aside / looked away] to hide her tears. // ~에서 참견하지 마라 Don't interfere [meddle]. / Don't poke your nose in [into] other people's business.

옆구리 the side; the flank. ¶오른쪽 ~가 쑤시다 [아프다] have a stitch [pain] in one's right side // ~를 쿡 찌르다 give a poke in (a person's) ribs / dig [poke] (a person) in the ribs // ~를 슬쩍 찌르다 nudge (a person) in the ribs.

옆길 1 〔큰길 옆으로 난 작은 길〕 a bypath; a byroad; a side road. 2 〔잘못된 방향〕 a wrong way; (토론 등의) a side issue; (a) digression. ¶그녀의 이야기는 자주 ~로 샌다 She digresses quite often. / She often gets off the subject. // 그의 강연은 본론에서 ~로 빗나갔다 His lecture wandered from the subject.

옆막이 a side cover [block].

옆면(-面) a side; sides.

옆모습 a profile; a face in profile; the side face. ¶그녀는 ~이 더 예쁘다 She looks better in profile. // ~을 찍은 사진이 있습니까 Do you have a photograph (of yourself) in profile?

옆문(-門) a side entrance [door] (of a house).

옆발치 ¶~에(서) at [close to] the feet of (a person) lying down.

옆방(-房) the next [adjoining] room.

옆얼굴 a profile; a face in profile; a face as seen from the side; the side face.

옆줄 a side line; (어류의) a lateral line.

옆질 a boat's rock(ing); rolling. **옆질하다** (a boat) rock; roll (from side to side).

옆집 the house next door; a neighboring [an adjoining / an adjacent] house. ¶~의 next

/ next-door // 한 집 건너 ~ (live) next door but one down // ~의 아이 our neighbor's child / the child next door // 저는 ~에 삽니다 I live next door. // 한 선생 댁은 우리 ~입니다 Mr. Han's house is next to ours.
●**옆집 사람** one's (next-door) neighbor.

옆쪽 the side; the flank.

예[1] 〔예전〕 old times; bygone days. ¶~나 지금이나 in all ages / ~로부터 from ancient [old] times // 100살까지 사는 사람은 ~로부터 드물다 Few people have ever lived to be one hundred years old.

예[2] 1 〔대답〕 yes(▶ 부정적인 대답일 경우에는 no); certainly. ¶~, 좋습니다 Yes, that will be [that's fine]. // ~, 물론 갑니다 Why yes, of course I'm coming. // ~, 사용하십시오 Why, certainly you may use it. // "벌써 끝냈습니까?" "~, 끝냈습니다." "Have you finished?" "Yes, I have." // "아직 안 끝났습니까?" "~, 안 끝났습니다." "You haven't finished yet?" "No, I haven't." // ~, 알았습니다 Yes, certainly. / All right. / (구어) O.K. 2 〔출석의 대답〕 yes; present; here. 3 〔재우쳐 묻는 소리〕. ¶~, 뭐라고요 What? What did you say? // ~? 그럴 수가 Really? That's impossible!

예(例) 1 〔실례·유례〕 an instance; a case; an example; an illustration. ¶~를 들면 for instance / for example / e.g. (▶ exempli gratia의 약어) / (… 같은) such as (▶ 예의 열거) / 〔말하자면〕 say // ~가 되다 serve as an example // ~를 들다 take [give] an example / cite an instance // 많은 위인이 가난에서 일어섰는데, ~를 들면 링컨이 있다 Many great men have risen from poverty — Lincoln, for example [instance].
2 〔관례〕 a habit; a custom. ¶~의 usual / customary / habitual // 그는 ~의 능변으로 상대방을 꼼짝 못하게 했다 He baffled his adversary with his usual eloquence.
3 〔이미 말한 바〕. ¶~의 the same / (문어) the said / (문제의) in question / (전술한) abovementioned // ~의 그 사람 the person in question // ~의 그 사건 the above-mentioned case.

예(禮) 1 salutation; a salute. ⇨경례 2 〔예법〕 etiquette; decorum; propriety; the proprieties(예절); politeness; courtesy. ¶~를 다하다 treat (a person) with the utmost courtesy / be polite and respectful to (a person) // ~를 갖추어 남을 초빙하다 engage (a person) with respect due to his worth / offer (a person) a position on most courteous terms // ~도 지나치면 실례가 된다 Excessive politeness lapses into impoliteness. 3 a ceremony. ⇨예식(禮式)

예각(銳角) 〔수〕 an acute angle.

예감(豫感) a foreboding; a presentiment; a premonition; a presage; (구어) a hunch(▶ 좋은 것에나 나쁜 것에나 씀). ¶불길한 ~ a gloomy foreboding / a previous sense of one's misfortune // 어머니께서 돌아가실 것 같은 ~이 들었다 I had a premonition [presentiment] that my mother would die soon. // 이 계획은 아무래도 잘되지 않을 것 같은 ~이 들었다 I had a feeling [hunch] that the plan would not work. // 그의 ~이 맞았다 His forebodings proved [came] true. **예감하다** have a foreboding [hunch] (of / that); feel a premonition [presentiment] (of / that); forebode. ¶죽음을 ~ forebode death / have a premoni-

예견(豫見) foresight; foreknowledge; prescience; precognition. **예견하다** foresee; foreknow; (문이) prognosticate. ¶그는 친구의 실패를 예견하고 있었다 He foresaw his friend's failure.

예고(豫告) a (previous) notice; an advance notice; a previous[preliminary] announcement; (경고) (a) warning. ¶~ 없는 시험 an unannounced examination / (구어) a popquiz / (구어) a pop test / a surprise examination // ~ 없이 without (previous) notice[warning] // ~ 없이 해고하다니 너무하다 It is outrageous that they should dismiss me without (previous) notice [warning] // 그는 ~도 없이 방문하였다 There was no advance notice of his coming. / He made[paid] a surprise visit. / He paid a visit without (previous) notice. / He made a surprise call. / He surprised me with a visit. **예고하다** notify[announce / inform / warn] beforehand[previously]; give [advance] warning[notice]; warn; (특히 영화·강연회 등의) give advance billing. ¶내일 방문하겠다고 예고해 두었다 I sent word I would call the next day. // 그만둘 경우에는 한 달 전에 예고해 주십시오 Please give us a month's notice before you[if you want to] quit[leave].
- **예고편** (영화의) a trailer; (영화·텔레비전의) a preview; a prevue.

예과(豫科) a preparatory course; a preparatory department; (의과 대학의) a premedical course.

예광탄(曳光彈) a tracer; a tracer bullet[shell]; a light[flame] tracer.

예규(例規) an established rule[regulation].

예금(預金) a deposit; money on deposit; a bank account. ¶당좌 ~ (미) a checking account / (영) a current account // 보통 ~ an ordinary[a general] deposit // 신탁 ~ a deposit in trust / a trust deposit // 은행 ~ a bank deposit[account] / a deposit in a bank // 저축 ~ a savings deposit[account] // 정기 ~ a fixed[time] deposit // 통지 ~ a deposit at notice[call] // 특별 ~ a special deposit // ~을 찾다 withdraw[draw] one's money[deposit] (from a bank) // 은행에 200만 원의 ~이 있다 I have two million won deposited[on deposit] in the bank[in my bank account]. / I have a bank account of 2,000,000 won. // 나는 ~을 30만 원 인출했다[찾았다] I withdrew three hundred thousand won from my (savings) account. // ~이 10만 원밖에 남지 않았다 I have only one hundred thousand won left in the bank. **예금하다** deposit (money in[with] a bank); make a deposit (in an account); place (money) on deposit (in a bank); bank (10,000 won). ¶나는 매월 20만 원씩 은행에 예금하고 있다 Every month I deposit[I make a deposit of] twenty thousand won in the bank. // 나는 그 은행에 예금했다 I have placed money on deposit with the bank.
- **예금 계좌** (미) savings account; (영) a deposit account. **예금액** the deposited amount; (money in) deposit. **예금자** / **예금주** a depositor. **예금 통장** a (deposit) passbook; a bankbook. **예금 통화** [경] deposit currency.

예기(銳氣) spirit; dash; mettle; ardor. ¶군사들은 크게 ~가 꺾였다 The soldiers were greatly dispirited.
예기(를) 지르다 break (a person's) spirits; dispirit; dishearten; damp[dampen] (a person's) enthusiasm[ardor].

예기(豫期) [기대] expectation(s); (an) anticipation; [희망] (a) hope; [예견] forecast; foresight. **예기하다** expect; anticipate; hope for; look for; look (ahead / forward) to; have in prospect; forecast; foresee. ¶예기치 않은 unexpected / unlooked-for / unanticipated / unforeseen / unthought-of // 네가 오리라고는 예기하지 못했다 I did not (in the least) expect to see you here. // 부모의 죽음은 그의 인생에 예기하지 못했던 변화를 가져왔다 His parents' death brought about an unexpected change in his life.

예끼 Damn it[you]!; Confound it[you].

예납(豫納) payment in advance; prepayment. ¶반납료 ~ 전보 a reply-paid telegram. **예납하다** pay in advance; prepay. ¶회비를 ~ pay the membership fee in advance.

예년(例年) 1 [어느 해] a normal[an ordinary] year; the average year. ¶금년 겨울은 ~에 없던 추위였다 This winter has been severer than usual. / It has been unusually[exceptionally] cold this winter. 2 [해마다] every year; annually. ¶~ 열리는 행사 an annual event[function].

예능(藝能) 1 [재주와 기능] accomplishments. ¶그녀는 여러 가지 ~에 능하다 She has a wide range of skills. / She has many accomplishments. / She is very accomplished. 2 [영화·미술·음악 등의 총칭] (public) entertainment; performing arts. ¶향토 ~ performing arts peculiar to a locality.
- **예능 교육** art education. **예능인** an entertainer; an artiste; a performing artist; (집합적) showfolk.

예니레 six or seven days.

예닐곱 six or seven.

예단(豫斷) (a) prediction; (a) presupposition; a foregone conclusion. ¶성공 여부는 ~을 불허한다 We can make no guess as to its success. / Whether it will succeed or not is unpredictable. **예단하다** predict; presuppose; guess. ¶다음에 무슨 일이 일어날지 예단할 수 없다 No one can predict[There is no knowing] what will happen next.

예도(藝道) an art; accomplishments.

예라 1 [아이들에게 그만 말라는 뜻으로 하는 소리] Stop!; Cut it out! ¶~ 그런 소리 작작해! Stop talking like that! 2 [확신 서지 않는 일을 결단할 때] all right; good; well. ¶~ 이젠 모르겠다 Well then. I'll have nothing more to do with it.

예레미야서(-書) The (Book of) Jeremiah(약어 Jer.).

예령(豫令) (구령의) a caution.

예리하다(銳利-) 1 (연장 등이) sharp; keen; pointed; sharp-edged. ¶예리한 날 a keen [sharp] edge // 예리한 무기 a sharp[trenchant / incisive] weapon // 예리한 날붙이 a sharp[keen-]edged tool[instrument]. 2 [두뇌·판단력이] acute; keen; sharp; shrewd; penetrating; piercing; (변설이) telling; incisive; pungent. ¶예리한 의론 a telling argument // 예리한 비판 (a) pungent criticism // 예리한 눈

piercing eyes // 그는 예리한 두뇌의 소유자다 He has a sharp mind. // 그것은 아주 예리한 통찰이다 That is quite a penetrating insight.

예매(豫買) advance purchase; purchase in advance; (purchase by) subscription. **예매하다** buy[purchase] in advance; subscribe for [to].

예매(豫賣) booking; (an) advance sale; sale in advance. **예매하다** sell in advance; book. ¶입장권을 ~ sell tickets in advance.
● **예매권** an advance ticket; a ticket sold in advance. ¶~을 신청하다 book a ticket.

예명(藝名) a stage name; (영화배우의) a screen name.

예문(例文) an illustration; an illustrative sentence; an example (sentence).

예물(禮物) 1 [사례물] a gift; a present; a return present (답례품). 2 (결혼의) a wedding present[gift] for the bride. 3 (신랑 신부의) wedding gifts exchanged between the bride and bridegroom.

예민하다(銳敏−) sharp; keen; acute; sensitive; subtle; fine; quick. ¶예민한 감각 a quick[keen / fine] sense / 감수성이 예민한 소녀 a sensitive girl // 그녀는 귀가 ~ She has a keen[an acute] ear. / She is keen [sharp / quick] of hearing. // 나는 코가 ~ I have a keen nose [smell]. / I am keen of scent.

예바르다(禮−) courteous; decorous; polite; civil; (서술적) be full of manners. ¶예바르게 with due courtesy / courteously / politely.

예방(豫防) prevention (of / against); protection (from / against); (a) precaution; [의] (a) prophylaxis. ¶질병의 ~ disease prevention // 화재의 ~ (take) precautions against fire // 범죄의 ~ the prevention of crime // ~은 치료보다 낫다 Prevention is better than cure. **예방하다** prevent; protect (from / against); ward off; keep off[away]; take preventive [precautionary] measures (against); take precaution (against); provide against. ¶전염병을 ~ prevent an epidemic // 이 병은 예방할 수 있다 This disease is preventable.
● **예방법** a method of prevention; a precaution; a preventive; [의] a prophylactic (against). **예방약** a preventive (medicine) (of / for / against); a prophylactic (medicine). **예방 의학** preventive medicine. **예방 접종** (a) vaccination; (an) inoculation. ¶~을 하다 inoculate / vaccinate. **예방 주사** a preventive shot[injection]. ¶장티푸스 ~ (anti)typhoid inoculation / (preventive) inoculation against typhoid // ~를 맞다 be inoculated against typhoid. **예방책** a precautionary [preventive] measure.

예방(禮訪) a courtesy visit [call]. **예방하다** pay a courtesy visit (to); make[pay] a courtesy call (at / on).

예배(禮拜) worship; (a) church[divine] service. ¶아침 ~ morning service / early church // 주일 ~ a Sunday service // ~ 중이다 be at church // (교회에서) 주일에 네 번 ~를 올리다 hold four services every Sunday // ~를 보다 attend church[divine] service / attend chapel / (구교) attend mass. **예배하다** worship (God); adore.
● **예배당** a chapel; a church.

예법(禮法) etiquette; manners; courtesy; decorum(s); propriety. ¶~을 배우다 learn good manners // ~을 지키다 observe the proprieties / 그는 ~을 모른다 He has [knows] no manners. / He is ill-mannered. // 그것은 ~에 어긋난다 It is a breach of etiquette [propriety]. / It goes against the canons of good behavior.

예보(豫報) a forecast; a prediction. ¶일기 ~ a weather forecast (for tomorrow) // 장기 (일기) ~ a long-range (weather) forecast // 오늘 밤에 비가 온다는 ~다 Rain is forecast for this evening. **예보하다** forecast; predict. ¶기상 통보관은 밤중에 홍수가 일어날 것이라고 예보했다 The weatherman forecasted flooding would occur during the night. → ¶예보된 대로 as (was) predicted / as (was) previously reported [announced].

예복(禮服) formal [ceremonial] dress(▶ formal dress는 일반 정장, ceremonial dress는 의식을 위한 복장); full dress; formal clothes; a dress suit. ¶결혼 ~ (남성의) a wedding suit / (여성의) a wedding dress // 궁중 ~ a court suit / full court dress // ~용 구두 dress shoes // ~을 입다 be dressed formal / wear [be in] formal [full] dress.

예봉(銳鋒) 1 [창·칼의 끝] a sharp [keen] point. 2 [정예한 선봉] the brunt (of an attack); an impetuous charge. ¶적의 ~을 꺾었다 We blunted [took off] the edge of the enemy's attack. / We broke the brunt of the enemy's attack. 3 [날카로운 논조] incisive reasoning; trenchant argument; the brunt (of an argument). ¶그의 ~은 당할 수가 없다 The force of his argument is irresistible.

예불(禮佛) [부처에게 경배하는 것] a rite offered before a statue of Buddha. **예불하다** worship before the image of Buddha.

예비(豫備) preparation; [마련] a reserve; a spare. ¶~의 [준비의] preliminary / preparatory / [따로 떼어 둔] spare / reserve / in reserve // ~ 식량 a reserve of food // 객실은 없습니다 We have no spare room for guests. **예비하다** prepare (for); provide (for); reserve; keep [have] (a thing) in reserve.
● **예비 검사 / 예비 점검** (a) preliminary examination [inspection]; a reconnaissance. **예비 교섭** preliminary negotiations. ¶~을 하다 negotiate beforehand / have a preliminary talk / hold preliminary negotiations [talks]. **예비군** (the) reserve forces. ¶직장 [지역] ~ workplace [regional] reserve forces // 향토 ~ the Homeland Reserve Forces // ~ 소집일 a reserve forces muster day. **예비금 / 예비비** a reserve [contingency] fund; an emergency fund; a reserve; money in reserve. **예비 선거** a preliminary election; (미) a primary (election). **예비 선수** a reserve (player). **예비 시험** a preliminary examination (for college entrance); a prelim. **예비역** service in the first reserve. **예비 지식** preliminary knowledge; background knowledge. **예비 타이어** a spare tire.

예쁘다 pretty; lovely; beautiful; fine; nice; comely; handsome; good-looking; fair; neat. ¶예쁜 얼굴 a fair [pretty] countenance [face] // 예쁜 아기 a cute baby // 예쁜 옷 fine [beautiful] clothes // 예쁜 목소리로 in a sweet voice // 예쁘게 차려입다 be finely dressed / dress oneself beautifully / (미국 속어) be dolled up // 글씨를 예쁘게 쓰다 write a pretty hand / write finely // 이렇게 예쁜 나비는 본 적이 없다 I've never seen such a pretty butterfly. / This is the most beautiful butterfly I've ever seen.

예사(例事) [보통의 일] a commonplace event; a common practice; an ordinary affair; a custom; [일상사] an everyday occurrence [affair]. ¶~로 **여기다** make little[nothing] / think nothing of / do not hesitate (to do) / make no scruple of (doing) / be indifferent (to) // 그는 거짓말하기를 ~로 안다 He tells lies without compunction[shame]. / He makes no scruple of lying. // 그는 마루에서 자는 것을 ~로 생각한다 He makes nothing of sleeping on the floor.

● **예삿일** a commonplace event. ⇨ ＝예사

예사롭다(例事-) common; commonplace; ordinary; usual. ¶예사로운 일 a common event[occurrence] / a commonplace event / an everyday occurrence[affair] / a matter of no consequence // 사태가 예사롭지 않다는 것을 알았다 I realized that the situation was serious[grave].

예산(豫算) [예정 경비] an appropriation; [견적] an estimate; [국가 등의 세입과 세출의 계획] a budget (for). ¶본~ the principal [original / main] budget // 수정 ~ a revised budget // 잠정 ~ a provisional budget // 추가 ~ the additional estimate / the supplementary budget // 내년도 ~ the budget for the coming (fiscal) year // ~의 범위 내에서 within the limit of budgetary appropriation // ~으로 at an estimated cost of // ~을 세우다[짜다] make[draw up] an estimate[a budget] / form a budget / budget (for the next year) // ~을 초과하다 go beyond the estimate / go over the budget / exceed[be in excess of] the budget[estimate] // ~에 넣다 include[appropriate / add] ... in the budget / set down ... in the budget[estimate] / provide for ... in the budget // 사회 복지 ~이 대폭 삭감되었다 The budget for social welfare was cut drastically. // 외국 여행을 할 ~이 없다 I can't afford to travel abroad. / My budget won't permit[allow] a trip abroad. // 그 계획은 ~ 범위 내에서는 무리다 With our budgetary limits, that plan is impossible. // 실제 지출은 ~을 월씬 초과했다 The actual expenditures surpassed[were far above] the estimate. // 집을 짓는 데 ~은 얼마로 잡고 있습니까 How much are you allowing for building your house? **예산하다** estimate; budget (for). ¶우리는 그 파티 비용을 100만 원으로 예산해 놓았다 We budgeted a million won for the party. // (점포에서) 어느 정도로 예산하셨습니까 May I ask what price range you had in mind?

● **예산 결손 / 예산 부족** a budgetary deficit. **예산 삭감** reduction of appropriation; a curtailment in the budget. **예산안** a draft budget; [의회의 심의 결정 전의 의안] a budget (bill); a bill of budget. ¶~을 국회에 제출하다 submit a budget (bill) to the National Assembly / present the estimates for the budget to the National Assembly / open the budget // ~을 심의하다 debate (on) [discuss] a budget bill. **예산 초과** an excess over the estimates. **예산 편성** compilation of the budget. ¶국가의 ~ the preparation[compilation] of the national budget.

예상(豫想) [예기] expectation(s); anticipation; [예측] a forecast; [어림] an estimate; [가상] supposition; presupposition. ¶경기 (景氣) ~ a business forecast // ~과는 달리 contrary to one's expectations / far from one's expectations // ~대로(의) [~과 같이] as (was) expected / as one expected / true to one's expectations / as might have been expected // ~이 들어맞다 be successful in speculation // ~이 빗나가다 [어긋나다] (사람이) be disappointed of one's expectations / have one's expectations defeated / be balked in one's expectations / (사물이) fall short [out] of one's reckoning // ~을 뒤엎다 go[be] against one's expectations / upset one's expectation[calculation] // ~과는 달리 자금이 필요한 만큼 모아지지 않았다 Contrary to our expectations, we could not raise the necessary funds. // 그는 ~ 문제를 맞혔다 He rightly[successfully] anticipated what kind of questions would be set on[(영) in] the exam. // 내 ~이 (들어)맞았다 My expectations proved right[came true]. / I guessed right. // 내 ~이 빗나갔다 My expectations proved wrong. / I guessed wrong. // 주가(株價)는 ~대로 되었다 The stock behaved as I expected. / The price of stock has ended up where I expected it to. // 우리 팀의 득점은 ~대로였다 [~에 어긋났다] Our team's score came up to[did not come up to / fell short of] our expectations. // 실제 비용은 ~을 웃돌았다 The actual cost surpassed[were above] the estimate. **예상하다** expect; forecast; anticipate; estimate; reckon. ¶그녀는 예년보다 훨씬 추운 겨울을 예상하고 두꺼운 코트를 샀다 She bought a heavy coat expecting[in anticipation of] an unusually cold winter. // 예상했던 대로 그들은 결혼했다 They got married, as (everyone had) expected. // 나는 혼잡을 예상하고 30분 일찍 집을 나섰다 Expecting[Anticipating] a crowd, I left home half an hour early. // 이 세상에서는 다음에 무슨 일이 일어날지 예상할 수가 없다 In this world we cannot foresee what will happen next. // 전문가들은 경기가 회복될 것으로 예상했다 The experts have predicted that business will recover. // 결과는 전혀 예상할 수가 없다 The outcome is anybody's guess [is completely unpredictable]. / How the result may turn out is beyond imagination. ➔!내일은 좋은 날씨가 예상된다 Fine weather is forecast for tomorrow.

● **예상액** an estimated amount; estimates. ¶**피해** ~ estimated damage. **예상외** ¶~의 unexpected / unlooked-for / unhoped(-for) / unanticipated / unforeseen // ~로 unexpectedly / beyond expectation(s) / contrary to [against] (one's) expectation // 그녀는 입시에서 ~로 좋은 성적을 거두었다 Contrary to (our) expectations, she did very well on[(영) in] the entrance examination. // 만년에 그에게 ~의 행복이 찾아왔다 An unexpected [unhoped-for] happiness came in his last years.

예서(隷書) an angular style of writing Chinese characters.

예선(豫選) 1 (경기 등의) a preliminary; a preliminary[an elimination] match[contest]; (레이스 등의) a preliminary[trial] heat; a preliminary[trial] race; (축구 등의) a quali-

fying round. ¶~을 통과하다 get through a preliminary[an elimination] match / qualify (for the semifinal)//그는 100미터 경주의 2차 ~을 통과했다 He got through the second heat in the 100-meter dash.//우리 팀은 ~에서 탈락했다 Our team was eliminated from the tournament. / Our team was rejected in an elimination match. / Our team failed to qualify in the heats. 예선하다 hold a preliminary match[contest].
2 (선거의) a provisional selection[election]; a preliminary election; a preelection; (미) a primary (election). 예선하다 select[elect] provisionally; preelect.

예속(隷屬) subordination. ¶~적 지위 a subordinate position. 예속하다 be subordinate [subject] (to); be under the control[authority] (of); come under the rule (of); subordinate oneself to; belong to.

예수 Jesus (Christ).
● 예수교 Christianity. 예수교인 a Christian.

예술(藝術) (집합적) art; (특정 부문의) an art; (the fine) arts(미술). ¶~의 artistic//~을 감상하다 appreciate art.
예술은 길고 인생은 짧다 Art is long and life is short.
● 예술가 / 예술인 an artist. ¶그는 ~ 기질이 있는 사람이다 He is an artistic type. / He is a man of an artistic nature[temperament]. 예술계 the art world; the world of art; artistic circles. 예술 대학 a university of arts; an art college. 예술미 beauty of art. 예술 사진 an artistic photograph. 예술 애호가 an art lover. 예술 지상주의 art for art's sake. 예술품 a work[an object] of art.

예술적(藝術的) artistic. ¶~으로 artistically // 비~ inartistic // ~ 재능 artistic genius [talent] // ~ 가치가 있는 작품 a work of great artistic value.

예스럽다 old; old-fashioned; antique; antiquated; archaic. ¶예스러운 생각 old-fashioned[outdated] ideas / antiquated views / outmoded[moss-grown] ideas//예스러운 말 an archaic word[expression].

예스맨 a yes-man; a person who agrees with everything that is said to him.

예습(豫習) preparation(s) (of one's lesson(s)). ¶~과 복습 preparations and reviews of one's lessons//내일 ~은 다 했니 Have you finished your preparations for tomorrow's lessons? 예습하다 prepare one's lesson(s); do one's homework; do preparation; (영국 구어) do prep. ¶예습하지 않고 등교하다 go to school without doing one's preparations / go to school unprepared.

예시(例示) illustration; exemplification. 예시하다 illustrate (by example); exemplify. ¶그들의 잔혹함을 ~ exemplify[illustrate] their cruelty.

예시(豫示) indication; adumbration. 예시하다 indicate beforehand; show signs of; shadow forth[out]; foreshadow; foreshow; adumbrate.

예식(例式) an established form.

예식(禮式) [예법에 따라 행하는 식] a ceremony; a celebration; [결혼식] a wedding (ceremony). ¶~을 올리다 hold a ceremony / (결혼의) celebrate[solemnize] a wedding//~은 가톨릭교회에서 거행되었다 The wedding was held at a Catholic church.

● 예식장 a ceremony hall. ¶결혼 ~ a wedding hall.

예심(豫審) a preliminary hearing[examination / investigation]; a pretrial hearing [examination / investigation]. ¶그는 ~에서 이를 부인하였다 He denied it in the pretrial interrogation.

예약(豫約) **1** (호텔·레스토랑·비행기·열차 등의) a reservation; (a) booking. ¶~을 받다 take reservations//~을 취소하다 cancel one's reservation(s)//이 방은 ~이 되어 있습니다 The room is bespoken for.//객실들은 모두 ~이 되어 있습니다 All the rooms are reserved. //~ 신청은 전화 719-9651로 해 주십시오 For reservations, please call 719-9651. 예약하다 make a reservation; reserve; (영) book [take] (a seat) in advance; have (a room) reserved; make a booking for (a room at a hotel); secure (a room) in advance; bespeak (a room). ¶특급으로 좌석 둘을 예약해 주십시오 Will you reserve[book] two seats on the limited express for me?//호텔[비행기]을 예약하지 못했다 I was not able to make a hotel[plane] reservation[booking].
2 (신문·잡지 등의) (a) subscription(▶ 정기 구독의 경우에 씀); (상품 등의) an advance order. ¶~ 없이 구입하실 수 없습니다 (잡지를) You can purchase it only by subscription[(상품을) by ordering in advance]. 예약하다 (출판물 등을) subscribe (to a weekly); (상품 등을) order (an article) in advance.
3 (병원·면접·미용실 등의) an appointment. ¶~ 없이 진찰받을 수 있는 의원 a walk-in clinic//면담하려면 ~을 해야 합니다 You have to make an appointment for an interview. / Interviews are by appointment. 예약하다 make an appointment. ¶목요일 2시에 그 치과 의사에게 가기로 예약했다 I made an appointment with the dentist[at the dentist's] for two o'clock on Thursday.
● 예약금 a deposit. 예약석 a reserved seat; (게시) Reserved. 예약 주문 an advance order.

예언(豫言) (a) prophecy; (a) prediction; a forecast. ¶그의 ~은 적중했다[빗나갔다] His prophecy[prediction] came true[did not come true]. 예언하다 foretell; predict; (종교적으로) prophesy. ¶그는 가까운 장래에 큰 재해가 일어날 것이라고 예언했다 He prophesied that there would be a great disaster in the near future.//그 사건은 나중에 일어날 대전쟁을 예언하고 있었다 The incident foretold [predicted / was prophetic of] the great war that would break out later.
● 예언서 [성] the prophets. 예언자 a foreteller; a prophet; (여자) a prophetess.

예외(例外) an exception. ¶~ 없이 without exception/거의 ~ 없이 with few exceptions //~적으로 exceptionally//이 경우에만은 ~로 하겠다 I'll make an exception in this case.//그들은 ~ 없이[한 사람의 ~자 말고는] 근면하다 They are hardworking without exception[with one exception].//그는 ~다 He is an exception[a special case].//~ 없는 규칙은 없다 There is no rule[There are no rules] without exceptions. / There are exceptions to every rule.

예우(禮遇) (an) honorable treatment; a cordial reception; privileges; honors. ¶각별한 ~를 하다 receive (a person) with marks of

예의 distinction // 전관(前官) ~를 받다 be accorded [granted] the privileges of one's former post [office]. **예우하다** receive (a person) courteously [cordially]; treat (a person) with respect.

예의(銳意) wholeheartedly; assiduously. ¶~ 주시하다 pay sharp attention to / watch up // ~ 검토하다 inquire into (a matter) assiduously / examine (a matter) in earnest // 그는 빈민 구제에 ~ 주력하였다 He concentrated his energy on [devoted himself to] the relief of the poor.

예의(禮儀) (good) manners; etiquette; courtesy; decorum(s); propriety; civility; politeness. ¶형식적인 ~ outward decorum / sham courtesy // ~ 바른 courteous / decorous / polite / civil // ~상 by [out of] courtesy [politeness] / as a matter of courtesy / for courtesy's sake // 그는 ~ 바른 태도로 말을 전했다 He ceremoniously delivered a message. // 그는 ~를 모른다 He has [knows] no manners. / He is ill-mannered [unmannered / unmannerly / ill-bred / impolite / discourteous / uncivil] // ~상 그를 방문하였다 I visited him out of [as a] courtesy. // 아무리 친해도 ~를 지킬 필요가 있다 Courtesy should not be forgotten even between close friends. // 넌 ~도 없니 Where's your manners?

● **예의범절** (the rules of) etiquette; manners; decorum(s); proprieties. ¶가정의 ~ etiquette [decorums] in the home // 식탁에서의 ~ table manners // 훌륭한 ~ good manners // ~이 바른 [바르지 못한] 아이 a well-bred [an ill-bred] child / a well-mannered [an ill-mannered] child / a well [badly] brought-up child // ~에 맞다 agree [be in accord] with the canons of good behavior [(the rules of) etiquette] / conform to (the rules of) etiquette // ~에 어긋나다 go against the canons of good behavior [(the rules of) etiquette] // ~을 가르치다 give (a person) lessons in manners [etiquette] / tell (a person) about the rules of etiquette.

예인선(曳引船) a tug; a tugboat; a towboat; a towing vessel.

예입금(預入金) a deposit; money on deposit.

예입하다(預入-) make a deposit (in a bank).

예장(禮裝) formal [ceremonial] dress. ⇨예복 ¶~을 의 넥타이 a dress tie // ~을 하고 in full [formal] dress. **예장하다** wear a ceremonial dress; be in full dress.

예전(옛날) the old days; ancient [old] times; [이전] former days [times]. ¶~의 old / old-time / ancient / [이전의] former / past / bygone // ~대로 as of old / as it was before // ~에 in old [ancient] times / in the old days / in former days / once // ~부터 from old times / from of old // 이 읍에는 ~ 모습이 없다 This town is not what it used to be. // 그에게는 ~의 섬세한 아름다움이 없다 She has lost the exquisite beauty she once had. // 그녀는 ~의 그녀가 아니다 She is not her former self.

예절(禮節) decorum(s); courtesy; manners; etiquette; propriety. ¶~을 지키다 observe the proprieties // ~을 모르다 have no sense of propriety / have no manners // ~을 중시하다 think much of propriety.

예정(豫定) [계획] a schedule; a program; a plan; [준비] (a) previous arrangement; pre-arrangement; (가격 등의) an estimate; [예상] expectation; anticipation. ¶출발[도착] ~ 시간 the expected time of departure [arrival] // ~대로 as expected [planned] / according to schedule // ~보다 일찍 earlier than expected / before (scheduled) time // ~보다 하루 일찍[늦게] one day ahead of [behind] time [the schedule] // ~ 시각에 at the appointed [set] time / on (scheduled) time // ~을 세우다 make a plan [program] // ~보다 출석자가 많았다 More people attended than we had expected. // 모임은 ~대로 잘되었다 The meeting proceeded just as planned. // 역에서 그와 만날 ~이다 I intend [plan] to meet him at the station. // 기차는 8시에 도착할 ~이다 The train is due (to arrive) at eight. // 총회는 4월 12일에 개최될 ~이다 The general meeting is to take place [to be held] on April 12. // 언제까지 이 도시에 체재할 ~입니까 How long do you plan [are you going] to stay in this city? **예정하다** plan; make a plan; schedule; arrange previously; estimate; expect; anticipate. ➔¶예정된 시간에 도착하다 arrive at the appointed [scheduled] time / (기차·비행기 등이) arrive on time.

● **예정일** a prearranged date; the scheduled date. ¶출산 ~ the expected date of confinement // 도착[출발] ~ the estimated [scheduled] date of arrival [sailing]. **예정자** an expectant; [입후보] an expectant candidate. ¶졸업 ~ an expectant graduate. **예정표** a schedule; a program; (여행의) an itinerary. ¶그것은 ~에 없다 It is not on the program [schedule].

예제 [여기저기] here and there; this place and that (place).

예제(例題) [보기] an example; [연습 문제] an exercise.

예증(例證) [예를 들어 증명함] illustration; an illustration; an instance; an example. ¶~으로(서) by way of illustration / as an example // 그것은 그의 근면함에 대한 ~이 된다 It illustrates [is illustrative of] his diligence. **예증하다** illustrate; exemplify. ¶이론을 예증하는 몇 가지 사실을 들다 mention [enumerate] facts in illustration of one's theory.

예지(豫知) [미리 앎] foresight; (지식·경험 등에 입각하는) prediction. ¶예언자는 ~ 능력이 있다고 한다 It is said that prophets have the power to foresee the future. **예지하다** [예언하다] foretell; [지식·경험 등에 입각하여 추론하다] predict; [예견하다] foresee. ¶예지하는 힘이 있는 사람 a man of foresight.

예지(叡智) [뛰어난 지혜] sagacity; wisdom; intelligence; [철] intellect.

예찬(禮讚) [숭배] worship; [칭송] admiration. ¶모성 ~ the glorification of motherhood // 미(美)의 ~ the cult of beauty. **예찬하다** worship; adore; idolize (a film star); glorify; sing the praises of. ¶사람들은 그의 위업을 예찬하였다 People were filled with admiration for his achievement [praised his great achievement].

예측(豫測) a preestimate; a forecast; presupposition; [예견] (a) prediction(▶ 과학적인 정확성을 뜻함); [어림] (an) estimate. ¶~이 틀리다 make a wrong estimate [forecast] // 우리는 ~을 잘못했다 We were mistaken in our

예치(預置) depositing. ⇨ 예탁
●예치금 a deposit; money on deposit.

예컨대(例—) for instance; for example; e.g.; […과 같은] such as; say. ¶~ 매나 독수리와 같은 맹금 birds of prey, such as the hawk and the eagle // 그는 이탈리아의 몇몇 도시들, ~ 로마, 밀라노를 찾았다 He visited several cities in Italy, for example Rome and Milan.

예탁(預託) depositing; deposition. ¶시중(市中) ~ the deposits of the Bank of Korea in city banks // 미국 ~ 증권 an American depositary receipt. 예탁하다 deposit (money in a bank).
●예탁금 a deposit; deposit money. 예탁자 a depositor.

예편하다(豫編—) transfer (a person) to the first reserve; place[register] (a person) on the reserve list. ➔예편되다 go into the first reserve / be placed on the reserve list // 예편되어 있다 be in the (U.S.) army reserve.

예포(禮砲) a salute (gun); a salvo. ¶21발의 ~ (fire) a 21-gun salute // ~를 쏘다 fire [give] a salute[salvo] / salute with cannon.

예풍(藝風) (개인의) the characteristic of one's performance; one's personal technique; [예술적인 전통] acting[artistic] tradition.

예항(曳航) towing. 예항하다 take[have] (a ship) in tow. ¶배를 항구로 ~ tow a ship into (a) harbor.

예행(豫行) a preliminary performance (of a play); a rehearsal. 예행하다 perform preliminarily; rehearse; have[give] a rehearsal; try out.
●예행연습 a rehearsal; a preliminary drill [training]; preliminary exercises; (연극 등의) a preliminary performance. ¶개회식의 ~을 하다 have[go through] a rehearsal for the opening ceremony.

예후(豫後) [병후의 경과·회복] convalescence; [의학에서, 병의 경과·결과의 예상] prognosis (pl. -ses). ¶그녀는 ~가 좋지 않다 She is not convalescing satisfactorily. // 그의 폐렴은 ~가 좋다 He is recovering well from pneumonia.

옐로카드 a yellow card.

옛 old; ancient; antique. ¶~ 모습 [자취] traces / remains / vestiges / (사람의) one's former self / one's former face[visage / looks / image / figure] // ~ 추억 the memory of one's early days / one's old memory // ~ 친구 an old friend (of mine) / (구어) an old pal // ~ 속담에 「침묵은 금」이라는 말이 있다 Silence is golden, as the old saying goes.

옛날 [옛적] antiquity; ancient[old] times; [지난날] old[bygone] days; former years [days]. ¶~의 old / (아주 옛날의) ancient / antique / [이전의] former / past / bygone // ~ (옛적)에 long ago / a long time ago / once upon a time // 먼 ~ the far past / the far-off days // ~부터 from old[ancient] times / since early times // 먼 ~부터 from the earliest times / from remote ages // 자신의 ~을 생각하다 look back upon one's past // ~을 그리워하다 sigh for the good old days // 그는 ~ 그대로의 모습이다 He is just as he used to be. / He has not changed. // 손 씨와는 ~부터 잘 아는 사이다 I have known Mr. Son since we were young. // 이 우물은 먼 ~부터 이곳에 있었다 This well has been here for countless generations. // ~ 옛적에 할아버지와 할머니가 살고 계셨습니다 A long, long time ago [Once upon a time] there lived an old man and his wife. // ~에는 전등이 없었다 Many years ago [Formerly] we had no electric lights. // 저것을 보니 ~ 생각이 난다 That reminds me of the past.
●옛날이야기 [옛날 민화] an old tale[story]; [회고담] one's past stories; stories of one's past[youth]. ¶한국의 ~ tales of old Korea // 아이들에게 ~를 들려주다 tell old tales to children.

옛말 1 [옛날에 쓰이던 말] an archaic[obsolete] word; an archaism. ¶이 말은 ~이다 This word is out of use now. 2 [격언] an old saying[proverb]. ¶~에 이르기를 「세월은 사람을 기다리지 않는다」라 하였다 As an old proverb says, [There is an old saying that] "Time and tide wait for no man." 3 [과거사]. ¶그 도시의 번영도 이젠 ~이 되고 말았다 The prosperity of the city is now a thing of the past.

옛사람 ancient people; men of old (times) [of former days]; (집합적) the ancients. ¶~이 가로되 as the ancients used to say / as they used to say in the old days / according to an old saying / as an old saying has it / an old saying goes[runs] (that).

옛사랑 [지난날 맺었던 사랑] a bygone romance; [옛 애인] (구어) one's old flame; an old flame of his[mine, etc.].

옛이야기 an old tale; one's past stories. ⇨ 옛날이야기(⇨옛날) ¶~ 를 하다 tell old tales to (children) / talk about[over] old times // 이젠 그것도 ~가 되었다 It is now an old story. // 그들은 노인의 ~에 귀를 기울었다 They listened to the old man's reminiscences.

옛일 a thing of the past; bygones; the past; a past event. ¶~을 생각하다 think of one's past [things of the past] // 그가 이사한 것은 지나간 ~이다 He moved away a long time ago. // ~은 ~이다 Let bygones be bygones.

옛적 antiquity; ancient[old] times. ¶옛날 ~을 생각하게 하는 소나무가 늘어선 길 an avenue of pines (which is) reminiscent of old times.

옛정(—情) (친구 간의) old friendship; (남녀간의) old love (affection). ¶~을 새롭게 하다 renew one's old friendship (with) / renew one's old love (for).

옛집 one's old[former] home[house]; one's late residence; an old nest[haunt]. ¶~을 그리워하다 long for one's old house // ~으로 돌아가다 return to one's old[former] haunt [place of work] / make a comeback.

옜다 (물건을 줄 때) Here it is!; Here you are!;

This [It] is for you! ¶~ 이것 가져라 Here, take this.

오¹ [아] Oh!; O dear!; Ah! ¶~ 슬프도다 Alas! Woe is me! // ~ 주여 O Lord! // ~ 생각난다 Aha! Now I remember! **2** [대답] Yes; Oh; All right.; Very well. ¶~, 곧 그리 갈게 All right, I'll be right there.

오(五) five; [제5] the fifth. ¶~분의 1 one fifth // ~ 배(의) fivefold / quintuple / 제~ 장 the fifth chapter / chapter five.

오가다 come and go; keep coming and going. ¶도심에서는 수많은 차들이 오간다 The traffic in the central part of the city is congested. // 갖가지 추억이 내 머릿속을 오갔다 All kinds of memories passed through my mind.

오가리 1 [호박의 살을 말린 것] dried slices [strips] of pumpkin [radish]. **2** [잎이 오글쪼글해진 것] all dried-up [잎이]; shriveled.
오가리(가) 들다 [오글쪼글해지다] dry up; curl up; wither; shrivel; be shriveled up.

오각(五角) five angles.
●**오각형** [수] a pentagon. ¶~의 pentagonal.

오갈 dried slices of pumpkin; all dried-up. ⇨오가리
오갈(이) 들다 1 dry up; curl up. ⇨오가리(가) 들다(⇨오가리) **2** [주눅 들다] shrink; be daunted; be in a funk.

오갈피 [한] the root bark of various araliaceous shrubs.

오감(五感) the (five) senses.

오감스럽다 [경망스럽다] imprudent; flippant; frivolous; thoughtless; heedless; rash; [괴벽하다] odd; queer; eccentric.

오거리(五-) a five-way crossing.

오경(五經) the Five Classics (of Ancient China); the Five Book of Confucianism.

오계(五戒) [불] the five Buddhist commandments (against murder, theft, adultery, falsehood and intemperance).

오곡(五穀) the five cereals [grains]; (집합적) all kinds of cereals; (staple) grains.
●**오곡밥** *ogokbap*; boiled rice with four other staple cereals.

오관(五官) the five sensory organs; the five organs of sense.

오그라들다 curl up; contract; wither; shrink; shrivel. ¶추워서 손이 오그라들었다 My fingers were numb with cold. // 말린 오징어는 구우면 오그라든다 A dried cuttlefish curls when grilled. // 몸이 오그라들 정도로 추웠다 It was cold enough to shrivel one up. // 이것은 빨아도 오그라들지 않는다 This does not shrink in the wash. / This is sanforized [shrink-resistant].

오그라뜨리다 make a dent (in). ⇨우그러뜨리다

오그라지다 1 [오므라지다] shrink; shrivel (up); curl up; contract. ¶나뭇잎이 ~ leaves shrivel [curl] up. **2** [옴폭해지다] dent; become indented. ¶오그라진 냄비 a dented pan // 생철은 잘 오그라진다 Tin dents easily.

오그리다 1 (몸을) curl up [roll] up (one's body); draw up [in] (one's legs). ¶몸을 오그리고 자다 sleep curled up // 다리를 오그리고 자서 방구석에 오그리고 있었다 It was so cold (that) we crouched [huddled up] in a corner (of the room). **2** (물건을) dent; indent; bend (something) out of shape; batter (in). ¶철사를 오그려 고리를 만들다 bend a piece of wire into a ring.

오글거리다 simmer; swarm. ⇨우글거리다

오글보글 [물·찌개가 끓는 소리] bubbling; simmering. ¶냄비 속에서 콩이 ~ 끓고 있다 The beans are simmering in the pot. **오글보글하다** bubble; simmer.

오글오글 in swarms. ⇨우글우글

오글쪼글하다 wrinkled; withered; shriveled; wilted; wizened; crumpled; rumpled. ¶오글쪼글한 손 a withered hand / a hand full of wrinkles // 오글쪼글한 노파 an old withered woman / a crone // 오글쪼글해지다 be crumpled / crumple / be wrinkled [rumpled / creased] // 내 옷에 주름이 오글쪼글했다 My clothes have gotten quite wrinkled. // 사과가 시들어 ~ The apple is all shriveled up.

오금 1 [무릎의 안쪽] the crook [hollow / inside curve] of the knee; the ham. ¶~을 펴다 stretch one's knees. **2** the bend [crook] of the arm. ⇨팔오금

오금(이) 뜨다 move about restlessly; be always on the gad.

오금(을) 박다 catch (a person) in contradiction; squelch; snub.

오금을 못 쓰다 be intimidated; be daunted; cower (down); be under (a person's) thumb; shrink inside oneself. ¶그는 아내 앞에서 오금을 못 쓴다 He is under his wife's thumb. / He is tied to his wife's apron strings. / He is a henpecked husband.

오금팽이 [굽어진 안쪽] an inner curve.

오긋하다 a little pressed [pushed] in; a little dented; nicely curved. ¶이 재료는 누르면 곧 오긋해진다 This material yields easily to pressure.

오기(傲氣) a competitive [an unyielding / an indomitable] spirit; emulation. ¶~로 [~가 나서] in a spirit of rivalry // ~가 있는 unyielding / spirited / strong-minded // ~가 있는 여자 아이 a strong-minded [a competitive / an unyielding / a spirited] girl / a girl of spirit // ~가 세다 be reluctant [unwilling] to admit defeat // ~를 부리다 be game enough to compete (another) / refuse to yield (to).

오기(誤記) a mistake [an error] in writing; (사소한) a slip of the pen; (철자의) a misspelling; (무기상의) misentry. **오기하다** write incorrectly; miswrite; make a slip of the pen; (철자를) misspell (a word).

오나가나 always; all the time; wherever one goes; everywhere you turn. ¶그는 ~ 아들 자랑이다 He always boasts about his son.

오나니슴 onanism; masturbation.

오냐 [아랫사람의 물음에 대답하는 말] Yes; [동의] all right; O.K. ¶~ 알았다 Yes, I see. // ~ 참 잘했어 Good! You did it very well. // ~ 그만하면 됐어 All right. That will do. // ~ 그렇게 해라 All right. You can do so. // ~ 울지 마라 There, there! Don't cry! // ~ 두고 보자 You shall soon smart for this. / Just wait! You'll catch it afterwards.

오너 an owner (of a professional baseball team).

오뇌(懊惱) (an) agony; anguish; a worry; trouble(s). **오뇌하다** be in agony; be anguished [worried / troubled].

오누이 brother and sister; siblings.

오뉴월(五六月) May and June. ¶~ 긴긴해 the live-long summer day.

오뉴월 염천 the hot weather of midsummer.
오늘 today; this day. ¶~따라 on this of all days / today of all days // ~부터 from today / from now on // ~까지 up to today [now] // ~ 오후 this afternoon // ~ 신문 today's newspaper // 내주[내년]의 ~ this day next week [year] // 지난주[작년]의 ~ a week [year] ago today // ~부터 1주일간 a week from today // ~은 무슨 요일[며칠]이냐 What day of the week [month] is it today? // ~ 있었던 일은 결코 잊지 않겠소 I will never forget what happened today.
● 오늘날 today; these days [times]; the present day. ¶~에는 nowadays / today / these days / at present // ~의 of the day / of the present time / contemporary // ~의 한국 Korea today / present-day Korea // ~의 학생 students of today // ~의 한국 여성의 지위 the present status of Korean women // ~에 이르기까지 until [to] the present / to this day // 컴퓨터[원자력] 시대의 ~ in this age of computers [atomic energy] // 생존 경쟁이 격심한 ~에 in these days of severe struggle for existence // ~에는 여자가 10대에 결혼하는 일이 거의 없다 Today [Nowadays / At present] few girls marry in their teens. // 그것은 ~의 젊은이들에게 인기가 없다 It does not appeal to [It has no appeal] the young people of today. **오늘내일** today or tomorrow; very soon. ¶~ 중에 끝내겠소 I will finish it in a day or two.

오니(汚泥) sludge. ¶활성 ~ (하수 처리장의) activated sludge.

오다¹ **1** [말하는 사람 쪽으로 움직이다] come. ¶오는 길에 on one's way here // 오고 가는 사람들 streams of people going and coming // 가까이 ~ come nearer / draw closer // 우연히 ~ happen to come / come by chance // 데리러[모시러] ~ call for (a person) // 이리 오너라 Come here. / Come this way. // 자 버스가 온다 Here comes our bus. / The bus is coming. // 그는 약속하고서도 오지 않았다 He never turned up in spite of his promise. // 이곳은 언젠가 온 일이 있다 I have been here once. // 무슨 일로 여기 왔느냐 What has brought you here? // 언제 여기에 오십니까 When are you coming here? / When will you be here? // 어서 오십시오 Welcome! // (점원이 손님에게) 어떻게 오셨습니까 May I help you? / What can I do for you? (▶ "Why did you come here?"라고 물을 수도 있으나 이는 잘 사용되지 않는 무례한 표현임) // 무슨 용건으로 오셨는지 여쭤 봐도 될까요 May I ask the nature of your business?
2 [도착하다] reach; arrive (at / in). ¶숙부님으로부터 편지가 왔다 I received a letter from my uncle. // 기차가 올 때까지 여기 있어라 Remain here till the train comes in. // 자, 목적지에 다 왔다 Here we are at our destination. // 편지 온 게 있느냐 Any mail for me? / 전화 왔습니다 There's a (telephone) call for you. / A phone for you. / You are wanted on the phone.
3 [찾아오다] call (on a person / at a house); come to see; visit. ¶미국에서 온 관광객 tourists from the United States // 네가 없는 사이에 어떤 여자가 왔었다 A lady came to see you during your absence. // 내일 손님이 두 분 오신다 We will have two guests tomorrow. // 박물관에는 매일 많은 방문객이 온다 Many people visit the museum every day. / There are many visitors in the museum every day. // 꼭 또 오십시오 Do come again. // 우리 집에 한번 놀러 오세요 Stop [Drop] by my house sometime. // 저의 집까지 와 주시겠습니까 May I ask you to come to my house? / Would you mind coming to my house? // 먼 길을 오시게 해서 죄송합니다 I'm sorry you had to come all this way.
4 [계절·때 등이 되다] come (round); draw near; set in; be due(기한이). ¶오는 20일에 on the 20th (of this month) // 오는 토요일에 파티가 있다 A party will be held next Saturday [on Saturday next]. / 3월이 오면 내 아들은 초등학생이 된다 My son will be a first-grader next march. // 올해는 겨울이 빨리 왔다 Winter is early in coming this year. / Winter has come early this year. // 단결해야 할 때가 왔다 The time came when we had to hang together. // 실행[행동]에 들어갈 때가 왔다 The time has come to go into action [to put it into practice].
5 [눈·비 등이 내리다] fall; rain; snow; come down. ¶비가 몹시 오고 있다 It's raining heavily. / It's pouring. // 눈이 몹시 오고 있다 It's snowing thick and fast. // 비가[눈이] 오기 시작했다 It began to rain [snow]. / It started raining [snowing]. // 비가 올 것 같다 It looks like rain. // 비가 오건 안 오건 가겠다 Rain or shine, we will go.
6 [유래·전래하다]. ¶그리스 어에서 온 말 a word derived from Greek / a word of Greek origin // 이 스포츠는 영국에서 온 것이다 This sport originated in England. // 이것은 프랑스에서 온 인형이다 This doll was brought from France. // 유럽에서 많은 식품이 와 있다 Many kinds of food are imported from Europe. // 불교가 한국에 온 것은 언제인가 When was Buddhism introduced into Korea?
7 [기인하다] come of [from]; be due to; be caused by. ¶이 사고는 그의 부주의에서 왔다 This accident was caused by his carelessness. // 회사의 도산은 그의 경영 부실에서 온 것이다 His clumsy management led the company into bankruptcy. // 이 병은 지나친 흡연에서 왔다 This disease is caused by excessive smoking.
8 [어떤 동작을 하고 돌아오다]. ¶신문을 가지고 오너라 Fetch me the newspaper. // 누구야 가서 보고 오너라 Go and see who is at the door. // 언제 그것을 가지러 올까요 When shall I call for it?
9 [잠·졸음이]. ¶졸음이 ~ become [feel] sleepy [drowsy].
10 [전기 등이] be lighted; come [go] on. ¶전깃불을 켤 때가 되었다 It is the time for the light to go on.

오는 말이 고와야 가는 말이 곱다(속담) A soft answer turns away wrath.
오는 정이 있어야 가는 정이 있다(속담) Scratch me and I'll scratch you.
왔다 갔다 하다 [정신이 맑았다 흐렸다 하다]. ¶정신이 왔다 갔다 한다 My mind wanders [strays].

오다² **1** [동작·작용의 계속]. ¶나는 20년 동안 그와 가깝게 사귀어 왔다 I have been on friendly terms with him for twenty years. // 지금까지 길러 온 개가 없어졌다 The dog I have had all this time is missing. **2** [근접하

다). ¶떠날 날이 자꾸 가까워 온다 The day is drawing near when we are to leave.// 방바닥이 따뜻해 온다 The floor of the room is getting warmer.

오다가다 [이따금] occasionally; at times; (every) now and then; once in a while; sometimes; [어쩌다가] casually. ¶~ 들르는 손님 (가게 등의) casual[stray] customer // ~ 만난 부부 a free-love couple / a case of free union // ~ 들르다 drop in every now and then // ~ 만나다 meet by chance // 그는 ~ 만난 여자와 결혼했다 He married a woman who came his way by mere chance.

오달지다 (성질이) shrewd; sharp; smart; (체격이) sturdy; stout; solid.

오답(誤答) an incorrect[a wrong] answer; an error. **오답하다** answer incorrectly[wrongly].

오대양(五大洋) the Five Oceans.

오대주(五大洲) the Five Continents.

오도독 1 [깨무는 소리] with a crunching [gnawing] sound. ¶~ 깨물다 champ / crunch. **오도독하다** crunch. ⇨**오도독거리다**1 2 [부러지는 소리] with a snap. **오도독하다** snap. ⇨**오도독거리다**2

오도독거리다 1 [깨물다] crunch; munch; make a crunching sound. 2 [부러지다] snap.

오도독뼈 a cartilage (bone); gristle.

오도방정 →오두방정

오도카니 vacantly; absently. ⇨우두커니

오도하다(悟道-) [불교의 진리를 깨닫다] attain (the) supreme wisdom (of Buddhism); be spiritually enlightened.

오도하다(誤導-) mislead; lead astray; [유혹하다] tempt. ¶이 영화는 젊은이들의 마음을 오도할 우려가 있다 This movie might lead young people astray. →¶군중은 헛소문에 오도되었다 The crowd was misled[deceived] by false rumors.

오독(誤讀) misreading. **오독하다** misread; read wrong. ¶암호 전보를 ~ 미사일 a telegram in code.

오돌오돌하다 hard (to chew); gristly; fibrous; tough.

오동나무(梧桐-) [식] a paulownia (tree); an empress tree. ¶~ 장롱 a chest of drawers made (wholly[entirely]) of paulownia wood.

오동통하다 plump; pudgy; chubby. ¶오동통한 빵 plump cheeks // 오동통한 소년 a chubby [plump] boy // 오동통한 얼굴 a bonny face / a buxom face.

오두막(-幕) (집) (-幕-) a hut; a shack; a shed; a hovel; a (humble) cottage; a shanty; (은둔자의 오두막집) a hermit's cell. ¶~ 을 짓다 put up a shanty[hovel] // ~이라도 좋으니 내 집을 갖고 싶다 I wish to have a house of my own, however humble it may be.

오두방정 flightiness; giddiness; frivolity; flippancy. ¶~을 떨다 act frivolously / behave in a giddy way.

오들오들 trembling; shivering; shuddering. ¶ ~ 떨다 quiver / tremble / shiver (with cold) // 두려워서 ~ 떨다 tremble with[for] fear / shudder at (the sight) // 추위에 ~ 떨다 shiver (all over) with[from] cold // 그 무서운 목소리에 그들은 ~ 떨었다 The horrible voice struck terror into them.

오디 (the fruit of) a mulberry.

오디션 [영화·라디오] an audition. ¶그들은 아가씨들에게 ~을 실시하였다 They auditioned [gave an audition to] the girls.

오디오 audio.

오독 →오뚝

오뚝 high; aloft. ⇨우뚝

오뚝이 a tumbling doll; a tumbler; a self-righting doll[toy].

오라 [포승] a (red) rope for binding a criminal. ¶죄인을 ~로 묶다 bind[tie up] a criminal (with a rope) / arrest[seize] a culprit // ~에 묶이다 be bound (with a rope) / be arrested[seized] // ~를 지우다 bind[tie] (a person's) hands behind his back // 한 오랏줄로 묶다 tie (person) in a row.

오라기 a bit[piece / strip / scrap] of thread [cloth]. ¶실 ~ a scrap of thread / 헝겊 ~ a piece[scrap] of cloth // 실 ~ 하나 걸치지 않은 stark-naked / with nothing on / without a stitch of clothing (on) // 옷에 실 ~가 붙다 have bits of thread on one's clothes.

오라버니 a girl's[woman's] older brother.
● **오라버니댁** the wife of a girl's older brother; woman's sister-in-law.

오라비 1 a girl's[woman's] older brother. ⇨오라버니 2 [여자가 자기 남동생을 지칭] my younger brother.

오라지다 have one's hands tied behind one's back; be trussed up.

오라질 Damn[Dash / Blast / Hang] it!; The devil!

오라토리오 [음] an oratorio (pl. ~s).

오락(娛樂) (an) amusement; (a) recreation; (an) entertainment; a pastime; pleasure; a hobby (취미). ¶건전한 ~ (a) wholesome entertainment[recreation / amusement] // 대중 ~ (a) popular[mass] entertainment // 실내 ~ indoor amusements // ~으로 for pleasure / for one's recreation[amusement] / by way of pastime / by pleasure / as a recreation.
● **오락물** a plaything; (영화의) a film for amusement. **오락 시설** recreation(al) [amusement] facilities; a means of public amusement. ¶우리 마을에는 ~이 부족하다 Our town needs more facilities for recreations[entertainment]. **오락실** an amusement hall; a recreation[rumpus / game] room; (군대의) a service club. **오락 프로** an entertainment program.

오락가락 coming and going; to and fro; back and forth; off and on. **오락가락하다** come and go; move[go] back and forth. ¶구름이 오락가락한다 The clouds come and go. // 정신이 오락가락한다 My mind wanders [strays]. // 비가 오락가락한다 It rains fitfully [on and off / by fits and starts].

오랑우탄 [동] an orang(o)utan(g).

오랑캐 a barbarian; [여진족] north[Manchurian] barbarians.

오랑캐꽃 [식] a violet. ⇨제비꽃

오래 [시간상으로 길게] long; for a long time [while]. ¶~ 계속된 습관 a custom of long standing // ~ 쓸 수 있는 가구 durable furniture // ~ 계속되다 last long / (날씨 등이 길게 계속되다) stay long / hold // ~ 걸리다 take long / take much [a long] time / require a lot [plenty] of time // 이 환자는 ~ 못 살 것 같아 걱정이오 I'm afraid this patient will not live much longer. // ~ 지나면 형편이 나아질 것이다 The situation may improve in the long run. // 밖은 추워서 ~ 있지 못했다 It was so cold outdoors that I couldn't stay there for

long [for a long time]. (▶ for long은 긍정적으로는 쓰지 않음) ¶나는 ~ 기다리고 있었다 I was kept waiting for a long time. // 너무 ~ 당신의 시간을 빼앗아 미안합니다 I'm afraid I have occupied too much of your time. // 우리는 결혼한 지 ~ 되지 않았다 We have not been married long. / It has not been long since we got married.

오래가다 (날씨 등이) hold; last; (옷이) wear(well); (기구 등이) stand long use; endure; be durable; keep [last] long. ¶오래가는 천 durable[serviceable] cloth // 오래가는 식품 food that can be kept[stored] for a long time // 오래가지 않다 do not last long[a long time] / be not durable // 이 식품은 오래 간다 [오래가지 못한다] This food keeps [doesn't keep] long. // 이 천은 오래간다 This fabric wears well. // 냉동식품은 냉동실에 넣어 두면 아주 오래간다 Frozen foods keep very long (when they are) in a freezer. // 이 냉장고는 오래가겠다 This refrigerator will be durable[last long]. // 이 면도칼은 참 오래갔다 This razor has withstood [stood up to] long use. // 나일론 로프는 면 로프보다 오래간다 Nylon ropes outlast cotton ones. // 처음에는 열성적이었지만 그는 오래가지 않아서 프랑스어 공부에 흥미를 잃었다 In spite of his early enthusiasm, he soon lost interest in the study of French. // 그들의 행복은 오래가지 않았다 Their happiness lasted but a short while. / Their happiness was short-lived. // 그의 아버지는 중병이어서 오래가지 못한다 His father is so ill that it is only a question of days with him.

오래간만 ¶~에 after a long time[interval / silence / absence / separation] / for the first time in a long time[while] // ~에 맞는 휴일 [~에 보는 좋은 날씨] the first holiday[fine day] in a long time // ~입니다 Long time no see. / I haven't seen you for a long time. / It is [has been] a long time since I saw you last. // 그는 ~에 학교에 나왔다 He returned to school after a long absence. // 최근에 중학교 시절의 친구로부터 ~에 편지가 왔다 A junior high school friend wrote to me recently after a long silence [(구어) for the first time in ages]. // 나는 ~에 옛 친구를 만났다 I met an old friend of mine after a long separation.

오래다 long; of long standing; long continued; of many years; (서술적) be a long time (since / ago). ¶오래지 않아 before long / not long after // 그 사람 만난 지가 ~ I have not seen him for a long time. // 아버지가 돌아가신 지 ~ My father died long ago[a long time ago]. / My father has been dead for a long time.

오래도록 for long; for a long time; [늦게까지] till late; a long while; [영원토록] eternally; forever and ever. ¶~ 기다리다 wait a long while // ~ 그로부터 소식이 없었다 I have not heard from him for a long time. // 그는 ~ 아내로부터 소식을 듣지 못했다 He hasn't heard from his wife for a long time. // 우리는 그렇게 ~ 기다릴 수 없다 We can't wait for him forever. // ~ 소식 전하지 못하여 미안합니다 I beg your pardon for my long silence.

오래되다 old; ancient; antique; time-honored; oldfashioned; time-worn; aged. ¶오래된 집 an old house[family] // 오래된 이야기 [친구] an old story[friend].

오래오래 very long; for a long long time; [영원히] forever; eternally; everlastingly. ¶~ 살다 live long / live to a ripe old age // 병을 ~ 앓다 be ill in bed for a long (long) time / suffer from a long[lengthy] illness // ~ 해로 (偕老)하다 live together in happy union till death parts them[you / us].

오래전 (-前) long ago [before]; long time ago. ¶그는 ~에 이사 가 버렸다 He moved away a long time ago. // 그는 ~에 생이별한 아버지를 다시 만났다 He met his father, from whom he had long been separated. // 그 문제는 ~에 벌써 해결이 난 것입니다 That question was settled once and for all long ago. // 저 사람을 ~부터 알고 있습니다 I have known him for a long time. // 존함을 ~부터 듣고 있습니다 I have been hearing of you for a long time. // ~부터 외국 여행을 하려고 생각하고 있었다 I have long wanted to travel abroad.

오랜 long; of long standing; long continued; of many years. ¶~ 경험 a long experience // ~ 습관 a habit of long standing / an old custom // ~ 옛날 great antiquity / time immemorial / the remote ages / the far-off days / the far past // ~ 친구 a longtime friend // ~ 세월의 신용 a reputation of long standing // ~ 옛날에 들은 이야기 a story I heard a long time ago // 나는 ~ 세월 여기 살고 있다 I have lived here for many years[for a long time]. // ~ 세월에 걸친 그의 연구가 완성되었다 He brought his years of research to completion. // ~ 세월의 노력이 수포로 돌아갔다 Long[Many] years of endeavor came to nothing. // 그 벽화는 ~ 옛날부터 발견되지 않고 묻혀 있었다 The mural painting has been buried undiscovered for a long time[since ancient times].

오랫동안 [썩 긴 동안] long; for a long time [while]; for ages[an age]. ¶~ 간직한 꿈 one's long-cherished dream // ~ 끌어 오는 문제 a long-standing problem // ~ 적조했습니다 (편지에서) Excuse my long silence. // ~ 편지를 못 드려 죄송합니다 I'm sorry I haven't written to you for such a long time.

오렌지 an orange.
● **오렌지 주스** orange juice.

오로라 aurora (pl. ~s, -rae).

오로지 solely; wholly; only; alone; entirely; exclusively. ¶~ 너를 위하여 solely for your sake // ~ 사회사업에 진력하다 give all one's energies [devote oneself] to social welfare work // ~ …을 연구하다 devote[apply] oneself to the study of ... // ~ 공상에만 잠기다 do nothing but indulge in idle fancies // 우리의 나아갈 길은 ~ 하나뿐이다 There is but one way open to us. // 그는 ~ 돈벌이만을 생각하고 있다 He is solely bent on making money. // 그녀는 ~ 자기 이익만을 차린다 She has an eye only to her own interests. // 그는 ~ 학문에 전념했다 He devoted himself solely to [was intent on] learning. // 친구라곤 ~ 너뿐이다 You are the only friend I have. // 제가 성공한 것은 ~ 당신 덕분입니다 It is wholly owing to you [It is entirely due to you] that I have succeeded. // 그는 ~ 논문 집필에만 몰두[전념]하고 있다 He spends almost all his time writing his thesis. / He is devoting himself solely to writing his thesis.

오롯하다 〔온전하다〕 perfect; complete; 〔모자라지 않다〕 sufficient.

오류(誤謬) a mistake; an error; a fallacy. ¶문법상의 ~ a grammatical mistake∥~를 범하다 make a mistake[an error] / fall into the error of …∥~를 시정하다 correct[rectify] an error / rectify a mistake∥네 작문에는 ~가 많다 Your composition has a lot of[is full of] mistakes.

오륜(五倫) the moral rules to govern the five human relations (of lord and vassal, father and son, husband and wife, young and old, and friends); the five cardinal principles of morality.

오륜기(五輪旗) the Olympic flag.

오르가슴(㊀orgasme) (an) orgasm. ¶~에 도달하다 reach orgasm / have an orgasm.

오르간 〔음〕 an organ. ¶리드 ~ a reed organ / a cabinet organ / a harmonium / an American organ∥전기 ~ an electric organ ∥파이프 ~ a pipe organ∥~을 치다 play (on) the organ.
● **오르간 연주자** an organist.

오르내리다 **1** (높은 곳을) go[walk] up and down (the steps); ascend and descend. ¶층계를 ~ go up and down the stairs∥많은 배들이 강을 오르내리는 것이 보였다 Many boats were (seen) going up and down the river.∥나는 하루에 열 번이나 계단을 오르내렸다 I went up and down the stairs ten times a day.∥우리는 엘리베이터를 타고 몇 번이나 오르내렸다 We went up and down in the elevator[(영) lift] several times. **2** (입에) be talked[gossiped] about. ¶남의 입에 ~ be talked about by people[others] / be on everybody's lips / be on the tongues of people∥그녀는 행실이 좋지 않아 남의 입에 오르내렸다 Her conduct gave rise to scandals. / Her conduct was on everybody's lips. **3** (먹은 음식이) sit[lie] heavy (in the stomach). **4** (물가·열 등이) fluctuate; rise and fall; go up and down. ¶야채 가격은 날씨에 따라 오르내린다 The prices of vegetables rise and fall [fluctuate] with the weather.∥온도계가 20도 선에서 오르내렸다 The mercury hovered around 20℃.∥내 혈압은 심하게 오르내린다 There have been drastic ups and downs in my blood pressure. / My blood pressure has been very unstable.∥온도는 20도에서 30도 사이를 오르내린다 The temperature varies [ranges] between 20℃ and 30℃ degrees.

오르다 **1** 〔아래에서 위로 움직여 가다〕 go [come] up; ascend; climb (up); rise. ¶산에 ~ go up a hill[mountain] / climb [ascend / make an ascent of] a mountain∥층계를 ~ go up a flight of stairs∥나무에 ~ go up [climb (up)] a tree∥지붕에 ~ climb (up) onto the roof∥사다리를 ~ scale [climb / mount] a ladder∥그는 천천히 단 위에 올랐다 He slowly stepped up[upon] the platform.∥막이 올랐다 The curtain rose.∥나는 하늘에라도 오른 듯한 기분이었다 I felt as if I were in (the) seventh heaven. **2** 〔지위·계급이 높아지다〕 rise (to); be promoted[advanced] (to); be raised (to). ¶권좌에 ~ rise to power∥그는 지위가 올랐다 He was promoted. / He rose in rank.∥그는 마침내 왕위에 올랐다 He finally became king [reached the throne / (문어) ascended to the throne].∥그는 50세에 수상의 지위에 올랐다 He rose to the post of Prime Minister at fifty. **3** 〔값·임금 등이 비싸지다〕 rise; advance; go [come / look] up. ¶물가가 올랐다 Prices have risen.∥석유 위기 직후에 물가가 급격히 올랐다 Prices soared[jumped / skyrocketed] right after the oil crisis.∥버스 요금이 550원에서 600원으로 올랐다 The bus fare went up from 550 won to 600 won.∥내년부터 세금이 오른다 Taxes will be raised next year.∥휘발유 세가 또 올랐다 There has been another advance in gasoline taxes.∥그의 봉급이 올랐다 He got his salary increased[raised]. / He got a raise[(영) rise] in salary.∥월급이 약간 올랐다 My salary has been raised[went up] just a little. **4** 〔성하여지다〕 be elated; be inflamed. ¶기세가 ~ be in high spirits∥선수들의 사기가 올라 있다 The players' morale is improving [rising].∥그 승전보로 그들의 사기가 크게 올랐다 Their morale soared at the report of the victory. **5** 〔나아지다〕 progress; make progress; improve. ¶성적이 ~ show a better school record∥능률이 ~ improve[increase] in efficiency∥인기가 ~ gain[rise / increase] in popularity / become more popular∥이번 학기에는 성적이 올랐다 (미) My grades went up this semester. / (영) I got higher marks this term.∥그의 학교 성적이 올랐다 His school[academic] record has improved. / He has shown some improvement in his grade. **6** 〔열·온도 등이 높아지다〕 rise; go up; get higher. ¶체온이 약간 올랐다 My temperature has risen slightly.∥어제 온도계는 30도까지 올랐다 The thermometer rose[went up] to 30℃ yesterday. **7** 〔술·약 기운 등이 몸 안에 퍼지다〕 be effective; work. ¶술이 ~ be flushed[dazed] (by liquor) / become[get] tipsy[intoxicated] / got into one's head∥약 기운이 ~ begin to feel the effect of a drug. **8** 〔연기·불길이 솟아 일어나다〕 rise; coil up. ¶굴뚝에서 가느다란 한 줄기 연기가 오르고 있다 A wisp of smoke rises from a chimney.∥나는 화산에서 연기가 오르는 것을 보았다 I saw smoke rising from the volcano.∥거리의 한 모퉁이에서 불길이 올랐다 A fire broke out in one corner of the town. **9** 〔말·차 등에 타다〕 mount; get[step] into [on]. ¶말에 ~ mount a horse∥배[비행기]에 ~ go aboard[on board] a ship[plane]∥차에 ~ get into car∥기차[버스]에 ~ get into [on] a train[bus]. **10** 〔상륙하다〕 land; go[come] on shore. ¶그들은 2개월 만에 뭍에 올랐다 They went ashore for the first time in two months. **11** 〔상류 쪽으로 나아가다〕 go up stream; go against the stream. ¶강을 ~ go up a river. **12** 〔울화가 치밀다〕 be offended; feel vexed [annoyed] (with / at); (고추 등의 약이) ripen to full flavor. ¶그의 행동에는 정말 약이 오른다 I am deeply offended by his conduct. ∥약이 올라 죽겠다 How vexatious! **13** 〔병균이나 독이 옮다〕 be infected (with); be affected (by). ¶옴이 ~ be infected with [affected by] the itch / have[suffer from] the itch∥옻이 ~ be poisoned with lacquer / get poison ivy.

14 [몸에 살이 많아지다] put on[gain] (flesh); flesh up[out]. ¶그의 볼에 살이 올랐다 His cheeks filled out.//이 계절에는 방어가 살이 오른다 In this season yellowtail put on fat.
15 [남의 이야깃거리가 되다] be gossiped about; become the talk of. ¶한창 세인의 입에 ~ be much talked about by people / be on everybody's lips//화망에 ~ be popularly [widely] expected//그것이 사람들의 화제에 올랐습니까 Was it talked about[discussed]?
16 [때가 묻다] get dirty (on one's back); become dirty[filthy].
17 [길을 떠나다] start; set; leave. ¶그는 유럽 여행길에 올랐다 He set out on a trip to Europe.//그들은 귀로에 올랐다 They started on their way home.
18 [기록에 적히다] be recorded[registered] (on / in); be put[placed] (in / on); be entered[included]. ¶블랙리스트에 ~ be put [placed] on the blacklist//지도에 ~ be represented on a map//그의 공적이 역사에 올라 있다 His achievement is recorded in history. //그의 이름이 전화번호부에 올라 있다 His name is put in the telephone directory.//후 보자들 명단에 그의 이름이 올라 있었다 His name was listed among the candidates [included on the list of candidates].
19 [회의·무대 등에 한몫 끼다] be placed before; be brought up; come up; be presented[put] on (the stage); (식탁에) be served on (the table). ¶회의 의제로 ~ be brought up at the meeting for discussion//춘향전이 그 무대에 올랐다 The story of Chunhyang is presented on the stage.//귀한 생선이 상에 올랐다 A rare fish was served.
20 [나무에 물이] rise. ¶나무에 물이 오른다 The sap rises.
21 [귀신 같은 것이 들리다] be possessed (by a spirit). ¶무당에게 신이 올랐다 A spirit entered into the (female) shaman.

오르되브르 (프) an hors d'oeuvre.
오르락내리락하다 go up down; rise and fall; (물가 등이) fluctuate. ¶요새는 물가가 오르락 내리락하여 몹시 변동이 심하다 Prices are fluctuating and very unstable these days.
오르막 1 [올라가는 길] an ascent; an upward slope; a rising hill; an uprise. ¶완만한[가파른] ~ a gradual[steep] ascent//그 길은 ~이다 The road goes uphill. ¶길은 거기서부터 ~이다 There the road is running uphill. **2** [기운·기세가 올라가는 상태] an upward trend; a rising turn; (운 등의) a lucky turn (in one's fortune); a rising fortune. ¶~ 시세 the upward trend of prices//그의 운세는 ~이 되었다 His luck took a turn for the better.
●**오르막길** an uphill road[path]; an ascent.
오른손 the right hand. ¶~에 우산을 들다 have an umbrella in one's right hand.
●**오른손잡이** [오른손을 쓰는 사람] a right-handed person; a right-hander; (구어) a righty. ¶~ 투수 a right-handed pitcher.
오른쪽 the right; the right side. ¶~의 right-hand / right (arm)//맨 ~의 rightmost//~ 에 on the right (of) / on[at] (its) right//~ 에 있는 사람 a person on one's right//~에 보이는 높은 산 the high mountain visible to [on] the right//…의 ~에 앉다 sit at the right of ... //~으로 돌다 turn right / turn to the right//~으로 가다 keep to the right//책 상의 ~에 서시오 Stand on the right (side) of the desk.//내 ~에 앉으시오 Please sit on my right.//~에 보이는 저 건물은 학교입니다 That building to the right is a school.
오른팔 1 [오른쪽의 팔] the right arm. **2** [심복] one's right-hand man; one's right hand. ¶… 의 ~이 되다 give assistance to a person / be a person's right hand//그는 수상의 ~이다 He is the Prime Minister's right-hand man [right hand].
오른편(-便) the right. ⇨*오른쪽 ¶~에 앉다 sit on one's right side//내 ~ 자리가 비어 있다 The seat on my right is unoccupied.
오름세(-勢) (물가의) an upward tendency (of the market); a rising trend; an advance; [증권] a bull (market). ¶~의 firm / bullish / strong//~를 보이다 show rising trends//수 입이 물가의 ~를 쫓아가지 못한다 My income cannot keep up with the rise in prices.
오름차(-次) [수] ascending powers. ¶~순으로 in ascending powers.
오리 [동] a (wild) duck; a mallard; (수컷) a drake. ¶새끼 ~ a duckling.
●**오리발** [물갈퀴] a web; a webbed foot; a web-fingered hand; a webfoot; (수영용의) a fin; a flipper. ¶~을 내밀다 pretend not to know[to be ignorant] / play innocent//~ 내 밀지 마, 자기가 한 일이란 걸 다 알고 있으면 서 Don't play innocent[look blank] — you know very well what you've done.
오리나무 [식] an alder; a black alder.
오리너구리 [동] a duckbill; a (duckbilled) platypus; a duckmole.
오리다 cut[clip] (out) (from). ¶오려 낸 신문 기사 (미) newspaper clippings / (영) press cuttings / scraps (from the Times)//둥글게 ~ cut a round piece (out of paper) / cut out round//참조용으로 기사를 ~ cut out [clip] an article for reference//신문의 미술란 을 오려 냈다 I clipped out the art column from the paper.
오리목(-木) [가늘고 길게 켠 목재] [건] a lath; a strip of wood[board].
오리무중(五里霧中) ¶~인 살인 사건 an unsolved murder mystery[case]//~이다 be in a fog[maze] / be at sea (in regard to) / be mystified//살인 사건은 여전히 ~에 빠져 있 다 The murder case is as much in the dark as ever.//그는 연구 방법을 알지 못하여 ~에 빠져 있다 He was at a complete loss[completely in the dark] as to how to proceed with his research.
오리엔테이션 orientation. ¶클럽 활동의 ~ orientation for extracurricular activities//신 입생에 대한 3일간의 ~ the obligatory three-day orientation course for the new students //입학식이 끝난 후 학생들은 교실에서 ~을 받았다 After the matriculation[entrance] ceremony the students were given orientation in the classrooms.
오리엔트 [동양] the Orient.
오리온자리 [천] Orion; the Hunter. ¶~의 세 별 Orion's Belt.
오리지널 [원형·원전·원본·원문] the original; an original; an original manuscript[picture / record].
오막살이(-幕-) **1** a hut; a shack. ⇨*오두막 (집) **2** [오두막집에서 사는 살림살이] life in a hut[shanty / (미) shack]. ¶~를 하다 lead a

오만 hut living / live a hut / be a hut-dweller.

오만(五萬) (잡다한) various; of every sort and kind; all sorts[kinds] of; (수많은) innumerable; countless; thousands; millions. ¶~ 가지 물건을 늘어놓다 display various kinds of articles∥~ 가지 수단을 다 써 보다 try every possible means / leave no stone unturned∥그 가게에서는 ~ 가지 물건을 팔고 있다 They sell all kinds[sorts] of things at that shop.

오만상(五萬相) a distorted[frowning / wry / puckered] face; a grimace; a scowl. ¶~을 짓다 distort one's face / make[pull] a (wry) face / make grimaces / pucker up one's face / screw one's face into wrinkles∥그녀는 아파서 ~을 찌푸렸다 She grimaced with pain.

오만하다(傲慢-) arrogant; haughty; insolent; overbearing. ¶오만하게 arrogantly / haughtily / proudly∥오만한 표정 big[proud] looks∥오만한 태도 a haughty attitude∥오만한 태도를 취하다 assume a haughty attitude / hold one's head high∥우리는 그가 오만하게 구는 것을 본 적이 없다 We never saw him behave haughtily[in an overbearing manner].∥"너 따위는 이해 못해."라고 그는 오만하게 말했다 He said haughtily, "You wouldn't understand."

오매불망(寤寐不忘) ¶~의 unforgettable / never-to-be-forgotten (event). **오매불망하다** cannot forget (something) waking or sleeping; bear in mind all the time; hold (the matter) in remembrance.

오메가 [그리스 어의 마지막 자모] omega (Ω, ω).

오면체(五面體) [수] a pentahedron.

오명(汚名) [더러워진 이름이나 명예] a disgrace; a bad name; dishonor; a stigma (pl. ~s, stigmata); a slur; a taint; a stain (on one's good name). ¶~을 씻다 remove the stigma[disgrace] that has (been) attached to one's name / wipe out a stain on one's name / clear one's name∥~을 남기다 leave a bad name behind (one)∥그는 마침내 ~을 씻었다 He finally cleared his name[vindicated his honor].

오목(五目) gobang; a game in which two players complete to line up five stones of their own color on a go board. ¶~을 두다 play gobang.

오목 거울 a concave mirror.
오목 렌즈 a concave lens.
오목조목 ¶~ 몰려 있는 섬들 a group of islands of various[all] sizes.

오목하다 dented; sunken; hollow; concave. ¶눈이 오목한 사람 a person with sunken [deep-set] eyes / a hollow-eyed person∥수저의 오목한 곳 the bowel[hollow] of a spoon.

오묘하다(奧妙-) profound; abstruse; deep; recondite. ¶오묘한 뜻 deep meaning∥그 성경 귀절의 오묘함 the profundity of the scripture.

오물(汚物) [더러운 것] filth; dirt; sewage(하수의); garbage(부엌의); [분뇨] night soil. ¶~의 처리 disposal of garbage.

오물거리다 squirm in swarm; mumble; falter; be tardy. ⇨ˁ우물거리다 ¶샌드위치를 오물거리며 먹다 mumble (on) sandwiches∥이 생선에는 구더기가 오물거린다 Maggots are wriggling in this fish.∥그는 오물거리며 변명을 했다 He mumbled (out) an excuse.

오물오물 wrigglingly; mumbling; mumblingly. ⇨ˁ우물우물 ¶~ 씹다 chew something with one's mouth closed∥~ 혼잣말을 중얼거리다 mumble to oneself∥그는 입 안에서 ~ 중얼거리며 변명을 했다 He mumbled (out) an excuse.

오므라들다 (벌어진 틈 등이) become narrow; narrow; (입이) pucker; purse; [줄어들다] shrink; contract; draw. ¶오므라든 입 a puckered[pursy] mouth / pursed lips∥상처가 오므라들고 있다 The wound is closing.

오므라이스 a rice omelet.
오므라지다 become narrower. ⇨ˁ오므라들다

오므리다 (벌어진 틈 등을) make narrower; shut; close; (입을) pucker; purse; (손바닥을) cup. ¶입을 ~ pucker up one's mouth / purse (up) one's lips∥발을 ~ draw in one's legs∥나는 손바닥을 오므려서 빗방울을 받았다 I hollowed the palm of my hand and caught a few raindrops.

오믈렛 (미) an omelet; (영) an omelette.
오미(五味) the five tastes(=the sweet, sour, salty, bitter, and pungent tastes).
● **오미자**(-子) yellow angel twigged magnolia.

오밀조밀하다(奧密稠密-) **1** (솜씨가) elaborate; exquisite; delicate. ¶오밀조밀한 세공품 an elaborate handiwork∥오밀조밀한 디자인 an elaborate design∥오밀조밀하게 꾸민 정원 an exquisite garden. **2** (마음씨가) minute; meticulous; scrupulous; sedulous.

오바이트하다(ˀovereat-) throw up; vomit up; puke up.

오밤중(午-中) midnight. ⇨ˁ한밤중
오발(誤發) accidental firing. **오발하다** fire (a gun) by accident[accidentally / by mistake].

오버 1 an overcoat. ⇨ˁ외투 **2** [초과]. **오버하다** go over; exceed. ¶만 원을 ~ exceed ten thousand won.

오버랩 [영] an overlap; (lap) dissolve. **오버랩하다** dissolve (into another scene). →스튜디오의 장면에 가두 장면을 오버랩시키자 Let's superimpose a street scene on the picture of the studio.

오버코트 an overcoat; (영) a greatcoat. ¶털 ~ a fur overcoat.
오버헤드 킥(ˀoverhead kick) a bicycle kick.
오벨리스크 [방첨탑(方尖塔)] an obelisk.

오보(誤報) an incorrect[an erroneous / a false] report; wrong information; misinformation. ¶그것은 ~였다 The report turned out (to be) incorrect. / The information was wrong.∥그 신문에는 가끔 ~가 실린다 That paper often gives wrong information.∥그들은 고의로 ~를 흘렸다 They deliberately circulated a fake report[misinformation]. **오보하다** give a false report; misreport; misinform (on).

오보에 [음] an oboe.
● **오보에 연주자** an oboist.
오복(五福) the five blessings(=longevity, wealth, health, virtue, and peaceful death).

오붓하다 substantial; sufficient; adequately enough; satisfactory; (살림이) moderately wealthy. ¶오붓한 살림 a comfortable living∥가족끼리의 오붓한 모임이었다 It was a family gathering[affair]. **오붓이** substantially; enough; sufficiently; in peace and competence; comfortably. ¶~ 살다 live in peace and competence / be well[comfortably] off / be well-to-do // 나는 가족끼리 ~ 살고 싶다 I want to live by ourselves without outsiders in the family.

오븐 an oven. ¶~에 케이크를 굽다 bake a cake in an oven.

오비이락(烏飛梨落) the casual[strange] coincidence arousing suspicion.

오빠 one's older[elder] brother; (구어) one's big brother(▶ 종종 어린이가 말하는 경우). (▶ 우리말에서는 여자의 손위 동기 남자를 「오빠」, 남자의 손위 동기 남자를 「형」으로 구별하여 말하고 있으나, 영어에서는 그런 구별이 없이 모두 older brother임)

오사리잡놈(-雜-) [온갖 못된 짓을 하는 잡놈] scoundrel; a blackguard; a thug; a no-good.

오산(誤算) [계산 착오] miscalculation; [잘못된 판단] misjudgment. ¶전략상의 ~ a strategical miscalculation // 그것은 내 ~이었다 I misjudged it. **오산하다** miscalculate; make a miscalculation; misjudge.

오색(五色) **1** [청·적·황·백·흑] the five cardinal colors. **2** [여러 빛깔] various colors. ¶~의 꽃 flowers of various colors

오색영롱하다(五色玲瓏-) resplendent; very colorful; (서술적) shine brilliantly in various colors.

오색잡놈(五色雜-) scoundrel. ⇨ "오사리잡놈

오색찬란하다(五色燦爛-) resplendent; very colorful. ⇨ 오색영롱하다 ¶보석을 박은 오색 찬란한 왕관 a brilliantly jeweled crown.

오서독스하다 orthodox. ¶오서독스한 방법 an orthodox method.

오선(五線) [음] the staff; the stave.
● **오선지** music[scoring] paper; a music [scoring] sheet.

오성 장군(五星將軍) (미) a five-star general(육군·공군); a five-star admiral(해군).

오세아니아 [대양주] Oceania. ¶~의 Oceanian / Oceanic.

오소리 [동] a badger; an old-world[a true] badger.

오손(汚損) a stain. **오손하다** stain; soil. → 오손되다 be stained / be soiled / be spoiled // 이 천은 오손되기 쉽다 This material gets soiled easily.

오솔길 a (narrow) path; a (lonely) lane; a trail. ¶숲 속의 ~ a path through a forest.

오수(午睡) a (midday) nap. ⇨ "낮잠 ¶~를 즐기다 nap / take a nap[siesta].

오수(汚水) dirty[filthy / foul] water. ⇨ "구정물¹
● **오수 처리장** a sewage treatment plant.

오순도순 intimately; harmoniously; in harmony; on good[friendly] terms. ¶~ 이야기하다 have a nice little tête-à-tête (with) // 그 부부는 ~ 잘 지내고 있다 That is a very harmonious couple.

오스카상(-賞) [영] an Academy Award. ⇨ "아카데미상(⇨아카데미)

오슬오슬 shivering. ⇨ <으슬으슬

오식(誤植) a misprint; a printer's[typographical] error; a typo. ¶~이 없는 책 a book free from[of] misprints // ~이 많다 teem with [be full of] misprints // ~을 정정하다 correct errors in proof[in printing] // (정오표에서) "fall"은 "fail"의 ~ For "fall" read "fail". **오식하다** misprint.

오신(誤信) (a) misbelief; a mistaken[wrong] belief; a fallacy. **오신하다** misbelieve; hold an erroneous belief[opinion]; (문어) be under a misapprehension.

오심(誤審) **1** [잘못 심판함] wrong refereeing. **오심하다** referee wrongly. **2** [법] a miscarriage of justice; misjudgment; mistrial. **오심하다** misjudge; judge wrongly.

오십(五十) fifty. ¶제~ the fiftieth // ~ 년 fifty years / half a century // ~ 분의 일 a fiftieth part // ~ 대에 in one's fifties // ~ 나이를 바라보다 be close[hard] upon fifty.

오십보백보(五十步百步) ¶~다 be six of one and half a dozen of the other / (미) be about and about / There is little [not much] difference between the two. / There is not much to choose between the two. // 그것은 ~ 격이다 It is a case of "a miss being as good as a mile[the pot calling the kettle black]."

오싹 with a chill. **오싹하다** feel[have] a chill; shudder (with horror); shiver; thrill; feel a thrill (of horror); feel creepy. ¶등골이 오싹해지는 공포 영화 a horror film // 등골이 ~ feel the (cold) shivers down the spine // 생각만 해도 ~ shudder[be horrified] at the mere thought (of) // 듣기[보기]만 해도 ~ shudder at the mere mention[sight] (of) // 오싹하게 하다 make one's blood run cold / send a thrill[chill] through one / give one cold shivers / freeze one with fright / make one shudder / make one's flesh creep[crawl] / give one goose flesh // 이상한 소리에 온몸이 오싹했다 At the strange noise a shiver ran through my whole body. // 그 소식을 듣고 온몸이 오싹했다 The news sent a chill to the marrow of my bones.

오싹오싹 shiveringly. **오싹오싹하다** (추위로) feel a chill; feel chilly; shiver (with cold); (공포 등으로) feel creepy. ¶몸이 오싹오싹한다, 열이 상당히 있는 것 같다 I have got the shakes. I'm afraid I have a high fever.

오아시스 an oasis (pl. oases). ¶사막의 ~ a desert oasis // 인생의 ~ an oasis in life // 양서는 마음의 ~다 Good books are an oasis for the mind.

오양 → 자두

오언 절구(五言絶句) a quatrain (in Chinese poetry) with five characters to a line.

오엑스문제(-問題) true-false questions.

오역(誤譯) a mistranslation; an incorrect translation; a mistake[an error] in translation. ¶~을 지적하다 point out mistakes in a translation // ~이 몇 군데 있다 You have made several slips in your translation. // 이 책에는 ~이 없다 There is not a (single) mistranslation in this book. / This book is free from errors in translation. **오역하다** mistranslate; make an error[a mistake / a slip] in translation. → ¶오역된 곳 a mistake[an error] in translation.

오열(五列) the Fifth Column. ⇨ 제오 열

오열(嗚咽) sobbing; weeping. **오열하다** sob; weep.

오염(汚染) pollution; contamination.(▶ 거의 같은 뜻으로 쓰이는 일도 있으나, 전자는 화학물질에, 후자는 세균에 오염된 경우를 말하는 일이 많음) ¶대기 ~ air pollution // 해양 ~ sea pollution // 방사능 ~ radioactive contamination // 환경 ~ environmental pollution // 공장 폐수로 인한 하천 ~ industrial pollu-

오욕(汚辱) [수치] disgrace; dishonor; [모욕] (an) insult. ¶~으로 얼룩진 생애 a life filled with shame[humiliation]//~을 당하다 suffer disgrace / be disgraced / incur disgrace//~을 참다 eat dirt[humble pie]//나는 이루 말할 수 없는 ~을 당했다 I was disgraced beyond all description. 오욕하다 disgrace; dishonor; stain (a person's name) with slander; bring disgrace upon (a person).

오용(誤用) misuse; wrong use; misapplication(적용상의). ¶말의 ~ incorrect[improper] use of language / misuse of a word / a catachresis (pl. -chreses)(어원의 오해에 의한) / a malapropism(어형 혼동에 의한, 우스팡스러운). 오용하다 misuse; misapply; use (a thing) for a wrong purpose; put (something) to an improper use.

오월(五月) May. ¶~의 여왕 a May queen//~의 축제 the May Festival(대학 등의).

오월동주(吳越同舟) bitter[implacable] enemies (placed by fate) in the same boat.

오이 [식] a cucumber.
오이 덩굴에서 가지 열리는 법은 없다(속담) An onion will not produce a rose.; Like breeds like.
오이를 거꾸로 먹어도 제멋(속담) Tastes differ.; Every man to his taste.
● 오이김치 cucumber *gimchi*(kimchi). 오이 소박이김치 stuffed cucumber *gimchi*(kimchi). 오이지 pickled cucumbers; cucumber pickles.

오이디푸스 [그리스 신화] Oedipus.
● 오이디푸스 콤플렉스 Oedipus complex.

오인(誤認) a mistake; misconception; misunderstanding; an erroneous assumption. 오인하다 mistake[take] (one thing) for (another); misunderstand; misconceive. ¶우군을 적으로 ~ mistake[taken]for a burglar//그는 안개로 신호를 오인했다 He mistook the signal in the fog.

오일 oil; petroleum; gasoline.
● 오일 달러 oil dollars; petrodollars. 오일 쇼크(*oil shock) the oil crisis; the oil squeeze.

오일장(五日葬) (have) a five-day funeral.

오입(誤入) illicit (sexual) intercourse; adultery. 오입하다 have illicit sexual intercourse (with); commit adultery.
● 오입쟁이 an adulterer.

오자(誤字) a wrong[miswritten] word; [잘못된 철자] a misspelling; [오식] a misprint; an erratum. ¶그의 작문은 ~투성이다 His composition is full of wrong characters [misspelled words](▶ 우리말의 경우는 wrong characters, 영어의 경우는 misspelled words).

오장(五臟) the five viscera(=liver, lungs, heart, kidneys and spleen).
● 오장 육부(─六腑) five viscera and six entrails; the internal organs and the bowels. ¶그 놈의 말을 들으니 ~가 뒤집힌다 His words make my blood boil.//~가 뒤틀리는 것 같았다 It was gut-wrenching.

오쟁이 a small straw bag.
오쟁이(를) 지다 be made a cuckold (of); wear the horns. ¶오쟁이 진 사내 a cuckold.

오전(午前) the forenoon; the morning; a.m. [A.M.]. ¶~ 8시 30분 열차 the 8:30 a.m. train//~ 9시에 at nine in the morning / at 9 a.m.//~(중)에 in the morning / on the morning (of August 7, of the third of September, etc.)/일요일 ~에 on Sunday morning//~ 중에는 집에 있다 I am at home in the morning.//3월 3일 ~에 그와 만났다 I met him on the morning of March 3.//열차는 ~ 10시에 도착한다 The train arrives at 10 a.m.

오점(汚點) [얼룩] a blot; a stain; [결점] a flaw. ¶~이 없는 stainless//그의 행동은 그의 경력에 ~을 남겼다 His behavior stained [cast a blot on / brought a stain on] his career.//그의 경력에는 아무런 ~이 없다 His record has no stain[blot] on it. / There is no stain[blot] on his record.//그 사건은 학교 이름에 ~을 남겼다 The affair left a stain on the school name.

오정(午正) (high) noon; midday; the meridian hour.

오존 [화] ozone. ¶~의[을 함유한] ozonous / ozonic//~으로 처리하다 ozonize.
● 오존층 an ozone layer.

오종 경기(五種競技) the pentathlon. ¶근대 ~ the modern pentathlon.

오종종하다 1 [빽빽하다] dense; thick; compact. ¶건포도가 오종종하게 박힌 케이크 a cake studded with raisins. 2 [얼굴이 옹졸스럽다] meager (face); mean. ¶오종종하게 생긴 사내 a mean man.

오죽 how; how much; very; indeed. ¶그것을 들으면 너의 어머니께서 ~ 기뻐하시겠니 How glad your mother will be to hear it!

오죽이나 how; how much. ⇨"오죽 ¶그 애가 ~ 아프면 울겠느냐 The child must be in dreadful pain, otherwise he wouldn't cry.//그것을 보고 그가 ~ 놀랐겠니 What was his surprise to see that!//~ 배가 고프겠니 You are very hungry, I dare say. / I can well imagine your hunger.//~ 낙담했겠니 I can well imagine your disappointment.

오죽잖다 trifling; trivial. ¶오죽잖은 녀석 a good-for-nothing fellow//그와 오죽잖은 일로 싸움을 했다 I had a quarrel with him over a trivial matter.

오줌 water(분뇨액으로서); (구어) pee; (비어) piss; (소아어) piddling; (마소의) stale. ¶~의 urinous / urinary//~을 누다 urinate / make [pass] water / (소아어) piddle / (비어) piss / (마소가) stale//~을 싸다 wet (the bed)//~을 참다 control one's need to urinate[to go the bathroom] / hold[retain] one's water//~을 지리다 be incontinent / lose control of one's bodily functions//~이 마렵다 have a desire[feel the urge] to urinate[pass water]

/ feel nature's call / want to piss∥길가에서 ~을 누다 urinate [relieve oneself] in the street∥나는 자주 ~이 마렵다 I have frequent need to urinate.∥내 need to go to the bathroom frequently.∥그 아이는 또 ~을 쌌다 The child had another toilet accident. / (자다가) The child wet the bed again.

● **오줌소태** 〔의〕 pollakiuria; sychnuria; micturition. **오줌싸개** a bed wetter. **오줌통** 〔방광〕 the bladder; 〔오줌 누는 통〕 a urine pail; a urinary; a urinal(변기).

오중주(五重奏) a quintet(te).

오지(奧地) the interior; the hinterland; upcountry; 〔미〕 the back country.∥아프리카의 ~ the heart [the innermost depths] of Africa∥아마존의 ~ the upper reaches of the Amazon∥~의 inland (town) / 〔미〕 back country.

오지그릇 glazed earthenware; pottery (with dark-brown glaze).

오지랖 the lapels of an outer garment.

오지랖(이) 넓다 〔참견이 많다〕 intrude; intermeddle; thrust [poke] (one's) nose into.

오직 simply; solely; merely; only; but; entirely. ¶~ 한 가지 이유 the only [sole] reason∥돈벌이만 생각하다 be solely bent on moneymaking∥그녀는 ~ 웃기만 했다 She did nothing but laugh.∥친구라고는 ~ 너뿐이다 You are the only friend I have.∥그는 ~ 학문에 전념했다 He devoted himself solely to [was intent on] learning.∥언어를 익히려면 ~ 연습뿐이다 Practice is the only way of mastering a language.∥나는 ~ 어머니께 감사할 따름이었다 All I could do was (to) [I could do nothing but] thank my mother.

오진(誤診) 〔의〕 misdiagnosis; an wrong [erroneous] diagnosis. **오진하다** misdiagnose; make a wrong diagnosis; make an error in diagnosis; diagnose erroneously. ¶그 의사는 폐렴을 감기로 오진했다 The doctor made a wrong diagnosis of a case of pneumonia, calling it a cold.

오징어 a cuttlefish(참오징어); a squid(뼈가 없는); an inkfish. ¶~는 먹물을 뿜는다 A cuttlefish ejects an inky liquid.

오차(誤差) 〔수〕 an (accidental) error; an aberration. ¶개인 ~ a personal error [equation]∥계산상의 ~ an (accidental) error in calculation∥**허용**(할 수 있는) ~ tolerance / the allowable margin of error∥1퍼센트 이내의 ~ an error of less than 1 percent∥~의 한계 a limit of error∥1퍼센트 이내의 ~는 면할 수 없다 Errors in the range of 1 percent are unavoidable.

오찬(午餐) a luncheon. ¶~을 들다 lunch / take lunch∥~에 초대하다 invite (a person) to a luncheon∥우리는 ~을 함께했다 We lunched together.

● **오찬회** a luncheon (party). ¶~를 열다 give [hold] a luncheon.

오촌(五寸) 〔종숙〕 a male cousin of one's father; 〔종질〕 a (first) cousin once removed.

오칭(誤稱) a misnomer. **오칭하다** call by a wrong name; call wrongly [erroneously].

오케스트라 〔음〕 an orchestra(▶ 고전 음악 전문의 오케스트라는 정식으로는 symphony orchestra). ¶실내 [심포니] ~ a chamber [symphony] orchestra∥~의 반주로 to an orchestral accompaniment.

오케이 OK; O.K.; All right. ¶"내일 꼭 오너라." "~." "Be sure to come tomorrow." "OK [Okay / All right]."

오탁하다(汚濁─) filthy and turgid. ➔¶자동차의 배기가스가 공기를 오탁시켜 버렸다 Exhaust from cars has polluted the air.

오토메이션 automation. ¶오피스 ~ office automation∥~으로 (bring down the cost of production) by automation∥~화한 공장 an automated plant[factory]∥~화하다 automate (a factory).

오토바이(*auto bicycle) a motorcycle. ¶~ 뒷좌석에 사람을 태우다 take a person on the pillion seat of one's motorcycle∥~를 급히 몰다 hurry by [on a] motorcycle.

오톨도톨하다 uneven; rough. ⇨ **우둘투둘하다**

오트밀 oatmeal; 〔영〕 porridge.

오판(誤判) misjudgment; a mistrial; miscarriage of justice [law]. ¶~으로 전쟁을 도발하다 provoke a war by miscalculation. **오판하다** misjudge; error in judgment; miscalculate.

오팔 〔광〕 opal.

오퍼 〔경〕 an offer. ¶구매 ~ a buying [buyer's] offer / a bid∥판매 ~ a selling offer / an offer∥확정 ~ a firm offer∥~를 내다 offer / submit an offer / make an offer (for goods) / put forward an offer∥~를 받다 receive an offer.

● **오퍼상**(─商) a commission agent.

오페라 (an) opera. ¶그랜드 ~ grand opera∥코믹 ~ a comic opera∥~의 operatic∥~는 노래, 기악, 무용 및 연극 등의 모든 무대 예술을 한데 모은 것이다 Opera is a blend of all the performing arts — song, instrumental music, dance, and drama.

● **오페라 가수** an opera singer. **오페라 극장** an opera house. **오페라단** an opera company [troupe].

오페레타 (an) operetta (pl. ~s, -retti).

오펙 〔석유 수출국 기구〕 OPEC(▶ Organization of Petroleum Exporting Countries의 약어).

오프사이드 〔축구·하키〕 offside. ¶~가 되다 be offside∥~ 반칙을 하다 be offside(s) / commit an offside penalty.

오프셋 인쇄(─印刷) offset printing [lithography]; offset. ¶사진 ~ photo offset printing∥~로 하다 print offset / offset.

오픈 게임 (*open game) an open event [tournament].

오픈카(*open car) a convertible; 〔구어〕 a ragtop.

오한(惡寒) a chill; a cold [shivering] fit; 〔의〕 rigor. ¶~이 나다 feel [catch / take / have] a chill∥아까부터 ~이 난다 I've been having chills for quite a while.

오합지졸(烏合之卒) a rabble; a disorderly crowd; a mob. ¶이 집단은 조직이라기보다 ~ 이다 This group is just a mixed bunch [a gathering of various types of people] rather than an organization.

오해(誤解) (a) misunderstanding; misapprehension; delusion; misconception. ¶이런 벽촌에 고급 호텔이 있다고 생각하시면 ~입니다 You cannot expect to find a high-class hotel in such an out-of-the-way place.∥그것은 그 쪽 사람의 ~이다 That's a misunderstanding on their part.∥이 편지는 ~를 불러일으키기 쉽다 This letter is misleading.∥아버지는 ~

오행 를 사기 쉬운 분이다 My father is apt to be misunderstood. // 그 일로 ~를 받았다 I was misunderstood on that point. // ~도 이만저만이 아니다 It is a gross misunderstanding.

오해하다 misunderstand; mistake; misapprehend; (어구를) put a wrong construction (on); misconstrue; [나쁘게 해석하다] take (something) amiss. ¶오해하지 마 Don't misunderstand me. / Don't get me wrong. / Don't take it the wrong way. // 뭔가 오해하고 있는 것 같다 You seem to have misunderstood something. / (구어) You have got hold of the wrong end of the sick. // 머리를 길게 하고 있어서 여자 아이로 오해했다 Because of his long hair I mistook him for a girl.

오행(五行) [민] the five elements (=metal, wood, water, fire, and earth).

오현금(五絃琴) a pentachord.

오호(嗚呼) Alas!; (고) Alack!; (고) Wo(e)! ¶~라 Alas! / 그녀는 이제 가고 없구나 Alas, she is dead and gone!

오후(午後) afternoon; p.m. ¶~ 이른 [늦은] 시간에 early [late] in the afternoon // 3월 10일의 ~에 on the afternoon of March 10 / in the afternoon on March 10 // ~에 오십시오 Please come in the afternoon. // 오늘 [내일/일요일] ~에 영화 보러 가자 Let's go to the movies this [tomorrow / Sunday] afternoon. // 그 열차는 ~ 한 시에 출발한다 The train leaves at 1 p.m.

오히려 1 [반대로] on the contrary; instead. ¶그 편이 ~ 낫다 That is better, though one may not have expected as much. // 도시에는 제 나름의 여러 가지 즐거움이 있지만 나는 조용한 시골 생활을 동경한다 The city has its own pleasures, but I long instead for a quiet country life.
2 [차라리] rather; [그래도 좀 더] all the more [better / worse]. ¶이 그림은 사실파적이라기보다는 ~ 인상파적이다 This picture is impressionistic rather than realistic. // 그녀는 가수라기보다는 ~ 여배우이다 She is not so much as a singer as an actress. / She is more of an actress than a singer. // 그가 보수파라고? 아니, ~ 실용주의자다 A conservative? No, if anything, he's a pragmatist.

옥(玉) 1 [보석] a precious stone; a gem; a jewel. 2 [광] jade.

옥에도 티가 있다(속담) No silver [gold] without its dross.

옥에 티(속담) a flaw in a precious stone; a fly in the ointment; a flaw in one's character; a blot on one's record [reputation]; a hole in one's coat. ¶그는 키가 작은 것이 ~다 The only defect [shortcoming] in his otherwise well-formed [perfect] figure is his short stature.

옥(獄) a prison; (미) a jail; (영) a gaol.

옥고(獄苦) the hardships of prison life. ¶~를 견디다 endure the hardships of prison life // ~를 치르고 나오다 serve out one's term of imprisonment.

옥내(屋內) the interior [inside] of a house. ¶~에서 indoors / within doors // ~의 indoor.
●**옥내 경기** an indoor game. **옥내 배선** interior wiring; house wiring.

옥니 an inturned tooth.
●**옥니박이** a person with inturned teeth.

옥답(沃畓) a rich [fertile] paddyfield.

옥도(沃度) [화] iodine. ⇨요오드

옥돌(玉-) a gem stone; jade.

옥돔(玉-) [동] a tilefish.

옥동자(玉童子) a (darling) baby boy; a cute [precious] son. ¶~가 태어났다 A perfectly lovely [adorable] baby boy was born.

옥문(獄門) a prison gate; the gate of jail. ¶~에 효수하다 expose a (decapitated) head at a prison gate.

옥바라지하다(獄-) supply a prisoner with clothes and food from outside the prison.

옥배(玉杯) 1 [옥으로 만든 잔] a jade cup. 2 [잔] a cup; a glass.

옥사하다(獄死-) die in prison.

옥살산(-酸) oxalic acid.

옥살이(獄-) penal servitude; a prison life. ⇨감옥살이(⇨감옥)

옥상(屋上) the rooftop; the top of the house. ¶그는 ~에 올라갔다 He climbed onto the roof.
●**옥상 정원** a roof garden.

옥새(玉璽) 1 [국새] the great seal made of jade. 2 [왕의 인장] the Royal [Imperial] seal; the privy seal.

옥색(玉色) light blue.

옥석(玉石) 1 a gem stone. ⇨옥돌 2 [옥과 돌] jades [gems] and stones. 3 [좋은 것과 나쁜 것] good and bad things; wheat and tares. ¶~을 가리지 못하다 fail to distinguish between good and bad / confuse good things and bad.
●**옥석구분**(-俱焚) [선악이 함께 멸함] indiscriminate destruction of good and bad alike.

옥소(沃素) [화] iodine. ⇨요오드

옥수(玉水) clear [crystal] water.

옥수(玉手) [임금의 손] the king's hand; [미인의 손] a woman's beautiful hand.

옥수수 Indian corn; (미) corn; (영) maize (▶(영)에서는 corn은 밀을 말함). ¶~ 한 알 a kernel of corn // ~의 속대 a corncob // ~의 술 a corn tassel // ~를 재배하다 grow corn.

옥신각신하다 argue [dispute / wrangle] (with); skirmish; altercate (with); squabble; have a (petty) quarrel (with). ¶서로 ~ wrangle with each other // 그녀는 이웃집 사람과 항상 옥신각신한다 She is constantly picking quarrels [causing trouble] with her next-door neighbor.

옥안(玉顏) 1 the king's face. ⇨용안(龍顏) 2 [미인의 얼굴] a woman's beautiful face.

옥양목(玉洋木) (영) calico; (미) muslin; (질이 좋은) cambric.

옥외(屋外) [집의 밖] the outdoors; the exterior of a house; the open (air). ¶~의 outdoor / open-air / outside // ~에서 outdoors / in the open / out of doors.
●**옥외 광고판** a billboard. **옥외 스포츠** outdoor sports. **옥외 집회** an open-air meeting; an out-of-door gathering.

옥잠화(玉簪花) [식] a hosta; a plantain lily.

옥좌(玉座) the Emperor's [Imperial] seat; the throne. ¶~에 앉다 sit on the throne / take the Imperial seat.

옥죄다 ¶코르셋은 몸을 옥죈다 A corset laces you in tight.

옥죄이다 be bound [fastened] tight; be clinched; (목을) be throttled [choked]; get tightened [cramped].

옥중(獄中) ¶~에 [에서] in prison [jail / (영) gaol / behind bars // ~에서 편지를 써 보내

다 write [send a letter] from prison.
● **옥중 일기** a prison diary.
옥체(玉體) **1** [임금의 몸] the person of the king; the Royal person; His Majesty's person. **2** your health. ⇨존체
옥타브 [음] an octave. ¶한 ~ 올려서[내려서] 노래하다 sing an octave higher[lower].
옥탄 [화] octane.
● **옥탄가 / 옥탄값** [화] the octane number [rating]. ¶~가 높은 휘발유 high-octane gasoline.
옥토(沃土) rich[fertile] soil; fertile land. ¶박토를 ~로 만들다 make barren soil fertile.
옥토끼(-) (달 속의) the rabbit[man] in the moon; [흰 토끼] a white rabbit.
옥편(玉篇) a dictionary of classical Chinese explained in Korean. ⇨`자전(字典)
옥황상제(玉皇上帝) the King of Heaven (of Taoism); Heaven.
온 [전부의] all; whole; entire; total. ¶~ 백성 the whole nation // ~ 세상 all (over) the world / the whole world // 나는 그것이 어디 있는지 ~ 집 안을 찾아봤다 I looked for it everywhere in [all over] the house. / I searched the whole house for it. // 그들과는 ~ 가족이 교제하고 있다 We socialize with them on a family basis.
온각(溫覺) [생] thermesthesia.
온갖 all; every; each and every; all kinds [sorts] of. ¶~ 빛깔의 꽃 flowers of various colors // ~ 수단을 쓰다 use every conceivable means / try every possible method / leave no stone unturned // ~ 고생을 다하다 go through all sorts of hardships // 이 가게에는 ~ 상품이 갖추어져 있다 They have every conceivable kind of merchandise in this shop. / They shock everything under the sun in this store. // 그는 ~ 노력을 했지만 헛수고였다 He failed in spite of his utmost efforts. // 독재자는 ~ 포학을 다했다 The dictator committed all kinds of atrocities. // 우리는 그가 꾸미는 ~ 익살맞은 얼굴을 보고 배꼽을 뺐다 We laughed hard at the variety of comic faces he made.
온건파(穩健派) a moderate faction; the moderates.
온건하다(穩健-) gentle; quiet; amicable; peaceful; moderate; sensible. ¶온건한 사상의 소유자 a person with[of] moderate views // 온건한 조치를 취하다 take a moderate step // 온건한 처리[해결]를 요망하다 request an out-of-court settlement [a peaceful solution to the problem] (▶ out-of-court는 「화해에 의한」의 뜻) // 그는 온건한 사람이다 He is a sensible [well-balanced] man. **온건히** gently; quietly; amicably; peacefully; sensibly. ¶일을 ~ 처리하다 settle a matter quietly / reach an amicable solution.
온고지신(溫故知新) reviewing the old and learning the new; carrying the knowledge gained into new fields.
온기(溫氣) warmth. ¶~가 있다 be warm // ~가 없다 be not warm / have no warmth // 이 물에는 아직도 ~가 남아 있다 The water is still a little warm. / There is some warmth in this water.
온난 전선(溫暖前線) [기상] a warm front.
온난하다(溫暖-) warm; mild; temperate. ¶이곳은 겨울철에도 ~ Even the winters here are mild.

온달 [아주 둥근 달] a full moon.
온당하다(穩當-) reasonable; proper; modest; just; right; moderate; appropriate; fitting. ¶온당한 인사 proper language // 온당한 요구 a reasonable claim // 온당한 조치 a just and proper measure // 사표를 내다니 온당하지 않다 Sending in your resignation was too drastic step [(구어) was going too far]. // 그의 발언은 온당하지 않다 What he said wasn't entirely reasonable. // 이쯤이면 온당한 조치라고 할 수 있겠지 If that's the case, then the action you took was proper [the steps you took were appropriate]. **온당히** reasonably; properly; modestly; justly; rightly.
온대(溫帶) the Temperate[Variable] Zone. ¶~성의 temperate.
● **온대 기후** a temperate climate. **온대 식물**[동물] the flora[fauna] of the temperate zone. **온대 지방** the temperate regions[latitudes].
온데간데없다 vanish; disappear; missing; vanish without leaving a trace; completely out of sight. ¶금고 속에 넣어 둔 보석이 ~ The jewel is missing[has disappeared] from the safe.
온도(溫度) temperature; heat. ¶실내 ~ room temperature / the indoor temperature // 절대 [표준] ~ [물] the absolute[standard] temperature // 체감 ~ sensible temperature // 평균 ~ the (annual) mean temperature // ~를 재다 take[measure] the temperature // ~를 조절하다 adjust[control] the temperature // ~가 높다[낮다] The temperature is high [low]. / It's hot[cold]. // ~는 45도이다 The temperature is 45 degrees. // ~가 올라간다 The temperature[mercury / thermometer] rises[goes up / climbs up]. // ~가 내려간다 The temperature[mercury / thermometer] falls[goes down].
● **온도계** a thermometer. ¶섭씨~ a centigrade thermometer // 화씨~ a Fahrenheit thermometer // 자기(自記) ~ a recording [self-registering] thermometer. **온도 조절 temperature control. 온도 조절기** a thermostat.
온돌(溫突·溫堗) ondol; a (Korean) floor heater; a hypocaust.
● **온돌방** a hot-floored room; an ondol room.
온라인 ¶~의 [컴] on-line // 본점과 지점은 ~으로 연결되어 있다 The head and branch offices are connected on-line. // 나는 부모님께 ~으로 약간의 돈을 부치려고 합니다 I'd like to wire some money to my parents.
● **온라인 시스템** (on) an on-line system. ¶은행은 모두 ~을 도입하고 있다 The on-line system has been adopted in all banks.
온랭(溫冷) warmth and coldness.
온면(溫麵) noodles served in hot soup; warm noodles.
온몸 the whole body. ¶~에 all over the body / from head to foot[heel] // ~이 멍투성이다 be black and blue all over // ~이 아프다 I feel pain all over my body. / I ache all over. // 독이 ~에 퍼졌다 The poison passed into his whole system. // 그는 ~에 햇살을 받으며 모래사장에 누워 있었다 He was lying on the sandy beach exposing his whole body to the sunshine.
온밤 the whole night; all night; all the night

온벽(-壁) 〔창·문이 없는 벽〕 a blank wall.
온상(溫床) a hotbed. ¶범죄의 ～ a hotbed of crime // 〔악〕[질병〕의 ～ a hotbed of vice [disease] // ～에서 묘를 기르다 raise seedlings in a hotbed.
온수(溫水) warm[hot] water. ⇨˚더운물 ¶～를 급수하다 supply (a bathroom with) hot water.
● **온수 공급** hot-water supply. **온수기** a water heater. ¶가스[순간] ～ a gas[an instantaneous] water heater.
온순하다(溫順-) gentle; genial; docile; meek; obedient; compliant. ¶양처럼 ～ be as meek as a lamb.
온스 〔중량의 단위〕 an ounce(기호 oz.).
온실(溫室) a hothouse; a greenhouse; 〔영〕 a glasshouse; a greenery. ¶～의 튤립 a greenhouse[hothouse] tulip // ～에서 재배하다 cultivate (a plant) under glass // 그는 ～에서 자랐다 He has been brought up on a bed of roses. / He has never tasted the bitter cup of life.
● **온실 재배** greenhouse cultivation; cultivation under glass. **온실 효과** the greenhouse effect.
온아하다(溫雅-) bland; graceful; amiable; affable; suave; kindly. ¶온아한 말 graceful language // 온아한 사람 a mild-mannered and refined person.
온 에어 〔방송 중〕 on the air. ¶～가 되다 (방송 프로 등이) be broadcast // 이 프로그램은 ～ 중이다 The program is on the air.
온열 요법(溫熱療法) thermotherapy.
온욕(溫浴) a warm[hot] bath.
온유하다(溫柔-) gentle; meek; mild; tender; sweet; docile. ¶기질이 온유한 사람 a person with mild[gentle] disposition.
온음(-音) 〔음〕 a whole tone.
● **온음계** the diatonic scale. **온음정** a whole tone[step]. **온음표** (미) a whole note; 〔영〕 a semibreve.
온장고(溫藏庫) a heating cabinet.
온전하다(穩全-) sound; whole; intact; unimpaired; perfect. ¶온전한 컵은 하나도 없다 There isn't a cup left whole. // 이 전집은 온전하지 못하다 This set of books is incomplete.
온전히 soundly; wholly; perfectly. ¶그는 사고 현장에서 기적적으로 ～ 돌아왔다 Miraculously, he came home unhurt from the scene of the accident. // 그 조각상은 ～ 도착했다 The statue reached us in perfect condition.
온정(溫情) a kindly feeling; kindliness; warm-heartedness; geniality. ¶～이 어린 판결 a merciful sentence // ～이 담긴 충고 kind advice // 판사는 피고에게 ～을 베풀었다 The judge showed sympathy to the accused.
온존하다(溫存-) keep; preserve; retain. ¶전통 기술을 ～ preserve traditional skills // 전력을 ～ retain one's war potential.
온종일(-終日) all day (long); the whole day; from morning till night. ¶그는 ～ 빈둥거리며 지냈다 He idled away the whole day.
온채 the whole[entire] house. ¶～를 전세로 내다 rent[〔영〕let] a house in whole.
온천(溫泉) a hot[thermal] spring; a spa(장소). ¶**온양** ～ the spa of Onyang / Onyang hot springs // ～욕을 하다 take a hot spring bath.
● **온천장** a hot springs resort; a spa.
온탕(溫湯) 〔온천의 따뜻한 물〕 the hot water of the spa[hot spring]; 〔적당한 온도의 탕〕 moderately warm bath.
온통 all; wholly; entirely; all over; bodily; in the gross[mass / lump]; every and all; any and every; the whole lot; (프) en masse [bloc]. ¶그는 벽에 ～ 그녀의 사진을 붙여 놓았다 He pinned pictures of her all over the wall. // 자동차가 튀기는 흙탕물을 ～ 뒤집어썼다 A passing car splashed muddy water all over me.
온풍(溫風) a warm breeze.
● **온풍기** a warm air circulator.
온혈(溫血) warm blood.
● **온혈 동물** a warm-blooded animal. ⇨˚정온 동물(⇨)정온.
온화하다(溫和-) 1 〔기후·날씨가〕 mild; temperate; clement; genial; benign. ¶온화한 기후 a mild[temperate] climate // 플로리다 반도는 기후가 ～ The Florida Peninsula has mild weather[a mild climate]. // 내일은 온화한 날씨가 될 것이다 We will have calm weather tomorrow. 2 〔성질·태도가〕 gentle; mild; genial. ¶온화한 인품 a gentle[pleasant / genial] personality // 그는 온화한 사람이다 He is a mild-mannered person.
온후하다(溫厚-) courteous; affable; mild-mannered; gentle; suave. ¶온후한 사람 a gentle[an affable] person.
올¹ 〔올해의〕 ～ 여름휴가 the coming summer vacation / the last summer vacation.
올² 〔가닥〕 a strand; a ply; (피륙의) warp. ¶머리털 한 ～ a strand of hair // ～이 성긴 coarse // ～이 고운 직물 close texture // 실크 스타킹은 간혹 ～이 풀린다 Silk stockings sometime run.
올가미 1 〔올무〕 a snare; a trap. ¶～를 놓다 lay[set] a trap (for) // ～로 잡다 catch (a rabbit) in[with] a trap / (en)trap / (en)snare // 족제비가 ～에 걸렸다 The weasel was caught in[fell into] a trap. 2 〔계략〕 a trap. ¶그 녀석은 쉽사리 ～에 걸렸다 The fellow walked straight into the trap.
올가미(를) 씌우다 trap[(문어) entrap] a person.
올곧다 1 〔마음이 곧다〕 honest; upright. ¶올곧은 사람 an honest[(문어) righteous] person // 그는 마음이 ～ He is upright at heart. 2 〔줄이 반듯하다〕 straight.
올나이트 ¶～의 all-night // ～로 영업하는 가게 an all-night store.
올되다 1 〔조숙하다〕 act too grown up for one's age; be precocious; be forward (for one's years). ¶올된 아이 a precocious [forward] child // 그는 나이에 비해서 올되었다 He was precocious[too wise] for his age. / He has an old head on young shoulders. // 그녀는 여중생치고는 올되었다 She is too forward for a junior high school girl. // 도시의 어린이는 시골 어린이보다 올되는 경향이 있다 Children in the cities have the tendency to act too grown up for their age, more than those in the country. 2 〔열매 등이 일찍 익다〕 ripen early. ¶올되는 품종 a variety of early ripening.
올드미스(*old miss) 〔노처녀〕 an old maid; a spinster; 〔영〕 a tabby.
올라가다 1 〔높이 오르다〕 go[walk] up; climb

(up); rise; ascend. ¶꼭대기까지 ~ climb to the top (of a tree) / 2층으로 ~ go upstairs // 하늘 높이 ~ soar [go up] in the air / soar skyward / 나는 사다리를 타고 지붕에 올라갔다 I climbed up the ladder to the roof. // 차는 천천히 언덕길을 올라갔다 The car drove up the slope slowly [crawled up the slope]. // 그는 층계를 달려서 올라갔다 He ran up the stairs. // 갑자기 그의 체온이 올라갔다 His temperature rose suddenly.
2 [강을 거슬러 상류로 가다] go [sail] up (a river); go upstream; (물고기가) run up (a river). ¶우리는 강을 따라 2킬로미터 올라갔다 We went upstream along [on] the river for two kilometers.
3 [지방에서 서울로 가다] go up to the capital [Seoul]. ¶올라가는 기차 an up train.
4 [지위 등이 높아지다] rise; be promoted [raised]. ¶그는 과장으로 올라갔다 He was promoted to chief of his section. // 내 딸은 금년에 5학년으로 올라갑니다 My daughter will enter the fifth grade [(영) go up to the fifth form] this year.
5 [값이 비싸지다] go up; rise; soar (크게); shoot up (급히). ¶물가는 계속 올라가고 있다 Prices have been rising steadily.
6 [없어지다] lose; (money) be lost; be spent uselessly. ¶도박을 하다가 전 재산이 ~ gamble away one's fortune / gamble oneself out of house and home.
7 [상륙하다] land; go [come] ashore. ¶승객들은 육지로 올라갔다 The passengers landed.
8 〈속〉 die; pass away [on]. ⇨죽다1
9 [진보하다] advance; progress; make progress [headway]; improve. ¶이번 학기에는 성적이 올라갔다 (미) My grades went up this semester. / (영) I got higher marks this term. // 그것으로 그의 명성이 올라갔다 That made him famous. // 내 영어 성적이 올라갔다 My grades in English improved [got better].

올라서다 1 [높은 데로 옮아 서다] step [get] onto; mount [ascend] (a platform). ¶그는 책상 위에 올라서서 천장의 먼지를 털었다 He stood on the desk to dust the ceiling. **2** [지위가 높아지다] rise to higher level of rank; [출세하다] rise in the world. ¶2위로 ~ move into the second place.

올라오다 come up. ¶2층에 ~ come upstairs // 그는 20세 때 서울로 올라왔다 He came to the capital [Seoul] at the age of twenty.

올라운드 플레이어 an all-round [(미) all-around] player.

올라타다 [탈것에 몸을 올려놓기] get into [on]; embark on [in] (a ship); step in to (a boat); mount [ride] (a horse); board (a train); go [come / get] on board [aboard (of)] (a ship). ¶말에 ~ sit astride a horse // 버스가 오자 몸을 날려 올라탔다 The bus came in and he swung into it. **2** [몸 위에 오르다] cover; line; tread (수탉이).

올려놓다 put (something) (up)on (a place / something). ¶손을 탁자 위에 ~ rest one's hands on a table / 그는 꾸러미를 선반 위에 올려놓았다 He put the package on the shelf.

올려다보다 look up (at); (시선을 들어서) raise one's eye toward; (고개를 들고) turn one's face up toward. ¶아이들은 어머니를 올려다보았다 The children looked up at [turned their face up toward] their mother.

올록볼록하다 uneven; rugged.

올리고세 -(世) [지] the Oligocene age.
올리다 1 [위로 오르게 하다] raise; lift (up); upraise; elevate; fly; put [get] up; hold up. ¶ 깃발을 ~ fly [hoist] a flag / 돌을 자기 머리 위로 들어 ~ raise a rock above one's head // 죄송합니다만 이 가방을 선반 위에 좀 올려 주십시오 Would you please put this suitcase up on the rack? // 그는 모자를 약간 들어 올려 부인에게 인사했다 He raised his hat a little to the lady. // 그는 간신히 100킬로의 바벨을 들어 올렸다 He finally lifted the 100-kilogram barbell.
2 [계급·등급·지위를 높이다] raise; promote. ¶계급을 ~ raise (a person's) rank / promote (a person) to a higher rank [grade].
3 [증가시키다] increase; [인상하다] raise; (구어) hike; (구어) boost. ¶봉급을 ~ increase a person's salary // 집세를 ~ raise the rent // 월급을 5퍼센트 ~ raise a person's salary by five percent // 노동조합은 봉급을 10퍼센트 올려 줄 것을 요구했다 The labor union demanded that wages be raised [increased] by 10 percent.
4 [성과를 얻다] achieve (good results); obtain; gain. ¶그들은 그 토지에서 100만 원의 수입을 올리게 될 것이다 There will be [They will make] a profit of one million won on the land. // 임대 가옥에서 집세로 나는 30만 원의 수입을 올린다 I have an income of 300,000 won from the houses I rent [(영) let]. / 우리는 그 밭에서 200만 원의 수익을 올렸다 We made a profit of 2 million won from those fields. // 그들은 훌륭한 성과를 올렸다 They obtained excellent results. / They did very well.
5 [바치다] give; offer; present. ¶잔을 ~ offer a cup (to one's senior) / "안녕히 주무셨습니까?" 하고 인사를 ~ greet (to one's senior) with a "Good morning" // 송 선생님께, 지은이 올림 To Mr. Song with the compliments of the author.
6 [차리다] serve; prepare. ¶상에 ~ serve [set] (a dish) on the table.
7 [상정·제출하다] bring up; present. ¶무대에 ~ put (a play) on the stage / stage (a play) / present [produce] (a play) // 우리는 다음 회의에 올릴 안건을 준비했다 We prepared a plan to submit at the next month's bill.
8 [기록하다] enter (a name); put (something) on record. ¶내달 청구서에 ~ put (the item) on next month's bill // 장부에 ~ enter (an item) in an account book // 나는 그것이 의사록에 올려지기를 바란다 I want it to be put in the minutes. // 이것은 기록에 올리지 않는다 This will be off the record.
9 [식을 거행하다] hold; observe; solemnize. ¶미사를 ~ read [say] Mass / 결혼식을 ~ hold a wedding ceremony / solemnize a marriage / 우리는 결혼식을 10월에 올릴 예정입니다 We plan to have [hold] our wedding (ceremony) in October.
10 [입히다] coat; [도금하다] plate; gild (금을). ¶구리에 주석을 ~ plate [wash] a ring with gold.
11 [기와 등을 이다] cover; roof. ¶기와를 올린 집 a tile-roofed house // 지붕에 기와를 ~ roof a house with tile / tile the roof of a house.
12 (기타). ¶약을 ~ grate on (a person's)

올리브 [식] an olive; an olive tree.
● **올리브색** olive (color). **올리브유** olive oil.
올림표 (—標) [음] a sharp(기호 #). ¶~를 붙이다 sharp.
올림피아드 the Olympiad.
올림픽 the Olympics; the Olympic Games. ¶국제 기능 ~ the International Vocational Training Competition/국제 장애자 ~ the International Paraplegics Olympic Games / Paralympics // 동계 ~ the Olympic Winter Games / the Winter Olympic Games / the Winter Olympics // 서울 ~ the Seoul Olympic [Olympic Games] // 프레~ the Pre-Olympics / the Pre-Olympics // 국제 ~ 위원회 the International Olympic Committee(약어 IOC) // 대한 ~ 위원회 the Korea Olympic Committee(약어 KOC).
● **올림픽 경기장** the Olympic stadium. **올림픽 마크** Olympic symbol. **올림픽 선수촌** an Olympic village. **올림픽 성화** the Olympic Flame; (릴레이의) the Olympic Torch. **올림픽 조직 위원회** the Olympic Organizing Committee(약어 O.O.C.).
올망 (—網) a deep-sea fishing net.
올망졸망 in lots of small units[pieces/lumps]; in a lovely huddle; in clusters. ¶진열창에는 인형들이 ~ 진열되어 있다 There are a lot of small dolls placed on display in the show window. // 산기슭에 집들이 ~ 모여 있다 There are little clusters of houses at the foot of a hill. **올망졸망하다** (서술적) be of various small sizes; come in lots of small units. ¶올망졸망한 아이들 a number of little children of uneven stature.
올무 a snare; a trap. ⇨ "올가미1
올바로 [진실되게] truthfully; [정직하게] honestly; uprightly; straight-forwardly; [합법적으로] lawfully; legally; [건전하게] soundly; [도덕적으로] morally. ¶~ 사는 사람 a righteous[an upright] man / a just[an honest] man // ~ 말하다 speak straight out // ~ 살다 lead an honest life / live straight // ~ 행동하다 behave properly[correctly] // 마음을 ~ 먹어라 Be a good man. // 그는 ~ 살아가고 있다 He is now living an honest life[honestly].
올바르다 [정당하다] right; [정의롭다] just; righteous; [잘못이 없다] correct; [정확하다] exact; accurate; [적절하다] proper; [합법적이다] lawful; legitimate; legal. ¶올바른 행위 right conduct // 그 문제에 대한 올바른 대답 the correct[right] answer to the question // 올바른 인간이 되다 reform oneself / become a new man // 올바른 일을 하다 do right / do the right thing // 그는 올바른 인간이 될 가망이 없다 He is incorrigible. / There's no hope of his ever becoming a respectable member of society. // 그는 돈을 올바르게 쓸 줄을 모른다 He does not know how to use money properly.
올밤 [일찍 익는 밤] an early(-ripening) variety of chestnut; early chestnuts.
올벼 [일찍 익는 벼] an early-ripening variety of rice plant; an early rice.
올빼미 [동] an owl. ¶~의 울음소리에 잠이 깼다 The hoot of an owl awoke me.
올새 (천의) texture; weave. ¶~가 거친[촘촘한] 천 cloth of loose[close] texture / cloth with a loose[close] weave / coarse-[close-]woven cloth // 이 스웨터는 ~가 촘촘하다 This sweater has fine weave.

올차다 1 [야무지고 기운차다] tough; firm; solid; vigorous; energetic. ¶올찬 사람 a tough guy / a man of steady[firm] character // 그 아이는 나이에 비해 ~ The boy is wise beyond years. 2 [곡식의 알이 일찍 들다] early-ripening. ¶올찬 벼이삭 an early-ripening ear of rice plant.
올챙이 a tadpole; (미) a polliwog.
● **올챙이배** a potbelly; a protruding belly.
올케 the wife of a girl's brother; a girl's sister-in-law.
올해 this year; the current[present] year. ¶~ 안에 in (the) course of this year / before the end of this year // ~는 윤년이다 This is a leap year. // 그 책은 ~ 안에 발행된다 The book will be published before the end of this year. // ~는 풍년이다 This is a bumper year. // ~도 며칠 남지 않았다 We have only a few days left before the end of the year.
옭걸다 [옭아서 걸다] fasten with a noose; hitch.
옭다 1 [잡아매다] tie (up); bind. ¶상자를 새끼로 ~ tie up a box with rope // 강도를 ~ truss a burglar up // 단단히 ~ tie firmly [tightly] / tie up (a luggage). 2 [올가미를 씌워 훔치다] secure by a noose; put a noose around; noose. ¶새끼로 개의 목을 ~ noose a rope round the neck of a dog. 3 [꾀로 걸려들게 하다] entrap; set a trap (for). ¶사람을 ~ entrap a person // 그는 기회 있을 때마다 나를 옭아 넣으려고 한다 He never lost an opportunity to set a trap for me.
옭매다 1 tie (a rope) in a square[reef] knot. ¶구두끈을 ~ reef-knot one's shoestrings. 2 cast[put] a noose round (the neck) and tie (to); make a false charge against (a person). ⇨ "옭아매다
옭매듭 a square[reef] knot.
옭아매다 1 [올가미로 잡아매다] cast[put] a noose round (the neck) and tie (to); (단단히) tie up (a package). ¶미친 개를 기둥에 ~ put the noose on a mad dog and leash[tie] it to a post. 2 [없는 죄를 꾸며 씌우다] make a false charge against (a person); charge (the guilt) on (a person) falsely; (구어) frame (a person). ¶그들은 그를 간첩으로 옭아맸다 They made a false charge of espionage against him.
옭히다 1 [잡아매이다] be tied (up); be bound [fastened]. 2 [올가미에 걸리다] be secured by a noose; be noosed; get roped; have the noose on; be caught in a snare. ¶산돼지가 옭혔다 A wild boar was caught in a snare. 3 [얽히다] be entangled; entangle; tangle. ¶옭힌 실을 풀다 untie entangled knots / unravel a thread. 4 [걸려들다] be ensnared [snared / entrapped]; be[get] entangled (in an affair).
옮기다 1 [자리를 다른 곳으로 바꾸다] move; remove; shift; transfer. ¶가구를 이 방에서 저 방으로 ~ shift furniture from one room to another // 책을 책상에서 선반으로 ~ transfer a book from a table to a shelf // 짐을 한 손에서 다른 손으로 ~ shift a bundle from one hand to the other // 책상을 한가운데로 ~ move the table to the center // 그녀는 가구의 위치를 여기저기로 옮겼다 She shifted the furniture around. // 나는 의자를 난로 가까이

로 옮겼다 I moved my chair nearer to the heater.∥주전자의 물을 보온병에 옮겼다 I emptied[poured] the (hot) water of the kettle into the vacuum flask.
2 [말·소문 등을 전하다] tell (at second hand); pass (words) on (to another). ¶소문을 ~ spread a rumor∥이 말은 절대로 남에게 옮기지 마라 Be sure to keep it all to yourself.
3 [숙소·소속 등을 바꾸다] move; remove; shift; transfer. ¶하숙을 ~ shift one's lodgings∥본사를 서울에서 부산으로 ~ transfer the head office from Seoul to Busan∥집을 인천으로 ~ remove one's residence to Incheon∥본적을 부산에서 서울로 ~ transfer one's legal domicile from Busan to Seoul∥그는 지방 학교에서 도시의 더 큰 학교로 옮겼다 He has transferred from the local school to the vaster one in the city.∥다음 학기에는 물리반에서 화학반으로 옮길 작정이다 Next semester I intend to transfer from physics to chemistry.∥우리는 최근에 거처를 옮겼다 We have just moved recently.∥그는 부산 지점으로 옮겼다 He was transferred to the branch office in Busan.
4 [병을 전염시키다] infect (a person with disease)(▶ 의학 용어로도 쓰임); give[pass / communicate] (a disease to another). ¶아기한테 감기를 옮기지 않도록 주의해라 Be careful not to infect the baby with your cold. / Be careful not to pass your cold on to the baby.∥공공장소에서 침을 뱉으면 병을 옮기게 될지도 모른다 Spitting in public places may lead to the communication of disease.∥네가 나한테 감기를 옮긴 것 같다 You seem to have given me your cold. / You seem to have infect me with your cold.
5 [돌리다] turn; divert; direct (to). ¶그는 내게서 시선을 옮겼다 He turned his eyes [glance] (away) from me.∥그들은 논의를 인구 문제로 옮겼다 They turned their discussion to the population problem.∥이야기는 이 화제에서 저 화제로 옮겨졌다 The conversation drifted from one topic to another.
6 [실천하다] carry out; execute; put (into); translate (into). ¶계획을 실행에 ~ put a plan into effect[practice]∥지식을 행동으로 ~ translate knowledge into action∥그 계획을 당장 행동으로 옮기자 Let's carry out [execute] the plan.
7 [번역하다] translate (into); put (into). ¶어떤 구를 프랑스 어로 ~ put a phrase into French∥이 책은 유명한 프랑스의 소설을 영어로 옮긴 것이다 This book is an English translation[version] of a famous French novel.∥다음 우리말을 영어로 옮겨라 Put [Translate] the following Korean in English.

옮다 **1** [이전하다] move[remove / shift / transfer] (to / into). **2** [병·버릇·사상 등이 전염되다] be infected (with); catch; take; contract (a bad cold). ¶이 병은 옮기 쉽다 This disease is contagious[catching / infectious]. (▶ infectious는 간접 전염, contagious는 직접 전염)∥아버지의 버릇이 내게도 옮았다 I got[picked up] the habit from my father. **3** [불·길이 번지다]. ¶불이 이웃집에 옮았다 The fire spread to the house next door. / The neighboring house caught fire, too. **4** [물들다]. ¶포장지의 색깔이 상자에 옮았다 The color of the wrapping paper rubbed off onto the box.

옮아가다 **1** [이전·이동하다] move[remove / shift / transfer] (to / into). ¶그들은 시골[새집]로 옮아갔다 They moved to[into] the country[a new house].∥그는 신민당에서 자유당으로 옮아갔다 He switched from the New Democratic Party to Liberal Party. **2** [퍼져 가다] spread (from one to another / to / into). ¶홍역이 이웃 마을로 옮아갔다 Measles spread to a neighboring village. **3** [다른 데로 미치다] pass (into / to); fall (to); turn (to). ¶화제가 사회 문제 쪽으로 옮아갔다 The conversation shifted to social problems.∥다음으로 우리의 화제는 야구로 옮아갔다 Then our talk turned to baseball.

옮아오다 **1** [전입하다] move in[into]; transfer (to this place). ¶부산에서 서울로 ~ move up to Seoul from Busan∥그가 지점에서 본점으로 옮아온다는 소문이다 Rumor has it that he will be transferred from the branch office to the head office here. **2** [퍼져 오다] spread (to this place / into Seoul here).

옳다[1] **1** [정의롭다] just; righteous; [정당하다] right; [합법적이다] lawful; legitimate; legal. ¶옳은 길 the right path[track] / the path of righteousness[virtue]∥옳은 말 a reasonable remark / an honest speech / the truth∥옳은 행위 right conduct∥옳은 말만 하는 사람 a person who always makes reasonable remarks∥옳은 길을 가다 tread the path of righteousness[virtue]∥옳은 길로 이끌다 guide (a person) into the right path / set (a person) on the right track∥옳은 일을 하다 do right / do the right thing∥어느 편이 옳은지 조사하다 find out on which side the right lies∥옳지 않은 짓을 하다 do wrong / commit an injustice∥그의 방법은 옳지 않다 He does not do it the right way.∥그는 옳지 않은 방법으로 이득을 보았다 He made profits by dishonest[unlawful] means.∥그들은 옳은 일을 위해 싸웠다 They fought in the cause of justice.∥그는 옳은 것은 옳다고 하고 그른 것은 그르다고 한다 He calls what is right right, and wrong wrong. / (구어) He calls a spade a spade.
2 [맞다] right; correct; proper; [정확하다] exact; accurate. ¶문제의 옳은 해답 the correct[right] answer to a question∥옳은 정보 correct[accurate] information∥수학 문제를 옳게 풀다 solve a problem in mathematics correctly[rightly]∥"이 해답은 옳습니까?" "아니오, 틀렸습니다." "Is this answer correct [right]?" "No, it's incorrect[wrong]."∥네 말이 전적으로 ~ You are perfectly right.∥네 판단이 ~ You are right in your judgment.∥내 추측이 옳았다 I guessed right.(▶ 이 right 는 부사)

옳다[2] Right!; All right!; OK!; Good! ¶~, 됐다 I've got it! / I am sure of my game! / I have got it in my power!∥~, 알았다 Eureka!

옳소 (미) Right on!; (영) Hear! Hear!
옳지 Right!; All right! ⇨옳다[2]
옴[1] [전염성 피부병; [의] scabies; (단수 취급); (동물의) mange. ¶~에 걸린 itchy / scabby∥그는 ~이 옮았다 He has[suffers from] scabies[the itch]. **2** [젖꼭지에 좁쌀처럼 돋은 것] a granular process on the papillary areola of a nursing mother.
옴[2] [전] an ohm(기호 Ω).
옴니버스 (an) omnibus.

●옴니버스 영화 an omnibus movie.
옴벌레 an itch mite.
옴실거리다 squirm; wriggle (about); swarm. ¶쓰레기통에 구더기가 옴실거리고 있었다 The garbage can was crawling [alive] with maggots.// 화분 밑에 지렁이가 옴실거리고 있었다 A lot of earthworms were wriggling under the flowerpot.
옴싹달싹 →옴짝달싹
옴씰하다 flinch (from). ⇨〈옴씰하다
옴의 법칙(一法則) Ohm's law.
옴질거리다 1 〔주저하다〕 hesitate; scruple (at); be hesitant [irresolute]; waver. ¶그가 모두가 떠난 다음에도 계속 옴질거리고 있었다 He lingered about after everyone else had left.// 옴질거리지 말고 털어놓으 Out with it! Never stand shilly-shallying. **2** squirm; wriggle (about); swarm. **3** 〔오물거리다〕 mumble. ¶그 노인은 단단한 건빵을 옴질거렸다 The old man mumbled hardtack.
옴질옴질 1 〔머뭇머뭇〕 hesitatingly; hesitantly; irresolutely. **옴질옴질하다** hesitate. ⇨〈옴질거리다1 ¶부탁하기 어려워 ~ be hesitating to ask a favor. **2** 〔옴실옴실〕 wrigglingly; squirmingly; crawling slowly. **옴질옴질하다** squirm. ⇨〈옴질거리다2 **3** 〔오물오물〕 mumblingly. ¶빵 껍질을 ~ 먹다 mumble on a crust. **옴질옴질하다** mumble. ⇨〈옴질거리다3
옴짝달싹 with a very slight [the slightest] move; budging slightly.
옴쭉 ¶~ 않다 do not move [budge / stir] (an inch) / stand as firm as a rock // 이 문은 아무리 밀어도 ~도 하지 않는다 No matter how I shoved, the door wouldn't budge an inch. // 나는 초만원인 버스 안에서 ~도 할 수가 없었다 I could not even move in the overcrowded bus. // 그는 아무리 욕을 먹었어도 ~도 하지 않았다 He remained calm [unmoved] in spite of abuse heaped on him.
옴쭉 못하다 cannot move at all; cannot stir [move / budge] an inch. ¶아내에게 옴쭉 못하는 남편 a henpecked husband // 옴쭉 못하게 하다 put (a person) into a strait jacket // 우리는 심한 눈보라 때문에 3일 동안 여기서 옴쭉 못하고 있다 We have been stuck here for three days by a heavy snowstorm. // 차량의 홍수로 옴쭉 못하게 되었다 We got tied up in traffic. // 그녀는 남편을 옴쭉 못하게 쥐고 흔든다 She dominates [henpecks] her husband. / She's got her husband under her thumb [firmly in control].
옴쭉달싹 →옴짝달싹
옴찔 with a flinch. ⇨〈옴찔
옴츠러들다 curl [huddle] oneself up; shrink (back). ⇨〈움츠러들다
옴츠리다 curl [huddle] oneself up. ⇨〈움츠리다
옴큼 a handful (of rice). ⇨〈움큼
옴파다 〔속을 오목하게 파다〕 scoop [gouge] out; hollow out; excavate. ¶통나무를 ~ hollow out a log.
옴팡눈 sunken [deep-set / retreating] eyes.
●**옴팡눈이** a person with sunken [deep-set] eyes; a hollow-eyed person.
옴패다 be hollowed [scooped / gouged] out; get excavated; 〔오목해지다〕 become hollow [depressed]; get sunken; sink.
옴폭 to a hollow. ⇨〈움폭
옴폭옴폭 in hollows. ⇨〈움폭움폭
옵서버 an observer; 〔집합적〕 an observer delegation. ¶~로서 참석하다 attend (a conference) as an observer [in the capacity of observer].
옵티미스트 〔낙천가〕 an optimist.
옵티미즘 〔낙천주의〕 optimism.
옷 〔의복〕 clothes(▶ 항상 복수형. 단, 수사와 함께 쓰지 않음); 〔집합적〕 clothing; a garment; 〔문어〕 dress(▶ 의류 전체의 뜻으로 관사 없이 쓰는 것은 예스러운 용법); (무대·가장용) costume; (주로 여성의 아이의) a dress; (한 벌의) a suit. ¶겉~ outer garments // 속~ underwear // ~ 한 벌 a suit of clothes // 헌 ~ worn [used] clothes // 한 번도 입지 않은 새 ~ brand-[bran-]new clothes // ~을 안 입고 naked / nude / stripped / unclothed // ~을 입다 put on one's clothes // ~을 벗다 take one's clothes off // 좋은 ~을 입고 be well dressed // ~이 많다 have a large wardrobe // 똑같은 ~을 입고 있다 be uniformly dressed // 아이의 ~을 벗겨 주다 help a child off with his clothes // 남의 ~을 벗기다 strip (a person) of his clothes // ~을 개다 fold one's clothes // ~을 걸치다 fling one's clothes on // ~을 입으[벗으]시오 Put on [Take off] your clothes. // 그녀는 흰~을 입고 있었다 She was dressed in white. / She was wearing a white dress. // ~을 갈아입을 때까지 기다려 주시오 Please wait I change (my clothes). // 그에겐 이 감색 ~이 잘 어울린다 This navy blue suit becomes him. // 그녀는 ~에 대하여 매우 까다롭다 She is very fussy [particular] about her clothes. // 그녀는 ~을 유별나지 않게 잘 입고 다닌다 She dresses well in an inconspicuous way. // 난 ~에는 관심이 없다 I don't care how I dress. // 나는 입고 갈 ~이 없다 I have nothing to go in. // 아이가 자라서 ~을 못 입게 되었다 The boy has outgrown [grown out of] his clothes.
옷이 날개라(속담) Fine clothes make [The tailor makes] the man.; Fine feathers make fine birds.
●**옷 가게** a clothing store [(영) shop]; a clothier's shop.
옷가슴 the breast; (셔츠의) the plastron. ¶~을 여미다 tidy oneself.
옷가지 〔몇 가지의 옷〕 several articles of clothing; garments. ¶~를 장만하다 provide oneself with necessary garments.
옷감 〔천〕 cloth; (재료로서) material; texture(직물). ¶바탕이 거친 [부드러운] ~ coarse [soft] cloth // 신사복 ~ suit material // ~의 견본 sample cloth / 《미》 a swatch // ~을 마르다 cut (out) cloth // ~의 바탕이 곱다[거칠다] be of fine [coarse] texture // ~이 2미터 듭니다 We need two meters of the cloth. // "이 양복의 ~은 무엇입니까?" "모(毛)입니다." "What material is this dress?" "It is wool."
옷거리 the appearance of one's clothes. ¶그는 ~가 좋다 He looks good in any type of clothes.
옷걸이 1 (삼각형의) a (clothes / coat) hanger. ¶양복을 ~에 걸다 hang a dress on a hanger. **2** (스탠드형의) a clothes tree; a coatrack.
옷고름 a breast-tie [breast ribbon] (of a Korean coat); a coat string. ¶~을 매다 [풀다] fasten [loosen] breast-ties / tie [untie] one's coat.
옷기장 the length of one's clothes; one's dress length. ¶이 치마는 ~이 좀 길다[짧다]

This skirt is a little too long [short] for me.
옷깃 〔한복의 동정〕 a neckband; 〔양복·와이셔츠의〕 a collar; 〔신사복의〕 a lapel. ¶~을 세우다 turn[pull] up the collar.
옷깃을 여미다 be awe-struck; be filled with awe. ¶그 초상화는 사람들로 하여금 옷깃을 여미게 한다 The portrait will inspire you with a feeling of reverence[awe]. // 불상 앞에 서면 옷깃을 여미게 된다 We feel awe-struck in front of a Buddhist image.
옷단 〔옷의 가장자리를 접은 것〕 (미) cuff; (영) a turnup; 〔옷의 가장자리를 감친 것〕 a hem. ¶~을 감치다 hem / overcast // 바지의 ~을 접다 turn up the hem of one's trousers.
옷맵시 the appearance of one's clothes. ¶~가 좋다[좋지 않다] wear one's clothes stylishly [badly / poorly] / dress oneself in good [bad] shape // 그녀는 ~를 내고 나타났다 She came all dressed up.
옷보(-褓) a wrapping cloth [kerchief] for clothes.
옷섶 a gusset; a gore.
옷소매 the sleeve [arm] of a coat. ¶~를 걷다 roll [turn] up one's sleeves // ~를 잡아당겨 남을 제지하다 hold (a person) by the sleeve.
옷솔 a clothesbrush. ¶~로 바지의 먼지를 떨다 brush the dust off one's trousers.
옷자락 〔허리 아랫부분〕 a skirt; 〔끝 부분〕 a hem; 〔길게 늘어진 치맛자락〕 the train; 〔양복 바지의〕 the bottom. ¶~을 들다 take the hem up // ~을 내리다 let the hem down // 그녀는 하얀 웨딩드레스의 ~을 질질 끌며 걸었다 Her white wedding dress trailed along the floor as she walked.
옷장(-欌) a clothes chest; a wardrobe.
옷차림 〔복장〕 clothing; dress; (문어) attire; 〔풍채〕 appearance. ¶~이 좋은[나쁜] 여자 a well-[poorly-]dressed woman // 화려한 ~을 한 여자 (경멸) a woman dressed to the teeth / a woman (who is) dressed up fit to kill // 화려한 ~을 하고 있다 be gaily dressed / be all[fully] decked out / be all dressed up // 훌륭한[초라한] ~을 하고 있다 be splendidly[shabbily] dressed // ~에 무관심하다 be careless about [indifferent to] one's dress [personal appearance] // 그는 ~이 언제나 단정하다 He always looks neat and tidy. // 그녀는 벌써 여름 ~을 하고 있었다 She was already wearing summer clothing. // 그녀는 수수한 ~을 좋아한다 She likes to be quietly dressed.
옷치레 dressing-up; rich attire. ¶~를 좋아하는 사람 a lover of finery // 그녀는 무척 ~를 좋아한다 She has a weakness for fine clothing. **옷치레하다** dress up; wear fine clothes.
옹(翁) 1 〔노인〕 an old [aged] man. 2 〔노인의 이름 밑에 붙이는 경칭〕 old Mr. …. ¶최 ~ the revered old Mr. Choe.
옹고집(壅固執) obstinacy; stubbornness; perversity; obduracy. ¶~을 부리다 be obstinate / be stiff-necked / do not give in // ~ 부리지 말게 Don't be so stubborn. // 그는 반대하면 반대할수록 ~을 부린다 If you oppose him, he becomes more and more obstinate.
● **옹고집쟁이** a person as stubborn as mule.
옹골지다 〔알차다〕 substantial; solid; meaty. ¶옹골지게 익은 보리 well-ripened [-filled] barley crop.
옹골차다 strong and firm; sturdy; tough. ¶옹골찬 몸 a solidly built body // 그는 옹골찬 사람이었다 The man was strong and firm. / He was a sturdy man.
옹글다 flawless; unbroken; unimpaired; intact; sound; perfect; whole. ¶옹근 재목 clean lumber [timber].
옹기(甕器) pottery with a dark brown glaze.
● **옹기장이** a pottery dealer. **옹기장이** a potter. **옹기전** a pottery shop.
옹기종기 in a knot; in a body group. ¶아이들은 ~ 텔레비전 앞에 앉아 있었다 Boys sat in a group [all bunched up] before the TV.
옹달샘 a small fountain [spring].
옹립하다(擁立-) 〔임금의 자리에 모시다〕 help (a young prince) to the throne. ¶그들은 어린 군주를 옹립했다 They supported [backed up] their young lord.
옹벽(擁壁) 〔건〕 a breast [retaining] wall; a revetment.
옹색하다(壅塞-) 1 〔군색하다〕 straitened; needy; reduced. ¶살림이 ~ be in needy [narrow / straitened] circumstances / be badly off // 돈에 ~ be pinched [pressed] for money / be hard up for money / be in straits // 저 집은 요즈음 생활이 옹색해졌다 That family has fallen on hard times. 2 〔비좁다〕 narrow and close; cramped; incommodious; (구어) poky. ¶식구가 늘어서 집이 옹색해졌다 Our family has outgrown our house. // 이 집은 4인 가족이 살기에는 좀 ~ This house is a little too small for a family of four live in. 3 〔옹졸하다〕 narrow [small]-minded; ungenerous; mean.
옹스트롬 〔물〕 〔단파장의 측정 단위〕 an angstrom unit (기호 Å).
옹알거리다 mutter. ⇨ 웅얼거리다
옹알옹알 mutteringly. ⇨ 웅얼웅얼
옹위(擁衛) guard; bodyguard; safeguard; escort. **옹위하다** guard; escort; (군대·군함이) convoy.
옹이 a knot; a knob; a knar; a gnarl; a knurl. ¶~가 있는 knarry / gnarled / knotty // ~가 많은 나무 knotty wood // ~가 많아 울퉁불퉁한 참나무 a gnarled oak.
옹졸하다(壅拙-) narrow-minded; illiberal; intolerant; ungenerous; hidebound; mean. ¶옹졸한 사람 a narrow-minded person // 생각이 ~ have a narrow(-minded) view (of).
옹주(翁主)· a daughter of a king's concubine; a princess by a concubine.
옹크리다 crouch (down). ⇨ 웅크리다
옹호(擁護) 〔보호〕 protection; defense; 〔변호〕 vindication; 〔원조·지지〕 support; assistance. ¶인권 ~ the protection of human rights [civil liberties]. **옹호하다** protect; safeguard; defend; stand by; support. ¶헌법을 ~ support the constitution // 그는 내 의견 [주장]을 옹호해 었다 He defended my opinion [claim]. // 그들은 소수파를 옹호했다 They stood by the minority. // 나를 옹호해 주는 사람은 아무도 없다 I've no one to speak up for me.
● **옹호자** a defender; a champion; a supporter.
옻 1 〔옻나무 진〕 lacquer; varnish; japan. 2 〔옻나무 진에 의한 피부병〕 lacquer poisoning. ¶~이 오르다 break out with lacquer poisoning / be poisoned by lacquer.
옻칠(-漆) 〔옻나무의 진〕 lacquer; japan; 〔옻칠하기〕 lacquering. **옻칠하다** lacquer (with japan); japan; varnish [cover] (with lac-

와 quer). ¶옻칠한 그릇 lacquer[japan] ware∥옻칠한 옷장 a japan cabinet.

와[1] 1 [기쁨의 환성] Hurrah!; [야] (미) Gee!; [놀람·감탄의 소리] Wow! ¶~, 우리가 이겼다 Hurray[Hurrah]! We've won.∥"이번 일요일에 서울 공원으로 놀러 가자." "~, 신 난다." "How about going to the Seoul Park next Sunday?" "Gee! That's nice! 2 [한목에 움직이거나 떠드는 모양] with a rush; loudly. ¶~ 밀려가다 advance with a rush∥~ 하고 큰 환성이 났다 A loud cheer[hurrah] went up.

와[2] 1 [열거] and. ¶너 ~ 나 you and I∥아버지 ~ 아들 father and son∥나는 사과 ~ 귤을 샀다 I bought apples and oranges.∥나는 영어 ~ 국어를 좋아한다 I like (both) English and Korean.(▶ 특히 양쪽을 강조할 때는 both ... and ...을 쓴다)∥나는 아침 식사로 토스트 ~ 커피 ~ 달걀 한 개 ~ 과일을 먹는다 I have [eat] toast, coffee, an egg(,) and fruit for breakfast.(▶ 3개 이상을 열거할 때는 마지막 명사 앞에 and를 넣고(넣지 않을 때도 있음), and 앞의 콤마는 있어도 되고 없어도 됨)
2 [함께] with; along[together] with; in company with; accompanied by. ¶친구~ 놀다 play with one's friends∥아버지~ 같이 가다 go with one's father / accompany one's father.
3 [대항] against; with. ¶친구~ 다투다 quarrel with one's friend∥추위 ~ 싸우다 struggle against the cold.
4 [합치·협력] with. ¶친구~ 협력하다 cooperate[collaborate] with one's friend.
5 [접촉] with. ¶본부~ 연락을 취하면서 행동하다 act in concert[conjunction] with the headquarters∥우연히 옛 친구~ 만났다 I happened to meet an old friend of mine.
6 [분리] with; from. ¶친구~ 헤어지다 part with[from] one's friend / [절교하다] break with[off from] one's friend.
7 [관계] with. ¶나는 그~ 거래가 있다 I have business relations[have dealings] with him.
8 [비교] with. ¶A~ B를 비교하다 compare A with B / set A against B∥나는 그~는 비교도 안 된다 I am no match for him.
9 [유사] as; like; (similar) to; [상이] (different) from. ¶어머니~ 같은 애정 motherly love / affection like a mother's∥여느 때~ 같이 as usual / as is usual (with a person) / as is one's wont∥이~는 달리 different from / in contrast with this.
10 [혼합] with. ¶우유 ~ 물을 섞다 mix water with milk / add water to milk / dilute milk with water.

와각거리다 clatter; rattle.
와그르르 with a crash; crashing; boiling up.
⇨와르르1·2·3
와글거리다 1 [북적이다] throng; crowd; swarm. ¶거리에는 사람들이 와글거렸다 The street was crowded[thronged] with people.∥그 행락지는 휴가를 즐기는 사람들로 와글거렸다 The tourist spot was overrun with the throngs of holiday makers. / Crowds of vacationers thronged the tourist spot. 2 [떠들다] make a noise; raise a clamor; be boisterous[clamorous]; clamor. ¶와글거려서 연설이 들리지 않는다 It is too noisy to hear the speech.∥선생님이 안 계셔서 교실 안이 와글거렸다 The classroom was noisy[in a commotion] because the teacher was away.
와글와글 [북적북적] in swarms[crowds / throngs]; [시끄럽게] noisily; clamorously; boisterously. ¶~ 떠들다 make a boisterous noise. 와글와글하다 throng; make a noise. ⇨"와글거리다 ¶회당 안은 와글와글하였다 There was a hum of voices in the audience.
와니스 →바니시
와닥닥 [급히] hurriedly; hastily; in a hurry. ¶그는 방에서 ~ 뛰쳐나갔다 He hurried [walked hastily] out of the room. / He rushed hurry-scurry[helter-skelter] out of the room.
와당탕 with a thump[bump]; [요란하게] boisterously; clamorously; noisily. ¶복도를 ~ 뛰어가다 run through a passage with clattering noise∥그는 계단을 ~ 내려갔다 He went bump down the stairs. 와당탕하다 make a thumping[bumping] sound; make a noise. ¶2층에서 와당탕하다가 어머니에게 야단 맞았다 We were scolded by mother because we make too much noise upstairs.
와드득 with a crunching sound. ¶호두를 ~ 깨물다 crunch a walnut.
와들와들 tremblingly; shiveringly. ¶~ 떨다 tremble all over[like an aspen leaf] / shiver (like a jelly) / be all of[in] a tremble / be (up) on the tremble∥무서워서 ~ 떨다 tremble[shake] with fear∥추위서 ~ 떨다 shiver with cold / quiver from cold∥나는 무릎이 ~ 떨렸다 My knees knocked together.∥갑자기 기온이 내려가서 우리는 모두 ~ 떨었다 The sudden drop in temperature made us all shiver.
와락 with a sudden jerk[tug]; [갑자기] with a rush[dash]; suddenly; all at once. ¶문의 손잡이를 ~ 돌리다 give a wrench at the doorknob∥남의 목을 ~ 껴안다 fling one's arms round a person's neck∥밧줄을 ~ 잡아 당기다 pull a rope with jerk / jerk[yank / tug] on[at] a rope∥그는 문을 ~ 열었다 He jerked open the door.∥그 개가 그에게 ~ 덤벼들었다 The dog sprang upon him.
와레즈 사이트 [소프트웨어를 무료로 배포하는 불법 사이트] a warez.
와룡(臥龍) a lying dragon; [재야의 큰 인물] a great man in obscurity; a great man with no opportunity to display his talent.
와르르 1 [무너지는 모양이나 소리] in a confused heap; with a crash. ¶~ 무너지다 fell (down)[collapse] with a crash / crash (down / through)∥지붕이 ~ 무너졌다 The roof fell in.∥그의 자신감은 ~ 무너져 내렸다 His self-confidence crumbled to dust. 2 [천둥소리] crashing; rolling; rumbling; thundering. 3 [물이 끓는 소리] boiling up; hubble-bubble. 4 [여럿이 동시에 몰려드는 모양] in crowds; in a rush. ¶사인을 얻으려고 ~ 몰려들다 storm[crowd around] (a person) for autographs∥많은 사람이 ~ 몰려나왔다 Many people came out in a rush.
와병하다(臥病-) be ill in bed; be laid up (with illness); be in one's sickbed; (미) be sick in bed.
와삭 with a rustle; with a rustling sound [noise]. 와삭하다 rustle; give (out) a rustle. ¶옷의 와삭하는 소리 the rustling of clothes.
와삭거리다 rustle; give (out) a rustle. ¶나뭇잎이 바람에 와삭거리고 있었다 The wind is rustling the leaves. / Leaves rustled in the wind.
와스스 [가벼운 물건이 떨어지는 모양] in

showers; thick and fast; with a rustling noise; [가벼운 물건이 무너지는 모양] asunder; to pieces. ¶가을에는 마른 잎이 ~ 떨어진다 In autumn dead leaves fall down in showers [thick and fast]. ¶나무 상자를 들어 올리려고 하자 ~ 부서졌다 When I tried to lift the wooden box, it fell apart.

와신상담(臥薪嘗膽) perseverance; endurance of hardship(s). ¶그는 3년의 ~ 끝에 사법 시험에 합격했다 After persevering for three years, he finally passed the bar examination. **와신상담하다** go through unspeakable hardships and privations. ¶와신상담하기 10년(후) after ten years of hard struggles against fortune.

와언(訛言) **1** [잘못 전해진 말] a false [an incorrect / an erroneous] report; wrong information; an unfounded [a groundless / a wild] rumor; a canard. **2** an [a provincial] accent. ⇨⇒사투리

와이더블유시에이 Y.W.C.A.(▶ Young Women's Christian Association의 약어).

와이드 스크린 [대형 영사막] a wide screen; [화면이 넓은 영화] a wide-screen movie.

와이셔츠(*white shirts) a shirt; a dress shirt(반소매 와이셔츠와 구별할 때). ¶반소매 ~ a short-sleeved shirts // ~ 차림으로 in one's shirt(-sleeves).

와이엠시에이 Y.M.C.A.(▶ Young Men's Christian Association의 약어).

와이퍼 a wiper; (자동차의) (미) a windshield [(영) a windscreen] wiper. ¶차의 ~를 움직이다 turn on the windshield wipers.

와이프 a wife; one's wife.

와인 [포도주] wine.
● **와인글라스** a wineglass.

와인드업 [야구] a windup.

와작와작 with a munching sound. ¶무를 ~ 먹다 munch at [on] a radish.

와전(訛傳) a false report; misinformation. **와전하다** give a false report; misinform.

와중(渦中) a vortex; a whirlpool. ¶싸움의 ~에 휩쓸려 들어가다 be drawn into the vortex of the struggle // 그는 사건의 ~에 말려들었다 He got dragged into [involved in] the incident [case]. // 나는 그들의 집안 싸움의 ~에 말려들었다 I got caught up in their family quarrel.

와지끈 with a crash [smash]; crash; smash. ¶~ 부수다 smash (up) (furniture) // 나뭇가지를 ~ 꺾다 break a twig with a snap // (밖에서) 문을 ~ 부수다 smash a door in // 돌이 유리창을 ~ 깨고 날아 들어왔다 A stone came crash through the window. **와지끈하다** crash; smash; go crash [smash]. ¶부엌에서 와지끈하는 소리가 났다 We heard a smash in the kitchen.

와트 [전] a watt; wattage. ¶60~의 전구 a 60-watt (light) bulb.

와해(瓦解) collapse; a (down)fall; a breakup. ¶정당의 ~ the collapse of a political party. **와해하다** collapse; break up; fall [go / crumble] to pieces; be smashed; be ruined. ➔내각은 조만간에 와해될 것이다 The Cabinet will soon be dissolved.

왁스 wax. ¶마루[스키]에 ~를 바르다 wax the floor [skis].

왁시글거리다 swarm (with); be crowded [thronged] (with); teem (with). ¶특매품 매장에는 사람들이 왁시글거렸다 A press of people seethed at the bargain counter.

왁자그르르 boisterously; uproariously; rowdily; with much noise. **왁자그르르하다** act boisterous [rowdy]; make a lot of noise. ¶왁자그르르한 웃음소리 roars of laughter // 왁자그르르한 모임 an uproarious assembly.

왁자지껄하다 talk boisterously [wildly]; wag one's tongue noisily.

왁자하다 1 [떠들썩하다] be boisterous [clamorous / uproarious / rowdy / tumultuous]. ¶왁자한 교실 an uproarious classroom // 왜 이리 왁자해 What a babel! **2** [소문이 퍼져 요란하다] much-talked-of [-about]; much-discussed; widespread; sensational. ¶세상을 왁자하게 만든 사건 a sensational [much-talked-about] affair.

완강하다(頑強-) tenacious; stubborn; obstinate; dogged; unbending; unyielding. ¶완강한 반대 unrelenting [stiff / stubborn / dogged / tenacious] opposition. **완강히** tenaciously; stubbornly; obstinately. ¶~ 반대하다 offer stiff [stubborn] opposition (to) // ~ 부정하다 deny persistently [obstinately] // 그는 그들의 간청을~ 거부했다 He turned an adamant ear to their entreaties. // 그는 나의 제안에 ~ 반대했다 He strongly opposed [took a strong position against] my proposals. // 적은 ~ 저항했다 The enemy resisted stubbornly [tenaciously].

완결(完結) conclusion; completion; an end. ¶~ [소설의 끝에 쓰는 말] Concluded. / The End. ¶다음 회 ~ To be concluded next time [week / month]. **완결하다** [마치다] conclude; complete; finish; end. ➔¶텔레비전의 연속 드라마가 이번 주 완결되었다 The serial TV drama was concluded [came to an end] this week. // 이 미술 전집은 50권으로 완결된다 This series of art books will be completed with the fiftieth volume. // 그의 마지막 소설은 완결되지 않고 말았다 He left his last novel unfinished.
● **완결 편** the last [concluding] program [episode] of a series.

완고하다(頑固-) stubborn; obstinate(▶ obstinate는 때로 고집스럽게 의견이나 방식을 굽히지 않음을, stubborn은 천성이 완고함을 내포); bigoted; headstrong; [끈질기다] persistent; dogged. ¶몹시 완고한 사람 a person as stubborn as a mule // 완고한 노인 an obstinate [a pigheaded] old man // 그는 지나치게 ~ He is too rigid [strait-laced]. // 그는 ~ 생각이 ~ He is obstinate [stubborn]. **완고히** stubbornly; firmly. ¶그는 ~ 자기의 견해를 고집한다 He sticks stubbornly to his own opinion. // 아무리 물어보아도 그는 ~ 입을 다물고 있었다 I asked him about it many times, but he would never open up. // 그는 ~ 내 청을 거절했다[전혀 들어주지 않았다] He turned a deaf ear [stubbornly refused to listen] to my request. // 그는 자기주장을 양보하기를 ~ 거절했다 He firmly [obstinately] refused to concede his point(▶ obstinately 는 막무가내로).

완곡어법(婉曲語法) [언] euphemism; periphrasis.

완곡하다(婉曲-) euphemistic; periphrastic; circumlocutional; roundabout. ¶완곡한 표현 a roundabout [periphrastic] expression / a euphemism // 「상상력이 풍부한 사람」이라는 것은 「거짓말쟁이」라는 말의 완곡한 표현이다

"An imaginative person" is a euphemism for "a liar". **완곡히** in a roundabout way; by euphemism. ¶~ 주의를 주었으나 그에게는 통하지 않았던 것 같다 He doesn't seem to have understood my indirect warning. ¶나는 불찬성의 뜻을 ~ 전했다 I indicated my disagreement in a roundabout way.

완공(完工) completion (of construction). **완공하다** complete (the construction). ➔¶완공되다 be completed / be finished ¶터널은 다음 달에 완공된다 The tunnel[Work on the tunnel] will be completed next month.

완구(玩具) a toy; a plaything. ⇨*장난감*(⇨*장난*)

● **완구점** a toy shop[(미) store].

완구(緩球) [야구] a slow ball. ⇨*슬로 볼*

완급(緩急) fast and slow motion; high and low speed. ¶당수된 자는 모름지기 정책의 ~을 알아야 한다 A party leader must know when to be lenient and when to be tough.

완납(完納) full payment; payment in full. **완납하다** pay (one's fine) in full; pay the whole amount of (one's tax). ¶나는 세금을 완납했다 I have paid all my taxes. / I have paid my taxes in full. ¶수업료를 완납하지 않은 학생이 있다 Some students have not completed the payment of school fees.

완두(豌豆) a pea; garden pea. ¶~를 **까다** shell peas.

완력(腕力) 1 [팔의 힘·체력] physical[muscular] strength; muscle. ¶~이 센 사람 a man of muscle∥그는 ~이 세다 He is a man of muscle[great strength]. / [팔의 힘이 세다] He has strong arms[a strong pair of arms]. ∥그는 ~에서는 누구에게 진 일이 없다 He never met his match in physical strength.∥ ~으로는 도저히 그를 당할 수가 없다 I am no match for him when it comes to muscle [physical strength]. 2 [폭력] (brute[brutal]) force; violence. ¶그들은 끝내 서로 ~을 휘두르게 되었다 They came to blows eventually.

완료(完了) completion. ¶준비 ~ Our preparations are complete[all set]. / We are quite ready now. **완료하다** [사물을 완성하다] complete; [마치다] finish. ➔¶완료되다 be completed / be finished / reach completion ∥식전의 준비는 완료되었다 The preparations for the ceremony are complete.∥건축 공사는 내일 완료될 예정이다 The construction work is to be completed[finished] tomorrow.∥여행 준비는 완료되었습니까 Are you ready for your journey? / Have you finished all the preparations for your trip?

● **완료 시제** [언] a perfect tense. ¶현재 [과거 / 미래] ~ the present[past / future] perfect tense.

완만하다(緩慢-) [속도가 느리다] slow (-moving[-going]); sluggish; [경사가 급하지 않다] gentle. ¶완만한 비탈길 a gentle slope ¶기복이 완만한 초원 an undulating meadow ∥완만한 플레이 (야구의) sloppy[careless] play∥사건의 완만한 조치 lax[sloppy] handling of a matter. **완만히** slowly; gently; inactively. ¶뜰에 연못 쪽으로 ~ 경사져 있다 The garden slopes gently down to the pond.

완벽(完璧) perfection. ¶~을 **기하다** aim at perfection. **완벽하다** perfect; flawless; impeccable(과실·죄 등이 없는). ¶완벽한 연기 a flawless[faultless] performance∥그는 교사로서 ~ As a teacher he is perfect.∥그녀의 연주는 실로 완벽했다 Her performance was virtually flawless[perfect / beyond criticism].∥연습을 해야 완벽해진다 Practice makes perfect.∥그의 알리바이는 ~ His alibi is perfect.∥그녀는 프랑스 어를 완벽하게 사용한다 She has a perfect command of French. / Her French is perfect.

완본(完本) a complete set of works. ⇨*완질본*

완봉(完封) 1 (항만 등의) complete blockade. **완봉하다** blockade completely. 2 [야구] a shutout. ¶그들은 자이언츠에게 ~ 승했다 They won by shutting out the Giants. **완봉하다** shut out.

완불(完拂) full payment. **완불하다** pay in full; pay up[off]; clear off. ¶자동차의 월부금을 ~ pay up one's installment on the car.

완비(完備) perfection; completion; full equipment. **완비하다** perfect; complete; equip [furnish / provide] completely. ➔¶완비된 (설비가) well-equipped / (아파트 등이) fully-furnished / ¶상하수도가 완비된 집 a house with both water and sewerage service∥이 학교는 급식 설비가 완비되어 있다 This school is completely equipped with catering facilities.∥이 건물은 냉방 시설이 완비되어 있다 This building is air-conditioned.∥시설이 완비된 대학이 반드시 좋은 대학은 아니다 A well-equipped university is not always a good university.

완상(玩賞) appreciation; enjoyment. **완상하다** appreciate; enjoy; savor. ¶추국(秋菊)을 ~ enjoy the autumn chrysanthemum.

완성(完成) completion; perfection; accomplishment; consummation; finish. ¶자기 ~ perfection of self∥신형 기관차가 드디어 ~에 가까워졌다 The new (locomotive) engine has now been nearly perfected. / The new (locomotive) engine has now neared[approached] completion[perfection]. **완성하다** [사람이 일을 마치다] finish; [완전한 것으로 되다] complete(▶ finish는 일상적인 사항에 대해서 씀); accomplish; perfect; bring (a thing) to completion[perfection]; finish up. ¶이 일을 연내에 완성하는 것은 무리이다 We can't complete this job by the end of the year.∥제 3권을 막 완성해 냈다 I've just finished the third volume.∥그는 3년간의 노력 끝에 연구를 완성했다 He completed his research after three years of effort.∥이 교량을 완성하는 데 5년이 걸렸다 It took five years to complete this bridge.∥그는 연내에 그림을 완성하려고 애쓰고 있다 He is endeavoring to finish the painting before the end of the year. ➔¶완성되다 be completed / be finished (off) / come to the finish / be accomplished / be brought to completion[perfection] / come to perfection / be perfected∥그 집은 다음 달에 완성된다 The house will be completed[ready] next month.∥새 청사는 근일 중에 완성된다 The new government office building will be completed in a few days.∥그 일은 내일 완성된다 The work will be finished tomorrow.∥그 공작품은 멋지게 완성되었다 The work turned out beautifully.

● **완성품** finished goods; a finished product.

완수(完遂) completion; accomplishment. **완수하다** accomplish; achieve; complete; carry out[through]; go through (with). ¶목적을 ~ accomplish one's aim[purpose] / attain one's object // 임무를 ~ carry out one's duty / fulfill one's duties // 나는 이 임무를 완수하려고 결심했다 I made up my mind to carry out[carry through / go through with] this task.

완숙하다(完熟-) **1** 〔음식 등을 완전히 익히다〕 boil hard. ¶완숙한 달걀 a hard-boiled egg // 달걀이 완숙했다 The eggs were boiled hard. **2** 〔과일 등이 완전히 익다〕 ripen into full maturity; attain[come to] (full[complete]) maturity. ¶완숙한 과일 a fully ripened fruit.

완승(完勝) a complete victory; a sweeping triumph. ¶~을 거두다 win out and out / have an out-and-out victory. **완승하다** win [score] a complete[total] victory (over one's opponent); make a clean score; (미) (경기에서) shut out.

완역(完譯) a complete translation. **완역하다** make a complete translation (of); translate completely[in full]. ¶그는 「춘향전」을 현대어로 완역했다 He translated the Tale of Chunhyang into modern Korean in its entirety.

완연하다(宛然-) distinct; obvious; clear; vivid. ¶봄이 ~ It has become quite spring-like. **완연히** distinctly; obviously; clearly; vividly. ¶실망한 빛이 그의 얼굴에 ~ 나타났다 His disappointment was obvious.

완자 a fried meatball.

완장(腕章) an armband; a brassard. ¶~을 두르다 wear an armband.

완전(完全) perfection; entirety; completeness; wholeness. ¶~에 가깝다 be nearly perfect // ~을 기하도록 최선을 다하자 Let's do our best, trying perfection. **완전하다** perfect; complete; entire; full; whole. ¶완전한 승리[패배] a complete victory[defeat] // 완전한 실패 an utter failure // 완전한 자유 absolute liberty / perfect liberty // 우리 팀은 완전(무결)한 수비를 자랑하고 있다 Our team is proud of its flawless defense. // 아직도 완전하다고는 할 수 없다 It is far[a long way] from perfect. // 그 불상은 완전한 형태로 남아 있다 That Buddhist image has been preserved intact. **완전히** perfectly; completely; entirely; fully; to perfection; quite; utterly; wholly; thoroughly; in its entirety; to the full; out and out. ¶~ 는 반대이다 quite the opposite[the reverse] // 나는 그의 의견에 ~ 동의할 수는 없다 I cannot wholly agree with him. // 이 시계는 ~ 고장 났다 This watch is completely out of order. // 이 정도의 과제는 ~ 알고 있어야 한다 You must understand lessons at this level completely[perfectly]. // 그는 ~ 잊혀지고 말았다 He was entirely[completely] forgotten. // 그것을 ~ 달성하려면 상당한 시간이 걸린다 It will take a long time to complete it. // 그녀는 그 시를 ~ 암송했다 She recited the poem to perfection.

● **완전 경쟁** [경] perfect competition. **완전 고용** full[perfect] employment. **완전 독점** [경] simple monopoly. **완전 범죄** a perfect crime. **완전 연소** [화] perfect[complete] combustion.

완제(完濟) **1** 〔빚을 완전히 갚음〕 payment in full; full[complete] payment. **완제하다** pay up; pay in full; complete payment of; clear off (one's debts); liquidate. ¶채무를 ~ pay off[clear (off)] one's debts / [법] fully satisfy the obligations / pay up the liabilities // 그는 채권자에게 채무를 완제했다 He settled [squared] with his creditor. **2** completion. ➡☞완료.

완제품(完製品) a finished product; finished goods.

완주하다(完走-) run[cover] the whole course[distance] (of).

완질본(完帙本) a complete set of works; complete works. ¶세익스피어의 ~ a complete [full] set of Shakespeare's works.

완충(緩衝) shock-absorbing; concussion-deadening; buffing. **완충하다** absorb shock; deaden concussion; buff.
● **완충국** a buffer state. **완충 장치** (철도 차량의) a buffer; (자동차 등의) (미) a bumper; (영) a fender; (기계의) a shock absorber. **완충 지대** a buffer[neutral] zone[area] (between two big powers).

완치(完治) (a) complete recovery; a perfect cure. **완치하다** recover completely; cure (a person, a disease, etc.) completely; heal (a person, a wound, etc.) completely. ➡¶완치되다 be completely cured[recovered] / heal completely // 완치될 때까지 한 달 동안 자택 요양을 해야 합니다 You need a month's convalescence at home for complete recovery[to recover completely]. // 그의 다리 부상은 완치 되었다 He has completely recovered from the wound in his leg. / The wound in his leg has healed completely.

완쾌(完快) complete recovery; complete cure. ¶우리는 아버님의 ~를 축하했다 We celebrated our father's recovery from his illness. **완쾌하다** recover (completely) (from one's illness); be completely cured (of a disease); be completely restored to health; get well. ¶그분은 완쾌하셨습니까 Has he recovered completely? // 하루 속히 완쾌하시기를 빕니다 I hope you will get well soon. / I wish you to recover in a short time. / Wishing for your speedy round. / (문어) I hope you will soon be restored to health. // 의사는 어머니께서 틀림없이 완쾌하실 거라고 내게 말했다 The doctor told me he was sure my mother would pull through. ➡그는 아직 몸이 완쾌 되지 않았다 He has not yet completely recovered (from her illness). / He is not yet completely restored to health. / He is not fully recovered. / He is not quite himself. // 그가 완쾌되려면 2주 더 치료를 받아야 합니다 Two more weeks' medical treatment is needed for him to make a complete recovery.

완투하다(完投-) pitch a complete game; go the (whole) distance; hurl [pitch] a whole game[the full nine innings].

완패(完敗) a complete[crushing] defeat; (미국 구어) a whitewash(경기에서의). **완패하다** suffer a complete[crushing] defeat; be crushingly[completely] defeated; (구어) be beaten (all) hollow; (미국 구어) take a shellacking. ¶그는 결승전에서 완패했다 He was defeated soundly[decisively] in the final match.

완하제(緩下劑) [약] a (mild) laxative; an aperient.

완행(緩行) **1** 〔느리게 감〕. **완행하다** go[run] slow. **2** a slow train. ➡☞완행열차(☞완행)
● **완행열차** a slow train; (미) a way train; a local train.

완화(緩和) relaxation; easing; (a) relief; alleviation; mitigation; (특히 국제간의 긴장의) a détente. ¶국제간의 긴장 ~를 목표로 삼다 aim at détente [a relaxation of tension between nations / an easing of strained relations between nations]. **완화하다** relax; ease; relieve; alleviate; lighten; soften; mitigate. ¶수입 제한을 ~ relax[ease] restrictions on imports // 교통난을 ~ ease[relieve] traffic congestion / ease a traffic jam / 규칙을 ~ make the rules less strict / 비평을 ~ tone down one's criticism / (구어) pull one's punches. → 새로운 제안으로 긴장이 어느 정도 완화되었다 The new suggestion helped relieve the strained situation to some extent.
● **완화 정책** an appeasement policy.

왈(曰) 1 [가로되] said; quoth. ¶공자 ~ Confucius[The Master] said (that) … 2 [소위] what is called; so-called. ¶~ 정치가 a so-called politician.

왈가닥 a tomboy; a hoyden; a romp; a kitten; (구어) a filly.

왈가왈부(曰可曰否) (옳다거니 그르다거니 함). ¶세상에서는 그 사람에 대해서 ~ 말이 많다 People are saying all kinds of things [this and that] about him. **왈가왈부하다** argue the rights and wrong (of matter); comment (on); criticize. ¶네가 왈가왈부할 처지가 아니지 않나 You don't have the right to say anything about it. / [관계없다] It's none of your business.

왈츠 a waltz. ¶~를 추다 dance a waltz / waltz.

왈칵 suddenly; all of a sudden; with a rush [jerk]. ¶저녁 먹은 것을 ~ 토해 내다 suddenly throw[bring] up one's dinner // ~ 뒤집히다 overturn[topple over] suddenly / be overturned[upset] all of a sudden // 문을 ~ 잡아당기다 pull a door with a jerk // ~ 성을 내다 burst into a furious rage // 눈물이 ~ 쏟아지다 gush / rush forth / flow out suddenly.

왈칵하다 [성미가 몹시 급하다] quick-[hot-]tempered; impatient; rash.

왈패(-牌) a hussy; a minx; (농조) a baggage; a nag.

왕(王) 1 [임금] a king; a monarch(군주); a ruler(지배자). ¶~을 옹립하다 enthrone a king / set a king on the throne // ~을 폐하다 dethrone a king // ~이 나라를 다스리고 있다 A king rules that country. 2 [제일인자] a king; a magnate; a baron; (미) a tycoon. ¶홈런 ~ a home-run king // 삼림의 ~ 떡갈나무 the oak, monarch of the forest // 사자는 백수의 ~이다 The lion is (the) king of beasts.

왕-(王) 1 [아주 큼] big; large; giant. ¶~ 감 a giant persimmon // ~뱀 a large[big] snake. 2 (항렬의) grand-; of one's grandfather.

왕가(王家) a royal family[house]; the blood royal. ¶그는 ~ 출신이다 He's from a royal family[house].

왕겨(王-) chaff; rice hulls[husks].

왕고모(王姑母) a grandaunt on one's father's side. ⇨대고모

왕골 [식] a sedge. ¶~에 sedgy.
● **왕골자리** a sedge mat.

왕관(王冠) the crown. ¶~을 쓰다 put on [wear] a crown / [왕이 되다] ascend[come to] the throne // ~을 벗다 take[throw] off a crown / [왕위에서 물러나다] abdicate[give up] the throne // 그는 ~을 버리고 사랑을 택했다 He threw away[(문어) forsook] the crown for the sake of love.

왕국(王國) 1 [왕이 다스리는 나라] a kingdom; a realm; a monarchy(군주국). ¶스웨덴 ~ the kingdom of Sweden // 네덜란드 ~ the realm of the Netherlands. 2 [어떤 현상·세력이 지배적으로 나타나는 영역] a kingdom; an empire. ¶미국은 참으로 야구 ~이다 The United States is truly a baseball-crazy country.

왕궁(王宮) the palace; a royal[king's] palace.

왕권(王權) sovereignty; sovereign power [right]; royal authority[powers]; the royal prerogative; the regal power. ¶~을 쥐다 hold regal sway.
● **왕권신수설** the doctrine of the divine right of kings.

왕녀(王女) a princess; a Royal princess.

왕년(往年) old times; the past; former times; the years gone by; those old days. ¶그녀는 ~의 유명한 아역 배우이다 She was once [formerly] a famous child star.

왕눈이(王-) a person with big eyes; a large-eyed person.

왕당(王黨) royalists; monarchists.
● **왕당파** the royalist faction.

왕대비(王大妃) the Queen Dowager; the Queen Mother.

왕도(王道) the rule of virtue[right]; righteous government; kingcraft. ¶~와 패도 the rule of right and the rule of mighty // 학문에는 ~ 없다 There's no royal road to learning.

왕도(王都) the (Royal) capital; the Royal metropolis.

왕래(往來) 1 [오고 감] coming and going; traffic. ¶사람의 ~ pedestrian traffic / comings and goings of people // ~가 잦은 거리 a busy street[road / thoroughfare] / a much frequented[traveled] road / a crowded [bustling] road // ~가 없는 거리 an empty street // 이 길은 사람의 ~가 많다 Many people pass this way. // 거리에는 사람의 ~가 끊겼다 The streets are deserted. / There is no one to be seen on the streets. // 요즈음 자동차의 ~가 늘었다 Recently traffic has increased. // 이 길은 차량의 ~가 적다 There is little traffic on[(영) in] this road. // 이 길은 사람의 ~가 거의 없다 Few people pass this way. / This street is almost deserted[empty]. // 사람과 차의 ~가 심하여 좀처럼 거리를 지나갈 수 없다 The street is so crowded with pedestrians and cars that it is hard to cross it. **왕래하다** come and go. ¶시내 중심부에는 왕래하는 차가 많다 The traffic in the central part of the city is congested.
2 [교제] intercourse; association; [서신의 교환] correspondence. ¶친척과의 ~도 끊고 있다 I am no longer having anything to do with my relatives. // 우리는 앞집과는 ~가 없다 We don't have anything to do[We are not on visiting terms] with our next-door neighbors. // 고향과의 ~가 끊겼다 My association with my hometown has ended. // 두 사람 사이에는 늘 편지의 ~가 있었다 They constantly exchanged letters. / Letters were going back and forth between them all the time. **왕래하다** visit[see] each other; have [hold] intercourse. ¶그들은 서로 왕래하는 사이다 They are on visiting terms with[They

often see] each other.∥그 사람들과는 왕래하지 않는 것이 좋겠다 You had better not mix with those people. / I would advise you not to associate with[to part company with] those people.

왕릉(王陵) a royal mausoleum (*pl.* -lea); a royal tomb.

왕림(枉臨) attendance; presence; a visit. ¶국무총리의 ~하에 with the Prime Minister in attendance / in the presence of the Prime Minister. **왕림하다** pay a visit to (a person / a place). ¶기념식에는 황태자가 왕림하셨다 We were honored by the presence of the Crown Prince at the commemoration ceremony.

왕립(王立)〔관형어적〕royal.
●**왕립 미술관** (영국의) the Royal Academy.

왕명(王命) a command[an order] of the king; a royal order[command]. ¶~을 하달하다 convey the command of the king∥그들은 ~을 기억하고 행동했다 They acted in defiance of orders of the king.

왕모래(王-) coarse sand.

왕밤(王-) a large chestnut.

왕방울(王-) a large bell. ¶~만 한 눈 a big eye / an ox eye∥눈이 ~만 하다 have big [ox] eyes / be big-[saucer-]eyed.

왕벌(王-)〔동〕a (ground) wasp. ⇨"말벌

왕복(往復)〔갔다 돌아오기〕going and returning;〔왔다 갔다 하기〕coming and going. ¶우주 ~선 space shuttle∥런던까지는 ~에 몇 시간 걸립니까 How long does it take to travel to and from London? / How many hours will it take to go to and come back [return] from London?∥~에 2시간 이상 걸릴 것이다 It will take more than two hours to get there and back.∥기차는 ~ 모두 초만원이었다 The train was jam-packed both ways[going and coming].∥경주까지 ~ 얼마입니까 How much[What is the fare] to Gyeongju and back? **왕복하다** go and come back[return]; make a round trip(교통기관을 이용하여); ply (between) (배가); shuttle (between) (전차 등이). ¶배가 하루에 세 번 강을 왕복한다 A boat goes up and down the river three times a day.∥저는 걸어서 학교를 왕복합니다 I walk to and from school.∥내가 회사를 왕복하는 버스는 언제나 붐빈다 The bus I take on my way to and from the office is always crowded.∥그 기차는 서울 인천 간을 왕복하여 운행한다 The train shuttles between Seoul and Incheon.
●**왕복 엽서** a prepaid postcard. **왕복 요금** round-trip[return] fare; the fare for a round trip; fare both ways; a round fare. **왕복표** / **왕복 승차권** / **왕복 차표**《미》a round-trip ticket;《영》a return ticket.

왕비(王妃) a queen; a queen consort. ¶~의 [다운] queenly.

왕생하다(往生-) go to Nirvana after death; go to[be reborn in] Paradise; die an easy and peaceful death. ¶그는 극락에 왕생할 것이 분명하다 There is no doubt he'll go to heaven.

왕성하다(旺盛-) flourishing; prime; high; excellent. ¶왕성한 욕망 an irresistible desire ∥혈기 왕성한 때에 in the prime of one's youth∥그는 언제나 원기(가) ~ He is always full of energy[vigor]. / He is always in high [fine] spirits.∥톰은 식욕이 ~ Tom has an excellent[a good] appetite.∥그는 지식[명예] 욕이 ~ He is very eager for knowledge [fame]. / He has a great thirst for knowledge[desire for fame].∥민주화를 향한 기운이 왕성하게 일고 있다 There was a rapidly growing trend toward(s) democratization.

왕세손(王世孫) the eldest son of the Crown Prince; the eldest grandson of a King (in the direct line).

왕세자(王世子) the Crown Prince; the Prince Royal; the Heir Apparent of the Throne. ¶~로 책봉되다 be proclaimed Crown Prince.
●**왕세자빈** the Crown Princess; the consort of the Crown Prince.

왕손(王孫)〔왕의 손자〕a royal grandson; a grandson of a king;〔왕의 후손〕a royal descendant. ¶~이다 be of Royal blood.

왕수(王水)〔화〕nitrohydrochloric acid; aqua regia.

왕실(王室) a royal family[house]. ⇨"왕가

왕업(王業) a Royal task. ¶~을 보좌하다 assist the Royal rule.

왕왕 ¶엔진이 ~ 돌아가기 시작했다 The engine started with a vroom.

왕왕(往往) sometimes; occasionally; (every) now and then; at times; from time to time; often; frequently;《구어》once in a while. ¶그가 말하는 것을 ~ 거의 알아듣지 못할 때가 ~ 있다 At times I hardly understand him.∥그것은 ~ 있는 일이다 It is a matter of no uncommon occurrence.

왕왕거리다 make a noise. ¶왕왕거리는 라디오 소리 the noisy sound of a radio∥그렇게 왕왕거리지 마라 Don't make so much noise.

왕위(王位) the throne; the crown. ¶~에 오르다 accede to[take] the throne / ascend [come to / mount] the throne / throne∥~에서 물러나다 abdicate the throne[crown]∥~를 잇다〔계승하다〕succeed to the throne [crown]∥~를 빼앗다 usurp the throne∥~에 있다 be on the throne∥~를 세자에게 물려주다 abdicate the throne in favor of the crown prince / make over the throne to the crown prince∥엘리자베스 1세는 1558년에 ~에 올랐다 Elizabeth I was crowned in 1558.
●**왕위 계승** succession to the throne. ¶~권 the right of succession.

왕자(王子) a (Royal) prince; a prince of the blood (royal).

왕자(王者) 1 a king. ⇨"임금 2〔통치자〕a ruler; a sovereign. 3〔제일인자〕the champion. ¶마라톤의 ~ the marathon champion.

왕정(王政) 1〔임금의 정치〕royal rule[government]. 2〔군주 정치〕monarchy; the royal regime.
●**왕정복고** (영국의) the Restoration.

왕조(王朝) a dynasty. ¶조선 ~ the Joseon dynasty∥빅토리아 ~ the reign of Queen Victoria / the Victorian Age∥~의 dynastic.

왕족(王族)〔집합적〕royalty; the Royal Family; the blood royal. ¶그는 ~이다 He is of royal blood.

왕좌(王座) 1〔임금의 자리〕the throne. ¶~에 앉다 come to[(문어) ascend] the throne. 2 〔으뜸가는 자리〕supremacy. ¶테니스계의 ~ 를 다투는 열전 heated match contesting supremacy in the tennis world∥~를 차지하다 come to the top / win the championship / hold the first place (among)∥이 회사는 지난

왕진 10년 동안 업계에서 ~를 차지하고 있다 This company has been at the top[has ranked first] in the business world for the past ten years.

왕진(往診) a call (on a patient); a house call; a (doctor's) visit (to a patient). ¶야간 ~ 의사 선생님은 지금 ~ 중입니다 The doctor is out making calls [seeing patients]. / The doctor is out[away] on his round of sick calls. **왕진하다** visit a patient in his home; go out to see a patient; pay a sick call on a patient; make a house call.
● **왕진료** a (doctor's) fee for a visit[house call]; doctor's visiting fee.

왕창 〈속〉 [엄청나게 큰 규모로]. ¶예산을 3분의 1이나 ~ 줄였다 A whole third of our budget was lopped[chopped] off. / We had a third of our budget cut in one fell swoop. // 그는 주식이 크게 올라서 돈을 ~ 벌었다 He hit the jackpot on the stock market and made a wad[pile / bundle].

왕초(王-) a (gang) leader; a boss. ¶암흑가의 ~ a boss of the underworld / an underworld boss // 소매치기의 ~ a master pickpocket.

왕통(王統) the Royal descendants; the Royal line.

왕후(王后) a queen. ⇨ 왕비

왕후(王侯) royalty and nobility; crowned heads; the king and peers; lords.

왜 1 [어째서] why; how; what; for what reason[purpose]; (구어) what for; (구어) how ... come; [무슨 까닭으로] on what ground. ¶~ 일찍 일어나지?" "조깅하기 위해서야." "Why do you get up early?" "Because I want to go jogging." / "What do you get up early for?" "To go jogging." // "그는 내게 몹시 화를 내고 있어." "~?" "모르겠어." "He's very angry with me." "How come?" "I don't know." // "~ 그녀는 오지 않았지요?" "잘 모르겠습니다." "How[Why] is it that she didn't come?" "I don't know." // ~ 미국에 갑니까 For what purpose are you going to America? / What are you going to America for?(▶ 후자는 구어적임) // "너는 ~ 웃었지?" "그녀의 말투가 우스웠기 때문입니다." "What made you laugh?" / "Why did you laugh?" "Because her way of saying it was funny."(▶ what을 써서 "무엇이 너로 하여금 …하게 했는가"를 나타내는 표현은 Why ...?보다 부드럽게 이유를 묻는 표현으로서 많이 쓰임. 예: "왜 여기에 왔지?" "What brought you here?") // ~ 화가 났지 What made you angry? // ~ 그녀를 의심하지 On what grounds do you suspect her?
2 [의문을 나타낼 때 쓰이는 말] why. ¶~, 담배 피우는 것이 뭐가 해로워 Why, what harm is there in smoking?

왜(倭) [왜국]; [왜인] Japanese.
왜가리 [동] a heron; an gray heron.
왜간장(倭-醬) Japanese soy (sauce).
왜건 1 [짐을 실을 수 있는 승용차] (미) station wagon; (영) an estate car. 2 [무개화차] (영) a waggon; a serving cart; [손수레] (영) a trolley. [식사용] ~ a dinner wagon.

왜곡(歪曲) distortion; perversion. ¶진실의 ~ 은 어떤 경우에도 용납되지 않는다 Distortion of the truth is unforgivable under any circumstances. **왜곡하다** strain; distort; pervert; contort; twist; warp. ¶사실을 ~ twist[distort] facts / give a fact a twist / falsify[misrepresent] the fact // 진실을 ~ strain[pervert] the truth // 규칙을 왜곡하여 해석하다 stretch[strain] the interpretation of a rule / 어떤 사항에 학설을 왜곡하여 적용하다 force a theory on an event // 그녀는 자기에게 유리하게 이야기를 왜곡했다 She distorted[twisted] the story of her own advantage.
➔ 사실이 왜곡되어 보도되었다 The facts were falsely represented in the news.

왜구(倭寇) Japanese pirates.
왜국(倭國) Japan.
왜냐하면 because; since; for(▶ 원인을 나타내는 강도는 위의 순서에 따라 약해짐). ¶고래는 포유 동물이다. ~ 태생(胎生)이니까 The whale is a mammal because it bears its young alive [is viviparous]. // 밤 사이에 비가 온 것 같다. ~ 길이 젖어 있으니까 It seems it [to have] rained during the night, because [since / for] the road is wet.
왜놈(倭-) a Jap.
왜병(倭兵) a Japanese soldier; (군대) the Japanese troops.
왜색(倭色) Japanese ways[manners / style]; things Japanese. ¶~을 일소하다 make a clean sweep of thing Japanese / sweep away Japanesque style.
왜소하다(矮小-) dwarf; dwarfish; undersized; diminutive; pygmy. ¶체구가 왜소한 사람 a dwarf / a dwarf-man.
왜식(倭式) Japanese style[fashion].
왜식(倭食) Japanese-style food; Japanese dish[cuisine / cooking].
● **왜식집** a Japanese restaurant.
왜인(倭人) a Japanese; (경멸) a Jap.
왜장(倭將) a Japanese commander[general].
왜적(倭敵) the Japanese invaders.
왜정(倭政) the Japanese rule[government].
● **왜정 시대** the period of the Japanese government in Korea; the Japanese rule days(1910-45).
왠지 I don't know why; without knowing why; somehow. ¶~ 나는 그가 싫다 Somehow I don't like him.
왱 1 [작은 날벌레가 날아갈 때 나는 소리] with a hum[buzz]. 2 [바람이 세차게 불 때 나는 소리] with a whistle[whiz(z) / hiss / sough]. 3 [돌팔매가 날아갈 때 들리는 소리] with a twang. 4 [소방차 등이 지나가는 소리]. ¶구급차가 ~ 하고 달려갔다 An ambulance scudded away with sirens wailing.
왱그랑댕그랑 tinkle-tinkle; ting-a-ling; with a jangle; clangorously. **왱그랑댕그랑하다** tinkle; clink; jangle-jangle; clangour.
외 [식] a cucumber. ⇨ 오이
외 single; sole; only. ¶~아들 an[the] only son.
외(外) [그 밖] except; but; with the exception of; (…이상은) beyond; (이외에) besides; in addition to. ¶그 사람 ~에는 아무도 그 질문에 대답하지 못했다 Nobody except[but] him could answer the question. // 네게 말한 것 ~에는 아무것도 모른다 I know nothing beyond what I told you. // 나 ~에 세 사람이 더 있었다 There were three more people besides me. // 그것 ~에는 아무것도 가지고 있지 않다 I have nothing but[besides] that. // 그는 만화책 ~에는 아무것도 읽지 않는다 He reads nothing save comic books. // 그는 이것 ~에는 아무 말도 없었다 He said nothing beyond this.

외-(外) **1** [외가] (related) on the mother's [daughter's] side; maternal. ¶~삼촌 one's maternal uncle. **2** [밖·표면] outside; outer; foreign. ¶~몽골 Outer Mongolia.

외가(外家) the mother's [maternal] (side of the) family; one's mother's old home. ¶~의 on the mother's [maternal] side / maternal // ~ 쪽 친척 a relative on one's mother's side.
● **외갓집** the mother's [maternal] (side of the) family. ⇨ˇ외가

외가닥 a (single) strand [ply].

외각(外角) **1** [수] an external [exterior] angle. **2** [야구] the outside corner (of the plate). ⇨ˇ아웃코너(⇨아웃)

외각(外殼) a crust; a shell; an integument; a case.

외갈래 a line.
● **외갈래 길** a road without a branch; a straight road.

외객(外客) a visitor; a guest; [외국 손님] a foreign visitor [tourist].

외견(外見) external [outward] appearance. ⇨ˇ외관(外觀).

외겹 one [a single] layer; one ply. ¶~의 single / one-ply / one-fold.

외경(外徑) an outside [external] diameter.

외경(畏敬) awe; dread. ⇨ˇ경외(敬畏)

외계(外界) the external [outside] world; the outside; [지구 밖] the outer space. ¶~의 사물 outward things // ~와의 교통이 끊어지다 be secluded [shut off] from the outer [external] world // ~와의 교신이 두절되었다 Communication with the outside world has been cut off.
● **외계인** a(n) (outer) space man; an extraterrestrial(약어 E.T.); extraterrestrial tourists.

외고집(-固執) (single-minded) stubbornness; obstinacy; perversity. ¶~인 obstinate / stubborn / headstrong / perverse // ~을 부리다 be obstinate [stubborn] / get stiff-necked // 그녀의 ~에 분통이 터졌다 I was exasperated by her willfulness [stubbornness].
● **외고집쟁이** a pigheaded person. ¶그는 ~ 다 He is a stiff necked person.

외곬 a single way [track / groove]. ¶~으로 with a single-mind / single-mindedly / in only one way / with only one purpose // ~으로 생각하는 사람 a person with a single-[one-]track mind / a single-minded person / a person whose mind runs on a single track // ~으로 생각하다 see things from only one point of view // 그녀는 평생을 ~으로 이 길을 걸어왔다 She spent her life single-mindedly in this line of work. // 그녀는 ~으로 그 사람만을 생각했다 She thought only of him.

외과(外科) [의학의 한 분과] surgery; (병원의) the department of surgery. ¶뇌 ~ brain surgery // 임상 [성형] ~ clinical [plastic] surgery // ~의 surgical.
● **외과 병동** a surgical ward. **외과 수술** (perform) a surgical operation. **외과 의사** a surgeon.

외과피(外果皮) [식] the epicarp; the exocarp.

외곽(外郭) **1** [성 밖으로 둘러쌓은 성] the outer wall; the outwall. **2** [바깥 테두리] the outer block [fence]; the contour. ¶수도권 순환선의 ~ 노선 the outer track of the Metropolitan Loop Line.

외관(外觀) external [outward] appearance; an outward show [aspect]; an exterior view. ¶~상 / 으로 externally / seemingly / apparently / in appearance / to all appearance // 건물의 ~ the exterior of a building // ~을 꾸미다 make outward show / put on a show // ~을 멋지게 꾸미다 put on a fair show // ~이 좋아지다 improve in appearance // 약간 ~을 바꾸어 상품의 판매를 시작하다 put the articles up for sale after making some changes [alterations] in their appearance // 그 집은 ~이 좋다 The house looks fine on the outside. // ~은 훌륭하지만 내부는 대단치 않다 The interior is not so fine as its outer appearance would suggest. // ~만 보고는 모른다 Appearances are deceptive. // 사람은 ~으로 판단하지 마라 You must not judge a person by his appearance. / Never judge from appearance.

외교(外交) [외국과의 교제] diplomacy; a foreign policy(정책); diplomatic relations [intercourse] (관계); (섭외) outside duty; canvassing. ¶강경 [약체] ~ a strong [weak / weak-kneed] foreign policy // 경제 ~ economic diplomacy (toward) // 공개 [비밀] ~ open [secret] diplomacy // 굴욕 ~ humiliating diplomacy // 달러 ~ dollar diplomacy // 다각 ~ multilateral diplomacy // 무력 ~ armed diplomacy // 문화 ~ cultural diplomacy // 민간(民間) ~ non-governmental [people-to-people] diplomacy // 실리 ~ diplomacy based on the national interest // 적극 ~ a positive [vigorous] foreign policy // 초당파 ~ a suprapary diplomacy / (양당 간의) (미) a bipartisan diplomacy // 초청 ~ diplomacy by invitation // 한국의 대미 ~ Korea's policy toward America // ~상(으로) diplomatically // ~상의 diplomatic // ~ 수완을 발휘하다 give full play to one's diplomatic skill // ~에 능하다 be quite a diplomatist // 정부의 ~가 서투르다는 이도 있다 Some say that the Government is wanting in diplomatic skill.
● **외교관** a diplomatic official; a diplomatist; a diplomat; (집합적) the diplomatic service. ¶~의 면책 특권 diplomatic immunity // ~이 되다 enter the diplomatic service // ~이다 be a diplomat / be in the diplomatic service. **외교 교섭** diplomatic negotiations. **외교 문서** a diplomatic document [note / paper]. **외교 문제** a diplomatic question [issue / problem / affair]. ¶그는 ~의 전문가이다 He is an expert in foreign affairs [diplomatic problems]. **외교 사절단** a diplomatic mission. **외교 정책** a diplomatic policy. ¶그들은 ~을 그르쳤다 They took a wrong diplomatic policy. **외교 통상부** the Ministry of Foreign Affairs and Trade. **외교 특권** diplomatic privileges (and immunities).

외교적(外交的) diplomatic. ¶필요한 모든 조치 all the necessary diplomatic steps // 분쟁을 ~으로 해결하다 settle a dispute diplomatically // ~ 절충으로 문제는 해결되었다 The problem was settled [resolved] through diplomatic negotiations [by diplomatic means].

외구(外寇) a foreign enemy. ⇨ˇ외적(外敵)

외국(外國) a foreign country [land]. ¶~의 foreign / alien / oversea(s) / exotic(외국풍의)

외근

// ~의 관습 foreign customs // ~산의 foreign-produced / of foreign production [growth / origin] // ~제의 of foreign manufacture [make] / foreign-made // ~제 기계류 machinery of foreign make // ~ 태생의 foreign-born // ~식으로 on foreign lines / in foreign style // ~으로 가는 배 a ship bound for abroad [bound outward] (from Korea) / a foreign-bound [an outbound / an outward-bound] ship // ~에 보낼[갈] 우편 outgoing mails // ~에 가다 go abroad [overseas] // ~을 여행하다 travel abroad // ~에 있다 be [stay] abroad // ~에서 돌아오다 return [come back] from abroad [from a foreign country] // ~에서 오다 come [be brought / be imported] from abroad // ~에서 죽다 die abroad // ~ 땅을 밟다 step [set foot] on foreign soil // ~의 침략을 받다 be invaded by a foreign country // ~의 영향을 받지 않다 be untouched by alien influences // ~의 지배하에 있다 be under foreign rule // 나는 한 달 전에 ~에서 돌아왔다 I returned from abroad a month ago.

●**외국 무역** foreign [overseas] trade. **외국 사절 / 외국 사신** a foreign envoy. **외국 상사** a foreign firm. **외국 상품** foreign goods. **외국 시장** an oversea(s) [a foreign] market. **외국어** a foreign language [tongue]. ¶제2 ~ a second foreign language // ~로[의] in a foreign language // ~를 배우기 시작하다 take up a foreign language // ~를 읽을 수 있게 되다 acquire a reading knowledge of [ability in] a foreign language // ~로 자기 생각을 말하기란 어렵다 It is very hard to express oneself in a language that is not one's own. // 당신은 어떤 ~를 말할 수 있습니까 What languages do you speak other than your mother tongue? // 그는 몇몇 ~에 능통하다 He is quite a linguist. / He's a polyglot. **외국 여행** a foreign travel. **외국인** a foreigner; a foreign national; an alien (▶ an alien은 그 나라의 시민권을 갖고 있지 않은 사람, 그 나라에 체류하고 있는 외국인이라는 뜻으로 쓰이는 경우가 많음. 법률적인 경우가 아니면 이 말은 사용하지 말 것). ¶재류 ~ aliens / foreign residents // ~ 전용 (게시) Foreigners only. **외국 자본** foreign capital [funds]. **외국풍** foreign manners [ways]; exotic fashion; exoticism. **외국환** foreign exchange.

외근(外勤) outside duty [service]; canvassing (외교원의). ¶~의 on outdoor service / on outside duty / (취재 근무) on reportorial duty // 당신은 내근입니까 ~입니까 Do you work inside or outside? **외근하다** work outside; do outside work; be on outside duty [service].

●**외근 기자** a reporter; a legman.

외기(外氣) the open air; the (outside) air. ¶…을 ~에 쏘이다 air (a thing) / expose (a thing) to the air // ~를 쐬다 air oneself / take the air // 그것은 ~에 닿으면 색이 변한다 The color changes when it is exposed to air [put out in the open air].

외길 an unforked road; a road without a fork all along.

외나무다리 a log bridge; a single-log bridge. ¶~를 건너다 cross (a stream) by a log bridge // ~에서 원수를 만나다 meet bad luck one cannot escape from.

외눈 one eye. ¶~인 one-eyed // ~인 사람 a one-eyed person.

●**외눈박이** a one-eyed person. ⇨애꾸눈이 (⇨애꾸)

외다 learn ... by heart; recite. ⇨외우다

외대다 [반대로 일러 주다] inform (a person) contrary to the facts; give (a person) a false report. ¶외대지 말고 사실대로 말해 주시오 Tell me the truth.

외도(外道) 1 [바르지 않은 길·노릇] evil principles; depraved doctrines; injustice. ¶그의 음악은 ~일 뿐이다 His music is too unorthodox. **외도하다** deviate [swerve] from (the right path). 2 illicit (sexual) intercourse. ⇨°오입

외돌다 keep [stand / remain] aloof (from).

외돌토리 a single person. ⇨°외톨이

외동딸 an only daughter.

외동아들 an only son.

외등(外燈) an outdoor lamp [light].

외따로 lonelily; solitarily; all alone; in isolation. ¶혼자 ~ 앉아 있다 sit all alone // ~ 살다 live in isolation (from others) / 들판 한가운데에 오두막집이 한 채 ~ 서 있다 In the middle of the field (there) stands a solitary cottage. // 그녀는 도시에서 떨어져 ~ 살고 있다 She lives a lonely life far away from town.

외딴 isolated; out-of-the-way; solitary. ¶나는 ~ 마을에 살고 있다 I live in a remote village. / I live in a village far from any city.

외딴섬 a remote [an isolated] island.

외딴집 a lonely house; a house remote from any village or town.

외딸 an only daughter.

외떡잎 [식] monocotyledon.

●**외떡잎식물** a monocotyledon; a monocotyledonous plant.

외떨어지다 out-of-the-way; remote; secluded; isolated; lonely.

외람되다(猥濫—) impertinent; impudent; forward; presumptuous. ¶외람된 말씀이오나 I dare [venture to] say ... / Allow me to tell you that ... / Excuse me, but .... // 외람된 짓을 하다 go beyond one's powers / exceed one's authority // 외람된 말을 하다 say pert things // 외람됩니다만 당신은 잘못 생각하고 계십니다 Excuse me, but you are mistaken.

외래(外來) ¶~의 foreign / imported / coming from abroad.

●**외래문화** foreign [imported] culture. **외래어** an adopted [a borrowed / a loan] word; a word of foreign origin. ¶이 말은 영어에서 온 ~다 We borrowed the word from English. / This is a loan word from English. / The word comes from English. **외래품** an imported [a foreign-made] article; (집합적) foreign [imported] goods. **외래 환자** an outpatient; a day-patient.

외력(外力) [물] external force. ¶~이 가해지다 be pressed by external force.

외로 1 [왼쪽으로] leftward(s); to [toward] the left (side). ¶~ 기울다 incline [lean] to the left (side) // ~ 가다 go to the left // 전선을 ~ 감다 coil wire counterclockwise. 2 [비뚤게] in the wrong direction; to the wrong path; to an evil course. ¶~ 가다 go astray / fall into evil ways // ~ 가도 서울만 가면 된다 The end justifies the means.

외로움 loneliness; lonesomeness. ¶~을 느끼다 feel lonely // 독서로 ~을 달래다 feel society in books / enjoy the companionship of books.

외롭다 lonely; lonesome; forlorn; (서술적) feel lonely[lonesome]. ¶외로운 고아 a desolate orphan // 외로운 사람 a solitary[lonely] person // 외로운 나그네 a lonely[solitary] traveler // 외로운 생활을 하다 lead a lonely [solitary] life // 도와줄 친구도 없이 나는 정말 외로웠다 Without friends to help, I felt quite forlorn. // 혼자 남게 되었으니 그녀는 얼마나 외로울까 How lonely and helpless she must feel left all by herself! // 그의 집은 외롭게 쓸쓸하게 언덕 위에 서 있었다 His house stood on a hill, alone and forsaken. **외로이** lonelily; alone; lonesomely. ¶~ 살다 live alone[a lonely life] / lead a lonely life // ~ 울다 cry all alone // 이국땅에서 ~ 죽다 die forlorn in a foreign land // 그녀는 남편이 죽은 뒤 ~ 살고 있다 Since her husband's death, she has been leading a lonely life.

외륜(外輪) [바깥쪽 바퀴] an outer ring; (차의) the rim (of a wheel); a tire; (기선의) a paddle wheel.
● **외륜산** [지] a somma; the outer rim (of a volcanic crater).

외마디 1 [한 동강] a single section[piece] (of a bamboo). 2 [한 마디의 소리] a short scream[outcry].

외면(外面) (an) outward appearance; the outside; the exterior. ¶~의 outside / outward / exterior / external // ~은[으로는] outwardly.
● **외면 묘사** an external description. **외면치레** a pretense; (영) a pretence; a show. ¶그의 친절은 ~다 His kindness is only a show.

외면하다(外面-) turn one's face away (from); look away (from); avert one's eyes (from); [무시하다] disregard. ¶그는 외면하며 지나갔다 He passed by, looking the other way. / 조지는 외면하고 나를 보지 않은 체했다 George looked away and pretended not to have noticed me. // 내가 오는 것을 보고 그는 급히 외면했다 He quickly looked the other way[turned away hastily] when he saw me coming.

외모(外貌) (an) outward appearance; external features; externals. ¶추악한 ~ an ugly appearance // 장사꾼 같은 ~ merchantlike appearance // ~는 거칠지만 마음은 착한 사람 a good man with a rough exterior // ~로는 outwardly / in appearance / to all appearances // ~로 사람을 판단하다 judge (of) a person by his appearances[looks] // ~가 닮다 resemble in appearance // 그는 ~가 단정한 사람이다 He is a man of decent appearance. / He is always neat in his person. // 사람을 ~로만 보아서는 안 된다 Appearances are deceptive[deceitful].

외무(外務) 1 [외국에 관한 정무] foreign[external] affairs. 2 [outside duty[service].
⇨°외근

외박(外泊) stopping[sleeping / staying] out (overnight). ¶~을 허가하다 permit staying out. **외박하다** stay out overnight; sleep out; (군인이) stop out of barracks. ¶무단 ~ be absent without leave(▶ 미군에서는 AWOL이라 약칭함) // 그는 어제 외박했다 He stayed [slept] out last night.

외배엽(外胚葉) [생] an ectoderm; an ectoblast.

외벌 a single set.

외벽(外壁) [건] an outer[external] wall.

외부(外部) [바깥쪽] the outside; the exterior; [바깥 세계] the outside world. ¶~의 outside / outer / external / exterior // ~의 압력 an external pressure // ~로부터 from without / from the outside // ~로부터의 원조 outside help // ~에 나타나다 appear on the outside // ~와 교통이 두절되다 be entirely isolated[cut off] from the outside world // 여승들은 ~와 전혀 교섭이 없다 The nuns have absolutely nothing to do with[are entirely secluded from] the outside world. // ~에 나타나지 않을 뿐 그 회사에는 늘 분쟁이 있었다 The firm has constant troubles, only they are not brought to light. // ~와의 교섭은 지배인이 한다 The manager attends to all matters which have to do with the public.
● **외부 감각** external sensation. **외부 사람 / 외부 인사** an outsider; a man on the outside. ¶그것은 ~의 짓이다 It was done by someone from outside. / It was the work of an outsider.

외분(外分) [수] external division. **외분하다** divide externally.

외분비(外分泌) [생] external secretion.
● **외분비선** an exocrine gland.

외빈(外賓) [외국 손님] a foreign guest[visitor]; [외부 손님] a guest[visitor].

외사촌(外四寸) a (first) cousin on the mother's side.

외삼촌(外三寸) an uncle; one's mother's [mom's] brother; (문어) a maternal uncle.

외상 credit; trust; (영국 구어) tick. ¶~으로 on credit[trust] / (미국 구어) on the cuff / ~으로 사다 buy (a thing) on credit[trust] / have (a thing) charged to one's account // ~으로 팔다 sell (a thing) on credit[trust] // ~을 주다 give credit // ~을 갚다 clear[pay] off one's credits[bills] // ~이 밀리다[늘다] run a credit / run up a score (at a grocery store) / ~을 장부에 기입하다 enter on the credit note // ~이 잘 안 걷혀 애먹다 be annoyed by a poor collection of bills // 나는 그것을 ~으로 샀다 I bought it on credit. // 이 물건을 ~으로 살 수 있습니까 May I purchase this on credit? // ~으로 해 주시오 Charge it to my account. // Put it on my bill. // 제 부친의 장부에 달아 주시오 Charge it to my father's account, please. / Please put it on my father's account. // 그 가게에 ~이 3,000원 있다 I owe the store a 3,000 won bill. // 이 가게는 ~이 통하지 않는다 They won't give me [allow] credit at this shop.
● **외상값** an account; a bill. ¶~을 받다 collect a bill. **외상 거래** credit transactions. **외상 매입** credit purchase; purchasing [buying] on credit. **외상 매출 / 외상 판매** credit sale; sale[selling] on credit. **외상 사절** (게시) No credit (given).; For cash only.; Sale on credit (absolutely) declined. **외상 손님** a charge[credit] customer.

외상(外相) the Foreign Minister.

외상(外傷) an external wound[injury]; [의] a trauma (pl. -ta, ~s). ¶~의[에 의한] traumatic // (신체 조직에) ~을 입히다 traumatize // 피해자에게는 전혀 ~이 없었다 The victim had[suffered] no external injuries.

외서(外書) a foreign book.

외선(外線) the outer line; (전기) outside wire; (전화의) an outside line.

외설(猥褻) obscenity; lewdness; indecency; licentiousness.
● **외설 문학** obscene[immoral] literature; pornography; salacious writings. **외설 행위** an obscenity; an indecent conduct[behavior].

외설스럽다(猥褻−) obscene; lewd; indecent; licentious; dirty; improper; nasty. ¶외설스러운 이야기 an indecent[filthy] talk / a risqué story // 외설스러운 그림 an obscene picture // 외설스러운 이야기를 하다 tell obscene jokes / talk dirty / 그 영화는 외설스러운 부분이 커트된 다음 상영이 허가되었다 The film was permitted to be shown after the obscene parts had[were] cut.

외세(外勢) 1 [바깥 형세] external situation[conditions]. 2 [외부의 세력] outside[foreign / alien] influence[power]. ¶~에 의존하다 depend on the power of a foreign country // ~를 배격하다 denounce[reject] the foreign power[influence].

외손 one hand.

외손뼉 a single palm.

외손뼉이 울지 못한다(속담) It takes two to quarrel.

외손(外孫) a child of one's daughter; a grandchild.

외손녀(外孫女) a daughter of one's daughter; a granddaughter.

외손자(外孫子) a son of one's daughter; a grandson.

외숙(外叔) an uncle; one's mother's[mom's] brother.

외숙모(外叔母) an aunt; the wife of one's mother's[mom's] brother.

외식(外食) eating[dining / boarding] out. **외식하다** eat[dine] out; (미) board out. ¶가족을 데리고 외식하러 가다 go to eat out with one's family // 오늘 밤에는 외식하러 가면 어떨까 Why don't we eat out tonight?
● **외식 산업** the food service industry.

외신(外信) a report from overseas; an overseas report; foreign[overseas] news. ¶~에 의하면 according to the report from overseas / An overseas report says ….

외심(外心) [수] a circumcenter.

외씨버선 slender Korean socks.

외아들 an only son.

외야(外野) [야구] the outfield.
● **외야석** (outfield) bleachers(▶ 보통 복수형). **외야수** an outfielder.

외양(外洋) the open sea; the ocean.
● **외양선** an ocean-going vessel[ship]; an ocean liner(정기선).

외양(外樣) outward appearance. ⇨겉모양 ¶~은 outwardly / in appearance // ~이 그럴듯하다 have a good appearance // ~을 꾸미다 make outward show / keep up appearances // 사람을 ~만으로 판단해서는 안 된다 You must not judge people by appearances. / Appearances are deceptive. // 이 아파트는 ~은 보기 좋으나 실은 아주 싸구려로 지은 것이다 This apartment building looks nice, but it was actually very cheaply constructed.

외양간(−間) (말의) a stable; (미) a (horse) barn; (소의) a cowhouse; a cowshed. ¶말을 ~에 넣다 put a horse in a stable / stable a horse.

외연(外延) [논] extension; denotation.

외연 기관(外燃機關) an external combustion engine.

외울 a single strand.

외용(外用) external use[application]. ¶이 약은 ~으로만 쓰인다 This medicine is for external application only. **외용하다** use[apply] externally.
● **외용약** a medicine[lotion] for external application[use]; an external remedy; [약병의 표서(表書)] "For outward only."

외우다 1 [암기하다] learn[know] … by heart; memorize; commit to memory. ¶영어 단어를 ~ memorize English words // 교과서의 문장을 ~ learn one's text by heart // 기도문을 기계적으로 ~ learn a prayer by rote // 나는 그 시를 외우고 있다 I know the poem by heart. // 나는 중요한 지명과 인명을 전부 외웠다 I've memorized all the important geographical and biographical names. / I've learned all the important geographical and biographical names by heart. // 그는 그 한 절을 기계적으로 외우고 있을 따름이다 He has only learned[memorized] the passage mechanically[by rote]. // 이 숫자들을 외울 수 있겠니 Can you carry these figures in your head?
2 [암송하다] recite; say … by heart; repeat … from memory. ¶염불을 ~ repeat[chant] the name of Buddha // 주문을 ~ make[utter] an incantation / chant a spell // 주기도문을 ~ chant the Lord's Prayer // 그는 그 긴 시를 줄줄 외웠다 He recited the long poem without any trouble[without stumbling] at all.

외유(外遊) a foreign travel[tour / trip]; a trip abroad; an overseas trip. ¶~의 길에 오르다 start on a tour abroad // ~에서 돌아오다 return home from one's foreign tour // 그는 ~ 중이다 He is (now) traveling abroad. / He is (now) on a foreign tour. **외유하다** go[travel / make a trip] abroad; go abroad.

외유내강(外柔內剛) being gentle in appearance, but sturdy in spirit; an iron hand in the velvet glove. **외유내강하다** ¶외유내강한 사람 a person who looks gentle but is tough inside // 어머니는 외유내강한 분이시다 My mother is gentle in appearance but quite strong in spirit[at heart]. / My mother looks gentle but is tough inside.

외음부(外陰部) external genital organs; genitalia.

외이(外耳) [생] the external ear; the concha (pl. -chae).

외인(外人) 1 a foreigner. ⇨외국인(⇨외국) 2 [밖의 사람] an outsider; a stranger. ¶이것은 ~만 알아서는 안 된다 This is between ourselves.
● **외인부대** a foreign legion. **외인 주택** foreign residents' houses. **외인 출입 금지** (게시) No admittance.; No trespassing.; Keep off!; (미) Keep out!

외인(外因) an external cause. ¶~성의 exogenous / exogenic // ~성 심장병 exogenous heart diseases // ~성 질환 an illness[(미) a sickness] with[which has] an external cause / an illness which has been caused externally.

외자(外資) foreign capital[funds]. ⇨외국 자본(⇨외국) ~ 계통의 회사 a foreign-affiliated firm.
● **외자 관리법** the foreign capital management law. **외자 도입** the induction[introduc-

외장(外裝) 〔겉 포장〕 wrapping(s); 〔겉칠〕 coating; 〔전〕 (전선의) sheathing; (자동차의) a trim; 〔바깥쪽 장식〕 an external ornament. ¶이 건물의 ~은 회반죽이다 The building was coated with plaster. / The building was plastered. // 그 차는 ~은 좋은데 내장이 좀 빈약하다 The car has a fine trim, but the interior is rather poor.
● **외장 공사** exterior work.

외적(外的) external; outward. ¶~인 이유 ostensible reasons.

외적(外敵) a foreign enemy[invader]. ¶~의 침입을 받다 suffer from a foreign invasion [attack / raid].

외접(外接) 〔수〕 circumscription. **외접하다** be circumscribed. ➔¶삼각형에 원을 외접시키다 circumscribe a circle about a triangle.
● **외접원** a circumscribed circle; a circum-circle.

외제(外製) ¶~의 of foreign make / foreign-made.
● **외제품** foreign-made articles; goods of foreign make; imported articles[goods].

외조모(外祖母) the mother of one's mother; a grandmother.

외조부(外祖父) the father of one's mother; a grandfather.

외족(外族) maternal relatives; a relative on one's mother's side.

외종 (사촌)(外從四寸) a cousin on one's mother's side; a maternal cousin.

외주(外注) an outside order. **외주하다** place an order with an outside supplier.
● **외주품** items ordered from outside suppliers.

외주(外周) 〔바깥쪽 둘레〕 the outer circumference.

외줄 a (single) line.

외줄기 a (single) stalk[stem].

외지(外地) **1** 〔타향〕 a place away from home; another country. ¶~로 일하러 가다 work away from home // ~로 돈 벌러 가다 go to another countryside to earn one's bread. **2** a foreign country[land]. ➪=외국 **3** 〔해외 영토〕 an external territory; an oversea(s) possessions.
● **외지 근무** overseas service.

외지(外紙) 〔외국 신문〕 a foreign newspaper; 〔집합적〕 the foreign press.

외지(外誌) a foreign magazine.

외지다 out-of-the-way; remote; secluded. ¶외진 곳 a remote[out-of-the-way] place // 외진 산길 a remote mountain trail[path].

외진(外診) 〔의〕 an external examination.

외짝 a fellow[companion] (to something); a counterpart. ¶~인 odd / mismatched // ~인 구두 an odd pair of shoes / mismatched shoes // 이 장갑은 ~이다 This glove is odd [mismatched / wrongly paired]. / This glove is not fellows.

외쪽 1 〔한쪽〕 one side(▶ 다른 쪽은 the other side). **2** 〔한 조각〕 a piece.

외채 a single house. ➪=외챗집(➪외채)
● **외챗집** a single[an independent] house.

외채(外債) 〔경〕 a foreign loan(차관); foreign bonds(증권); foreign debt(부채). ¶~를 줄이다 reduce foreign liabilities // ~를 모집하다 raise[float] a foreign loan / place a loan on the foreign market // ~를 상환하다 redeem [refund] a foreign loan // ~를 상환하지 못하다 default on foreign loans //무거운 ~부담을 줄이다 curtail[reduce] the heavy foreign debt burden.
● **외채 상환 기금** a redemption fund for foreign[external] bonds.

외척(外戚) a maternal relative; a relative on one's mother's side.

외출(外出) going out; an outing. ¶~을 싫어하는 사람 a stay-at-home / a homebody // (군인이) ~을 금지당하다 be confined to the barracks // ~을 허가받다 be allowed out // 그는 용무가 있어 ~ 중이다 He is out on business. // 그것이 그의 ~ 중에 일어난 일이다 It happened during his absence[while he was out]. **외출하다** go out. ¶외출하지 않다 stay at home / keep[stay] indoors // 외출할 채비를 하다 get ready to go out / get dressed for going out // 외출했다가 돌아오다 come home [back] from a visit // 좀처럼 외출하지 않다 seldom stir abroad[outside] // 잠시 외출해도 되겠습니까 May I go out for a while? // 그가 어디로 외출했는지 압니까 Do you know where he has gone? // 이런 폭풍우에는 외출할 수 없다 There is no going out in such a storm.
● **외출 금지** (군인의) confinement (to the barracks). **외출복** street clothes[wear].

외출혈(外出血) 〔의〕 external hemorrhage.

외측(外側) the outside. ➪=바깥쪽(➪바깥)

외치(外治) **1** diplomacy; a foreign policy. ➪=외교(外交) **2** 〔의〕 external[surgical] treatment. **외치하다** apply external[surgical] treatment; treat externally.

외치다 shout; cry (out); yell; shriek; scream; (감격해서) exclaim. ¶사람 살리라고 ~ cry for help // 고통을 못 이겨[기쁜 나머지] ~ cry out in pain[for joy] // 목이 쉬도록 ~ shout oneself hoarse // 소리 높이 ~ give a shout / scream / let out a yell // "도둑이야!" 하고 ~ cry "Thief!" // "불이야! 불이야!" 하고 ~ cry "Fire, fire!" // 찬성이라고 ~ shout approbation // 반대라고 ~ clamor against // 찢어지는 소리로 ~ utter a piercing shriek // 핵무기 금지를 ~ appeal for a nuclear ban[a ban on nuclear weapons] // 수업료[등록금] 인상 반대를 ~ clamor against a raise in tuition[fees] // 남북통일을 ~ cry out for the unification of Korea.

외침 a shout; a cry; an outcry; a yell; a clamor; a shriek; a scream. ¶개혁의 ~ a cry [clamor] for reform // 민족의 ~ the voice of the race.

외탁하다(外-) take after one's mother's side in appearance[character]. ¶그녀는 외탁했다 She takes after her mother's side of the family.

외톨 1 (밤송이 등의) a single ripened chestnut [garlic bulb]. **2** a single person. ➪=외톨이

외톨이 〔홀몸〕 a single[solitary / lonely] person. ¶~가 되다 be left alone[to oneself] // 나는 ~가 되어 쓸쓸했다 I felt lonely. // 남녀 짝짓기를 했는데 나만이 파트너를 차지하지 못해 ~가 되었다 When we divided up into couples I was left without a partner[left over].

외투(外套) 《미》 an overcoat; 《영》 a great-

외투막(外套膜) (연체동물의) a mantle.
외판(外販) (a) traveling sale; (a) house-to-house sale. **외판하다** travel (in); make [pay] house-to-house call [visit] for sale; visit from door to door for sale. ¶가정용품을 ~ travel in domestic appliances / make [pay] house-to-house call selling domestic appliances.
● **외판원** a salesman; (여자) a saleswoman; (지방 순회의) a commercial traveler; a traveling salesman; (방문 판매의) a house-to-house salesman [saleswoman]. ¶서적 ~ (house-to-house) salesman in books // 그는 유능한 ~이다 He is an able salesman.
외팔 one arm.
● **외팔이** a one-armed person.
외풍(外風) 1 [밖에서 들어오는 바람] a draught; a draft. ¶~이 있는 drafty (room) // ~을 막다 cut off the drafts // 우리 집은 ~이 세다 My house gives free passage to draughts. // 이 방에는 ~이 있다 There is a draft in this room. 2 [외국 풍속] foreignism; exotic fashion; foreign [Western] style. ¶~에 물들다 be affected in Western style.
외피(外皮) (피부의) an integument; a skin; (과일 씨·옥수수 등의) a husk; (곡식의) a hull; [동물·알·견과 등의 딱딱한 껍질] a shell; [빵·파이 등의 거죽] a crust.
외할머니(外─) a mother of one's mother; a grandmother.
외할아버지(外─) a father of one's mother; a grandfather.
외항(外港) an outer port for a large city; an outport.
외항(外項) [수] an outer term; the extreme.
외항선(外航船) an oceangoing ship [vessel]; an ocean liner(▶ 특히 호화로운 객선).
외향성(外向性) [심] extroversion. ¶~인 extrovert(ed) / extroversive // ~인 사람 an extrovert.
외형(外形) 1 [사물의 겉모양] an outward form [shape]; outward appearance. 2 [경] the gross sales [proceeds]; the turnover. ¶우리 회사는 최근 ~이 연 100억 원으로 급격히 신장했다 The sales figure of our firm recently soared to an annual total of ten billion won.
외화(外貨) 1 [외국의 화폐] foreign currency [money]. ¶우리 ~ (Korea's) foreign exchange holdings // ~를 벌어들이다 earn foreign currency [money] // 우리나라의 보유 ~는 계속 줄어들고 있다 Korea's foreign-exchange holdings are continuing to decrease. 2 [외국 화물] foreign [imported] goods.
● **외화 가득률** foreign-exchange earnings [earning rate]. **외화 관리** management of foreign currency holdings. **외화 보유고** foreign currency holdings; foreign exchange reserve. **외화 유출** the diversion [outflow] of foreign currency. **외화 획득** the acquisition of foreign currencies.
외화(外畵) [외국의 영화] a foreign film [movie].
외환(外患) fear of foreign [outside] invasion; foreign [external] troubles; troubles from without; the pressure [invasion] of foreign enemy. ¶내우~ internal and external troubles / trouble from within and without / troubles at home and abroad.
외환(外換) foreign exchange. ⇨ "외국환(⇨외국)
● **외환 관리법** [법] the Foreign Exchange Control Law. **외환 시장**[시세] a foreign exchange market [rate]. **외환 은행** a foreign exchange bank.
왼 left; left-hand(ed). ¶~ 다리 a left leg / ~ 무릎 a left knee.
왼나사(─螺絲) a left-handed screw [thread].
왼손 the left hand. ¶그녀는 ~으로 젓가락질을 한다 She uses chopsticks in [with] her [the] left hand. / She eats left-handed.
● **왼손잡이** a left-handed person; a left-hander; a lefty. ¶~ 투수 a left-handed pitcher / a left-hander / (미) a southpaw // 그는 ~이다 He is left-handed. / He is a left-hander. **왼손 타자** [야구] a left-handed batter.
왼쪽 the left side. ¶~ 눈 the [one's] left eye // 맨 ~의 the leftmost // ~에 on the left (hand) (of) / left // ~ 길 ~에 on the left(-hand) side of the road // ~에 핸들이 있는 차 a car for left-hand steering // ~에 앉다 sit on (a person's) left // ~으로 돌다 turn to the left / turn left // 나사를 ~으로 돌리다 turn a screw counterclockwise // 다음 모퉁이에서 ~으로 도시오 Make a turn to the left at the next corner.
왼팔 the left arm.
왼편(─便) the left side. ⇨ "왼쪽 ¶강의 ~ 기슭 the left bank of a river // ~에 언덕이 보인다 You can see a hill to the left. / There is a hill on the left.
요[1] a Korean mattress placed on the floor for use as a bed; a sleeping mat. ¶~와 이불 beddings // ~를 깔다 lay a Korean mattress / make the bed // ~를 개다 put away the Korean mattress.
요[2] this; these; present; current. ⇨ "이[5] ¶~ 녀석 this fellow [guy] // ~ 며칠 (동안) these few days / for the last few days // ~ 근처에 in this neighborhood.
요(要) [중요한 골자] the main [essential] point; the point. ¶~는 The point is (that) ... // ~는 무리를 하지 않는 것이다 It is essential that you should not overdo it. // ~ 기본을 파악하는 것이다 The essential [main / most important] thing is to grasp the fundamental principles.
요가 (범) yoga. ¶~의 수련자 a yogi // ~를 하다 practice yoga.
요강(要綱) a summary [an outline] of essential points; the gist; the main principle; [취지서] a prospectus. ¶입시 ~ a list of the entrance requirements (for a college) // 모집 ~ guidelines for applicants / an application guidebook [handbook].
요건(要件) 1 [중요한 일] an important matter [business]. 2 [필요조건] a condition; a requisite; an indispensable [essential] factor; essentials. ¶~을 구비하다 meet [satisfy] the necessary [essential] conditions [requirements] // 관용은 평화의 첫째 ~이다 Tolerance is the first requisite for peace.

요격(邀擊) an ambush; intercept; interception. ¶공중 ~ air interception. **요격하다** lie in wait[ambush] (for); ambush; waylay; intercept. ¶적을 ~ meet[confront] the (approaching) enemy // 침입하는 미사일을 ~ intercept an incoming missile // 아군은 적기를 요격할 태세를 갖추었다 Our forces prepared to intercept enemy airplanes.
● **요격기** an interceptor (fighter). **요격 미사일** an interceptor; an intercept(or) missile.
요결(要訣) 1 [비결] a key; a secret. ¶성공의 ~ the secret of success; the key to success // 성공의 ~은 노력이다 The secret of success lies in hard work. // 건강의 ~은 일찍 일어나는 것이다 Early rising in the morning is a key to good health. 2 [긴요한 뜻] an essential meaning; a vital point (of).
요괴(妖怪) 〔요망스러운 마귀〕 a ghost; an apparition; a specter[(영) spectre]. **요괴하다** wicked and bizarre; eerie; weird.
요구(要求) (권리로서의, 또는 강력한) a demand; (당연한 권리로서의) a claim; 〔요청〕 a request; 〔필요〕 needs. ¶임금 인상 ~ a demand for higher wages // 시대의 ~ the needs[requirements] of the times // 정당한 ~ a reasonable claim // 부당한[터무니없는] ~ an unreasonable[inordinate] demand // ~에 응하다 admit (a person's) claim / accede to[meet] (a person's) demand / comply with (a person's) request // 시대의 ~를 충족하다 fulfill the needs[requirement] of the times // 노동자들의 임금 인상 ~는 거절되었다 The workers' demands for higher pay were rejected. // 그 집이 자기 것이라는 그의 ~는 무효가 되었다 His claim to ownership of the house was invalid. // 우리는 너의 ~에 응해서 여기에 왔다 We came here at your request. // 당장의 ~를 만족시켜 주는 집이면 되겠습니다 I shall put up with the house if it answers my immediate needs. **요구하다** require; claim (damaged); demand; request; call (for); call upon (a person to do); ask [make a demand] for (money). ¶손해 배상을 ~ put in a claim for the damage / claim (100 dollar) for damages // 법의 보호를 ~ claim the protection of the law // 그는 터무니없는 값을 요구했다 He asked[wanted] a preposterous price. // (구어) He jacked up the price to a preposterous level. // 그 땅이 정말로 너의 것이라면 왜 권리를 요구하지 않는가 If the land really belongs to you, why don't you lay claim to it? // 사회는 인재를 요구하고 있다 Society needs the talented. // 그들은 사장의 퇴진을 요구했다 They demanded that the president should resign. / They demanded[called for] the resignation of the president. // 노조는 회사 측에 임금 인상을 요구했다 The union demanded more pay from the company.
● **요구불 예금** a demand deposit. **요구액** amount demanded[claimed]. **요구 조건** the terms desired.
요구르트 yogurt; yogh(o)urt.
요귀(妖鬼) a ghost. ⇨ 요괴
요금(料金) a charge; a rate; 〔수수료·입장료·전문직에 대한 사례〕 a fee; 〔탈것의〕 a fare. ¶전기[전화 / 가스 / 수도] ~ the power [telephone / gas / water] rate // 우편 ~ postal charges[rates] // 입장 ~ an admission fee // 택시[버스] ~ a taxi[bus] fare // 비싼[싼] ~으로 at high[low] rates // ~을 받다 make a charge (for admission) // ~을 받지 않다 make no charge (for) // ~을 내다 pay a charge[rate] // 비싼 ~을 물다 pay high rates (to) // ~을 올리다[내리다] raise[lower] the charge[rate] // 가스[전기 / 수도] ~을 지불하다 pay the gas[power / water] bill // ~ 없이 배달하다 deliver goods free of charge[for nothing] // 주차 ~은 2,000원이었다 They charged 2,000 won for parking. // ~은 필요 없습니다 It is free of charge. // ~은 후불해도 됩니다 You need not pay now. / You may pay later.
● **요금 별납** charges paid separately. ¶~으로 100통의 편지를 부쳤다 I mailed a hundred letters postpaid. **요금표** a list of charges[rates]; a price list; a tariff.
요기(妖氣) a weird[ghostly] air. ¶이 집에는 ~가 서려 있다 There is something weird and ghostly about this house. // 그녀에게서는 어떤 ~가 감돌고 있다 There is something ghostly[unearthly] about her. / She exudes a weird atmosphere.
요기(療飢) 〔시장기를 겨우 면함〕. ¶그것은 잠시 동안의 ~가 되었을 뿐이다 It just cheated hunger for a while. **요기하다** stave[keep] off hunger; allay[stay] hunger; keep the wolf from the door. ¶그는 치즈 한 조각으로 요기했다 He staved off his hunger with a piece of cheese. // 그들은 바다거북의 알로 요기하며 굶주림을 면했다 They ate turtles' eggs to stave off starvation.
요긴하다(要緊一) important; of vital importance. ⇨ 긴요하다
요까짓 this kind of. ⇨ 이까짓 ¶~ 일로 화를 내다니 그도 어른답지 못하다 It's childish of him to get angry over such a trivial matter [little thing].
요녀(妖女) 〔요망한 계집〕 a temptress; an enchantress; a vamp; a witch; a siren.
요담(要談) a talk on important matters; an important talk. ¶~ 중이다 be the middle of an important consultation. **요담하다** have an important talk (with a person on something); talk over the important matter.
요도(尿道) 〔생〕 the urethra (pl. -thrae, ~s). ¶~의 urethral.
● **요도 검사** urethroscopy. **요도관** the urethral canal. **요도염** urethritis; inflammation of the urethra.
요독증(尿毒症) 〔의〕 uremia; urine [uremic] poisoning.
요동(搖動) shaking; (배의) pitching(전후의); rolling(좌우의); (수레의) jolting. ¶이 길은 차의 ~이 심하다 The car jolts badly on this road. // 배의 ~이 그치지 않았다 The boat kept pitching[rolling]. **요동하다** tremble; shake; quake; wobble; (수레가) jolt; (배가) pitch and roll; rock. ¶배는 전후좌우로 심하게 요동했다 Our ship rolled and pitched [rocked] heavily.
요들 a yodel. ¶~을 부르다 give a yodel // ~ 창법으로 노래하다 yodel (a song).
● **요들 가수** a yodeler.
요란하다(搖亂一·擾亂一) 1 〔시끄럽고 떠들썩하다〕 noisy; loud; boisterous; uproarious; clamorous; tumultuous; shrill. ¶여자의 요란한 비명 소리 shrill[piercing] scream of a woman // 요란한 벨 소리 the alarming sound of a bell // 열차가 요란한 소리를 내며 지나갔

요람 다 The train thundered past.// 대포가 요란한 소리와 함께 불을 뿜었다 The artillery belched fire with a deafening roar. **요란히** noisily; clamorously; with a roar. ¶누군가가 ~ 문을 두드리는 소리를 들었다 I heard someone knocking wildly at the door.// 소방차가 사이렌을 ~ 울리며 달려갔다 A fire engine raced past with its siren screaming. **2** [지나치게 화려하다] showy; gaudy; garish. ¶요란한 장식품 gaudy decorations. **요란히** showily; gaudily; garishly. ¶그녀는 ~ 차려입고 있다 She is gaudily[showily] dressed.// 그 방은 ~ 장식되어 있었다 The room was ostentatiously decorated.

요람(要覽) a summary; an outline; [안내서] a handbook; a manual. ¶회사 ~ a general survey of a company// 대학 ~ a college bulletin[(미) catalog].

요람(搖籃) a swinging cot; a cradle. ¶~을 흔들다 rock (a child) in a cradle.
요람에서 무덤까지 from (the) cradle to (the) grave(▶ 사회 복지의 표어).¶복지 국가에서는 ~ 생활이 보장된다 In a welfare state the people are guaranteed security from (the) cradle to (the) grave.
● **요람기** the cradle; babyhood; infancy; the inchoate stage.

요량(料量) [잘 헤아려 생각함] a thought; a conception; an intention; [판단] judgment; discretion. ¶내 ~으로는 in my thought [conception]// 당신 ~대로 하시오 Act on your own judgment[discretion]. **요량하다** consider carefully; use one's discretion. ¶그 일은 당신이 요량해서 하시오 I will leave the matter to your discretion.// 과연 그가 그렇게 했는지 어떤지 나로서는 요량할 수가 없다 I cannot tell[It is difficult for me to say] whether he did so or not.

요령(要領) **1** [요점] the point; the gist; the sum and substance; [개요] an outline; [요지] the purport; the import. ¶~ 있는 강의 a pointed lecture// ~ 있게 말하다 speak to the point.// 이 해설은 ~이 있다[~이 없다] This explanation is to the point[not to the point].
2 [비결·기교] a knack; the trick; tact; (미) know-how. ¶사람을 다루는 ~ the art of handling people// ~ 있는 사람 a tactless man// ~이 필요하다 require tact[skill]// ~을 터득하다 get the hang[knack] (of)// ~이 생기다 get the hang[knack] of it// 그는 ~이 좋다 [잘 처신하다] He is very clever.// 아내는 돈을 취급하는 ~을 알고 있다[알지 못한다] My wife handles money matters very efficiently [ineptly / clumsily].// 나는 이 일의 ~을 아직 파악하지 못하고 있다 I haven't got the knack[(구어) hang] of this job yet.// ~만 터득하면 말 타기는 쉽다 It's easy to ride a horse once you get the knack[the hang] of it.// 그는 갓난아이를 달래는 ~을 알고 있다 He knows the knack of playing with [amusing] a baby.// ~만 익히면 간단하다 It's easy once you get the knack[hang] of it.// 그는 판매의 ~을 익히는 데 상당한 시간이 걸렸다 It took him a long time to learn the art of salesmanship.// 그녀는 ~ 있게 그 신청을 거절했다 She tactfully refused the offer.
● **요령부득** ¶~한 이야기 a rambling[pointless] story// ~하다 be pointless / be not to the point / be beside the point// ~한 대답을 하다 give a noncommittal[an ambiguous / an evasive] answer// 너의 질문은 ~이다 Your question isn't to the point.// 그의 이야기는 나로서는 ~이었다 I missed the whole point of his talk.// 그의 말은 모두 ~이어서 알 수가 없다 Everything he says is so vague [indefinite] that I can't tell what he means. // 당신의 제안은 ~이다 Your suggestion is not to the point.

요령(鐃鈴·搖鈴) a handbell.
요로(尿路) the urinary tract.
요로(要路) **1** [주요 도로] a main[an arterial] road; a main artery (of traffic). ¶한국의 교통 ~ the main arteries of the Korean highway system. **2** [중요한 지위] an important[influential] position; [당국] the authorities. ¶~에 있는 사람들 those in authority[important positions]// (사람이) ~에 있다 be in authority / hold an important position.

요리(料理) **1** [음식 만들기] cooking; cookery (일반 요리법); cuisine(특정 요리법); [음식] a dish; food. ¶간단한 ~ simple dishes// 고급 ~ haute cuisine// 고기[생선 / 야채] ~ a meat[fish / vegetable] dish// 서양[중국] ~ a Western[Chinese] food[cuisine]// 일품 ~ one-course dinner// 1인분의 ~ a plate// 한국 ~를 먹다 have a Korean meal// ~를 내놓다 serve dishes / set dishes on the table// 그녀는 ~를 잘한다 She is a good cook.// ~ 솜씨가 서툽니다 I am no good at cooking.// 이 ~는 맛이 없다[좋다] This is a poor[delicious / palatable] dish.// ~가 준비되었다 The dishes are ready. **요리하다** cook (food); prepare (a dish). ¶고기[야채]를 ~ cook meat[vegetables].
2 [처리함] handling; management. **요리하다** manage; administer; handle. ¶국정을 ~ manage[conduct] state affairs / administer the affairs of state// 일을 ~ manage the work// 나 혼자서는 도저히 그 일을 요리할 수 없을 것 같다 I think I cannot manage the work by myself.
● **요리법** cookery; cooking; a recipe(개개 요리의 조리법). **요리사** a cook; (프) a chef; a cooky(여자). **요리 책** (미) a cookbook; (영) a cookery book. **요리 학원** a cooking school. **요릿집** a gisaeng house; a (Korean style) restaurant. ¶고급 ~ a fashionable restaurant// 중국 ~ a Chinese restaurant.

요리조리 like this way and that; this way and that. ⇨^{이리저리}

요마 **1** [요만한] trifling; trivial; small. ¶~ 일 a trifle / a trifling[trivial] matter// ~ 일로 놀랄 내가 아니다 I am not the [a] man to be startled by such a trifle.// ~ 일로 결심을 바꿀 생각은 없다 I would not change my mind for so little. **2** by this (much). ⇨^{이만2}

요만큼 about this [so] much. ⇨^{이만큼}

요망(妖妄) ¶~을 떨다[부리다] act[behave] frivolously[capriciously]. **요망하다** frivolous; capricious; fickle; flippant. ¶이 요망한 년 You wicked hussy!

요망(要望) a cry (for); a demand (for); a request; [소망] a desire; a wish. ¶~에 따르다 meet the demand (of the age)// 학장은 학생들의 ~에 응하려고 노력했다 The president tried to meet[comply with] the wishes [demands] of the students.// 정부는 국민의 ~에 귀를 기울여야 한다 The Government

요면(凹面) a concave surface; concave; concavity. ¶~의 concave/양쪽 ~의 concavo-concave.
● **요면경** a concave mirror. ⇨ 오목 거울
요목(要目) **1** principal[important] items; [적요] an epitome. **2** [교] a syllabus (*pl.* -bi, ~es); a conspectus. ¶교수~ a syllabus of lectures.
요물(妖物) [요사스런 물건] an uncanny[weird] one; [간악한 사람] a wicked[crafty and malicious] person. ¶여우는 ~이라고 한다 The fox is regarded as a mysterious animal [magic-creature].
요번(一番) this time. ⇨ 이번
요법(療法) a (method of) medical treatment; a remedy; a cure; therapy. ¶정신 ~ mental treatment // 전기 ~ electrotherapy // 민간 ~ a folk remedy // 방사선 ~ radiotherapy // 지압 ~ finger-pressure therapy // 물리 ~ 사 a physical therapist // 나는 식이 ~을 하고 있다 I am on a diet.
요변(妖變) [요사스런 사건] a mystery; a mysterious event; [요사스런 행동] strange [mysterious / uncanny] behavior. ¶~을 떨다[부리다] act[behave / work] suspiciously [strangely].
요부(妖婦) an enchantress; a temptress; a vamp(ire); a siren; a witch; a jilt(닿녀). ¶~형의 여자 a vamp type woman // 그녀는 이 영화에서 ~ 역으로 나온다 In the film she plays the part of a seductive woman who ensnares men.
요부(要部) the principal[important / essential] part.
요부(腰部) the waist; the hips; the loins; the lumbar[pelvic] region. ¶~의 lumbar.
요사(妖邪) capriciousness; fickleness; treacherousness; wickedness; craftiness. ¶~를 떨다[부리다] behave in a capricious[treacherous / wicked] way / act capriciously[treacherously / weirdly]. **요사하다** capricious; fickle; treacherous; weird; uncanny; wicked; evil; vicious; crafty; cunning.
요사이 [최근] recently; lately; of late(▶ of late는 좀 딱딱한 표현. 완료 시제에나 과거 시제에나 모두 쓰임); [요즈음] these days; [지금] nowadays; (구어) now; [지난 며칠간] the past few days. ¶~는 그를 보지 못했다 I haven't seen him lately. // ~는 경기가 어떻습니까 How is (your) business these days? // ~ 며칠 동안 앓아누워 있었다 I have been sick in bed for several days. // ~는 계속 날씨가 좋다 We have had a spell of fine weather lately.
요산(尿酸) [화] uric acid.
요새 recently. ⇨ 요사이 ¶~ 사람 men of the present-day // ~ 청년 the young men of today / today's youth // ~ 학생 기질 the way of thinking of the students of these days // ~ 일어난 일 a recent event // ~ 어떻게 지내십니까 How have you been (lately)?
요새(要塞) a fortress; a stronghold; fortifications(▶ 보통 복수형). ¶난공불락의 ~ an impregnable fortress // ~가 함락되어 적의 수중에 넘어갔다 The fortress fell to the enemy.
● **요새지 / 요새 지대** a fortified zone.
요석(尿石) [의] a urolith; a urinary calculus.
요소(尿素) [화] urea.
요소 an important[key] point[position]; [군] a strategic point. ¶~~에 at important points[positions] / at every strategic point // ~~를 설명하다 explain the important points (of) // 그는 논문의 ~~에 밑줄을 쳤다 He underlined the important parts of the article. // ~를 군인이 지키고 있었다 Soldiers were stationed at the strategic points. / Troops fortified the points of strategic importance.
요소(要素) 〔성분〕 an element; 〔구성 요소〕 a constituent; 〔요인〕 a factor; a requisite(필요 조건). ¶구성 ~ a constituent element / a component (element) // 생물체의 구성 ~ the elements of living bodies // 생산의 3~ the three requisites for production // 행복의 ~ a factor of happiness // 그의 부주의가 실패한 주요 ~ 중 하나였다 His carelessness was one of the main factors behind his failure. // 건강은 행복에 불가결한 ~이다 Health is a requisite for[an indispensable factor in] happiness.
요술(妖術) conjuring tricks; jugglery; magic. ¶~을 부리다 conjure / juggle / do[perform] a conjuring trick / use magic / perform sleight-of-hand tricks // 그는 ~을 잘 부린다 He is good at conjuring[magic] tricks. // 그는 트럼프 ~을 잘한다 He is good at card tricks. // 그는 모자 속에서 비둘기를 꺼내는 ~을 했다 He conjured a pigeon out of his hat.
● **요술 방망이** a mallet of luck; the Aladdin's lamp. **요술쟁이** a magician; a juggler; a conjurer.
요시찰인(要視察人) a person under (close) surveillance; a person on a surveillance list [blacklist]. ¶그는 경찰의 ~이다 The police are keeping an eye on him.
요식(要式) (the necessary) formalities.
● **요식 행위** a formal act. ¶비~ an informal act.
요식업(料食業) restaurant business.
● **요식업자** a restaurant owner[keeper].
요실금(尿失禁) [한] the incontinence of urine.
요약(要約) summing-up (*pl.* summings-up); a summary; an outline; a digest; a résumé; an abstract(논문 등의); a synopsis(내용의 특징을 간추린 것). **요약하다** sum up; summarize; digest; give a summing-up; abridge; (미) brief. ¶요약하면 to sum up / to make a long story short / to put it shortly[briefly] / in short / in brief / in a word / in sum // 사건을 요약해서 설명하다 give a concise[brief] explanation of an incident // 상황을 요약해서 말하다 sketch[outline / give an outline of] the situation // 다음 이야기를 200자 이내로 요약하라 Summarize[Give a summary of] the following story in less than two hundred words. // 문제를 요약해서 말씀드리겠습니다 I will summarize[touch on the essentials of / sum up] the problem.
요양(療養) medical treatment[care]; [병의 조리] recuperation. ¶자택 ~ home treatment / recuperation at home // 전지 ~ a change of air // 어머니는 병원에서 ~ 중입니다 My

요업

mother is under treatment in hospital.∥그는 지금 집에서 ~ 중이다 He is now recuperating[convalescing] at his home. **요양하다** receive[get] medical treatment; recuperate (oneself / one's health). ¶의사는 내게 1개월 가량 병원에서 요양하라고 말했다 The doctor told me to receive medical treatment in the hospital for a month or so.
● **요양원** a sanatorium (*pl.* ~s, -ria); (미) a sanitarium (*pl.* ~s, -ria). **요양지** a health resort.

요업(窯業) the ceramic industry; ceramics (단수 취급).
● **요업가** a ceramist. **요업 공학** ceramic engineering. **요업 제품** ceramic manufactures; a ceramic(개개의).

요엘서(-書) [성] (The Book of) Joel.

요연하다(瞭然-) clear; evident; plain; obvious; manifest. ¶그것은 일목~ It is clear at a glance. / It jumps to the eyes.

요염하다(妖艷-) fascinating; bewitching; (문어) voluptuous; erotic; (구어) sexy; coquettish; seductive. ¶요염한 자태 an enticing[a charming / a bewitching] figure∥요염한 미소 an enticing[a bewitching] smile∥요염한 여자 an alluring[attractive] woman / a sexy girl / a charmer∥요염한 눈길을 보내다 give a come-hither look / cast a coquettish [voluptuous] glance (at)∥그녀는 그에게 요염하게 웃음было지 She smiled at him bewitchingly. / She flashed a fascinating smile at him.∥그녀는 요염한 눈으로 그를 쳐다보았다 She looked up at him with seductive [amorous] eyes.

요오드(⑤Jod) [화] iodine; iodin(기호 I).
● **요오드팅크** iodine tincture; (구어) iodine. **요오드포름** iodoform; tri-iodomethane. **요오드화**(-化) iodation. **요오드화나트륨** sodium iodide.

요요 a yo-yo (*pl.* ~s, ~es). ¶~를 가지고 놀다 play with a yo-yo.

요원(要員) (necessary) personnel(▶ 단수형으로 복수 취급). ¶보안 ~ security personnel∥노동 ~ workers needed∥대타 ~ [야구] a pinch-hitting specialist.

요원(燎原) a prairie on fire.
요원의 불길 wildfire. ¶대학의 소요가 ~처럼 번졌다 Campus disturbances spread like wildfire.

요원하다(遙遠-·遼遠-) remote; faraway; far-off. ¶목표에 이르려면 아직 ~ We are yet far from our object[goal].

요인(要人) a very important person; a V.I.P. (*pl.* V.I.P's); (구어) a VIP (*pl.* VIPs); a leading[key] figure. ¶정부 ~ a VIP in the government / key figures in the government ∥ ~석 seats (reserved) for VIPs.

요인(要因) a (primary) factor; a main[chief] cause; a cause. ¶최근에 있었던 폭동의 ~ the cause of a recent disturbance∥청소년 비행에는 많은 ~이 깔려 있다 There are a number of factors underlying juvenile delinquency.∥성실함이 그가 성공한 최대의 ~이었다 Honesty was the most important factor in his success.

요일(曜日) a day of the week. ¶그날은 무슨 ~입니까 What day (of the week) is that?∥무슨 ~이든 좋습니다 Any day (of the week) will do (for me).∥"오늘은 무슨 ~입니까?" "수~입니다." "What day (of the week) is it today [What is today]?" "It's Wednesday."(▶ 영어에서 What day?로 물어 오면 요일을 대답해야 한다. 이 요일이 선행하는 습관은 우리말과 다르니 주의할 것)

요전(-前) the other day; some[a few] days ago; some[a short] time ago; recently; lately. ¶~ 약속을 잊지 않도록 하시오 Don't forget what you promised the other day. ∥ ~부터 그를 보지 못했소 I have not seen him for several days.∥~ 날 밤 음악회에서 그를 만났다 I met him at the concert the other evening.∥바로 ~에 그의 편지를 받았습니다 I had a letter from him only the other day[only a few days ago]. / A letter came from him quite recently.∥나는 바로 ~까지 앓아누워 있었다 I was ill until quite recently.

요절(夭折) a premature[an early / an untimely] death. **요절하다** die young; die prematurely; die[suffer] an early[an untimely / a premature] death; die before one's time; meet an untimely death; be nipped in the bud; be brought[sent] to an early grave. ¶그는 요절했다 He died (quite) young. / He died at an early age.∥그는 교통사고로 요절했다 He met a premature death in a traffic accident.

요절(腰折·腰絕) ¶그의 이야기가 너무도 우스워서 우리는 ~복통했다 His story was so funny that we were all in convulsions[we all laughed till our sides began to ache].∥원숭이의 재주를 보고 관객은 ~복통했다 The spectators were all in fits of[thrown into convulsions of] laughter at the funny tricks of the monkey. **요절하다** hold[burst / split] one's sides with laughter; have a sidesplitting laugh; laugh oneself into convulsions; be convulsed with laughter.

요절나다(橈折-) 1 [물건이 못 쓰게 되다] break; be broken; be demolished; come[go] to pieces; be damaged; be destroyed; break [come] down. ¶지진으로 많은 집이 요절났다 Many houses were destroyed[demolished] by the earthquake.∥그의 차는 충돌로 요절났다 His car was badly smashed up[(미) was totaled] in the crash. 2 [일이 실패하다] be spoiled; be ruined; fall through. ¶그 계획은 인력 부족으로 요절났다 The plan fell through due to the shortage of manpower.

요절내다(橈折-) break (down); spoil; ruin; smash; destroy; demolish; break up. ¶그는 화가 나서 컵을 마루에 던져 요절냈다 He threw[flung] a glass to the floor angrily and smashed it to pieces.

요점(要點) the point; the main[essential / vital / principal / crucial] point; the gist (of a lecture); the crux; the essentials; the highlight; the pivot; (미) the nub. ¶강연[강의]의 ~ the main point of a lecture∥논의의 ~ the main points of an argument∥~만 말하십시오 To the point, please. / Come to the point at once. / Cut it short.∥자 잘 들어요, 여기가 ~입니다 Now, listen. This is the point.∥내가 말하고자 하는 것의 ~은 이렇다 The long and short of what I have to say is this.∥~을 추려서 설명드리겠습니다 Let me give you a summary of it.∥이것이 원작과 위작을 구별하는 ~이다 This is the vital point in distinguishing between an origin and a counterfeit.∥네가 말하는 ~을 모르겠다 I

요정(了定) 〔결판〕 (a) decision; (a) settlement; 〔종료〕 an end; a close; (a) conclusion. **요정하다** 〔끝내다〕 end; finish; complete; conclude; bring (it) to a close [an end]; put an end to; 〔결정짓다〕 decide (on); determine; settle; fix (upon).

요정(妖精) a fairy; (작은 요정) a sprite; an elf (*pl.* elves). ¶~의 fairy / elfin //~의 나라 fairyland / an elfland //꽃의 ~ the sprite of a flower / 눈의 ~ a snow fairy / 숲의 ~ a dryad (*pl.* ~(e)s) / 물의 ~ a (water) nymph // 바다의 ~ an ocean[a sea] nymph / a sea fairy.

요정(料亭) a gisaeng house. ⇨ 요릿집(⇨요리)

요조숙녀(窈窕淑女) a lady of refined manners; an elegant[a graceful] lady; a chaste and modest woman.

요주의(要注意) ¶나는 흉부 X선 검사에서 ~를 선고받았다 After the chest X-ray I was told that I needed special medical attention. // 그 후 그는 학급에서 ~ 인물이 되었다 Since then, he has become a student to be watched in the class.
●**요주의자** (건강상의) a person who needs special medical attention; (형법상의) a person under (close) surveillance.

요즈음 〔오늘날〕 now; these days; nowadays; today; at present; 〔최근〕 recently; lately; of late(▶ 이 셋은 과거·현재 완료 시제에도 쓰임. of late는 조금 딱딱한 말). ¶~ 젊은이들 the young people of today[of these days] / today's youth / youngsters[young fellows] (of) today / present-day youths / young people today // ~의 유행 fashions of late / the latest fashion // ~의 경향 present-day trends // ~은 긴 스커트가 유행이다 Long skirts are in fashion now. // ~ 세상에 그렇게 욕심 없는 사람은 드물다 These days we seldom meet with such an unselfish person. / Such an unselfish man is rarely to be met with nowadays. // ~ 본 영화 중에서 어떤 영화가 제일 괜찮던가요 Of the films you have seen recently, which did you like (the) best? // ~ 날씨가 꽤 추워졌습니다 (편지에서) There's a nip in the air these days. / It has been getting colder lately[of late]. // ~ 나는 몸이 좋지 않다 Recently I have not been well. // ~ 젊은이들이 항상 겸손하지 못한 것은 아니다 Today's young people are not always very polite. // ~ 그를 통 보지 못했다 I seldom see him now. / I haven't seen much of him lately. // ~ 보기 드문 큰 눈이 왔다 We had the heaviest snowfall in recent years. // ~ 한국 경제가 세계의 주목을 끌고 있다 The Korean economy today is attracting the world's attention. // ~은 물가가 높다 Prices are high these days. // ~ 아이들은 조숙하다 The children of today are precocious.

요즘 now; these days. ⇨ 요즈음

요지(要地) an important place. ¶상업상의 ~ a place of great commercial importance // 군사상의 ~ a strategic point.

요지(要旨) 〔요점〕 the point; the gist; the major[essential / important] points; 〔대요〕 an outline; 〔요약〕 a summary; 〔취지〕 the purport; the keynote. ¶신 박사의 강연 ~ the gist[main points] of Dr. Sin's lecture // 너는 ~를 전혀 파악하지 못하고 있다 You cannot see the point of your talk. / I can not get[catch] the point of your remarks. have completely missed[failed to catch / failed to grasp] the point. // 강연의 ~를 말씀해 주십시오 Tell me the gist[(문어) purport] of the lecture. // 이 장(章)의 ~는 다음과 같다 The summary[outline] of this chapter is as follows. // 나는 질문의 ~를 노트에 적었다 I wrote down the essential points of the questions in my notebook.

요지경(瑤池鏡) a device for peep[raree] show. ¶~ 같은 정국 the kaleidoscopic political situation // 인생은 ~ 속이다 Life is kaleidoscopic.

요지부동하다(搖之不動-) do not stir[budge / move] an inch; be unshakable[adamantine / steadfast / unyielding / invincible]; stand as firm as rock. ¶그는 한번 마음을 정하면 요지부동한다 Once he has made up his mind, he won't budge an inch. // 무슨 일이 있어도 우리의 단결은 요지부동할 겁니다 We will stick together no matter what happens.

요직(要職) (be in) an important post[office]; (a man in) a key[responsible] post[position]; a post[position] of importance [responsibility / authority]. ¶정부의 ~에 있다 hold an important post[portfolio] in the government // 그는 회사에서 ~에 앉았다 He assumed[was appointed to] an important[a key] post in his company.

요철(凹凸) unevenness; irregularities. ¶지구 표면의 ~ the irregularities of the earth's surface // ~이 있는 uneven / irregular / rugged // ~이 심한 해안선 an irregular coastline.

요청(要請) a request; a demand(강한 요구). ¶ 시대의 ~에 부응하다 meet the demands of the times // 그녀는 참석한 모든 사람들의 ~으로 피아노를 연주했다 She played the piano at the request of all the people there. // 시청자의 열화와 같은 ~에 따라 이 프로를 재방송합니다 This program is being rerun in response to the fervent requests of our viewers. // 협력해 달라는 그들의 ~을 우리는 무시할 수밖에 없었다 We had no choice but to disregard their appeal for cooperation. // 나는 그런 ~에는 응할 수가 없다 I cannot agree to such a demand. // 그는 내게 무리한 [부당한] ~을 했다 He made an unreasonable request of me. // 나는 그 기획을 설명해 달라는 ~을 받았다 I was called upon to explain the project. **요청하다** request; demand; call on[ask] (a person) for (something). ¶몇 번이나 원조를 ~ make many requests for assistance // 정부는 포로의 즉각 석방을 요청했다 The government called for [requested] the immediate release of the prisoners of war. // 우리는 그에게 원조를 요청했다 We asked for his help. // 요청하신 대로 항공 편으로 보내 드렸습니다 We sent the goods by air as requested. // 요청하시는 대로 보내 드리겠습니다 It will be sent on request. // 그들은 사장과의 면담을 요청했다 They requested an interview with the president.

요체(要諦) the secret; the key. ¶선거 운동의 ~는 민중의 마음을 사로잡는 데 있다 The important point in an election campaign is to win the hearts of the people.

요추(腰椎) 〔생〕 the lumbar vertebrae (*sing.* -bra).

요충(蟯蟲) 〔동〕 a threadworm; a pinworm.

요충(지)(要衝地) a place of strategic importance; a strategic point [place]. ¶천연의 ~ a natural stronghold [fortress].

요컨대(要−) in a word; to sum up; in short; in brief; in sum; in fine; to be brief [short]; to make [cut] a long story short. ¶~ 그것을 할 수 있는 사람은 그밖에 없다 In point of fact [When all is said and done / In the final analysis], he is the only one who can do it. ∥ 그는 속은 거야 In short [To make a long story short], he was deceived. ∥ 네 이야기는 ~ 우리의 제안을 거절한다는 말이지 What you are saying amounts [comes down / boils down] to a rejection of our proposal, doesn't it? / ~ 그는 기회주의자이다 In short [In a word], he is an opportunist. ∥ ~ 그녀는 그에게 홀딱 빠지기 시작했던 거야 To make a long story short, she began to fall for him.

요크셔종(−種) (돼지의) a Yorkshire.

요통(腰痛) (suffer from) lumbago (pl. ~s).

요트 (유람용) (미) a sailboat; (영) a sailing boat; a boat; (경기용) a racing yacht; a racer (▶ 한국에서 말하는 요트는 sailboat에 해당하는 경우가 많음). ¶~에 타다 yacht / cruise in a yacht ∥ ~를 타러 가다 go yachting.

● **요트 경기 / 요트 레이스** a yacht race; yachting. (대회) a regatta.

요판(凹版) (인) an intaglio.

● **요판 인쇄** intaglio printing.

요하다(要−) need; require; want; take; call for; demand. ¶이 기계는 수리를 요한다 This machine needs repairing [to be repaired]. ∥ 이 일을 끝내는 데는 꼬박 이틀을 요한다 It will take two whole days to finish this work. ∥ 이 기계의 조작에는 주의를 요한다 You should [want to] be careful in operating this machine. ∥ 이것은 긴급을 요한다 This is urgent. ∥ 이런 수술은 세심한 주의를 요한다 Operations of this kind demand the utmost care. ∥ 그 계획은 많은 시간을 요한다 That project wants plenty of time.

요한 계시록(−啓示錄) [성] The Book of the Apocalypse of St. John(가톨릭교); The Book of Revelations of St. John(기독교).

요한복음(−福音) [성] (The Gospel according to St.) John.

요항(要項) the important [principal] items; the main [essential / important] points; the staple; the gist.

요행(僥倖·徼幸) chance luck; luck by chance; fortune; a godsend; a windfall (▶ 특히 의외의 금전상의); a fluke; a lucky [happy] chance. ¶~을 바라다 trust to chance [luck] / leave (a matter) to chance / take the risk / lean on a false hope / trust to ∥ ~을 바라고 해 보다 take the [one's] chance (of) ∥ ~을 믿고 주식을 사다 buy stocks at a venture ∥ 그것은 ~에 지나지 않는다 It was just good luck [a mere fluke]. ∥ 그의 승진은 정말 ~이었다 His promotion was really godsend [a piece of good luck]. ∥ 이전 같은 ~는 이 계속되는 것은 아니다 Things won't go as luckily [well] as (they did) before. ∥ 그는 ~을 믿고 그런 행동을 한 것이다 He took that action, hoping against hope. ∥ 제가 성공한 것은 순전히 ~입니다 It was by mere chance [by a fluke] that I succeeded. / I owe my success to (good) luck. **요행하다** (서술적) be lucky [fortunate]. **요행히** by (a stroke of good) luck; luckily; by good fortune; as (good) luck would have it. ¶~ 얻은 이익 unexpected [windfall] profits ∥ ~ 얻은 승리 an accidental victory ∥ 나는 ~ 그 사고를 면했다 I was lucky [fortunate] enough to escape unhurt from the accident.

● **요행수**(−數) good fortune [luck]; a fluke; a chance success. ¶~로 남을 이기다 defeat a person by a fluke [through pure luck] ∥ 나는 ~를 바라고 시험을 쳤다 I guessed on [(영) in] the exam. ∥ ~를 바라고 일을 해서는 안 된다 You must not do a thing in hopes of good fortune.

요혈(尿血) [의] bloody urine; h(a)ematuria. ⇨혈뇨

욕(辱) 1 an insulting remark. ⇨**욕설 2** [나무라거나 꾸짖음] (a) scolding; a reprimand; a rebuke. 3 [수치·모욕] shame; disgrace; humiliation; insult. ¶시정의 쇄신을 위해서라면 나는 어떤 ~도 달게 받을 각오가 되어 있다 I am perfectly willing to be called names [eat dirt / eat humble pie / pocket an insult] if what I do helps advance the reform of city government. / I don't even mind being vilified for the reform of city government. 4 [수고] trouble; labor; toil; pains.

-욕(欲·慾) a desire; a thirst; a hunger; an appetite. ¶명예~ a desire for fame ∥ 소유~ a desire to possess / the possessive instinct ∥ 지식~ a thirst for knowledge / hunger after learning / a desire to learn [for knowledge] ∥ 독서~ an appetite for reading.

욕구(欲求·慾求) (a) desire [wish / craving] (for); wants. ¶살고자 하는 ~ the will to live / craving for life ∥ 성적 ~ sexual desire ∥ ~를 억누르다 repress [overcome] one's desires ∥ ~를 채우다 gratify [satisfy] one's wants [desire] ∥ 그의 부모는 그의 물질적 ~를 모두 채워 주었다 His parents supplied all his material wants. ∥ 지적 ~에는 한이 없다 There is no limit to our desire to learn. **욕구하다** desire; want; wish; crave (for).

● **욕구 불만** [심] frustration. ¶~이 되다 [~에 빠지다] feel frustrated / fall into a state of frustration ∥ 그는 ~에 빠져 있다 He is feeling frustrated. / He is irritated because he's not getting what he wants. ∥ ~으로 그런 행동을 하는 사람이 있다 Some people behave like that out of frustration.

욕되다(辱−) be a dishonor [disgrace / shame] (to); bring disgrace upon. ¶나는 내 자신을 욕되게 하는 짓을 할 수 없다 I can't do anything that would hurt my reputation [disgrace my name]. ∥ 그런 짓을 하면 네 가문을 욕되게 하는 것이 된다 You will disgrace [shame] your family if you do anything like that. / If you do so, you will bring disgrace [dishonor] on your family. ∥ 욕되게 사느니 죽는 편이 낫다 I would rather die than be disgraced. / I don't want to live in disgrace.

욕망(欲望·慾望) greed (for); (a) desire (for money / to do / that); a craving; an ambition. ¶~이라는 이름의 전차 (희곡 작품명) A Streetcar Named Desire ∥ ~을 품다 harbor an ambition ∥ ~을 채우다 [억누르다] satisfy [subdue] one's desire ∥ 육체적 ~에 불타다 be consumed with [by] lust ∥ 그는 권력에 대한 강한 ~을 가지고 있었다 He had a lust for power. ∥ 그는 ~을 이루기 위해서라면

무슨 일이든지 한다 He is ready to do anything [resorts to any means] to satisfy [gratify] his desires[ambition].
욕먹다(辱-) 1 [욕설을 듣다] be abused; be reviled; be called (bad / rough) names. 2 [야단맞다] be scolded; get[have] a scolding; catch[get] it; [비난받다] be blamed (for); be criticized (unfavorably); be reproached. ¶그녀는 늑장을 부리다가 어머니에게 욕먹었다 She got a scolding from her mother for her tardiness.// 그는 욕먹을 짓을 했다 His conduct deserves criticism.
욕보다(辱-) 1 [고생하다] have trouble[difficulty]; have a hard time; take pains; go through[undergo / suffer] hardships. ¶그동안 욕보았네 Thank you very much.// Many thanks for your trouble! / I thank you for your kind labor. / You have done a fine job! 2 [치욕을 당하다] be put to shame; disgrace oneself; be humiliated; be disgraced; be shamed; be dishonored; be insulted. 3 [강간을 당하다] be raped; be violated; be outraged; be attacked [(미) assaulted].
욕보이다(辱-) 1 [폐를 끼치다] put (a person) to trouble; give (a person) trouble. 2 [치욕을 주다] disgrace; dishonor; humiliate; insult; put (a person) to shame; bring shame on (a person). 3 [능욕하다] violate; outrage; rape; commit a rape on; abuse; ravish; attack; assault.
욕설(辱說) an insulting remark; abuse; a word of abuse; abusive language; (구어) a swearword. ¶~을 퍼붓다 abuse a person / shower abuse on a person / call a person all names / curse (and swear)(▶ curse는 저주하며 욕하다) / swear at a person / revile at a person // 지독한 ~을 퍼붓다 heap cruel abuse on a person // 군중은 그에게 ~을 퍼부었다 The crowd abused him. / The crowd showered abuse on him.// 갑자기 그에게 마구 ~이 날아왔다 He was greeted with a shower of abuse.// 그는 여러 사람 앞에서 나에게 ~을 퍼부었다 He abused me[called me names] in public.// 의사당 안은 온통 서로 고함치는 ~로 시끄러웠다 The floor of the chamber was in an uproar with abuse being hurled back and forth on all sides.// 그는 우리에게 온갖 ~을 해 대었다 He called us all kinds of names. **욕설하다** abuse; swear (at); revile; use abusive[bad] language (to / against).
욕실(浴室) a bathroom; a bath; (미) a toilet (room). ¶~이 딸린 셋집 a house to let with a bathroom.
욕심(慾心·欲心) [탐욕] greed; avarice; avariciousness; covetousness; cupidity; selfishness; self-interest; [욕망] desire. ¶~을 부리다 be avaricious / be covetous / be greedy / rapacious // 너는 지나치게 ~을 부리는구나 You are asking too much. / You are so grasping[avaricious]. / You are expecting [wanting] too much.// 그는 ~이 많다 He is a greedy[(문어) an avaricious / grasping] man.// 아내는 ~이 없는 여자다 [갖고 싶어 하는 것이 별로 없다] My wife is a woman of few wants. / [욕심꾸러기가 아니다] My wife is far from greedy[(문어) avaricious].// 그는 ~이 많기로 이를 데 없다 He is as greedy as he can be. / He is bursting with avarice.// ~을 버려라 Rise above self-interest.// 그는 ~을 버리지 못한다 He can't resist seeking selfish gain.// ~ 같아서는 조금 더 키가 크면 좋겠다 I wish he were a little taller. / (구어) If I could have my druthers, I'd make him a little taller.
욕심(이) 사납다 be grasping; be sordid; be blind with avarice. ¶그는 욕심이 사나웠다 He was blind with greed[avarice]. / He was so grasping[avaricious].
● **욕심꾸러기 / 욕심쟁이** a grasping[grabby / greedy] fellow[man]; a grabber.
욕쟁이(辱-) a foul-mouthed [-tongued] person; a slanderer; a fishwife(여자); (미국 속어) a knocker; (험담꾼) a scandalmonger; a scandal-bearer. ¶그는 ~다 He is foul-mouthed[-tongued]. / (미국 속어) He is a knocker.
욕정(欲情·慾情) 1 [충동적으로 일어나는 욕심] greed; avarice. 2 [색욕] passion; sexual desire [love]; lust; carnal desire [appetite]; sensual[fleshly] appetites. ¶~을 일으키는 영화 movie that arouses sexual desire // 그녀가 입은 가슴이 깊이 팬 드레스가 그의 ~을 자극했다 Her low-cut[revealing] dress aroused him.
욕조(浴槽) a bathtub. ¶~에 몸을 담그다 have [take] a bath / bathe oneself in the bathtub.
욕지거리(辱-) 〈속〉 an insulting remark. ⇨ 욕설
욕지기 nausea; qualm; retch; a sickly feeling; (미) sickness at the stomach. ¶~를 참다 stifle[repress] a feeling of nausea. **욕지기하다** feel like vomiting; retch; have nausea; feel nauseated; feel sick (at[to] the stomach); feel queasy.
욕지기나다 feel like vomiting; retch. ⇨ 욕지기하다(⇨욕지기) ¶욕지기나는 냄새 a nauseating[nauseous / sickening] smell // 욕지기나게 하다 make one sick at[to] the stomach / turn one's stomach / provoke [cause] nausea / nauseate// 그 냄새를 맡으니 욕지기났다 The smell made me sick.// 보기만 해도 욕지기난다 The mere sight of it was enough to turns my stomach. / My stomach turns at the mere sight of it.
욕창(縟瘡) a bedsore; [의] a decubitus (pl. -ti). ¶그는 ~을 앓고 있다 He has bedsores.
욕탕(浴湯) a bath; a bathhouse. ⇨ 목욕탕(⇨목욕)
욕하다(辱-) abuse; swear (at); call (a person) names; speak ill of (a person); revile (at / against); scold.
욥기(-記) [성] (The Book of) Job.
용(龍) a dragon.
-용(用) use. ¶가정~ 비누 soap for home use / 직원~ 화장실 a lavatory for the staff / a staff toilet // 수출~ 도자기 chinaware for export // 청소년~ 만화 comics for boys // 남자 [여자]~ 우산 umbrellas for gentlemen [ladies] / gentlemen's[ladies'] umbrellas // 부인~ 장갑 ladies' gloves // 업무[가정]~ 의 for business [family] use [purpose] // 일반~ 으로 제공하다 (장소를) open a place to the public / (물건을) put a thing to public use.
용감무쌍하다(勇敢無雙-) be unmatched [unparalleled] in bravery [valor].
용감성(勇敢性) bravery; valor; heroism; gallantry.
용감하다(勇敢-) brave; courageous; gallant;

용건

(문어) valiant(▶ brave는 위험이나 고통에 자진해서 맞서는, courageous는 위험이나 어려움을 당했을 때 두려움을 이길 수 있는, gallant는 용감함에 외관상의 화려함이 따르는, valiant는 특히 싸움에서 불굴의 용기를 보이는); heroic; daring; plucky. ¶용감한 병사 a brave soldier // 그의 용감한 행위 his courageous[heroic] deed // 그는 용감하게도 대통령에게 직소(直訴)했다 He was courageous enough[had the courage] to make a direct appeal to the President. **용감히** bravely; courageously; gallantly; valiantly; heroically. ¶그는 조국을 위해 ~ 싸웠다 He fought bravely for his country. // ~ 전진했다 I moved forward undauntedly.

용건(用件) business; affairs. ⇨불일 ¶급한 ~ urgent[pressing] business // ~은 없습니까 Can I do anything for you? / Can[May] I help you? // 무슨 ~입니까 What can I do for you? / What do you want with[of] me? // 형님은 외출 중인데 무슨 ~이신지요 My brother is away now. Can I take a message for him? // ~이 있으신 분은 건너편 스미스 상회로 (게시) Inquire At Smith & Co. Across The Street. // 바로 ~으로 들어갑시다 Let's get down to business at once. // 나는 곧장 ~을 말했다 I went to the point at once.

용골(龍骨) 1 [고생대의 화석] mastodon bones. 2 (선박의) the keel.

용공(容共) [공산주의 또는 그 정책을 용인함]. ¶~의 pro-communist.

● **용공 분자** a pro-communist. **용공 사상** pro-communist thought.

용광로(鎔鑛爐) [공] a blast furnace; a smelting furnace.

용구(用具) [손으로 쓰는 기구] a tool; [연장] an instrument; (요리·청소 등의) a utensil; (전반적인) an implement; a (tool) kit(도구 일습). ¶운동 ~ sporting goods // 골프[스키] ~ a golf[skiing] outfit // the things one needs for golf[skiing] // 주방 ~ kitchen utensils // 재봉 ~를 가져오너라 Bring something to sew with.

용궁(龍宮) the Sea God's Palace.

용기(用器) [기구를 사용함] use of an instrument[a tool]; [사용하는 기구] an instrument; a tool.

용기(勇氣) courage; valor; bravery; (미) grit; (구어) spunk; nerve; prowess; pluck. ¶술김에 내는 ~ (구어) Dutch courage // 대단한 ~ high courage // ~ 있는 courageous / brave / plucky / gritty // ~ 없는 pluckless / cowardly / timid / fainthearted / lily-livered / nerveless // ~를 잃다 [~가 꺾이다] lose courage[heart] / be discouraged // 용케도 여기에 올 ~가 있었군 How dare you come here? // 나는 거역할 ~는 없었다 I did not dare to disobey him. / I did not have the courage[nerve / heart] to disobey him. // I did not have it in me to disobey him. // 그는 마지막 순간에 ~가 사라졌다 His courage failed him at the last minute. // ~를 내어 다시 한번 해 보게 Call (up)[Summon up / Screw up / Muster up] all your courage and try it once more. / Get up your[the] nerve to try it once more. / Take[Collect] courage[heart] and try it once more. // 그는 아무리 지독한 일을 당해도 ~를 잃는 법이 없었다 The most trying experience did not discourage him. // 당신의 말에 ~를 얻었습니다 Your words have encouraged me. // 사람들은 모두 장군의 ~를 칭송했다 Everybody admired the general for his bravery.

용기(容器) (상자·깡통 등의) a container; (문어) a receptacle; (특히 액체를 담는) a vessel; a case. ¶~의 무게 tare weight / actual tare // 그것을 담아 갈 ~가 없다 I have nothing to carry it in. // 그 빈 깡통을 ~로 쓸 수 있다 The empty can[(영) tin] will serve as a container. // 이것은 ~의 무게를 포함해서[빼고] 1 킬로그램입니다 This weighs one kilogram gross[net]. / This weighs one kilogram gross[net] weight.

용꿈(龍−) a lucky[an auspicious] dream; a good and prosperous dream. ¶~을 꾸다 dream[have] a lucky dream / see a dragon in one's dream as a good omen.

용납(容納) permission; allowance; approval; admission; toleration; [용서] pardon; forgiveness. **용납하다** permit; allow; approve; admit; tolerate; pardon; forgive. ¶지연을 용납하지 않다 admit of no delay // 아버지는 내가 그 일에 참여하는 것을 용납하지 않을 것이다 Father will not permit me to take part in it.

용녀(龍女) 1 [용왕의 딸] the princess of the Sea God. 2 [용궁에 산다는 선녀] a nymph of the Sea God's Palace.

용단(勇斷) a resolute decision; a resolute [decisive] step; a drastic measure; a (manly) resolution; a courageous decision. ¶~을 내리다 make[give] a courageous[resolute] decision / make a (manly) resolution / take a resolute[decisive] step // 사장의 ~으로 그는 해고를 면했다 He escaped being fired thanks to the president's decision. // 경찰서 서장은 폭도 진압에 관해서 ~을 내리지 않을 수 없었다 The police chief was obliged to take decisive steps to suppress the mob.

용달(用達) delivery; delivery service. **용달하다** deliver.

● **용달업** the delivery business. **용달차** a delivery van.

용도(用途) a use; service. ¶~가 다양하다 have many[various] uses / be used [utilized] for various purposes[in various ways] // 돈의 ~를 밝히다[분명히 해 두다] keep a record of how money was spent[what the money was spent for](▶ for what은 사용한 목적을 나타냄) / keep account of the money spent / make known[account for] how the money was spent // 돈의 ~가 불분명하다 It is not clear how the money was spent. // 이 기계는 어떤 ~에 쓰입니까 What is this machine used for? / What use does this machine have?

용돈(用−) pocket money(▶ 영국에서는 어린이가 받는 용돈을 말함); spending money; (미) an allowance(▶ 영국에서는 학생, 장성한 딸이나 아들이 받는 용돈); pin money(▶ 아내·딸·누이의 용돈). ¶심부름을 하고 ~을 얻다 earn pocket money by running errands // 그는 ~으로 아내에게 줄 선물을 샀다 He bought a present for his wife out of his own pocket. // 나는 아이에게 1주일에 5천 원씩 ~을 준다 I give[allow] my child 5,000 won a week for pocket money[his own use]. / I give my child an allowance of 5,000 won a month.

용두사미(龍頭蛇尾) an anticlimax; a tame

용두질 masturbation; onanism; self-abuse. **용두질하다** masturbate; perform masturbation[onanism]; commit self-abuse.

용량(用量) [약의 사용량] the amount of medicine to be taken; dosage; (1회의) a dose.

용량(容量) capacity; volume. ¶열~ thermal capacity∥전기 ~ electric capacity∥이 그릇의 ~은 3리터이다 This container can hold [has a capacity of] three liters.
● **용량 분석** [화] volumetric analysis (*pl.* -ses); volumetry.

용렬하다(庸劣-) stupid; silly; senseless; absurd; [옹졸하다] illiberal; intolerant; mean. ¶용렬한 사람 fool / a simpleton / a blockhead∥용렬한 짓을 하다 do a stupid act / act foolishly.

용례(用例) an example; an illustration(실례). ¶문장을 ~로 인용하다 cite [quote] a sentence in illustration (of)∥이 사전에는 ~가 풍부하다 This dictionary has many examples.

용마루(龍-) the ridge (of a roof).

용매(溶媒) [화] a solvent; a dissolvent; a menstruum (*pl.* ~s, -strua).

용맹(勇猛) dauntlessness; intrepidity; valor; bravery; lionheartedness. ¶~무쌍한 군인 a dauntless [brave and daring] soldier / a valiant warrior. **용맹하다** bold; undaunted; plucky; lionhearted; (문어) valiant; (문어) intrepid; (문어) dauntless.
● **용맹심** a dauntless spirit; intrepid courage. ¶그는 ~을 발휘하여 싸웠다 He fought with an intrepid spirit[courageously].

용모(容貌) appearance; looks; features; the face; a countenance. ¶~가 수려한 beautiful / handsome / good-looking / (문어) fair / (문어) comely(▶ handsome은 보통 남자에게, 여자에게는 beautiful을 씀)∥~가 수려한 남자 a man with handsome features∥~보다 마음씨 Better a good heart than a fair face. ∥그녀는 ~가 수려하다 She has good looks. ∥그는 ~가 단정하다[형편없다] He has good [terrible] looks. / He is good-looking[ugly].

용무(用務) business; a thing to do. ¶급한 ~ urgent[pressing] business∥일상 ~ one's daily round / one's routine work∥~를 마치다 finish[execute / carry out] one's business∥무슨 ~지요. May I ask your business?∥네게 잠깐 ~가 있다 I have some work for you (to do).

용법(用法) usage; the way to using; how to use; the directions (for use). ¶전치사의 ~ the uses of prepositions∥기계의 ~ how to use a machine∥~을 잘 알고 있다 be familiar with the use (of)∥이 약은 ~을 잘 모르면 해가 된다 This medicine is harmful if you use it[if used] in the wrong way.

용변(用便) easing nature; going to the lavatory[bathroom]. ¶~ 후 after stool∥나는 ~을 보고 싶다 I have to go to the bathroom [loo].(▶ bathroom은 (미), loo는 (영))/ (멋을 부려) Nature calls. **용변하다** wash one's hands; relieve oneself; ease nature; go to stool[the closet]; go to the lavatory[(미) bathroom]; (여성의 경우) go to the ladies' room[bathroom].

용병(用兵) [군사를 부리는 것] manipulation of troops. ¶~에 능한 사람 an able commander∥~에 통달하다 be well versed in tactics / be a tactician∥전투에서 ~이 뛰어나다 be good at battle tactics. **용병하다** employ [manipulate / maneuver] the troops.
● **용병술** tactics; strategy(▶ tactics는 전술을 말하며 단수 취급, strategy는 전쟁 전체에 관한 전략); the science of war.

용병(勇兵) a brave soldier.

용병(傭兵) a mercenary (soldier); a hired soldier.

용불용설(用不用說) [생] the theory of use and disuse; Lamarckism.

용사(勇士) 1 [용맹스러운 사람] a brave man; a hero. ¶제2차 세계 대전의 ~ a veteran of World War Ⅱ / a World War Ⅱ veteran∥역전의 ~ an experienced soldier. 2 a brave soldier. ⇨⁼용병(勇兵)

용상(龍牀) the King seat; the (royal) throne.

용상(聳上) [역도] the clean and jerk.

용서(容恕) pardon; forgiveness; mercy. ¶~못할 말 an unforgivable remark∥~ 없는 merciless / unsparing∥~를 바라다 beg for mercy∥그들은 적에게 아무런 ~도 없었다 They showed little mercy to their enemies. ∥~를 빌면서 한 말씀 드리고자 합니다 With your permission [(문어) By your leave], I would like to say something to you. **용서하다** pardon; forgive; excuse(▶ pardon은 잘못을 용서하다, forgive는 잘못을 책망하지 않고 상대방에 대한 악감정을 품지 않다, excuse는 책망하지 않고 너그럽게 봐주다); have mercy on (a person); [눈감아 주다] overlook; pass over. ¶그를 용서해라. 네 형제이다 Forgive him. He is your brother.∥아들은 어머니에게 잘못을 용서해 달라고 빌었다 He asked his mother to forgive him for his mistake.∥이제는 용서할 수 없다 I cannot tolerate it any longer. / I cannot let it pass any longer.∥소소한 잘못은 용서해 주자 We'll overlook small mistakes.∥한 번만 용서해 주십시오. Pardon[Forgive] me just this once.∥그는 아들의 잘못을 용서하였다 He excused his son's misbehavior.∥그는 사소한 잘못도 용서하지 않았다 He did not excuse[pardon] even the smallest errors.∥부디 용서해 주십시오 I beg your pardon.

용선(傭船) [배를 세내어 얻음] chartering; hiring; charterage; [세낸 배] a chartered vessel[boat / ship]. **용선하다** charter a ship; hire out a ship. ¶이 유조선은 대형 석유 회사에 5년간 용선하기로 되어 있었다 This tanker was to be chartered[hired] by a big oil company for five years.
● **용선 계약** a charter. ¶~을 맺다 charter a ship. **용선료** charterage; a charter fee (for a boat). **용선자** a charterer.

용설란(龍舌蘭) [식] an agave.

용소(龍沼) the basin of a waterfall; a linn.

용솟음(湧-) [끓어오름] boiling; seething; bubbling up; [분출] gush; leaping up; a spout (of water). **용솟음하다** boil; gush. ⇨⁼용솟음치다

용솟음치다(湧-) [끓어오르다] boil; seethe; bubble up; [분출하다] gush out; leap out; rise up; spurt; spout. ¶용솟음치는 정열 surging passion / an outpouring of passion [enthusiasm]∥피가 용솟음치게 하다 cause

용수 the blood to tingle / inflame the blood (of) / stir one's blood.

용수(用水) (수도의) city water; (관개용의) water for irrigation; (소방용의) water for extinguishing fires. ¶공업[농업] ~ water for industrial[agricultural] use.
● 용수로 (관개의) an irrigation canal[channel]; (발전용 또는 목재 등을 흘려보내는) a flume.

용수철(龍鬚鐵) a (coil / hair) spring. ¶~이 든 매트리스 a spring mattress // ~ 장치가 된 장난감 a windup[spring-driven] toy // 이 인형은 ~로 움직인다 This doll moves if you wind it up.

용신(龍神) the Sea King[God]. ⇨ 용왕
● 용신제 the Sea God festival.

용쓰다 1 [기운을 쓰다] put forth strength; muster (up) [summon] strength; bend one's energy (on / upon). 2 [참다] endure forcibly.

용안(龍顔) the King's face. ¶~을 배알하다 be received in audience by His Majesty[the King]; be granted an audience with His Majesty[the King].

용암(鎔巖) lava. ¶화산에서 ~이 흘러나왔다 Lava gushed[shot] from the volcano.
● 용암 대지 a lava plateau. 용암층 a lava bed.

용액(溶液) a solution. ¶진한 ~ a concentrated[strong] solution // 묽은 ~ a dilute[weak] solution // 3천 배의 질산은 ~ a silver nitrate solution with a concentration[strength] of 1/3000[1 to 3,000] // ~을 만들다 bring (salt) into solution // 석탄산 ~을 만들다 make a solution of carbolic acid.

용어(用語) [술어] a term; phraseology; (집합적) terminology; [어휘] (a) vocabulary. ¶과학 ~ scientific terms // 관청 ~ official language // 법률 ~ legal terms[terminology / phraseology] // 전문 ~ technical terms[terminology] // 의학[군대] ~로 in medical language[military parlance] // 이 책의 ~는 너무 어렵다 The terminology in this book is too difficult.

용언(用言) [언] a word with declined or conjugated endings(▶ declined는 형용사, conjugated는 동사의 경우).

용역(用役) service.
● 용역단(-團) service corps. 용역 수출 service export.

용왕(龍王) the Sea King[God].

용원(傭員) 1 [임시 고용인] a temporary employee. 2 a piecework man. ⇨ 품팔이꾼

용융(鎔融·熔融) [물] fusion; melting. ⇨ 용해
● 용융점 a melting[fusing] point. ⇨ 녹는점

용의 1 [의향] an intention; [생각] an idea; a thought. 2 [준비] preparedness; readiness. ¶그는 목숨을 걸 ~가 있다 He is ready to risk his life.

용의(容疑) suspicion. ¶남에게 ~를 두다 fix one's suspicion on a person // 살인 ~가 걸리 be suspected of murder // 그는 횡령의 ~로 구금되었다 He was detained for suspected embezzlement[on suspicion of embezzlement].
● 용의자 [법] a suspected person. ⇨ 피의자

용의주도하다(用意周到-) be very careful; be cautious; be prudent; be circumspect. ¶용의주도한 계획 carefully laid plan.

용이하다(容易-) easy; simple; facile; plain. ¶그 다리를 놓는 것은 용이한 일이 아니다 It will be no easy task to build that bridge. // 최근, 여러 물가의 상승으로 살기가 용이하지 않게 되었다 Recently, because of the rise in prices, it has become difficult to make both ends meet. // 회사의 재정 상태가 용이하지 않다 The company is in financial difficulties.

용이히 with ease; easily. ¶그런 일은 ~ 믿을 수 없다 It's hard to believe.

용인(容認) admission; approval; acceptance; toleration (of). 용인하다 approve; admit; allow; accept; tolerate. ¶너의 이기적인 행동은 용인하기 어렵다 I can't accept your selfish conduct. // 그들은 그 계획을 용인했다 They approved[gave their approval to] the project.

용자(勇者) a hero (pl. ~es); a brave [courageous] man; a man of valor[courage]; (집합적) the brave.

용자(容姿) the face and features[form]; figure; one's appearance[look / form / style]. ¶꽃다운 ~ a blooming face // 우아한 ~ a graceful figure.

용장(勇將) a brave general[leader]. ¶카르타고의 ~ 한니발 the great Carthaginian general Hannibal // ~ 밑에 약졸(弱卒) 없다 Like master, like man.

용재(用材) [재료] material; [목재] timber; (미) lumber. 건축 ~ building materials.

용적(容積) [용량] capacity; [부피] volume. ¶~ 3리터의 병 a bottle with a capacity of three liters // 이 상자의 ~은 1m³이다 The volume of this box is one cubic meter.
● 용적량 the measure of capacity. 용적률[건] floor space index; floor area ratio.

용접(鎔接) welding. ¶산소[전기] ~ oxyacetylene[electric] welding. 용접하다 weld (together); weld (A to B). ¶축의 파편을 ~ weld the pieces of an axle (together).
● 용접공 welder. 용접기 a welding machine; a welder. 용접봉 a welding rod.

용제(溶劑) a solvent. ¶벤젠은 유지의 ~이다 Benzene is a solvent for grease.

용지(用地) a lot; a site. ¶공장 ~ a factory site // 건축 ~ a building lot[site] // 농업 ~ farmland // 철도 ~ a railway land // ~를 선정하다 choose a site (for a new school).

용지(用紙) [서식으로 된 종이] a (blank) form; a blank; [...용 종이] paper. ¶신청 ~ an application form[blank] // 시험 ~ an examination paper // 답안 ~ an answer sheet // 투표 ~ a ballot // 주문 ~ an order blank // 인쇄된 ~ a printed form // ~에 기입하다 fill out[(영) in] a form.

용질(溶質) a solute.

용출(湧出) eruption; gust. ¶석유의 연간 ~량 the annual output of oil. 용출하다 gush[spring] out; erupt; well up.

용출(溶出) [화] elution. 용출하다 flow out.
● 용출액 [화] an effluent.

용태(容態) one's condition. ¶그 소녀의 ~가 갑자기 호전되었다 The condition of the sick girl took a sudden turn for the better. // 어제 그의 ~가 갑자기 악화됐다 Yesterday he became suddenly worse. // "그의 ~는 어떻습니까?" "별로 좋지 않습니다." "How is he?" "He isn't in very good condition."

용퇴(勇退) voluntary[willing] retirement[resignation]. 용퇴하다 retire voluntarily;

용 resign one's post with good grace; withdraw gracefully; (미) bow out. ¶정계에서 ~ retire from political life // 그는 이제 용퇴하도 될 나이이다 He is old enough to resign his post. // 그는 후진에게 길을 열어 주기 위해 용퇴했다 He retired[resigned his post] voluntarily in order to open the way for younger men.

용트림(龍-) a loud belch forced out on purpose. **용트림하다** force out a loud belch on purpose.

용품(用品) supplies(필수품); goods(물품); a utensil(용구). ¶사무~ office supplies // 주방 ~ kitchen utensils / kitchenware // 가정~ household wares / domestic articles // 우리는 여행~을 모두 샀다 We bought everything we needed for our trip.

용하다 1 [재주가 뛰어나다] skillful; dexterous; adroit; mastery. ¶용한 의사 a skilled physician[doctor] // 용한 점쟁이 a fortuneteller who makes good hits // 그림에 ~ draw deftly well. 2 [장하다] admirable; praiseworthy; laudable; commendable; great. ¶네가 혼자서 그런 큰 일을 다 했다니 참 ~ It is admirable that you did such a great work by yourself. // 그 아이가 주운 지갑을 임자에게 돌려주었다니 참으로 ~ How admirable of the boy to returned the wallet he had found to its owner.

용해(溶解) dissolution; melting; solution; liquefaction. ¶기계적[화학적] ~ mechanical [chemical] solution. **용해하다** melt; dissolve; liquefy. ¶소금은 물에 용해한다 Salt dissolves in water. // 그것은 물에 용해한다[용해하지 않는다] It is insoluble [insoluble] in water.
● **용해도** solubility. ¶~ 곡선 a solubility curve. **용해액** a solution. ⇨ᵘ용액 **용해열** heat of solution. **용해점** the melting point. **용해제** [화] a solvent. ⇨ᵘ용매 **용해질** [화] a solute. ⇨ᵘ용질

용해(鎔解) (금속의) smelting; fusion. **용해하다** smelt; fuse. ¶용해하기 쉬운[어려운] fusible [infusible].
● **용해로** a smelting furnace. **용해점** the smelting point.

용호상박(龍虎相搏) a well-matched contest; a Titanic struggle; diamond cut diamond. ¶~의 결전 a decisive battle fought between two mighty rivals.

우 1 [일시에 몰리는 모양] all at once; with a rush; in a body[crowd]. ¶~ 나오다 come out with a rush / rush out // 사람들이 현장에 ~ 몰려갔다 A crowd of people rushed to the scene. // 사람들이 가게로 ~ 몰려왔다 People stormed the shop. 2 [비·바람이 몰아치는 모양·소리] with a rushing sound; briskly. ¶비가 ~ 쏟아졌다 The rain was lashing down.

우(右) the right.

우(愚) folly; foolishness. ¶~를 범하다 commit a folly.

우각(牛角) a bull's[cow's] horn. ⇨ᵘ쇠뿔
우각(優角) [수] a reflex[major] angle. ¶~의 reflex / major.

우거지 1 [푸성귀의 겉껍질] outer leaves (of a cabbage, etc.). 2 [절인 것의 위쪽의 품질이 낮은 곳] the top layer of pickles.
● **우거지상**(-相) a wry[scowling] face; a sullen face; a scowl; a grimace; a frown. ¶~을 하다 make a wry face / grimace / scowl.

우거지다 grow thick[dense / rampant]; grow rank(▶ rank는 바람직하지 않은 식물에 씀);

우기다 be overgrown with(장소가); be rampant [luxuriant / thick]; flourish. ¶잡초가 우거진 뜰 a garden overgrown[rank] with weeds // 나무가 우거진 산 a thickly-wooded hill // 나무가 우거져 있다 be overgrown [thickly covered] with trees / be thickly wooded // 산에 소나무가 우거져 있다 The mountain is overgrown with pine trees. // 정원은 온통 잡초로 우거져 있다 The garden is overgrown with weeds.

우격다짐 forcing; compulsion; coercion. ¶~으로 by force / forcibly / high-handedly / coercively / (미) by a strong-arm method // 남에게 ~으로 어떤 일을 하게 하다 force a person to do something // 그들은 그 법안을 ~으로 국회를 통과시켰다 They forced the bill through the National Assembly. // 너의 방법은 좀 ~이다 You are a little too high-handed in this matter. **우격다짐하다** force [compel] (a person) to (do); coerce[force] (a person) into (doing); resort to high-handed measures.

우격으로 by force; forcibly; high-handedly.
우경(右傾) inclination to the right; veering [turning / tending] to the right side. **우경하다** lean[drift] toward(s) the right; become [turn] rightist.
우계(雨季) the wet[rainy] season. ⇨ᵘ우기
우골(牛骨) cow bones. ⇨ᵘ쇠뼈
우국(憂國) patriotism.
● **우국지사**(-之士) a patriot; a public-spirited man. **우국충정** patriotism; patriotic sentiment; [열정] a fire of patriotism. ¶~에서 by intense concern for the welfare of the country / out of patriotism.

우군(右軍) the right wing of an army. ⇨ᵘ우익군(우익군)
우군(友軍) [아군] a friendly army[force]; [동맹군] an allied army. ¶~기 a friendly plane.
우그러들다 curl up; contract. ⇨ᵘ오그라들다
우그러뜨리다 make a dent (in); dent. ¶물통을 ~ dent a bucket // 자동차의 펜더를 ~ dent a fender of the car // 새 주전자를 식탁 모서리에 부딪쳐 우그러뜨렸다 I hit the new kettle against the edge of the table and made a dent in the side.
우그러지다 shrink; dent. ⇨ᵘ오그라지다
우그리다 curl[roll] up (one's body); dent. ⇨ᵘ오그리다

우글거리다 1 [물이 끓다] simmer; boil (up). 2 [한곳에 모여 움직이다] swarm; be crowded [thronged]; be alive (with). ¶물고기가 우글거리는 연못 a pond alive with fish // 개미가 설탕에 우글거린다 Ants are swarming about [around] the sugar.

우글우글 in swarms; alive with. **우글우글하다** swarming; alive[crawling] (with); teeming. ¶쓰레기통에는 구더기가 우글우글했다 The garbage can was crawling[alive] with maggots. // 화분 밑에는 지렁이가 우글우글했다 A lot of earthworms were wriggling under the flowerpots. // 이 나라에는 실업자가 ~ There are an enormous number of unemployed people in this country.

우글쭈글하다 wrinkled; withered. ⇨ᵘ오글쪼글하다
우기(雨期) the wet[rainy] season; (열대 지방의) the rains. ¶~에 접어들었다 The wet season has set in. / The rains came.
우기다 insist (on / that); persist (in); de-

우는소리 mand one's own way; force (one's ideas on); assert oneself; impose (one's views upon). ¶자기 말을 ~ persist in one's ideas // 사실이라고 ~ allege as a fact / 자기 의견이 옳다고 ~ stick to one's own opinion / hold fast to one's own views / carry one's point // 그는 자기만 옳다고 우겼다 He insisted he was the only one who was right. // 그는 여전히 모른다고 우긴다 He keeps saying that he does not know. // 그는 자기의 의견이 옳다고 우겨 댔다 He insisted that his opinion was right. / He insisted on the correctness of his opinion. / He persisted in his opinion.

우는소리 a whine; a complaint; a grumble; a grievance; (미국 속어) beef. ¶~를 **하다** grumble (at) / complain (of / about) / (미국구어) gripe // 그는 불경기라고 끝없이 ~만 늘어놓는다 He is constantly complaining about the hard times. // 나에게 ~를 해 봐야 소용없다 It's no use whining about it to me.

우단(羽緞) velvet. ¶그녀는 검은 ~ 옷을 입고 있었다 She was wearing a black velvet dress. / She was dressed in black velvet.

우당(友黨) an allied (political) party.

우당탕 with a thud [thump / bump]; heavily. ¶빈 드럼통이 ~ 소리를 내며 굴러 갔다 An empty oil drum was banging along down the road. // 그는 층계를 ~ 내려갔다 He went bump down the stairs. **우당탕하다** thump. ⇨"우당탕거리다

우당탕거리다 thump; stamp [stomp] (about / along). ¶아이들이 위층에서 우당탕거리며 뛰어놀고 있다 The kids are romping [thudding] away upstairs.

우대(優待) 1 [특별히 잘 대우함] (a) courteous [generous] treatment; (a) warm reception; hospitality. ¶우리는 멀리서 온 손님이라고 하여 ~를 받았다 We received kind [good] treatment as visitors from afar. // 이 나라에서는 외국인은 ~를 받고 있다 In this country foreigners are treated very well. // 그들은 가는 곳마다 ~를 받았다 They were treated courteously wherever they went. **우대하다** treat a person courteously [with courtesy]; receive a person warmly.

2 [특별히 유리하게 취급함] preferential treatment. **우대하다** give preferential treatment; [무료로 대우하다] entertain a person (free of charge). ¶극장은 고령자를 우대했다 The theater offered elderly people complimentary tickets. → ¶유경험자는 급여상 우대받을 것이다 An experienced man will be paid a good salary [be well-paid].

● **우대권** a complimentary ticket. ¶할인 ~ a discount coupon. **우대 금리** prime rate.

우두(牛痘) [의] cowpox; vaccinia. ¶~의 백신 cinic // ~를 놓다 vaccinate / inoculate (a person) for [against] smallpox // ~를 맞다 take [undergo] vaccination.

● **우두 자국** a (large) vaccination scar.

우두둑 with a crunching [gnawing] sound; with a snap. ⇨오도독

우두머리 1 [물건의 꼭대기] the top. 2 [단체·조직의 장] the chief; the head; the leader; the boss. ¶혁명 운동의 ~ the leader of a revolutionary movement // 도적의 ~ the head of a gang of bandits // 여러 사람의 ~가 되어 앞장서다 take the lead at the head of a large group of people // 이 집의 ~는 어머니다 The mother is the boss of this house. / The mother is the head of this house. // 그는 남들의 ~가 될 만한 남자가 아니다 He is not a man to lead others. / He's not cut to be a leader.

우두커니 vacantly; absent-mindedly; absently; blankly; abstractedly; with a blank look. ¶~ 바라보다 look [gaze] vacantly [blankly] (at) / moon (over) / (허공을) stare into space // ~ 서[앉아] 있다 stand [sit] idle // ~ 보고만 있다 remain an idle spectator // ~ 생각에 잠겨 있다 be in a brown study // 그는 출입구[대문간]에 ~ 서 있었다 He was standing stolidly in the doorway.

우둔하다(愚鈍-) stupid (as an owl); silly; asinine; dull; thick-headed. ¶그는 정말 ~ He's real dunce [dummy / blockhead].

우둥퉁하다 plump; pudgy. ⇨°오동통하다

우등(優等) (등급 등의) excellence. (학업의) honors. ¶그는 학력 ~을 인정받았다 He was recognized for excellence in scholarship. // 그녀는 대학을 ~으로 졸업했다 She graduated from college with honors [(미) cum laude]. / (영) She graduated with honours [got an honours degree].

● **우등상** a honor (prize). ¶나는 ~을 받았다 I was awarded an honor prize. **우등생** an honor student.

우뚝 high; aloft. ¶~ 솟은 산 a soaring [towering] mountain // ~ 솟다 rise (high) / soar (up) / tower // 그 산은 구름 위로 ~ 솟아 있다 The mountain rises (high) [towers] above the clouds. **우뚝하다** high; tall; lofty; towering; soaring; [뛰어나다] eminent; prominent; conspicuous; outstanding. ¶우뚝한 코 a high nose // 키가 ~ be tall (in stature).

우라늄 [화] uranium(기호 U). ¶천연[농축] ~ natural [enriched] uranium.

우락부락하다 rude; rough; wild; rowdy; violent. ¶우락부락한 사내 a rough / a rowdy [wild] fellow // 우락부락한 행동[태도] rude [rough] behavior [manner] // 우락부락하게 굴다 behave rudely [wildly] // 그는 성질이 ~ He has a violent temper.

우랄·알타이 어족(-語族) the Ural-Altaic (languages).

우랄 어족(-語族) Uralian; Uralic.

우람하다 stately; imposing; grand; magnificent. ¶체격이 우람한 남자 a big brawny [muscular] man.

우량(雨量) (the amount of) rainfall. ⇨"강우량(⇨강우)

● **우량계** a rain gauge.

우량(優良) superiority; excellence. **우량하다** superior; excellent; choice. ¶품질이 우량한 차 tea of superior quality / high quality tea.

● **우량 기업** a top-ranking company. **우량도서** good books (for the general reader / for children). **우량아** a very healthy child; a child in excellent health. ¶~ 선발 대회 a baby contest [show]. **우량주**(-株) a blue chip; a blue-chip stock; (영) gilt-edged share; (영) gilts. **우량품** superior [excellent] goods; choice goods.

우러나다 soak out; come out. ¶이 미역은 국물이 맛있게 우러난다 This seaweed makes good stock. // 이 차는 향이 잘 우러난다 This tea draws [infuses] well. / This tea produces a lot of flavor. // 이 차는 잘 우러나지 않는다 This tea doesn't draw well.

우러나오다 spring up; well up; soak out. ¶진심에서 우러나온 감사의 말 heartfelt words of gratitude / warm [cordial / heartfelt] thanks // 그의 편지 지면에는 딸에 대한 깊은 사랑이 우러나와 있었다 His letter was permeated with his deep affection for his daughter.

우러러보다 1 [높은 데를 쳐다보다] look up (at); turn one's face upward (to). ¶(힘없이) 하늘을 ~ look up at the sky (helplessly). 2 [존경하다] look up to (a person); respect; revere. ¶우러러볼 만한 인물 an admirable [a laudable / a praiseworthy] person / a person worthy of respect // 나는 그의 용기를 우러러본다 I admire his courage. // 나는 그를 스승으로 우러러보았다 I looked up to [respected] him as my teacher. // 시민들은 그를 우러러보았다 He was respected [held in high esteem] by the townspeople.

우러르다 1 [고개를 높이 쳐들다] raise one's head; look up. ¶하늘을 우러러 한 점 부끄러움이 없다 I am not morally ashamed of myself before God. / I have no sin on my conscience. 2 [존경하다] look up to (a person); respect; revere.

우렁우렁 with a ringing [resounding] sound. ¶~ 울리다 ring / reverberate / resound / roll. **우렁우렁하다** ringing; resounding; reverberating; rolling. ¶그의 목소리는 ~ His voice is deep, rolling and resonant.

우렁이 [동] a pond [mud] snail.

우렁잇속 inscrutability; impenetrability; mystery. ¶그의 마음은 ~ 같다 What he has in his mind is a mystery to me. / I cannot fathom his intention.

우렁차다 sonorous; rotund; resonant; rich and full; resounding. ¶우렁찬 목소리 a rotund [sonorous] voice // 우리는 우렁차게 애국가를 불렀다 We sang the national anthem with a sonorous voice.

우레 thunder. ⇨`천둥 ¶~와 같은 환성 thundering [vociferous] cheers.

우레(와) 같은 박수 ¶사람들은 그에게 ~를 보냈다 He received thunderous applause. // 그는 ~를 받으며 홀을 빠져나갔다 He left the hall amid a storm of applause.

●**우렛소리** a peal of thunder. ⇨`천둥소리(⇨ 천둥)

우레탄 urethane.

우려(憂慮) worry; anxiety; (문어) apprehension; concern. ¶앞으로의 전망에 관해서는 관계 당국 사이에 ~의 빛이 있다 The authorities concerned are very anxious about the outlook for the future. // 선장은 깊은 ~를 하며 어두운 바다를 바라보고 있었다 The captain looked over the dark sea with intense concern [deep anxiety]. **우려하다** be worried [anxious] (about); be concerned (about). ¶나는 교내 폭력의 증가를 우려한다 I am concerned [worried / anxious] about the increase of violence at schools. // 도시 어린이의 건강 상태는 우려할 만한 것이다 The physical condition of city children is deplorable. // 그의 장래를 우려하지 않을 수 없다 I am very concerned about his future. / I am filled with anxiety [concern / apprehension] about [as to] his future. // 의사는 그의 병세를 우려하고 있다 The doctor is anxious about his condition. / The doctor has fears for his recovery. // 우리는 나라의 재정 상태를 우려하고 있다 We are sorried over the financial situation [condition] of our country.

우려먹다 1 [진액 등을 우러내어 먹다] infuse; steep (in a liquid). ¶약초를 ~ infuse herbs in water. 2 [착취하다] screw (out); squeeze; exact; exploit; milk (a person); extort. ¶남에게서 돈을 ~ screw money out of a person / screw a person out of his money / milk a person // 국민으로부터 세금을 ~ wring taxes from the people // 그 고리대금업자는 가난한 학생으로부터 돈을 우려먹었다 The loan shark squeezed money out of the poor student. 3 [다시 써먹다] reuse; reutilize.

우로나란히(右-) [구령] Dress right!

우롱(愚弄) mockery; derision; ridicule; scoff. **우롱하다** make fun of; ridicule; fool; make a fool [an ass] of; make sport of; play with; jeer at; mock at. ¶사람을 우롱하는 데도 분수가 있지 There's a limit to ridicule. // 나를 우롱할 생각이냐 Are you laughing at [trying to make fun of] me? // 그것은 순전히 독자를 우롱하는 짓이다 It is simply trifling with the readers.

우뢰 →우레

우르르 1 [한꺼번에 몰려가는 모양] in crowds [droves]; in great numbers; thronging; rushingly. ¶학생들이 ~ 강당으로 들어왔다 [에서 나갔다] The students thronged into [poured out of] the auditorium noisily. // 소가 우리에서 떼를 지어 ~ 달아났다 The herd of cattle stampeded out of the corral. // 군중이 ~ 광장으로 밀려들었다 People surged in crowds to the square. // 사람들이 ~ 현장으로 모여들었다 People rushed [thronged] to the spot.

2 [물 등이 끓는 모양] boiling up [over]; [물 등이 끓어오르는 소리] (boil) noisily. ¶물이 ~ 끓고 있다 The water is boiling up.

3 [쌓인 물건이 무너지거나 떨어지는 모양] (fall) in a confused heap; together; [그 소리] rumbling; hurtling; rattling; with a crash [crashing noise]. ¶~ 무너지다 fall down all of a heap / collapse (and fall) with a crash / fall rumbling [hurtling / rattling] / crash down // ~ 떨어지다 rumble [rattle] down // 담이 ~ 무너졌다 The wall fell with a heavy thud. / The wall collapsed with a crash.

4 [천둥 치는 소리] rumbling; thundering; booming. ¶~ 울리다 rumble / boom / thunder / grumble // 멀리서 천둥이 울린다 Thunder grumbles [growls] in the distance.

우리 (짐승의) a cage; (가축의) a pen; (작은 동물의) a hutch; (동물원 등에서 새를 기르는 커다란) an aviary. ¶돼지 ~ a pigsty / a pigpen // 사자 ~ a cage for lions / a lion's cage // ~ 에 갇힌 곰 a caged bear // 호랑이를 ~에 가두다 cage a tiger.

우리다 1 [물에] infuse; steep [soak] (herbs) in water. 2 [우려내다] extort; wring; squeeze.

우리(들) [1인칭 복수 대명사] we(주격); our(소유격); us(목적격); ours(소유 대명사); ourselves(재귀 대명사). ¶~ 아버지 my father (▶ 우리나라에서는 때로「나」를「우리」로 표현하는 경우가 있음) // ~ 회사 사장 the president of our company / (구어) our boss // ~ 일동 all of us // ~ 대학에서는 at our [this] university // ~ 연구소의 연구원 research

우리말 our language; the vernacular; Korean.

우마(牛馬) horses and cattle; oxen and horses.

우마차(牛馬車) a horse cart and an oxcart; (집합적) a cart.

우매하다(愚昧-) stupid; silly; ignorant; benighted; asinine. ¶우매한 백성 ignorant[unenlightened] people/우매한 백성을 선동하다 instigate the mob / agitate the mob// 우매한 사람들을 깨우치다 enlighten the ignorant.

우모(羽毛) a feather; a plume; (집합적) feathering; plumage; [솜털] down.

우무 agar(-agar). ⇨"한천(寒天)1

우묵하다 dented; sunken. ⇨오목하다

우문(愚問) a stupid[silly / foolish] question.
● **우문현답** a wise answer to a silly question.

우물 a well. ¶~ 파는 사람 a well sinker[digger] // ~을 **파다** dig[sink] a well // ~을 **치다** clean a well // 이 ~은 깊다[얕다] This well is deep[shallow]. // 오랜 가뭄으로 ~이 말랐다 Because of a long drought, the wells dried up.

우물 안 개구리(속담) a person of narrow outlook; a man of limited scope.

우물에 가 숭늉 찾는다(속담) He seeks wool on an ass.

우물을 파도 한 우물을 파라(속담) Every man must walk[labor] in his own calling[trade].; He that hunts[who runs after] two hares will catch neither.; A rolling stone gathers no moss.
● **우물가** a well side. ¶~에서 at the well. **우물물** well water. ¶~을 **긷다** draw water from a well.

우물거리다 1 [벌레 등이 모여 몸을 꾸물거리다] squirm[wriggle about] in swarm; (장소에서) be alive (with fish); swarm[be crowded] (with). ¶땅에는 벌레가 우물거리고 있었다 The ground was simply crawling with worms.
2 [음식물을 씹지 못하고 이리저리 굴리다] mumble; chew ineffectively. ¶빵껍질을 ~ mumble on a crust.
3 [말이 막히다·더듬다] falter; stammer; speak haltingly; [중얼거리다] speak indistinctly; mumble. ¶그는 무슨 말을 하려고 하다가 우물거렸다 He started to say something but faltered[hesitated]. // 소년은 그 전날 결석한 이유를 대지 못하고 우물거렸다 The boy hesitated[was reluctant] to tell (the teacher) why he had been absent the day before. // 우물거리지 말고 대답해라 Answer me quickly.
4 [행동을 꾸물대다] be tardy; linger; dally; dawdle (over); be sluggish; idle about; [주저하다] hesitate; waver; dilly-dally. ¶우물거리다가 기회를 잃다 dally away one's opportunity // 우물거리고 있으니까 버스가 가 버렸으 You were so slow that we missed the bus. // 우물거리고 있을 때가 아니다 There's no time to lose. / We mustn't dilly-dally. // 모두들 가 버리고 나서도 그는 우물거리고 있었다 He lingered about after everyone else had left.

우물우물 1 (벌레 등이) wrigglingly; in swarms. **우물우물하다** squirm in swarm. ⇨ 우물거리다1 2 (입속에서) mumbling. ¶~ 먹다 chew something with one's mouth closed / mumble. **우물우물하다** mumble. ⇨"우물거리다2 3 (말을) mumblingly. ¶~ 혼잣말을 하다 mumble to oneself / 노부인은 뭔가를 ~ 말했다 The old woman mumbled (out) something. **우물우물하다** falter; mumble. ⇨"우물거리다3

우물쭈물 irresolutely; indecisively; hesitantly; hesitatingly; vaguely; indistinctly; half-heartedly. ¶~ 말하다 mumble / mouth one's words / speak ambiguously // 그는 말꼬리를 흐렸다 He mumbled the end of his words[sentence]. **우물쭈물하다** be irresolute[indecisive]; be hesitant: hesitate; be tardy[slow]; linger. ¶우물쭈물하는 사람 an indecisive man / a person who is always shilly-shallying // 아직도 결정을 않았어? 왜 우물쭈물하는군 Haven't you decided yet? You do shilly-shally. // 우물쭈물하지 마라 No hanging back!

우뭇가사리 [식] an agar(-agar).

우므러들다 become narrower. ⇨오프라들다

우므리다 make narrower. ⇨오므리다

우미하다(優美-) graceful; elegant; refined. ¶ 고아(高雅)하고 우미한 자태 a refined and elegant figure.

우민(愚民) the ignorant masses.
● **우민 정책** policies to keep the people ignorant (and easy to rule).

우박(雨雹) hail; (한 알의) a hailstone. ¶알이 큰 ~ a large hailstone // ~의 피해 hail damage / ~을 동반한 폭풍 a hailstorm // 어제는 ~이 내렸다 It hailed yesterday. / We had[There was] a hailstorm yesterday. / 농작물은 ~의 피해를 입었다 The crops were damaged by[suffered damage from] hail.

우발(偶發) accidental[incidental] occurrence. **우발하다** happen accidentally; occur[come out] by chance. ¶사고가 계속해서 우발했다 Unforeseen accidents happened in succession.
● **우발 사건** a contingency; an accident. **우발성** contingency; eventuality.

우발적(偶發的) accidental; incidental; casual; contingent. ¶~인 사건 an (unforeseen) accident // ~인 일이 없는 한 unless an unforeseen accident occurs // 그것은 순전히 ~인 사건이었다 It was a pure accident.

우방(友邦) [친한 나라] a friendly nation; [동맹국] an ally; an allied nation.

우범(虞犯) [죄를 저지를 우려가 있는 것] liability to crime.
● **우범 소년** a juvenile liable to committing a crime. **우범자** a person liable to committing a crime. **우범 지대** a crime-ridden district; a crime-prone area.

우변(右邊) 1 [오른편쪽] the right side. ¶장부의 ~에 기입하다 enter the right side of the book. 2 [수] the right side of an equation.

우비(雨備) 1 [오른편쪽] a rain outfit; rainwear(입는 것). ¶~를 **입다** put on a rainwear // ~를 **갖추다** prepare for rain.

우비다 dig up; grub. ⇨"후비다

우비적거리다 keep scooping[scraping] out. ⇨"후비적거리다

우사(牛舍) a stable. ⇨외양간

우산(雨傘·雨繖) an umbrella. ¶자동 ~ self-

opening[jump] umbrella // 접는 ~ a folding [collapsible] umbrella // ~의 천 cloth / gore / panel / ~을 쓰다[받다] put up an umbrella / hold an umbrella // ~을 쓰고 걷다 walk under an umbrella // ~을 펴다[접다] open [close / fold] an umbrella // ~을 갖고 가거라 Take an umbrella with you. // 낯선 사람이 내게 ~을 받쳐 주었다 A stranger let me under his umbrella. // 바람이 ~을 뒤집어 버렸다 The wind blew[turned] my umbrella inside [wrong side] out. // 저 여자분에게 ~을 받쳐 드려라 Hold your umbrella over that woman.
● 우산꽂이 an umbrella stand. 우산살 umbrella ribs.

우상(偶像) an idol; an image. ¶~적인 가수 an idol[idolized] singer // ~을 숭배하다 worship an idol // ~을 파괴하다 break idols / smash idols / throw down the idols // 그 가수는 십 대 청소년의 ~이었다 The singer was an idol of the teenagers.
● 우상 숭배 idol worship; idolatry. 우상 숭배자 idol worshiper; idolater. 우상 파괴 iconoclasm. 우상화 idolization. ~하다 idolize.

우색(憂色) 〔근심하는 빛〕 a worried[an anxious] look; a melancholy[gloomy] air. ¶짙은 ~을 띠고 with deep anxiety[intense concern] / ~을 띠다 wear a worried look / wear an anxious look / look concerned [anxious / gloomy / worried].

우생(優生) ¶~의 eugenic.
● 우생학 eugenics. ¶이 결혼은 ~상 바람직하지 않다 Eugenically (speaking)[From a eugenic point of view], this marriage is undesirable. 우생학자 a eugenist.

우선(優先) priority; precedence; 〔선택에서의 우선권〕 preference. ¶부속 고등학교의 졸업생은 대학에 ~적으로 입학이 허가된다 Graduates of the senior high school attached to the university are given priority in admission. 우선하다 have priority (over); take precedence (over). ¶이 일이 다른 무엇보다도 우선한다 This work takes first[top] priority. → ¶우선시키다 give priority[precedence / preference] (to)(▶ 우선권을 부여하는 것이 주어) // 인명 존중은 무엇보다도 우선되어야 한다 Respect for human life should have [take] priority[precedence] over all other things. / The highest priority should be given to human life. / 정부는 이재민 구제를 우선시키겠다는 견해를 밝혔다 The Government expressed the view that relief for the victims should be the first consideration.
● 우선권 (the right of) priority[preference]; a preferential[prior] right; precedence; the first claim. ¶통행의 ~ the right of way // ~을 갖다[~이 있다] have priority (rights) (to / over) / have preference (to) / have a prior lien (on) / have the prior claim (to) // ~을 얻다 acquire a priority / take precedence (over / of) / acquire the first claim (to) // ~을 주다 give priority (to) / give[afford / offer] preference (to). 우선 배당 preference[preferred] dividends. 우선순위 the order of priority[precedence]. ¶~를 매기다 prioritize. 우선주(-株) preferred stocks; 〔영〕 preference shares.

우선(于先) 1 〔먼저〕 first (of all); 〔무엇보다도〕 above all; in the first place; to begin with. ¶~ 사건의 원인부터 조사해 봅시다 In the first place[First of all / To begin with], let's investigate the cause of the accident. // ~ 아이들을 놓아 줘라 Let the children go first. // ~ 돈이 필요하다 We need funds above all [before anything] else. / The first thing we need is money. // ~ 가족에게 알려야겠다 First of all, I must let my family know. // ~ 필요한 자금은 확보되었다 We've secured enough funds for the present.
2 〔아쉬운 대로〕 for the time being. ¶~ 그것으로 족하겠다 It'll do for the time being. // ~ 안심이 된다 Well, that's relief. / At least that's a relief for the moment. / We are safe for the moment, at any rate. // ~ 사례의 말씀만 드립니다 (▶ 답례로 하는 편지의 끝맺음) With many thanks. / Yours gratefully. // ~ 이만하면 되겠다 This will do for the present [time being].
우선 먹기는 곶감이 달다(속담) I don't care what happens afterwards.; The consequence are not my concern.

우성(優性) 〔생〕 dominance; dominant (character). ¶~의 dominant.
● 우성 유전 prepotence. 우성 형질 a dominant trait[characteristic].

우세 〔남에게 비웃음을 당함·비웃음〕 derision; ridicule; sneer. 우세하다 bring[draw] ridicule upon oneself; provoke[evoke] the derision (of); make a laughingstock of oneself; become a butt for ridicule.

우세(優勢) 〔남보다 나은 형세〕 superiority; preponderance; ascendancy; predominance. ¶의회에서는 보수당이 ~를 차지하고 있다 The Conservative Party holds sway in the National Assembly. / The National Assembly is dominated by the Conservatives. // 시장 선거에서 존슨 씨는 처음부터 ~를 지켰다 Mr. Johnson had been in the lead from the start for the mayorship[(영) mayoralty]. 우세하다 〔우위에 있다〕 superior; 〔지배적이다〕 predominant; leading. ¶적은 물량적으로 우세했다 The enemy was superior to us materially. / The enemy was far better supplied than we were. // 그의 견해가 우세해지고 있다 His opinion has gained predominance. // 그들 쪽이 수적으로 우세했다 They were superior (to us)[surpassed us] in numbers.

우세스럽다 〔서술적〕 be shameful[scandalous]. ¶이번 사건으로 내 꼴이 우세스럽게 되었다 This incident made me a laughingstock. / With this incident I was laughed at by everybody.

우송(郵送) mailing; posting. 우송하다 〔미〕 mail; 〔영〕 post; send by mail[post]. ¶서류는 별도로 우송하겠습니다 I will mail[post] you the documents under separate cover. // 이 소포를 한 씨대로 우송해 주십시오 Please send this parcel to Mr. Han by mail[post].
● 우송료 postage; 〔미〕 mailing costs; postal charges[rates]. ¶소포 ~ postage on a parcel.

우수(右手) the right hand. ⇨ 오른손
우수(雨水) 1 rainwater. ⇨ 빗물 2 〔24절기의 하나〕 usu; "the first rainfall of the year" (as one of the 24 seasonal divisions according to the lunar calendar that falls about 18th of February).
우수(偶數) an even number. ⇨ 짝수 ¶~ 페이지 an even-numbered page // ~의 even /

우수 even-numbered.

우수(憂愁) melancholy; gloom; grief; dumps. ¶~의 melancholy / grievous / gloomy // 그들 일가족은 ~에 잠겨 있었다 A melancholy [gloomy] atmosphere had settled over the family members. / The whole family was in a melancholy mood.

우수리 1 [끝수] a fraction; an odd sum(금액). ¶10을 3으로 나누면 ~ 1이 남는다 Ten divided by three leaves a remainder of one. // ~는 버리시오 Round off to the nearest whole number. // ~를 떼어 주세요 Make it a round sum. // ~ 300원을 떼어 버리고 5,000원으로 하겠다 I'll knock off the odd 300 won and make it a round[an even] five thousand won. 2 [거스름돈] change. ¶천 원짜리를 내고 받은 ~ change from a thousand-won note // ~를 내어 주다 make change / give (a person) change // ~를 받다 get the change.

우수성(優秀性) excellency; prowess.

우수수 in great masses; in a multitude; in large[great] numbers. ¶~ 무너지다 crumble[tumble] down // 바람에 나뭇잎이 ~ 떨어졌다 A gust of wind shook a multitude of leaves off the trees.

우수하다(優秀-) superior; excellent; superb; distinguished. ¶우수한 작품 an excellent work // 우수한 법률가 a brilliant[an able] lawyer // 가장 우수한 젊은이들 the pick of young men // 우수한 성적을 올리다 get excellent results / establish a fine record // 그는 우수한 성적으로 졸업했다 He graduated from school with an excellent record[high marks]. // 그녀는 역사에서 우수한 성적을 올렸다 She did very well in history. // 그는 각 과목에서 우수함을 나타냈다 He showed his excellence[superiority] in every subject.

우스개 comicality; drollery; waggery; jocularity; [농담] a joke; a jest; (a) pleasantry; fun. ¶~로 삼다 make fun[sport] of / turn (a thing) into ridicule / laugh away (something) // 냥 ~로 한 말이 그녀의 마음에 거슬린 것 같다 What I said just for fun seems to have offended her.
●**우스갯소리** a short funny story[tale]; a joke. **우스갯짓** clownery; buffoonery; comicality; drollery; waggery.

우스꽝스럽다 ridiculous; ludicrous; funny; comic(al); droll. ¶그는 늘 우스꽝스러운 시늉을 하여 우리를 웃기곤 했다 He used to play the fool and entertain us. // 그 꼴이란 참으로 우스꽝스러웠다 He cut the funniest figure imaginable.

우습다 1 [웃을 만하다] funny; laughable; comical; ludicrous. ¶우스운 이야기 a funny story // 우스운 말을 하다 crack a joke / say funny things // 뭐가 그리 우습나 What makes you laugh so much? // 그의 농담은 조금도 우습지 않았다 His joke wasn't funny at all. / His joke didn't make us laugh at all. // 그는 말하는 투가 아주 ~ The way he talks is very funny[humorous]. // 그가 이 모자를 쓰면 우습겠다 It must be very funny when he wears this hat. / He must look comical in this hat. // 어찌나 우스운지 웃음을 참을 수가 없었다 It was so funny that I could not help laughing.
2 [가소롭다] ridiculous; laughing. ¶그가 사장에 선임되다니 우습기 짝이 없다 How ridiculous[What nonsense] it is that he should be elected as president. // 그런 이야기를 내가 믿을 줄 알다니 우습기 그지없다 It is ridiculous to expect me to believe such stories.
3 [하찮다] trifle; trivial; small; slight; insignificant. ¶우스운 것이지만 받아 주십시오 This is nothing wonderful, but I hope you like it.

우습게 보다 [얕보다] make[think] light of; make little account of; think lightly of; treat lightly; [업신여기다] scorn; disdain; look down (up)on (a person). ¶문제를 ~ treat [take] a matter lightly / 인명을 ~ make light of human life / set human life at nothing[naught] / place low value on human life / 손윗사람을 ~ slight[be disrespectful to] one's superiors // 그는 아무리 작은 일이라도 우습게 보지 않았다 He never made light of small[little] things. // 그는 우습게 볼 수 없는 사람이다 He is not a person to be trifled with[made light of]. // 그가 어린애라고 우습게 보지 마라 Don't underestimate him, just because he is a boy.

우승(優勝) [승리] a victory; (선수권의) a championship; a title. ¶준~ a runner-up (pl. runners-up) // 두 팀이 ~을 다투고 있다 The two teams are vying[competing] for the championship. // 그는 2초의 차로 ~을 놓쳤다 He lost by two seconds. **우승하다** win the victory[championship]; come off[out] winner[victor]; win the title. ¶그녀는 단식에서 우승했다 She won the singles title[championship]. // (수영에서) 원정 팀이 우승했다 The visiting team won the championship (in swimming). // 금년에는 그들이 우승할 것으로 생각한다 I think they will win the pennant [the league] this year.(▶ the pennant는 야구에서, the league는 일반적으로 리그전에서 씀)
●**우승기**(-旗) a championship flag; (미) a pennant. **우승자** [선수권 보유자] a champion; a title holder; [승리자] a winner; a victor. ¶~ 명단 the honor roll. **우승컵 / 우승배** a championship cup; a trophy (cup); (영) cup. **우승 팀** the champion(ship) team; [승리 팀] the winning team. **우승 후보** a (title) favorite.

우시장(牛市場) a cattle fair[market].

우심방(右心房) [생] the right atrium (of the heart) (pl. -ria).

우심실(右心室) [생] the right ventricle (of the heart).

우썩 vigorously; rapidly; noticeably; remarkably. ¶~ 늘다 make a remarkable improvement // ~ 줄다 decrease rapidly // 지난번보다 키가 ~ 자랐구나 You've really grown since I last saw you.

우아 [기쁨의 소리] Hurrah!; Hurray!; Wow!; (미) Gee! ¶~, 우리가 이겼다 Hurray [Hurrah]! We've won. // ~, 신 난다 Gee! That's nice.

우아하다(優雅-) elegant; graceful; refined; polished; tasteful. ¶몸가짐이 우아한 여자 a woman who moves gracefully / (문어) a woman of graceful carriage // 우아한 모습 a graceful[delicate] figure[appearance] / a gentle and elegant figure // 우아한 태도로 in a graceful manner // 태도가 ~ be graceful (and gentle) in manner // 숙모는 언행이 우아

하신 분이다 My aunt has an elegant [a graceful] manner. / My aunt is elegant [graceful] in manner. // 그녀는 우아하게 절을 했다 She bowed gracefully. // 그녀는 우아하게 춤을 추었다 She danced gracefully [elegantly].

우악스럽다 (愚惡-) rough; wild; violent. ¶우악스러운 사람 a wild fellow / a rowdy / a rough / (미국 속어) a rough neck // 우악스럽게 생기다 have a ferocious look // 우악스럽게 다루다 handle roughly / bang [knock] (a thing) about // 그는 일을 우악스럽게 한다 He does a crude job.

우안 (愚案) [어리석은 안건] a foolish plan; [자기의 안] my opinion [plan].

우애 (友愛) 1 [형제간의 사랑] brotherly love; fraternal affection. ¶그 형제는 ~가 두터웠다 The brothers love deeply each other. 2 [친구 사이의 정분] friendship; fellowship; (문어) fraternity. ¶~의 정 a feeling of fellowship // ~를 돈독히 하다 promote good friendship.

우어 [마소를 멈추게 할 때 내는 소리] Whoa; Wo; Woa.

우엉 [식] a burdock; a cocklebur(r).

우여곡절 (迂餘曲折) turns and twists; vicissitudes; complications. ¶인생의 ~ the vicissitudes [ups and downs] of life // ~ 끝에 그 사건은 간신히 결말을 보았다 The matter was settled at last after many twists and turns [many complications].

우연 (偶然) a chance; an accident. (▶ chance 쪽이 일반적, accident는 우연성이 강함) ¶~의 일치 a (strange) coincidence / a coincidental conjunction // 참으로 ~의 일치군 What a coincidence! // 그를 공항에서 만난 것은 순전히 ~이었다 It was purely by chance [accident] that I met him at the airport. // 그 모임에서 그의 옆에 앉게 된 것은 순전히 ~이었다 It was pure chance [It was by mere chance] that I sat next to him at the meeting. **우연하다** accidental; chance; casual; haphazard. ¶우연한 사건 an accident // 우연한 만남 an accidental [a chance] meeting // 그와는 우연한 일로 서로 알게 되었다 I got acquainted with him by chance. **우연히** by chance; by accident; as chance would have it. ¶나는 ~ 그 가게에 들렀다 I dropped in at the store quite by chance. // ~도 그들은 현장에 있었다 They happened [chanced] to be on the spot. // ~ 어떤 생각이 떠올랐다 An idea crossed my mind. / An idea occurred to me. // 나는 ~ 그를 만났다 I happened to meet him. / (구어) I ran [bumped] into him by chance. // 신기하게도 친구가 빠뜨린 지갑을 ~ 내가 주웠다 By a curious [strange] coincidence, I picked up the wallet a friend had dropped. // 사람들은 곧잘 그 두 사람을 형제로 보지만 실은 아주 ~ 서로 닮은 것이다 People often take them for brothers but they resemble each other purely [quite] coincidentally. / People often take them for brothers but it's pure coincidence that they resemble each other. // 나는 ~ 지나가다가 그 노인이 쓰러지는 것을 보았다 I just happened to be passing by and saw the old man fall. // 나는 ~ 그 사실을 알게 되었다 I happened to find out the truth. / I found out the truth by accident.

우열 (優劣) superiority or inferiority; merits and [or] demerits. ¶~을 **가리다** put [place] (one thing) above (the other) / discriminate (between A and B) // ~**이 없다** be equal [level] (with) / be evenly matched (with) // 두 사람 사이에는 ~이 없다 There is no difference between the two. // 그 두 바이올리니스트의 ~을 가린다는 것은 어려운 일이었다 It was hard to tell which of the two violin players was better. // 학업 성적의 ~로 인간의 가치가 결정되는 것은 아니다 Scholastic ability has nothing to do with a person's worth as a human being. // 20명의 참가자가 ~을 겨루었다 Twenty participants vied [strived] for superiority. / Twenty participants struggled [contended] for mastery. // 그 안(案)들의 ~을 논해 봅시다 Let's discuss the advantages and disadvantages [the merits and demerits] of the plans. / Let's discuss the comparative merits of the plans.
● **우열의 법칙** the law of dominance.

우왕좌왕하다 (右往左往-) run about in confusion; go hither and thither [this way and that]; run pell-mell; rush about to no purpose. ¶사람들은 방 안에서 우왕좌왕하며 어쩔 줄 몰라 하고 있었다 People were rushing around the room in total confusion. // 관객들은 출구를 찾아서 홀 안을 우왕좌왕했다 Looking for a way out, the spectators ran about in confusion [went this way and that / went hither and thither] in the hall.

우우 1 [세찬 바람 소리]. ¶바람이 ~ 분다 The wind is whistling [hissing]. / The wind is high filling the air with whistling sounds. 2 [몰려오는 모양] in crowds; in a rush. ¶그들은 문간으로 ~ 몰려갔다 They rushed to the door. // 많은 사람이 ~ 몰려나왔다 Many people came out in a rush. 3 [야유하는 소리] boo; hiss. ¶청중은 ~ 야유를 퍼부어 연사를 하단시켰다 The audience booed and hissed [shouted] the speaker down.

우울 (憂鬱) melancholy; depression; gloom; (구어) the blues. ¶~을 떨쳐 버리다 dispell one's melancholy [gloom]. **우울하다** (기분이) melancholy; (be) dispirited. ¶기분이 우울해지는 음악 gloomy [depressing] music // 기분이 ~ I feel gloomy. / I am depressed in mind [spirits]. / I feel down [blue / low]. // 퍽 우울한 이야기로군요 It's a very depressing story, isn't it? // 그는 아내와 헤어진 뒤로는 우울한 얼굴을 하고 있다 He has looked gloomy [depressed] since he separated from his wife. // 우울해 보이는군 You look depressed [blue / down]. // 왜 우울한 얼굴을 하고 있니 Why the long face? / Why so blue [down]? // 무슨 일로 그리 우울해 있느냐 What makes you feel so gloomy? / What has you put in such a bad mood? // 아버지께서는 성적표를 보시고 우울한 얼굴을 하셨다 When I showed my father my report card he made [drew / pulled] a long face. // 또 한 번의 실패로 그는 우울해졌다 He was [felt] dispirited by his second failure. // 몸의 상태가 나빠 우울해요 I feel depressed about my health. / Something is wrong with me, and it has me very depressed. // 그가 도산했다는 소식을 듣고 우울했다 The news of his going bankrupt made me dejected [(구어) gave me the blues]. // 온통 우울한 일뿐이다 I have had a lot of depressing things happen to me. // 요즘엔 우울한 날씨가 계속되는군 Recently we have been having gloomy weather. // 우울한

얼굴을 하지 마라 Don't pull such a long face.
● **우울증**(-症) depression; melancholia. ¶~환자 a melancholiac.

우월감(優越感) a sense of superiority; a[the] superiority complex. ¶그는 급우들에게 ~을 가졌다 He felt superior[his own superiority] to his classmates.

우월하다(優越-) superior; supreme; predominant; dominating. ¶그들은 다른 팀보다 우월하다는 것을 증명해 보였다 They proved their superiority over[to] the other teams.

우위(優位) predominance; superiority; ascendancy; ascendency (over others); a dominant [prominent] position; a position of advantage. ¶~를 차지하다 get[gain] an advantage (over) / gain[get / obtain] the ascendency / hold a dominant position / attain[establish / realize] superiority (over) / gain[get / have] the upper hand (of) // 이 곳에서는 여성이 ~에 있다 Here women are predominant over men. // 그는 처음부터 다른 사람들보다 ~에 서 있었다 From the beginning he had the advantage over[of] the others. // 군사력에서 이 나라보다 ~에 있는 나라가 없다 This country is inferior to none in military power. // 우리 팀이 ~를 차지하고 있었다 Our team gained[got] the upper hand.

우유(牛乳) milk(▶ 모유·양젖 등과 특별히 구별할 필요가 있을 때는 cow's milk라고 함). **살균 ~** pasteurized milk // **무균 ~** bacteria-free milk // **쉰 ~** sour milk // **~로 자란 아기** a bottle-fed baby / a hand-reared baby // **~를 짜다** milk a cow // **~를 배달하다** deliver milk // **~ 한 잔 주세요** Give me a glass of milk. / A glass of milk, please. // **나는 개를 ~로 키웠다** I fed the dog on milk. / I brought up the dog on the bottle. / I fed milk to the dog.
● **우유 배달부** a milkman; a milk roundsman. **우유병** a milk bottle.

우유부단하다(優柔不斷-) indecisive; irresolute; (weak and) vacillating; wavering; (구어) shilly-shallying. ¶우유부단한 사람 an irresolute[indecisive] man / a man of indecision // 그는 끝까지 우유부단했다 He could not make up his mind[was indecisive] to the last. // 그는 우유부단한 사람이다 He is indecisive[irresolute]. / He is a waverer [shilly-shally / shilly-shallyer]. / He backs and fills. / He does not know his own mind. / He lacks decision.

우의(友誼) [우정] friendship; fellowship; fraternity; comradeship. ¶~를 다지다 promote friendship (between) / form a fast[close] friendship (with) // 그는 ~가 두터운 사람이다 He is a faithful[very kind] friend. / He is faithful[kind / warm] to his friends.

우의(雨衣) a raincoat. ⇨ *비옷

우의(寓意) an allegory; a hidden meaning; [교훈] the moral of the story. **우의하다** satirize; innuendo; lampoon(혹독하게); squib.

우이독경(牛耳讀經) ¶~이다 It's like preaching to deaf ears[to the wind] // 어머니의 간청도 그에게는 ~이었다 All his mother's pleas fell flat on him. / He would not listen to his mother's pleas.

우익(右翼) 1 [비행기의 오른쪽 날개] the right wing.
2 the right wing of an army. ¶우리는 적의 ~을 공격했다 We made an attack on the right flank of the enemy.
3 (주의상의) the right (wing). ¶그는 ~이다 He is a right-winger. // 그는 ~의 색채를 띠고 있다 He has right inclinations. / His political views are conservative. // 그는 어느 쪽인가 하면 ~이다 If anything, he is somewhat conservative.
4 [야구] [우익수] a right fielder.
5 [야구] the right field. ¶그는 ~을 맡고 있다 He is the right fielder.
● **우익군** the right wing of an army. ⇨ *우익2 **우익 단체** a right-wing[rightists] organization. **우익수** [야구] a right fielder.

우장(雨裝) [우비를 차림] preparation against [for] rain; [우비] rain gear; rainwear; a rain outfit; a raincoat. **우장하다** equip[provide] oneself with rain gear; prepare for rain.

우적우적 1 [서두는 모양] vigorously; rapidly. 2 [씹는 모양] munching; with a munching sound. ¶~ 씹다 munch / eat with a munching sound. 3 [무너지는 모양] squeaking; creaking.

우정(友情) friendship; friendly feelings. ¶~을 맺다 contract[form] friendship with (a person) // 나는 그 사람과의 ~을 돈독히[두터이] 했다 I cultivated[promoted] my friendship with him. / I advanced a friendly feeling with him. // 그녀는 ~이 두터운 사람이다 She is kind[warm] to her friend(s). / She is cordial[tender] in friendship.

우주(宇宙) [모든 천체를 포함하는 전 공간] the universe; [질서 있는 통일체로서의 세계] the cosmos; [지구 대기권 밖] space; outer space. ¶대~ macrocosm // 소~ microcosm // ~의 universal / cosmic // 태양과 별은 ~의 일부이다 The sun and stars are parts of the universe.
● **우주 개발 계획** a space developing project. **우주 공학** space engineering. **우주 로켓** a space[cosmic] rocket. **우주론** cosmology. **우주복** a spacesuit. **우주 비행** (a) space flight. **우주비행사** an astronaut; (특히 구소련의) a cosmonaut; (우주 소설 등에 등장하는) spaceman. **우주선**(-船) a spacecraft; a spaceship; a space shuttle(왕복선). **유인[무인] ~** a manned[an unmanned] spacecraft. **우주여행** a space trip; space travel. ¶~자 an astronaut / a space traveler / a traveler in space // ~을 하다 travel through space. **우주 왕복선** a space shuttle. **우주 유영** a spacewalk; a walk in space. ¶~을 하다 spacewalk. **우주인** (지구인에 대해서) an alien; (외계에서 온) a being[creature] from outer space; a spaceman. **우주 정류장 / 우주 스테이션** a space station; a space platform.

우중(雨中) ¶~에 in the rain // ~에도 불구하고 in spite of the rain / ignoring the rain / though it is raining // 이런 ~에 외출을 하시렵니까 Are you going out in this rain[rainy weather].

우중충하다 dark; somber; dull; drab; subdued. ¶우중충한 날씨 gloomy[dull / depressing] weather // 우중충한 색 a dark[subdued] color // 우중충한 하늘 a dull[gloomy / leaden] sky / an overcast sky.

우지 a crybaby. ⇨ *울보

우지(牛脂) (beef) tallow. ⇨ *쇠기름

우지끈 with a crash. ¶강풍으로 돛대가 ~ 부

러졌다 The strong wind brought[blew] down the mast with a crash. **우지끈하다** crash.

우지끈거리다 make successive crashing noises. ¶기둥이 우지끈거리며 쓰러졌다 The pillar collapsed[fell] with a crashing noise.

우지직 1 [타는 소리] cracking; sputtering; with a sputter. ¶~ 타는 불 a snappy fire // ~ 타다 crackle / burn crackling / burn with a crackling sound. **우지직하다** crack; make a crackling sound[noise]; sputter; splutter. 2 [부러지는 소리] with a snap[crack]. ¶나뭇가지를 ~ 꺾다 break a twig with a snap. **우지직하다** snap; crack.

우지직거리다 1 [타다] crackle; crack; pop. ¶우지직거리며 타다 burn with a crackle. 2 [부러지다] creak; crack. 3 [물 등이 졸아붙다] seethe.

우직하다 (愚直-) honest to a fault; (simple and) stupidly honest; too honest. ¶그는 정말 우직한 사람이다 He is natively honest. / He is honest to a fault.

우짖다 1 [새가 지저귀다] sing; chirp; chirrup; twitter; warble. 2 [사람이] cry in tears. ⇨°울부짖다

우쭐거리다 [몸짓을 하며 바삐 움직이다] shake[sway] (oneself) rhythmically; keep dancing[swaying]; [뽐내다] keep strutting [swaggering]. ¶우쭐거리는 태도 a cocksure attitude // 나는 그 녀석의 우쭐거리는 태도가 마음에 들지 않는다 I don't like him because he is so conceited[too sure of himself]. / 그녀는 미인 콘테스트에서 입상하더니 우쭐거린다 She has become conceited[gotten a swollen head] since she won that beauty contest. / 너무 우쭐거리지 마라 Don't be presumptuous[cheeky / so sure of yourself]. / 그녀는 상을 몇 개나 받아도 조금도 우쭐거리지 않는다 She has won several prizes, but she is not at all puffed up (with pride). / 그를 한 번 이겼다고 그렇게 우쭐거리는 거냐 Are you acting so arrogant[haughty / (속어) stuck-up] (just) because you beat him once? / 그들은 우승을 한 뒤 다소 우쭐거렸다 They have been a bit puffed up since their victory.

우쭐우쭐 (몸체를) swaying; dancing; (걸음을) swaggering; strutting. ¶~ 걷다 strut along // ~ 춤추다 dance up and down. **우쭐우쭐하다** shake[sway] (oneself) rhythmically. ⇨° 우쭐거리다

우쭐하다 be proud (of); be pompous; be[get] stuck-up (about); be[get] puffed up (by / with); puff oneself up (with); be[get] (self-)conceited; be[feel] elated (with / by); be inflated[exultant] (over); be self-complacent; have a swelled head; swell with pride (at). ¶조그만 성공에 우쭐해서는 안 된다 Don't become complacent[smug] over your small success. / Don't become too proud of your small success. / Don't be elated over a minor success. / 그는 뻔한 공치사에도 금세 우쭐해진다 He is easily pleased by hollow compliments. // 선생이 한 마디 칭찬해 주기만 하면 그는 곧 우쭐해졌다 A word of praise from the teacher immediately puffed him up. // 그는 첫 번째 표적이 명중하자 지나치게 우쭐해하며 다시 하더니 무참하게 실패했다 Having hit the mark the first time, he carried a good thing too far and tried again, only to fail miserably. // 그녀는 미모라고 아주 우쭐해한다 She is quite proud of her own beauty. // 아무도 반론을 펴지 않자 그는 우쭐해져서 자기주장을 마구 늘어놓았다 Since nobody contradicted him, he just complacently rattled about his idea[theory]. // 이런 일로 우쭐할 것 없다 This is nothing to be proud of. // 그녀는 너무 칭찬해 주면 우쭐해한다 She will get a swollen head[grow arrogant] if we praise her too much.

우천 (雨天) rainy[wet] weather; a rainy[wet] day. ¶2주간 계속된 ~ a wet spell lasting two weeks / two weeks of rain // ~으로 시합은 중지되었다 The game was rained out. / The game was called off because of[on account of / owing to] rain. // 운동회는 ~일 경우 순연됨 In case of rain[If it rains], the athletic meet will be put off until the next fine day.

● **우천순연** (게시) To be postponed until the first fine day in case of rain.

우체국 (郵遞局) a post office; (영) a post. ¶간이 ~ a postal agency // 군사 ~ an army post office(약어 A.P.O.) // 선내 ~ a ship post office // 중앙 ~ (한국의) the Central Post Office / (런던의) the General Post Office(약어 G.P.O.) // 철도 ~ a traveling[railway] post office // ~ 사무원 a post-office clerk / (미) a mail[mailing] clerk / (영) a postal clerk.

● **우체국장** a postmaster; a postmistress(여자).

우체부 (郵遞夫) a postman. ⇨°우편집배원(⇨° 우편)

우체통 (郵遞筒) (미) a mailbox; (영) a postbox; a letter box; a pillar box(▶ 기둥 모양의); a post. ¶~에 편지를 넣다 mail a letter (at a mailbox) / post a letter / put a letter into a mailbox.

우측 (右側) the right. ⇨°오른쪽 ¶거리의 ~에 있는 집 the house on the right-hand side of the street // 당신의 ~에 앉은 사람은 누군가요 Who is the man on your right?

● **우측통행** (게시) Keep to the right.; Walk on right side facing traffic. ¶한국에서 자동차는 ~이다 Traffic keeps to the right in Korea.

우툴두툴하다 uneven; rough; rugged; bumpy; ragged; scraggy; granulated. ¶우툴두툴한 도로 a bumpy[rough] road // 표면이 우툴두툴한 가죽 granulated leather // 표면을 우툴두툴하게 만들다 roughen the surface (of) / (가죽을) granulate.

우파 (右派) the right wing[wingers]; the Right; the rightists; the right-wing faction.

우편 (右便) the right. ⇨°오른쪽

우편 (郵便) [제도] mail[postal] service; (미) mail; (영) post; [우편물] mail; postal matter. ¶국내[외국] ~ domestic[foreign / overseas] mail // 등기 ~ registered mail // 유치 ~ (미) general delivery / (口) poste restante // 군사 ~ military mail // 항공 ~ air mail // 제1[2]종 ~ first-[second-]class mail // 만국 ~ 연합 the Universal Postal Union(약어 UPU) // ~으로 보내다 send (a parcel) by post[mail] / post / mail / consign (a letter) to the post // 신청서를 ~으로 보내다 send (in) one's application by mail // 회신은 왕복 ~으로 해 주십시오 Please reply by return mail[(영) of post]. / 그 편지는 항공 ~으로 부쳐졌다 The letter was sent by air[airmail].

● **우편낭** (미) a mailbag; (가죽의) a mail pouch; (천의) a mailsack; (영) a postbag. 우

우편물 postal matter; (미) mail; (영) post. ¶배달 불능 ~ a dead letter // 광고 ~ advertising matter // ~을 분류하다 sort mail // ~이 많이 왔다 I had a lot of mail. // 오늘 ~은 엽서 뿐이다 There are only postcards in today's mail[post]. **우편배달** mail delivery. **우편 번호** (전체) the postal[(미)] zip] code; (개개의) a postal[(미)] zip] code number (of a postal delivery zone); a (postal) zone number(▶ zip은 zone improvement program의 약어). ¶~는 몇 번입니까 What is your postal code number? **우편 사서함** a post-office box(약어 P.O. Box). **우편 소인** a postmark; a post-office stamp. **우편엽서** a postal card; a post-card. **우편 요금** postage; postal charges [rates]. ¶국내[외국행] ~ domestic[foreign] postage // ~ 수취인 지급 payment of postage by addressee // 미납 postage unpaid // 미납으로 보내다 send (a parcel) (with) postage unpaid // ~ 후납 (표시) Postage will be paid by the licensee[addressee]. // ~ 무료 [불요] (표시) Post-free. / Postage-free. / Free of postal charge. / Postage included. // ~ 지불필 (표시) Postage paid. // ~ 부족 (표시) Insufficient[Short] postage. / Postage due. // ~이 80원 부족합니다 There is 80 won postage due. // 이 편지의 ~은 얼마입니까 What is the postage for[of] this letter? **우편 제도** the postal system. **우편 주문** a mail order. **우편집배원** a postman; (미) a mailman. **우편통** (미) a mailbox; a letterbox. **우편환** (미) a postal[post] money order(약어 P.M.O.); a money order. ¶내국[외국] ~ an inland[international] money order // ~을 발행하다 draw a postal money order // ~을 지불하다 cash a postal money order // ~을 현금으로 받다 have a postal money order cashed / 1만 원짜리 ~을 한 장 끊어 주시오 Give me a postal money order for ten thousand won. // ~을 현금으로 바꾸었다 I cashed a money order. // 그 사람 앞으로 5천 원의 ~을 발급받았다 I had a postal money order for 5,000 won issued to be sent to him. // 5만 원을 ~으로 보내고 싶은데요 I would like to send fifty thousand won by postal money order.

우표(郵票) a (postage) stamp; (미국 속어) a sticker. ¶기념 ~ commemorative stamp // 200원짜리 ~ two hundred won stamp // ~를 붙이지 않고 낸 편지 a letter posted unpaid // ~를 붙이다 put a stamp on (the envelope) / affix[stick / attach] a stamp (to a letter) / stamp (a letter) // ~를 여기에 붙여 주시오 Put[(문어) Affix] the stamp here. // (봉투에 인쇄된 문구) Place postage here. // 이 편지는 얼마짜리 ~를 붙입니까 What is the postage for this letter? // 반신용 ~를 동봉하여 조회하십시오 Inquiries must be accompanied with [by] return postage.

●**우표 수집** stamp collecting; [우표 수집 연구] philately. **우표 수집가** a stamp collector; [우표 수집 연구가] a philatelist. **우표첩** a stamp album[book / booklet]; a stock book.

우피(牛皮) leather. ⇨⁼쇠가죽

우향앞으로가(右向~) 〔구령〕 Right wheel!

우향우(右向右) 〔구령〕 Right face!; (영) Right turn!

우현(右舷) starboard; the right side of a boat. ¶~으로 키를 돌리다 starboard the helm / put the helm starboard // ~ 전방에 선체 출현 Ship sighted starboard ahead! // 배가 ~으로 기울었다 The boat listed to starboard.

우호(友好) friendship; (문어) amity. ¶양국의 ~를 강화하다 promote friendship[amity] between the two nations / cement friendly relations[a friendly understanding] between the two nations.

●**우호 관계** friendly[cordial / amicable] relations; (a) friendship. ¶세계 여러 나라와 ~를 유지하다 maintain friendly relations with all the nations of the world. **우호국** a friendly nation[state / power]. **우호 조약** a treaty of friendship[amity]; a friendship treaty.

우호적(友好的) friendly; amicable; fraternal. ¶~으로 대하다 treat (a person) in a friendly way[an amicable manner] // 우리나라는 그 나라와 ~인 관계에 있다 We are on friendly terms with that country. // 두 당수 간의 회담은 극히 ~으로 열렸다 The talk between the two party leaders was held in a very amicable atmosphere.

우화(寓話) an allegory; a fable(▶ fable은 보통 동물을 주인공으로 한 것). ¶이솝 ~ Aesop's Fables // 동물 ~ an animal fable.

●**우화 작가** a fable writer; a fabler.

우환(憂患) 1 [복잡한 일로 생긴 걱정] troubles; cares; worry; anxiety; distress; (불행) a calamity; a misfortune. ¶집안에 ~이 있다 have troubles in one's family // ~이 끊이지 않다 suffer a series of misfortunes. 2 [질병] illness. ¶집안의 ~ family illness // 그 집에는 ~이 그칠 새가 없다 Someone is always laid up in that family.

우황(牛黃) ox bezoar.

우회(迂廻) a roundabout way; a circuit; a detour. ¶~적 방법 an indirection // ~적 방법을 취하다 use an indirect method. **우회하다** take a long way around; make[take] a circuit (round); make a detour; detour; make [go (to a place)] by] a roundabout[circuitous] way[route]; skirt round; go out of one's way. ¶우리는 우회하여 집으로 돌아왔다 We came home by a roundabout route. / We took a roundabout way home. // 그렇게 하면 멀리 우회하게 된다 That will be a long way round. // 우리는 그를 집까지 바래다주기 위해 우회했다 We went out of our way to see him home. // 그 마을은 산을 우회해서 가야 한다 You have to go around a mountain to get to the village.

●**우회 도로** a bypass; a road bypassing a town. **우회로** a roundabout[circuitous] way [route / course]; a circuit; a detour. **우회 생산** circuitous production; a roundabout method of production.

우회전(右回轉) ¶~ 금지 (게시) No Right Turn. **우회전하다** make a right turn; turn (to the) right; turn toward right.

우후죽순(雨後竹筍) ¶~처럼 새로운 빌딩이 선다 New buildings are sprouting up like mushrooms after rain. // 새 집들이 ~처럼 들어섰다 New houses sprang up like so many mushrooms[weeds] after rain. // 유사품들이 ~처럼 나타났다 Copycat products appeared [cropped up] like so many mushrooms[(속어) like crazy].

욱기(-氣) [욱하는 성질] an inflammable [impulsive] nature; hotheadedness. ¶~가 있다 be hot-tempered[hot-headed / hot-

욱다 1 [안으로 우그러지다] dent; become dented [hollow/depressed]; form a hollow; get a dent in [on]. 2 ((기운이)) 줄이지다] sink; wane; collapse; slacken; become weak; lose vigor; be enfeebled; be weakened; be enervated.

욱시글거리다 swarm (with); be crowded [thronged] (with); teem (with). ¶광장에는 사람들이 욱시글거렸다 The public square was crowded with people.

욱시글욱시글 swarming together. **욱시글욱시글하다** swarm (with). ⇨욱시글거리다

욱신거리다 1 [(머리·상처 등이) 쑤시다] shoot; sting; have a shooting pain (in); tingle [throb] (with pain). ¶팔이 욱신거렸다 Pain shoot up my arm. / I have a shooting pain in my arm.//충치가 밤새 욱신거렸다 My bad tooth [My cavity] ached all night.//아침부터 골치가 욱신거린다 My temples have been throbbing [pounding] since morning. 2 [북적거리다] swarm; throng; hustle and jostle [bustle]; mill about; push and shove; be in a bustle. ¶그 근처에 군중이 욱신거리고 있었다 Crowds were swarming about the place.

욱이다 bend [turn/batter] (a thing) in; dent (a thing). ¶양철을 욱이어 넣다 bend a tin plate in.

욱지르다 intimidate; browbeat; cow. ¶욱질러 말을 못하게 하다 shut (a person) up.

욱질리다 be intimidated; get browbeaten.

욱하다 get impetuous; burst forth; rouse up; flare up; excite oneself; be stirred; lose one's head. ¶욱해서 in a fit of passion / in a (fit of) rage//욱하기 쉬운 성질 an explosive temper // 욱하는 성질이 있는 hot-tempered // 욱하고 성을 내다 be roused to anger / flare up (in anger) / burst into a sudden anger // 그는 욱하여 책을 집어던졌다 He threw a book in a fit of rage.

운(運) fortune; luck; [운명] fate; destiny; (a) lot; [기회] chance. ¶~ 좋게[나쁘게] fortunately [unfortunately] / luckily [unluckily] / ~이 나쁘다 be out of luck // ~이 트이기 시작했다 Fortune is smiling on me. / Luck has turned my way. / My luck has turned.//앨리스는 남편 ~이 없다 Alice has had no luck with husbands.//나는 ~이 다했다 I ran out of luck.//~을 하늘에 맡기고 나는 바다에 뛰어들었다 I jumped into the sea, leaving my fate to Heaven [trusting to Providence].//~ 좋게 위원의 한 사람으로 선출되었다 I was fortunate enough to be chosen a member of the committee.//~ 좋게 순풍이 불었다 Fortunately, a favorable wind arose.//~ 나쁘게 지갑을 잃었다 I had the misfortune to lose my wallet.//~ 나쁘게 눈보라로 열차가 불통이 되었다 Unfortunately [As luck would have it], railroad service was suspended owing to a blizzard.//~에 맡기고 해 보아라 Trust to chance [Providence] and try it. / Give it a try and see what happens. / (구어) Have a go [bash] at it.//가장 ~이 나쁜 사람은 나였다 I was the most unlucky of all.//참 ~이 좋군 How lucky!//이제 우리 집도 ~이 트이나 봅니다 Fortune [The tide] is now turning in our family's favor. / Things are finally starting to look up for family.//내가 그때 그를 만날 수 있었던 것은 ~이 좋았기 때문이다 I was lucky to be able to see him then.

운(韻) rhyme; (미) a rime. ¶~을 맞춘 시 a rhyme / a rhymed verse//~을 달지 않은 시 rhymeless [blank] verse.

운(을) 달다 rhyme; (미) rime.

운(을) 떼다 [말을 시작하다] begin to talk. ¶운을 멘 김에 다 말해 버려라 Don't stop in the middle of what you were saying.

운각(韻脚) (시의) a (metrical) foot (*pl.* feet). ¶5~ five feet / [보격] a pentameter.

운동(運動) 1 [보건을 위하여서 신체를 움직임] (physical) exercise; [경기] athletics; [스포츠] sports; [체조] gymnastics. ¶옥내 ~ an indoor sport // 옥외 ~ an outdoor sport / field sports // 적당한 ~은 건강에 좋다 Moderate exercise is good for the health.//그는 ~으로 조깅을 한다 He jogs for exercise.//테니스는 내가 좋아하는 ~이다 Tennis is my favorite sports.//개는 날마다 ~을 시킬 필요가 있다 Dogs need to have exercise [to be exercised] every day.//이 책을 읽으면 머리의 ~이 된다 This book provides good exercise for the mind. **운동하다** take [get] exercise; exercise. ¶적당히 ~ take moderate exercise. 2 [목적을 위한 집단의 활동] a movement; a campaign; a drive; (의회의) lobbying. ¶모금 ~ a fund-raising drive / a drive to raise funds // 학생 [정치/노동] ~ a student [political/labor] movement // 금주 ~ a temperance movement // 금연 ~ an antismoking [a nonsmoking] movement // 선거 ~ an election campaign // 여성 해방 ~ Women's Liberation [Lib] / the women's movement // 교통안전 ~ a traffic safety campaign / a campaign for traffic safety // ~을 벌이다 set a movement on foot / start a movement / launch a drive [campaign] // 나는 취직 ~을 시작했다 I have started looking for a job. **운동하다** conduct [carry on] a campaign (for/against); canvass (for/against); agitate, lobby (a bill). ¶우리는 국회의원을 상대로 열심히 운동했다 We did a lot of lobbying among Members of Parliament. 3 [물체의 움직임] motion; movement. ¶파상(波狀)[직선] ~ a wavy [straight-line] motion // 상하 ~ an up-and-down motion // 회전 ~ a rotary [rotatory] motion // 행성의 ~ the movement of the planets // 모든 힘은 ~에 변화를 주는 작용을 한다 All forces act to cause a change in motion.//흔들이의 ~이 정지되었다 The motion of the pendulum has stopped. / The pendulum has stopped swinging. **운동하다** move; be in motion.

● **운동가** an athlete; a sportsman. **운동 경기** athletic sports; athletics. **운동권 학생** a student political activist. **운동복** sports clothes; sportswear; a gym suit. **운동부** (학교의) an athletic club. **운동 부족** lack [want] of exercise; underexercise. ¶그는 ~으로 살이 찌기 시작했다 He began to get fat through lack [want] of exercise. **운동선수** an athlete. **운동 시설** sports facilities. **운동 신경** [생] the motor nerves. ¶그는 ~이 발달해 있다[둔하다] He has quick [slow] reflexes. / He is quick [slow] in his movements. **운동 에너지** [물] kinetic energy. **운동원** (어떤 목적을 위한) a campaigner; (선거의) a canvasser; an electioneer [electioneering agent]; (정치상의) an agitator. **운동의 법칙** the laws of motion. 운

운두

운동장 (학교의) a playground; [경기장] a (sports) field. **운동 정신** sportsmanship. **운동화** (스포츠용의) sports[gym] shoes; [고무 바닥의 즈크화] sneakers. **운동회** an athletic meeting[meet]. ¶**학교 ~** the school sports // **~를 개최하다** hold a sports meeting.

운두 the height of shoes[bowls]. ¶**~가 높은[낮은] 신** a high-[low-]cut shoes // **~가 깊은 접시** a deep dish // **~가 높은 모자** a tall hat.

운명 (運命) (신 등의 힘에 의한) (a) fate; (초자연적인) (a) destiny; (나쁜) doom; [주로 행운] (a) fortune; (우연에 의한) a lot; [숙명] kismet. ¶**~의 여신** the (three) Fates / Fortune // **그 장난** a quirk of fate // **~을 지배하다** control fate / sway fortune // **~을 결정하다** determine one's destiny[fate] // **~을 개척하다** carve out one's own fortune / be the master of one's own destiny / shape one's own future // **승무원은 전원 배와 ~을 함께했다** All the crew went down with the ship[shared the fate of the vessel]. // **그 결과가 우리의 ~을 좌우할 것이다** The results will affect our fate. / The outcome will either make us or break us. // **~이라고 체념하기에는 너무 이르다** It is too early to give up and call it fate [resign ourselves to it]. // **그들은 다시 만날 수 없는 ~이었다** They were (destined) never to meet again. // **우리는 결국 죽는 ~이다** We are all doomed[destined / fated] to die eventually. // **~의 여신은 우리 편인 것처럼 생각되었다** Fortune[Lady Luck] seemed to favor us[be on our side / be smiling on us]. // **그 총아란 그를 두고 하는 말이다** Fortune's favorite, that's him. // **신기한 ~으로 두 사람이 부부로 맺어졌다** It was a strange turn of Fortune's wheel that brought husband and wife together. // **이렇게 된 것도 ~이겠지요** This must be the hand of Fate. // **그 전투가 그 나라의 ~을 결정했다** The battle decided the fate of the country.
● **운명론** fatalism. **운명론자** a fatalist.

운명하다 (殞命-) die; pass away; breathe one's last.

운모 (雲母) [광] mica. ¶**흑~** biotite // **백~** muscovite / talc / **금~** phlogopite.
● **운모지** (-紙) mica paper. **운모 편암** mica schist[slate].

운무 (雲霧) cloud and mist[fog]. ¶**~에 싸인 산꼭대기** a mountaintop veiled in cloud and mist.

운문 (韻文) 1 (산문에 대하여) verse. ¶**산문을 ~으로 고치다** versify a piece of prose. 2 [시] poem; (집합적) poetry.

운반 (運搬) transportation; conveyance; transport carriage. **운반하다** [나르다] carry; [수송하다] transport, convey. ¶**철도로 자재를 ~ carry[transport / convey] the material by rail** // **가구를 전부 운반하는 데 큰 밴이 필요했다** It took a large van to transport all the furniture. → **그 채소는 트럭에 의해 시장으로 운반된다** The vegetables are conveyed in trucks to market. // **부상자는 병원으로 운반되었다** The wounded were carried in(to) a hospital.
● **운반비** [수송비] freight; (영) carriage; (화물의) cartage; portage; (철도 화물의) haulage. **운반인** a carrier; [역의 포터·호텔의 보이 등 손님의 짐을 손으로 운반하는 사람] a porter; (광산의) a putter; a headsman. **운반차** [트럭] a truck[(영) a lorry]; [2륜 짐차·짐마차] a cart; [4륜 짐마차] a wagon. ¶**환자[부상자] ~** an ambulance (car) / **이삿짐 ~** a remove[removal] van.

운봉 (雲峯) [산봉우리같이 피어오르는 구름] a highest column of clouds; a cloud bank; [구름을 인 산봉우리] a mountain top[peak] veiled in clouds.

운석 (隕石) [별똥별] a meteorite; a meteoric [falling] stone. ¶**석질** (石質) **~** an aerolite.

운성 (隕星) [천] a shooting star. ⇒**유성** (流星)

운송 (運送) transportation; (영) transport; conveyance; carriage; forwarding; (미) freight. ¶**철도에 의한 화물의 ~** rail freight / **육상** [해상] **~** transportation by land[sea] / **여객 ~** passenger transportation // **트럭 ~ 중의 사고** an accident in transit. **운송하다** transport; convey; carry; forward. ¶**물품은 트럭으로 운송합니다** We will send the goods by truck. / We will truck the goods.
● **운송료 / 운송비** a (passenger) fare; a charge. ⇒**운임** **운송선** a transport (ship); a cargo vessel; a freighter. **운송업** the transport[freight / shipping] industry; the transportation business. **운송업자** (이삿짐 전문의) a mover; (영) a remover. **운송인** a forwarding[shipping] agent; a carrier; (미) an expressman.

운수 (運數) one's star; luck; fortune; chance. ¶**~가 좋은 해** a good[lucky] year // **~가 좋다** be fortunate / be lucky // **나는 ~가 길하다** [불길하다] I was born under a lucky[an unlucky] star. // **그녀는 금년 ~가 좋다**[사납다] Her star is in a favorable [unfavorable] position this year. / Her star is visiting [falling] this year. // **나는 점쟁이한테 ~를 보아 달랬다** I had my fortune told by a fortune-teller. / I had a fortune-teller tell my fortune. // **신년의 복권에 당첨되었으니 금년은 ~ 대통일 것이다** I've won a prize in the New Year('s) lottery. I'm sure this will be my year.

운수 (運輸) transportation; (영) transport; conveyance. ¶**해상 ~** marine transportation / shipping // **육상** [철도] **~** overland[rail] transport(ation) // **여객 ~** passenger[railway] traffic.
● **운수업** the transportation business. **운수회사** a transportation[an express] company.

운신 (運身) a movement; a stir. ¶**그는 중병이라 ~도 못 한다** He is so ill that he can hardly sit up on his bed. **운신하다** move (about); stir.

운영 (運營) [관리] management; [조직을 움직임] administration; operation. ¶**그는 그 회사의 ~에 실패했다** He failed in the management of the company. **운영하다** manage; run; administer, steer; conduct. ¶**사업을 ~ manage[operate / run] a business** // **학교를 ~ run a school** // **국사를 ~ conduct state affairs** // **그 회사를 실제로 운영하고 있는 것은 사장 비서이다** It's the president's secretary who actually runs[controls] the company. → **이 조직은 30명으로 구성된 이사회에 의해 운영되고 있다** This organization is administered by a board of trustees consisting of thirty members.
● **운영비** working expenses; operational [operating] costs. **운영 위원회** (국회 등의) a steering committee; (미국 하원의) the

Committee of Rules. 운영 자금 working [operating] funds [capital].

운용(運用) application; working; (practical) use; operation. ¶그들은 그 법률의 ~을 잘못 했다 They made a wrong application of the law.∥자금의 ~을 그에게 맡겼다 The use of the funds was left up to him.∥문학적 지식은 언어의 ~ 면에 도움이 되는가 Is literary knowledge helpful in the practical use of a language? **운용하다** make; use; work; employ; put in practice; apply. ¶자금을 ~ employ funds / invest one's money shrewdly ∥법률을 ~ apply a law∥이 돈을 어떻게 운용할 셈인가 How do you plan to use this money?
● 운용 자금 working[functioning] capital; operational funds.

운우지정(雲雨之情) [남녀간의 육체적으로 관계하는 사랑] erotic love; sensual love.

운운(云云) and so on; and so forth; and such; and the like. ¶~의 such and such / certain (reason)∥남성의 입장 ~이 문제의 핵심은 아니다 Men's position and so forth [and the like / and so on] is not the core of the problem. **운운하다** [이러쿵저러쿵 말하다] say something or other (of / about); say thus and thus; say such and such; [비판하다] criticize; comment (on). ¶지금은 그것을 운운할 때가 아니다 Now is not the time to criticize [comment on] it.

운율(韻律) [시학] (a) meter [(영) (a) metre]; (a) rhythm. ¶~의 metrical∥~적인 [가락] 있는] rhythmical∥~이 없는 시 rhythmless [lame] verse.

운임(運賃) [여객의] a (passenger) fare; [요금] a charge; (화물의) freight (rates / charges); (영) goods rates; carriage; [짐수레의] cartage; (해운의) shipping expenses. ¶국내 [해양 / 항공] ~ inland [ocean / airway] freight∥반액 ~ a half fare∥편도 [왕복] ~ a single [return] fare∥할인 ~ a reduced fare∥~ 지불필 freight [carriage] paid∥~은 이쪽에서 부담합니다 We pay the freight. / (게시) Carriage Free. ∥철도 ~이 5% 인상되었다 Railroad [(영) Rail(way)] fares were raised five percent.
● 운임 무료 (게시) Carriage Free. 운임 보험료 포함 가격 cost, insurance and freight (약어 CIF); the cost with insurance and freight charges included. 운임 포함 가격 cost and freight (약어 C&F); the cost with freight charges included. 운임표 (철도의) a table of railroad fares; (화물의) a table of freight charges.

운전(運轉) (자동차의) driving; (열차·버스 편의) running; (기계의) operation; working. ¶시운전 a trial run [operation] / (자동차의) a road test∥음주 ~ drunken driving∥그는 ~을 잘한다 [잘 못한다] He is a good [bad] driver. **운전하다** drive (a car); run (a train); operate [put / set] (a machine). ¶자기 차를 손수 ~ drive one's own car∥기계를 ~ operate [run] a machine∥자동차를 ~ drive a car / take [beat] the wheel.
● 운전대 a steering wheel; a wheel. 운전면허 시험 (자동차의) (take) a driving test. 운전면허증 a driver's license; (영) a driving license. 운전사 (자동차의) a driver; (자가용의 고용된) a chauffeur; (전차의) a motorman; (택시의) a cabdriver [cabman]; (구어) a cabbie [cabby]. ¶교대 ~ a codriver / (속어) a spare driver∥모범 ~ an exemplary driver. 운전석 (자동차의) a driver's seat; (전차의) a motorman's seat. 운전수 ➡운전사 (↔운전)

운지법(運指法) [음] fingering.

운집하다(雲集—) crowd; gather [assemble] in crowds; throng. ¶역전 광장에는 군중이 운집해 있었다 A crowd (of people) had gathered at the square [plaza] in front of the station.

운철(隕鐵) [광] iron meteorite; meteoric iron.

운치(韻致) [고아한 품위가 있는 기상] elegance; refinement; grace; daintiness. ¶~ 있는 tasteful / [우아한] elegant∥그것이 방에 한층 ~를 더해 주었다 It made the room all the more attractive [charming].

운크타드 UNCTAD(▶ United Nations Conference on Trade and Development의 약어).

운필(運筆) [획] strokes of the brush [pen]; [붓을 놀리는 법] the use of [manner of handling] the brush [pen]. ¶~ 연습 brush-stroke practice∥힘 있는 ~ powerful brush strokes∥그의 ~에는 힘이 없다 There's no force in his brush strokes.

운하(運河) a canal; a waterway. ¶갑문식 ~ a lock canal∥~를 파다 dig [build / cut] a canal∥파나마 ~가 폐쇄되었다 The Panama Canal was blocked [closed].
● 운하 통행료 a canal toll.

운항(運航) navigation; operation; service; passage. ¶제트기의 ~ 계획 plans for flying jet planes [establishing jet service]∥시계(視界) 불량으로 그 비행 편 [선박 편]은 ~이 중지되었다 Owing to poor visibility, the flight [boat] has been canceled. **운항하다** operate; run; ply. ¶두 항구 사이를 연락선이 운항하고 있다 A ferryboat plies between the two ports.

운해(雲海) 1 [바다처럼 널리 깔린 구름] a sea of clouds. 2 [구름이 덮인 바다] a clouded [overcast] sea.

운행(運行) 1 [천체가 궤도를 돎] movement; revolution(자전·공전). ¶천체의 ~ the movement of heavenly bodies. **운행하다** move [revolve / travel] (round the sun); (궤도 상을) orbit (around / round). ¶위성은 행성의 주위를 운행한다 Moons revolve [orbit / move / travel] around planets.
2 (열차·버스 등의) running; operation; service. ¶폭우로 버스의 ~이 중단되었다 Bus service was suspended [Buses stopped running] because of the heavy rain.∥엘리베이터는 ~이 정지되고 있다 The elevator isn't running [is out of service]. **운행하다** run; operate. ➡¶8월에는 임시 열차 [버스]가 운행된다 Special trains [buses] run [are run] in August.∥버스는 15분 간격으로 운행되고 있다 There is a bus every fifteen minutes.
● 운행 정지 the suspension of operation (for 3 days). 운행표 (철도의) a (train) schedule; a timetable. ¶열차는 ~대로 운행하고 있다 Trains are running on schedule [according to the timetable].

운형자(雲形—) [수] curved rule; a French curve.

운휴(運休) suspension [stoppage] of the (bus) service. ¶버스의 ~ suspension of all bus service∥홍도행 선편은 현재 ~ 중입니다 Steamer service to Hongdo has been (temporarily) suspended. **운휴하다** [편의 하

나를 취소하다] be canceled[(영) cancelled]; [열차·버스·노선이 정지되다] stop running; [편 전체가 일시 정지하다] be suspended. → ¶사고로 상행 열차 3편이 운휴되었다 Because of an accident three up trains have been canceled.// 경부선은 사고로 일시 운휴되었다 The Gyeongbu[Seoul-Busan] Line stopped running[was stopped] for a while due to an accident.

울[1] [친척] kinsmen; kin; relatives; one's people; folks. ¶~을 믿고 행패하다 play the bully, relying on his family to back him up.

울[2] a fence. ⇨울타리

울[3] [양모] wool. ¶~로 짠 카펫 a woolen carpet.

울걱거리다 gargle; rinse out one's mouth. ¶소금물을 울걱거려 양치질하다 gargle with salt water.

울걱울걱 gargling. ¶~ 양치질하다 gargle (one's mouth). **울걱울걱하다** gargle. ⇨˚울걱거리다

울고불고하다 cry[shout / yell] in tears; howl; scream. ¶지나간 일을 울고불고해 봐야 소용없다 It's no use crying over spilt ((미)spilled) milk.

울근불근하다 1 [서로 불화하여 맞서다] be on bad terms (with); be at daggers drawn (with); be at odds[outs] (with); (미) be at loggerheads (with). ¶늘 울근불근하며 지내다 lead a cat-and-dog life. 2 [여위어 앙상하다] bony; scraggy; rawboned; barebonded; very lean. ¶뼈가 울근불근한 사람 a skinny person / a bag of bones.

울긋불긋 colorfully; picturesquely. ¶뜰에는 꽃이 ~ 피어 있었다 The garden was riot of color. **울긋불긋하다** colorful; varicolored; picturesque. ¶울긋불긋한 옷 colorful[varicolored] clothes// 가을의 산들은 단풍이 져 울긋불긋했다 The hills are aflame with autumn colors.

울꺽 1 [갑자기 토하려는 모양] kecking; retching. ¶~ 토하다 vomit / throw up. 2 [격한 감정이 치미는 모양] all at once; suddenly. ¶화가 ~ 치밀다 have a fit of anger / fly into a rage ¶그는 ~ 화가 치밀어 내게 컵을 던졌다 He threw a cup at me in a fit of rage.

울다 1 (사람이) cry; weep; shed tears; sob(흐느끼며); blubber(훌쩍거리며); wail(비통하게); whimper(낮게). ¶악을 쓰며 우는 아기 a squalling baby// 몹시 ~ cry one's eyes [heart] out// 아파서 ~ cry with pain// 슬퍼서 ~ weep from sorrow// 기뻐서 ~ cry [weep] for joy / shed tears of joy// 감동해서 ~ be moved to tears// 슬픈 소식을 듣고 ~ weep at sad news// 마음속으로 ~ weep at heart// 울면서 말하다 sob out (one's story) // 우는 체하다 pretend to weep / [거짓 눈물을 흘리다] shed sham[false / crocodile] tears // 울며 겨자 먹기로 reluctantly / unwillingly / against one's will // 그는 울며 겨자 먹기로 그 제안에 동의했다 He gave his reluctant consent to the proposal.// 아기가 울고 있군 The baby is crying.// 슬프면 실컷 울게나 If you are sad, have a good[long] cry[weep to your heart's content]. / 실컷 울게 내버려 둬라 Let him cry it out.// 나는 울고 싶은 것을 이를 악물고 참았다 I clenched my teeth to hold back the sobs[tears]. // 그 돈을 잃어버린 것을 알고 나는 울고 싶었다 I felt like crying when I discovered I lost the money.// 나는 그에게 가지 말라고 울며 애원했다 I begged him in tears not to go.

2 (새·벌레) sing; chirp; twitter; (고양이) mew; meow; purr(가르랑거리며); (소) moo; low(낮고 길게); (말) neigh(길고 크게); whinny(낮고 부드럽게); (양·염소) bleat; (나귀) bray; (쥐) squeak; (개구리) croak; (오리) quack; (부엉이) hoot; (비둘기) cook; (까마귀) caw; (수탉) crow; (암탉) cackle; cluck; (병아리) peep. ¶어딘가에서 뻐꾸기가 울고 있다 Somewhere a cuckoo was calling.// 밖에서는 매미가 울고 있었다 There were cicadas singing out side. // 여치는 여름 내내 즐거운 듯이 울고 있었다 Grasshoppers chirped happily all summer.

3 [우글쭈글해지다] wrinkle; crumple; cockle; pucker; become crumpled[wrinkled]. ¶다리미가 뜨거워서 비단이 울었다 The hot iron make puckers in (the piece of) silk.// 벽지를 잘못 바르면 운다 Wallpaper cockles when you paste it wrongly.

4 [진동하여 소리 나다] whistling; whizzing; with a whistle[whiz(z)]. ¶바람에 전깃줄이 윙윙 운다 The wind sets up a humming in the wires.// 바람에 문풍지가 울었다 The wind whistled through the crack in the door.

5 [종·천둥 등이 소리를 내다] sound; ring. ¶뱃고동이 울었다 The steam whistle blew.

6 [귀에서 저절로 소리가 나다] ring; buzz. ¶귀가 운다 My ears are ringing. / I have a ringing[buzzing] in my ears.

우는 아이 젖 준다(속담) The squeaking wheel gets the grease.

울지 않는 아이 젖 주랴(속담) There's no such thing as a free lunch.

울대 [동] the syrinx. ⇨˚명기(鳴器)

울뚝불뚝 roughly; wildly; rashly. **울뚝불뚝하다** rough; wild; rash. ¶울뚝불뚝한 태도 a rude[rough] manner.

울렁거리다 1 [두근거리다] beat (fast); pound(심하게); throb; thump; palpitate. ¶울렁거리는 가슴 a throbbing heart // 나는 기뻐서 가슴이 울렁거렸다 I felt my heart beating with joy.// 그녀의 가슴은 기대감에 울렁거렸다 Her heart fluttered[beat fast] in anticipation.// 나는 울렁거리는 가슴을 진정시킬 수가 없었다 I could not control the thumping of my heart. 2 [물결이 연해 흔들리다] surge; roll; swell. 3 [메슥거리다] feel sick; feel like vomiting; feel nausea; be sick at the stomach. ¶그 냄새를 맡자 속이 울렁거렸다 The smell made me sick.

울렁울렁 (가슴이) pit-a-pat; (물결이) surging; rolling; tossing; (속이) heaving. **울렁울렁하다** beat (fast); surge; feel sick. ⇨˚울렁거리다

울리다 1 [사람을 울게 하다] let (a child) cry; move[touch] (a person) to tears. ¶아이를 ~ set a child crying// 심금을 울리는 이야기 a touching[moving] story// 그의 연설은 청중을 울렸다 His eloquence moved the audience to tears.

2 [소리를 내다] ring (a bell); sound (a trumpet); beat (a drum); jingle (bells); chime (bells); clang (a gong); blow (a whistle). ¶경적을 ~ blow a warning whistle / (자동차의) blow a horn// 종을 ~ ring a bell / (교회 등에서 천천히) toll a bell// 초인종을 ~ ring a doorbell / [초인종의 단추를 누르다] push the button// 땅을 울리며 나아가다 (차 등이) rumble along// 폭음을 울리면서 화산이 분화했다 The volcano erupted with a

resounding boom.
3 [소리가 나다] sound; ring; peal(방울 등이); go bang(쾅 하고); roar; [울려 퍼지다] thunder; rumble; roll(녀성이); boom(대포가); [소리가 반향하다] echo; resound; reverberate. ¶울려 퍼지는 소리 a reverberating sound∥멀리서 울리는 천둥소리 a peal of far-off thunder∥진진 나팔이 울렸다 The bugle sounded for the advance.∥종이 울렸다 The bell rang[pealed]. (▶ peal은 크게 울림)∥사이렌은 정오에 울린다 A siren goes[rings/sounds/blows] at noon.∥초인종이 울리고 있다 There goes the doorbell.∥천둥이 멀리서 울리고 있다 It's thundering in the distance. / There is a roll of thunder in the distance. ∥나는 귀가 울린다 I have a ringing in my ears.∥박수 소리가 천장에 울렸다 The roof resounded with their applause.∥총소리가 울렸다 We heard the report of a gun.∥경보가 울렸다 The alarm went off.∥대포 소리가 전쟁터에 울려 퍼졌다 The roar of the cannon reverberated over the battlefield.∥환호 소리가 거리에 울려 퍼졌다 Shouts of joy reverberated[resounded] in the streets.∥북소리가 홀 가득히 울려 퍼졌다 The sound of a drum reverberated[resounded] throughout the hall.∥전화가 한밤중에 요란하게 울렸다 The telephone rang alarmingly[loudly] in the middle of the night.
4 [세력이 드날리다] wield; sway; dominate; [평판이 알려지다] be widely[well] known; resound; be famous[celebrated]. ¶세도가 쩡쩡 ~ wield influence[power]∥그의 명성이 방방곡곡에 울려 퍼졌다 His fame resounded[rang / spread] far and wide.
울림 [반향] an echo (*pl.* ~es); (a) reverberation. ¶산~[언] 울린다 Echoes resound.
울림소리 [언] a voiced sound.
울 마크 a wool mark.
울컥거리다 be close to tears. ⇨**울먹이다**
울먹이다 be close to tears; be on the verge of tears; be about[ready] to cry. ¶그 아이는 울먹이고 있었다 The boy was ready to burst into tears.
울보 a crybaby; blubberer.
울부짖다 cry[shout / yell] in tears; scream; wail; (바다·바람이) howl; roar; rave. ¶울부짖는 부녀자들 screaming women and children∥그녀는 아버지의 시신을 붙잡고 울부짖었다 She wailed over her father's remains.
울분(鬱憤) pent-up anger[frustration]; resentment; wrath; grudge. ¶~을 참다[억누르다] control one's anger∥~을 풀다[터뜨리다] vent[give vent to] one's pent-up anger / wreak one's wrath (on a person) / (구어) let off the steam∥그는 그들에 대한 ~을 터뜨렸다 He gave vent to his feeling of bitterness against them.∥그는 ~을 풀 길이 없어 입술을 깨물었다 Barely able to contain anger [restrain his resentment], he bit his lip.
울상(-相) a face ready[about] to cry; a tearful face. ¶~을 짓다[~이 되다] be close to tears / be on the verge of tears / be ready [about] to cry.
울새 [동] a Swinhoe's red-tailed robin.
울쑥불쑥하다 protruding here and there; jagged; indented. ¶울쑥불쑥한 고층 빌딩군 jagged sky scrapers.
울안 a fenced-in lot; an enclosure; a precinct.
울울하다(鬱鬱-) **1** [마음이 답답하다] de-

pressed; melancholy; gloomy; heavy-hearted. ¶울울하게 gloomily / moodily / melancholily∥울울하게 세월을 보내다 mope away one's time. **2** thick; dense.
울음 weeping; crying; a cry. ¶~을 터뜨리다 burst[break] into tears / burst out[fall to] crying / be moved[give way] to tears∥~을 그치다 stop crying[weeping] / cry oneself out / have one's cry out∥~을 참다 gulp down[hold back] one's tears / repress one's tears∥~을 그치고 눈물을 닦아라 Stop crying. Dry[Wipe away] your tears!
●**울음보** ¶~를 터뜨리다 burst[break] into tears. **울음소리** (조수·개 등의) a cry; (새의) a song; a call; a note; a twitter; (벌레의) the chirping of insects. ¶까마귀의 ~ a caw / the cawing of a crow∥부엉이의 음침한 ~ the gloomy hoot of an owl∥이웃집 강아지의 ~ 때문에 나는 잘 수가 없었다 I couldn't sleep because of the yelping of my neighbor's puppies.
울적하다(鬱寂-) melancholy; gloomy; dejected; out of[in low] spirits. ¶울적한 기분으로 with a heavy heart / in a depressed mood / in a melancholy frame of mind∥요 며칠 동안 비가 와서 기분이 몹시 ~ These rainy days depress me[put me out of sorts].∥기분이 몹시 ~ I'm[I feel] awfully depressed.
울증(鬱症) melancholia; [의] hypochondria.
울짱 1 [죽 늘여 박은 긴 말뚝] a fence stake. **2** a fence. ⇨**울타리**
울창하다(鬱蒼-) thick; dense; luxuriant (growth); exuberant. ¶울창하게 thickly / densely / luxuriantly / exuberantly∥울창한 숲 a thick[dense] forest∥수목이 울창하게 자랐다 The trees have grown thickly[luxuriantly].
울컥 kecking; all at once. ⇨**울컥**
울타리 a fence; an enclosure; a hedge(산울타리); a hurdle(엮은 것); railings(목책). ¶**대나무** ~ a bamboo fence∥~를 친 정원 a fenced-off garden∥~를 **치다** enclose (a house) / with a fence / fence round (a house) / make a fence / fence in[up] of∥~를 **뛰어넘다** jump over a fence / clear a fence∥정원에 ~를 치다 fence a garden / put up [build] a fence around garden∥그는 자기 농장을 ~로 둘러쳤다 He surrounded his farm with a fence. / He ran a fence around [fenced] his farm.
울퉁불퉁하다 uneven; bumpy (road); rugged (features); jagged (rocks). ¶울퉁불퉁한[울퉁불퉁하지 않은] 땅 uneven[even / level] ground∥울퉁불퉁한 길 a bumpy[rough] road∥근육이 울퉁불퉁한 남자[팔] a muscular man[brawny arm].
울혈(鬱血) [의] congestion [engorgement] (of blood). ¶~(성)의 congestive∥~이 **되다** be congested with blood∥나의 간은 ~이 되어 있다 My liver is congested.
울화(鬱火) pent-up anger[resentment]; wrath; rancor; a grudge; vexation. ¶~가 **치밀다** feel the surge of anger[resentment].
●**울화병** a disease caused by pent-up rage.
울화통 pent-up anger. ⇨**울화** ¶~이 **터지다** burst into a fit of rage / explode with anger / (미국 속어) blow one's top∥그는 끝내 ~을 터뜨리고 말았다 Finally he burst[flew] into a fit of rage.
움[1] [초목의 어린싹] a tiller; a sprout; a shoot

움

(from the stump of a tree); an offshoot. ¶~이 트다 sprout / shoot / tiller // ~이 돋다 bud / shoot / sprout / put forth shoots // 작약이 ~이 돋기 시작했다 The peony started to sprout.

움² [땅을 파서 만든 집] a dugout; (화초·채소의) a pit. ¶~을 파다 dig out a pit / ~에 저장[preserve] vegetables in a pit / pit / ~에서 살다 live in a dugout.

움라우트 [언] umlaut.

움막(-幕) a dugout. ¶~에서 살다 live in a dugout.
● **움막살이** life in a dugout.

움실거리다 squirm. ➪ 움실거리다

움씰하다 flinch (from); draw back (with fear / fright); shrink (from); wince (at); recoil (from). ¶강도가 든 칼을 보고 ~ flinch [shrink] at the sight of the burglar's knife.

움직거리다 [자꾸 움직이다] keep moving; budge; stir. ¶잠자던 곰이 움직거리기 시작했다 The bear began to stir from his sleep. / 움직거리지 말고 가만히 있어 Don't move a muscle.

움직이다¹ [타동사] **1** [이동시키다] move; shift; remove; budge; stir. ¶책상을 왼쪽으로 ~ move [shift] a desk to the left / 기둥을 오른쪽으로 조금 ~ move [shift] a pole [post] a little farther to the right / 그는 몸을 뒤로 움직여 고쳐 앉았다 He shifted [sat] back in the chair. // 우리 셋으로도 그 바위를 움직일 수 없었다 Not even the three of us could budge [move] the rock. // 손발이 묶여서 몸을 움직일 수 없었다 Bound hand and foot, I was quite helpless. // 환자는 입술을 조금 움직였다 The patient moved his lips slightly.
2 [기계 등을 가동시키다] set [put] in motion; run; drive; operate; work. ¶차를 ~ run [drive / roll] a car / 전기는 기계를 움직인다 Electricity moves a machine. // 이 기계는 움직이기 쉽다 This machine is easy to work [operate / handle]. // 바퀴를 한 번만 움직이면 타성으로 한참 동안 돌아간다 Once you set a wheel in motion, it will keep turning for quite a while because of inertia. // 당신은 이 기계를 움직일 수 있습니까 Can you operate this machine?
3 [사람의 마음을 끌거나 흔들다] move; touch; inspire; affect; influence; have influence on. ¶남의 마음을 움직여 …하게 하다 move [incite] (a person) to do / 사람들을 움직여 난민을 구제하다 move people to provide relief for the refugees // 많은 계약금으로도 그를 움직일 수가 없었다 He was not tempted [swayed] even by the high contract fee. // 사람의 마음을 움직이는 것은 성실이다 Sincerity is what moves [touches] people. / Sincerity is what wins [stirs] people's hearts.
4 [동원하다]. ¶군대를 ~ mobilize troops.
5 [부정하다] deny. ¶움직일 수 없는 증거 a positive [an incontestable] proof // 그것은 움직일 수 없는 사실이다 It is an undeniable [indisputable] fact.
6 [변경하다] change; alter; [흔들다] shake. ¶움직일 수 없는 결심 an unshakable [a firm / an immovable] resolution.
7 [경영하다] run; manage. ¶이곳 공장은 종업원이 움직이고 있다 The factory here is run [managed] by the workers. // 그는 한국의 재계를 움직이는 사람이다 He is a man who moves [pull the strings of] Korean finance.

움직이다² [자동사] **1** [동작·이동하다] move; stir; budge; shift. ¶움직이고 있다 be in motion / be moving [stirring] // 움직이지 않다 do not move [stir] / be at rest / remain still / (구어) stay put / sit tight // 움직이지 않게 되다 stop moving / come to a standstill // 움직이지 마라 Don't move. / Stay there. / Keep still. / (구어) Stay put. / Freeze. (▶「움직이면 쏜다」「밑이 위험하다」등, 움직이면 안 되는 경우의 말) // 움직이면 죽는다 Stir [One move], and you are a dead man.
2 [흔들리다] stir; shake; swing; sway. ¶(나뭇잎 등이) 바람에 ~ tremble in the breeze / sway to the wind // 바람이 없어 나뭇잎 하나 움직이지 않았다 The air was breathless and not a leaf stirred.
3 [기계가] work; operate; run; go. ¶전기로 ~ go by electricity // (전차 등이) 움직이지 않게 되다 break down / come [be brought] to a standstill / be tied up // 이 차는 휘발유로 움직인다 The car runs on [is run by] gasoline. // 이 기계는 전기로 움직인다 This machine goes [is worked] by electricity.
4 [행동하다] work; [행동하다] move. ¶남의 뜻대로 ~ move at another's beck and call // 마침내 경찰이 움직이기 시작했다 Finally the police went into action. // 이젠 남의 명령대로 움직이는 것은 질색이다 I have had enough of taking orders from others [being at another's beck and call].
5 [좌우되다] be influenced; be swayed; [동요하다] waver; fluctuate; vacillate; be shaken. ¶감정에 ~ be swayed by sentiment // 그런 일로는 그가 움직이지 않을걸 It will have scarcely any influence on him. // 나는 돈으로는 움직이지 않는다 I will not be influenced by money. / You cannot tempt [sway] me with money.
6 [마음이 흔들리다] be moved; be touched; be affected. ¶움직이지 않다 be immovable / remain firm // 그녀의 친절이 마침내 그의 마음을 움직였다 Her kindness finally touched him [won his heart]. // 아무리 호소해도 그의 마음은 움직이지 않았다 He was unmoved by our pleas.
7 [변하다] vary; change. ¶움직일 수 없는[확고한] 결론 a foregone conclusion // 그 방침은 움직이지 않는다 The plan will not be changed. // 세계 정세가 움직이고 있다 The world situation is changing.
8 [전임하다] be transferred (to another position). ¶당분간 나는 (지금 직책에서) 움직이지 않을 것이다 (남의 의사로) I won't be transferred for a while. / (자기 의사로) I will remain at my present job for a while.

움직임 [이동] a movement; motion; [활동] activity; [동향] a trend; a drift; a movement; a development. ¶여론의 ~ the drift [trend] of public opinion // 세계 경제의 ~ trends in world economics // 피곤해서 선수들의 ~이 둔해졌다 Because they're tired, the players' movements have grown sluggish. // 그는 테니스를 칠 때의 발의 ~이 아주 좋다 His footwork in playing tennis is quite good. // 그 지역의 주민들 사이에 불온한 ~이 있었다 There were signs of trouble among the residents of that area. // 경찰은 그 일당의 ~을 엄중히 감시하고 있다 The police are keeping a close watch on the gang's activities [movements].

움질거리다 hesitate; squirm; mumble. ➪

질거리다
움질움질 hesitatingly; wrigglingly; mumblingly. ⇨움질움질
움집 a dugout; a mud hut. ¶~살이를 하다 dwell in a dugout.
움쭉 ⇨움쭉
움쩔 with a flinch. **움찔하다** start; be jumpy; be startled (at); flinch; shrink back; wince. ¶그는 강도의 칼을 보고 한순간 움찔했다 He flinched[shrank] for a moment at the sight of the burglar's knife.//누가 내 어깨를 두드러서 움찔했다 I started[jumped] when someone tapped me on the shoulder.
움츠러들다 1 (몸이) curl[huddle] oneself up; squeeze oneself (in). ¶추워서 ~ be huddled up with cold//몸이 움츠러들 정도로 춥다 It is cold enough to shrivel one up. 2 (무서움 등으로) shrink (back); cower. ¶무서워서 ~ shrink with fear//그녀는 화가 난 그의 얼굴을 보고 움츠러들었다 She cowered[shrank back] before his angry looks.
움츠리다 curl[huddle] oneself up; shrink (up). ¶목[머리]을 ~ duck one's head//내가 캐물어도 그는 어깨를 움츠릴 뿐이다 When I questioned him, he only shrugged.//나는 몸을 움츠리고 위험이 지나가기를 기다렸다 I shrank[drew] back and waited for the danger to pass.//그는 많은 청중 앞에 나오면 긴장해서 몸을 움츠린다 He shrank before the large audience.//큰 불도그를 보고 나는 몸을 움츠렸다 I cowered[drew back] at the sight of the big bulldog.
움켜잡다 grasp; clasp; grip; grab (up); take hold of; seize. ¶멱살을 ~ seize[grab] a person by the collar[lapels]//그는 내 손을 움켜잡았다 He clasped[grasped / gripped] my hand firmly.//그는 칼을 움켜잡고 달려들었다 Grabbing a knife, he closed in on me.
움켜쥐다 hold (a thing) tight(ly) (in one's hand); grip; grasp; squeeze; clutch; clasp; clench; take fast[firm] hold (of). ¶(남의) 손을 ~ squeeze (a person's) hand//주먹을 ~ clench[double up] one's fist//그 아이는 헝겊을 움켜쥐고 있었다 The child held a piece of cloth tight(ly) in his hand.//그는 치기 전에 배트를 단단히 움켜쥐었다 He took a good hold on the bat[grasp the bat firmly] before swinging it.
움큼 a handful (of rice); a fistful (of sand); a grasp. ¶한 ~ 쥐다 make a grip (of something).
움키다 1〔잡다·쥐다〕grasp; grip; clench; clutch; clasp; hold; seize. ¶땅콩을 한 움큼 ~ grasp a handful of peanuts in one's hand. 2〔짐승이 발로 힘 있게 잡다〕 claw hold of; seize (with the claws); grasp; grip. ¶솔개가 병아리를 움켜 채어 갔다 A kite caught a chick.
움트다 1〔싹이 나다〕sprout; shoot; bud; germinate; put forth[shoot out] buds. ¶새싹이 움트는 무렵 when plants bud in the spring//날씨가 따뜻해서 밀이 빨리 움텄다 The warm weather has caused the wheat to sprout early. 2〔사물이 생기다〕arise; begin to grow. ¶두 사람 사이에 사랑이 움텄다 Love grew up between the two.//젊은이들 사이에 새로운 사상이 움터 가고 있다 A new way of thinking is appearing among young people.
움파 a Welsh onion grown in an pit.
움파다 scoop[gouge] out. ⇨움파다

움패다 by hollowed out. ⇨움패다
움푹 to a hollow[dent / depression]. ¶~ 들어가다 become hollow / become dented / sink//길이 ~ 팼다 The road caved in.//그 자동차는 충돌 때문에 ~ 들어갔다 The car was banged up[badly dented] in a collision.//이 재료는 누르면 ~ 들어간다 This material yields easily to pressure. **움푹하다** hollow; concave; sunken; dented. ¶움푹한 눈 sunken[deep-set] eyes//눈이 ~ have deep-set eyes.
움푹움푹 in hollows[pits / depressions]. ¶비에 땅이 ~ 패었다 The ground was washed out in small hollows by the rain.
웃- upper; above; outer.
웃거름 (an) additional manuring.
웃기다 make (a person) laugh; set (a person) laughing; excite one's laughter; cause a laugh; provoke laughter[a smile]; 〔재미나게 하다〕amuse (a person). ¶그는 농담으로 여러 차례 청중을 웃겼다 He often set the audience laughing with his jokes.//그만 웃겨요 Please don't make me laugh any more.//그것은 웃기는 이야기다 That is a ludicrous[ridiculous] story.//네가 내게 충고를 하겠다고? 정말 웃기는군 You to offer advice to me? How ridiculous.//그가 배우라니 웃기는군 What a laugh[How laughable] that he's an actor! **웃기지 마** Don't be ridiculous[silly]! / You're talking nonsense.
웃다 1〔기뻐서 소리를 내다〕laugh(소리 내어); smile(미소 지으며); chuckle(조용하게); giggle(깔갈거리며); grin(싱긋); smirk(히죽히죽); simper(싱글싱글). ¶잘 웃는 사람 a good [an easy] laugher//~ 웃는 얼굴 a smiling face//웃으면서 with a laugh[smile] / laughingly / smilingly//배꼽을 잡고 ~ hold[burst / split] one's sides with[for] laughing[laughter] / be convulsed with laughter (at)//자지러지게 ~ laugh one's head off / (미국구어) laugh fit to kill/억지로 ~ smile a forced smile / force a laugh/눈물이 나도록 ~ laugh till one cries / laugh oneself to tears//방긋[방글방글] ~ smile sweetly / beam (upon) / smile radiantly (at)//왁자그르르 ~ roar[howl] with laughter/너털웃음을 ~ give a horselaugh/쓴웃음을 ~ smile a bitter[wry] smile//웃으며 승낙[거절]하다 laugh one's consent[dissent]//경멸의 웃음을 ~ smile a smile of contempt//웃으며 헤어지다 part good friends//나는 웃지 않을 수 없었다 I couldn't help laughing[but laugh].//(사진 촬영 때) 자 웃어요 Say cheese! 2〔비웃다〕ridicule; laugh at; jeer[sneer / scoff] at; laugh at. ¶남의 불행을 보고 ~ make merry over another's mishap//울지 마라, 남들이 웃는다 Don't cry and make yourself ridiculous.//웃을 테면 웃어 봐라, 나는 끝까지 해 볼 작정이다 You cannot laugh me out of my resolution.
웃는 낯에 침 뱉으랴(속담) Laugh and the world laughs with you.; Docility disarms anger.
웃더껑이 a lid(뚜껑); a cover(덮개); a flap(호주머니의).
웃도리 →윗도리
웃돈 〔차액〕a difference; a margin; 〔할증금〕an extra; a premium. ¶~을 치르다 pay the difference in cash / make up a difference in cash//그는 ~을 얹어 주고서야 그 집을 살 수

웃돌다

있었다 He had to pay a premium before he could buy the house.

웃돌다 exceed; be better (than); surpass. ¶지난 수년간 출생률이 사망률을 웃돌고 있다 In the last few years the birth rate has exceeded the death rate.// 올해 수확은 예상을 웃돌았다 This year's crop has exceeded the expected amount.

웃목 →윗목

웃물 1 →윗물 **2** supernatant fluid [liquid]. ⇨겉물

웃사람 →윗사람

웃어넘기다 laugh away [off]. ¶이건 웃어넘길 일이 아니다 It's no laughing matter.// 그는 나의 잘못을 웃어넘겼다 He laughed away [off] my mistake. / He let my mistake pass with a smile.

웃어른 one's elder; a senior.

웃옷 [겉옷] an outer garment; outerwear.

웃음 a laugh; laughing; laughter(큰 웃음); a smile(미소); a chuckle(킬킬거리는 웃음); a giggle(주로 여자 아이가). ¶억지 ~ a forced [strained] laugh / a feigned [forced] smile// 만면에 ~을 띠고 with a broad smile on one's face / beaming with a smile// ~을 짓다 wear a smile// ~을 참다 suppress [repress / resist] a smile / swallow a laugh// ~을 웃다 smile a smile / have a laugh// ~을 참지 못하다 chuckle in spite of oneself// 저절로 ~이 나왔다 Laughter rose within me before I was aware of it.// 나는 간신히 ~을 참았다 I suppressed [swallowed] my laughter with difficulty. / I barely managed to keep myself from bursting into laughter.// 좌중은 와 하고 ~을 터뜨렸다 The party burst into a roar of laughter.// 그 여자는 억지 ~으로 근심의 빛을 감췄다 She hid her anxiety with a forced smile.

웃음을 사다 incur laughter; be laughed at; make a show [fool] of oneself; draw ridicule upon oneself.

웃음을 팔다 [여자가 화류계 생활을 하다] live as a prostitute; walk the streets.

●**웃음거리** a laughingstock; a byword; a butt for [of] ridicule; a standing joke; (구어) a laugh. ¶세상의 ~ 가 되다 become a laughingstock for others / become the butt of ridicule// 마을의 ~가 되다 become the laughingstock of the village// 그의 행동은 그 고장의 ~였다 His behavior was a standing joke in the town.// 남의 ~가 되지 않도록 하라 Try not to make a laughingstock [fool] of yourself. / Try not to get yourself laughed at. **웃음꽃** a cheerful laugh; a happy [joyous] laughter. ¶~을 피우다 laugh a cheerful laugh / give a happy [joyous] laughter. **웃음보** suppressed laughter. ¶~를 터뜨리다 explode with laughter// 그 농담을 듣고 그들은 ~를 터뜨렸다 They exploded with laughter at the joke. **웃음소리** a laughing voice; laughter. ¶방 안에서 ~가 들려왔다 The sound of laughter came from the room. **웃음판** a scene of boisterous laughter. ¶그의 이야기를 듣고 좌중은 이 ~이 되었다 At his story the whole party burst into laughter [broke out laughing / burst out laughing].

웃자라다 overgrow. ¶보리가 웃자랐다 The barley overgrew itself.

웃통 the upper part of the body. ¶~을 벗다 strip oneself to one's waist / take off one's coat.

웅거하다(雄據-) hold and defend one's own territory; stand one's ground. ¶천혜의 요새에 ~ betake oneself to a mountain fastness.

웅담(熊膽) bear's gall.

웅대하다(雄大-) grand; magnificent; majestic. ¶한라산의 웅대한 경치 a grand [magnificent / majestic] view of Hallasan(Mt. Halla)// 웅대한 구상 a grand conception// 새 개발 계획은 규모의 웅대함을 자랑하고 있다 The new development plan boasts a grand scale.

웅덩이 puddle; a pool. ¶~가 많다 be boggy / be swampy / be puddly.

웅덩이지다 form a puddle.

웅도(雄圖) an ambitious [a daring] enterprise; an ambitious plan. ¶~를 펴지 못하다 fail to realize one's great ambition// 그들은 ~를 펴기 시작했다 They have launched a daring [an ambitious] enterprise.

웅변(雄辯) eloquence; fluency (of speech); (a flood of) oratory. ¶~의 eloquent / fluent / silver-tongued// ~을 토하다 speak fluently [eloquently / with eloquence] / put forth one's eloquence// 그는 그 계획에 대해서 ~을 토했다 He spoke eloquently [with eloquence] about the project.// 이 기록은 국가의 번영을 ~으로 말해 주고 있다 The record is eloquent of national prosperity.// 결과가 이 사실을 ~으로 말해 주고 있다 The result eloquently speaks of [bears eloquent witness to] this fact.

웅변은 은, 침묵은 금 Speech is silver [silvern], silence is gold [golden].

●**웅변가** an eloquent [a fluent] speaker; an eloquent orator. **웅변대회** an oratorical [a speech] contest. ¶교내 ~ an intramural oratorical contest (of a university). **웅변술** oratory; the art of public speaking.

웅비(雄飛) a great leap [flight]; a flying jump; launching out. **웅비하다** take a flying jump; soar up; launch (out) (into); embark on (a career). ¶해외로 웅비한 한국인 the Korean people who were actively engaged in various enterprises abroad// 해외로 ~ leave for abroad full of ambition// 정계에 ~ play an active part in politics.

웅성(雄性) maleness. ¶~의 male.

●**웅성 배우자** [생] male gamete.

웅성거리다 be noisy; be excited; be in commotion; hum. ¶여럿이 웅성거리는 소리 the deep hum of a thousand voices / a babel of voices// 선생님이 안 계셔서 교실 안은 웅성거렸다 The classroom was noisy [in a commotion] because the teacher was away.// 그녀가 입장하자 장내는 웅성거렸다 There was a general stir as she entered. / Her entrance created a general stir in the audience.

웅얼거리다 mutter; murmur; mumble (out). ¶혼자서 ~ mutter [murmur] to oneself// 찬이 나쁘다고 ~ grumble over the food// 그는 대우가 나쁘다고 웅얼거렸다 He complained about the treatment he had received.// 그 노부인은 뭔가를 웅얼거렸다 The old woman mumbled (out) something.

웅얼웅얼 mumblingly; mutteringly; murmuringly. ¶그는 무어라고 ~ 혼잣말을 하며 갔다

He went away muttering something to himself.
웅장하다(雄壯-) grand; magnificent; majestic; splendid. ¶웅장한 저택 a magnificent [an imposing] mansion // 웅장한 경치 a magnificent view / a grand sight / a spectacular scene // 웅장한 구상 grand conception // 웅장한 건물 a splendid [magnificent] building // 기상에서 본 알프스의 산들은 웅장했다 The Alps looked magnificent from the airplane. // 노트르담 대성당은 ~ Notre Dame is an imposing cathedral. // 우리는 나이아가라 폭포의 웅장함에 감탄했다 We were struck with [by] the grandeur of Niagara Falls.
웅지(雄志) (a) noble ambition [aspiration]; (a) heroic spirit. ¶~를 품다 cherish [have] a noble ambition // 그는 ~를 이루지 못하고 죽었다 He died before he could realize his noble aspiration.
웅크리다 crouch (down); huddle [curl] oneself up. ¶웅크린 자세 in a crouch / in a crouching posture // 웅크리고 앉다 sit crouching [hunched up / squat] / squat oneself (on the ground) // 웅크리고 자다 sleep huddled [curled] up // 길가에 웅크리고 앉다 crouch by the roadside // 그는 구석에 몸을 웅크리고 있었다 He was cowering in a corner. // 고양이가 양달에 웅크리고 앉아 있다 A cat is crouching in the sun. // 그녀는 그 자리에 웅크리고 앉았다 She squatted down on the spot [right there].
워낙 1 [본디] originally; [처음부터] from the outset [beginning]; [태생이] by nature; naturally. ¶그는 ~ 게으름쟁이다 He is inherently a lazy creature. // 그는 ~ 몸이 약하다 He is constitutionally weak. / He was born weak. // 그는 ~ 그림을 잘 그린다 He is a good painter by nature. / He is a born painter. 2 [아주] too; too much; excessively; to excess; [미] overly; [몹시] very [quite / much]. ¶이 책은 ~ 어려워서 읽을 수가 없다 This book is too difficult for me to read. // ~ 멀어서 사흘에는 못 간다 It lies too far afield [away] for a three days' trip.
워드 프로세서 a word processor.
워밍업 a warm-up; warming up.
워커(˚walker) [군화] combat [army] boots.
워크숍 [교] a workshop.
워크아웃 [기업 개선 작업] workout.
워키토키 a walkie-talkie.
원¹ [우리나라의 화폐 단위] a won (약어 ₩, W). ¶천 ~짜리 지폐 a thousand won note // 귤을 천 ~어치 주세요 Please give me 1,000 won worth of oranges. // 이 구두를 2만 ~에 샀다 I bought this pair of shoes for 20,000 won.
원² [놀라거나 언짢을 때의 말] Well!; Indeed!; What!; How! ¶~, 덥기도 하다 How hot it is! // 내 ~, 할 수 없지 Well, it cannot be helped. // ~ 저런 (정말이야) (미국 구어) I want to know. // ~, 이럴 수가 What a surprise! / It's indeed a surprise (to me)! // ~, 이렇게 고마울 수가 How kind of you! / It's awfully [(속어) awful] kind of you.
원(圓) [원형] a circle; [작은 원] a circlet. ¶~의 circular // 주어진 삼각형 주위에 ~을 그려라 Draw [Describe] a circle around a given triangle. // 솔개가 하늘에 ~을 그리며 날고 있다 A kite is flying in a circle high up in the sky.

원(願) [소원] a wish (for / to do / that); [강한 소망] a desire (for / to do / that); [간청] an entreaty (for / to do); [부탁] a request (for / that). ¶~을 들어주다 grant a person's wish / (間투) comply with a person's request // 평생의 ~을 이루다 realize one's dearest wishes / have one's cherished hope fulfilled // 모든 일이 ~대로 되었다 Everything came out as I hoped it would.
원-(元·原) [원래의] original; primitive; [전의] former; previous; ex-. ¶~계획 one's original plan // ~주인 the former owner // ~주소 an out-of-date address.
-원(員) a member (of). ¶편집~ a member of the editorial staff.
-원(院) [보호 시설] an asylum; [국회] the House. ¶양로~ an asylum for the aged // 상[하]~ the Upper [Lower] House.
원가(原價) the cost (price); the prime [first] cost. ¶공장 ~ the manufacturing cost // 구입 ~ the purchasing cost // 생산 ~ the production cost / the cost of production // ~의 3할 할인 30% less than the purchasing price // ~로 팔다 sell [offer] at cost // ~ 이하로 팔다 sell with loss on cost / sell below (the) cost.
● **원가 계산** cost accounting; costing.
원거리(遠距離) a long [great] distance; a long range. ¶~의 long-distance / long-range // ~에 at a long distance // ~에 쏘다 shoot at a long range // 이 마을 어린이들은 ~를 걸어서 통학하기 때문에 고생한다 The children in this village have a hard time because they must walk long distances to school.
원격(遠隔) [관형어적] distant; remote; far; faraway; far-off.
● **원격 조작/원격 제어** remote control. **원격지** a remote [distant] place. **원격 진료** telemedicine.
원경(遠景) a distant view; perspective. ¶이 산의 ~은 아름답다 See from afar, [The distant view of] this mountain is beautiful.
원고(原告) [법] (민사 소송의) the plaintiff; complainant; (형사 소송의) a prosecutor; [고발자] a accuser. ¶그 증거는 명백히 ~에게 불리하다 The evidence tells plainly against the accuser.
원고(原稿) (인쇄용의) a manuscript (약어 MS., pl. MSS.); a copy; [초고] a draft; notes. ¶타이프로 친 ~ a typescript // 손으로 쓴 ~ a handwritten manuscript // 자필 ~ a manuscript written in one's own hand // ~를 쓰다 manuscript / prepare one's copy // ~를 써서 생활하다 live by writing [by one's pen] // ~ 없이 이야기하다 speak without notes // ~를 채택[거절]하다 accept [reject] (a person's) contribution // 나는 잡지에 ~를 쓰고 있다 I am writing (an article) for a magazine. // 그 책은 인쇄가 되었는가 또는 ~ 그대로인가 Is the book in print or in manuscript? // ~를 보라 (교정의 지시) Follow copy (약어 FC).
● **원고료** a manuscript fee; pay (for the writing); copy money. **원고(용)지** manuscript paper; a writing pad (철해 있는); (신문 기자용의) (미) a scratch pad; (영) a scribbling block. ¶2백자 ~ manuscript paper with squares two hundred characters.
원광(原鑛) a raw ore; an ore; unprocessed [crude] ore.
원광(圓光) a glory. ⇨=후광(後光)

원군(援軍) a relief; rescue forces; reinforcement(증원 부대의 뜻으로는 복수형). ¶~을 기다리다 wait for reinforcements // ~을 보내다 reinforce / send reinforcements (to) // ~을 요청하다 ask for reinforcements // 우리는 5만의 ~을 보냈다 We sent a reinforcement of fifty thousand men.

원귀(冤鬼) a vengeful [vindictive] spirit [ghost]. ¶~에 씌다 be possessed by a vengeful spirit // ~를 달래다 lay [appease] a vindictive ghost.

원근(遠近) **1** [먼 곳과 가까운 곳] places both near and far. ¶~을 불구하고 regardless of distance // ~에서 많은 팬들이 모여들었다 Countless fans gathered from far and near. **2** [멀고 가까움]. ¶밤 화재는 ~을 알 수 없기 때문에 불안하다 A night fire is disturbing because I can't tell whether the fire is near (by) or not.
● **원근법** [미] perspective; perspective representation; scenography. ¶이 그림은 ~에 의해 그려진 것이다 This picture is drawn in perspective.

원금(元金) [밑천] capital; [본전] the principal. ¶~과 이자 the principal and interest // ~[~ 100만 원]에 대한 이자 interest on the principal [a principal of one million won].

원급(原級) [언] the positive degree. ¶"farther"의 ~은 "far"이다 "Far" is the positive degree of "farther."

원기(元氣) vigor; energy; vitality; spirits; dash; stamina; (구어) go; pep. ¶~ 왕성한 full of vitality [energy / (구어) pep] / in high [good] spirits // 남의 ~를 북돋우다 encourage a person / cheer a person up // 그들은 ~ 왕성하다 They are full of energy [in high spirits].
● **원기 부족** lack of vigor.

원기둥(圓─) [수] a (circular) cylinder. ¶직~ a right cylinder // ~의 cylindric(al).

원내(院內) ¶~에 inside the House [National Assembly].
● **원내 총무** the leader of the House; (미) the floor leader; (영) the (party) whip.

원년(元年) the first year (of an era, a king's reign, etc.).

원님(員─) a local governor. ¶그는 ~ 덕에 나팔 분다 He is just an ass in a lion's skin.

원단(元旦) New Year's Day; the first day of the year. ¶~에 on New Year's Day // ~에 그 해의 계획을 세우다 make one's plans for the year on New Year's Day.

원대(原隊) one's (original) unit. ¶그는 상처가 아물어 ~로 복귀했다 When his wound had healed, he returned to his unit.

원대하다(遠大─) [광범위하다] far-reaching; [앞을 내다보다] farseeing; [장기간에 걸치다] long-range. ¶원대한 계획 [뜻] a great [long-range] plan [ambition] // 원대한 목적 far-reaching aims // 원대한 이상 a lofty ideal // 일을 원대하게 꾀하다 formulate a far-reaching program / take a long view (of) // 그들은 원대한 계획을 세웠다 They have made a far-reaching [an ambitious] plan.

원도(原圖) the original drawing [plan / map].

원동기(原動機) a motor; a prime mover.

원동력(原動力) **1** [기계의 근원적인 힘] motive power. **2** [일의 추진력] a driving [an impelling] force. ¶활동의 ~ the mainspring of activity // 행동의 ~ the motive of one's action // 사회의 ~ the driving force of the world // 이 연구의 ~이 된 것은 고대에 대한 그의 강한 관심이었다 His strong interest in ancient times impelled him to do this research. // 애국심이 그 운동의 ~이었다 Patriotism was the motive power of [behind] the movement.

원두막(園頭幕) a shed on stilts for a melon patch [field] guard.

원둘레(圓─) [수] circumference. ⇨ 원주(圓周)

원래(元來·原來) [본디] originally; by origin; [본질적으로] essentially; [선천적으로] by nature; naturally; [처음부터] from the first [beginning / outset / start]. ¶~의 목적을 이루다 achieve [attain / accomplish] one's (original) purpose [object] // 사람은 ~ 이기적인 동물이다 Man is selfish by nature. // 차(茶)는 ~ 중국에서 왔다 Tea originally came from China. // 「아름다움」이란 ~ 주관적인 것이다 "Beauty" is essentially [in itself] subjective. // 대개의 어린이들은 ~ 곤충을 좋아한다 Most children are by nature lovers of insects.

원로(元老) an elder; a senior (member); an old-timer; a veteran; a doyen (of a body). ¶정계의 ~ an elder [a senior] statesman // 언론계의 ~ an old-timer in journalism // 당의 ~ the grand old man of the party // 법조계 [연극계]의 ~ a veteran of law [stage] // 실업계의 ~급 an elder [old-timer] in business circles.
● **원로원** [역] the senate; the senate house.

원로 정치 government strongly influenced by elder statesmen.

원론(原論) the principles (of). ¶사회학 ~ the principles of sociology.

원료(原料) [가공하지 않은 재료] raw materials; [천연 그대로의 재료] crude materials. ¶우리나라는 ~를 수입하고 제품을 수출한다 We import raw materials and export manufactured goods. // 이 약은 곰팡이를 ~로 하여 만든 것이다 This medicine is made from a mold. // 나일론의 ~는 무엇인가요 What is nylon made of [from]?

원룸 아파트(×one-room apartment) a studio; (미) a studio apartment; (영) a studio flat.

원리(元利) principal and interest. ¶~ 합계로 약 10만 원이 된다 The amount with interest added comes to about a hundred thousand won.

원리(原理) [원칙] a principle; [이론] a theory; [근본 법칙] fundamentals. ¶근본 ~ the underlying [root] principles // 종교 [수학]의 ~ the fundamentals of religion [mathematics] // 생활 지도의 ~ the ruling [guiding] principle of life // 발전기의 ~ the principle of the dynamo // …과 같은 ~로서 on the same principle as … / on a similar principle to … // …을 처신의 ~로 삼다 base one's principles of conduct on … // 주권이 국민에게 있다고 하는 민주주의의 ~를 수호하다 defend the democratic principle that sovereignty lies with the people // 다수결은 민주주의의 가장 중요한 ~이다 Decision by the [a] majority is one of the most important principle of democracy.

원만하다(圓滿─) perfect; integral; complete; [조화적이다] harmonious; amicable; peaceful; [만족스럽다] satisfactory; [용모·인격 등이 부드럽다] well-rounded; bland; suave. ¶원만한 해결 an amicable [a peaceful] settlement / a satisfactory settlement //원만한 인물 a person who is easy to get along with // 그의 가정은 매우 ~ His home is a very happy one. //톰과 메리 사이는 원만하지 못했다 Tom and Mary did not get along well with each other. //그의 성격이 원만해졌다 His character has been rounded off. 원만히 harmoniously; smoothly; peacefully; amicably. ¶파업은 ~ 해결되었다 The strike was settled peacefully [to everyone's satisfaction]. // 그들은 부부로서 40년 동안 ~ 지냈다 They lived in perfect harmony [harmoniously] as man and wife for forty years.

원망(怨望) [탓함] resentment; reproach; [원한] a bitter [an ill] feeling; a grudge; a spite; [불평] a grievance; a complaint. ¶그는 사람들의 ~의 대상이 되었다 He became the object of public resentment. //그녀는 나에 대해 쌓였던 ~을 늘어놓았다 She enumerated all the grudges she held against me. //나는 남의 ~을 살 만한 일은 한 적이 없다 I don't remember having done anything to incur the resentment of others. //그는 모친에게 ~의 말을 했다 He grumbled at his mother. **원망하다** [원한을 품다] have [hold / bear] a grudge (against); [비난하다] blame; [분개하다] resent. ¶어떤 결과가 되든지 원망하지 않겠다 There'll be no hard feelings whatever happens. //하늘을 원망해도 소용없다 It's no use cursing heaven. //이 계획의 실패에 대해서는 나를 원망하는 수밖에 없다 I have only myself to blame [thank] for the failure of this project.

원망스럽다(怨望-) reproachful; regrettable; hateful. ¶원망스러운 [비난하는 듯한] reproachful / [원한을 품은] spiteful //원망스러운 눈초리 a reproachful glance //그녀는 원망스러운 눈으로 나를 보았다 Her eyes reproached me. //나는 그의 배반을 정말 원망스럽게 생각한다 I feel bitter against him for his betrayal. / I resent his betrayal. //나 자신의 부주의가 몹시 원망스러웠다 I bitterly regretted my own carelessness. //나는 비가 몹시 원망스러웠다 I was terribly disappointed by the rain. / It was a great pity that it rained.

원매인(願買人) a buyer; a purchaser. ¶그는 ~이 없어서 농장을 세놓았다 Failing a purchaser, he rented the farm.

원매인(原賣人) a seller; a vendor; a bargainer; a bear(거소); [법] a bargainor.

원맨쇼 a solo [one-man] show.

원면(原綿) raw cotton.

원명(原名) the original name.

원모(原毛) raw wool.

원목(原木) material [raw] lumber; (펄프의) pulpwood.

원무(圓舞) **1** [윤무] a round dance. **2** a waltz. ⇨ 원무곡(⇨원무)
●**원무곡** a waltz.

원문(原文) [원래의 문장] the original; (번역 등에 대하여) the original (text). ¶판결의 ~ the (original) text of a decision //그리스 어의 ~에서 번역하다 translate from the original Greek //그녀는 「안나 카레니나」를 ~으로 읽었다 She read Anna Karenina in the original. //이 번역은 ~에 충실하다 This transla-tion is faithful to the original.

원반(圓盤) [크고 둥근 소반] a disk; (영) disc; (경기용의) a discus (*pl.* ~es, disci). ¶하늘을 나는 ~ a flying saucer.
●**원반던지기** the discus throw.

원병(援兵) a relief. ⇨ 원군

원본(原本) the original (work); the original copy [text]; [법] the script (copy에 대하여). ¶증서의 ~을 복사하다 make a copy of the original document.

원부(原簿) (회계의) a ledger; (등기·호적의) the original register. ¶~에 기입하다 make an entry in a ledger //~와 대조하다 check 《the account》 with the ledger in which the original entry was made.

원뿔(圓−) a (circular) cone. ¶직~ a right cone / ~(형)의 conic(al).
●**원뿔 곡선** a conic (section). **원뿔대** a truncated cone; a frustum of a cone.

원사이드 게임 a one-sided [lopsided] game. ¶오늘의 시합은 타이거스의 ~이었다 Today's game was all the Tigers. / The Tigers were on top all the way.

원산(原産) the origin of a product. ¶아프리카 ~의 새 a native African bird //키위는 중국 ~이다 The kiwi fruit came from China originally.
●**원산지** [물건의 생산지] the place of origin; [동식물의 본래의 산지] the (original / natural) home; the habitat. ¶담배의 ~ the (original) home of the tobacco plant // ~ 불명의 of doubtful provenance.

원상(原狀) the original [former] state [condition]. ¶손상된 조각을 ~복구하다 restore a damaged sculpture to its former state //이러한 충격적인 경험을 하고 난 그가 ~대로 회복될 수는 없겠다 He can never again be his former self after such a traumatic experience. //파괴된 시가가 ~으로 회복되기까지는 10년은 걸릴 것이다 It will take the ruined town ten years to return to its original condition.

원색(原色) [색의 기본색] a primary color. ¶삼~ the three primary colors.
●**원색 사진** a color picture; a colored picture; pictures in color.

원색동물(原索動物) [동] a protochordate.

원생(原生) [생] abiogenesis. ¶~의 prim(a)eval / primordial.
●**원생대** the Proterozoic era. **원생동물** a protozoan; 《집합적》 the Protozoa. **원생림** a prim(a)eval [virgin] forest. **원생생물** a protist. **원생식물** a protophyte.

원샷(*one shot) [건배] bottoms up.

원서(原書) [원본] the original (book / work). ¶영어 [불어] ~ an English [a French] book in the original //루소를 ~로 읽었다 I read Rousseau in the original.

원서(願書) an application; a written request. ¶입학 ~를 내다 submit [send in] an application for admission to a school //~를 접수하다 receive [accept] an application //~를 쓰다 fill out [《영》 in] an application form //이 직종에 대한 ~는 3월 1일부터 접수합니다 Applications for the job will be accepted starting [beginning] March 1.

원석(原石) **1** a raw ore. ⇨ 원광(原鑛) **2** [가공하지 않은 보석] rough (stone); gemstone. ¶다이아몬드의 ~ a rough diamond.

원성(怨聲) a grudge; a grievance; a reproach-

원소(元素) 〔화〕 an element; a chemical element; 〔수〕 an element. ¶동위 ~ an isotope // 불안정 ~ an unstable element // ~의 elemental // 물은 두 ~로 분해된다 Water is resolved into two elements.
● 원소 기호 the symbol of element. 원소 주기율 the periodic law of the elements.

원손(元孫) the eldest son of the Prince Royal.

원수(元首) the chief[head] of state; a sovereign. ¶일국의 ~ the head[sovereign] of a nation.

원수(元帥) (육군의) a (field) marshal; (미) a general of the army; (해군의) an[a fleet] admiral; (영) an admiral (of the fleet); (공군) a general of the air force; (영) a marshal of the Royal Air Force. ¶맥아더 ~ General of the Army Douglas MacArthur.

원수(怨讐) 〔원한이 맺힌 사람〕 a foe; an enemy; (사물) the object of one's grudge [grievances]. ¶~지간 mutual enemies // 불구대천의 ~ a deadly enemy[foe] // ~를 갚다 revenge oneself (on) / avenge (a person) (on / upon) // 은혜를 ~로 갚다 return evil for good // 그는 나의 친절을 ~로 갚았다 He returned my kindness [My kindness was rewarded] with ill will[hostility]. // 그들은 서로 ~지간이다 They are enemies to each other. // 그녀는 아버지의 ~를 갚았다 She avenged her father (on his enemy).She took revenge on her father's enemy. // 저들에게 죽은 아내의 ~를 갚아 주겠다 I will avenge my dead wife on them.

원수지다(怨讐-) make an enemy of (a person). ¶너와 원수질 일을 한 적이 없다 You have no case to be spiteful against me. // 그 둘은 서로 원수진 사이다 They are enemies to each other.

원숙하다(圓熟-) mature; mellow; ripe. ¶원숙한 사상 mature ideas // 원숙한 문체 a mature style // 원숙한 솜씨 mature[consummate / masterly] skill // 원숙한 솜씨의 목수 a skilled carpenter // 그는 원숙한 사상가[피아니스트]이다 He is a mature thinker[pianist]. // 저 선생은 나이가 들면서 원숙해졌다 That teacher has mellowed with age. // 그의 기예는 원숙해졌다 His art has matured [has attained maturity].

원숭이 〔동〕 a monkey; 〔유인원〕 an ape. ¶곡예 a monkey show // ~ 흉내 indiscriminate imitation // ~가 깩깩 소리 지르고 있다 A monkey is chattering[gibbering].

원숭이도 나무에서 떨어진다(속담) Even Homer sometimes nods.

원시(原始·元始) 〔관형어적〕 primitive; primeval; pristine; 〔비문명적인〕 uncivilized.
● 원시림 a primeval[virgin] forest. 원시 사회 primitive society. 원시생활 a primitive [primeval] life. 원시 시대 the primitive ages; primitive times. 원시인 primitive man.

원시(遠視) 1 〔멀리 봄〕 looking far-off at. 2 〔의〕 (미) farsightedness; (영) long-sightedness; hypermetropia; hyperopia. ¶~인 사람 a long-sighted person / a hypermetrope / a hyperopic.
● 원시경 glasses for farsightedness[farsighted people / hyperopia]. 원시안 a farsighted [long-sighted] eye.

원시적(原始的) primitive; primeval. ⇨원시 (原始) ~ 본능 a primitive instinct.

원심(原審) 〔원재판〕 the original trial; 〔원판결〕 the original judgment[verdict / decision]; 〔원법원〕 the court of original judgment. ¶~대로 as originally decided // ~을 파기하다 overturn[set aside] the original verdict.

원심(圓心) 〔수〕 the center (of a circle).

원심(遠心) ¶~(성)의 centrifugal.
● 원심력 centrifugal force. 원심 분리기 a centrifugal machine[separator]; (우유에서 크림을 분리하는) a centrifuge. 원심 탈수기 a centrifugal hydroextractor.

원아(園兒) 〔유치원에 다니는 아이〕 a kindergarten child; a kindergartener.

원안(原案) (의안의) the original bill; (계획의) the original plan. ¶~을 작성하다 prepare a draft (of) / ~을 수정하다 amend the original bill // 법안은 ~대로 가결되었다 The bill passed in its original form.

원앙(鴛鴦) 1 〔동〕 a mandarin duck. 2 〔의좋은 부부〕 a happily-married[loving] couple; a couple of lovebirds. ¶두 사람 사이는 ~의 사이이다 Those two are as devoted as a pair of lovebirds.
● 원앙금침 a quilt and a pillow with an embroidered pair of mandarin ducks; the marriage bed. ¶~을 나누다 share the marriage bed.

원액(原液) an undiluted solution.

원양(遠洋) the open sea far from land; an ocean.
● 원양 어선 a deep-sea fishing vessel; a pelagic-fishing vessel. 원양 어업 deep-sea [pelagic] fishing[fishery]. 원양 항해 ocean navigation; an ocean voyage.

원어(原語) the original language[word]. ¶소설을 ~로 읽다 read a novel in the original.

원영(遠泳) a long-distance swim.

원예(園藝) 〔정원 손질〕 gardening; floriculture(꽃 재배); horticulture. ¶가정 ~ gardening as a pastime.
● 원예과 the department of horticulture. 원예사 / 원예가 a gardener; a horticulturist. 원예술 the art[technique] of gardening; horticulture. 원예 식물 a garden plant. 원예학 horticulture.

원외(員外) a nonmembership.

원외(院外) ¶~의 nonparliamentary / outside (the House / Congress / Parliament).
● 원외 세력 outside influence. 원외 운동 lobbying. ¶~을 하다 lobby. 원외 투쟁 a conflict outside the Parliament; an out-of-the-House struggle.

원용(援用) claim; 〔인용〕 quotation. 원용하다 claim; 〔인용하다〕 quote; (법률 등을) invoke. ¶조항을 ~ invoke a clause.

원운동(圓運動) circular motion.

원유(原油) crude oil [(영) petroleum].

원유회(園遊會) a garden party.

원음(原音) 〔본디의 음〕 the original sound; 〔원어에서의 발음〕 the original pronunciation; 〔음〕〔음〕 a fundamental tone. ¶외국어의 ~을 충실하게 표기하다 faithfully transcribe the pronunciation of a foreign language.

원의(原義) the primary[original] meaning.

원인(原人) 〔원시인〕 a primitive[primeval] man. ¶베이징 ~ a Sinanthropus / Peking man.

원인(原因) (어떤 결과를 낳는) (a) cause (of);

(직접적인 계기가 되는) (문어) (an) occasion (for); (발단이 되는) the origin (of); [요인] a factor. **간접[직접]~** an indirect[a direct] cause // **근본~** the root cause // **주요~** a major cause (for) // **~과 결과** cause and effect // **싸움[언쟁]의 ~** the seeds of a quarrel // **재난의 ~** the seeds of trouble // **사고의 ~** the cause of[the factors behind] an accident // **프랑스 혁명의 ~** the cause [origins] of the French Revolution // **문제가 생긴 ~** the source of the trouble // **…에 ~을 두다** be caused by / originate in / arise [start / result] from // **~을 규명하다** trace (a thing) to (its) origin // **불명의 화재** a fire of unknown origin // **그들은 교통 체증의 ~을 분석했다** They analyzed the factors leading to traffic jams. // **그가 우연히 한 말이 ~이 되어 오랜 정책 논쟁이 되었다** His chance remark caused[(문어) occasioned] a long policy dispute. / **(문어)** His chance remark was the occasion for a long policy dispute. // **말다툼이 벌어진 ~은 사소한 오해였다** The cause of the argument was[The argument was caused by] a small misunderstanding. // **그 큰 화재의 ~은 담뱃불의 부주의한 취급이었다** The great fire was caused by careless handling of a cigarette. // **회사 공금 횡령이 ~이 되어 그는 퇴직당했다** He was dismissed because he had misappropriated company funds.

원인(猿人) [고고] an ape-man; a pithecanthropus (*pl.* -pi). ¶**직립~** Pithecanthropus erectus / a pithecanthrope.

원일점(遠日點) [천] the aphelion (*pl.* -lia); the higher apsis.

원자(元子) [임금의 맏아들] the eldest son of the king; the Prince Royal.

원자(原子) [물] an atom. ¶**~의** atomic.
● **원자가** atomic value; valence; valency. **원자 구조** atomic structure. **원자량** an atomic weight. **원자력** atomic[nuclear] energy [power]. ¶**~의** atomic // **~의 평화적 이용** the peaceful use of nuclear energy. **원자력 발전** nuclear (electric) power generation. ¶**~소** a nuclear power plant[station]. **원자력 산업** nuclear power industry. **원자력 연구소** the Institute of Atomic Energy Research. **원자로** an atomic[a nuclear] reactor[furnace]. **원자론** atomic theory; atomism. **원자 물리학** atomic[nuclear] physics. **원자 번호** an atomic number. **원자병** an atomic[A-bomb] disease; radiation sickness. **원자 폭탄** an atomic[a fission / a nuclear] bomb; an A-bomb; an atom bomb. ¶**~ 탑재기** an atomic bomber // **~에 의한 공격** atomic bombing // **~으로 공격하다** bomb (a target) with an atomic bomb / atom-bomb. **원자학** nucleonics; atomics. **원자핵** an atomic nucleus. ¶**~의** nuclear. **원자핵 공학** nucleonics. **원자핵 반응** a nuclear reaction. **원자핵 분열** atomic fission.

원자재(原資材) raw material(s).

원작(原作) the original (work). ¶**괴테의 ~으로부터의 번안** an adaptation from the original (story) by Goethe // **~ 민상수, 각색 홍민원** written by Min Sangsu and adapted [dramatized] by Hong Minwon.
● **원작자** the (original) author; the writer.

원장(元帳) a ledger(약어 led.). ¶**총계정 ~** the general ledger // **~에 기입[기장]하다** enter (an item)[make an entry] in a ledger // **~과 대조하다** check (the account) with the ledger.

원장(院長) (병원의) the director (of a hospital); (학원의) the principal[president] (of an academy).

원장(園長) ¶**동물원의 ~** the director of a zoo // **유치원의 ~** the director of a kindergarten [nursery school] // **학원의 ~** the president [director / head] of an educational institution.

원재료(原材料) raw material(s).

원저(原著) the original work.

원저자(原著者) the writer; the author.

원적(原籍) a domicile; an original domicile; a permanent abode.
● **원적지** the place of one's domicile; [법] the domicile of origin.

원전(原典) the original text (of the Bible).

원점(原點) 1 [기본점] the starting point; the origin; the beginning. ¶**~에서 다시 시작하다** start again from square one // **~으로 돌아가다** be[go] back to square one // **~으로 돌아가서 생각하다** consider a thing again from the beginning. 2 [수] the origin. ¶**좌표의 ~을 지나는 직선** a straight line which passes through the origin of the coordinates.

원정(遠征) an expedition; a campaign; an invasion(침입); (군대의) a military expedition; (운동선수의) a playing tour; a visit. ¶**~의** expeditionary // **그 야구 팀은 제주도에 ~ 중이다** The baseball team is on the road in Jejudo. **원정하다** go on[make] an expedition; make[go on] a foray; make a playing tour of. ¶**그들은 북극까지 원정했다** They went on an expedition to the North Pole. // **우리 고교 팀은 광주까지 원정했다** Our high school team went to Gwangju to play against local teams there.
● **원정군**(군대 등의) an expedition; an expeditionary force; (경기의) a visiting team; a visitor. ¶**우리는 ~을 파견했다** We dispatched an expedition. **원정 시합** an out match.

원제(原題) the original title.

원조(元祖) [창시자] the originator; the founder. ¶**국제법의 ~** the father of international law // **우리 가게는 한국 슈퍼마켓의 ~이다** Our store was the (very) first[This store was the forerunner] of the supermarket of Korea.

원조(援助) [조력] assistance; aid; [지원] support. ¶**정신적[물질적] ~** moral [material] support // **재정적 ~** financial aid // **그에게 ~를 청하자** Let's ask[appeal to] him for help. // **당신의 ~가 우리의 마지막 희망입니다** Your aid is the only thing we have to depend on. **원조하다** assist; help; aid; support. ¶**우리는 그가 입후보하면 원조하기로 했다** We agreed to back him up if he decided to run [(영) stand] for election.
● **원조국** a donor country; an aid donor; an aid country. **원조 물자** aid goods. **원조자** a supporter.

원종(原種) 1 [씨앗을 받기 위해 뿌리는 종자] seed stock; seed grain. 2 [변종·개량종에 대하여] the ancestor; the original[wild] strain [breed]; a pure breed.

원죄(原罪) original sin.

원죄(冤罪) a false charge[accusation]. ¶**살인**

원주

의 ~를 쓰다 be falsely charged with murder // ~를 벗다 clear oneself of a false charge [accusation].

원주(圓周) [수] circumference; the circumference of a circle. ¶~가 500미터이다 It is five hundred meters in circumference. // 원의 지름 곱하기 원주율은 ~이다 π times the diameter equals the circumference (of a circle).
● **원주율** pi(기호 π); the ratio of the circumference of a circle to its diameter.

원주(圓柱) ➡원기둥

원주민(原住民) (외국인에 대하여) a native; (식민에 대하여) aborigines; an aboriginal(원주민의 한 사람 한 사람). ¶아프리카의 ~ the natives[aborigines] of Africa.

원지(原紙) (등사판용의) a stencil; stencil paper. ¶~를 긁다 cut a stencil.

원지점(遠地點) [천] an apogee.

원채(原-) [건] the main house[building].

원천(源泉) the source; the origin. ¶악의 ~ the source of evil // 수면이야말로 활동의 ~이다 It is sleep that is the wellspring of our activity.
● **원천 과세** taxation at the source; pay-as-you-earn(약어 P.A.Y.E.). ¶~를 하다 tax [withhold taxes] at the source. **원천 소득세** a withholding income tax. **원천 징수** withholding[deducting] taxes[at the (income) source].

원체(元體) originally. ⇨²워낙

원초(原初) the origin(s); the source; the first; the (very) start. ¶~의 first / original // ~의 지구에는 생물이 없었다 Originally[At first] there was no life on earth.

원촌(原寸) [실물 치수] actual[natural / life / full] size. ¶~ 크기의 사진 a full-scale[life-size] photograph.

원추(圓錐) ➡원뿔

원추리 [식] a day lily.

원칙(原則) [원리] a principle; [일반적으로 공통된 법칙] a general rule. ¶근본 ~ a basic [fundamental] principle // 경제학의 ~ the principles of economics // ~적으로 as a (general) rule / in principle / on general principles // ~**에서 벗어나다** be against the principle // 기본 ~에 입각하여 행동하다 act on the basis of fundamental rules // 우리는 어떤 ~을 세워야 한다 We ought to establish [to lay down / to formulate] some rules. // 나는 ~적으로 남에게 간섭을 하지 않기로 하고 있다 I make it a rule[My rule is] not to interfere with others. // ~적으로 신청금은 반환하지 않습니다 As a (general) rule we do not refund the reservation fee. // 나는 ~적으로 찬성이다 I agree in principle. // ~적으로는 네가 하는 말이 옳다 You are right theoretically. // ~과 실제는 때로는 일치하지 않는다 Principle and practice often differ.

원컨대(願-) I pray you; I hope; May ...; I wish (I could ...). ¶~ 그날은 비가 오지 않기를 I pray it won't[hope it doesn't] rain (on) that day.

원탁(圓卓) a round table. ¶~의 기사들 the Knights of the Round Table // ~**에 둘러앉다** sit at[around] a round table.
● **원탁회의** a round-table conference.

원통(圓筒) 1 [둥근 통] a cylinder. 2 ➡원기둥

원통하다(冤痛-) 1 [분하다] vexatious; vexing; mortifying. ¶원통해하다 be chagrined (at / by) / be frustrated / be vexed / feel chagrined // 원통해서 눈물을 흘리다 shed tears of vexation // 우리는 시합에 저서 원통했다 It chagrined us to lose the game. // 놈에게 모욕을 당하다니 원통해 죽겠다 What a shame that I must take such an insult from him! // 이 원통함은 평생 잊지 못할 것이다 I'll never forget how bitterly vexed I was. **원통히** vexatiously.
2 [유감이다] regrettable; deplorable. ¶그렇게 젊은 나이에 죽다니 참으로 ~ What a pity [It's too bad / It's shame] that he should have died so young. **원통히** regrettably; deplorably. ¶~ 여기다 regret / feel sorry (that).

원판(元-) [본디의 판국] the original state (of a thing); [원래] from the first[beginning / outset]; originally.

원판(原板) a (photographic) negative.

원판(原版) 1 (활자 조판의) a form; (영) a forme; (사진 인쇄판의) the original plate. 2 the first edition. ⇨²초판(初版)

원폭(原爆) an atomic bomb. ⇨원자 폭탄(⇨원자(原子))
● **원폭 기지** an atomic base. **원폭 실험** (conduct) an atomic[A-bomb] test. **원폭 투하** atomic bombing. **원폭 희생자** an A-bomb victim.

원 풀이 하다(怨-) vent one's spite; be avenged; avenge oneself; pay off old scores (with); be even (with).

원풀이하다(願-) have one's desire fulfilled; have one's wish realized.

원피스 a dress; a one-piece (dress).(▶ dress 가 일반적인 말로서 널리 쓰임. one-piece는 그다지 잘 쓰이지 않으며, 쓰이는 경우에도 위아래가 이어진 여성 수영복을 가리킬 때가 많음.

원하다(願-) 1 [바라다] want[wish / (문어) desire] (to do / a person to do / that) (▶ want that ...라고는 하지 않음); [좋아하다] like (to do / doing / a person to do). ¶자유를 ~ wish for[want] liberty // 그는 화가가 되기를 원하고 있다 He wants to be an artist. // 자네가 원한다면 가겠다 If you wish, I will go. // 그것이야말로 제가 원하던 것입니다 I could ask nothing better. / That's exactly what I wanted[desired]. // 여러분이 전력을 다해 주실 것을 원합니다 I'd like you to do your best. // 네가 원하는 것을 사 주겠다 I will buy you anything you like. // 그는 딸이 원하는 사람과 결혼시켰다 He let his daughter marry the man she had chosen[of her choice]. // 나는 명성 따위는 원하지 않습니다 I don't care for fame.
2 [기대하다] expect a person (to do / that); hope (to do / that). ¶그는 아들에게 너무 많은 것을 원하고 있다 He is expecting too much of his son. // 지구 상에서 전쟁이 없어지기를 우리는 원한다 We hope there will be no more war on the earth.

원한(怨恨) [원망하는·원망하는 마음] a grudge (against); [악감정] ill will (against); [미움] hatred (of / for). ¶~에 의한 범행 a crime born of a desire for revenge / a crime resulting from a grudge // ~이 사무친 적 one's bitterest[mortal / sworn] enemy // 남의 ~을 사다 incur other's ill will / make enemies // 옛날의 ~을 풀다 pay off an old score // 나는 그에게 ~이 있다 I have[hold] a grudge against him. / I bear him a grudge. // 네게

은 없다 I have nothing against you. / I bear you no ill will.// 그의 모욕에 대한 나의 ~은 영원히 풀리지 않을 것이다 His insult will rankle in my mind for the rest of my life.// 나는 그놈에 대해 ~이 뼈에 사무쳐 있다 I hate him from the bottom of my heart.// 여기에 잠들어 있는 사람들은 ~을 품고 죽었을 것이다 The people, sleeping here must have died full of rancor[hatred].

원해(遠海) the open sea.
● **원해 어업** pelagic[deep-sea] fishery.

원형(原形) 〔본디의 모양〕 the original form. ¶~을 유지하다 keep[retain] its original form / remain intact // ~을 잃다 have no trace of the original form / lose the original form // ~으로 복귀하다 be restored to the original form // 이 조각상은 ~을 유지하지 못하고 있다 This statue retains nothing of its original form.// 그것은 ~을 알아볼 수 없을 만큼 파괴되었다 It was so badly damaged that it could not be recognized.

원형(原型) 〔기본이 되는 모형〕 a model; a prototype; an archetype.

원형(圓形) a circle; a round shape. ¶~의 circular / round // ~ 건물 a circular[round] building / (둥근 지붕의) a rotunda // 종이를 ~으로 오리다 cut paper into a circle.
● **원형 경기장 / 원형 극장** an amphitheater.

원형질(原形質) protoplasm; plasma. ¶~의 protoplasmic.
● **원형질체** a protoplast.

원호(援護) support; backup; help; relief. **원호하다** support; back(up); help; give relief [support] to.
● **원호 기금** a relief funds. **원호 대상자** a relief recipient.

원호(圓弧) a circular arc. ¶~를 그리다 describe[draw] an arc.

원혼(冤魂) a revengeful[a vindictive / an ireful] spirit[ghost]; furies. ¶~을 달래다 lay [appease] a revengeful spirit[ghost].

원화(-貨) the won (currency). ¶~의 하락 the fall of the won // ~로 환산하다 convert (dollars) into won[Korean currency].

원화(原畵) the original picture. ¶렘브란트의 ~ a Rembrandt original.

원활하다(圓滑-) smooth; 〔융화적·협화적〕 harmonious; amicable. ¶그들은 서로 원활하지 못하다 They don't get along well together. **원활히** smoothly; harmoniously; peacefully. ¶일은 ~ 진행되고 있다 The work is going smoothly[without a hitch]. // 나는 일이 ~되어 가기를 바라고 있다 I hope things will go smoothly.

원흉(元兇) a ringleader; the chief instigator; the prime mover; the head[leader]《of a gang》. ¶반정부 운동의 ~ the ringleader of an antigovernment movement // 공해의 ~ the main culprit behind pollution // 각성제 밀수단의 ~을 체포하다 arrest the ringleaders of the stimulant drug smuggling ring.

월(月) 〔달〕 the moon; (달력의) a month; 〔월요일〕 Monday. ¶우리는 ~ 1회[2회] 모입니다 We meet together once[twice] a month.// 집세는 ~ 30만 원입니다 The rent is 300,000 won per[a] month.

월간(月刊) monthly publication. ¶~ 출판물 a monthly (publication) // 이 잡지는 ~이다 This magazine is issued[published] monthly.
● **월간 잡지** a monthly (magazine).

월경(月經) menstruation; menses; a (menstrual) period; (구어) one's period. ¶~이 있다[없다] have one's[no] period // 그녀는 ~ 중이다 She is menstruating[(구어) having her period].// 그녀의 ~은 순조롭다 Her periods are regular. // ~이 1주일 이상이나 늦어지고 있다 My period is more than a week late.
● **월경 불순** irregular menstruation; menstrual irregularity. **월경 주기** a menstrual cycle. **월경통** menstrual pain; (미국 구어) the cramps.

월경(越境) a border violation. **월경하다** cross [transgress] the border; violate a frontier. ¶그는 월경해서 도망쳤다 He escaped over [across] the border.// 게릴라들은 종종 월경해 왔다 Guerrillas often transgressed the border.

월계(月計) a monthly account. **월계하다** cast accounts monthly.

월계관(月桂冠) a laurel crown; a crown of laurel[honors]; the laurel; laurels. ¶승리의 ~을 쓰다 be crowned with the laurel of victory / carry off the honors.

월계수(月桂樹) 〔식〕 a laurel; a bay tree.

월광(月光) moonlight. ⇨달빛 ¶베토벤의 「~ 소나타」 Beethoven's Moonlight Sonata.

월권(越權) abuse of confidence; a stretch of authority; arrogation; (문어) exceeding one's prerogatives. ¶상사가 부하의 사생활에 참견하는 것은 ~이다 Superiors have no right to say anything about the private lives of their men. // 내 수입을 조사하는 것은 ~이다 You exceed your authority[overstep yourself] in checking into my income. **월권하다** exceed[overstep] one's authority; go beyond[exceed] one's powers[competence]; override one's commission.
● **월권 행위** (an act of) arrogation.

월급(月給) a (monthly) salary; monthly pay. ¶첫 ~ starting pay / a starting salary // 낮은 ~ a small[low] salary / 많은 ~을 받는 사람 a high-salaried man // ~이 오르다[깎이다] get a raise (or 《영》 rise)[take a cut] in one's salary // 그는 100만 원의 ~을 받고 있다 He draws[receives] a salary of 1,000,000 won a month.
● **월급날** (a) payday. **월급봉투** a pay envelope. **월급쟁이** a salaried employee[worker]; 〔샐러리맨 층〕 the salaried classes.

월남하다(越南-) (경계를 넘어) come south over the border; (북한으로부터) come from North Korea (over the 38th parallel); cross the 38th parallel into South Korea.

월내(月內) ~에 〔이달 안에〕 before this month is out / 〔한 달 안에〕 within a month.

월동(越冬) passing the winter; wintering. **월동하다** pass the winter; winter; hibernate(동물이 동면하여). ¶그들은 남극 대륙에서 월동했다 They passed the winter on the Antarctic Continent.
● **월동 준비** preparations for the winter. ¶~로 바쁘다 be busy preparing for winter.

월드 와이드 웹 the World Wide Web(약어 WWW); the Web.

월드컵 (축구·미식축구의) the World Cup.

월등하다(越等-)《서술적》 stand in different levels; be not in a class《with》; be widely apart《in ability》. ¶월등한 상대와의 싸움 an uneven battle // 수에 있어 ~ exceed in number // 그는 이 학교에서 성적이 ~ He is by far the best student in the whole school. // 그는 독서력에 있어서는 우리 중 누구보다도 ~ He excels[surpasses] all of us in reading ability. // 그는 어릴 때부터 남보다 월등한 재능을 보였다 He began to show outstanding ability in his childhood. **월등히** by far; far and away; by long[all] odds; outstandingly. ¶힘이 ~ 세다 be far stronger (than) // ~ 잘 하다 be beyond comparison more skillful (than) / outclass[outdo] (another) in skill // 그는 나보다 연설을 ~ 잘한다 As a public speaker, he's in a completely different class from me. // 이 책이 다른 책보다 ~ 재미있다 This is by far the most interesting book of (them all). // 이것이 ~ 좋다 This is far [much] better. / This is far and away the better.

월력(月曆) a calendar. ⇨달력
월령(月齡) [천] the age of the moon.
월례(月例) ¶~의 monthly.
● **월례 행사** a monthly event. **월례회** a monthly meeting.
월리(月利) a monthly interest. ⇨달리(-邊) ¶~ 2부로 돈을 빌려 주다 lend money at two percent a[per] month.
월말(月末) ¶~에[까지는] at[by] the end of the month.
● **월말 계산** a month-end settlement.
월면(月面) the surface of the moon; the moon's surface. ¶~에 발자국을 남기다 walk [leave one's footprints] on the moon's surface // 로켓은 ~에 착륙했다 The rocket landed on the moon.
● **월면도** a selenographic chart. **월면차** a moon buggy.
월반하다(越班-) skip a grade. ¶그는 1학년에서 3학년으로 월반했다 He skipped his first grade to third.
월변(月邊) a monthly interest. ⇨달리(-邊)
월별(月別) ¶~ 지출 monthly expenses // 가스·전기 요금은 ~로 지불하고 있다 I pay for the gas and electricity by the month.
월보(月報) a monthly bulletin[report]; a monthly newsletter; monthly returns. ¶무역 ~ monthly trade returns.
월부(月賦) (미) a monthly installment plan; an easy payment plan; (영) a (monthly) hire-purchase system. ¶나는 ~로 가구를 샀다 I bought furniture on the monthly installment plan[in monthly installments]. // 매월 2만 원씩 6개월 ~이다 That will be six monthly payments of 20,000 won each.
● **월부액** the amount allocated per month. **월부 판매** the (monthly) installment sale [plan]; (영) the hire-purchase system.
월북하다(越北-) (경계를 넘어) go north over the border; (북한으로) go to North Korea (over the 38th parallel); cross the 38th parallel into North Korea.
월사금(月謝金) a (monthly) school[tuition] fee; a monthly fee.
월색(月色) moonlight. ⇨달빛
월석(月石) a moonrock.
월세(月貰) monthly rent. ¶이 집은 ~ 30만 원이다 This house rents for[at] 300,000 won a month.
월세계(月世界) 1 [달의 세계] the moon; the lunar world. ¶~ 여행 a lunar [moon] journey[flight]. 2 [달빛이 비친 천지] the moonlit world; a moonlit landscape.
월수(月收) 1 [월수입] a monthly income. ¶그는 ~가 100만 원이다 He has a monthly income of 1,000,000 won. / He earns 1,000,000 won a month. 2 [본전에 이자를 얹어 갚아 가는 빚] (make) a monthly installment loan.
월식(月蝕·月食) an eclipse of the moon; a lunar eclipse. ¶개기 ~ a total eclipse of the moon / 부분 ~ a partial eclipse of the moon.
월야(月夜) a moonlight night. ⇨달밤
월요병(月曜病) depression on Monday (after the weekend).
월요일(月曜日) Monday(약어 Mon.). ¶~에는 수업이 6시간 있습니다 We have six classes on Mondays. // 지난 ~에는 영어 시험이 있었다 We had a test in English last Monday. // 다음 ~에는 야구 시합이 있다 We('ll) have a baseball game next Monday[on Monday].
월일(月日) [달과 날] months and days; [달과 해] the moon and the sun; [날짜] the date.
월정(月定) [관형어적] monthly; month-to-month.
● **월정 구독료** monthly subscription.
월차(月次) 1 [달의 위치] a phase of the moon. 2 every[each] month. ⇨매달
● **월차 휴가** a day's leave of absence per month (with pay).
월척(越尺) [한 자가 넘는 물고기] a fish over one *ja*; a big fish. ¶~을 올리다 catch a big fish.
월초(月初) (at) the beginning of the month.
월평(月評) a monthly review (of). ¶문단 ~ a monthly survey of the literary world.
월하(月下) [달빛 아래]. ¶~의 향연 a banquet under the moon[in the moonlight] // ~의 정원 a moonlit garden.
● **월하노인** [남녀의 인연을 맺어 준다는 중매인] a matchmaker; a go-between.
웨딩드레스 a wedding dress.
웨딩 마치 a wedding march.
웨이스트 the waist (of a dress). ¶~가 가늘다 have a slim waist // 그녀의 ~는 24인치이다 Her waist measurement is 24 inches. / She is 24 inches around[(영) round] the waist.
웨이터 a waiter.
웨이트리스 a waitress.
웨이트 트레이닝 weight training.
웨이퍼 [양과자의 일종] a wafer.
웨하스 ⇨웨이퍼
웬 [어찌 된] what kind[sort] of; what ... like; [어떤] a certain; some. ¶~ 사람이냐 Who is the man? / What is he here for? // ~ 사람이 저렇게 많이 모였지 What a hell of a lot of people!
웬 떡이냐 ¶이게 ~ What an unexpected piece of good luck[a windfall] it is!
웬걸 Oh!; Why!; Well!; on the contrary; far from that. ¶"수고하셨습니다." "~요." "I thank you for your trouble." "Not at all[(미)] You're welcome." // "이제 끝났냐?" "~, 지금 막 시작했을 뿐이야." "Have you finished?" "Why, I have only just begun." // ~, 나 같은 건 어림도 없어 Oh, I'm nothing compared with him. // 그는 겁쟁이로 보이지만, ~ 여간 용감하지 않아 He looks timid, but actually he is quite courageous.
웬만큼 1 [어느 정도] to some degree[extent];

within bounds; [알맞게] moderately; reasonably. ¶~ 마시다 drink temperately / be moderate in drinking // 운동도 ~ 해야지 지나치면 오히려 해롭다 An excessive amount of exercise will do you more harm than good. // ~ 해 둬요 You must keep within bounds. / I warn you not to go to excess. // 농담도 ~ 해 두게 Don't carry your jokes too far!
2 [어지간히 제법] fairly; pretty; tolerably; passably. ¶~ [구어] so-so. ¶그녀는 영어를 ~ 한다 She speaks passable [fairly good] English. / She speaks English pretty [passably] well. // 그의 책치고는 ~ 팔렸다 The book was a so-so seller by his standards.

웬만하다 [어지간하다] not very bad; (구어) so-so; tolerable; passable. ¶머리가 웬만한 아이 a boy of average intelligence // 웬만하면 if you could arrange it / (참석을 부탁할 때 등) if you are not engaged // 수입이 ~ have a handsome income // 내 성적은 웬만했다 My grades were neither good nor bad. // "요즘 장사는 잘됩니까?" "예, 웬만합니다." "How is your business (doing)?" "Well, it's so-so." // 음향 효과는 ~ The sound effects are tolerable [fairy good]. // 웬만하면 내일 모임에 나와 주시지요 Couldn't you arrange to attend [make time] the meeting tomorrow?

웬일 what matter [business]. ¶~로 on what business // ~로 이런 밤중에 오셨습니까 What have you come here for tonight? / What business has brought you here tonight? // ~로 여기 왔지 What is your business here? // ~이지 Have you any business with me? / What do you want with me? // 이렇듯 조용하니 ~이지 What does this silence mean?

웰터급 (一級) the welterweight division. ¶~ 선수 a welterweight.
웹 the Web; the World Wide Web.
웹 디자이너 the web designer.
웹마스터 a webmaster.
웹 브라우저 a web browser.
웹 사이트 a web site; a website; a Web site; a Website.
웹 서버 a web server.
웹 서핑 web surfing; Web surfing.
웹진 [잡지 스타일의 웹 사이트 페이지] a webzine.
웹 프로듀서 a web producer.
웽그렁뎅그렁 tinkle-tinkle. ⇨왱그랑댕그랑
위 1 [위쪽] the above; the upside; the topside; the upper part. ¶바로 ~에[의] right [just] above // ~를 보다 look upward(s) / cast an upward glance // 손을 ~로 올리다 hold up [raise] one's hand // 그 테라스 ~에 발코니가 있었다 There was a balcony over the terrace. // 비행기가 구름 ~를 날았다 The airplane flew above the clouds. // 식탁 ~에는 샹들리에가 늘어져 있었다 A chandelier hung over [above] the table. // 그는 3층 ~에 살고 있다 He lives three floors up. // ~로 가면 갈수록 공기가 희박해진다 The higher we go up, the thinner the air becomes. // 그가 던진 공이 내 머리 ~를 날아갔다 The ball he threw flew over my head.
2 [표면] surface; [책상 등의 윗면] top. ¶마루 ~에 융단을 깔다 spread a carpet over the floor // 그녀는 식탁 ~에 식탁보를 씌웠다 She spread a tablecloth over the table. // 그 책은 선반 ~에 있다 The book is in on the shelf. // 물 ~에 뭔가가 떠 있다 There is something floating on the surface of the water.
3 [꼭대기] the top; the summit; [가장 윗부분] the head. ¶맨 ~의 topmost / uppermost // ~에서 아래까지 from top to bottom / 남산 타워 ~에서 한강을 바라보다 look at the Hangang (Han River) from the top of Namsan Tower // ~에 올라가다 climb to the top of a hill // 그 책은 책장의 ~에서 3번째 선반에 있다 The book is on the third shelf from the top in [영] of] the bookcase. // 언덕 ~에서 바라본 경치는 그만이었다 We can have a splendid view from the top [summit] of the hill. // 그의 이름은 페이지의 맨 ~에 있었다 His name was at the head of the page.
4 [나은 쪽] superiority; predominance; [선두] lead. ¶그의 그림이 내 그림보다 ~였다 His picture was better than mine. // 질에 있어서는 이것이 그것보다 훨씬 ~이다 In quality this is far superior to [much better than] that. // 수영은 그녀가 나보다 한 수 ~이다 She can swim better than I (can). // 영어에서는 그의 실력이 나보다 ~이다 He is more proficient in English than I (am). // ~를 바라보면 한이 없다 Ambition knows no bound. / There is always something higher to aim for.
5 [많은 쪽]. ¶그는 나보다 3살 ~이다 He is three years older than I [(미) me]. / He is older than I [(미) me] by three years. / He is senior to me by three years. // 두 사람 중 내가 나이가 ~이다 I am the older [elder] of the two. // 그녀는 나보다 1학년 ~였다 She was a year ahead of me in school.
6 [상급의 위치나 기관]. ¶~의 지위 a higher position // 남의 ~에 서다 lead people // 그는 학교에서는 나보다 아래였으나, 회사에서는 ~가 되었다 He didn't do as well as I did at school, but in the firm he has a higher position than mine. // 그는 남의 ~에 설 지도자적 인물이 아니다 He is not of leadership caliber. / He lacks leadership ability. // ~로부터의 명령에 복종해야 한다 You must obey an order from above.
7 [앞에 든 내용]. ¶~와 같은 이유로 나는 반대한다 I am opposed to it for the above reasons. // ~와 서의 상위 없음 I swear the above is a true statement.

위 (位) **1** [등수·등급] position; grade; rank. ¶2~ (석차) the second place / (사람) a runner-up // 제1~가 되다 take [win] first place / head [top / lead] off the list (of) // 제4~로 떨어지다 drop to fourth (place) // 나는 100미터 경주에서 3~를 했다 I finished the hundred-meter race in third place. // 그는 콘테스트에서 2~로 입상했다 He won (the) second prize in the contest. **2** [지위] a position; a place; rank. ¶천자의 ~ the (Imperial) throne. **3** [위패로 모신 신의 수]. ¶영령 8~ eight heroic souls.

위 (胃) [생] the stomach. ¶반추 동물의 제1[2/3/4]~ the paunch [honeycomb / manyplies / read] of a ruminant // ~의 gastric // ~가 아프다 have a stomachache // ~가 튼튼하다 [약하다] have good [poor / weak] digestion // ~가 나쁘다 have a stomach disorder / have [suffer from] stomach trouble // ~를 세

위경 척하다 wash out the stomach // ~를 튼튼히 하다 strengthen a weak stomach // 어제 저녁 식사로 ~의 상태가 나빠졌다 The dinner last night upset my stomach.

위경(危境) [위태로운 처지] a critical situation; a crisis. ¶~에 직면하다 face [be confronted with] a crisis // ~에서 벗어나다 tide over [pass through] a crisis.

위경(胃鏡) [의] a gastroscope. ¶~ 검사법 gastroscopy.

위경련(胃痙攣) [의] stomach cramps; a gastrospasm. ¶~을 일으키다 have stomach cramp(s) / have cramp(s) in the stomach.

위계(位階) grade of rank(s); a (court) rank. ¶~가 높은 사람 a person high in rank // ~를 높여 주다 promote (a person) to a higher rank.
● 위계질서 the order of rank.

위계(僞計) [거짓 꾀] a deceptive plan; a fraudulent scheme. ¶~를 쓰다 use a deceptive scheme.

위공(偉功) a distinguished service; a great deed. ¶의학에서 ~을 세우다 render distinguished services in medicine.

위관(胃管) a stomach tube.

위관(尉官) (육·공군의) officers below the rank of major; (해군의) officers below the rank of lieutenant commander; (미) company officer.

위구(危懼) [염려하고 두려워하는 것] apprehensions; misgivings(▶ 두 단어 모두 장래에 대한 불안); anxiety(걱정); fear(두려움). ¶일말의 ~심을 품다 have [(문어) harbor] vague misgivings (about). **위구하다** be [feel] apprehensive [uneasy] (about).

위국(危局) a crisis (pl. -ses); a critical situation.

위궤양(胃潰瘍) [의] a gastric [stomach] ulcer.

위급(危急) [긴급 사태] an emergency; [중대 국면] a crisis. ¶~을 알리다 raise [give] the alarm // 우리는 항상 ~ 시에 대비해야 한다 We should always be prepared for emergency. **위급하다** critical; exigent; imminent; crucial. ¶위급한 경우에 in case of (an) emergency // 그는 회사가 위급할 때 구해 주었다 He came to the rescue of the company at a time of crisis. // 정계가 더욱 위급해지고 있다 The political situation is becoming more and more threatening [tense].
● 위급존망지추 a critical [crucial] time.

위기(危機) a crisis (pl. crises); an emergency; a critical situation; a crucial juncture; a pinch. ¶~의 국면 a critical phase // 정치 [재정]적 ~ a political [financial] crisis // 식량 [에너지] ~ a food [an energy] crisis // ~에 처하여 at a critical moment / in the moment of crisis // ~를 넘기다 pull through [survive] a crisis // ~가 박두하다 be on the verge [on the brink] of a crisis / be very close to a crisis // ~에서 헤어나다 get over [through] a crisis // 우리는 (재정적) ~에 직면해 있다 We are now [confronting] a (financial) crisis.
● 위기감 ¶~을 갖다 [불러일으키다] have [produce] a sense of impending crisis // 이 높아 가고 있다 There is a growing sense of crisis. **위기일발** a critical moment. ¶~의 순간에 at a critical moment / in the very nick of time // ~을 모면했다 (구어) I escaped by the skin of my teeth. // 아! ~이었다 Oh, that was close!

위난(危難) danger; a peril. ¶~을 당하다 [~이 닥치다] encounter a dangerous situation // 그는 구사일생으로 ~을 모면했다 He had a narrow escape from death.

위대하다(偉大-) great; grand; mighty. ¶위대한 작곡가 a great composer // 위대한 업적 a great achievement [performance / work] // 그는 응용과학 분야에 위대한 공헌을 했다 He made great contributions in the field of applied science. // 그는 한국이 낳은 가장 위대한 정치가이다 He is the greatest statesman (that) Korea (has) ever produced.

위도(緯度) latitude(약어 lat.). ¶고[저] ~ (be in) a high [low] latitude // ~의 latitudinal // ~상(으로) latitudinally // ~를 달리하다 be in different latitudes (from) // 그 지방의 ~는 몇 도인가 What is the latitude of the place? // 그 지방은 서울과 같은 ~이다 That district is in [at] the same latitude as Seoul.

위독하다(危篤-) serious; critical; grave(최악 상태인). ¶그의 아버지는 위독하시다 His father is in a critical [serious] condition. // 부친이 위독하다는 전보를 받았다 I got a wire informing me of [announcing] my father's critical condition.

위력(威力) power(힘); authority(권위·권력); influence(세력·지배력). ¶돈의 ~ the power of money [wealth] // ~이 있는 powerful // ~을 떨치다 [나타내다] display one's great power / exercise [wield] one's power [authority] (over) / make one's influence felt // 그는 돈의 ~으로 그 지위를 얻었다 He used the power of money [wealth] to gain his position. // 그 신형 폭탄은 ~을 전 세계에 과시했다 The new bomb displayed its power to the world. // 돈의 ~이 만사를 해결한다 Money is almighty. / Money talks. // 그는 ~ 직책의 ~을 빌려서 그들을 복종시켰다 He took advantage of his title to make them obey him.

위력(偉力) great power; mighty force.

위령(違令) [명령을 어기는 것] violation of an order [command]. **위령하다** disobey an order; act contrary to (a person's) orders; violate a command.

위령제(慰靈祭) a memorial service. ¶전몰장병 ~ a memorial service for the war dead.

위령탑(慰靈塔) a cenotaph; a memorial tower.

위로(慰勞) 1 [위안] consolation; solace; comfort. **위로하다** console; solace; comfort; give comfort to (a person). ¶남의 불행을 ~ console a person for his misfortune // 슬픔에 잠겨 있는 사람을 ~ comfort a person who is in sorrow // 그는 나를 위로하려고 그렇게 말하고 있을 뿐이다 He is saying so merely to comfort [console] me. // 부친을 잃은 한 친구를 위로하기 위해 그들은 소풍을 계획했다 They planned a picnic to cheer up one of their friends who had lost her father. // 나로서는 뭐라고 위로해야 할지 몰랐다 I found myself at a loss for words of consolation. / I did not know what to say to comfort him.
2 [수고를 치하함] appreciation of the services rendered; recognition [acknowledgment] of (a person's) services. **위로하다** acknowledge [recognize / appreciate] (a person's) services. ¶선수의 노고를 ~ show one's appreciation for a player's efforts // 1년에 두 번 1박 여행으로 종업원을 ~ provide recreation for employees with twice-yearly

overnight trips // 우리는 종업원들의 노고를 위로하기 위해 휴가를 주었다 We granted a holiday to our employees in recognition [appreciation / acknowledgment] of their services.
● **위로금** a bonus.
위명(僞名) pseudonym; 〔가명〕 a false [an assumed / a fictitious] name; (범죄인 등의) an alias.
위무(慰撫) 〔위로하고 어루만짐〕 appeasement; pacification. **위무하다** pacify; soothe; appease(▶ 상대편에게 양보하고 요구를 들어줌으로써 달래는 뜻을 나타냄). ¶사고 희생자 가족을 ~ try to calm the families of the accident victims.
위문(慰問) 〔위로하려고 문안함〕 consolation; comfort; 〔병문안〕 an inquiry; a visit (to). **위문하다** 〔위로하다〕 console; comfort; 〔병문안하다〕 inquire after 《a person's》 health; visit. ¶환자를 ~ visit a sick person // 시장은 사고의 부상자를 위문하기 위해 병원을 찾았다 The mayor went to the hospital to console the people injured in the accident.
● **위문편지** a consolatory letter; a letter of sympathy; (문안의) a letter of inquiry after 《a person's》 health. **위문품** (little) comforts; a comfort article; a present 《to a sick person》.
위반(違反) (법령·규칙의) violation; contravention; infringement; (계약·약속의) breach. ¶교통 ~ traffic violation / violation of traffic regulations // 속도 ~ violation of the speed limits / speeding(속도를 내기) // 주차 ~ parking violation // 학칙 ~ violation of the school rules [regulations] // 헌법 ~ (a) violation of the constitution / unconstitutionality // 너의 행위는 학칙 ~이다 You have acted against [violated] the school regulations. **위반하다** break; violate [infringe / contravene] 《law》; act contrary to 《instructions》; run counter to 《rules》. ¶규칙을 ~ infringe [violate] a rule / run counter to the regulation // 법률을 위반하는 자는 처벌된다 Anyone who breaks the law [A lawbreaker] will be punished. →¶그것은 올림픽 정신에 위반된다 It runs counter to the Olympic spirit.
● **위반자** an offender; a violator. ¶교통 ~ traffic offender.
위배(違背) violation. ⇨ °위반
위법(違法) illegality; unlawfulness; lawbreaking. ¶~적인 illegal / unlawful // ~적으로 illegally / unlawfully / against the law // 마약 매매는 ~이다 It is against the law [illegal] to buy or sell narcotics. **위법하다** break the law; violate [infringe / contravene] the law.
● **위법성** illegality. **위법자** a lawbreaker; an offender (against the law). **위법 행위** an illegal [unlawful] act; an illegality; 〔법〕 a delict; (남의 권리에 대한) an injury; (관리 등의) an irregularity; a malfeasance.
위벽(胃壁) the walls of the stomach; stomach walls.
위병(胃病) a stomach trouble [disorder]. ¶~을 앓다 suffer from a stomach trouble.
위병(衛兵) a guard; 〔보초〕 a sentinel; a sentry. ¶~의 교대 the changing of the guard // ~을 두다 [세우다] post a guard // ~을 서다 be on guard.
● **위병 근무** guard duty. ¶~ 중이다 be on guard. **위병 장교** an officer (in charge) of the guard.

위본(僞本) a forged [an apocryphal] book; a pseudograph; a forgery; 〔해적판〕 a pirated edition.
위부(委付) 〔법〕 abandonment.
위산(胃酸) 〔생〕 gastric acid.
● **위산 과다증** gastric hyperacidity.
위상(位相) 〔물〕〔전〕 a phase; 〔수〕 topology.
● **위상 수학** topology; analysis situs.
위샘(胃-) 〔생〕 a gastric gland.
위생(衛生) sanitation; hygiene. ¶공중 ~ public health // 보건 ~ hygiene / sanitation(▶ hygiene은 주로 청결함에, sanitation은 오물의 제거 등에 주안점을 둠) // 학교 ~ school hygiene // 정신 ~ mental hygiene. // ~에 주의하다 be careful of one's health // 이 식당은 ~ 상태가 좋다 [나쁘다] This restaurant is sanitary [insanitary]. / This restaurant has good [poor] sanitation.
● **위생 공학** sanitary engineering. **위생병** 〔군〕 a hospital [medical] orderly; a medical [hospital] corpsman; (미국 속어) a [an army] medic. **위생복** disinfected overgarment. **위생 시설** sanitary [health] facilities; (특히 하수 등) sanitation. **위생학** hygienics; hygiene. ¶공중 ~ sanitary science.
위생적(衛生的) hygienic; sanitary. ¶비~인 insanitary // 〔불결한〕 unclean // ~인 식품 (a) wholesome food // ~인 하수 설비 sanitary sewerage // 이것은 ~[비]~이다 This is a sanitary [insanitary] wrapper.
위서(僞書) 1 〔가짜 편지〕 a forged letter. 2 a forged book. ⇨ °위본 3 a forged document. ⇨위조문서(⇨위조).
위선(胃腺) 〔생〕 a gastric gland. ⇨ °위샘
위선(僞善) hypocrisy; pharisaism. ¶~적인 hypocritical // ~을 행하다 play the hypocrite / behave hypocritically.
● **위선자** a hypocrite; a pharisee; a wolf in sheep's clothing.
위선(緯線) 〔지〕 a parallel (of latitude); a latitude line.
위성(衛星) 〔천〕 a satellite. ¶인공~ a man-made [an artificial] satellite // 통신 ~ a communications satellite // 방송 ~ a telecommunications satellite // 기상 ~ a weather satellite // 정지 ~ a stationary satellite // 정찰 ~ a reconnaissance satellite // 지구 물리 관측 ~ the orbiting Geophysical Observatory // 첩보 ~ a spy(-in-the-sky) satellite // ~의 궤도 the orbit of a satellite // 달은 지구의 ~이다 The moon is a satellite of the earth. // 토성은 10개의 ~을 가지고 있다 Saturn has ten satellites [moons].
● **위성국** a satellite; a satellite [client] state. **위성 도시** a satellite city [town]. **위성 전송** satellite transmission. **위성 중계** satellite relay; transmission via satellite. ¶올림픽의 열전이 ~로 방송되었다 The heated contests in the Olympic Games were broadcast via [by] satellite relay.
위세(威勢) 1 〔복종시키는 힘〕 power; might; influence; authority. ¶~를 보이다 make a show of one's power / make a display of one's influence // 그는 재계에서 ~를 떨치고 있다 He is gaining influence [(미국 구어) clout] in financial circles. // 그의 ~에 눌려 말 한마디 못했다 I was overwhelmed by his authority that I couldn't say a word. 2 〔위엄 있는 기세〕 high spirits; dash. ¶~ 당당한

위세척 high-spirited / full of high spirits / gallant / dashing / spanking // 우리는 ~ 당당히 떠났다 We plucked up our spirits and set out.

위세척(胃洗滌) (a) gastrolavage. ¶~을 하다 use a stomach pump on a person.

위수(衛戍) a garrison; board guard(국경 경비).
● **위수령** Garrison Decree. **위수병** garrison troops. **위수지** a garrison town.

위스키 whisky; whiskey(▶ bourbon 등 미국산이나 아일랜드산은 whiskey, 스코틀랜드산은 whisky로 구분하여 철자함). ¶스카치 ~ Scotch whisky // ~ 소다 a whisk(e)y and soda /(미) a highball // ~ 잔 a whisk(e)y glass // 물을 타지 않은 ~ straight[neat] whisk(e)y // 물을 탄 ~ whisky and water // ~를 스트레이트로 마시다 drink whisky straight[(영) neat] // ~에 얼음을 넣어 주세요. I'd like a whisky on the rock.

위시하다(爲始-) begin; commence; start. ¶위시하여 including ... ¶국무총리를 위시한 각 각료 the Cabinet Members, including the Prime Minister[from the Prime Minister down] // 송 박사를 위시해서 많은 인사가 파티에 초대되었다 Many dignitaries, including Dr. Song, were invited to the party. // 교장을 위시해서 다섯 명의 선생이 그 모임에 참석했다 Five teachers, including the principal, attended the meeting.

위신(威信) [위엄과 신망] authority and confidence; dignity; prestige. ¶~의 실추 lose of prestige // ~을 지키다 maintain[preserve] one's dignity[prestige] // ~을 잃다 lose authority[prestige] / lose[lower] one's dignity / let oneself down // ~을 되찾다 restore one's prestige / recover one's lost prestige // 그에게 사정한다는 것은 내 ~을 떨어뜨리는 일이다 It is beneath my dignity to ask a favor of him. // 그것이 당신의 ~을 떨어뜨린다고는 생각지 않소 I don't think it will discredit you. // 그런 사소한 일로 싸운다는 것은 네 ~에 관한 문제다 You are lowering yourself by picking a quarrel over such a trifling matter.

위아래 (신분의) high and low; the upper and lower; up and down; above and below. ¶~가 뒤바뀌다 be upside down / be topsy-turvy // 남을 ~로 훑어보다 look (a person) up and down / survey (a person) from head to foot // 그 소년은 기를 ~로 흔들었다 The boy waved the flag up and down. // 배는 ~로 몹시 흔들렸다 The boat pitched heavily. // 너는 ~를 거꾸로 놓았다 You've put it upside down.

위안(慰安) (a) comfort; (a) consolation; solace.(▶ comfort는 남의 불행을 덜고 기운을 돋우는 일, consolation은 슬픔이나 실의를 경감하는 일, solace는 슬픔·괴로움 등을 달래 주는 일) ¶아름다운 경관을 바라보면서 나는 ~을 얻는다 Looking at beautiful scenery is a consolation to me. // 나는 음악을 들으면 ~이 된다 I find solace[consolation / comfort] in listening to music. // 딴 사람들도 실패했다는 것을 알아도 ~이 되지 않는다 It is cold [small] comfort to find that others have also failed. // 내 딸이 나의 유일한 ~이오 My daughter is my sole[only] consolation. // 그녀는 종교에서 ~을 얻었다 She sought solace[comfort / consolation] in religion. / She went to religion for solace. / She took refuge in[at / behind] religion. / She solaced herself with religion. // 그는 그림 그리기에서 ~을 찾았다 He found amusement in painting. **위안하다** comfort; console; solace; give [bring] comfort (to); [기분을 돋우다] cheer up. ¶그 사나이는 술로 자신의 불행을 위안했다 The (unhappy) man consoled himself with drinking.
● **위안부** a comfort girl[woman]. **위안처** an oasis.

위암(胃癌) [의] a stomach[gastric] cancer; a cancer of the stomach.

위압(威壓) coercion; high-handedness; overpowering; browbeating; [법] (폭력적인) duress. ¶~적(인) coercive / high-handed / overbearing / domineering / browbeating // 그는 종종 ~적인 태도를 취했다 He often assumed a coercive[domineering] attitude. // 나는 장관 앞에서 ~을 느꼈다 I felt overawed in the presence of the director. **위압하다** coerce; overpower; overawe; overbear; browbeat. ¶군대는 발포해서 군중을 위압했다 The army coerced the crowd by firing into it.
➔ **위압당하다** be overawed (by) / be cowed (before).

위액(胃液) [생] gastric juice[fluid]. ¶~의 분비 the secretion of gastric juices.
● **위액 분비선**(-分泌腺) a gastric gland.

위약(胃弱) dyspepsia; indigestion; weak [poor] digestion. **위약하다** dyspeptic; (서술적) have (a) weak[poor] digestion; suffer from indigestion; have a weak stomach. ¶위약한 사람 a dyspeptic.

위약(違約) a breach of a promise[a contract / an agreement]; a default(의무·채무의 불이행·태만). **위약하다** break a promise[a contract / an agreement / an appointment]; break[go back on] one's word[promise]; default. ¶그가 위약하지는 않을 것이다 He will keep[be faithful to] his promise. / He will not break the contract.
● **위약금** a penalty[damage] for breach of contract(▶ damage는 손해 배상금). ¶계약을 파기하면 ~을 물어야 한다 If I break[violate] a contract, I have to pay the breach-of-contract damages.

위엄(威嚴) dignity; majesty; stateliness. ¶~ 있는 dignified / majestic(al) stately // ~을 보이다 stand on one's dignity / show one's dignity // ~을 지키다 maintain[keep] one's dignity / keep (up) one's state / (법관 등이) keep one's gravity // ~을 잃다[손상시키다] impair[compromise / damage / lower] one's dignity // ~ 있는 얼굴을 하고 있다 be severe in countenance / look as grave as a judge // 그의 태도에는 어딘지 ~이 있다 There is something dignified in his bearing.

위업(偉業) a great achievement[work / feat]. ¶~을 이루다 achieve a feat[great work] / accomplish a great feat.

위염(胃炎) [의] gastritis; inflammation of the stomach.

위용(威容) [위엄 찬 모습] a dignified [a commanding / a grand / a majestic] appearance; a dignified mien. ¶~을 갖추고 in a dignified attitude // ~을 갖추다 assume a dignified attitude / compose one's appearance // ~을 보이다 present [offer] a grand spectacle [a magnificent appearance] // 그 도시의 중심부에 의사당이 높이 솟아 그 ~을 자랑하고 있다

In the center of the town the assembly hall rises in state.

위원(委員) a member of a committee; a committee member; a committeeman; (집합적) a committee; a commissioner. ¶국무 ~ a cabinet member / a minister // 논설 ~ (신문의) an editorial writer / an editorialist /(영) a leader writer // 상임 ~ a standing[permanent] committee // 집행 ~ an executive committee // 나는 운영 ~에 선출되었다 I was elected to the steering committee. // 나는 재무 ~입니다 I am on [a member of] the finance committee. // 각 학급에서 집행 ~이 나와 있다 Each class is represented on the executive committee. // 의사들이 ~으로 되어 있다 Medical doctors constitute the committee. // 이 위원회는 7명의 ~으로 되어 있다 This committee is made up[consists] of seven members.
● **위원장** a chairperson; (남성) a chairman; (여성) a chairwoman. **위원회** a committee; (특히 정부의) a commission; a board; (회의) a committee meeting. ¶교육 ~ a board of education // 분과 ~ a subcommittee / a subcommission / (회의) a sectional committee meeting // 상임 ~ a standing committee // 운영 ~ a steering committee // 전문 ~ an expert committee // 조사 ~ an investigation committee // 준비 ~ an arrangement committee / 창립 ~ an organizing committee / ~ 결정 사항 committee findings // ~를 개최하다 hold a committee meeting // ~를 소집[해산]하다 call[adjourn] a committee meeting // ~가 개최 중이다 The committee is in session.

위의(威儀) [위엄 있는 태도] a dignified mien; a solemn manner. ¶~를 갖추고 in a dignified[solemn] manner / with a solemnity of manner / solemnly // 사람들은 ~를 갖추고 식에 참석했다 The people attended the ceremony in a dignified[solemn] manner.

위인(爲人) [사람의 됨됨이] one's personality [character]; [됨됨이로 본 사람] a person. ¶그는 도둑질할 ~이 아니다 He is not a [the sort of] man to commit a theft. // 이번에 새로 온 선생은 어떤 ~이냐 What kind of (a) man is the new teacher? // 이런 행위는 그의 ~을 말해 준다 Such conduct is characteristic [typical] of him.

위인(偉人) a great man; [영웅] a hero (pl. ~es). ¶과거의 ~들 the great names of past ages // ~이 되다 attain greatness.
● **위인전** the life[biography] of a great man.

위임(委任) [맡김] trust; commission; charge; (권한의) delegation; (권한의) authorization; commitment; [법] mandate. **위임하다** entrust (a person) with (a thing); entrust (a thing) to (a person); charge (a person) with (a thing); charge (a thing) to (a person); leave (a thing) to (a person); commit (a thing) to (a person); commission (a person) to (do something); (권한을) delegate (authority / power) to (a person). ¶우리는 그 문제의 결정을 위원회에 위임했다 We left[entrusted] the problem to the decision of the committee. // 대통령은 그 대사에게 이 건에 대한 전권을 위임했다 The president has entrusted the ambassador with full power regarding this matter. // 나는 그 문제를 그에게 위임했다 I have left the matter to him. // 사무상의 일은 모두 그에게 위임하고 있다 I put all business matters under his charge. // 이 문제는 교무 회의에 위임해야 한다 We have to refer this question to the faculty meeting. ➜¶그는 양자 사이의 조정을 위임받았다 He was commissioned to mediate between the two parties.
● **위임 명령** a delegated[an instructed] order. **위임자** the mandator. ¶피~ a trustee. **위임장** a letter[warrant / power] of attorney; (증권) a proxy. ¶백지 ~ a carte blanche. **위임 통치** mandate; mandatory rule[administration]. ¶~를 하다 carry out a mandate // ~하에 놓여 있다 be placed under the United Nations mandate. **위임 통치령** territories under mandate; mandated territories.

위자료(慰藉料) consolation money; a solatium (pl. -tia); (이혼의) a (cash) settlement; (구어) heart[love] balm; [고통·피해에 대한 배상금] compensation. ¶부상자들은 ~를 청구했다 The injured demanded compensation. // 그녀는 그에게 ~를 달라고 요구했다 She demanded that he pay consolation money (when he wanted to leave her).

위작(僞作) a forgery; a fake. ¶르누아르 그림의 ~ forged Renoir.

위장(胃腸) the stomach and intestines [bowls]; the gastrointestines. ¶~의 gastrointestinal / gastroenteric / ~을 해치다 hurt[upset] the stomach (and bowls) // 나는 ~이 튼튼하다[약하다] I have good[poor / weak] digestion.
● **위장병** a gastroenteric[digestive] disorder. ¶그의 ~이 좀처럼 낫지 않는 듯하다 His stomach disease does not seem to be getting any better. **위장약** digestive medicine; (소화제) a digestive. **위장염** gastroenteritis.

위장(僞裝) (a) camouflage; [변장] (a) disguise. ¶~을 하고 in disguise / in[under] the disguise (of). **위장하다** camouflage a thing (as); disguise oneself (as). ¶상선으로 위장한 군함 a warship disguised as a merchant ship.
● **위장 귀순** defection in disguise. **위장 전입** a false resident registration.

위정자(爲政者) [정치가] an administrator; a statesman. ¶~는 국민의 소리를 들어야 한다 Those who govern the people must listen to their voice.

위조(僞造) forgery; fabrication; counterfeiting. ¶공문서 ~ the forgery of official papers // 문서 ~죄 forgery of documents // 화폐 ~자 a coiner. **위조하다** forge; counterfeit(▶ 진짜와 비슷하게 만드는 것); fabricate; commit forgery. ¶위조한 counterfeit / forged / 1만 원짜리 지폐를 ~ counterfeit ten thousand-won bills[(영) notes] // 수표를 ~ forge a check // 문서를 ~ fabricate a document.
● **위조문서** a forged document; false papers; a fake document. **위조지폐** a counterfeit [forged / false] (bank) note. **위조품** a forgery; a counterfeit; a fake; a spurious article. **위조 화폐** a forged[counterfeit] coin; fake money.

위족(僞足) [생] a pseudopodium (pl. -dia).

위주(爲主) ¶자기 ~의 사고방식 self-centered way of thinking // 아동 ~의 교육 child-centered education // 경제 성장 ~의 정책 growth-oriented policy // 이 학교는 어학을 ~

로 하고 있다 Language takes the central place in [forms the foundation of] the curriculum of this school. // 우리 회사는 실력 ~로 사람을 고용한다 "Ability first" is our motto in employing men. // 그는 품질을 ~로 하는 영업 방침으로 사업에 성공했다 His "quality first" policy brought him success in business.

위중하다(危重-) be seriously [critically] ill; be in a critical condition. ¶어머니가 위중하시다는 전보를 받았다 I got a wire informing me of [announcing] my mother's critical condition.

위증(僞證) [법] false witness; false evidence [testimony] (법정에서 선서한 후의). **위증하다** give false witness; give false evidence [testimony]; perjure oneself; commit perjury; swear [testify] falsely (against). ¶그는 위증했다가 위증죄로 기소되었다 He gave false witness [evidence / testimony] and was accused of perjury.
● **위증자** a perjurer. **위증죄** (the crime of) perjury.

위쪽 the upper direction [part]. ¶강을 ~으로 100킬로미터 올라가다 go a hundred kilometers up a river // 벽 ~에 틈새가 있다 There is a crack in the upper part of the wall.

위촉(委囑) [직권 등의 위임] commission; entrusting; [임명] appointment; [의뢰] request. ¶~으로 [~에 의하여] by request / at a person's request. **위촉하다** entrust; commission; [임명하다] appoint. ¶그 일은 존슨 씨에게 위촉했다 I entrusted the matter to Mr. Johnson. →¶스미스 씨는 시 당국으로부터 식전(式典) 음악의 작곡을 위촉받았다 Mr. Smith was commissioned by the municipal authorities to compose music for the ceremony. // 신 박사의 전기(傳記) 편집을 위촉받았다 I was placed in charge of compiling Dr. Sin's biography. // 그는 운영 위원으로 위촉되었다 He was appointed to the steering committee.

위축(萎縮) withering; shrinkage; shriveling; contraction; (영양 불량 등에 의한) atrophy. ¶간[신장]의 ~ atrophy of the liver [the kidneys] // ~성의 atrophic. **위축하다** (물체가) wither; wilt; shrivel; shrink; (사람이) shrink (from); be daunted (by failure); be dispirited; [공포·부끄러움 등으로 움츠리다] cower. →그녀의 깔보는 눈초리에 그는 위축되고 말았다 She withered him with a scornful look. // 사자는 맹수 조련사의 회초리 앞에서 위축되었다 The lion shrank from its trainer's whip.

위층(-層) the upper floor [story]; upstairs. ¶~의 사무소 an upstairs office // ~으로 가다 go upstairs // 침실은 ~에 있다 The bedrooms are upstairs [on the upper floor]. // 나는 ~에서 나는 발소리를 들었다 I heard footsteps upstairs.

위치(位置) **1** [장소] a place; (a) position; (a) location; a situation; a site. ¶~를 잡다 [바꾸다] take [shift] one's position // 배의 ~를 재다 fix a ship's position // 북극성은 ~가 바뀌지 않는다 The pole star always stays in one (and the same) position. // 지도에 x표로 나타낸 것이 극장의 ~입니다 The x on the map indicates the location of the theater. // 그 상점은 ~가 좋다 The store is favorably located [situated]. / The store is located in an advantageous position. // 그 도로 표지는 ~가 나쁘다 That road sign is ill-located. **위치하다** be situated [located]; lie (도시·국가 등이); stand (산·건물 등이). ¶그 나라의 수도는 약간 북쪽에 위치하고 있다 The nation's capital is located [is situated / lies] somewhat to the north. // 대전은 서울과 부산의 중간에 위치한다 Daejeon lies midway between Seoul and Busan.
2 [입장] a place; [처지] a situation; [지위] a position. ¶네가 내 ~에 있다면 어떻게 하겠나 If you were in my place [position], what would you do? // 그는 그 회사에서 높은 ~에 있다 He holds a high position in the company.
● **위치 에너지** potential energy.

위탁(委託) trust; commission(임무 등의); consignment(판매의); committal; commitment. ¶~하에 있다 be held in trust. **위탁하다** entrust; consign (to); put (a thing) in a person's charge; commit; commission. ¶나는 이 계획의 실행을 그의 그룹에 위탁했다 I entrusted the group with the implementation of this plan. / I entrusted the implementation of this plan to his group. // 이 물품의 판매를 대리점에 위탁했다 We have consigned these goods to our agent. // 나는 그 일을 변호사에게 위탁했습니다 I have left that matter to my lawyer. →¶그는 그 건에 관한 교섭을 위탁받았다 He was commissioned [given a commission] to negotiate over the matter.
● **위탁 가공** processing of brought-in materials; processing on commission. **위탁금** money in trust; trust money. **위탁물** consignment goods. **위탁인 / 위탁자** a client; [위탁 판매인] a consignor; [법] a settlor; a trustor. ¶피~ a trustee / a principal. **위탁 판매** consignment [commission] sale; sale on commission [consignment]. ¶~로 on consignment // ~를 **하다** sell (goods) on commission [consignment].

위태롭다(危殆-) dangerous; hazardous; perilous; risky(모험적인); precarious(불안정한); (병세가) critical; grave; serious. ¶위태로운 장난 a dangerous game // 위태로운 짓을 하다 run [take on] a risk / make a risky attempt // 나라를 위태롭게 하다 compromise the safety of the country // 이 토대는 ~ This foundation is not stable [secure]. // 이건 위태로운 도박이다 It's a risky [hazardous] bet. // 아버지의 용태가 ~ My father is in critical condition. // 그의 목숨이 ~ His life is in danger [threatened].

위태위태하다(危殆危殆-) dangerous; hazardous. ⇨ 위태롭다 ¶보기만 해도 ~ It makes me feel uneasy [nervous] just to see it.

위태하다(危殆-) dangerous; hazardous. ⇨ 위태롭다

위턱 the upper jaw.
● **위턱뼈** the upper jawbone; maxillary bone.

위통(胃痛) a stomachache; [의] gastralgia. ¶~이 있다 have a stomachache.

위트 wit. ¶~가 풍부한 대화 a witty conversation // 그는 ~가 있는 사람이다 He is a wit [a witty man].

위패(位牌) a (Buddhist) mortuary [memorial] tablet. ¶조상의 ~ a family mortuary [memorial] tablet.

위폐(僞幣) counterfeit[fake] money.
위풍(威風) dignity; majesty; an imposing[a majestic] air; a commanding presence. ¶그 장군은 주위를 압도하는 ~을 지니고 있었다 The general gave an impression of majesty[great dignity]. / The general had a commanding presence[an awe-inspiring air about him].
위풍당당하다(威風堂堂-) majestic; imposing; commanding; awe-inspiring. ¶위풍당당한 인물 a man of commanding presence // 위풍당당하게 in a majestic[a dignified / an imposing] manner // 그 우승 팀은 위풍당당하게 큰 거리를 행진하였다 The championship team triumphantly paraded through the main street.
위필(僞筆) forged (hand)writing. ¶~의 forged // ~로 in a forged hand // 이 왕당의 글씨는 ~이다 This Wandang is a forgery[fake]. **위필하다** forge; counterfeit.
위하다(爲-) **1** [이롭게 하다] do for the good[benefit] of; do in favor[behalf] of. ¶예술을 위한 예술 art for art's sake // 초보자를 위한 영어책 an English book for beginner // 나라를 위하여 죽다 die for one's country // 공익을 위하여 일하다 work for the common good // 가는 것이 당신을 위하여 좋을 것이오 It is to your interest to go. // 그것은 당신을 위하여 좋을 것이 없소 It will do you no good. // 그런 환자를 위할 병원이 부족하다 We are short of hospitals that can handle such cases. // 그 대학에서는 외국인을 위한 한국어 강좌를 개강하고 있다 The university offers Korean language courses for students from abroad. // 그렇게 위하는 체하는 소리는 이제 듣기 지겹다 I'm tired of hearing about how it'll be good for me[how it's all for my own good] (when in fact it's you who's going to benefit). // 손 씨를 위한 송별회가 열렸다 A farewell party was given in honor of Mr. Son. // 그는 토론을 위한 토론을 좋아한다 He likes to argue just for argument's sake.
2 [사랑하다] care for; love; [공경하다] serve; honor; revere; respect; worship. ¶부모를 ~ be devoted to[take good care of] one's parents // 아이들을 ~ be kind to children // 그는 아내를 몹시 위한다 He thinks of his wife before himself.
3 [소중히 하다] have regard for; take good care of; esteem; value; make[think] much of. ¶건강을 ~ take (great) care of one's health // 돈보다 명예를 더 ~ care for one's honor more than for one's money.
4 [(목적 등을) 이루려고 하다] ¶살기 위하여 싸우다 fight for one's life // 노후를 위하여 저금하다 save money for one's old age // 시간에 대어 열차를 잡아타기 위하여 일찌감치 집을 나왔다 I left home early in order to[so that I could] catch the train. // 모임에 늦지 않기 위하여 급히 서둘렀다 I hurried so as not to be late for the meeting. // 그는 그녀를 기쁘게 해 주기 위하여 그렇게 말했다 He said that to please her. // 그녀는 무엇을 위하여 사는지 모르겠다 I wonder what she lives for. // 그들은 문제 해결을 위하여 노력했다 They worked toward(s) a solution of the problem.
위해(危害) (an) injury; harm. ¶남에게 ~를 가하다 injure[harm] a person / do harm to a person / 《문어》 inflict (an) injury on a person // ~를 입다 suffer an injury // ~를 모면하다 escape injury / be unhurt.
● **위해물** a dangerous[hazardous] article.
위헌(違憲) (a) violation of the constitution; unconstitutionality. ¶이 결정은 ~이다 This decision is unconstitutional.
위험(危險) (a) danger; (사람의 힘으로는 회피할 수 없는) (a) hazard; (생명에 관계되는) peril; (모험·도박에 따르는) (a) risk. ¶직업상의 ~ occupational hazards // ~에 빠지다 be in danger / fall into a dangerous situation / 《문어》 be endangered // 닥쳐오는 ~을 느끼다 sense[apprehend] imminent danger // ~을 무릅쓰다 run a risk / take risks / brave a danger // ~! 폭발물 《게시》 Caution: Explosives. // 더워서 이 음식은 썩을 ~(성)이 있다 It is so hot that this food is in danger of going bad[I'm afraid this food won't keep]. / It is so hot that there is some danger this food may go bad. // 그는 생명의 ~을 무릅쓰고 그 아이를 구했다 He saved the child at the risk of his life. // 등산가들은 엄청난 ~에 직면해 있었다 The climbers were in great peril. // 어디든 도난당할 ~이 없는 곳에 숨겨 두게 Please keep it somewhere there's no danger of its being stolen. **위험하다** dangerous; perilous; risky; hazardous; critical; breakneck (speed). ¶위험한 놀이 a dangerous game // 위험한 내기를 하다 take a risk // 위험한 처지에 놓이다 be exposed to danger / have a dangerous experience // 태풍이 접근해 오므로 바다에서 수영하는 것은 ~ It's dangerous to go swimming in the sea as a typhoon is approaching. // 그녀의 생명은 위험한 상태에 있다 Her life is in danger. // 이 강에서 헤엄치는 것은 ~ It's dangerous to swim[bathe] in the river. // 그것은 위험한 내기다 It's a risky[hazardous] bet. // 내 심장으로는 조깅이 위험하다는 말을 들었다 I was told[warned] that with my heart, jogging would be risky. // 위험해 Look out! / Watch out! // 그의 거래는 매우 ~ His business is very risky. // 위험하므로 귀중품은 몸에 지녀 주십시오 Keep your valuables on you because it is not safe to leave them lying around.
● **위험물** a dangerous substance[article]. ¶~ 지입(持入) 금지 《게시》 No Dangerous Objects. / Dangerous Objects Prohibited. **위험 부담** [법] risk bearing. **위험성** a possibility of danger; dangerousness; riskiness. ¶~이 많은 risky / dangerous // ~이 없는 safe / sure / secure. **위험 신호** a danger signal. **위험인물** a dangerous person; a security risk(국가 안보상).
위험천만하다(危險千萬-) extremely dangerous. ¶위험천만한 짓을 하다 perform a hazardous feat / sleep on a volcano.
위협(威脅) a menace; a threat(▶ menace가 더 강하며, 적의도 포함됨); intimidation. ¶~적인 태도를 취하다 take a threatening[menacing] attitude // 갑자기 ~적인 태도로 변하다 change suddenly to a threatening attitude // 그의 말투는 ~적이었다 There was menace[a threat] in his tone. // 깡패들에게 ~을 당해 돈을 빼앗겼다 The gangsters used threats to get money from him. / 《미국 구어》 He was shaken down by gangsters. // 그것은 단순한 ~에 지나지 않아 It's just[nothing but] a bluff. // 죽이겠다는 ~을 받고 서명했다 I signed it under threat of death. // 인구의 급

위화감

격한 증가는 이 나라의 경제에 대한 심각한 ~이 될 것이다 The rapid increase in population will prove a great[serious] menace to the economy of this nation.∥우리나라는 전쟁의 ~에 직면하고 있다 Our country is threatened[menaced] by war. / Our nation is faced with the thread[menace] of war. **위협하다** intimidate; threaten; scare; menace(▶ 약간 문어적). ¶학문[언론]의 자유를 위협하는 짓 a threat to academic freedom[freedom of speech]∥위협하는 말 threatening remarks[language]∥칼로 ~ threaten a person with a knife∥그를 위협해서 자백시켰다 Frighten[Scare] him into confessing.∥그는 난폭한 행위로 소년을 위협했다 He threatened the boy with violence.∥도둑은 들키자 가족을 위협했다 When he was detected, the housebreaker resorted to threatening the family.∥그는 우리를 그냥 두지 않겠다고 위협했다 He threatened us with a suggestion of violence. →¶그는 생명을 위협받고 있다 His life is threatened[in jeopardy].
●**위협사격** a warning shot. ¶경관은 도주하는 사나이를 향해 ~을 했다 The policeman fired a warning shot at the man running away. **위협자** an intimidator; a scaremonger.

위화감(違和感) a sense of incongruity. ¶우아한 부인의 거친 말투에서 나는 ~을 느꼈다 Such a harsh tone of voice, coming from such an elegant woman, struck me as incongruous.∥그는 어떤 자리에 가나 ~을 느끼지 않는다 He never feels out of place no matter what company he finds himself in.

위훈(偉勳) a great service[achievement]; a brilliant exploit; a distinguished merit. ¶~을 세우다 accomplish a great deed / render distinguished service(s).

윈도 1 [진열장] a window. 2 [컴] [사각형의 화면 구조] a window.
●**윈도 브러시**(˝brush) a wiper; (미) a windshield wiper; (영) a windscreen wiper. **윈도쇼핑** window-shopping. ¶~을 하다 window-shop / go window-shopping.

윈드서핑 windsurfing.

윗누이 an elder sister.

윗눈썹 upper eyelashes[lashes].

윗니 the upper teeth.

윗도리 1 [상체] the upper part of the body; the upper body; the bust. 2 〈속〉 a coat. ⇨윗옷 ¶~를 벗다 take off one's coat.

윗목 the upper part of an *ondol* floor.

윗물 the water of the upper stream (of a river); the upper waters (of a river).

윗물이 맑아야 아랫물이 맑다(속담) Like master, like man.; As is the king, so is the people.

윗방(-房) the upper room. ¶그는 내 바로 ~에 살고 있다 He lives in the room just above mine.

윗사람 1 [연장자] one's elders; one's seniors. 2 [지위 등이 자기보다 높은 사람] one's superior(s); one's better(s).

윗옷 a coat; a jacket. ¶~을 벗고 일하다 work in one's shirtsleeves.

윗입술 the upper lip.

윗자리 [상좌] an upper[a higher] seat; the top seat; [주빈의 자리] the seat[place] of honor; [높은 지위] a high position[rank]. ¶~에 앉다 sit at the head (of the table) / take the top seat / (높은 지위) be highly placed / attain a high rank.

윙(윙) [벌레 소리] with a buzz[hum]; [기계 소리] with a whir; [바람 소리] with a whistle[whiz(z)]. ¶비행기가 ~ 머리 위를 날아간다 A plane is droning overhead.∥바람이 ~ 불어 댔다 The wind hissed and raged. **윙윙하다** buzz and buzz. ⇨˝윙윙거리다

윙윙거리다 (벌 등이) buzz and buzz; hum; make humming sounds; drone; (바람 소리가) whizz; whistle. ¶벌이 내 귀 주위에서 웡윙거리고 있다 A bee is buzzing around my ears.∥모터가 윙윙거리며 돌고 있다 The motor is purring(▶ pur는 비교적 작고 매끄러운 소리).∥전기면도기의 윙윙거리는 소리가 들렸다 I heard the hum(ming)[buzzing] of an electric razor.∥북풍이 윙윙거리며 불고 있다 The north wind is whistling.

윙크 a wink. **윙크하다** wink (at); give a wink (to).

유(有) 1 [존재함] existence; being. ¶무에서 ~를 창조해 내다 make something out of nothing. 2 [있음]. ¶~자격자 a qualified [licensed] person∥~의의(意義) significant.

유(類) 1 [무리] a group. 2 [종류] a kind; a sort; a type; a class; the like (of it). ¶이런 ~의 책 this kind of books / books of this kind∥이런 ~의 물건 goods in this line / articles of this kind[brand / description]∥이런 ~의 상품은 현재 품절이다 The goods in this line are now sold out.∥나는 그런 ~의 음악을 좋아하지 않는다 I don't like music of that sort.∥이 ∥ 작품은 독창성에서 그 ~가 없다 This work is unequaled[unparalleled] in originality.∥저런 ~의 기계는 값이 비싸다 Machines of that type[sort / kind] are expensive. 3 [생] [강(綱)] a class; [목(目)] an order. 4 [논] a genus. ⇨유개념

유가(儒家) a Confucianist; a Confucian scholar.

유가(有價) ¶~의 valuable / negotiable.
●**유가물** valuables. **유가 증권** securities; negotiable securities[instruments].

유가족(遺家族) a bereaved family. ¶군인 ~ a war-bereaved family.

유감(遺憾) 1 [섭섭함] regret; a pity. ¶~으로 생각하다 regret / be sorry (for) / feel sorry (that)∥~이다 It is a pity that ....∥~천만이다 It is a thousand pities that ....∥~이지만 I regret[am sorry] to say, but ... / to my regret∥어제 모임에 네가 나오지 않아 ~천만이다 I regret it very deeply that you did not attend the meeting yesterday.∥생전에 그 아이에게 아무것도 못 해 주어서 ~이다 I regret [I'm sorry] that I could do nothing for the boy in his lifetime.∥~이지만 이 프로는 중지됩니다 I regret[am sorry] to say that this program will be discontinued.
2 [좋지 않은 감정] a grudge; resentment. ¶너 나한테 ~ 있나 Do you have a grudge against me? / Are you harboring a grudge against me?

유감스럽다(遺憾—) 1 [섭섭하다] regrettable; deplorable. ¶유감스럽게 생각하다 regret / feel sorry (that)∥유감스럽게도 몸이 약하다 Unfortunately[It is unfortunate that] I am not very strong.∥유감스럽게도 국무총리는 피해 지역을 들르지 않고 지나가 버렸다 Much to our vexation[chagrin], the Prime Minister passed by the stricken area without stop-

ping.//사상자를 낸 것은 유감스런 일이다 We regret[It is regrettable] that there were some casualties.//나는 유감스럽지만 초대를 거절했다 I regretfully declined the invitation.//유감스럽게도 그의 강의는 병 때문에 중지되었다 To our regret, his lecture was canceled because he was ill.//그가 입상(入賞)하지 못했다는 것은 유감스러운 일입니다 It is a matter for regret that he did not win the prize./It is to be regretted that he was not awarded the prize.//그가 본회의에 참석하지 못한다는 것은 유감스러운 일이다 It is deplorable[regrettable] that he should be absent from this meeting.(▶ deplorable은 애석하다는 느낌뿐만 아니라 비난의 뜻도 포함됨)
2 [불만족하다] unsatisfactory.

유감없다(遺憾-) [완전하다] perfect; (most) satisfactory; [충분하다] thorough. **유감없이** perfectly; fully; most satisfactorily; to one's heart's content. ¶그의 특질은 이 시에 나타나 있다 His characteristics are fully revealed in this poem.//그녀는 재능을 발휘했다 She displayed her abilities to the full.//그는 시험에서 실력을 ~ 발휘했다 He fully showed his real ability in the examination.

유개(有蓋) ¶~의 covered/roofed/lidded.
● **유개차** a covered cart[wagon].

유개념(類槪念) [논] a genus.

유객(遊客) **1** [유람객] a tourist; a man on a pleasure trip. **2** [건달] a playboy; a loafer. **3** [탕아] a libertine; a rake; a debauchee.

유격(遊擊) [군] a search-and-kill[destroy] mission; a hit-and-run attack; an attack by a mobile unit.
● **유격대** a guer(r)illa unit; a flying column [corps/army]; a commando unit; mobile forces; a corps of rangers. **유격수** [야구] a shortstop; a short. **유격전** guer(r)illa warfare.

유고(有故) [사고] an accident; an incident; (a) trouble; a mishap; [사정] reasons; circumstances. ¶~ 시에는 at the time of an accident. **유고하다** 《서술적》 have (some) trouble; have a reason (for it); be owing to some trouble.

유고(遺稿) posthumous works[manuscripts]; literary remains. ¶이 책은 최 교수의 ~집이다 This book is a collection of manuscripts left unpublished in professor Choe's lifetime.

유곡(幽谷) [깊은 골짜기] a deep ravine. ¶심산~의 고장 a place with high mountains and secluded deep valleys.

유골(遺骨) ashes; the (skeletal) remains. ¶전사자의 ~ the remains of the war dead//~을 줍다 [항아리에 거두다] gather (a person's) ashes[put a person's ashes in an urn]//~을 봉안하다 place (a person's) remains in (a temple).

유공(有功) ¶~의 meritorious.
● **유공자** a man of merit. **유공 훈장** the order of merit.

유곽(遊廓) [미] a (licensed) red-light district; licensed[gay/prostitute] quarters. ¶~에 드나들다 frequent houses of ill fame.

유관(有關) being related[concerned]; having relation[concern]. ¶~ 업체 a concern interested/its associated company//~ 기관의 상호 협조 cooperation of the agencies[or-gans] concerned.

유괴(誘拐) kidnapping; abduction. **유괴하다** kidnap (a child); abduct (a person from his home). ¶어린아이는 몸값을 목적으로 집에서 유괴되었다 The child was kidnapped [abducted] from his home for ransom.//그 외교관은 유괴되었고, 유괴범은 100만 달러의 몸값을 요구했다 The diplomat was kidnapped and the kidnapper demanded a ransom of one million dollar.
● **유괴범** (사람) a kidnapper; an abductor; (죄) abduction. **유괴 사건** a kidnapping case.

유교(儒敎) Confucianism. ¶~의 (감화) Confucian (influence).
● **유교 사상** Confucian ideas.

유구무언(有口無言) [항변할 말이 없음]. ¶~이다 have no word in excuse//참으로 ~입니다 There is no excuse whatever.

유구하다(悠久-) eternal; everlasting; perpetual; permanent. ¶유구한 역사의 흐름 the eternal flow of history//그것은 유구한 옛날부터 변하지 않았다 It has not changed from time immemorial.

유권자(有權者) the holder of a right; (선거의) a (qualified) voter; an elector; 《집합적》 the electorate. ¶~의 총수는 6백만에 달한다 The electoral roll amounts to 6 million.

유권 해석(有權解釋) an authoritative interpretation. ¶중앙 선거 관리 위원회의 ~ the ruling of the Central Election Control Committee.

유급(有給) ¶~의 paid/salaried.
● **유급 휴가** a paid holiday[vacation]; paid leave. ¶나는 1주일간 ~를 얻었다 I took a week off with pay.

유급하다(留級-) remain[stay] in the same class for another year. ¶그는 고등학교 때 2년 유급했다 He stayed for[(영) in] in the high school two years longer than his classmates. →¶유급되다 be kept in the same class.

유기(有期) [관용어적] terminable; for a definite period.
● **유기 공채** a fixed-term[terminable] loan [bond]. **유기형** a sentence for imprisonment for a definite period[term]. ¶그는 ~에 처해졌다 He was sentenced to prison for a definite term.

유기(有機) [관용어적] organic; systematic.
● **유기 농업** organic farming. **유기물** organic matter; an organism. **유기체** an organism; an organic body; an organized matter. **유기 화학** organic chemistry. **유기 화합물** an organic compound.

유기(遺棄) [내다 버림] abandonment; dereliction(선박 등의); desertion(배우자 등의); exposition. ¶직무 ~ neglect of duty. **유기하다** abandon; desert; leave (a dead body) unattended. ¶사체를 ~ abandon a corpse//그녀는 갓난아기를 정거장의 벤치에 유기하다가 붙잡혔다 She was arrested for leaving her baby on a station bench.
● **유기물** an abandoned article; (해상의) a derelict.

유기(鍮器) brassware. ⇨놋그릇

유기음(有機音) [거센소리] [언] an aspirated sound; an aspirate.

유기적(有機的) organic; systematic. ⇨유기(有機) ¶~으로 organically//~ 세계관 the organic view of the world.

유난 [보통과 다름] unusualness; uncommonness; extraordinariness; [괴상함] singularity; eccentricity; peculiarity; oddity. ¶~을 떨다 behave fastidiously // 아무것도 아닌 일에 ~을 떨다 make much ado [a great fuss] about nothing / make mountain out of a molehill. **유난하다** unusual; uncommon; extraordinary; exceptional; singular; eccentric; peculiar; odd; fantastic. ¶옷차림이 유난한 여자 an odd-looking woman / a fantastically dressed woman // 유난한 옷차림을 하고 있다 be dressed in singular fashion // 오늘은 더위가 ~ It's exceptionally hot today. / Today's heat is exceptional. // 이 일에 대한 그의 흥미는 ~ His interest in this matter is extraordinary. // 그는 음식에 대해서 ~ He is very particular [fussy] about his food. // 그에게는 좀 유난한 데가 있다 He has something peculiar about him. / He is a bit eccentric in some of his way. **유난히** unusually; extraordinarily; [현저히] remarkably. ¶~ 크다 extraordinary large / amazingly big // 그녀의 미모가 ~ 눈에 띄었다 She attracted much attention by her good looks.

유네스코 [유엔 교육 과학 문화 기구] UNESCO(▶ the United Nations Educational, Scientific, and Cultural Organization의 약어).

유년(幼年) (early) childhood; infancy. ¶~용 그림책 picture books for little children.
●**유년기** infancy; childhood. ¶~에[부터] in [from / since] one's childhood [infancy] // 나의 ~는 행복했다 I spent a happy childhood.

유념(留念) attention; consideration; regard; mindfulness. **유념하다** bear[keep / fix] (something) in mind; be mindful of; take (a matter) to heart. ¶부탁하신 건은 유념하겠습니다 I will bear your request in mind. // 잊지 말고 그것을 유념하게나 Keep it in mind.

유능하다(有能-) able; capable; competent; talented; efficient. ¶유능한 사람 a man of ability / an able [a capable] man // 유능한 변호사 an able lawyer // 유능한 타자수 a good typist // 이 팀의 아이들은 모두 ~[유능한 선수들이다] The boys on this team are all talented [good] players. // 아버지는 유능한 사업가였다 My father was a capable businessman. // 그에게는 유능한 부하가 없다 He has no able [useful] men under him. // 그는 매우 유능한 기자이다 He is a very able [capable / competent] reporter.

유니버시아드 [국제 학생 경기 대회] the Universiade.

유니세프 [국제 연합 아동 기금] UNICEF(▶ the United Nations International Children's Emergency Fund의 약어).

유니섹스 unisex. ¶~의 옷 unisex clothes.

유니언 잭 [영국 국기] the Union Jack.

유니크하다 [독특하다] unique; [비길 데 없다] unusual. ¶유니크한 사람 an unusual person // 그녀의 복장은 아주 ~ She dresses in a most unique fashion.

유니폼 a uniform. ¶~을 입은 선수들 players in uniform.

유다르다(類-) uncommon; unusual; extraordinary; [별나다] odd; peculiar. ¶유다른 취향 a new departure // 유다른 행동 peculiar behavior // 유다른 사람 a unique person / a rare man. **유달리** conspicuously; remarkably; exceptionally; particularly; especially; extraordinarily. ¶오늘 밤은 ~ 춥다 It's particularly [especially] cold tonight. // 그녀는 그 구절을 ~ 큰 소리로 읽었다 She read the passage aloud in an exceptionally loud voice. // 헬렌의 모자가 ~ 눈에 띄었다 Helen's hat stood out from the rest. / Helen's hat attracted the most attention. // 올해는 ~ 비가 많이 내렸다 We have had an exceptional amount of rain this year.

유다서(-書) (The General Epistle of St.) Jude.

유단자(有段者) a holder of a rank (in judo, baduk(go), etc).

유당(乳糖) [화] lactose; milk sugar. ⇨젖당

유대 Jud(a)ea. ¶~의 Jewish / Judaic(al).
●**유대교** Judaism. ¶~ 예배당 a synagogue. **유대 민족** the Jewish[circumcised] race; the children of Israel. **유대 인** a Jew; a Hebrew; (집합적) the Jews. ¶~ 거리 a ghetto (pl. ~s, ghetti) / the Jewish quarter.

유대(紐帶) a band; a tie; relation(관계). ¶동맹제국의 ~ the bond of allied nations // 부모 자식 간의 ~ the ties that bind parents and child together // 긴밀한 ~를 맺다 come[be brought] into close relation (with) // ~를 강화하다 strengthen the ties (between) // 한미 ~를 공고히 하다 place Seoul-Washington ties on a firm foot // 상업적 ~를 강화하다 strengthen one's commercial ties (with) // 그들 사이에는 강한 애정의 ~ 관계가 있었다 There was a close bond of affection between them.

유대 목(有袋目) [동] the marsupials; a pouched animal.

유덕(遺德) [죽은 사람이 끼친 덕] the influence[virtue] of the departed. ¶~을 기리다 speak highly of the virtue of the departed.

유덕하다(有德-) virtuous. ¶유덕한 사람 a virtuous man / (문어) a man of virtue.

유도(柔道) judo. ¶~를 하다 practice judo // 시합을 하다 have a judo match (with a person) // 그는 ~ 5단이다 He is a judo expert of the fifth dan.
●**유도복** a suit for judo practice. **유도 사범** an instructor of judo.

유도(誘導) inducement; guidance; [전][생] induction; [화] derivation. ¶원격 ~ tele-guidance // 자기(自己) ~ self-induction // 전자(電磁) ~ electromagnetic induction // 관제사의 ~는 완벽했다 The instructions from the control tower were perfect. / The air controllers gave perfect instructions. // 시계 불량으로 비행기는 관제탑의 ~를 받아 착륙했다 As visibility was poor, the plane made a landing[landed] following the instructions from the control tower. **유도하다** lead; guide; [전][생] induce; [화] derive. ¶~(지상 전파로) 비행기를 ~ vector a plane // 불이 났을 때, 판매원이 손님을 밖으로 능숙하게 유도했다 At the time of the fire the salesgirls skillfully guided[led] the customers out of the shop. // 나는 그녀에게 말을 하도록 유도해 보았다 I tried to lead her to talk.
●**유도 신문** a leading question. ¶~을 하다 lead (a criminal suspect) to the point in question // ~에 걸려들다 be led (against one's will) to make a disadvantageous statement by deliberate questions // 그는 ~을 당했다 He was asked leading questions. // 이의 있습니다. 그 질문은 ~입니다 I object to the

question as a leading question.//용의자는 검사의 교묘한 ~에 걸려서 자백하였다 The suspect led to confess to his crime by the public prosecutor's skillful question. **유도 장치** a guidance system; guidance control. **유도 전기** induced electricity. **유도탄** a (guided) missile.

유독(有毒) poisonousness; noxiousness. **유독하다** poisonous; toxic; venomous; [해롭다] noxious. ¶유독한 폐기물 poisonous[toxic] waste//유독한 착색제 a toxic[poisonous / noxious] coloring agent//약도 잘못 섭취하면 유독할 때가 있다 Taken in the wrong way, medicine may prove toxic.
● **유독 가스** a poisonous gas.

유독(唯獨) solely; only; alone; singly. ¶~ 너만이 그렇게 생각하고 있다 Nobody thinks so but[except] yourself.// ~ 돈벌이만이 인생의 목적은 아니다 Money-making is not the sole end and aim of existence.// ~ 너만이 이것을 할 수 있다 You alone[No body but you. / You are the only one who] can do this.

유동(流動) a flow; flowing; floating; [물] flowage(점성 물질의). ¶정세는 아직 ~적이다 The situation is still fluid[unsettled].//인구는 ~적이다 The population is mobile. **유동하다** flow; float; circulate; be liquid.
● **유동성** fluidity; mobility. ¶~ 있는 fluid / mobile. **유동식** liquid food; a liquid; a liquid diet. **유동 인구** a floating population. **유동 자본** circulating[floating] capital. **유동 자산** floating[liquid / current] assets[fund / money].

유두(乳頭) [생] a nipple; a mammilla (*pl.* -lae); a papilla; (동물 어미의) a teat.
● **유두염** acromastitis.

유들유들 impudently; shamelessly; brazen-facedly. **유들유들하다** impudent; audacious; brazen-faced; barefaced; shameless; (구어) cheeky. ¶저런 유들유들한 녀석은 질색이다 I hate such an impudent[a cheeky / a shameless] fellow.//그는 유들유들하게도 다시 찾아왔다 He had the impudence[effrontery] to come again./(구어) He had the nerve[cheek] to come again.

유라시아 Eurasia; Europe and Asia. ¶~의 Eurasian / European and Asiatic.
● **유라시아 대륙** the Eurasian Continent. **유라시아 사람** [유럽과 아시아의 혼혈인] a Eurasian.

유람(遊覽) sightseeing; an excursion. ¶아버지는 빈을 ~ 중이시다 My father is seeing[doing] the sights of Vienna.//나의 외국 여행은 ~이 아니다 The object of my trip abroad is not to have a good time[fun]. **유람하다** go sightseeing; (미) sightsee. ¶워싱턴 시를 ~ go sight-seeing[sightsee] in Washington, D.C.//그는 우리나라 전국을 유람했다 He made[took] a sightseeing trip throughout Korea.
● **유람객** sightseers; tourists; excursionists; a vacationist. **유람선** an excursion ship; a pleasure boat; a barge; a sightseeing boat.

유랑(流浪) wandering; roaming. ¶~의 길에 오르다 go wandering. **유랑하다** wander[roam] about[from place to place]; rove. ¶유랑하는 wandering / vagrant / nomadic(유목하는)//유랑하는 나그네 a wandering traveler//그는 여러 날 황야를 유랑했다 He wandered over the wilderness for days.

● **유랑민** a nomadic people; nomads. **유랑 생활** a wandering[nomadic / Bohemian] life; vagabondage; nomadism. **유랑자** a wanderer; a roamer; a vagabond; a vagrant.

유래(由來) [기원] the origin; the genesis; [내력] the history; [출처] the source; the derivation. ¶~가 있는 집 a family with a history// ~를 캐다 trace (a custom) to its source[origin]//그들은 그 지명의 ~를 조사했다 They traced the history[They inquired into the origin] of the name of the place.//이 표현의 ~는 무엇일까 Where does this expression come from. **유래하다** result (from); originate (in); be derived (from); date back (to the time of ...). ¶그 싸움은 강력한 두 집안 사이의 다툼에서 유래한다 The strife between the two strong clans brought about the battle.//이 축제는 15세기에서 유래한다 This festival dates back to the fifteen century.

유량(流量) (하천의) stream flow; flow rate; quantity of flow; [물] flux.
● **유량계** a flow meter; a current meter.

유러달러 [경] a Eurodollar.

유럽 Europe. ¶~의 European //~화하다 Europeanize / Westernize// ~을 여행하다 go over[make a trip] to Europe.
● **유럽 경제 공동체** the European Economic Community(약어 EEC). **유럽 사람** a European. **유럽 연합** the European Union(약어 EU).

유려하다(流麗-) flowing; elegant; refined; fluent. ¶유려한 문체 a flowing, elegant style.

유력자(有力者) an influential man.

유력하다(有力-) 1 [권세가 있다] powerful; [강력하다] strong; [영향력이 있다] influential. ¶유력한 정당 a powerful political party//유력한 후보자 a strong candidate//유력한 정치가 an influential politician//협회의 유력한 회원 a leading member of the society//그 제안은 그들의 유력한 지지를 얻었다 The proposal gained influential[powerful / strong] support among them.

2 [효력이 있다] strong; [설득력이 있다] convincing; [신용할 수 있다] reliable; [가능성이 있다] likely. ¶그것은 유력한 근거에 의거하고 있다 It has a strong foundation.//우리는 유력한 증거를 발견했다 We've found convincing proof.//우리는 목격자에게서 유력한 증언을 얻었다 We obtained valuable testimony from the witness.//국회는 가을에 해산될 것이라는 견해가 ~ The prevailing view is that the National Assembly will be dissolved in the fall.

유령(幽靈) [망령] a ghost; [갑자기 나타나는 유령] an apparition; [환영] a phantom; [요괴] (미) a specter; (영) a spectre. ¶살해된 여자의 ~ the apparition[ghost] of a murdered woman// ~이 나오는 집 a haunted house// ~ 같은 ghostly / ghostlike// ~이라도 나타날 것 같은 밤이었다 It was a ghostly night.//이 뒷골목은 ~이 나타난다는 곳이다 People say a ghost appears in this alley.
● **유령선** a phantom ship; a flying Dutchman. **유령 회사** a bogus company; (영) a long firm.

유례(類例) a similar example[instance / case]; a parallel case. ¶세계에 ~가 없는 사건 an incident unparalleled anywhere in the world// ~없는 unparalleled / without paral-

유료

lel / unique / [선례가 없는] unprecedented // 이 사업은 고금에 그 ~가 없는 규모의 것이다 This undertaking is unprecedented in scale. / The scale of the work has no equal in history.

유료(有料) a charge. ¶~인 charged / feed / toll / paid // 입장은 ~입니까 무료입니까 Is the admission free or charged? // 그 동물원은 어린이는 무료이나 어른은 ~이다 Admission to that zoo is free for children, but adults are charged a fee.
● **유료 도로** a toll road. **유료 변소** a pay toilet. **유료 주차장** a toll parking place[lot].

유루(遺漏) 1 [누락] (an) omission; oversight. ¶~ 없이 without a slip / with nothing omitted / [철저하게] exhaustively / thoroughly // ~ 없이 조사하다 make an exhaustive investigation (of). **유루하다** be omitted; overlook; pass over[by]; miss (seeing). 2 [새어 나옴] (a) leakage; a leak. ¶가스의 ~ a gas leak // ~를 막다 stop[plug] a leak. **유루하다** leak; escape; run out.

유류(油類) [집합적] oil.
● **유류 파동** an oil crisis.

유류품(遺留品) an article left (behind); a lost article. ¶범행 현장에는 많은 ~이 있었다 There were a lot of things left behind at the scene of the crime.

유리(有理) [관형어적] [수] rational.
● **유리수**[식] [수] a rational number[expression]. **유리 함수** [수] a rational function.

유리(琉璃) glass; [유리창] a pane, a windowpane; (시계의) a crystal. ¶광학 ~ optical glass // 판[색] ~ plate[stained] glass // 젖빛 ~ frosted glass // 안전 ~ safety glass // 한 장의 ~ a sheet of glass // ~ 같은 glassy // 창에 ~를 끼우다 put glass in a window // ~는 광선과 열을 통과시킨다 Glass is pervious to light and heat. // ~는 잘 깨진다 Glass breaks easily.
● **유리그릇** glassware. **유리병** a glass bottle; (작은) a vial. **유리창** a glass window.

유리(遊離) 1 [떨어짐] isolation; separation. ¶속세로부터의 ~ isolation[separation] from the secular world. **유리하다** isolate; separate. ¶영혼은 신체와 유리해도 존재할 수 있다고 그는 믿고 있다 He believes that the soul can exist apart[separate] from the body. ➔ ¶유리시키다 liberate / educe / let[set] free // 그것은 현실과 유리된 정책이었다 It was an unrealistic policy. // 정부가 국민으로부터 유리된 것이 혁명의 원인이었다 The revolution was caused by the alienation of government from the people. 2 [물] [화] isolation; extrication. **유리하다** isolate; extricate.

유리걸식하다(流離乞食-) beg one's way.

유리하다(有利-) [이익이 있다] profitable; paying; [편리·유익하다] advantageous; favorable. ¶유리한 거래 a profitable deal // 유리한 사업 a profitable enterprise / a paying business // 유리한 지위 a vantage ground / a coign of vantage // 한국에 유리한 조건 terms advantageous[favorable] to Korea // 유리해지다 turn (out) to one's advantage // 이 성채(城砦)는 지세가 ~ This fortress has the advantage of strategic position. // 그는 어떤 상황도 자기에게 유리하게 돌려놓는다 He turns every circumstance to his advantage. // 그 제의는 유리한 조건이었다 It was proposed on advantageous[favorable] terms. // 그 아파트의 유리한 점은 정거장에서 가깝다는 것이다 The advantage of that apartment house is that it is near the station. // 상대방 입후보자는 자금 면에서 그 사람보다 유리한 입장에 있었다 The rival candidate had an advantage over him[the upper hand] in funds. // 전쟁의 국면은 우리에게 유리하게 전개되었다 The war situation turned to our advantage.

유린(蹂躪) [침해] (an) infringement; [겁탈] violation; [짓밟음] trampling down; devastation. ¶인권 ~ an infringement upon personal rights // 적의 ~에 내맡기다 be left to the enemy's devastating advance. **유린하다** infringe upon; violate; trample upon[on]; tread down; devastate; ravage; override. ¶기본적 인권을 ~ violate[infringe upon] fundamental human rights // 개인의 자유를 ~ trample on the right of personal liberty // 남의 권리를 ~ ride roughshod over the rights of others. ➔ ¶적국이 침략군에게 유린당하였다 The whole country was left at the (tender) mercy of the invading army.
● **유린자** a devastator.

유림(儒林) Confucianists; Confucian scholars.

유망(有望) promise; a bright prospect[future]. **유망하다** promising; hopeful; full of promise; favorable. ¶유망한 청년 promising young man // 유망한 영화 스타 an up-and-coming movie // 유망한 전도 a bright[rosy] future / rosy prospects / a promising career // 유망한 투자 분야 a promising field for investment // 그는 전도가 ~ He has bright prospects before him. / The chances for his future success are very great. / He has a bright future. // 그는 입상이 ~ The prospects of[for] his winning a prize are good. // 우리의 장사는 앞날이 ~ Our business prospects are bright.
● **유망주**(-株) (주식) active stocks; (사람) an up-and-comer; (미국 구어) a comer. ¶그는 이 과(課)의 젊은이 중에서는 첫째를 달리는 ~다 He is the most promising of all the young men in this department.

유머 humor[(영) humour]; a joke(농담). ¶~가 풍부하다 be highly humorous / be full of [rich in] humor // ~가 있다 have a (fine) sense of humor // 그는 ~를 아는[모르는] 사람이다 He has a[no] sense of humor. // 그녀는 ~가 넘치는 대화를 한다 Her conversation is full of humor[wit]. (▶ humor는 남의 마음에 호소하는 익살인 데 비해, wit는 지적인 재치가 있는 익살) // 그의 이야기에는 ~가 있다 His talk is full of humor[highly humorous]. / There is a spice of humor in his talk. // 그는 ~가 풍부하다 He is very witty.
● **유머 감각** a sense of humor.

유머러스하다 humo(u)rous. ¶그 전말을 유머러스하게 이야기하다 tell the whole story with a humorous touch[amusingly] // 그는 유머러스한 사람이다 He is a very funny[amusing / humorous] person. / He has a good sense of humor.

유명(幽明) [어둠과 밝음] light and darkness; [저승과 이승] this and the other world.
유명을 달리하다 pass away; depart this life; die. ¶저 용감한 사람도 마침내 유명을 달리했다 That valiant man has at last died.

유명(遺命) one's last[dying] wish[words / request]. ¶선왕의 ~에 따라 according to

유복하다

one's late king's will.
유명론(唯名論) [철] nominalism.
유명무실하다(有名無實-) (only) nominal; titular; in name only; (a scholar) in nothing but the name. ¶유명무실한 사장 a nominal [figurehead] president// 유명무실한 지도자 a titular leader without any power// 그 조약은 지금은 유명무실해졌다 The treaty has now become a more scrap of paper.// 이 규정은 ~ Nobody follows that rule.
유명세(有名稅) the price of fame.
유명인(有名人) a celebrity; a notable; a big name. ¶다음 모임에는 많은 ~이 올 것이다 There will be many big names at the next meeting.
유명하다(有名-) [이름 높다] famous; famed; noted; notable; [꽤 알려지다] well-known; [저명하다] celebrated; renowned; distinguished; [악명 높다] notorious. ¶유명한 음악가 a famous[noted / famed] musician// 유명한 물리학자 a celebrated physicist// 세계적으로 유명한 화가 a world-famous artist / an artist of world-wide fame// 최근에 급속히 유명해진 가수 a singer who has become popular very rapidly / a singer who has jumped[leaped] into fame of late// 전 세계적으로 유명한 상품 a brand noted throughout the world// 유명해지다 become famous / acquire[earn] fame / gain renown / win a reputation / come to fame / [악평을 얻다] gain notoriety// 일약 유명해지다 leap to fame// 무명에서 유명해지다 lift oneself out of obscurity// 그녀는 아름다운 목소리로 유명했다 She is famous[noted] for her beautiful voice.// 그곳은 피서지로 ~ The place is well-known as a summer resort.// 그녀는 뛰어난 오페라 가수로서 유명해졌다 She rose to fame [won a reputation] as an excellent opera singer.// 그는 국제적으로 유명해졌다 He became internationally famous.// 이 도시는 세계 최대의 제철소로 ~ This town is famous for the world largest ironworks.// 그는 이 작품으로 유명해지기 시작했다 This book first won him public notice.
유모(乳母) a wet nurse; (소아어) a nanny. ¶아이를 ~에게 맡기다 leave a baby with a nurse.
● 유모차 (미) a baby carriage; (미국 구어) a buggy; (영) a perambulator; (영국 구어) a pram. ¶~를 밀고 가다 push a baby carriage// ~에 아이를 태우고 가다 wheel a child in a pram.
유목(遊牧) nomadism. ¶~의 nomadic. 유목하다 lead[live] a nomadic life; nomadize.
● 유목민 a nomad(▶ 종종 복수형으로). 유목 민족 nomadic tribes.
유무(有無) [있음과 없음] existence and nonexistence. ¶오늘의 결석자의 ~를 확인한다 check and see if anyone is absent today// 경험의 ~에 따라 너의 급료는 달라진다 Your salary depends on your experience [whether you are experienced or not].
유문(幽門) [생] the pylorus (pl. -ri).
유물(遺物) [역사상 유물] a relic (of the past); remains(▶ relic은 도구·무기 등, remains는 동굴·건조물 등); [유증물] a legacy; a bequest; [유품] an article left by a deceased person; [추억이 되는 물건] a memento (pl. -s). ¶석기 시대의 ~ a relic from the Stone Age// 조상의 ~ the mementos[relics] of the family's ancestors// 구시대의 ~ antiquities / a survival of olden days// 그는 전세기의 ~이다 He is quite a museum piece. / He has outlived his time.
유물(唯物) [관형어적] [철] materialistic.
● 유물론 materialism. ¶사적[변증법적] ~ historical[dialectical] materialism. 유물론자 a materialist. 유물 사관(-史觀) the materialistic conception[interpretation] of history.
유미주의(唯美主義) (a)estheticism.
유민(流民) wandering people; (전쟁으로 인한) displaced persons(약어 DP, D.P.).
유밀과(油蜜菓) oil-and-honey pastry.
유발(乳鉢) a mortar. ⇨"막자사발(⇨막자)
유발(誘發) induction. 유발하다 induce; cause [arouse] (one's anger); give rise to[touch off / trigger] (a war). ¶무력 충돌은 ~ invite an armed conflict// 과식은 여러 가지 병을 유발한다 Overeating can cause[induce / bring about] all kinds of illnesses.// 무엇이 제3차 세계 대전을 유발할지 알 수 없다 Anything may touch off[trigger / set off] a third world war.// 증세(增稅)는 격렬한 반정부 데모를 유발했다 The tax increase gave rise[led] to violent antigovernment demonstrations.
유방(乳房) a breast; (문어) a bosom; (속어) boobs; (속어) tits. ¶~의 mammary// ~이 큰[작은] large-[small-]breasted (girl).
● 유방암 [의] cancer of the breast; breast cancer; mammary cancer; a mastocarcinoma (pl. -mata, -s). ¶~ 환자 a patient with breast cancer / a breast cancer case// 그녀는 ~에 걸렸다 She has breast cancer.
유배(流配) banishment; exile; deportation. 유배하다 banish[exile] (a person to an island); condemn (a criminal) to exile; deport. ➔유배되다 be exiled / be banished / be deported// 그는 머나먼 섬으로 유배되었다 He was exiled to a far-off island.// 그는 고국에서 이 고장으로 유배되었다 He was exiled [banished] from his native country to this place.
● 유배자 an exile; deportee; a deported criminal. 유배지 a penal colony[settlement]; a place of exile.
유백색(乳白色) ¶~의 milk-white / milky.
유별(有別) (a) distinction; (a) discrimination. ¶남녀 ~이다 There is a distinction between man and woman.
유별(類別) classification; assortment. 유별하다 classify; grade; assort.
유별나다(有別-) [보통이 아니다] uncommon; extraordinary; unusual; [기묘하다] peculiar; eccentric; odd; singular. ¶유별난 기동 eccentric behavior// 그는 좀 ~ He is peculiar[an eccentric] fellow in a way.// 그의 사고방식은 좀 ~ His way of thinking is quite peculiar.// [독특하다] His ideas are quite unique.// 그 가게의 장식은 ~ The store is decorated original designs. / The shop has an unusual decor.
유보(留保) 1 reservation. ⇨"보류 2 [법] (권리의) (a) reservation. 유보하다 reserve; withhold. ¶뒷날 변경할 권리를 ~ reserve the right to make changes later.
유복자(遺腹子) a posthumous child.
유복하다(裕福-) rich; wealthy; well-to-do; well-off(▶ well-off는 안정된 수입이 있는 정도, 그 밖의 말은 부자를 의미함); affluent; opulent. ¶그는 유복한 생활을 하고 있다 He

유부 is well-off[living in affluence].// 어린 시절에 그녀는 유복하게 자랐다 She was brought up in affluent[easy] circumstances.// 그는 유복한 가정에서 태어났다 He was born rich.

유부(油腐) (a piece of) deep-fried bean curd.
● **유부국수** noodles in soup with fried bean curd.

유부남(有婦男) a married man.
유부녀(有夫女) a married woman.

유비무환(有備無患) Lay up for[against] a rainy day.; Forewarned is forearmed.; Providing is preventing.

유사(有史) the beginning of history. ¶ ~의 historic // ~ 이전의 prehistoric / of prehistoric time // ~ 이전에 in prehistoric times / before the dawn of history // ~ 이전의 시대 prehistoric times / the prehistoric age // ~ 이래 since the dawn[beginning] of history // ~ 이래의 대전쟁 the greatest war in history // 인류의 달 착륙은 ~ 이래의 사건이었다 Man's landing on the moon was one of the greatest events in recorded history. // ~ 이래 그와 같은 일이 일어난 선례가 없다 Such a thing has not taken place since the dawn of history.

유사(流沙) quicksand; drift sand.

유사(類似) [관형어적]. **유사하다** similar; like; alike; (성질·기능 등이) analogous; (서술적) resemble. ¶음악회, 강연회 기타 유사한 행사 a concert, a lecture and similar events // 저 그림과 이것이 아주 ~ That painting has a strong resemblance to this. // 양자는 아주 ~ The two are just alike. // 이 차는 모양이 그것과 ~ The car resembles that one in shape.
● **유사성** (a) resemblance; (a) similarity; (a) likeness; an analogy. ¶식물과 동물의 생활의 ~ the affinity[likeness] between plant and animal life // 인간성의 ~ the kinship of human nature. **유사점** a point of similarity [resemblance]. ¶이 두 논문 사이에는 ~이 많다 The two theses have many points in common. **유사품** [모조품] an imitation; [비슷한 물건] a similar article. ¶이것이 ~이 나돌고 있다 There are articles similar to this on the market.

유사 분열(有絲分裂) [생] mitosis; karyokinesis; mitotic cell division.

유사시에(有事時-) in time[case] of emergency; in an emergency. ¶ ~ 대비하다 provide for an emergency // ~는 군대가 출동한다 The army will be mobilized in case of emergency. // ~는 반드시 이것을 상기해 주십시오 Please remember this in time of emergency[need].

유산(乳酸) [화] lactic acid. ⇒락트산
● **유산균** lactic acid bacteria.

유산(流産) (태아의) (a) miscarriage; (an) abortion; [실패] failure. ¶인공 ~ artificial abortion[miscarriage]. **유산하다** miscarry; abort; have a miscarriage; (계획 등이) prove abortive. ¶그녀는 유산했다 She had a miscarriage. → **유산시키다** produce an abortion / procure abortion // 유산되다 be given up / be called off(모임 등이) // 계획이 유산되고 말았다 Our plans miscarried[fell through / were aborted].

유산(遺産) 1 [사후에 남겨진 재산] property left (by a deceased person); an inheritance; [특히 유언에 의해 상속하는 재산] a legacy; (문어) a bequest(금전); [법] an estate. ¶ ~을 상속받다 inherit a fortune [property / an estate] // ~을 분배하다 divide one's property (among one's children) // ~을 빼앗다 seize an inheritance // ~을 노리다 be after the inheritance // 그가 살고 있는 이 집은 삼촌의 ~이다 The house he lives in is the property left by his uncle. // 그가 죽자 손녀가 많은 ~을 받았다 On his death his granddaughter came into a rich inheritance[received a rich legacy]. // 그는 딸들에게 많은 ~을 남겼다 He left [(문어) bequeathed] a large fortune to his daughters. // 그녀는 숙모의 ~을 상속했다 She inherited [succeeded to] her aunt's property. // 그는 3억 원 상당의 부동산을 ~로 물려받았다 He inherited real estate worth three hundred million won.
2 [남겨진 사물] a vestige; a heritage. ¶그 나라에는 훌륭한 문화적·역사적 ~이 있다 The country has a glorious cultural and historical heritage. // 그 풍습은 봉건 시대의 ~이다 This custom is a vestige of the feudal age.
● **유산 상속** succession to property. **유산 상속인** an heir[heiress(여자)] to property; an inheritor.

유산 계급(有産階級) the propertied classes; the bourgeoisie; the bourgeois class. ¶ ~의 사람 a bourgeois / a man of property // 그는 ~ 출신이다 He comes from a bourgeois family.

유산자(有産者) a propertied man.

유상(有償) compensation; consideration. ¶ ~의 onerous // ~으로 취득하다 obtain (something) for counter value // 이것은 ~입니까, 무상입니까 Do we have to pay for this[Does this have to be paid for], or is it free?
● **유상 계약** a contract made for a consideration; an onerous contract. **유상 취득** acquisition for value.

유상(油狀) ¶ ~의 oily (matter) / oillike.
유색(有色) ¶ ~의 colored.
● **유색 인종** colored races; non-white people [nations].

유생(幼生) [동] a larva (pl. -vae).
● **유생 기관**(-器官) a larval organ.

유생(儒生) a Confucian (scholar); a student of Confucianism.

유서(由緖) [내력] a history; a story. ¶ ~ 깊은 historied / great-historied // ~ 깊은 곳 a spot with its old associations / a place with a historic background // ~ 있는 사찰 a temple with a (long) history // 그는 ~ 있는 집안 출신이다 He comes from a noble[ancient] family. / He is of noble [high] birth.

유서(遺書) [유언장] a note left behind by a dead person; (자살자의) a suicide note; [유언] a will. ¶ ~를 쓰다 make[draw up] one's will [testament] // ~를 남기고 죽다 die testate // 자살자의 ~는 없었다 The suicide left no note behind.

유서(類書) similar books. ¶구상의 기발함에 있어 ~가 없다 This book is unique[unparalleled] in the originality of its conception.

유선(有線) wire. ¶ ~의 wire / wired / cabled.
● **유선 방송** cable broadcasting[broadcasts]. **유선 전화** a (wire) telephone; wire telephony. **유선 텔레비전** cable television; cable TV.

유선(乳腺) [생] the mammary gland. ⇒젖샘
유선형(流線型) a streamline shape[form]. ¶

~의 열차 a streamliner / a streamlined train // 차를 ~으로 만들다 streamline a car.
유성(有性) [관형어적] gamic; sexual.
● 유성 생식 sexual reproduction.
유성(有聲) ¶~의 voiced / vocal.
● 유성 영화 a talking film[picture]; a talkie.
유성음 [언] a voiced sound. ⇨ ˉ울림소리
유성(油性) [관형어적] oily; greasy.
● 유성 도료 an oil paint.
유성(流星) [천] a shooting[falling] star; a meteor.
● 유성우 a meteor shower.
유성(遊星) a planet. ⇨ ˉ행성(行星)
유성기(留聲器) a gramophone. ⇨ ˉ축음기
유세(有稅) ¶~의 taxable.
● 유세품 taxable goods; goods subject to duty[taxation].
유세(有勢) ¶~를 떨다 wield[exercise] influence[power] (over) / hold[bear] sway // 좋은 자리에 있다고 너무 ~ 떨지 마라 Don't be so high-hatted under the shelter of your post.
유세(遊說) a canvassing[an electioneering] tour; (미) stumping. ¶~에 나서다 go canvassing[campaigning] (for votes) / (미) go on the stump // 그의 충청 지방에서의 ~는 성공적이었다 His campaign tour of the Chungcheong district was successful. // 그의 지방 ~는 반응이 없었다 His canvassing[(미국 속어) barnstorming] in local areas fell flat. **유세하다** go canvassing; canvass; make an electioneering tour; barnstorm(지방을); (미) take[go on] the stump; stump (it). ¶나는 전국을 유세했다 I canvassed[stumped] the whole country. // 후보자들이 선거구를 유세하고 있다 The candidates are stumping the election[electoral] district.
유소년(幼少年) children and infants; older and younger children.
유소하다(幼少−) young; juvenile.
유속(流速) the velocity[speed] of a moving [running] fluid. ¶조류의 ~ the speed of a current / the drift of a current // ~은 초속 5미터이다 The current is flowing at five meters per second.
유속(遺俗) old traditions; hereditary customs.
유수(有數) [두드러짐]. ¶~의 eminent / prominent / leading / distinguished / foremost // 국내 ~의 두 은행 the two leading banks in the country // 그는 세계 ~의 과학자이다 He is one of the world's most eminent[prominent] scientists. **유수하다** eminent; prominent; leading; distinguished; foremost.
유수(幽囚) imprisonment; confinement. ¶바빌론의 ~ [성] the Babylonian captivity[exile].
유수(流水) running[flowing] water. ¶세월은 ~와 같다 Time flies (like an arrow).
유수 정책(誘水政策) [경] a pump priming policy. ¶~을 쓰다 prime the pump.
유숙하다(留宿−) lodge (at); put up (at); stay (at / in). ¶고모 댁에 유숙하고 있다 I'm staying with my aunt.
유순하다(柔順−) obedient; submissive; [얌전하다] gentle; meek; [다루기 쉽다] docile. ¶유순한 여성 a docile woman // 그녀는 마치 양처럼 ~ She is (as) meek as a lamb. **유순히** obediently; submissively; gently; meekly; tamely. ¶그녀는 평생 동안 ~ 남편 시중을 들었다 She served her husband submissively [obediently] all her life.

유스타키오관(−管) [생] the Eustachian tube.
유스 호스텔 a youth hostel.
유시(諭示) admonition; injunction; instruction; a message. ¶대통령의 ~ a presidential instruction[message]. **유시하다** admonish; give admonition (to); instruct.
유식하다(有識−) learned; educated; well-informed; knowledgeable. ¶유식한 체하다 pretend to know much / assume an air of wisdom / set up for a wise man.
유신(維新) renovation; the Revitalizing Reform. ¶10월 ~ the October Revitalizing Reforms // (일본의) 메이지 ~ the Meiji Restoration.
유신론(有神論) theism.
● 유신론자 a theist. ¶그는 결코 ~가 아니었다 He never believed in God.
유실(流失) washing[carrying] away. **유실하다** wash[carry / sweep] away. →¶홍수로 수백 채의 집이 유실되었다 Hundreds of houses were washed[swept] away by the flood.
● 유실 가옥 houses carried[washed] away by the floods.
유실(遺失) loss. **유실하다** lose; leave behind.
● 유실물 a lost article; lost property. ¶~은 여기서 보관되고 있다 Lost articles are kept here.
유심론(唯心論) spiritualism; idealism.
● 유심론자 a spiritualist; an idealist.
유심하다(有心−) attentive; careful; mindful; cautious. **유심히** attentively; with attention [care / caution]; carefully; mindfully; cautiously. ¶~ 귀를 기울이다 listen attentively (to) / give[lend] an ear (to) / hear attentively[mindfully] // ~ 바라보다 look hard[mindfully] (at) / gaze earnestly[intently] (at / on) / get a good look (into).
유아(幼兒) an infant; a small child; (구어) a (tiny) tot. ¶~의 infant / infantile / infantine // 이것들은 ~용 장난감입니다 These are toys for small children[tiny tots / infants].
● 유아원 a nursery school; (미) preschool.
유아(乳兒) a suckling; a nursling; a baby.
● 유아 세례 infant baptism. **유아식** baby food.
유아독존(唯我獨尊) 1 [자기 혼자 잘남] self-conceit; self-satisfaction; complacency. ¶~적인 태도 (독선적인) a self-righteous[holier-than-thou] attitude / (자만하는) a conceited attitude // ~적으로 처신하는 일이 많다 I often behave self-righteously[complacently / in self-centered way]. 2 [자기보다 귀한 것이 없음] Only I am holy.; I am my own Lord [Holy am I alone] throughout heaven and earth.
유아등(誘蛾燈) a light trap (for destroying insects).
유아르엘 [인터넷 주소] a URL(▶ Uniform [Universal] Resource Locator의 약어).
유암(乳癌) [의] cancer of the breast. ⇨ ˉ유방암(⇨유방)
유압(油壓) oil[hydraulic] pressure. ¶~의[식인] hydraulic.
● 유압계 an oil pressure gauge[governor].
유액(乳液) 1 [식] (고무나무 등의) latex (pl. ~es, latices); [유상(乳狀) 액체] (a) milky liquid. 2 [화장용의 크림] a milky lotion.
유야무야하다(有耶無耶−) noncommittal; indefinite. ¶이 일을 유야무야해서는 안 된다 We must not leave this matter unsettled

유약

[undecided]. // 그 독직 사건은 유야무야하는 사이에 잊혀졌다 The corruption case was hushed up and eventually forgotten. ➔ 유야무야되어 버리다 be dropped / become hazy / end in smoke // 결론은 유야무야되고 말았다 We were unable to come to any definite conclusion.

유약(釉藥) (도자기에 칠하는) glaze; (법랑) enamel. ¶~을 칠한 도자기 glazed ware // ~을 칠하다 glaze / put glaze on 〔pottery〕/ enamel.

유약하다(幼弱−) juvenile and weak; young and fragile.

유약하다(柔弱−) ladylike; girlish; weak; weak-kneed; effeminate; enervate. ¶유약한 소년 an effeminate boy // 유약한 태도 a weak-kneed attitude // 그는 유약한 사람이다 He has a weak personality.

유어(幼魚) a young fish; a fry.

유어(類語) a synonym; an associate [a kindred] word. ¶「기쁨」과 「즐거움」은 ~이다 "Joy" is a synonym of [is synonymous with] "delight."

유언(遺言) a will (▶ 정식으로는 one's last will and testament); (구두(口頭)의) one's last words. ¶~ 없이 죽은 사람 an intestate // ~대로 [~에 의해] in accordance [conformity] with one's will [last wish] / at one's (last) wish // ~을 집행하다 administer [carry out] a will // ~을 남기지 않고 죽다 die intestate [without a will] // 고인의 ~대로 장례식은 올리지 않았다 In accordance with the (express) wishes of the deceased, no funeral was held. // 아내에게 남긴 그의 ~은 아이들을 잘 부탁한다는 것이었다 His last words to his wife were "Take good care of our children." / On his deathbed he asked his wife to take good care of their children. 유언하다 express one's dying wish; leave [make] a (verbal) will (that ...); will (that ...). ¶그는 거액의 돈을 병원에 기증한다고 유언했다 He willed a huge sum of money to the hospital. / He left a huge sum of money to the hospital in his will.

● 유언장 a (written) will; one's last will and testament. ¶자필의 ~ a holograph [holographic(al)] will // ~을 쓰다 [작성하다] make one's will [testament] / draw (up) [execute] a will // 변호사에게 ~을 만들게 하다 have a lawyer draw up [prepare] one's will.

유언비어(流言蜚語) a groundless [wild] / rumor; a canard; a false report. ¶~를 퍼뜨리는 사람 a rumormonger // ~를 퍼뜨리다 spread a sensational rumor / spread [circulate] a false rumor / set a false rumor afloat [abroad] / put a rumor into currency / circulate canards // 각종 ~가 횡행하고 있다 All sorts of rumors are going round [are in the air / (문어) are abroad]. / Rumors of every kind are rife [abroad].

유업(乳業) the dairy business; dairy farming.

유업(遺業) work left after a person's death. ¶아버지의 ~을 계승하다 carry on [take over] the work of one's dead father.

유엔 U.N. (▶ United Nations의 약어).

유역(流域) a basin; (큰 강의) a (river) valley. ¶테네시 강 ~ the Tennessee Valley // 한강 ~에 in the Hangang(Han River) basin // 그러한 소도시들은 모두 낙동강 ~에 있다 All those towns are (located) on the Nakdonggang(Nakdong River).

유연(油煙) lamp soot [smoke]; lampblack; carbon. ¶~으로 까맣게 된 램프의 등피 a lamp chimney blackened with soot.

유연(類緣) 1 a relative. ⇨친척 2 [생] affinity.

유연성(柔軟性) suppleness; flexibility; pliability; pliableness; softness. ¶저 사람은 이 부족하다 That man needs a little more flexibility.

유연하다(柔軟−) (물건이) soft; pliable; pliant; flexible (▶ pliant, pliable은 「구부리거나 비틀 수 있음」, flexible은 「꺾이지 않고 휘어짐」을 강조. pliable, pliant, flexible 이 세 단어는 비유적으로도 쓰임); (몸(의 부분)이) supple; lithe (▶ supple은 「근육·동작 등이 탄력 있고 부드러움」을 강조); (몸이) limber. ¶유연한 몸 a lithe [limber / supple] body // 유연한 동작 (부드러운) lithe movements / (우아한) graceful movements // 유연한 자세를 취하다 take a flexible attitude // 그녀는 몸이 ~ She has a pliant [supple] body.

유연하다(悠然−) calm; composed; serene. 유연히 calmly; composedly; with composure; serenely.

유열(愉悅) joy. ¶사는 데 ~을 느끼다 feel the joy of life.

유영(游泳) swimming. ¶우주 ~ a space walk. 유영하다 swim; have a swim; (물고기·물새 등이) sail.

유예(猶豫) 1 [망설임] hesitation. 유예하다 hesitate; delay. ¶유예하지 말고 단행하라 Carry it out without a delay. // 한시도 유예할 수 없다 There is not a moment to lose. / There is no time to lose [to be lost]. / It admits [permits] of no delay. / We cannot afford to wait (any longer).

2 [연기] (a) postponement; (a) delay; (a) deferment; (형의) a suspension; (의무·처형의) a stay; (의무 수행·지불 등의) grace. ¶집행 ~ a stay of execution / (사형의 집행 유예) a reprieve / suspension of a sentence // 지급 ~ indulgence / grace of payment // 더 이상의 ~는 허용할 수 없다 No further postponement [delay] can be allowed. // 1주일간의 ~를 주십시오 Please grant us an extension of one week [a week's extension]. 유예하다 put off; postpone; allow [grant] delay [grace / respite]; give (a day's) grace; (형의 집행을) reprieve. ¶그들은 형의 집행을 유예했다 They postponed [delayed] the execution. // 채권자는 지불을 하루 유예했다 The creditor allowed [granted] a day's grace for payment.

● 유예 기간 a period of grace; a grace period; (영) days of grace; (준비 기간) time in advance. ¶(채무 이행의) 법정 ~ [법] a legal delay // 새 법률의 발효까지는 3년의 ~이 있다 It will be another 3 years [There is a three year grace period] before the new law goes into effect [takes effect].

유용(流用) (a) diversion; (an) appropriation; (a) misappropriation. ¶공금 ~ misappropriation [embezzlement] of public money / peculation. 유용하다 divert [apply / appropriate] (the money) to 〔some other purpose〕; (부정으로) misappropriate. ¶그들은 수리비의 일부를 접대비로 유용했다 They diverted part of the repair allowance to entertainment expenses. / They appropriated part of the repair allowance for entertainment expens-

유임하다

es.// 그는 공금을 유용했다 He misappropriated[made use of] Government funds. ➔ ¶공금이 지사의 사저(私邸) 건축에 유용되었음이 밝혀졌다 It came to light that public money had been diverted to the construction of the governor's private residence.

유용성(有用性) usefulness; utility.

유용하다(有用-) useful (to / for); helpful; good (for something); serviceable; valuable; of use[service / avail]. ¶유용한 도구 a valuable tool// 돈을 유용하게 쓰다 put money to a good use// 전쟁으로 인해 국가에 유용한 인재를 많이 잃었다 The war killed many able men who would have been useful[valuable] to the state.// 그녀는 회사에 유용한 인재다 She is useful to our company.// 이 책은 상당히 유용했다 This book was very helpful.// 말은 짐을 운반하는 데 유용한 동물이다 The horse is a useful[valuable] animal for carrying loads.// 그 도구는 여러 가지 점에서 ~ The tool serves us[is of use to us] in many ways.

유원지(遊園地) an amusement park; 《영》 a recreation[pleasure] ground; a pleasure resort. ¶어린이 ~ an amusement park for children.

유월(六月) June(약어 Jun.).

유월절(逾越節) 〔종〕 the Passover.

유유낙낙하다(唯唯諾諾-) 〔명령대로 하다〕 do as told without objection; be obedient [submissive]; 〔선뜻 응하다〕 give a ready [willing] consent (to). ¶유유낙낙하게 〔시키는 대로〕 obediently / submissively / at a person's beck and call / 〔기꺼이〕 (quite) willingly / readily// 그는 아버지의 분부에 유유낙낙했다 He readily obeyed his father's orders.

유유상종(類類相從) Birds of a feather flock together.; Like draws to like.; Like attracts like.

유유자적하다(悠悠自適-) live in easy[comfortable] retirement; live free from worldly cares. ¶아버지는 퇴직 후 유유자적하게 살고 계시다 My father has been enjoying a free life[leading an easy life] since he retired.

유유하다(悠悠-) 1 〔움직임이 한가하다〕 slow; leisurely; deliberate; 〔침착하다〕 quiet; calm; composed; sedate. ¶지진이 일어났어도 그는 유유했다 Even when the earthquake hit he remained quite calm[composed]. **유유히** 〔마음 편히〕 at ease; in comfort; 〔여유 만만하게〕 slowly; in a leisurely way[manner]; deliberately; 〔침착하게〕 quietly; calmly; composedly; with composure; serenely in a quiet[self-possessed] manner. ¶떠날 시간인데도 그는 ~ 신문을 읽고 있었다 He was reading a newspaper in a leisurely manner even though it was time to leave.// 그는 모자를 쓰고 나서 ~ 걸어갔다 Putting on his hat, he walked away in a leisurely manner with slow[deliberate] steps.// 우리는 적을 눈앞에 두고도 ~ 식사를 했다 We sat down composedly to a hearty meal in the face of the enemy.// 나는 ~ 담배를 피우고 있었다 I was smoking at ease.

2 〔멀고 아득하다〕 eternal; endless; boundless; vast; remote; far-off. **유유히** eternally; endlessly; remotely; vastly.

유의(留意) attention; heed; regard. **유의하다** note; pay attention to; be mindful[regardful] (of); bear[keep] (a thing) in mind. ¶유의하여 듣다 listen attentively to / give ear to / be all ears[attention] // 이 점을 유의하시오 Please note[pay attention to] this point.// 그의 건강 상태에 특히 유의하시기 바랍니다 Please pay special attention to[take good care of] his health.// 그들이 어린이의 심리에 충분히 유의했다고는 보지 않는다 I don't believe they gave enough thought to the child's psychology.// 이 점에 유의하고 그 책을 다시 읽어 보게 Read the book again, keeping this point in mind.

유익하다(有益-) 〔유용하다〕 helpful; useful; serviceable; 〔이익이 있다〕 beneficial; 〔교육적이다〕 instructive; edifying; 〔건전하다〕 wholesome; 〔유리하다〕 profitable; advantageous. ¶선생님이 유익한 이야기를 해 주셨다 The teacher told us a helpful[a beneficial / 《문어》 an edifying / instructive] story.// 이 설명은 문외한에게 매우 ~ This explanation is very helpful[useful] for laymen.// 유익한 말씀 감사합니다 Thank you for your instructive[《문어》 edifying] talk.// 지나치게 엄격한 것은 학생들에게 유익하지 않다 It doesn't help the pupils to be too hard on them.// 시찰 여행은 유익하였다 The inspection tour proved quite useful[helpful].

유인(有人) 〔관형어적〕 manned; piloted.
● **유인 우주선** a manned spaceship.

유인(誘引) enticement; allurement; temptation. **유인하다** entice; allure. ¶적을 위험한 곳으로 ~ lure the enemy into a dangerous position// 사람을 나쁜 길로 ~ tempt a person into wrongdoing// 그들은 그 여자를 그 집으로 유인했다 They lured her into the house.

유인(誘因) a motive; a cause; an incitement; an incentive. ¶~이 되다 cause / induce // 과로는 종종 병의 ~이 된다 Overwork often causes[induces] illness. / Illness is often caused[induced] by overwork.// 선생님의 경솔한 말이 학생들이 반항하게 된 ~이 되었다 The teacher's careless words triggered [brought about / led to] the students' revolt.

유인물(油印物) a mimeographed copy.

유인원(類人猿) 〔동〕 an anthropoid (ape); a troglodyte.

유일무이하다(唯一無二-) one and only; unique; peerless. ¶나의 유일무이한 친구 the one and only friend I have / my best friend.

유일신(唯一神) 《worship》 the one and only God.

유일하다(唯一-) only(▶ the를 붙여서); sole; one (and only); 〔독특하다〕 unique. ¶나의 유일한 벗 the only friend of mine / my sole friend// 고대 페르시아의 이 유리 접시는 세계에서 유일한 것이다 This glass plate from ancient Persia is unique.// 사직하는 것만이 그가 할 수 있는 유일한 길이다 The only way open to him is to resign.// 그를 설득하는 유일한 방법은 그의 인정에 호소하는 일이다 There is no other way of persuading him than to pull at his heartstrings.// 그림 그리는 것이 그녀의 유일한 낙이다 Painting is the only pleasure She has (in life).

유임하다(留任-) remain[stay / continue] in office. ¶그는 한 기를 더 회장 자리에 유임할 것이다 He will remain in office as chairman for another term. ➔ ¶그가 그 모임의 회장에 유임되기로 결정되었다 It was decided that he

유입(流入) inflow; influx. ¶외국 자본의 ~ an inflow[influx] of foreign capital // 난민의 ~ 이 당면 사회 문제이다 The influx of refugees is a social problem at present. **유입하다** flow [come / stream] in[into].

유자(柚子) [식] a citron; a Chinese lemon.

유자격자(有資格者) a qualified person; a qualifier; an eligible (person); [면허를 딴 사람] a person with a license. ¶**약사** ~ a licensed pharmacist // **입후보** ~ people eligible[qualified] to be candidates // 우리는 간호사[교사] ~ 를 찾고 있다 We want a trained nurse [licensed teacher].

유자녀(遺子女) [죽은 사람의 자녀] bereaved children; children left by the deceased.

유작(遺作) one's posthumous work(s).

유장하다(悠長-) 1 [길고 오래다] long; of long standing. ¶유장한 세월 a long time / a long stretch of time / many years. 2 [성미가 느릿하다] leisurely; slow; deliberate; easygoing.

유저(遺著) a posthumous book.

유적(遺跡) a site; remains; ruins; vestiges; (historic) relics. ¶고대 로마의 ~ the remains[ruins] of ancient Rome // 성곽의 ~ 을 보존하다 preserve the ruins of a castle // 석기 시대의 ~ 이 발견되었다 A Stone Age site was discovered.

유전(油田) an [a petroleum] field; oil land. ¶해저 ~ a submarine oil field // ~ 을 **발견하다** discover an oil field / strike[hit] oil.

● **유전 지대** an oil (producing) region. **유전 탐사** oil exploration.

유전(流轉) 1 [떠돎] vagrancy; wandering. **유전하다** wander (about); rove; roam. 2 [변천] constant mutation; perpetual motion; vicissitudes. **유전하다** change[mutate] constantly; move perpetually. ¶만물은 유전한다 All things are in flux. / Everything is constantly changing. 3 [불] [인과의 연결] transmigration. **유전하다** transmigrate.

유전(遺傳) heredity; inheritance; (hereditary) transmission. ¶**우성**[열성] ~ dominant [recessive] inheritance // ~ 적인[성의] hereditary / of hereditary nature / transmissible / transmittable / heritable / inheritable // ~ 적인 영향 genetic effects // 그녀의 음악적 재능은 어머니로부터의 ~ 이다 She has inherited her musical talent from her mother. // 이 병은 우리 집의 ~ 이다 This disease runs in my family. / There is a taint of this disease in my family. **유전하다** be inherited; be passed down[on] (to); be transmitted; be hereditary; run in the blood[family]. ¶아버지의 병이 아이들에게 유전했다 The father's disease was passed down[on] to his children. // 이 병은 유전하지 않는다 This disease is not hereditary.

● **유전 공학** genetic engineering. **유전병** a hereditary [family / constitutional] disease. **유전자** [생] a gene. ¶**성 결정** ~ a sex determining gene // **열성**[우성] ~ a recessive [dominant] gene // **인공** ~ an artificial gene // **합성** ~ a synthesized gene // ~ 에 의한 genetic / genic. **유전학** genetics.

유정(油井) an oil well; (미) an oiler. ¶~ 을 **뚫다** drill for oil / sink an oil.

유제(油劑) a greasy medicine; an oil-based medicine; [연고] (an) ointment.

유제(乳劑) (an) emulsion. ¶**석유** ~ a petroleum emulsion.

유제(類題) [흡사한 문제] a similar question; [흡사한 제목] a similar title.

유제류(有蹄類) [동] the ungulates; an ungulate (animal); a hoofed animal. ¶**말은** ~ **이다** The horse is an ungulate[a hoofed] animal.

유제품(乳製品) dairy goods[products].

유조(油槽) an oil tank.

● **유조선** a[an oil] tanker; (대형의) a supertanker. **유조차** an oil truck; (영) a tanker.

유족(遺族) the bereaved (family); the family of the deceased; a surviving family. ¶**전사자** ~ the war bereaved // 그의 ~ 으로는 아내와 딸 하나가 있다 He was survived by his wife and one daughter. / He left his wife and one daughter (behind [to mourn his death]).

유족하다(裕足-) affluent; opulent; rich; wealthy; well-off. ¶**석유와 석탄이 유족한 나라** a country rich in oil and coal. **유족히** affluently; wealthily; opulently. ¶~ **살다** live well / be well [comfortably] off / live in easy [affluent] circumstances / live in opulence [abundance / affluence / plenty] // 그녀는 어릴 때 ~ 자랐다 She was brought up in affluent[easy] circumstances.

유종(有終) having an end; consummation. **유종의 미** crowning glory; consummation (of wisdom and virtue); swan song. ¶~ 를 **거두다** carry (a thing) to perfection / bring (a matter) to a successful conclusion // 그는 마지막 시합에서도 완승하여 오랜 선수 생활에 ~ 를 두었다 He rounded off[crowned] his long playing career with a complete victory in his last match. / He brought his long playing career to a fine finish by winning a complete victory in his last match. // 그는 노벨상을 받아 생애에 ~ 를 거두었다 He rounded off his career by winning the Nobel prize.

유종(乳腫) [의] mastitis.

유죄(有罪) guilt. ¶~ 를 **선고하다** convict (a person) of a crime / give (a person) the verdict of guilty / declare (a person) guilty // **수회죄로** ~ 가 **되다** be convicted of bribery // **배심원은 그를** ~ **로 평결했다** The jury found him guilty. / The jury brought in a verdict of guilty against him. // **그녀는 아직** ~ **로 확정되지 않았다** Her guilt has not been established yet. / She has not yet been proved guilty. **유죄하다** guilty; culpable.

● **유죄 판결** a judgment of guilty; (get) a conviction. ¶~ 를 **받다** be convicted // 그는 ~ 을 **받았다** He was found guilty.

유즙(乳汁) milk.

유증(遺贈) the disposition of property under a person's will; testation; (동산의) bequest; bequeathal; (부동산의) devise. **유증하다** leave (a thing to a person) in one's will; will (to); (동산을) bequeath; leave a bequest; legate; (부동산을) devise. ¶**숙부는 그에게 저택을 유증했다** His uncle left him a big house. // 그는 모교에 거액의 돈을 유증했다 He bequeathed an enormous sum of money to his alma mater.

● **유증물** a bequest; a legacy. **유증자** a legator; a devisor.

유지(有志) 1 [뜻 있는 사람] an interested person; a volunteer; those[people] interested (in a matter). ¶~들이 모두 장학 기금을 기탁했다 All those interested contributed some money to the scholarship fund. 2 [영향력을 지닌 사람] an influential person; a man of influence[power]; [요직자] (구어) a big man. ¶그는 그 고장의 ~이다 He is quite influential in the town.

유지 (乳脂) butterfat; milk fat.
● 유지 비누 curd soap.

유지 (油脂) oils and fats.
● 유지 공업 the oil and fat industry.

유지 (油紙) oilpaper; oiled paper.

유지 (維持) maintenance; preservation; support; conservation; upkeep(집 등의). ¶평화의 ~ the maintenance of peace // 현상 ~ 정책 the policy of maintaining the present condition[status quo]. 유지하다 maintain (peace, order, etc.); keep (one's health); sustain (an institution); support (life). ¶현상을 ~ maintain the status quo // 체면을 ~ keep up appearances / save face / 건강을 ~ preserve one's health / keep oneself in good health // 생명을 ~ sustain[support] life / keep a person alive // 한 집안의 생계를 ~ support one's family // 실내 온도를 일정하게 ~ keep a room at a fixed temperature // 사회 질서[무역의 균형]를 ~ maintain public order[the trade balance] // 환자의 생명을 유지하기 위한 장치가 설치되었다 Life-support apparatus was attached to the patient. ¶그들은 자금이 모자라 회[클럽]를 유지할 수 없게 되었다 They became unable to maintain the club [keep the club going] for lack of funds. → ¶그 협회는 거의 기부금으로 유지된다 The society is supported almost entirely by contributions.
● 유지비 the cost of maintenance; upkeep.

유지 (遺志) the desire[wish / intention / will] of a deceased person; one's dying wishes [will]. ¶아버지의 ~에 따라 in conformity with the wishes of one's deceased father / according to one's father's last wishes[dying wish] // 고인의 ~를 실천하다[따르다] carry out[follow] the intention of the deceased.

유질 (流質) foreclosure; a mortgage forfeit. 유질되다 be forfeited; be foreclosed; run out. → ¶유질된 카메라 an unredeemed camera // 저당물이 유질되었다 The mortgage was foreclosed.

유착 (癒着) 1 [의] (상처 등의) adhesion; conglutination. ¶그녀는 맹장 수술 후의 ~으로 고생을 했다 She had painful adhesions after her appendectomy. 유착하다 adhere (to); stick[knit] together. 2 [서로 깊은 관련을 지님]. ¶정경 ~ a close relationship between political and business circle. 유착하다 have a cozy relationship (with). ¶대통령은 일부 자본가와 유착해 있다는 비난을 받았다 The president was accused of having a cozy relationship with a certain group of capitalists.

유창하다 (流暢−) fluent (in English); smooth. ¶말이 유창한 사람 an eloquent[a fluent] speaker // 그는 유창한 연설을 했다 He made a fluent speech. // 그녀의 입에서 유창한 프랑스 어가 흘러나왔다 She spoke fluent French. // 그는 중국어가 유창하다 He speaks Chinese fluently[with ease]. / He is a fluent speaker of Chinese. // 이 일에는 유창한 영어가 요구된다 Fluency in English is required for this job. 유창히 fluently; eloquently. ¶~ 말하다 speak fluently.

유채 (油菜) [식] a rape (plant); a cole.
유채색 (有彩色) an chromatic color.
유체 (有體) ¶~의 tangible / [법] corporeal.
● 유체물 a materiality; [법] a corporeal thing.

유체 (流體) [물] a fluid.
● 유체 압력 fluid pressure. 유체 역학 hydrodynamics; hydromechanics.

유추 (類推) analogical inference; (an) analogy. ¶~적인 analogical / analogic / ~에 의하여 [through] analogy. 유추하다 analogize; infer; use analogy. ¶…으로 유추하여 on the analogy of ... // 부분 전체를 ~ analogize the whole out of a part // 목소리로 유추하면 그는 상당한 연배인 것 같다 Judging from his voice, he seems to be pretty old.
● 유추 해석 analogical interpretation.

유출 (流出) an outflow; an effluence; (an) effluxi; a drain(재화 등의). ¶석유의 ~ an oil spill // 두뇌 ~ a brain drain // 미술품의 해외 ~ the drain of the works of fine arts into foreign countries. 유출하다 flow[run] out; issue; discharge; drain out; overflow(넘쳐서).

유충 (幼蟲) [동] a larva. ⇨ 애벌레.
● 유충기 the larval stage. ¶~의 누에 a silkworm in the larval stage.

유층 (油層) an oil stratum.

유치 (乳齒) a milk tooth. ⇨ 젖니.

유치 (留置) 1 [억류] detention; custody. 유치하다 detain; hold (a person) in custody; lock up. ¶피의자로서[음주 운전으로] ~ detain a person[lock up a person / keep a person in custody] as a suspect [for drunken driving]. → ¶그 남자는 도둑질한 혐의로 경찰에 유치되었다 The man was detained at the police station on suspicion of theft. 2 (우편 등의). 유치하다 leave until called for.
● 유치장 a house of detention; (구어) a lock up. ¶그는 ~에 갇혔다 He was jailed. / He was locked up in jail.

유치 (誘致) attraction; invitation. ¶섬에 새로운 다리가 생겨 관광객 ~에 도움이 되고 있다 The newly-constructed bridge helps attract tourists to the island. 유치하다 lure; attract; invite. ¶외국인 관광객을 한국에 ~ attract foreign tourists to Korea // 어촌에 공장을 ~ invite factories to a fishing village // 그들은 원자력 발전소를 시에 유치하려 하고 있다 They are trying to lure a nuclear power plant [facility] into their city.

유치원 (幼稚園) a kindergarten; a nursery school; (미) a preschool. ¶막내 아이가 ~에 다니고 있다 My youngest son[daughter] goes to[is in] kindergarten.(▶ 이 경우는 관사를 붙이지 않음)
● 유치원생 a kindergarten pupil; a kindergartener.

유치하다 (幼稚−) [어린애 같다] childish; [어려서 미숙하다] infantile; [미숙하다] crude; unrefined; [원시적이다] primitive. ¶유치한 생각 childish[immature] ideas // 유치한 놀이 infantile[babyish] games // 유치한 디자인 a crude[an unrefined] design // 그 계획은 ~ The plan is puerile.

유쾌하다 (愉快−) pleasant; enjoyable; merry; delightful; joyful. ¶유쾌한 사람 a jolly [cheerful / pleasant] fellow // 유쾌한 기질 a pleasant[cheerful] disposition // 나는 기분이

유탄

유쾌하지 않다 I feel depressed. / I am low spirits. 유쾌히 pleasantly; merrily; delightfully; joyfully; cheerfully. ¶~ 웃다 laugh cheerfully [delightedly] / smile a happy smile // 자, ~ 놉시다 Let's have a good time. / Let's make a day [night] of it.

유탄(流彈) a stray bullet; (엽총의) a stray shot. ¶그는 ~에 맞았다 He was hit by a stray bullet.

유탄(榴彈) a high-explosive projectile; a shell.
유태(猶太) 〈음역〉 Jud(a)ea. ⇨유대
유택(幽宅) a grave. ⇨"무덤
유턴 (자동차 등의) (make) a U-turn.
●유턴 금지 (게시) No U-turn.
유토피아 (a) Utopia. ¶~의 Utopian.

유통(流通) 1 [활기] ventilation; [순환] circulation. ¶공기가 ~이 잘되다 [안 되다] be well [poorly] ventilated / 공기의 ~을 잘되게 하다 facilitate ventilation / facilitate the circulation of air. 유통하다 circulate; ventilate; flow. 2 (돈의) circulation; currency; (어음의) negotiation. 유통하다 circulate; pass current; (어음 등이) float. ¶유통하고 있다 be in circulation / (어음이) be afloat. →¶새 지폐는 내달부터 유통된다 The new bill [(영) note] will be put into circulation next month.
●유통 경로 a distribution channel. 유통 구조 distribution structure. ¶~를 개선하다 improve [upgrade] the marketing structure (for agricultural and fishery products). 유통 산업 the distribution industry. 유통 시장 a circulation market. 유통 혁명 a distribution revolution; (a) distribution upheaval.

유파(流派) a school. ¶새 ~를 세우다 create [found] a new school (of painting).

유폐(幽閉) confinement. 유폐하다 confine (a person in a place); shut [lock] up. →¶그는 지하 감옥에 유폐되었다 He was confined in a dungeon.

유포(流布) circulation; spread. 유포하다 [퍼지다] be circulated; be current; spread; get about [afloat]; go around; (퍼뜨리다) circulate; spread. →¶유포되고 있다 be in circulation / be current / be prevalent / be going around // 소문을 유포시키다 circulate [disseminate] a rumor / set a rumor afloat // ¶풍설은 부산에 꾸준히 유포되고 있었다 The rumor was persistently circulated in Busan. // 이상한 소문이 유포됐다 A strange rumor got about.

유품(遺品) a relics; an article left by the departed. ¶이 시계는 아버지의 ~이다 This watch was left to me by my father.

유풍(遺風) [옛날 풍속] old traditions (and customs); a remnant; a survival. ¶이 고장에는 봉건 시대의 ~이 아직 존재한다 The traditions of the feudal age still alive in this town.

유피아이 [미국의 통신사] UPI; U.P.I.(▶ United Press International의 약어).

유하다(留-) [머물러 묵다] stay (at / in / with); stop (at / in / with); lodge (in / with); put up (at a hotel). ¶하룻밤 ~ stay overnight / stop (for) the night / take a lodging for the night // 친구 집에 ~ stay at a friend's (house) / stay with a friend.

유하다(柔-) 1 [부드럽다] soft; mild; gentle; genial; tender; sweet; amiable. ¶유한 사람 a man of sweet temper / a gentle [genial] person / a tender-hearted [gentle-mannered] person // 성격이 ~ be mild of temper / be of a gentle nature. 2 [걱정이 없다] carefree; easy(going); happy-go-lucky. ¶유한 성질 an easygoing disposition.

유학(留學) study(ing) abroad. ¶이탈리아 ~ 중에 during one's stay in Italy as a student. 유학하다 study abroad; go abroad for [to] study. ¶국비 [사비] 로 ~ study abroad at a government expense [by private means] // 그는 사회학을 공부하기 위해 미국에 유학했다 He went to the United States to study sociology.

●유학생 a student studying abroad; (해외에서 온) a foreign student. ¶한국에 있는 영국인 ~ British students in Korea // 미국에 있는 한국인 ~은 5만 명이라고도, 10만 명이라고도 한다 Some say the number of Korean students studying in the United States is about fifty thousand, and some say a hundred thousand. // 서울 대학교에는 많은 ~이 있다 There are many foreign students in Seoul University.

유학(遊學) [타향에서 공부하는 것]. ¶서울 ~ 중에 while studying in Seoul / during one's period of study in Seoul. 유학하다 study [pursue knowledge / prosecute one's studies] far away from (one's) home.

유학(儒學) Confucianism.
●유학자 a Confucian scholar.

유한(有限) limitedness; finiteness. 유한하다 limited; [수] finite; [식] definite; determinate. ¶유한한 생명 a mortal life // 인간의 힘은 ~ There is a limit to man's power.
●유한급수 a finite series. 유한 (책임) 회사 (미) a corporation; (영) a limited(-liability) company(▶ 회사명 다음에 (미) Incorporated의 약어 Inc., (영) Limited의 약어 Ltd.를 붙임).

유한(有閑) [관형어적] leisure(d).
●유한계급 the leisured classes; the leisure class. 유한마담 / 유한부인 a lady of leisure; a leisured woman.

유한(遺恨) the grudge [rancor / spite / enmity / malice] of a deceased person. ¶고인의 ~을 풀다 gratify [satisfy] the spite of the deceased.

유합(癒合) [의] agglutination; conglutination; healing. 유합하다 agglutinate; conglutinate.

유해(有害) [관형어적] noxious. ¶~ 가스 noxious gas. 유해하다 harmful (to); injurious (to); bad; noxious; hurtful. ¶농작물에 ~ be harmful to the crops // 풍기상 ~ be prejudicial [destructive] to public morals // 심신에 ~ affect both mind and body // 과음은 건강에 ~ Excessive drinking is injurious to [bad for / harmful to] health.
●유해물 a toxic substance. 유해 식품 harmful food.

유해(遺骸) a (dead) body; a corpse; remains. ¶~를 인수하다 claim (a person's) body [mortal remains] // 그녀의 ~는 향리에 묻혔다 Her remains [mortal body / All that is mortal of her] was buried [resting] in her old home.

유해무익하다(有害無益-) (서술적) do more harm than good. ¶이 규칙은 ~ This rule is not only useless but simply bad [harmful]. // 편파적인 견해를 학생들에게 강조하는 것은 ~ It does more harm than good to force one-sided opinions on the pupils.

유행(流行) **1** (복장 등의) (a) fashion; a vogue; mode; (한때의 열광적인) a craze; (일시적인) a fad; (인기) popularity. ¶~이 지난 모자 an old-fashioned hat∥최신의 ~ the latest fashion / the latest mode in fashion∥파리의 ~ Paris fashion∥일시적인 ~ a passing fad∥오래가는 ~ a long-lived fashion∥~을 좇다 follow the fashion[mode]∥~에 뒤지다 be behind the fashion∥~의 첨단을 걷다 lead [set] the fashion∥~을 만들어 내다 set [create] the fashion (of the hour)∥~이 지나다 go out of fashion[style]∥그녀는 최신 ~의 옷을 입고 있다 She is dressed in the latest fashion.∥지금은 긴 스커트가 ~이다 Long skirts are the vogue[fashion] now. / Long skirts are in now.∥이 스타일의 옷은 ~을 타지 않는다 A suit of this style is not subject to changes in fashion.∥굽 높은 구두가 ~이다 High-heeled shoes are the vogue[are the rage / are in fashion].∥그녀는 최신 ~의 머리형을 하고 있었다 She wore her hair in a modish [the latest] style. **유행하다** be in fashion [vogue]; (인기가 있다) be popular. ¶요즘 유행하는 주간지 a trendy weekly magazine∥유행하게 되다 come into fashion [vogue] / become fashionable [a craze / a fad]∥가죽 코트가 유행하게 되었다 [유행하지 않게 되었다] Leather coats have come into [have gone out of] fashion [vogue].∥이런 종류의 음악이 현재 유행하고 있다 This type of music is popular now.∥그와 같은 의견이 젊은이들 사이에 유행하고 있다 That sort of opinion is prevalent among young people.∥비디오 게임이 어린이들 사이에 크게 유행하고 있다 Video games are all the rage among children.∥한때 학생들 사이에 마르크시즘이 유행했다 Marxism prevailed[was popular] among students at one time. ➔그 머리형이 젊은 여성들 간에 유행되고 있다 The hair style is in fashion[vogue] among young women.

2 [전염병이 만연함] prevalence. **유행하다** prevail; be prevalent. ¶이질이 유행하기 시작했다 Dysentery has broken out.∥작년에는 전국에 독감이 유행했다 Last year influenza was prevalent all over the country.∥역병이 유행하고 있다 An epidemic is raging.(▶ 맹위를 떨치고)∥그곳에는 아직도 콜레라가 유행하고 있습니까 Is cholera still prevalent in the area? / Is the cholera epidemic still going on in the area?

● **유행가** a popular song. **유행 가수** a popular singer. **유행병** a fashion (disease). **유행성** [의] epidemicity. ¶~의 epidemic. **유행성 감기** influenza; (구어) the flu. ¶~에 걸리다 catch[get] the flu. **유행어** a cant; a word in fashion.

유혈(流血) bloodshed. ¶~의 참사 an affair of bloodshed / a bloody affair∥~이 낭자하다 be smeared[covered] with blood∥~극을 벌이다 have a bloody fight∥군대는 더 이상의 ~을 보지 않고 그 도시를 점령했다 The army occupied the city without further bloodshed.∥데모는 ~ 참사로 발전했다 The demonstration developed into a bloody affair.

유형(有形) materiality; concreteness. ¶~의 material / tangible / (문어) corporeal∥~화하다 materialize / embody.

● **유형 무역** visible trade. **유형 문화재** tangible cultural properties. **유형물** a concrete object. **유형 재산** tangible[corporeal] property.

유형(流刑) exile; deportation; banishment; transportation. ¶종신 ~ transportation for life / ~에 처하다 condemn (a person) to exile / banish / exile / transport / deport.

유형(類型) a type; a pattern. ¶그것은 세 가지 ~으로 분류된다 They can be divided into three types.

유형무형(有形無形) [형체의 유무가 분명하지 아니함]. ¶~의 material and immaterial [moral] / visible and invisible / tangible and intangible∥나는 그로부터 ~의 많은 도움을 받았다 I received great support, both material and moral, from him.

유혹(誘惑) temptation; allurement; enticement; seduction. ¶대도시의 ~ the allurements [temptations] of a big city∥바다의 ~ the lure[call] of the sea∥술의 ~ the temptation of drink(ing)∥~을 물리치다 overcome temptation∥~에 빠지다 yield to temptation / be tempted∥~과 싸우다 fight [resist] temptation∥조심성 없이 돈을 방치해 두는 것은 ~의 원인이 된다 Money left carelessly about is a temptation.∥그는 처녀에게 ~의 손길을 뻗쳤다 He tempted the girl.∥그는 나쁜 친구들의 ~에 빠져 못된 길에 발을 들여놓았다 Tempted by bad companions, he fell into evil ways. **유혹하다** […하고 싶은 마음이 들게 하다] tempt (a person to do / a person into doing); lure (a person into doing); [부추기다] entice (a person to do / a person into doing); [꾀어서 타락시키다] seduce (a girl)(▶ seduce는 거의 sex에 대해서 씀). ¶나쁜 친구가 그에게 담배를 피우라고 유혹했다 Bad friends tempted him to smoke [into smoking].∥그는 그녀를 유혹하여 돈을 훔치게 했다 He enticed her to steal money.

● **유혹물** a temptation; a lure; an invitation (to death); a bait; (미국 구어) a come-on.

유화(乳化) emulsification.

유화(油畵) (그림) an oil painting.

● **유화가** an oil painter.

유화(宥和) appeasement. ¶반대파에 대한 ~를 고려하고 있다 We want to appease [placate / conciliate] our opponents. **유화하다** appease; placate; propitiate; pacify.

● **유화 정책** an appeasement policy; a policy of appeasement.

유화하다(柔和-) mild; gentle; meek(▶ mild는 엄격하지 않은, gentle은 인정이 있고 상냥한, meek는 얌전하고 순종함을 말함). ¶유화한 눈매 meek[gentle] eyes∥기질이 유화한 사람 a person with mild[gentle] disposition.

유황(硫黃) [화] sulfur. ⇨=황(黃)2

● **유황천** a sulfur spring.

유회(流會) cancellation of a meeting. **유회하다** cancel a meeting. ➔정원 미달로 유회되었다 For want of a quorum, the meeting was canceled[called off].∥의장의 결석으로 유회되었다 The meeting was canceled due to the absence of the chairman.

유효(有效) validity(법규 등의); availability(표 등의); effectiveness; efficiency. **유효하다** [효과가 있다] effective; (어떤 기간·조건하에서) available; good; profitable. ¶유효한 담보 a good security∥유효한 표 an available ticket∥이 약은 심한 두통에 ~ This medicine works well for stubborn headaches.∥이 법

유훈

규는 교통사고를 줄이는데 유효할 것이다 These regulations will help to decrease the number of[effectively cut down] traffic accidents.∥이 계약은 5년간 ~ This contract is valid[effective] for five years.∥그 법률은 아직 ~ That law still stands.∥불가침 조약이 유효한 동안, 우리나라는 안전하다 Our country is safe while the nonaggression treaty remains in force.∥신청은 8월 31까지 유효합니다 Your application must be postmarked no later than August 31(st)[31 August]. **유효히** effectively; effectually; efficaciously; profitably.

● **유효 기간** the term[period] of validity; the available period. ¶차표의 ~ the period for which a ticket is valid∥ ~ 3개월 effective [valid] for three months∥이 표의 ~은 며칠입니까 How long is the ticket valid? **유효 사거리** the effective range; the effective distance. **유효 수요** (an) effective demand.

유훈(遺訓) [죽은 사람이 남긴 훈계] the instructions[teachings] of the departed. ¶그들은 은사의 ~을 충실히 지켰다 They faithfully followed their late teacher's instructions [teachings].

유휴(遊休) [관형어적] idle; unused.

● **유휴 시설** idle[unused] facilities [equipment]. **유휴 자금** idle assets. **유휴 자본** idle capital[funds]. **유휴지** idle land.

유흥(遊興) pleasure (seeking); merrymaking; amusement. ¶~에 빠지다 pursue [indulge in] pleasures∥그는 ~에 돈을 아끼지 않았다 He didn't mind spending money to have fun. ∥그는 ~에 푹 빠져 있다 He does nothing but play around.∥그는 젊었을 때 ~에 빠졌다 In his youth he was given[addicted] to the pursuit of pleasure. **유흥하다** make merry; make pleasures; amuse oneself; be [go] on the spree.

● **유흥가** an amusement center[quarter]; gay quarters; (미) a red-light district. **유흥비** amusement expenses; (영국 구어) beer money. **유흥업소** a merrymaking [an entertainment] place; an amusement spot. **사치성 ~** a luxurious[an extravagant] entertainment spot.

유희(遊戲) a game; sports; (어린이의) play; [오락] a pastime; amusements. ¶~를 즐기다 enjoy a game / amuse oneself at a game∥그녀는 연애를 일종의 ~로 생각하고 있었다 She regarded love as a sort of game.∥유치원생들은 원을 그리며 ~를 하고 있었다 The kindergarten children were playing and dancing in a circle. **유희하다** make merry; play; play (at) game.

육(六) six. ¶제 ~ the sixth∥~분의 1 one-sixth∥~ 개월 six month.

육(肉) [살] flesh; [고기] meat; [육신] the flesh. ¶영과 ~ flesh and spirit / body and soul.

육각(六角) **1** six angles. ⇨육모¶~의 hexagonal / sexangular. **2** (악기) the Six Musical Instruments.

● **육각형** a hexagon; a sexangle.

육감(六感) a sixth sense; intuition; hunch. ¶ ~으로 (guided) by the sixth sense / (act) on one's hunch∥그것이 거짓말이라는 것을 ~으로 알았다 I knew by intuition[My sixth sense told me] that it wasn't true.∥나의 ~으로는 그녀가 가까운 장래에 결혼할 것 같다 I have a hunch that she will get married in the near future.∥나는 ~으로 그 남자가 수상하다고 생각했다 I sensed that there was something fishy about him.∥내 ~이 맞았다 My hunch proved right.

육감(肉感) [육체가 풍기는 느낌] the senses of the flesh; [성적인 느낌] sexual feeling. ¶그 그림에는 ~을 돋우는 것이 있다 There is something suggestive[that incites sexual feelings] about that painting.

육감적(肉感的) sensual; voluptuous; (구어) sexy. ¶~인 여자 a sexy[sensual] woman∥그녀의 입은 ~이다 She has a sensual mouth.

육갑(六甲) the sexagenary cycle. ⇨육십갑자

육개장(肉-) spicy beef soup.

육계(肉界) the physical[sensual] world.

육교(陸橋) an overhead bridge; (미) an overpass; a crossover; (철도의) an overbridge; (도시의) (미) a pedestrian overpass[(영) bridge]; (영) flyover.

육군(陸軍) the army. ¶미국[영국] ~ the United States[British] Army∥한국 ~ the Republic of Korea Army / ROKA∥~의 military / army∥~에 입대하다 (지원하여) enter [enlist in / join] the army / (징집되어) (미) be drafted[(영) conscripted] into the army ∥~에서 제대하다 leave the army.

● **육군 대장** a general; an army general. **육군 본부** the Headquarter of the Army. **육군 사관학교** (미) the U.S. Military Academy; (영) the Royal Military Academy. ¶~ 생도 a military cadet. **육군 장교** an army [a military] officer. **육군 참모 총장** the Army Chief of Staff.

육대주(六大洲) the Six Continents.

육두문자(肉頭文字) an abusive word. ¶~를 늘어놓다 use abusive language / abuse a person.

육로(陸路) a land[an overland] route. ¶~로 by land / by an overland route / overland.

● **육로 수송** overland[land] transportation.

육류(肉類) meat; flesh; flesh-meat. ¶~를 멀리하다 abstain from flesh and meat.

육면체(六面體) [수] a hexahedron (*pl.* ~s, -hedra). ¶정~ a regular hexahedron / a cube∥~의 hexahedral.

육모(六-) six angles.

육묘하다(育苗-) raise seedlings[saplings].

육박전(肉薄戰) bitter fighting at close quarters; (경기) a close contest[game].

육박하다(肉薄-) come close (to); [바싹 다가붙다] press hard (on); (경쟁에서) tread close on (a person's) heels; run (a competitor) hard[close]. ¶우리는 적의 진영에 육박했다 We closed in (up)on the enemy camp. ∥도전자는 챔피언에게 육박했다 The challenger pushed the champion hard.

육발이(六-) a six-toed person.

육법(六法) the six codes (of laws).

● **육법 전서** a Compendium of Laws; the Statute Books; a complete book of the six Major Laws.

육봉(肉峯) [낙타의 등에 난 큰 혹] a hump.

육분의(六分儀) a sextant.

육상(陸上) **1** land; ground; shore. ¶~의[으로 / 에서] on land[shore] / ashore∥~으로 가다[수송하다] go[transport] by land. **2** track and field. ⇨육상 경기(⇨육상)

● **육상 경기** track and field; an athletic

sport. 육상 운송 land transportation; transportation by land.

육서(陸棲) living on land. ¶~의 terrestrial.
● **육서 동물** a land [terrestrial] animal.

육성(肉聲) a natural voice; a (human) voice. ¶비록 ~이었으나 그의 목소리는 홀의 구석구석까지 잘 들렸다 Though he did not use a microphone, his voice reached every corner of the hall.∥나는 그녀의 ~을 들은 적이 없다 I haven't heard her voice.

육성(育成) rearing; upbringing; raising; (문어) nurture. ¶영재의 ~ the bringing up [rearing] of gifted children. **육성하다** bring up; rear; raise. ¶그는 전쟁 고아들을 여러 가지 직업으로 육성하는 데 힘썼다 He devoted himself to taking care of war orphans and training them in various trades.∥그는 많은 신종 식물을 육성했다 He cultivated a number of new species of plants.
● **육성 재배** rearing and cultivating. **육성회비** (학교의) school supporting fees.

육손이(六─) a six-fingered person.

육송(陸送) land transportation [(영) transport]. **육송하다** transport by land. ¶감자를 ~ transport potatoes by land.

육수(肉水) meat[beef] stock; gravy; meat juice; broth.

육순(六旬) sixty years old.

육식(肉食) [사람이 고기붙이를 먹음] a meat diet; meat-eating; [동물이 다른 짐승의 고기를 먹이로 함] flesh-eating; (음식) animal food; meat food. ¶~을 피하다 abstain from fish and meat. **육식하다** (사람이) eat meat; (새·짐승이) eat flesh; live on flesh. ¶그는 체력을 증강시키기 위해 육식하고 있다 He is on a meat diet to increase his physical strength.
● **육식가** a meat-eater. **육식 동물** a predatory animal. **육식조** a bird of prey; a predatory bird.

육신(肉身) the body. ⇨ⁿ육체

육십(六十) sixty. ¶제~ the sixtieth∥~ 년 기념제 the sixtieth [diamond] anniversary∥~대의 사람 a sexagenarian / a sexagenary / a person in his sixties∥~ 년대에 in the (nineteen) sixties [1960's / 1960s].

육십갑자(六十甲子) the sexagenary cycle.

육아(肉芽) (a) granulation.
● **육아종** a granuloma (pl. ~s, -mata).

육아(育兒) child care; nursing; upbringing of a child. ¶그녀는 ~에 전념하고 있다 She devotes herself to (the care of) her children. **육아하다** rear [bring up] a child; take care of a child; nurse (직업으로서).
● **육아법** the way one rears children; how to bring up children. **육아원** a children's home; (기아의) a foundling hospital; (고아의) an orphanage.

육안(肉眼) the naked eye; (망원경 등을 사용하지 않는) the unaided eye. ¶~으로 보이는 별들 stars visible to ordinary sight∥~으로 보다 see with the naked eye∥~으로 보이다 can be observed by the naked eye∥박테리아는 ~으로는 보이지 않는다 Bacteria are invisible to the naked eye.∥그 별은 ~으로는 보이지 않는다 You can't see that star with the naked [unaided] eye.

육영(育英) education (for bright young people). **육영하다** educate.
● **육영 사업** educational work.

육욕(肉慾) sexual [carnal] desires; (문어) the lusts of the flesh. ¶~을 채우다 satisfy one's sensual appetites / gratify one's lusts∥~을 억제하다 restrain one's passions / be continent∥~에 빠지다 indulge in [give oneself over to] sexual desires [pleasures].

육우(肉牛) beef cattle.

육이오 전쟁(六二五戰爭) the Korean War.

육정(肉情) sexual desires. ⇨육욕

육종(肉腫) [종양] a tumor; [의] a sarcoma (pl. ~s, -mata). ¶등뼈에 ~이 생겼다 A sarcoma [(malignant) tumor] has formed on the backbone.

육종(育種) breeding. ¶교배 ~ breeding by crossing∥교잡 ~ breeding by hybridization. **육종하다** breed.

육중주(六重奏) [음] a sextet(te).

육중하다(肉重─) (부피가) bulky and heavy; massive; ponderous; (체격이) heavily built; stout. ¶참나무로 만든 육중한 문 a stoutly-built oak door / a heavy tread / a clamp∥체격이 육중한 사람 a massively built man.

육지(陸地) land; (배에서 본) the shore. ¶~ 쪽으로 landward∥지구의 ~ 면적 the land area of the Earth∥~에 사는 동물 a land [terrestrial] animal∥~가 보이는 곳에서 within sight of land∥(배가) ~에 접근하다 stand in for the shore / approach land∥~에 오르다 land / go ashore [on shore] / get to land∥~로 둘러싸이다 be landlocked∥~가 눈에 들어왔다 [보였다] We came in sight of land. / Land was within sight.∥그들은 2개월 만에 ~를 밟았다 They went ashore for the first time in two months.

육질(肉質) 1 [살이 많은 성질] fleshiness. 2 [고기의 품질] the quality [grade] of meat.

육체(肉體) the body; the flesh; flesh and blood. ¶~와 정신 the body and the spirit∥영혼과 ~의 갈등 a conflict between the spirit and the flesh∥그의 ~는 흙으로 돌아갔다 His body [flesh] returned to dust.
● **육체노동** physical [manual] labor. ¶~을 하다 do physical [manual] laborer / work with one's hands. **육체미** physical beauty; the beauty of the body. ¶그녀는 ~의 소유자이다 She has a well-proportioned figure [body].

육체적(肉體的) physical; bodily. ¶~인 고통 bodily [physical] pain∥~인 쾌락 pleasures of the flesh / sensual pleasure∥~ 충동 the body urge.

육촌(六寸) [재종(再從)] a second [secondary] cousin; [친등] the sixth degree of consanguinity.

육친(肉親) [혈족 관계의 사람] a blood relative [relation]; (가족) one's people. ¶~의 정 love for one's (blood) relations∥그는 ~에게 부터도 버림을 받았다 He has been given up by his own family [people].

육탄(肉彈) a human bullet [bomb].
● **육탄전**(─戰) a battle in which man hurl [fling] themselves at the enemy; a hand-to-hand struggle.

육포(肉脯) a slice of dried meat [beef]; jerked meat; jerk.

육풍(陸風) [지] a land wind [breeze].

육필(肉筆) one's own handwriting; an autograph. ¶아버지의 ~ 유서 a will in my father's own handwriting / my father's auto-

육해공군 graph[holograph] will // 추사의 ~ 병풍 a folding screen painted by Chusa himself[in Chusa's own hand].

육해공군(陸海空軍) land, sea and air forces; the army, navy and air forces; the armed forces[services].

육해군(陸海軍) the army and navy; military and naval forces; the land and sea forces. ¶~의 확장 expansion of armaments on land and sea.

육혈포(六穴砲) a six-chambered revolver; a six-shooter.

육회(肉膾) a dish of minced[sliced] beef.

윤(潤) gloss; luster. ⇨˝윤기(潤氣)¶이 돌은 진주 같은 ~이 난다 This stone has a pearly luster. // 이 책상은 ~이 잘 난다 This table has a good polish.

윤간(輪姦) multiple rape (of a girl by teenagers); gang rape. **윤간하다** commit gang rape; rape[violate] (a girl) by turns.

윤곽(輪廓) 1 [겉모습] outline; contours (of a human body); profile (of a face). ¶얼굴의 ~ the contour of one's face // ~이 뚜렷한 얼굴 clear cut[well-defined] features / 고층 빌딩이 하늘에 그리는 ~ the outline of tall buildings against the sky / a skyline formed by tall buildings // 인체[언덕]의 ~을 그리다 draw the contour of a body[hill] // 나는 그 사람의 ~밖에 보지 못했다 I only saw the man's figure in silhouette. 2 [개략] an outline; a rough[general] idea. ¶~을 파악하다 grasp the general idea[outline] (of) / get a picture (of) // 기획의 ~을 말하다 outline [give an outline of] a plan.

윤기(潤氣) gloss; luster[(영) lustre]; brightness; glaze; polish; shine; brilliance(보석 등의). ¶~가 있는 lustrous // ~가 흐르는 검은 머리 glossy black hair // ~가 없다 be lusterless [dry / dull / dim / dingy] // 저 말은 털에 ~가 흐른다 That horse has a glossy coat. / 그는 항상 얼굴에 ~가 흐른다 He always has a bright complexion.

윤나다(潤-) be glossy; be lustrous; be bright; be polished. ¶윤나는 종이 glossy paper // 잘 문지르면 마루가 윤난다 The floor gets a polish from good rubbing. / Good rubbing gives a polish to the floor.

윤내다(潤-) gloss; glaze; polish up; bring out the luster. ¶윤내는 약 polishing wax // 보석을 갈아서 ~ polish a jewel to bring out the shine[its luster] // 종이[천]에 ~ calender paper[cloth].

윤년(閏年) a leap year; a bissextile[an intercalary] year. ¶~은 4년마다 든다 A leap year occurs[comes] every four years.

윤달(閏-) a leap month; a bissextile[an intercalary] month (in the lunar calendar).

윤락(淪落) ruin; fall; corruption. **윤락하다** be ruined; go to the bad; be corrupted; ruin oneself (by dissipation).
● **윤락가** a red-light district; gay quarters; whoredom; a brothel. **윤락 여성** a ruined [fallen] woman; a delinquent girl.

윤리(倫理) ethics; morals; a code of conduct. ¶정치 ~ morality in politics // 변호사가 의뢰인에 관한 정보를 흘리는 것은 ~에 반한다 It is not ethical for a lawyer to reveal information about his clients. // 그것은 의사의 ~에 어긋나는 일이 아닐까 Isn't it an offense against medical ethics?

● **윤리학** ethics; moral philosophy[science]. **윤리학자** an ethicist; a moral philosopher.

윤리적(倫理的) ethic(al); moral. ¶~인 행위 a moral act // 내게 ~인 책임은 있을지 모르나 법률적인 책임은 없다 Though I may be morally at fault, I am not legally responsible.

윤무(輪舞) a round dance. ⇨˝원무1

윤번(輪番) turn; rotation. ¶~으로 alternately / in turn / by turns / by [in] rotation // ~으로 망을 보다 keep watch by turns[alternately / in turn]. **윤번하다** take turns (at driving) in rotation; rotate.
● **윤번제** a rotation system. ¶~로 의장이 되다 take turns as chairman // 당번은 ~이다 We are on duty by[in] rotation.

윤색(潤色) embellishment; coloring. **윤색하다** embellish; color. ¶이야기를 ~ embellish one's story. → ¶많이 윤색된 이야기 a colorful narrative.

윤생(輪生) [식] verticil; verticillation. **윤생하다** leaf in verticil.

윤일(閏日) a leap day.

윤작(輪作) [농] crop rotation; rotation of crops. **윤작하다** rotate crops. ¶그들은 토마토와 밀을 윤작하고 있다 They rotate tomatoes with wheat.

윤전(輪轉) rotation; revolving. **윤전하다** rotate; revolve; turn round.
● **윤전기** a rotary press[machine]. ¶초고속도 ~ a super-high speed rotary press.

윤창(輪唱) [음] a troll. ⇨˝돌림 노래

윤택(潤澤) 1 [광택] (a) gloss; (a) luster. **윤택하다** (서술적) glossy; shiny. 2 [풍부] abundance; richness; [유복] affluence; wealth. **윤택하다** abundant; ample; affluent; rich; well-to-do. ¶생활이 그다지 윤택하지 않은 사람 a man of limited means of support // 윤택하게 richly / abundantly / in affluence // 윤택해지다 be made rich / become [be made] prosperous // 그들은 윤택한 사회에서 자랐다 They were brought up in an affluent society. // 아파트를 여러 채 세 주고 있어 그는 윤택한 생활을 하고 있다 He lives comfortably since he owns a number of apartment house that he rents out. // 수출의 증가로 서민의 호주머니도 윤택해질 것이다 The increase of exports will enrich[benefit] ordinary people as well.

윤허(允許) royal sanction[grant / permission]. ¶~를 바라다 ask for[submit (a matter) for] royal sanction. **윤허하다** be pleased to give sanction (to); grant (royal) sanction.

윤형(輪形) [바퀴 같은 모양] a circle; a ring (shape). ¶~의 ring(-shaped) / wheel-shaped / round / circular.

윤화(輪禍) a traffic[an automobile] accident. ¶~를 입다 meet with a traffic accident // 그는 ~로 죽었다 He was killed in a traffic accident.

윤활(潤滑) [관형어적]. **윤활하다** lubricous; smooth; lubricative.
● **윤활유** lubricating oil; lubricant; (미) lube (oil). **윤활제 / 윤활액** a lubricant.

윤회(輪廻) 1 [차례로 돌아감] rotation; constant mutation. **윤회하다** rotate; mutate constantly. 2 [불] samsara; metempsychosis; transmigration (of souls); cycle of life. **윤회하다** transmigrate.

●윤회설 doctrine of transmigration of souls; transmigrationism.
율(律) **1** [법규] a law; a regulation; [계율] (Buddhist) commandments. ¶인과~ the law of causality // 불문~ an unwritten law. **2** [음률] (a) rhythm; meter.
-율(率) (a) ratio; proportion; rate. ¶백분~ (a) percentage // 출산~ a birthrate.
율동(律動) (a) rhythm; (a) rhythmic movement.
● 율동 체조 rhythmic gymnastics.
율동적(律動的) rhythmic; rhythmical. ¶~으로 rhythmically // ~인 발걸음 소리 rhythmical footsteps.
율령(律令) a statute; a mandate; a law; an ordinance.
율무(식) Job's-tear; tear-grass; adlay.
율법(律法) [법률] (the) law; [신이 내린 규범] commandments; [계율] religious precepts.
융(絨) (피륙의 하나) cotton flannel.
융기(隆起) **1** [돌기] (a) protuberance; a sharp rise. 융기하다 rise. **2** [지] (an) upheaval; an uplift. ¶지층의 ~ an uplift of strata. 융기하다 rise up; upheave; uplift.
● 융기 해안 an uplifted coast.
융단(絨緞) a carpet; a rug; [집합적] carpeting; [작은 것] a scatter[(미) throw] rug. ¶페르시아 ~ a Persian rug // 마루에 ~을 깔다 carpet the floor / lay[put down] a carpet [rug] on the floor // 온 마루에 ~이 깔려 있다 The room has wall-to-wall carpeting.
● 융단 폭격 carpet bombing.
융모(絨毛) [생] [식] a villus. ⇨융털
융비술(隆鼻術) plastic surgery of the nose; rhinoplasty.
융성(隆盛) prosperity. ¶국운(國運)의 ~ national prosperity. 융성하다 prospering; flourishing; thriving. ¶융성해지다 prosper / grow prosperous / thrive // 가운(家運)이 융성해지고 있다 The fortunes of the family are looking up. // 이 지방에서는 제철업이 ~ The iron industry is prospering in this district.
융숭하다(隆崇-) cordial; hospitable. ¶융숭한 대접 a cordial[warm / hospitable] reception // 우리는 융숭한 대접을 받았다 We were warmly[hospitably] received. 융숭히 cordially; hospitably. ¶~ 대접하다 entertain (a person) cordially.
융자(融資) [자금을 융통하기] financing; [자금의 대출] lend; [융통되는 자금] a fund. ¶단기 ~ a short(-term) loan / a call loan(은행 간의 요구불) // 은행은 그 회사에 대한 ~를 중단했다 The bank cut off its financing to the firm.
융자하다 finance; furnish (a company) with funds; [대출하다] lend; loan (a person three million won). ¶인천 은행은 그 회사에 5억 원을 융자했다 The Incheon Bank provided 500,000,000 won to the company. // 나는 은행에서 주택 자금을 융자받았다 I obtained a housing[building] loan from the bank. / I borrowed money from the bank to build a house.
● 융자금 a loan.
융점(融點) a melting point. ⇨융해점(⇨융해점)
융털(융단의 보풀) pile; [생] [식] a villus (pl. -li).
융통(融通) [돌려씀] borrowing. ¶돈의 ~이 되지 않는다 I am having a hard time raising the money. 융통하다 [돌려쓰다] borrow. ¶내게 10만 원 융통해 줄 수 없겠습니까 Could you accommodate me with a loan of 100,000 won? / Could you lend me 100,000 won? // 돈을 조금 융통해 주십시오 Please lend[(미) loan] me a little money. // 건축 자금은 내가 융통해 주지 I will finance the construction of the building.
● 융통성 adaptability; elasticity; flexibility. ¶~이 있는 adaptable / elastic / flexible // ~이 없는 unadaptable / inelastic / inflexible // 그는 ~이 없다 He lacks flexibility. / He's incapable of adapting to changing circumstances. // 좀 더 ~이 있는 규칙을 만들자 Let's make the rules a little more elastic [flexible]. 융통 어음 an accommodation bill [draft]; a negotiable paper.
융합(融合) fusion; [조화] harmony. ¶핵 ~ nuclear fusion // 민족의 ~ a blending of races // 두 나라의 ~은 무척 어렵다 Harmony between the two nations is hard to bring about. 융합하다 fuse[blend] into one; merge; unite; become merged (with); [융화하다] harmonize. ¶앵글로·색슨 어와 노르만·프랑스 어가 융합해서 초기 근대 영어가 되었다 Anglo-saxon and Norman French merged in Early Modern English. ➔¶민중의 분노와 불만이 융합되어 폭동이 일어났다 The anger and discontent of the people fused[united] and resulted in a riot.
융해(融解) [물] fusion; melting; dissolution; liquefaction. 융해하다 fuse; melt; dissolve; liquefy; thaw. ¶융해한 금속 metals in fusion // 이 금속은 고온에서 융해한다 This metal melts[liquefies] at high temperatures.
● 융해열 the heat of fusion. 융해점 a melting point. ⇨녹는점
융화(融化) [화] deliquescence. 융화하다 deliquesce; soften.
융화(融和) [조화] harmony; [화해] reconciliation; [통일] integration. ¶인근 국가들과 ~를 유지해 나가는 것이 중요하다 It is important to maintain harmonious relations with neighboring countries. // 두 파 간의 ~가 마침내 이루어졌다 The two factions were finally reconciled. 융화하다 [조화하다] harmonize [get along] with; [화목하다] be melted together; [융해하다] be reconciled (with). ¶국제 정세는 융화하는 방향으로 움직이고 있다 International affairs are moving toward greater harmony. // 그는 누구와도 쉽게 융화한다 He makes[becomes] friends with anyone easily. ➔¶그들의 사고방식은 새로운 시대 풍조와 융화되고 있다 Their ideas are in harmony with new trends.
윷 **1** [네 쪽의 나무로 만든 놀이감] a *yut*; the four sticks used in playing *yut*. **2** [끗수] 4 points made by throwing a *yut* so that all four faces come up.
윷놀이 a *yunnori*; a game of *yut*. 윷놀이하다 play *yut*.
윷판 [말판] a *yut* board; [윷 노는 자리] the scene of a *yut* game.
으깨다 [부수다] crush (up / down); grind (down) [갈아서]; [짓이기다] mash; squash. ¶(서양 요리의) 으깬 감자 mashed potatoes // 포도주를 만들기 위해 포도를 ~ crush grapes for wine // 감자를 ~ mash potatoes.
-으나 but; though; (whether ...) or; quite. ⇨-나 ¶좋~ 싫~ whether you like it or not // 크나 작~ regardless of its size // 있~ 없~ whether there is[was] or not // 넓~ 넓은 바

다 a sea that is ever so wide.∥높~ 높은 산 such a[a really] high mountain / ever so high a mountain.∥깊~ 깊은 물 water ever so deep.∥나이는 젊~ though (he is) young / young as he is.∥가고 싶~ 시간이 없다 I'd like to come, but I haven't got the time.∥그는 나이는 많~ 아주 정정하다 He is quite vigorous although (he is) very old.∥그는 열의는 있~ 재주가 없다 He has enthusiasm but no talent.∥그는 돈은 많~ 불행하다 Though he is rich, he is unhappy.∥생각은 좋~ 실행하기가 곤란하다 A good plan, to be sure, but it is hardly practicable.

-으나 마나 [그러하거나 아니거나] as well ... as; whether ... or. ¶그건 있~ 마찬가지다 I am just as well without it as with it. / It doesn't matter whether I have it or not.∥우유 같은 건 있~ 마찬가지다 Milk is not enough to satisfy my hunger.

-으나마 though; however. ⇨ -나마 ¶변변치 않~ 내 차를 쓰십시오 You may use my car, such as it is.∥그는 돈은 있~ 불행하다 In spite of[For all / With all] his riches, he is unhappy.

-으니 since; because; and also; and; or. ⇨ -니 ¶이제 늦었~ 돌아가자 As[Since] it is (getting) late, let's go home.∥그게 발각되었~ 우리는 어쩌할 수도 없다 Since[Now that] it has been discovered, we can do nothing about it.∥돈을 잃었~ 나는 외국에 갈 생각을 버려야 한다 Since[As] I have lost my money, I have to give up the idea of going abroad.∥그 소식을 들으~ 마음이 놓인다 Now that I hear the news, I feel better.∥그해에 그는 과거에 급제하였으~, 그때 그의 나이 겨우 열여섯이었다 He passed the civil service examination in that year, when he was only sixteen years old.

-으니까 now that; since; because. ⇨ -니까 ¶자네의 의견이 받아들여졌~ 그것으로 만족해야 할 것이다 Since your proposal has been accepted, you should be more than satisfied.∥나이가 젊~ 그런 실수를 저지르는 것도 당연하다 Young as he is, it is natural for him to commit such a mistake.∥한 서너 달 더 남았~ 천천히 일해도 된다 As there are about three more months, we can take our time on the job.

-으니만큼 because (of); since; as; for. ⇨ -니 만큼 ¶그는 수많은 곤란을 겪어 왔~ 인생에 대한 많은 경험을 쌓았다 As he has seen [gone through] many difficulties, he knows a lot about life.

-으되 but; (even) though; if; and that. ⇨ -되 ¶나이는 먹었~ though he is old / old as he is.

으드득 1 [깨무는 소리] crunching; with a crunching sound. **으드득하다** crunch. ¶그는 밤을 으드득하고 깨물었다 He crunched chestnuts. 2 [이 가는 소리]. ¶말이 재갈을 물고 이를 ~ 갈았다 The horse champed at the bit. **으드득하다** grate[gnash / grind] one's teeth.

으드득거리다 [깨물다] crunch; crump; [이를 갈다] grind[grit / grate] the teeth.

으뜸 1 the first (place); number one; No. 1; [최고·최상] the head; the best; the top. ¶그녀는 항상 반에서 ~이었다 She was always at the top of her class. 2 [기본·근본] the root; the basis (*pl.* bases); the foundation. ¶건강은 인간의 행복의 ~이다 Health is the foundation of human happiness.
●**으뜸음** [음] a tonic; a keynote.

으뜸가다 be at the head (of); occupy the first place; stand[rank] first (among); be top. ¶당대에 으뜸가는 피아니스트 the greatest pianist of our time.∥그녀는 학교에서 으뜸가는 인기를 얻고 있다 She is the most popular girl at school.∥이 나라 국민의 근면함은 세계에서 으뜸간다 The diligence of the people of this nation stands out above others.∥그들의 업적은 세계에서 으뜸가는 것이다 Their achievements are by far the most outstanding[remarkable] in the world.

-으라 ⇨ -라² ¶많이 먹~ Take as much as you wish. / Help yourself freely.∥신의 은총이 있~ May God bless you!

-으라고 ⇨ -라고 ¶그에게 앉~ 해라 Tell him to sit down.∥그녀에게 옷을 입~ 해라 Tell her to put on her clothes.

-으라는 ⇨ -라는 ¶내가 받은 명령은 그 자리에 머물러 있~ 것이었다 The orders given to me were to stay where I was.∥그 물은 식사를 마친 후 손을 씻~ 것이었다 The water was to wash your hands after you'll finished your dinner.

-으라니 ⇨ -라니
-으라니까 ⇨ -라니까
-으라든지 or; whether[either] ... or. ⇨ -라든지
-으라면 ⇨ -라면²
-으락 ⇨ -락 ¶그는 그것을 보자 얼굴이 붉~푸르락했다 His color came and went[He was alternately flushed and pale] at the spectacle.

-으란 ⇨ -란 ¶네게 그 편지를 읽~ 말이 아니었다 I didn't mean ((미국 구어) for) you to read the letter.

-으람 ⇨ -람¹
-으래 they say; I hear. ⇨ -래
-으래서 ⇨ -래서
-으래서야 ⇨ -래서야
-으랴 ⇨ -랴 ¶어찌 내가 그런 일을 할 수 있~ How on earth[ever] can I do such a thing?∥어떻게 그것이 사실일 수 있~ How can it have been true?∥그가 설마 어제 집에 있었~ He cannot have been at home yesterday.∥내가 어찌 알고 있~ How do[should] I know?∥만사가 잘되어 갈지 누가 알 수 있~ Who knows but that everything will come out right?∥우리가 어찌 불만을 품지 않을 수가 있~ How is it possible but that we should be discontented?

-으러 for the purpose of. ⇨ -러 ¶사람을 찾~가다 go looking[hunting] for a person.∥그는 늘 점심을 먹~ 집에 간다 He always goes home for lunch.

으레 1 [당연히] (as a matter) of course; to be sure; naturally; without question; no doubt. ¶그것은 ~ 우리가 할 일이다 Needless to say it is our duty to do so.∥~ 이렇게 되는 법이다 This is quite in the nature of things.∥빚진 것은 ~ 갚아야 한다 One ought to pay what one owes.∥자식은 ~ 부모를 사랑해야 한다 It is natural for a child to love its parents.∥저런 인간은 ~ 처벌을 받아야 한다 Such a person well deserves the punishment.
2 [언제나] always; usually; [변함없이] invariably; [규칙적으로] regularly. ¶~ …하

다 be in the habit of (doing) / make it a rule to (do) // 나는 식전에는 ~ 산책한다 I make it a rule to take a walk before breakfast. // 그 일에는 ~ 위험이 따른다 It is invariably attended by danger. // 그들은 만나기만 하면 ~ 싸운다 They never meet without quarreling. / They quarrel whenever they meet. // 네가 한 마디 하면 그는 ~ 말대꾸를 한다 If you say anything to him, he always talks back.

-으려고 with the intention of (doing). ⇨ˉ-려고 ¶지위를 얻~ 하다 try for a position // 석 달 더 있~ 한다 I intend [am prepared] to stay another 3 months. // 그는 곤충을 잡~ 나무에 올라갔다 In trying [in an effort] to catch the insect, he climbed up the tree. // 그는 늦지 않~ 서둘렀다 He hurried up so as not to [so that he wouldn't] be late.

-으려기에 on account of; owing to; as. ⇨ˉ-려기에

-으려나 I wonder (if, whether, what, who, where, when, etc.). ⇨ˉ-려나

-으려네 I will (do); I intend [mean / purpose] to (do). ⇨ˉ-려네

-으려느냐 ⇨ˉ-려느냐

-으려는 ⇨ˉ-려는

-으려는가 ⇨ˉ-려는가

-으려는데 ⇨ˉ-려는데 ¶그가 듣지도 않~ 어떻게 설복시킬 수 있겠나 How can I convince him when he will not listen?

-으려니 ⇨ˉ-려니

-으려니와 not only ... but; as well as; and. ⇨ˉ-려니와

-으려다가 ⇨ˉ-려다가

-으려면 ⇨ˉ-려면 ¶국수를 먹~ 젓가락이 있어야 한다 You need chopsticks to eat noodles.

-으려무나 be pleased to ...; may. ⇨ˉ-려무나

-으려야 ⇨ˉ-려야 ¶웃지 않~ 않을 수 없었다 I could not help laughing. / I could not but laugh. // 잊~ 잊을 수 없다 I shall never forget.

-으려오 (I) will (do); intend to (do). ⇨ˉ-려오

-으련다 ⇨ˉ-련다

-으련마는 ⇨ˉ-련마는 ¶갈 수만 있다면 좋~ If I could go, I should be glad.

-으렵니까 ⇨ˉ-렵니까 ¶함께 영화 구경 가시지 않~ Won't you go to the movies with me?

-으렵니다 ⇨ˉ-렵니다

-으렷다 be sure [bound / agreed] to happen. ⇨ˉ-렷다 ¶너는 그 일을 알고 있~ You must be aware of it. / You know it, don't you?

으례 →으레

으로 [수단·방법] by; through; with; in; [원료·재료] out of; [방향] to; into; [원인·동기·이유] for; because; with; [지위·신분] as; [시간·경과] by. ⇨ˉ-로 ¶힘~ by sheer strength / by (brute) force // 금력~ through the power of money // 밤낮~ by day and (by) night / day and night // 진흙~ 더러워진 구두 shoes covered with mud // 역~ 가는 도중에 On the way to the station // 석탄~ 만들다 make (a thing) out of coal // 펜~ 쓰다 write with a pen // 건물 안~ 들어가다 go into a building // 사전~ 그 단어를 찾아봐요 Look up the word in a dictionary. // 스위스는 그 경치의 아름다움~ 유명하다 Switzerland is famous for its scenic beauty. // 우천~ 모임이 연기되었다 The meeting was postponed because of [on account of / owing to] rain. // 저분을 스승~ 받들고 있습니다 I look up to him as my teacher. / I consider him my teacher.

으로나 ⇨ˉ-로나 ¶어느 면~ in all aspects // 힘 ~ 속력~ in strength and [or] in speed.

으로는 ⇨ˉ-로는 ¶학력~ 내가 그보다 낫다 As for [to] academic background, I am ahead of him. // 이것~ 이 책을 살 수 없다 This is not enough for [to buy] the book. // 손해의 변상만 ~ 너를 놓아줄 수 없다 Merely paying for the damage won't absolve you. // 다소의 비난 ~ 그는 끄떡도 안 한다 Just a little criticism won't bother him in the least. // 확실치는 않지만, 소문~ 그가 길에서 큰돈을 주웠다고 한다 I don't know for certain, but they say he found a large amount of money on the road.

으로부터 from; out of. ⇨ˉ-로부터 ¶10미터 떨어진 곳~ from a distance to ten meters // ···~ 독립하다 become independent of ... // 계단 [지붕] ~ 떨어지다 fall off the staircase [roof] // 자네 이야기를 송 군~ 들었다 I heard of you through [from] Mr. Song.

으로서 as; for; from; out of. ⇨ˉ-로서 ¶여흥~ by way of entertainment // 선물에 대한 보답 ~ in return for a present // 그것은 장관~ 하신 말씀입니까 Did you say so in your capacity as minister? // 그는 겨우 15세인데 그 나이의 소년~ 매우 침착한 것이 놀랍다 Considering that he is only fifteen, I marvel at his poise.

으로써 with; by (means of). ¶사상을 행동~ 나타내다 express an idea in terms of action.

으르다 [위협하다] menace; intimidate; threaten; blackmail; browbeat; scare; bully; (구어) bulldoze. ¶으르고 달래고 하여 what with threats and (what with) entreaties // 을러서 자백시키다 frighten [scare] (a person) into confession // 그는 나에게 권총을 들이대며 을렀다 He threatened me with a pistol. // 그는 나를 을러서 정보를 빼냈다 He blackmailed me into giving information.

으르렁 [짐승이 성내어 우는 소리] snarl; growl; roar.

으르렁거리다 1 [짐승이 성내어 울부짖다] snarl; growl; roar. ¶개가 낯선 사람을 보고 으르렁거렸다 The dog growled [snarled] at a stranger. // 이리가 낮게 으르렁거렸다 The wolf growled low [gave a low growl]. 2 [다투다] quarrel [squabble] (with); brawl; feud (with); bicker. ¶서로 으르렁거리며 살아가다 lead a cat-and-dog life // 그 형제는 항상 서로 으르렁거리고 있다 The brothers are always quarreling [squabbling] with each other. / The brothers are always at each other's throats.

으름장 a threat; a menace; a scare; [위협하는 말] threatening remarks. ¶아이들도 영리해져서 이제 ~을 놓아도 먹혀들지 않는다 The children are too smart now for threats to work. // 그는 내게 ~을 놓았다 He uttered threats against me.

-으리다 I will. ⇨ˉ-리다 ¶내가 읽~ I'll be glad to read it.

-으리라 may [might] (be / do); I will. ⇨ˉ-리라 ¶그는 오늘 오지 않~ I don't think he will come today. // 두 번 다시 잡히지 않~ I will not be caught again.

-으리만큼 enough to (do); so ... that. ⇨ˉ-리만큼 ¶눈앞의 내 손이 보이지 않~ 어둡다 It is so dark that I can't see my hand before me. // 이 책은 여섯 살 먹은 아이도 읽을 수 있~ 쉽다 This book is easy enough for a six-year-old child to read.

-으리요 ⇨ -리요

으리으리하다 grand; stately; majestic; magnificent; imposing. ¶으리으리한 대법원 건물 the imposing building of the Supreme Court // 으리으리한 대저택 an imposing [magnificent] mansion // 으리으리한 생활을 하다 live like a prince [lord] / live in fine [grand] style // 그 방은 으리으리하게 장식되어 있었다 The room was gorgeously decorated.

-으마 I will gladly (do). ⇨ -마

-으며 and; or; while; as. ⇨ -며 ¶귀로는 들 눈으로는 본다 We hear with our ears, and see with our eyes.

-으면 if; when; whenever. ⇨ -면 ¶요즘은 젊은이들을 말할 것 같으(as for) the young people of today / when it comes to today's young people // 말을 듣지 않으 과자를 주지 않을 테다 If you don't do as you're told I won't give you any cake. // 바로 입원했으 는 살았을지도 모른다 He might have been saved if he had been hospitalized at once. // 나는 더 돈이 있었으 하고 언제나 생각하고 있었다 I always wished I had more money. // 모두 준비가 되었으 출발하자 When everybody is ready, let's start. // 저의 집에도 좀 오셨으 합니다 I wish you would come and see us, too. / Won't you come and see us, too?

-으면서 while; as; though; but. ⇨ -면서 ¶웃으 말하다 speak with a smile // 음악을 들으 고향을 생각하다 think of home while listening to the music // 그는 라디오를 들으 편지를 쓰고 있다 Half listening to the radio, he is writing a letter.

-으므로 on account of; owing to; as. ⇨ -므로 ¶돈이 없으 since I have no money // 날이 어두워지기 시작했으 as it was getting dark // 온갖 대비를 다 했으 우리는 성공할 것으로 안다 All precautions have been taken, so that we expect to succeed.

-으소서 please do. ⇨ -소서 ¶제 말씀을 들으 Pray listen to me.

으스대다 be arrogant [proud / overbearing]; swagger (about); square [perk up] one's shoulders; give oneself [put on] airs; assume a haughty attitude. ¶으스대며 걷다 swagger / strut / walk with an air // 재산 좀 있다고 으스대다 swagger about one's possession // 으스대는 꼴을 보고만 있지는 않겠다 I will not be lorded over.

으스러뜨리다 smash; crush; crack; break (in pieces). ¶호두를 으스러뜨리다 crack a nut // 이 기계는 목재를 으스러뜨려서 펄프로 만든다 This machine crushes (wooden) logs into pulp.

으스러지다 be crushed to pieces; be grazed. ⇨ 아스러지다

으스름하다 [침침하고 흐릿하다] hazy; misty; clouded; vague. ¶으스름한 달 a clouded [dim / hazy] moon.

으스스 shivering with cold; with one's blood running cold. ¶~ 추워지다 feel a chill / feel chilly / shiver with cold // ~ 추워서 일찍 잤다 I felt cold and shivery, (and) so I went to bed early. **으스스하다** [춥다] chill; chilly; rather cold; coldish; [무시무시하다] ghastly; spooky; weird; uncanny. ¶으스스한 날씨 chilly weather // 으스스한 장소 a spooky place // 으스스한 정적 an eerie stillness // 오늘 아침은 으스스했다 It was shivering(ly) this morning. // 여기는 귀신이라도 나올 것 같아서 ~ I am afraid. Maybe there are ghosts here. // 그 일을 생각만 해도 몸이 ~ It chills my blood to think of it.

으슥하다 retired (and quiet); sequestered; secluded; covert; lonely; deep. ¶으슥한 구석 a covert nook // 으슥한 산길 a remote [lonely] mountain path [trail] // 으슥한 숲 속에서 in the gloom [depths] of a forest // 밤이 으슥해졌다 The night was getting on [well advanced].

으슬으슬 shivering. ¶~ 춥다 feel chilly / feel [have] a chill (with) // 오늘은 ~ 춥다 The weather is chilly today. **으슬으슬하다** chilly; somewhat cold. ¶으슬으슬한 날씨 chilly weather // 몸이 ~. 열이 상당히 있는 것 같다 I have got the shakes. I'm afraid I have a high fever.

으슴푸레하다 hazy; dim; misty; clouded; vague. ¶으슴푸레한 달빛 아래서 in the misty moonlight // 달빛이 ~ The moon shines dimly. // 복도에 등불이 으슴푸레하게 비치고 있었다 A light shone dimly in the passage.

으쓱[1] [추위·무서움으로 몸이 움츠러드는 모양] with a shudder. **으쓱하다** [춥다] cold; chilly; [무섭다] frightful; grim; grisly; horrible; chilling; blood-curdling; hair-raising.

으쓱[2] 1 [어깨를 들어 올리는 모양] with a shrug (of one's shoulders). **으쓱하다** perk up one's shoulders. ⇨ 으쓱거리다1 2 [우쭐하는 모양]. **으쓱하다** be conceited. ⇨ 으쓱거리다2

으쓱거리다 1 [어깨를] perk up one's shoulders. ¶그는 내 질문에 대답은 않고 어깨를 으쓱였을 뿐이다 He just shrugged his shoulders without answering my question. // 내가 추궁해도 그는 어깨를 으쓱거렸을 뿐이다 When I questioned him, he only shrugged. 2 [우쭐대다] be conceited; be vain; fancy oneself; flatter oneself; be puffed up. ¶톰은 자기 반에서 머리가 가장 좋다고 으쓱거리고 있다 Tom flatters himself that he is the most intelligent boy in his class. // 그녀는 제 딴에는 아름답다고 으쓱거리고 있다 She fancies herself (to be) beautiful.

으악 [놀래 줄 때 지르는 소리] Boo; Bo; Boh; [놀랐을 때 지르는 소리] Ugh; Wow; Gee; [갑자기 토하는 소리] Puke!; with a puke. ¶~ 소리를 지르다 shriek / scream // ~ 놀랐다 Wow! You gave me a start.

윽박지르다 put down with threats; treat with a high hand; browbeat [bully] (a person into [out of]). ¶제안을 승낙하도록 ~ browbeat (a person) into accepting a proposal // 토론에서 그를 윽박질렀다 I drove him into a corner in argument [discussion].

은 1 [주제 표시·보편 속성]. ¶달~ 지구의 위성이다 The moon is a satellite of the earth. // 사람~ 죽기 마련이다 Man is mortal. 2 [대조·배타]. ¶그는 술~ 마시지만 담배는 피우지 않는다 He drinks but doesn't smoke. 3 [강조]. ¶가끔~ 아들과 함께 테니스도 친다 I have an occasional game of tennis [Sometimes I play tennis] with my son.

-은 1 [형용사 어간에] ... that [which / who] is. ¶작~ 나무 a tree that is little / a little tree // 매우 낡~ 모자 a hat which is very old / a very old hat. 2 [동사 어간에] ... that [which / who] (one) did [has done]. ¶내가 어제 읽~ 책 the book that I read yesterday // 잘 닦~ 구두 well-polished shoes // 보물을 묻~ 곳 the place where the treasure is buried // 하고 싶~ 사람은 누구나 신청할 수 있다 Any one who chooses can apply.

은(銀) [금속 원소] silver(기호 Ag). ¶순~ fine [pure / refined] silver // ~(제)의 silver // ~같은 silvery // ~을 입힌 silver-plated // ~을 **입히다** silver / plate (a thing) with silver // 이 접시는 ~제이다 This plate is (made of) silver.

은거(隱居) retirement (from the active handling of business[family] affairs); a secluded life. **은거하다** retire (from the handling of practical affairs); go into[live in] seclusion; retire from the world. ¶산중에 ~ retire to hermitage in the mountain // 그는 정계에서 은퇴하여 고향에 은거했다 He retired from politics to a secluded life in his hometown.

은공(恩功) a favor and (meritorious) service; an obligation. ¶부모의 ~ parental love // 스승의 ~ one's debt to one's teacher // ~을 **잊다** lose one's gratitude.

은광(銀鑛) 1 [은을 채굴하는 광산] a silver mine. 2 [은이 들어 있는 광석] silver ore.

은괴(銀塊) [막대 모양의 은 덩어리] a silver ingot[bar]; bar silver; 《집합적》 silver bullion.

은그릇(銀-) 《집합적》 silver; 《미》 silverware.

은근하다(慇懃-) 1 [정중하다] gentle; polite; courteous; civil. ¶은근한 태도 a polite[courteous] manner // 은근한 말씨 polite language. **은근히** politely; courteously; with much courtesy.
2 [은밀하다] quiet; inward; implicit; suggestive; indirect; secret; private. ¶은근한 미소 a quiet smile // 은근한 협박 a veiled threat. **은근히** quietly; in one's heart; indirectly; secretly; privately; in confidence[private]. ¶~ 걱정하다 feel anxious in one's heart[inwardly] // (남의 마음을) ~ 떠보다 beat about the bush / sound (a person about) // ~ 비추다 hint (at something) / drop a hint / suggest // 네가 오기를 ~ 기다리고 있었다 I have been expecting you. // 나는 그를 ~ 비꼬아 주었다 I had a quiet dig at him. // 그 일로 ~ 걱정했습니다 I felt anxious about it in my heart.
3 [그윽하다] soft; gentle; mild; (색깔 등이) sober; sedate; quiet; subdued. ¶은근한 색깔 a sober[sedate / quiet / soft] color / a subdued color(엷은) // 은근한 불로 끓이다 stew / cook over a slow fire / simmer. **은근히** softly; gently; mildly; soberly.
4 [다정하다] intimate. ¶은근한 사이다 have an intimate relationship with (a person) // 그는 그 여자와 은근한 사이다 He has a clandestine relationship with that woman. **은근히** intimately.

은닉(隱匿) concealment; secretion. ¶장물 ~ 죄 secretion of stolen goods // 그는 장물 ~ 죄로 기소되었다 He was charged with sheltering[harboring] a criminal. **은닉하다** conceal; hide; secrete; shelter; harbor (a criminal). ¶ 범인을 ~ harbor a culprit.
● **은닉처** a hiding place.

은덕(恩德) a favor, a benefit; favor and indebtedness. ¶~을 **베풀다** confer a benefit (upon) // ~을 **입다** receive benefits // 기도를 했더니 ~이 있었다 God has answered my prayers. / My prayers have been answered.

-은데 and; but; when; while. ⇨ -ㄴ데 ¶아버지는 키가 작~ 어머니는 크다 My mother is tall, while my father is short.

은도금(銀鍍金) silver plating; silvering. **은도금하다** plate with silver; silver. ¶은도금한 silver-plated / silver gilt.

은둔(隱遁) retirement[seclusion] (from the world); sequestration; withdrawal from ordinary life. **은둔하다** retire form the world; live in retirement[seclusion]; leave[떠나다] / renounce the world; seclude[isolate] oneself from society.
● **은둔 생활** a sequestered[retired] life, a life in seclusion. ¶그는 ~을 하고 있다 He leads a secluded life. / He lives in a secluded place. **은둔자** a recluse; a hermit. **은둔처** a place of seclusion; a hermitage; a retreat.

-은들 granted that; though; even though[if]. ⇨ -ㄴ들 ¶칭찬을 많이 받~ 무슨 소용이 있으랴 So he received much praise—what good is it?

은딱지(銀-) a silver case.

은막(銀幕) 1 [영사막] a (projection) screen. 2 [영화계] the film[cinema] world; filmdom; the movies.

은메달(銀-) a silver medal.

은밀하다(隱密-) covert; secret; private; confidential; privy. **은밀히** covertly; secretly; privately; confidentially; in confidence[private / secret]. ¶~ 해결하다 settle (a matter) privately[out of court] // ~ 이야기하다 tell confidentially // ~ 만나기를 요청하다 ask a private interview (with a person) // ~ 말씀드릴 것이 있습니다 I should like to speak to you confidentially[in private]. // 이건 너에게만 ~ 하는 이야기야 This is for your private ear.

은박(銀箔) silver foil[leaf] (▶ leaf는 보통 foil 보다 얇음); beaten silver.
● **은박지** aluminum[《영》 aluminium] foil; tinfoil. ¶영계를 ~에 싸서 굽다 bake chicken wrapped in foil[tinfoil].

은반(銀盤) 1 [은 쟁반] a silver plate. ¶~에 옥 구르는 소리 a tinkling[musical] voice. 2 [달] the (silvery) moon; [스케이트장] a skating [ice] rink. ¶~의 여왕 the queen on the ice.

은발(銀髮) silver(-gray) hair. ¶~의 silver-haired // ~의 노신사 an old gentleman with silvery hair.

은방울꽃(銀-) [식] a lily of the valley.

은배(銀杯) a silver cup.

은백색(銀白色) silver(y) white.

은분(銀粉) powdered silver; silver dust.

은붙이(銀-) 《집합적》 silverware.

은빛(銀-) silver; silveriness; silver color. ¶~의 silver-colored / silvery.

은사(恩師) the teacher one has studied under; one's former teacher.

은사(隱士) a retired scholar; a recluse.

은상(銀賞) a silver prize.

은색(銀色) silver. ⇨ 은빛

은세계(銀世界) a silver world; the (whole) landscape covered[blanketed] with snow; a vast snowy scene. ¶바깥은 온통 ~였다 The whole place was covered with[mantled in] snow.

은세공(銀細工) [은으로 장식품 등을 만듦] silverwork; [그 세공품] silverware. **은세공하다** work silver.

은수저(銀-) a silver spoon.

은신처(隱身處) [숨는 곳] a hiding place; (범죄인의) a hideout; [피난처] a refuge. ¶경찰은 범인의 ~를 찾아냈다 The police tracked

은신하다 (隱身-) hide[conceal] oneself; tuck oneself away (somewhere); [피신하다] take [seek] refuge[shelter].

은실 (銀-) silver thread[strand]; spun silver.

은어 (隱語) a secret language; [직업 용어] jargon; (특정 계급·직업인끼리의) cant; (도둑 등의) argot. ¶~로 **이야기하다** talk in secret language // 그들은 ~로 이야기하고 있었다 They were talking in the jargon of their trade.

은연중 (隱然中) tacitly; implicitly; by implication; indirectly; in a roundabout way. ¶친구를 ~에 돕다 help a friend on the quiet[on the "Q.T."] / ~ 사의를 비치다 hint at one's resignation // 그는 공직에서 은퇴했으나 아직도 정계에서 ~에 영향력을 행사하고 있다 Although retired from public office, he still exercises great influence behind the scenes in politics.

은유 (隱喩) (a) metaphor.
● 은유법 a metaphor.

은은하다 (隱隱-) 1 [어슴푸레하다] hazy; mist; [흐릿하다] dim; dusky. ¶은은한 향기 a subtle perfume // 안개 속에서 은은한 불빛을 보았다 I saw a dim light in the mist. 은은히 hazily; dimly; duskily. ¶라일락 꽃향기가 ~ 풍겼다 There was a faint smell[fragrance] of lilac. 2 [소리가 가늘다] dim; faint; vague; distant (to the ears). ¶은은한 포성의 distant booming of cannons. 은은히 faintly; vaguely. ¶종소리가 ~ 들려왔다 There came the dim sound of a bell to my ears.

은인 (恩人) a benefactor; a benefactress(여자); [후원자] a patron; a patroness(여자). ¶그녀는 나의 ~입니다 I owe her a great deal. / I am very much indebted to her. / 이분은 나의 생명의 ~입니다 This is the man who saved my life.

은자 (隱者) a hermit; a recluse; an anchorite; a solitary.

은잔 (銀盞) a silver (wine) cup.

은장도 (銀粧刀) a silver-decorated knife.

은전 (恩典) a special favor; a special privilege. ¶특별 ~으로 by special grace // ~을 입다 receive[be granted] a special favor // 학비 면제의 ~을 입다 receive a special tuition exemption.

은전 (銀錢) a silver coin.

은제 (銀製) ¶~의 (made of) silver // ~ 컵 a silver cup.

은종이 (銀-) silver paper; tinfoil.

은총 (恩寵) grace(신의); favor(사람의). ¶신의 ~으로 by divine favor / by the grace of God // ~을 잃다 lose (a person's) favor / fall into disfavor / fall from grace(신의) // 신의 ~을 빌다 pray for God's grace // 하느님의 ~이 당신에게 내리기를 God bless you! / 제가 구제된 것은 신의 ~이라고 생각합니다 I think what saved me was the grace of God.

은테 (銀-) a silver rim.
● 은테 안경 silver-rimmed glasses.

은퇴 (隱退) retirement (from active[public] life); seclusion (from the world). 은퇴하다 retire (from one's profession); seclude (oneself from the world). ¶은퇴한 정치가 a retired politician // 은퇴하여 시골에 가다 go into seclusion in the country / retire to the country // 은퇴해 있다 be in retirement / 정계에서 ~ retire from active politics[from the political world] // 그는 28세에 프로 테니스에서 은퇴한다고 공언했다 He announced his retirement from professional tennis at 28. / 그가 선수에서 은퇴한 것은 몇 살 때입니까 How old was he when he retired as an active player?
● 은퇴 경기 a farewell match.

은파 (銀波) the silvery waves; white waves.

은폐 (隱蔽) concealment; hiding; suppression; coverture; cover-up. 은폐하다 conceal; hide; cover (up); suppress; draw a veil (over); keep (a matter) secret[dark]. ¶사실을 ~ suppress[cover up] a fact / slur a fact over // 학교 당국은 사건의 진상을 은폐하려 했다 The school authorities tried to conceal[cover up] the facts[truth] about the case. / 그는 범죄를 은폐하기 위해 집에 불을 질렀다 He set fire to the house to cover up his crime.

은하 (銀河) the Milky Way; the Galaxy; (라) the Via Lactea. ¶~(계)의 galactic.
● 은하계 the galactic system. ¶~ 내 성운 a galactic nebula // 외 성운 an extragalactic nebula. 은하수 the Milky Way; the Galaxy.

은행 (銀行) a bank. ¶국립 ~ a national bank / 국책 ~ a national[state] policy bank // 발권 ~ a bank of issue // 보통 ~ an ordinary commercial bank // 상업 ~ a commercial bank // 수출입 ~ an export-import bank // 시중 ~ a city bank // 신탁 ~ a trust bank // 안구 ~ an eye bank // 예금 ~ a deposit money bank // 외환 ~ a foreign exchange bank // 저축 ~ a savings bank // 중앙 ~ the central bank // 지방 ~ a local[provincial] bank // 학교 ~ a school bank // 혈액 ~ a blood bank // ~에서 돈을 빌리다 get[take out] a loan at a bank / borrow money from a bank // ~에 많은 예금이 있다 have a big bank account / have a large sum of money in the bank // ~과 거래가 있다 have an account with a bank // ~에서 100만 원을 찾았다 I withdrew[drew out / took out] a million won from the bank. / ~에 1,000달러 예금했다 I deposited[placed / put] a thousand dollars in the bank. / I banked a thousand dollars.
● 은행권 a bank bill[(영) note]. 은행 예금 a bank deposit. 은행원 a bank clerk; (집합적) the staff of a bank. 은행 이자 bank interest [rate]. 은행장 the president of a bank. 은행 창구 bank windows.

은행 (銀杏) a ginkgo nut.
● 은행나무 a ginkgo[gingko] (tree).

은혜 (恩惠) a favor; a benefit; a blessing; an obligation; moral indebtedness; a boon(이익). ¶스승의 ~ one's debt to one's teacher / obligations[what] one owes to one's teacher // ~를 **입다** receive benefits[favors] / enjoy benevolent influence // ~를 **베풀다** favor / do (a person) a favor / bestow a favor on (a person) // ~를 **알다** be grateful (to a person / for a person's kindness) / have a sense of gratitude // ~를 **모르다** be ungrateful[thankless] // ~를 **잊다** be ungrateful // ~를 **갚다** repay[return] (a person's) kindness / repay an obligation // ~를 원수로 갚다 repay kindness with evil / bite the hand that feeds one // 내 아들은 그 여자에게 많은 ~를 입고 있다 My son owes that woman a great deal. // ~는 결코 잊지 않겠습니다 I will [(영) shall] never forget your kindness [what you have done for me]. // 그는 ~를 원수로 갚은 녀석이다 When you pat him, he snaps at you.

은혼식(銀婚式) a silver wedding (anniversary). ¶~을 올리다 celebrate (their) silver wedding.

은화(銀貨) a silver coin; white money.

은화식물(隱花植物) a cryptogam; a flowerless plant.

은회색(銀灰色) silver gray. ¶~의 silver-gray.

을 1 [타동사의 목적]. ¶신문을 ~ 보다 read [look at] the newspaper // 사람을 ~ 찾다 visit [find/look for] a person // 돈을 ~ 빼앗다 rob (a person) of his money // 컵에 물을 ~ 채우다 fill a glass with water // 돈을 ~ 원한다 I want money. // 나는 바다보다 산을 ~ 좋아한다 I like the mountains better than the sea.

2 [수동태의 목적]. ¶약점을 ~ 잡히다 have one's weakness seized [played] upon // 발목을 ~ 차이다 get a kick [get kicked] on the ankle // 물건을 ~ 빼앗기다 be robbed of a thing // 손목을 ~ 잡히다 be taken [seized] by the wrist.

3 [동작의 기점]. ¶[열차가] 역을 ~ 떠나다 leave [quit] the station // 서울을 ~ 떠나다 leave Seoul // 직장을 ~ 이탈하다 desert [quit] one's job / walk off one's job / (미) walk out on one's job.

4 [동작의 목적·방향]. ¶세계 일주 여행을 ~ 떠나다 set out on a round-the-world trip // 영화 구경을 ~ 가다 go to see a movie // 언제 시장을 ~ 갈 셈이냐 When will you go shopping?

5 [경과 장소]. ¶산을 ~ 넘다 go over [cross] a mountain // 하늘을 ~ 날다 fly (in) the sky.

6 [동안]. ¶달을 ~ 넘기지 않고 before the month is over // 사흘을 ~ 굶다 starve for three days // 두 시간을 ~ 자다 sleep (for) two hours // 하루 8시간을 ~ 일하다 work for eight hours a day.

7 [차례]. ¶수석을 ~ 하다 go first / rank first / 첨단을 ~ 가다 [걷다] be in the van (of the new era).

8 [동족 목적어]. ¶꿈을 ~ 꾸다 dream (a dream) // 숨을 ~ 쉬다 breathe (a breath) // 잠을 ~ 자다 sleep (a sleep).

9 [구이적]. ¶마음을 ~ 먹다 have a mind (to) / make up one's mind // 앞장을 ~ 서다 lead (the van of) / stand at the head (of) / be in the lead / act as leader (to).

10 [관계]. ¶병을 ~ 구실로 under the pretext of illness // 결혼을 ~ 조건으로 with the condition that should unite in marriage / under the promise of marriage.

11 [생략·강조]. ¶하늘에는 영광~, 땅에는 평화를 Glory be in the heaven, and peace on earth! // 나에게 자유가 아니면 죽음을 ~ 달라 Give me liberty, or give me death.

-을 ⇨ ˉ-ㄹ ¶울고 있을 ~ 때가 아니다 This is no time for weeping.

을(乙) [제2] the second; B (급수의); [후자] the latter; (등급의) second grade; grade [class] B.

-을걸 I dare say; perhaps; probably. ⇨ ˉ-ㄹ걸 ¶네가 그것을 보았으면 좋았~ You should have seen it. / If only you could [If you could only] have seen it. // 이 세상에 태어나지 않았으면 좋았~ I wish I had never been born. //

그렇지는 않~ I am afraid not. / I should say not. // 내일은 아마도 날씨가 좋~ It will probably be fine tomorrow. // 그는 부상당했~ He may have been hurt.

-을게 ⇨ ˉ-ㄹ게

-을까 ⇨ ˉ-ㄹ까 ¶지금 몇 시나 되었~ I wonder what the time is now. // 내가 이것을 먹어도 괜찮~ Is it all right to eat this? // 도대체 그런 일이 있을 수 있~ How can that be, I wonder? // 그가 어떻게 해서 그것을 손에 넣었~ How did he get hold of it? // 누가 그런 일을 알고 있~ Who would know such a thing? // 늦지나 않~ I am afraid of being late. // 금년에도 또 실패하지 않~ I am afraid I shall fail again this year. // 내가 오래 살 수 있~ Shall I live long? // 전화번호를 가르쳐 주실 수 있~요 Will you kindly give me your phone number? // 우산을 빌려 주실 수 있~요 Would you lend me an umbrella?

-을까 보다 ˉ-ㄹ까 보다(⇨ˉ-ㄹ까) ¶책이나 읽~ I would rather read.

-을는지 if ...; whether ... (or not). ⇨ˉ-는지

-을라 ⇨ˉ-라 ¶서둘러라, 학교에 늦~ Hurry up, or you will be late for school.

-을라치면 when; whenever. ⇨ˉ-라치면

-을락 말락 barely; almost. ⇨ˉ-ㄹ락 말락 ¶당~ close to (the housetops) / (pass) by a (close) shave.

을러대다 threaten; menace; browbeat; (미) bulldoze. ¶을러대어 by threats / by intimidation // 죽인다고 [투옥한다고 / 체포한다고] ~ threaten (a person) with death [imprisonment / arrest] // 을러대어 승낙을 받다 threaten (a person) into compliance // 그는 경찰에 알리겠다고 을러댔다 He threatened to report the matter to the police.

을러메다 threaten. ⇨ˉ을러대다

을러방망이 threatening with one's fists.

-을망정 (even) though; although. ⇨ˉ-ㄹ망정 ¶늙었~ though he is old / old as he is // 죽~ 그 짓은 못하겠다 I would rather die than do it. // 굶어 죽~ 도둑질은 안 한다 I'd rather starve than steal. // 그녀는 나를 실망시켰~, 어머니로서 나는 희망을 버리지 않을 것이다 She disappointed me. However, as a mother I shall not give up hope. // 빌어먹~ 그에게 손을 벌리지는 않겠다 Even if I were brought to begging, I would never ask a favor of him.

-을밖에 cannot (choose) but (do). ⇨ˉ-ㄹ밖에 ¶그의 말이 하도 어이없으니 웃~ His remark is so absurd that I can't do anything but laugh [I can't help laughing].

-을뿐더러 not only [merely] ... but (also). ⇨ˉ-ㄹ뿐더러 ¶그것은 품질이 좋~ 가격도 싸다 It is both good and cheap.

-을세라 lest (should); for fear (that). ⇨ˉ-ㄹ세라

-을수록 the more [less] ..., the more [less]. ⇨ˉ-ㄹ수록

을씨년스럽다 1 [날씨 등이 스산하다] dreary; dismal; gloomy; [쓸쓸하다] (서술적) look miserable [shabby / wretched]. ¶을씨년스러운 날씨 gloomy weather // 옷이 너절해서 을씨년스럽게 보이다 look wretched with shabby clothes. **2** [살림이 군색하다] poor; miserable. ¶살림이 ~ live in poverty / live poor.

-을이만큼 →ˉ-으리만큼

을종(乙種) grade [class] B; second grade.

-을지 whether (... or); if. ⇨ˉ-ㄹ지 ¶그가 집에

-을지나 있~ 모르겠군 I wonder if he is at home(or not).

-을지나 though ... must[should] .... ⇨-ㄹ지나 ¶그녀는 마땅히 벌을 받~ 그가 관대히 그 잘못을 용서해 주었다 She ought to be punished, but he was generous enough to pardon her fault.

-을지니라 must; should. ⇨-ㄹ지니라

-을지라도 though; even if[though]. ⇨-ㄹ지라도 ¶꼭 맞지는 않았~ 네가 꽤 근접하였다 Though[Although] not exactly right, you are fairly close. / That is not too wide of the mark.

-을지언정 even if[though]. ⇨-ㄹ지언정 ¶죽을지언정 노예로 살진 않겠다 I would sooner [rather] die than live in slavery.//굶어 죽을지언정 아버지 신세는 안 지겠다 Even if I starve to death, I won't ask a favor of my father.

-을진대 if; in case; suppose. ⇨-ㄹ진대 ¶네 도움이 없~ 내가 어찌 성공하겠는가 If it were not for your help, I should fail.

읊다 [시를 짓되] compose (a poem); [시가를 소리 높이 노래하다] recite [chant] (a poem). ¶망향의 정을 시로 ~ express one's yearning for his home in a poem//가을 화초를 시로 ~ write [(문어)] sing) about autumnal flowering plants in a poem.

읊조리다 recite (a poem); chant (a hymn).

음 (音) 1 [소리] a sound; [음조] a note; a tone. ¶높은[낮은] ~ a high[low] sound//아름다운 ~ a melodious[musical] sound//~의 높낮이 pitch//~의 강약 loudness//~을 내다 emit[produce] a sound//~을 조정하다 (연주 전에) tune (up)//그는 ~에 까다롭다 He has a critical ear. / He is particular[(구어)] fussy] about sound quality.//이 피아노는 ~이 맞는다[안 맞는다] This piano is in [out of] tune.
2 [자음(字音)] the sound [pronunciation] of a letter[character]. ¶한자에 ~을 달다 give the reading of Chinese characters in *Hangeul* alphabet//이 한자의 ~은 무엇이냐 What is the pronunciation of this Chinese characters?

음 (陰) 1 [철] Yin; the negative[female] principle in nature. 2 [수][물] [음수] negative [minus] number [quantity]. ¶~의 부호 a negative[minus] sign//~의 수 a negative [minus] number.

음으로 양으로 implicitly and explicitly; openly and covertly; publicly and privately. ¶~ 은혜를 입다 be favored directly and indirectly// ~ 도와주다 help (a person) openly and secretly//그는 나를 ~ 도와주었다 He helped me both publicly[openly] and privately.

음가 (音價) [언] a phonetic [sound] value; [음] a note value.

음각 (陰刻) an intaglio; (depressed) engraving [carving]; [미] a white line. **음각하다** intaglio; engrave.

음감 (音感) a sense of sound. ¶절대 ~ (have) perfect pitch//저 사람은 ~이 좋다 He has a good sense of pitch.

음경 (陰莖) [생] the penis (*pl.* penes, ~es); the phallus (*pl.* -li, ~es); [미국 비어] the cock.

음계 (音階) [음] the (musical) scale; the gamut. ¶단[장] ~ the minor[major] scale// 반[온] ~ a chromatic[diatonic] scale//~ 연습을 하다 practice the scales.

음곡 (音曲) [음률의 곡조] a tune; a melody.

음극 (陰極) (전기의) the cathode(▶ 양극 anode에 대해); the negative pole (of electric current).
● **음극선** cathode rays.

음기 (陰氣) [음침한 기운] a chill; cold; chillness; gloominess; dreariness.

음낭 (陰囊) [생] the scrotum (*pl.* -ta, ~s); [미국 비어] the balls.

음녀 (淫女) [음탕한 계집] a lewd[wanton / dissolute] woman; an unchaste woman; a woman of easy virtue [of loose morals]; a vamp; a bitch.

음담 (淫談) indecent [an obscene / a foul / an improper] stories; dirty[smutty] stories. ¶~을 하다 tell obscene [indecent] jokes.
● **음담패설** indecent jokes. ⇨음담

음덕 (陰德) [숨은 덕행] a stealthy benefaction; good done by stealth; a secret act of charity(자선 행위). ¶~을 베풀다 do good secretly.

음독 (音讀) reading aloud. **음독하다** read aloud.

음독 (飮毒) taking poison. **음독하다** take poison.
● **음독자살** suicide by taking poison. ¶~을 하다 kill oneself[commit suicide] by taking poison / poison oneself to death//그는 ~을 했다 He committed suicide[killed himself] by taking poison.

음란 (淫亂) lewdness; lasciviousness; lechery; salacity; incontinence. **음란하다** lecherous; lewd; incontinent; lustful; obscene; salacious; lascivious; indecent. ¶음란한 그림 an obscene picture//음란한 이야기 an indecent talk / a dirty story//음란한 여자 a loose woman / a woman of easy virtue / a slut // 음란한 생활을 하다 lead a promiscuous[loose] life.

음량 (音量) (musical) volume; sound volume. ¶라디오의 ~을 줄이다[높이다] turn down [up] the volume on the radio//스테레오의 ~을 최고로 높이다 turn a stereo all the way up[on full blast].

음력 (陰曆) the lunar calendar. ⇨태음력(太陰曆) ¶~ 4월 1일 April 1 by[according to] the lunar calendar//~을 쓰다 use[follow] the lunar calendar//~으로 날을 세다 reckon according to the lunar calendar.

음료 (飮料) a drink; a beverage; drinkables. ¶알코올 ~ an alcoholic drink//비(非)알코올 ~ a nonalcoholic drink//청량 ~ (미) a soft drink//혼합 ~ concoctions / cocktail / (미) highball//이 물은 ~로 적합하지 않다 This water is unfit to drink[(문어) is not potable].//무슨 ~를 드릴까요 What kind of drink[beverage] would you like?
● **음료수** drinking water; potable water; water to drink.

음률 (音律) [음조] a tune; a note; a melody; [고저] a pitch; [운] a rhythm.

음매 [소 우는 소리] a moo; (소아어) (소) moo-cow. ¶~ 울다 moo / low / bellow / bleat(송아지가).

음모 (陰毛) [의] pubic hair; pubes.

음모 (陰謀) a plot; an intrigue; [책략] machinations; (도당을 짠) (a) conspiracy; [미국 구어] a frame-up. ¶암살 ~ designs against (a

person's) life / a conspiracy to kill (a person) // ~에 가담하다 be implicated [initiated] in a plot // ~를 꾸미다 plot / lay [hatch / brew / frame / weave / concoct] a plot / form a conspiracy against (a person's life) / intrigue against (a person) // ~를 적발하다 expose [lay bare] a plot / unmask a conspiracy // 정부에 대하여 ~를 꾸미다 form [frame] a plot against the government // 수상 암살 ~가 발각되었다 A plot [conspiracy] to assassinate the Premier was bared. // 그들은 테러리스트와 짜고 국왕 살해 ~를 기도했다 They conspired with the terrorists to murder the king. // 그들은 대통령의 살해 ~를 꾸몄다 They plotted to murder the President. / They attempted to take the life of the President. **음모하다** plot; conspire; intrigue. ¶암살을 ~ plot against (a person's) life // 정부 전복을 ~ conspire [intrigue] against the government.
● **음모자** a plotter; a conspirator; an intriguer.

음문 (陰門) [생] the vulva.
음미 (吟味) 1 [감상] appreciation. **음미하다** appreciate; savor; enjoy. ¶숙독 ~ read with appreciation // 시를 ~ enjoy poems. 2 [맛봄] sampling; tasting. **음미하다** sample; taste; enjoy. ¶술맛을 ~ taste [take a taste of] liquor // 수프의 맛을 ~ sample [taste the seasoning of] soup // 그 말은 세월이 갈수록 음미해 볼 만한 것이 되었다 The words became more and more meaningful [significant] as the years passed.

음반 (音盤) (a copy of) a record; a disc; a disk. ¶엘피 ~ an LP [a long-playing] record // 스테레오 ~ a stereo record // 베토벤의 ~ a record of Beethoven's music // ~에 녹음하다 cut a record // ~에 노래를 취입하다 make a record of one's singing / ~을 걸다 play a record // ~으로 노래를 듣다 listen to a song on a record.

음복하다 (飮福-) partake of sacrificial food and drink.
음부 (陰部) [생] the pubic [genital] region; (완곡) the private parts; the privates; genitals. ¶외~ external genital organs / genitalia / (특히 여성의) pudenda (▶ pudendum의 복수형) / ~의 pudental.
음부 (淫婦) a lewd woman. ⇨음녀
음산하다 (陰散-) cloudy and gloomy; dreary; dismal. ¶음산한 날씨 gloomy [dismal] weather // 겨울 동안 내내 음산한 날이 계속되었다 Dark and gloomy days continued for most of the winter.
음색 (音色) a tone color; (프) timbre; clang tint. ¶~이 곱다 sound beautiful / have a good timbre // 하프와 플루트는 ~이 다르다 The harp and the flute differ in timbre. // 피아노와 바이올린은 ~이 다르다 Pianos and violins have different timbres.
음서 (淫書) [음탕한 내용의 책] an erotic book; a foul [lascivious] book; (집합적) obscene literature; pornography.
음성 (音聲) a voice. ⇨목소리
● **음성 기관** the vocal organs. **음성 기호** a phonetic sign [symbol]; a phonetic notation. **음성 다중 방송** multiplex transmission [broadcasting]; the multichannel sound system. **음성학** phonetics.
음성 (陰性) 1 [음침한 성격] (a) somber character; [음침한 기질] (a) gloomy disposition. ¶~인 [적인] gloomy / dismal. 2 a negative reaction. ⇨음성 반응 (⇨음성) ¶~인 negative // 그의 투베르쿨린 반응은 ~이었다 His reaction to the tuberculin test was negative. / He showed no reaction to the tuberculin test.
● **음성 거래** unlawful [illicit / under-the-table] deal [transaction]. **음성 반응** a negative reaction. **음성 수입** / **음성 소득** ill-gotten [illicit] gains; (관리의) spoils; (get) a perquisite. **음성 콜레라** dormant cholera.
-**음세** I will gladly (do it for you). ⇨-ㅁ세 ¶곧 갚~ I'll pay you back pretty soon.
음소 (音素) [언] a phoneme.
음속 (音速) sound speed; the speed of sound. ¶초~ 수송 여객기 a supersonic transport // ~의 sonic // ~의 벽 the sonic [sound] barrier // ~의 벽을 돌파하다 break the sound barrier // ~의 2배 빠른 비행기 an airplane that goes (at) twice the speed of sound // 이 비행기는 ~의 2배로 비행한다 This plane flies at double the speed of sound [Mach 2].
음수 (陰數) a negative number.
음순 (陰脣) the labia (*sing*. labium); (구어) the lips. ¶대 [소] ~ the labia majora [minora] / (구어) the outer [inner] lips (of the vulva).
음습하다 (陰濕-) shady and dampish. ¶이 식물은 음습한 땅에서 자란다 This plant grows in damp, shady places.
음식 (飮食) (a) food; (일상의) a diet; (식탁의) a table; a meal; food and drink; refreshments. ¶상하기 쉬운 ~ perishables // 먹다 남은 ~ leftover food // ~을 들다 eat food // ~을 절제하다 be moderate in eating and drinking // ~ 대접을 받다 receive (a person's) hospitality / partake of hospitality / be feasted [entertained] / be treated (to macaroni) // ~ 대접을 하다 entertain / give (a person) hospitality / give (a person) a dinner [feast] / give a feast [dinner] // ~에 손도 대지 않다 leave the food [dish] untouched // 그는 ~에 까다롭다 He is particular [finicky / fussy] about his food. // 환자의 ~은 우유로 제한되었다 The patient's diet was restricted to milk. // 저 호텔은 ~이 좋다 [나쁘다] That hotel sets a good [poor] table. // 여름철에는 ~에 조심해라 Be careful about your food [what you eat] during the summer. // 그 ~은 소화가 잘된다 [안 된다] That is digestible [indigestible] food. // 우리는 영양이 있는 ~을 섭취해야 한다 We must eat [take] nourishing food. // 무슨 ~을 가장 좋아하세요 What's your favorite food [dish]?
● **음식물** (a) food; a diet. ⇨음식 **음식점** a restaurant; [대중 식당] an eating house; (속어) an eatery.
음심 (淫心) sexual [carnal / lustful] desire; lust; lewdness. ¶~이 발동하다 feel lewd [whorish (여자가)] // ~을 품다 have a zest for lechery.
음악 (音樂) music. ¶고전 ~ classical music // 구체 ~ concrete music / (프) musique concrète // 교회 ~ church music // 극장 ~ scenic music // 레코드 ~ recorded [transcribed] music // 민속 ~ folk music // 실내 ~ chamber music // 전자 ~ electronic music // 절대 ~ absolute [abstract] music //

표제 ~ program music // 피아노 ~ piano music // 한국 ~ Korean music // ~의 [적인] musical / melodious // ~의 밤 a musical evening [soiree] // ~의 대가 a great musician // ~을 배우다 take lessons in music // ~을 연주하다 play [perform] music // ~을 이해하다 [이해하지 못하다] have an [no] ear for music // ~에 취미가 있다 have a taste for music // ~에 맞추어 노래하다 [춤추다] sing [dance] to music // 그는 ~을 아주 좋아한다 He likes music very much. / He love music. / He is a great music-lover. // 그녀는 ~을 배우고 있다 She is learning [studying] music.
●음악가 a musician. 음악 감상실 a music hall. 음악당 a concert hall; a bandstand (옥외 연주용). 음악성 musicality; musicianship. 음악 애호가 a music lover. 음악학 musicology. 음악회 a concert; a recital. ¶야외 ~ an outdoor concert // ~를 개최하다 give a concert [recital].

음양(陰陽) 1 [역학의 음과 양] the principles of Yin and Yang; the positive and negative; [남성과 여성] the male and female. ¶~의 조화 the harmony of the male and female // 그는 그들을 ~으로 도와주었다 He helped them both openly and secretly. 2 [전] [음극과 양극] the negative and positive terminals; the cathode and anode.
●음양가 a fortune-teller; a diviner. 음양각 [-刻] [미] relievo and intaglio.

음역(音域) [음] a range [register].

음역(音譯) transliteration. 음역하다 transliterate. ¶한국어를 로마자로 ~ transliterate Korean writing into Roman letters.

음영(陰影) 1 [그림자] a shadow; a silhouette. 2 [그늘] shade. ¶가로의 ~이 진 쪽 the shady side of the street // ~이 지다 be shaded (from the sun by a tree).

음욕(淫慾) sexual [carnal] desire; lust. ¶~에 빠지다 indulge in sensual pleasures // ~을 억누르다 restrain one's sexual desire.

음용(飮用) ¶~의 [마시기 위한] for drinking / potable / [내복용의] for internal use / [마실 수 있는] drinkable / fit to drink // ~에 적합하지 않다 be not good to drink / be unfit to drink / be undrinkable. 음용하다 drink. ¶이 물은 음용할 수 있다 This water is drinkable [good for drinking / (문어) potable].
●음용수 drinking water; 《게시》 Drinking [Potable] Water.

음운(音韻) [언] a phoneme.
●음운론 phonemics; phonology. 음운 조직 a phonemic system; the sound system (of a language).

음울하다(陰鬱-) gloomy; dark; black; dreary; cheerless; depressed; melancholy; moody. ¶음울한 이야기 a sad [melancholy] story // 음울한 날씨 gloomy weather // 음울한 얼굴을 하고 있다 look melancholy [dismal / depressed] // 방에는 음울한 분위기가 차 있었다 A gloomy atmosphere pervaded the room.

음원(音源) a sound source.

음위(陰痿) impotence. ¶~의 impotent.

음유 시인(吟遊詩人) a wandering minstrel; (이탈리아·남프랑스의) a troubadour.

음이온(陰-) [화] an anion; a negative ion.

음자리표(音-標) [음] a clef. ¶낮은~ the bass clef / the F clef // 높은~ the treble clef / the G clef // 다~ the C clef.

음전(音栓) [음] a stop (knob).

음전기(陰電氣) negative electricity.

음전자(陰電子) a negatron; a negative electron.

음전하(陰電荷) (a) negative (electric) charge.

음전하다 modest; decent; genteel; elegant; refined. ¶음전한 색시 a nice young girl // 말씨[태도]가 ~ be decent in speech [manner].

음절(音節) a syllable. ¶~의 syllabic // 단[이 / 삼 / 다]~어 a monosyllabic [disyllabic / trisyllabic / polysyllabic] word // ~의 분철법 syllabication / syllabification // 단어를 ~로 나누다 write [divide] a word in syllables / syllabify.
●음절 문자 a syllabic (character [symbol]); a syllabary (표).

음정(音程) [음] an [a musical] interval; a step. ¶단[장]~ a minor [major] (interval) // 반~ a semitone / a half step // 온~ a tone / a whole step // 정확한 ~ the correct interval // ~이 맞지 않게 노래하다 sing off key // 이 바이올린은 ~이 잘못되어 있다 This violin is out of tune.

음조(音調) (말할 때의) intonation; accent; [곡조] a tune; [음색] a tone; [운율] (a) rhythm; [가락] (a) melody; [소리의 높낮이] a pitch. ¶~가 맞다 [틀리다] be in [out of] tune // 그녀는 바이올린의 ~를 맞추었다 She tuned the violin. // 그녀는 높은[낮은] ~의 목소리다 She has a high-pitched [low-pitched] voice. // 그들은 목소리의 ~를 올렸다 [내렸다] They raised [lowered] their voices. // 배우들은 목소리의 ~를 수월히 고칠 수 있다 Actors can easily modulate their voices. // 그녀는 갑자기 ~를 바꾸었다 She suddenly changed her tone.

음주(飮酒) drinking. ¶~의 해독 evil effects of drinking / ~에 빠지다 be given [addicted] to drinking / indulge in drinking // ~로 패가망신하다 drink one's fortune away // ~를 삼가다 be of sober habits. 음주하다 drink; take wine.
●음주가 a drinker. 음주벽 a habit of drinking. 음주 운전 driving while intoxicated; drunk(en) driving. ¶~을 하다 drive when drunk // ~ 하지 마라 Don't drink and drive. / Drinking and driving don't mix. 음주 측정기 (영) a breathalyzer; (미) a drunkometer.

음지(陰地) a shaded lot [ground].
음지도 양지 될 때가 있다 (속담) Every cloud has a silver lining.; Fortune knocks at our doors by turns.; After the rain comes fair weather.

-음직하다 probable; likely; not unlikely. ¶음직한 이야기 a likely story // 먹~ look delicious / be tempting [appetizing] // 믿~ be reliable / be trustworthy // …은 흔히 있~ It is quite probable that …. // 네가 음직했을 곳을 모두 찾았다 I looked for you in every likely place.

음질(音質) the quality of sound; timbre. ¶이 음반은 ~이 좋다 [나쁘다] This record has good [poor] sound quality.

음차(音叉) [물] a tuning fork. ⇨ 소리굽쇠 (소리).

음치(音癡) (상태) tone deafness; (사람) a tone-deaf person. ¶~인 tone-deaf // 그는 ~다 He is tone-deaf. / He has no musical sense [ear for music].

음침하다(陰沈-) [음산하다] gloomy; dismal; dreary; melancholy; cheerless; dark; [의뭉

럽다) tricky; sly. ¶음침한 방 a dismal room // 음침한 날씨 gloomy[dismal] weather // 음침한 이야기 dismal talk // 음침한 얼굴을 하고 있다 look gloomy[melancholy].

음탕하다(淫蕩-) lewd; lustful; lecherous; dissipated; dissolute. ¶음탕한 말을 하다 say improper[indecent] things // 음탕한 눈초리로 보다 give (a person) a lecherous[lewd] look // 음탕한 생활에 빠지다 lead a promiscuous [loose] life // 그는 그녀에게 음탕한 짓을 했다 He did something dirty[indecent] to her.

음파(音波) a sound[sonic] wave. ¶초~ an ultrasonic wave // 수중 ~ 탐지기 a sonobuoy.
● 음파 측정기 a phonometer.

음표(音標) [음] a (musical) note. ¶겹점 ~ a double dotted note // 온~ a whole note / (영) a semibreve // 점~ a dotted note / 2분~ a minim / a half note / 4분~ a quarter note / (영) a crotchet / 8분~ an eighth note / (영) a quaver / 16분~ a sixteenth note / (영) a demisemiquaver // ~를 단 noted.

음표 문자(音標文字) 1 a phonetic sign. ⇨ 음성 기호(⇨음성(音聲)) ¶만국 ~ the international phonetic alphabet[signs]. 2 a phonogram. ⇨ 표음 문자(⇨표음)

음해하다(陰害-) do (a person) harm[an injury] secretly; [중상하다] stab (a person) in the back; backbite.

음핵(陰核) [생] the clitoris; the phallus (pl. -li).

음행(淫行) an obscene act; lewd[immoral / unchaste] conduct. ¶~을 일삼다 take liberties with (a woman) / commit obscene acts upon (a woman).

음향(音響) (a) sound; a noise(소음). ¶~을 흡수하다 absorb sound / be sound-[noise-] absorbent // 강당은 ~ 상태가 좋지 못하다 The auditorium is bad for sound.
● 음향 탐지기 a sound detector; a sound detection gear. **음향 효과** sound effects; (건물 내부의) acoustics.

음험하다(陰險-) tricky; sly; wily; crafty; dark; snaky; treacherous; double-dealing [-faced]. ¶음험한 사람 an insidious man / a person who might knife you in the back / (구어) a person who is waiting for a chance to do you in // 음험한 눈매 a sinister look in a person's eyes // 그는 음험한 수법으로 동료를 모함했다 He used a dirty trick to entrap his colleague. // 그녀는 음험한 수단으로 원하는 것을 손에 넣었다 She obtained what she wanted by underhand[(미) underhanded] means.

음화(陰畫) [사진] a negative.

음훈(音訓) [언] the pronunciation and the meaning (of a Chinese character).

음흉하다(陰凶-) black-hearted; wicked; treacherous; crafty; viperous. ¶음흉한 사람 a treacherous person // 음흉한 웃음 a wicked smile.

읍(邑) a *eup*; a town; (영) a county. ¶여주~ the town of Yeoju // ~에 가다 go up to town.

읍(揖) a polite bow with one's hands in front. **읍하다** bow with one's hands locked together in front of the chest.

읍내(邑內) (in) a town.

읍소하다(泣訴-) implore[supplicate / appeal to] (a person for mercy) with tears in one's eyes.

-**읍시다** let us (do). ⇨ -ㅂ시다 ¶불 좀 먹읍시다 Let's have something to eat. // 담뱃불 좀 얻~ Give me a light, please. / May I have a light?

응 1 [대답할 때 하는 소리] yes; (구어) yeah; all right; OK. ¶~, 그래 Yeah, I guess so. // "배가 고프니?" "~, 배가 고파." "Are you hungry?" "Yes, I am." // "너 안 가니?" "~, 안 가." "Don't you go?" "No, I don't." 2 [대답을 촉구할 때의 소리] OK?; eh? ¶정말 멋있었지, ~? Wasn't it splendid, eh?

응결(凝結) (기체의) condensation; (액체의) congelation; (우유 등의) curding. **응결하다** (기체가) condense; (액체가) congeal; coagulate; curd. → 증류수는 수증기를 응결시켜 만든다 Distilled water is produced by condensing steam.
● 응결물 a congelation (of). 응결점 the freezing point. ¶액체에 따라 ~이 다르다 Every liquid has a different freezing point.

응고(凝固) congelation; (특히 생물의 체액의) coagulation; [물][화] solidification. **응고하다** (액체가 얼거나 하여) congeal; (액체가) coagulate; (우유 등이) curdle; (액체·기체가) solidify. ¶시멘트가 응고했다 The cement has solidified[set]. // 피가 응고하여 딱지가 되었다 The blood congealed and formed a scab.
● 응고열 the heat of condensation. 응고점 a coagulating[setting] point; [물][화] solidifying point.

응급(應急) ¶~의 (긴급한) emergency / [임시의] temporary / [임시 변통의] makeshift // ~ 작업 emergency operations // 부상자를 위해 ~으로 침대를 만들었다 They made makeshift beds for the injured.
● 응급실 a first-aid room; an emergency room. **응급조치** / **응급 수단** an emergency[a makeshift / a temporary] measure. ¶~를 취하다 adopt temporary measures. **응급 치료** first aid; first-aid treatment. ¶야전 ~ field dressing / first-aid dressing // 화상의 ~(법) the first-aid treatment of burns // ~ 훈련을 하다 train (a person) in first aid // ~를 하다 give first aid[treatment] (to a person) / apply first-aid dressing (to) // ~를 받다 be medically aided. **응급 환자** a first-aid patient.

응낙(應諾) consent; assent; compliance; acceptance. **응낙하다** consent (to); give one's consent (to); agree (to)(▶ consent는 agree보다 딱딱한 표현); assent (to); accept. ¶취임[사임]을 ~ accept the post[one's resignation] // 고개를 끄덕이며 ~ nod assent (to) // 그들은 권고를 응낙했다 They accepted the recommendation.

응달 (the) shade; the shady place[side]. ¶~의 shady // ~에서 in the shade // ~이 지다 be shaded (by) // (수목 등이) ~을 만들다 give [provide / afford] shade (from the warm sun) // ~에서 쉬다 take a rest in the shade // 그 나무가 마침 좋은 ~을 만들고 있었다 The tree makes a very good shade. // 이것은 ~에서 말리세요 Dry it in the shaded[out of the sun].

응답(應答) a reply; an answer; a response. ¶질의~ questions and answers // ~이 없다 receive no reply[response] // 몇 번인가 그에게 전화를 했으나 ~이 없었다 I called him several times, but there was no answer [nobody answered]. **응답하다** reply; answer;

응당(應當) [당연히] necessarily; as a matter of course; [반드시] for sure; without fail. ¶~ 해야 할 일 a thing one ought to do [should do] // 그것은 ~ 있는 일이다 That is a matter of course.

응당하다(應當-) 1 [당연하다] just; natural; deserved. ¶그런 인간이 벌을 받는 것은 응당한 일이다 Such a person well deserves the punishment. // 빌린 것을 돌려주는 것은 응당한 일이다 One ought to pay what one owes. 2 [알맞다] proper; suitable. ¶능력에 응당한 봉급 a salary proportionate to one's ability.

응대(應待) (a) reception. ⇨응접

응대(應對) [상대함] address. ¶~를 잘하는[못하는] 사람 a man of good [awkward] address // 그녀는 전화를 잘한다 She handles phone calls well. / She has a good telephone manner. **응대하다** deal (with); (점원이) serve; wait on. ¶저 여점원은 손님을 친절히 응대한다 That saleswoman is very helpful to the customers. // 나는 그녀의 응대하는 품이 싫다 I don't like her manner of dealing with people and talk (with). // 사장님은 지금 손님을 응대하고 계십니다 The president is engaged with a visitor.

응등그러지다 [뒤틀리다] be awry; warp; get twisted; [움츠러지다] shrink (up); dry up; shrivel.

응등그리다 shrink (up); huddle [curl] (oneself) up.

응력(應力) [물] stress.

응모(應募) (주식 등의) (a) subscription; [지원] (an) application; (지원병의) enlistment; (현상·경기에의) (an) entry; (광고 등에의) response; an answer. ¶광고를 냈더니 많은 ~가 있었다 There were a lot of responses [was a great deal of response] to our advertisement. **응모하다** [신청하다] apply (for); make an application for; (기부 등에) subscribe (for / to); (경쟁 등에) enter (for). ¶공채 모집에 ~ subscribe for government bonds // 회원 모집에 ~ apply for membership in an association // 현상에 ~ enter a prize contest // 나는 그 직장에 응모해서 결과를 기다리고 있다 I have applied [made an application] for the job and am waiting for the result. // 응모한 원고는 돌려 드리지 않습니다 We will not return (the) manuscript sent in.

●**응모자** (입학·취직 등의) an applicant (for); (공채 등의) a subscriber (for). [현상 등의] ~ a prize essayist // ~ 전원에게 T셔츠를 증정하다 A T-shirt to be presented to every contestant.

응보(應報) retribution; nemesis(천벌). ¶인과 ~ retribution / karma // 나쁜 짓에는 무서운 ~가 따른다 An evil deed calls forth fearful retribution. // 대학 시절 학업을 태만히 한 것에 대한 ~를 받아 나는 지금 그 죗값을 치르지 않으면 안 된다 Now I have to pay (the penalty) for having neglected my studies in my college days. // 그것은 너의 나쁜 짓에 대한 ~이다 It's a punishment for the wrong you did. / That's what you get for doing wrong.

응분(應分) accordance with one's circumstances[ability / means]. ¶~의 [분수에 맞는] according to one's ability [status] / [알맞은] due / appropriate // ~의 기부를 하다 contribute according to one's means // 그는 ~의 칭찬을 받았다 He was given the praise he (so rightly) deserved. // 그는 자기 일에 대해 ~의 보수를 받았다 He received appropriate [reasonable] remuneration [(미) just compensation] for his work.

응사(應射) a return shot; return fire. ¶~를 받다 [초래하다] bring [draw / invite] return fire (from the enemy). **응사하다** fire [shoot] back; respond to another's firing; return another's fire.

응석 (a child's) playing on another's affection; playing the baby (to). ¶이 아이는 ~이 심해서 야단이야 This is quite a spoilt child. / This boy is quite spoiled. // 그녀는 지나치게 아들의 ~을 받아 준다 She indulged [pampered] her son too much. / She was overindulged with her son. / She spoiled her son. // 아이들은 지나치게 ~을 받아 주면 안 된다 Children must not be indulged too much. // 아저씨께 ~을 부리면 못써요 Don't make up to your uncle like that. // 그녀는 ~을 부리는 그 남자에게 바짝 달라붙었다 She nestled up to the man in a coquettish manner. **응석하다** play the baby (to); behave like a baby [spoiled child].

●**응석꾸러기** / **응석둥이** / **응석받이** a spoiled [spoilt] child; a pampered child. ¶자식을 ~로 키르다 bring up one's child indulgently // 자넨 아들을 지나치게 ~로 만들고 있다 You are babying your son too much.

응소(應召) answer the call; be drafted [conscripted]; obey the call-up. ¶그는 응소하여 해군에 입대했다 He was conscripted [(미)] drafted] into the navy.

응수(應手) [바둑·장기] a countermove; a response. ¶그는 강공을 당하여 ~에 고심했다 He was under strong attack and had few countermoves available to him [had difficulty in finding a way to respond]. **응수하다** (make a) countermove; answer a move (with a countermove).

응수(應酬) [대답] a reply; an answer; a response; [말대꾸] a retort; a repartee; return. **응수하다** answer; retort; respond; reply; return. ¶지지 않고 주먹으로 ~ return an unyielding blow / (구어) give as good as one gets.

응시(凝視) a stare; a gaze. **응시하다** stare at; look hard at; gaze at[on]; watch (a thing) intently. ¶남의 얼굴 [눈]을 ~ gaze [stare] into a person's face [eyes] (▶ stare의 대상이 사람인 경우, 몹시 무례한 느낌이 따름) // 그 남자는 바다를 응시했다 The man gazed [stared / looked hard] at the sea. / The man fixed his eyes on the sea.

응시자(應試者) a participant in an examination; an applicant (for).

응시하다(應試-) apply for an examination; take [(영)] sit for] an examination. ¶내년에는 어느 대학에 응시할 생각인가 Which university are you going to apply [take the entrance examination] for next year? // 나는 작년에 K대학에 응시했으나 실패했다 Last year I failed (to pass) the entrance examination for K

University.

응애응애 mewling; whimpering. ¶(갓난아이가) ~ 울다 mewl / whimper.

응어리 1 (근육 등의) stiffness; a lump. ¶겨드랑이에 ~가 생겼다 A growth has developed under my armpit. 2 (과실·사물의) the core; a kernel; the heart (of a matter). 3 (맺힌 감정) a bad [an unpleasant / an ill] feeling. ¶이것으로 간신히 가슴에 맺힌 ~가 풀렸다 At last the things that have been weighing on me have been settled. / Now all my anxieties [worries] have been removed.∥그들 사이에는 아직 풀리지 않은 ~가 남아 있다 They still harbor ill feelings for [toward] each other. / Their ill will hasn't decreased.

응용(應用) 〔적용〕 (practical) application; 〔실용〕 practice. ¶원리의 실지 ~ the application of a principle∥~ 범위가 넓은 원리 a principle of wide application. **응용하다** 〔이론 등을 적용하다〕 apply (to); 〔실용하다〕 put to practical use; adapt. ¶응용할 수 있는 practicable∥과학을 일상 생활에 ~ apply science to daily life∥학설을 실제로 ~ put a theory to practical use∥널리 ~ have wide application∥이 과에서 배운 것을 응용해 보아라 Put to use what you have learned in this lesson.
● **응용문제** an applied problem [question]. **응용 물리학**[화학] applied physics [chemistry]. **응용 미술** applied fine arts. **응용 프로그램** an application program.

응원(應援) 1 〔도와줌〕 aid; (an) assistance; help; 〔지지〕 support; 〔후원〕 backing. ¶~을 청하다 ask for help / call for a person's help. **응원하다** aid; assist; support; back (up). ¶남을 응원하러 오다[가다] come [go] to a person's aid∥후보자를 ~ support a candidate. 2 (경기의) cheering. ¶~의 함성 a cheer / cheering. **응원하다** cheer; (미국 구어) root (for). ¶자기 팀을 ~ cheer[(미국 구어) root] for one's team∥우리는 모두 K대학을 응원했다 We all cheered [rooted for] the K University team.
● **응원가** a rooter's song; a fight song; (영) a supporters' song. **응원단** a cheering squad [party]; (미국 구어) rooters. **응원단장** a cheerleader; (미국 구어) a head rooter.

응전(應戰) (a) response; a reply. **응전하다** accept battle [a challenge]; (포화로) return the fire [shot]; return to the enemy fire; fight back(반격하다). ¶맹렬한 펀치로 ~ counter [fight back] with a hard punch∥우리는 응전했다 We returned the fire [responded to their fire / fought back].

응접(應接) (a) reception. **응접하다** receive. ¶손님을 응접하느라 바쁘다 be busy receiving visitors∥그들은 손님을 정중히 응접했다 They treated [received / entertained] the guest politely.
● **응접실** (학교나 회사의) a reception room; (개인 집의) a living room; a drawing room(▶다소 예스러운 느낌).

응집(凝集) cohesion; agglutination. **응집하다** cohere. ¶응집시키다 agglutinate.
● **응집력** cohesive force; cohesion (power). ¶~이 있는 cohesive. **응집소** agglutinin.

응징(膺懲) chastisement; punishment. **응징하다** chastise; punish. ¶악을 ~ chastise vice / punish the wicked.

응찰하다(應札-) tender a bid (for).

응축(凝縮) condensation. **응축하다** condense. ¶증기가 응축하여 물이 된다 Steam condenses into water. ➔¶그의 평생의 연구 결과가 이 한 책에 응축되어 있다 His lifework is condensed in this (single) book.
● **응축기** a condenser.

응하다(應-) 1 〔대답하다〕 answer; reply to; respond to; (소집에) muster; 〔순종하다〕 meet; obey. ¶질의에 ~ respond to [answer] questions∥호출에 ~ obey a summons∥미소로 ~ respond with a smile∥그의 부름에 응하여 전국에서 동지가 모여들었다 In response to his call men of like mind gathered from all over the country.∥의사는 나의 전화 연락에 응하여 곧 와 주었다 The doctor came at once in answer [response] to my telephone call.
2 〔승낙하다〕 comply with; accede to; grant (a demand / a request); consent to; agree to. ¶제안에 선뜻 ~ consent readily [give ready consent] to a proposal∥주문[초대 / 도전]에 ~ accept an order[an invitation / a challenge]∥응하지 않다 decline (to do something)∥나는 그의 도전에 응했다 I responded to [accepted] his challenge.∥자네의 초대에 기꺼이 응하겠네 I shall be delighted to accept your invitation.
3 〔응모하다〕 subscribe for; apply for; make application for; enter. ¶주식 공모에 ~ subscribe for shares∥학생 모집에 ~ apply for admission to a school∥지원병 모집에 ~ enlist for a volunteer∥현상 소설 모집에 ~ enter a prize-contest for stories∥사원 모집에 ~ apply for a job with a company / respond to a help-wanted ad.
4 〔충족하다〕 meet; satisfy(수요 등에); fulfill(기대 등에); supply(요구 등에); answer(희망 등에). ¶당장의 필요에 ~ meet the exigencies of the hour∥수요에 ~ meet [supply] the demand∥새 시대의 필요와 요구에 ~ meet the needs and demands of a new age.

응혈(凝血) 〔피의 덩어리〕 a blood clot; 〔응고된 혈액〕 clotted [coagulated] blood. **응혈하다** curdle; coagulate. ➔¶상처 주변이 응혈되어 있다 The blood has clotted around the wound.

의 1 〔소유〕 …'s; of; belonging to. ¶아버지~ 집 my father's house∥우리~ 소원 our wishes∥톰~ 아버지 Tom's father∥나무~ 뿌리 the root of a tree∥그는 아이~ 머리를 때렸다 He struck the child on the head.∥그~ 영어 공부는 단지 취미에 지나지 않는다 (Studying) English for him is nothing but a pastime.∥이 모자는 누구~ 것입니까 Whose hat is this? / (문어) To whom does this hat belong?
2 〔소재〕 at; in; on. ¶역~ 신문 판매소 the newsstand at the station∥부산~ 내 친구 my friend in Busan∥뜰~ 벚나무 a cherry tree in the garden∥해변~ 호텔 a seaside hotel / a hotel on the seaside∥호남선~ 역 a station on the Honam [Daejeon-Mokpo] Line∥양양~ 포도 grapes from Anyang∥강~ 다리 a bridge over a river.
3 〔시간〕 in; on. ¶오후~ 수업 classes in the afternoon / afternoon classes∥수요일~ 모임 the meeting on Wednesday∥3개월~ 휴가 a three months' [three-month] vacation∥오전 6시~ 부산행 급행 the 6 a.m. express for

Busan // 어제~ 저녁 식사 last night's supper.

4 [분량] of. ¶한 줌~ 모래 a handful of sand // 한 병~ 포도주 a bottle of wine // 두 켤래~ 구두 two pairs of shoes.

5 [모양·성질]. ¶네모꼴~ 상자 a square box // 포도~ 계절[수확기] a vintage // 백발~ 노인 an old man with white hair / a white-haired old man / 꿈~ 나라 a dreamland / the land of dreams // 영어~ 연설 an address [a speech] in English.

6 [···을 위한] for. ¶내 친구에~ 선물 a present for a friend of mine // 사장님~ 심부름으로 그는 외출했다 He went out on an errand for the president.

7 [내용] in; on; for. ¶영어~ 텍스트 a text in English / an English text // 10만 원~ 수표 a check for 100,000 won.

8 [주격]. ¶시간~ 흐름 the passage of time.

9 [대상]. ¶한국 제품~ 선전 advertisement of [an advertisement for] Korean products // 도어~ 열쇠 a key to the door // 수수께끼~ 실마리 a clue to a mystery // 그 사태~ 수습에 오랜 시간이 걸렸다 It took a long time to settle the matter.

10 [소속] of; for; to. ¶학교~ 선생 a schoolteacher // 서울 대학교~ 교수 a professor at Seoul National University // 영국 대사~ 비서 a secretary to the British Ambassador / the British Ambassador's secretary // 우리 회사~ 긍지 the pride of our company / a credit to our company // 이달~ 봉급 salaries for this month(▶ 회사 측) / this month's salary(▶ 봉급을 받는 측).

11 [···에 관한] on; of; in. ¶아동 심리학~ 권위자 an authority on child psychology // 물고기~ 연구 a study of fish / research on fish // 농업~ 기술 혁신 the technological revolution in agriculture // 어렸을 때~ 이야기를 해 주십시오 Please tell me about your childhood.

12 [···에 의한] by; of. ¶헤밍웨이~ 소설 Hemingway's novels / novels (written) by Hemingway // 세잔~ 그림 a picture (painted) by Cezanne / a Cezanne // 춘원의 작품 the works of Chunwon(▶ 작품 전체) / a work by Chunwon (▶ 한 작품).

13 [사회적·친족적 관계] between; with. ¶아버지와 어머니~ 관계 the relationship between my father and mother // 그는 학급~ 인기인이다 He is a favorite with[among] his classmates. // 그녀에게는 전남편~ 자식이 한 사람 있다 She has a child by her former husband.

14 [···로부터의] from. ¶부친~ 편지 a letter from my father // 친구~ 전갈 a message from one's friend.

의(義) 1 [정의] justice; righteousness; [신의] faith; [충의] loyalty; [도의] morality; [명예] honor. ¶~를 위해 죽다 die in the cause of justice[honor] // ~를 중히 여기다 value honor / put great importance on doing what is right // ~를 위해 일어서다 stand for a good cause // ~를 보고 행하지 않음은 용기가 없음이니라 To see what is right without doing it argues[bespeaks] an absence of courage.

2 [관계·의리] relationship; relations; ties; bonds. ¶형제의 ~를 맺다 swear to be brothers / 부자의 ~를 맺다 contract the relations of father and son / swear to enter into the father-and-son relationship // (부모가) 자식과의 ~를 끊다 disown one's son[daughter] / cut off relationship with one's son [daughter].

3 [뜻] meaning; significance.

의(誼) [친한 사이] relations; relationship; terms; [정의] friendship; intimacy; good will; [화합] harmony; concord. ¶~가 상하다 break (with) / quarrel [fall out] (with) / be estranged (from) // 그 부부간은 ~가 좋지 않다 The husband and wife are estranged [alienated] from each other. // 그 일로 우리는 ~가 상했다 It has set us at odds.

의거(義擧) a noble [worthy] undertaking; a heroic deed [act]. ¶4·19 ~ the Student Revolution on April 19th // 압제에 대항해서 ~를 일으키다 rise against oppression.

의거하다(依據-) **1** [어떤 것에 근거하다] be based (on / upon); be founded (on); be grounded (on / upon / in); (미) be predicated (on / upon); confirm (to); accord (with); depend (on). ¶자료에 의거해서 on the basis [authority] of the data // 아버지의 유언에 의거하여 under the provisions of my father's will // 세금은 수입에 의거한다 Taxation is based on income. // 당신의 주장은 무엇에 의거하고 있습니까 On what do you base [found] your argument? / What is the basis of your argument? // 우리는 그의 지시에 의거하여 행동하였다 We acted in accordance with his instructions. // 봉급은 근속 연수에 의거해서 지불된다 Wages are paid according to years of service.

2 [의존하다] depend (on).

의견(意見) (an) opinion; an idea; a view(견해). ¶다수[소수] a majority [minority] opinion // 반대 ~에 opposing opinion / (상반되는) a contrary [an opposite] opinion [view] // 전문가의 ~ an expert opinion / expert [professional] advice / 온건한 [과격한] ~의 소유자 a man of moderate [extreme] opinions / ~의 일치 [상위] the coincidence [difference] of opinions // 내 ~으로는 in my opinion // 남의 ~을 묻다 [청하다] ask a person's opinion [view] / [자문하다] consult a person's opinion // ~을 말하다 give [express] one's opinion [views] (on / about) // 어떤 문제에 대하여 남과 ~을 교환하다 [나누다] exchange views with a person on [about] a matter // ~을 같이하다 [~이 같다] be of the same opinion / be of an opinion / share a person's views // 남의 ~을 존중하다 respect [reverence] a person's opinion // 이 점에 관해서는 ~이 구구하다 Opinions vary [differ] on this point. / They are divided (in opinion) [Opinion is divided] on this point. / 무슨 ~이라도 있으십니까 Do you have any comment to make about it? / Do you have anything to say about it? // 내 교육 문제에 대해 어머니는 아버지와 ~이 맞지 않았다 My mother disagreed [did not agree] with my father about my education. / My mother had different views from my father's about my education. / My mother differed [dissented] from my father in opinion on my education. / My mother was at issue [variance] with my father on my education. // 그의 아내와 어머니는 늘 ~이 맞지 않는다 His wife and mother are constantly locking horns [always

at odds] with each other.// 이 문제에 있어서는 그와 나는 ~을 달리한다 He and I don't see eye to eye[aren't on the same wavelength] when it comes to that matter.// 그들은 끝까지 ~의 일치를 보지 못했다 They were unable to[failed to] reach an agreement to the very end.// 우리는 각각 ~이 다르다는 점에 동의했다 We agreed to differ. // 서슴지 말고 ~을 말씀해 주십시오 Please state[tell / express] your ideas freely.
● **의견서** a written opinion; a statement of one's views.

의결 (議決) a decision; a resolution. ¶…의 ~을 거쳐야 한다 be subject to the decision of …. **의결하다** decide; resolve; (투표로) pass a vote (of); vote (for / against / on a bill). ¶위원회는 한국이 제출한 결의안을 의결했다 The committee voted for[adopted] the resolution submitted by Korea. ➔¶그 문제는 출석자의 과반수로 의결되었다 The issue was decided by a majority of those present.// 내각 불신임안이 의결되었다 A motion of non-confidence in the Cabinet was passed.
● **의결권** a voting right; the right to vote. ¶~을 행사하다 exercise one's vote // ~이 있다 have a voting rights. **의결 기관** a legislative [deliberative] organ.

의고 (擬古) imitation of classical[ancient] style. **의고하다** write[constitute / compose / form / construct] in (imitation of) classical style.
● **의고주의** [고전주의] classicism; (언어·미술상의) archaism; (가짜의) pseudoarchaism; pseudoclassicism. **의고체** classicism.

의과 (醫科) a medical department[school].
● **의과 대학** a medical college.

의관 (衣冠) 1 [옷과 갓] clothes and a crown. 2 [옷차림] attire. ¶~을 갖추다 be in full dress / be decently dressed // ~을 정제하다 dress oneself neatly / tidy[(미) fix] oneself up.

의구 (疑懼) apprehensions; misgivings; suspicion; doubt; uneasiness. ¶~를 느끼다 feel apprehensive[uneasy] (about) / feel[have] misgivings (about). **의구하다** apprehend; suspect; doubt.
● **의구심** misgivings; apprehensions; fear. ¶일말의 ~을 품다 have[harbor] vague misgivings (about) // 실험의 성패에 관해서 ~이 있었다 There were some misgivings[doubts] about the outcome of the experiment.// ~이 풀렸다 My suspicion has been cleared away. / My doubts have been dispelled.

의구 (依舊-) (remain) unchanged; (서술적) remain as it was; be as (it was) before. ¶산천은 의구하되 인물은 간 곳 없다 As the mountains and rivers of one's hometown are unchanged from old times, but men of the day are dead and gone.

의기 (意氣) [기운] spirits; heart; (미) grit; vigor; [사기] morale. ¶그는 한 번의 실패로 ~가 꺾일 사람이 아니다 He is not a man to be daunted by a single failure.

의기 (義氣) [의협] chivalrous spirit; chivalry; heroism; [공공심] public spirit. ¶~ 있는 chivalrous / heroic / public-spirited.

의기소침하다 (意氣銷沈-) be dispirited [disheartened]; be depressed in spirits; be in low spirits; be despondent. ¶의기소침해진 패자 despondent losers // 실패한 그들은 의기소침해 있다 They are depressed[in low spirits] due to their failure.

의기양양하다 (意氣揚揚-) triumphant; exultant. ¶의기양양하게 exultingly / exultantly / elatedly / proudly / triumphantly / in triumph / in good[high] spirits // 의기양양한 승리자 high-spirited winners // 그들은 의기양양했다 They were in high spirits.

의기충천하다 (意氣衝天-) one's spirits rise to the skies; be in high[roaring / towering / royal] spirits. ¶첫 시합에 이긴 그들은 의기충천했다 After winning the first game, their spirits soared.

의기투합하다 (意氣投合-) be of congenial temper; be of a mind; find a kindred [congenial] spirit in (a person). ¶나와 그녀는 의기투합했다 I have found a congenial spirit in her.

의논 (議論) consultation; talks; conference(협의). **의논하다** talk (with); consult; confer (with); seek[ask] (a person's) advice. ¶변호사와 ~ consult a lawyer // 이마를 맞대고 ~ lay[put] heads together (about a matter) // 우리는 그 일에 대해서 의논했다 We consulted (with each other) about the matter. / We talked over the matter.// 좀 의논할 일이 있는데요 I'm sorry to trouble you, but I've got something that needs your advice[help].

의당 (宜當) naturally; duly; justly; properly; deservedly; (as a matter) of course. ¶~ 받아야 할 벌 deserved punishment // 그것은 ~ 내 돈이다 It is my money by right.// 그는 ~ 벌을 받아야 한다 He must be deservedly punished.// ~ 모든 학생이 도와야 한다 Every student ought to help.// 그의 일에 대해 ~ 돈이 지불되어야 한다 Money is due (to) him for his work. **의당한** right; proper; just; justifiable; reasonable; natural; deserved; merited; due. ¶자식이 부모를 사랑하는 것은 의당한 일이다 It is natural for child to love its parents.// 학생이 열심히 공부해야 하는 것은 ~ It is proper that students should[ought to] work hard.

의대 (衣帶) clothes and belts.

의대 (醫大) a medical college. ⇨**의과 대학**(⇨ 의과)

의도 (意圖) an intention; intent(▶ 다소 격식 차린 말); [생각] an idea; a design; [목적] a purpose. ¶그는 외유할 ~로 영어 공부를 열심히 하고 있다 He is studying English hard with the intention of going abroad. // 매사가 나의 ~대로 되지 않았다 Everything I did was contrary to my own intentions. // 나의 원래 ~는 그를 설득하는 것이었다 My original intent was to persuade him. // 그런 ~로 말한 것은 아니다 I did not mean it that way. // 무슨 ~로 그런 말을 하는가 What do you mean by that? // 그의 ~는 우리를 이간시키려는 것이다 His design is to separate[drive a wedge between] us. **의도하다** intend; design; aim (at). ¶그에게는 의도하는 바가 있었다 He had a plan ready. / He had everything mapped out.// 그가 의도한 대로 그는 그 여행으로 유명해졌다 Just as he had planned, the trip won him a great deal of publicity.// 나는 ~가 의도하는 바가 무엇인지 궁금하다 I wonder what he is aiming at.

의례 (儀禮) courtesy; etiquette; [예식] formality; [의식] a ceremony. ¶가정~ 준칙 (the) family rite rules // 외교 ~ diplomatic courtesy[etiquette] // 일정한 ~에 따라 with a

의례적(儀禮的) ceremonious; ceremonial; formal. ¶~인 방문 (pay) a duty[courtesy] call // ~으로 out of courtesy / by courtesy / ceremoniously.

의론(議論) [토의] an argument; a discussion; [논쟁] a controversy; a dispute; [토론] a debate. ¶~을 펴다 go on[proceed] with one's argument // ~을 벌이다 join[take] issue (with a person on a point) / engage in wordy warfare / cross[bandy] words (with a person) / engage in a verbal battle[a battle of words] // ~이 분분하다 Contending voices are heard on all sides. **의론하다** argue; discuss; dispute; debate; controvert; contend; make an argument.

의롭다(義-) righteous; rightful; just. ¶의로운 사람 a righteous man / (집합적) the righteous // 의로운 싸움 a righteous war / fighting for a rightful cause // 의로운 일을 하다 do a right thing / do right // 대의를 위해 의롭게 죽다 sacrifice oneself for the sake of justice.

의뢰(依賴) 1 [의지] dependence; reliance. **의뢰하다** depend[rely] on; lean on; turn[look] to (a person for). ¶너는 내게 지나치게 의뢰하고 있다 You depend too much on me. 2 [부탁] a request; solicitation; [위탁] trust; commission. ¶~에 의해서 at a person's request. **의뢰하다** ask (a person to do); request; make (a person) a request; entrust (a person with a matter); commission (a person to do); place (a matter) in (a person's) hands; leave (something) to (a person / a person's charge). ¶변호사에게 (사건을) commit[leave] (a matter) to a lawyer // [변호사를 대다] retain a lawyer.
● **의뢰서** / **의뢰장** a letter of request; a letter asking a favor; a written request. **의뢰인** (변호사 등의) a client.

의료(衣料) clothing; clothes.

의료(醫療) medical treatment[care / attention]; health care; medical service. ¶국립~원 the National Medical Center // 불법~행위 (conduct) unauthorized medical treatment // ~의 medical // 그는 지난 여름 이후 내내 ~를 받고 있다 He has been receiving [undergoing / getting] medical treatment since last summer.
● **의료계** the medical world; medical circles. **의료 기관** a medical institution. **의료 보험** ➡ 국민 건강 보험(⇨국민) **의료비** medical expenses; a doctor's bill; a fee for medical treatment. **의료 시설** medical facilities.

의류(衣類) (집합적) clothing; clothes; [경] a garment; (개인 소유의) one's wardrobe. ¶~ 한 점 an article of clothing / 한 벌 a suit of clothes // 저의 가게에서는 어린이용으만 취급하고 있습니다 We specialize in children's wear.

의리(義理) [의무] justice; [의무] duty; obligation; [신의] faith; fidelity; loyalty. ¶~가 있다 be faithful[dutiful] / have a keen[strong] sense of honor[duty] // ~가 없다 have no sense of duty / fail in one's duty // ~를 지키다 be[remain] loyal[faithful / true] (to) / keep faith (with) // 그는 친구에 대해 ~를 지켰다 He kept faith with his friends. / He was faithful to his friends. // 그는 ~를 아는 사람이다 He is man of honor. // 그는 ~와 인정을 중히 여긴다 He places a high value on moral obligations and personal relationships.

의무(義務) (a) duty; an obligation(▶ duty는 자기 자신 또는 남에 대해서 당연히 해야 한다고 생각되는 것, obligation은 외부 사정에 구속되어 남을 위해 해야 하는 것); [책임] (a) responsibility. ¶병역의 ~ liability for military service // 납세의 ~ liability for tax payment // 국가에 대한 ~ a duty to one's country // 법률상의 ~ legal obligation[responsibility] // ~를 다하다 carry out[perform / do] one's duty // ~를 지다 owe a duty (to one's country) // ~를 게을리 하다 neglect[fail in] one's duty // 남편에겐 아내를 부양할 ~가 있다 A husband has a duty[an obligation] to support his wife. // 우리는 세금을 낼 ~가 있다 We are under obligation[have an obligation] to pay our taxes. // 내게는 그를 돌봐야 할 ~가 없다 I am under no obligation to look after him. // 환자를 돌보는 것이 우리의 ~이다 We ought to[must] care for the sick. // 운전자는 면허증을 휴대하는 것이 ~로 되어 있다 Drivers are required[It is compulsory for drivers] to carry a driver's license. // 권리를 주장하기 전에 ~를 다하여라 You must do[perform / fulfill] your duties before you assert your rights.
● **의무감** a sense of duty[obligation]. ¶~이 부족하다 have a poor sense of duty / lack a sense of duty. **의무 교육** compulsory education. ¶~을 받다 receive compulsory education // ~을 마치다 finish one's compulsory education.

의문(疑問) [질문] a question; an interrogation; [의심] a doubt. ¶~의 죽음 a mysterious death // ~을 품다 have doubts (about) / be skeptical about / doubt // ~을 제기하다 pose[set up / raise / present] a question / throw[cast] a doubt (on) / express a doubt // 그런 일이 가능할는지 ~이다 I doubt whether such a thing is possible. // 그의 신뢰성에 대해서는 ~의 여지가 있다 His reliability is open to question[doubt]. / I have some doubts about his reliability. // 그가 스파이라는 점은 ~의 여지가 없다 There is no doubt that he is a spy. // 그 숫자에 대해서 ~이 있다 I have some doubts about that figure. // 무엇이든지 ~이 있으면 질문하시오 Ask me whatever questions you may have. // 그의 명쾌한 설명으로 나의 모든 ~이 풀렸다 His lucid explanation drove away[dispelled] all my doubts.
● **의문 대명사** an interrogative pronoun. **의문문** an interrogative sentence. **의문사** an interrogative. **의문점** a doubtful[moot] point; a point in question; a doubt. ¶~을 해결하다[풀다] resolve[clear / dispell] one's doubts.

의뭉스럽다 [교활하다] sly; wily; dark; disingenuous; [표리가 있다] double-dealing; double-faced[-hearted]. ¶의뭉스러운 웃음 a sly smile // 의뭉스러운 사람 a double-dealer // 의뭉스러운 아이 a precocious child.

의미(意味) a meaning; a sense; [의의] significance; [주지(主旨)] the import; [함축] an implication; a connotation. ¶문자 그대로의 ~ literal meaning // 낱말의 ~ the meaning of a word // 그의 행동의 진정한 ~ the real significance of his action // 대통령의 말의 ~ the import of the President's words // ~ 있는 표정 a meaning[significant / suggestive]

의사

look / a look full of meaning // ~ 없는 meaningless / devoid of meaning / empty (words) / senseless / pointless / [하찮은] insignificant / nonsensical / foolish / absurd // 넓은 ~로 in a broad [large] sense / in a wide meaning // 좁은 ~로 in a narrow [limited / restricted] sense // 어떤 ~에서 in a (certain) sense / in one [some] sense / in a way [manner] // ~를 **파악하다** grasp [catch / seize] the meaning // 나쁜 ~로 말한 것은 아니다 I meant no ill will. / My meaning was quite innocent. 그 일은 전혀 ~가 없다 The matter is of no significance. **의미하다** mean; signify; purport; imply; stand for. ¶LP는 무엇을 의미하느냐 What does LP stand for?
●**의미론** [언] semantics.
의미심장하다(意味深長-) very meaningful; full of meaning; profound in meaning; (서술적) have a [be of] profound significance; mean much [a great deal]. ¶**의미심장한 시선** [눈길] a meaning [an expressive] glance / a significant look // 의미심장한 표정을 짓고 with some significance in one's face // 그녀는 내 얼굴을 의미심장한 눈빛으로 쳐다보았다 She looked at me with eyes full of meaning [as if she knew something]. // 그는 의미심장한 말을 남기고 갔다 He said something very significant as he left.
의법(依法) (in) accordance [conformity] with law. **의법하다** be in accordance [conformity] with law.
●**의법 조치** measures [disposition] according to law.
의병(義兵) a patriotic [loyal] soldier; [의용병] a volunteer; (집합적) an army raised in the cause of justice; a loyal [righteous] army. ¶~을 **일으키다** raise an army in the cause of justice / raise a loyal army.
의복(衣服) clothes (▶ 항상 복수형. 단, 수사(數詞)와 함께 쓰지 않음); dress; [문어] garments; (미) apparel; (종종 복합어) wear; suit; (집합적) clothing. ¶~을 **갈아입다** change into proper [decent] clothes / change (one's clothes) // ~을 **갖추다** [장소에 어울리는 복장을 하다] dress [clothe] oneself properly // ~을 **단정히 하다** tidy oneself up // 무기 소지 여부를 알기 위해 ~을 검사하다 inspect a person's clothes for weapons / search a person for weapons.
의부(義父) **1** a stepfather. ⇨"**의붓아버지 2** [수양아버지] an adoptive [a foster] father. **3** [의로 맺은 아버지] a sworn father.
의분(義憤) indignation; righteous angry. ¶나는 그를 속인 사람에 대해 ~을 느꼈다 I burned with (righteous) indignation against the man who had swindled him. // 나는 그 잔인한 행위에 강한 ~을 느꼈다 I felt strong indignation at the cruelties. / I was filled with righteous anger at the cruelties. / The cruelties made me indignant.
의붓딸 a stepdaughter.
의붓아들 a stepson.
의붓아버지 a stepfather.
의붓어머니 a stepmother.
의붓자식(-子息) a stepchild; [아들] a stepson; [딸] a stepdaughter. ¶~을 **냉대하다** ill-treat one's stepchild.
의붓자식 다루듯(속담) treat (a person) like a stepchild [like a Cinderella / as an outsider]; leave (a person) neglected [in the cold].
의사(義士) a righteous [high-principled] man; a martyr.
의사(意思) 〔생각〕 a mind; an idea; 〔의향〕 an intention; an intent; a purpose. ¶~가 **통하다** come to an understanding / understand each other // ~를 **밝히다** speak one's mind / express one's intention // ~를 **묻다** ask a person's intention // …할 ~가 있다 have a mind [an intention] to do // 나는 선생이 될 ~는 추호도 없다 I do not have the slightest intention of becoming a teacher. // 그는 부모의 ~를 어기고 결혼했다 He married against his parent's wishes. // 양자 사이에 ~소통이 없었기 때문에 그 계획은 좌절되었다 Through a lack of understanding between the two parties, the project fell through.
●**의사 결정** decision-making. **의사 표시** an expression [indication] of one's intentions; [법] a declaration of intent. ¶~를 **하다** indicate [express / declare] one's intentions / make a declaration of intention // 별다른 ~가 없을 때에는 in the absence of any different declaration of intention // 당신은 ~를 분명히 해야 한다 You must express your intentions [ideas] clearly.
의사(擬似) 〔관형어적〕 false; suspected; quasi.
●**의사 콜레라** a suspected case of cholera; false cholera.
의사(醫師) a (medical) doctor; (내과의) a physician; (개업의) a (medical) practitioner; (외과의) a surgeon; (전문의) a specialist; (구어) a medico (pl. ~s); (구어) a doc. ¶**단골 ~** a one's (regular / family) doctor // **개업 ~** a general practitioner (약어 G.P.) // **돌팔이 ~** a quack (doctor) // ~의 치료를 받고 있다 be under medical treatment [a doctor's care] // ~**로서 개업하다** practice medicine / become a medical practitioner // 눈이 아파 ~의 진찰을 받다 [~에게 보이다] see [consult] a doctor about one's eye trouble // 환자를 ~에게 보이다 commit a sick person to a doctor's care / get a sick person medical treatment // ~를 **부르러 보내다**[가다] send [go] for a doctor // ~를 **부르다** call in a doctor / get a doctor // ~의 진찰을 받아 보겠다 I will consult [see / have] a doctor. / I will seek medical advice. // 그는 작년에 ~로 개업했다 He set up [began practicing] as a doctor last year. // 심장 전문의 ~에게 보이는 것이 좋겠다 You should see a heart specialist. // 저 ~는 환자가 많다 That doctor has (established) a large [an extensive] practice.
●**의사 면허** medical license; a license to practice medicine.
의사(議事) 〔의논〕 deliberation; conference; consultation; (그 사항) proceedings. ¶~에 **들어가다** [~를 끝내다] commence [close] the proceedings // (회의 전에) ~를 **정리하다** arrange the proceedings (for a conference) // 지금부터 ~에 들어가겠습니다 [~를 진행하겠습니다] We shall now proceed to business. / Business is now in order.
●**의사당** an assembly hall. ¶**국회 ~** (한국의) the National Assembly Building / (미국의) the Capitol / (영국의) the Houses of Parliament / (일본 등의) the Diet Building // **지방 의회 ~** an assembly hall. **의사록** the minutes [a record] (of the proceedings). ¶~

을 만들다 take minutes of (the proceedings) // ~에 올라 있다 be on the minutes. **의사일정** the agenda; the order of the day. ¶~에 오르다 be placed on the agenda / (미) go on the calendar // 의제를 ~에[에서] 넣다[빼다] include[exclude] an item in[from] the agenda // ~을 변경해야 한다 We have to make a change in the agenda. // 그 사항은 ~에 들어 있다 The item is on the agenda. **의사 진행** the progress of the proceedings. ¶~을 촉진하다 expedite the proceedings. // ~에 관하여 발언을 요구하다 ask for the floor on a point of order // ~을 방해하다 obstruct the proceedings / (미) filibuster.

의상(衣裳) clothes; (주로 여성의) dress; (집합적) clothing; wardrobe; (무대용) costume. ¶한국의 민속 ~ the national costume of Korea // 대여 ~ clothes[costumes] for hire [(미) rent] // 무대 ~ theatrical[stage] costume / dress for a part // 신부 ~ a wedding dress // 화려한[검소한] ~을 입고 있다 be gaily[simply] attired[dressed] // 그는 카우보이[인디언]의 ~을 입고 나타났다 He appeared in a cowboy[an Indian] costume. // 그녀는 ~이 꽤 많다 She has an extensive [a large] wardrobe.
● **의상실** [양장점] a dressmaker's (shop).

의생활(衣生活) clothing habits.

의서(醫書) a medical book; a book on medicine.

의석(議席) a seat (in an assembly hall); [의사당의 의원석] the floor. ¶나는 시 의회에 ~을 가지고 있다 I have a seat on the City Council. // 신당은 선거에서 30석의 ~을 얻었다 The new party won thirty seats[places] in the election. // 그는 ~을 잃었다 He lost his seat.

의성어(擬聲語) an onomatopoeic[echoic] word; an onomatopoeia; an onomatope. ¶~의 onomatopoeic / onomatopoetic.

의수(義手) an artificial arm[hand].

의술(醫術) the medical art; medicine. ¶~의 medical // ~을 베풀다 give (a person) medical care / give medicine to (a person) // ~은 인술이다 Medicine is a benevolent art.

의식(衣食) food and clothing. ¶~이 족해야 예절을 안다 Well fed, well bred. / A sharp stomach makes short devotion. / It is hard for an empty sack to stand straight.

의식(意識) 1 [감각] consciousness; one's sense. ¶~이 있는 conscious // ~을 잃다 lose consciousness[one's senses] / faint (away) // ~을 회복하다 recover consciousness / come to one's senses / come to (oneself) // ~을 회복시키다 bring a person around[(영) round] // 그는 3일 동안 ~이 없었다 He remained unconscious for three days. // 환자는 서서히 ~을 되찾았다 The patient gradually became conscious[recovered consciousness]. // 그녀의 ~은 마지막 순간까지 또렷했다 Her mind was clear to the end. // 그녀는 ~ 불명인 채로 죽었다 She died without regaining consciousness.
2 [자각·자의식] consciousness; awareness. ¶계급[민족] ~ the class[race] consciousness // 사회 ~ the social consciousness // 죄 ~ consciousness of guilt // ~의 흐름 the stream consciousness // 그에게는 도덕적 ~이 부족하다 He lacks moral sense. / He has no sense of morality. **의식하다** be conscious (of); be aware (of). ¶그녀는 남들이 보고 있다는 것을 의식하고 있었다 She was conscious of being watched[that she was being watched]. // 그는 위험을 의식하고 있었다 He was aware of the danger.
● **의식 구조** one's way of thinking; a line of thinking. ¶~를 바꾸다 change one's point of view / view (a thing) from a different angle.

의식(儀式) (식전) a ceremony; (축전) function; (종교의) a service; a rite; a ritual. ¶~을 거행하다 perform a ceremony[service] // 그 ~은 내일 거행된다 The ceremony will be held [carried out] tomorrow. // ~은 순조롭게 진행되었다 The ceremony went off without a hitch. / The ceremony was completed smoothly.

의식적(意識的) conscious; intentional; deliberate. ¶~으로 consciously / deliberately / intentionally / on purpose // 호흡을 하는 데는 ~인 노력이 필요 없다 Breathing does not require conscious effort. // 나는 ~으로 그것을 했다 I did it intentionally[deliberately].

의식주(衣食住) food, clothing and shelter. ¶~에 필요한 것 the necessaries[necessities] of life / living necessaries // ~를 제공하다 feed, lodge and clothe (a person) // 그들은 ~의 걱정이 없는 생활을 한다 They are well fed, well clothed[clad] and well housed.

의심(疑心) [의혹] (a) doubt; [의문] a question; [불신] (a) distrust; [혐의] (a) suspicion. ¶당치 않은 ~ petty suspicions / bigoted distrust // ~을 품다 have doubts / ~을 풀다 clear oneself of[from] suspicion / dispel[clear away] suspicion / dispel[remove / clear away] doubts / 너는 (매사에) ~이 너무 많다 You are too suspicious (about everything). // ~이 풀렸다 My doubts has disappeared[vanished]. // 그의 당황한 태도에 ~이 갔다 His flurried manner aroused my suspicion. // 그는 그 돈을 훔치지 않았나 하는 ~을 받았다 He was suspected of having stolen the money. // 그런 행동은 ~을 받기 쉽다 Such conduct is likely to arouse suspicion. // 그는 낯선 사람에 대해서는 ~이 많다 He doesn't readily trust strangers. / He takes a distrustful attitude toward(s) strangers. / He is suspicious of strangers. // 그의 행동은 그들의 ~을 샀다 His behavior incurred their suspicion. / His behavior gave rise to their suspicion. // 내가 범인일 것이라는 ~을 받았다 I was suspected to be the criminal. // 남의 ~을 받을 짓은 하지 마라 Don't lay yourself open to suspicion / Don't do anything that would excite [rouse] people's suspicion. **의심하다** [의혹을 품다] doubt (of); be doubtful of; have[entertain / feel] a doubt (as to / about); [믿지 않다] distrust; mistrust; [혐의를 걸다] suspect; be suspicious of[about]. ¶많은 사람이 그의 결백을 의심했다 Many have expressed their doubts as to his innocence. // 그의 성공을 의심하는 사람은 아무도 없다 No one doubts his success. // 이 약품은 그 안정성을 의심해 볼 필요가 있다 There is some doubt about[We are doubtful of] the safety of this medicine. // 그가 그것을 했다는 것은 의심할 여지가 없다 There is no room for doubt that he did it. // 그 서명의 신빙성에 대해서는 의심할 여지가 없다 There is no question about the authenticity of the signature.

// 그는 의심할 나위 없이 성공할 것이다 I have no doubt that he will succeed. / He is sure to succeed. / It is [I am] certain that he will succeed. // 이것은 의심할 나위 없이 진짜다 There is no doubt [question] (but) that this is the real thing. / This is unquestionably [undoubtedly] the real thing. // 급우들은 나를 의심하는 눈으로 보았다 I was looked upon with suspicion [suspicious eyes] by my classmates. // 그들은 내가 돈을 가져갔다고 의심하고 있는 것 같다 They seem to think [suspect] that I took the money. // 그들은 그의 말을 의심했다 They would not believe [They had doubts about] what he said. // 나는 그가 약속을 지킬 것을 믿어 의심하지 않는다 I do not have the slightest doubt [I am confident] that he will keep his word. // 그의 능력을 의심하지 않을 수 없다 I can't help being doubtful [skeptical] of his ability. // 우리는 그가 돈을 횡령하지 않았나 하고 의심했다 We suspected that he had embezzled the money. / We suspected him of embezzlement [embezzling the money]. // 그녀는 사람을 의심할 줄 모른다 She always takes people at their word.

의심스럽다(疑心-) doubtful; questionable; dubious; [수상쩍다] suspicious. ¶그의 성실성이 ~ I doubt his integrity. // 그가 성공할지 ~ I doubt if he will succeed. / I am doubtful of his success. // 그의 의도가 ~ I suspect his intentions. // 그의 의도가 좋은지 ~ I doubt whether his intentions are good. // 그의 알리바이가 ~ I have doubts about his alibi. // 그렇게 의심스러운 눈으로 나를 보지 마라 Please don't look at me so suspiciously [with such suspicious eyes]. // 그 신빙성이 ~ Its reliability is doubtful [open to question]. // 그가 제 시간에 올지 ~ I doubt [It is doubtful] whether he will make it [arrive in time]. // 그 정보는 ~ I am doubtful [suspicious] of that information. // 그는 의심스러운 듯이 고개를 저었다 He shook his head doubtfully. // 그의 상식이 ~ I'm inclined to doubt his commonsense. / It makes you wonder whether he has any common sense. // 나는 (아무래도) 그가 ~ I suspect him (to be guilty).

의심쩍다(疑心-) doubtful; questionable. ⇨의심스럽다 ¶의심쩍은 판정 a questionable [debatable] decision // 그는 그 결정을 의심쩍어 했다 He doubted the wisdom of the decision. / He couldn't understand the decision. / The decision made no sense to him. // 그는 그 안(案)을 좀 의심쩍게 생각했다 He was a little dubious of the plan.

의아스럽다(疑訝-) (be) doubtful; dubious; suspicious. ¶의아스러운 시선으로 with a suspicious look [glance] // 그는 의아스러운 표정을 지었다 He looked dubious [suspicious]. / He gave a dubious look. // 내가 그 임무를 맡기에는 너무 어려 보여 그녀는 의아스러운 눈으로 나를 바라보았다 She looked at me dubiously, as I appeared too young for the task.

의아하다(疑訝-) dubious; suspicious. ¶그녀의 행동에는 의아한 점이 있다 There's something suspicious about her actions. // 나는 도대체 무슨 일인가 하고 의아해했다 I wondered what had happened. **의아히** dubiously; suspiciously; doubtingly. ¶그녀는 무슨 일이냐고 ~ 물었다 She asked dubiously what was the matter.

의안(義眼) a glass eye; an artificial [a false] eye. ¶~을 하고 있다 have a false eye // 그는 오른쪽 눈이 ~이다 His right eye is false [glass].

의안(議案) (법률의) a bill; a measure; [회의의 의제] a question. ¶정부 제출 ~ a government bill // 새 ~을 의회에 제출하다 submit a new bill to [introduce a new bill in] the National Assembly / present a bill in [to] the Congress // ~을 기초하다 draw up a bill // ~을 통과시키다 pass [approve / carry] a bill // ~을 채택하다 adopt a bill // ~을 부결하다 reject [kill / vote down / vote against] a bill // ~이 의회를 통과했다 The bill passed [went through] the House. // ~은 부결되었다 The bill [measure] was rejected [defeated / negatived]. // 그 ~을 표결에 붙입시다 Let's put the question to a vote. // 그 ~은 국회에 제출되었다 The bill was laid before the National Assembly.

의약(醫藥) 〔약〕 medicine; 〔의술과 약〕 medical treatment [care] and dispensary.
●**의약 분업** the separation of pharmacy and clinic. **의약품** medical supplies.

의역(意譯) (a) free [loose] translation; a rude version. **의역하다** translate freely; give [make] a free [loose] translation. ¶다음 글을 축어역(逐語譯)이 아니라 의역하시오 Give the general meaning of the following passage, not a word-for-word translation. // 이것은 지나치게 의역했다 This translation is too free.

의연금(義捐金) a contribution; a subscription; a donation; a gift of money; alms. ¶수재 ~ subscriptions to relieve the flood victims [sufferers] // ~을 모으다 collect [gather / invite] contributions / raise subscriptions / pass around the hat // 그는 난민 구제 ~으로 10만 원을 내놓았다 He donated a hundred thousand won toward(s) refugee relief [to help the refugees].

의연하다(依然-) usual; unchanged; 〔구어〕 inevitable; 〔서술적〕 be in the same state. ¶구태 ~ remain as it was [as before] / remain unchanged. **의연히** as it was; as before; as it used to be; as ever; still; as usual.

의연하다(毅然-) resolute; dauntless; firm. ¶의연한 태도로 with a resolute attitude // 그는 끝까지 의연한 태도를 잃지 않았다 He never lost his fortitude. // 그녀의 의연한 태도는 우리에게 깊은 감명을 주었다 Her firm [resolute / dauntless] attitude impressed us deeply. **의연히** resolutely; firmly; with fortitude. ¶그는 그 제안을 ~ 거절했다 He declined the offer firmly [resolutely]. // 그는 자기주장을 ~ 굽히지 않았다 He stuck firmly to his contention.

의예과(醫豫科) the premedical course; 〔구어〕 premed.

의외(意外) unexpectation; surprise; an accident; an unexpected [unforeseen] matter. ¶~의 unexpected(우연한) // ~로 unexpectedly / surprisingly / to one's surprise / contrary to [beyond] one's expectation // 시험은 ~로 어려웠다 [쉬웠다] The examination was harder [easier] than I had expected. // 이익은 ~로 적다 The profit will be much less than you think. // 일이 ~로 잘되어 간다 Things went more smoothly than I had expected. // ~로 여성의 몸이 장거리 경주에 적합하다는

것이 입증되었다 Contrary to general belief, women have proved to be physically well adapted for long-distance races.∥사건은 ~의 방향으로 발전했다 The case took an unexpected turn.∥너를 여기서 만나다니 참으로 ~이다 I never expected thought [imagined] I would see you here.∥그가 낙제하다니 ~이다 I am surprised to hear that he failed (in) his examination.∥~의 결과였다 The results were surprising.

의욕(意慾) will; volition; zest; (a) desire. ¶근로 ~ the will to work∥삶에 대한 ~ the will to live∥그에게는 모든 것을 배우고 싶은 강한 ~이 있다 He is eager [has a strong desire] to learn everything.∥그녀는 남편이 죽은 뒤 삶의 ~을 잃었다 She lost all interest in life after her husband's death.

의욕적(意慾的) highly motivated; keenly enthusiastic. ¶~인 사람 a highly [strongly] motivated person∥~인 대작 an ambitious piece of work on a grand scale∥그들은 ~으로 이 새로운 기획에 착수했다 They started on this new enterprise with a will [with enthusiasm].∥그는 ~으로 일하고 있다 He is working with enthusiasm [a will].∥그는 지나치게 ~이다 He is too ambitious.

의용(義勇) loyalty and courage; heroism.
● **의용군** a volunteer army.

의용(儀容) manners; bearing; a mien; presence.

의원(醫院) a doctor's [medical practitioner's] office; (영) a doctor's surgery. ¶최 ~ Dr. Choe's office.

의원(醫員) (집합적) the medical staff; (개인) a member of the medical staff; a physician; a doctor.

의원(議院) (한국) the National Assembly; (일본) the Diet; (미국) the Congress; (영국) the Parliament.
● **의원 내각제** the parliamentary government system.

의원(議員) (일반적인) a member (of an assembly); an assemblyman; a representative. ¶국회 ~ (한국의) a member of the National Assembly / (일본·덴마크의) a member of the Diet / (영국의) a Member of Parliament / an MP / (미국의) a Congressman / a Congresswoman / an MC∥상원 ~ (미) a Senator(약어 Sen.) / (영) a member of the House of Lords∥하원 ~ (미) a member of the House of Representatives / a representative(약어 Rep.) / (영) a member of the House of Commons∥서울특별시 의회 ~ a member of the Seoul Metropolitan Assembly∥도[시 / 구] ~ a member of a prefectural [municipal / ward] assembly∥평 ~ an ordinary [average] M.P. [member]∥~으로 당선되다 be elected a member (of)∥~ 직을 사퇴하다 resign one's membership [seat] (in the National Assembly).
● **의원석** a seat (in the House); (집합적) the floor. **의원 총회** a general meeting of the National Assembly; a party caucus.

의의(意義) 1 [의미] a meaning; a sense. 2 [중요성·가치] (a) meaning; importance; significance. ¶인생의 ~ the meaning [significance] of life∥~ 있는 일 worthwhile [meaningful] work∥중대한 역사적 ~가 있는 사건 an event of great historical significance∥고등학교에서의 외국어 교육의 ~ the significance [importance] of foreign language teaching in senior high school∥~ 있는 significant / useful / worthwhile∥~ 없는 meaningless / insignificant∥~ 깊은 of deep significance∥~ 있는 생활을 하다 lead a life worth living / lead a significant [useful] life / live to some purpose.

의인(義人) a righteous [an upright] person; a person of high principles.

의인(擬人) personification. ¶~화하다 personify∥~화된 것 the personification (of)∥이솝은 동물을 ~화했다 Aesop personified [anthropomorphized] animals (in his fables). **의인하다** personify; impersonate.
● **의인법** personification.

의자(椅子) (등받이 있는 1인용의) a chair; (등받이·팔걸이 없는) a stool; [회전의자] a swivel chair; [흔들의자] a rocking chair. ¶긴 ~ a bench / a sofa / a lounge / a couch / a divan(벽에 붙인) ∥ **안락** ~ an easy chair∥**어린이용**(높은) ~ a high chair∥접는 ~ a folding chair / (간편한 것) a camp chair / (범포제) a hammock chair∥**팔걸이** ~ an armchair∥**회전** ~ a revolving [swivel] chair∥**흔들** ~ a rocking chair∥**전기** ~ an electric chair / (미국 속어) a hot chair∥~의 등[팔/다리/바닥] the back [arms / legs / seat] of a chair∥~에 앉다 sit on [in] a chair / take a seat on [in] a chair (▶ in은 안락의자 등에 깊이 앉을 때) / take a chair∥~에서 일어서다 rise [get up] from the chair [seat]∥~를 앞으로 당기다 pull [draw] up a chair / drag one's chair forward∥~에 앉기를 권하다 offer (a person) a chair.

의장(意匠) (a decorative [an artistic]) design. ¶참신한 ~ a novel design / a creation∥등록된 ~ a registered design∥정교한 ~의 가구 elaborately designed furniture∥~을 고안하다 think [work] out a design∥그는 참신한 ~을 고안해 냈다 He thought out an original design.
● **의장 등록** registration of designs.

의장(儀仗) implements [arms] used in the national ceremonies.
● **의장대**(一隊) a guard of honor; an honor guard. ¶~를 **사열하다** inspect [review] an honor guard.

의장(議長) the chairman(▶ 여성에게도 씀); the chairwoman(여성); the chairperson(▶ 남녀의 구별 없이 씀); (미국 하원의) the Speaker; (영·미 상원의) the president. ¶임시 ~ an acting chairman∥~이 되다 take [be in] the chair∥~! (호칭) Mr. [Madam] Chairman!∥그녀는 ~이 되었다 She took the chair.∥누가 ~을 맡고 있었느냐 Who was in the chair?

의장(議場) an assembly hall; a chamber; [장내 의원석] the floor. ¶~이 혼란에 빠졌다 The floor was thrown into confusion.∥그는 ~의 질서를 회복하러 애썼다 He tried to restore order on the floor.

의적(義賊) [의로운 도적] a Robin Hood figure; a chivalrous robber; a benevolent picaroon.

의전(儀典) a ceremony; function. ⇨의식(儀式)
● **의전실** the Office of Protocol.

의절(義絶) a rupture; cutting off relationship; a breach (of friendship); (자녀와의) disowning; disinheritance. **의절하다** break off rela-

의정하다 stately; dignified; grand; imposing; commanding. ¶의젓한 태도 a stately manner // 의젓한 풍채 commanding presence / imposing appearance // 너도 이제는 의젓한 어른이다 You've grown into a fine adult. / You're now ready to take your place in adult society. // 그는 어디로 보나 의젓한 청년이다 He is very presentable young man. // 그는 나이는 어리지만 의젓한 핵물리학자이다 He is young, but he is a distinguished nuclear physicist. // 그때의 그의 태도는 의젓했다 The attitude he took then really commanded our admiration. **의젓이** stately; in state; dignifiedly; with dignity; in a dignified manner. ¶~ 걷다 walk in grand style // 좀 ~ 앉아 기다려라 Sit and wait patiently. // 사절단은 그 나라 수도에 ~ 들어갔다 The delegation entered the capital of the country in state.

의정(議定) an agreement. **의정하다** confer and agree upon; confer and decide.
● **의정서** a protocol.

의정(議政) parliamentary government. ⇨ 의회 정치(⇨의회)

의제(義弟) a sworn (younger) brother.

의제(議題) a topic [subject] (for discussion); a problem; the agenda. ¶그 안건은 오늘의 ~로 상정되었다 That came [was brought] up for discussion today. // 그것은 중요한 ~로 되어 있다 That is high [That is a very important item] on the agenda. // 그 회의에서는 여러 가지 ~가 토의되었다 Various topics [subjects] were dealt with at the conference. // 그것은 ~에 포함되어 있지 않다 It is not on the agenda.

의제(擬制) [법] a (legal) fiction. ¶~의 fictitious / [법] constructive.
● **의제 자본** a watered [fictitious] capital.

의족(義足) an artificial leg; (구어) a wooden leg. ¶~을 한 사람 a wooden-legged person // 그의 왼쪽 다리는 ~이다 His left leg is an artificial one. / He has an artificial left leg.

의존(依存) reliance; dependence. ¶상호 ~ interdependence // 두 도시는 여러 가지 점에서 상호 ~ 관계에 있다 These two cities are interdependent in many ways. **의존하다** depend (on); be dependent (on); rely (on). ¶이 나라의 경제는 석유 수출에 의존하고 있다 The economy of this country depends [is dependent] on the export of oil. // 이 도시는 관광에 의존한다 The town is dependent on tourism. / Tourist resources are what keep this town going. // 나라의 재정은 국채에 의존하는 바 크다 The financing of the nation depends greatly on government bonds. // 그렇게 매사를 내게 의존하지 말게 Don't rely [depend] on me for everything. // 언제까지 부모에게 의존하고 있을 것인가 It's high time you were independent of your parents.

의좋다(誼-) (서술적) be on good [intimate] terms (with); be good friends (with); be friendly (with). ¶의좋은 부부 a devoted [happy] couple / a couple who dote on each other // 의좋게 on good [friendly / cordial] terms / in harmony / like good friends // 그들은 의좋게 지내고 있다 They live together in harmony.

의중(意中) one's inmost feelings. ⇨ 마음속(⇨마음). ¶~의 사람 the person one has in mind // 남의 ~을 헤아리다 read a person's mind [thoughts] // ~을 털어놓다 open one's heart (to a person) // 그들은 그의 ~을 떠보려고 몹시 애썼다 They strove hard to sound out his intentions [what was in his mind].

의지(依支) 1 [몸을 기댐] leaning; [그 대상] a support. **의지하다** recline (on a couch); lean [rest] (against the wall). ¶그는 지팡이에 의지하면서 걸어갔다 He walked leaning on [with the help of] his stick. // 나는 류머티즘 때문에 지팡이에 의지하지 않고는 걷지 못한다 Since I have rheumatism, I cannot walk without leaning on [using] a cane [(영) stick].

2 [의존] reliance; dependence; [의지의 대상] a support; a prop; a staff. ¶성경은 그의 생애에서 최대의 ~가 되었다 The Bible was his greatest support throughout his life. // 이 아들만이 나의 ~가 됩니다 This son is my sole support. **의지하다** depend [rely] (on); place [put] reliance (on / in); trust (on); turn [look] to (a person) (for help); fall back on. ¶송 씨에게 ~ rely [depend] on [(문어) upon] Mr. Song // 의지하지 않다 depend [reply / count] upon oneself // 당신은 내게 지나치게 의지하고 있다 You depend too much on me. // 나는 오로지 너를 의지하고 있다 I rely entirely on you. // 그는 의지할 사람이 못 된다 He is unreliable. / He is untrustworthy. // 그들은 수입을 목축에 의지했다 They depended [relied] on stock-farming as a source of income. // 숙모는 아버지를 의지하고 우리 집에 오셨다 My aunt came to our house counting on my father's help [support]. // 그는 그 나이에도 부모에게 의지하여 살고 있다 He still lives [depends] on his parents, even at his age. // 나는 늙어서도 아들에 의지하지 않을 작정이다 I am determined not to be dependent on [be a burden to] my son in my old age. // 신앙에 의지하지 않았던들 나는 살 수 없었을 것이다 If I had not been supported by my faith, I would not have been able to go on living. // 이 당이 의지하고 있는 기반은 노동자이다 This party has the working class as its base. / Working men and women make up the base of this political party.

의지(意志) will; volition. ¶자유 ~ free will // 불굴의 ~ an indomitable [iron] will // 굳은 [박약한] ~ a strong [weak] will // ~가 강한 사람 a person of strong [iron] will / a strong-willed man // ~가 약한 사람 a man of weak will / a weak-willed person // ~의 힘으로 by willpower / by the (sheer) force of one's will // ~가 박약하면 무슨 일에나 성공하기 어렵다 You will never succeed in anything if you don't have a firm purpose.
● **의지력** willpower; force of will.

의지가지없다(依支-) [조금도 의탁할 곳이 없다] forlorn; alone; helpless; lonely; (서술적) have no one to depend upon [to turn to for help]. ¶의지가지없는 사람들 the lonely and the helpless // 의지가지없는 노인들 old people with no relatives to look after them [to turn to] // 나는 의지가지없는 신세다 I have no place to go. / I have nobody to turn to (for help).

의처증(疑妻症) a morbid suspicion of one's

wife's chastity; a groundless doubt of one's wife's faithfulness.

의치(義齒) an artificial[a false] tooth; (한 벌의) a dentures; false teeth. ¶총[부분] ~ a full[partial] denture // ~를 하나 해 넣었다 I had an artificial[a false] tooth put in. // 그의 이는 모두 ~이다 He wears a full set of false teeth[dentures].

의타심(依他心) (a propensity to) dependence; reliance. ¶그는 ~이 강하다 He relies[depends] too much upon others.

의탁(依託) 〔의지〕 reliance; dependence; 〔맡김〕 entrust; trust. **의탁하다** entrust to (a person's) care; trust (to); rely[depend] (on). ¶몸을 ~ entrust oneself to a person's care // 의탁할 곳 없다 have no place to go to / be helpless[homeless] // 그는 외아들을 내게 의탁하고 외국에 갔다 He went abroad committing his only son to my care. ➔ ¶의탁받다 be entrusted.

의태(擬態) 〔생〕 mimicry; mimesis. ¶~의 mimic.
● **의태어** 〔언〕 an imitative word; a mimetic word.

의표(意表) a surprise; unexpectedness. ¶남의 ~를 찌르다 take a person by surprise / do something quite unexpected // 나는 그의 책략의 ~를 찔렀다 I outwitted[outsmarted] my opponent by doing just the opposite of what he expected.

의하다(依-) **1** 〔의거하다〕 be based[founded / grounded] on[upon] (something). ¶노동에 의한 결론 a conclusion based on experimental results // 소문에 의하면 as report has it [goes] / according to rumors // 전하는 바에 의하면 reportedly // 그의 의견은 그의 경험에 의한 것이다 His opinion is based[founded / grounded] on his experience. // 들은 바에 의하면 그는 유능한 사람인 것 같다 Judging from reports, he seems to be an able man. // 이야기에 의하면 그는 전사했다고 한다 The story goes that he was killed in war.
2 〔말미암다〕 be due to; be caused by; be owing to[attributable to]. ¶승리를 천우에 의한 것으로 돌리다 attribute[refer] one's victory to Providence // 그 화재는 누전에 의한 것이었다 The fire was caused by a short circuit. // 그 사고는 그의 부주의한 운전에 의한 것이었다 The accident was due to his careless driving. // 암에 의한 사망률이 증가하고 있다 The death rate from cancer is rising. // 짙은 안개에 의한 결항이 계속되었다 Ships were prevented from sailing every day because of[on account of / by] dense fog.

의학(醫學) medicine; medical science. ¶~의 medical // ~적으로 medical(ly) // ~을 **연구하다** study medicine // 병원에서 ~ 실습을 하다 walk the hospital(s) / (미) act as an intern / intern (at the Memorial Hospital).
● **의학계** the medical world; medical circles. **의학도** a medical student. **의학 박사** a doctor of medicine; (학위) a Doctor of Medicine(약어 M.D.). **의학자** a medical man; a doctor.

의합하다(意合-) **1** 〔의좋다〕 friendly; amicable. **2** 〔뜻이 맞다〕 congenial.

의향(意向) 〔의도〕 an intention; 〔생각〕 an idea; views; 〔소망〕 wishes. ¶~을 **비치다** disclose one's intention // ~을 **타진하다** sound (a person's) opinion[views] // 상대방의 ~을 알아봐 주시겠습니까 Could you sound out the other party's intentions for me? / May I ask you to find out what the other party intends to do? // 이 문제에 대한 당신의 ~은 어떤 것입니까 What are your views on this question? // 나는 부모의 ~에 따라 대학 진학을 포기했다 Obeying my parents' wishes, I gave up the idea of entering a university. // 그를 만날[결혼할] ~은 없습니다 I have no intention of seeing him[getting married].

의협심(義俠心) (a) chivalrous spirit. ¶~이 있는 chivalrous / heroic // ~이 강한 사람 a chivalrous person / a man of chivalrous spirit.

의형(義兄) a sworn[pledged] elder brother.

의형제(義兄弟) a sworn brother[friend]. ¶두 사나이는 ~를 맺었다 The two men took a pledge of brotherhood. / The two men swore themselves brothers.

의혹(疑惑) suspicion (of / that); doubt (about / as to / that). ¶~을 **풀다** clear oneself of suspicion // ~에 싸여 있다 be wrapt in a shroud of suspicion // ~을 **품다** entertain[have] doubts (about) / be in doubt / harbor suspicion / have misgivings (about) // 그런 행동은 ~을 초래하기 쉽다 Such conduct is likely to arouse suspicion. // 그의 알리바이에 대해서 나는 ~을 품고 있다 I have doubts about his alibi. // ~의 눈으로 사물을 보면 의심스럽게 보이는 법이다 When you regard things with suspicion, they begin to look suspicious.

의회(議會) **1** 〔한국의〕 the National Assembly; (일본·덴마크의) the Diet; (영국의) Parliament; (미국의) Congress. ¶국민 ~ the National Assembly // 금번[제40차] ~ the present[the 40th] session of the National Assembly // ~의 지지를 받다 receive congressional support // ~를 **해산[소집]하다** dissolve[convene / convoke] Parliament // ~는 개회 중이다 The House is now sitting[in session]. // ~는 어제부터 1개월의 회기로 개회되었다 The assembly was convened yesterday and will be in session for a month.
2 (지방의) an assembly. ¶특별시 ~ the metropolitan assembly // 도[시] ~ prefectural [municipal] assembly.
● **의회 정치** parliamentary government [politics]; parliamentarism. **의회 제도** the parliamentary system.

이[1] **1** (사람·동물의) a tooth (*pl*. teeth). ¶썩은 ~ a decayed[bad] tooth // 고른 ~ even teeth // ~가 **좋다** have good[bad] teeth // ~를 **갈다** 〔새 이가 나다〕 lose one's baby[milk] teeth and get one's second teeth // ~를 **빼다** draw[pull out] a tooth / have a teeth pulled[drown] (out) // ~가 **고르다**[고르지 않다] have a regular[irregular] set of teeth // ~를 해 박다 have a false tooth put in // ~가 **들뜨다** set one's teeth on edge // loose one's teeth // ~를 **닦다**[쑤시다] brush [pick] one's teeth // ~를 **치료하다** have one's teeth treated / take[undergo] dental treatment // (사람이) ~가 **나다** cut one's teeth // ~를 **드러내다** bare[show] one's teeth // 어제 ~를 한 개 뺐다 I had a tooth pulled[(문어) extracted] yesterday. / I had a tooth out yesterday. // ~가 **아프다** I have a toothache. / My tooth aches. // 이 아이는 ~가 나기 시작했다 This child is teething[cutting a tooth].

이 아이는 ~가 늦게 난다 This child's teeth are slow to come in. // 앞쪽 ~가 흔들린다 My front teeth are loose. // ~가 한 개 빠졌다 A tooth came out[fell out]. // 그녀는 ~가 고르게 나 있다 Her teeth are even. // 나는 공포[추위]로 ~가 덜덜 떨렸다 My teeth chattered with fright[cold]. // 단것을 지나치게 먹으면 ~가 상한다 Too much indulgence in sweets decays the teeth.

2 (기구 등의) a cog; a tooth; a dent. ¶톱날의 ~ the teeth of a saw // ~ 빠진 칼 a knife with a broken blade // 기어의 ~가 잘 맞물리지 않는다 The cogs[gears] do not engage properly. // 이 칼은 ~가 빠졌다 The edge of this knife is nicked.

3 (사기그릇 등의) a chip. ¶~ 빠진 찻잔 a chipped teacup.

이 없으면 잇몸으로 살지 (속담) You can get along without something if necessary.

이(를) 갈다 [벼르다] be eager; for revenge; grind one's teeth with vexation. ¶이를 갈며 분해하다 grind one's teeth with vexation / grit one's teeth // 그는 이를 갈며 내 의견을 공박해 왔다 He leaped to attack my argument with evident hostility.

이를 악물다 clench[clamp] one's teeth; set one's teeth. ¶나는 이를 악물고 아픔을 참았다 I clenched[gritted] my teeth to bear the pain. / I bore the pain with clenched teeth. // 그녀는 이를 악물고 역경을 극복했다 She overcame her difficulties with fortitude.

이² [동] a louse (pl. lice). ¶~투성이의 lousy (head) // ~가 들끓다 become infested with lice // ~를 잡다 hunt[crush] a louse / get rid of lice.

이 잡듯이 in every nook and corner; everywhere. ¶~ 뒤지다 leave no stone unturned / go over with a fine toothcomb // 탈주자를 찾아 그 지역을 ~ 하다 comb the area for the deserter // 경찰은 그 집을 ~ 수색했다 The police searched all over the house[every nook and corner of the house].

이³ [사람] a person; a man; one. ¶최 씨라는 ~ a (certain) Mr. Choe / one Choe / a man named[by the name of] Choe // 저기 있는 ~가 누구지 Who is that man?

이⁴ this; it; these. ¶~ 밖에 besides / above this // ~와 같은 편지 such a letter as this // ~와 같은 이유로 for such reason (as mentioned) // ~와는 반대로 on the contrary to this // 내가 하면 ~처럼 잘된다 See how well I do it. // ~처럼 와 주셔서 고맙습니다 Thank you for coming like this. // ~처럼 재미있는 일은 없다 Nothing is more interesting than this. // ~처럼 잘되리란 기대하기 어렵다 You can't expect anything to go like this. // ~처럼 많은 비는 여기서는 드문 일이다 It is rare to have so much rain[such a heavy rainfall] here.

이⁵ this; these; present; current. ¶당신의 ~ 책 this book of yours // ~ 귀로 다 들었다 I heard it with my own ears. // ~ 일을 잊어서는 안 된다 Do not forget this. // ~ 책은 누구 겁니까 Whose book is this? (▶ Whose is this book?라는 표현은 쓰이지 않음) // 나는 ~ 도시에서 10년 동안 살고 있다 I have been (living) in this town for the past ten years.

이 핑계 저 핑계 this excuse or that; (on) one excuse or another; (on) some pretext or other. ¶~ 대며 일을 자꾸 미루다 keep putting the matter off with one excuse after another // 그는 ~ 대며 집세를 내지 않는다 He avoids paying the rent on some pretext or other[for one reason or another].

이 (二·貳) [둘] two; [둘째] the second. ¶~ 대(代) two generations // 8에 ~를 더하면 10이 된다 Two added to eight makes ten. / Eight and two make[are] ten. / Eight plus two is ten. // ~ 삼은 육이다 Two times three makes [is] six.

이 (利) **1** [나은 점] an advantage. ¶서로 ~가 되다 be mutually advantageous. **2** [이득] gain; profit. ¶~가 많은 장사 a profitable [lucrative] business // ~를 보다 make a profit / profit (from the sale) // ~가 남다 bring profits / yield a profit // ~가 박하다 give little profit / do not pay much // 그는 상당한 ~를 보고 그것을 팔았다 He sold it at a considerable profit. // 그런 짓은 해서 무슨 ~가 되나 What is the profit of doing that? **3** [이자] interest (on a loan).

이가 (二價) [화] bivalence; divalence. ¶~의 bivalent / divalent / diatomic / dyadic.

이간 (離間) alienation; estrangement. **이간하다** alienate[estrange] (a person from another); separate[sever] (husband and wife); come between (the two); cause an estrangement (between two old friends). ➔¶그녀는 두 사람 사이를 이간시키려고 한다 She intends to alienate them from each other. // 그는 두 당을 이간시키려 했다 He tried to estrange[alienate / drive a wedge between] the two parties.

● **이간책** a scheme to provoke estrangement [alienation]; a discord-producing intrigue.

이감하다 (移監—) transfer (a convict) to another prison[cell / ward].

이같이 like this; thus; so; in this way; so much; in such a manner. ¶~ 된 이상 now that things have come to this pass // ~ 많이 so many[much] / (구어) this many[much] // ~ 많은 돈 such a big sum of money / so much money // ~ 추운 날씨는 처음이다 I have never seen such cold weather as this. // 그는 ~ 말했다 He spoke like this[to this effect].

이것 1 this (pl. these); this one; this thing. ¶~은 말하자면 that is (to say) // ~은 제쳐 두고 leaving this aside // 사과는 ~이 마지막이다 This is the last of the apples. / These are the last apples we have. // 이 인생이다 Such is life. // ~으로 저의 이야기를 끝냅니다 Let me conclude my speech with this. // "~이다!"라고 그는 외쳤다 "That's it!" he cried. / "I've got it!" he cried. // ~이면 되겠습니까 Will this do? // ~이면 그도 반대하지 않을 것이다 If you give him this, he will not raise any objection. // ~만은 확실하다 This much is certain. // ~만은 아무에게도 주지 않겠다 I will never give this to anybody. // ~가지고 있는 것이 ~뿐입니까 Is this all you have? // ~이야말로 스포츠맨십의 귀감이다 This is a true example of sportsmanship. // ~으로 내 인생은 끝장이다 This will ruin me. / This will be the end of me. // ~도 오로지 당신 덕분입니다 I owe this entirely to you. // 돈은 ~이 전부다 That is all the money I have. // 기회는 ~이 마지막이다 This is our last chance.

2 [사람을 얕잡아 부르는 말]. ¶~ 봐 Look

이것저것 [See] here. / Listen. / I say. // ~ 봐 어디 가나 Here[Say], where are you going?

이것저것 this and that; this, that and the other (thing); (for) one thing and another. ¶~ 생각한 끝에 after thinking this way and that over the matter / after much thinking // ~ 다 everything / every and all // 어머니는 외동아들의 일을 ~ 걱정했다 The mother worried about her only son over one thing or another. // 그는 ~ 농담을 하면서 우리를 웃었다 He made us laugh about this and that[with his endless repertoire of jokes]. // 그는 언제나 어렵다고 ~ 불평만 한다 He is always grumbling, saying this or that is too hard for him. // 그는 친절하게 ~ 충고해 주었다 He gave kindly advice about this and that.

이견(異見) a different view[opinion]; a dissenting opinion; [이의] a protest; an objection. ¶~을 내세우다 present a different view (from) / [문어] give a dissenting opinion (from) / raise an objection (to).

이고 1 [두 가지 이상의 사물을 아울러 설명] and (also); and; or. ¶이것은 펜~ 그것은 연필이다 This is a pen and that is a pencil. // 한 분은 의사~ 한 분은 변호사이다 One is a doctor and the other is a lawyer. 2 […이나 …이든] any; ... ever. ¶무엇~ whichever / anything // 누구~ whoever // 정말~ 아니고 간에 whatever (it may be) true or not // 아무 연필~ 다 좋다 Any pencil will do. // 그것을 빼놓고는 무엇~ 하겠다 I'll do anything but that.

이골 [몸에 밴 버릇] an acquired[a fixed] habit.
이골(이) 나다 be accustomed[used] to; be well acquainted with; become habituated [inured] to. ¶형편없는 식사에는 이골이 나 있다 I am accustomed[used] to poor meals. // 그는 가난했기 때문에 곤궁에는 이골이 나 있었다 His experience of poverty inured him to hardship.

이곳 this place; here. ¶~ 사람들 the people here / (그 지방의) the people of this district // ~에(서) here / in this place // ~으로 here / to this place // ~을 지나실 때는 한번 들러 주시오 Drop in please When you come this way. // ~은 이미 벚꽃이 만발해 있습니다 The cherry blossoms are already in full bloom here.

이곳저곳 here and there.

이공(理工) science and engineering.
●**이공 대학** a college of science and engineering.

이과(理科) 1 [학문·교과] science; natural science. ¶~는 내가 좋아하는 과목이다 Science is my favorite subject. 2 (학과) the science course[department]. ¶나는 ~로 진학 생각이다 I intend to take the science course in college.
●**이과 대학** a college of science.

이관(移管) transfer (the management of). **이관하다** transfer. ➔¶이 사업은 시에서 도로 이관되었다 This work[project] was transferred from the municipal authorities to the control of the province. // 그 건은 건설국으로 이관되었다 That case has been transferred to the control of the construction bureau.

이교(異敎) [자기가 믿는 이외의 종교] a different religion; [기독교에서 본 이단] a heresy; paganism; heathenism. ¶~의 heathen / pagan / heretical // 그들은 ~를 믿고 있다 They believe in a heathen[pagan] religion.
●**이교도** a heathen; a pagan; a heretic. ¶~를 개종시키다 convert the heathen.

이구동성(異口同聲) a unanimous voice; common consent. ¶~으로 with one voice / in unison / in chorus (만장일치로) unanimously // 그들은 ~으로 그를 비난했다 They all censured him with one voice. // 노조원들은 ~으로 임금 인상을 요구했다 The member of the labor union unanimously demanded a wage increase.

이국(異國) a foreign country[land]; a strange land. ¶~의 foreign // ~에 묻히다 die in a foreign land // 그들은 ~에서 떠돌고 있다 They are exiles from home. // 이곳은 ~의 언어가 혼재하는 항구 도시이다 This is a port town, where many foreign languages mingle on the streets.
●**이국인** a foreigner. **이국정서** exoticism.

이국적(異國的) exotic. ¶그곳에는 ~인 정서가 있어 좋다 I like that place because it has an exotic atmosphere about it.

이군(二軍) [야구] a farm[scrub] team; a farm.
●**이군 선수** a farm hand; a scrub.

이권(利權) rights (and interests); (광산 발굴 등의) a concession. ¶은광 개발의 ~ a concession to develop a silver mine // ~을 획득하다 acquire concessions[rights] // ~을 포기하다 renounce one's interests // 신 씨가 운영하던 사업의 ~을 모두 당사가 인수하였음을 알려 드립니다 We have the pleasure to inform you that we have taken over all the business interests carried on by Mr. Sin.
●**이권 운동** graft(ing); hunting for a concession.

이글 [골프] eagle. ¶9번 홀에서 ~을 쳤다 He shot an eagle on the ninth hole.

이글거리다 glare; blaze; dazzle(눈부시게). ¶이글거리는 태양 a glaring sun / 정욕으로 이글거리는 눈 eyes burning with passion // 그는 분노로 이글거리는 눈을 내게 돌렸다 He glared anger at me. // 그의 눈은 노여움으로 이글거렸다 His eyes glared with anger.

이글루 [얼음집] an igloo; an iglu.

이글이글 [불타는 모양] (burning) briskly; [빛나는 모양] glaringly; (얼굴이) deeply flushed. ¶숯불이 ~ 타고 있다 The charcoal burns lively. // 태양이 머리 위에서 ~ 내리쬐고 있었다 The sun was blazing[glaring] down on us. **이글이글하다** blazing; burning; glaring; glowing.

이급(二級) the second class[grade]. ¶~의 second-class // ~ 호텔 a second-class hotel.

이기(利器) 1 [잘 드는 기구] a sharp-edged tool. 2 [실용에 편리한 것] a convenience; facilities. ¶문명의 ~ modern conveniences.

이기다[1] [승리하다] win; win[gain] a victory (over); triumph (over); [처부수다] beat; defeat. ¶싸움에 ~ win a battle[a war] // 소송에 ~ win a suit / 3점의 차로 ~ win by three points[runs] (▶ runs는 야구의 경우) / 경쟁 상대에게 ~ beat one's opponent // 토론에서 ~ defeat[get the better of] (a person) in a debate // 적을 ~ overcome[defeat] one's enemy / 가까스로 ~ win a close victory (over) // 우리는 이길 가망이 없다 We have little chance of winning. // 우리 학교는 야구

시합에서 B교를 이겼다 Our school beat[won a victory over] B school at baseball.// 이 시합에서는 내가 이긴다 This game is mine.// 그는 모든 시합을 다 이겼다 He won every event.// 네가 이겼다 The game [day] is yours. / You win.// 우리 팀은 그들에게 7대 5로 이겼다 Our team won the game against them (by a score of) 7 to 5.// 1회전에서 상대방을 넘어뜨리고 이긴 여세를 몰아 우승했다 Flushed with success after beating his first round opponent, he went on to win the championship.// 신진 권투 선수가 챔피언을 이겼다 The new boxer outboxed the champion.// 누가 이기나 해보자 We will see which of us is master. **2** [극복하다] overcome[surmount] (obstacles); get[tide] over (difficulties).

이기다² **1** [반죽하다] knead (dough); work (mortar); temper(점토 등을). ¶되게 이긴 재료 a stiffly kneaded[beaten] material// 진흙을 잘 ~ knead the clay thoroughly// 회반죽을 ~ mix plaster thoroughly// 물감을 기름으로 ~ temper paints with oil// 밀가루와 물을 섞어 이겨서 밀가루 반죽을 만들다 mix flour and water and knead into dough// 어린이가 진흙을 이기며 놀고 있었다 A child was enjoying squeezing the mud through his fingers. **2** [잘게 짓쩧다] mince; chop[cut] up. ¶고기를 ~ mince meat.

이기심(利己心) egoistic[selfish / egocentric / self-centered] mind. ¶그녀는 ~의 덩어리다 She is egoism personified. / She is selfishness itself.

이기적(利己的) selfish; egoistic(al). ¶~이 아닌 unselfish / [이타적인] altruistic// ~인 요구 a self-centered demand// ~인 사고방식 a selfish way of thinking.

이기주의(利己主義) egoism.
● **이기주의자** an egoist.

이기죽거리다 make provoking[invidious] remarks[jokes]; grate on (a person's) nerve; go against the grain.

이까짓 this kind of; such a; so trifling[slight / little / small]. ¶~ 것을 두려워해서는 안 된다 You should not fear such a little thing. / You shouldn't let such a small thing worry you.// ~ 것쯤이야 This is nothing.// ~ 일로 떠들지 마라 Don't make a fuss about such a little thing.// 그는 ~ 돈으로는 만족하지 않을 것이다 He won't be satisfied with such a small[so small a] sum of money.// ~ 일로 걱정할 것 없다 You needn't worry about such a little thing.// ~ 것 하고 깔본 게 잘못이었다 I did wrong in making light of the matter.

이끌다 **1** [거느리다] lead; head (a party); be at the head (of); [지휘하다] command (an army); [데리고 가다] take[bring / have] (a person) along[with one]. ¶그는 선수단을 이끌고 유럽으로 원정을 갔다 He visited European countries leading[at the head of] delegation of athletes.// 나는 학생을 이끌고 박물관에 갔다 I went to the museum with my students. / I took my students to the museum.// 그는 내각을 이끌고 가고 있다 He heads the Cabinet. **2** [지도·인도하다] guide; lead; shepherd (a crowd). ¶남을 바른길로 ~ guide a person's steps in the path of righteousness// (사람을) 잘못 ~ fail to lead (a person) properly / lead (a person) astray// 공식을 이용해서 답을 이끌어 내다 arrive at [get / find] an answer by using the formula// 선생이나 부모나 그 학생을 바른길로 이끌려고 했다 The teacher and the parents were trying to guide the student into the right path.// 그를 파멸로 이끈 것은 그녀였다 It was she that[who] led him to ruin.

이끌리다 **1** [지휘를 받다] be led; be headed; be commanded. **2** [인도되다] be led; be conducted; be guided to. ¶이끌려 가다 be led away / be taken along. **3** [정에] be tied [fettered] (by); be drawn (by); (감정·호기심에) be driven (by); be carried away (by one's feelings). ¶호기심에 이끌려 under the impulse of curiosity / out of curiosity// 감정에 이끌려서는 안 된다 Don't let your feelings run away with you.

이끼 moss; [지의류] lichen. ¶~의 mossy / lichened// 솔~ hair moss// 물~ bog moss// 우산~ liverwort// ~ 낀 정원 a moss-covered garden / a garden overgrown with moss// ~ 낀 고목 the lichened trunk of an old tree / an old tree trunk covered with lichen// 바위에 ~가 끼어 있다 Moss has formed on the rock.

이나 **1** [그러나] but; (and) yet; [한편] while; meanwhile; [⋯하기는 하나] though; although; nevertheless; however; still. ¶그의 말은 사실~ 표현이 나빴다 He spoke the truth, but expressed himself poorly. **2** [정도·비교] as many[much] as; no less [fewer] than; as long as; nearly; about. ¶이 물건은 만 원~ 했다 This article cost all of 10,000 won. / This article cost no less than 10,000 won.// 그가 그것을 완성하는 데는 10년~ 걸렸다 It took him ten long years to complete it.// 10명~ 같은 실수를 했다 As many as ten people made the same mistake. **3** [선택] either … or; or; any. ¶어느 것~ 마음에 드는 것을 택해라 Take whichever [whatever] you like.// 손 군~ 내가 가야만 한다 Either Mr. Son or I must go.// 어느 방법~ 별 차이는 없다 It makes no difference either way. / There is no major difference between the ways. **4** [어느 것을 막론하고] and; as well as; (두 가지 물건일 때) both … and. ¶그는 밤~ 낮~ 일했다 He worked night and day.

이나마¹ [이것이나마] although it is. ¶~ 없는 것보다는 낫다 This is better than nothing.

이나마² [우선 아쉬운 대로] although; though; even if; however. ¶변변치 못한 선물~ 받아 주십시오 Kindly accept my trifling gift. / I hope you will accept this little present.// 어머니를 한 번 ~ 뵙고 싶다 How I long to have a look of my mother!// 낡은 자가용~ 한 대 있었으면 좋겠다 I wish I had a car of my own however old it might be.

이남(以南) **1** [남쪽] south (of) …; … and southward. ¶38선 ~ south of the 38th parallel// 서울 ~ Seoul and southward / south of Seoul// 이 종류의 식물은 대전 ~에 생육한다 This kind of plant grows south of[does not grow north of] Daejeon. **2** [남한] South Korea.

이남박 a rice-washing bowl.

이내 1 [곧] at once; directly; immediately; (구어) right away; [얼마 후] soon; presently; shortly. ¶(약 등이) ~ 듣다 have an instant

이내 effect (on) / work at once // ~ 돌아오겠다 I'll be back in a moment. // 일이 끝나면 ~ 와 주시오 Come to see me as soon as you finish your work. // 그는 ~ 돌아왔다 He came back shortly. **2** [그후 내처] ever since. ¶헤어지고 ~ 감감소식이다 I have not heard from him since I saw him last.

이내(以內) [어떤 기준을 포함해서 그보다 적은 범위] within; less than; not more than. ¶역에서 학교까지는 걸어서 10분 ~입니다 Our school is less than ten minutes' walk from the station. // 그 일은 1주일 ~에 마칠 수 있습니다 The work will be finished within [in less than] a week. // 비용은 5,000원 ~입니다 The expenses will not exceed 5,000 won. // 내 딸은 10개월 ~에 걷기 시작했다 My daughter began to walk before she was ten months old. // 다음 기사를 500단어 ~로 요약해서 쓰시오 Write a summary of the following article in not more than 500 words.

이년생(二年生) a second-grade[-year] pupil [student]; (미) a second grader; (4년제 대학·고교의) (미) a sophomore; (3년제 고교의) a junior; (2년제 전문대의) a senior.

이념(理念) [철학상의 개념] an idea; [이데올로기] (an) ideology; [신조로서의 생각] a philosophy (of). ¶~적인 ideological // 사회주의 ~ socialist ideology // 스미스 박사의 교육 ~ Dr. Smith's educational philosophy [philosophy of education] // 그들은 ~을 달리한다 They have different ideology.

이놈 this man[fellow]; this (damn) guy. ¶~ 아 You rascal ! / You villain [scoundrel] !

이농(離農) rural exodus. **이농하다** abandon [give up] farming (in favor of another occupation).

이뇨(利尿) [오줌이 잘 나오게 함] diuresis. **이뇨하다** urinate; pass water.
● **이뇨제** a diuretic.

이니 [사물을 열거할 때 씀] and so on [forth]; and; or; and the like; and others. ¶쌀 ~ 된장 ~ 그 밖의 여러 가지 것 rice, soybean paste, and various other food stuffs // 수업 ~ 저술 ~ 하여 조금도 틈이 없다 Between [What with] teaching and writing, my time is wholly taken up.

이니셔티브 [주도권] (the) initiative. ¶그가 ~를 취해서 자원자 그룹을 조직했다 He took the initiative in organizing a volunteer group.

이니셜 initials. ¶그는 보통 ~로 서명한다 He usually signs documents with his initials. / He usually initials documents.

이닝 [야구] an inning.

이다¹ **1** [머리에 얹다] put (a thing) on the head. ¶눈을 이고 있는 산들 snow-capped mountains // 물동이를 이고 가다 carry a water jar on one's head // 그 산은 만년설을 이고 있다 The mountain is perpetually covered with snow. / The mountain is capped [crowned] with eternal snow. **2** [지붕을 덮다] cover; thatch(짚으로); tile over(기와로); shingle(판자로); slate(슬레이트로). ¶그 농가는 볏짚으로 이어져 있다 The farmer's cottage is thatched. // 우리 집은 기와[지붕널]로 이어져 있다 The roof of my house is covered with tiles [shingles].

이다² **1** [단정의 말] be. ¶그는 학생 ~ He is a student. // 그의 태도는 우호적 ~ His attitude is friendly. // 오늘은 어머니가 돌아가신 날 ~ Today is the anniversary of my mother's death. **2** [...이 되다] come; make; be. ¶이번 생일이 되면 스무 살 ~ I shall be [am coming] twenty years old next birthday. // 둘 더하기 셋은 다섯 ~ Two and three make(s) five. **3** (수량이) number(수); weigh(무게); measure(도량); cover(면적). ¶그는 키가 6피트 ~ He is 6 feet tall. // 그는 체중이 60킬로 ~ He weighs 60 kilograms.

이다음 next. ¶아버지는 ~ 수요일에 돌아오신다 My father comes back next Wednesday. // 이 이야기의 계속은 ~에 하자 I will tell you the rest of this story some other day. // 나는 ~까지 기다릴 수 없다 I cannot wait for another occasion [till next time].

이다지(도) this much; so much; to this degree [extent]; so; thus. ¶~ 오래 살 것 같이 this // 그가 ~ 바보인 줄은 몰랐다 I didn't know he was such a fool. / I thought he was much wiser. // 눈이 ~ 많이 오리라고는 생각지 못했다 I did not think of so much snowfall here. // 외국어가 ~ 힘들어서야 어디 배우겠나 With a foreign language as tough [hard] as all this, how can I ever learn it! // ~ 아름다운 경치를 나는 본 적이 없다 I have never seen such beautiful scenery (as this).

이단(異端) (정통파에 대한) (a) heresy; (크리스트교에서 본) paganism. ¶~의 heretical // 당시 그의 학설은 ~으로 간주됐다 At that time his theory was regarded as unorthodox [a deviation from orthodoxy] // 그의 음악은 지나치게 ~적이다 His music is too unorthodox.
● **이단시** ¶~하다 treat [regard] (an idea) as heresy [unorthodox]. **이단자** a heretic; [반대자] a dissenter.

이달 this month. ¶~ 호 잡지 the current number [issue] of the magazine // ~ 초[2일]에 at the beginning [on the second] of this month // 나는 ~ 중에 끝내고 싶다 I will finish it this month [within the month]. // ~ 15일은 휴일이다 The 15th of this month is a holiday.

이대로 as it is [stands]; as one is; like this. ¶의사를 불러요, 환자를 ~ 방치할 수는 없으니까 Call [Send for] a doctor — we can't leave the sick man like this. // 서류에는 손대지 말고 ~ 놓아 두어라 Don't touch the papers; leave them just as they are. / Leave the papers alone [untouched]. // 나는 ~도 만족한다 I am contented as I am. // 이 문장은 ~도 의미가 통한다 The sentence does make sense even as it stands now. // 조사도 하지 않고 문제를 ~ 둘 작정이냐 Are you going to pass over the problem without looking into it at all? // ~ 이 도시에서 살기는 싫다 I don't want to go on living in this city. // ~라면 금주 말까지는 일을 끝낼 수 있겠다 At this rate, the work will be finished by this weekend. // ~라면 만사가 끝장이다 If things go on like this, everything will be ruined [lost].

이데아 1 [이상] an ideal. **2** [철] an idea.

이데올로기 an ideology. ¶~의 ideological // ~의 논쟁 an ideological dispute // 그와 나는 ~가 다르다 He and I have different philosophies. / He and I hold to different ideologies.

이동(以東) east of ...; ... and eastward. ¶춘천 ~은 비가 오고 있다 It is raining in Chuncheon and eastward.

이동(異動) [지위·직책의 변동] (personnel)

이동(移動) (a) movement; [이주] migration. ¶인구의 ~ the movement of population / the population movement // 민족의 ~ racial migration // 게르만 민족의 대~ [역] the Germanic [Gothic] migration // 그들의 ~ 범위는 넓다 They travel far and wide. **이동하다** move; get around; shift (one's position). ¶유목민은 풀을 찾아 끊임없이 이동하고 다녔다 The nomads were constantly on the move looking for grass. // 휴식 시간에는 다른 교실로 이동해야 한다 We have to move to another classroom during the recess.

● **이동 경찰** mobile police; riot police. **이동도서관** an itinerant library. ⇨순회도서관(⇨순회) **이동 병원** a hospital on wheels. **이동성** ¶~의 rambling / roving. **이동성 고기압** a migratory anticyclone. **이동 통신** mobile communication.

이득(利得) 1 [이익] (a) profit; (a) gain; [유리] (an) advantage; benefit. ¶부당 ~ ill-gotten gains / (행위) profiteering / [법] unjust enrichment // 부당 ~자 a profiteer // ~이 되는 profitable / [유리한] advantageous / [경제적인] economical // ~을 보다 profit / gain / benefit / economize // 원화의 상승으로 몇몇의 대회사가 ~을 보았다 Some big companies profited [gained] by the raise [rise] of the won. // 그는 작년에 산 땅을 팔아서 상당한 ~을 보았다 He made a great profit on the sale of the land he bought last year. // 지금 이것을 사 두면 1할의 ~을 볼 겁니다 You can save [economize] 10%, if you buy this now. // 서로 싸워 봐야 누구의 ~도 되지 않는다 Nobody benefits from a quarrel.

2 [물] a gain.

이든(지) whether ... or; either ... or; or; [무엇이나 가리지 않고] any; -ever. ¶그것이 사실 아니든 간에 whether it is true or not / whether or not it is true // 잭~ 나든 가기는 가야 한다 Either Jack or I must go. // 네가 가장 적절하다고 생각하는 조치를 취하라 Take whatever [any] measures you think best. // 어느 책~ 괜찮다 Any book will do.

이듬해 the next [following] year; the year after. ¶~로의 이월 the balance carried forward to the next year // 그 ~ 이른 가을에 그는 세상을 떠났다 Early in the autumn of the following year he passed away. // 그는 그 ~에 태어났다 He was born the year after that [(in) the following year].

이등(二等) [등급의 둘째] the second class. ¶~의 second-class // (여객선의) 특별 ~ the cabin class // ~으로 가다 travel second-class / (구어) go second.

● **이등병** (육군·해병) a private; (해군) a seaman apprentice; an ordinary seaman; (공군) an airman. **이등품** second-grade articles [goods].

이등변 삼각형(二等邊三角形) [수] an isosceles triangle.

이등분(二等分) bisection. **이등분하다** divide [cut] into two (equal parts); (수학에서) bisect. ¶그녀는 그 케이크를 이등분했다 She divided the cake into two equal parts [pieces]. // 토지를 형제끼리 이등분했다 The land was divided equally between the two brothers. // 주어진 원 [각]을 이등분하라 Bisect the given circle [angle].

이디엄 [숙어] (an) idiom.

이따(가) a little [bit] later; after a while [short time]; a short time later. ¶~ 다시 오겠습니다 I will come again after a while. // ~ 전화를 하겠습니다 I'll call you later (on).

이따금 sometimes; occasionally; (every) now and then; (구어) once in a while. ¶그는 ~ 찾아온다 He drops in sometimes [once in a while / from time to time]. // 이 지방에서는 ~ 지진이 일어난다 In this district we have earthquakes once in a while. // 그는 ~ 편지를 보내 준다 He writes to us at long intervals.

이따위 such (a thing / a person) as this; a thing [person] of this sort [kind]; this kind [sort] (of). ¶~ 일 a job of this kind // ~ 책 this kind [sort] of book(s) // ~ 녀석은 생전 처음 보겠다 I've never seen such an odious fellow like him before. // ~ 일은 두 번 다시 하지 않겠다 I'll never do such a thing again.

이때 this; now. ¶~에 at this time [juncture / moment / point] / here / then / thereupon / 바로 ~(에) at this very moment [instant] / just in (the nick of) time // ~까지 그렇게 훌륭한 사람을 본 일이 없다 I have never seen such a great man. // 집이 흔들린 것은 바로 ~였다 It was just then [at this very moment] that the house began to shake. // 우리는 8시에 귀가했는데, ~까지는 비가 멎어 있었다 We reached home at eight. By this time it had stopped raining.

이때껏 until [up to] now; till now.

이라 1 ⇨ 이라고 ¶이 물고기는 영어로 무엇~ 합니까 What do you call this fish in English? 2 […이기 때문에]. ¶그는 워낙 용감한 사람~ 조금도 두려워하지 않았다 He felt no fear, for he was very brave. // 그는 고생한 사람~ 인정이 많다 He is sympathetic, as he has seen much of life.

이라고 1 [인용]. ¶이것이 표범 ~ 하는 동물이다 This is an animal called the leopard. // 의사는 신경 쇠약~ 진단했다 The doctor diagnosed the case as a mental breakdown. // 80~는 하지만 머리는 맑은 상태다 Though he is eighty, his mind is clear. // 3월~ 하지만 북쪽 지방의 바람은 아직 매우 차다 Although it is March, the wind is still very cold up [in the] north. 2 [얕잡아 지적하는 투]. ¶그것도 성공 ~ 할 수 있을까 Can we call it a success? // 아무리 그의 책임~는 하지만 그 한 사람의 책임으로 돌려서는 안 된다 However that may be, he shouldn't be held solely responsible.

이라는 named; called; titled. ¶제인~ 소녀 a girl called [named] Jane.

이라도 if; even if [though]; although; however. ¶내일~ 가 볼까요 Let's go tomorrow, shall we? / How about going tomorrow? // 제1권만~ 인쇄를 했어야 했는데 We should have printed the first volume, at least. // 아무리 멍한 사람~ 알아차릴걸 Even the most inattentive person would notice. // 그것을 옮

게 말 할 수 있을 때까지 몇 번~ 발음 연습을 하시오 Practice pronouncing it as many times as necessary till you can say it correctly. // 어느 것 ~ 좋다 Either will do. // 사과, 귤, 무엇~ 좋아하는 것을 가져요 You can have whatever you like — an apple, an orange, or anything.

이란 ⇨ "란 ¶존~ 아이 a boy named[called] John / a boy, John by name // 명동~ 번화가 shopping areas called "Myeongdong" // 1천만 원~ 거액 such a large sum as 10 million won // 몇 천 명~ 사람 thousands of people // 길~ 길은 사람으로 꽉 메워졌다 Every street was filled with people. // 청춘~ 무엇인가 What is youth? // 인생~ 이런 것이다 Such is life. / This is life. // 운명~ 아무도 알 수 없는 것이다 No one can tell about his destiny. // 아이들~ 역시 어쩔 수 없어 Children are children. // 돈~ 나에게 있어서 하찮은 것이다 Money means nothing to me. // 현재 내가 해야 할 일~ 걷는 일뿐이다 All I have to do now is to walk.

이란성 쌍둥이 (二卵性雙─) fraternal [biovular / dizygotic] twins.

이랑¹ (밭의) the ridge and the furrow. ¶밭에 ~을 만들다 (가래로) make furrows in a field / furrow a field.

이랑² and; or. ⇨ "랑 ¶그녀는 문방구에서 연필 ~ 공책~ 많이 샀다 She bought pencils, notebook, etc.[and what not] at a stationery shop. // 이것~ 저것~ 무엇이 다르죠 What's the difference between this and that? // 나는 그 사람~ 아무 관계도 없다 I have nothing to do with him.

이래 (以來) since; from. ¶그때 ~ since then / from that time on [onward / downward] / ever since(그때부터 줄곧) // 16세기 ~ from the 16th century downward [onward] // 지난 10년 ~ these ten years / in [for] the last [past] ten years // 그녀는 출산 ~ 건강이 좋지 않다 She has not been well ever since she had the baby [ever since her baby's birth]. // 그가 총독이 된 ~ 5년이 된다 It has been five years since he became governor.

이래라저래라 ordering (a person) to do this and to do that; ordering (people) about. ¶나로서는 그에게 ~ 할 수가 없다 I am not in a position to tell him what to do. // 나한테 ~ 하지 마라 Stop bothering [(구어) bugging] me about everything.

이래서 so; This is why .... ¶~ 그는 믿을 수가 없다 This is why we cannot trust him. / As you see, he is not reliable. // ~ 우리 팀의 에이스다 This is what the ace of our team can do [is made of]! // ~ 내가 가기 싫다고 한 것이다 This is why I did not want to go.

이래저래 with this, that or the other; for one thing or another; what with this and (what with) that. ¶~ 만 원은 있어야겠다 I need 10,000 won for this and that. / ~ 나는 바쁘다 I am busy with one thing and another.

이랬다저랬다 this way and that way. ¶~ 하는 사람 a man of variable temper // 그녀는 ~ 변덕이 심하다 She is so whimsical. / She easily changes her mind. // 너무 ~ 하지 마라 Don't be so fickle. // 그는 말을 ~ 한다 He says first one thing and then the opposite.

이랴 [마소를 몰 때 하는 소리] Get up!; Giddap!; (계속 몰 때) Gee-up!; Gee-ho!; (빨리 몰 때) Gee-(h)up!; Gee-(h)up!; (오른쪽·앞으로 몰 때) Gee!; (왼쪽으로 몰 때) Haw!; Gee wo!

이러구러 (in the) meantime; meanwhile. ¶~ 3년이 지났다 Three years have passed all too soon. / Meanwhile, three years went by. // ~ 해가 저물었다 In the meantime [Meanwhile] the sun went down.

이러나저러나 at any rate; in any case [event]; anyway; anyhow; at all events. ¶~ 그것은 내게 매한가지다 It is all one [the same] to me. // ~ 그것은 어리석은 이야기다 Anyhow [At any rate], it is an idiotic story.

이러니저러니 this and [or] that. ⇨이러쿵저러쿵 ¶~ 하지 말고 따라와라 Just shut up and follow me. // 당신은 ~ 말할 권리가 없소 You don't have the right to say anything about it. / (상관 마라) It's none of your business. // ~ 해도 그는 정계에서 위대한 인물이다 After all he is the greatest star [figure] in the political world.

이러다(가) as things go; under the circumstances. ¶서둘러라, ~ 기차 놓칠라 Hurry up, or we will miss the train. // 이러다가는 일을 오전 중에 도저히 끝마치지 못하겠다 You'll never finish the work before noon if you work at this rate.

이러면 이 채면이 말이 아니다 If this is the case, I'll lose face.

이러이러하다 so and so; such and such. ¶이러이러한 사람 such and such a person // 이러이러한 이야기 such and such a story // 사건의 경과는 ~ The affair developed like this. // 그는 이러이러한 구실로 돈을 갚지 않았다 He avoided paying on [under] some pretext (or other).

이러저러하다 so and so. ⇨이러이러하다

이러쿵저러쿵 this and [or] that; one thing or another; something or other. ¶~ 잔소리는 그만둬 Stop nagging. / (미국 속어) Quit your bitching. / (영국 속어) Give your tongue a rest. // ~ 하지 말고 하라는 대로 하는 편이 좋다 You'd better do what you're told without further ado. // 그는 ~ 불평만 하고 있다 He is always complaining about this and that [one thing or another]. // 이 문제에 대해서 ~ 말할 권리가 없다 I have no right to say anything about the matter. // 항간에서는 그에 대해서 ~ 말이 많다 People are saying all kinds of things [this and that] about him. // 사람들이 ~ 말할 테면 말하게 내버려 둬 If people want to criticize us, let them. // ~ 말이 많은 세상이다 People is gossiping. / People will talk. // 나한테 ~ 말하지 마라 Stop bothering me about everything.

이러하다 such; this. ⇨이렇다 ¶이러한 사람 such a one / a person like this // 이러한 행위는 용서할 수 없다 Such behavior is unpardonable. // 이러한 일은 좀체로 나타나지 않는 법이다 Such things seldom happen. / Things like this seldom happen. // 그 정원은 극락도 이러할까 싶을 정도로 장려했다 The garden is so magnificent that it makes one think, "Paradise must be like this!". // 사정은 ~ This situation is as I have stated above.

이럭저럭 somehow or other; one way or another; somehow; [어느덧] before one knows; unnoticed; in no time. ¶~ 해 나가다 get along somehow // ~ 살아가다 eke out a living / manage to keep the pot boiling // ~ 생계를 꾸려 나가다 scrape a living // ~ 날이

저물었다 In the meantime[Meanwhile] the sun went down.∥~ 위기는 모면했다 We somehow managed to ride out[get through] the crisis.∥~ 대학은 졸업했다 He graduated from college somehow or other.∥~ 하는 동안에 1주일이 지났다 A week passed as they tried this and that[one thing after another].∥문제는 ~ 해결되었다 The matter has been settled somehow or other.

이런[^1] [이러한] such; this; like this; such ... as this; of this kind[sort]. ¶~ 정세 아래 under these (special) circumstances∥~ 편지 such a letter as this / a letter of this sort∥~ 때[경우]는 in a case like this∥~ 곤란한 때에는 in these hard times / in hard times such as these∥~ 실정이니 양해해 주시기 바랍니다 Such being the case, please understand our position.∥~ 일은 좀처럼 일어나지 않는다 Such things seldom happen. / Things like this seldom happen.∥~ 종류의 범죄는 드물다 This sort of crime is rare.∥나는 ~ 것을 들어 본 적이 없다 I have never heard of such a thing[anything like this].∥~ 좋은 기회가 다시는 없을 것이다 There will never be such a good chance as this again.∥~ 까닭에 나는 하루 종일 집에 있었다 Such being the case, I stayed home all day. / That was why I was at home all day.

이런[^2] [놀랄 때 내는 소리] Oh; oh dear!; (남자가 하는 말로) Oh, damn!; (여자가 하는 말로) Good gracious[heavens]!; Oh, my! ¶~, 또 실수를 했군 Oh, damn! I've made a mistake again.∥~, 어처구니없군 Oh, how stupid!∥~, 벌써 돌아갈 시간인걸 Why! It's time to go home already.(▶ 「이런」이라고 말하고 다음 말에 이을 때, Why! Well!을 씀)∥~, 웬 소동일까 What's that noise, I wonder.∥~, 벌써 10시인가 My, is it already ten o'clock?

이런저런 this and that; one thing and[or] another; something or other. ¶~ 생각 끝에 after fully considering the matter / after fully thinking this way and that over the matter / after much thinking∥우리는 모닥불을 둘러 싸고 앉아서 ~ 이야기를 나누었다 We sat around the fire talking about this and[or] that.∥아버지는 ~ 일로 항상 바쁘시다 My father is busy with one thing and another.

이렇게 like this; in this way[manner]; thus; [이 정도로] this much; so much; so; such; to this extent. ¶~ 좋은 기회는 다시없을 것이다 There will never be such a good chance as this again.∥내가 ~ 하는 것은 오직 너를 위해서이다 I behave like this simply because I am concerned about you.∥사정이 ~ 된 이상 최악의 경우를 생각해야 한다 Since it has come to this, we must be prepared for the worst.∥~ 하면 성공할 것이다 If you do it like this[this way], you will succeed.∥나는 ~ 해서 회사의 재건에 성공했다 In this way [(문어)] Thus], I succeeded in rebuilding the company.∥~ 묶으면 풀어지지 않는다 If you tie it this way[like this], it won't come loose.∥나는 ~ 늦은 줄은 몰랐다 I didn't realize it was so[this] late.∥~ ~ 재미나는 이야기는 들어 보지 못했다 I've never heard anything so funny. / This is the funniest thing I've ever heard.∥네가 ~ 노력했는데도 실패했다니 이상하다 It is strange that you should have failed after[in spite of] all your efforts.∥~ 그는 위대한 사람이었다 As I have said, he was a great man.∥~ 해 보아라 Try to do it like this[in this way].∥만사가 ~ 잘돼 가고 있다 As you (can) see everything is all right.∥자루 안에 ~ 많은 감자[설탕]가 있었다 We found all these potatoes[all this sugar] in the bag.∥~ 밤늦게 거리를 배회하면 안 된다 You shouldn't wander around town at this late hour[at such late hour / at this time of night].

이렇다 such; this; of this kind[sort]; like this. ¶그의 이야기는 ~ His story runs like this. / His story is as follows.∥나는 ~ 할 이유도 없이 꾸지람을 들었다 I was scolded without any[for no] particular reason.∥내게는 ~ 할 장점도 없다 I don't really have any particularly strong points. / I have no strong points to speak of.∥~ 할 성과는 없었다 There were no significant results. / There were no results of any significance[worth mentioning].∥그림은 ~ 할 만한 것이 못 된다 The picture is not worth mentioning.∥그는 아직 ~ 할 작품을 내지 못했다 He has produced no works to speak of.

이래 봬도 I may not look as much, but ...; you may not take (me) as such but .... ¶~ 내가 젊었을 때는 플레이보이로 통했었다 Though I may not look it now, I was considered a playboy when I was young.

이렇든 저렇든 whether it is this or that; anyhow; anyway; in any way[case / event]; at any rate.

이렇듯 like this; thus; in this way[manner]. ¶~는 ~ 위대한 사람이었다 As I have said, he was a great man.

이레 1 [일곱 날] seven days. ¶~ **동안** for seven days. 2 the seventh day (of a month). ⇨**초이렛날**
● **이렛날** the seventh day. ¶섣달 스무 ~ the 27th of December.

이력(履歷) one's personal history; [경력] one's background; one's career(직업상의); one's record. ¶~이 좋은[훌륭한] 사람 a man with a good record / a man of sound background / a man of good antecedents∥남의 ~을 조사하다 check up on[look into] a person's background / (문어) inquire into a person's antecedents∥그는 어떤 ~이 있는 사람입니까 What sort of a career has he had? / What is his background[past record]?∥후보의 ~을 간단히 말씀해 주십시오 Please state briefly the candidate's personal history[background].

이력(이) 나다 get used[accustomed] (to); become experienced; get skill. ¶나는 형편없는 식사에는 이력이 나 있다 I am used[accustomed] to poor meals.∥그는 하도 가난을 겪어서 어려움에도 이력이 났다 His experience of poverty inured him to hardship.
● **이력서** a personal history; a curriculum vitae (pl. curricula ~, ~s ~); (미) a résumé. ¶회사에 ~를 제출하다 submit one's curriculum vitae to a company / present one's personal history to a company.

이례적(異例的) exceptional; unprecedented; singular. ¶~인 행운 singular good luck∥그가 우리 회의에 참석한다는 것은 ~인 일이다 It's very unusual for him to attend our meeting.

이론(異論) [다른 이론] a different[dissenting] opinion; [이의] an objection; a protest. ¶그는 그 결정에 ~을 제기했다 He objected [raised an objection] to the decision. / He protested the decision.∥나는 그것에 대해 ~이 없다 I have no objection to it. / I take no particular exception to it.∥선생님들 사이에서는 ~이 있었다 There were different opinions among the teachers.∥이 문제를 놓고 여러 가지 ~이 나왔다 Opinion was divided on this point. / Differing views were aired on this point.

이론(理論) (a) theory. ¶~(상)의 theoretical∥~상으로는 theoretically / in theory / in reason / on paper∥~과 실천 theory and practice∥~만 내세우는 사람 an argumentative person∥~을 세우다 theorize / frame a theory∥~을 실천에 옮기다 put[reduce] a theory into[to] practice∥~과 실제를 일치시키다 reconcile theory and practice∥그는 그 분야에 많은 ~을 세웠다 He formed [founded] a lot of theories in his field.∥~과 실제는 반드시 일치하지는 않는다 Theory and practice do not always coincide[go together].

● **이론가** a theorist; a theoretician. **이론 경제학** theoretical economics.

이롭다(利-) profitable; advantageous; beneficial; good (for); helpful (to / for); favorable; instructive. ¶이로운 조건 advantageous[remunerative] terms∥어린이에게 이로운 책 a book good for children∥학생에게 이로운 교훈 an instructive lesson to students∥남을 이롭게 하다 benefit the public∥be of service to the public∥그 경험은 나에게 이로운 점이 많았다 That experience was very beneficial[taught me a lot].∥그의 강연은 이로운 점이 하나도 없었다 I gained[learned] nothing from his lectures.∥그렇게 하는 것이 그녀에게 이로울 것이다 It would be to her benefit to do so.∥그렇게 해도 이로울 것이 하나도 없다 There is no advantage in doing so.∥복종하는 것이 너에게 이로울 것이다 Submission will pay you better.∥입을 다물고 있는 것이 네 신상에 ~ It is to your own interest to keep silence.

이루 (not) by any means; by no means; (not) at all; (cannot) possibly. ¶~ 다 말할 수 없는 beyond description / surpassing description / indescribable / indefinable / inexpressible / unspeakable / ineffable∥~ 다 헤아릴 수 없는 numberless / innumerable / countless∥그 노동자들의 비참한 양상은 ~ 다 표현할 수가 없다 The laborers' miserable conditions are beyond description.∥그 경치는 ~ 다 말할 수가 없다 The scene is indescribably beautiful.∥사람의 마음에는 ~ 헤아릴 수 없는 그 무엇이 있다 There is something inscrutable[unfathomable] in men's heart.

이루(二壘) [야구] 1 second (base); (미국 속어) the keystone (sack). ¶~를 지키다 act as second baseman∥그는 ~에 닿기도 전에 아웃이 되었다 He was put out before he reached second (base). 2 a second baseman. ⇨²이루수(⇨²이루).

● **이루타** a second baseman; a second. **이루타** a two-base hit; a double; (구어) a two-bagger. ¶~를 치다 get a two-base hit / double / hit a two-bagger∥그는 ~를 쳐서 주자를 삼루에 보냈다 He doubled the runner to third.

이루다 1 [형성하다] form; make; constitute. ¶원을 ~ form a circle∥사회를 ~ form society∥행복한 가정을 ~ make[build / establish / start] a happy home∥어시장이 성황을 이루고 있었다 The fish market was bustling with activity.∥폭발 현장은 참상을 이루고 있었다 The scene of the explosion presented[was] a tragic sight.∥내 생각은 아직 형태를 이루지 못하고 있다 My idea have not taken shape yet.∥이 조사는 우리 계획의 일부를 이루고 있다 This investigation forms (a) part of[is included in] our project.
2 [성취하다] accomplish; achieve; attain; [완성하다] complete; fulfill; finish; [실행하다] perform; realize; do; effect. ¶이루지 못한 사랑 unfulfilled love / hopeless[forlorn] love / unreturned[unrequited] love∥큰일을 ~ accomplish[achieve] a great thing / perform a great deed / execute a great task∥목적을 ~ achieve[reach] one's goal / attain one's object / gain one's end / accomplish[achieve / effect] one's purpose∥뜻을 ~ have one's wish[desire] fulfilled / realize one's desire / have one's will / gratify one's wishes / attain one's ambition∥명예와 명성을 ~ achieve distinction and fame∥내 꿈을 이룰 수가 없다 I cannot realize my dream.∥이 벽화는 세 화가가 이루어 놓은 것이었다 This mural was done by three artists.

이루어지다 1 [뜻대로 되다] be achieved[attained / effected / completed / realized / fulfilled]; be[get] accomplished[done]. ¶내 소원이 이루어졌다 My wish was fulfilled.∥그의 오랜 숙원이 이루어졌다 His long-cherished desire was realized. / He attained his long-cherished desire.∥그의 사랑은 도저히 이루어질 것 같지 않다 His love for her seems hopeless.∥그의 기도가 이루어졌다 His prayer was answered.∥그 철교 건설이 이제야 이루어졌다 The railway bridge has been completed.
2 [어떤 상태·결과가 되다] be formed[composed] of; be made up of; (타협·계약 등이) be made[concluded / settled / arrived / arranged]. ¶5장(章)으로 이루어진 논문 a thesis consisting of five chapters∥그 집단은 여러 직업의 사람들로 이루어져 있었다 The group was composed[made up] of people of various occupations.∥양가의 혼담이 이루어졌다 A marriage has been arranged between two families.

이룩하다 1 [(어떤 현상·사업을) 이루다] accomplish; achieve; complete; gain. ¶그는 마침내 큰 사업을 이룩했다 He accomplished [completed / went through with] the great undertaking at last.∥그는 일곱 번의 도전 끝에 드디어 에베레스트 산 정복을 이룩했다 After six attempts, he finally managed to conquer Mt. Everest.∥한국인의 근면성이 오늘의 경제 발전을 이룩한 것이다 The diligence of the Korean has brought about [given rise to] the country's present level of economic development.∥과학은 괄목할 만한 발전을 이룩했다 Science has made remarkable advances.
2 [세우다·수립하다] found; establish; erect; set up; build. ¶나라를 ~ found[establish] a country[state].

이류(二流) second rate[class]. ¶~의 second-class / second-rate / [보다 못한] minor.
- **이류 작가** a minor[second] writer.

이륙(離陸) a takeoff; a hop-off; taking[flying] off; leaving the ground. ¶~ 시의 소음 takeoff noise. **이륙하다** take off; hop off; take the air; leave the ground. ¶비행기는 미끄러지듯이 이륙했다 The plane made a smooth takeoff. / The plane took off smoothly.
- **이륙 지점** a takeoff point. **이륙 활주** a takeoff run.

이륜차(二輪車) a two-wheeled vehicle; a two-wheeler; a bicycle; a motor bicycle. ¶자동 ~ a motorcycle // (구어) a motorbike // 원동기 부착 ~ a motorized two-wheeled vehicle.

이르다[1] **1** [(어떤 장소·시간 등에) 닿다] reach; arrive; get to; go; lead. ¶산꼭대기에 ~ reach the summit of a mountain // 목적지에 ~ reach[get to / arrive at] one's destination // 성숙기[고령]에 ~ reach maturity[old age] // 이 길은 바다에 이른다 This road leads[goes down] to the sea. // 그 길로 가면 국경에 이른다 The road leads[goes] to the border. // 내 아들이 이제 성년에 이르렀다 My son came of age. / My son has reached adulthood[manhood]. / My son has attained to man's estate. // 이 길은 한계령을 넘어 설악산에 이른다 This road leads to Seoraksan(Mt. Seorak) via Hangyeryeong. // 여기서 속초에 이르는 길이 폐쇄되었다 The road from here to Sokcho was closed. // 우리는 아직 그들과 합의에 이르지 못했다 We have not yet been able to reach[arrive at] an agreement with them. **2** [미치다] extend (to); come to; get to; [(결과가 …이) 되다] result (in); end (in); lead (to). ¶높은 예술의 경지에 이른 사람 a master of an art / a person who has mastered an art // 대장에서 사병에 이르기까지 from the general down to the common soldiers // 한밤중에 이르기까지 until the middle of the night // 지금에 이르기까지 until now / (down) to this day / up to the present (time) / (미) to date // 10월에 이르러서도 협상이 타결되지 않았다 It was already October and negotiations has not yet been concluded. // 지금에 이르기까지 그에게서 소식이 없었다 I have not heard from him since. // 일이 이에 이르러서는 사태를 수습할 아무런 방도가 없다 Now that things have come to this (pass), nothing can be done to save the situation. // 그 도시의 인구는 500만 명에 이르렀다 The population of the city reached five million. // 그 손해는 1억 원[억대]에 이르렀다 The damage amounted to a hundred million won[ran into hundreds of millions of won]. // 그 건축비는 5,000만 원에 이를 것이다 The building expenses will reach[amount] to 50million won. // 정국(政局)은 중대한 국면에 이르렀다 Political developments have reached an important stage[entered a crucial phase]. // 그의 기법[기술]은 아직 완벽의 경지에 이르지 못했다 His technique has not yet reached[(문어) attained to] perfection. // 오래지 않아 그의 작업도 수준에 이를 것이다 It will not be long before his work comes up to the standard. // 나는 그의 청렴결백을 의심하기에 이르렀다 I came to doubt his integrity.

이르다[2] **1** [말하다] say. ¶성경에 이르기를 The Bible says that …. / It says in the Bible that …. // 너에게 일러둘 말이 있다 I have got something to say to you. **2** [알아듣거나 깨닫게 말하다] explain; teach; advise; tell; bid. ¶그에게 어떻게 해야 하는지를 일러 주십시오 Please explain to him how to do it. // 어머니는 결혼을 너무 서두르지 말라고 일러 주셨다 My mother advised me against marrying in haste. // 무엇을 해야 하는지는 선생님이 일러 주실 거야 Our teacher will tell us what to do. // 그에게 가라고 일렀다 I bade him to go. **3** [알려 주다] make known (in advance); tell; inform; report. ¶미리 일러 주다 give (a person) previous notice / forewarn (a person of a matter) // 넌지시 일러 주다 suggest / hint (at) / drop a hint // 길을 일러 주다 show (a person) the way (to) / direct (a person) to a place // 어머니는 내게 요리하는 법을 일러 주셨다 My mother taught me how to cook. // 언제 파리를 떠날지 내게 일러 주시오 Tell me when you will leave Paris. // 그는 자신이 결정한 내용을 내게 일러 주었다 He informed me of his decision. **4** [고자질하다] tell[squeal] (on a person); tell[carry] tales (about). ¶그는 아버지께 이르지 않겠다고 약속했다 He promised not to tell father on me.
- **이를 데 없다** ¶슬프기 ~ be inexpressibly sad // 그가 살아 있다는 소식을 들으니 기쁘기 이를 데 없었다 I was overjoyed to hear that he was alive.

이르다[3] **1** [늦지 않고 빠르다] early. ¶이른 봄 early spring // 우리는 이른 아침에 출발했다 We departed early in the morning[day]. // 그는 평소보다[예정 시간보다] 2시간 이르게 도착했다 He came home two hours earlier than usual[ahead of time]. **2** [아직 그 시기가 되지 않다] premature. ¶결과를 발표하기에는 아직 ~ It would be premature to announce the results now. // 네가 그 책을 읽기에는 아직 ~ You are not old enough to read that book. // 개막하기엔 아직 시간이 ~ We have plenty of time before the curtain rises. // 봄은 아직 ~ It's still early in the spring. / (문어) The spring is still young.

이른바 what is called; what you[we / people] call; as it is called; so-called; as they say. ¶~ 벼락부자 a so-called upstart // 이런 남자가 ~ 신사다 Such a man is what you[people] call a gentleman. // 그는 ~ 우등생이다 He is what you call[what is called] an honor student. / He is one of those so-called honor students.

이를테면 1 [말하자면] so to speak; as it were; [어떤 의미에서] in a sense; [어떤 점에서] in a way; so to call it; as it were; [실제로는] practically. ¶그는 ~ 살아 있는 사전이야 He is, so to speak, a walking[living] dictionary. // 그는 ~ 나의 제2의 아버지다 He is, so to speak, a second father. / He has been a father to me in a way. **2** [가령] for example; for instance; such as. ¶~ 매나 독수리 같은 맹금 birds of prey, such as the hawk and the eagle // ~ 당신 같은 젊은이들이 이 일에는 필요하다 Young men, such as you, are needed for this work.

이름 1 a name; [성을 제외한 이름] a given [personal / Christian] name; a forename; (미) a first name; [성명] a full name. (▶ 영미인의 이름은 「이름+중간 이름+성」의 순서

이름나다

로 나타냄. 가령, "Charles Robert Darwin"의 경우, Charles는 given name이고, Darwin은 성(姓)으로서 family[last] name이며 Robert는 middle name임. 한편, 우리나라 사람의 이름은 영미의 경우와 반대로 「성+이름」의 순서로 나타내는데, 이는 로마자로 나타낼 때에도 그대로 유지됨. 곧, 「송나리」는 "Song Nari [Nari]"로 나타냄. ¶제사라는 ~의 여자 a woman named[called] Jessie / a woman by[of] the name of Jessie / a woman, Jessie by name // ~을 **부르다** call[address] (a person) by name / ~을 **대다** tell[mention] one's name / give[announce] one's name (as) / name oneself / introduce oneself (as) // ~을 **짓다** [이름을 붙이다] name / give a name / [세례명을 붙이다] christen // ~을 **사칭하다** assume (a person's) name / make a fraudulent use of (a person's) name / masquerade under (a person's) name // ~을 **속이다** assume a false name / give a wrong name / misrepresent oneself (as) / ~이 무엇입니까 May I have your name, please? / May I ask your name? / What's the name, please? / (전달해야 할 때) What name shall I say? (▶ "What's your name?"보다 "May I have[ask] your name, please?"가 공손한 표현임) // 그 사람의 ~은 알고 있다 I know him only by name. // 투서자의 희망에 따라 ~은 밝히지 않는다 The contributor wants his name withheld. // 그는 ~도 대지 않고 가 버렸다 He left without giving his name. // ~을 부르면 대답해라 Answer when you are called by name [your name is called]. // 누군가 내 ~을 사칭한 자가 있다 Somebody has used my name. // 나는 사람들 ~을 잘 잊어 먹는다 I have a bad[poor] memory for names. // 그들은 아기의 세례명으로 존이라는 ~을 지어 주었다 They christened their baby by John. // 그 아이들의 ~은 역대 대통령들의 ~을 따서 지은 것이었다 The children were named after successive Presidents. // 아기에게 ~을 지어 주었나요 Have you named the new baby yet? **2** [명칭] a name; a designation; [책 등의 제목] a title. ¶음 [거리]의 ~ the name of a town[street] // 거리 ~ 변경 renaming a street // 그는 「깍쟁이 빌」이라는 ~으로 통했다 He went by the name of[was known as] "Bill the Miser". // 그들은 회사 ~으로 그에게 부조금을 주었다 They gave him a gift of money in the name of the company. // 그 책은 「현대 회화」라는 ~으로 출판되었다 The book was published under the title Modern Painting. // 그는 「동인」이란 ~으로 책을 썼다 He wrote a book under the pseudonym [pen name] of Dongin. // 서울의 옛 ~은 무엇입니까 What is the old name for Seoul? **3** [평판] (a) reputation; a name; fame; renown; distinction; eminence. ¶아버지의 ~을 욕되지 않게 하여라 Live up to your father's reputation. // 그는 그 ~에 어긋나지 않는 훌륭한 정치가였다 He was a distinguished statesman who deserved[was worthy of] the name. // 그는 그 사건으로 학교의 ~을 더럽혔다 That incident tarnished [harmed] the reputation of the school. // 자기 ~을 소중히 여기는 사람은 그런 치사한 일을 할 수 없다 One who values his good name cannot do such a cheap thing. **4** [구실·명분] a pretext; a plea; a pretense. ¶~뿐인 nominal // 종교라는 ~ 아래 under the color[mask] of religions / 자선이라는 ~으로 in the cloak of charity // 그는 그 회사의 사장이라지만 ~뿐이다 He is president of the company in name only. / He is a figurehead [nominal] president of the company. // 그는 ~뿐인 감독이었다 He was (but) a nominal manager. // 그는 자기 부친의 ~을 빌려 그 안에 맹렬히 반대했다 (구실로 삼아서) On the pretext of his father's objecting, he opposed the plan violently. / (이름을 들어서) He strongly opposed the plan in the name of his father.

이름(을) 날리다 win[gain] fame; make[gain / win / obtain] a reputation; win[make] a name for oneself; win[get] oneself a name; gain[earn / obtain / win] distinction. ¶그는 당시 크게 이름을 날린 실업가였다 He was a much renowned[noted] businessman at the time. // 그는 그 작품으로 이름을 날렸다 He established distinction by work. / The work gained him a reputation.

이름(을) 남기다 leave one's name behind; leave[make] one's mark (on the history of ...); live in the memory of men. ¶그는 발견으로 후세에 이름을 남겼다 He immortalized himself[made himself immortal] with that discovery.

이름(이) 없다 be nameless; be obscure; be unknown. ¶이름 없는 사람 an obscure man / a man unknown to fame / a nameless [an insignificant] man / a man of no mark / a nobody // 이름 없는 가난한 화가 a poor obscure[nameless / unknown] painter.

이름(이) 있다 be famous[noted / eminent / celebrated / well-known / renowned / reputed]; be good repute.

이름(을) 팔다 [이름·명성을 이용하다] trade on one's name[reputation]; take advantage of one's name[publicity].

●**이름표** a nameplate; a name card. ¶어린이의 ~ a child's identification tag // ~를 **달다** attach[affix] a name tag (to) / attach an identification tag (to a child).

이름나다 become famous[renowned] (for); have a name (for); make[win] a name for oneself; win oneself a name; make a fame for oneself; become noted[celebrated] (for). ¶그 강둑은 벚꽃의 명승지로 이름나 있다 The banks of the river have become a popular cherry-viewing site. / The riverbanks have become famous for the beautiful cherry blossoms. // 그는 세계적으로 이름난 외교관이다 He enjoys worldwide fame as a diplomatist. / He is a world-famous diplomat. // 그는 구두쇠로 이름나 있었다 He had the name of miser.

이리[1] (물고기의) milt; soft roe.

이리[2] [동] a wolf (pl. wolves). ¶~ 떼 a pack of wolves // ~가 짖는 소리 a wolf's cry[howl] // 양의 가죽을 쓴 ~ a wolf in sheep's clothing, a wolf in a lamb's skin.

이리[3] **1** [이곳으로·이쪽으로] this way [direction]; here. ¶~ 오너라 Come here! / (남의 집을 방문했을 때) Hello! // ~ 앉으시 Sit here. // ~ 오십시오 This way, please. / Please come this way. // ~ 앉으십시오 Will you sit over here, please? // ~ 가면 바다가 나옵니다 This path leads[goes] to the sea. **2** [이러하게] in this way[manner]; like this; such; thus. ¶~ 될 줄 알았다 I know things would

이리듐 [화] iridium(기호 Ir.)
이리저리 1 [이러하고 저러하게] like this way and that; thus and thus. ¶~ 핑계를 대고 on some pretext or other∥그는 ~ 핑계를 대고 후원자를 밝히지 않았다 He used excuses and evasions to avoid giving the name of his sponsor. **2** [이쪽으로 저쪽으로] this way and that; to and fro; back and forth; from one place to another; here and there. ¶~ 둘러보다 look this way and that∥나는 방 안을 ~ 둘러보았다 I looked here and there about my room.∥그 남자는 ~ 떠돌아다녔다 The man wandered from one place to another[from place to place].
이리하여 accordingly; therefore; thus. ¶~ 나는 회사 재건에 성공했다 Thus I succeeded in rebuilding the company.
이마 (얼굴의) the forehead; the brow. ¶넓은[좁은] ~ a broad[narrow] forehead / a high[low] brow / 툭 튀어나온 ~ a beetle[prominent] brow / a projecting[bulging] forehead∥~가 튀어나온 여자 아이 a girl with a prominent forehead∥~를 맞대고 의논하다 lay[put] (their) heads together / (구어) go into a huddle / huddle together∥그는 ~가 훤하다 He has a broad forehead.
● **이맛살** wrinkles in[on / across] the forehead. ¶~을 찌푸리다 wrinkle (up) one's forehead / produce wrinkles in the forehead / knit one's brows / frown∥~을 찌푸리고 with a furrowed[ridged] brow / with knitted brows∥모두 그녀의 머리 모양을 보고 ~을 찌푸렸다 Everyone looked askance[frowned] at her hair style.
이만 1 [이 정도의] this much[many]. ¶~ 일로 손하지는 않는다 This isn't enough to discourage me.∥~ 짐은 아무것도 아니다 This much baggage is just nothing. **2** [이만하고서] by this (much); this far. ¶오늘은 ~ (합시다) So much[That's all] for today. / This is all for today.∥그럼 ~ 가 보겠습니다 I must say good-bye now. / Now I ask you excuse myself.∥오늘 일은 ~ 끝냅시다 Let us leave off work. / Let's call it a day.
이만저만 to this extent[point] or that; this much or that; so so; tolerably. ¶그 일을 끝내기가 ~ 힘든 일이 아니었다 It was a hard strain to finish the work.∥~ 놀라지 않았다 I was not a little surprised.∥그녀의 고생은 ~이 아니었다 She went through many hardships.∥그는 노래 솜씨가 ~이 아니다 No one can match him in singing. **이만저만하다** tolerable; fair; ordinary; commonplace. ¶아이를 기른다는 것이 이만저만한 일이 아니다 It is no easy thing[task] to bring up a child.∥예산 내에서 해 나간다는 것은 이만저만한 일이 아니다 It is hard to get along within the budget.∥그의 재능은 이만저만한 것이 아니다 He is a man of uncommon ability.∥그는 이만저만한 거짓말쟁이가 아니다 He is a colossal liar.
이만큼 (분량) about this[so] much; (수) about so many; (크기) about so large; about this size; (길이) about so long; about this length; (폭) about so wide; about this width; (정도) this far; to this degree[extent]. ¶그 연못의 깊이는 ~이다 The pond is about so[this] deep.∥~ 훌륭한 시를 쓸 수 있는 사람은 드물다 Few (people) can write poems so well[such fine poems].∥~ 야단쳤으니 그도 정신을 좀 차릴 거야 I believe so much scolding will open his eyes to his faults.
이만하다 this much[many]; as much[many] as this. ¶작년에도 이만한 인원이 모였었다 About this many people gathered last year.∥이만한 돈이면 당분간은 견디겠다 This much money will do for the time being.∥이만한 속력으로는 저 차를 따라잡지 못하겠다 You can't over take that car driving at this speed.∥이만하면 충분할 거야 This much may be enough. / This will do.∥이만한 추위 쯤 대단한 게 뭐냐 What does this amount of cold matter? / Surely you can stand cold weather like this.∥그의 키는 ~ He is (about) this tall.
이맘때 about[around] this time; at this time of (the) day[night / year]; at this hour of the day[morning / evening / night]. ¶바로 ~ at this point of time∥진달래는 해마다 ~ 핀다 Azaleas bloom about this time every year[at this time of (the) year].∥해마다 ~는 비가 아주 많이 온다 Every year about this time we have a great deal of rain.∥내년 ~ 우리는 무엇을 하고 있을까 I wonder what we'll be doing at this time next year.∥내일 ~ 면 그는 서울에 도착했을 것이다 He will have arrived in Seoul by this time tomorrow.∥작년 ~에는 첫눈이 왔었다 We had the first snow about this time last year.
이메일 (an) email; (an) e-mail; (an) E-mail.
이며 and; or. ¶제비꽃∼ 튤립과 같은 꽃들 flowers, such as violets and tulips∥책∼ 연필∼ 하는 것들을 샀다 I bought books, pencils and the like.
이면 (裏面) **1** [속·안] the back; the reverse (side); the other side. ¶어음의 ~ the back of a bill∥음반의 ~ the reverse side[Side Two] of a record∥달의 ~ the other side of the moon∥책의 ~에 작자의 약력이 쓰여 있다 A brief outline of the author's life is given on the back of the book.∥~을 보시오 Over / Please turn over(약어 P.T.O.)(▶ 영국에서는 약자로 씀). / Continued overleaf. / Please see the other side.
2 [내부의 면] the inside; the background; [어두운 면] the dark[seamy] side. ¶~에 숨은 진상 the truth behind the facts∥~의 생활 one's intimate[private] life∥~의 사정에 밝은 사람들 those on the inside∥이 사건의 ~은 나도 전연 모른다 I have no inside knowledge about this event.∥그 ~에는 여러 가지 사정이 있다 There is more to it than meets the eye.∥그가 ~에서 활발히 움직이고 있었다 He was very active behind the scenes.∥양당은 ~에서 거래를 한 듯하다 The parties appear to have arranged a deal behind the scenes[a behind-the-scenes deal].∥이 사건의 ~에는 이 여자가 있다 She is at the bottom of this affair.
● **이면공작** behind-the-scene[backstage] maneuvering[maneuvers]; underground activities; undercover work; wirepulling. ¶누가 ~을 하고 있는가 Who is pulling the strings (backstage)?
이면각 (二面角) [수] a dihedral angle.
이명 (耳鳴) ear noises; earringing; [의] tinnitus. ¶~이 있다 I have a ringing[buzzing] in my ears. / My ears are ringing.

이명

이명(異名) [별명] a nickname; [다른 이름] another name; a second name; an alias.

이모(姨母) an aunt; one's mom's[mother's] sister; [문어] a maternal aunt. (▶ 영미에서는 우리나라와 달리 「이모 / 고모 / 숙모 / 외숙모」 등을 aunt로 총칭해서 쓰는 것이 일반적이며, 그것을 굳이 구별하고자 할 때, 「이모」의 경우 "mom's sister / maternal aunt" 등을 씀)
● **이모부** an uncle; the husband of one's mother's[mom's] sister.

이모작(二毛作) [농] double cropping. ¶~을 하다 raise two crops a year / double-crop // 이 지역은 여름에는 벼, 겨울에는 보리의 ~이 가능하다 It's possible to grow two crops a year in this area: rice in summer and wheat in winter.
● **이모작 지대** a two-crop area.

이모저모 every side[aspect] (of a matter); this way and that. ¶~로 생각하다 view (a matter) from every angle[different angles] // 나는 ~로 망설인 끝에 전직하기로 작정했다 After vacillating this way and that, I finally decided to change jobs.

이모티콘 [채팅 등에서 감정·표정 등을 나타내는 기호] an emoticon; a smiley.

이목(耳目) 1 [귀와 눈] the eye and ear. 2 [남들의 주의] public attention[notice]. ¶세상의 ~을 피하다 avoid public notice / slip from the sight of the world // 전 세계의 ~이 극동에 집중되어 있다 The eyes of the world are centered on the Far East. // 국민의 ~은 또다시 국내 정치 문제로 쏠렸다 The center of public interest has again shifted to political affairs at home.
이목을 끌다 attract[arrest] people's[public] attention; catch the public eye. ¶남들의 이목을 끄는 광고 an eye-catching advertisement // 이목을 끄는 사건 a sensational incident // 그 사건은 크게 세상의 이목을 끌었다 The event caused[created] a great sensation.

이목구비(耳目口鼻) [귀·눈·입·코] ear, eye, mouth, and nose; [용모] features; looks. ¶~가 수려한 얼굴 a well-shaped face // ~가 수려하다 have a regular[even] features / have a handsome face(남자) // ~가 또렷하다 have well-defined[clearly-marked / clean-cut] features.

이무기 [거대한 뱀] a monster serpent; a giant snake; a boa.

이문(利文) a margin of profit; a (profit) margin; [이익] profits; returns. ¶많은[적은] ~ a large[small] margin of profit // ~이 박한 장사 a low-profit business // (사업 등이) ~이 많다[박하다] yield much[little] profit / have a large[small] margin of profit / pay well[badly] // 이 상품은 ~이 박하다 These goods bring in small returns. // 이 가격이면 ~이 없다 The price leaves (me) no margin (of profit). // ~은 적지만 수량으로 메워 나갑니다 The profit is small, but we make it up by the number[quantity] we sell.

이물 [배의 머리] the bow; the prow; the stem. ¶~에서 고물까지 from stem to stern // 보트는 ~에서부터 가라앉기 시작했다 The boat sank bow first.

이물(異物) an alien substance; a foreign body; an extraneous matter. ¶엑스레이 사진에 위 속의 ~이 나타났다 An X-ray photo showed a foreign body in the stomach.

이미 already; before; previously. ¶~ 내가 말한 바와 같이 as I have already stated / as stated above // 때는 ~ 늦었다 It is too late now. // 내가 거기 갔을 때는 ~ 그들이 떠난 뒤였다 When I got there, they had already left. // 나는 ~ 약속이 있다 I have a previous engagement. // 그것은 ~ 해결이 난 것이다 It has already been taken care of[settled]. // 나는 그것을 ~ 각오하고 있었다 I was already prepared for that. // 추적대가 ~ 우리 뒤를 바싹 뒤쫓아 왔다 A party of pursuers was already close behind us[at our heels].

이미지 1 [심] an image. ⇨ **심상**(心象) 2 [사물·사람에게서 받는 인상] an image; an impression. ¶~를 바꾸다 give a new impression / change the image (of) // 이것은 우리 당의 ~를 높여 줄 것이다 This will improve the image of our party. // 그 사건은 회사의 ~를 손상시켰다 The incident harmed[damaged / lowered / hurt] the image of the company. / The incident was detrimental to the reputation[image / name] of the company. // 나에게는 21세기의 ~가 떠오르지 않는다 I cannot imagine what the 21st century will be like.

이미지즘 imagism.

이민(移民) [외국으로 이주하기] emigration; [외국에서 이주해 오기] immigration; [외국으로의 이주자] an emigrant; [외국으로부터의 이주자] an immigrant. ¶아시아에서 온 immigrants from Asia / 그는 미국으로의 ~이 허가되었다 He has been granted permission to immigrate to America. **이민하다** emigrate (from / into / to). ¶그들은 한국에서 브라질로 이민했다 They emigrated from Korea to Brazil.

이바지하다 1 [공헌하다] contribute (to); make a contribution (to); render services to; conduce to; make for; do much for[toward]. ¶증기 기관의 발명은 산업 발달에 이바지하는 바 컸다 The invention of the steam engine contributed greatly to the development of industry. // 그는 한국 학계에 크게 이바지했다 He rendered great services in the academic world of Korea. // 국제 연합은 세계 평화에 크게 이바지하고 있다 The United Nations have been doing a great deal for world peace. 2 [공급하다] provide; furnish; supply.

이발(理髮) a haircut; hairdressing. **이발하다** have one's hair cut[cropped / trimmed]; have[get] haircut; (남의 머리를) dress[trim / cut] (a person's) hair; barber (a person). ¶이발해야겠다 I must have a haircut. / I must go to a barber's (shop). / I must have my haircut.
● **이발사** a barber; a haircutter; (영) a hairdresser. **이발소** (미) a barbershop; (영) a barber's (shop).

이방(異邦) a foreign country.
● **이방인** a foreigner; an alien; a stranger.

이번(-番) [금번] this time; [현재] now; [다음번] next time; [머잖아] shortly; soon; [최근] recently; lately. ¶~ 시험 (미래) the next examination // ~ 회기 중에 during this session // ~에 부산으로 전근했습니다 I have been transferred to Busan. // ~ 사고에서는 부상자가 없었다 There were no injuries in the recent[this] accident. // ~에 아래 장소로 이사했습니다 I have (recently) moved to the address given below. // 우리는 ~에 한해서 특례를 인정하겠다 We will grant an exception just this once. // ~에는 신청자가 적었다 This time there have been few applicants.〃에는 꼭 이기겠다 I will win this time for sure.〃~만은 보내 주세요 Let me go just this once.〃~에는 네 차례다 It's your turn. / Your turn now.〃~에 발굴된 고분은 석기 시대의 것이다 The recently excavated burial mound[The tumulus (that was) excavated recently] dates from the Stone Age.〃~에 프랑스에 갑니다 I'm going to France shortly.〃~에 또 거짓말을 하면 용서하지 않겠다 I'll never forgive you if you tell another lie.〃~시험에는 합격하고 싶다 I hope to pass the next[coming] examination.〃~ 일요일에 놀러 오시오 Come and see me next[this] Sunday.〃~만큼은 정말 화를 못 참겠다 This time I really can't suppress my anger.〃~만은 용서해 주겠다 I will forgive you just this once.

이법 (理法) [원리와 법칙] principles and rules; a law; [도리와 예법] propriety and decorum. ¶자연의 ~에 맞다 It is in accord with law of nature.

이벤트 [사건·행사] an event. ¶메인~ a main event.

이변 (異變) [사고] an accident; [이상한 일] something unusual; [재변] a disaster; a calamity; a catastrophe. ¶뜻밖의 ~을 당하지 않나 have an accident /아버지의 신변에 무슨 ~이 일어난 것이 아닌가 하고 걱정했었다 I was afraid that something had happened to [some accident had befallen] my father.〃큰 ~이 발생했다 An extraordinary event took place.〃작년은 기상 ~의 해였다 We had unusual weather (all) last year.

이별 (離別) separation; parting; farewell. ¶~의 슬픔 the sorrow of parting /〜의 눈물 tears at parting /두 사람은 ~을 아쉬워하고 있었다 The couple were unwilling to part[to say their good-byes].〃우리는 ~을 앞두고 술잔을 나누었다 We had a drink together before parting[we parted].〃**이별하다** separate from (a person); part from (a person). ¶두 사람은 이별한 후 다시는 만나지 못했다 They never saw each other again.〃그는 어렸을 때 어머니와 이별했다 He was separated from his mother when he was a child.

● **이별가** a farewell song; a song of farewell.
● **이별주** a farewell[parting] drink.

이복 (異腹) a different mother; a half-brother[sister]; a brother[sister] by a different mother(▶ 이부(異父)의 경우도 같음). ¶그들은 ~ 자매이다 They are half-sisters[sisters by a different mother].

● **이복형제** a brother[sister] by a different mother; a half brother[sister].

이봐 hello; hey; hi; say; listen; look here. ¶~, 조심해 Hey, look out!〃~, 일어나 Hey, wake up.〃~, 그만해 Stop it, I tell you!〃~, 조용히 해 Hey[Come on], be quiet!

이부 (二部) [야간부] the evening school [division]. ¶그는 이 대학의 ~ 학생이다 He is a student in this university's evening division.

● **이부제** (학교의) the double-shift school system; a two-shift system. ¶~ 수업 instruction in two sessions[a double session]〃~로 일하다 work on the two-shift system.

이부 (異父) a different father.

● **이부형제** a half-brother[-sister]; a brother[sister] by a different father. ¶우리는 ~이다 We are half-brothers[brothers by different fathers].

이부자리 bedding; bedclothes (and mattress). ¶~를 깔다[펴다] spread the bedding (on)〃~를 개다 fold up the bedding.

이북 [전자책] an e-book; an eBook.

이북 (以北) 1 [북쪽] north (of); ... and northward. ¶38선 ~ north of the 38th parallel〃폭설로 인해 한강 ~의 교통이 마비되었다 All road and rail traffic north of the Hangang(Han River) has been paralyzed by the heavy snow. 2 [북한] North Korea. ¶~에 계시는 어머니 one's mother in North Korea〃그는 ~에서 왔다 He came from North Korea.

이분 this gentleman[lady]. ¶~에게 차를 올려 주십시오 Please give[bring] this lady[gentleman] a cup of tea.〃~은 송 씨입니다 This is Mr. Song.〃~들은 모두 60세 이상입니다 These people[ladies and gentlemen] are all over sixty.

이분 (二分) division into two parts; a half. ¶~의 일 a half / one-half /승객 중의 ~의 일은 한국인이었다 Half the passengers were Korean. **이분하다** divide (a thing) in two [into two parts]; halve. ¶이익은 당신과 이분하자 I will halve the profits with you.〃선생은 학생을 A그룹과 B그룹으로 이분했다 The teacher divided the students into two groups, A and B.

● **이분법** [논] dichotomy. **이분음표** (미) a half note; (영) a minim note.

이분자 (異分子) a foreign element; an outsider. ¶~를 배제하다 eliminate[exclude] alien elements

이불 bedclothes; a quilt(누빈 것); (깃털의) an eiderdown; (미) a comforter(▶ 주로 깃털 이불). ¶~을 개다 fold up the bedding〃~을 치우다 put away the bedding〃~을 덮다 pull a quilt over oneself /침대에 ~을 덮다 put a quilt on a bed〃~ 속에 들어가다 get into bed〃어머니는 아이에게 ~을 덮어 주었다 The mother covered[wrapped] her child in a blanket.

● **이불보** a wrapping cloth for quilt.

이브 [하와의 영어명] Eve.

이브닝드레스 an evening dress[gown].

이비인후과 (耳鼻咽喉科) otorhinolaryngology; (구어) the ear, nose and throat department.

이쁘다 →예쁘다

이사 (理事) a director; (대학 등의) a trustee. ¶대표 ~ a representative director〃상임 ~ an executive director〃전무 ~ a (senior) managing director〃상무 ~ a managing[an executive] director〃판매 담당 ~ a chief sales executive〃~가 되다 become a member of the board of directors.

● **이사국** a member of a council. ¶안전 보장 이사회 상임[비상임] ~ a permanent[non-permanent] member of the UN Security Council. **이사장** the chief director; the chairman[chairperson] of the board of directors [trustees]. **이사회** (기구) a directorate; a council; (회의) a directors' meeting. ¶국제 연합 안전 보장 ~ the United Nations Security Council.

이사 (移徙) a move; a removal; a change of address. ¶~ 가는 곳 one's new address〃새로 ~ 온 이웃 my new neighbor〃언제 ~ 갑

이사야서

니까 When are you moving?// 언제 ~ 읍니까 When are you moving in?// 사무소는 ~ 준비로 바쁘다 They are busy preparing to move their office. **이사하다** move (to / into); remove (to / into); change one's abode (to). ¶우리는 내주에 새집으로 이사한다 We are moving to [into] a new house next week (▶ into는 아파트 등에 씀).// 그녀는 편지로 이사했다는 것을 알려 왔다 She wrote to tell me her change of address.// 그 집은 서울로 이사했다 The family moved to Seoul.
● **이사 비용** moving expense. **이삿짐** the goods to be moved.

이사야서 (~書) [성] (The Book of) Isaiah (약어 Is., Isa.).

이삭 1 (벼·보리 등의) an ear; a head; a spike. ¶벼 ~ an ear of rice // 보리의 ~이 패다 The barley is putting forth [forming] ears. / The barley has come into ear.// 벼 ~이 다 나왔다 The heads of the rice are all out. 2 (땅에 떨어진) fallen ear (of grain) gleaning. ¶~을 줍는 사람 a gleaner // ~을 줍다 glean.

이산 (離散) dispersion; separation; scattering. ¶일가가 ~의 비운에 처했다 The family had the misfortune to be broken up. **이산하다** disperse; scatter; be dispersed [scattered]. ¶회사가 파산하여 사원들은 이산했다 After the bankruptcy of the company, the employees scattered [dispersed].
● **이산가족** dispersed [separated] families. ¶~ 찾기 운동 a campaign for reunion of dispersed family members // 그 가족은 ~이 되었다 The family broke up.

이산화탄소 (二酸化炭素) carbon dioxide.
이산화황 (二酸化黃) sulfur dioxide.

이삼 (二三) two or three; a few; some; a couple of. ¶~ 차 two or three times // 명의 어린이 a few [some] children // ~ 일 기다려 주실 수 없겠습니까 Couldn't you wait (for) a few [two or three / a couple of] days?

이상 (以上) 1 [위에서 말한 것] the above (-mentioned); the above (-stated). ¶~의 사항 the above-mentioned items / the items mentioned above // ~의 이유로 for the reasons stated above // ~으로 오늘 모임을 마칩니다 That concludes today's meeting. / That's all for today's meeting.
2 [일정한 기준보다 많음] more than; over; above; beyond; past (▶ 이들 단어를 쓸 때에는 우리말로 나타낸 숫자는 포함되지 않음에 주의. 곧, more than three는 3을 포함하지 않되, 그보다 큰 수를 가리킴); [일정한 표준으로부터 위] not less than; or more; and over [up] (▶ three or more 는 three and over는 3을 포함하되, 그보다 큰 수를 가리킴). ¶10 ~ 100까지 from 10 to 100 // 두 사람[두 종류] ~ two or more persons [kinds] // 70세 ~ 인 people seventy and over / elderly people over sixty-nine (years of age) // 25세 ~ 30세까지의 사람 people between (the ages of) 25 and 30 // 30분 ~ 기다리다 wait (for) more than half an hour // 수입 ~의 생활을 하다 live beyond one's income [means] // 이 트럭은 4톤 ~은 실을 수 없다 This truck [(영) lorry] cannot carry more than four tons (▶ 최대 4톤).// 이 전차는 시속 200킬로 ~으로 달릴 수 있다 This train can travel at more than 200 kilometers per hour.// 버스의 정원 ~ 승차는 엄격히 금지시켜야 한다 Overloading buses should be strictly forbidden.// 그녀는 체력 ~의 일을 하고 있다 She is working harder than her physical strength permits. / She is overworking.// 시험은 예상 ~으로 어려웠다 The exam was much harder than I (had) expected.// 이 ~은 일할 수 없다 I can't work any longer. / I can work no more.// 이 ~ 논의해도 소용없다 It's no use arguing any further.// 이 ~ 폐를 끼치지 않겠습니다 I won't trouble you any further [anymore / (영) any more].// 이 ~의 불평은 듣고 싶지 않다 I don't want to hear any more complaints from you.// 그렇게 충분히 배당되었는데 이 ~ 무엇을 바라는가 When you are so well supplied, what else do you need [can you ask for]?// 그는 열 권 ~의 책을 펴냈다 He has published more than ten books.
3 [이미 그렇게 된 바에는] now that; since; if ... at all. ¶거기서 급료를 받는 ~ 일하지 않을 수 없다 As long as I am paid by them, I have to work. / 취직을 한 ~ 열심히 일해야 한다 Now that you've got a job you must work hard (▶ now that은 어떤 사정의 변화가 있었을 때 씀).// 그것을 본 ~ 믿지 않을 수 없다 Since I have seen it, I cannot help believing it.// 약속한 ~ 가야만 한다 Since I've promised, I have to go.// 일단 일을 시작한 ~ 끝까지 해내야 한다 Once you have started on your work, you have to complete [stick to] it.
4 [끝] The end (▶ 보고 등의 끝에 적음); [완결] concluded (▶ 시리즈물의 끝 등); [이것으로 끝] (구어) That's all.

이상 (異常) extraordinariness; singularity; abnormality; uncommonness; oddity. ¶그는 몸에 ~이 생겼다 He has not been well.// 의사는 환자의 상태에 ~이 생길까 걱정해서 면회를 금지시켰다 The doctor forbade visitors for fear that patient's condition might change [take a turn] for the worse.// 절차에 ~이 있었다 There was some confusion in the procedure. **이상하다** [생소하다] strange; novel; [보기 드물다] uncommon; unusual; singular; abnormal; [기이하다] odd; peculiar; [상궤를 벗어나다] eccentric; [괴상하다] grotesque; [불가사의하다] mysterious; unaccountable; [수상하다] suspicious. ¶이상한 외모 a peculiar [grotesque] appearance // 이상한 외모의 여인 an odd-looking woman / a fantastically dressed woman // 이상한 집안 a strange [an eccentric] family // 이상한 사람 a funny [an eccentric] person / an odd fish // 이상하게 unusually / extraordinarily / remarkably / strangely // 이상하게도 strangely [oddly] enough / strange to say // 그 그림은 내게 이상한 느낌을 주었다 The picture struck me as strange [(구어) weird].// 나는 일종의 이상한 공포를 느꼈다 I experienced an indescribable horror.// 오늘은 아침부터 머리가 ~ 해 I have not been myself since this morning.// 그가 아직 오지 않은 것이 이상하다고 생각하지 않니 Don't you think it strange that he hasn't come yet?// 오늘은 그의 태도[상태]가 어쩐지 ~ He is not quite himself today. / There's something wrong with him today.// 남을 이상한 눈으로 보지 마라 Don't be prejudiced against others.// 그는 이상하게 서먹먹한 태도를 취하기 시작했다 He has grown strangely distant.// 이상한 사나이가 서성거리고 있다 A suspicious-looking man is hanging about.∥그는 이상하리만큼 열심히 일에 착수했다 He set to work with extraordinary zeal.∥저 빈 집에 대해 이상한 이야기가 나돈다 A strange story is told about that deserted house.∥그는 이상하게 창백해 보였다 He looked strangely pale.∥요즈음은 이상하게도 사고가 많다 For some reason, there have a lot of accidents recently.∥이상하게 들릴지 모르지만, 나는 누구나 대학 교육을 받을 필요는 없다고 생각한다 Strange as it may sound, I don't believe everyone needs a university education.∥그가 오지 않은 것은 정말 이상한 일이었다 His absence was incomprehensible.∥그가 갑자기 병에 걸렸다는 것은 이상한 일이다 It seems strange [odd] that he became ill so suddenly.∥그의 실패는 이상할 것 없다 It's natural that he failed. / No wonder (that) he failed.∥그녀는 이상한 눈으로 나를 봤다 She gave me a queer [an odd] look. / She looked at me in a strange way.∥어딘가 좀 ~ 하다 I feel (that) something is strange [wrong / out of the ordinary].∥별로 이상한 일은 없었다 Nothing unusual happened.∥무슨 이상한 일이라도 생기지나 않았을까 I'm afraid something has gone wrong.∥동물원에서는 이상한 동물을 많이 봤다 I saw many strange animals in the zoo.

● **이상 건조** (주의보) (a warning of) extremely dry weather (condition). **이상 난동**(-暖冬) an abnormally warm winter.

이상(異狀) [고장] a malfunction; the matter; an accident; something wrong; [변화] a change; (정신의) disorder; derangement; abnormality; (신체의) (an) indisposition. ¶아무 ~이 없다 Nothing unusual has happened. / There's nothing wrong. / Everything is all right [O.K. / in perfect order].∥엔진에 뭔가 ~이 있다 Something is wrong [the matter] with the engine.∥소리가 이상해서 기계에 ~이 있음을 알았다 A change in the sound it made told us that the machine was malfunctioning.∥기계에 ~이 있다 The machine is out of order.∥그는 목의 ~을 호소하고 있다 He is complaining that something is wrong with his throat.∥그는 몸에 ~이 있다 He isn't well. / (구어) He is indisposed.∥그의 용태에 ~은 없는 것 같다 I don't see any change (for the worse) in his condition.∥그는 정신에 ~이 생겼다 He became mentally deranged.∥전원 ~없습니다 We are all unharmed. / None of us were [was] injured.∥수확에는 ~이 없었다 No damage was done to the crops.

이상(理想) an ideal. ¶~과 현실 the Ideal and the Real∥~에 불타는 사람 a man of ideals∥높은 ~을 품다 have lofty ideals∥~을 좇다 follow [pursue] an ideal∥~에 맞다 meet [measure up to] one's ideal∥그는 ~을 실현했다 He realized his ideal.

● **이상주의** idealism. ¶~적인 idealistic. **이상주의자** an idealist. **이상향** Utopia; an ideal land. **이상화** idealization. ¶~하다 idealize / sublimate.

이상야릇하다(異常-) queer; odd; funny; absurd. ¶이상야릇한 모자 an absurd [a funny-looking] hat∥기분이 ~ feel queer. **이상야릇이** queer; oddly; funnily.

이상적(理想的) ideal. ¶~인 가정 an ideal home∥~인 남편[아내] an ideal husband [wife]∥그는 나의 ~인 남성이다 He is a man after my own heart. / He is the right man for me.∥바람이 없고 따뜻한 날이 낚시하기에 ~이다 A warm windless day is ideal for fishing.

이색(二色) two colors.
● **이색 인쇄** two-color printing.
이색(異色) 1 [다른 색] a different color. 2 [색다름] novelty.
● **이색 인종** a race of a different color.
이색적(異色的) unique; novel. ¶~인 작가[화가] a unique novelist [artist]∥~인 작품 a novel [unique] work∥그는 낭만파 작곡가 중에서도 ~이다 Among romantic composers he is a unique figure.
이생(-生) this life(-time); this present life.
이서(以西) [어떤 지점을 기준하여 그 서쪽] west (of); ... and westward. ¶추풍령 ~에는 큰비가 온다는 예보이다 Heavy rain is forecast (in the area) west of Chupungnyeong.
이서(裏書) (an) endorsement. ⇨*배서(背書).
이설(異說) a divergent [different] view; [이단] a heterodoxy; a heresy. ¶그는 정설에 대해 ~을 내세운다 He dissents from the established view. / His view differs from the established one.∥사고의 원인에 대해 ~이 분분하다 Opinion is divided on the cause of the accident.∥그는 이 건에 대해 ~을 내세웠다 He put forward a different view of [aired a divergent opinion on] this matter.
이설하다(移設-) move [remove / shift / transfer] (in / into). ¶사무실을 지방으로 ~ move the office to the local district.
이성(異性) 1 [다른 성질] different nature; [화] isomerism. 2 [다른 성] the opposite [other] sex. ¶~을 알다 have one's first sexual experience∥~ 교제가 넓다 have a large acquaintance of the opposite sex∥그에게는 ~의 친구가 많다 He has a lot of girlfriends.∥~ 사이에 참다운 우정이 있을 수 있을까 Can't boys [girls] find real friendship with the opposite sex?
● **이성 관계** relations with opposite sex. **이성애** heterosexuality.
이성(理性) reason; reasoning power; rationality; [철] Logos. ¶순수[실천] ~ pure [practical] reason∥논쟁에서 ~을 잃지 않는 사람 a rational type of man in an argument∥~적 (으로) rational(ly)∥~이 있다 have reason [a logical mind] / have good sense∥~에 호소하다[따르다] appeal to [listen to] reason∥~을 잃다 lose control of oneself / (속어) blow one's cool∥인간은 ~을 지닌 동물이다 Man is a rational animal [rational]. / Man has reasoning power [the power to reason].∥그 때 나는 ~을 잃고 있었다 At that time I was distracted.
이세(二世) 1 [이민 간 사람의 자녀]. ¶재미 교포 ~ an American-born Korean / a Korean∥~의 second-generation.
2 [2대] the second. ¶찰스 ~ Charles Ⅱ(▶ the second라고 읽음).
3 [아버지와 같은 이름의 자식] junior. ¶폴 윌슨 ~ Paul Wilson, Jr. [Junior].
4 [자식] a son. ¶그에게 ~가 태어났다 He now has a son.
5 [현세와 내세] this world and the next.
이솝 이야기 Aesop's Fables.
이송(移送) transfer; removal. ¶사건의 ~ [법] removal [transfer] of a case. **이송하다** trans-

이수 fer; remove. ➜이 사건은 대법원으로 이송되었다 This case was sent[transferred] to the Supreme Court.// 용의자는 법원으로 이송되는 도중에 도주했다 The suspect escaped while he was being taken to the courthouse.

이수(履修) completion. **이수하다** (학과·과정을) take; (수료하다) finish. ¶작년에 몇 과목을 이수했습니까 How many courses did you take last year?// 그는 3년 동안에 필수 과목을 모두 이수했다 He finished all the required courses in three years.

이순(耳順) the sixtieth year (of age). ¶~인 사람 a sexagenarian // ~에 달하다 attain one's sixtieth year of age.

이스트 [효모균] yeast.

이슥하다 far advanced; late. ¶이슥해지다 grow late // 밤이 이슥하여 late at night // 밤이 이슥했으므로 그는 마지못해 떠났다 It had grown so late that he left with reluctance.// 밤이 ~ It is very late. / (문어) The night is far advanced.// 그는 밤이 이슥하도록 공부한다 He sits up studying till late at night.

이슬 1 dew. ¶밤~ nightly dew // 아침 ~ morning dew // ~이 맺힌 dewy (flowers) / bedewed // **이 내린다** It dews. / The dew [Dew] falls.// 풀잎에 ~이 내려 있었다 There were drops of dew on the grass. // 잔디가 ~에 젖어 있었다 The lawn was wet with dew. 2 [눈물의 비유] a tear. ¶그녀의 눈에 ~이 맺혔다 Tears welled up in[sprang to] her eyes. **이슬로 사라지다** die on the scaffold [gallows]; die in the battle. ¶단두대의 ~ die on the guillotine // 전장의 ~ die in battle / be killed in action[battle].
● **이슬방울** a dewdrop; a dew gem; a drop of dew. **이슬비** (a) drizzle; a drizzling rain; a misty rain; a fog rain; a mizzle. ¶~가 내리고 있다 It is drizzling. // 하루 종일 ~가 내렸다 It drizzled all day. **이슬점** [물] the dew point.

이슬람교(-教) Islam. ¶~의 Islamic / Muslim / Moslem.
● **이슬람교도** a Muslim; a Moslem; an Islamite; (집합적) Islam (▶ a Muslim은 이슬람교도 자신이 쓰는 말).

이승 this life; this world; this (present) life. ¶~의 worldly / earthly / mundane // ~을 떠나다 die / pass away / depart this world // 이것이 그와의 ~에서의 이별이 될지도 모른다 This may turn out to be the (very) last time in my life that I see him.// 그는 아버지에게 ~에서의 마지막 이별을 고했다 He bid his father a last farewell. / He took his last leave of his father.

이식(利息) interest. ⇨이자(利子)

이식(移植) (식물·장기 등의) transplantation; (피부·근육의) grafting. ¶피부 ~ a skin graft // 각막 ~ a corneal graft // 내장의 ~ an organ transplant // 심장 ~ 수술 a heart transplant operation. **이식하다** (식물을) transplant; replant; (외국산 식물을) implant; (피부·뼈를) graft; transplant. ¶다른 화분에 ~ plant in another pot / repot // 묘목을 정원에 이식했다 I transplanted seedlings (in) to the garden.

이실직고(以實直告) reporting the truth; telling the truth. **이실직고하다** state a fact just as it is; give an honest statement [account] of fact; not to put too fine a point on it.

이심(二心) 1 [두 마음] duplicity; a double heart. ¶~을 품은 double[two]-hearted / double[two]-faced / double-dealing // ~이 없는 faithful / sincere // ~이 있는 사람 a double-dealer // **를 품다** be double-faced [two-faced] / play a double game. 2 [변덕] fickleness. 3 [배반] treachery.

이심(二審) [법] the second (judicial) trial; retrial(재심).

이심(異心) 1 any other intention. ⇨딴마음 2 ~. ⇨이심(二心)[1]

이심전심(以心傳心) direct communication from mind to mind; mental communication; telepathy. ¶그들은 ~으로 서로의 기분을 잘 아는 것 같다 They seem to understand each other by a sort of telepathy. **이심전심하다** communicate telepathically.

이십(二十) [스물] twenty; a score; [스무째] the twentieth. ¶~ 세기 the twentieth century // ~분의 일 one twentieth // ~ 대의 젊은이 a young man in his twenties.

이쑤시개 a toothpick. ¶~로 이를 쑤시다 use a toothpick / pick one's teeth with a toothpick.

이악하다 1 [끈덕지다] persevering; tenacious; pertinacious. ¶이악하게 일하다 work perseveringly / stick to one's work. 2 [이익을 위하여 아득바득하다] shrewd; sharp; wide-awake; (서술적) be wide-awake to one's own interest. ¶이악한 아이 a smart boy // 그는 ~ He is alive[wide-awake] to his own interests. / He has a quickeye for profit.

이앓이 (a) toothache. ⇨치통

이앙(移秧) rice planting.
● **이앙기**(-期) the rice planting season. **이앙기**(-機) a rice planting machine.

이야 [강조] the very; just; indeed; [제한] only. ¶말~ 바른 말이지 to be plain[frank / honest / candid] (with you) / plainly speaking / to conceal nothing from you // 남~ 뭐라 하든 상관없다 I don't care a bit what other people say. // 그쯤~ 나도 알고 있다 I know as much. // 그 사람~ 얼마나 화가 났겠니 I can imagine how angry he must have been.

이야기 1 [담화] a talk; [대화] (a) conversation; [한담] a chat; a gossip; [화제] a topic (of conversation); the subject; [연설] a speech; an address. ¶쓸데없는 ~ idle talk / gossip // 근거 없는 ~ groundless talk // 뒷~ an inside story / greenroom talk // ~를 시작하다 begin to talk // ~를 그치다 stop talking // ~를 계속하다 keep (on) talking / continue [keep up] a conversation // ~를 가로막다 interrupt[break into] a conversation // ~를 꺼내다 bring up a subject[topic] // 우리는 오랫동안 ~를 했다 We had a long talk. / We talked for a long time. // 그가 또 설교조의 ~를 늘어놓기 시작했다 He has begun his usual lecturing again. / He has started holding forth again. // 제 ~를 끝까지 들어 보세요 Hear me out, please. (▶ 대화 도중에 상대방이 말을 자르려고 할 때 하는 말임) // 그는 말이 적어서 ~를 끌고 가는 데에 고생했다 Since he was a quiet man, I had a hard time trying to keep the conversation going. // 우리는 즐거운 ~를 했다 We had a pleasant talk. // 국제 정세에 관해서 그와 ~를 나누었다 I talked with him about the international situation. // 모두 새 시장에 대한 ~를 하고 있었다 Everyone was talking about the new mayor.∥저 배우는 ~를 조리 있게 잘한다 That actor narrates well.∥아니 넌 무슨 ~냐 What do you mean? / What are you talking about?∥이상한 ~입니다만… It may sound strange, but ….∥이건 다른 ~입니다만 여행 일정은 정하셨습니까 Not to change the subject, but have you decided on the itinerary of your trip?∥이건 너와 나만의 ~다 This is (just) between you and me [ourselves].∥그 문제로 그와 여러 번 ~를 했다 I have had several talks with him about that matter.∥~만 무성하고 일은 진전이 없다 There is too much talk and not enough work being done.∥그렇다면 전혀 ~가 다르다 That's not our understanding.∥~를 하자면 깁니다 It's a long story. **이야기하다** [담화하다] talk; speak; converse; chat (over); have a talk[chat] (with); [진술하다] state; mention; explain; relate; narrate. ¶함께 ~ talk together∥그는 그 사고의 자초지종을 우리에게 이야기했다 He told us the whole story of the accident.∥그는 진상을 이야기했다 He told the truth.∥그는 경험담을 이야기했다 He related his experiences.∥그는 그 사건을 보고 온 듯이 이야기했다 He described the incident as if he had been an eyewitness to it.∥이야기하던 것으로 화제를 돌립시다 Let's get back to what we were talking about.

2 [설화] a tale; a story; [전설] a legend; [소설] a novel; a fiction; [우화] a fable; [삽화] an episode. ¶어린이를 위한 ~ stories[tales] for children∥**역사** ~ a historical novel∥**사랑** ~ a love story∥「캔터베리 ~」 The Canterbury Tales∥「이솝 ~」 Aesop's Fables∥한라산을 둘러싼 옛 ~ a legend[folk tale/folk story] concerning Hallasan(Mt. Halla)∥아주 재미있게 꾸민 ~ a highly-embellished story∥효도하는 아들의 옛~ an old tale of a dutiful son∥토끼와 거북이의 ~ the fable of the hare and the tortoise∥그의 전기에는 우스운 ~가 몇 군데에 나온다 Some funny episodes are related in his biography.∥믿을 수가 없는 ~다 It is an incredible story.∥그는 민화 ~를 잘한다 He is a good folk story teller. **이야기하다** tell a story[tale]; relate; narrate; give an account (of); make a description (of).

3 [소문] a rumor; a report; news; gossip. ¶…라는 ~다 People[They] say that …./ It is said that ….∥~인즉 …하다 The story goes that ….∥그 ~는 들어서 알고 있다 I know it by hearsay.∥곧 정변이 일어날 것이라는 ~가 있다 Rumor has it[says] that there will be a change of government before long.∥그가 해외에 파견된다는 ~가 들린다 They say[I've heard] that he will be sent abroad.∥학교에 그 ~가 파다하다 The whole school is full of it. **이야기하다** speak[talk / gossip] about; talk of; rumor. ¶그렇게들 이야기한다 It is so rumored. / So I understand. / People[They] say so. / So I am told.

4 [상의] consultation; [교섭] negotiations. ¶~가 되다[이루어지다] come to[arrive at] an understanding (with) / reach (an) agreement (with) / come to terms (with) / reach (an) agreement (with) / come to terms (with) / (상업상의) strike[close] a bargain / 그 문제로 그와 수차례 ~를 나눴다 I have several talks with him about that matter.∥어떻게 좀 ~가 될 수 없을까요 Can't you arrive at some understanding?∥~는 아직 거기까지 진전되지는 못했다 The negotiations are not yet so far advanced.∥그것은 ~가 다르다 That is not[against] our understanding[agreement]. **이야기하다** [상의하다] talk (with); consult (a person); [교섭하다] negotiate (with); arrange (with). ¶아들의 문제로 선생님과 이야기했다 I consulted the teacher about my son.∥이 문제에 대해 철저히 이야기해 보자 Let's talk out this problem.

5 [사정] the facts; reasons. ¶그렇게 되면 ~가 달라진다 That's another story.∥이제는 ~가 달라졌다 It's quite another story now.∥그렇게 되었더라면 ~는 많이 달라졌을지도 모른다 It might have made all the difference in the world. / The story might have been very different then.

이야기가 났으니 말이지 I take this occasion [opportunity] to say ….; I merely mention (this) in passing. ¶~ 지진이라면 어젯밤에도 한 번 있었어 Apropos[Talking] of earthquake, we felt one last night.

● **이야기꽃** ¶~을 피워 2시간이 금방 지나갔다 Two hours passed by quickly while we talked[chatted] about this and that. **이야기깃거리** a topic[subject] (of conversation). ¶~가 되다 become the topic[subject] of a talk[conversation] / come up in conversation∥~가 떨어지다 find one's topics of conversation exhausted / have nothing more to talk about∥그건 좋은 ~다 It's a good topic for conversation.∥그의 영웅적 행위는 사람들의 ~가 되었다 His daring exploits became legendary.

이야말로[1] [이것이야 참말로] the very; just; indeed. ¶이것 ~ 내가 쭉 찾고 있던 것이다 This is the very thing[This is just the thing] that I have been looking for.∥그 사람 ~ 비난 받아야 한다 It is he that[who] should be blamed.∥그 사람 ~ 진짜 미식가다 He is a gourmet if ever there was one.

이야말로[2] [이것이야말로] just; exactly; very. ¶~ 내가 원하던 물건이다 This is the very thing[just the thing] that I wanted.∥~ 인생의 비극이다 This is indeed[in truth] one of tragedies of life.∥~ 천재가 아니면 할 수 없는 일이다 This is nothing less than a work of genius.

이양(移讓) transfer; turning over; relinquishment. **이양하다** transfer; turn over; hand over; relinquish. ¶권리를 ~ transfer one's right (to another) / devolve rights upon (a person)∥정권을 ~ hand over the reins of government[power] / transfer the government∥그 왕은 왕위를 조카에게 이양했다 The king abdicated in favor of his nephew.

이어받다 [계승하다] succeed to; accede to; inherit (the property); take over; be[fall] heir to. ¶아버지의 일[회사]을 ~ take over one's father's work[company]∥나는 우리 집의 전통을 이어받았다 I carried on the traditions of my family.∥장남이 그의 작위를 이어받었다 His eldest son succeeded to his title.∥그는 부친의 재능을 이어받고 있다 He has inherited his father's talent.

이어서 [계속하여] continuously; successively; [다음으로] subsequently; soon after. ¶윤씨가 최 씨에 ~ 사장이 되었다 Mr. Yun has succeeded Mr. Choe as (the) president.∥강

이어지다

연에 ~ 질의응답이 있었다 The lecture was followed by a question-and-answer session. // ~ 모차르트의 교향악 30번이 연주되었다 Then[Next] the 30th symphony by Mozart was performed. // ~ 교장 선생님의 말씀이 있으시겠습니다 Next[Now] our principal is going to make an address to you.

이어지다 be[get] connected; be joined[linked] together. ¶이 기사의 나머지는 25페이지에 ~된다 This article is continued on page 25. // 이 길은 100미터 전방에서 고속도로와 ~된다 The road connects with[is connected to] the superhighway 100 meters ahead.

이어폰 earphones. ¶~으로 라디오를 듣다 listen to the radio with[through] an earphone.

이엉 (straw) thatch. ¶~ 지붕 a straw-thatched roof // 그 집은 ~으로 이어져 있다 The cottage is thatched with straw.
● **이엉집** a straw-thatched house.

이에 [이리하여 곧] hereupon; thereupon; at this point; to this; hence; accordingly. ¶나는 (음악에 대한) 귀도 목소리도 없다. ~ 노래를 부를 줄 모른다 I have neither ear nor voice, hence I can not sing.

이여 ¶신~ 우리를 불쌍히 여기소서 Oh, God! Have pity on us.

이역(二役) a double role. ¶1인 ~을 하다 play a double role / act two characters / play[double] the parts of (A and B).

이역(異域) [외국] a foreign country[land]; [타향] a strange land. ¶~에서 살다 live far away from home / be a stranger in a strange land // 그는 ~에 뼈를 묻었다 He died in a foreign land. / He spent[lived] his last year in a foreign country.

이열치열(以熱治熱) resort to an evil measure to destroy other evils; fight fire with fire.

이오니아식(-式) the Ionic order. ¶~ 건축 Ionic architecture.

이온 [물] an ion. ¶수소 ~ a hydrogen ion // 양 ~ a cation / a positive ion // 음~ an anion / a negative ion.
● **이온 결합** an ionic bond. **이온층** [천] ionosphere. **이온화** electrolytic dissociation; ionization. ¶~ 경향 ionization tendency // ~ 하다 ionize.

이완(弛緩) relaxation; [의] atony; [규율 등의] laxity. ¶괄약근의 ~ relaxation of a sphincter. **이완하다** relax; slack (off). ¶이완된 사지 flaccid limbs. →¶병사들의 규율이 좀 이완되어 있다 There is some laxity in discipline among the soldiers.

이왕(已往) 1 [과거·이전] the past; bygones. 2 [이미] already; now that; since; if … at all. ¶~ 할 바엔 큰일을 해라 If you do anything at all, do something great. // ~ 가기로 했으면 가야지 Once you have decided to go, you had better go. // ~ 2시간이나 기다렸으니 그가 올 때까지 있는 게 어때 Why don't you stay until he comes, since you've waited for two hours already?

이왕이면(已往-) [어차피 할 바에는] If … must[should]; if … at all. ¶~ 철저히 해라 If you do it at all, do it thoroughly. // ~ 나하고 같이 가자 As long as you are going anyway, come along with me. // ~ 영어를 배우겠다 As long as I am about it[While I'm at it], I might as well take English. // ~ 끝까지 싸우 라 If you do fight, fight it out [to a finish].

이왕지사(已往之事) 1 [지나간 일] (a thing of) the past; bygones. 2 already; now that. ⇨이왕2

이외(以外) ¶~에 […을 제외하고] except / […말고는] besides / in addition to // 그는 소설 ~에는 아무것도 읽지 않는다 His reading is limited[confined] to novels. / He reads nothing but[except] novels. // 이 아이가 몸에 걸치고 있는 것은 신발 ~에는 모두 어머니가 손수 만든 것이다 Except for her shoes, everything this child has on was made by her mother. // 저는 약간 피곤하다는 것 ~에는 별로 이상이 없습니다 There's nothing wrong with me except that I am a little tired. // 본교 생 ~에는 학교 밖으로 나가 주십시오 Those other than the students of this school are requested to leave the (school) premises. // 이 회사의 종업원들은 거의가 서울 ~의 사람들이다 Most of the employees of this firm are from outside (of) Seoul. // 유럽 여행에서 프랑스 ~에 어느 나라에 갔었습니까 What countries besides France did you visit while on your tour of[in] Europe? // 우리는 필수 과목 ~에 선택 과목을 최소한도 5과목 이수해야만 한다 In addition to required subjects, we must take at least five electives.

이용(利用) 1 [이롭게 씀] utilization; use; [쓸모있게 씀] good use; profitable employment; improvement. ¶폐물[폐품] ~ utilization of waste material. **이용하다** [활용하다] utilize; [선용하다] make (good) use of; take advantage of; (태양열·물 등을) exploit; harness. ¶어둠을 이용하여 under cover of darkness // 잘[더 잘 / 최대한] ~ make good[better / the best] use of // 태양 에너지를 ~ harness [make use of] solar energy // 기회를 ~ use [take advantage of] an opportunity // 여가를 최대한 ~ turn one's spare time to the best possible advantage // 지형을 ~ take advantage[make good use] of the lay of the land[topography] // 조합은 휴양 시설을 다른 조합도 공동 이용하도록 해 놓았다 The unions let members of other unions use their resort facilities. // 정부는 이 기회를 이용해서 정책을 수립해야 한다 The government should find a way to take advantage of this opportunity. // 우리는 우리나라의 자원을 충분히 이용해야 한다 We must exploit fully our country's natural resources. // 그들은 그 강을 이용해서 발전소를 건설할 것을 계획하고 있다 They are planning to harness the river to generate electricity. →¶이 과정에는 중력의 법칙이 이용되고 있다 The law of gravity is utilized in this process.

2 [자기 자신을 위한 수단으로 씀]. **이용하다** avail oneself of; take advantage of; [우려먹다] exploit. ¶특권을 ~ exploit[trade on / take advantage of] one's privileges // 그는 우리의 약점을 이용하여 터무니없는 값으로 그것을 강매했다 Taking advantage of our weakness[helpless situation], he forced it upon us at an exorbitant price. →¶그는 쉽게 남에게 이용당한다 He is easily taken advantage of. / (구어) He is a sucker[an easy mark]. // 그는 상사에게 늘 이용당하고 있었다 He was always being made a cat's paw of[being used] by his boss.
● **이용 가치** utility value. ¶~가 있다[없다] be of[be no] utility value. **이용법** utiliza-

tion; a use; a way to use; how to use. **이용자** a user; (도서관 등의) a visitor.

이용(理容) haircutting; (주로 여성의) hairdressing.

이울다 1 [시들다] wither (away); droop; wilt; fade (away). ¶꽃이 이울었다 The flower has withered[faded]. / 꽃과 아름다움은 이우는 법이다 Flowers and beauty wither. 2 (달이) wane. ¶달이 이울어 간다 The moon is on the wane. 3 [쇠약해지다] decline; decay; fall (off / away); sink; wane; fail. ¶이울어지다 be on the decline / 〔구어〕 be on the skids // 운세가 ~ be down on one's luck // 그 이후 그의 가운은 이울게 되었다 Since then the fortunes of his family have been on the wane [decline].

이웃 [근처] the neighborhood[vicinity]; [접한 곳] the next door; [이웃집 사람] a (next-door) neighbor. ¶~ **나라들** the surrounding [neighboring / adjoining] countries // ~ **읍** [고을] the nearest[next] town / a neighboring town // ~ **돕기 운동** a help-your-neighbor campaign // ~ **사랑** love of one's neighbor / good Samaritanism // ~에 있는 neighboring / nearby // ~과 사이가 좋다[나쁘다] get along well[badly] with one's neighbors // 양 씨가 ~에 이사해 왔다 Mr. Yang has moved into the neighborhood. // 저 집 개는 밤에 짖어 대기 때문에 ~ 사람들이 모두 싫어한다 Their dog barks at night, and bothers everyone in the neighborhood. **이웃하다** neighbor (to); adjoin (each other); be next door to each other. ¶나는 그와 이웃해서 살고 있다 I live next door to him.

● **이웃사촌** a good neighbor. **이웃집** a next-door[a neighboring / an adjacent] house; a neighbor's house; the house next door.

이원(二元) duality. ¶~적 dual.
● **이원론** dualism.

이원제(二院制) a bicameral system. ⇨*양원제 (⇨양원)

이월(二月) February(약어 Feb).

이월(移越) a transfer; (전기로부터의) bringing forward; (차기로의) carrying forward. ¶이자의 ~이 있었기 때문에 원금이 늘어났다 With the transfer of the interest, the amount of the principal increased. **이월하다** transfer; (전기로부터) bring forward[over]; (차기로) carry forward[over]. ¶가계비의 잔액을 다음 달로 ~ carry forward[over] the balance from last month's household expenses. →¶이번 달에는 5만 원이 이월되었다 There was a fifty thousand won balance carried forward this month.

● **이월금** (전기로부터의) the balance[amount of money] brought forward (from the previous account); (차기로의) the amount of money carried forward (to the next account).

이유(理由) 1 (a) reason; [근거] grounds; [원인] a cause; [동기] a motive. ¶**존재** ~ the justification for the existence (of a thing / of a person)/ 〔프〕 the raison d'être // 표면상의 ~ an ostensible reason // 자살한 ~ a motive for a suicide // 충분한 ~ a good reason // 빈약한 ~ a weak[poor] reason // ~ 있는[없는] 반대 well-grounded[groundless] opposition // 그는 ~가 있어 직장을 그만두었다 He quit the job with reason[for some reason]. / 그럴 만한 충분한 ~가 있다 There is every reason to do so. // 지각한 ~를 말하시오 Tell me why you were late. / Give the reason (why) you were late. // 그는 ~ 없이 해고되었다 He was fired unreasonably. // 그는 게으르다는 ~로 강등되었다 He was demoted because of his laziness[because he was lazy]. // 그는 건강상의 ~로 정년 전에 퇴직했다 He retired early for reasons for health. // 직무 태만의 ~로 퇴직을 명한다 You are dismissed from office on the grounds that you neglected your duties. // 그토록 좋은 일자리를 그만두다니 무슨 ~라도 있었느냐 Did you have some reason of your own for giving up such a good job? // 네가 오지 않을 ~가 없다 There is no reason why you should not come.

2 [구실] an excuse; a pretext. ¶이런저런 ~를 붙여서 on some pretext or other / on one pretext or another // 그런 것은 ~가 되지 못한다 That is no excuse. // 그런 ~는 통하지 않는다 Such an excuse won't do.

이유(離乳) weaning; ablactation. **이유하다** wean (a baby from the breast[its mother]); be weaned.
● **이유기** the weaning period. ¶그 아기는 지금 ~에 있다 The baby is being weaned. / The baby is going through the weaning period. **이유식** weaning food; baby food.

이윤(利潤) (a) profit; (a) gain. ¶한계[초과] ~ marginal[excess] profits // ~이 많은 장사 a profitable[paying] business // 돈을 회전시키지 않으면 ~은 생기지 않는다 Money needs to be turned over quickly if it is to produce profits. // 그는 그 거래에서 상당한 ~을 얻었다 He made a good[fair] profit on the transaction.
● **이윤율** a profit rate; a rate of profit.

이율(利率) the rate of interest; the interest rate. ¶**법정** ~ the legal rate of interest // **은행** ~ the bank rate // ~을 **인상하다** raise [increase] the rate of interest // ~을 **인하하다** lower[decrease / reduce] the rate of interest // 연 7푼 5리의 ~로 돈을 빌려 주다 lend [〔미〕 loan] money at the rate of 7.5 percent per year // 정기 예금의 ~이 내렸다[올랐다] The rate of interest on fixed deposits has been reduced[raised]. // 그 융자의 ~은 상당히 높다 The rate of interest on the loan is pretty high.

이율배반(二律背反) 〔철〕 antinomy.

이윽고 soon afterward(s); in a (little) while; after a while; before long. ¶해가 지고 ~ 달이 떴다 The sun set, and soon[by and by / in a short time] the moon appeared. // ~ 성이 나타났다 It was not long before the castle came into view. // ~ 비가 그쳤다 By and by it stopped raining.

이음매 [이은 자리] a joint; a juncture; a seam. ¶2개의 철관의 ~ a joint connecting two lengths of iron pipe // ~가 없는 seamless / jointless // ~ 없는 레일 a welded rail // 파이프의 ~에서 물이 새어 나왔다 Water leaked from where the two pipe were joined [connected].

이음새 →이음매

이의(異義) a different meaning; another meaning. **동음**~**어** a homonym.

이의(異議) 〔반대〕 an objection; 〔항의〕 a protest; 〔불찬성〕 dissent; 〔법〕 a demurrer. ¶ ~**가 있다[없다]** have an[have no] objection (to) // ~**를 제기하다** make an objection (to)

이익 / object (to) / protest (against) / dissent (from) / (재판에서) impeach (a witness) // 그의 제안에 몇 사람이 ~를 제기했다 Several people objected to [opposed / raised objections against] his proposal. // 뉴욕으로의 전근에는 ~가 없다 I have no objection to being transferred to New York. // 전원 ~ 없이 그 안을 채택했다 All present accepted the proposal unanimously [with one accord]. // 그는 그 결정에 대해 ~를 제기했다 He protested against the decision. // (의장이) ~ 없습니까 ~ 없다고 인정합니다 Does anyone has any objection? I see no objection. // (회의에서) ~ 있소 Objection! // ~ 없소 No objection!

● 이의 신청 an exception; a formal objection. ¶~을 하다 file [make] an objection // (재판장이) ~을 인정 [각하]합니다 Objection sustained [overruled]. 이의 신청인 [법] a demurrant.

이익(利益) 1 [벌이·수입] (a) profit; (a) gain. ¶큰 ~ a large profit // 부당한 ~ (an) undue profit / ill-gotten gains // 이 적은 장사 low-profit [unprofitable] business // ~이 생기는 거래 a profitable job // ~ 위주의 profit-minded // ~이 있는 profitable // ~이 없는 unprofitable // ~을 얻다 make a profit (on a transaction / by selling stocks) // 사회에 ~을 환원하다 return one's profits to society // 그것은 팔면 2,000달러의 ~이 있다 It will fetch a profit [gain] of 2,000 dollars. // 그것은 별로 큰 ~이 안 된다 It won't yield much profit. / It won't pay well. // 그들은 부당한 [비정상적인] ~을 올렸다 (구어) They made a killing. // 이 장사는 ~이 많다 [적다] This business is [is not] very profitable. // 이 장사는 별로 ~이 없다 This business doesn't pay very well [isn't making much of a profit].
2 [유익하고 도움이 됨] benefit; profit; advantage; good; interests. ¶…의 ~을 위하여 for the benefit of ... // 사회의 ~을 위해 힘쓰다 work hard for the public good // 그런 책은 읽어 봐야 아무 ~이 안 된다 It is of no use [It does no good] to read such a book. / You won't gain anything by reading a book like that. // 그것은 나의 ~이 된다 It is to my advantage. // 그는 늘 자기의 ~만 생각하고 있다 He always looks after his own interest. / He is always thinking of his own advantage. // 이 일은 ~이 있다 This job has its advantages. // 그는 ~에 밝다 He has a quick eye for profit. / He is very alert to his own interests.

● 이익금 earnings; a profit. 이익 배당 distribution of profit; profit-sharing.

이인(異人) 1 [비범한 사람] a man of unusual ability. 2 [다른 사람] a different person. ¶그것은 동명~이다 That is a different person with the same name.

이인삼각(二人三脚) a three-legged race.
이인칭(二人稱) [언] the second person.
이임하다(離任-) leave one's office [post].
이입(移入) introduction; import; shipping in. ¶감정 ~ [심] empathy // 외국인 노동자의 ~ the introduction of foreign labor. 이입하다 introduce; import; bring in [from]; ship in. ➡¶이 논문은 집필자의 감정이 지나치게 이입되어 있다 The writer has put too much personal feeling into this thesis.

이자(利子) interest. ¶미불 ~ interest unpaid [accrued / in arrears] / accrued [outstanding] interest (payable) // 연체 [은행 / 확정 / 미수 / 사채] overdue [bank / fixed / accrued / debenture] interest // 정기 예금의 ~ interest on a fixed deposit // 무~의 interest-free // 무~로 free of interest / without interest // 높은 [낮은] ~로 at high [low] interest // 8퍼센트의 ~로 돈을 빌려 주다 lend [(미) loan] money at 8 percent interest // ~를 붙여서 갚아 주다 pay back the money with interest // ~를 받고 돈을 빌려 주다 lend [put out] one's money at interest // 이 저금은 5푼의 ~가 붙는다 This deposit bears [yields] 5 percent interest. // ~가 ~를 낳아 원금의 배가 되었다 Interest bore interest and doubled the principal.

● 이자 소득 the income from interests. 이자 수입 interest receipts.

이자(膵子) [생] the pancreas; (양·송아지 등의 식용의) a sweetbread. ¶~의 pancreatic.

● 이자액 pancreatic juice.

이장(里長) the head (man) of a village; a village headman.

이장하다(移葬-) exhume and bury elsewhere [in another place]; remove a grave to another place.

이재(理財) finance; economy; management of financial affairs; financial management. ¶그는 ~에 밝다 He is a good financier. / He is clever at making money. 이재하다 manage financial affairs.

● 이재국 the Financial (Management) Bureau.

이재(罹災) suffering (from a calamity); affliction. 이재하다 suffer (from a calamity); fall a victim (to a calamity); be hit [visited] (by a typhoon). ¶그의 일가는 최근의 홍수로 이재했다 His family fell victim to the recent flood.

● 이재 구조 기금 a (disaster) relief fund. 이재민 the sufferers (from); the afflicted people; the victims (of). ¶홍수의 ~ flood victims // 공습의 ~ a victim of an air raid / 전쟁 ~ war victims // ~을 구호하다 carry out the relief of victims of a disaster.

이적(利敵) benefiting the enemy. 이적하다 benefit [help] the enemy.

● 이적 행위 an act advantageous to the enemy. ¶우리의 약점을 공표하는 것은 ~이다 Publicizing our weakness will just profit [help] the enemy.

이적(移籍) transfer of registration. 이적하다 transfer one's registration (from / to). ➡¶그는 내년에 브레이브스로 이적된다 He will transferred to the Braves next year.

● 이적료 (프로 야구의) a waiver.

이적하다(離籍-) have one's name removed from the family register. ➡¶그는 방탕한 아들을 이적시켰다 He has his profligate son's name removed from the family register.

이전(以前) 1 [그보다 전에] before. ¶이보다 ~ before this time // 홍 씨 ~에는 누가 지사였습니까 Who was the governor prior to Mr. Hong? // 아침 8시 ~에는 전화를 걸지 마세요 Please do not telephone me before eight in the morning.
2 [예전] former times [days]. ¶~(에) formerly / in former times / in days gone by / of old / previously / before / [한때] once / on an earlier occasion // ~의 수상 an ex-

premier ~의 장관 a former minister.∥~의 동료 a former colleague.∥그 위대한 스타도 ~에는 시골 처녀에 지나지 않았다 The great star had originally been just a country girl.∥~에 여기는 황무지였다 This was once wasteland.∥~에 나는 거기에 자주 가곤 했었다 I used to go there often.∥그는 ~의 건강을 되찾지는 못했다 Though his life was saved, he never regained his health.∥~에는 이곳에 초가집이 있었다 There used to be a (straw-)thatched house here.

이전(移轉) 1 [이사] a move; a removal; a change of address[residence]. ¶그들은 사무소의 ~ 준비로 바쁘다 They are busy preparing to move their office. **이전하다** move; remove; shift home; move one's residence (from ... to ...). ¶위 주소로 이전했습니다 We have moved to the above address.∥그 회사는 이전했음을 편지로 알려 왔다 The company wrote to tell me their change of address.
2 [권리 등을 넘겨주거나 넘겨받음] (a) transfer; demise. ¶권리의 ~ a transfer of rights / 재산의 ~ a transfer of property. **이전하다** transfer; change hands. ¶이전할 수 있는 권리 transferable rights / 토지의 소유권을 아내에게 ~ transfer a land deed to one's wife's name.
● **이전 등기** registration of a (land) transfer.

이전투구(泥田鬪狗) throwing[slinging / flinging] mud at one another.

이점(利點) an advantage. ¶이 제품은 가볍고 튼튼하다는 ~이 있다 This article has the advantage of being light and durable.∥그것이 다른 상점에 비해 이 상점의 ~이다 That is the advantage of this store over the others.∥그는 작가로서의 명성을 ~으로 해서 지사에 당선했다 Taking advantage of his fame as a writer, he won the gubernatorial election.∥그곳은 시골과 도시의 ~을 겸비하고 있다 the location combines advantages of country and city.

이정(里程) mileage; (a) distance. ¶경주까지의 ~ the distance to Gyeongju / 10킬로의 ~ a distance of 10 kilometers.
● **이정표**(-表) a table of distances. **이정표**(-標) a milestone; a milepost.

이제 now. ¶~ 막 just (now) / a moment ago ∥~는 now / at the present time / nowadays / [이미] already∥그는 ~ 다시 일어설 기력을 잃었다 He has already lost the will to get up again. / He no longer has the will to get up[get to his feet] again. / He no longer has the strength to stand up.∥우리는 ~ 끝장이다 It's all up with us now. / It's all over now. ∥~ 결혼식 날짜가 정해졌으므로 그 준비로 자네가 바빠지겠군그래 Now that the date of your wedding has been fixed, I expect you will be busy with preparations.∥병이 ~ 다 나으셨습니까 Have you recovered from your illness? / Are you well now? ∥~ 돌아가야겠습니다 I must be off[going] now.

이제껏 till[by] now; until[up tp] now[the present]; up[down] to date; hitherto; so [thus] far; to[by] this time; yet. ¶~ 어디에 가 있었니 Where have you been all this while? ∥~ 뭘 하고 있었니 What have you been doing all this time?

이제나저제나 impatiently. ¶우리 모두가 경기의 시작을 ~ 기다리고 있었다 We were all waiting impatiently for the game to begin.

이제야 now. ¶싸움은 ~ 끝났다 The battle is now over.∥~ 승부를 걸 때이다 This is the moment to go for victory.∥~말로 청년이 일어설 때이다 Now is the time for the younger generation to rouse themselves to action.

이종(異種) [다른 종류] a different kind[sort / species]; [변종] a variety. ¶이것은 저것과는 ~의 곤충이다 This is an insect of a different kind[species] from that.∥이 꽃은 난초의 ~이다 This flower is a variety of orchid.
● **이종 교배** hybridization; crossbreeding.

이종(사촌)(姨從四寸) a cousin who is the child of one's mother's sister.

이주(移住) [이사] a move; a removal. **이주하다** move (to); remove. ¶경기도로 ~ move to Gyeonggido. 2 (외국으로의) emigration; (외국으로부터의) immigration(▶ 정착); [사람의 옮겨 삶·동물의 이동] migration(▶ 반복되는 이주나 집단의 이동에도 쓰임). **이주하다** emigrate (from a place to a place); immigrate (to a place from a place); migrate (from a place to a place). ¶형은 브라질로 이주했다 My brother emigrated to Brazil.∥그는 독일에서 (이 나라로) 이주해 온 사람이다 He is an immigrant from Germany.
● **이주자** (외국으로의) an emigrant; an immigrant; (이주민) a settler; (외국으로부터의) an immigrant.

이죽거리다 make provoking[invidious] remarks[jokes]. ⇨ˇ이기죽거리다

이중(二重) duplication; double(ness). ¶~의 [둘이 겹쳐진] double / [두 부분으로 된] dual∥~의 화장지 two-ply toilet paper∥이 용기에는 ~의 뚜껑이 붙어 있다 This container has a double lid.∥이 기계는 ~의 목적으로 쓰일 수 있다 This machine serves [fills] a double purpose.∥상자는 ~으로 포장되어 있었다 The box was wrapped with a double layer.∥술에 취하면 물건이 ~으로 보인다 When I am drunk I see double.∥회비를 ~으로 청구해 왔다 I was asked to pay the fee twice.∥그 토지에는 ~의 소유권이 있음을 알았다 The land proved to be under dual ownership.
● **이중 가격** a double price. **이중고**(-苦) a double torture. ¶파산과 병과의 ~에 시달리다 be under the double torture of bankruptcy and illness. **이중과세**(-課稅) double taxation. **이중 구조** [경] dual industrial structure. **이중 국적** dual nationality[citizenship]. ¶~자 a dual national. **이중 모음** [언] a diphthong. **이중생활** a double life. ¶아버지는 일 때문에 서울에, 가족은 부산에 살고 있어, 우리는 ~을 하고 있다 We maintain two households — my father is working in Seoul, and the rest of the family live(s) in Busan. **이중성**(-性) dualism; duplicity. **이중인격** a dual[double] personality / a Jekyll and Hyde. **이중주** a duet. ¶바이올린 ~ a violin duet. **이중창**(-唱) a duet. **이중창**(-窓) a double window. ¶~이 있는 방 a double-windowed room.

이즈음 now; these days. ⇨ˇ요즈음
이즘 now; these days. ⇨ˇ이즈음
이지러지다 1 [한 귀퉁이가 떨어지다] chip

이지적(理智的) intellectual. ¶그는 ~인 사람이다 He is an intellectual man.// 그녀는 ~으로 보인다 She looks intelligent.

이직(移職) change of occupation. ⇨전직(轉職)

이직률(離職率) the unemployment rate.

이직하다(離職-) 〔직장을 그만두다〕 leave [quit] one's job; 〔실업하다〕 lose one's job. ¶불황 때문에 많은 사람이 이직했다 Many lost their jobs because of the recession.

이진법(二進法) 〔수〕 the binary system [scale].

이질(姨姪) a nephew [niece] who is the child of one's wife's sister.

이질(痢疾) 〔의〕 dysentery; (bloody) flux. ¶아메바성 ~ amoebic dysentery.

이질적(異質的) heterogeneous; disparate; of a different nature [kind]. ¶그것은 ~인 사람들이 모인 집단이었다 It was a group of heterogeneous people.// 이 사건은 완전히 ~인 것이다 This incident is of an entirely different nature.

이쪽 1 〔화자(話者)에게 가까운 쪽〕 this side. ¶~으로 here / this way // ~으로 오십시오 Come here. / This way, please.// 화장실은 ~입니다 Here's the bathroom.// ~으로 앉아 주십시오 Will you sit over here, please?// 차는 거리의 ~에 세워 주십시오 Please park your car on this side of the street.// 복도의 ~에 상자가 쌓여 있다 There is a pile of boxes on this side of the corridor [(미) hall].// 강의 ~에 집이 몇 채 있다 There are a few houses on this side of the river.// 우리는 ~저쪽 찾아 보았으나 그 집을 찾지 못했다 We looked here and there, but couldn't find the house.
2 〔화자에게 가까운 것〕 this (one). ¶~ 사과가 더 크다 This apple is bigger.// 그쪽보다 이 좋다 This (one) is better than that (one). // ~은 헨리 밀스 씨입니다 This is Mr. Henry Mills.
3 〔자기(편)〕 we; us; our party. ¶~ 사정도 생각해 주십시오 Please take our convenience into consideration, too.// 그 건은 ~에서 처리하겠습니다 We will take care of the matter.

이쯤 about this [so] much. ⇨이만큼 ¶오늘은 ~에서 끝낸다 So much for today. / We'll stop here for today. / That's all for today.// ~에서 화해해야 한다 It's time you make up. // 어린아이라도 ~은 알고 있다 Even a child knows this much.

이차(二次) 1 〔부차〕 secondary. 2 〔차수가 2인 것〕. ¶~는 〔수〕 quadratic.
●**이차 감염** secondary infection. **이차 방정식** a quadratic equation.

이차원(二次元) two dimensions. ¶~의 two-dimensional // 평면은 ~이다 A plane has two dimensions [is two-dimensional].

이차적(二次的) subsidiary; secondary. ¶그것은 ~인 문제다 That is a matter of secondary importance. / That is a secondary consideration.

이착륙하다(離着陸-) take off and landing.

이채(異彩) a conspicuous color. ¶~를 띠다 be conspicuous / cut a conspicuous [brilliant] figure / stand out from others // 그는 현대 음악계에서 ~를 띠고 있다 He stands out [is conspicuous] among contemporary musicians.// 그는 전위 영화 제작으로 영화계에서 ~를 띠고 있었다 He made his presence in the film world felt with his avant-garde movies.

이채롭다(異彩-) conspicuous; shining; brilliant; distinguished; striking. ¶그는 자기 반에서 이채로운 존재이다 He is quite different from the other students in his class.

이첩(移牒) notification to the authorities concerned; communication. **이첩하다** transmit (an order / the information) to the office [official] concerned; pass (the information) on (to); notify (of / that); refer (to); communicate (to).

이체(異體) 1 〔다른 체재·형상〕 an unusual form. 2 〔생〕 a variant. ¶자웅 ~ dioecism.
●**이체동심**(-同心) perfect harmony between two persons. ¶그들은 ~이다 They are of one mind.

이촉 the root of a tooth.

이층집(二層-) a two-story [-storied] house; a house of two stories.

이치(理致) 1 〔논리〕 (a) theory; 〔도리〕 reason. ¶~에 맞는 [맞지 않는] 이야기 a reasonable [an unreasonable] story // 네 말은 ~에 맞지 않는다 What you say does not stand to reason [make sense / hold water].// ~로는 그렇지만 실제로는 불가능하다 It is true in theory but impossible in reality.// 남녀 관계는 ~만으로 설명할 수 없다 There is something about the relationship between man and woman that can't be defined logically. / The relationship between man and woman is beyond reason or logic.// 그가 아버지의 사업을 이어받는 것은 당연한 ~다 It is only natural [stands to reason] that he should succeed to his father's business.// 그 요구는 ~에 맞는다 [맞지 않는다] The demand stands to [is contrary to] reason. / That is a reasonable [an unreasonable] demand.// 그에게 ~를 따져도 소용없다 It is no use reasoning with him.
2 〔원리〕 a principle. ¶자연의 ~ a natural law // …의 ~를 탐구하다 go [inquire] into the principles of // 자식을 사랑하는 것은 자연의 ~다 It is in the nature of things that parents should love their children.

이칭(異稱) another name; another [a different] title.

이키(나) Oh!; Oh my (goodness)!; Dear me!; Gosh!; 《미국 속어》 Gee! ¶~ 놀랐다 Oh, what a surprise!

이타(利他) altruism. ¶~적인 altruistic / unselfish.
●**이타주의** altruism. **이타주의자** an altruist.

이탈(離脫) (a) secession; (a) separation; a breakaway. ¶국적 ~ the renunciation of one's nationality **이탈하다** secede (from); break [drift] away (from); leave (a party). ¶ 당적(黨籍)을 ~ secede from a party // 구식 사고방식에서 ~ get rid of an old-fashioned idea // 그들은 연맹에서 이탈했다 They left [seceded from / broke away from] the league.// 노동자들은 오전 중 직장을 이탈했다 The workers walked out during the morning.
●**이탈자** a seceder.

이탓저탓 with this excuse [complaint] and that; on one pretext or another; on some

이태 two years. ¶~ 동안 for two years.
이탤릭(체)(-體) [인] italics; italic type. ¶~으로 인쇄하다 print in italics∥외국어는 ~으로 하시오 Italicize foreign words.
이토(泥土) mud; clay. ⇨진흙
이토록 this much; so much; so; like this. ¶~ 부탁하는데도 for all my request∥~ 잘될 줄은 미처 몰랐다 Little did I expect to succeed so well.∥~ 늦으리라고는 생각지 못했다 I didn't realize it was so [this] late.
이튿날 1 [다음 날] the next [following] day; the day after. ¶~ 아침 the next morning∥~인 5월 1일 우리는 인천항을 떠났다 On the next day, May (the) first, we departed from Incheon Harbor. **2** [둘째 날] the second day. ¶열 ~ the twelfth day (of) the month.
이틀[1] [2일간] two days. ¶~마다 every two days / every other day∥~째에 on the second day∥~ 간격을 두고 every third day / every three days∥하루 ~에 in a day or two. **2** the second day (of a month). ⇨초이튿날
이틀[2] [치조(齒槽)] the socket of a tooth; [생] an alveolus (pl. -li); an alveole.
이파리 [잎] a leaf (pl. leaves); (풀의) a blade. ¶파란 ~가 있는 채소 green vegetables.
이판사판 ¶~ 해 보겠다 I'll take a chance on it / I'll give it a try, sink or swim. / (구어) Let's go for broke!∥~**이다** What have I got to lose (or win)?
이판암(泥板巖) [광] shale.
이팔청춘(二八靑春) sixteen years of age; the prime of youth; sweet sixteen; (사람) a maiden of sixteen.
이편(-便) **1** [이쪽 편] this side[way]; [이것] this (one). ¶~으로 오십시오 This way, please.∥정거장은 길 ~에 있다 The station is on this[our] side of the street.∥~이 더 고급이다 This is of better quality.∥저편보다 ~이 마음에 든다 I prefer this to that one.∥~에 은행이 있습니까 Is there a bank around [about / near] here? **2** [자기] I; we. ¶~의 잘못 my[our] fault / a fault on my[our] part∥~으로서는 이의가 없습니다 There is no objection as far as we are concerned.
이하(以下) **1** (수량이) ... (and) downward; not exceeding. ¶10개 회사 ~ (최대 10사) ten or fewer companies∥50 ~ 50 and less / 50 and below∥부모의 연간 수입이 5백만 원 ~인 학생 a student whose parent's annual income does not exceed five million won. **2** [정도] under; below; beneath; less[lower] than. ¶보통 ~ below the general level / below the average [mark / standard]∥중류 ~ below the middle class∥총액은 예상 ~다 The sum total falls under what was expected.∥그의 성적은 보통 ~이다 His grades are below [lower than] average.∥우리는 이것들을 원가 ~로 판매하고 있습니다 We are selling these below [at less than] cost. **3** [나머지] the following. ¶~와 같음 the same as follows∥~ 동(同) and so on [forth]∥~ 동문(同文) the same as above∥123페이지 ~를 참조하라 See page 123f. [pp. 123ff.]. (▶ f.는 (and the) following (page), ff.는 (and the) following (pages)의 약어). **4** [다른 것] other. ¶총리 ~ 여러 장관 및 관리들 the prime minister and other ministers and officials beneath him / the prime minister and lesser ministers and officials∥사장 ~ 수위에 이르기까지 전 사원이 그 식전에 참석했다 The ceremony was attended by all members of the company from director (down) to watchman.
이하선(耳下腺) the parotid (gland).
●**이하선염** parotitis; mumps(▶ 단수 취급). ¶~에 걸리다 catch[come down with] the mumps.
이학(理學) science.
●**이학 박사** (사람) a doctor of science; (학위) Doctor of Science(약어 D.Sc.). **이학부** the department of science.
이합집산(離合集散) meeting and parting. ¶정당의 ~ changing alignment of political parties / vicissitudes in alignment of political parties∥정당인의 ~이 심하다 Party men are constantly changing their factions.∥~은 흔히 있는 세상사다 It is the way of the world to meet and part.
이항(二項) ~의 binomial / binominal.
●**이항 방정식** a binomial equation. **이항식** a binomial expression [formula]; a binomial.
이해(利害) loss and gain; profit and loss; advantages and disadvantages; interest(s); concern. ¶공통의 ~ common interests∥~가 없는 거래 an even bargain∥~를 초월한 사랑 disinterested love∥~에 관계되다 affect one's interests∥나는 ~ 따위를 따지지 않는다 I don't care a bit about making a profit. / It doesn't matter whether I make money (on it) or not.∥그는 자기의 ~만 생각하고 있다 He thinks of nothing but his own interests [advantage].
●**이해관계** interests; concern; stake. ¶상충하는 ~의 조절 the adjustment of conflicting interests∥~가 있다 have an interest [a concern] (in)∥그 나라는 한국에 큰 ~를 가지고 있다 That country has a vital interest in Korea. **이해관계자** the persons [those] interested [concerned]; the interested party. **이해득실** loss and gain; profit and loss; advantages and disadvantages; interests; [좋은 점과 나쁜 점] merits and demerits. ¶새 제도의 ~ the advantages and disadvantages [the plus and minuses] of the new system∥~을 따지다 calculate [reckon] the loss and gain (of) / balance the profits and loss (of)∥그는 ~에 밝다 He knows where his interests lie. **이해타산** [계산] calculation [reckoning] of the loss and gain [the profits and losses]; [욕심] self-interest; interestedness. ¶~을 떠나서 apart from the consideration of gain / unfettered by one's self-interest∥그 행위는 ~을 넘어선 것이었다 He did it from disinterested motives.∥당신은 항상 ~만 생각하여 행동한다 You are always acting from selfish motives.
이해(理解) understanding; comprehension; grasp; apprehension; appreciation. ¶충분한 ~ a full understanding∥상호 (간)의 ~ mutual understanding∥~가 곤란하다 be incomprehensible / be hard to understand / be beyond one's comprehension∥~가 부족하다 do not fully understand / want sympathy∥~가 빠르다[느리다] be quick [slow] to understand [comprehend]∥상호 간의 ~를 도모하다 promote [increase / deepen] mutu-

이행

al understanding / know each other better // 그는 ~가 빠르다 He is perceptive[quick to understand]. / [지각·분별이 예민하다] He is sensible. // 그는 ~가 둔하다 [머리가 나쁘다] He is dull-witted[obtuse]. / [지각·분별이 둔하다] He is imperceptive. / He isn't sensitive. // 그의 말은 ~가 안 간다 What he does not make sense. // 그는 ~가 빠르므로 크게 도움이 된다 He is a great help because he is quick to understand. **이해하다** understand; comprehend; apprehend; appreciate; grasp; make out; see. ¶이해하기 힘든 incomprehensible / hard[difficult] to understand // 이해하기 쉬운 easy to understand / easily understandable // 이해할 수 있는 understandable / comprehensible // 다른 것으로 잘못 ~ mistake[take] one thing for another // 자유의 뜻을 잘못 ~ have a mistaken[wrong] idea of freedom // 한 씨는 내 말을 잘 이해해 주었다 Mr. Han understood me quite well. // 아무도 그녀의 업적을 이해하지 못했다 Nobody appreciated her work. // 그 때는 그의 의도를 이해하지 못했다 I could not make out his intentions at that time. // 그의 시는 나로서는 이해할 수 없다 His poems are beyond my comprehension. / I don't understand his poems. // 그녀가 왜 내 제안에 동의하지 않았는지 이해하기 어렵다 I can hardly understand why she hasn't agreed to this proposal. // 무슨 생각을 하고 있는지 그의 진의를 이해하지 못하겠다 I cannot understand [make out] what he has in mind. // 나는 그의 침묵을 찬성으로 이해했다 I construed his silence as agreement. // 그것은 인간으로서는 이해할 수가 없다 It is beyond human understanding. // 너는 그의 성의를 이해해 주어야 한다 You should take his sincerity into consideration. / You should appreciate his sincerity. ➔ **이해시키다** make (a person) understand.

● **이해력** the comprehensive faculty; the understanding; the power to understand; sense. ¶~이 좋은 사람 a person quick to understand (things) / a sensible person // 이 모자라다 have a poor understanding / ~이 없다 lack understanding // ~을 기르다 cultivate the power of understanding. **이해심** understanding; consideration; sympathy. ¶~이 있는 어머니 an understanding mother // ~이 없는 어머니 a mother who lacks understanding // ~이 있다 be considerate (of other people's feelings) / be sympathetic (about) // ~이 없다 be unsympathetic / be inconsiderate (of) // 그는 남의 고통에 대한 ~이 부족하다[없다] He lacks consideration for [He is insensitive to] the suffering of others.

이행(移行) [물] translation; a switchover; a shift. ¶새 제도로의 ~은 원활히 이루어졌다 The switchover[shift] (from the old) to the new system was carried out[(문어) effected] smoothly. **이행하다** move[proceed] (to); shift (to). ¶평화 산업으로 ~ switch over to peace industry // 우리 회사는 감속(減速) 경영으로 이행했다 Our company shifted to a slow-growth policy.

이행(履行) performance (of a duty); fulfillment (of a promise); discharge (of an obligation); execution (of a contract); observance (of a rule); implementation (of a treaty). ¶계약[조약] ~ the execution[implementation] of a contract (treaty) // 약속의 ~ fulfillment of a promise. **이행하다** fulfill (a promise); carry out (a pledge); perform (a duty); discharge (an obligation); execute (a contract); put (one's principle) into practice; live up to (one's principle); observe (a rule); implement (a treaty). ¶의무를 이행하지 않다 fail to perform a duty // 계약을 ~ perform[carry out] a contract // 약속을 ~ fulfill[keep / carry out] a promise // 채무를 이행하지 않다 default on debt payments // 그는 명령을 충실히 이행했다 He carried out the order faithfully[to the letter].

● **이행자** a performer; an executer.

이형(異形) [생] heteromorphy; heteromorphism.

● **이형 세포** an idioblast. **이형 색체** a heterochromosome.

이혼(離婚) a divorce; divorcement. ¶법정 ~ a judicial divorce // 합의[협의] ~ a divorce by consent[agreement] // ~을 요구하다 seek [claim] a divorce. **이혼하다** divorce (one's wife); be divorced from (one's husband); have one's marriage annulled(법적으로). ¶이혼한 사람 a divorced person / (남자) a divorcé / (여자) a divorcée // 이혼하여 갈라지다 be separated by divorce // 그녀는 마침내 이혼할 수 있었다 She finally got[obtained] a divorce. // 그는 아내와 이혼했다 He divorced his wife. // 그의 딸은 이혼했다 His daughter has been divorced[has got(ten) a divorce] (▶ 후자는 여자 쪽에서 이혼을 요구했을 경우). ➔ **이혼당하다** be divorced (by one's husband).

● **이혼 소송** a divorce suit. ¶~을 제기하다 sue for a divorce. **이혼 절차** divorce procedure.

이화명나방(二化螟−) [동] a pearl-moth; a grass moth.

이화 작용(異化作用) [생] dissimilation; catabolism.

이화학(理化學) physics and chemistry. ¶~의 physicochemical.

이후(以後) [금후] after this; from now on [this time (on)]; [그 후] after that time; since then; from that time on; afterward(s); [그 후 지금까지] ever since. ¶그때 ~지금까지 from that time down to this day // 밤 10시 ~에는 텔레비전의 소리를 줄여 주십시오 Please turn down your TV after ten p.m. // 내주 수요일 ~에는 집에 없습니다 I shall not be (at) home on or after next Wednesday [from next Wednesday on]. // 7월 ~는 부산에 있을 겁니다 I shall be in Busan from July on. // 나는 정월 ~ 건강이 좋지 않다 I haven't been well since New-Year's (Day).

익년(翌年) the next[following] year; the year after.

익다¹ 1 (열매·과일이) ripen; become ripe. ¶익은 ripe // 너무 익은 overripe // 익지 않은 과일 unripe[green] fruits // 복숭아는 아직 익지 않았다 The peaches have not ripened yet. // 이 버찌는 아직 먹을 수 있을 정도로 익지 않았다 These cherries are not ripe enough to eat. // 밭에서 익은 토마토는 달다 Garden-ripened tomatoes have better flavor.

2 (날것이) boil; be boiled; be done; cook; cooked. ¶잘 익은 well-done[-cooked] // 너무 ~ be overdone / be cooked two much // 잘 익었니 Is it cooked well? / Is it well done? /

이것은 잘 익지 않았다 This is only half boiled[half done]. / This is underdone.// 고기가 익어 가고 있다 The meat is boiling. **3** (술·장·김치 등이) ferment; mature; be[get] matured; be aged(술이); become seasoned. ¶포도주는 세월이 지나야 익는다 Wine is softened by age.// 김치가 잘 익었다 The *gimchi* (kimchi) has picked up flavor[has become seasoned].// 이 포도주는 잘 익지 않는다 This wine has not matured[aged] properly. **4** (살갗이) turn red; redden; color. ¶(난로의 열 등으로) 발갛게 익은 얼굴 a glowing face (with heat)// 목욕을 하고 나니 몸이 온통 익은 것 같았다 I was all of a glow after the bath.

익다² **1** [능숙하다] skilled; skillful; trained; experienced; practiced; expert. **2** [설지 않다] familiar; accustomed. [서술적] used (to); become accustomed to; become familiar (with); become experienced in. ¶귀에 익은 [익지 않은] 목소리 a familiar [strange] voice // 손에 익은 펜 the pen one is used to writing with// 눈[귀]에 ~ get used to seeing [hearing] / be accustomed to see[hear] // 이 광경은 눈에 익은 것이다 This is a familiar scene to me.

익명(匿名) [본이름을 숨김] anonymity; [가명] a pseudonym; a cryptonym; an anonym(e). ¶~의 anonymous / innominate / (a prince) incognito // ~의 투서[투고] an anonymous letter[contribution] // ~의 작가 an anonymous author[writer] // ~의 기부인 a donor whose name was withheld// ~의 독지가 an anonymous benefactor // ~으로 비평하다 criticize (another) under cover of a false name// 그는 ~으로 서평을 했다 He reviewed books anonymously.// 기증한 분은 ~을 바라고 있습니다 The donor wishes to remain anonymous.

● **익명자** an incognito (*pl.* ~s) (남자); an incognita(여자); an anonym(e).
익모초(益母草) [식] a motherwort.
익사(溺死) drowning. ¶~ 직전의 어린이 a drowning child// ~을 모면하다 escape a watery grave. **익사하다** be drowned (to death); drown; drown oneself(자살하다). ¶나는 익사할 뻔했다 I (was) nearly drowned.// 그는 바다[강]에서 익사했다 He was drowned[He drowned] at sea[in the river].

● **익사자** a drowned person. ¶올여름에는 많은 ~가 생겼다 Many people were drowned this summer. / There were many cases of drowning this summer. **익사체** a drowned body.

익살 comicality; drollery; waggery; clownery; jocularity; [농담] a joke; a jest; (a) pleasantry; [우스꽝] humor. ¶~을 떨다[부리다] clown (around) / play the buffoon[fool] / be funny// 좌석의 분위기를 맞추려고 ~을 부리고 있다 I am clowning around in order to keep everybody entertained.// ~ 좀 떨지 마라, 진정이야 Don't be funny — I'm serious.

● **익살꾸러기** / **익살꾼** / **익살쟁이** a joker; a jester; a jokester; a buffoon; a clown; a wag; a droll[facetious] person.
익살맞다 comic(al); funny. ⇨**익살스럽다** ¶그의 말투는 아주 ~ The way he talks is very funny [humorous].
익살스럽다 comic(al); funny; humorous; waggish; jocular; jocose; jesting; clownish;

droll. ¶익살스러운 몸짓 droll[comical] behavior // 익살스러운 이야기 a funny [humorous] story// 그의 말에는 언제나 익살스러운 데가 있다 What he says always sounds humorous. / There is a comic touch in his words.// 그는 익살스러운 짓을 하여 우리를 웃겼다 He amused us by acting [playing] the fool.// 그는 익살스러운 말로 우리를 웃겼다 He kept us laughing with his funny remarks.

익숙하다 **1** [친숙하다] familiar; accustomed; experienced. ¶익숙한 일 a familiar job// 익숙한 길 the familiar road[path / trail] // 익숙하지 않은 일 unaccustomed work// 익숙하지다 get[be] used (to) / become[be] accustomed (to) / grow familiar (with) / become injured (to hardships) / become habituated (to dangers) // 추운 날씨에 익숙해지다 accustom oneself to cold weather// 그 역할을 여러 번 되풀이하는 사이에 나는 많이 익숙해졌다 In the process of repeating the role many times, I got quite used to it.// 그녀는 여러 사람들 앞에서 이야기하는 데 아주 익숙해진 것 같다 She looks quite at home even speaking in front of large groups.// 그 여배우가 무대에 익숙해지기까지는 꽤 시일이 걸렸다 It took the actress a long while to get over her stage fright.// 그는 외국어를 알아듣는 데 익숙하지 않다 He is not used[accustomed] to hearing foreign languages.// 이주자들은 곧 새 고장에 익숙해졌다 The immigrants soon acclimated [영] acclimatised] themselves to the new land.// 그는 이 고을에 익숙하지 않다 He is a stranger in this town. / He is unfamiliar with this town.// 그는 이제 자기 일에 익숙해졌다 He is quite settled in his job.// 그녀는 무대에서 노래하는 데에 익숙한 것 같다 She seems quite at home singing on the stage.// 그는 어려운 일에 익숙하지 않았다 He was not accustomed[used] to hard work.// 그는 곧 외국의 관습에 익숙해졌다 He soon became familiar with[picked up] foreign customs.// 그는 겨우 새로운 방식에 익숙해졌다 He finally got[became] accustomed [used] to the new method. **2** [능숙하다] skilled; skillful; experienced; practiced; expert. ¶익숙한 사회자 an experienced emcee// 익숙한 솜씨로 with practiced [clever] hands / skillfully // 익숙한 태도로 in a practiced [an experienced] manner // 교수법에 ~ be an experienced teacher// 그는 익숙한 솜씨로 나이프와 포크를 다루었다 He managed his knife and fork with practiced hand.// 그것은 기술이 익숙해져야 할 수 있는 일이다 It requires great deal[amount] of skill.// 나는 자동차 운전에 아직 익숙하지 않다 I don't have much experience in driving. / I'm not an experienced driver.// 그는 익숙한 솜씨로 그 시계를 분해했다 He took the watch apart with a practiced [skilled] hand. **익숙히** skillfully; expertly; with skill; with practiced [clever] hands; like an old hand [an old-timer / a veteran]. ¶영어를 ~ 쓰다 have a good command of English// ~ 노래하다 sing with skill.

익월(翌月) the next [following] month.
익일(翌日) the next [following] day. ¶편지를 낸 ~ 그는 도착했다 He arrived the day after the letters was posted.
익조(益鳥) a useful [beneficial] bird.

익충(益蟲) a useful[beneficial] insect.
익히 ¶~ 알다 know well[fully / thoroughly].be well aware[informed] of (a fact) / be familiar[well acquainted] with (a matter) / be at home in[on] (things America)//이 점은 너희들도 ~ 알고 있을 줄 안다 I think you are all well aware of it.
익히다¹ [열매 등을 익게 하다] make ripe; ripen; mellow; mature. ¶인공열로 과일을 ~ ripen fruit by artificial heat // 햇볕이 과일을 익힌다 The sun ripens fruit. **2** [날것을 익게 하다] boil; cook. ¶익힌 생선 boiled[cooked] fish // 달걀을 ~ boil an egg // 고기를 잘 ~ get the meat well done. **3** [술·장 등을 발효시키다] mature; ferment; brew; age. ¶포도주를 ~ let wine mature // 김치를 ~ get *gimchi* (kimchi) seasoned[flavored]. **4** (살갗을) redden; color.
익히다² [익숙하게 하다] make oneself familiar with; familiarize oneself with; habituate oneself to; inure oneself to; acclimate oneself to; accustom oneself to; acquaint oneself with; get (a person) accustomed to; accustom (a person) to; [습득하다] learn; practice; acquire (French). ¶음악을 ~ practice music / take[have] lessons in music / study music (under a person) // 장사를 ~ train (a person) to a trade // 차의 운전을 익혀라 Learn how to drive a car. // 그 설명서를 읽으면 사용 방법을 곧 익힐 수 있을 것이다 Read the explanation, and you will understand at once how to use it[how it works]. // 태권도를 완전히 익히는 데 그는 여러 해가 걸렸다 He spent many years (in) mastering *taegwondo*. // 영어는 시작은 쉽지만 완전히 익히기는 어렵다 English is easy to begin, but hard to master.
인 [몸에 밴 습관] a (personal) habit; a peculiarity; [악습] a vice.
인(이) 박이다 get[fall] into a habit of (doing); become addict (to). ¶인이 박인 사람 a habitual user (of) // 그는 담배[마약]에 인이 박였다 He is addicted to smoking [drug].
인(仁) **1** [유교의 중심적 도덕 이념] perfect virtue; [인애(仁愛)] benevolence; humanity; philanthropy; charity. **2** [식] [핵] a core; [씨] a stone; a kernel. **3** [생] a nucleolus.
인(印) [도장] a seal; [스탬프] a stamp. ¶일부를 찍다 stamp the date.
인(燐) [화] phosphorus(기호 P). ¶~의 phosphorous(3가의) / phosphoric(5가의) / (속어) phossy.
-인(人) a person; a man. ¶한국~ a Korean / 경제~ a financier // 신문~ a newspaper man.
인가(人家) a house; a dwelling. ¶~가 밀집한[드문드문한] 지역 a densely[sparsely / thinly] populated area // ~가 없는 deserted / desolate / uninhabited // ~가 많다 be crowded with houses / be thickly inhabited / be densely populated // 우리는 여러 시간을 걸었지만 ~는 한 집도 보이지 않았다 We walked for hours without coming upon a single house [(문어) human habitation]. // 그는 ~에서 떨어진 숲 속에 살고 있었다 He lived in the woods far from any human dwelling.
인가(認可) [승인] approval; [허가] permission; [행정상의 허가] authorization. ¶무~ 보육원 an unauthorized day-care center // ~를 받고 under license // ~를 얻다[받다] obtain[secure / get] sanction [authorization] (from) / obtain a license[permit] (from) / be authorized[sanctioned] (by) // 당국의 ~를 신청하다 apply for the approval of the authorities // 구청장에게 ~를 신청하십시오 You should apply to the head of the ward for approval[permission]. // 음식점을 개업하려면 보건 복지부의 ~가 필요하다 You must obtain[get] authorization[sanction] from the Ministry of Health and Welfare in order to open a restaurant. // 이 교과서는 교육적 자원부의 ~를 받은 것이다 These textbooks are authorized by the Ministry of Education and Human Resources Development. **인가하다** approve; [허가하다] permit; authorize; give permission [license]. ¶교육 인적 자원부 장관은 종합 대학교의 신설 계획을 인가했다 The Minister of Education and Human Resources Development approved the plan for building a new university. ➔ 이 학교는 정식 인가된 전문학교이다 This school is authorized as a vocational school.
인각하다(印刻-) engrave (a seal); carve; cut; inscribe; sculpture.
인간(人間) **1** [사람] a human being; a man (*pl*. men); a mortal; [인류] man; mankind. ¶~의 human / mortal // ~의 탈을 쓴 악마 a demon in human shape[form] // ~의 존엄성 human[man's] dignity // 지구 상의 ~ men on earth // 제대로 된 ~ [인격자] a man of character / [원숙한 사람] a very mature man // ~으로서의 약점 human weaknesses / a human weak point // ~은 원숭이와 다르다 Human beings are different from apes. // ~은 말을 할 수 있는 유일한 동물이다 Man is the only animal that can talk. // ~은 하나의 갈대에 불과하며 자연 속에서 가장 약하다. 그러나 ~은 생각하는 갈대이다 (Pascal의 말) Man is but a reed, the weakest in nature, but he is thinking reed. // ~은 죽기 마련이다 Man is mortal. // 그런 실수는 ~이면 다 있을 수 있는 일이다 Such an error is very human. // 그 침팬지는 ~과 같은 지혜를 가지고 있다 했다 It was said that chimpanzee was as intelligent as a man. // 그것은 ~으로서는 도저히 할 수 없는 일이다 It is beyond human power.
2 [사람의 됨됨이] character; nature; personality. ¶그는 어떤 ~입니까 What is he like? / What sort of man he is? // 그는 ~이 되지못했다 He is ill-natured. // 그는 ~이 아주 변했다 He is quite another man now. / He is not what he used to be. // 그에게는 ~을 보는 눈이 없다 He is a poor [no] judge of character.
인간 만사는 새옹지마라(속담) Inscrutable are the ways of Heaven.
● **인간 관계** human relations. **인간미** (touches of) humanity; a human touch; humaneness. ¶~가 있는 재판관 a warm-hearted judge // ~가 있다 be humane / be warmhearted // 그에게는 ~가 없다 He lacks humane feelings. / He is a coldhearted man. / There is not a touch of humanity about him. **인간 사회** human society; the community of men. **인간성** human nature; humanity. ¶~을 말살하다 dehumanize / divest (a person) of human qualities // 언어의 연구는

바로 ~의 연구이다 The study of language is the study of human nature.// 그는 ~이 나쁘다 He is ill-natured. **인간애** human love; (인류애) philanthropy.

인감(印鑑) 〔인발〕 a registered seal impression.
- **인감도장** one's registered[legal] seal. **인감증명서** a document certifying that a seal is registered.

인건비(人件費) personnel expenses[expenditure]; 〔봉급 지급 비용〕 payroll costs; 〔노동에 대해 지급하는 비용〕 labor costs. ¶학교 예산의 70퍼센트가 ~이다 Seventy percent of the school budget goes to pay salaries. ¶요즘은 ~가 늘어나고 있다 Personnel expenses are increasing these days.

인걸(人傑) a remarkable[outstanding] man [character]; a hero.

인격(人格) character; personality; individuality. ¶ ~의 whole personality // ~적인 감화 moral influence // 훌륭한 ~ a fine character // ~을 갖춘 사람 a man of character // ~을 함양[도야]하다 build up one's character // ~을 존중[무시]하다 respect[ignore] a man's individuality.
- **인격 교육** character building. **인격자** a man of character. **인격화** personification. ¶ ~하다 personify // 그리스 인은 자연계의 모든 것을 ~했다 The Greeks personified everything in nature.

인견(人絹) artificial silk. ⇨ˋ인조견⊕인조

인계(引繼) a transfer (of duties); turning [handling] over (one's duties). ¶사무 ~가 끝났다 Transfer of business has been completed. **인계하다** transfer (one's business); take[hand] over. ¶후임자에게 사무를 ~ transfer[hand over] one's business to one's successor. →선임자로부터 사무를 인계받다 take over one's duties from one's predecessor // 그는 홍 씨의 일을 인계받기로 되어 있다 He is supposed to take over Mr. Hong's job.

인고(忍苦) endurance; stoicism. ¶ ~의 생애 a stoic life // ~의 일생 a life of patient endurance.

인골(人骨) a human bone.

인공(人工) human work[labor]; 〔자연물에 가공하는 일〕 art; human skill; artificiality. ¶ ~의 artificial / man-made [-created] / unnatural // ~적으로 artificially // ~의 미(美) the beauty of human art / man-made beauty // 자연과 ~ nature and art // 자연계에는 ~으로 모방할 수 없는 것이 많다 There are many things in nature which defy human ingenuity to imitate them. // ~적으로 비를 오게 하는 일이 가능하다 It is possible to make rain fall artificially.
- **인공 강우** rainmaking. **인공 수정** artificial insemination[fertilization]. **인공 심장** a mechanical heart. **인공위성** an artificial[a man-made] satellite. ¶ ~을 발사하다 launch an artificial satellite. **인공 유산** artificial abortion. **인공 지능** artificial intelligence. **인공호흡** artificial breathing[respiration]. ¶ ~기를 ~을 해 주다 practice[try] artificial respiration (on) / try mouth-to-mouth respiration (on).

인과(因果) 1 ¶ 〔원인과 결과〕 cause and effect. 2 〔불〕 karma; a retribution.
- **인과 관계** a causal relationship; causation. ¶이 두 사건 사이에는 아무런 ~가 없다 There is no causal relationship between these two incidents. **인과율** / **인과 법칙** the law[principle] of causality[causation]; the law of cause and effect. **인과응보** retribution; karma; a reward in accordance with a deed. ¶그의 ~이다 He got exactly what he deserved.

인광(燐光) 〔물〕 phosphorescene. ¶ ~을 발하다 phosphoresce / emit phosphorescence.

인광(燐礦) mineral phosphate.
- **인광석** phosphate ore.

인구(人口) (a) population. ¶노동 ~ the working population // 과잉 ~ surplus population // 실업 ~ the jobless[unemployed] population // ~의 증가[감소] an increase[a decrease] in population // 8만의 도시 a city of 80,000 people // 급격한 ~의 증가 a population explosion // ~가 조밀[희박]하다 be densely[sparsely] populated / be thickly [thinly] peopled // ~가 많다[적다] have a large[small] population // 서울은 1,000만의 ~를 갖고 있다 Seoul has a population of 10,000,000.
- **인구 과잉** overpopulation. ¶ ~ 지대 an overpopulated area. **인구 동태** dynamic trends in (a) population. **인구 통계** dynamic population statistics. **인구 밀도** population density. ¶ ~가 높은[낮은] 지역 a densely [sparsely] populated area // 이 나라는 ~가 높다[낮다] This country is densely [sparsely] populated. // 이 지방의 ~는 1평방킬로미터당 100명이다 The density of population in the region is 100 persons to a square kilometer. / The per-square-kilometer population density of the region is 100. **인구 정태**(-靜態) static trends in (a) population. **인구 통계** static population statistics. **인구 조사** (take) a census.

인권(人權) human[personal] rights; the rights of man; (미) 〔시민권·공민권〕 civil rights. ¶기본적 ~ fundamental human rights // ~을 유린하다 infringe upon personal [human] rights // ~을 옹호하다 depend human rights // ~을 박탈하다 proscribe (a man) // 남의 ~은 존중해야 한다 We must respect the human rights of other people. // 그것은 ~에 관한 문제이다 That's a question of[touching upon] human rights.
- **인권 선언** the Declaration of Human Rights. ¶세계 ~ the International Declaration of Human Rights. **인권 옹호** the protection of human rights[civil liberties]. **인권 유린** / **인권 침해** a violation of[an outrage against] human rights. ¶그것은 ~이다 That's an infringement on our human rights.

인근(隣近) the neighborhood; the vicinity. ¶ ~ 주민들 neighbors // ~의 neighboring / nearby (hospital) // ~ 사람들에게 호소하다 appeal to the people in one's neighborhood / appeal to one's neighbors.

인기(人氣) popularity; public interest. ¶ ~ 있는 소설 a popular novel // ~ 있는 사람 a favorite / a popular figure[person] // 사교계의 ~ 최고의 인사 the most popular member of society // 대중 사이에 ~ 있는 정치가 a politician popular among the people / a politician enjoying the confidence of the people // ~를 높이다 heighten[increase] one's popularity // ~를 잃다 lose one's popularity / become

인기척

인기 /~를 되찾다 regain one's popularity // 여자에게 ~가 있다 be a favorite with women / receive the attention of women // 그의 기부는 ~를 얻기 위한 시도인 것 같다 He seems to have made the donation in an effort to win public favor. // 저 학생은 학급에서 ~가 좋은 사람이다 The student is popular [a favorite] with the class. // 그녀는 친구들 사이에 ~가 좋다 [없다] She is popular [unpopular] with her friends. // 그 소설은 주부들의 ~를 얻었다 The novel won [enjoyed] popularity among housewives. // 그 선생은 학생들에게 ~가 없다 The teacher is not popular with the students. // 저 가수는 젊은이에게 ~가 있다 [없다] That singer is [is not] popular among [with] young people. // 이 만화 잡지는 초등학교 아동에게 ~가 있다 This comic magazine is a favorite with schoolchildren. // 그 프로는 ~가 오르고 [떨어지고] 있다 The program is rising [falling] in popularity. // 저 여배우는 지금 ~ 절정이다 That actress is at the height of her popularity. // 이 음반은 십 대들의 ~를 휩쓸고 있다 This record is top of the pops among teenagers. / This record is all the rage [[속어] the hottest thing going] among teenagers. // 그는 지금 ~가 오르고 있는 작가이다 He is a writer of rising fame [popularity]. // 그는 급우들에게 ~가 없다 He is unpopular among his classmates. // 그 작품은 ~가 없다 That performance has little appeal. // 그 상품은 ~가 없다 There isn't much demand for that article. // 그는 소설가로서 한창 ~가 있다 He is a very popular novelist.

● **인기 가수** a pop singer; a star singer; a pop idol. **인기 배우** a popular actor [star]; a screen [stage] idol; a film [stage] favorite. **인기 소설** a sensational [catching] novel. **인기 작가** a popular writer. **인기투표** a popularity vote [poll].

인기척(人-) an indication [a sign] of a person being around. ¶교정에는 ~이 없었다 The campus was deserted [empty]. // 누가 따라오는 ~이 있다 I hear someone following me. // 그 집에는 ~이라고는 없었다 The house gave no sign of life.

인내(忍耐) [참고 견딤] patience; endurance (▶ endurance는 특히 장기간에 걸친 인내); [끈질김] perseverance. ¶그것을 해내는 데는 대단한 ~심이 필요하다 It takes a lot of perseverance to accomplish it. // 그는 ~심이 강한 사람이다 He is a man of great patience. / He is very patient [persevering]. **인내하다** be patient (with / about); persevere (at / in / with); have patience (with); stand; endure; bear; put up with. ¶그는 마침내 인내할 수 없게 되었다 His patience was worn out at last.

● **인내력** [참을성] endurance; patience; [지구력] staying power; [끈질김] perseverance; fortitude. ¶~이 있다 have staying power [perseverance] // ~이 없다 lack patience.

인대(靭帶) [생] a ligament.

인덕(人德) [인복] blessedness with friendly people; natural [innate] virtue. ¶그는 ~이 있다 He has been blessed with people who are willing to help him.

인덕(仁德) benevolence; goodness; humanity. ¶~이 있는 국왕 a benevolent king.

인덱스 [색인] an index (*pl.* ~es, -dices).

인도(人道) **1** [지켜야 할 도리] humanity; morality. ¶~를 유린하다 [짓밟다] commit an outrage against humanity // 그들의 행위는 ~에 어긋나는 것이다 Their actions are against humanity. **2** [보도(步道)] a footpath; a footway; (미) a sidewalk; (영) a pavement. ¶~와 차도의 구별이 없는 장소 a place without distinction of footway and carriageway.

● **인도교**(-橋) a footbridge; (영) a pedestrian bridge; (미) a pedestrians' overpass. **인도주의** humanitarianism; humanism. **인도주의자** a humanitarian; a humanist.

인도(引渡) [물품의] (a) delivery; (특히 동산·부동산의) (a) transfer; (범죄인·점거물의) (a) surrender; (국가간 또는 미국의 주(州) 사이에서의 도망자의) extradition. ¶공장 ~ ex works [factory / mill] // 도착항 ~ free port of destination // 화차 ~ free on rail [truck] (F.O.R. [F.O.T.]) / (미) free on board (약어 F.O.B., f.o.b.) // 증권의 ~ 체결 transaction settlement by delivery of share certificates // 대금 상환 ~ payment on delivery of / COD (▶ collect [cash] on delivery의 약이) // 포로의 ~ delivery of prisoner-of-war // 물품의 ~를 완료하다 complete delivery of goods // 우리는 그것을 대금 상환 ~로 보내겠습니다 We will send it C.O.D. // 대금 상환 ~로 지불해 주시오 Please pay cash on delivery. // 짐의 ~는 차질 없이 수행됐다 The packages were delivered without a hitch. / The delivery of the packages was carried out smoothly. // 프랑스는 공중 납치 범인의 ~를 요구했다 France requested extradition of the hijacker [that the hijacker be extradited]. **인도하다** deliver (to); transfer; hand [turn] over; (포로·범인을) surrender; extradite(국제간의 지명수배자를). ¶화물을 ~ deliver goods // 소유자에게 ~ hand over a thing to the owner. → ¶그 남자는 경찰에 인도되었다 The man was handed over to the police. // 그의 유해는 가족에게 인도되었다 His remains were handed over to his family.

인도(引導) [지도] guidance; (a) lead; [안내] showing the way. ¶신의 ~ divine guidance. **인도하다** guide; lead; conduct. ¶후진을 ~ give guidance to the younger generation // 남을 바른길로 ~ lead a person into the right path // 선생이나 부모나 그 학생을 바른길로 인도하려고 했다 The teacher and the parents were trying to guide the student into the right path.

인도·게르만 어족(-語族) the Indo-Germanic (family of) languages. ▷ 인도·유럽 어족

인도양(印度洋) the Indian Ocean.

인도·유럽 어족(-語族) the Indo-European (family of) languages.

인도적(人道的) [인정이 있는] humane; [인도주의적인] humanitarian. ¶~ 견지에서 from a humanitarian point of view [viewpoint] // ~으로 문제를 해결하다 solve a problem in a humane way // 90세의 죄수는 ~ 견지에서 석방되었다 The ninety-year-old prisoner was released on humanitarian grounds.

인동(덩굴)(忍冬-) [식] a (Japanese) honeysuckle.

인두 (다림질용) an iron; (납땜용) a soldering iron. ¶~로 주름을 펴다 smooth the creases with a hot iron.

● **인두질** ironing.

인두(咽頭) 〚생〛 the pharynx (*pl.* ~es, -rynges). ¶~의 pharyng(e)al.
● **인두염** pharyngitis.

인두겁(人-) human shape[form]; a human face; the covering of a human. ¶~을 쓴 짐승 a brute in human shape∥그는 ~만 썼지 짐승이나 다름신다 He is man in face, (but) brute in mind.

인두세(人頭稅) a poll[per capita] tax; a capitation (tax); 〚미〛 a head tax.

인들 […라 할지라도 어찌] even; whatever; however; granted that it is[be]; even though it is[be]. ¶그런 욕을 듣고는 아무리 착한 사람 ~ 가만 있겠느냐 Anyone, however gentle, would get angry at such abusive language. ∥공자 같은 성인~ 결점이 없겠는가 Confucius himself had some faults.∥낙화 ~ 꽃이 아니랴. 쓸어 무삼하리요 Fallen blossoms are still blossoms. — Do not sweep them away.

인디언 an (American) Indian; a Native American(▶ Indian은 경멸적인 어감이 있는 말이라 하여, 최근에는 완곡어인 Native American이 널리 쓰이고 있음).

인디오(⑩Indio) an Indian; a Central[South] American Indian.

인력(人力) 〚사람의 힘〛 human power [strength]; human agency(자연력에 대하여); 〚인간의 노동력〛 manpower. ¶고급 ~ (the development of) high-quality human resources∥~으로 할 수 없는 일도 있다 Some things are beyond human power.∥자연현상은 ~으로 어찌할 수가 없다 Natural phenomena are beyond the (control of) human power.
● **인력거** a jinrikisha; ricksha; a rickshaw. ¶~에 타다 ride in a ricksha∥~를 끌다 draw [pull] a ricksha. **인력거꾼** a ricksha man; a rickshaw man; a ricksha-puller. **인력난** manpower problems. **인력 수출** manpower export; export of labor force.

인력(引力) 〚끄는 힘〛 (an) attractive force; (물체 간의) attraction; (원자 간의) affinity; (우주·천체의) gravitation; (자기(磁氣)의) magnetism. ¶만유~ universal gravitation∥지구 ~ terrestrial gravitation[gravity] / the earth's gravitational force[pull]∥보세관[분자] ~ capillary[molecular] attraction∥~이 있는 attractive / magnetic∥조수의 간만은 달의 ~ 때문에 일어난다 The ebb and flow of the tide are due to the gravitational pull of the moon.

인류(人類) mankind; the human race; humanity; humankind; man; Homo Sapiens. ¶~의 행복 human happiness[welfare]∥여기서는 ~의 기원에 대해서 약간 언급하겠다 Here I would like to say a few words about the origin of man[the human race / Homo Sapience].∥그것은 ~의 역사상 가장 끔찍한 참사 중 하나였다 It was one of the most disastrous incidents in human history[the history of man].∥1969년 7월, ~는 처음으로 달에 도달했다 In July, 1969, man reached the moon for the first time.∥"이것은, 한 인간에게 있어서는 작은 일보이지만 ~에게 있어서는 위대한 비약이다."라고 암스트롱은 월면(月面)에 내려섰을 때 말했다 "That's one small step for man but one great leap for mankind," said Armstrong as he stepped on the moon's surface.
● **인류애** love of mankind. **인류학** anthropology.

인륜(人倫) 〚인도〛 humanity; human duties; 〚도덕〛 morality; moral principles. ¶~에 벗어난 행위 an act contrary to morality∥~을 어기다 go contrary to morality / transgress moral laws∥너의 행위는 ~에 어긋난다 Your behavior is immoral[inhuman].
● **인륜대사** the important[grave] matter of life(=a wedding, a funeral, etc.).

인맥(人脈) a group of men (having the same financial or political interest); 〚파벌〛 a clique; a faction. ¶학계 ~ an academical clique∥~을 형성하다 form a clique[faction].

인면수심(人面獸心) a brute with a human face.

인멸(湮滅·埋滅) 〚없앰〛 destruction; 〚없어짐〛 extinction; disappearance. ¶피의자는 증거의 ~을 도모했다 The suspect tried to destroy the evidence. **인멸하다** destroy; make away with; be extinct.

인명(人名) a person's name; the name of a person.
● **인명록** a directory. **인명사전** a biographical dictionary.

인명(人命) (human) life. ¶~을 희생하여 at the sacrifice [cost / expense] of life∥~을 존중하다 have respect[regard] for human life / hold life sacred∥~을 가볍게 보다 make light of human life∥~을 구조하다 save (a) life∥그것에~의 희생은 없었다 It caused no injury to human life.∥그것은 ~에 관계되는 중대한 문제다 It is a serious matter affecting people's lives.∥~은 재천(在天)이다 Life and death are providential.
● **인명 구조** lifesaving; the saving of a life. **인명 손실** a loss of lives; the toll of lives.

인문(人文) 1 〚문화〛 civilization; culture. 2 〚윤리·질서〛 humanity.
● **인문 과학** cultural sciences; (독) Kulturwissenschaft. **인문주의** humanism. **인문주의자** a humanist.

인물(人物) 1 〚사람〛 a person; 〚구어〛 a character; 〚거물〛 a figure. ¶중요~ an important person[figure] / a VIP∥역사상의 ~ a historical figure∥위험 ~ a dangerous person[character]∥요주의 ~ a person on the blacklist / a person to keep one's eye on∥그는 바람직한[바람직하지 않은] ~로 인정되었다(외교관 등이 상대방 국가에 있어서) He was declared persona[persona non] grata.∥그는 상당한 ~이 될 것이다 He will become something[somebody] in the world.∥그는 역사상 위대한 ~로 간주되고 있다 He is considered to have been a great man[character / figure] in history.

2 〚인품·성격〛 a character; personality. ¶~을 보다 read a person's character∥~을 보증하다 answer for a person's character∥그는 어떤 ~입니까 What sort of man is he?∥그의 ~은 나무랄 데가 없다 His character leaves very little to be desired.∥그는 ~을 보는 눈이 있다 He is a good judge of character.

3 〚소설·극 중의〛 a character; a personage; a person; (그림의) a human figure; a figure subject. ¶등장~ the characters in the drama[novel] / (라) dramatis personae∥작중(作中) ~ the characters in the story∥그녀는 자기가 소설 속의 한 ~이 된 것 같은 느낌이 들었다 She felt as if she were a character in a novel.

인민

4 [인재] a man of ability; a talented man; an able man; a talent; a person to be reckoned with; a person of some standing. ¶실업계에서 가장 유능한 ~ the most efficient man in business circles

5 [용모] features; looks; personal appearance. ¶~이 잘생기다 be good-looking / have good[attractive] looks / be handsome[well-favored / beautiful] / ~이 못생기다 be plain-looking[ill-favored / (미) homely] / be ugly.
● **인물 묘사** a portrait; a character sketch; a description[portrait / sketch] of a character. **인물화** a portrait; a figure painting; [초상화] a portrait.

인민 (人民) the people; the citizens; [민중] the public; (영) the subjects(신민). ¶~의 권리 civil rights // ~의 적 an enemy of the people / a people's enemy // ~의, ~에 의한, ~을 위한 정치 government of the people, by the people, for the people // ~을 보호하다 protect the people // ~의 권리는 존중되어야 한다 Civil[People's] rights should be respected.
● **인민공사** (중국의) a (people's) commune. **인민 공화국** a people's republic. **인민 전선** the Popular Front // 나라에 따라 다른 명칭이 있을 수 있다. **인민 해방군** the People's Liberation Army.

인보이스 [경] an invoice.

인복 (人福) blessedness with friendly people.

인본주의 (人本主義) humanism. ⇨"인문주의(⇨인문)
● **인본주의자** a humanist. ⇨"인문주의자(⇨인문)

인부 (人夫) a labo(u)rer; a coolie; a hand; a navvy. ¶철도 ~ a lineman / a railway worker // 공사판의 ~ a construction laborer / a navvy.

인분 (人糞) feces; excrement; ordure; stool.
● **인분 비료** human manure; night soil (for manure).

인사 (人士) a man of good breeding; a gentleman; (사람들) people; men. ¶거물급 ~ an important figure / a VIP // 반정부 ~ an antigovernment personage // 재야 ~ an opposition personage // 각계각층의 ~ people of all social standings.

인사 (人事) **1** (사교상의) a greeting; recognition; the time of day(아침·저녁의); (말) compliments; (연설) an address. ¶~를 나누다 exchange greetings [salutations / the time of day] // 아침[작별] ~를 하다 say good morning[goodby(e)] / 신임 ~를 하다 [연설을 하다] make an inaugural address / (돌아다니며) make one's inaugural calls // 그들은 초면의 ~를 했다 They introduced themselves to each other. // 그는 ~도 없이 바로 용건을 꺼냈다 Without any formalities he plunged directly into the matter at hand. // 결혼식이 끝난 후 양가 친척 간에 ~가 교환되었다 After the wedding ceremony, the members of the two families and their relatives were formally introduced to one another. // 몇 마디 ~ 말씀을 드리겠습니다 Allow me to say a few words of greetings. **인사하다** greet; salute; say hello; pay one's respects; meet; recognize; present one's compliments; pay a visit of courtesy. ¶모자를 벗고[에 손을 대고] ~ raise[touch] one's hat to // 손을 흔들어 ~ greet a person with a wave (of the hand) / wave in greeting // 새로 온 과장에게 아직도 인사하지 못했다 I have not yet paid my respects [said hello] to the new chief of my section.

2 [절] a bow; a kowtow; a salute; a courts(e)y(여자의). ¶~를 받다 receive the bows of (one's students). **인사하다** make a (polite) bow (to); kowtow; bow (low / politely); bow[incline] one's head; make [do] one's manners. ¶어른에게 ~ make a bow to one's elder.

3 [예의] manners; etiquette; civility; decorum; courtesy. ¶계절의 ~ (특히 크리스마스·세해의) Season's Greetings // 새해 ~를 보내다 send New Year's greetings // 내일 이사하기 때문에 이웃들에 가서 ~를 하고 와야겠다 As I'm moving away tomorrow, I'll come and pay my respects[make my farewells] in the neighborhood.

4 [감사] thanks; gratitude; acknowledgement; appreciation; a present (in acknowledgment). ¶선물을 받았는데 무엇으로 ~를 할까 What shall I give him in return for his present? // 뭐라고 ~를 드려야 할지 모르겠습니다 I don't know how to thank you. **인사하다** thank[give thanks to] (a person for something); express [offer] one's thanks [gratitude] (to a person for something).

5 [사람이 해야 할 일] human business. ¶~를 다하다 try every possible means // 우리는 ~를 다하고 천명을 기다릴 뿐이다 [진인사 대천명(盡人事待天命)] We can only do our best and leave the rest to Providence.

6 [의식] consciousness; senses.

7 [개인의 의식·능력·신분에 관한 일] personnel matters[affairs]; personnel changes. ¶그는 ~를 맡고 있다 He is in charge of personnel (affairs[matters]).
● **인사 고과** (~考課) performance rating; merit rating. **인사과** [국/부] the section [bureau / division] of personnel; the personnel (affairs) section[bureau / division]. **인사 관리** personnel management. **인사권** the right of personnel management. **인사말** expressions used in greetings[in exchanging courtesies]; [식사(式辭)] an address. ¶~을 하다 deliver a prologue / make an introductory speech on the stage // 중매인은 신부의 부모에게 결혼 축하의 ~을 했다 The go-between offered words of congratulation to the bride's parents. // 그는 졸업식에서 ~을 했다 He gave an address at the graduation ceremony[(미) (the) commencement]. **인사 불성** [기절] unconsciousness; loss of consciousness; stupor; insensibility. ¶~의 unconscious // ~에 빠지다 faint / become unconscious / (구어) pass out // 그는 3일 동안 ~이었다 He was in a coma for three days. // 그는 ~에서 깨어났다 He came to [regained consciousness]. // 그는 과음해서 ~이 되었다 Having drunk too much, he fall unconscious. **인사성** good manners; etiquette; decorum. ¶~이 밝다[없다] have good[bad] manners / be well[ill-] mannered. **인사이동** personnel transfers[changes]; a (sweeping) shake-up(대이동). ¶~를 하다 reshuffle / reorganize / shake up / transfer / ~에 불만이 있다 I don't like the way they handle personnel transfers[changes]. // 이번에 직원의 ~이 있었다 There was a change

in[of] personnel[the staff] recently. **인사치레** ¶~의 웃음 a polite[an insincere] laugh∥당신은 ~로 그렇게 말하고 있다 You say so out of politeness. / You are just saying so to be nice[kind].∥그들은 ~로 마지못해 딱 한 번 나를 찾아왔다 They paid us a visit once just out of a sense of duty.

인산(燐酸) [화] phosphoric acid.
● **인산 비료** (a) phosphatic fertilizer. **인산칼슘** calcium phosphate.

인산인해(人山人海) a great crowd (of people). ¶그곳은 ~였다 People crowded there. / A crowd gathered there. / There was a large crowd of onlookers there.

인삼(人蔘) insam; ginseng(▶ "ginseng"은 일본어에서 온 말임).
● **인삼주**[차] insam liquor[tea].

인상(人相) looks; features; an appearance. ¶~이 좋지 않은 사람 an evil-looking man∥~을 보고 범인을 판단하다 judge a person by his looks∥범인은 어떤 ~이었지 Describe the looks[features] of the criminal.
● **인상착의**(一着衣) features and clothes (of a criminal suspect). ¶범인의 ~에 꼭 맞는 사람 a person answering[meeting] the description of the criminal.

인상(引上) **1** [끌어 올림] pulling[drawing] up. **인상하다** pull[draw] up.
2 [물가 등의 올림] a raise; [영] a rise; an increase; raising; [구어] a hike. ¶철도 운임의 ~ an increase in train fares∥물가[세금]의 ~ a raise[rise] in prices[taxes]∥가격 ~ a price increase[(구어) hike]∥목수들은 임금 ~을 요구했다 The carpenters demanded higher wages.∥그들은 약 30퍼센트의 임금 ~을 획득했다 They won a wage increase of around 30 percent. **인상하다** raise; (영) rise; increase; (구어) hike; (구어) up. ¶운임을 2할 ~ raise fares by 20 percent. ➔전화 요금이 8프로 인상되었다 The telephone rates were raised[increased] (by) 8 percent.∥버스 요금이 50원 (550원에서 600원) 인상되었다 The bus fare was raised by 50 won (from 550 won to 600 won).
3 [역도] the snatch. ¶~에서 120킬로그램을 들다 lift 120 kilogram in snatch.

인상(印象) (an) impression. ¶좋은[나쁜] ~ a good[bad] impression∥첫 ~ one's first impression∥~이 좋은[나쁜] 사람 a pleasant [an unpleasant] person∥~을 해치다[좋게 하다] damage[improve] a person's impression of one∥그는 청렴한 사람이라는 ~을 준다 He impresses me as a man of integrity. ∥어머니의 웃는 얼굴이 내 기억 속에 강하게 ~지어져 있다 My mother's smiling face is strongly impressed on my memory.∥그녀의 신비스러운 미소가 내 ~에 남았다 I was enchanted by her mysterious smile. / Her mysterious smile took possession of my heart.∥그의 ~은 좋았다 He made a good impression on me. / He impressed me favorably.∥이 책은 한국의 그릇된 ~을 준다 The book gives a misleading impression of Korea.∥광주의 ~은 어떠했습니까 What were your impressions of Gwangju? / What did you think of Gwangju?∥내가 받은 ~은 결코 잊을 수가 없다 I shall never forget the impression made upon me.
● **인상주의** impressionism. **인상파** the impressionists. ¶후기 ~ the postimpressionists.

인상적(印象的) impressive; memorable; imposing. ¶~인 광경 an impressive scene∥그녀의 우아한 태도가 매우 ~이었다 I was deeply impressed by her graceful carriage.∥그의 연설은 확실히 ~이었다 His speech was certainly striking.

인색하다(吝嗇—) stingy; tightfisted; closefisted; cheap; miserly; niggardly; parsimonious. ¶인색한 사람 a stingy[cheap] person / a miser / a niggard. (구어) a tightwad / a cheapskate / a skinflint∥돈에 ~ be stingy with one's money / be tightfisted[closefisted] / be grasping / be greedy about money∥그는 돈에 인색하지 않다 He is liberal in spending money. / He is generous [free] with his money.∥그는 돈에 대해서는 ~ He is mean[nasty] about money[when it comes to money matters]. / He is disgustingly greedy[grasping]. / 정말 인색하군 What a tightwad[(미) cheapskate]. **인색히** stingily; cheaply; miserably; niggardly; parsimoniously. ¶~ 굴다 be stingy / be parsimonious / stint on[oneself] / skimp (on)∥그렇게 ~ 굴지 마라 Don't be such a skinflint[(미) cheapskate].

인생(人生) (man's) life; [일생] one's life. ¶~의 가시밭길 the thorny path of life∥~의 흥망성쇠 ups and downs of fortune∥~의 종말 the end of one's life / one's journey's end∥~의 목적[의미] the aim[meaning] of life∥~의 덧없음 the frailty[transience] of human life∥~을 낙관[비관]하다 look on the bright [dark] side of life / take a cheerful[gloomy] view of life∥~을 즐기다 enjoy life∥~을 꿈결처럼 보내다 dream away one's life∥나는 행복한 ~을 보내고 싶다 I want to live happily [a happy life].∥그는 ~ 경험이 풍부한 사람이다 He has seen a good deal in his life.∥~이란 그런 거야 Such is life. / This is how life [the world] wags on.∥~은 나그넷길과 같다 Life is compared[likened] to a journey.∥~은 고달프다 Life's journey is full of hardships.

인생철십고래희(一七十古來稀) Men seldom [Few people] live to be seventy.
● **인생관** one's view of life; one's outlook on life. **인생무상** the frailty of human life. **인생철학** the philosophy (of life).

인서트 [영] an insert.

인선(人選) the selection of a suitable person; the choice of men[the personnel]. ¶각료의 ~ the selection of Cabinet members∥~난에 빠지다 find difficulty in choosing a right person (for a position)∥그의 후임자를 지금 ~ 중이다 They are now looking for his successor. **인선하다** select[choose] a suitable person (for a post); make a choice from a list of names. ¶나는 잘못 인선했다 I chose [selected] the wrong person (for the position).

인성(人性) [사람의 성품] character; [본성] human nature. ¶~은 본래 착한 것이다 All men are born good. / Man is intrinsically good.
● **인성론** ethology.

인성(靭性) [물] tenacity. ¶~이 있는 tenacious / tough.

인세(印稅) a royalty(▶ 보통 복수형으로 씀); [인지세] the stamp duty. ¶그는 저서의 ~로

인솔(引率) leading; guiding. **인솔하다** lead; head; guide. ¶여행단을 ~ guide a tourist party // 학생을 인솔하여 박물관에 견학 가다 lead a party of schoolchildren on a study-visit to a museum // 누가 인솔하고 갑니까 Who will take care of the group? ➔ ¶교사에게 인솔된 아동들 a group of schoolchildren headed[led] by their teacher.

● **인솔자** a leader; (관광 여행단 등의) a tour conductor[guide]. ¶좋은 ~가 있어서 다행이었다 We were lucky to have a good leader.

인쇄(印刷) print; [인쇄하기] printing; (인쇄 기술 등) press. ¶4색 ~ four-color printing // ~의 잘못 printer's[typographical] errors ; misprints // ~에 부치다 send[put] (a book) to press // 그 논문은 지금 ~ 중이다 The treatise is now being printed[at the printer's]. / 이것은 ~가 선명하다 This is clearly[neatly] printed. / 이 글자는 ~가 분명치 않다 This letter had[did] not come out well. **인쇄하다** print; put into print. ¶손으로 인쇄한 포스터 posters run off by hand[on a hand-press] // 우리는 초판을 4,000부 인쇄했다 We printed four thousand copies of the first edition. // 나는 연하장을 인쇄하게 했다 I had some New Year('s) cards printed. ➔ ¶그 논문은 절반쯤이 인쇄되고 있다 About half of the thesis has gone to press.

● **인쇄공** a printer. **인쇄기** a (printing) press; (영) a printing machine. **인쇄물** printed matter. **인쇄소** a printing office; a print shop. **인쇄술** (the art of) printing; typography. **인쇄업** printing (business).

인수(引受) 1 [물품·권리 등을 넘겨받음] taking over; charge; [법] subrogation; [권리 등의 이전] a transfer. ¶사무의 ~인계 transfer of business. **인수하다** take over (a person's responsibility); shoulder (a person's debt); undertake; assume. ¶사무를 ~ take over a business (from another) // 사건을 ~ take (up) an affair in hand // 새 경영자가 그 가게를 인수했다 The new manager took over the store.

2 [수락] (어음 등의) acceptance; (채권·주식 등의 발행의) underwriting; (주식의) subscription; (보증) a guarantee. ¶어음의 ~를 거절하다 dishonor a bill. **인수하다** accept; honor; (회사채의 발행을) underwrite. ¶어음의 지불을 ~ accept[honor] a bill // 장기 채권의 발행을 ~ underwrite a long-term bond issue // 비용의 지불을 ~ underwrite the cost // 주식을 ~ subscribe for shares // 남의 부채를 ~ shoulder a person's debts.

● **인수 어음** an accepted[acceptable] bill. **인수 은행** an accepting bank. **인수인**(-人) (분실물 등의) a claimant; (고아 등의) a caretaker; (포로의) a ransomer; (환어음의) an acceptor; (공채·사채 모집의) an underwriter; [보증인] a surety; a guarantor.

인수(因數) [수] a factor. **소~** a prime factor // **공통 ~** a common factor.

● **인수 분해** factorization; resolution into factors. ¶~를 하다 factor / factorize.

인술(仁術) [어진 덕을 베푸는 행위] a benevolent act; [의술] the healing art. ¶의술은 ~이다 Medicine is a benevolent art. / Medicine is a caring[humanitarian] profession.

인슈트 [야구] an inshoot.

인슐린 [생] insulin.

인스턴트 instant. ¶~커피 instant coffee.

● **인스턴트식품** instant food; convenience food. ¶최근에는 여러 가지 ~이 나돌고 있다 Various kinds of instant foodstuffs are sold these days.

인스피레이션 (an) inspiration. ¶…에서 ~을 얻다[받다] get[receive] an inspiration from ... // ~이 떠오르다 have an inspiration [(구어) a bright idea].

인습(因習) (a) convention; conventionality; a long-established custom; [관습] usage. ¶~적인 conventional // ~을 타파하다 break down an old[a long-established] custom / do away with conventionalities / break down an old[a long-established] usage // ~에 얽매이다 be a slave to[of] convention // ~에 얽매이지 않다 be unconcerned about conventionalities.

● **인습주의** conventionalism; traditionalism; Grundyism.

인식(認識) awareness; recognition; cognition; cognizance; perception; understanding. ¶너는 그것에 대한 ~이 아직 피상적이다 You still have only a superficial understanding of it. // 우리는 그 사람들에 대한 ~을 새롭게 할 필요가 있다 We have to look at those people in a new[fresh] light. // 일반 대중이 이 문제에 대한 ~을 더욱 깊이 하도록 유도해야 한다 It is necessary to lead the public to a better understanding of this matter. **인식하다** recognize; perceive; understand; be aware of; know. ¶나는 그 사실의 중요성을 잘 인식하고 있다 I know[understand] very well how important that fact is // 나는 I am fully aware of the importance of the fact. // 우리는 그것이 잠정적인 결정임을 인식하고 있다 We understand that it is a provisional agreement.

● **인식론** [철] epistemology. **인식 부족** lack of understanding[knowledge]. ¶그는 ~으로 큰 실수를 했다 He made a great mistake from a lack of understanding[knowledge]. // 그것은 나의 ~이었다 I lacked proper understanding of it. / It was my fault for not being properly aware of the problems involved.

인신(人身) 1 [사람의 몸] the human body. 2 [개인의 신상·신분] one's person.

● **인신공격** personal remarks; a personal attack. ¶~을 하다 be personal (in a dispute) / make a personal attack (on a person) / indulge in personalities // 그들은 나에 대해서 ~을 했다 They made a personal attack on[against] me. **인신매매** human [flesh] traffic; traffic in human beings; [노예매매] the slave trade. ¶~를 하다 trade [traffic] in human beings.

인심(人心) 1 [사람의 마음] a man's mind [heart]. 2 [인정] humane feeling; humaneness; sympathy; the heart. ¶~이 후한 사람 a liberal [generous] giver // ~이 좋다[후하다] be generous / be liberal / have an open hand // ~이 박하다 be coldhearted / be heartless / be inhumane // ~을 쓰다 give freely[generously] / give with an open hand // 이런 비상 시계를 주시다니 참으로 ~이 후하시군요 It's

very generous[How generous] of you to give me such an expensive watch.// 그는 그 연구소에 ~ 좋게 100만 불을 기부했다 He generously gave a million won to the institute.
3 [백성의 마음] the sentiments of the people; people's hearts[minds]; public feeling. ¶~의 동요 general unrest//~을 얻다[잃다] win[lose] the hearts of the people//~을 현혹시키다 mislead the public//~의 향배를 살피다 perceive the drift of the public sentiments//정부는 ~을 잃었다 The government lost the supports of the people.//이 동요되었다 The people were agitated.//~이 흉흉하다 The people are panic-stricken[are in alarm].

인양(引揚) pulling[drawing] up; (시체 등의) recovery; (난파선의) salvage. ¶선체 ~ the salvage of the ship. **인양하다** pull[draw] up; (시체를) recover; (난파선을) salvage; (그물을) pull in. ¶난파선을 ~ salvage wrecked ship. → ¶그 침몰선은 해면으로 인양되었다 The sunken ship was raised to the surface of the sea.
● **인양 작업** a salvage operations[work].

인어(人魚) 1 [상상의 동물] (여자) a mermaid; (남자) a merman. 2 [동] a dugong; a sea pig.

인연(因緣) 1 [연분] connection; relation; affinity. ¶부부의 ~ the conjugal[nuptial / marriage] ties[knot]//부모 자식 간의 ~ the ties that bind parent and child together//그 도시는 이 시(詩)와 깊은 ~이 있다 The town is closely connected with this poem. / The town has a close connection with this poem.//그와 나는 ~이 깊다 He and I are closely bound up together.//이 회사와 이 지역 간에는 깊은 ~이 있다 There are close ties[There is a close connection] between this company and the local community.//남녀를 부부로 맺는 ~이란 기이하고도 놀라운 일이다 Strange and wonderful are the ties that bind two people together (in marriage).//그는 우리와는 전혀 ~이 없는 사람이다 He is a perfect stranger to us.//그는 돈과 ~이 없는 사람이다 [인연이 멀다] He has never had much money. / He is unlucky in moneymaking. / Money and he are strangers.
2 [인과] cause and occasion; [불] karma; [운명] fatality; fate; destiny. ¶~이 있으면 if fate so ordains//우리가 서로 알게 된 것도 무슨 ~이었을 것이다 We were no doubt predestined to become acquainted with each other.//이것도 전생의 ~이다 This is our destiny. / This was predestined. / There is an act of providence in it.//그들은 테니스가 ~이 되어 친해졌다 Playing tennis brought them together.

인연을 끊다 break (off) with ...; cut [sever] one's connections (with). ¶부부의 ~ divorce one's husband[wife] / get a divorce//부모 자식[형제]의 ~ disown one's child [brother]//주종의 ~ break the ties between master and servant.

인연을 맺다 form a connection (with); form ties (with). ¶부부의 ~ tie the nuptial [marriage] knot / get married//의형제의 ~ become sworn brothers//그는 내 누이동생과 부부의 인연을 맺었다 He married my sister.

인연이 멀다 bear little relation (with); not closely related. ¶화학과는 인연이 먼 과학 sciences unrelated to chemistry//나는 철학 하고는 ~ I don't know much about philosophy. / I've never read much philosophy.

인용(引用) (a) quotation; (a) citation. **인용하다** (책·연설 등의 말을) quote; (확증하기 위해 문장·책·작가 등을) cite; take (a line) from; adduce. ¶인용할 가치가 있는 quotable / quoteworthy//밀턴에서 인용한 구절 a quotation[a phrase quoted] from Milton//한 문장을 ~ cite a passage//초서의 한 절을 ~ quote a passage from Chaucer//이것은 밀턴으로부터 인용한 것이다 This phrase is a quotation[is quoted] from Milton.//그는 자주 성경을 인용한다 He often quotes the Bible.
● **인용구 / 인용문** a quotation; a quoted passage; (구어) a quote. ¶~의 출처를 밝히다 identify a quotation / trace a quotation to its original source. **인용부** quotation marks. ⇨*따옴표

인원(人員) [인원수] the number of persons; [집합적] the staff; the personnel. ¶가동 ~ available hands//~을 늘리다 increase personnel / ~을 줄이다 reduce personnel / cut the number of employees / curtail the personnel (of the office) / decrease the working force//~이 너무 많다 be overstaffed//~이 부족하다 be short of hands / be shorthanded / be short-staffed / be understaffed//필요한 ~을 급히 보충할 필요가 있다 It is necessary to supply the needed number of people immediately.
● **인원 감축** downsizing. ¶~을 하다 downsize. **인원 구성** personnel setup. **인원 점검** a roll call; the muster. ¶~을 하다 call the roll / hold a muster.

인위(人爲) an act of man; human work; [인공] artificiality.

인위적(人爲的) artificial. ¶~으로 artificially//~인 재해 a disaster caused by man//~ 시세 artificial[manipulated] market price.

인의(仁義) [인과 의] humanity and justice; [도덕] morality; morals. ¶~가 땅에 떨어졌다 Public morality is completely gone.
● **인의예지신**(一禮智信) benevolence, righteousness, propriety, wisdom, and sincerity.

인자(仁者) a humane[benevolent / kindhearted] person; a man of virtue; a man of goodwill.
● **인자무적**(一無敵) The benevolent know no enemy.; Virtue[Benevolence] disarms opposition.

인자(因子) a factor; [생] a gene; a factor. ¶가속도 ~ [경] an accelerator.

인자하다(仁慈-) benign; benignant; benevolent; merciful. ¶인자한 국왕 a benignant sovereign.

인장(印章) a seal. ⇨*도장(圖章) ¶~을 찍다 affix[set] one's seal (on) / put one's seal [stamp] (on) / seal//~을 위조하다 counterfeit[forge] a seal.
● **인장 위조** forgery of a seal.

인재(人材) [일 등에 유능한 사람] a competent person; [능력이 있는 사람] a man of ability; [재능 많은 사람] a man of talent; [유능한 직원 전체] an efficient staff. ¶~를 발탁하다 select talented people/~를 모으다 call in the best brains / gather talented people / ~를 찾다 look out for talent//그는 유능한 ~이다 He is a competent person[man of ability]. / He is an able man.//우리에게는 ~

가 부족하다 We are short of talented people. // 우리 회사의 기술진에는 ~가 많다[부족하다] Our firm has[does not have] an efficient staff of engineers.

인적(人的) human. ¶그것은 큰 화재였지만 ~피해는 없었다 Though it was a big fire, no one was hurt. // 그 전투에서 그들은 큰 ~손해를 입었다 In the battle they lost a great many men.
● **인적 자원** human resources; man power. ¶~의 부족 lack of human resources // ~이 풍부하다 be rich in human resources.

인적(人跡) human traces[footsteps]. ¶~이 드문 unfrequented / trackless / out-of-the-way / (a place) away from the haunts of men / off the beaten track // ~이 드문 산길 unfrequented mountain path // ~이 끊어진 황야 a deserted[an uninhabited] wilderness.

인절미 injeolmi; a square cake made from glutinous rice (coated with bean flour).

인접(隣接) [관형어적] neighboring; adjoining; adjacent; contiguous. **인접하다** adjoin; be adjacent[contiguous] to; be[stand / lie] close by. ¶인접한 마을들 neighboring[nearby] villages // 학교에 인접한 공원 a park adjacent to a school // 캐나다는 미국에 인접해 있다 Canada adjoins the United States. // 그의 토지는 간선 도로에 인접해 있다 His land adjoins to the highway. // 톰의 집은 존의 집에 인접해 있다 Tom's house is next to John's. // 그 공장의 폭발로 인접한 주택들이 파괴되었다 The explosion in the factory destroyed the adjoining[adjacent] houses.
● **인접 국가** a neighboring[adjoining] country; a country having a common boundary.

인정(人情) 1 [동정심] sympathy; compassion; fellow feeling; [연민] pity; [자비심] mercy; charity; benevolence; [친절] kindness. ¶따뜻한 ~ kindly feelings // 세상의 메마른 ~ the hardness of the world // ~사정없이 without unrelenting sternness / without mercy[pity] // ~에 끌리다 be moved with compassion / be touched with pity // 그는 ~이라고는 없는 사람이다 He has no heart[tender feelings]. / He is lost[dead] to pity. // 그는 ~이 많다 He is warmhearted[kindhearted / tenderhearted]. / He has a feeling heart. // 그는 ~이 없다 He is coldhearted[heartless / unfeeling]. / He has an unfeeling heart. // 상사는 부하에게 ~을 베풀어야 한다 Those in high positions must be considerate of their subordinate. // 판사는 그 피고에게 ~을 베풀었다 The judge showed sympathy[mercy] to the accused. // 이 고장 사람들은 ~이 없다 People here are very cold. // 너는 참 ~머리가 없구나 You are really ruthless[merciless].
2 [인간적 감정] human feelings; [인간성] human nature; humanity. ¶어디서나 ~에는 변함이 없다 Human nature is the same everywhere. // 나는 ~상 차마 그런 일을 할 수가 없다 I can't find it in my heart to do so. / How can I do such a thing as a man.
● **인정미** [인간미] a human touch; humanity; [따뜻함] humane feelings; [친절] kindness. ¶그는 ~가 있다 He has the heart in the right place. / He has (plenty of) heart. / He has a (fine) human touch. // 그에게서는 ~를 찾아볼 수 없다 He has not a touch of human feeling.

인정(仁政) benevolent government[rule]; humane government. ¶~을 베풀다 govern[rule] with benevolence.

인정(認定) [인식] recognition; acknowledgment; [승인] approval; [인가] sanction; authorization; [허가] permission. ¶자격시험 a qualifying test / a qualification test // 그의 위업은 세상의 ~을 받았다 His great achievement was recognized by the public. **인정하다** (진실·유효성 등을) admit; acknowledge; (정당·정상을) accept; [좋다고 평가하다] approve of; recognize; [허가하다] allow; permit; [인가하다] authorize; sanction. ¶그것을 사실이라고 ~ acknowledge the truth of it / acknowledge it as true[to be true / that it is true] // 부채가 있음을 ~ acknowledge a debt // 자기의 잘못을 ~ acknowledge one's mistakes / admit[allow / (미) concede] that one was wrong / admit[own / avow] oneself (to have been) in the wrong // 패배를 ~ recognize defeat // 요구를 ~ allow a request[claim] // 그가 과연 천재임을 인정한다 I allow him to be a genius. / I allow that he is a genius. // 우리는 그를 의장으로 인정한다 We acknowledge him our chairman. // 그는 그 아기가 자기 자식임을 인정했다 He acknowledged[owned / recognized] the baby as his child. / He avowed the baby for his child. // 그는 패배를 인정했다 He recognized that he was lost / He acknowledged himself beaten. // 그는 자기의 잘못을 인정했다 He admitted his mistake[that he was wrong]. // 선생님은 시험에 연필 사용을 인정했다 The teacher allowed[permitted] the students to use pencils in the exam. // 그는 범행을 인정했다 He confessed to the crime. // 학교에서는 두 가지 교복을 인정하고 있다 The school authorizes two kinds of uniforms. // 내가 그만 못하다는 것을 인정한다 I know he's better than I am. // 우리는 그의 노력을 인정한다 We think highly of his efforts. → [일반적으로 인정되어 있는 사실 the generally accepted fact // 그는 유죄[무죄]로 인정되었다 He was found guilty[innocent]. // 속어 중에는 관용상 정당한 것으로 인정된 것도 있다 Some slang is authorized by usage. // 그들은 피폭자임을 인정받았다 They have been certified as atomic bomb victims.
● **인정서** a certificate; a written recognition.

인정스럽다(人情-) kindhearted; warmhearted; tenderhearted; sympathetic. ¶그는 한 인정스러운 노인에게 구조되었다 He was saved by a kindhearted old man.

인제 [이제] now; [곧] soon; before long; by and by; in (course of) time; [앞으로] from now on. ¶~라도 늦지 않다 It is not too late to do so. // ~ 와서 그런 말을 해야 소용없다 There's (of) no use saying such a thing now when it's too late. // 그는 ~ 막 돌아왔다 He came back just now.

인조(人造) artificiality. ¶~의 (대용으로 만든) artificial / (사람이 만든) man-made / (모조의) imitation / (합성된) synthetic.
● **인조견** artificial silk; rayon. **인조 고무** synthetic[artificial] rubber. **인조 비료** chemical fertilizer. ⇨ 화학 비료(⇨화학) **인조 섬유** (a) synthetic[chemical] fiber. **인조인간** a robot. ⇨ 로봇

인종(人種) a race; an ethnic group(한 나라 안

에서의 인종적 집단). ¶황색[백색] ~ the yellow[white] race // ~적 편견 race[racial] prejudice // 다른 ~ 간의 결혼 intermarriage (between people of different races) / interracial marriage / (특히 백인과 흑인 간의) miscegenation // ~의 racial // 이 도시의 주민은 세 ~으로 이루어져 있다 The population of this town consists of three ethnic group. // ~이나 종교를 이유로 사람을 차별해서는 안 된다 We must not discriminate against a person because of race or religion.
● 인종 문제 the race problem; the color question[problem]. 인종 차별 racial discrimination; (미국의 흑인에 대한) segregation; (남아프리카의) apartheid. ¶~ 철폐 abolition of racial discrimination / (미국의) desegregation / integration(인종적 무차별 대우) // 학교에서의 ~ 철폐 school desegregation / 흑인을 ~ 하다 segregate[discriminate against] black people. 인종 차별주의 racism.

인종(忍從) (patient) submission; resignation. **인종하다** submit (to); resign oneself (to). ¶인종하는 생활 life of (patient) submission // 운명에는 인종하는 도리밖에 없다 We must submit[resign ourselves] to our fate.

인주(印朱) an ink(ing)[a stamp] pad; cinnabar[red] seal-ink.
● 인주갑 a seal wax case.

인출(人-) an exorcistical rope. ⇨ 금줄(禁-)
인중(人中) the philtrum (pl. -tra).
인즉 [으로 말하면] speaking of; to speak of; as far. ¶기회~ 아주 좋소 As for the opportunity, it is a good one. // 사실~ 그 편지 부치는 것을 깜박 잊고 있었소 To tell (you) the truth, I forgot about mailing the letter.

인증(引證) quotation; citation. **인증하다** (말·문장·통계 등을) quote; (사실·사례 통계 등을) cite.

인증(認證) certification; attestation; authentication. **인증하다** certify; attest; authenticate.
● 인증서 a certificate of authentication.

인지(人指) a forefinger. ⇨ 집게손가락
인지(人智) human intelligence[knowledge]; human understanding. ¶~의 발달 the advancement of human knowledge // 그것은 ~가 도저히 미치지 못하는 것이다 It is far beyond human understanding[intelligence].

인지(印紙) a stamp. ¶200원짜리 수입 ~ a 200-won revenue stamp // 영수증에 ~를 붙이다 put a stamp a receipt / affix a stamp upon a receipt / stamp a receipt // 세금은 ~로 납부해 주십시오 Pay the tax in stamps.
● 인지세 the stamp duty; the stamp tax.

인지(認知) 1 [인정하여 앎] recognition; perception; 2 cognition. **인지하다** see; witness; sight; discern; perceive; recognize. 2 [법] recognition; (legal) acknowledgment. ¶사생아의 ~ filiation / affiliation // 사생아 사건 a paternity case. **인지하다** recognize [acknowledge / own] (a child) as one's own. ¶그는 그 아이를 인지했다 He acknowledged (paternity of) the child. / He recognized the child as his own.

인지상정(人之常情) human nature; human feelings; humaneness; humanity. ¶쾌락을 추구하는 것은 ~이다 The desire to pursue pleasure is but too natural to the human nature. // 우는 아이를 보면 달래 주고 싶어 하는 것이 ~이다 It is human nature[only human / quite natural with all men] to want to comfort a crying child. // 부모가 자기 자식을 사랑하는 것은 ~이다 It is natural that parents love their own children.

인질(人質) a hostage. ¶그들은 약 2개월 동안 ~로 잡혀 있었다 They were held hostage [as hostages] for about two months. // 게릴라들이 대사관 직원을 ~로 잡았다 The guerrillas took[held] the embassy staff hostage[as hostages].
● 인질극 taking of hostage. ¶~을 벌이다 take[hold] a person as (a) hostage.

인책하다(引責-) assume the responsibility (for); take the responsibility on oneself; hold oneself responsible (for). ¶그는 부하 직원의 스캔들로 인책하여 사직했다 He assumed the responsibility for the scandal among the subordinates and resigned.

인척(姻戚) a relative by marriage; one's inlaw(▶ 보통 복수형으로 쓰임). ¶여동생이 결혼하면 나는 저 사장과 ~이 된다 As a result of my sister's marriage I'll be related to that company president. // 우리는 송씨 가문과 ~이 되었다 We became connected[allied] with the Song's. // 그녀는 이제 우리 집의 ~입니다 She is related to my family by marriage.

인체(人體) the human body. ¶~를 해부하다 dissect[anatomize] a human body // ~에 무해하다 be harmless to humans / have no ill effects on the human body // 그 실험은 ~에 위해를 가하지 않아 안 된다 The experiment should not inflict injury[bodily injury] on anyone.
● 인체 구조 the structure of the human body. 인체 실험 an experiment on a human body; a living-body test. 인체 해부학 human anatomy.

인출(引出) (a) withdrawal. ¶은행 예금의 ~ bank withdrawals // 초과 ~ overdraft // (국제 통화 기금의) 특별 ~권 special drawing rights(약어 SDR). **인출하다** draw out; withdraw. ¶은행에서 저금을 ~ withdraw one's savings from the bank // 그는 은행에서 100만 원을 인출했다 He drew out one million won from his bank account.

인치 an inch (2.540cm)(약어 in.; 기호 "). ¶3 피트 6~ three feet six inches / 3ft. 6in. / 3′ 6″ // 1피트는 12~이다 There are twelve inches in a foot.

인치하다(引致-) take (a person) into custody.

인칭(人稱) [언] person. ¶1[2 / 3]~ the first [second / third] person.
● 인칭 대명사 a personal pronoun. ¶1[2 / 3]~ a pronoun in the first[second / third] person / a first[second / third] person pronoun.

인커브 [야구] an incurve; an in. ¶~를 던지다 throw an inside breaking curve (ball)[a curve that break to the inside].

인코너 [야구] the inside corner (of the plate). ¶~로 공을 던지다 pitch a ball close to a batter.

인큐베이터 [보육기] an incubator.
인터넷 the Internet; the Net. ¶나는 ~에서 정보를 얻었다 I got the information from the Internet.
● 인터넷 방송 Internet broadcasting. 인터넷 서비스 제공자 an Internet service provider (약어 ISP).

인터뷰 an interview. ¶단독 ~ (have) an exclusive interview (with)//전화 ~ a telephone interview//기자와의 ~ a press interview//~를 받는 사람 an interviewer//외무장관은 ~에 응해 주었다 The foreign minister gave [agreed to give] an interview. **인터뷰하다** interview. ¶인터뷰하는 사람 an interviewer.

인터셉트 (축구·농구·럭비 등에서) an intercept.

인터체인지 (고속도로 등의) an interchange.

인터폰 an intercom(정식 명칭은 an intercommunication system. 인터폰은 상표명 an interphone에 유래하나, 영어에서는 보통 intercom을 씀). ¶집에다 ~을 장치했다 I had an intercom installed in my house(남을 시켜서).//사장은 ~으로 비서와 통화하게 되어 있다 The President can speak to his secretary over the intercom.

인터폴 [국제 형사 경찰 기구] Interpol; (정식 명칭) the International Criminal Police Organization(약어 ICPO).

인턴 (미) an intern(e); (영) a houseman. ¶~으로 근무하다 intern [serve one's internship (at)]//그는 성 마리아 병원에 ~으로 있다 He is interning [He is doing his internship / He is an intern] at St. Mary's Hospital.

인테리어 (디자인) [실내 장식] interior design.
● **인테리어 디자이너** an interior designer.

인텔리(겐치아) (러) intelligentsia; [지식인] an intellectual; [교양인] an educated person; (미국 속어) an egghead; (미국 속어) a double-dome; [집합적] the intelligentsia (▶ 단수·복수 취급); the intellectuals. ¶그는 인텔리이다 He is an intellectual. / He is intelligent.

인토네이션 (an) intonation. ¶그의 ~은 이상하다 He speaks with a strange intonation.

인파(人波) a surging crowd (of people); a crowd [throng] (of people). ¶우리는 ~를 헤치고 나아갔다 We pushed [elbowed / forced] our way through the crowd. / We jostled through a crowd.//나는 ~를 누비듯이 나아갔다 I threaded my way through the crowd.//박람회에는 많은 ~가 모여들었다 There was a large turnout at the exposition. / The exposition grounds were crowded with people [jammed with a crowd of people].//나는 ~에 시달렸다 I was jostled in [among / by] the crowd. / I was buffeted by the waves of humanity.

인파이팅 [권투] infighting.

인편(人便) (through) the agency of a person. ¶~에 [~으로] by someone / by means of someone / through the agency of person//~에 보내다 send (a thing) by someone//~에 편지를 보내다 request a person to carry a letter / send a letter by a person.

인품(人品) character; one's personality; [품격] a dignity; (a) grace; nobility. ¶그의 ~을 잘 알고 있다 I know him very well.//그녀의 ~은 어떠냐 What sort of person is she?//그는 ~이 빼어나다 He is a wonderful person [an excellent man].

인프라 [기반 시설] an infrastructure.

인플레(이션) inflation [overissue] (of currency); currency inflation [expansion]. ¶악성 ~ an inflationary spiral / vicious [unsound / spiral] inflation//정체성 ~ stagflation//잠재적 ~ latent inflation//~의 악화 aggravation of the inflation [the inflationary trend]//~의 둔화 slowdown of the inflationary trend / disinflation//인플레를 초래하다 [일으키다] cause [bring on] inflation//인플레를 억제하다 check [curb] inflation//이것은 악성 ~이다 This inflation is vicious.
● **인플레이션 대책** an anti-inflation measure [policy].

인플루엔자 [유행성 감기] influenza; (구어) (the) flu; [지독한 감기] a bad cold.

인하(引下) (a) reduction; lowering; a cut. ¶가격 ~ the reduction [lowering] of prices / (동제에 의한) a rollback//운임 ~ a reduction [cut] in fare. **인하하다** lower; bring down; reduce; cut down; (통제하여) roll back. ¶가격 [임금] ~ reduce [lower / cut] the price [wages]//세금 ~ put through tax reductions.

인하다(因-) be caused by; be due to; be owing to; result from; start [arise] from; originate in. ¶운전 부주의로 인한 사고 an accident due to [caused by] careless driving//그녀는 부상으로 인하여 목숨을 잃었다 Her death resulted from injuries.//불결로 인하여 병이 생기는 경우도 있다 Some diseases are attributable to lack of cleanliness.//사고는 부주의로 인하여 생긴다 Accidents arise from carelessness.//폭설로 인하여 기차가 연착되었다 Owing to a heavy snowfall the train was delayed.

인해 전술(人海戰術) human sea [wave] tactics; the strategy of throwing waves of men into action. ¶~을 쓰다 send out more and more people / pour in one wave of reinforcements after another.

인허(認許) approval; permission. **인허하다** approve; permit; authorize. ¶정부는 그 계획을 인허했다 The government approved the plan.

인형(人形) a doll. ¶꼭두각시 ~ a puppet / a marionette//손가락 ~ a hand puppet / a glove doll//옷을 갈아 입히는 ~ a dress-up doll//밀랍 ~ a wax doll [figure]//말하는 ~ a talking doll//솜을 넣고 꿰맨 ~ a rag [stuffed] doll//~을 놀리는 사람 a puppeteer / a puppet player [manipulator]//~ 같은 얼굴 a doll's face//~ 같은 소녀 a doll-faced girl//~을 가지고 놀다 play (with) dolls//~을 놀리다 work [marionette] puppets (by wires).
● **인형극** a puppet [marionette] show; a marionette performance.

인형(仁兄) dear friend; dear Mr. ~.

인화(人和) harmony [concord] among men; unity between the members; peace and amity among people. ¶~를 도모하다 promote the harmony among men. **인화하다** be harmonious among men; be in perfect harmony [concord] among men.

인화(引火) ignition. **인화하다** ignite; catch [take] fire. ¶이 가스는 매우 인화하기 쉽다 This gas is highly inflammable.//담뱃불이 휘발유에 인화했다 The gasoline [(영) petrol] caught fire from a lighted cigarette.
● **인화물** the inflammables. **인화성** inflammability; ignitability.

인화(印畵) [사진] [인화하기] printing; [인화된 것] a print. ¶이중 ~ double printing. **인화하다** print (off / out); make a print (of). ¶사

진은 몇 장 인화하시겠습니까 How many photographs do you want printed? ➡¶사진이 인화되었다 The pictures have been printed. / The printers are ready[done].
  ● **인화지** photographic (printing) paper; sensitized paper(감광지).
인환(引換) exchange. ⇨**상환**(相換).
  ● **인환권** an exchange ticket; a coupon.
인후(咽喉) [생] the throat. ¶~의 jugular / guttural.
  ● **인후염** [의] a sore throat.

일 1 (놀이에 대하여) work; (오래고 고된 일) labor; (과해진 임무) a task; (직) a job; employment; (업무) business; (도직) one's job; (임무) a duty; (직업) one's occupation. ¶손으로 하는 ~ manual work // 세탁이나 청소 등의 집안 ~ household chores such as washing and cleaning // 손에 익지 않은 ~ unaccustomed work[employment] // ~의 분량 work load // 벌이가 신통치 않은[좋은] ~ a bad[good] job // ~을 빨리 해치우는 사람 a quick worker[hand] // 번역 ~을 하다 do a job of translating / do translations[translation work] / work as a translator // ~이 없다 have nothing to do / have no work on hand / have no business to attend to / be out of work[employment / a job] / be without work / be jobless / be unemployed / be unoccupied / be free / be disengaged / 《구어》 be at a loose end / 《구어》 be on the beach(선원 등이) // ~에 착수하다 fall to work / take up work / get (down) to business / set to work / go into harness // ~을 맡기다 entrust (a person) with a task / give work to (a person) // ~을 적당히 하다 do one's work in rough-and-ready way / (날림으로) scamp[skip] one's work // ~을 그만두다 quit [leave off / get away from] work / relinquish one's work / (직장을) throw up one's job // 하루 ~을 쉬다 take a day off from work // 남의 ~을 대신 해 주다 take a person's duty // 할 ~이 무척 많다 I have a great many[a lot of] things to do. // 오늘 내가 할 ~이라도 있습니까 Is there anything[any work] for me to do today? // 그녀는 ~을 아주 잘한다 She is quite able[capable]. / She is good in her job. / She makes a fine job of it. // 오늘은 일찍 ~을 마쳤다 I got my work done early today. / I finished my work early today. // 아내의 병이 걱정되어 ~이 손에 잡히지 않는다 I'm so anxious about my wife's illness that I can't settle down to[concentrate on] my work. / I am so concerned about my wife's illness that I am unable to get myself to work. // 오늘은 ~이 전혀 진척이 되지 않는군 My work isn't going at all well today. // 8시에 ~을 시작해 주시오 Please set to[begin to / start / commence] work at eight. / Please get on the job at eight. / Please go to business at eight. // 나는 하루 종일 ~에 쫓겼다 I have been swamped with work[pressed with business] all day long. / I have had a pressure of business all day long. // 나는 엄청난 ~을 떠맡았다 I have taken on a monstrous task. / I have undertaken an awful job. // 저 처녀는 ~을 아주 열심히 한다 The girl works very hard. // 나는 식탁의 좌석을 배열하는 ~을 맡았다 I undertook the job[role] of seating arrangements for the meal. // 오늘 ~은 끝났다 My work is over for the day. // 오늘 ~은 이것으로 끝내자 Let's call it a day. // 죄송하지만 그 ~만은 못하겠습니다 I'm sorry, but that is something I just cannot do. // 매일 하는 ~이라 아무것도 아니요 It is my daily routine, so I don't mind at all. // 자기 ~은 자기가 하도록 해라 Learn to do things for yourself.

2 (문제) a thing; a matter; an affair; (구어) a concern. ¶중대한 ~ a serious matter [affair] // 가장 중요한 ~ the most important thing // 불쾌한 ~ an unpleasant matter / something unpleasant // 돈에 관한 ~ money [pecuniary] matters / a matter of money // 생사에 관한 ~ a matter of life and death // 교육[사업]에 관한 ~ an educational[a business] matter // 남의 ~ other person's affairs // ~을 그르치다 make matter worse // 무슨 ~에 대해서 말하고 있는가 What are you talking about? / What do you mean? // 그의 연애 사건은 누구나 알고 있는 ~이다 His love affair is something that everyone knows about. // 그것을 듣자 나의 개에 관한 ~이 생각났다 When I heard it I thought of my dog. // 그것은 내가 관여할 ~이 아니다 That's none of my concern[business]. / That has nothing to do with me. // 네가 상관할 ~이 아니다 None of your affair[business]. / That's no affair[business] of yours. // 다른 ~은 그만두고 당면한 계획을 짜자 Let's put other things aside and polish our plans for this project. // 그것은 성가신 ~이다 It's an awkward business. // 이것은 무슨 ~인지 도무지 모르겠다 I can't understand this business at all. // 네가 그를 때리지 않은 것은 참 잘한 ~이다 It's a good job you didn't hit him.

3 (사정·형편) circumstances; a case; things. ¶무슨 ~이 있어도 under [in] any circumstances / at any cost / on all accounts / in any case // ~이 잘 풀리면 under favorable conditions[circumstances] / if nothing intervenes // 모든 ~이 잘되어 가고 있다 Things are getting better. // 무슨 ~이 있어도 거기에는 두 번 다시 가지 마라 Under no circumstances should you go there again. // ~이 여기에 이르고 보니 나는 모든 것을 고백할 수밖에 없다 Since things have come to this, there is nothing I can do but confess everything. // 나는 ~이 뜻대로 되지 않아 실패했다 Things did not go as I had wanted them to, and I failed.

4 (용무) business; an engagement. ¶무슨 ~로 왔지 What's your business here? / What have you come here for? // 무슨 ~이든 분부만 내리십시오 I'm always at your service. / I will place myself at your service any time you want. // 무슨 ~입니까 What do you want with[of] me? / What do you want me for? // 오늘 밤에는 ~이 있어 나가지 못한다 Business prevents me from going out this evening.

5 (사고) an accident; (사건) an incident; an occurrence; an event; a happening; an affair; (귀찮은 일) trouble. ¶무서운[끔찍한] ~ a terrible affair // 그 ~은 크리스마스 날 밤에 일어났다 The incident took place on Christmas night. // 그의 신상에 이상한 ~이 일어났다 A strange thing happened to him. // 무슨 ~이 있을 때는 전화를 해 다오 Call me[《영》Ring me up] in case of emergency [if

일

anything happens / in an emergency]. ¶그는 또 ~을 저질렀다 He caused trouble again. // 도중에 그에게 무슨 ~이 생겼는지도 모르겠다 Perhaps something has happened to him on the way. // 그의 집에 무슨 ~이 있었던 모양이다 Something unusual seems to have happened at his home. / He seems to have had some trouble at home.
6 [계획·사업] a plan; a program(me); a project; a scheme; an undertaking; [음모] a plot; a trick. ¶~을 꾸미다 make [form / lay] a plan / form [forge] a scheme / (음모를) hatch [brew] a plot / conspire [intrigue] (against) // ~을 추진하다 [진행시키다] carry a program forward / carry forward a scheme / work a scheme / proceed (with) / go ahead (with) / carry on (with) // ~이 척척 진행된다 The plan is on a fair way to success.
7 [경험] an experience. ¶판다를 본 ~이 있니 Have you ever seen a panda? / Did you ever see panda? // 그는 영화를 보러 가는 ~이 거의 없다 He hardly ever goes to the movies. // 나는 아직 외국에 나가 본 ~이 없다 I have never been abroad. // 나는 한 번도 그를 만난 ~이 없다 I have not seen him once. // 비행기를 타 본 ~이 있니 How you ever traveled by plane?
8 [업적] an achievement; merits; services. ¶훌륭한 ~을 하다 render distinguished services (to) / distinguish oneself (in).
9 [물] work. ¶~함수 work function // 열을 ~로 바꾸다 convert heat into work.

일(一) one; [첫째] the first; [로마 숫자] Ⅰ; (주사위·카드 등의) an ace. ¶1 ~ 세기 a century / one hundred years // (카드놀이에서) 다이아몬드의 ~ the ace of diamonds // 5분의 ~ a fifth part / one fifth // ~ 인 ~ 표 one man one vote.

일(日) a day. ¶2, 3~ 전 a few days earlier // 6월 2~에 on the 2nd of June / on June 2.

일가(一家) **1** [가정] a home; a household; [가족] one's family; (미) one's folks [people]. ¶민씨 ~ the Min family / the Mins // ~의 주인 the master of a house / the head of a family // 그는 젊지만 벌써 ~를 이루었다 Though (he is) young, he has already established [made] a home of his own. / Young as he is, he has already kept house. // 부친이 돌아가신 뒤 장녀가 ~를 부양했다 After her father's death, the eldest daughter supported the family.
2 [친척] a relative; a relation; (남자) a kinsman; (여자) a kinswoman; (집합적) kinsfolk. ¶가까운 [먼] ~ a near [distant] relative // 그는 당신의 ~입니까 Are you related to him? // 그는 나의 먼 ~입니다 He is a distant relative of mine. / He is distantly related to me.
3 [독자적 경지·체제를 이룬 상태] (형식) a style; (유파) a school; (권위) an authority. ¶~를 이루다 develop a style of one's own / make a name / establish one's fame // 그녀는 문인으로서 ~를 이루고 있다 She is a writer of established reputation [of some standing]. / She has established her fame as a novelist. // 그는 고전 무용에서 ~를 이루었다 He created a style of his own in classical dancing.
● **일가문중** one's kinsfolk; one's clan. **일가붙이** family relations; relatives; one's kinsfolk.
¶그녀에게 ~라고는 조카 하나뿐이었다 Her niece was the only relative she had. **일가친척** one's relatives in blood and law [by blood and marriage]. ¶그는 회사의 요직에 ~을 앉혔다 He filled the main posts of the company with the member of his own family.

일가(一價) [화] monovalence; univalence. ¶~의 monovalent / univalent / monatomic.
● **일가 원소** a monad.

일가견(一家見) one's own opinion; a personal view; an (independent) opinion of one's own. ¶그는 낚시에 관해 ~이 있다 He has views of his own on fishing. // 그 문제에 대해 그는 ~이 있다 He has well-informed opinions on the problem.

일가족(一家族) a family; a household; [전가족] the whole family; all the family. ¶~ 집단 자살 a family suicide // ~을 몰살하다 murder the whole family.

일각(一角) **1** [한 귀퉁이] a corner; a nook. ¶정계의 ~ a section of political circles // 이번 밀수 사건은 빙산의 ~에 지나지 않는다 This smuggling case is just the tip of the iceberg.
2 [하나의 뿔] a [one] horn.
● **일각수**(-獸) a unicorn.

일각(一刻) a moment; a minute; an instant. ¶~을 다투어 그 아이의 부모에게 연락을 취해야 한다 We must get in touch with the child's parents without a moment's delay [as soon as possible / at once / in no time / immediately]. // 우리는 ~을 다투어 그 환자를 수술해야 한다 We must lose no time in operating on the patient. // ~을 다투는 사태이다 The situation is urgent. / There is not a moment to lose.

일각이 여삼추 A minute is like three years [seems like a lifetime]. ¶한 달 동안 그가 돌아오기를 기다렸는데 ~였다 I waited a month for his return, it was an eternity for me.

일간(日刊) daily publication [issue]. ¶이 신문은 ~이다 This paper is published daily. / This paper is a daily.
● **일간 신문 / 일간지** a daily (newspaper).

일간(日間) **1** [하루 동안] a[one] day. ¶~ 작업량 a day's work amount. **2** [얼마 안 있어] one of these days; someday; some other time; [문어] in due course; [조만간] sooner or later; (문어) in time. ¶~ 그로부터 연락이 있을 것입니다 You'll hear from him sooner or later [one of these days / later on] (▶ later on은 나중에). // ~ 송 씨에게 자세한 내용을 보고드리겠습니다 I will give Mr. Song the full particulars in due course. // ~ 또 천천히 이야기하자 Let's talk it over when we have more time. // ~ 다시 편지드리겠습니다 I will write to you again soon.

일갈(一喝) a thundering cry; a roar. **일갈하다** cry in a voice of thunder; thunder (out); roar.

일감 a piece of work. ⇨ 일거리

일개(一介) ¶~의 mere / only // ~ 서생 a mere student // 나는 ~의 가난한 학생에 지나지 않는다 I am nothing but [no more than] a struggling student. // 그녀는 ~ 고용인에 불과하다 She is only an [a mere] employee.

일개인(一個人) [한 사람] an individual; [사인(私人)] a private person. ¶~으로서 as an individual / as a man [private person] // ~의 생각 one's personal [private] view // ~의 자격

일거(一擧) one effort; one action. ¶~에 once (and) for all / at[by] one charge / at a stroke / at a stretch // 문제를 ~에 해결하다 solve a problem at a stroke // 적을 ~에 무찌르다 defeat an enemy by one charge // 그의 체포로 사건은 ~에 해결되었다 His arrest cleared up the case once (and) for all.
● **일거양득** killing two birds with one stone. ¶그는 출세와 재산의 ~을 노리고 사장의 딸에게 접근했다 He had his eye on both success and a fortune, so he approached the president's daughter. // 이 방법으로 하면 ~이다 This method enables us to kill two birds with one stone. / This method serves two ends. **일거일동** one's every move(ment). ⇨ 일거수일투족

일거리 a piece of work; a job; business; [임무] a mission; a task. ¶~가 있다 have work to do / have a business to attend to // ~가 없다 be out of work / have nothing to do // 그는 내게 편한 ~을 주었다 He gave me an easy task. // 요새는 ~가 많다 We have plenty[a lot] of work to do for today.

일거수일투족(一擧手一投足) one's every move(ment). ¶[자기의] ~에 주의하다 be prudent in doing every little thing // 나는 그녀의 ~을 놓치지 않으려고 지켜보았다 I watched her, trying not to miss even the slightest movement. // 세상 사람들은 그의 ~을 지켜보고 있다 His movement are being carefully watched by the public.

일건(一件) an affair; a matter; a case.
● **일건 서류** (all) the papers[documents] relating[relative] to the case; a dossier (of a criminal case).

일격(一擊) a blow; a stroke. ¶~에 by a (single) blow / at a[one] blow[stroke] / at a brush / with one stroke[blow] // 그는 ~을 얻어맞고 쓰러졌다 He was felled with a single blow. // 그는 상대방에게 강력한 ~을 가했다 He struck his opponent a mighty blow. // 그 사나이는 그의 이마에 ~을 가했다 The man dealt him a blow on the forehead. // 그 증인의 증언은 그에게 중대한 ~을 가했다 The testimony of the witness was a severe blow to him.

일견(一見) **1** [한 번 보기] a look; a glance. **일견하다** cast a glance (at); have[take] a look (at). ¶일견한 바(로는) at first sight[glance] // 나는 일견하여 그의 진의를 알아차렸다 I saw his true motive at a glance[at once]. **2** [보기에] apparently; seemingly. ¶그 두 사람은 ~ 오랜 친구 사이 같았다 The two looked like old friends. // 그녀는 ~ 행복한 것 같지만 실지는 그렇지 않다 She is not as happy as she seems to be. / She looks happy, but actually she is not.

일계(一計) a plan. ¶~를 생각해 내다 think[work] out a plan.
일계(日計) daily account; daily expenses.
● **일계표** daily trial balance.

일고(一考) consideration; a thought. ¶이 일에는 ~의 여지가 있다 This matter leaves room for consideration. **일고하다** consider; give a thought (to); think of[about]. ¶이 문제에 대해 일고해 주시기 바랍니다 Please think it over and let me know.

일고(一顧) a notice; a glance. ¶남의 경고를 ~도 하지 않다 pay no attention to a person's warning // 그는 그 계획을 ~도 하지 않았다 He didn't give the slightest consideration to the plan. // 이 작품은 ~의 가치도 없다 This work isn't even worth a glance[one's notice].

일곱 seven. ¶~ 살 seven years of age // ~ 살 먹은 아이 a child of seven years old / a child of seven (years) / a seven-year-old (child).
일곱이레 the 49th day after a baby's birth.
일곱째 the seventh.

일과(一過) ¶태풍 ~ 후에 after the passage of typhoon // ~성의 fleeting / transient // ~성의 열 a transient fever // 그녀는 테니스에 미쳐 있지만 그래 봐야 ~성인 것임에 틀림없다 She's crazy about tennis, but it's bound to be a short-lived enthusiasm. **일과하다** [지나가다] pass away; [눈을 거치다] run one's eyes through (a book); glance[run] (one's eyes) over (the papers).

일과(日課) (학과) a daily lesson; (일) a daily task; daily work. ¶~를 마치다 do one's daily stint[task] // 그는 매일 아침 가벼운 운동을 하는 것을 ~로 하고 있다 He makes a point of doing light exercises every morning.
● **일과표** [매일 같은 일과] a daily schedule; [그날 하루의 예정] one's[a] schedule for the day.

일관(一貫) consistency; coherence. ¶그는 시종~ 노동자의 편이었다 He remained a stalwart friend of working people all his life. **일관하다** be consistent[coherent]. ¶나는 일관하여 사장파였다 I was on the president's side from start to finish[all the way]. // 그는 평생을 일관하여 과학 발전을 위해 헌신했다 He devoted himself to the development of science throughout his life. ➔ **일관된** 사상 a consistent thought.
● **일관성** consistency. ¶~이 없는 이야기 a disconnected story // 그의 논의에는 ~이 없다 His argument is (self-)contradictory[illogical]. **일관 작업** continuous[nonstop] operation. ¶~의 공장 an assembly plant // ~으로 제품을 만들다 manufacture goods on an assembly line.

일괄(一括) a bundle; a lump. ¶이 다섯 개 법안이 ~ 상정되었다 These five bills were brought before Congress as one lump package. **일괄하다** [한데 묶다] lump things together (under one head); [요약하다] sum up; summarize. ¶자동차 값을 일괄하여 치르다 pay for a car in one lump sum // 일괄해서 보내다 send (things) in a bundle // 이와 같이 다종다양한 문제를 일괄하여 처리하기는 불가능하다 It's impossible to deal with such a variety of problems collectively.
● **일괄 계약** a bulk contract; a contract in bulk; a blanket contract. **일괄 구입** a blanket purchase. ¶일용품을 ~을 하다 buy daily necessities in bulk. **일괄 사표** a wholesale resignation; a resignation en bloc [in a body]. **일괄 처리** [컴] batch processing.

일광(日光) sunlight; sunshine. ¶직사 ~ direct sunlight // 이 약은 ~이 들지 않는 곳에 두시오 Keep this medicine out of the sun.
● **일광 소독** disinfection by sun-light; sterilization by sunning. ¶침구를 ~을 하다 disinfect the bedding by sunning it. **일광욕** a sun bath. ¶해변에서 ~을 하다 take a sun bath

일교차 on the beach / sunbathe on the beach.
일교차(日較差) [기상] diurnal range.
일구다 1 [개간하다] bring (waste land) under cultivation; reclaim (waste land); open ground; break up the soil. ¶밭을 쟁기로 ~ plow[(영) plough] a field // 땅을 ~ turn the ground (over). 2 [두더지가] (a mole) raise a mound; burrow in.
일구이언(一口二言) double-dealing; duplicity; equivocation. **일구이언하다** be double-tongued; [약속을 어기다] break one's word [promise]. ¶나는 일구이언하지 않는다 I mean what I say. / I never go back on[fail to keep] my word. / I am as good as my word [promise]. // 그는 늘 일구이언한다 He always speaks with a forked tongue.
일국(一國) [한 나라] a country; a nation; [나라 전체] the whole country. ¶~의 재상 a prime minister of a country // ~을 뒤흔든 사건 an event that shakes[jolts] the whole country.
일군(一軍) 1 [온 군대] an army; the whole army. ¶~을 거느리고 at the head of an army. 2 [제일 야전군] the First Army. 3 [야구] the first team. ¶그는 아직 2군에서 1군으로 올라오지 못했다 He still hasn't made it (up) from the farm to the first team.
● **일군 사령관** the Commander of the First Army.
일군(一群) a group. ¶~의 난민 a group of refugees // ~의 들새 a flock of wild birds // ~의 가축 a herd of cattle.
일그러지다 be distorted; be contorted; be twisted. ¶고통으로 일그러진 얼굴 a face drawn[contorted / twisted] with pain // 그들의 얼굴은 긴장으로 일그러져 있었다 Their faces were drawn[taut] with tension.
일금(一金) (the sum of) money. ¶~ 5천 원 (the sum of) five thousand won // ~ 5만 원 정히 영수하였음 Received (of Mr. Han) the sum of 50,000 won(▶ 영수증에 쓰는 말).
일급(一級) [첫째 등급] the first class. ¶그녀의 연기는 ~이다 Her acting is first-class.
● **일급품** the finest[choicest] articles; first-class goods. ¶이 천은 ~입니다 This material is of the highest quality.
일급(日給) daily wages.
일기(一技) an art; a skill. ¶1인 ~ one man, one skill.
일기(一期) 1 [한 기간] a [one] term; [반 년] a half-year; (3개월) a quarter. ¶그는 ~를 더 근무하게 되어 있다 He is to be in office for another term. 2 [한평생] one's span of life; one's whole life; one's lifetime. ¶50세를 ~로 죽다 die at the age of fifty / die aged 50.
일기(一騎) [한 명의 기병] a (single) horseman. ¶이들 세 청년은 각기 ~ 당천의 용사들이다 Each of these three young men is a match for a thousand.
일기(日記) a diary. ¶그림~ a picture diary // 여행~ a travel diary / an itinerary // 학생~ a student diary // ~를 쓰다 keep a diary / write (in) one's diary // ~에 적다 record [write down] in one's diary / make an entry (of a matter) in one's diary / diarize (a matter).
● **일기장** a diary; [부기] a daybook.
일기(日氣) the weather. ¶~를 예보하다 make a weather forecast / forecast the weather // 요즘은 ~가 고르지 못하다 The weather is changeable these days.
● **일기 예보** a weather forecast. ¶내일의 ~ the weather forecast for tomorrow // ~에 의하면 according to the weather forecast / the weatherman says … // ~가 맞았다[틀렸다] The weather forecast was right[wrong]. // ~에 의하면 오늘 밤부터 비가 올 것이라고 한다 The forecast says it will begin to rain tonight. // ~에 의하면 내일은 맑다고 한다 According to the weather forecast, it will be fine tomorrow.
일깨우다 1 [깨닫게 하다] awaken; open (a person's) eyes; arouse; [계몽하다] enlighten (a person on). ¶잘못을 ~ convince (a person) of his error // 민중을 ~ enlighten [educate] the public. 2 [잠에서 깨우다] wake (a person) up early in the morning.
일껏 with much trouble[effort]; with great pains. ¶~ 애썼으나 after all one's efforts / after much trouble // 그는 ~ 모은 돈을 몽땅 써 버리고 말았다 He spent all the money he had saved up. // ~ 애썼으나 수포로 돌아가고 말았다 All my pains went for nothing. // 그의 어머니가 ~ 만드신 음식이 식탁 위에서 식어 가고 있다 The dinner his mother prepared so carefully is getting cold on the table.
일꾼 1 [일하는 사람] a worker; [품팔이꾼] a wage earner; a wageworker; [노동자] a laborer; a workman; a hand. ¶집안의 ~ the breadwinner / the supporter // 수리 때문에 집에 ~이 와 있다 We have a man in the house doing repair work. // 그는 많은 ~을 거느리고 있다 He has a lot of workers in his employ.
2 [유능한 사람] an able person; a man of ability[capacity / resources]; [부지런한 사람] a hard[a good / an energetic] worker. ¶나라의 ~ a[the] pillar of the state // 그는 우리 회사에서 없어서는 안 될 ~이다 His work is indispensable to our firm.
일년생(一年生) a first-year[-grade] student [boy]; a first grader; (대학·고교의) a freshman.
일념(一念) [결의] determination; resolution; [열의] zeal; [열렬한 소원] a wholehearted [an ardent] wish. ¶살려고 하는 환자의 ~이 병을 회복으로 향하게 했다 The patient's determination to live led to his recovery. // 그녀는 어머니를 만나고 싶은 ~에서 상경했다 She came to Seoul out of a sheer desire to see her mother.
일다¹ 1 [파도 등이] run high; (바람이) rise; get up; spring up; (사건 등이) happen; break out. ¶이 비누는 거품이 잘 인다 This soap lathers well. // 가을바람이 일었다[일기 시작했다] An autumn breeze has risen[begun to blow]. // 자동차가 지나가자 먼지가 일었다 A cloud of dust rose when the cars passed. // 태풍이 다가와 파도가 일고 있다 The waves are high because a typhoon is coming. // 바람이 불어 먼지가 일었다 The wind raised [stirred up / whirled up] the dust.
2 [왕성해지다] grow violent[fierce]; rise [increase] in violence; [번창하다] prosper; grow prosperous; flourish. ¶살림이 ~ rise to fortune / come to wealth / spring into affluence(갑자기) // 세력이 ~ increase in power / gain in influence // 거리의 한 모퉁이에서 불길이 일었다 A fire broke out in one corner of the town.

3 (보물 등이) be nappy[fluffy]. ¶보풀이 인 천 cloth with a rough nap.

일다² (쌀 등을) wash; clean by washing. ¶사금을 ~ wash for gold / (냄비로) pan gold // 쌀을 ~ wash rice to remove stones / clean rice.

일단(一段) **1** [단계] a stage. ¶(자동차의) ~ 기어 first[bottom] gear // 기어를 ~ 넣다 put a car in[into] first[bottom] gear // 로켓을 ~을 분리하여 detach the first stage of a rocket.
2 (층계의) a step (of a staircase).
3 [등급] the first grade(초단).
4 [문장의] a passage; a paragraph.
5 (신문 등의) a column. ¶~ 광고 a one-column ad.

일단(一團) a body; a group; a party; a company.(▶ body는 공동으로 무엇인가를 하는 단체, group은 비교적 소수의 집단, party는 공통의 목적을 위한 일시적 단체, company는 함께 있거나 혹은 함께 무엇인가를 하는 집단을 나타내는 경우가 많음) ¶악당의 ~ a pack[gang] of scoundrels[rascals / (구어) no-goods] // 지방 순회 배우의 ~ a troupe[company] of traveling performers / 관광객의 ~ a party[(구어) batch] of tourists // ~이 되어 in a body[group] // 10명이 ~이 되어 in groups of ten // 불만을 품은 사람들은 ~이 되어 퇴장했다 The discontented elements walked out of the meeting en masse.

일단(一端) [사물의 한 끝] one end; [한 부분] a part. ¶이 시에 대해서 감상의 ~을 말하겠습니다 Let me state a few[some] of my impressions of this poem. // 이 한 가지 사실에서 사정의 ~을 알 수가 있다 From this one fact we can get some idea of the circumstances. // 그는 실력의 ~을 보여 주었다 He showed a glimpse of his real ability.

일단(一旦) [한번] once; [우선 먼저] first; beforehand; in advance (to). ¶~ 유사시에는 in case of (an) emergency // ~ 한 약속은 지켜야 한다 A promise once made should be kept. / A promise is a promise! / 그는 ~ 정하면 한 치도 양보하지 않는다 Once he has decided on a matter, he will not yield an inch. // 나는 ~은 대학 진학을 포기했다 For a time[At one point] I gave up the idea of going to a university. // 철도 건널목에서는 ~ 정지해야 한다 You must come to a (complete) stop at railroad crossing. // 내 펜을 쓰려면 사전에 ~ 내게 물었어야 마땅하다 You ought to have at least asked me whether you used my pen. // 나는 ~ 그 제의를 받아들였다 I accepted the offer tentatively. // 오늘은 ~ 이것으로 끝냅시다 So much for today. / Let's stop here today.

일단락(一段落) a pause. ¶~을 짓다 settle a matter for the time being / 이것으로 ~ 지었다 We have come to the end of a chapter. / We have gotten successfully through one big part of the work. // 그들은 교섭을 ~ 지었다 They have finished[wound up / wrapped up] the first phase of the negotiations.

일당(一黨) [한 패거리] an unsavory group; a gang; a ring (of thieves). ¶그는 강도의 ~으로 오인받았다 He was mistaken for one of the burglars. // 그 밀수단 ~은 체포를 모면했다 The whole gang of smugglers[The whole smuggling ring] escaped arrest. // 경찰은 ~ 4명을 체포했다 The police arrested a group of four man.

●**일당 독재** one-party dictatorship[rule].

일당(日當) [하루의 수당] a daily allowance; [일급] daily wages. ¶~으로 지급하다 pay (a person) by the day / 그는 임금을 ~으로 계산하여 지급받았다 He was paid by the day [at a daily rate]. // 나는 ~ 40,000원에 일했다 I worked for the daily wage of 40,000 won. / I was paid 40,000 won a day.

●**일당제** a day-rate system.

일당백(一當百) ¶~의 용사 a match for a hundred / a matchless[mighty] warrior // 이들 세 청년은 모두 ~의 용사들이다 Each of these three young men is a match for a hundred.

일대(一代) a[one] generation; a lifetime. ¶일생 ~의 큰 실수 the greatest mistake of one's life // 그의 ~에 쌓아 올린 재산 a fortune built up in his lifetime // 그는 ~의 영웅이었다 He was the greatest hero of his[the] day.

●**일대기** a biography; a life. ¶출세 ~ a success story.

일대(一帶) [어떤 지역의 전부] the whole place[area / district]. ¶밀밭이 펼쳐진 ~ a stretch of wheat fields // 호남 지방 ~에 all over[throughout] the Honam / 경찰이 부근 ~를 뒤졌다 The police searched the whole neighborhood. / The police hunted all over the place. // 그 ~는 온통 습지이다 The whole district is swampy. // 동대문 ~는 모두 스모그로 뒤덮여 있었다 The entire Dongdaemun area was covered with smog. // 부근 ~가 눈으로 덮여 있었다 There was a coat of snow over everything. / There was snow all around.

일대(一大) [대단한] great; grand; remarkable; wonderful; [중요한] very important; of great importance. ¶~ 발견 a discovery of great importance[consequence] / ~ 성황을 이루다 (모임이) be a great success / be well attended / (장사가) do a thriving[roaring] business // ~ 용단을 내리다 take a decisive step[a drastic measure] // ~ 장관을 이루다 present[offer] a grand sight[spectacle].

일대사(一大事) a serious[grave] affair; a matter of great consequence; a matter of grave concern. ¶이것은 국가의 ~다 This is a matter of great consequence to the state.

일대일(一對一) one to one. ¶~의 대화 a person-to-person[one-to-one] talk // ~의 승부[대결] a single combat / a man-to-man fight / ~로 승부를 겨루다 fight in single combat / fight man to man.

일도양단(一刀兩斷) ¶~의 조치 a drastic [decisive] measure / an incisive policy / ~의 조치를 취하다 take a drastic measure / resort to a rough[kill-or-cure] method. **일도양단하다** cut (a person / a thing) in two with a single stroke of the sword.

일독(一讀) a perusal; a (single) reading. **일독하다** peruse; read (a book) (through / once); run one's eyes over (a paper). ¶일독할 가치가 있다 be worth reading / 일독한 것만으로 저자의 역량에 압도되었다 Just a glance through the book was enough to impress on me the power of the author. // 일독한 것만으로는 그 문장의 뜻을 알 수가 없었다 I couldn't make out what the sentence meant at first reading.

일동(一同) all; everyone. ¶우리들 ~ all of us / we all // 가족 ~ all one's family // 참석자 ~

all those present // 교직원 ~ the whole school // ~이 함께 in a body / en masse [bloc] // ~을 대표하여 중심으로 감사드립니다 On behalf of us all, I would like to express our sincere thanks.

일되다 1 [열매 등이 일찍 익다] mature early; grow[ripen] early; mature young. 2 [조숙하다] be precocious[premature].

일등 (一等) [첫째 등급] the first class[rank / grade].
- **일등국** a first-class power. ¶~이 되다 rank among the greatest powers of the world. **일등병** (육군·해병) a private first class(약어 Pfc.); [해군] (미) a seaman; (영) a leading seaman; [공군] (미) an airman second class; a senior aircraftman. **일등 선실** a first-class cabin. **일등품** a first-class article.

일란성 쌍둥이 (一卵性雙—) identical twins(▶ 그 한쪽은 an identical twin).

일람 (一覽) 1 [한 번 죽 읽어 봄] a look; a glance; [점검] an inspection. ¶~ 후 3개월 불의 어음을 발행하다 draw a draft on (a person) at three months' sight[at three months after sight] // 그 계획서는 이사회의 ~에 돌려졌다 The program was presented at the board meeting for inspection. **일람하다** have a look (at a thing); take a look [glance] (at); take a view (of). ¶그는 그 명부를 일람한 후 내게 되돌려 주었다 After glancing through the list, he returned it to me. 2 [편람]. ¶「서울 명소 ~」 (A List of) Places to See in Seoul.
- **일람표** [체계적으로 나열한 것] a table; [항목을 열거한 것] a list; [카탈로그] a catalog; (영) a catalogue. ¶졸업생 ~ a list of graduates.

일러두기 explanatory notes; introductory remarks; a legend(지도·도표 등의).

일러두다 [지시하다] tell[instruct] (a person to do something); bid (a person do something); [부탁하다] ask; request. ¶그는 아들에게 매일 아침 정원에 물을 뿌리라고 일러두었다 He told[instructed] his son to water the garden every morning. // 나는 그에게 집을 잘 보라고 일러두고 외출했다 I went out, leaving the house in his charge.

일러바치다 tell tales (about / against / upon a person); tell on (a person). ¶일러바치는 사람 a taleteller / a talebearer / a telltale // 일러바치지 마라 Don't tell on me. // 한 번만 더 그런 짓을 하면 선생님께 일러바치겠다 If you do it again, I'll tell on you to the teacher[the teacher on you]. // 그녀가 내 일을 선생님께 일러바쳤음에 틀림없다 She must have told on me to our teacher.

일러스트레이션 [삽화] (an) illustration; [선화·데생] a drawing. ¶책의 ~을 그리다 draw [do] illustration for a book.

일렁거리다 (배가) sway; toss (on the waves); rock; pitch(앞뒤로); roll(옆으로). ¶(배가) 몸시 ~ roll or pitch heavily // 배가 일렁거려 속이 언짢다 The pitch and roll makes me sick.

일력 (日曆) a daily pad[block] calendar. ¶~을 메어 내다 tear a leaf off a calendar.

일련 (一連) a series (of); a chain (of); a sequence (of); a string (of); a train (of). ¶~의 핵 실험 a series of nuclear tests // ~의 살인 사건 a chain of events // ~의 사건은 1992년에 시작되었다 The whole train[chain] of events began in 1992.
- **일련번호** consecutive numbers. ¶표에 ~를 매기다 print the tickets with consecutive numbers // 나는 ~로 된 복권 열 장을 샀다 I bought ten lottery tickets with consecutive numbers. // 각주는 각 장마다 ~로 되어 있다 The footnotes are numbered consecutively chapter by chapter.

일렬 (一列) [세로 또는 가로의 한 줄] a line; (가로의) a row; (세로의) a file. ¶~ 횡대로 서다 form a row // ~ 종대로 나아가다 march in a (single) file // ~로 늘어서다 (버스 정류소 등에서) stand in (a) line / line up / (영) form a queue / queue up.

일례 (一例) an example; an instance. ¶~를 들면 for example[instance] / to give[cite / mention] an example[instance] // …의 ~가 되다 afford an example of … / serve as an example of … // 이 사건은 교내 폭력의 ~에 지나지 않는다 This incident is just one example[illustration] of violence in schools.

일로 (一路) [곧장 가는 길] a straight road. ¶환자는 회복 ~에 있다 The patient is on the road of recovery. // 인구는 증가 ~에 있다 The population is steadily increasing.

일로매진하다 (一路邁進—) go[advance] straight; [노력하다] strive only for (a matter). ¶이상의 실현에 ~ make a great effort to reach one's ideal.

일루 (一縷) [한 오리의 실] a single thread; [줄] a faintish line; [희미한 형세] a thin wisp (of smoke); a faint gleam (of hope). ¶~의 희망 a ray of hope // 그의 실패로 ~의 희망도 사라졌다 His failure deprived me of my last hope. // 성공에 대한 ~의 희망도 없다 There is not the faintest hope of success.

일루 (一壘) [야구] 1 first base. ¶~로 나아가다 get on first base // 포볼로 ~에 나가다 get to first on balls. 2 [야구] a first baseman. ⇨ 일루수⇨일루
- **일루수** [야구] a first baseman. **일루타** a single.

일류 (一流) [제1급] the first class[rank]. ¶~의 first-class [-rank / rate] / top-rank [-ranking / -drawer] / topflight / of the first class [rank / rate / order] // ~의 극작가 a playwright of the first rank // ~의 메이커 one of the leading manufactures // 그는 현대의 ~ 지휘자다 He is one of the best conductors of today.
- **일류 가수** a top class singer. **일류 극장** a first-class theater. **일류 선수** a ranking player. **일류 작가** a first-rate writer; one of the best[leading] writers (of Korea).

일륜차 (一輪車) [손수레] a (wheel) barrow.

일률적 (一律的) [균일한] flat; uniform; [동등한] even; equal; [무차별의] indiscriminate. ¶~으로 [균등하게] uniformly / evenly / [무차별로] indiscriminately // ~의 속도로 나아가다 proceed at a uniform speed // 전체 인원을 ~으로 대우하다 treat everyone equally [exactly the same] // 임금은 ~으로 12퍼센트 인상되었다 Their wages were raised across the board by 12 percent. / There was an across-the-board wage hike of 12 percent. // 이 규칙을 ~으로 적용시킬 수는 없다 This rule cannot be applied in all cases.

일리 (一理) some truth; some reason. ¶너의 말에도 ~가 있다 There is some truth[some-

thing] in what you say. / You have a point there. // 그의 불평에도 ~가 없는 것은 아니다 He complains and not without reason.

일막극(一幕劇) a one-act play; a one-acter.

일말(一抹) 〔약간〕 a touch (of); a tinge (of). ¶~의 불안 a vague feeling of anxiety / a faint sense[a tinge / a shadow] of uneasiness // 나는 내 아들의 앞날에 ~의 불안을 느낀다 I feel somewhat uneasy about my son's future. // 그녀에게는 ~의 고적함이 있다 There is a touch[hint] of loneliness about her. // 그녀를 혼자 돌려보내는 데는 ~의 불안감이 있었다 I felt slightly uneasy at the thought of letting her go home alone.

일망타진하다(一網打盡-) make a wholesale arrest (of); arrest (persons) in one bold raid; make a roundup; round up. ➔마약 밀매단은 일망타진되었다 The gang of narcotics smugglers were arrested wholesale.

일맥상통하다(一脈相通-) have a thread of connection (with); have something to do with. ¶…과 일맥상통하는 데가 있다 have something in common with … // 두 사람은 일맥상통하는 바가 있다 The two have something in common. // 그의 의견은 전체주의와 일맥상통하는 데가 있다 His opinion has something to do[in common] with totalitarianism.

일면(一面) **1** 〔한쪽 면〕 one side. ¶사물의 ~만을 보는 태도〔방식〕 a one-sided way of looking at things // 사물의 ~만을 보고 판단하다 pass judgment by looking at only one side[aspect] of things // 그 사건에는 우스꽝스러운 ~도 있었다 The incident had a comic side to it. // 이 허황되고 터무니없는 이야기에도 ~의 진리는 있다 This story, though wild and preposterous on the face of it, has some [a grain of] truth in it. // 그 뉴스는 세상의 어두운 ~을 엿보게 하는 것이었다 The news revealed the dark side of the world. // 자네 말에도 ~의 진리는 있다 There is some truth in what you say. // 그는 문제의 ~밖에 보지 않는다 He sees only one side of an issue [part of the picture]. // 우리는 그 이야기에서 그의 성격의 ~을 엿볼 수 있다 We can get a glimpse of his character from the story.
2 〔한편〕 on the other (hand); while. ¶그는 엄격하지만 ~ 부드러운 데도 있다 On one hand he is stern, but on the other he is tender. // 외국에서 자란 한국 아이들은 국내에서의 대학 진학에 불리하지만 ~ 국제적 시야를 지니고 있다는 이점도 있다 Korean children raised overseas are at a disadvantage in entering Korean universities, but on the other hand they have the advantage of having acquired a cosmopolitan outlook.
3 〔처음 만남〕 the first meeting. **일면하다** meet for the first time.

일면식(一面識) 〔한 번 만나 본 정도로 아는 일〕 a sight acquaintance; a bowing [nodding] acquaintance. ¶~도 없는 사람 an utter[an entire / a perfect] stranger // …과 ~이 있다 be slightly acquainted with (a person) / be on bowing terms with (a person) / know (a person) by sight // 송 씨와는 ~도 없습니다 I have never met Mr. Song. / Mr. Song is a total stranger to me.

일명(一名) 〔별명〕 another name; an alias. ¶잭 앨런 ~ 빅 조 Jack Allen, also known as Big Joe / Jack Allen, alias Big Joe.

일모(日暮) 〔일몰〕 nightfall; sunset; (미) sundown; 〔황혼〕 dusk; twilight; 〔초저녁〕 evening.

일모작(一毛作) a single crop. ¶이 지방에서는 벼의 ~을 하고 있다 They raise a single crop of rice in this district.

일목요연하다(一目瞭然-) be clear at a glance; be (quite) obvious; be as clear as day.

일몰(日沒) (at) sunset; (at) sundown. ¶~전〔후〕 before[after] sunset / before[after] dark // 일출에서 ~까지 from sunup to sundown // ~이 되자 거리에는 인적이 끊겼다 As soon as the sun set the street became empty. // 오늘의 ~은 오후 6시이다 The sun will set at six this evening.

일문(一門) 〔한 집안〕 a family; the (whole) clan; one's folks. ¶민씨 ~ the Min clan.

일문(日文) 〔일본 글〕 Japanese script[writings]. ¶~으로 옮기다 translate into Japanese.

일문일답(一問一答) a series of questions and answers. ¶시장은 연설을 한 뒤 ~에 응했다 After the mayor's speech there was a question and answer period[session]. **일문일답하다** give an immediate answer to each question; have a question and answer session.

일미(一味) 〔첫째가는 좋은 맛〕 a good flavor; relish. ¶이 요리는 맛이 ~다 This dish is far from bad. / (미국 속어) This dish eats like a million dollars. // 이 술은 천하 ~다 This liquor is unrivaled[beyond compare]. / This wine is superb[excellent].

일박(一泊) a night's lodging; an overnight stay. ¶1인 ~ 2만 원 twenty thousand won a night per head[person] // 3식의 숙박제도 the American plan // ~ 2일로 경주에 갈 작정이다 I am planning to make an overnight trip to Gyeongju. **일박하다** stay overnight; stop for the night; put up (at a hotel) for the night; pass[spend] a night (at / in). ¶어젯밤에는 대전에서 일박했다 We stayed in Daejeon last night. // 그날 밤은 산장에서 일박했다 We stayed at a mountain hut for the night.
●**일박 여행** an overnight trip (to).

일반(一般) **1** 〔전체·전반〕. ¶~의 general / universal / generic / widespread / 〔보통의〕 common / ordinary / average / usual // ~ 학생 average[ordinary] students // ~용으로 popular use // ~에게 알리다 make (it) generally known.
2 〔보통의 사람들〕 the public. ¶~에 공개하다 open (a garden) to the public // 이 도서관은 ~에게 공개되어 있지 않다 This library is not open to the public. // 여기는 ~ 사람이 오는 장소가 아니다 This is not a place for the general public. // 이 카메라는 ~용이다 This camera is made[suitable] for the general user.
3 〔마찬가지의 상태〕. ¶~의 the same / one and the same / identical.
●**일반 교서** (미국 대통령의) the State of the Union Address[Message]. **일반 교양 과목** liberal arts; a general education subject. **일반 대중** the general public; the public (at large). ¶~이 흥미를 가지는 일 a matter of general interest. **일반론** a generality; a generalization. ¶이 문제는 ~으로 끝낼 문제가

일발

아니다 This problem cannot be settled [disposed of] with generalizations. / Generalities won't solve this problem. **일반미** (一米) traditional rice; rice of traditional breed. **일반 사면** a general pardon. **일반 원칙** broad [general] principles. **일반직** (公務員の) regular government service. **일반화** generalization; popularization. ¶~하다 generalize / popularize. **일반 회계 예산** a general account budget.

일발(一發) a (single) shot [charge]. ¶~의 총성 the report of a gun (shot) // ~로 at a shot [at the first fire] // 사냥감을 ~에 쓰러뜨리다 down one's quarry with a single shot.

일방(一方) 1 [한쪽] one side [hand]; [다른 쪽] the other side [hand]. 2 [편도] one way.
● **일방통행** one-way traffic; (게시) One Way.

일방적(一方的) 1 [한쪽으로만 치우친] one-sided. ¶~으로 one-sidedly // ~인 의견 a one-sided view [opinion] // 우리 팀이 ~으로 승리했다 Our team won a runaway [lopsided] victory. 2 [자기 쪽만 생각하는] unilateral; [한 방향만으로의] one-way. ¶~인 계약 an unilateral contract // ~인 대화 a one-way conversation // ~으로 계약을 파기하다 unilaterally renounce a treaty // 그들은 내게 ~으로 책임을 미루었다 They laid all the responsibility on me.

일벌 [동] a worker (bee); a working bee.

일벌백계(一罰百戒) an exemplary punishment. ¶~로 다스리다 punish a person as a warning to all the others.

일변(一變) a (complete) change. ¶형세의 ~ a drastic [sweeping] change of the situation. **일변하다** change completely [entirely / altogether]; undergo a (complete) change; turn round. ¶유럽의 지도는 일변했다 The map of Europe changed completely [underwent drastic changes]. // 그의 성격은 일변했다 He became another man. ➔ ¶근년의 기술 발달은 일상생활을 일변시켰다 The progress of technology in recent years has revolutionized everyday life.

일변(日邊) daily [a daily rate of] interest. ¶~으로 빌린 돈 money loaned at daily interest.

일변도(一邊倒) wholehearted [complete] devotion to one side; doing the utmost for one side alone. ¶미국 ~ exclusive devotion to [support for] the interests of the U.S.A. // 그는 친미 ~다 He is pro-American through and through. // 그는 스카치위스키 ~다 He is a devotee of [sticks to] Scotch whisky.

일별(一瞥) a glance; a look; a glimpse. ¶아무에게 ~도 주지 않고 without taking any notice of a person. **일별하다** glance (at); cast a glance (at); have a glimpse (of); give (a person or thing) a glance. ¶일별하여 at a glance // 나는 일별하여 그림을 알았다 I recognized him at a glance [first sight]. // 일별하여 무가치한 것임을 알 수 있었다 A single glance was enough to convince me of its worthlessness.

일보(一步) a [one] step; a pace. ¶~ 전진하다 take a step forward [ahead] // ~ 후퇴하다 take a step back / retreat [back off] a step / ~를 양보하면 내가 옳다고 해도… Even admitting that you are (in the) right, … // 여기서 ~를 그르치면 대참사가 된다 A false step at this point would lead to disaster. // 적군을 궤멸시키기 ~ 직전까지 몰아붙였다 We drove the enemy to the brink of total defeat. // 탱크는 폭발하기 ~ 직전이었다 The tank was on the verge of explosion [about to explode].

일보(日報) 1 [매일의 보고·보도] a daily report [bulletin]. 2 a daily (newspaper). ⇨ 일간 신문(⊙)일간(日刊) ¶D ~ (신문명) the D Daily News.

일복(一福) [일거리가 늘 많음]. ¶~을 타고나다 be destined to a life of work through life // ~이 많다 have plenty [a lot] of work to do // ~이 터지다 be assigned interminable task (of).

일본(日本) Japan. ¶~의 Japanese // ~식의 Japanesque // ~식으로 in Japanese style.
● **일본 사람** a Japanese; (집합적) the Japanese (people). **일본어** Japanese; the Japanese language. **일본 요리** Japanese-style dish; Japanese-style cuisine.

일부(一部) (a) part; a portion; a section; a division. ¶제~ part I [One] // 재산의 ~ a portion of the family property // ~의 partial / sectional // 그의 일기의 ~는 프랑스어로 씌어 있다 Part of his diary is written in French. // 재해를 입은 지역으로 보내는 보급품의 ~는 헬리콥터로, ~는 트럭으로 수송되었다 The supplies for the stricken area were transported partly by helicopter and partly by truck [(영) lorry]. // 그 법안은 ~ 수정을 거쳐 통과되었다 The bill was passed after being amended in parts [after the amendment of certain sections]. // 이러한 나쁜 습관은 사회 ~에서 공공연히 행해지고 있다 This vice is a common practice in some sections of society. // 눈은 ~ 지역에만 내렸다 Snow fell in only certain areas. / There were local snow flurries.

일부(日附) a date; dating. ¶5월 10일 ~의 편지 a letter dated May 10 // ~가 없는 undated (letter) // 이 편지는 ~가 잘못되었다 This letter is wrongly dated.
● **일부 변경선** the (international) date line. **일부인**(日附印) a date stamp; a dater (회전식의).

일부(日賦) daily installment. ¶~로 갚다 pay by daily installments.
● **일부금** daily installment payment.

일부다처(제)(一夫多妻制) polygamy. ¶~의 polygamous.

일부러 1 purposely; deliberately. ⇨ 짐짓 ¶~한 짓은 아니지만 그녀의 감정에 상처를 주었다 I unknowingly [unwittingly] hurt her feelings. // 그는 ~ 내 이름을 말했다 He mentioned my name on purpose. // 그는 ~ 대답을 틀리게 했다 He gave the wrong answer on purpose. // 당신을 ~ 피했던 건 아니었습니다 I had no intention of avoiding you. // 그랬던 것이 아닙니다 I didn't do it intentionally [on purpose]. // 먼 곳까지 ~ 와 주셔서 감사합니다 Thank you for coming all the way to see me.
2 [특히 마음을 내어] specially; expressly. ¶너를 만나려고 ~ 여기 온 거야 I came here expressly to see you [with the express purpose of seeing you]. // 그녀는 너를 위해 ~ 이 케이크를 만든 거야 She made this cake specially for you.

일부분(一部分) one part [portion / section / division].

일부일처(제)(一夫一妻制) monogamy. ¶~의

일부종사(一夫從事) serving but a single husband. **일부종사하다** serve but one husband.

일부종신(一夫終身) having but a single husband during life. **일부종신하다** have but one husband during [throughout] one's life.

일사(一死) 1 [한 목숨을 버림]. 2 [야구] one (man) out. ¶~ 만루 One [It's one] out with the bases loaded.
● **일사보국**(一報國) dying for one's country.

일사(一事) one thing; a single item.
● **일사부재리** [법] (the principle of) prohibition against double jeopardy. **일사부재의** [법] the principle of not taking up an item once voted on during the same session.

일사병(日射病) sunstroke; heatstroke; siriasis. ¶~에 걸리다 have [be affected by] sunstroke / be sunstruck.

일사분기(一四分期) the first [1st] quarter (of the year).

일사불란하다(一絲不亂一) well-ordered; thoroughly consistent; (서술적) be in perfect [strict] order. ¶**일사불란한** 논조 a thoroughly logical [consistent] argument // **일사불란한** 팀워크 fine team work // **일사불란하게** in perfect order // 그들은 **일사불란하게** 행진했다 They marched on in strict order [in an orderly line].

일사천리(一瀉千里) dashing flow of torrents; rapid advance. ¶~로 with great rapidity / at full gallop / with a force of an avalanche // 일을 ~로 해치우다 rush through one's work // 의안을 ~로 통과시키다 rush a bill through // 기사를 ~로 쓰다 dash off an article // 우리는 5마일의 도정을 ~로 주파했다 We covered five miles at top [great] speed.

일산화질소(一酸化窒素) nitrogen monoxide.

일산화탄소(一酸化炭素) carbon monoxide. ¶그들은 ~ 중독으로 죽었다 They died from [of] carbon monoxide poisoning.

일삼다 [직무로 삼다] make it one's business to 《do something》; engage in; [전념하다] devote oneself to; [탐닉하다] give oneself up to; abandon oneself to. ¶향락을 일삼고 의무를 소홀히 하다 [집안을 돌보지 않다] indulge in amusements to the neglect of one's duties [family] // 그는 젊었을 때 음주를 일삼았다 He indulged in drinking when young.

일상(日常) daily; every day; usually; always. ¶~의 [적인] daily / everyday (▶ 형용사로 쓸 때만 한 단어로 철자한다) / usual / routine // ~적인 일 one's daily [routine] work // ~에 없어서는 안 되는 것 something indispensable to everyday // 자동차 사고는 ~ 겪는 사건이다 Car accidents are daily [everyday] happenings. / Car accidents occur almost everyday.
● **일상사** an everyday experience [occurrence]. **일상생활** everyday [daily] life. **일상회화** daily conversation.

일색(一色) 1 [한 가지 색] one color; a solid color. ¶빨강 ~의 융단 a solid-red carpet // 그녀는 노랑 ~의 옷차림이었다 She was dressed all [entirely] in yellow.
2 [뛰어난 미인] a distinguished beauty. ¶천하~ a matchless beauty in the world.
3 [한 가지로만 된 모양]. ¶그 도시는 어디를 가나 선거 ~이었다 It was impossible to forget about the election no matter where you went in the town. // 그 위원회는 민주당 ~이었다 The committee seats were exclusively occupied by Democrats. // 온 나라 안의 화제가 새 대통령에 관한 소문 ~이었다 The whole nation [Everybody in the country] talked about nothing but the new President.

일생(一生) [평생] one's (whole) life; a lifetime. ¶~의 lifelong / for life // ~ 동안에 in the whole course of one's life / in [during] one's lifetime [life] // ~의 사업 one's lifework // ~에 한 번 once in one's life // ~에 한 번 있는 기회 the chance of a lifetime // ~을 통하여 from the cradle to the grave / from birth to death / during one's lifetime // ~을 걸다 stake one's life (for) // ~을 마치다 end [close] one's life / finish one's life // ~을 그르치다 make a failure of one's life / wreck one's chances in life / ruin one's career // 사람의 ~은 짧다 One's span of life is short.

일석(日夕) evening. ⇨저녁1
● **일석 점호** the evening roll call.

일석이조(一石二鳥) killing two birds with one stone. ¶그것은 ~다 It serves a double purpose. / It's a two-bird-one-stone solution.

일선(一線) 1 [줄] a line. ¶~을 긋다 draw a line // 동정과 연민 사이에 명확한 ~을 긋다 draw a clear [neat] line between sympathy and pity. 2 [제일선] the front; the first line. ¶~에 서다 stand [be] in the fire front (of) // 그는 실업계의 ~에서 활약하고 있다 He is on the front line in business. // 나는 아직 ~에서 물러날 생각은 없다 I am not yet thinking of retiring from the front line [taking a less active role].
● **일선 근무** field [active] service.

일설(一說) [다른 설] another opinion [view / version]; [다른 소문] another report. ¶~에 의하면 according to another report [version] // ~에 의하면 그는 부하에게 살해되었다고 한다 There is another version of the story [another report] which holds that he was killed by one of his followers.

일세(一世) 1 [그 시대] the time; the age; the day. ¶~의 영웅 the greatest hero of the age [a day] // ~를 풍미하다 command [rule] the world [age] // 그 사상은 ~를 풍미했다 That was the ruling idea of the day [age / time]. / The idea took hold of the world in those days. 2 [일대] a [one] generation; [일생] a lifetime; one (whole) life. ¶재미 교포 ~ the first-generation Korean-Americans in the U.S. 3 [이름이 같은 군주의 초대]. ¶엘리자베스 ~ Elizabeth I [the first].

일소(一笑) 1 [한 번 웃음] a laugh; a smile. **일소하다** laugh a laugh; smile (at). 2 [업신여기는 웃음] a scornful laugh; ridicule; sneer. **일소하다** give a scornful laugh; ridicule.

일소에 부치다 laugh (a matter) off [down / away]; dismiss (a matter) with a laugh. ¶의사는 암에 대한 나의 의심을 일소에 부쳤다 The doctor laughingly dismissed my fears of cancer. // 나의 제안은 일소에 부쳐졌다 My proposal was laughed down.

일소(一掃) a (clean) sweep; a cleanup. **일소하다** sweep (away); drive away [out]; clear (away [out]); wipe out; stamp [root] out; eradicate; uproot. ¶악습을 ~ stamp [root] out a bad custom // 주자를 ~ [야구] clear the bases / drive in all the runners // 시 당국은 빈민가를 일소할 계획을 세웠다 The

일손 1 [일하는 사람] a hand; a worker; [도움] help; assistance. ¶농촌의 ~ 돕기 운동 a (nationwide) drive to help farmers (in their busiest harvest season) // ~의 부족 a shortage of help [hands] // ~을 돕다 provide a helping hand // 농장에서는 ~이 부족해서 어려움을 겪고 있었다 They had a hard time on the farm because of a shortage of hands. // 이 작업장은 ~이 부족하다 This workshop is shorthanded. // 이 병원은 ~이 부족하다 This hospital is understaffed. // 하녀가 그만둬서 ~이 달린다 As the maid has quit, we are shorthanded.
2 [일하는 손] work in hand. ¶~을 붙들다 start work(ing) / begin to work // ~을 쉬다 take a (work) break.
3 [일하는 솜씨] a skil(l)ful hand; skill at a job. ¶~이 거칠다 be of inferior workmanship / do a poor job (of something) / be clumsy (at something).

일손(을) 놓다 [떼다] (잠시) stop one's work; lay one's work aside; (그만두다) quit [leave off / get away from] work; (사직하다) throw up one's job. ¶자, 일손을 놓고 한 대 피웁시다 Let's stop here and have a smoke. // 일손을 뗀 지 오래 된다 It is a long time since I got away from work.

일손이 잡히지 않다 be unable to make oneself settle down to work; cannot concentrate on one's work. ¶아내의 병이 걱정이 되어 도무지 일손이 잡히지 않는다 I am so anxious about my wife's illness that I can't settle down to [concentrate on] my work at all.

일수 (日收) 1 [본전 및 이자를 며칠에 나누어 일정액을 날마다 거둠] a daily installment [payment]. ¶~로 5,000원씩 갚다 pay back by daily installments of 5,000 won // ~을 돈을 빌려 주다 [빌리다] lend [borrow] money by daily installments. 2 [하루의 수입] a daily income.
● **일수놀이** moneylending by [in] daily installments. **일수쟁이** a moneylender who collects by daily installments.

일수 (日數) 1 [날의 수] (the number of) days. ¶치료 ~ days of treatment // 많은 ~가 걸리다 take many days. 2 [그날의 운수] one's luck for the day. ¶~가 좋다 [사납다] have a lucky [an unlucky] day // 오늘은 ~가 사납다 It's my unlucky day.

일순 (一巡) a round; a tour; a patrol(경관의). **일순하다** make a round [tour] (of); walk over [round] (a museum); (경관이) go on one's beat; make one's rounds; patrol.

일순 (간) (一瞬間) an instant; a moment; a flash; a twinkling. ¶~의 momentary // ~에 in an instant [a moment / a flash / a wink] / in the twinkling of an eye // 그것은 ~에 벌어진 일이었다 It happened in an instant [a moment].

일습 (一襲) a kit; a (complete) set; a suit(e). ¶개인용 컴퓨터 ~ a personal computer kit / a kit for building a personal computer // 세면 도구 ~ a toilet kit // 등산 용구 ~ (a complete set of) equipment for mountain climbing.

일승일패 (一勝一敗) one win and [against] one defeat. ¶지금까지 우리 팀은 ~다 So far our team has won one game and lost one.

일시 (一時) 1 [한때] once; at one [a] time. ¶나는 ~ 전직을 진지하게 생각했었다 At one time I seriously thought of changing jobs. // 이 도시는 ~ 수출 산업의 중심지로서 번영했다 This town once enjoyed prosperity as the center of the export industry.
2 [동시] one time; the same time.
3 [잠시] for a time; momentarily; temporarily. ¶산사태로 인해서 경춘선 전 구간이 ~ 불통되었다 Owing to a landslide, train service was temporarily suspended on the whole of the Gyeongchun [Seoul-Chuncheon] Line. // 기숙사가 만원이어서 근처에 ~ 하숙하기로 했다 Since the student dormitory is full, I have decided to stay in a rooming house nearby for the time being.
● **일시불** payment in a lump sum. ¶~로 지불하다 pay in a lump sum. **일시 정지** (표지) Stop. ¶철도 건널목에서 ~를 하다 stop before crossing the railroad tracks. **일시 해고** a layoff.

일시 (日時) [날과 때] the day and hour; [날짜와 시간] the date and hour. ¶출발 ~는 변경 [지정]할 수 없다 The date and time cannot be changed [fixed]. // 모임의 ~를 변경합니다 We will put off the date of the meeting.

일시에 (一時−) at the same time; all at once; simultaneously (with). ¶학생들이 ~ 떠들기 시작했다 The students got noisy all at once. // 모든 청중이 ~ 일어섰다 Simultaneously the whole audience stood up. // 선거의 개표가 전국에서 ~ 시작된다 Ballot counting will begin simultaneously throughout the country.

일시적 (一時的) temporary; casual; transient; momentary; transitory. ¶~ 인기 ephemeral [short-lived] popularity // ~ 생각 [유행] a passing thought [fashion] // ~ 현상 a passing phenomenon // ~인 충동으로 그녀는 그에게 많은 돈을 주었다 Carried away by the impulse of the moment, she gave him a large sum of money.

일식 (日蝕·日食) [천] a solar eclipse; an eclipse of the sun. ¶개기 [부분] ~ a total [partial] eclipse of the sun // 지난달에 ~이 있었다 A solar eclipse occurred last month. / There was an eclipse of the sun last month.

일신 (一身) 1 [자기 한 몸] oneself; one's self. ¶~의 이해관계를 생각지 않고 regardless of one's own interests // ~의 이익만을 도모하다 consult one's own [personal] interests only // 그는 ~의 영달만을 꿈꾸다 죽었다 He only dreamed all his life of distinguishing himself. 2 [온 몸] the whole body. ⇨온몸.
● **일신상** [한 개인의 형편]. ¶~의 personal // ~의 일로 상담하다 consult (a person) about one's personal affairs // 이것은 나의 ~의 일입니다 This is personal to myself. / The matter is my business. // 그녀는 ~의 사정으로 사직했다 She resigned from her post for

personal reasons.

일신(一新) renovation; renewal. **일신하다** [새로워지다] be renovated [renewed / reformed]; change completely; [새롭게 하다] renovate; renew; reform; make a striking change (in policies). ¶생활을 ～ begin a new life / (생활양식을) reform one's way of living // 그는 그 일이 있은 이후로 면목을 일신했다 He became quite another person after that event.

일신교(一神敎) [종] monotheism. ¶～의 monothestic.
● 일신교도 a monotheist.

일심(一心) **1** [한마음] one mind; a whole mind. ¶～이 되다 unite in one mind / become one in mind[spirit] // ～협력하여 일을 하다 work in close cooperation // 우리는 ～ 단결하여 난국에 임했다 We united together to deal with the difficulties. **2** [일념] a single heart; wholeheartedness; a determined mind[soul]. ¶～으로 with all one's mind / heart and soul // ～으로 …하다 set one's heart on ... / devote oneself to ....
● 일심동체 being one in body and mind. ¶～가 되다 become one flesh / [부부가 되다] become man and wife // 부부는 ～다 Man and wife are one in body and mind[spirit]. / Man and wife are of one mind[soul] and flesh.

일심(一審) a first-instance trial. ⇨제일심(⇨제일(第一)) ¶그는 ～에서 유죄가 되었다 He was found guilty in the first trial.

일심전력하다(一心專力一) concentrate one's thoughts and energies (on); devote all one's energies (to). ¶그는 일신전력하여 이 사건을 해결하려 하고 있다 He has thrown himself completely into[is deeply absorbed in] solving this case.

일쑤 habitual practice. ¶…하기가 ～이다 be always doing (something unpleasant) // 그는 남을 비웃기 ～다 He's always sneering at others. // 그는 지각하기가 ～다 It is usual with him to be late. // 그는 거짓말하기가 ～다 He tells a lie every time he turns around.

일약(一躍) at a (single) bound; at a jump; (all) of a sudden; at[with] a leap. ¶～ 유명해지다 spring[leap] into fame[eminence] // 그는 ～ 국장이 되었다 He leaped to the head of the bureau. / He became the head of the bureau in one jump. // 그는 그 한 곡으로 일약 단에서 유명해졌다 He won[leaped into] fame as a musician with that one work. / With that one work he became famous overnight.

일어(日語) Japanese. ⇨일본어(⇨일본)
● 일어 회화 Japanese conversation.

일어나다 1 [잠을 깨다] wake up; awake; (잠·병석에서) rise from one's bed; get up. ¶일찍 일어나는 사람 an early riser // 일찍 ～ get up early / rise early // 그가 잠자리에서 일어난 것은 정오를 지나서였다 It was past noon when he got out of bed. // 자, 일어나요 Wake up! / Get up! // 언제나 아침 일찍[늦게] 일어난다 I am an early[a late] riser. // 잠을 깼을 때는 모두 일어나 있었다 When I awoke, everybody was up. // 어젯밤은 자지 않고 일어나 있었다 I sat[stayed / was] up all night (last night).
2 stand up. ⇨일어서다¹ ¶그녀는 노인에게 자리를 양보하기 위해 일어났다 She stood up to give her seat to an old man. // 그는 비틀비틀하면서 일어났다 He staggered to his feet. // 다리가 저려 일어날 수가 없다 I can't stand up because my legs have gone to sleep.
3 [발생하다] happen; occur; take place; come about; arise; break out. ¶내각 퇴진을 요구하는 운동이 국민들 간에 일어났다 A movement arose among the people to demand the Cabinet to resign en bloc. // 전쟁이 곧 일어날 것 같다 It looks as if a war is imminent. / War fires are beginning to smolder. // 무슨 일이 일어나도 당황해서는 안 된다 You must not be upset whatever may happen. // 엄청난 사고가 일어났다 A terrible accident has occurred. / There has been a terrible accident. // 학교에서 폭력 사건이 일어났다 Violence broke out at the school. // 이웃 간에 말썽[다툼 / 싸움]이 일어났다 Trouble[A dispute / A quarrel] arose among the neighbors. // 군중 사이에서 감탄의 소리가 일어났다 Voices of surprise rose among the crowd. / There were cries of surprise from the crowd. // 이 도시에 커다란 변화가 일어나고 있다 A great change has taken place in this city.
4 [발흥하다] spring up; come into being; arise. ¶최근 각종 신흥 공업이 일어났다 Various new industries have sprung up lately.
5 [성하게 되다] rise; flourish; prosper; be prosperous; revive. ¶나라가 크게 일어났다 A nation rode the wave of a great prosperity. // 그의 집안은 그의 대에 이르러 크게 일어났다 In his days, the family prospered.
6 [불이 발생하다] be kindled; be made; (a fire) burn; get lively; (a flame) rise. ¶불이 잘 일어난다 The fire is burning lively.
7 [바람이 불다] rise; blow; come up. ¶별안간 큰 바람이 일어났다 All of a sudden, a great wind came up.
8 [열·전기가 생기다] be produced[generated]. ¶나무토막을 비벼 대니 열이 일어났다 Heat was generated by rubbing the pieces of wood together. // 화학 섬유의 속옷에서는 정전기가 곧잘 일어난다 Underwear of synthetic fibers easily generates static electricity.
9 [기인하다] come of; originate (in); have its origin (in); arise[spring / result] (from). ¶그것은 모두 나의 오해에서 일어났다 It was all caused by[due to] my misunderstanding. // 분쟁은 주민들의 이기주의적 태도에서 일어났다 The trouble originated in the self-centered attitude of the residents. // 이번 실패는 과신(過信)에서 일어난 것이다 The failure resulted from overconfidence. // This failure came of overconfidence. // 그들의 불화는 무엇 때문에 일어났느냐 What started [triggered off] their hostility? // 우리들의 싸움은 사소한 오해로 일어났다 Our quarrel originated in a trivial misunderstanding.

일어서다 1 [기립하다] stand up; rise (to one's feet); get up (on one's feet); get to one's feet; pick oneself up. ¶자리에서 ～ rise from one's seat // 가려고 ～ rise to go // 벌떡 ～ spring[jump / leap] to one's feet // 간신히 ～ struggle[scramble / climb] to one's feet // 일제히 ～ stand up all at once / rise as a one // 그 아기는 이제 혼자 일어서게 되었다 The baby can now stand up by himself. // 그가 들어오자 그들은 반쯤 일어서서 인사했다 When he came in, they half rose to their feet and

일어탁수

greeted him.
2 [분기하다] be up (and doing); rise (up) (against); rouse oneself (to action). ¶그들은 굶주린 사람들을 구하기 위해 일어섰다 They took action to save the starving. // 무기를 들고 우리가 일어서야 할 때가 왔다 The time has come for us to take up arms [stand up and fight].

일어탁수(一魚濁水) One man's mistake [error / misconduct] does damage [injury / mischief] to many.

일언(一言) a (single) word; one word. ¶그는 일구도 소홀히 하지 않고 말을 신중히 한다 He weighs his words carefully. // 그녀는 나의 부탁을 ~지하에 거절했다 She flatly refused my request. / She turned me down flat [point-blank. (구어) cold].
● **일언반구** a single word. ¶나는 ~도 놓치지 않으려고 정신을 바짝 차렸다 I was all ears [attention] so as not to miss a single word.

일언이폐지하다(一言以蔽之一) boil down to one word; express in a single word. ¶일언이 폐지하면 너의 잘못이다 To sum up the story, it is your fault.

일없다 1 [필요 없다] unwanted; needless; uncalled-for; (서술적) do not want. ¶이 편지에 답장은 ~ You need not reply to this letter. // 옷은 일없으니 돈이나 주시오 I don't want clothes, give me money. **2** [상관없다] (서술적) need not worry (about); do not mind; be all right. ¶맥주 한 잔쯤이야 일없겠지 I should not mind a glass of beer. // 이 물은 마셔도 일없겠지요 Is this water good to drink?

일엽편주(一葉片舟) [조그만 조각배] a (small) boat; a lighter; a skiff. ¶~를 젓다 row a little boat / pole a skiff.

일요일(日曜日) Sunday. ¶다음 [지난] ~에 next [last] sunday / on Sunday next [last] // 오늘은 ~이다 It is Sunday today. // 나는 ~에는 교회에 간다 I go to church on Sunday(s). // 나는 ~도 없는 바쁜 생활이다 I am so busy I can't take even a day's rest.

일요판(日曜版) (신문의) a Sunday supplement.

일용(日用) daily [everyday] use. ¶~의 everyday / daily. **일용하다** use everyday. ¶일용하는 잡화 miscellaneous goods for daily use // 일용할 양식 one's daily bread.
● **일용품** daily necessities.

일원(一元) ¶~의 [적인] unified / unitary. [철]monistic.
● **일원론** [철]monism. **일원론자** a monist. **일원화** [통일] unification; [집중화] centralization.

일원(一員) a member. ¶클럽의 ~ a member of the club / 폭력단의 ~ a member of a gang / a gangster.

일원(一圓) the whole place. ⇨ˉ일대(一帶)

일원제(一院制) a one-chamber [unicameral] system.

일월(一月) January(약어 Jan.). ¶~ 상[하]순에 early [late] in January.

일월(日月) [해와 달] the sun and the moon; [날과 달] the day and the month; [세월] time; days; years.
● **일월성신** the sun, the moon and the stars.

일으키다 1 [세우다] pick (a person) up; raise [set] up; set upright; lift up; (먼지 등을) raise. ¶일으켜 세우다 raise (a person) up / help (a person) to his feet // 트럭이 먼지를 크게 일으켰다 The truck raised [stirred up] a cloud of dust. // 그는 몸을 일으켰다 He raised himself (in bed). / He sat up. // 나는 쓰러진 화병을 일으켜 세웠다 I set up [righted] a vase that had fallen. // 나는 넘어진 아이를 일으켜 주었다 I helped the child who had fallen get to his feet. / I picked up the child who had fallen.

2 [야기하다] raise (a commotion); create; cause; make; give rise to; stir up (a trouble); [촉발·유인하다] provoke; invite. ¶범죄 사건을 ~ commit a crime / 일대 센세이션을 ~ create a great sensation / 연쇄 반응을 ~ cause [trigger] a chain reaction / 사회 불안이 폭동을 일으켰다 Social unrest led to rioting. // 당신의 부주의가 사고를 일으켰다 Your carelessness caused the accident. / The accident occurred because of your carelessness. // 차가 엔진 고장을 일으켰다 The car's engine stalled. / The car had engine trouble. // 그 연설은 사람들에게 얼마간의 소동을 일으켰다 The speech made [caused] a bit of a turmoil among the people. // 저런 사람은 문제를 일으키고 만다 Such a man would cause [give rise to] trouble.

3 [설립하다] set up; establish [found] (a school); [발기하다] promote; organize; [창시하다] start (a movement); begin; launch [undertake] (a new enterprise). ¶새로운 사업을 ~ start a new enterprise / 모금 운동을 ~ launch a fund raising campaign [drive] // 그녀는 지사를 상대로 소송을 일으켰다 She sued the governor. / She started a lawsuit against the governor.

4 [흥하게 하다] bring to prosperity; revive; restore; make prosperous; promote. ¶나라를 ~ bring a nation to prosperity / 쓰러진 집안을 ~ resuscitate a ruined family / 산업을 ~ promote industry.

5 [불을 피우다] make; kindle. ¶난로에 불을 ~ make a fire in the stove.

6 [발생시키다] generate; produce (heat); raise; excite. ¶(정)전기를 ~ generate (static) electricity // 열을 ~ generate [produce] heat.

7 [발병하다] fall [get / be taken] ill with; be seized with; be attacked with; (원인이) cause; set up. ¶뇌빈혈을 ~ have an attack of cerebral anaemia // 두통을 일으키기 쉽다 be subject to headaches // 그는 발작 [심장 발작 / 복통]을 일으켰다 He had a fit [a heart attack / a stomachache].

일의대수(一衣帶水) [한 줄기의 띠와 같은 강물] a narrow strip of water; a narrow strait. ¶한국과 일본은 ~를 사이에 두고 있을 뿐이다 Korea is separated from Japan by only a narrow strip of water. / Only a narrow channel lies between Korea and Japan.

일익(一翼) a part [role] (to play). ¶~을 담당하다 act [perform] a part [role] (of) / bear a part (in) // 우리 회사는 개발도상국의 산업 개발에 ~을 담당하고 있다 Our company is playing a role [part] in the industrial development of the developing nations.

일익(日益) day by day; from day to day; as day follows day; daily; every day. ¶사태가 ~ 악화되고 있다 The situation is getting worse and worse every day.

일인(一人) one person.

●**일인당** for each person; per capita[head]. ¶~ 경작 면적 the cultivated acreage per person∥회원의 회비는 ~ 5,000원이다 The membership fee is five thousand won per capita. **일인 독재** one-man dictatorship. **일인분** a portion (for one person). ¶~의 of one man∥~의 식사 a plate∥~에 5,000원 five thousand won per head[each]∥카레라이스를 ~ 부탁합니다 One order of curry and rice, please. **일인이역** (play)a double role.

일인(日人) a Japanese.

일인자(一人者) the first man (in). ⇨제일인자(⇨제일(第一)) ¶그는 기타 연주의 ~다 He is an A1 [the No. 1] guitar-player[guitarist].

일인칭(一人稱) [언] the first person.
●**일인칭 소설** a first-person novel; an "I" story.

일일(一日) one day. ⇨ 하루3 ¶제~ the first day∥~ 3회 three times a day∥~에 in a day∥~ 일선(一善)을 행하다 do some little good each day / do one good turn a day.
●**일일생활권** a living space of a day. **일일여삼추**(一日如三秋) ¶~로 애타게 기다리다 feel as if the days were three years long∥나는 ~로 아버지의 귀국을 기다렸다 I waited impatiently for my father to come home. **일일지장**(一之長) superiority; be a little ahead of (a person). ¶나는 그 일에서 너보다 ~이 있다 I am a little superior to you in that line.∥프랑스는 항공기 산업에 있어 이탈리아보다 ~이 있다 France is a little ahead[a step in advance] of Italy in its aircraft industry.

일일이 [일마다] in everything; in every case; every single thing; without omission. ¶~ 간섭하다 meddle in everything∥그는 내가 하는 일을 ~ 트집 잡는다 He finds fault with everything I do.∥들은 이야기를 네가 ~ 보고할 필요는 없다 You don't have to report everything you hear.

일일이(一一) **1** [하나하나] one by one; severally; separately. ¶~ 조사하다 examine (things) one by one∥~ 열거하다 mention one by one / enumerate / itemize∥그것을 ~ 세고 있을 수만은 없다 If you start counting them one by one, there will be no end to it. **2** [상세히] in detail; in full; fully. ¶~ 말하다 particularize / give full particulars∥~ 보고하다 report in full∥당신이 ~ 설명하지 않아도 된다 You don't have to[It's not necessary to] go into details.

일임하다(一任-) leave (a matter) entirely [up] to (a) person[in a person's hand]; entrust (a person) with the task (of). ¶이 문제는 의장에게 일임하는 것이 어떻겠습니까 What do you say to leaving this matter to the chairman's discretion? ➔¶이 지점의 경영은 내게 일임되어 있다 I am entrusted with the management of this branch (of the firm).

일자(日字) a date; (the number of) days. ⇨ 날짜.

일자리 [직업] employment; a job; [직장] a place; a position; a situation. ¶일정한 ~ a fixed job / fixed employment / a regular occupation∥~가 없는 unemployed / jobless∥~를 얻다 obtain[secure] employment / find[get] work / get a job[구하다] seek employment[work] / look[hunt] for a job[place]∥~를 주다 give (a person) work [something to do] / afford employment (to)∥~를 구해 주다 find work for (a person) / get (a person) a job∥~를 잃다 lose one's employment[job / position]∥그가 슈퍼마켓에 ~을 얻어 주었다 He found me employment[a job] in a supermarket.∥아버지는 ~를 얻지 못하고 있다 My father is out of work [a job].∥나는 친구의 친절한 주선으로 마침내 ~을 얻었다 I got a job at last with the kind help of my best friend.∥~는 얼마든지 있다 There are plenty of jobs[posts] available.∥당신의 회사에 타자수의 ~는 없습니까 Is there any vacancy[opening] for a typist in your firm?∥나는 ~를 찾고 있다 I'm looking for a job.∥이 회사에는 ~가 없다 There is no opening[vacancy] in this firm.

일자무식(一字無識) dense illiteracy[ignorance]. ¶~의 unlettered / illiterate / ignorant.
●**일자무식꾼** an densely illiterate person; an ignoramus.

일장(一場) a round; a bout; a (short) spell; a scene. ¶~ 연설을 하다 make[deliver] a speech[an address]∥학생들에게 ~ 훈시를 하다 give an address of instruction to students.
●**일장춘몽** [헛된 영화·덧없는 일] an empty dream; a crushed hope. ¶~ 같은 인생 transient[ephemeral] life[existence] / mutable life∥~으로 돌아가다 vanish like a vision [dream] / end in an empty dream∥~으로 사라지다 vanish like a dream∥인생은 ~이다 Life is but an empty dream. / How brief is the span of (human) life.

일장기(日章旗) 〔일본의 국기〕 the national flag of Japan.

일장일단(一長一短) merits and demerits; advantages and disadvantages. ¶이 안은 ~이 있다 This plan has both good points and bad points[advantages and disadvantages].∥어느 후보나 ~이 있다 All of the candidates have their strong points and shortcomings.

일전(一戰) 〔전투〕 a battle; a fight; an engagement; 〔승부〕 a game; a contest; a bout. ¶~을 벌이다 fight a battle / (승부) have a game[bout] (with) (bout는 권투·씨름 등에서)∥우리는 국경 가까이서 적의 전초 부대와 ~을 벌였다 We encountered an advance unit of the enemy near the border.∥상대방이 나의 제안을 거절하면 나는 ~을 불사하겠다 If the other party rejects my proposal, I shall not hesitate to fight.

일전(日前) 〔며칠 전〕 the other day; (부사적) some days[a few days] ago. ¶~에 그를 만났을 때는 아주 건강했다 The last time I saw him, he was in excellent health.∥~에 한 약속을 잊지 마라 Don't forget what you promised the other day.

일절(一切) all; wholly; entirely; absolutely. ¶그런 일은 ~ 모릅니다 I don't know anything (at all) about it.∥나는 그들과 ~ 관계가 없다 I don't have anything[have nothing] to do with them.∥이 방 안에서는 ~ 금연입니다 Smoking is absolutely[strictly] prohibited in this room.∥외상은 ~ 사절합니다 We never sell on credit. / (게시) No credit given.

일정(日程) **1** (그날의) a day's program [schedule]; a daily routine. ¶여행 ~ an itinerary∥경기 ~ a fixture∥꽉 찬 ~ a tight[crowded] schedule∥~을 짜다 form a

일정불변하다

schedule / make a program / make out the schedule (for one's trip) // ~을 마치다[마쿠다] complete [alter] a day's program [schedule] // 시험 ~을 발표하다 announce the dates of the examination // 오늘은 무슨 ~이 있느냐 Do you have any plans for today? // 그의 ~은 항상 꽉 차 있다 His schedule [program] is always tight [crowded]. // 내일의 ~은 아직 미정이다 The schedule [program] for tomorrow has not been worked out yet. // 그는 지금 여행 ~을 짜기에 바쁘다 He is now busy in making out the itinerary.
2 (의사 진행의) the order of the day; the agenda; (미) the calendar. ¶ 이 사항을 ~에 올려[~에서 빼] 주십시오 Please put this item on [exclude this item from] the agenda. // 그러면 오늘의 ~에 들어가겠습니다 Now let us proceed with the order of the day.
● **일정표** (그날의) a program; (일정 시간마다의) a schedule; (영국 의회의) an order paper; (여행의) an itinerary.

일정불변하다(一定不變一) invariable; constant; permanent. ¶ 일정불변한 방침 a definite and unchanging policy // 지구는 일정불변한 속도로 자전한다 The earth revolves on its axis at a uniform speed.

일정하다(一定一) [정해져 있다] fixed; definite; [한결같다] regular. ¶ 일정한 곳 the fixed [right / proper / correct] place // 일정한 직업 a regular job // 일정한 수입 a regular [fixed] income // 일정한 기간에 for a given period / [지정된 기간에] for a specified period of time // 일정한 조건하에서 under certain conditions // 일정한 비율로 at a fixed rate (of) // 일정한 간격을 두고 at regular intervals // 일정한 온도를 유지하다 maintain an even [a uniform] temperature // 신청서는 일정한 서식에 따라 쓰게 되어 있다 Applications are to be written out according to the prescribed form. // 그는 일정한 견해가 없다 He has no definite opinion. **일정히** fixedly; definitely; regularly.

일제(一齊) [관형어적] simultaneous; unanimous. ¶ ~ 등귀 [증권] an all-round advance [spurt] / a general rise // ~ 호출 [통] a general calling. **일제히** [어린이 한꺼번에] all together; in a body; [동시에] all at once; simultaneously; [이구동성으로] in chorus [unison / concert]; with one voice; unanimously. ¶ ~ 환성을 올리다 cheer in chorus // 그들은 ~ 웃었다 They laughed all together. // 선거의 개표는 전국에서 ~ 실시된다 Ballot counting will begin simultaneously throughout the country. // 사람들은 무어라고 외치면서 ~ 우리 쪽으로 달려왔다 The people ran toward(s) us in a body shouting something. // 그들은 ~ "아니요!"라고 외쳤다 They shouted "No!" with one voice.
● **일제 검거** a wholesale arrest; a sweeping roundup [wholesale arrest] of (a gang of robbers). **일제 사격** a burst of shots; a salvo; a volley. **일제 하락** [증권] an all-round fall [decline]; a general slump.

일제(日帝) [일본 제국] the Japanese Empire; [일본 제국주의] Japanese imperialism; imperialist Japan. ¶ ~의 침략 an aggression of the Japanese Empire // ~하에 under the rule of Japanese imperialism.

일제(日製) Japanese make; Japanese manufacture. ¶ ~ 자동차 cars made in Japan / cars of Japanese make / Japanese cars.

일조(一助) a help; an aid. ¶ 빈민 구제의 ~로서 toward the relief of the poor // ~가 되다 be a help (to) / be of a help (toward).

일조(一朝) 1 a brief space of time. ⇨ **일조일석** (☆일조) ¶ ~에 in a day / in a short time. 2 [만약] ¶ ~ 유사시 in case of (an) emergency.
● **일조일석** [짧은 시일] a brief space [span] of time. ¶ 이것은 ~에 해결될 문제가 아니다 This is not a problem that can be solved in a short time.

일조(日照) sunshine.
● **일조권** a right to sunshine [sunlight]. ¶ 그 건물이 들어서면 ~을 위협받을[빼앗길] 우려가 있다 I'm afraid that building will threaten our right to sunlight [deprive us of sunlight]. **일조 시간** [일출부터 일몰까지의 시간] the hours between sunrise and sunset; daylight hours; [해가 비치고 있는 시간] hours of sunshine. ¶ 가을부터 겨울에 걸쳐 ~이 짧아진다 We have fewer daylight hours from autumn through winter.

일족(一族) [일가족] the whole family; one's people [folks]; [문중·집안] the clan; [친척] one's relatives [kinsmen / kin] (kin은 집합적으로 씀). ¶ ~의 웃어른 the head of a clan // ~ 권솔을 이끌고 with one's family and followers / with one's whole clan // 조부의 미수(米壽)~이 모여 축하했다 All my relatives met to celebrate my grandfather's eighty-eighth birthday.

일종(一種) 1 [한 종류] a kind; a sort; [변종] a variety. ¶ 이것은 백합의 ~이다 This is one variety of lily. // 밀은 풀의 ~이다 Wheat is a kind [sort] of grass. // 늑대는 개의 ~입니까 Is the wolf a kind [species] of dog? 2 [어떤 종류] ¶ ~의 귀금속 a kind of precious metals // ~의 독특한 향기 a unique aroma / an aroma all its own // 이 책은 ~의 안내서이다 This is a kind [sort] of guidebook. // 그는 말하자면 ~의 이상주의자다 He is a kind [sort] of (an) idealist.

일주(一周) [한 바퀴 돎] one [a] round; [1회전] a revolution. **일주하다** make a round (of); go round (a track); [회전하다] revolve; make a revolution. ¶ 세계를 ~ travel round the world / make a round-the-world trip // 지구는 1년 걸려 태양을 일주한다 The earth goes [revolves] around the sun once a year. // 식후에 내 차를 타고 시내를 일주했다 After dinner we took a spin around town in my car.
● **일주 여행** the round trip. ¶ 세계 ~ a round-the-world trip / a tour [trip] around [round] the world / globe-trotting // 제주도 ~을 했다 I made a circuit (tour) of Jejudo.

일주기(一週忌) the first anniversary of the death of a person. ⇨ **소상**(小祥) ¶ 오늘은 돌아가신 아버님의 ~다 Today is the first anniversary of my father's death.

일주 운동(日週運動) diurnal motion.

일지(日誌) a diary; a journal. ¶ 학급[작업] ~ a diary record of one's class [work] // 항해 ~ a log(book) // 병상 ~ a diary written on one's sickbed / a patient's diary // 임상 ~ a physician's diary // 여행 ~ a travel diary // ~를 적다 keep a diary [journal].

일직(日直) day duty. ¶ 오늘은 ~이다 I am on

day duty today.
●일직 사령 / 일직 장교 an officer of the day; (영) an orderly officer.

일직선(一直線) a straight line. ¶~으로 in a straight line / in a beeline∥~으로 나아가다 go straight on / make a beeline (이) 그것들은 ~으로 늘어서 있었다 They were arranged in a straight line. / They were lined up straight.∥그는 초원을 ~으로 가로질렀다 He cut straight across the field. / He made a beeline across the field.∥우리 집은 여기서 ~으로 1킬로미터 간 곳에 있다 My house is about a kilometer from here as the crow flies.

일진(一陣) 1 [선진(先陣)] the van (of an army); the vanguard; [선발대] an advanced party. ¶제~이 출발했다 The first group set out. 2 [한바탕 불기] a gust[blast] (of wind); a puff[whiff] (of breeze); a gale (of wind) (강풍). ¶~광풍이 일었다 A raging wind arose [sprang up].

일진(日辰) [민] 1 [날의 간지] the binary designation of the day according to the sexagenary cycle. 2 [운수] the day's fortune. ¶~을 잡아 결혼하다 choose a lucky day for one's wedding∥오늘은 ~이 좋다 This is a lucky day for me.∥오늘은 ~이 사납다 This is not a lucky day for me.

일진일퇴(一進一退) advance and retreat; ebb and flow. ¶~의 now advancing and now retreating / (시세 등이) fluctuating / seesaw ∥~의 경기 a seesaw game[match] ∥승부는 ~로 어느 쪽이 이길지 예상할 수 없다 It is a seesaw game and we cannot predict which side will win.∥~의 접전에 관객은 흥분했다 The spectators were excited by the seesaw [closed] game. **일진일퇴하다** advance and retreat; ebb and flow; fluctuate.

일찌감치 a little early; rather early. ¶~ 떠나다 make[get off to] a little earlier start∥~ 오면 더 좋다 If you come a bit earlier, all the better.∥오늘은 ~ 돌아가려고 생각한다 I want to leave earlier (than usual) today.

일찍 early. ⇨"일찍이 ¶아침 ~ early in the morning / in the early morning∥~ 일어나는 사람 an early riser[(구어) bird] / ~ 자고 일어나다 keep early[good / regular] hours / 저녁을 ~ 먹다 have an early supper∥좀 더 ~ 그 말을 했더라면 좋았을걸 You should have said so earlier[long ago].∥우리는 조금 ~ 목적지에 도착했다 We arrived at our destination in good time [ahead of schedule].

일찍이 1 [이르게] early. ¶나는 여느 때보다 ~ 저녁 식사 준비를 했다 I prepared supper a little earlier than usual.∥그는 ~ 부모를 여의었다 He lost his parents at an early age. **2** [전에] once; one time; before; (의문) ever; (부정) never. ¶그는 피아니스트로서 ~ 이름이 높았다 He became famous as a pianist long ago.∥그런 위대한 사람은 ~ 본 적이 없다 He is the greatest man I have ever seen.

일차(一次) 1 [관형어적] primary; fundamental. 2 [방정식에서]. ¶~의 linear / of the first degree.
●**일차 방정식** a linear equation; an equation of the first degree. **일차 산업** a primary industry.

일차원(一次元) ¶~의 one-dimensional / unidimensional.

일착(一着) [첫째로 도착함] the first arrival; the first (in the race). ¶짐이 ~이었다 Jim came in[finished] first. / Jim won (the) first placed (in the race). **일착하다** finish[come in] first; be the first to come in; win the first place; breast the tape.

일처다부(一妻多夫) polyandry. ¶~의 polyandrous.

일천하다(日淺-) short; not long (since ...). ¶ 취직한 지 아직 ~ It is not long since he got his job.∥회사는 창립한 지 아직 ~ It is only a short time since the company was founded.∥서울에 이사온 지 ~ It hasn't been long since we moved to Seoul.

일체(一切) [모든 것] all; every thing; the whole; [모두·죄다] wholly; entirely; absolutely. ¶~의 all / entire / whole∥~의 비용 the total cost[expenses] / 사건의 진상은 ~ 비밀로 되어 있다 Absolute secrecy is preserved as to the actual state of the matter.∥본건에는 ~ 관계가 없다 I have nothing whatever to do with this affair.

일체(一體) [한 몸] a[one] body; [동일체] (a) unity. ¶~가 되어 in one / in a body / as one body / in one united body / as a man∥부부는 ~다 Husband and wife are one flesh.∥온 국민이 ~가 되어 국난에 대처했다 The whole nation rose as a man in the national crisis.
●**일체감**(一感) ¶양자 사이에 ~이 생겼다 A sense of unity[oneness] developed between the two. **일체화** unification; integration. ¶~하다 unify / integrate.

일촉즉발(一觸卽發) a touch-and-go[an explosive] situation; a situation full of dynamite [ripe for explosion]; a hair-trigger crisis. ¶~의 중동 the tinderbox of the Middle East∥국경 부근은 ~의 상황이다 The situation near the border is strained to the point where any slight incident could touch off open hostilities.∥두 나라의 관계는 ~의 전운이 감돌고 있었다 The relations between the two countries were such that war could have broken out at the slightest provocation.

일촌광음(一寸光陰) a moment; a minute; an instant. ⇨촌음

일축하다(一蹴-) [걸어차다] kick; [거절하다] turn down; refuse[reject] flatly; [이기다] beat[win] easily. ¶상대를 가볍게 (경기에서) beat easily / brush off lightly∥그의 제안을 일축했다 I spurned[turned down] his proposal.∥경영자 측은 조합의 요구를 일축했다 The management rejected the demands of the union. ➔우리의 임금 인상 요구는 일축되었다 Our demand for higher wages was turned down flat.

일출(日出) sunrise; (미) sunup. ¶~에서 일몰까지 from sunup to sundown / between sunup and sundown.

일취월장(日就月將) [날로 달로 진보함] rapid progress; steady advance. **일취월장하다** make rapid progress[steady advance]. ¶과학 기술은 일취월장하고 있다 Technology is making rapid progress.

일층(一層) [한결 더] more; still[much] more; the more; all[only] the more. ¶~ 힘이 드는 일 a (much) harder work∥~ 노력하다 make greater efforts / work harder (than ever).

일치(一致) 1 [합치] agreement; accord; concurrence; consensus (of opinion); conformity; consistency; congruence; congruity; [언]

일침 concord; agreement. ¶시제의 ~ 〔언〕 sequence of tenses / 여론의 ~ a unified public opinion / 우연의 ~ a casual [strange] coincidence (of). **일치하다** 〔합치하다〕 agree (with); (be in) accord (with); concur [consist] (with); conform (to); be conformable (with); be congruous (with). ¶내 생각은 이 점에서 그의 생각과 일치했다 I agreed with him on this point. // 그들의 견해는 완전히 일치하고 있다 Their views are in perfect harmony [total accord]. // 나의 의견은 당신의 의견과 일치한다 I agree with you. / I am at one with you. // 당신의 말과 행동은 일치하지 않는다 What you say and what you do are two entirely different things. / What you do is not consistent with what you say. // 아버지와 어머니는 내가 진학할 학교에 대해서 의견이 일치하지 않는다 My father and mother differ as to what school I should go on to.
2 〔부합〕 coincidence; 〔대응〕 correspondence. **일치하다** coincide (with); be identical (to); correspond (to). ¶금고에 남은 지문은 그의 지문과 일치한다 The fingerprint left on the safe are identical to his. // 그의 은퇴와 그의 아들의 귀국이 시기적으로 일치했다 His retirement coincided with his son's return from abroad. // 한국의 도와 미국의 주는 완전히 일치하는 것은 아니다 The Korean province does not quite correspond to the state in the United States.
● **일치단결** union; solidarity; harmonious cooperation. ¶~하다 unite (with) / act in union (with) / be united. **일치점** a point of agreement. ¶양자 사이에 ~을 발견하기가 어렵다 It is hard to find any common ground [point of agreement] between the two.
일침(一鍼) 〔충고〕 advice; (an) admonition; 〔간함〕 dissuasion. ¶그는 건방진 아들에게 ~을 가했다 He reproved his son for his impoliteness. // 그들은 그의 어리석은 행동에 ~을 가했다 They remonstrated with him about [on] his foolish behavior.
일컫다 **1** 〔칭하다〕 call; name; designate; 〔자칭하다〕 claim. ¶존이라고 일컫는 남자 a man named [called / who calls himself] John // 스스로 대학자라고 ~ style oneself as a great scholar // 하와이는 흔히 태평양의 낙원이라 일컬어진다 Hawaii is often referred to as the Paradise of the Pacific. // 고인의 손자라고 일컫는 사람이 나타났다 A man appeared who claimed to be the grandson of the deceased. **2** 〔칭찬하다〕 praise; laud; extol; admire; speak highly of. ¶모든 사람이 그의 덕을 일컬었다 Everybody extolled his supreme virtue.
일탈(逸脫) (a) deviation; (a) departure; a breakaway (from). ¶오랜 습관으로부터의 ~ a radical departure [deviation] from longstanding customs. **일탈하다** deviate (from); depart (from); break away (from); overstep (the bounds). ¶이 안은 당초의 목적에서 일탈하고 있다 This plan is a departure from our original aim. / This plan does not reflect our original idea faithfully.
일터 one's place of work; one's job (site); 〔공장〕 a workshop; (회사·사무실) one's office.
일파(一派) 〔유파〕 a school; 〔파당〕 a party; a faction; 〔종파〕 a sect; denomination(큰). ¶송씨 ~ Song faction [followers / adherents] // ~를 세우다 create [found] a school of one's own / 〔종교상의〕 found a new sect // 그는 젊어서 ~를 이루었다 While still young, he established [formed] a school of his own. // 감리교는 프로테스탄트의 ~이다 The Methodists are a denomination of the Protestant church.
일패도지(一敗塗地) 〔여지없이 패함〕 a complete [crushing] defeat. **일패도지하다** meet with complete defeat; suffer a crushing [an overwhelming] reverse [defeat] (at the hands of); be humbled to the dust.
일편단심(一片丹心) single-heartedness; single-mindedness; a sincere heart. ¶~으로 single-mindedly / devotedly / with single-minded devotion // ~으로 섬기다 serve faithfully // 그는 나라의 통일을 위해 ~으로 노력하다 He devoted himself [was devoted] to the unification of his country.
일평생(一平生) a lifetime; one's (whole) life. ⇨ **한평생**(一平生) ¶~의 소원 one's lifelong desire / a desire cherished for life // ~에 한 번 once in one's life // ~을 독신으로 지내다 remain single throughout [all] one's life / live and die a bachelor(남자가) // 그는 그 일에 ~을 바쳤다 He devoted his (whole) life to the work.
일폭(一幅) a scroll; a piece (of picture). ¶~의 명화 a notable painting // 논을 거니는 백로들의 모습은 ~의 그림 같았다 The white herons in the rice fields were very picturesque.
일품(一品) **1** 〔최고〕 an article of top quality; a superior article. ¶천하 ~ a unique article / a non(e)such. **2** 〔역〕 the first court rank.
● **일품요리** a one course dinner; dishes à la carte. ¶식사는 ~를 주문했다 I ordered a meal à la carte.
일품(逸品) an excellence article [piece]; a (real) gem; a rarity; a masterpiece(걸작). ¶이 한 권은 전 수집품 중의 ~이다 This volume is the gem of the whole collection.
일필(一筆) one stroke of a pen [brush]. ¶~을 적어 보내다 write [drop] (a person) a line.
● **일필휘지** dashing off with one stroke of a brush.
일하다 〔노동하다〕 work; labor; do one's work [job / task]; 〔근무하다〕 serve (at); be in the service [employ] (of). ¶열심히 ~ work hard / be hard at work // 부지런히 ~ work diligently / work away / toil and moil // 지나치게 ~ overwork oneself / work too hard // 돈 [생활]을 위하여 ~ work for money [one's living] // 일하기를 싫어하다 be work-shy / be lazy // 그는 일한 만큼의 보수를 요구했다 He asked for a salary commensurate with his achievements [work]. // 그녀는 호텔로 일하러 나갔다 She went to work [got employment] in a hotel. // 그녀는 연중 내내 무섭게 일하고 있다 She is working like a horse all the year round. // 부하들이 제대로 일하지 않는다 My men don't work as they should. // 이 회사에서 일하고 싶다 I would like to be employed by [get a job in] this firm. // 형은 공장에서 일하고 있다 My brother works in a factory. // 그는 지나치게 일하여 건강을 해쳤다 He overworked and made himself ill.
일행(一行) a party; 〔배우·예능인 등의 일단〕 a troupe; a company. ¶관광단 ~ a tourist party / a party of sightseers // 봅 호프 ~ Bob Hope and his troupe // ~에 참가하다

join the party / be a member of the party / ~이 몇 분이세요. How large is your party? // ~은 6명이다 There are six of us in the party. / The party is made up of six in all. // 대사 ~은 오늘 아침 이곳에 도착했다 The Ambassador and his suite[staff] arrived here this morning.

일화(逸話) an anecdote. ¶~의[가 많은] anecdotal // 그녀에게는 재미있는 ~가 있다 An amusing anecdote is told of her. / There's an interesting story about her.
● **일화집** an anecdotage.

일확천금(一攫千金) making a big fortune on a single occasion[with one swoop]. ¶~의 (미) get-rich-quick // 그는 ~을 꿈꾸고 있다 He dreams of making a fortune at one swoop. / He wants to get rich quick.

일환(一環) a link; [연관된 여러 사물 중 일부] (a) part. ¶그것은 일련의 사건의 ~에 불과하다 It is only one link in a continuing chain of events. // 도시 계획의 ~으로서 쓰레기 처리장이 만들어졌다 As part of the city planning, a garbage disposal plant was built.

일회용(一回用) ~의 throwaway / disposable // ~의 종이 냅킨[기저귀] throwaway[disposable] paper napkins[diapers] // 현대는 ~ 시대이다 This is the age of throwing away things after use.

일회전(一回戰) [첫 번째 시합] the first game; (토너먼트의) the first round.

일흔 seventy. ¶~ 번째 the seventieth.

일희일비(一喜一悲) alternation of joy and sorrow. **일희일비하다** be now glad, now sad (at); be alternately happy and miserable (at). ¶우리는 3월 한 달을 일희일비하며 보냈다 We spent most of March in suspense, now optimistic, now pessimistic.

읽다 1 (책 등을) read; peruse; [독송하다] recite (an ode); chant (a sutra). ¶읽기와 쓰기 reading and writing // 식사를 ~ read out an address // 악보를 ~ read music // 암호를 ~ decipher a code // (컴퓨터에서) 정보를 ~ read a (computer) print-out // 큰 소리로 ~ read (a) loud[loudly] // 급히 ~ read hurriedly / glance over // 술술 ~ read fluently / read on without pause // 따라 ~ echo [follow] (one's teacher) in reading // 대충 ~ look through[over] / skim / run one's eye(s) over // 아이들에게 동화를 읽어 주다 read a fairy story to[for] the children // 책을 읽다가 잠들다 read oneself to sleep // 나는 그 책을 처음부터 끝까지 읽었다 I read the book from beginning to end[cover to cover]. // 그의 자서전은 마치 모험 소설을 읽는 것 같다 His autobiography reads like an adventure story. // 그 다음 몇 장은 건너뛰고 읽었다 I skipped over the next few chapters. // 그런 책은 대충 읽으면 된다 You can just scan [skim through] such a book. // 이런 점에 유의하며 그 기록을 읽었다 I examined the records with these points in mind. // 이 책은 읽기 쉽게 씌어 있다 This book is written in an easy style[in plain language].
2 [알아차리다] read; guess(추측하다); understand(이해하다). ¶남의 마음을 ~ read other people's minds / tell what other people are thinking // 남의 표정을 ~ read a person's attitude from his expression[the look on his face] // 나는 그의 마음을 읽을 수가 없었다 I couldn't read his thoughts. / I couldn't tell what he was thinking. // 그녀는 그의 표정에서 마음의 혼란을 읽었다 She grasped his inner confusion from his look.
3 [바둑 등의 수를 생각하거나 헤아려 알다] see; guess; figure. ¶상대방의 수를 ~ guess one's opponent's move // 잘 두기 위해서는 몇 수 읽을 줄 알아야 한다 To improve the quality of your play, you have to learn to read[see] several moves through.

읽을거리 reading (matter); a book; a story. ¶좋은[시시한] good[dull] reading // 어린이의 ~ juvenile reading / a book for children // 나는 비행기 여행 때 가벼운 ~를 가지고 갔다 I took along some light reading for the flight.

읽히다 1 [읽게 하다] get (a person) to read; set (a person) to reading; have (a book) read (by a person). 2 [읽혀지다] be read. ¶널리 ~ be widely read // 성경은 모든 책 중에서 가장 많이 읽히고 있다 The Bible is the most read of all books. // 이 소설은 고교생 사이에서 널리 읽히고 있다 This novel is widely read by high school students.

잃다 1 [없어지다] lose; miss; be deprived of(빼앗겨서). ¶노름으로 전 재산을 ~ lose one's entire fortune at the gambling table / gamble away one's entire fortune // 직장을 ~ lose one's job / be dismissed // 수천 명의 사람들이 태풍으로 집을 잃었다 Thousands of people were left homeless by the typhoon. // 그는 경마에서 돈을 잃었다 He lost his money betting on horses. // 그는 전 재산을 잃었다 He lost[was deprived of] his whole property. // 그는 독직 사건으로 장관 자리를 잃고 말았다 He lost[was forced to resign] his position as minister because he had taken a bribe. // 그는 야심 때문에 목숨을 잃었다 His ambition cost him his life.
2 [상실하다] lose. ¶시력[청력]을 ~ lose sight[hearing] // 나는 아직도 희망을 잃지 않고 있다 I have not given up hope. // 나는 영문학에 흥미를 잃었다 I have lost interest in English literature. // 어머니는 너무 걱정해서 식욕을 잃었다 My mother is so worried (about it) that she has lost her appetite. // 그는 노름에 넋을 잃고 있다 He is lost in[is hooked in] gambling. // 이번 일로 완전히 신용을 잃고 말았다 I've entirely lost my credit as a result of this affair.
3 [죽음을 당하여 이별하다] lose; be deprived [bereft] of. ¶부모를 잃은 아이 an orphan / an orphaned child // 그 남자는 사랑하는 아내를 잃었다 The man lost[was bereaved of] his beloved wife. // 나는 부모를 한꺼번에 잃었다 I lost[was deprived of] both my parents at the same time. // 그는 절친한 친구를 잃고 슬픔에 잠겼다 He grieved over the loss of his close friend. // 나는 5살 난 아들을 잃었다 I lost my son when he was five.
4 [방향·길을 찾지 못하게 되다] lose; miss; stray. ¶길 잃은 아이 a lost child // 길 잃은 양 lost sheep // 길을 ~ lose[miss] one's way // 방향 감각을 ~ lose one's sense of direction / lose one's bearings // 나는 길을 잃고 낯선 곳을 헤맸다 I lost my way and wandered into a strange place. // 잠자리가 길을 잃고 내 방으로 날아들었다 A dragonfly strayed into my room.
5 [분실하다] lose; forget; leave(두고 오다). ¶지갑을 ~ lose one's purse.

잃어버리다

6 [잡지 못하게 되다] lose; miss; neglect. ¶기회를 ~ lose[miss / neglect] an opportunity.

잃어버리다 lose. ⇨°잃다 ¶나는 그 돈을 잃어버렸다 I have lost the money.// 우산을 잃어버릴 뻔했다 I was forgetting my umbrella.// 한번 잃어버린 것은 거의 되찾을 수 없다 One rarely recovers what he has lost.

임 〔연인〕 a lover(남자); a sweetheart(여자). ¶옛 ~ (속어) one's old flame // ~ 그리운 마음 a heart pining for an absent love // ~을 그리워하다 miss one's love.

임도 보고 뽕도 딴다(속담) killing two birds with one stone.

임간 학교(林間學校) an open-air [outdoor] school; a camp(ing) school.

임검(臨檢) 〔검사〕 an (official) inspection; an on-the-spot investigation; 〔수색〕 a raid; a search; (선박의) boarding. **임검하다** 〔검사하다〕 inspect (a hotel); make an official inspection; 〔수색하다〕 visit and search (a house); (선박을) (board and) search (a ship). ¶세관원은 마약 밀매의 혐의로 그 외국선을 임검했다 Suspecting that it was involved in drug traffic, customs officers searched the foreign ship.

● **임검반** a raiding party; (선박의) a boarding party.

임계(臨界) ¶~의 〔물〕〔수〕 critical.

● **임계각** critical angle. **임계 압력**[온도] the critical pressure [temperature].

임관(任官) an appointment (to an office); a commission. **임관하다** appoint (a person to an office). ➜¶임관된 장교 a commissioned officer // 소위로 임관되다 be commissioned second lieutenant.

● **임관식** (hold) an inaugural ceremony.

임균(淋菌·痲菌) a gonococcus (pl. -cocci).

임금 〔군주 국가의 왕〕 a king; 〔군주〕 a monarch; 〔지배자〕 a ruler.

임금(賃金) 〔노임〕 wages(▶ 보통 복수형); pay(급료). ¶기본 ~ basic wages // 기아 ~ starvation wages // 기준 ~ the standard wages // 능률 ~ efficiency wages // 생활 ~ living wages // 시간제 ~ time wages // 실질[명목] ~ real[nominal] wages // 작업량제 ~ piece wages // 전시 특별 ~ war wages // 최고[최저] ~ maximum[minimum] wages // 최저 ~제 the minimum wage system // 할증[가외] ~ extra wages // 싼 ~으로 at low wages // 하루 30,000원의 ~으로 일하다 work for[at] a wage of 30,000 won a day // ~을 올리다 increase[raise] a person's wages // ~을 내리다 cut (down)[reduce / lower] a person's wages // 그는 후한 ~을 받고 있다 He earns [gets / receives] good wages. // 우리 회사는 ~이 낮다[높다] My office pays low[high] wages.

● **임금 격차** a wage differential. ¶지역별 ~ regional wage differentials. **임금 노동자** / **임금 생활자** a wage earner; (미) a wageworker. **임금 동결** a wage freeze. **임금 인상** a wage increase; (미) a wage [pay] hike; a wage[pay] raise [(영) rise]; raise [(영) rise] (in wages). ¶종업원은 고용주에게 ~을 요구했다 The employees asked their employer for a pay [wage] raise. / The employees demanded a wage increase [higher wages] from [of] their employer. // 노동조합은 20퍼센트의 ~을 요구했다 The labor [trade] union demanded a 20 percent pay raise. // 그들은 ~을 위한 파업에 돌입했다 They went on strike for higher wages. **임금 정책** a wage policy. **임금 제도** a wage system. **임금 투쟁** a wage struggle; a (labor) struggle for a wage hike.

임기(任期) one's term of office[service]; one's tenure (of office); (의원의) a term of membership. ¶나머지 ~ the remainder[unexpired portion] of one's term of office // ~를 연장하다 extend one's term // 그 시장의 ~는 다음 달에 만료된다 The mayor's term of office expires [comes to an end / ends] next month. // 그는 지사의 ~를 마쳤다 He finished (up)[came to the end of] his term as governor. / He served out his term as governor. / 이 대학 학장의 ~는 4년이다 The term of the president of this college is four years. / The president of this college serves a four-year term. // 대통령은 ~ 중에 사망했다 The president died during.

● **임기 만료** completion[expiration] of one's term of office. ¶~ 전에 해임되다 be dismissed before one's term expires.

임기응변(臨機應變) adaptation to circumstances. ¶~의 expedient / emergency // ~으로 as the occasion demand / according to circumstances // 그에게는 ~의 재치가 있다 He has the talent of accommodating [adapting / suiting] himself to the occasion [circumstances]. / He is full of resources in an emergency. // 그것은 ~의 조치였다 They were the proper steps [measures] to meet the situation. / That was what was required of the moment. // 그는 ~의 조치를 취했다 He employed means suited [geared] to the occasion. **임기응변하다** act according to the circumstances.

임대(賃貸) lease; hire; (부동산의) location; (물품의) hiring out; (배의) charter. ¶사무실의 ~ lease of an office building. **임대하다** (토지·건물·기계 등을) lease; (토지·건물 등을) rent; (집·방 등을) rent; (영) let; (자전거 등을) (미) rent (out); (영) hire (out)(▶ (미)에서는 hire를 쏨. 단, 텔레비전은 rent); (큰 배·비행기 등을) charter. ¶방을 ~ rent[(영) let] a room // 건물을 ~ lease[rent] a building // 자전거를 시간제로 ~ rent [(영) hire] bicycles (out) by the hour / let bicycles out on hire by the hour // 정부는 피난민에게 싼 값의 아파트를 임대했다 The government rented inexpensive apartments to the refugees.

● **임대 계약** a lease contract. **임대료** (a) rent; (문어) a rental; (자동차 등의) hire; (배의) charterage. ¶보트의 ~는 얼마입니까 How much does it cost to rent a boat? / How much is the hire of a boat? **임대 아파트** a rental apartment; an apartment on lease; (영) flats to let. **임대업** leasing service. **임대인** a lessor.

임대차(賃貸借) rental; leasing.

임면(任免) 〔임명과 해임〕 appointment and dismissal [removal]. **임면하다** appoint and dismiss [remove].

● **임면권** power to appoint and dismiss [remove] (members of the staff). ¶이 회사에서는 누가 ~을 가지고 있습니까 Who has the right[power] to appoint and dismiss [hire and fire] the employees in this company?

임명(任命) appointment; (무관의) commission. ¶이 관직은 ~에 의하여 결정된다 This office is filled by appointment. / This is an appointive office. **임명하다** appoint (a person to an office). ¶남을 회사의 이사로 ~ make a person a (company) director / appoint a person director // 대통령은 윤 판사를 대법원 판사로 임명했다 The President appointed Judge Yun to the Supreme Court. ➡그는 지점장에 임명되었다 He was appointed (to the post of) branch manager. // 그는 교장으로 임명되었다 He was appointed (to be) principal.

● **임명권** appointive power; the power to appoint. ¶대사의 ~은 대통령에게 있다 The President has the power to appoint[name] ambassadors. **임명권자** a person who has the appointive powers.

임무(任務) a duty; an office; a task; [사명] a mission. ¶중대 ~ an important duty / a great task[mission] // ~를 **다하다**[수행하다] accomplish[fulfill / discharge] one's duty / accomplish one's task / fulfill one's mission // 그는 ~에 충실하다 He is faithful to his duties. // 그는 경찰관으로서의 ~를 태만히 했다 He neglected his duty as a policeman. // 그들은 각자 맡은 바 ~를 잘 수행했다 Each of them discharged his duty[did his own part] well. // 그에게는 특별한 ~가 없다 He has no particular duty to perform[no particular function]. // 나에게는 그 ~가 너무 버겁다 The task is too much for me. // 그는 특별한 ~를 띠고 프랑스에 왔다 He came to France on a special mission.

임박하다(臨迫-) impend; draw near; be close[near] at hand; be imminent; approach. ¶시험이 임박했다 The examination is near[close] at hand. // 전쟁이 임박했다 War is imminent. // 출발할 날이 임박했다 The day for departure is near at hand[is drawing near]. // 선거가 임박했다 The election has approached[is now close at hand].

임부(妊婦·姙婦) a pregnant woman; an expectant mother(처음 임신한); a woman in the family way; a woman in pregnancy[in a delicate condition].

임산물(林産物) forest products.

임산부(妊産婦) pregnant women and nursing mothers.

임상(臨床) ¶~의 clinical.

● **임상 강의** a clinical lecture; a clinic. **임상 병리학**[심리학] clinical pathology[psychology]. **임상 실험** a clinical testing. ¶그 약은 ~중이다 The medicine is undergoing clinical testing (on patients). **임상 의학** [의] clinical medicine.

임석(臨席) attendance; presence; company. ¶…의 ~하에 with (a person) in attendance / in the presence of (a person) // 선수들은 대통령 ~하에 시합을 하게 되었다 The players were honored to play in the presence of the President. **임석하다** attend; be present (at). ¶저희의 만찬회에 임석해 주시면 영광이겠습니다 We request the honor of your company at the dinner.

임시(臨時) 1 [필요에 따라 그때그때 정한 것]. ¶~의 special / extra / extraordinary / emergency // ~로 specially / extraordinarily. 2 [일시적인 동안]. ¶~의 temporary / provisional / interim / expedient / makeshift // ~로 for the time being / temporarily / provisionally / as a makeshift // ~로 내가 의장 직을 맡겠다 I'll take the chair for the time being. 3 [어떤 시기]. ¶…할 ~에 on the point of … / just before // 그녀가 그 전화를 받은 것은 파리를 출발할 ~였다 It was when she was on the point of leaving Paris that she got the phone call.

● **임시 고용인** a temporary employee; a part-time worker; a part-timer. **임시 국회** an extraordinary session of the National Assembly. **임시변통** a makeshift; a stopgap; a shift; a patchwork. ¶~을 **하다** make shift (with) / temporize / make (a thing) do (for the present) / fill[stop / supply] a gap // 우리는 의자 대신 ~으로 나무 상자를 사용했다 We used wooden boxes as substitutes for chairs[as makeshift chairs]. // 책이 도착할 때까지 ~으로 이 복사물을 쓰겠습니다 We will make do with these xeroxed copies until the books arrive. // 그러면 당분간 ~이 되겠다 It will serve (our purpose) for the present. / It will do for the present. / It will be enough [sufficient] for the current need. // 이 돈이면 4, 5일 동안 ~이 된다 This money will tide me over the next few days. // ~으로 이것을 쓰십시오 Use this as a makeshift. **임시 소집** an emergency call-up. **임시 열차** a special [extra] train. ¶~로 **떠나다** leave (Seoul) by a special train. **임시 정부** a provisional government; (미승인의) a de facto government. **임시 총회** an extraordinary general meeting.

임신(妊娠·姙娠) pregnancy. ¶자궁 외 ~ extrauterine[ectopic] pregnancy // ~ 중에 during the period of pregnancy[maternity] // 그녀는 ~ 6개월[24주]이다 She is in the twenty-four weeks of pregnancy. / She is twenty-four weeks pregnant.(▶ 영어에서는 달이 아니라 주로 말하는 것이 보통임) **임신하다** become pregnant[impregnated]; be[get] pregnant; (구어) get[be] in the[a] family way; [의] (문어) conceive. ¶그녀는 임신하고 있다 She is pregnant. / She is going to have a baby. ➡그는 애인을 임신시키고 말았다 He got his girl friend pregnant[into trouble].

● **임신복** maternity wear[clothes]. **임신부** a pregnant woman. **임신 중절** (an artificial) abortion. ¶~을 **하다** have an abortion.

임야(林野) forests and fields; a forest land.

임업(林業) forestry.

● **임업 시험장** a experimental forestry station.

임연수어(林延壽魚) [동] an Atka mackerel [fish].

임용(任用) appointment. ¶공무원 ~령 the Official Appointment Regulations // ~ 후보자 명부 a list of eligible candidates for appointment. **임용하다** appoint. ➡요직에 임용되다 be appointed an important position.

임원(任員) a person holding a managerial[an executive] post; an executive; an official; an officer; a person in charge; (전체) the board; the staff. ¶조합 ~ a union official[officer] // 그는 ~ 중 한 사람이다 He is on the board [on the staff / a member of the board]. // 나는 육상 경기 대회의 ~이다 I am on the committee in charge of the athletic meet.

● **임원석** seats reserved for the officials [officers]. **임원회** an officers'[executives'] meeting.

임의(任意) option; discretion; voluntariness.

¶~의 option / discretionary / voluntary / arbitrary∥~의 장소 any place∥이 과목은 ~로 선택할 수 있다 This subject is optional [(미) elective]. / You have the choice [option] of taking this subject or not.∥이 돈은 네 ~대로 써도 좋다 This money is at your disposal. / You can use this money as you please [like]. / This money is within [in] your discretion to dispose of it.∥~대로 해석 하십시오 You are free to give any interpretation to it you like.∥기부는 ~로 합니다 Contributions are voluntary.∥위원은 회장에 의해서 ~로 선정되었다 The committee members were chosen arbitrarily by the president.∥경찰서까지 ~ 동행해 주십시오 I ask you to come with me to the police station voluntarily [of your own accord].
●**임의 선택** option; free choice. **임의 추출법** [수] random sampling. **임의 출두** voluntary appearance [attendance]. ¶나는 경찰서에 ~를 하라는 요구를 받았다 I was requested to appear at the police station voluntary [to make a voluntary appearance at the police station].

임자¹ [소유한 사람] the owner. ¶~ 없는 개 an ownerless [a stray] dog∥~ 없는 집 a vacant [deserted] house∥~ 있는 여자 a married woman∥저 여자 ~ 있니 Is she spoken for?∥이 집은 ~가 바뀌었다 This house has changed hands. / This house now has a new owner.∥이 땅의 ~는 누구입니까 Whose land is this? / Who owns this land?

임자² 1 [자네] you; old fellow [man]. 2 [부부간의 호칭] (my) dear; darling; (my) honey.

임전(臨戰) presence at a battle. **임전하다** go into action.
●**임전무퇴** knowing no retreat at the battlefield. **임전 태세** preparations for action; military preparedness; clearing the decks [ship] for action. ¶~를 갖추다 be prepared for war / be ready for a fight.

임종(臨終) 1 [죽음에 임함] one's end; one's deathbed; [목숨이 끊어질 때] one's last moment; the time [hour] of death. ¶~의 고통 death agonies∥~의 자리 one's deathbed∥~ 때에 at the point of death / on one's deathbed∥~에 하신 아버지의 훈계 my father's deathbed [dying] admonition∥그가 ~에 한 말 what he said on his deathbed [with his last breath] / his dying words∥그의 ~이 가까워졌다 He is on his deathbed. / He is at death's door. / He is near death. / His hour [time] has come. / His end is nearing.∥그녀는 ~ 때까지 딸에 대해 걱정했다 She was concerned about her daughter until her dying hour [to her last moment / until she has breathed her last / to her dying day / until her dying day].∥그는 ~을 맞이하여 자기 딸을 용서했다 He forgave his daughter in the hour of his death [on his deathbed].∥아버지의 ~의 말씀은 무엇이었습니까 What were my father's dying [last] words? / What did my father say on his deathbed [with his last breath / in his last moments]? **임종하다** be on one's deathbed; be at the moment of death; be dying. ¶그는 80세의 나이에 조용히 임종했다 He died peacefully [died a peaceful death] at the age of eighty.
2 [종신] attendance [presence] at one's parent's deathbed. ¶나는 아버지의 ~을 했다 I attended my father on his deathbed.∥가슴 아프게도 아버지의 ~을 못 했다 I am really sorry I could not take a last look at my dying father [attend my father on his deathbed / have a last look at my father in life]. **임종하다** attend [be at] one's parent's deathbed; be with (a person) at (his) death.

임지(任地) one's post. ¶~에서 죽다 die at one's post∥그는 어제 새 ~로 떠났다 He set out for [left for / proceeded to] his new post yesterday.

임질(淋疾·痳疾) [의] gonorrhea; (영) gonorrhoea; (속어) the clap. ¶~의 gonorrheal∥~에 걸리다 suffer from gonorrhea / get the clap.
●**임질균** a gonococcus (pl. -cocci).

임차(賃借) hire; hiring; (부동산의) lease; (토지·가옥의) renting. ¶~용 가옥 house for rent [(영) to let]. **임차하다** rent; (영) hire (hire는 자동차 등의 일시적인 것에, rent는 장기간의 것에 씀); lease (land); take [hold] (land / a house) by [on] lease; charter (a ship). ¶임차한 자동차 rented [(영) hired] car∥방을 ~ rent a room.
●**임차권** the right of lease; a lease. **임차료** (a) rent; (the charge for) hire; rental. **임차인** a hirer; a lessee; a leaseholder; a borrower; a debtor. ¶아파트 ~ the tenant of an apartment.

임치(任置) deposition; bailment.
●**임치인** a depositor; a truster; a bailor.

임파(淋巴) 〈음역〉 [생] lymph. ⇨림프
●**임파선**(-腺) a lymphatic gland. ⇨림프샘(⇨림프)

임하다(任-) 1 [떠맡다] take (a mission) upon oneself; assume. ¶목사를 천직으로 알고 ~ find out one's mission to the ministry.
2 [임명하다] appoint (a person to a post).

임하다(臨-) 1 [윗사람이 아랫사람을 대하다] deal with. ¶학생에게 임하는 그의 태도는 훌륭했다 His attitude toward(s) the students was admirable.
2 [임석하다] attend; be present (at). ¶졸업식에 ~ attend [be present at] the graduation ceremony.
3 [직면하다] meet; face; be confronted (by). ¶위기에 임하여 in (the) face of danger / in the presence of danger / 죽음에 임하여 on one's deathbed / at the moment of death∥침착하게 난국에 ~ face a difficult situation unperturbed∥아버지는 태연히 죽음에 임했다 My father met his death calmly.
4 [면하다] look out on [upon]; face (on / to); front (on / to). ¶바다에 임한 집 a house facing [fronting (on)] the sea∥학교는 호수에 임하고 있다 The school fronts a lake.∥우리 집은 공원에 임하고 있다 Our house fronts on [looks out upon] the park.∥런던은 템스 강에 임하고 있다 London stands on the Thames.

임학(林學) forestry. ⇨삼림학(⇨삼림)
●**임학자** a dendrologist; a forestry expert.

임해(臨海) [바다에 임하는 것]. ¶~의 seaside.
●**임해 공업 단지** a seaside [coastal] industrial park.

입¹ (사람·동물의) a mouth; [입술] lips; [의] an os (pl. ora). ¶꽉 다문 ~ a firm(ly)-set mouth / a mouth turned down at the

corners ~의 oral // ~이 큰 big mouthed // ~ 안의[안에] in the mouth // ~을 크게 벌리다 open one's mouth wide / gape // ~을 크게 벌리고 웃다 laugh with one's mouth wide open[with an open mouth] // ~을 오므리다 purse (up) one's lips / pucker up one's mouth // ~에 잔뜩 넣고 먹다 eat in big mouthfuls // ~에 음식을 넣은 채 말하다 talk with one's mouth full // 손으로 ~을 가리다 clap one's hand to one's mouth // ~을 삐죽 내밀다 pout one's mouth[lips] // ~을 비죽거리다 curl one's lip / make a wry mouth[wry mouths] at a person // ~에서 ~으로 전해지다[퍼지다] pass[be whispered / spread] from mouth to mouth // 그녀는 ~이 예쁘다 She has a cute mouth. // 그는 ~을 딱 벌리고 서 있었다 He was standing with his mouth wide open. // 그는 ~에서 냄새가 난다 He has (a) foul[bad] breath. / He suffers from halitosis. // 그 소문은 ~에서 ~으로 전해졌다 The rumor passed from mouth to mouth. // 아픔을 호소하는 말은 그녀의 ~에서 한 번도 나오지 않았다 No complaints of pain have ever passed her lips. // 모두 ~을 딱 벌렸다 Every mouth dropped open. // 개는 뼈다귀를 ~에 물었다 The dog seized a bone with the mouth. // ~이 화근이다 Out of the mouth comes evil. / The mouth is the gate of misfortune. // 심한 말이 그의 ~에서 튀어나왔다 Violent words poured from his lips. // 그런 일을 하면 ~이 열둘이라도 할 말이 없다 Such action admits of no excuse[is unjustifiable]. 2 [사람·식구] a mouth to feed; a dependent. ¶~이 많다 have a large family to support // ~을 줄이다 reduce the number of mouths to feed.
3 [말] tongue; speech; words; [소문] gossip; rumor. ¶~을 조심해라 Be careful what you say. / Watch your tongue. // 그는 ~으로는 그렇게 말하지만 사실은 너에 대해 정말 걱정하고 있다 Though he talks that way, he is really worried about you. // 내 ~으로 말한다는 것은 우습겠지만, 이 아들은 정말 믿음직스럽다 It may sound odd coming from me, but this son of mine is thoroughly dependable.
4 [미각] (one's) taste; (one's) palate. ¶~이 고급인 사람 a gourmet // 그녀는 ~이 까다롭다 She has a delicate palate. // 그는 ~이 고급이다 He is quite an epicure. / He has a dainty tooth[has a pampered taste]. / He is a gourmet.

입(이) 가볍다 be talkative; be loose-[glib-]tongued; be loose-lipped. ¶저 여자 아이는 정말 ~ That girl is a regular chatterbox[is a real blabbermouth].

입(을) 놀리다 say at a venture; talk at random. ¶그는 아무렇게나 입을 놀리지 않는다 He weighs[picks / spares] his words.

입(을) 다물다 close[shut] one's mouth; [말을 않다] be[keep] silent; keep one's mouth shut; hold one's tongue; keep dumb[mum] (about); button (up) one's lips. ¶그 문제에 대해서 나는 입을 다물 수밖에 없다 I can only hold my tongue[be silent] on the matter. / I cannot but keep mute and silent about it. / I cannot but keep a tight lip on the matter. // 그는 입을 꼭 다물고 아무 말도 하지 않았다 He pursed (up) his lips and remained silent. / He (obstinately) kept his lips tight shut. // 입 다물어라 Button (up) your lips! / Shut up your mouth! / Silence! // 입 다물고 있으면 중간은 한다 Silence never makes mistakes. / Least said, soonest mended.

입(을) 떼다 begin to talk; start a talk; broach (a subject); break the silence; [말하기 어려운 일을 말하다] break the ice. ¶그는 술에 취하자 마침내 입을 떼기 시작했다 At last under the influence of wine he began to talk. // 오늘 아침에 그는 통 입을 떼지 않았다 I haven't heard a peep out of him this morning.

입(을) 막다 silence; put[reduce] a person to silence. ¶돈으로 남의 ~ buy a person's silence // 그들은 나의 상관을 통해서 내 입을 막으려고 했다 They tried to silence me with the aid of my superior. // 세상 사람들의 입을 막을 수는 없다 People will talk. / We cannot stop gossip.

입만 살다 be all talk and no deed; be bold in word only. ¶그는 입만 살아 있는 놈이다 He is all talk and no deed. / His big talk belies him. / He is bold in word only.

입만 아프다 be in vain; be useless; go for nothing. ¶그에게는 충고를 해 봐야 ~ It is useless to advise him. / My advice was lost on him.

입(을) 맞추다 1 kiss; press one's lips against. ¶남의 손에 ~ kiss another's hand // 남의 볼에 ~ kiss a person on the cheek / kiss a person's cheek. 2 [말이 일치되게 하다] sing from the same hymn[song] sheet.

입(을) 모으다 입을 모아 with one mouth [voice] / in chorus[unison] / unanimously / all (speaking) together / with one accord // 학생들은 입을 모아 아무것도 모른다고 말했다 The pupils said in chorus that they knew nothing about it.

입 밖에 내다 speak[talk] (of); mention; mouth (a word). ¶남이 그 이름을 입 밖에 내기만 해도 그는 기분 나빠한다 The mere mention of that name hurts his feelings. // 그것을 한 마디라도 입 밖에 내서는 안 된다 Say nothing to any one. / Breathe not a syllable of it to any one.

입(이) 싸다 be talkative. ⇨"입(이) 가볍다(⇨입)

입(을) 씻다 feign innocence[ignorance]; dissimulate. ¶그는 입을 씻고 애써 개의치 않는 체하고 있다 He is feigning innocence and trying to look unconcerned.

입에 담다[올리다] speak[talk] (of); mention; refer[allude] (to); mouth. ¶그 문제는 입에 담기도 싫다 I cannot bear to refer to the subject. // 그런 사람에 관한 일은 입에 담기도 싫다 It's unpleasant for me to talk about such a man.

입에 대다 taste; touch; eat; have; take. ¶그는 술은 입에 대지도 않는다 He does not touch a drop of liquor. // 그녀는 그 요리를 일체 입에 대지 않았다 She left all the dishes untouched. / No dishes passed her lips.

입에 맞다 suit one's taste[palate]; be nice to the palate; be palatable; be to one's taste. ¶입에 맞는 떡 an agreeable food[thing] // 멕시코 요리는 내 입에 맞지 않는 것 같다 I'm afraid Mexican food is not to my taste[does not agree with me].

입에 발린 소리 lip service; mere praise; mere [left-handed] compliments. ¶~를 하다 pay

lip service (to a person) // 그가 너에게 하는 칭찬은 ~쯤으로 듣는 게 좋을 거다 When he praises you, you'd better take it as a kind of lip service.

입에서 신물이 나다 be bored (by / with); (구어)be fed up (with). ¶그런 이야기에는 입에서 신물이 난다 I've heard enough of that kind of talk. // 그녀의 우는 소리는 이제 입에서 신물이 난다 I'm disgusted with[sick and tired of] (hearing) her complaints.

입에 오르다[오르내리다] be talked by people [others]; be a topic of conversations (among); be the talk of the town. ¶시장(市長)의 부정이 시민의 입에 오르고 있다 The mayor's irregularities are being talked about by the citizens. // 인사이동을 둘러싼 이야기가 사원들 입에 오르내리고 있었다 The personnel changes were a topic of conversation among the staff members.

입에 풀칠(을) 하다 make one's living; gain a livelihood; win one's daily bread. ¶간신히 ~ gain a bare livelihood / live from hand to mouth // 그는 잡문을 써서 입에 풀칠을 하고 있다 He managed to get enough to eat by writing miscellaneous essays.

입을 열다 tell; open one's mouth; confess; let out; disclose [reveal / betray] (a secret); squeal. ¶마침내 그가 입을 열었다 At last he began to talk. // 그녀는 입을 열기만 하면 시어머니 험담이다 She never opens her mouth without speaking ill of her mother-in-law. // 용의자는 마침내 입을 열었다 The suspect confessed at last. // 결국 그는 입을 열어 사실대로 털어놓았다 Eventually he came out with the truth. // 그는 입을 열기가 무섭게 진술을 부인했다 No sooner were the words out of his mouth than he denied what he said. // 그는 입을 열자마자 은사를 칭송했다 He began his speech by paying tribute to[with words of praise for] his teacher.

입이 거칠다 have a dirty tongue; be foul-mouthed.

입이 걸다 be foulmouthed; have a violent-tongued; have a foul mouth; have a sharp [spiteful / venomous / bitter / foul] tongue. ¶그는 ~ He has a sharp[venomous / scathing / cutting] tongue.

입이 궁금하다 wish[want] to eat. ¶담배를 끊었더니 입이 궁금해서 견딜 수가 없다 Since I gave up smoking I just have to have something to put in my mouth.

입이 근질근질하다 be dying to tell. ¶신디는 남편에게 아기를 가졌다는 말을 하고 싶어 입이 근질근질했다 Cindy was dying to tell her husband she was pregnant.

입이 닳도록 over and over again. ¶담배는 몸에 해롭다고 ~ 말했지만 그는 듣지 않는다 I have told him over and over again the smoking is bad for his health, but he only turns a deaf ear to my warning[to me].

입이 더럽다 abuse; be abusive; swear at. ¶그는 ~ He is abusive. // 그는 때로 아내에게 입이 더러운 말을 쓴다 He sometimes uses abusive language to his wife.

입이 무겁다 be slow of speech; be close mouthed; be tight-mouthed; be tight-lipped; be close-lipped; discreet; be uncommunicative; be reticent; be reserved in speech. ¶그는 ~ He is a man of few words.

입이 쓰다 be bitter[sorry / unpleasant / displeased / unhappy]. ¶입이 쓴 경험 a bitter experience // 그 생각을 하니 ~ It makes me sick to think of it. // 그 소식을 들으니 ~ I am displeased at the news.

입이 짧다 have a small appetite; eat like a bird; do not eat much; be fussy about foods; [편식하다] have an unbalanced diet. ¶입이 짧은 사람 a small [light / poor] eater // 너는 몹시 입이 짧구나 You eat no more than a little bird. / What a small eater you are!

입가 the sides of the mouth; at one's lips. ¶~에 미소를 띠고 with a smile playing about one's mouth [lips] / with a smile at the corner(s) of one's mouth / with a smile on one's lips // 수수께끼 같은 미소가 그녀의 ~에 감돌았다 A mysterious smile played around [hovered round] her lips[mouth]. / She had a mysterious smile on her lips.

입가심 a savo(u)ry. ¶나는 쓴 약을 먹고 ~으로 사과를 먹었다 I ate an apple to get rid of [take away] the bitter taste of the medicine.

입가심하다 kill[take off] the aftertaste.

입각(入閣) entry into the Cabinet. **입각하다** join[enter] the Cabinet; become a member of the Cabinet; take a seat in the Cabinet; receive a portfolio.

입각하다(立脚-) be based [grounded / founded] on; take one's ground on; rest on the basis of. ¶그것은 사실에 입각한 논의였다 The arguments were based on facts. // 우리는 스포츠 정신에 입각하여 정정당당히 싸울 것이다 We will play fairly, conforming to the rules of good sportsmanship. // 우리는 선거법에 입각하여 국회의원을 선출했다 We elected the National Assembly members according to [in accordance with] the election law.

입간판(立看板) a billboard; a standing signboard.

입감(入監) imprisonment; incarceration. ¶~중이던 be in jail [prison] / be behind the bars. **입감하다** be sent [put in] to prison [jail]; be jailed; be imprisoned.

입거하다(入渠-) lie up; enter a dock; come [go / get] into (a) dock; dock; be docked. ¶수리를 위해 배가 입거하고 있다 The ship is docked [in dock] for repairs.

입건하다(立件-) book (a person) for [on a charge of]. ¶경찰은 그를 절도 혐의로 입건했다 The police booked him on suspicion of theft. → ¶형사 입건되다 be criminally booked (on charge of) // 그는 강도 혐의로 입건되었다 He was booked on a charge of burglary.

입경하다(入京-) enter [arrive in] the capital; come up to Seoul. ¶지방 선수단이 속속 입경했다 The local team came up to Seoul one after another.

입고(入庫) (상품 등의) storage in warehouse; (차 등의) entering the (car) shed. **입고하다** (상품을) stock; warehouse; (차를) enter the (car)shed. ¶상품을 창고에 ~ store goods in a warehouse. → ¶상품이 입고되었다 The goods were stocked [warehoused]. / The goods were stored in a warehouse. // 자동차[보트]가 입고되었다 Automobiles [Boats] entered the shed.

입관(入棺) placing[putting] a body in a coffin. **입관하다** lay a dead person in a coffin; place [put] a person's body in a coffin.

●**입관식** the rite of placing a body in a

입당

coffin.
입교(入校) entrance into a school. ⇨ 입학
입구(入口) an entrance; a way in; the door (to a room); doorway; (미) an entry (to a river); the mouth (of a harbor); the approach (to a bridge). ¶터널의 ~ the beginning of a tunnel / the approach to a tunnel // 항구의 ~ the mouth of a harbor // 공원의 ~ the gate to[of] a park / the approach to a park / a park gate // ~의 초인종 the doorbell // 강당 ~에서 at the entrance to a hall // ~를 막지 마라 Don't block the entrance[doorway / entry]. // ~를 못 찾겠다 I can't find my way in.
입국(入國) entry[entrance] (into a country); [이민·이주] immigration. ¶불법 ~ illegal entry // 불법 ~자 an illegal entrant // 그는 ~이 허가되었다 He was admitted to the country. // 그는 ~을 거절당했다 He was refused entrance[entry] to the country. **입국하다** enter a country; be admitted to[into] a country; (이민인) immigrate into a country. ¶미국에 입국하려면 여러 가지 절차가 필요하다 There are many formalities to be gone through before you enter[are admitted into] America.
● **입국 사증** entry visa. **입국 절차** formalities for entry; entry formalities. **입국 허가서** an entry permit.
입국(立國) 1 [나라를 세움] the founding [establishment] of a nation. **입국하다** found [establish] a nation. 2 [국력을 길러 번영하게 함]. ¶산업 ~ the prosperity of a nation on the basis of industries // 한국은 무역 ~이다 Korea is a trading nation.
입궐(入闕) a visit to the Royal Palace; attendance at[entry into] the Royal Court. **입궐하다** go to the Royal Palace; proceed[go] to the Royal Court.
입금(入金) [돈이 들어옴] receipt of money; [그 돈] money received; receipts; [돈을 넣음] depositing; [예금] a deposit. **입금하다** [받다] receive (money); [치르다] pay (money). →¶은행에 50만 원이 입금되었다 Five hundred thousand won was deposited in[paid into] the bank. / The bank received five hundred thousand won. // 지난달에 그 회사로부터는 20만 원이 입금되었다 I received two hundred thousand won from the company last month. // 돈은 3월 1일에 입금시켜야 한다 The payment is due on March 1.
● **입금 전표** a deposit[credit] slip.
입김 1 [입에서 나오는 김] the steam of breath; puffs of one's breath. ¶아버지의 ~이 어린 담뱃대 my father's favorite pipe // ~을 불다 breathe upon / blow one's breath on // 나는 ~을 불어 손을 녹였다 I blew on my hands to warm them. // 그는 안경에 ~을 불어 닦았다 He breathed on his glasses and wiped them. 2 [영향력] (an) influence. ¶저 사람에게는 어느 장관의 ~이 작용하고 있다 He is backed up by[has the backing of] a minister. // 그는 장 씨 부인의 ~으로 과장이 되었다 He gained the position of section chief on the recommendation[through the influence] of Mrs. Jang.
입내¹ [소리·말로 내는 흉내] mimicry. ¶~를 내다 mimic a person's speech / imitate a person's way of speaking / imitate / mimic a person[a person's talk] // 그가 선생님의 ~를 내자 모두들 웃었다 Everyone laughed when he mimicked[imitated] his teacher's speech [way of speaking].
● **입내쟁이** a mimic; a mimicker; an imitator.
입내² [구취] bad[foul] breath; [의] halitosis. ¶그는 ~가 난다 He has bad[foul] breath. / His breath smells[foul / stinks].
입다 1 (옷을) put on; get on; slip on(걸치다); rush[throw] on(급히); wear; have on; be dressed in. (put on은 입는 동작, wear는 입은 상태를 나타냄) ¶한복을 입은 여인 a woman in Korean clothes // 치마를 ~ put on a skirt // 승마복을 ~ dress oneself for a ride // 제일 좋은 옷을 입고 나가다 go out in one's best (clothes) // 옷을 입은 채로 자다 sleep in one's clothes / go to bed without changing clothes / (구어) turn in all standing // 그는 상의를 입었다 He put his jacket on. / He put on his coat. // 그는 파자마를 입었다 He got into his pajamas. // 그녀는 치마를 벗어버리고 슬랙스를 입었다 She took off her skirt and put on slacks. // 그 옷이 맞는지 한번 입어 보아라 Try[Put] it on to see if it fits (you). // 그녀는 교복(횐옷)을 입고 있었다 She was dressed in her school uniform[in white]. // 외투는 그대로 입고 계십시오 Keep your (over)coat on, please. // 파자마를 입고 밖에 나가면 안 된다 You mustn't go outside in your pajamas. // 이 옷을 벌써 10년 동안이나 해질 정도로 입고 있다 I've been wearing these old clothes for ten years. / These old clothes are worn out after ten years of wear. // 그는 서둘러 바지를 입었다 He put on his trousers. // 이 타이츠는 아직 입을 수 있다 These tights can still be worn[still have some wear in them]. // 그녀는 멋진 드레스를 입고 나타났다 She appeared in a beautiful dress[all dressed up]. / She came wearing a very nice dress. // 그는 연미복을 입고 있었다 He wore[was wearing / was dressed in] a swallowtail coat. // 너는 그 드레스를 입으면 근사하다 You are wonderful in that dress.
2 (손해 등을) sustain; suffer; incur. ¶큰 손해를 ~ sustain a heavy losses / suffer a serious loss / suffer[receive] a great damage // 부상을 ~ be[get] wounded[injured] / get hurt / suffer[sustain] an injury (to a knee) // 사고로 상처를 ~ be injured in an accident // 전투에서 부상을 ~ be wounded in action // 그는 어깨에 상처를 입었다 He was injured in the shoulder.
3 (은혜·도움 등을) get[receive] (a favor); be favored (with); bask (in). ¶은혜를 ~ receive benefits[favors] // 그녀에게 은혜를 많이 입고 있다 I am greatly indebted to her.
4 (상을). ¶상을 ~ take to[go into] mourning / observe mourning // 나는 어머니의 상을 입고 있다 I am in mourning for my mother.
입단하다(入團−) join[enter] an organization. ¶그 소년은 소년단에 입단했다 The boy joined[enrol(l)ed in] the Boy Scouts. // 그는 자이언츠에 입단했다 He joined the Giants.
입담 volubility; skill at talking; the gift of (the) tongue. ¶~이 좋다 be good at talking / be glib-tongued / be voluble-tongued / be a glib talker / have the gift of the gab / have a candied tongue.
입당(入黨) joining a political party. **입당하다**

입대 join [become a member of] a political party. ¶그는 민주당에 입당했다 He joined [became a member of] the Democratic party.

입대 (入隊) joining the army; enlistment; enrollment. **입대하다** join [enlist in] the army; enroll [be enrolled] in a unit [corps / regiment]; (징병에 의해) be conscripted [drafted] into the army.
● **입대자** a recruit.

입덧 morning sickness; nausea accompanying pregnancy. ¶~이 나다 have morning sickness // ~이 심하다 suffer greatly from morning sickness.

입도선매 (立稻先賣) selling rice before the harvest. ¶~를 하다 sell rice before it is reaped.

입동 (立冬) [24절기의 하나] ipdong; the beginning of winter; the first day of winter according to the lunar calendar.

입력 (入力) 1 [전] (power) input. 2 [컴] input. **입력하다** input. ¶정보를 컴퓨터에 ~ input information // 컴퓨터에 데이터를 ~ feed data into a computer / feed a computer with data // 프로그램을 입력할 때 종종 오류를 범한다 We often make errors when we enter [key in] a program.
● **입력 장치** input equipment; an input unit.

입막음하다 make a person keep quiet [silent] (about); forbid a person to mention (it); stop a person's mouth; muzzle (a person); tie (a person's) tongue; bind (a person) to secrecy. ¶나는 그녀에게 그 일을 말하지 않도록 입막음했다 I made her promise to keep quiet [silent] about the matter. / I stopped her mouth on the matter. →그 사건에 대해서 우리는 단단히 입막음당했다 We were strictly forbidden to talk about the incident. / We were pledged to strict secrecy about the incident.

입맛 (an) appetite; one's taste; one's palate. ¶~이 나다 have a good appetite // ~을 잃다 lose one's appetite // ~이 없다 have no appetite / lack appetite // ~을 돋우다 stimulate [arouse] one's appetite / tickle one's palate / make one's mouth water // 나는 오늘 ~이 없다 I don't want to eat anything today. / I have no [little] appetite today. // 과로로 ~이 사라졌다 Overworking spoiled my appetite.

입맛(을) 다시다 1 (못마땅하여) click [clack] one's tongue; tut-tut. ¶남의 행동이 못마땅하여 ~ click one's tongue at a person's behavior. 2 [욕심을 내다] have an itch [a desire] (for / to do); want. ¶그는 그 지위에 입맛을 다셨다 He wanted the post very badly.

입맛(이) 떨어지다 1 [입맛을 잃다] lose one's appetite. ¶그런 말을 들으면 입맛이 떨어진다 Such talk spoils my dinner. 2 [흥미가 나지 않다] be spoiled [dampened] (by). ¶그 사건으로 입맛이 완전히 떨어지고 말았다 We lost all our interest in it after the incident.

입맛(이) 쓰다 be bitter [unpleasant / displeased]. ¶속았다고 생각하니 ~ I am vexed to think that I was cheated. // 그 생각을 하니 ~ It makes me sick to think of it.

입맞춤 a kiss (on the cheek); a smack. ➪키스

입매 (the shape of) a mouth. ➪입모습 ¶그녀는 ~가 예쁘다 She has a lovely [sweet] mouth.

입모습 (the shape of) a mouth. ¶~이 예쁘다 have a pretty [sweet / lovely] mouth // 그의 ~은 어머니의 그것을 닮았다 His mouth looks like his mother's.

입목 (立木) [땅 위에 서 있는 산 나무] a living [standing / growing] tree.

입문 (入門) 1 [문하생으로 들어감] entrance; admission. **입문하다** enter a private school; become a person's pupil. ¶그는 15세 때 유명한 프로 기사(棋士) 문하에 입문했다 At the age of fifteen he became a disciple [pupil] of a well-known professional go player. ¶그는 홍참 씨 아래 입문해서 배웠다 He studied under the tutorship of Mr. Hong Cham. 2 [초심자 지도] a guide. ¶스키 ~ (저서명) A Guide to Skiing // 철학 ~ (저서명) An Introduction to Philosophy.
● **입문서** a primer; a guide; an introduction. ¶바둑 ~ a primer [guide] of baduk(go).

입바르다 be frank; be outspoken [plainspoken]; be straightforward. ¶입바른 소리 plain speaking / a straight talk // 입바른 소리를 하다 speak plainly [frankly] / in a straightforward manner] / talk straight / call a spade a spade.

입방 (立方) ➡세제곱

입방아 small talk; a gossip; a (society) chat; idle chatter. ¶~를 찧다 chat / have a chat / gossip // 새색시를 두고 동네 아낙네들이 ~를 찧고 있다 The new bride is on the subject of housewives' gossip.

입버릇 [말버릇] a way [habit] of saying; [자주 입에 담는 말] a pet [favorite] phrase [saying]. ¶~이 되다 be in the habit of saying / never fail to say / be often on one's lips // ~이 고약하다 be foulmouthed / be violent-tongued / have a sharp tongue // 그는 ~처럼 돈이 없다고 말한다 He always says that he has no money.

입법 (立法) legislation; lawmaking. ¶교육 ~ educational legislation // ~의 legislative / legislatorial // ~ 정신에 위배되다 be contrary to the spirit of legislation. **입법하다** legislate; make [enact] laws.
● **입법권** legislative power. **입법 기관 / 입법부** a legislative organ [body]; the legislature. **입법자** a legislator; a lawmaker. **입법화** legalization.

입사 (入社) joining [entering] a company. **입사하다** join [enter] a company [firm] (as a salesman); become a member of a company; obtain a position in a concern. ¶당신은 언제 입사했습니까 When did you join us [this company]? / How long have you been working for [with] us?
● **입사 시험** an employment exam(ination); [면접시험] an interview. ¶대회사의 ~을 치다 [에 합격하다] go in for [succeed in] the examination [test] for service in a big firm.

입사 (入射) [물] incidence. ¶~의 incident.
● **입사각** an angle of incidence; an incidence angle; an entrance angle. **입사 광선** incident light; an incident ray.

입산 (入山) 1 [산에 들어감]. **입산하다** enter a mountain range; climb [go up] a mountain. 2 [절에 들어감]. **입산하다** enter a monastery; come to live in one's temple; enter the priesthood; become a bonze.
● **입산수도** mountaineering asceticism. ¶

승 a monk who leads an ascetic life in the mountains.

입상(入賞) winning a prize. **입상하다** win a prize; (경마에서) finish in the money. ¶입상한 사진[개] a prizewinning photograph[dog] // 그는 경주에서 1등에 입상했다 He won [carried off] (the) first prize in the race. / He first placed[finished first] in the race.
● **입상자** a prizewinner; (올림픽 등의) a medalist.

입상(立像) a statue of a standing figure. ¶아폴로의 ~ a standing figure of Apollo.

입상(粒狀) [알갱이 모양]. ~의 granular / granulous / graniform // ~으로 만들다 granulate.

입석(立席) (극장의) the gallery; (극장·버스 등의) (미) standing room; room for standing. ¶~도 만원이다 There's no room even for standing. // 이외 만원 (게시) Standing Room Only(약어 S.R.O.).
● **입석 손님** a standee.

입선(入選) winning; being selected[accepted] for a competition. **입선하다** [응모 출품한 것이 뽑히다] be accepted; be selected. ¶1등에 ~ be selected for the first prize // 그의 그림이 미술 전람회에 입선했다 His picture was accepted for the art exhibition.
● **입선자** a winner. **입선작** a winning work.

입성 (속) clothes. ⇨옷

입성하다(入城-) enter a castle[fortress] (▶fortress는 종종 소도시까지 포함하는 큰 요새지); make a triumphal entry into a fortress [castle].

입소(入所) 1 [연구소 등에 들어감] entrance (into); admission (to). ~ 훈련 initiatory training // 신병(新兵) ~식을 거행하다 hold an entrance ceremony of the new soldiers [recruits]. **입소하다** enter[be admitted to] (an institute). 2 [교도소에 들어감] imprisonment; incarceration; (수용소에서) internment; confinement. **입소하다** (교도소에) be put in[into] prison; be imprisoned; (수용소에) be put into[sent to] a (concentration) camp; be interned.

입속말 [입속으로 중얼거리는 말] a mumble; a murmur. **~을 하다** mumble / mutter / murmur (at / against) // 그 노부인은 ~로 뭐라고 중얼거렸다 The old woman mumbled (out) something.

입수(入手) acquisition; procurement. **입수하다** [손에 넣다] get; (보통 노력하여) obtain; (재산·권리 등을) acquire. ¶세무서가 어디선가 탈세 정보를 입수했다 The tax office got information from somewhere about tax evasion. / Somehow the tax office got wind of tax evasion. // 이 그림은 최근에 입수한 것이다 This picture is my latest aquisition.
● **입수 경로** means of acquisition. ¶경찰은 그의 총의 ~를 조사하고 있다 The police are investigating how he came to possess the gun[the gun came into his possession].

입술 a lip. ¶윗[아랫] ~ the upper[lower] lip // 얇은[두터운] ~ thin[thick] lips // ~을 내밀다 pout one's lips // ~을 오므리다 purse up one's lips // ~을 핥다 lick one's lips // 그녀는 심부름을 시키자 뾰로통해서 ~을 내밀었다 She pouted when she was given an errand to run. // 그는 그녀의 ~을 훔쳤다 He snatched a kiss from her.

입술을 깨물다 bite one's lips; gnaw one's lips. ¶분해서 ~ bite one's lips in vexation // 그는 입술을 깨물고 참았다 He gnawed his lips to control his temper.
● **입술소리** [언] a labial (sound). **입술연지** [립스틱] (a) lipstick; a lip pencil; [루주] rouge. ~를 짙게 칠한 아가씨들 girls with lips thickly painted // ~를 바르다 put on lipstick.

입시(入試) an entrance exam(ination). ⇨입학시험(⇨)일람
● **입시 지옥** the entrance examination evil; exam hell.

입신(入神) divineness. ¶그의 피아노 연주는 ~의 솜씨였다 He played the piano to perfection. / He showed consummate skill in playing the piano.

입신(立身) advancement in life; a rise in the world. ¶~을 꾀하다 seek one's fortune. **입신하다** rise in the world; succeed[get ahead] in life.
● **입신양명** rising in the world and winning [gaining] fame; achieving glory. ¶그는 ~하고 은퇴했다 Having won success and fame, he retired. **입신출세** success in life. ¶그는 능란하게 ~했다 He made his way skillfully in life[the world].

입실하다(入室-) enter[go into] a room.

입심 loquacity; talkativeness; volubility. ¶~이 좋은 사람 a glib talker / a talkative person / a chatterbox(여자) // **~이 좋다** be loquacious[talkative / voluble / glib] / have a facile tongue.

입씨름 1 [말을 주고받기] exchange of words. **입씨름하다** exchange words; talk back and forth. ¶장사꾼과 가격 문제로 ~ bargain [make a bargain] with the merchant over the price. **2** [말다툼] a quarrel; an argument; a dispute. ¶공연한[끝없는] ~만 벌이다 have a fruitless[an endless] dispute [argument]. **입씨름하다** quarrel; wrangle; dispute.

입안(立案) [안을 정하는 것] drawing up a plan; [초안 작성] drafting. ¶정부는 새로운 세법을 ~ 중이다 The government is drafting [drawing up] a new tax bill. **입안하다** plan; make[draw up] a plan; draft (a plan). ¶그것은 그가 입안했다 He made [drafted] the plan for it. // 이 계획은 누가 입안했지 Who planned this? / Who made[drew up] this plan?
● **입안자** a planner; a framer (of a project). ¶정책 ~ a policy maker.

입양(入養) (an) adoption. **입양하다** adopt (a child) as one's son; receive into one's family as a son; affiliate. ¶우리는 그를 양자로 입양했다 We have adopted him (as our son).

입어권(入漁權) the common of piscary; fishing rights in waters belonging to another.

입영(入營) enrollment; enlistment. ¶~ 중이다 be in the army / be serving with the colors. **입영하다** (지원하여) enlist in the army; join the army; (징병되어) be drafted [(영)] conscripted] into the army.

입욕(入浴) a bath; bathing. ¶그는 ~ 중이다 He's bathing. / He's having a bath. **입욕하다** take[have] a bath. ➔환자를 입욕시키다 give a patient a bath.

입원(入院) admission (in)to a hospital; hospitalization. ¶~ 중이다 (미) be in the hospi-

입자 tal / (영) be in hospital // ~ 신청을 하다 apply for admission to a hospital. **입원하다** be hospitalized; enter [go into] a hospital. ¶그는 2주일 전에 입원했다 He was hospitalized [admitted to a hospital] two weeks ago. // 그는 2주 동안 입원하고 있다 He has been in (the) hospital for two weeks (▶ (미)에서는 the를 붙이는 것이 보통). →¶어제 그를 입원시켰다 He was sent to (the) hospital yesterday.
- **입원비 / 입원료** hospital charges. **입원 수속 / 입원 절차** hospital admission procedures [formalities / red-tape]; formalities connected with hospital treatment. **입원실** a sickroom; a ward. **입원 치료** hospital treatment. ¶그는 ~가 필요하다 He needs [requires] hospital treatment. **입원 환자** a patient; an inpatient.

입자(粒子) a particle; a grain. ¶반-[물]- an antiparticle //경~ a lepton //중~ a heavy (atomic) particle / a baryon // 빛의 ~ particles of light // 모래의 ~ grains of sand // ~가 굵은 음판 a grainy negative.
- **입자량** particle weight.

입장(入場) entrance; [관람객 등이 장내로 들어감] admission; admittance. ¶~을 허락하다 admit (a person) to [into] (a place) / give [grant] (a person) admission [admittance] (to / into) // ~을 거절당하다 be denied [refused] admittance / be turned away // ~은 성년자에 한함 Only adults are admitted. / Only adults are allowed to enter. // 12세 미만의 어린이는 ~ 불가 (게시) No Admission to Children under 12 (years of age). // 관계자외 ~ 금지 (게시) No Admittance Except on Business. **입장하다** enter; go [come] in; (관람객이) be admitted (to); get (in). ¶무료~ have a free pass / be allowed in free // (선수가) 경기장에 ~ enter the stadium // 이 표로는 한 사람만 입장할 수 있다 This ticket admits one person only. // 늦었기 때문에 입장할 수 없었다 As I was late, I was unable to gain admittance.
- **입장권**(-券) an admission ticket; (역의) a platform ticket. ¶무료~ a complimentary ticket. **입장료** an entrance [admission] fee. ¶~를 (3,000원) 받다 charge admission (3,000 won for admission). **입장 무료** (게시) Admission Free. **입장식** an entrance ceremony; an opening ceremony.

입장(立場) 1 [당면한 처지] a situation; a position. ¶우리나라는 지금 어려운 ~에 놓여 있다 Our country is in a difficult situation [delicate position] now. // 자네의 조심성 없는 말 때문에 나는 거북한 ~에 놓였다 Your careless remark put me in an awkward position. // 나는 이 일에 대해서는 명확한 것을 말할 ~에 있지 않다 I am not in a position to say anything definite about this case. // 내가 당신의 ~이라면 그 돈은 받지 않을 것입니다 If I were you, I would not take the money. // 내 ~이 되어 보시오 I wish you to put yourself in my position [place].
2 [견지·관점] a viewpoint; a standpoint; [보는 각도] angle. ¶그는 다른 ~에서 그 일을 논했다 He discussed the matter from a different point of view [viewpoint / angle]. // 그는 자기 ~을 밝히지 않았다 He did not make his standpoint clear. // 이것은 내 정치적 ~ 때문에 반대하지 않을 수 없다 My political stand being what it is, I have to oppose this. // 그의 ~에서 보면 그것은 시간의 낭비이다 From his viewpoint, it is a waste of time. // ~을 바꿔 볼 필요도 있다 It is necessary to look at it from a different angle [point of view].

입적(入寂) [불] the passing away of a Buddha [a revered priest]; entering Nirvana. **입적하다** pass into [enter] Nirvana.

입적(入籍) an entry in the family register; registration (등록). **입적하다** have one's name entered in the family register. →¶부모는 아기를 호적에 입적시켰다 The parents had their baby's name entered in [on] the family register.

입정 [입버릇] a way [habit] of saying; [입놀림] a move of the mouth.
입정(을) 놀리다 keep one's mouth busy to eat; eat frequently between meals.

입정 사납다 be foulmouthed [abusive]. ¶입정 사납게 욕하다 call a person (bad) names / revile a person / abuse a person // 쌍방이 입정 사납게 서로 욕했다 Both parties exchanged abuse.

입정(入廷) admission to [entrance into] the courtroom. **입정하다** enter [appear in] the courtroom.

입주자(入住者) a dweller; an occupant of a house.

입주하다(入住-) move into (an apartment / a flat); (가정에) live in (a house); live with (a family). ¶새로 지은 집에 ~ move into a new(ly)-built house // 이 아파트에는 10세대가 입주하고 있다 This apartment house [apartment building / (영) block of flats] is occupied by ten families. / Ten families live in this apartment house. // 그는 가정교사로 그 집에 입주하고 있었다 He lived in the house [with the family] as tutor.

입증(立證) proof; demonstration; establishment (of a fact); substantiation (of one's statement). **입증하다** give proof; prove (a person's guilt [innocence]); establish (a fact); [일이 정당함을 증명하다] testify (a fact); attest to (a fact); corroborate; confirm; support; bear out. ¶…을 입증하기 위해 in support [corroboration / proof] of ... // 무고함을 ~ prove one's innocence / vindicate oneself // 유죄를 ~ prove (a person) guilty // 그의 유죄를 입증하는 것은 아무것도 없다 There is nothing to prove his guilt. / There is no proof [evidence] of his guilt. // 그 상품은 한국의 광학 공업의 우수성을 입증했다 The article demonstrated the excellence [superiority] of the optical industry in Korea.
- **입증 자료** supporting evidence.

입지(立地) location (of industry).
- **입지 조건** conditions of location; geographical conditions. ¶이 은행은 ~이 좋다 [나쁘다] This bank is conveniently [favorably] [inconveniently / unfavorably] located. // 나는 ~이 좋은 점포용 부지를 찾고 있다 I am looking for a site suitable for building a store.

입지(立志) fixing one's aim in life; determination to make a success in life; decision of purpose in life. **입지하다** fix one's aim in life; determine to make a success in life.
- **입지전**(-傳) the biography of a self-made

man; a success story. ¶그는 ~적 인물이다 He is a self-made man.

입질 a bite; a strike. ¶(낚시꾼이) ~을 느끼다 have[feel] a bite[strike] // 고기의 ~이 좋다 [시원찮다] The fish are biting well[badly]. // 낚싯줄에 센 ~이 왔다 I felt a tug on the line. // ~이 많이 있었다 We had a lot of bites [strikes]. / Many fish bit[took bait]. **입질하다** bite; take a bait.

입차다 [장담하다] talk big[boastfully]; talk in large terms.

입찬말 tall[big] talk; boasting; bragging. ¶~을 하는 것 같지만, 그 일을 할 수 있는 사람은 나밖에 없습니다 I may sound presumptuous [boastful], but I would say that there is no one besides myself who could do this job. // ~을 하는 것이 아니다 You shouldn't talk so big.

입찬소리 tall[big] talk. ⇨ °입찬말

입찰(入札) a bid; a tender. ¶지명[경쟁] ~ a private[public] tender // 비공개 ~ a closed bid[tender] // 최고[최저] ~ the highest [lowest] tender[bid] // ~에 부치다 (경매 입찰) sell (articles) by (public) tender / (공사 등의) invite tender / call for bids // ~을 모집하다 invite[call for] bids[tenders] (for) // 교사 건축의 ~이 있었다 Bids were invited for the construction of the school building. // 그는 그 집을 ~로 낙찰시켰다 His bid for the house was accepted. **입찰하다** bid(▶ 과거·과거 분사 모두 bid); tender; put in a tender [bid] (for).(▶ bid는 경매나 일의 하청을 위한 입찰에도 쓰이지만, tender는 일의 하청을 입찰하는 데 쓰임) ¶교량 공사를 ~ bid[tender] for a bridge construction job // 그 회사는 다른 어느 회사보다 높게[낮게] 입찰했다 The firm outbid[underbid] the others. / The firm made the highest[lowest] bid.

● **입찰 가격** the price tendered; a bidding price. **입찰 공고** a bid announcement; a notice of tender (for engineering work). **입찰 보증금** a bid bond; security (money) for a tender. **입찰자** a bidder; a tenderer.

입천장(-天障) the palate; the roof of the mouth. ¶~의 palatal / palatine // ~이 헐었다 My palate has become sore.

입체(立體) a solid (body). ¶~의 cubic / solid / three-dimensional.

● **입체감** a cubic effect. ¶~ 있는 three-dimensional (사진·영화 등의) stereoscopic // 그는 그림에 ~을 내려고 고심했었다 He worked hard to give his painting a three-dimensional effect. **입체 도형** a solid figure. **입체 영화** a three-dimensional[three-dimensioned / three-dimension] film; a 3-D[three-D] film[movie / picture].

입체적(立體的) cubic; solid; three-dimensional. ¶그의 그림은 ~이다 His pictures look three-dimensional. // 그는 사회의 구조를 ~으로 설명했었다 He explained the structure of society from all angles.

입체하다(立替-) pay (for another). ¶그가 입장료를 ~해 주었다 He paid the admission for me.

입추(立秋) [24절기의 하나] ipchu; the beginning of autumn; the first day of autumn [(미) fall] according to the lunar calendar.

입추의 여지가 없다(立錐-餘地-) be densely crowded; be filled to capacity; be packed like sardines. ¶회장은 입추의 여지도 없었다 There wasn't even standing room left in the hall.

입춘(立春) [24절기의 하나] ipchun; the beginning of spring; the first day of spring according to the lunar calendar.

입하(入荷) arrival[receipt] of goods. ¶오늘의 정어리 ~량은 30톤이다 The shipment of sardines received today was thirty tons. / Thirty tons of sardines came in today. // 비 때문에 딸기의 ~는 없었다 Because of the rain, we received no fresh supply of strawberries. **입하하다** arrive; be received.

입하(立夏) [24절기의 하나] ipha; the beginning of summer; the first day of summer according to the lunar calendar.

입학(入學) entrance into[admission to] a school; (대학의) matriculation. ¶재 ~ reentrance[readmission] into a school // ~ 준비를 하다 prepare for a school[college] // ~을 허가하다 grant admission (to). **입학하다** enter (a) school; [입학이 허가되다] be admitted to a school; (대학에) be admitted to [enter] a university. ¶내 동생은 내년에 초등학교에 입학한다 My brother enters elementary school next year.

● **입학금** an entrance[admission] fee. **입학생** a new[newly enrolled / newly registered] student. ¶금년의 대학 ~은 이십만 명이다 There are 200,000 new undergraduates this year. / (미) There are 200,000 freshmen this year. **입학시험** an entrance[admission] exam(ination). ¶대학의 ~ college entrance exams // ~을 치다 take [(영) an entrance examination] // ~에 합격하다[떨어지다] pass[fail in] an entrance examination // ~의 준비를 하다 prepare for an entrance examination // ~ 과목은 영어·수학·국어이다 The entrance examination covers English, math and Korean. **입학식** an entrance ceremony. **입학 원서** an application for admission. ¶~ 용지 an application blank[form] // 대학원에 ~를 냈다 I sent in an application for[I applied for] the graduate school. **입학 자격** requirements[qualifications] for admission.

입항(入港) arrival (of a ship) in port; entry into port. ¶배는 ~ 중이다 The ship is in (the) port. **입항하다** enter (a) port[harbor]; arrive in[come into] port. ¶배는 내일 부산에 입항할 예정이다 The ship is due at Busan tomorrow. / The ship is scheduled to make [put in at] Busan tomorrow.

● **입항선** a ship entering port. **입항세** port [harbor] dues. **입항 절차** the clearance inwards.

입향순속(入鄕循俗) ¶~하라 When you are at [in] Rome, do as Rome does[the Romans do]. / Do as they do at[in] Rome.

입헌(立憲) constitutionalization; establishment of a constitution.

● **입헌 군주국** a constitutional monarchy. **입헌 정치** constitutional government. **입헌주의** constitutionalism.

입헌적(立憲的) constitutional. ¶~으로 constitutionally // ~ 수단으로 through constitutional means.

입회(入會) admission; joining; entrance. ¶클럽에 ~를 신청하다 apply for admission to a club / apply for membership in a club // ~를 원하다 desire membership in a society // ~를

입회 허락하다 admit (a person) to membership [into a society] // 협회의 ~가 허락되다 be admitted to [enrolled in] a society / be admitted to membership in a society. **입회하다** enter; join; become a member (of a club); be admitted into an association. ¶나는 테니스 클럽에 입회했다 I have become a member of the tennis club. / I have joined the tennis club. // 누구든지 입회할 수 있다 Membership is open to all. / Everybody is welcome to join (the club).
● **입회금** an entrance [admission / enrollment / initiation] fee. ¶~을 내다 pay (for) one's footing. **입회자** a new member.

입회 (立會) [참석] presence; attendance; witnessing(증인으로서의); (감사·세무 조사의) observation. ¶증인 ~하에 in the presence of a witness // 남의 ~를 요구하다 ask for a person's presence (at). **입회하다** attend; be present (at); (증인으로서) witness; be (a) witness (to). ¶나도 선거 개표에 입회했다 I was among the witnesses at the opening of the ballot. // 그 유언장은 유족 전원이 입회한 자리에서 개봉되었다 The will was opened in the presence of all the relatives. // 부검(剖檢)에 입회하시기 바랍니다 Your presence is requested at the autopsy.
● **입회 경관** a policeman in attendance. **입회인** an observer; a witness(증인).

입후보 (立候補) (미) candidacy; (영) candidature. ¶~를 선언하다 announce [declare] one's candidacy (for) // ~를 등록[취소]하다 file [withdraw] one's candidacy // ~를 사퇴하다 withdraw one's candidacy. **입후보하다** be a candidate for; come forward as a candidate for; (미) run for (President / the Presidency); (영) stand for. ¶서울에서 run as a candidate in Seoul // 그는 국회의원에 입후보했다 He ran for the National Assembly. / (미) He ran for Congress. / (영) He stood for Parliament. // 이번 겨울의 대통령 선거에는 누가 입후보하는가 Who is going to be a candidate for President in the election this winter.
● **입후보 등록** registration of one's candidacy. **입후보자** a candidate (for).

입히다 1 [옷을 입게 하다] dress; clothe; put on [over]. ¶옷을 ~ put clothes on (a person) // 저고리를 입혀 보다 try a coat on (a person) // 어린이에게 옷을 ~ dress a child // 나는 딸을 거들어 옷을 입혔다 I helped my daughter on with [put on] her dress.
2 [물건의 거죽에 한 꺼풀 바르거나 씌우다] plate; coat; gild; (표면에) cover; veneer. ¶금을 입힌 액자 a gilded frame // 은을 입힌 (watch chain) / of plated silver / silver-plated (handle) // 고무를 입힌 rubber-coated // 주석을 ~ coat (copper) with tin / 정원에 잔디를 ~ lay the garden with turf / turf [sod] the garden // 그 메달에는 금이 입혀 있다 The medal is gold-plated.
3 [해를 주다] cause (damage to); inflict (an injury on); subject (a person)to; do (harm). ¶화를 ~ do (a person) an evil // 그는 인질에게 깊은 상처를 입혔다 He inflicted a severe injury on the hostage.

잇 [이불 등의 거죽을 싸는 피륙] a cover. ¶베갯 ~ a pillow cover / a pillowcase / 욧 ~ a mattress cover.

잇다 1 [맞붙이다] join [link] (a thing to another); piece together; put together; connect (a thing with another); combine; piece (a thing to another). ¶두 점을 잇는 직선 a (straight) line that links two points / 줄을 ~ link strings together // 파이프를 ~ join pipes (to each other) / connect pipes with a joint // 두 가닥의 실을 ~ tie two pieces of thread together // 저 독채는 복도로 몸채와 이어져 있다 The detached room is connected with [to] the main house [building] by a corridor. // 나는 두 널조각을 이었다 I joined two pieces of board together. // 나는 천조각을 이어 방석을 만들었다 I sewed pieces of cloth together and made a cushion.
2 [계속하다] continue; keep [go] on (with); carry [hold] on (with). ¶끼니를 ~ live from hand to mouth // 그는 빵과 물만으로 목숨을 이었다 He sustained himself on bread and water. // 그는 다음과 같이 말을 이었다 He continued as follow. // 그는 목청을 가다듬은 후 말을 이었다 After clearing his throat, he took up the thread of the story again. // 아직도 그의 무덤을 찾는 사람들이 줄을 잇고 있다 A lot of people still visit his grave. / There is still no end to the throng of people who visit his tomb. // 그는 유 씨에 이어 말했다. He spoke after Mr. Yu. // 폭풍우의 뒤를 이어 좋은 날씨가 계속되었다 A long spell of fine weather followed the storm. // 그의 뒤를 이어 내가 사표를 제출했다 After him, I was the next to hand in my resignation.
3 [계승하다] succeed to; carry on; inherit; take over. ¶아버지의 뒤를 ~ succeed one's father // 가업을 ~ succeed to the family business // 장남이 전 재산을 이어받았다 The eldest son inherited [succeeded to] all the property. // 엘리자베스가 메리의 뒤를 이어 여왕이 되었다 Elizabeth succeeded Mary as Queen. // 패거리의 우두머리가 죽자 누가 그 뒤를 잇는가를 둘러싸고 분쟁이 있었다 After the head of the gang died, there was trouble over who would take his place.

잇달다 [연달다] continue; keep; occur in succession; succeed one another; follow one after another. ¶잇단 참사 [비보] the successive disasters [bad news] // 잇단 가뭄 a long spell of dry weather // 잇달아 continually / successively / in succession / one after another [the other] // 10시간 잇달아 for ten hours running [at a stretch / on end / together] // 잇달아 손해보다 suffer a series of losses // 병사들은 잇달아 쓰러졌다 The soldiers fell one after another. // 뜻밖의 사건이 잇달아 발생했다 Unexpected events occurred in succession. // 나는 잇달아 불행을 당했다 I had a series [succession] of misfortunes. // 사람들이 잇달아 다방 안으로 들어왔다 People streamed [filed] into the coffeehouse in droves. // 그 시험에서는 영점이 잇달아 나왔다 There were a lot of zeros [(미국 속어) There was a whole slew of zeros] on that test. // 우리에게 잇달아 문의가 왔다 We had one inquiry after another. / We received inquiries in rapid succession. // 아이들은 잇달아 병이 났다 The children became ill one after another. // 잇달아 세 명의 손님이 왔다 I had three visitors in succession [in a row]. // 마약 밀매자 일당은 잇달아 한사람씩 체포되었다 The police arrested [(구어) pulled in] the members of the drug ring one after another.

// 요즘 항공기 사고가 잇달았다 There have been a lot of airplane accidents recently.

잇닿다 be connected; adjoin; be adjacent to. ¶(호텔의) 잇닿은 두 방 two adjacent [adjoining] rooms // 거실은 침실에 잇닿아 있다 The sitting room comes onto a bedroom. // 그 공원은 강가로 잇닿아 있다 The park reaches [stretches] down to the river.

잇대다 [연결하다] join; link; connect; couple; attach; put together; piece up [together]; patch together. ¶두 책상을 ~ put two tables together // 기관차를 객차에 ~ couple a locomotive with passenger cars // 거리에는 작은 집들이 잇대어 있다 The street is lined with small houses.

잇따르다 occur in succession; follow one after another. ¶잇따라 in succession / one after another [the other (둘인 경우)] // 잇따라 다섯 번 이기다 win five consecutive victories // 잇따라 한 선생의 말씀이 있겠습니다 Next Mr. Han will speak to you. // 전쟁 뉴스가 잇따라 들어왔다 News items about the war came in rapid succession. // 그 집안은 잇따라 불행을 겪었다 The family was hit by one misfortune after another. / One misfortune visited the family on the heels of the last. // 외국 원수가 5명이나 잇따라 서울을 방문했다 Five foreign heads of state visited Seoul one right after another [in rapid succession].

잇몸 the gum(s); the teethridge; the gingiva (pl. -vae). ¶~의 종기 a gumboil / a small abscess on the gum // ~을 드러내고 웃다 (show one's teeth and) grin.

잇새 gaps in the [one's] teeth. ¶~에 낀 음식을 제거하다 remove bits of food lodged [from] between the teeth // ~가 떴다 His teeth are loose. // ~에 고기가 끼었다 I got a shred of meat stuck between my teeth.

잇소리 [언] a dental sound [consonant].

잇수 [치수] the pulp of teeth; [치형] the shape of teeth. ¶~이 좋다 [나쁘다] have a good [bad] set of teeth / have a regular [an irregular] set of teeth.

잇속 (利-) (a) profit; (a) gain; (이기적인) self-interest. ¶~이 있는 장사 a profitable [paying] business / ~이 없는 unprofitable / gainless // ~을 차리다 make a profit // 그는 ~에 밝다 He has a quick eye for profits. / (미국 구어) He's always trying to make a profit. // 그는 항상 자기 ~만 차린다 He always puts self first. / He is always self-centered [selfish].

잇자국 a toothprint; a teethmark. ¶~이 나다 have a toothprint.

있다¹ **1** [위치하다] be; be situated; (미) be located; stand (건물 등이); lie (도시 등이); run (산맥·강이). ¶강가에 있는 절 a temple standing by the river // 한국은 중국의 동쪽에 ~ Korea lies to the east of China. // 그 도시는 서울의 북서쪽에 ~ The town lies to the northwest of Seoul. // 꽃병이 탁자 위에 ~ The vase is on the table. // 우리 학교는 서울의 교외에 ~ Our school is [is situated / is located] in the suburbs of Seoul. // 강 건너편에 목장이 있었다 There was a pasture on the other side of the river. // 이 마을에는 성터가 있다 This village contains the ruins of a castle.

2 [존재하다] there is [are]; be; exist; be in existence; [발견되다] be found. ¶책상 위에 책이 한 권 ~ There is a book on the desk. // 그 책은 책상 위에 ~ The book is on the desk. // 우리에 소가 세 마리 ~ There are three cows in the shed. // 너는 귀신이 정말로 있다고 생각하니 Do you really think ghosts exist? // 한국의 산에는 곰이 ~ Bears live [are found] in the mountains of Korea. // 이 호수에는 물고기가 많이 ~ This lake is full of [abounds in] fish. // 그녀의 도움이 오늘의 그를 있게 했다 Thanks [Owing] to her help he has become what he is today. / He owes what he is today to her. // 광주리 안에 사과가 몇 개 ~ There are some apples in the basket. // 그것은 지금도 ~ It is still in existence. // 원래 있던 곳에 갖다 두어라 Put it back where it was [where you found it]. // 카페인은 커피나 차에도 ~ Caffeine is found in coffee and tea.

3 [발생하다] happen; occur; take place; break out. ¶사고가 있었던 곳 the scene of a disaster // 어젯밤에 바로 저 교차로에서 교통사고가 2건 있었다 Two road accidents happened [occurred] at the crossing near here last night. // 무슨 일이 있어도 당황하면 안 된다 You must not be upset whatever may happen. // 어제 강한 지진이 있었다 A severe earthquake was felt yesterday. // 간밤에 화재가 있었다 A fire broke out last night. // 그 부부 사이에 무슨 일이 있었는지 나는 모르겠다 I don't know what has passed between that couple. // 뉴스는 9시에 ~ The news comes on [There is a news bulletin] at nine. // 정직한 것이 손해인 때가 더러 ~ It often happens that honesty does not pay.

4 [열리다·행해지다] be held; take place. ¶우리 시험은 3월에 ~ We have examinations in March. / Examinations take place in March. // 올림픽 경기는 4년마다 한 번 ~ The Olympic Games are held every fourth year [every four years]. // 그 모임은 언제 있습니까 When is the meeting to be held? // 수업은 5시까지 ~ We have school until 5 o'clock.

5 [거주하다] live; dwell; reside; [머무르다] stay; remain. ¶나는 1주일 가량 친구 집에 있었다 I stayed with a friend of for a week or so. // 이 방은 너무 무더워서 있을 수가 없다 This room is so sultry that I can't possibly remain here. // 최 군 있습니까 Is (Mr.) Choe there [in]? // 그는 1주일 동안 있을 예정으로 부산에 도착했다 He arrived in Busan on [for] a week's visit. // 그것은 내가 파리에 있을 때의 일이었다 It happened during my stay [while I was staying] in Paris. // 좀 더 여기 있어라 Stay here a bit longer. // 한국에는 얼마나 오래 있을 예정이지 How long do you intend to stay in Korea?

6 [근무하다] serve; work. ¶우리 집 아이는 보험 회사에 ~ My son is in [with] an insurance company. // 왜 그런지 그는 어떤 직장에나 오래 있지 못한다 Somehow he is unable to hold down any job for long. // 내가 있는 회사는 봉급이 괜찮다 Our company pays good salaries.

7 [소유하다] have; possess; own; [부여받고 있다] be endowed [gifted] with. ¶재산이 ~ be rich / be wealthy // 있는 힘을 다 내다 put forth all one's strength // 그에게는 돈과 시간이 ~ He has money and time to spare. // 그는 시골에 농장이 ~ He has [owns] a farm in

있다

the country.∥우리에게는 투표권이 ~ We have the right to vote.∥그에게는 천부의 재능이 ~ He has[is endowed with] natural gifts.∥그에게는 그 일을 할 수 있는 충분한 자격이 ~ He is fully qualified to do the work.∥그는 그 일을 할 every qualification for the work.∥그녀에게는 손자가 여섯 명 ~ She has six grandchildren.∥그는 있는 힘을 다하여 잡아당겼다 He pulled at it with all his might[strength].

8 [부유하다] be rich[wealthy]; be well-off [well-to-do]. ¶있는 나라와 없는 나라 haves and have-nots∥그녀는 있는 집안에 태어났다 She was born rich[with a silver spoon in her mouth]. / She was born into a wealthy family.∥그는 있는 집안에서 자라났다 He was brought up a rich[wealthy / well-to-do] family.

9 [경과하다] pass by[away]; go by; elapse. ¶그는 1시간만 있으면 돌아옵니다 He will be back in an hour('s time).∥2, 3년만 있으면 만사가 잘될 것이다 A few years more[out], and everything will be all right.

10 [부속되어 있다] have (a thing) attached to (it); (설비가) be equipped[fitted / provided] with. ¶최근에 항공기에는 라운지와 침대가 있다 Airplane nowadays are equipped with lounges and berths.∥우리 학교에는 기숙사가 ~ Our school has a dormitory attached to it.

11 [포함되어 있다] be contained; be included. ¶그들 중에는 3명의 여성도 있었다 Three women were included among them.∥이 책에는 재미있는 이야기가 많이 ~ This book contains many interesting stories.

12 [입수되다] be got; be had. ¶저 가게에는 담배가 있습니까 Do they sell cigarettes at that store?∥그것은 백화점에 ~ It can be got at a department store. / You can get it at the stores.∥이것은 아무 데나 있는 물건이 아니다 This article is of no ordinary type.

13 (경험이). ¶거기에 가 본 일이 있니 Did you ever visit the place? / Have you ever been there?∥설악산에 두 번 오른 적이 ~ I have climbed Seoraksan(Mt. Seorak) twice.∥나는 자주 무서운 꿈을 꾸는 수가 ~ I often have frightening dreams.∥그는 이 고장에 여러 번 와 본 적이 ~ He has been to this town several times.

14 […에 있다] consist (in); lie (in); […에 달리다] depend (on). ¶이 사전의 장점은 사용하기 편한 데 ~ The strong point of this dictionary lies[consists] in the ease with which it can be used.∥그 시의 매력은 형용사의 사용법에 ~ The charm of this poem consists in its use of adjective.∥행복은 만족에 ~ Happiness consists in contentment.

15 [자체에 지니거나 가지다] have; cherish; conceive. ¶실력이 ~ have real capacity∥바람기가 ~ be an unfaithful wife[husband] / play with love∥배 속에 아이가 ~ be (big) with child / be pregnant∥마음속에 비밀이 ~ cherish the secret∥누구에게나 양심은 ~ Everyone has a conscience.

16 [가능하다] can; be able to (do); be capable of. ¶그녀는 프랑스 어를 말할 수 ~ She can speak French.∥이 엘리베이터는 30명이 탈 수 ~ This elevator can carry[is capable of carrying] 30 people.∥나는 학생 때 100미터를 11초에 달릴 수 있었다 I could [was able to] run 100 meters in 11 second, when I was in school.

17 (관하여). ¶…에 있어서 in … / as for … / as to … / as regards … / in point of … / in the matter of …∥이 경우에 있어서 in this case∥학력에 있어서는 그보다 낫다 As for [to] academic background, I am ahead of him.(▶ as for는 문두에만 씀)∥그 물품은 질에 있어서 떨어진다 The goods are inferior in quality.

있다² [상태의 계속] be; go; keep; remain; [동작의 계속] be doing. ¶보고 ~ keep watching∥울고만 ~ keep crying / do nothing but cry∥먹지 않고 ~ go without food∥일을 하고 ~ be working / be at work∥그들은 야구를 하고 ~ They are playing baseball.∥그는 의학을 연구하고 ~ He does medical research.∥지금 그는 일을 하고[놀고] ~ He is working[playing] now.∥He is at work [play] now.∥문은 닫혀 ~ The door is shut.∥자네는 무슨 신문을 구독하고 있는가 What newspaper do you subscribe to[take]?∥우리는 언제나 갖추어져 ~ We're ready.∥그는 이 근처에서 살고 ~ He lives near here.∥그는 언제나 불평만 늘어놓고 ~ He is always complaining of something.

잉꼬 [동] a parakeet.
잉어 [동] a carp (pl. ~, ~s).
잉여 (剩餘) **1** [쓰고 난 나머지] a surplus; an overplus; the remainder; [잔액] a balance. ¶이 나라는 작년에 3만 톤의 농산물의 ~가 생겼다 Last year this country had a surplus of thirty thousand tons of agricultural produce. **2** [수] ➡나머지3
● **잉여 가치** [경] surplus value. **잉여금** a surplus (fund); balance in hand.

잉잉 with whimpers. ¶~ 울다 whimper / blubber. **잉잉하다** buzz; hum. ⇨잉잉거리다
잉잉거리다 buzz; hum; make a humming sound; drone. ¶전깃줄이 바람에 잉잉거렸다 The wind set up a humming in the wires.∥모기 한 마리가 귓가에서 잉잉거렸다 A mosquito buzzed about my ear.

잉카 Inca. ¶~의 Incan / Incaic.
● **잉카 문명** the Incan Civilization. **잉카 제국** the Incaic Empire.

잉크 ink. ¶~ 묻은 손가락 inky fingers∥만년필용 ~ ink for the fountain pen∥활판[동사/인쇄] ~ typographic [copying / printing] ink∥빨간[검은] ~ red[black] ink∥~로 쓰다 write in ink∥펜과 ~로 쓰다 write with pen and ink∥손가락에 ~를 묻히다 get ink on one's fingers∥~를 흘리다 spill ink.
● **잉크병** an ink bottle; an inkpot. **잉크스탠드** an inkstand.

잉태 (孕胎) conception; pregnancy. **잉태하다** get[become] pregnant (with child); (구어) get in the[a] family way.

잊다 1 [망각하다] forget; be forgetful (of); (일을) slip one's mind; escape[slip] one's memory. ¶그녀의 전화번호를 잊었다 I forget [have forgotten] her phone number.(▶ forget은 당장은 생각이 나지 않는 경우, forgotten은 완전히 잊어버린 경우를 말함)∥오늘 약속이 있는 것을 잊고 있었다 I forget that I had an appointment today.(▶ forget that은 that절의 내용을 잊고 있었던 것을 지금 생각이 났다는 뜻)∥그녀를 만난 일이 있는 것을 잊었니 Have you forgotten[Don't you remember] meeting her?(▶ 과거에 있었던 일

잊었다는 뜻으로는 이와 같이 동명사를 씀) ∥서류를 제출할 것을 깜박 잊었다 I carelessly forgot to hand in the papers.(▶ forget to do는「잊었기 때문에 하지 않았다」의 뜻)∥잊지 말고 부모에게 편지를 써 보내라 Remember[Don't forget] to write to your parents.∥나는 그것을 까맣게 잊고 있었다 It had entirely slipped my mind. / It entirely escaped my memory.∥이 일을 잠시도 잊지 마라 Always keep[bear] this in mind.∥숙제를 잊지 마라 Don't neglect your homework.∥그것은 잊을 수 없는 추억이 되었다 It has become a lasting memory.∥그것은 잊을 수 없는 사건이었다 It was a memorable[an unforgettable] event.∥이 은혜는 결코 잊지 않겠습니다 I will never forget your kindness to me.∥당신을 영원히 잊지 않겠습니다 You are ever in my mind[thoughts].
2 〔깨닫지 못하다〕 do not mind[notice]; be unaware of; forget. ¶추위를 ~ forget the cold∥독서에 열중하다 보니 시간이 가는 것도 잊고 있었다 I was so absorbed in my book that I had forgotten all about the time.∥그는 침식을 잊고 연구에 몰두했다 He devoted [buried] himself to his research.∥그는 더위를 잊고 공부했다 He was too absorbed in study to mind heat.
3 〔단념하고 생각을 하지 않다〕 dismiss (a thing) from one's mind; think no more of; put (a thing) out of one's mind. ¶그녀는 술로 시름을 잊으려고 했다 She tried to drown her worries in drink.∥일을 하면 슬픔을 잊을 수 있습니다 I can forget my sorrow[grief] when I am working.∥이 원한은 죽어도 못 잊겠다 I shall carry the resentment to the grave.∥그녀는 슬픔을 잊은 듯했다 She looks as if she has got over her grief.
4 〔두고 오다〕 leave (something) behind; forget (something); 〔잊고 가져오지 않다〕 forget to bring[take] (something). ¶역에다 가방을 깜박 잊고 왔다 I have left my bag at the station.(▶ 장소를 나타내는 부사(구)가 있으면 leave를 씀)∥짐을 잊고 오는 일이 없도록 하라 Don't forget your baggage. / Don't leave your baggage behind.∥카메라를 (어딘가에) 깜박 잊고 왔다 I have mislaid my camera (somewhere).∥열차에 우산을 깜박 잊고 왔다 I left my umbrella in the train. / I forgot my umbrella when I got off the train.∥내리실 때는 잊으시는 물건이 없도록 하십시오 Don't forget anything when you leave the train.

잊어버리다 〔모두 잊다·아주 잊다〕 entirely [completely] forget. ¶그 일은 이제 잊어버려라 Dismiss the matter from your mind.

잊히다 be forgotten; pass out of mind[one's memory]. ¶잊히지 않는 일 a memorable[an unforgettable] event∥세상에서 ~ be sunk [lost] in oblivion / die from the memory of the world∥그녀가 잊히지 않았다 She was always on my mind.∥그는 곧 세상에서 잊혀졌다 He was soon forgotten. / In time he sank into oblivion.∥그 문명은 세상에서 잊혀졌다 The civilization was forgotten (by the world). / The civilization passed[sank] into oblivion.

잎 a leaf (*pl*. leaves); a needle(침엽); (풀의) a blade; (양치 등의) a frond; 〔집합적〕 foliage. ¶무성한 ~ thick foliage∥**나뭇**~ leaves of the tree∥풀~ blades of grass∥~이 우거진 leafy∥병든 ~ diseased[blighted] leaves∥~의 겉면[뒷면] the upper[under] surface of a leaf∥~이 없는 leafless / bare∥~이 무성한 가지 a leafy branch∥~이 보기 좋은 나무 a tree with handsome foliage∥~이 질 무렵 the fall of the leaf∥~**이 나오다** come into leaf∥~**이 떨어지다** become leafless∥느릅나무는 지금 ~이 나오고 있다 The elms are now in leaf.∥벼의 ~이 10센티미터 자랐다 The rice blades are ten centimeters high.∥~이 피었다 The leaves are out.

잎나무 brushwood.
잎담배 leaf tobacco.
잎맥(-脈) 〔식〕 the veins (of a leaf).
잎사귀 a leaf; a leaflet.
잎자루 〔식〕 a leafstalk; a petiole.
잎줄기 〔식〕 a cladophyll; a phylloclade; phyllocladium.

ㅈ

자[1] [길이·높이를 재는 기구] a ruler; a rule; [측정기] a measure. ¶T~ a T-square // 삼각(ㅁ)~ a triangle / [영]~ a set square / 운형[곡선]~ a French curve // 미터~ a meter measure[rule] // 야드~ a yardstick / a yard measure // ~로 잰 듯이 as precisely as a square / like clockwork // ~를 대고 선을 긋다 draw a line with a ruler // 판자의 길이를 ~로 쟀다 I measured[took the measurements of] the board with a ruler[rule]. **2** [길이의 단위] a ja; a foot. ¶한 ~에 얼마로 팔다[사다] sell [buy] (a thing) by the ja[foot] // 이 옷감은 꼭 다섯 ~다 This cloth measures five ja exactly.

자[2] [행동을 재촉할 때 내는 소리] come on; come now; come; now (then); well (now); [달랠 때의 소리] there; please; pray. ¶~, 안으로 들어가자 Come on, let's go in. // ~, 이제 슬슬 떠날 준비를 해 볼까 Now then, shall we get ready to leave[go]? / ~, 이제 한숨 돌리는 게 어때요 Well, how about taking a break now? // ~, 조용히 해 주세요 Now, be quiet, please. // ~, 이것 잡아 Here, catch it! // ~, 간다 Here goes! / ~ ~ 진정하시오 Come, come, calm[compose] yourself.

-자 1 [권유] let (us); let's. ¶기다려 보~ Let's wait and see. // 어디 보~ Let's see now.
2 [···을 하는 것과 동시에] as soon as; no sooner ... than ...; hardly[scarcely] ... when ...; the moment[instant] .... ¶나는 호텔에 도착하~ 곧 그에게 전화했다 I telephoned him as soon as I arrived at the hotel. // 그 청년은 내 모습을 보~ 달아났다 No sooner had the young man caught sight of me than he ran away. // 방에 한 발짝 들어서~ 악취에 숨이 막혔다 The moment I stepped into the room, I was choked by a foul odor. // 홍 군이 나가~ 최 군이 들어왔다 As soon as Hong went out, Choe came in. / Choe came in just as Hong was leaving[left]. // 숲을 지나~ 넓은 목장이 나타났다 Beyond the forest there was a large pasture.
3 [어떤 자격과 함께 다른 자격이 있음] and. ¶그는 배우이~ 감독이다 He is an actor and (a) director.

자(子) **1** [자식] a son; a child. **2** [공자] Confucius. ¶~ 왈 Confucius says ....

자(字) **1** [글자] a character; [표음 문자] a letter(a, b, c 등); [표의 문자] an ideograph(한자 등). ¶한~ a Chinese character // 200~ 원고지 manuscript paper with squares for two hundred characters // 영어의 에이 ~도 모르다 do not know a word of English. **2** [낱말] a word. ¶도착하거든 몇 ~ 적어 보내 주게 Drop me a line[a few lines] when you get there. **3** [본이름 외에 부르는 이름] a name received upon reaching adulthood.

자(者) a person; one; a fellow; a guy. ¶어리석은 ~ a fool / a simpleton / an ass // 민이란 ~ one[a] Min / a man named Min // 가난한 ~는 복이 있도다 Those who are poor shall be blessed. // 학식이 적은 ~는 말이 많다 Who knows little says much.

자가(自家) one's own house; [자기] (one's) self. ¶~ 재배의 home-grown / (tomatoes) of one's own growing.

● **자가당착** self-contradiction. ¶~의 self-contradictory // ~에 빠지다 contradict oneself // 잘 설명하려 했으나 그는 ~에 빠지고 말았다 He contradicted himself in spite of his efforts to explain well. **자가발전 장치** a private electric generator; a power plant of one's own. **자가 수정**(-受精) self-fertilization; autogamy.

자가용(自家用) **1** [개인용·가정용]. ¶~의 for private use / for home consumption / private / personal // 수확한 쌀의 절반은 ~입니다 Half of the crop of rice is for home[our own] consumption. **2** [자가용 차] a privately-owned car; an owner-driven car; one's own car. ¶~으로 부산까지 갔다 I went to Busan in my own car.

자각(自覺) (self-)awareness; (self-)consciousness; (self-)awakening. ¶그들은 자기 책임에 대한 ~이 없었다 They didn't realize[were unaware of / were not conscious of] the responsibilities that lay upon them. **자각하다** be conscious[aware] of (one's duty); realize; awake (to). ¶그는 교장으로서의 책임을 자각하고 있다 He is fully aware [conscious] of his responsibility as principal. // 나라의 대표라는 것을 자각하기 바란다 I'd like you to realize that you are representing our country (and behave accordingly). ➔ 죄를 자각시키다 wake[awake] (a person) to a sense of sin.

● **자각 증상** subjective symptoms.

자간(子癇) [의] eclampsia. ¶~의 eclamptic.
자간(字間) the space between letters. ¶~을 좀 더 떼시오 Leave a little more space between the letters.

자갈 gravel; (small) pebbles; shingle(해안 등의). ¶~의[이 많은] gravelly // 도로에 ~을 깔다 gravel a road / lay[cover] a road with gravel.

● **자갈길** a gravel road[path]; (공원·정원 등의) a gravel walk. **자갈밭** a gravelly [stony] place[field].

자갈색(紫褐色) purplish brown.
자개 jagae; (a lamina of) mother-of-pearl [nacre]. ¶~를 박다 inlay (a cabinet) with mother-of-pearl.

● **자개그릇** a wooden vessel inlaid with mother-of-pearl. **자개 세공** (an article of) mother-of-pearl work.

자객(刺客) an assassin; a killer. ¶~의 손에 쓰러지다 fall (a) victim to an assassin / be assassinated.

자격(資格) **1** [일정한 신분·지위] capacity; [권리] a right. ¶그는 무슨 ~으로 회의에 참석했지 In what capacity did he attend the meeting? // 그는 대표의 ~으로 답변했다 He replied in his capacity as delegate. // 국민

모두 법률의 보호를 받을 ~이 있다 Every citizen has the right to enjoy the protection of the law. **2** [어떤 신분·지위에 반드시 필요한 조건] qualification(s); [증명] certification; a license; (영) a licence; [능력] competence; capability. ¶유[무]~자 a qualified [an unqualified] person // 선거~ qualifications for an elector / the elective franchise / 피선거~ eligibility // ~을 부여하다 grant (a person) qualification [certification] (as) / certify (a person as) / qualify (a person as [to do]) // ~을 박탈하다 strip (a person) of his qualification [certification] (as) / disqualify (a person from) // 그는 변호사 ~을 땄다 He qualified [obtained certification] as a lawyer. // 그는 교장으로서의 ~이 없다 He is incompetent as a principal. // 나는 영어를 가르칠 ~을 갖고 있다 I am qualified [I have a license] to teach English. // 그는 그 연구회의 회원이 될 ~이 있다 He has the qualifications [is eligible] for membership in [(영) of] the study group. // 그가 대통령이 될 ~이 있는지 의심스럽다 His eligibility for the presidency is doubtful.
● **자격 상실** disqualification. **자격시험** a screening [qualifying] examination. **자격증** a certificate of qualifications.

자격지심 (自激之心) (a feeling of) self-reproach [-accusation / -reproof / -condemnation]; a guilty conscience. ¶그것은 ~에서 나온 말이다 He said that out of self-accusation.

자결 (自決) **1** [자기가 결정함] self-determination. ¶민족 ~주의 the principle of racial self-determination. **자결하다** determine by [for] oneself. **2** [스스로 목숨을 끊음] suicide. **자결하다** kill oneself; commit suicide.

자경단 (自警團) (미) a vigilance committee; a vigilante corps (▶ 이에 해당하는 것이 영국에는 없음).

자계 (磁界) [물] a magnetic field. ⇨ **자기장** (⇨ 자기(磁氣))

자고 (鷓鴣) [동] a partridge.

자고로 (自古-) from old(en) [ancient] times; from remote ages; from of old; from time immemorial; since early times; traditionally. ¶~ 한국인은 흰옷을 즐겨 입는다 Koreans traditionally prefer to wear white clothes.

자괴지심 (自愧之心) a sense of shame. ¶~이 있다 have [feel] a sense of shame / be sensible to shame // ~이 없다 have no sense of [be quite without] shame.

자구 (字句) [문자와 어구] words and phrases; [표현] expression; wording. ¶~상의 잘못 mistakes in words and phrases // ~의 해석 the interpretation of words and phrases // ~대로의 [에 구애받지 않는] 번역 (a) literal [free] translation // ~를 **수정하다** make some changes in the wording // 이 문장은 ~대로 해석해서는 안 된다 You should not take [interpret] this sentence literally.

자구 행위 (自救行爲) [법] self-help.

자국 1 [닿은 자리] a mark; a print; an imprint; an impression; [더럼] a stain. ¶손가락 ~ a finger mark / a finger print / 신발 ~ the print of shoes / 핏~ a bloodstain / 잉크 ~ an inkstain / 눈물 ~이 있는 얼굴 a tear-stained [-streaked] face // ~을 **남기다** [~이 남다] leave a mark (on).
2 [발자국] a footprint; a footmark; [지나간 자리] a track; a trail. ¶차가 지나간 ~ the trace [track] of a car // 소가 지나간 ~ cow tracks / tracks of a cow.
3 [흔적] a mark; a trace; a stamp; a sign; a vestige; a scar (상처의); a wale [weal] (매로 때린). ¶우두 ~ a vaccination scar // 이빨 ~ tooth marks / 긁힌 ~ a scratch / 물린 ~ a bite / a mark made by biting // 모기에 물린 ~ a mosquito bite.

자국 (自國) [자기 나라] one's own country; [고국] one's native land; one's homeland; one's motherland. ¶~ 제품의 homemade.
● **자국인** one's fellow countrymen.

자궁 (子宮) [생] the womb; the uterus (pl. -ri).
● **자궁병** a uterine disease. **자궁암** uterine cancer. **자궁염** metritis. **자궁 외 임신** extrauterine pregnancy; ectopic pregnancy.

자귀 [나무를 깎아 다듬는 연장] an adz(e).
● **자귀질** adzing. ¶~을 하다 adz(e).

자귀나무 [식] a silk tree.

자그마치 1 [자그마하게] somewhat small [little]; in a smallish way. ¶농담도 ~ 하시오 Don't carry your joke too far. **2** [적지 않게] not a little; no less [fewer] than; as much [many] as. ¶그는 ~ 3천 권의 책을 가지고 있다 He has fewer than [no less than / as many as] three thousand books. // 빚이 ~ 천만 원에 이르렀다 The debt reached a surprising amount of ten million won.

자그마하다 smallish; tiny; somewhat [rather] small [little]; of a somewhat small size; small-sized. ¶키가 자그마한 사내 a man short(ish) in stature [height] / a short(ish) [little] man / 몸집이 자그마한 여성 a woman of small stature [build] // 자그마한 꽃무늬가 있는 블라우스 a blouse with a pattern of small flowers.

자그맣다 smallish; tiny. ⇨ **자그마하다**

자극 (刺戟) **1** [감각 기관에 대한 작용] a stimulus (pl. -li); stimulation; [따끔따끔하거나 얼얼한 느낌] irritation. **자극하다** stimulate; irritate. ¶포도주가 식욕을 자극했다 Wine stimulated my appetite. // 강렬한 햇빛은 눈을 자극한다 Strong sunlight irritates the eyes. // 이 생선은 혀를 자극하는 듯한 맛이 있다 This fish has a sharp taste. // 그녀의 새된 목소리는 그의 신경을 자극했다 Her shrill voice got on his nerves.
2 [마음에 작용함] stimulation; [자극을 일으키는 것] a stimulus; an nerves; [유인] an incentive; [고무하는 것] a spur. ¶~이 없는 dull / boring / monotonous // 그의 성공이 내가 공부하는 데 ~이 되었다 His success served as the stimulus [incentive] for my study. // 형의 성공으로 ~을 받아 그도 더욱 노력했다 His brother's success spurred [incited] him to greater effort. // 그는 오토바이에서 ~을 찾았다 He sought excitement [thrills] in riding a motorcycle. // 그는 ~이 없는 생활을 하고 있다 He is leading a dull [monotonous / boring] life. **자극하다** stimulate; spur; give an impulse (to); give [provide] an impetus [a stimulus] (to); excite; stir up. ¶그는 화를 잘 내니까 자극하지 마라 Don't excite him, he is touchy. // 그것은 상대국의 감정을 자극했다 It antagonized the other nation. // 그는 나를 자극해 죄를 범하게 했다 He put me up to [incited me to commit] a crime. / (계략적으로) He

자극

tricked me into committing a crime. ¶그 음악가의 망명에 자극되어 많은 지식인들이 외국으로 망명했다 Stimulated by the musician's defection, many intellectuals sought refuge in other countries.
* **자극 요법** stimulation therapy. **자극제** a stimulant; an irritant; an excitant.

자극(磁極) [물] a magnetic pole. ⇨자기극(⇨자기(磁氣))

자극적(刺戟的) [자극을 주는] stimulative; [두근거리게 하는] thrilling; [선정적인] sensational; [도발적인] provocative. ¶~인 영화 sensational movie∥~인 태도로 in provocative manner.

자금(資金) funds; a fund; (a) capital. ¶운동 ~ a campaign fund∥구제 ~ a relief fund∥사업 ~ an enterprising fund∥선거 ~ an election campaign fund / electoral funds∥운전[준비 / 회전] ~ working[reserve / revolving] funds∥정치 ~ money for political activities / political funds[contributions]∥풍부한 ~ ample funds∥~이 있다 have funds / be in funds∥~이 떨어지다 be out of funds∥~이 풍부[부족]하다 have ample[be short of] funds∥운동~을 조달하다 raise campaign funds∥~을 마련하려고 동분서주하다 busy oneself in searching for funds / go around trying to raise money∥~을 회전시키다 turn money∥~을 융통해 주다 accommodate (a person) with money∥~ 출처를 조사하다 probe into the sources of money∥그의 백부가 그에게 ~을 대 주었다 His uncle furnished[provided] funds for him. / His uncle funded[financed] him.∥이 회사는 지금 ~에 쪼들리고 있다 This company is now pressed for[short of] money.
* **자금난** financial difficulty; stringency of capital; lack of funds. ¶새 도서관 건설 계획은 ~으로 중단 상태에 있다 The planning for the new library building has come to a stop because of financial difficulties[for lack of funds]. **자금 동결** freezing of funds. **자금 압박** the financial strains. **자금 조달** fund raising; financing. ¶~이 어렵다 have difficulty[a hard time] raising funds∥그는 ~의 수완이 좋다 He is a good fund-raiser.

자급(自給) self-support; self-sustenance. **자급하다** support oneself; provide for oneself; make one's own supply. ¶자급하는 self-supporting[-supplying] / self-sustained[-sustaining].
* **자급자족** self-sufficiency; self-sufficing. ¶~의 self-sufficient[-sufficing / -sustaining / -contained]∥경제적 ~ economic self-sufficiency / autarky∥이 나라는 식량을 ~하고 있다 This country is self-sufficient in food [able to feed itself].

자긍(自矜) [자만] self-conceit; self-importance; [긍지] pride; dignity; self-respect. **자긍하다** [자만하다] be conceited; [선정적인] flatter [fancy] oneself; [긍지를 가지다] pride oneself (on); have (one's) pride.

자기(自己) (one's) self; oneself. ¶~ 스스로 oneself / personally / by[for] oneself / single-handed∥~ 생각만 하다 think only of oneself∥~ 마음대로 하다 do as one pleases [likes]∥~ 자신을 알다 know oneself∥~의 이익만을 생각하다 think only of[look only to] one's own interests∥~을 돌아보다 reflect on oneself∥그는 ~밖에 모른다 He

thinks only of himself. / He is self-centered [full of himself]. / He is a selfish devil.∥~일은 ~가 돌봐야 한다 We must mind our own business.∥~ 일은 ~가 해라 Look after yourself.
자기 얼굴에 침 뱉기(속담) disgrace oneself.
* **자기 과시** self-display. **자기기만** self-deception. **자기도취** self-absorption; narcissism; (구어) an ego trip. **자기만족** self-contentment[-satisfaction / -complacency]. **자기~의** self-satisfied / complacent∥~을 하다 satisfy[gratify / content] oneself / be complacent∥그런 것으로 ~을 해서는 안 된다 You should not be satisfied with such a thing. **자기모순** self-contradiction. **자기반성** self-reflection. **자기 부정** self-denial. **자기비판** (a) self-criticism. **자기소개** self-introduction. ¶~를 하다 introduce oneself (to)∥여러분 ~를 해 주세요 Everybody, please introduce yourselves. **자기 암시** autosuggestion. ¶~에 걸리다 be subject to autosuggestion. **자기앞 수표** a cashier's check; a bank [banker's] check. **자기애** self-love. **자기주장** self-assertion. **자기중심** egocentricity. ¶~적인 egocentric / self-centered / selfish∥그는 ~주의다 His motto is "self first". **자기 최면** autohypnotism; autohypnosis; self-induced hypnotism. ¶~에 걸리다 become autohypnotic / subject oneself to hypnotism. **자기혐오** self-hate; self-hatred. ¶그는 ~에 빠져 헤어나지를 못하고 있다 He is sunk hopelessly in self-hatred.

자기(自記) 1 [스스로 기록함] writing by oneself. **자기하다** write by oneself. 2 [기계의 자동 기록] self-register. **자기하다** register automatically.
* **자기 온도계**[우량계] a self-registering thermometer[rain gauge].

자기(瓷器·磁器) porcelain. ⇨사기그릇(⇨사기(沙器)) ¶고려 ~ Goryeo ceramics[pottery / porcelain].

자기(磁氣) [물] magnetism. ¶유도[감응] ~ induced magnetism∥잔류 ~ residual magnetism∥지 ~ terrestrial magnetism∥~의 magnetic∥~를 띠게 하다 magnetize∥~를 띠다 become magnetized∥~를 없애다 demagnetize
* **자기극** [물] a magnetic pole. **자기 나침반** a magnetic compass. **자기 디스크** [컴] a magnetic disc. **자기력** magnetic force; magnetism. **자기 유도 / 자기감응** magnetic induction. **자기장** [물] a magnetic field. ¶~의 강도[방향] the strength[direction] of a magnetic field. **자기 테이프** [컴] a magnetic tape. **자기 폭풍** a magnetic storm. **자기학** magnetics.

자꾸 [잇달아] frequently; repeatedly; again and again; [끊임없이] incessantly; constantly; [열심히] eagerly; intently; strongly. ¶~ 생각하다 think hard[intently]∥~ 권하다 strongly urge (a person to do)∥그녀는 새 옷을 ~ 맞춘다 She has new dresses made one after another.∥매상이 ~~ 늘어났다 Our sales rose steadily and rapidly).∥머리가 ~ 아팠다 My head kept aching.

-자꾸나 let us; let's; how about[shall we] ...? ¶한잔 하~ Let's have a drink, shall we? / How[What] about a drink?

자낭(子囊) [식] an ascus (pl. -ci).
* **자낭균** an ascomycete; a sac fungus.

자네 you; old boy(호칭). ¶~들 you fellows

[people / chaps] ～ 이것 잠깐 빌려 주게 Hey, old buddy, can I borrow this for a minute?

자녀(子女) sons and daughters; children; offspring. ¶～ 교육 the education of one's children/양가의 ～ boys and girls from good families / young men and women of respectable families/그들은 양가의 ～들이다 They come of a good family[a gentle birth].

자다 1 〔잠자다〕 sleep; 〔잠들다〕 go[get] to sleep; fall asleep. 〔낮잠을 ～ take [have] a nap/한숨 못 ～ do not sleep a wink/세상 모르고 ～ sleep like a log [top]//옷을 입은 채 ～ sleep with one's clothes on/자리 가다 to bed//자지 않고 있다 sit[stay] up (till late at night) / keep vigil//자지 않고 간호하다 sit up with (a patient) / attend on (a sick person) all through the night / watch with (an invalid)//밤늦도록 자지 않고 공부하다 burn the midnight oil//일찍[늦게] 자고 일찍 [늦게] 일어나다 keep early[late] hours/아직 안 자니 Are you still up?//그는 아직 자고 있다 He's still in bed. / He's still sleeping.//이제 잘 시간이다 It's time (for you) to go to bed now. / It's time that you went to bed.//어젯밤은 잘 잤니 Did you sleep well last night? / Did you have a good sleep last night?//늦게까지 안 자면 내일 아침 일찍 못 일어날 거다 If you stay up late, you will not be able to get up early tomorrow morning.//그의 제의를 받아들일 것인지 하룻밤 자면서 잘 생각해 보아라 Sleep on the question of whether to accept his offer or not.//푹 자라 Sleep well [soundly].//아주 푹 잘 잤다 I slept like a dog[baby]. / I slept very soundly.//하루 이틀 자지 않는다고 죽지는 않아 A sleepless night or two will not kill a person.

2 〔동침하다〕 go to bed with; sleep with; share the bed with. ¶피고는 그녀와 잤다는 것을 시인했다 The defendant admitted that he had slept [had had sexual intercourse] with her.

3 〔물결·바람이 잠잠해지다〕 calm down; die down; abate; get lulled; subside. ¶바람이 잤다 The wind died [went / calmed / sank] down. / The wind has subsided.//오늘 저녁에는 파도가 좀 잤다 The sea has gone down a little this evening.

4 〔머릿결 등이 착 붙어 자리가 잡히다〕 get pressed [smoothed] down; take a set. ¶머리가 이제 잔다 My hair has set now.

5 〔기계가 멈추어 서다〕 stop; run down. ¶시계가 잔다 The clock stops [runs down].

자나 깨나 〔잠들었거나 깨었거나〕 asleep or awake; 〔항상〕 all the time; always; twenty-four hours a day. ¶～ 그녀는 환자 간호만 하였다 She attended the patient day and night.//그녀는 ～ 그를 생각했다 Asleep or awake, she thought of him.//그렇게 ～ 술만 마시면 건강을 잃게 거야 You will ruin your health if you go on drinking day in, day out.//그녀는 ～ 자식 걱정이다 She is worrying about her son every single moment.

자단(紫檀) 〔식〕 a red sandalwood; a rosewood. ¶～ 탁자 a rosewood table / a table of rosewood.

자담하다(自擔－) take care[charge] of one's own share; 〔비용을 스스로 부담하다〕 pay one's own expenses.

자당(自黨) one's (own) party.
자당(慈堂) 〔남의 어머니에 대한 존칭〕 your [his / her] esteemed mother.
자당(蔗糖) 〔화〕 sucrose.
자동(自動) automatic action [movement / operation]; automatism; self-motion. ¶～의 automatic//반～의 semiautomatic.
●**자동 감지기** an automatic sensing device. **자동문** an automatic door. **자동 변속 장치** (an) automatic transmission [drive]. **자동 소총** an automatic (rifle). **자동식** ¶～의 automatic//반～의 semiautomatic. **자동식 전화** an automatic telephone. **자동 응답기** a ((tele)phone) answering machine. **자동 이체**(移替) automatic payment; 〔영〕 direct debit. **자동 제어** automatic control[regulation]. **자동 제어 장치** an automatic controller. **자동판매기** a slot[vending] machine; an automat. ¶커피 ～ a coffee vending [slot] machine. **자동 화재경보기** an automatic fire alarm.

자동사(自動詞) 〔언〕 an intransitive verb (약어 v.i., vi.). ¶불완전 〔완전〕 ～ an incomplete [a complete] intransitive verb.

자동적(自動的) self-moving[-operating]; automatic. ¶～으로 움직이다 move automatically[of itself] / (기계적으로) work mechanically//～으로 기록하다 register (five degrees of frost)//이 문은 ～으로 열린다 This door opens automatically.//부친이 사망했으므로 ～으로 외아들이 저택을 상속했다 As the father died, his only son inherited the estate as a matter of course.

자동차(自動車) a car; 〔영〕 a motorcar; 〔미〕 an automobile; 〔미국 구어〕 an auto. ¶고물 ～ a used car / a flivver / a jalopy / 〔영〕 an old banger//영업용 ～ motorcars for business use / trade cars//임대 ～ a rent-a-car / a rental car//소형 [중형 / 대형] ～ a compact [medium-sized / large] car//유개 [무개] ～ a closed [an open] car (▶지붕을 접을 수 있는 자동차는 a convertible car)//장갑(裝甲) ～ an armored car/전기 ～ an electromobile / an electric motorcar//포장형 ～ a convertible (coupé [sedan])//화물 ～ 〔미〕 a truck / 〔영〕 a (motor) lorry// ～로 가다 go by (motor) car// ～로 여행하다 make a motor trip// ～로 드라이브 가다 go (out) for a drive // ～에 타다 ride a car / take [go for] a ride in a car// ～로 운반하다 motor (goods)//휴일에 ～로 놀러 가다 drive out on one's holiday tour// ～에 태워 주다 give (a person) a ride [lift] (in a car)// ～를 운전하다 drive a car [an automobile]// ～를 세워 두다 park a car//지금은 ～ 시대다 This is an [the] age of motorcars.//댁까지 ～로 모셔다 드리지요 (자기 차로) I'll drive you home. / (택시로) I'll take you home in a cab.

●**자동차 경주** a motor[an auto] race. ¶～ 선수 a racing driver// ～장 a motor racecourse / a motordrome. **자동차 공업** / **자동차 산업** an automobile industry; 〔미〕 the auto [car] industry; 〔영〕 the motor [car] industry. **자동차 도로** (전용의) a driveway; a motorway; an auto [a motor] road; a road for motoring; a turnpike (road) (유료 고속도로). **자동차 보험** motor [〔미〕automobile] insurance. **자동차 사고** a car [an automobile] accident. **자동차 운전면허증** 〔미〕 a driver's license; 〔영〕 a driving licence. **자동차 전시회** / **자동차 쇼** an auto (mobile) show. 자동

자두 [자두나무 열매] a plum.
● 자두나무 [식] a plum tree.

자디잘다 very small; tiny; fine; (사람이) meticulous; overscrupulous. ¶자디잔 사람 a petty-minded person / a meticulous [an overscrupulous] person // 자디잔 글자 a very small [a microscopic(al)] character [letter] // 파를 자디잘게 썰다 chop a scallion fine.

자라 [동] a snapping [mud / soft-shelled] turtle; a terrapin.
자라 보고 놀란 가슴 소댕[솥뚜껑] 보고 놀란다(속담) Once bitten, twice shy.; The burnt child dreads the fire.

자라다[1] [성장하다] grow (up); [양육되다] be brought up; be bred. ¶한창 자라는 아이 a growing child // 빨리[더디] 자라는 나무 a tree of rapid [slow] growth // 자람에 따라 as one grows up [becomes older] // 무럭무럭 ~ grow up quickly and healthily / (초목이) grow rapidly // 너무 ~ be overgrown / overgrow oneself // 너무 자라서 옷이 작아지다 outgrow one's clothes // 내 머리털이 길게 자랐다 My hair has grown [gotten long]. // 그녀는 얌전하게 [버릇없이] 자랐다 She is well-bred [ill-bred]. // 나는 시골[도시]에서 자랐다 I grew [was brought] up in the country [in a city]. / I am country-bred [city-bred]. // 그는 크게 자랐다 (몸이) He has grown much bigger. / (사람됨이) He has matured greatly. // 이 토양에서는 야채가 잘 자란다 Vegetables grow well in this soil. // 저 아이는 모유로 자랐지만, 이 아이는 우유로 자랐다 That child was breast-fed, but this one was bottle-fed. // 그녀의 아들은 훌륭한 젊은이로 자랐다 Her son has grown into a fine young man.
2 [발전하다] improve; develop; progress; make progress. ¶그의 영어 실력이 부쩍 자랐다 His English has improved a great deal. // 그 제조업이 자라서 성대한 산업이 되었다 The manufacture developed into a large and flourishing industry. // 부산은 세계 최대의 항구 중 하나로 자랐다 Busan has grown [developed] into one of the largest port cities in the world.

자라다[2] 1 [족하다] enough; sufficient; suffice. ¶식량은 충분히 자란다 We have enough [sufficient] provisions. // 10만 원가량이면 자랄 것이다 A hundred thousand won or so will do [suffice].
2 [미치다] reach; get [attain] to; come up to (the standard). ¶손이 자라지 않는 곳에 beyond [out of] one's reach / where one can't get at (it) // 힘이 자라는 데까지 as much as lies in one's power / to the best of one's ability // 환자의 손이 자라는 곳에 라디오를 두었다 I put the radio within reach of the sick man. // "저 가지까지 손이 자랄까?" "그렇게 높은 데까지는 자라지 않아." "Can you reach that branch?" "No, I can't reach so high."

자락 the skirt; the (dress) hem; the bottom (바지 등의); the trail (여성복의 긴 자락). ¶치마의 ~ the hem of a skirt // 바지 ~을 걷어올리다 tuck up one's trousers // 그녀는 치맛~을 당겨서 무릎을 가렸다 She pulled the hem of her skirt over her knees. / She pulled down her skirt to hide her knees. // 그녀는 흰 웨딩드레스의 ~을 끌며 걸어갔다 Her white wedding dress trailed along the floor as she walked.

자랑 pride; boast; boasting; brag; bragging. ¶제고장 ~ boasting of [pride in] one's home town // ~삼아 for show [display] / for one's boast // 그녀는 부모의 ~이다 She's the pride (and joy) of her parents. // 자기 ~은 아니지만 내 강연은 대성공이었다 My lecture was a great success, even if I do say so myself! // 그렇게 제 ~ 하는 사람은 처음 본다 I've never seen anyone who praised himself so much! // 그녀가 아들 ~ 하는 것은 무리가 아니다 She may well be proud of her son. // 그는 항상 아버지가 부자인 것을 ~삼고 있다 He is always boasting of his rich father. **자랑하다** be proud of; boast [brag] of; make a boast of; be boastful. ¶자랑하는 사람 a braggart / a boaster // 자랑하지 않는 사람 a modest person // 자랑해 보이다 make a display [show] of (a thing) // 솜씨를 ~ brag [vaunt] of one's skill // 그는 예쁜 딸이 있는 것을 자랑하고 있다 He is proud of having a beautiful daughter. // 그는 좋은 가문에서 태어났음을 자랑하고 있다 He takes pride in his high birth. / He is proud of good family background. // 그들은 자기 도시의 깨끗한 거리를 자랑하고 있다 They pride themselves on their town's clean streets. // 그녀의 이 업적은 마땅히 자랑할 만한 것이다 She can rightly take pride in [She can be justly proud of] this achievement. // 그것은 자랑할 만한 것이 못 된다 That's nothing to be proud of [to boast about]. // 이것이 그가 자랑하는 그림이다 This is picture he is proud of. // 그녀는 자기 아들을 곧잘 자랑한다 She often boasts of [about] her son.
● **자랑거리** something to brag about [of]; a feather in one's cap; a source of pride. ¶우리 학교의 ~ the pride of our school / a credit to our school // 그녀는 목소리가 ~다 She is vain of her voice. // 이 장미는 그의 ~다 This rose is his boast. // 그것은 별로 ~가 못 된다 It is nothing to be proud of. / It is not much to boast of [about].

자랑스럽다 proud (of); boastful. ¶자랑스러워 하는 아버지 the proud father // 자랑스러운 듯이 proudly / boastfully / boastingly // 자랑스러운 얼굴[태도] (with) a proud look [air] // 자랑스러워 보이다 look proud // 자랑스럽게 말하다 speak boastingly (of) // 우리는 그가 우리 학교의 졸업생임을 자랑스럽게 생각한다 We are proud that he is a graduate of our school. // 그는 아들의 성공 소식을 듣고서 크게 자랑스러웠다 He was filled with pride [felt very proud] on hearing of his son's success. // 그들은 자기 학교를 자랑스럽게 여긴다 They take pride in [are proud of] their school. // 주장은 한의 묘기를 자랑스럽게 이야기했다 The captain spoke proudly of [talked proudly about] Han's feat. // 소년은 종이비행기를 자랑스럽게 보여 주러 왔다 The boy proudly brought the paper airplane to show us. // 그는 자랑스러운 듯 미소 지었다 He looked proud as he smiled.

자력(自力) one's own strength [efforts / exertions]. ¶~으로 하다 do single-handed / do without help / do by [for] oneself / do by one's own strength [ability] // ~으로 서다 lift [pull] oneself up by one's own bootstraps

[boottags]//~으로 인생을 개척하다 carve out career for oneself//환자는 ~으로 회복했다 The patient recovered without medical treatment.
● **자력 구제** [법] self-help.
자력(資力) [여유를 갖고 쓸 수 있는 돈] means; [자금] funds; (financial) resources; the wherewithal. ¶~이 있는[없는] 사람 a man of[without / with no] means//~ 부족으로 for lack of funds//~**이 충분하다** have enough[plenty of] funds (for)//자동차를 가질 만한 ~이 없다 I can't afford[can ill afford] a motorcar.//그에게는 그것을 완성할 만한 ~이 없었다 He lacked the wherewithal to bring it to completion.
자력(磁力) magnetic force. ⇨자기력(⇨자기(磁氣)) ¶~의 magnetic.
● **자력계** a magnetometer. **자력선** a line of magnetic force.
자력갱생하다(自力更生-) start a new life through one's own efforts[single-handedly].
자료(資料) materials (for study); [데이터] data (on)(▶ data는 datum의 복수형. (미)에서는 종종 단수 취급을 함); (조사 결과) findings. ¶**연구[통계]~** materials for study [statistics] / research [statistics] materials [data] // 인구 문제에 관한 ~ data on the population problem // 연구 ~를 모으다 collect research material(s) // 고문서를 연구 ~로 쓰다 use old documents as the material for one's research // 이 ~는 매우 유용하다 These data are[This data is] very useful. // 이 시안을 토의의 ~로 제출합니다 As a material[basis] for discussion, I present this tentative plan. // 그의 보고서는 믿을 만한 조사 ~에 입각한 것이다 His report is based on reliable findings.
● **자료실** (특히 신문사 등의) a morgue.
자루¹ a bag; a sack; (주로 가죽으로 된 작은 자루) a pouch. ¶**쌀~** a rice bag // **한 ~ 가득** a bagful / a sackful // ~ **같은** baggy // **한 ~의 감자** a sack of potatoes // ~**에서 꺼내다** take (something) out of a bag // ~**를 비우다** empty a bag // 그것을 ~에 담아 주시오 Will you put it[them] in[into] a bag?
자루² [손잡이] a handle; a grip(▶ 손으로 잡는 모양을 하고 있으며 보통 handle의 일부; [빗자루의]) a broomstick; (창 등 긴 무기나 골프채 등의) a shaft; (도끼·단도 등의) a haft. ¶~가 긴 국자 a long-handled ladle // ~를 **달다** put a handle[haft] (to[on] a sickle).
자루³ [기름한 물건의 낱개를 세는 단위] a piece[stick] (of India ink); a pair (of scissors); a stand (총 등의). ¶**연필 두 ~** two pencils // **분필 다섯 ~** five pieces of chalk // **총 세 ~** three pieces [stands] of rifles // **칼 한 ~** a sword.
자르다 1 [끊어 내다] cut; chop(도끼 등으로); saw(톱으로); clip(가위로); shear(큰 가위로); carve(식탁에서 요리한 고기를); hash(고기 등을 잘게); slice(빵을). ¶**잘게~** cut (a thing) fine [into small pieces] // **잘라 내다** cut off [out / away] / whittle down(작은 칼로) / tear off(손으로) / [외과] resect(일부를) // 가지를 잘라 내다 cut off[prune] a branch // 가위로 머리칼을 ~ cut hair with scissors // 이 케이크를 둘로 잘라 주시오 Please cut the cake into two. // 그 빵을 한 조각 잘라 주실 수 있겠습니까 Will you slice that bread for me? // 당근은 큼직하게 자르고 양파는 잘게 자릅니다 Chop carrots and mince onions. // 이 나무를 자르는 데 5시간이 걸렸다 It took me five hours to cut down[fell] the tree.
2 [해고하다] dismiss; discharge; (구어) fire. ¶사장은 당장에 그의 목을 잘랐다 Boss fired him out in no time.
3 [단호하게 행하다]. ¶**딱 잘라 거절하다** refuse flatly / give (a person) a flat[a point-blank / a square / an outright] refusal // 그녀는 그의 제의를 딱 잘라 거절했다 She flatly refused his offer. // 그의 부탁을 딱 잘라 거절할 수가 없었다 I couldn't give a flat refusal to his request.
잘라 말하다 state clearly[definitely]; make a definite statement (of); declare; affirm; assert. ¶잘라 말할 수는 없지만 3일까지는 회답이 올 것으로 생각한다 I cannot say for sure that the answer will come by the third, but I think it will. // 그의 친구들은 그가 결백하다고 잘라 말했다 His friends affirmed that he was innocent.
자르르 1 [윤기 등이 흐르는 모양] greasily. ¶**기름기가 ~ 흐르는** greasy / oily // **얼굴에 기름기가 ~ 도는 40대 남자** an oily-faced fleshy man in his forty. 2 [저린 느낌이 일어나는 모양] with a dull pain (in the joints). ¶**전기가 ~ 오르다** get an electric shock.
자리¹ 1 [공간] room; space. ¶~를 **차지하다** take up[occupy] much room[space] // 이 옷장은 ~를 너무 많이 차지한다 This wardrobe takes up too much room[a lot of space]. // 이제는 텔레비전을 놓을 ~가 없다 There's no room left for a TV set. // 접을 수 있는 침대는 ~를 별로 차지하지 않는다 A folding bed takes[requires] little room[space]. // 모두가 앉을 ~는 없다 There is not enough room for everyone to sit down. // 이 페이지에는 더 써 넣을 ~가 없다 There is no more space to write in on this page. // 주차할 ~를 찾는 데 힘이 들었다 We had a hard time finding a parking space[place].
2 [흔적] a mark; a print; a trace; a scar(상처의); an old[former] site(건물 등의); ruins(유적). ¶**총알이 박힌 ~** a mark of a bullet // 그녀의 등에는 수술한 ~가 남아 있다 She has a scar from an operation on her back. // 이것이 옛날에 성이 있던 ~이다 This is the old [former] site of the castle. // 그 마을에는 폭격을 당한 ~가 남아 있다 There are bombsites in the village.
3 [좌석] a seat; a place(지정된). ¶**빈 ~** a vacant seat // ~**에 앉다** sit (down) / take [have] one's seat / seat oneself (at a table) // ~를 **잡다** take a[one's] seat / be seated / seat oneself (at a table) / sit down // ~**에서 일어서다** rise (up) from one's seat // 남에게 ~를 양보하다 give one's seat to a person // 상석에 ~를 잡다 take the top seat // ~에 앉아 주십시오 Please sit down. / Please take your seat. / Please be seated. // 그는 버스에서 그 노인에게 ~를 양보했다 He gave his seat on the bus to the old man. // 그는 두 사람 몫의 ~를 차지하고 있다 He occupies enough space for two (people). // 네가 돌아올 때까지 ~를 잡아 두지 I'll keep your seat (for you) until you come back. // "~를 잡을 수 있을까?" "다음 기차를 기다리면 틀림없어." "Do you think we can get our seats?" "I'm sure we can if we wait for the next train." // "이 ~는 비어 있습니까?" "아니요, 사람이 있습니다."

자리

"Is this seat [place] vacant [free / open / taken]?" "No, it's taken [occupied]." // 옆에 앉은 사람이 담배를 권했다 The man sitting next to me offered me a cigarette. // 그는 지금 ~에 없습니다 He isn't at his desk right now. // 그 강당에는 ~가 1,000개 있다 The auditorium seats a thousand person [has a thousand seats]. // 그는 ~를 박차고 나가 버렸다 He flung out of the room. // 내 ~를 비워 두시오 Please make room for me. // 모두들 ~를 잡고 앉았다 Everybody took a seat.

4 [직위·지위] a position; a post; a situation. ¶빈~ a vacancy / a vacant post // 장관[각료] ~ a portfolio (of a Minister) / a ministerial post / a seat in the cabinet // 높은 ~에 있는 사람 a very important person / a VIP // 권력의 ~에 오르다 reach a position of authority // 그는 시장 ~를 노리고 있다 He has an eye on the office of major. // 부사장 ~가 하나 비어 있다 One post for a vice-president is vacant. // 그 학교에 선생 ~가 하나 났다 There is an opening for a teacher at that school. // 나는 은행에 ~를 얻었다 I found a position with a bank. // 자리가 나면 자네 문제를 고려해 보지 You will be considered when there is a vacancy. // 그는 권력의 ~를 지키기 위해서는 무슨 일이나 한다 He would try anything to keep himself [remain] in power.

5 [특정한 기회] an occasion; an opportunity; [특정한 장소] a spot; [현장] the scene. ¶사고[범죄]가 일어난 ~ the scene of accident [crime] // 그는 그 ~에 어울리는 말을 했다 He said things suitable for the occasion. // 너는 그 ~에 어울리는 옷을 입고 있었다 She was properly dressed for the occasion. // 그는 그 ~에서 사건을 해결했다 He settled down the matter on the spot [at once]. // 이 ~를 빌려 한 말씀 드리겠습니다 Let me take this opportunity to tell you a word. / On this occasion I will tell a word. // 왜 당신은 그 ~에서 항의하지 않았소 Why didn't you protest then and there? // 그의 약속은 그 ~에서 뿐이니 신용할 수가 없다 He makes promises just for the occasion, so he can't be trusted. // 이 옷은 어느 ~에서나 입을 수 있다 This dress can be worn on all occasions. // 그의 연설은 그 ~에 있던 사람들에게 깊은 감명을 주었다 His speech impressed those present. // (제삼자에게) 잠시 ~ 좀 비켜 주시겠어요 Will you excuse us for a minute?

6 [위치] a position; a location; a situation. ¶~가 좋다[나쁘다] be well [badly] situated // 그 가게는 ~가 좋다 The store is favorably located [situated]. / The store is located in an advantageous position. // ~가 좋으면 장사가 잘된다 The locality brings a great deal of business. // 나는 무대 전체가 잘 보이는 ~에 있었다 I was in a good position to see the whole stage. // 여기는 성이 ~ 잡고 있던 곳이다 This is the place where a castle formerly stood. // 그 공원은 시의 동쪽에 ~ 잡고 있다 The park lies in the east of the city.

7 [숫자의 위치]; (소수점 이하의) a figure; a place. ¶두[세 / 네] ~의 숫자 double [three / four] figures / a two-[three-/four-]digit number // 소수점 이하 두 ~까지 계산하다 calculate it to two decimals [decimal places] // 계산이 한 ~ 틀렸다 My calculation was one digit off. / I miscalculated by one digit.

8 [별자리]. ¶큰곰~ the Great Bear / the Big Dipper.

자리를 같이하다 [옆에 같이 앉다] sit (side by side) together; [참석하다] attent (a meeting); be present (at); participate in; meet; take part in.

자리를 뜨다 leave one's seat. ¶그는 급한 볼일이 있어 자리를 떴다 He left (his seat) on urgent business.

자리(를) 잡다 1 [정착하다] settle (down); fix [take up] one's residence; make one's home; establish oneself. ¶서울에 ~ settle down in Seoul // 여관에 ~ get settled [put up] at an inn // 그는 마침내 교사로서 자리를 잡았다 At last he settled down as a teacher [to teaching]. // 고기압이 한반도 상공에 자리 잡고 있다 A high pressure area has settled over the Korean Peninsula. // 결혼을 해서 자리 잡을 때가 되었다 It is time for you to get married and settle down. **2** [뿌리내리다] take root; take firm hold. ¶한국에서는 민주주의가 아직 자리 잡지 못하고 있다 Democracy is not yet deeply rooted in Korea. // 사악한 생각이 그의 마음속에 자리 잡고 있었다 A wicked idea had lodged itself in his mind [heart].

자리(가) 잡히다 1 [익숙해지다] become skillful [expert]; get skilled. ¶아직 자리 잡히지 않은 기술 a half-learned skill // 그는 일이 자리 잡혔다 He is good at his job. **2** [어수선하던 것이 가라앉다] be started along the right lines; get going. ¶일이 자리 잡혔다 My work is on the right track. / My business has gained its footing [ground].

자리² 1 [왕골 등으로 짠 깔개] a mat; (집합적) matting. ¶못~ a rush mat // ~를 깔다 spread a mat (on the floor) // ~를 잡고 눕다 lie down on the mat. **2** [이부자리] bedding; bedclothes. ¶~를 펴다 put down bedding / spread [lay out] bedding (on the ondol) // ~를 걷다 put away the bedding. **3** [잠자리] a bed. ¶~에 들다 go to bed.

자리(를) 보다 make [prepare / lay] a bed.

●**자리끼** nighttime drinking water.

자리보전하다 (-保全-) lie in one's sickbed; be sick in bed; be laid up in bed; be bedridden. ¶그는 2개월째 자리보전하고 있다 He's been sick [ill] in bed (for) the last two months. / He's been lying in his sickbed (for) these two months.

자린고비 a very stingy [(구어) cheap] person; a notorious miser; a skinflint; (속어) a tightwad; (속어) a cheapskate.

자립 (自立) [독립] independence; self-reliance; [자활] self-support. **자립하다** become independent; establish oneself; rely on oneself; stand [get] on one's own legs [feet]; set oneself up (in business); [자활하다] support oneself. ¶자립하여 independently / on one's own // 그는 이제 자립했다 He is on his own now. / He is now his own man [master]. // 그의 아들은 이미 자립하고 있다 His son is already supporting himself. // 그 일로 해서 그는 부모로부터 자립할 수 있었다 The job made him independent of his parents. // 그는 벌써 35세인데도 아직 자립하지 못하고 있다 He is already thirty-five years old, but he still cannot stand on his own feet.

●**자립 경제** self-supporting economy; eco-

자발적

nomical independence. 자립어 an independent word. 자립정신 an independent spirit.

-자마자 as soon as; no sooner ... than ...; hardly[scarcely] ... when[before] ...; directly; immediately; the very moment[instant]. ¶나서~ 비가 오기 시작했다 As soon as I set out[went out], it began to rain.∥그는 돈을 받~ 방에서 뛰쳐나갔다 No sooner had he received the money than he rushed out of the room.∥차가 출발하~ 어떤 사람이 내 이름을 부르는 소리가 들렸다 The car had hardly started when I heard a man call my name.∥그는 대학을 나오~ 결혼했다 He married directly he left the university.∥자명종이 울리~ 그는 침대에서 뛰쳐나왔다 The instant[moment] the alarm clock rang, he leaped out of bed.∥그는 대학을 졸업하~ 실업계에 투신했다 Immediately on graduating from the university, he went into business.∥그가 외출하~ 눈이 오기 시작했다 Scarcely had he gone out when it began to snow.

자막(字幕) 〔화면에 비쳐 보이는 대화〕 superimposed dialogue; 〔원작자·협력자 등의 이름이 나오는 자막〕 (credit) titles(▶ 보통 복수형); 〔외국 영화 대사의 번역〕 subtitles; 〔제목명이나 설명적인 것〕 a caption. ¶설명[보조]~ a cut-in / a subtitle / an insert title∥우리 말이 있는 이탈리아 영화 an Italian film with Korean subtitles∥영화에 ~을 넣다 superimpose (a caption / dialogue) on a film / title a film / add titles to movies.

자막대기 〔잣대〕 a (measuring) rule[rod]; a yardstick.

자만(自慢) conceit; self-conceit; 〔허영심〕 vanity; 〔자랑〕 pride. **자만하다** be conceited [self-conceited]; be vain (about); flatter oneself; fancy oneself; think (too) highly of oneself; 〔구어〕 have a swelled head. ¶그녀는 자기 딴에는 아름답다고 자만하고 있다 She fancies herself[to be] beautiful.∥톰은 반에서 자기가 가장 머리가 좋다고 자만하고 있다 Tom flatters himself that he is the most intelligent boy in his class.∥그는 반드시 성공한다고 자만하고 있다 He is cocksure of his success. **자만하지 마라** Don't be conceited[vain].
● **자만심** ¶그는 ~이 강하다 He is full of conceit. / He thinks very highly of himself.

자망(刺網) a gill net.
● **자망 어선** a gill netter.

자매(姉妹) sisters. ¶친~ sisters-german∥이복~ half sisters∥양~ foster sisters∥홍 씨~ the Hong sisters∥~의[같은] sisterly∥~같은 애정 sisterly love∥~는 몇 분입니까 How many sisters do you have?
● **자매결연** establishment[setting up] of sisterhood relationship[ties]. ¶~을 맺다 set up sisterhood relationship (with). **자매 기관** sister agencies. **자매 학교** a sister school. **자매 회사** an affiliated company; an affiliate.

자맥질 diving; ducking. **자맥질하다** dive (into / in / under) water; dip into (the river); duck; go[swim] underwater.

자멸(自滅) self-destruction; self-ruin. ¶정치적 ~ (commit) political suicide∥~적인 self-destructive / suicidal∥그들의 행위는 ~을 초래할 것이다 Their acts will lead to self-destruction.∥그의 태만이 ~을 가져왔다 His idleness resulted in self-ruin. **자멸하다** destroy[ruin] oneself; bring destruction upon oneself; 〔망하다〕 perish (naturally). ¶그 한 마디로 그는 정치적으로 자멸했다 He ruined himself politically[brought about his own political downfall] with that one word. ∥적은 실제로는 자멸했던 것이다 In effect, the enemies destroyed themselves.

자명종(自鳴鐘) an alarm (clock). ¶~ 소리에 잠을 깨다 wake to the alarm (at five o'clock) ∥~을 5시 30분에 맞추어 두다 set an alarm clock for half past five∥~이 울릴 시간에 울리지 않았다 The alarm did not go off at the set time.

자명하다(自明-) 〔명백하다〕 self-evident; 〔설명이 필요 없다〕 self-explanatory; 〔분명하다〕 obvious. ¶자명한 이치 a self-evident[an obvious] truth / a truism / an axiom∥그렇게 되는 것은 자명한 일이다 It is self-evident that it will turn out that way.∥그가 아버지의 사업을 잇는다는 것은 자명한 이치다 It is only natural[stands to reason] that he should succeed to his father's business.

자모(字母) **1** 〔언〕 an alphabet; a letter (of the alphabet); a syllabic. **2** 〔활자의〕 a matrix (pl. matrices, matrixes); a (font of) printing type. ¶~를 주조하다 cast a font[(영) fount] of type.

자모(慈母) an affectionate[a loving] mother; 〔존칭〕 one's mother.

자모음(子母音) 〔언〕 consonants and vowels.

자못 very (much); ever so much; greatly; 〔적잖이〕 not a little. ¶그에 대한 기대가 ~ 크다 I expect much from him.∥그 이야기를 듣고 나는 ~ 놀랐다 I was not a little surprised to hear the story.∥그들은 우리에게 ~ 친절했다 They were exceedingly kind to us.

자몽 a grapefruit.

자문(諮問) a request for advice; (a) consultation. ¶~에 응하다 provide advice and suggestions as requested∥그들은 정부의 ~에 응했다 They responded to the government's request for advice. **자문하다** consult (a person about a matter); submit[refer] (a matter to); seek advice. ¶문제를 위원회에 ~ refer a problem to a committee.
● **자문 기관** a consultative body; an advisory organ. **자문 위원회** an advisory[a consultative] committee.

자문자답(自問自答) a soliloquy. **자문자답하다** wonder to oneself; answer one's own question; think aloud; talk to oneself; soliloquize(독백하다).

자문하다(自問-) question[ask] oneself.

자물쇠 a lock; a padlock(맹꽁이 자물쇠); a snaplock(자동 자물쇠). ¶~ 수선업자 a locksmith∥~를 채우다[열다] lock[unlock] (a door)∥~를 고치다 repair[fix] a lock∥이 문은 ~가 잘 안 잠긴다 This door won't lock.

자바라(啫哱囉) 〔음〕 small cymbals.

자박 with a light footstep.

자박거리다 walk with light footsteps.

자반 salted fish. ¶고등어 ~ a salted mackerel.

자반뒤집기하다 〔몹시 아파 엎치락뒤치락하다〕 writhe in agony; toss[fling] about in great pain. ¶그는 복통으로 자반뒤집기했다 He lay turning from side to side, his stomachache.

자발성(自發性) spontaneity; spontaneousness.

자발적(自發的) spontaneous; voluntary. ¶~인 원조 voluntary aid∥~으로 spontaneous-

자배기 a large-mouthed round pottery.
자백(自白) [고백] (a) confession; penance; [자인] admission. ¶고문에 의한 ~은 증거가 되지 못한다 Confessions extracted by torture cannot be accepted as evidence.// 우리는 그의 ~을 얻지 못했다 We failed to produce confession from him. **자백하다** confess (to); make (a) confession; own (up); admit. ¶범죄를 ~ confess to an offense [a crime] / confess one's guilt // make a confession of one's crime//그는 죄를 남김없이 자백했다 He made a full confession of his crime. / He made a clean breast of his crime.//그는 자신이 간첩이었음을 자백했다 He admitted[owned up to] having been a spy.//용의자는 쉽사리 자백하지 않았다 The suspect would not own up.
자벌레 [동] a looper; an inchworm; a measuring worm; a canker worm; a spanworm.
자본(資本) (a) capital, a fund. ¶가변 ~ variable capital // 고정 [외국] ~ fixed [foreign] capital // 공칭 ~ nominal capital // 금융 [독점] ~ financial [monopolistic] capital // 매판 ~ comprador capital // 자기 [수권(受權)] owned [authorized] capital // 불변 [의제(擬制)] ~ constant [fictitious] capital // 사회 [타인] ~ social overhead [borrowed] ~ // 산업 ~ industrial capital // 운전 ~ working capital [funds] // 유동 [유통] ~ floating [circulating] capital // 유휴 ~ unemployed [idle] capital // 주식 ~ share capital // 투하 ~ invested capital // 미국 ~ 계열의 회사 a company funded by American capital // ~의 축적 the accumulation of capital // ~의 자유화 liberalization of the capital (market) // ~이 많이 소요되는 사업 an enterprise which requires heavy investment // ~ 부족의 capital-short // ~ 부족에 시달리다 suffer from a lack of funds // ~을 투하하다 invest capital (in an enterprise) // ~을 전하하다[회전시키다] revolve capital // ~을 사장해 두다 allow capital to lie idle // 그는 3,000만 원의 ~으로 책방을 시작했다 He started a bookstore with a capital of 30 million won. // 아버지가 내 기획에 ~을 대 주셨다 My father financed [provided the money for] my project. // 그들은 외국 ~의 유치에 열을 올리고 있다 They are working hard to attract foreign investment(s).
● **자본가** a capitalist; a financier. ¶~와 노동자 capital and labor. **자본금** (a) capital; (주식) (영) a share capital; (미) capital stock. ¶미불입 ~ outstanding [uncalled] capital // 그 회사의 ~은 20만 달러이다 The company had a capital [was capitalized at] $200,000. **자본 시장** the capital market. **자본재**(-財) capital goods. **자본주** a financier; a financial supporter. **자본주의** capitalism. ¶~의 capitalistic // 국가 ~ state capitalism // 독점 ~ monopolistic capitalism // 산업 ~ industrial capitalism // 수정 ~ modified [revised] capitalism. **자본 회전율** capital turnover.
자봉틀(自縫-) →재봉틀(⇨재봉)

자부(子婦) [며느리] a daughter-in-law; one's son's wife.
자부(自負) self-confidence; pride. **자부하다** [자신이 있다] be self-confident; [자랑스럽게 생각하다] take pride in; be proud; think highly of oneself. ¶나는 여성의 지위 향상에 공헌했다고 자부한다 I take pride in having contributed to the elevation of the status of women. // 자부하지만 자만하지는 않습니다 I am self-confident, but not conceited. // 그는 자신이 대단하다고 자부하고 있다 He is really high on himself. / He is puffed up with self-importance [-conceit]. / (구어) He thinks he's really something. // 그녀는 자신이 아름답다고 자부하고 있었다 She had a very high opinion of her own beauty.
● **자부심** self-confidence; self-esteem [-importance]; pride. ¶~이 있는 [강한] self-confident (person) / self-important / proud // 그는 ~이 대단하다 He has a very high opinion of himself. / He thinks highly of himself.
자북(극)(磁北極) the magnetic north pole.
자비(自費) one's own expense [charge]. ¶~로 출판하다 publish one's book at one's own expense // 그는 ~로 시집을 출판했다 He published a book of poems at his own expense. // 나는 ~로 연구 여행을 해야 했다 I had to pay for the study tour out of my own pocket.
● **자비생** a private [self-paying] student. **자비 유학생** a student studying abroad at his [her] own expense.
자비(慈悲) [인정] mercy; benevolence; [연민] compassion; pity; clemency; [자선] charity. ¶~를 빌다 beg for mercy / beseech charity // ~를 베풀다 have mercy on (a person) / show mercy [clemency] to (a person) / [적선하다] do (a person) an act of charity. **자비하다** merciful; charitable (to the poor); benevolent; compassionate. ¶자비하신 국왕 a merciful [benevolent] king.
● **자비심** a merciful heart; mercy. ¶~이 깊은 사람 a benevolent [charitable / merciful] person // 그는 ~이라고는 없는 인간이다 He is a stranger to (pity or) mercy. / He has a heart of stone. / He has only an unfeeling heart.
자비롭다(慈悲-) merciful. ⇨ **자비하다**(⇨자비(慈悲))
자빠뜨리다 (사람을) make (a person) fall on his back; knock [push / throw] (a person) down on his back; (물건을) knock [push / pull / throw] (a thing) down. ¶쳐서 [밀어서] ~ knock [push] (a person) down (on his back) // 의자를 ~ tip over a chair.
자빠지다 1 [뒤로 넘어지다] fall on one's back; go [fall] over; tumble over backward; tumble down. ¶얼음판 위에 ~ fall down on the ice. **2** [일에서 손을 떼고 물러나다] drop away [off]; fall away. **3** 〈속〉 lie down. ⇨자다
자산(資産) property; a fortune; means; assets; [부] wealth. ¶고정 ~ fixed [permanent] assets // 부외(簿外) ~ unlisted [hidden] assets // 유동 ~ current assets / (즉시 환금할 수 있는) liquid [available] assets / (단기성의) current [circulating / floating] assets // 유형 ~ tangible assets [property] // ~과 부채 assets and liabilities // ~의 동결 freezing of (European) assets //

그는 고향에 약간의 ~이 있다 He has some property in the area where he was born.// 그는 주식 중개인으로 ~을 이루었다 He made his fortune as a stockbroker.// 너 정도의 ~이면 무엇이든 할 수 있다 A man of your means can do anything.
● **자산가** a wealthy[rich] person; a man of property[wealth / fortune / means]. **자산 부채표** a statement of assets and liabilities. **자산 상태** one's financial standing. **자산 소득** assets income. **자산 평가** revaluation of property.
자살(自殺) (a) suicide; self-murder. ¶집단 ~ mass suicide// 음독 ~ suicide by taking poison// 투신 ~ suicide by drowning// 가스 ~을 하다 gas oneself to death// 분신 ~을 하다 burn oneself to death// ~을 기도하다 attempt suicide. **자살하다** commit suicide; kill oneself; take one's own life. ¶자살할 목적으로 with suicidal intent// 목을 매어 ~ hang oneself (to death)// 그는 권총으로 자살했다 He shot himself fatally with a pistol.
● **자살 미수** an attempted suicide. **자살 방조** aiding and abetting a suicide. **자살자** a suicide.
자상(刺傷) a stab (wound); a pierced[puncture] wound.
자상하다(仔詳-) [상세하다] minute; detailed; full; [생각이 깊다] thoughtful; considerate. ¶자상한 배려 attentive consideration// 아내에게 자상한 남편 a thoughtful husband. **자상히** thoughtfully; in detail; minutely; in full; at (full) length. ¶~ 설명하다 explain (a matter) in detail[minutely] / give (a person) a detailed explanation (of).
자새 a reel.
● **자새질** reeling.
자색(姿色) [여자의 고운 얼굴] a fair face; good looks; [아름다운 자태와 안색] a fair face and a beautiful figure. ¶~이 뛰어난 여인 a woman of rare personal beauty// ~이 뛰어나다 have a fair face and a beautiful figure / surpass (others) in beauty.
자색(紫色) purple. ⇨ 자주색
자생(自生) spontaneous generation; autogenesis; abiogenesis; [야생] wild[natural] growth. **자생하다** grow wild[naturally / spontaneously]. ¶자생하는 autogenous / spontaneous / [야생하는] wild// 이 지방에는 포도가 자생하고 있다 Grapevines grow naturally in this district.
● **자생 식물** a wild[native] plant.
자서(自書) one's own handwriting. ⇨ 자필
자서(自署) an autograph; a signature. ¶저자의 ~가 있는 책 an autographed[inscribed] copy / a copy with the author's autograph [signature]. **자서하다** sign (one's name); affix one's autograph; autograph. ¶문서에 ~ sign one's name to a document / sign a document.
자서전(自敍傳) an autobiography. ¶~적(으로) autobiographical(ly)// ~적 소설 an autobiographical novel / a fictionized autobiography// ~을 쓰다 write the story of one's own life / write one's life story.
● **자서전 작가** an autobiographer.
자석(磁石) a magnet; (자철광) magnetite; magnetic iron ore. ¶~ 막대[발굽] ~ a bar [horseshoe] magnet// 영구 ~ a permanent magnet// 천연 ~ a natural magnet / a loadstone / a lodestone// ~(성)의 magnetic// ~의 인력 magnetic attraction// ~은 철을 끌어당긴다 A magnet attracts iron.
● **자석 발전기** a magnetogenerator; a magneto.
자석영(紫石英) amethyst. ⇨ 자수정
자선(自選) 1 [자신의 작품에서 골라 뽑음] personal choice; self-selection. **자선하다** select by oneself; select out of one's works. 2 [자신을 택함] self-election. **자선하다** choose [elect] oneself (to be a director).
자선(慈善) charity; benevolence; beneficence; philanthropy; [구휼] almsgiving. ¶~의 charitable / benevolent / philanthropic// ~을 목적으로 for charitable purpose. **자선하다** give to charity; practice charity[philanthropy]. ¶가난한 사람에게 ~ give alms to the poor.
● **자선가** a charitable person; philanthropist. ¶숨은 ~ a good Samaritan. **자선 기금** a charity fund. **자선냄비** a charity pot. **자선 단체** a charity (organization). **자선 사업** charitable[philanthropic] work; charities. ¶그는 전 재산을 ~에 기증했다 He left all his property to charities. **자선시**(-市) a charity baza(a)r.
자성(自省) self-examination; reflection; self-reflection. ¶~을 촉구하다 ask (a person) to reflect on himself. **자성하다** examine[reflect on] oneself; introspect.
자성(磁性) magnetism. ¶~의 magnetic// ~을 띠게 하다[제거하다] magnetize[demagnetize].
● **자성체** a magnetic body. ¶반(反) ~ a diamagnetic body / a diamagnet.
자성(雌性) [생] femini(ni)ty; femaleness.
자세(姿勢) a posture; a pose; a physical position[stance]; [몸가짐] a carriage; [태도] an attitude; bearing. ¶방어 ~ a posture of defense / (펜싱 등에서) (on) guard// 발레의 기본 ~ basic positions in ballet// 저[고] ~ a low[high] attitude[posture]// ~가 흐트러지다 lose one's balance// ~가 좋다[나쁘다] have good[bad] posture// ~를 바로 하다 straighten up / sit[stand] up straight// 차려 ~를 취하다 come[snap] to attention// 쉬어 ~를 취하다 stand at ease// 편한 ~로 앉다 sit in a comfortable position// 저 ~를 취하다 assume a low profile[posture]// 그녀는 우스운 ~로 춤을 추고 있었다 She was dancing in a funny posture.// 사진작가는 모델에게 소파에 기대고 있는 ~를 취해 달라고 부탁했다 The photographer asked the model to pose in reclining posture on the sofa.
자세하다(仔細-) minute; detailed; full. ¶사건에 관한 자세한 보고서를 작성하다 make a minute[detailed] report on[of] a case// 자세한 설명을 하다 give a detailed account// 이 계획에 관한 더 자세한 내용은 추후에 알려 드리겠습니다 I will give you further details [particulars] on[about] this project later.// 자세한 내용은 면담할 때 이야기할 것입니다 Details will be discussed in person[be settled at a personal interview].// 나는 자세한 것은 모릅니다 I don't know the details. **자세히** minutely; in detail; in particular; fully; in full; closely. ¶~ 보고하다 report in detail [minutely]// ~ 조사하다 examine (a thing) minutely / check thoroughly / investigate (a case) very carefully// 현재 상황을 ~ 보고하

다 report how things stand down to the minutest detail / give a detailed[full] report of how things stand // 나는 일의 경과를 ~ 기록해 두었다 I have put down the course of events in detail[in full / minutely]. // 그 자동차 사고에 대해서 ~ 들려주십시오 Tell us about the car accident in detail. / Tell us the details of the car accident. // 그는 나에게 ~ 설명해 주었다 He gave me a detailed[minute / careful] explanation of it.

자속(磁束) 〖물〗 magnetic flux.
● **자속 밀도** magnetic flux density; magnetic induction.

자손(子孫) 1 [아들과 손자] sons and grandsons. 2 [후손] a descendant; 《집합적》 posterity; offspring. ¶~ 대대로 전해 내려오는 보물 a treasure handed down to posterity [from generation to generation] // 그 가문도 ~의 대에 와서 기울기 시작했다 The family began to decline in subsequent generations. // 그 형제는 유명한 정치가의 ~이다 The brothers are descended from[the descendants of] a famous politician.

자수(自首) self-surrender; self-denunciation; voluntary denunciation[surrender]. **자수하다** surrender[deliver] oneself; give oneself up[turn oneself in]. ¶그는 경찰에 자수했다 He surrendered[delivered] himself to the police. / He gave himself up to the police.

자수(刺繡) embroidery. ¶~를 놓은 블라우스 an embroidered blouse // ~를 **놓다** embroider / do[lay] embroidery (on) // 그녀는 앞치마에 작은 새들의 ~를 놓았다 She embroidered some birds on her apron[her apron with birds]. **자수하다** embroider; do[lay] embroidery (on).
● **자수본 / 자수 무늬** embroidery designs. **자수실** embroidery thread. **자수틀** an embroidery frame; a tabo(u)ret.

자수성가하다(自手成家-) rise from one class to another on one's own merits; make one's fortune by one's own efforts; make a career for oneself. ¶자수성가한 사람 a self-made man.

자수정(紫水晶) amethyst; violet quartz.

자숙(自肅) self-restraint[-control]; self-discipline. **자숙하다** restrain oneself; exercise self-control[-discipline]; discipline[control] oneself. ¶두 회사는 광고에 관해 자숙하기로 합의했다 Both companies agreed to use self-control over their advertising. // 병을 앓고 난 뒤로부터 술과 담배를 자숙하고 있습니다 Since my illness I have restrained myself from drinking and smoking.

자습(自習) self-teaching; studying[learning] by oneself. **자습하다** study for[by] oneself; teach oneself; study without a teacher; practice oneself. ¶그는 영어를 자습했다 (혼자서) He studied English by himself. / (독학으로) He taught himself English.
● **자습서** a self-teaching[teach-yourself] book[manual]; a crib; 《미국 구어》 a pony; 《미국 속어》 a horse. ¶독어 ~ (저서명) German Self-Taught // ~의 사용을 금하다 The use of cribs is prohibited. **자습 시간** study time. ¶2교시는 선생님이 부재중이어서 ~으로 바뀌었다 The second period was changed into a study-room hour because the teacher was absent.

자승(自乘) ➡제곱

자승자박하다(自繩自縛-) fall in a trap set by oneself; be caught in one's own trap; forge fetters for one's own bondage. ¶너무 세밀한 규칙을 만들면 자승자박하게 된다 If you make too many detailed regulations, you will end up entangled in your own net.

자식(子息) 1 [아들 딸] a child (*pl.* children); offspring (단수·복수 동형); sons and daughters. ¶사람의 ~ a human being // **전처** ~ a child by one's former[first] wife // 아내가 데리고 온 ~ a child brought by a second wife // ~이 없다 be childless / be without issue / have no child[issue] // ~을 **낳다** give birth to a child / bear a child // ~을 끔찍이 사랑하다 care very much for[be very fond of] one's children // 그는 누구의 ~인지 모른다 His paternity is unknown. // 나는 내가 누구의 ~인지 오랫동안 모르고 있었다 I did not know who my parents were for a long time. // 그는 화가의 ~이다 He was born in[into] a painter's family. / His father is a painter. // 그는 ~이 많다 He has many children [a large family]. // 그들에게는 ~이 없다 They have no children. / (문어) They have not been blessed with children.
2 [남자에 대한 욕] a chap; a fellow; (미국 구어) a guy; (비어) a bastard; (꼬마) a kid; an urchin; (경멸) a brat; an imp. ¶이 후레~ You son of a whore! // 이 개~아 You son of a bitch[gun]! // 이 ~아 (아이에게) You little imp! / You kid!

자신(自身) (one's) self; oneself. ¶나 ~ myself // ~이 (몸소) in person / (혼자서) by oneself // 자기 ~을 위해 for one's own sake // 자기 ~도 돌보지 못하다 cannot look after oneself // 네 ~이 생각하라 Think for yourself. // 왜 내가 그런 짓을 했는지 나 ~도 모르겠다 Even I don't know why I did such a thing. // 나 ~은 이 그림이 좋습니다 Personally I prefer this picture. // 너 ~의 의견은 어떤가 What is your (own) personal opinion?

자신(自信) (self-)confidence; assurance. ¶~이 넘치는 젊은 공무원 a self-assertive young official // ~을 **잃다** lose confidence (in one's own ability) // 나는 프랑스 어에 ~이 없다 I don't have any confidence in my French. // 나는 요리에 있어서는 ~이 있다 I am confident of my ability in cooking. // 나는 이 계획에서 성공할 ~이 있다 I feel confident that I will succeed in this project. // 그 사람이라면 ~을 갖고 당신에게 추천할 수 있습니다 I can confidently recommend him to you. / I can recommend him to you with confidence. **자신하다** have confidence (in); be confident (of / that).

자신만만하다(自信滿滿-) have plenty of confidence in oneself; be full of self-confidence; have great faith in oneself. ¶자신만만한 태도 a confident[an assured] manner.

자심하다(滋甚-) worse; more serious; aggravated. ¶자심해지다 get[grow / become] worse / go from bad to worse / be aggravated // 추위가 자심해진다 It is getting colder.

자아(自我) (the) self (*pl.* selves); (the) ego (*pl.* ~s). ¶~가 강한 self-assertive / (자기 중심의) egotistic / (이기적인) egoistic / (자기 본위의) selfish // ~의 형성 the formation of one's ego // ~의 해방 the emancipation of self // ~를 **주장하다** assert oneself // ~에 눈을

다 become conscious of oneself.
● **자아비판** self-criticism. **자아실현** self-realization. **자아 억제** self-repression. **자아의식** self-consciousness.

자아내다 1 (실을) draw out; reel off; spin. ¶고치에서 실을 ~ reel silk off cocoons // 솜에서 실을 ~ spin cotton into thread / spin thread [yarn] out of cotton. 2 (액체·기체를) draw (liquid) from; suck out; pump out. 3 (느낌 등을) evoke; draw out; provoke; create. ¶동정심을 ~ evoke (a person's) sympathy // 물의를 ~ evoke much criticism // 의심을 ~ create [arouse] suspicion // 그 광경은 관중들의 눈물을 자아냈다 The scene moved the crowd to tears. // 그는 유머 있는 이야기로 다정한 분위기를 자아내었다 He created a friendly atmosphere with his humorous remarks.

자아올리다 suck [draw] up (water); pump up (펌프로). ¶펌프로 우물물을 ~ pump water (up) from a well.

자애 (自愛) 1 [자신을 아낌] self-love; self-regard. **자애하다** take care of [look after] oneself [one's health]. ¶자애하시기 바랍니다 I hope you will take good care of [look after] yourself. / Please be careful of your health. 2 [이기적임] selfishness; egoism.

자애 (慈愛) affection; love; kindness; benevolence. ¶어머니의 ~ motherly love [affection].

자애롭다 (慈愛-) affectionate; loving; fond (parents); benevolent; tender. ¶자애로운 격려 affectionate encouragement // 그는 그 어린아이들을 자애로운 눈으로 지켜보고 있었다 He was watching the small children with fond eyes.

자양 (滋養) nourishment; nutrition; alimentation. ¶~이 있는 [많은] nourishing / nutritious.
● **자양분** a nutritious [nutritive] element; nutritive material; (a) nutriment; sustenance. ¶~이 많은 nutritious / nutritive / nourishing // ~이 적은 lean / innutritive / innutritious // ~을 섭취하다 take nutritious food.

자업자득 (自業自得) the natural consequence of one's (mis)deeds; the natural outcome of one's acts. ¶네가 불행해진 것은 ~이다 You brought on [invited] your own misfortunes. // 그것은 ~이다 You asked for it. / It's no more than you deserved. **자업자득하다** reap the fruits of one's actions; reap the harvest of one's own sowing.

자연 (自然) 1 [천연의 모습] nature. ¶~ (그대로)의 natural // ~을 벗하다 take nature for a friend / make a friend of [be close to] nature // ~을 가까이하다 commune [converse] with nature // 우리는 ~의 품에 안겨 휴식을 취했다 (문어) We rested in the bosom of nature. // 우리는 계곡의 아름다운 ~경관을 즐겼다 We enjoyed the wonderful natural view of the ravine. **자연히** naturally; unaffectedly. ⇨자연2 ¶그분 앞에서는 ~ 예의 바르게 된다 I can't help behaving properly in his presence. // 그는 과묵하니까 ~ 친구도 적다 He is so reserved that naturally he has few friends.
2 naturally; unaffectedly; spontaneously; automatically.
● **자연계** the natural [physical] world; (the realm of) nature. **자연 과학** natural science. **자연도태** natural selection. **자연력** [자연계의 작용] (a) natural agency; (풍력·수력 등) the force of nature; elemental forces. ¶~을 이용하다 harness nature (for). **자연물** a natural object. **자연미** natural beauty; the beauty of nature. **자연 발화** [연소] spontaneous combustion [ignition]. **자연법칙** the law of nature; the natural laws. **자연보호** protection [conservation / preservation] of nature; protection of natural environment. ¶~ 운동 [단체] a conservation movement [group]. **자연사** (-死) (a) natural death. ¶~하다 die a natural death. **자연석** (-石) a living [native] rock. **자연수** [수] a natural number. **자연 숭배** nature worship [cult]. **자연식품** natural foods. **자연인** a natural [an unspoiled] man [person]. **자연재해** a natural disaster. **자연주의** naturalism. **자연현상** a natural phenomenon.

자연스럽다 (自然-) natural; unaffected; unstudied. ¶자연스럽게 이야기하다 speak unaffectedly // 자연스럽게 행동하다 behave naturally // 그의 말하는 태도는 아주 ~ His way of speaking is very natural. // 그의 행동은 자연스럽지 않다 His behavior is unnatural [affected]. // 그녀가 어머니를 그리워하는 것은 자연스러운 일이다 It is only natural that she should be deeply attached to her mother.

자영 (自營) self-management; self-sustenance. ¶~의 self-employed. **자영하다** do business on one's own. ¶그는 요릿집을 자영하고 있다 He runs a restaurant of his own.
● **자영 사업** an independent enterprise. **자영업자** an independent businessman; a self-employed person (▶ an independent businessman 은 회사·상점을 소유하고 있는 경우).

자오선 (子午線) [천] the meridian. ¶본초 ~ the prime [standard] meridian.
자오의 (子午儀) [천] a meridian [transit] instrument.
자오환 (子午環) [천] a meridian [transit] circle.
자외선 (紫外線) [물] ultraviolet rays.
● **자외선 요법** ultraviolet treatment [therapy].

자욱하다 dense; thick; heavy. ¶안개가 자욱한 산들 misty [hazy] mountains // 방에는 연기가 자욱했다 The room was filled with smoke. // 아침 안개가 마을에 자욱했다 The morning mist hung (low) over the village. **자욱이** thickly; densely; heavily.

자웅 (雌雄) 1 male and female. ⇨암수 ¶~을 감별하다 determine the sex (of chickens). 2 [승부·우열] victory or defeat. ¶일찍이 두 나라는 ~을 겨루고 있었다 The two nations once struggled for supremacy [fought for superiority]. // 양군은 이 싸움에서 ~을 결판 내려 하고 있었다 The two armies were ready to fight to a finish [fight a decisive battle].
● **자웅 감별사** a (chicken) sexer. **자웅 동주** (-同株) monoecism. **자웅 이주** (-異株) dioecism.

자원 (自願) volunteering. ¶그 병원은 ~ 봉사에만 의존하고 있다 The hospital is entirely dependent on voluntary support. **자원하다** volunteer (for). ¶자원하여 of one's own accord / voluntarily.

자원

●자원 봉사자 a volunteer. ¶정화 운동에 참가할 ~를 환영합니다 Volunteers are welcome to join the clean-up campaign.

자원(資源) resources. ¶광물 ~ mineral resources // 물적 ~ material resources // 미개발 ~ undeveloped [dormant] resources // 석유 ~ oil resources // 수력 ~ water resources // 인적 ~ manpower resources // 지하 ~ underground [subterranean] resources // 천연 ~ natural resources // 유한한 ~ finite resources // 전쟁은 나라의 ~을 고갈시킬 것이다 The war will drain [be a drain on] our national resources.
●자원 개발 resource development. 자원 보호 conservation of resources.

자위(自慰) 1 [스스로 위로함] self-consolation. 자위하다 console [solace] oneself. ¶마음을 ~하여 to ease one's mind [conscience] / (분이) to allay one's anxiety // …이라 생각하고 ~ comfort oneself with the thought (that). 2 masturbation. ⇨ ~수음

자위(自衛) self-defense; self-protection; self-preservation. 자위하다 defend [protect] oneself.
●자위권 the right of self-defence. 자위대 (일본의) the Self-Defense Force.

자유(自由) [구속으로부터의 해방] freedom; [권리로서의 자유] liberty. ¶개인의 ~ personal liberty // 언론 [신앙 / 출판] 의 ~ freedom of speech [religion / the press] // 통행의 ~ freedom of transit // ~의 천지 a land of freedom // ~의 여신상 Statue of Liberty // ~의 몸이 되다 [죄수가 석방되다] be set free / [직장 등을 그만두다] become one's own master // 우리는 ~와 방종을 혼동해서는 안 된다 We should not take freedom and license to be the same thing. // 많은 사람이 ~를 위해 싸우다가 죽었다 A lot of people fought and died for freedom [liberty]. // ~ 아니면 죽음을 달라 Give me liberty, or give me death. // 게시든 가시든 ~입니다 You are free to stay or leave, as you like. // 어디에 가건 자네의 ~일세 You may [you are free to] go wherever you like. // 토론회의 참가는 ~입니다 The discussion is open to all [everyone].
●자유 결혼 free marriage [union]; common-law marriage. 자유 경쟁 free [open] competition. ¶~ 시장 a free competitive market. 자유 경제 free economy. 자유권 civil liberties. ¶~을 박탈당하다 be deprived of one's civil liberties. 자유 낙하 [물] free fall(ing). 자유 무역 free trade. ¶~항 a free port. 자유민 (a) free people. 자유방임 noninterference; [경] laissez-[laisser-]faire. ¶~하다 leave (a person) to himself / give [leave] (a person) a free hand. 자유방임주의 a noninterference [hands-off] policy; (the principle of) laissez-faire; a let-alone policy. 자유세계 (공산권에 대하여) the free world. 자유시(-詩) free verse. 자유의사 free will. ¶그것은 그가 ~에 따라 한 것이다 He did it of his own free will. / It was purely voluntary on his part. 자유 의지 free will [volition]; spontaneity. ¶~론 the doctrine [theory] of free will / [철] indeterminism. 자유인 a free man. 자유자재 ¶~로 freely / with perfect freedom / at will / as one pleases [likes] // 사람을 ~로 다루다 lead a person by the nose / have a person at one's beck and call // 그는 ~로 시를 쓸 수 있다 He can compose poems at will. // 그는 영어를 ~로 구사한다 He has a good [perfect] command of English. 자유재량 latitude; discretion; a free hand. ¶~에 맡기다 leave (a matter) to the discretion of (a person) / give (a person) a free hand (in). 자유주의 liberalism. ¶~ 국가 a free nation / ~자 a liberalist. 자유직업 / 자유업 a free-lance profession. 자유 진영 the Free World; the Western Camp. 자유투 [농구] a free throwing. 자유형 [수영] (the) freestyle. 자유화(-化) liberalization; freeing (of trade). ¶한국의 무역을 90퍼센트까지 ~하다 liberalize 90 percent of Korea's trade / free Korea's trade up 90 percent.

자유롭다(自由-) free; liberal; unrestrained. ¶상상력의 자유로운 활동 the free play of imagination // 자유로운 몸이 되다 be set at liberty / [해방되다] be set free / be liberated // 자유로운 행동을 하다 take [go] one's own way // 우리는 자유로운 나라에 살고 있다 We live in a free country. 자유로이 freely; at (one's) will; as one please [likes / wishes]. ¶~ 사용하다 make free use of (something) // 그는 에스파냐 어를 ~ 구사한다 He is fluent in Spanish. // 새처럼 공중을 ~ 날아 봤으면 I wish I could fly in the sky as freely [easily] as a bird.

자유스럽다(自由-) free; liberal. ⇨ 자유롭다

자율(自律) 1 [자기 억제] self-control [restraint / -regulation]. ¶~적인 self-controlling / self-regulating // 학생들의 ~ 학습 independent work on the part of students. 2 [철] autonomy. ¶~적인 autonomous / autonomic.
●자율 신경 [생] an autonomic nerve.

자음(子音) [언] a consonant. ¶무성 ~ a voiceless [an unvoiced] consonant // 유성 ~ a voiced consonant // ~의 consonantal.

자음(字音) the sound [pronunciation] of a letter [character].

자의(字義) the meaning [signification / sense] of a word. ¶~대로의 해석 a literal [word-for-word] interpretation / ~대로 해석하다 interpret (a word) literally [in a literal sense].

자의(自意) one's own will [volition]. ¶~로 voluntarily / of one's own will [accord] / on [upon] one's own initiative // 나는 ~로 사직했다 I resigned of my own free will.

자의(恣意) arbitrariness. ¶~적인 선택 [결정] an arbitrary choice [decision] // 이 교과서는 그가 ~로 채택한 것이다 He adopted this textbook on his own authority.

자의식(自意識) self-consciousness. ¶~을 발달시키다 develop a consciousness of self.

자이로스코프 a gyroscope.
자이로컴퍼스 a gyrocompass.

자인(自認) (self-)acknowledgment; admission. 자인하다 acknowledge (oneself beaten); own (oneself to be inferior); admit. ¶실패를 ~ acknowledge one's own failure / acknowledge oneself to have failed / admit (to) having [that one has] failed // 그는 자기가 두려워하고 있음을 자인했다 He admitted to his fears. // 그는 패배를 자인했다 He owned his defeat. // 내가 그보다 한 수 아래임을 자인한다 I acknowledge his superiority.

자일 (독) a Seil; a (climbing) rope. ¶~을 바위에 잡아매다 belay a rope round [to] a rock // 그들은 ~로 몸을 서로 묶었다 They roped

자자손손(子子孫孫) descendants; posterity; offspring. ¶~에 이르기까지 to one's remotest descendants//~에 전하다 transmit [hand down] (printed treasures) to (all) posterity.

자자하다(藉藉) (서술적) be widely spread; be spread abroad; be widely known. ¶천하에 명성이 자자한 정치가 a world-famous statesman//칭찬이 ~ win wide admiration//명성이 ~ be highly reputed [renowned]//그는 젊었을 때 염문이 자자했다 In his youth there were many rumors about his romances.//그 학설은 한국에서 평판이 ~ The theory is creating a sensation in Korea.

자작(子爵) a viscount.
●**자작 부인** a viscountess.

자작(自作) one's own work [making]. ¶~의 음악 a score of one's own composition / music written by oneself//이 드레스는 ~입니다 I made this dress myself.//나는 그의 자연(自演)의 연극을 보았다 I saw him acting in a play he wrote himself. **자작하다** make (a thing) by [for] oneself; (농작물을) cultivate one's own farm; farm on one's own land.
●**자작농** an independent [an owner / a landed] farmer; an owner. **자작시** one's own poem.

자작(自酌) self-service in liquor drinking. **자작하다** help oneself to liquor; pour liquor [wine] for oneself; drink liquor by self-service.

자작나무(식) a white [silver] birch.

자잘하다 (all are) small [little / tiny / fine / minute]. ¶자잘한 꽃무늬가 있는 블라우스 a blouse with a pattern of small flowers//자잘한 빚부터 갚다 pay off the small debt first.

자장(磁場) [물] a magnetic field. ⇨자기장(⇨자기(磁氣))

자장가(-歌) a lullaby; a cradlesong; a hushaby(e); a nursery song. ¶~를 불러 아기를 재우다 lullaby [sing] a baby to sleep / sing a lullaby to make a child go to sleep.

자장자장 hushaby(e). ¶~ 잘도 잔다 Hushaby, my dear.

자재(資材) materials. ¶건축 ~ building [construction] materials//포장 ~ packing materials.
●**자재난** (a) shortage of materials; material shortage. **자재부** a materials department.

자저(自著) one's own book; one of one's own books.

자전(字典) a dictionary of classical Chinese explained in Korea.

자전(自傳) an autobiography. ⇨자서전

자전(自轉) rotation. ¶지구의 ~ 주기 the earth's rotation period. **자전하다** rotate [revolve / turn round] (on its own axis).//지구는 서쪽에서 동쪽으로 자전한다 The earth rotates from west to east.//지구는 태양 주위를 공전하면서 지축을 중심으로 자전한다 The earth rotates on its axis while revolving around the sun.

자전거(自轉車) a bicycle; (구어) a bike; a cycle; (속어) a wheel. ¶2인승 ~ a tandem bicycle//경주용 ~ a racing bicycle//~ 타는 사람 a bicycle rider / a cyclist / a cycler//~로 가다 go by bicycle / go on a bicycle//~의 페달을 밟다 pedal a bicycle//~를 탈 줄 압니까 Can you ride a bicycle? / Can you cycle?
●**자전거 경기장** a bicycle race track; a cyclodrome; a velodrome. **자전거 경주** bicycle racing; a bicycle race. **자전거포** a bicycle shop.

자절(自切) [동] (도마뱀 따위의) autotomy; self-amputation.

자정(子正) midnight. ¶~에 at midnight.

자정(自淨) self-purification; self-cleansing.
●**자정 작용** the self-cleansing action (of nature).

자제(子弟) 1 [남의 아들] a son. 2 [남의 집안의 젊은이] children; young ones. ¶양가의 ~ children of good families.

자제(自制) self-control [-restraint]; self-command [-mastery]. **자제하다** control [restrain] oneself; contain oneself; check oneself (from doing).
●**자제력** the power of self-control; command over one's temper. ¶~이 없는 사람 a person with no control over himself / an incontinent person//~을 잃다 lose one's self-control / lose control over [of] oneself.

자제(自製) one's own manufacture [making]. ¶~의 homemade / (a boat) made by oneself / (chairs) of one's own making.

자조(自助) self-help; self-reliance. ¶~는 최선의 도움 Self-help is the best help. **자조하다** help oneself; rely on oneself.
●**자조 정신** the spirit of self-help.

자조(自嘲) self-deprecation; self-scorn; self-mockery. ¶~적인 self-mocking. **자조하다** sneer [laugh] at oneself.

자족(自足) 1 [자급하여 넉넉함] self-sufficiency. **자족하다** self-sufficient. 2 [자기 만족] self-satisfaction; self-contentment. **자족하다** be satisfied.
●**자족 경제** a self-sufficient economy.

자존(自存) self-existence. **자존하다** exist of [by] itself. ¶자존하는 self-existent.

자존(自尊) [스스로 자기를 높임] self-respect; self-esteem; pride. **자존하다** respect [esteem] oneself; have self-respect [-esteem]; be proud.
●**자존심** pride; self-respect. ¶~이 있는 사람 a self-respecting person//~을 잃다 lose one's self-respect//내 비판에 그의 ~은 크게 상했다 My criticism hurt [wounded] his pride badly.//그는 ~이 강하다 He has much self-respect [pride]. / He thinks very highly of himself.//그의 용서를 바라다니 나의 ~이 허락하지 않는다 I am too proud to ask him for forgiveness.//~을 잃지 마라 Don't hold yourself cheap.

자주 frequently; often; [여러 번 반복하여] repeatedly; [여러 번 잦게] many times. ¶이 지방에서는 그러한 일이 ~ 일어난다 Such things happen very often [frequently] in this district.//그는 나를 ~ 만나러 왔다 He came to see me again and again.//요 며칠 동안 방화 사건이 ~ 일어났다 There have been many cases of arson in the last few days. / There has been a rash of incendiary fires in the last few days.//이런 기회는 그렇게 ~ 오지 않는다 You won't have such a chance very often.

자주(自主) independence; self-reliance.
●**자주 국방** self-reliance of national defense. **자주권** autonomy; (지방 자치 단체의) legislative [political] autonomy. **자주독립** sovereign independence. **자주성** independency. ¶~이

자주(색)

있다 be independent. **자주정신** an independent spirit.

자주(색) (紫朱色) purple; red purple.
● **자주빛** purple. ⇨ **자주** ¶짙은 ~ dark [deep] purple // ~으로 물들이다 dye (a thing) (in) purple.

자주적 (自主的) [자립적] independent; [자발적] voluntary. ¶~으로 independently / voluntarily / of one's own will / on one's own judgment // 그녀의 사고방식에는 ~인 데가 없다 She lacks independence in her way of thinking. // ~외교 정책을 펼 필요가 있다 It is necessary to further an independent foreign policy.

자주포 (自走砲) a self-propelled gun.

자중 (自重) [언행을 신중하게 함] prudence; caution. **자중하다** be cautious; be prudent. ¶자신의 처지를 생각해서 자중하기 바란다 I hope you will consider your own position and not act rashly. // 앞으로는 더욱 자중하겠습니다 I will be more prudent[cautious] from now on.

자중지란 (自中之亂) a fight among themselves; (an) internal strife[dissension].

자지 a penis (pl. penes, ~es); the male sex organ; (금기) a cock; (속어) a dick; (속어) a pecker; (금기) a prick.

자지러지다 [움츠러지다] shrink; cower; crouch; wither; cringe. ¶자지러지게 놀라다 shrink with fright / be frightened[startled] out of one's wits // 자지러지게 비명을 지르다 give a shrill cry / let out a screech // 자지러지게 웃다 hold[split] one's sides with laughter / double up with laughter.

자진 (自進) [관형어적] voluntary; spontaneous. **자진하다** volunteer (oneself). ¶자진하여 돈을 기부하다 contribute money voluntarily [willingly] // 그는 언제나 자진해서 어려운 일을 맡는다 He is always ready to undertake difficult tasks. // 그는 자진해서 그 일을 했다 He volunteered to do the work. / He did it voluntarily [of his own accord / of his own free will] // 학생들이 자진하여 교실 청소를 했다 The pupils cleaned the room on their own initiative [choice].
● **자진 신고** a voluntary report.

자질 (資質) [천성] nature; disposition; [기질] a temperament; [재능] a gift. ¶타고난 ~ one's natural disposition // 저 피아니스트는 ~이 좋다 That pianist has a natural gift (for music). // 그는 화가로서 뛰어난 ~을 갖고 있다 He is highly talented[gifted] as an artist [a painter].

자질구레하다 all in small size; petty; trifling; slight. ¶자질구레한 일 sundry jobs / [사소한 일] trifling matters[things] / the trifles // 가정의 자질구레한 일들을 부지런히 하다 go about the household chores.

자찬 (自讚) self-praise. **자찬하다** praise oneself; sing one's own praises.

자책 (自責) self-reproach. **자책하다** reproach oneself.
● **자책감** a guilty conscience; pangs[pricks / twinges] of conscience; remorse. ¶~에 사로잡히다 suffer from a guilty conscience / be conscience-stricken. **자책점** (-點) [야구] an earned run.

자처 (自處) 1 suicide. ⇨**자결**2 2 [체함] pretension; assumption. **자처하다** pretend (to be a hero); look upon[regard] oneself (as); consider[profess] oneself (to be). ¶영웅으로 ~ pretend to be a hero // 시인으로 ~ [시인인 체하다] pose as[pretend to be] a poet / [시인을 자칭하다] profess to be a poet / [제 멋에는 시인인 줄로 알다] fancy oneself a poet.

자천 (自薦) self-recommendation. **자천하다** recommend oneself (for a position / for a job).

자철 (磁鐵) [광] magnetic iron.

자철석 (a) lodestone; magnetite.

자청하다 (自請-) volunteer (for); offer oneself (as). ¶그는 양자 사이의 중재역을 자청하고 나섰다 He took it upon himself [volunteered] to mediate between the two parties. // 그는 계획 실행에 한몫을 하겠다고 자청해 나섰다 He offered his services in carrying out the plan.

자체 (自體) one's (own) body; oneself; itself. ¶어린 시절에는 축제 그 ~가 내게는 즐거운 것이었다 When I was young, the festival was in itself a happy occasion. // 그의 목적 ~는 훌륭했다 His motive in itself was admirable. // 감 ~는 좋으나 스타일이 싫다 The material itself is all right, but I don't like the style.
● **자체 감사** self-inspection.

자체 (字體) the form of a character; (활자의) a typeface. ¶큰 ~로 인쇄된 책 a book printed in large type // 이 단어의 ~는 이탤릭으로 해야 한다 The typeface of this word must be italic. / This word must be italicized.

자초지종 (自初至終) [상세한 내용] the whole story; everything (about an affair); a complete[full] account (of); [처음부터 끝까지] from beginning to end. ¶~을 말하다 tell the whole story / tell the story from beginning to end // 그는 ~을 알고 있다 He knows everything about it. // 그는 그 사건의 ~을 이야기했다 He gave a full [detailed] account of the incident.

자초하다 (自招-) bring[draw] upon oneself; incur (blame); court (danger). ¶화를 ~ bring a misfortune on oneself // 너는 파멸을 자초한 것이다 You have brought ruin upon yourself. // 그는 무모한 행동으로 재난을 자초한 것이나 다름없다 He has in a sense, courted disaster by his own reckless conduct. // 그것은 자네가 자초한 거야 You asked for it.

자축 (自祝) celebration by oneself. **자축하다** celebrate by oneself. ¶가족끼리 ~ have a family celebration // 성공을 ~ celebrate one's own success.

자취 1 [흔적] a mark; a track; a trace; a vestige; a sign. ¶그 작가의 정신적 성장을 ~를 더듬다 follow the track of the writer's mental growth // 우리 옛집의 ~는 아무 데도 없었다 Not a trace[nothing] remained of our old house. // 그는 ~ 하나 남기지 않고 사라졌다 He disappeared like smoke [without leaving a trace]. // 많은 사람들이 지나간 ~가 보였다 There were tracks indicating that a large number of people had passed. // 옛 영화의 ~는 하나도 없었다 There was not a vestige of its former prosperity (remaining). 2 [수] a locus (pl. -ci). ¶~를 구하다 find a locus.

자취를 감추다 disappear without a trace; cover one's tracks.

자취 (自炊) cooking food for oneself. **자취하다** cook one's own meals; do one's own

cooking; cook for oneself; board oneself. ¶나는 자취하고 있다 I am my own cook.
● 자취방 a room with cooking facilities. 자취생 a self-boarding student.

자치(自治) self-government; self-administration; autonomy; home rule. ¶지방 ~ local autonomy // ~의 self-governing / autonomous // 시민들에게 ~를 허용하다 allow citizens to govern themselves. **자치하다** govern oneself.
● 자치권 autonomy; the right of self-government. 자치 단체 a self-governing community [body]. ¶지방 ~ a local government. 자치령 a (self-governing) dominion. 자치회 (학생의) a student council; (지역의) a neighborhood self-governing body.

자치기 tipcat; pussy. ¶~의 (치는) 막대기 a (striking) bat // ~의 나무토막 a tipcat / a cat / a pussy.

자친(慈親) one's mother.

자침(磁針) (자석의) a magnetic needle; (나침반의) a compass needle.

자칫 ¶~ 잘못되다 if the worst happens / if things go wrong [go against one] // 말을 ~ 잘못하면 make a slip of the tongue // ~ 잘못되면 너는 모가지야 If the worst comes to the worst, you will be dismissed. // ~ 잘못되면 너의 목숨이 위태로울 거야 If things go wrong, your life will be in danger.

자칫하면 at [on / with] the slightest slip [provocation]; (very) nearly; almost; barely; narrowly. ¶~ 반대 방향의 열차를 탈 뻔했다 I almost took a train going in the opposite direction. // ~ 사다리에서 떨어질 뻔했다 I was on the point of falling off the ladder. // 그의 차는 ~ 정면 충돌할 뻔했다 His car barely [narrowly] escaped a head-on collision (with another car). // ~ 죽을 뻔했다 I came within an inch of being killed. // ~ 기차를 놓칠 뻔했다 I was nearly [near] missing the train. // 나는 장마철에는 ~ 병이 들기 쉽다 I am apt [prone / liable] to become ill during the rainy season. // 그는 ~ 화를 낸다 He gets angry at [on] the slightest provocation.

자칭(自稱) [관형어적] self-styled [-appointed]; would-be. ¶~ 신사 a self-styled gentleman // ~ 화가 [시인] a would-be [self-styled / self-professed] artist [poet] // ~ 존이라는 사람 a man named [called / who calls himself] John. **자칭하다** style [call / describe / profess] oneself; [주장하다] claim to be. ¶예술가라고 ~ style [call] oneself an artist // 고인의 손자라고 자칭하는 사람이 나타났다 A man who claimed to be the grandson of the deceased. // 그는 자기가 변호사라고 자칭했다 He passed himself off as [professed to be] a lawyer.

자켓 →재킷

자타(自他) oneself and others; [철] subject and object. ¶~ 공히 (both) oneself and others // ~의 구별을 분명히 하다 draw a line of demarcation between oneself and others // 그는 ~가 인정하는 일류 화가다 He is generally admitted to be a first-rate artist [painter]. // 그가 우리나라 최고의 골퍼임은 ~가 공인하는 바다 He is acknowledged (to be) the best golfer in this country.

자탄하다(自歎−) complain of oneself; lament oneself. ¶그는 손실을 당하고는 자탄했다 He lamented over his loss.

자태(姿態) a figure; a shape. ¶한라산의 우아한 ~ the graceful shape [figure] of Hallasan (Mt. Halla) // 그녀의 요염한 ~ her bewitching [coquettish] figure // 그녀는 아름다운 ~를 하고 있다 She has a beautiful figure.

자택(自宅) one's (own) house; one's home. ¶~의 전화번호 one's home telephone number // ~에서 at one's home // ~에 있다 be (at) home / be in // ~에 없다 be not (at) home / be away [absent] from home / be out.
● 자택 연금 (be under) house arrest; domiciliary confinement. 자택 요양 convalescing at home; home treatment.

자퇴(自退) voluntary retirement [resignation]; (입후보 등의) voluntary withdrawal. **자퇴하다** retire voluntarily [willingly]; resign [leave] one's post of one's own accord; relieve oneself of one's post. ¶입후보를 ~ withdraw one's candidacy of one's own free will [own accord] // 그는 후진에게 길을 열어 주려고 자퇴했다 He retired [resigned his post] voluntarily in order to open the way for younger men.

자투리 odds and ends (of yard goods); the remnants (of dress goods); waste pieces (from cutting cloth). ¶~를 싸게 팔다 hold a remnant sale // ~로 인형을 만들다 make a doll with odds and ends of cloth

자파(自派) one's own party [faction].

자판기(自販機) a vending (slot) machine. ¶커피 ~ a coffee vending [slot] machine.

자폐증(自閉症) [의] autism. ¶~에 걸린 아동 an autistic child.

자포자기(自暴自棄) desperation; despair; self-abandonment [-negligence]. ¶~의 desperate / self-abandoned // 범인은 ~가 되어 닥치는 대로 발포했다 The desperate criminal fired indiscriminately. // 그는 친구에게 배신당하고 ~가 되었다 His friend's betrayal drove him to desperation. / He became desperate at his friend's betrayal. // 그는 실연한 후 ~가 되었다 He gave himself up [abandoned himself] to despair after his disappointment in love. // 그는 시험에 실패하여 ~가 되었다 His failure in the examination put him in a devil-may-care mood. **자포자기하다** become desperate; give oneself up to despair. ¶자포자기한 desperate.

자폭(自爆) a suicidal [self-blasting] explosion. **자폭하다** (배가) scuttle one's ship; (비행기가) dash one's plane into an enemy position; crash one's plane against the target. ¶그의 비행기는 적함에 돌진해서 자폭했다 He crashed his plane into an enemy warship.

자필(自筆) one's own handwriting; a holograph. ¶~ 문서 an autograph document / a holograph // 그의 ~ 편지 a letter (written) in his own hand // ~의 autograph(ic) / written by oneself / of [written in] one's own hand (writing) // ~로 in one's own hand [handwriting] / in holograph / autographically // 그것은 월탄의 ~ 원고이다 The manuscripts are in Woltan's own hand (writing).
● 자필 서명 an autograph. 자필 이력서 one's personal history in one's own handwriting.

자학(自虐) self-torment; self-torture. ¶~적인 self-tormenting. **자학하다** torment [torture] oneself; be cruel to oneself.

자해(自害) 1 [자기 몸을 스스로 해침] self-wrong; self-injury. **자해하다** do self-wrong; injure[hurt] oneself. 2 (a) suicide. ⇨자살

자행하다(恣行-) have one's own way; do as one pleases; commit. ¶살인을 ~ commit murder / murder[kill] (a person) // 살육을 ~ kill recklessly / massacre[butcher] brutally.

자형(字形) the form of a character.

자형(姉兄) one's elder sister's husband. ⇨매형(妹兄)

자혜롭다(慈惠-) charitable; benevolent. ¶빈민에게 ~ be charitable to[toward] the poor.

자화상(自畵像) a self-portrait. ¶~을 그리다 paint one's own portrait.

자화 수분(自花受粉) self-pollination.

자화자찬(自畵自讚) self-praise. ¶그는 늘 ~만 한다 He always blows his own trumpet. **자화자찬하다** sing one's own praises; praise oneself; (구어) blow one's own horn[trumpet]. ¶그는 자기가 참 잘했다고 자화자찬했다 He told everyone how well he had done it.

자활(自活) self-support. ¶~의 길 a means of earning one's own living. **자활하다** support [sustain] oneself; earn[make] one's (own) living; provide for oneself; shift[fend] for oneself. ¶그녀는 어린이들에게 피아노를 가르쳐 자활하고 있다 She earns her own living by giving piano lessons to children.

자회사(子會社) a subsidiary (company); an affiliated company; a daughter firm.

자획(字畵) the strokes in a Chinese character.

작(爵) a title of nobility; peerage; court rank.

작(作) 1 [제작(품)] a work; a production. ¶셰익스피어 ~ 햄릿 Hamlet written by Shakespeare // 소월 ~의 시 a poem written by Sowol // 이 조각은 로댕 ~이다 This sculpture is (a work) by Rodin. 2 [수확·경작] a harvest; a crop; a yield. ¶일[이]모 ~ single-[double-] cropping // 평년 ~ an average crop.

작가(作家) 1 [소설가] a novelist; [저술가] a writer; [저자] an author. ¶여류 ~ a woman novelist[writer] / an authoress // 신진 ~ a rising[young] novelist / a budding writer // 인기 ~ a popular writer. 2 [예술품을 창작하는 사람] an artist. ¶도예 ~ a ceramic artist // 사진 ~ a photo artist.

작고(作故) death; decease. **작고하다** decease; die; pass away. ¶작고한 the late ... / the (late) lamented ... / the deceased ... // 작고한 사람 the deceased.

작곡(作曲) (musical) composition. ¶홍난파 ~ composed by Hong Nanpa // 슈베르트 ~, 실러 작시 Music by Schubert, Words by Schiller. **작곡하다** write music; compose (an opera). ¶시에 붙여 ~ set a poem to music / write the music for a poem // 이 노래는 그가 작사·작곡한 것이다 He wrote both words and music for this song.
● **작곡가** a (musical) composer.

작금(昨今) now; these days. ¶~의 더위 the hot weather these days / the recent hot weather // ~에는 nowadays / lately / recently // ~에는 천 원으로는 거의 아무것도 못 산다 You can hardly buy anything for one thousand won nowadays.

작년(昨年) last year. ⇨지난해 ¶~ 겨울 last winter // ~ 5월 last May / May of last year // ~ 오늘 this day last year / a year ago today.

작다 1 [길이·넓이·부피가 얼마 안 되다] small; little (▶ little은 종종 «귀여운» 등의 뜻을 가지며, 숙어로 쓰이는 경우는 드묾); tiny(아주 작다). ¶작은 집[방] a small house[room] // 작은 책상 a small[small-sized] desk // 작은 알갱이 a small grain // 작은 벌레 a tiny insect // 작은 활자 small[fine] print // 몸집이 작은 사람 a small person / a person of slight build[small stature] / a small-boned person // 이 신발은 내게 좀 ~ These shoes are a little too small for me. // 그는 나보다 키가 훨씬 ~ He is much shorter than I (am). // 그는 나이에 비해서 ~ He is small for his age. // 글씨가 작아서 읽을 수가 없다 The letters are too small for me to read.

2 [정도·범위·규모가 크지 않다] small; low(낮다). ¶8보다 작은 수 numbers smaller[lower] than eight // 작은 나라 a small country // 작은 목소리로 이야기하다 speak in a low[small] voice // 그 사업도 애초에는 규모가 작았다 The enterprise started from small beginnings.

3 [보잘것없다] small; trifling; trivial; slight; petty. ¶작은 일 a small[trivial] matter [affair] / a trifle // 작은 잘못 a small error // 싸움은 작은 일에서 비롯되는 일이 많다 Many quarrels have a petty beginning. // 그런 작은 일로 속을 썩이지 마라 Don't worry about such trivial matters.

4 [인물·도량이 좁다] small-minded; narrow-minded; petty. ¶작은 인물 a small-minded [petty] person / (스케일이) a man of small caliber // 그는 지도자로서는 인물이 ~ He is not a leadership caliber. / He lacks the qualities a leader needs.

작달막하다 short and thick; dumpy; stocky; stumpy. ¶키가 작달막하고 어깨가 떡 벌어진 남자 a stocky man.

작당하다(作黨-) form a group[clique / gang]; gang together; conspire. ¶작당하여 남을 죽이려 하다 conspire[form a conspiracy] against a person's life // 그는 친구들과 작당해서 그 노인한테서 큰돈을 우려냈다 He teamed up with his friends to swindle a large sum of money out of the old man.

작대기 1 [긴 막대기] a stick; a rod; a pole; a staff. ¶대나무 ~ a bamboo stick // ~를 휘두르다 wield a stick. 2 [잘못된 곳에 긋는 줄] the mark of failure (in a test).

작도(作圖) 1 [지도·설계도 등을 그림] drawing figures. **작도하다** draw a figure[chart / diagram]. 2 [수] construction. **작도하다** construct (a parallelogram).
● **작도법** drawing; draftmanship.

작동하다(作動-) run; work; operate. ¶기계가 작동하는 소리 the (operating) noise of a machine // 자동차의 엔진이 작동하지 않는다 The car engine is not running. // 스프링클러 설비는 발화와 동시에 작동했다 The sprinkler system began to function[work] as soon as the fire started. → 이 기계는 전력으로 작동된다 This machine is run[works] by electricity. // 그는 엔진을 작동시켰다 He started the engine.

작두 a straw[grass] cutter; a fodder chopper.
● **작두질** chopping; cutting.

작두콩 [식] a sword bean; a saber bean.

작렬(炸裂) (an) explosion. **작렬하다** explode; go off. ¶그 순간 폭탄이 작렬했다 At that moment a bomb exploded.

작명(作名) naming. **작명하다** give a name; name; christen(세례명을).

작문(作文) [글을 지음] composition; [지은 글] a composition. ¶자유 ~ free composition // ~을 짓다 write a composition. **작문하다** make a composition; write (a theme) composition.
● **작문 시간** a composition lesson.

작물(作物) the crops. ⇨ 농작물(農-). ¶원예 ~ garden stuff // 특용 ~ industrial crops // ~을 재배하다 raise[grow] crops // ~을 심다 plant a crop // 그들은 ~을 거둬들였다 They harvested[gathered in] the crop(s). // 이 지방의 주된 ~은 쌀이다 Rice is the principal crop in this area.

작법(作法) how to write[compose]. ¶시나리오 ~ how to write scenarios.

작별(作別) a farewell; a good-by(e); (a) parting; (a) separation. ¶~을 고하다 take (one's) leave / say good-by(e) (to) / say[bid] farewell[good-by(e)] (to) // ~을 아쉬워하다 be loath to part / express regret at parting // ~의 키스를 하다 kiss good-by(e) (to) // 우리는 선생님과 ~의 인사를 나누었다 We exchanged good-by(e)s with our teacher. // 고향으로 돌아가게 되어 ~ 인사차 왔습니다 As I am going to return to my native town, I have come to say[bid] good-by(e). **작별하다** take one's leave; bid farewell; part (from / with); say good-by(e). ¶부산으로 향하는 그와 역에서 작별했다 I saw him off at the station when he left for Busan. // 그는 손을 흔들며 그들과 작별하였다 He waved goodby(e) to them.

작부(作付) [작물을 심음] planting. **작부하다** crop[plant / sow] (a field with barley); put seeds in the ground.
● **작부 면적** the planted (rice) area[acreage]; the acreage under (rice) cultivation; the area under crop.

작부(酌婦) a waitress; a barmaid.

작사(作詞) ¶홍난파 ~ 작곡 words and music by Hong Nanpa. **작사하다** write words; write the lyrics (for a song).
● **작사자** a songwriter.

작살 a harpoon; a fish spear; a gig. ¶고래를 ~을 쏘다 harpoon a whale.

작살나다 be smashed to atoms; break[be broken] to splinters.

작살내다 break[crush / smash] (a thing) to pieces[atoms].

작성(作成) preparation; framing; drawing up. ¶연설문의 원고를 ~ 중이다 I am preparing [writing] a speech. **작성하다** make (out); prepare; frame; draw up; write out; [법] execute. ¶예산안을 ~ draw out a budget / 예정표를 ~ make out[prepare] a schedule // 초안을 ~ make[prepare / work out] a draft / 계약서를 2통 ~ draw up[prepare] a contract in duplicate.

작시(作詩) verse writing; versification. ⇨ 작(詩作)

작심(作心) a resolve; (a) resolution; (a) determination. **작심하다** resolve; determine; be determined; decide; make up one's mind.
● **작심삼일** a short-lived resolution; a resolution good for only three days. ¶그는 무슨 일에나 ~이다 He can't stick to anything. / He can't keep his resolutions longer than a day or two.

작약(芍藥) [식] a (herbaceous) peony.

작약(炸藥) an explosive; a bursting charge; bursting[blasting] powder.

작업(作業) work; operation. ¶공동 ~ cooperative work // 구조 ~ rescue operations // 그들은 일제히 ~을 시작했다 They all started work at once. // 우리는 매일 9시에 ~ 시작해서 6시에 마친다 Every day we start working at nine and stop (working) at six. // 그 공장은 ~이 중단되고 있다 Operations at the plant have been suspended. / The plant has suspended operations[has shut down]. // ~ 중 출입 금지 (게시) No Admittance During Working Hours. **작업하다** work; conduct operations.
● **작업 능률** operation[work] efficiency. **작업량** amount of work (to be) done; (어치) a man-day; (시간당) a manhour. **작업모** [군] a fatigue cap. **작업반** a work[working] party; (군대의) a fatigue party. **작업복** working dress[clothes / garments]; a working uniform; (선원의) a jumper; [가슴받이가 있고 멜빵이 달린 옷] overall. ¶~을 입은 젊은이 a youth in overalls. **작업 시간** working hours. **작업실** a workroom; an operation room. **작업장** a workshop; one's place of work. **작업 환경** working environment[surroundings].

작열(灼熱) incandescence; red[torrid] heat; broiling[scorching] heat. **작열하다** become red-hot. ¶작열하는 scorching / burning / red-hot / white-hot / incandescent // 하늘에는 작열하는 태양이 비치고 있었다 A scorching sun was shining in the sky.

작용(作用) (an) action; a working; (an) operation; (a) process; [영향] an effect; [기능] a function. ¶화학 ~ (a) chemical action // 동화 ~ the process of assimilation // 인력의 ~ the influence of gravity / a gravitational effect // 자연의 ~은 불가사의하다 The workings of nature are a mystery. **작용하다** act (on); work (on); operate (on); affect; function. ¶계략은 멋지게 작용했다 The strategy worked excellently. // 어떤 초자연적인 힘이 작용하고 있는 것 같다 Some supernatural power seems to be at work. // 산(酸)은 금속에 작용한다 Acids act on metals.
● **작용 반작용의 법칙** [물] the law of action and reaction. **작용선** [물] a line of action. **작용점** [물] a point of application.

작위(作爲) 1 [의도적으로 행동함] artificiality. ¶~적인 [의도적인] deliberate / intentional / [인공적인] artificial / contrived // 그때의 그의 행동은 우연인지 ~인지 판단하기 어렵다 It is difficult to decide whether his action at the time was accidental or deliberate. 2 [법] commission; feasance. ¶부(不)~ [법] nonfeasance / omission.
● **작위범** [법] a crime of commission.

작위(爵位) a title[degree] of nobility; peerage; court rank. ¶~를 가진 사람 a titled man / a man who has[with] a title // ~를 **수여하다** grace (a person) with a title.

작은곰자리 [천] the Little[Lesser] Bear; the Ursa Minor; the Little Dipper.

작은말 [언] a light insotope of a word.

작은아버지 an uncle; a younger uncle; one's father's[dad's] younger brother.

작은어머니 an aunt; a younger aunt; the wife of one's father's[dad's] younger brother.

작은집 1 [아들 · 동생의 집] one's son's[young-

작자(作者) 1 a tenant(farmer). ⇨ˆ소작인⇨소작) 2 [저자] an author; (소설 등의) a writer; (시인) a poet; (그림·조각 등의) an artist; (각본가) a dramatist; a playwright. ¶ 불명의 anonymous / authorless // 이 소설의 ~는 하디이다 This novel was written by Hardy. 3 [남을 업신여겨 이르는 말] a fellow; a guy; (영국 속어) a bloke. ¶그 ~는 어디로 갔을까 Where has the guy gone away? 4 [물건을 살 사람] a needy person (for a thing); a buyer; a purchaser. ¶~가 없다 find no buyer / have no demand // 그 집은 ~가 곧 나타났다 A buyer for the house was soon found.

작작 [대강·어지간하게] not too much; properly; moderately; in moderation; within measure. ¶술 좀 ~ 해라 Don't drink too much. / Be moderate in drinking. // 바보 같은 소리 ~ 해라 Stop your silly talk! / Cut out your nonsense!

작전(作戰) [군] (military) operations; [전략] strategy; [전술] tactics. ¶공동[합동] ~ concerted operations / combined [joint] action // 공세 [수세] ~ active [passive] operations / offensive [defensive] operations // 양동(陽動) ~ a feint operation // ~상의 strategic / operational // ~을 짜다 plan one's strategy / elaborate [work out] a plan of operations // 일대 ~을 개시[강행]하다 launch [undertake] a major action // ~을 그르치다 commit a strategic [a tactical / an operational] error // 거기는 ~상 중요한 지점이다 That place is of strategic importance. // ~이 딱 들어맞았다 Our plan [(구어) ploy] worked remarkably well. **작전하다** launch (military) maneuvers; carry out military operations.

● **작전 개시일** the D-day. **작전 계획** (make out) a plan of operations. **작전 기지** [center] of operations. **작전 타임** [체] a time-out.

작정(作定) 1 [결정] decision; determination; resolution. **작정하다** decide; determine; resolve; make up one's mind; fix upon [on]. ¶그는 술을 끊기로 작정했다 He decided [resolved] to quit [give up] drinking. // 그는 아들을 후계자로 삼기로 작정했다 He fixed upon his son as his successor. // 그는 의사가 되기로 작정했다 He determined [is determined] to become [be] a doctor. // 그는 직장을 그만두기로 작정했다 He made up his mind to resign from his job.
2 [의향] an intention; a plan; a design; an idea; a thought; a notion; [목적] a purpose; a goal. ¶그럴 ~으로 for that purpose / with that intention // 나는 그럴 ~이오 That's what I intend to do. // 내일 돌아올 ~이다 I intend [am planning] to come back tomorrow. // 어쩔 ~으로 그렇게 말했습니까 In [With] what spirit did you say so? **작정하다** intend to (do); plan.

작중 인물(作中人物) a character who appears in the work.

작파하다(作破-) stop; cease; give up; put an end (to); cancel; call off; withdraw. ¶계획을 ~ lay aside [drop] a scheme.

작폐(作弊) making trouble; making a nuisance. **작폐하다** give [cause] (a person) trouble [annoyance / worry]; make trouble [a nuisance]; exert an evil [a baneful] influence (upon); embarrass; annoy.

작품(作品) a (piece of) work; a product; a production; [음] an opus (*pl.* opera). ¶문예[문학] ~ a literary work // 예술 ~ a work of art // 현대 조각가 ~ 전 an exhibition of works by contemporary sculptors // 셰익스피어의 ~집 the works of Shakespeare // 훌륭한 ~ a marvelous piece of work // 피카소의 ~ (a work of) Picasso // 이 곡은 누구의 ~입니까 Who was the composer of this music? / Who composed this piece of music?

작풍(作風) a style; (문학의) a literary style; (어떤 작가·작곡가·미술가·시대 등의) (an) idiom. ¶베토벤의 ~ the idiom of Beethoven // 그는 헤밍웨이의 ~을 모방하여 글을 쓴다 He writes in the style of Hemingway. / His style is an imitation of Hemingway's.

작황(作況) (한 지역·한 종류의) a crop; a harvest; a yield; (한 지방·한 계절의) the crops. ¶올해는 ~이 좋다[나쁘다] The crops are good [poor] this year. // 올해는 벼의 ~이 좋다[나쁘다] We have a good [poor] crop of rice this year.

잔(盞) a cup; a glass; a teacup(찻잔); [술잔] a winecup; a wineglass. ¶~을 비우다 empty [drain] one's winecup (to the last drop) // ~을 거듭하다 drink one cup (of wine) after another / drink many cups of wine // ~을 주고받다 exchange cups (of wine) // ~을 들어 건강을 축복하다 drink to a person's health / toast (to) a person's health / raise one's glass to (a person) // ~을 가득 채우다 fill the cup [glass] to the brim.

잔가지 a twig; (꽃이나 잎이 달린) a sprig; (꽃이나 열매가 달린) a spray. ¶~를 치다 trim [prune] a tree / lop off twigs.

잔걸음 [가까운 데를 자주 왔다 갔다 하는 걸음] walking back and forth within a short distance; [발걸음을 작게 떼면서 걷는 걸음] walking with short steps. ¶~을 치다 walk back and forth within a short distance.

잔고(殘高) money left over. ⇨ˆ잔액

잔광(殘光) [해가 질 무렵의 약한 햇빛] an afterglow. ¶석양의 ~ the afterglow of a sunset. 2 [물] afterglow.

잔교(棧橋) 1 [계곡의 절벽 사이에 높이 걸친 다리] a suspension bridge. 2 [부두에 만들어진 구조물] a (landing) pier; a jetty. ¶군용 ~ a military pier // 목조[석조] ~ a wooden [masonry] pier // ~ 부(浮) ~ a floating pier / a floating stage.

잔구(殘丘) [지] a monadnock.

잔글씨 a small [fine] letter; a small character. ¶~로 쓰다 write small [closely].

잔금 a fine [small] line.

잔금(殘金) 1 [쓰고 남은 돈] (the) surplus (money); (the) money left (over). 2 [못다 갚은 돈] the remainder (of a payment); the balance (due). ¶~은 즉시 갚아 주시오 Please pay the balance [remainder / remaining sum] immediately. // 이번 주말까지는 빚의 ~을 갚아야 한다 I have to pay the remainder of my debt [what I owe] by the end of this week.

잔기(殘期) the remaining period [time]; the unexpired period.

잔기침 a slight cough; a hacking cough; a hack. **잔기침하다** hack; have a hacking [dry] cough.

잔꾀 (petty) tricks; shallow cunning; wiles; (an) artifice. ¶~ 부리는 사람 a tricky person / a petty trickey [trickster] // ~를 부리다 use tricks / work out a cunning [shrewd] scheme / play cheap tricks (on) / resort to petty tricks / be tricky / employ petty shifts / (미) frame up / (속이다/조작하다) manipulate / (구어) cook // 몰래 [뒤에서] ~를 부리다 play tricks [use trickery] behind the scenes // ~를 부리지 마라 None of your stupid [cheap] tricks!

잔당(殘黨) the remnants (of a defeated party). ¶과격파의 ~ 몇 명이 체포되었다 A few of the remaining radicals were arrested.

잔돈 [액수가 적은 돈] small coins [money]; (small) change. ¶잔갑 coin purse / a small change purse // ~으로 지불하다 pay in small change [with small money] // 지폐를 ~으로 바꾸다 break [change] a bill [(영) a note] into small money // ~ 없으세요 Have anything smaller? / ~이 하나도 없다 I don't have any small money [change] with me. // ~이 떨어졌다 I have run out of change. // ~으로 바꾸어 줄 수 있으세요 Can you change [break] this? / Can I have change for this?

잔돈(殘-) [거스름돈] change. ¶~ 여기 있습니다 Here's your change.

잔돌 a pebble. ¶~이 많은 pebbly.

잔디 [식] a lawn; turf; sod; (a patch of) grass. ¶마른 ~ dry turf / 깎는 기계 a lawn mower / (수동식) a hand mower / (동력식) a power [motor] mower / 뜰에 ~를 심다 turf [sod] the garden / lay the garden with turf // ~를 깎다 mow the grass [lawn].
● **잔디밭** a lawn; (a) turf; a grassplot. ¶~에 물을 뿌리다 sprinkle over the lawn // ~에 들어가지 마시오 《게시》 Keep off the grass.

잔뜩 1 [꽉 차게] full; fully; to the full; to capacity; 〔많이〕 a lot; in plenty; abundantly; heavily; amply. ¶~ 마시다 drink heavily [deep] / drink one's fill / 빚을 ~ 지고 있다 be under a heavy debt / be deeply indebted (to a person) / 빵에 잼을 ~ 바르다 spread a lot of jam on the bread / spread the bread thickly with jam // 어제는 ~ 쇼핑 했다 I did a lot of shopping yesterday. / 나는 레코드를 ~ 샀다 I bought many records. // 그는 돈을 ~ 모았다 He saved a lot of money. // ~ 먹었습니다 / I have had (more than) enough now. / I have eaten well.

2 [몹시] intensely; heavily; extremely; exceedingly; hard. ¶~ 찌푸린 날씨 dull [thick] weather / a heavily leaden [sullen / overcast] sky / ~ 취하다 be heavily [hopelessly / dead] drunk // 어제 그는 ~ 골이 났다 He got [became] hot with anger [rage] yesterday. // 어제는 ~ 일을 했다 I worked very hard yesterday.

잔루(殘壘) ¶2명의 주자가 ~로 끝났다 Two runners were left [stranded] on base.

잔류(殘留) remaining; staying behind. **잔류하다** remain [stay] behind.
● **잔류물** a residual substance; a residue; a residuum (pl. -dua); leavings; remnants; (a) sediment; (액체 등의) dregs.

잔말 small talk; useless talk; a small [an idle] complaint. ¶~ 마라 Stop complaining about every little thing. / Cut your bitching. / Shut up! **잔말하다** twaddle; say useless things.

잔망스럽다(孱妄-) feeble and narrow minded; weak and light-headed.

잔무(殘務) remaining [unfinished] business; unsettled affairs. ¶~를 정리하다 wind up the affairs (of) / settle [clear up] the remaining [pending] business / (미) close out [down / up] / 회사의 ~를 정리하다 wind up [liquidate] a company.

잔물결 ripples; rippling waves; wavelets. ¶~ 하나 없는 호수 면 the rippleless [glassy] surface of the lake // ~이 일다 ripple // 이따금 산들바람이 수면에 ~을 일으킨다 Now and then a gentle breeze ripples the surface of the water. // 잔잔한 수면에는 ~ 하나 없었다 Not a ripple disturbed the glassy surface of the water.

잔병(-病) a slight [minor] sickness [illness]; a slight indisposition; a minor ailment. ¶그는 아직 ~ 한번 앓은 적이 없다 He's never had [known] a day's illness.
● **잔병치레** getting sick frequently.

잔상(殘像) 〔심〕 an afterimage.

잔설(殘雪) the remaining snow; unmelted snow; lingering snow. ¶골짜기에는 아직도 ~이 남아 있었다 There was still some unmelted snow in the valley.

잔셈 a small [trifling] account. ¶~을 치르다 settle small accounts.

잔소리 1 [잔말] useless [small] talk; empty [idle] talk; empty prattle; tittle-tattle. ¶~가 심한 여자 a faultfinding woman / a nagging woman / a shrew / a termagant / 어머니는 ~가 많은 시어머니를 깍듯이 받들었다 My mother served her faultfinding mother-in-law faithfully. // 그는 몇 번이고 ~를 듣지 않으면 아무 일도 안한다 He does nothing unless he is told five hundred times. // 나는 그 여자의 그칠 줄 모르는 ~에 질렸다 I was fed up with [I got sick and tired of] her endless carping. // 그녀는 늘 아이들에게 ~를 늘어놓는다 She keeps grumbling at her children. // 그는 방음(防音)에 대해서 ~가 많다 He is very particular [finical] about sound-proofing. **잔소리하다** talk idle; say useless things; tittle-tattle; 〔종알거리다〕 nag (at); find fault (with); (미) gripe (at / about); 〔불평하다〕 complain (of); grumble (at / over). ¶그녀는 늘 남편의 귀가 시간이 늦다고 잔소리했다 She kept nagging her husband for coming home late.

2 [꾸중] (a) scolding; a rebuke; a lecture; preaching; (속어) a talking-to. ¶~ 그만 해 Enough of your preaching! / 넌 ~ 들을 거야 You'll catch it! / You'll be scolded. / You'll get [receive] a scolding. **잔소리하다** scold; lecture; give (a person) a scolding; give [read] (a person) a lecture [lesson]; rebuke; reprimand; reprove; (속어) jaw.
● **잔소리꾼** a chatterbox; prattler; a nag(ger); a carper; a faultfinder; a scolder; a preacher; a lecturer.

잔손 minute attention [care / trouble]; elaborate [detailed] handwork. ¶~이 가다 take [require] (much) manual effort / take (a lot of) trouble // ~이 가는 일 a piece of work requiring elaborate care / laborious [troublesome] handwork.
● **잔손질** working in detail [with much care]; [마무리 손질] (give) the finishing [final] touches.

잔솔 a young pine tree.
- **잔솔밭** a grove of young pines.

잔술(盞−) liquor in a cup[glass]; a glassful of liquor.
- **잔술집** a pub[tavern] that sells liquor by the cup[glass].

잔심부름 sundry errands[jobs]; odd jobs; miscellaneous services.

잔악하다(殘惡−) cruel; atrocious; brutal; inhuman; cold-blooded; outrageous. ¶온갖 잔악한 짓을 다하다 employ every means of atrocity[brutality] that one can think of.

잔액(殘額) [남은 돈] money left over; [예금 등의 잔고] the balance; [미불금] the remainder. ¶이월 ~ (차기로의) the balance carried forward / (전기로부터의) the balance brought forward // 은행 예금 ~을 알아보다 check one's bank balance[one's balance in the bank] // ~을 이월하다 have the balance carried forward (to) // ~을 전액 인출하다 draw the balance to nothing // ~은 얼마입니까 How much money is left?

잔업(殘業) overtime work; extra work. **잔업하다** work overtime[extra hours]; work after the usual hours[beyond office hours].
- **잔업 수당** overtime pay; an allowance for overtime work.

잔여(殘餘) the rest; [화학 처리 등의 잔류물이나 유산의 나머지 부분] the residue.
- **잔여액** the balance; the remainder. **잔여 재산** remaining[surplus] assets; [법] the residue[residuum] (of one's estate); residuary estate; residual property.

잔영(殘影) traces; remnants. ¶이 일대에는 옛 도읍의 ~이 남아 있다 Traces of the old capital remain in this area.

잔인성(殘忍性) (a) brutality; cruelty; a brutal[cruel] nature. ¶~을 드러내다 show the brutal side of one's nature / give rein to one's brutality // ~을 띠다 be cruel / have a brutal nature // ~을 띤 범행 a brutal crime.

잔인하다(殘忍−) brutal; cruel; merciless; cold-blooded; hardhearted; coldhearted; ruthless. ¶잔인한 성격 a brutal[cruel] nature / 잔인한 사람 a brutal[savage] man / a brute / 잔인한 짓 a cruel act / a brutality.

잔일 [자질구레한 일] a trifling[minor] matter; a matter of detail; [잔손 가는 일] troublesome work; sundry jobs; (household) chores.

잔잔하다 still; quiet; calm; tranquil; placid; peaceful; serene; smooth. ¶잔잔한 바다[호수] a calm[placid / serene] sea[lake] // 잔잔한 수면 calm water // 잔잔한 미소 a serene smile / 잔잔해지다 (바다가) become (grow) calm / calm[quiet] down / be lulled / (바람이) abate / drop / subside / die away / (바람·물결이) fall / blow itself out / (일시적으로) lull.

잔재(殘滓) 1 [찌꺼기] leavings; leftovers; remnants; (액체의) dregs. 2 [흔적] a vestige. ¶군국주의의 ~ (remaining) vestiges of militarism.

잔재미 a bit of pleasure[amusement]; subtle pleasure; (낚시질 등에서의) a nice bit of take [catch]. ¶~를 보다 have a nice little time of it / get a subtle pleasure (from it) / (성공) make a hit in a small way / (낚시질 등에서) fish up a nice bit of[not a few of] catch [take] / (이익을) turn a tidy profit // 도박에서 한 번 ~를 보면 발을 빼기가 어렵다 Once one is successful in gambling, it's hard to give it up.

잔재주 a cheap[petty] trick. ¶~을 부리다 play[resort] cheap tricks // 그는 ~로 세상을 살아가고 있다 He gets by on[with] his wits. // ~는 부리지 않는 게 좋다 You shouldn't play petty[cheap] tricks.

잔적(殘敵) remaining enemy; surviving enemy[soldiers]; enemy remnants[survivors]; stragglers(낙오자들). ¶~을 소탕하다 clear away the remnants of the enemy army / mop up enemy remnants.

잔존(殘存) [없어지지 않고 남아 있음] survival. **잔존하다** remain; survive; subsist. ¶이것은 오늘날 잔존하는 최고(最古)의 사본이다 This is the oldest extant manuscript. / This is the oldest manuscript existing today.
- **잔존 동물[식물]** relic fauna[flora]. **잔존물** a hangover; a survival. **잔존자** a survivor.

잔주름 fine wrinkles; (눈가의) crow's-feet. ¶~이 진 얼굴 a face lined with fine wrinkles / a finely wrinkled face // 그녀는 눈가에 ~이 있다 She has crow's-feet.

잔챙이 a small one of inferior quality; small fry. ¶물고기 ~ small fry[fish] // ~를 골라 내다 pick[sort] out a small, inferior one.

잔치 party; a feast; a banquet(공식적인). ¶돌 생일 ~ a birthday party for one-year old baby / 생일 ~ a birthday party // 혼인 ~ a wedding reception[banquet] / (영) a wedding breakfast(주간의 회식) / 환갑 ~ a banquet on one's sixtieth birthday // ~를 베풀다 hold [give] a party[feast] // ~에 참석하다 attend [be present at] a party // ~가 한창이다 The party is in full swing[is at its height].
- **잔칫집** a banqueting house.

잔털 fine hair; [솜털] downy hair.

잔품(殘品) the remaining stock(s); unsold goods; the stock left; remnants. ¶~이 얼마 없다 The stock is running short[low].

잔학하다(殘虐−) cruel; brutal; inhuman; ruthless. ¶잔학한 행위 a cruel[brutal] act / (문어) an atrocity.

잔해(殘骸) (배·건물 등의) a wreck; (집합적) wreckage; [잔류물] ruins; [무너진 것] debris. ¶그 비행기의 ~는 정글 속에서 발견되었다 The wreckage from[of] the plane was found in the jungle. // 배의 ~는 인양될 것이다 The wreck[wreckage / remains] of the ship will be salvaged.

잔향(殘響) (a) reverberation. ¶절의 종소리의 ~ the reverberation(s) of a temple bell.

잔허리 the small of the back.

잔혹하다(殘酷−) cruel; brutal; merciless; atrocious. ¶잔혹하게 다루다 treat (a person) cruelly[brutally].

잘 1 [익숙하고 은란하게] well; skillfully; cleverly; expertly. ¶그녀는 피아노를 ~ 친다 She plays the piano well. / She is a good piano player[pianist]. / She is good at playing the piano. // 그는 글씨를 ~ 쓴다 He is good at handwriting. / He writes well. // 이 상의는 ~ 만들었다 This jacket is well made. / This is a well-made jacket. // 그녀는 춤을 ~ 춘다 She is skillful at[in] dancing. // 그는 말을 아주 ~ 다룬다 He is very clever with horses. // 그는 문장을 ~ 쓴다 He is a good writer.
2 [주의해서] carefully; attentively; cautious-

ly.¶자동차를 ~ 몰고 가라 Drive your car carefully.// ~ 듣고 있다네 I'm listening carefully.// ~ 생각하고 답을 써라 Think carefully before you write the answer.// 이 사진을 ~ 보아라 Look at this picture carefully [well / closely]. / Have a good look at this picture.

3 [탈 없이·무사히] safely; in safety; well; all right.¶무사히 ~ 돌아왔구나 How lucky you got back safe and sound!// 컴퓨터는 ~ 작동하고 있다 The computer is working well.// 재봉틀이 ~ 돌아가지 않는다 Something is wrong[the matter] with the sewing machine.

4 [좋게] favorably; well; good; nice; [훌륭하게] finely; admirably.¶아이를 ~ 키우다 bring up one's child the way a child should be brought up// 남을 ~ 말해 주다 speak well[favorably] of a person / say good things about a person / say a good word for a person// 그는 언제나 자기만 ~ 보이려고 한다 He always tries to take all the credit for himself[make himself look good (at the expense of others)].

5 [충분히] fully; perfectly; thoroughly; well; [만족스럽게] successfully; favorably. ¶~ 자다 sleep well / have a good sleep / pass [have] a good night// 나는 내 기분을 ~ 표현할 수 없다 I can't express my feelings well.// 교섭은 ~ 마무리 지어졌다 The negotiations ended successfully.// ~ 먹었습니다 I have enjoyed my dinner very much. / Thank you for your hospitality [your hospitable entertainment].// ~ 모르겠는데요. 다시 한 번 말씀해 주십시오 I didn't quite get it. Please say it again.// 그것을 ~ 생각해 보고 결심해라 Make up your mind after you have thought it over thoroughly.

6 [정확히] closely; exactly. ¶네 비밀을 내가 ~ 알고 있어 I know exactly what your secret is.// ~ 알고 있습니다 I am well aware of it.// ~ 알았습니다 Certainly[Very good], sir[ma'am].// 그를 ~ 알고 있다 I know him very well.// 그녀가 한 말을 ~ 기억하고 있다 I remember exactly what she said.

7 [적절히] properly; [때·기회] opportunely; in good time; just in time. ¶마침 ~ 왔군 You've come at the right[a timely] moment.// 그것을 ~ 부탁하네 I leave it to your judgment. / I trust it to your discretion [good offices].

8 [예쁘게·멋지게] beautifully; prettily; charmingly; smartly. ¶~ 차려입다 be in one's (Sunday) best / wear [put on] fine clothes / dress oneself beautifully.

9 [자주] (very) often; frequently; [걸핏하면] readily; easily. ¶~ 웃다 laugh readily// 그는 눈물을 ~ 흘린다 He is easily moved to tears. / He cries easily.// 그는 화를 ~ 낸다 He often gets angry.// 내가 어릴 적에 어머니는 책을 ~ 읽어 주셨다 When I was a child, my mother used to read me books.

10 [맞는 모양·어울리는 모양] well; properly. ¶~ 맞다 fit nicely[to a T]// 그 그림은 이 방에 ~ 맞지 않는다 That picture does not suit [go well with] this room.// 그와 그의 아들은 서로 뜻이 ~ 맞지 않았다 He and his son did not get along well with each other.// 그의 생각은 현대와 ~ 맞지 않는다 His ideas are outdated[out-of-date].

11 [쉽게] easily; with ease; handily; without difficulty. ¶이 고기는 ~ 썰린다 This meat cuts[carves] easily.// 이 철사는 ~ 구부러진다 This wire is easy to bend.

12 [분명히] clearly; distinctly; plainly; obviously. ¶내 목소리가 ~ 들려요? Can you hear me distinctly?// 그의 목소리는 전화에서 ~ 들렸다 His voice was clear and plain over the telephone.// 사진 속의 인물들은 아주 ~ 나와 있다 All the figures in the photograph are very clear[easily recognized / clearly identifiable].

잘 자랄 나무는 떡잎부터 안다(속담) Genius displays itself even in childhood.

잘가닥 1 [부딪는 소리] with a click[snap]. ¶자물쇠가 ~ 잠겼다[열렸다] The lock clicked shut[open]. **2** [들러붙는 모양]. ¶~ 들러붙다 stick fast[hard] (like wax).

잘그랑 with a clang[clank / clink].

잘나다 1 [뛰어나다] eminent; excellent; [비범하다] extraordinary; remarkable. ¶잘난 사람 an extraordinary character / (속어) a bigwig / (속어) a big name // 자기를 잘났다고 생각하다 think much[highly] of oneself / have a high opinion[a great idea] of oneself // 잘난 체하다 put on[assume] airs/an air of importance] // 잘난 체하고 with an air of importance // 나는 그가 잘난 체하는 것이 싫다 I don't like the way he acts important.// 그는 자기가 잘났다고 생각한다 He thinks he is (a) somebody.

2 [모양이 보기에 좋다] good-looking; comely; fair; pretty; handsome; beautiful.

3 (반어적) useless; worthless; trifling; unworthy. ¶그는 늘 그 잘난 지식을 과시한다 He always shows off his poor knowledge.// 너 참 잘났어 You're a fine one!

잘다 1 [작다] small; fine(가루 등이); [가늘다] slender. ¶글씨를 잘게 쓰다 write closely// 그녀는 천을 잘게 찢었다 She tore the cloth to shreds.// 이 해안은 모래가 ~ The beach has fine sand.// 그녀는 양파를 잘게 썰었다 She chopped the onions up. **2** [생각·성질이 좀스럽다] small; narrow-minded; mean. ¶잔 사람 a small-minded person / a mean fellow// 그런 말을 하다니 너도 사람이 잘구나 It is small of you to say so.// 그는 사람이 ~ He has a narrow mind. / He is narrow-minded [a narrow-minded man].

잘되다 1 [성공하다] get on in the world[in life]; rise[succeed] in the world; make a success in life[the world]; make one's way [get on] in life; [승진하다] win[get / obtain] promotion. ¶그의 부모님은 아들이 잘된 것을 보고 기뻐했다 His parents were glad of their son's success[glad that their son had succeeded] in life.

2 (일이) go well[right]; work well; work out; go on smoothly; (결과가) come[turn] out all right; pay off. ¶늘 그렇게 잘되는 것은 아니다 Things do not always go well.// 그가 나타날 때까지는 만사가 잘되어 가고 있었다 Everything was going well[smoothly] until he appeared on the scene.// 일이 잘되지 않을 때는 어떻게 하려느냐 What will you do if things don't work out?// 일은 잘되었다 Things have gone well. / Things have come out well.

3 (장사·사업이) prosper; be prosperous; thrive; flourish. ¶요즈음은 장사가 잘되지 않

는다 These days my business has not been going well.∥장사가 잘되었다 The business was[proved] a success.∥그의 사업이 잘되고 있다 His business is thriving[flourishing]. / He is enjoying good business.

4 (만든 것·솜씨가) be done[made] well; be of fine make; be of excellent workmanship. ¶밥이 잘되었다 The rice is done well.∥이 수프는 아주 잘되었다 This soup is well made[very good].∥이번 퍼머는 썩 잘되지 못했다 My perm didn't take very well this time.

5 (농사가) have a good[fine] crop (of wheat); be fruitful(과실이); (작황이) be growing[doing] well. ¶올해는 벼농사가 잘되었다[잘되지 않았다] We had a good[poor] rice crop this year.∥이 지방에서는 복숭아가 잘된다 Peaches grow well in this part of the country.∥이 농장에서는 속성 재배의 야채가 잘된다 This farm produces good crops of forced vegetables.

6 (완전하다) be thorough[perfect / complete]; be well attended[tended]. ¶우리 학교는 위생 시설이 잘되어 있다 Our school has complete sanitary facilities.∥뜰의 손질이 잘돼 있다 The garden is tended with great care.

잘되면 제 탓 못되면 조상 탓(속담) One puts credit[merit] upon oneself when things go well, and blames one's ancestors when not.

잘라먹다 bilk[jump] (a bill / a person). ⇨떼어먹다

잘래잘래 shaking (one's head). ¶머리를 ~ 혼들다 shake one's head (several[many] times).

잘록하다 constricted[compressed] (in the middle); narrow; slim; slender. ¶잘록한 아가씨 a slim-waisted girl∥표주박의 잘록한 부분 the neck[narrow part] of a gourd∥그 꽃병은 중간 부분이 ~ The vase is narrow in the middle.

잘리다 [끊어지다] be cut (off); be chopped; be severed; be torn; (나무가) be felled[hewed]; be cut down. [목이] ~ be decapitated[beheaded] / [해고되다] be dismissed[discharged] / (구어) be fired / (구어) get the ax(e) / (속어) get the boot∥나무가 잘린 곳 the cleaved space∥내 손가락이 잘렸다 I had my finger cut.∥강풍으로 전깃줄이 잘리었다 The gale tore up telegraph wire.

잘못 1 [과실] a fault; an error; a misstep; a slip; [오류] a mistake; [죄과] a blame. ¶[작은] ~ a gross[slight / minor] error∥인쇄의 ~ a printer's error / a misprint / (구어) a typo [계산의] ~ a misspelling[miscalculation]∥판단의 ~ an error in judgment∥~을 저지르다 make a mistake[an error]∥~을 인정하다 admit[acknowledge] a mistake∥자기 ~을 깨닫다 see[(문어) perceive] one's error∥네 작문에는 ~이 많다 Your composition has a lot of[is full of] mistakes.∥내 기억에 ~이 없는 한 그녀는 미국이 아니라 캐나다로 유학을 갔다 If I remember correctly[(구어) right], she went to Canada to study, not the U.S.A.∥~이 있으면 고쳐다 Correct errors if (there are) any.∥그렇게 생각한 것이 ~이었다 I was mistaken in thinking so.∥그가 돈을 빌려 주리라고 생각하면 큰 ~이야 If you think he's going to lend you money, you are badly[very much] mistaken[you're terribly wrong / you are making a big mistake].∥그의 계산에 ~이 있었다 There were some mistakes in his calculations.∥그의 ~이 아니다 It's not his fault. / He is not to blame.∥그는 자기 ~을 인정하려고 들지 않았다 He would not admit[acknowledge] that he was wrong[to blame]. **잘못하다** make a mistake[an error]; err; do wrongly[improperly / amiss]; misdo; blunder. ~을 by mistake / in error; mishandle one's car∥판단을 ~ err in one's judgment∥해석을 ~ misinterpret / take a thing in a wrong sense∥계산을 ~ make a mistake[an error] in calculation / miscalculate∥그는 직업의 선택을 잘못했다 He chose the wrong job.∥자칫 잘못하다가는 네 목숨이 위태롭다 If things go wrong, your life will be in danger.∥어서 잘못했다고 해라 Come on, now, and say you're sorry. ➔**잘못되다** go wrong[badly] / be unsuccessful / make a mess of∥잘못된 생각 a mistaken[an erroneous] thought∥잘못된 정의감 a false sense of justice∥그 벽칠은 분명히 잘못되어 있다 The wall is obviously not painted well.∥이 편지는 주소가 잘못되어 있다 The address on this letter is wrong. / This letter is addressed wrongly.∥엔진이 어딘지 잘못되어 있다 Something is wrong with the engine.

2 [틀리게] by[through] mistake; in error; through one's fault; misguidedly; mistakenly; wrong(ly). ¶첫발을 ~ 디디다 make a wrong start / start off on the wrong foot∥정책을 ~ 세우다 adopt a misguided policy∥나는 길을 ~ 들어[잡아] 헤맸다 I took the wrong road and got lost.∥전화가 ~ 걸려 왔다 It was a wrong number.∥사람을 ~ 보신 게 아닙니까 Aren't you taking me for somebody else? / You must be mistaking me for someone else.∥하마터면 아가씨의 언니로 볼 뻔했다 I almost took you for your sister.∥운전사가 교통 신호를 ~ 보았기 때문에 사고가 발생했다 The accident occurred because the driver misread the signal.∥그녀는 내 핸드백을 ~ 가져갔다 She took my bag home with her by mistake.∥그는 기차를 ~ 탔다 He took a[the] wrong train.∥그는 그녀의 말을 ~ 들었다 He misunderstood her.

잘못짚다 guess wrong; make a wrong guess[estimate]; misjudge (the result); make a miscalculation (about); shoot at the wrong mark. ¶그가 힘이 되어 주리라 생각했는데, 내가 잘못짚은 것이었다 I thought I could depend on him, but he did not come up to[fell short of] my expectations.

잘바닥 with a splash[slosh]. **잘바닥하다** splash. ⇨잘바닥거리다

잘바닥거리다 splash; slosh.

잘살다 live in affluence[opulence]; have a comfortable living; be well-off; live happily. ¶잘사는 농부 a wealthy[substantial] farmer∥잘살게 되다 become[grow] rich / come to wealth.

잘생기다 good-[nice-]looking; beautiful; pretty; handsome; comely; fair. ¶잘생긴 남자 a handsome[good-looking] man∥잘생긴 여자 a beautiful[pretty] woman∥얼굴이 ~ have a handsome[pretty] face∥조지는 잘생긴 소년이다 George is a good-looking boy.∥그녀는 잘생긴 편이 못된다 She is rather

homely [plain-looking]. / She has plain features. (▶ 모두 ugly의 완곡한 표현임)

잘잘 1 [더운 모양] simmeringly; boilingly; bubblingly. ¶ ~ 끓다 simmer / boil / seethe / stew / bubble // 방바닥이 ~ 끓는다 The floor of the hypocaust is piping hot. // 환자는 열이 있어 몸이 ~ 끓었다 The patient was hot with fever.
2 [흔드는 모양] shakingly. ¶약병을 ~ 흔들다 shake a bottle of medicine // 동전을 손에 쥐고 ~ 흔들다 jingle coins in one's hand.
3 [쏘다니는 모양] bustlingly; busily. ¶매일 밤 어디를 그렇게 ~ 쏘다니냐 Where do you gad about every night?
4 [끌리는 모양] draggingly. ¶그녀는 드레스의 자락을 ~ 끌었다 Her long dress was trailing along behind her.
5 [기름기가 도는 모양] oilily; greasily. ¶개기름이 ~ 흐르는 40대 남자 an oily-faced fleshy man in his forties // 기름이 ~ 도는 생선 an oily fish // 그녀의 머리는 까마귀의 깃털처럼 새까맣고 윤기가 ~ 흘렀다 Her hair was black and glossy as the raven's wing.

잘잘못 right and [or] wrong. ¶ ~의 판단 discrimination of right and wrong // ~을 가리다 distinguish between right and wrong / tell [distinguish] right from wrong // 이 경우 ~을 밝히기는 어렵다 In this case we cannot tell right from wrong. // 법정에 가서 ~을 가려보자 Let's argue the rights and wrongs of the case in court. // ~간에 그것은 사실이다 It may be right or wrong, but it is a fact.

잘하다 1 [올바르게 하다] do a right thing; do right; [훌륭히 하다] do well; do (a thing) successfully. ¶길에서 주운 지갑을 파출소에 갖다 준 것은 아주 잘한 일이었다 It was quite right of you to take the purse you had found on the road to the police box. // 네가 판단을 잘했다 You were right [correct] in your judgment. // 잘했다 Well done!
2 [능란하게 하다] be skillful (in); be good (at / in); be expert (in / at); be a good hand (at). ¶노래를 ~ sing well // 요리를 ~ be good at cooking / be a good cook // 거래를 ~ have a flair for bargains // 이야기를 ~ be a good talker // 공부를 ~ be doing well at school // 그는 영어를 아주 잘한다 He is very good at English. // 그녀는 영어를 잘하지만 수학은 잘하지 못한다 She is good at [does well in] English but (is) no good [poor] at math. (▶ does well을 사용할 때는 but 다음의 is가 필요함) // 그는 자기 반에서 잘하는 축에 속한다 He ranks high in his class. // 그는 자기 반에서 가장 잘한다 He is at the top of his class. // 그는 수영을 잘한다 He is good at swimming. / He is a good swimmer. / He swims well. // 당신은 영어를 잘하는군요 You speak good English. // 그는 골프를 꽤 잘한다 He can play golf pretty well. // 그는 술을 잘한다 He is a drinker.
3 [만족하게 하다] satisfy; gratify; please; give (a person) satisfaction. ¶그 녀석은 언제나 사장에게 잘하려고 한다 He is always trying to please the president. / (구어) He is always sucking up to the president. // 그녀는 내게 아주 잘해 주었다 She was very good [kind] to me.
4 [자주 하다] do often [frequently]. ¶거짓말을 ~ be a habitual liar // 그는 결석을 잘한다 He is often absent.
5 [기타]. ¶그들은 잘하면 큰돈을 벌 수 있다고 생각하고 있다 They figure that they can make a mint of money if all goes well. // 잘하면 내일은 일이 끝난다 With luck [If things go well], we will finish the work tomorrow.

잘해야 at best; at the very best; at (the) most; at the very most. ¶정확히는 모르지만 ~ 2분 정도일 것으로 생각됩니다 I don't know exactly, but I should think about two minutes at the most.

잠 1 [수면] (a) sleep; (a) slumber(숙면); [졸기] a nap; a doze. ¶선 ~ a light sleep // 깊은 [편안한 / 불안한] ~ a deep [restful / uneasy] sleep // ~을 깨우다 awake / wake up / [각성시키다] awaken / bring (a person) to (his) senses // ~이 깨다 wake (up) / awake / be awakened / [비유] come [be brought] to one's senses / have one's eye opened // ~을 설치다 sleep badly / not sleep well / toss and turn all night // 어젯밤에는 ~이 모자랐다 I didn't get enough sleep last night. // 나는 좀처럼 ~이 들지 못했다 I did not get to sleep easily. // 그는 곧 ~이 들었다 He soon fell asleep. // 따뜻한 날씨 때문에 그는 ~이 왔다 The warm weather made him sleepy. // 요란한 모터사이클 소리가 내 ~을 방해했다 My sleep was disturbed by the screech of motorbikes. // 아래층에서 나는 소리에 ~이 깼다 I was awakened by a noise downstairs. // 나는 밤중에 ~이 싹 깨어 새벽까지 통 자지 못했다 I awoke completely in the middle of the night and couldn't get back to sleep till dawn. // 차를 너무 마셨더니 ~이 오지 않았다 Too much tea kept me awake.
2 [누에의] sleep (of the silkworm). ¶누에의 한 [두 / 석] ~ the first [second / third] sleep of the silkworm.
3 [솜 등의] the state of being pressed. ¶ ~을 재운 이불솜 pressed wadding for bedquilt.

잠을 자야 꿈을 꾸지(속담) You must sow before you can reap.; Larks do not fall ready-roasted into your mouth.; No cause, no effect.

잠결 ¶ ~에 while (one is) asleep / in one's sleep / while dozing(졸며) // ~에 듣다 hear while asleep [half asleep] // ~에 나는 훌쩍훌쩍 우는 소리를 들었다 In my sleep I heard someone sobbing. // 나는 ~에 "불이야!" 하는 소리를 들었다 Half asleep and half awake, I heard the cry, "Fire!"

잠귀 ¶ ~가 밝은 사람 a light [bad] sleeper // ~가 밝다 be easily awakened / be wakeful / be a light sleeper // ~가 어둡다 [질기다] be a heavy [sound / good] sleeper / hard to arouse from sleep // 노인은 대개 ~가 밝다 Old people are mostly light sleepers.

잠그다[1] 1 (문 등을) lock (up); fasten (with a lock [latch]). ¶문을 ~ lock [fasten] a door // 창고 [가게] 잠그는 것을 잊지 마라 Don't forget to lock up the warehouse. // 문과 창문을 모두 잠갔어요 Have you fastened all the doors and windows? 2 (수도 등을) turn off. ¶수도를 ~ turn off the tap [water] // 가스를 ~ turn off the gas / turn the gas out // 수도 잠그는 것을 잊어버렸다 I forgot to turn off the water.

잠그다[2] (액체 속에) soak; immerse (in) (충분히); dip (in) (잠깐); steep (in) (잠가 두다). ¶탕 안에 몸을 ~ soak in the bath // 더운물에 발을 ~ dip one's feet in hot water.

잠기다

잠기다[1] 1 [문·자물쇠 등이] be locked; lock; be fastened. ¶자물쇠가 잠긴 문 a locked door // 문의 자물쇠가 잠기지 않는다 The door won't lock. // 이 블라우스의 단추는 잘 잠기지 않는다 The buttons on this blouse are hard to fasten. 2 [목이 쉬다] get[become / grow] hoarse[husky / harsh]; hoarsen; have a frog in the throat. ¶너무 소리를 질러 목이 ~ shout[shriek] oneself hoarse // 감기 때문에 목이 꽉 잠겼다 I lost my voice because of a cold. // 그는 목이 잠겨 있다 His voice is hoarse.

잠기다[2] 1 [물속에] soak[be soaked] (in); be immersed[steeped] (in); [수몰되다] be submerged (in); be flooded (with water); be under (water). ¶물에 잠긴 배 a waterlogged boat // 온 마을이 물에 잠겼다 The whole village was submerged[flooded]. / The whole village was under water. // 우리 집이 방바닥 밑[위]까지 물에 잠겼다 Our house was flooded below[above] the floor level. // 나는 욕조 물에 잠겨 위스키를 마셨다 I drank whisky while soaking[I soaked] in the bath. // 고래는 오랜 시간 물속에 잠겨 있을 수 있다 The whale can remain[stay] underwater for a long time.
2 [열중하다] be absorbed[engrossed / immersed] in; be intent[bent] on; give oneself [be given] to. ¶생각에 ~ be lost[sunk] in thought // 그녀는 슬픔에 잠겨 있다 She is sunk in sorrow. // 온 도시가 슬픔에 잠긴 것처럼 보였다 The whole town had a grief-stricken look about it. // 그는 비탄에 잠겨 있었다 He was overwhelmed by[with] grief. / Grief overwhelmed him. // 그는 명상에 잠겨 있다 He is lost in meditation[contemplation]. // 나는 추억에 잠겼다 I lost myself in reminiscences.
3 (돈 등이) be tied up; be locked up. ¶자본이 토지에 잠겨 있었다 The capital was locked up in land.

잠깐 [명사] a while; a short time; [부사] just a minute[moment]; for a moment[while]; briefly. ¶~의 momentary / brief // 그들의 즐거운 생활은 아주 ~이었다 Their happy life together lasted but a short while. // 오래 기다렸던 휴일도 ~으로 끝나 버렸다 My long-awaited holiday was over in a moment [flash]. // ~ 사이에 마을이 완전히 변했다 The village changed completely in a very short time. // ~만 기다려 주세요 Just a moment, please. // ~ 뵙고 싶은데요 May I see you for just a moment[for a (little) while]?

잠꼬대 1 [수면 중의 헛소리] talking in one's sleep; somniloquy(습관적인). **잠꼬대하다** talk while asleep in one's sleep]. ¶큰 소리로 ~ cry out in one's sleep // 내 누이동생은 매일 밤 잠꼬대한다 My sister talks in her sleep [while asleep] every night. 2 [사리에 닿지 는 말] silly talk; nonsense; rot. ¶~ 같은 네 말을 누가 들어 주겠니 No one will listen to your nonsense. / It is useless to talk such nonsense. // ~ 같은 소리 작작 해라 Don't talk rubbish! **잠꼬대하다** talk nonsense[rot / rubbish].

잠꾸러기 a sleepyhead; a late riser; a lie-abed. ¶그는 ~다 He gets up late. / He is a late riser.

잠동무 a bed fellow; a bedmate.

잠들다 1 [잠을 자는 상태가 되다] fall asleep; go off to sleep; sink [fall] into a slumber [sleep]. ¶아기는 어머니 품 안에서 잠들었다 The baby fell asleep in its mother's arms. // 그는 곧 잠들었다 Soon he fell asleep. // 그는 몹시 술에 취해 홀에서 잠들어 버렸다 Quite drunk, he dropped off to sleep[fell asleep] in the hall. // 그는 자리에 눕자마자 잠들어 버렸다 No sooner had he gone to bed than he was asleep.
2 [죽다] die; pass away; go to one's rest. ¶영원히 ~ sleep the eternal[last] sleep / go to one's long sleep / take one's last sleep // 그의 영혼이여 고이 잠드소서 May his soul rest in peace! // 많은 병사가 바다 밑바닥에 잠들어 있다 Many soldiers lie beneath the sea.

잠망경 (潛望鏡) a periscope.
잠바 a (zip-up) jacket. ⇨ 점퍼
잠방이 knee-length pants (for men); short pants[trousers] (for men); unlined shorts [pants] (for men).
잠버릇 ¶그는 ~이 나쁘다 He moves[rolls] around on his bed while asleep. / He tosses around[about] in his sleep.

잠복 (潛伏) 1 [숨음] hiding; concealment; an ambush. ¶그는 ~ 중이다 He is in hiding. **잠복하다** conceal oneself; go into hiding; be in hiding; lie low. ¶잠복하고 있다가 행인을 습격하다 waylay a passerby // 3명의 형사가 건너편 아파트에 잠복하고 있었다 Three detectives were staked out in an apartment across the street. // 범인은 시내에 잠복했음에 틀림없다 The criminal must be in hiding in the city.
2 [병의 증상이 밖으로 나타나지 않음] latency. **잠복하다** lie latent[dormant]. ¶결핵균이 어린 시절부터 그녀의 몸 안에 잠복해 있었던 것 같다 She appears to have been carrying the tubercle bacilli since her childhood.
● **잠복근무** (be on the) ambush (sentry) duty. **잠복기** [의] the incubation[latent] period. ¶그 병은 ~가 길다[짧다] The disease has a long[short] incubation period.
잠사 (蠶絲) silk thread.
● **잠사업** the silk-reeling[sericultural] industry.
잠수 (潛水) diving. **잠수하다** dive; go underwater; submerge. ¶진주 채취를 위해 ~ dive for pearls.
● **잠수 모함** a submarine tender[carrier / depot ship]. **잠수복** a diving suit[dress]. **잠수부** a diver. **잠수함** a submarine; (구어) a sub; an underwater boat. ¶공격형 ~ a hunter-killer submarine // 원자력 ~ an atomic(-powered) submarine / a nuclear-powered[-propelled / -driven] submarine // ~으로 습격하다 submarine (a convoy).

잠시 (暫時) [명사] a little[short] while; a moment; [부사] for a (little[short]) while; for some time; for a (period of) time; for a moment. ¶~의 기쁨 (a) transient joy // ~의 사랑 passing[short-lived] love // ~만 기다려 주십시오 Please wait a while. / Please wait (for) a few minutes. // ~ 후 그가 나타났다 He appeared after a short time[presently]. (▶ presently는 (미)에서는 조금 딱딱한 느낌) // ~ 후에 그가 올 것이다 He will come in a few minutes[before long]. // ~라도 이 일을 잊어서는 안 된다 Do not forget this for even a moment. / Don't ever forget this.∥그는 ~ 있다가 대답했다 He answered after a short pause.∥이 아이는 ~도 눈을 뗄 수가 없습니다 The child needs constant watching.

잠식(蠶食) encroachment; aggression. **잠식하다** [서서히 침입하다] encroach (on); make inroads (into / on / upon). ¶한국 상품이 이 나라의 시장을 잠식하기 시작했다 Korean goods began to make inroads on[eat into] this country's markets.∥수입품이 국내 시장을 잠식했다 Imports took over the domestic market.∥두 후보는 표밭을 서로 잠식하다가 둘 다 떨어졌다 The two candidates stole each other's votes and both lost.

잠실(蠶室) a silkworm-rearing[-raising] room.

잠언(箴言) **1** [훈계의 말] a maxim; a proverb; an aphorism; an adage. **2** [성] the Book of Proverbs(약어 Prov.). ¶솔로몬의 ~ the Proverbs Solomon.

잠업(蠶業) the sericultural industry. ⇨양잠업(⇨양잠)

잠열(潛熱) [물] latent heat. ⇨숨은열

잠옷 night clothes; (헐렁한 여성·어린이용의) a nightgown; (남자용 셔츠형의) a nightshirt; [과자마] (a pair of) pajamas. ¶~ 바람으로 in one's night clothes[pajamas]∥빨리 ~로 갈아입어요 Change[Get ready] for bed quickly.

잠입(潛入) infiltration. **잠입하다** infiltrate (the enemy country)(▶ 주로 군대 용어); [숨어 들어가다] sneak[steal] into; [밀항하여 들어가다] smuggle oneself into (a country). ¶무장간첩들이 서울에 잠입했다 Some armed agents infiltrated Seoul. ➔적국에 스파이를 잠입시키다 infiltrate enemy territory with spies / smuggle a spy into the enemy country.

잠자다 1 [사람·동물이] sleep; have a sleep. ¶잠자는 사자 a sleeping lion∥잠자는 숲 속의 미녀 (the) sleeping Beauty. **2** [부푼 것이] lie down; be smoothed[pressed] down. ¶이불솜이 잠잤다 The (cotton) wadding for bedquilt was well set. **3** [자본 등이] lie idle; [상품이] remain unsold (on the shelf). ¶잠자고 있는 자본 dead capital∥잠자고 있는 물자 idle commodities∥막대한 자원이 지하에 잠자고 있다 Vast resources lie idle[untapped / unexploited] under the ground.

잠자리[1] [자는 자리] a bed; a kip; a crib[(영) cot] (유아용의); a berth(기차·기선 등의); a pallet(짚을 넣은). ¶온돌방에 ~를 깔다 spread the bedding in an ondol room∥~에 들다 go to bed / turn in / (구어) hit the sack∥~에서 나오다 get out of bed∥~에서 담배를 태우다[책을 읽다] smoke[read] in bed∥~를 개다 fold (up) the bedding∥그는 여느 때보다 일찍 ~에 들었다 He went to bed earlier than usual.

잠자리를 같이하다 sleep together; sleep with (a person); sleep double; sleep in the same bed (with).

잠자리(를) 보다 (밤에 자기 전에) prepare a bed; make a bed.

잠자리[2] [동] a dragonfly; a devil's darning needle.

잠자코 dumbly; silently; without a word; without comment; without saying anything; obediently; without objection. ¶~ 있다 be [remain] silent / say nothing∥~ 열심히 일하다 work hard in silence∥그 점에 대해서 그는 ~ 있었다 He said nothing[kept silent / held his tongue] on the point.∥그것에 대해서는 ~ 있는 게 좋아 You had better keep it to yourself.∥그는 ~ 나가 버렸다 He went out without saying a word. / (인사도 없이) He took French leave.∥~ 하란 대로 해 Do as you are told without any questions.∥그런 모욕에는 ~ 있을 수 없다 I cannot take such an insult lying down.∥이렇게 많은 사람들이 피로워하고 있는데 내가 ~ 있을 수는 없다 I cannot remain indifferent when so many people are suffering.∥이런 부당한 처사에 ~ 있을 수 없다 I cannot put up with such unfair treatment.

잠잠하다(潛潛-) silent; (deathly) quiet; still; hushed. ¶잠잠해지다 become still[quiet] / fall silent∥분쟁은 마침내 잠잠해졌다 The dispute finally subsided[calmed down / was finally settled].∥거리는 ~ All is quiet in the street. / The street looks deserted.∥청중은 물을 끼얹은 듯이 잠잠해졌다 A hushed [dead] silence[A hush] fell over the audience.∥교수가 들어오자 학생들은 모두 잠잠해졌다 All the students fell silent when the professor entered the room.

잠재(潛在) latency; potentiality; dormancy. ¶그 대학에는 좌익 사상을 갖고 있는 자들이 ~ 세력을 이루고 있다 Leftists have a strong latent influence in[(미) at] that university. **잠재하다** be latent[dormant]; lurk; lie hidden. ¶기계 문명에는 많은 폐해가 잠재하고 있다 Many potential evils lurk in industrialized civilization.

●**잠재력** potential[latent] power[strength] (▶ potential은 존재하지만 아직 이용되지 않은 것, latent는 존재하지만 표면에 나오지 않은 것). **잠재 수요** a potential demand. **잠재의식** a subconscious awareness; subconsciousness.

잠재우다 [자게 하다] put (a person) to sleep [bed]. ¶나는 간신히 아기를 잠재웠다 I finally managed to put the baby to sleep.

잠재적(潛在的) [가능성이 있는] potential; [숨어 있는] latent; [휴식 상태인] dormant; [잠재의식적인] subconscious; [밑바닥에 있는] underlying. ¶~ 에너지 potential energy∥~ 위협 a latent threat.

●**잠재적 실업** invisible[potential / latent] unemployment.

잠적하다(潛跡-) disappear; vanish; abscond; conceal oneself; cover one's traces. ¶그 점원은 이튿날 매상금을 갖고 잠적했다 The next morning the clerk absconded[vanished] with the proceeds.∥그녀는 갑자기 잠적해 버렸다 She suddenly disappeared.

잠정 예산(暫定豫算) a provisional budget.

잠정적(暫定的) temporary; provisional; tentative. ¶~ 합의 a provisional agreement∥~으로 provisionally / tentatively / temporarily / for the time being∥집세를 ~으로 동결해 둡시다 Let's leave the rent unaltered for the time being.

잠투정 a baby's peevishness before[after] sleeping. **잠투정하다** fret[get peevish] before [after] sleeping. ¶아기들은 대개 잠이 오면 잠투정한다 Young children fret[get fretful] when they are sleep.

잠함(潛函) a caisson; a pontoon. ¶목조 ~ a wood pneumatic caisson.

잠항

- **잠함 공법**(-工法) a caisson method; an open caisson method. **잠함병** the caisson [diver's] disease; (구어) the bends.

잠항(潛航) a submarine voyage; navigation under water. ¶~의 기록을 세우다 make [create] a new immersion record of (60 hours). **잠항하다** navigate [cruise] under water.
- **잠항 시간** underwater time. **잠항정** a submarine; an underwater boat.

잠행하다(潛行-) go [travel] incognito; make a secret visit (to).

잡가(雜歌) a popular folk song.

잡것(雜-) 1 [여러 가지가 섞이어 있는 물건] miscellaneous articles; odds and ends; [불순물] impurities. 2 [잡스러운 사람] a low [mean] fellow.

잡곡(雜穀) miscellaneous cereals; minor cereals [grains]; (영) corn.
- **잡곡밥** boiled rice and cereals.

잡귀(雜鬼) minor demons [fiends]; sundry evil spirits.

잡균(雜菌) various germs [bacteria]; germs of various sorts.

잡기(雜技) [노름] gambling of various kind; [재주] various arts and craft.

잡기(雜記) [여러 가지 일을 질서 없이 적은 것] miscellaneous notes [records / writings]; miscellanies; miscellanea. **잡기하다** write miscellaneous matter disorderly.
- **잡기장** a notebook.

잡년(雜-) a loose woman; a woman of easy virtue; a slut.

잡념(雜念) idle [stray] thoughts; earthly [worldly] thoughts. ¶나는 ~을 떨쳐 버리고 일에 몰두했다 I put all other thoughts out of my mind and threw myself into my work.

잡놈(雜-) a low [mean] man; a fast liver; a profligate.

잡다 [손으로 쥐다] grasp; clasp; grip(▶ 이 세 단어는 뜻은 거의 같으나 뒤로 갈수록 힘을 주는 느낌이 강함); seize(▶ seize는 행동의 갑작스러움을 강조); hold; take hold of. ¶남의 손을 ~ grasp a person's hand // 연필을 ~ take a pencil in one's hand // 소매를 ~ catch [seize] (a person) by the sleeve // 자동차의 핸들을 ~ grip the steering wheel (of a car) // 그 사람은 내 멱살을 잡았다 The man grabbed [seized] me by the lapels of my coat. // 그는 내 손을 꼭 잡았다 He squeezed my hand. // 나는 밧줄을 꽉 잡았다 I caught [took hold of] the rope. // 그 아이는 내 소매를 잡고 가지 못하게 했다 The child held [seized / took hold of] my sleeve and wouldn't let me go. // 그는 땅볼을 잘 잡는다 He make a good pickup of a grounder.

2 [체포하다] arrest; make an arrest; catch; nab. ¶범인을 ~ catch [arrest] a criminal // 소매치기를 현장에서 ~ catch [arrest] a pickpocket in the act // 경찰은 유괴범을 잡았다 The police arrested [caught / captured] the kidnapper.

3 [포획하다] catch; capture; seize. ¶족제비를 ~ catch a weasel // 토끼를 덫으로 ~ trap [snare] a rabbit // 그 소년은 맨손으로 큰 물고기를 잡았다 The boy caught [captured] a big fish with his bare hands. // 나는 예쁜 나비를 잡았다 I caught a beautiful butterfly.

4 [만류하다] keep; prevent (a person) from going [leaving]. ¶오래 잡아 두지는 않겠습니다 I won't keep you long. // 잡지 마십시오 Please let me go. // 아무리 해도 그를 잡아 둘 수가 없었다 Nothing could keep [prevent] him from leaving.

5 [자동차를 세우다] pick up; take; get. ¶택시를 ~ pick up [take] a taxi // 나는 역 앞에서 택시를 잡았다 I got a taxi in front of the station. // 그는 지나가는 택시를 잡았다 He hailed [flagged down] a cruising taxi(▶ hail은 손을 쳐서, flag down은 손을 드는 동작을 말함).

6 [정권·세도를 차지하다] seize; dominate; rule; control. ¶정권을 ~ take power / come into power // 영국에서는 지금 보수당이 정권을 잡고 있다 In Britain the Conservative party is now in power. // 그들은 권력을 잡으려 하고 있다 They are trying to seize [come into] power. // 여기서는 그가 모든 것을 잡고 있다 He controls everything here.

7 [돈·재물을 가지다] make [build up] a fortune; make a (one's) pile. ¶그는 석유로 한 밑천 잡았다 He made a fortune out of oil. // 그는 이 사업으로 한몫 잡았다 He is making very good money out of this enterprise.

8 [담보·인질을 맡거나 붙들다] take (security); take [hold] (as); secure. ¶인질을 ~ take [hold] (a person) (as) hostage // 담보를 ~ take security / secure oneself from loss / 그 은행이 땅을 담보로 잡고 있다 The bank hold a mortgage on the land. // 그 고리대금업자는 담보를 잡고 돈을 빌려 주었다 The usurer lent money on mortgage. // 그는 그 소녀를 인질로 잡았다 He took the girl (as) a hostage.

9 [정하다] decide (on); fix (up); set; appoint; [차지하다] hold; take (up); occupy. ¶방향을 ~ decide on [upon] one's course // 날짜를 ~ fix [appoint / set] a date (for) / name a date (for) // 상좌에 자리를 ~ take the top seat // 자리를 잡고 앉다 take a seat / be seated // 우리는 모임의 장소와 날짜를 잡았다 We fixed [settled] the date and place for the meeting. // "결혼식 날짜는 잡았습니까?" "아직입니다." "Has the date for the wedding been fixed?" "No, not yet." // 그 집안이 이 도시에 자리를 잡은 지 3년이 된다 Three years has passed since the family settled down in this town. // 새로 지은 집에서는 서재를 넓게 잡았다 I used a lot of space in my newly built house for a study.

10 [확보하다] put aside; reserve. ¶남을 위해 자리를 잡아 두다 reserve a seat for a person // 지금이라도 좋은 자리를 잡을 수 있어 If you start now, you will be able to get a good seat. // 당신 자리를 잡아 두었소 We have saved a seat for you. // 반도 호텔에 남향 방을 하나 잡아 주세요 Please reserve [take] a southward room at the Bando Hotel.

11 [···으로 일을 하다] do. ¶붓을 ~ write / put pen to paper // 도화를 ~ draw [make] a picture / paint (a water color) // 그는 택시의 핸들을 잡고 있다 He is a taxi driver. // 나는 몇 해 동안 화필을 잡지 않았다 I have not painted for several years.

12 [찾아내다] find (fault with); point to (a shortcoming); take advantage (of) (이용하다). ¶남의 흠을 ~ find fault with a person // 남의 말꼬리를 ~ catch a person in his own words // 남의 약점을 ~ take advantage of another's weak point / avail oneself of

another's disadvantage // 단서를 ~ have [find] a clue (to / for) / have a key (to) // 문제의 핵심을 ~ go[get] to the heart of a matter // 그는 노상 그녀의 흠만 잡으려 한다 He is always finding fault with her. // 문제 해결의 실마리를 잡을 수 없다 I can't find the key to the problem. // 그 형사는 우연히 새로운 단서를 잡았다 The detective happened to find a new clue.

13 [제 가락을 찾아 부르다] tune (a piano); put (a piano) in tune. ¶그는 언제나 음정을 잡고 노래한다 He always sings in tune.

14 [물을 괴게 하다] store; save; reserve. ¶저수지에 물을 ~ store water in reservoir // 논에 물을 ~ water a rice field.

15 [유지하다] keep; hold. ¶몸의 중심을 ~ keep one's balance // 한 발로 서서 몸의 중심을 ~ balance oneself on one leg // 나는 서프보드 위에서 몸의 균형을 잡을 수가 없다 I cannot keep my balance [balance myself] on a surfboard.

16 [마음을 바로잡다] calm [compose] oneself; collect one's scattered mind; steady oneself. ¶들뜬 마음을 ~ hold the rein over one's erratic mind / keep a firm hand on oneself // 마음을 잡고 공부하다 study in a settled frame of mind // 그는 마음을 잡고 열심히 일하기 시작했다 He began to work earnestly, reforming himself [with new resolution].

17 [불을 끄다] put out; extinguish; get (a fire) under control. ¶물로 불길을 ~ put out a fire with water // 우리는 낙엽에 옮겨 붙은 불을 밟아서 잡았다 We stamped out the fire that had started in the fallen leaves. // 1시간이나 걸려 불을 잡았다 The fire was put out [gotten under control / extinguished] in about an hour.

18 [물가 등을 안정시키다] check; stop; curb; halt. ¶인플레를 ~ check[curb] an inflation // 정부는 물가를 잡는 데 실패했다 The government failed to keep prices down [stabilize prices]. // 정부는 물가의 상승을 연 5퍼센트 이내에서 잡으려 하고 있다 The government is trying to limit price increase to five percent a year [to an annual rate of five percent].

19 [만들다] make. ¶계획을 ~ make a plan // 일정을 ~ make a schedule // 초안을 ~ prepare [make out] a draft // 나는 여름 방학의 일정을 잡았다 I made a schedule for the summer vacation. // 나는 세계를 일주할 계획을 잡고 있다 I am planning to make a tour around the world.

20 [어림하다] estimate (at); make an estimate (of). ¶아무리 많이 잡아도 at the highest estimate / at most / at the outside // 아무리 적게 잡아도 at the lowest estimate / at least // 손해를 얼마로 잡고 있습니까 What is the estimated loss? // 그 목수는 집의 신축 비용을 1억 원으로 잡았다 The carpenter estimated the cost of (building) the new house at a hundred million won. // 그는 비용을 대충 잡았다 He made a rough estimate of the expenses.

21 [주름을 잡다] crease; rimple; goffer. ¶주름을 깨끗이 잡은 바지 well-creased [neatly-pressed] trousers // 주름 잡은 치마 a pleat skirt // 바지에 주름을 ~ crease one's trousers.

22 [도살하다] slaughter; butcher. ¶소를 ~ slaughter [butcher] a cow.

23 [헐뜯다] blame; slander. ¶생사람 ~ lay the blame on a person // 생사람 잡지 마 Don't slander me.

잡다하다 (雜多－) miscellaneous; mixed; sundry; of various kinds[sorts]. ¶잡다한 물건 sundries // 거기에는 잡다한 사람들이 모여 있었다 There were all [various] sorts of people gathered there.

잡담 (雜談) a chat; idle [small] talk; a gossip; (a) light conversation. ¶그들은 ~을 즐기고 있었다 They were enjoying a chat [(구어) some chitchat]. // 민 선생은 수업 중에 자주 ~을 한다 Mr. Min often makes digressions during [in] class. // 이웃 사람들이 거리에서 ~을 하고 있다 The neighbors are having a chat in the street. **잡담하다** chat; have a chat (with); make small [idle] talk; gossip. ¶나는 그 사람과 잠깐 잡담했을 뿐이다 I only exchanged some small talk with him. / I only had a casual conversation with him.

잡동사니 miscellaneous articles; sundries; odds and ends; all [various] sorts of articles. ¶다락에는 ~만 있다 There is all sorts of articles in the attic.

잡되다 (雜－) [천하다] vulgar; low; mean; indecent; [난잡하다] loose; dissolute; dissipated; wanton; lewd; licentious; immoral. ¶잡된 사람 a low [dissolute] person // 잡된 생각 licentious [lewd] thoughts // 잡되고 방탕한 생활을 하다 lead a dissipated [fast / loose] life.

잡목 (雜木) miscellaneous small trees; scrubs.
● **잡목림** a growth of (miscellaneous) trees; a copse; a coppice; a thicket of assorted trees.

잡무 (雜務) [사소한 일] trivial (routine) duties; [잡다한 일] miscellaneous duties [tasks]; [자투리 일] odd jobs. ¶~를 정리하다 finish off miscellaneous tasks // 교사는 수업 외에 ~가 너무 많다 Teachers have too many things to do besides teaching. // 요즈음은 이런저런 ~에 쫓기고 있습니다 I am occupied with trivial routine duties [one thing and another] these days.

잡문 (雜文) a literary miscellany; miscellaneous writings; random jottings.
● **잡문가** a writer of odd subjects; a miscellanist.

잡물 (雜物) **1** [잡것] miscellaneous things [article]; sundries. **2** [불순물] foreign ingredients; impurities.

잡배 (雜輩) [잡된 무리] a low fellow; vulgar people; small fry; trash.

잡범 (雜犯) all kinds of crime [criminals] except political crime [criminals].

잡부 (雜夫) a handyman. ⇨ =잡역부(⇨)잡역.

잡부금 (雜賦金) miscellaneous fees. ¶~을 일소하다 prohibit the collection of miscellaneous fees.

잡비 (雜費) sundry [miscellaneous / petty] expenses; general expenses; sundries; [임시비] incidental expenses; incidentals; [용돈] petty cash. ¶~가 늘었다 The miscellaneous expenses mounted up to quite a sum.
● **잡비 계정** a petty expenses account.

잡상인 (雜商人) miscellaneous traders; petty tradesmen; pedlars. ¶~ 출입 금지 (게시) Nothing bought at the Door. / No Peddlers or Salesmen. / (영) No Hawkers or

잡색 Salesmen.

잡색(雜色) [여러 가지 빛깔] various colors; variegated color(특히 꽃·잎 등의); [온갖 종류의 사람] all kinds of people; a motley crew. ¶~의 parti-colored / variegated / varicolored.

잡서(雜書) [어떤 분류에도 들지 않는 책] miscellaneous books; [잡다한 책] books on various subjects; books of every sort and kind.

잡석(雜石) broken stones; rubble.

잡세(雜稅) miscellaneous taxes.

잡소리(雜-) 1 [잡된 소리] an obscene[a dirty] talk; an indecent[a filthy] talk; [잡말] silly talk; idle talk; hokum. 2 noise; jarring. ➪잡음2

잡수다 eat; have. ➪먹다1 ¶진지 잡수셨습니까 Do you have a meal?

잡수입(雜收入) miscellaneous revenue [receipts]; miscellaneous[odd] incomes.

잡스럽다(雜-) vulgar; low. ➪잡되다

잡식(雜食) a mixed diet. ¶~의 omnivorous / polyphagous. **잡식하다** live on a mixed diet; be omnivorous.
● **잡식 동물** a polyphagous[omnivorous] animal; an omnivore. **잡식성** [동] polyphagia.

잡신(雜神) minor demons. ➪잡귀

잡아가다 take[walk] (a suspect to a police station); haul[bring] (a person) before (a police authority). ¶경관이 그를 잡아갔다 The policeman took him to the police station.

잡아내다 1 [밖으로] take (something) out; [골라내다] pick[single] out; sort out. ¶용의자 중에서 범인을 ~ pick out a criminal in the suspects. 2 [잘못 등을] find out; discover; pick out ¶남의 흠을 ~ find fault with a person / pick[point] out another's defects // 나는 그 책에서 오식을 20군데나 잡아냈다 I have discovered twenty misprints in this book.

잡아당기다 [끌어당기다] pull; draw; tug(세게); jerk(갑자기). ¶남의 손[귀]을 ~ pull a person's hand[ear] // 밧줄을 ~ pull at[on] a rope // 와락 ~ pull with a sudden jerk // 서로 ~ pull at each other // 양쪽에서 ~ tug from both side // 줄이 끊어질 정도로 ~ strain a rope at the breaking point // 나는 그 끈을 잡아당겼다 I pulled (at) the cord. // 그녀는 내 소매를 잡아당겼다 She pulled me by the sleeve.

잡아들이다 take[walk / haul / bring] (a person) in. ¶범인을 ~ bring a criminal in.

잡아떼다 1 [붙어 있는 것을] tear off; peel. ¶상자에 붙은 라벨을 ~ tear a label off a box // 봉투에 붙은 우표를 ~ peel a stamp from an envelope // 우리는 벽에 붙인 포스터를 잡아떼는 데 애먹었다 We worked hard to tear off the bills posted on the walls.
2 [모르는 체하다] pretend not to know[to be ignorant]; feign[pretend] ignorance. ¶그는 그것은 모르는 일이라고 잡아뗐다 He pretended not to know it and would not admit that he knew it. // 당국은 그런 사실이 없다고 끝내 잡아뗐다 The authorities were positive in denying the fact. // 끝끝내 모른다고 잡아뗄 셈이냐 How dare you feign ignorance all this time? // 잡아떼도 소용없어 There's no use pretending ignorance.

잡아매다 1 [한데 매다] bind[tie] up; lash together. ¶책을 한데 ~ bundle up books // 잔가지를 잡아매어 다발을 지었다 I bound twigs in[into] faggots[bundles]. 2 [고정시키다] tie[fasten / leash] (to). ¶나는 개를 기둥에 잡아맸다 I tied the dog to a pole. // 나는 말을 나무에 잡아맸다 I hitched[fastened] the horse to a tree. // 나는 끈 두 개를 잡아맸다 I tied two strings together.

잡아먹다 1 (사람이 동물을) butcher[slaughter] and eat; (동물이 동물을) devour; prey on. ¶물고기를 ~ catch and eat fish // 고양이는 쥐를 잡아먹는다 Cats catch mice[rats]. // 어떤 종류의 동물은 서로 잡아먹는다 Some animals prey[feed] on one another. / Some animals are cannibalistic.
2 [요하다] take; need; occupy [차지하다]; [소비하다] consume; [낭비하다] spend. ¶이것은 꽤 많은 시간을 잡아먹는다 This takes so much time. // 이 책장은 장소를 많이 잡아먹는다 This bookshelf takes up too much space. // 그녀는 화장을 하는 데 시간을 많이 잡아먹는다 She spends a lot of time in making up (her face). // 이 새 차는 휘발유를 많이 잡아먹는다 This new car consumes lots of gasoline. // 이 사업은 돈을 많이 잡아먹는다 This enterprise eats money. / This is a very costly enterprise.
3 [못살게 굴다] be hard on; [학대하다] ill-treat; torment. ¶그녀는 며느리를 잡아먹을 듯이 대한다 She is hard on her daughter-in-law. // 그는 나만 보면 언제나 잡아먹을 듯이 군다 He picks on me all the time.

잡아채다 snatch[switch] (away) (from); twitch. ¶그 남자는 그에게서 돈다발을 잡아채어 도망갔다 The man snatched a bundle of notes from him and ran away. // 오토바이를 탄 젊은 남자가 내 손[어깨]에서 핸드백을 잡아챘다 A young man on a motorcycle snatched my purse out of my hand[off my shoulder].

잡아타다 get; take; pick up. ¶택시를 ~ get a taxi / pick up a taxi // 나는 공항으로 택시를 잡아타고 갔다 I went to the airport by taxi. / I took a taxi to the airport.

잡어(雜魚) [자질구레한 물고기] small fish of various kinds; offal; small fry.

잡역(雜役) [잡다한 일] miscellaneous work; [뜨내기 일] odd jobs; chores; [군] fatigue duty; sundry services.
● **잡역부**(-夫) a handyman; an odd-job man; a jobber.

잡음(雜音) 1 [소음] noise; [의] (기관의) souffle; murmur. ¶거리의 ~이 시끄러워서 이야기를 할 수 없다 The traffic outside is so noisy that it's hard to talk.
2 [전신·라디오 등의] noise; jarring(혼선); [전파 장애] static; (공전(空電)에 의한) atmospherics. ¶라디오의 ~ (radio) noise / static // 이 음반을 틀면 ~이 많이 난다 This record makes a lot of noise when you play it. // 텔레비전에서 ~이 났다 The television program was affected by noises[static / atmospherics]. // 마이크에서 ~이 났다 The mike was picking up noises.
3 [주위의 쓸데없는 의견] interference; (an) irresponsible criticism (of an outsider). ¶남의 이야기에 쓸데없는 ~ 넣지 마 Don't interfere in our talk. / Stop putting irrelevancies from aside.

잡인(雜人) an outsider. ¶~ 출입 금지 (게시)

No Admittance Except On Business. / No Trespassing.

잡일(雜-) miscellaneous[various / assorted] affairs; (미) (routine household) chores(일상의). ¶가정의 ~ household chores∥신변의 ~을 정리하다 put all one's trifling[minor] personal affairs in order / straighten out all one's personal affairs∥나는 ~에 얽매어 있었습니다 I have been caught up in all sorts of routine work.∥나는 ~에 쫓겨 가장 중요한 일이 진척되지 않습니다 I am so busy with miscellaneous trifles that I cannot get on with the work that concerns me most.

잡종(雜種) a cross (breed); a hybrid; half-breed; a mongrel(특히 개의); (접목에 의한) a graft hybrid. ¶~의 cross[half-]bred / hybrid / mongrel∥~을 만들다 cross one breed with another / cross two breeds / interbreed∥이 진달래는 재래종과 유럽종의 ~이다 This azalea is a cross between a native stock and a European one.∥우리 집 개는 ~입니다 Our dog is a mongrel.

잡지(雜誌) a magazine; (학회 등의) a journal; [정기 간행물] a periodical. ¶주간[월간 / 계간] ~ a weekly[monthly / quarterly] magazine(▶ magazine을 생략할 경우가 흔함)∥종합 ~ a general magazine / a (highbrow) review magazine∥평론 ~ a review (magazine)∥대중[여성] ~ a popular[women's] magazine∥문예 ~ a literary magazine∥소년 소녀 ~ a teen-age magazine∥의학 ~ a medical journal∥연 4회 발행하는 ~ a quarterly∥월 2회 간행하는 ~ a semimonthly magazine∥~를 편집하다 edit a magazine∥~를 발행하다 bring out[publish] a magazine∥~를 구독하다 take (in)[subscribe for] a magazine∥~에 기고하다 write for a magazine / contribute an article to a magazine.
● **잡지 광고** magazine advertising. **잡지 기자** a magazine reporter[writer]; a journalist. **잡지사** a magazine house.

잡채(雜菜) chop suey; a mixed dish of Chinese noodle, vegetables and sliced beef [pork].

잡초(雜草) weeds. ¶~가 무성하게 자란 땅 land overgrown[thick] with weeds∥뜰의 ~를 뽑나 weed a garden∥뜰에는 ~가 무성했다 The garden was overgrown[overrun] with weeds.

잡치다 1 [그르치다] fail; spoil; ruin; mar; make a mess of; mess up. ¶일을 ~ make bungling work of / make a mess of it∥일생을 ~ blast one's career / make a failure of one's life∥사업을 ~ fail in one's undertaking∥나는 시험을 잡쳤다 I failed (in) the examination.∥공을 헛쳤을 때 나는 이제 이 시합을 잡쳤다고 생각했다 When I missed the ball, I thought I had lost the game.∥단 한 번의 실수로 그는 일생을 잡치고 말았다 Just a single failure ruined his life.
2 [기분 등을 상하다] hurt; harm; injure. ¶남의 기분을 잡쳐 놓다 hurt a person's feeling / offend a person∥나는 버릇없는 말을 해서 아버지의 기분을 잡쳐 버리고 말았다 My rude remark offended[hurt the feelings of] my father.

잡탕(雜湯) 1 [여러 가지 재료를 썰어 넣고 끓인 음식] a hotchpotch. 2 [뒤범벅] a jumble; a hodgepodge; (영) a hotchpotch; a medley. ¶~의 medley / mixed / promiscuous∥~을 만들다 jumble together / mix up.

잡풀(雜-) weeds. ⇨"잡초

잡혼(雜婚) promiscuity. ⇨"난혼

잡화(雜貨) miscellaneous goods; general merchandise; sundries; (미) notions; (식료품을 포함하는) groceries.
● **잡화상** grocery business; (상인) a grocer. **잡화점** (주로 시골의) a general store; (식료품의) a grocer's (shop); (미) a grocery (store).

잡히다¹ 1 [고름이 괴다] form; rise. ¶엄지발가락에 물집이 잡혔다 A blister formed on my big toe. / I have a blister on my big toe. 2 [얼음이 얼기 시작하다] form. ¶물에 살얼음이 잡혔다 A thin sheet of ice has formed on the water.∥오늘 아침 연못에 얼음이 잡혔다 The ice formed on the pond this morning. 3 [꽃망울이 생기다] put forth; shoot out. ¶꽃망울이 ~ put forth[shoot out] buds / have buds.

잡히다² 1 [손에 쥐어지다] be taken (up); be held[seized / caught / grabbed]. ¶그는 손에 잡히는 대로 한껏 동전을 쥐었다 He seized all the coppers that his fist could hold.∥그는 책상 위에 있는 것을 손에 잡히는 대로 도둑에게 던졌다 He picked up whatever came to hand on the desk and began throwing things at the thief.
2 [체포되다] be arrested; be caught[captured]. ¶그 강도는 마침내 잡히고 말았다 The rubber was arrested[captured] at last.∥도망친 사자는 아직 잡히지 않고 있다 The escaped lion is still loose[at large].∥그는 추적자에게 잡혔다 He was caught by his pursuers.∥나는 속도위반으로 순찰차에 잡혔다 I was stopped by a police[patrol] car for speeding.
3 [포획되다] be caught[captured / seized]. ¶며칠 전에 이 근처에서 이상한 물고기가 잡혔다 The other day a strange fish was caught near here.∥물고기가 많이 잡혔다 I had a big catch of fish.∥오늘은 꿩이 많이 잡혔다 I've had a good bag of pheasants today.∥비가 온 뒤에는 항상 물고기가 잘 잡힌다 Fish always take best after rain.
4 [만류당하다] be kept[tied up]; be prevented from going. ¶그녀에게 가면 잡혀서 좀처럼 돌아갈 수가 없다 When you (go to) visit her, it is really hard to get away.∥그에게 잡혀서 올 수가 없었다 I was tied up with him.
5 (자동차가) be taken[got / caught]. ¶이 시간에는 택시가 좀처럼 잡히지 않는다 It's hard to get[catch / flag down] a taxi at this time of day.
6 (담보·인질이) be taken[held]. ¶그들은 약 2개월 동안 인질로 잡혀 있었다 They were held hostage[as hostages] for about two months.∥대사관원이 인질로 잡혔다 The embassy people were taken[held] hostage.∥보석을 저당 잡히고 10만 원을 빌렸다 I pawned a jewel for a hundred thousand won.∥그의 집은 은행 대출금의 담보로 잡혀 있다 His house has been mortgaged (to) the bank for[against] a loan.
7 [결정되다] be decided[fixed]; [차지하다] be occupied; [정착되다] be settled. ¶날짜가 잡히는 대로 알려 드리겠습니다 I'll tell you when[after] the date is[has been] fixed.∥앞으로의 방침은 잡혔습니까 Have you decided on you future course?∥그는 간신히 교사로서 자리가 잡혔다 At last he settled down as a teacher[to teaching].

잡히다

8 (약점 등을) be found; be pointed to. ¶트집을 ~ be found fault with // 흠을 ~ be spoken ill of / be caviled at // 적에게 약점이 ~ give a handle to the enemy // 그는 부하에게 약점이 잡혀 있는데 부하가 그의 비밀을 알고 있기 때문이다 He is in the power of his subordinate, who knows his secret.
9 (액체나 기체 등이) be stored[saved]; be reserved. ¶논에 물이 잡혔다 The rice field has watered adequately.
10 [유지되다] be kept[held]. ¶균형이 잡힌 몸매 a well-proportioned figure // 균형이 잡혀 있다 be well-balanced / be kept in an equilibrium // 이 나라는 수입과 수출의 균형이 잡혀 있다 This country has an even balance of imports and exports.
11 (불길이) be put out[extinguished]. ¶불이 저절로 잡혔다 The fire burnt itself out.
12 (일정 등이) be included; be (counted) among. ¶스케줄에 잡혀 있지 않은 unscheduled (flight) // 의사 일정에 잡혀 있다 be on the day's agenda // 오늘은 스케줄이 꽉 잡혀 있다 My schedule today is very tight.
13 (주름이) become creased; be wrinkled [crumpled]. ¶주름이 잡힌 얼굴 a wrinkled [lined] face // 이 옷감은 주름이 잘 잡힌다 This material [cloth] wrinkles easily. // 그의 이마에는 노령과 고생으로 깊은 주름이 잡혔다 Age and care have made deep lines on his forehead.

잡히다[3] [손으로 잡게 하다] let (another) take hold of one's hand. ¶어머니는 아이한테 연필을 잡혔다 The mother gave the child a pencil to hold.

잣 pine nuts.
잣나무 [식] a Korean nut pine.
잣눈 [눈금] a scale; a graduation[division] (on a ruler).
잣다 1 [뽑다] spin. ¶실을 ~ spin thread [yarn] // 목화에서 실을 ~ spin cotton into yarn / spin thread[yarn] out of cotton // 고치에서 명주실을 ~ reel silk off cocoons // 그녀는 실을 잣고 있다 She is spinning. **2** (물을) draw (up) (water); (펌프로) pump (up) (water).
잣대 a (measuring) rule [rod]. ⇨ 자막대기
잣죽 (—粥) porridge[gruel] made of rice and pine nuts.
장(丈) [길이의 단위] a jang (=10 ja =3.314 yds.).
장(長) **1** [우두머리] a leader; a chief; a boss; a head. ¶일가의 ~ the head of a family // 그는 ~이 될 인물이 못된다 He is not a man to lead others. / He isn't cut out to be a leader.
2 [긴·오랜] long.
장(章) [문장의 단위] a chapter. ¶제2~ Chapter Ⅱ / the second chapter // 이 문제는 다른 ~에서 검토하겠다 We will discuss this problem in another chapter.
장(張) a leaf (of a book); a sheet (of paper); a piece (of paper). ¶종이 다섯 ~ five sheets [pieces] of paper // 판유리 두 ~ two panes [sheets] of glass // 20원짜리 우표 다섯 ~ five twenty-won stamps // 표 두 ~ two ticket // 접시 네 ~ four plates // 천 원짜리 열 ~ ten one-thousand-won notes[bills] // 얇게 썬 치즈 한 ~ a thin slice of cheese // 그 사진을 한 ~ 더 인화해 줄 수 있습니까 Can you print an extra copy of that photograph for me?

장(將) **1** a commander. ⇨ 장수(將帥) **2** (장기의) the King; [장군] check; checkmate. ¶~이야 Check (to your King)! / Mate!
장(場) **1** [시장] a market; [영] (매일 등의 정기적인) a fair. ¶5일~ a five day interval town market // 농작물을 ~에 내다 장 [bring] crops to market // ~이 서는 날 [고장] a market day [town] // ~이 있다 The market is held. // 이 읍에서는 5일에 한 번 ~이 선다 A fair is held on [(영) in] this town every five days.
2 [장소] a place; a spot; a ground. ¶사격~ a rifle range // 골프 ~ a golf course / the golf links // ~내 [외]에 in [out of] the hall [ground] // 토론의 ~ a place for debating [discussion].
3 [물] a field. ¶중력의 ~ a gravitational field // ~의 이론 field theory.
4 [연극의 장면] a scene. ¶3막 7~의 연극 a play in three acts and seven scenes // 제3막 제2~ Act Ⅲ Scene Ⅱ.
장마다 망둥이[꼴뚜기] 날까 (속담) Good luck does not always repeat itself.
장(을) 보다 sell[buy] (a thing) in the market; market. ¶장 보러 가다 go to market / (미) go marketing // 어머니는 장을 보러 가셨다 Mother went shopping.
장(腸) [생] the intestines; the bowels (장 전체·내장); (속어) the guts. ¶~이 나쁘다 have something wrong with one's intestines / have an intestinal disorder.
장(醬) (간장) soy (sauce); (된장) soy bean paste; (고추장) soybean paste with pepper.
장(欌) a wardrobe; a chest of drawers; a cabinet; a closet; a cage. ¶새~ a bird cage // 옷~ a wardrobe / a chest of drawers // 단층 [이층] ~ a single [double] chest of drawers // 붙박이 ~ a built-in wardrobe.
장(臟) the viscera.
-장(丈) [존칭] an esteemed elder. ¶노인~ an elderly person // 춘부~ your venerable father.
-장(狀) a letter. ¶소개~ a letter of introduction // 초대~ a letter of invitation / an invitation // 추천~ a letter of recommendation.
장가 a marriage; a wedding; taking a wife; getting a bride.
장가가다 marry [wed] a woman; take a woman in marriage; take a woman to wife. ¶그 사람 언제 장가갔나 When did he get married?
장가들다 marry [wed] a woman. ⇨ 장가가다 ¶자네 장가들었나 Are you married? / Do you have a wife?
장가들이다 marry (a son) to a woman; get (a son) married. ¶그는 아들을 의사의 딸한테 장가들었다 He married his son to doctor's daughter.
장갑(掌匣) (a pair of) gloves; [벙어리장갑] (a pair of) mittens; [긴 장갑] a gauntlet (glove). ¶고무~ rubber gloves // 권투 ~ a boxing glove // ~을 낀 손 a gloved hand // ~을 끼다 [벗다] put on [pull off / take off] gloves // 그녀는 흰 ~을 끼고 있었다 She had white gloves on. // ~을 낀 채 악수하는 것은 실례이다 It is impolite to shake hands with your gloves on. // (악수할 때) ~을 끼어 죄송합니다 Excuse my glove.
장갑(裝甲) armoring. **장갑하다** armor.
●**장갑 부대** an armored corps. **장갑차** an

장거(壯擧) a grand[great] project; a heroic [daring] attempt. ¶세계 일주 비행의 ~ the grand project of a round-the-world flight∥그는 요트에 의한 세계 일주의 ~를 이루어 냈다[에 올랐다] He completed[is on] a grand round-the-world voyage on a yacht.

장거리(長距離) a long distance; (사정(射程) 등의) a long range. ¶~의 long-distance / long-range.
● 장거리 경주 a long-distance race. 장거리 전화 a long-distance call; (영) a trunk call. ¶~를 걸다 call (a person) up long distance / make a long-distance call (to a person) // 하와이에 ~를 신청하다 put in call to Hawaii // 부산으로 ~를 부탁합니다 I want a long-distance call to Busan. 장거리포 a long-range gun[cannon].

장검(長劍) a long sword.

장결핵(腸結核) [의] tuberculosis of the intestine.

장고하다(長考-) think about (a matter) for a long time; ponder. ¶장고한 끝에 마침내 그는 결론에 도달했다 After thinking it over for a long time, he finally arrived at a decision.

장골(腸骨) [생] the ilium (*pl.* ilia); the hipbone.

장과(漿果) [식] juicy fleshy fruit; a berry; a bacca (*pl.* -ae).

장관(壯觀) a grand[magnificent / splendid] sight; a great spectacle; grandeur. ¶~을 이루다 present a grand sight[fine spectacle] // 비행기에서 본 설악산은 ~이었다 Seoraksan (Mt. Seorak) looked magnificent from the airplane. // 대양에서의 일몰은 ~이다 The sun setting on the ocean is a grand sight [presents a grand spectacle].

장관(長官) (미) a secretary; (영) a minister; a cabinet member. ¶국무 ~ (미국의) Secretary of State // 국방부 ~ the Minister of Defense // 급 공무원 an official of (Cabinet) rank // ~이 되다 be appointed a (Cabinet) Minister / enter the Cabinet / be given a Cabinet post // 그는 재정 경제부 ~에 임명되었다 He was appointed as the Minister of Finance and Economy.
● 장관 직 / 장관 자리 a portfolio (*pl.* ~s); ministership; a Cabinet position.

장관(將官) (육군·공군·해병대의) a general (officer); (해군) a flag officer; an admiral.

장관(腸管) [생] the intestinal canal[tract].

장광설(長廣舌) a long talk[speech]; (길고 지루한) a lengthy speech. ¶후보자는 ~을 늘어놓았다 The candidate gave a long(-winded) speech.

장교(將校) an officer; a commissioned officer. ¶육군[해군 / 공군 / 해병대] ~ a military [naval / air force / marine] officer // 고급 ~ a high-ranking officer / (미국 구어) the brass 《집합적》 // 사병 출신 ~ a commissioned officer promoted[risen] from the ranks / a ranker // ~와 사병 officers and men // ~로 임관되다 be commissioned / receive commission.
● 장교단 an officer corps.

장구 a *janggu*; an hourglass-shaped drum. ¶~를 치다 tap the *janggu* with a stick.
● 장구채 a *janggu* stick.

장구(裝具) [몸에 지니는 기구] equipment(s); an outfit. (▶ outfit에는 개인 소지품도 포함되지만, equipment에는 포함되지 않음) ¶그들은 겨울 등산용 ~를 갖추지 못하고 있었다 They were not equipped for mountain climbing in the winter. // 우리는 설상(雪上) 캠핑용 ~를 가지고 있다 We have the right equipment [We are properly outfitted] for camping in the snow.

장구벌레 a mosquito larva (*pl.* ~s, -vae); a wriggler.

장구하다(長久-) eternal; permanent; everlasting; perpetual; long. ¶장구한 역사 a long history // 장구한 시일이 지난 후 after the lapse of many a year // 장구한 시일을 요하다 require a long period of time. **장구히** eternally; permanently; perpetually.

장국(醬-) [맑은장국] clear soup; [간장을 타서 끓인 국] soup flavored with soy (sauce).
● 장국밥 rice in beef soup.

장군(將軍) 1 [대장] a general. ¶5성 ~ a five-star general / a General of the Army // 동 ~ General Winter. 2 [장기] a check; a mate. ¶겹 ~ a double check // 멍군 ~ a check in return // ~! Check (to your King)! / Checkmate!
장군(을) 받다 make a defensive move against a checkmate; get out of check.

장군풀(將軍-) [식] a rhubarb; a wine plant.

장궤양(腸潰瘍) [의] an intestinal ulcer.

장기(長技) one's forte; one's speciality; one's strong point. ¶~…이다 be good at ... / be strong in ... / be a good hand at ... // 그 노래가 그의 ~가 되었다 That song has become his party piece. // 꽃꽂이는 그녀의 ~다 Arranging flowers is her specialty. // 수리하는 일이라면 나의 ~입니다 I'm an expert at repairing things. / (구어) Repairing things is right up my alley. // 속구가 저 투수의 ~다 His fast ball is that pitcher's strong point.

장기(長期) [장기간] a long term; [장시일] a long (period of) time. ¶~의 임대 계약 a long-term lease // 인체에 대한 ~적 영향 the long-term health effects // ~의 long / long-term (transaction) / long-dated (debenture) / long-range (study) / of long duration // ~적으로는 for the long run // ~적으로는 유리하게 될 것이다 It will turn out to our advantage in the long run. // 이 지역의 개발에는 ~적인 계획이 필요하다 Long-term plans are needed for the development of this region. // 나는 파리에 ~ 체재할 예정이다 I'm planning to stay in Paris for a long time.
● 장기 거래 long-term transaction. 장기 근속 long service; years of labor. 장기 예보 a long-range forecast. 장기전 [long prolonged / protracted] war; [장기 경쟁] a long-range contest. ¶전쟁은 ~이 되었다 The war was long drawn out. 장기화 하다 extend over a long period[space] of time / be protracted / be prolonged // 분쟁은 ~했다 The dispute extended over a long period. // 이 교섭은 ~될 것 같다 I'm afraid it will be quite a long negotiation. / It'll take quite a long time before the negotiations are concluded. 장기 흥행 a long run.

장기(將棋·將棊) *janggi*; Korean chess. ¶~를 두다 play *janggi*[chess] (with) / have a game of *janggi* (with) // ~에 이기다[지다] win [lose] a game of *janggi* // ~ 둘 줄 압니까 Do you know how to play *janggi*?

장기짝 a chessman; a piece(하나 하나). 장기판 a chessboard.

장기(臟器) [생] internal organs; the viscera; the intestines. ¶인공 ~ artificial (internal) organs.
●**장기 이식** internal organ transplant(ation).

장꾼(場-) marketeers and marketers; market crowds.

장끼 a male pheasant. ⇨수평

장난 (약간 악의가 있는) mischief; (악의가 없는) a practical joke; a prank; [희롱] fun; a trick. ¶운명의 ~ a trick of fortune[fate] // 실없는 ~ wanton mischief // 이 한창 심한 아이런이 a child at the mischievous age // ~스런 표정으로 with a mischievous[an impish] look // ~삼아 half in fun / for[in / out of] fun / in jest / for amusement / (오락으로) as a pastime[hobby] // ~을 못 하게 하다 keep (a boy) out of mischief // 그는 ~이 지나쳐 상사의 역정을 샀다 He carried his jokes too far and fell into disfavor with his boss. // 저는 그저 ~삼아 그 항아리를 구웠습니다 I baked that pot just for fun [half in fun]. // 그는 ~삼아 선생의 흉내를 냈다 He mimicked the teacher in fun[in sport]. // 나는 이것을 ~삼아 하고 있는 것이 아니다 I am not doing this just for the fun of it. // ~삼아 해 본 웃음을 이다 I did it merely for the fun of it. **장난하다** do mischief; be mischievous. ⇨장난치다
●**장난감** a toy; a plaything. ¶~ 권총 a toy pistol[gun] // ~ 기차 a toy train // 어른의 ~ marital aids // 그 소년은 ~을 가지고 놀고 있었다 The boy was playing with his toys. // 너는 ~을 가지고 놀 나이가 아니다 You have outgrown your playthings. **장난기** playfulness; mischievousness. ¶~가 있는 playful / sportive / full of play[fun] / mischievous / impish // ~가 어린 눈으로 with mischievous [impish] eyes // ~가 많은 사람 a person full of fun and mischief // ~가 어린 웃음 an impish smile. **장난꾸러기** [장난이 심한 어린이] a mischievous[naughty] boy; an urchin; an imp; a little demon of a child; [장난이 심한 사람] a mischief(-maker); a rogue; a frolicker; (미국 구어) a prankster.

장난치다 do mischief; be mischievous; do a naughty thing; play[pull] a trick[prank] (on a person); play a (practical) joke (upon); [가지고 놀다] play[tamper / fool / toy / trifle] (with); (미국) monkey (with). ¶장난치기 좋아하는 mischievous / (어린이가 장난스런) naughty // 한창 장난치는 나이의 사내아이 a boy at his most mischievous age / a boy brimful of mischief // 장난치다가 들키다 be caught in mischief // 어린이들이 장난치지 못하도록 지켜보고 있어라 Watch the children and be sure they don't cause any mischief. // 초인종을 가지고 장난치지 마라 Don't play[fool about] with the doorbell. // 대여섯 살이면 한창 장난칠 나이다 Boys are most mischievous at five or six.

장날(場-) a market day; a fair day.

장남(長男) the [one's] eldest [(미) oldest] son; the first (born) son; (아들이 둘일 때) one's elder[older] son. ¶그에게는 아들이 둘 있는데, ~ 쪽이 그를 쏙 닮았다 He has two sons. The elder one is just like him[resembles him very much].

장내(場內) the inside of the hall[grounds / premises]. ¶~에서 in the hall / in the grounds / on the premises // ~는 입추의 여지도 없다 There is no standing room in the hall. // ~는 점점 더 혼잡해졌다 The place got more and more crowded. // ~는 흥분의 도가니에 빠졌다 (연설 회장 등에서) The audience was filled with intense excitement. / (스포츠 등에서) The spectators grew more and more excited.

장녀(長女) the [one's] eldest [(미) oldest] daughter; the first (born) daughter; (딸이 둘일 때) one's elder[older] daughter.

장년(壯年) (the prime of) manhood; the prime of life; [중년] middle age. ¶~의 남자 a man in the prime // ~에 달하다 reach manhood / attain the prime of manhood // 그는 이미 ~이 지났다 He is already past his prime.
●**장년기** (in one's) manhood; (in) the prime of the life.

장뇌(樟腦) camphor; [방충제 알약] a camphor ball. ¶~의 camphoric // ~를 넣다 camphorate.
●**장뇌유** camphor oil.

장님 a blind person; (집합적) the blind; blind men[people]. ¶~인 blind / sightless / eyeless // 눈뜬 ~ an unlettered[illiterate] person // ~이 되다 go[become] blind / lose one's sight // ~으로 태어나다 be born blind // 그는 9세 때에 ~이 되었다 He lost his sight [eyesight] at the age of nine.

장님 코끼리 만지는 격(속담) It's like the blind men who touched only one part of an elephant and claimed that what it was like.

장님 코끼리 말하듯 한다(속담) One cannot see the wood for the trees.

장다리 [꽃줄기] a flower stalk (of radishes, cabbages, etc.); a scape. ¶~가 나다 go[run] to seed.

장단 beat; time; rhythm; tempo. ¶흥겨운 ~ exciting beat // 북으로 ~을 치다 beat time with a drum.

장단(이) 맞다 1 [가락이 맞다] be in time. ¶장단이 맞는 노래 a rhythmical song // 장단이 맞지 않다 be out of time // 그녀의 노래는 장단이 맞지 않는다 Her singing is off beat. / She can't keep time when she sings. **2** [동작에 생각이 맞다] get along[on] well. ¶그녀는 한방 친구와 장단이 잘 맞는 것 같다 She seems to be getting along nicely with her roommate.

장단(을) 맞추다 1 [박자를 맞추다] beat [keep] time (with). ¶메트로놈에 ~ keep time with metronome // 발로 장단을 맞추고 있다 I am beating time with my feet. // 그들은 손뼉을 쳐서 장단을 맞추었다 They clapped their hands to keep time. **2** [남의 기분을 돋우다] attune oneself (to); play in another's key. ¶그는 남들과 장단을 잘 맞추어 간다 He gets on well[nicely] with others. // 때로는 남들과 장단을 맞추는 것도 좋다 It's good idea to go along with what others want once in a while.

장단(長短) **1** [길고 짧음] (relative) length. ¶(2개의) 끈의 ~을 재다 measure the relative length of (two) strings. **2** merits and demerits. ⇨장단점

장단점(長短點) merits and demerits; strengths and weaknesses; good and bad points. ¶사람마다 ~이 있다 Every man has his merits and demerits. / Each man has

장담(壯談) an [a positive] assertion; affirmation; a positive statement. **장담하다** assert; affirm; state positively. ¶의사는 내 병이 다 나았다고 장담했다 The doctor pronounced that I was cured.∥그것은 반드시 일어나리라고 장담한다 I assure you that it will happen.∥그것이 사실임을 나는 장담한다 I affirm it to be a fact.∥장담할 수는 없지만 그는 시험에 합격하리라 생각한다 I cannot say positively [for certain], but I believe he will pass the examination.∥그 말이 옳다고 장담할 수 있습니까 Can you affirm[vouch for] the truth of the statement?

장대(長-) a pole; a rod. ¶대나무 ~ a bamboo pole.

장대로 하늘 재기(속담) attempting[trying to do] the impossible; making ropes of sand; trying to put a quart into a pint pot.

● **장대높이뛰기** the pole vault; the pole jump. ¶~용 장대 a vaulting pole∥~를 하다 pole-vault∥그는 ~에서 5미터를 거뜬히 뛰어 넘었다 He easily cleared the five-meter bar in the pole vault. **장대높이뛰기 선수** a pole-vaulter.

장대하다(壯大-) big and strong[stout]; large and robust; husky. ¶장대한 체격 a large and robust build.

장도(壯途) an ambitious undertaking [course]. ¶~에 오르다 start on the ambitious course∥세계 일주 비행의 ~에 오르다 embark on the ambitious enterprise of a round-the-world flight∥그들은 남극 탐험의 ~에 올랐다 They started on an ambitious expedition to the Antarctic.

장도(長途) [먼 길] a long way[distance].

장도(粧刀) an encased ornamental knife. ¶은~ a knife ornamented with silver.

장도리 a hammer. ¶노루발 ~ a claw hammer∥~ 대가리 a hammer-head∥~의 자루 the handle of a hammer∥~로 못을 뽑다 extract [pull out] a nail with a claw hammer∥그는 ~로 못을 박았다 He drove a nail in with a hammer.

장독(醬-) a *jangdok*; a crock[jar] of soy sauce.

● **장독대** a *jangdokdae*; a soy-jar stand; a terrace where soy sauce crocks are placed.

장돌림(場-) an itinerant market trader; a roving marketeer.

장돌뱅이(場-) an itinerant market trader. ⇨ 장돌림

장두(長頭) [고고] dolichocephaly; dolichocephalism. ¶~의 dolichocephalic / dolichocephalous.

장두(檣頭) [돛대의 맨 꼭대기] a masthead.

장딴지 the calf (of the leg) (*pl.* calves).

장래(將來) the future; [전망] the prospect. ¶한국의 ~ the future of Korea∥밝은 ~ a bright[brilliant] future / bright prospects∥어두운 ~ a dark future / gloomy prospects∥~가 유망한 청년 a young man with bright prospects / a promising young man∥~의 서울을 위한 계획 plans for the Seoul tomorrow∥가까운 ~에 in the near future∥먼 ~에 in the remote[distant / far-off] future∥~의 계획을 세우다 make a plan for one's future∥~를 점치다[예상하다] predict[forecast] the future (of)∥~를 **생각하다** think of the future (of) / look far into the future (of)∥먼 ~를 생각해서 계획을 세우다 plan for the distant future∥그는 ~에 대한 희망에 넘쳐 있다 He is full of hope for the future.∥그의 ~는 보장되어 있다 His future is assured.∥이 아이의 ~가 걱정된다 I am worried about this child's future.∥나는 그녀의 ~가 어떻게 될지 모른다 I don't know what will become of her in the future.∥나는 ~에 대한 희망이 전연 없다 I have no hope for the future. / The future looks grim[bleak] to me.∥이 사업의 ~는 밝다 The outlook for this business is bright.

● **장래성** future; possibility; prospect. ¶~ 있는 청년 a promising young man∥이 직업은 ~이 있다 This job is promising. / There is a future in this job.∥이런 시골에 있다가는 ~이 없다 No career is possible in this small village.∥그녀는 ~ 있는 과학자이다 She is a promising scientist[a scientist with great promise].∥그 장사는 ~이 있다[없다] The business looks[doesn't look] promising.

장려(獎勵) encouragement; stimulation; [촉진] promotion. **장려하다** encourage; stimulate; promote; [추천하다] recommend. ¶운동을 ~ encourage athletic sports∥산업[학문]을 ~ encourage[promote] industry[learning]∥우리는 그들에게 저축을 장려했다 We encouraged them to save.∥그것이 어린이들의 독서를 장려하는 결과가 되었다 It served as an incentive for the children to read.∥우리 학교에서는 모든 종류의 스포츠를 장려하고 있다 Our school encourages all kinds of sports.∥그것은 그다지 장려할 만한 것이 못된다 It's not a thing to be recommended.

● **장려금** (특히, 국가가 단체에게 주는) a bounty; a subsidy; a grant; (생산성 향상을 위한) an incentive. ¶수출 ~ a bounty on exports / an export bounty∥증산 ~ a bounty for increased production.

장려하다(壯麗-) splendid; [장대하고 아름답다] magnificent; [웅대하다] grand. ¶석양을 등신 설악산의 장려한 모습 the magnificent sight of Seoraksan(Mt. Seorak) against the setting sun.

장력(張力) [물] tension; tensile force; tensility. ¶표면 ~ surface tension.

장렬(葬列) a funeral procession[train].

장렬하다(壯烈-) heroic; brave; gallant. ¶장렬한 죽음 a heroic[glorious] death (in the battle)∥그는 그 전투에서 장렬한 최후를 마쳤다 He died a heroic death in the battle.∥그들은 적을 향해 장렬한 돌격을 감행했다 They launched a brave[valiant] charge at the enemy. **장렬히** heroically; bravely; gallantly.

장례(葬禮) a funeral. ¶~에 **참례하다** attend a funeral / be (present) at a funeral∥~를 **지내다** hold a funeral (for) / perform[conduct] a funeral service[the last offices] (for)∥우리는 그를 위한 성대한 ~를 치렀다 We held a big funeral for him.

● **장례비** funeral expenses. **장례식** a funeral (service / ceremony); a burial service(매장). ¶성대한 ~ an elaborate funeral∥~을 **치르다** hold a funeral (service) (for)∥~은 불교식으로 치러졌다 The funeral was in accordance with Buddhist rites.∥그의 ~에 참석

할 작정이다 I plan to attend his funeral.//아저씨의 ~에 다녀왔다 I have been at[to] my uncle's funeral.//홍수산 씨의 ~이 10시에 거행된다 The funeral service[Funeral services] for Mr. Hong Susan will be held at ten o'clock.

장로 (長老) 〔고로(古老)〕 an elder; a senior; (교회의) a presbyter; an elder; (집합적) the presbytery. ¶정계의 ~ a senior statesman // 교회의 ~ the elders of a church.
● **장로교** Presbyterianism. **장로교회** a Presbyterian church.

장롱 (欌籠) a chest (of drawers) (서랍만 여러 개 겹친 것); a wardrobe(양복장); (미) a bureau(거울이 달린 침실용).

장르 a genre. ¶시의 ~ a genre of poetry.

장마 the rainy spell in (early) summer; a long spell of rainy weather. ¶~가 들었다[그쳤다] The rainy season has set in [is over].
● **장마 전선** a seasonal rain front. **장마철** the rainy season.

장막 (帳幕) 1 〔천막〕 a tent; (큰 것) a pavilion; a marquee. ¶~을 치다 pitch[set up] a tent // ~을 걷다 strike[pull down] a tent. 2 〔막〕 a curtain; hangings. ¶밤의 ~ the veil [mantle] of darkness // 철[죽]의 ~ the iron [bamboo] curtain // 신비의 ~에 싸이다 be wrapped[shrouded] in (a veil of) mystery // 밤의 ~이 드리워졌다 Night fell.

장만 〔준비〕 preparation; 〔구입〕 purchase. **장만하다** prepare; purchase; get; buy. ¶옷을 새로 ~ buy a new suit / have a new suit made // 낚시 도구를 ~ buy fishing tackle[a rod and reel] // 집을 ~ get[buy] a house // 그녀는 오늘 새 모자를 장만했다 She got a new hat today. // 신축 가옥에 들일 가구를 몇 가지 장만했다 I bought some furniture for the new house. // 어머니는 저녁 식사를 장만하고 계셨다 My mother was preparing supper[getting supper ready].

장면 (場面) 1 〔연극·영화 등의 정경〕 a scene; a situation. ¶연애 ~ a love scene // 아슬아슬한 [숨 막히는] ~ a thrilling[an intense] situation // 영화의 한 ~ a scene in a movie // ~이 바뀌었다 The scene changed[shifted]. 2 〔광경〕 a scene; a sight. ¶극적인 ~ a dramatic scene // 우리는 어제 이 거리에서 범인이 체포되는 극적인 ~을 목격했다 Yesterday we witnessed the dramatic scene of a criminal being arrested on this street. // 그것은 영화의 한 ~ 같았다 It was like a scene out of a movie.

장모 (丈母) one's wife's mother; one's mother-in-law.

장모음 (長母音) a long vowel.

장문 (一門) a wide-open gate[door].

장문 (長文) a long sentence; a long passage; a long article(기사·논문). ¶~의 전보[편지] a long telegram[letter].

장물 (贓物) stolen goods[articles]; (속어) hot goods; (속어) a swag. ¶~을 은닉하다 conceal stolen goods.
● **장물아비** a dealer in stolen goods; a hot goods broker; a receiver; a fence. **장물 취득** fencing; receiving stolen goods.

장미 (薔薇) 〔식〕 a rose (tree); a rose bush of the prairie(별명). ¶들~ a wild rose / a brier // ~의 봉오리 a rosebud.
● **장미꽃 / 장미화** a rose. **장밋빛** rose color; rose pink. ¶~의 rosy / rose-colored[-tinted]

~ 입술[뺨] rosy lips[cheeks] // ~ 인생관 a rose-colored[an optimistic] view of life // ~ 미래를 마음에 그리다 imagine rosy future // 인생이 언제나 ~인 것은 아니다 Life is not always a bed of roses.

장바구니 (場-) a shopping basket.

장발 (長髮) long hair. ¶~의 long-haired / (a young man) wearing (his) hair long // 그는 ~을 하고 있다 He wears his hair long.
● **장발족** a "hippie" style long-haired youth; longhairs.

장방형 (長方形) 〔수〕 a rectangle. ⇨=직사각형

장벽 (腸壁) the intestinal wall.

장벽 (障壁); 〔막은 벽〕 a fence; a wall; a barrier; 〔방해물〕 an obstacle. ¶관세 ~ a customs barrier / a tariff wall // ~을 구축하다 build[set up] a barrier[wall] (between) // 언어의 ~을 극복하다 overcome the language barrier // ~을 제거하다 remove[demolish / break down] a barrier (between) // 그들은 민족의 ~을 넘어 결혼했다 They formed a union across the boundaries of race.

장병 (長病) a long[protracted] illness; a lingering[chronic] disease. ¶그는 ~ 끝에 죽었다 He died after a lingering illness.

장병 (將兵) officers and men.

장보기 (場-) selling[buying] in the market.

장복 (長服) constant use (of a medicine); habitual use (of a medicine). **장복하다** use (a medicine) constantly; take (a medicine) habitually; take (a medicine) for a long time.

장본인 (張本人) the ringleader; the author (of a plot); the prime mover; the originator. ¶반정부 운동의 ~ the ringleader of an antigovernment movement // 이 사건의 ~은 거물 의원인 듯하다 The person at the center of this case appears to be an important Assemblyman. // 그가 그 폭동의 ~이다 He is the bottom of the riot.

장부 〔건〕 a tenon.
● **장붓구멍** a mortise; a mortice.

장부 (丈夫) 1 〔장성한 남자〕 a full-grown man; a grown-up. 2 a man; a manly man. ⇨=대장부

장부일언중천금 A man's word is as good as a bond.

장부 (帳簿) a book; an account book; 〔원장(元帳)〕 a ledger; (호적 등의) a register. ¶상업 ~ trade books // 외상 ~ a charge account // 이중 ~ double bookkeeping // ~를 적다 keep accounts // ~를 속이다 cook the books / tamper with the accounts // 나날의 매출을 ~에 적다 enter the daily proceeds in the (account) book // ~상의 숫자를 맞추다 make the accounts balance / balance the books // ~가 맞지 않는다 The accounts don't balance. // ~에 달아 놓으세요 Charge this against me [to my account]. // ~는 꼭 맞아떨어진다 The books balance exactly.
● **장부 가격** book value. **장부 계원** a bookkeeper; an accountant. **장부 정리** adjustment of accounts.

장비 (裝備) equipment; (여행 등의) an outfit (for); rigging(배의). ¶야영 ~ a campequipage // 중~의 heavily equipped (division) // 우수한 ~를 갖춘 군함 a well-equipped warship // 병사들은 완전한 ~를 갖추고 있었다 The soldiers were fully outfitted[equipped]. // 저 산에 오르려면 여름에도 겨울 ~가 필요

하다 You need a winter outfit to climb that mountain even in summer. **장비하다** equip [outfit / fit] oneself; fit out (a ship). ¶그 군함은 10인치 포 9문을 장비하고 있다 The warship carries nine 10-inch guns. ¶그 비행기에는 레이더가 장비되어 있다 The airplane is equipped with radar. / The aircraft has radar equipment.

장사 business; commerce; trade; [거래] a transaction; a deal. ¶음식 ~ the restaurant business // 술~ the liquor business // 수지가 맞는 [괜찮은] ~ a profitable [paying] business // 수지 안 맞는 ~ a nonpaying business // ~의 요령 [비결] a trick of the trade // ~의 경쟁자 a business [trade] rival // ~를 시작하다 go into [start in] business // ~를 배우다 learn a trade // ~를 그만두다 close [give up / wind up] one's business // 그의 ~는 번창하고 있다 He is succeeding in his business. / He's doing good business. // 작년에는 ~가 잘되었다 Business [Trade] was good [brisk] last year. // 그는 가구 ~를 하고 있다 He is in the furniture business. / He deals in furniture. // ~는 어떻습니까 [잘됩니까] How is your trade? / How goes it with your business? // 요즈음 도무지 ~가 되지 않습니다 There is no business doing these days. / Our business is in low water nowadays. // ~가 전혀 안 된다 I'm doing no business at all. **장사하다** (물건을) trade [deal] in; [경영하다] engage in business; do business; run a business.
● **장사꾼 / 장사치** a merchant; a tradesman; a dealer (in rice). **장삿속** a commercial spirit; a mercantile mind; a profit-making motive. ¶~으로 for mercenary reasons / for mere gain // ~을 떠나서 from a noncommercial motive / apart from gain // 그는 ~으로 그 일을 맡았다 He took on the job from mercenary motive.

장사 (壯士) a man of great strength; a strong man; a man of Herculean strength. ¶그는 힘이 천하~다 He is a man of unparalleled [matchless] physical strength. / He has the strength of a horse [lion].

장사 (葬事) a burial. ¶~를 **시내다** hold a funeral / perform a funeral service // 우리는 그를 위해 성대하 ~ 지냈다 We held a big funeral for him. **장사하다** bury; inter; entomb. ¶우리는 그의 유해를 땅속 깊이 장사했다 We buried [interred] his remains deep under the ground.

장사진 (長蛇陣) a very long line [(영) queue]. ¶~을 치다 form (up) a long line [queue] // 그들은 고기를 사기 위해 ~을 이루었다 They stood in a long line [queue] to buy meat.

장삼 (長衫) [승려의 옷옷] a broad-sleeved Buddhist robe.

장삼이사 (張三李四) ordinary [common] men; every "Tom, Dick, and Harry".

장색 (匠色) a handicraftsman. ⇨**장인**(匠人)

장생 (長生) long life; longevity. ¶불로~의 비결 the secret of perpetual youth and longevity. **장생하다** live long; live a long life; be long-lived.
● **장생불사** (-不死) eternal life; eternal longevity; immortality. ¶~의 영약 the elixir of life // ~하다 enjoy eternal life / share immortality.

장서 (藏書) a collection of books; (개인의) one's (private) library; [도서관 등의] the book stock. ¶천 권의 ~가 있다 have a collection [library] of 1,000 volumes // 그의 ~는 약 2만 권이라고 한다 His library is said to contain 20,000 volumes. // 이 도서관에는 3백만 권의 ~가 있다 This library houses three million books.
● **장서가** a book collector. ¶홍 교수는 ~이다 Professor Hong has [owns] a large library [great many books]. **장서 목록** a library catalog(ue); (개인의) a catalog(ue) of one's books [the books in one's library].

장석 (長石) [광] feldspar; (영) felspar. ¶정~ orthoclase // 사~ plagioclase.

장선 (腸腺) a catgut; a gut.

장성 (長城) a long wall. ¶만리~ the Great Wall of China.

장성 (將星) generals. ¶육해군 ~ army and navy celebrities.

장성하다 (長成-) grow up (to be a man [woman]); reach [attain] manhood [womanhood]; come of age. ¶장성한 grown-up (son) // 장성하여 어른이 되다 grow into an adult // 그에게 장성한 아이가 셋이나 있다 He has three grown-up children.

장소 (場所) 1 [곳] a place; [특정한 곳] a spot; [정확한 지점] a point; [현장] a scene. ¶분쟁이 일어날 듯한 ~ a trouble spot // 모임의 ~ a place of [for] meeting // 불이 난 ~ the scene of a fire // ~를 가리지 않고 regardless of where one is / with no thought of the character of the place // 오아시스란 사막에서 물이 있는 ~이다 An oasis is a spot [place] in a [the] desert where water can be found. // 조용히 이야기할 수 있는 ~를 찾아보자 Let's find a quiet corner for our talk. // 이곳에서 그런 의논을 하는 것은 ~에 어울리지 않는다 Such an argument is out of place here. // 원래 있던 ~에 두어라 Put it where you found it.

2 [위치] a position; a situation; a location. ¶~가 좋다 [나쁘다] be well [badly] situated // ~가 좋아야 장사가 번창한다 The locality brings a great deal of business. // 그의 가게는 편리한 ~에 있다 His store is conveniently located [situated]. // ~를 가려서 말을 해라 Suit your words to the situation.

3 [터] a site. ¶우리 집을 짓기에 알맞은 ~ a suitable building site for our house // ~를 고르다 select a site (for an exhibition) // 새 공장을 지을 알맞은 ~가 필요하다 We want a suitable site for a new factory.

4 [여지] room; space. ¶좁은 ~ narrow space // ~를 차지하다 take up [occupy] much room [space] // 너희 두 사람에 ~는 있다 There is room [space] enough for you two. // 이제는 텔레비전을 둘 ~가 없다 There is no room left for TV set.

장손 (長孫) one's firstborn grandson by one's eldest son. ⇨**맏손자**

장송 (長松) a tall pine tree. ¶낙락~ a tall pine with graceful [shapely] branches.

장송곡 (葬送曲) a funeral [dead] march.

장수 [상인] a merchant; a trader; a tradesman; a seller; [소매점의 주인] (미) storekeeper; (영) shopkeeper. ¶도붓~ a peddler / a hawker // 생선 ~ a fishmonger // 책 ~ a bookseller.

장수 (長壽) a long life; longevity. ¶~의 비결 the secret of longevity // ~를 **누리다** live to a

장수 great age // 그는 90세의 ~를 누렸다 He lived to be ninety. **장수하다** live a long life. ¶그는 부인보다 장수했다 He outlived his wife. // 그녀는 85세까지 장수했다 She lived to be eighty-five. // 그의 집안은 장수하는 혈통이다 He comes of a long-lived family.
● **장수 마을** a village where many people live to an advanced age.

장수(將帥) a commander; a commandant; a general.

장수(張數) the number of leaves [sheets]. ¶엽서의 ~를 세다 count (the number of) postcards // 필요한 표의 ~를 말씀하십시오 Please tell me how many tickets you want.

장승 1 [동리 어귀의 기둥] a *jangseung*; a totem pole (at the village entrance). 2 [키가 멋없이 큰 사람] a lanky man; (미) a gangling fellow.

장시간(長時間) many hours; long time. ¶~에 걸쳐 이야기하다 have a long talk (with) // 우리는 그 문제를 ~에 걸쳐 논의했다 We discussed the matter for (many) hours. // 나는 그 서류를 ~에 걸쳐 검토했다 I looked over the papers for a long time [many hours].

장시세(場時勢) the market price [value]. ¶~의 변동 market fluctuations // ~가 올랐다 [내렸다] The market advanced [declined].

장시일(長時日) a long (period [space] of) time; years. ¶50년이란 ~에 걸쳐서 for the long space of fifty years // ~을 요하다 require a long period of time // 그는 ~에 걸쳐서 그 사건의 원인을 구명했다 He spent many years investigating the cause(s) of the incident.

장식(裝飾) ornament; decoration; (집합적) ornamentation; adornment; (의복 등의) trimmings; dressing. ¶무대 ~ stage decoration // 실내 ~ interior decoration [design] // 머리 ~ an ornament for the hair / a hair ornament // 크리스마스 ~ Christmas decoration(▶ 크리스마스 장식의 경우 개개의 장식을 말할 때 a Christmas tree ornament) // 가게의 ~ shop decorations / window dressing // ~이 없는 옷 a simple dress / simple [plain] clothing // ~이 없는 벽 a bare wall // 블라우스에 프릴 을 달았다 I trimmed the blouse with frills. // 그는 거실의 ~을 끝마쳤다 He has finished putting up the decorations in the living room. // 쇼윈도의 ~은 세련되어 있었다 The window was tastefully dressed [decorated]. **장식하다** decorate; ornament; adorn. ¶방을 ~ put up decorations in a room // 진열장을 ~ decorate [dress] a shop window // 탁자를 꽃으로 ~ adorn a table with flowers // 그녀는 상자를 리본으로 장식했다 She decorated the box with a ribbon. // 대관식의 사진이 제1면을 장식했다 A picture of the coronation ceremony appeared on the front page. // 그는 승리로 첫날을 장식했다 He started off on the right foot [He got off to a good start] with a win on the first day (of the tournament). ➔ ¶방은 빅토리아 시대풍으로 장식되어 있었다 The room was decorated in Victorian style. // 그 방에는 도자기와 그림이 아름답게 장식되어 있었다 Ceramic pieces and pictures were beautifully arranged in the room.
● **장식 미술** decorative art. **장식용** ¶~의 목적으로 / for decoration / ~ 전구 a decorative light bulb // 이 꽃병은 ~이다 This vase is ornamental. **장식음** [음] an ornament; a grace. ⇨꾸밈음 **장식품** [장식물] an ornament; a decoration; [명목뿐인 것] a figurehead; a dummy. ¶우리 회사의 사장은 ~에 불과하다 The president of our company is just a figurehead. // 그들은 위원장을 ~으로 만들고 말았다 They made a dummy of the chairman.

장신(長身) a tall figure [stature]. ¶~의 남자 a tall man / a man of great [high] stature.

장신구(裝身具) accessories; personal ornaments; (신사용의) (미) haberdashery.

장아찌 a *jangajji*; sliced vegetables preserved in soy sauce [soybean paste].

장악(掌握) hold; grasp; command. **장악하다** hold; grasp; command; have control over. ¶제해권을 ~ secure the command of the sea / command the sea // 그는 부하를 완전히 장악하고 있다 He is in complete control of his men. // 노동당이 정권을 장악했다 The Labor Party came in [into] power. // 장군은 전국에 걸쳐 권력을 완전히 장악하고 있었다 The General had a firm grip on the whole country.

장안(長安) the capital; Seoul. ¶~의 화제가 되다 become the topic of conversation in Seoul.

장암(腸癌) [의] intestinal cancer.

장애(障礙) 1 [방해] an obstruction; a hindrance; [방해물] an obstacle; [어려운 일] a difficulty. ¶무역의 ~ a trade barrier // ~가 되다 be an obstacle (to) / be deterrent (to) // 뜻하지 않은 ~에 부딪히다 come up against a snag // ~를 극복하다 surmount an obstacle [a difficulty] // 유연성의 결여는 진보의 ~가 된다 Lack of flexibility is an obstacle to one's progress. // 그는 무엇이 그의 출세의 ~가 되고 있는지 몰랐다 He did not understand what was in the way of his success in life. // 너의 앞날에는 여러 가지 ~가 있을 것이다 You will meet with various obstacles in your way [path]. // 큰 나무가 쓰러져서 교통의 ~가 되고 있었다 A big fallen tree obstructed the road. // 회원이 되기 위해서는 당신의 국적이 ~가 될 것이다 You will be barred from membership because of your nationality. 2 (신체상의) a handicap; a disorder. ¶언어 ~ a speech impediment [defect] // 위장 ~ a gastrointestinal disorder // 정서 [갱년기] ~ an emotional [a menopausal] disorder.
● **장애물** an obstacle; a hurdle. ¶~을 뛰어넘다 (장애물 달리기에서) clear [jump over] a hurdle / (추상적으로) hurdle an obstacle. **장애물 달리기 / 장애물 경주** (운동회의) an obstacle race; (허들의) a hurdle race; (경마의) a steeple chase. ¶~를 하다 run the hurdles / run an obstacle course. **장애인** a physically challenged [handicapped] person(▶ handicapped보다 challenged가 완곡하고 부드러운 말임. 한편, a disabled person은 직설적인 말로 가급적 사용하지 않는 것이 좋음). ¶시각 [청각 / 정신] ~ a visually [hearing / mentally] challenged person.

장액(腸液) [생] intestinal juice.
장어(長魚) [동] an eel. ⇨뱀장어
● **장어구이** broiled eels.

장엄하다(莊嚴-) solemn; impressive; sublime; majestic. ¶장엄한 음악 solemn music // 장엄한 경치 sublime [majestic] scenery. **장엄히** solemnly; sublimely; magnificently; majestically. ¶의식은 ~ 행해졌다 The cere-

장염(腸炎) [의] inflammation of the intestines; enteritis.
장옷 a jangot; a lady's veil; a cloak.
장외(場外) ¶~의[에] outside the hall [grounds / room] / ~에 넘쳐 있는 청중 an overflow audience / (스포츠에서) an overflow crowd of spectators.
● **장외 거래** over-the-counter trading; off-board transactions. **장외 시장** the off-board [over-the-counter] market. **장외 주식** unlisted stocks; an over-the-counter stock. **장외 홈런** an out-of-the-park homer.
장원(壯元) 1 [수석 합격] passing a examination first on the list. **장원하다** win the first place in a state examination; pass (the civil service examination) first on the list; head the list in a contest. 2 [시험에서 첫째로 합격한 사람] a person who has won the first place in a state examination; the first place winner in a contest.
장원(莊園) [역] a manor. ¶~의 영주 the lord of a manor // ~ 영주의 저택 a manor house.
● **장원 제도** the manorial system.
장유(長幼) young and old.
● **장유유서**(-有序) The young must honor their elders.; Precedence should be given to older people.
장음(長音) [긴소리] a long[prolonged] sound; [장모음] a long vowel.
장음계(長音階) a major scale.
장의(葬儀) a funeral. ⇨=**장례**(葬禮)
● **장의사** a funeral home[parlor]; (영) an undertaker's (shop).
장인(丈人) one's wife's father; one's father-in-law (*pl.* fathers-in-law).
장인(匠人) a handicraftsman; a craftsman; an artisan.
● **장인 기질** the artisan spirit.
장자(長子) the firstborn son. ⇨=**맏아들**
● **장자 상속권** the right of primogeniture.
장자(長者) 1 [윗사람] one's superior; one's betters; [연장자] one's elder; one's senior. 2 [덕망가] an elder of virtue; a man of moral influence. 3 [큰 부자] a wealthy[rich] man. **백만~** a millionaire.// **억만~** a billionaire.
장작(長斫) firewood. ¶불을 패다 split wood// ~을 지피다 put more wood on the fire / add more wood to the fire.
● **장작개비** a piece of (fire)-wood; a billet. **장작불** wood fire.
장장(長長) very long; at great length; lengthily. ¶회의는 ~ 6시간이나 계속되었다 The meeting went on and on[dragged on] for six long hours.
장전(裝塡) [탄약을 잼] loading; a charge. **장전하다** load[charge] (a gun). ¶그는 총에 탄환을 장전했다 He loaded his gun with bullets. ➔¶그 권총에는 탄환이 모두 장전되어 있었다 The gun was fully loaded.
장절(章節) chapters and sections.
장점(長點) a strong[good] point; a merit; [이점] an advantage. ¶사람에게는 누구나 ~과 단점이 있다 Everybody has his merits and demerits.// 당신의 ~을 살리도록 하세요 Try to develop your strong points.// 나는 남의 ~을 보려고 애쓰고 있다 I try to see the good in others.// 그의 ~은 인정해 주어야 한다 You must give him his due.//그것이 바로 그 ~이다 That's the charm[beauty] of it. / That's the good thing about it.// 성실성만이 그의 ~이다 His only merit[recommendation / strength] is his earnestness.// 조작이 아주 간단하다는 것이 이 기계의 ~이다 The advantage of this machine is that it is very easy to operate.// 그는 잘생기지 않았지만 재빠른 유머 감각이 ~이었다 He wasn't good-looking, but he did have the virtue of a quick sense of humor.
장정(壯丁) 1 [젊고 기운이 좋은 사람] a vigorous youth[young] man. ¶두 사람 몫의 일을 하다 do the work of two vigorous youth. 2 [징병 적령자] a man of enlistment[military] age.
장정(長征) a long march.
장정(長程) a long[great] distance. ¶~에 오르다 start on a long journey.
장정(裝幀) [제본] binding; (표지의) design. ¶이 책의 ~은 훌륭하다 This book is very beautifully bound. **장정하다** bind; (표지를) design. ¶책을 천[가죽]으로 ~ bind a book in cloth[leather].
장조(長調) [음] a major (key). ¶가[다]~의 교향곡 a symphony in A[C] major.
장조림(醬-) beef boiled down in soy sauce.
장조카(長-) the eldest son of one's eldest brother.
장족(長足) [진보 등이 빠름]. ¶언어의 습득에 ~의 진보를 이룩하다 make rapid progress [remarkable progress / great strides] in learning languages // 의학은 최근에 ~의 진보를 이룩했다 Medical science has made remarkable [rapid] progress of late.
장죽(長竹) a long (tobacco) pipe. ¶~을 입에 물다 stick one's long pipe in one's mouth.
장중(掌中) ¶~에 있다 be in the hollow[palm] of one's hand / be in one's hands / be in one's power // ~에 떨어지다 fall into (a person's) power[hands / possession] / slip into (a person's) grasp[clutches] // ~에 들어오다 fall under the power (of).
● **장중보옥**(-寶玉) the apple of one's eye; one's jewel. ¶~을 잃다 lose a prize within one's grasp // 그는 딸을 ~으로 아낀다 His daughter is the apple of his eye.
장중하다(莊重-) solemn; sublime; grave. ¶장중한 음악 solemn music // 메시지는 장중한 어조로 낭독되었다 The message was read out in a solemn tone (of voice). **장중히** solemnly; with solemnity.
장지(障-) [칸막이 문] a jangji; a paper sliding door[screen]. ¶유리 ~ a sliding glass door // ~를 열다[닫다] open[shut] a sliding door // ~에 종이를 바르다[갈다] paper[repaper] a sliding door.
● **장지문** a jangjimun; a paper sliding door.
장지(長指) the middle[second] finger.
장지(葬地) a burial[burying] ground; [묘지] a cemetery; a graveyard.
장지(壯志) a grand ambition; a lofty aspiration. ¶~를 품다 entertain a great ambition.
장질(長姪) the eldest son of one's eldest brother. ⇨=**장조카**
장질부사(腸窒扶斯) typhoid(fever). ⇨=**장티푸스**
장차(將次) [장래에] in future(막연히 금후); in the future(미래에); [언젠가] someday. ¶~ 어떤 일이 일어날지 아무도 모른다 Nobody can tell[We never can tell] what will happen

장창(長槍) a long spear[lance].
장총(長銃) a (long-barreled) rifle.
장축(長軸) [수] the major axis. ⇨˚긴지름
장출혈(腸出血) [의] enterohemorrhage.
장치(裝置) equipment; a device; (an) apparatus.(▶ equipment는 집합 명사로서 기기의 가장 일반적인 말. a device는 특히 기계 등의 일부·부품의 뜻. apparatus는 특정한 목적을 가진 한 벌의 기계로서 복수형은 드물다) ¶기동 ~ a triggering device // 난방 ~ a heater / a heating apparatus[system] // 냉방 ~ an air conditioner // 무대 ~ a stage setting // 무전 ~ a radio / radio equipment / a wireless apparatus // 발화 ~ an ignition device // 방화(防火) ~ fire prevention equipment // 스테레오 ~ a stereo equipment // 안전 ~ a safety device // 이 시계는 전기 ~입니다 This is an electric clock. / This clock is worked by electricity. **장치하다** equip[fit / furnish] (with); install. ¶배에 레이더를 ~ equip a ship with a radar // 시한폭탄을 ~ set a time bomb. ➔ ¶실험실에는 온갖 기구가 장치되어 있다 The laboratory is fully equipped.
장침(長枕) an elbow rest; an armrest.
장침(長針) 1 the minute [long] hand. ⇨˚분침(分針) 2 [긴 바늘] a long needle.
장카타르(腸-) [의] inflammation of the intestines. ⇨˚장염
장쾌하다(壯快-) stirring; thrilling; exciting. ¶정상을 정복한 기분은 참으로 장쾌했다 It was indeed a stirring feeling to reach the top of the mountain.
장타(長打) [야구] a long hit; an extra-base hit; hit for extra bases.
●**장타자** a long-ball hitter; a power hitter.
장탄하다(裝彈-) load[charge] (a gun) (with shot); put a charge in (a gun).
장터(場-) a market place[site].
장티푸스(腸-) typhoid (fever); (영) enteric.
●**장티푸스 예방 주사** antityphoid inoculation. **장티푸스 환자** a typhoid patient[case].
장파(長波) a long wave.
장판(壯版) 1 [기름 먹인 종이로 바른 방바닥] a floor covered with oilpaper. ¶~을 닦다 wipe the floor of oilpaper. 2 (a sheet of) oilpaper (for floor). ⇨˚장판지(⇨장판).
●**장판지** (a sheet of) oilpaper (for floor).
장편(長篇) a long piece[work].
●**장편 소설** a long novel.
장폐색증(腸閉塞症) [의] ileus; intestinal obstruction.
장하다(壯-) admirable; praiseworthy; creditable; laudable; splendid. ¶장한 어머니 a respectable[an honorable] mother // 장한 행동 a praiseworthy deed / an admirable conduct // 그녀가 동생들을 돌보고 있다니 장하기도 하다 It is quite a praiseworthy[an admirable] thing that she is looking after her younger brothers. // 그의 행동은 ~ His conduct is worthy of praise. // 내 아들은 장하게도 우등상을 탔다 I'm proud of my son who was awarded a honor prize. // 정말 ~ Well done! / Bravo! / I'm proud of you. **장히** admirably; praiseworthily; creditably; laudably; splendidly.
장학(獎學) encouragement of learning. **장학하다** encourage learning.
●**장학관** a school inspector[commissioner]. ¶도[시] ~ a provincial[municipal] school inspector. **장학금** a scholarship; (대학원생·연구자의) a fellowship. ¶풀브라이트 ~ (미국 정부가 주는) Fulbright-Hays grant // ~을 받는 학생 a scholarship student / a fellowship recipient // 그는 ~을 받고 있다 He is on (a) scholarship. // 그는 많은 ~을 받았다 He was awarded[granted] a large scholarship. // 그는 전액 ~을 받고 대학에 들어갔다 He went to college[a university] on a full scholarship. **장학생** a student on a scholarship; a scholarship student.
장해(障害) an obstacle; a hindrance.
장화(長靴) (a pair of) boots; rain boots(진 땅에 신는). ¶고무 ~ rubber boots / (영) gum boots / (영) wellingtons // 반~ half boots // 승마용 ~ riding boots // 그는 ~를 신고 있다 He is wearing boots.
장황하다(張皇-) lengthy; long-winded; [지겹다] long and boring; tedious; prolix. ¶장황한 연설 a lengthy[long-winded] speech // 장황한 이야기 a tedious[long and tiresome] talk // 장황한 설명 a long-winded explanation // 이 문장은 좀 ~ This passage is a little too lengthy[wordy]. **장황히** lengthily; at length; long-windedly. ¶~ 이야기하다 speak long-windedly // ~ 설명하다 make a long-winded explanation / describe tediously // 그는 자기의 경력을 ~ 늘어놓았다 He spoke of his own career at length.
잦다[1] (물 등이) become less; decrease; lessen.
잦다[2] (뒤로 기울다) lean[bend] back(ward).
잦다[3] [빈번하다] frequent; incessant; [간격이 짧다] short. ¶잦은 기침 a hacking cough // 잦은 걸음으로 with quick steps / at a quick pace / at a trot // 겨울에는 화재가 ~ Fires are frequent in wintertime. // 7월에는 비가 잦았다 Rainy weather prevailed in July. // 요즘 아버지로부터 전화가 잦았다 My father has called up very often[many times] recently.
잦뜨리다 throw back(ward). ⇨˚젖뜨리다
잦아들다 (물이 서서히 말라 가다) become less; decrease; lessen; boil down(끓어서). ¶우물물이 잦아들었다 The water in the well has got low.
잦아지다[1] (말라서) dry up; go down; be boiled down. ¶가뭄에서 못의 물이 잦아졌다 The pond has dried up because of dry weather. // 수프가 잦아지지 않도록 불을 약하게 해라 Turn down the fire so that the soup will not boil down.
잦아지다[2] [자주 있게 되다] occur frequently[at short intervals]; be frequent. ¶요즘 이 도시에서 교통사고가 잦아지고 있다 These days traffic accidents have occurred frequently in this town.
잦혀지다 1 [뒤집히다] be overturned; be upset; be turned upside down. 2 (뒤로) bend back(ward); lean backward; be pulled back. 3 [열리다] be flung[thrown] open.
잦히다[1] (밥을) ripen[steam] (boiled rice); allow boiled rice to settle by a slow fire.
잦히다[2] bend back(ward); turn out; fling open. ⇨˚젖히다
재[1] (타고 남은 것) ash(es). ¶연탄[석탄] ~ briquet[coal] cinders // 담뱃 ~ cigarette

ash(es) // 화산~ volcanic ash(es) // 죽음의 ~ the lethal fallout (from an atomic test) / ~ 투성이의 full of ashes / ashy // 나무를 태워서 ~를 만들었다 I made ash by burning wood. // 내 장서가 모두 ~가 되어 버렸다 All my books were reduced to ashes[went up in smoke]. // 그는 죽어서 ~가 되었다 He was cremated.

재² 〔고개〕 a (mountain) pass; a ridge. ¶박달~ the Bakdal Pass // ~를 넘다 cross (over) a (mountain) pass // 우리는 ~를 넘어 차를 몰았다 We drove our car over the mountain pass.

재 (齋) 〔불〕 a Buddhist memorial service; a Buddhist mass[service]. ¶~를 올리다 hold a Buddhist service for the dead / have a Buddhist mass read for the repose of (a person's) soul.

재- (再) re-; again; once more. ¶~조사 reexamination // ~투자 reinvestment.

재가 (再嫁) remarriage(of a woman). ⇨ 개가 (改嫁)

재가 (裁可) sanction; (official) approval. ¶대통령의 ~를 바라다 submit a matter for Presidential sanction[approval] // 대통령의 ~를 얻다 obtain Presidential sanction. 재가하다 sanction; approve; give sanction (to).

재가하다 (在家-) **1** 〔집에 있다〕 be (at) home; be in; keep[stay] at home. **2** 〔불〕 lead the ascetic life of Buddhism at one's home; practice Buddhist austerities at one's home.

재간 (才幹) 〔능력〕 ability; talent; capability; 〔재주〕 skill. ¶~ 있는 〔유능한〕 able / talented / 〔일을 감당하는〕 capable // ~ 있는 사람 an able[a capable] person // 말~ the gift of gab // 손~ manual skill / dexterity.

재간 (再刊) republication; reissue. 재간하다 republish; reissue.

재갈 〔말의 입에 물리는 물건〕 a bit; 〔임마개〕 a gag. ¶말에 ~을 물리다 put a bit in a horse's mouth // 남에게 ~을 먹이다 gag a person.

재갈매기 〔동〕 a herring gull.

재감 (在監) imprisonment; staying in prison. ¶~ 중인 in prison // ~ 중이다 be in prison[jail].
●**재감자** a prisoner; a prison inmate; 〔집합적〕 the criminal population.

재감염 (再感染) reinfection. 재감염하다 infect again.

재강 〔술찌끼〕 liquor lees; dregs; draff.

재개 (再開) reopening; resumption. 재개하다 (일단 종료했던 것을) reopen; (일시적인 중단 후에) resume; 〔경기를 ~〕 resume play. →¶회의는 오후 1시에 재개된다 The meeting will be resumed[reopened] at 1 p.m. // 한미 교섭이 재개되었다 The negotiations between Korea and America were reopened [resumed]. // 국회는 12일에 재개된다 The National Assembly is to resume work on the 12th.

재개발 (再開發) redevelopment. 재개발하다 redevelop.
●**재개발 지역** a redevelopment area[zone].

재건 (再建) rebuilding; reconstruction. ¶전후의 ~ postwar reconstruction // 그는 회사의 ~에 나섰다 He set out to reconstruct the company[put the company back on its feet]. // 그들은 황폐한 조국의 ~에 힘썼다 They worked for the reconstruction of their devastated country. 재건하다 rebuild; reconstruct; reestablish; restore(복구). ¶그들은 도산 직전의 회사를 재건하는 데 성공했다 They succeeded in restoring the nearly bankrupt company. →¶그 도시는 지진이 있은 지 1년 후에 완전히 재건되었다 The town was completely reconstructed[rebuilt] (from ruin) one year after the earthquake.

재검토 (再檢討) 〔다시 한 번 더 조사함〕 (a) reexamination; restudying; 〔다시 한 번 생각함〕 a reconsideration; a review; 〔재평가〕 (a) reappraisal; reevaluation. ¶대통령은 국방 계획의 ~를 지시했다 The President ordered a defense review. 재검토하다 reexamine; reconsider; review; restudy; reappraise; reevaluate. ¶그것을 재검토하겠다 We'll study it again. // 그 계획은 재검토할 필요가 있다 The plan needs to be reexamined[reconsidered].

재결 (裁決) a decision; (법적인) a verdict; (a) judgment(▶ decision과 동의어로 쓰이는 수도 있음). ¶~을 바라다 submit[leave] a matter to a person's judgment / await a person's verdict // ~에 따르다 abide by a decision // 그에게 유리한 ~이 내려졌다 A decision[judgment] was given in his favor. / They rendered a verdict favorable to him. 재결하다 decide; judge; pass[give] judgment (on); bring in verdict.
●**재결권** authority to decide; a casting vote. ¶가부 동수일 때는 의장에게 ~이 있다 When the votes equally decided, the chairman has the casting vote.

재결합 (再結合) reunion; recombination. ¶이산가족의 ~ reunion of one's dispersed family members. 재결합하다 reunite (with); recombine; rejoin together; return to the former relations (with). ¶전남편과 ~ be reconciled[reunited] with her former husband / be reinstated as wife.

재경 (在京) staying[being / residing] in Seoul. 재경하다 stay in Seoul; be[reside] in Seoul.
●**재경 동창생** alumni in Seoul. **재경 외국인** foreign residents in Seoul.

재경 (財經) finance[financial administration] and economy. ¶국회 ~ 위원회 the finance and economy committee of the National Assembly.

재계 (財界) 〔금융계〕 the financial world; financial circles; 〔경제계〕 the economic world; economic circles; 〔실업계〕 the business world; business circles. ¶~의 거물 a leading financier[businessman] / (미) a tycoon // ~의 위기 a financial crisis // ~의 안정〔불안〕 financial stability[unrest] // ~가 활기를 띠고 있다 The financial world shows signs of activity.
●**재계 인사** a financier; a big businessman.

재계 (齋戒) purification. ¶목욕~ purification by ablution / lustration. 재계하다 purify oneself; perform purification.

재고 (再考) reconsideration. ¶~를 촉구[요청]하다 urge[ask] (a person) to reconsider // ~를 요함 (라) ad referendum // ~의 여지가 없다 There is no room for reconsideration. 재고하다 reconsider; think over again. ¶재고한 결과 on reflection / on second thought // 재고해 보겠습니다 I will consider it once more.

재고 (在庫) stock; the stockpile. ¶적정 ~ proper stock // 유통 ~ distributor's stock //

재교
~가 있다[없다] be in[out of] stock // ~를 조사하다 take stock[inventory] / check the stock // ~를 조정하다 adjust the stock // 등유의 ~는 이제 없습니다 We have no more stock of kerosene. // 이 텔레비전은 ~가 4대 밖에 없다 We have only four of these televisions in stock[on hand]. // 저 가게는 ~가 풍부하다 That store has a large stock of articles. // 저 회사는 ~가 부족하다 That firm is low on[short of] stock. 중고차의 ~가 떨어졌다 Used car have run out of stock.
● 재고 관리 inventory management[control] 재고량 the total stock. 재고 정리 clearance of the goods in stock. ~ 세일 a clearance sale. 재고 조사 (take) inventory; stocktaking. 재고품 goods in stock; stored goods; goods in store.

재교(再校) the second proof. ¶~를 보다 read the second proof // ~를 요함 Second proof required. **재교하다** read the second proof; proofread a second time.

재교부(再交付) (a) reissue; (a) renewal; (a) regrant. ¶그는 그 증명서의 ~를 신청했다 He applied for the reissue of the certificate. **재교부하다** reissue; regrant.

재교육(再敎育) reeducation; retraining; (현직의) in-service training. **재교육하다** reeducate; retrain. → ¶점원을 재교육시키다 train again[retrain] clerks.

재구성(再構成) reconstruction; recomposition; reconstitution. **재구성하다** reconstruct; recompose; reconstitute.

재귀(再歸) recurrence; return. **재귀하다** return; come[go] back.
● 재귀 대명사[동사] [언] a reflexive pronoun [verb].

재규어 [동] a jaguar; an American leopard.

재기(才氣) talent. ¶~가 있는 quick-witted / gifted / resourceful / (very) witty[brilliant] // ~ 발랄한 brilliant / extremely clever / (a man) of great resources.

재기(再起) 1 [복귀] a comeback. ¶그는 ~ 불능인 것 같다 He seems to be little chance of his comeback. **재기하다** come back; make a comeback; rise again. ¶테너 가수로서 ~ stage a comeback as a tenor. 2 [회복] recovery; restoration. ¶그는 ~ 불능이다 He's finished[through]. / He'll never recover sufficiently to resume a normal life. **재기하다** recover; be restored. → ¶그녀의 부모는 그를 충격으로부터 재기시키려고 심혈을 기울였다 Her parents racked their brains trying to think of a way to help her get over her shock.

재깍[1] [물건이 부러지거나 부딪칠 때에 나는 소리] with a click[clack / snick]; with a snap. ¶자물쇠가 ~ 잠겼다 The lock clicked shut. // 시계가 ~ ~ 소리를 내고 있다 Click, click, click ... goes the watch. **재깍하다** keep clicking. →재깍거리다

재깍[2] [일을 빠르게 해치우는 모양] quickly; speedily; with dispatch; instantly; on the spot; at once. ¶일을 ~ 해치우다 do a thing quickly[with dispatch] / be prompt in one's work // (꾸물대지 말고) 해치워라 Be quick about it! / Make short work of it!

재깍거리다 keep clicking[snapping]. ¶시계가 재깍거린다 The clock is ticking.

재난(災難) [재해] a disaster; a calamity; [불행] (a) misfortune; a mishap; [돌발 사고]

an accident; a catastrophe. ¶~을 겪다[당하다] meet with misfortune / have bad luck // ~을 모면하다 escape a disaster // 뜻밖의 ~을 당했다 I met with an unexpected calamity [misfortune]. // ~의 연속이다 One calamity has followed on the heels of another. / We have suffering a series of misfortunes. // 그는 산사태로 집이 무너지는 ~을 당했다 He had the great misfortune of having his house destroyed by a landslide.

재능(才能) [능력] ability; (타고난) talent; (천재적인) a gift; [천분] a genius; (선천적·후천적인) faculty. ¶어학적[음악적] ~ linguistic [musical] talent // 숨은 ~ a hidden talent // ~이 있는 사람 an able[a talented / a gifted] man // ~이 없는 사람 an ungifted person / a person without talent // 자기의 ~을 펼쳐 나가다 develop one's talent // ~을 십분 발휘하다 fully display one's genius // 그에게는 이 연구를 수행할 ~이 있다 He has the ability to carry out this research. // 그는 태어나면서부터 ~이 있다 He is naturally gifted. / He was born with talent. // 그녀는 음악에 ~을 발휘했다 She has showed[displayed] a talent for music. // 그녀는 화가로서의 최고의 ~을 지닌 사람이다 She has great talent as a painter.

재다[1] [잘난 체하다] put on airs; give oneself airs; make a boast of; assume an air of importance; wear a high hat. ¶존은 1등 상을 탔다고 재고 있었다 John boasted of having won the first prize. // 그것은 하나도 젤 만한 일이 못 된다 That is nothing to be proud of. // 그렇게 재지 마라 Don't be so puffed up.

2 (길이·크기·양을) measure; (무게를) weigh; (소요 시간을) time; (수심을) sound; [일반적으로 계측하다] gauge; gage; [측정하다] take. ¶키를 ~ measure one's height // 몸무게를 ~ weigh oneself / take one's weight // 각도를 ~ take[measure] the angle (of) // 막대기의 길이 [집의 높이]를 ~ measure the length of a stick[the height of a house] // 강의 수심을 ~ sound[fathom] the depth of a river // 경주의 시간[주자의 속도]을 ~ time a race [the speed of a runner] // 체온을 ~ take one's temperature // 나는 거리를 쟀다 I measured the distance. // 재단사는 내 새 코트의 치수를 쟀다 The tailor took my measure[measurements] for a new coat.

3 [따져 보다] think over; consider carefully; ponder (up)on[over]; deliberate over. ¶이것저것 재어 본 후에 after a great deal of thinking / after putting two and two together // 앞뒤를 ~ take every possible consequence [situation] into consideration // 모든 각도에서 재어 보다 survey[study] (a problem) from every angle[all view point].

4 [장전하다] load; charge. ¶탄알을 잰 총 a loaded gun // 그는 총에 탄환을 쟀다 He loaded his gun with bullets.

재다[2] →재우다

재다[3] heap (up); pile up. ⇨ 쟁이다

재다[4] 1 [빠르다] fast; quick; [날래다] nimble; agile; alert; prompt. ¶손이 ~ have nimble fingers / be skillful[quick] with one's hand // 그는 걸음이 ~ He walks very fast. / He is a fast walker. 2 [입이 가볍다] talkative; voluble; glib. ¶그는 입이 재서 곤란하다 His tongue wags too freely. 3 [쉬 더워지다] easy[quick] to warm up.

재단(財團) a foundation. ¶포드 ~ the Ford

Foundation // ~을 설립하다 establish an endowment [a foundation] / found a fund.
● 재단 법인 a foundation; a (foundational) juridical person; (미) a nonprofit corporation.
재단 (裁斷) 1 a decision. ⇨ "재결 2 cutting (out). ⇨ "마름질 ¶~이 잘되어 있다 [신통찮다] be well [ill] tailored [cut]. **재단하다** cut (out). ¶드레스를 ~ cut out a dress // 옷감을 ~ cut (the) cloth / cut cloth for sewing / cut out a pattern // 우리는 치수에 맞추어 와이셔츠 감을 재단했다 We cut (out) shirts to measure.
● 재단기 a cutter; a cutting machine; (종이의) a paper cutter; a guillotine. **재단사** a cutter.
재담 (才談) a witticism; a witty remark; a joke; a pun; a quibble; a play upon [on] words. **재담하다** make a witty remarks; play upon words; make a joke [pun].
● 재담꾼 a joker; a quibbler.
재당숙 (再堂叔) a male second cousin of one's father. ⇨ 재종숙 (⇨재종)
재당질 (再堂姪) a son of one's second cousin. ⇨ 재종질 (⇨재종)
재덕 (才德) talent and virtue. ¶~을 겸비한 사람 an able and virtuous person // ~을 겸비하다 be both talented and virtuous.
재독 (再讀) a second reading. **재독하다** read (a book) again; reread. ¶이 책은 재독할 만하다 This book is worth a second reading.
재돌입 (再突入) (로켓의) reentry. **재돌입하다** reenter. ¶로켓은 대기권에 재돌입했다 The rocket reentered the atmosphere. // 기동대는 시위대 속으로 재돌입했다 The riot police broke (into) the ranks of the demonstrators again.
재동 (才童) a clever child; a child of talent.
재두루미 [동] a white-naped [-necked] crane.
재떨이 an ashtray; (다리가 달린 것) a smoking stand. ¶담뱃재를 ~에 떨다 knock [tip] off the ashes of one's cigarette into the ashtray // ~에 담배를 비벼 끄다 put out one's cigarette in an ashtray.
재래 (在來) ¶~의 [보통의] ordinary / common / usual / [옛날부터의] conventional / customary / [전통적인] traditional / [그 고장 원산의] native // ~의 방법에 따르다 follow the usual [customary] procedures // 새 제품은 ~의 것보다 경비가 싸게 먹힌다 The new product requires less overheads than the existing [old] one.
● 재래식 a conventional type. ¶~ 무기 conventional weapons // ~ 공법으로 집을 짓다 build a house using traditional construction methods. 재래종 a native species [kind]. ¶~ 옥수수 the native species of corn.
재래 (再來) a second coming [advent]; a reincarnation. ¶그는 모차르트의 ~이다 He is a second Mozart. **재래하다** come again.
재략 (才略) [책략] a clever scheme; [재치] resource(s). ¶~이 뛰어난 사람 a very resourceful person / a man of great resource.
재량 (裁量) discretion; a free hand. ¶자유~권 (have no) discretionary power [authority] / 자기의 ~으로 at one's discretion // ~에 맡기다 leave (a matter) to (a person's) discretion / give (a person) a free hand (in a matter) // 그 건을 그의 ~에 맡겼다 I left the matter to his discretion. // 그를 사직시키는 것은 너의 ~에 달려 있다 It is within your discretion to have him dismissed.
● 재량 처분 discretional [discretionary] disposition.
재력 (財力) 1 [금력] financial power [ability]; [재산] means; wealth. ¶~이 있는 사람 a man of means [wealth] // ~의 힘을 빌려서 through the power of money / by letting one's money talk. 2 [재원] (financial) resources; funds; wherewithal; [채무 이행 능력] solvency. ¶~이 없어 금전적으로 아무 것도 도와 드릴 수 없습니다 I am afraid I have no funds with which to help you. // 그에게는 그것을 완성할 만한 ~이 없다 He has not the wherewithal to bring it to completion.
재론 (再論) reargument; rediscussion. **재론하다** reargue; rediscuss; redispute; argue [discuss] again. ¶이 문제는 재론할 가치도 없다 This problem is not worth rediscussing.
재롱 (才弄) (baby's) cute movements. ¶~스럽다 cute / sweet // ~을 떨다 [부리다] act cutely / do cute movements / make sweet gesture.
● 재롱둥이 an adorable [a cute] baby doing cute movements.
재료 (材料) material(s); matter; stuff; [원료] raw material(s); (요리 등의) ingredients; [자료] data. ¶건축 ~ building [construction] materials // 생물학의 실험 ~ materials for biological experiments // 이 집은 좋은 ~를 써서 지었다 This house is built of good materials. // 그는 그 이야기를 다음 소설의 ~로 삼으려고 생각하고 있다 He is thinking of using this story as material for his next novel. // 케이크의 ~로 밀가루와 설탕 외에 무엇이 필요합니까 What do we need as ingredients of a cake besides flour and sugar?
● 재료비 the cost of materials (for).
재류 (在留) residence. ¶나는 파리 ~ 중에 그를 만났다 I met him when I was living in Paris. **재류하다** live (in / at); reside (at / in); dwell; stay. ¶재류하는 resident / living (in / at).
● 재류민 residents. ⇨ 거류민 (⇨거류)
재림 (再臨) a second coming [advent]; a reincarnation. ¶예수의 ~ the Second Coming [Advent] of Christ // 예수 ~ 설 Adventism. **재림하다** come again; be reincarnated. ¶그는 마치 공자님이 재림한 것 같은 사람이다 He is a second Confucius.
재목 (材木) wood; (미) lumber; (영) timber; a log (통나무). ¶쌓아 놓은 ~ piled lumber // 산에서 ~을 베어 내다 bring down lumber [timber] from the mountains // ~을 건조시키다 season the wood.
● 재목상 a lumber [timber] dealer [merchant].
재무 (財務) financial affairs. ¶그는 ~ 담당 이사이다 He is a [the] director in charge of financial affairs. (▶ 이사가 한 사람일 때는 정관사를 씀)
● 재무 관리 financial management. 재무제표 (─諸表) financial statements.
재무장 (再武裝) rearmament; remilitarization. ¶도덕 ~ moral rearmament. **재무장하다** rearm (itself); remilitarize (a country).
재물 (財物) property; riches; means; effects; wealth; goods; one's valuables. ¶~에 눈이 어두워지다 be dazzled by riches // 남의 ~을

빼앗다 rob a person of his property.

재미 1 [즐거움] (a) pleasure; amusement; enjoyment; fun; [흥미] interest. ¶소설을 읽는 ~ the pleasure of reading novels // 가정생활의 ~ the amenities of home life // 물건을 직접 손으로 만드는 ~ the pleasure of making things by hand // 그는 스포츠에서 아무런 ~도 느끼지 못했다 He derived no pleasure from sporting. // 그녀는 무슨 ~로 살고 있을까 I wonder what she lives for. // 그의 강의는 ~라고는 조금도 없다 His lectures are very dull [boring]. // 나는 ~로 그림을 그리고 있는 것이 아니다 I don't paint pictures for pleasure [fun / amusement]. // 나는 수학의 ~를 잃었다 I lost interest in mathematics. // 그는 인생에 ~를 잃었다 He grew weary of life. / He lost interest in life.
2 [형편] a condition; a state. ¶요즘 ~가 어때 How are you getting along with your business? / How is your business going? // ~가 좋아 All is going well. / Every thing turning out all right.
3 [좋은 성과] a good result; good fruit.

재미 보다 1 [즐거움을 맛보다] make a merry time of it; have a good time; enjoy [amuse] oneself; have fun. ¶재미 좀 보았니 Did you have a good time? / Did you enjoy yourself? 2 [성과를 올리다] obtain [get] good results; be rewarded with good fruits. ¶나는 그 거래에서 재미를 보았다 I made [gained] a profit on the deal. / 낚시에서 재미 좀 보았습니까 Did you get (any) good fishing? // 그들은 수출에서 재미를 톡톡히 보았다 They made large profit from exports.

재미(를) 붙이다 get [come] to like; become fond of; begin to love; take a fancy to. ¶그는 요즈음 공부에 재미를 붙였다 Recently he has come to enjoy his studies. // 나는 요즈음 테니스에 재미를 붙였다 I have recently become fond of [come to like] tennis.

재미(在美) [관용어적] (living) in America. ¶~중에 during one's stay in America / while in America.
● **재미 교포** a Korean living in America. **재미 유학생** Korean students studying in America.

재미나다 be interesting [amusing]; be funny [jolly]. ¶재미나는 이야기 잘 들었습니다 We have enjoyed your interesting talk.

재미없다 uninteresting; dull; unamusing. ¶재미없는 시합 a dull game [match] // 재미없는 책 a boring [an uninteresting] book // 정말 재미없는 이야기다 It's utterly unromantic. / What a prosaic story! // 회사에 나가는 ~ Working at a business firm isn't interesting [any fun]. // 너 이러면 재미없어 You'll pay for it.

재미있다 interesting; amusing; entertaining; funny; jolly; exciting. ¶재미있는 책 an interesting book // 재미있는 이야기 an amusing [a good] story / an entertaining [interesting] talk // 재미있는 경기 an exciting [a lively] game // 재미있는 착상 a good [happy] idea / an intriguing idea // 어제는 아주 재미있었다 I had a very good time yesterday. / I enjoyed myself very much yesterday. // 이 소설은 재미있었다 The novel was interesting. / I found the novel interesting. // 그것은 재미있는 영화였다 It was an exciting [entertaining] movie. // 소풍은 아주 재미있었다 We had a lot of [great] fun at the picnic. // 잘 낚이기만 하면 낚시는 아주 ~ Fishing is great fun when there is a good catch. // 재미있었니 Did you have a good time? / Did you enjoy yourself? // 나는 이 소설을 재미있게 읽었다 I read the novel with interest. // 나는 친구들과 재미있게 놀았다 I had a good [pleasant] time with my friends.

재발(再發) 1 [다시 생김] a recurrence; (병의) a return; (먼저보다 더 나빠지는 재발) relapse. ¶전쟁의 ~ the recurrence of war // 대홍수의 ~을 방지하다 prevent a recurrence of disastrous floods // 한반도에서의 전쟁의 ~을 방지하다 prevent the recurrence of war on the Korean Peninsula. **재발하다** (병·문제가) recur; come back; flare up again; (사람이) have [suffer] a relapse; relapse (into). ¶중동 전쟁이 재발했다 The Arab-Israeli War broke out again. // 그는 암이 재발했다 He got cancer again. / The cancer reappeared [flared up again]. / He had a recurrence of cancer. // 이 병은 재발하면 위험하다 A second attack of this illness will be serious.
2 [재발송] resending; reforwarding. **재발하다** resend; reforward; send (out) again.

재발견(再發見) rediscovery. **재발견하다** rediscover. ¶처음으로 외국 여행을 하여 한국의 좋은 점을 재발견했다 I traveled abroad for the first time and rediscovered the good things about Korea.

재발급(再發給) (a) reissue. **재발급하다** reissue. ¶증명서를 ~ reissue a certificate (to).

재발행(再發行) reissue. **재발행하다** reissue.

재방송(再放送) rebroadcasting; a repeat; a rebroadcast. ¶이것은 어젯밤 프로그램의 ~입니다 This is the repeat [rebroadcast] of a program from yesterday evening. **재방송하다** rebroadcast; broadcast (a program) again; show a rerun (of an old movie).

재배(再拜) 1 [두 번 하는 절] bowing twice; a second bowing [obeisance]. **재배하다** bow twice. 2 (편지 끝에) "As ever"; "Sincerely yours".

재배(栽培) cultivation; culture; raising; growing. ¶커피 [담배] ~ coffee [tobacco] growing // **수경**(水耕) ~ hydroponics / aquiculture // **속성** ~ forcing [intensive] culture / forcing // 온실 ~를 하다 raise (tomatoes) in a hothouse [a greenhouse] // 그 지방에서는 사탕수수의 ~가 성하다 Sugarcane is widely cultivated in that region. **재배하다** cultivate; grow; raise. ¶온실에 재배한 장미 a hothouse rose // 비닐하우스에서 채소를 ~ grow vegetables in a plastic greenhouse // 그는 장미를 여러 종류 재배하고 있다 He grows [raises] many kinds of roses. → ¶재배되고 있다 be in cultivation.
● **재배법** a method of cultivation. **재배자** a grower; a cultivator.

재배치(再配置) reassignment; relocation; realignment. ¶군의 전국적인 ~ the relocation of army units throughout the country. **재배치하다** reassign; relocate; realign.

재벌(財閥) a financial combine [group / clique]; a zaibatsu (단수·복수 동형); (집합적) the plutocracy. ¶일송 ~ Ilsong financial group [clique] / Ilsong interests.
● **재벌 기업** a (business) conglomerate; a

business group.

재범(再犯) repetition of an offense; a second conviction; [죄를 두 번째 지은 사람] a second offender; a repeater. **재범하다** repeat an offense; commit a second offense.

재변(災變) a calamity; a disaster.

재보험(再保險) reinsurance; (영) (특히 생명 보험의) reassurance. **재보험하다** reinsure; (영) (특히 생명 보험을) reassure.

재복무(再服務) (군인의) renewed enlistment; reenlistment. **재복무하다** reenlist; extend one's military service.

재봉(裁縫) [바느질] sewing; needlework; [옷을 짓기] tailoring; dressmaking. ¶이 잘된 옷 a well-tailored suit // ~을 잘[못]하다 be good[poor] at needlework[tailoring] // ~을 배우다 take lessons in sewing[needlework]. **재봉하다** sew; do needlework; sit at needlework.

● **재봉사** (신사복의) a tailor; (숙녀복의) a dressmaker; (여성) a seamstress. **재봉틀** a sewing machine. ¶발[손] ~ a treadle[hand-operated] sewing machine // 전기 ~ an electric sewing machine // ~을 밟다 run a sewing machine by foot // ~로 스커트를 박다 sew a skirt by machine // 그녀는 드레스를 ~로 박고 있다 She is sewing[making] dress with a sewing machine.

재분배(再分配) redistribution; reallotment. ¶부의 ~ redistribution of wealth. **재분배하다** redistribute; reallot.

재분할(再分割) redivision; repartition. **재분할하다** redivide; repartition; partition again.

재빠르다 quick; swift; agile; nimble; alert; prompt. ¶재빠른 움직임 an agile[alert] movement // 재빠른 대답 a prompt reply[answer] // 손이 ~ have nimble fingers // 그는 행동이 ~ He is quick[nimble] in action. // 그는 기회를 포착하는 데는 ~ He is alert in seizing[quick to seize] the opportunity. **재빨리** quickly; agilely; rapidly; nimbly; promptly. ¶그는 군중 속에서 ~ 친구를 찾아냈다 He quickly picked out[spotted] his friend in the crowd. // 그는 일어서서 노인에게 자리를 양보했다 He immediately stood up and gave his seat to the old man. // 그 사고의 뉴스를 듣자 그는 ~ 현장으로 달려갔다 On hearing of the accident, he hurried to the scene at once. // 개는 ~ 도망쳤다 The dog ran away quickly. // 그는 ~ 그것을 알아차렸다 He was quick to notice it.

재사(才士) [재주가 있는 남자] a man of talent[ability]; a talented[gifted / clever] person; a wit.
● **재사가인**(一佳人) wit and beauty.

재산(財産) property; (one's) possessions; a fortune; an estate.(▶ property는 주로 법률 용어로 쓰이, fortune은 비교적 큰 재산에, estate는 법률 용어로서 유산으로 상속되는 동산·부동산에 쓰임) ¶기본 ~ income-producing assets / [법] principal / 사유[공유] ~ private[public] property // 국유 ~ state-owned[national] property // 세습[상속] ~ hereditary[heritable] property // 유형[무형] ~ tangible[intangible] property // 증여 ~ a settlement // 막대한 ~ a large fortune // ~을 노리고 결혼하려는 남자 a fortune hunter // 백만 달러의 ~ a million dollars' worth of property // 약간의 ~이 있다 have a small fortune // 먹고살 ~이 있다 have enough to live on // ~을 상속하다 inherit[succeed to / come into] a fortune // ~을 압류하다 seize[attach] (a person's) property // ~을 다투다 claim[lay claim to] (a person's) property // ~을 몰수하다 confiscate (a person's) property // ~을 탕진하다 squander[run through] one's fortune / spend all one's wealth (on) // 남의 ~을 관리하다 manage a person's property // 아버지는 주식으로 ~을 모았다[잃었다] My father made[lost] his fortune on the stock market. // 최 씨는 10억 원의 ~이 있다 Mr. Choe is worth a billion won[has a billion won (to his name)]. // 그는 전 ~을 조카에게 양도했다 He made over all his property to his nephew. // 그는 전 ~을 잃었다 He lost every cent he had. // 성실은 최대의 ~이다 Integrity is the greatest asset a person can have.

● **재산가** a man of wealth[fortune / means / property]; a wealthy[rich] person. **재산권** the right to own property; property rights. ¶~의 설정[이전] settlement[transfer] of the title to a property. **재산 목록** an inventory (of property); a list of property. **재산 상속** succession to property; inheritance of property. **재산세** a property tax; (영) rates. **재산 압류** attachment[seizure] of property; [법] a levy of attachment.

재삼(再三) more than once; again and again; over and over (again); many times; often; repeatedly. ¶그에게 위험하다는 ~ 경고했으나 아무 소용이 없었다 I warned him of the danger over and over[time and time] again but it was useless. // 그는 재촉을 받고 나서 겨우 의사에게 갔다 He went to see a doctor after he was urged again and again[repeatedly].

재상(宰相) the prime minister; the premier (under the king).

재상영(再上映) a rerun; a revival. **재상영하다** rerun; revive; show again. ➔ ¶이 영화는 내달에 재상영됩니다 This film will be rerun[shown again] next month.

재색(才色) wit and beauty. ¶~을 겸비한 부인 a lady equipped with wit and beauty / a beautiful and talented woman // 그녀는 ~을 겸비하고 있다 She is endowed[gifted] with both beauty and intelligence[brains].

재생(再生) **1** [되살아남] revival; resuscitation. **재생하다** revive; resuscitate; come to life again; be restored to life.
2 [갱생] regeneration; reformation. **재생하다** regenerate; make a fresh start in life; turn over a new leaf. ¶그 소년은 완전히 재생하여 훌륭한 사회인이 되었다 The boy completely reformed himself[came back to normal] and became a respected citizen.
3 [폐물의 재생산] reclamation; regeneration; reproduction. ¶~ 가능한 reclaimable / recyclable / reproducible. **재생하다** reclaim; regenerate; reproduce; recycle. ¶고무를 ~ reclaim rubber.
4 (음·영상의) reproduction; (테이프의) playback; replay. ¶음의 ~ sound reproduction. **재생하다** reproduce; play back; replay. ¶테이프리코더로 음악을 ~ play[reproduce] music on the tape recorder // 요즈음은 텔레비전 방송을 비디오로 재생하여 보는 것이 유행하고 있다 Nowadays it is quite popular to watch a television program played back[repro-

재생산

duced] on a videotape recorder.
5 [생] regeneration; reproduction. ¶모발의 끊임없는 ~ constant regeneration of hair. **재생하다** regenerate; reproduce. ¶어떤 동물은 신체의 없어진 부분을 재생할 수 있다 Some animals can regenerate lost parts of the body. ➔ ¶도마뱀은 꼬리가 잘려도 재생된다 The lizard is able to reproduce a tail when it's torn off.
● **재생고무** reclaimed rubber. **재생 산업** the reproductive industry. **재생 장치** (녹음·녹화의) playback equipment; (기계의) regeneration equipment. **재생품** a recycled article.

재생산 (再生産) reproduction. ¶축소[확대] ~ reproduction on a regressive [progressive] scale. **재생산하다** reproduce.

재선 (再選) **1** (a) reelection. ⇨ 재선거 **2** [두 번째의 당선] reelection. ¶그는 국회의원 ~을 노리고 있다 He is seeking reelection to the National Assembly. **재선하다** reelect. ➔ ¶그는 학장에 재선되었다 He was reelected president of the college [university].

재선거 (再選擧) (a) reelection; a recall election. **재선거하다** reelect; hold a reelection.

재소자 (在所者) a prisoner; a prison inmate; (집합적) the criminal population.

재송 (再送) [다시 보냄] resending; reforwarding. **재송하다** send again; resend; reforward.

재수 (財數) luck; fortune. ¶~ 좋은 사람 a lucky [fortunate] person // ~ 없게 unluckily / unfortunately / by ill luck // ~가 좋다 be fortunate / be lucky // ~가 없다 be unlucky / be unfortunate / be out of[off one's] luck / have no luck // ~가 트였다 Fortune has begun to smile upon me. / The wheel of fortune has begun to roll my way. // 오늘은 정말 ~가 좋군 I'm very lucky today. / Luck is on my side today. // 오늘은 ~가 없군 I'm out of luck today! / My luck is out today. // 요즘은 ~가 옴 붙듯 한다 The luck runs terribly against me these days.
재수 없는 놈은 (뒤로) 자빠져도 코가 깨진다 (속담) The bread never falls but on its buttered side.

재수생 (再修生) a high school graduate who is waiting for another chance to enter a college. ¶그는 ~이다 He failed (in) this year's college entrance exams and is preparing for the next chance.

재수입 (再輸入) reimport; reimportation. **재수입하다** reimport.
● **재수입품** reimports; reimported articles.

재수출 (再輸出) reexport; reexportation. **재수출하다** reexport.
● **재수출품** reexports; reexported articles.

재수하다 (再修-) prepare oneself for the college entrance exams for the next chance.

재스민 [식] a jasmin(e); a jessamine; [향유] jasmin(e) oil.

재시합 (再試合) rematch; replay; [설욕전] a return match [game]. **재시합하다** replay; play a game again; have a match again.

재시험 (再試驗) (a) reexamination; retesting. ¶~을 치다 take a reeaxmination / (구어) make up an examination(불합격 과목의). **재시험하다** reexamine; retest; examine[test] again.

재심 (再審) **1** (a) reexamination. ⇨ 재심사 **2** (재판의) a retrial; a new trial; (a) review; (a) renewal of procedure.(▶ retrial은 같은 사건을 다시 심사하는 일, review는 상소의 경우 판사가 이미 행한 재판에 대해서 심사하는 일) ¶~을 청구하다 [명령하다] apply for [order] a new trial. **재심하다** try [hear] again; review; retry. ¶하급 법원의 판결을 ~ review decisions of a lower court.
● **재심 청구** a petition for a retrial.

재심사 (再審査) (a) reexamination; (a) review; (a) retest. **재심사하다** reexamine; examine again; review; retest. ¶응모자의 자격을 ~ retest the qualification of an applicant.

재앙 (災殃) [재난] a disaster; a calamity; a woe; [불행] a misfortune; mishap; [사고] an accident. ¶거듭되는 ~ a series [spell] of misfortunes // ~을 당하다 meet with a calamity / suffer a disaster [misfortune] // 그의 부주의가 ~을 몰고 왔다 His carelessness invited [brought on / caused / was the cause of] the disaster. // 그에게 ~이 내렸다 He had bad luck. / Misfortune befell him. // 그는 간신히 ~을 모면했다 He narrowly escaped the disaster [accident].

재야 (在野) ¶~의 [관직에 없는] out of office / [권좌에 없는] out of power / [정당이 야당의 입장에 있는] in opposition // 이 법안은 ~ 각 당의 조정이 어려울 것이다 It will be difficult to get arrangement from the various opposition parties on this bill. // 장관은 ~의 유능한 인재를 등용할 방침이다 The minister intends to appoint talented people from outside government. **재야하다** be in private life; remain out of public office; be out of office [power].
● **재야인사** distinguished men out of office; a prominent figure outside [out of] government.

재언하다 (再言-) say [speak] again. ¶그 계획이 실패로 끝나리라는 것은 재언할 필요도 없다 It is needless to say that the plan will end in failure.

재연 (再演) **1** [재상연] a repeat [second] performance. **재연하다** repeat (the same play); stage [present / perform] (a play) again. ¶로열 셰익스피어 극단은 「맥베스」를 재연하고 있다 The Royal Shakespeare Company is presenting [performing] "Macbeth" again. **2** [반복] reenactment. **재연하다** reenact. ¶살인 현장을 ~ reenact the scene of the murder // 범행을 재연해 보다 reconstruct one's crime.

재연 (再燃) recurrence; revival; recrudescence; (불의) reignition; resuscitation. ¶문제의 ~ resuscitation of a problem // 인플레의 ~ recurrence of inflation. **재연하다** revive; resuscitate; be resuscitated; come to the fore again. ¶인플레가 재연할 것 같다 Inflation is likely to recur. ➔ **재연시키다** revive (an old quarrel) / reignite (a dispute) / reheat (the crisis) // 그 문제가 재연되었다 The problem has come to the fore again. // 그 케케묵은 논쟁이 재연되고 있다 That old controversy has been brought up again [revived].

재외 (在外) [관형어적] overseas; (거주) resident abroad; (주재) stationed abroad; (보유) held [kept] abroad.
● **재외 공관** diplomatic establishments abroad; embassies and legations abroad. **재외 교포** Korean residents overseas [abroad]; overseas Koreans.

재우 [매우 재게] quickly; nimbly; agilely;

alertly. ¶발걸음을 ~ 떼어 놓다 walk at a quick[brisk] pace.

재우다 1 [자게 하다] end[put] (a child) to sleep[bed]. ¶책을 읽어 주며 ~ read (a child) to sleep // 나는 언제나 아기를 노래를 불러 주어 재운다 I usually sing[lull] my baby to sleep. // 할머니는 요람을 흔들어 아기를 재운다 The grandma rocked the baby to sleep. // 우리 집에서는 아이들을 9시에 재운다 We send our children to bed at nine (o'clock). 2 [묵게 하다] lodge (a person); give (a person) shelter[a bed]; put (a person) up; accomodate (a person)(호텔 등에서). ¶남을 하룻밤 ~ give a person a night's lodging / give a person a bed overnight / put a person up for the night // 우리는 하룻밤 재워 달라고 부탁했다 We asked for a night's lodging. 3 (솜 등을) press; (머리 등을) smooth (down); settle. ¶솜을 ~ press cotton flat // 그는 들뜬 머리를 재웠다 He smoothed his fluffy hair down.

재우치다 push (a person) to do; press (a person) to do; urge. ¶남에게 빨리 대답하라고 ~ urge a person to answer promptly / press a person for a prompt reply // 변호사는 사실을 이야기하라고 증인을 재우쳤다 The lawyer urged[pressed] the witness to tell the truth.

재원 (才媛) a talented[an intelligent] girl [woman]; an accomplished young lady. ¶그녀는 대학 출신의 ~이다 She's a talented university graduate.

재원 (財源) a source of revenue[income]; economic[financial] resources; finances(재력); funds(자금). ¶새로운 ~을 찾다 seek a new source of revenue[income] // ~을 고갈시키다 drain[exhaust] the resources // 그들은 ~이 풍부하다[부족하다] Their financial resources are very secure[exhausted]. // 우리는 도서관을 세울 만한 ~이 없다 We do not have enough funds[money] to build a library.

재위 (在位) a reign. ¶…의 ~ 중에 during[in] the reign of … // 20년 ~ 후에 after a reign of 20 years. **재위하다** be on the throne; reign. ¶그 왕은 불과 2년 재위했다 The king reigned[was on the throne] (for) only two years.
● **재위 기간** the period of (Queen Victoria's) reign.

재음미하다 (再吟味-) appreciate[enjoy] again. ¶그 시를 ~ appreciate the poem again.

재인 (才人) 1 [재능 있는 사람] a man of talent [ability]; a clever person. 2 [광대] a clown; a comic; (미국 구어) a funnyman.

재인식 (再認識) recognizing[appreciating] anew (the merit of a thing). ¶자연식품의 ~ rediscovering (the value of) natural foods. **재인식하다** have a new understanding (of); realize again; recognize anew. ¶정세를 ~ have a new understanding of the situation // 나는 이 문제의 중요성을 재인식했다 I realized again the importance of the problem. // 이로써 그것의 가치와 사명을 재인식하게 되었다 This led to a renewed appreciation of its value and mission.

재일 (在日) [관형어적] (stationed [staying / resident]) in Japan.
● **재일 교포** Korean residents in Japan. ¶~ 모국 방문단 a homevisiting group of Korean residents in Japan. **재일 한국 거류민단** the Korean Residents Association in Japan.

재임 (在任) ¶~ 중에 during one's term of office / during one's service (as managing director with the Han Il Bank) / while in office // ~ 중인 사람 an incumbent // 송 씨는 미국에 ~ 중이다 Mr. Song holds a post in America. // ~ 중에는 신세가 많았습니다 Thank you for the help you gave me while I was in office. // 그 일은 내 ~ 중에 일어났다 It happened during my term in office. **재임하다** hold office [a post]; be in office.

재임 (再任) reappointment; reinstatement. **재임하다** get reappointed. →¶재임시키다 reappoint (a person to an office) / (한 번 해임된 후에) reinstate (a person in an office) // 그는 이전의 자리에 재임되었다 He was reinstated in his former position.

재입국 (再入國) (a) reentry (into a country). **재입국하다** reenter (into a country).
● **재입국 허가(서)** a reentry permit.

재입학 (再入學) readmission (to a school); reentrance. ¶~을 허가하다 readmit (a boy to a school). **재입학하다** reenter.

재자가인 (才子佳人) a wit and a beauty.

재작년 (再昨年) the year before last; two years ago. ¶~ 겨울 the winter before last.

재잘거리다 chatter; prattle; gab; gabble; rattle; wag one's tongue[jaws]. ¶재잘거리는 사람 a chattering [prattling] person / a chatterer // 재잘거리는 여자[아이] a chatterbox / 한 시간 동안이나 ~ rattle on for an hour // 그녀는 입담 좋게 잘도 재잘거린다 She is such a chatterbox. / How her tongue runs on! / What a talkative[gabby] woman she is! // 계집애들이 즐겁게 재잘거리고 있다 The girls are chattering away happily.

재잘재잘 chatteringly; tattlingly; volubly; glibly; garrulously. ¶~ 지껄이다 wag one's tongue[jaw] / gabble / jabber / prattle / rattle / chatter // ~ 잘도 지껄인다 What a glib talker he is! / What a glib tongue he has!

재재거리다 chatter; prattle. ⇨재잘거리다

재적 (在籍) enrollment. ¶그 학교의 ~ 학생은 3천 명이다 The school has 3,000 students on the register. / The school has a total enrollment of three thousand. **재적하다** be on the register[roll]; be registered. ¶그 학교에는 많은 외국인 학생이 재적하고 있다 The school has a large enrollment[registration] of foreign students. // 그 학생은 재적하고 있지 않다 That student is no longer enrolled [on the register].
● **재적자** (단체 등의) a registered person; (학생) students on the register[roll]; a registered student.

재정 (財政) finance(s); financial affairs (of a company); (고) economy. ¶건전[흑자] ~ sound[balanced] finance // **국가** ~ national finance // 시(市) ~ the city finance[purse] // 적자 ~ red-ink[deficit / unbalanced] finance // 지방 ~ local (government) finance // ~(상)의 financial / fiscal / ~상의 위기 (be in) the financial crisis [(구어) bind] // ~의 경직화 rigidification[inflexibility] of public finance // ~의 핍박 financial straits [pressure / stringency] // 국가 ~의 재건 reestablishment of national economy / reconstruc-

재정

tion of the government finances // ~이 곤란하다 be in financial difficulty // ~을 확립하다 put the finances (of a company) on a firm basis // ~을 긴축하다 tighten one's belt[purse strings] // 그 나라는 ~이 풍부하다 The national economy is healthy. // 그 나라 [회사]의 ~은 건전하다 The country's [company's] finances are sound. // 그 회사는 ~이 단단하다 The firm has good financial standing. // ~ 기반이 약한 회사는 금년 내에 쓰러질 것이다 Financially weak firm will go bankrupt within this year.
- **재정 경제부** the Ministry of Finance and Economy. **재정 고문** a financial advisor. **재정난** financial difficulties[trouble]. ¶~에 빠지다 get into financial trouble. **재정 보증** financial guarantee. **재정 보증인** a financial guarantor. **재정 정책** a financial [fiscal] policy. ¶긴축 ~ a tight money policy / a tight-financing policy. **재정학** the science of finance; (the study of) public finance.

재정(裁定) [옳고 그름을 따져 결정함] a decision; (a) judgment; [판결] a verdict; a ruling. ¶~에 (마지못해) 따르다 accept a decision[ruling] (reluctantly). **재정하다** decide (on) (a case / an issue); (법정이) rule (on) (that...should...).
- **재정안** [법] an arbitration draft[proposal]. **재정자** an adjudicator.

재정적(財政的) financial; fiscal. ¶~ 원조 (a) financial support[help] // ~인 이유로 on financial grounds // ~으로 financially / fiscally // ~으로 파탄에 빠져 있다 be financially insolvent // ~으로 건전하다 be financially solvent // 그는 ~으로 어려움에 빠져 있다 He is in a bad way financially. / He is hard up. / He is badly off.

재조사(再調査) reexamination; review; reinvestigation; resurvey. **재조사하다** reexamine; review; reinvestigate; resurvey.

재조정(再調整) readjustment; reregulation. **재조정하다** readjust; reregulate. ¶금리를 ~ readjust the rate of interest // 경기 일정을 ~ reschedule a fixture.

재조직(再組織) reorganization. **재조직하다** reorganize (a company); restructure. ¶노동조합을 ~ reorganize a labor union.

재종(再從) a second cousin.
- **재종간** second-cousinship. **재종고모** a female second cousin of one's father. **재종숙** a male second cousin of one's father. **재종질** a son[daughter] of one's second cousin.

재주 1 [재능] ability; talent; gifts; genius; an aptitude. ¶말~ oratorical talent / (속어) the gift of (the) gab // 발명의 ~ an inventive brain // 뛰어난 ~ a brilliant talent // 숨은 ~ a hidden[latent] talent // ~ 있는 able / talented / gifted // ~ 있는 사람 a talented [clever] man / a man of talent[ability] // ~ 없는 talentless // ~가 있다 have [possess] a talent [an aptitude] (for) // 어학에 ~가 있다 have a linguistic aptitude / have an aptitude [gift] for languages // ~가 없다 lack ability / have no ability[talent] // 제 ~를 너무 믿다 have too much confidence in[be overconfident of] one's (own) talent[ability] // ~를 충분히 발휘하다 give full play to one's ability // ~를 보이다 show[display] one's ability [talent] // 그녀는 ~가 비상하다 She has eminent talents. // 그는 가르치는 일 외에는 ~가 없다 All he can do is just (to) teach. 2 [기술·손재간] skillfulness; dexterity. ¶손~ manual skill / handicraft // ~ 있는 skillful (in) / handy / dexterous (in / at) / be skilled (in the use of) // ~가 비상한 사람 a man of wonderful skill // ~가 뛰어나다 excel at[in] one's skill[thing] // 그는 연장을 다루는 ~가 있다 He is handy with tools. // 그녀는 소질도 있고 ~도 있다 She's talented and has great skill. 3 [곡예] a feat; a trick; a stunt(아슬아슬한). ¶개에게 ~를 가르치다 teach a dog tricks // 돌고래에게는 여러 가지 ~를 가르칠 수 있다 Dolphins can be taught to do[perform] many tricks.

재주는 곰이 넘고 돈은 되놈이 받는다(속담) One beats the bush and another catches the birds.

재주(를) 부리다 do[perform] acrobatic feats. ¶재주를 부리는 곡예사 an acrobat // 아슬아슬한 ~ perform a risky feat[stunt].

재주(를) 피우다 play[resort to] cheap tricks. ¶재주 피우지 마라 None of your cheap tricks!
- **재주꾼** a person of remarkable talents; a skillful[dexterous / smart / clever] person. ¶그는 처세하는 데 있어 아주 ~이다 He goes along[makes his way] very cleverly in the world. / He knows very well how to swim in the sea of life.

재주껏 to the best of one's ability; as much as one can do. ¶~ 살아가다 live by one's wits.

재주넘다 turn[make] a somersault; tumble. ¶그는 잔디 위에서 재주넘었다 He turned a somersault on the lawn.

재중(在中) ¶인쇄물 ~ (게시) Printed matter (only). // 사진 ~ (게시) Photo(s). / Photographs. // 견본 ~ Samples (only).

재즈(樂) jazz (music). ¶모던 ~ modern jazz // ~(풍)의 jazzy // ~를 연주하다 play jazz / jazz // ~(음악)에 맞추어 춤추다 dance to jazz // 곡을 ~풍으로 편곡하다 (구어) jazz up a tune.
- **재즈 가수** a jazz singer. **재즈 밴드** a jazz band. **재즈 음악** jazz music.

재직(在職) ¶~ 중인 검사 an incumbent public prosecutor // ~ 중인 a public prosecutor in office // ~ 중에 during one's tenure[term] of office / while (one is) in office // ~ 중에 사망하다 die in office. **재직하다** hold office [a post]; be in office[service]. ¶회사에 20년 ~ serve twenty years with a company // 공무원으로서 5년 ~ hold a government post for five years // 그는 이 학교에 재직한 지 30년이 된다 He has served[taught] in this school for thirty years.
- **재직 기간** the period of one's service. **재직자** an incumbent; the holder of a post

재질(才質) natural gifts[endowments]; talent. ¶풍부한 ~ rich endowments // ~이 풍부하다 be highly gifted[richly endowed] // ~이 없다 be untalented / be endowed with no genius // ~을 살리다[발휘하다] make the best use of one's talent.

재질(材質) 1 [목재의 성질] the quality of the lumber[wood]. 2 [재료의 성질] the quality of the material. ¶이 가구는 ~이 단단하다 This furniture was made with durable materials.

재차(再次) [거듭하여] twice; again; [두 번째로] for the second time; [한 번 더] once more; once again. ¶~의 second/another/~의 방문 (pay) one's second visit / 시도하다 try again / make another[a second] attempt // 나는 ~ 주의[경고]를 받았다 I was warned for the second time. / I got a second warning. // ~ 해[시도해] 보십시오 Try (it) again[once more]. / Give it another try. // ~ 부탁의 말씀을 드리려고 찾아왔습니다 I've come to ask you once again.

재채기 sneezing; a sneeze. **재채기하다** sneeze; do one's sneezing; have a fit of sneezing(연발아). ¶그는 크게 재채기했다 He gave a violent sneeze. / He sneezed violently.

재천(在天) [~의 in heaven / blessed / heavenly / 인명은 ~이다 Life and death are providential.

재청(再請) [다시 청함] a second request; an encore; [동의에 대한] seconding. **재청하다** request a second time; encore; [동의에] second (a motion).

재촉 pressing; urging. ¶한 달이라도 집세가 밀리면 ~이 성화같다 They come pressing hotly for the house rent, if it is even a month behind. **재촉하다** press (a person for a thing); urge (a person to do); hurry (up); (빚을) dun. ¶확답을 ~ urge a person to answer definitely // 일을 ~ hasten[hurry up] the work / 걸음을 ~ hurry one's way / quicken one's pace[steps] // 그는 그녀에게 집세를 재촉했다 He pressed[(구어) hounded] her for the rent. // 변호사는 진실을 말하라고 증인을 재촉했다 The lawyer urged[pressed] the witness to tell the truth. // 그들은 그 일을 끝내라고 그를 재촉했다 They rushed[pushed] him very hard to finish it. // 그들은 우리에게 빚을 갚으라고 재촉하고 있다 They are dunning us for payment of the debt. // 나는 개회식 시간에 대어 도착할 수 있도록 택시 운전사를 재촉했다 I urged the taxi driver to hurry so that I would arrive in time for the opening ceremony. // 그렇게 재촉하지 말아 주게 Don't hurry[rush] me so.

재촬영(再撮影) [사진] a retake. **재촬영하다** rephotograph; retake; take (a picture) over again.

재출발(再出發) a restart; a fresh start. **재출발하다** restart; make a fresh[new] start; start a fresh. ¶그녀는 인생을 재출발하기로 작정했다 She made up her mind to make a fresh start of life.

재취(再娶) a second marriage; remarriage; [후처] a second wife. ¶~ 소생 a child by one's second wife // ~를 맞다 marry a second wife // ~로 맞이하다 take (a woman) for[as] a second wife. **재취하다** remarry (after the death of one's first wife); marry again.

재치(才致) quick wit; tact; resources. ¶~ 있는 사람 a quick-witted person / a tactful man / a man of sense // ~ 있는 농담 a nimble jest // ~가 없는 사람 a slow-witted person / a man of slow wits // ~ 있는 quick-witted / witty / tactful // ~가 있다 be quick-witted / be tactful[resourceful] // ~ 있는 말을 하다 make a witty remark // ~ 있는 대답을 하다 give an adroit[a tactful] answer // ~가 없다 be slow-[dull-]witted / be not tactful // 그는 매우 ~ 있는 사람이다 He is really a quick-witted man. / (구어) He's really on the ball. // 그의 이야기는 ~가 넘친다 His talk is full of wit. // 그녀는 ~ 있게 화제를 바꾸었다 She tactfully changed the subject.

재킷 [상의] a jacket; [음반의 커버] a jacket.

재탕(再湯) 1 [다시 달임] a second decoction (of medicinal herb). **재탕하다** decoct again; make a second decoction (of medicinal herb). 2 [재이용] a rehash; an adaptation. **재탕하다** make a rehash (of); adapt. ¶그의 제2작은 처녀작을 재탕한 것에 불과하다 His second work is nothing but a rehash of his first one. // 그 연극은 프랑스의 원작을 재탕한 것이다 The play is adapted from a French original.

재투자(再投資) reinvestment. **재투자하다** reinvest; plow back (the profits of a business). ¶토지에 ~ reinvest one's money in land // 이윤을 설비에 ~ plow back profits into equipment.

재투표(再投票) revoting. **재투표하다** take a vote again; renew voting.

재판(再版) 1 [개정판] a second[revised] edition. ¶책의 ~을 찍다[발행하다] print[publish] a second edition of a book. 2 [제2쇄] a second impression[printing]; [중판] a reprint. ¶~ 3천 부 a second impression of 3,000 copies // 그의 저서는 한 달도 지나기 전에 ~이 나왔다 His book ran into a second printing in[was reprinted within] less than a month. **재판하다** reprint. ¶재판하게 되다 run into a second impression. 3 [되풀이] (a) repetition (of a past event). ¶그것은 1950년의 ~이 될 것이다 It will be 1950 over again. **재판하다** repeat.

재판(裁判) justice; [공판] a trial; a hearing; [판결] judgment; decision. ¶민사[형사] ~ a civil[criminal] trial // 결석[궐석] ~ judgment by default // 모의 ~ a mock[sham] trial // 약식 ~ a summary trial // 인민 ~ (린치식의) (미국 구어) a kangaroo court // 정식 ~ a formal trial // 확정 ~ final judgment // 공정한 ~ fair justice / impartial judgment // ~의 공시 publication of a judgment // ~의 일정을 결정하다 assign a day for trial // ~에 부치다[회부하다] put (a case) on trial / bring (a matter) to trial[judgment] / bring (a person) to justice // ~에 회부되다 be tried / be brought to trial / be put on trial / come to court // ~에 이기다[지다] win[lose] a suit[case] // ~을 받다 be tried / face a trial / stand one's trial / be on trial // ~을 걸다 lay (a case) before the court / submit (a case) to the court / bring a suit (against a person) / sue (a person) // ~을 열다 hold a court // ~이 진행 중이다 The court is in session. / A case is being tried. // 곧 그의 ~이 열린다 He is going to be tried[stand trial] soon. // 그 사건은 ~ 중이다 The matter is pending in court. / The case is on trial. // 그는 공금 횡령 혐의로 ~에 회부되어 있다 He is being tried on a charge of embezzling public money. // 그 ~은 피고가 승소했다 The case was decided in favor of the defendant. **재판하다** judge [try] a person[a case].

● **재판관** a judge; [집합적] the court. ¶~ 기피 a challenge of a judge. **재판권** jurisdiction. ¶…에 대하여 ~이 있다 have jurisdiction over ... // ~을 행사하다 exercise jurisdiction. **재판소** a court of law[justice]; a law

재편(성) court. **재판장** the presiding judge; (미) the chief justice.

재편(성)(再編成) reorganization; a reshuffle; rearrangement (of classes). **재편(성)하다** reorganize; reshuffle; (미국 구어) revamp. ¶학급을 ~ rearrange classes // 위원회를 ~ reorganize a committee.

재평가(再評價) revaluation; reassessment; reappraisal. ¶자산 ~ revaluation [reassessment] of property. **재평가하다** revaluate; reevaluate; reassess. → ¶그 제도의 좋은 점이 재평가되기에 이르렀다 Recently people have come to a new understanding of [have taken a fresh look at] the good points of the system.

재학(在學) ¶~ 중에 while one is a student / 현재 ~ 중인 학생은 1만 명이다 Ten thousand students are currently enrolled. // 아버지는 내가 대학 ~ 중에 돌아가셨다 My father died when I was in college [a college student]. **재학하다** be in[at] school[college]; be a student (at); be enrolled (at).

● **재학생** a (registered) student; an enrolled student; (대학의) an undergraduate. ¶~을 대표하여 on behalf[representing] the whole student body. **재학 증명서** a certificate of studentship; a student registration certificate; a certificate of student registration.

재할인(再割引) [경] a rediscount (of a bill). **재할인하다** rediscount (a bill).

● **재할인 어음** a rediscount bill. **재할인 이율** a rediscount rate.

재해(災害) a disaster; a calamity(큰 재해); an accident(사고). ¶~를 입다 suffer from a disaster // 이 지역은 폭우로 지독한 ~를 입었다 This region suffered great damage from the heavy rains. // 올해는 여러 가지로 ~가 많았다 We have suffered many disasters this year.

● **재해 대책** countermeasures against natural calamities. ¶중앙 ~ 본부 the Central Anti-Calamity Headquarters(약어 CACH) // ~을 강구하다 prepare [draw up / devise] measures for dealing with disasters [emergencies]. **재해 방지** prevention of disasters; disaster prevention. **재해 복구비** natural disaster relief expenditure[fund]. **재해지** a disaster [a stricken] area; a suffering [devastated] district.

재향 군인(在鄕軍人) (퇴역의) an ex-soldier; an ex-serviceman; (미) a veteran; (예비역의) a reservist; (집합적) soldiers on the reserve list.

● **재향 군인회** the association of reservists; (미) the American Legion(약어 A.L.). ¶대한민국 ~ the Korean Veterans Association.

재현(再現) [다시 나타남] reappearance; reemergence; [다시 나타냄] reenactment; (a) reproduction. **재현하다** reappear; reemerge; appear again; reenact; reproduce. ¶살인 현장을 ~ reenact the scene of the murder // 이것은 다빈치의 모나리자를 재현한 것이다 This is a reproduction of da Vinci's Mona Lisa.

재혼(再婚) a second marriage; remarriage. ¶~을 권하다 advise (a woman) to remarry. **재혼하다** marry again[second time]; remarry. ¶그는 아이들을 위해서 재혼하기로 했다 He decided to remarry for the sake of his children.

● **재혼자** a remarried person.

재화(災禍) a disaster; a (natural) calamity; an accident.

재화(財貨) property; riches. ⇨ 재물

재확인(再確認) reconfirmation; reaffirmation. **재확인하다** reconfirm; reaffirm; confirm again. ¶아시아에 있어서의 한반도의 전략적 중요성을 ~ reaffirm the strategical importance of the Korean Peninsula in Asia // 예약을 재확인하고 싶은데요 I would like to reconfirm my reservation.

재활용(再活用) recycling. **재활용하다** recycle. ¶종이를 ~ recycle paper.

● **재활용 센터** a recycling center.

재회(再會) reunion. ¶이산가족의 ~ the reunion of the separated families // ~를 기약하다 promise to meet again // ~는 기약하기 어렵다 We may not meet again. / God knows when we may be brought together again. / 우리는 ~를 기약하고 헤어졌다 We parted with a promise to meet again. **재회하다** meet [see] (a person) again.

잭 1 [기중기의 한 가지] a jack. ¶~으로 차를 들어 올리다 jack up a car. **2** [카드놀이] the knave; the jack. **3** [전] a jack.

잭나이프 a jackknife.

잼 jam. ¶딸기 ~ strawberry jam // ~을 바른 빵 bread and jam / 빵에는 (두껍게) ~이 발라져 있었다 The bread was spread with (a thick layer of) jam.

잼버리 a jamboree.

잽 [권투] a jab. ¶라이트[레프트] ~ a right (hand) [left(hand)] jab // ~을 먹이다 jab (one's opponent).

잽싸다 quick; agile; nimble. ¶잽싸게 nimbly / agilely / quickly / with alacrity // 잽싸게 달아나다 run away [escape] quickly // 일을 잽싸게 해치우다 rattle a piece of business through // 그녀는 맞지 않으려고 잽싸게 몸을 피했다 She nimbly dodged the blow. // 그는 일을 잽싸게 해치웠다 He finished his work briskly [with alacrity].

잿더미 a heap of ashes. ¶~로 만들다 reduce to ashes / burn up[down] // 나의 장서가 모두 ~가 되고 말았다 All my books were reduced to ashes[went up in smoke].

잿물 1 [재를 우려낸 물] lye. ¶~을 받다 [내리다] render lye from ashes // ~에 담그다 soak in lye. **2** caustic soda. ⇨ 양잿물

잿밥(齋-) (boiled) rice offered to Buddha. ¶부처님께 ~을 올리다 offer (a bowl of) rice to Buddha.

잿빛 ash color; gray[(영) grey] (color). ¶~이 도는 grayish / ashy // 그녀의 안색이 ~으로 변했다 Her face went ash-pale [turned ashen].

쟁(箏) [현악기의 하나] a jaeng; a kind of harp with thirteen silk string.

쟁기 a plow[(영)plough]. ¶~로 갈다 plow [plough] (the fields).

● **쟁기꾼** a plowman. **쟁기질** plowing. ¶~을 하다 plow.

쟁론(爭論) a dispute; an argument; a controversy. ¶~을 시작하다 get into an argument with (a person) over (a matter). **쟁론하다** dispute[argue] (with); have a dispute[an argument] (with).

쟁반(錚盤) a tray; a server; a salver(금속제의); a platter(대형의). ¶음식을 ~에 얹어 갖다 주다 bring a person his dinner on a tray.

쟁의(爭議) a dispute; a strife; a trouble; [파

업] a strike; a walkout. ¶노동 ～ a labor dispute∥소작 ～ disputes between landowners and tenant farmers / tenant disputes∥～를 **일으키다** (일이) beget[cause] a dispute[strife] / (사람이) go on (a) strike / walk out∥～를 **조정하다** mediate[adjust] a dispute∥～를 **해결하다** settle a dispute [strike]∥～를 **끝내다** stop a dispute / halt [call off] a strike∥～ 중이다 be on strike [(口) a strike]∥회사와 종업원 간에 ～가 일어났다 A dispute arose between the management and the employees.∥～는 원만히 해결되었다 The dispute was settled amicably.
● **쟁의권** the right of strike. **쟁의 행위** a direct action; [파업] a strike.

쟁이다 [물건을 차곡차곡 쌓다] heap (up); pile up; stack; put[lay] one thing on another; make a neat pile; accumulate. ¶김을 ～ lay pressed seaweed sheets one on top of another (so that seasonings may soak through)∥고기를 ～ leave sliced meat in piles[stacks]∥입구에 쌀가마가 쟁여져 있었다 Bags of rice were piled up at the entrance.

쟁쟁하다(琤琤-) **1** [소리가 매우 맑다] clear; sonorous; resonant. ¶그는 쟁쟁한 목소리로 한시를 읊었다 He recited Chinese poems in a clear, resonant[sonorous] voice. **2** [귀에 울리는 듯하다] ring (in one's ears). ¶아버지의 말씀이 지금도 귀에 ～ My father's words still ring in my ears[linger in my heart / haunt my memory].

쟁쟁하다(錚錚-) [여럿 중에서 뛰어나다] prominent; eminent; outstanding; distinguished; leading. ¶쟁쟁한 학자들 eminent [distinguished] scholars∥정계의 쟁쟁한 사람들 the leading figures of the political world∥쟁쟁한 음악가 a prominent musician∥그의 명성은 온 천하에 쟁쟁하다 The whole world resounds[rings] with his fame. / His fame resounds throughout the whole world.

쟁점(爭點) an issue; the point (at issue). ¶법률상의 ～ an issue of law∥～을 벗어난 논쟁 dispute off the point∥오랫동안 논의하다 보니 ～이 흐려졌다 We argued so long that we lost track of the issue.∥당신의 말은 ～을 벗어나 있다 Your remarks are off the point.

쟁취하다(爭取-) win; gain; obtain; secure; score. ¶독립을 ～ win one's independence∥승리를 ～ gain[win] a victory∥그들은 연습에 연습을 거듭하여 우승을 쟁취했다 They achieved victory through practice and more practice.

쟁탈(爭奪) a scramble; a struggle; a contest; a competition. **쟁탈하다** scramble (for); struggle (for); compete (for). ¶장관 자리를 ～ fight[compete] for a Cabinet post∥선수들은 공을 쟁탈하기 위해 필사적으로 연습을 거듭하여 우승을 쟁취했다 The players scrambled for the ball.∥양팀이 1위의 자리를 두고 쟁탈했다 The two teams contended against each other for the first place.
● **쟁탈전** a scramble (for); a fight (for). ¶**선수권** ～ a championship tournament; a pennant race∥**우승배** ～ a contest for a trophy∥**정당 간의 권력** ～ the scramble [struggle] for power among (political) parties∥양국은 그 섬을 두고 ～을 벌였다 The two countries vied for possession of the island.

저[1] [가로 불게 되어 있는 악기] a flute; a fife.
저[2] (a pair of) chopsticks. ⇨**젓가락**
저[3] **1** [1인칭 겸양어] I. ⇨**나** ¶～의 my∥～로서는 for my part / as for me∥그것은 ～입니다 It's me.(▶ It's 뒤에는 주격 보어로서 I가 오는 것이 문법상 옳지만, 일반적으로는 me가 널리 쓰임)∥잘못을 저지른 것은 ～입니다 It is I that[who] made the mistake.(▶ 이 경우는 me보다 주격인 I를 쓰는 것이 보통임) **2** [자기] oneself; self. ¶～ 혼자서 by oneself / (독력으로) for oneself∥그는 ～로서는 옳다고 여기고 있다 He believes himself to be in the right.
저[4] [좀 떨어져 있는 것을 가리켜서] that (pl. those). ¶～ 남자 that man∥～ 건물을 보아라 Look at the building over there.∥～ 부인[신사] 누구죠 who might that lady[gentleman] be?
저[5] [얼른 생각이 나지 않을 때의 소리] well; let me see; say; uh. ¶～, 실례지만 역이 어디인지 가르쳐 주십시오 Excuse me, but could you tell me where the station is?∥～, 그렇게는 안 될 것입니다 Well, no, that won't do. / Well, I'm afraid that won't do.∥그의 이름은, ～ 홍 씨였지 His name is — er — Hong, isn't it?

저(著) one's writings (저술); (written) by. ¶한 박사 ～ (written) by Dr. Han.
저가(低價) a low price. ¶**최** ～ the lowest [bottom] price∥～**품** low-priced goods.
저간(這間) then; that time[occasion]; [요즘] recent[these] days. ¶～의 사정 the circumstance of the occasion[days]∥그의 ～ 소식을 알고 있습니까 Do you know his whereabouts? / Do you know how he is getting along lately?
저개발(低開發) underdevelopment. ¶～의 underdeveloped.
● **저개발국** a developing country. ⇨**개발도상국**(☞**개발**)
저것 that; that thing; that one; that person. ¶"～이 뭣입니까?" "시청입니다." "What's that (over there)?" "It's the city hall."∥이것보다 ～이 더 좋다 That one is better than this.∥～이야말로 전형적인 한국식 가옥이다 That's a typical Korean-style house.∥～은 정말로 성능이 좋은 차다 That car really performs well.∥말해 봐야 ～이 알 리 없지 You can't expect that man to understand it if you try.
저격(狙擊) snipe; sniping shot; sharpshooting. ¶～**용 소총** a sniper rifle∥～**을 당하다** be sniped[at] (by). **저격하다** shoot[fire] (at); snipe (at). ¶누군가가 옥상에서 대통령을 저격했다 Someone shot[shot at / sniped at] the president from the rooftop.(▶ shot은 총알이 맞았다는 것, shot at, sniped at 은 겨누어 쏘았다는 것을 뜻함)
● **저격대** a sharpshooting squad. **저격범** a sniper. **저격병** a sharpshooter; a sniper.
저고리 a *jeogori*; a Korean-style (short) coat (for women); a Korean-style jacket. ¶**양복** ～ a coat / a jacket∥**치마** ～ a coat and skirt∥～**을 입다[벗다]** put on[take off] one's coat.
저곳 that place; there. ⇨**그곳**
저공(低空) a low altitude[sky]. ¶～**으로 비행하다** fly low / fly at a low altitude.
● **저공비행** a low-altitude flight; low flying. **저공 폭격** low-altitude bombing.
저금(貯金) [돈을 모음] saving; [절약하여 모은 돈] savings; [은행 예금] a deposit. ¶**우편** ～

저금리 postal savings // 적립 ~ installment savings // ~이 있다[없다] have some [no] savings // ~을 다 써 버리다 exhaust one's savings [bank deposit] // 우체국에서 ~을 찾았다 I withdrew my savings from the post office. // 그녀는 노후를 위한 ~이 거의 없다 She has very little money saved (up) for her old age. **저금하다** save (money); deposit (money in a bank). ¶나는 수입의 일부를 저금하고 있다 I save a part of my income. ¶나는 은행에 500만 원 저금해 둔 것이 있다 I have five million won (deposited) in the bank.
● **저금통** a moneybox; (어린이용의) a piggy bank. **저금통장** a passbook.

저금리(低金利) low interest. ¶~로 at a low rate of interest / at low interest (rates).
● **저금리 정책** a cheap-money policy.

저급(低級) low grade; low class; inferiority **저급하다** [정도가 낮다] low-grade; low-class; [저속하다] vulgar; [값싸다] cheap. ¶저급한 책 a lowbrow book // 저급한 취미 vulgar tastes // 그는 저급한 잡지를 잘 본다 He often reads cheap magazines.

저기 [저곳] that place; [저곳에] over there. ¶여기서 ~까지 from here to there // ~서 뭘 하고 있었지 What were you doing over there? // ~서 기다려 주게 Wait for me in [over] there. // 나는 ~가 좋다 I like that place. // ~ 보이는 것이 북한산이다 The mountain over there is Bukhansan(Mt. Bukhan).

저기압(低氣壓) 1 [낮은 기압] low (atmospheric) pressure; a[an atmospheric] depression. ¶열대[온대] ~ a tropical[an extratropical] cyclone // ~의 중심 the center of a depression[a low pressure area] // ~이 발생했다 A low pressure developed. // ~이 동중국해를 동남으로 이동하고 있다 A low pressure area[zone] is traveling southeast across the East China Sea. // 제주도 남쪽 해상엔 980 헥토파스칼의 ~이 있다 There is a low pressure of 980 hectopascals over the sea south of Jejudo.
2 [기분이 좋지 못함] a bad temper. ¶그녀가 오늘은 ~이다 She is in a bad temper today. / She is out of sorts [in a bad mood] today.

저까짓 so trivial; so trifling; [저런 정도] that much. ¶~ 것[일] such a trivial thing [matter] / so trifling a thing[matter] / such trifles // ~ 놈이 뭐가 대수야 I am flattering myself that I can rival with that guy. / Why should I be afraid of a person like that? // ~ 일은 나라도 할 수 있을 것 같다 I'm flattering myself that I can do that much.

저나마 although it is (nothing more than) that. ¶~는 좀 나아진 편이다 It is a considerable improvement as it is. // ~ 있다는 게 다행이다 That is better than nothing. / Half a loaf is better than no bread.

저널리스트 a journalist.
저널리즘 journalism.
저네(들) those people (over there); they.
저녁 1 [해가 질 무렵부터 밤이 오기까지의 사이] evening; nightfall; dusk. **¶내일[오늘/어제] ~** tomorrow[this / yesterday] evening // ~ 종 the evening bell / the curfew // ~마다 every evening // ~ 6시쯤 눈이 오기 시작했다 It began to snow about six in the evening. // 그는 내일 ~ 한국을 떠난다 He leaves Korea tomorrow evening. // 어제 ~ 그녀로부터 전화가 왔다 She called me yesterday evening. // 그 일은 2월 28일[수요일] ~에 일어났다 It happened on the evening of Feb. 28th [Wednesday evening]. **2** an evening meal. ⇨"저녁밥(⇨저녁)

● **저녁노을** a glow of the sky at sunset; the evening glow; the afterglow. ¶~이 진 하늘 the sky at sunset / the sky aglow with the setting sun // 하늘에는 ~이 졌다 There is a sunset. / (문어) The sky is aglow with the setting sun. **저녁때** evening; nightfall; sunset; dusk. ¶~에 at nightfall [sunset] // ~까지 집에 돌아오너라 Come home before it gets dark. // 우리는 ~에 마을에 도착했다 We arrived in town toward(s) evening. // ~가 되면 바람이 한층 차가워진다 As dusk falls the wind becomes colder. **저녁밥** an evening meal; (a) supper; (a) dinner.(▶ (미)에서는 저녁밥이 가벼운 것이면 supper, 성찬으로 차린 것이면 dinner라고 함. (영)에서는 보통 저녁밥이 dinner이며, supper는 야식) ¶~을 짓다 prepare supper // 나는 ~을 가볍게 마쳤다 I had a light supper. / 나는 ~으로 비프스테이크를 먹었다 I ate[had] steak for supper. // 그는 지금 ~을 들고 있다 He is at supper now. // ~은 무엇으로 할까 What shall we have for supper? // ~이 다 되었다 Supper is ready. // 일찌감치 ~을 먹자 Let's have an early supper[dinner]. // 그는 ~을 먹지 않고 잠자리에 들었다 He went to bed supperless.

저놈 that fellow[chap]; (미국 구어) that guy; (영국 구어) that broke.

저능(低能) weak-mindedness; feeblemindedness. **저능하다** feebleminded; weak-minded [-headed]; softheaded; mentally deficient [weak / feeble]; (속어) daffy.
● **저능아** a mentally retarded child. ⇨"정신지체아(⇨정신(精神))

저다지 so; so much; [저 정도로] to that extent[degree]; (구어) that. ¶~ 아름다운 그림 so fine a picture // 손님이 ~ 많이 오리라고는 예상치 못했다 We did not expect to have so many visitors. // 영어 시험이 ~ 어려우리라고는 생각지 못했다 I never expected that the English exam would be so[that] hard. // ~도 대담한 사람은 본 적이 없다 I have never seen such a daring man. / He is the most daring man I have ever seen.

저당(抵當) (a) mortgage; security. ¶근-fixed collateral // 동산 ~ chattel mortgage // 1번[2번] ~ a first[second] mortgage // 이중 ~ a double mortgage // 땅을 1,000만 원에 ~ 잡히다 mortgage land for ten million won // 땅을 ~ 잡고 돈을 빌려 주다 take land as security for a loan / lend money with land as security // 은행은 내 부동산을 ~ 잡고 있다 The bank holds my estate in mortgage[a mortgage on my estate]. // 이 집은 3,000만원의 ~에 들어 있다 There is a mortgage of thirty million won on the house. / This house is mortgaged for thirty million won.
저당하다 mortgage (a house / land); give [put / lay] (a thing) in pledge. ¶나는 집을 저당하고 2,000만 원을 빌렸다 I borrowed twenty million won on my house. / I gave [used] my house as security for a twenty million won loan.
● **저당권** mortgage; right of pledge; [법] hypothec. **저당권자** a mortgagee; an encum-

brancer. 저당물 a security; a pledge; a thing mortgaged. ¶~을 도로 찾았다 The mortgage was redeemed.

저대로 as it is[stands]; like that; in that condition. ¶~가 좋다 I like that better as it is. // 그 사건을 ~ 두어서는 안 된다 The matter cannot be allowed to stand as it is. / We cannot afford to leave[let] the matter alone.

저돌적(猪突的) reckless; headlong; foolhardy; rash. ¶~으로 headlong / precipitately / recklessly // ~인 사람 a reckless[foolhardy] person // ~으로 돌진하다 make a headlong rush // 그의 ~인 운전이 사고의 원인이었다 His reckless driving was cause of[caused] the accident.

저들 [저이들] those people (over there); they. ¶그것은 ~의 것이다 That's theirs.

저따위 that sort[kind] of; such; that. ¶~ 인간과는 상종하고 싶지 않다 I don't want to be friends with that sort[kind] of person. // 뭐 ~가 다 있어 What a man! / That fellow is impossible!

저러하다 like that. ⇨저렇다

저런[1] [저러한] such; that; that sort[kind] of; like that. ¶~ 남자 a man like that / such a man as that // ~ 나쁜 짓은 반드시 드러나고야 만다 Such evildoing as that never fails to come out. // ~ 사람들은 참을 수가 없다 I cannot endure those like them[men of that sort]. // 이런 일 ~ 일로 바쁘다 I am very busy with one thing or other.

저런[2] [가볍게 놀라는 모양] Dear me!; Oh, dear!; Great[Good] heavens!; Good[My] gracious!; My god! ¶~, 야단났군 Mercy on me! / Good gracious! // ~, 또 시작했군 There you go again!

저렇게 [저와 같이] like that. ¶~ 비쌀 줄은 몰랐다 I didn't think it would cost so[that] much. // 그는 말은 ~ 해도 마음씨는 상냥한 사람이다 He is kind at heart in spite of his harsh way of speaking. // 설마 ~ 될 줄은 몰랐다 I never thought it would turn out that way. // 그가 ~ 심한 말을 할 줄은 몰랐다 I never thought he would say a terrible thing like that. / What an awful thing for him to say!

저렇다 like that; that way. ¶이렇다 ~ 말이 많다 say this and that / say things / be critical (about) / make complaints // 이렇다 ~ 참견하지 말게 Stop bothering[(구어) bugging] me about everything. // 젊은이들이란 저렇단 말이야 Such is the way with young people.

저력(底力) potential[latent] energy; underlying strength. ¶~이 있는 사람 an energetic person / a person who has hidden power within him / a man of real ability // 그는 머리는 잘 돌아가지만 ~이 없다 He is clever but has no inner resources. / He's (superficially) clever but underneath he lacks what it takes. // 그의 ~을 보여 줄 좋은 기회였다 It was a good chance to show his real ability [to show what he could do]. // 그는 ~을 발휘해서 우승했다 He did himself justice and won the first prize.

저렴하다(低廉-) cheap; inexpensive; low [moderate] in price. ¶저렴한 호텔 an inexpensive hotel / a hotel with moderate tariff // 이쪽이 ~ This is less expensive.

저류(底流) 1 [바다의 흐름] an undercurrent; underflow. 2 [표면에 드러나지 않는 세력]. ¶의식의 ~ subconscious current // 표면상의 평화의 ~에는 웬지 험악한 공기가 있다 There is some sort of threatening atmosphere underlying the seeming peace.

저리[1] [저렇게] so; like that; (in) that way; to that extent[degree]. ¶그는 어째서 ~도 못 살까 Why is he so poor, I wonder? 2 [저곳으로] to that place; over there; [저쪽으로] that way; to that direction. ¶~ 가 Go away! / Away[Get along] with you! // ~ 비켜라 Get out of my way! / Don't stand in my way.

저리(低利) low interest. ¶~로 돈을 빌리다 borrow money at low interest.

● **저리 자금** a low-interest fund. **저리채**(－債) a low-interest debt.

저리다 (서술적) become[go] numb; be numbed; (오래 앉아 있어서) go to sleep; be asleep. ¶추위로 손발이 저려 왔다 My hands and legs were numb with cold. // 마루에 오랫동안 앉아 있었더니 발이 저렸다 I have been sitting on floor for a long time, and my legs are asleep. / My legs are numb from sitting on floor too long.

저마다 each (one); every one; respectively. ¶~ 제가 옳다고 한다 Every man claims that he himself is right. // 사람에게는 ~ 호불호가 있다 Each man has his own likes and dislikes. // 그들은 ~ 다른 길을 가기로 했다 They each have decided to go their separate ways.

저만큼 [저만한 정도로] to that extent[degree]; (구어) that. ¶~ 열심히 연습하지 않으면 숙달하지 않는다 You will not make progress unless you practice that hard. // 나는 피아노를 ~ 잘 치지 못한다 I can't play the piano so well as that[that well]. // ~은 나도 할 수 있을 것같이 생각된다 I'm flattering myself that I can do that much.

저만하다 1 [크기·정도가 서로 비슷하다] that much; as much[many / big / large / long / wide] as that. ¶저만한 크기의 것을 보여 주시오 Show me the one as large as that. // 저만한 재능이 있는 사람에게 어디를 가나 실직하는 일은 없을 것이다 Such a talented man[A man of his talent] will never be out of job wherever he goes. // 저만하면 충분할 거야 That much may be enough. // 저만한 미인은 본 적이 없다 She is the most beautiful girl I've ever seen. 2 [대단하지 않다] not so serious[too bad]. ¶상처가 저만하니 다행이다 It is really fortunate of him to be injure slightly.

저맘때 (at) that time of (the) day[month / year]; (at) that hour of the day[morning / evening / night]. ¶아이들은 ~에는 장난이 심하다 Children usually are naughty at about that age. // 나는 ~는 희망에 불탔었다 When I was his age, I was full of hope.

저명(著名) prominence; distinction; eminence; celebrity. **저명하다** famous; well-known; prominent; eminent; celebrated. ¶저명한 학자 a celebrated scholar.

● **저명인사** a celebrity; a famous person.

저물가(低物價) low prices.

● **저물가 정책** a low-price policy.

저물다 1 [해가 져서 어두워지다] grow[get] dark. ¶날이 저물기 전에 before dark[nightfall] // 날이 저물어 가고 있다 It is growing [getting] dark. / The sun is about to set. / Night is falling. // 날이 완전히 저물었다 Night

저미다 // 친구의 집을 찾아 헤매는 동안에 날이 저물었다 Night fell while I was wandering around looking for my friend's house. // 날이 저물기 전에 집에 돌아가거라 Hurry home before it gets dark. / Hurry home while it is light. // 요새는 일곱 시에 날이 저문다 It grows dark at seven these days.
2 [계절이나 한 해가 다 지나다] end; come to an end [a close]; close; run [be] out. ¶저물어 가는 봄을 아쉬워하다 regret the passing of spring // 가을이 저물었다 Autumn is over. // 그해가 저물어 가고 있었다 The year was coming [drawings] to an end.

저미다 slice; cut (meat) thin [into thin pieces]. ¶생선의 살을 ~ slice raw fish.

저버리다 1 [신의·기대 등을] go [act] against; go back on; run counter to. ¶은혜를 ~ go back on one's obligation / be ungrateful / lose one's gratitude // 기대를 ~ be contrary to a person's expectations // 그는 나를 도와주겠다고 약속했으나 막판에 가서 나의 기대를 저버렸다 He promised to help me, but at the last minutes he let me down.
2 [버리다] forsake; desert; give up; abandon. ¶처자를 ~ desert [(문어) forsake] one's wife and children // 나를 저버리지 말아 주세요 Don't abandon me. / Please stand by me. // 파산하자 친구들은 모두 그를 저버렸다 All his friends walked out on [(문어) forsook] him when he went bankrupt.

저벅거리다 walk with heavy footsteps; walk with a thud; tramp; trample. ¶군인들이 저벅거리며 지나가는 소리가 들렸다 Soldiers were heard tramping by.

저벅저벅 with a crunch [thud]; with a heavy footstep. ¶얼어붙은 눈을 ~ 밟고 가다 crunch through frozen snow. **저벅저벅하다** make a tramping sound; tramp.

저번(這番) the other day; a few days ago; some time ago; lately. ¶내가 ~에 왔을 때 the last time I came here // ~에 한 약속을 잊지 마 Don't forget what you promised the other day.

저변(底邊) **1** [수] ➔밑변 **2** [밑바탕을 이루는 층]. ¶사회의 ~ 사람들 people at the lower levels of society // 그는 사회의 ~에서 기어오르고 애쓰고 있다 He is struggling to climb up from the bottom of the social ladder.

저서(著書) a book; a work; one's writings. ¶예술에 관한 ~ a book on art // 그는 정치관계 ~가 많다 He has written many books on politics. // 그는 1990년에 처음으로 ~를 출판했다 He published his first book [work] in 1990.

저소득(低所得) a small income.
● **저소득층** the lower income bracket; the lower brackets of income.

저속(低速) [저속도] (a) low speed. ¶~으로 차를 운전하다 drive a car at low speed.

저속하다(低俗-) vulgar; base; lowbrow; coarse; indecent. ¶저속한 영화 a vulgar film // 저속한 오락 lowbrow entertainment // 저속한 말 vulgar [coarse / bad] language // 저속한 사람 a lowbrow / a mean [base] person / a (man of) mean [base] character // 그녀의 복장은 ~ Her clothing is in vulgar taste. // 그 영화는 ~ That film is dirty. // 그의 취미는 ~ He has bad taste.

저수(貯水) [물을 모아 둠] storage of water; [모아 둔 물] reservoir water. **저수하다** keep water in store; store water; impound. ➔빗물은 탱크에 저수된다 Rainwater is (collected and) stored in a tank (기수).
● **저수량** pondage; the volume of water kept in store. **저수지** a reservoir.

저수위(低水位) the low-water level. ¶~ 경보기 a low-water alarm.

저술(著述) [쓰기] writing; [책] a book; [작품] a work; [문학 작품] writings. ¶위생법에 관한 ~ a work on hygiene // 이것은 누구의 ~인지 모른다 This is of unknown authorship. **저술하다** write (a book). ¶그는 10권의 소설을 저술했다 He wrote ten novels. / He is the author of ten novels.
● **저술가** a writer; an author; (여성) an authoress [a woman writer [author].

저습하다(低濕-) low(-lying) and damp. ¶저습한 소택지 a low marshy place.

저승 the other world; the world of the dead; the next world; the land of the dead; (문어) the netherworld. ¶~길을 떠나다 leave this world / leave one's journey to the next world / die. // 그는 ~으로 떠나기 전에 신부 차림의 딸의 모습을 보는 것이 소원이라고 말했다 He said that he only wished he could have seen his daughter in her bridal finery before he died. // 저는 ~길을 떠날 때가 되었습니다 I am ready for my journey to the other [next] world.

저압(低壓) [낮은 압력] low pressure; [낮은 전압] low tension [voltage].
● **저압선** a low tension [voltage] cable. **저압 전류** a low-tension current.

저액(低額) a small sum.

저어새 [동] a spoonbill.

저어하다 fear; be afraid of [to go]; be apprehensive of. ¶…하지 않을까 저어하여 for fear of (doing) / for fear that [lest] (...should do) / fearful of (getting infected) // 무슨 일이 일어나지 않을까 ~ fear what will happen.

저열(低熱) low heat.

저온(低溫) a low temperature. ¶~에서 at low temperature.
● **저온 냉동** low temperature refrigeration. **저온 살균** (low temperature) pasteurization. **저온학** cryogenics.

저울 a scale; [천칭] (a pair of) scales [balances]; [막대저울] a steelyard; lever scales; [용수철저울] a spring balance; [체중계] a (weighing) scale; (bathroom) scales. ¶물건을 ~에 달다 weigh the goods in the balance [on the scales] // 그것을 ~로 달아 봅시다 Let's weigh it. // 이 ~은 고장 났다 These scales are not working properly.
● **저울눈** the notches of a beam. ¶~을 속이다 cheat weight / give short weight / weigh with the thumb. **저울대** a balance beam. **저울질** ¶~을 하다 weigh (something in the balance [on the scales]) / scale / put on the scales / [비유] compare (A) with (B) // 그는 득실을 ~해 보고 그 일을 거절했다 After weighing the pros and cons, he declined (to take) the job. // 그녀는 가정과 직업을 ~한 끝에 직업을 선택했다 She compared home with career [weighted home against career] and chose the latter. **저울추** a weight. **저울판** a scale; a pan; (양쪽) a pair of scales.

저위(低位) a low position [rank]. ¶저 나라의 생활수준은 극히 ~에 있다 The standard of living in that country is very low. // 우리 팀은

줄곧 10위라는 ~에 있었다 Our team was all the way down in tenth place.

저위도(低緯度) low latitudes.

저유(貯油) storage of oil.
●저유 탱크 a storage tank.

저율(低率) a low rate[ratio]. ¶~의 low-rate / low가 2,000명에 한 사람이라는 ~로 at the low rate of one person out of two thousand.

저음(低音) (음조의) a low tone; (피치의) a low-pitched sound; (목소리의) a low voice; [음] bass. ¶~으로 노래하다 sing bass / sing in the lowest register.
●저음 가수 a bass; a low-voiced singer.

저의(底意) one's original purpose; one's real intention; one's will[motive]; one's inmost thought; an ulterior motive. ¶그의 ~를 헤아릴 수 없었다 I could not make out his true[underlying] motives[intentions]. // 그가 하는 말에는 ~가 없다 He means what he says. // 그는 무엇인가 다른 ~가 있어서 그 말을 한 것임에 틀림없다 He must have said that with some ulterior motive.

저이 that person; he; she. ¶~는 내 누이요 She is my sister. // "~는 누구요?" "그는 한 씨요." "Who's that?" "That's Mr. Han."

저인망(底引網) a trawl (net). ¶~으로 고기를 잡다 trawl (for fish).
●저인망 어선 a trawler; a dragnet fishing boat. 저인망 어업 fishing with a trawl; trawl[dragnet] fishery.

저임금(低賃金) low wages; (급료) low pay.
●저임금 근로자 a low-wage earner.

저자 (가게) a market[grocery] stand; [장] a fair; a market. ¶~가 서다 A fair is held[opened].
●저잣거리 the streets (of a city, town, etc.); the downtown.

저자(著者) an author; a writer. ¶~ 목록[색인] an author catalog[index] // ~ 불명의 우화집 an anonymous book of fables // ~임을 주장하다 claim the authorship (of) // 그가 이 소설의 ~이다 He's the author of this novel. / He wrote this novel.

저자세(低姿勢) a low profile; a modest[low] attitude. ¶~를 취하다 assume a low posture / take a low[humble / modest] attitude // 입후보자는 모두 ~였다 All the candidates maintained a low profile[a low-keyed stance]. // 몰고 늘어지는 기자들에 대해 수상 ~였다 The Prime Minister adopted a moderate tone toward(s) the persistent reporters.

저작(咀嚼) [음식물을 씹음] mastication; chewing. **저작하다** masticate; chew.
●저작근(一筋) a muscle of mastication.

저작(著作) writing; authorship; [저서] a (literary) work; a book. ¶~으로 생활하다 live by one's pen / live by writing. **저작하다** write (a book); do writing for books.
●저작권 a copyright; literary property. ¶국제 ~ international copyright // ~을 소유하다[획득하다] hold[secure] the copyright (of) // ~을 침해하다 pirate (a book) / infringe a copyright // 이 책은 ~이 있다 This book is copyrighted. **저작권법** a copyright law; the Copyright Act. **저작물** a (literary) work; a book. **저작자** an author; a writer.

저장(貯藏) storage; [보존] preservation. **저장하다** store (up); lay by; preserve; conserve. ¶저장하고 있다 have (things) in store / have a store[stock] of (things) // 냉동 ~ keep a thing in cold storage // 야채를 움막에 ~ preserve[keep] vegetables in the cellar // 오래 저장하기 어렵다 be of limited storage life // 과실은 설탕절임으로 저장한다 Fruit is preserved with sugar. ➔¶창고에는 묵은 쌀이 50톤 저장되어 있다 We have fifty tons of old rice stored[in store] in the warehouse.
●저장고 a storehouse; a storage house. **저장품** stores; stock; stored goods. **저장실** a storeroom.

저절로 of[by] itself; of its own accord; naturally; [자동적으로] automatically. ¶노력하면 길은 ~ 열린다 If you work hard, thing'll work out by themselves[look after themselves]. // 나이가 들면 인생 철학도 ~ 바뀐다 As you grow older, your philosophy of life changes naturally. // 문이 ~ 열렸다 The door opened by itself. // 정면에 있는 문은 앞에 서면 ~ 열린다 The front door opens automatically when you step in front of it. // 내버려 두었더니 상처가 ~ 나았다 I left the cut alone and it healed all by itself.

저조(低調) 1 [낮은 가락] a low tone; an undertone. **저조하다** low-toned; low-pitched; low-keyed. 2 [침체함] dullness; lowness; a slump(운동선수의). **저조하다** inactive; inanimate; dull; slow; sluggish; slack. ¶완전히 저조한 시합이었다 The game was really dull. // 학생들 공부하려는 의욕이 저조했다 The pupils' desire to learn was at a low ebb. // 시황이 ~ The market is sluggish[dull]. // 저조한 작품뿐이었다 They were all low-grade works.

저조(低潮) (an) ebb tide. ⇨간조(干潮)

저주(詛呪) a curse; cursing; (an) imprecation; (a) malediction; (an) execration; damnation(신의). **저주하다** curse; call down a curse upon (a person); imprecate evil upon (a person); execrate; wish ill of (a person). ¶세상을 ~ curse the world // 그는 나를 저주하고 있다 He wishes me evil. // 그는 사랑의 경쟁자를 저주했다 He cursed his rival in love. // 그는 자신의 불행을 저주했다 He cursed his own misfortune. ➔¶저주받은 cursed / doomed // 그녀는 저주받은 자기의 운명을 한탄했다 She lamented over her cursed[ill-fated] life.

저주파(低周波) [전] (a) low frequency(약어 LF, l.f.); [통신] (a) audio frequency(약어 AF).

저지 [심판원] a judge.
●저지 페이퍼 a judge paper.

저지(低地) low land; low-lying ground.

저지(沮止) prevention; obstruction; hindrance; a check; blocking. **저지하다** stop; prevent; obstruct; hinder; impede; check; hold[set] back. ¶콜레라의 전염을 ~ check the spread of cholera // 행동을 ~ stop (a person) from acting[an action] // 우리는 간신히 적군을 저지하고 있다 We are barely keeping the enemy at bay[holding the enemy in check]. // 우리는 적기의 침입을 저지할 수 없었다 We could not stop[intercept] the enemy planes. // 그들은 실력으로 그 법안의 통과를 저지했다 By resort to force, they held back the passage of the bill. ➔¶데모대는 경찰에 의해 저지당했다 The demonstrators were held back by the police.
●저지선 (데모대 등의) a police line. ¶~을 뚫

저지르다 다 break through a police line.

저지르다 commit; make (a mistake); do (a bad act). ¶죄를 ~ sin / commit a crime (sin 은 도덕상의, crime은 법률상의 죄)//일을 ~ cause trouble[a disturbance] / spoil a program//그는 온갖 범죄를 저질렀다 He committed many kinds of crimes.//그가 도 대체 무슨 일을 저질렀지 What on earth did he do?//그는 어처구니없는 실수를 저질렀다 He made[committed] an awful blunder.//나는 돌이킬 수 없는 잘못을 저지르고 말았다 I have made an irreparable mistake.

저질 (低質) low quality. ¶~의 low / low-grade / of inferior quality/~의 신문 a gutter press/~의 인간 vulgar people.
●**저질탄** coal of low quality.

저쪽 1 [저편] that side[direction]; [반대쪽] the other side[direction]. ¶~에 over there / yonder//강 ~에 on the other side of the river / across the river//바다 ~에서 from beyond[across] the sea//길 ~에 서 있는 사 람 the man standing on the other side of the street//갠 날에는 ~에 인천이 보입니다 On a clear day, you can see Incheon in that direction.//~으로 가시오 Get out of here. / Go away.//비행기는 눈 깜짝할 사이에 산 ~으로 사라졌다 In an instant the plane vanished beyond the hills.//~에서 무슨 일이 일어나고 있느냐 What's going on over there?
2 [상대방] the other party; he; she; they. ¶ ~에서 먼저 시비를 걸어온 거다 They started the argument, not us.//~ 의견도 들어 보도 록 하자 Let's hear the opinions of the other side.//여비는 ~에서 맡는다 They will pay our traveling expenses.

저촉 (抵觸) conflict; infringement; contravention. **저촉하다** conflict[be in conflict] with; be contrary to. →¶법에 저촉되다 be contrary to law / be against the law//법률에 저촉될 만 한 일은 하지 않는다 I have done nothing against[(문어) that contravenes] the law. //그의 견해는 종래의 학설에 저촉되는 것이었 다 His view conflicted with the existing theory.//그의 행위는 규칙에 저촉된다 His act is against the rules.

저축 (貯蓄) saving; [저금] savings. ¶[재형] (workers') property accumulation savings ¶ ~의 날 the Savings Day/~이 있다[없다] have some[no] savings / have some[no] money saved//~을 장려하다 encourage savings. **저축하다** save (up); store up; put [set] by[aside]. ¶만일의 경우에 대비해서 ~ save against a rainy day//수입에서 얼마를 ~ save something from[out of] one's income//그는 연수입의 1할을 으레 저축한다 He regularly puts aside ten percent of his annual income.//그는 해외여행을 위해 돈을 저축하고 있다 He is saving (up) money for a trip abroad.//그는 저축한 돈을 전부 은행에 맡겨 두고 있다 He keeps all his savings in the bank. →¶절약하면 한 달에 10만 원은 저 축할 수 있다 If I cut but on expenses, I can save one hundred thousand won a month.
●**저축 성향** a propensity to save. **저축 예금** a savings deposit. **저축 운동** a savings campaign.

저탄 (貯炭) a stock of coal. **저탄하다** store (up) coal.
●**저탄소 / 저탄장** a coal yard[depot]; a coaling station; a bunker(배의).

저택 (邸宅) a residence; a mansion(대저택). ¶ 호화 ~ a palatial residence//으리으리한 ~ a lordly[stately] mansion / a fine house [home]//그는 시골에 훌륭한 ~을 갖고 있다 He has a fine country home[estate].

저편 (-便) that side[direction]; the other party. ⇨`저쪽

저하 (低下) [낮아짐] falloff; a decline; a drop; lowering; (품질의) deterioration; (가격의) depreciation. ¶능률의 ~ a lowering of efficiency//도덕적 관심의 ~ a decline in concern about morals. **저하하다** fall off; decline; drop; lower; go down (in price); deteriorate. ¶능률이 ~ show a drop in efficiency / drop off in efficiency//밤에는 기온이 영하로 저하 한다 The temperature falls[drops] below zero at night.//수위가 5미터 저하했다 The water level dropped (by) five meters. →¶저하 시키다 let fall / lower / reduce / deteriorate// 요즘 아이들은 체력이 저하되어 있다 The children of today have declined in strength. / Children of today have less strength than those of the past.//의료의 질이 저하되어 있 다 The quality of medical care has been deteriorating.//이와 같은 표현이 작품의 질을 저하시키고 있다 These expressions debase [lower] the quality of his work.

저학년 (低學年) the lower grades. ¶~ 아동 schoolchildren in the lower grades.

저항 (抵抗) **1** [대항] resistance; opposition(반 대). ¶최후의 ~ the last-ditch stand/~을 받다 meet with[run into] resistance. **저항하 다** resist; offer[make] resistance[opposition] (to); oppose; stand[struggle / fight] against. ¶저항할 수 없는 세력 an irresistible force//저항하기 어려운 irresistible//공격에 ~ resist an attack / withstand an attack// 유혹에 ~ resist temptation//그들은 우리에 게 전혀 저항하지 않았다 They didn't resist us at all. / They made no resistance to [against] us.//그들은 적군에 완강히 저항했 다 They put up[offered] stubborn resistance to the enemy.//운명에 저항해도 소용없 다 It's no use resisting[striving against] destiny. / (미국 구어) You can't buck fate.
2 [물][전] resistance; drag(항력). ¶마찰 ~ frictional resistance//공기 ~ air resistance //전기 ~ electrical resistance//공기의 ~을 줄이다 lessen[reduce] the air resistance//이 종류의 금속은 열에 ~하는 힘이 있다 This kind of metal has heat resistant properties.
●**저항기** (-器) a resistor. **저항력** (power of) resistance; resisting power[force]. ¶병에 대 해 ~이 있다 have resistance to diseases//~ 을 잃다 lose the power of resistance//그녀 는 세균에 대한 ~이 약하다 She has little resistance to germs. **저항 운동** the Resistance movement; the Resistance (2차 대전 때의 지 하 조직 등).

저해 (沮害) a check (on); (an) obstruction (to); an impediment (in / to); a hindrance (to). (▶ check은 갑자기 정지시키는 일, obstruction은 진행을 방해하는 것, impediment 는 진로에 있는 장애물, hindrance는 방해하여 더디게 하는 것) **저해하다** check; obstruct; impede; hinder. ¶평화를 저해하는 것 an obstruction to peace//발달을 ~ hamper [impede / check] development//언론의 자유 를 ~ infringe on the freedom of speech//인 종의 대립이 그 나라의 발전을 저해하고 있다

The antagonism among the races has hindered [impeded] the development of the country.

저혈압(低血壓) low blood pressure; hypotension. ¶나는 ~이다 I have low blood pressure.

저희 [우리] we; [저 사람들] they; those people. ¶~들 we / they / ~들의 소망 our [their] hope // ~는 그런 물건을 다루지 않고 있습니다 We do not deal in such things.

적 1 [때] the time (when); (on) the occasion. ¶어릴 ~에 in one's childhood [early days] // 젊었을 ~에 while one was young. 2 [경험] an experience. ¶서울에 가 본 ~이 있습니까 Have you ever been to Seoul? / 그는 경주에서 이긴 ~이 없다 He has never once won a race.

적(敵) 1 [원수] an enemy; a foe (▶ foe 쪽이 뜻이 강함). ¶인류의 ~ an enemy of mankind // 평화 [사회]의 ~ an enemy to peace [society] // 많은 ~ a numerous enemy / an enemy of large force // ~과 싸우다 fight with the enemy // ~이 되다 become an enemy / turn against (another) // ~에게 붙다 go over to the enemy // ~의 수중에 떨어지다 fall into the enemy's hands // ~을 소탕하다 clear (the land) of the enemy // ~은 뜻하지 않은 곳에 있다 The enemy will be found where you least expect him. // 오늘의 친구가 내일의 ~이 될지도 모른다 A friend today may turn against you tomorrow. 2 [경기 등의 상대방] an opponent; an adversary (▶ 둘 다 적개심을 반드시 포함하지는 않으나, adversary의 경우는 적의를 포함하는 경우가 있음); [경쟁자] a rival; a competitor; [필적하는 상대] a match; an equal. ¶사업상의 ~ one's business rival / a rival [competitor] in business.

적(積) → 곱²

적(籍) 1 [호적] one's family register; [본적] one's domicile. ¶~에 올리다 [빼다] have one's name entered in [removed from] the family register // 내 ~은 서울에 있다 Seoul is registered as being my legal home. / (구어) I am domiciled in Seoul. 2 [단체의 적] membership. ¶단체에 ~을 두다 be a member of a group [society] // 대학에 ~을 두다 be enrolled at a college // 이 학교에는 2,000명의 학생이 ~을 두고 있다 The school has 2,000 students on the register. / The school has a registration [an enrollment] of 2,000 students.

-적(的) -al; -ic(al); -like. ¶경제~ economical / 교육~ from an educational point of view // 금전~으로는 monetarily / financially / as far as money goes [is concerned] // 귀족~인 태도 an aristocratic manner // 그 모임은 가정~인 분위기였다 The party was held in [had] a homely atmosphere. // 그는 논리~으로 생각하는 기질이다 He is the sort of man who thinks logically.

적갈색(赤褐色) reddish brown; (특히 모발의) auburn. ¶~ 머리 auburn hair.

적개심(敵愾心) a hostile feeling; hostility; (문어) enmity. ¶~에 불타다 influenced by a hostile feeling // ~을 품다 feel an enmity (toward(s) a person) / be hostile (to a person) // 나는 그들에 대해서 ~을 품었다 I harbored enmity against them.

적격(適格) (a) proper qualification; eligibility; competence. ¶그는 법관으로서는 ~이다 He is qualified to be a judge. // 그는 교사로서 ~이 아니다 He is not cut out to be a teacher. / He doesn't have what it takes to be a teacher. // 간사장(幹事長)이 그에게는 ~이다 The post of chief secretary is just right for him.
● **적격자** a qualified person; the right [very] person (for). ¶그는 그 일에 ~다 He has the right [necessary] qualifications for the job. / He is qualified [eligible] for the job.

적국(敵國) a hostile country [power]; the enemy.

적군(敵軍) enemy troops; a hostile army [force].

적극(積極) 1 [관형어적] the positive. 2 [부사적] positively; actively; constructively; progressively.
● **적극성** positiveness; enterprising spirit. ¶~이 있는 positive / ~이 있는 남자 an enterprising man // 그 사람은 ~이 없다 He never takes the initiative. **적극 외교** the positive diplomacy.

적극적(積極的) positive; active; constructive; progressive. ¶~인 사람 a man of [with] enterprising spirit / an active [a positive] person // ~인 인생관 [자세] a positive view of life [attitude toward life] / ~인 태도를 취하다 take a positive attitude // 기획에 ~으로 참여하다 take an active part in a project // ~으로 활동하다 be in full activity / be full of activities // ~으로 검토하겠다 We will consider it in a positive light. // 그의 ~인 자세가 호감을 얻었다 His forward-looking approach was welcomed. // 정부는 ~으로 정책을 밀고 나갔다 The Government was aggressive in pursuing its policy. // 그녀는 ~인 사람이다 She is a woman of action. / (구어) She is a real go-getter.

적금(積金) installment savings; an installment deposit. ¶~을 붓다 save up [deposit] by (monthly) installments.

적기(赤旗) [빨간 깃발] a red flag; [공산당의 상징 기] the Red Flag; [위험 신호의 기] a red flag (of warning); an emergency [a warning] flag.

적기(適期) a suitable [fit / proper] time; a good season (for). ¶~의 seasonable / well-timed / timely / opportune // ~에 in due [good] season // 지금이 등산의 ~이다 This is a good climbing season. // 그 책은 ~에 나왔다 The publication of the book was timely [well-timed].

적기(敵機) an enemy [a hostile] plane.

적나라하다(赤裸裸-) naked; nude; bare; frankness; plainness; frank; plain; outspoken. ¶적나라하게 frankly / plainly / candidly / ~적나라한 사실 a plain [bald / bare] fact // 일의 진상을 적나라하게 말하다 frankly tell the truth of the matter / give the naked face of the case // 나는 빈민가의 생활을 적나라하게 그리려고 했다 I attempted to describe life in the slums just as it is.

적다¹ [글로 쓰다] write [note / put / jot] down; make [take] notes (of / on). ¶그가 하는 말을 적어 두었다 I wrote down [I took notes on] what he said. // 일의 경과를 적어 두어야겠다 I will write [note] down how it happened. // 나는 그들의 이야기를 노트에 적었다 I recorded their conversation in a note-

적다

book.∥나는 그의 주소를 물어 수첩에 적었다 I asked his address and wrote it down[made a note of it] in my pocket notebook.∥그녀는 산 물건을 하나하나 적어 두었다 She wrote down every item she had bought.∥번호를 적어 두어라 Jot down the number.∥그는 요점을 주의 깊게 적어 두었다 He made careful notes of the main points.∥나는 마음에 떠오르는 것은 무엇이든지 적어 두었다 I jotted down whatever came to mind.∥수첩에 지난 번 모임의 내용을 적어 놓았다 I noted down what happened at the last meeting in my notebook.

적다² (수가) few; (양이) little; (수·양이) small; [변약하다] scarce; [불충분하다] scanty; [부족하다] short; [드물다] rare. ¶적은 수입 a small income∥말수가 적은 사람 a man of few words∥칼로리가 ~ be low[poor] in calories∥이것을 할 수 있는 사람은 아주 ~ Very few can do it.∥이 나라에서 80세 이상 되는 사람은 극히 ~ In this country, people over eighty years old are rare[few and far between].∥작년에는 비가 적었다 We didn't have much rain last year.∥We had little rain last year.∥용돈이 5,000원이면 너무 ~ An allowance of five thousand won is far too little[far from sufficient]. / Five thousand won isn't nearly enough pocket money.∥연료가 적었다 Fuel was limited[scarce].∥이 방법이 위험이 ~ This method is safer[less risky].∥그는 연수를 실제보다 약간 적게 신고했다 He reported his annual income somewhat below the actual figure.∥내 차에는 설탕을 약간 적게 넣어 주세요 Please put just a little sugar in my tea.

적당하다 (適當—) 1 [알맞다] suitable; proper; suited; adequate; fit; appropriate; [지나치지 않다] moderate. ¶적당한 운동 moderate exercise∥적당한 직업 a suitable job∥적당한 조건으로 on fair terms∥적당한 때에 at a [the] proper time∥적당한 속도로 at a moderate speed∥적당한 가격으로 at a reasonable[moderate]price∥그는 적당한 치료를 받지 않으면 안 된다 He has to get proper medical treatment.∥어린이들에게 적당한 놀이터가 아쉽다 We need a suitable place for our children to play.∥그 자리에는 그 사람이 가장 ~ He is the best person for the post.∥이 질문은 어린이들에게 적당하지 않다 This question is not suitable for[good for / suited to ask] children.∥이 표현은 학교의 교과서에 싣기에 적당하지 않다 This expression is not proper[appropriate] to be used in school textbooks. **적당히** suitably; properly; appropriately; reasonably; moderately. ¶~ 운동하다 take moderate exercise∥취향에 따라 ~ 설탕을 넣으세요 Add sugar to suit your taste. / Add sugar as you like.∥그 통닭이 ~ 구워졌다 The roast chicken is done to a turn.(▶ to a turn은 특히 요리에 대해 쓰임) 2 [애매하게] vague; [태도가 분명치 않다] non-committal. **적당히** vaguely; noncommittally. ¶나는 ~ 대답해 주었다 I made a vague answer.∥그 여자는 ~ 구슬러 두면 된다 You needn't deal with her seriously.∥일을 ~ 해치우지 마라 Don't be slack on your work. / Don't give your work a lick and a promise.

적대 (敵對) hostility; antagonism; contention. **적대하다** [맞서다] turn (against); fight (against); [반대하다] oppose; be hostile to; confront; be antagonistic to. ¶우리와 적대하는 나라 a nation hostile to our country / a hostile country.

● **적대국** a nation hostile to our country; a hostile country. **적대시** hostility; enmity. ¶~하다 be hostile to / look upon (a person) as an enemy / regard (a person) with hostility / show enmity toward∥그는 나를 ~하고 있다 He is hostile to me. / He shows enmity toward me.∥두 집안이 서로 ~하고 있다 The two families are at odds with each other. **적대 행위** a hostile act[action]. ¶일본에 대하여 ~를 취하다 take hostile action against Japan / behave in a manner hostile to Japan.

적도 (赤道) the equator; the line. ¶지구[천구]의 ~ the terrestrial[celestial] equator∥~의 equatorial∥~ 직하에(서) right on the equator∥~ 직하의 남미 equatorial South America∥~를 횡단하다 cross the equator [line].

● **적도 기단** an equatorial air mass. **적도 무풍대** the doldrums. **적도의**(—儀) an equatorial telescope. **적도 해류** the equatorial currents.

적동석 (赤銅石) [광] cuprite; red copper [ore].

적란운 (積亂雲) [기상] a cumulonimbus (pl. —es, -bi).

적량 (適量) a proper quantity; (약의) a (proper) dose. ¶~을 넘다 take too much / eat [drink] to excess / (약의) overdose oneself.

적령 (適齡) a proper[fit] age (for). ¶결혼 ~ the marriageable age∥징병 ~ the conscription age∥징병 ~의 젊은이들 young men of draft age∥수영을 시작하는 데 특별한 ~은 없다 There is no specially suitable age at which to begin[start] learning swimming.

● **적령기** ¶결혼 ~에 달하다 reach[attain] the marriageable age / be old enough to marry∥결혼 ~의 딸이 있다 I have a daughter of marriageable age.

적례 (適例) a good[an apposite] example; an apt[a typical] instance; a case in point. ¶~를 들다 cite a happy illustration[an apt example] / quote a case in point∥다음은 한 ~이다 The following is a good example.

적록 색맹 (赤綠色盲) red-green blindness.

적리 (赤痢) [의] dysentery. ¶아메 바성 ~ amoebic dysentery.

● **적리균** a dysentery bacillus.

적립 (積立) accumulation; reserving; laying [putting] by. **적립하다** save up (money); lay [put] by[aside]; accumulate; amass; reserve. ¶나는 한 달에 100,000원씩 적립하고 있다 I lay aside 100,000 won every month.∥그녀는 급료의 일부를 결혼 자금으로 적립하고 있다 She saves[lays aside / sets aside] a part of her salary for her marriage.

● **적립금** a reserve (fund); (영) the rest. ¶별도[법정] ~ a special[legal] reserve.

적막 (寂寞) loneliness; desolation. **적막하다** lonely; lonesome; dreary; desolate; deserted. ¶적막한 산속 lonely[lonesome / dreary] mountain recesses∥적막한 곳 a lonely place∥적막한 광경 a dreary[desolate] sight∥비철의 관광지는 ~ A tourist resort is quite deserted[is as lonesome as a graveyard] in the off-season. **적막히** lonelily; desolately; drearily.

● **적막감** a feeling of loneliness.

적멸(寂滅) [불] Nirvana; [죽음] death. **적멸하다** enter into Nirvana; die; pass away.

적반하장(賊反荷杖) ¶그는 ~으로 내게 대들었다 He got at me just like he was trying to carry the war into the enemy's camp. // 그 사기꾼은 ~으로 나를 사기꾼이라 주장했다 That swindler had the brazen cheek to call me one. // ~도 유분수지 How brazen-faced [audacious] he is about his wrong doing!

적발(摘發) exposure; disclosure. **적발하다** expose; disclose; lay bare [open]; uncover. ¶부정 사건을 ~ expose [lay bare] a scandal / 특정 외래품을 ~ uncover contrabands. →¶마약 밀수단이 경찰에 적발되었다 The narcotic smuggling gang was unearthed by the police. // 그 은행의 부정행위가 적발되었다 The financial irregularities at that bank were exposed [disclosed / laid bare].

적법(適法) legality; lawfulness. ¶~**이다** be lawful [legal] / ~**이 아니다** be unlawful [illegal] // 이 운동은 ~으로 인정받고 있다 This movement is allowed by (the) law [perfectly legitimate]. **적법하다** lawful; legal. ¶경찰관이 취한 조치는 적법했다 The measures the policemen took were lawful.

● **적법 조치** a lawful measure. **적법 행위** a legal [lawful] act.

적병(敵兵) an enemy; an enemy soldier; 《집합적》 the enemy.

적부(適否) (일의) propriety; (사람의) suitability; fitness. ¶인물의 ~ the fitness of a person // 그 수단의 ~는 차치하고라도 setting aside the question of the propriety of the measure / setting aside the question (of) whether the measure is proper or not // ~를 **판단하다** judge whether a thing is proper or not // 그들의 행동의 ~에 대해서 논의가 있었다 The propriety of their action was disputed.

● **적부 심사** review of the legality (of the detention).

적분(積分) [수] integral. ¶**정**[**부정**]~ definite [indefinite] integral / ~**이 가능한** integrable. **적분하다** integrate. ¶F를 X에 대하여 A에서 B까지 ~ integrate F with respect to X from A to B.

● **적분 방정식** an integral equation. **적분법** integration. **적분 상수** a constant of integration.

적산(敵産) enemy property (in one's land). ¶~**을 몰수하다** confiscate the enemy property.

적산(積算) addition; integration. **적산하다** add up; integrate.

● **적산법** integration. **적산 전력계** a watthour meter; an integrating wattmeter.

적삼 jeoksam; a Korean-style unlined summer jacket.

적색(赤色) 1 [붉은색] red (color). ¶~**의** red // ~ **리트머스 시험지** red litmus paper. 2 [공산주의를 상징하는 빛깔] communism.

● **적색분자** a Red; Red elements. **적색 혁명** a Red revolution.

적서(嫡庶) legitimate and illegitimate children. ¶~**를 구분하다** draw a line between legitimate and illegitimate.

적선(敵船) an enemy ship [vessel].

적선(積善) 1 [착한 일을 많이 함] accumulation of virtuous [good] deeds. **적선하다** accumulate virtuous [good] deeds. 2 [동냥질에 하는 행위] almsgiving; charity. **적선하다** give alms (to a person); give in charity.

적설(積雪) (an accumulation of) snow; snow (on the ground); snowdrifts. ¶~**에 갇힌 지역** a snowbound area / ~**로 갇히다** be snowbound / be snowed up // ~**은** 1미터**에 달했다** The snow was one meter deep. / We had a snowfall of one meter. // 열차는 ~로 10시간 동안 꼼짝 못하고 있었다 The heavy (fall of) snow halted the train for ten hours.

● **적설량** a snowfall (of six centimeters).

적성(適性) fitness; aptitude. (▶ fitness는 성격, aptitude는 주로 능력에 대해서 말함) ¶교사로서의 ~**이 있다** have the qualities a teacher needs / have the qualities needed in a teacher // 그는 음악에 대한 ~**이 있다** He has musical aptitude [an aptitude for music]. // 법관으로서의 그의 ~을 알아볼 필요가 있다 We must examine his fitness as a judge.

● **적성 검사** an aptitude test. ¶**직업** ~ a vocational aptitude test. ¶~**를 받다** undergo an aptitude test.

적성(敵性) inimical [enemy] character.

● **적성 국가** a hostile country.

적세(敵勢) the strength of the enemy; [기세] the morale of the foe [enemy]. ¶~**를 꺾다** shatter the enemy's morale.

적소(適所) the right [proper] place; a proper [suitable] position. ¶**적재**~ the right man in the right place [for the right job] // 인재를 ~**에 배치하다** place men of ability in the right positions.

적송(積送) [경] shipment; (위탁 판매를 위한) consignment. ¶**철도** ~ shipment [forwarding] by rail. **적송하다** ship; send; consign. ¶주문하신 부품은 선편으로 적송합니다 We will ship [send] the parts you ordered by sea [ocean freight].

● **적송인** a shipper; a consignor; a consigner; a sender. **적송품** consigned [consignment] goods; a consignment.

적수(赤手) an empty hand. ⇨**맨손**

적수(敵手) [경쟁자] a competitor; [필적하는 사람] a match; an equal; [적대자] an opponent. ¶**호**~ a good rival [match] / a worthy opponent // 나는 그의 ~가 못 된다 I am no match for him. // 아무리 해 봐도 도저히 자네의 ~는 못 되겠네 Try what I will, I do not think I am quite a match for you.

적시(適時) [알맞은 때] ¶~**의** timely / opportune.

● **적시 안타** [야구] a timely hit. ¶그는 ~를 날렸다 He got a timely hit.

적시다 wet; [축이다] moisten; drench; dampen. ¶**옷을** ~ get one's clothes wet // 스펀지를 물에 ~ moisten a sponge (with water) // 눈물로 소매를 ~ wet one's sleeves with tears // 그는 눈물로 뺨을 적시면서 용서를 빌었다 He begged their pardon with tears streaming down his cheeks. // 그녀는 다리미질을 하기 전에 그 천을 적셨다 She dampened the cloth before ironing it.

적신호(赤信號) 1 [교통 신호] a red (traffic) light; a stoplight. ¶~**를 무시하다** go through [ignore] a stoplight // ~**로 바뀌어 정지하다** stop at [for] a red light // ~ **때는 길을 건너서는 안 된다** Don't cross the street on the red light [when the (traffic) light is red]. 2 [위험 신호] a danger signal. ¶**고혈압은** ~**이다**

High blood pressure is a danger signal.

적실(嫡室) one's lawful wife. ⇨ 본처

적십자(赤十字) 1 [붉은 십자] a red cross. 2 the Red Cross (Society). ⇨ 적십자사(⇨ 적십자). ¶청소년 ~ the Red Cross Youth(약어 R.C.Y.) / 남북 ~ 회담 talks between the South and North Korean Red Cross Societies.
● **적십자사** the Red Cross (Society). ¶만국 ~ the International Red Cross.

적어도 at least; in the least; not less than; to say the least. ¶~ 파리만은 보고 싶다 I want to see Paris at least. // ~ 한 시간만 더 머물 수 있다면 좋으련만 I wish I could stay at least one hour longer. // ~ 학자라는 사람이 그런 짓을 하리라고는 믿어지지 않는다 It is unbelievable that any scholar worthy of the name should do such a thing. // ~ 대학생이라면 그런 것쯤은 알고 있어야 한다 Any university student[If you are a university students, you] ought to know that much at least. // ~ 5만 원[2시간은 들겠다[걸리겠다] It will cost at least fifty thousand won[take at least two hours]. // 하루에 ~ 20달러는 필요할 것이다 You'll need at least[a minimum of] twenty dollars a day.

적어지다 diminish; decrease; lessen.

적역(適役) [알맞은 배역·직임] a suitable[fit] post; (연극·영화의) a fit[suitable] role. ¶그런 자리에는 그가 ~이다 He is the very[just the right] person for such a post. / The job is tailor-made for him. // 그는 이 중재역에 ~이 있다 He was well cast for this mediating role. // 햄릿에는 그가 ~이다 He is the right man for the role of Hamlet.

적역(適譯) a proper[suitable] translation; (최고의) the most appropriate translation.

적열(赤熱) red heat. **적열하다** heat (iron) to red heat; make red-hot. ¶적열한 쇠 red-hot iron.

적외선(赤外線) [물] infrared rays.
● **적외선 분광기** an infrared spectrometer. **적외선 사진** an infrared photograph; infrared photography(사진술). **적외선 요법** infrared therapy.

적요(摘要) a summary; an outline; a résumé; an epitome; a synopsis; a digest. ¶강연의 ~ a summary[an outline] of a lecture. **적요하다** summarize; sum up; epitomize; outline; give a summary of.
● **적요란**(-欄) a space for notes[explanatory remarks].

적용(適用) (an) application. ¶그들은 생활 보호법의 ~을 받고 있다 The Livelihood Protection Law has been applied in their case. // 이 말의 ~ 범위는 매우 넓다 This word has a very wide application. **적용하다** apply (a rule) to (a case). ➔ ¶법규 제2조가 이 경우에 적용된다 The second article of the regulations can be applied[is applicable] to this case. // 그 방법이 모든 사례에 적용되지는 못한다 The method cannot be applied to all cases.

적운(積雲) [기상] a cumulus (*pl.* -li); a cumulus cloud.

적응(適應) 1 [잘 어울림] adaptation; accommodation; adjustment; conformity. **적응하다** adapt[accomodate / adjust / acclimate] oneself; confirm(일치하다). ¶새 환경에 ~ acclimate[acclimatize] oneself to a new environment // 시대의 요구에 ~ meet the needs of the times // 환경의 변화에 ~ adapt oneself to the change in one's surroundings // 그녀는 환경의 변화에 잘 적응할 수 있다 She can easily adapt herself to[fit herself into] her surroundings. // 나는 환경에 잘 적응하지 못한다 I am slow adjust to my surroundings. // 그녀는 한국에서의 바쁜 생활에 그럭저럭 잘 적응했다 She managed to accommodate herself to the busy life in Korea. // 당신은 사회에 적응하도록 노력해야 한다 You should try to conform to the way of the world. ➔ **적응시키다** adapt / accommodate.
2 (동식물의) adaptation.
● **적응성** adaptability; flexibility.

적의(敵意) a hostile feeling; hostility; enmity. ¶~ 있는 hostile / antagonistic // 남에게 ~를 품다 harbor[entertain] a hostile feeling against a person / feel hostility against (a person) / bear (a person) grudge // ~를 나타내다[보이다] manifest[show] a hostile feeling against (a person) // 나는 그에게 ~를 갖고 있지 않다 I have no hostility[enmity] toward him.

적이 [꽤 어지간히] a little; a bit; slightly; somewhat; to some extent; to a certain degree; rather. ¶그것에는 우리도 ~ 놀랐다 That came as a bit of surprise to us. // 그 소식에 나는 ~ 당황했다 I was somewhat embarrassed at that news.

적이나 [얼마간이라도] a little at least; if any; at the very least. ¶그가 ~ 후회하다니 다행이다 I'm glad he is sorry a little at least.

적임(適任) 1 [알맞음·알맞은 임무] fitness; suitability; competence. ¶~이 아닌 unfit (for) / inadequate / unqualified / incompetent / inept // ~이다 be fit[suitable] (for the post) / be suited (to the office) / be well qualified (for a teacher) / be competent (for) // 수학 교사로서 ~이다 be competent teacher of mathematics // 그는 교장 자리에 ~이다 He is competent for the head of a school. // 그는 교사로서 ~이다 He is well suited for teaching. / (구어) He has what it takes to be a teacher. 2 a well-qualified person. ⇨ 적임자(⇨ 적임)
● **적임자** a well-qualified person; a person well suited (for the job); a competent person; the right man (for the task). ¶최~다 be the very man[just the man] for (the post) // 그는 ~다 He is the right[very] man for the position. // 이 일에는 그녀가 최고의 ~다 She is the best woman for the job.

적자(赤字) [공식 회계의 부족액] a deficit; [손실] the red; a loss; [빨간 숫자] red figure. ¶~ 예산 a budget deficit // 수지의 ~ an adverse balance of payments // 상당한 ~ a sizable deficit // ~를 보다 show a loss [deficit] / go into the red // ~를 내고 있다 be in the red (figures) / have a deficit // 20억 원에 달하는 ~를 내다 go into the red to the extent of two billion won // show a red-ink figure of two billion won // ~를 메우다 cover [make up] a deficit // 우리 집 가계는 ~다 Our household is in the red. // 시의 재정은 ~가 났다 Our municipal finances went into the red[a deficit]. // 그는 ~가 나지 않도록 했다 He kept out of the red. // 우리는 50만 원의 ~를 보았다 We are five hundred thousand

won in the red. / We have gone five hundred thousand won into the red.
● **적자 경영 / 적자 운영** deficit operation. ¶그 회사는 ~이다 The company is operating in the red[at a loss]. **적자 재정** deficit [red-ink] financing; a financial deficit.

적자(嫡子) [정실의 아들] a legitimate child [son].

적자(適者) those fit; the fit; a fit person. ¶~만이 성공하는 사회 a society in which only the fit succeed.
● **적자생존**(-生存) the survival of the fittest. ¶그것은 ~의 원리에 합치된다 It conforms to the principle that only the fittest can survive[the principle of the survival of the fittest].

적잖다 not a little; not a few; no small(강조); [상당하다] considerable. ¶적잖은 사람이 현장에 있었다 Not a few[Quite a few] people were on the spot. // 적잖은 위험이 있다 There is no small danger. // 그는 적잖은 손해를 보았다 He has suffered a considerable loss. **적잖이** in no small quantities(양이); in no small numbers(양이); not a little(정도가); a great deal. ¶그 소식을 듣고 우리는 ~ 놀랐다 We were not a little[greatly] surprised at the news. // 나는 그녀에게 ~ 신세를 지고 있다 I owe a great deal to her.

적장(敵將) the enemy general[commander].

적재(積載) loading; carrying. **적재하다** load; carry. ¶화물을 적재한 트럭 a loaded truck / 배에 화물을 ~ load a ship with goods / load cargo on a ship.
● **적재량** loadage. **적재 화물** cargo on board.

적재적소(適材適所) the right man in the right place[for the right job]. ¶~가 아니다 be a case of a square peg in a round hole // ~에 배치하다 put the right man in the right place.

적적하다(寂寂-) lonely; lonesome; forlorn; deserted. ¶적적한 느낌 (a feeling of) loneliness[lonesomeness] // 적적한 곳 a lonely [deserted] place // 나는 말벗이 없어서 ~ I feel lonely having no one to talk to. // 아이들이 없으니 집 안이 ~ The house is lonely without children. // 네가 없으면 적적할 거야 I'm going to miss you when you're gone. / When you go away, I'm going to be very lonely. **적적히** lonelily; lonesomely; forlornly. ¶~ 살다[지내다] lead[live] a lonely life.

적전(敵前) ¶~의[에 / 에서] in the presence [face] of the enemy / before the enemy / facing the enemy // ~에서 도망치다 turn one's way back to the enemy / be a deserter under fire.
● **적전 도하**(-渡河) forced crossing of a river (against an enemy).

적절하다(適切-) suitable; good; appropriate; proper; happy; [당면 문제에 꼭 맞다] relevant; pertinent; adequate; [시기가] well-timed; timely. ¶적절한 말 a happy[fitting] remark // 적절한 표현 a suitable expression // 적절한 예 an apt[appropriate] instance / a good example // 적절한 평 an apt[a pertinent] criticism // 적절한 비유 a fitting simile // 전치사의 적절한 용법 the proper use of prepositions // 적절한 조치를 취하다 take proper measures // 적절한 대답을 하다 answer relevantly // 그녀의 발언은 적절한 것이었다 Her remarks were appropriate. // 비평은 적절했다 The criticism was apt[to the point]. // 이 제목은 시의 내용으로 볼 때 ~ The title suits the content of the poem. // 이 감동을 표현할 적절한 말이 떠오르지 않는다 I cannot find the right words to express how moved I am. **적절히** pertinently; suitably; fitly; appropriately. ¶송 선생이 아주 ~ 말한 바와 같이 As Mr. Song so aptly stated, ... // 그것[그 말]은 이 생각을 ~ 나타내 주고 있다 That is a happy[(문어) felicitous] expression for this idea.

적정(適正) [관형어적]. **적정하다** proper; right; just; reasonable; fair. ¶적정한 분배 fair [just] distribution.
● **적정 가격** the right[reasonable / fair] price. ¶~으로 매매하다 buy and sell (goods) at reasonable[right] prices. **적정 수준** optimum level.

적정(敵情) the movements[conditions / situation] of the enemy. ¶~을 정찰하다 reconnoiter the enemy position / spy on the enemy's movements.

적조(赤潮) a red tide; red water.

적중(的中) a (good) hit. **적중하다** [과녁에 맞다] hit the mark[target]; (예언 등이) come true; (추측 등이) guess right. ¶적중하지 않다 miss[be wide of] the mark / (상상이) guess wild[wrong] // 총알은 모두 적중했다 Every shot hit the mark. // 나의 예상[예언]은 적중했다 My prediction proved right[came right]. // 그의 상상은 적중했다 He was right in his conjecture. / He guessed right. // 그의 상상은 적중하지 않았다[빗나갔다] He guessed wrong. // 나의 예감이 적중했다 My hunch was right on the nose.
● **적중률** a hitting ratio.

적지(適地) suitable land. ¶그 땅은 밀 경작의 ~이다 The soil is suited to the cultivation of wheat.

적지(敵地) enemy land[territory country]. ¶~에 깊숙이 들어가다 penetrate deep into the enemy territory // ~를 정찰하다 make a survey of the enemy-held area / reconnoiter the enemy territory.

적진(敵陣) [적의 진영] the enemy's camp; [적의 진지] the enemy's position; the enemy line. ¶~을 돌파하다 break through the enemy line // ~을 공격하다 attack the enemy's position // ~을 빼앗다 dislodge the enemy from its[their] position / carry [capture] the enemy's position // 병사들은 ~을 급습했다 The soldiers raided the enemy's camp.

적철석(赤鐵石) [광] hematite; red iron ore.

적체(積滯) stagnation; a tie-up; retention; accumulation; congestion. ¶화물의 ~ a congestion[an accumulation] of goods. **적체하다** be stagnant; stagnate; congest; accumulate; pile up. ¶폭풍우로 화물이 적체해 있다 Freight has piled up owing to the storm.

적출(摘出) 1 [끄집어냄] extraction; removal. ¶그녀는 난소 ~ 수술을 받았다 She had an operation for the removal of an ovary. **적출하다** extract; remove. ¶그들은 상처에서 유리 파편을 적출했다 They extracted[removed] a small piece of glass from the wound. 2 [들추어냄] exposure. **적출하다** expose; disclose; bring to light. ¶부정을 ~ expose injustice.

적출(嫡出) a legitimate child; a child of legitimate birth. ¶~의 born in wedlock // ~이다

적출 be born in wedlock.
적출(積出) shipment. ⇨출하(出荷)
●적출항 a port of shipment. ¶석탄 ~ a coal loading port.
적치하다(積置-) pile up; amass; heap.
적탄(敵彈) [적이 쏘는 총탄] enemy('s) bullet; [적이 쏘는 포탄] enemy('s) shells. ¶~을 무릅쓰고 in the face of the enemy's fire // ~에 쓰러지다 be killed by an enemy's bullet / be shot dead by the enemy // 그는 ~에 맞아 부상했다 He was wounded by an enemy bullet.
적평(適評) a just[apt] criticism; an appropriate[a pertinent] comment. ¶그는 그녀의 작품에 ~을 했다 He made an apt comment on her works.
적폐(積弊) a deep-rooted[-seated] evil; an evil of long standing. ¶~를 일소하다 clean up[eradicate] deep-rooted evils.
적포도주(赤葡萄酒) red wine.
적하(積荷) loading; a load. ⇨적화(積貨)
적함(敵艦) a hostile[an enemy] ship; (집합적) hostile craft.
적합하다(適合-) fit; suitable; proper; befitting; adequate; appropriate; compatible. ¶노인에게 적합한 식사 a diet suitable for the old // 젊은 사람들에게 적합한 일 a job suitable for young people // 혼자 살기에 적합한 집 a house suitable for living alone // 목적에 ~ serve one's purpose // 그는 교사로서 적합하지 않다 He is not fit to be a teacher. // 그 사람이야말로 분쟁을 조정하는 데 적합한 사람이다 He is the very man to mediate the dispute. // 이 강둑은 캠핑하기에 적합하지 않다 This riverbank is not a good place for camping.
적혈구(赤血球) [생] a red (blood) cell; a red corpuscle; an erythrocyte.
적화(赤化) communization; Bolshevization; sovietization. ¶~의 위험 the red menace // 한반도 ~ 통일의 망상 fantastic dream of communizing the entire Korean Peninsula // ~를 방지하다 check the spread of communism. 적화하다 [빨갱이가 되게 하다] communize; Bolshevize; sovietize; make (a person / a country) communistic; [빨갱이가 되다] turn[become] red[communist / Bolshevik].
●적화 운동 a red[Bolshevik] movement; communist[red] activities.
적화(積貨) [적재] loading; shipment; [화물] a load; (미) a freight; (미) goods(철도·도로 등에 의한); a cargo(배·비행기에 의한). ¶그 트럭의 ~는 곡물이었다 The truck had a load of[was loaded with] grain. 적화하다 load; (배가) take in cargo.
●적화 목록 a manifest(기선의); a freight list. 적화 보험 cargo insurance.
적확하다(的確-) accurate; exact; precise. ¶말의 적확한 뜻 the exact meaning of a word // 적확한 묘사 an accurate description // 적확한 증거 a positive proof / proof positive // 적확한 숫자 exact figures // 본건은 적확한 판단을 요한다 This case needs a precise judgement. 적확히 accurately; with accuracy; exactly; precisely. ¶사건을 ~ 묘사하다 describe an event accurately.
적황색(赤黃色) reddish yellow (color).
적흑색(赤黑色) reddish black (color).
적히다 be written[put] down; be recorded; [기술되다] be described. ¶이름이 ~ have one's name noted down // 편지에 이렇게 적혀 있다 The letter says[reads] that .... // 유언장에는 다음과 같이 적혀 있다 The will runs as follows. // "그 메모에는 뭐라고 적혀 있었습니까?" "중요 서류라고 적혀 있었습니다." "What did the note say?" "It said 'important papers'."

전 [물건의 가장자리] a brim; a rim; an edge. ¶~이 넓은 꽃병 a vase with a broad brim.
전(田) a (dry) field; a farm. ⇨밭
전(全) all; whole; entire; total; complete; full; pan-. ¶~ 세계 the whole world // ~ 국민 the whole nation // ~ 20권 a complete set of 20 volumes // ~ 페이지 삽화 a full-page illustration // 그는 화재로 ~ 재산을 잃었다 He lost all his property in a fire.
전(前) 1 [막연한 과거] before; once; formerly; previously. ¶~처럼 as before // ~부터 for some time (past) // ~에 말한 바와 같이 as previously stated // 그는 ~처럼 열심히 일하지 않는다 He doesn't work hard as before. // 타이는 ~에 시암이라고 불렀다 Thailand was formerly called Siam. // 당신에 관해서는 ~부터 많이 듣고 있었습니다 I've heard a lot about you for some time. // ~에는 이 근방에 은행이 있었다 There used to be a bank around[(미) about] here. // 그는 ~과는 완전히 딴사람이 되었다 He is not what he used to be. / He has become quite another man. // 그는 ~에 선생이었다 He was formerly a teacher. // ~에 한 번 그것을 본 적이 있다 I have seen it once (before).
2 [일정한 때보다 앞] ago; before; prior to. ¶이틀 ~의 신문 a newspaper of two days ago // 30 ~의 젊은 여자 a young woman who is not thirty yet / a young woman on the right side of thirty // 2, 3일 ~에 (지금부터) a few days ago / (그때부터) a few days before // 지금으로부터 5년 ~에 five years ago[since] // 7시 15분 ~에 at a quarter to[(미) of] seven // 6월 30일 ~에 before the 30th of June // 출발하기 ~에 before[prior to] one's departure // 날이 새기 ~에 before daybreak // 오래-부터 since a long time[while] ago / from long ago [way back] // 10월 3일 ~에 회답해 주십시오 Please give your answer before[not later than] October 3. // 1시 5분 ~이다 It's five (minutes) to[(미) of] one. // 아침 8시 ~에는 전화를 하지 마세요 Please do not call[(미) ring] me before eight in the morning. // 그는 아직 40 ~이다 He is yet under forty. / He is on this side[the right side] of forty.
3 [편지에서] Dear; Sir. ¶어머님 ~ 상서 Dear Mother.
4 [이전의] former; ex-. ¶~ 미국 대통령 the former President[ex-President] of the United States // ~ 국무총리 an ex-Prime Minister / a one-time prim minister // ~ 국회 의원 an ex-member of the National Assembly / an ex-M.P. // ~ 교장 an ex-principal.
5 [이전·앞] previous; pre-. ¶~세기 the previous century // ~ 크리스트교 시대 pre-Christian era // ~ 주소 one's former[previous] address // ~ 근대적인 premodern / old-fashioned
전에 없이 unusually; unwontedly; by way of exception. ¶그는 ~ 기운이 없었다 He was in unusually low spirits. // 그녀는 ~ 상냥하게 말을 걸어왔다 She spoke to me more kindly than usual.

전(煎) jeon; fried food. ¶~을 부치다 fry / prepare a fried[fry] dish // 생선을 ~ 부치다 fry fish.

전(廛) (미) a store; (영) a shop; [노점 등] a stall; a booth. ¶쌀~ a rice store.

전(錢) [화폐 단위] a jeon(=1/100 won).

-전(展) an exhibition; an exhibit. ¶개인~ a private(one-man) exhibition // 학생 작품~ an exhibition of the pupils' works // 사진~ a photo exhibition.

-전(傳) [전기] a biography; a life. ¶위인~ the lives of great men // 에디슨~ a life[biography] of Edison.

-전(戰) **1** [전쟁] a war; warfare; [전투] a battle; a fight. ¶공중~ an air battle[war] // 근대~ modern warfare // 시가~ street fighting / 육박~ a hand-to-hand fight / a close combat. **2** (경기의) a game; a match. ¶1회~ the first game / (토너먼트의) the first round / 리그~ league competition / (한 시합) a league game // 대학 대항~ intercollegiate games.

전가(傳家) ~의 hereditary / ancestral / successive / handed down.

전가의 보도(寶刀) [비장의 수단] a trump card; one's last resort. ¶~를 빼다 play one's trump card / resort to one's last measure // ~를 빼기에는 아직 이르다 It's too early to resort to my last trick[to play my trump card].

전가(轉嫁) [죄·책임 등을 넘기어 맡김] imputation. **전가하다** impute; blame; lay[put] the blame on (a person); shift; transfer. ¶그는 내게 죄를 전가했다 He put the crime on me. // 자신의 책임을 남에게 전가하지 마라 Don't shift the responsibility onto someone else. // 그는 책임을 동생에게 전가했다 He put the blame on[upon] his brother. / He shifted the responsibility onto his brother's shoulders. // 그들은 돈이 없어진 책임을 그 청년에게 전가했다 They shifted the blame for the loss of the money onto the young man. ➔¶국가 재정의 핍박이 세금이란 형태로 우리에게 전가된다 The financial difficulties of the nation are passed on to us in the form of taxes.

전각(全角) [인] an em. ¶~ 대시 an em dash.
전각(殿閣) a (royal) Palace.
전각(篆刻) [인장을 새김] seal engraving.
전간(癲癇) [의] epilepsy. ⇨"간질(癇疾)
전갈(全蠍) [동] a scorpion.
●**전갈자리** [천] the Scorpion; Scorpio.

전갈(傳喝) a message; word. ¶~을 보내다 send word[message] // ~을 전하다 deliver [give] a (verbal) message // ~을 받다 receive a message / get word // 다음 주에 방문하겠다고 그에게 ~을 보냈다 I sent him word[a message] that I would visit him next week. // 민 씨로부터 ~이 있었습니다 I have a message for you from Mr. Min. **전갈하다** send word[a message] (to); give a (verbal) message.

전개(展開) **1** [열려서 펼쳐짐] spread; expand; unfolding. **전개하다** spread[open / roll] out; unfold. ➔¶끝없이 전개되는 태평양 the boundless expanse of the Pacific // 아름다운 경치가 눈앞에 전개되었다 Beautiful scenery unfolded[spread out] before my eyes.

2 [진전시켜 펼침] unfolding; development; [연] discovery. ¶국면의 ~ the development of the situation // 이 사건의 앞으로의 ~가 기다려진다 We are waiting to see how this case will develop[unfold]. **전개하다** unfold; develop. ¶새 국면을 ~ take a new turn / make a fresh development // 이론을 ~ unfold[state] one's theory / build up logic // 그는 독특한 새 이론을 전개했다 He developed a new theory of his own. ➔¶이 사건은 앞으로 어떻게 전개될까 What will be the future developments of the affair?

3 (군대의) deployment. **전개하다** deploy; fan out.

4 [수] expansion; development. **전개하다** expand; develop.

●**전개도** a development figure. **전개식** [수] an expansion.

전갱이 [동] a horse mackerel; a saurel.

전거(典據) authority; [출전] a source. ¶믿을 만한 ~ reliable authority // ~가 있는 authentic / authorized / authenticated // ~ 있는 학설 an authoritative[an authenticated / a well-documented] theory // ~가 확실한 of good[right] authority // ~가 없는 unauthorized / unauthenticated / without authority // ~를 들다 [밝히다] name[give / cite] the authority (for) / indicate the source (of) // 명백한 ~을 들다 give chapter and verse (for) // 이 논문은 ~가 제시되어 있지 않다 This article[essay] does not cite any authority[source].

전거(轉居) a move; a removal; a change of address. **전거하다** remove; move; change one's abode[address]; transfer one's residence (to).

전격(電擊) [전기의 충격] an electric shock; [급습] a lightning attack; a blitz.
●**전격 작전** blitz(krieg) tactics. **전격전** a lightning war; a blitz(krieg).

전격적(電擊的) lightning; blitz. ¶~인 속도로 with lightning speed // ~으로 공격을 받다 be attacked with a blitz // 상원은 그 의안을 ~으로 통과시켰다 The Upper House[Senate] has passed the bill with lightning speed.

전결(專決) [결정권자의 의사만으로 결정] an arbitrary decision. ¶사장 ~ 사항 a matter of arbitrary decision by the president. **전결하다** decide arbitrarily; make an arbitrary decision.

전경(全景) a complete[a panoramic] view; a panorama (of). ¶경기장의 ~ a panoramic view of the grounds // 서울의 ~을 보다 see the whole[a panorama] of Seoul // 이 산정에서는 호남평야의 ~이 바라보인다 This mountaintop commands a view of the entire Honam Plain.
●**전경 사진** a panoramic photograph.

전경(前景) (the scenery in) the foreground.
전경(戰警) the combat police (force). ⇨"전투경찰(⇨전투)

전고(前古) [지난 옛날] remote antiquity; ancient[old] times; the old days. ¶그것은 ~에 없는 사고였다 It was an unprecedented accident.

전곡(田穀) dry-field grain.
전곡(錢穀) money and grain.
전골 jeongol; Korean-style chowder.
●**전골냄비** chowder pan.

전공(專攻) one's specialty[(영) speciality]; one's special study; (미) one's major. ¶부(副)~ a minor. **전공하다** specialize (in his-

전공 tory); (영) make a special study (of); (미) major (in). ¶그는 대학에서 무엇을 전공했습니까 (미) What did he major[specialize] in college? / (영) What did he specialize in [read] at the university?//그는 역사를 전공하고 있다 (미) He is a history major. / (영) He is reading history.//그는 Y대학에서 경제학을 전공하고 작년에 졸업했다 He graduated from Y University last year, with a major in economics.
- 전공과목 one's special subject; (미) one's major. 전공 분야 one's major field.

전공(電工) an electrician.

전공(戰功) distinguished war services; meritorious services in war. ¶~이 있는 장교 an officer with a fine war record//~을 세우다 distinguish oneself in war[on the field of battle]//~에 의하여 무공 훈장을 받다 be decorated with the Order of Military Merit for one's distinguished services in war//그는 2차 대전에서 ~을 세웠다 He distinguished himself in World War Ⅱ.

전과(全科) [학교에서 규정한 모든 과목] all (the) subjects; [학교에서 규정한 모든 과정] the whole[full / complete] course; all (the) courses (of). ¶~를 이수하다 complete the whole course.

전과(前科) a previous conviction[offense / crime]; a criminal record. ¶~ 5범인 사람 a person with five previous convictions//~가 없는 사람 a person with no criminal record//그는 ~가 있다 He has a criminal record.//그는 ~ 3범이다 He has been convicted three times previously. / He has three previous convictions.//그는 소매치기 ~가 한 번 있다 He has been convicted once for pickpocketing.
- 전과자 / 전과범 an ex-convict; a man with a criminal record; (속어) an ex-con; (영국 속어) an old lag.

전과(戰果) [전투에서 거둔 성과] war results; military achievements[gains]. ¶혁혁한 ~를 거두다[~가 혁혁하다] achieve brilliant war results / make marked military achievements//아군은 혁혁한 ~을 올렸다 Our troops made brilliant[remarkable] military gains.

전과(轉科) [학과나 병과 등을 옮김] a change of (academic) courses. 전과하다 change one's course (to). ¶영문과로 ~ change to the English department.

전관(前官) the predecessor (in a post). ¶고관들은 퇴임 후에 ~예우를 받는다 High-ranking officials, after their retirement, are granted the privileges of their former posts.

전관(專管) [그 일만을 전적으로 책임지고 관리함] exclusive jurisdiction[competency]. 전관하다 have the exclusive jurisdiction (over).
- 전관 수역(-水域) waters under exclusive jurisdiction; an exclusive offshore zone; (한국의) Korean territorial water; waters within Korea's exclusive jurisdiction.

전광(電光) 1 lightning. ⇨번갯불 ¶~석화(石火)와 같이 like a flash of lightning / with lightning speed//그는 ~석화와 같이 그 소설을 완성했다 He finished (writing) the novel in no time.//그들은 ~석화처럼 잽싸게 텐트를 쳤다 They pitched their tents with lightning speed. 2 [전등의 불빛] electric light.
- 전광판 an electric bulletin board; (경기장의) an electric(al) scoreboard.

전교(全校) [학교 전체] the whole school. ¶~에서 가장 열심히 공부하는 학생 the most diligent[hardworking] student in the whole school//그는 항상 ~에서 1등이었다 He was always at the top[head] of the whole school.
- 전교생 the whole student body; all the students of the school. ¶~이 소풍을 갔다 The whole school[All the pupils] went on an excursion.//~을 대표하여 송 군이 환영사를 했다 On behalf of[Representing] all the students, Song made a welcome speech.

전교(轉交) [다른 사람을 거쳐 받게 함] care of(약어 c/o). ¶남궁 씨 ─ 선우 씨 앞 Mr. Seonu, c/o[care of] Mr. Namgung//편지는 민 선생 ~로 보내라 Write (to) me (in) care of Mr. Min. 전교하다 send (a letter) in care of[to the care of] (a person).

전구(前驅) a forerunner; a precursor; an outrider; the van; the vanguard.
- 전구 증상 prodromal[premonitory] symptoms (of); [의] a prodrome.

전구(前球) an electric[a light] bulb; an electric-light bulb; a bulb. ¶가스 ~ a gas-filled bulb//반투명[젖빛] ~ a frosted bulb//백열 ~ an incandescent light bulb//색 ~ a colored bulb//섬광[플래시] ~ a flash bulb//소형[꼬마] ~ a miniature bulb//100와트짜리 ~ a 100 watt bulb//끊어진 ~ a burntout light bulb//~를 소켓에 끼우다[에서 빼내다] screw a bulb into[out of] a socket//부엌의 ~가 끊어졌다 The (light) bulb in the kitchen has burnt out.

전국(全國) the whole country[land]; [전국 각지] all parts of the country. ¶~의 national / nationwide / countrywide//~에서[으로부터] from all over the country//~ 체육 대회 the National Sports[Athletic] Meet//한파가 ~을 덮쳤다 A cold wave hit the whole country[land].//대통령의 연설은 오늘 밤에 방송된다 President's speech[address] will be broadcast nationwide tonight.//응모자는 ~에서 모여들었다 Applicants gathered [came] from all parts of[all over] the country.
- 전국 경제인 연합회 the Federation of Korean Industries(약어 FKI). 전국구 the national[nationwide] constituency. 전국 대회 a national conference; (정당 등의) a national convention. ¶~를 개최하다 hold a national meeting[conference].

전국(戰局) [전쟁이 되어 가는 판국] the state[tide] of the war; the war situation. ¶~이 호전되었다 The tide of war turns in one's favor.//~은 일진일퇴이다 The war situation hangs in the balance[is very uncertain].//~은 하룻밤 사이에 변했다 The tide of the war has turned in a single night.//~이 아군에 불리해졌다 The (tide of) war turned against us.

전국(戰國) [역] the Warring States.
- 전국 시대 [역] the Age[Period] of the Warring states.

전국적(全國的) national; nationwide; countrywide. ¶~인 파업 countrywide strikes//~으로 all over the country[land] / throughout the country / in all parts of the country//~으로 유명한 사람 a man with national reputation//경찰은 교통사고를 방지하기 위하여

전군(全軍) the whole army [force]. ¶~을 지휘하다 command the whole army.

전권(全卷) 〔한 권의 책 전체〕 the whole volume; 〔여러 권 전체〕 a complete set. ¶~을 통하여 from cover to cover / through the book // ~을 통독하다 read the book from cover to cover / read through the book // 이 책은 ~에 기지가 넘친다 This book is full of wit from cover to cover. / The whole volume is full of wit.

전권(全權) full [plenary] power; absolute authority. ¶그들은 그 교섭의 ~을 그에게 위임했다 They invested [entrusted] him with full powers to carry out [on] the negotiations. // 그가 이 문제에 있어서는 ~을 쥐고 있다 He holds full power in this matter. // 송 씨는 이 문제의 ~을 위임받았다 Mr. Song was invested with complete authority [given carte blanche] on this issue.
● **전권 공사** a minister plenipotentiary. **전권 대사** an ambassador plenipotentiary. ¶특명 ~ an ambassador extraordinary and plenipotentiary.

전권(專權) an exclusive right; arbitrary power. ¶그는 ~의 비난을 면할 수가 없다 He is to blame for wielding his power arbitrarily. **전권하다** exercise [wield] arbitrary power (over).

전극(電極) an electrode; a pole. ¶양 [음] ~ a positive [negative] pole.

전근(轉勤) a transfer (to another's office); transference (to another's office). **전근하다** be transferred to. ➡ 그는 최근에 포항 지사로 전근되었다 He has recently been transferred to the Pohang branch (office). // 나는 본점으로 전근되었습니다 I was transferred to the head office.

전근대적(前近代的) 〔근대 이전의〕 premodern; 〔시대에 뒤진〕 old-fashioned; outdated. ¶그의 사고방식은 ~이다 He is out of date [behind his age] in thought.

전기(前記) ¶~의 foregoing / aforesaid / abovementioned / the said (person) // ~와 같은 이유로 for the abovementioned [aforesaid / foregoing] reasons // ~와 같은 사정이오니 such being the case. **전기하다** mention [say / refer to] above. ¶전기한 대로 이것은 중대한 문제다 As mentioned above, this is a serious problem. // 전기한 금액을 내 은행 계좌로 입금해 주십시오 Please pay the said amount into my bank account.

전기(前期) 〔1년의 전반기〕 the first half year; 〔앞의 시기〕 the preceding [last] term; (2학기제 대학의) the first term [semester]. ¶이것은 고려 ~의 토기이다 This earthenware belongs to the earlier Goryeo period.
● **전기 결산** settlement for the first half year. **전기 이월금** the sum brought [carried] over from the last account.

전기(傳記) a life (story); a biography. ¶슈바이처의 ~ a life of Albert Schweitzer // 보스웰이 쓴 존슨의 ~ Boswell's biography of Johnson // 나는 채플린의 ~을 읽고 감동했다 I read the biography [life] of Charles Chaplin and was very impressed.
● **전기 문학** biographical literature. **전기물** biographical writings. **전기 작가** a biographer.

전기(電氣) electricity; an electric current (전류). ¶동(動)~ current [dynamic / kinetic] electricity // 마찰 ~ frictional electricity // 수력 ~ hydroelectricity // 양~ positive electricity // 음~ negative electricity // 열(熱)~ thermal electricity // 정(靜)~ static electricity // ~의 electric / electrical / (연결형의) electro- // ~를 일으키다 generate electricity // ~를 통하다 [끊다] turn on [cut off] an electric current // ~를 절약하다 save electricity [current] // 이 전선에는 ~가 통하고 있다 This wire is live [charged with electricity / electrically charged]. / This is a live wire. // 차고에는 ~가 들어옵니까 Do you have electricity in your garage? // 이 기계는 ~로 움직인다 This machine works by electricity. // 이 자동차는 ~로 달린다 This automobile runs on electricity.
● **전기 검침원** an electricity checker [inspector]. **전기 공사** electric work. **전기 공학** electrical engineering. **전기 기구** an electric appliance. ¶가정용 ~ household electric appliance. **전기난로** an electric heater [(영) fire]. **전기다리미** an electric iron. **전기담요** an electric blanket. **전기료** electric charges; power rates. **전기면도기** an electric shaver [razor]. **전기 분해** electrolysis. **전기 역학** electrodynamics. **전기 용접** electric weld. **전기장** 〔물〕 an electric field. **전기 저항** electric(al) resistance (약어 R). **전기 절연체** an electric insulator. **전기 청소기** vacuum cleaner; (영) a hoover. ¶거실 양탄자를 ~로 청소하다 run a vacuum cleaner over the carpet in the sitting room. **전기 통신** telecommunication; electric communication. **전기 회로** an electric circuit. **전깃불** electric light. **전깃줄** an electric wire. ⇨ 전선(電線)

전기(電機) 〔전기의 힘으로 움직이는 기계〕 a piece of electric(al) machinery [equipment]. ¶중~ heavy electrical equipment.
● **전기 공업** electric machinery industry.

전기(戰記) a record of a war; a military history. ¶갈리아 ~ Commentaries on the Gallic Wars.

전기(戰機) 〔전쟁·전투가 일어나려는 기미〕 the time for fighting [battle]. ¶마침내 ~가 무르익었다 The moment has come to open hostilities [go into battle].

전기(轉記) posting. **전기하다** post; transfer.

전기(轉機) a turning point. ¶이것이 내 생애의 한 ~가 되었다 This was the turning point of my career. // 산업계로서는 대공황이 일대 ~가 되었다 The Great Depression was [proved to be] a major turning point for the industrial world. // 한국의 경제는 지금 ~에 서 있다 The economy of Korea is now at the turning point.

전나무 〔식〕 a fir (tree).

전날(前-) 1 〔바로 앞의 날〕 the previous [preceding] day; the day before. ¶크리스마스 ~ the day before Christmas // ~ 밤 the previous night / the night before / an eve (축제의) // 결혼식 ~에 on the day before the wedding. 2 〔지난날〕 the past (days); former days. ¶~의 일들 things of the past.

전남편(前男便) one's former husband; 〔이혼

전납 한 남편) one's ex-husband. ¶~의 자식 a child by her former husband.

전납(全納) full payment; payment in full. 전납하다 pay in full; pay the whole amount of (one's tax).

전납(前納) prepayment. ⇨선납(先納)

전년(前年) 1 last year. ⇨지난해 **2** [지나간 해] past years; a few years ago; former years. ¶그 ~ the year before // 이 공사는 ~부터 계속되고 있었다 The construction work had been going on since the previous year.
● **전년도** (회사 등의) the last fiscal [financial] year; (학교의) the last academic year. ¶~의 회계 보고 the financial report for the last year.

전념(專念) concentration of mind; undivided attention. **전념하다** be devoted (to) [absorbed (in)]; devote oneself (to); be intent (on); concentrate (on); devote one's mind (to); attend (to); apply oneself (to). ¶차분히 연구에 ~ settle down to one's research // 일에 ~ concentrate on one's work // 그는 공부에 전념했다 He applied his mind to study. // 나는 이 일에 전념하고 있습니다 I am putting my heart and soul into this job. // 그는 평생을 인도에서 전도에 전념했다 He devoted [dedicated] his life to missionary work in India.

전뇌(前腦) [생] the prosencephalon; the forebrain.

전능하다(全能-) almighty; omnipotent. ¶전지전능한 omniscient and omnipotent // 전능하신 하느님 Almighty God / the Almighty / God Almighty.

전단(全段) (신문의) a whole [an entire] page; the whole space. ¶~이 대지진 뉴스로 메워져 있었다 The whole [entire] page was taken up by news of the severe earthquake.
● **전단 표제** a banner (headline); a bannerline.

전단(剪斷) [잘라서 끊음] a shear; shearing. **전단하다** shear; cut with scissors.

전단(專斷) an arbitrary decision. **전단하다** act arbitrarily [on one's own authority].

전단(傳單) a bill; (손으로 주는) a handbill; (미) a handout; (접은 것) a leaflet; (벽보) a placard; a poster. ¶~을 돌리다 distribute handbills // ~을 뿌리다 distribute bills / broadcast leaflets // ~을 붙이다 stick [paste up] a bill / put up a poster / stick [put] up a placard // 비행기에서 ~을 뿌리다 drop leaflets from a plane // 괴상한 옷차림을 한 사람이 ~을 돌리고 있었다 A man in a strange costume was distributing [giving out] handouts [handbills]. // 조간신문에 광고 ~이 들어 있었다 Advertising bills were inserted between the pages of the morning paper.

전달(前-) 1 [어느 달의 바로 앞의 달] the previous [preceding] month; the month before. ¶그는 그 ~에 귀국했다 He had come home the previous month. // 나는 그가 죽기 ~에 그를 방문했다 I called on him the month before his death. **2** last month. ⇨지난달 ¶~에서 넘어온 이월금이 3만 원쯤 있다 There is about thirty thousand won carried over from last month.

전달(傳達) (메시지·생각·전기 등 일반적인) transmission; (정보 등의) communication; (생각 등의) conveyance. ¶음향의 ~은 광선보다 느리다 Sound travels slower than light. **전달하다** transmit; communicate; convey. ¶우리는 언어를 사용해서 사상이나 감정을 전달한다 We communicate ideas and feelings by means of language. // 이 일에 대해서는 그에게 편지로 전달하겠습니다 I will communicate with him by mail about the matter. // 이 감명을 말로는 전달할 수 없다 I cannot convey in words the deep impression this has made on me. ➔내 의도[이 뉴스]가 모든 사람에게 전달되기를 바란다 I would like my intentions [this news] to be correctly conveyed [transmitted] to everyone.
● **전달 경로** an avenue of communication.
전달자 [사자] a messenger.

전담(全擔) full [entire / whole] charge. **전담하다** assume [take] full charge; be wholly charged (for). ¶비용을 ~ bear [shoulder] the whole expenses // 사업의 운영을 ~ assume full charge of a business // 비용은 그가 전담했다 (구어) He picked up the entire check. // 그가 그 학교의 운영을 일체 전담하고 있다 He runs solely all the business end of the school.

전담(專擔) exclusive charge. ¶소매치기 ~반 a pickpocket squad. **전담하다** take [bear / assume] exclusive charge (of); be exclusively charged (for).

전답(田畓) rice paddies and dry fields. ⇨논밭

전당(典當) pawn; pledge; (미국 속어) hock.
전당(을) 잡다 take (a thing) in pawn [pledge]. ¶전당 잡는 사람 a pawnee / a pledgee // 전당 잡고 있다 hold (a thing) in pawn.
전당(을) 잡히다 pawn; pledge; give [put] (something) in pawn; give to [lay in / put in] pledge; (미국 속어) hock. ¶전당 잡히는 사람 a pawner / a pledger // 전당 잡혀 있다 be in [at] pawn // (미국 속어) be in hock // 시계를 전당 잡혔다 I have given [put] my watch in pawn. // 보석을 전당 잡히고 10만 원을 빌렸다 I pawned a jewel for ₩100,000.
● **전당포** a pawnbroker's shop; a pawnshop; (미국 속어) a hock shop; (영국 속어) a popshop. ¶~에 드나들다 frequent a pawnshop. **전당품** a pawn; an article for pawning. ¶~을 도로 찾다 take [get / redeem] out of pawn.

전당(殿堂) 1 [훌륭한 건물] a palace; a hall; a grand building. ¶예술의 ~ a sanctuary [magnificent repository] of the fine arts // 야구의 ~ the Baseball Hall of Fame. **2** [신불을 모시는 건물] a shrine; a temple. ¶신의 ~ a sanctuary of God.

전당 대회(全黨大會) the national convention of a party; a party convention. ¶2002년의 민주당 ~ the 2002 Democratic Party Convention.

전대(前代) [앞의 세대] the previous generation; [지난 시대] the last period.
● **전대미문(-未聞)** ¶~의 unheard-of / unprecedented / unparalleled / record-breaking // ~의 대사고 an accident of unprecedented magnitude [scale] // 그는 금메달 6개라는 ~의 일을 해냈다 He pulled off the unheard-of [unprecedented] feat of winning six gold medals. // 이번 독직 사건은 금액에 있어서 ~이다 This bribery [corruption] case exceeds all records in the amount of money involved.

전대(戰隊) 〔함대〕 a squadron; a flotilla(▶ 둘 이상의 squadron으로 이루어짐). ¶~를 짜다 assemble [form] a squadron.

전대(轉貸) (토지의) underlease; sublease; (가옥의) underletting; subletting. **전대하다** sublet [subrent] (a house); sublease [underlease] (land). ¶집을 ~ sublet [sublease] a house // 빌딩 [토지]을 ~ sublease a building [land].
● **전대인** a sublessor.

전대(纏帶) a money bag; (허리에 차는) waist porch.

전도(全圖) a complete map. ¶대한민국 ~ a complete map of Korea // 세계 ~ a world map.

전도(前途) 1 〔나아갈 길〕 the way one has still to go; the distance yet to cover. ¶~는 아직 멀다 I have a long way to go. 2 the future. ⇨ ＊장래 ¶~가 암담하다 have a gloomy prospect // 우리는 신혼부부의 ~를 축하하여 건배했다 We drank to a happy future for the newly married couple. // 그의 ~는 험난하다 Various problems lie in his way [ahead of him]. // 자동차 산업의 ~는 어둡다 The prospects for the automobile industry are dark [black].

전도(前渡) (돈의) advance payment; payment in advance; (물건의) delivery in advance. **전도하다** pay [deliver] in advance.
● **전도금** advanced money; an advance; an advancement.

전도(傳道) mission (work); gospel preaching; evangelical work. ¶국내 [국외] ~ home [foreign] mission work // 크리스트교의 ~ (문어) the propagation of Christianity. **전도하다** be engaged in mission [missionary] work(▶ 주로 비(非)크리스트교 국가에서 하는 경우); spread [preach] the gospel; propagate one's religion. ¶크리스트교를 ~ preach [(문어) propagate] Christianity / missionize / evangelize // 그는 한국 각지에서 크리스트교를 전도하고 다녔다 He preached Christianity throughout Korea.
● **전도사** 〔선교사〕 a missionary; 〔복음 전파자〕 an evangelist. **전도 사업** missionary work.

전도(傳導) 〔열·전기의〕 conduction; transmission. ¶열의 ~ heat conduction. **전도하다** conduct; transmit. ¶구리는 전기를 가장 잘 전도한다 Copper conducts electricity best. // 금속은 열을 전도한다 Metals transmit heat.
● **전도성** conductibility. ¶~이 있는 conductible / conductive. **전도율 / 전도도** conductivity. **전도체** a conductor. ¶비~ a nonconductor.

전도(顚倒) 1 〔엎드러짐〕 a fall; overturn. **전도하다** fall (to the ground); overturn; tumble (down). 2 〔거꾸로 함〕 the reverse; inversion. **전도하다** reverse; invert (상하가). → ¶그것은 본말이 전도된 이야기다 That is putting the cart before the horse [mistaking the means for the end]. // 주객이 전도되어 미국 여자가 김치를 담가 주었다 Reserving our positions, the American girl fixed us gimchi(kimchi).

전도요원하다(前途遙遠─) (사람이) have a long [far] way to go; have a long way before one; (일이) be far [a long way] off. ¶목적지까지는 ~ We are still far from our destination [goal]. / We still have a long way to go before we reach our goal. // 우주선을 타고 화성으로 여행할 수 있기까지는 아직 ~ The day is still far off when we can take a spaceship to Mars.

전동(電動) 〔관형어적〕 electromotive; electric-powered.
● **전동기** an electric motor; an electromotor; a motor. ¶교류 ~ an AC [alternating current] motor // 직류 ~ a DC [direct current] motor // 유도 ~ an induction motor. **전동력** electromotive force. ⇨ ＊기전력(⇨ 기전) **전동발전기** a motor generator. **전동차** a train run by electricity; a [an electric] train.

전두(前頭) 〔머리의 앞부분〕 the front (of the head); the forehead (이마); 〔의〕 the sinciput.
● **전두골** the frontal bone. **전두엽**(─葉) the frontal lobe.

전등(電燈) an electric light [lamp] (▶ 자명할 때는 단순히 a light [lamp]). ¶~의 갓 a lampshade // 회중~ an electric torch / 《미》 a flashlight // ~을 켜다 turn [switch] on the light // ~을 끄다 turn [switch] off the light // ~이 밝다 [어둡다] The light is bright [dim]. // 갑자기 ~이 꺼졌다 The light went out suddenly. // ~이 들어오지 않는다 The light won't come on.

전라(全裸) stark nakedness. ¶~의 stark naked // ~의 여성 a woman in the nude // ~의 그림 a nude picture // 그는 ~로 거기에 누워 있었다 He lay there stark naked [with nothing on].

전락(轉落) 〔타락〕 degradation; 〔영락〕 ruin; downfall. **전락하다** degrade; be ruined; go to ruin. ¶우리 팀은 최하위로 전락했다 Our team fell into last place [the cellar]. // 잭은 마약 상습자로 전락했다 Jack became a drug addict [(미국 구어) a junkie].
● **전락자** a ruined person.

전란(戰亂) 〔전쟁〕 war; 〔전투〕 battle; 〔동란〕 disturbances. ¶~의 유고슬라비아 war-torn Yugoslavia // 아름다운 전원이 ~의 도가니로 변했다 The beautiful countryside was turned into a battlefield.

전람(展覽) exhibition; show; display. **전람하다** exhibit; put [place] (paintings) on exhibition [display]; display; show.
● **전람실** a showroom. **전람회** an exhibition; an exhibit; a show. ¶미술 ~ an art exhibition // ~에 그림을 출품하다 put a painting on display at an exhibition // ~를 개최하다 [보러 가다] hold [visit] an exhibition // 저 백화점에서는 피카소의 ~가 열리고 있다 That department store is holding [having] a Picasso exhibition. **전람회장** an exhibition gallery [hall].

전래(傳來) 1 〔전해 내려옴〕 transmission. ¶조상 ~의 가업 a hereditary occupation // 그는 조상 ~의 땅을 팔았다 He sold the family estate. // 이것이 조상 ~의 비술이다 This secret has been handed down [transmitted] from our ancestors. **전래하다** be transmitted; be handed down.
2 〔도래〕 introduction; importation; influx. ¶중국 ~의 문자 letters [writing] of Chinese origin. **전래하다** be imported [introduced]. ¶불교는 4세기에 한국에 전래했다 Buddhism was first introduced into Korea in the fourth century. → ¶이것은 조선 시대에 전래된 것이다 This was introduced into Korea in the Joseon dynasty period.

전략(前略) 〔앞부분을 줄이는 것〕 omission of

전략

what precedes. **전략하다** omit the preface. ¶전략하옵고 (편지에서) I hasten to inform you that ... / Just a line to tell you that ....

전략(戰略) (a) strategy; a stratagem. ¶~을 세우다 plan[work out / map out] a strategy / devise a stratagem // ~을 짜내다 elaborate a strategy // 그 ~을 세운 것은 그 사람이다 It is he who worked[mapped] out the strategy. // 그 섬은 ~상 중요하다 The island is strategically important[important from the strategic point of view].

● **전략가** a strategist. **전략 무기** strategic arms. **전략 무기 제한 협정** the Strategic Arms Limitation Talks(약어 SALT). **전략 물자** strategic goods[materials]. **전략 산업** a strategic industry. **전략 핵무기** strategic nuclear arms. **전략 회의** a strategy meeting.

전략적(戰略的) strategic; strategical. ¶~ 후퇴 a strategic retreat // ~ 거점 a strategic point // ~으로 strategically.

전량(全量) the whole quantity.

전력(全力) all one's power[strength / might / energy]; one's best[utmost]. ¶~을 다하여 with all one's might / to the best of one's ability / to the utmost (of one's power) // ~을 다하다 do one's best[utmost] / do all one can / do everything in one's power / devote [apply] all one's energies (to) // 그는 ~을 다해서 밧줄을 당겼다 He pulled on the rope with all his strength[might]. // 나는 문제의 해결에 ~을 다했다 I tried[did] my best [utmost] to solve the problem. // 그녀는 장애아의 양육에 ~을 기울였다 She devoted all her energies to bringing up handicapped children.

전력(前歷) one's past[previous] record; one's past history[life]; a past(수상한). ¶경찰은 그의 ~을 조사했다 The police checked [inquired into] his past record[history]. // 너는 ~을 감추고 그 자리에 응모했다 She concealed her past when she applied for the position. // 그녀는 수상한 ~을 갖고 있다 She is a woman with a past.

전력(電力) electric power. ¶공업용 ~ industrial electric power // 도시에 ~을 공급하다 supply a city with electric power // ~을 절약하다 save electricity // ~이 낭비되고 있다 Electricity is being wasted. // ~ 소비량이 상승했다 The consumption of electricity has taken a jump[leap] (upward).

● **전력계** a wattmeter. **전력 부족** a power shortage. ¶그 지방은 ~으로 시달리고 있다 They are suffering from an electric power shortage in that area. **전력 사정** the (electric) power situation. **전력 제한** power restrictions; restrictions adopted to save electricity.

전력(戰力) [병력] military strength; (잠재적인) war potential; [전투력] fighting power [strength]. ¶어느 나라나 ~의 증강을 도모하고 있다 Each nation is attempting to strengthen[build up] its war potential. // 두 선수가 합류하여 우리 팀의 ~이 크게 강화되었다 The two new players have proved a real asset to the team. / Since the two players joined our team, our strength has greatly increased.

● **전력 유지**[상실] the maintenance[loss] of war potential. **전력 증강** the strengthening of war potential.

전력(戰歷) war career[record]. ¶~이 혁혁한 군인 a veteran of many campaigns.

전령(傳令) a messenger; a message runner. ¶기마 ~ a despatch rider // 사령부에 ~을 보내다 send a messenger[a runner] to headquarters.

전령(電鈴) [전종] an electric bell. ¶~을 누르다 ring an electric bell.

전례(前例) a precedent; a previous instance. ¶~ 없는 일 an unprecedented matter / an unheard-of affair // ~에 의해서 according to a precedent // ~가 되다 become[give] a precedent // ~를 만들다 set[make / create] a precedent // ~를 깨다 violate[depart from] the precedent / break the precedent // ~로 삼다 take (a matter) as a precedent // ~를 따르다 follow a precedent // 그것에는 ~가 없다 There is no precedent for it. / It is without a precedent. // 그것은 ~가 없는 일이다 It is an unprecedented matter.

전류(電流) an electric(al) current; a flow of electricity. ¶고압 ~ a high voltage[tension] current // 교류 ~ an alternating current(약어 A.C.) // 직류 ~ a direct current(약어 D.C.) // 무효 ~ a wattless current // ~의 세기 the intensity of an electric current / current intensity // ~가 통하고 있는 전선 a live wire // 전선에 ~를 통하다 send electric current into a wire / pass electric current through a wire / charge a wire with electricity // 텔레비전에 ~를 통하다 connect a television to electricity // ~를 끊다 shut off the current / turn off the electricity // ~가 끊어졌다 The current was off. // 콘센트에 플러그를 꽂으면 ~가 통한다 Put the plug into the outlet, and the current will be on.

● **전류계** an ammeter.

전륜(前輪) a front wheel.

● **전륜 구동**(―驅動) front-wheel drive. ¶~의 차 a car with front-wheel drive.

전리(電離) [물] electrolytic dissociation. **전리하다** ionize. 2 ionization. ⇨ 이온화(⇨이온)

● **전리층** the ionosphere.

전리품(戰利品) a trophy (of war)(▶ 종종 복수형); [노획품] spoils (of war); booty.

전립(戰笠) [무관이 썼던 벙거지] a soldier's felt hat.

전립선(前立腺) [생] the prostate (gland). ¶~의 prostate / prostatic.

● **전립선 비대증** prostatomegaly. **전립선염** prostatitis.

전말(顚末) [자초지종] everything (about); [전체적 경과] the whole story; [자세한 설명] the full account; [사정] the whole circumstance; [경위] the course of events. ¶그는 사건의 ~을 이야기했다 He gave a full [detailed] account of the event. // 그가 사과하게 된 ~은 이렇다 This is how he came to apologize.

전망(展望) 1 [조망] a view; a prospect; an lookout. ¶이 언덕에서는 김제평야의 ~이 좋다 This hill commands a fine view of the Gimje plains. / We can get a fine view of the Gimje plains from this hill. // 높은 담이 가리고 있어 ~이 좋지 않다 The view is obstructed by a high wall. // 창에서 보는 ~이 좋다 There is a fine view from the window. / The window commands a fine view. // 2층 창문에서 보는 산의 ~이 매우 좋다 From my upstairs window I have a wide view of the

mountains. **전망하다** look out (over); take an extensive view (of); [둘러보다] survey; look around. ¶언덕 위에서는 전 시가지를 전망할 수 있다 The hill commands a view of the whole town. **2** [장래를 내다봄] a prospect; an outlook (for); [예측] a forecast (for). ¶내년도의 경제 ~ the prospects for the economy next year // 사업의 ~은 좋지 않다 Business prospects are discouraging. // 일의 ~이 아직 서지 않는다 The outlook for the work is still vague. // 경기 회복의 ~이 보이지 않는다 There is no knowing when the economy will recover [(구어) pick up again]. // 마침내 연구를 완성할 ~이 보인다 At last the completion of my research is in sight. **전망하다** survey; make a survey of; forecast (the future). ¶우리나라의 식량 사정을 ~ survey [make a survey of] the food situation in our country // 그는 독특하게 정계를 전망했다 He gave his unique views on the political world.
● **전망대** an observatory; an observation platform; a lookout. **전망탑** an observation tower; (잠수함의) a conning tower.

전매(專賣) [독점 판매] a monopoly; monopolization. **전매하다** have [maintain] a monopoly (on tobacco); monopolize.
● **전매권** monopoly; exclusive right(s). **전매특허** a patent. ¶~를 얻다 [출원하다] get [apply for] a patent (on) // ~를 인가하다 grant a patent // ~ 출원 중 (게시) A patent applied for. / Patent pending. **전매특허권** patent rights. **전매특허품** a patented article. **전매품** articles under monopoly; monopoly goods. ¶이 나라에서는 담배가 정부의 ~이다 Tobacco is a government monopoly in this country.

전매(轉賣) (a) resale; (증권의) a liquidation sale. **전매하다** resell. ¶그는 토지를 전매하여 큰돈을 벌었다 He made a fortune by repeatedly buying and selling land.

전면(全面) **1** [면 전체] the whole [entire] surface. ¶벽 ~에 페인트칠을 하다 paint the wall all over. **2** [모든 방면] all sides [aspects]. ¶~에 걸쳐 연구하다 study (a subject) in all its aspects // 이 문제는 ~에 걸쳐 조사가 이루어지고 있다 This question is being considered from all sides. / (문어) The matter is being studied in all its aspects. **3** [신문의 전 지면] the whole space (of a newspaper). ¶그 뉴스가 ~을 메웠다 The whole page was covered with the news.
● **전면 광고** a full-page advertisement. **전면전 / 전면 전쟁** (an) all-out war; (a) full-scale war; a general war.

전면(前面) the front; the frontage; (건축물의) the facade. ¶~에 in front (of) / in the foreground // ~으로 나오다 come to the fore [front] // ~에 적군의 참호가 있었다 The enemy trenches were directly in front of us. // 그 집의 ~은 희게 칠해져 있었다 The front of the house was painted white.

전면적(全面的) all-out; whole; entire; overall; general; complete; sweeping. ¶~인 임금 인상 [삭감] an across-the-board wage hike [cut] // ~인 통제 full control // ~으로 wholly / entirely / sweepingly // 핵무기의 ~ 금지를 주장하다 advocate the complete [overall] abolition of nuclear weapons // ~인 규약 개정이 이루어졌다 There was a complete [sweeping] revision of the rules. // 그의 제안은 ~으로 거부되었다 His proposal was rejected in its entirety. / All the terms of his proposal were turned down.

전멸(全滅) complete [total] destruction; annihilation; extermination. ¶그 야생의 새는 ~ 직전에 있다 That species of bird is on the verge of extinction. **전멸하다** be wiped out; be completely destroyed; be annihilated; be exterminated; be crushed. ¶수비대는 폭격으로 전멸했다 The defenders were bombed and wiped out. // 우리 팀은 전멸했다 Our team suffered a total defeat. / The other team annihilated us. // 이 살충제면 흰개미는 전멸할 것이다 This insecticide will exterminate the termites. ➔ **전멸시키다** wipe out / destroy completely / annihilate / exterminate / crush 우리는 적을 전멸시켰다 We crushed our enemy.

전모(全貌) [전체의 모양] the whole [entire] picture (of); the whole aspect; the full [whole] story; details (상세). ¶그 사건의 ~가 차차 밝혀지기 시작했다 The whole picture [story] of what had happened gradually became clear. // 그는 이 보고서에서 그 음모의 ~를 밝히고 있다 He reveals the secret plot in its entirety in this report. // 그는 계획 ~를 말해 주었다 He told me the details of his project.

전몰(戰歿) death in battle [action]. ⇨전사(戰死)
● **전몰장병** (개인) a fallen soldier; 《집합적》 the war dead.

전무(專務) **1** [전문적으로 맡아보는 사무] one's principal duty. **2** (사장을 보좌하여 업무를 관장하는 사람) a (senior) managing director.

전무하다(全無—) wholly lacking [wanting]. ¶그가 승진할 기회는 ~ He has no chance whatever of being promoted. // 그는 책임감이라고는 ~ He has no sense of responsibility whatsoever. // 그녀는 교사로서는 적성이 ~ She has absolutely no right to be a teacher. // 나는 우주 과학의 지식이 ~ I know nothing at all about space science.

전무후무하다(前無後無—) unprecedented; unheard-of; unparalleled; record-breaking; all-time. ¶전무후무한 기록 an all-time record // 그것은 전무후무한 쾌거다 It is the first and probably the last brilliant achievement. // 매출액은 전무후무한 고액에 달했다 Sales have reached an all-time high. // 그 전람회는 전무후무한 성황을 이뤘다 The exhibition was an unprecedented [unparalleled] success. // 이와 같은 베스트셀러는 전무후무한 것이라 해도 좋을 게다 We have never had and never again will have such a best seller as this.

전문(全文) [문장의 전체] the whole sentence [passage]; [연설 등의 본문 전체] the full [whole] text. ¶헌법 [조약]의 ~ the full [complete] text of the Constitution [a treaty] // 편지의 ~ the whole letter // ~을 인용하다 quote the whole sentence [passage].

전문(前文) **1** [앞에 쓴 글] the above [foregoing] sentence. ¶~에서 언급한 바와 같이 as is stated [mentioned] above. **2** [서문] a preamble.

전문(專門) a specialty; (영) a speciality; (구어) line; [연구 과제 [분야]] subject [field] of study. ¶~의 [특별한 분야의] special / [특별한 기술·지식을 필요로 하는] technical / [특

전문

별한 직업의] professional // …의 ~ 메이커 manufacturers specialized in the production of … // 소비의 연구를 ~으로 하다 make a special[specialize in the] study of consumption // 역사학을 ~으로 하다 specialize in [make a specialty of] history // 대학에서 역사를 ~으로 공부하다 (미) major in history at college / (영) read history at university // 그것을 연구하는 데는 물리학의 ~ 지식이 필요하다 That research requires a special[technical] knowledge of physics. // 그는 ~ 음악가이다 He is a professional musician. // 화학은 나의 ~이 아니다 Chemistry is not in my line[field]. // 이 가게는 수입품을 ~으로 취급하고 있다 This store specializes in imported goods. // 그것은 내 ~이 아니다 It is not in my line [outside my (specialized) field].
● **전문가** a specialist; a professional; (특히 숙련된) an expert (in). ¶농업 ~ an expert in agriculture // 요리의 ~ [직업으로 하는 사람] a professional cook / [달인] an expert in cooking // 이 그림은 ~ 뺨치는 그림이다 This picture puts even a professional to shame. // 우리는 이 방면의 ~의 의견을 들어야만 한다 We must seek expert[professional] advice. // 그의 노래는 ~가 무색할 정도다 He sings like a professional. / He sings so well that he puts professionals to shame. **전문 교육** (기능을 가르치는) technical training; (고도의) professional education. **전문대학** a college. **전문어** a technical term. **전문 위원** an expert advisor; a technical expert. **전문의**(-醫) a medical specialist. ¶안과 ~ an eye specialist / an ophthalmologist // 심장병 ~ a heart specialist. **전문점** a specialty store[(영) shop]; a store specializing in (men's wear). **전문지** a technical journal[magazine]. ¶의학[경제] ~ a medical[an economic] journal. **전문 지식** expert knowledge. **전문학교** ➡전문대학(⇨전문) **전문화** specialization. ¶~하다 specialize // 오늘날 많은 분야의 학문이 고도의 ~되어 있다 These days study in many fields is highly specialized.

전문(電文) [전보] a telegram; [전보에 의한 통신문] a telegraphic message; (해외로부터의) a cablegram. ¶즉시 오라는 ~이었다 The telegram said to come at once. // ~의 뜻을 알 수가 없다 The (wording of the) telegram makes no sense.

전문(傳聞) [전하여 들음] hearsay; a report. ¶나는 ~으로 알고 있을 뿐이다 I know about it only from [by] hearsay. **전문하다** hear [learn] from others; know by report; learn [know] by hearsay. ¶전문한 바에 의하면 각료가 독직 사건에 연루되어 있다고 한다 I hear [It is said] that cabinet ministers are involved in a bribery case.
● **전문 증거** hearsay evidence. **전문 증인** a hearsay witness.

전문적(專門的) [특별한 분야의] special; [특별한 기술·지식을 필요로 하는] technical; [특별한 직업의] professional. ¶~ 지식 expert [technical / special] knowledge // 그것은 고도로 ~인 일이다 It's highly technical matter.

전미(全美) [관형어적]. ¶~의 all-American // ~ 선수권 an all-American championship.

전반(全般) the whole. ¶사회 ~ the world at large // 미술사 ~ art history in general // 한국의 교육 ~ Korean education on the whole // ~에 걸쳐서 generally / by and large / across the board // 과학 ~에 걸치다 cover the whole field[range] of science // ~의 ~에 걸쳐 연구하다 make a general study (of) / study (a subject) in all its bearings[aspects] // 그것은 학생 ~의 문제이다 It is a problem of students in general.

전반(前半) [앞의 절반] the first half; (럭비 등) the first period. ¶그해의 ~은 일기가 불순했다 The weather was unsettled during the first half of the year. // 그녀는 30대 ~이다 She is in her early thirties.
● **전반기** the first half year. **전반전** the first half of the game.

전반사(全反射) total reflection.

전반적(全般的) whole; general; overall. ¶~으로 [일반적으로] generally / [전체적으로] on the whole / overall // 내년의 경기에 대한 우리의 ~인 견해 our general opinion of how thing will go next year // ~으로 논하다 make a general comment (on) // ~으로 고찰하다 consider (a matter) by and large / study (a matter) in all its aspects // 금년에는 ~으로 비가 많다 On the whole we have had a lot of rain this year.

전방(前方) 1 [앞쪽] the front. ¶~의 front / forward / ~에 ahead / in front of / before // 백 미터 ~에 선로가 있다 There are tracks 100 meters ahead. // ~에 곰이 나타났다 A bear appeared before[in front of] us. // ~에 인가의 지붕이 보였다 Roofs of houses appeared ahead of us. 2 [제일선] the front (line). ¶~의 병사들 the men on the front line.
● **전방 기지** an advanced base; an outpost. **전방 부대** a forward unit; a unit on the front line.

전방(廛房) a store; (영) a shop.

전번(前番) the last time. ⇨¬지난번

전범(戰犯) (범죄) war crimes; (사람) a war criminal.
● **전범 용의자** a suspected war criminal; a war criminal suspect.

전법(戰法) [낱낱의 전술] tactics(▶ 단수·복수 취급); [종합적인 전략] (a) strategy. ¶그들은 기습 ~으로 이겼다 They won by surprise tactics.

전변(轉變) [변하여 바뀜] constant change; mutation; vicissitude. ¶인생의 ~ the vicissitudes of life // ~ 무상의 vicissitudinous / ever-shifting[-changing] / changeful / inconstant. **전변하다** change constantly; mutate.

전별(餞別) [서운하여 잔치를 베풀고 작별함] a send-off. **전별하다** see (a person) off; give (a person) send-off.
● **전별연**(-宴) a farewell[send-off] party; a farewell dinner.

전병(煎餅) a kind of cake made by mixing various flours. ⇨¬부꾸미

전보(電報) a telegram; a telegraphic message; (구어) a wire; a telegraph; a dispatch. ¶국내[국제] ~ a domestic[an international] telegram // 발신[수신] ~ an outgoing [incoming] telegram // 시간 외 ~ a late telegram[message] // 암호[친전] ~ a code [confidential] telegram // 외국 ~ a foreign telegram / a cable // 지급 ~ an urgent [express] telegram // ~로 by wire[telegraph / cable / telegram] // ~를 치다 send[dispatch] a telegram (to) / telegraph (to) /

(영) wire (to) / send a wire // ~를 배달하다 deliver a telegram // 송금 의뢰의 ~를 치다 telegraph [wire] (a person) for money // 나는 그녀에게 ~를 쳤다 I sent her a telegram. // 도착 시간은 ~로 알려 주게 Telegraph [Wire] me the time of your arrival. / Let me know the time of your arrival by telegraph [wire]. // 형에게서 어머니 위독이라는 ~가 왔다 My brother telegraphed [wired] me that my mother was seriously ill.
● **전보료** a telegram fee [charge]. **전보용지** a telegram form [(미) blank].

전보(塡補) [부족을 채움] compensation; making up. **전보하다** compensate for; make up for; make good. ¶결손을 ~ make up for [cover] the deficit.

전보(轉補) transference; shuffling. ¶~를 명하다 transfer (a person). **전보하다** transfer. ➔ ¶전보되다 be transferred (to another position).

전복(全鰒) an abalone; an ear shell.
● **전복죽** abalone porridge.

전복(顚覆) an overthrow; an overturn; an upset; subversion; capsizal. ¶그들은 정부의 ~을 기도했다 They plotted to overthrow the government. **전복하다** be overthrown [overturned]; be capsized. ¶열차는 탈선으로 전복했다 The train (was) overturned when it derailed. / The train jumped the tracks and overturned. // 보트는 큰 파도에 밀려 전복했다 A boat was capsized by [A boat capsized in] high waves. ➔ ¶전복시키다 overthrow / overturn / subvert / capsize // 반란군이 정부를 전복시켰다 The rebels overthrew [overturned] the government.

전봇대(電報-) (전선용) an electric (light) pole; (전신용) a telephone pole.

전부(全部) [전체] the whole; [합계] the total; (부사) all; entirely; in all; altogether; all told. ¶~의 all / whole / total // 그 시는 ~ 외우고 있다 I can recite the whole poem by heart. / I have memorized the entire poem. // 사과는 ~ 썩고 말았다 All (of) the apples have gone bad. // 내 이야기를 ~ 듣기 전에는 돌아가면 안 된다 You may not leave until you have heard me out [to the end]. // 내가 할 수 있는 일은 ~ 해 보았다 I have tried every possible [conceivable] means. // 그의 책이 ~ 재미있다고는 할 수 없다 Not all of his books are interesting. // 나는 목수 연장은 ~ 갖추고 있다 I have a complete set of carpenter's tools. // 부상자는 ~ 13명이었다 All told, thirteen persons were injured. // 여비는 ~ 5만 원 들었다 The travel expenses totaled fifty thousand won. // 내게는 그녀가 ~다 She is everything to me. // 그들의 안(案)은 ~ 각하되었다 All their proposals were rejected.

전부(前部) [앞의 부분] the front (part); the fore; the forepart. ¶배의 ~ the fore part of a ship.

전부(戰斧) [옛날에 전쟁할 때 쓰던 도끼] a battle-ax [(영) -axe].

전분(澱粉) starch. ⇨ "녹말

전비(前非) [이전에 저지른 잘못] one's past misdeed [sin]. ¶~를 뉘우치다 repent of one's past misdeeds [sins].

전비(戰費) war expenditure; the cost of war.

전비(戰備) preparations for war; war [warlike] preparations. ¶그들은 ~를 갖추느라 정신이 없었다 They were hastily preparing for war.

전사(戰士) 1 [전투하는 병사] a warrior; a combatant; a fighter. ¶무명~(의 묘) (the tomb of) the unknown soldier. 2 [제일선에서 활약하고 있는 사람] a frontline worker. ¶산업 ~ an industrial worker // 자유의 ~ a champion of liberty.

전사(戰史) the history of a war; a war history. ¶이 작전은 ~에 남을 것이다 This battle strategy will live in the annals of war [go down in history].

전사(戰死) death in battle [action]. **전사하다** die in a war; be killed in action [battle]; die [fall] in battle. ¶명예롭게 ~ die a glorious [heroic] death on the field of battle / meet glorious death in action.
● **전사자** a person killed in action [battle]; (집합적) the war dead.

전사(轉寫) [옮기어 베낌] transcription; copying. **전사하다** copy; transcribe (▶ 다른 문자·기호로 바꾸어 쓰는 것도 포함). ¶신문에서 이 한 구절을 전사했습니다 I copied this paragraph from a newspaper. // 테이프를 발음 기호로 전사하시오 Transcribe the tape in(to) phonetic signs [symbols].
● **전사 잉크** transfer ink. **전사지** transfer paper.

전산(電算) computation [calculation] by computer.
● **전산기** a [an electronic] computer. ⇨ 전자계산기(⇨)전자(電子) **전산화** computerization. ¶사무 처리가 ~되었다 The clerical work has been taken over by computers.

전상(戰傷) a war wound. **전상하다** be wounded in battle [action].
● **전상병** a wounded soldier. **전상자** a person wounded in a war; a wounded serviceman; (집합적) the war wounded.

전생(前生) [불] a previous [former] existence [life]. ¶~의 인연 karma relations (from a previous life) / predestination / fate // 이렇게 된 것도 ~에서 지은 죄의 갚음인지도 모른다 The miserable plight I am in may be punishment for sins I committed in a former existence [life]. // 우연한 사귐도 ~의 인연이다 Even a chance acquaintance is clue to the karma in a previous life.

전서(全書) a compendium (pl. ~s, -dia); a complete book. ¶육법~ a compendium of laws // 백과~ an encyclop(a)edia.

전서(前書) [전에 보낸 편지] one's last [previous] letter. ¶고린도 ~ The First Epistle of St. Paul to the Corinthians / I Corinthians(약어 I Cor.).

전서(篆書) an ancient style of writing Chinese characters (still in use for seals).

전서구(傳書鳩) [통신에 이용되는 훈련된 비둘기] a carrier [homing] pigeon. ¶본부로 ~를 날려 보내다 release a carrier [homing] pigeon in the direction of headquarters // ~로 메시지를 보내다 send a message by carrier pigeon.

전선(全線) the whole [entire] line; all line; (전장의) the whole battle line. ¶경부선은 ~에 걸쳐 불통이다 Train service has been stopped along the whole (length) of the Gyeongbu [Seoul-Busan] Line. // ~이 개통되기까지는 아직 두 시간쯤 걸린다 It will be about two hours before the whole [entire] line is reopened.

전선(前線) 1 [전장의 제1선] the front. ¶~으로 돌아오다 return to the front // ~에서 격한 전투가 있었다 There was a fierce battle at the front. 2 [기상] a front. ¶한랭[온난]~ a cold[warm] front // 장마~ a seasonal rain front // ~이 통과할 때 돌풍이 불었다 As the front passed, strong winds blew.
● **전선 기지** an advance base. **전선 부대** a unit at the front.

전선(電線) an electric wire; (전등의) electric light wire; (전신용의) telegraph wire [line]. ¶고압~ a high-tension wire [line] / (미) high-voltage cable // 해저~ a cable // ~을 끌다 put up electric wires // 집에 ~을 끌다 wire a house for electricity // 폭풍우로 ~이 끊어졌다 Power lines were broken[snapped] by the storm.

전선(戰船) [전투에 사용하는 배] a war vessel; a fighting ship.

전선(戰線) 1 [전장에서] a (battle) front; the fighting line. ¶서부~에서는 on the western front // ~에 가다 go to the front // 그는 ~에 나가 있다 He is at the front. // 영국은 독일에 대하여 프랑스와 공동~을 폈다 England and France formed a united front against Germany. 2 (사회 운동 등의). ¶통일~ a united front // 인민~ a popular front.

전설(傳說) a legend; a tradition; [민화] a folktale. ¶민간~ a popular tradition / folk-lore // 고대 한국의 ~ an early Korean legend // 예로부터의 ~ a tradition handed down (by word of mouth) from old times // ~로 유명한 도시 a fabled city / a city celebrated in fable[legend] // 고장의 ~에 의하면 옛날 이 호수에 용이 살았다고 한다 A local legend has it that [According to a local legend] a dragon lived in this lake long ago. // 그것은 마을의 ~에 남아 있다 It has been handed down among the villagers. // 그는 우리나라의 ~적 인물이다 He is a legend in our country.

전성(全盛) the height [zenith] of prosperity [power]. ¶당시 그 일족이 ~을 이루고 있었다 At that time the family was at the height of its prosperity. **전성하다** flourish. ¶사실주의가 전성하고 있었다 Realism was in all its glory.
● **전성기 / 전성시대** the period[age] of prosperity; the golden age; the heyday; (사람의) one's best days. ¶철강업의 ~에 in the heyday[golden age] of the steel industry // 그는 지금 ~에 있다 He is now in his prime [at the peak of his career].

전성(展性) (금속의) malleability. ¶~이 있는 malleable.

전성(轉成) [바뀌어 다른 것이 됨] transformation; transmutation. **전성하다** be transformed (into); change (into).
● **전성어** [파생어] a derivative; [외래어] a loanword.

전세(前世) 1 the previous generation. ⇨ 전대(前代) 2 [불] a previous existence. ⇨ 전생(前生)

전세(專貰) charter; chartering. ¶관광 여행을 위해 버스를 ~내다 charter a bus for sightseeing // 그들은 버스를 ~내어 여행길에 나섰다 They went on a trip in a chartered bus. // 우리는 하와이까지 비행기를 ~냈다 We chartered a plane for a flight to Hawaii.
● **전세 버스[비행기]** a chartered bus [plane].

전세(傳貰) the lease of a house[room] on a deposit basis. ¶~를 놓다 lease a house [room] on a deposit basis // ~를 들다 take a lease of a house[room] on a deposit basis.
● **전세금** deposit money (for the lease of a house[room]). **전세방** a room which lease on a deposit basis. **전세집** a house which lease on a deposit basis.

전세(戰勢) [싸움의 형세] the war situation; the aspect of a war. ¶~가 역전해서 우리에게 유리해졌다 The war situation reversed in our favor. // 시시각각으로 ~가 악화된다 Every time we blink, the map changes.

전세기(前世紀) (그 세기의 앞의) the preceding[foregoing] century; (금세기의 앞의) the last century. ¶~적인 사고방식 an outdated [old-fashioned] way of thinking // 그는 ~의 유물 같은 사람이다 He is a leftover from the days before the Flood. / He is a museum piece.

전소(全燒) [모조리 타 버림] total destruction by fire. **전소하다** be totally [completely] destroyed by fire; be burnt down; be razed [consumed] to the ground. ¶그 집은 화재로 전소했다 The house was totally destroyed by fire[burned (down) to the ground]. // 그 유명한 사원은 작년에 전소했다 The famous temple was reduced to ashes [totally destroyed by fire / burned down] last year.

전속(專屬) [오로지 한곳에만 속함] exclusive belongingness. ¶그는 그 극장의 ~ 배우이다 He is an actor under contract to[attached to] the theater. // 임금님에게는 ~의 이발사가 있다 The king has a barber who serves him exclusively. **전속하다** belong exclusively (to); be under the exclusive contract (of).
● **전속 가수** a singer attached to[under exclusive contract with] (the MBC). **전속 부관** the aide-de-camp. **전속 악단** an orchestra attached to (the MBC); the (MBC) studio orchestra.

전속(轉屬) transfer (to). **전속하다** be transferred (to); transfer (to). → ¶그는 영업부로 전속되었다 He was transferred to the business[commercial] section.

전속력(全速力) [최고 속도] full speed; top speed. ¶자동차가 ~으로 지나갔다 A car drove[rushed] past me at full[top] speed. // 배는 ~을 냈다 The ship put on full steam. // 나는 ~으로 달렸다 I ran as fast as I could.

전손(全損) [전체에 걸쳐 입은 손실] total loss. ¶추정~ constructive total loss // ~을 보다 suffer a total loss.
● **전손 담보** free from all average; security for total loss only.

전송(電送) electrical transmission; facsimile. ¶~사진 telephotography / phototelegraphy / radiophotography / facsimile // 사진 ~ 장치 a facsimile telegraphy. **전송하다** send [transmit] in facsimile; (텔레타이프로) teletype; (텔렉스로) telex. ¶기자는 사고 현장 사진을 전송했다 (무선으로) The reporter sent a picture by wireless[sent a radiophoto] from the scene of the accident. / (유선으로) The reporter sent a picture by wire[sent a Wirephoto] from the scene of the accident.
● **전송 사진** (유선의) a phototelegraph; (상표명) a Wirephoto; (무선의) a radiophoto(graph); a facsimile.

전송(餞送) a send-off; seeing off. ¶신혼부부

사람들의 따뜻한 ~을 받았다 The newlywed couple were given a warm send-off. **전송하다** see (a person) off; give (a person) a send-off. ¶대문[역]까지 ~ see (a person) to the door[station] // 많은 친구들이 공항까지 전송해 주었다 A lot of my friends came to the airport to see me off. // 서울역에서 친구를 전송해 주고 오는 길이다 I've been to Seoul Station to see off a friend of mine.

전송 (轉送) transmission; (우편물 등의) forwarding; (전신의) translation. ¶~을 부탁드립니다 (봉투에 쓰는 말) Please forward. **전송하다** transmit; (우편물 등을) forward; send on [forward]; (전신을) translate. ¶저에게 오는 편지는 모두 전송해 주십시오 Kindly forward all the letters addressed to me.

전수 (全數) **1** [전체의 수] the whole [total] (number). **2** [모두] all; in all; totally; altogether.

전수 (專修) [오로지 한 가지 일만을 닦음] specialization. **전수하다** specialize in; make a special study [specialty] (of); take a special course (of); (미) major in.
● **전수 학교** a special-vocational school.

전수 (傳受) being instructed [initiated]. **전수하다** be instructed [initiated]; receive instruction. ¶예술의 비결을 ~ be initiated into the secrets [mysteries] of an art.
● **전수자** an initiate; (집합적) the initiated.

전수 (傳授) (기술 등의) instruction; initiation. **전수하다** instruct; give instruction (in); initiate. ¶남에게 골동품 수집의 비결을 ~ initiate a person in(to) the mysteries of antique-collecting. ➔¶비전(祕傳)은 아버지로부터 아들에게 대대로 전수되었다 The secret of the art passed [was handed down] from father to son.
● **전수자** an initiator.

전수금 (前受金) an advance received.

전술 (前述) ¶~의 above / abovementioned / foregoing / aforesaid. **전술하다** ¶전술한 논거 the above(-mentioned) argument // 전술한 이유로 초대를 거절하지 않을 수 없습니다 For the reason mentioned above [above-mentioned reason], I have to decline your invitation. // 전술한 바와 같이 필자는 그 의견에 동의할 수 없다 As stated [mentioned] above, the writer cannot agree with that view.

전술 (戰術) tactics; strategy.(▶ strategy는 대규모의 장기에 걸친 종합적 전술. tactics는 실전에 있어서의 개개의 전략) ¶고등 ~ grand tactics // 교묘한 ~ clever tactics / a clever tactical move // ~상의 tactical / strategic(al) // ~적인 tactical // ~상의 잘못 a tactical error // ~적으로 tactically // 침묵 ~을 쓰다 adopt a strategy of silence // 군대는 ~상 그 도시에서 철수했다 The army made a strategic withdrawal from the city.
● **전술가** a tactician; a strategist. **전술 전환** a shift in tactics. **전술 핵무기** a tactical nuclear weapon.

전습 (傳襲) inheritance. **전습하다** inherit (one's father's habits); follow (the traditions). ¶아버지로부터 강건한 체질을 ~ inherit a strong constitution from one's father.

전승 (全勝) a complete victory; a clean score [record]. ¶그 레슬링 선수는 ~ 우승했다 The wrestler won the championship without losing a single match. **전승하다** win a complete victory; make a clean score; leave [make] a clean record; make straight wins. ¶우리 팀은 전승했다 Our team won all its games [finished with a perfect record].

전승 (傳承) transmission; (구전) (an) oral tradition; a tradition. ¶민간 ~ folklore. **전승하다** hand down; transmit. ¶그 고장 사람들은 전승한 설화 folktales handed down from generation to generation among the natives. ➔¶이 족자는 우리 조부의 대(代)부터 전승된 가보이다 This scroll is a family treasure handed down from our grandfathers time.
● **전승 문학** oral literature; folk literature.

전승 (戰勝) a victory. ¶~을 축하하다 celebrate (a) victory. **전승하다** win [gain] a victory (over); come out victorious; carry [win] the day; bring a war to a victorious conclusion [issue].
● **전승국** a victorious nation [country].

전시 (展示) display; exhibition(▶ display는 「남의 눈을 끄는」의 뉘앙스가 강함). **전시하다** put (a sculpture) on show [display]; exhibit; display. ¶일류 화가의 그림을 ~ exhibit the paintings of first-rate artists. ➔¶전시되어 있다 be on show [display] / be on exhibition // 진열장에 값비싼 항아리가 전시되어 있다 An expensive vase is being displayed [is on display] in the showcase. // 그 고문서는 이 박물관에서 일반에게 전시되고 있습니다 The ancient manuscript is on display for public viewing in this museum. / The ancient manuscripts may be viewed by the public in this museum.
● **전시관** a pavilion. **전시 물품** an exhibit; (집합적) exhibition. **전시실** a gallery; an exhibit hall [room]; an exhibition hall. **전시장** an exhibition hall [room]. **전시회** an exhibition; a display. **전시 효과** demonstration effect.

전시 (戰時) [전쟁이 벌어진 때] wartime; time of war. ¶~의 wartime // ~ 중에 during the war / in wartime // ~에나 평화시에나 both in time of peace and in time of war // 그는 ~에 지도자 중 한 사람이었다 He was one of the wartime leaders.
● **전시 내각** a war cabinet. **전시 상태** ¶~에 돌입하다 enter into a state of war / ~에 있다 be in a state of war. **전시 체제** a war(time) regime. ¶~로 on a war footing [basis].

전신 (全身) the whole body; (그림·사진 등에서) the full length. ¶~에 화상을 입다 get burns over one's whole body // ~이 아프다 I am aching from head to foot [all over]. // 그는 ~의 힘을 모두 쏟아 잡아당겼다 He pulled at it with all his strength. // ~이 흠뻑 젖었다 I got soaked to the skin.
● **전신 마취** general an(a)esthesia. ¶~를 하다 put (a patient) under general anesthesia. **전신 불수** total paralysis. **전신상** (~像) a full-length portrait. **전신 운동** exercise of the whole body.

전신 (前身) one's former self; one's past; one's past life [history]. ¶그녀의 ~은 가수이다 She used to be a singer. // 그의 ~을 아는 사람은 거의 없다 Few people know his past history. // 이 대학의 ~은 사숙(私塾)이었다 The forerunner of this college was a private school. // 이 회사의 ~은 작은 유리 공장이었다 This company was originally a small glass factory.

전신(前信) one's last letter. ¶~에서 말씀드린 바와 같이 as I informed you in my last (letter).

전신(電信) telegraphic communication; telegraph; wire; cable(해외 전신); telegraphy(전신술). ¶무선 ~ wireless (telegraphy) / radiotelegraphy // 해저 ~ submarine telegraphy // ~의 telegraphic // ~으로 by telegraph // ~을 보내다 telegraph (to) / wire (to) / cable // ~이 두절되었다 Telegraphic communication was interrupted [cut off / suspended]. // 본토와 낙도 사이에 ~이 개통되었다[회복되었다] Telegraph(ic) service between the mainland and the isolated island has begun [resumed].
● **전신국** a telegraph office [station]. **전신 약호** a telegraphic [cable] address. **전신주** a telegraph pole. **전신환**(-換) a telegraphic transfer [remittance] (약호 T.T.). ¶~으로 송금하다 remit money (to a person) by telegraphic transfer.

전실(前室) a person's former [divorced] wife. ¶~ 자식 the children of a person's former wife.

전심(全心) one's whole heart. ¶~을 기울여 with one's whole heart / wholeheartedly // 그는 ~전력 교무에 몰두했다 He devoted himself to school affairs heart and soul [wholeheartedly]. // 그는 ~전력 이 사건의 해결에 몰두하고 있다 He has thrown himself completely into [is deeply absorbed in] solving this case.

전심(專心) concentration of mind; undivided attention. **전심하다** devote oneself to; concentrate one's thoughts [energies] on. ¶그는 그 문제에 전심하고 있다 His thoughts are centered on the problem.

전압(電壓) [전] voltage. ¶높은[낮은] ~ a high [low] voltage // ~을 올리다[내리다] increase [decrease / reduce] voltage // ~이 높다[낮다] The voltage is high [low].
● **전압계** a voltmeter. **전압 조절기** a [an automatic] pressure regulator.

전액(全額) the total [full] amount; the (sum) total. ¶신청금 ~을 환불하다 refund the entire [(문어) the whole of the] application fee // ~부채를 ~ 반제했다 I repaid my debt in full. // 그 피해자는 자기가 요구한 보상액을 ~ 지급받았다 The victim was paid the full amount of the damages he had demanded. // 치료비는 ~ 보험에서 지불된다 All the medical expenses will be covered by insurance.
● **전액 담보** full coverage.

전야(前夜) 1 last night. ⇨어젯밤(⇨어제) 2 [그 전날 밤] the previous night; the night before; the eve (of). ¶크리스마스 ~ Christmas Eve // 졸업식의 ~에 on the eve of graduation.
● **전야제**(一祭) an eve. ¶우리는 독립 기념일의 ~를 지냈다 We celebrated the eve of Independence Day.

전어(錢魚) [동] a gizzard shad.

전언(前言) [이전에 한 말] one's previous words [remarks / statement].

전언(傳言) [전하는 말] a (verbal) message; word. ¶~을 남겨 놓다 leave word [a message] (with) // 그로부터 ~을 부탁받았습니다 I have a message from him. // 그녀는 내일 오겠다는 ~을 아들 편에 보내왔다 Her son brought me word that she would come the next day. **전언하다** send (a person) word (that ...); give a message (to).

전업(專業) a special [principal] occupation; a speciality; a profession. ¶~을 ~으로 하다 make a speciality of (foreign trade) / specialize in ... // 이 농가는 벼농사를 ~으로 하고 있다 On this farm they concentrate on the cultivation [production] of rice. / This farm specializes in rice cultivation. // 그는 화훼 재배를 ~으로 하고 있다 He is a floriculturist by profession.
● **전업농가** a full-time farmer. **전업주부** (미) a homemaker; (영) a housewife.

전업(轉業) a change of occupation [employment / career]. **전업하다** change one's job [profession]; switch jobs.

전역(全域) the whole area [region]. ¶호남 ~이 태풍 20호의 피해를 입었다 The whole Honam area was hit by typhoon No. 20. // 그의 발견은 자연 과학 ~에 영향을 미쳤다 This discovery of his affected every field of natural science.

전역(全譯) a complete translation. ¶그는 세익스피어의 ~을 시도했다 He attempted to translate all the works of Shakespeare.

전역(戰役) war; warfare. ⇨전쟁

전역(戰域) [전쟁 구역] a war [battle] area [zone]; a theater of operations. ¶~이 확대되었다 The theater of operations was expanded.

전역(轉役) [군] transfer (from active service to the first reserve); [제대] discharge from military service. **전역하다** be transferred (from the active list to the reserve list); [제대하다] be discharged [dismissed] from military service. ➔**전역시키다** transfer (a person) to the first reserve / place [register] (a person) on the reserve list.

전연(全然) quite; entirely. ⇨전혀

전열(前列) the front row. ¶그는 ~의 왼쪽에서 두 번째에 있다 He is the second from left in the front row.

전열(電熱) electric heat.
● **전열기** an electric heater [(영) fire]; (취사용) an electric range [(미) stove / (영) cooker].

전열(戰列) a line of battle; a battle line. ¶~에 가담하다 join the line of battle // ~에서 벗어나다 withdraw [retire] from battle // 그녀는 반전 운동의 ~에 가담했다 She joined an anti-war activity.

전염(傳染) 1 (접촉에 의한 질병의) contagion; (간접적인) infection. ¶자가(自家) ~ autoinfection // 접촉 ~ contact infection // 직접 [간접] ~ direct [indirect] infection // 이 병은 공기 ~으로 발생한다 This disease occurs as a result of aerial infection. **전염하다** (병이) be contagious [infectious / catching]; (사람이) be infected (with); catch. ¶이 병은 전염한다 This disease is catching [contagious / infectious] (▶ contagious는 접촉에 의해, infectious는 공기·물 등에 의해 발생한다는 뜻이나 실제로는 이 두 말이 같이 쓰이는 경우가 많음). ➔**200명의 아동이 독감에 전염되었다** Two hundred pupils caught the flu. 2 [버릇 등이 옮아서 물이 듦]. ¶그런 유행은 ~되기 쉽다 Such fashions catch on fast.
● **전염 경로** the route of infection. ¶그 병의 ~는 알 수 없었다 They were not able to

trace the disease. / The source of the disease was unknown. **전염병** a contagious disease(▶ 접촉 전염에 의한); an infectious disease(▶ 간접 전염에 의한); 〔유행병〕 an epidemic. ¶〔법정〕 ~ a legally designated〔an official〕 contagious disease∥~이 그 지방에서 크게 번지고 있다 There is an epidemic in that area. / An epidemic is raging in the area.∥이 피부병은 접촉 ~이다 This dermatitis is contagious. **전염병 환자** a person who has caught a contagious disease. **전염원**(-源) a source of infection.

전와(轉訛) (linguistic) corruption. **전와하다** be corrupted (from one spelling to another).
●**전와어**(-語) a corrupted word (form); a corruption.

전용(專用) exclusive〔private / personal〕 use. ¶~의 exclusive / private / for one's private use∥한글 ~ the exclusive use of *Hangeul*∥대통령 ~ 비행기 the presidential plane∥야간 ~ 전화 a night line∥자동차 ~ 도로〔표지〕 Motor Vehicles Only. / Pedestrians and Bicycles Prohibited.∥종업원 ~ 엘리베이터 an elevator for the exclusive use of employees〔only for the employees〕∥그는 자기 ~의 비행기를 가지고 있다 He has a plane for his personal use∥**여성 ~**〔게시〕 Ladies Only. **전용하다** have a thing for one's exclusive use; use exclusively.
●**전용기** a personal plane. **전용차** a private〔personal〕 car; a car for one's personal〔exclusive〕 use.

전용(轉用) diversion. **전용하다** divert (to); convert. ¶우리는 교육비를 식비로 전용하지 않을 수 없었다 We had to divert〔redirect〕 part of the educational budget to pay for food.∥낡은 공장을 전용해서 새 쇼핑센터로 만들었다 The old factory was converted into a new shopping center.

전우(戰友) a fellow soldier; a comrade in arms; a war comrade; 〔미〕 a war buddy.

전운(戰雲) war clouds. ¶그 군도(群島)에는 ~이 감돌았다 War clouds〔The threat of war〕 hung over the islands.

전원(田園) 〔논밭〕 fields; 〔시골〕 rural districts; the country. ¶~의 rural / pastoral∥여기는 한때 조용한 ~이었으나 지금은 공업도시가 되었다 This once quiet rural district has turned into an industrial city.
●**전원 교향곡** the Pastoral Symphony. **전원도시** a rural〔garden〕 city. **전원생활** (enjoy) country〔rural〕 life. **전원시**(-詩) a pastoral; an idyll. **전원 풍경** a rural landscape.

전원(全員) all the members; the entire staff. ¶교직원 ~이 토의에 참가했다 The whole faculty〔All the members of the faculty〕 participated in the discussion.∥추락 사고로 ~이 사망했다 All aboard the plane were killed in the crash.∥스미스 씨를 ~ 일치로 회장으로 추대했다 They proposed Mr. Smith unanimously as the president of the society.∥~ 이상 없음 All are safe and sound.

전원(電源) 1〔전력 공급의 원천〕 a power source; a power supply. ¶~을 개발하다 develop power sources∥~을 끊다 shut〔cut〕 off the power supply. 2〔콘센트〕 an (electric) outlet. ¶코드를 ~에 꽂다 put a plug in a socket〔(미) an outlet〕∥텔레비전을 ~에 연결하다 plug in a television (set).

전위(前衛) 1〔위위대〕〔군〕 the vanguard; an advance guard. 2 (구기에서) a forward; 〔테니스〕 an forward〔net〕 player; 〔미식축구〕 〔미〕 a linesman. 3 (예술에서). ¶~적인 avant-garde.
●**전위 문학**〔미술 / 음악〕 avant-garde〔vanguard〕 literature〔art / music〕. **전위 영화** an avant-garde picture.

전위(電位) electric potential. ¶양〔음〕~ positive〔negative〕 potential.
●**전위 강하** a potential drop. **전위계** an electrometer. **전위차** potential difference.

전위(轉位) 1〔위치가 바뀜〕 transposition. 2〔물〕 dislocation. 3 (태아 위치의) version. 4〔화〕 rearrangement.

전유(專有) exclusive〔sole〕 possession (of). **전유하다**〔독점권을 갖다〕 monopolize; 〔자기만의 것으로 하다〕 take sole possession (of).
●**전유권** a monopoly (of); an exclusive right (to).

전율(戰慄) a shudder; a shiver. **전율하다** shudder; shiver; tremble with fear. ¶전율할 광경 a horrible sight∥그 얼굴을 보기만 해도 그녀는 무의식중에 전율했다 One look at the face, and an involuntary shudder ran through her.∥또 어린이가 유괴되었다는 말을 듣고 어머니들은 전율했다 When they heard that yet another child had been kidnapped, the mothers shivered.

전음(顫音) 〔음〕 trill.

전의(戰意) fighting spirit; the will〔intention〕 to fight. ¶~를 잃다 lose one's fighting spirit∥왕성한 ~를 보이다 show real〔a lot of〕 fight∥~가 없다 have no will to fight / have no fight in one.

전의(轉義) a figurative〔transferred〕 meaning.

전이(轉移) (a) change; 〔물〕 transition; 〔의〕 metastasis; 〔정신 의학〕 transference; 〔화〕 transformation. **전이하다** change; spread (by metastasis); transfer. ¶유방암이 림프샘으로 전이하고 있다 The breast cancer has spread〔metastasized〕 to the lymph nodes.
●**전이 원소**〔화〕 a transition element.

전인 교육(全人敎育) all-round education.

전인미답(前人未踏) ¶~의〔발을 들여놓은 일이 없는〕 untrodden /〔전례가 없는〕 unprecedented /~의 극지(極地) a polar region previously untrodden by man∥~의 원시림 a trackless primeval forest.

전일(前日) the previous day; the past (days). ⇨**전날**.

전일제(全日制) 〔교〕 the full-time schooling system. ¶~ **고등학교** a full-time (senior) high school.

전임(前任) (사람) one's predecessor; a former official. ¶~의 preceding∥~ **교장** the preceding principal.
●**전임자** one's predecessor. ¶바로 직전의 ~ one's immediate predecessor.

전임(專任) exclusive duty; full service; sole charge. ¶~의 full-time∥회사의 ~ 상담역 a full-time adviser to a company∥그녀는 우리 학교의 음악 ~ 선생님이다 She is a full-time teacher of music at our school. **전임하다** be in full service; do exclusive duty.
●**전임 강사** a full-time lecturer. (대학의) (미) instructor.

전임(轉任) a change of post; transference. **전임하다** be transferred to〔another post〕; change one's post. ¶해리스는 파리에서 뉴욕으로 전임했다 Harris was transferred to New

전입 York from Paris.// 그는 교육 인적 자원부에 연구소로 전임했다 He was transferred from the Ministry of Education and Human Resources Development to a research institute.
- **전임지** one's new post. ¶홍 씨의 ~는 부산이라고 한다 I hear Mr. Hong's new post is Busan.

전입(轉入) transference; moving in(to). **전입하다** be[get] transferred; move in. ¶민 씨네는 광주에서 서울로 전입했다 The Mins moved to Seoul from Gwangju.
- **전입생** a student transferred from another school. ¶저 아이는 ~이다 The child transferred to this school. **전입신고** a moving-in notification. ¶~의 절차 the procedure for filing notice that one has moved.

전자(前者) 1 [후자에 대하여 앞의 것] the former(the latter에 대하여); (구어) the first (the second에 대하여). ¶~의 예는 후자의 예보다 낫다 The former example is better than the latter.// 이 두 기계 중 ~는 국산이고 후자는 미국제이다 Of these two machines, the former is of Korean make and the latter the first is of Korean make and the second is of American make. 2 the last time. ⇨ *지난번* ¶~에는 고마웠습니다 Thank you for the other day.

전자(電子) [물] an electron. ¶~의 electronic.
- **전자계산기** a[an electronic] computer. **전자 공업** electronics industry. **전자 공학** electronics. **전자레인지** a microwave oven. **전자오락** an electronic game[amusement]; a video game. **전자오락실** an electronic game [amusement] room; a video game room; video games. **전자 오르간** an electronic organ. **전자 우편** an electronic mail(약어 EM). **전자 음악** electronic music. **전자 장치** an electronic device. **전자 출판** electronic publishing. **전자 현미경** an electron microscope. **전자 화폐** electronic money; e-money.

전자(電磁) electromagnetism. ⇨ *전자기*
- **전자석** an electromagnet.

전자(篆字) a seal character.

전자기(電磁氣) electromagnetism. ¶~의 electromagnetic.
- **전자기력** electromagnetic force. **전자기 유도** electromagnetic induction. **전자기장** an electromagnetic field. **전자기파** an electromagnetic wave; (통신의) a radio wave.

전작(田作) (농사) dry field farming; (작물) dry field crop; harvest from upland fields.

전작(前酌) [딴 술자리에서 이미 마신 술] drinks taken before joining (a party). ¶~이 있습니다 I had a few drinks before I came here.

전장(全長) the full[total / overall] length. ¶다리의 ~은 60피트이다 The total length of the bridge is sixty feet. / The bridge is sixty feet long.// 그 배는 ~ 30미터이다 The ship has an overall length of 30 meters. / The ship is 30 meter (long) from stem to stern.

전장(前章) (in) the preceding[foregoing] chapter; (바로 앞의) the last chapter.

전장(前場) (증권 거래에서) the morning session; the first session[call].

전장(電場) [물] an electric field. ⇨ *전기장*(⇨ *전기*(電氣))

전장(戰場) a battlefield. ⇨ *전쟁터*(⇨ *전쟁*)

전재(戰災) [전쟁으로 인한 피해] war damage; [전쟁으로 인한 황폐] war devastation. ¶~를 입다 suffer war damage / be damaged during [in] a war// 이 지역은 ~을 면했다 This part escaped damage during the war.
- **전재민** a war victim; a victim of war. **전재지구** an area devastated by a war; a war-damaged area.

전재(轉載) reprinting; reproduction. ¶신 교수의 승인 아래 ~ Reprinted[Reproduced] by courtesy of professor Sin. **전재하다** reprint; reproduce. ¶이 기사는 타임지에서 전재한 것입니다 This article was reprinted from the Times.
- **전재 금지** Reproduction forbidden.; All rights[Copyright] reserved.; No part of this book may be reproduced in any form (without permission).

전쟁(戰爭) war; warfare; (개개의 싸움) battle. ¶국지 ~ a limited war// 세계 ~ a global [world] war// 소규모 ~ a brush-fire war// 장기 ~ a protracted[long-drawn(-out)] war// 전면 ~ a total[an all-out] war// 침략 ~ an aggressive war// 핵~ a nuclear war// ~의 참화 the calamity of war / war calamities// ~에 이기다[지다] win[lose] a war// ~을 일으키다 go to war (against) / make war (on) // ~에 휩쓸리다 be involved in a war// ~에 개입하다 intervene in a war// ~에 대비하다 prepare for war// ~에 참가하다 enter[participate in] a war// 양국은 ~ 중이다 The two countries were at war with each other.// 양국은 ~에 돌입했다 The two countries rushed into war.// 그 ~으로 많은 희생자를 냈다 The war cost heavily in human life. **전쟁하다** make war (with); go to war (with); wage (a) war (against); war (with); [전투하다] fight (a battle). ¶나치스는 세계의 열강과 전쟁했다 Nazis waged war against the great powers of the world.
- **전쟁고아** a war orphan. **전쟁 공포증** war-phobia. **전쟁놀이** ¶~를 하다 play at soldiers. **전쟁 도발자** a warmonger. **전쟁미망인** a war widow. **전쟁 범죄** war crimes. **전쟁 범죄자** a war criminal. **전쟁 영화** a war movie [film]. **전쟁터** a battlefield; a battleground; a field of battle; the seat[theater] of war; the front(전선). ¶그의 아버지는 ~에서 죽었다 His father died in battle.// 그 도시는 ~가 되었다 The town turned into a battlefield [scene of battle].// 이곳은 2차 대전 때 ~였다 A battle was fought her[in this place] in World WarⅡ.

전적(全的) overall; complete; whole; the full. ¶~으로 wholly / totally / entirely / completely / fully// ~으로 동의하다 give a blanket consent (to)// 그 물품의 인도에 대하여 저희가 ~으로 책임을 집니다 We take complete responsibility for the delivery of the goods.

전적(戰跡) (visit) an old battlefield; the scene of old battle.

전적(戰績) (전쟁의) a war record; (시합·경기의) results(▶ 보통 복수형); a record; a score. ¶그 팀은 지난 1년 동안 빛나는 ~을 남겼다 The team had a brilliant record[had scored a series of brilliant victories] in the past year.

전적(轉籍) (본적의) transfer of one's domicile; (학적의) transfer of the school register of a student. **전적하다** transfer one's domicile [family register] (from / to). ¶광주에서 현

주소로 전적했습니다 I have transferred my permanent domicile from Gwangju to my present address.

전전(戰前) prewar days[times]. ¶~의 prewar // ~에는 in (the) prewar days[times] / before the war.

전전(前前) ¶~년 (올해의) the years before last / two years ago / (어느 해의) two years before // ~달(이달의) the month before last / (어느 달의) two months before // ~날(오늘의) the day before yesterday / (어느 날의) two days before // 그것은 ~ 번 위원회에서 결정되었다 It was decided two meetings ago[at the meeting before last]. // 그는 ~ 주에 퇴원했다 He left ((미) the) hospital the week before last[two weeks ago].

전전긍긍하다(戰戰兢兢−) be terribly[awfully / dreadfully] afraid; be trembling with fear. ¶그는 전전긍긍하며 그곳에 서 있었다 He stood there in fear and trembling. // 도둑은 경찰에 발각될까 봐 전전긍긍하며 며칠을 보냈다 The thief passed several days in fear of being discovered by the police.

전전하다(輾轉−) toss[roll] about. ¶그는 잠을 못 이루고 밤새도록 전전했다 He could not sleep a wink and tossed and turned all night long. / He had a sleepless night, rolling[tossing] about on the bed.

전전하다(轉轉−) [굴러다니다] roll about; go rolling; [헤매다] wander from place to place; roam about. ¶이 직장 저 직장을 ~ change jobs many times // 그 남자는 각지를 전전했다 The man wandered from one place to another[from place to place].

전정(前庭) [앞뜰] a front yard[garden].

전정(剪定) (생육·결실을 좋게 하기 위한) pruning; (다듬기 위한) trimming. **전정하다** prune; trim. ¶장미를 ~ prune rose bushes.

● **전정가위** (a pair of) pruning shears.

전정 기관(前庭器官) a vestibular organ.

전제(前提) [논] a premise. ¶대[소] ~ the major[minor] premise // 그는 잘못된 ~로 논의를 하고 있다 He is arguing from false premises. // 내 이름을 밝히지 않는다는 ~로 정보를 제공하기로 승낙했다 I contented to give information on condition that my name would not be used. // 우리는 조기 해결을 ~로 협상에 들어갔다 We entered into negotiations on the assumption that an early solution would be reached. **전제하다** set (something) forth as a premise; premise.

● **전제 조건** a precondition (for / of); a prerequisite (to / for).

전제(專制) [전제 정치] despotism; [독재 정치] autocracy; dictatorship; [절대주의] absolutism. ¶~적인 despotic / autocratic / dictatorial / absolute. **전제하다** be despotic; be autocratic; be arbitrary; tyrannize; act the tyrant to[over].

● **전제국** an absolute monarchy. **전제 군주** a despot; an autocrat; an absolute monarch. [ruler]. ¶~ 정치 an absolute monarchy. **전제 정치** despotic[autocratic] government; autocracy. **전제주의** absolutism; despotism.

전조(前兆) an omen (of disaster). ⇨정조

전조(前條) [앞의 조항 또는 조문] the preceding[foregoing] clause[item].

전조(轉調) [음] modulation. ⇨=조바꿈

전조등(前照燈) a headlight; a headlamp. ¶~을 켜다[끄다] turn on[off] the headlight(s).

전주(前奏) [음] a prelude; an introductory part. ¶식은 오르간의 ~로 시작되었다 The ceremony began with a prelude of organ music [an organ prelude].

● **전주곡** (前奏曲) a prelude. ¶쇼팽의 ~ Chopin's Preludes // 사소한 발포 사건이 대전쟁의 ~이 될 줄은 아무도 몰랐다 Nobody thought the minor shooting incident would lead to a great war.

전주(前週) last week. ⇨지난주

전주(電柱) an electric (light) pole. ⇨=전봇대

전주(電鑄) electroforming.

전주(錢主) 1 [밑천을 대 주는 사람] financier; capitalist. ¶~가 되다 give (a person) financial support[monetary aid] / finance (an enterprise) // 이 사업의 ~는 홍 씨다 This enterprise is financed[financially backed up] by Mr. Hong. 2 [빚 준 사람] a creditor.

전지(全紙) [전 지면] the whole space (of a newspaper); [잘라 내지 않은] a whole sheet (of paper).

전지(剪枝) trimming. ⇨=가지치기(⇨가지¹)

● **전지가위** (a pair of) pruning shears. ⇨=전정가위(⇨전정(剪定))

전지(電池) [전류를 일으키는 장치] a battery; a[an electric] cell(▶ cell이 모인 것이 battery). ¶건~ a dry battery[cell] // 축~ a storage battery // 수은~ a mercury battery // 알칼리 ~ an alkaline battery // 태양 ~ a solar cell[battery] // 1차[2차] ~ a primary [secondary] battery // 화학 ~ a chemical cell // ~를 다 써 버리다 run down a battery // ~가 다되었다 The battery is dead.

● **전지 개폐기** a battery switch. **전지 용량** battery capacity. **전지 충전** battery charging.

전지(戰地) a battlefield. ⇨=전쟁터(⇨전쟁)

전지 요양(轉地療養) treatment by a change of air; going away for one's health. ¶~을 하다 go away (to some place) for one's health / try a change of air for one's health // 어머니는 진해에 ~을 하러 가셨다 My mother was gone to Jinhae for a change (of air).

전지전능하다(全知全能−) omniscient and omnipotent[almighty]. ¶전지전능하신 하느님 Almighty God / God Almighty / the Almighty.

전직(前職) a former post[office].

● **전직 교사** a former teacher. **전직 형사** an ex-detective.

전직(轉職) change of occupation. **전직하다** change one's occupation[job / employment / profession]; take up another job. ¶그는 은행원에서 농부로 전직했다 He resigned his post as bank clerk and became a farmer.

전진(前進) [앞으로 나아감] an advance; a forward movement. ¶~! [구령] Forward! **전진하다** advance; step[march / move] forward; go ahead; proceed; (배 등이) make headway. ¶1보 ~ take a step forward // 그들은 국경을 넘어서 전진했다 They advanced beyond the border. // 우리는 눈 때문에 전진할 수가 없었다 The snow prevented us from going forward[ahead].

● **전진 기지** an advance base; [전초 기지] an outpost.

전진(戰陣) [전투를 위한 진영] battle formation; battle array; [전장] a battlefield; the front.

전질(全帙) a complete set (of books).

전집(全集) one's complete[collected] works.

¶디킨스 ~ the complete works of Dickens // 세계 미술[문학] ~ the complete series of world art[literature] // 단권으로 된 셰익스피어 ~ 이 현재 편집 중이다 A new one-volume edition of Shakespeare's complete [collected] works is now in preparation.
- 전집물 a complete works series.

전차(前借) 〔앞당겨서 빚으로 씀〕 an advance; borrowing in advance. **전차하다** borrow [draw] (money) in advance; get an advance. ¶월급의 절반을 ~ receive half one's salary in advance.
- 전차금 money borrowed in advance.

전차(電車) 〔시가 전차〕 (미) a streetcar; (영) a tram(car). ¶~를 운전하다 run [operate] a streetcar [tram(car)].
- 전차 선로 / 전차 궤도 a streetcar line [track]; (미) a car line; (영) a tramline; (영) a tramway.

전차(戰車) a tank. ¶경[중] ~ a light [heavy] tank // 수륙 양용 ~ an amphibian tank.
- 전차병 a tankman. 전차 부대 tank forces; a fleet of tanks. 전차포 a tank gun. ¶대~ an antitank gun.

전차(轉借) 〔남이 빌려 온 것을 다시 빌림〕 subtenancy; a sublease; underletting. **전차하다** borrow (a book) secondhand; rent (a room) secondhand; sublease (land); underlet. ¶친구의 아파트를 전차하고 있습니다 I am subleasing my friend's apartment.
- 전차인 an undertenant; a subtenant; a sublessee.

전채(前菜) an hors d'oeuvre (pl. ~~, ~~s) (⇨ 보통 복수형).

전처(前妻) one's former [first] wife; one's ex-wife.
- 전처 소생 a child by a former wife. ¶~이 셋 있다 have three children by one's previous marriage.

전천후(全天候) ¶~(용)의 all-weather // ~ 비행기 an all-weather airplane // ~ 테니스 코트 an all-weather tennis court.
- 전천후기(-機) all-weather plane. 전천후 농업 all-weather agriculture.

전철(前轍) ruts left by (the wheels of) vehicles that have passed before.
전철을 밟다 repeat the mistakes [errors] of one's predecessors. ¶스미스 씨의 전철을 밟지 않도록 하시오 Don't make the same mistake as Mr. Smith. / Don't repeat Mr. Smith's mistake. // 작년의 전철을 밟고 싶지 않다 I don't want to commit the same error [fall into the same trap] as I did last year.

전철(電鐵) an electric railroad [railway].

전철(轉轍) 〔철도〕 (미) switching. **전철하다** shunt [(미) switch] (a train).
- 전철기 (미) a (railroad) switch; a shunt; (영) points.

전체(全體) the whole; (문어) the entirety. ¶~의 whole / all / entire // ~에 걸쳐 all over / throughout // 그 여행 ~에 걸쳐서 during the entire trip / all through the trip // 나라 ~를 통하여 throughout the country // 우리는 그 제안 ~를 각하했다 We rejected the whole proposal. / We rejected the proposal in its entirety. // 마을 ~에 악취가 가득했다 There was a bad smell all over the town. / The whole town was filled with a terrible smell. // 학급 ~로 볼 때 이 아이는 결코 성적이 나쁘지 않다 His performance is not bad at all, considered in relation to that of the class as a whole. // ~로 볼 때 이 모임은 성공적이었다 On the whole, this event was a success.
- 전체주의 totalitarianism. 전체 회의 a plenary session; (총회) a general meeting.

전체적(全體的) whole; all; entire. ¶~으로 generally / in general / on the whole / as a whole // 여비는 ~으로 30만 원 들었다 The traveling expenses amounted to three hundred thousand won all told [all together / in all].

전초(前哨) an outpost; an advanced post.
- 전초 기지 an advanced base. 전초 부대 an outpost unit [troops]. 전초전 an outpost action; a preliminary skirmish. ¶선거는 이미 ~에 들어섰다 The election campaign has already entered its preliminary stages.

전축(電蓄) an electric phonograph [(영) gramophone]; a record player. ¶라디오 겸용 ~ a radiophonograph / (영) radiogramophone // 스테레오 [하이파이] ~ a stereophonic [hi-fi / high-fidelity] phonograph // ~을 틀다 play [turn on] a electric phonograph.

전출(轉出) 1 〔다른 근무지로 옮겨 감〕 transfer; transference. **전출하다** be [get] transferred (to a new post). ¶방계 회사로 ~ be transferred to a subsidiary company. →그는 지방으로 전출되었다 He was transferred to a local office. 2 〔다른 곳으로 이주함〕 a move; a removal. **전출하다** move (to); change one's place. ¶서울에서 시골로 ~ move from Seoul to the country.
- 전출 신고 report of a change of address. 전출지 a place of moving out; a new address.

전치(全治) (a) complete recovery. ⇨"완치 ¶그는 ~ 2주의 부상을 입었다 He suffered an injury that would take [(문어) require] two weeks to heal completely.

전치(轉置) transposition. **전치하다** transpose; dislocate; displace.

전치사(前置詞) a preposition. ¶이 동사에는 어떤 ~가 붙는가 What preposition is required after this verb?
- 전치사구 a prepositional phrase.

전토(全土) 〔국토 전체〕 the whole land [country]. ¶유럽 ~에 all over Europe // 우리나라 ~에 한파가 내습했다 A cold wave hit the whole of Korea. // 피해는 ~에 미치고 있다 The whole country suffered damage.

전통(傳統) (a) tradition; (인습) (a) convention; 〔유산〕 a heritage; 〔역사〕 a history. ¶오랫동안 가꾸어 온 ~ a long-established tradition // ~을 존중하는 사람들 those who cherish tradition(s) // ~에 따르다 [~을 지키다] follow [maintain] the tradition // ~을 깨다 break a tradition [convention] / break with tradition [convention] // 우리 회사는 80년의 ~을 갖고 있다 Our company has a tradition [history] of eighty years.
- 전통문화 a cultural heritage. 전통주의 traditionalism.

전통적(傳統的) traditional; conventional. ¶~인 것 conventionality // ~으로 traditionally / conventionally // 이 축제는 그 나라의 ~인 행사의 하나로 꼽힌다 This festival is one of the traditional events of the country. // 이 학교는 ~으로 규율이 까다롭다 They are traditionally [by tradition] strict in their discipline at this school.

전투(戰鬪) a battle(▶ 주로 대규모의 전투); a fight 《against / with》; [전투 행위] combat; an action. ¶공격[방어] ~ offensive [defensive] operations // 야간 ~ night fighting // ~를 개시하다 commence hostilities / go into battle // ~를 중지하다 suspend hostilities / break off a battle // ~에 참가하다 see action [combat] / take part in a battle [an action]. **전투하다** fight (a battle); engage in battle.
● **전투 경찰** the combat police (force); (구성원) a combat policeman. **전투기** a fighter; a combat plane. **전투 대형** (form) (a) battle formation. **전투력** fighting [combat] power. **전투모** a field [fatigue] cap. **전투복** a combat uniform; a battle jacket [dress]; (미) battle fatigues; battle dress. **전투 부대** a combat unit; fighting forces [troops]. **전투원** a combatant; (집합적) combat personnel. ¶비 ~ a noncombatant / a civilian. **전투 준비** preparation for action; [구령] To arms! **전투 폭격기** a fighter-bomber. **전투화** combat shoes.

전파(全破) [전부 파괴함] complete destruction [collapse]. **전파하다** destroy completely; raze; demolish. ➜¶이 마을에서는 태풍으로 집 다섯 채가 전파되었다 Five houses in this village were completely destroyed by the typhoon.

전파(電波) an electric [radio] wave. ¶~를 통해서 이야기하다 talk on [over] the radio // (목소리가) ~를 타다 go out over the airwaves.
● **전파계** a wavemeter. **전파 망원경** a radio telescope. **전파 방해** jamming. ¶이웃 나라가 24시간 ~를 했다 A neighboring country jammed our broadcast for 24 hours. **전파 탐지기** a radar.

전파(傳播) [널리 전하여 퍼뜨림] spread; propagation; transmission. ¶음[빛]의 ~ the propagation of sound [light] // 병균의 ~ dissemination of disease germs. **전파하다** spread; propagate. (음 등을) transmit. ¶물은 음을 잘 전파한다 Water easily transmits [conducts] sound. ➜¶빛은 음보다 훨씬 빨리 전파된다 Light travels much faster than sound.
● **전파 속도** propagation velocity.

전패(全敗) a complete defeat; a crushing [total] defeat; a rout. ¶그들은 마지막 시합에 이김으로써 ~는 면했다 As they won their final game, they were spared a winless season. **전패하다** be completely defeated (in); sustain a crushing defeat; lose all games. ¶프랑스 축구 팀은 전패했다 The French soccer team lost all its matches [games].

전편(全篇) the whole book [volume]; the whole reel(영화의). ¶~을 통해서 from cover to cover / throughout the volume // 소설 ~에 넘쳐흐르는 반전 감정 the antiwar feelings pervading the whole story.

전편(前篇) the first part [volume]; (후편에 대하여) the first half.

전폐(全廢) [아주 그만두거나 없앰] total abolition. ¶공창(公娼)의 ~ the abolition of licensed prostitution // 그들은 핵무기의 ~를 요구했다 They demanded the total abolition of nuclear weapons. **전폐하다** abolish totally [completely]; do away with; lift. ¶정부는 식료품 수입에 대한 제한을 전폐했다 The Government lifted all restrictions on food imports. ➜¶차별적인 제도는 전폐되었다 All discriminatory institutions were abolished [done away with].

전폭(全幅) the overall [full] width; the whole breadth. ¶이 비행기는 ~이 26미터이다 This airplane [aircraft] has a wing span of twenty-six meters.

전폭기(戰爆機) a fighter-bomber.

전표(傳票) a slip; a ticket(약식의). ¶대체 ~ a transfer slip // 매출 ~ a sales slip [ticket] // 수납[입금] ~ a receiving [receipt] slip // 예금 ~ a deposit ticket // 지불 ~ a payment [paying-out] slip // 주문 ~ an order slip // ~를 떼다 write out [issue] a slip // ~와 교환으로 돈을 지불하다 pay money in exchange for a slip.

전하(殿下) His [Her] Imperial [Royal] Highness(▶ Her는 여성, Royal은 영국 왕족의 경우); [호칭] Your Imperial [Royal] Highness(▶ 여기에 따르는 동사는 제3인칭을 씀). ¶황태자 ~ His Imperial Highness [H.I.H.] the Crown Prince // 황태자비 ~ Her Imperial Highness [H.I.H.] the Crown Princess // ~께서도 알고 계십니까 Has Your Royal [Imperial] Highness been informed of it?

전하(電荷) [전] (an) electric charge. ¶양[음] ~ (a) positive [negative] charge.

전하다(傳-) 1 (소식이나 물건 등을) tell; communicate; deliver; hand (over). ¶전갈을 ~ deliver a message // 비보를 가족에게 ~ break the sad news to the family // 사장에게 내가 왔다고 전해 주시오 Will you tell the president that I'm here? // 한 씨에게 전갈을 전해 주시겠습니까 Can I leave a message with you for Mr. Han? // 내일 이곳에 오도록 그 사람에게 말 좀 전해 주십시오 Please tell him to come here tomorrow. / Please send him word telling him to come here tomorrow. // 그녀에게 무슨 전하고 싶은 말씀이 있습니까 Is there any message you would like me to give her? // 전하신 말씀의 취지를 잘 알아들었습니다 We understand perfectly the message you conveyed to us. // 이 편지를 그 사람에게 전해 주십시오 Please deliver this letter to him in person. // 이 서류를 그에게 전해 주십시오 Please hand these papers (over) to him. // 내 전갈을 그에게 전해 주셨으면 좋겠습니다 I'd like (for) you to give him a message. / (문어) Please convey my message to him. // 그에게 안부를 전해 주세요 Give my best regards [wishes] to him. / Kindly remember me to him. // 전하는 바에 의하면 그는 상당한 빚을 지고 있는 모양이다 There is a rumor that he is deep in debt.
2 [물려주다] hand down; transmit; leave; bequeath. ¶자손[후세]에 ~ hand down to posterity // 이 의식(儀式)은 아버지에게서 아들로 전해 내려온 것이다 Knowledge of this ritual has been handed down from father to son. // 이것은 대대로 전해 내려오는 가훈이다 This is a family precept transmitted [handed down] from generation to generation.
3 [전수(傳授)하다] teach; [전하여 보내다] pass (knowledge) on to; impart; initiate. ¶지식을 ~ impart knowledge to (the young) // 비법을 ~ initiate (a person) in the mysteries of an art // 내가 알고 있는 것은 이제 모두 제자들에게 전했다 I have taught my pupils everything I know. / (문어) I have imparted all my knowledge to my pupils. //

전학

그는 포도주 양조의 비밀을 아들에게 전해 주었다 He passed the secrets of wine-brewing on to his son.
4 〔들여오다〕 introduce 《into》. ¶한국에 기독교를 ~ introduce Christianity into Korea.
5 〔열·빛·소리 등을 전도(傳導)하다〕 transmit; conduct; propagate; convey. ¶진동을 ~ propagate vibration∥구리는 전기를 전한다 Copper conducts[transmits] electricity.∥공기는 소리를 전한다 Air conveys sound.

전학(轉學) change[transfer] of schools. **전학하다** change[transfer] to another school; change one's school. ¶부산에 있는 학교로 ~ change[transfer] to a school in Busan∥그는 한국의 대학에서 미국의 대학으로 전학했다 He changed[transferred] from a college [university] in Korea to an American college [university].
● **전학생** a transfer student (from another school).

전함(戰艦) a battleship; a warship.

전항(前項) **1** 〔앞에 든 조항〕 the preceding clause; 〔앞의 절〕 the previous paragraph. ¶상세한 것은 ~ 참조하라 For the details, refer to the preceding clause[paragraph]. **2** 〔수〕 the antecedent.

전해(前─) **1** 〔바로 앞의 해〕 the previous year; the year before. ¶나는 그가 죽기 ~에 그를 처음으로 만났다 I met him for the first time the year before his death. **2** last year. ⇨"지난해.

전해(電解) electrolysis. ⇨"전기 분해(⇨전기(電氣))
● **전해액** an electrolytic solution; an electrolyte. **전해질 / 전해물** an electrolyte.

전향(轉向) a turn; a conversion; 〔구어〕 an about-face. ¶~을 맹세하다 swear to renounce one's views. **전향하다** turn[swing / switch (over)]《to》; be converted《to》; abandon one's idea (in favor of); do an about-face. ¶저 청년은 좌파에서 우파로 전향하고 말았다 That young man has switched (his politics)[has undergone a conversion] from the left to the right.∥그들은 당국의 탄압에 굴복하여 마침내 전향하고 말았다 Submitting[Yielding] to oppression by the authorities, they finally gave up their (political) ideals[deserted their camp].∥그는 우리를 배반하고 적 쪽으로 전향했다 He betrayed us and went over to the enemy.
● **전향자** a convert; 〔배신자〕 a turncoat.

전혀(全─) 〔아주〕 quite; entirely; utterly; completely; wholly; totally; altogether; 〔부정문에서〕 not at all; not in the least. ¶~ 말도 안 되는 소리다 It is too absurd for words. / It is entirely[utterly] out of the question.∥사건과는 ~ 관계가 없다 I have absolutely nothing to do with the affair.∥그 일에 대해서는 ~ 모릅니다 I know nothing about it. / I don't know anything at all about it.∥그런 일은 ~ 생각해 본 일도 없다 That was the furthest thing from my mind.∥그의 말은 ~ 알 수가 없었다 I didn't understand even a word what he said.∥그것이 무엇인지 대충 잡을 수가 없다 I don't have the faintest[slightest / least / remotest] idea what it is.∥세금에 관하여는 나는 ~ 아는 바가 없다 I know absolutely nothing about taxes.∥아무리 비평을 받는다고 하더라도 나는 ~ 개의치 않는다 I don't give a damn[I don't care a jot] how much they criticize me.∥그녀는 유행에 관심이 ~ 없다 She doesn't care a bit about fashion.∥나는 술을 ~ 못 한다 I can't drink at all.∥나는 돈과는 ~ 인연이 없다 I never had much money.∥그것에 대하여는 ~ 아는 바가 없소 I know nothing (at all) about it.∥그는 그 소식을 듣고도 ~ 놀라지 않았다 He was not at all surprised to hear the news.∥그 두 그림 사이에는 비슷한 점이 ~ 없다 There is not the slightest resemblance between the two pictures.∥이 작품은 ~ 값어치가 없다 This work is quite[completely / perfectly] worthless.∥그런 계략인 줄은 ~ 모르고 그의 요구를 승낙했다 Entirely unaware of the trick, I complied with his request.∥그런 일에는 ~ 마음을 쓰지 않는다 I am not in the least worried about it.∥내가 들은 바와는 ~ 달랐다 It was entirely different from what I had heard.∥요즈음 나는 외출을 ~ 하지 않았다 I haven't been out at all lately.∥나는 ~ 아프지 않소 I have no pain at all.

전형(典型) 〔기준이 되는 형〕 a type; a pattern; a specimen; a model(모범). ¶여성의 ~ a model of womanhood∥그녀는 도덕적 한국 여성의 ~이었다 She was a model[paragon] of feminine virtue in Korea.∥그는 전후 작가의 ~이다 He is representative postwar writer.

전형(銓衡) selection; choice; screening. ¶그는 ~에서 누락되었다 He was rejected[turned down]. / He was not selected[chosen]. / He was passed over.∥그녀는 응모자 중에서 서류 ~으로 채용되었다 She was selected from among the applicants after a screening of documents. **전형하다** select; make choice; screen.
● **전형 기준** criteria for selection.

전형적(典型的) typical; model; ideal. ¶그는 ~인 영국 신사다 He is a typical English gentleman.

전호(前號) 〔앞의 호수〕 the last[preceding] issue[number]. ¶~까지의 줄거리 an outline of the story up to the last[preceding] number∥~에서 계속 《표시》 Continued from the last issue (of the magazine).

전화(電化) electrification. ¶농촌의 ~ rural electrification. **전화하다** electrify.

전화(電話) a telephone; 〔구어〕 a phone; a phone call; 〔영〕 a ring. ¶공중 ~ a public (tele)phone / 〔영〕 a pay phone / 〔공중 ~ 박스 a telephone booth / 〔미〕 a pay station∥구내 ~ 〔직통 전화〕 an interphone / 〔교환 전화〕 an extension (telephone) / 국제 ~ an international telephone call / 누름단추식 ~ a pushbutton phone / 〔영〕 a keyphone∥다이얼식 ~ a dial phone / 벽걸이식 ~ a wall telephone / 시내[시외] ~ a local[an out-of-town] telephone call∥자동 ~ a dial phone / 장거리 ~ a long-distance call / 〔영〕 a trunk call / 직통 ~ a direct telephone line / (정부 수뇌 간의) a hot line / 탁상 ~ a desk phone / 텔레비전 ~ a videophone / a videotelephone / 부재 중 녹음 ~ an answering machine / 장난[악의가 없는] a prank [crank] call / (외설한) an obscene phone call / a dirty[nasty] phone call / (괴롭히는) a harassing phone call / 잘못 걸린 ~ a wrong number∥~를 끊다 ring off / hang up∥~를 오래 하다 make a long phone call / talk for a

long time on the phone // 남과 ~로 연락하다 contact a person by phone // ~를 받는 분은 누구입니까 Who's speaking? // ~가 잘 들리지 않습니다. 조금 더 큰 소리로 말씀하세요 I can't hear you. — Will you speak louder, please? // ~를 써도 되겠습니까 May I use your telephone? // 누이와 ~로 이야기하다 I talked to my sister over the telephone. // 이렇게 이른[늦은] 시간에 ~를 드려 죄송합니다 I'm sorry to call you at this early[late] hour. // 결과는 ~로 알려 주십시오 Please let me know the results by phone. // 누가 좀 받아 주어요 Will somebody answer the telephone? // 미스 민을 대 드릴까요 Shall I put Miss Min on [call Miss Min to] the phone? // 당신에게 ~가 걸려 왔습니다 You are wanted on the phone. // ~왔습니다 There's a telephone call for you! // 이 ~는 잡음이 많다 This phone has lots of static. // 겨우 그와 ~가 통했다 I finally got him on the phone. // ~가 혼선되어 있다 The lines are crossed. // 이 ~는 통화 중입니다 (미) The line is busy. / (영) The number's engaged. // ~를 교장 선생님과 연결해 드리겠습니다 I'll put you through to the principal. // 그에게 ~를 걸었다 I called him. / I rang him up. // ~ 잘못 거셨습니다 You've got the wrong number. / You have the wrong number. // ~가 끊기었다 The connection was broken. / I was cut off. // ~를 끊지 말고 기다려 주세요 Please hold the line. // ~를 받으세요 Please answer the phone. // ~가 나왔습니다 (교환원이) You are connected. // 어머니는 지금 ~중이십니다 My mother is on the phone now. // 이 ~는 불통입니다 This telephone line is interrupted. / This telephone is out of order. / The line[wire] is dead. **전화하다** telephone; phone; (미) call (up); (영) ring (up); make a phone call (to); dial (다이얼을 돌려서). ¶112번에 ~하여 police / call 112 // 기상 예보는 131번에 전화하면 알 수 있다 Dial 131 for the weather forecast. // 내일 아침에 전화하겠다 I'll call you [give you a call] tomorrow morning. // 나한테 전화해 다오 Give me a call [ring / buzz]. / Call [Ring / Buzz / Phone] me. // 오늘은 못 간다고 홍 군에게 전화하겠다 I'll telephone Mr. Hong to say that I cannot come today.
●**전화 교환원** a telephone operator; (미국 구어) a hello girl(여성). ¶장거리 ~ a long distance operator. **전화국** a telephone office. **전화기** a telephone (set); (구어) a phone. **전화료** / **전화 요금** telephone charges. **전화번호** a (tele)phone number. ¶~가 잘못되었습니다 I have the wrong number. **전화번호부** a telephone directory; a (tele)phone book. ¶업종별 ~ a classified telephone directory / the Yellow Pages // ~를 찾아보다 consult the telephone directory. **전화선** a telephone wire [line].

전화(戰火) a fire caused by war. ⇨ ⁺병화(兵火).
전화(戰禍) the devastation[horrors / ravages / disasters] of war; war damage. ¶~를 입은 나라 a country devastated[ravaged] by war // ~를 입다 suffer the ravages of war // 그 도시는 심한 ~를 입었다 The town was severely damaged in the war.
전화(轉化) (a) change; (a) transformation. **전화하다** change; be transformed; (수크로오스가) be inverted.

전화위복(轉禍爲福) ¶이것을 ~의 기회로 삼자 Let's turn the misfortune to our advantage. **전화위복하다** turn a misfortune into a blessing.
전환(轉換) 1 [바꿈] conversion; switch; [변환] turnover; switchover. ¶성~ a change of sex / a sex change // 사고방식의 ~ a mental switchover / psychological reorientation // 군수 산업의 평화 산업으로의 ~ the switchover of war industries to peace industries // 외교 정책의 근본적 ~이 필요하다 A drastic switch [changeover] in foreign policies is necessary. // 그 방식으로의 ~은 간단히 됩니다 A conversion [switch / change] to that system can easily be made. **전환하다** convert; switch (from ... to ...); turn; change (over).
2 (마음의) diversion. ¶기분~으로 산책이라도 하지 그래 Why don't you take a walk for a change of air[a little diversion]? **전환하다** divert; turn. ¶주의를 딴 데로 ~ divert oneself from (cares) / turn one's attention (from something) to another // 노래를 불러 기분을 ~ divert oneself in singing.
●**전환기**(-期) a turning point; a transition period[stage]. ¶역사적 ~ a turning point in history // 당시 한국은 ~에 있었다 Korea was at a turning point [undergoing a transition] then. **전환기**(-器) a commutator; a switch. **전환점** a turning point. ¶그것이 내 인생의 ~이었다 That was the turning point of my career.

전황(戰況) the war [military] situation; the progress of a battle. ¶~을 보고하다 report on the military situation // ~은 아군에 불리하다 The war was not going in our favor.
전회(前回) the last time. ⇨ 지난번.
전회(轉回) 1 (a) revolution. ⇨ 회전(回轉) 2 [자리바꿈] [음] (an) inversion.
전후(前後) 1 [앞과 뒤] front and rear. 2 [순서·질서] order; sequence. ¶~가 뒤바뀌다 be inverted / be reversed // ~가 뒤바뀌어 있다 The order is inverted [reversed]. // 이야기가 ~가 뒤바뀌어 있다 The story lacks sequence. 3 [가량] about; around; or so; thereabout. ¶그녀는 20세~다 She is around twenty. // 40세 ~의 남자가 나를 찾아왔다 A man of about forty came to see me. // 나는 한 달에 100만 원 ~의 수입이 있다 I have an income of 1,000,000 won or so a month. / I have an income of around[about] 1,000,000 won a month.
●**전후좌우** four sides; all direction. ¶~에 all direction // (배가) ~로 흔들리다 pitch and roll // 나는 ~를 둘러보았다 I looked all around me.

전후(戰後) the postwar period [days / years / era]. ¶~의 postwar / afterwar / postbellum / (프) après guerre // ~에 after the war // 그의 집안은 ~에 완전히 몰락했다 His family has been reduced to poverty since the war.
●**전후파** the après guerre [postwar] generation [school]. ¶~의 청년들 young men of the postwar generation.
전후하다(前後-) 1 [거의 잇달아 일어나다] succeed on another; come one after another. ¶2개의 태풍이 그 섬을 전후하여 덮쳤다 Two typhoons hit the island one after another. // 형과 아우가 전후해서 도착했다 The brothers arrived within a few minutes of each other.

2 [일정한 때를 중심으로 그 안팎을 이루다]. ¶그 전람회는 크리스마스를 전후해서 개최될 예정이다 The exhibition is to be held before or after[sometimes around] Christmas. // 지진을 전후해서 화재가 발생했다 A fire broke out almost simultaneously with the earthquake. // 그는 9시 전후해서 왔다 He came about [around] nine o'clock.

전희(前戲) (sexual) foreplay.
절¹ (사찰) a (Buddhist) temple. ¶~에 불공을 드리러 가다 go to worship at a temple / visit a temple for worship.
절² (인사) a bow; an obeisance; a curtsy(여성의). ¶큰~ a (ceremonial) deep bow // 그들은 서로 공손히 ~을 했다 They bowed deeply at each other. // 그는 ~을 하고 자리를 물러났다 He bowed himself out. // 나는 여왕 폐하에게 ~을 했다 I curtsied to the queen. **절하다** bow (to); bow down (to); make a bow[an obeisance] (to). ¶공손히 ~ bow politely / make a low[polite] bow (to) / 가볍게 ~ bow slightly / 무릎을 꿇고 ~ bow down upon one's knees / 고맙다고 ~ bow one's thanks // 선생님에게 ~ bow to[salute] one's teacher.
절(節) 1 (글의) a paragraph; a passage; (시의) a stanza; (성경의) a verse. ¶제1장 제2~ Chapter I, Paragraph Ⅱ // 제1장 제1~ 을 번역하다 translate the first paragraph in chapter I // 나는 이 한 ~을 읽은 기억이 있다 I remember reading this passage. **2** (언) a clause.
-절(節) (명절) a (national) holiday; (구어) a red-letter day; a festival (day); (철) a season. ¶개천~ the National Foundation Day // 단오~ the *Dano* Festival.
절감(節減) reduction; curtailment; retrenchment. ¶경비의 ~ the retrenchment of expenditure. **절감하다** cut (down); cut down on; trim; reduce; curtail; retrench. ¶예산을 ~ make a retrenchment in the budget // 우리는 경비를 절감해야만 한다 We have to cut (down on) [trim] (our) expenses. / We have to reduce[curtail] our expenses. // 우리는 에너지 소비를 절감해야 한다 We have to cut down on[economize in] our consumption of energy.
절감하다(切感-) feel[realize] keenly[acutely]; become keenly aware (of). ¶외국어의 필요성을 ~ feel keenly the necessity of knowing some foreign language // 우리는 사회적 책임을 절감하고 있다 We keenly realize our social responsibility. // 나는 영어를 마스터하는 어려움을 절감했다 I acutely felt the difficulty of mastering English. // 이 실패로 평소의 연습이 얼마나 중요한가를 절감했다 This failure brought home to me[made me realize keenly] how important daily practice was.
절개(切開) (an) incision; an operation(수술). ¶복부 ~ an abdominal incision // 위 ~술 gastrotomy. **절개하다** cut open[out]; incise; make an incision (in); operate. ¶종기를 ~ incise a tumor // 환부를 ~ cut out an affected part.
● **절개 수술** a surgical operation; incision. ¶제왕 ~ a Caesarean operation // 나는 유방암의 ~을 받았다 I was operated on for breast cancer.
절개(節槪) constancy; fidelity; integrity; (신조) a principle; (정조) chastity. ¶~를 지키다 keep[remain faithful to] one's principles / (의자가) keep one's chastity // 그는 ~가 있는 사람이다 He is a man of integrity (principle). // 그녀는 ~가 없다 She is a loose woman. / She is a woman of questionable [dubious] character.
절거덕 1 (부딪는 소리) with a click[snap]. ¶문의 걸쇠를 ~ 잠그다 latch a door click // 그는 문을 ~ 닫았다 He clapped the door to. / 자물쇠가 ~ 잠겼다[열렸다] The lock clicked shut[open]. **절거덕하다** click; clank; clang; make a snap. **2** (들러붙는 모양). ¶벽에 포스터를 ~ 붙이다 paste[stick] a poster to the wall.
절거덕거리다 make snap[click] away; slap and slap. ¶절거덕거리는 쇠사슬 clanking chains.
절경(絶景) a wonderful sight; a superb view; beautiful[picturesque] scenery. ¶천하~ scenery beyond description[unparalleled in the world] // 참으로 ~이군 What a grand sight this is! // 이곳은 천하~이다 The view [scenery] here is unparalleled in its grandeur[beauty].
절교장(絶交狀) a letter breaking off one's relationship (with a person); (미국 속어) a Dear John (letter)(여자가 남자에게 보내는).
절교하다(絶交-) break off[sever] relations (with); cut[drop] one's acquaintance (with); cut with (a person). ¶창식이는 복동이와 절교했다 Changsik broke off his friendship with Bokdong. // 나는 그녀와 절교했다 I am through[finished] with her. / I'm done with her.
절구 a *jeolgu*; a (stone / wood) mortar. ¶~에 쌀을 찧다 pound rice in a mortar // 우리는 ~로 떡을 쳤다 We pounded boiled rice in a mortar to make rice cakes.
● **절구질** pounding grain in a mortar. **절구통** the body of a mortar; (뚱뚱한 사람) a plump fellow; a fat person. **절굿공이** a mallet; a pounder.
절구(絶句) (한시(漢詩)의 근체시 형식의 하나) a Chinese quatrain. ¶오언(五言) ~ a Chinese quatrain with five-character lines.
절규(絶叫) a scream; a shriek; an exclamation. ¶피맺힌 ~ the painful outcries. **절규하다** cry out; shout; scream; shriek; exclaim (at the top of one's voice). ¶정계의 정화(淨化)를 ~ cry loudly for the purification of the political world // "사람 살려!"라고 한 여인이 절규했다 A woman cried out[shouted] at the top of her voice for "help." / "Help!" a woman shrieked[screamed].
절그렁 with a clang[clank / clink]. ¶쇠사슬의 ~ 소리 the clang of chains // 그녀가 걸어가자 손에 든 열쇠 다발이 ~ 소리를 냈다 The keys in her hand clinked as she walked. **절그렁하다** clink. ⇨ 절그렁거리다
절그렁거리다 clink; jingle; rattle.
절기(節氣) (절후) the 24 divisions of the year (in the lunar calendar); the subdivisions of the seasons.
절다¹ (소금에) be[get] salted; be seasoned with salt. ¶이 배추는 알맞게 절었다 This cabbage is moderately salted.
절다² (다리를) limp; hobble; walk lame[with a limp]. ¶심하게[약간] ~ limp heavily [slightly] / have a bad[slight] limp // 오른쪽

다리를 ~ limp in the right leg // 절면서 걷다 limp along / walk lame [with a limp] / hobble (along) // 부상한 선수는 다리를 절며 벤치로 물러갔다 The injured player limped to the bench.

절단(切斷) cutting; severance; disconnection (전선 등의); amputation(손발의). **절단하다** cut; cut off; sever; disconnect; amputate. ¶둘로 ~ cut (a thing) in two // 전선을 ~ cut (off) a wire // 칼로 밧줄을 ~ sever a rope with a knife // 의사는 그의 왼쪽 다리를 무릎 위에서 절단했다 The doctor amputated his left leg above the knee. ¶절단된 손가락을 붙이다 rejoin a severed finger to the hand.
● **절단기** a cutting machine; a cutter; a shredder(서류 등의). **절단면** a (cross) section. [제도] a cutting plane.

절대(絶對) absoluteness. ¶~의 absolute / positive / unconditional / categorical // 불변의 immutable / permanent.
● **절대 개념** absolute concept. **절대 군주국** absolute monarchy. **절대다수 (win)** an absolute majority. **절대량** an absolute quantity. **절대 안정** a complete[an absolute] rest. ¶환자는 ~을 요한다 The patient must be kept absolutely at rest. ¶의사는 그녀에게 ~을 지시했다 She was ordered by the doctor to remain absolutely quiet[take complete bed rest]. **절대 온도** [물] absolute temperature. **절대 음악** absolute[abstract] music. **절대자** [철] the Absolute; the absolute being. **절대주의** [철][경] absolutism. **절대치** ➡**절댓값** [수] an absolute value.

절대로(絶對-) absolutely; positively; unconditionally. ¶~ 필요[불가능]하다 be absolutely necessary[impossible] // 그에게 말하지 마라 No matter what[Whatever you do], don't mention it to him. / Don't mention it to him under any circumstances. // ~ 가르쳐 줄 수 없다 I can't tell you for the life of me. // 나는 거기에 ~ 다시 가지 않겠다 I will never go there again. / (속어) [갈까 보냐] I'll be damned if I go there again! // 나는 그런 말을 한 적이 ~ 없다 I have never said such a thing. // 댁에 폐를 끼치지 않겠다는 것을 약속드립니다 I promise that I will cause [give] you no trouble whatever. / I promise I will not inconvenience you in any way. // ~ 뇌물을 받지 않았다는 것을 맹세합니다 I swear to God I never took a bribe.

절대적(絶對的) absolute; unconditional; positive; imperative; categorical. ¶~으로 absolutely / unconditionally / positively.

절도(節度) moderation. ¶~를 지키다 use [exercise] moderation (in) // 좀 ~ 있는 생활을 해 보는 것이 어떠냐 How about trying to put a bit of order in your life? / How about trying to lead a more ordered[a better regulated] life?

절도(竊盜) theft; stealing; pilferage(좀도둑질); [법] larceny; [범인] a thief (*pl.* thieves). **절도하다** commit a theft; steal; pilfer; filch. ¶시계를 절도한 혐의로 on a charge[the suspicion] of the larceny of a watch.
● **절도죄** theft; [법] larceny. ¶그는 ~로 체포되었다 He was arrested on a charge of theft.

절뚝거리다 limp; hobble. ➪**절다**²
절뚝발이 a lame person. ➪**절름발이**
절레절레 shaking one's head. ¶그녀는 그것은 싫다고 고개를 ~ 흔들었다 She shook her head to show she didn't like it.

절로 1 of[by] itself. ➪**저절로 2** [저리로] that way[direction] over there.
절룩거리다 limp; hobble. ➪**절다**²
절름거리다 limp; hobble. ➪**절다**²
절름발이 a lame person; a cripple. ¶~가 되다 become lame[crippled] / go[fall] lame // 그는 심한 ~다 He is badly lame. / He is a bad cripple.

절망(絶望) despair; hopelessness. ¶~에 빠지다 give way to despair // ~ 상태에 있다 be in a desperate situation // ~의 구렁텅이에 빠져 있다 be (sunk) in the depths of despair. **절망하다** despair of (one's future); be driven to despair; give up (all) hope. ¶절망 끝에 out of despair / driven[overcome] by despair // 절망하여 in despair / despairingly // 그는 절망한 끝에 자살을 기도했다 He attempted to suicide out of despair. // 그는 도시 생활에 절망하고 있었다 He had despaired of city life. // 그는 인생에 절망했다 He has lost faith in life. ➔¶**절망시키다** make (a person) despair / drive (a person) to despair.

절망적(絶望的) hopeless; desperate; despairful. ¶환자의 생명은 이미 ~이다 The patient's life is despaired of. // 전황은 ~이다 The war situation is hopeless. // 이달의 우리 집 가계는 ~인 상태이다 Our household budget is in a desperate state[in a bad way] this month. // 전도는 아주 ~이다 There is not a slim chance[a gleam of hope] before us. // 그는 이제 ~이다 (위독하여) He is past hope. / (조난당하여) He has been given up for lost.

절멸(絶滅) [아주 없어짐] extinction; [아주 없앰] extermination; annihilation; eradication. ¶~ 직전까지 (be hunted) nearly to the point of extinction // 성병의 ~을 도모하다 try to exterminate venereal diseases // 따오기는 ~ 직전에 있다 The crested ibis is on the verge of extinction. **절멸하다** become extinct; go out of existence; die out; exterminate; annihilate. ¶절멸한 민족 a lost[an extinct] race // 도도새는 절멸했다 The Dodo has become extinct.

절명(絶命) death. **절명하다** die; expire; pass away; breathe one's last. ¶그렇게 말하고 그는 절명했다 With these words, he breathed his last.

절묘하다(絶妙-) superb; exquisite; miraculous. ¶절묘한 재주 a miraculous feat // 절묘한 필치 an exquisite touch // 그 곡예사는 절묘한 연기로 관객을 흥분시켰다 The acrobat thrilled all the spectators with his marvelous performance. // 이 시는 서정성과 이성(理性)이 절묘한 조화를 이루고 있다 This poem exhibits an exquisite balance between lyricism and reason.

절미(節米) economy in rice consumption; rice saving. **절미하다** economize (in) rice; save rice.
● **절미 운동** a movement for rice saving.

절박하다(切迫-) 1 [시급하다] urgent; pressing; impending; imminent. ¶절박한 문제 a pressing question // 절박한 위기 imminent crisis // 절박한 필요성 an urgent[a pressing] need // 시일이 ~ Time presses. / There is no time to lose. / There is very little time left. // 입학시험 기일이 ~ The entrance examina-

절반(折半) a half. ¶컵의 ~ half a cup /~의 크기[값] half the size[price] // ~씩 나누ى go halves[shares] / share (something) half and half (with a person)//저녁 식사대를 ~ 씩 나누다 go fifty[split the bill] on the cost of a dinner//벌써 ~은 왔다 We have already covered half the distance[come half the way]. // 과일의 ~은 썩었다 Half (of) the fruit is bad. /계란의 ~은 상했다 Half (of) the eggs are rotten(▶ 동사는 half (of) 뒤의 명사 와 일치).

절버덕 with a splash[slosh]. 절버덕하다 splash. ⇨ ~절버덕거리다

절버덕거리다 splash; slosh. ¶아이들은 절버덕거리며 시냇물로 들어갔다 The children walked into the stream, splashing as they went. / The children sloshed into the stream.

절벅 with a splash. ⇨ ~절버덕

절벽(絶壁) a cliff; a precipice. ¶깎아지른 듯한 ~ a mural[vertical] cliff// ~을 기어오르다 scale[climb] a cliff/~에서 추락하다 fall off a cliff.

절삭(切削) cutting. 절삭하다 cut.
● 절삭 공구 a cutting tool.

절상(切上) (평가의) revaluation (of the currency). 절상하다 revaluate. ¶평가[원]를 ~ revaluate the currency[the won] (upward).

절색(絶色) a rare beauty; a woman of matchless[peerless] beauty; the fairest of the fair.

절세(絶世) [뛰어남]. ¶~의 peerless / matchless / unequaled (in beauty) / unsurpassed.
● 절세미인 a rare beauty; a woman of matchless[peerless] beauty. ¶그녀는 ~이다 I have never seen such a beautiful woman as she. / She is a woman of matchless [peerless] beauty. / She is unequaled in beauty.

절수(節水) economization of water; water saving. ¶시 당국은 시민들에게 ~를 호소했다 City officials called on the people to conserve water[cut back on their use of water]. 절수하다 economize (in) water. ¶우리는 여름 내 절수해야 했다 We had to use water sparingly all through the summer.

절식(絶食) a fast. ⇨ ~단식(斷食)

절식(節食) moderation in eating; an abstemious[a spare] diet. 절식하다 be moderate in eating; eat moderately; control one's eating; (병·미용 등으로) be on a diet. ¶그녀는 너무 뚱뚱해져서 절식하고 있다 As she is overweight, she is on a diet[dieting].

절실하다(切實하다) [중대하고 심각하다] serious; severe; [정세가 긴박하다] acute; [진정이다] earnest; [절박하다] pressing; urgent. ¶절실한 소원 an earnest desire/ 절실한 요구 a pressing need//식량 부족은 절실한 문제이다 Food shortage is a serious[severe] problem. //주택 (부족) 문제는 여전히 ~에 ever. 절실히 acutely; keenly; fully; urgently. ¶…의 필요성을 ~ 느끼다 feel keenly the necessity of ... // 나는 사태의 중대성을 ~ 느끼고 있었다 I was keenly[acutely] aware of the seriousness of the situation.

절약(節約) economy; saving; frugality; thrift. ¶경비의 ~ reduction of overhead[costs / expenditures] // 시간 ~ the saving of time. 절약하다 economize; spare; save; be frugal [economical / thrifty]; [절감하다] curtail; cut (down). ¶전기를 ~ economize on electric power/ 경비를 ~ cut down expenses // 시간과 돈을 ~ save[be frugal of] time and money//이 방법으로 하면 시간을 절약할 수 있다 This method will save time. → 그것은 경비가 절약된다 That will cut down on [reduce] expenses. // 이것은 많은 시간[노력] 이 절약된다 This will save a great deal of time[labor]. // 그렇게 하면 다달이 2,000원이 절약된다 It will save me two thousand won a month. // 나는 비용이 절약되었다 I was spared the expense. // 지름길로 가면 10분이 절약된다 You can save ten minutes by taking a shortcut.
● 절약가 a thrifty[an economical] person; an economist.

절연(絶緣) 1 [인연·관계를 끊음] disconnection; divorcement. 절연하다 break (with); break off[sever] relations (with); (미) be through with. ¶그 사람과는 절연했다 I have broken (off) relations with him. / I have done with him. / I am through with him. 2 [전] insulation; isolation. 절연하다 insulate; isolate. ¶절연한 insulated / isolated.
● 절연기(~器) an insulator; a (cut-off) switch. 절연선 an insulated wire. 절연 재료 / 절연물 an insulating material. 절연체 [전] an insulator; an isolator.

절연(節煙) temperance[moderation] in smoking. 절연하다 be temperate[moderate] in smoking; cut down on one's smoking. ¶ 나는 지금 절연하고 있는 중이다 I'm trying to smoke less[cut down on my smoking]. // 좀 절연하는 것이 좋겠다 Don't smoke too much.

절의(節義) fidelity to one's principle; constancy; honor. ¶~를 중히 여기다 adhere to one's principles / stick to one's colors.

절이다 salt (vegetables); preserve (fish) in [with] salt. ¶절인 배추 salted cabbage //생선을 소금에 ~ salt fish (down) / preserve fish in salt.

절전(節電) economy in power consumption; power saving. 절전하다 economize (in) power; save electricity.
● 절전 운동 a power-savings campaign.

절절 simmeringly; shakingly; bustlingly. ⇨ 잘잘·1·2·3

절절하다(切切하다) earnest; eager; ardent. ¶절절한 사랑의 편지 an ardent love letter. 절절히 earnestly; eagerly; ardently. ¶~ 호소하다 appeal earnestly[ardently].

절정(絶頂) 1 [산꼭대기] a mountaintop; the summit[top] of a mountain. 2 [정점] the peak; the height; the acme; the climax. ¶번영의 ~에 있다 be at the zenith of prosperity/ 융성의 ~에 이르다 attain the acme of prosperity/ 그 여배우는 지금 인기가 ~에 있다 The actress is at the top[peak] of her popularity. // 가을이 그 ~에 있다 Autumn is at its height. / We're getting to the best part of autumn. / 선거 운동이 지금 ~에 있다 The election campaign is in full

절제(切除) (외과에서) excision; a resection(조직 일부의). ¶위 ~ the resection of a person's stomach // 폐 ~술 pneumonectomy.
절제하다 remove surgically; cut off[out]; excise; resect. ¶폐엽을 ~ remove one lobe of a lung / perform a lobectomy.

절제(節制) moderation; temperance; abstinence; self-restraint; continence(성욕의). ¶음식의 ~는 가장 좋은 약이다 Temperance is the best medicine. / Moderation is everything to the health. / Feed by measure and defy the physician. **절제하다** be moderate [temperate] (in); abstain (from); restrain; be continent. ¶술을 ~ be temperate [moderate] in drinking // 욕망을 ~ control one's passion(성욕을) // 의사는 내게 음식을 절제하도록 권했다 The doctor advised moderation in eating and drinking[advised me to cut down on my eating and drinking].
● **절제 생활** temperate living.

절조(節操) principle; constancy. ⇨ˇ지조(志操)

절주(節酒) moderation in drinking. **절주하다** be moderate in drinking; cut down on one's drinking.

절지동물(節肢動物) 〔동〕 an arthropod.

절차(節次) 〔순서〕 a procedure; a process; 〔법률·규칙상 필요한 것〕 formalities; 〔단계〕 steps; (소송의) proceedings. ¶소송 ~ legal proceedings // 수출 ~ export procedure // 법률상의 번거로운 ~ the cumbersome processes of the law // ~상의 문제 a procedural issue // ~에 따라서 according to[in accordance with] procedure // ~를 **밟다** go through (due) formalities / take proceedings // 공항에서 입국 ~를 밟아야 한다 You have to go through the entry procedure[formalities] at the airport. // 입국 ~는 이달 중으로 완료해야 한다 The entrance procedures must be completed by the end of this month. // 나는 정식 ~를 밟아 이 아이를 양녀로 했다 I followed the prescribed legal procedures and took this child as my adopted daughter. // 외국에 가려면 어떤 ~를 밟아야 하는지 알려 주십시오 Please tell me what steps I must take (in order) to go abroad. // 그 물품을 수입하는 데는 복잡한 ~가 있다 You have to go through complicated formalities to import that article.
● **절차법** 〔법〕 the law of procedure; procedural law; an adjective law.

절찬(絶讚) high praise; great admiration. ¶그의 연기는 전례 없는 ~을 받았다 His acting won[received] unprecedented praise. // 그들의 협력 정신은 ~을 받을 만하다 Their spirit of cooperation is highly admirable. // ~리에 판매 중 Widely acclaimed[Rave reviews]! Now on sale. // ~리에 상영 ~ 중 Now showing amid enormous popular acclaim! **절찬하다** praise highly; admire greatly; speak in the highest terms of; be loud in one's praise; extol. ¶그는 그녀의 용기 있는 행위를 절찬했다 He extolled her courageous deed to the skies.

절창(絶唱) 1 〔뛰어난 시가〕 a superb song [poem]; an excellent piece of poetry. 2 〔뛰어난 명창〕 a superb singer.

절충(折衷) a compromise; a cross; blending.

¶~적인 eclectic // 정치적 ~을 모색하다 seek political compromise. **절충하다** arrange [make] compromise (between); blend; compromise. ¶내 안과 그의 안을 절충하여 최종적 제안을 결정했다 He and I combined our ideas and decided on a final compromise proposal. // 이것은 회화와 조각을 절충한 것 같은 작품이다 This work is, so to speak, a cross between a painting and a sculpture.
● **절충안** a compromise (plan). **절충주의** eclecticism.

절충(折衝) negotiation(s). ¶~을 거듭한 결과 after protracted negotiation // 현재 노사간에 ~ 중이다 Negotiations are now under way [going on] between labor and management. // 그 일은 양국 사이에서 외교적 ~을 하고 있다 It is under diplomatic negotiation between the two nations. **절충하다** negotiate (with). ¶영토 문제로 이웃 나라와 ~ negotiate with a neighboring country on[over] the territorial issue.

절취(竊取) 〔훔쳐서 제 것으로 함〕 theft; stealing; pilferage(좀도둑질). **절취하다** steal; commit a theft; pilfer.

절취선(切取線) the line along which to cut (a section) off; 〔접선〕 a dotted line; 〔바늘구멍〕 a perforated line.

절치부심하다(切齒腐心−) gnash[grind] one's teeth with vexation[chagrin]; grit one's teeth.

절친하다(切親−) intimate; familiar; close. ¶절친한 친구 a close[one's best] friend // 나는 그와 ~ I am intimately acquainted with him. / He and I are good friend. // 그는 나의 절친한 친구 중 한 사람이다 He is one of my good[close / best] friends.

절터 a temple site; the site[ruins] of a temple.

절판(絶版) going out of print. ¶그 책은 ~입니다 The book is out of print. **절판하다** print no more copies of (the book). ➔¶**절판되다** go out of print.

절편 *jeolpyeon*; a flat[round] rice cake with flower pattern imprinted.

절편(截片) 〔수〕 an intercept.

절품(絶品) absence of stock. ⇨ˇ품절(品切)

절품(絶品) 〔아주 뛰어난 물건·작품〕 an article of superb[unrivaled] quality; 〔비길 데 없이 독특한 물건〕 a unique article; a rare object. ¶이것은 목판화의 ~이다 This is an excellent [a rare] wood-block print.

절필(絶筆) 1 〔마지막 글〕 a person's last piece of writing[written composition]; a person's last printed effort. ¶이 수필이 그의 ~이 되었다 This essay was the last thing he wrote before his death. 2 〔글 쓰기를 그만둠〕 giving up writing; putting down one's pen. **절필하다** give up (further) writing; break the pencil.

절하(切下) (a) cut[reduction] (in price). ¶평가 ~ 〔경〕 devaluation (of the currency). **절하하다** cut (down) (to); reduce (to). ¶평가를 ~ devaluate[(미) devalue] (the currency) // 원을 30퍼센트 ~ devalue the won by 30 percent. ➔¶그 나라의 통화는 50% 절하되었다 The currency of the country was devalued by 50 percent.

절호(絶好) ¶~의 best / ideal / perfect / capital / splendid / grand / excellent / golden // ~의 기회 the best chance / a golden[rare]

절후(節候) the 24 divisions of the year(in the lunar calendar). ⇨절기(節氣)

젊다 young; youthful. ¶젊은 사람들 young people // 젊었을 때에 when (one is) young / in one's youth // 젊었을 때부터 from one's youth[early years] // 그의 아버지는 아직 ~ His father is still young. // 당신은 나이보다 훨씬 젊어 보이는군요 You looks much younger (than your age). // 너는 아직 젊으니까 괜찮다 You have still a number of hopeful years to live. // 그는 나이는 젊지만 생각은 깊다 He has an old head on young shoulders. // 비록 늙었어도 그는 마음만은 ~ Though old, he has a youthful spirit. // 그는 정치가로서는 젊은 편이다 He is young as statesmen go. // 그녀는 이제 40대이지만 젊었을 때의 모습 그대로이다 She has kept her youthful figure, though she is already in her forties. // 그는 젊어서 죽었다 He died young. // 그는 한국의 젊은 작가 중에서는 최고에 속한다 He is among the best of the younger generation of Korean writers.

젊디젊다 quite young. ¶그녀는 젊디젊은 나이에 과부가 되었다 She became a widow when she is still quite young.

젊어지다 grow younger; restore youth; rejuvenate. ¶화장을 하면 다섯 살은 젊어진다 Makeup will take at least five years off your age. / You will look at least five years younger if you use makeup. / 아이들과 놀면 다시 젊어진 듯한 기분이 든다 When I play with children, I feel young again. // 새로운 일이 그를 젊어지게 했다 His new job has rejuvenated him.

젊은이 [젊은 남자] a young man; a youth; a lad; [젊은 남녀] a young person; a youngster(특히 나이 어린 사람·소년 등에 씀);〔집합적〕 the young; young people; young men and women; the youth. ¶마을의 ~들 the young people in the village // ~의 피를 끓게 하다 inflame the blood[ardor] of youth / stir young men's blood // 그 전투에서 많은 ~가 죽었다 Many young men were killed in the battle. // 그녀는 10대 ~의 우상이다 She is the idol of teen-age youngster.

젊음 youth; youthfulness. ¶그는 아직 ~을 잃지 않고 있다 He still keeps[retains] his youthfulness[youth]. / 여자는 ~이 생명이다 Youth is a woman's life. // ~은 보배다 Youth is a treasure.

점(占) fortune-telling; divination. ¶관상 ~ divination by the features // 카드로 ~을 치다 tell fortunes with cards // 혼자 ~을 치다(남자로) play solitaire // ~을 쳐 달라고 하다 have one's fortune told / consult a fortune-teller // ~에서 …고 나오다 The fortune-teller[My fortune] says that ….

점(點) **1** [반점] a dot; a spot; a speck; a speckle. ¶갈색 ~이 박인 흰 개 a white dog with brown spots // ~을 찍다 mark with a dot / spot / dot // 연필로 ~을 찍었다 I made a dot with a pencil. // i자의 ~ 찍는 것을 잊지 마라 Don't forget to dot the i's. // 그녀의 은제 식기에는 한 ~의 얼룩도 없었다 Her silver plate is spotless. // 어제저녁에는 바람 한 ~ 없었다 There was not a breath of air last evening. // 하늘엔 구름 한 ~ 없었다 There is not a speck of cloud in the sky. // 나는 그 산의 위치를 나타내기 위해 지도에 빨간 ~을 찍었다 I put a red dot on the map to mark the position of the mountain.
2 (기호로서의) a point. ¶온 ~ a full stop [point] / a period // 가운뎃 ~ the middle point // 구두 ~을 찍다 punctuate.
3 [논점] a point; [견지] a standpoint; a point of view; a viewpoint; 〔사항〕 respect. ¶어떤 ~에서는 in some respects[points] // 문제가 되는 ~을 먼저 밝히기로 합시다 Let us first clarify the point in question. // 인간은 말을 할 수 있다는 ~에서 동물과 다르다 Human beings are different from animals in that they can speak. // 그 ~에서 말한다면 나로서는 빠를수록 좋겠소 From that point of view[standpoint], I would say the sooner the better. // 그 ~에서는 당신과 완전히 동감입니다 In that respect, I agree with you completely. // 색깔은 좋지 않으나 그 밖의 ~은 아주 좋다 The color(ing) is not too good, but otherwise it is quite satisfactory. // 그게 그의 좋은 ~이다 That is his good[strong] point. // 그는 모든 ~에서 나보다 낫다 In every respect[way] he is superior to me.
4 [피부의] a mole; [의] a tache; [모반] a birthmark; [의] a nevus. ¶~을 빼다 remove a mole.
5 [수] a point; a dot; 〔소수점〕 a decimal point. ¶3.14퍼센트 three point one four percent.
6 [성적의 평가] marks; grades. ¶60~으로 시험에 합격하다 pass an examination with a score[(미)grade / (영)mark] of 60 // 그는 물리 시험에서 100~ 만점 중 95~을 받았다 He got 95 percent in the physics exam. / He got 95 marks out of 100 in the physics exam. // "너는 몇 ~ 받았니?" "40~이야." "How much[What / What mark / What percent] did you get?" "40 (marks[percents])." // 100~ 만점이다 A perfect score is a hundred.
7 [경기의 득점] a point; [총득점] a score; (야구·크리켓의) a run. ¶1~도 얻지 못하고 물러나다 be put out without a run // 2회에 2 ~을 따다 score two runs in the second inning // 우리 팀이 3~ 땄다 Our team scored 3 points. / (야구에서) Our team earned [scored] 3 runs.
8 [물품의 수] an item; a piece. ¶가구 3~ three pieces of furniture // 의류 10~ ten items[pieces] of clothing // 시계, 목걸이, 양복 등 4~을 도둑맞았다 Four items including a watch, a necklace, and a suit were stolen.
9 [바둑판 돌의 수] a stone; a piece; [바둑판의 눈] a cross. ¶한 ~ 두다 put[place] a stone.
10 [고기·생선 등의 작은 조각] a piece (of meat); a cut; a slice. ¶포커커틀릿 한 ~ a bite-sized piece of pork cutlet.

-점(店) [가게] a store; (영) a shop. ¶양복~ a tailor's (shop).

점감(漸減) [점점 줄어듦] a gradual decrease; (a) diminution. **점감하다** decrease[diminish] gradually; dwindle; be on the decrease.

점거(占據) occupation. ¶불법 ~ unlawful [illegal] occupation. **점거하다** occupy. ¶그는 방 2개를 점거하고 있다 He has two rooms all to himself.

●**점거자** an occupant; an inmate. **점거지** an

점검(點檢) 1 (물건의) (an) inspection; (an) examination; (a) check. ¶불시 ~ a spot check[test] // 엔진 ~ an engine checkup // 피복 ~ inspection of clothing // (자동차의) 정기[6개월] ~ a periodical[semiannual] inspection (of a car). 점검하다 inspect; examine; check. ¶기계를 ~ inspect[check] a machine // …을 점검하겠습니다 Please let me check …. 점검하다 call the roll. ¶그는 작업 인원을 점검했다 He took a[the] roll call of the workers.

점고(漸高) [차차 높아짐] a gradual rise [elevation]. 점고하다 rise [ascend / increase] gradually. ¶…에 대한 관심이 ~ take[have] a gradual growing[increasing] of interest in …

점괘(占卦) a divinatory sign. ¶~가 좋다[나쁘다] have a good[an ill] divination sign.

점근(漸近) [점점 가까워짐] a gradual approach. 점근하다 approach gradually; get nearer (to).
● 점근선 an asymptote; an asymptotic line.

점대(占一) [점칠 때 쓰는 대오리] divining sticks.

점대칭(點對稱) [수] point symmetry.

점도(粘度) [물] viscosity. ⇨ ~점성도⇨점성(粘性))

점두(店頭) [가게의 앞쪽] (미) a store front; (영) a shop front; [쇼윈도] (영) a shopwindow. ¶~의 물건 things on sale (in a shop) // ~에 장식되어 있는 옷 a clothes displayed in the shopwindow // 이 물건은 ~에서는 팔지 않고 직접 손님에게 우송한다 These articles are not sold over the counter, but are sent to customers directly by mail.
● 점두 거래 / 점두 매매 over-the-counter transactions[trading]. 점두 장식 window dressing[trimming].

점등(漸騰) [시세가 점점 오름] a gradual rise (in prices). 점등하다 rise gradually[little by little]; make a gradual rise. ¶주가(株價)가 점등하고 있다 Stock is rising gradually.

점등(點燈) [등에 불을 켬] lighting. 점등하다 turn[switch] on a light; light a lamp.
● 점등 시간 lighting-up time.

점락(點落) 1 [시세가 점점 내려감] a gradual fall (of prices). 점락하다 fall[decline] gradually. 2 [증권] a gradual decline; sagging; a droop. 점락하다 ease off; recede; sag.

점령(占領) [점거] occupation; [공략] capture; [점유] possession. ¶도시의 ~ capture of a town // 그곳은 프랑스 군의 ~하에 들어갔다 It was occupied by the French. 점령하다 occupy; capture; take; take possession of. ¶적의 군대는 그 소도시를 점령했다 Enemy troops occupied[took] the town.
● 점령군 the occupation forces[troops / army]. 점령지 (an) occupied territory.

점막(粘膜) a mucous membrane.

점멸(點滅) flickering. 점멸하다 [켰다 껐다 하다] turn[switch] on and off; blink; [켜였다 꺼졌다 하다] go[come] on and off. ¶크리스마스트리에 걸린 장식용 꼬마전구가 점멸하고 있다 The fairy lamps hung on the Christmas tree flash[blink] on and off. ➔¶경찰관은 회중전등을 점멸시켰다 The policeman switched his flashlight on and off.
● 점멸기 a switch. 점멸등 an on-and-off light; a flasher.

점묘(點描) a sketch. ¶인물 ~ a character sketch / a personal profile. 점묘하다 sketch.
● 점묘 화가 a pointillist. 점묘 화법 pointillism.

점박이(點─) [큰 점이 있는 사람] a person with a birthmark[mole]; [큰 점이 있는 동물] a spotted[speckled] animal.

점방(店房) a store. ⇨ ~가게

점보 1 [특대의 것]. ¶~인 huge / (구어) jumbo. 2 (사진 인화의) a jumbo-sized print.
● 점보제트기 a jumbo jet.

점서(占書) [점술에 관한 책] a fortune(-telling) book; a book on divination.

점선(點線) [점 구멍이 나 있는 떼어 내는 선] a dotted line; a broken line; a perforated line. ¶~을 긋다 draw a dotted line // ~을 친 글에 주의하시오 Pay attention to the sentence with the dotted line. // ~에서 떼어 낼 것 Tear off along the perforated line.

점성(占星) divination by the stars; horoscope.
● 점성가 / 점성술사 an astrologist; an astrologer. 점성술 / 점성학 astrology.

점성(粘性) [차지고 끈끈한 성질] viscosity. ¶~의 viscous.
● 점성도(─度) [물] viscosity.

점수(點數) 1 [성적을 나타내는 숫자] (merit) marks; (미) grades. ¶~를 매기다 give marks / give (a student) his percentile score / rate (80%) / award points // 나는 좋은 ~를 따고 싶다 I'd like to get good marks. // 우리 선생님은 ~가 후하다[짜다] Our teacher is an easy[a hard] marker. / Our teacher is lenient[strict] in evaluating his students. // 나는 낮은 ~로 시험에 합격했다 I passed the test with a low mark. // 그는 ~를 따려고 상사에게 알랑거렸다 He flattered his boss in order to score points with him.
2 (경기 등의) points; a score; (야구의) runs. ¶~를 많이 따다 make a good score // 라이온스는 ~ 차를 벌렸다[좁혔다] The Lions widened[closed] the gap. // 호루라기를 부는 동안에 들어간 공은 ~가 된다 A shot scored while the whistle is blowing counts (as a point).
3 points. ⇨ ~끗수

점수(를) 따다 [좋게 평가받다] get on (a person's) good[right] side. ¶그 사람에게 점수 좀 따 봐 Try to get on his good side.

점술(占術) the art of divination; fortunetelling.

점신세(漸新世) [지] the Oligocene age. ⇨ ~올리고세.

점심(點心) (a) lunch; (a) luncheon(다소 격식을 차린 것). ¶가벼운 ~ a light lunch // ~을 먹다 eat[have] lunch // 나는 ~에 샌드위치를 먹었다 I had sandwiches for lunch.
● 점심때 lunch time; noontime; noon. 점심 시간 lunch time; a lunch break. ¶~은 한 시간이다 We have an hour's lunch break.

점안(點眼) dropping lotion in the eyes. 점안하다 apply eyewash (to); drop (eye) lotion in the eyes. ¶하루 3번 이 약을 점안한 Use these eye drops three times a day.
● 점안수 eye drops; eye wash.

점액(粘液) [끈끈한 액체] (a) viscous liquid; (동식물의) mucus; (식물의) mucilage. ¶~의 mucous / (식물의) mucilaginous // ~을 분비하다 secrete viscous liquid[mucus].

점액 분비 secretion of mucus. **점액선** a mucous gland; (괄태충 등의) a slime gland.
점액질 [심] a phlegmatic temperament. ¶~인 사람 a person of phlegmatic temperament.

점원(店員) (남자) a shop assistant; (미) a (store) clerk; (여자) a saleslady; a saleswoman; salesgirl; a shopgirl. ¶그는 식료품점의 ~이다 He is a clerk in a grocery store.

점유(占有) occupation; [소유] possession; (특히 토지·가옥의) occupancy. ¶불법 ~ [법] detention / deforcement / detinue /그 토지의 ~는 불법이다 The occupation of the land is illegal. **점유하다** occupy; possess; take possession of. ¶그 회사는 시장의 30퍼센트를 점유하고 있다 The company has a 30% market share.
● **점유권** the right of possession; a possessory right. ¶토지의 ~ a possessory title to land /~을 획득하다 [법] acquire possession (of). **점유물** a possession. **점유율** ¶시장 ~ market share / percentage of the market. **점유자** the owner; a possessor.

점음표(點音標) [음] a dotted note.

점입가경(漸入佳境) approaching the climax. ¶이야기가 ~이다 The story become more and more interesting. **점입가경하다** approach a climax; get more interesting; grow in fascination.

점자(點字) [맹인용 문자] Braille (braille) (dots); braille points [type]; raised letters. ¶~를 읽다 read braille // ~로 옮기다 put into braille.
● **점자 도서관** a braille library. **점자 책** a book in braille.

점잔 a dignified air. ¶~을 부리다 [빼다 / 피우다] assume a dignified air / behave in a genteel way /그는 남들 앞에서는 ~을 뺀다 He puts on [assumes] a look of studied composure in public. // 아무리 ~을 빼 봐야 우리는 그의 내력을 알고 있다 It doesn't make any difference what airs he put on — we know his background.

점잖다 [품격이 높다] gentle; decent; respectable; [의젓하고 바르다] dignified; grave; (빛깔이) quiet; sober. ¶점잖은 사람 a man of polished manners and good taste // 점잖지 못한 [품위 없는] indecent / [호색적인] lascivious / [버릇없는] improper(완곡한 표현) /점잖은 체하다 put on airs // 말씨가 ~ use refined language / be refined in one's speech /그녀는 점잖게 차려입고 있다 She is dressed elegantly [in good taste]. // 그는 여자 분에게 점잖지 못한 행동을 했다 He took liberties [behaved indecently] with a woman.

점재하다(點在-) [점점이 있다] be dotted (with); [간격을 두고 있다] be studded (with). ¶만(灣) 안에는 작은 섬들이 점재해 있다 The bay is dotted [studded] with islets. // 풀밭 속에 꽃이 점재해 있다 The grass is starred with flowers.

점쟁이(占-) a diviner; a soothsayer; a fortuneteller; a palmist(손금을 보는). ¶거리의 ~ a street / [미] sidewalk / (경) pavement] fortuneteller // ~에게 미래를 점쳐 달라고 하다 consult a fortuneteller about one's future.

점점(漸漸) [서서히] gradually; [조금씩] little by little; [차례차례] one after another; step by step. ¶~ (더) more and more // ~ 적어져 가다 /지구의 자원은 ~ 적어져 가고 있다 The earth's natural resources are getting [becoming] less and less. // 그는 ~ 지반을 굳혀 갔다 He gained ground him by inch [by degrees]. // 날이 ~ 더워졌다 It is getting hotter and hotter. // 소리는 ~ 멀어졌다 The sound died away. // 환자는 ~ 회복되고 있다 The patient is gradually gaining strength. // 그의 용태가 ~ 나빠진다 His condition is going from bad to worse. // 그의 모습은 ~ 어둠 속에 사라져 갔다 His figure gradually disappeared into the darkness. // 형세는 그에게 ~ 불리해지고 있다 Things are getting less and less favorable for him. // 물가가 ~ 올라가고 있다 Commodity prices are going up all the time.

점점이(點點-) [여기저기에] here and there; [흩어져서] scattered; sporadically. ¶들판에는 작은 집들이 ~ 있다 Small houses stand here and there in the plain. // 마루에는 피가 ~ 떨어졌다 Blood fell in drops on [dripped onto] the floor. // 하늘에는 ~ 별이 반짝이고 있었다 The sky was studded [strewn / strewed] with twinkling stars. // 호수에는 ~ 보트가 떠 있었다 The lake was dotted with boats.

점주(店主) [가게의 주인] (미) a storekeeper; (영) a shopkeeper; a proprietor [an owner / a proprietress] of a store [shop] (▶ proprietress는 여주인).

점증(漸增) [점점 증가함] gradual increase. **점증하다** increase gradually [by degrees / little by little]; be on the increase. ¶그의 지지자는 점증하고 있다 The number of his supporters is increasing gradually [little by little]. →정부는 군사력을 점증시킬 방침이다 The government is planning to increase the nation's military strength by degrees.

점지하다 bless (a person) with a baby. ¶이 아이는 하늘이 점지해 주신 아이다 This child is a blessing [a gift from God].

점진(漸進) gradual progress; steady advance. ¶이 방면의 기술은 ~적으로 발달하고 있다 Techniques in this field are being gradually improved [showing gradual progress]. // 위원회는 ~적인 개혁안을 가다듬었다 The committee has worked out a moderate reform plan. **점진하다** advance gradually; make gradual progress.
● **점진주의** gradualism; a moderate [slow-and-steady] policy. **점진주의자** a gradualist.

점찍다(點-) have [keep] one's eye(s) [an eye] on; mark out [down] for; (골라서) pick out (a house for hire); spot. ¶(마음속에) 점찍어 놓은 사람 the person one is thinking of / a man [girl] of one's heart / the choice of one's heart /범인은 점찍어 놓았다 The culprit is spotted. // 저 세 사람이 수상하다고 점찍고 있다 I have an eye to those three, whom I suspect to be offenders. // 경찰은 그를 점찍어 놓고 있었다 The police were keeping their eyes on him.

점차(漸次) gradually. ⇨ 점점

점착(粘着) adhesion; cohesion. **점착하다** stick (to); adhere (to).
● **점착력** adhesive power [strength]. **점착제** (an) adhesive.

점철하다(點綴-) dot; stud; intersperse.

점치다(占-) tell fortunes; do horoscopes. ¶운명 [미래]을 ~ tell [read / foretell] (a person's) fortune[future]//우리는 이번 상품으로 회사의 장래를 점칠 계획이다 We plan to gamble the company's future on the next product.//누가 앞날을 점칠 수 있는가 Who can read the future?

점토(粘土) clay. ¶내화(耐火) ～ fireclay/〔～의〕 〔～질의〕 clayey / clayish/그는 ～로 물건 만들기를 좋아한다 He likes clay work[to make things with clay].
● **점토암** 〔광〕 clay stone; argillite.

점판암(粘板巖) 〔광〕 clay slate.

점퍼(ˇjumper) a (zip-up) jacket; (스포츠용) a windbreaker. (▶ jumper는 (영)에서는 스웨터를, (미)에서는 점퍼스커트를 가리킴)
● **점퍼스커트** (미) a jumper; (영) a pinafore dress.

점포(店鋪) a store. ⇨가게
● **점포 정리 판매** a winding-up sale.

점프 a jump. ¶스키 ～에 관한 한 그에게 견줄 사람은 없다 No one can compete with him in ski jumping. **점프하다** jump.

점하다(占–) occupy; hold; have; get; take; form. ¶수출의 3할을 전기 제품이 점하고 있다 Electric appliances form[make up] thirty percent of our exports.

점호(點呼) a roll call; (a) call-over. ¶일조(日夕) 〔일석〕 the morning[evening]//임시〔불시〕 ～ a check[surprise] roll call. **점호하다** call the roll (of); roll-call; call (over) the names (of). ¶종업원을 ～ take the roll call of the employees//그는 인원을 점호했다 He called the roll.

점화(點火) ignition; lighting. **점화하다** light; ignite; kindle; set off. ¶그들은 다이너마이트에 점화했다 They ignited[set off] a charge of dynamite. →등대는 일정한 시간에 점화된다 A beacon lamp is lighted regularly.
● **점화기** a lighter; an igniter. **점화 장치** (총포 등의) an igniter; an ignition device [system]; (차의) the ignition.

접 a [one] hundred (persimmon / cabbages). ¶마늘 한 ～ one hundred bulbs of garlic.

접(接) grafting. ¶～을 붙이다 graft.

접각(接角) 〔수〕 an adjacent angle.

접객(接客) reception of a guest; entertainment. **접객하다** receive[entertain] a guest.
● **접객업** the service trade; hotel and restaurant business. **접객업자** a caterer; hotel and restaurant keepers.

접견(接見) an audience; an interview; a reception. **접견하다** grant an audience (to); receive (a person) (in audience); have an interview with (a person); give an interview (to). ¶전하는 나를 접견해 주셨다 His royal Highness received me in audience.
● **접견실** an audience chamber; a reception room.

접경(接境) a border; a boundary; the confine; a frontier(국경). **접경하다** border (on); be contiguous (to). ¶미국은 캐나다와 접경하고 있다 The United States borders on[upon] Canada.

접골(接骨) bonesetting. ¶나는 병원에서 ～ 치료를 받았다 I had my broken bone set at the hospital. **접골하다** (골절을) set a (broken) bone; (탈구를) set a dislocated bone[joint]. ¶뺀[부러진] 다리를 ～ set a dislocated [broken] leg bone.
● **접골사** a bonesetter. **접골의**(－醫) an osteopath.

접근(接近) approach; access; approximation. **접근하다** approach; make an approach (to); come close (to); draw[come / get] near; 〔교제하다〕 (try to) associate with. ¶접근하기 힘든 사람 a person difficult of access[hard to approach] / an unapproachable person//보트가 접근해 왔다 A boat approached[drew near].//태풍이 서울에 접근해 오고 있다 A typhoon is approaching[advancing on] Seoul.//화성이 지구에 가장 가까이 접근하는 때는 언제입니까 When does mars come nearest (to) the earth?//그에게는 사람들을 접근하지 못하게 하는 무언가가 있다 There is something in him that keeps people at a distance.//폭발물에 접근하지 마시오 Keep away from an explosive!
● **접근전** a close combat; 〔권투〕 infighting.

접다 1 〔겹치다〕 fold (up); turn back[down] (구석 등을); double(반으로). ¶그는 편지를 반으로[두 번] 접었다 He folded the letter in [into] two[four].//그녀는 종이를 접어 학을 만들었다 She folded a piece of paper into the shape of a crane. / She made a folded paper crane.//그는 지도를 접었다 He folded up the map.//그는 페이지의 구석을 접었다 He turned down the corner of the page. / He dog-eared his book.//그 서류를 접으면 안 된다 Don't fold the papers.

2 (폈던 것을) shut; close; fold. ¶우산을 ～ close[shut / fold] an umbrella//(새가) 날개를 ～ furl the wings//부채를 접어서 앞에 놓으시오 Shut off the fan and place it in front of you.

3 〔보류하다〕 lay [set / put] aside; shelve; (미) table. ¶이 문제는 당분간 접어 두기로 했다 We decided to put aside the question for sometime.//그 계획은 당분간 접어 두게 되었다 The plan has been shelved for the time being.

4 overlook; give odds (to). ⇨접어주다

접대(接待) 〔응대〕 reception; 〔대접〕 entertainment. ¶나는 매우 성의 있는[따뜻한] ～를 받았다 I received a hearty welcome. / I was received very warmly. / I was given a warm reception.//그녀는 손님 ～가 능하다[서툴다] She's good[poor] hostess.//저 호텔은 손님 ～를 잘한다 That hotel gives good service. **접대하다** receive; entertain. ¶손님을 ～ receive guests//그 대사 부인은 수요일 밤에 언제나 손님을 접대한다 The ambassador's wife is at home [receives] every Wednesday evening.
● **접대부** a barmaid; (미국 속어) a B-girl. **접대비** reception expenses. **접대원** a receptionist.

접두사(接頭辭) 〔언〕 a prefix.

접때 the other day; some time ago; a few [several / some] days ago; (최근) recently; lately. ¶그녀는 ～부터 병원에 입원하고 있다 She has been in (the) hospital recently [lately].//～ 너한테 이야기하지 않았던가 Haven't I told you before?

접목(接木) 〔나무를 접붙임〕 grafting; 〔접붙인 나무〕 a grafted tree. **접목하다** graft[engraft] (in / into / onto / upon); put a graft into (a stock). ¶동백나무를 접본에 ～ graft a shoot of a camellia onto a (parent) stock.

접미사(接尾辭) 〔언〕 a suffix.

접변(接變) 〔언〕 assimilation (of sounds). **접변하다** be assimilated (to neighboring sounds).

접본(椄本) the (parent) stock.

접붙이다(椄—) graft. ¶접지를 접본에 ~ graft a cutting onto a stock.

접선(接線) 1 [수] a tangent (line). 2 [접촉] contact; touch. **접선하다** contact; touch; come into[in] contact[touch] (with); make contact (with). ¶적과 접선하고 있다 keep in contact with the enemy.

접속(接續) 1 [맞대어서 이음] connection; joining; junction; [전] a joint. **접속하다** connect (to / with); join (with / to); link (up). ¶난로를 가스관에 ~ connect a stove to [with] a gas hose[[영] gas pipe]// 두 파이프를 ~ join one pipe to another. ➔¶이 열차는 수원에서 특급 열차에 접속된다 This train connects with a super-express at Suwon. 2 [컴] an interface.
● **접속곡** [음] a medley; a potpourri. **접속사**(—詞) a conjunction. ¶등위 ~ a coordinate [coordinating] conjunction// 종속 ~ a subordinate conjunction.

접수(接收) [권력 기관이 국민의 소유물을 강제로 인수함] requisition. **접수하다** requisition; take over. ¶정부가 그 고장 주민의 가옥을 접수했다 The government requisitioned the houses of the townsfolk. ➔¶그 건물은 군용으로 접수되었다 The building was requisitioned for army use.//그 극장은 한때 미국에 접수되어 있었다 The theater was once under requisition by[of] the U.S. forces.
● **접수 가옥** a requisitioned house.

접수(接受) acceptance; receipt. ¶원서 ~ 기간 the time for application / the application period// 담당관은 서류의 ~를 거부했다 The official in charge refused to accept the papers. **접수하다** accept (a proposal, an application, etc.); receive (a petition, an application, etc.). ¶주문은 ~ take an order // 입학 원서는 2월 1일부터 접수합니다 Applications for admission will be accepted on or after February.
● **접수계원** a receptionist; [미] a reception [an information] clerk. **접수 번호** a receipt number. **접수처** a reception[an information] desk.

접시 a plate(평평한); a dish(깊은); a saucer(받침의); a platter(큰); [식사의 한 접시] a course; [음식의 한 접시분] a helping. ¶수프 ~ a soup plate// 한 ~의 고기 a dish of meat// 여섯 ~의 요리 a six-course dinner// 맨 처음[맨 나중]의 ~ the first[last] course // 요리를 ~에 담아 put the food on a plate // 그는 샐러드를 세 ~ 먹었다 He ate up three helpings of salad. ¶~를 몇 개 깼느냐 How many plates did you break?
● **접시꽃** [식] a hollyhock; a rose mallow. **접시닦이** a dishwasher; (영) a washer-up. **접시저울** a balance; a pair of scales.

접신(接神) being possessed of a spirit. **접신하다** be possessed of a spirit.

접안경(接眼鏡) an eyepiece. ⇨ 접안렌즈.

접안렌즈(接眼—) an eyepiece; an ocular; an eye lens; an eyeglass.

접안하다(接岸—) come alongside the pier [quay]. ➔ 배를 접안시키다 bring a ship alongside the pier[quay].

접어들다 1 [어떤 장소·시기에 다가가다] come upon[to]; approach; draw near. ¶우리는 산길로 접어들었다 We came to a mountain path.//정마철로 접어들고 있다 The rainy season has set in.//역으로 접어들고도 그 열차는 속력을 늦추지 않았다 The train did not slow down as it approached[neared] the station. 2 (방향·목표로) take; pick up (a road). ¶숲 속으로 ~ take to the woods//북으로 길을 ~ turn[take a route] to the north.

접어주다 1 [너그럽게 봐주다] overlook; pass over; shut[close] one's eye (to a person's mistake). ¶자네 행위를 이번만은 접어주겠네 I will overlook your behavior for this once. 2 (바둑에서) give[lay] odds (of); give (one stone) advantage (over a person). ¶다섯 점 ~ give a five-stone handicap // 몇 점 접어주시겠습니까 What handicap will you give me?

접영(蝶泳) the butterfly stroke.

접의자(—椅子) a folding[collapsible] chair; a camp chair.

접자 a carpenter's rule; a zigzag rule; a folding scale[rule].

접전(接戰) [싸움의] a close fight[combat]; (경기의) a close contest[game]; a seesaw game. ¶양팀은 ~을 벌였다 The two teams played a tight match[game].// 그들은 한창 ~ 중이었다 They were in close combat.//이번 선거는 민 씨와 홍 씨의 ~이다 This election is a close race between Mr. Min and Mr. Hong. // 그 시합은 1점을 다투는 ~이 되었다 The match[game] was closely contested. / The game turned into a struggle for one point [run]. (▶ 야구에서)//끝에 우리 팀이 이겼다 After (playing) a seesaw game, our team (finally) won. **접전하다** fight a close fight; come to close combat; [경쟁하다] be in keen competition (with); (경기에서) have a close contest[game] (with); have a seesaw game.

접점(接點) [수] a point of contact.

접종(接種) [의] (an) inoculation; (a) vaccination(백신, 특히 종두의). ¶비시지 ~ inoculation of BCG// 소아마비의 예방 ~ a polio vaccination / (a) vaccination against polio //그는 콜레라 예방 ~을 받았다 He was inoculated [had an inoculation] against cholera. **접종하다** inoculate; vaccinate (a person against).

접지(接地) [전] (미) grounding; (영) earthing. **접지하다** ground; earth.
● **접지선** (미) a ground wire; (영) an earth wire.

접지(摺紙) [종이 접기] paper folding; [제책] folding printed sheets (for binding). **접지하다** fold printed sheets (for binding).
● **접지공** [제책] a folder. **접지기**(—機) a folding machine; a folder.

접질리다 sprain; wrench; wrick; have[get] a sprain[wrench]. ¶그는 스케이트를 타다가 발목을 접질렸다 He sprained[wrenched] his ankle while skating.

접착(接着) [화] adhesion. **접착하다** glue; stick to; adhere to. ¶깨진 접시의 파편을 ~ glue the fragments of a plate back together.
● **접착력** adhesive strength. **접착제** glue; (an) adhesive; bond. ¶순간 ~ (a) quick-drying glue. **접착테이프** adhesive tape.

접촉(接觸) 1 [물체의] touch; contact; [전] (electrical) contact; [수] tangency; contingence; osculation. ¶(전류의) ~을 끊다 break contact // 전기의 ~이 나쁘다 The (electrical) contact is bad.// 그 병은 ~에 의해서 전염한다 The disease is contagious by touch. **접촉하다** contact; make contact (with); come in

[into] contact (with); touch(가볍게). ➜¶접촉시키다 contact / bring [throw / put] (a thing) into contact (with)//휘발유에 불을 접촉시키면 폭발할 것이다 Bringing fire into contact with gasoline may cause an explosion.
2 [교제] contact; touch; communication. ¶공식 ~ an official contact//~을 유지하다 keep in touch [contact] (with)//~을 끊다 break off [get out of] contact (with) / lose touch [contact] (with)//개인적인 ~이 있다 have a personal contact (with a person)// 예비 ~을 갖다 make preliminary contacts (with)//남북의 ~에서 큰 진전을 보다 make good progress in the south-north contacts// 그는 많은 사람과 ~이 있다 He has contact(s) with many people. **접촉하다** touch; contact; come in [into] contact [touch] (with); make contact (with). ¶그는 유력한 사람들과 접촉하고 있다 He is in touch with some influential [powerful] men.//그는 사업상 온갖 부류의 사람들과 접촉한다 His business throws him into contact with all sorts of people.
●**접촉각** [수] a contact angle. **접촉 반응** [화] (a) contact catalytic reaction. **접촉 변성암** a contact metamorphic rock. **접촉 사고** a minor collision; (미국 구어) a fender bender. ¶~를 일으키다 cause a collision// 내 자동차는 하마터면 트럭과 ~를 일으킬 뻔했다 My car nearly collide with a truck. **접촉 전염 / 접촉 감염** contact infection.

접치이다 be folded; receive odds. ⇨ ¶접히다
접칼 a clasp knife; a pocketknife; a jackknife.
접하다(接-) **1** [인접하다] abut (on); border (on); be close (to); be adjacent (to); stand [lie] next (to)//도로에 접한 땅 the land abutting on the road / a lot fronting on a road//국경에 접한 지역[지대] the area close to the border [(영) frontier]//북쪽은 만주와 접해 있다 be bordered on the north by Manchuria//두 집이 서로 접하고 있다 Two houses adjoin each other.
2 [소식 등을 받다] receive; accept; get. ¶부음(訃音)을 ~ receive the news of (a person's) death / hear of (a person's) death// 아버지가 위독하다는 전보를 접하고 나는 급히 고향으로 내려갔다 On receipt of a telegram informing me that my father was in critical condition, I hurried to my hometown.//아직 상세한 보고는 접하지 못했다 Particulars are not yet to hand.
3 [사귀다·대하다] contact; touch; come in [into] contact [touch] (with). ¶많은 사람과 ~ come in (to) contact with many people// 여자를 ~ know a woman//환자와 ~ come in contact with sick people//문학에 ~ have [get] access to literature//나는 직업상 저명 인사와 접하는 기회가 많다 I have many opportunities to meet [come in contact with] well-known people because of my profession.
4 [수] be tangent (to). ¶두 원은 C에서 서로 접한다 The two circles are tangent to each other at C.

접합(接合) **1** [한데 붙임] joining. **접합하다** join; unite; put together. ¶철판 2장을 ~ join two iron plate together / join one iron plate to another//벽돌과 돌을 시멘트로 ~ unite bricks and stones with cement. **2** [생] conjugation; zygosis. **접합하다** conjugate.
●**접합자 / 접합체** [생] a zygote. **접합재** a binder. **접합제** cement; a bonding agent.
접히다 **1** [종이 등이] be folded; be doubled (up). ¶네 겹으로 ~ be folded in four//융단의 모서리가 밑으로 접혀 있었다 The corner of the rug was folded under. **2** [바둑 등에서] have (one stone) advantage (over a person); receive odds. ¶네 점 ~ receive a four-stone handicap.

젓 *jeot*; salted [pickled] seafood. ¶새우[멸치 / 조개] ~ salted [pickled] shrimps [anchovies / clams]//~을 담그다 salt [souse] (shrimps).
젓가락 (a pair of) chopsticks. ¶~으로 먹다 eat with chopsticks//그는 ~질이 서툴다 He cannot use chopsticks well.
젓갈 *jeotgal*; salted seafood. ⇨젓
젓다 **1** (액체를) stir; (도구를 써서 계란 등을) beat; (급격히) whip. ¶달걀 3개를 거품이 일 때까지 ~ beat three eggs until they are frothy//커피에 넣은 설탕을 스푼으로 저으시오 Stir the sugar in your coffee with a spoon.//크림을 저어서 거품을 일게 하라 Whip the cream.
2 (배를) row; pull an oar; (카누 등을) paddle. ¶노를 잘[잘못] 젓는 사람 a good [bad] oarsman//배를 ~ row a boat//힘껏 ~ row with all one's might / bend to the oar//우리는 배를 저어 기슭에 닿았다 We rowed the boat ashore [to the shore].//그들은 바다로 저어 나갔다 They rowed out into the ocean [sea].
3 (손을) wave (one's hand); (머리를) shake (one's head). ¶그녀는 손을 저어 조용히 하라고 했다 She waved her hand for silence.//그는 내 질문에 머리를 가로저었다 He shook his head in answering my question.

정[1] [돌을 쪼는 연장] a chisel. ¶~으로 돌을 쪼다 cut a stone with chisel / chisel a stone.
정[2] [정말로] truly; really; actually; very; quite; indeed; (미국 구어) real. ¶~ 싫다면 할 수 없지 There is no help for it, if you really don't like it.//그가 ~ 혼자서 간다면 할 수 없지 We cannot help it if he really wants to go alone.
정(丁) [넷째 등급] the fourth grade; D grade.
정(情) **1** [감정·마음] feeling(s); [세련된 심정] sentiment; [인정] human nature. ¶연민의 ~ (a sentiment of) pity//~이 많은[없는] 사람 a warmhearted [coldhearted] person//~이 많다 be warmhearted [tenderhearted / kindhearted] / have a kind [warm] heart//~에 약하다 be susceptible [tenderhearted / sentimental]//그는 ~에 무르다 He is easily moved [softhearted / sentimental].
2 [애정] heart; affection; attachment; a tender feeling; love(이성 간의). ¶부부의 ~ conjugal affection//부모 자식 간의 ~ the affection [love] between parent and child//~을 쏟다 give (a person) great affection//~을 통하다 have a love affair [an amour] with (a person) / become intimate with (a man / a woman)//여자한테 ~이 들다 become attached to [grow fond of] a girl//함께 일을 하는 동안에 그녀에게 ~이 들기 시작했다 After working with her for some time, I gradually began to love [be attached to / care for] her.//그녀는 그 아이에게 ~이 쏠렸다 Her heart went (out) to the child.

정-(正) **1** (副)에 대하여 original. **2** [정식의] regular. ¶~회원 a regular member // ~사원 a full-fledged [regular] employee of a company. **3** [똑바른] due; exactly. ¶~남향인 집 a house facing due south.

-정(亭) [정자] a bower (in a garden); an arbor; a bower; a pavilion. ¶팔각~ an octagonal pavilion / an octagon.

-정(整) ¶십만 원~ (the sum of) one hundred thousand won / (우수리 없는) clear[net] 100,000 won / 100,000 won flat.

-정(錠) [알약] a (diazine) tablet; a pill. ¶비타민~ a vitamin pill[tablet].

-정(艇) [배] a boat. ¶경비~ a guard ship.

정가(定價) (일반적으로) a price; [정해진 가격] a fixed price; [정규의 가격] a regular price; [가격표에 있는 가격] a list price. ¶~로 팔다 sell at a fixed price // ~를 매기다 set a price on (an article) // ~를 올리다 raise[increase] the price // ~를 내리다 reduce[lower / cut (down)] the price // ~의 2할을 할인하여 팔다 make a discount of 20 percent off[on] the fixed price // 이 모자는 ~가 얼마요 What is the price of this hat? // 이 모자는 ~ 10,000 원입니다 This hat is priced at 10,000 won. // 이 책을 ~의 20프로를 할인해서 샀다 I bought this book at 20 percent off its regular[list] price.
● **정가표** a price tag. ¶물건에 ~를 붙이다 fix a price tag to an article.

정가극(正歌劇) a grand opera.

정각(正刻) [바로 그 시각] the exact time. ¶~에 exactly / precisely / just / sharp // 5시 ~에 just[exactly] at five (o'clock) / at five sharp / on the dot of five // ~ 10시에 와 주게 Come at ten sharp[at exactly ten o'clock]. // 회의는 ~ 10시에 시작되었다 The meeting began promptly[punctually] at ten. // 그는 여느 때처럼 ~ 3시에 강의를 마쳤다 As usual he finished his lecture exactly at 3 o'clock.

정각(定刻) [정해진 시간] the appointed [fixed] time; [예정된 시간] the scheduled time.

정각(頂角) ➡꼭지각

정간(井間) a checker square; a check; a square.

정간(停刊) temporary prohibition[suspension] of publication. ¶신문의 ~을 해제하다 release the suspension of a newspaper. **정간하다** prohibit[suspend] publication temporarily. ➔그 잡지는 정간당했다[정간되었다] Publication of the magazine was temporarily discontinued[suspended].

정갈스럽다 neat; trim. ⇨정갈하다

정갈하다 neat; trim; tidy; snug. ¶그녀는 항상 옷차림이 정갈했다 She always dresses neatly (and cleanly). // 그의 방은 ~ His room is tidy. // He keeps his room tidy.

정감(情感) emotion; sentiment. ¶~ 있는 사람 a man of emotion // ~ 있게 말하다 speak with emotion[feeling] / speak soulfully[feelingly] // 이것은 ~이 넘치는 문장이다 This is a very emotional passage.

정강(政綱) [정치의 근본] a political principle; (정당의) a (party) platform. ¶사회당의 ~을 채택하다 accept[adopt] the socialist platform.

정강마루 [생] the ridge of the shin.

정강이 the shank; the shin. ¶~가 까지다 have one's shin barked // ~를 바위에 부딪다 shin oneself against a rock // 그는 나의 ~를 걷어찼다 He kicked me in the shin.
● **정강이받이** (경기용) leg[shin] guards. **정강이뼈** the shinbone; the tibia (*pl.* -ae, ~s).

정객(政客) a statesman; a politician.

정거(停車) a stop. ⇨~정차
● **정거장** a station; (미) a railroad [(영) railway] station; (미) a depot; a stop. ¶갈아타는 ~ a junction station / a (railway) junction // ~을 떠나다 (열차가) leave[go out of] the station // 쏜살같이 ~을 통과하다 dash through a station // 다음 ~은 어딥니까 What is the next station[stop]? // "부산까지는 앞으로 몇 ~ 남았습니까?" "다섯 ~입니다." "How many stations[stops] is it from here to Busan?" "It's five stations[stops]." **정거장 대합실** a station waiting room.

정격(正格) regularity. ¶~의 regular / correct / orthodox / [음] authentic.
● **정격 활용** [언] a regular conjugation.

정견(定見) [일정한 주견] a fixed[definite] opinion[view]; [지론] a settled[firm] conviction. ¶~이 없다 have no definite opinion [views] of one's own / have no fixed views of one's own // 시장은 전혀 ~이 없는 사람이다 The mayor is a man without fixed[firm] principles.

정견(政見) a political view[opinion]. ¶~의 차이 differences in political opinions // ~을 발표하다 state one's political views // ~을 달리하다 have different political views / differ (from a person) in political views
● **정견 발표회** a campaign meeting; a meeting for the announcement of one's political views.

정결하다(貞潔−) chaste and pure. ¶정결한 부인 a chaste [faithful / virtuous] wife.

정결하다(淨潔−) clean; neat; undefiled; pure. ¶방을 정결하게 하다 keep one's room neat as a pin.

정경(政經) politics and economics. ¶~ 분리의 원칙 the principle of separation of political matters from economic matters.
● **정경 유착** the cozy relations between politics and economics.

정경(情景) a scene; a sight. ¶애통한 ~ a sorrowful[heartbreaking] sight // 그 ~은 지금도 분명히 생각난다 I can still remember the scene[sight] vividly.

정계(政界) the political world[arena]; political circles. ¶~의 움직임 a political trend // ~의 불안 unrest in political world / a political unrest // ~의 소식통 informed political circles // ~의 정화(淨化) a cleanup of political circles // ~에 들어가다 [~로 진출하다] enter the political world / go into politics as a career / go in for politics // ~의 사정에 정통하다 be familiar[conversant] with political affairs / be familiar with the political situation // 그의 아버지는 ~의 거물이었다 His father was a big figure in politics. / His father was one of the political leaders of Korea. // 아버지는 70세에 ~에서 물러났다 My father retired from political life[politics] at the age of seventy.

정곡(正鵠) the point; the mark. ¶~을 찌른 발언 a relevant [pertinent] remark // 그의 답변은 ~을 찔렀다 His answer was to the point. // 그의 논거는 ~에서 벗어나 있었다 His arguments missed the point [were wide of the mark].//그 고찰은 바로 ~을 찌르고 있다 That observation is right to the point [hits the (right) nail on the head].

정공(正攻) [정면 공격] a frontal attack; [정정당당한 공격] a fair (and square) fighting; a fair play. **정공하다** make a frontal attack (against); [정정당당히 싸우다] fight fairly (and squarely); fight openly and squarely; play fair.
●**정공법** the regular tactics for attack. ¶~을 쓰다 adopt [employ] standard [straightforward] tactics.

정과(正果) various fruits preserved in honey [syrup].

정관(定款) the articles of association. ¶주식회사의 ~ the articles of incorporation // 회사의 ~ 제1조 Art.[Article] I of the Statutes of the Company [Corporation].

정관(精管) [생] a spermatic duct. ⇨ 수정관
●**정관 절제술** vasectomy. ¶~을 받다 undergo vasectomy.

정관(靜觀) contemplation. ¶~적인 태도를 취하다 take [assume] a wait-and-see attitude (toward). **정관하다** contemplate; watch; wait and see. ¶좀 더 사태를 정관하는 편이 좋을 것 같군 I think we had better watch the development of the situation a little longer.
●**정관주의** a wait-and-see policy.

정관사(定冠詞) [언] the definite article ¶부정관사 indefinite article // 그 단어는 ~를 붙여야 한다 The word must take the definite article before it.

정교(正敎) 1 (사교(邪敎)에 대하여) orthodoxy. 2 the Greek Orthodox Church. ⇨ 그리스 정교회

정교(政敎) 1 [정치와 종교] religion and politics; Church and State. 2 [정치와 교육] politics and education.
●**정교 분리** the separation of religion and politics [Church and State]. **정교 일치** the unity [union] of Church and State.

정교(情交) 1 [친교] close friendship; intimacy. **정교하다** become intimate with; have friendly relations with; be on friendly terms with; be friendly with. 2 (남녀의) sexual intercourse; (구어) sex. **정교하다** have sex [sexual intercourse] (with); make love (to / with).

정교사(正教師) a regular [qualified] teacher.

정교하다(精巧-) elaborate; exquisite; sophisticated; delicate. ¶정교한 기계 a sophisticated [delicate] machine / a machine of excellent mechanism // 정교한 작품 an elaborate work / a work showing elaborate workmanship // 이것이 현재로서는 가장 정교한 카메라라고 생각한다 I suppose this is the most elaborate camera available. // 이건 정말 정교한 솜씨다 This is of exquisite [elaborate] workmanship.

정교회(正敎會) the Greek Orthodox Church. ⇨ 그리스 정교회

정구(庭球) (lawn) tennis. ⇨ 테니스

정국(政局) the political situation. ¶~의 위기 a political crisis / a critical development in the political situation // ~의 안정 [불안정] the stability [instability] of a political situation / ~의 타개책 a measure to break a political deadlock // 그는 총선거에 의해서 ~의 안정을 도모하려고 했다 He attempted to stabilize [save] the political situation by calling a general election. // 현 정권은 ~을 타개할 수 있을까 Can the present government break the political situation?

정권(政權) [정치권력] political [administrative] power; a government; an administration (특히 미국); [정치 조직] a regime. ¶괴뢰 ~ a puppet government // 군사 ~ a military regime / a junta // 독재 ~ a dictatorial regime // 중국의 공산당 ~ the Communist regime in China // ~을 쥐다 come into power / take the helm of state affairs // ~을 잃다 go out of power // ~을 유지하다 stay in power // ~을 이양하다 turn over the reins of government // ~을 수립하다 establish a [one's] regime // ~을 연장하다 prolong the life one's regime.
●**정권 교체** the change of regime; a power change. ¶평화적인 ~ a peaceful turnover [transfer] of political power. **정권 다툼** a struggle [scramble] for political power. **정권욕** ambition [desire] for political power. ¶~에 불타다 burn with ambition for political power / be hungry [thirsty] for power. **정권이양** a transition [transfer] of power (to).

정규(正規) formality; regularity. ¶~의 regular / formal // ~의 수업 a regular lesson // ~의 절차를 밟는 것이 좋을 겁니다 It is advisable to go through the regular procedure(s) [due formalities].
●**정규 교육** regular [formal] school education. ¶~을 받다 have regular school education // 그는 ~을 받지 못했다 He has not received formal school education. **정규군** a regular army(약어 RA, R.A.). **정규 분포** [수] normal distribution.

정근(精勤) 1 [근면] diligence; industry. **정근하다** work hard; be diligent; be industrious; be assiduous; attend to one's duties diligently. 2 (근무자의) good [regular] attendance. ¶10년간의 ~ one's 10-year service with a laudable record. **정근하다** attend (office) regularly.
●**정근상** a prize for regular attendance. **정근자** (회사·학교 등의) an employee [a student] with a good attendance record.

정글 a jungle.

정글짐 a jungle gym.

정금(正金) 1 pure gold. ⇨ 순금 2 [금화·은화] specie.

정기(正氣) 1 [천지의 원기] the spirit which animates and controls the universe. 2 [바른 기풍] the fair and equitable spirit; righteousness.

정기(定期) a fixed period [term]. ¶~의 regular / periodic(al).
●**정기 간행물** a periodical publication; a periodical; a journal. **정기 검진 / 정기 진단** a seasonal health examination [medical check-up]. **정기 공연** (오케스트라의) a subscription concert. **정기 국회** an ordinary [a regular] session of the National Assembly. **정기선**(一船) a liner. ¶원양 항로의 ~ an ocean liner. **정기 예금** a fixed deposit; a time deposit. **정기 총회** a regular general meeting (of the stockholders). **정기 항로** a regular line [service]. **정기 휴가** regular [periodic] holidays. **정기 휴일** a regular holiday [day-off]; a shop-holiday(상점의).

정기(精氣) 1 [만물의 기운] the spirit of all

정기적 [the] creation. 2 [기운] energy; vigor; vitality.

정기적(定期的) regular; periodic(al). ¶~으로 periodically / at regular intervals at stated periods / regularly / at fixed times [~으로 있다 [행해지다] occur at fixed [stated] periods / (모임이) be held at regular intervals // 검침원은 ~으로 가스 미터[가스 계량기]를 조사하러 온다 A meterman comes at regular intervals [regularly] to check [read] the gas meter. // 그들은 풀장의 물을 ~으로 검사한다 They make regular examinations of the water in the (swimming) pool.

정나미(情-) [애착] attachment; affection. ¶~가 떨어지다 become disgusted (with) / fall out of love (with) / be disaffected (toward) // 그 사람에게는 이제 완전히 ~가 떨어졌다 I'm totally disgusted with that man. / I've completely given up on that man. // 그 사람이 저따위 짓을 하다니 ~가 떨어진다 How disgusting to see him act that way!

정남(방)(正南方) due south. ¶집에서 1킬로~에 공원이 있다 There is a park one kilometer directly south of my house. // 비행기는 ~을 향해서 날고 있다 The plane is flying due south.

정낭(선)(精囊腺) [의] a seminal vesicle [cyst]; a spermatic sac.

정년(丁年) [성인이 되는 나이] full age; [법정 연령] majority. ¶~에 이르다 come of age / attain [reach] one's majority // ~에 이르지 않다 [미달이다] be underage / be in one's minority // 우리는 20세면 ~에 이른다 We come of age at twenty.

정년(停年) age limit; retirement age. ¶~으로 퇴직하다 retire under the age limit // ~에 이르다 reach the age limit // 공무원의 ~을 60세로 하다 set the retirement age of government officials at 60 // 교사의 ~은 62세다 The teachers retire at 62. // 그는 금년에 ~이다 He is due to retire this year.

● **정년제** the age-limit system. **정년퇴직** retirement under the age limit. ¶아버지는 금년 3월에 ~을 하신다 My father will reach retirement age and leave his job this March.

정념(情念) sentiments; passions; emotion. ¶~에 불타다 be burning with emotion.

정녕(丁寧·叮嚀) [꼭] surely; certainly; for sure; for certain. ¶봄은 ~ 오려는가 Has spring come surely? // 네 말이 ~ 사실이냐 Are you sure? / Is it true? // 그는 ~ 떠나려 한다 He wants to leave for sure.

정다각형(正多角形) a regular [an equilateral] polygon.

정다면체(正多面體) a regular polyhedron.

정담(政談) a discourse on politics; a political talk. ¶~을 하다 talk politics.

정담(情談) [다정한 이야기] a friendly talk; (남녀의) a tête-à-tête; lover's talk. ¶나는 그와 오랫동안 ~을 나누었다 I have a long friendly talk with him.

정답(正答) a correct answer. ¶문제의 ~을 대다 get the correct answer to a question.

정답다(情-) [친밀하다] friendly; familiar; intimate; close; [다정하다] affectionate; loving; warm-hearted; [화목하다] happy (family). ¶정다운 친구 a good [great / close / bosom] friend / (구어) a chum // 정다운 고향 a sweet home // 정답게 살다 live happily together / be happy with (one's wife) // 정다운 노부부를 보는 것은 즐거운 일이다 It is pleasant to watch a loving old couple. // 그녀는 정답게 웃었다 She smiled affably [amiably]. / She smiled in a friendly way. // 그녀는 자기 딸의 머리를 정답게 쓰다듬었다 She stroke her daughter's head tenderly [affectionately]. // 두 사람은 아주 ~ (친구가) The two are on very friendly terms. / (부부가) There is perfect conjugal harmony between them.

정당(政黨) a political party. ¶보수[혁신] ~ a conservative [reformist] party // 진보[급진] ~ a progressive [radical] party // ~의 출신의 각료 [수상] a party minister [premier] // ~에 적을 두다 [소속되다] belong to [be a member of] a political party / ~에 가입하다 join [enter] a political party / affiliate oneself with a political party // 그는 새 ~을 결성했다 He formed [organized] a new political party.

● **정당 강령** (미) a party platform; (영) a party programme. **정당 내각** a party cabinet. **정당 정치** party politics [government].

정당(精糖) [화] [정제하는 일] sugar refining; [정제된 설탕] refined sugar.

정당방위(正當防衛) (lawful) self-defense; legal defense. ¶~로 (kill a man) in self-defense / [법] se defendendo.

정당하다(正當-) [공정하고 옳다] just; fair; right; [알맞다] proper; [이치에 닿다] reasonable; [적절하다] good; [합법적이다] lawful / legal / legitimate. ¶정당한 요구 a reasonable [legitimate] demand // 정당한 보상 just compensation // 정당한 왕위 계승자 the legitimate heir to the throne // 정당한 절차를 밟다 go through the proper channels // 정당한 법적 절차를 밟지 않고 without due process of law // 그녀가 거절하는 데는 정당한 이유가 있다 She has (a) good reason to decline it. / She is fully justified in rejecting it. // 이것은 정당한 거래입니다 This is an aboveboard deal. / There is nothing illegal [shady] about this deal. // 그는 정당한 이유 없이 결석했다 He was absent without a good reason. // 이 돈은 정당한 수단으로 얻은 것이다 I got this money by fair means. **정당히** justly; rightly; properly; duly; fairly; reasonably; legitimately. ¶나를 ~ 평가해 주었으면 한다 I'd like you to do me justice [do justice to me].

정당화(正當化) justification. **정당화하다** justify. ¶그는 자기의 행위를 정당화하려고 했다 He tried to justify himself. ➔ ¶그 같은 폭력은 어떤 이유로도 또는 어떤 명분으로도 정당화될 수 없다 Such violence cannot be justified by any excuse or under any pretext.

정대하다(正大-) fair; upright; just

정도(正道) the right path [way / track]. ¶~에 어긋나는 행위 an unrighteous [unjust] act // ~를 밟다 tread the path of righteousness [virtue] / be righteous [upright] // ~로 이끌다 guide (a person) into the right path // 그는 어쩌다가 ~에서 벗어났다 On the spur of the moment he strayed [deviated] from the right path.

정도(定都) the foundation of a capital. ¶서울 ~ 600주년 the six hundredth anniversary of the capital Seoul. **정도하다** found a capital.

정도(程度) 1 [양·우열 등의] (a) degree; extent; a level; rate; (a) grade; (a) standard. ¶생

~ the standard of living / living standard.∥**지능** ~ the intellectual standard.∥손해의 ~ the extent of loss [damage].∥고교 졸업 ~의 학력 academic ability equal to that of a high school graduate.∥**~가 높다[낮다]** be of high [low] standard [grade].∥이것과 저것은 ~의 차이지 종류의 차이는 아니다 The difference between this and that is one of degree, not kind.∥이것은 ~의 문제이다 It's a matter [question] of degree.∥그 두 학생의 학력은 ~는 거의 같다 The two students are more or less at the same scholastic level.∥이 교재는 대학 ~의 학생을 위해서 쓴 것이다 The textbook was written for the students at the college level [for the college level students].∥그들의 생활 ~는 높다[낮다] Their standard of living is high [low].∥그는 강의를 청중의 ~에 맞추었다 He adapted his lecture to the level of the audience.∥그가 한 말은 어느 ~ 사실이다 There is some truth in what he said. / What he said is true to some extent.∥그를 어느 ~까지 신용할 수 있습니까 To what extent [degree] can he be trusted?∥이 ~에서 그만두자 Let this be enough.

2 [한도] limit; bounds. ¶죽지 않을 ~로 훈련시키다 push a person to the very limit of his endurance in training.∥모든 일에는 ~라는 것이 있다 There is a limit to everything.∥참는 것도 ~가 있다 I can no longer put up with it.∥농담하는 것도 ~가 있다 You have carried your joke too far.∥추운 ~가 아니다 Cold is not the word [is no fame for it].

3 [가량]. ¶전동차는 5분 ~의 간격으로 발착한다 Trains arrive and depart every five minutes or so.∥비용은 대체로 어느 ~일까요 At about how much do you put the expense? / What is your rough estimate of the cost?∥비용은 5만 원 ~를 생각하면 된다 You may estimate the expenses at about [around] 50,000 won.

정독(精讀) intensive [careful] reading; perusal. **정독하다** read intensively [carefully / with care]; peruse.

정돈(停頓) [한때 멈춤] a deadlock; a standstill; a stalemate; a impasse. ¶외교상의 ~ 상태 a diplomatic stalemate.∥~ 상태를 타개하다 break the deadlock [stalemate] / bring a deadlock [an impasse] to an end / find a way out of the impasse.∥자금 부족 때문에 운동은 ~ 상태에 빠져 있다 The movement is at a standstill for lack of funds. **정돈하다** come to a standstill [deadlock]; be held up; (인) bog down.

정돈(整頓) order; proper arrangement. **정돈하다** put [set] in order; straighten up; tidy up; arrange properly. ¶그는 책꽂이를 깔끔히 정돈해 놓았다 He keeps his bookcases in order.∥그녀는 무엇이든 잘 정돈해 둔다 She keeps everything shipshape. ➔ 정돈된 서랍 a well-ordered [tidy] drawer∥정돈되지 않은 방 an untidy [a disorderly] room∥방이 말끔히 정돈되어 있었다 The room was all tidied up.∥모든 것이 잘 정돈되어 있다 Everything is in its place.

정동(방)(正東方) due east. ¶~으로 침로를 잡아라 Head due east.

정들다(情−) (남에게) become familiar (with); get intimate (with); grow fond (of); become attached (to); (장소 등에) get used to living in (a house). ¶정든 임 (미) one's steady / (남자) one's lover / her (young) man / (여자) one's love [sweetheart]∥정든 고국산천 one's dear fatherland∥그녀와 ~ fall in love with [become fond of] a girl∥두 사람은 마침내 서로 정들게 되었다 The couple finally opened their hearts to each other.

정떨어지다(情−) become disgusted (with); be disaffected (toward); fall out of love (with); grow sick [tired] (of). ¶그 생각을 하면 정떨어진다 It makes me sick to think of it.∥그녀는 그의 촌스러운 몸가짐에 정떨어졌다 She was repelled by his rustic manners.∥그녀의 얼굴을 보면 정떨어진다 Her face quite puts me off.∥네놈에게는 정떨어졌어 I've had just about enough of you.∥독재자의 정책에 국민들은 곧 정떨어졌다 The dictator's policies had soon disaffected the people.

정략(政略) **1** [정치상의 책략] political tactics; a political maneuver [strategy]. ¶~적인 political∥그것은 일시적인 ~에서 나온 조치다 It is a measure dictated by political expediency. **2** [방책] a policy; [대책] a measure; a step. ¶정부는 재정의 재건 ~을 발표했다 The Government has announced measures [steps] to improve the finances of the country.

● **정략가** a clever political tactician; (특히 이권을 찾아다니는) a politician. **정략결혼** (정치적인) a political marriage; (당사자의 타산적인) a marriage of convenience.

정량(定量) a fixed quantity [amount]; (내복약의) a dose. ¶~의 quantitative∥~ 이상의 술을 마시다 overdrink oneself∥환자에게 ~ 이상으로 약을 처방하지 않도록 주의하시오 Take care not to overdose [prescribe overdoses of medicine for] your patients.

● **정량 분석** [화] quantitative analysis.

정력(精力) energy; [생명력] vitality; [활력] vigor; 《미국 구어》 hustle. ¶~적(으로) energetic(ally) / vigorous(ly)∥~을 다 써 버리다 exhaust one's energy∥나이를 먹으며 그는 ~을 잃었다 He has grown old and lost his vigor.∥더울 때 장어를 먹으면 ~이 생긴다고 한다 They say eels invigorate us [give us energy] during the hot season.∥그는 물리학 연구에 ~을 기울였다 He applied his energies to the study of physics.∥그는 아주 ~적인 작가다 He is a very active writer.

● **정력가** a man of (great) energy [vigor]; an energetic person.

정련(精練) [실·천 등에서 불순물을 제거함] scouring. **정련하다** scour. ¶원모를 ~ scour raw wool∥생사를 ~ degum raw silk.

정련(精鍊) [광석에서 금속을 뽑아 정제함] smelting. **정련하다** smelt (copper).

정렬(整列) an array; a line up. ¶~ [구령] Fall in! **정렬하다** stand in (a) line; (영) form a queue; (가로로) stand in a row; line up; form a line. ¶길 양쪽에 ~ line be drawn up on] both sides of the road∥승객들은 플랫폼에 세 줄로 정렬하 있었다 They formed [stood in] three lines on the platform.∥그들은 카메라 앞에 3열로 정렬했다 They lined up in three rows in front of the camera.∥정렬해서 기다려 주십시오 Please wait in line [a queue].

정령(政令) [내각이 제정하는 명령] a cabinet order; [정부의 명령] a government ordinance.

정령(精靈) **1** [초목 등에 깃든 혼령] a spirit; a

정례 sprite(요정). ¶꽃의 ~ the spirit of a flower // 물의 ~ a water nymph[sprite] // 숲의 ~ a dryad. 2 [혼백] the spirit of a dead person.
- **정령 숭배** animism.

정례(定例) an established usage. ¶~의 regular / ordinary / usual // ~에 따라 총회가 지난달에 소집되었다 According to regular practice a general meeting was convened last month.
- **정례 기자 회견** a regular press conference [interview].

정론(正論) a sound argument[reasoning]. ¶~을 펴다 make sound remarks / put forth a sound argument // 그의 말은 ~이다 What he said is quite reasonable.

정론(定論) [확고한 이론] an established theory; [합의된 의견] a decided[an agreed] opinion.

정론(政論) political argument[discussion]. ¶~을 벌이다 have political discussions (with) / discuss current political affairs.

정류(停留) a stop; (a) stoppage. **정류하다** stop; pull up.
- **정류장** a station; a stop; (미) a depot. ¶버스 ~ a bus stop // 어느 ~에서 내리십니까 Where[At which stop] do you (want to) get off?

정류(精溜) [화] rectification; refinement. **정류하다** rectify; purify; refine. ¶알코올[주류]을 ~ rectify alcohol[spirits].
- **정류탑** a rectifying column.

정류(整流) [전] rectification; commutation. **정류하다** rectify; commute; commutate.
- **정류관** a rectifying tube. **정류기** a rectifier.
정류 작용 rectifying action.

정률(定率) [일정한 비율] a fixed rate. ¶20퍼센트의 ~로 at a fixed rate of 20 percent.
- **정률세** proportional taxation.

정리(廷吏) [법원의] a sergeant; a (law) court clerk.

정리(定理) a theorem; a proposition. ¶이항[다항] ~ the binomial[multinomial] theorem // 피타고라스 ~의 새로운 증명법 a new demonstration of the Pythagorean theorem [proposition].

정리(情理) [인정과 도리] reason and sentiment.

정리(整理) 1 [흐트러져 있는 것을 질서 있게 함] arrangement; regulation; adjustment; order. ¶경지 ~ the adjustment of arable land // 재정[행정] ~ financial[administrative] adjustment // 교통~ traffic regulation [control] // 미~의 서류 unfiled papers // 가사의 ~는 그녀에게 맡기고 있다 I have entrusted the management of household affairs to her. **정리하다** arrange; adjust; regulate; tidy (up); straighten (up / out); (생각 등을) put [throw / get] (one's idea) into shape[in order]. ¶자료를 ~ classify[pigeonhole] data / arrange data / put data in order // 서류를 ~ sort out papers // 장부를 ~ adjust accounts // 나는 이 일을 가능한 한 속히 정리하고 싶다 I'd like to have this matter disposed of as soon as possible.
2 [감원] reduction; curtailment; a shake-up; [매각·처분] disposition; clearance. ¶회사의 인원 ~로 그는 해고되었다 As a result of personnel cuts[staff reductions] in his company, he was dismissed. **정리하다** reduce; curtail; cut down; [처분하다] dispose of; sell. ¶불필요한 것을 ~ dispose of[throw away] unnecessary things // 가재를 ~ dispose of one's household goods and furniture // 그 회사는 인원을 정리했다 The company cut down (on)[reduced] its staff.
3 [해소·해체] liquidation; (지불 관계의) full payment; settlement. **정리하다** liquidate; wind up; (지불 관계를) clear away; pay off; settle (one's debts). ¶회사를 ~ liquidate [wind up] a company // 나는 모든 부채를 정리하고 싶다 I want to clear (away)[pay off] all my debts.
- **정리함** a filling cabinet. **정리 해고** downsizing. ¶~를 하다 downsize.

정립(定立) [논] a thesis (pl. theses).

정립(鼎立) [세 사람 또는 세 개의 세력이 서로 대립함] a triangular position. **정립하다** be in a three-cornered[triangular] contest; stand in a trio. ¶그 당시 세 세력이 정립하고 있었다 At that time three powers were opposing to one another.

정말(正−) 1 truth(거짓에 대해 진실); a fact(사실); reality(현실). ¶~ 같은 [있을 법한] likely / [외양뿐인] seeming / [그럴듯한] specious / plausible // ~ 같은 거짓말 a plausible [specious] lie // 농담을 ~로 여기다 take a joke seriously // 남의 말을 ~로 여기다 take a person at his word(s) / believe a person // ~일까 Can it be true? / I wonder if it is true. // ~이야 That[It] is true. / Yes, indeed. / So it is. / Believe me. // 그 소문은 ~이었다 The rumor proved[turned out] (to be) true. // 그의 말은 ~같이 들린다 His words ring [sound] true[like truth]. / He seems to be telling the truth. // 너 그거 ~이냐[진심이냐] Do you mean what you say?
2 truly; really. ⇨ 정말로

정말로(正−) [참으로] truly; really; indeed; [확실히] certainly; assuredly; surely; to be sure; [마음속으로부터] heartily; sincerely; [매우] very; quite; greatly; (구어) awfully. ¶~ 고맙습니다 Thanks a lot. // ~ 죄송합니다 I'm very sorry. / I sincerely apologize. / I beg your forgiveness. // 요전 날엔 ~ 신세를 많이 졌습니다 Thanks for (everything) the other day. // ~ 수고했습니다 (일해 준 사람에게) Thanks a lot. / Thank you very much. // 그는 ~ 깜짝 놀랐다 He was quite frightened. // 그렇게 한다면 넌 ~ 사나이다 If you do that, then you will really be a man. // 그는 ~ 다루기 힘든 사람이다 He is so[terribly] hard to handle. // 이건 ~ 괘씸한 일이다 This is absolutely[simply] unpardonable. // 나는 ~ 말문이 막혔다 I was at a complete loss for words. / (구어) I was utterly flabbergasted. // ~ 뻔뻔스러운 놈이구나 How utterly brazen he is! / What gall he has! // 그것은 ~ 재미있는 책이다 It is indeed[really] an interesting book to read. // ~ 그렇다면 나는 어떻게 하면 좋을까 If it's true I wonder what I should do? // ~ 네 말대로다 Exactly (as you say)! / Yes, indeed. // ~ 영리한 아이로구나 What a clever child she is!

정맥(精麥) scoured barley[wheat]. **정맥하다** scour barley[wheat] (▶ barley는 보리, wheat은 밀).

정맥(靜脈) a vein. ¶경~ the jugular (vein) // 소~ a veinlet // ~의 venous.
- **정맥류**(−瘤) a varix (pl. varices). ¶그는 다리에 ~가 나와 있다 He has varicose veins

정면(正面) the front[face]; the frontage; the front part; the facade(건물의). ¶호텔의 ~ 현관[입구] the front entrance [door] of a hotel // ~으로 [직접] directly / [똑바로] straight / [마주 대하여] to one's face / right in one's face // 적을 ~에서 공격하다 make a frontal attack on the enemy // 계획을 ~으로 반대하다 oppose a plan squarely[openly] // …의 얼굴을 ~으로 쳐다보 look a person (straight / full) in the face // 어려운 문제에 ~으로 부딪치다 tackle a difficult problem head-on[squarely] // 그 대성당의 ~은 조각으로 장식되어 있다 The facade of the cathedral is decorated with carvings. // 우리는 바람을 ~으로 받고 달렸다 We ran directly against[into the teeth of] the wind. // 나는 ~으로 머리를 한 대 얻어맞았다 I was hit squarely on the head. // 그들은 ~으로 대립했다 They clashed head-on concerning the tax question. // 그는 선생님에게 ~으로 반대하였다 He directly opposed his teacher. / He opposed his teacher outright.
● **정면도** a front view. **정면충돌** a head-on collision; a head-on car clash. ¶~을 하다 collide[clash] head-on (with / against) / come into a head-on collision (with) // 그 트럭은 승용차와 ~하였다 The truck had a head-on collision[collided head-on] with a passenger car. // 두 대의 자동차가 ~했다 The two cars collided head-on[had a head-on collision]. // 두 사람의 의견은 ~하였다 They had a violent clash of opinion.

정모(正帽) a ceremonial hat(예모); a regulation[uniform] cap(제모).

정무(政務) state[political] affairs; government[official] business. ¶~를 보다 attend to government affairs / administer the affairs of state.

정문(正門) the front[main] gate; [입구] the main entrance. ¶성의 ~ the front gate of a castle // ~으로 들어가다 go in by the front [main] gate / enter premises by the main gate.

정문(頂門) the crown of the head. ⇨정수리
● **정문일침**(ーー鍼) a finger on the sore spot; a home thrust. ¶아버지의 말씀은 바로 ~이었다 My father's words really hit home [touched a sore spot].

정물(靜物) still life.
● **정물화** a still life (pl. ~s); a still-life picture[painting].

정미(精米) **1** [쓿어 쌀을 만듦] rice polishing. **정미하다** polish rice. **2** polished rice. ⇨정백미
● **정미기** a rice-polishing machine. **정미소** a rice(-cleaning) mill.

정밀(精密) minuteness; precision; accuracy. **정밀하다** minute; precise; accurate. (▶ minute는 세밀한 데까지 주의가 미치고 있는, precise는 세밀한 데까지 정확함. accurate는 모델이나 정해진 기준에 충실함을 뜻함) ¶정밀한 지도 a detailed[minute] map // 나는 정밀한 건강 진단을 받았다 I underwent a minute [close] health[medical] examination. **정밀히** minutely; in detail; precisely. ¶~ 조사하다 investigate closely[minutely].
● **정밀 검사** a close[thorough / minute] examination. **정밀 (기계) 공업** the precision (machinery) industry. **정밀도**(-度) precision; accuracy. ¶~ 높은 렌즈 a lens of great precision / a high-precision lens // 이 측정치는 ~가 높다 These measurements are highly[very] precise.

정박(碇泊·渟泊) anchorage; mooring. ¶~ 중인 배 a ship at anchor. **정박하다** anchor; lie; berth; come to anchor. ¶정박하고 있다 be [lie] at anchor // 배는 인천항에 정박해 있다 The ship is at anchor[is moored] in Incheon Harbor. // 여객선 1척이 항구에 정박하고 있다 A passenger ship is lying at anchor in the harbor.
● **정박 기간** lay days. **정박료** anchorage fees; berthage. **정박항** an anchorage harbor.

정박아(精薄兒) a mentally deficient[retarded] child. ⇨정신박약아(⇨정신(精神))

정반대(正反對) the exact[direct] opposite; the exact reverse; just the opposite. ¶~의 directly [diametrically] opposite // ~에 in direct opposition to // 그의 의견은 네 의견과 ~다 His opinion is directly opposite to yours. // 그는 말하는 것과 하는 짓이 ~다 He says one thing and does another. // 나는 본심과는 ~되는 말을 하고 말았다 I said just the opposite of what I meant. // 호언장담과는 ~로 그의 호주머니 상태는 아주 어렵다 His boastful remarks to the contrary, he is really hard up. // 그것은 우리의 기대와는 ~의 결과를 초래했다 It produced[brought about] results exactly the opposite of what we had hoped for. // 그는 소문과는 ~로 극히 검소하게 살고 있다 Contrary to rumor, he leads a very frugal life.

정반합(正反合) [철] thesis-antithesis-synthesis.

정방(精紡) (fine) spinning.
● **정방기** a spinning machine.

정방형(正方形) [수] a regular quadrilateral. ⇨정사각형

정배(定配) banishment; exile; deportation. **정배하다** condemn (a person) to exile; banish [exile / deport] (to).

정백미(精白米) polished rice.

정벌(征伐) conquest; subjugation. **정벌하다** conquer; [지배하에 두다] subjugate.

정범(正犯) the principal offense.
● **정범자** the principal offender.

정변(政變) [정권의 변동] a political change; [혁명] a revolution; [쿠데타] (프) a coup d'état; [내각 경질] a change of[in] government. ¶그 나라에서 ~이 일어난 것 같다 It is reported that a revolution[coup d'état] has taken place in that country.

정병(精兵) [우수하고 강한 군사] elite soldiers; crack troops; picked men. ¶~ 5천 a crack troop of 5,000 strong.

정보(情報) (a piece[bit] of) information; intelligence; a report; [자료] data; (외교·거래상의) information(s); news; [슬쩍 알려 주는] a tipoff. ¶귀중한 ~ a valuable piece[bit] of information // 거짓 ~ a false[wrong] tip // 최신 ~ the latest news // ~를 얻다[수집하다] get[collect] information (on / about) // ~를 누설하다 leak information // …에게 ~를 흘리다 tip a person off / feed information to a person // 관계자로부터 ~를 얻으려고 동분서주하다 run around getting information from the people concerned // …라는 ~가 있다 it is reported that ... // ~를 제공하다 give infor-

정복

mation // 그는 주식에 관한 유익한[내부] ~를 내게 주었다 He gave me useful[inside] tips about the stock market.

● 정보 검색 information retrieval. 정보기관 a secret[an intelligence] service. 정보망 networks of intelligence[information]; a intelligence network. ¶~을 치다[~에 걸리다] set up[be caught in] an intelligence[information] network. 정보 산업 the information [communication] industry. 정보 시대 the age of information; the information age. 정보원(-員) an informer; an (intelligence) agent. 정보원(-源) a source of information. ¶~은 어디냐 Where did you get this information? / Who did you get this information from? 정보 처리 data[information] processing. ¶~ 산업 data processing industry. 정보 통신부 the Ministry of Information and Communication. 정보화 사회 the informationalized society.

정복(正服) [의식 때에 입는 정식의 옷] (in) (full) dress; a full-dress uniform(군대의).

정복(征服) conquest; subjugation; mastery. ¶알렉산더 대왕의 근동 ~ Alexander the Great's conquest of the Near East. **정복하다** conquer; subjugate; overcome; master; subdue. ¶정복할 수 없는 unconquerable // 산을 ~ conquer a mountain // 자연을 ~ subdue nature // 그는 독일어를 정복했다 He mastered German. // 그녀는 정복하기 어려운 여자다 She is adamant to affection. / She is love-proof.

● 정복자 a conqueror.

정본(正本) [공문서의 등본] an officially certified copy; (법률 용어) an exemplification; [원본] the original copy. ¶~과 부본 the original and a copy.

정부(正否) right or wrong. ¶~를 **분별하다** tell [know / distinguish] right from wrong // ~를 생각하지 않고 계획에 착수했다 I joined in the plan without stopping to consider the rights and wrongs of it.

정부(正副) (지위의) principal and vice[assistant]; (서류의) original and copy.

● 정부의장 the speaker and vice-speaker; the chairman and vice-chairman.

정부(政府) the government(▶ 자기 나라의 정부를 가리킬 때는 the Government로 대문자를 쓰는 일이 많음); (미) the administration; [내각] a cabinet(▶ 자기 나라나 특정 국가의 내각을 가리킬 때는 대문자로 시작하는 일이 많음). ¶임시 ~ a provisional government // 중앙 ~ the central government // 미국 연방 ~ the United States Government / the Federal Government / the Administration // 프랑스 ~ the French Government // 그 당시의 ~ the then government / the government of the[at that] time // ~의 governmental // 현 ~하에서 (hold a post) under the present government // ~를 지지[타도]하다 support [overthrow] the government // ~를 공격하다 attack the government // ~의 예산안이 국회를 통과했다 The government-drafted budget passed the National Assembly.

● 정부 당국 the government authorities. 정부미 government-stock rice. 정부안 the government bill. 정부 종합 청사 the Unified [Integrated] Government Building.

정부(情夫) a lover; (속어) a fancy man. ¶그녀에게는 ~가 있는 것 같다 She seems to have a lover.

정부(情婦) a mistress; a sweetheart; a (lady) love. ¶~를 **두다** keep a mistress.

정북(방)(正北方) due north. ¶바람이 ~에서 불어온다 The wind is blowing directly from the north. // 그 온천은 마을의 ~에 있다 The spa lies due north of the town.

정분(情分) intimacy; familiarity; close friendship; affection. ¶이웃 간의 ~ the sentiment of neighborliness // 그들은 ~이 두터운 사이다 They are close friends.

정비(整備) 1 [가다듬어 비교함]. **정비하다** set (a thing) in good condition[working order]; improve(개선하다). ¶진용을 ~ array the formation (of troops) // 그라운드를 ~ get an athletic field ready (for a game) / put the grounds in good condition // 각종 법령을 시민 생활의 현실적인 필요에 맞게 ~ improve various laws and regulations in such a way to meet the realistic needs of civil lives // 민주당은 진용을 정비해서 다가올 대선에 대비하고 있다 The Democratic Party are in battle formation for the forthcoming Presidential election.

2 [유지·보전] maintenance; [판매 후의 수리] service. ¶차량 ~ vehicle maintenance // 저 차는 ~가 잘 되어 있다 That car is in good repair. // 나는 차의 정기적인 ~를 받고 있다 I have my car serviced regularly. // 그는 자동차의 ~ 기술을 배우고 있다 He is studying automobile mechanics. / He's learning how to fix[repair] cars. **정비하다** [차 등을 수리하다] repair; [부품] fix; [판매 후 수리·점검하다] service; [손질하여 유지하다] maintain. ¶비행기를 ~ service an airplane.

● 정비공 (비행장의) a member of a ground crew; (기계의) maintenance man; repairman; a mechanic. ¶자동차 ~ a car mechanic.

정비례(正比例) [수] direct proportion[ratio]. **정비례하다** be in direct proportion[ratio] (to); be directly proportional (to). ¶…에 정비례하여 in direct[exact] proportion[ratio] to // 국민의 비만과 심장병의 발생률은 그 나라의 부유의 정도와 정비례한다 The incidence of obesity and heart disease in a country is directly proportional to the wealth of that country.

정사(正史) [올바른 역사] authentic[true] history.

정사(正邪) right and wrong; good and bad [evil]. ¶~를 구별할 줄 알다 know[can tell] right from wrong / discriminate between right and wrong.

정사(政事) political affairs; administrative business. ¶~를 **돌보다** manage the administrative business.

정사(情死) a love[lovers'] suicide; a love for love; a (lovers') double suicide. **정사하다** die together for love; commit a lover's [double] suicide. ¶불행한 두 연인은 정사하고 말았다 The two unhappy lovers killed themselves. / The unhappy lovers ended their affair by killing themselves.

정사(情事) [연애] a romance; [연애 사건] a love affair; [간통] adultery; an illicit intercourse. ¶혼외 ~ extramarital intercourse.

정사(精査) a minute investigation; a careful survey[examination]. **정사하다** [자세히 조사하다] investigate thoroughly; [정성들여 검사

하다] examine carefully; [면밀히 검사하다] scrutinize.

정사각형(正四角形) [수] a regular quadrilateral[tetragon]. ¶~인 탁자 a square table // 종이를 ~으로 자르다 cut a sheet of paper into a square.

정사면체(正四面體) [수] a regular tetrahedron.

정사영(正射影) [수] an orthographic[orthogonal] projection; an orthograph.
● **정사영법** orthography.

정사원(正社員) a regular[full-fledged] employee (of a company); a regular member.

정산(精算) [개산(概算)에 대하여] exact calculation; accurate reckoning; [차감 예산] adjustment; [결산] settlement of accounts. **정산하다** [정밀히 계산하다] calculate exactly; [조정하다] adjust; [결산하다] settle [(구어) fix] accounts. ¶그 표를 출구에서 정산해 주십시오 Please show the ticket at the exit and pay the adjusted fee.// 내가 전부 지불할 테니 나중에 각자가 정산하기로 하자 I'll pay for all of us, and we can settle up later.
● **정산액** the amount due; the adjusted amount. **정산표** a working sheet.

정삼각형(正三角形) an equilateral[a regular] triangle.

정상(正常) normality; (미) normalcy. ¶~인 [으로] normal[-ly] // 비~인 abnormal // ~으로 돌아오다 be restored to normal condition [return to normal(ity)] // 인체의 ~ 체온은 36.5이다 The normal temperature of the human body is 36.5 degrees. // 그의 머리는 ~이 아니다 He is off his head. / He is not in his right mind. // ~ 상태의 그는 이렇지 않다 He is another person when he is in normal condition. // 경인선은 오후부터 ~ 운행으로 돌아섰다 The Gyeongin[Seoul-Incheon] Line was put back into normal operation in the afternoon. // 그 투수는 ~ 컨디션이 아니다 The pitcher is not playing up to form[is not in form]. // 그가 ~ 궤도에 오르기까지는 시간이 걸린다 It takes him some time to get into [hit] his stride.
● **정상 가격** a normal price. **정상아** a normal child. **정상화** normalization. ¶국교 ~ normalization of the diplomatic relations (between Korea and Japan) // ~하다 normalize / be normalized // 관계를 ~하다 put (diplomatic) relations back on course / normalize [restore] one's relations [links] with. / renew diplomatic relations with.

정상(定常) regularity; constancy. ¶~의 regular / stationary / steady // ~적으로 steadily.
● **정상류**(-流) a steady flow. **정상파** [물] a stationary wave.

정상(頂上) 1 [산의 꼭대기] the top; the summit; the (highest) peck. ¶산의 ~에 at the top of the mountain // 그들은 마침내 ~에 올랐다 They gained the summit at last. 2 [극점] the peak; the top; the zenith. ¶그는 번영의 ~에 있다 He is at the peak of his prosperity. // 이 나라의 의학은 세계의 ~ 수준에 있다 Medical science in this country ranks [is on a level] with the best in the world.
● **정상 외교** summit diplomacy. **정상 회담** a summit conference [meeting / session / talk].

정상(情狀) [사실의 상태] circumstances;

conditions. ¶~ 참작 extenuation // ~을 참작하다 make allowances[allow] for circumstances / take the circumstance into consideration / extenuate // 나는 ~을 참작하여 용서했다 I took the circumstances into consideration and[As there were extenuating circumstances], I forgave him. // 그의 잔인한 범죄에는 ~을 참작할 여지가 없다 There is no room to take the circumstances of his cruel crime into consideration. / We cannot extenuate his cruel crime.

정상배(政商輩) a businessman who has connections with politicians[political affiliations].

정색(正色) [얼굴빛을 바꾸어 엄정한 빛을 보임] a serious countenance; earnestness. **정색하다** become serious[grave]; assume [put on] a serious look[countenance]; put on a serious[grave]face; straighten one's face. ¶정색하고 with a serious[grave] look / with a straight face // 남을 정색하고 나무라다 reprove a person with a solemn air // 그는 언제나 정색하고 말한다 He always speaks in a stiff[(구어) starchy] manner. // 그녀가 정색하고 그렇게 말했어 She said that with a perfect straight face.

정서(正書) square-hand[printed-style] characters. **정서하다** write square hand.
● **정서법** orthography.

정서(淨書) [글씨를 깨끗이 씀] copying fair; [글씨를 깨끗이 쓴 것] a fair[clean] copy. **정서하다** make a fair[clean] copy (of one's notes); copy[write out] fair. ¶그녀는 원고를 정서해 주었다 She helped me in making [make] a fair copy of the draft.

정서(情緒) emotion; feeling; sentiment. ¶이국 ~ an exotic mood / exoticism // ~가 넘쳐흐르다 be overcome with emotions / have a tender feeling (for a person) // 그녀는 ~가 불안정하다 She is emotionally unstable.
● **정서 장애** emotional disturbance. ¶~아 emotionally disturbed children.

정서(방)(正西方) due west. ¶여기서 ~에 역이 있다 There is a station directly west of here.

정석(定石) 1 [바둑·장기] a standard move (in go); a formula in the game of go. ¶~대로 두다 play (go) by the standard move. 2 [정해진 방식] ¶우리는 모든 것을 ~대로 했다 We did everything by the book[in the usual way]. // 그것이 ~이다 That's standard practice[the usual method].

정선(停船) [배를 멈춤] stoppage of a ship; (검역을 위한) quarantine. ¶~을 명하다 stop a ship / order a ship to stop (검역을 위해) quarantine. **정선하다** stop; (a ship) be brought to stop. ¶배는 검역을 위해 정선했다 (환자가 발생했으므로) The ship was quarantined. / (일반적인 검사를 위해) The ship was stopped for a medical examination. // 배는 부득이 항구 밖에서 일시 정선했다 The ship was held up temporarily outside the port.

정선(精選) careful selection. **정선하다** select [pick out] carefully. ¶정선한 사과 select [carefully selected] apples // 이것은 재료를 정선해서 만든 것입니다 These articles are (made) of carefully selected materials. →¶여기에 있는 모든 것은 많은 것 중에서 정선된 것이다 All of these have been selected carefully out of many articles.
● **정선품** choice goods. ¶통조림의 ~ choice

정설(定說) 〔학문상의〕 an established theory; 〔널리 인정된 의견〕 a widely-accepted notion; 〔일반적 의견〕 a general opinion. ¶새로운 실험은 ~를 뒤집었다 The new experiment overturned the established theory.// 이 언어는 셈계라는 것이 일반의 ~로 되어 있다 It is the accepted view[The generally accepted opinion is] that this language belongs to the Semitic family.

정성(精誠) one's true heart; sincerity; devotion; wholeheartedness; earnestness(열성). ¶~ 어린 충고 earnest advice // ~을 다하여 하느님께 기도하다 pray to God intently [fervently / wholeheartedly] // 그는 모든 ~을 기울여 일을 했다 He did his work with all his heart.// 더 ~ 들여 일해라 Put more spirit into your work. / Do your work with more spirit.// 나는 처가에서 장인 장모의 ~을 다한 대접을 받았다 My wife's parents gave me a very warm reception.// 그녀의 병간호는 나무랄 데 없을 정도로 ~이 어린 것이다 Her nursing is perfect[leaves nothing to be desired].// 그는 자기 연구에 온 ~을 기울였다 He put his heart and soul into his research.// ~ 어린 선물을 보내 주셔서 대단히 감사합니다 Thank you very much for sending me the kind present.

정성 분석(定性分析) 〔화〕 qualitative analysis.

정세(情勢) the situation; the state of affairs; conditions. (▶ situation은 사람·사물이 놓인 특정 상황, state of affairs는 사태를 나타내는 일반적인 말, condition은 원인이나 상황에 관계된 그때의 상태) ¶국제〔국내〕 ~ the international[domestic] situation // 세계 ~ the world situation // ~의 변화 changes in the situation[state of affairs] // ~를 판단〔파악〕하다 assess[take in] the situation // ~를 관망하다 watch the development of the situation // ~를 주시하다 observe the situation // ~를 분석하다 analyze the situation // 이제는 ~가 바뀌었다 This is no longer the case.// 전쟁이 일어날 듯한 ~였다 Conditions looked toward war.// 현재의 ~로는 성공할 것 같지 않다 As things stand now[Under the present conditions / Under the present circumstances], we are not likely to succeed.

● **정세 판단** (a correct) analysis (and judgment) of the situation.

정소(精巢) a testicle; a spermary(고환).

정수(定數) 1 〔일정한 수〕 a fixed[stated] number; 〔정족수〕 a quorum. 2 ➡상수(常數)1 3 〔정해진 운수〕 destiny; fate.

정수(淨水) clean water.

● **정수기** a water purifier. **정수장** a filtration plant; a water purification plant.

정수(精髓) 1 〔골수〕 the marrow (of a bone). 2 〔본질〕 the essence; the quintessence; the cream; the best. ¶학문의 ~ the essence of learning // 동양 문화의 ~ the essence of the Eastern Culture // 현대 과학 기술의 ~를 모으다 gather the best that advanced modern technology has to offer // 그의 작품은 한국 민속 예술의 ~를 나타내고 있다 His work embodies the quintessence of Korean folk art.

정수(靜水) standing[stagnant / still] water.

정수(整數) 〔수〕 an integral number; an integer.

정수리(頂-) the crown[top] of the head; 《속어》 the pate. ¶그는 ~을 한 대 맞았다 He received[took] a blow on the top of the head.

정숙하다(貞淑-) chaste; virtuous. ¶정숙한 아내 a chaste[virtuous] wife // 정숙하지 못한 아내 an unfaithful wife // 그녀는 정숙한 아내였다 She was faithful to her husband.

정숙하다(靜肅-) silent; still; quiet. ¶지휘자가 손을 들자 연주회장은 정숙해졌다 As the conductor raised his hand a hush fell over the hall. **정숙히** silently; quietly. ¶~ 해라 Keep[Be] quiet. / Don't make a noise. / (회의 등에서) Order! Order!

정승(政丞) a minister of State; a prime minister (in the Joseon dynasty).

정시(正視) 1 〔똑바로 봄〕 looking straight; 〔생〕 stigmatism. **정시하다** look (a person) in the face; look straight (at). 2 〔생〕 emmetropia. ➪정시안(➪정시)

● **정시 렌즈** an orthoptic lens. **정시안** 〔생〕 emmetropia.

정시(定時) 〔정해진 시간〕 the[a] fixed time; 〔예정된 시간〕 the scheduled time; 〔규칙적인 시간〕 regular hours. ¶~의 regular / periodical // ~에 at the fixed time / 〔예정대로〕 on schedule // ~에 운행하다 move on schedule / operate regularly // 그는 매일 ~에 출근한다 He goes to work at a fixed time every day.// 비행기는 ~에 도착합니다 The plane will arrive on time[schedule].// 회의는 ~에 시작되었다 The meeting started at the scheduled time.

정식(正式) formality. ¶~의 〔형식이 완비된〕 formal / 〔공식의〕 official / 〔적법한〕 legal / 〔정규의〕 regular // ~으로 formally / officially / legally / regularly // ~ 모임 a formal meeting // ~으로 결혼하다 be legally married // 남을 ~으로 방문하다 make[pay] a formal visit to a person // 그것의 ~ 발표는 언제입니까 When is it to be officially released [announced]? // 관공서에서 ~ 통보가 있었다 I received formal[official] notification from the government office.// 그녀는 ~으로 요리를 배운 것이 아니다 She has not taken formal cooking lessons.// 한국은 1991년 9월 18일 유엔에 ~ 가입했다 Korea became a regular member of the United Nations in Sept. 18, 1991.

● **정식 결혼** legal[formal] marriage. **정식 재판** (apply for) a formal trial. ¶~을 요구하다 〔신청하다〕 demand[appeal to the court for] a formal trial.

정식(定式) 〔규정〕 a formula (pl. ~s, -lae); an established form. ¶~의 formula / regular / formal.

정식(定食) a regular[set] meal; 〔정해진 메뉴〕 a fixed menu; (호텔·레스토랑 등의) table d'hôte; 《영》 an ordinary. ¶낮의 ~ set lunch // "무엇으로 하시겠습니까?" "B ~을 주십시오." "What would you like (to have), sir?" "Give me dinner B, please."// 오늘의 ~ (게시) Today's[Chef's] Special.

정식(整式) 〔수〕 an integral expression.

정신(艇身) a boat's length. ¶2~〔반 ~〕의 차로 이기다 win (a race) by two lengths[half a length].

정신(精神) 1 (지성) mind; (육체에 대한 마음) spirit; (영혼) soul; (의지) will; (마음의 상태·기분) mentality. ¶희생 ~ a self-sacrificing spirit // 협동 ~ a cooperative spirit // 박애

an exemplary spirit // 군인 ~ military spirit // 한국의 국민~ the Korean national spirit // ~의 mental / spiritual / [감정적인] emotional // [훌륭한] a noble mind [sentiment] // 비열한 ~ a base mind / a mean spirit // ~이 건전한 사람 a man of sound mind // ~에 이상이 있다 be mentally ill [unbalanced] / be out of one's mind // ~을 함양하다 train [nourish / cultivate] one's mind // ~을 가다듬다 brace oneself up / pull oneself together / straighten oneself out // 그 너는 아들의 죽음으로 ~이 이상해졌다 Her son's death affected her mind. // 그는 그 문제에 ~을 집중했다 He concentrated his attention on the question. // 그는 ~은 멀쩡하다 He is sane / He is in his right mind.

2 [사물의 근본적인 의의·사상] the spirit. ¶시대 ~ the spirit of the time [age] // 독립 ~ the spirit of independence // 입법 ~ the spirit of legislation // 헌법 ~ the spirit of the constitution // 그러면 법률의 ~은 죽고 만다 It violates the spirit of the law.

정신(이) 나가다 be upset; be flurried; lose presence of mind; [바보스러워지다] become foolish; grow absent-minded. ¶정신 나간 얼굴 a vacant look / (미국 속어) a moony face // 너 정신 나갔니 Are you crazy? // 정신 나간 소리 집어치워 Don't talk nonsense! // 그건 정신 나간 짓이다 It's sheer madness.

정신(이) 들다 come to oneself; come to (one's sense); recover [regain] consciousness [one's senses]. ¶5분 후에, 그는 정신이 들었다 He came to his senses after five minutes. // 정신이 들고 보니 도랑 속에서 자고 있었다 When I came to, I found myself lying in a ditch.

정신(을) 잃다 faint (away); swoon; lose consciousness [one's senses]; be stunned (by the news). ¶열이 높아 ~ be delirious with fever // 환자는 고열로 정신을 잃고 헛소리를 내고 있다 The patient is talking in the delirium of a high fever. // 그는 술을 마셔도 정신을 잃지 않는다 Even when he drinks he doesn't lose control of himself.

정신(을) 차리다 collect one's mind; pay attention. ¶정신 차려 Clean up your act! / Get your act together! // 그는 마침내 정신을 차려서 일에 열중하게 되었다 He came to his senses at last and began to throw himself into his work. // 그가 기절했을 때 정신 차리게 보드카를 먹였다 When he fainted, I made him drink some vodka to bring him around [to revive him].

정신(이) 팔리다 be silly over (a woman); be absorbed in; be intent on. ¶그는 텔레비전을 보는 데 정신이 팔려 있었다 He was completely absorbed in watching television. // 오만 가지 일에 정신이 팔려 있었다 I have been caught up in all sorts of work. // 나는 다른 일에 정신이 팔려 있었다 I was thinking about [preoccupied with] something else.

●**정신 감정** a psychiatric test; a mental examination. ¶~을 하다 carry out [conduct] a psychiatric examination. **정신과의사** a psychiatrist. ¶~ 의사 a psychiatrist. **정신 교육** moral education. **정신력** mental [spiritual] strength. ¶(환자가) ~으로 버티고 있다 stay alive by the sheer force of (his) will to live. **정신문화** moral [spiritual] culture. **정신박약** mental retardation. ⇨"정신 지체(⇨정신) 정

신박약아 a mentally deficient [retarded] child; a weak-minded [feebleminded] child. **정신병** a mental disease [illness]; a psychosis (pl. -ses); psychopathy. ¶그는 ~에 걸려 있다 He is mentally ill [deranged]. // 그 집에는 ~의 유전이 있다 There is a taint of insanity in his family. / Insanity runs in the blood of his family. **정신 병원** a mental hospital [institution]; an insane asylum; a madhouse. **정신병자** a mentally deranged person; an insane [a demented] person; a lunatic; a psychopath; (미국 속어) a psycho. **정신 분석(학)** psychoanalysis. ¶~자 a psychoanalyst // ~을 하다 psychoanalyze. **정신 분열증** schizophrenia. ¶~ 환자 a schizophreniac. **정신 상태** a mental condition; a state of mind. ¶남의 ~를 의심하다 doubt (a person's) sanity. **정신 안정제** a tranquil(l)izer. **정신 요법** psychotherapy; mental healing. **정신 위생** mental hygiene. **정신 이상** mental derangement [disorder]. **정신 이상자** an insane person; a lunatic; a psycho. **정신 지체** mental retardation. **정신 지체아** a mentally retarded child. **정신 착란** a mental disorder.

정신없다 (精神－) be out of one's senses; [산만하다] be distracted [absent-minded / blank]; (바쁘거나 하여) be upset [flurried]. **정신없이** ¶~ 취하다 get blind [dead] drunk / drink oneself dead drunk // 나는 ~ 걸어 다녔다 I walked about like a man in a trance. // 그는 아침까지 ~ 잤다 He slept like a log [soundly] until morning.

정신적 (精神的) mental; spiritual; psychical; moral. ¶~ 피로 mental exhaustion // ~ 사랑 Platonic love // ~ 유산 spiritual [mental] heritage // ~ 원조 moral support // ~ 학대 mental cruelty // ~으로 mentally / spiritually / morally // ~으로 지쳐 버리다 be mentally tired out / suffer from a nervous breakdown // 그의 ~ 타격은 컸다 He received a great emotional shock [mental blow].

정실 (正室) [본처] a lawful [legal] wife. ¶(관계가 있던) 제인을 ~로 삼다 make an honest woman of Jane.

정실 (情實) [사사로운 정] personal [private] considerations; [편애] favoritism. ¶~을 배제하다 set aside personal considerations (in public matters) // 그는 ~에 좌우되었다 He was influenced by personal considerations. // 그는 실력보다도 ~ 덕분에 그 지위를 얻었다 He got that position more through favoritism than on the basis of merit.

●**정실 인사** (－人事) personnel changes through favoritism.

정압 (定壓) [일정한 압력] constant pressure. **정액** (定額) a fixed amount [sum]; the specified [required] amount. ¶~에 달하다 [달하지 않다] come up to [come short of] the specified amount // ~의 학비를 부모에게서 받다 receive a fixed sum of money for school expenses from one's parents // 기부금은 ~에 달했다 [미달했다] Donations reached [fell short of] the required amount.

●**정액세** a fixed amount tax. **정액 소득** a fixed income. **정액제** a flat [fixed] sum system; (전기료 등의) flat-rate tariff.

정액 (精液) semen; sperm (▶ a sperm은 정자의 뜻). ¶~의 spermatic / seminal.

●**정액관** a spermaduct. **정액 사출** a seminal

정양(靜養) 〔안정하여 휴양함〕 (a) rest. ¶병후의 ~ recuperation (after an illness) // ~차 for a rest / for (the benefit of) one's health // 당신은 3개월의 ~이 필요합니다 You need three months of quiet rest. // 그는 병후 자택에서 ~ 중이다 He is resting at home after his illness. // 그는 ~차 온양으로 갔다 He went to Onyang for his health [to recuperate]. **정양하다** rest quietly; take a rest.

정어리 〔동〕 a sardine (pl. ~, ~s).

정언적(定言的) 〔논〕 categorical.
● **정언적 명령** categorical imperative. **정언적 명제** a categorical proposition.

정역학(靜力學) 〔물〕 statics. ¶~적인 static(al).

정연하다(整然-) 〔말끔하다〕 order; well-ordered; regular; 〔체계적이다〕 systematic. ¶모든 것이 질서 ~ All are arranged in good order. // 그녀는 정연한 이론의 소유자이다 She has logical mind. **정연히** in good order; in an orderly manner [fashion]; systematically. ¶그들은 ~ 늘어서 있었다 They stood in an orderly line. // 그의 논문은 ~ 짜여져 있다 His thesis is well-organized.

정열(情熱) 〔강한 감정〕 (a) passion; 〔유별난 열정〕 ardor; 〔오래 계속되는 열정〕 fervor; 〔뭔가를 추구하는 열심〕 enthusiasm; 〔아주 강한 열정〕 zeal. ¶~에 불타다 burn with passion // ~을 쏟다 put one's heart (into) // 창작에 ~을 불태우다 have a passion for creative writing / 그녀는 음악에 대한 ~을 가지고 있다 She has a passion for music. / She is enthusiastic over [about] music. // 그것으로 그의 ~은 식어 버렸다 It chilled [cooled] his ardor.

정열적(情熱的) passionate; ardent; fervent; enthusiastic; zealous. ¶~ 성격 a passionate personality // ~으로 passionately / with enthusiasm // 그는 ~인 사람이다 He is a man of passion. / He is a passionate man.

정염(正鹽) 〔화〕 a normal salt.

정염(情炎) 〔불같이 타오르는 욕정〕 flaming desire; burning passion. ¶~을 불태우다 kindle the passions // ~에 불타다 burn with passions.

정예(精銳) the pick [best] (of the men); the cream of the crop; the elite. ¶미 공군의 ~ the pick of the United States Air Force // 소수 ~의 과학자 집단 a small elite group of scientists.
● **정예 부대** an elite troop; a crack unit.

정오(正午) (high) noon; twelve (o'clock) noon (시간을 좀 엄밀히 나타낼 때); midday. ¶~의 사이렌 the noon siren [whistle] // ~의 뉴스 a midday report / twelve o'clock news // 지금 ~입니다 It's twelve o'clock noon. // 우리는 ~에 점심을 먹는다 We have lunch at noon.

정오(正誤) 〔잘못을 바로잡음〕 correction [rectification] of errors. **정오하다** correct an error; rectify.
● **정오표** (a list of) errata; (출판물의) (a list of) corrigenda (▶ 본래 복수형이나 an errata, a corrigenda라고 하는 사람이 많음).

정온(定溫) a fixed [constant] temperature.
● **정온 동물** a warm-blooded [homoiothermic] animal.

정욕(情慾) sexual [sensual] desire; passions; lust. ¶~의 노예 a slave of passions // ~을 억누르다 repress one's sexual appetites / control one's sex drive // ~에 빠지다 indulge [give in to] one's passions // ~을 채우다 gratify one's lust // ~은 억제하기 어렵다 Passions are hard to control.

정원(定員) 1 〔규정된 인원수〕 the [a] fixed number; 〔지정된 인원수〕 prescribed number; 〔할당된 인원수〕 a quota. ¶~의 감축 a decrease [cut] in the fixed [regular] number // ~의 증가 an increase in the fixed [regular] number // ~에 도달하다 reach the fixed number // 이 나라 하원의 ~은 85이다 The Lower House of this country is composed of eighty-five members. // 위원회는 아직까지도 ~ 미달이다 Some seats on the committee are still unfilled. // 사학과는 학생 수 150명의 ~에 훨씬 미달되어 있다 The history department is far short of its full quota of 150 students. // 응모자는 ~을 훨씬 초과했다 The number of applicant was much greater than the fixed [prescribed] number (of openings [places]).
2 〔수용력〕 a (seating) capacity; the rated capacity. ¶~ 200명의 배 a ship with a capacity of 200 passengers // 이 극장은 ~ 1,500명이다 This theater seats 1,500 people [has a seating capacity of 1,500]. // 이 버스는 ~을 초과하고 있다 This bus is carrying more passengers than the seating capacity allows. / This bus is overloaded.

정원(庭園) a garden; a park (넓은). ¶옥상 ~ a roof garden // ~을 꾸미다 make [lay out] a garden / engage in landscape gardening // ~을 손보다 work in [on] one's garden // ~의 풀을 뽑았다 I weeded the garden.
● **정원사** a gardener. **정원수** a garden tree. ¶~를 손질하다 trim garden trees.

정월(正月) 〔1월〕 January (약어 Jan.); the first month of the year. ¶~ 초하루 New Year's Day // ~ 보름 the 15th of the New Year according to the lunar calender.

정유(精油) 1 (식물성의) an essential oil. 2 〔정제한 석유〕 refined oil.
● **정유소** an oil refinery. **정유 회사** an oil refining company.

정육(精肉) (good quality) meat.
● **정육점** a butcher('s) [meat] shop.

정육면체(正六面體) a regular hexahedron; a cube.

정의 a definition. ¶정확한 ~ an exact definition // 사전에 나와 있는 ~ a dictionary definition (of a word) // ~를 내리다 give [formulate / frame / lay down] a definition (of) / define // 신사의 ~는 예의를 아는 사람이다 A gentleman is defined as one who knows manners. / Good manners define the gentleman. **정의하다** define (as); give a definition (of). ¶그는 자유를 자기가 하고 싶은 일을 하는 것으로 정의했다 He defined freedom as doing what he wanted. // 이 용어를 명확히 정의할 수 있습니까 Can you clearly define [give a clear definition of] this term?

정의 justice; right; righteousness. ¶~의 편 a champion [friend / lover] of justice // ~를 위해 싸우다 fight in the cause of justice // ~를 옹호하다 defend the right // ~는 끝내는 승리한다 Right will prevail in the end.
● **정의감** a sense of justice. ¶그는 ~이 강하다 He has a strong sense of justice.

●**정의역** [수] the domain.
정의(情誼) [서로 사귀어 친해진 정] friendly feelings; (ties of) friendship; good-fellowship. ¶깊은 ～ deep friendship // ～가 두텁다 be very faithful[friendly] / be kind and warmhearted // 나는 오랜 ～ 때문에 그에게 거절의 말을 할 수 없었다 Because of our long-standing friendship, I could not say no.
정의롭다(正義―) just; righteous. ¶정의로운 싸움 a righteous war / fighting for a rightful cause.
정자(正字) [똑똑하고 체가 바른 글자] a correct letter; [한자의 속자·약자가 아닌 본래의 글자] the correct form of a Chinese character. ¶글자를 흘리지 말고 ～로 써라 Write correctly not in the running style[in a simplified form].
●**정자법** [언] orthography.
정자(亭子) a *jeongja*; a pavilion; a summerhouse; [휴식처] an arbor; a bower.
●**정자나무** [그늘 나무] a shade tree.
정자(精子) [동] a spermatozoon (*pl.* -zoa); (집합적) a sperm.; [식] a spermatozoid. ¶～의 spermatoid.
●**정자은행** a sperm bank.
정작 [진짜인 것] a real fact; truth; actuality; reality; [실지로] truly; really; actually; practically. ¶～ 알아보니 거짓말이었다 Upon actual investigation, it turned out to be a false report. // ～ 출발할 때가 되자 그는 병이 나 버렸다 When it was time to go[At the moment when he was actually to start] he became sick[(영) ill]. // 이것은 간단한 규칙이지만 ～ 하면 그다지 간단하지가 않다 This is a simple rule, but in practice, it is far from simple. // ～ 사려고 하면 살 수가 없다 When you actually try to buy one, it is not to be had.
정장(正裝) fulldress; formal dress; a full(-dress) uniform(군인의). ¶～을 요하는 파티 a dress-up party // ～은 필요 없습니다 (초대장에서) (Dress) Informal. / No dress. **정장하다** (일반인이) dress up; (군인 등이) be in full dress. ¶오늘 파티에는 정장하고 가야 한다 You have to dress up for today's party.
정장(艇長) [작은 함정을 지휘하는 우두머리] a coxswain; [구어] a cox; a skipper; [잠수정·수뢰정 등의 장] a captain; a commander.
정장석(正長石) [광] orthoclase.
정장제(整腸劑) medicine for intestinal disorders.
정쟁(政爭) a political strife[controversy / dispute]; political warfare. ¶그는 딸의 결혼을 ～의 도구로 이용했다 He made a political issue of his daughter's marriage.
정적(政敵) a political opponent[rival / enemy]. (▶ opponent는 대항자, rival은 같은 목적으로 맞서는 상대, enemy는 증오심을 품고 있는 상대)
정적(靜的) [움직임이 없다] static; [고요하다] still. ¶～으로 statically // 그의 작품은 ～이면서도 동적인 힘이 훌륭한 조화를 이루고 있다 In his work stillness and movement are beautifully harmonized.
정적(靜寂) [고요하여 괴괴함] silence; still(ness); quiet(ness). ¶호수는 평소의 ～으로 돌아갔다 The lake regained its usual calmness[tranquility] // 집 안은 죽은 듯 이 감돌았다 Dead silence reigned over[in / throughout] the house. // 돌연 폭음이 밤의 ～을 깼다 All of a sudden an explosion broke the silence[stillness] of the night.
정적분(定積分) [수] definite integral.
정전(停電) a stoppage[breakdown] of electric current; a power failure[outage]; (파업·절전을 위한) a power cut; (전등이 꺼지는 일) a blackout. ¶전면 ～ a general failure of power supply // 낙뢰로 인한 ～으로 전동차가 멎었다 Trains stopped[Train runs were disrupted] owing to the power failure caused by lightning. **정전하다** (the electricity) be off[cut]; (the power) be gone off[give out]. ➔¶내일 오전 1시부터 5시까지 정전됩니다 The electric current will be off[cut] from 1 a.m. to 5 a.m. tomorrow.
정전(停戰) a cease-fire(군대 용어); an armistice(일정 기간의); a truce(협정에 의한). **정전하다** cease fire; stop fighting; suspend hostilities; have a truce.
●**정전 위원회** a cease-fire committee. **정전 협정** a cease-fire agreement; a truce. **정전을 맺다** conclude a cease-fire agreement / agree to stop fighting. **정전 회담** a cease-fire conference; cease-fire talks.
정전기(正電氣) [물] positive electricity. ⇨⁼양전기(陽電氣)
정전기(靜電氣) [전] static electricity. ¶～의 electrostatic // 스웨터를 벗을 때 지직 하고 ～가 일어났다 When I took off my sweater it crackled[snapped / popped] with static electricity.
●**정전기 유도** electrostatic induction.
정절(貞節) [여자의 곧은 절개] fidelity; (conjugal) faithfulness; [정조] chastity. ¶～을 지키다 maintain chastity // 그녀는 남편에 대하여 ～을 지켰다 She was faithful[a faithful wife] to her husband.
정점(頂點) 1➔ 꼭짓점 2 [꼭대기] the top; the peak; the summit. 3 the peak. ⇨⁼절정2 ¶그의 인기는 이제 ～에 달했다 He has reached the peak of his popularity. // 그 야구 시합은 ～에 달했다 The baseball game reached its most exciting point. // 기온은 대개 팔월에 가서 ～에 이른다 Temperatures usually reach their peak in August.
정정(訂正) (a) correction. ¶～을 많이 한 원고 a manuscript full of corrections // '가다'를 '갔다'로 ～ (정오표에서) For "go" read "went". **정정하다** correct; make correction. ¶잘못이 있으면 정정하시오 Correct errors, if any. // 전부 읽은 다음에 정정해 주시오 Please make correction after you have read it through. // 붉은 잉크 부분이 교사가 정정한 곳입니다 The parts in red ink are the corrections made by the teacher.
정정(政情) a political situation; political conditions[affairs]. ¶～이 불안하다 Political conditions become acute[grow strained]. // 그는 현재의 한국 ～에 정통해 있다 He is familiar[well acquainted] with the political situation in present-day Korea. // 대정치가라도 나오지 않는 한 이 ～ 불안은 계속될 것 같다 Unless a great statesman appears, this political unrest will persist.
정정당당하다(正正堂堂―) fair; fair and square; open and aboveboard. ¶정정당당한 승부 a fairly contested match // 그의 태도는 항상 ～ His manner is fair and square all the time. // 그의 협상 방법은 정정당당한 것이었다 His way of negotiating was fair and

정정하다 square. **정정당당히** fairly (and squarely); openly; aboveboard. ¶우리 ~ 싸우자[승부하자] Let's play fair[make it a fair fight].∥~해 보자 Come on and play fair.

정정하다(亭亭-) 1 (나무 등이) tall; high; towering. ¶정정한 소나무 a tall[high] pine tree. 2 (노인이) vigorous; hale and hearty. ¶정정한 노인 a hale old man∥그는 80세의 고령이지만 아직 ~ He is still vigorous[hale and hearty] at the advanced[ripe old] age of eighty.

정제(精製) 1 [물질을 순수하게 함] refinement; purification. **정제하다** refine; purify. ¶정제한 설탕[석유] refined sugar[petroleum]∥알코올을 ~ purify alcohol∥설탕이나 석유는 정제한 후에 사용된다 Sugar and oil are refined before they are consumed. 2 [정성 들여 만듦] careful manufacture. **정제하다** manufacture carefully.

정제(錠劑) (둥그스름한) a pill; (원판형의) a tablet.

정조(貞操) chastity; virtue; (female) honor; [처녀성] virginity; maidenhood. ¶~를 지키다 keep one's chastity∥여자의 ~를 더럽히다 rape a woman / violate the chastity of a woman∥남자에게 ~를 바치다 surrender one's chastity to a man / give oneself to a man∥그녀는 끝까지 ~를 지켰다 She remained chaste[virtuous] to the last.∥그녀는 ~를 팔았다 She sold her chastity[herself].

● **정조 관념** a sense of virtue. ¶~이 약하다 have a weak sense of virtue / be a woman of easy virtue. **정조대**(一帶) a chastity belt. **정조 유린** violation of chastity.

정조(情操) sentiments. ¶미적(美的)[도덕적] ~ aesthetic[moral] sentiments.

정족수(定足數) a quorum. ¶~에 달하다 achieve a quorum∥참석자는 ~에 미달했다 There were not enough people present for a quorum. / The number of those present did not reach a quorum.∥이 회의의 ~는 회원의 3분의 2이다 Two-thirds of the members of this society constitutes[forms] a quorum for a meeting.

정종(正宗) refined rice wine.
정좌하다(正坐-) sit erect on one's knees.
정좌하다(靜坐-) sit quietly[still]; sit in meditation.

정주(定住) settlement. **정주하다** live; be living; reside permanently; settle down. ¶그들은 한 곳에 정주하는 법이 없다 They never settle down in one place.∥우리가 여기에 정주한 지 10년이 된다 Ten years have passed since we settled here.

● **정주자** a permanent resident.
정중(正中) the very middle.
● **정중선** a median line.

정중하다(鄭重-) [예의바르다] polite; [공손하다] courteous; [사교상의 예법에 맞다] civil; [경의가 많다] respectful; [대접이 좋다] hospitable. ¶정중한 환영 a cordial[warm] reception∥정중한 말을 쓰다 use courteous [polite] language / be courteous in wording ∥그들은 우리에게 아주 정중했다 They were very polite to us.∥나는 정중한 대접을 받았다 I was courteously entertained.∥그는 말씨가 ~ He has a polite manner of speaking. / He is polite[courteous] in speaking. **정중히** politely; courteously; civilly; respectfully; hospitably; with hospitality. ¶~ 사과하다 make a polite apology / apologize civilly∥~ 인사하다 give (a person) a polite greeting / [절을 하다] bow deeply[politely / courteously]∥그들은 우리를 ~ 맞이했다 We were received with hospitality[hospitably].

정지(停止) [멎음] stoppage; a stop; a halt; a standstill. **정지하다** stop; come to a stop; halt. ¶교차로에서 일단 ~ stop before crossing the intersection∥기계가 정지했다 The machine stopped[came to a halt].∥일은 정지함이 없이 계속되었다 The work continued without stoppage(s)[stopping].∥행렬이 정지했다 The procession halted[came to a standstill].∥그의 차가 내 집 앞에서 정지했다 His car drew[pulled] up in front of my house. ➔ 총파업으로 버스와 지하철이 정지되었다 The general strike has halted buses and subway.

2 [금지] suspension; temporary prohibition; ban. ¶영업[지급 / 발행] ~ suspension of business[payment / publication]∥신문의 발행 ~를 해제하다 release the suspension of a newspaper. **정지하다** suspend. ¶영업[지급]을 ~ suspend business[payment]. ➔그는 운전면허를 1개월간 정지당했다 He was disqualified from driving for a month. / He has his driving license suspended for a month.∥그 식당은 1개월간 영업을 정지당했다 The restaurant was ordered to suspend its business for one month.

● **정지 신호** a stop signal; a stoplight.

정지(靜止) a standstill; rest; repose; stillness. ¶~ 상태 a stationary state∥내 맥박은 ~ 상태에서 70이었다 My resting pulse (rate) was 70. / My pulse (rate) was 70 when I was at rest. **정지하다** stand still; rest; come to a standstill[halt]. ¶정지하고 있는 물체 the bodies at rest∥정지하고 있다 be at a standstill / remain stationary.

● **정지 궤도** (a) stationary orbit. ¶~에 위성을 쏘아 올리다 launch a satellite to be placed in stationary orbit around the earth. **정지 위성** a stationary satellite.

정지(整地) (건축을 위한) leveling of land [ground]; (경작을 위한) soil preparation. **정지하다** (땅을 택지용으로 정돈하다) prepare the land for the construction of a house; [땅을 고르다] level[grade] the land[the ground]; (경작자용으로 정비하다) prepare the soil (for planting). ¶이곳은 택지용으로 ~ 중이다 This place is being prepared as a residential area. / This area is being developed for residential purposes.

정직(正直) honesty; [성실] integrity. **정직하다** honest; upright. ¶정직한 사람 an honest man / a man of honesty[integrity]∥그는 정직한 소년이다 He is an honest boy.∥이것은 정직한 사람이 손해를 보는 좋은 예다 This is a good example of a case in which honesty doesn't pay. **정직히** honestly; squarely. ¶~ 살다 live an honest life∥나는 나 자신이 ~ 번 돈을 원한다 I want my own, honestly-earned money.∥~ 숨기지 소용없이 말해 Be honest and tell me everything about it.

정직(定職) a permanent[fixed] job; a regular occupation; fixed employment. ¶~이 없는 불규칙한 생활 a desultory life without regular occupation∥~이 없다 have no regular occupation[employment].

정직(停職) suspension from duty [office]. ¶~을 명하다 suspend (a person) from office // 그는 1개월의 ~ 명령을 받았다 He was suspended from duty for a month. // 그는 ~을 당했다 He was suspended from office.

정진(精進) earnest [close] application; 〔전념〕 devotion. **정진하다** devote oneself (to); apply oneself (to). ¶문학 연구에 ~ devote oneself to the study of literature // 그는 학문에 정진했다 He devoted [applied] himself to his studies.

정차(停車) a stop; stoppage. ¶급~ a sudden stop / 비상 [일시] ~ an emergency [a temporary / a short] stop / ~ 금지 〔게시〕 No stopping. / 〔영〕 No standing. **정차하다** 〔서다〕 stop; halt; come to a stop; 〔구어〕 pull up; 〔세우다〕 make a stop; bring (a car) to a halt; 〔구어〕 pull up. ¶사고로 ~ be held up by an accident // 그 차는 교문 앞에 정차했다 The car pulled up in front of the school gate. // 기차는 10분간 정차했다 The train made a ten-minute stop. // 이 열차는 역마다 정차합니다 This train stops at every station. / This train is a local train. / 다음에 정차하는 역은 어디입니까 What is the next station we stop at? ➔ ¶경찰이 그 트럭을 신호 있는 데서 정차시켰다 The policeman stopped the truck at the traffic light.

● **정차 시간** stoppage time. ¶~은 몇 분입니까 How many minutes will the train be stopped?

정착(定着) 1 〔정주〕 settlement. ¶~ 생활 settled life. **정착하다** settle (down). ¶그 가족이 이 읍에 정착한 지 3년이 된다 Three years have passed since the family settled down in this town.
2 (관습 등이). **정착하다** come to stay; 〔뿌리내리다〕 take root; 〔확립되다〕 become established. ¶민주주의는 한국에 정착할 것인가 Has democracy come to stay [been established / taken root] in Korea? // 이 표현은 이미 젊은이들 사이에 정착해 있다 This expression has already become established among the younger generation. // 불교는 한국에 깊이 정착했다 Buddhism planted its roots deeply in Korean soil. ➔ ¶이 관습은 농촌에 확고히 정착되지는 않았다 This custom is not firmly established in agricultural districts.
3 〔사진〕 fixation; (photographic) fixing. **정착하다** fix.

● **정착금** resettlement funds. **정착액** 〔사진〕 a fixing solution. **정착제**(-劑) 〔사진〕 a fixing agent; a fixative; a fixer.

정찰(正札) a price tag [mark / label]. ¶상품에 ~을 붙이다 put a price tag on an article // 5,000원의 ~이 붙어 있다 It is marked [priced at] 5,000 won. // It carries a price tag of 5,000 won. // 저희는 ~ 판매를 하고 있습니다 We don't make reduction in price. / We sell only at the prices marked.

● **정찰 가격** (at) a fixed [labeled] price. **정찰제** a price-tag system; a fixed price system. ¶~를 실시하다 enforce a price-tag system.

정찰(偵察) scouting; (군사상의) reconnaissance. ¶공중 ~ aerial reconnaissance // ~ 임무를 띠고 나가다 go out on a scouting mission. **정찰하다** scout; spy upon; reconnoiter. ¶적정(敵情)을 ~ spy on the movement of the enemy // 그 비행기는 우리나라의 기지를 정찰하고 항공 사진을 찍었다 The plane reconnoitered the bases in our country and took aerial photos. // 잠깐 상황을 정찰하고 올게 I'll go and see what's happening.

● **정찰기** a reconnaissance [spy] plane. **정찰대** a reconnoitering [scouting] party; scouts. **정찰병** a reconnoiter; a scout; 〔미〕 a scouter. **정찰 비행** (make) a reconnaissance flight.

정채(精彩) brilliance; colorfulness; 〔생기〕 life; vitality.

정책(政策) (a) policy. ¶경제 ~ an economic policy / 사회 [상업 / 산업] ~ an social [a commercial / an industrial] policy / 선린 ~ a good-neighbor policy / 외교 [대외] ~ a diplomatic [foreign] policy / ~상의 문제 a matter of policy / a policy issue // 미국의 아시아 ~ American [U.S.] policy toward(s) Asia // ~을 채택하다 employ [adopt] a policy // ~을 결정하다 fix [decide on] a policy // ~을 바꾸다 change one's policy // ~을 변경하지 않다 make no departure from one's policy // ~을 실행하다 carry out a policy // ~을 지지하다 support a policy // ~을 심의하다 deliberate on a policy // 새 ~을 발표하다 announce [publish] a new policy // 당의 ~에 따르다 follow the party line / be a faithful party liner // 금융 긴축 ~을 취하다[실행하다] adopt [carry out] a tight money policy // 농업 ~을 세우다 formulate an agricultural policy.

● **정책 강령** (정당의) a (party) platform. **정책 노선** a line of policy; 〔미〕 party line. **정책 수립** / **정책 입안** policy-making.

정처(正妻) a lawful [legal] wife.

정처(定處) 〔정한 곳〕 a fixed place; 〔처소〕 one's dwelling place; one's (place of) residence; one's abode. ¶~ 없는 나그네 a wandering traveler // ~ 없이 떠돌아다니다 wander [roam] about aimlessly / wander from place to place // 그는 ~ 없이 떠돌아다녔다 He wandered aimlessly [here and there].

정체(正體) 〔본디의 모습〕 the identity (of); 〔본성〕 one's true character [colors]; one's real nature. ¶~불명인 사람 an unidentified man / a man with dubious backgrounds // ~를 알 수 없는 병 a mysterious [an unidentified] illness // ~를 드러내다 reveal one's true self / show oneself for what one really is / show one's true colors // ~를 감추다 hide one's real identity // ~를 벗기다 unmask; 〔구어〕 debunk // 그것이 그녀의 ~다 That's what she really is like. // 나는 그의 ~를 파악할 수가 없다 I can't make out his true character. // 저 덜컹덜컹하는 소리의 ~는 무엇일까 I wonder what the cause of that rattling is. // 내가 저 협잡꾼의 ~를 벗기고야 말겠다 I'll unmask that imposter.

정체(政體) a form of government; political system; government. ¶공화 [민주 / 군주] ~ a republican [democratic / monarchical] form of government // 입헌 [전제] ~ constitutional [absolute] government // 입헌 군주 ~ constitutional [limited] monarchy // 절대 군주 ~ an absolute [a despotic] monarchy.

정체(停滯) (일 등의) stagnation; (화물 등의) accumulation; (자금 등의) a tie-up; (지불의) falling into arrears. ¶화물의 ~ an accumulation of goods. **정체하다** accumulate; be tied up; fall into arrears; pile up (우편물이); congest (교통 등이). ¶이 거리는 늘 차가 정체

정초 해 있다 This street is always congested [crowded]. →¶폭풍우로 화물이 정체되어 있다 Freight has piled up owing to the storm.// 지난 주에는 업무가 정체됐다 Office[Desk] work piled up[accumulated] last week.// 퇴근 시간에는 교통이 정체된다 Traffic piles up at rush hour. / Traffic jams develop in the rush hour.// 전쟁으로 무역이 정체되었다 The war caused a paralysis of trade.

● **정체 전선** [기상] a stationary front.

정초(正初) the beginning of January. ¶~에 early in January.

정충(精蟲) [동] a spermatozoon. ⇨ 정자(精子)

정취(情趣) [기분] a mood; [분위기] an atmosphere; [아취] an artistic effect; charms; a touch. ¶이국 ~ an exotic mood[atmosphere] / exoticism // ~ 있는 뜰 an elegant[a tasteful] garden / a garden with true character // 옛 도시의 ~와 위용이 넘치는 행사 a ceremonial event full of charm and dignity in an ancient city // 그것이 그 방의 ~를 한결 돋우어 준다 It made the room all the more attractive[charming].

정치(定置) [일정한 장소에 놓임] fixing; stationing. **정치하다** fix; station.

● **정치망** a fixed net; a stationary net. **정치망 어업** fixed shore net fishing; stationary net fishery.

정치(政治) politics (단수·복수 동형); [통치] government; [시정] administration. ¶과두 ~ oligarchy // 관료 ~ bureaucratic government // 금권 ~ plutocracy // 독재[전제] ~ despotism // 무단 ~ the rule of the saber // 민주 ~ democratic government // 의회 ~ parliamentary government // 정당 ~ party politics // 깨끗한 ~ clean politics // ~의 빈곤 lack of political ingenuity / lack of good government // ~ 의식이 강한 사람들 politically conscious people // ~에 손대다[관여하다] take up[engage in] politics / meddle in politics // ~에 관여하지 않다 let [leave] politics alone / keep out of politics // ~를 하다 take the reins of government / administer[conduct] the affairs of state // ~를 논하다 talk[discuss] politics / politicize // ~를 불신하다 have a distrust of politics // 그는 ~에는 전혀 무관심하다 He is utterly indifferent to politics. / He is utterly apolitical. // 그들은 술을 마시면서 ~를 논했다 They talked[discussed] politics over wine. // ~를 하는 사람은 국민의 소리를 들어야 한다 Those who govern the people must listen to their voice. // 국회의원은 나라의 ~에 관여한다 Assemblymen take part in the affairs of state. // 그는 ~ 의식이 발달해 있다 He is politically-minded.

● **정치가** a politician; a statesman. (▶ 이 두 단어를 대조적으로 쓸 때는, 전자는 당리당략을 일삼고 사리를 도모하는 정치꾼이라는 나쁜 뜻으로, 후자는 훌륭한 정치가라는 좋은 뜻으로 쓰인다. 그러나 보통 직업으로서의 정치가를 가리킬 때는 중립적인 뜻에서 전자를 쓴다) **정치계** political circles. **정치 공작** political maneuvering. **정치권력** political authority. **정치 단체** a political body[organization]. **정치력** political power[influence]. **정치 문제** a political issue[problem]. **정치범** (범죄) political offense; (사람) a political offender [prisoner]. **정치사** a political history. **정치열** political fever. **정치 자금** a political fund; [선거 자금] campaign funds[money]. **정치 투쟁** a political struggle; political strife. **정치 풍토** the political climate. **정치학** political science; politics. **정치 헌금** a political donation; political contribution. **정치 활동** political activity.

정치적(政治的) political. ¶~ 망명 political exile // ~ 수완 political ability[ingenuity] / statecraft // ~ 보복 political retaliation // ~ 해결 settlement (of a problem) through the political channel // ~ 무관심 political apathy // ~으로 politically // 그는 ~ 수완이 있다 He is an able politician. / He is a tactical politician.

정치하다(精緻—) [미세하다] minute; [섬세하다] delicate; [미묘하다] nice; subtle; [철저하다] exhaustive. ¶정치한 솜씨 delicate workmanship // 그의 연구는 유례가 없을 정도로 ~ No other study is more exhaustive and detailed than his.

정칙(正則) a regular system[method]. ¶~의 regular / proper / formal / systematic / normal // ~으로 영어 연구[공부]를 하다 study [learn] English systematically / take a regular course in English.

정칙(定則) [정한 규칙] an established rule; a law. ¶회(會)의 ~에 반하다 be against the established rules of an association.

정크 [중국의 배] a junk.

정탐(偵探) spying; espionage; scouting(정찰). **정탐하다** spy out (a region); spy into (a secret); scout. ¶적정을 ~ spy on the enemy's movements // 회사의 내정을 ~ spy out the inside affairs of a company.

● **정탐꾼** a spy; a secret agent; a scout(정찰자).

정태(靜態) stationariness. ¶~의 static / statical / stationary.

● **정태 경제학** static economics.

정토(淨土) [불] the Pure Land; Paradise; the Buddhist Elysium. ¶서방 ~ the Western Paradise.

정통(正統) [정당한 계승] legitimacy; [일반 또는 공적으로 인정된 것] orthodoxy. ¶임금의 ~ 적자 the king's legitimate son // ~의 legitimate / orthodox // 그는 ~적인 예술관을 가지고 있다 He has an orthodox concept of art. // 그의 서예는 추사(秋史)의 ~ 유파에 속하는 것이었다 His calligraphy belonged to the orthodox Chusa school.

● **정통주의** legitimism. **정통파** ¶그는 인상주의의 ~로 자처하고 있다 He claims to be the legitimate descent of the Impressionists.

정통하다(精通—) [친숙하여 잘 알고 있다] be familiar (with); [경청하여 잘 알고 있다] be well acquainted (with); [특정한 분야에 밝다] be (well) versed (in); [경험이나 지식이 있다] be conversant (with). ¶정통한 소식통 a well-informed person[source] // 출판계의 내정을 ~ be familiar with the internal affairs of the publishing world // 노동 문제에 ~ have a thorough knowledge of labor problems // 우리 선생님은 미국 문학에 ~ Our teacher is well-versed in[has a thorough knowledge of] American literature. // 그는 회사의 내부 사정에 ~ He knows very well[knows everything about] what's going on inside the company. // 그는 중근동의 정세에 ~ He is well informed about[as to] the Middle and Near East situation.

정파(政派) a faction (within a political party).
정판(整版) [인] justification. **정판하다** justify.
● **정판공** a justifier.

정평(定評) an established reputation. ¶~이 나 있는 acknowledged / recognized // ~이 나 있는 인물 a recognized figure / a man of established reputation[fame] // 좋다는 ~을 얻다 be recognized as good // …이라는 일반의 ~이다 it is generally agreed that … // 저 대학은 화학의 연구로 ~이 나 있다 That university enjoys an established reputation for chemical research. // 민 교수는 지진학자로서 ~이 나 있다 Professor Min is an acknowledged authority on seismology. // 우리 회사 제품의 품질이 뛰어나다는 ~이 있다 We enjoy a high reputation for the quality of our goods. // 저 고등학교는 야구가 강한 것으로 ~이 나 있다 Everybody knows that high school has a strong baseball team. // 저 회사는 일류 기업으로서 ~이 나 있다 That company is generally[widely] recognized as one of the leading[first-rate] firms.

정표(情表) a token; a keepsake; a memento. ¶감사의 ~ (as) a token of one's gratitude [appreciation] // 하찮은 물건이지만 저의 감사의 ~입니다 This is a small token of my gratitude. // 숙모는 ~로서 이 반지를 주셨다 My aunt gave me this ring as a keepsake.

정하다(定-) 1 [결정하다] decide (on); determine; [문제를 해결하고 조화시켜 결정하다] settle (on); [분명히 결정하다] fix; [선택하여 결정하다] choose; fix upon[on]; [타협 등을 하여 결정하다] arrange; [특히 날짜를 정하다] appoint. ¶정한 시간에 at the stated [appointed] time // 목적지를 ~ decide where to go // 출발 날짜를 ~ fix a date for (one's) departure / set the day of (one's) departure // 목표를 ~ set up a goal // 방침을 ~ decide on[upon] one's course // 값을 ~ fix the price // 태도를 ~ define one's attitude // 직업을 ~ fix one's occupation / decide upon one's profession // 무엇을 해야 할지를 ~ determine what is to be done // 평생의 일을 천문학으로 ~ make astronomy one's career // 미리 정한 대로 그들은 6시 열차를 탔다 They got on the 6 o'clock train as previously arranged. // 그들은 정한 시간에 만났다 They met at the appointed [prearranged] time. // 그들은 혼례일을 10월 10일으로 정했다 They have fixed October 10 as the date of their wedding. / Their wedding has been set for October 10. // 클럽의 회원들은 알파벳순으로 앉기로 정했다 They decided that the club members should sit in alphabetical order. // 그것은 네가 정할 일이다 It is up to you to decide. // 그는 9월에 이집트로 가기로 정했다 He decided[made up his mind / (문어) determined] to go to Egypt. // 어느 것으로 정하실까요 Which will you choose?
2 [결심하다] decide; determine; resolve; make up one's mind (구어). ¶그는 술을 끊기로 마음을 정했다 He decided[resolved] to quit[give up] drinking. / He decided [resolved] that he quit[give up] drinking. // 그는 의사가 되기로 마음을 정했다 He determined[is determined] to become[be] a doctor. (determine은 「결심한다」는 동작, be determined는 「결심하고 있다」는 심리적 상태에 뜻의 중점이 있음) // 그는 직장을 그만두기로 마음을 정했다 He made up his mind to resign from his job.
3 [규정하다] provide(법률·조약이); stipulate(조항으로서). ¶법이 정하는 바에 따라 as provided by law // 규정을 ~ lay down rules.

정하다(淨-) [깨끗하다] clear; pure; clean. ¶정한 물 clear[pure] water. **정히** clearly; cleanly; purely. ¶옷을 ~ 입다 keep oneself neat and trim / be neat in one's dress.

정학(停學) suspension from school[college]; (영) rustication(대학의). ¶1주일간의 ~ one week's suspension from school // ~을 당한 학생 a suspended student // ~을 **당하다** be suspended (from school) // ~을 **명하다** [~에 처하다] suspend (a student) from school [(영) rusticate] // 그는 무기~ 처분을 받았다 He was suspended from school for an indefinite period.

정한(定限) [기한] a definite period of time; a limited time; [한도] a fixed limit; a fixed degree.

정해(正解) [올바른 대답] a correct[right] answer; [바른 풀이] a correct solution. ¶~는 51페이지를 보시오 Turn to page 51 for the (correct) answer. **정해하다** [바르게 대답하다] answer right; give a right answer; [바르게 풀다] solve correctly; give a correct solution.

정해지다(定-) 1 [결정되다] be decided; be settled[fixed]; be determined; [합의되다] be arranged. ¶다음 회의는 4월 10일로 정해졌다 April 10 was fixed as the date of next meeting. / We decided on April 10 as the date of the next meeting. // 최우수 영화는 터키의 작품으로 정해졌다 The prize for the best film was awarded to a Turkish movie. / It was decided that the award for the best movie should go to a Turkish film. // 내 운명은 이미 정해져 있다 My destiny is already decided[determined]. // 공급은 수요에 따라 정해진다 Demand determines supply. // 각자는 정해진 것을 지켜야만 한다 Everyone should stick to what we've decided[what has been decided].
2 [규정되다] be provided; be stipulated; be laid down. ¶법률로 ~ be established[stipulated] by law // 20부터 선거권이 있다는 것은 법률로 정해져 있다 The law provides [specifies] that everyone acquires the vote at twenty.

정향(丁香) [한] dried clove buds; clove.
● **정향나무** (교목) a clove (tree); (관목) a kind of lilac bush.

정형(定刑) [법] capital punishment.
정형(定形) [일정한 형태] a fixed form; a regular shape.
● **정형 동사** a finite verb.
정형(定型) [일정한 형식] a set pattern; a (fixed / regular) type; a fixed form; standard(표준).
● **정형시** poetry[verse] with a fixed form.
정형(整形) [몸의 외형을 바르게 고침] restoration of bone structures that are defective or damaged by injury or disease.
● **정형 수술** (undergo) orthopedic treatment; an orthopedic operation. **정형외과** orthopedics; orthopedic surgery; (병원의 과) the orthopedics department.

정혼(定婚) betrothal. **정혼하다** betroth[affiance] oneself (to a person); become be-

정화(正貨) [본위 화폐] specie. ¶~의 유출[유입] an outflow[inflow] of specie.
● **정화 보유고** specie holdings. **정화 준비** specie[gold] reserve.

정화(淨化) 1 [깨끗이 하기] purification; purgation; elutriation. **정화하다** purify; cleanse; deterge; elutriate. 2 [불순분자의 숙청] a purge; [정치 부패 등의 일소] a cleanup. **정화하다** purge; clean up. ¶현재의 정계를 정화하려면 발본적인 개혁이 필요하다 Drastic reforms are needed to clean up the present political world.
● **정화기** / **정화 장치** a purifier. **정화 운동** a cleanup movement[campaign / drive]; a purge. **정화조** a water-purifier tank (for drinking water); (하수의) a septic tank (for sewage).

정화(精華) the essence; the quintessence; the flower; the glory. ¶기사도의 ~ the flower of chivalry.

정화수(井華水) water drawn from the well at daybreak.

정확(正確) [바르고 확실함] correctness; exactness; accuracy; precision. **정확하다** correct; exact; accurate; precise. ¶정확한 시간 correct[exact] time // 정확한 치수 precise[exact] measurements // 정확한 조준 폭격 pinpoint bombing // 말의 정확한 뜻 the exact meaning of a word // 정확한 답을 하다 give a correct[a precise / an exact] answer // 그는 정확한 영어를 말한다 He speaks correct English. // 그의 기억은 ~ He has an exact[accurate] memory. // 내 시계는 ~ [지금 시간이 맞다] My watch is right. / [언제나 시간이 맞다] My watch keeps good[accurate] time. **정확히** correctly; exactly; accurately; precisely; punctually(시간적으로). ¶~ 말하면 exactly[precisely] speaking / to be exact // ~ 발음하다 pronounce correctly // 시간을 ~ 지키다 be punctual (to the moment) // 그가 어떤 모습이 있는지 ~ 말해 주시오 Tell me exactly how he looked. // ~ 말하자면 5밀리미터 부족하다 To be precise, it is five millimeters short. // 그녀는 약속한 대로 ~ 7시에 왔다 She came punctually[precisely] at seven, just as she had promised. / (구어) She came at seven on the dot as she had promised.
● **정확성** ¶보도의 ~ the accuracy of information // 뉴스 보도는 ~이 생명이다 Accuracy is very important in news reporting. // 그는 시계 장치와 같은 ~으로 폭탄에서 신관을 제거했다 He removed the fuse from the bomb with clockwork precision.

정황(情況) [사물의 정세와 형편] the state of things[affairs]; conditions; a situation; circumstances. ¶현재의 ~으로는 as matters stand / in the present situation / under these circumstances.
● **정황 증거** [법] circumstantial evidence.

정회(停會) suspension of a meeting; [휴회] adjournment; (의회의) prorogation. **정회하다** suspend a meeting; adjourn; prorogue.

정회원(正會員) a full[regular] member. ¶~의 자격 full membership.

정훈(政訓) troop information and education (약칭 TI&E).

정히(正-) surely; certainly. ¶일금 십만 원 ~ 영수함 K 씨 귀하 Received from[of] Mr. K the sum of 100,000 won.

젖 1 [유즙] milk; [모유] mother's milk; [우유] cow's milk. ¶소의 ~을 짜는 사람 a milkman (여자) a milkmaid / a dairymaid // 과 꿀이 흐르는 땅 land of milk and honey // ~이 많이[안] 나오는 유방 a milky[dry] breast // (아이에게) ~을 먹이다[빨리다] suckle (a child) / give the breast to (a child) / give (a baby) suck / nurse // ~이 잘 나오다[나오지 않다] (사람이) have plenty of[little] milk // 아이를 ~으로 기르다 (모유의 경우) nourish a baby on mother's milk / (인공유의 경우) bring up a baby on the bottle // ~을 떼다 wean a child // ~이 많다 have plenty of milk // ~을 먹고 싶어 하다 want to be fed / want the breast // ~ 먹던 힘까지 다하여 to the utmost of one's power // 소의 ~을 짜다 milk a cow // 이 소는 ~이 많다 This cow milks well. // 아기가 엄마의 ~을 먹고 있다 The baby is sucking milk from its mother.
2 a breast. ⇨ ⁼유방(乳房) ¶아이에게 ~을 물리다 give the breast to a child // 아이가 엄마의 ~을 빨고 있다 The baby is sucking at its mother's breast. // ~이 붓었다 The breast is swollen. / The breasts fill.
3 [식물의 진] milk (of a plant); latex.

젖(을) 떼다 [이유시키다] wean. ¶아이를 ~ wean a baby from the breast.

젖가슴 the breast; the bosom.

젖꼭지 (포유동물, 특히 여성의) a nipple; a teat; [생] a mam(m)illa (pl. -lae); (젖병의) (미) a nipple; (영) a teat. ¶~ 모양의 nipplelike / mastoid.

젖내 [젖냄새] the smell of milk.

젖내(가) 나다 [유치하다] be babyish[puerile]; [미숙하다] be green. ¶젖내 나는 [유치한] babyish / [미숙한] green / raw / inexperienced // 그는 아직도 젖내가 난다 He is still green[immature]. / He is still wet behind the ears.

젖니 a milk[baby / deciduous] tooth.

젖다 1 (물 등에) get wet[drenched]; be wet; be damp[moistened]. ¶젖은 옷 [땅] wet clothes[ground] // 비에 ~ get wet in the rain // 흠뻑 ~ be drenched[soaked] to the skin / get dripping[wringing] wet (from the rain) // 땀으로 흠뻑 젖어 있다 be dripping wet with perspiration // 젖은 걸레로 닦다 wipe with a wet[damp] cloth // 잎들이 이슬로 젖어 있었다 The leaves were wet with dew. // 셔츠가 온통 땀에 젖었다 My shirt was thoroughly soaked with sweat. // 온몸이 비에 흠뻑 젖었다 I was wet through and through [I was soaked to the skin] with (the) rain. // 옷이 흠뻑 젖었다 My clothes are dripping wet. // 신문이 비에 흠뻑 젖어 있었다 The newspaper had gotten soaked in the rain. // 소녀의 눈은 눈물에 젖어 있었다 The girl's eyes were wet[moist] with tears.
2 [빠지다] be addicted[given / taken] to; indulge in; be immersed; give oneself up to. ¶행복에 ~ swim in bliss // 즐거운 분위기에 ~ steep oneself in the merry atmosphere // 술에 젖어 살다 be[become] the slave of drink / give oneself over to drinking / lose oneself in liquor / (구어) be a wino.
3 [귀에 익다] get used to hearing; be accustomed to hear; become familiar with. ¶귀에 젖은 목소리 a familiar voice.

젖당(-糖) [화] lactose; milk sugar.

젖떼기 a child [an animal] of the weaning age.

젖뜨리다 throw [bend] back (ward); lean backward. ¶몸을 ~ throw [stick] out one's chest / hold one's head high// 고개를 젖뜨리고 의자에 앉다 sit in a chair with one's head thrown back.

젖먹이 a nursing baby; a suckling; an unweaned child.

젖몸살 mastitis. ¶~을 앓다 have inflamed mammary glands / suffer from mastitis.

젖병(-甁) a baby [nursing / feeding] bottle; a nurser.

젖비린내 the smell of milk. ⇨ ̄젖내

젖빛 milk white. ¶~의 milk-white.
● **젖빛 유리** frosted [ground] glass.

젖산(-酸) 〔화〕 lactic acid. ⇨락트산

젖샘 〔생〕 the mammary gland.

젖소 a milch [milk] cow; 〔집합적〕 dairy cattle. ¶~의 무리 a herd of dairy cattle.

젖어머니 a wet nurse. ⇨ ̄유모

젖통 〈속〉 tits; boobs. ¶~이 큰 여자 a girl with big boobs / 〈속어〉 a blowsy [bosomy] girl / 〈속어〉 a bust-bomb.

젖퉁이 〈속〉 tits. ⇨젖통

젖히다 1 〔뒤로〕 bend back (ward); lean backward; pull back. ¶몸을 뒤로 ~ bend oneself back / lean oneself backward / throw one's head back// 가슴을 뒤로 ~ throw [stick] out one's chest// 어깨를 ~ put back one's shoulders// 그는 거만하게 몸을 뒤로 젖히고 앉아 있었다 He sat [leaned] back arrogantly [pompously / self-importantly] in his chair. // 그는 가슴을 젖히고 자기의 상대자를 노려보았다 He straightened himself up and glared at his opponent.

2 〔뒤집다〕 turn out [over]; 〔옷 등을〕 turn inside out; turn outside in; 〔카드 등을〕 turn up (a card). ¶저고리를 ~ turn a coat inside out.

3 〔열다〕 fling open; open wide. ¶창문을 활짝 ~ fling a window open.

제[1] 1 〔1인칭 겸양어〕 I. ⇨내¶~가 하겠습니다 I'll do.// ~가 이 집 주인입니다 I am the owner of this house. 2 〔자기〕 self; oneself. ¶ ~가 좋아서 하는 일 a self-imposed work.

제[2] 1 my. ⇨내¶~ 생각으로는 for my part / as for me. 2 〔자기의〕 one's own; personal; private. ¶~멋대로 of one's own accord [own free will] / on one's own advice // ~ 이익만 생각하다 look to one's own interests / take care of number one // ~ 생각만 하다 think of oneself only / be self-centered // ~ 일은 제가 하다 mind [look after] one's own business.

제 눈에 안경이다 Love blinds us to all imperfections; Love is blind.

제(諸) 〔많은〕 many; 〔몇 개의〕 several; 〔여러 가지의〕 various; 〔모든〕 all. ¶~ 국가 various [many] countries // ~ 경비 sundry [miscellaneous] expenses // ~ 문제 various problems.

제-(第) ¶~1과 the first lesson // ~2 number two (약어 No. 2) / the second (약어 2nd) // ~5조 ~항 the second clause of Article Five [V] // 브람스의 교향곡 ~1번 Brahms's Symphony No. 1.

-제(制) 〔제도〕 a system. ¶〔국회의〕 양원~ the bicameral system // 의원 내각~ the parliamentary cabinet system // 4년~ 대학 a four-year college [university] // (노동의) 주 40시간~ a forty-hour (work) week.

-제(祭) 〔의식〕 a ceremony; a service; 〔축제〕 a festival; a fete (day). ¶기념~ a commemoration.

-제(製) 〔물건을 제조한 곳·재료〕 make; manufacture. ¶외국~의 foreign-make / (articles) of foreign manufacture // 영국~의 자동차 a car of English make / a British-made car / a car made in England // 한국~의 완구 Korean-made toys / toys made in Korea // 강철~의 made of steel.

-제(劑) 〔조제한 약품〕 a medicine; a drug. ¶소화~ a digestive / 진통~ an anodyne.

제가(齊家) wise government of one's family. **제가하다** govern one's family wisely; manage [regulate] one's household.

제가(諸家) 〔여러 학자〕 many masters; all the schools (of art); 〔친척들〕 the whole family.

제각각(-各各) each; severally. ⇨제각기

제각기(-各其) 1 〔각자〕 each. ¶소년들은 ~개를 기르고 있다 Each boy [Each of the boys] keeps a dog. / The boys each keep a dog. // 그 아이들은 ~ 자리에 앉았다 Each of the children took his (own) seat. // 학생들은 ~ 불만을 토로했다 Each of the pupils voiced his own complaints. 2 〔따로따로〕 severally; separately; respectively; individually. ¶~ 집으로 돌아가다 return to (their) respective homes / go home individually // ~ 살다 live separately (from) // 톰과 창식이와 필립은 ~ 영어, 한국어, 프랑스 어를 말했다 Tom, Changsik, and Philip spoke English, Korean, and French respectively.

제강(製鋼) steel manufacture; steelmaking. **제강하다** make steel.
● **제강소** a steelworks; a steel mill. **제강업** the steel industry.

제거(除去) removal; elimination; exclusion. ¶수술에 의한 난소의 ~ an operative removal of the ovary. **제거하다** get rid of (something); clear (something of); take away; remove; eliminate; exclude. ¶장애물을 모두 ~ remove [eliminate / get rid of] all obstacles // 원인을 ~ remove a cause // 무능한 자를 ~ weed out [get rid of] the incompetent // 사회의 병폐를 ~ eradicate the social diseases // 광석에서 불순물을 ~ remove impurities from the ore // 수준 이하의 물건을 ~ eliminate articles (that are) below standard // 이 장치로 유해 물질을 제거할 수 있다 We can eliminate harmful materials with this device.

제격(-格) becoming to one's status. ¶~이다 〔~에 어울리다〕 be suitable (for / to) / be suited (to) / become / be fit / be proper (for) // 그 일은 그에게 ~이다 It's a suitable position for him. // 그 핑크색 새 옷은 그녀에게 ~이다 The new pink dress becomes [is becoming to] her. // 이 코트는 너에게 아주 ~이다 This coat suits [becomes] you very nicely [well].

제고장 one's native place; the (original) home.

제고하다(提高-) raise; heighten; elevate; lift; 〔증진하다〕 increase; enhance. ¶생산성을 ~ raise [increase] the productivity // 중동의 긴장이 세계 전쟁의 불안을 제고하고 있다 Tension in the Middle East are increasing the fear of another world war.

제곱 [수] a square. ¶2의 5~ the 5th power of $2/2^5$ (▶ two to the fifth power라고 읽음) // 50~ 피트 50 square feet // 5의 ~은 25이다 The square of 5 is 25. / Five squared is twenty-five. **제곱하다** square (a number); multiply (a number) by itself. ¶10을 ~ raise ten to the second power.
● **제곱근** [수] a square root. ~을 구하다[~을 풀다] extract[find] the square root (of) // 16의 ~은 4이다 The square root of sixteen is four. **제곱근풀이** [수] evolution; the extraction of a square root. **제곱비** (a) subduplicate ratio.

제공(提供) an offer; supply. ¶실비 ~ offered at cost // 이 프로는 맥주 회사의 ~입니다 This program is sponsored by a beer company. **제공하다** [내놓다] offer; make an offer; [주다] give; [필요한 것을 공급하다] provide; [모자라는 것을] supply; [광고주가 되다] sponsor. ¶그에게 200만 원을 ~ offer him two million won // 그 물건을 만 원에 [2할 할인하여] ~ offer the article at ten thousand won[at 20% reduction] // (라디오 등의) 프로를 ~ sponsor a program // 그는 자기 집을 회의장으로 제공했다 He offered his house as a meeting place. // 그는 우리에게 모든 정보를 제공해 주었다 He gave us[provided us with] all kinds of information. // 그는 귀중한 자료를 제공해 주었다 He supplied valuable data to us. / He supplied us with valuable data.
● **제공자** an offerer; a donor.

제공권(制空權) the command[control / mastery] of the air; air domination[supremacy]. ¶~을 잡다[잃다] win[lose] the air / secure [lose] the command[mastery] of the air // 그들은 ~을 장악하고 있었다 They had command of the air.

제과(製菓) confectionery. **제과하다** make confections.
● **제과업** the confectionery industry. **제과점** a confectioner's shop; a confectionery.

제구(祭具) [제사 도구] implements and other paraphernalia used in religious rites; ritual implements.

제구력(制球力) [야구] control (of the ball). ¶~이 있다 have good control of the ball / have fine ball control // ~이 없다 lack control of the ball // 그 투수는 ~이 있다 The pitcher has good control.

제구실 1 [해야 할 책임] one's function; one's duty; one's part. ¶~을 하다 discharge [fulfill] one's duties / do one's part / be worth one's salt // ~을 못 하다 fail in one's duty / fail to do one's duty / be not worth one's salt // 교육자로서 ~을 하다 fulfill its function as educator // 그는 ~을 다했다 He has fully performed his duties[task]. // 그는 경찰로서 ~을 못 했다 He failed his duties as a policeman. 2 [천연두·홍역 등] the usual epidemic diseases that every child has to go through.

제국(帝國) an empire. ¶로마[대영] ~ the Roman[British] Empire // ~의 imperial.
● **제국주의** imperialism. ¶반~ anti-imperialism // ~적(인) imperialist(ic). **제국주의자** an imperialist.

제국(諸國) various[many / all] countries. ¶해외 ~ foreign countries // 그 회의에는 동남아 ~에서 온 대표들이 참석했다 Representatives from Southeast Asian countries attended the meeting.

제군(諸君) gentlemen; my friends; you. ¶학생 ~의 말을 나는 이해할 수가 없다 I don't understand what you students are talking about.

제금(提琴) a violin. ⇨ 바이올린

제기¹ (놀이 기구) a jegi; a shuttlecock kicking on the inside of a foot; (놀이) a kicking shuttlecock game. ¶~를 차다 kick shuttlecock with a foot.

제기² God damn (it). ⇨ 제기랄

제기(祭器) [제사 때 쓰는 그릇] vessels, for memorial service of the deceased.

제기랄 God damn (it).; Gosh!; Hell!; Hang it!; Confound it!; God darn it! ¶~ 또 비가 온다 Gee, it's raining again! // ~ 비싸기도 하다 It's damn expensive! // ~ 앞바퀴가 펑크 났다 Oh, gosh, the front wheel has flat.

제기하다(提起—) (문제 등을) bring up [forward]; raise; (소송 등을) institute; lodge; submit. ¶(문제를) 회의에 ~ bring (a matter) before a meeting // 소송을 ~ institute [lodge / file] a lawsuit // 이의(異議)를 ~ raise an objection (to) // 제안에 이의를 ~ object[raise objections / be opposed] to a proposal // 그는 문제를 제기했다 He presented[brought forward] a problem. / He raised [posed] a question. // 그들은 위헌 소송을 제기했다 They instituted an unconstitutionality suit.

제꺽 with a click; quickly. ⇨ 재깍¹·²

제단(祭壇) an altar.

제당(製糖) sugar manufacture. **제당하다** make sugar.
● **제당 공장** a sugar manufactory.

제대(除隊) [군] discharge from military service; (해산에 의한) demobilization; (영국구어) demob. ¶만기[명예] ~ an honorable discharge // 불명예 ~ a dishonorable discharge. **제대하다** be discharged from military service; get one's discharge; leave the army[colors]; (해산에 의해) be demobilized. ¶만기로 ~ be honorably discharged.
● **제대병 / 제대 군인** a discharged soldier; an ex-serviceman.

제대(梯隊) [군] an echelon.

제대로 1 [격식대로] formally; regularly; squarely; in a formal way; in style; in due [proper] form. ¶영어를 ~ 배우다 study English systematically[by an orthodox method] // 기왕 할 바에는 ~ 하자 Let us do the thing in style if we do it at all. // 나의 바이올린은 ~ 배운 것이 아니다 I have not taken regular violin lessons.
2 [마음먹은 대로] as one thinks[desires]; to one's fancy[satisfaction]. ¶만사가 ~ 되었다 Everything went just as I'd hoped[wanted]. // 계획이 ~ 진행되었다 The plan worked as desired.
3 [충분히] well; enough; sufficiently; fully; properly; decently. ¶~ 보지도 않고 그것을 사 버렸다 I bought it without looking at it well. // 그는 편지를 ~ 못 쓴다 He can't write a letter properly. // 그는 소심해서 사람들 앞에서는 ~ 말도 못한다 He is so timid that he scarcely opens his mouth in public. // 어젯밤에는 잠을 ~ 못 잤다 I did not sleep well last night.

제도(制度) (체계적인) a system; (관습적인) an

institution; [기구] an organization. ¶교육 ~ an educational[a school] system // 사회 ~ a social system [institution] // 의회 ~ the parliamentary system [institution] // 군대의 ~ the organization of the armed forces // 현행 ~ 하에서는 under the existing system // ~를 확립하다 establish[build up] a system // ~를 폐지하다 abolish a system // ~를 시행하다 enforce a system / put a system [an institution] in operation[practice] // 현재의 ~ 하에서 이것은 용납되지 않는다 This is not allowed under the present[current] system.
● 제도화 systematization; institutionalization. ¶~하다 systematize / institutionalize.

제도 (製圖) drafting; drawing; (지도의) cartography. 제도하다 draft; draw.
● 제도가 a draftsman; (지도의) a cartographer. 제도실 a drafting[drawing] room.

제도 (諸島) an archipelago; a group of islands. ¶하와이 ~ the Hawaiian Islands // 에게 해 ~ the Aegean Islands.

제도 (濟度) [극락세계로 인도함] salvation; redemption. 제도하다 save; redeem. ¶제도하기가 어려운 사람들 lost souls / people who are beyond redemption // 중생을 ~ work the salvation of all creatures.

제독 (提督) [해군의 장관] an admiral(▶ a fleet admiral(해군 원수), an [a full] admiral(해군 대장), a vice admiral(해군 중장), a rear admiral(해군 소장)의 네 계급을 포함함); [함대의 사령관] a fleet commander. ¶넬슨 ~ Admiral Nelson.

제독하다 (除毒-) neutralize[counteract] poison.

제동 (制動) [공] braking; [전] damping; [스키] stemming. ¶~을 걸다 apply[put on] the brake. 제동하다 brake; damp.
● 제동기 [공] a brake. 제동 장치 a brake system; a damping device; [항] an arresting gear. 제동 회전 [스키] a stem turn.

제등 (提燈) a (paper) lantern.
● 제등 행렬 (hold) a lantern parade[procession / march].

제때 a fixed[scheduled / proper / right] time; the right occasion[moment]. ¶~에 just at the right moment / just in time (for) / in the nick of time(아슬아슬한 때에) // ~에 식사하다 have regular meals / be regular in one's diet // ~에 끝내다 get (a thing) done by the time appointed // ~에 거기 도착할 수 있을까 I doubt if I can get there in time.

제라늄 [식] a geranium (pl. ~s).

제련 (製鍊) refining; smelting. ¶~용 용광로 a smelting[reducing] furnace. 제련하다 refine (metals); smelt (copper).
● 제련소 a refinery; a smelting works; a smeltery.

제례 (祭禮) memorial services; sacrificial rites; religious ceremonies.

제로 zero; nothing; [영] nought. ¶이 나라의 경제 성장률은 작년에 ~였다 The rate of economic growth in this country last year was zero. // 나의 화학 지식은 ~에 가깝다 I know practically nothing about chemistry.
● 제로 게임 [테니스] a love game[set].

제록스 (상표명) Xerox. ¶~로 복사하다 xerox (a copy) / make a Xerox copy.

제막식 (除幕式) a ceremony of unveiling; an unveiling (ceremony); 《미》 an unveiling exercise. ¶그 동상의 ~은 어제 거행되었다 The bronze statue was unveiled yesterday.

제멋 one's own way [style / fancy]. ¶그는 ~에 겨워서 산다 He lives just as the fancy takes him.

제멋대로 [제 마음대로] of one's own accord [free will]; [제 하고 싶은 대로] at one's will; as one pleases[likes]; at one's own pleasure; [독단으로] on one's own authority. ¶~ 하다 [좋아하는 일만 하다] do just what one wants / do anything one likes / [하고 싶은 대로 하다] have one's own way // ~ 하게 내버려 두게 Let him do as he pleases. / Let him go his own way. // 그는 왕으로서 권력을 ~ 휘둘렀다 He exercised his powers as king to the full. // 저 녀석이 ~ 하게 내버려 두지 않을 거야 I won't let him get[have] his own way in everything. / I won't allow him to do things just as he pleases. // 그가 ~ 결정한 일이다 He decided it without consulting anyone.

제면 (製麵) noodle making. 제면하다 make noodles.
● 제면기 a noodle-making machine.

제명 (除名) expulsion. ¶당은 한 씨의 ~을 결의했다 The party decided to expel Mr. Han. 제명하다 strike[take] a person's name off the list[roll]; remove (a person's) name (from the membership list); withdraw (a person's) name; expel a person (from). ➔¶그는 회원 명단에서 제명되었다 His name was removed from[dropped from / struck off] the list of members.

제명 (題名) a title. ¶「유혹」이라는 ~의 영화 a picture entitled "Temptation" // 「…」이라는 ~으로 출판되다 be published under the title "…" // 책에 ~을 붙이다 entitle a book.

제모 (制帽) a regulation [uniform] cap; (학교의) a school cap. ¶제복 ~ 차림의 장교 an officer in uniform.

제목 (題目) a title; [주제] a subject; a theme. ¶「민주주의」라는 ~의 논문 an article entitled "Democracy" // 리포트 [토론] 의 ~을 주다 assign a theme [subject] for a report [discussion] // 그는 자신의 소설에 「초록의 대지」라는 ~을 달았다 He entitled his novel "The Green Earth". / He gave the title "The Green Earth" to his novel.

제문 (祭文) a message [letter] of condolence; (연설) a memorial address. ¶~을 읽다 read one's message of condolence / make a memorial address.

제물 (祭物) 1 [제사에 쓰는 음식] an offering; a sacrifice; a sacrificial offering. ¶동물을 ~로 바치다 offer an animal in sacrifice // 신에게 ~을 바치다 offer a sacrifice to the gods / make a sacrifice on the altar / immolate a sacrificial victim to God. 2 [희생물] a victim; a scapegoat. ¶그는 이번 부정 사건의 ~이 되어 면직되었다 He was made a scapegoat in [for] the recent scandal and was discharged from his post.

제물낚시 a fly; an artificial fly; a fishing fly; a flyhook; a governor; (미끼 달린) a feather and lure.

제물로 of [by] itself. ⇨ ²저절로

제물에 of its [one's] own accord; of itself; by itself. ¶상처가 ~ 나았다 The wound healed of itself.

제반 (諸般) different kinds [sorts]; various kinds; all sorts. ¶~의 various / all / every //

제발

~ 사정을 고려하여 all things considered / taking all the circumstances into consideration.//우리는 ~ 준비를 갖추었다 We have made all the necessary preparations.
● **제반사** various matters[affairs]; all things.
제발 for God's[Heaven's] sake; for goodness' [mercy's / pity's] sake; please. ¶~ 그 일을 잊어 주십시오 Won't you please forget all about it?//~ 나를 가만히 놔 줘 Please leave [let] me alone.//~ 저리 가 주게 Won't you please go? / I beg of you that you go[to go].// ~ 열흘만 더 참아 주십시오 For pity's sake, please wait ten days more.//~ 그만두 어라 Stop it, for heaven's sake!//~ 목숨만 살려 주십시오 For God's[Christ's] sake spare my life.
제발 덕분에 for mercy's[God's] sake; please; I pray[entreat]. ¶~ 이 복권이 맞아 주었으면 Let[Please let] this be a winning ticket.
제방(堤防) a (river) bank; an embankment; a dike; a levee(특히 홍수 방지용). ¶~을 쌓다 build an embankment[a dike]//홍수로 ~이 무너졌다 The flood (waters) broke down the riverbank[levee].//~을 더 높이 쌓아야겠다 We must build a higher bank.
제방 공사 bank revetment; banking.
제법 fairly; pretty; rather; passably; quite; considerably. ¶오늘은 ~ 춥다 It's rather [pretty] cold today.//저 아이도 ~ 쓸모가 있다 That child is up to the job.//그는 영어를 ~ 자유롭게 말한다 He speaks English fairly well.//그녀는 노래 솜씨가 ~이다 She is a fine[good] singer.
제보(提報) giving information. **제보하다** give [furnish] information.
● **제보자** an informant.
제복(制服) a uniform; (하인·고용인의) (a) livery. ¶학교 ~ a school uniform//~을 입은 장교 a uniformed officer//~을 입고 등교하다 wear a uniform to school / go to school in uniform//경찰관이나 소방관은 ~을 입고 있다 Policemen and firemen wear uniforms.//그 빌딩 앞에는 ~을 입은 경비원이 있었다 There was a watchman in uniform[an uniformed watchman] in front of the building.
제복(祭服) (liturgical) vestments; sacrificial robes.
제복(除服) [상복을 벗음]. **제복하다** leave off mourning; go out of mourning.
제본(製本) (book) binding. ¶가~ temporary binding//이 책은 ~이 잘되어 있다 This book is well[tightly] bound.//그 잡지는 지금 ~ 중이다 The magazine is now at the binder's. / The magazine has been sent out for binding. **제본하다** bind (a book). → ¶잘 [서투르게] 제본된 책 a well[poorly] bound book//이 책은 가죽으로 제본되어 있다 This book is bound in leather.
제분(製粉) flour milling. **제분하다** mill; grind (corn) into flour.
● **제분기** a flour mill. **제분소** a flour mill.
제비[1] [추첨] a lottery; [추첨식 판매] a raffle; (한 장의) a lot; a lottery ticket; a raffle ticket. ¶당첨된 ~ a prize lot / a lucky [winning] number//~를 뽑다 draw[cast] lots//그는 ~를 뽑았으나 I drew a blank.//나는 ~를 뽑아 자전거[1등 상]를 탔다 I won a bicycle[drew the prizewinning ticket] in a lottery.//~를 뽑아 갈 사람을 정하자 Let us draw lots and decide who shall go.//(경기의) 대진은 ~로 결정되었다 The teams were paired[The pairings were determined] by lot.
● **제비뽑기** drawing lots. ¶~로 정하다 settle [decide] (a thing) by lots.
제비[2] [동] a swallow; (미) a barn swallow; (영) an eastern house swallow.
● **제비족** a young lover (of an older woman); a gigolo.
제비꽃 [식] a violet.
제비추리 beef from the inside ribs.
제빙(製氷) ice manufacture. **제빙하다** make ice.
● **제빙 공장** / **제빙소** an ice plant[manufactory]. **제빙기** an ice machine; an ice-maker.
제사(祭祀) (a) sacrifice; sacrificial rites; (죽은 사람의) a memorial service. ¶조상의 영혼에 ~ 지내다 hold a ceremony (to pray) for the repose of one's ancestors//우리는 아버지의 6주기 ~를 지냈다 We held a memorial service on the sixth anniversary of our father's death.
● **제삿날** a memorial service[sacrifice] day; (a person's) deathday; the anniversary of (a person's) death.
제사(製絲) [방적] spinning; [명주실을 만듦] silk-thread manufacture; silk reeling.
● **제사 공장** a spinning[silk] mill. **제사업** the spinning[silk] industry.
제사장(祭司長) the chief officiating priest.
제산제(制酸劑) [의] an antacid[antiacid] (agent).
제살붙이 one's relatives[kinsfolk]; one's own people.
제삼(第三) the third; number three; the tertiary. ¶~의 third / tertiary.
● **제삼 계급** the third class[estate]; (프랑스 혁명 당시의) the bourgeoisie. **제삼국**(-國) a third power. **제삼 세계** the Third World. **제삼 인칭**[언] the third person. ⇨삼인칭 **제삼자** [당사자 이외의 사람] a third party; [국외자] an outsider. ¶~의 위치에 서다 stand outside//그들은 ~에게 조정을 부탁했다 They asked for mediation of a third party.
제상(祭床) a table used in a memorial service; a sacrificial table.
제설(除雪) snow removing[removal]; snow clearings. **제설하다** remove[clear away] the snow (from the street); clear (a street) of snow.
● **제설기** / **제설차** a snowplow. **제설 작업** snow-removal work.
제설(諸說) [여러 가지 의견] various views [opinions]; [여러 사람의 학설] various theories. ¶그 문제에 대해서는 ~이 분분하다 Opinion is divided[Various views are being expressed] on the subject.
제세(濟世) salvation of the world; promotion of social[national] welfare. **제세하다** save the world.
제소(提訴) instituting (a lawsuit). **제소하다** bring a case before the court; present a case to the court; institute a lawsuit; take action [file an action] (against a person). ¶손해 배상 청구 소송을 ~ file a suit in a court for compensatory damages (against [to] a person). →¶마침내 그 분쟁은 법원에 제소되었다 Finally the dispute was brought into court.

●제소자 a suitor; a complainant.

제수(弟嫂) a younger brother's wife; a sister-in-law.

제수(除數) [수] divisor. ¶피~ a dividend.

제수(祭需) ritual food; sacrifices.

제스처 1 [몸짓] a gesture. ¶과장된 ~로 이야기하다 speak with exaggerated gestures. **2** [시늉] a gesture. ¶다만 ~로 말했을 뿐이다 I only said so as a gesture. // 그의 사과는 단지 ~에 불과하다 His apology is a mere gesture.

제습(除濕) dehumidification. **제습하다** dehumidify.
●**제습기** a dehumidifier. **제습제** a dehumidifying agent.

제시(提示) presentation. **제시하다** present; show. ¶나는 입구에서 신분 증명서를 제시하라는 말을 들었다 I was asked to show[present] my identification card at the gate. // 여권을 제시해 주십시오 Show[Produce] your passport.

제시간(-時間) [지정된 시간] the appointed time; [일정한 시간] the fixed[regular] time; [예정된 시간] the scheduled time. ¶~에 at the appointed[fixed] time / on time / on schedule time // ~보다 10분 늦어지다 be ten minutes behind time[schedule] // 열차는 ~에 도착했다 The train arrived on time [schedule]. // ~에 일을 시작해야 한다 A man should always be on time for his work. // 그는 ~까지 오지 않았다 He did not come by the appointed time.

제씨(弟氏) (a person's) younger brother. ⇨ 계씨(季氏).

제씨(諸氏) [여러분] gentlemen; you; Messrs. ¶독자 ~ my readers.

제안(提案) a proposal; a proposition; a suggestion; (회의 등에서의) a motion. ¶반대 ~ a counterproposal / a counteroffer // ~에 응하다 agree to a proposal // 그에게 그 ~을 꺼내 보았다 I approached him with the proposal. / I broached him on the subject. // 양국 간의 무역 증가 ~이 가결[부결]되었다 The proposals for increasing trade between the two countries were adopted[rejected]. // 존슨 씨로부터 동의의 ~이 있었다 The motion was proposed[made] by Mr. Johnson. **제안하다** propose (doing / that); suggest; (동의를) move. ¶빨리 출발할 것을 제안합니다 I suggest an early start. / I propose[suggest] starting early[that we (should) start early]. // 의장 선출 방법에 대해서 제안하게 해 주십시오 Let me make a proposal concerning the method of electing the chairman.
●**제안자** a proposer; (동의(動議)의) a mover.

제압(制壓) control; ascendancy; supremacy; mastery. **제압하다** gain control (of); bring (a thing) under one's control. ¶바다를 ~ gain control of the seas // 폭도를 ~ bring rioters under control // 암을 ~ find a cure for cancer // 반란을 ~ suppress a revolt // 우리는 적의 기선을 제압하려고 그 항구를 공격했다 We attacked the harbor to forestall the enemy force.

제야(除夜) New Year's Eve. ¶~의 종 the watch-night bell // ~의 종소리 the tolling of the bells on New Year's Eve // ~의 종을 치다 ring out the old year.

제약(制約) **1** [한정된 범위 내에 제한하기] a restriction; [행위 등의 구속] a restraint; a constraint; [한정] a limitation. ¶우리는 많은 ~을 받고 있다 We are under many restrictions. // 이것은 사회적 ~을 받지 않는다 This is free from social restraints. // 시간의 ~을 받아 만족하게 만들지 못했다 Because of the time limit[Limited in time], we could not do it satisfactorily. // 예산상의 ~이 있어서 그것을 살 수가 없다 We cannot afford to buy it because of budgetary limitations. // 그것은 아무런 ~이 없는 자유로운 투표였다 It was a free vote without constraint. **제약하다** restrict; restrain; constrain; limit. ¶자유를 ~ restrict a person's freedom.
2 [제한하는 조건] a condition. ¶~이 너무 많으면 응모자가 오지 않을 것이다 If you set up too many conditions, no one will apply.

제약(製藥) [약의 제조] medicine[drug] manufacture; pharmacy; [제조된 약] a manufactured medicine[drug]. **제약하다** manufacture drugs[medicines].
●**제약 공장** a pharmaceutical factory. **제약업자** a drug[pharmaceutical] manufacturer. **제약 회사** a pharmaceutical company; a drug manufacturing company.

제어(制御) control; governing; management. ¶비행기의 자동 ~ (장치) the automatic control(s) of an aircraft. **제어하다** control; bring under control; govern; restrain; manage; hold in check. ¶제어하기 쉬운 easy to control / controllable / manageable / docile // 제어할 수 없다 be out of control / be beyond one's control // 이 기계는 제어하기 쉽다[어렵다] This machine is easy[hard] to control.
●**제어기** a controller. **제어 장치** a control system; a control device; a control unit.

제언(提言) a suggestion; a proposal. ¶일을 즉시 개시해야 한다는 ~ the suggestion[advice] that the work (should) be started at once. **제언하다** suggest (that / doing); propose (doing / that).

제염(製鹽) salt manufacture[making]. **제염하다** make salt.
●**제염소** a saltern; a saltworks. **제염업** the salt industry.

제오 열(第五列) the Fifth Column; the Fifth Columnists.

제왕(帝王) an emperor; a sovereign; a monarch. ¶~의 imperial.

제왕 절개 수술(帝王切開手術) (a) Caesarean section[operation]. ¶~로 아이를 분만시키다 deliver a child by Caesarean section.

제외(除外) exclusion; exception; [면제] exemption. **제외하다** exclude; except; make an exception (of a person's case); [면제하다] exempt (a person from service). ¶…을 제외하다 except / excepting / but / with the exception of / exclusive of // 그런 경우는 제외해야 할 것이다 We may have to exclude [except] such a case. // 이 법률은 미성년자를 제외하고 모든 국민에 적용된다 This law is applied to all the citizens except minors. // 어린이를 제외하고 모두 5명이다 We are five in all, excluding children. ➔ 이 나라에 거주권이 없는 사람은 회원에서 제외된다 Non-resident in this country are excluded[excepted] from the membership. // 외국인은 이 규칙의 적용에서 제외된다 Aliens are exempt from the application of these regulations. / These regulations are not applied to aliens.

제우스 [그리스 신화] Zeus.

제위

제위(帝位) the (Imperial) throne; the crown. ¶~에 오르다 ascend [accede to / come to] the throne // ~에 있다 be [sit] on the throne // ~를 잇다 succeed to the throne // ~를 물려주다 abdicate the throne in favor of (another) // ~를 다투다 pretend to [fight for] the throne // ~를 노리다 aspire to [have designs on] the throne / aim at the crown.

제위(諸位) (회사 등에 부치는 편지에서) Gentlemen; Dear Sirs; [여러분] all; everyone. ¶관련자 ~ (증명서·추천장 등에서) To whom it may concern. // 참석자 ~ all the participants / 출석자 ~의 찬성으로 송 씨가 회장으로 취임했습니다 Mr. Song has assumed the chairmanship with the approval of all (those / the members) present.

제유(製油) oil manufacturing [manufacture].
● 제유 공장 an oil factory [refinery].

제육 [돼지고기] pork; hog flesh [meat].
● 제육구이 roast pork.

제의(提議) a proposal; a proposition; a suggestion; an offer; (회의 등에서의) a motion. ¶…의 ~로 at the instance [motion] of … / ~에 응하다 accept (a person's) offer / consent to (a person's) proposal // ~를 거절하다 decline (a person's) offer / reject (a person's) proposal // 그의 ~는 채택[부결]되었다 His motion was adopted [rejected]. **제의하다** propose; make a proposition [proposal]; suggest; offer. ¶나는 그들을 원조하겠다고 제의했다 I offered to help them. // 재단은 의학 연구자에게 보조금을 주겠다고 제의했다 The Foundation proposed giving grants to medical researchers. // 우리는 그들에게 시합을 제의했다 We challenged them to a game. // 나는 다른 방법을 제의합니다 I'd like to suggest a different plan [doing it in a different way].
● 제의자 a proposer; (동의(動議)의) a mover.

제이 인칭(第二人稱) [언] the second person. ⇨ ⁼이인칭

제이 종 운전면허(第二種運轉免許) a second category driver's license.

제일(祭日) a memorial service day. ⇨ ⁼제삿날 (제사(祭祀))

제일(第一) 1 [첫째가는 것] the first; number one. ¶~의 [첫째가는] the first / [주요한·일차적인] primary / [주요한] main / [최고의] the best / [일류의] leading / [앞서는] foremost / [으뜸의] 문제 the first [main] problem // 세계 ~의 시인 the greatest poet in the world // 이 기획의 ~ 목표는 무엇입니까 What is the primary [chief / principal] aim of this project? / 사전은 이것이 ~이다 This is the best dictionary. // 건강이 ~이다 Health is the most important thing. / Health is above everything else. // 안전 ~ (게시) Safety First. 2 most; extremely. ⇨ ⁼가장
● 제일보 the first step (to). ⇨ ⁼첫걸음 ¶성공에의 ~를 내딛다 make [take] the first step toward(s) success // 나는 ~를 그르쳤다 I got off to a bad start. / I started off on the wrong foot. **제일선** [최전선] the first [foremost] line; [일선] the front. ¶~의 화가 an artist actively at work / a painter active at the forefront of the artistic world // 아직은 ~에서 물러날 생각이 없다 I am not yet thinking of taking a less active role. **제일심** a first-instance trial; a trial in the court of first instance. ¶~에서 무죄가 되다 be acquitted at the first trial. **제일 야당** the major opposition party. **제일인자** the first man (in); the leading person; the authority; the first among one's peers. ¶국제법의 ~ a recognized authority on international law // 그는 그 당시 문학 평론의 ~였다 He was the leading [foremost] literary critic of the day. // 그는 재계의 ~이다 He is a topflight [topnotch] businessman. **제일 인칭** [언] the first person. ⇨ ⁼일인칭

제자(弟子) [문하생] a pupil; [고교·대학의 학생] a student; (어떤 선생 또는 학설에 관한) a disciple; [도제] an apprentice. ¶예수와 그 ~들 Christ and his disciples // 그는 윤 교수의 특별히 촉망하고 아끼는 ~이다 He is a favorite student [pupil] of professor Yun. // 부디 ~로 받아 주십시오 Please take me on as your pupil. // 그는 소목장이의 ~가 되었다 He was apprenticed [became an apprentice] to a cabinet maker.

제자(題字) [표제] the title; (신문의) a heading; (비석의) an inscription.

제자리 [본디 있던 자리] the former place; [마땅한 자리] the proper place. ¶책은 다 읽었으면 ~에 갖다 놓으시오 When you had finished a book, return it to where it was. // 가구는 모두 ~에 놓여 있지 않았다 All the furniture was out of place.
● 제자리멀리 [높이] 뛰기 a standing broad [high] jump. **제자리표** [음] a natural.

제자리걸음 1 [선 채로 걷는 동작]. **제자리걸음하다** mark time. ¶군인들은 행진을 멈추고 제자리걸음했다 The soldier halted their forward progress and marched in place. ➜선생은 학생들을 제자리걸음시켰다 The teacher made the students mark time.
2 [사물이 정체하여 진보하지 못함] a standstill; a stalemate. **제자리걸음하다** come to [be at] a standstill; mark time. ¶그 연구는 제자리걸음했다 The research came to a standstill. / We were getting no where with our research.
3 (물가 등의) pegging. **제자리걸음하다** peg; mark time; remain stationary. ¶물가는 4월 현재 제자리걸음하고 있다 The prices are pegged on the April basis. // 시세는 제자리걸음하고 있다 The quotations are quite stationary.

제작(製作) manufacture; production. ¶공동 ~ (a) co-production / 전기 기구의 ~ the manufacture of electrical appliances // ~ 중이다 be in the work. **제작하다** make; manufacture; produce. ¶그들은 기계를 제작하고 있다 They manufacture machines. // 그는 새로운 영화를 제작하고 있다 He is producing a new film.
● 제작비 the cost of production; production costs. **제작소** a factory; a manufactory; a works; a plant; a mill; a workshop(소규모의). ¶국립 영화 ~ the National Film Production Center // 영화 ~ a movie studio [lot]. **제작자** a maker; a manufacturer; (영화·연극 등의) a producer. ¶공동 ~ [영] a co-producer.

제재(制裁) sanctions; punishment(벌). ¶사회적 [도덕적] 인 ~ social [moral] sanction // 법의 ~ legal sanction // ~를 풀다 lift one's sanctions (against) // ~를 가하다 apply sanctions (against) / punish / inflict punishment upon (a person) // EC의 여러 나라는 그 나라에 대하여 경제상의 ~를 가했다

The EC nations applied economic sanctions against the country.∥그는 이미 충분한 사회적 ~를 받았다 He has already suffered good[great] social punishment[sanction]. **제재하다** apply sanction (against); punish; inflict punishment (upon).

제재(製材) [벌채한 나무로 재목을 만듦] sawing; (미) lumbering. **제재하다** saw (up) logs (into planks).
● **제재공**(-工) a logger; a lumberjack; a sawyer. **제재소** a sawmill; a lumbermill.

제재(題材) [주제가 되는 자료] a subject; a theme; the subject matter. ¶계절에 관한 ~ a seasonal theme (in poetry) / a theme of nature.

제적(除籍) removal of a person's name from (the register). ¶학교에서 ~을 당하다 be expelled from school∥~ 학생을 복귀시키다 reinstate the students expelled from school. **제적하다** remove[cross out / cross off] name from (the register); strike a person's name off (the membership list). ➔그 학생은 수업료 미납으로 제적되었다 The name of the student was removed[crossed out] from the school register because he did not pay the school fees.

제전(祭典) [일반적인] a festival; [종교적인] a feast; a fete. ¶성탄절과 부활절은 교회의 ~이다 Christmas and Easter are church festivals.

제절(諸節) 1 [댁내 여러분] all the family; all of you; everybody. ¶댁내 ~이 무고하신지요 How are your people? / How is[are] your family? 2 [여러 가지 일] various affairs[matters]; everything; all things.

제정(制定) establishment; enactment. **제정하다** establish; enact; legislate. ¶법률을 ~ enact laws / legislate (against / for) / 새 헌법을 ~ establish [set up / enact] a new constitution∥새로운 교통 법규를 제정할 필요가 있다 It is necessary to establish new traffic regulations.

제정(帝政) imperial government[rule / regime]; monarchical rule.
● **제정 러시아** Czarist[Tsarist] Russia. **제정시대** the monarchical days.

제정(祭政) [제사와 정치] the church and state.
● **제정일치** the unity of the church and state; theocracy(정치 형태).

제정(提呈) [바침] presentation. **제정하다** present; offer (to a high personage). ¶(신임 대사가) 신임장을 ~ present one's credentials (to).

제정신(-精神) senses; (right) mind. ¶~이 아니다 be out of one's senses[mind] / be insane[mad] ∥그가 ~으로 그런 짓을 했다고는 생각되지 않는다 He must be out of his mind to do such a thing. ∥설마 ~으로 하는 말은 아니겠지 Surely you don't mean it? / 뜻밖의 성공으로 그는 ~이 아니다[몹시 흥분되어 있다] The unexpected success has gone to his head.

제조(製造) manufacture; production. ¶그는 가방을 ~ 판매하고 있다 He is a manufacturer and seller of bags. / He manufactures and sells bags. **제조하다** [공장 등에서 대규모로 만들다] manufacture; [상품을 생산하다] produce; turn out; [일반적으로 물건을 만들다] make. ¶영국에서 제조한 English-made / of English make∥펄프로 인조 섬유를 ~ make staple fiber from pulp∥넝마로 종이를 ~ manufacture rags into paper∥이 공장에서는 하루에 1,000대의 텔레비전을 제조한다 This factory turns out a thousand television sets a day.∥이 파이프는 영국에서 제조한 것이다 This pipe is of English make.
● **제조법** (공정) a manufacturing process; (기술) a manufacturing technique; how to make. ¶이 빵의 ~을 가르쳐 주십시오 Please show me how to bake[make] this bread. / Please give me the recipe for this bread. **제조업** the manufacturing industry. **제조업자** a manufacturer; a maker. **제조원**(-元) the maker; the manufacturer. **제조 원가** the cost of production; manufacturing[production] cost. **제조 회사** a manufacturing company.

제주(祭主) [상제] the chief mourner; [종교의식의 주재자] the master of religious rites.

제주(祭酒) sacrificial wine; wine for use in a sacrificial rite. ¶~를 올리다 offer wine to the spirit of a dead person[before the altar].

제지(制止) (a) restraint; control; check. ¶~를 받다 be under[subject to] restraint / be restrained∥~를 받지 않다 be free from restraint∥그는 차장의 ~를 무릅쓰고 움직이는 열차에 뛰어올랐다 He jumped on to a moving train, defying the conductor. **제지하다** restrain; control; check; stop; keep (a person) from (doing); hold[keep] back (a crowd). ¶제지할 수 없게 되다 (사물이) get beyond[out of] one's control / go out of hand / (사람이) lose control (of) / 경관은 군중을 제지했다[제지할 수 없었다] The police controlled[lost control of] the crowd. ∥ 선생이 제지하려 했지만 그들은 들으려 하지 않았다 They didn't pay any attention to the teacher's attempts to restrain them[hold them back].

제지(製紙) paper-making; paper manufacture. ¶~용 펄프 paper pulp. **제지하다** make [manufacture] paper.
● **제지 공장** a paper mill; a paper manufactory. **제지업** the paper (manufacturing) industry. **제지 회사** a paper manufacturing company.

제차(諸車) various kinds of vehicles. ¶~ 통행금지 (게시) Closed to all vehicles. / No thoroughfare to vehicles.∥이 거리는 ~ 통행금지로 되어 있다 No wheeled traffic is allowed in this street.

제창(提唱) advocacy; proposal(제의). **제창하다** advocate; bring forward; propose. ¶새로운 학설을 ~ advocate[bring forward] a new doctrine∥인류의 평등을 ~ proclaim[advocate] the equality of men / 자유주의를 ~ advocate liberalism∥그들은 핵무기의 금지를 제창했다 They advocated[proposed] the abolition of nuclear weapons[nuclear disarmament].∥학자들은 새로운 외교 정책의 필요성을 제창하고 있다 Scholars preach[advocate] the necessity for new foreign policies.
● **제창자** an advocate.

제창(齊唱) a unison; a chorus(합창). **제창하다** sing in unison[chorus]. ¶애국가를 ~ sing the Korean national anthem in unison.

제척하다(除斥-) exclude; expel; reject; [법] challenge (the juror).

제철 [알맞은 때] the right[best] season. ¶~

제철

인[이 아닌] 과실 fruits in[out of] season // ~이 아닌데 핀 꽃 a blossom out of season / a flower coming out unseasonably // ~을 만나다 be in one's heyday[prime] / be in one's palmy days / be in one's element / have one's own way // 버섯은 지금은 ~이다 Mushrooms are now in season. // 굴은 이제 ~이 지났다 Oysters are now out of season.

제철(製鐵) iron manufacture. ¶종합 ~ 공장 an integrated steelworks. **제철하다** manufacture iron.
- **제철소** an iron mill; an ironworks. **제철업** the iron industry. **제철 회사** an iron (manufacturing) company.

제청(提請) [추천] recommendation; [지명] nomination. **제청하다** recommend; nominate. ¶총리는 신 박사를 교육 인적 자원부 장관으로 제청했다 The Prime Minister recommended[nominated] Dr. Sin as the Minister of Education and Human Resources Development.

제초(除草) weeding. **제초하다** weed (a garden).
- **제초기** a weeder; an eradicator. **제초제** a weed killer; a herbicide. ¶논에 ~를 뿌리다 dust herbicide on paddy fields.

제출(提出) presentation; (의안 등의) introduction. **제출하다** (의안 등을) present; introduce; submit; lay[bring] (a bill before the Parliament); (의견을) offer; advance; (항의를) lodge[file] (a protest with the authorities); (사표를) tender; (증거를) produce; bring forward; (문제를) pose (a problem); (원서·답안을) give[send / hand] in; turn in. ¶신청서를 ~ present an application // 보고서를 submit a report // 그는 사장에게 사표를 제출했다 He tendered[sent in] his resignation to the president. // 그들은 회의에 제출할 서류를 작성 중이다 They are drawing up the documents for submission[to submit / to be presented] to the conference. // 원서는 2월 5일까지 제출해야 합니다 Applications should be [to be] submitted by February 5. // 시간이 다 되었습니다. 답안을 제출해 주십시오 The time is up. Hand in[(미) Turn in] your answer sheets[examination papers]. // 그는 증거를 제출할 것을 요구받았다 He was asked to produce proof[evidence]. // 야당은 불신임안의 동의를 제출했다 The opposition party moved a vote of[introduced a motion of] nonconfidence. ➔¶논문이 모조리 제출되었다 All the theses have been presented[handed in]. // 그것은 참고로 제출되어야 한다 It should be submitted for reference.
- **제출자** (서류의) a presenter; (안건의) a proposer.

제취(除臭) deodorization. **제취하다** deodorize.
- **제취제** (a) deodorizer; (a) deodorant.

제치다 1 [거치적거리지 않게 치워 놓다] remove (an obstacle); put (a thing) out of the way; get rid of. ¶거치적거리는 물건을 제쳐 놓다 remove[get rid of] an obstacle / get obstacles out of the way.
2 [빼놓다] put[lay] aside; reserve. ¶경비 문제는 제쳐 놓고 apart from the question of expense // 돈 문제는 제쳐 놓더라도 그러한 여행은 매우 피곤하게 됩니다 Apart from[To say nothing of] the question of money, such a trip would be very tiring. / Setting aside the question of money, such a trip would be very tiring.
3 [나중에 하려고 미루다] let (a matter) wait; put off; hold over. ¶만사를 제처 놓고(우선) before everything[anything else] / first of all // 하던 일을 제쳐 놓고 친구를 맞으러 일어서다 get up to meet a friend, laying aside what one was doing // 만사 제쳐 놓고 그 일을 그에게 알리시오 Inform him about it first of all[before anything else]. // 그는 일을 제쳐 놓고 마작에 온 정신이 팔려 있다 He lets his work hang and is completely wrapped up in mah-jongg.

제토제(制吐劑) [구토를 멈추게 하는 약] an antiemetic (medicine).

제트 a jet.
- **제트기** a jet (plane). **제트 기류** the jet stream. **제트 여객기** a jet-propelled airliner; a jetliner.

제판(製版) [인] plate making. ¶사진 ~ (술) photoengraving.
- **제판공** a platemaker; a photoengraver.

제패(制霸) 1 [정복] conquest; (지배) domination; mastery. ¶세계 ~ world conquest [hegemony] / domination of the world. **제패하다** conquer; dominate. ¶세계를 ~ conquer[dominate] the world // 하늘 [바다] 을 ~ secure the control of the air[sea]. 2 [경기의 우승] championship. **제패하다** win[gain] the championship (of). ¶그는 한국 스키계를 제패했다 He won an all-Korea skiing championship.

제풀로 [자기 스스로] at one's own discretion; of one's own will; [저절로] of itself[oneself].

제풀에 at one's own discretion. ⇨제풀로

제품(製品) a product; [물건] an article; [상품] good; [공장에서의 대량 생산물] manufactures; manufactured goods. ¶국내 ~ home[domestic] products // 한국 ~ articles of Korean make / goods made in Korea // 면 [견] ~ cotton[silk] manufactures // 유리 ~ glassware // 전기 ~ electric appliances // 석유 화학 [낙농] ~ petrochemical[dairy] products // 반(半) ~ semifinished goods // 그는 새 ~을 소개하기 위해 미국에서 이곳에 와 있다 He's here from the United States to introduce a new product to us. // 저희는 외국 ~을 취급하지 않습니다 We don't deal in foreign products[imported goods].
- **제품 가격** prices of manufactured goods. **제품 원가** the cost of product.

제하다(除一) 1 [공제하다] take off[away]; deduct; subtract (from); subduct (from). ¶세금을 제하고 100만 원의 월수 a monthly income of 1,000,000 won after taxes // 봉급에서 ~ deduct (a sum) from one's salary // 집세는 봉급에서 제해진다 The rent is deducted from my salary[pay]. // 필요 경비를 제하고도 아직 100만 원이 남는다 Even after we take off[deduct] (the) necessary expenses, we'll have a million won left. 2 [나누다] divide.

제한(制限) (a) restriction; (a) restraint; [한계] a limit; (a) limitation. ¶군비 ~ armament limitation // 산아 ~ birth control // 수입 ~ import restrictions (on) // 연령 ~ an age limit // 전력 (소비) ~ restriction on (electric) power consumption // ~ 없이 unrestrictedly / without limitation[restriction] // ~ 내[밖]에 within[beyond] the limits // 스페이스에 ~이 있기 때문에 because of space limitations // 시간 ~이 있다 be restricted in time // 수에

~이 있다 be limited in number // ~을 받다 be subjected to restriction // ~을 완화하다 relax restrictions (on trade) // ~을 해제[철폐]하다 lift [remove / withdraw] restriction (on) // 참가에 남녀의 ~ 없음 Participation is open to either sex. // 회원 자격의 ~을 완화했다 The qualifications for membership have been relaxed. // 그들은 최고 가격과 최저 가격의 ~을 두었다 They set [established] a price floor and a price ceiling. // They limited [held] the increase of capital stock to 30 percent. 제한하다 restrict; limit; confine. ¶(건강을 위하여) 식사를 ~ place [put] (a person) on a diet // 그들은 증자액을 30%로 제한했다 They limited [held] the increase of capital stock to 30 percent. ➔ ¶행동을 제한받다 be restricted in one's movements // 방청인은 10명으로 제한되어 있다 The number of auditors is limited [restricted] to ten. // 그들은 행동이 제한되어 있다 They are restricted in their actions. // 그녀는 고혈압 때문에 식사가 제한되어 있다 She is on a restricted diet because of high blood pressure. // 이 일에는 시간이 제한되어 있다 This work has to be finished in a limited length of time.
● 제한 구역 a restricted area. 제한 속도 a speed limit. ¶여기서의 ~는 시속 60킬로미터입니다 The speed limit here is 60 kilometers per hour.

제해권(制海權) the command of the sea; naval supremacy. ¶~을 잡다[잡고 있다] secure [hold / have] the command of the sea / command the sea // ~을 잃다 lose the command of the sea // ~을 되찾다 regain the lost command of the sea.

제헌(制憲) establishment of the constitution. 제헌하다 establish the constitution.
● 제헌 국회 the Constituent National Assembly. 제헌절 Constitution Memorial Day.

제혁(製革) tanning; leather manufacturing. 제혁하다 tan hides; make hides into leather.
● 제혁 공장 a tannery. 제혁업 the tanning industry.

제현(諸賢) gentlemen.
제형(諸兄) (부르는 말로) (my) dear friends.
제형(蹄形) [말굽 모양] U-shape. ¶~의 hoof-shaped / U-shaped.
제호(題號) the title (of a book). ¶~를 붙이다 give a title (to a book) / entitle (a book).
제화(製靴) shoemaking.
● 제화공 a shoemaker. 제화업 the shoe industry.
제후(諸侯) feudal lords.
제휴(提携) cooperation; concert; coalition. ¶기술 ~ a technical cooperation [tie-up] (between) // 우리는 귀사와의 ~를 희망하고 있습니다 We hope to link up [affiliate] with your company. / We hope to obtain the cooperation of your company. 제휴하다 cooperate with; act in concert with; move in harmony; go hand in hand with; join [clasp] hands with; tie up with. ¶…과 제휴하여 (work) in concert [cooperation] with // 제휴하고 있다 be aligned (with) / be bound in the same camp.
● 제휴 회사 an affiliated concern.
제힘 one's own efforts.
젠체하다 make an affected pose; assume airs [an air of importance]; put on airs (and graces); be proud [arrogant]. ¶젠체하는 affected / conceited // 젠체하는 사람 an affected person / a snob // 그는 언제나 젠체한다 He always puts on airs. // 그렇게 젠체하지 마라 Don't give yourself such airs. // 그는 쓸데없는 것을 젠체하고 말하는 버릇이 있다 He has a way of talking nonsense with an air of importance. // 그는 젠체하므로 학급 친구들이 싫어한다 He is disliked by his classmates for being pretentious [self-important].

젤라틴 [화] gelatin(e).
젤리 jelly; [반고체의 과자] (a) jelly. ¶~ 모양이 되다[으로 만들다] jelly / jellify // 수프를 식혔더니 ~가 되었다 The soup jellied when it chilled.
젯메(祭―) [제사 때 올리는 밥] sacrificial rice; rice offering.
젯밥(祭―) [제사에 쓰고 물린 밥] boiled rice that has been used as a sacrificial offering; rice left over from a rite.
조¹ [식] foxtail [Italian / German] millet. ¶~의 낱알 a grain of foxtail millet.
조² that (pl. those). ⇨<저⁴
조(兆) [수] [미] a trillion; [영] a billion. ¶5~원 five trillion [billion] won.
조(條) 1 [조목] a provision; an article; a clause; an item. ¶제1~ Article [Section] 1 / 소년법 24~ 1항 1호 Paragraph [Para.] 1 of Sub-Section 1 of section [sec.] 24 of the Juvenile Act // 헌법 제11~에 의거하여 under Article 11 of the Constitution // 국제 연합 헌장 제51~에 의거한 집단 안전 보장 a collective security based on Article of 51 of the United Nations Charter. 2 [특정한 조건]. ¶…~로 as / for / by way of // 여흥[사과]~로 by way of entertainment [apology] // 원고료 ~로 일금 50만 원정을 정히 영수하였음 I acknowledge receipt of the sum of 500,000 won as the contribution fee.
조(組) [작은 집단] a company; a party; a band; a group. ¶2인 ~ a pair / a duet / a duo // 3인 ~ 강도 a trio of robbers // ~를 만들다[짜다] form [make up] a group // 카드놀이에서 나는 그녀와 한 ~가 되었다 She and I were partners [I was on her side] in card game.
조(調) 1 [음조] tune; a tone; (가락을 이룬) a meter. 2 [어조] a tone; [방식] a way; a manner; [태도] an air; an attitude. ¶비난~로 (speak) with a tone [an air] of censure / critically // 농담[장난]~로 jokingly / half in jest // 시비~로 in a defiant attitude / defiantly // 연설~로 in an oratorical tone // 변명~로 in a tone of apology.
-조(朝) 1 [왕조] a dynasty. ¶명(明)~ the Ming dynasty // 조선~ the Joseon dynasty. 2 [치세] a reign. ¶빅토리아~ the reign of Queen Victoria / the Victorian Age.
조가(弔歌) [죽음을 애도하는 노래] a dirge; an elegy.
조가비 a shell. ¶~를 줍다 gather [pick] shells.
조각 a piece; a bit; a fragment; a slip; a strip; a slice (얇은 조각); a scrap (자투리); a cut (베어 낸). ¶빵 ~ piece of bread // 유리 ~ a broken piece of glass / a glass splinter // 종잇 ~ bits [scraps] of paper // 케이크 한 ~ a cut [piece / slice] of cake // 깨진 꽃병의 ~ the fragments of a broken vase // ~으로 in pieces [scraps] // 두 ~으로 깨지다 break [be broken] in two // 천을 작은 ~으로 자르다

조각 cut cloth (up) into small pieces // 유리 ~에 손을 베다 cut one's hand on a fragment [broken piece] of glass // 그 증서는 이제 한 ~의 휴지에 지나지 않는다 That bond is now a mere [nothing more than a] scrap of paper.
- **조각달** a crescent (moon); a waxing moon(상현의); a waning moon(하현의).

조각(組閣) [내각을 조직함] formation of a cabinet [ministry]. **조각하다** form a cabinet; organize [construct] a ministry.

조각(彫刻·雕刻) sculpture; engraving; carving. (▶ sculpture는 금속·돌·나무 등을 새겨서 상을 만드는 일. engraving은 같은 재료의 단단한 표면에 문자나 무늬를 새기는 일. carving은 두 가지 경우에 다 쓰임) ¶~처럼 윤곽이 뚜렷한 얼굴 clear-cut features // ~처럼 균형이 잡힌 몸 a sculpturesque body. **조각하다** carve; sculpture; engrave; chase(금속에); chisel(끌로). ¶나무에 조각한 상 an image carved in wood // 대리석으로 상을 chisel a statue out of marble // 그는 대리석으로 상을 조각했다 He carved [sculpted / sculptured] a statue out of marble. // 그는 비석에 가문을 조각했다 He engraved the family crest on the tombstone.
- **조각가** an engraver; a sculptor. **조각도** a chisel; (동판의) a graver; a burin. **조각물** / **조각품** a sculpture; a carving; an engraving.

조각나다 1 [갈라지다] split (in [into] pieces); cleave; splinter; [부서지다] break (into pieces); be broken (to pieces). ¶둘로 ~ (부서져서) break [be broken] in two / (갈라져서) split in two // 산산이 ~ break [be broken] to pieces / smash [be smashed] to pieces // 그 정당은 여러 파벌로 조각났다 The political party split into factions. 2 [의견이 맞지 않다] have a split in opinion; be divided in opinion.

조각조각 in (broken) pieces; all to pieces; in fragments; in strips. ¶~ 되다 become broken to pieces // 부수다 [찢다] break [tear] (a thing) in [to / into] pieces // 헝겊을 ~ 잇다 piece together odds and ends of cloth // 헝겊을 ~ 이어서 이불을 만들다 make [piece together] a patchwork quilt.

조간(朝刊) a morning paper; (석간에 대하여) a morning edition. ¶오늘자 A일보 ~ this morning's A.
- **조간신문** a morning paper.

조갈(燥渴) a raging thirst; a parched throat. ¶~이 나다 suffer from thirst.
- **조갈증** [한] a disease symptomized by thirst. ⇨=소갈증

조감도(鳥瞰圖) a bird's-eye view; an air [aerial] view(항공 사진); an airscape(하늘에서 본 경치); an airplane view.

조감독(助監督) [영] an assistant director.

조강(粗鋼) [가공이 안 된 강철] crude steel.

조강지처(糟糠之妻) one's wife married in poverty; one's old life partner. ¶그녀는 나의 ~이다 She is my wife, my helpmate throughout all the struggles of my life.

조개 a shellfish; [대합조개] a clam. ¶~를 줍다 gather shellfish // ~를 캐다 dig out shellfish [clams].
- **조개더미** / **조개무지** a shell heap; a shell mound.

조객(弔客) a person calling to condole; a caller for condolence.

조건(條件) 1 [조항] an item; a stipulation. 2 [제약 사항] a term; a qualification(제한). ¶**강화**[화해] ~ the terms of peace [settlement] // **계약** ~ the terms of a contract // **매매**[거래] ~ the terms of sale [trade] // 무리가 없는 ~ reasonable terms // …을 고르는 세 가지 ~ the three terms for choosing (a spouse, a job etc.). 3 [어떤 일의 성립에 필요한 사항] a condition. ¶**노동** ~ labor [working] conditions // **부대** ~ a collateral [an incidental] condition // **전제** ~ a prior condition // **필수** ~ a sine qua non (condition) / a precondition // **제1** [**첫째**] ~ the first prerequisite // **필요충분**[**수**] ~ the necessary and sufficient condition // **악** ~ unfavorable conditions // **지급** ~ terms of payment // **해제** ~ a condition subsequent // **입지** ~ location requirements (for a factory) // 평등한 ~으로 on equal terms // 무(~으로) without condition // 유리한 ~으로 on favorable terms // 불리한 ~으로 on unfavorable condition // 극히 가혹[안이]한 ~으로 [아래] under the toughest [easiest] conditions // …이라는 ~으로 on condition of [that] / provided [on the understanding] that // 분배에 참여한다는 ~으로 on condition of sharing (in) // 적어도 한 달 전에 통고한다는 ~으로 subject to at least a month's previous notice // 좋은 ~으로 계약을 맺다 conclude a favorable contract / close a contract at good terms // …이라는 ~으로 허용하다 give permission on condition that (she shall return it in a day) // …을 ~으로 하고 있다 be subject to (your consent) / be contingent on (your agreement) // …을 ~으로 하다 make it a condition that … // ~을 **붙이다** attach [annex] a condition (to one's proposal) / saddle (a person) with condition / set terms // 까다로운 ~을 붙이다 set [lay down] iron-bound conditions // 일정한 ~을 설정하다 stipulate for certain terms // ~을 **변경하다** modify the terms // …을 지키게 하다 hold (a person) to ~ // ~을 **채우다**[만족시키다] meet the qualification // 제기한 ~을 철회하다 waive conditions mentioned // ~을 가급적 완화하다 make the condition as easy as possible // ~을 정하고 약속하다 promise on fixed condition // 기부에 아무 ~도 붙이지 않다 tie no strings to one's gift // 건강은 성공의 ~이다 Health is a condition [prerequisite] of success. // 선불 ~으로 합시다 I make it a condition that you pay in advance. // 이 융자에는 ~이 붙어 있다 There are some strings [conditions] attached to this loan. // 어둡기 전에 귀가한다는 ~으로 그는 딸의 외출을 허가했다 He allowed his daughter to go out on condition that she would come back before dark. // 네가 도와준다는 ~으로 그것을 맡겠다 I will undertake it on condition that you help me. // 그는 유리한 ~으로 채용되었다 He was employed on favorable terms. // 더 좋은 ~을 다른 바이어가 제의했다 Better terms were offered by other buyers. // 철도 회사는 땅 임자에게 매우 좋은 ~을 제시했다 The railroad offered the landowner excellent terms.
- **조건문** [언] a conditional (sentence). **조건반사** [생] a conditioned reflex [response]. ¶~를 **일으키다** cause a conditioned reflex / condition. **조건부**(-附) ¶~의 conditional /

qualified / [조건이 붙은] with some strings attached (to it) // ~로 conditionally / with conditions attached / with (a) proviso // ~로 승낙하다 give a qualified consent // 채용은 모두 ~로 한다 Any initial appointment shall be considered conditional. // 이 제의는 ~다 This offer is conditional. // 그의 제안에 ~로 찬성한다 I agree to his proposal conditionally. // 정부 보조금은 언제나 ~이다 Government grants always have strings attached. 조건절 [언] a conditional clause.

조견표(早見表) a chart; a table. ¶전화번호 ~ telephone numbers at a glance // 칼로리 ~ a simplified calory chart // 표준 체중 ~ Your Recommend Weight at a Glance.

조경(造景) landscape gardening.
● 조경사 a landscape architect.

조계(早計) [이른 계획] a premature scheme; (경솔) rashness; [시기 상조] prematurity. ¶~ premature / too hasty / overhasty / rash // 그렇게 생각하는 것은 ~이다 This is too hasty a conclusion. / Don't jump to that conclusion. / It would be premature to think so.

조고(祖考) one's deceased grandfather.

조곡(弔哭) wailing in mourning; keening. 조곡하다 wail in mourning; keen.

조곡(組曲) [음] a suite. ¶바흐의 프랑스 ~ the French Suites by Bach.

조공(朝貢) bringing a tribute (to a country). 조공하다 bring a tribute (to a country); pay tribute (to a country with something).
● 조공국 a tributary state.

조관(朝官) ⇨조신(朝臣)

조광권(租鑛權) a mining right [concession].

조교(弔橋) a suspension bridge. ⇨현수교(吊현)

조교(助敎) an assistant teacher [instructor]; a coadjutor.

조교수(助敎授) (미) an assistant professor. ¶영문학과 ~ an assistant professor of English literature.

조국(祖國) one's homeland [fatherland / motherland]; one's mother [native] country. ¶~을 지키다 [위해 싸우다] defend [fight for] one's fatherland // ~을 떠나다 leave one's native country // 해외에서 ~을 그리다 be nostalgic of one's mother country while on foreign soil.
● 조국애 love of [for] one's motherland [(own) country]; [애국심] patriotism. ¶~에 불타다 burn with love for one's country.

조규(條規) [조문의 규정] a stipulation; articles [provisions / regulations] (of a law).

조그마하다 teeny-weeny.

조그만큼 (수·양) just a few[little]; (정도) to a slight degree.

조그맣다 teeny-weeny. ⇨조그마하다

조금 1 (양) a small quantity; a little; a dash. ¶아주 ~ just a little [bit] // ~ 더 a little [bit] more // 술을 ~만 마시다 just drink a little / (구어) go light on the liquor // 저녁 식사를 ~ 먹다 have a bite of supper // 물을 ~ 탄 위스키 whisky with a splash [dash] of water // 돈이 ~이라도 있다면 if one has any money // 소금을 ~ 쳐서 간을 맞추다 season (food) with a dash of salt // 돈이 ~ 필요하다 I want some money. // 돈이 ~밖에 없다 I have only a little money. // 항아리에는 설탕이 ~ 들어 있었다 There was a little sugar in the pot. // 차를 ~ 더 드시겠습니까 Would you like some more tea?

2 (수) a small number; a few; some. ¶아주 ~ just a few // ~ 더 a few more // 그에게 친구가 ~은 있다 He has a few friends. // 나는 영어책을 ~ 갖고 있다 I have a few [some] English books. // 오렌지를 ~ 보내 드렸습니다 I sent you a few oranges. // 이 작문에는 오류가 ~ 있다 There are some mistakes in this composition. // 독일어 책은 ~밖에 갖고 있지 않다 I have only a few German books. // 이 책에는 오식이 ~밖에 없다 There are only a few [but few] misprints in this book. // 그 집회에는 사람이 ~밖에 모이지 않았다 Only a small number of people came to [attended] the rally.

3 (정도) something; somewhat; a little; a trifle; slightly; to a slight degree; a shade. ¶~ 쓴 [사용한] partially used (matchbook) // ~의 slight // ~ 화가 나서 a little offended // ~ 놀라서 in some surprise / a little surprised // ~이라도 친절한 마음이 있다면 if you have a spark [touch / drop] of kindness in you // 머리가 ~ 아프다 I have a slight headache. // 오늘은 기분이 ~ 좋다 I feel a little [shade] better today. // 그의 병세가 ~ 나아졌다 His condition improved a little. / He is slightly better. // 이 장대는 ~ 길다 This pole is a bit too long. // 그는 ~ 살찐 편이다 He is a little on the heavy side. // 창문을 ~만 열어 다오 Open the window a crack. // ~만 더 노력해라 Make one more effort. // 이 책이 저것보다 ~ 더 두껍다 This book is a little [a bit] thicker than that one. // 나는 ~ 놀랐다 I was somewhat taken aback. // 그는 ~ 거북한 모양이었다 He looked somewhat discomfited. // 그에게는 ~ 우스꽝스런 데가 있다 There is something comical about him. // 그의 태도가 ~ 부드러워진 것 같다 His attitude seems to have softened to some extent. // 그것은 우리를 ~ 놀라게 했다 That came as bit of a surprise to us. // 방에 들어섰을 때 그의 얼굴이 ~ 상기되어 있었다 He looked somewhat flushed when he entered the room. // 그녀는 머리를 ~ 숙이며 말하기 시작했다 She began to talk with her head slightly lowered. // "당신은 프랑스 어를 할 줄 아십니까?" "네, 아주 ~ 합니다." "Do you speak French?" "Yes, I do, but just a little." // 그녀의 독어는 ~ 미흡한 데가 있다 Her German leaves something to be desired. // 그는 ~은 학식이 있다 He is something of a scholar. // 그가 ~ 이상하다고 생각하지 않으세요 Don't you think there is something wrong with him? / Don't you think he is a little strange? // 그 그림을 ~만 오른쪽으로 옮기는 것이 좋겠다 It would be better to move the picture just a bit [a shade] to the right. // 그것이 ~이라도 도움이 된다면 기쁘겠습니다 I shall be happy if it serves some useful purpose. // 그의 태도가 ~이라도 나아졌습니까 Has he shown any improvement in his attitude? / Is he behaving any better?

4 (시간) a moment; a minute; a (little) while. ¶~ 전(에) a little while ago // ~ 있으면 [지나면] in a little while / in a short time / a little later / shortly / soon // ~만 기다려 주십시오 Please wait a minute [moment]. / Just a moment, please. / One moment, sir [madam]. / (구어) Hold on a minute [second].

조금 please.∥~ 있다가 다시 한 번 전화해 주세요 Please call again a little later.∥~ 더 기다리고 있었더니 그가 나타났다 We waited a little longer, and he turned up.∥저녁 식사 준비가 되려면 ~ 더 걸린다 It will be sometime [It will take a little while longer] before dinner is ready.∥그는 바로 ~ 전에 산책 나갔습니다 He has just (this minute) gone out for a walk.∥바로 ~ 전에 텔레비전으로 보도되었다 It was reported on TV only a few minutes ago. **5** (거리) a little way; a short distance. ¶~ 떨어져서 a little way off∥강을 따라 ~ 가다 go a little way along the river∥~ 가니까 강이 나왔다 A little way on, we came to a river.∥역은 ~만 가면 됩니다 It is but a short way from here to the station. / The station is right up ahead. / We're almost at the station.∥학교까지는 ~만 가면 됩니다 It is only a short distance to the school.

조금(潮─) the neap tide; (at) the neap.

조금도 (not) in the least; (not) at all; (not) in any degree; (not) a bit; (not) the slightest. ¶~ 쓸모가 없다 be of no use at all / be good for nothing∥~ 효과가 없다 take no effect whatever [at all]∥~ 허점을 드러내지 않다 allow (the opponent) no opportunity to seize∥나는 그것에 관해 ~ 의심하지 않는다 I have not the least [slightest] doubt about it.∥나는 ~ 상관 없다 I don't care twopence [a straw] about it.∥그런 일은 ~ 개의치 않는다 I don't care a bit about it.∥그것에 관하여는 ~ 의심스러운 점은 없다 There is no doubt whatever about it.∥그녀는 독어 지식이 ~ 없다 She has not the least [slightest] knowledge of German.∥그는 양심이라고 는 ~ 없다 He has not an ounce [atom] of conscience.∥그것은 ~ 예상하지 못했다 That is the last thing I expected.∥그런 생각 은 ~ 없다 Nothing is farther from my intention.∥이 둘은 ~ 틀리지 않다 These two are absolutely identical.∥이건 저것에 비하여 ~ 못하지 않다 This is every bit as good as that.∥그는 ~ 양보를 하지 않았다 He hasn't budged an inch.∥그는 ~ 동요되지 않았다 He wasn't in the least disturbed.∥그는 ~ 기죽지 않았다 He was not at all daunted. / He was not daunted in the least. / It didn't bother [faze] him at all.∥상대는 ~ 빈틈을 보이지 않았다 My opponent gave me no chance to attack.∥My opponent never dropped [let down] his guard.∥양심의 가책 을 받을 일은 ~ 없다 I haven't done anything [I have nothing] to be ashamed of.∥모두가 식욕이 왕성해서 음식을 ~ 남기지 않았 다 Everyone had a good appetite so there wasn't a bit of food left.∥~ 도움이 되어 드 리지 못했습니다 I was of no use.

조급하다(躁急─) quick-[hot-]tempered; impatient; impetuous; hasty. ¶조급한 사람 a person of impetuous disposition / a hasty person / a hothead∥마음이 ~ be eager (to do) / be driven by impetuosity∥조급한 마음 을 가라앉히다 control oneself / hold one's horses∥조급한 마음을 어쩔 수 없었다 I can't control my impatience. I cannot help being very impatient.∥네가 지금 사표를 낸다면 조 급했다는 비판을 면할 수 없을 것이다 If you send in your resignation now, you will be criticized for being precipitate [too hasty]. **조급히** impetuously; impatiently. ¶그렇게 굴지 마라 Don't be so impatient. / What's the [your] hurry?

조기 [동] a croaker; a yellow corbina.

조기(弔旗) **1** [조의를 뜻하는 기] a mourning flag; a flag draped in black. ¶~를 달다 hang out [fly] a mourning flag / put out [hang] a flag draped in black. **2** a flag at half-mast. ⇨ 반기(半旗)

조기(早起) early rising. **조기하다** rise [get up] early; rise with the sun [lark].
● **조기회** an early risers club [meeting].

조기(早期) [이른 시기] an early stage. ¶~에 발견하다 detect [spot] (a disease) in its early stages∥암의 치료에는 ~ 발견이 매우 중요하다 Early discovery [detection] is of vital importance for the successful treatment of cancer.∥교섭은 ~ 타결을 보았다 The negotiations came to an early settlement.
● **조기 교육** early education; (학령 전의) preschool education. ¶음악의 ~은 효과가 있 다 Music lessons at an early stage are effective. **조기 상환** advanced redemption. **조기 진단** early diagnosis [checkup]. **조기 치료** early treatment.

조깅 [천천히 달리기] jogging. ¶~은 살을 빼고 건강을 증진시키는 좋은 방법이다 Jogging is a good way to lose weight and improve one's health. **조깅하다** jog (one's mile and a quarter). ¶아버지는 아침마다 공원에서 조깅하신 다 Father jogs in the park every morning.

조끼¹ [소매 없는 옷] (미) a vest; (영) a waistcoat.
● **조끼삼** a sleeved vest [waistcoat].

조끼² [손잡이가 달린 컵] a mug; a jug. ¶맥주 한 ~ a mug [jugful] of beer.

조난 a disaster; an accident; (배의) (a) shipwreck; a distress. **조난하다** meet with a disaster; (배가) be wrecked; be in distress. ¶산에서 ~ [길을 잃다] get lost [disappear] in the mountains / [사고 등으로 죽다] be killed in a mountaineering accident∥태풍으로 배 가 조난하였다 The ship sank [was wrecked] in the typhoon.∥눈사태로 다섯 사람이 조난 하였다 Five persons were lost in the avalanche.
● **조난선** a ship in distress; a wrecked ship. ¶~을 구조하다 go to the rescue of a ship in distress. **조난 신호** a distress signal; a signal of distress; an SOS; a distress call(무전의). ¶~를 보내다 [받다] send [pick up] a distress call [an SOS]∥우리는 ~를 보냈다 We sent out an SOS.∥근처를 항해하던 어선이 ~를 수신하였다 A fishing boat sailing nearby picked up the SOS. **조난자** a victim; a sufferer. ¶올겨울에는 산에서의 ~가 50명을 넘었 다 Over fifty people lost their lives in the mountains this winter.

조달(調達) supply; (군대의) procurement; (식 량·일용품의) provision; (영) purveyance; (돈 의) raising; (주문의) fulfillment; execution. **조달하다** supply; provide; furnish (a person with a thing); (영) purvey [cater] (provisions); raise (a fund for); fill [fulfill / execute] (an order). ¶토지를 저당하여 돈을 ~ raise money on one's land∥당시는 우유를 조달하기가 어려웠다 It was hard to procure milk in those days.
● **조달청** the Supply Administration.

조도(照度) luminous intensity; (intensity of)

illumination; illuminance. ¶럭스는 ~의 단위이다 A lux is a unit of illumination.
● **조도계** an illuminometer; a photometer.
조동사(助動詞) [언] an auxiliary verb. ⇨ ⁼보조동사(⇨보조(補助))
조락(凋落) [시들기] [몰락] decline; decay. ¶자연주의 문학의 ~ the decline of the naturalist school in literature. **조락하다** wither; decline; decay; fall.
조란(鳥卵) an egg (of a bird).
조력(助力) help; aid; assistance; support(후원); cooperation(협력). ¶…의 ~으로 with a person's help / with [through] a person's assistance / 남의 ~을 받지 않고 unaided / without another's help // ~을 청하다 seek assistance (from a friend) / ask (a person) for his help / 네 ~이 필요하다 I stand in need of your assistance. / I need your assistance. // 너의 ~으로 어려움을 벗어났다 You helped me out of the difficulty. **조력하다** help; aid [assist] (in a person's work); give [render] (a person) aid (in doing / to do). ¶그는 기꺼이 조력해 주러 왔다 He gladly came to my aid.
● **조력자** a helper; an assistant; a supporter; a friend.
조력 발전소(潮力發電所) a tidal (power) plant.
조련(操鍊) 1 (military) drill. ⇨ ⁼교련(敎鍊) 2 [괴롭힘]. **조련하다** torment; harass; afflict; torture.
조령모개(朝令暮改) an unsettled course of action; lack of principle. ¶~의 정책 a fickle [an inconstant] policy.
조례(弔禮) condolence etiquette; the manners [forms] for condolence.
조례(條例) [규칙이나 법령] regulations; rules; a law; an act; an ordinance.
조례(朝禮) a morning gathering [meeting].
조로(早老) premature old age. ¶~의 prematurely aged [old]. **조로하다** ¶조로해 보이다 looks older than one's age.
● **조로 현상** symptoms of premature old age.
조로(朝露) the morning dew. ¶인생은 ~와도 같다 Man's life vanishes like the dew. / Life is but a span.
조로아스터교(-敎) Zoroastrianism. ¶~도 a Zoroastrian.
조록조록 with wrinkles; sprinklingly. ⇨ ⁼주룩주룩
조롱(鳥籠) a birdcage. ⇨ ⁼새장
조롱(嘲弄) mockery; ridicule; derision; raillery; scoffing; jeering. **조롱하다** make a fool (of); make sport [fun] (of); mock at; ridicule; deride; scoff [jeer] at; rail at [against]. ¶~조롱하듯이 derisively / scoffing(ly) / mocking(ly) / …을 조롱하여 in ridicule of … // 조롱하지 마 (구어) You're pulling my leg! → **조롱당하다** be ridiculed / be sneered [scoffed] at / be held in derision. / 나는 조롱당하고서는 못 참는다 I can't afford to be fooled. // 그는 남에게 조롱당할 짓을 했다 He laid himself open to ridicule.
조롱박 1 [식] a bottle gourd. ⇨ ⁼호리병박(⇨호리병) 2 [쪽박] a dipping gourd.
조루(早漏) [의] premature ejaculation.
조류(鳥類) [동] birds; fowls; bird life; the feathered tribe.
● **조류 보호** bird protection. **조류학** ornithology; birdlore. **조류학자** an ornithologist.

조류(潮流) 1 [해류] a tide; a (tidal) current. 2 [풍조] a tendency; a current; a trend. ¶시대 ~에 따르다 [거스르다] swim with [against] the stream [current of the times] // 시대의 ~는 거스를 수가 없다 There is no swimming [fighting] against the current [tendency] of the times.
조류(藻類) [식] algae; [해조] seaweeds. ¶~의 [비슷한] algal / algoid.
● **조류학** phycology; algology. **조류학자** an algologist; a phycologist.
조르개 a tightening string [cord].
조르다 1 [죄다] tighten; strangle; constrict; choke(목을). ¶허리띠를 ~ tighten one's belt // 졸라 죽이다 strangle (a person) to death // 레슬링에서 상대방의 목을 조르는 것은 반칙이다 In wrestling a strangle hold is against the rules.
2 [요구하다] tease [importune / press] (a person for something); ask (a person) importunately (for money); coax (something) out of (a person). ¶과자를 달라고 ~ clamor for candy // 결혼하자고 졸라 대다 tease (a person) to marry (one) // 사탕을 달라고 졸라 대다 clamor for candy // 그는 내게 돈을 달라고 졸랐다 He pressed me for money. // 마누라는 내게 모피 코트를 사 달라고 졸랐다 I was pressed by my wife [My wife kept begging me] to buy her a fur coat. // 아버지에게 레코드플레이어를 사 달라고 졸랐다 I pestered [badgered / (구어) kept after] my father to buy me a record player. // 그는 그녀를 졸라 서류에 서명케 했다 He badgered [hounded] her into signing the paper. // 그는 아버지를 졸라 동물원에 데려다 주도록 만들었다 He wheedled his father into taking him to the zoo.
조르르 1 [액체가 흘러내리는 모양] tricklingly; dribbling; running. 2 [미끄러지는 모양] slidingly; slipperily. 3 [빠르게 내닫는 모양] at a dash; with one rush.
조르륵 dribbling; trickling.
조리(笊籬) [쌀을 이는 기구] a (bamboo) strainer; a meshwork ladle.
조리(條理) logical sequence; logic; reason. ¶~가 있는 [닿는] reasonable / logical / consistent // ~가 없는 [닿지 않는] unreasonable / illogical / incongruous // ~가 없는 말 an incoherent account [remark] // ~에 맞다 stand to reason / square with reason / be reasonable // ~ 있게 말하다 speak logically / state one's ideas in logical order // 네가 하는 말은 ~가 닿지 않는다 What you say isn't logical [doesn't make sense]. // 좀 더 ~ 있게 [~에 맞게] 말을 해 주게 Talk more coherently [logically].
조리(調理) 1 [조섭] care of (one's delicate) health; nursing oneself. **조리하다** take care of one's health; nurse oneself. 2 [요리] cooking; cookery. **조리하다** cook (food); prepare (a dish); dress (fish).
● **조리대** a kitchen table; a dresser. **조리법** the art of cooking; cookery; cuisine. **조리사** a cook. **조리실** a cuisine; a kitchen.
조리개 [사진기의 기계 장치] an iris diaphragm; an iris (pl. ~es, irides). ¶(카메라의) ~ 5.6으로 셔터를 누르면 shot at F 5.6 // ~ 3.5로 사진을 찍었다 I shot at F 3.5. / I took a picture with an aperture [a lens] opening of 3.5.

조리다

조리다 boil down. ¶생선을 간장에 ~ boil fish down in soy // 과일을 설탕과 함께 조려서 잼을 만들다 boil fruit with sugar into jam.

조림 food boiled down in soy; hard-boiled food. ¶고기~ hard-boiled beef (in soy) // 생선~ fish boiled in soy with spices // 통~ canned food.

조림(造林) afforestation; forestation; reforestation(재식림). **조림하다** afforest (a mountain / a valley); plant trees; reforest (a nuded land).
● **조림 계획 / 조림 사업** a tree-planting[an afforestation] project. **조림지** an afforested land; [삼림] a plantation.

조립(組立) [맞추어 짬] (일반적인) constructing; fabrication; (기계의) assembling; assembly; assemblage. ¶모형의 ~이 나의 취미이다 My hobby is putting together models. **조립하다** construct; fabricate; frame; assemble; fix up; erect; put[fit / piece] together. ¶라디오[자동차]를 ~ assemble a radio[an automobile] // 가옥을 ~ fabricate a house / set up a prefab // 부품품을 조립하여 완성품으로 만들다 assemble the parts into a complete unit // 그는 모형 비행기를 조립했다 He put together [assembled] a model plane.
● **조립식** ¶~의 fabricated (ship / house) / knock down // ~ 주택 a prefabricated house // ~ 책장 a sectional[knockdown] bookcase. **조립 주택** a prefabricated house; a prefab.

조마(調馬) horse training[breaking]. **조마하다** train[break (in)] a horse.
● **조마사**(一師) a horse trainer.

조마조마하다 (서술적) feel nervous[timid / uneasy]; be in great fear (of); be kept in suspense; be in a fidget[flutter]. ¶조마조마한 마음으로 (불안으로) in great fear / in thrilling[breathless] suspense / with bated breath / (기대 등으로) with breathless interest // 조마조마하게 하다 put (a person) into a flutter / keep (a person) in suspense / make[drive] (a person) nervous // 나는 불안으로 가슴이 조마조마했다 I felt ill at ease. / My heart was filled with misgivings[anxiety]. // 내가 무슨 말을 꺼낼까 마음이 조마조마했다 I was anxious[uneasy] about what you were going to say. // 보고만 있어도 ~ It makes me feel uneasy[nervous] just to see it. // 나는 들킬까 봐 조마조마했다 I was afraid[was in fear] of being found out. // 나는 경기의 처음부터 끝까지 조마조마했다 The game kept me in suspense from start to finish. // 그녀는 무대의 막 뒤에서 조마조마한 마음으로 딸의 연기를 지켜보고 있었다 She was watching her daughter's performance with bated breath from behind the curtain.

조막 ¶~만 하다 be about the size of a fist / be of a fist size / be very small.

조막손 a claw hand; a clubhand.
● **조막손이** a claw-handed person.

조만간(早晚間) sooner or later; (at) some time or other; in (the course of) time; by and by; in the near future. ¶내각은 ~ 총사직하게 될 것이다 The general resignation of the Cabinet is only a question of time. // ~ 알게 될 거다 Wait and see. / Time will show[tell]. / You shall see. // 교육 제도는 ~ 개선되게 되어 있다 The educational system is to be revised one of these days[sooner or later]. // 이 집은 ~ 철거될 것이다 This house will be pulled down in due course.

조망(眺望) a view; a prospect; a lookout; an outlook. ¶~이 좋은 곳 a place commanding [with] a fine view (of) // ~이 좋은 호텔 a hotel with a fine view // **~이 좋다** have a fine view[prospect] // 언덕 위의 저 집은 ~이 좋다 That house on the hill commands a fine view. // 나무숲이 ~을 가린다 The cluster of trees shuts out the prospect. // 이 호텔에서는 호수의 ~이 훌륭하다 This hotel commands [has] a fine view of the lake. // 그 언덕 꼭대기에서의 ~은 대단하다 The view[(문어) prospect] from the hilltop is splendid. **조망하다** take a view of; have a distant view of.

조망(鳥網) a fowling[bird / fowler's] net.

조명(照明) illumination; lighting(무대의). ¶무대 ~ stage lighting // 직접 [간접] ~ direct [indirect] illumination // ~이 잘된[잘 안 된] well-[ill-] lit // **~이 불충분하다** be poorly illuminated // 건물을 밝은 ~을 비추다 illuminate[light up] a building brightly // 남에게 국부[집중] ~을 비추다 spotlight[turn a spotlight on] a person // 무대 전체에 푸른 ~을 비추다 flood the stage with blue light // 이 방은 ~이 좋다[나쁘다] This room is well[poorly] lighted.
● **조명 기구** an illuminator; (집합적) lighting apparatus; (프) luminaire. **조명등** (street / tunnel) lighting. **조명탄** a flare (bomb); a light bomb; a star shell.

조명(嘲名) ¶**~이 나다** get[have] a bad reputation / have an ill name / be notorious (for).

조모(祖母) a grandmother. ⇨할머니1

조목(條目) a head(ing); an item. ⇨항목

조목조목(條目條目) item by item; in items.

조몰락거리다 work and press with the hands. ⇨주물럭거리다

조무래기 1 [자질구레한 물건] small articles; petty goods; sundries; odds and ends. 2 [어린아이] small children; little kids; small fry.

조문(弔文) a funeral[memorial] address; a letter of condolence.

조문(弔問) [상주를 위문함] a call of condolence; a condolatory call. ¶**~을 받다** receive callers for condolence / receive callers who (have) come to express their sympathy. **조문하다** make a call of condolence[sympathy]; make a condolatory call.
● **조문객** a caller for condolence; a condolence caller; a condoler.

조문(條文) [본문] the text (of the regulation / of a law); the letter (of the statute); [조항] a provision. ¶저작권법의 ~ the provisions of the Copyright Law // 조약의 ~ the provisions of a treaty // 헌법의 ~ the provisions of the Constitution // **~에 있는 바와 같이** as stipulated in the text // **~에 명기되어 있다** be expressly stated in the provisions (of the statute).

조물주(造物主) the Creator (of the Universe); the Maker; the Great Artificer[Architect]; God.

조미(調味) seasoning; flavoring. **조미하다** season; flavor; spice; give flavor to. ¶소금으로 ~ season with salt.
● **조미료** a seasoning; a flavoring; (집합적) spice. ¶화학~ a synthetic flavoring matter.

조밀하다(稠密-) dense; crowded; thick; populous; close. ¶인구가 조밀한 나라[지방]

densely[thickly] populated country[district] // 이 나라는 인구가 ~ This country is densely populated. // 그 부근에는 인가가 ~ Houses are closely crowded in that neighborhood.

조바꿈(調-) [음] modulation; a change of key. **조바꿈하다** modulate; change keys.

조바심 [마음 졸임] fidgets; fret; uneasiness; nervousness. ¶~ 나게 하다 worry / fret (a person's) heart / keep[hold] (a person) in suspense // 그녀가 무사하였다는 것을 알기까지 몹시 ~이 났다 I had a very anxious time until I knew that she was safe. **조바심하다** worry (oneself); be anxious[nervous] (about); bother (oneself) (about); fidget [jitter] (about). ¶(남이) 돌아오기를 조바심하며 기다리다 wait in anxious suspense for (a person's) arrival.

조바위 [여자 방한모] a women's winter hat (with earflaps).

조반(朝飯) breakfast. ⇨아침밥(⇨아침) ¶~을 먹다 eat[take] breakfast / eat[have] one's breakfast // ~으로는 토스트와 과일을 먹습니다 I have toast and fruit for breakfast. // 나는 다섯 시에 벌써 ~을 먹고 있었다 I was already at breakfast at five.

조발(調髮) [머리를 땋음] plaiting hair; [이발] a hair cut; hairdressing. **조발하다** [땋다] plait[braid] one's hair; make one's hair into a plait; [이발하다] have a haircut.

조발성 치매(早發性癡呆) schizophrenia. ⇨정신 분열증(⇨정신(精神))

조밥 boiled millet; boiled rice with millet.

조방농업(粗放農業) extensive agriculture [farming].

조변석개(朝變夕改) changefulness; changeableness; inconstancy; fickleness; capriciousness. **조변석개하다** change constantly; take an unsettled course of action; be full of whims; be fickle[instant / capricious].

조병창(造兵廠) an arms factory; an arsenal; (미) an armory.

조복(朝服) a court suit; a (full) court dress.

조부(祖父) a grandfather. ⇨할아버지₁ ¶증~ a great-grandfather // ~의 [다운] grandfatherly.

조부모(祖父母) grandparents. ¶~의 grandparental.

조붓하다 [서술적] be somewhat[rather] narrow; be a bit narrow; be on the narrow side.

조비(祖妣) one's deceased grandmother.

조사(弔詞·弔辭) [죽음의 슬픔을 나타낸 글] words[a letter] of condolence; [장례식에서의] a memorial[funeral] address. ¶~를 하다 express one's condolence / [연설을 하다] make a memorial address.

조사(早死) a premature[an untimely / an early] death. **조사하다** die young; die an early[a premature] death; die at an early age; die before one's time.

조사(助詞) [언] a postpositional word functioning as an auxiliary to a main word; a postposition.

조사(助辭) [언] a particle (in classical Chinese). ⇨어조사

조사(照查) [대조하여 조사함] (an) examination by reference (to); a check (up); verification; collation. **조사하다** check; (미) check up (on); examine by reference (to); verify; collate.

조사(照射) irradiation. **조사하다** irradiate. ¶엑스선을 ~ apply X-rays to (a person's neck) / X-ray (a person's chest).

조사(調査) (an) investigation; (an) examination; (an) inquiry; (a) survey. ¶시장 ~ a market research // 현지 ~ an on-the-spot investigation // 당국의 ~에 의하면 according to the investigation made by the authorities // ~ 중이다 be under investigation // ~를 위탁하다 entrust investigation (to) // 그 사건은 지금 ~ 중이다 The case is under investigation. // 사고의 원인은 현재 ~ 중임 The cause of the accident is under investigation. // 그의 배후 관계를 ~ 중이다 We are checking up on his background. // 이 건에 대한 ~는 다 되어 있다 We've already found out all about this matter. / We've finished our investigation of this case. / We know all the facts of this case. // 자세한 ~ 없이 결론을 서둘러서는 안 된다 Don't jump to conclusions without close inquiry. // 그 후의 ~로는 그의 병이 악성이 아니라는 것이 판명되었다 On further examination they found his disease was not malignant. // 회사의 간부들까지 독직 혐의로 ~를 받았다 Even the executives of the company were investigated on suspicion of bribery. // ~ 결과 그것은 단순한 소문으로 판명됐다 Upon investigation it was found to be a mere rumor. **조사하다** investigate; examine (into); inquire [look / search] into; survey; look[go] over. ¶조사하면 보니 inquiry[investigation] // 철저히 ~ make a thorough[an exhaustive] investigation / investigate[examine into] (a matter) thoroughly / probe (a matter) to the bottom // 면밀히 ~ inquire into (a matter) closely // 원인을 ~ investigate the cause / inquire into the cause // 사건을 ~ investigate an affair // 표[어컨]를 ~ check[examine] a ticket[a passport] // 물건을 일일이 ~ look over the articles one by one // 사실을 ~ investigate [look into] the facts (of a case) // …의 가능성을 ~ conduct an inquiry into the possibility of … // (회의의) 장부를 ~ look into the books // 인물을 ~ inquire into[check up on] a person's character // 인구를 ~ take a census // 토지를 ~ survey an area // 남의 신원을 ~ make an investigation of a person's background // 사고 원인을 철저히 ~ make a thorough investigation of[into] the causes of the accident // 그들의 불화의 원인을 ~ look[inquire] into the cause of the dissension between them // 검사는 그 원인을 조사했다 The prosecutor looked into the cause. // 경찰은 그의 신원을 철저히 조사했다 The police made a thorough investigation of his past. // 경찰은 그 살인 사건을 조사했다 The police investigated the murder. // 특별 위원회가 4개월 동안이나 암살 사건을 조사해 오고 있다 A special commission has been probing the assassination for four months. // 나는 그 뜬소문의 근원을 조사했다 I investigated [looked into] the source of the rumor. // 조사한 후에 회답을 드리겠습니다 We will give an answer after due inquiry. // 그 문제는 더 깊이 조사해 볼 필요가 있다 We need to look into the matter more deeply. ➔그의 신원은 철저히 조사되었다 A thorough investigation was made into his background.

● **조사 결과** [판명된 일] findings. ¶위원회는

조산 ~를 발표했다 The committee announced its findings. **조사관** an examiner; an investigator. **조사단** an investigation committee. **조사서** a written investigation. **조사 자료** data for investigation; research data.

조산(早産) a premature birth. **조산하다** (산모가) be prematurely delivered of a child; (아이가) be born prematurely. ¶그녀는 조산하였다 She gave birth prematurely.
● **조산아** a premature (baby); a prematurely-born baby.

조산사(助産師) a midwife.

조삼모사(朝三暮四) 〔어리석음〕 being easily fooled; knowing only one side of the story; 〔간교로 속여 희롱함〕 swindling (a person) by means of a clever trick.

조상(弔喪) 〔조의를 표함〕 condolence; a visit of condolence. **조상하다** condole (with a person on his bereavement); offer one's condolence (to a person on a sad event).

조상(祖上) an ancestor; a forefather; 〔집합적〕 ancestry. ¶인류의 ~ the progenitor of the human race // ~ 대대로 전하여오는 ancestral / hereditary / ~ 대대로 내려오는[전래의] 물건[재산] an heirloom handed down in the family for generations // ~으로부터 전하여오다 descend from ancestors // ~을 숭배하다 worship ancestors // ~의 이름을 욕되게 하다 bring disgrace upon the good name of one's fathers // ~ 전래의 땅을 상속하다 inherit the land passed down from one's ancestors / inherit the ancestral lands.
● **조상굿** 〔민〕 an exorcism for one's ancestors. **조상 숭배** ancestor worship.

조상(彫像) a (carved) statue; 〔집합적〕 statuary. ¶대리석 ~ a statue in marble.

조생종(早生種) 〔농〕 a precocious species.

조서(詔書) (임금의) a Royal edict[rescript].

조서(調書) 〔법〕 a protocol; a written evidence; a record; a report. ¶~의 작성 drawing up of a protocol // ~를 꾸미다 put (a deposition) on record // 경찰은 용의자를 신문하여 ~를 작성했다 The police drew up a report by questioning the suspect.

조석(朝夕) 1 〔때〕 morning and evening. ¶~으로 in the mornings and evenings // [늘] day and night // [늘] day in, day out // 목숨이 ~에 있다 be on the brink[verge] of death // ~으로 식사를 제한하다 cut back on food intake in the morning and evening / diet at breakfast and dinner // 앞으로 2, 3일간은 ~으로 매우 쌀쌀해질 것 같다 For the next two or three days, it will probably be quite chilly in the mornings and evenings. 2 breakfast and supper. ⇨조석반

조석(潮汐) the flowing tide and ebbing tide. ⇨조석수
● **조석수** 〔밀물과 썰물〕 the flowing[rising] tide and ebbing[falling] tide; the tide.

조석반(朝夕飯) breakfast and supper.

조선(造船) shipbuilding. **조선하다** build a ship.
● **조선공** a shipbuilding worker; 〔배 목수〕 a shipwright; a ship[shipbuilding] carpenter. **조선소** a dockyard; a shipbuilding yard; a shipyard. **조선업** the shipbuilding industry.

조성(助成) 〔도와서 이루게 함〕 furtherance; fostering; conducement; aid. **조성하다** 〔도와주다〕 help; aid(▶ 흔히 공적으로); assist(▶ 보조적으로); 〔촉진하다〕 further; foster; promote; conduce[contribute] to (national welfare).
● **조성금** a subsidy; a grant; a bounty; a grant-in-aid.

조성(造成) 〔만들어 이룸〕 creation; preparation (of a housing site). ¶택지 ~ development of building lots / preparation [reclamation] of land for building lots(▶ reclamation은 주로 매립의 경우). **조성하다** create; clear; prepare; reclaim; stabilize. ¶산림을 ~ make a woodland / afforest a mountain // 사회 불안을 ~ create social unrest // 공포 분위기를 ~ produce[create] a terror atmosphere.

조성(組成) 〔짜 맞추거나 만듦〕 composition; constitution; make-up; formation. **조성하다** constitute; make up; form; compose.

조세(租稅) taxes; 〔과세〕 taxation.
● **조세 부담** the burden of taxation; a tax burden. **조세 수입** tax revenues. **조세 징수** the collection of a tax.

조소(彫塑) 〔미〕 〔조형 미술〕 the plastic arts; carving and modeling[〔영〕 modelling]; 〔소상〕 a plastic image; a clay[plaster] figure. ¶~를 만들다 mold[model] a plastic image.

조소(嘲笑) 〔비웃음〕 a derisive[sardonic] smile; a scornful laugh; a gibe; derision; ridicule(▶ 비웃는 일을 포괄적으로); sneer(▶ 일순간 비죽 웃는 일). ¶~거리가 되다 make a laughingstock of oneself // 세인의 ~를 사다 excite the public derision / bring ridicule upon oneself // 그의 실패는 사람들의 ~를 샀다 His blunder incurred people's ridicule [provoked people's derision]. // 그는 전교의 ~의 대상이 되었다 He made himself the laughingstock of the whole school. **조소하다** laugh scornfully [mockingly / derisively] (at); deride; ridicule. ¶조소하여 sneeringly // 그들은 나의 소심을 조소했다 They mocked me for[laughed at] my cowardice. / They ridiculed my cowardice. // 그들은 그 낡은 사고방식을 조소했다 They jeered[scoffed / laughed scornfully] at the old-fashioned idea.

조속히(早速-) immediate(ly); prompt(ly); as soon as possible; at the earliest possible moment; at your earliest convenience. ¶우리는 ~ 회신해야 한다 A prompt answer is required. / We are required to answer immediately[promptly / without delay / at once]. // 그 문제는 ~ 해결할 필요가 있다 The matter should be settled as soon as possible.

조수(助手) 〔일을 보조하는 사람〕 a helper; a help; an assistant. ¶연구 ~ a research assistant // 외과 ~ a surgeon's mate / a surgical assistant // 운전 ~ an assistant driver // 대학의 ~ a tutor.
● **조수석** (자동차 등의) the seat next to the driver.

조수(鳥獸) 〔새와 짐승〕 birds and beasts; fur and feather.
● **조수 보호** wild life conservation. **조수 보호구** a wildlife sanctuary.

조수(潮水) the tide; tidewater. ¶~의 간만 the ebb and flow of the tide // ~가 들어오고 있다 The tide is rising[coming in]. // ~가 차 있다 [빠졌다] It's high[low] tide. // ~가 바뀌고 있다 The tide is turning.

조숙하다(早熟-) mature young[early]; grow [ripen] early; be precocious[premature]. ¶

조숙한 아이 a precocious child.// 그는 나이에 비해서 ~ He is precocious [too wise] for his age. / He has an old head on young shoulders.
조시 (弔詩) 〔애도의 뜻을 실은 시〕 an elegy.
조식 (朝食) breakfast. ⇨아침밥(⇨아침)
조식 (粗食) 〔검소한 음식〕 a plain diet; coarse [simple] food; poor [meager] fare; a frugal meal. ¶~에 익숙해지다 become accustomed to plain fare.// 조식(粗衣)에 만족하다 be content with plain living [a simple life].
조신 (朝臣) a courtier; (집합적) the court.
조신 (操身) carefulness of conduct [behavior]; circumspection. **조신하다**[1] 〔몸가짐을 조심하다〕 be careful of oneself; behave with discretion [caution]; behave discreetly; exercise circumspection.
조신하다[2] (操身−) 〔얌전하다〕 gentle; well-behaved. ¶저 아이는 ~ That child has such a good manners.
조실부모하다 (早失父母−) lose one's parents early in life. ¶그는 조실부모했다 He lost his parents at an early age.
조심 (操心) 〔주의〕 care; carefulness; heed; 〔경계〕 caution; precaution; guard; vigilance; 〔신중〕 prudence; discretion; circumspection. ¶~ precaution against fire / (게시) Watch out for fires! / Fire danger! / Flammable!// ~은 용기의 태반이다 〔군자는 위험한 일에 가까이하지 않는다〕 Discretion is the better part of valor.// 화재만은 일으키지 않도록 온갖 ~을 다했다 I took every precaution (imaginable) against fire. **조심하다** take care (of); be careful [cautious] (of); take precautions (against); beware (of); guard (against); be watchful (against); use prudence; be circumspect. ¶몸가짐에 ~ be careful about one's personal appearance// 불을 ~ be careful with fire// 자동차를 ~ watch [look] out for cars// 말을 ~ be careful of one's language [in what one says] / mind one's language// 언동을 ~ be discreet in word and deed// 앞으로 이런 일이 없도록 조심하겠습니다 I will be careful not to do such a thing again.// 길을 건널 때는 차를 조심해라 Watch [Look] out for cars when you cross a street.// 조심해라 Watch out! / Be careful! / Heads up!// 언제나 부품이 떨어지지 않도록 조심해라 See that we always have parts in stock. 조심해서 다녀오시오 Good-bye! / Have a nice day [trip]. (▶ trip은 여행을 떠나는 사람에게)// 병에 걸리지 않도록 조심해라 Take care not to get sick.// 저 남자에게는 조심해야 한다 You must watch out for [be careful of] that man.// 지나치게 적극적이지 않도록 조심했다 I guarded against becoming too aggressive.// 소매치기에 조심해라 Beware of pickpockets. / Pickpockets operate here.// 발밑을 조심해라 Watch [Mind] your step!// 조심하지 않으면 사고를 일으킨다 If you are not careful [If you let your attention wander], you may cause an accident.// 그 꽃병은 조심해서 다루세요 Please handle the vase carefully [with care].// 자넨 조심하지 않으면 본전마저 잃게 될 것이다 You'll lose the principal, too, if you're not careful.// 우리가 그에게 말을 할 때는 조심해야 한다 We must be diplomatic [careful] when we speak to him.// 말할 때는 조심해라 Be careful when [Think twice before] you speak.// 물을 흘리지 않도록 조심하시오 Take care that you don't spill the water. / Be careful not to spill the water.// 자동차를 조심하시오 Look out for cars. / (미) Watch out for cars.// 그는 건강에 조심하고 있다 He takes care of himself [his health].// 말을 좀 더 조심해서 하시오 Be more careful about your language [in your choice of word].// 한 번 사고를 일으킨 후부터는 나는 조심해서 운전해 왔다 I caused an accident once, and ever since I have driven very carefully [with caution].// 이건 국제회의이니까 제발 말에 조심해 주기 바란다 It's an international conference. Please be careful about what you say.
●**조심성** cautiousness; carefulness; discretion; prudence; circumspection. ¶~이 없는 careless / thoughtless // ~이 많은 thoughtful / careful / scrupulous / cautious / alert / prudent / circumspect // ~ 없는 말을 함부로 하다 speak careless words / make a slip of the tongue // 그는 일에 ~이 없다 He is careless with [over] his work.// 네가 ~이 있었더라면 그런 남자에게 뒤를 밟히지 않았을 것이다 If you hadn't been careless, you wouldn't have been followed by such a man.
조심스럽다 (操心−) cautious; careful. ¶조심스럽게 cautiously / carefully// 그녀는 인형을 종이에 조심스럽게 쌌다 She carefully wrapped the doll in paper.// 그는 만사에 ~ He is conscientious in [careful about] everything.// 그의 대답 [말씨]은 매우 조심스러웠다 He was very guarded [careful] in his answers [speech].// 그들은 조심스럽게 얼음 위를 걸었다 They walked cautiously on the ice.// 나는 계단 하나하나를 조심스럽게 내려갔다 I went down each step (of the staircase) carefully.
조심조심 (操心操心) 〔주뼛주뼛〕 timidly; 〔조심하여〕 gingerly. ¶나는 ~ 창문으로 안을 들여다보았다 Timidly I peeped in through the window.// 나는 ~ 얼음이 언 연못에 내려섰다 Gingerly, I stepped onto the frozen pond.// 어린이는 ~ 상자 안을 들여다보았다 The child looked into the box with fear [hesitatingly].
조아리다 knock (one's forehead) on the floor [ground]; kowtow; give a deep bow (in reverence). ¶머리를 ~ give a deep bow / kowtow.
조아팔다 〔조금씩 팔다〕 sell in small lots (of); break (it) up into small lots to sell.
조악품 (粗惡品) an inferior article; goods of poor quality.
조악하다 (粗惡−) coarse; crude; bad; inferior. ¶조악한 물품 crude [shoddy] goods / goods of inferior quality [make] // 조악한 직물 coarse [rough] cloth.
조야 (朝野) 〔조정과 민간〕 the government and the people; the (whole) nation. ¶~의 명사 men of distinction both in and out of government// ~ 모두 그의 죽음을 애도했다 The whole nation mourned (over) his death.
조야하다 (粗野−) 〔세련되지 못하다〕 crude; 〔예절을 모르다·거칠다〕 rude; 〔난폭하다〕 rough; coarse(ly). ¶조야한 [상스러운] 사람 a vulgar [rude] person(▶ vulgar는 저속하고 상스러움을 뜻하고, rude는 무례하고 예절을 모름을 뜻함)// 조야한 언동을 삼가다 avoid coarse speech [language] and (bad) manners.
조약 (條約) a treaty; a pact; a convention; an

조약돌 a pebble(stone); a small stone; (물가의) a shingle.

조어(祖語) [근원이 되는 언어] a parent language.

조어(釣魚) [물고기를 낚음] angling; fishing (with rod and line). **조어하다** angle; fish.

조어(造語) [신어를 만들기] coinage; [새로 만들어진 언어] a coined word; [임시 대용어] a nonce word. **조어하다** coin a word.

조언(助言) [문어] counsel; a hint; a suggestion. ¶전문가의 ~ professional advice // ~을 구하다 ask advice (of a person) // 나는 민 군에게 ~을 구하러 갔다 I went to Min for advice. // 자네가 내게 ~을 좀 해 주지 않겠나 Will you give me some advice? // 이것은 법률가의 ~을 요청하는 편이 낫겠다 We'd better ask[seek] a lawyer's advice on this. // 오늘날 결혼에 있어서 부모의 ~을 따르는 젊은이는 거의 없다 Nowadays few young people will listen to [follow] their parents' advice about marriage. // 우리가 성공할 것은 당신의 ~ 덕분입니다 Thanks to your advice we were able to succeed. **조언하다** advise; counsel; give (a person) advice[counsel]; suggest. ¶그는 내게 그 시험을 치르라고 조언해 주었다 He advised me to take the examination. // 조언해 주셔서 감사합니다 Thank you for speaking on my behalf.

● **조언자** an adviser[advisor]; a counselor, (영) a counsellor.

조업(操業) [기계를 움직여 일함] operation(s); work. ¶8시간 ~ an eight hour run (of a factory) // 완전 ~ (be in) full operation // ~을 시작[중지]하다 begin[cease] operations // ~을 단축하다 cut back on[curtail] operations. **조업하다** operate; run; work. ¶조업하고 있다 be in operation // 그 공장은 완전 조업하고 있다 The plant is in full operation.

● **조업 개시** a[the] start-up [beginning] of operations. **조업 단축** a[the] short-time [curtailed] operation; reduction[curtailment] of operation[working hours]. **조업 일수** days operated. **조업 중지** a[the] shut-down of operations; a[the] cessation of work.

조역(助役) [도와주는 일] an assistant action; [보좌하는 사람] a supporting role; an assistant stationmaster(역의); a helper. **조역하다** help[assist] (a person).

조연(助演) [남자 조연] a supporting actor; [여자 조연] a supporting actress. **조연하다** assist[support] (the leading actor); play support. ¶그는 최근의 공연에서 조연하였다 He was the supporting actor [played the supporting role] in the recent stage performance.

조영(造營) [집 등을 지음] building; erection; construction. ¶대성당은 현재 ~ 중이다 The cathedral is now under construction. **조영하다** build; erect; construct.

● **조영물** buildings; structures.

조예(造詣) attainments; scholarship. ¶학문에 ~가 깊은 사람 a man of great erudition // 음악에 ~가 깊다 be well versed in music // 그는 습자(붓글씨)에 ~가 깊다 He is accomplished in penmanship. // 그는 한국 문학에 ~가 깊다 He has a profound [deep] knowledge of Korean literature. / He is well versed in Korean literature.

조옮김(調-) [음] (a) transpose; (a) transposition. **조옮김하다** transpose. ¶내림마조에서 라조로 ~ transpose from E flat to D.

조용하다 [잠잠하다] quiet (place); silent (audience); still; [고요하다] calm; placid; tranquil; serene; [격하지 않다] soft; gentle (voice). ¶조용한 밤 a quiet[still] night // 조용한 태도 quiet[calm] manners // 조용한 시골 a tranquil country place // 조용한 바다 a calm[placid] sea // 조용한 음악 soft music // 말소리가 조용한 사람 a quiet-spoken person // 쥐 죽은 듯이 ~ be as silent as death [the grave] // 조용한 생활을 보내다 lead a serene life // 온 집 안이 쥐 죽은 듯이 조용했다 Dead silence reigned throughout the house. // 청중이 쥐 죽은 듯 조용해졌다 A hush fell over the audience. // 집 안은 아주 조용했다 All was still in the house. // 내가 살고 있는 곳은 조용합니다 I live in a quiet neighborhood. **조용히** quietly; silently; still; calmly; softly; gently. ¶~ 하다 keep quiet[still] // 자고 있다 sleep quietly[in peace] // ~ 살다 live in quiet[peace] / lead a quiet life // ~ 이야기하다 speak in a quiet tone[gentle voice] // ~ 걷다 walk slowly[quietly] // ~ 해 Be quiet! / Silence! // ~ 있어 Keep still! // ~ 이야기하자 Let's talk about it calmly. // ~ 제발 ~ Don't get so excited, please. / Calm down! / (구어) Take it easy! // 그 노인은 인적이 드문 숲 속에서 ~ 혼자 살고 있었다 The old man lived a quiet, solitary life in a forest far from any human settlement. // 그들은 그의 말을 ~ 듣고 있었다 They listened to him quietly. // 그녀는 자기 내력을 ~ 이야기했다 She talked quietly about her background. // 그는 ~ 담배를 피우고 있다 He is smoking sedately. // 여기는 사람 눈이 많아서 ~ 이야기할 수도 없다 There are too many eyes around here to have a personal talk.

조우(遭遇) 1 [우연히 만남] an encounter. **조우하다** encounter (the enemy); meet with (an accident). ¶사람은 언제 어떤 운명에 조우할지 모른다 We never know what fate we may encounter[what may be in store for us]. 2 [임금의 신임을 받음]. **조우하다** win royal confidence.

● **조우전** an encounter; an engagement.

조울병(躁鬱病) [의] a manic-depressive insanity[psychosis].

● **조울병 환자** a manic-depressive.

조원(造園) [정원을 만듦] landscape gardening; the art of landscaping. **조원하다** lay out [make] a garden; landscape; do the landscaping.

조위(弔慰) 〔조문과 위문〕 condolence; sympathy. **조위하다** condole with (a person); offer [express] one's condolence(s) to (a person over his bereavement).
● **조위금** condolence money; a monetary token of condolence.

조율(調律) tuning. ¶그 오케스트라는 ~ 중이었다 The orchestra was tuning up. **조율하다** tune (up); key; put (a piano) in tune. ¶이 피아노는 조율해야겠다 This piano needs tuning.
● **조율사** a (piano) tuner.

조음(調音) 〔소리를 고름〕 intonation; modulation; 〔악기의〕 tuning; 〔음〕 a tone; 〔언〕 articulation. **조음하다** tune (a piano); articulate (sound).

조응(照應) 〔서로 일치하게 대응함〕 correspondence; agreement; accordance. **조응하다** agree [accord] (with); correspond (to); be in accordance (with).

조의(弔意) 〔남의 죽음을 슬퍼하는 뜻〕 condolence; mourning; sympathy. ¶~를 표하여 as a mark of respect to the deceased / out of respect for the deceased // 장관은 유족에게 ~를 표했다 The minister offered his condolences [expressed his sympathy] to the bereaved. // 삼가 ~를 표합니다 Please accept my sincere condolence.

조인(調印) 〔서명〕 signing; sealing. **조인하다** ¶조약에 ~ sign a treaty // 협정에 ~ seal an agreement / affix one's seal to an agreement.
● **조인국** a signatory (power). **조인식** a ceremony of signing; a signing ceremony. ¶~을 **거행하다** hold a signing ceremony.

조작(造作) 〔제작〕 making; 〔날조〕 fabrication; invention; concoction; framing up. ¶이건 완전한 ~이다 It is a pure fabrication [mere fake]. **조작하다** 〔제작하다〕 make; manufacture; 〔날조하다〕 make up; fabricate; concoct; invent (a story); fake; forge; 〔미〕 cook up. ¶나는 출장 여비를 조작하여 여자 친구에게 선물을 사 주었다 I juggled [inflated] my traveling expenses and bought my girlfriend a present. →**조작된 이야기** a made-up [an invented] story / a fiction // **조작된 재판** a frame-up trial // **조작된 민의(民意)** falsified will of the people.
● **조작 기사** a fabrication; a fabricated report. ¶~투성이의 신문 newspaper full of inventions.

조작(操作) **1** 〔기계 등의〕 (an) operation; handling; a mechanism; the works. ¶뻐꾸기시계의 ~ the works of a cuckoo clock // 인위적 ~ artificial manipulation // 원격 ~ remote control // 이 기계의 기어 ~은 복잡하다 The working of the gears of this machine is quite complex. // 이 장치는 교묘한 ~으로 작동하고 있다 This device works by an ingenious mechanism. **조작하다** operate [work] (a machine); manipulate (the market); handle. ¶실로 조작하는 인형 a windup [mechanical] doll // 기계를 ~ operate [work] a machine.
2 〔자금 등의〕 manipulation. ¶**금융**[**시장**] ~ money [market] operation / monetary [market] manipulation // 그는 주식 시장의 교묘한 ~으로 큰 부자가 되었다 He made a fortune by clever manipulation of the stock market. **조작하다** manipulate.

조잡하다(粗雜−) coarse; rough; crude; gross. ¶조잡한 계획 a crude scheme // 조잡한 문장 a slipshod style // 조잡한 사고방식 a loose way of thinking // 조잡하게 지은 집 a poorly [carelessly] built house // 조잡하게 놓은 책들 books lying in disarray // 조잡하게 그리다 draw roughly // 조잡하게 만들어져 있다 be roughly made // 조잡한 글을 쓰다 write sloppy prose / write in a slipshod style // 이 제품은 조잡하게 만들어졌다 This article has been sloppily [carelessly] made. // 이것은 조잡한 그림이다 It's a crude [roughly-executed] painting. // 이런 조잡한 계획으로는 성공 못 한다 You won't succeed with such a crude [rough] plan. / You won't succeed with a plan like that / It's full of holes.

조장(助長) 〔도와서 더 자라게 함〕 promotion; furtherance. **조장하다** 〔촉진하다〕 promote; 〔발전시키다〕 encourage; 〔악화시키다〕 aggravate. ¶악폐를 ~ aggravate [promote] evils // 그런 일을 하면 오히려 그들의 악습을 조장하게 된다 That would only prove an incentive to their evil ways. // 그것은 대중의 불만을 조장하는 것이 된다 That will foster discontent among the general public. // 정부는 국내 산업을 조장할 대책을 세웠다 The government took measures to promote domestic industry.

조장(組長) 〔조의 책임자〕 a head; a foreman; a boss.

조전(弔電) 〔조상의 뜻으로 전하는 전보〕 a telegram of condolence [sympathy]; a condolatory telegram. ¶~을 **치다** send a telegram of condolence (to) / telegraph one's condolence // 나는 그에게 ~을 쳤다 I telegraphed him my condolences [sympathy].

조절(調節) regulation; adjustment; control; governing; 〔조정〕 modulation; tuning(악기의); tuning in(라디오의); 〔언〕 articulation. ¶목소리의 ~ the modulation of one's voice // 물가의 ~ the regulation [control] of price // **미가**(米價) ~ the regulation [control] of the price of rice // 남북 회담 ~ 위원회 the South-North Coordinating Committee. **조절하다** regulate (a machine); adjust (prices); control (birth); fix; (음조 등을) modulate (one's voice); tune (a piano); tune in (the radio). ¶의자의 높이를 ~ adjust the height of a chair // 라디오를 ~ [**선국**(選局)] **하다** tune a radio // 밸브를 ~ control a valve // 음량을 ~ adjust the volume // 이 스위치로 방의 온도를 조절하세요 Regulate the temperature of the room with this switch.
● **조절기** a regulator; an adjuster; a governor; a modulator(라디오의). **조절판** 〔공〕 a regulator [control] valve.

조정(朝廷) the (Royal) Court; the government.

조정(漕艇) 〔운동·오락으로 보트를 저음〕 rowing; boating. ¶~**용 보트** a rowboat. **조정하다** row a boat.
● **조정 경기** a boat race; a regatta.

조정(調停) 〔분쟁을 화해시켜 그치게 함〕 mediation; arbitration(▶ 당사자가 선정한 자 또는 법적으로 지정된 자에 의한); intercession; peacemaking. ¶**강제** ~ compulsory arbitration // ~을 **제의하다** offer to mediate // ~**에 나서다** undertake mediation // ~**에 맡기다** refer (a case) to arbitration / submit a dispute for arbitration // ~**에 부치다** resort to mediation / submit (a matter) to arbitration

조정 //~으로 해결하다 settle (a matter) by arbitration// 그 문제는 ~에 부쳐질 것이다 The matter will go to arbitration.// 그들은 ~지를 표결하였다 They voted to suspend negotiations. **조정하다** mediate (between two persons); arbitrate (a case / in a matter / between two); intercede (with B for A); intervene (in a strike); make peace. ¶분쟁을 ~ mediate a quarrel// 양자 사이에서 ~ mediate [arbitrate] between two parties// 쟁의[파업]를 ~ negotiate a dispute [a strike].
● **조정안** a mediation [compromise] plan; an arbitration proposal. **조정자** a mediator; an arbitrator; an intervener; a peacemaker.

조정 (調整) regulation; adjustment; (분쟁 등의) reconciliation; control; coordination; (음조 등의) modulation; tuning. ¶고도 ~ (항공에서) altitude control// 연말 ~ (소득세의) a year-end adjustment// 노사 관계의 ~ labor-management adjustment// 미(微)(라디오·TV) fine tuning// 고장으로 ~ 중 (게시) Out of Order.// 그의 ~으로 일이 잘 진행되었다 Thanks to his mediation the matter went well. **조정하다** (바람직한 상태로 하다) adjust; [일정한 수준·상태로 유지하다] regulate; control; coordinate; fix up; (음조 등) modulate; tune. ¶가격을 ~ adjust price// 텔레비전의 화상을 ~ adjust the picture// 시계를 ~ adjust a watch// 재~ readjust// 그는 기계의 속도를 조정했다 He regulated the speed of the machine.// 의장은 이견을 조정해야 한다 The chairman should iron out differences of opinion.// 그들은 면접을 원했지만 나는 시간을 조정할 수 없었다 They wanted an interview, but I couldn't work it in [work it into my schedule].// 나는 그의 결혼식에 참석할 수 있도록 시간을 조정했다 I arranged [worked] it so I could attend his wedding.
● **조정기** a regulator; (가스의) a governor. **조정실** [라디오·TV] a control room. **조정자** a coordinator.

조제 (調劑) [여러 가지 약을 적절히 조합하여 약제를 만듦] compounding [preparation] of medicines. ¶약의 ~를 잘못하다 compound a medicine in a wrong way. **조제하다** prepare [compound] a medicine; (처방에 따라) fill [make up] a prescription. ¶처방대로 ~ make up [fill] a prescription / dispense a prescription// 약국에서 감기약을 조제했다 I had my prescription for the cold filled in the drugstore. →¶**조제시키다** have the prescription filled.
● **조제법** pharmacy. **조제실** a dispensary. **조제약** a mixture; a preparation.

조조 (早朝) early morning.
● **조조할인 영화** (see) a movie shown at reduced admission fees for (early) morning.

조족지혈 (鳥足之血) a mere smidgen [particle]; (be) practically nothing.

조종 (弔鐘) (애도의) a funeral bell; (sound) a death knell. ¶~이 울리고 있다 Funeral bells are tolling.

조종 (祖宗) the royal ancestors; forefathers of a king.

조종 (操縱) 1 [기계·탈것을 다룸] operation; handling. **조종하다** manage; operate; handle. ¶기계를 ~ operate [handle / work] a machine// 비행기를 ~ pilot [fly] a plane// 배를 ~ steer a ship.
2 [남을 제 식대로 부림] manipulation. **조종하다** maneuver [(영) manoeuvre]; manipulate. ¶막후에서 조종하는 사람 a wirepuller// 여론을 ~ manipulate public opinion// 그녀는 남편을 마음대로 조종할 수 있다 She knows how to maneuver her husband into doing what she wants.// 그가 뒤에서 조종하였다 He pulled the wires [strings] behind the scenes.// 그는 부하를 마음대로 조종했다 He had his men completely under control. / He controlled his men like puppets on strings.// 그는 실업계를 조종하고 있다 He pulls the strings in the business world.// 그녀는 남편을 아주 잘 조종한다 She handles her husband quite well.
● **조종사** a pilot. ¶부~ a copilot. **조종석** a cockpit. **조종자** a manipulator; an operator.

조주 (助奏) [음] an o(b)bligato.

조준 (照準) aiming; (an / one's) aim. ¶상하 ~ laying for elevation// 직접 ~ direct laying //~에 총의 ~을 맞추다 aim a gun at ... //~에 ~을 맞추다 take aim at ... / aim at ... / set one's sight on ... //~이 맞지 않아 그는 표적을 빗맞추었다 His aim was off and he missed his mark.// 그는 올림픽에 ~을 맞추어 연습하고 있다 He is practicing so that he will be in top condition for the Olympics. **조준하다** aim (at); take aim [sight] (at); sight (a target); lay (a gun).
● **조준기** (-器) a sight. **조준선** a line of sight.

조지다 1 [단단히 맞추다] fix tightly; tighten up; screw up. ¶사개를 ~ screw [make / fix] a joint tight. 2 [단속하다] exercise strict control (over); make double-sure; hold (a person) to; bear down on. 3 [호되게 때리다] beat (a person) soundly; [미국 구어] give (a person) a good hiding. 4 〈속〉 spoil; mar. ⇒**망치다**

조직 (組織) 1 [통일체·조성된 것] an organization; [결성하는 일] formation; construction. ¶마약 밀매 ~ a drug-smuggling ring [organization]// 폭력[비밀] ~의 두목 the leader of a gang [secret] organization. **조직하다** organize; form. ¶다시 ~ reorganize// 노동조합을 ~ organize a labor union / organize workers into a union// 새 내각을 ~ form a new cabinet// 협회를 ~ organize a society [an association].
2 [구성] constitution. ¶이 도표는 우리 협회의 ~을 나타낸 것입니다 This diagram shows the structure [makeup / setup] of our association. **조직하다** compose; constitute; set up. →¶이사회는 11명으로 조직되어 있다 The Board of Trustees is composed [made up] of eleven members. / The Board of Trustees consists of eleven members.
3 [계통] a system.
4 [세포의 집단] tissue; texture. ¶세포 ~ cellulation / cellular texture// 신경[근육] ~ nervous [muscular] tissue.
● **조직력** organizing ability; systematizing talent; capacity for organization. ¶그에게는 ~이 있다 He has organizing ability.// 저 조합은 큰 ~을 자랑하고 있다 That union boasts of the strength of its numbers. **조직망** the network of a system. **조직책** a chief organizer. **조직체** an organism; an organic body. **조직 폭력** gangsterism; organized violence. **조직화** systematization. ¶~하다 systematize.

조직적(組織的) systematic. ¶~으로 systematically // ~ 연구 a systematic study // 그의 방식은 ~이다 His way of doing things is methodical. // 그들은 이들 사건을 ~으로 검토하고 있다 They are examining those cases systematically.

조짐(兆朕) 〔길조〕 a good omen; 〔전조〕 an omen; 〔문어〕 a portent; 〔징후〕 symptoms; signs. ¶불길한 ~ a bad omen // 회복의 ~ indications[signs] of recovery // …라니 ~이 나쁘다 〔제수가 없다〕 It is a bad sign that .... / 〔문어〕 It augurs ill (for him) that .... // 그는 ~이 좋은 출발을 보여 주었다 He got off to a good start. // 맨 처음부터 홈런이라니 ~이 좋다 It is a good sign [〔문어〕 augurs well] that he hit a homer at the very beginning. // 옛날 사람은 까마귀가 이상하게 울면 불행의 ~이라고 말했다 The ancients said that when crows cawed in an unusual way it portended a misfortune. // 장사가 잘될 좋은 ~이 보인다 The business has begun to look promising.

조차 〔…도〕 even; 〔게다가〕 besides; in addition. ¶이름~ 못 쓰다 cannot so much as sign one's own name // 그~ 모르고 있다면 아무도 모른다 If even he doesn't know, then nobody does. // 그는 ABC~ 쓸 줄 모른다 He can't even write the alphabet. / He cannot so much as write the alphabet. / 한 방울의 물~ 없다 There is not a drop of water (to be had[found]). // 이렇게 쉬운 한자~ 못 쓰는 대학생이 있다 There are some university students who cannot even write a simple character like this. / Even this simple character is too difficult for some college students. // 선생님~ 그 문제를 풀지 못했다 Even the teacher could not solve the question.

조차(租借) 〔빌림〕 a lease (of territory). ¶~ 기한을 연장하다 extend the lease (for 99 years / from ... to ...). **조차하다** lease; hold (lend) by lease. ¶영국은 99년의 계약으로 이 지역을 조차하고 있었다 England had a 99-year lease on this territory.
● **조차권** a lease; a leasehold. **조차지** leased land; (a) leased territory.

조차(潮差) the range of the tide; tide range.

조차(操車) 〔철도〕 marshaling. **조차하다** marshal (locomotives).
● **조차계** a (train) dispatcher. **조차장** a marshaling yard; a switchyard.

조찬(朝餐) breakfast.
● **조찬 기도회** a breakfast prayer meeting.

조처(措處) a measure; a step; 〔처리〕 management; arrangement; disposal. ¶적절한 ~ a measure suited to the occasion / a proper step[measure] // 강경한 ~를 취하다 take strong measures[action] (against). **조처하다** take a step[measure]; take action; manage; arrange; dispose (of); conduct; settle. ¶잘못 ~ take a wrong step[measure] // 재빨리 ~ take prompt action (on) // 그 일을 적절히 조처해 주시오 Arrange the matter as you think best[fit]. // 조처하겠습니다 I will see to it [make it / fix it] all right. // 어두워지기 전에 일이 끝나도록 조처해 주시오 See (to it) that the work is done before dark. // 내 독단으로는 어느 쪽으로도 조처하기가 어렵습니다 I can't decide it either way on my own responsibility.

조청(造清) grain syrup; glucose.

조촐하다 〔아담하다〕 snug; cozy; neat; 〔단정하다〕 dapper; refined; elegant; tidy; decent; 〔해사하다〕 graceful; fair; handsome. ¶조촐한 가게 a tidy [spiffy] little shop // 조촐한 정원 a tidy little garden // 조촐하고 아담한 집 a cozy [〔영〕 cosy / snug / neat] little house (▶ cozy 는 살기 편한, snug는 조촐하고 아담한, neat 는 깨끗한 느낌). **조촐히** snugly; cosily; neatly; elegantly; decently; fair.

조총(弔銃) a volley of rifles at a funeral service. ¶~을 발사하다 fire a volley for the dead.

조총(鳥銃) a fowling piece; a matchlock; a firelock.

조총련(朝總聯) the pro-Pyeongyang federation of Korean residents in Japan; the pro-north Korean residents' league in Japan; Jochongnyeon.

조충(條蟲) a tapeworm; a taenia (*pl.* ~s, -niae).
● **조충 구제약** a taeniacide; a taeniafuge; a tapeworm remedy.

조치(措置) a measure. ⇨¨조처 ¶보완 ~ (take) complementary measures // 후속 ~ (take) follow-up measures // 오토바이 갱들에 대해 단호한 ~를 취하다 take strong measures[take strong action] against motorcycle gangs // 경찰은 마약의 밀매에 대해 단호한 ~를 취했다 The police cracked down on drug smuggling. // 네가 취한 처음 ~는 잘못되어 있었다 The first step you took[Your very first move] was wrong.

조카 a nephew; a niece. ¶…의 ~ a nephew [niece] to [of] … // ~의 아들 a grandnephew // 처~ a wife's nephew[niece].
● **조카딸** a niece. **조카며느리** a nephew's wife. **조카뻘** the relation of nephew. ¶그는 내 ~이다 He stands to me in the relation of nephew. **조카사위** a niece's husband.

조타(操舵) steering; steerage. **조타하다** steer; helm.
● **조타기** the steering gear. **조타수** a steerman; a quartermaster; a helmsman. **조타실** a pilot house; a steering house; a wheelhouse.

조탁(彫琢) 〔보석 등의〕 carving and polishing; 〔문장의〕 elaboration. **조탁하다** carve and polish; elaborate.

조탄(粗炭) coarse[low-grade] coal.

조퇴(早退) leaving office[school] early. **조퇴하다** leave the class before it is dismissed; leave office earlier than usual. ¶나는 학교를 조퇴하였다 I came home before school was out. // 오늘은 회사를 조퇴하고 치과에 갔다 I left my office early[earlier than usual] and went to the dentist. // 그는 머리가 아파서 학교에서 한 시간 일찍 조퇴했다 He left school an hour earlier than usual because of a headache.

조판(組版) 〔인〕 〔조판함〕 composition; 〔조판판〕 a form; 〔영〕 a forme. ¶~은 아직 해판되지 않았다 The type is not yet distributed. // ~이 잘 안 되었다 The print is badly set up. **조판하다** set up in type; make into a form; compose[set] type. →¶책은 조판되어 있다 The book is in type.

조폐(造幣) coinage; mintage. **조폐하다** mint; stamp coin.

조포(弔砲) a funeral salute. ¶대통령 장례식의

조표 ~가 울렸다 A funeral salute was fired in honor of the late President.

조표(調標) [악보의 표] a key signature.

조합(組合) an association; a society; (근로자의) a union; (동업 조합) a guild. ¶공제~ a benevolent society // 노동~ a labor [trade] union // 산업별~ an industrial [a vertical] union // 생산[소비]~ a producers' [consumers'] co-operative // 신용~ a credit association // 어용~ a company [kept] union // 협동~ a cooperative association [union] / a co-op // ~을 조직하다 organize [form] an association [a union] // ~에 가입하다 join an association [a union] // 소비자~을 조직하다 organize a consumer's cooperative society // ~에 가입시키다 take (a person) into partnership / admit (a person) into the association.
● **조합원** a partner; a syndicate member; a copartner; a union member; a unionist. ¶비~ a nonunion man [worker] / a nonunionist. **조합장** a union president.

조합(調合) 1 seasoning. ⇨ 조미(調味) 2 [섞음] compounding; mixing; preparation. **조합하다** compound; (make up) (a medicine); mix (together); prepare. ¶이것과 저것을 ~ compound this and that // 처방대로 ~ fill a prescription / dispense [make up] a prescription.

조항(條項) articles (and clauses); (계약의) stipulations; clauses; [각항·항목] a provision; terms; an item. ¶계약~ a contract clause // 인수~ the provisions for acceptance // 계약의 제3~ the third clause [article] of the contract // 인권에 관한 헌법상의~ the constitution's provisions on human rights // ~을 변경하다 alter a clause // ~을 삭제하다 erase [eliminate] a clause.

조혈(造血) blood formation; h(a)ematogenesis. ¶~성의 h(a)ematogenous.
● **조혈제** a blood-forming medicine; a h(a)ematic drug.

조형(造形) molding; (영) moulding; modeling; (영) modelling. **조형하다** mo(u)ld; model; shape.
● **조형 예술** / **조형 미술** formative [plastic] arts.

조혼(早婚) an early marriage. **조혼하다** marry young. ¶옛날에는 여자들이 조혼했다 Women used to marry early [(quite) young].

조홍(潮紅) flush (in the face).

조화(弔花) funeral [funerary] flowers; (화환) a funeral wreath. ¶~ 사절 No flowers.

조화(造化) creation; nature; the universe. ¶신의~ work of God / divine work / providence / a miracle / (be done by) the fingers of God // ~의 신 the Creator / the Maker [Great Artificer] (of the Universe).

조화(造花) an artificial [imitation] flower.

조화(調和) harmony; accord; agreement; (a) reconciliation; symphony. ¶음의~ consonance [harmony] of sounds // 신구 사상의~ harmony between the old and new ideas // ~가 안 되다 lack harmony / be at odds [variance] with / be out of keeping [place] with // ~가 잘된 배색이다 The coloring is harmonious. / The colors harmonize well. // 그것은 그 장소의 분위기와 ~가 되지 않았다 It was out of tune with the atmosphere of the place. **조화하다** harmonize (with); be in harmony [keeping] (with); match (with); agree [accord] (with); be harmonious (with); be consonant (with / to); go well (with). ➜ 스웨터와 스커트를 조화시키다 match a sweater and skirt / match a sweater with skirt // 사중창은 잘 조화되어 있었다 [있지 않았다] The quartet(te) harmonized [didn't harmonize] well. // 그녀는 조화된 복장을 갖추고 있다 She is properly dressed.

조회(朝會) a morning gathering. ⇨ 조례(朝禮)

조회(照會) [인적 사항 등을 알아봄] (an) inquiry; a reference. ¶그 건은 ~ 중이오 We are waiting for an answer to our letter requesting information about it. // 그 회사로부터 그에 관한 ~를 받았다 We have received inquiries about him from that firm. **조회하다** refer a matter to a person; ask [(문어) inquire of] (a person about a matter). ¶그 건에 관해서는 사무소로 직접 조회해 주시오 Please apply [refer] directly to the office for information about it.
● **조회처** (신원·신용 등의) a reference.

족 in a row; tearing; (recede) utterly; all during; straight; at a gulp; roughly. ⇨ 죽

족(足) 1 [발] the foot (of a cow) (used for food); trotters(양·돼지 등의); pettitoes(돼지의). 2 a pair. ⇨ 켤레²

족(族) (원소 등의) a group. ¶백금~ the platinum group.

-족(族) 1 [종족] a race; a tribe. ¶고사(高砂)~ the native Formosan tribe [tribesmen]. 2 [종속] a class; a tribe; a race; a set; a lot; a party. ¶히피~ hippies.

족내혼(族內婚) endogamy. ¶~의 endogamous / endogamic.

족대기다 [볶아치다] torment; badger; harass; worry; put the screw(s) on; [우겨 대다] insist; force (one's idea). ¶며느리를 족대기어 내쫓다 torment [tease / worry] a daughter-in-law out of the house // 남을 족대기어 일을 시키다 force a person to work.

족두리 a jokduri; a bride's headpiece (worn at a wedding); a bridal tiara [crown].

족발(足一) [돼지의 발] pettitoes; (pig's) trotters.

족벌(族閥) a clan; a clique.
● **족벌 정치** clan government. **족벌주의** nepotism.

족보(族譜) a jokbo; a genealogy; a pedigree; a genealogical [family] tree; a table of descent. ¶문중의~ a clan genealogy // 집안의~ a family pedigree // ~를 캐다 trace [look into] one's genealogy / genealogize // ~를 만들다 [편찬하다] draw up [compile] a genealogy (of).

족속(族屬) [일가붙이] kinsmen; relatives; a clan; clansmen; [패거리] a party; a set; a lot(무리); fellows. ¶저런~ such (base) fellows.

족쇄(足鎖) leg irons; fetters; shackles; hampers. ¶~를 채우다 fetter / shackle / put (a person) in the stocks / lay (a person) by the heels // 그에게는 ~가 채워져 있었다 He was put in fetters [irons].

족자(簇子) a hanging scroll [picture]; a scroll (picture).

족장(族長) [우두머리] a patriarch; the head of a family; a matriarch(여성). ¶~의 patri-

archal / (여성) matriarchal.

족적(足跡·足迹) a footprint; a footmark; an impression[imprint] of a foot. ¶~을 남기다 leave one's footmarks[an impress] (on one's age).

족제비 [동] (일반적인) a (yellow) weasel; (한국산) a Siberian mink.

족족[1] [하나하나마다] whenever; every time; as often as; whatever time. ¶하는 ~ 실패하다 fail in every attempt[at every step] / 배우는 ~ 잊어버린다 I forget as soon as I learn. // 그 둘은 만나는 ~ 싸움이다 Every time those two meet, there is a quarrel.

족족[2] in rows; in sheets; into shreds; (draw through a clasping hand) briskly. ⇨<죽죽

족집게 (a pair of) tweezers; nippers. ¶~로 뽑다 tweeze (a thorn out of the finger) / pluck (a hair) out with tweezers / use tweezers on (a hair).

족치다 1 [작게 만들다] chop; hack. 2 [결딴내다] destroy; mangle. ¶탁자를 ~ break a table. 3 [몹시 볶아치다] torture severely; (미국 속어) put the squeeze (to a person); (미국 속어) put the screws (on a person).

족탕(足湯) soup made with foot and knuckle (of beef); beef-foot soup.

족편(足−) calf's-hoof jelly[gelatin / agar-agar].

족하다(足−) [충분하다] enough; sufficient; adequate; (서술적) suffice; [충족하다] serve; answer; do. ¶~이라고 말하면 ~ Suffice it to say that .... / 5천 원 정도면 ~ Five thousand won or so will suffice[do]. // 이 한 가지 사실로 그의 성격의 견실함을 증명하기에 ~ This single fact suffices to prove[serves to show] that he is a man of sound character. // 그 방에 대해서 말한다면 단지 호화롭다는 한 마디로 ~ The room is simply gorgeous.

족히 enough; sufficiently; fully; easily; well. ¶~ 볼[읽을] 만하다 be well worth seeing[reading] // 그는 신장이 ~ 6피트는 된다 He stands a full six feet. / He is all of six feet tall. // ~ 1시간은 기다렸다 I waited for a good hour. // 그 극장은 ~ 5천의 관중을 수용할 수 있다 The theater is spacious enough to accommodate more than five thousand audiences. // 그와는 ~ 문학을 논할 만하다 He is well worth talking literature with.

존경(尊敬) respect; esteem; reverence; veneration; deference. ¶그는 ~을 받을 만한 사람이다 He is a man we should all respect[look up to]. / He is an admirable man. // 그 정치가는 민중의 ~을 받았다[잃었다] The statesman earned[lost] the esteem of the public. // 그는 전교생의 ~의 대상이었다 All the students in the school revered[venerated] him. / He was an object of veneration among the students. **존경하다** respect; esteem; revere; honor; venerate; hold (a person) in respect[esteem / veneration]. ¶선생님을 ~ show respect[deference] to one's teachers / be deferential to one's teachers / 나는 어렸을 때 형을 존경했다 As a child I used to look up to my older[(영) elder] brother. // 나는 노인을 존경하도록 교육을 받았다 I was taught to respect[honor] elderly people. // 나는 그녀의 용기를 존경한다 I esteem[admire / respect] her for her courage. →¶그녀는 동네 사람들로부터 존경받고 있었다 She was respected [held in high esteem] by the townspeople. // 그는 하느님처럼 존경받았다 He was revered [looked up to] like a god.

존귀하다(尊貴−) high and noble.

존대(尊待) ¶~를 받다 be held in esteem (by) / be highly thought of (by). **존대하다** treat with respect[politeness]; be polite (to); hold (a person) in esteem.
● **존대어** an honorific (expression / word); a term of respect.

존득거리다 keep sticking.

존 디펜스 zone defense.

존립(存立) existence; subsistence. ¶학교의 ~을 위태롭게 하는 사건이다 The incident threatens the continued existence of the school. **존립하다** exist; subsist.

존망(存亡) life and death; existence; fate; destiny. ¶국가 ~의 위급한 시기에 in this time of national crisis // 이것은 국가의 ~에 관한 일이다 It is a matter of life and [or] death for the nation.

존부(存否) existence and inexistence. ¶생존자의 ~는 분명치 않다 It is not known whether there are survivors or not. // 네스 호의 피물의 ~에 대해서는 여러 가지 설이 있다 There are various views about whether Nessie really exists or not.

존비(尊卑) aristocrats and plebeians; high and low; the upper and the lower classes.
● **존비귀천** high and low. ¶~의 구별 없이 irrespective of rank / without distinction of rank / high and low alike / from palace to hovel.

존속(存續) continuance; continuation; duration; retention. **존속하다** continue (to exist [be]); endure; last. ¶새 제도가 적용된 후에도 수년 동안 구제도가 존속했다 The old system was retained for several years after the new system came into use. →¶존속시키다 continue / maintain / retain / keep up.
● **존속 기간** a term of existence.

존속(尊屬) [법] an ascendant; an ancestor. ¶직계[방계] ~ a lineal[collateral] ascendant.
● **존속 살해** the killing[homicide / murder / manslaughter] of a lineal ascendant.

존안(尊顏) your face. ¶~을 뵈옵다 have the honor[pleasure] of seeing you.

존엄(尊嚴) dignity; majesty; prestige. ¶인간의 ~성 the dignity of man / ~을 손상하다 impair the dignity (of). **존엄하다** dignified; august; venerable.

존영(尊影) your[his] portrait[picture].

존의(尊意) [남의 의견] your opinion[view]; [남의 의사] your will[idea].

존장(尊長) a (venerable) elder; you (sir).

존재(存在) existence; being; subsistence(생존). ¶불쌍한 ~ a wretched being // 그 작품의 ~는 무시되어 있었다 The work was buried in oblivion. // 그는 마침내 ~를 인정받았다 He finally won recognition. // 그는 위대한 ~였다 He was a great man. // 유령의 ~를 정말로 믿고 있습니까 Do you really believe ghosts exist[believe in the existence of ghosts]? **존재하다** exist; subsist; be in existence[being]; [잔존하다] subsist; remain; be extant. ¶존재하지 않는 nonexistent // 지구가 존재하는 한 as long as the earth exists // 함께 ~ coexist (with something else).
● **존재론** ontology. **존재 이유** one's reason for being[living(사람의 경우)]; (프) raison d'être.

존중(尊重) respect; esteem; deference. ¶인권의 ~ respect for human rights. **존중하다** respect; esteem; hold (a person) in respect [esteem]; hold (a matter) in great account [honor]; value; prize; set much value on; [진지하게 고려하다] pay serious attention (to); give (a matter) serious consideration. ¶여론을 ~ pay regard to public opinion // 사생활을 ~ respect[have respect for] (a person's) privacy // 나는 돈보다 청빈을 존중한다 I value honest poverty above money. // 젊은 사람들은 부모가 존중하는 가치를 무시하는 경향이 있다 Young people tend to disregard the values that are important to their parents. // 메이커는 좀 더 소비자의 의견을 존중해야 한다 Manufacturers should pay more attention to the opinions of consumers. // 충고는 존중하겠습니다 We value[(문어) esteem] your advice.

존체(尊體) your health.

존치(存置) maintenance (of a system). **존치하다** maintain.

존칭(尊稱) an honorific title. ¶그는 「전하」의 ~으로 불리고 있다 He is called by the honorific title of "Your Highness."

존폐(存廢) maintenance[continuation] or abolition. ¶~ 문제 the question of maintenance or abolition (of the institution) // 그 제도의 ~를 재고할 때가 되었다 It is now time to reconsider whether to continue the system or abolish it.

존필(尊筆) your writing[hand].

존한(尊翰) your letter[favor].

존함(尊銜) your name. ¶~은 많이 들었습니다 I have often heard of[about] you.

존형(尊兄) you sir.

졸 [화] a sol; a colloidal solution.

졸(卒) [장기] a pawn. ¶~을 잡다[때리다] take[place] a pawn.

졸개(卒-) a servant; an attendant; a retainer.

졸고(拙稿) unworthy manuscript of mine; my (humble) manuscript.

졸공(拙工) a clumsy[an awkward] workman.

졸깃졸깃하다 gummy; rubbery; tough; chewy; sticky. ¶졸깃졸깃한 맛이 없는 떡 rice cake without much chewiness // 이 떡은 ~ This rice cake is chewy. / This rice cake has a chewy texture.

졸년(卒年) [죽은 해] the year of (a person's) death. ¶~월일 the date of (a person's) death.

졸다[1] (졸려서) doze; nap (in one's seat); drowse; snooze; slumber. ¶기차 안에서 ~ fall asleep on the train // 졸면서 운전하다 fall asleep at the wheel / drift[doze] off while one is driving // 나는 깜빡 졸았다 I was dozing off. // 오후의 수업에서 학생들은 꾸벅꾸벅 졸기 시작했다 The pupils started to nod during the afternoon class. // 꾸벅꾸벅 졸고 있었는데 그녀가 깨웠다 I was dozing off, when she awakened me.

졸다[2] (끓어서) get boiled down; be boiled dry; boil[simmer] down.

졸도(卒倒) a faint; a swoon; a fainting fit. **졸도하다** fall down in a swoon; fall into a swoon; fall in a dead faint; (속어) keel over. ¶그는 출혈 과다[공포]로 졸도했다 He fainted from loss of blood[fear]. // 그들은 더위 때문에 졸도했다 They passed out because of the heat. // 그녀는 허기져 길바닥에서 졸도했다 Faint with hunger, she collapsed by the roadside.

졸때기 1 [규모가 작은 일] a petty job; being petty. ¶~ 장사 small trade. 2 [지위가 변변하지 못한 사람] a petty[an unimportant] person; (집합적) small fry. ¶~ 공무원 a petty official.

졸라매다 fasten tight(ly); bind; tie; lace (up); brace; draw. ¶허리띠를 ~ draw a belt tighter / tighten one's belt // 구두끈을 ~ lace (up) one's boots // 끈으로 허리를 ~ lace one's waist in // 그녀는 몸을 너무 졸라맸다 She is too tightened.

졸래졸래 flippantly; forwardly; pertly; frivolously. ¶꼬마는 ~ 엄마 뒤를 따라갔다 The child trotted along after his mother.

졸렬하다(拙劣-) clumsy; awkward; bungling; unskillful; inexpert; poor. ¶졸렬한 작품 a poor[rubbish] work // 그것은 외교상 졸렬한 방식이었다 It is diplomatically an unwise measure.

졸론(拙論) 1 (졸렬한) a poor opinion[view]; a clumsy argument. 2 (자기의) my (humble) opinion[view]; my argument.

졸리다[1] [잠이 오다] become[fell / get] sleepy [drowsy]; have a sleepy spell; (구어) gather [pick] straws. ¶졸린 눈 drowsy eyes // 자넨 졸린 얼굴이군 You look sleepy. // 그의 강의는 아주 지루해서 모두 졸리게 한다 His lectures are utterly dull and boring[put everyone to sleep]. // 졸려 죽겠다 I suffer from sleepiness.

졸리다[2] 1 [조름을 당하다] be badgered; get pestered; get teased[pressed / importuned]; be solicited[entreated / urged]. 2 [단단하게 매이다] be[get] tightened; be fastened tight. ¶끈으로 목이 졸린 시체 the body of a person who was strangled with a cord // 목이 졸려 죽다 be strangled[throttled].

졸막졸막하다 of various sizes; various[irregular / uneven] in size. ¶졸막졸막한 집들 houses of various sizes / a cluster of irregular houses.

졸망졸망 1 [울퉁불퉁] unevenly; roughly; bumpily. **졸망졸망하다** uneven; rough; bumpy. 2 [옹기종기]. **졸망졸망하다** small and irregular in size. ¶졸망졸망한 아이들 a bunch of children of all sizes.

졸문(拙文) 1 [서툰 글] poor writing; a poor composition; a poor[bad] style of writing. 2 [자기 글] my writing[composition].

졸병(卒兵) a common soldier; a private; a soldier of the lowest rank. ¶~들 the ranks / the rank and file.

졸부(猝富) an upstart. ⇨벼락부자(⇨벼락).

졸사(猝死) a sudden death. **졸사하다** die suddenly; (구어) pop off (unexpectedly).

졸사간에(猝私間-) in a moment[an instant].

졸서(卒逝) passing (away); dying; decease. **졸서하다** pass away; depart this life; decease.

졸속(拙速) ¶~의 rough-and-ready / hasty // ~으로 일을 처리하다 handle a matter with more haste than caution.

●**졸속주의** a rough-and-ready[helter-skelter] method; a speed-before-quality policy. ¶그들은 ~로 그 일을 끝마쳤다 They rushed through that job just to get it done[without enough attention to quality].

졸아들다 (끓어서) be boiled down[dry]; boil

down. ¶수프가 졸아들었다 The soup has boiled down.
졸아붙다 be boiled dry; boil down to nothing.
졸업(卒業) graduation; completion of a course (of study). ¶~ 전[후] before[after] graduation / before[after] leaving school. **졸업하다** graduate (from); finish(finish은 초등학교, 중학교, 고교 등에 쓸 수 있음. graduate from은 (미)에서는 초등학교·중학교 이외의 학교에 쓰지만, (영)에서는 대학만 씀); complete the whole course (of a school) ; pass through (a school). ¶우등으로 ~ graduate with honors // 1등으로 ~ graduate first in one's class [on the list] (in high school) // 그는 하바드 대학을 졸업했다 He graduated from Harvard. // 언제 고교를 졸업했습니까 When did you finish [graduate from] high school? // 내가 너보다 먼저 졸업했다 I graduated from school earlier than you.
● **졸업 논문** a graduation essay [thesis (pl. -ses)]. **졸업반** (students of) the graduating class. **졸업생** a graduate; (미) (남자) an alumnus (pl. -ni); (여자) an alumna (pl. -nae). ¶~ 명부 a list of graduates / 천 명의 ~을 내다 turn out 1,000 boys [girls] // 2002년도의 서울 대학교 ~ a graduate of Seoul National University, in the class of 2002. **졸업 시험** a graduation examination. **졸업식** a graduation ceremony; (미) a commencement. ¶~ 날 the graduation day / (미) the commencement day / (영) the speech day // ~을 거행하다 hold the graduation ceremony [commencement exercises]. **졸업장** a diploma; a graduation certificate.(▶ diploma 는 (미)의 주로 고교·대학의 졸업장, (영)에서는 전반적으로 씀. graduation certificate는 (미)에서는 고교·대학 이외의 학교에, (영)에서는 대학에만 씀)
졸음 drowsiness; sleepiness. ¶~이 오는 눈 heavy[sleepy] eyes // ~이 오는 봄날 a drowsy[(영) somnolent] spring day // 점차로 ~이 나를 엄습했다 I was gradually overcome with drowsiness. // 나는 몹시 ~이 왔다 I became very sleepy. // 그는 눈을 비벼 ~을 쫓았다 He wiped[rubbed] the sleep out of his eyes. // 나는 ~을 쫓기 위해 홍차 한 잔을 마셨다 I had a cup of tea to keep myself awake.
졸이다 1 (끓여서) boil down; boil (salt) dry; condense (milk). ¶간장에 ~ boil (fish, vegetables, etc.) hard with soy // 과일즙을 바짝 졸이면 시럽이 된다 The fruit juice may be boiled down into a syrup.
2 (마음을) worry (oneself); feel anxious [uneasy / nervous]. ¶마음을 ~ worry (oneself) (about) / be anxious (about) / (불안하게) feel nervous [timid / uneasy] / be afraid (of) // 마음을 졸이게 하다 bother / worry / fidget / [불안한 마음을 갖게 하다] keep [hold] (a person) in suspense // 돌아올 기를 마음 졸이며 기다린다 wait in anxious suspense for (a person's) return // 그녀는 아들의 비행에 가슴을 졸이고 있다 She is grieved over her son's misconduct.
졸자(拙者) 1 [나의 겸사말] I. 2 [용렬한 사람] a stupid [foolish] fellow.
졸작(拙作) 1 [서투른 작품] a poor work. 2 [자기 작품에 대한 겸양어] my (humble) work.
졸장부(拙丈夫) a small-minded man; a petty little fellow; an unmanly man; a sissy; a mouse.
졸저(拙著) 1 [졸렬한 저작물] a poor composition; a poor book [work]. 2 [자기 저작의 겸손한 말] my (humble) work.
졸졸 1 [흐르는 모양] (flow) ceaselessly in a stream; in streams; profusely; running; gurgling; murmuring; purling; babbling. ¶시냇물이 ~ 흐르고 있다 The brook is flowing with a murmuring sound. 2 [따라다니는 모양] (follow a person) closely and persistently; tagging; tailing. ¶~ 따라다니다 tag after (a person's) heels / tail after.
졸지에(猝地-) [갑자기] abruptly; suddenly; on a sudden; all of a sudden; unexpectedly; all at once. ¶~ 사고를 당하다 have an accident all of a sudden / ~ 당하는 일이라 당황했다 I was perturbed, for it was all too sudden.
졸책(拙策) 1 [서투른 꾀] an inadequate [unsatisfactory] policy; an awkward [a clumsy] step [measure]. 2 [자기 방책을 겸손히 이르는 말] my (modest) plan.
졸필(拙筆) 1 [악필] poor (hand)writing; a poor [bad] hand; [글씨를 잘 쓰지 못하는 사람] a poor [bad] penman; a poor writer. 2 [자기 글씨를 겸손히 이르는 말] my (humble) handwriting.
졸하다(拙-) 1 [서투르다] unskillful; poor; clumsy; inexpert; bungling; awkward; inapt. ¶글씨가 ~ write a poor hand. 2 [옹졸하다] narrow-minded; petty; illiberal; mean. ¶졸한 사람 a narrow-minded person.
좀¹ [동] a moth; a clothes [fish] moth; a bristletail; a bookworm; a silverfish. ¶~이 먹은 책 a moth-eaten book / 모직물에 ~ 방지 가공을 하다 mothproof woolen material [clothing]
좀이 쑤시다 be itching (to do); have [get] itchy feet; have ants in one's pants. ¶그 소식을 모두에게 알리고 싶어서 좀이 쑤셨다 I was itching to tell everybody the news.
좀² 1 a small quantity; a small number; something; a moment; a little way. ⇨조금 ¶~ 아는 사이 a slender [slight] acquaintance // 상체를 ~ 앞으로 굽히고 bending slightly forward // 상점에서 물건을 ~ 사다 make a small purchase at [in] a store // 환자는 오늘 ~ 나아진 것 같다 The patient seems to be a little [slightly] better today. // 어딘지 ~ 다르다 There certainly is some difference, though indescribable (between the two). // 자네와 ~ 이야기할 것이 있네 I want to have a word with you. // ~ 궁금한 것이 있어 물어봅니다 I'm asking just to make sure. // ~ 부탁할 것이 있습니다 I want to ask you a little favor. // (좌석 등을) ~ 좁혀 앉아 주실까요 Will you please move up a little and make room for me? // 그건 ~ 재미있군 It's kind of interesting, isn't it? // ~ 더 큰 소리로 말해라 Speak a little louder. // ~ 더 드시지요 Won't you have some more? // ~ 더 기다려 주십시오 Kindly wait a little longer. // ~ 더 걷자 Let's do more walking.
2 [제발] kindly; (if you) please; pray; I beg; [꼭] by all means. ¶문 ~ 닫아 주세요 May I trouble you to shut the door? / I will thank you to shut the door. // 확답을 ~ 주십시오 Please give us a definite answer.
3 [그 얼마나] how; what; how much [many]. ¶세계 일주를 할 수 있으면 ~ 좋을까 How I

좀- petty; small. ¶~놈 a petty fellow / ~생원 a narrow-minded person / a petty poltroon.

좀것 a petty person[thing]; small things; (집합적) small fry.

좀꾀 little[shallow / cheap] tricks; petty wiles. ¶~를 부리다 play cheap tricks / resort to petty wiles // ~가 많다 be full of little tricks.

좀노릇 a petty job; trifling work; a chore.

좀도둑 a sneak thief; a petty thief; (구어) a sneak; a pilferer; a filcher; (미국 속어) a porch climber. ¶집을 비운 사이에 ~이 들었다 We had our house robbed in our absence. / Our house was robbed while we were away.
● **좀도둑질** petty larceny; pilfering; filching. ¶~을 하다 pilfer / filch / (구어) sneak.

좀먹다 be worm-[moth-]eaten; be eaten by worms; [먹어 들어가다] eat in; gnaw at (one's life); [해를 입히다] spoil; ruin; undermine. ¶좀먹은 스웨터[책] a moth-eaten sweater[book] // 마음을 좀먹는 근심 a gnawing anxiety // 동심을 ~ destroy the innocence of a child's mind // 부정부패가 나라를 좀먹고 있다 Corruption is eating [gnawing] at our country.

좀생원 (一生員) a narrow-minded person; a petty poltroon.

좀생이 1 [묘성] the Pleiades. 2 [좀것] small [petty] things.

좀스럽다 1 [성질이 옹졸하고 잘다] small-minded; petty. ¶좀스러운 사람 a petty person // 좀스럽게 굴다 be too meticulous // 남자는 좀스러우면 못쓴다 A man should not trouble himself with small matters. 2 [규모가 작다] small; petty; minor; trifling. ¶좀스러운 일[사물] a trifling matter // 좀스러운 직업 a petty job.

좀약 (一藥) a mothball.

좀처럼 [여간해서는] seldom; rarely; hardly; scarcely; [쉽사리] (not) easily; (not) readily. ¶~ 성내지 않다 be slow to take offense // ~ 안 열린다 The door will not open. // 그는 ~ 그곳에 가지 않는다 He hardly[scarcely] ever goes there. // 그는 일요일에 ~ 집에 없다 He is seldom at home on sunday. // 그것은 ~ 얻기 어려운 기회다 It is a rare chance. / (일생 단 한 번의) It is the chance of a lifetime. // 그런 사람은 ~ 없다 He is one in a thousand. // 그는 ~ 승낙하지 않을 걸세 I don't think he will give a ready consent. // 나는 ~ 남에게 속지 않는다 I am not easily fooled.

좀팽이 1 [몸집이 작고 좀스러운 사람] a petty short person; a small-minded person. 2 [보잘것없는 물건] a petty[small] thing; a thing too small to be worth looking at.

좁다 [폭이 작다] narrow; [면적이 작다] small; [범위가 작다] limited; [옹색하다] close; tight. ¶좁은 길 a narrow path[lane] // 좁은 방[정원] a small room[garden] // 좁은 틈 a narrow opening // 좁은 문 a narrow gate / [성] a strait gate // 좁은 활동 무대 a limited sphere of activity // 좁은 소견 a small [narrow] mind // 시야가 좁은 shortsighted / nearsighted / (a person) of narrow[limited] views // 소견이 ~ be narrow-minded / be narrow in one's opinion // 교제 범위가 ~ have a small circle of friends // 이 옷은 겨드랑이가 ~ This coat is tight under the arm. // 가구가 많아서 방이 ~ The room is crowded with furniture and we are cramped for room. // 그는 시야가 ~ He takes a narrow view of things. // 한국은 땅이 좁은 데 비해 인구가 많다 Korea has a large population in its limited area. // 이 대학교의 입시는 좁은 문이다 Only a few can pass the entrance examination of this college. / It is most difficult to be admitted to this college.

좁다랗다 narrow and close; narrowish; somewhat[rather] narrow; (서술적) be a little too narrow.

좁쌀 [조] hulled millet; [비유] a tiny[petty] thing.
● **좁쌀뱅이** a petty person. **좁쌀영감** a petty old man.

좁쌀풀 [식] 1 (취란화과의) a loosestrife. 2 (현삼과의) an eyebright.

좁아지다 become[get] narrow; narrow. ¶끝으로 갈수록 ~ narrow toward the end / taper (off) // 그 도로의 너비는 여기서 좁아진다 The road narrows[gets narrow] here. // 그 계곡은 올라갈수록 좁아진다 The valley contracts as one goes up it. // 식구가 불어나서 집이 좁아졌다 Our family has outgrown our house.

좁히다 [넓이·범위를] narrow; make narrow; straiten; reduce (the width); (사이를) close; compact. ¶행간을 ~ crowd the lines // 열과 열 사이를 ~ [군] close the ranks (of troops) // 좁혀 앉다 sit close[closely] // 좀 (자리를) 좁혀 주세요 Please crush up a little. // 선두의 두 주자 사이가 좁혀지고 있다 The gap between the front runners is narrowing. // 문제를 한 가지 범위로 좁혀서 생각해 보자 Let's limit ourselves to a consideration of[Let's focus on] just one phase of the problem.

종¹ (宗) [마늘 등의 꽃줄기] (the end of) a stalk (of garlic).

종² [노비] a slave; a servant. ¶여 [계집] ~ a slave girl / a female slave // ~같이 부리다 put (a person) to a practical slave labor / use (a person) like a slave // ~같이 일하다 work like a slave / drudge // ~으로 삼다 enslave / make a slave (of) // ~으로 팔리다 be sold for a slave.

종 (宗) [종파] a (religious) domination[sect]. ¶천태 ~ Cheontae sect (of Buddhism).

종 (種) 1 a kind; a sort. ⇒ °종류 ¶여러 ~의 every variety[sort] of ... // 이 형의 것은 세 ~이 있습니다 This model is available in three sizes. 2 [생] a species (단수·복수 동형). ¶~의 기원 (저서명) the origin of species. 3 [종자] a seed; a grain; [품종] a breed; a stock. ¶잡~ hybrid / crossbred // 몽고~의 말 a horse of Mongolian breed.

종 (縱) length; height. ⇒ °세로

종 (鐘) a bell. ¶(학교에서의) 예비~ the first bell / the warning bell // 하학(下學)을 알리는 ~ the closing bell // 시간을 알리는 ~ the time bell // ~ 치는 사람 a bell ringer // ~을 치다 strike[toll] a bell // ~을 울리다 ring [toll] a bell // ~을 달다 put a bell (on) // ~이 울린다 A bell tolls[rings]. // 교회의 ~이 11시를 알렸다 The church bell rang out eleven.

종-(從) [존수]. ¶~형 one's(elder) cousin // ~형제[자매] cousins.

종가(宗家) 〔문중의 큰집〕 the head family[house]. ¶그의 집은 민씨 집안의 ~이다 His family is the main branch of the Min family.
종가(終價) 〔증권〕 a closing price[quotation]. ¶~가 2만 원이 되었다 (주식 시장에서) The stock market has closed at 20,000 won.
종가래 a small spade.
종가세(從價稅) an ad valorem duty.
종각(鐘閣) a pavilion for a bell.
종간(終刊) cessation of publication. ¶이 잡지는 이번 호로 ~됩니다 With this issue, this magazine will cease publication.
종견(種犬) a breeding-dog.
종결(終結) (a) conclusion; (a) termination; an end; a close. ¶전쟁의 ~ the end of the war // 토론의 ~ the conclusion of a discussion. **종결하다** end; close; terminate; be concluded; come[be brought] to a close [an end]. ¶토의를 종결하고 표결에 부칠 것을 제의합니다 I move that we close the debate and put this to a vote. ➔¶**종결시키다** conclude / close / terminate / put an end (to) / bring to a conclusion // 전쟁을 종결시키다 bring the war to a conclusion[an end] // (의회에서) 토론을 종결시키다 invoke closure [(미) cloture] // 마침내 양국 간의 분쟁은 종결되었다 The dispute between the two countries finally come to an end.
종곡(終曲) 〔음〕 the finale.
종관(縱貫) traversing; running[penetrating] lengthwise. **종관하다** run[run through / penetrate] lengthwise; traverse (a desert) (from one end to the other).
종교(宗敎) (a) religion. ¶기성 ~ established[existing] religions // 민족 ~ the religion of a people // 자연[계시] ~ natural[revealed] religion // ~적인[상의] religious / spiritual // ~적 감정 religious feeling // 비(非)~적(인) nonreligious // ~를 믿다 believe in a religion / profess[embrace] a religion // ~를 버리다 abjure[renounce] one's religion // ~를 박해하다 persecute a religion // ~를 금하다 ban[proscribe] a religion // 신앙하는 ~가 없다 profess no religion // ~에(서) 위안을 찾다 seek solace[consolation] in religion // 그는 ~를 버렸다 He gave up[abandoned] his faith. // 무슨 ~를 믿으십니까 What religion do you profess?
● **종교가** a man of religion; a religionist; a religious man. **종교 개혁** religious reformation; 〔역〕 the Reformation. **종교계** the religious world; religious circles. **종교 단체** a religious body[organization]. **종교 문제** a religious question[problem]. **종교 음악** sacred music. **종교인** a believer. **종교 재판** the Inquisition.
종국(終局) 〔끝장〕 an end; a close; a conclusion; a termination; a denouement; a finale. ¶~의 final / ultimate / eventual // ~에 가서는 after all / ultimately / in the long run // ~에 가까워지다 draw to a close[an end] // ~을 고(告)하다 come[be brought] to an end[a close / a conclusion] / be concluded // 전쟁은 ~에 가까워졌다 The war drew to a close[an end].
종군(從軍) service in a war. ¶~을 지원하다 petition[apply] for a permission to go to war // ~ 중이다 be at the front / be in the field. **종군하다** follow[join] the army; go to the front; serve in the war. ¶그는 제2차 세계 대전에 종군했다 He served[saw active service] in the world war Ⅱ.
● **종군 기자[기장]** a war correspondent [medal].
종극(終極) the extreme; the final; the ultimate. ¶~의 ultimate / final / extreme // 인생의 ~의 목적 the ultimate purpose[object] of[in] life.
종기(終期) the closing days[period]; the end; the close.
종기(腫氣) a swelling; a boil; a tumor; an abscess. ¶악성 ~ a malignant tumor // 좀체로 가라앉지 않는 ~ an obstinate swelling // ~를 삭히는 약 a resolvent / a resolutive // ~가 나다 have a boil (on) / ~가 났다 A boil has formed on my back. / I have got a boil on my back.
종내(終乃) 〔끝내〕 to the end[last]; 〔드디어〕 at (long) last; finally; after all.
종년 〈비〉 a servant girl. ⇨계집종(⇨)계집)
종노릇 slavery; servitude. **종노릇하다** serve as a slave; be a slave (to).
종놈 〈비〉 a servant. ⇨사내종(⇨사내)
종다리 〔동〕 a skylark; a lark. ¶~가 하늘 높이 날아올랐다 A lark soared up into the sky.
종단(宗團) an order; a religious order.
종단(縱斷) 〔세로 자르기〕 vertical section; 〔분할〕 a division; a split. **종단하다** cut[divide] (something) vertically[longitudinally]; (국토 등을) run through (the land); travel[run] across; traverse. ¶일본을 종단하는 화산맥 a volcanic chain that runs through Japan // 산맥이 그 반도를 종단하고 있다 A mountain range runs through the peninsula.
종달새 〔동〕 a skylark. ⇨종다리
종답(宗畓) clan fields; the ritual land of a clan.
종당에(從當-) as a matter of course; from the very nature of things; at last; after all; in the end. ¶그는 도박을 일삼더니 ~ 재산을 날려 버렸다 He went on gambling until at last he lost all his fortune.
종대(縱隊) a column; a file. ¶일렬~ a (single) file / an Indian file // 2열 ~ double file[column] / a double file column // 4열 ~ a quarter column / a column of fours // 중대 ~ a company column // 소대 [중대 / 분대] ~ a column of platoons [companies / sections] // 일렬~로 행진하다 march in single file / defile.
종돈(種豚) 〔수컷 씨돼지〕 a boar; 〔암컷 씨돼지〕 a breed[brood] sow.
종두(種痘) (a) vaccination; (an) inoculation. ¶~를 맞다 take[undergo] vaccination / be vaccinated[inoculated] for[against] smallpox.
종래(從來) ¶~에는 hitherto / heretofore / up to now[this time] / so far // ~대로 [~과 같이] as in the past / as usual [before] / as of old // ~의 former (method) / usual / old / 〔현존의〕 existing // ~의 사고방식 traditional ways of thinking // ~의 악폐를 뿌리 뽑다 make away with the existing evils // 이 기계는 ~의 것과 비교하여 격리 발전된 것이다 This machine is a remarkable improvement on[over] those currently in use.
종량세(從量稅) a specific duty.
● **종량세율** a specific tariff.
종려(棕櫚) 〔식〕 a hemp palm; a palm.
● **종려나무** a palm tree.

종렬(縱列) a column; a file; a train. ¶~ 행진 a defile∥소대[중대/분대] ~로 in column of platoons[companies / sections]∥~ 행진을 하다 defile∥~을 짓다[이루다] form a file / queue up.

종료(終了) [끝남] an end; a close; (a) conclusion; [완료] completion; (기한의) expiration. 종료하다 end; conclude; terminate; come to an end; be over; be completed; expire.

종루(鐘樓) a belfry; a bell tower; a campanile.

종류(種類) a kind; a sort; a variety; a class; a species (단수·복수 동형); a description; [형태] a type; [성질] nature. ¶모든 ~의 all kinds[sort] of / of every kind[description]∥같은 ~의 of the same kind[sort]∥여러 ~의 것 things of various kinds∥모든 ~의 것 things of every kind[description] / all kinds [sorts] of things∥온갖 ~의 과일 all kinds of fruit∥갖가지[여러] ~의 꽃 various species[kinds] of flower∥온갖 ~의 사람 all manner[kinds] of people∥저런 ~의 것 things of that kind∥이런 ~의 범죄 crimes of this nature∥~를 가르다 classify / sort∥세 ~로 가르다 divide (things) into three classes∥어떤 ~의 사람과 사귀고 있는가 What sort of people do you mix with?∥온갖 ~의 사람이 모여 있었다 (문어) All manner of people were gathered there.∥이런 ~의 연구는 많은 시간이 걸린다 Research of this nature takes a great deal of time.∥이 ~의 기계는 내구력이 있다 This type of machine is very durable.∥포장지는 두 ~가 있습니다 We have two kinds of wrapping paper.∥나는 이런 ~의 종이는 싫다 I don't like this kind [sort] of paper.∥그런 ~의 것이라면 많이 있다 We have plenty of those[of that kind / like that].

●**종류별** classification; assortment. ¶~로 나누다 classify / assort.

종마(種馬) a stud (horse); a breeding horse; a stallion.

종막(終幕) an end; a close; (연극의) curtain-fall; the finale; [대단원] (프) the dénouement. ¶~이 다가오다 draw to a close[an end].

종말(終末) an end; a close; a conclusion. ¶비참한 ~이었다 It came to a tragic end.∥전쟁도 ~에 가까워졌다 The war is drawing to a close.

종말을 고하다 come[be brought] to an end.

●**종말론** [종] eschatology.

종매(從妹) a younger female cousin.

종목(種目) an item; an event(경기의). ¶영업 ~ items of business∥당일의 주요 ~ [체] main events for the day∥제품을 ~별로 목록을 작성하다 list products by item∥지출을 ~[항목]별로 쓰다 itemize the expenditures [(영) expenditure]∥그는 두 ~에 출전했다 He took part in two events.

종묘(宗廟) the Royal Ancestors'[Ancestral] Shrine.

종묘(種苗) seeds and saplings; seedlings.

종무(宗務) religious affairs.

종무(終務) the closing of offices for the year; the end of the year's business.

종물(從物) [법] an accessory (thing).

종반(전)(終盤戰) [바둑·장기] the end game; (선거 등의) the last[final] phase[stage] (of an election campaign). ¶선거전은 ~에 들어섰다 The General Election campaign has entered its last days.

종발(鐘鉢) a small bowl.

종범(從犯) [법] participation in a crime; aiding and abetting; accessory. ¶사전[사후] ~ an accessory before[after] the fact∥살인죄의 ~ an accessory to murder∥~의 (a man) accessory (to a crime).

●**종범자** an accessory[accessary] (to a crime); an accomplice.

종별(種別) (a) classification; (an) assortment. 종별하다 classify; divide into classes; assort. ¶도구를 용도에 따라 ~ classify implements according to use.

종복(從僕) [사내 종] a servant; an attendant; a valet.

종사(從死) [뒤를 따라서 죽음] self-immolation on the death of a person. 종사하다 immolate oneself on the death (of a person); follow (a person) to the grave.

종사하다(從事-) engage (oneself) in (business); pursue (a calling); follow (a profession); practice (medicine); attend to[work at] (a business); carry on (trade). ¶…에 종사하고 있다 be engaged in[be occupied with]∥…에 열심히 ~ devote oneself to (book writing)∥실무[공무/무역]에 종사하고 있다 be engaged in business[official duties / trade]∥저작[교육]에 ~ employ oneself in writing[on education]∥그 주민은 주로 농업에 종사하고 있다 The inhabitants are occupied mainly with agriculture.∥그는 무슨 업에 종사하고 있습니까 What business is he engaged in?∥그는 신문 사업에 종사하고 있습니다 He is engaged in newspaper work.

종서(縱書) vertical writing. ➪ 세로쓰기

종선(縱線) vertical line. ➪ 세로줄(㉿)세로)

종성(終聲) [언] a final consonant.

종소리(鐘-) the sound[ringing / peal] of a bell.

종속(從屬) subordination; dependency. ¶~적인 subordinate / dependent / auxiliary. 종속하다 be subordinate[subject] (to a foreign rule); depend[be dependent] (upon[on]).

→¶**종속시키다** subordinate (one thing to another)∥광고과를 판매부에 종속시키다 subordinate the advertisement section to the sales department.

●**종속 관계** subordinate relationship. **종속절** [언] a subordinate clause.

종손(宗孫) the eldest grandson of the head family.

종손(從孫) the grandson of one's brother; a grandnephew.

종숙(從叔) a male cousin of one's father.

종식(終熄) cessation; an end. 종식하다 cease; end; come to an end; be brought to a close.

→¶**종식시키다** put an end[a stop] to (war)∥마침내 전란은 종식되었다 Finally the war ended[came to an end].∥천연두는 종식되었다 Smallpox has been stamped out.

종신(宗臣) **1** [원훈] a distinguished minister of state. **2** [벼슬하는 종친] a minister from the royal family.

종신(終身) [일생] a whole life; one's life; [죽음] the end of life; one's death; [임종] being at one's parent's deathbed. ¶~의 life / life-long. 종신하다 [죽다] end one's life[days]; finish[live out] one's life; be on [at] one's parent's deathbed.

●**종신 고용 제도** the life(long) employment

system. 종신 연금 a life pension[annuity].
종신형 imprisonment for life.
종실(宗室) the Royal family; a member of the royal clan.
종심(終審) [법] the final[last] examination [trial].
● 종심 법원 the court of last instance.
종씨(宗氏) a clansman (of the same surname).
종아리 [생] the calf (pl. calves).
종아리(를) 맞다 get whipped on the calf.
종아리(를) 치다[때리다] lash[whip] (a person) on the calf.
● 종아리뼈 a fibula; a splint bone. 종아리채 a switch; (미) a cane.
종알거리다 [잽싸게 지껄이다] spatter; prate; prattle; babble; [중얼거리다] grumble (at); murmur.
종알종알 babblingly; prattlingly. 종알종알하다 spatter. ➪ 종알거리다
종양(腫瘍) [의] a tumo(u)r; a neoplasm. ¶뇌~ a cerebral tumor // 양성[악성] ~ a benign [malign / malignant] tumor // ~이 생긴 tumorous / tumoral // 그는 뇌에 ~이 생겼다 He developed a brain tumor.
종언(終焉) [임종] the end (of life); death; [종말] an end; a close; expiration; completion; finish. ¶대제국은 ~을 고했다 The great empire ceased to exist[came to an end]. 종언하다 die; end; come to an end; finish; complete.
종업(從業) [업무에 종사함] work in service. 종업하다 be employed; be in the service; (쉬고 있던 사람이) return to work.
● 종업 시간 working hours. 종업원 (한 사람) an employe(e); an operative; a (service) worker; (집합적) men; (all) hands; a working staff.
종업(終業) the close of work[school]. 종업하다 end one's work.
● 종업 시간 the closing hour. 종업식 the closing ceremony[exercises].
종연(終演) the end of a show; the close[end] (of a run of performances). ¶~은 9시 30분입니다 The curtain falls at nine-thirty. 종연하다 end; finish; close (a theater / the performance); be over.
종요롭다 important; vital; essential; indispensable; pivotal. 종요로이 importantly; vitally; indispensably; essentially.
종용(慫慂) [권고] advice; suggestion; [설득] persuasion; [유발] inducement. ¶…의 ~으로 at (a person's) suggestion[instance] // 친구의 ~으로 생명 보험에 들었다 I took out [bought] a life insurance policy at my friend's suggestion. 종용하다 [권고하다] advise; suggest; counsel; [유발하다 : 설득하다] persuade; prevail upon. ¶나는 그에게 자수를 종용했다 I advised him to surrender himself to police officers.
종우(種牛) a (seed) bull.
종유굴(鍾乳窟) a stalactite grotto.
종유석(鍾乳石) [광] a stalactite.
종이 paper. ¶~ 한 장 a sheet of paper // 색 ~ colored paper // ~ 한 첩[연] a quire[ream] of paper // ~로 만든 made of paper / papermade // ~에 싸다 wrap[do up] (a thing) in paper // ~에 쓰다 write[put down] on paper // ~를 바르다 paper (a wall / a box) // ~를 만들다[뜨다] make paper // ~를 접어 비행기

를 만들다 fold a piece of paper into the figure of an airplane / 상자에 빨간 ~를 바르다 paper a box red // 책을 ~로 싸다 wrap a book (up) in paper // 이 ~에 주소와 이름을 쓰시오 Write your name and address on this paper.
● 종이 한 장 차이 a very slight difference (between); (by) a paper-thin majority [margin]. ¶천재와 미치광이는 ~다 There's only a very fine line between a genius and a madman.
● 종이 냅킨 a paper napkin[serviette]. 종이쪽 a piece[scrap / strip] of paper. 종이컵 a paper cup; a Dixie (cup). 종이호랑이 a paper tiger. 종잇조각 a piece of paper.
종일(終日) all day (long); the whole day (over); for a whole day; throughout [all through] the day; from morning till [to] night. ¶~ 독서를 하다 read books all day // 그는 ~ 잠을 자고 보냈다 He spent the whole day in bed. // ~ 기다려도 아무 일도 일어나지 않았다 We waited all day (long), but nothing happened. // 그는 ~ 그 방에 있었다 He stayed in the room from morning till night[throughout the day]. // 하루 ~ 서 있어서 피로했다 I was exhausted, having been on my feet all day. // 그녀는 ~토록 환자를 간호했다 She attended the patient all day[day and night].
종자(從者) a follower; a retainer; an attendant; (봉건 시대의) a vassal; (집합적) (the lord's) retinue; a servant. ¶~로 삼다 take a person into one's service / accept a person as a retainer / ~가 되다 enter a person's service / take up service under a person.
종자(種子) 1 (식물의) a seed; (복숭아 등의) a stone; a pip; (미) a pit; (동물의) a breed; a stock; a strain. 2 [사람의 혈통] an offspring; a son-of-a-gun; a bastard.
● 종자식물 a seed plant.
종자매(從姉妹) female cousins.
종작없다 pointless; desultory; senseless; nonsensical; absurd. ¶종작없는 말 senseless remarks / nonsense // 그가 하는 말은 ~ He speaks incoherently. / He talks in a rambling way.
종잡다 [대중으로 헤아려 잡다] get the gist; get a rough idea; get at the main idea; get the point; roughly understand. ¶종잡을 수 없는 공상에 빠지다 indulge in whimsical fancy // 네 이야기는 이랬다저랬다 해서 종잡을 수가 없다 Your rambling way of talking is getting us nowhere. // 그의 말은 종잡을 수 없다 You can't see what he's driving at. / There is no logic in his remark.
종장(終章) the last of the 3 verses of a (sijo) poem; the last part of a song.
종적(蹤跡·蹤迹) traces; vestiges; whereabouts. ¶~을 감추다 cover one's tracks / leave no trace behind / disappear // 소년이 ~을 감춘 지 며칠 된다 The boy has been missing from his home for some days.
종적(縱的) longitudinal; lengthwise; vertical(수직의).
● 종적 연락 vertical contact.
종전(宗田) [종중 소유의 밭] those dry fields that produce the crop used in the ancestral sacrifices of the clan that owns them.
종전(從前) ¶~의 previous / former / old / usual // ~에 hitherto / heretofore / formerly

종전 / before // ~의 관계 one's past connections (with a person) // ~과 같이 as in the past / as usual / as before / as heretofore / as hitherto / as ever / as of old / as of yore // ~과 같다 be same as before // 그는 모든 것이 ~ 그대로이기를 원했다 He wanted everything to be the way it had been.

종전 (終戰) the end [termination] of the war; the termination [cessation] of hostilities. ¶~ 후 after the end of the war / postwar // ~후의 혼란 postwar confusion // ~이 되다 the war comes to an end.

종점 (終點) the end of the line; the last stop; the terminal (station); (영) the terminus (*pl.* -ni, ~es). ¶버스 ~ the last stop of a bus / the end of the bus line // 열차 ~ a rail(road) terminal // 경부선의 ~은 부산이다 The end of the line for [The terminus of] the Gyeongbu [Seoul-Busan] Line is in Busan. // ~의 바로 전에서 내리세요 Get off at the next to the last stop.

종정 (宗正) [종파의 우두머리] the superintendent priest; the head of a Buddhist sect.

종제 (從弟) younger male paternal cousins.

종조 (宗祖) the founder of a religious sect; the father; the originator.

종조모 (從祖母) a grandaunt; a great-aunt.

종조부 (從祖父) a granduncle; a great-uncle.

종족 (宗族) kindred; a clan; a family.

종족 (種族) 1 [인종] a race; [부족] a tribe. 2 [동·식물의 종] a species (*pl.* ~). ¶~의 racial / tribal // 북미 인디언의 대~ major North American Indian tribes // ~의 전쟁 a tribal [an intertribal] war.
● **종족 보존** preservation of the species.

종종 with short quick paces; with hurried steps.

종종 (種種) 1 [물건의 가지가지] several [various / diverse / different] kinds. 2 [가끔] occasionally; [자주] frequently; often; every now and then. ¶~ 친구를 찾다 visit a friend every now and then // 이 지역에서는 그런 일이 ~ 일어난다 Such things happen very often [frequently] in this district. // 요즈음 한국인 중에는 ~ 영양 과잉의 예를 볼 수가 있다 These days one can often see Korean who are overnourished. // 그에게서는 ~ 소식이 있습니다 I hear from him once in a while.

종종거리다 walk with hurried steps.

종종걸음 short and quick steps; a quick pace; hurried [mincing] steps; tripping. ¶그녀는 ~으로 나를 따라왔다 She followed behind me with short, quick steps. // 그 소녀는 ~으로 길을 걸어왔다 The girl came tripping down the road.

종주 (宗主) a suzerain.
● **종주국** a suzerain state. **종주권** suzerain power; suzerainty.

종주하다 (縱走-) [능선을 따라 걷다] walk along the (mountain) ridges. ¶섬을 종주하는 산맥 the mountain range which traverses the island [which runs from one end of the island to the other] // 한국을 강원도에서 제주도까지 종주했다 We drove through Korea from Gangwondo to Jejudo. / We traveled the length of Korea from Gangwondo to Jejudo by car.

종중 (宗中) the families of the same clan.
● **종중논 / 종중답** the paddy fields owned by a clan.

종지 (宗旨) 1 [종문의 취지] the tenets [doctrines] of a religious sect. 2 [근본이 되는 요지] the main purport; the fundamental meaning.

종지 (終止) termination; cessation; an end; a stop. **종지하다** terminate; end; come [bring] to an end.

종지부 (終止符) a period. ⇨ 마침표
종지부(를) 찍다 put an end to .... ¶이젠 이 문제에도 종지부를 찍어야 할 때가 왔다 It is time we put an end to this matter. // 이제 이런 생활에 종지부를 찍고 싶다 I want to put a period to this kind of life. // 그 사건이 그의 출세에 종지부를 찍었다 The incident put a stop to his rise in the world.

종지뼈 [슬개골] a kneecap; the patella.

종진 (縱陣) a column; a line ahead. ¶~으로 in a line ahead / in single file // ~을 짓다 [펴다] form a column.

종질 (從姪) a male cousin's son.

종질녀 (從姪女) a male cousin's daughter.

종착역 (終着驛) (미) a terminal (station); (영) a terminus (*pl.* -ni, ~es). ¶~이 수원인 열차 a train that goes only as far as Suwon // 이 열차는 여기가 ~입니다 This train does not go any further [terminates here].

종창 (腫脹) [몸의 한 부분이 부어오름·그 상처] a swelling; a boil; an intumescence.

종축 (種畜) breeding stock.
● **종축장** a livestock breeding farm.

종축 (縱軸) ➡ 세로축(⇨세로)

종친 (宗親) 1 [임금의 친척] kindred of the king; royal clansmen. 2 [일가] clansmen; kindred.
● **종친회** a clan [family] meeting.

종탑 (鐘塔) a bell tower; a belfry.

종파 (宗派) 1 [종교의 분파] a denomination; a (religious) sect. (▶ denomination은 sect보다도 큰 경우가 많음. sect는 본산(本山)에 대한 분파를 말함) 2 [지파(支派)에 대한] the main branch of a family [clan]. ¶~적(인) sectarian / denominational // 당신은 (기독교의) 어느 ~에 속합니까 Which (Christian) denomination do you belong to?
● **종파 싸움** a sectarian strife.

종파 (縱波) a longitudinal wave; (지진의) a P wave (▶ a primary wave의 약어).

종파 (種播) sowing; seeding. ⇨ 씨뿌리기

종피 (種皮) a testa (*pl.* -tae).

종합 (綜合) (a) synthesis (*pl.* -ses); generalization; [논] colligation. ¶~ 운영 integrated [well-coordinated] management. **종합하다** synthesize; generalize; unite; put [piece] together. ¶이런 각종의 보고를 종합해 보니 putting these various reports together // 종합해서 생각하다 think of collectively // 각 종목의 득점을 ~ total [add up] the points scored in individual events // 모든 점을 종합하여 이 같은 결론에 도달했다 After considering all the factors [After taking everything into consideration], we reached this conclusion.
● **종합 경기** all-round games [events]; (체조의) combined exercises. ¶개인 [단체] ~ individual [team] combined (exercises). **종합 대학** a university. **종합 병원** a general hospital; a polyclinic (hospital). **종합 소득세** a composite income tax. **종합 예술** composite art.

종합적 (綜合的) [통합적] synthetic; composite; all-round; (미) overall; [포괄적] com-

종헌(終獻) the last[third] libation in a sacrifice.

종형(從兄) an older (male) cousin.

종회(宗會) a clan[family] meeting. ¶~를 열다 hold a family meeting.

종횡(縱橫) perpendicular and [or] horizontal; length and breadth. ¶~으로 lengthwise and crosswise / [사방팔방으로] in all directions / throughout the length and breadth (of) / [자유자재로] freely/철도는 국토를 ~으로 달리고 있다 A network of railways covers the country. // 그는 시국을 ~으로 논했다 He commented freely on the present situation. // 그는 ~으로 정계에서 활약하고 있다 He moves about most energetically in the political world.

●**종횡무진** ¶그는 ~의 분전(奮戰)을 했다 He fought his enemies right and left. // 그는 ~의 대활약을 했다 He played a very active[remarkable] part in it.

좆 a cock. ⇨자지

좇다 1 [그대로 따르다] follow; conform oneself to; act on[upon]. ¶관습을 좇아서 in conformity with custom / according to custom/선례를 ~ follow a precedent/유행을 ~ follow the fashion // 대세를 ~ conform to the times // 충고를 ~ take[follow] (a person's) advice // 남이 하는 대로 좇아 하다 follow (another's) example / follow in (another's) steps/공자의 가르침을 ~ follow Confucius teachings/원칙을 좇아 행하다 act on a principle.

2 [복종하다] obey; abide by; submit[give in] to. ¶아무의 지시를 ~ follow[take] a person's direction/명령을 ~ obey (a person's) orders[commands] // 법을 ~ obey[be obedient to] the law/아무의 뜻을 ~ submit to a person's will.

좋다¹ 1 (상태·성질 등이) good; nice; fine; (마음씨가) good; good-natured; nice; gentle; (머리가) bright; clever; smart. ¶좋은 소식 welcome[encouraging / good] news/유아에게 가장 좋은 그림책 ideal picture books for little children // 좋은 선물 a nice[handsome] present/~ 상태가 ~ 「나쁘다」 be in good[bad / poor] condition/좋든 나쁘든 (whether it is) good or bad // 좋지도 나쁘지도 않다 be neither good nor bad / be just tolerable // 그거 참 좋은 생각이다 That's a good idea. // 이 책은 나의 가장 좋은 벗이다 This book is my best friend. // 그에게는 좋은 소식이었다 That was welcome news to him. // He was very glad[happy] to hear that. // 이 탄광의 석탄은 질이 ~ The coal from this mine is of good quality. // 저 청년은 머리가 ~ He is an intelligent[a bright / (구어) a smart] young man. // 그에게 좋은 점이라고는 하나도 없다 He has absolutely nothing to recommend him. // 그에게는 꽤 좋은 점이 있다 He has some fine qualities. // 그녀의 어디가 좋은지 모르겠다 I don't know what you[people] see in her. // 그 아이는 학교 성적이 ~ The boy does well at school. // 그녀의 쇼팽 연주는 참 좋았다 She played Chopin very well. // 그는 좋은 급료를 받고 있다 He is well-paid. // He gets a good salary. // 이 도시는 살기 좋은 곳이다 This town is a pleasant[comfortable] place to live. // 이 책은 이해하기 ~ This book is easy to understand. // 학창 시절의 그의 성적은 별로 좋지 않았다 The results of the experiment were not encouraging. // 그의 평판은 좋지 않다 He has a bad[an unsavory] reputation.

2 (날씨가) fine; fair; bright; lovely; pleasant; (기후가) mild; (경치가) fine; beautiful; fine; (냄새·맛·소리 등이) sweet; nice; good; pleasing; agreeable. ¶좋은 목소리 a sweet voice // 좋은 냄새 [향기] a nice[sweet] smell // 좋은 기후 a mild climate // 날씨가 ~ It's fine weather. // 이 지대는 참으로 경치가 ~ This district has truly lovely scenery. // 차 맛이 참 좋군요 This tea tastes excellent[very good]. // 장미는 냄새가 참 ~ A rose smells very sweet.

3 (기분·건강이) well; fine; good; all right; agreeable; pleasant; joyful. ¶기분 좋은 일 a glad[delightful] thing / cream and sugar // 좋아서 정신을 못 차리다 be beside oneself[be transported] with joy/기분을 (사람이) feel[find] (something) pleasant / feel good / (사물이) be comfortable[pleasant / agreeable] // 기분이 매우 ~ I feel wonderful[(구어) great].

4 [귀하다] precious; valuable; (집안이) noble; good. ¶좋은 자료 valuable[precious] materials // 그는 좋은 집안의 태생이다 He comes of a noble family. // 좋은 정보를 알려주셔서 고맙습니다 Many thank for your valuable information.

5 (행운의) good; lucky; fortunate; opportune; happy; auspicious(상서로운); favorable. ¶좋은 전조 a good[lucky] omen // 좋은 팔자를 타고나다 be born under a lucky star // 비가 멎어서 좋았다 Fortunately it stopped raining. // 운이 좋게도 그는 그 전차를 타지 않았다 Luckily, he did not take that train. // 오늘은 특히 좋은 날인가 봐. 결혼식장은 어디나 예약이 꽉 차 있어 (문어) This seems to be a specially auspicious day. Every banquet hall is booked full with wedding receptions.

6 [이롭다] good (for); efficacious; beneficial. ¶(약이) 천식에 ~ be efficacious[good] for asthma // 매일 아침 산책하는 것은 건강에 ~ It is good for the health to take a walk every morning.

7 [알맞다] proper; right; good; suitable; fitting; [유리하다] profitable; advantageous; favorable; [유용하다] useful. ¶좋은 사업 a profitable[paying] business // 좋은 조건 remunerative terms // 좋은 경험 a useful experience // 좋은 때에 at a favorable moment / opportunely // 그는 마침 좋은 때에 왔다 He came at the right moment. // 내 바둑에는 그가 좋은 맞수이다 He would make a very good baduk(go) opponent for me. // 이런 이야기를 듣는 것보다 책을 읽는 편이 훨씬 좋겠다 You would be better off reading a book than listening to such talk.

8 [정당하다] right; justifiable; warrantable. ¶…이라고 해도 ~ we may rightly[safely] say that ... / it may safely be said that ... // 그것으로 좋다고 생각하는가 Do you think you are justified?

9 [충분하다] good; well; all right; enough; (서술적) will do; serve the purpose. ¶"내일 대답해 드리면 되겠습니까?" "좋습니다." "Will it be all right if I give you my answer tomorrow?" "Certainly." // "하나 더 어떻습니까?" "아

좋다

니요. (이 상태로) 좋소." "Won't you have one more?" "No, thank you (I've had plenty)."
10 (소망) 〖내일 비가 오면 좋을 텐데 I hope it will rain tomorrow.〗〖좀 더 시간이 있으면 좋을[좋았을] 텐데 I wish I had[had had] more time.〗〖그런 일을 안 했으면 좋았을 텐데 You should not have done such a thing.〗〖그가 곧 나았으면 좋겠다 I hope he may recover soon.
11 [바람직하다] desirable; preferable; [좋아하다] (서술적) like (something better than ...); love; prefer (a thing to ...); choose. 〖좋아서 by[from] choice / by[for] preference / for the love[fun] of it〗〖좋을 대로 하세요 Suit yourself. / Do as you like.〗〖아무 때나 당신 좋을 때 오세요 Come (and see us) any time (you like).〗〖무엇이 좋아서 그런 짓을 했느냐 Why did you choose to do such a thing?〗〖어느 쪽이 좋습니까 Which do you prefer? / Which do you like better?〗〖어느 쪽이나 좋습니다 Either will do.〗〖그는 나를 좋게 생각하지 않는 것 같다 He seems to be displeased with me. / He doesn't seem to like[approve of] me.〗〖네가 갈 수 있다면 그것보다 더 좋은 일은 없다 If you can go, that would be the best possible thing.〗〖신중함이 제일 ~ It is best to be careful.〗〖그는 좋아서 그녀와 결혼한 것은 아니었다 It was not of his own free will[of his own accord / by choice] that he married her.
12 (비교) better; superior (to); [···하는 편이 낫다] (서술적) had better (do). 〖훨씬 ~ (be) much[far] better〗〖너는 바닷가로 가는 편이 좋겠다 You had better[I advise you to] go to the seaside.〗〖환자는 오늘 다소 좋은 편이다 The patient is a little better today.〗〖그에게는 좋았던 시절이 있었다 He has seen his better days.
13 [(···해도) 괜찮다] (서술적) may; be at liberty to (do); be welcome to (do). 〖문을 열어도 ~ You may open the door.〗〖여기서는 담배를 피워도 ~ It's all right to smoke here.〗〖이젠 돌아가도 ~ You can[may] go home now.〗〖사과 안 해도 ~ You need not apologize.〗〖"전화를 좀 써도 좋습니까?" "물론이지요. 어서 쓰세요." "May I use your telephone?" "Certainly, go right ahead[Yes, please do]."
14 [(···하지 않아도) 괜찮다] do not have to; need not (do); do not need to (do). 〖역까지 마중 나오지 않아도 좋소 You don't need to meet me at the station.
15 (상관·지장 없다) (서술적) do not mind (doing); do not care (if); have no objection to (doing); be game (to / for); may (do); might as well (do). 〖"한잔하세." "좋아." "Let's have a drink." "Sure."〗〖좋다면 내일 테니스를 치지 않겠니 How about playing [Would you like to play] tennis tomorrow?〗〖그런 일은 어찌 되어도 ~ It doesn't matter.〗〖또 와도 좋습니까 Do you mind my coming here again?〗〖만일 그 기차를 못 타면 다음 차라도 ~ If you should miss the train, you might take the next.〗〖"이 아기 좀 잠깐만 봐 주시겠습니까?" "좋습니다." "Will you look after the baby for a little while?" "Certainly [With pleasure]."
16 [쉽다] easy. 〖그의 글씨체는 읽기가 ~ His writing is easy to read.
17 [친하다] intimate; friendly; [사랑스럽다]

dear; sweet. 〖좋은 사람[애인] a lover(주로 남자) / a sweetheart(주로 여자) / lovers(연인들) / (속어) a sweetie / one's flame / 사이좋은 부부 a devoted[happy] couple〗〖그 둘은 매우 사이가 ~ They are great[very good] friends. / They are hand and[in] glove with each other. / (구어) They are (as) thick as thieves[glues].〗〖우리는 이웃집 사람들과 사이가 ~ We are on good terms with our next-door neighbors.
18 [능란하다] skillful; good; clever; fine; expert; crack. 〖말솜씨가 ~ be a good talker〗〖글씨가 ~ write a good hand〗〖문장이 ~ write a good style / be an able[a talented] writer.
19 [부럽다] enviable. 〖좋은 지위 an enviable position〗〖그런 훌륭한 자식을 두셔서 참 좋겠습니다 Such a fine child you have. How I envy you!
좋은 약은 입에 쓰다.(속담) Good medicine is bitter to the mouth.; Bitter pills may have blessed effects.
좋다² Good!; Well! ⇨ᆞ좋아
좋아 Good!; Well!; All right!; O.K.!; [환성] Whoopee!; Goodie!; Oh boy!; Whee!; [찬성] Agreed!; (미국 구어) Check!; [통신] Roger! 〖~, 아주 잘했어 Good! You did it very well.〗〖~, 그러면 됐어 All right. That will do.〗〖~, 해 주지 O.K. I'll do it for you.
좋아지내다 be on intimate terms (with); be good friends (with). 〖그 둘은 서로 좋아지낸다 The two of them are hand and[in] glove with each other. / They love each other.
좋아지다 1 (상태가) improve; become [get] better; (병세가) get better; take a turn for the better; (날씨가) clear up; [아름다워지다] become finer[more beautiful]. 〖날씨가 좋아진다 The weather clears up. / The weather becomes better[improves].〗〖수학 성적이 많이 좋아졌다 My grades in mathematics improved[rose].〗〖그녀의 운은 좋아지기 시작하고 있었다 Her luck was beginning to turn. / Things were looking up for her.〗〖경기가 좋아져 가고 있다 The market is[Business conditions are] picking[looking] up.〗〖2, 3일 쉬면 좋아질 것입니다 A few days' rest will put you all right.〗〖그녀는 건강이 이제 완전히 좋아진 것 같다 She seems to be quite all right now.
2 [좋아하게 되다] get[come / learn] to like (a thing); become fond of; take a fancy[liking] to. 〖···이 점점 ~ develop a liking for ...〗〖나는 이 집이 좋아졌어요 I've become fond of this house.〗〖두 사람 사이는 다시 좋아질 것 같지 않다 They are alienated beyond all hope of reconciliation.
좋아하다 (기호) like; (사랑) love; be fond (of); have a liking[fancy / taste] for; (특별히) be partial to; (주로 음식을) have a weakness for (apples); prefer (a thing) to (another); (주로 부정문·의문문에서) care (for something / to do). 〖좋아하는 옷 one's favorite dress〗〖좋아하지 않는 녀석 an unpleasant[a disagreeable] fellow〗〖바나나를 좋아한다 I like bananas.〗〖나는 음악을 대단히 좋아한다 I love[am very fond of] music.〗〖나는 혼자 있는 것을 좋아한다 I like to be alone. / I enjoy being alone.〗〖커피보다 홍차를 좋아한다 I prefer tea to coffee. / I like tea better than coffee.〗〖연극은 크게 좋아하지 않

습니다 I'm not particularly interested in plays.∥그녀를 첫눈에 좋아하게 되었다 I fell in love with[took (a fancy) to] her at first sight.∥저런 형의 얼굴은 좋아하지 않는다 I don't care for that type of face.∥그는 그 레슬링 선수를 좋아한다 He is a fan of that wrestler.∥모두가 그를 좋아한다 He is liked[loved] by everybody.∥그런 종류의 그림은 별로 좋아하지 않는다 I don't care much for that kind of painting.∥특별히 좋아하는 것은 없습니다 I have no particular preference.∥그는 개를 매우 좋아한다 He is crazy about dogs.∥그는 우표 수집을 매우 좋아한다 He has a passion for collecting stamps.∥(구어) He is a stamp nut.∥나는 재즈를 별로 좋아하지 않는다 Jazz isn't my cup of tea.

좌(左) the left; the following; (사상) a leftist; (집합적) the left. ¶~에서 우로 from left to right.

좌(座) a seat; [지위] a position; a status. ¶권력의 ~에 있는 사람들 men in power∥권력의 ~에 오르다 come to[into] power.

-좌(座) [천] constellation. ¶대웅~ the Great Bear / Ursa Major.

좌경(左傾) inclination to the left; radicalization; Bolshevization; leftism. ¶~적(的) leftist / radical / Red / Bolshevized∥~ 색채가 농후한 잡지 a journal of pronouncedly leftist color∥이 정당은 약간 ~이다 This party is a little to the left. **좌경하다** lean [drift] toward(s) the left; swing to the left; become [turn] leftist[radical].
● **좌경 문학** leftist literature. **좌경 사상** leftist thinking[views]; radical thinking.

좌고우면(左顧右眄) a look to left and right. ⇨**좌우고면**

좌골(坐骨) the hipbone; [의] the ischium (pl. -chia).
● **좌골 신경** the sciatic nerve. **좌골 신경통** hip gou; [의] sciatica.

좌담(座談) a table talk; [대화] (a) conversation; a colloquy; [토의] a discussion. ¶~의 명수 an excellent conversationalist∥~식으로 이야기하다 talk (about a matter) informally.
● **좌담회** a discussion (meeting); a round-table talk [conference]; a symposium (pl. ~s, -sia). ¶~를 가지다 hold a symposium (on) / have a discussion meeting.

좌르르 with a great rush; with a splash. ¶물이 ~ 쏟아졌다 Water came rushing out.∥콩이 ~ 탁자 위에 쏟아졌다 The beans spilled on the table with a rattling sound.

좌방(左方) the left side.

좌변(左邊) the left side. ¶(수학에서) ~의 항 the left side of a mathematical equation.

좌불안석(坐不安席) [불안·근심 등으로 가만히 앉아 있지를 못함] being unable to sit comfortably (from anxiety, etc.). **좌불안석하다** be unable to rest; fidget; squirm anxiously. ¶두려움 때문에 좌불안석했다 Fear kept me restless.∥그는 흥분하여 좌불안석했다 He was very nervous and couldn't sit still.∥그녀는 좌불안석하고 있었다 She was in a fidget.

좌상(坐商) [앉은장사] keeping a shop; [앉은장수] a shopkeeper (as contrasted with a hawker).

좌상(坐像) a sedentary [seated / sitting] figure [image / statue]. ¶원효 대사의 ~ a seated figure of the Saint Wonhyo.

좌상(座上) 1 [좌중] (in) the company; the party; all those present. 2 [연장자] the elder in a company [party].

좌상(挫傷) [좌창] a contusion; a sprain; a wrench; a fractural injury; a fracture. ¶그는 어깨에 ~을 당했다 He suffered shoulder contusions.

좌석(座席·坐席) [자리] a seat; a cockpit(비행기의); a pew(교회의); (sitting) room(여지). ¶앞[뒷] ~ a front[back / rear] seat∥~에 앉다 take one's seat / seat oneself (at a table / in a chair) / (미) have one's seat∥남을 위해 ~을 확보하다 secure a seat for a person∥속히 ~에 앉아 주십시오 Please take your seat [be seated] quickly.∥버스가 주행 중일 때는 ~을 일어서지[떠나지] 마십시오 Don't stand up[leave your seat] while the bus is running.∥이 극장에는 300명분의 ~이 있다 [~이 300석 있다] There are seats for three hundred people in this theater.
● **좌석권** a place card. **좌석 만원** (극장의 게시) Standing Room Only(약어 S.R.O.). **좌석 버스** a seat bus. **좌석 번호** the seat number. **좌석수** seating capacity[accommodation].

좌선(坐禪) [불] Zen meditation; sitting in Buddhist meditation; *Dhyāna Pāramitā* (Sans.). **좌선하다** sit in meditation; practice Zen meditation (in a temple).

좌시(坐視) watching idly [with indifference]. **좌시하다** look on idly [with indifference]; remain a mere spectator [looker-on]; watch in silence; [눈감다·못 본 체하다] overlook; wink at. ¶피난민의 곤경을 좌시해서는 안 된다 We must not look on unconcernedly [idly] at the plight of the refugees.∥숙부님이 도산의 위기에 처해 있는 것을 나는 좌시할 수가 없다 I cannot (just) sit (idle) and watch my uncle tottering on the verge of bankruptcy.∥그들의 비참한 처지에 내가 어떻게 좌시할 수 있겠는가 How can I remain indifferent to their miserable state?

좌안(左岸) [하천의 왼쪽 물가] the left bank (of a river).

좌약(坐藥) a suppository.

좌완 투수(左腕投手) a lefthander; a south paw (pitcher); (미국 속어) a lefty.

좌욕(坐浴) a sitz [hip] bath.

좌우(左右) 1 [왼쪽과 오른쪽] right and left. ¶길의 ~에 on either side [both sides] of the road∥~에 수행원을 거느리고 with retainers on either side∥~로 흔들리다 roll from side to side∥~를 둘러보다 look around / glance about∥~를 잘 살피고 길을 건너가시오 Look both ways carefully before you cross the road.∥다리가 있는 곳에서 우리는 ~로 헤어졌다 At the bridge we parted and went off in opposite directions.
2 [측근자] one's attendants; people in attendance. ¶~를 물리치고 밀담을 하다 keep one's attendants away and have a closed-door conference (with).
3 [지배·영향] sway; influence; control. **좌우하다** [지배하다] command; govern; control; gain control of; dominate; sway; have (a thing) under one's control; have (a person) under one's thumb; [영향을 끼치다] affect; influence; have[exert] an influence upon. ¶시장을 ~ control[gain control of] the market∥한 나라의 운명을 ~ control[de-

cide] the fate of a nation // 신문은 여론을 좌우한다 Newspapers influence the current of thought. ➔¶좌우되다 be under the control (of) / be swayed (by) / be influenced (by) // 감정에 좌우되다[사로잡히다] be carried away by one's emotions // 친구들에게 좌우되기[영향을 받기] 쉽다 be easily influenced by one's friends.
● 좌우 대칭 symmetry. ¶~의 symmetrical.

좌우간(左右間) at any rate; in any event; anyhow; (미) anyway; in any case; at all events. ¶~ 나가 보겠다 I'll go out anyway [in either case]. // ~ 정오까지는 그를 기다리고 있겠다 Well, at any rate, I'll wait for him till noon. // ~ 무슨 대책을 강구해야지 After all, a measure should be taken to it. // ~ 준비만은 해 두자 In any case [At all events], I'll make preparations for it.

좌우고면(左右顧眄) [이리저리 돌아봄] a look to left and right; looking around; irresolution; vacillation. **좌우고면하다** waver (in one's attitude); vacillate; be irresolute; sit on the fence. ¶좌우고면하며 갈 바를 모르다 look this and that way / waver in one's attitude.

좌우명(座右銘) one's motto; a favorite proverb[maxim].

좌우익(左右翼) 1 [군] left and right wings of the army; the left and right column. 2 [좌익과 우익] left-wing and right-wing.

좌익(左翼) 1 [비행기의 왼쪽 날개] the left wing.
2 the left wing of an army. ¶적의 ~을 공격하다 attack the enemy's left wing.
3 (주의상의) the left (wing); (급진적·과격적 당파·인물) the leftist; the left-winger. ¶~적 (인) leftist / left-wing // 신~ the New Left // 극~ the extreme left (wing) // 이 단체는 ~으로 기울어져 있다 This organization has leftist leanings. // 그는 ~이다 He is a leftist. / He is left-wing. / He is a left-winger. // 저 그룹은 다소 ~으로 생각된다 The group is considered mildly leftist.
4 [야구] [좌익수] a left fielder.
5 [야구] the left field.
● 좌익군 the left wing of an army. ➪=좌익2 **좌익 단체** a leftist organization; a group of radicals. **좌익분자** a left-wing element. **좌익 사상** leftism. ¶~에 물들다 be tinctured with radicalism. **좌익수** [야구] a left fielder. **좌익 운동** a leftist movements; a left [radical] movement.

좌장(坐杖) a T-shaped armrest.
좌장(座長) the senior person present (in a seated group).
좌절(挫折) 1 (계획의) a breakdown; ruin; collapse; a reverse; [계획·일이 실패로 돌아감] a setback; [용기·희망 등이 꺾임] (a) frustration. **좌절하다** miscarry; be baffled; get ruined; be upset; break down; collapse; fall through; fall to the ground; suffer a setback; get frustrated; be frustrated. ➔좌절시키다 frustrate (a person's plan) / balk (a person in his plan) / disappoint (a person's plans / hopes) // 계획이 좌절되다 a plan is ruined [upset] // 불경기의 여파로 그의 사업이 좌절되었다 Hit by the depression, his business had[suffered] a setback. // 음악가가 되려는 그의 희망은 전쟁 때문에 좌절되었다 His desire to become a musician was frustrated by the war.
2 (마음·기운의) discouragement. **좌절하다** get discouraged[disheartened / daunted].
● **좌절감** frustration; disappointment. ¶~에 빠지다 feel frustrated // 여러 번 ~을 맛보다 experience frustration (before completing a project).

좌정하다(坐定-) sit; be seated; take a seat.
좌종(坐鐘) a table clock.
좌중(座中) ¶~을 둘러보다 look over the whole assembly (of people) // ~은 순식간에 혼란에 빠졌다 The gathering was instantly thrown into confusion. // ~이 모두 감동의 눈물을 흘렸다 All present were [The whole company was] moved to tears. // 그는 겁을 먹은 듯 슬금슬금 ~을 둘러보았다 He looked timidly around at everyone present [there].

좌지우지하다(左之右之-) turn[twist] (a person) round one's little finger; turn, twist, and wind (a person); lead; control; take the lead (in); have (a person) at one's beck and call; lead (a person) by the nose. ¶당을 좌지우지하는 것은 그다 He is the leader of the party. / He is in control of the party.

좌천(左遷) degradation; relegation; downgrading; demotion. ¶그의 이번 전임(轉任)은 ~이다 His new appointment is a change for the worse. **좌천하다** relegate (to); demote (to); transfer (a person) to a lower position; be downgraded[demoted]. ➔¶그는 지방 지점의 지배인으로 좌천되었다 He was demoted to manager of a local branch.

좌초(坐礁) running aground; stranding. **좌초하다** strike[run on] a rock; strand; be stranded[aground]; run aground[ashore]. ¶좌초한 배 a stranded ship // 우리 배는 아산만 부근에서 좌초했다 Our boat ran aground [was stranded] near Asan Bay. ➔¶폭풍우로 배는 좌초되었다 The tempest drove the ship on the rock.

좌충우돌하다(左衝右突-) dash this way and rush that; plunge forward on this side and dash in on that.

좌측(左側) the left-hand side; the left. ¶~으로 세 번째가 당신 자리입니다 The third chair on the left is your seat. / Your seat is the third on the left.
● **좌측통행** (게시) Keep to the left.

좌파(左派) the left; a left-wing party[faction]; (사람) the left wingers; the leftists. ¶~의 leftist / left-wing // **사회당** ~ the leftist Socialists / the Left-Wingers of the Socialists.

좌판(坐板) a low bench; a board to sit on.
좌편(左便) the left side; the left.
좌표(座標) [수] coordinates. ¶극~ polar coordinates // 곡선~ curvilinear coordinates // 데카르트[평행] ~ Cartesian coordinates // 세로 ~ the ordinate // 직각 ~ rectangular coordinates // 가로 ~ the abscissa (pl. -s, -cissae).
● **좌표계** [수] a system of coordinates; a coordinate system. **좌표축** an axis of coordinates; a coordinate axis.

좌하(座下) [편지에서 이름 아래에 쓰는 말] Esquire(약이 Esq.); Mr. ….
좌향(坐向) [민] geomantic aspect; a prospect. ¶묘의 ~을 잡다 determine the exact direction in which the grave must face // 이 집은 ~이 나쁘다 This house has a bad aspect.

좌향앞으로가(左向-) 〔구령〕 Left wheel!
좌향좌(左向左) 〔구령〕 Left turn[face]!
좌현(左舷) port; the port side. ¶~에 on the port side / aport // ~ 앞[뒤]쪽에 on the port bow[quarter] // ~으로 기울다 list to port // (선수를) ~으로 돌리다 turn (the bow / the ship) to port / port // ~에 배가 보였다 A ship was visible to port[off the port beam].
좌회전(左回轉) left(-hand) turn. **좌회전하다** turn (to the) left; make a left (at).
●**좌회전 금지** 〔게시〕 No left turn.
좌흥(座興) amusement[entertainment] of the company; fun. ¶~으로 in[for] fun / by way of joke / to amuse[entertain] the company // ~을 돋우기 위해 한마디 하다 tell a short story for the entertainment of the company // 그는 연회의 ~을 위해 민요를 불렀다 He sang a folk song for entertainment at the banquet. / He entertained the company at the banquet with folk songs.

좍 1 [퍼지는 모양] far and wide; widely; (spread) suddenly. ¶소문이 ~ 퍼졌다 The rumor has spread[got abroad] in a fish[like wildfire]. // 그 소식은 나라 안에 ~ 퍼졌다 The news was flashed over the country. 2 [거침없이] fluently; with ease. ¶~ 외다 recite fluently. 3 [흐르는 모양] in a quick stream; (stream out) suddenly; with a splosh[splash].
좍좍 1 (비 등이) heavily; in torrents. ¶~ 물을 끼얹다 pour[shower] water on[over] (the grass) // 비가 ~ 쏟아진다 It's pouring. / It's raining heavily[hard / cats and dogs]. // 이 위에 물을 ~ 끼얹으시오 Pour lots of water over this. 2 [거침없이] easily; with ease; fluently. ¶~ 외다 recite (a poem) fluently[easily].
좔좔 (flow) freely[forcibly]; with a swilling sound. ¶~ 흐르다 (water) run freely / swill // 시냇물이 ~ 흐른다 The brook flows with a lively current.
죄(罪) (법률상의) a crime; (종교·도덕상의) a sin; [악덕] a vice; [과오] a fault; [죄책] blame; charge; [반칙] an offense; [벌] (a) punishment; a penalty; [유죄] guilt. ¶~ 있는[많은] guilty / blamable / sinful // ~ 없는 not guilty / blameless / crimeless / sinless / free from guilt / innocent // 극악한 ~ a crime of the deepest dye // 죽을~ a grave offense / a crime deserving of death // ~ 많은 생활을 하다 lead a life of sin[guilt] // ~를 묻다 accuse (a person) of a crime / bring a charge against (a person) // ~를 규명하다 inquire into (a person's) crime // ~를 용서하다 condone[forgive] an offense // ~를 인정하다 plead guilty / submit to a sentence / admit an offense // ~가 없다고 항변하다 plead innocent / plead one's innocence // ~를 자백하다 confess one's guilt // ~를 쐬우다 put[throw / lay] the blame on[upon] (a person) // (거짓 증거로) make a false charge against (another) // ~를 거듭 짓다 commit one crime after another // ~을 짊어지다 take the guilt upon oneself / hold oneself blamable // ~에서 구하다 save[deliver] (a person) from sin // ~를 감하다 mitigate[reduce] (a person's) punishment // ~도 없는데 죽이다 kill (an animal) without provocation // 그는 ~가 없다 He is innocent. // 그는 ~를 범해서 체포되었다 He committed a crime and was arrested. // 그것은 인도에 어긋나는 ~다 It is an offense against humanity. // 그는 ~를 다른 사람에게 씌웠다 He pinned the guilt on someone else. // 내 마음의 ~를 용서하소서 Forgive my sins. // 그들은 같은 ~로 갇혀 있다 They are in prison for the same crime. // 비록 ~가 있다고 판정되어도 사형에 처해지지는 않겠지 Even if he should be found guilty, he would not be sentenced to death. // ~는 미워해도 사람은 미워하지 마라 Condemn the offense and not its perpetrator. // 이 실패는 누구의 ~냐 Who is responsible[to blame] for the failure? // 내 ~는 아니다 I am not to blame for it. / It's not my fault.

죄과(罪科) [죄와 허물] an offense; a sin; a crime; blame; guilt. ¶~를 묻다 inquire into (a person's) crime // ~가 없는 사람 an innocent[a guiltless] person // ~가 없는 사람을 처벌하다 punish (a person) for nothing.
죄과(罪過) [그릇된 허물] an offense; [죄악] a sin; [과오] a fault.
죄다¹ 1 (느슨한 것을) tighten; make tight(er); strain; draw in; stretch; [수축시키다] contract; [조르다] strangle; wring. ¶볼트를 ~ tighten (up) a bolt // 나사로 ~ screw // 바이올린의 줄을 ~ screw up[stretch] the strings of a violin // 느슨한 줄을 ~ tighten[strain] a loose rope / stretch a loose rope tight // 고삐를 ~ tighten[pull up] the reins // 혁대를 ~ tighten a belt // 기타의 줄을 ~ tighten the strings of a guitar // 나사돌리개로 나사를 ~ tighten a screw with a screwdriver.
2 [벌어진 사이를 좁히다] put[place] close; (자리를) sit up; sit close[closely]. ¶열과 열 사이를 ~ close the ranks // 자리를 더 죄어 앉다 sit up a little closer / sit closer together.
3 (마음을) feel anxious[uneasy / nervous] (about); be fidgety; be worried (about); worry (oneself) (about). ¶결과가 어찌 될까 마음을 ~ be worried over the result / be worried over how it will turn out // 돌아오기를 마음 죄며 기다리다 wait in anxious suspense.
죄다² [전부] all; wholly; entirely; all through [together]; in all; altogether. ¶~ 털어놓다 confess everything // 용돈을 ~ 써 버리다 spend the last penny of one's pocket money // 가지고 있는 것을 ~ 주다 give (a person) everything that one has // 내가 알고 있는 것은 ~ 말했습니다 I have told you all I know. // ~ 고백해라 Make a clean breast of it. / Own up! / Confess everything!
죄명(罪名) the name of a crime[an offense]; charge. ¶사기의 ~으로 on a charge of fraud / charged with fraud // 애매한 ~으로 on no definite charge // 절도의 ~을 썼다 He was charged with theft. // 그는 방화의 ~으로 기소되었다 He was indicted on a charge of arson [was charged with arson]. // 그의 ~은 모릅니다 I do not know the name of his offense [what he is accused of].
죄목(罪目) [죄과] a charge; [혐의] suspicion. ¶…의 ~으로 (be indicted / be wanted) on a charge of ... // 그는 살인의 ~으로 체포되었다 He was arrested on a charge of murder.
죄받다(罪-) [지은 죄에 대해 벌을 받다] suffer[incur] punishment[a penalty]; be punished. ¶죄받을 짓 a sinful act // 그런 짓

죄상

을 하면 죄받는다 Heaven will punish you for it.
죄상(罪狀) [범죄의 실상] (the nature of) an offense [a crime]; guilt; criminality; charges. ¶~을 인정[부인]하다 plead guilty [not guilty] to a (criminal) charge // ~을 자백하다 confess one's crime [guilt] // ~이 명백해지다 stand convicted of a crime // 4개 항목의 ~으로 기소되다 be indicted on four counts // 피고인에게 ~의 시인 여부를 묻다 arraign the accused for [for] his crime // 그는 강도와 살인의 두 가지 ~으로 기소되었다 He was indicted on the two counts of burglary and murder.

죄송하다(罪悚−) (be) sorry [regrettable]. ¶죄송하다 be [feel] sorry (for) / regret / [송구해하다] feel small / be [feel] ashamed // 죄송하지만[죄송합니다만] I am sorry to trouble you, but .... / Excuse me, but ... / I beg your pardon sir, but .... // 오래 기다리게 해서 죄송합니다 I am very sorry to have kept you waiting so long. // 폐를 끼쳐서 대단히 죄송합니다 (이제부터 부탁할 때) I'm very sorry to trouble you. / (무엇을 해 받고서) I'm very sorry to have troubled you. // 죄송합니다만 다시 한 번 말씀해 주십시오 I am very sorry, but would you repeat it once more? // 죄송합니다만 버스 정류장이 어디입니까 Excuse me, but where is the bus stop? // 말씀 도중에 죄송합니다만 그건 작년 일을 말씀하시는 것입니까 Excuse me for interruption, but are you talking about last year? // 죄송합니다만 좀 천천히 말씀해 주시겠습니까 Would you mind speaking a little more slowly? // 죄송합니다만 오늘은 좀 쉬겠습니다 I am sorry, I will be absent today. // 죄송합니다만 오늘은 동행하지 못하겠습니다 (권유에 대하여) I am sorry for not going with you today. // 죄송합니다만 이 가방을 좀 지켜봐 주시겠습니까 I am sorry to trouble you, but could you watch this bag for me?

죄수(罪囚) a prisoner; a convict; (미국 구어) a jailbird.
● **죄수복** a prison uniform.

죄악(罪惡) (법률상의) a crime; (도덕·종교상의) (a) sin; a vice. ¶~의 소굴 a sink of iniquity // ~을 범하다 commit a sin [crime].
● **죄악감** the sense [feeling] of sin [guilt]; guilt feelings. ¶~을 느끼다 feel guilty. **죄악시~하다** consider (adultery) a sin.

죄어들다 tighten; become narrower [tighter]; get tightened [drawn up]. ¶수사망이 죄어들었다 The police dragnet moved in. // 양손을 묶은 밧줄이 살에 죄어들었다 The rope with which his hands were tied cut into the flesh. // 그 광경을 보고 그는 가슴이 죄어드는 것 같았다 The sight wrung his heart.

죄어치다 (바짝) tighten; [몰아치다] put spurs (to); urge (a person) on [forward]; [재촉하다] press; urge; rush; dun. ¶수사망을 ~ tighten the police dragnet // 일을 빨리 하라고 ~ urge (a person) to do a quick job / rush (a person) along to get job done faster // 빚을 갚으라고 ~ dun [press / push] (a person) for payment of a debt / urge (a person) to pay a debt.

죄업(罪業) [불] a sin; a sinful act. ¶~이 많은 사람 a sinful man / a sinner // ~을 쌓다[거듭하다] commit one sin after another / live a sinful life / live in sin.

죄의식(罪意識) the sense of sin [guilt]. ¶~있는 guilt-conscious / [ridden].

죄이다 1 (물건이) tighten; be tightened; be constricted; stiffen. ¶가슴이 죄이는 느낌 a constriction in the chest. 2 (마음이) feel anxious [uneasy / nervous]; be held [kept] in suspense.

죄인(罪人) (법률상의) a criminal; an offender; a lawbreaker; a convict(기결의); a culprit(미결의); (종교·도덕상의) a sinner; a transgressor; a delinquent.

죄적(罪迹) [범죄 증거가 될 만한 흔적] proofs [traces] of guilt; evidence [traces] of a crime.

죄증(罪證) [범죄의 증거] evidence [proofs] of a crime.

죄질(罪質) the nature of a crime [an offence].

죄짓다(罪−) (법률상으로) commit a crime [an offense]; (종교·도덕상으로) commit a sin; sin; trespass (against).

죄책(罪責) the liability of the accused. ¶~을 묻다 accuse (a person) of a crime // ~감을 느끼다 feel guilty / have a guilty conscience // 그가 ~감이 있으니까 고분고분하게 구는 것이다 He behaves submissively [maintains a low profile] because he has a guilty conscience [has something to hide].

죄형 법정주의(罪刑法定主義) the principle of "nulla poena [nullum crimen] sine lege"; the principle of legality.

죔쇠 a buckle; a clasp; a clamp.

죔틀 a press; a vise. ¶~에 걸어 죄다 put to a press.

죗값(罪−) wages of sin.

주(主) 1 [하느님] the Lord; God; [그리스도] our Lord. ¶~기도문 [기] the Lord's Prayer. 2 [주된 부분] the chief [principal] part; the main part. ¶누가 ~가 되어 이 계획을 추진했는가 Who took the initiative [lead] in carrying out the plan?

주(州) [옛 행정 구획] a province; (미국의) a state. ¶미시간 ~ the state of Michigan // 하와이는 1959년에 ~가 되었다 Hawaii attained statehood in 1959. // 수사는 ~ 전역에 걸쳐 실시됐다 They made a statewide search.

주(洲) 1 [퇴적으로 이루어진 땅] a sandbank; a (sand) bar. ¶삼각~ a delta. 2 [대륙] a continent. ¶아시아 ~ the continent of Asia // 오대~ the Five continents.

주(株) 1 stocks; shares. ➪주식(株式) ¶우량~ bluechip [gilt-edged] stocks // 우선~ preference [preferred] shares // 보통~ an ordinary [a common] share // 성장~ (미) growth [special] stock / (영) a growth [special] share // 인기~ active [leading / popular / favorite / glamor] stocks // 투기~ speculative stocks // ~의 가격 상승 [하락] a rise [fall] in shares // ~를 사다 buy [invest in] stock(s) / buy an interest (in a business) // 석유 회사의 ~를 2,000~ 사다 buy two thousand shares in an oil company // ~를 처분하다 liquidate shares // ~의 시세가 변동하다 shares fluctuate in price // 한 ~에 대해 …의 특별 배당을 받다 receive an extra dividend of ... a share // 최근에 철강~가 올랐다 Steel stocks [(영) shares] have been rising [going up] of late. 2 [그루] a root. ¶밤나무 세 ~ three chestnut trees // 장미 한 ~ a rose plant.

주(週) a week. ¶금[내 / 전] ~ this [next / last]

week // 2~간 two week / (영) a fortnight // 몇 ~ 동안 for (many) weeks // ~초에 at the beginning of the week // ~의 중간쯤에 at midweek // 지난 ~의 오늘 this day last week // 우리는 ~ 40시간 노동을 한다 We are on a forty-hour (work) week.

주(註·注) an annotation; (explanatory) notes; a commentary; comment. ¶~가 붙은[~를 단] annotated / with notes // ~를 **붙이다**[**달다**] annotate / add [annex] notes (to a book) / make [write] notes (on) // ~를 단 햄릿 신판 a new, annotated edition of Hamlet // 그 책에는 상세한 ~가 붙어 있다 The book is fully annotated.

주-(駐) ¶~한 resident [stationed] in Korea // ~미 한국 대사 the Korean Ambassador to [in] the United States.

주가(株價) the price of a stock; a stock price. ¶~가 오르다[내리다] one's stock rises [falls / goes down].
주가가 오르다 raise one in public esteem.
● 주가 지수 the price index of stocks. ¶종합 ~ the composite stock exchange index.

주간(主幹) (편집국의) the chief editor; the editor in chief. 주간하다 edit (a magazine).

주간(週刊) weekly publication; [간행물] a weekly (periodical). ¶~의 published weekly / weekly (paper).
● 주간지 / 주간 잡지 a weekly magazine. ¶시사 ~ a weekly newsmagazine / a newsweekly // 여성 ~ a women's weekly.

주간(週間) a week. ¶2~ (for) two weeks / a fortnight // 교통안전 ~ Traffic Safety Week // 전국 독서 ~ National Book Week // 2~의 휴가 fortnight's holiday
● 주간 논평 a weekly review.

주간(晝間) the daytime; day. ¶~에 in the daytime / during the day / by day // ~에는 일하고 야간에 학교에 다니다 work by day and attend school by night.
● 주간 근무 day-duty; daywork.

주객(主客) [주인과 손님] host and guest; [주(主)가 되는 것과 종(從)이 되는 것] principal and auxiliary; [언] subject and object. ¶순식간에 ~이 전도되었다 (형세의 역전) Very soon the tables were turned.

주객(酒客) [술을 좋아하는 사람] a drinker; a tippler.

주거(住居) [거주하는 집] a dwelling (house); a residence; an abode; [거주하는 것] living; residence. ¶~가 일정하지 않은 사람들 [문어] people of no fixed abode // ~를 **정하다** take up one's abode [residence] / settle (down) // ~를 **옮기다** move one's residence (to) // 이 읍에 ~를 정하기로 하겠다 I'll settle down in this town. // 그는 ~가 일정하지 않다 He is homeless. / He has no fixed residence.
● 주거비 housing expenses [expenditure]. 주거 지역 a residential district [area]. 주거 침입 housebreaking; violation of domicile.

주격(구둣주걱) a shoehorn; [밥주걱] a rice scoop.
● 주걱턱 a protruding chin; a spoonlike chin.

주검 a corpse. ⇨²시체(屍體)

주격(主格) [언] the nominative [subjective] case.
● 주격 보어 a subjective complement.

주견(主見) [자기주장이 있는 의견] one's own opinion [view]; a firm conviction; a fixed opinion. ¶~이 없다 have no fixed views [definite opinion] of one's own.

주경야독하다(晝耕夜讀-) work by day and study by night; grab every opportunity to better oneself.

주고받다 give and take reciprocally; exchange; interchange; reciprocate. ¶인사를 ~ exchange greetings // 편지를 ~ exchange letters (with) // 선물을 ~ give presents to one another [each other] // 술잔을 ~ exchange cups of wine // 아침 인사를 ~ exchange morning greetings / say good morning to one another // 그들은 심한 말을 주고받았다 They exchanged harsh words. // 그들은 악수를 주고받았다 They shook hands with each other. // 그들은 서로 미소를 주고받았다 They smiled at each other.

주곡(主穀) staple food-grains; main food staple.

주공(鑄工) a caster; a cast-iron worker.

주관(主管) supervision; superintendence; management. 주관하다 superintend; supervise; manage; have [be in] charge of.
● 주관자 a superintendent; a supervisor; a manager.

주관(主觀) (객관에 대하여) subjectivity; [주체] the subject; [자아] the ego. ¶~에 **치우치다** be too subjective // 점수는 심사원의 ~에 따라 가지각색이었다 The subjectivity of the judges' opinions resulted in a variety of scores.
● 주관론 [철] subjectivism. 주관성 subjectivity.

주관적(主觀的) subjective. ¶~ 비평 subjective criticism // ~으로 subjectively // ~으로 말하면 subjectively speaking // ~으로 보다 take a subjective view of (things).

주광성(走光性) [생] phototaxis. ¶~의 phototactic.

주교(主教) 1 [가] a bishop. ¶대~ an archbishop / a primate. 2 [주장으로 삼는 교] a dominant [major] religion.

주교(舟橋) a pontoon bridge. ⇨배다리

주구(走狗) 1 [사냥개] a hound. 2 an agent. ⇨²앞잡이2 ¶공산당의 ~ a mere tool of communists // 남의 ~가 되다 be made a cat's-paw of a person // 그는 한동호 씨의 ~에 지나지 않는다 He is a mere tool (in the hands) of Mr. Han Dongho.

주군(主君) one's (liege) lord; one's master.

주권(主權) sovereignty; sovereign power. ¶~을 **침해하다** violate the sovereignty (of) // ~을 **포기하다** yield [give up] (one's) sovereignty (over an island to another country).
● 주권국 / 주권 국가 a sovereign nation [power]. 주권자 a sovereign; a supreme ruler.

주권(株券) a share [stock] certificate; a share; a stock. ¶기명 ~ a registered share // 무기명 ~ a share certificate to bearer // ~의 명의를 변경하다 transfer a share [stock] certificate // ~으로 백만 원을 가지고 있다 have 1,000,000 won in share certificates // ~을 현금으로 바꾸다 cash stocks.

주근깨 a freckle; a fleck; a lentigo (pl. -tigines). ¶~가 낀 freckled / freckle-faced (girl) // ~가 있는 얼굴 a freckled face // ~**가 끼다** freckle / get freckled // 그는 ~투성이다 He has a lot of freckles.

주급(週給) a weekly pay; weekly wages. ¶~백 달러를 받다 draw a salary of 100 dollars a week (from a firm) / get $100 a week wages∥ ~ 2백 달러로 일하고 있다 I am employed at a weekly salary of 200 dollars.
● **주급 제도** the weekly payment system. ¶여기서는 ~를 실시하고 있다 We are paid by the week here.

주기(酒氣) the smell of liquor. ⇨"술기운" ¶~를 띠고 있다 be drunk / be intoxicated / be under the influence of liquor∥그는 ~를 띠고 있다 He is drunk. / He smells of liquor.∥그는 ~를 띤 채 쳐들어왔다 He came barging in reeking of alcohol.

주기(周忌·週忌) an anniversary of (a person's) death. ¶아버지의 8~ the eighth anniversary of one's father's death.

주기(週期) a period; a cycle. ¶경기의 ~ a business cycle∥행성의 ~ the period of a planet.
● **주기성**(-性) periodicity. **주기율** [화] the law of periodicity; the periodic law.

주기도문(主祈禱文) the Lord's prayer; (say) a pater [paternoster].

주기억 장치(主記憶裝置) main memory; main storage.

주낙 a fishing reel with longline. ¶~으로 고기를 잡다 fish with a reel and longline.

주년(週年) a whole year; an anniversary. ¶10~ the tenth anniversary∥2백 ~ 축제 the bicentennial festival∥미 독립 2백 ~을 기념하다 celebrate the American bicentennial [America's 200th birthday].

주눅 〔움츠러듦〕 diffidence; self-distrust; timidity; backwardness; 〔언죽번죽함〕 impudence; shamelessness.

주눅(이) 들다 become [be] diffident; lose heart [one's nerve]; shrink (from); be daunted (at / by); feel timid [small]. ¶나는 그 사람 앞에 나가기만 하면 주눅이 든다 I feel small in his presence. / I lose my nerve in front of him.

주니어 〔연소자〕 a junior.

주다¹ 1 〔제공하다〕 give; present (a person) with (something). ¶거저[공으로] ~ give (a person something) without charge [for nothing]∥남몰래 〔슬쩍〕 ~ slip (a 1,000-won note) into (a person's) hand [pocket]∥먹을 것을 ~ feed (a child) / give (a person) something to eat∥환자에게 약을 ~ administer [give] a medicine to a patient∥어린이에게 용돈을 ~ allow one's child pocket money∥아기에게 젖을 ~ give suck [the breast] to a child∥꽃에 물을 ~ water flowers∥닭에게 모이를 ~ feed the chickens∥거지에게 동냥을 ~ give to beggars∥그는 내게 선물을 주었다 He gave me a present.∥이 책을 너에게 주겠다 I'll give this book to you.∥이 책을 저에게 주시는 겁니까 Is this book for me?∥이 시계를 네게 주겠다 I will give you this watch. / This watch is for you. / You can have this watch.∥쇠고기를 1킬로그램 주십시오 Give me [I would like] a kilogram of beef.∥그것을 내게 주지 않겠니 Will you give it to me? / Will you let me have it? / May I have it?∥어머니는 내게 상당한 액수의 돈을 주었다 My mother gave me a considerable sum of money.∥금붕어에게 먹이를 주었니 Have you fed [given food to] the goldfish?∥나는 아침마다 나무에 물을 준다 I water the plants every morning.∥네가 갖고 싶다면 전부 주겠다 You can have them all if you want them.∥커피를 한 잔 주지 않겠소 Can I have a cup of coffee?

2 〔수여·부여하다〕 give; award (a person a medal); bestow (a favor on a person); confer (a title on [upon] a person); grant (a person a privilege). ¶박사 학위를 ~ confer a doctorate [a doctor's degree] on (a person)∥노벨상을 ~ bestow a Nobel prize on (a person)∥훈장을 ~ confer [award] a decoration [an order] (on a person)∥기회를 ~ afford [give / allow] an opportunity (of) / give (a person) a chance [break]∥승자에게는 금메달이 주어졌다 The winner was given [presented with] a gold medal. / A gold medal was given [presented] to the winner.∥그에게는 옥스퍼드 대학으로부터 박사 학위가 주어졌다 He was awarded [granted / given] a doctor's degree by Oxford. / A doctor's degree was conferred upon him by Oxford.∥우리에게 다시 한번 해 볼 기회를 주십시오 Please give us one more chance to try it.∥우리는 자연이 우리에게 주는 혜택에 감사해야 한다 We should be grateful for the favors bestowed on us by nature.

3 〔대다〕 give (rations to); provide; furnish; supply. ¶일[일거리]을 ~ provide (a person) with work∥자금을 ~ furnish with funds∥(보수로서) 월 100만 원을 ~ pay a monthly salary of 1,000,000 won∥나는 그에게 외투와 양복을 주었다 I provided him with an overcoat and a suit.∥급료를 많이 주는 일자리를 얻고 싶다 I want to get a job that pays well.

4 〔할당·부과하다〕 allot [assign] (work to a person); impose (a task on a person); set (a pupil a problem). ¶…에게 주어진 일 work assigned to (a person) / a task imposed on (a person)∥학생에게 주어진 문제 a problem set to a student∥과업을 ~ assign (a person) a task∥각자에게 몫을 ~ allot a share to each∥내게 중요한 지위가 주어졌다 I was assigned to an important post.

5 〔끼치다·가하다〕 cause; inflict; bring about; bring to bear; occasion (anxiety to …); exert [exercise] (influence upon); inflict (an injury on …). ¶나쁜 영향을 ~ exert a bad influence (upon)∥고통을 ~ cause pain (to)∥타격을 ~ give a blow (to a person's business)∥모욕을 ~ insult (a person)∥태풍이 벼농사에 큰 피해를 주었다 The typhoon did [caused] great damage to the rice crop. / The typhoon inflicted heavy damage on the rice crop.∥친구의 사망 소식은 내게 큰 충격을 주었다 The news of my friend's death was a shock to [shocked] me.

6 〔마음을 터놓다〕. ¶마음을 ~ open one's heart (to) / open up one's mind.

7 〔(줄을) 풀리게 하다〕 let loose; pay out. ¶연줄을 ~ let loose [pay out] the string of a kite.

8 〔힘을 미치게 하다〕 put (strength / force) in; put forth (one's strength). ¶힘을 주어 말하다 emphasize one's words / accentuate / speak with emphasis.

9 〔박다〕 drive [knock] in (a nail). ¶침을 ~ apply acupuncture.

주거니 받거니 〔주고받거나 건네는 모양〕 exchanging (wine cups). ¶~ 하며 마시다 hobnob [have a hobnob] (with).

주다² […에게 베풀다] do something for (a person); do a favor for (a person); take the trouble to (do). ¶거들어 ~ help / lend one's help (to) // 책을 빌려 ~ lend [loan] a book // 책[장난감]을 사 ~ buy (a person) a book [toy] / buy a book[toy] for (a person) // 상의를 입혀[벗겨] ~ help (a person) on[off] with his coat // 문을 열어 ~ open the door for (a person) // 이 편지를 부쳐 주게 Go mail this letter for me. // 그는 아이들에게 책을 읽어 주었다 He read a book for the children. // 네게 해 줄 재미있는 이야기가 있다 I have an interesting story to tell you. // 그것을 보여 주세요 Let me see[have a look at] it. / Show it to me. // 그녀는 내게 그 편지를 읽게 해 주었다 She let me [allowed me to] read the letter. // 그에게도 보여 주어라 Let him see it, too. // 그는 내 말을 들어 주지 않았다 He wouldn't listen to me. // 송 여사가 이 숄을 짜 주셨습니다 I had this shawl knit(ted) by Mrs. Song. // 그는 일부러 나를 만나러 와 주었다 He took the trouble to come and see me. // 그렇게 해 주신다면 정말 기쁘겠습니다 I should be very happy if you would[could] kindly do so.

주단(紬緞) [명주와 비단] silks and satins; silk fabrics [goods / stuff].

주당(酒黨) a drinker; a bacchant; a votary of Bacchus.

주대 [낚싯줄과 낚싯대] a (fishing) rod and line.

주도(主導) leading; initiative. ¶민간 ~의 경제 private-initiated economy // ~ 역할을 하다 play a leading role (for) / play a leading part (in) // 자동차 산업이 불황 탈피의 ~적 역할을 했다 The auto industry played the trigger role in getting the economy out of recession. **주도하다** lead (a movement); take the lead (in educational reform).
● **주도권** leadership; initiative; hegemony (동맹국들에 대한). ¶~ 다툼 a struggle for leadership / a leadership struggle // ~을 쥐다 [잡다] take the leadership [initiative] (in) // ~을 빼앗다 wrest [take] away the initiative (from) // ~을 잡기 위한 싸움을 벌이다 vie for the (party) leadership // 외교 교섭의 ~을 쥐다 take the initiative [leadership] in diplomatic negotiations // 그가 ~을 잡고 자원 봉사대를 조직했다 He took the initiative in organizing a volunteer group. **주도자** the leader; the prime mover.

주도(酒道) a drinking manner; a drinker's etiquette.

주도하다(周到-) [주의가 두루 미쳐서 빈틈없다] scrupulous; cautious; careful; circumspect; thoroughgoing. ¶주도한 계획 a carefully worked-out plan / a well-laid scheme // 주도하게 circumspectly / scrupulously / carefully / cautiously // 주도한 주의를 기울이다 pay close attention (to) // 주도한 주의를 요한다 It requires meticulous[scrupulous] care. // 모임은 주도하게 계획되어 있었다 The meeting had been carefully planned.

주독(酒毒) alcohol poisoning. ⇨"숙독(-毒)

주동(主動) 1 [어떤 일에 주장이 되어 행동함] leadership. **주동하다** take the lead [leadership] (of). 2 the prime mover. ⇨"주동자(⇨주동)
● **주동자** the prime mover; the moving spirit; the leader. ¶데모 ~를 검거하다 arrest the leader of the demonstration.

주되다(主-) ¶주된 chief / principal / main / major / prime / leading / important // 주된 원인 a major cause (for) // 주된 산물 principal [staple] products // 주된 과업 the principal task // 라이트와 브레이크가 이 차의 주된 점검 부분이다 The lights and brakes are the main points to be checked on this car.

주두(柱枓) [건] [대접받침] a capital; a chapiter; a cap (piece).

주두(柱頭) [식] [암술머리] a stigma (pl. -mata, ~s).

주둔(駐屯) [머무름] stationing; posting; staying; a stay. **주둔하다** be stationed (in / at); stay; occupy(점령). ¶한국에 주둔하고 있는 미군 U.S. troops stationed in Korea // 외국 군대가 그 나라에 주둔하고 있다 Foreign troops are stationed in that country. // 거기에는 500명의 병사가 주둔하고 있었다 Five hundred soldiers were stationed[quartered] there. (▶ be quartered는 막사를 짓고 숙영하다) ➔ 군대를 주둔시키다 station [post] troops.
● **주둔군** [수비대] a garrison; [점령군] stationary troops; occupation forces. **주둔지** a post; an army post.

주둥아리 〈속〉 a mouth. ⇨입1

주둥이 1 〈속〉 a mouth. ⇨입1 2 (개 등의) a muzzle; (새의) a bill; (육식조의) a beak. 3 (물건의) a mouthpiece; a mouth; a spout; (호스의) a nozzle.

주둥이를 놀리다 wag one's tongue[jaw]. ¶누구 앞에서 함부로 그런 주둥이를 놀리느냐 How dare you talk to me like that!

주둥이(가) 싸다 be a glib (talker); be talkative; be voluble; be a chatterbox.

주량(酒量) one's drinking [alcoholic] capacity. ¶~이 세다 drink much / be a heavy drinker // ~이 늘다[줄다] come to drink more[less] than before [one used to] // 그는 ~이 세다 He is a heavy drinker. // 나는 ~이 별로 세지 않다 I am not very much of a drinker. // 나는 요즈음 ~이 늘었다 I drink more liquor lately. // ~을 줄이는 게 좋겠다 You'd better cut down on your drinking.

주렁주렁 in clusters; in full bearing. ¶열매가 ~ 열린 나무 a tree in full bearing // 나무에 ~ 열린 과실 the load of fruit on a tree // (열매가) ~ 열리다 grow in clusters // 감나무에 감이 ~ 달려 있다 The persimmon tree is loaded with fruit. // 그에게는 처자가 ~ 딸려 있다 He has many mouths to feed. / He has a large family to feed.

주력(主力) [중심이 되는 힘] the main force [strength]. ¶~을 쏟다 concentrate one's efforts (on) / devote oneself (to) // 적의 ~은 아군의 좌측을 맹렬히 공격했다 The enemy's main force pressed on our left flank.
● **주력 부대** main-force units. **주력 업종** a core[central] business. **주력주** leading[key] shares[stocks]. **주력 함대** the main squadron[fleet].

주력(注力) [온 힘을 기울임] concentrating one's efforts; putting forth one's strength [effort]. **주력하다** concentrate[focus] one's efforts [energies] (on); throw energy into; devote oneself (to); exert oneself (for / in). ¶기타의 습득에 주력했다 I concentrated (all) energy on learning the guitar.

주렴(珠簾) bead blinds; a bead screen.

주례(主禮) (일) officiating at a wedding ceremony; (사람) an officiator. ¶그들의 결혼식은 목사에 ～로 행해졌다 Their wedding ceremony was conducted by the minister. / Their marriage was solemnized by the minister.
주례(를) 서다 officiate at a marriage.
● **주례 목사** an officiating minister.

주로(主-) mainly; principally; chiefly; primarily; in the main; [대개] mostly; for the most part; generally. ¶그가 하는 일은 ～ 수금(收金)이다 His job is mainly [chiefly] collecting money. / Collecting money is the main part of his job. ¶여름은 ～ 바닷가에서 지냅니다 I spend the summer mostly at the seaside. // 그것은 ～ 기후의 변화 때문이다 It is mainly due to climatic changes. // 회원은 ～ 학생들이었다 Most of the members were students. / The members were mostly students. // 이 소설은 ～ 유대 인 문제를 다루고 있다 The chief [main] concern of this novel is the Jews. / The novel deals principally [mainly] with the Jewish problem. // 이 책의 독자는 ～ 주부이다 Most of the readers of this book are housewives. / The readers of this book are mostly [for the most part] housewives.

주로(走路) (경기장의) a track; (마라톤 등의) a course.

주루(走壘) [야구] base running. ¶～를 잘하다 be good at base running // ～에서 실책을 범하다 make an error in base running.

주룩주룩 1 (주름이) with wrinkles [rumples / folds]. ¶～ 주름이 가다 become full of wrinkles [lines]. 2 (비 등이) sprinklingly; pattering; pitter-patter. ¶～ 오는 비 a sprinkling [sprinkle] of rain / a sprinkling rain // (비가) ～ 오다 sprinkle / patter / fall pitter-patter (on).

주류(主流) the main current; the main stream. ¶미국 문학의 ～ the main current of American literature.
● **주류파** the leading [mainstream / main-current] faction; the faction in power. ¶반～ anti-mainstream group [faction] // ～와 반～의 다툼 a struggle between the mainstream faction and the opposing factions.

주류(酒類) alcoholic liquors [beverages]; intoxicating drinks; (미) wet goods. ¶비～ 음료 a soft drink.
● **주류 판매점** a liquor shop.

주르르 1 [액체가 흘러내리는 모양] tricklingly; dribbling; running. ¶～ 흐르다 trickle down [out / along] // 눈물이 ～ 그녀의 뺨을 흘러내렸다 Tears streamed [rolled] down her cheeks. 2 [미끄러지는 모양] slidingly; slipperily. ¶～ 미끄러져 내리다 slide [slip] down (a tree) // (허리띠 등이) ～ 풀리다 slip off. 3 [빠르게 내닫는 모양] at a dash; with one rush. ¶～ 달려가다 make a dash (for) / go off at a dash.

주르륵 dribbling; trickling.

주름 [구김살] wrinkles; crumples; furrows; [접은 줄] pleats; folds; creases. ¶잔～ fine wrinkles [lines] // 이마에 ～ wrinkles [lines] on one's forehead // 나이 들어 ～ 진 얼굴 a face wrinkled with age // 눈가의 ～ a crow's-foot // ～을 잡다 pleat / fold / take a tuck / gather in // 바지에 ～을 잡다 crease [put a crease in] one's trousers // ～을 펴다 smooth (down) / iron out wrinkles // 바지의 ～을 펴다 take creases out of the trousers / smooth [press] out wrinkles from [in] the trousers // 종이의 ～을 펴다 smooth out crumpled paper.
● **주름살** [구김살] wrinkles; [접은 줄] pleats; folds; creases. ¶나는 눈 ～이 생겨나고 있다 I have begun to develop wrinkles round my eyes. // 노령과 걱정이 그의 이마에 ～을 지었다 Age and care have made deep lines on his forehead. **주름치마** a pleated skirt.

주름잡다 [세력을 떨치다] overwhelm; dominate; predominate; sway. ¶전국을 ～ sway the whole nation // 세상을 ～ take the world by storm // 그는 당대를 주름잡는 정치가다 He is a most powerful [influential] politician now.

주리 the leg-screw torture.
주리(를) 틀다 twist (a suspect's) legs (as a torture).

주리다 [배 곯다] be [go] hungry; starve; famish; be famished; [갈망하다] be hungry [avid] (for / after); hunger [starve / hanker / thirst] for [after]. ¶사랑에 ～ hanker after love / be hungry for affection // 처자를 주리게 하다 let one's family go hungry // 배를 채우다 satisfy one's appetite (with some food) / gratify one's hunger // 그는 배를 주리며 아들을 교육시켰다 He gave his son an education, denying himself all the comforts of life.

주립(州立) [관형어적] (an institution, an organization, etc.) established [founded] by the state; state-established [-founded].
● **주립 대학** a state university.

주마가편(走馬加鞭) inspiring [urging] (a person) to further efforts.

주마간산(走馬看山) taking a cursory view (of); giving a hurried glance (to / over); running one's eyes over.

주마등(走馬燈) [영등] a revolving lantern; [비유] kaleidoscopic change. ¶～ 같은 kaleidoscopic / ever-changing [shifting] // 어린 시절의 추억이 ～처럼 떠올랐다 Many memories of my childhood were brought back in rapid succession.

주막(酒幕) an inn. ¶～에 들다 put up at an inn.

주말(週末) the weekend. ¶나는 ～에 친구에게 갈 거야 I'm going to visit a friend over the weekend. // 그는 ～이 되면 골프만 친다 He does nothing but play golf on [(영) at] weekends. // 이번 ～엔 예정이 어떻습니까 What are your plans for this coming weekend?
● **주말여행** a weekend trip. ¶～을 떠나다 go away for the weekend.

주맥(主脈) 1 [으뜸이 되는 줄기] the main range. 2 (잎맥의) the main vein.

주머니 1 [물건을 넣는 것] a bag; a sack; a pouch. ¶～에 넣다 put into a bag / bag // ～를 비우다 empty a bag. 2 a pocket. ⇨ 호주머니
● **주머니 사정** one's financial [pecuniary] condition; one's finances [funds]. ¶～이 좋다 have a heavy purse / have plenty of money / be in funds // ～이 나쁘다 have a light purse / be short of money / be out of funds / be badly off. **주머닛돈** pocket money.

주먹 a (clenched) fist; the knuckles; (속어) dukes; the bunch of fives. ¶빈～ an empty

hand∥~만 한 돌 a fist-size(d) stone[rock] ∥~을 휘두르다 wave[shake] one's fist at (a person)∥~을 쥐다 clench one's fist∥남에게 ~을 먹이다 hit a person with one's fist∥맨~으로 싸우다 fight (against the enemy) with naked fists∥그는 소년에게 ~세례를 퍼부었다 He rained blows on the boy. / He hit the boy again and again.∥그는 나에게 ~을 휘둘러 보였다 He shook his fist at me.∥학생 시절에는 나도 ~으로 이름을 날렸다 I was known as a tough when I was in school.
●주먹구구 [손가락 셈] finger counting; counting (something) on one's fingers; [어림] rule of thumb; a rough estimate[calculation]; approximate figures. ¶~로 어림잡다 estimate by rule of thumb / make a rule-of-thumb estimate / make a rough estimate [calculation] (of). 주먹다짐 [주먹질] blows (with the fist); fisting; fisticuffs; [옥박지름] threats with one's fists; the menace of violence; an intimidatory measure. ¶마침내 ~이 벌어졌다 Finally they came to blows. / They ended up exchanging blows. / At last they got into a fight. 주먹밥 a rice ball. 주먹심 the power of one's fist (to hit grasp figure); [완력] physical strength; force. 주먹질 [때리기] blows with the fists; fisting; fisticuffs; [위협] threats with the fists; [옥] fist shaking. ¶~을 하다 strike (a person) with the fists / fist (each other) / fight / threaten[menace] with the fists / shake [raise] one's fist at (a person) from behind.
주먹코 a bulbous[potato] nose; a snub nose.
주명곡(奏鳴曲) [음] a sonata. ⇨소나타
주모(酒母) [술을 파는 여자] the hostess of an inn; an innkeeper.
주모자(主謀者) a ringleader; a leader; a moving spirit; a prime mover; the author of (a mischief); the originator. ¶폭동의 ~는 누구인가 Who instigated[was behind] the riot? ∥그가 ~임에 틀림없다 He must be the mastermind[at the bottom] of the affair.∥그가 개혁안의 ~다 He is the chief mover in the scheme of reform.
주모하다(主謀―) lead[head] (a conspiracy, a movement, etc.); take the lead (in); organize.
주목(朱木) [식] a yew (tree).
주목(注目) attention; observation; notice; remark. ¶세인의 ~의 대상이 되다 become the center[focus] of public attention∥~ (구령) Attention!∥그 책은 누구에게도 ~을 받지 못했다 Nobody took any notice of the book. / The book went unnoticed.∥공해 문제는 최근 적지 않은 ~을 끌고 있다 The pollution problem has lately attracted considerable attention. 주목하다 pay[give] attention (to); direct[turn] one's attention (to); observe; watch; take notice (of). ¶주목할 만한 현상 a noteworthy[remarkable] phenomenon∥금년의 주목할 만한 문학 작품은 the notable literary works of this year∥그의 작품은 주목할 만하다[주목할 가치가 없다] His work is[not] worthy of note. / His work deserves[doesn't deserve] our attention.∥세계가 (대단한) 관심을 갖고 한국의 공업을 주목하고 있다 Korea's industry is watched by all the world with (keen) interest.∥경찰관은 그 남자의 수상한 행동에 주목했다 The police-

man noticed the man's suspicious conduct. ➔¶그 일의 귀추가 매우 주목된다 The development is being watched with keen interest.
주무(主務) [행위] chief control of affairs; [사람] the chief official in charge of affairs. 주무하다 be in charge of; have[take] charge of; have control over; have competence (over a matter).
●주무 관청[장관] the competent authorities[Minister].
주무르다 1 (물건을) rub and press with the fingers; fumble with; tamper[tinker] with. ¶흙을 ~ play[finger] with mud / make mud pies. 2 (몸을) massage; knead(근육을). ¶어깨 [다리]를 ~ massage (a person's) shoulders [legs]∥어깨를 주무르게 하다 have one's shoulders massaged. 3 [농락하다] sport[toy / trifle / fool] (with); make sport[a plaything / a fool] (of). ¶…을 마음대로 ~ have (a person) completely under one's control / make a dummy of (a person) / keep (one's husband) under one's thumb.
주무시다 sleep. ⇨자다 ¶할아버지는 벌써 주무신다 My grandfather has already gone to bed.∥아버지 안녕히 주무십시오 Good night, Father!
주문(主文) 1 (문장 속의) the main clause. 2 (판결문의) the text (of a judicial decision).
주문(注文) 1 [맞춤] an order; a commission; [주문하는 일] ordering. ¶견본 ~ a sample order∥구두 ~ a verbal order∥대량 [소량] ~ a large[small] order∥추가 ~ a reorder∥화급한 ~ a rush order∥~에 응하여 [따라] on the order of / to order∥~에 응하다 accept [take] an order∥~을 맡다 [받다] accept [take (up)] an order / take[book] orders (from) / secure an order∥~을 받는 대로 곧 upon receipt of your order∥그 물품에 ~이 쇄도했다 Orders came pouring in[flooded in] for that article. / We were swamped with orders for that article.∥백과사전은 ~ 중이다 The encyclopedia is on order.∥저 가게에서는 베테랑 점원이 손님의 ~을 받고 있다 At that store experienced clerk[assistants] attend to customers.∥이제 마지막 ~을 받습니다 (식당 등에서) This is the last chance to make an order. / We are now taking last orders. / Last orders, please. 주문하다 order (an article from a firm); give an order (for an article to a firm); place[put in] an order (with a firm for an article / in a country). ¶추가 ~ reorder / make[place] a supplementary[an additional] order∥영국[외국]에 책을 ~ order books from England[abroad]∥주문한 것이 드디어 왔다 I got my order at last.∥(음식점에서 종업원이) 주문하시겠습니까 May I take your order?∥나는 종업원에게 커피를 주문했다 I gave the waitress an order for (a cup of) coffee. / I ordered (a cup of) coffee from a waitress.∥나는 그것을 저 회사에 주문했다 I placed an order for it with that company.∥주문해 놓고 있습니다 It is on order.∥그들은 야근하는 사람들에게 제공할 식사를 주문했다 They ordered dinner to be sent in to the people working late.∥오늘은 주문하실 것이 없으십니까 Have you any order today, Madam[Sir]?
2 [요구] a request; a demand; [조건] a condition. ¶~을 달다 make a request∥그는 무리한 ~을 해 왔다 He has made an unrea-

주문

sonable request of us.∥집은 남향으로 해 달라는 한 가지 ~만을 달고 집을 짓게 했다 I had a house built with only one condition attached: that it should face south.∥모든 것이 ~대로 되는 것은 아니다 You cannot have everything your own way. **주문하다** request; demand.
● **주문서** an order sheet. **주문자** [주문한 사람] the orderer. **주문품** an article made to order.

주문(呪文) an incantation; a spell. ¶액막이의 ~ an incantation against bad luck∥~을 외우다 utter an incantation∥~을 걸다 cast a spell (on a person)∥~으로 병을 고치러 하다 try to cure a disease with an incantation∥고인의 영혼을 ~으로 불러내다 conjure up the spirit of the deceased.

주물(呪物) a fetish.
● **주물 숭배** fetishism.

주물(鑄物) casting; cast-iron ware; a cast-iron product. ¶~의 상 a cast-metal statue∥~용 선철 foundry pig iron.
● **주물공** a founder; a caster. **주물 공장** a foundry.

주물럭거리다 work and press with the hands; fumble with; finger; knead; massage.

주물럭주물럭 kneadingly; fumbling; fingering. **주물럭주물럭하다** work and press with the hands. ⇨주물럭거리다

주미(駐美) [관형어적] resident[stationed] in America.
● **주미 한국 대사** the Korean Ambassador to [in] the United States[at[in / to] Washington].

주민(住民) an inhabitant; resident; citizen. ¶그는 이 아파트의 ~이 아니다 He is not a resident of[He does not live in] this apartment house.
● **주민 등록** resident registration. **주민 등록 번호** a resident registration number. **주민 등록증** a resident card; a certificate of residence. **주민세** a residence tax.

주발(周鉢) [놋쇠로 만든 밥그릇] a (brass) bowl. ¶한 ~의 죽 a bowl of porridge.

주방(廚房) a kitchen; a cookroom; a cookery; a cuisine; (배 안의) a galley; a cookhouse.
● **주방용품** kitchen utensils. **주방장** a head cook; (프) a chef.

주번(週番) weekly duty. ¶금주는 ~이다 I am on duty this week.

주범(主犯) the principal (offender); a principal in the first degree. ¶그가 ~이다 He committed the offense as the principal.

주법(走法) [체] (a form of) running. ¶그가 마라톤의 ~을 가르쳐 주었다 He taught me how to run a marathon.

주법(奏法) execution. ⇨연주법(⇨연주) ¶바이올린 ~ a way of playing the violin.

주벽(酒癖) one's behavior[(영) behaviour / mood] when drunk; a drinking habit. ¶그는 (나쁜) ~이 있다 [심하다] He turns nasty [quarrelsome] when he drinks.

주변 initiative; resourcefulness; nous; versatility. ¶~이 좋은 resourceful / versatile∥~이 없는 clueless / resourceless / incompetent / not adaptable∥말~이 좋다 be a glib talker / be fair-spoken / be glib-[silver-/ smooth-]tongued∥나는 ~이 없어 재치 있게 인사말도 못 한다 I am too inept to pay clever compliments.
● **주변머리** 〈속〉 initiative. ⇨주변 ¶돈도 없고 ~도 없다 I am neither rich nor versatile.

주변(周邊) [주위] the circumference; the surroundings; the periphery; (도회의) the environs; the outskirts. ¶~에 [언저리에] around / [근처에] in the neighborhood[(영) neighbourhood / vicinity](▶neighbourhood는 사는 사람들을 의식하고, vicinity는 장소를 의미함)∥이 ~에 around here / in this neighborhood∥역 ~에 near the station∥서울 ~에 in the vicinity of Seoul / in and around Seoul∥~에는 아무도 없었다 There was no one around.∥~ 일대에 꽃이 피어 있었다 Flowers were in full bloom all around us.∥그는 한 마디 말도 않고 ~을 살피고 있었다 He was looking about him without saying a word.

주보(酒甫) [술에 결은 사람] a (heavy) drinker; a (confirmed) drunkard.

주보(週報) [한 주일마다 발행하는 신문] a weekly (paper); (공보) a weekly (bulletin); (보고) a weekly report.

주봉(主峯) [최고봉] the main[principal] peak; the highest peak.

주부(主部) [주요한 부분] the main[principal] part; [언] the subject.

주부(主婦) (한 집안의) a housewife; a mistress; a materfamilias; (미) a homemaker(▶housewife와 househusband를 총칭하는 말로, 최근에는 housewife가 성 차별적인 말이라 하여 대신 이 말을 많이 쓰고 있음); [안주인] the hostess. ¶알뜰한 ~ a good [practical] housewife∥~가 되다 manage [run / mother] one's household∥그녀는 이제 아주 ~티가 난다 She is now every inch a housewife.

주부코 a whisk(e)y nose; a drinker's nose.

주비(籌備) [계획하여 준비함] arrangement; preparation.
● **주비 위원회** a preparatory committee; an arrangements committee.

주빈(主賓) the guest of honor[(영) honour]. ¶…을 ~으로 만찬회를 열다 give a dinner in honor of ….
● **주빈석** the seat of honor.

주뼛주뼛 hesitantly; diffidently; hesitatingly; in a hesitant[diffident] manner; in a hesitating way. **주뼛주뼛하다** shy and hesitant; nervous; timorous. ¶그는 쭈뼛쭈뼛하며 아무 말도 못 하고 서 있었다 He stood there timidly without saying a word.

주사(主事) 1 (관리의) a junior official; (집합적) the clerical staff. 2 (경칭) Mr.; Esq. ¶홍~ Mr. Hong.

주사(主辭) [논] the subject.

주사(朱砂) [광] cinnabar.

주사(走査) [TV] scanning. **주사하다** scan.
● **주사기** a scanner.

주사(注射) (an) injection; (구어) a shot; [접종] an inoculation; a vaccination. ¶근육[정맥] ~ (an) intramuscular [intravenous] injection∥모르핀 ~ an injection of morphine∥예방 ~ a preventive injection[shot] (against influenza)∥피하 ~ (a) hypodermic [subcutaneous] injection∥1회의 ~량 a syringeful∥팔에 모르핀 ~를 맞다 get[have] a morphine shot in[on] the arm∥그녀에게 ~가 효험이 있었다[없었다] The injection worked[didn't work] on her.∥그 환자는 ~로 겨우 목숨을 부지하고 있었다 The patient was barely kept alive by injections. **주사하다** inject; give [make / administer / apply] an injection; syringe. ¶포도당을 ～ administer an injection of glucose // 캠퍼 2대를 ～ give [administer] (a person) two camphor injections.

● **주사기** an injector; a syringe. **주사액 / 주사약** an injection. **주삿바늘 / 주사침** an injection syringe; a needle.

주사(酒邪) [술 마신 뒤의 나쁜 버릇] a drunken frenzy. ¶～가 있는 사람 a bad drunk / a vicious drinker // ～가 있다 be an obnoxious drunk.

주사위 a die (*pl.* dice) (▶ 속담 외에는 보통 one of the dice로 씀). ¶～를 던지다 cast [roll / throw] dice.

주사위는 던져졌다 (속담) The die is cast.; There's no turning back now.

● **주사위 놀이** diceplay. ¶～를 하다 play dice.

주산(主山) the guardian hill (located north of a town or grave).

주산(珠算) calculation on the abacus. ¶～을 잘하다 be good at abacus calculation. **주산하다** reckon [count] on the abacus; do sums [calculate] on an abacus.

주산물(主産物) staple products [produce]; main [chief / principal] products.

주산지(主産地) a chief producing district [center].

주상(主上) (His Majesty) the King.

주상(主喪) the chief mourner.

주색(朱色) a vermilion color; vermilion; cinnabar red.

주색(酒色) wine and women; wine and idle dalliance. ¶～에 빠지다 be addicted [given] to sensual pleasures / abandon [yield] oneself to wine and women / indulge in debauchery // 그는 ～에 빠져 있다 He leads a life of dissipation [a dissolute life].

● **주색잡기** wine, sex, and gambling.

주생활(住生活) housing life [habits].

주서 a juicer.

주서(朱書) rubrication. **주서하다** write in red (ink); rubricate.

주석(主席) the head; the chief; (중국의) the Chairman.

주석(朱錫) tin (기호 Sn). ¶～을 입히다 [～으로 싸다] tin.

● **주석박** tin foil.

주석(柱石) 1 [기둥과 주춧돌] pillars and cornerstones. 2 [가장 중요한 구실을 하는 사람] a pillar; a mainstay; a (main) prop; a support; a cornerstone. ¶국가의 ～ the cornerstone of a nation // 사회의 ～ the pillars of society.

주석(酒石) [화] (crude) tartar.

● **주석산** tartaric acid.

주석(酒席) a banquet; a feast; a drinking party. ¶～을 마련하다 hold a party // ～에서 시중들다 serve at a party.

주석(註釋·注釋) (explanatory) notes; comments; a commentary; [주석 붙이기] annotation; explanation; exposition. ¶～이 붙은 책 an annotated book / a book with explanatory notes // 한시에 ～을 붙이다 annotate Chinese poems // 이것에는 다소의 ～이 필요하다 This needs some explication.

● **주석자** an annotator.

주선(周旋) [알선] good [kind] offices; [추천] recommendation; [중개] mediation; agency. ¶우리는 사장님의 ～으로 결혼하게 되었다 We got married thanks to the help [[문어] through the kind offices] of the president. // 그의 친절한 ～으로 모든 일이 잘되어 갔다 Everything went smoothly thanks to [through] his kind arrangement. // 이 모임은 최 선생의 ～으로 이루어졌다 This meeting came about as a result of Mr. Choe's leadership. **주선하다** act as one's agent; use one's good offices. ¶나는 친구가 주선해 주어 취직했다 Through the good offices of a friend, I got a job. // 그는 고맙게도 아들의 취직을 주선해 주었다 He was so kind as to help my son get a job [use his influence in getting a job for my son].

● **주선료** a brokerage fee; a commission. **주선인** a broker; an agent; (고용의) an employment agent.

주섬주섬 ¶～ 줍다 pick up piece by piece [one by one] / gather // 방바닥의 장난감을 ～ 줍다 gather one's toys from the floor.

주성분(主成分) the chief [main] ingredient(s); the main component(s). ¶이 약의 ～은 요오드이다 The chief ingredient of this medicine is iodine.

주세(酒稅) a liquor tax.

● **주세법** [법] the Liquor Tax Law.

주소(住所) one's dwelling (place); one's residence [abode]; one's quarters; [법] a domicile. ¶현 ～ one's present address // ～가 일정하지 않다 have no fixed abode [address] / have no definite domicile / (미국 구어) be a floater // ～를 정하다 take up one's residence [abode / quarters] (at) / make one's home (at) / settle down (at) // ～를 변경하다 change one's place of residence // ～가 틀리다 be wrongly addressed / make misaddressed // 겉봉에 ～를 쓰다 [적다] address an envelope [a letter] (to a person) // ～가 바뀌었습니다 I have changed my address. / I have moved. // ～가 어디입니까 May I have your address? / What is your address?

● **주소록** an address book; a directory. **주소 불명** the address unknown. **주소 성명** one's name and address. ¶～을 말하시오 Give me your name and address. // ～을 기입하십시오 Write (down) your name and address.

주술(呪術) incantation; enchantment; magic; the black art; spell.

주스 juice; fruit juice; fruit-flavo(u)r soft drink. ¶깡통에 든 ～ canned juice // 프루트 ～ fruit juice // 농축 환원 ～ concentrated reconstituted juice.

주시(注視) a steady gaze; close observation; scrutiny. ¶만인의 ～의 대상이 되다 become the cynosure of the world [of all eyes]. **주시하다** gaze steadily (at); fix one's eyes (on); observe (a person) closely; watch [look at] (a thing) carefully. ¶그는 그녀를 주시했다 He fixed his eyes on [upon] her. // 경찰관은 그의 행동을 주시했다 The policeman watched him [observed his behavior] closely.

주식(主食) the staple [principal] food; the chief article of food. ¶～ **대용음** a substitute for staple food // 한국 사람은 쌀을 ～으로 한다 The staple [principal] food of the Koreans is rice. / The Koreans diet is built around rice.

주식(株式) 〔미〕 stocks; 〔영〕 shares. ¶~을 발행하다 issue stocks // ~을 모집하다 invite subscriptions for shares / offer stocks for subscription // ~을 양도하다 transfer shares [stocks] // ~을 매매하다 deal in stocks [shares] // ~에 손을 대다 speculate[dabble] in stocks / play[dabble on] the stock market // ~으로 돈을 벌다[손해 보다] make [lose] money on[in] the stock market.
● 주식 거래 stock dealings; a deal in stock (1회의 경우); an operation in stock(대규모의). 주식 공개 offering of stock to the public; going public. 주식 매매 dealing in stocks [shares]; stockjobbing(부정한). 주식 발행 a stock issue. 주식 배당 a stock dividend; a (share) dividend. 주식 시세 / 주식 시황 (stock exchange) quotations; stock[share] prices. 주식 시장 the stock market; stock exchange. 주식 중매인 a stockbroker; 〔영〕 a sharebroker. 주식 투자 investment in stocks. 주식 회사 〔미〕 a joint-stock corporation(약어 Inc.); 〔영〕 a joint-stock company(약어 & Co., Ltd.).

주식(畫食) 〔점심밥〕 lunch; luncheon; a midday meal.

주심(主審) 〔야구에서〕 the head[chief] umpire; 〔권투 등에서〕 the referee.

주악(奏樂) a musical performance.

주안(主眼) 〔주되는 목표〕 the prime[principal] object; the chief aim[end]; the object in view; the principal point. ¶인격 양성을 ~으로 하여 with an eye to character-building // 그것은 경제 성장을 ~으로 하고 있다 It aims principally at economic growth.
● 주안점 〔요점〕 the point; 《문어》 the purport; 〔주목표〕 the main object. ¶계획의 ~은 아동 복지이다 The main object[point] of the plan is child welfare.

주안상(酒案床) a drinking table. ⇨"술상"

주야(晝夜) day and night. ¶~로 일하다 work day and night[around the clock] // ~ 교대로 일하다 work in night and day shifts // ~로 골몰하다 be busy day and night // 부상병은 일~ 의식이 없었다 The wounded soldier remained unconscious for twenty-four hours.

주야장천(晝夜長川) 〔밤낮으로·늘〕 day and night ever passing; unceasingly.

주어(主語) 〔언〕 the subject (of a sentence).

주역(主役) 1 〔주인공의 역〕 the leading [starring / principal] part[role]; 〔주연하는 배우〕 the star; the leading actor[actress]. ¶~을 맡다 play the lead // 그는 ~로 영화에서 ~을 했다 He played the leading role[part] in the film. / He starred in the film. 2 〔중심 인물〕 a leader. ¶그녀는 깨끗한 선거 운동의 ~이었다 She was the leader of the clean-elections campaign. // 쿠데타의 ~은 공군 장교들이었다 The leading figures in the coup d'état were air force officers.

주역(周易) (저서명) the Book of Changes.

주연(主演) a star; 〔남자 주연〕 the leading actor; 〔여자 주연〕 the leading actress. 주연하다 play the leading part; star (in a play [film]). ¶그 영화에서는 러셀 크로가 주연했다 The movie starred Russell Crowe. / Russell Crowe starred[played the lead] in the movie.
● 주연 배우 a star; the leading actor[actress].

주연(周延) 〔논〕 distribution.

주연(酒宴) a feast; (공식적인) a banquet; a drinking bout[party]. ¶~을 베풀다 hold a banquet // ~을 벌이다 have[go on] a spree [drunken frolic] // ~이 한창이다 The banquet is at its height now.

주열성(走熱性) thermotaxis. ¶ ~의 thermotactic / thermotaxic.

주영(駐英) 〔관형어적〕 resident[stationed] in England.
● 주영 한국 대사 the Korean Ambassador to the United Kingdom.

주옥(珠玉) a gem; a jewel; (집합적) jewelry. ¶~같은 글 a literary gem / a writing of rare beauty // ~의 명편 a literary gem / a masterpiece / a jewel of a literary work.

주요(主要) 〔관형어적〕 principal; chief; main; major; leading; important; staple. ¶~ 수출국 the principal exporting nations. 주요하다 principal; chief; main; major; leading; important; staple. ¶스위스의 주요한 산업은 시계 제조이다 The key industry of Switzerland is watchmaking. // 커피는 브라질의 주요한 산물의 하나이다 Coffee is one of the staples[staple products] of Brazil.
● 주요 경기 종목 the main events (of today). 주요 도시 major cities. ¶한국의 ~ chief cities of Korea. 주요 산물 staple products. 주요 산업 key industries. 주요 성분 the main [principal] ingredients. 주요 시장 a primary market. 주요 원인 main cause[reason]. 주요 인물 the leading[key] figures; (연극이나 소설 등의) the main characters.

주워대다 quote[mention] this and[or] that; enumerate glibly. ¶이유를 ~ pick excuses [reasons] from the air // 거짓말을 ~ make up lies.

주워듣다 happen to hear (of / about); learn (something) by chance; pick up (a bit of information). ¶남에게서 주워들은 지식 knowledge picked up from others // 남에게서 이야기를 ~ pick a story up from others.

주워섬기다 chatter; rattle on; spiel; shoot off one's mouth; carry tales.

주위(周圍) 1 〔둘레〕 the circumference; the girth; (기하에서) the periphery. ¶~의 숲 the surrounding woods // 대학 캠퍼스 ~에는 방풍림이 둘러싸고 있다 The campus is surrounded by a windbreak.
2 〔환경〕 the surroundings(▶ 복수형); the environment; 〔근처〕 the neighborhood; 〔영〕 the neighbourhood. ¶~의 마을들 neighboring towns // 집 ~를 치우다 tidy up a yard / tidy up the area around a house // ~에서 사람들이 몰려왔다 People gathered from all around // 그들을 바라보는 ~의 눈초리가 차가웠다 Those around them looked coldly on them.
3 〔주위의 사정·부대 상황〕 circumstances. ¶~의 상황에 따라 depending on the circumstances // ~의 사정으로 할 수 없이 그렇게 했다 I did so through force of circumstance.

주유(注油) oiling; lubrication; 〔급유〕 oil supply. 주유하다 oil; lubricate; fill; feed. ¶차에 ~ gas up one's car.
● 주유기(−器) a lubricator; an oiler. 주유소 an oil[a filling] station; 〔미〕 a gas[service] station.

주유(周遊) 〔돌아다니면서 유람함〕 a (circular) tour; a round trip; (할인 요금에 의한, 보통 당일치기의) an excursion. ¶세계 ~ a round-the-world tour // ~를 **떠나다** go on a tour 주유하다 make a circular tour. ¶제주도를 ~ tour through Jejudo.

주의(主義) [행동의 지침] (a) principle; [교리] a doctrine; [신념] a belief; [방침] a line; a system; a basis. ¶감각~ sensationalism // 객관~ objectivism // 공화~ republicanism // 비관~ pessimism // ~가 있는[없는] 사람 a man of principle [no principle] // 현금~로 (do business) on a cash // ~를 **지키다** act [live] up to one's principle / stick to one's principle // 나에게 ~ 따위는 없다 I have no set beliefs. / I follow no particular doctrines. // 안전 제일~로 나가자 Let's go by the motto of "Safety First".

주의(注意) **1** [유의·주목] attention; observation; note; notice; heed; [경계·조심] care; watch; caution. ¶(남의) ~를 끄는 attractive / catching // ~가 **부족하다** be careless [inattentive / incautious] // ~를 **기울이다** pay attention (to) // ~를 **끌다** draw [attract / catch / command] (a person's) attention // ~를 다른 곳으로 돌리다 call away the attention // 공부에 ~를 집중해라 You must concentrate on your study. // 새로운 사태에 대해 그의 ~를 촉구했다 I brought the new situation to his notice. // 한 마디 말씀을 드리겠습니다 Just a word of caution. // 일할 때는 ~ 깊게 하여야 한다 You must be attentive to your work. **주의하다** give attention [heed] to; observe; take note [notice] of; mind; take care of; be careful of; beware of; be cautious [watchful] of; look out for. ¶사소한 일에도 ~ pay attention to detail // 건강에 ~ take care of oneself [one's health] // 교통 신호에 ~ look [pay attention] to traffic signals // 감기에 걸리지 않도록 주의해라 Mind (that) you do not take cold. // 이 사실에 특히 주의해 주기 바란다 I want to call your special attention to this fact. // 그는 남이 말하는 것에 주의하지 않는다 He takes no heed of [gives no heed to / pays no attention to] what others say.

2 [충고] (a piece of) advice; counsel; [경고] (a) warning. ¶의사의 ~에도 불구하고 in spite of the doctor's warning // 나는 그에게 약간의 ~를 주었다 I gave him a piece of advice. // 담배를 너무 많이 피우지 말도록 ~를 주었다 I warned him against smoking too much. **주의하다** advise; counsel; give advice to; [경고하다] warn; give warning; caution (a person) against. →¶가벼운 몸짓으로 주의시키다 make a slight warning gesture.

3 [일깨움] suggestion; [타이름] admonition. ¶남의 잘못에 ~를 주다 remind a person of his error // 집에 돌아가거든 그 일에 대한 가족들을 ~를 환기시켜 주시오 When you go home, please remind your people of the matter. **주의하다** [일깨워 주다] remind (a person) of; put (a person) in mind of; [타이르다] admonish (a person).

4 [준칙(準則)] rules; hints. ¶위생상의 ~ sanitary rules // 작문상의 ~점 hints toward [on] prose composition.

●**주의력** the power of attention; attentiveness. ¶~을 **집중하다** concentrate (one's attention) (on). **주의보** [기상] a (storm) warning. ¶폭풍 ~ a storm warning // 파랑 ~가 제주에 내려졌다 A heavy seas warning is in force [has been posted] for Jeju. **주의사항** suggestions; hints; matters that require attention; N.B.(▶ 문장 등에 쓰는 약어로 「요! 주의」의 뜻). **주의 인물** a suspicious [dangerous] character; a person under observation [the eyes of the police].

주인(主人) **1** [가장] the master (of a house); the head (of a family); (손님과 대칭으로) the host; the hostess(여자). ¶~과 손님 host and guest // ~ 노릇을 하다 play the host / act as host.

2 [임자] the owner; the proprietor; (여관 등의) the landlord; the landlady(여성). ¶집 ~ the owner of a house // 생선 가게 ~ the owner of a fish shop // ~이 없는 고양이 an ownerless cat // 여관 ~ an innkeeper / the owner of an inn // 이 집 ~은 누굽니까 Who owns this house? // 걸려 온 전화 목소리의 ~은 정 씨었다 The person on the other end of the line was Mr. Jeong. / The voice I heard when I answered the phone was Mr. Jeong's.

3 [고용주] an employer; the master; [경영주] the proprietor. ¶~ 행세를 하다 behave like a master.

4 [남편] one's husband [man].

●**주인공** a hero (pl. ~es); a heroine(여자). ¶그 소설은 귀환 병사를 ~으로 하고 있다 The novel has a returned soldier as its hero. **주인집** one's employer's [master's] house. ¶~에서 **쫓겨나다** be out of one's master's favor / be dismissed.

주인(主因) the primary [principal] cause; the main factor. ¶사고의 ~은 운전자의 부주의였다 The main cause of the accident was the driver's carelessness. // 불황의 ~은 생산 과잉에 있다 The trade depression is mainly due to overproduction.

주일(主日) the Lord's day; Sunday.

●**주일 학교** a Sunday school.

주일(週日) a weekday; a week. ¶이번[지난 / 다음] ~ this [last / next] week // 2~ 후[전] 의 오늘 today [this day] fortnight // 한 서너 ~ 걸리겠다 It will take a few weeks. // 크리스마스까지는 아직 3~ 남았다 We have still three weeks left until Christmas.

주일(駐日) [관형어적] resident [stationed] in Japan.

●**주일 한국 대사관** the Embassy of the Republic of Korea to Japan.

주임(主任) a chief; a head; a person in charge (of); a manager. ¶회계 ~ the chief treasurer // 홍보부 ~ the public relations [P.R.] manager // 수사 ~ a chief investigator // 영어과 ~ the head of the English department // 물리학과의 ~으로 있습니다 I am chairman of the Physics Department.

●**주임 교사** the teacher in charge. ¶그는 2학년의 ~이다 He is in charge of the second year class. **주임 교수** the chairman [head] (of a department).

주입(注入) pouring into; (약액 등의) injection; (신사상 등의) infusion; instillation; (교육의) cramming. **주입하다** [부어 넣다] pour [put] into; (약액을) inject; (사상 등을) infuse (a spirit into a person's mind); instill (a sentiment in a person); implant (a principle in a person's mind); [되풀이하여 가르치다] (문어) inculcate (a person with a doctrine). ¶지식을 ~ stuff [cram] one's head with knowledge // 정맥에 약을 ~ inject medicine

주자 into a vein / inject a vein with a drug//그는 과격한 사상을 학생들에게 주입하고 있다 He inculcates the students with radical ideas.
● **주입식 교육** cramming education.

주자(走者) a runner; [야구] a (base) runner. ¶제1 ～ (계주의) the first runner//최종 ～ an anchorman//단거리 ～ a sprinter//일루 ～ (야구의) a first-base runner//～를 일루로 보내다 get a runner on first//～를 2루로 나아가게 하다 advance a runner to second//～를 두 사람 두고서 안타를 날리다 smack a hit with two runners[men] on (base).

주자(奏者) a performer. ⇨연주자(⇨연주)

주자(鑄字) [활자를 만드는 일] type-founding [-casting]; [그 활자] a metal (printing) type.

주자학(朱子學) orthodox Neo-Confucianism; the Zhu Xi[Chu Hsi] school of Neo-Confucianism.

주장(主張) insistence; (an) assertion; persistence; [논점] one's contention; one's point; [지론] one's opinion[stand / doctrine]. ¶～을 관철하다 carry[gain] one's point//～을 굽히다 concede a point / compromise//～을 굽히지 않다 stand firm (for a thing) / stick to one's opinion[guns]//그는 자기～이 강하다 He is extremely self-assertive.//우리의 ～은 수락되지 않았다 Our contention was not accepted. **주장하다** insist (on / upon); assert; [강조하다] emphasize; lay stress (on); [주장하다] advocate. ¶권리를 ～ assert[insist on] one's rights//무죄를 ～ assert[maintain / insist] that one is innocent / plead innocence[not guilty]//평화론을 ～ advocate pacificism//군비(軍備) 축소의 필요성을 ～ preach[urge] the necessity of arms reduction//끝까지 모른다고 ～ persist in pleading one's ignorance//그는 작품 중에서 자유의 중요성을 주장하였다 In his work he emphasized[laid stress on] the importance of freedom.//그는 자기가 그 땅의 소유자라고 주장하였다 He claimed to be the owner of the land[that he owned the land].//그는 개혁을 주장하였다 He advocated reform.//그는 끝까지 결백을 주장했다 He persisted in asserting his innocence.//그는 이 문제와는 아무런 관련도 없었다고 주장했다 He insisted that he had had no part whatever in this matter.//그는 법정에서 무죄를 주장했다 He pleaded not guilty in court.//그는 결백하다고 주장했다 He asserted that he was innocent.

주장(主將) 1 (팀의) the captain (of a baseball team). 2 (군대의) the supreme commander; the commander-in-chief.

주재(主宰) superintendence; supervision. ¶…의 ～하에 under the superintendence [supervision] of …//서 씨의 ～로 under the supervision[superintendence] of Mr. Seo. **주재하다** [감독하다] supervise; superintend; [사회보다] preside (over). ¶최 씨가 주재하는 잡지 a magazine edited[run] by Mr. Choe//독서회를 ～ preside over a reading circle//이것은 황 씨가 주재하는 계간지이다 This is the quarterly that Mr. Hwang edits.//그는 오늘의 모임을 주재할 예정이다 He is to chair today's meeting.
● **주재자** the president; the leader; (회의의) the chairman; (동인지 등의) an editor.

주재(駐在) residence; a stay. ¶～의 residing [resident] (in a country)//한국 ～ 프랑스 대사 the French Ambassador to Korea. **주재하다** reside (at / in); be resident (at / in); be stationed (at / in); stay.
● **주재관** a resident official. **주재국** the country of residence; the country in which a person is stationed. **주재원** (신문사의) a resident reporter.

주저(躊躇) [망설임] hesitation; [우유부단] indecision; irresolution; (의견·방침 등의) vacillation; (양심의 가책에 의한) scruples. **주저하다** hesitate; [흔들리다] waver; scruple (at); think twice (about doing); vacillate; be irresolute[hesitant]. ¶주저하여 hesitantly//주저하지 않고 without hesitation / [결연히] resolutely / [망설이지 않고] without scruple//주저하지 않고 의견을 말하다 tell[give] one's opinion frankly[without reserve]//그는 갈까 어떻게 할까 아직 주저하고 있다 He is still hesitating about going[whether he should go].//그는 어느 쪽 의견을 취할까 주저했다 He wavered[vacillated] between the two opinions.//그는 남의 돈을 쓰는 것을 주저하지 않는다 He has no scruples about spending other people's money.//그는 친구로부터 돈을 빌리고 떼먹기를 주저하지 않았다 He didn't hesitate to borrow[had no scruples about borrowing] money from his friends without paying it back.//잘못을 고치는 데는 주저할 것 없다 It is never too late to mend one's ways.//나는 저 큰 집을 사기를 주저하고 있다 I'm hesitating to buy[about buying] that big house.//그는 양자의 선택에 주저하고 있다 He is vacillating between two choices.//묻는 말에 주저하지 않고 대답했다 I answered without a moment's hesitation.//그는 주저하지 않고 그 문을 두드렸다 He knocked at[on] the door without any[with no] hesitation.//그것은 틀렸다고 주저하지 않고 말했다 I felt no hesitation in saying that it was wrong.

주저(主著) [주가 되는 저서] one's main [chief] (literary) work.

주저앉다 1 [맥없이 앉다] fall[sink] down; drop (on one's knees); lapse (on the floor); [털썩 앉다] sit down plump. ¶그녀는 소파에 털썩 주저앉았다 She sat back in[sank into] the sofa.//그는 무릎에 힘이 빠져 맥없이 마루 바닥에 주저앉아 버렸다 His knees went from under him[His knees crumpled like pastry. / His knee joints turned to water] and he sank weakly to the floor.
2 [내려앉다] sink; fall[cave] in; go under; collapse; subside. ¶주저앉은 코 a bashed-in nose//내가 앉으면 이 의자는 주저앉을 거야 This chair will collapse under my weight.
3 [머물다] stay on; sit on; settle down; plant oneself. ¶그는 사직하려다 그대로 주저앉았다 He stayed on in his office and gave up the idea of resigning.
4 [포기하다] give up; abandon; leave[lay / cast] off. ¶무슨 일이 있어도 주저앉지 않겠다 Nothing shall hinder[deter] me.

주저앉히다 (의자 등에) cause (a person) to sit down; sit (a person) down (hard); (못 떠나게) make (a person) stay on.

주전(主戰) 1 [전쟁하기를 주장함] advocacy of war; pro-war. **주전하다** advocate[clamor for] war. 2 [주력이 되어 싸움] fighting as the main force. **주전하다** fight[play games] as the main force[strength / body].

● **주전 투수** an ace pitcher[hurler].
주전부리 snacking between meals. **주전부리하다** gobble[take] snacks between meals.
주전자(酒煎子) a (copper / brass) kettle; a teakettle; (아가리가 큰) a ewer; (손잡이가 달린) a jug. ¶~에 물을 끓이다 boil water in a kettle.
주절(主節) [언] main[principal] clause.
주점(酒店) a wine seller's; 《미》 a package[liquor] store; a bar; a barroom; a saloon; a tavern; [영국 구어] a pub.
주접 [생물체가 쇠하여지는 상태] stunting; abortion.
주접(이) 들다 1 [발육이] get stunted[dwarfed]; (생기가) languish. ¶주접이 든 나무[짐승] a stunted[scrubby] tree[animal] // 영양 부족으로 ~ be in bad shape through lack nourishment. 2 [살림살이가] be reduced to poverty; (옷·몸치례가) get[become] shabby[dirty / slovenly].
주접스럽다 greedy; voracious; ravenous; starving; gluttonous.
주정(舟艇) [소형 배] a boat; a craft. ¶상륙용 ~ a landing boat[craft].
주정(酒酊) drunken frenzy[wrench]; disorderly behavior caused by liquor. ¶그는 ~이 심하다 He is a troublesome drinker. / He is a bad drunk. **주정하다** lose control of oneself in drink; become a bother to others in one's cups. ¶그는 주정하는 법이 없다 He carries his drink like a gentleman. / He is a good drunk.
● **주정꾼 / 주정뱅이 / 주정쟁이** a troublesome drunkard; a bad drunk.
주정(酒精) [화] ethanol. ⇨에탄올 ¶공업용 ~ industrial alcohol.
주제 1 shabby appearance. ⇨주제꼴(⇨주제) 2 [변변치 않은 처지·형편] a wretched situation. ¶풋내기인 ~에 though (one is) only a beginner // 의사도 아닌 ~에 As if you were a doctor// 할 줄 모르는 ~에 무턱대고 좋아하다 be crazy about (a thing) at which he is poor hand / be enthusiastic (for a thing) though a poor hand at it // 그는 ~ 사납게 이래저래라 한다 He has the effrontery to keep telling me what to do. // 너는 아무것도 모르는 ~에 무엇이든 알고 있는 것처럼 말한다 You talk knowingly without knowing a thing.
● **주제꼴** shabby[humble / wretched] appearance[looks]. ¶~이 사납다 have a shabby appearance / be impertinent[cheeky] / 이런 ~로 남 앞에 나갈 수가 없다 I simply cannot appear before company looking like this. // 그런 ~을 하고 가면 업신여길 거야 You will be slighted, if you go so poorly[ill] dressed.
주제(主題) a subject; a theme; (음악 등의) a leitmotif. ¶~의 thematic // 도시 생활이란 ~로 작문을 하다 write a composition[an essay] on the subject[theme] of city life // 또 ~에서 벗어났군 You've gotten off the subject again.
● **주제가** a theme song (of a motion picture).
주제넘다 forward; meddlesome; presumptuous; cheeky; impertinent; impudent; saucy; pert; sassy. ¶주제넘은 놈 an impertinent[a saucy / a presumptuous] fellow / a forward person // 주제넘게 말을 하다 talk impudently[fresh / smart] // 주제넘게 presumptuously / forwardly / impertinently / impudently // 주제넘은 충고 uncalled-for[uninvited / impertinent] advice // 그러한 비평은 ~ Such comments are presumptuous[uncalled-for]. // 주제넘은 제의인 것 같습니다만 제 집에 묵으시면 어떨지요 It may sound impertinent of me to suggest it, but you're welcome to stay at my house if you like. // 그녀는 주제넘은 짓은 전연 하지 않는다 She never pushes herself forward. // 그는 초대받지도 않았는데 그 모임에 주제넘게 끼어들었다 Uninvited he thrust himself into the party.
주조(主潮) the main tide; the main current. ¶유럽 문예의 ~ the main current of European literature // 근대 음악의 ~ the main current of modern music.
주조(酒造) making[the production of] alcoholic beverages; (양조주의) brewing; (포도주의) wine-making; (증류주의) distilling. **주조하다** brew; distill [(영) distil] (whisky).
● **주조업** brewing; wine-making; distilling; the brewing[wine-making / distilling] industry[business].
주조(鑄造) casting; founding; (화폐의) minting; coinage. **주조하다** cast (metal types); found (a bell); mold[(영) mould]; coin; mint (money); strike (coins). ¶상(像)을 청동으로 ~ cast a statue in bronze.
● **주조소** a foundry; a mint(화폐의). **주조 화폐** metallic currency; a struck coin.
주조음(主調音) [음] the dominant note(s); the keynote.
주종(主從) [주인과 종자] master and servant[man]; employer and employee; lord and vassal; [주체와 종속] the principal and the subordinate[accessory].
● **주종 관계** the relation between master and servant. ¶그들은 ~였다 They were master and man.
주주(株主) 《미》 a stockholder; 《영》 a shareholder. ¶대[소] ~ a large[small] stockholder.
● **주주 총회** a general meeting of stockholders[(영) shareholders]; a general shareholders' meeting.
주지(主旨) [중심이 되는 생각] the (general) purport; the (main) meaning; the gist; the drift. ¶담화의 ~ the drift[gist] of a discourse // 그의 연설의 ~를 알 수 있었다[없었다] I got[missed] the point[purport / drift] of his speech. // 그러한 ~의 편지를 받았다 He wrote me[His letter was] to that effect.
주지(住持) the chief priest (at a Buddhist temple).
주지(周知) common[universal] knowledge. ¶~으로 known to all[everybody] / universally[widely / well] known // ~의 사실 a matter of common knowledge / a well-known fact.
주지하다 everybody knows; be known to everybody. ¶주지하는 바와 같이 as everyone knows / as is generally known.
주지사(州知事) the governor of a state.
주지육림(酒池肉林) [호사스러운 술잔치] a sumptuous feast[banquet]; obscene orgies; a debauch.
주지주의(主知主義) [철] intellectualism.
주차(駐車) parking. ¶무료 ~ free parking // 불법 ~ illegal parking // ~ 중인 자동차 a parked car. **주차하다** park (a car).

주차

●**주차 금지** (게시) No Parking. **주차 금지 구역** a no-parking area. **주차 위반** a parking violation; illegal parking. ¶나는 ~으로 벌금을 물었다 I was fined for parking my car improperly[a parking violation]. **주차장** (많이 주차하는 곳) (미) a parking lot; (영) a car park; (차 한 대분의) a parking space. ¶전시회장에는 무료 ~이 있습니까 Is there free parking at the exposition?

주착(主着) →주책

주창(主唱) advocacy; promotion. **주창하다** advocate (peace); promote. ¶생물학상의 새 학설을 ~ advance a new theory in biology // 그녀는 남녀 동등 임금 제도를 주창해 왔다 She has long advocated equal pay for men and women.

●**주창자** an advocate; a promoter.

주책 [일정하게 자리 잡힌 생각] a definite view[opinion]; a fixed opinion.

●**주책망나니** / **주책바가지** a wishy-washy [spineless / indecisive / injudicious / indiscreet] person.

주책없다 indecent; immodest; dishonorable; shameful; frivolous. ¶주책없는 짓을 하다 behave disgracefully[indecently]. **주책없이** ¶~ 말을 하다 talk senselessly[pointlessly] / talk nonsense / talk without rhyme or reason // 여자에게 ~ 굴다 take liberties with a woman.

주철(鑄鐵) cast iron.

●**주철소** an iron foundry.

주청하다(奏請一) petition the king for sanction (of).

주체 coping with one's burden. **주체하다** cope with[take care of] one's burden.

주체(를) 못하다 do not know what to do (with); find (a person) unmanageable; be too much[many] (for); be beyond[out of] one's control; be unmanageable[uncontrollable]. ¶나는 한가한 시간을 주체 못하고 있다 I don't know what to do with my free time. // 그녀는 아이들을 주체 못하고 있었다 The children were too much of a handful for her[too much for her to handle]. // 그는 뚱뚱해서 내 몸을 주체 못한다 He is so fat (that) he can hardly get along with himself.

●**주쳇덩어리** [주체하기 어려운 일·물건·사람] a thing[person] that is hard to handle [manage]; "a real problem (on one's hands)". ¶집안의 ~ the black sheep of[in] the family.

주체(主體) the main[principal] body; [철] the subject. ¶~적 subjective / independent // ~적 행동 independent action // 그 조직은 개업의사 ~가 되어 있다 It is an organization made up mainly of practicing physicians.

●**주체성** (establish) subjectivity; [자주성] independence; [개성] individuality; selfhood. ¶그들은 ~이 결여되어 있다 They lack self-direction. **주체 세력** the main group [body] (of a movement).

주체스럽다 unmanageable; unwieldy; burdensome; cumbersome. ¶그는 큰 몸뚱이가 주체스러운 듯이 어기적거리고 있었다 He walked away awkwardly as if his big body were more than he could manage. // 그 원숭이는 주체스러운 존재가 되어 버렸다 The monkey became a nuisance. / The monkey got to be more than we could handle. // 이 아이는 거칠어서 데리고 다니기가 ~ The child

is beyond my control to take him with me.

주최(主催) sponsorship; auspice. ¶…의 공동 ~로 under the joint auspices of ... // 오늘 모임은 총리실 ~이다 The meeting today is sponsored by [(문어) being held under the auspices of] the Prime Minister's Office. // 대모는 20개 여성 단체의 공동 ~였다 The demonstration was jointly sponsored by [under the joint sponsorship of] twenty women's organizations. **주최하다** sponsor; promote. ¶모임을 ~ sponsor a meeting.

●**주최국** the host nation. **주최자** the sponsor; the promoter. ¶여행단의 ~ a tour organizer // 참가자는 ~ 측 발표에 따르면 2만 명이었다 The participants numbered twenty thousand, according to the sponsor[promoter].

주추 a foundation stone; a cornerstone.

●**주춧돌** a foundation stone; a cornerstone.

주축(主軸) the principal[main] axis (pl. axes); [공] the main shaft[spindle]. ¶그는 팀의 ~으로 활약했다 The team revolved around[his play]. / He held the team together. // 방위 문제를 ~으로 하는 여야당의 공방이 전개되었다 There were heated exchanges between the ruling and opposition parties (centering) on national defence.

주춤거리다 hesitate; be hesitant; waver; hold back (from); boggle (at). ¶주춤거리면서 hesitatingly / hesitantly / falteringly / waveringly // 살까 말까 ~ hesitate to buy // 명확히 대답하지 못하고 ~ hesitate to give a definite answer // 주춤거리며 말하다 speak in a halting way / stammer out // 결단을 짓지 못하고 ~ be hesitant to make a decision // 그는 잠시 주춤거린 후 그것을 사기로 했다 He decided to buy it after a short period of hesitation.

주춤주춤 hesitatingly; hesitantly; falteringly; waveringly. **주춤주춤하다** hesitate. ⇨ 주춤거리다

주치의(主治醫) the physician in charge (of); one's (family) doctor.

주택(住宅) a house; a residence(▶ house 보다 새로운 말투로 비교적 큰 저택을 가리킴); (집합적) housing. ¶간이[조립] ~ a prefabricated house / (미) a prefab // 공영 ~ a city-built[-owned] house // 근로자용 ~ houses for the working class // 모델 ~ a model dwelling // 문화 ~ a modern dwelling // 호화 ~ a luxurious[deluxe] house[mansion] / a palatial mansion // ~이 부족한 한국에서 in house-short Korea // 그 건물은 ~으로는 적합치 않다 The building is not fit to live in. // 이 곳은 ~이 부족하다 We are short of housing.

●**주택가** a residential street. **주택난** (a) shortage of houses; housing shortage [trouble]; a house famine. ¶~으로 고생하다 suffer from scarcity of houses[the housing shortage] // ~은 큰 사회 문제가 되어 있다 The house famine poses[forms] a big social problem. **주택지** a residential quarter [district / area / section]. **주택 청약 예금** an apartment-application deposit.

주파(周波) [물] a (wave) cycle. ¶고[저] ~ high [low] frequency.

●**주파수** frequency. ¶~ 20 a frequency of 20 cycles (per second) // 가청 ~ audible frequency / audio frequency(약어 A.F., a.f.) // 방송국은 ~ 500킬로헤르츠로 방송하고 있다

This station broadcasts at[on] a frequency of 500 kilohertz. 주파수 변조 frequency modulation(약어 FM).

주파하다(走破-) run[cover] the whole distance(between). ¶참가자 전원이 10킬로 코스를 주파하였다 All the participants ran the whole course of ten kilometers[completed the ten-kilometer course]. //그는 1킬로를 3분에 주파하였다 He covered one kilometer in three minutes.

주판(籌板·珠板) an abacus. ⇨＝수판

주포(主砲) the main[principal] gun[battery]; 〔야구〕 a big slugger[gun]. ¶9회에는 우리(팀) 주포가 돌아온다 We will have our big guns coming to the plate in the ninth inning.

주피터 〔로마 신화〕 Jupiter.

주필(主筆) the (chief) editor; the editor in chief. ¶부~ an assistant editor /(영) a subeditor.

주한(駐韓) 〔관형어적〕 resident[stationed] in Korea.
●**주한 미국 대사** the United States[American] Ambassador to Korea. **주한 미군** U.S. armed forces in Korea.

주항(周航) 〔여러 곳을 두루 항해함〕 circumnavigation; sailing round. **주항하다** circumnavigate; sail[cruise] round. ¶여객선은 3개월 동안에 세계를 주항했다 The passenger boat sailed around[(문어) circumnavigated] the world in three months.

주해(註解) (an) annotation; an explanatory note; comments; a commentary. ¶상세한 ~ copious notes //~를 단 책 an annotated book / a book with notes //~를 **달다** annotate (a book) //~가 달린 초서의 시집 an annotated edition of Chaucer's poems / Chaucer's poems with notes. **주해하다** annotate; comment (on); make[give] notes (on).
●**주해서** (학생용) a key; (학생 속어) a crib; (미국 속어) a horse. **주해자** an annotator; a commentator.

주행(走行) traveling; covering. ¶~ 중의 차 a moving car //~ 중에는 이유 없이 운전사에게 말을 걸지 마십시오 〔게시〕 Don't speak to the driver without good reason when[while] the bus is running. **주행하다** travel (from A to B); cover (100 miles in an hour).
●**주행 거리** the distance covered (in a given time); 〔마일수〕 mileage. ¶~가 짧은 차 a gas guzzler //~ 리터당 ~는 얼마입니까 How many kilometers per liter do you get from this car? //이 차는 ~가 길다 This car gets good mileage. **주행계** an odometer. **주행 시간** time taken in traveling (from A to B); (기차의) rail time.

주행성(晝行性) 〔낮에 활동하는 성질〕. ¶~의 diurnal (insect) / daytime (animal).

주형(鑄型) a mold; a cast; (활자·레코드 등의) a matrix (pl. -rices, ~es). ¶~을 뜨다 cast (a mold).

주호(酒豪) a hard[heavy] drinker; a tippler.

주홍(色)(朱紅色) scarlet; cinnabar(red); vermilion.
●**주홍빛** scarlet. ⇨＝주홍 ¶~으로 저녁놀이 진 하늘 the sky dyed vermilion[bright red] with the evening glow //~의 cinnabar red / vermilion.

주화(鑄貨) minting; mintage; coinage.

주화론(主和論) advocacy of peace.

주황(色)(朱黃色) orange color.
●**주황빛** orange color. ⇨＝주황

주효(奏效) efficacy; (an) effect; fruitfulness; virtue. **주효하다** show efficacy; be effectual; be effective; (약이) take effect; work well; be fruitful; (미) pay off. ¶그의 시도는 주효하지 않았다 His attempt yielded no results. / His attempt proved ineffectual. //우리의 정치 운동은 주효했다 Our political campaigning paid off. //이 위협은 군중에게 크게 주효했다 This threat had a noticeable effect on the crowd. //그의 교묘한 조작이 주효했다 His manipulations proved effective.

주효(酒肴) 〔술과 안주〕 wine and refreshments; wine and food.

주휴(週休) a weekly holiday. ¶우리 (회사)는 ~ 2일제이다 We are on a five-day workweek.

주흥(酒興) 〔술자리의 여흥〕 entertainment at a drinking party; elation from drinking; feeling high; conviviality; 〔들떠서 신 나는 기분〕 merrymaking; 〔술 생각〕 yen[craving] for alcohol. ¶~에 겨워 under the influence of wine / in one's drunken exhilaration / heated by wine //그들은 ~을 돋구기 위해 노래를 불렀다 They sang songs to heighten the gaiety of the party. //그 일 때문에 모처럼의 ~이 깨고 말았다 That brought a chill over the merrymaking party.

죽¹ 〔열 벌〕 ten pieces; ten (plates, garments, etc). ¶접시 한 ~ ten plates.

죽² **1** 〔늘어선 모양〕 in a row[line]. ¶~ 늘어서다 stand in line //~ 늘어앉다 be seated in a row / form a line //~ 늘어놓다 make an array of (toys) / display //보트는 스타트 라인에 ~ 늘어서 있다 The boats are lined up at the starting line.

2 〔찢는 소리〕 tearing; ripping; with a rip. ¶편지를 ~ 찢다 tear a letter across //손수건을 ~ 찢다 rip a handkerchief //그는 손수건을 ~ 찢어 상처에 감았다 He tore off his handkerchief and bandaged the wounded part.

3 (물·기운 등이) (recede) utterly; completely; all the way; all down the line; readily; easily. ¶큰물이 ~ 빠졌다 The flood recedcd completely. //기운이 ~ 빠졌다 I am utterly exhausted. //열이 ~ 내렸다 The fever has entirely left me.

4 〔줄곧〕 all during; throughout; all the time; straight (through). ¶3일 동안 ~ for three consecutive[successive] days / for three days running[on end] //그날부터 ~ from that day on //일 년 동안 ~ all the year round //지금까지 ~ 기다렸습니다 I've been waiting for you all this while. //역에서 집까지 ~ 걸어왔다 I've walked home all the way from the station. //그때부터 ~ 여기서 살고 있습니다 I have lived here ever since.

5 〔곧게〕 straight; direct(ly). ¶수직선을 ~ 긋다 draw a perpendicular line //양손을 뻗고 등을 ~ 펴시오 Throw your arms way up and stretch your back. //~ 들어오십시오 Come right in. //이 길을 ~ 가면 바로 공회당이 나옵니다 This road will lead you straight [directly] to the public hall.

6 〔단숨에〕 at a gulp[draught]; 〔빠는 모양〕 (suck) hard; 〔키스 소리〕 Smack! ¶나는 찬 소주 한 잔을 천천히 ~ 들이켰다 I finished a cup of cold *soju* in a single long draught.

7 〔대강〕 roughly; quickly; briefly. ¶~ 훑어보

죽다 look[glance / run] through / look over / 편지를 ~ 훑어보다 pass one's eyes over a letter // 한눈에 청중의 얼굴을 ~ 둘러보다 sweep the faces of an audience with a glance.

죽(粥) juk; (rice) gruel; porridge; hot cereal; (유아용) pap. ¶~을 끓이다 cook hot cereal // 겨우 ~이나 먹고살다 live on a crust // ~을 마시다 eat[sip] rice porridge.

죽(竹) bamboo.

죽기(竹器) bamboo ware; a bamboo bowl.

죽는소리 〔엄살〕 talking[making a] poor mouth; exaggeration[pretension] of one's pain[hardship]; feigned[overdone] dismay; 〔불평〕 a complaint; a grievance; a whimper; a grumble. **죽는소리하다** exaggerate[pretend] pain[hardship]; make complaints (to a person about something); complain (about / of). ¶죽는소리하지 마라 Stop talking poor mouth.

죽다 1 〔사망하다〕 die; pass away[on]; be gone; (구어) pop off (the hooks); 〔목숨을 잃다〕 meet one's end[death]; lose one's life; kick one's bucket; perish(▶ 죽다 경우에는 좀 문어적인 말로 굶거나 얼어 죽을 경우에 흔히 씀); 〔생을 마치다〕 close one's day[life]; end one's career; 〔저승으로 가다〕 leave this world; go to the better world; join the majority; sleep the eternal[final] sleep; 〔자살하다〕 kill oneself; commit suicide; take one's own life. ¶죽은 dead / the late (Mr. A) / departed / deceased // 죽을 각오로 at the risk of one's life // 죽느냐 사느냐의 문제 a matter of life and death // 죽은 사람들 the dead // 죽어도 말 못하겠다 cannot tell for one's life // 병[암]으로 ~ die of a disease[cancer] // 부상으로 ~ die from a wound(▶ 병이나 굶주림 등 외의 그 밖의 원인으로 죽을 때는, 부상이나 그 밖의 원인으로 죽을 때는 from을 씀) // 교통사고로 ~ die[be killed] in a traffic accident // 죽어 가고 있다 be dying // 그가 죽은 지 5년이 된다 He has been dead for five years. / It has been five years since he died. // 나는 이대로는 결코 죽을 수 없다 I can't die and leave things in this state. // 그는 죽을 각오로 그곳에 갔다 He went there knowing full well that it might cost him his life. // 부끄러워서 죽을 지경이었다 I was so embarrassed I could have just died. // 나는 언제 죽을지 모르는 몸이다 I may meet my fate[end] at any moment. // 그는 스스로 목을 베어 죽었다 He killed himself by cutting his throat. // 죽기 전에 자서전이라도 써 두고 싶다 I'd like to write my autobiography before I die. // 집에 가고 싶어 죽을 지경이었다 I was dying to go home. / I wanted to go home so badly I couldn't contain myself. // 목이 말라 죽을 지경이다 I'm dying for a glass of water. // 죽어 버리고 싶다 I wish I were dead. // 나는 죽어도 그런 짓은 하고 싶지 않다 I would rather die than do a thing like that. // 그는 죽은 거나 마찬가지다 He is as good as dead. // 그는 딸이 죽은 것이라고 체념했다 He gave his daughter up for dead. // 그는 원자 폭탄 공격으로 죽었다 He was killed in the atomic bomb attack. // 우리가 어떻게 그를 이대로 죽게 할 수 있겠는가 How can we just stand around and let him die? // 부모의 부주의가 자식을 죽게 하는 수도 있다 Sometimes the parents' carelessness results in a child's death. // 발견했을 때 노인은 이미 죽어 있었다 When the old man was found he was already dead. // 돈이 없어 죽을 지경이다 I am very hard up for money.
2 〔기가〕 get deflated[crestfallen / downcast / out of spirits]; have the blues; be depressed; be (down) in the dumps. ¶죽어 가는 목소리 a faint[weak] voice // 이 글씨는 죽었다 There is no life in this writing. // 이 말을 빼면 이 문장은 죽어 버린다 The sentence falls flat if you cross that word out. // 그는 실연을 하고 완전히 풀이 죽었다 Having lost in love, he was completely dejected.
3 (초목이) wither; die; perish; be dead; be blasted(서리 등으로). ¶죽은 withered / dead / dry / sphacelated.
4 (풀기가) lost its starch; wilt.
5 (불이) die out; go out. ¶죽어 가는 불 a dying fire // 불이 죽지 않게 하다 keep the fire alive / keep the light burning.
6 〔동작이 멎다〕 run down; stop. ¶시계가 죽었다 The clock has stopped.
7 〔바둑〕 be captured.
8 〔야구〕 be (put) out.

죽은 자식 나이 세기(속담) There is no point in dwelling on might-have-beens.; It is like crying over spilt milk.

죽어라 하고 desperately; frantically; like hell; for life; as hard as one can; with utmost effort; tooth and nail. ¶~ 달리다 run as fast as one's legs can carry one // ~ 도망치다 run for one's (dear) life // ~ 일하다 work away like one possessed.

죽은 목숨 (살길이 없는) a life as good as dead; a person beyond the realm of hope [help] (such as a sick person); a hopeless case; a person as good as dead; a person who might as well be dead. ¶너는 인제 ~이다 You are a dead[marked] man now. // 나는 ~처럼 느껴졌다 〔살아 있다는 생각이 들지 않았다〕 I felt more dead than alive.

죽을 둥 살 둥 desperately; frantically; life and death; tooth and nail. ¶~ 덤비다 go it as if one's life depends on it / go after at it tooth and nail.

죽자 사자 with all one's strength[might]; with might and main; to the best of one's power. ¶~ 일하다 work at[up to] capacity / work with all one's strength / work hard as one can // 그는 그것을 자기가 하게 해 달라고 ~ 내게 매달렸다 He begged me fervently [ardently] to let him do it. // 그 둘은 ~ 한다 Those two are mad about each other.

죽데기 〔통나무의 겉쪽에서 떼어 낸 조각〕 side splits from whole logs (used as firewood).

죽도(竹刀) a bamboo-knife.
죽렴(竹簾) a bamboo blind[screen]. ⇨대발
죽림(竹林) a bamboo thicket. ⇨대숲
죽마(竹馬) a child's hobbyhorse; stilts; a bamboo horse (for children). ¶~를 타다 walk on stilts.
● **죽마고우** an old friend; a childhood friend; an old playmate. ¶~들이 한데 모였다 Old familiar faces[Old friends] got together at the reunion.

죽세공(竹細工) (a piece of) bamboo work.
● **죽세공품** bamboo ware.
죽순(竹筍) a bamboo shoot[sprout].
죽술(粥-) 〔몇 숟갈의 죽〕 a few spoonful of porridge. ¶~이나 먹고 살아가다 lead a meager life // ~연명하다 scratch a living / eke out

a precarious living.

죽어지내다 live under oppression; live a life of subjugation. ¶그는 아버지[아내] 앞에 죽어지낸다 He lives under his father's[wife's] thumb.

죽을병(-病) a fatal[mortal] disease; a deadly malady. ¶~에 걸리다 contract[suffer from] a fatal disease.

죽을상(-相) an agonized look; a frantic [desperate] look. ¶그는 그 소식을 듣자 ~이 되었다 He turned deadly pale at the news.

죽을힘 the last effort; a frantic[desperate] effort. ¶~을 다해서 frantically / desperately / for one's life / ~을 다해서 헤엄치다[도망치다] swim[run] for one's life // ~을 다해서 싸우다 fight a desperate fight / fight to the death.

죽음 death; decease; (왕의) demise. ¶암에 의한 ~ death from cancer // ~의 공포 the fear of death // ~에 임하여 on one's deathbed // ~을 무릅쓰고 at the risk of one's death // ~같은 고요 a deathlike silence // ~에 대한 각오를 하다 prepare oneself for death / be ready to die / ~에서 다시 살아나다 return from the dead / resurrect // ~**으로 속죄하다** atone for (a crime) with death // ~**이 다가오다** be near[approach] one's final hour / 개~을 하다 die a dog's death / die to no purpose [avail] // 영광스러운 ~을 하다 die a glorious death // 간신히 ~을 모면하다 have[make] a narrow escape / escape death (by a hair's breadth) / be snatched from the jaws of death // 그는 용기를 갖고 ~에 임했다 He faced death with courage.

죽음의 재 atomic[radioactive] dust.

죽의 장막(竹-帳幕) the Bamboo Curtain.

죽이다 1 (살해) kill; slay; put (a person) to death; take (another's) life; put an end to (another's) life; make[do] away with (a person); murder; (학살) massacre; slaughter; (도살) butcher. ¶목을 졸라 ~ strangle to death // 때려 ~ beat to death // 돌로 쳐 ~ stone (a person) to death // 독약을 먹여 ~ dose (a person) to death // 사람을 죽이려고 꾀하다 conspire against[have designs upon] a person's life // 남을 칼로 베어 ~ kill a person with a sword[knife] // 사람을 죽이고 사형을 당하다 be executed[hanged] for murder[homicide] // 죽여 버리다 do away with (a person) / do (a person) in / put (a person) to death / kill (a person) off // 죽여 버린다고 위협하다 threaten (a person) with death // 한 걸음이라도 움직이면 죽여 버린다 Stir a step, and you shall die. / Stick[Stay] right where you are, or you're a dead man. // 죽일 놈 Rascal! / Wretch! / S.O.B.! // 죽일 놈아 Damn you! / Be damned to you. // 그는 죽일 놈이군 He is a rascal, indeed. // 죽여 버려 (속어) Finish him off! // 너를 죽이겠다 You shall die. // 미친 말이 아이를 차[짓밟아] 죽였다 The crazed horse kicked[trampled] the child to death. // 그는 사람을 죽였다 He committed murder[homicide / manslaughter] (▶ manslaughter는 과실에 의한 살인).
2 (잃다) suffer the death[loss] of; lose (a son / a chessman). ¶졸 하나를 ~ lose a pawn // 전쟁에 아들을 ~ lose a son in the war.
3 [억제하다] hold back; restrain; deaden; muffle. ¶감정을 ~ restrain one's feeling // 소리를 죽여 말하다 speak under one's breath / speak in a low (tone of) voice // 발소리를 ~ muffle one's footsteps // 나는 숨을 죽이고 싸움을 지켜보았다 Holding my breath, I watched the fight.
4 (동작을) stop (a timepiece / a top / a motor); allow (it) to stop.
5 (불을) put out (a fire / a light); let (it) go out.

죽장(竹杖) a bamboo stick[cane].

죽죽 1 (줄을) in rows[lines]; row after row; in streaks. ¶줄을 ~ 긋다 draw line after line.
2 (비가) in sheets; in showers; (거침없이) briskly; directly; vigorously; rapidly; steadily(착착). ¶~ 나아가다 go on and on / go ahead at a rapid pace // ~ 늘다 (성적이) make steady[rapid] progress / (사업이) make steady expansion // 비가 ~ 내리다 It rains[The rain comes down] in sheets.
3 (찢기는 모양) into shreds; in[to] pieces. ¶~ 찢다 tear to pieces.
4 [기운차게] (draw through a clasping hand) briskly. ¶나뭇가지의 잎을 ~ 훑다 strip leaves off a twig briskly // 주스를 빨대로 ~ 빨다 suck up juice through a straw.

죽지 a shoulder blade; a scapula; the shoulder joint. ¶날갯 ~ the joint of a wing // 어깻 ~ the shoulder joint // 팔 ~ the upper arm.

죽지(를) 떼다 1 [활을 쏘고 어깨를 내리다] lower one's shoulder after shooting an arrow. 2 [배후를 믿고 위세를 부리다] act overbearing; be imperious; be stuck-up; put on airs.

죽창(竹槍) a bamboo spear.

죽책(竹柵) a bamboo fence[palisade / stockade].

죽치다 [한곳에만 들어박히다] stay put at home; confine[shut] oneself in one's house; keep oneself indoors. ¶그는 집 안에 죽치고 있다 He is a regular stay-at-home. // 그는 아직도 말단에서 죽치고 있다 He is still an obscure underling. // 그는 얼마 동안 시골에서 죽치고 있었다 He stayed in the country doing nothing for some time.

죽침(竹針) a bamboo[knitting] needle.

죽통(竹筒) a bamboo tube.

죽통(粥筩) [구유] a feeding trough.

준-(準) [의사(擬似)의] quasi-; [반] semi-; associate. ¶~결승 a semifinal / ~사법적 권력 quasi-judicial power // ~현행범 a quasi-flagrant offense // ~회원 an associate member.

준거(準據) authority cited; standard referred to; going to a standard[reference]; referring to a precedent[rule]. **준거하다** be based upon; follow; go to. ¶~에 준거해서 on the authority of / in accordance with / in conformity to / pursuant to // …의 준거하는 바를 밝히다 give the authority of … // 법률에 ~ comply with the law // 준거할 규정이 없다 want no rule to go by // 그 분석이 준거한 바를 보여 주시오 Give your authority for that analysis. / What is that analysis based on? // 준거하는 선례가 있으면 편리하다 It's useful to have some precedents to go by.

준걸(俊傑) a man of eminent[great] ability; a great man; a hero.

준결승(전)(準決勝戰) a semifinal (game); the semifinals. ¶~ 출전자 a semifinalist // ~에 진출하다 go on to the semifinals // ~에 나가

준골 다 play[run] in the semifinals // 그들은 ~에서 패했다 They were defeated in the semifinals.

준골(俊骨) 〔준수하게 생긴 골격〕 an eminent physique; (그런 사람) a man of eminent physique[ability].

준공(竣工) completion. ¶~이 가깝다 be nearing completion (of a house). **준공하다** be completed; be finished. ➔¶새 교사가 준공되었다 The new schoolhouse has been completed.
● **준공식** the ceremony for the completion; a dedication ceremony; a ceremony to celebrate the completion (of).

준교사(準敎師) an assistant teacher; a teaching assistant.

준동(蠢動) wriggling (like worms); squirming; activities. ¶빨치산의 ~ activities of the partisans // 불평분자들의 ~ 따위는 개의할 것 없다 You will do well to ignore the (behind-the-scenes) maneuvering of the discontented elements. **준동하다** (벌레가) crawl; wriggle; (무리가) be active; stir; infest.

준령(峻嶺) a steep mountain pass; a dangerous high range.

준론(峻論) a serious discussion; stringent criticism.

준마(駿馬) a noble[an excellent] horse; a swift horse; a fleet steed.

준말 a shortened word; an abbreviation; an abbreviated word; a shortening. ¶"can't"란 낱말은 "cannot"의 ~이다 The word "can't" is a shortened form of "cannot". // U.S.A.는 무엇의 ~입니까 What do the letters U.S.A. stand for?

준법(遵法) 〔법령을 지키는 것〕 law-abiding; obeying the law. **준법하다** abide by[obey / observe] the law.
● **준법정신** a law-abiding spirit; respect for law; the spirit of obeying laws[of law observance]. ¶~이 있다 be law-abiding // ~을 앙양하다 promote law-abiding spirit. **준법 투쟁** a law-abiding labor struggle; a work-to-rule struggle.

준별(峻別) 〔몹시 엄격한 구별〕 a sharp[nice] distinction; a discrimination. **준별하다** make a sharp distinction (between A and B).

준봉(峻峯) a steep peak; a lofty peak.

준봉(遵奉) 〔전례·명령을 좇아서 받듦〕 observance. **준봉하다** observe; obey; follow; adhere to; conform to; abide by; live up to. ¶국법을 ~ obey[abide by] the laws of the country // 어버이의 가르침을 ~ observe one's parents' teachings.

준비(準備) preparation(s); preliminary arrangements; preparedness; readiness(▶ preparation이 상태·행위를 나타낼 때에는 단수, 결과를 나타낼 때에는 복수형을 씀). ¶시험 ~ preparations for examinations // 여행 ~ preparations for a trip // 정화(正貨) ~ a gold reserve // ~ 없는 연설 an extempore [(미국속어) off-the-cup] speech // ~ 부족의 ill-prepared (attempt) // 돌아갈 ~ 가 되어 있다 get ready to go back // 마음의 ~가 되어 있다 be ready[prepared] (to do) // 잠자리의 ~를 하다 make a bed // 환영 ~를 하다 make arrangements for the reception // ~에 차질이 생겨 우리는 갈 수 없게 되었다 The arrangements went wrong, so we could not go. // 장례식의 모든 ~가 되었다 All the arrangements have been made[Everything has been arranged] for the funeral. // 어머니는 저녁 식사 ~를 하고 계셨다 My mother was getting supper ready[preparing supper]. // 손님이 언제 도착해도 되게끔 ~가 다 되어 있었다 Everything was ready for the guests whenever they should arrive. // 돌아갈 ~는 다 되었니 Are you ready to leave for home? // ~가 끝나면 출발이다 We'll start as soon as we are ready[our preparations are completed]. // 모두 ~가 되었는가 Are you all set? // 이번 겨울의 석유 부족에 대비한 ~는 되어 있는가 Have you provided against an oil shortage this winter? // 숲 속의 짐승들은 겨우살이 ~를 서두르고 있다 The beasts of the forest are busy preparing[with preparations] for winter. // 회의는 많은 사전 ~를 요했다 The conference required a great deal of preparation[spadework]. (▶ spadework는 회의 장소 물색과 식사 준비 등을 말함) // 제자리에 ~ (스타트에서) On your mark(s)! Get set! Go! / Ready! Set! Go! // 사격 ~ Ready your gun. // 만루가 되어 1루타로 역전시킬 ~가 되어 있었다 The bases were loaded, and things were all set up for a turnaround. **준비하다** prepare (for); ready; arrange (for); make preparations (for); get ready (for). ¶준비해 둔 담배 a stock[reserve stock / supply] of cigarettes // 실험실에 많은 기계를 준비해 놓았다 We provided the laboratory with a lot of equipment. // 차를 준비하지 않았기 때문에 그들은 존을 나무랐다 They blamed John for not having provided transportation.
● **준비금** a reserve fund; a reserve supply of money; money to cover the cost of getting ready[preparing] for something; (이전(移轉)의) a moving allowance. ¶법정 ~ a legal reserve fund. **준비 운동** warming[limbering] up; warming-up[limbering-up] exercises; (경주에서) sweating; a sweat. ¶~을 하다 warm[limber] up // 경주에 대비해 다리의 ~을 하다 warm up[train] one's legs for a race (▶ warm up은 경주 직전의 준비 운동, 경주를 위한 오랜 준비 운동은 train). **준비 은행** a reserve bank. **준비 절차** [법] preparatory proceedings; preliminaries.

준사관(准士官) a warrant officer.

준설(浚渫) dredging. **준설하다** dredge. ¶강바닥을 ~ dredge up mud at the bottom of a river / dredge the river bottom.
● **준설기** a dredging machine. **준설선** a dredger; a dredging vessel. **준설 작업** dredging operations[work].

준수(遵守) observance; compliance; conformity. **준수하다** observe (rules, the law, etc.); obey; abide by; follow; comply (with); conform to. ¶준수하는 사람 an observer // 법률을 잘 준수하는 국민 a law-abiding people // 법률[규칙]을 ~ observe the law[rules].

준수하다(俊秀-) excel in talent and elegance; superior and refined. ¶준수한 젊은이 a young man of outstanding talent / (외모가) a well-set, handsome youth.

준엄하다(峻嚴-) stringent; severe; rigorous; stern; strict. ¶준엄하게 strictly / sternly // 준엄한 검사 a relentless prosecutor // 준엄한 태도 a stern attitude // 준엄한 얼굴을 하다 look stern // 당국의 단속은 더할 수 없이 준엄했다 The enforcement of regulations by the authorities was strictness itself. // 그는 부하

에게 지나치게 준엄했다 He was too hard on his subordinates.

준열하다(峻烈-) rigorous; stern; severe; sharp; relentless. ¶준열한 논고 a scathing argument // 준열한 비판 sharp[scathing] criticism // 검사의 논고는 아주 준열했다 The prosecutor's address was most unsparing. / The prosecutor's summary could not have been harsher.

준용(準用) applying (a rule, etc.) correspondingly (to a case); adapting; adaptation. **준용하다** apply (a rule, etc.) with appropriate modifications; make[extend] (a rule) to cover a case; adapt. ¶법을 ~ apply the law mutatis mutandis / fit the law (to the case) // 이 경우에는 …에 관한 본조(本條)의 규정을 준용한다 The provision of this article shall apply in this case.

준우승(準優勝) a victory in the semifinals.
●**준우승자** a winner of the semifinals.

준위(准尉) a sub-officer; a warrant officer(약어 WO).

준장(准將) [미 육군] a brigadier general; [영 육군] a brigadier; [미·영 해군] a commodore; [미 공군] a brigadier general; [영 공군] an air commodore.

준재(俊才) [아주 뛰어난 재주] eminent ability [talent]; [뛰어난 재주를 가진 사람] a brilliant[talented] person; a man of talent; a genius.

준족(駿足) [걸음이 빠른 말] a swift horse; [잘 달리는 사람] a swift[fast] runner. ¶~의 야구 선수 a fleet-footed[fast] baseball player / a speedster // ~이다 be swift[fleet] of foot / be a fast runner.

준준결승(전)(準準決勝戰) a quarterfinal (game / match / round); the quarterfinals.
●**준준결승 출전자** a quarterfinalist.

준칙(準則) a standing rule; working rules; [기준] a standard; a criterion (pl. ~s, -ria); [지켜야 할 규칙] a rule; a regulation. ¶법률은 행위의 ~이다 Law is the rule to action.

준평원(準平原) [지] a peneplain.

준하다(準-) [따르다] act on (a rule, precedent, etc.); [본보기에 따르다] follow; go by; conform to; apply correspondingly (to); [모방하다] model after; [비례하다] be proportionate (to); be in proportion (to). ¶…에 준하여 in accordance with … / in proportion to (one's exertion) / in proportion as (one exerts oneself) // 회원에 ~ be treated the same as a regular member // 정회원에 준하는 대우를 받다 receive the same treatment as regular members // 이하 이에 준한 This also applies to the following cases.

준행하다(遵行-) follow in accordance with an order[the rule]; observe; obey; comply with; conform to. ¶법을 ~ observe laws.

준험하다(峻險-) steep; precipitous.

준현행범(準現行犯) [법] a quasi-flagrant offense.

준회원(準會員) an associate member.

줄¹ 1 [끈] a string; a cord; a rope; a line. ¶갖가지 색실로 꼰 ~ a multicolored cord / a cord made by entwining threads of various colors // 낚싯 ~ a fishing line // 사다리 ~ a roe ladder // 연 ~ a kite string / a string[twine] for a kite // ~을 두른 구역 a roped-off area // 상자를 ~로 묶다 tie up a box with rope / rope a box // 짐의 ~을 풀다 untie a package // 가는 ~을 꼬다 make a rope // 건축 현장을 ~로 격리하다 rope off a building site.
2 (악기의) a string; a chord; gut(재료로서). ¶바이올린에 ~을 달다 string[restring] a violin // ~을 죄다 tighten the string // ~이 끊어졌다 The string snapped. / The line gave way[broke].
3 [선] a line. ¶가는[굵은] ~ a thin[thick] line // ~을 긋다 draw a line / line[rule] (paper) / line through / run a line through / underline // 종이 한복판에 ~을 내리그으시오 Draw a line down the middle of the paper.
4 [행] a line; a row; (시의) a line (of verse); a verse; (편지 등의) a line. ¶~과 ~ 사이를 떼다 leave space between lines / space out // 한 ~씩 건너 쓰다 write on every other line.
5 [열] a row; a line; a string; a file(종렬); a rank(횡렬); a queue(차례를 기다리는). ¶한 ~로 늘어선 자동차 a string of cars // 한 ~로 in a straight line / ~을 서다 stand in (a) line / form a line // ~에서 새치기하다 break[barge / cut] into a line / jump the queue // 아이들을 ~을 서게 하다 line up children // 새 우표를 사려고 사람들이 ~ 서 있었다 People had lined up[(영) had queued] to buy the new stamp. // 그들은 세로 4~로 서서 행진했다 They marched four abreast. // 그 길 양편에는 은행나무가 ~ 서 있다 The road is lined on both sides with ginkgo trees.
6 [무늬] a stripe; a streak; a stria; a band. ¶금 ~ gold stripes // ~이 진 바지 striped trousers // 녹색 ~이 진 유니폼 a uniform with green stripes.
7 [인연·관계] a connection; a concern; relations. ¶~을 대어 두다 maintain certain useful contacts with (the underworld) // 이로써 마지막 믿던 ~도 끊기고 말았다 This put an end to my last hope. / My last hope has gone.
8 (나이의). ¶50~의 남자 a man in his fifties // 40~에 접어들다 enter the forties / pass one's forty-year milestone.
9 [광맥] a vein (of ore); a mineral vein; a lode.
10 [엮어 묶은 두름] a string (of). ¶담배 한 ~ a sheaf of tobacco (leaves) // 마른 생선 한 ~ a string of dried fish.

줄(을) 대다 [끊이지 않고 죽 이어 대다] continue; go on; keep on; follow one after another; run[follow] without intermission [interruption / a break]. ¶줄 대어 continuously / uninterruptedly / in succession / in a row[line] // 줄 대어 서다 stand in a row[line / queue] / line[queue] up.

줄(이) 풀리다 strike a better vein of ore.

줄² [연장] a file; a rasp(이가 굵은); a grail(빗 제조용 반원형의); a raspatory(외과용). ¶마무리 ~ a smooth file // 밥 filings // 그는 ~질을 하여 철판의 모서리를 다듬었다[매끄럽게 했다] He filed off the edge of the griddle[filed the edge of the griddle smooth].

줄³ 1 [방법] how to (do); the way. ¶요리할 ~ 알다 know how to cook // 그는 아무것도 할 ~ 모른다 He is good for nothing. 2 [셈속] (the fact) that. ¶그런 일이 있을 ~ 꿈에도 몰랐다 I never dreamed[Little did I dream] of such a thing. / That was the last thing I expected to happen. // 그는 내일 올 것이니

줄 1666

그런 ~ 아시오 He will come tomorrow, so please be prepared. / Please hear in mind that he is coming tomorrow.//네가 이것을 쓴 ~을 그가 어찌 알겠는가 How should he know that you wrote this?

줄⁴ [일 또는 에너지의 단위] a joule.

줄거리 1 [줄기] a stalk; a stem; a caulis; a leafstalk; a petiole. 2 [골자] an [a brief / a rough] outline; a summary; a synopsis (pl. -ses); (소설·연극의) a plot. ¶연극의 ~ the plot [synopsis] of a play//복잡한 ~의 극 a play which has a complicated plot//~를 말하다 give an outline [a summary] (of)//이야기의 ~를 더듬다 follow the thread of a story//이 이야기는 어떤 ~인가 What is the plot of the story?

줄곧 all the time; all the way; in season and out; at all hours; night and day; constantly; continually. ¶침대에 ~ 누워 있어야 하는 노인 a bedridden old man / an old man confined to bed//~ 재잘거리다 keep chattering all the time//~ 비가 온다 It rains day in and day out.//너 여기에 ~ 있었니 Have you been here all the time?//대전에서부터 ~ 서 있어야 했다 I had to stand all the way from Daejeon.//그녀는 수업 중 ~ 자고 있었다 She slept through the whole class.//그는 일생을 ~ 독신으로 지냈다 He remained single throughout [all through] his life.//인질은 ~ 감시를 받았다 The hostage was constantly watched. / Constant watch was kept over the hostage.

줄기 1 (나무의) a trunk; (풀 등의) a stem; a stalk; a cane; a haulm. ¶~의 지름이 2미터 되는 나무 a tree with a trunk two meters in diameter//샐러리 [아스파라거스]의 한 ~ a stick [stalk] of celery [asparagus].
2 (물 등의) a course; a stream. ¶강 ~ the course of a river//(강이) 두 ~로 갈라지다 fork / divide into two branches//홍수는 강 ~를 바꾸어 놓는다 Floods turn rivers out of their course.
3 (산 등의) a range. ¶산 ~ a range of mountains.
4 (소나기의) a shower; a downpour; a rainfall. ¶소나기가 한 ~ 올 것 같다 It looks like we're in for a bit of a downpour.
5 [줄] a line; a stripe; a streak; a column [wisp] (of smoke). ¶한 ~의 불빛 a streak of light//한 ~ 희망의 빛이 보였다 A ray of hope appeared.//두 ~의 눈물이 주르르 볼 타고 흘러내렸다 Tears streaked down both cheeks. / A line of tears ran down each [either] cheek.//한 ~의 흰 길이 들 가운데 뻗어 있었다 A white road ran through the fields.

줄기줄기 1 (시냇물이) in streams [streamlets]. ¶물이 ~ 흐른다 Water flows in streamlets. 2 (산이) in ranges [chains]. ¶산이 ~ 뻗어 나간다 A mountain spreads out into ranges.

줄기차다 vigorous; exuberant; bursting [streaming] with vitality. ¶줄기찬 비 a driving [pouring / sheeting] rain / a drenching shower//4일 동안 줄기차게 내린 비 the down pour of rain which persisted for four days//줄기차게 비가 내리다 rain hard [incessantly]//줄기차게 항거하다 offer a stout resistance//시냇물이 줄기차게 흘러간다 The stream rushes along exuberantly.//세계는 여성 해방을 향하여 줄기차게 움직이고 있었다 The world was moving steadily and swiftly towards women's liberation.

줄넘기 [줄을 돌리는 놀이] rope skipping; [돌리는 줄] a skipping [jump] rope; [줄을 뛰어 넘는 놀이] rope jumping. **줄넘기하다** skip [jump] rope; turn a skipping rope.

줄다 become [get] smaller [less]; decrease; diminish; lessen; be reduced; go down; fall (off); dwindle(차차); run low; abate; subside; shrink(의복 등이); [단축되다] be shortened [abbreviated.].¶가치 [수 / 양]가 ~ decrease in value [number / quantity]//체중이 ~ lose weight//3분의 1로 ~ be reduced to one-third//(빨래가) 줄지 않는 unshrinkable//강물이 준다 The river sinks.//우물물이 줄었다 The water in the well has got low.//구두가 줄어 버렸다 My shoes have tightened [become tight].//체중이 5킬로 줄었다 I have lost weight by five kilograms. / I have lost five kilograms (in weight).//세수(稅收)가 줄어 버렸다 Tax revenues fell (off).//회원 수가 줄었다 The membership has decreased.//수익이 줄었다 The profit has diminished [decreased]//수출이 5퍼센트 줄었다 Our exports showed a decrease of [decreased by] five percent.//이 옷감은 빨면 준다 This material shrinks when washed.//이것은 빨아도 줄지 않는다 This is sanforized [shrink-resistant]. / This does not shrink in the wash.//스웨터를 빨았더니 기장이 5센티나 줄었다 The sweater shrank five centimeters in length when I washed it.//이번 달에는 수입이 갑자기 줄었다 My income plunged [took a nose dive / dropped / plummeted] this month.//고무는 온도에 따라 늘거나 준다 Rubber expands and contracts according to the temperature.//등유의 저장량이 줄고 있다 We are running short [out] of kerosene.

줄다리기 juldarigi; a tug of war. **줄다리기하다** play at a tug of war.

줄달다 continue; occur in succession; follow one after another. ¶줄달아 continuously / without intermission [a break] / in succession / successively / one upon the heels of another / in a row [line]//불행이 줄달아 일어났다 One misfortune followed (on the heels of) another.//오전에는 손님이 줄달았다 We received a cascade [stream] of visitors through the morning.

줄달음(질) running fast; dashing; darting **줄달음(질)하다** run fast [hard] ; rush; dash dart.

줄달음치다 run fast [hard] ; rush; dash dart. ¶줄달음쳐 달아나다 run away for one's life / run dead away / take to one's heels.

줄담배 ¶~를 피우다 chainsmoke//~를 피우는 사람 a chainsmoker//그는 ~를 피운다 He is a chainsmoker. / He chainsmokes.

줄모 rice seedlings transplanted in check rows. ¶~를 심다 transplant rice seedlings in check rows.

줄목 the key [essential / vital] point; the highlight.

줄무늬 stripes; a striped pattern. ¶~가 있는 striped//~ 바지 striped trousers//~의 천 striped cloth//~ 셔츠 a striped shirt//~의 드레스 a dress with a striped pattern//~지게 짜다 weave in stripes.

줄바둑 a poor game of Baduk (simply putting stones in rows). ¶~을 두다 play [have] a

poor game of *Baduk*.
줄밥 (줄질할 때의) filings.
줄방귀 a succession of flatuses; successive farts.
줄사다리 a rope ladder.
줄어들다 〔크기가 작게 되다〕 shrink; contract; shorten; dwindle (away); diminish (in size); 〔수량이 적게 되다〕 decrease; lessen; fall (off); run low. ¶줄어들지 않는 shrink-proof[nonshrinkable] 《fabrics》/ 〔상/품명〕 Sanforized 《cottons》// 〔빨아도〕 줄어들지 않다 be unshrinkable // 점점 줄어들어 없어지다 dwindle away into nothing // 이것은 세탁해도 줄어들지 않습니다 This won't shrink in the wash[when washed]. // 그 나라는 기근 때문에 인구가 몹시 줄어들었다 Famine depopulated the country greatly. // 우리는 줄어든 예산으로 지내고 있다 We are on a reduced budget.
줄이다 〔감소하다〕 reduce; decrease; diminish; lessen; 〔단축·절감하다〕 shorten; cut short; cut (down); curtail; 〔절약하다〕 economize; 〔축소하다〕 contract; boil down; 〔생략하다〕 abbreviate; abridge. ¶비용을 ~ reduce[cut down] expenses // 속도를 ~ slow down / reduce one's speed // 예산을 ~ make a retrenchment in the budget // 생산량을 ~ curtail productions // 생활비를 ~ reduce one's living cost // 목숨을 ~ shorten one's life // 기간을 ~ reduce the term // 적자를 ~ hold down the deficit // 교제비를 ~ cut back on entertainment expenses // 수면 시간을 ~ shorten[cut down] one's hours of sleep // 문장(文章)의 길이를 3분의 1로 ~ condense [cut down] a passage to a third of its length // 스커트 길이를 2센티 ~ shorten the length [take up the hem] of a skirt by two centimeters // 기록을 0.4초 ~ shave[clip] 0.4 seconds (in a race) // 그는 이야기를 조금 줄였다 He shortened[cut] his story a bit. // 코트가 내게는 너무 길어서 줄였다 The coat was too long for me so I shortened it. // 다이어트[식이 요법]를 하여 나는 체중을 줄이고 있다 I am reducing[losing weight] by dieting. // 의사에게서 술을 줄이라는 충고를 받았다 The doctor advised me to drink less. // 우리는 수습 기간을 3개월로 줄였다 We cut down[reduced] the probationary period to three months. // 그는 휴가를 하루 줄였다 He cut short his vacation by one day. // 맨 먼저 연료비를 줄이기로 결정했다 We decided to cut down on our fuel bills first. // 그녀는 생활비를 줄이지 않으면 안 되었다 She had to cut down[reduce] her living expenses. // 그해의 국가 예산을 줄였다 They retrenched[cut down] the national budget for the year. // 염분의 섭취를 줄이시오 Do not take too much salt. / Cut down on your intake of salt. // 우리는 금년에는 쌀의 생산을 줄이지 않을 수 없었다 We had to reduce[cut back on] the production of rice this year.
줄임표(-標) 〔인〕 ellipsis; leaders.
줄자 a tape (measure); a tapeline. ¶~로 재다 tape-measure.
줄잡다 make a conservative[moderate] estimate (of); estimate (a cost) low; underestimate. ¶줄잡아서 on a conservative estimate / at a moderate estimate / moderately // 최하로 줄잡아서[아무리 줄잡아도] at the lowest estimate // 비용을 ~ make a rock-bottom estimate of the expenses // 비용은 줄잡아도 20만 원은 들겠다 It will cost at least 200,000 won. // 그의 재산은 줄잡아도 10억은 된다 A conservative estimate of the value of his property is about 1,000 million won. // 손해는 줄잡아 5백만 원이다 The (amount of) damage is conservatively estimated at five million won. // 초대자는 줄잡아 100명은 밑돌지 않아야 한다 By moderate estimates, at least a[one] hundred people have to be invited.
줄줄 1 〔흐르는 모양〕 (flow) ceaselessly in a stream; in streams; profusely; running; gurgling; murmuring; purling; babbling. ¶땀을 ~ 흘리다 perspire profusely / swelter // 침을 ~ 흘리다 drivel freely / dribble // 그의 얼굴에서 많이 ~ 흐르고 있다 His face is dripping with perspiration. // 수돗물에서 ~ 나온다 Water trickles down (from the faucet). // 그의 손바닥에서 피가 ~ 흐르고 있었다 Blood was running from his palm. // 눈물이 ~ 그녀의 뺨에 흘러내렸다 Tears ran[streamed] down her cheeks.
2 〔막힘없이〕 smoothly (and easily); without a hitch; fluently; flowingly. ¶시를 ~ 외다 recite a poem fluently.
3 〔따라다니는 모양〕 《follow a person》 closely and persistently; tagging; tailing.
줄줄이 in row after row; in rows; all lines [rows].
줄짓다 〔정렬하다〕 be in a row; stand in (a) line; 〔줄을 짓다〕 line up; rank. ¶일렬로 ~ stand in a line // 두 줄로 ~ form[stand in] two lines // 줄지어 서다 stand in a row / 〔차례를 기다려〕 queue[line] up // 노점이 줄지어 선 거리 a street lined with stalls // 줄지어 서게 하다 have (them) get into[stand in] line // 자동차들이 줄지어 달려갔다 Cars ran past in a line. // 그 거리에는 멋진 집들이 줄지어 있다 A row of buildings lines the street.
줄타기 (tight) rope dancing[walking]; a tightrope feat[act]. ¶위태위태한 ~를 하다 run a risk / walk a high wire / make a risky attempt / engage in touch-and-go business // 그의 거래는 위험한 ~이다 He is walking a tightrope in his business dealings. **줄타기하다** walk a tightrope; walk[dance] on a tightrope.
● **줄타기 광대** / **줄타기 곡예사** a tightrope walker[dancer]; a funambulist.
줄행랑(-行廊) 1 〔행랑채〕 the front wing of a house; the servants' quarters. 2 〈속〉 (an) escape; (a) flight. ⇨도망
줄행랑치다(-行廊-) abscond; decamp; run away[off]; make off; take flight. ¶범인은 남미로 줄행랑쳤음에 틀림없다 The suspect must have fled to South America. // 우리는 그가 시내에서 줄행랑치기 전에 붙잡지 않으면 안 된다 We must arrest him before he runs away from[(구어) skips] town.
줌 1 a (clenched) fist. ⇨주먹 2 a handful (of rice). ⇨움큼
줍다 〔집어 올리다〕 pick up; 〔채집하다〕 gather (shells); 〔발견하다〕 find (a purse). ¶떨어진 이삭을 ~ glean[gather] ears of corn (after the reapers) // 밤을 ~ gather chestnut // 정원에 흩어져 있는 종잇조각을 ~ pick up the scraps of paper scattered about in the garden // 주워 넣다 pick up and put in // 이것저것 주워 먹다 grab a bite of this and

thar/나쁜 것들을 주워 냈다 He took out those of worse ones.//돈을 바닥에서 주워 포켓에 넣었다 I picked up the money on the floor and put it in his pocket.//그는 돌을 주웠다 He picked up a stone.//거리에서 지갑을 주웠다 I picked up[found] a wallet on the street.//그녀는 흩어진 성냥개비를 상자에 다시 주워 담았다 She picked up scattered matches and put them back into the box.

줏대(主-) a definite view[opinion]; a fixed principle; (the) backbone; moral fiber; firmness[strength] of character. ¶~ 있는 사람 a man of principle / a man of firm[strong] character//~ 없는 사람 a man without settled convictions / a spineless [back] boneless] fellow//그는 ~가 없다 He lacks firmness of character. / He has no backbone [moral fiber].

중 a Buddhist priest. ⇨ 승려 ¶~이 되다 become a priest[monk] / enter the priesthood.

중이 제 머리를 못 깎는다(속담) You cannot scratch your own back.

중¹(中) 1 [중앙] the center; the middle. 2 [중위] medium; average. ¶~ 정도의 middling / medium / mediocre//~ 이상이 되다 rise above mediocrity[(the) average]//~ 이하로 떨어지다 fall below mediocrity[the average]//그녀의 학교 성적은 ~이다 She is medium in scholarship[studies].//그의 성적은 ~보다 조금 상[하]이다 His marks are slightly above[below] average.

중²(中) 1 [···가운데] in; between; among; amidst; out of. ¶왕 ~의 왕 the king of kings//공기 ~의 산소 the oxygen in the air //그 ~의 하나 one of them//둘 ~의 어느 하나 either of the two//승객 ~의 한 사람 one of[among] the passengers//많은 후보자 ~에서 선출하다 select out of[from among] many candidates//나는 미국인 친구 ~에서 그가 가장 사귀기 무난하다 I find him the easiest of my American friends to get along with.//이 책은 그의 대표작 ~에 든다 This book counts among his major works.//너희들 두 사람 ~ 한 사람은 뒤에 남지 않으면 안 된다 One (or the other) of you has to stay behind.//이 병에 걸리는 사람은 1만 명 ~에서 한 사람뿐이다 Only one out of[in] ten thousand people develops[contracts] this disease.//나는 1년 ~ 4개월밖에 집에 있지 않는다 I am home only four months out of the year.//불행 ~ 다행이었다 It was the (only) redeeming feature in the whole unhappy affair.

2 [···의 속] in; through.

3 [···동안에] during; in (the course of); throughout; while; for. ¶1년 ~ 내내 all the year round / 오전 ~ 내내 in[all through] the morning//휴가 ~에 during the vacation //여행 ~에 on one's journey//부재 ~에 during[in] one's absence//수업 ~에 (while) in class//금주 ~에 in the course of[within] the week//오늘 ~에 sometime today / in the course of today//내달 ~에 some time during next month//나는 오전 ~에 세탁을 마쳤다 I finished washing in the morning [before noon]./수업 ~에는 조용히 해라 Don't talk during class.//오전 ~에는 집에 있겠습니다 I will be (at) home all morning.//나는 지난 1년 ~에서 3개월은 외국에서 보냈다 I spent three months abroad during the past year.//한창 바쁘신 ~에 이렇게 와 주셔서 감사합니다 Thank you very much for coming right in the middle of your day.

4 [진행 중] under; in process[course] of. ¶건축 ~인 다리 a bridge under construction //집필 ~인 책 a book one has on hand [is engaged on]//토의 ~인 문제 the question under discussion//식사 ~이다 be at table // 지금 시험 ~이다 The examinations are going on now.//아버지는 지금 여행 ~이시다 My father is (away) on a trip.//모든 사람은 지금 식사 ~이다 Everyone is eating now.//그녀는 근무 ~이다 She is on duty.//그는 독서 ~에 잠이 들었다 While (he was) reading he fell asleep.//그 계획은 진행 ~이다 The project is under way.//그것은 아직 쓰는 ~이다 I have not yet finished writing it.//통화 ~입니다 The line is busy[(영) engaged].//그 사건은 지금 조사 ~이다 The matter is under[in course of] investigation.

중간(中間) the middle; midway. ¶~의 middle / mean / halfway / intermediate / interim / ~ 굵기의 medium-fine (woolen yarn) / medium-point(ed) (fountain pen)//~(의) 입장을 취하다 take a middle position (between)//~ 에 in[at] the middle (of) / halfway / midway//방 ~에 있는 책상 a desk in the middle[center] of the room//···의 ~에 있다 lie (midway / halfway) between ... //···의 ~에 서다 mediate between ... / act as go-between for (two parties)//두 점의 ~(쯤)에 있다 be somewhere in between the two points//그 ~에 섬이 하나 있다 An islands lies between them.//수원은 서울과 대전의 ~에 있다 Suwon lies halfway between Seoul and Daejeon.//우리 학교는 역과 공원의 ~쯤에 있다 Our school is situated about halfway between the station and the park.//철도역과 백화점 ~에 은행이 있다 There is a bank halfway[midway] between the station and the department store.//그녀의 드레스 색깔은 파란색과 자주색의 ~쯤 되는 색이었다 The color of her dress was somewhere between blue and purple.//저기 집들이 늘어선 ~에서 약간 왼쪽의 하얀 집이 내 집이다 My house is the white one a little to the left of the center of that row of houses.//그의 석차는 학급에서 ~보다 조금 아래다 He ranks a little below the middle of his class.

● **중간고사** / **중간시험** a midterm examination. **중간노선** a middle-(of-the-)road line; neutrality. ¶~을 취하다 take[follow] the middle-road course / steer a middle course. **중간보고** an interim report. **중간 상인** a middleman; a broker. **중간자**(-子) [물] a meson; a mesotron. ¶~의 mesonic / mesotronic. **중간층** the middle class(es); the middlebrows. **중간치** medium[in-between] things[sizes / prices / quality]; a medium; middlings; middles. **중간파** neutrals; the middle-(of-the-)roaders.

중갈이(中-) vegetables out of season.
중갑판(中甲板) the middle deck.
중개(仲介) intermediation; mediation(조정); agency. ¶···의 ~로 through the (inter)mediation of ... //~의 역할을 하다 act as a go-between[intermediary]//그의 ~로 거래가 성사됐다 A deal was concluded through his intermediation.//K 상사(商社)의 ~로 그 두

회사는 계약을 맺었다 The two firms struck a bargain through the intermediation of K and Co.//우리나라가 이 두 나라의 ~ 역할을 하기를 나는 바라고 있다 I hope our nation will act as a go-between for those two powers.//미국은 양국 간의 휴전 교섭에 ~ 역할을 할 용의가 있다 The United States is ready to act as an intermediary in cease-fire talks between the two countries.//그는 두 집안의 화해를 위해 ~를 자청했다 He offered to mediate between the two families to help them mend their differences.//그는 부동산의 ~를 하고 있다 He is a real estate agent[(영) an estate agent]. **중개하다** mediate [intermediate] (between two parties].
- **중개 무역** merchant [commission / intermediary] trade. **중개 수수료** brokerage (commission). **중개업** brokerage (business); agency. **중개인 / 중개자** a mediator; an intermediary; a go-between; (주선인) an agent; a commission agent[broker]; a broker; agent. ¶~을 통하여 through an agent // ~을 통하지 않고 without[minus] a middleman.

중거리(中距離) a middle distance.
- **중거리 경주** a middle-distance race. **중거리 선수** a middle-distance runner. **중거리 탄도탄** an intermediate range ballistic missile(약어 IRBM).

중견(中堅) [중심이 되는 사람] the backbone; the mainstay; the nucleus; [군] the main body; [야구] center (field). ¶회사의 ~이 되다 form[prove oneself] the backbone of a company // 이 사람들은 한국 경제계의 ~이다 These people form the core[nucleus] of the Korean economic world.//중산 계급은 국가의 ~이다 The middle class forms the backbone of the nation.
- **중견 간부** a leading[principal] member (of a company). **중견수** [야구] a center fielder. **중견 작가** [야구] a (lady) writer of medium [intermediate] standing.

중경상(重輕傷) a serious or slight injury [wound]; a major or minor injury. ¶~을 입다 be seriously or slightly injured[wounded] / suffer a major or minor injury // 승객 10명이 ~을 입었다 Ten passengers were injured either slightly or seriously.
- **중경상자** the seriously and slightly injured [wounded]; major and minor casualties.

중계(中繼) **1** [중간에서 이어 줌] relay. **2** relay broadcasting. ⇨중계방송(⇨중계) ¶무대 ~ a stage relay broadcast / a drama relayed from the stage // 실황 ~ relay of actual conditions // 우주 ~ (via) the space relay // 현장 ~ relay from the spot. **중계하다** relay; rebroadcast; translate.
- **중계국** a relay station. **중계 무역** transit [intermediate] trade. **중계방송** relay broadcasting; rebroadcasting; a relay broadcast; a rebroadcast; (미) hookup. ¶전국 ~ broadcasting over a nationwide hookup[network] //전국에 ~을 하다 broadcast over a nationwide hookup[network] //한국 전역에 남극 기지 실황 ~이 실시되었다 The actual scene at the Antarctic base was relayed throughout Korea over a nationwide network.

중고(中古) **1** [역] [중고기(期)] the Middle Ages; medieval times. ¶~(기)의 medieval. **2** a (slightly) used article. ⇨중고품(⇨중고)
- **중고차** a used car. ¶~ 시장 a used car market. **중고품** a (slightly) used article; secondhand goods. ¶~의 slightly used[old] / secondhand // ~ 옷가지 worn clothes //신품 같은 ~ an article slightly used but almost brand-new[as good as new] // ~을 사다 buy a thing secondhand[at second hand].

중고기 [동] a kind of freshwater carp.
중공(中共) **1** the Chinese Communist Party. ⇨중국 공산당(⇨중국) **2** [중화 인민 공화국] the People's Republic of China.
- **중공군** the Communist Chinese Army.

중공업(重工業) heavy industries.
중과부적(衆寡不敵) ¶~이다 We are outnumbered [overcome in number]. / There is no contending against such heavy[big] odds.// ~으로 패했다 We were outnumbered and defeated.

중과세(重課稅) heavy taxation.
중과(실)(重過失) gross negligence.
중구난방(衆口難防) You can't shut the doors of people's mouths.; There is no silencing Mrs. Grundy.; Grundyism is an annoying thing indeed.

중국(中國) China; [정식 국호] the People's Republic of China(중화 인민 공화국). ¶~의 Chinese
- **중국 공산당** the Chinese Communist Party; (당원) the Chinese Communists. **중국 사람** a Chinese; (집합적) the Chinese. **중국어** Chinese; the Chinese language. **중국 요리** Chinese dishes[food]; (요리법) Chinese cooking[cookery].

중궁(전)(中宮殿) a queen.
중권(中卷) the middle[second] volume[book] (of a set of three).

중근동(中近東) the Middle and Near East.
중금속(重金屬) [화] a heavy metal.
중금주의(重金主義) [경] the mercantile system.

중급(中級) (an) intermediate level; middle [medium] class[(미) grade]. ¶~의 intermediate / medium / of the middle class [intermediate rank] //「~ 영문법」(저서명) An English Grammar for Intermediate Students // 그의 검술 솜씨는 ~이다 He is a middle grade fencer.
- **중급 영어** intermediate English.

중기(中期) the middle period; [생] (세포 분열의) the metaphase. ¶18세기 ~ the mid-eighteenth century // 조선 ~에 in the middle of the Joseon dynasty.

중기(重機) **1** [중공업용 기계] heavy machinery. **2** [군] a heavy machine gun. ⇨중기관총
중기관총(重機關銃) [군] a heavy machine gun.

중남미(中南美) Central and South America.
- **중남미 사람** a Latin American.

중년(中年) middle age[life]; one's middle years. ¶~을 넘은 여자 a woman past middle age / an elderly woman // ~의 middle-aged / in middle life.
- **중년기** the middle years of one's life. **중년 신사** a middle-aged gentleman. **중년층** the middle-aged; the middle generation.

중노동(重勞動) heavy[hard] labor. ¶~을 하다 engage[be engaged] in heavy labor.
중농(中農) a middle-class[-scale] farmer. ¶~의 가정 a medium-scale farm family.
중농 정책(重農政策) an agriculture-first policy.

중농주의(重農主義) [경] physiocracy; physiocratism.
- ●**중농주의자** a physiocrat.

중뇌(中腦) [생] the midbrain; the mesencephalon (pl. -la).

중늙은이(中一) an elderly man; a person in advanced middle age.

중단(中段) 1 (계단의) the middle of the stairs; (침대의) the middle berth[bunk]. 2 (글의) the middle part of a writing[book].

중단(中斷) interruption; discontinuance; suspension; a break. ¶**시효** ~ [법] interruption of prescription // 대화[교통]의 ~ a lull in the conversation[traffic]. **중단하다** discontinue; interrupt; suspend; break (off). ¶연설[교섭]을 ~ break off a speech[negotiations] // 손님이 있어서 나는 일을 잠시 동안 중단했다 I stopped working[laid aside my work] for a while because I had a guest. // 정부는 대미 교섭을 중단했다 The Government broke off the negotiations with America. // 그는 쓰던 편지를 중단하고 나갔다 He went out leaving the letter unfinished. // 우리는 여행을 중단하고 즉시 되돌아왔다 We cut our trip short and came back at once. →¶**중단되다** be interrupted[suspended / discontinued] // 재판이 중단되었다 The trial was suspended. // 판매가 중단되었다 The sale was discontinued. // 그 계획이 중단되었다 The plan was frustrated. / The plan was brought to a halt. // 그의 연설은 야유로 중단되었다 His speech was interrupted by boos and hisses. // 이 프로그램의 방영은 사흘째 되던 날에 중단되었다 This TV program was discontinued[canceled] on the third day. // 그 사건의 수사는 중도에서 일단 중단되었다 The investigation of the affair was temporarily suspended. // 이야기가 중단될 때마다 나는 빗소리를 의식했다 Whenever there was a lull in the conversation I noticed the sound of the rain. // 그의 공격은 중단되지 않고 계속되었다 His verbal attack went on without a break.

중대(中隊) company(보병·공병); squadron (비행 중대); a battery (포병). ¶**~를 편제[편성]하다** form a company.
- ●**중대장** a company[battery / troop] commander; a squadron leader.

중대(重大) [관형어적]. **중대하다** important; serious; grave; (a matter) of great[vital] importance. ¶**중대한 문제** an important problem / a serious[vital] question / a grave issue[subject] // **중대한 과실** gross negligence / a gross mistake / a vital error // **중대한 사태** a grave situation // **중대한 책임** weighty[serious] responsibility // **중대한 결과** grave consequences // **중대한 결과를 가져오다** lead to a grave consequence // …에게 중대한 영향이 있다 have an important influence upon … // …만큼 중대하지 않다 be of less importance than (that) // **중대한 사태가 되었다** The situation has become grave. // 그것은 중대한 실책이다 It's a serious[awful] blunder. // 그는 중대한 사명을 띠고 있다 He is charged with an important mission. // 이것은 우리 회사로서 매우 중대한 문제이다 This is a serious[crucial] problem for our company. // 그의 오해가 중대한 결과를 초래했다 His misunderstanding had[brought about] grave consequences.
- ●**중대 관심사** a matter of the utmost [gravest] concern. **중대사 / 중대 사건** a serious affair[happening / case]; an important[a grave] matter. **중대 성명** an important statement[announcement].

중대가리 [중처럼 빡빡 깎은 머리] a shaved [shaven] head; [중처럼 빡빡 깎은 사람] a person with a shaved head.

중도(中途) halfway; midway; mid-course. ¶~에서 halfway / midway / in the middle // 일을 ~에서 그만두다 stop in the middle of (work) / do things by halves / stop working halfway // ~에서 되돌아오다 turn back halfway // 일의 ~에서 쓰러지다 break down in the middle of one's work // ~에서 퇴학하다 give up school / leave school in mid-course [without finishing the whole course] // 그는 일[이야기]을 ~에서 그만두었다 He stopped in the middle of his work[speech].

중도(中道) (도로의) the middle of a road; the middle path; [중용] the middle road (between two extremes); mean; moderation. ¶~를 걷다[취하다 / 지키다] take the golden mean / take the middle-of-the-road course / take a moderate course.
- ●**중도 정치** (미) a middle-(of-the-)road politics.

중독(中毒) poisoning; toxication; [의] intoxication. ¶수은 ~ mercurial[mercury] poisoning / hydrargyrism // 식~ food poisoning / poisoning from eating // 아편 ~ opiumism / opium poisoning // 알코올 ~ alcoholism / addiction to alcohol / alcoholic poisoning // ~의 intoxicative // ~성의 poisonous / toxic // 그는 ~ 증세를 나타냈다 He showed[had] symptoms of poisoning. **중독되다** be[get] poisoned. ¶복어에 ~ be[get] poisoned by globefish // 코카인을 상용하면 중독된다 Habitual use of cocaine causes toxicosis.
- ●**중독자** an addict. ¶마약 ~ a drug addict // 알코올 ~ an alcoholic.

중동(中) [사물의 중간 부분] the middle part (of a thing); the central part; the middle; [허리 부분] the waist (of the garment). ¶~이 가는[좁은] slender[narrow] in the middle // (옷이) ~이 긴[짧은] long-[short-]waisted // ~을 두 토막으로 자르다 cut in two in the middle.
- ●**중동끈** a waistband; a waist sash.

중동(中東) the Middle East; the Mideast. ¶~의 Middle Eastern.

중동(仲冬) [겨울의 한창 추울 때] the eleventh lunar month; midwinter.

중동무이(中一) [중간에서 흐지부지함]. ¶~의 half-finished / unfinished / halfway / incomplete // 일을 ~인 채로 놔두다 leave a matter pending[half done / in suspense]. **중동무이하다** do (things) by halves; leave (things) unfinished[half done]; stop[give up] (working) halfway.

중등(中等) [가운데 등급] the middle[second] class; the secondary grade; [가운데 질] medium[average] quality; [중위] common standard; mediocrity; the average. ¶~의 middle(-class) / medium / moderate / middling / mediocre / average // (성적 등이) ~ 이상[이하]이다 be above[below] mediocrity [the average].
- ●**중등 교육** secondary education. **중등학교** a secondary school; a school of secondary grade.

중략(中略) an ellipsis (*pl.* -lipses); an omission (of interior parts); [언] a syncope; syncopation. ¶K 씨는 말했다, "나는 (~) 그 사건과 관계가 없다." Mr. K said, 'I ... have nothing to do with that matter.'"(▶ 생략을 나타내는 점은 언제나 3개임) **중략하다** omit; skip; syncopate. ¶그의 진술은 다 읽기는 너무 길기 때문에 중략해서 읽겠습니다 Please allow me to omit part of his statement, as it is too long to read in full.

중량(重量) weight. ¶총[정미] ~ gross [net] weight // 항공 우편물의 ~ air mail poundage // ~ 한도를 초과한 화물 an overweight luggage [(영) baggage] // ~가 있는 massive / weighty // ~이 모자라다 be short of weight / be underweight / weigh less than (it) should // ~을 속이다 give short weight [measure] // 돌의 ~을 달아 보다 weigh a stone // ~이 3파운드 나간다 It weighs three pounds. // 당신의 짐은 제한 ~을 초과하고 있습니다 Your luggage is over the weight limit. // "그 생선의 ~은 얼마나 됩니까?" "5파운드입니다." "What is the weight of the fish [How much does the fish weigh]?" "It weighs five pounds." // 설탕의 ~이 모자라다 The sugar is underweight [short-weighted]. (▶ short-weighted는 일부러 모자라게 했을 경우) // 저 가게에서는 ~을 속이지 않는다 They give honest weight in that store.
● **중량급**[체] the heavyweight division [class]. **중량 부족**[초과] short weight [overweight]. **중량 제한** weight [(미)] load] limits.

중력(重力) gravity; (terrestrial) gravitation. ¶무 ~ 상태 [the condition] of nongravitation [weightlessness] / a gravity-free state // ~의 법칙 the law of gravity // ~의 중심 the center of gravity.
● **중력 가속도** the acceleration of gravity. **중력장**(-場) the gravity field.

중령(中領) (육군·해병) (미) a lieutenant colonel; (영) a lieutenant-colonel; (해군) a commander; (공군) (미) a lieutenant colonel; (영) a wing commander.

중론(衆論) [다수인의 의론] consultation; public discussion; [다수 의견] a majority opinion; a consensus of opinion. ¶~에 의하여 결정되다 be unanimously decided (on) [agreed on] // ~에 따르다 act according to a majority opinion // ~에 묻다 refer (a matter) to public discussion.

중류(中流) **1** (강의) midstream; (상류·하류에 대한) the middle reaches [courses]. ¶~는 강폭이 넓다 The river is broad in its middle course. // 배는 ~에 정박하고 있었다 The boat was anchored in midstream. **2** (사회의) the middle class(es).
● **중류 가정** a middleclass family. **중류 계급(의 사람)** middle-class people; the middle classes.

중립(中立) neutrality; neutralization. ¶무장[비무장] ~ armed [disarmed] neutrality // ~의 neutral / (의원 등의) independent // ~을 선언하다 declare [proclaim] neutrality // ~ 노선을 따르다 follow [take] the neutral [neutralist] line // ~을 지키다 observe [keep / maintain] neutrality // ~을 어기다 violate (a country's) neutrality.
● **중립국** a neutral power [state / country]; a neutral; a neutralist [an unaligned / a noncommitted] nation. **중립성** neutrality; impartiality. **중립주의** neutralism. ¶~의 neutralist. **중립주의자** a neutralist. **중립 지대** a neutral zone. **중립화** neutralization. ¶~하다 neutralize / (국가가) turn neutralist.

중립적(中立的) neutral; (의원 등의) independent. ¶~인 태도를 취하다 stand neutral / take a neutral attitude // ~인 입장을 취하다 be on neutral ground / occupy middle ground // 나는 언제나 ~인 입장을 취하고 있다 I always stay on neutral ground.

중매(仲買) broking; brokerage. **중매하다** act as (a) broker.
● **중매 구전 / 중매 수수료** (a) brokerage (on bills); a commission. **중매인** a broker; a middleman; a commission merchant [agent].

중매(仲媒) matchmaking. ¶~의 ~로 through (a person's) good offices / through the good offices of ... // 남에게 ~를 부탁하다 ask another to act as (a) go-between // 친구의 ~로 결혼하다 get married through a friend's matchmaking // 그들은 안 씨 부부의 ~로 결혼했다 They got married through the good offices of Mr. and Mrs. An. // 신랑의 상사가 두 사람의 ~를 섰다 The groom's boss arranged their marriage. **중매하다** arrange a match (between); act as (a) go-between [a middleman]; go between (two parties). ¶내가 그들을 중매했다 I arranged a match [marriage] between them. // 숙모가 그들 두 사람을 중매했다 My aunt acted as a go-between for the two of them.
● **중매결혼** a marriage made up by a go-between; a marriage by arrangement; an arranged match. **중매인 / 중매쟁이** a matchmaker; a go-between; a middleman. ¶그는 그녀를 그렇게 말하시니까 ~이니까 그런 거다 He is saying all those nice things about her, as matchmakers will.

중문(中門) an inner gate.
중문(重文) [언] a compound sentence.
중미(中美) Central America. ¶~의 Central American // ~의 나라 a Central American country // ~의 사람들 Central Americans.

중바랑 a monk's knapsack [shoulder pack].

중반(전)(中盤戰) (선거 등의) the middle phase (of an election campaign); (바둑·장기의) the middle game. ¶~에 들어가다 (선거 등이) reach the peak (of the election campaign) / (바둑의) get into the thick of a game // 게임은 ~에 들어섰다 The game was now in its middle stages. // 선거전은 ~을 넘어섰다[맞이했다] The election campaign was approaching the final stages [at its height / in full swing].

중방(中枋) [건] a horizontal wall strut. ⇨ 중인방.

중배(中-) **1** [중복] the bulging part (of); the belly; the bilge. ¶독의 ~ the belly of a pot // 통의 ~ the bilge of a barrel // ~가 부르다 be bulged out [swollen] in the middle / have a bulge [swelling] in the middle / be "pot bellied." **2** (짐승의) a middle litter (of pigs, etc.).

중벌(重罰) a heavy [severe] punishment. ¶~에 처하다 punish (a person) severely / inflict a severe punishment (on a person) // 그는 ~에 처해졌다 He was punished severely.

중범(重犯) **1** [중대 범죄] a major offense;

중병(重病) a serious [severe] illness [disease]; a disease of a serious nature. ¶~이다 be very [seriously / dangerously / critically] ill / ~에 걸리다 get [fall / be taken] seriously ill // 그는 ~이다 He is seriously [critically] ill. // 그는 ~을 앓고 있다 He is suffering from a serious illness.

중복(中伏) the second 10-day period of the dog days; a mid dog days.

중복(中腹) [산의 중턱] the mountain's breast; the midslope of a mountain. ¶~에 halfway up [down] (a hill) / 지리산의 ~ 윗부분은 구름에 싸여 있었다 The upper half of Jirisan(Mt. Jiri) was enveloped in clouds.

중복(重複) [겹침] duplication; overlap; overlapping; [되풀이] repetition; redundancy(군말). ¶~을 피하다 avoid duplication [overlapping] // 한 문장 중에서 같은 말의 ~은 피해야 한다 You should avoid the repetition of the same word in a sentence. // 이 문장은 ~이 많다 This passage is full of redundancies. 중복하다 duplicate; overlap; double; repeat; be repeated. →¶중복된 duplicate / overlapping / repeated / redundant / (어구 등의) tautological / pleonastic // 호텔 측의 실수로 예약이 중복되어 있었다 The reservation was duplicated because of a mistake on the hotel's part.

중부(中部) (in) the central part [district].
● **중부 전선** the central forward area [region]; the central frontline areas. **중부 지방** the central districts [area / region]. ¶영국 잉글랜드] ~(의 여러 주) the Midlands.

중뿔나다(中-) [주제넘다] meddlesome; intrusive; officious; forward; pert; impertinent. ¶중뿔난 사람 an intruder / an obtruder / an intermeddler / an interloper / a forward person / a busybody // 중뿔나게 말하다 make an uncalled-for [impertinent / uninvited] remark / break [cut / butt] in / interfere in [meddle with] (another's business) // 중뿔나게 나서지 마라 This is no business of yours. / Mind your own business.

중사(中士) (영) a sergeant; (속어) a sarge; [미 육군] a sergeant first class; [미 해군] a chief petty officer; [미 공군] a master sergeant.

중산 계급(中産階級) the middle class(es); (경멸) the petite bourgeoisie; [중산 계급의 사람들] the middle classes; middle-class people. ¶~의 사람 a middle-class citizen / a bourgeois.

중산모(中山帽) (미) a derby (hat); (미국 속어) a pot hat; (영) a bowler (hat).

중상(中傷) (a) slander; (a) calumny; defamation.(▶ calumny는 공적인 일이나 인물에 관해서 쓰는 일이 많음. defamation은 명예를 손상시키는 일을 강조함) ¶~적 slanderous / defamatory / calumnious // ~이 심하다 be (a) gross slander. / It's nothing but (a) slander. // 그는 내게 대해서 ~적인 기사를 썼다 He wrote a defamatory [slanderous] article about me. **중상하다** slander (a person); malign (a person); calumniate; traduce; stab (a person) in the back. ¶그는 남을 중상하기 좋아하는 사람이다 He is given to slander. / He is a scandalmonger. // 당원끼리 서로 중상하고 있다 The party members are throwing mud at one another [are engaged in mudslinging].
● **중상자** a slanderer; a detractor; a maligner.

중상(重喪) losing one's parents one after another within three years.

중상(重傷) a serious [severe] wound [injury] (▶ wound는 고의에 의해 입은 부상, injury는 주로 사고의 결과로 입은 부상). ¶머리 [얼굴 / 발]에 ~을 입다 be seriously wounded [injured] in the head [in the face / in both legs] / receive [suffer] serious head [face / leg] wounds [injuries] // ~을 입히다 cause serious injury (to a person) / injure a person seriously // 그 전투에서 그는 ~을 입었다 He was seriously wounded in the battle. // 부상자 8명 중 1명은 ~이다 Eight persons were injured, one seriously.
● **중상자** a severely wounded [injured] person. ¶사망자 1명, ~ 8명 One was killed and eight were severely wounded.

중상주의(重商主義) mercantilism.
● **중상주의자** a mercantilist.

중생(重生) [가] a rebirth; a second birth. **중생하다** be born again; be [get] reborn.

중생(衆生) [불] [일체의 생물] living things; sentient beings; [인간] the people; mankind; the world. ¶일체 ~ all sentient beings / all creatures / all life // ~을 제도하다 save the world / deliver mankind.

중생대(中生代) [지] the Mesozoic (era). ¶~의 Mesozoic.

중서부(中西部) (미국의) the Middle West; the Midwest.

중석(重石) [화] tungsten. ⇨텅스텐

중석기 시대(中石器時代) [고고] the Mesolithic period [era]; the Middle Stone Age. ¶~의 mesolithic.

중선거구(中選擧區) a medium constituency [electoral district].
● **중선거구제** the system of having medium-sized constituencies [electoral districts].

중성(中性) 1 [화] neutrality. ¶~의 neutral. 2 [언] the neuter gender. ¶~의 neuter. 3 [생] sexlessness. ¶~적인 여자 a sexless woman.
● **중성 반응** a neutral reaction. **중성 세제** a neutral detergent. **중성자** [물] a neutron. ¶광~ a photoneutron // 반~ an antineutron // 열~ a thermal neutron // 중(重)~ a dineutron. **중성화**(-化) neutralization. **중성화**(-花) a neutral flower.

중성(中聲) [언] the medial of a Korean orthographic syllable; the vowels (and semivowels) of a Korean syllable.

중세(中世) the middle [medieval] ages. ¶~의 medieval.
● **중세기** the Middle Ages. **중세사** (the) medieval history.

중세(重稅) [무거운 세금] a heavy tax [duty]; [무거운 과세] heavy taxation. ¶~를 부과하다 impose a heavy tax (on) // ~에 시달리다 groan under heavy taxation // 월급쟁이는 ~에 시달리고 있다 Salaried workers are laboring under a burden of heavy taxation.

중소(中小) [관형어적] medium and small.
● **중소기업** medium and small-sized enterprises [businesses]; smaller [minor] enter-

prises[business]. ¶그는 ~에서 일하고 있다 He works for[is employed in] one of the smaller firms.// 정부는 ~ 육성책 강화를 다짐했다 The government pledged to step up measures to help development of medium and small enterprises. **중소기업 은행** the small and Medium Industry Bank. **중소기업 자금** bank loans for small-medium industries. **중소기업청** Small and Medium Business Administration. **중소 상공업자** merchants and industrialists of small and medium-sized enterprises.

중수(重水) [화] heavy water; deuterium oxide.

중수(重修) restoration; improvement; remodel(l)ing; repairing (a building). **중수하다** repair; improve (a road).

중수소(重水素) [화] heavyhydrogen; deuterium. ¶3~ tritium.

중순(中旬) the middle ten days of a month. ¶4월 ~에 around the middle of April / in mid-April / 5월 ~부터 since mid-May / 9월 ~경 about the middle of September.

중시(重視) serious consideration. **중시하다** attach (great / much) importance to (something); take a serious view of (a matter); lay stress on (a point); think much of (a person). ¶양보다 질을 ~ attach greater importance to quality than to quantity / 나는 인품을 가장 중시하고 사람을 고용한다 I regard character as most important when I choose employees.// 당국은 그 사건을 중시했다 The authorities took the incident very seriously. ➔그의 발언은 중시되었다 His statement was taken very seriously.

중신(重臣) [원로] a senior statesman; [중직에 있는 신하] a chief retainer.

중심(中心) 1 [한가운데] the center; (영) the centre. ¶~의 central / 축을 ~으로 해서 회전하다 revolve around a central pivot / revolve on an axis // 그의 집은 도시 ~에 있다 His house is in the center of town[the heart of the city].// 은행은 그 고장에서도 번화한 ~에 자리 잡고 있다 The bank is situated in the main part[business center] of (the) town.

2 [중추] the pivot. ¶~이 되어 일하다 work in a central[key] role / take the lead in the work // 서울은 정치의 ~이다 Seoul is the center of politics. / Seoul is the political center.// 그 이야기는 젊은 남녀의 연애를 ~으로 전개된다 The story centers round[on] the love of a young man and woman.// 사람들은 그를 ~으로 모여들었다 People gathered around him.

3 [중점] the central point; the focus (pl. ~es, foci). ¶당신의 의견은 문제의 ~에서 벗어나 있다 Your opinion is off[beside] the point.

4 [균형] balance. ¶~을 잡다[잃다] keep [lose] one's balance / ~을 잃고 넘어지다 lose one's balance and stumble // ~이 잡히있지 않다 be out of balance / be ill-balanced // 한 발로 서서 몸의 ~을 잡다 balance oneself on one leg.

5 [줏대] a definite view[opinion]; a fixed principle. ¶~이 서 있는 사람 a man of fixed principle.

●**중심가** the main street; (영) the high street; the midtown area. **중심부** the central part. **중심 사상** the central idea. **중심선** the center line. **중심 세력** a central force. **중심인물** a central[focal] figure; a key man; the leading[guiding] spirit; a leader of the pack; the leader; the (life and) soul (of the party); the brain; the ringleader; the dominant personality. ¶그는 우리 그룹의 ~이다 He is the central figure in our group. **중심점** the central point. **중심지** the center; the metropolis; the omphalos. ¶상업[공업]의 ~ a commercial[an industrial] center // 재해의 ~ a district hardest hit by a disaster / the center of the ruined area // 학문의 ~ a seat of learning // 서울은 한국의 교통 ~이다 Seoul is the center of transportation[the hub of the transportation system] in Korea. **중심 타선** leading batsmen (of a team).

중심(重心) [물] the center of gravity. ⇨ 무게중심(⇨무게).

중압(重壓) strong pressure. ¶~을 가하다 put [exert] pressure upon (a person) / bring pressure to bear upon (a person) / (구어) pressure (a person). **중압하다** press hard.

●**중압감** an oppressive feeling. ¶국민은 높은 세금에 ~을 느끼고 있다 The people felt a sense of oppression under the burden of heavy taxation.// 그의 말투에는 ~이 있다 He has an overbearing way of speaking.

중앙(中央) the center; the middle; the heart; [수도] a metropolis. ¶~의 central / middle // 시의 ~에 in the center[heart] of the city // ~에 모으다[모이다] concentrate / centralize // 정원의 ~에 분수가 있다 There is a fountain in the center of the garden.

●**중앙난방** central heating. ¶~식 a central heating system // ~의 건물 a centrally heated building. **중앙선** the central line of the highway; (철도의) the Central Line. **중앙 아시아[아메리카]** Central Asia[America]. **중앙 우체국** the Central Post Office(약어 CPO). **중앙은행** a central bank. **중앙 정부** the central government. **중앙 집권** centralization of power. **중앙 집권제** centralism. **중앙청** the Capitol Building (in Seoul).

중언부언(重言復言) repetition; reiteration. **중언부언하다** repeat; reiterate; say over again; harp on the same string. ¶중언부언하지 말고 빨리 다녀와라 Quit going on and on about the same old thing and get going!

중얼거리다 mutter; murmur; (불평을) grumble. ¶무어라고 혼자 ~ mutter something to oneself.

중얼중얼 muttering; murmuring; grumbling. ¶그는 ~ 혼잣말을 하고 있다 He is muttering[mumbling] something to himself. **중얼중얼하다** mutter. ⇨중얼거리다.

중역(重役) a director; an executive(▶ director 는 총괄적으로 경영 관리에 임하며 executive 는 업무 집행에 관계함); (집합적) the board (of the directors). ¶~ 자리 [지위] a directorship // ~이 되다 obtain a seat on the board of directors // 그는 ~ 타입이다 He has the look[the assurance and dignity] of a director.// 그는 회사의 ~이다 He is on the board of directors. / He is on the executive board of the corporation.

●**중역 회의** a meeting of the board of directors; a directors' meeting.

중역(重譯) (a) retranslation. **중역하다** retranslate.

중엽(中葉) [중간쯤 되는 시대] the middle part (of a period). ¶17세기 ~ the mid-sev-

중외(中外) 1 〔나라의 안과 밖〕 the inside and outside of the country; home and abroad. ¶~의 domestic[home] and foreign / internal and external∥~에 (at) home and abroad / inside and outside the country / (announce) to the world∥~에 독립을 선언하다 declare independence to the world∥~에 명성을 떨치다 be known both at home and abroad / gain a world-wide reputation. 2 〔정부와 민간〕 the government and the people; 〔서울과 지방〕 the capital and the provinces.

중요(重要) 〔관형어적〕. ¶역사상의 ~ 사건 some highlights[salient events] of history∥군사상의 ~ 지점 places of military importance. **중요하다** important; of importance [consequence / moment]; momentous; weighty; essential; 〔주요하다〕 principal; cardinal. ¶중요하지 않은 of no[little] importance[consequence] / unimportant∥정부의 아주 중요한 지위를 차지하다 hold a very important position in the Government∥공기는 사람이 살아가는 데 있어 절대 없어서는 안될 중요한 것이다 Air is essential to human life.∥그는 매우 중요한 역할을 했다 He played a vital role.∥그는 중요한 용건으로 외출했다 He went out on important business.∥그는 시험을 앞둔 중요한 시기에 감기에 걸렸다 He caught a cold before the examination, just when it was most important for him to be fit[in good health].∥중요한 점에서 의견이 갈렸다 Opinions differed on a crucial point.∥환자에게는 지금이 가장 중요한 때다 This is the most critical time for the patient.∥그는 항상 중요한 때에 없다 He is never here when he is needed most.∥무리를 하지 않는 것이 가장 ~ It is essential that you should not overdo it.∥중요한 점은 그 사람이 거기에 있었는가이다 The main point is whether he was there at that time or not.∥나는 가장 중요한 때 병이 들어 버렸다 I was taken ill at the critical moment.
● **중요 무형 문화재** an important intangible cultural heritage[asset]. **중요 문화재** an important cultural property. **중요 사항** an important matter; a matter of consequence [moment]. **중요성** importance; gravity; materiality (of the fact). ¶~이 있다〔없다〕 be of[no] importance∥그 대책의 ~을 강조하다 urge (upon a person) the importance of the measure. **중요 인물** an important person; (속어) a VIP.

중요시하다(重要視-) regard[consider / look upon] a person[a thing] as important. ¶그들은 명예를 대단히 중요시했다 They regarded personal honor very highly. / They held personal honor in high esteem.∥중매결혼에서는 가문이나 학력을 중요시하는 경우가 많다 Family background and schooling are considered very important in many arranged marriages. ➡¶유사한 책 중에서 가장 중요시 되는 것은 이 책이다 This book is the most highly regarded among those of the same type.

중용(中庸) 1 〔중정(中正)〕 the (happy / golden / constant) mean; the middle path[way / course]; (미) the middle-of-the-road; 〔알맞음〕 moderation. ¶~을 이룬 moderate∥~을 이룬 생각 a moderate opinion∥~을 벗어난 immoderate / aberrant∥~을 취하다 take a moderate course[the golden mean]∥그는 언제나 ~을 지키고 있다 He is always moderate. / He never goes to extremes.∥~에서 벗어난 행동은 삼가야 한다 You must avoid going to extremes. / You must keep to a moderate course. 2 〔경서의 하나〕 the Doctrine of the Mean; the Right Path.

중용(重用) promotion to a responsible post. **중용하다** give[assign] (a person) an important position[a responsible post]; appoint (a person) to a position of trust; promote (a person) to a responsible post. ➡¶중용되다 be taken into confidence (by one's superior)∥중용되고 있다 hold an important position (in a company).

중우(衆愚) 〔많은 어리석은 사람〕 the vulgar masses; an ignorant crowd.
● **중우 정치** mob rule; mobocracy.

중원(中原) 〔들판의 중앙〕 the center of a field; 〔경쟁의 마당〕 the field of contest. ¶~의 패권을 다투다 compete for supremacy in a country.

중위(中位) medium; mediocrity; average. ¶~의 medium / middling / middle / average / moderate / passable∥~ 이상〔이하〕이다 be above[below] the average.

중위(中尉) 〔미 육군〕 a first lieutenant; (영) a lieutenant; 〔미 해군〕 a lieutenant junior grade; (영) a sublieutenant; 〔미 해병대〕 a first lieutenant; 〔미 공군〕 a first lieutenant; (영) a flying officer.

중유(重油) heavy[thick] oil; crude[raw] petroleum; fuel oil.

중은(重恩) 〔크고 두터운 은혜〕 great favor [kindness]; obligations; indebtedness. ¶~을 입다 receive[meet with] great kindness / owe (a person) great obligations / lie under deep obligations (to).

중음(中音) 〔음〕 (여성의) mezzo-soprano; (남성의) baritone; 〔가온음〕 a mediant.

중음(重音) 〔언〕 a double sound.

중의(衆意) 〔여러 사람의 의견〕 a majority opinion; a consensus of opinion. ¶~가 일치하다 be unanimously decided (on)[agreed on]∥~에 따르다 act according to a majority opinion.

중의(衆議) consultation. ⇨중론

중이(中耳) 〔생〕 the middle ear; the tympanum (pl. ~s, -na).
● **중이염** inflammation of the middle ear; 〔의〕 otitis media.

중인(衆人) 〔뭇사람〕 the people; the public. ¶그들의 기발한 복장은 ~의 표적이었다 Their unconventional clothes became the focus [object] of public attention.

중인방(中引枋) 〔건〕 a horizontal wall strut.

중일 전쟁(中日戰爭) the Chinese-Japanese War.

중임(重任) 1 〔중대 임무〕 an important duty [mission]; 〔중책〕 a heavy responsibility [trust]. ¶~을 떠맡다 take a heavy burden on oneself∥~을 완수하다 fulfill an important[a weighty] duty. 2 〔재임〕 reappointment; 〔재선〕 reelection. ¶~도 무방하다 One may hold the office[be reappointed] for a second term. **중임하다** reappoint (a person to an office); reelect.

중장(中章) the middle part of a *sijo* poem.

중장(中將) 〔미 육군〕 a lieutenant general;

(영) a lieutenant-general; [미 해군] vice admiral; (영) a vice-admiral; [미 해병대] a lieutenant general; [미 공군] a lieutenant general; (영) an air marshall.

중장비(重裝備) heavy equipment. ¶~의 heavily equipped (division).

중재(仲裁) arbitration; mediation; intervention; intercession. ¶강제[임의] ~ compulsory[voluntary] arbitration//이 건은 ~에 붙여졌다 This case was submitted[referred] to arbitration.//제3자에 의한 ~ 신청은 모두 거부되었다 All offers of mediation by a third party were rejected.//그의 ~로 그 문제는 해결되었다 The matter was settled privately through his intercession[mediation]//두 국가는 제3국의 ~로 화해했다 The two nations made peace with each other through the mediation of the third nation.//마침내 장관이 문제의 해결을 위해 ~에 나서게 되었다 The Minister finally intervened to solve the problem. / In order to solve the problem, the Minister eventually had to get involved. **중재하다** arbitrate; mediate [intervene / intercede] (between); act as (a) peacemaker. ¶쌍방 간에 들어서서 ~ mediate between two parties / make peace between the two//두 사람의 이야기를 듣고 중재해 주었다 I listened to what both of them had to say and arbitrated[mediated] between them.

● **중재 위원회** an arbitration committee; (정당 등의) a trouble shooting committee. **중재인 / 중재자** an arbitrator; an arbiter; a mediator.

중전(中殿) a queen; a queen consort.
● **중전마마** Her Majesty the Queen.

중전기(重電機) heavy electric equipment.
중전차(重戰車) a heavy tank.

중절(中絶) [중도에서 끊어짐] (an) interruption; [일시 중지] (a) suspension. ¶임신 ~ an abortion//임신 ~을 하다 have[get] an abortion. **중절하다** be interrupted; be suspended; [계획 등이 연기되다] be postponed; [계획 등이 보류되다] be held up; 《구어》 be put on hold; 《구어》 be put on the back burner.

중절모(자)(中折帽子) a soft[felt] hat; a homburg; (미) a fedora (hat); (영) a trilby (hat); [테가 넓은 모자] a wide-awake (hat).

중점(中點) [인] a centered period; [수] the middle point (of a line); the midpoint.

중점(重點) an important point; [강조] emphasis; stress; [중요] importance; [우위] priority. ¶군비보다 국민의 복지에 ~을 두는 정책 a policy which gives priority to the welfare of the people rather than to armaments//우리 학교는 과학에 ~을 두고 있다 Our school places great importance[stress] on science.//그의 연설은 인화의 필요성에 ~을 두고 있었다 His speech emphasized [stressed / placed emphasis on] the need of harmony among people.//소방서는 관내의 호텔을 ~적으로 점검했다 In making inspections, the fire department concentrated [focused its attention] on the hotels in its jurisdiction.//우리 회는 회원 상호 간의 친목에 ~적인 목표를 두고 있다 It is the chief aim of our society to promote friendship among the members.

중정(重訂) a second revision; a re-revision. **중정하다** revise twice.

중조(重曹) sodium bicarbonate. ⇨=탄산수소나트륨(⇨탄산).

중죄(重罪) a grave offense[(영) offence]; a grave crime; [법] (a) felony. ¶~의 felonious //~를 범하다 commit a felony.
● **중죄인** a felon.

중주(重奏) a duet(t). ¶현악 사 ~ a string quartet.

중중거리다 grumble; complain; mutter; 《미국 구어》 grouch.

중증(重症) a serious illness. ¶~이다 be seriously ill.
● **중증 환자** a serious case.

중지(中止) discontinuance; discontinuation; suspension; abeyance; stoppage; interruption; a standstill. ¶업무의 일시적인 ~ a temporary suspension of business//그 기계는 지금 가동 ~ 중이다 That machine is not running[is out of operation] now.//그들의 계획에 ~ 명령이 내려졌다 They were ordered to suspend[give up] the project. / Someone put a stop to their plans. **중지하다** discontinue; suspend; interrupt; stop; drop; call off (a game); break off (a meeting); leave off; give up (trying). ¶건축을 ~ stop [discontinue] construction//지불을 ~ suspend payment / stop payment (on) / [부금을 거르다] let one's payments lapse//싸움은 당분간 중지하자 Let's stop quarreling for a while. ➔¶오늘 예정의 회합[시합]은 중지되었다 Today's meeting[match] has been called off[canceled].//버스 운행이 중지되고 있다 Bus service has been suspended.//부당한 차별은 중지되어야 한다 Unlawful discrimination should be ended[be brought to a end].

중지(中指) the middle[second] finger.

중지(衆智) the wisdom of the many. ¶~를 모으다 ask advice[seek counsel] of many people.

중직(重職) a responsible[an important] post [position]. ¶대학 내의 ~을 맡다 hold a responsible post in[within] a university.

중진(重鎭) 1 [영향력 있는 중요한 인물] a man of influence; a prominent[an influential / a leading] figure; a protagonist; [학계 등의 중요 인물] an authority; [사회의 기둥] a pillar; a mainstay. ¶문단의 ~ the most prominent figure in the literary world / the dean[doyen] (of Korean) men of letters//재계의 ~ grand old man (a tycoon) in the financial world//그는 화단의 ~이다 He is a leading figure in painting circles.

중진국(中進國) a developing country[nation]; semideveloped country[nation].

중창(重唱) [음] a part song. ¶2[3 / 4 / 5] ~ a duet [trio / quartet(et) / quintet(te)].

중채(中−) a building erected between the main quarters; a building inside the main enclosure.

중책(重責) 1 [중대한 책임] a heavy responsibility; an important mission. ¶~을 지다[맡다] assume[take / incur] a heavy responsibility//~을 완수하다 carry out[fulfill] an important mission. 2 [엄한 책망] a severe rebuke[reprimand].

중천(中天) midair; the midheaven; the middle sky; the zenith. ¶달이 ~에 떠 있다 The moon is shining overhead.

중첩하다(重疊−) lie one upon[on top of]

another; overlap each other[one another]; be piled one above[on] another; pile up. ¶중첩어 in piles[layers] / one above the other // 산이 중첩해 있다 Mountains rise one above another.

중추(中樞) **1** [중요한 부분] the nucleus (*pl.* -clei, ~es). ¶사회의 ~ the mainstay of a society / a mainstay of society // 그는 회사의 ~에서 일하고 있다 He works at the hub of the company. // 그 세 사람은 운동의 ~를 이루고 있다 Those three people form the nucleus of the movement. **2** the nerve center. ⇨¨신경 중추(⇨신경(神經))
● **중추 산업** a pivotal[key] industry. **중추 신경** the central nerves.

중추(仲秋) midautumn; the middle of autumn; the eighth lunar month.
● **중추명월** the harvest moon.

중축(中軸) **1** [중앙의 축] the axis (*pl.* axes). **2** [중심이 되는 사람·것] // 이 새로운 운동의 ~은 장 씨이다 Mr. Jang is the central figure in the new movement.

중층(中層) **1** [중간에 있는 층] the middle stratum[layer]; (건물의) the middle story [floor]; (바다 등의) the middle depths; the mid-depths. **2** the middle class(es). ⇨¨중류2

중치(中-) medium[in-between] things. ⇨¨중간치(⇨중간) ¶~ 크기의 달걀 a medium-sized egg // ~ 사이즈 medium size.

중침(中針) a medium-sized needle; a needle of medium size.

중크롬산나트륨(重-酸-) sodium dichromate.

중크롬산칼륨(重-酸-) potassium dichromate.

중키(中-) average[middle / medium] height; middling[mean / medium] stature. ¶~의 중간 일 a matter of no small [of the utmost] magnitude // (a man) of mean[middle] stature / (a man) of middle[medium] height.

중탄산소다(重炭酸-) sodium bicarbonate; (일반적으로) baking soda.

중탄산염(重炭酸鹽) bicarbonate.

중탕하다(重湯-) heat[warm] (something) in a water bath (in boiling water).

중태(重態) a serious[grave] condition; a critical state[stage]; the seriousness of one's illness. ¶~에 빠지다 become seriously [critically] ill / take a critical turn(▶ serious보다 critical 쪽이 더 위중함) // 그는 폐렴으로 이다 He is seriously ill with pneumonia. // 아버님은 ~이시다 My father is in critical condition. // 그는 부상을 입었는데 ~였다 He was wounded and in a serious condition.

중턱(中-) [산허리] the mountain's breast; the mid-slope of a mountain; a hillside. ¶~에서 halfway up[down] (a mountain) // 산 ~에 찻집이 있다 There is a teahouse halfway up the mountain. // 언덕 ~까지 내려왔을 때 비가 오기 시작했다 It began to rain when we were halfway down the hill.

중톱(中-) a medium-size(d) saw; a saw of medium size.

중퇴(中退) leaving school in midcourse; dropping out of school. **중퇴하다** drop out of school; quit school. ¶그녀는 1년으로 대학을 중퇴했다 She quit[left] college [the university] after a year.
● **중퇴자** a school dropout. **대학[고교] ~** a college[high school] dropout.

중파(中波) [물] a medium frequency[wave].
● **중파 방송** medium-wave broadcasting.

중판(中判) [종이의 중간 판] a medium size. ¶~의 medium-sized.

중판(重版) [거듭 인쇄] a second [an another] impression; [개정판] a second edition; an additional printing. **중판하다** reprint; print the second edition. ➡그의 책은 중판되었다 His book was reprinted.

중편(中篇) **1** [제2권] the second part; the middle [2nd] volume. **2** a novelette. ⇨¨중편소설(⇨중편)
● **중편 소설** a novelette; a medium-length novel [story].

중평(衆評) [여러 사람의 평] public [general] opinion. ¶그가 그 자리에 적임자라는 데 ~이 일치되어 있다 It is universally admitted that he is just the man for the post.

중포(重砲) a heavy gun; (집합적) heavy artillery.
● **중포병** a heavy artilleryman.

중폭격기(重爆擊機) a heavy bomber; a heavy bombing plane; (속어) a heavy.

중품(中品) fair average quality; an article of medium quality.

중풍(中風) [떨리는 증세가 있는 것] palsy; [마비] paralysis; (집합적) apoplexy. ¶~의 apoplectic / paralytic // ~에 걸리다 have a stroke of paralysis / be stricken[taken] with paralysis
● **중풍 환자** a paralytic.

중하(仲夏) midsummer; the height of summer; the fifth lunar month.

중하다(重-) **1** [중요하다] important; weighty; serious; grave; [소중하다] valuable; of (great / much) value; dear. ¶상당히 [극히] 중한 일 a matter of no small [of the utmost] magnitude // 중한 손님 [친구] a valued customer [friend]. **중히** importantly; valuably. ¶명예를 ~ 여기다 respect [have a deep sense of] honor // 건강을 무엇보다 ~ 여기다 set health before everything else // ~ 여기지 않다 have no regard for / make little [light] of / slight / think slightly of.
2 [책임·임무 등이 무겁다] severe; serious; grave; weighty. ¶중한 벌 a heavy [severe] punishment. **중히** weightily; severely.
3 [위중하다] serious; critical; bad. ¶중한 병에 걸리다 get seriously [critically] ill.

중학교(中學校) (미) a junior high school(▶ 7~8 또는 7~9 학년의 학생이 다니는 학교); middle school(▶ 주로 사립학교에서 5~8 또는 5~9 학년의 학생이 다니는 학교를 가리킴. 한편, (영)에서는 8, 9세부터 12, 13세 아동이 다니는 학교를 가리킴). ¶공[사]립 ~에 다니다 attend a public [private] junior high school.

중학생(中學生) (미) a junior high school student [boy / girl]; (영) a (lower) secondary school pupil.

중합(重合) [화] polymerization. **중합하다** polymerize.
● **중합체** a polymer.

중항(中項) internal [inner] terms. ¶비례 ~ a mean proportional.

중핵(中核) the kernel; the core; the nucleus (*pl.* -clei, ~es). ¶사회주의가 이 운동의 ~을 이루고 있다 Socialism is at the core of this movement. // 가정은 사회의 ~을 이룬다 The family is the nucleus of the community.

중형(中型) a medium [middle] size. ¶~의

medium- [middle-] size.
● 중형차 a medium vehicles; a medium-size passenger car.
중형(重刑) a severe sentence [punishment]; a heavy penalty. ¶남에게 ~을 과하다 punish a person severely // ~에 처하다 sentence (a person) to a severe punishment / inflict a heavy penalty up (a person).
중형(仲兄) [자기의 둘째 형] one's second eldest brother.
중혼(重婚) bigamy; double marriage. ¶~의 bigamous // ~의 죄를 범하고 있다 be guilty of bigamy. 중혼하다 commit bigamy; marry (a person) bigamously.
● 중혼자 a bigamist.
중화(中和) [화] neutralization; (독 등의) counteraction. ¶~성(性)의 counteractive. 중화하다 neutralize; (독 등을) counteract; antagonize. ¶독성을 ~ neutralize the effects of poison. ➔¶산을 염기로 중화시키다 neutralize an acid with a base.
● 중화제 a counteragent; a counteractive.
중화기(重火器) heavy weapons [firearms].
중화요리(中華料理) Chinese dishes [food]; (요리법) Chinese cooking [cuisine].
중환(重患) a serious illness. ⇨중병
중환자(重患者) a serious case.
중후하다(重厚一) serious; grave; solemn; profound; imposing; dignified. ¶중후한 태도 a grave and serious attitude // 중후한 성격 solid character // 중후한 문체 a dignified style // ~하게 with an important air / weightily / seriously / gravely / with profoundness [depth] // 사장실의 집기는 전체적으로 ~ The furnishing of the president's room are wholly dignified. // 그는 나이가 듦에 따라 중후한 인물이 되었다 As he grew older, his character gained depth.
중흥(中興) restoration; revival. ¶그는 민족의 주역이었다 He was the father of the national restoration. 중흥하다 revive; be restored; be rehabilitated.
쥐¹ [동] a rat; (생쥐) a mouse (pl. mice). ¶들~ a field mouse // 집~ house rat // ~가 찍찍 울고 있다 Mice are squeaking [squealing].
쥐 숨듯 without leaving any trace.
쥐 잡듯이 violently; rudely; roughly. ¶(남을) ~ 하다 treat (a person) roughly [rudely] / ride roughshod over / handle (a person) roughly.
쥐 죽은 듯이 as still as can be; all hushed and still; as quiet as a mouse; deathly quiet; dead. ¶~ 조용하다 be (as) silent as the grave / quiet enough to hear a pin drop // 집안은 ~ 고요하였다 A profound [deep] silence reigned within the house. // 거리는 ~ 조용하였다 A great quiet reigned over the city.
쥐² [근육 경련] (a) cramp; (미국 구어) charley horse. ¶~가 나다 have a cramp // 발에 ~가 나다 have a cramp in the leg // 내 다리(근육)에 ~가 났다 My leg muscles are stiff. / I have cramps in my leg muscles.
쥐구멍 a mousehole; a rathole. ¶~을 찾다 wish one could disappear for a moment / seek a loophole // 나는 창피해서 ~을 찾고 싶을 지경이다 I'm so embarrassed that I wish the earth would swallow me up.

쥐구멍에도 별 들 날 있다 (속담) Every dog has his day.; Everything comes to him who waits.
쥐꼬리 ¶~만 한 월급 a small [low / meager] salary / a small stipend / a (mere) pittance / a poor [paltry] pay // ~만 한 월급으로 일하다 [생활하다] work at [live on] a meager salary // 갓 입사했기 때문에 보너스는 ~만 했다 Since I just joined the company, I got only a very small [a tiny / (구어) an itsy-bitsy] bonus.
쥐다 1 clasp; clench; grasp; grip; clutch; [붙잡다] hold; seize; take [get] hold of. ¶주먹을 ~ clench one's fist // 멱살을 ~ seize (a person) by the neck // 단단히 ~ take a firm grip (of) // 나는 그가 100미터 경주를 할 때 손에 땀을 쥐었다 I was breathless with excitement when he ran in the hundred-meter race. // 그는 무엇이든 한번 쥐면 내놓지 않는다 Once he gets hold of something, he never lets go. // 그는 문의 손잡이를 쥐고 돌렸다 He grasped the knob of the door and turned it. // 그녀는 편지를 받아 쥐기가 무섭게 봉투를 뜯었다 No sooner had she been handed the letter than she burst it open. // 어머니는 아기에게 딸랑이를 쥐어 주었다 The mother gave the baby a rattle to hold.
2 (권력 등). ¶패권을 ~ hold the supremacy (of) // 권력을 ~ seize [come into] power / have access to power // 증거를 ~ have [get] a proof / get hold of evidence // 남의 비밀을 ~ get [have] hold of a person's secret // 남편을 쥐었다 놨다 하다 dominate one's husband / keep one's husband under one's thumb // 그는 권력을 한손에 쥐게 되었다 He seized power for himself. / He consolidated power in his own hands. // 실권은 그가 쥐고 있다 He holds the actual power. / The real power is in his hands. // 그들은 무엇인가 우리의 비밀을 쥐고 있는 것 같다 They seem to have something on us [be in possession of some secret about us].
쥐어 주다 (돈을) slip (money) into (a person's) hand [pocket]; (팁을) tip (a porter); (뇌물을) grease [tickle] (a person's) palm; oil (a person's) hand; bribe. ¶만 원을 ~ give (a person) a 10,000 won bribe // 그에게 돈을 쥐어 주면 기꺼이 할 것이다 You can easily bribe him to do it. // 하인에게 조금 쥐어 주고 비밀을 알아냈다 I tipped the servant into telling me the secret. // 나는 그 사내에게 돈을 쥐어 주어 입을 막았다 I bribed the man into silence. / I bought the man's silence.
쥐덫 a rattrap; a mousetrap. ¶~을 놓다 set a trap for rats // ~으로 쥐를 잡다 catch a mouse with a mousetrap.
쥐똥나무 [식] a wax tree; a privet.
쥐라기(一紀) [지] the Jurassic (period); the Jura.
쥐락펴락하다 have (a person) under one's thumb; twist (a person) around one's little finger; boss [push] (a person) around. ¶그 여자는 남편을 쥐락펴락한다 She bosses her husband around.
쥐며느리 [동] a sow [pill] bug; a wood louse.
쥐뿔 [보잘것없는 것] a trifling thing; trivial [wretched] stuff; the merest trifle; (구어) a fiddle-faddle. ¶~도 모르는 사람 an (utterly) unlettered [illiterate] person / an ignoramus.
쥐뿔도 없다 be penniless; have not a penny

쥐뿔같다 [brass farthing] in the world; be as poor as a rat. ¶쥐뿔도 없는 사람 a penniless person / a pauper.

쥐뿔같다 worthless; good-for-nothing; useless; (속어) rotten; corny.

쥐새끼 [쥐의 새끼] a young rat. ¶~ 같은 놈 a paltry fellow / a mean rat.

쥐색(-色) dark gray; a slate color. ¶~의 dark gray / slate-colored.

쥐약(-藥) rat poison; ratsbane. ¶~을 먹다 swallow[take] rat poison.

쥐어뜯다 tear; rend; scratch off; pluck off; tear[rip] off. ¶창자를 쥐어뜯는 것 같은 heartrending // 머리털을 ~ rend[tear] one's hair // 새털을 ~ pick[pluck] a fowl / 닭털을 ~ pluck (feather from) a chicken // 회한이 가슴을 쥐어뜯는 듯했다 My heart was torn [was wrung] with regret. / I felt my heart torn to pieces by remorse. // 그녀는 그 소식을 듣고 가슴이 쥐어뜯기는 것 같았다 It wrung her heart to hear it. / Her heart was surcharged with grief at the news.

쥐어박다 strike (a person) with one's fist; give[deal / deliver] (a person) a blow with one's fist; use one's fist on (a person); punch. ¶머리를 ~ rap (a person) on the head / give a punch on the head.

쥐어지르다 [주먹으로 힘껏 지르다] smash (a person) with the fist; slug; give (a person) a hard punch (on the head).

쥐어짜다 1 (액체를) press[squeeze] out; extract; wring. ¶수건을 ~ wring a towel (out / dry).
2 (머리·목소리 등을) press out; squeeze. ¶머리를 ~ rack[cudgel / beat / puzzle] one's brains (about / over / to do) / split one's head / strive hard to think out (a plan) // 목소리를 ~ strain one's voice / raise one's voice to the highest possible pitch // 시를 지으려고 머리를 ~ work on[craft] a poem // 종일 머리를 ~ rack one's brains all day long // 그들은 대책을 생각해 내느라고 머리를 쥐어짜고 있다 They are racking their brains to devise a counter measure. // 그는 애써 머리를 쥐어짰지만 타개책을 발견하지 못했다 He thought hard[racked his brains] but could find no solution.
3 [몹시 조르다] importune[press] (a person for money); ask (a person) importunately for (money). ¶그는 돈을 더 달라고 어머니를 쥐어짰다 He pressed his mother for more money.

쥐어흔들다 1 [잡고 흔들다] grab and shake. ¶어깨를 ~ shake (a person) by the shoulder. 2 have (a person) at one's beck.

쥐엄나무 [식] a honey locust.

쥐엄발이 [발] a shriveled foot; (사람) a person with a shriveled foot.

쥐엄쥐엄 "grab it! grab it!"

쥐여지내다 be under the control[dominion / yoke] of ...; live under (a person's) thumb; live in the grips of ... ¶아내에게 쥐여지내는 남편 a henpecked husband // 지금도 쥐여지내는 몸입니다 I am not my own master [mistress].

쥐이다 be caught[held]; get grabbed.

쥐치 [동] a filefish; a leatherfish.

쥘부채 a (folding) fan. ¶~의 살 the ribs of a fan // ~를 쓰다 use a fan / fan oneself.

쥘손 [손잡이 부분] a handle; a handgrip; a grip; a gripe; (주전자 등의) a catch; an ear.

즈런즈런 [살림살이가 넉넉한 모양] abundantly; richly; plentifully; amply; in affluence [opulence]. **즈런즈런하다** abundant; rich; plentiful; ample; affluent; opulent. ¶살림이 ~ be well[comfortably] off / live in plenty [abundance / comfort] / be well-to-do.

즈봉 →바지¹

즈음 →[일이 어찌 될 무렵] when ...; about the time when .... ¶요~ these days / lately / recently / nowadays // 그~ in those days / at that time / then // 매년 이~에는 at this time of (the) year // 1990년 ~부터 since around 1990 // 배꽃이 지려는 ~이다 The pear blossoms are on the verge of falling.

즈음하여 when; at the time (of); in case (of); on the occasion (of). ¶이때에 ~ at this time [juncture] // 위험에 ~ in case of danger // 어려운 때 ~ in time of need // 이별에 ~ at parting from you // 출발에 ~ at the time of one's departure // 이 백과사전의 간행에 ~ on the occasion of the publication of this encyclopedia // 그는 사임에 ~ 연설을 하였다 Upon resigning[On resigning / When he resigned], he made a speech.

즈크 (cotton) duck; (cotton) canvas.
●**즈크화** canvas[duck] shoes.

즉(卽) 1 [곧] namely; that is (to say); or; (문어) viz.(▶ 보통 namely로 읽음); (문어) i.e.(▶ [áiː] 또는 that is로 읽음). ¶1파운드 ~ 100펜스 one pound, or one hundred pence // 그의 조부 ~ 고(故) 심 대장 his grandfather, that is, the late General Sim // 작문의 법칙 ~ 문법 the rules of composition, or grammar // 이 기간 ~ 전시의 수년간에 in this period, that is, during the several war years // 너의 성공이 ~ 나의 성공이다 Your success means my success. // 한국의 중등 교육은 두 학교 ~ 중학교와 고등학교에서 행해진다 In Korea secondary education is provided in two schools, namely, the junior high school and the (senior) high school. // 성공자가 ~ 부자일 수는 없다 A successful man is not necessarily rich.
2 [바로] just; precisely; exactly; [다름 아닌] nothing but; neither more nor less. ¶그것이 ~ 내가 바라는 것이다 That's just the thing I want. // 그 사람이 ~ 장군(將軍) 자신이었다 It was the general himself[no less than the general].

즉각(卽刻) on the spot; at once; right away; instantly; immediately; in a moment; without delay. ¶~적인 immediate / instant / instantaneous / prompt // ~ 행동을 취하다 take immediate action // ~ 승낙하다 give a ready consent (to) // 우리는 ~ 그들에게 전보를 쳤다 We cabled them immediately. // 환자는 ~ 수술을 받아야 한다 The patient must be operated on without delay. // 그는 ~(즉석에서) 결심을 했다 He made up his mind on the spot. // 나는 ~ 출발했다 I left immediately[(구어) right away]. / I started at once. // 우리는 ~ 국외로 퇴거하라는 명령을 받았다 We were ordered out of the country on the spot. / We were ordered to leave the country immediately. // 이 약은 ~ 효험을 나타낸다고 한다 This medicine is supposed to take immediate effect[to work immediately].

즉결(卽決) a prompt[an immediate / a quick] decision; (재판의) a summary decision; (영)

a snap judgment. ¶사태는 ~을 요한다 The situation calls for an immediate decision. **즉결하다** decide promptly [immediately / on the spot]; [법] try (a case) summarily.
●**즉결 재판** a summary decision [trial]. ¶~을 하다 decide summarily on a case / try (a case) summarily. **즉결 처분** summary conviction.

즉답(卽答) a ready [an immediate / a prompt] answer. ¶~을 요구하다 ask for a prompt reply // ~은 무리다 I can't give an answer right now [here and now / without considering the matter]. // 수상은 ~을 피했다 The Premier did not give an immediate answer. / The Premier avoided answering the question immediately [just then]. **즉답하다** give a ready answer; answer offhand.

즉사(卽死) (an) instant [instantaneous] death; death on the spot. **즉사하다** be killed instantly [instantaneously]; be killed outright [on the spot]. ¶그 소년은 차에 치여 즉사했다 The boy was hit by a car and died instantly [an instantaneous death].

즉석(卽席) ¶~의 immediate / ready / instant / prompt / impromptu / improvised / offhand(ed) // ~에서 offhandedly / instantly / immediately / promptly / at once / outright / (미) right away [off] / at short [a moment's] notice / [간단히] readily / easily / on the spot / (미국 구어) off the cuff // 그 일은 ~에서 될 수 없다 The work can't be done at a moment's notice. // ~에서 대답할 수 없다 I cannot give him an answer offhand [so easily / lightly]. // 나는 ~에서 결정할 수 없다 I can't decide readily [(구어) off the bat]. // 그렇게 큰 일을 ~에서 떠맡을 수 없다 I can't undertake such a big job just like that. // 그는 ~에서 승낙했다 He consented on the spot [immediately]. // ~에서 신청하지 않으면 기회를 놓친다 Unless you apply promptly, you'll miss your chance. // 그 문제는 ~에서 결정되었다 The matter was decided on the spot [without any discussion]. // 나는 ~에서 그 제의를 거절했다 I declined the offer on the spot. // 그는 ~에서 연설을 했다 He made an impromptu [an extemporaneous] speech. / He spoke impromptu. // 나는 ~에서 노래를 지었다 I improvised [made up] a song.
●**즉석연설** an impromptu [extemporaneous] speech; an off-the-cuff speech. **즉석요리** a light, quickly prepared dish; an instant [improvised] dish.

즉시(卽時) instantly; promptly; at once; on the spot [instant]; (미국 구어) right away [off]. ¶…하자 ~ as soon as ... / no sooner ... than / directly // ~ / scarcely [hardly] ... when [before] // 구호물자가 ~ 발송되었다 Relief goods were sent off at once. // 이것은 ~ 조사를 요한다 This calls for an immediate investigation. / This should be investigated promptly. // 그것은 ~ 해결되었다 It was settled on the spot. // 계획을 세우는 ~ 실행하기로 하자 Let's put the plan into action as soon as it's drawn up. // 물건이 도착하는 ~ 송금하겠습니다 I will send the money on receipt of the goods. // 홍 선생, 접수부로 ~ 와 주십시오 Mr Hong, you are wanted immediately at the information desk. // ~ 알려 드리겠습니다 I'll lose no time in letting you know. // 운동을 하니 효과가 (내게) ~ 나타났다 Physical exercise had an instant [immediate] effect (on me). // ~ 그에게 전해 드리겠습니다 I will tell him immediately. // 거기에 도착하면 ~ 전화를 울리겠습니다 I will phone you as soon as I arrive there.
●**즉시불** spot [immediate] payment; cash on the spot. ¶20만 원 ~로 해 주십시오 Pay me 200,000 won in cash, please. **즉시 인도** spot delivery.

즉위(卽位) accession to the throne; enthronement; coronation. **즉위하다** accede to [ascend] the throne; (왕이) become king [emperor]; (여왕이) become queen [empress].

즉응(卽應) conformity; agreement; adaptation. **즉응하다** [곧 응하다] conform to; agree with; adapt oneself to; [대처하다] cope with; meet. ¶즉응하여 in immediate conformity with / in immediate response to // 시대에 즉응한 교육 education adapted to the times // 시대적 요구에 ~ meet the needs [demands] of the times.

즉행(卽行) [곧 떠남] prompt departure; [곧 행함] prompt execution [action]. **즉행하다** depart at once; go promptly; execute [carry out] promptly; act at once. ¶옳다고 생각하는 일을 즉행하라 Do at once what you think is right.

즉효(卽效) immediate effect (of medicine). ¶치통에 ~가 있다 have an immediate effect on toothaches / [즉시 고통을 제거하다] give immediate relief from pain cause by toothaches // 이 알약은 환자에게 ~가 있었다 The pill had a prompt [an immediate / an instant] effect on the sick man.
●**즉효약** a quick remedy; a quick-acting medicine.

즉흥(卽興) impromptu amusement. ¶~의 improvised / impromptu / extempore.
●**즉흥곡** an improvisation; an impromptu. **즉흥시** an improvised [impromptu] poem; impromptu poetry [verse].

즉흥적(卽興的) impromptu; extempore; extemporary; improvisatory. ¶~으로 만들다 improvise // ~으로 시를 지을 수 있습니까 Can you compose poetry impromptu [(구어) off the cuff / (구어) off the top of your head]? // 그는 ~인 경영 방식으로나마 그런 대로 가게를 유지하고 있다 He manages to keep his store afloat even with his haphazard manner of running it. // 나는 그런 ~인 생활 방식에는 찬성할 수 없다 I don't approve of your happy-go-lucky way of life.

즐거움 joy; delight; pleasure; [행복] happiness; enjoyment. ¶독서의 ~ the pleasure of reading // 인생의 ~ the pleasure [joy / enjoyment] of life // 가정생활의 ~ the amenities of home life // ~이 없는 사람 a man of few pleasures // 자녀 교육을 유일한 ~으로 삼다 find one's sole comfort in the education of the young // ~을 실컷 맛보다 enjoy oneself to the full // 인생의 ~을 실컷 맛보다 enjoy all the amenities [pleasure] of life / drain the cup of pleasure to the dregs // 인생에 ~이 없어졌다 The charm of life is gone. // 독서가 유일한 ~이다 Reading is my only pleasure.

즐겁다 merry; pleasant; happy; cheerful; delightful; enjoyable; joyous; joyful; sweet. ¶즐거운 크리스마스 a merry Christmas // 즐거운 추억 a pleasant [happy / sweet] memory

즐기다

//즐거운 가정 a happy home//괴로운 때나 즐거운 때나 in pain or pleasure//즐겁게 놀다 [보내다] have a good [pleasant / fine] time (of it) / (미국 속어) have a ball // 즐겁게 하다 [해 주다] amuse (a child with story) / entertain [delight] (a person) with (something) / give pleasure to // 아주 즐겁게 지냈습니다 (떠날 때 하는 말) I've had a wonderful time. / This has been most enjoyable. / I've enjoyed myself very much.//청중은 강사의 이야기를 즐겁게 들었다 The audience listened to the lecture with interest.//그는 계속 농담을 하여 모든 사람을 즐겁게 했다 He told a lot of jokes and made everyone laugh [amused everybody].//우리는 즐거운 한때를 보냈다 We had a pleasant [nice] time.//그녀는 여행의 즐거운 추억을 깊이 간직했다 She cherished the delightful [happy] memories of her journey.//그는 함께 있으면 즐거운 사람이다. He's good company. / He's fun to be with.// 우리는 해변에서 2시간 동안 즐겁게 지냈다 We passed two hours pleasantly at the seashore.//그녀는 친구들과 이야기하는 것이 참 즐거웠다 She took [found] great pleasure in chatting with her friends.//그와 함께 걷는 것이 즐거웠다 It was a pleasure to walk with him.//파티는 정말 즐거웠다 I enjoyed the party a great deal.//그는 즐거운 얼굴이었다 He looked happy.//아이들은 즐겁게 놀고 있었다 The children were playing happily.//봄에는 갖가지 색깔의 꽃이 공원을 찾아오는 사람들의 눈을 즐겁게 해 주었다 In spring, flowers of various colors delight [please] the eyes of visitors to the park.//감미로운 음악이 우리 귀를 즐겁게 해 주었다 We feasted our ears on the sweet music [melodies]. **즐거이** pleasantly; delightfully; merrily; cheerfully; joyfully; joyously; gaily. ¶하루를 ~ 보내다 have a nice day // ~ 지내다 live [lead] a happy life // ~ 놀다 enjoy oneself // ~ 맞이하다 welcome with joy / receive (a person) with open arms.

즐기다 [즐거워하다] take [find] pleasure [delight] in; enjoy (an evening); enjoy oneself (over something / by doing); have a good [pleasant / fine] time (of it); have fun; [재미로 하다] amuse oneself (with something / by doing); make sport of (something). ¶물놀이를 즐기는 아이들 children playing [having fun] in the water // 즐겨 그림을 그리다 care to paint a picture frequently / draw a picture very often // 즐겨 독서하다 take pleasure in reading // 인생을 ~ enjoy life // 드라이브 [낚시]를 ~ enjoy oneself driving [fishing] // 그는 옛 가구를 모으는 것을 즐겼다 He took delight in collecting antiques.//나는 때때로 만화 읽기를 즐긴다 I sometimes amuse myself by reading comics.//그는 즐겨 이른 아침에 산책했다 He liked taking walks early in the morning.//그녀는 즐겨 언니의 아이를 돌보았다 She looked after her sister's children willingly [gladly].//차를 샀으니 일요일에는 드라이브를 즐기게 되었다 As I have bought a car, I can enjoy going for a drive on Sundays.//새 레코드가 있으면 나는 1주일은 즐길 수 있다 A new record would keep me amused for the next week.//남자도 여자도 유쾌하게 즐기고 있다 Both men and women are making merry.//그는 혼자 카드놀이를 즐기고 있었다 He amused himself by playing solitaire.//그는 술이나 담배를 즐기지 않는다 He neither drinks nor smokes.

즐비하다(櫛比-) 〔서슴히〕 stand in a row; line (a street). ¶창고가 즐비한 거리 a street lined with warehouses//도심에는 고층 빌딩이 즐비하게 늘어서 있었다 There were skyscrapers standing in a row in the center of the city.

즙(汁) (과실의) juice; (초목의) sap; (고무나무 등의) latex. ¶고기 ~ meat juice // **과일 [사과]** ~ fruit [apple] juice // ~**이 많다** be juicy [succulent] // ~**을 내다** extract [squeeze / press] juice // 사과를 ~을 내다 juice [press the juice out of] an apple // 포도의 ~을 짜다 press out the juice of grapes // 레몬의 ~을 짜내다 squeeze juice from a lemon.

즙액(汁液) juice. ¶~이 풍부한 [없는] juicy [juiceless].

증(症) 〔증세〕 symptoms; 〔화증〕 anger; 〔싫증〕 disgust; dislike. ¶중독 ~ toxic symptoms / 자각 ~ subjective symptoms // 무섬 ~이 나다 show signs of fear // 싫 ~이 나다 feel a repugnance (to).

-증(證) a certificate; a warrant; a bill. ¶학생 ~ a student's (identification) card // 영수 ~ a receipt.

증가(增加) (an) increase; addition; (an) increment; augmentation; gain; rise. ¶인구의 ~ (an) increase in population // 자연 ~ (a) natural increase [increment] // 응모자의 ~로 경쟁이 격심해졌다 Owing to the increase [rise] in the number of candidates, competition has become keener.//그것은 작년에 비해서 30퍼센트의 ~이다 It shows an increase of 30 percent over last year.//한국으로부터의 자동차 수출은 ~ 일로에 있다 The number of cars exported by Korea continues to grow steadily. / Korean automobile exports go right on increasing. **증가하다** increase; augment; rise; grow; swell. ¶수가 ~ increase in number.//65세 이상의 인구가 꾸준히 [급속히] 증가하고 있다 The number of people over sixty-five is rising steadily [rapidly].//지난 선거에서 여당의 의석이 15석 증가했다 The Government party gained fifteen seats in the last election. / The party in the power increased its number of M.P.'s by fifteen in the last election. ➔**증가되고 있다** be on the increase // **인원을 증가시키다** increase [augment] the staff [personnel] // **공급을 증가시키다** reinforce the supply.
● **증가액** the amount of increase; an increment. **증가율** the rate of increase.

증간(增刊) an extra number [issue / edition]; a special number (of a magazine / for the New Year). ¶춘계 ~(호) a special spring number / a special [an extra] issue for spring. **증간하다** issue an extra number.
● **증간호** a special issue.

증감(增減) increase and [or] decrease; 〔변화〕 variations; fluctuation(s). ¶체중의 ~ variation in one's weight / gains and losses in weight // 매상은 월별로 ~이 있다 Our sales vary from month to month. / Our sales fluctuate each month.//대도시의 인구는 ~이 별로 없다 The population of large cities does not change [increase or decrease] very much. **증감하다** increase and [or] decrease; 〔변화하다〕 vary; fluctuate.

증강(增強) reinforcement; augmentation; (an) increase; (a) buildup. ¶공급 물자의 ~ increase of supplies // 군사력의 ~ a military buildup. **증강하다** reinforce; increase; augment; build up (their military strength). ¶국방력을 ~ strengthen national defense // 적은 병력을 증강했다 The enemy built up [(미국 속어) beefed up] their army. // 나라의 방위력을 증강하려면 막대한 돈이 든다 It requires a huge sum of money to bolster [build up] the nation's defenses.

증거(證據) proof (of / that); evidence (of / for / that)(▶ proof는 의심할 여지없이 입증할 수 있는 증거, evidence는 주장을 뒷받침하는 데 필요한 문서, 증언, 물건 등에서 얻어지는 증거); witness; (a) testimony. ¶상황 ~ circumstantial evidence // 간접 ~ indirect evidence // 물적 ~ material evidence // 충분한 [불충분한] ~ sufficient [insufficient] evidence // ~ 불충분으로 for lack [want] of good evidence / on the ground of insufficient evidence // …을 증명하기 위해 ~를 제시하다 give [produce / bring forward] evidence to prove that … // …이라는 충분한 ~가 있다 There is sufficient evidence [ample proof] that …. // 나는 확실한 ~를 가지고 있다 I have certain [positive] proof of it. // 범인은 모든 ~를 인멸하였다 The criminal destroyed all the evidence. // ~를 대자 그녀는 얼굴이 빨개졌다 As proof [a sure sign] of it, she blushed. // 그는 물적 ~ 불충분으로 석방되었다 For want of material evidence he was released [set free] // 우리는 뚜렷한 ~가 있었다 There was [We had] clear-cut evidence. // 우리는 벌써 자네에 대한 ~를 잡고 있는 거야 (속어) We've got the goods (on you). // 검사는 피고를 불리하게 하는 유력한 ~를 찾아내지 못했다 The prosecutor could find no evidence strong enough to clinch his case against the accused. // 이 편지는 그의 배신의 ~가 되기에 충분하다 This letter provides adequate proof of his betrayal. // 그의 진술을 뒷받침할 만한 ~가 없다 He has no evidence to back up his statement.

● **증거물 / 증거품** (a piece of) evidence; an exhibit (of evidence); a voucher. **증거 보전** preservation of evidence. **증거 인멸** destruction of evidence. ¶~을 꾀하다 try to hide traces of the crime. **증거 자료** corroborative facts. **증거 조사** taking of evidence.

증권(證券) [증거가 되는 문권] a document; [채무 증서] a bond; [주식 증권] a certificate; [환어음] a bill; [공채·주권 등의 유가 증권] securities(▶ 보통 복수형); [상업 증권] a commercial [financial] instrument; [보험 증권] an insurance policy. ¶국고 ~ an exchequer bond // (미) a treasury bond // 대용 ~ collateral securities // 선화 ~ a bill of lading(약어 B/L) // 유가 ~ securities // 유통 ~ a negotiable instrument // 정부 발행 ~ government securities // 창고 ~ warehouse receipt // 그는 ~에 손을 댔다가 실패했다 He lost money on the stock market.

● **증권 거래소** a stock exchange; the Securities Exchange. ¶한국 ~ the Korea Stock Exchange. **증권 매매** dealing in bonds and securities. **증권 시장** the securities market. **증권 투자** securities investment. **증권 회사** the security corporation.

증기(蒸氣) steam; vapor; (영) vapour. ¶포화 ~ saturated steam // ~를 내다 [멈추다] turn on [off] the steam / turn the steam on [off] // ~로 움직이다 be driven by steam // ~를 쐬다 steam (cloth) / moisten (cloth) by steam.

● **증기 기관** a steam engine. **증기 기관차** a steam locomotive. **증기선** a steamer. **증기 소독** steam disinfection. **증기압** steam [vapor] pressure [tension].

증대(增大) enlargement; augmentation; (an) accretion; (an) increase; (an) increment; a step-up. ¶생산의 ~ a step-up in production // 인구의 ~ a swell [an increase] in population. **증대하다** [커지다] become [grow] larger; [커지게 하다] enlarge; increase; augment; swell (the total); enhance; step up (the amount). ¶수요가 ~ the demands rise (for it) / be more in demand // 흉악 범죄가 증대하고 있다 Brutal crimes are increasing [on the increase]. // 최근에 여자 입학자가 증대하고 있다 Recently there has been a great increase in the enrollment of female [girl] students.

● **증대호(-號)** an enlarged number.

증량(增量) (an) increase in quantity. **증량하다** increase the quantity (of). ¶소화제를 ~ increase the dosage of digestive medicine.

증류(蒸溜) distillation. **증류하다** distill. ¶바닷물을 증류하여 민물을 만들다 distill fresh water from seawater.

● **증류기** a distiller; a retort. **증류수** distilled water. **증류주** distilled [spirituous] liquor; spirits.

증명(證明) (a) proof; evidence; testimony(▶ evidence는 완전하지는 않지만 증거가 되는 사실, proof는 의심할 여지가 없는 완전한 증거, testimony는 진위를 증명할 수 있는 공공연한 증언을 뜻함); attestation; demonstration; corroboration; substantiation; certification; verification. ¶정리(定理)의 ~ the demonstration of a theorem [proposition]. **증명하다** prove; testify to (a fact); attest (to) (a fact); witness; bear witness [testimony] to (a fact); evidence; demonstrate; corroborate; substantiate; show; confirm; certify; verify; authenticate. ¶무죄를 ~ prove [establish] one's innocence // …임을 증명함 (증명서에서) This is to [I hereby] certify that … // 정리를 ~ demonstrate a proposition // 학설을 ~ demonstrate a theory // 범죄를 ~ bear witness to a crime // 문서를 ~ attest a document // 이 사실은 바로 그의 무죄를 증명한다 This fact is indeed proof of his innocence. // 이 기하 문제를 증명해 봐라 Demonstrate this geometrical proposition. // 그는 그 소문이 진실임을 증명하였다 He testified to the truth of the rumor. ➔ ¶이 이론은 아직 과학적으로 증명되지 않았다 This theory is not yet scientifically established.

● **증명서** a certificate; a testimonial(인물·자격 등의). ¶건강 ~ a health certificate / a (medical) certificate of health // 신분 ~ an identification card // 원산지 ~ [경] a certificate of origin // 사망 [결혼] ~ a death [marriage] certificate // ~를 교부하다 grant a certificate (to) / confer a certificate (on a person) // ~를 발급하다 issue a certificate (to).

증모(增募) an increased recruiting [enrolling]; raising extra (troops / labo(u)rers / subscriptions). **증모하다** (군인 등을) recruit larger enlistment; raise extra troops; (학생 등을) receive larger enrollment; increase the number (of students) to be admitted; raise extra.

증발(蒸發) **1** (액체의) evaporation; vaporization; volatilization. ¶~성의 vaporable / vaporific / volatile // ~의 evaporative. 증발하다 escape [fly off] in vapor; evaporate; be volatilized; (수증기로) steam away. ¶증발하기 쉬운 액체 a volatile liquid.
2 [사람·물건이 없어짐] mysterious disappearance; evaporation. 증발하다 disappear mysteriously [into thin air]; evaporate. ¶그녀의 남편은 3년 전에 증발한 뒤로 소식이 없다 Her husband disappeared [ran away / vanished into thin air] three years ago and has not been heard from since. / Her husband has been missing for the last three years. // 잠깐 눈을 뗀 사이에 내 가방이 증발하였다 During the instant I had taken my eyes off it, my bag disappeared.

증발(增發) (열차의) operation of an extra train; (통화의) an increased issue. 증발하다 (열차를) operate an extra train; increase the railway service; (통화를) issue additional paper money. ¶정부는 공채를 증발하였다 The government issued additional bonds. → ¶그 기간에는 임시 열차가 증발된다 They run [put on] extra trains during that period.

증배(增配) [배급량을 늘림] an increased ration; [주식 배당을 늘림] an increased dividend; a bonus; an extra distribution. 증배하다 declare [pay] an increased dividend; increase the ration (of rice). ¶회사는 이익이 났으므로 다음 기에 증배할 것이다 As the company's profits have risen, it will pay a larger dividend on stocks next term.

증병(增兵) reinforcement; an increase (in the number) of soldiers (at the front). 증병하다 reinforce the troops; dispatch reinforcements.

증보(增補) enlargement; supplementation; enlarged; supplemented. ¶개정 ~판 a new edition revised and enlarged / a revised and enlarged edition // ~ 개정하여 재판하다 produce a reprint with additions and emendations. 증보하다 enlarge; supplement.

증빙(證憑) proof; evidence; testimony.
● 증빙 서류 documentary evidence.

증산(增産) increased output [production] (of cars); a production increase; (농산물의) an increased yield. ¶생사의 ~ 계획은 중지되었다 The plan for increasing the output of silk was dropped. // 식료품 ~이 급선무다 It is of burning necessity to turn out foodstuffs in increasing amount. 증산하다 increase [boost] production (of); increase the yield. ¶강철을 ~ increase [step up] the production of steel // 곡물을 ~ increase the yield of grain.

증산(蒸散) (수분·식물의) transpiration. ¶식물은 기공으로 ~ 작용을 한다 Most plants transpire through their stomata. 증산하다 (수분·식물이) transpire.

증상(症狀) symptoms. ⇨ 증세(症勢)

증서(證書) [재무 등의 문서] a bond; [양도 등의 문서] a deed; [증거 서류] a document; a paper; [영수증] a voucher; [증명서] a certificate; (졸업의) a diploma. ¶차용 ~ an I.O.U. // 공정 ~ (공증서) a notary deed // 국채 ~ government bonds // 예금 ~ certificate of deposit // ~의 때늦은 제출 belated presentation of a deed for evidence // ~를 작성하다 draw up a bond // ~에 날인하다 seal a deed // 나는 ~를 받아 놓고 있다 I hold a deed.

증설(增設) (an) increase (of buildings); enlargement; extension. 증설하다 increase; establish (five) more (schools); install more (telephones). ¶병원을 ~ build more hospitals // 이 대학은 새 학과를 증설했다 This university opened [established] a new department. → ¶이 병원에 최근 소아 병동이 증설되었다 A children's ward has recently been added to this hospital.

증세(症勢) symptoms; the condition of illness. ¶학질(의) ~가 있다 have [show] the symptoms of malaria // 환자는 ~가 좀 어떻습니까 How is the patient progressing? // 가벼운 류머티즘 ~가 있다 have a touch of rheumatism // 그에게 콜레라의 ~가 보인다 He shows [has] symptoms of cholera. // 자각 ~가 있습니까 Have you noticed any symptoms yourself? // 그 환자의 ~는 예사롭지가 않다 The patient's condition is grave. // 그 환자의 ~는 급속히 악화됐다 The patient has taken a sudden turn for the worse.

증세(增稅) a tax increase; increased taxation. ¶1할의 ~ a ten percent increase in taxation. 증세하다 increase [raise] taxes (on a thing / on a person).

증손(曾孫) a great-grandchild; a great-grandson.

증손녀(曾孫女) a great-granddaughter.

증손자(曾孫子) a great-grandchild. ⇨ 증손

증쇄(增刷) (an) additional printing. 증쇄하다 print in addition. ¶급히 5,000부를 증쇄했다 An additional five thousand copies of the book were printed in a hurry.

증수(增水) the rise of a river; flooding. 증수하다 rise; swell. ¶오랜 비가 내린 후이므로 강은 증수하고 있다 The river is rising after the heavy rain. // 한강이 증수했다 Hangang (Han River) is swollen. // 어젯밤의 호우로 강이 1m 증수했다 Because of last night's heavy rain, the river has risen one meter.

증수(增收) [수입이 늚] an increase of receipts [income / revenue] (▶ revenue는 주로 국가·공공 단체·회사 등의 세입); [수확이 늚] an increased yield; an increase of crop. ¶세금의 자연 ~ automatic increases in tax revenues // 쌀의 ~를 도모하다 increase the yield of rice // 작년의 같은 달에 비하여 약 5퍼센트의 ~이다 Our balance sheet shows an increased profit of about five percent over the same month of last year. 증수하다 (one's income / the revenue / the crop) increase (by 5%). → ¶소득세 수입은 작년보다 5% 증수되었다 There was an increase of 5 percent over last year in the revenue from income tax.

증식(增殖) increase; multiplication; (문어) propagation; [생] proliferation. ¶병적 ~ (피부 조직의) vegetation // 세포의 이상 ~ hyperplasia of cells. 증식하다 increase; propagate; multiply; proliferate.

증액(增額) the increased amount of money; increment; increase. ¶임금의 ~ an increase in wages // 국방비의 ~에 반대하다 oppose an increase in the national defense budget // 여비의 ~을 요구하다 ask an additional sum for one's travel // 그들은 임금의 ~을 요구하며 파업에 들어갔다 They went on strike demanding higher wages. // 우리는 교육 예산의 ~을 요구했다 We demanded that they increase the amount budgeted for education. / We demanded an increase in the budget for education. **증액하다** increase (the amount); raise; augment. ➔¶가족 수당이 증액되었다 The family allowance has been raised.

증언(證言) (verbal) evidence; testimony; witness; attestation. ¶목격자의 ~ the testimony of an eyewitness // 허위 ~을 하다 give false evidence[testimony] / commit perjury // 피고에게 유리[불리]한 ~을 하다 testify in favor of[against] the accused // 남에게 ~을 부탁하다 call a person as a witness. **증언하다** testify; attest; bear witness; depose; give evidence; (문어) bear witness (to). ¶그녀는 그가 무죄라고 증언하였다 She testified[bore witness] to his innocence. / She testified that he was innocent. // 나는 그 사건에서 증언하도록 소환당했다 I was called to give testimony in the case.
● **증언대** the witness box; (미) the witness stand. ¶~에 서다 take the witness stand.

증여(贈與) donation; presentation; gift. **증여하다** [물건을 주다] [격식을 차려, 상·기념품 등을 주다] present(개인적인 선물에는 쓰지 않음); make a present of; confer; donate. ¶남에게 시계를 ~ make a person a present of a clock / give a person a clock (as a present) // 그는 시에 5천만 원을 증여하였다 He donated[presented] fifty million won to the town.
● **증여세** a donation[gift] tax. **증여자** a giver; a donator; a donor. **증여 재산** a donated property.

증오(憎惡) hatred; loathing; abhorrence(▶ hatred는 적의나 악의가 따르는 극도의 증오, loathing은 사람이나 물건에 대한 몸서리칠 정도의 증오, abhorrence는 도덕적인 혐오를 나타내는 일이 많으나, 구체적인 것에 대해서도 쓰임); detestation. ¶~를 사다 incur (a person's) hatred // ~의 마음을 품다 feel animosity (toward(s)) // 그는 ~에 찬 눈으로 그 남자를 노려보았다 He stared at the man with loathing[hatred]. // 그는 아버지에 대해서 ~를 품고 있다 He hates his father. / He has feelings of hate[hatred] toward his father. // 그들에 대한 ~도 이제는 벌써 없어졌다 My resentment against them is now gone. **증오하다** hate; detest; loathe; abhor; bear[have] a grudge (against). ¶증오할 행위 a detestable[a hateful / an abhorrent / an odious] deed.

증원(增員) an increase of personnel[the staff]; an increase in (the number of) personnel. **증원하다** increase the personnel[staff]. ¶직원 50명을 80명으로 ~ increase the staff of fifty to eighty. ➔¶연안 경비대가 50명 증원되었다 The coast guard contingent has been increased by fifty men.

증원(增援) reinforcement. **증원하다** reinforce. ¶수비대를 ~ reinforce a garrison.
● **증원 부대** reinforcements.

증인(證人) a witness; an eyewitness; an attestor; a testifier; a deponent; [보증인] a surety. ¶산~ a living witness // ~이 되다 testify (to a fact) / bear witness (to a fact) / (법정에서) give evidence / (신원의) stand surety (for a person) // ~으로 내세우다 call a person as a witness // ~을 소환하다 summon a witness (to appear in court) // 한 남자가 ~으로서 출두했다 A man presented himself as a witness.
● **증인석** the witness box[stand]. ¶~에 서다 be in the (witness) box / (미) be on[take] the (witness) stand // 그 재판에서 그는 선서를 하고 ~에 섰다 At the trial he took the stand under oath. **증인 신문** (an) examination of a witness. ¶~을 하다 examine a witness.

증인(證印) a seal affixed to a document; a notary seal.

증자(增資) an increase of capital; a capital increase. ¶과대 ~ stock watering. **증자하다** increase capital; (주식회사가) increase its [their] (capital) stock.
● **증자 신주** additional stocks; newly issued stocks.

증정(增訂) supplementing[enlarging] and correcting[revising]; enlarged and revised. **증정하다** supplement and correct; enlarge and revise.

증정(贈呈) presentation; proffering; (저서에) "With the author's compliments"; (선물 등에) To[Presented to] (Mr. A) (with best wishes from ...). ¶꽃의 ~ a floral gift / (조화(弔花)의) a floral tributes // 목록 무료 ~ (게시) Catalog offered free. // ~(저자 또는 기증자의 말) With the compliments of the author[publisher]. **증정하다** present (a person with a thing / a thing to a person); make a present[gift] of (a thing to a person); proffer; give. ¶저서를 ~ send a person a complimentary copy of one's book // 그녀는 유치원에 피아노를 증정했다 She presented [made a present of] a piano to a kindergarten.
● **증정본** a presentation copy; a keepsake; a gift book; an author's copy; a complimentary copy (of a book). **증정식** the ceremony of the presentation (of). **증정품** a present; a gift.

증조모(曾祖母) a (paternal) great-grandmother.

증조부(曾祖父) a (paternal) great-grandfather.

증지(證紙) a stamp; (검사필의) an inspection stamp[sticker]; (금전 영수의) a stamp certifying receipt of payment.

증진(增進) (an) increase; promotion; advance; furtherance. ¶식욕 ~ improvement[an increase] in one's appetite // 문화 교류의 ~ the promotion of cultural exchanges // 그는 국제간의 이해 ~에 노력했다 He worked hard to further[(문어) for the furtherance of] international understanding. // 그는 조깅을 하여 건강의 ~을 도모했다 He tried to improve his health by jogging. // 나는 감기에 대한 저항력 ~을 위해 항상 노력하고 있다 I always try to raise[increase] my resistance to colds. **증진하다** promote; increase; further. ¶사회 복지를 ~ extend social welfare services // 능률을 ~ increase efficiency.

증차(增車) a raise in the number of cars [vehicles].

증축(增築) extension[addition / enlargement]

증파 of a building. ¶강의 제방 높이의 ~ raising of riverbanks // 지금 교사를 ~ 중입니다 An addition is being made to the school. // 저 은행은 지금 ~ 중이다 They are now enlarging the building at that bank. / An extension is now under construction at that bank. **증축하다** extend [enlarge / add to] a building; build an annex [extension] to (the main building); make an enlargement of (a building). ¶새로이 증축한 건물 a new extension building // 집을 ~ enlarge [add onto] a house / build an annex [extension] onto the main house (▶ annex는 복도 등으로 본동과 연결된 별동) // 우리는 방 하나를 증축했다 We built one more room. / We added one more room onto the house.
● **증축 공사** extension work.

증파 (增派) reinforcement; additional dispatch. **증파하다** send as reinforcements; send [dispatch] additional troops. ¶의사와 간호사를 ~ dispatch more doctors and nurses // 소방대를 ~ reinforce the fire brigade // 함대를 ~ send naval reinforcements (to).

증편하다 (增便-) [정기 편의 횟수를 늘리다]. → ¶관광철에는 여행기가 증편된다 There will be an increase in the number of passenger flights during the tourist season. / Flights of passenger planes will be increased during the tourist season.

증폭 (增幅) [전] amplification. **증폭하다** amplify.
● **증폭기** an amplifier.

증표 (證票) a certificate; a voucher.

증회 (贈賄) giving a bribe; bribery; graft. **증회하다** give bribes; grease [oil / tickle] (a person's) palm [hand]. ¶그는 총리에게 1억원을 증회했다 He gave a bribe of a hundred million won to the Prime Minister.
● **증회 사건** a bribery [(미)) graft] case. **증회자** a briber. **증회죄** bribery.

증후 (症候) symptoms. ⇨ ~증세 (症勢)
● **증후군** symptoms; a syndrome. ¶다운 ~ Down's syndrome.

지 [...부터 ...까지의 동안] (the time) since; from the time when. ¶고향을 떠난 ~ 벌써 10년이나 된다 It is already ten years since I left home. / Ten years have passed since I left home. // 햇빛을 본 ~ 가 오래다 It's been a long time since we saw any sunshine. // 여기 오신 ~ 가 얼마나 됩니까 How long have you been here? // 그분과 작별한 ~ 얼마나 되죠 How long is it since you saw him last? // 동생이 미국에 간 ~ 가 벌써 5년이나 된다 My little brother has been in America five years already. // 편지를 받은 ~ 두 달이나 된다 It's been two months since I got a letter.

-지 **1** [확인]. ¶오늘은 몹시 춥~ It is very cold today, isn't it?
2 [말끝]. ¶오늘은 누가 오겠~ Someone may come to see me today. // 부(否)가 3표에 가(可)가 10표였~ There were ten ayes against three noes.
3 [부정]. ¶저 배에는 사람이 타고 있~ 않다 The steamer has no passengers on board. // 사람이 많은데도 능률이 오르~ 않는다 Sufficient efficiency is not obtained in spite of the large numbers of workers. // 덥~도 춥~도 않다 It is neither hot nor cold.
4 [여러 상황의 나열]. ¶비가 오면 길은 질~, 날씨가 좋으면 먼지는 나~, 여기 생활은 조금도 유쾌하지 않다 Rain makes the roads muddy, and fine weather (makes them) dusty. Indeed, life here is not at all comfortable. // 재산은 없어지~, 채권자에게는 시달리~, 그는 죽을 지경이다 What with the loss of his fortune, and (what with) the pressure of his creditors, he is in great distress.
5 [대조]. ¶그는 기사이~ 사무원은 아니다 He is an engineer, (and) not a clerk.
6 [청유]. ¶집으로 가~ Let's go home.

지가 (地價) [토지 가격] the price [value] of land; a land value. ¶법정 ~ the assessed land value // ~의 등귀 [하락] the rise [fall] of land prices.

지가 (紙價) the price of paper.

지각 (地殼) the (earth) crust; the lithosphere.
● **지각 변동** diastrophism; crustal movements [disturbances]. **지각 운동** crustal activity.

지각 (知覺) **1** [알아서 깨달음] perception; [그 능력] perceptivity; sensory [sense] perception; sensation. **지각하다** perceive; feel. ¶지각할 수 있다 [없다] be perceptible [imperceptible].
2 [철] discretion; sense; judg(e)ment; wisdom. ¶~이 들다 attain one's years of discretion / cut one's wisdom teeth // 나이가 그만하면 ~이 날 때도 되었다 You are old enough to have more sense than that.
● **지각 동사** [언] verbs of perception. **지각력** perceptivity.

지각 (遲刻) being late; tardiness; lateness. **지각하다** be late; be behind time; come late. ¶학교에 ~ be late for school / (미) be tardy // 지각하지 않고 회사에 가다 get to work on time // 첫 시간에 지각했다 I came to school late for the first period. // 그는 늘 지각한다 He is always behind time. / He always comes late. // 지각하지 않도록 학교에 가거라 Go to school on time.

지각없다 (知覺-) be thoughtless; be unthinking; be rash. ¶지각없는 짓을 했군 How imprudent he is to have done such a thing! // 그는 아직도 ~ He doesn't have sense enough to know better. **지각없이** ¶그는 ~ 정체불명의 여자와 결혼했다 He was rash enough to marry a woman of doubtful background.

지갑 (紙匣) [동전 지갑] a (coin) purse; a pocketbook; [지폐·카드 등을 넣는 지갑] a wallet; a billfold. ¶가죽 ~ a leather pocketbook / 두둑한 ~ a well-lined purse / a plump purse // ~이 가볍다 have a light purse // ~을 채우다 fill a purse (with money) / replenish one's purse (빈 지갑을).

지검 (地檢) the District Public Prosecutor's Office. ⇨ ~지방 검찰청 (⇨ 지방(地方))

지게 [짐 지는 기구] a jige; a coolie rack (for carrying things); an A-frame (carrier); a carrying rack; a back rack. ¶~를 지다 carry the A-frame on one's back // 물건을 ~에 얹다 put [load] (things) on the A-frame carrier.
● **지게꾼** an A-frame coolie; a burden carrier; a bearer. **지게차** a forklift truck.

지게미 **1** [술 찌꺼기] residue left after rice wine is drained; wine lees. **2** [눈의 눈곱] gum collecting in the eyes as a result of heavy drinking [fever].

지겹다 [너더리 나다] tedious; wearisome;

tiresome; [지긋지긋하다] loathsome; detestable; provoking; disgusting; repulsive; horrible. ¶지겨운 사람 an odious[a loathsome] person//지겨운 듯이 disgustedly//지겨워하다 be vexed (at/by) / feel disgusted (at)//할 일 없이 기다리는 것이 이젠 ~ I am tired of waiting around, doing nothing [hanging around waiting].//아이고 지겨워 Confound it! / Damn it!//지겨운 비다 Damn this rain!

지경(地境) **1** [경계] a boundary; a border. ¶인접 토지와의 ~ the boundary with the neighboring land. **2** [형편] a situation; a condition; circumstances. ¶…할 ~에 있다 be on the point[verge / brink] of / be about to / [직면하다] face//죽을 ~이다 be in a bad fix/[파멸한 ~] 이 stand on the brink of ruin//죽을 ~에 이르다 be dying / hang [hover] between life and death//그 회사는 파산 ~에 있다 The company stands face to face with bankruptcy.

지계(地階) [건] a basement; a cellar.

지고(至高) [더할 수 없이 높음] sublimity; supremacy. **지고하다** highest; most sublime; supreme.

지골(肢骨) [팔다리뼈] bones of the extremities.

지골(指骨) [손가락뼈] a phalanx (pl. ~es, langes); a phalange.

지관(地官) a geomancer. ¶~을 찾아가서 묏자리를 물어봤다 I went and found a geomancer and asked him for a lucky site for burials.

지괴(地塊) [지] a block; a landmass.
● **지괴 운동** the block movement.

지구(地球) the earth; the globe(▶ 둥근 모양임을 강조함). ¶~의 자전 the rotation of the earth//~의 인력 terrestrial gravitation / the earth's gravity//~의 뒤쪽[반대쪽]에 on the other side of the globe / half a world away // ~ 최후의 날 doomsday//~로의 (귀환) 궤도 a transearth trajectory//~의 공전 the revolution of the earth//~는 지축을 중심으로 자전한다 The earth revolves on its axis.
● **지구 과학** (an) earth science. **지구 궤도** the earth orbit. **지구 물리학** geophysics. **지구본** a (terrestrial) globe. **지구 온난화** global warming. **지구촌** a global village.

지구(地區) a district; a zone; a region; an area; (미) a section. ¶상업[오락 / 주택] ~ a business[an amusement / a residence] zone//풍치 ~ a scenic zone.
● **지구당** a (electoral) district party chapter; a (party's) constituency chapter. ¶~ 위원장 the chairman of a district party chapter / (미) a district leader.

지구(地溝) [지] a rift valley; a graben; a trough (between two parallel faults).

지구력(持久力) [체력] stamina; [인내력] staying power; endurance; persistence; tenacity.

지구전(持久戰) **1** [오랫동안 싸우는 전투] a war of attrition; a holding action; a protracted[drawn-out] struggle[war]; (진지전) position warfare. ¶~의 태세를 갖추고 있다 They are prepared to hold out (in the war)//~으로 돌입하다 get into the stage of position warfare. **2** [오랫동안 싸우는 시합] a contest [game] of endurance; an endurance contest [game]. ¶~으로 끌고 가다 bring (it) into a game of endurance.

지국(支局) a branch office. ¶신문사 ~ a branch office of a newspaper.
● **지국장** the head[manager] of a branch; the branch manager. ¶런던 ~ the head of the London branch office.

지그러디다 grumble to one's annoyance.
지그럭지그럭 grumbling; complaining; whining. **지그럭지그럭하다** grumble to one's annoyance. ⇨ 지그럭거리다

지그시 1 [참는 모양] patiently; perseveringly; persistently; doggedly; without letup. ¶고생을 ~ 견디다 endure one's hardship stoically // 모욕을 ~ 참다 patiently put up with the insult//나는 이가 아픈 것을 ~ 참았다 I bore the toothache with stoical resignation. **2** [누르거나 당기는 모양] gently; softly; quietly. ¶여자 손을 ~ 당기다 pull a girl's hand stealthily//소매를 ~ 잡아당기다 tug gently at (a person's) sleeve//눈을 ~ 감다 close one's eyes gently.

지그재그 zigzag. ¶~로 in zigzags//~로 나아가다 (go) zigzag / follow[trace] a zigzag course//~ 코스를 잡다 take a zigzag course.

지극하다(至極-) extreme; utmost; exceeding. ¶그는 어머니에 대한 효성이 ~ He is extremely devoted to his mother. **지극히** extremely; exceedingly; very. ¶~ 잔인한 행위 an extremely cruel deed//~ 아름다운 경치 a scene of exceeding beauty//~ 중요한 문제 a very important matter / a problem of the greatest importance//~ 검손하다 be extremely modest / be modest to a degree[in the extreme]//그는 ~ 만족스런 모양이었다 He looked highly pleased.//그것은 ~ 당연한 일이다 It's quite natural.

지근거리다 1 [집적거리다] annoy; tease; make a nuisance (of); needle. ¶남을 ~ needle a person//지근거리며 돈을 달라다 pester (a person) for money//여자에게 dangle about[after] a woman. **2** (머리가 아프다) have a shooting pain (in one's head). ¶아침부터 관자놀이가 지근거리며 아프다 My temples have been throbbing[pounding] since morning. **3** [씹다] chew softly.

지근덕거리다 annoy; molest; pester; bother; tease. ¶여자한테 ~ annoy a woman.

지근(덕)지근(덕) annoying; molesting; pestering; bothering; teasing. **지근(덕)지근(덕)하다** annoy; molest. ⇨ 지근덕거리다

지글거리다 sizzle; simmer; bubble[foam] up; seethe.

지글지글 sizzling; simmering; bubbling [foaming] up; seething. ¶~ 끓다 sizzle//미움으로 속이 ~ 타다 one's mind seethes with hatred//고기가 ~ 타고 있다 The meat is sizzling. **지글지글하다** sizzle; simmer. ⇨ 지글거리다

지금(只今) **1** [현재] the present; the present day[time]; this time[moment]; now. ¶~의 학생 students (of) today / today's students // ~부터 10년 전[후] ten years ago[from now / (문어) hence]//~의 주지사 the present governor//~은 옛날과 다르다 Things are not what they used to be.//~의 프랑스 어는 라틴 어와 아주 다르다 Current[Present-day] French is quite different from Latin.//~으로서는 서울을 떠날 생각이 없다 For the present I have no intention of leaving Seoul.

지금 //~에 와서는 그런 모자를 쓰는 사람이 아무도 없다 Nobody wears hats like that nowadays[these days]. // ~ 조사 중입니다 It is now under investigation. //~으로서는 이것으로 별 지장이 없겠습니다 This will do for the time being. //~의 시각은 12시 15분 전이다 It is now a quarter to[(미) of] twelve. //그는 ~쯤 뉴욕에 도착했을 것이다 He must have arrived in New York by this time[by now]. // 도대체 너는 ~까지 어디를 돌아다니고[어디에 가] 있었니 Where on earth have you been until this hour? //~은 그의 상태에 변화가 없다 At the moment, there is[Recently there has been] little change in his condition. //~부터 여기를 당신의 집으로 생각해 주십시오 Please consider this your home from now on. //~까지도 그것은 수수께끼이다 It is still a mystery. //더 늦기 전에 ~이라도 그에게 사과해야 할 것이다 You should apologize to him before it is too late. //대관절 ~까지 어디 가 있었니 Where have you been all this while? //~까지는 모든 것이 순조롭다 Everything has worked well so far. //~까지 내가 읽은 것 중에서는 이것이 가장 재미있는 책이다 This is the most interesting book I have ever read. / I have never read such an interesting book (as this). //그것은 ~까지 내가 잊지 못하는 사건이다 I cannot forget that event even now. //~까지 들은 것을 이야기해 주십시오 Tell me what you have heard so far [thus far / until now]. //~까지 이렇게 행복했던 일은 없다 Never have I been so happy in my life.
2 [방금] just (now); only[but] just; but [even] now; a moment ago; [지금 곧] soon; at once; (just) in a moment; this very moment; this minute[instant]; (미) right away[off]; right now; immediately. ¶~ 막 이 책을 다 읽었다 I have just finished reading it. / I finished reading it a moment ago[just now]. //~ 곧 와 주게 Come at once[right away]. //~ 갑니다 I'm coming. //~ 지불해 주시오 Pay me this very instant. / Pay right down. //~ 곧 오너라 Come here this very minute.

지금(地金) ingot gold; free gold; (토대가 되는) ground metal; (화폐의) bullion.

지금거리다 chew gritty; be gritty to the teeth. ¶밥이 지금거린다 The rice is gritty.

지금지금 gritty. ¶~ 씹히다 chew gritty. **지금지금하다** chew gritty. ⇨지금거리다

지급(支給) [공급] purveyance; provision; supply; furnishment; [지불] payment. **지급하다** supply [provide] (a person) with (a thing); [군인 등에게 의복 등을 내줌] issue; furnish; give; pay; grant; allow. ¶의식을[학비를] ~ supply (a person) with food and clothing[schooling] //여비를 ~ grant (a person) traveling allowance / pay (a person's) fare (to Pusan) //월급 100만 원을 ~ pay a salary of one million won. ➔나는 한 달에 30만 원씩의 용돈을 지급받았다 I was given an allowance of 300,000 won a month. //헬리콥터로 도민(島民)에게 식료품이 지급되었다 The islanders were supplied with food by helicopter.
● **지급 거절** refusal of payment. **지급 기한** the due date; the date of payment. ¶~이 된 어음 a mature bill /집세의 ~은 언제입니까 When is the rent due? /이 어음은 ~이 되었다[지났다] This bill is due[overdue]. **지급 보증** certification of payment; (provide) payment guarantee. **지급 불능** insolvency. **지급 어음** a bill payable. **지급 유예** postponement of payment; (법령으로 인정된) a moratorium (pl. ~s, ria). ¶~를 허락하다 grant a moratorium. **지급인** a payer. **지급 정지** suspension of payment. **지급 준비금** a reserve fund for payment; payment reserves.

지급(至急) utmost urgency; exigency. ¶~ 편으로 보내다 send by express //~ 회신을 바랍니다 I am waiting for your prompt[early] answer. /「~ 친전」이라고 씌어 있는 편지 a letter marked "private and urgent" //~을 요한다 The matter is pressing. **지급하다** urgent; pressing; immediate. **지급히** urgently; promptly; immediately; at once; without delay; with dispatch; with all haste[speed]; as soon as possible.
● **지급 전보[전화]** an urgent telegram[call].

지긋지긋하다 1 [넌더리 나다] tedious; wearisome; tiresome. ¶지긋지긋한 일 a tedious [boring / wearisome] task //비도 지긋지긋하게 온다 We have had enough of rain. //이젠 정치 싸움에는 지긋지긋해졌다 I am fed up with political bickering. 2 [지겹다] loathsome; detestable; tedious; repulsive; horrible. ¶지긋지긋한 광경 a horrible sight //지긋한 날씨 abominable weather //생각만 해도 ~ It makes me sick even to think of it.

지긋하다 〔서술적〕 be advanced in years; be well up in years. ¶나이가 지긋한 부인 an elderly woman / a woman advanced in age // 꽤 나이가 지긋한 (a person) well on in life.

-지기¹ [논밭의 넓이] a stretch[plot / patch] of paddy good for planting .... ¶닷 마 ~ a plot of paddy good for planting five mal of seed //두 섬 ~ a stretch of paddy good for planting two seom of seed.

-지기² [지키는 사람] a keeper; a watchman; a watch; a guard. ¶능~ a grave caretaker [keeper] //등대~ a lighthouse keeper //문~ a gatekeeper / a doorkeeper //산~ a (forest) ranger / a forester //별장~ a villa keeper / a lodge keeper.

지기(地氣) [토양 중의 공기] air in the earth; [땅의 눅눅한 기운] vapor from the earth.

지기(志氣) [의지와 기개] will and spirit. ¶애국의 ~ spirit of patriotism.

지기(知己) an acquaintance. ⇨지기지우 ¶~가 많다 have a wide circle of acquaintances / know many people //그녀를 처음 만났을 때부터 오랜 ~처럼 친근감을 느꼈다 Even when I first met her I felt as if she had been a close friend[I had known her] for years.

지기(紙器) a paper container; papier-mâché [paper] ware.

지기지우(知己之友) 〔아는 사람〕 an acquaintance; 〔친한 친구〕 a bosom friend; an intimate (friend); a close[great] friend; one's best friend.

지껄이다 talk; chat; chatter; gabble; wag one's tongue. ¶잘 지껄이는 사람 a great talker / a chatterbox / a prattler / a rattler // 쉴 새 없이 ~ talk and talk / talk without ceasing / reel off / rattle on //뜻을 알 수 없는 말을 ~ talk jargon[nonsense] / gibber // 허튼소리를 ~ talk nonsense / talk rot //함부로 ~ talk too freely / (미국 속어) shoot off one's mouth //너무 지껄여서 목이 쉬다 talk

지나다

oneself hoarse. // 그는 연방 지껄여 댔다 He went on talking with a flow of eloquence. // 그 소녀는 정말 재잘재잘 잘도 지껄였다 The girl just rattled on [jabbered away]. // 그녀는 숨도 돌리지 않고 지껄여 댔다 She kept talking [rattled on] without pausing for breath. // 도대체 무슨 소리를 지껄이는 거야 What the deuce are you talking about? // 그만 좀 지껄여라 Hold your tongue.

지끈 with a snap; snappingly. **지끈하다** snap; give a snap; crack; crash. ¶지끈하고 부러지다 break with a snap / snap off / snap short // 지끈하고 두 토막으로 부러뜨리다 snap (a stick) in two // 돛대 부러지는 소리가 지끈했다 There was the sound of the mast snapping.

지끈지끈 1 [부러지는 소리] with a snap; snappingly. ¶~ 부러지다 snap in [to] pieces. 2 [머리가 아픈 모양]. ¶머리가 ~ 아프다 have a splitting [racking] headache.

지끔거리다 chew gritty. ⇨ 지금거리다

지나가다 go [run] past; go [pass] by; go [pass] along [through]; pass (a place); (세월이) pass. ¶지나가는 사람 a passerby (*pl.* passersby) // 차창을 지나가는 풍경 the scenery passing by the (train) window // 집 앞을 ~ pass [go past / walk past] a house // 숲을 ~ go through a forest // 우연히 ~ happen [chance] to pass (by) / pass by casually / happen along // 지나가게 하다 let (a person) pass / let (a thing) through // 지나가는 길에 as one passes / when passing / on the way // 태풍은 지나갔다 The typhoon has passed. // 우리는 옆 골목으로 지나갔다 We passed along [through] a side street. // 방금 지나간 것이 플라자 호텔이다 The hotel we just passed is the Plaza Hotel. // 우리는 군중 속을 지나갔다 We went through a crowd. // 사건이 일어났을 때 마침 그 장소를 지나가는 길이었다 I happened to be passing by the place when the incident occurred. // 병원 앞을 지나가면 사거리가 나온다 Passing the hospital, you will come to a crossroads. // 천둥은 곧 지나갈 거다 The thunder will soon pass [be over]. // 그는 길에서 만나도 못 본 체하고 지나갔다 When we met in the street, he passed me by with no sign of recognition. // 그는 지나가는 길에 그녀에게 말을 걸었다 [인사를 했다] He spoke to [greeted] her as he passed (by). // 지나가던 부인이 우산을 빌려 주었다 A woman who happened to pass by lent me an umbrella. // 지나가는 사람들이 깜짝 놀라 발걸음을 멈추었다 Passersby stopped in surprise. // 지나가는 택시를 세웠다 I stopped a passing taxi. // 지나가는 길에 그의 집에 들렀다 I dropped in at his house on the way. // 이 길은 지나갈 수 없다 The road is blocked. // 좀 지나갑시다 Let me by [pass / through], please. / Would you let me pass [through], please?

지나다 1 [통과하다] pass (by); go [run] past; pass through. ¶문전을 ~ pass (a person's) door // 숲 속을 ~ pass through a wood // 안양을 지나서 가다 go beyond Anyang // 동경을 지나 미국에 가다 go to America by way of Tokyo / pass [go] through Tokyo on the [one's] way to America // 인도를 지나서 중근동(中近東)에 가다 go to the Near East via India // 교회 앞을 지나서 갔다 I went past the church. // 지나는 길에 들렀습니다 I have just dropped in as I was passing. // 터널을 지나서 차는 해안으로 나왔다 Passing [After passing] through a tunnel, the car came to a beach. // 지금 지난 역의 이름은 무엇입니까 What is the name of the station we have just passed [left behind]? // 대전은 천안을 지나서 얼마나 됩니까 How far is Daejeon beyond Cheonan? 2 [경과하다] pass; elapse; pass by [away]; go [roll] by; (기한이) expire; be out. ¶1, 2년만 지나면 in a year or two // 조금 더 지나서 a little later / later on // (그로부터) 닷새 지나서 five days later [after that] / at the expiration [end] of five days / after the lapse of five days // 지난 일들 (things of) the past / bygones // 지난 5월 9일 May 9 last / last May 9 // 지난 5년간 for the last [past] five years // 시간이 지남에 따라 as time goes by [passes] / with the lapse [passage] of time // 한 달도 지나기 전에 in less than a month / within a month // 얼마 지나지 않아서 before long // 몇 년 지나는 사이에 in the course of the years // 지금부터 10년이 지나면 in ten years from now // 5년 기한이 ~ exceed the limit of five years / be over a period of five years // 오랜 세월이 지났다 A long time has passed. // 여름이 지나고 가을이 왔다 Summer has passed [is over] and autumn is here. // 5년이란 행복한 세월이 순식간에 지났다 Five years of happiness passed in an instant [a twinkling]. // 그 후로 5년이 지났다 Five years have passed since then. / It has been five years since then. // 1개월이 지나도 아무 소식이 없다 A month has passed [elapsed] and we have had no news. // 네 리포트 제출 기한이 지났다 Your paper is overdue. // 그가 여기에 이사를 온 [이사 와 산] 지 3년이 지났다 Three years have passed [It has been three years] since he came here (to live). // 시간이 지남에 따라 통증이 사라졌다 The pain died away as time went by. // 이 건 이제 지난 일이다 It is a thing of the past. // 3일도 지나기 전에 그는 여행에서 돌아왔다 It was not three days before he returned from his journey. // 약속 시간이 지났는데도 그녀는 아직 오지 않았다 It is past the appointed time, but she hasn't come yet. // 이 표에 적힌 기한이 지났으니 이것은 무효다 The time limit indicated on this ticket has passed, so it is no longer valid. / The validity of this ticket has expired. // 지난 일은 다 잊어버리자 Let bygones be bygones. // 지나 버린 일은 돌이킬 수 없다 What is done cannot be undone / What's done is done.

3 [초과하다] exceed; be above [over]; be more than; go beyond; go too far [to excess]. ¶도가 지나면 if carried to excess [to the extreme] // 그 문제는 이제 논의의 단계가 지났다 The problem has gone beyond the stage of argument.

지나지 아니하다 be nothing but ...; be no more than ...; [다만 …뿐] only; merely. ¶그것은 단지 추측에 지나지 않는다 It is no more than a guess. // 그는 이름만의 사장에 지나지 않는다 He is nothing but [no more than] a figurehead [nominal] president. // 이것은 수많은 예(例) 중의 하나에 지나지 않는다 This is only one instance out of many. // 그것은 구실[평계]에 지나지 않는다 It is a mere excuse. / That is an excuse, and nothing more. // 그저 해야 할 일을 한 데 지나지 않습

지나새나

니다 I only have done what I ought to (do). // 단순한 코감기에 지나지 않으니 걱정하지 마시오 It is just[only] a head cold, so please don't worry.

지나새나 night in (and) day out; night and day; day and night; around[round] the clock; always; constantly; all the time. ¶그녀는 ~ 남편한테 바가지를 긁있다 She yapped at her husband morning and night. // 그는 ~ 담배만 피우고 있다 He is smoking all the time.

지나오다 1 [거쳐서 오다] pass (by); pass through; come by[along / through]. // 숲을 ~ come through a forest // 벌써 그 집을 지나온 것 같다 We must have passed that house. // 지금 지나온 정거장 이름은 무엇입니까 What is the name of the station we have just passed? // 기차가 자는 동안에 대전을 지나왔다 Our train passed Daejeon while I was asleep. 2 [겪다] experience; go through. ¶지나온 일 bygones / (a thing of) the past // 지나온 일을 생각하다 think of the past[bygone days].

지나치다 1 [정도를 넘다] exceed (in); (서술적) go too far[to excess]; be too much; break[go beyond] bounds; be excessive; be immoderate[intemperate] (in drinking). ¶지나친 요구 inordinate demands // 지나친 음주 excessive[inordinate] drinking // 지나치게 excessively / immoderately / to excess // 말이 ~ say too much / go too far in talk / criticize too severely // 지나치게 하다 carry (something) to excess / go[run] to excess / overdo / overdo it // 지나치게 먹다 overeat oneself / eat too much // 일을 지나치게 하다 work too hard[much] / overwork oneself // 지나치게 일해서 병나다 fall ill from overwork / overwork oneself ill // 지나치게 술을 마시다 overdrink (oneself) / drink too much[to excess] / 운동을 지나치게 하다 take excessive exercise / take too much[overdo] exercise / exercise to excess // 지나치게 똑똑하다 be too clever to a fault[weakness] // 지나치게 걱정을 하다 be overanxious[too anxious] (about) / worry oneself too much (about) // 지나치게 검약하다 be thrifty to a fault // 그는 지나치게 관대하다 He is too generous. // 너는 지나치게 일한다 You are overworking (yourself). / You are working too hard. // 그는 지나치게 친절하다 He is overly kind. // 그는 자의식이 ~ He is too self-conscious. // 그는 일을 지나치게 하여 병이 났다 He got ill because of overwork. / He overworked and made himself ill. // 너는 네 병에 대해서 지나치게 걱정한다 You worry too much about your illness. // 그는 종종 술을 지나치게 마신다 He often drinks too much [문어] to excess]. / He often drinks more than he should. // 그녀는 그에게 거의 지나치다고 할 수 있을 정도로 관심을 보였다 She showed almost excessive concern for him. // 그의 출입을 막는 것은 ~ You are going too far in refusing him admittance to your home. // 말다툼은 무방하지만 주먹다짐은 ~ You may argue as much as you like, but exchanging blows is overdoing it. // 그는 좀 지나친 경향이 있다 He tends to go too far[go to extremes]. // 매사에 지나친 것은 좋지 않다 Don't overdo anything. / It's not wise to go to extremes in anything. // 자네가 그런 말을 하다니 좀 지나치네 It is rather forward of you to say a thing like that. // 농담이 좀 지나쳤군 You carried your joke a bit too far. // 그건 좀 지나쳤다 That's going too far.

2 [지나가다] go [walk] past; pass by; pass (a place); (내려야 할 곳을) ride past[be carried beyond] (one's destination); (들르고 않고) pass through (a place) without stopping; pass (a person's door) without dropping in. ¶내려야 할 곳을 ~ pass[ride past] one's destination // 두세 집 ~ go past two or three doors beyond // 열차는 플랫폼을 지나쳐서 정거했다 The train ran past (the whole length of) the platform before it stopped. // 깜박 잊고 역을 지나쳐 버렸다 I was so absentminded that I went right past the station. // 나는 버스 정거장 하나를 지나쳐 버렸다 I was carried one (bus) stop beyond my destination. / I went one stop too far.

지난날 the past[old] days; the past; (the) bygone days; (the) days gone by. ¶~의 일 things of the past / ~이 그립다 I long for the days past. / Give me the good old times. // 나는 ~의 내가 아니다 I am not what I used to be.

지난달 last month; ultimo(약어 ult.). ¶~ 10일에 on the 10th (of) last month.

지난밤 last night.

지난번 (-番) the last time[occasion / session]; (부사적) last (time); before this; previously. ¶~의 the last (session) / preceding / previous // ~에 받은 편지 the last letter received // ~에 알려 드린 바와 같이 as I let you know last time / as previously announced // ~에 만났을 때 when I saw him last / the last time I met him // ~ 수업에는 출석하지 않았다 I didn't attend the last class. // 이 우산은 ~에 부산에서 산 것입니다 I bought this umbrella in Busan the other day. // ~에도 말했지만 올해는 외국에 가지 않을 겁니다 As I said before[mentioned previously], I won't go abroad this year. // ~에 만난 것이 언제였더라 When did I see you last? / When was it that I saw you last? // ~에 부산에 간 것은 추석 때였다 The last time I went to Busan was the day of *chuseok* (Harvest Moon Day). // ~에 너에게 말하지 않았던가 Haven't I told you before? // 그 일에 대해서는 ~ 편지에 알려 드렸습니다 I wrote about it in my last[latest] letter.

지난주 (-週) last week. ¶~의 오늘 this day (last) week / today week / a week ago today // ~의 수요일 last Wednesday (week) / a week ago last Wednesday.

지난하다 (至難-) most[extremely] difficult. ¶지난한 일 a task of extreme difficulty // 서서 잔다는 것은 나로서는 지난한 일입니다 It is almost[next to] impossible for me to sleep in a standing position.

지난해 last year.

지날결 (부사적) as one passes; when passing; on the way. ¶~에 들렀습니다 I have just dropped in as I was passing.

지남철 (指南鐵) [자석] a magnet; [자침] a magnetic needle.

지남침 (指南針) a magnetic needle.

지낭 (智囊) [지혜가 많은 사람] a man of great wisdom; the brain; [지혜의 주머니] a fountain of wisdom. ¶~을 쥐어짜다 cudgel[rack] one's brains.

지내다 1 [때를 보내다] pass; spend; pass one's time. ¶하루[하룻밤]를 ~ pass a day [night]//하는 일 없이 ~ waste time / idle [dawdle] one's time away//독서로 ~ spend one's time reading//휴가를 해변에서 ~ spend one's holidays by the seaside//외투 없이는 겨울을 지낼 수 없다 I cannot go through the winter without an overcoat.//그는 여름 방학을 책을 읽으면서 지냈다 He spent his summer vacation reading books.//그날 밤은 역 대합실에서 지냈다 We spent the night in the waiting room of the station. 2 [살아 나가다] live; get on[along]; lead [live] a (dog's) life. ¶편안히 ~ live comfortable[in comfort] / be comfortably[well] off / be in easy circumstances//어렵게 ~ make a poor[bare / scanty] living / be badly off//행복하게 ~ live happily[a happy life]//호화롭게 ~ live in luxury//사이좋게 ~ get along[on] well (with)//과부로 ~ live in widowhood//식모 없이 ~ get along[do / manage] without a housemaid//(요즈음) 어떻게 지내십니까 How are you getting along[on]?//무사히 지내고 있습니다 We are (getting along) quite well, thank you.//그녀는 적은 수입으로 그럭저럭 지내고 있다 She gets[rubs] along on her small income.//한 달에 10만 원으로 지낼 수는 없다 I can't make do with[live on] 100,000 won a month.//물 없이는 하루도 지낼 수 없다 We can't do without water even for a single day.//난 어떻게든 지낼 수 있어요 I can get by somehow. 3 [교제하다] associate (with); keep company (with); mix[mingle] (with). ¶친하게 ~ be on intimate terms (with)//그와는 아주 잘 지낸다 I get along very well[fine] with him.//그녀는 새 동료들과 잘 지내고 있는 것 같다 She seems to be getting along all right with her new colleagues. 4 [어떤 지위를 누리다] serve (as); hold (a post); follow a career. ¶오랫동안 외교관을 지낸 사람 a man of long diplomatic career//외무 장관을 지낸 사람 a former Minister[an ex-Minister] of Foreign Affairs//그는 한때 국회의원을 지냈다 He was once[at one time] a member of the National Assembly.//그는 3대 시의회 의원을 지냈다 He served as the third member of the city[municipal] assembly. 5 [치르다] hold; celebrate; observe. ¶제사를 ~ perform ancestral rites//장례를 ~ hold a funeral service.

지내듣다 listen to (a person) inattentively; take no notice (of); pay no attention (to); give no heed (to); be deaf to (a person's) remonstrances. ¶남의 충고를 ~ turn a deaf ear to (a person's) advice / disregard [give no heed to] (a person's) advice.

지내보다 1 [사귀어 보다] keep company with; associate[have relations] with; get on [along] with. ¶사람은 지내봐야 안다 It takes time to really get to know a person.//지내보니 그는 좋은 친구였다 On further[a closer] acquaintance I found him a jolly fellow. 2 [주의하지 않고 보다] pass by[over]; lose sight of; let (something) escape one's notice; fail to notice; overlook. ¶너무 졸려서 가장 재미있는 장면을 지내보고 말았다 I was so sleepy that I lost sight of the most interesting scene. / I was so sleepy that I missed seeing the most interesting scene.

지네 [동] a centipede; a scolopendrid; a chilopod.

지느러미 a fin; a pinna (*pl.* ~s, -nae). ¶등[가슴/배/꼬리]~ a dorsal[pectoral / ventral / caudal] fin.

지능(知能) intellectual[mental] faculties; mental capacity; intelligence; intellect.(▶ intelligence는 두뇌의 활동으로, 지적인 일에 흥미가 있어 두뇌를 활동시키는 힘이 있음) ¶~적인 intellectual//~이 뒤떨어진 어린이 (두뇌의 발육이 뒤져 있는) a mentally retarded child / (보통의 교육을 받을 수 없는) a mentally deficient child//~이 우수한 사람들 men of high intellectual power//~을 계발하다 develop intellectual faculties[the intellect]//그는 ~이 높다 He is very intelligent [brainy].//그는 ~이 뛰어난 사람이다 He is a man of keen[penetrating] intelligence. / He is a very brilliant man.//그 아이의 ~은 15세 이상이다 His I.Q. age is above 15. ●**지능 검사** an intelligence[a mental] test; an I.Q. test. ¶~를 하다 give an intelligence test (to). **지능범**(범죄) an intellectual[a mental] offense[crime]; (범인) an intellectual[a mental] offender[criminal]. **지능 지수** an intelligence quotient(약어 IQ, I.Q.). ¶~ 135다 have an IQ of 135.

지니다 1 [휴대하다] carry; have. ¶무기를 ~ carry[be armed with] a weapon//시계를 ~ carry[wear] a watch//몸에 권총을 ~ carry a pistol with one//지니고 다니다 carry (a thing) about one//돈을 지니고 있지 않다 I have no money with[about / on] me.//이 책은 지니고 다니기에 편리하다 This book is handy to carry.//도적은 흉기를 지니고 있지는 않았다 The robber had[carried] no weapon with him. 2 [가지다] have; possess; keep; own. ¶풍부한 자원을 ~ have ample resources//장서를 많이 ~ have a large library//병독을 ~ carry a poisonous virus//중대한 의의를 ~ bear great significance//어떤 의미를 ~ bear a meaning//재능을 ~ have[possess] a talent (of)//인간은 이성을 지니고 있다 Man is endowed with reason. 3 [간직하다] have; hold (an opinion); retain (youth); entertain (an idea); harbor (hatred); cherish (hopes); bear (a grudge against). ¶비밀을 ~ cherish a secret//나쁜 감정을 ~ have[bear] ill feelings//…이 되려는 꿈을 ~ be ambitious to become ...//그는 신념을 지니고 나가리라 믿습니다 I believe he will hold to his convictions.

지다¹ 1 (그늘 등이). ¶그늘진 길 a shady path//그늘이 ~ be shaded//그 나무 때문에 집이 너무 그늘이 진다 The tree shades the house too much. 2 (얼룩이). ¶얼룩이 ~ become stained [blotted / smudged]//너의 옷깃에 얼룩이 져 있다 Your collar has a stain on it.//천장은 비가 새어 얼룩이 져 있었다 The ceiling was patched with damp.//살인범의 와이셔츠는 피로 얼룩이 져 있었다 The murderer's shirt was blotched with blood. 3 (장마 등이). ¶홍수가 ~ be flooded[inundated]//장마가 졌다 The rainy season has set in. 4 (원수 등이). ¶원수~ incur an enmity /

지다

make an enemy of (a person) / bear constant enmity[spite] against (a person) // 그 둘은 서로 원수진 사이다 They are enemies to each other.

지다² **1** (해·달이) sink; set; go down. ¶지는 해 the setting sun // 해 질 무렵에 at dusk[nightfall] / toward evening // 해가 지고 나서 after dark[sunset] // 해가 지기 전에 before (it is) dark / before sundown[sunset] // 달이 졌다 The moon set[sank / went down]. // 해가 (지평선 너머로) 졌다 The sun has set[has sunk below the horizon]. // 해는 동쪽에서 떠서 서쪽으로 진다 The sun rises in the east and sets in the west. // 해가 서산에 졌다 The sun has sunk behind the western mountains.

2 (꽃·잎 등이) fall; scatter; be scattered [shed]. ¶지기 시작하다 begin to fall // (꽃이) 지지 않고 남아 있다 remain[be still] in bloom // 곧 꽃이 지겠지 The flowers will soon be gone. // 벚꽃이 다 졌다 The cherry blossoms are gone[have fallen]. // 나뭇잎은 모두 졌다 The leaves have all fallen from the trees.

3 [묻었던 것이 없어지다] come out; be taken off[out]; be removed. ¶이 잉크 얼룩은 빨아도 잘 지지 않는다 This ink stain will not wash out. // 아무리 빨아도 때가 지지 않는다 The dirts will not come out, however hard I may try to wash them off.

지다³ **1** [패배하다] be defeated; suffer a defeat (at the hands of); be beaten; have[get] the worst of (an argument); lose (a game / a battle / a lawsuit / the day); be worsted; go under; bow (to); be outdone; come out[off] second best (in a battle). ¶지기 싫어하는 unyielding / unbending // 시합에 ~ lose [drop] a game // 토론에 ~ come down[be worsted] in an argument / be argued down // 경쟁에 ~ lose in a contest[competition] // 경주에 ~ lose a race / (미) lose out in a race // 일부러 져 주다 throw a match[game / race] (to one's opponent) // 졌다고 말하다 admit defeat / admit[own] oneself beaten // 내가 졌다 I am beaten[beat / under]! / I've lost! / You win! / The game is yours. // 그는 시합[재판]에 졌다 He lost the game[case]. // 그들은 한국 시리즈의 첫 게임에 졌다 They lost the first game of the Korean Series. // 그들은 경주[경쟁]에서 졌다 They lost in the race[competition / contest]. // 그는 아무한테도 진 일이 없다 He has never met his match yet. // 그에게 질까 봐서 한층 더 분발했다 Not to be outdone by him, I worked harder. // 우리 팀은 10대 6으로 부산 팀에게 졌다 Our team lost the game to the Busan team by a score of 10 to 6. // 이것은 지는 싸움이다 We are fighting a losing battle. // 지는 것이 이기는 것이다 To lose is to win.

2 [굴복하다] be overcome (with); yield (to); surrender (to); submit (to); give in (to); bow (to); give way (to); succumb (to). ¶유혹에 ~ yield[succumb] to temptation // 감정에 ~ give way to one's feelings / be overcome with emotion // 더위에 ~ succumb to the heat / be affected[upset] by hot weather // 그는 어이없이 저 버렸다 How easily he gave in! // 그녀는 유혹에 졌다[넘어갔다] She yielded[succumbed] to temptation. // 저런 건 방진 놈한테 질소냐 I'll never give in to such a boor.

3 [뒤지다] be second (to); be inferior (to); fall behind; yield (the palm) (to); play second fiddle to. ¶수적으로 ~ be overwhelmed in number / be outnumbered // 재주로는 누구한테도 지지 않는다 As far as talent is concerned, he is second to none. // 그는 아직도 젊은이에게 지지 않는다 He can still keep up with young people. // 영어에서 황 군은 반의 누구에게도 지지 않는다 In English Hwang is second to none in the class. // 완력으로는 그에게 지지 않는다 I equal him in physical strength.

지다⁴ **1** (등에) bear; carry[have / take] (something) on one's back; shoulder. ¶짐을 지고 with a load on one's back // 무거운 짐을 ~ bear a heavy burden // 쌀 가마니를 등에 ~ carry a bag of rice on one's back // 그 여자는 큰 보따리를 등에 지고 있었다 The woman was carrying a big bundle on her back.

2 (빚을) fall[run] into (debt); incur [contract] (a debt). ¶남의 빚을 대신 ~ shoulder[assume] another's debts // 빚을 지고 있다 be in debt (to / with) / owe // 빚을 지지 않고 살다 keep[be] out of debt / keep one's head above water // 그는 많은 빚을 졌다 He ran up a lot of debts. // 그는 아버지의 빚을 대신 졌다 He shouldered[took responsibility for] his father's debts. // 그녀에게 빚을 얼마나 졌나 How much money do you owe her? // 그에게 진 빚을 갚을 도리가 없었다 I didn't have the means to pay for what I owed to him.

3 (의무 등을) undertake; be charged with (a duty); bear[assume / take / shoulder] (the responsibility for[of]); (죄를) be accused of; bear (the blame). ¶책임을 ~ take[assume] responsibility (for) / be responsible (for) // …할 의무를 ~ be obliged to (do) / be under obligation to (do) // …의 책임은 일체 지지 않다 hold no liability for ... // 나는 그런 일에 책임을 질 수 없습니다 I cannot take the responsibility for something like that. // 그는 학장으로서 모든 책임을 져야 했다 As the president of the university, he had to assume full responsibility. // 그 책임은 그가 져야 한다 The blame lies at his door. // 그는 책임을 지고 물러났다 He took the responsibility on himself and resigned. // 사고의 책임을 지고 사장은 사임했다 Called to account [Held responsible] for the accident, the president resigned.

4 (신세를) (사람이) owe; be placed under an obligation; be indebted to (a person) for (something); be in (another's) debt; (물건이) be due to. ¶신세를 많이 졌습니다 I am greatly indebted to you for your help. // 나는 그에게 신세를 많이 지고 있다 I owe him much. / I am under a heavy debt to him.

지다⁵ [되어 가다] become; grow; get; come to (be / do). ¶추워 ~ get cold // 좋아 ~ [호감을 가지게 되다] begin[get] to like (a thing) / take a fancy to (a man) / [호전되다] take a favorable turn / improve // 싫어 ~ cease to like (a thing) / 나빠 ~ (병세 등이) take a serious turn / change for the worse // 피로해 ~ get[grow] tired // 어두워 ~ become[get] dark // 엷어 ~ become thin / become light [pale] (빛깔 등이) / become dim[faint] / fade away // 밤이 길어진다 The nights are growing longer. // 날씨가 아주 따뜻해지고 있다 The weather [It] is getting quite warm.//그는 그녀가 싫어졌다 He has fallen out of love with her.//이제는 수학이 좋아졌다 Now I've come to like mathematics.

지당하다(至當−) reasonable; right; rational; proper; fair; just; justifiable; warrantable; natural. ¶지당한 조처 a proper measure//지당한 말씀이십니다 You are (quite) right./Your opinions are right enough./It's just as you say.//지당하신 질문입니다 You may well ask that.//그 말도 지당하기는 하다 There is some truth in what you say.//그가 금세기의 최대 화가로 불리고 있는 것은 지당한 일이다 It is most natural[right and proper] that he should be called the greatest artist of the present century. **지당히** properly; reasonably; justly; fairly; naturally.

지대(地代) ground [land] rent; rent; rental(총수입). ¶~가 비싼[싼] high-[low-]rented//~로 생활하다 live on revenue from land//~를 올리다 raise ground rents.

지대(地帶) a zone; an area; a region; a belt. ¶~의 zonal (frontier)//공장[주택] ~ an industrial[a residential] area[zone]//녹화 ~ a green belt//미작 ~ a rice-producing district//비무장 ~ a demilitarized zone//사막[산림] ~ a desert[forest] area//산악 ~ a mountainous area//안전 ~ a safety zone//(가로의) a safety island[isle] / an islands 완충 ~ a buffer[neutral] zone//요새 ~ a fortified[strategic] zone//위험 ~ a danger spot[zone / area]//중립 ~ a neutral zone.

지대(址臺) [건] a foundation; a stereobate.
●**지댓돌** a foundation stone.

지대공(地對空) ground-[surface-]to-air.
●**지대공 미사일** a ground-[surface-]to-air missile.

지대지(地對地) ground-[surface-]to-ground [-surface].
●**지대지 미사일** a ground-to-ground missile; a surface-to-surface missile.

지대하다(至大−) (the) greatest possible (responsibility); vast; enormous; immense; very great. ¶지대한 관심사 a matter of great interest[concern]//그 문제에 대해서 지대한 관심을 갖다 be greatly interested in the matter//청년들에 대한 그의 영향력은 ~ He has an enormous[a great] influence over young people.

지덕(地德) the benign influence of a (housing / grave) site.

지덕(知德) knowledge and virtue. ¶~을 갖춘 사람 a man of (wide) knowledge and (high) virtue//~을 겸비하다 combine knowledge with virtue.

지도(地圖) a map; a chart(해도); a plan(도시 등의). ¶도로 ~ a road map//등고선 ~ a contour map//모형 ~ a model map//relief map//백 ~ a blank map//역사 ~ a historical map//축척 ~ a map on a reduced scale//항공 ~ an air map / an aeronautical map / an aerial chart//백분의 1 ~ a map (drawn) on a scale of one to one hundred//(벽에) 거는 ~ a wall map//자세한[간단한] ~ a detailed [rough] map//정확한 ~ an accurate map//~에서 찾다 search a map for (a place) / look up [out] (a place) on [in] a map//~에 있다[없다] be [be not] on maps [the map]//~를 그리다 draw a map [plan]//~를 보다[찾다] consult [refer to / read] a map//~ 보는 법을 배우다 take lessons in map-reading//~ 보는 법을 잘 알고 있다 be good at reading maps.
●**지도 책** an atlas.

지도(指導) guidance; leading; lead; leadership; direction; coaching(경기 등의). ¶개인 ~ personal guidance//…의 ~하에 under (a person's) guidance / under the leadership of …//양 씨의 ~ 아래[−하에] under the guidance [leadership / direction] of Mr. Yang ~적 역할을 하다 play the part of the leader / play a leading part (in)//~를 바라다 look to (a person) for guidance//선생님의 ~를 받다[바라다] receive [ask for] a teacher's guidance//~적 입장[위치]에 있다 be in a position of leadership//그는 스포츠 클럽에서 ~적 역할을 하고 있다 He plays a leading part[role] in the sports club.//앞으로도 계속 ~를 바라겠습니다 I hope you will continue to guide me in the future. **지도하다** guide; lead; take the lead; give a lead (to a person); pilot; direct; coach. ¶공부를 ~ guide (a student) in his studies//연구를 ~ guide (a person's) research work / guide (a person) in his research//잘못 ~ misdirect / misguide//후진을 ~ give guidance to the younger generation//연극을 ~ coach a play.
●**지도 교사** a guidance teacher. **지도 교수** (대학에서 과목 선택의) an academic adviser. **지도력** leadership; the capacity as a leader. ¶위대한 ~을 지니다 have great leadership. **지도서** a guide (book); a manual. **지도 원리** / **지도 방침** a principle of guidance; a guiding [governing] principle. **지도자** a leader; a guide; a director; a pilot; a coach; a rudder. ¶유능한 ~ 밑에서 under competent direction//~가 되다 become a leader / assume leadership (of / in)//그는 민권 운동의 ~였다 He was a leader of the civil rights movement. **지도층** the leadership. ¶~ 인사 people in the leadership class.

지도리 [건] pivots; hinges.

지독스럽다(至毒−) severe; terrible; exorbitant; cruel. ⇨지독하다

지독하다(至毒−) [심하다] severe; violent; sharp; intense; hard; bitter; serious; heavy; foul(병이); [무섭다] terrible; dreadful; frightful; fearful; awful; gross; ghastly; [엄청나다] exorbitant; outrageous; [잔인하다] cruel; harsh; hard; inhuman. ¶지독한 감기 a bad [nasty] cold//지독한 구두쇠 an awful miser//지독한 게으름쟁이 a hopeless idler//지독한 냄새 a bad [a nasty / a repulsive / a nauseous / an offensive] smell//지독한 추위 severe [intense / bitter] cold//지독한 눈[비] a heavy snow [rain / rainfall]//지독한 폭풍 a severe [heavy / violent] storm//지독한 말을 하다 use strong language//그는 지독한 근시이다 He is dreadfully nearsighted.//지독한 날씨였다 We have had nasty weather. **지독히** severely; violently; heavily; terribly; awfully; bitterly; excessively; harshly; hard. ¶~ 공부하다 study awfully hard//남을 ~ 부려 먹다 drive a person hard / sweat a servant//~ 덥다[춥다] be terribly [awfully / bitterly] hot [cold]//~ 붐비는군 What a crowd [crush]! / Hell of a crowd, isn't it?

지동설(地動說) the heliocentric theory; the Copernican theory [system].

지둔하다(至鈍−) extremely stupid[dull].
지둔하다(遲鈍−) dull; stupid; stolid; torpid; slow-witted; backward. ¶지둔한 아이 a slow-witted child.
지드럭거리다 tease; harass; (속어) needle; vex; beset(붙어 다니며); pester.
지드럭지드럭 teasing; harassing. **지드럭지드럭하다** tease; harass. ⇨지드럭거리다
지등롱(紙燈籠) a paper-covered lantern.
지라 [생] the spleen; the milt.
지란지교(芝蘭之交)〔벗 사이에 맑고도 높은 교제〕good and noble friendship.
지랄 1 [의] epilepsy. ⇨지랄병(⇨지랄) **2** [미친 짓] an act of madness; an insanity; a crazy [frantic / wild] action; [난폭한 짓] outrageous[riotous] behavior. **지랄하다** get hysterical; go crazy; run[go] wild; do violence; behave rudely[outrageously]; commit an outrage.
● **지랄병** [의] epilepsy; an epileptic fit. **지랄쟁이** [간질 환자] an epileptic; [못된 놈] a wild fellow; a rowdy; a madcap.
지략(智略)〔슬기로운 계략〕resources; practical ingenuity; artifice; strategy. ¶~이 풍부한 사람 a resourceful mind / a man (fertile) of resources // ~이 풍부하다 be resourceful / be full of resources.
지렁이 [동] an earthworm; (낚시의 미끼) a fishworm; a fishing worm.
지렁이도 밟으면 꿈틀한다(속담) Even a worm will turn.; Tread on a worm and it will turn.
지레¹ [지렛대] a lever; a handspike. ¶~의 작용 the action of levers / leverage // ~로 들어 올리다 raise (something) with a lever / lever up / (영) prise / prize.
● **지레질** levering. ¶~을 하다 lever up / raise (something) with a lever.
지레² [미리] beforehand; in advance; prematurely; [성급히] overhastily; without due consideration. ¶~ 판단하다 make a hasty conclusion / jump at[rush to] a conclusion.
지레짐작(−斟酌)〔미리 넘겨짚는 짐작〕a guess[conjecture] made in advance; presupposition; a hasty conclusion[deduction]. **지레짐작하다** guess[conjecture] beforehand; presuppose; form[come to] a hasty[rash] conclusion; make a hasty deduction. ¶…라고 ~ run off[away] with the idea that …// 그는 지레짐작하여 그녀가 죽었다고 믿었다 He jumped to the conclusion that she was dead.// 내가 지레짐작한 대로였다 It was just as I had guessed.
지력(地力) fertility (of soil); [물] terrestrial gravitation. ¶~이 떨어졌다 The productivity of the soil has dropped[decreased].
지력(智力)〔사물을 헤아리는 능력〕intellectual[mental / brain] power; mental capacity[faculties]; intellect; intelligence; mentality; brains. ¶~이 발달된 intelligent / intellectual //그의 ~은 12세 된 아이와 같다 He has a mentality of a 12-year-old child. / His I.Q. [mental] age is not above 12.//그는 나보다 체력은 떨어지지만 ~은 훨씬 뛰어나다 She is physically weaker than I am, but mentally far superior.
지력선(指力線) [물] lines of force; [자력선] a line of magnetic force.
지령(指令) an order; a directive; instructions. ¶비밀 ~ a secret order // 파업의 ~을 내리다 order[call on] (the union members) to go on a strike // 무전으로 ~을 받다 receive radio instructions (from). **지령하다** order; issue an order; instruct; give instructions; dictate.
지령(紙齡)〔신문이 발행된 호수〕the issue number of a periodical.
지론(持論)〔늘 가지고 있는 의론〕a cherished opinion[view]; a pet opinion[theory]; a stock argument. ¶~대로 실행하다 act up to one's opinion // ~이라는 것이 나의 ~이다 I am of (the) opinion that …. / My theory is that …. / I hold that …. // 여성도 직업을 가져야 한다는 것이 내 ~입니다 My theory is [I firmly believe] that women should have jobs, too.// 그는 자기 ~을 고수하고 있다 He sticks to his own pet view[opinion].
지뢰(地雷)〔땅속에 묻는 폭약〕a (land) mine; a ground torpedo. ¶~를 묻다[매설하다] lay[charge] a mine // ~를 건드리다 strike a mine // ~를 제거[회수]하다 remove[retrieve] (unexploded) mines // 적의 ~를 폭파하다 spring a mine laid by the enemy.
● **지뢰밭** a mine field. **지뢰 탐지기** a mine detector.
지루하다 bored; tedious; tiresome; wearisome; (서술적) have a dull time; find (something) very dull. ¶지루한 장마 a long and tiresome rain // 지루한 일상생활 an insipid daily life // 지루한 이야기 a tedious discourse // 지루한 강연 a tedious lecture // 지루한 연설 a monotonous address // 지루한 줄 모르게 without any sense of boredom // 지루한 듯이 보이다 look bored / wear a bored look // 지루하게 tediously / repeatedly(되풀이하여) // 지루하게 긴 연설 a long and boring speech // 지루하게 만들다 bore / tire / weary // 지루해 죽겠다 I am bored to death. / Time hangs heavy on my hands.// 이 책은 ~ This book bores me.// 그의 강의는 정말 지루했다 His lecture was quite tedious[(구어) a real bore].//그의 이야기는 항상 장황하고 ~ His speeches are always long and tedious [boring].//그의 연설은 못 견딜 정도로 지루했다 His speech bored me to death.// 연설은 지루하게 계속되었다 The speech dragged [droned] interminably on.// 나는 지루한 나머지 산책에 나섰다 I went for a walk to kill time.// 지루한 나머지 나는 옛 일기장을 꺼내 읽었다 I took out my old diaries and read them to pass the time.
지류(支流) **1**〔강의〕a tributary (river [stream]); a feeder; a branch (of a river); an affluent(본류로 흘러 들어가는); an effluent (stream) (본류로 흘러나오는). ¶이 강은 한강의 ~다 This river is a tributary to Han-gang(Han River). **2** a branch. ⇨분과 ¶역사의 ~ the bypaths of history.
지르다 1 (소리를) cry aloud; yell; scream. ¶공포의 비명을 지르다 with yells of horror // 소리를 ~ give a cry / raise one's voice // 고함을 ~ yell / shout / bawl / give a loud cry // 비명을 ~ utter[give] a shriek / scream / shriek // 살려 달라고 소리를 ~ scream[cry / call] for help // 아파서 소리를 ~ give a cry of pain / shriek[shout] with pain // 그는 아파서 소리를 질렀다 He gave[uttered] a cry of pain. // 그것을 보고 모두 환성을 질렀다 They shouted for joy at the sight. // 그는 갑자기 기성을 질렀다 He suddenly uttered[gave / let

out〕 a strange cry.
2 〔치다〕 beat; strike; hit; punch; kick (at); 〔박아 넣다〕 drive in; hammer; wedge in. ¶주먹으로 한 대 ~ give a blow/strike[hit] (a person) with one's fist∥발로 정강이를 ~ kick (a person) in the shin∥공을 ~ give a kick at a ball.
3 〔불을〕. ¶불을 ~ set fire to (a shed)/set (a house) on fire∥적이 성에다 불을 질렀다 The enemy set fire to the castle[set the castle on fire].
4 〔꽃다〕 pass〔run/put〕 (a thing) through; insert; put into. ¶빗장을 ~ bar[bolt] the gate∥머리에 비녀를 ~ stick an ornamental pin in the hair.
5 〔지름길로 가다〕 take a shorter way[shortcut]; cut across. ¶도로를 질러서 가다 cut across the road.
6 〔자르다〕 cut off; clip; nip; snip (off). ¶순을 ~ nip the bud.
7 〔기운을 꺾다〕 crush; damp; cast a damp over. ¶기를 ~ cast a damp over (a person's) spirits.
8 〔노름에서 돈을 걸다〕 bet; stake; wager. ¶만 원 지르겠다 〔구어〕 I'll go[lay] you 10,000 won.

지르르 1 〔윤기 등이 흐르는 모양〕 greasily. **2** 〔저린 느낌이 일어나는 모양〕 with a dull pain (in the joints).
지르박 a jitterbug. ¶~을 추다 jitterbug.
지르잡다 wash (only) the soiled part of (a frock). ¶얼룩을 ~ wash the stain out/wash out the stain.
지르코늄 〔화〕 zirconium(기호 Zr).
지르콘 〔광〕 zircon.
● **지르콘산** zirconic acid.
지름 a diameter; the distance across. ¶반~ a radius (pl. -dii, ~es) a semidiameter.
지름길 a shorter way; a shortcut. ¶마포로 가는 ~ a shorter road to Mapo∥~로 가다 take a shortcut/take a shorter route∥이것이 ~이오 This is the[a] shorter way.∥들을 가로지르는 ~이 있다 There is a shortcut across the field.∥You can cut across the field.∥영어에 숙달하는 ~은 없다 There is no shortcut to the mastery of[easy method for mastering] English.∥우리는 ~로 왔다 We came by a shortcut.
지리(地利) **1** 〔지세의 이로움〕 a geographical advantage; vantage ground. ¶~를 얻다 occupy an advantageous position∥~가 좋다 be advantageously located. **2** 〔땅에서 얻는 이익〕 profit from the land.
지리(地理) **1** 〔지리학〕 geography. ¶인문〔자연/정치/상업〕 ~ human[physical/political/commercial] geography. **2** 〔지세·지형〕 geographical features; topography. ¶~에 관한〔상의〕 geographical/topographical∥그는 이 주변의 ~에 밝다 He is familiar with this neighborhood./He knows the neighborhood very well.∥나는 이 주변의 ~에 어둡다 I am a stranger here./I don't know my way around.
● **지리책** a geography (book).
지리다¹ 〔오줌 등을〕 wet[soil] one's pants.
지리다² 〔냄새 등이〕 urinous; smelling of urine.
지리멸렬(支離滅裂) incoherence; inconsistency; 〔사분오열〕 disruption; chaos. **지리멸렬하다** become incoherent; lose (its) consistency; 〔분열하다〕 split[divide] into many small fractions; be torn asunder; 〔혼란에 빠지다〕 be thrown into utter confusion. ¶그의 의논은 ~ His argument lacks coherence[is full of inconsistencies].
지리하다(支離─) → 지루하다
지린내 the smell of urine; a urinous stink.

-지마는 but; however; though; although; still; (and) yet; nevertheless; notwithstanding; while; all the same. ¶여러 가지로 충고를 했~ after all my advice/온갖 치료를 베풀었 ~ in spite of all medical care∥결점은 있~ with all one's faults∥그렇기는 하~ for all that/nonetheless/nevertheless/유감스럽~ I am sorry, but .../to my regret∥그는 젊~ 이해심이 있다 Young as he is, he is considerate./Though[Although] (he is) young, he is considerate.∥전력을 다했~ 실패로 끝났다 For all[In spite of] my efforts, it ended in a failure.∥그는 아이이~ 얕보지 못한다 Child though he is[Though he is a child], We cannot make light of him.∥나쁘다는 것을 알~ 그는 그것을 한 것 같다 It seems that he did it knowing it was wrong.∥그는 백만장자~ 금전 기부를 늘 거절한다 He is a millionaire, nonetheless[a millionaire, but even so] he always refuses to donate money.∥부자~ 행복하지는 않다 I am rich but not happy.

-지만 but; however. ⇨ -지마는
지망(志望) **1** 〔바람〕 a wish; a desire; an ambition.(▶ wish는 좀 소극적인 바람, desire는 wish보다 강한 바람, ambition은 자기의 장래 목표·일 등에 관한 강한 바람) ¶~대로 as one wishes. **지망하다** 〔원하다〕 want (to do); 〔계획하다〕 plan (to do); 〔신청하다〕 apply for; 〔희망하다〕 wish (to do). ¶그는 화가를 지망하고 있다 He wishes[plans] to be a painter.∥그는 정치가를 지망하고 있다 He has an ambition to be a statesman.∥나는 A 대학을 지망했다 〔원서를 냈다〕 I applied for A university./〔입학하려고 한다〕 I want to go to A university.
2 〔선택〕 one's choice. ¶제1~ 학교[학과] the school[department] of one's preference∥나의 제1~은 이 대학이었다 My first choice was this college.∥제1~은 어디로 했니 What school did you apply for as your first choice?
● **지망자** an applicant; an aspirant. ¶소설가 ~ an aspiring novelist∥여배우 ~ a woman aspiring to a screen career/a would-be actress∥많은 ~가 있었다 There were many applications (for a post). **지망 학교** the school of one's choice.
지망지망 carelessly; heedlessly; imprudently; hastily; lightly; thoughtlessly; (act) indiscreetly.
지맥(支脈) **1** 〔산의〕 an offset. **2** 〔혈관·잎맥의〕 a veinlet.
지맥(地脈) **1** 〔지층의 연속한 맥락〕 the contiguous line of a (terrestrial) stratum. **2** 〔지하수의 통로〕 a subterranean water channel.
지면(地面) 〔땅의 표면〕 the surface (of land/the earth); the ground(땅바닥). ¶~에서 3미터 위에 three meters above the ground∥~에는 눈이 30센티나 쌓여 있다 The snow lies thirty centimeters deep on the ground.∥비행기가 ~에 부딪혔다 The airplane crashed to the ground.∥비가 와서 ~이 젖어 있다

지면 The ground [The surface of the land] is wet after rain.

지면(知面) acquaintance. ¶~이 있는 well-acquainted / familiar.

지면(紙面) (신문의) paper; a sheet; [여백] space. ¶~ 관계로 on account of space consideration [limited space] // ~이 허락하는 한 to the limit of space // ~을 늘리다 increase the printed columns (of a paper) // …에 많은 ~을 할애[할당]하다 devote a good deal of space to … // 국무총리의 사임 뉴스가 온통 ~을 장식했다 News of the prime minister's resignation was all over the papers. // ~ 관계로 상세히 말할 수는 없다 I cannot go into detail because of limited space.

지면(誌面) the space of a magazine [journal / periodical]. ¶~을 통해 through a magazine // ~에서 in a magazine // ~에 글을 기고하고 있다 be getting space (in the journal) // 상세한 것은 본지 8월 호의 ~을 보십시오 For details, see the August issue (of this magazine).

지명(地名) a place name.
●**지명 사전** a geographical dictionary; a gazetteer.

지명(知名) [이름이 널리 알려져 있음] prominence; eminence; distinction; celebrity. ¶~의 well-known / celebrated // ~도가 높은 well-known.
●**지명인사** a noted [well-known] person; a celebrity; a man of distinction [mark / note]; a notable.

지명(知命) 1 [천명을 앎] knowing the decrees of Heaven. 2 [50세] one's fiftieth year; (at) the age of fifty.

지명(指名) [후보로서 추천하기] nomination; [임명] designation. ¶~순으로 in the order of the persons called [mentioned] // 그는 선생님의 ~을 받아 일어섰다 He stood up when the teacher called on him. **지명하다** nominate; designate; name. ¶당은 그를 대통령으로 지명하기로 했다 The party decided to nominate him for the Presidency. // 그를 그 자리에 지명한 것은 누구인가 Who designated [named] him for the position? ➔¶시장에 지명된 사람은 안 씨입니다 The nominee for mayor is Mr. An.
●**지명 수배** the institution of a search for a wanted man. ¶~ 중인 wanted by the police // 경찰은 그를 전국에 ~를 했다 The police started an open search for the criminal (throughout the country). **지명 수배자** a criminal on the most wanted list; a person wanted by the police; a fugitive from justice. **지명 타자** a designated hitter (약어 DH).

지모(智謀) [슬기로운 꾀] ingenuity; resourcefulness. ¶~가 모자라는 lacking in [without] resource // ~가 풍부한 사람 a resourceful man // ~를 짜내다 plot and scheme.

지목(地目) the classification of land (into categories based on use).
●**지목 변경** reclassification of land; a change in the category of land.

지목하다(指目-) fasten [keep] one's eyes on (a person); mark out [down] (a thing / a person) for (some purpose); point out; indicate; spot; put the finger on; suspect. ¶그것을 훔친 것은 그 사람이라고 나는 처음부터 지목하고 있었다 From the beginning I suspected him of stealing it. ➔¶그는 유력한 간첩 용의자로 지목되었다 He was marked as a probable spy. // 지목되는 용의자를 찾아냈는가 Have you found a likely suspect?

지문(地文) physiography. ⇨지문학(⇨)지문)
●**지문학** physiography; physical geography. **지문학자** a physiographer.

지문(指紋) a fingerprint; a finger mark; a dactylogram; a thumb print(엄지손가락의). ¶범인의 것인 듯한 ~ fingerprints supposed to be the criminals / fingerprints attributable to the criminal // ~을 확인하다 identify (a criminal's) fingerprints // ~을 남기다 leave one's fingerprints (on a thing) // ~을 남기지 않도록 장갑을 끼다 wear gloves to avoid leaving fingerprints // ~을 채취하다 take [get] (a person's) fingerprints / fingerprint (a person).
●**지문 채취** fingerprinting.

지물(紙物) paper goods.
●**지물포** a paper goods store [shop].

지반(地盤) 1 [지면] the ground. ¶단단한[약한] ~ firm [soft] ground // ~이 약하다 The ground is not firm.
2 [기초·토대] the foundation; base; [성공의 발판] a foothold; position. ¶~을 확립하다 establish a footing // ~을 얻다 secure a position / gain [get] a footing [foothold] (in society) // ~을 다지다 solidify the foundation // ~을 잃다 [유지하다] lose [keep] one's foothold // 그는 변호사로서의 ~을 굳혔다 He established himself as a lawyer. // 그는 주류파 안에서 확고한 ~을 가지고 있었다 He was securely entrenched [He has a secure foothold] in the main stream faction. // 그는 장차 발전할 ~을 구축했다 He laid the foundation for future progress.
3 [세력 범위] one's sphere of influence. ¶그는 농촌을 ~으로 하여 입후보했다 He ran for the National Assembly in an agricultural district. // 그들은 민주당의 ~을 잠식했다 They cut into the Democratists' support. // 이곳에서는 최근에 공화당의 ~이 흔들리고 있다 The Republicans have been losing support here recently. / The Republicans' strength here has been eroding of late.
●**지반 침하** subsidence of ground.

지방(地方) a locality; a district; a region; an area; a section; (수도 이외의) the provinces; [시골] the country; […부근] neighborhood; vicinity. ¶~적 provincial / local(▶ provincial은 도시에 대하여 「시골」이라는 의미로 쓰이나, local은 도시를 포함하여 「어떤 특정 지역에 관련된」의 의미로 쓰임) // 영남 ~ the Yeongnam districts // 산악 ~ a mountainous region [area] // 이 ~에서는 in this part of the country // ~ 사람 country people // ~에 [으로] 가다 go into [down to] the country // ~을 여행하다 make a provincial tour / make a tour of the country // 이 ~의 명물은 무엇입니까 What is this place known for?
●**지방 검찰청** the District Public Prosecutor's Office. **지방 공무원** a local public employee; a provincial government official. **지방 공연** a provincial tour. **지방 관청** a local government; (영) a local authority. **지방 법원** a district court. **지방 분권** decentralization of power. **지방 사투리** a local accent; a brogue. **지방색** local color. ¶~이 풍부한 산물 a product characteristic of a region // 이 소설은 ~이 짙다 This novel is full of [strong in]

local color. 지방 선거 a local election. 지방세 (미) local taxes; (영) local rates. 지방 순회 a provincial [country] tour (of a theatrical troupe); (영) a tour of the country. ¶~를 하다 make a country tour / make a tour of the provinces / go round the country. 지방 의회 a local assembly. 지방 자치 local autonomy. 지방 자치 단체 a self-governing body. 지방 행정 local administration.

지방(脂肪) 〔동·식물의〕 fat; 〔부드러운 수지〕 grease; 〔돼지의〕 lard; 〔고래 등 바다짐승의〕 blubber; 〔양·소의 단단한〕 suet. ¶**동물성**〔식물성〕 ~ animal [vegetable] fat // ~이 많은〔적은〕 고기 fatty [lean] meat.
● **지방 조직** adipose tissue. **지방질** fat; sebaceous constitution. ¶~의 fatty / sebaceous // ~이 많다 be fatty.

지방(紙榜) 〔종이로 만든 신주(神主)〕 an ancestral tablet made of paper.

지배(支配) 〔처리〕 management; 〔관리〕 control; superintendence; 〔통치〕 rule; government; domination; sway; overlordship; 〔지휘〕 direction; guidance; 〔심〕 ascendance; 〔언〕 government. ¶환경의 ~를 받다 be at the mercy of one's circumstances [environment]. **지배하다** manage; control; assume control (of); rule (of); rule (over); govern; reign (over); dominate; have under one's rule; lay hold (on); hold sway (over). ¶운명을 ~ control one's destiny / be master of one's destiny // 여론을 ~ sway [lead] public opinion // 이들 지방은 모두 로마 제국이 지배하고 있었다 All these regions were controlled [ruled / governed] by the Roman Empire. // 바다를 지배하는 자가 세계를 지배한다 Those who have command of the seas have control of the world. →¶그는 감정에 지배되기 쉽다 He is apt to be influenced by personal feelings. // 이 나라의 농업은 전에는 전적으로 날씨에 지배되어 있었다 The agriculture of this country used to be totally at the mercy of the weather. // 모든 생물은 자연의 법칙에 지배되고 있다 All living things are subject to the laws of nature.
● **지배 계급** the governing [ruling] classes. **지배 능력** physical intelligence. **지배력** controlling power; control. **지배인** a manager; an executive. ¶부~ an assistant manager / a submanager // 여자 ~ a manageress // 총~ a general manager // 호텔 ~ the manager of a hotel / a hotel manager. **지배자** a ruler; a master; a dominator.

지배적(支配的) dominant; overriding. ¶그는 우리 그룹에서 ~인 입장에 있다 He occupies a dominant position in our group. // 이 나라에서는 보호주의적 생각이 ~이다 In this country protectionism views are predominant.

지벅거리다 〔휘청이며 걷다〕 falter; stagger; totter; teeter; reel; walk with difficulty; walk unsteadily.

지벅지벅 falteringly; totteringly; staggeringly. ¶~ 걷다 stagger [totter] along / walk with an unsteady gait. **지벅지벅하다** falter; stagger. ⇨ 지벅거리다

지번(地番) 〔토지를 구획지어 매긴 번호〕 a lot number. ¶~의 정리 renumbering of lots.

지범거리다 pick up one by one [piece by piece]; grab food here and there.

지변(地變) a terrestrial upheaval; an extraordinary geographical phenomenon; a natural disaster that changes the face of the earth.

지병(持病) a chronic [constitutional] disease; an old complaint; (미) an old spell. ¶~으로 자리에 눕다 be confined to bed by an attack of one's chronic disease // ~이 도졌다 An attack of my chronic disease has set in. // 관절염이 나의 ~이다 Arthritis is a chronic disease with me. / I am subject to arthritis.

지보(至寶) 〔지극히 중요한 보배〕 the greatest treasure. ¶그는 예술계의 ~다 He is the pride of the art world.

지복(至福) supreme bliss; beatitude.

지부(支部) a branch office; (노동조합 등의) a local (branch). ¶이 협회의 부산 ~ the Busan branch [chapter] of this association.
● **지부장** the manager of a branch office; the president of a chapter.

지부럭거리다 peck at (a person); annoy; vex; bother; tease; make sport [fun] of; (속어) rib.

지분(持分) a share; a portion. ¶그 비용 중 내 ~은 얼마입니까 What is my share of the cost?

지분(脂粉) 〔연지와 백분〕 rouge and powder; cosmetics. ¶~을 바르다 put on [apply] makeup / (정성 들여) put on makeup carefully.

지분거리다 1 〔건드려 귀찮게 하다〕 annoy; vex; pester; bother. 2 chew gritty. ⇨ 지금거리다

지불(支拂) 〔돈을 치름〕 payment; payoff; defrayment; defrayal; disbursement; discharge. ¶전액 ~ payment in full // 현금 ~ payment in cash // ~을 연기하다 put off [postpone] payment // ~을 독촉하다 press (a person) for payment // 그는 집세 ~을 않고 있다 He is behind with the rent. // ~은 월말에 하겠다 I'll settle the account at the end of this month. // 나는 이미 50만 원의 ~을 받았다 I have already received payments totaling five hundred thousand won. // 그 은행은 ~을 정지〔거절〕했다 The bank has stopped [refused] payment. **지불하다** pay (out); make payment; pay [meet] one's bills; settle one's account's; (어음을) meet. ¶계산을 ~ pay (off) the bills [accounts] // 어음을 ~ honor a bill // 현찰〔크레디트 카드 / 수표〕로 ~ pay in cash [with a credit card / with a check] // 이달에 지불해야 할 것이 많다 I have many bills to pay this month. // 내 회비는 모두 지불했다 My dues are all paid up.
● **지불액** the amount paid [due].

지붕 a roof. ¶기와 ~ a tiled [slated] roof // 둥근 ~ a dome / a cupola // 슬레이트 ~ a slated roof // 초가 ~ a (straw-)thatched roof // 자동차의 ~ the roof [top] of a car // 세계의 ~ the roof of the world // ~ 이는 사람 a roofer / (영) a tiler // ~을 임시로 이다 cover a hut with a temporary roof // 기와〔슬레이트 / 이엉 / 판자〕로 ~을 이다 cover a roof [roof a house] with tiles [slates / thatch / shingles] / tile [slate / thatch / shingle] a house // 한 ~ 밑에 3세대가 함께 살고 있다 Three generations of the family live together in one house [under one roof]. // 도둑은 ~을 타고 도망쳤다 The thief fled along the rooftops.

지브 (요트에서) a jib (sail).
지사(支社) a branch office.
지사(志士) a man of noble ideals. ¶애국~ a

지사 patriot // 근왕(勤王)의 ~ a loyalist / a royalist / a loyal supporter of the Emperor.

지사(知事) a (prefectural) governor. ¶경기도 ~ the Governor of Gyeonggi-do.
● **지사 직** governorship.

지사제(止瀉劑) an antidiarrhea; a binding medicine.

지상(地上) (on) the ground. ¶~ 50피트 fifty feet above (the) ground // 12층 지하 3층인 빌딩 a building with twelve stories above ground and three beneath ground level // ~에[에서] on the ground / on (the) earth // ~에서 3백 미터 되는 곳에 at 300 meters above the ground // ~에서 모습을 감추다 disappear off the face of the earth.
● **지상 관제** ground control. **지상군**(~軍) ground [land] army; ground troops. **지상권** surface rights. ¶~을 가지다 hold[enjoy] superficies. **지상 낙원** a heaven[paradise] on earth; the Earthly Paradise. **지상 병력** ground force [strength]; land power.

지상(至上) supremacy. ¶~의 영광 the supreme glory / the supreme honor // 예술 ~ 주의 (the doctrine of) art for art's sake.
● **지상 명령** categorical imperative. ⇨ 정언적 명령(⇒정언).

지상(地相) 1 [토지의 감정] geomancy. 2 [지형] topography; geographical features.

지상(地象) a terrestrial phenomenon.

지상(紙上) ¶~에 on paper / in the newspaper // 본 ~에서 in our columns // ~의 토론 discussion in the newspapers // ~의 공론 a mere theory // ~의 계획 a paper plan // 그 사건은 1주일 동안 ~을 메웠다 The papers were full of the incident for a whole week.

지상(誌上) [잡지의 지면 위]. ¶~에서 in a magazine // 본지 3월 호의 ~에서 in the March issue of this magazine // 다음 호 ~에 발표하다 make (in) public in the next number[issue].

지새다 1 [달이 지면서 밤이 새다] the day dawns[breaks / cracks]; it dawns. ¶지새는 달 a wan morning moon / the morning moon. 2 → 지새우다

지새우다 [밤을 고스란히 새우다] pass a night without sleep; sit up all (through the) night; stay up all night[the whole night]. ¶뜬눈으로 ~ do not sleep a wink / be wakeful all night // 술로 ~ drink all night long / drink the night[feast a night] away // 독서로 ~ sit up all night reading[over a book] // 그녀는 몇 날을 눈물로 지새웠다 She spent many days in tears.

지서(支署) a branch office[station]; a substation; a local branch; (경찰의) a police substation[box].

지석(誌石) a memorial stone.

지석묘(支石墓) [고고] a dolmen; a cromlech.

지선(支線) (철도의) a branch line; a feeder (line); a local line(지방 철도); (항공로의) a feeder (line / route); (전주의) a supporting wire.

지선(至善) [견줄 데 없이 착함] the highest [supreme] good.

지성(至誠) [지극한 정성] perfect[absolute] sincerity; [헌신] devotion; wholeheartedness.
지성이면 감천(感天) (속담) Sincerity moves [can move] heaven.

지성(知性) intellect; intelligence; mentality. ¶~에 호소하다 appeal to the intellect // 그는 높은 ~을 갖고 있다 He is highly intellectual. // 그 사람에게 ~이 있는지 의심스럽다 I suspect he is not very intellectually oriented.
● **지성미** beauty enhanced by intellect. **지성인** an intellectual; a highbrow.

지성껏(至誠-) sincerely[devotedly]; with all one's heart.

지성소(至聖所) [성] the sanctuary; the hold of holies.

지성적(知性的) intellectual; intelligent. ¶~인 여자 an intellectual woman / a woman of intellect.

지세(地貰) ground[land] rent.

지세(地稅) a land tax.

지세(地勢) topography. ⇨ 지형(地形) ¶한국의 ~ the physical aspect of Korea // ~상의 topographical.

지소(支所) a branch (office); a substation.

지소사(指小辭) [언] diminutive.

지속(持續) continuance; continuation; maintenance. ¶~적 lasting / continuous / sustaining. **지속하다** [지탱하다] maintain; sustain; support; keep up; [계속하다] continue; last; remain; [견디다] endure; hold [stand] out. ¶전쟁을 ~ keep up[continue] a war. →¶평화로운 상태가 얼마 동안 지속됐다 Peace lasted for a while. // ¶이 좋은 날씨가 지속될 것으로 보인다 It looks as if[(미) looks like] this good weather will hold.
● **지속 기간** duration. **지속력** endurance; staying power. **지속성** durability. **지속음** a continuant sound.

지수(指數) an index; (거듭제곱의) [수] an exponent. ¶물가 ~ a price index // 불쾌 ~ the discomfort index // 지능 ~ an[one's] intelligence quotient(약어 I.Q.).

지순하다(至純-) absolutely pure.

지순하다(至順-) meek; gentle; (서술적) be as meek as a lamb.

지스러기 refuse; waste; trash; odd-come-shorts; odds and ends; cuttings. ¶헝겊 ~ waste pieces of cut cloth / cuttings // ~ 솜 waste[refuse] cotton / (cotton) waste.

지시(指示) indication; denotation; pointing out; instructions; directions; (구어) a pointer; [명령] orders; commands; dictation. ¶당국으로부터의 ~에 따라 according to the notice from the authorities // 나는 ~대로 복용했다 I took the medicine as directed. // 그는 시말서를 제출하라는 ~를 받았다 He was told[ordered / required] to send in a written apology. // 그는 내 ~하에 그 일을 했다 He did the work under my direction. // 나는 자네 ~ 따위는 받지 않겠다 I won't take orders from you. / I won't be dictated to by you. // 도와 드리라는 ~를 받았습니다 I was told to help you. **지시하다** indicate; denote; show; point to; index (out); direct; [지적하다] point out; [명령하다] order; command. ¶그는 아침 일찍 출발하도록 그들에게 지시했다 He gave them instruction[instructed them / directed them] to leave early in the morning. →¶지시된 대로 사용하시오 (게시) Use only as directed.
● **지시서** directions; an order. **지시약** [화] an indicator. **지시판** a signboard; a notice board. ¶행선 ~ a sign indicating the destination (of a bus or train). **지시 형용사** [언

명사 [언] a demonstrative adjective[pronoun].

지식(知識) knowledge; acquaintance; (미) knowhow; information(견문); learning(학문); attainment(소양); understanding(이해). ¶기초 ~ a basic[foundation] knowledge // 예비 ~ a preliminary[previous] knowledge // 전문 ~ an expert[a professional] knowledge [information] // 일반적 ~ general knowledge [information] // 산~ a working knowledge // 실용적인 ~ serviceable[practical] knowledge // 정확한 ~ an accurate knowledge / definite information // 무턱대고 얻어들은[최신] ~ secondhand[up-to-date] knowledge // 신문에서 얻은 ~ newspaper learning // ~의 습득 acquirement[acquisition] of knowledge // ~이 많은 사람 a well-informed person // ~을 얻다 acquire[get / gain] knowledge // ~을 넓히다 broaden one's knowledge / add to one's stock of knowledge // ~을 쌓다 accumulate[store up] knowledge / stock one's mind with knowledge // ~이 모자라다 lack knowledge[information] // 법률 ~이 있다 have legal knowledge / be legally enlightened // 영어 ~이 다소 있다 have some knowledge of English // ~을 향상시키다[닦다] improve one's mind[knowledge] // ~을 뽐내다 parade[air] one's knowledge // 문법 ~이 별로 없다 know little grammar // 그는 영어의 초보 ~조차 없다 He doesn't know even the ABC of English. // 그는 경제학의 ~이 많다 He has a good knowledge of economics. // 이 책은 캐나다에 관한 ~을 많이 전해 준다 This book gives a lot of information on[about] Canada.
- **지식 계급** the intelligentsia; the educated [intellectual] class; [지식층] the intellectuals. **지식 산업** the knowledge industry. **지식욕** [지식을 추구하는 욕망] a desire to learn; an appetite for knowledge; intellectual appetite; love of learning. ¶~이 왕성하다 have a great desire to learn / have a thirst for knowledge // ~을 만족시키다 gratify one's thirst for knowledge. **지식인** an intellectual; [교양 있는 사람] an educated person.

지신(地神) the god of the earth.

지실(知悉) [죄다 앎] complete knowledge [information]. **지실하다** know everything [all] (about); have a full[thorough] knowledge (of); be fully informed (of).

지심(地心) [지구의 중심] the center [(영) centre] of the earth.

지싯거리다 ask (a person) importunately for; importune (a person) for; press[tease] (a person) for; keep begging.

지아비 my husband.

지아이 a GI (*pl.* GI's, GIs)(▶ Government Issue의 약어).

지악스럽다(至惡-) heinous; assiduous. ⇨ 지악하다 ¶지악스럽게 일하다 toil and moil / plod away / work hard.

지악하다(至惡-) 1 [극악하다] heinous; atrocious; most wicked; brutal; villainous. ¶지악한 놈 an accomplished villain / a devil / a fiend // 지악한 수단 knavish tricks / villainous measures. 2 [억척스럽다] assiduous; sedulous; hell-bent.

지압(地壓) a ground pressure; an earth pressure.
- **지압 요법** a finger-pressure therapy; manual therapeutics; acupressure treatment[therapy].

지약(持藥) a medicine for one's habitual use.

지양(止揚) [철] sublation; (독) aufheben. **지양하다** sublate.

지어내다 [꾸며 내다] cook up; coin; frame up; make up (a story); fabricate; invent; forge. ¶지어낸 말 a made-up[cooked-up / fabricated] story // 지어낸 기사 a cooked-up report // 이야기를 ~ make up a story // 그것은 지어낸 이야기가 아니고 엄연한 사실이다 It is no fable, but the grim truth.

지어먹다 gather (one's wits); apply[gather] (one's mind). ¶마음을 ~ gather one's wits / give[apply] one's mind (to) / keep one's mind (on).

지어미 [아내] a wife.

지언(至言) [당연한 말] a wise[good] saying; most reasonable remarks; a wise saying.

지엄하다(至嚴-) extremely strict[stern / rigorous].

지역(地域) an area; a region; a district (▶ area는 어떤 범위의 구역, region은 기후적·지리적·문화적 등의 특징에 의해 다른 것과 구별되는 구역, district은 행정·사법 등의 목적으로 구분된 구역을 가리킴); a zone. ¶공업 ~ a manufacturing area // 방화(防火) ~ a fire zone // ~적(인) local / regional // ~별로 by regional groups // 강수량이 많은 ~ a region with a great deal of precipitation // 개발 촉진 ~ development promoted district // 개발 제한 ~ limited development district // 따라 다르다 vary a different localities // 전염병의 만연을 ~에 한정시키다 localize the spread of an epidemic.
- **지역구** (선거의) local[district] constituencies[electorates]. **지역난방** district heating. **지역 단체** a local[regional / territorial] society. **지역 사회** a community. ¶~ 개발 community development // ~ 학교 a community school. **지역 주민** a local resident; 《집합적》 local citizenry[populace].

지역권(地役權) [법] (an) easement; servitude.
- **지역권자** a servitude holder.

지연(地緣) regional relation; regionalism. ¶~이나 혈연을 따지다 stick to regionalism and kinship // ~, 학연 및 혈연을 배격하다 reject regionalism, school relations, and kinship // 사람들은 혈연이 아닌 ~으로 굳게 뭉쳐 있었다 The people were bound together not by blood but by a shared territorial bond. // 혈연, ~에 따른 정실은 공직자 사회에서 완전히 뿌리 뽑아야 한다 Any favoritism out of blood relations, regionalism should be totally eradicated in the bureaucratic society.

지연(遲延) delay; retardation; procrastination; postponement. **지연하다** [늦추다] delay; [연기되다] be postponed; be put off; [늦어지다] be delayed; be late; be retarded; be behind time; be overdue. ¶예정보다 1시간이나 지연하여 one hour behind the schedule. →오래 지연된 long-deferred // 지연시키다 delay / retard / occasion[cause] delay // 출발이 지연되다 be delayed in one's departure // 열차가 지연되어 아직 도착하지 않았다 The train is overdue. // 그의 출발이 상당히 지연되었다 His departure was postponed[was put off] for a long time. // 날씨가 나빠 비행기의 이륙이 지연되고 있다 The bad weather has delayed the takeoff of the plane.

지열(止熱) the abatement of temperature (in sickness); dropping of temperature. **지열하다** [열이 내리다] one's temperature falls [goes down]; [열을 내리게 하다] lower the temperature; allay [bring down] the fever.

지열(地熱) terrestrial [subterranean] heat; [지] geotherm. ¶~ 에너지의 개발 development of geothermal energy // 여기서 ~ 에너지는 발전으로 활용되고 있다 Geothermal energy is utilized here for power generation.

지엽(枝葉) **1** [가지와 잎] branches and leaves. **2** [중요하지 않은 일] minor details; unessentials; side issues. ¶그런 문제는 가장 ~적인 일이다 It is a matter of the least important. / 당신은 ~적인 문제를 논하고 있다 You are discussing a side issue. / Your argument concerns a subject of minor [secondary] importance.

지옥(地獄) hell (▶ 흔히 Hell); Hades; the inferno. ¶교통~ a (terrific) traffic jam // 생~ a hell on earth / a living hell / an earthy [a mundane] hell / an inferno (pl. ~s) // 시험~ the torture of examination / the examination evil // ~ 같은 hellish / infernal / a hell of a (place) // ~의 고통 the tortures of hell // ~에 보내지다 be turned into hell // ~에 떨어지다 go to hell / descend into hell // ~에서 부처를 만난 심정이었다 It was a godsend (to me in my distress).

지온(地溫) soil [ground] temperature.

지용(智勇) wisdom and courage [valor / (영) valour]. ¶~의 무장(武將) a wise and valiant general // ~을 겸비한 명장 a great general remarkable for both wisdom and valor.

지용성(脂溶性) [화] fat-solubility; liposolubility. ¶~의 soluble in fats / fat-soluble / liposoluble.

지우(知友) [친한 벗] an acquaintance; a close [good] friend.

지우(知遇) favor; warm friendship. ¶~에 보답하다 requite (a person's) favor // ~를 입다 be favored with (a person's) warm friendship / enjoy (a person's) favor.

● **지우지감**(-之感) gratitude for (a person's) warm friendship.

지우개 an eraser. ¶고무~ an eraser [a rubber] / an india rubber / a rubber // 칠판~ a chalk [blackboard] eraser / a wiper // ~로 지우다 rub out (a pencil mark) with an eraser.

지우다¹ [문질러 없애 버리다] rub out; wipe away [out]; erase; efface; strike [cross out]; delete. ¶칠판의 글자를 ~ erase the words on the blackboard // 벽의 낙서를 ~ rub out [clear off] the scribblings on the wall // 맨 끝 줄을 ~ cross out the last line // 카세트테이프의 잡음을 ~ remove the noise from a cassette tape // 페인트[녹]를 ~ remove the paint [rust] (from) // 화장을 씻어 ~ wash off one's makeup // 옷의 진흙을 씻어 ~ wash the mud out of one's clothing // 과거의 추억을 지워 버리다 erase [efface] the memories of the past // 악취를 ~ remove a bad odor // 내 이름이 명단에서 지워졌다 My names was struck [taken] off the list. // 검열관이 3단어를 지웠다 Three words were deleted by the censor. // 세월이 그 쓰라린 기억을 지워 주었다 The passage of time erased the bitter memory. // 그 무시무시한 광경을 나는 기억에서 지워 버릴 수가 없다 I can never blot out [wipe out / efface] the memory of that horrible scene. // 그의 목소리는 노호 속에 지워졌다 His voice was lost in the roar of angry shots [was drowned out by the angry roar]. // 나는 벽의 낙서를 지워 버렸다 I wiped the scribblings off the wall.

지우다² **1** [짐을 지게 하다] burden (with); put (something) on (a person's) back; make (a person) carry [bear]. ¶짐을 ~ lay a burden upon (a person) / burden (a person) // 말에 짐을 ~ load a horse up // 그에게 [그의 등에] 륙색을 지웠다 I had him carry a rucksack (on his back).
2 [부담시키다] charge (a person with a duty); lay (a duty on a person); put (the responsibility for something) on. ¶남에게 의무를 ~ charge a person with a duty // 남에게 죄의 책임을 ~ fix [pin] a crime on a person / fix [lay] the blame on a person // 중대한 임무를 ~ entrust (a person) with an important mission // 비용을 ~ make (a person) bear the expenses // 그는 자기 책임을 나에게 지웠다 He shuffled off his responsibility upon [onto] my shoulders.

지우다³ **1** [떨어지게 하다] cause to fall; scatter (flowers); (아이를) have a miscarriage; have an abortion. ¶그녀는 사랑의 씨를 배었으나 지워 버렸다 She received the dear pledge of his love, but she had it aborted. **2** [눈물을 흘리다] bring tears to (a person's) eyes. **3** [숨 거두다] die; expire; breathe one's last.

지우다⁴ [형성하다] form; shape; make. ¶그림자를 ~ cast [throw] (its) shadow (on / over) / project a shadow // 그늘을 ~ shade / cast shade upon.

지원(支援) support; backing; aid. ¶적극적 ~ active [positive] support // 정신적 ~ moral support // ~하에 with the support (of) / under the auspices [sponsorship] (of) // ~을 청하다 ask (a person's) support (in) // 그는 노동조합의 ~을 받고 있다 He is backed (up) by the union. **지원하다** support; back [bolster] (up). ¶나라의 농업을 정부가 지원하고 있다 The agriculture of the country is protected by the government.

● **지원 부대** backup [support] forces. **지원자** a supporter; a patron.

지원(志願) [지망] (a) desire; (an) aspiration; [신청] (an) application; [자진함] volunteering. ¶~을 받아들이다 grant (a person's) application. **지원하다** desire; wish; aspire to; apply (for); volunteer (for). ¶대학에 입학을 ~ apply for admission to a university // 병역을 ~ volunteer for military service / enlist in the army // 그는 안내역을 지원했다 He offered himself [his services] as a guide.

● **지원병** a volunteer. **지원서** a written application. **지원자** an applicant; a candidate; a volunteer; an aspirant. ¶입학 ~ an applicant for entrance (to a school).

지위(地位) (a) rank; [위계] (a) court rank; [신분] (a) position; (다른 것과의 관계에서 본 상대적인 지위) status. ¶~가 높은 사람 a man of high rank // 높은 ~에 오르다 rise to a high rank // ~가 높다 [낮다] be high [low] in rank // ~를 높이다 [낮추다] raise [lower] a person in rank / promote [demote] a person // 사회적인 ~가 높다 [낮다] be of high [low] social standing // 중요한 ~를 차지하다 occupy an important position.// 여성의 ~를 향상시키다 improve[elevate] women's status in society.// 그는 경사의 ~로 승진했다 He rose to the rank of (police) sergeant.// 수회(收賄) 사건에 연루되어 그는 ~를 잃었다 Involvement in the bribery case has cost him his position.// 그는 나보다 ~ 위다 He is superior to me in rank.// 그는 신하가 오를 수 있는 가장 높은 ~에 올랐다 He rose to the highest rank that an ordinary citizen could attain.// 네 ~를 생각해라 Consider your own position.// 그는 그 회사에서 높은 ~에 있다 He holds a high position in the company.// 그는 ~도 있고 돈도 있다 He has both position and money.// 나는 지금의 ~로 만족한다 I am very well where I am.

지육(智育) intellectual[mental] training; mental education[culture]. ¶~에 치우치다 overemphasize mental education.

지은이 an author; a writer.

지의류(地衣類) [식] lichen.

지인(知人) an acquaintance; a friend(▶ acquaintance is friend보다 교제가 얕은 사람). ¶부친의 ~ an acquaintance of my father's// 나의 ~인 영국인 an Englishman of my acquaintance.
● 지인지감(-之鑑) good judgment of human nature[character].

지인용(智仁勇) wisdom, benevolence and valor.

지일(至日) [천] the solstices; [동지] the winter solstice; [하지] summer solstice.

지자(智者) a wise man; a man of wisdom; a sage; 《집합적》 the wise.
● 지자불혹(-不惑) A wise man knows his own mind[never wavers].

지자(知者) a man of intellect; a learned and experienced man; a well-informed person; 《집합적》 the intellect.

지자기(地磁氣) [물] terrestrial[earth] magnetism; geomagnetism.

지장(支障) [장애] a hindrance; an impediment; [방해] an obstacle; interference; [불편] inconvenience; [곤란] (a) difficulty; trouble. ¶~ 없이 without hindrance[a hitch] / smoothly// ~이 없는 한 if nothing interferes// ~을 초래하다 cause one inconvenience / hinder one / impede / interfere with …// ~이 없다 [불편이 없다] experience no inconvenience / [곤란이 없다] have no difficulty[trouble] (in doing) / [선약이 없다] be disengaged / be free / be at liberty / [없어도 되다] can do without / [해가 없다] be harmless// ~이 있다 be hindered[impeded] / be engaged(불일·선약으로) / [불편스러움을 느끼다] experience inconvenience / [곤란하다] have trouble (in doing) // 모든 것이 아무 ~이 없이 진행되었다 Everything went off smoothly[without a hitch]. / 손님이 많아 일에 ~을 초래했다 I was delayed in my work by so many guests. / I had so many guests that I got behind in my work.// 오른손에 붕대를 감고 있어서 글을 쓰는 데 ~이 있다 I have trouble in writing, as my right arm is bandaged.// 결근한 교사가 많아서 수업에 ~이 있다 The absence of so many teachers interferes with classwork.// 야당의 야유가 심하여 의사 진행에 ~을 주었다 The proceedings were obstructed[hindered] by the violent jeering from the Opposition benches.// 안경이 없으면 잔글씨를 읽는 데 ~이 있다 Without glasses I have trouble (in) reading small letters.// 일찍 자지 않으면 내일의 일에 ~을 받게 됩니다 Going to bed late will have an adverse effect on your work tomorrow.// 상처는 입었지만 걷는 데 ~은 없다 I got hurt, but the injury doesn't prevent me from walking[《구어》 but I can walk all right].// 과음하면 내일의 일에 ~이 생깁니다 If you drink too much, it'll interfere with your work tomorrow, you know.

지장(指章) a thumbmark; a thumbprint. ¶~을 찍다 seal (a document) with the thumb// 서류에 ~을 찍었다 I affixed my thumbprint to the papers. / I put my thumbmark on the papers.

지장(智將) a resourceful general.

지저귀다 (새가) sing; chirp; chirrup; twitter; warble; (사람이) prattle; chatter.

지저귀다 twitter; [쩍쩍 울다] chirp; chatter; chirrup; [목소리를 떨면서 노래하다] warble (꾀꼬리 등). ¶지저귀는 새소리 a bird's twitterings[chirpings]// 종달새가 지저귀고 있다 Larks are warbling[singing].

지저분하다 [불결하다] filthy; foul; smutty; dirty(-looking); unclean(ly); [어수선하다] scattered about; in disorder[confusion]; messy; untidy. ¶지저분하게 in confusion [disorder] // 지저분한 방 a room in a mess / a messed-up room// 지저분한 거리 a dirty street// 지저분한 지역 a squalid district// 지저분한 글씨로 씌어진 편지 a letter written in an awful scrawl// 서툰 글씨로 지저분하게 씌어 있다 It is written in an irregular [awkward] hand.// 사무실 안은 지저분하게 어질러져 있었다 The office was in a mess.// 그 아이는 밥을 지저분하게 먹어서 자주 꾸지람을 듣는다 The boy is often scolded for his messy way of eating.// 그 방은 항상 ~ That room is always a mess[in disorder].

지적(知的) intellectual(▶ intellectual은 지능이 높을 뿐 아니라 고도로 지식에 대한 흥미가 있음을 말함); [정신적] mental. ¶~인 인적 자원 educated manpower// 사물을 ~으로 이해하는 것만으로는 불충분하다 It is not enough to understand a thing in one's mind.
● 지적 교류 intellectual interchange. 지적 능력 mental faculties. 지적 소유권 intellectual property rights. 지적 활동 mental[intellectual] activity.

지적(地積) [땅의 면적] acreage.
● 지적 측량 a cadastral survey.

지적(地籍) a land register.
● 지적도 a cadastral map.

지적(指摘) indication. **지적하다** point out; indicate; lay a[one's] finger (on). ¶위에 지적한 바와 같이 as pointed out above// 문제점을 ~ indicate a controversial point / point out the controversial issue// 오류를 ~ indicate an error / point out a mistake// 다음 문장의 잘못을 지적하시오 Point out the mistakes in the following sentences.// 의사는 병의 원인을 정확하게 지적하였다 The doctor put his finger correctly on the cause of the illness.

지전(紙錢) paper money. ⇨지폐

지절(志節) principle and constancy[faith]; integrity.

지절거리다 chatter; prattle. ⇨재잘거리다

지점(支店) (은행 등의) a branch (office); (가게의) a branch (store). ¶해외 ~ overseas

branches[offices]//이 은행의 종로 ~ the Jongno branch of this bank//~을 개설하다 open a branch//~에 전근되다 be transferred [assigned] to a branch office//이 가게는 주요 도시에 ~을 가지고 있다 This store has branches in the main cities.
- **지점장** the manager of a branch office; a branch manager.

지점(地點) a spot; a point; a place. ¶중추적인 [유리한] ~ a pivotal [vantage] point//예정된 ~ the intended spot//사고가 일어난 ~ the spot where the accident took place//지도[도로] 상의 한 ~ a point on a map[road]//출발 ~ the starting point//그녀는 4킬로미터 ~에서 선두가 되었다 She was in first place at the four-kilometer mark.

지정(指定) appointment; designation; assignment; specification. ¶학교 ~ 서점 the bookshop designated[specified] by the school// 전 좌석 ~ (게시) All Seats Reserved.//학교 ~ **여관** a hotel designated by the school. **지정하다** appoint; designate; assign; name; specify; earmark. ¶지정한 대로 as specified //미리 ~ designate beforehand / specify in advance//면회 장소[시간]를 ~ appoint the place[hour] of meeting//만날 시간과 장소를 지정해 주십시오 Please designate[name] a time and place to meet. ➔¶지정된 시간과 장소에서 at the fixed[appointed] time and place//그는 지정된 시간보다 30분 늦게 왔다 He arrived thirty minutes past the appointed time.
- **지정 가격** the limits. **지정석** a reserved seat; (게시) Reserved.

지정거리다 [조금 지체하다] loiter[tarry] on the way; waste one's time on the way; dawdle along the road; linger.

지정학(地政學) geopolitics. ¶~의 geopolitic(al).
- **지정학자** a geopolitician.

지조(志操) principle; [절조] constancy; fidelity; integrity; honor. ¶~가 고결한 사람 a man of high principle and firm will//~가 굳다 be faithful to one's principle(s)//~를 지키다 keep[remain faithful to] one's principles //~를 버리다 desert one's colors.

지족(支族) a branch family[tribe].

지존(至尊) [임금] his Majesty the King.

지주(支柱) [기둥] a prop; a stay; [지주가 되는 사람] a support; a mainstay. ¶한 집안의 ~ the prop and stay of a family//~를 대다 prop[shore] up / strut//두개의 통나무를 ~로 삼아 담을 떠받쳤다 The wall was propped up by two logs.//그는 한 집안의 ~이다 He is the chief support[mainstay] of the family.

지주(地主) [토지의 소유자] a landowner; (소작인 쪽에서 본 경우) a landlord; a landholder. ¶대 ~ a large landowner//부재 ~ an absentee landlord.

지주(持株) [소유주] one's stock holdings; one's shares.
- **지주 회사** a holding company.

지중(地中) ¶~의 subterranean / underground //~에 in the earth / under the ground.

지중해(地中海) the Mediterranean Sea.
- **지중해성 기후** the Mediterranean climate.

지지 〈소아〉 Dirty! ¶에이 ~, 아가 만지지 마 Oh, it's dirty — Baby mustn't touch.

지지(支持) [지원] support; backing; [애고] patronage. ¶여론의 ~ the backing of public opinion//일반 대중[국민]의 ~ popular support//정신적 ~ (give) moral support// 의회와 여론의 강력한 ~를 받다 receive strong congressional and public support//그녀는 급우[여론]의 ~을 받았다 She had the backing[support] of her classmates[public opinion].//신당은 여성을 사이에 ~를 얻고 있다 The new party has been gaining support among women. **지지하다** support; back (up); give[render] support (to); uphold; stand by; hold up; sustain; prop (up). ¶남의 주장을 ~ support[second] a person's claim //모두 ~ line up behind (a person)//전폭적으로 ~ throw one's full support behind (a person)//나는 될 수 있는 대로 너를 지지하겠다 I will stand by you[back you up] as much as I can. ➔¶지지받다 have (a person) at one's back / get[gain] support (from)//지지받지 못하게 되다 lose the support (of).
- **지지율** an approval rating. ¶현 내각에 대한 ~이 30퍼센트 이하로 떨어졌다 The percentage of those supporting the present cabinet fell under 30 percent. **지지자** a supporter; a backer. ¶그는 재계에 유력한 ~가 있다 He has an influential supporter in the financial world.

지지(地誌) a topography; a geographical description. ¶~의 topographic(al).
- **지지학** (the science of) topography.

지지난달 the month before last.

지지난밤 the night before last.

지지난번(-番) the time before last.

지지난해 the year before last.

지지다 1 [끓이다] stew. ¶생선을 ~ stew fish //내 손가락에 장을 지져라 Broil me! **2** [지짐질하다] pan-fry; (프) sauté; grill. ¶고기를 기름에 ~ pan-fry meat//저냐를 ~ make fish sauté//빈대떡을 ~ make green-pea griddle-cake. **3** (인두 등으로) cauterize; sear; scorch; brand. ¶인두로 상처를 ~ sear a wound with a hot iron.

지지르다 1 [무거운 것으로 내리누르다] press (something) under[with]; put a weight on (something). ¶돌로 ~ press (a thing) under a stone. **2** [기운·의견을 꺾어 누르다] repress; hold[put] down; crush; daunt; depress (a person's spirit). ¶사람의 기를 ~ cow (a person)//그는 내가 제기하는 이의를 모조리 지질렀다 He overbore whatever objections were raised by me. / He overbore all my objections.

지지리 terribly; dreadfully; awfully; frightfully; unbearably. ¶~ 못나다 [못생기다] be awfully ugly(-looking)//[어리석다] be downright stupid//~ 고생하다 go through terrible[unbearable] hardships.

지지부진하다(遲遲不進-) make slow[little] progress; make time; go at a snail's pace. ¶작업이 ~ The work is making slow progress.//협상이 지지부진하고 있다 The negotiations have made little progress. / The negotiations have not gotten very far.//그 운동은 ~ The movement is not going well at all.//건설 공사는 ~ The work of construction is making progress at a snail's pace.

지지하다 [시시하다] trivial; worthless; rubbishy; trashy. ¶지지한 것[일] trash / garbage//지지한 소리를 하다 talk nonsense[rot / rubbish] / say silly things.

지지하다(遲遲-) slow; lagging; tardy. ¶지지

하게 slowly / tardily.

지진(地震) an earthquake (shock); a seismic [terrestrial] tremor. ¶~의 중심 a seismic / seismal // ~의 중심 a seismic center / 대 ~ a big [great] earthquake / a macroseism // 해저 ~ a submarine earthquake // 화산 ~ a volcanic earthquake // 단층[심발(深發)] ~ a dislocation [deep-focus] earthquake // 군발~ a series of earthquakes // ~을 느끼다 feel an earthquake [an earth tremor] // ~이 나다 an earthquake occurs / there is an earthquake / have an earthquake // 오늘 아침 상당한 [가벼운] ~이 있었다 We had [There was] a pretty strong [a slight] earthquake this morning. // 그 ~은 진도 6이었다 The quake was 6 [registered a magnitude of 6] on the Richter scale.
●**지진계** a seismometer; a seismograph. **지진대** an earthquake zone [belt]. **지진학** seismology. **지진학자** a seismologist.

지진아(遲進兒) a (mentally) retarded [backward] child. ¶이 아이는 ~이다 This child is a late developer. / He is a backward [retarded] child. (▶ retarded 쪽이 backward 보다 뜻이 강함)

지질(地質) geology; geological features; [토질] the nature of the soil. ¶~의 geological.
●**지질 공학** geotechnology. **지질 분석** a soil analysis. **지질학** geology. ¶구조 ~ structural [tectonic] geology.

지질(紙質) the quality of paper. ¶이 노트의 ~은 대단히 좋다[나쁘다] The paper in this notebook is of excellent [poor] quality.

지질리다 [무거운 것에 내리눌리다] be pressed under [with]; [기가 꺾이다] be crushed [daunted]; be held down.

지질하다 1 [변변치 못하다] worthless; useless; good-for-nothing; poor; trashy. ¶지질한 놈 a good-for-nothing / 지질한 소리를 하다 talk nonsense / say silly things. 2 [따분하다] tedious; dull; boring; wearisome; tiresome. ¶지질한 것[사람] a bore // 지질한 소설 a boring novel.

지짐이 a stew. ¶고기 ~ meat stew.

지짐질 making griddlecakes; panfrying. **지짐질하다** panfry.

지참금(持參金) a dowry; a dot. ¶~이 많은 여자 a woman with a large dowry / 딸에게 ~을 주다 dower [endow] a daughter at marriage // 그는 딸을 시집보낼 때 ~을 주었다 He gave his daughter a dowry when she married.

지참인(持參人) a bearer.

지참하다(持參-) [가져오다] bring (a thing) (with one); [가져가다] take (a thing) with one; carry; bear. ¶주문하신 책을 지참했습니다 I have brought you the book you ordered. // 필기도구 반드시 지참할 것 Don't forget to take [bring] your pen with you.

지척(咫尺) a very short distance; an inch. ¶~을 분간할 수 없는 어두운 밤 a pitch-dark night.

지척거리다 shuffle along; scuff; scuffle; drag one's way.

지척지척 dragging; plodding; trudging. ¶~걷다 plod along / walk with dragging feet. **지척지척하다** shuffle along. ⇨~지척거리다

지천(至賤) 1 [매우 천함]. **지천하다** humblest; very humble. ¶그는 지천한 집안에서 태어난 사람이었다 He was a man of very humble birth. 2 [풍부] abundance. ¶~으로 in great abundance / ever so much [many] // 돈이 ~으로 많다 (속어) stink of money. **지천하다** abundant.

지청(支廳) a branch (government) office.

지청구하다 carp; find fault (with); complain needlessly.

지체 [문벌] lineage; pedigree; the (social) standing of a family; (family) stock; [위계] a rank. ¶~가 높은[낮은] 사람 a person of high [low] birth / a person of high [low] standing.

지체(肢體) the limbs; the hands and feet; [몸 전체] the body (as a whole). ¶그의 ~는 균형이 잡혀 있다 He is well-proportioned [has a well-proportioned body].
●**지체부자유아** a physically handicapped child; a crippled child.

지체(遲滯) (a) delay; [지불의 의무를 지연] arrears; retardation; procrastination. ¶~ 없이 without delay / promptly / immediately // ~ 없이 보고하다 lose no time in reporting (something) // 세금을 ~ 없이 납부하는 사람 one's taxes on time // 본 건은 잠시의 ~도 허용되지 않는다 The matter will not bear any delay [admits of no delay]. **지체하다** delay; tarry; defer; hold off; procrastinate; be in arrears. ¶어째서 그가 이렇게 지체하는 것일까 I wonder what detains [is keeping] him so long. ➔¶큰 눈으로 지체된 우편물이 쌓여 간다 More and more mail is piling up undelivered because of the big snowfall.

지축(地軸) the earth's axis. ¶~을 뒤흔드는 듯한 요란한 소리 a deep, earthshaking rumble.

지출(支出) [지불함] (an) expenditure; disbursements; [경비] expenses. ¶부당 ~ an unjust disbursement // 예산 외 ~ disbursements not provided for in the budget // 정부 [재정] ~ government expenditure // 총~ total expenditure // 경상[임시] ~ ordinary [extraordinary] expenditure // 수입과 ~ revenue and expenditure / income and outgo // 막대한 ~ a heavy [an enormous] expenditure // 국고로부터의 부정 ~ an illegal disbursement from the National Treasury // ~이 많다[적다] have many [few] expenses // ~을 억제하다 hold down expenditure [expenses] // 물가가 올라 ~이 자꾸 늘어 간다 Owing to rising prices, our expenses keep growing. // 이달에는 이것저것 생각지 않았던 ~이 많았다 This month I have had various unexpected expenses to meet. **지출하다** pay [out]; spend; (문어) expend; disburse. ¶준비금에서 ~ pay out of the reserve fund // 군비에 다액을 ~ spend large sums of money on arms // …달러를 ~ make an appropriation of $ ....
●**지출액** the amount disbursed; the expenditure; the disbursement; the outlay.

지층(地層) a stratum (pl. -ta); a layer; a geologic formation; measures. ¶~(상)의 stratigraphic // ~의 경사 dip of a stratum.

지치 [식] a gromwell.

지치다[1] [피로하다] be [get / become] tired; be fatigued; grow weary. ¶지칠 줄 모르는 [만족할 줄 모르는] insatiable / [끈질긴] persistent / [끊임없는] unceasing // 지칠 줄 모르는 야망 insatiable ambition // 인생에 지친 표정

지치다

a world-weary air [expression] // 지칠 줄 모르는 인내력 tireless perseverance / unflagging effort // 나는 지쳐 버렸다 I'm worn out [tired out / (영) fagged (out)]. // 무거운 짐을 운반하느라 나는 지쳐 버렸다 I wore myself out carrying heavy luggage. / I was exhausted [dead tired] from carrying heavy luggage. // 그의 수다에 나는 완전히 지쳤다 He talked my head off. // 나는 살기에 지쳤다 I'm weary [tired] of life. // 성공에 대한 지칠 줄 모르는 노력이 오늘의 그를 있게 했다[만들었다] His unceasing efforts to achieve success have made him what he is today. // 나는 철야를 하여 매우 지쳤다 I stayed up all night and am worn out [terribly tired]. / I am very tired because I was up all night.
2 [마소 등이 기운이 빠져 똥을 싸다] have a watery stool (from fatigue).

지치다² [얼음을] slide [skate] on the ice; do skating. ¶얼음지치기 skating // 얼음을 지치러 가다 go skating // 스케이트를 신고 얼음을 ~ glide over the ice on skates / skate // 얼음이 얇아서 지치지 못한다 The ice is not thick enough to skate upon.

지치다³ [문을 잠그지 않고 닫아만 두다] close (a door) without locking; leave (a door) closed but unlocked; close (a door) softly [lightly].

지친 (至親) **1** [아주 친함] very close friendship [relationship]; intimacy. **지친하다** [서술적] be on intimate [the best] terms (with). **2** [부자지간 (등)] very near relationship (by blood).

지침 (指針) **1** [계기의 침] an indicator; a pointer; an index (*pl.* ~es, -dices); [자석의 침] a compass needle. **2** [길잡이] a guide; a guiding principle. ¶그는 내게 생애의 ~을 주었다 He has given me the principle that guides my life.

지칭하다 (指稱-) call; name; designate. ➔¶하와이는 태평양의 낙원으로 지칭된다 Hawaii is often referred to as the Paradise of the Pacific.

지켜보다 watch (intently); stare [gaze] (at); watch [keep watch] (over); (wait and) see (관망). ¶아이들을 지켜보는 어머니 a mother watching over her children // 나는 새가 새끼에게 먹이를 주는 것을 지켜보았다 I was gazing at a bird feeding its little ones. // 내가 하는 것을 지켜보시오 Watch what I (am going to) do. // 그들은 그 사업의 진전을 지켜보기로 했다 They decided to (wait and) see how the business would go. // 나는 그가 서명하는 것을 지켜보고 확인하였다 I watched to make sure that he signed his name. // 그의 죽음을 지켜보았다 I saw him die with my own eyes. / I was with him when he died. / [죽음을 확인하다] I made sure that he was dead.

지키다 1 [살피다] watch; keep a watch; [호위] stand guard; guard; [보호] protect; [방어] defend. ¶적으로부터 나라를 ~ defend the country against the enemy // 문을 ~ guard the gate // 위해로부터 몸을 ~ protect oneself from harm // 집을 ~ look after [take care of] a house // 양 떼를 ~ watch a flock of sheep // 제 몸을 ~ protect oneself / (구어) save one's own skin // 그들은 성채를 단단히 지켰다 They defended the fort tenaciously. // 그는 흉한으로부터 아내를 지키려고 앞으로 나섰다 He stepped forward to protect his wife from [against] the ruffian. // 내가 없는 동안 가게 [가방]를 지켜 주십시오 Please tend the store (or Watch the counter)[Keep an eye on this bag] while I'm away.
2 [준수하다] keep; fulfill; observe; obey; abide by; follow; stick [adhere] (to) (주의 등을). ¶약속을 ~ keep one's promise [word] // 지조를 ~ hold [stick] to one's principles // 규칙을 ~ obey [follow / observe] the regulations // 침묵을 ~ maintain one's silence // 독신을 ~ remain single all one's life // 법을 ~ abide by the law // 비밀을 ~ keep a secret // 중립을 ~ observe neutrality // 본분을 ~ fulfill one's duty / stick [keep] to one's lot in life // 절개를 ~ remain faithful to one's allegiance [loyalty] / keep one's integrity / follow [observe] one's principles / stick to one's colors [guns] / maintain chastity // 교통 신호를 ~ [지키지 않다] observe [neglect] traffic signal // 시간을 엄격히 ~ be punctual to the minute // 우리 팀은 지금까지 1패를 지켜 왔다 We've managed to prevent our team from being beaten more than once so far. // 누구든지 이 규칙은 지켜야 한다 This regulation is binding on everybody. // 우리는 법률을 지키지 않으면 안 된다 We must observe the laws.

지탄 (指彈) [비난] (an adverse) criticism; blame; (a) reproach; reprobation; (a) censure. ¶~을 받다 be made a focus of [be subjected to] criticism / incur a censure / lay oneself open to censure / be blamed [censured] (for) // 모든 사람들로부터 ~을 받다 be scorned [shunned / left] by all / be in disgrace with all others / be ostracized // 그는 마을 사람들의 ~을 받고 있다 He is the pest to the villagers. **지탄하다** [배척하다] snap one's fingers (at); shun; disdain; scorn; [비난하다] criticize unfavorably [adversely]; censure; blame; reproach; denounce.

지탱하다 (支撐-) [버티다] prop; bolster [prop] up; [유지하다] support; maintain; sustain; hold; keep; bear up. ¶지붕을 ~ hold up the roof / receive the weight of the roof // 집안을 ~ maintain one's family // 봉급으로는 생활을 지탱해 나갈 수 없다 I cannot make a living [get along] on my salary. // 경영 방침을 바꾸지 않으면 회사가 지탱해 나갈 수 없다 The firm cannot keep going unless management policy is changed. // 그는 대가족을 지탱해 나가야만 한다 He has to support a large family. // 그는 약으로 목숨을 지탱하고 있는 상태다 He is being kept alive by medication. // 그 상점은 그의 힘으로 지탱하고 있다 He is the prop [mainstay] of the store.

지파 (支派) [지손] a branch family; [부족] a branch tribe; [분파] a branch; a subbranch; an offshoot; (당내의) a faction; a splinter party.

지팡이 (미) a cane (▶ 일반적으로 가는 것); (영) a (walking) stick; (양치기가 사용하는 자루가 굽은) a crook; (마법의) a magic wand. ¶대 ~ a bamboo cane // 등산용 ~ an alpenstock // ~ 속에 칼을 넣은 a sword cane // ~를 짚고 걷다 walk with a stick [a cane] // ~에 의지하다 lean [hang] on a stick // ~를 짚다 use a stick // ~를 가지고 다니다 carry a cane [stick].

지퍼 (미) a zipper; (영) a zip (fastener). ¶~ 달린 자루 a bag with a zipper / (영) a zip

bag // 드레스 등의 ~를 올리다 zip up a dress at[in] the back // 가방의 ~를 열다 unzip a bag / undo the zipper of a bag / zip a bag open // (동의) ~를 좀 채워 주시겠어요 Zip me up, will you?

지편 (紙片) a piece[scrap / slip / bit] of paper; a strip of paper(길쭉한).

지평 (地平) 1 [대지의 평면] the surface of the earth. 2 the horizon. ⇨ 지평선(⇨지평)
- **지평선** the horizon; the skyline. ¶~ 상의 horizontal / ~ 위에 above (or on)[below] the horizon(▶ on은 「지평선에 닿은 위에」의 뜻) / ~ 위로 떠오르다 rise above [the] horizon // ~ 밑으로 가라앉다 sink below the horizon // 해가 ~ 쪽으로 기울었다 The sun sank toward the horizon.

지폐 (紙幣) paper money; (미) a bill; (영) a (bank-)note. ¶불환 ~ an inconvertible note // 소액 ~ a bank note of low denomination / small paper money / (미) a shinplaster // 위조 ~ a counterfeit [forged] note // 태환 ~ a convertible note // 1만 원권 ~ a 10,000 won bill[note] // ~ 뭉치 a sheaf[bundle] of (bank) notes / (미국 구어) a wad of bills // 천원권 ~로 2만 원 twenty thousand won in thousand-won bills[notes] // 고액 ~를 잔돈으로 바꾸다 break a large-denomination bill [note] // ~를 남발하다 inflate paper currency.
- **지폐 발행 은행** a note-issuing bank; a bank of issue. **지폐 본위** paper standard.

지폭 (紙幅) the width of paper.
지표 (地表) the surface of the earth.
- **지표수** surface water.

지표 (指標) an index (pl. -es, indices); [수] a character(istic). ¶경기 ~ a business indicator[barometer] // 세계 평화의 ~ a guidepost to world peace // 일국의 경제 상태의 ~ an index of a nation's economic conditions // 그는 장래 외교 정책의 ~를 분명히 밝혔다 He made clear his guidelines on future foreign policy.

지푸라기 bits of straw; a straw.
지프 a jeep.
지피다¹ (불을) make (a fire); (장작 등을) put (fuel on fire); feed (a fire with coal); supply with fuel; stoke; replenish. ¶모닥불에 장작을 ~ feed a bonfire with wood // 화덕에 불을 ~ light a fire in an oven / a stove / a range // 석탄을 좀 더 지펴 주십시오 Put more coal on the fire.

지피다² [신통하다] get inspiration from a divine power; be inspired.

지필 (紙筆) paper and pens[writing brushes].
지필묵 (紙筆墨) paper, pens[writing brushes] and ink[India(n) ink].

지하 (地下) 1 [땅속]. ~의 underground / subterranean // 5미터 five meters below [under] (the) ground // ~의 세력 underground influences // ~에서 일하는 사람 an underground worker // ~ 3층 지상 10층 건물 a building with three stories below and ten above the ground // ~ 30미터를 파다 dig thirty meters (underground) / go 숨다 [잠입하다] go underground / go into hiding. 2 [저승] Hades; the other world; the underworld; [무덤] a grave. ¶~에 잠들다 sleep in the grave.
- **지하 경제** the underground economy. **지하 공작** underground activities. **지하도** an un-

derground passage; (영) a subway; [군] a gallery. **지하상가** an underground shopping center [(영) centre]. **지하수** subterranean [underground] water. **지하실** a basement; (식료품 등을 저장하는) a cellar. **지하 ½반** a semibasement. **지하 운동** underground activities. ¶반나치 ~ the anti-Nazi underground movement. **지하자원** underground resources. **지하 창고** a cellar. **지하철** (미) a subway; (영) an underground (railway); (런던의) the Tube; (파리의) the Metro. ¶~을 타다 take a subway train // ~로 가다 go by subway // ~이 가장 빨리 도착합니다 The fastest way to get there is by subway. **지하층** the basement.

지학 (地學) (an) earth science. ⇨ 지구 과학(⇨지구(地球))

지함 (紙函) [종이 함] a carton; a cardboard box.

지핵부 (地核部) the center [(영) centre] of the earth.

지행 (知行) knowledge and conduct[deed].

지향 (志向) (an) intention; (an) inclination; an aim. ¶권력 ~ an innate respect for authority // 브랜드 ~ a weakness for the products of well-known makers // 미래 ~형의 future-oriented // 가족 ~의 젊은이가 늘고 있다 We have more and more family-oriented young men these days. **지향하다** intend[aspire] (to do); aim.

지향성 (指向性) directivity.
지향하다 (指向-) point (to). ¶목하의 정세는 더욱 험한 국면을 지향하고 있다 The present situation points to more serious developments ahead.

지혈 (止血) stopping of bleeding; stanching; hemostasis; (영) haemostasis. **지혈하다** check the bleeding; control hemorrhage.
- **지혈대** a tourniquet. **지혈제** a styptic; a hemostatic.

지협 (地峽) an isthmus (pl. -es, -mi); a neck of land. ¶~의 isthmian // 파나마[수에즈] ~ the Isthmus of Panama[Suez].

지형 (地形) (한 지역의) topography; geographical features; (땅의 형상) landform. ¶~상의 topographical // ~의 이용 utilization of topographical [geographical] features // 그는 이 근방의 ~에 밝다 He is familiar with the lie [(미) lay] of the land around here.
- **지형도** a topographical map. **지형학** geomorphology; topography.

지형 (紙型) [종이판] a papier-mâché; a paper mold [(영) mould]. ¶~을 뜨다 make[take] a papier-mâché mold / make a paper mold.

지혜 (智慧) wisdom; sense; wits; brains; sagacity; intelligence; resourcefulness. ¶생활의 ~ wisdom for living[of life] // ~가 있는 wise / sensible / intelligent / sagacious / ingenious / witty // ~가 없는 brainless / unwise / dull / foolish / stupid // ~가 모자라는 shallow-brained / half-witted / slow-witted // ~를 짜내다 draw on one's resources / strain one's wits / rack[beat / tax / puzzle / cudgel] one's brains // ~를 발휘하다 show wisdom.

지혜롭다 (智慧-) be wise[sagacious].
지호 (指呼) [손짓을 하여 부름]. ¶~간에 있다 be within hail[call / hailing distance]. **지호하다** beckon (to a person).

지화자 a shout to mark time in accompany-

지환(指環) a set of two rings. ⇨가락지
지효(至孝) [지극한 효성] the utmost filial piety.
지휘(指揮) command; [지시] direction(s); instructions; [감독] superintendence; supervision. ¶송 씨의 ~ 아래 under the command[direction] of Mr. Song // 민 씨의 ~로 conducted by Mr. Min / under the baton of Mr. Min / ···의 ~하에 두다 place (a troop) under the command of ... / ~ 감독하다 direct and supervise // ~를 받다 be under (a person's) command / be presided over (by a person) / be superintended (by a person) // ~를 청하다 ask orders // 만사를 그의 ~에 따라야 한다 You must follow[ask for] his directions in everything. **지휘하다** command; lead; head; direct; instruct; preside over (a meeting); superintend; take [assume / hold] command (of an army); (악단을) direct; conduct; lead; baton. ¶일군을 지휘하여 at the head[in command] of an army // 오케스트라를 ~ conduct an orchestra // 그는 그 군단을 지휘했다 He commanded[took command of] the corps.
● **지휘관** a commander; a commanding officer[generals]. ¶최고 ~ the supreme commander / a captain general (pl. captains general). **지휘권** authority (to command); the right to command. ¶~을 발동하다 exercise (the Attorney General's) directional authority. **지휘대** a podium (pl. -dia); a raised platform. **지휘봉** a baton. **지휘자** a commander; a director; a leader; (음악의) a conductor. ¶현악단의 ~자 an orchestral conductor.
직(職) **1** a government post. ⇨관직(官職) **2** an occupation. ⇨직업 **3** one's duty. ⇨직책
직각(直角) [수] a right angle. ¶~의 right-angle(d) / rectangular / orthogonal // ···과 ~으로 at a right angle to ... / perpendicular [normal] to ... // 두 개의 선은 ~을 이루고 있다[으로 엇갈려 있다] The two lines are[meet / cross] at right angles to each other.
● **직각 삼각형** a right triangle; a right-angle(d) triangle.
직각적(直覺的) intuitive; intuitional. ¶~으로 intuitively / intuitionally // ~으로 알다 know intuitively[by intuition].
직간(直諫) [바른말로 간함] personal admonition; direct remonstration. **직간하다** reprove (a person) to his face; remonstrate directly. ¶나는 사장의 어리석은 행동에 대해 직간했다 I remonstrated with the president about his foolish conduct.
직감(直感) intuition; (미국 구어) hunch. ¶나는 그것을 ~으로 알았다 I knew it by intuition. // 내 ~이 맞았다[빗나갔다] My intuition[hunch] was right[wrong]. // 내 ~에 의하면 이 계획은 실패할 것이다 I have a hunch (that) this plan will fail. **직감하다** perceive intuitively; feel (a thing) in one's bones. ¶나는 위험이 다가오고 있음을 직감했다 I knew by intuition[felt in my bones] that danger was approaching. // 사태를 직감했다 I sensed what the situation was.
직감적(直感的) intuitive. ¶나는 상대가 권총을 주머니에 넣고 있다는 것을 ~으로 알았다 Intuition told me the man had a revolver in his pocket.
직거래(直去來) a direct transaction; direct dealing. **직거래하다** transact direct(ly) (with); make a direct deal (with).
직격(直擊) [곧바로 침] direct hit.
● **직격탄** a direct hit[shot]. ¶~을 맞다 be hit directly by a bomb.
직결(直結) direct connection; [전] direct coupling. **직결하다** connect[link] directly (with). ➔ **¶직결되다** be connected directly (with) // 시민에게 직결되어 있다 be linked directly with the citizen // 과일은 산지와 직결된 구매를 하고 있다 We buy fruit directly from the districts where it is produced.
직경(直徑) ➡지름
직계(直系) a direct line. ¶~의 lineal // ~의 자손 a direct descendant // 그는 19세기의 유명한 정치가의 ~이다 He is directly descended from[is a direct descendant of] a famous statesman of the nineteenth century.
● **직계 가족** family members in a direct line. **직계 존속**[비속] a lineal ascendant[descendant].
직고하다(直告-) inform[report / tell] truthfully.
직공(職工) a workman; a factory hand; (특히 기계공) a mechanic; an operative.
직관(直觀) intuition; insight.
직구(直球) [야구] a straight ball.
직권(職權) one's official authority. ¶~에 의하여 in[by] virtue of one's office // ~ 밖의 일을 하다 overstep one's authority // ~을 행사[남용]하다 exercise[abuse] one's authority // 사장은 새 공장 부지를 선정하는 ~을 그에게 주었다 The president authorized him to decide on a site for the new factory. // 의장은 ~을 행사하여 폐회를 선언했다 The chairman declared the meeting closed by virtue of his authority.
● **직권 남용** abuse of one's authority; misfeasance. ¶네가 그런 결정을 하면 ~이 될 거야 If you make such a decision, it will be an abuse of authority.
직급(職級) the class of one's position.
직기(織機) a weaving machine; a loom.
직녀(織女) **1** [피륙 짜는 여자] a woman waver. **2** [천] Vega; 직녀성(⇨직녀)
● **직녀성** [천] Vega; the Weaver.
직능(職能) **1** [직업상의 능력] professional [occupational] ability. **2** [직업에 따른 고유 기능] function. ¶판사의 ~ the function of a judge.
● **직능 대표(제)** vocational[professional] representation (system).
직답(直答) **1** [직접 대답함] a direct answer. **직답하다** personally answer. ¶나는 상사에게 직답했다 I answered my boss directly[in person]. **2** a ready answer. ⇨즉답
직렬(直列) [전] a series. ¶전지를 ~로 잇다 connect cells in (a) series.
● **직렬 회로** a series circuit.
직로(直路) a straight road; a direct route.
직류(直流) [전] direct current(약어 D.C.); continuous current; series flow. ¶~은 direct-current.
● **직류 발전기** a D.C. generator[dynamo]. **직류 회로** a direct current circuit.
직립(直立) ¶~의 straight / upright / [수직의] perpendicular. **직립하다** stand up straight. ¶직립한 텔레비전 탑 a television tower rising

straight into the sky // 직립한 절벽 precipices rising perpendicularly
- 직립 원인 a pithecanthrope; a Java man.

직매 (直賣) direct sales. **직매하다** sell directly [on the spot]; carry out direct sales. ¶이 의자는 메이커에서 직매하고 있다 These chairs are sold directly by the manufacturer. // 달걀은 농가에서 직매하는 것을 사면 싸게 치인다 We get eggs cheaper if we buy them directly (from the farm).
- 직매점 a direct sales store.

직면하다 (直面-) face (up to); confront; be confronted with [by]; be faced with; come face to face with; be up against. ¶위기에 ~ be at a critical moment / be facing a crisis // 파멸에 직면하고 있다 be on the verge [brink] of ruin / 그들은 극복하기 어려운 난관에 직면하였다 They were face-to-face [were confronted] with almost insurmountable difficulties. // 그는 죽음에 직면해서도 침착했다 He remained calm in the face of [imminent] death. // 그들은 지금 위험에 직면하고 있다 They are now faced [confronted] with danger. // 우리 당은 분열의 위기에 직면하고 있었다 Our party was on the point [verge] of splitting (into factions).

직명 (職名) [직업명] (the exact name of) one's occupation; (공무원의) an official title. ¶당신의 ~은 정확히 말해서 무엇입니까 What exactly is your title [position]?

직무 (職務) (a) duty; an office; a function; a job. ¶~를 수행하다 [태만히 하다] perform [neglect] one's duty // ~에 충실하다 be faithful to one's duties [job] // ~를 분담하다 divide duties (among) // 나는 ~상 위험한 일을 당해야 하는 일도 있다 Sometimes I have to face danger as a matter [in the line] of duty. // 그는 ~상 공해 문제를 잘 알고 있다 Because of his duties [job] he is familiar with the problems of pollution. // 우리는 각각 다른 ~를 맡고 있소 We work in different areas. // 그는 ~의 성격상 출장이 잦다 The nature of his office [duties] requires that he make frequent business trips. // 그는 ~에 충실하다 He is faithful to his duties.
- 직무 규정 office regulations. 직무 방해 interference with one's work [a person's duty]. 직무 수당 a service allowance; an allowance attached to a post. 직무 수행 performance of one's duty. 직무 유기 dereliction [delinquency] of one's duty. 직무 태만 neglect [dereliction] of duty; culpable neglect [negligence]; delinquency. ¶그는 ~으로 견책 처분을 받았다 He was reprimanded for neglect of duty.

직물 (織物) textiles; (textile) fabrics; [천] cloth.
- 직물 공업 the textile industry. 직물상 (미) a dealer in dry goods; (영) a fabric dealer. 직물업 the textile trade; (제조) textile manufacture.

직배 (直配) [배달] direct delivery; [배급] direct distribution. **직배하다** deliver [distribute] directly. → 달걀은 양계장에서 직배된다 Eggs are delivered directly from a poultry farm.

직분 (職分) one's duty; one's job. ¶~을 다하다 do [fulfill] one's duty // ~을 알다 know one's duty // 공무원으로서의 ~을 망각하다 neglect one's duty as a public servant / commit deeds unworthy of a public official.

직사 (直射) 1 (광선의) direct rays. **직사하다** (the sun) shine [beat] directly (upon). ¶태양이 내 얼굴을 직사하고 있다 The sun is shining directly on [in] my face. 2 (총포의) direct fire; frontal fire. **직사하다** fire direct (upon); fire point-blank (at).
- 직사광선 a direct ray of light. ¶이 식물은 ~을 피해 주세요 Keep this plant out of the direct rays of the sun. / Don't expose this plant directly to the sun. 직사포 a direct-firing gun.

직사각형 (直四角形) [수] a rectangle; a right-angled tetragon. ¶~의 rectangular.

직삼각형 (直三角形) a right triangle. ⇨"직각 삼각형 (⇨직각(直角))

직선 (直線) a straight [right] line; a beeline. ¶~ (모양)의 straight(-line) / rectilineal // ~으로 in a straight line / ~을 긋다 draw a straight line // (사람이) ~적이다 be thoroughly straight / be straightforward
- 직선거리 a lineal distance; a distance in a straight line. ¶~로 in a straight line / in a beeline [a crow line / (미) an air line] / as the crow flies // 서울까지 ~로 얼마나 됩니까 How far is it to Seoul as the crow flies? // 서울까지는 ~로 약 30킬로다 It is about thirty kilometers to Seoul in a straight line [a beeline]. 직선 운동 a rectilineal [straight-line] motion. 직선 코스 a straight course.

직설 (直說) straight talk; plain speaking; frankness. **직설하다** talk frankly [straight from the shoulder]; speak out; speak up; speak without reserve.
- 직설법 [언] the indicative mood.

직성 풀리다 (直星-) be satisfied [gratified]; feel relieved. ¶이것으로는 직성이 풀리지 않는다 This is not enough to satisfy. // 그녀는 무엇이건 자신이 직접 하지 않고선 직성이 안 풀린다 She is not satisfied with anything unless she does it by herself.

직소 (直訴) a direct appeal [petition]. ¶~를 기도하다 attempt a direct appeal (to the King). **직소하다** make a direct appeal (to the King); appeal directly (to the King).

직속 (直屬) ¶대통령 ~의 연구 기관 a research institute directly responsible [responsible directly] to the President // 그 기관은 내각 ~이다 That organization is under direct [immediate] control of the Cabinet. // 그는 나의 ~상관이다 He is the senior officer I directly belong to. **직속하다** be under the immediate [direct] control (of).
- 직속 부하 a subordinate under one's direct control.

직송 (直送) directly delivery. ¶산지 ~의 야채 vegetables direct [fresh] from the growing district. **직송하다** send direct(ly) (to).

직수입 (直輸入) direct import [importation]. **직수입하다** import (goods) direct(ly) (from). ¶미국에서 직수입한 원료 raw materials imported direct(ly) from the United States.
- 직수입품 direct imports; articles imported direct from abroad.

직수출 (直輸出) direct export [exportation]. **직수출하다** export (goods) direct(ly) (to). ¶기계를 ~ export machines direct to a foreign country.
- 직수출품 direct exports.

직시 (直視) looking (a person) in the face. **직시하다** look (a person) in the face; look

직언(直言) plain speaking; a straight talk; outspoken advice. **직언하다** speak plainly [frankly]; speak without reserve; speak one's mind; speak out. ¶상사에게 ~ speak plainly [frankly / without reserve] to one's boss.

직업(職業) an occupation; a calling; a vocation; (전문적인 사회 활동) a profession; (장사·수공 등의) a trade. ¶…을 ~으로 삼다 be (a physician) by profession / be (a carpenter) by trade // ~이 없는 jobless / unemployed / ~에 종사하다 follow [engage in] an occupation (of ...) // ~을 구하다 seek employment / look for a position [job] // ~을 선택하다 choose one's profession [trade] // ~을 가지다 take up an occupation / adopt (teaching) as a profession // ~을 바꾸다 change one's occupation // ~을 얻다 get [obtain] a job [position / situation] / be employed // ~을 바꾸지 않다 stick to one's occupation // ~을 전전하다 work at a variety of occupations // 아버지의 ~을 계승하다 succeed one's father in his occupation // 당신의 ~은 무엇입니까 What do you do (for a living)? / What is your occupation? / What business are you in? / What line of work are you in? // 아버님의 ~은 무엇입니까 What is your father's job [occupation]? / What line of business is your father in? / What does your father do? // 아버지의 ~은 목수[의사]였습니다 My father was a carpenter by trade [a medical doctor by profession]. // 그는 ~이 문필가이다 He is a writer by profession. // 그에게는 일정한 ~이 없다 He has no regular job [occupation]. / (구어) He is at loose ends [a loose end]. // 직업은 모든 ~이 여성에게 개방되어 있다고 생각하십니까 Do you think all careers are open to women? // 서적 외관이 내 ~이다 The sale of [Selling] books is my business. // 나는 ~상 여행을 많이 해야 됩니다 My calling requires a good deal of traveling.

●**직업 교육** vocational education. **직업회** a professional [(미) career] soldier. **직업병** an occupational disease. **직업 보도** vocational guidance [training]. **직업소개소** an employment [a placement] agency. **직업여성** a working [career] woman; a woman worker. **직업의식** professional consciousness; professionalism. ¶그에게는 ~이 없다 He does not take his job seriously. **직업학교** a vocational [trade] school. **직업 훈련** vocational training. ¶~원[소] a vocational training center.

직역(直譯) literal [verbatim / word-for-word] translation. **직역하다** translate literally [word-for-word]. ¶문장을 ~ translate a passage word-for-word / translate a passage literally.

직영(直營) direct management [control]. ¶L 백화점의 ~ 식당 a restaurant under direct management of the L Department Store // 정부의 ~ 사업 an enterprise under government management // …의 ~이다 be under direct management of ... // 이 가게는 A 제과의 ~이다 This store is under the direct management of A Bakery. **직영하다** manage [control / operate] directly.

직원(職員) (전체) the staff; the personnel; the faculty(대학의); (개인) a member of the staff. ¶철도청 ~ the staff of the office of Railways // ~의 이동 a personnel change / a change in the staff / a reshuffle of personnel // 50명의 ~ a staff of 50 men // 회사 ~이다 be on the staff of a company // ~은 몇 사람입니까 How many people do you have on your staff? // 나는 이 사무실의 ~입니다 I am a staff member [on the staff] at this office. // 그는 그 고등학교의 ~이다 He is on the staff of the high school.

●**직원 명부** a staff list; a personnel directory. **직원회** (학교의) a staff meeting.

직유(直喩) [문] a simile. ¶~를 쓰다 similize.

직육면체(直六面體) a rectangular parallelepiped.

직인(職印) an official seal; [정부의 도장] a government seal.

직임(職任) one's office [official] duties; one's professional duties.

직장(直腸) [생] the rectum (pl. -ta). ¶~의 rectal.

●**직장암** cancer of the rectum. **직장염** rectitis; proctitis.

직장(職場) [일터] one's place of work; one's job(site); one's post; a workshop(공장). ¶~을 그만두다 desert [quit] one's post / walk out (on one's job) // ~에서 쫓겨나다 be forced [compelled] to leave one's position // ~으로 돌아가다 return [be back] to work // ~을 자주 바꾸다 [옮기다] change one's employment with (great) frequency // ~을 찾다 [구하다] seek employment / look for a position / ~을 얻다 obtain employment / get a job / find a place / ~을 알선하다 help (a person) (to) find a job / ~을 구해 주다 find (a person) a place [situation] / 나의 ~은 도심지에 있다 My place of work [office] is in the heart of the city. // 우리 ~에는 여성이 많다 There are many women in my office [workshop / factory]. // 나는 새 ~을 얻었습니다 I've taken [got] a new job. // 그는 매일 ~에 나갑니다 He goes to work [his office] every day. // 그는 작년에 ~을 바꾸었다 He changed his job last year. // 형은 지금 다른 ~에서 일합니다 My brother works at a different place now. // 그의 ~은 어디입니까 Where does he work? // 제 남편은 아직 ~에서 돌아오지 않았습니다 My husband has not returned from work yet.

●**직장 대표** (노동 쟁의의) a shop deputy.

직재(直裁) **1** [즉석 결재] a prompt decision [approval]; the decision [approval] on the spot. **직재하다** give a prompt decision [approval]; approve [decide] on the spot. **2** [직접 결재] a personal [direct] decision. **직재하다** give personal [direct] decision; decide personally [directly].

직전(直前) ¶끓는 ~의 물 water just short of boiling // ~에 just [right] before / just prior to // 시험 ~에 just before the examination / on the eve of the examination // 죽기 ~에 just before one's death // 본루 ~에서 아웃되다 be touched out right short of home // 비행기가 이륙 ~에 폭발하였다 The plane exploded just before takeoff. // 그는 시험 ~에 병이 들었다 He fell ill just before [on the eve of] the examination. // 그녀는 결혼식 ~에 앓게 되었다 She became ill just before the wedding.∥나는 결승선 ~에서 상대를 앞질렀다 I overtook my rival just in front of the finish line.∥그는 파산 ~이다 He is on the verge[brink] of bankrupt.∥그의 원고는 마감시간 ~에 도착했다 His manuscript arrived just before the deadline.

직접(直接) [관형어적] direct; immediate; personal; firsthand. ¶~(으로) direct(ly) / immediately / at firsthand / firsthand / [몸소] personally / in person∥~ 얻은 firsthand information (about)∥~ 간접으로 directly or indirectly∥~ 듣다 hear at firsthand∥~ 말하다 tell (it) with one's own lips∥~ 면회하다 see (a person) personally∥~ 인도하다[주다] deliver[hand over] (a thing) personally∥~ 조사하다 investigate at firsthand∥~ 행동을 취하다 take direct action∥…에 ~ 영향을 미치다 have a direct influence on …∥~ 과 관계가 있다 have direct connection with …∥~편지를 건네주다 deliver a letter in person[personally]∥본인이 ~ 신청하다 apply in person∥이것은 그에게서 ~ 들은 이야기이다 I heard this directly from him.∥This is what I heard from him at first hand.∥나는 그와 ~ 이야기했다 I talked with him in person.∥~ 그에게 말하는 것이 좋다 You had better speak to him personally[yourself].∥이 눈으로 ~ 보았다 I saw it with my own eyes.∥그 일에 대해서 나는 그와 ~ 협상했다 I negotiated directly with him about the matter.∥네가 가는 것이 좋겠다 You'd better go in person [yourself].∥~ 본 일을 말하고 있는 것이다 I speak from actual observation.∥그에게는 ~ 간접으로 신세가 많다 I owe him many obligations, direct and indirect.∥이 사건은 그것과 ~ 관계가 없다 This case does not have a direct bearing on that one. / This case is not directly related to that one.

● **직접 경험** direct experience. **직접 목적어** [언] a direct object. **직접 선거** a direct election. **직접세** a direct tax. **직접 조명** direct illumination. **직접 화법** [언] direct narration [speech].

직제(職制) the organization[setup] of on office. ¶~를 개편하다 reorganize an office.

직조(織造) weaving. **직조하다** weave.
● **직조공** a weaver. **직조기**(-機) a loom; a weaving machine.

직종(職種) a type of occupation; an occupational category. ¶~별로 (classify) by [according to] (the) occupation.

직직 1 [신발을 끄는 모양] shuffling; scuffling. ¶신을 ~ 끌다 scuffle one's shoes. 2 [찢는 모양] tearing; rending. ¶~ 찢다 tear[rend] (papers) to pieces. 3 [획·선을 긋는 모양] with (repeated) random strokes (of the pen). ¶~ 그어 지우다 scratch out.

직직거리다 (신발 등을) scuff; scuffle; shuffle.

직진하다(直進-) go straight on[ahead]; make straight for; advance in a beeline; make a straight drive[advance] (to). ¶빛은 직진한다 Light travels straight.

직책(職責) responsibilities pertaining to one's work[job]; one's duty. ¶~을 다하다 do [perform] one's duties∥~을 중시하다 have a strong sense of duty[responsibility]∥그는 ~을 완수하지 못했다 He failed in his duty.∥그는 ~을 수행하기 위해서는 어떠한 위험도 두려워하지 않았다 He was ready to face any danger when duty called.∥그는 ~상 경제 문제에 정통하다 He is well versed in economic affairs because of his duties.∥~상 방치해 둘 수 없다 I can't pass it over in silence, considering my duty[position].

● **직책 수당** an allowance for the post attached.

직통(直通) direct communication[service]; (교통 기관의) through service[traffic]. ¶~으로 …에 가다 go to … without changing cars [without transfer]∥이 열차는 부산까지 ~입니다 This train goes direct[through] to Busan. **직통하다** communicate directly (with); be in direct communications (with).

● **직통 전화(선)** a direct telephone line; (정부 수뇌 간의) a hot line.

직필(直筆) 1 [사실대로 쓰기] uncolored writing; straight reporting. **직필하다** write plainly (on a matter); write in frank language. 2 [붓을 세워서 쓰기] holding the brush upright while writing. **직필하다** write holding a brush upright.

직하(直下) 1 [바로 아래]. ¶~의[에 / 에서] directly under (a thing) / directly below∥적도 ~ right at the equator. 2 [수직 강하] a vertical descent; a perpendicular fall. ¶사건은 급전~으로 해결되었다 The matter has come to an abrupt settlement. **직하하다** fall perpendicularly[plumb down]; descend vertically. ¶급전직하하여 suddenly / all of a sudden / precipitately.

-**직하다** ¶굵~ somewhat thick[big] / thickish∥묵~ rather heavy[massive / weighty]∥죽이 되~ The gruel is rather thick.

직할(直轄) direct control[jurisdiction]. ¶…의 ~로 옮기다 transfer (a matter) to the direct control of …∥본교는 교육 인적 자원부 ~이다 This school is under the direct control [supervision] of the Ministry of Education and Human Resources Development. **직할하다** control directly; hold under direct jurisdiction.

● **직할시** ➡ 광역시 (⇨) 광역

직함(職銜) a title; (구어) a handle (to one's name). ¶~이 있는 사람 a man of title∥겉만 번지르르한 ~ a pretentious title∥어마어마한 ~ a high-sounding title∥국무총리의 ~ the title of Prime Minister∥~이 있는 with a title [handle] to one's name / titled∥~이 없는 untitled / without any title∥그는 아무 ~도 없다 He has no handle to his name.

직항(直航) (배의) a direct voyage[service]; (비행기의) a nonstop flight. **직항하다** (배가) sail direct[straight] (for / to); (비행기가) make a nonstop flight (to); fly nonstop (to / for). ¶이 비행기[배]는 샌프란시스코로 직항하고 있다 This plane is flying[This ship is sailing] direct[nonstop] to San Francisco.

● **직항로** a direct line.

직행(直行) going straight[direct]; through running; [정차하지 않음] nonstop. **직행하다** go straight[direct] (to); run[go] through (to). (기차가). ¶사고 현장으로 ~ rush straight to the scene of the accident∥갈아타지 않고 ~ go[run] through without making a change∥이 열차는 경주까지 직행한다 This train goes direct[straight] to Gyeongju.∥서울로 직행했다 I went direct[directly] to Seoul.

● **직행 버스** a nonstop bus. **직행 열차** a

진후 (直後) ¶~에 immediately [just / directly / right] after // 회의 ~에 immediately after the meeting // 종전 ~에 directly after the end of the war / just after the war's end // 사건 발생 ~에 경찰관이 현장에 급히 갔다 Immediately [Directly] after the incident, the police rushed to the spot.

진 [술의 일종] gin. ¶드라이 ~ dry gin // ~ 피즈 gin fizz // ~ 토닉 gin and tonic.

진(津) (나무의) resin; gum; sap; (담배의) nicotine; tar. ¶담뱃~ (tobacco) tar // 송~ pine resin // 담뱃~으로 누렇게 된 손가락 a nicotine-stained finger // (나무에서) ~이 나오다 exude [excrete] gum [resin] // 담뱃대가 ~으로 막혀 있다 The pipe is stopped up with tar.

진(이) 빠지다 (사람이) be exhausted; be spent up; be wrung out.

진(陣) [진형] battle [camp] formation; battle array; [대열] lines; ranks; [진영] a camp; [진지] a position.
진(을) 치다 take up a position; encamp; pitch [make] a camp; form in [make] battle array.

진-(眞) [참된] real; true; [진짜의] genuine. ¶~면목 one's true self [character] // ~품 a genuine article.

-진(陣) [무리·그룹] a group; a band; a party. ¶교수~ the teaching staff (of a university) // 보도~ a news front / (미) a press corps // 장사~ a long line [file / row] / a long queue.

진가(眞價) real [true / intrinsic] value [merit]; real worth; true merit. ¶교육의 ~ the true value of education // ~가 있다 have intrinsic value // ~를 인정하다 appreciate [recognize] the worth (of) // ~를 발휘하다 prove one's merits [worth] / do oneself justice // ~를 의심하다 doubt the true worth // 작품의 ~를 인정하다 recognize [appreciate] the true value of a work // 내 ~를 알아주지 않는다 They deny me justice. // 어떤 물건의 ~는 외견이 아니라 실질에 있다 The true value of a thing lies in its substance, not in its appearance.

진간장(津-醬) aged soy sauce.
진갈이하다 plow a wet [watered] field.
진갑(進甲) the 61st anniversary of one's birth; one's 61st birthday.
●진갑 잔치 a feast on one's 61st birthday; a 61st birthday feast.

진객(珍客) a least-expected visitor [guest]; a welcome guest.

진격(進擊) a march onward; a charge; a drive; a push; an attack; an attack. 진격하다 charge (at / on); attack; make an attack (on); make a drive [push] (on / upon); march (upon); advance (on / against); assault.
●진격 명령 an order to advance; (미국 구어) a go-ahead.

진경(眞境) 1 [참다운 지경] the real condition; the actual state of things. 2 [실지 그대로의 경계] the actual border (line).

진공(眞空) a vacuum (pl. ~s, vacua). ¶~의 vacuous / hollow / empty / evacuated // ~ 상태에서 under vacuum // ~으로 하다 make vacuous // ~으로 되다 form a vacuum.
●진공관 a (vacuum) tube. ¶2 [3] 극 ~ a two- [three-] electrode vacuum tube // 4극 ~ a tetrode // 5극 ~ a pentode. 진공청소기 a vacuum cleaner [sweeper].

진공(進攻) a march onward. ⇨진격(進擊)
진과(珍果) rare [uncommon] fruits.
진과(珍菓) rare confectionery [sweet stuff].
진구렁 a bog; a slough; a quagmire; a morass. ¶~에 빠지다 bog (down) / be [get] bogged / [비유] be bogged down / get stuck in a bog // ~에서 빠져나오다 find a way out of the swamp // ~에 보다 깊숙이 빠지다 get bogged deeper in the mud.

진국(眞-) 1 [참되어 거짓이 없는 사람] a true [truthful] person; an honest [a sincere] person. 2 [물을 타지 않은 진한 국물] pure [undiluted] liquor [soy sauce].

진군(進軍) march; marching; (an) advance. ¶~나팔을 불다 sound the march / bugle on march // ~을 명하다 order the advance (to) // ~ 중이다 be on the march. 진군하다 march [advance] (on a town / against the enemy). ¶보무당당하게 ~ march [advance] in fine array.
●진군가 a marching song.

진귀하다(珍貴-) rare and precious [valuable]. ¶진귀한 책 a rare book.

진급(進級) (a) promotion; remove(학교의). ¶~이 빠르다 [늦다] be rapid [slow] in promotion. 진급하다 be promoted; win promotion. ¶대령으로 ~ be promoted to (be) a colonel // 그는 2학년으로 진급했다 He moved up [was promoted] to the second-year class [grade]. (▶ the second grade는 (미)에서 초등학교 2학년) ➔ ¶진급시키다 promote (a person) to a higher position / advance.
●진급 시험 an examination for promotion.

진기(津氣) stickiness; viscosity; glutinousness; glutinosity. ¶~가 있는 sticky / viscid / viscous / glutinous // 이 쌀은 ~가 있다 This rice is rich in gluten.

진기(珍器) a rare vessel; a curio; a curiosity.
진기하다(珍奇-) quaint; queer; strange; singular; extraordinary. ¶진기한 현상 a strange phenomenon // 진기한 것 a rarity / a curiosity / a novelty // 진기한 새 [동물] a rare bird [animal] // 그것은 아주 진기한 사건이다 The case is a singular one. // 그 당시는 모두들 그것을 아주 진기해했다 It was then a great novelty.

진날 a rainy [wet] day. ¶~에 대비하다 provide for a rainy day // ~ 개 사귀기 meeting with an unpleasant and troublesome affair.

진 댁 나막신 찾듯 (속담) asking a long-neglected friend for help in time of need.

진노(震怒) wild rage; wrath; fury. ¶신의 ~를 사다 excite [arouse] the wrath of God // 신의 ~를 달래다 appease the wrath of God. 진노하다 rage; be enraged; be inflamed with rage.

진눈 [짓무른 눈] blear eyes.
진눈깨비 sleet. ¶~가 내리는 날 a sleet day // ~가 내린다 It sleets. / Sleet is falling.

진단(診斷) (a) diagnosis (pl. -noses); diagnostication. ¶건강 ~ a medical [physical / health] examination [(미) checkup] // 조기 ~ (make) an early diagnosis (of) // 종합 ~ a comprehensive medical testing // ~을 받다 have (one's case) diagnosed // ~을 내리다 pronounce a diagnosis // ~을 잘못하다 make a wrong diagnosis // 정 박사의 ~으로는 유방암이다 Dr. Jeong's diagnosis [In Dr. Jeong's opinion, it] is breast cancer. // 저 의사는 ~을 잘한다 That doctor seldom fails in his

diagnosis. 진단하다 diagnose; make a diagnosis (of); give one's diagnosis (of). ¶옳게 ~ make a correct diagnosis // 폐암으로 ~ diagnose (a case) as cancer of the lungs // 심장병으로 인한 사망으로 ~ pronounce (a person) dead of heart attack // 의사는 잘못 진단했다 The doctor made an incorrect diagnosis. // 의사는 폐렴으로 진단했다 The doctor diagnosed the case as pneumonia.
● **진단서** a medical certificate; (a written) diagnosis.

진달래 [식] an azalea.

진담(眞談) a serious [an earnest] talk. ¶농담을 ~으로 듣다 take a joke seriously // 내 말은 ~이다 My talk is not a joke. / I mean business [what I say]. // 너 그 말 ~이냐 Do you really mean it? // 이번에는 ~이다 I mean business this time.

진답(陳畓) a paddy field in fallow; a fallow (rice) paddy.

진대 1 [떼쓰다시피 괴롭힘] annoyance; pestering; molestation. ¶~를 **붙이다** annoy [harass / pester] (a person) // 그녀가 ~ 붙여 그는 할 수 없이 결혼했다 She pestered him until he married her. **2** →뱀

진도(進度) progress. ¶**학과** ~ progress of classwork // 이런 ~로 간다면 if things go at this rate // 반에 따라 ~가 다르다 Progress is different from class to class. // 이 반(班)은 수학의 ~가 빠르다[늦다] This class is forward [backward] in mathematics.
● **진도표** (학과의) a teaching schedule (for the term); (일의) a progress chart.

진도(震度) seismic intensity. ¶~ 5의 강진 a very strong earthquake of five degrees intensity / a tremor of the 5th degree on the seismic scale // ~ 8.7을 기록하다 register 8.7 on the Richter scale // 지금의 지진은 ~ 3이었다 The earthquake we had just now registered 3 on the seismic scale.

진동 [소매의 겨드랑이 밑의 넓이] the (lengthwise) width of an armhole (of a sleeve).

진동(振動) (an) oscillation; (a) vibration; a swing. ¶~을 **일으키다** set up a vibration [a swing motion] // ~을 **멈추다** stop the vibration. **진동하다** oscillate; swing; vibrate; librate; move to and fro.
● **진동계** a vibration gauge; a vibrometer; a vibrograph. **진동수** the number of vibrations; an oscillation frequency; a pitch. **진동판** a diaphragm; a tympanum (pl. ~s, -na) (전화기의).

진동(震動) a shock; tremor; concussion. ¶지진의 ~ the shocks of an earthquake // ~을 느끼다 feel a shock // 약간의 ~을 깨닫다 notice a slight tremor // 갑자기 ~이 왔다 There was suddenly a tremor. // 이 차는 ~이 심하다 [적다] This car bumps horribly [moves smoothly]. **진동하다** shake; quake; tremble; quiver. ¶집이 심하게 진동하였다 The house rocked violently. // 대지가 진동하여 갈라졌다 The earth quaked [shook] and cracked. // 대형 트럭이 지나갈 때마다 집이 진동했다 The house shook [trembled] whenever a big truck passed. →¶진동시키다 shake.

진두(陣頭) (at) the head (of an army); the front. ¶~에 **서다** lead the van (of) / be the front / be at the head (of a unit) // ~에 서서 말을 몰다 ride at the head (of an army).
● **진두지휘** command exercised by the head of army. ¶~를 **하다** lead one's men [take the lead] (in doing).

진득근하다 very staid; sedate; sober; earnest; quite quiet; patient. **진득근히** very sedately; soberly; earnestly; most quietly; patiently.

진드기 [동] a tick; a mite; an acarid; an acarus (pl. -ri). ¶개 ~ a dog tick // ~ 같은 사람 a barnacle / a hanger-on // ~처럼 끈질긴 tenacious // ~에 **물리다** be bitten by a tick // ~처럼 물고 늘어져 떨어지지 않는다 He sticks to me like a leech.

진득거리다 1 [들러붙다] keep sticking [holding on / adhering]. **2** [검질겨 끊어지지 않다] resist cutting.

진득진득 [끈적끈적] stickily; adhesively; [검질긴 모양] stubbornly (ly); unyieldingly (ly). ¶옷이 몸에 ~ 달라붙는다 My clothing clings to my body. **진득진득하다** sticky; gluey; stubborn; tough; tenacious. ¶(표면이) 진득진득한 잎 a viscid leaf // 검고 진득진득한 진흙 black sticky mud.

진득하다 staid; sedate; sober; dignified; grave; earnest; quiet; patient. ¶진득한 성격 a staid character // 그는 언제 보아도 ~ He always appears dignified. / He is a deep-seated person. **진득이** gravely; sedately; with dignity; in earnest; soberly; quietly; patiently. ¶~ **앉아 공부하다** settle [set] down to one's studies // ~ 한곳에 머무르다 stay in one place for a long time.

진디 [동] **1** an aphid. ⇨ **진딧물 2** a tick. ⇨ 진드기

진딧물 [동] an aphid; a plant louse (pl. plant lice); a swarm of aphides.

진땀(津-) sweat of anxiety; sticky sweat. ¶~ **나다** sweat hard.

진땀(을) **빼다** have a hard time; have an awful [a hell of a] time. ¶시험 치르느라 ~ sweat out an exam.

진력(盡力) endeavo(u)r(s); efforts; exertion(s); [알선] assistance; service(s); good offices. **진력하다** endeavor; make efforts; exert oneself; render services. ¶교육 사업에 ~ render service to the cause of education // 인류를 위하여 크게 ~ do [render] great service to mankind.

진력나다(盡力-) **1** [싫증이 나다] be sick [sick and tired] (of); be bored (with / by); (속이) be fed up (with). ¶진력나지 않는 경치 a sight [view] one never tires of seeing / a view one can never see too often // 진력나지 않는 책 a book one never tires of reading // 진력나는 강의 a boring [tedious / tiresome / wearisome] lecture. **2** [힘이 다하다] one's strength is gone [ebb].

진로(進路) a course (to advance); the way ahead; one's path in life. ¶~를 **정하다** fix one's way // ~가 **막히다** be blocked the way // 졸업 후의 ~를 결정하다 decide what (one is going) to do after graduation // ~를 **가로막다** block the way / stand in (a person's) way // ~를 **개척하다** hew [cut] one's way / make way (for) // 인생의 ~를 그르치다 take a false [wrong] course in life // 후진을 위해 ~를 열어 주다 make way for one's juniors // 태풍의 ~에 놓여 있다 be in the path of the typhoon // 행렬은 ~를 바꾸었다 The procession changed its course. // 태풍은 ~를 동쪽으로 바꿨다 The typhoon shifted its course towards the east.

진료
- **진로 지도** guidance counseling.

진료(診療) medical examination and treatment. ¶~를 받다 receive (medical) treatment / be treated // ~ 신청서 작성하는 곳 (게시) Fill out medical treatment application form here. // 외래 환자는 이곳에서 ~를 받을 수 있음 Diagnosis and treatment are available to outpatient here. // 그는 지금 병원에서 폐렴의 ~를 받고 있다 He is under treatment for pneumonia in ((미) the) hospital. / He is in (the) hospital being treated for pneumonia. **진료하다** give medical treatment; treat.
- **진료소** a clinic; a medical office. **진료 시간** consultation hours. **진료실** an examination [a consultation] room; a medical office.

진루하다(進壘-) 〔야구〕 advance. ¶2루에 ~ advance [move up] to second base.

진리(眞理) truth; true principles. ¶~의 추구 pursuit of truth // 만고불변의 ~ an eternal [a permanent] truth // 보편적인 ~ a universal truth // 움직일 수 없는 ~ an uncontrovertible [unquestionable] truth // ~의 탐구자 a seeker of the truth // ~를 **탐구하다** seek (after) truth.

진맥(診脈) feeling the pulse (for diagnosis). **진맥하다** feel the pulse (of).

진면목(眞面目) one's true character. ¶~을 **발휘하다** (능력을) give full play to one's abilities / (진가를) prove one's real worth // 이 쾌거는 그의 ~을 보여 주고 있다 This heroic achievement is entirely characteristic of [is just like] him.

진무르다 → 짓무르다

진문(珍聞) 〔귀한 소문〕 extraordinary news; a curious story; rare news; an interesting story.

진물(津-) ooze from a sore; colloid. ¶~이 나다 a sore oozes [waters].

진미(珍味) a delicacy; a gourmet delight; a delicate flavo(u)r; rare dainties; delicacies; a rich diet; "goodies". ¶계절의 ~ delicacies of the season // 산해 ~ dainties of many [all] kinds / dainty foods of every kind / all sorts of delicacies // 이건 ~로구나 What a delicacy this is!

진미(眞味) 〔참된 맛〕 true taste; 〔진정한 취미〕 genuine appreciation. ¶음악의 ~ the charm of music // 인생의 ~ the real taste [the zest] of life // 동양화의 ~를 알다 appreciate what oriental painting is all about.

진미(陳米) old stale rice.

진발 muddy feet [shoes]. ¶~로 마루에 올라오다 soil the floor with muddy feet [shoes] / carry dirt into the floor.

진배없다 〔서술적〕 be equal (to); be as good as; be on a level (with); be on a par (with); be no worse (than). ¶죽은 거나 ~ be virtually [as good as] dead // 새것이나 ~ be as good as new // 그런 모욕이나 ~ Such a speech amounts almost to insult.

진버짐 eczema; a watery ringworm.

진범(인)(眞犯人) the true culprit; the real offender [criminal]. ¶~은 아직 잡히지 않고 있다 The real criminal is still at large.

진법(陣法) 〔군〕 disposition of troops; plan of campaign; tactics. ¶방어 [공격] ~ defensive [offensive] disposition.

진보(珍寶) precious things; a treasure.

진보(進步) 〔진척〕 progress; 〔전진〕 (an) advance; 〔개선〕 (an) improvement (in). ¶놀라운 ~ marvelous [wonderful] progress // ~가 빠른 [더딘] 학생 a quick [slow] learner // ~가 빠르다 [느리다] make rapid [slow] progress // ~를 **저해하다** hinder [retard / impede] progress // 과학이 눈부신 ~를 이룩했다 Science has made remarkable progress [advances]. **진보하다** (make) progress; advance; improve. ¶착착 ~ make steady progress // 그의 작문이 크게 진보했다 He has improved greatly in composition. →¶그의 생각은 당시의 사람들보다 진보된 것이었다 His were ahead of his time.
- **진보주의** progressivism. **진보주의자** a progressive; 〔집합적〕 the progressive; the progressive faction [camp].

진보적(進步的) progressive; advanced. ¶~인 사람 a man of progressive ideas [advanced views] / a forward-looking [-thinking] man / a person with progressive ideas // ~인 사상 a progressive idea.

진본(珍本) a rare book. ⇨*진서

진본(眞本) an authentic [unforged] piece of writing [painting].

진부(眞否) truth (or falsity); truth or falsehood; genuineness; truth; authenticity. ¶~를 **확인하다** ascertain whether it is true or not / ascertain the truth // 일의 ~를 캐다 [묻다] look [inquire] into the truth of a matter.

진부하다(陳腐-) stale; hackneyed; old-fashioned; antiquated; commonplace; worn-out; trite. ¶진부한 생각 an old-fashioned [outdated] idea // 진부한 익살 a stale [trite] joke // 생각이 진부한 사람 an old-fashioned person / (구어) a fossil / a back number / 〔보수적인 사람〕 conservative person // 진부한 학설 an outdated theory // 진부한 라디오 프로그램 a stereotyped radio program // 진부한 표현이지만 세상은 정말 좁은 것이다 It's a trite [stereotyped] saying, but it's really a small world. // 그 학설은 이제 ~ That theory is dated. // 그 진부한 농담은 그만 집어치워 No more of your tired old [those same old] jokes! // 그의 이론은 모두 진부하고 평범하다 His arguments are all cut and dried.

진분수(眞分數) a proper fraction.

진사(辰砂) 〔광〕 cinnabar.

진사(珍事) a strange event; a rare incident; an odd event; a marvel.

진사(陳謝) 〔사과함〕 an apology. ¶~의 편지 a letter of apology. **진사하다** apologize (for); express one's regret. ¶진사할 것을 요구하다 demand an apology (from) // 아들의 무례한 말에 대해 진사합니다 I beg your pardon [apologize to you] for my son's impolite remark.

진사(進士) a person who has passed the primary state examination only.

진상(眞相) 〔진실〕 the truth; 〔사실〕 a fact; the real facts of a case; the actual state of things; the real situation; the true picture (of). ¶~을 **밝히다** disclose the real state / reveal the truth / probe [reveal] the true picture of (the incident) // 일의 ~을 알다 know the truth about an affair / see a matter in its true light // 일의 ~을 규명하다 inquire into the truth of the matter / inquire into the real state of affairs / reach [get down] to the bedrock // ~을 **말하다** lay bare the truth of (a matter) // ~을 **파악하다** get at

진상 the truth; real state of affairs / bottom of an affair. ¶~을 가리다 put a false color on (a matter) // 불원 ~이 알려지겠지 The truth will be out some day.
● **진상 조사단[위원회]** a fact-finding mission[committee].

진상(進上) presenting to the king the local products as tribute from the country. **진상하다** present to the king; offer up.
● **진상물** a present to the king.

진서(珍書) a rare book; a treasured book.

진선미(眞善美) truth, good(ness) and beauty.

진성(眞性) 1 [천성] one's inborn nature. 2 [의] genuineness. ¶~의 (병을 말할 때) genuine.
● **진성 뇌염** a genuine encephalitis. ¶~ 환자 a genuine encephalitis case / a genuine case of encephalitis. **진성 콜레라** (a case of) genuine cholera; true cholera.

진세(陣勢) the position of troops; the disposition of forces; military strength.

진세(塵世) this world; this mortal life. ¶~를 버리다 renounce the world.

진속(塵俗) this world; this earthly life.

진솔 1 [새 옷] brand-new clothes. 2 ramie-cloth garments made in spring or fall. ⇨ ⁻진솔옷(⑤진솔).
● **진솔옷** ramie-cloth garments made in spring or fall.

진수(珍羞) rare dainties; delicacies; food of delicate flavo(u)r.
● **진수성찬** rich viands and sumptuous fare. ¶야! 오늘 밤은 ~이로구나 Wow, it looks like a great dinner tonight!

진수(眞髓) [사물의 본질적인 골자] the essence; [정수·중심적 요점] the quintessence; [핵심] the soul; the gist; the core. ¶평화주의의 ~ the quintessence of pacifism // 화랑도의 ~ the spirit of *Hwarangdo* // 기사도의 ~ the soul of knighthood[chivalry] // 이것이 바로 크리스트교의 ~이다 This is the soul of Christianity.

진수(進水) launching (a vessel). **진수하다** launch. →¶진수되다 be launched / take the water.
● **진수대** the launching platform[way]. **진수식** a launching ceremony.

진술(陳述) a statement; a deposition(증인의). ¶거짓 없는[허위의] ~을 하다 make a true [false] statement // ~을 취소하다 withdraw [retract] one's case // ~을 듣다 take a deposition // 변호사는 상세한 ~을 했다 The lawyer made [presented] a detailed statement. // 그는 피고에 불리[유리]한 ~을 했다 He testified against[for] the accused. **진술하다** state (one's case); set forth; give [make] a statement; expound [explain] (one's views on a subject); lay (one's views) before (another). ¶의견을 ~ state [set forth] one's views // 그는 그 남자가 집에서 나오는 것을 목격했다고 진술했다 He deposed to having [that he had] seen the man leave the house.
● **진술서** a deposition; a (written) statement [declaration]; (선서 진술서) an affidavit. ¶~를 제출하다 send[hand] in a statement / present a statement.

진신발 muddy shoes.

진실(眞實) (the) truth; truthfulness; sincerity. ¶~을 말하자면 to tell the truth / the fact is ... // ~을 말하다 [왜곡하다] tell [bend / twist] the truth // ~을 밝히다 [추구하다] reveal [search for] the truth // ~을 증명하다 prove the truth (of) // 안됐지만 그것은 ~이다 That is only too true. // ~은 밝혀지기 마련이다 The truth is bound to come to light anyway. **진실한** true; truthful; sincere; genuine. ¶진실하지 않은 insincere / faithless / unfaithful / false. **진실히** truly; really; in truth; in reality; sincerely; heartily. ¶~ 대하다 act sincerely (towards a person) // ~ 하다 work in earnest.
● **진실성** [충실성] fidelity; allegiance; loyalty; devotion; [신빙·믿음성] the authority (of a report); credibility; the truth (of a statement); veracity. ¶보고의 ~ the veracity of a report // ~을 의심하다 doubt the truth (of a report) // 그의 말에는 ~이 없다 There is no truth in what he says. // 이 소설에는 ~이 있다 There is an air of reality about this novel.

진실로(眞實─) really; truly; indeed. ¶~ 이 세상이 싫증이 난다 I am heartily sick of this world.

진심(眞心) sincerity; earnestness; seriousness; a true heart. ¶~ 어린 sincere / hearty / heartfelt / wholehearted / cordial / warm // ~으로 with one's whole heart / wholeheartedly / sincerely / seriously / in earnest // 너 ~으로 그렇게 말하는 거야 Do you (really) mean it? // 나는 ~으로 이렇게 말하는 것입니다 I am saying this in all seriousness. // ~이 담긴 네 선물 고맙다 Thank you for your thoughtful gift. // 그는 ~으로 친구에게 충고했다 He advised his friend from the heart. // 당신의 성공을 ~으로 축하합니다 Let me [Allow me to] congratulate you most heartily on your success. (▶ all me to 쪽이 격식 차린 표현임) // 결례를 ~으로 사과드립니다 I sincerely apologize. // 나는 그에게 한 일에 대하여 ~으로 미안하게 생각하고 있다 At bottom [heart] I feel very bad about what I did to him.

진압(鎭壓) suppression; repression; subjugation. **진압하다** suppress; repress; subdue; quell; subjugate; put down. ¶폭동을 ~ suppress [put down / quell] a riot [rioters] // 기동대가 소동을 진압했다 The riot squad quelled the disturbance. // 경찰이 데모 군중을 진압했다 The police crushed the demonstrators [put down the demonstration].
● **진압책** a repressive measure.

진앙(震央) [진원 바로 위의 지표 상의 위치] the seismic epicenter[(영) epicentre].

진애(塵埃) dust; dirt. ¶~ 속에 버려두다 expose (a thing) to dirt.

진액(津液) 1 resin; sap. ¶~이 많은 resinous // 포도나무를 베면 ~이 나온다 A grape vine bleeds when cut. // 사탕단풍의 ~이 흐르기 시작하면 줄기에 칼금을 그어 그것을 받는다 Sugar maples are tapped when the sap begins to flow. 2 extract. ¶인삼의 ~ *insam*(ginseng) extract.

진언(進言) offering one's views; advice; counsel. **진언하다** advise; (문어) counsel; offer one's views; suggest. ¶그는 수상에게 양국 사이의 무역 증진에 대해 진언했다 He made a proposal to the Prime Minister about increasing [He advised the Prime Minister to increase] trade between the two countries.

진언(眞言) [불] the words of Buddha; holy words.

진역(震域) an old name for Korea.

진연(塵煙) [티끌] a cloud of dust; dust rising like a cloud.

진열(陳列) [예술 작품·제품 등의 전시] (an) exhibition; [죽 벌여 보이기] (a) display; show; arrangement. ¶~ 중인 상품 wares on show[display] // 화랑에 ~ 중인 그림 the paintings on exhibition[display] at the art gallery. **진열하다** exhibit; display; put on show; arrange. ¶가게에 상품을 ~ display articles in a shop // 선생님은 어린이들의 그림을 벽에 진열했다 The teacher exhibited the children's pictures on the wall. ➔¶우리들의 새 작품은 이 방에 진열되어 있다 Our new works are displayed[are on display] in this room.

●**진열관** a museum; an exhibition hall. ¶상품 ~ a commercial museum // 회화 ~ a (picture) gallery / an art gallery. **진열대** a display stand[counter]. **진열실** a showroom; a display room. **진열장**(-欌) a showcase; a display case; a show window. **진열창** a show window; a display window.

진영(陣營) [군대의 주둔지] a camp; a military encampment; an encampment. ¶자유 ~ the liberal camp // 동서 양 ~ 간의 긴장 the tension between the two camps of the East and the West[the East-West camps / the two power blocks of the world] // ~을 치다 encamp / pitch a camp // 양쪽 ~으로부터의 중립을 유지하다 stand aloof from both camps.

진영(眞影) a true image; a portrait; a picture; a likeness. ¶세종 대왕의 ~ a portrait of King Sejong.

진옥(眞玉) genuine jade.

진옴(한) watery itch.

진외가(陳外家) the parents' home of one's paternal grandmother.

진용(陣容) (a) battle formation; [배치] battle array; a disposition; a line-up. ¶신내각의 ~ the makeup of the new cabinet / the new cabinet lineup // 교사의 새 ~ a new lineup of teachers // ~을 재정비하다 reorganize the battle front // 공격의 ~이 정비되었다 The troops are arrayed[in position] for the attack. // 위원회의 새로운 ~이 발표되었다 The new members of the committee were announced. // 이 대학의 교수 ~은 훌륭하다 This university has a fine faculty. // 내각의 ~이 달라졌다 The Cabinet has been reshuffled.

진원(震源) [지] the seismic center[focus]; the center of an earthquake.

●**진원지** the seismic center; [비유] the center of the disturbance. ¶오늘의 ~는 목포 부근이었다 The center of today's earth quake lay near Mokpo. // 문제의 ~는 그였다 He was the originator of the trouble. // 소동 ~는 울산이었다 The disturbance originated in Ulsan.

진위(眞僞) truth and[or] falsehood; truth; authenticity; genuineness. ¶~를 확인하다 ascertain the truth (of) // 일[소문]의 ~를 확인해 보다 make sure of the truth of the matter[the story] // ~를 조사하다 examine [look into] the genuineness (of an article) // ~를 분별하다 discriminate truth from error // 그 ~는 분명하지 않다 It is of dubious authenticity.

진의(眞意) the real intention; the true motive [meaning]; the ultimate purpose. ¶그의 ~가 무엇인지 알 수 없다 I cannot see what he really means. // I cannot make out what he is driving at. // 내 ~는 거기에 있어 That is what I really mean. // 그의 ~는 배우가 되는 것이다 His real intention is to become an actor. // 그녀의 ~를 모르겠다 Her true motive is unknown. / I don't know what she really has in mind.

진의(眞義) the true meaning[signification].

진인(眞因) [사실상의 원인] the true cause; [사실상의 동기] the true motive; the real reason[ground]. ¶죽음의 ~ the real cause of (a person's) death.

진일 [물을 써서 하는 일] wet housework; chores in which one's hands get wet. ¶~로 손이 거칠어졌다 My hands chapped owing to the washing and scullery work.

진입(進入) entry (into a place); penetration. ¶제차(諸車) ~ 엄금 (게시) No thoroughfare. **진입하다** enter; go[penetrate] into; make one's way (into). ¶궤도에 ~ achieve[go into / enter into] orbit // 데모대[시위대]는 역전 광장으로 진입하였다 The demonstrators marched[made their way] into the square in front of the station. // 열차가 2번 선으로 진입해 오고 있었다 The train was approaching [coming in] on Track Two.

●**진입 금지** (게시) Do not enter. **진입등** an approach light. **진입로** (비행기 등의) an approach; an access road; (고속도로의) a ramp; (영) a slip road.

진잎 leaves of vegetables (esp. salted).

진자(振子) [물] a pendulum. ¶~의 진폭 the swing of a pendulum // ~가 원 위치로 돌아갔다 The pendulum swung back to its original position.

●**진자 시계** a pendulum clock.

진자리 1 [애를 갓 놓은 자리·갓 죽은 자리] the spot where a child was just born[a person just died]. 2 [똥오줌 싼 자리] a spot soiled by a child's urine[feces]. 3 [그 자리] the place; the spot. ¶~에서 then and there / on the spot / on that occasion.

진작 [그때에] then and there; on the spot; at once; on that occasion; [좀 더 일찍] earlier. ¶왜 ~ 말하지 않았니 You might have said so then and there. // ~ 말씀 못 드려 죄송합니다 I apologize for not having said this before. // ~ 갔어야 했다 You should have gone earlier. // ~부터 그를 만나고 싶었었다 I have long wanted to see him.

진작(振作) stimulation (to action); rousing. **진작하다** stir up; stimulate to action; rouse; shake up. ¶국민정신을 ~ arouse the national spirit. ➔¶사기를 진작시키다 stir up the morale (of troops).

진장(珍藏) keeping as treasure; treasuring. ¶~의 서(書) one's treasured[prized] books. **진장하다** treasure (up).

●**진장품** a treasured possession.

진재(震災) an earthquake disaster. ¶~의 지역 a district hit by an earthquake / an earthquake-stricken district // ~ 예방 (건물 등의) prevention of damage from earthquakes / (화재의) prevention of the disasters which result from earthquakes.

진저 〔생강과의 여러해살이풀〕 ginger.

진저리 〔몸을 떠는〕 a shiver after urinating; a quiver; a shudder; disgust; repugnance; aversion.

진저리(가) 나다 have a sudden feeling of disgust. ¶이 더위에는 진저리가 난다 I'm sick of this heat. / I've had enough of this heat. / This heat is too much for me.∥그의 끊임없는 불평에 나는 진저리가 났다 I was fed up with his perpetual complaining. / I was sick and tired of his perpetual complaining.∥이런 음식은 보기만 해도 진저리가 난다 The mere sight of such food revolts me.

진저리(를) 치다 shiver after urinating; shudder; be horrified. ¶전쟁 소리는 듣기만 해도 진저리를 치게 한다 The mere mention of a war makes me shudder.

진전(進展) 〔발전〕 development. ¶연구에 ~을 보다 advance in one's studies∥해는 과학에 큰 ~을 보았다 Science made great progress this year. **진전하다** progress; develop. ➔¶원활하게 진전되다 go on smoothly / make good progress∥사업을 진전시키다 develop one's business∥도시화가 진전됨에 따라 이 지방에서도 자연이 급속도로 사라져 간다 With the advance of urbanization, the natural environment is rapidly disappearing even from this district.∥협상은 급속히 진전되었다 The negotiations have made rapid progress.

진절머리 a shiver after urinating. ➪**진저리**

진정(眞情) 1〔진실한 마음〕 sincerity; true heart; genuine sentiment; true feelings. ¶~의 true / sincere / earnest / sane / ~으로 sincerely / truly / seriously∥~으로 사랑하는 사람 a person one likes from the bottom of one's heart∥자기 ~을 털어놓다 reveal one's true feelings∥~을 토로하다 express[show] one's true heart∥당신의 친절에 ~으로 감사 드립니다 I heartly[sincerely] thank you for your kindness.∥그 말씀은 ~입니까 Do you mean what you say[to say so]? 2〔진실한 사정〕 the true facts of a case; the true state; the true picture.

진정(陳情) a representation; a petition; an appeal. ¶~을 받아들이다 grant a petition / recognize a representation∥~을 각하하다 reject[spurn / turn down] a petition[representation]. **진정하다** 〔청원하다〕 make a representation (to / against); lay (the case) before (the authorities); petition (the authorities); make a plea[an appeal] (to); appeal (to the authorities). ¶그들은 그 법안을 철회하도록 정부에 진정했다 They petitioned the government to withdraw the bill.

● **진정서** a (written) representation; a petition. ¶~를 작성하다 draw up a petition∥우리는 정부에 ~를 제출했다 We presented [sent in / hand in] a petition to the government. / We filed a petition with the government authorities. **진정자** a petitioner.

진정(進呈) 〔자진하여 드림〕 presentation. ¶견본 무료 ~ 〔광고〕 Write for free samples. / Samples sent free on application. **진정하다** give; present (a person) with (a thing); present (a thing) to (a person); make (a person) a present of (a thing). ¶무료로 ~ be presented free∥홍 씨에게 진정함 To [Presented to] Mr. Hong∥신청하는 대로 견본을 진정함 Samples sent on application.

진정(鎭定) suppression; repression; subdual. **진정하다** suppress; repress; subdue; pacify; quell; tranquil(l)ize. ¶반란을 ~ suppress [put down / quell] a revolt.

진정(鎭靜) calm; quiet; tranquil(l)ity; appeasement; pacification. **진정하다** calm; quiet; (고통 등을) soothe; allay; appease; abate; (소동 등을) tranquil(l)ize; pacify. ¶마음을 ~ calm oneself (down)∥노여움을 ~ (자기의) quell[appease] one's anger / (남의) calm[appease] (a person's) anger∥제발 진정하게 Calm down. / Take it easy. / Don't be [get] so excited. / Cool it. / Simmer down. / Chill out. ➔¶그녀는 다시는 그런 일을 하지 않겠다는 약속을 하여 아버지의 노여움을 진정시켜 드렸다 She appeased her father's anger by promising never to do it again.∥소란이 진정되었다 The commotion subsided[died down].∥그의 조용한 어조는 그들의 흥분을 진정시켰다 His quiet tone cooled their excitement.∥그의 노여움은 진정되었다 His anger cooled off. / He calmed down.∥인플레는 진정되어 평년처럼 3퍼센트 내외가 되었다 Inflation has settled down at an annual rate of about three percent.

● **진정제** a sedative; a calmative; a tranquil(l)izer.

진정(眞正) 〔참으로〕 genuinely; authentically; truly. ¶그는 아들을 ~ 사랑했다 He truly loved his son.

진정하다(眞正-) genuine; authentic; real; true; pure. ¶진정한 의미에서 in the true sense of the world∥진정한 친구 one's bosom friend∥진정한 우정 true friendship∥진정한 인류에 genuine love for humanity∥진정한 민주주의를 고찰하다 consider what true democracy is[what a true democracy should be]∥그는 진정한 크리스트교도이다 He is a real[genuine] Christian.∥그는 진정한 신사다 He is a gentleman to the score.∥나는 그에게 진정한 축하의 말을 보냈다 I sent sincere words of congratulation to him. / I sent him my heartfelt congratulations.

진종일(盡終日) all day (long). ➪**온종일**

진주(眞珠) a pearl. ¶모조[양식] ~ an imitation[a culture(d)] pearl∥인조 ~ an artificial[a false / an imitation] pearl∥흑 ~ a black[pink] pearl∥핑크색 ~ pink pearl∥~ 같은 pearly∥~ 박은 반지 a ring set with a pearl∥~ 캐는 사람 a pearl diver[fisher]∥~를 채취하다 fish[dive] for pearls / pearl∥그것은 돼지에게 ~를 던져 주는 것과 같다 That's like casting pearls before swine.

● **진주 목걸이** a pearl necklace. **진주 양식** pearl culture; the culture of pearls. **진주 양식장** a pearl farm[bed]. **진주잡이** / **진주 채취** pearl fishery; pearling; (채취자) a pearl diver [fisher]; a pearler. **진주조개** a pearl oyster [shell]; a pearl-oyster's shell.

진주(進駐) 〔진군하여 주둔함〕 occupation; stationing; stay; 〔진입〕 an entry (into). **진주하다** stay; be stationed (at); advance (into); make an (armed) entry (into).

● **진주군** stationary troops; (점령지의) occupation forces

진중(陣中) ¶~에 in camp / in the ranks / in the field / at the front∥적의 ~으로 돌격하다 rush (bravely) into the ranks of the enemy.

● **진중 일기** a staff diary; a field [war] diary.

진중하다(鎭重─) sedate; gentle; grave; dignified. ¶진중한 발걸음으로 with a dignified step / with a solemn pace∥그는 행동이 ~ He is prudent in his behavior. **진중히** sedately; gently; gravely.

진중하다(珍重─) valuable; precious; treasured. **진중히** valuably; preciously. ¶~ 여기다 highly esteem[value] / prize / treasure / set great store by / make[think] much of∥기념물으로 ~ 여기겠습니다 I shall prize it as a keepsake.∥우리는 그 꽃병을 ~ 여겼다 We prized[valued] the vase highly. / We treasured[cherished] the vase.

진지 a meal. ⇨¹밥2 ¶~ 잡수셨습니까 Have you had your breakfast[dinner / supper]?

진지(陣地) [군] a military camp site; a position; an encampment. ¶아군 ~ one's own position[encampment]∥가설 ~ a temporary position∥본 ~ the main position∥포병 ~ an artillery position∥견고한 ~ a stronghold∥~를 점령하다 occupy[carry] a position∥~를 잃다 lose the field∥~를 철수하다 evacuate[withdraw from] a position / decamp / break camp∥~를 고수[탈환]하다 hold[recover] a position∥~를 사수하다 defend a position to the last∥적의 ~를 빼앗았다 We dislodged the enemy from their position.∥저 ~를 공략하면 적은 우리 손안에 들게 된다 If we take that position we'll have the enemy within our grasp.∥완강한 저항을 시도한 끝에 적은 ~를 철퇴했다 After stubborn resistance the enemy evacuated its [his] lines.
● **진지전** position operations; position warfare; position-war.

진지하다(眞摯─) serious; earnest; sober. ¶진지하게 earnestly / in earnest / single-mindedly∥진지한 얼굴 an intense[a serious] face∥진지한 태도 a sincere attitude∥진지한 사람 a sincere person / a serious(-minded) person∥진지한 경기 a game played in real earnest[(구어) for keeps]∥진지한 얼굴로 with a serious[an earnest] look∥진지하게 생각[고려]하다 give (a matter) a serious consideration / take (a matter) seriously∥진지하게 살다 live honestly / live straight∥그는 아주 진지한 사람이다 He is sobriety itself.∥허튼소리 그만하고 그것을 진지하게 읽어 보게 Stop your nonsense, and read it seriously.∥나는 인생에 관하여 진지하게 생각한다 I think seriously[earnestly] about life.∥나는 진지합니다 I am serious[in earnest / (구어) in dead earnest].∥ / I mean what I say [(구어) business].∥그는 항상 진지하지 못하다 He never takes things seriously enough. ∥그는 진지하게 연구에 몰두하고 있다 He is completely absorbed in his research. / He is intent upon[on] his studies.∥그 일은 진지하게 생각할 필요가 있다 It requires grave [sober] reflection.∥그런 농담은 그만 하고 좀 진지한 얘기를 하자 I have had enough of such jokes. Let's talk sense.

진진하다(津津─) overflowing; brimful; brim with; (서술적) be full of. ¶맛이 ~ be tasteful∥흥미는 be highly interesting / be an unfailing fountain of interest.

진집 [가늘게 벌어진 틈] a gap; a crevice; an opening; an aperture; a crack. ¶~이 나다 develop[have] a crack[an opening].

진짜(眞─) 1 [참된 것] a genuine article; the real stuff[thing]. ¶~의 genuine / real / true / [전거(典據)가 있는] authentic∥~ 진주 a natural[genuine] pearl∥~ 루벤스(의 그림) an authentic[a genuine] Rubens∥파리 사람[토박이] a Parisian to the core[born and bred]∥~ 와 똑같은 초상화 a lifelike portrait∥~ 16세기의 고문서 authentic manuscripts of the 16th century∥~와 같이 만들다 imitate to the life∥~와 가짜를 가리다 tell the real[originals] from the false [imitations]∥~와 모조품을 분간하는 것은 전문가가 아니면 할 수 없다 It takes an expert to tell an imitations from the original[real thing].∥그 사람의 피아노 솜씨는 ~다 He play the piano like a real[professional] artist.
2 truly; really; heartly. ¶그는 ~ 화를 냈다 He flew into a genuine rage.

진짜로(眞─) truly; really. ⇨²진짜2

진찰(診察) (a) medical examination. ¶세밀한 ~을 받다 have oneself carefully examined∥의사의 ~을 받다 consult a physician / see a doctor (for his medical advice)∥나는 적어도 1년에 한 번은 의사의 ~을 받는다 I have to consult a doctor at least once a year.∥의사의 ~을 받는 편이 좋겠다 You'd better see[consult] a doctor.∥~ 무료 (게시) Consultation free. **진찰하다** examine[see / have a look at] (a patient). ¶의사가 환자를 진찰했다 The doctor examined the patient.∥오늘은 어느 선생님이 진찰하십니까 Which doctor is seeing patients [on duty] today?
● **진찰권** a consultation ticket. **진찰료** a consultation fee; a doctor's bill. ¶~는 얼마입니까 (진찰 후에) How much do I owe you? / What's the fee, please? / (일반적으로) How much do you charge for a consultation? **진찰실** a consultation[consulting] room.

진창 mud; a muddy place[spot] (in a road); mire; a quagmire. ¶~에 발을 들여놓다 step into the mud∥~에 빠지다 get stuck in the mud∥~ 속을 걷다 trudge in the mud∥~에서 빠져나오다 pull oneself out of the mire∥발이 ~에 빠졌다 My feet got stuck in the mud.∥빗물이 흘러들어 봉당은 ~이 되어 버렸다 The dirt floor was turned to mud by the rainwater which had run in. / Rainwater had run in and turned the dirt floor to mud.
● **진창길** a muddy road; a sloppy road.

진척(進陟) 1 (일의) progress; (an) advance. ¶~ 중이다 be under way / be in progress∥~이 없다 make no[little] progress / be slow in progress∥현저한 ~을 보이다 show marked progress. **진척하다** advance; progress; make (good) progress; make headway. →¶진척시키다 hasten / speed up / accelerate∥공사를 빨리 진척시키다 speed up construction∥그의 연구는 진척되고 있다[진척되지 않고 있다] His research is making rapid [little] progress.∥일은 만족스럽게 진척되고 있다 The work is making satisfactory progress.∥만사가 순조롭게 진척되고 있다 Everything is going very smoothly[well].∥일은 그 단계까지 진척되지 않았다 It has not reached that stage yet.∥공사는 순조로이[급속도로] 진척되고 있다 The (construction) work is making steady[rapid] progress. / The work is moving ahead steadily[rapidly].∥건축 공사가 잘 진척되지 않아 비용이 늘어났다 The construction work progressed very slowly

and costs mounted up. // 한미 협상이 진척되고 있다 The Korea-American negotiations are making good progress. // 그 교량 공사가 진척되고 있다 The construction of the bridge is under way [in progress].
2 [벼슬이 올라감] promotion; advancement; rise (in rank). **진척하다** be promoted [advanced] (to).

진출(進出) advance; march; [군] debouchment. ¶한국 제품의 해외 ~ the advance of Korean-made goods into foreign markets // 여성의 사회 ~ participation of women in public affairs. **진출하다** advance (into); go [launch] (into); find one's way (into); branch out (into); [군] debouch. ¶해외 시장에 ~ [판로를 개척하다] find a market abroad / [파고들다] make inroads into foreign markets // 정계에 ~ go into politics // 실업계에 ~ enter the business world // 그녀는 이 작품으로 문단에 진출했다 With this work, she made her debut in literary circles. // 그녀는 정구 시합에서 준결승에 진출했다 In the tennis tournament, she advanced to the semifinals. // 그는 큰 슈퍼마켓을 개점하여 그 도시의 상업 지역에 진출했다 He moved in on the business section of the city by opening a large supermarket there.

진취(進就) making gradual achievement [progress]. **진취하다** make gradual progress.

진취성(進取性) a progressive [an enterprising] spirit.

진취적(進取的) progressive; enterprising; 《미국 구어》 go-ahead. ¶~인 기상 an enterprising spirit. // 그는 ~인 기상이 넘치고 있다 He is full of enterprise.

진탕(-宕) to one's heart's content; as one likes; freely. ¶~ 먹다[마시다] eat [drink] one's fill.

진탕(震盪·振盪) concussion; a shock. ¶뇌~ cerebral concussion / the concussion of the brain. **진탕하다** get a shock [concussion]; give a shock; shake.

진토(塵土) dust and dirt.

진통(陣痛) labor pains; travail; throes; pangs of childbirth(분만 시의). ¶~ 중이다 be in travail [labor] / ~을 겪다 suffer throes [pangs] (of childbirth) / feel pains // ~이 시작되다 begin to labor / have [feel] labor pains / suffer the pains [throes] of childbirth // ~이 일어나고 있다 be in labor // 그녀의 ~이 시작되었다 Her labor has started. / She has begun to have labor pains. / She has gone into labor.

진통(鎭痛) alleviation [soothing] of pain.
●**진통제** an anodyne; an analgesic; a painkiller; a pain-killing drug; a balm. ¶~를 주세요 Give me something for [to relieve] the pain.

진퇴(進退) **1** [나아감과 물러감] advance and retreat; movement. ¶~의 자유를 잃다 be unable to move / [오도 가도 못하다] get stalled (in the mud) / be stranded. **2** (사임이나 유임이냐의) resigning and remaining in office. ¶나의 ~ 여부는 오로지 이 시도의 결과 여하에 달려 있다 Whether I must resign or I can continue in my office all depends on the result of this attempt.
●**진퇴양난** a dilemma; a (tight) fix; a predicament. ¶~이다 [~에 빠지다] be driven to the wall [corner] / be in a dilemma [fix] / be on the horns of a dilemma / find oneself between two fires / 《구어》 be up a (gum) tree // 인파 속에 파묻혀 나는 ~이었다 In the crowd of people I was unable to move. // 우리는 ~에 빠졌다 We were caught between Scylla and Charybdis [between the devil and the deep blue sea].

진펄 a bog; a swamp; a marsh.

진폐(증)(塵肺症) [의] pneumoconiosis.

진폭(振幅) [물] amplitude (of vibration). ¶진자의 ~ the swing of a pendulum.
●**진폭 변조** [전] amplitude modulation(약어 AM).

진폭(震幅) a seismic amplitude; the amplitude of an earthquake.

진풀 wet starch.

진품(珍品) a rare article; a rarity; a curio; a curiosity. ¶벽감에는 밀레의 ~이 걸려 있다 A rare painting by Millet is hanging in the alcove.

진품(眞品) a sterling [genuine] article.

진피(眞皮) [생] the thick skin; the true [inner] skin; the dermis.

진하다(盡-) [다하다] be exhausted; be spent; be used up; come to an end; run out. ¶기운이 ~ feel exhausted // 운이 ~ run out of luck.

진하다(津-) **1** (빛깔이) dark; deep; saturated. ¶진한 빛 a dark color // 진한 갈색 dark [deep] brown color / a dark shade of brown // 진한 빛깔의 커튼 a curtain of deep colors // 진하게 화장한 여자 a thickly painted woman. **2** (액체가) thick; heavy; strong(맛이). ¶진한 수프 thick [rich] soup // 진한 차[커피] strong tea [coffee] // (요리에서) 진하게 하는 것 a liaison / 맛이 진한 요리 a filling [rich] dish(▶ filing 은 만복감(滿腹感)을 주다, rich는 기름지거나 단맛이 많다는 뜻) // 고깃국물 소스를 진하게 하는 재료 a thickening [thickener] for gravy // 이 커피는 너무 ~ This coffee is too strong for me.

진학(進學) entrance into a school of higher grade. **진학하다** go on to the next stage of one's education. ¶그는 대학으로 진학할 작정이다 《미》 He intends to go to college [a university]. / 《영》 He intends to go to university. // 이 학교 학생의 80프로가 대학에 진학한다 Eighty percent of the students at this school go on to [enter] universities.
●**진학률** the ratio of students who go on to a higher stage of education. **진학 지망자** a student wishing to go on to a school of higher grade.

진항(進航) sailing; navigation. **진항하다** make headway [seaway]; steam; sail.

진해제(鎭咳劑) a cough remedy [mixture].

진행(進行) progress; progression; (an) advance; march; onward movement. ¶공사의 급속한 ~ the rapid progress being made in the construction work // ~ 중이다 be in progress / be on the move / be going on / be under way // ~이 빠르다[느리다] make rapid [slow] progress // ~을 계속하다 continue in one's course / (의사(議事)의) proceed with (the business) // ~을 방해하다 hinder [impede] the progress (of) / 의사(議事)의 ~을 도모[방해]하다 facilitate (or expedite) [obstruct] proceedings. // 사건의 조사가 현재 ~ 중이다 An investigation of the

진형 matter is now under way.∥논문의 ~ 상태가 어떻습니까 How are you getting on with your thesis?∥이 길을 죽 가면 ~ 방향에서 오른편에 은행이 있습니다 As you go along this street, you'll find a bank on your right. **진행하다** advance; be advanced; progress; make progress; proceed; go on [forward]; make headway; (탈것이) run; move; be in motion; (배가) proceed; steam; sail; head (for); make seaway. ¶순조롭게 ~ progress favorably [smoothly]∥그는 진행하는 열차에서 뛰어내렸다 He jumped off a moving train.∥일이 순조롭게 진행하고 있다 The work is progressing [going] smoothly [well]. ➔¶의사를 진행시키다 expedite the proceedings∥자기에게 편리하도록 일을 진행시키다 proceed with things to suit one's own convenience∥시합을 제 페이스에 맞추어 잘 진행시키다 move a game [match] forward at one's own pace∥회의는 원활히 진행되었다 The conference went forward [proceeded] very smoothly.
● **진행계**(-係) a program director; [사회자] the master of ceremonies. **진행형** [언] the progressive form. ¶현재 [과거 / 미래] ~ the present [past / future] progressive form.

진형(陣形) (battle / camp) formation; battle array. ¶방어 [공격] ~ a defensive [an offensive] disposition∥~을 갖추고 전진하다 move forward [advance] in formation.

진혼(鎭魂) repose of souls.
● **진혼곡** a requiem. **진혼 미사** a requiem [Requiem] (mass). **진혼제** a service for the repose of the deceased [departed soul].

진홍(색) (眞紅色) crimson; cardinal (red); (deep) scarlet. ¶~의 crimson / cardinal∥~ 옷을 입다 wear scarlet / be dressed in crimson [scarlet].

진화(進化) [생] evolution; progress. ¶정향~ orthogenesis∥인류의 ~ human evolution / the evolution of man∥~적인 evolutional / evolutionary∥~적으로 evolutionally. **진화하다** evolve [develop] (from ... into ...). ¶인간은 원숭이에서 진화했다고 한다 Man is said to have evolved from the ape. ➔¶진화시키다 evolve.
● **진화론** [생] the theory [doctrine] of evolution; the evolution(ary) theory. ¶~적 [상의] evolutionistic / evolutionary. **진화론자** an evolutionist.

진화(鎭火) extinguishment of a fire; putting out a fire. ¶~에 힘쓰다 fight a fire. **진화하다** (불이) be extinguished; be put out; (불을) extinguish; put out; bring under control. ➔¶마침내 산불은 3시에 간신히 진화되었다 The forest fire was finally brought under control [finally died down] at three.∥이웃집의 작은 화재는 쉽게 진화되었다 The small fire next door was easily put out [extinguished].

진휼(賑恤) relief; almsgiving. **진휼하다** relieve (famine).
● **진휼금** alms.

진흙 1 [물기 섞인 흙] mud; mire; dirt. ¶~투성이의 구두 muddy shoes / shoes covered [caked] with mud(▶ caked는 마른 진흙)∥~투성이의 길 a muddy road∥~투성이가 되다 be covered with mud [dirt] / get muddy∥~에 빠지다 stick in the mud∥구두의 ~을 털다 scrape the mud from one's shoes∥아이들은 ~투성이가 되어 돌아왔다 The children came home covered with mud. 2 [점토] clay. ¶~ 덩어리 a lump of clay∥~의 clay∥~ 같은 clayey∥~으로 만든 상(像) a figure in clay / a clay figure.
● **진흙탕** (morasses of) mud. ¶~이다 be muddy [miry].

진흥(振興) promotion; furtherance; rousing; awakening. ¶무역 ~ the promotion of foreign trade∥산업 [수출]의 ~을 꾀하다 promote the development of industry [exports]∥그 협회는 과학의 ~을 목적으로 설립되었다 The association was established for the advancement of science [to further scientific] research. **진흥하다** [조성하다] promote; help forward; further; advance; encourage; [진작하다] arouse; awaken; stir up; inspire.
● **진흥책** measures for the promotion [advancement / furtherance] (of).

질 potter's clay; unglazed clay.

-질 [노릇·짓의 뜻] (the act of) doing. ¶양치~ rinsing the mouth∥톱~ sawing∥바느~ sewing∥서방~ adultery.

질(帙) 1 [책갑] a folding case (for a book [books]); a wrapper. 2 [책의 한 벌] a set of books. ¶이 책은 5권으로 한 ~이다 This book is complete in five volumes.

질(質) 1 [품질·소질] quality. ¶~이 좋다 [나쁘다] be of good [bad] quality / be superior [inferior] in quality∥~이 다르다 differ in quality∥~을 높이다 [떨어뜨리다] improve [lower] the quality∥양보다 ~ Quality over quantity. / Quality is more important than quantity. 2 [자질] nature; disposition; [체질] constitution; [특질] characteristic; [본질] property; [품성] character. ¶~이 나쁜 범죄 a vicious crime∥뛰어나게 ~이 좋은 학생 an exceptionally brilliant student∥~이 좋은 [나쁜] good [ill-]natured / well-[ill-]disposed / (일의) of good [bad] character [nature] / (병 등의) benignant [malignant]∥~이 나쁜 장난 a mean trick∥~이 다르다 be cast in different molds / be of another [a different] stamp∥~이 같다 be cast in the same mold.

질(膣) [생] the vagina (pl. ~s, -nae).

질겁하다 be appalled; be astounded; be frightened; be scared; start; take fright; be surprised; be startled; be taken aback. ¶질겁해서 말을 못 하다 be struck dumb with consternation∥그 소식을 듣고 ~ be shocked at [by / to hear] the news∥총소리에 ~ start at the sound of a rifle shot∥그 소리에 그녀는 질겁했다 The noise brought her heart up into her mouth.

질겅질겅 chewing; gnawing. ¶~ 씹다 chew away at (it)∥껌을 ~ 씹다 chew gum noisily.

질경이 [식] a (broad-leaved) plantain; a whiteman's foot.

질곡(桎梏) fetters; bonds; a yoke. ¶~을 벗어나다 break [shake off] the fetters [bonds] (of) / cast [fling / shake / throw] off the yoke (of) / break away from the yoke (of)∥독재 정치의 ~에서 벗어나다 break the fetters [chains] of autocracy∥그들은 인습의 ~에 사로잡혀 있다 They are fettered by convention.

질권(質權) the right of pledge; (주로 부동산의) the mortgage right. ¶~을 설정하다 establish the right of pledge.

●**질권 설정자** a pledger; a pledg(e)or. **질권자** a pledgee; a pawnee.

질그릇 a pottery (ware); (집합적) unglazed pottery; earthenware.

질근질근 [꼬는 모양] weave (a string / a rope) slowly[leisurely]; [씹는 모양] chewing.

질금거리다 trickle; dribble. ⇨ˮ찔끔거리다

질기다 1 (고기 등이) tough; leathery. ¶질긴 고기 tough meat // 이 스테이크는 ~ This (beef) steak is tough. // 이 고기는 너무 질겨서 씹을 수 없었다 The meat was too tough to chew. **2** [내구성이 있다] durable; lasting; enduring. ¶질긴 천 coarse cloth / 질긴 종이 paper that does not tear easily // 이것은 질긴 옷감이다 This is sturdy cloth. **3** (성질이) tenacious; pertinacious; persistent; persevering; tough. ¶성질이 질긴 남자 a man of tenacity / (미) a tough guy.

질기와 an earthen (roofing) tile.

질깃질깃하다 gummy; rubbery. ⇨ˮ졸깃졸깃하다

질끈 (tying) tight; firmly; fast. ¶머리에 ~ 동여맨 수건 a twisted towel worn around one's head // 허리띠를 ~ 매다 gird oneself tight.

질녀(姪女) a niece. ⇨ˮ조카딸(⇨조카)

질다 1 (반죽·밥이) soft; slushy; watery. ¶밥이 너무 질게 되었다 The rice has come out too soft[slushy]. **2** (땅이) muddy; slushy; messy; wet. ¶진 길 a muddy road.

질동이 a clay[an earthen] jar.

질뚝배기 a large clay bowl.

질량(質量) [물] mass; quantity of matter. ●**질량 단위** (원자의) a mass unit. **질량 보존[불변]의 법칙** the law of conservation [constancy] of mass. **질량수** mass number.

질러가다 take a short way[shortcut]; cut across (a field). ¶길을 ~ go by a shorter way.

질러오다 come by a short way[shortcut].

질름거리다 brim over; give in small amounts. ⇨ˮ찔름거리다¹·²

질리다¹ **1** [진력나다] be disgusted[bored] (with); be sick (of); be fed up (with); have had enough (of); [혼나다] have a bitter experience. ¶이번 일에 질려서 this taught me a lesson and ... // 그는 한 번의 실패에 질려서 두 번 다시 손댈 엄두가 안 났다 A single failure discouraged him from another trial[made him shy of trying it again]. // 그 수수께끼에는 질렸어 That riddle had me stumped[(영) flummoxed]. // 그가 늘 하는 허튼소리에 질리고 말았어 All his usual nonsense got on my nerves. // 날카로운 질문에 그는 질렸다 The pointed question put him on the spot. / He was at his wit's end how to answer the pointed question. / (영국 구어) The pointed question flummoxed him. // 나는 그의 집요함[끈질김]에 질렸다 I am annoyed by his persistence. / (구어) I can't stand the way he keeps bugging me. // 그 철학 책에 나는 질렸다 That book on philosophy was too much for me. // 그의 옹고집에는 질렸다 His pigheadedness was just too much (to take). **2** (기가) be amazed[stunned / aghast / dumfounded]; [겁내다] be cowed; cower; (파랗게) be overawed; turn (ghastly) pale. ¶무서워서 파랗게 ~ turn deadly pale[as white as a sheet] with fright / blanch with fear // 질려서 말도 못하다 be (struck) dumb with amazement / be dumfounded (at) // 그는 아버지 앞에서는 기가 질려서 말 한마디 못한다 When his father is present, he loses his nerve and can't say a thing. // 사람들이 공포에 질려 달아났다 Seized with[Caught up by] panic, the people fled. **3** (물감이) dye unevenly; (값이) cost.

질리다² [채다] get a kick; get kicked; be booted; be struck; be hit. ¶영구리를 ~ get a kick on the side / 정강이를 ~ be[get] kicked on the shin.

질문(質問) a question; a query; an inquiry; an interrogation; a quiz; an interpellation(국회에서의). ¶긴급 일반 ~ (국회에서의) an emergency[a general] interpellation // 날카로운 ~ a pointed[poignant] question // 짓궂은 ~ a captious question / 급소를 찌른 ~, a home[very pertinent] question // ~에 답변하다 answer a question // ~ 공세를 당하다 face a barrage[volley] of questions // ~을 퍼붓다 rain[shower] questions on (a person) / deluge[pelt] (a person) with questions // ~을 받다 be questioned / ~을 끝내다 put an end to questions / bring interpellations to a close // ~을 되풀이하다 repeat one's question // ~ 없습니까 Are there[Have you] any questions? // 학생들은 선생님에게 ~을 퍼부었다 The students rained questions on the teacher. // 나는 ~ 공세를 당하여 매우 난처했다 I was hit by a barrage of questions and didn't know how to deal with the situation. // ~을 하나 하겠습니다 I will ask you a question. **질문하다** ask (a person) a question; put a question (to a person); question; interrogate; (미) quiz; (국회에서) interpellate. ¶성가시게 ~ pester[plague / persecute] (a person) with questions // 잇달아 ~ fire (off) questions (at) / discharge[fire off] a volley of questions (at) / ask question after question in quick succession / fling rapid-fire questions // 질문해도 좋습니까 May I ask you a question? // 그는 질문하다가 그만두었다 He started asking, but stopped.
●**질문서** a written inquiry; an interrogation; (프) a questionnaire(조사용의). **질문자** a questioner; an interrogator; interpellator(국회에서의).

질물(質物) a pawn; a pledge.

질박하다(質樸-·質朴-) simple and unadorned; (마음이) simple (and honest); simple-hearted[-minded]; unsophisticated.

질벅거리다 be wet and soft; be muddy. ¶길이 패 질벅거렸다 It was a very muddy walk.

질번질번하다 abundant; plentiful; affluent; wealthy; well-to-do. ¶질번질번하게 살다 live in clover / be well-to-do.

질병(疾病) a disease; a sickness; a malady; a disorder. ¶소화기 계통의 ~ a disorder of the digestive system // ~과 싸우다 combat [fight] a disease.

질부(姪婦) a nephew's wife. ⇨ˮ조카며느리(⇨조카)

질빵 a shoulder-pack strap; a backstrap. ¶~을 지다 have a back-sack strapped across one's chest.

질산(窒酸) [화] nitric acid.
●**질산염** nitrate. **질산은** silver nitrate; lunar [common] caustic. **질산칼륨** potassium nitrate.

질색(窒塞) [아주 싫음] disgust; detestation;

abhorrence; abomination; dismay; shock; horror. ¶나는 부정을 ~이다 I abhor[have an abhorrence of] injustice.∥그런 방법은 ~이다 That way of doing it is detestable.∥나는 그런 일을 한다는 것은 ~이야 I wouldn't do such a thing for anything.∥그녀를 불러내면 어때? 그녀는 네게 반했어." "그 여자 말이야 난 ~이야." (구어) "Come on, why don't you ask her out? She's got a real crush on you." "Her? No way!"∥그런 녀석하고 어울리는 것은 딱 ~이다 I don't want his company on any account. / I don't want anything to do with him, no matter what!∥자네 설교는 그만 하지, 난 ~이야 No more your lectures, please! / I've had enough of your lectures!∥그는 재즈라면 딱 ~이다 He has an instinctive dislike of jazz. / He has an antipathy to [against] jazz.∥나는 전쟁은 ~이다 I hate war. / No more war.∥그 사람은 ~이다 I don't want anything to do with him.∥그 녀석은 다루기 까다로워 내게는 ~이다 I just can't handle him, so I avoid him like the plague. **질색하다** hate; detest; loathe; abhor.(▶ hate, loathe는 일반적으로 심한 증오를 나타내고, detest는 경멸감을 내포함. abhor는 증오와 반감, 거부감 등을 나타냄) ¶남을 질색하고 싫어하다 hate a person like poison∥그녀는 그 사나이를 독사 대하듯 질색했다 She abhorred[detested / loathed] the man as if he were a viper.

질서(秩序) (public) order; [규율] discipline; [체계] system; regularity; method. ¶사회의 ~ public[social] order∥새 ~ a new order∥~ 있는 orderly / methodical / systematic∥~ 없는 disorderly / disordered / unsystematic / unmethodical / unorganized / irregular / confused / undisciplined∥~ 정연하게 in good[perfect] order∥**정연하다** be in good[perfect / apple-pie] order∥~가 문란해 있다 be in disorder / be in a state of confusion∥~를 확립[회복]하다 establish [restore] order∥~를 어지럽히다 disturb [upset] order∥사회의 ~를 유지하다 maintain[keep / preserve] public order∥그들은 ~ 정연하게 일한다 They work systematically.

질소(窒素) [화] nitrogen(기호 N). ¶공중 ~ atmospheric[air] nitrogen∥과산화~ nitrogen proxide∥산화~ nitric oxide∥석회~ nitrolime[calcium cyanamide].
● **질소 가스** nitrogen gas. **질소 폭탄** a nitrogen bomb. **질소 화합물** a nitrogenous compound.

질솥 an earthen pot[oven].

질시(嫉視) jealousy; regarding with jealousy [dislike]; jealous looks. ¶~를 받다 be regarded with jealousy. **질시하다** regard (a person) with jealousy; keep a jealous eye on (a person).

질식(窒息) suffocation; asphyxiation; asphyxia; asphyxy. ¶~성의 suffocative / asphyxiating. **질식하다** be suffocated[choked / stifled / smothered]; be asphyxiated.∥질식해서 죽다 be suffocated[choked] to death / die from[by] suffocation∥그는 질식하여 죽었다 He died from[of] suffocation.∥He suffocated[choked] to death. ➔¶**질식시키다** suffocate / asphyxiate / choke (off) / stifle / smother∥갓난아기는 무거운 담요 밑에 깔려 질식되어 죽었다 The baby had been smothered under the heavy blankets.
● **질식사** death from suffocation.

질염(膣炎) [의] vaginitis; colpitis.

질의(質疑) a question; an interrogation; an inquiry; an interpellation(국회에서의). ¶대정부 ~ (국회의원의) a parliamentary interpellation∥~에 답하다 answer a question∥강사는 청중의 ~에 답(변)했다 The lecturer answered the question asked by the audience.∥이것으로 ~를 마치겠다 With this, we will bring the questions to an end.
● **질의 연설** (국회에서의) an interpellation. ¶~을 하다 address an interpellation (on a matter to a minister). **질의응답** question and answer. ¶~이 있은 후 의안이 표결되었다 After questions and answers the bill was put to the vote. **질의자** a questioner; an interrogator; an interpellater.

질적(質的) qualitative. ¶~ 변화 a qualitative change∥~으로 qualitatively / in quality∥~으로나 양적으로나 quantitatively as well as qualitatively / both in quality and in quantity∥~으로 다르다 differ in quality / (성질 등이) be cast in different molds∥이 물건은 ~으로 별로 좋지 않다 Qualitatively (speaking) [In (terms of) quality], this article is not very good.

질주(疾走) a scamper; a scud; a scuttle. **질주하다** scuttle; scamper; scud; spank; run at full speed[like a shot]; dash. ¶질주하는 자동차 a speeding motorcar∥그는 내리막길을 질주했다 He dashed[tore] down the slope.

질질 1 [물건을 끄는 모양] draggingly; trailingly. ¶지친 발을 ~ 끌다 drag[shuffle] one's weary feet∥치맛자락을 ~ 끌며 걷다 walk with a trailing skirt / trail one's skirt∥그들은 무엇인가 무거운 것을 ~ 끌고 갔다 They were dragging something heavy.∥그녀는 치맛자락을 ~ 끌고 갔다 The bottom of her dress was dragging (along)[trailing along] on the floor.
2 [오래 끄는 모양] long; draggingly; lingering. ¶~ 끄는 병 a lingering disease∥(시간·행사 등이) ~ 오래 끌다 trail on / drag on∥재판은 ~ 끌었다 The trial dragged on [along].∥전쟁이 ~ 오래 끌었다 The war dragged on.
3 [흐르는 모양] tricklingly; dribbling. ¶기름기가 ~ 흐르는 얼굴 an oily face∥콧물을 ~ 흘리다 run at the nose / snivel∥침을 ~ 흘리다 drivel freely / dribble (at the mouth)∥오줌을 ~ 싸다 dribble urine.

질질거리다 [이리저리 쏘다니다] roam around; gad about; (미국 속어) bum around.

질책(叱責) (a) reproof; reproach; rebuke; reprimand. **질책하다** scold; reprove; reproach; rebuke; reprimand; call (a person) to task; give (a person) a talking-to; call (a person) on the carpet. ¶부주의를 ~ reproach [reprimand / reprove] (a person) for his carelessness∥그는 아들을 심하게 질책하였다 He scolded his son severely. / He gave his son a sharp reprimand. ➔¶**질책받다 [당하다]** receive a reprimand (from) / be scolded (by).

질책(帙冊) [한 벌의 책] a set of books; a set in (several) volumes; books enclosed in a case.

질척거리다 (길이) be muddy; be miry; (눈이 녹아) be slushy; (죽 모양으로) mushy; soppy;

sloppy. ¶눈이 녹아 질척거리는 길 a muddy road caused by melting of snow / a slushy road∥길은 몹시 질척거렸다 It was a very muddy walk.

질척질척 muddily; like mush; sloppily; slushily. **질척질척하다** muddy; sloppy; sludgy; slushy. ¶질척질척한 경마장 a sloppy racetrack∥질척질척해지다 become sloppy.

질척하다 soft and wet; muddy; sludgy; slushy; sloppy; soppy; mushy.

질컥하다 muddy; gooey; sludgy; slushy; sloppy.

질타(叱咤) (a) scolding. **질타하다** scold; rate; give (a person) a (good) scolding.

질탕관(－湯罐) a pipkin.

질탕하다(跌宕・佚蕩－) riotous; racketing; bacchanal(ian); saturnalian. ¶질탕하게 놀다 go on a racket[the spree] / revel it.

질투(嫉妬) jealousy; envy; heartburning. (▶ envy는 자기도 같은 것을 갖고 싶은 기분, jealousy는 자기가 갖고 있지 않은 것을 남이 갖고 있을 때 증오하는 마음의 뜻으로 보다 강한 감정을 나타냄) ¶~로 인한 싸움 a quarrel caused by jealousy∥~가 많은 jealous / envious / green-eyed∥~가 나서[~ 끝에] from jealousy / out of envy∥~에 눈이 어두워[멀어] blinded by jealousy / in a fit of jealous rage∥나는 그에게[그의 성공에] ~를 느꼈다 I felt jealous[envious] of him[his success]∥그는 ~가 나서 그렇게 말하는 것이다 He says so out of envy. **질투하다** be [feel] jealous (of / over); envy (a person); be[become] envious (of); be green with envy. ¶그녀는 늘 미인인 여동생을 질투하고 있었다 She was always jealous of her sister for her good looks[envious of her sister's good looks].

●**질투심** jealousy; envy. ⇨질투 ¶~에 불타다 burn with jealousy / be eaten up with envy∥그것을 보고 그는 ~이 불같이 일어났다 Green envy filled his heart at the sight of it.∥그녀는 두 사람이 손에 손을 잡고 공원을 거니는 것을 ~에 불타 바라보았다 Green-eyed with jealousy, she watched the pair of them walking hand in hand through the park.

질퍽거리다 be sloppy[soppy]; be squashy; be muddy; be miry; [눈이 녹아서] be slushy. ¶길이 몹시 질퍽거렸다 It was a very muddy walk.∥비가 많이 와서 땅이 질퍽거린다 The ground is sloppy[sloshy] after a heavy rain.

질퍽질퍽 sloppily; slushily; sloshily; with squishing noises. **질퍽질퍽하다** sloppy; soppy; squishy; slushy; sloshy. ¶질퍽질퍽한 길 a sloppy road.

질퍽하다 sloppy; soppy; squishy; slushy; sloshy. ¶비가 와서 질퍽한 길 a road soppy with the rain.

질펀하다 1 [넓고 평평하다] broad and level; wide and even. ¶질펀한 들 a broad expanse of fields / a wide (spread of) plain. **질펀히** wide(ly) and even(ly). 2 [게으르다] sluggish; slovenly; lazy; idle. **질펀히** sluggishly; slothfully; sprawlingly; idly. ¶방바닥에 ~ 누워서 소일하다 spend one's time idly sprawled on the floor. 3 [그득하다] numerous; enormous. **질펀히** numerously; enormously.

질풍(疾風) a gale; a strong[swift] wind; [기상] a fresh breeze. ¶~같이 like a whirlwind / swiftly.

●**질풍노도** the storm and stress.

질항아리(－缸－) an earthenware jar; a clay jar.

질화물(窒化物) [화] a nitride.

질환(疾患) a disease. ⇨질병

질흙 1 mud; clay. ⇨진흙 2 [질그릇 만드는 흙] clay; potter's clay.

짊어지다 1 [등에 짐을 메다] take (a burden) on one's[the] back; shoulder; bear. ¶무거운 짐을 ~ bear a heavy burden∥등에 짊어지고 가다 carry on one's back∥그녀는 보따리를 짊어지고 있었다 She had a bundle on her back.∥그는 배낭을 짊어지고 계속 걸어갔다 He shouldered his knapsack and walked on. 2 [부담 등을 맡다] encumber[saddle / burden] oneself (with); be saddled (with). ¶장래의 국가 운명을 짊어질 사람들 those who will shoulder the future destiny of our country∥무거운 책임을 ~ have a heavy responsibility thrust on one / shoulder [assume] the heavy responsibility (of)∥빚을 ~ be encumbered[saddled] with debts∥남의 빚을 ~ shoulder[assume] another's debts∥성가신 일을 ~ be saddled with an encumbrance∥한국의 앞날을 ~ bear the destiny of future Korea on one's shoulders.

짐 1 [하물] a load; a burden; [뱃짐] a cargo (pl. ~es, ~s); a freight; [화물] goods; [미] a freight; [수화물] luggage; [미] baggage; [포장 하물] a pack; a package. ¶무거운[가벼운] ~ a heavy[light] load∥~을 만재한 배 a heavily laden ship∥~을 싣다 load (a cart) / pack (a horse) / (배가) take in cargo∥~을 과중하게 싣다 overload (a cart)∥~을 부리다 unload (a ship / a cart) / unpack (a horse) / clear (a ship) / (배가) discharge her cargo∥~을 덜다 lighten the load∥~을 풀다 unpack (a package / a box)∥~을 꾸리다 pack (up) / (미) package∥~을 부치다 send [consign] goods (to a person)∥~을 지다 bear a load on one's shoulders∥그 배는 그 항구에서 ~을 실었다 The ship took on cargo at the harbor.∥그들은 배에서 ~을 내렸다 They unloaded the ship. / The ship discharged its cargo.∥그 트럭에는 너무 ~이 많이 실려 있다 The truck is overloaded.∥배는 ~이 무거워서 가라앉았다 The boat sank under the load.∥너한테는 이 ~이 좀 무겁겠구나 I'm afraid this is too much for you. 2 [부담] a burden; a load; an encumbrance (특히 어린이). ¶마음의 ~ a load[weight] on one's mind∥~이 되다 be a burden to one∥~을 벗다 unburden / be relieved[ease oneself] of a burden / discharge a burden∥남에게 ~을 지우다 impose a burden[heavy charge] on a person∥~이 되므로 그것은 가지고 가지 않겠다 I won't take it, because it will weigh me down[(문어) encumber me].∥그 소년은 가족을 부양해야 하는 ~을 지지 않으면 안 되었다 The boy had to take on the burden of supporting his family.∥등에서 ~을 벗은 것 같은 기분이다 I feel as if a load had been taken off my back.∥처자식은 그의 ~이었다 His wife and children were a burden to[(속어) a drag on] him.∥그녀의 친절이 점점 무거운 ~이 되었다 Her kindness is gradually becoming a burden.∥변변치 못한 동생이 그녀의 평생의 ~이었다 Her good-for-nothing brother was a burden[an encumbrance] she had to bear for life.

짐(朕) [임금의 자칭] I. ⇨나¹

짐꾼 a burden-bearer; a carrier; a porter; a cooly[coolie].

짐마차 (-馬車) a wagon; a dray; a cart. ¶~로 나르다 carry (goods) in a cart / cart (things away).

짐바리 a load (on a pack animal); a pack. ¶노새의 ~ a mule's pack.

짐배 [화물선] a cargo boat; a freighter; [거룻배] a lighter; a barge.

짐수레 [손수레] a cart; [짐마차] a wagon; a dray; a van. ¶~ 한 대분의 야채 a cartload [wagonload] of vegetables // ~에 싣다 load a cart (with goods) // ~를 끌다 draw[pull] a cart // ~로 건초를 나르다 carry hay in a cart [wagon].

짐스럽다 burdensome; cumbersome; troublesome. ¶짐스럽게 여기다 find (it) burdensome / treat[regard] (a person) as a nuisance.

짐승 a beast; a brute; an animal. ¶~ 같은 bestial / brutal / beastly / brutish / animal // ~ 같은 인간 a beast of a man / a brute // ~ 같은 행위 a brutal[bestial] act / a brutality // 그는 ~ 같은 놈이다 He is a beast of a man. // 이 ~ 같은 놈아 You brute! / You rat! // 그 녀석은 ~만도 못한 놈이다 He is worse than a brute.

짐자동차 (-自動車) (미) a truck; a motor truck; an autotruck; an automobile truck; (영) a (motor) lorry.

짐작 (斟酌) [어림] guess; guesswork; (a) presumption; (a) conjecture; (an) inference; (an) estimation; (a) surmise; [판단] judgment. ¶눈~ eye measure / measuring by (the) eye // 손~ measuring roughly with one's hands // 내 ~으로는 in my estimation // ~이 가다 can guess[(구어) imagine] / have in mind / have an idea (of) // ~이 가지 않다 cannot imagine / have no idea (of) / (미) be unable to figure (it) out // ~이 맞다 guess right / be right in one's conjecture // ~이 어긋나다 make a wrong guess / be [go / fall] wide of the mark // 그가 갔을 만한 데가 ~이 간다 (가지 않는다) I have an[no] idea where he might be. // ~으로 대답했는데 맞았다 I answered with a guess and found I was right. // 이제 대충 ~이 간다 I have formed some idea of it. / I've got the rough idea (of it). // 나는 그들의 생각을 ~ 못 하겠다 I cannot guess what they are thinking. **짐작하다** guess; presume; conjecture; infer; surmise; estimate; [판단하다] judge; gather. ¶짐작하신 대로입니다 You have guessed right. / It is just as you have imagined[(문어) surmised / conjectured]. // 그의 얼굴을 보고 나는 모든 것을 짐작했다 I read the whole story in his face. // 겉으로 보아 나이 스물은 될 것으로 짐작했다 From his appearance I guessed his age at 20. // 그가 얼마나 기뻐했을까는 짐작하고도 남는다 It can easily be imagined how glad he was. // 그게 뭔지 전혀 짐작할 수가 없다 I cannot form any idea of what it is. ➔ 그녀의 실종의 원인에 대해서 짐작되는 바가 있다[없다] I have an[don't have any] idea why she disappeared.

짐짐하다 1 [맛이 없이 찝찝하다] salty and untasty[tasteless] ; salty without any flavor. 2 feel awkward. ⇨ 찜찜하다

짐짓 purposely; deliberately; advisedly; intentionally; on purpose; by (deliberate) design; knowingly; wittingly. ¶~ 냉정한 태도를 취하다 deliberately assume an indifferent attitude // 그 사람은 ~ 못 알아듣는 체했다 He would not understand me. // 그는 ~ 모르는 체했다 He affected ignorance. // 그는 ~ 아무렇지도 않은 투로 그렇게 말했다 He said so in a carefully casual tone.

짐짝 a package; a pack; a parcel; a piece of baggage; an item of freight.

짐차 (-車) a truck; a motor truck. ⇨ 짐자동차

집 1 [가옥] a house; (미) a home; [집합적] housing; a dwelling; an abode; a residence; a mansion(대저택). ¶기와~ a tile-roofed house // 초가~ a thatch-roofed house // 넓은[좁은] ~ a large[small] house // 좋은[초라한] ~ a fine[shabby] house // 쓰러져 가는 ~ a house ready to tumble down // 빈 ~ an unoccupied[untenanted] house / a vacant [an empty] house // 아담한 ~ a modest house // 제 ~ a house of one's own / one's own house // ~ 밖에서 out of[outside] the house / out-of-doors / outdoors // ~ 안에(서) inside the house / indoors // ~ 없는 homeless / houseless / shelterless / vagrant // ~ 없는 사람들 houseless[homeless] people // ~ 없는 신세가 되다 be rendered homeless // ~에 있다 stay[sit / be] at home / be in // ~에 없다 be out[not at home] / stay[be] away from home // 한~에 살다 live under the same roof // ~을 비우다 leave one's house empty / (이사를 가서) move out / quit[vacate / empty] a house // ~을 짓다 build[erect / put up] a house / (자기의) build oneself a house // ~을 헐다 take a house to pieces / pull down a house // ~을 빌리다[세들다] rent a house / take a house (for the summer) // ~을 세놓다 let[rent] a house // ~을 보다 take care of[look after] the house (during a person's absence) // ~을 구하러 다니다 go house hunting / look about for a house // ~까지 바래다주다 walk (a person) home // 일요일에는 ~에 있습니다 I'll be (at) home on Sunday. // 그 남자는 ~이 없었다 The man was homeless. // ~이 어디냐 Where do you live? / Tell me your home address. // 아버지는 ~에 계신가 Is your father at home [in]? // 내 ~은 이 근처에 있다 My home is near here. // 나는 대전에서는 숙부의 ~에서 묵었다 In Daejeon I stayed at my uncle's. / I stayed with my uncle in Daejeon. // 며칠이든 우리 ~에 머물러 주십시오 Please stay with us as long as you like. // 다음 달에는 우리 ~에서 모입시다 Let's meet at my place next month. // 그것을 장 씨 ~에 두고 왔다 I left it at Mr. Jang's house. // 전쟁으로 많은 사람이 ~을 잃었다 Many people were left homeless by the war[lost their homes in the war].

2 [가정·집안] a home; a family; a household. ¶우리 ~ our home // 우리 ~ 아이들 my[our] children // 우리 ~ 사람 my (good) wife // 우리 ~ 양반 my good man / my husband // ~ 돌아가다 go[come / get / return] home // ~을 나가다[떠나다] leave home (at the age of 13) // ~을 뛰쳐나가다 run away from home // 가난한 ~에 태어나다 be born poor[of a poor family] // 부잣~에 태어나다 be born rich // ~ 생각이 나다 get homesick / think of home // 우리 ~ 아이들은 수영을 잘한다 Our children are good at

swimming.// 우리 ~은 5인 가족입니다 We are a family of five. / There are five in my family.// 내 ~보다 좋은 곳은 없다 There's no place like home.// 지난달 이후로 ~에서 소식이 없다 I haven't heard from home since last month.// ~으로 돌아가게 I advise you to go home.
3 [영업 장소] a place; a house; [상점] a store; (미) a shop; [음식점] a restaurant. ¶빵~ a bakery / (미) a bakeshop // 술~ a bar / a saloon / a tavern // (영) a public house // 국숫~ a noodle restaurant[shop] // 중국~ a Chinese restaurant // 일식~ a Japanese restaurant.
4 [새의 보금자리] a nest; [벌의 보금자리] a hornets'[wasps'] nest; a comb; a beehive(꿀벌의); [거미의 보금자리] a (cob)web; [짐승의 보금자리] a lair; a den. ¶개~ a kennel / a doghouse // 새~ a bird's nest // (벌을) 벌~에 넣다 hive // (비둘기가) ~으로 돌아가다 home (to its cote).
5 [케이스] a box; a case; an incasement; a protector; a sheath. ¶두꺼비~ a fuse box // 칼~ a sheath / a scabbard // 아기~ the womb.
6 [바둑의 빈 칸] crosses; captured territory. ¶다섯 ~ 이기다[지다] win[lose] by five crosses.
집(이) 나다 1 [팔 집이 생기다] a house is offered[put up] for sale; [이사 가서 집이 비다] a house is vacated. **2** [바둑에서 집이 되다] a territory is acquired[formed].

집(輯) a series. ¶제1~ the first series.

-집(集) [시가·문장 등을 모은 책] a collection. ¶단편 소설~ a collection of short stories / collected short stories (of O. Henry) // 서간~ a collection of letters / collected letters // 수필~ a collection of essays.

집게 tongs; flat pliers; pincers; nippers; clamps; clampers. ¶~로 **집다** pick up with tongs // ~로 못을 뽑다 pull a nail out with pliers.

집게발 claws; nippers; pincers; forceps(집게벌레의). ¶(게가) ~로 집다 nip with its claws // 게가 ~로 무언가를 집었다 A crab nipped [pinched] something with its claws.

집게벌레 an earwig.
집게뼘 a span. ¶폭이[길이가] ~으로 한 뼘이다 be a span broad[long].
집게손가락 a forefinger; an index finger; the first finger.
집결(集結) concentration; collection; (군대의) assembly; buildup. **집결하다** [모으다] concentrate; collect; gather; assemble; build up; [모이다] be concentrated; gather; assemble. ¶병력을 ~ concentrate[build up] troops // 국경에 군대를 ~ mass[gather / assemble] troops on the border(▶ mass는 대군을 집결하다).
●**집결지** an assembly place; a marshaling area.
집계(集計) totalization; [합계] a categorized[classified] total; an aggregate. ¶~를 내다 find[compute] the classified total (of). **집계하다** totalize; combine into a total. ¶투표를 ~ collect votes into one sum.
●**집계표** a tabulation; a summary sheet.
집광기(集光器) a condenser.
집괭이 a house cat; a pet cat.
집괴(集塊) a mass; a cluster; an agglomerate.

집구석 the interior[inside] of a house. ¶~에 inside the house / within doors / indoors // ~에 틀어박혀 있다 keep[stay] indoors / keep (to) the house / confine oneself in one's house.
집권(執權) assuming[taking] the reins of government; coming into power[office]. ¶~ 중에 while in power // 한 사람에 의한 장기~을 막다 prevent long-term seizure of power by one man. **집권하다** assume[take(over)] the reins of government; take[win / attain] power; come[get] into power[office]; come in; take the helm of state affairs.
●**집권당** the party in power[office]. ¶공화당은 마침내 ~에서 물러났다 The Republican Party went out of power at last.
집권(集權) centralization of power. **집권하다** centralize the power.
집기(什器) an article of furniture. ⇨집물
집념(執念) [집착심] a deep attachment (to); tenacity of purpose; [복수심] spite; vindictive feeling. ¶~이 강한 tenacious of one's purpose / [복수의 집념이 강한] revengeful / spiteful // 나는 새로운 형의 시의 창조에 ~을 불태우고 있었다 I devoted myself to the creation of a new type of poetry. **집념하다** [집착하다] be deeply attached (to); [전념하다] be intent (on); keep[have] one's mind (on); concentrate one's mind (to).
집다 pick[take] up (a thing). ¶집게로 ~ pick up with tongs // 길에 떨어진 돈을 ~ pick up a coin on the street // 젓가락으로 콩을 ~ pick up the beans with chopsticks // 손으로 집어 먹다 eat with the fingers // 돈을 집어 주고 입막음하다 bribe (a person) into secrecy[to hush up] // 그는 케이크를 손가락으로 집어 먹었다 He ate the cake with his fingers.
집단(集團) a group; a mass. ¶~으로 in a group // ~적으로 collectively / as a group // ~을 이루다 form a group // 식중독이 ~적으로 발생했다 There was a mass outbreak of food poisoning.
●**집단 검거** a mass arrest. **집단 농장** a collective farm; (구소련의) a kolkhoz (pl. ~y. ~es); (이스라엘의) a kibbutz (pl. ~im). **집단 생활** living[life] in a group. **집단 심리** group [mass] psychology. **집단 안전 보장** collective security. **집단의식** group consciousness. **집단 지도** collective[group] guidance [leadership]. **집단 폭행** mob violence. **집단화** collectivization. ¶~하다 collectivize.
집달관(執達官) a bailiff.
집달리(執達吏) ⇨집달관
집대성(集大成) ¶그것은 윌리엄 포크너 연구의 ~이다 It is a compilation of all of the studies made so far on William Faulkner. **집대성하다** compile (all available data) into one book; make[give] a comprehensive[complete] survey of (past studies on a subject). ¶한국의 민화를 ~ compile all the folktales in Korea into a book[a single work].
집도(執刀) performance of an operation. ¶수술[해부]은 최 박사의 ~로 행해졌다 The operation[dissection] was performed by Dr. Choe. **집도하다** perform[conduct] an operation.
●**집도자** (수술의) an operator.
집들이 a housewarming (party). ¶~는 언제

집무 할 거니 When are you going to have a house-warming? **집들이하다** hold[have] a house-warming (party).

집무(執務) performance of one's official duties; execution of one's business. ¶~ 중이다 be at one's desk / be on duty // 사장은 ~ 중입니다 The president is at work[his desk] now. **집무하다** attend to one's business[duties]; work. ¶오전 9시부터 오후 5시까지 ~ 한다 work from 9 a.m. to[till] 5 p.m.
● **집무 시간** office[business / working] hours. ¶~ 중 면회 사절 〈게시〉 All visits declined during office hours. / ~ 중에 담배를 피우지 마십시오 Don't smoke during office hours[while you are at work].

집문서(-文書) a house deed; a title deed; deed[title] papers. ¶~를 잡히고 돈을 차용하다 make a loan with the deed for security / borrow money[secure a loan] on one's house.

집물(什物) (하나) an article[piece] of furniture; a utensil; an appliance; (집합적) household furniture[articles] (and utensils); (고정시킨) fixtures; fittings. ¶사무(실)용 ~ office fixtures.

집배(集配) collection and delivery. ¶우편 ~원 a postman / (미) a mailman. **집배하다** collect and deliver (the morning mail). ¶화물을 ~ collect and deliver freight[(영) goods].

집비둘기 a domestic pigeon.

집사(執事) a steward; a butler; (기독교의) a deacon; a deaconess(여자).

집사람 my wife.

집산(集散) collection and distribution. **집산하다** collect[gather / receive] and distribute.
● **집산지** a collecting[receiving] and distributing center; a trading center.

집산주의(集産主義) collectivism. ¶~의 collectivistic / collectivist.

집성(集成) collection; compilation; codification. **집성하다** collect; compile; gather together into a whole; codify.

집세(-貰) a (house) rent; a rental(집세의 수입액). ¶비싼[싼] ~ a high[low] rent // 밀린 ~ back rent / rent in arrears // ~를 내다[치르다] pay the rent (on a house) / pay for the house // ~를 올리다[내리다] raise[lower] the rent // ~가 오르다[내리다] the rent rises[falls] // ~를 내지 않고 살다 live rent-free (in a house) / live in a house free of rent // 네가 있는 집의 ~는 얼마냐 What is the rent on your house? / 이렇게 큰 집인데도 ~는 싸다 I pay a low rent for this large house. / 집주인이 ~를 올렸다[내렸다] The landlord raised[lowered] the rent. / 그는 ~가 3개월 이상이나 밀렸다 He got more than three months behind with his rent. // 이 집은 ~가 월 30만 원이다 This house rents for[at] 300,000 won a month.

집시 a gypsy[gipsy]. ¶~족 the Gypsies.

집안 1 [가정] a family; a household; a[one's] home. ¶온 ~ the whole family / all the family // ~ 사람들 [식구] one's family / members of a family / one's people / (구어) one's folks // 한 ~ 사람들 those who are of the same family / ~에서[끼리] among one's people / in private / privately // ~의 family / domestic / household // ~의 큰일 a matter of great concern to the family // ~의 기둥 the support of a family // ~의 보배 an heirloom / a household treasure // ~의 명예 an honor[a credit] to one's family // ~의 화목 domestic harmony // ~을 꾸려나가다 manage a household / keep house // ~을 빛내다 raise the reputation of one's family // ~을 다시 일으키다 rebuild[restore] the family fortunes // ~의 수치를 드러내다[드러내지 않다] wash one's dirty linen in public[at home] // ~ 식구들이 모두 함께 일했다 The whole family worked together. // 그는 온 ~ 사람들에게 인기가 있다 He is the favorite of all (the members of) the family. // 스미스 씨 댁의 ~ 사람들은 모두 함께 여행을 떠났다 All the Smiths have gone on a trip. / The Smiths have all gone on a trip together. // ~이 모두 평안합니다 All my family are well.
2 [일가] a family; a clan; [친척] one's relatives; one's kindred; [가문] the (social) standing[status] of a family. ¶양씨 ~ the Yang's clan[family] // 오래된 ~ a family of pedigree // 좋은[천한] ~에 태어난 사람 a person of good[low / humble] birth // ~이 좋다 come of (a) good stock[a good family] / be of good lineage[birth] / be of high descent[birth] // ~이 좋지 않다 be of low birth / come of a poor family // 그녀는 ~이 좋다[나쁘다] She comes of a good[lowly] family. / She is wellborn[lowborn]. // 내 딸은 ~의 수치다 My daughter is a disgrace to the family.
● **집안 사정** one's family circumstances[reasons]. **집안 싸움** [내분] an internal trouble[discord / squabble]; [한 집안의 싸움] a family[domestic] trouble[discord]; a family quarrel[dispute]. ¶~을 하다 have a family quarrel // ~을 일으키다 cause[give rise to] an internal trouble / 그들은 상속 문제로 ~을 하고 있다 They are quarreling[disputing] among themselves over the inheritance. **집안일** a family[private / domestic] affair; household matters. ¶~은 일체 아내가 맡아 보고 있다 My wife is in charge of all the household affairs.

집알이 a courtesy call on (a person) in his new house. **집알이하다** call on (a person) to congratulate his moving house.

집약(集約) ¶~적(인) intensive // ~적(인) 방법 an intensive method. **집약하다** do (something) intensively; adopt an intensive method.
● **집약(적) 농업** intensive agriculture.

집어넣다 put[take / bring] in; throw[cast / fling] in[into]. ¶가방에 서류를 ~ stuff the documents into a briefcase // 계란을 끓는 물에 ~ put an egg into boiling water // 휴지통에 ~ throw (a thing) into the wastebasket // 도둑놈을 감옥에 ~ throw a thief into prison / put a thief in jail // 그는 주머니에 손을 집어넣었다 He put his hand into his pocket.

집어등(集魚燈) a fish-luring light; a fishing lamp.

집어먹다 [착복하다] embezzle; peculate; pocket. ¶큰 돈을 ~ pocket[peculate] a large sum // 공금을 ~ embezzle part of official money // 그는 그 돈의 반 이상을 집어먹었다 More than half of the money stuck to his fingers.

집어삼키다 1 [입에 넣어 삼키다] swallow;

eat. ¶한입에 꿀꺽 ~ gulp down / swallow at one gulp. **2** [가로채다] embezzle; appropriate (unlawfully); swallow up. ¶남의 물건을 ~ appropriate the belongings of another // 남의 돈을 ~ embezzle money from a person // 남의 재산을 ~ dispossess a person of his property // 그는 내 재산을 집어삼켰다 He has taken liberties with my property.

집어세다 1 [먹어 치우다] eat up; eat (it) clean. ¶순식간에 국수 세 그릇을 ~ dispose of three bowls of noodles in a short time // 밥을 네 공기나 ~ eat up [empty] four bowls of rice. **2** [착복하다] pocket; embezzle; misappropriate; appropriate (to oneself); peculate. ¶공금을 ~ divert public money into one's own pocket. **3** [닦아세우다] scold away; rebuke (a person) strongly; give (a person) a severe rating.

집어치우다 give [throw] up; quit; abandon; leave [lay] off. ¶일을 ~ leave off the work // 공부를 ~ give up one's studies // 학교를 ~ leave [give up / withdraw from] school // 장사를 ~ quit one's business // 직장을 ~ throw up one's job // 의사 노릇을 ~ relinquish one's (medical) practice // 법학을 집어치우고 미술을 하다 abandon law for art // 그런 이야기는 집어치워 Cut (it) out!

집어타다 take; get on. ¶택시를 ~ pick up [grab] a taxi.

집오리 a (domestic) duck; a drake(수컷). ¶~가 꽥꽥거리고 있다 Ducks are quacking.

집요하다(執拗-) [완고하다] obstinate; stubborn; [끈덕지다] tenacious; pertinacious; persistent. ¶집요한 질문 tenacious questions // 집요하게 stubbornly / obstinately / persistently / tenaciously / with tenacity // 집요하게 물고 늘어지다 give stubborn resistance (to) / stubbornly refuse to give up // 그는 집요하게 자기 의견을 고집한다 He clings obstinately [tenaciously] to his opinions.

집적(集積) accumulation; [물] integration. **집적하다** accumulate; pile (up); heap up [together]; amass; [물] integrate.
●**집적 회로** an integrated circuit(약어 I.C.). ¶초대규모 ~ very large scale integration(약어 VLSI).

집적거리다 1 [손대다] meddle with [in]; have a hand [finger / concern] in; dip one's fingers into; turn [put] one's hand to. ¶쓸데없이 ~ have a finger in the pie // 그는 이것저것 집적거리고만 있을 뿐 일정한 직업을 찾으려고 하지 않는다 He has a go at this and that but never tries to find [get] a steady job. **2** [건드리다] tease; harass; rag; peck at (a person); (속어) needle. ¶누이를 ~ needle one's sister.

집정(執政) administration; governing; government; [나라의 정권을 잡은 사람] an administrator; a dictator; [프랑스 역사] a director(혁명 정부의); a consul(제1공화 정부 시대의). **집정하다** rule [reign] over (a country); govern [administer] (a country); take the helm of state affairs; be in power.
●**집정관** [로마 역사] a consul.

집주(集註) a variorum (edition).

집주인(-主人) **1** [가장] the master of a house; the head of a family. **2** [집임자] the owner of a house; a house owner; a landlord(남자); a landlady(여자).

집중(集中) concentration; convergence; centralization. ¶인구의 ~ gravitation of the population (toward) // 공부에 정신 ~이 안 된다 I can't concentrate on study. **집중하다** [모으다] concentrate (upon); focus (upon); centralize (upon); mass (troops); [모이다] converge (into / on); focus (on); center (on / around). ¶그에게 ~ concentrate one's attention [mind] on (one's work) // 그는 주의를 그것에 집중했다 He concentrated his attention on it. // 우리는 그 일에 전력을 집중했다 We concentrated [focused] our energies on the job. // 언제나 전방에 주의를 집중하라 Keep your attention on the road ahead. →¶논의는 그 점에 집중됐다 The discussion centered on that point.
●**집중 공격** a concentrated attack. **집중력** one's ability to concentrate all one's energies (upon); one's (power of) concentration. ¶그의 ~은 칭찬할 만하다 His ability to concentrate all his energies upon anything he does is quite admirable. **집중 사격** concentrated [converging] fire. **집중 안타** [야구] an avalanche [a rally] of hits. **집중 호우** a localized torrential downpour.

집쥐 [동] a house rat.

집진기(集塵機) a dust collector.

집집이 at every door [house]; from door to door. ¶~ 방문하다 call from door to door // ~ 국기가 휘날리고 있다 The national flag is fluttering over [at] every door.

집착(執着) [애착] attachment (to / for); [고집] persistence (in); tenacity; pertinacity. ¶생에 대한 ~ tenacity for [clinging to] life. **집착하다** be attached (to); adhere [stick / cling] (to); hold fast (to). ¶그는 구습에 몹시 집착하고 있다 He has a deep attachment to old customs. / He is attached to old customs. // 나는 지금의 지위에 집착하지 않는다 I feel no attachment for my present post.
●**집착력** tenacity; pertinacity; adhesive power.

집찰(集札) [개찰한 표를 모으는 것] ticket collection. **집찰하다** collect tickets.
●**집찰계원** a ticket collector.

집채 (the bulk of) a house. ¶~만 한 황소 a bull about the size of a house / an enormous bull // ~만 한 파도 a mountainous [huge] wave / a mountain of a wave // ~만 하다 be as large as a house / be of great size [bulk].

집치레 the (interior) decoration of a house. ¶~가 잘되어 있다 be nicely decorated. **집치레하다** decorate (the interior of) a house; do the interior decoration.

집터 a house [home / building] site; a housing [building] lot; a site for a house; land for housing(여러 주택의). ¶옛 ~ the site of an old building // ~를 닦다 level the ground for a house // ~를 물색하다 look for a site for a building.

집토끼 a house rabbit.

집필(執筆) writing. ¶기사의 ~을 의뢰받다 be asked to contribute an article. **집필하다** write; contribute. ¶잡지에 ~ write for a magazine // 그는 몇몇 잡지를 위해 집필하고 있다 He writes for several magazines.
●**집필자** the writer; the author; (잡지 기사 등의) a contributor.

집하(集荷) collection of cargo. **집하하다** collect cargo.

집합(集合) (a) gathering; (a) meeting; (an) assemblage; (a) muster; [수] a set; concurrence. ¶무한[유한] ~ an infinite [a finite] set∥~! [구령] Everyone, come here. / Gather around. **집합하다** gather; collect; assemble; meet; rendezvous; congregate; flock; throng. ¶10시에 운동장에 집합할 것 Assemble on the (athletic) field at ten.∥전원이 강당에 집합해 있었다 All the members were assembled in the hall.
● **집합 나팔** a muster call. **집합론** [수] set theory; the theory of sets. **집합 명사** [언] a collective noun. **집합체** an aggregate.

집행(執行) execution; performance; conduct; enforcement. ¶가~ provisional execution∥강제 ~ forcible execution∥영장 ~ commitment∥~을 중지하다 suspend execution. **집행하다** execute; discharge; perform; hold; carry into effect[execution]; put into effect; carry out; exercise; conduct. ¶형을 ~ execute a sentence∥사형을 ~ carry out the death sentence / execute (a criminal).
● **집행관** an executor. **집행 기관** an executive organ. **집행부** the executives. **집행 영장** a writ of execution. **집행 위원회** an executive committee. **집행 유예** a suspended sentence(▶ 집행 유예부 판결); probation(▶ 보호 관찰 기관부 판결); a stay of execution. ¶~ 중에 있다 be on probation∥~ 2년에 처하다 give a person a suspended sentence of two years / place[put] (a person) on two years' probation∥그는 징역 1년 6개월, ~ 4년의 선고를 받았다 He was sentenced to a year and a half in prison with four years' suspension of sentence. **집행자** an executor; (유언의) the executor of a will; (사형의) an executioner; (회사 업무의) (미) an executive. **집행 정지** suspension of execution. **집행 처분** an executive measure.

집형(執刑) [형을 집행하는 것] the execution of a sentence. **집형하다** execute a sentence.

집회(集會) a meeting; an assembly; (비공식의) a gathering. ¶불법 ~ an unlawful assembly∥옥외 ~ an open-air meeting∥정치 ~ a political rally∥친목을 위한 ~ a social gathering∥~를 방해하다 thwart [disturb / interrupt] an assembly [rally]∥학생들이 1시에 ~를 열었다 The students opened a meeting at one. **집회하다** assemble; gather; meet together; hold a meeting.
집회의 자유 freedom of assembly.
● **집회 신고** a notice of an assembly; gathering permits. **집회 장소** meeting place; an assembly hall.

집히다 get picked up; be held [picked up] between one's fingers [thumb and fingers]. ¶손에 집히는 대로 먹다 eat anything one can put[get] one's hands on∥손에 집히는 대로 가지다 take all that one's fist can hold∥바늘이 잘 집히지 않는다 The needle is hard to pick up.

짓 [행위] an act; a deed; behavior; conduct; [소행] a work; (one's) doings. ¶눈~ a sign with the eyes / a look / an eye-signal / eyeing / giving the eye (to)∥몸~ a gesture / individual mannerisms∥손~ a motion of the hand / a wave / a gesture / a hand signal∥저놈의 하는 ~이 마음에 안 든다 I don't like his behavior. / (구어) I can't take [stand] the way that guy acts.∥그것은 미친 [정신 나간] ~이다 It's an act of madness.∥바보 같은 ~은 하지 마라 Don't act like a fool.∥나는 그런 ~은 하지 못한다 I cannot do a thing like that. / I cannot behave like that.∥그것은 위험한 ~이다 That's a dangerous game.

짓거리 1 [홍겨워서 멋으로 하는 짓] a gesture [an act] out of merriment; a bit of fun; one's sportive doings. 2 〈속〉 an act; a work. ⇨짓

짓궂다 [악의에 차 있다] ill-tempered; ill-natured; cross-grained; spiteful; crabbed; malicious; [귀찮게 놀리다] (mildly) mischievous; prankful; [달갑지 않다] unlucky; unfortunate. ¶짓궂은 전화 a harassing (phone) call / (난잡한) an obscene [a dirty] call∥짓궂은 편지 a poison-pen [harassing] letter∥그는 자네에게 짓궂게 굴고 싶을 뿐이야 He is just trying to annoy you. / (구어) He is just giving you a bad [hard] time.

짓누르다 weigh down; press down; press upon (a thing); [억누르다] put down; (마음을) weigh heavily on (one's mind). ¶아버지의 존재가 늘 나의 마음을 짓눌렀다 The existence of my father always weighed heavy on me.

짓눌리다 be weighed down; be crushed [squashed]. ¶근심 걱정에 ~ be oppressed with [by] worry.

짓다 1 [만들다] make; manufacture; fashion; tailor. ¶잘 지은 옷 well [handsomely] tailored [cut] clothes / 구두를 ~ make shoes (직공이)∥그는 내 옷을 여러 벌 지었다 He tailored me several suits.
2 [건조하다] build; erect; construct. ¶집을 ~ build a house∥절을 ~ build [erect] a Buddhist temple∥나는 최근에 집을 지었소 (남이) I recently had a house built. / (자기가) I built a house recently.∥이 나무에 새가 둥우리를 지었다 Birds have built a nest in this tree.∥이 집은 새로 지을 때가 되었다 It is about time to rebuild this house.
3 [작성하다] write; compose; make. ¶시[소설]를 ~ write a poem [novel]∥작문을 ~ write a composition∥(그것은) 자기가 지은 것이 아니라고 그는 말했다 He denied the authorship.∥당신이 시를 짓기 시작한 것은 언제쯤입니까 When did you start [begin] composing poems?
4 (밥을) boil; cook; prepare. ¶밥을 ~ cook [boil] rice∥저녁밥을 ~ prepare [cook] supper∥밥이 지어졌느냐 Has the rice cooked? / Is the rice ready?∥점심을 3인분 지어 주세요 Prepare lunch for three, will you?
5 (열을) form; make. ¶줄을 ~ form a line∥줄을 지어 (march) in a line∥그들은 행렬을 지어 행진했다 They marched in procession.∥학생들은 떼를 지어 강당으로 향했다 The students headed for the auditorium in groups.
6 (농사를) cultivate; farm; crop; grow; raise. ¶농사를 ~ do farm work / till the soil / engage in farming / 벼농사를 ~ grow [raise] rice / till a paddy field∥여기서는 밀농사를 많이 짓는다 Here much wheat is grown.
7 (죄를) commit; do. ¶죄를 ~ commit a crime [sin]∥내가 무슨 죄를 지었단 말이오 In what have I offended?
8 [표정 등을 나타내어 보이다] show; express; look (glad / sad). ¶미소를 ~ smile

wear[put forth] a smile // 눈물~ moisten at one's eyes // 슬픈 표정을 ~ give[take on] a sad look // 이상한 표정을 ~ make a strange expression.
9 [확정하다] settle; solve. ¶(일의) 결말을 ~ settle[wind up] (a matter) / bring (a matter) to an end[to a conclusion] / clinch // 결론을 ~ draw[form] a conclusion // 투쟁 중의 쌍방은 타협을 짓기로 합의하였다 The conflicting parties agreed to compromise.
10 [조제하다] prepare; compound; dispense; administer; prescribe. ¶약을 ~ prepare [compound / dispense] medicines / fill [make up] a prescription (처방전대로).
11 [거짓 꾸미다] make up; invent; fabricate; manufacture. ¶지어낸 이야기 a made-up[an invented] story / an invention.

짓무르다 be gangrenous; inflame; blister; fester. ¶빨갛게 짓무른 살 an inflamed raw skin // 짓무른 눈 blear[sore] eyes // 손의 화상이 짓물렀다 The burn on my hand has turned into a running sore[has become infected].

짓밟다 **1** [밟아서 뭉개다] trample[tread] (flowers) under foot; stamp down (to the ground). ¶군중이 공원의 화초를 짓밟았다 The crowd trampled on the flowers in the public garden. / The crowd crushed the flowers in the public garden[underfoot]. **2** [유린하다] trample upon[down]; tread down; override; infringe (upon); ravage. ¶남의 감정을 ~ trample on a person's feelings / hurt a person's feelings // 국토를 ~ ravage a country // 법을 ~ violate the law.

짓밟히다 be trampled down[upon]; be trodden down[on]; get trampled under foot; be downtrodden; get overridden. ¶…의 짓밟혀서 trodden under foot by ... / under the heel [hoof] of ... // 짓밟혀 죽다 be trampled [trodden] to death (by).

짓씹다 chew thoroughly; masticate; triturate; fletcherize.

짓이기다 mash; squash; knead to (a) mash; (밟아서) stamp down (to the ground). ¶진흙을 ~ knead mud // 포도를 밟아서 ~ trample grapes // 사람을 ~ beat a person to a jelly / thrash a person.

짓찧다 **1** [아주 세게 찧다] pound[crush] up; grind down[up]; pulverize. ¶절구에 고추를 ~ pulverize red pepper in a mortar. **2** [부딪치다] strike[hit / bump] hard; batter. ¶돌담에 머리를 ~ batter one's head against a stone wall.

징¹ [대야 모양의 국악기] a *jing*; a gong. ¶~을 울리다 strike a *jing* // ~이 울리고 있다 There goes the *jing*. / The *jing* is sounding.

징² [구두에 박은 쇠못] a clout (nail); (대가리가 큰) a hobnail; (장식용) a stud. ¶~을 박은 장화 hobnailed boots // 구두에 ~을 박다 put [get] heel and toe plates on one's shoes.

징건하다 (서술적) feel bloated (with food); oppress the stomach; sit[lie] heavy on the stomach.

징검다리 a stepping-stone. ¶~를 따라 뜰을 가로지르다 follow the stepping-stones across the garden.

징계(懲戒) disciplinary action; [견책] a reprimand. **징계하다** reprimand; take disciplinary action.
●**징계 위원회** a disciplinary committee. **징계 처분** a disciplinary measure; disciplinary action. ¶~을 받다 be submitted to disciplinary punishment // 회사는 파업 참가자를 전원 ~을 했다 The company took disciplinary action against all the employees who had taken part in the strike.

징그럽다 creepy; crawly; disgusting; loathsome; abhorrent; revolting; detestable; repulsive; (서술적) feel a chill creep over one. ¶징그러운 녀석 a disgusting fellow / (미국 속이) a creep // 징그럽게 웃다 grin a gruesome smile // 그 남자는 어쩐지 ~ There is something creepy about him. // 동생은 뱀을 징그러워한다 My brother detests snakes. // 보기만 해도 ~ The mere sight makes me feel crawly.

징두리 [건] the foundation[lower part] of a wall.

징모(徵募) enlistment. **징모하다** enlist; recruit. ¶병사를 ~ enlist[recruit] men for the army[for military service] / raise an army.

징발(徵發) requisition; commandeering; levy; forage(마초 등의). ¶식량 ~ requisition of provisions. **징발하다** requisition (from); put (a thing) in requisition; lay (a thing) under requisition; (병사를) levy. ¶군은 시민의 차를 징발했다 The army requisitioned the people's cars. →¶그 건물은 군용으로 징발되었다 The building was seized[commandeered] for military purposes.
●**징발권** the right of requisition. **징발령** a requisition order.

징벌(懲罰) punishment; (교정의 뜻을 내포하여) discipline; chastisement. ¶그들은 그를 ~에 처하기로 결정했다 They decided to punish[discipline] him. **징벌하다** punish; discipline; castigate; chastise.

징병(徵兵) [군무에 강제 모집] conscription; (미) the draft; (compulsory) military service. ¶~을 기피하다 evade military service / (미) evade the draft // ~으로 나가다 serve in the army. **징병하다** conscript; enlist; recruit; (미) draft; enroll; call up.
●**징병 검사** an examination for conscription. ¶~를 받다 be given a physical examination for conscription // ~에 합격하다 pass an examination for conscription / be found eligible for conscription. **징병 기피** evasion of conscription[military service]; (미) evasion of the draft; draft evasion[dodging]. **징병 제도** the conscription[draft] system.

징세(徵稅) [세금을 거두어들임] tax collection; taxation. **징세하다** collect taxes (from a person); levy taxes (on a person).

징수(徵收) [조세·수수료 등을 거둠] a levy; [대금 등을 거둠] collection. ¶원천 ~ collection at the source **징수하다** levy; collect. ¶3 퍼센트의 수수료[1인당 10,000원의 회비]를 징수합니다 We will collect a three percent commission[a fee of 10,000 won per person]. →¶교통 위반으로 많은 벌금을 징수당했다 I was fined heavily[They levied a heavy fine on me] for a violation of traffic rules.
●**징수액** the amount collected.

징역(懲役) penal servitude; imprisonment (with hard labor). ¶무기 ~ life imprisonment // 그는 3년의 ~에 처해졌다 He was sentenced to three year's imprisonment. // 그

는 ~을 살았다 He served a term in prison. // 그는 5년의 ~을 마쳤다 He finished his five-year prison term.
● **징역살이** a prison life; a life behind bars; imprisonment.

징용(徵用) 〔국가의 힘으로 사람을 불러 씀〕 commandeering; drafting; requisition; impressment. ¶나는 ~으로 공장에서 강제 노동을 당했다 I was forced to work in a factory as a conscript laborer. **징용하다** commandeer; conscript; (미) draft. →¶트럭은 전부 군에 징용되었다 All the trucks were commandeered [requisitioned] by the army.

징조(徵兆) an omen (of disaster); a portent (흉조); 〔조짐〕 a precursor; a presage; a warning; a premonition; a symptom. ¶좋은 [나쁜] ~ a good [an evil] omen //…의 ~가 되다 (fore)bode a happy ending) / presage / betoken / foreshadow / be ominous of / portend / signify (fine weather) // 먹구름은 흔히 폭풍우의 ~가 된다 A dark cloud often betokens[portends / presages] a storm. // 날씨는 회복될 ~가 안 보인다 The weather shows no sign of improvement.

징집(徵集) levy; enlistment; enrollment; (미) draft; conscription; recruitment. **징집하다** levy; enlist; conscript; conscribe; enroll; recruit; call up[out]; raise; summon to colors. →¶그는 군에 징집되었다 He was recruited[(미) drafted] (into the army).
● **징집 면제** exemption from conscription [enlistment]; (미) exemption from the draft. ¶~의 특전 the privilege of exemption from conscription. **징집영장** a draft card.

징크스 a jinx. ¶~를 깨다 smash[break] a jinx // 우리 팀은 결승전에서 지게 된다는 ~가 있다 There is saying that our team always loses in the finals.

징후(徵候) a sign; 〔병의 조짐〕 a symptom. ¶인플레가 악화될 ~가 보인다 There are signs that inflation is worsening. // 저 구름은 심한 뇌우의 ~이다 The clouds threaten a thunderstorm. // 그 환자는 디프테리아의 ~를 보여 주고 있다 The patient shows[has] the symptoms of diphtheria.

짖다 (개가) bark (at a stranger); (사냥개가) bay; (까막까치가) caw; croak. ¶개는 한 번 길고 슬프게 짖었다 The dog set up a long, mournful howl. // 사냥개가 멀리서 짖는 소리가 들린다 We can hear the distant baying of the hounds.

짖는 개는 물지 않는다(속담) A barking dog seldom bites.; Great barkers are no biters.

짙다 1 〔빛깔이 강하다〕 deep; rich; dark. ¶짙은 빨강 dark[deep] red // 짙은 빛깔 a rich color // 그녀의 화장은 ~ She is heavily made up [is wearing a lot of makeup].
2 〔농도·밀도가 높다〕 thick; heavy. ¶짙은 안개 a dense [thick] fog // 그 소년의 눈썹[머리털]이 ~ The boy has thick eyebrows [hair].
3 〔맛이 강하다〕. ¶차가 ~ The tea is strong. // 이 스튜는 맛이 ~ This stew is strongly seasoned.
4 〔정도가 강하다〕. ¶패색이 ~ The outlook is dark. / The specter of defeat looms large. // 저 남자가 그를 죽인 혐의가 ~ There seems to be little doubt [There is a strong possibility] that that man killed him. / There is a strong suspicion that he committed the murder. // 그들의 짙은 키스에 나는 어리둥절했다 I was embarrassed by their hot[passionate] kiss.

짙푸르다 deep blue; azure. ¶짙푸른 초원 a lush green field // 하늘은 짙푸르게 개어 있었다 The sky had cleared to a deep blue color.

짚 (a) straw. ¶밀[볏] ~ wheat[rice] straw // ~으로 만든 인형 a straw man / a man of straw // ~으로 싸다 wrap up in straw // ~을 썰다 cut straw into chaff / chaff // ~을 깔다 spread straw / (마구간에) litter (a stall) down / cover (a sty) with straw.

짚가리 a strawstack; a pile [stack] of straw; a rick. ¶~를 쌓다 rick / stack / pile straw (sheaves) in a stack / head up in a rick.

짚다 1 〔지팡이·손을 바닥에 대고 의지하다〕 rest (on); lean (on); support by; place[put] one's hand (on a cane) for support. ¶지팡이를 ~ use a cane[stick] // 테이블을 손으로 ~ place one's hand on the table // 나는 목발을 짚으면 걸을 수 있다 I can walk if I use crutches.
2 〔손을 대어 살며시 누르다〕 touch; feel; pat. ¶맥을 ~ take[feel / examine] (a person's) pulse / have one's fingers on (a person's) pulse // 의사가 그의 맥을 짚었다 The doctor took his pulse.
3 〔지적하다〕 point out [finger] (a word).
4 〔짐작하다〕 guess; give [take / make] a guess (at); have a shot. ¶그는 시합의 결과를 잘못 짚었다 He made an error in judging how the game would go.

짚단 a sheaf of straw. ¶~을 만들다 tie up straw in sheaves.

짚신 a *jipsin*; straw shoes. ¶~을 신다 wear [put on] straw shoes // ~을 삼다 make straw shoes.

짚신도 제 짝이 있다(속담) Every Jack has his Jill.

짚신벌레 〔동〕 a paramecium (*pl.* -cia).

짚이다 〔짐작이 가다〕 (happen to) know of; have in mind; suspect. ¶전혀 짚이는 데가 없다 have not faintest [slightest] idea (of) // 당신 시계를 누가 훔쳤는지 짚이는 데가 있습니까 Have you any idea who stole your watch?

째개다 split; break.

째깁기 invisible mending. **째깁기하다** mend (the trousers) invisibly. ¶양복을 ~ do invisible mending.

짜다¹ 1 〔만들다〕 put[piece / fit] together; assemble; construct; make; frame; fix up. ¶발판을 ~ put up scaffolding // 그는 통나무를 짜서 오두막집을 지었다 He put some logs together and built a cabin. / He built a hut out of some logs. // 그녀는 쇳조각을 짜 맞추어 오브제를 만들었다 She put together some pieces of steel and created a work of art.
2 〔조직·편성하다〕 form; organize; compose. ¶배구 팀을 ~ form a volleyball team // 2, 3명씩의 여러 조를 ~ form groups of two or three // (축구 등의) 편을 ~ choose sides // 편을 짜서 놀자 Let's play sides. // 우리는 학생의 그룹을 다시 짰다 We regrouped the students. / We rearranged the grouping of the students.
3 〔짜서〕 weave; inweave; interweave; net (a hammock). ¶금실을 짜 넣은 허리띠 a belt interwoven with gold thread // 무명[모직]을 ~ weave cotton[woolen] cloth // 베틀로

work[weave] at the loom//이 천은 털실로 짠 것이다 This cloth is woven of wool.
4 [뜨개질하다] knit; crochet. ¶털실로 양말을 ~ knit wool into stockings / knit stockings out of wool//이 양말은 손으로 짠 것이다 These stockings are hand-knitted.
5 [공모·결탁하다] collude; conspire (with); plot together (with); arrange. ¶미리 짜고 하는 경기 a fixed[put-up] match[game]//그것은 둘이서 사전에 짜고 한 일이다 It was a prearranged thing between the two.//There was some collusion between the two.//나는 그녀와 짜고 그를 파멸시키기로 했다 I conspired with her to bring about his ruin.//그는 그녀와 짜고 그 아이를 유괴했다 He kidnapped the child in collusion[(구어) cahoots] with her.//그는 두세 명의 동료와 짜고 교장을 궁지에 빠뜨렸다 He conspired with a few colleagues to drive the principal into a corner.
6 [입안·구성하다] form; draw up; frame; conceive; [안출하다] hammer[work] out (a plan); contrive. ¶장래의 계획을 ~ lay plans for the future//예정표를 ~ prepare a schedule//여행 일정을 다시 ~ rearrange the schedule for the trip//공사의 예산을 다 ~ finish[draw up] the budget for the work.
7 [조판하다] compose; set a copy; set (up) in (7-point) type; set type in a case. ¶활자를 다 ~ finish setting type//9포인트로[소문자로] ~ set (up) in 9-point type[in lower case letters].
8 [상투를 만들다] wear[tie] (a topknot).

짜 다² **1** [물기를 빼려고 비틀다] wring; squeeze. ¶수건을 ~ wring (water from) a towel / give a towel a wring / squeeze out water from a towel//그의 옷은 짜야 할 만큼 젖어 있었다 His clothes were wringing [dripping] wet.
2 [액체를 내다] squeeze; press; extract. ¶레몬 즙을 ~ press juice out of a lemon//우유를 ~ milk a cow//튜브에서 치약을 ~ squeeze toothpaste out of a tube//상처에서 고름을 ~ squeeze pus from a wound//포도 즙을 짜서 컵에 넣다 squeeze the juice of some grapes into a glass//바짝 짜내다 squeeze to the utmost.
3 (머리를) press out; squeeze. ¶머리를 ~ rack one's brains//없는 지혜를 짜내어 생각하다 (cudgel] what little brains one has//아무리 머리를 짜 봐도 답이 나오지 않았다 I racked my brains for an answer but came up with none.
4 [착취하다] extort; squeeze; exploit; (속어) soak. ¶국민으로부터 세금을 짜내다 wring taxes from the people//그들은 서민에게서 짜낸 세금을 낭비하고 있다 They are wasting the tax money squeezed out of the people.
5 (눈물을) shed[weep] tears.

짜다³ **1** [소금 맛이 있다] salty; salt; briny; (서술적) taste[be] salty. ¶짠 음식 salty food//짜게 담근 야채절임 salty pickles//이 생선은 약간 ~ This fish tastes a bit salty.//이 야채절임은 ~ These pickles are salty. **2** [인색하다] grudging; stingy; (서술적) grudge; begrudge; (점수가) strict; severe. ¶그는 점수가 너무 ~ He is a hard marker[grader].//우리 선생님은 항상 점수가 ~ Our teacher is always rather strict in grading.//그는 돈에 ~ He is tightfisted[closefisted]. / He is particular about money.

짜르르 greasily; with a dull pain (in the joints). ⇨'자르르
-짜리 [···값어치의 물건] a thing worth .... ¶천 원~ (지폐) a 1,000-won bill[note] / (물건) an article worth[valued at] 1,000 won / one-thousand-won article. **2** [···수·양의 물건] a thing weighing ...(무게); a thing containing .... ¶열 알~ (약봉지) a package containing ten pills//10파운드~ a ten-pounder. **3** [···복장을 한 사람] a person in[wearing] .... ¶양복~ a person in[wearing] western clothes. **4** [···나이의 사람]. ¶다섯 살~ 아이 a five-year-old child.
짜릿하다 [저린] benumbed; [쑤시는] tingling; smarting; [쏘는] pungent; piquant; [오싹하게 하는] thrilling. ¶짜릿한 풍자 pungent[piquant] sarcasm//그녀의 해학에는 짜릿한 맛이 있다 She has a biting sense of humor. / There is a touch of spice in her jokes[humor].
짜부라뜨리다 deflate; (눌러서) crush; [으깨다] squeeze to a pulp; crumple; make shrivel; wither. ¶갓을 ~ crush a hat//그는 내 모자를 짜부라뜨렸다 He squashed [crushed] my hat flat.
짜부라지다 get deflated[crushed / crumpled]; shrivel; wither. ¶그 개구리는 모터사이클에 치어 짜부라졌다 The frog got squashed by a motorcycle.//자동차가 납작하게 짜부라졌다 The car was crushed[(미국 속어) was totaled].//지진으로 집이 짜부라졌다 The house collapsed[was flattened by] the earthquake.//그놈의 콧대가 짜부라지게 해주겠다 (구어) I'm going to bash in[flatten] that guy's nose.
짜이다 1 (피륙 등이) be[get] woven; be[get] knitted. ¶그 천은 면사로 짜여 있다 The fabric is woven of cotton.
2 (규구·규모 등이) be[get] fitted[pieced] together; (조직·이론 등이) be[get] formed[framed / structured / organized / arranged]. ¶그 논문은 잘 짜여져 있다 The thesis is well arranged.//이 극은 잘 짜여져 있다 This play is well constructed.//이 팀은 잘 짜여져 있다 This team is unified.//우리 팀은 강한 상대와 경기 대전이 짜여졌다 Our team was pitted against[matched with / matched against] a powerful opponent.//그 정당은 잘 짜여져 있지 않다 The party is divided.
3 [어울리다] be well-matched; become.
짜임 being put[fitted / pieced] together; [조직] system; organization; [구성] composition; constitution; [구조] construction; structure; framework; makeup.
●**짜임새** structure; make; makeup; constitution. ¶~ 있는 보고 a well-organized report//~가 시원찮다 The make is poor. / It is of bad make.
짜장 [과연·정말로] really; truly; indeed; in (good / very) sooth.
짜증 (-症) fret; irritation; vexation; anger; annoyance. ¶나는 교통 체증에 휘말려서 ~이 났다 Caught in a traffic jam, I grew impatient.//옆집 피아노 소리에 그녀는 ~이 났다 She was irritated by the sound of her next-door neighbor's piano. / Her nerves were set on edge by the sound of the piano from next door.//그는 걸핏하면 ~을 낸다 He is very

짜하다 irritable.// 그녀의 수다스러운 이야기에 나는 ~이 났다 I listened to her chatter in irritation. / Her chatter irritated me[got on my nerves].// 빌어먹을, ~이 나 죽겠다 Confound[Damn] it!

짜하다 〔소문이 자자하다〕 widespread (rumor); spread abroad; well circulated. ¶소문이 짜하게 퍼졌다 The rumor went about [got abroad]. / The rumor spread like wildfire.

짝¹ 〔쌍을 이룬 것 중의 하나〕 one of a pair [couple]; a counterpart; a parallel; (사람의) one's pal [partner / mate / fellow]; one's spouse(배우자). ¶양말[구두 / 장갑]의 odd sock[shoe / glove]// ~**이 맞다** match with another / pair / make[form] a pair[set] / form a counterpart[parallel] (to)// 이 장갑은 그것과 한 ~이 아니다 This glove does not match that one.// 그와 그녀는 좋은 ~이다 They make a good couple.// 그들은 각각 ~을 지었다 They paired off into couples.// 나는 그와 ~을 지었다 I paired with him. / He and I formed a pair.// 결혼하려 해도 알맞은 ~이 없다 I wish to marry but cannot find a fit mate.// 아들에게 적당한 아내를 ~지어 주다 find one's son a suitable wife// 춤추는 사람은 둘씩 ~을 지었다 The dancers were paired off.

짝(을) 맞추다 make a pair of (two things); pair (two things); match (colors).

짝(이) 없다 〔비길 바 없다〕 incomparable; matchless; extreme; be without a peer. ¶건방지기 짝이 없는 태도 an extremely impolite attitude// 가엾기 ~ I am very[exceedingly] sorry.// 그는 비겁하기 ~ He is a hopeless coward.// 그것은 난처하기 짝이 없는 일이다 It has[You have] caused me a great deal of trouble. / This has put me in an extremely embarrassing[awkward] position.// 네가 사자를 기르다는 위험하기 짝이 없는 일이다 It's terribly dangerous for you to keep a lion.// 입상하여 나는 기쁘기 ~ I am overjoyed [thrilled] to have won the prize.

짝² 〔곳〕 〔아무 ~에도 쓸모가 없다〕 be quite useless[of no use] / be good for nothing / be no good (for).

짝³ 〔갈비를 세는 단위〕 a one side (of beef /pork) ribs); 〔짐을 세는 단위〕 a pack (of loads); a bale (of dried fishes).

짝⁴ 1 〔찢는 소리〕 ripping; tearing. ¶종이를 ~ 찢다 tear up paper// 그는 봉투를 ~ 찢어 편지를 꺼냈다 He ripped the letter open. 2 〔활짝〕 wide-open; abroad. ¶입을 ~ 벌리다 open one's mouth wide / gape// 다리를 ~ 벌리고 앉다 sit with one's legs spread apart.

짝귀 (a person with) mismatched ears.

짝눈 mismatched eyes.

● **짝눈이** a person with mismatched eyes.

짝사랑 unrequited [unanswered / unreturned / one-sided] love. ¶나의 사랑은 ~이었다 My love was not returned. **짝사랑하다** be in love without return; love one-sidedly; carry a torch for (a person). ¶그녀는 친구의 보이프렌드를 짝사랑하고 있다 She feels a secret love for her friend's boyfriend.

짝수(-數) an even number. ¶~의 even / even-numbered.

짝신 〔제 짝이 아닌 신〕 an unmatched[a mismated] pair of shoes; wrongly paired shoes.

짝짓기 mating. **짝짓기하다** mate.

짝짜꿍 a baby's hand-clapping game; "pat-a-cake". ¶~ 곤지곤지 죔죔 도리도리 "Clap it, clap it, mark it, mark it, grab it, grab it, roll it, roll it!"

짝짜꿍이 1 〔다툼〕 a clash; a fight; a commotion; a scene. **짝짜꿍이하다** clash[fight] with each other. 2 〔밀계〕 a secret scheme. **짝짜꿍이하다** secretly scheme.

짝 1 〔찢기거나 갈라지는 소리·모양〕 ripping; tearing (up); 〔신발을 끄는 소리〕 dragging; scuffing; shuffling. ¶옷을 ~ 찢다 rip up one's clothes// 옷의 솔기를 ~ 뜯다 rip open a seam// 종이를 ~ 찢다 tear up a paper into scraps[pieces]// 심한 가뭄으로 논바닥이 ~ 갈라졌다 The rice paddies were splintered all over due to a long draught. 2 (끈끈한 것이) clinging fast [close / tight]; stickily. ¶엿은 이에 붙는다 A taffy sticks on the teeth. 3 〔입맛 다시는 소리〕 smacking; licking. ¶입맛을 ~ 다시다 smack one's lips / lick one's chops [lips].

짝짝거리다 1 〔혀로 소리 내다〕 smack[lick] (one's lips). ¶(입을) 짝짝거리며 먹다 smack one's lips while eating. 2 (신발 등을) scuff. 3 〔찢다〕 rip; tear up; scrap up.

짝짝이 an odd[unmatched] pair (of shoes [socks]); a wrongly matched[mismatched / mismated] pair. ¶~의 odd / mismatched // 그녀는 ~ 장갑을 끼고 있었다 She was wearing an odd pair of gloves.// 그 어린아이는 신을 ~로 신고 있었다 The little child was wearing odd[mismatched] shoes.// 이 구두는 ~다 These shoes are wrongly paired.// 그는 눈이 ~다 One of his eyes is bigger than the other.

짝하다 become a partner; partake.

짠물 seawater. ⇨`바닷물(⇨바다)

● **짠물고기** a sea fish. ⇨`바닷물고기(⇨바다)

짠지 radish preserved with salt.

짠하다 (서술적) feel depressed [sad / blue].

쨀그랑 with a clang. ⇨`쨀가랑

쨀까닥 with a click. ⇨`쨀가닥

짤끔거리다 1 (물 등이) trickle; dribble. 2 〔찔름거리다〕 give in small amounts.

짤끔짤끔 1 (물 등이) trickling; dribbling. 2 〔조금씩〕 piecemeal; in dribs and drabs.

짤따랗다 shortish; rather short; (서술적) be on the short side.

짤라뱅이 a short object; an undersized thing; a dwarf; a runt; a midget; a miniature.

짤랑거리다 clink; jingle; tinkle. ¶방울을 ~ jingle[tinkle] a bell// 그는 호주머니의 돈을 짤랑거렸다 He jingled the coins in his pocket.// 열쇠 뭉치가 짤랑거렸다 The bundle of keys clinked together.

짤래짤래 shaking one's head. ⇨`잘래잘래

짤막짤막 (severally) short; choppy. **짤막짤막하다** small; cut-off; choppy; be all short. ¶짤막짤막한 단어들 short words// 오이를 짤막짤막하게 썰다 cut cucumbers in small pieces// 글을 짤막짤막하게 쓰다 write choppy sentences.

짤막하다 shortish; choppy; (서술적) be on the short side. ¶짤막한 인사말 a brief address.

짤짤 simmeringly; shakingly; bustlingly; draggingly; oilily. ⇨`잘잘

짤짤거리다 〔돌아다니다〕 go around hurriedly; dart about.

짤짤이 a person who dashes about uncere-

짧다 1 [시간·길이가] short; brief; abbreviated (costume). ¶짧은 생애 a short life / a brief span of life ¶짧은 이야기 a brief talk / a short story ∥ 짧은 바지 shorts ∥ 짧은 스커트 a short skirt ∥ 짧게 말하면 in short / to be brief ¶짧게 하다 shorten / make short ∥ 머리를 짧게 자르다 have one's hair cut short ∥ 손톱을 짧게 자르다 trim one's fingernails close ∥ 배트를 짧게 잡다 shorten up on the bat ∥ 겨울에는 해가 짧아진다 The days get shorter in winter. ∥ 내각의 수명은 짧았다 The cabinet was short-lived. ∥ 그 노인의 여생은 ~ The old man has not long to live. ∥ 사람의 일생은 ~ Our life is but a span. ∥ 식사(式辭)는 짧은 편이 환영받는다 Most people prefer a brief address. / A brief address is welcomed by [is welcome to] everyone.
2 [부족하다] wanting; short; lacking; deficient; insufficient; poor. ¶짧은 밑천 a small capital / 《미국 구어》 a shoestring ∥ 짧은 영어로 이야기하다 speak in poor [broken] English ∥ 밑천이 ~ be short in funds ∥ 그는 영어가 ~ He is a poor speaker of English.

짧은지름 [수] the minor axis.

짬 1 [겨를] spare [free] time; leisure; [연극에서 대사나 동작의 중단 시간] a pause; an interval. ¶~이 없다 have no time to spare / ~을 내다 make time (to do) ¶아버지는 ~만 있으면 독서하신다 My father spends all his spare time (in) reading. ∥ 그녀는 ~만 있으면 스웨터를 짰다 She made use of [used] her leisure to knit a sweater. ∥ ~이 있는 대로 그림을 그리곤 했었다 I used to paint pictures in my spare moments. ∥ ~을 내어 한두 시간 잠을 잤다 I snatched a few hours of sleep. 2 [틈] an opening; a chink.

짬짜미 [짜고 하는 약속] a secret promise [agreement / contract / pact]; undercover negotiations [bargaining]. **짬짜미하다** promise secretly; indulge in undercover negotiations.

짬짬이 in one's spare time; in the intervals (between).

짭새 〈속〉 a cop.

짭짤하다 1 [맛이] nice and salty; have a good salty taste (to); tasty. ¶짭짤한 고기 반찬 a nicely salted meat dish ∥ 짭짤하고 달큼한 salted and sweetened. 2 [쓸 만하다] nice; good; passable; fair; fine. ¶짭짤한 수입 a good [fair] income.

짭짭 licking one's chops. ⇨ ²쩝쩝

짱구 [머리] a bulging head; (사람) a bulging-headed person.
● **짱구머리** a bulging head.

짱짱하다 sturdy; stout; strong.

-째 1 [순서·등급] a rank; a grade; -th; ahead; beyond; off; away. ¶첫[둘 / 셋]~ first [second / third] ∥ 첫[둘 / 셋]~로 firstly [secondly / thirdly] ∥ 두 번~의 결혼 a second marriage ∥ 둘~ 형(兄) the second oldest brother ∥ 세계에서 다섯~로 큰 산 the fifth highest mountain in the world ∥ 입원하서 7일~ on the seventh day after one's admission to a hospital ∥ 둘~를 차지하다 take the second place / rank second ∥ 그는 열 번~로 가입했다 He was the tenth member to join. ∥ 약국은 은행에서 셋~ 번 집이다 The pharmacy is the third shop from the bank.

2 [통째로·그대로] and all; together with; inclusive of; as it is. ¶사과를 껍질~ 먹다 eat an apple, peel and all ∥ 생선을 가시~ 삼켜 버리다 devour a fish, bones and all ∥ 폭풍으로 나무가 뿌리~ 뽑혔다 The tree was uprooted by the storm.

째깍¹ with a click. ⇨ ¹재깍¹
째깍² quickly; speedily. ⇨ ²재깍²
째다¹ [짓다] cut open (a boil); open; lance; incise. ¶종기를 ~ lance a boil ∥ 소매치기가 주머니를 칼로 째고 돈을 훔쳐 갔다 A pickpocket cut my pocket open with a knife and took my money.

째다² 1 [부족하다] be insufficient; be short of. ¶살림이 ~ be in want / be needy ∥ 일손이 쩬다 We are short of hands. 2 [작다] be too small (to wear comfortably). ¶이 옷은 너무 째다 The suit is too tight for me.

째리다 look disapprovingly out of the corner of one's eyes (at). ⇨ '흘기다 ¶째려 봤다가 해서 깡패에게 공갈당할 뻔했다 Saying that I had given him a dirty [malicious] look, a hoodlum tried to shake me down.

째마리 (물건) trash; rubbish; junk; waste; (사람) a good-for-nothing; a scum; a human waste [debris].

째보 [언청이] a harelipped person.

째(어)지다 split; rend; tear; rip; cleave. ¶길게 째진 눈 long slanted eyes ∥ 깃발이 바람에 갈가리 째졌다 The flag was torn to ribbons by the wind. ¶이런 종이는 쉽게 째어지다 Paper of this quality tears easily.

짹짹거리다 tweet; twitter; chirp. ¶새들이 짹짹거리고 있다 Birds are chirping [twittering]. / Birds are going tweet-tweet [cheep-cheep].

쨍 with a clank [clink]. ¶칼과 칼이 ~ 부딪쳤다 The swords clanked. ∥ 나는 귀가 ~ 하고 울린다 I have a ringing in my ears. / My ears ring.

쨍그랑 with a clink [clank / clang]. ¶접시가 마룻바닥에 ~ 떨어졌다 The dishes fell on the floor with a crash. **쨍그랑하다** clink; clang; give a clink [clank]. ¶유리창에 공이 맞아 쨍그랑하고 깨졌다 The ball crashed against the window and broke it.

쨍쨍 (the sun shines) blazing(ly); bright(ly); glaring(ly). ¶해가 모래 위에 ~ 내리쬐었다 The sun glared down upon the sand. ∥ 해가 ~ 내리쬐고 있었다 The sun was blazing [glaring] down on us. **쨍쨍하다** bright; blazing.

쨍쨍거리다 snap [nag / snarl] (at); speak snappishly [snarlingly] (to); be snappish (with); give the rough side of one's tongue.

쩌렁쩌렁하다 resonant. ¶그는 목소리가 쩌렁쩌렁했다 He has a resonant voice.

쩌렁거리다 go clang; clang; clang and clang.

쩌렁쩌렁 with clang after clang. **쩌렁쩌렁하다** go clang. ⇨ ²쩌렁거리다

쩌릿하다 benumbed; tingling. ⇨ ²찌릿하다 ¶코드에 닿았더니 전기가 쩌릿했다 When I touched the cord I felt [got] an electric shock.

쩨쩨 1 [혀 차는 소리] Tsk tsk tsk! 2 [소를 왼쪽으로 몰 때 내는 소리] Haw!

-쩍다 feel; give [have] a feeling (of). ¶겸연~ be abashed [shamefaced] ∥ 괴이~ be queer [strange] ∥ 미심~ be doubtful [suspicious] ∥ 의심~ be doubtful [questionable] ∥ 미안~

쩍쩍 be embarrassed.
쩍쩍 ripping; stickily; smacking. ⇨ 짝짝
쩍하면 [툭하면] on the slightest movement; easily; with the slightest provocation.
쩔쩔매다 fluster oneself; be all in a hurry; be flurried; be thrown into consternation; be at a loss. ¶바빠서 ~ be so busy that one doesn't know the left from the right // 시험장에서 ~ be snowed under by the examinations // 상관한테 ~ be shaken up by one's superior // 쩔쩔매며 어쩔할 바를 모르다 be at a loss to know what to do // 문제가 산적해서 쩔쩔맬 지경이다 I am almost overwhelmed by the mountain of problems confronting me.
쩝쩝 [입맛을 다시는 모양] licking one's chops; smacking one's lips. ¶입맛을 ~ 다시다 lick one's chops / smack one's lips. **쩝쩝하다** lick one's chops. ⇨ 쩝쩝거리다
쩝쩝거리다 lick one's chops; smack one's lips. ¶쩝쩝거리며 먹다 smack one's lips while eating.
쩡쩡 1 [권세가 대단한 모양] resounding; powerful; mighty. ¶~한 정치가 an influential statesman // 세력이 ~ 울리다 enjoy resounding influence. **2** [갈라지는 소리] cracking. ¶얼음이 ~ 갈라졌다 The ice cracked. / The ice broke [gave way] with a crack.
쩨쩨하다 1 [인색하다] stingy; niggardly; miserly; close-[tight-]fisted; illiberal. ¶쩨쩨한 사람 a miser / a stingy person // 쩨쩨한 생각 a narrow-minded idea [way of thinking] / a shabby thought // 쩨쩨하게 stingily / niggardly // 쩨쩨한 소리 하지 마라 Don't be stingy. / Be liberal. **2** [치사하다] mean; [초라하다] poor; shabby; [옹졸하다] narrow-minded; small (mind). ¶그는 쩨쩨한 녀석이다 He is small-minded fellow. // 그는 심성이 ~ He has a mean spirit. // 그의 쩨쩨한 방식은 알고 있다 We know his little ways.
쩽그렁 with a clink. ⇨ 쨍그랑
쪼개다 split; break; divide. ¶둘로 ~ split [divide] (a thing) in [into] two // 땅을 쪼개어 팔다 sell one's land in lots // 용돈을 쪼개어 책을 사다 use part of one's pocket money to buy books // 손도끼로 판자를 두 조각으로 쪼갰다 The hatchet cut [split] the board in two.
쪼개지다 split; break; divide; get split.
쪼그라지다 get pressed out of shape; get lean. ⇨ 쭈그러지다
쪼그랑박 a stunted gourd.
쪼그랑할멈 a withered old woman.
쪼그리다 press out of shape; crouch. ⇨ 쭈그리다
쪼글쪼글하다 withered. ⇨ 쭈글쭈글하다
쪼다 1 (새가) pick (at); pick up; peck (at); dab. ¶쪼아 먹다 peck at and eat // 새가 빵을 쪼고 있다 The bird is pecking at the bread. **2** (정 등으로) chisel; cut; carve. ¶돌을 쪼아 이름을 새기다 carve one's name in a stone // 정으로 돌을 ~ cut a stone with a chisel // 그는 돌을 쪼아 상을 만들었다 He chiseled the statue from a rock.
쪼들리다 be hard pressed; be oppressed. ¶돈에 ~ be pressed [strapped] for money // 가난에 ~ be pinched with poverty // 빚에 ~ be harassed with debts // 생활에 ~ be in straitened circumstances / be hard up for living.
쪼르르 tricklingly; slidingly; at a dash. ⇨ 조르르 ¶수도에서 물이 ~ 흐른다 Water dribbles from the faucet. // 마루 위를 쥐가 ~ 달리고 있었다 A mouse was running about on the floor.
쪼르륵 dribbling. ⇨ 조르륵
쪽¹ [식] an indigo plant.
쪽² (머리의) a knot of hair (on the back of the head); a chignon; a coiffure. ¶~ 찐 머리 a (round) chignon // ~을 찌다 do one's hair up in a chignon // ~을 찌고 있다 have a chignon (of black hair).
쪽³ [조각] a piece; a slice; a cut; a plank. ¶마늘 한 ~ a clove of garlic // 참외 한 ~ a slice of melon.
쪽⁴ 1 [방향] a direction; a way; [측면] a side; [곳] a part; a quarter. ¶왼 ~ the left side // 오른 ~ the right side // 강 ~으로 가다 go toward the river // 그는 문 ~으로 걸어갔다 He walked to the door. // 나도 그 ~으로 간다 I am going that way, too. **2** (당사자 사이의) a side; a part. ¶내 ~의 [에서는] on my part [side] // 방송 [청중] ~에서 at the broadcasting [listening] end // 우리 ~ our side // 어머니 ~의 친척 a relative on one's mother's side // 그 ~ 사람들도 와서 우리와 함께 합시다 You over there, come join us. // 네 ~이 나쁘다 You are to blame. / You are in the wrong. / The fault is on your side. // 지팡이는 굵은 ~이 좋다 I prefer a walking stick on the thick side. // 그 ~에서 먼저 말한 거지 You started it. / You said it first. / You brought up the subject.
쪽⁵ [페이지] a page.
쪽마루 a veranda of one or two floorboards [planks].
쪽매 a thing made by putting together small thin pieces of wood; parquetry-work; parquet. ¶~ 붙임하다 inlay parquet strips on (a base board) // ~질하다 make [decorate] (a wooden vessel) with parquet strips / make a parquet vessel.
쪽문(-門) a side door [gate]; a wicket gate; a small side gate (which one must duck to enter).
쪽박 a small gourd; a gourd dipper.
쪽발이 1 [외발] a thing which has only one leg left; a one-legged thing. **2** (발통이 두 갈래진) a cloven foot. **3** [일본인의 비칭] a Jap.
쪽빛 indigo (blue); indigotin. ¶~의 indigo-blue / deep blue // ~으로 물들이다 dye (a dress) deep blue.
쪽자(-字) [인] a single piece of printing type made by combining parts taken from other pieces.
쪽지(-紙) a slip of paper; a tag; a note [message] left behind. ¶~에 몇 자 적다 jot a few words down on a slip // 그가 집에 없어서 ~를 부인에게 맡기고 왔다 As he was not at home, I left a message with his wife.
쫀득쫀득 sticky; glutinous; adhesive; elastic; rubbery; tough.
쫀쫀하다 (서술적) be finely woven; be of fine weave.
쫄깃쫄깃하다 gummy; rubbery. ⇨ 졸깃졸깃하다
쫄딱 completely; wholly; altogether; utterly. ¶~ 망하다 go completely to the dogs.
쫄래둥이 a frivolous urchin.
쫄쫄 (flow) ceaselessly in a stream; (follow a person) closely and persistently. ⇨ 졸졸

쫑그리다 ¶파수 보는 개가 귀를 쫑그렸다 The watchdog pricked up its ears.

쫑긋 ¶귀를 ~ 세운 개 a dog with ears cocked.

쫑긋거리다 1 (입술을) work (the mouth); move the lips. ¶입을 ~ move the lips / curl one's lips / make a lip. 2 (귀를) move the ears; cock [prick up / strain] one's ears. ¶그 말은 양귀를 쫑긋거렸다 The horse cocked up the ears.

쫑알거리다 spatter; grumble (at). ⇨ 종알거리다

쫓겨나다 [내쫓기다] be expelled; be turned [got / put / sent / driven] out; be routed out (of); be hustled out (of town); be kicked out (of); (지위에서) be ousted [expelled / dislodged] (from a position); (해고당하다) be dismissed; lose one's place. ¶집에서 ~ be thrown out of the house // 클럽[학교]에서 쫓겨났다 I was expelled from the club [from school]. // 직장에서 쫓겨났다 I was dismissed fired from one's post. // 고향에서 쫓겨났다 I was driven out of my hometown.

쫓기다 [뒤쫓기다] be pursued [chased] (after); be run [taken] after; be trailed; be hunted (up); be coursed; be hounded. ¶쫓기는 사람 the pursued // 몹시 ~ be heavily pursued // 일[시간]에 ~ be pressed by work [for time] // 나는 공부[가사]에 쫓기고 있다 I am busy with my studies [housework].// 잡무에 쫓겨 그를 잊고 있었다 Under the pressure of routine business, I had forgotten about him. // 바쁜 일에 쫓겨 회답을 드리지 못해서 정말 죄송합니다 (편지에서) Excuse [I must apologize to you for] my delay in answering, because I have been extremely busy. // 무엇인가에 쫓기는 듯한 기분이다 I feel as if I were being hastened [urged] on by something. // 도둑은 쫓겨 골목으로 뛰어 들어갔다 The hunted robber rushed into an alley. // 그는 경찰에 쫓기고 있다 He is wanted by the police. / The police are after him.

쫓다 1 (물리치다) drive out [away]; shoo away; expel. ¶새를 ~ shoo birds away // 파리를 ~ drive [fan] flies away // 재액(災厄)을 쫓아 주기 바란다 I want to be rid of my ill luck. // 그들은 그녀에게서 악귀를 쫓기 위해 빌었다 They prayed to exorcise [drive] the evil spirit from her. // 그는 음식에 꾀는 파리 떼를 손으로 쫓고 있었다 With his hands he was swishing [beating] away the flies that swarmed around the food. 2 (특히 범인·사냥감 등을) pursue; chase; run after. ¶쫓는 사람 the pursuer // 사냥감을 ~ chase game // 도둑[범인]을 ~ pursue a thief [criminal].

쫓아가다 1 (뒤쫓아서) go in pursuit; pursue; follow; run after. ¶도망하는 적을 ~ give chase to the retreating enemy // 도둑을 ~ run after a robber // 아이들이 나비를 쫓아간다 Children run after butterflies. // 먼저 가시오 개를 데리고 쫓아가리다 You go on ahead, and I will follow with the dog. // 그녀는 쭉 그의 뒤를 쫓아갔다 She followed a long way behind him. 2 (앞선 것을) catch up with; keep up with. ¶앞서 가는 사람을 ~ catch up with a person ahead. 3 [함께 ~ follow; accompany; go with. ¶사절단을 ~ accompany a delegation / join the retinue of a mission.

쫓아내다 drive out; expel; evict; dismiss; fire; sack. ¶학생들을 학교에서 ~ expel a student from school // 식모를 ~ give a maid the sack // 선동자를 모임에서 쫓아냈다 We ejected an agitator from the meeting. // 고양이를 집 밖으로 쫓아냈다 I drove the cat out of the house. // 끈질긴 외판원을 쫓아냈다 I sent the persistent salesman packing. // 그는 화나서 손님을 쫓아냈다 In anger, he showed his guest the door. // 그를 쫓아내라 Throw him out!

쫓아다니다 [여기저기 뒤쫓다] chase; run [chase] after; [뛰어다니다] run about [round]; [붙어 다님] follow about [around]; dangle about [after]. ¶여자 뒤를 ~ dangle after girls // 그는 노상 여자의 뒤를 쫓아다니고 있다 He is always chasing girls.

쫓아오다 1 (추적해 오다) come in pursuit; follow at (a person's) heels. ¶나를 쫓아오너라 Follow me. // 아이가 내 뒤를 쫓아왔다 A child came running after me. 2 (바싹 따라오다) keep up with; catch up. ¶너무 빨리 걸어서 그는 쫓아오지 못했다 I walked too fast for him to catch up with me.

쫙 far and wide; fluently; in a quick stream. ⇨ 확

쬐다¹ [햇빛이 비치다] shine on [over]; beat [strike] (down) on. ¶볕이 쬐지 않는 장소 a place out of the sun.

쬐다² 1 [불기운을 몸에 쬐다] warm oneself (at [by] the fire); have a warm [heat] (by [at] the fire); take warmth; put (a thing) over the fire; hold up to the heat. ¶손을 불에 쬐어 녹이다 warm one's hands over a fire // 옷을 난로 앞에 쬐어 말리다 dry one's clothes in front of a fire // 난로 앞에 앉아서 불을 ~ sit at the stove and have a warm.
2 [볕을 몸에 받다] expose (a thing) to the sun; bathe [bask] in the sun; [말리다] dry (a thing) in the sun. ¶햇볕을 ~ bask [bathe] in the sun / sun oneself / take the sun / get some sun // 이불을 햇볕에 ~ expose bedding to the sun / air bedding // 나는 햇볕을 쬐는 것을 좋아한다 I like to bask in the sun [to sun myself].

쭈그러뜨리다 press [squeeze] out of shape; crush. ¶모자를 납작하게 ~ crush a hat flat.

쭈그러지다 1 [우그러져 작아지다] get pressed [squeezed] out of shape; be crushed. ¶쭈그러진 모자 a battered hat. 2 [쪼글쪼글해지다] get lean; grow gaunt; wither; shrivel. ¶쭈그러진 얼굴 a worn face.

쭈그렁이 1 [쭈그러진 물건] a thing crushed out of shape. 2 [쭈글쭈글한 늙은이] a withered old person.

쭈그리다 1 press [squeeze] out of shape; crush. 2 [우그리다] crouch; squat; bend low; stoop. ¶쭈그린 자세로 in a squatting position // 몸을 ~ bend oneself low / stoop (over a desk) // 난로 앞에 쭈그리고 앉아 있는 사람이 있었다 A squat figure sat in front of the fire.

쭈글쭈글하다 withered; wrinkled. ¶쭈글쭈글하게 구겨진 옷 crumpled clothes // 쭈글쭈글한 노인 a wrinkled old man // 노파의 쭈글쭈글한 손 the old woman's wrinkled hand // 스커트는 ~ The skirt is terribly wrinkled. // 차의 앞부분이 쭈글쭈글하게 찌그러졌다 The front of the car was crushed [smashed] out of shape. // 그녀가 너무 세게 쥐고 있었기 때문에 모자가 쭈글쭈글해졌다 She held her hat

쯔르르 so tightly that it became crumpled out of shape.

쯔르르 tricklingly; slidingly; at a dash. ⇨ 주르르

쭈뼛하다 (서술적) be bulged out; (one's hair) be standing on end. ¶머리끝이 쭈뼛해지다 feel a shudder // 머리카락이 쭈뼛해지다 I felt a cold chill pass through me. / A shiver ran through my limb. // 어두운 뜰 가운데서 사람의 그림자를 보고 쭈뼛했다 My blood ran cold as I saw a figure in the dark garden. // 보기만 해도 머리가 쭈뼛해진다 The mere sight of it makes my hair stand on end.

쭉 in a row; with a rip; (recede) utterly; all during; straight; at a gulp; roughly. ⇨ 죽²

쭉정이 empty heads of grain; blasted ears. ¶벼 ~ an immature ear of rice.

쭉쭉 in rows; in showers; into shreds; (draw through a clasping hand) briskly. ⇨ 죽죽

-쯤 1 [정도] about (so much); approximately; around; nearly; ... or so; some (▶ some은 주로 수사에 붙음: some 20 boys). ¶30~ 되는 신사 a gentleman of about thirty / a thirty-ish gentleman // 오늘은 온도가 30도~입니다 The temperature today is 30° or so [or thereabouts]. // 내가 할 수 있는 것은 기껏해야 그~이다 At most, what I can do is something of that sort. / That's just about all I can do. // 10분~ 기다려 주겠니 Will you wait ten minutes or so? // 너는 그~에서 그만두었어야 했어 You should have stopped (it) at that point. // 그것을 만드는 데 3일~ 걸릴 것이다 It will take three days or so to make it. // 90프로~ 완성이 됐다 The work is nearly completed.

2 [무렵] at about (a certain time). ¶한 시~ about one o'clock / 4월 중순~ around mid-April // 모임이 끝날 때~ toward(s) the end of the party // 몇 시~ 해서 about what time // 이때~ 떠나야 한다고 판단했다 I judged it was about time for me to leave. // 내주~ 또 오겠습니다 I will come again some time next week. // 다음 일요일~ 벚꽃이 필 것이다 The cherry blossoms will come out around next Sunday. // 3시~에 손님이 올 예정이다 I'm expecting a guest around three.

3 [적어도] at least. ¶잡지 하나~ 거저 준다 I can give you at least a copy of a magazine for nothing. // 사과의 말~은 해야 할 게 아닌가 At any rate, you have to apologize for what you have done.

쯧쯧 tut-tut; tsk tsk.

찌개 a pot stew. ¶된장~ a pot stew with doenjang(=bean paste) as its main ingredient // 생선~ a fish pot stew // ~ 그릇 a stew bowl.

찌그러지다 get pressed [squeezed] out of shape; be crushed. ¶찌그러진 [비틀린] distorted / warped / [타원형이 된] oval // 이 원은 찌그러졌다 This circle is misshapen. // 구두 모양이 찌그러졌다 My shoes have lost their shape. // 이런 식으로 만든 옷은 모양이 잘 찌그러지지 않습니다 A coat of this style will keep [retain] its shape.

찌그렁이 stubborn insistence. ¶~를 부리다 stubbornly insist on one's own way.

찌긋거리다 1 [눈을 자꾸 찌그리다] wink (an eye) at (a person). ¶남에게 눈을 ~ wink at a person / give a person an eye-signal. 2 [연해 당기다] pull at.

찌꺼기 1 [침전물] dregs; (주류의) lees; (버캐) scum; (커피 등의) grounds; sediment; residuum. ¶커피 ~ coffee grounds // 밥 ~ residue of rice // 컵에 붙은 ~ dregs left in a glass // 수면의 ~(버캐)를 걷어내다 skim off the scum on the water // 아무 ~도 남기지 않고 다 마시다 drink[drain] ... to the dregs. 2 [나머지] leavings; remains; remnants; leftovers; waste. ¶~ 사과 the worst of the apples (in a basket) / 먹다 남긴 ~ leftovers (of food) // 턱~ the remnants of a good meal / the leftovers.

찌다¹ [살이 올라서 뚱뚱해지다] grow fat; gain weight; put on flesh. ¶그는 너무 살이 쪘다 He is overweight.

찌다² [날씨가 더워지다] get steaming hot; be sultry; be humid. ¶찌는 듯한 더위 the sweltering heat // 오늘은 푹푹 찐다 It is sultry today. // 날이 찌는 듯이 덥다 It is steaming hot.

찌다³ [뜨거운 김에 익히다] steam. ¶찐 고구마 steamed sweet-potatoes // 찬밥을 ~ steam boiled rice // 조미(調味)를 하지 않고 그냥 ~ steamed food without any water or seasoning added.

찌들다 1 [더러워지다] get dirty. 2 [여위다] be hardened (by bitter experiences). ¶살림에 ~ be [look] worn with domestic [family] cares.

찌르다 1 [뾰족한 것으로 세차게 들이밀다] pierce; prick; stab; thrust. ¶음식을 젓가락으로 콕콕 ~ pick at the food with chopsticks // 나는 실수로 손가락을 바늘로 찔렀다 I pricked my finger with a needle [I ran a needle into my finger] by mistake. // 악한이 단도로 그의 등을 찔렀다 The ruffian stabbed him in the back with a knife. // 창으로 적병을 찔렀다 He pierced [transfixed] an enemy soldier with his spear. // 그 남자는 밀짚 매트에 칼을 찔렀다 The man stuck a knife into the straw mat. // 질투에 사로잡혀 그는 아내를 찔러 죽였다 Driven by jealousy, he stabbed his wife to death.

2 [쑤시다] poke(막대기로); prod(손가락 등으로); jab; [팔꿈치로 가볍게 밀치다] nudge; elbow. ¶옆구리를 ~ poke[give a poke] in the ribs // 주의를 끌기 위해 그는 팔꿈치로 나를 콕콕 찔렀다 He nudged[jogged] me with his elbow to attract my attention. // 나는 그를 팔꿈치로 쿡 찌르며 인사를 하라고 알려 주었다 I nudged[poked] him to remind him to bow. // 경찰은 경찰봉으로 내 옆구리를 쿡 찔렀다 The policeman jabbed me in the ribs with his club.

3 [꽂아 넣다] pass [put / run] (a thing) through; insert; put into. ¶주머니에 손을 찔러 넣고 with one's hands buried in the pockets.

4 [후각을 자극하다] be pungent. ¶소독약 냄새가 코를 찔렀다 The smell of disinfectant caught [문어] assailed] my nose. // 코를 찌르는 듯한 암모니아의 역겨운 냄새가 부근에 가득했다 The sharp, offensive smell of ammonia filled the air.

5 [닿을 듯하다] strike against. ¶사납게 날뛰는 파도가 마치 하늘을 찌를 듯했다 The raging waves leaped[reached] high into the sky.

6 [감정·초점 등을 건드리다] strike; touch; come home to (a person). ¶가슴을 찌르는 듯한 말 words that pierce the heart // 그 한 마

다가 나의 가슴을 찔렀다 That one word cut me to the quick.// 상대자는 내 이론의 허점을 찔렀다 My opponent seized upon the weak point in my logic.// 나는 그 사건의 핵심을 찌르는 데 필요한 증거를 찾았다 I found the evidence we needed to get at[to reach the heart of] the case.

7 [밀고하다] inform (on / against); lay [lodge] information (against); turn information (on a person); report[tell] (on a person). ¶경찰에 ~ denounce (a person) to the police // 공범자를 ~ betray one's accomplices.

찌르레기 [동] a (gray) starling.
찌르르 greasily; with a dull pain (in the joints). ⇨′지르르
찌륵 with a slurp (as through a straw). **찌륵하다** give[make] a slurp.
찌부러지다 get deflated. ⇨′짜부라지다
찌뿌드드하다 (서술적) feel uncomfortable; be out of sorts. ¶몸이 ~ feel uncomfortable / be unwell.
찌푸리다 1 [날씨가 흐리다] get cloudy; cloud over. ¶찌푸린 날씨 cloudy weather. **2** [얼굴을 찡그리다] let (one's face) cloud over; frown; scowl; wrinkle up. ¶그는 눈살을 찌푸리며 이야기했다 He talked with his brows knitted.// 그녀의 머리 모양을 보고 모두는 눈살을 찌푸렸다 Everyone looked askance[frowned] at her hair style.// 어머니는 내 이야기를 들으시며 눈살[이맛살]을 찌푸리셨다 My mother knitted her brows as she listened to me.// 그는 얼굴을 잔뜩 찌푸리고 있었다 He looked sour[displeased].// 그는 아파서 얼굴을 찌푸렸다 His face was distorted with pain.

찍 1 [미끄러지는 모양]. ¶~ 미끄러지다 get a slip / slip. **2** [긋는 모양]. ¶선을 ~ 긋다 draw a line with a (vigorous) stroke. **3** [찢는 소리]. ¶~ 찢다 rip up (one's clothes) / tear up (paper). **4** [쥐 등의 울음소리]. ¶~ 하고 울다 squeak.

찍다 1 (인쇄물·도장 등을) imprint; impress; stamp. ¶패스포트에 검인을 ~ stamp a passport // 책에 자기 도장을 ~ stamp one's name in a book // 편지에 소인을 ~ imprint a postmark on a letter // 서류에 도장을 ~ affix one's seal to a document // 지폐를 ~ print money.
2 [묻히다] dip (into). ¶펜을 잉크에 ~ dip the pen into the ink // 설탕을 찍어 먹다 eat (a thing) with sugar.
3 [점을 표시하다] place (a dot); mark with a point; dot; point; earmark; designate. ¶소수점을 ~ place a decimal point // 그녀는 i의 점을 찍는 것을 잊었다 She forgot to dot the i [put a dot on the i].
4 [눈여겨 두다] pick out; have an eye (on); spot(범인 등을).
5 [도끼 등으로 내리치다] chop (with an ax); hew; hack; cut. ¶도끼로 나무를 찍어 넘기다 chop a tree down with an ax.
6 [차표 등에 구멍을 내다] punch.
7 [사진을 박다] take (a photograph); shoot; snap. ¶사진을 찍었다 I had my picture taken. // 위 엑스레이 사진을 찍었다 I had my stomach x-rayed.
8 [찔러 꿰다] catch with a hook; pierce; thrust. ¶갈고리로 나무를 ~ hook a log // 멧돼지를 창으로 ~ spear a wild boar.

찍소리 a chirp; a tweet; a word; a syllable. ¶그는 ~도 못했다 There was nothing he could say.// 이렇게 하면 그는 ~ 못할 테지 This will shut him up. / He will be completely nonplus(s)ed by this.// 그는 약점을 찔려서는 ~도 못했다 There was no answer he could give[He was at a loss to reply], for he had been touched on a weak point.// 그의 논리 정연한 주장에는 ~도 못했다 I was utterly silenced by his logical argument.

찍어매다 sew (up); stitch (two pieces of cloth) together lightly; stitch (a thing) onto; tack (a ribbon to a hat). ¶터진 데를 ~ stitch up a tear[rip].
찍찍 shuffling; tearing; with (repeated) random strokes (of the pen). ⇨′직직
찍찍거리다¹ scuff; scuffle. ⇨′직직거리다
찍찍거리다² tweet; twitter. ⇨′쩍쩍거리다
찍히다 get imprinted[impressed / stamped]; get dipped (into); get pointed off[earmarked / designated]; get punched[hacked / cut]; get taken(사진이); get hooked.
찐득거리다 keep sticking; resist cutting. ⇨′진득거리다
찐빵 steamed bread.
찐쌀 rice processed by steaming unripe grains.
찔끔거리다 trickle; dribble; fall[run down] off and on. ¶걸핏하면 눈물을 ~ be maudlin / (구어) be sloppy / slobber.
찔끔찔끔 trickling; piecemeal. ⇨′짤끔짤끔 ¶돈을 ~ 주다 give money out piecemeal // 돈을 ~ 쓰다 use one's money in dribs and drabs.
찔끔하다 get struck with fear; be intimidated. ¶아버지의 묻는 말에 찔끔했다 My heart stood still at father's question.// 나는 그의 말에 찔끔했다 His word came home to me.
찔레(나무) [식] a wild[multiflora] rose; a brier.
찔름거리다¹ [넘치다] brim over; flow over the brim.
찔름거리다² [조금씩 주다] give in small amounts[in driblets]; give a little at a time; give off and on.
찔름찔름¹ [넘치도록] brimfully. **찔름찔름하다**¹ brim over. ⇨′찔름거리다¹
찔름찔름² [조금씩] piecemeal; in dribs and drabs. **찔름찔름하다**² give in small amounts. ⇨′찔름거리다²
찔리다 [남에게 찌름을 당하다] get (something) pierced[stabbed / pricked / thrust into]; (가슴에) go home to one's heart. ¶가시에 손을 ~ get a hand pricked by a thorn // 칼에 등을 찔려 죽다 be stabbed in the back to death // 그의 목에 생선 가시가 찔렸다 He had a fishbone stuck in his throat.// 그의 말에 가슴이 찔렸다 I had[felt] a prick of conscience at what he said.

찔찔 draggingly; long; tricklingly. ⇨′질질
찜 a steamed dish. ¶닭 ~ steamed chicken.
찜질 fomentation; applying a poultice[a compress / an ice pack]. ¶더운 ~ a hot compress / a stupe // 모래 ~ (take) a (hot) sand bath / treatment by the sand bath // 얼음 ~ applying an ice pack. **찜질하다** foment; poultice; apply a hot[cold] pack to. ¶더운 물수건으로 무릎을 ~ apply a hot towel to the knee.
찜찜하다 (서술적) feel awkward[embar-

찝찔하다

rassed]; feel ill at ease. ¶돈 문제는 말하기가 ~ It is awkward to speak about money matters.

찝찔하다 nice and salty. ⇨ ²짭짤하다1

찡그리다 twist up (one's face / eyes) into a scowl. ¶얼굴[눈]을 ~ frown / scowl / make a wry face / knit one's brow / make a grimace // 그는 화가 나서 얼굴을 찡그렸다 His brow was crinkled with anger. // 그는 고통을 견디지 못해 얼굴을 찡그렸다 His face was distorted with pain.

찡긋거리다 twist[wrinkle up] one's face at (a person); make a mouth at; wink at.

찡얼거리다 [애가 보채다] whimper; fuss; whine. ¶애가 왜 이렇게 찡얼거릴까, 어디가 아픈가 The baby is quite fretful today, I wonder whether he[she] is sick.

찡찡거리다 grumble; murmur; whine; whimper.

찡찡이 a habitual sniffer. ⇨ ¯코찡찡이

찡찡하다 1 feel awkward. ⇨ ¯찜찜하다 2 [코가 막혀 숨 쉬기가 거북하다] 〈서술적〉 be odd-sounding because of a nasal polyp.

찢기다 get torn[rent / ripped]. ¶갈기갈기 ~ be torn to ribbons // 그의 옷이 가시 철망에 찢겼다 His clothes were rent on barbed wire. // 깃발은 갈갈이 찢겨 있다 The banner is rent to pieces.

찢다 tear; rend; rip. ¶입장권을 둘로 ~ tear an admission ticket in two // 편지를 갈기갈기 ~ tear a letter to pieces // 공책을 한 장 찢어 내다 tear off a sheet from a notebook // 자루를 찢어서 열다 rip a bag open // 찢어 죽이다 tear (a person) limb from limb // 갈가리 찢어 죽여도 시원치 않을 놈이다 Nothing could appease my anger against him. // 그는 손수건을 찢어 붕대로 썼다 He tore off his handkerchief and bandaged the bruise.

찢어발기다 tear to threads; rip to ribbons.

찢어지다 tear; rend; rip. ¶가슴이 찢어지는 듯한 heart-rending // 찢어지기 쉽다 tear easily // 그 헝겊은 너무 잡아당기면 찢어진다 If you pull on the cloth too hard, it will split. // 이 천은 좀처럼 찢어지지 않는다 This cloth will not tear.

찧다 pound; ram. ¶떡쌀을 ~ pound glutinous rice // 절구에 쌀을 ~ pound rice in a mortar // 쿵방아를 ~ fall flat on the ground // 벽에 이마를 ~ ram one's head against a wall // 엉덩방아를 ~ plop down with a thud.

차- [찰기가 있는] glutinous. ¶~좁쌀 hulled [polished] glutinous millet.

차(此) [이(것)] this; these; present; current. ¶~로써 now / with this / hereby.

차(車) 1 [탈것] a vehicle; a carriage; a conveyance; [자동차] a motorcar; an automobile; a car; [택시] a taxi; (화물용의) a van; a wagon; a lorry; a truck. ¶~에서 내리다 get off a car / step out of [alight from] a car / ~를 타다 take a motorcar / ride in a car [taxi] / go in a car [taxi] // ~에 태워 주다 give (a person) a ride / pick (a person) up / (보행자를) give (a person) a lift // ~로 붐비다 be crowded with (auto) traffic // ~로 운반하다 carry [transport] (goods) in a car [truck] / ~로 여행하다 travel by (a) vehicle // ~를 몇 대나 갖고 있다 possess [have] several cars / keep a stable of cars // ~를 멈추다 bring a car to a halt [to rest] / ~를 세우다 (손을 들어) stop [hold up / (미) flag (down)] a cab / 우리는 극장까지 ~로 갔습니다 We went to the theater by car [in the car]. (▶ in the car는 자기의 차로) / We drove to the theater. // 집까지 ~로 태워다 드리죠 I will give you a lift to your home. // 역에서 ~를 탈 수 있습니다 You can get a taxi at the station. // ~를 부를까요 Shall I get a car for you? / ~를 잡아 [전화로 불러] 주시겠습니까 Would you get [call] me a taxi? // 그 호텔은 역에서 ~로 10분도 안 걸린다 The hotel is situated within ten minutes' ride from the station. // 문 앞에 ~가 대기하고 있습니다 The car is waiting (for you) at the gate. // 10시 정각에 호텔까지 ~를 보내겠습니다 I'll send a car to the hotel at ten sharp. // 이 길에는 ~가 들어갈 수 없다 Traffic is not [No cars are] allowed on this road.
2 [장기] a castle; a rook.

차(茶) 1 a tea plant. ⇨차나무
2 [차나무의 잎] tea (leaves). ¶~ 산지 a tea-growing district / a tea-producing center.
3 [차나무의 잎을 달인 음료] tea. ¶녹~ green tea / 홍~ black tea / 진한 [멀건] ~ strong [weak] tea // ~ 찌끼 used tea leaves / tea grounds [dregs] // ~ 거르개 a tea strainer / ~ 한 잔 a cup of tea // ~를 끓이다 make [brew / draw / prepare] tea / fix tea // ~를 따르다 pour tea into a cup // ~를 마시다 drink tea / tea // ~를 대접하다 serve (a person) with tea // ~를 마시면서 이야기하다 talk over (a cup of) tea // ~가 나왔다 Tea was served. // ~나 마십시다 Let's have some tea. // 이 ~는 진한 [엷은] ~를 좋아한다 He likes his tea strong [weak]. / 이 ~는 잘 우러난다 [우러나지 않는다] This tea draws [doesn't draw] well. // ~를 마시면서 의논했다 We discussed the matter over tea. // 이 ~는 여러 잔 끓여서 이제 싱겁다 This tea is weak because I've already made several cups with the same leaves.

차(差) 1 [차이] (a) difference; variance; [변화] variation; [격차] (a) disparity; (a) discrepancy; inequality; odds; a gap; (가격상의) a margin; (득표의) a majority; a plurality (차점 득표자와의); (액수상의) balance; [천] equation. ¶A와 B의 ~ the difference between A and B // 세대 ~ a generation gap // 견해의 ~ a difference in view / 지위 [신분]의 ~ (a) disparity [difference] in rank [social standing] // 연령의 ~ difference [disparity] in [of] age / age difference // 품질의 ~ difference in quality // 임금의 ~ wage differentials // ~가 있다 there is a difference (between) / differ (from) / vary (from) // ~가 없다 there is no difference (between) // 근소한 ~로 이기다 win by a narrow margin [small majority] // 200표의 ~로 당선하다 win an election by a majority [plurality] of 200 (votes) // 꽤 큰 ~로 당선하다 be elected by a handsome margin // 1점 ~로 지다 [이기다] lose [win] the game by one point // 근소한 ~로 2위가 되다 make a close second (in a race) // ~를 두다 [차별하다] discriminate (between A and B) / make a discrimination / [등급을 매기다] grade / graduate // ~를 내다 [벌이다] (경기에서) establish [build up / open] a lead (on one's opponent) // 그 두 사람의 의견에는 큰 ~가 있다 There is a great gap between the views of the two. / Their opinions differ greatly. // 둘 사이에 큰 ~는 없다 There is no great difference between the two. // 우리는 두 점 ~로 졌다 [이겼다] We lost [won] the game by two points [runs] (▶ runs는 야구에서). // 7표 ~로 그가 의장으로 선출되었다 He was elected chairman by (a margin of) seven votes. // 5초의 ~로 그는 2위를 앞질렀다 He beat the runner-up by five seconds. / He finished five seconds ahead of the runner-up. // 그 나라는 빈부의 ~가 심하다 [심하지 않다] There is a [no] big gulf [cleavage] between (the) rich and (the) poor in that country.
2 [수] the remainder. ¶~를 구하다 find the remainder.

차(次) 1 […한 김에] while; when; as; by the way; while one is at [about] it. ¶서울로 가는 ~에 on the way to Seoul // 부산에 내려온 ~에 들러 봤습니다 I just dropped in while I was in Busan.
2 […하려던 참] time; moment; just as. ¶(막) …하려던 ~였다 was going to (do) / was (just) about to (do) / was on the point [brink / verge] of (doing) // 막 외출하려던 ~에 그녀가 왔다 I was just going out, when she came to see me.
3 [순서] order; sequence; [수] degree; [횟수] time. ¶1~ 방정식 a linear [simple] equation / an equation of the first degree // 1 [2] ~ 코일 [전지] a primary [secondary] coil [battery] // 제2~ 발표 the second announcement // 제2~ 세계 대전 World War Ⅱ // 제3~ 내각 the third cabinet // 그는 1~ 시험에 합격했다 He passed the primary examination.

-차(次) […하려고] for the purpose of; with

차가 (借家) [빌려 든 집] a rented [leased / hired] house; [세듬] renting a house. **차가하다** rent [hire / take] a house.

차가다 snatch (away) (from / off); catch away. ⇨채다¹

차간 거리 (車間距離) the distance between (two) cars going in the same direction. ¶~를 지키다 observe the proper distance between cars // ~를 충분히 두다 leave enough room between one's car and the car in front // 앞차와의 사이에 안전한 ~를 유지하다 maintain a proper [safe] distance between one's car and the car ahead.

차감 (差減) 1 [빼기] (a) deduction; (a) subtraction; [법] (a) recoupment. **차감하다** deduct; subtract; recoup. 2 (계정의) a balance; [차액] a margin. **차감하다** balance (an account). ¶수입과 지출을 차감하면 다소의 이익이 있다 When earnings and disbursements are balanced, some profit is left.
● **차감 잔액** the balance.

차갑다 (온도·기온이) cold; frigid; icy; chill(y); [매몰차다] cold-hearted; cold-blooded. ¶차가운 사람 a cold-hearted [an icy] person / a man of gelid reserve // 차가운 태도 a cold [frosty / frigid] manner // 차가운 대접 a cold reception [treatment] // 몹시 차가운 공기 sharp air // 얼음처럼 차가운 icy / as cold as ice / ice-cold // 차가운 눈으로 남을 보다 look at a person coldly / cast a cold eye [steely glance] on a person / give a person a stony stare // 차가워지다 become [get] cold [chilled] / (태도가) cool off (toward one's lover) / [죽다] be cold in death / die // 그녀의 태도는 요즘 퍽 차가워졌다 Her attitude toward me has lately got indifferent.

차고 (車庫) a car shed; a carbarn; (a carriage) shed; (전차의) a tram depot [shed]; (자동차의) a garage; a carport. ¶~에 넣다 put (a streetcar) into a barn / put (an automobile) into a garage / garage (a car) // ~에 넣어 두다 keep (a bus) in a barn / garage (a car).

차곡차곡 in orderly fashion; in a neat pile; (lay) one thing on another. ¶벽돌을 ~ 쌓다 lay one brick on another // 접시를 ~ 쌓아 놓다 stack the dishes into neat piles // 침구를 ~ 개다 fold bedding up in piles // 옷을 장에 ~ 넣다 put one's clothes one by one in a wardrobe.

차관 (次官) a vice-minister; an undersecretary; (미) a deputy secretary. ¶사무 ~ a permanent vice-minister // 정무 ~ a parliamentary vice-minister // ~급의 (a person) of the vice-minister class.
● **차관보** (-補) (미) an assistant secretary. **국방** ~ the Assistant Secretary of Defense.

차관 (借款) a loan. ¶개발 ~ a development loan [credit] // 공공 [재정] ~ a public [financial] loan // 상업 [민간] ~ a commercial [private] loan // 장기 [단기] ~ a long-term [short-term] loan // ~을 신청하다 ask [apply] for a loan // ~을 얻다 obtain a loan [credit] // ~을 제공하다 grant [extend / give] a credit (to) // 50억 원의 ~을 체결하다 contract a loan of five billion won.
● **차관단** a consortium (*pl.* -tia, ~s).

차광 (遮光) shading the light. **차광하다** shield [shade] the light.
● **차광막** (등화관제용) a blackout curtain (창문의); a shade (등불 둘레의); a flag (텔레비전 카메라의).

차근차근 scrupulously; methodically; systematically; (서두르지 않고) step by step. ¶~ 설명하다 give full particulars // 일을 ~ 처리하다 dispose of a matter carefully [step by step] // 어려운 문제를 ~ 해결하다 settle (up) a difficult problem by going at it systematically // 그는 그녀가 잘못을 깨닫도록 ~ 설득하려 했다 He tried patiently to convince her of her error. **차근차근하다** careful; methodical; scrupulous; slow but steady.

차금 (借金) a debt; a loan.

차기 (次期) the next term.
● **차기 대통령** the president for the next term; the next President; the President-elect. **차기 정권** the next Administration.

차꼬 [옛날, 죄인의 발을 채우던 형틀] shackles; fetters. ¶~를 채운 (a criminal) in fetters // ~를 채우다 shackle / fetter.

차나무 (茶—) a tea plant.

차남 (次男) one's [the / a] second son.

차내 (車內) the inside of a car [train]. ¶~에서 (자동차) in the car [bus] / (기차) in [on] the train / (전차) in the tram // 이 ~에서는 금연입니다 Smoking is prohibited in this car. / This is a nonsmoking car [(영) carriage]. // ~에서는 담배를 삼가 주십시오 (게시) Passengers are requested to refrain from smoking. / Please don't smoke in the car.

차녀 (次女) one's [the / a] second daughter.

차다¹ 1 [가득하게 되다] fill (up); become full (of); be filled [replete] (with); brim (with); (시간·일·자리 등이) be engaged; be occupied. ¶책이 꽉 찬 책꽂이 a bookcase filled [stuffed] with books // 활기에 가득 찬 젊은이들 young men full of vitality // 독에 물이 ~ water fills a jar / a jar is filled (up) with water // 배가 ~ one's stomach is full // 꽉 꽉 [빽빽이] 들어 ~ be jammed / be tightly packed / be overcrowded / be packed full // 앞날이 희망에 차 있다 one's future is full of hope // 활기에 차 있다 be full of vigor // 예정이 꽉 차 있다 have a heavy [close packed] schedule // 연못에는 물이 가득 차 있었다 The pond was full of water. // 물통에 물이 가득 차 있다 The bucket is full of water. / The bucket is brimful of [brimming with] water. // 공원은 인파로 가득 차 있다 The park is crowded with [is full of] people. // 좌석은 학생들로 가득 찼다 The seats were filled with students. // 그들의 마음은 행복감으로 가득 차 있었다 A happy feeling pervaded their hearts. / Their hearts were filled with happiness. // 그 방은 차 있다 The room is occupied. // 결원은 이미 찼다 The vacancy has been filled. // 나는 예정이 차 있다 My schedule is tight [jam-packed]. // 직장에 자리가 차서 내가 들어갈 자리가 없다 All the positions are filled and there is no vacancy for me.
2 [흡족하다] be satisfied [pleased] (with); be content (with); (사물이) be satisfactory. ¶마음에 ~ meet with satisfaction / prove satis-

factory / be satisfied (with) / be content (with) // 며느리가 마음에 ~ be satisfied with one's daughter-in-law // 밥이 양에 ~ have enough rice (to satisfy one's appetite) // 마음에 차지를 않다 (사람이) be dissatisfied [displeased] (with) / (사물이) do not please / be [prove] unsatisfactory / leave something [much] to be desired // 나는 어쩐지 마음에 차지 않았다 I felt somehow dissatisfied. **3** [정한 수효가 되다] measure up to (a certain quantity); come (up) to; amount to; be as much as. ¶정족수에 ~ form [make / constitute] a quorum // 정족수에 차지 않다 be short of necessary quorum / lack a quorum // 일정 액수에 차지 않다 be short of a certain amount.
4 [만기가 되다] expire(임기가); (어음 등이) mature; reach maturity; fall [be / become] due. ¶임기가 ~ one's term of office expires // 임신부의 달이 ~ one's time (of delivery) comes // 어음의 기한이 ~ a bill matures [is due for payment] // 그는 형기가 차서 출감했다 On the expiry of the term he was discharged from prison. // 그의 임기는 내달에 찬다 His term of office will expire next month. // 내달로 지급 기한이 찬다 The payment will come due next month. // 그녀는 달이 차서 어린아이를 분만했다 Her time came and she gave birth to a baby.
5 [달이 둥글게 되다] wax; (미) full. ¶달이 찼다 The moon is (at the) full. / There is a full moon. // 달도 차면 기운다 Every flood [tide] hath its ebb.

차다² 1 [발로] kick (at); give (a person) a kick on the shin. ¶되받아 ~ kick back / return a kick // 서로 ~ kick at each other // 차 넣다 kick in // 차올리다 kick up / give an upward kick / send (a thing) over // 의자를 차서 넘어뜨리다 kick over a chair // 공을 되받아 ~ kick a ball back / return a ball a kick // 문을 발로 차서 열다 kick a door open // 그는 문을 찼다 He gave a kick at the gate. // 그는 양동이를 차서 우그러뜨렸다 He kicked a hole in the bucket. // 그는 병을 도랑에 차 넣었다 He kicked the bottle into a ditch. // 그는 자리를 차고 회의실에서 나왔다 He stamped out of the conference room. // 그는 문을 차서 부수고 [열고] 방으로 들어갔다 He kicked the door down [open] and went in.
2 [거절하다] reject; refuse; turn down; (미국구어) kick (a request); (애인 등을) jilt (a person); discard; throw (a person) over. ¶애인을 차 버리다 jilt one's lover.
3 [혀를] click. ¶혀를 ~ click [clack] one's tongue / tsk / go tsk.

차다³ 1 [패용하다] attach; fasten on; wear. ¶시계를 ~ put [strap] on a watch / wear a (wrist-)watch // 칼을 ~ wear [carry] a sword at one's side // 훈장을 ~ pin on [wear] a decoration [medal] // 패물을 ~ wear trinkets // 권총을 허리에 ~ wear a gun at one's side [on one's hip] // 그 기병 장교는 군도를 허리에 차고 있었다 The cavalry officer wore a saber [(영) sabre] at his side. **2** (쇠고랑을) be handcuffed [manacled]; (차꼬를) be fettered [shackled]; be put in shackles. ¶쇠고랑을 찬 죄수 a handcuffed prisoner.

차다⁴ 1 [온도·날씨가] cold; chilly; icy; frosty; freezing; cool. ¶찬 날씨 cold weather // 찬밥 cold boiled rice // 찬물 cold water // 찬 바람 a cold [chilly] wind // 차게 한 cooled (water) / iced (drinks) // 차게 하다 cool / (얼음으로) ice / (냉장 장치로) refrigerate // 차게 해 두다 keep (a thing) cool on ice // 우유를 냉장고에 넣어서 차게 해 두다 keep milk cool in a refrigerator // 차지다 become [get] cold [chilled] / go cold // 얼음장같이 ~ be icecold / be (as) cold as ice // 바깥 날씨가 몹시 ~ It is freezing cold outside. // 공기가 몹시 ~ There is a nip in the air. // 오늘 아침은 날씨가 꽤 차군요 It's rather chilly this morning. // 오늘 아침은 공기가 ~ There is a chill in the air this morning.
2 (마음 등이) coldhearted; cold-blooded; cold; frigid. ¶찬 사람 a coldhearted [an icy] person // (태도가) 차지다 cool off (toward one's lover).

찬 이슬 맞는 놈 (속담) a night thief; a burglar; a night prowler [walker].

차단(遮斷) interception; isolation; quarantine(전염병 방지를 위한); [전] break. ¶교통 ~ roadblocking / quarantine(검역 등으로 인한). **차단하다** intercept; isolate; cut off; shut off; quarantine; [전] break. // 외부의 음향을 ~ exclude (the) outside sounds // 교통을 ~ cut off from all communication with the outside world // 퇴로을 ~ intercept [cut off] the [a person's] retreat / block the way of retreat // 보급로를 ~ block the supply route // 도둑의 도주로를 ~ cut off a thief's escape // 이 벽은 외부의 음향을 차단하기에 충분하다 These walls are thick enough to shut out outside sounds. → 그 거리의 교통이 한 시간 동안 차단되었다 Traffic on the street was stopped [interrupted] for an hour. / The street was closed for an hour.

● **차단기**(一器) (전류의) a (circuit) breaker.
차단기(一機) (건널목의) a crossing gate; (오르내림식의) a lifting gate.

차대(次代) the coming [oncoming] generation.

차대(車臺) a car body; a chassis (*pl.* ~(es)) (자동차의).

차도(車道) a roadway; a carriageway; (미) a driveway.

차도(差度) improvement (of illness); convalescence. ¶~이 있다 get better / improve / convalesce / (병세가) be progressing favorably / take a turn for the better / take a favorable turn // 환자는 완연히 ~를 보이고 있다 The patient is well on toward [on the road to] recovery.

차돌 quartz; quartzite. ¶~ 같은 사람 a tough fellow / a man of steadfast character.

차등(差等) gradation; graduation; (a) difference. ¶~이 있다 be different in grade(s) // ~을 두다 grade / graduate / discriminate.
● **차등 세율** a graded [differential] tariff.

차디차다 [매우 차다] very cold; freezing; frigid; icy; ever so cold; as cold as ice; cold as cold can be.

차라리 rather (than); better (than); sooner (than); before; first; preferably. ¶수치를 당하느니 ~ 죽는 것이 낫다 I would rather [sooner] die than suffer disgrace. / Death is preferable to dishonor. // ~ 학교를 그만둬 버릴까 보다 I wonder if I had(n't) better leave school. // 굴복하느니 ~ 죽어 버리겠다 I'll die before giving in. // 너는 가지 않는 편이 ~ 낫다 You had better not go there. // 이런 일을

차량

하느니 ~ 죽어 버릴 테다 I would rather [sooner] die than do such work.

차량(車輛) vehicles; cars; a (railway) carriage; (철도·운송 회사의) the rolling stock. ¶~ 한 대분의 화물 a carload (of goods) // ~에 의한 수송 wheeled transport // ~의 정비 불량 poor maintenance of the vehicles ●**차량 검사** vehicle (maintenance) inspection; vehicle safety inspection. **차량 등록** vehicle registration. **차량 번호판** (자동차의) a license plate. **차량 정비** vehicle maintenance. **차량 통행금지** (게시) No thoroughfare for vehicles.; Closed to all vehicles.

차려 [구령] Attention!; Shun! ¶~ 자세 attention // ~ 자세를 취하다 come to attention / stand at[to] attention // 벌떡 일어나 ~ 자세를 취하다 spring to attention.

차력하다(借力−) boost one's strength (with a physical or by spiritual tonic).

차례(次例) **1** [순서] order; [순번] a turn. ¶[내[네] ~ my[your] turn / 줄지어 ~를 기다리는 people people standing in queues awaiting their turn // ~로 in (regular) order / in turn / by turns / by[in] rotation / one by one / one after another / 나이 ~로 by priority of age / according to seniority // ~를 따라 in due order[course / succession] / in regular sequence / through regular grades // ~가 뒤바뀌다 be out of order / be in wrong order // ~로 서다 stand in order / stand in a queue (줄지어) / 키 ~로 서다 stand in order of height // ~가 오다[되다] one's turn comes round // ~로 돌리다 pass (a thing) (a)round [from hand to hand] // 술잔을 ~로 돌리다 pass the winecup around // ~대로 늘어놓다 put things in order // ~로 하다 take one's turn (to do) / (번갈아) take by spell / take spell and spell // ~로 일하다[망을 보다] work [watch] by turns // ~로 노래를 부르다 sing by turns[in turn] / take turns at singing // ~를 기다리다 await[wait (for)] one's turn / (이발소에서) wait for attention // 배우 휴게실에서 (무대에) 나갈 ~를 기다리다 wait in the green room for one's turn to go on // ~를 앞당기다 move up (something) in order // ~를 바꾸다 change the order // 그들을 한 사람씩 ~로 때려 주었다 I beat them one by one. // 우리는 ~로 교장실에 불려 갔다 We were summoned to the principal's office one by one. // 그는 책을 한 권씩 ~로 읽었다 He read one book after another. // 우리는 ~로 파수를 보았다 We took turns watching. / We watched by turns. // 그들은 ~로 각자의 의견을 말했다 They gave their opinions by turns [in turn]. // 마침내 ~가 돌아왔다 At last my turn came. / Finally it come to my turn. // 누구 ~입니까 Whose turn is it? / Who is next? / (바둑 등에서) Whose move is it? // 이번에는 누가 이야기할 ~죠 Who is the next speaker? // 이번에는 내가 읽을 ~다 It's my turn to read now.

2 [횟수] time; round. ¶한 ~ once // 두 ~ twice // 세 ~ thrice / three times // 여러 ~ several times // 책을 몇 ~ 읽다 read a book several times // 두 ~ 이기다 win two rounds (of a game) // 술잔을 네 ~째 돌리다 pass the winecup for the fourth round of drinks.

3 [목차] a table of contents. ¶~를 달다 attach a table of contents to (a book).

차례(茶禮) a *charye*; ancestor-memorial rites.

¶~를 지내다 observe a worship service for family ancestors on (*chuseok* morning).

차례차례(次例次例) in due[regular] order; in order; in turn; by turns; in regular sequence; [하나하나] one by one; one after another; successively. ¶~ 키대로 서다 stand (one after another) in order of height // 사람을 ~ 불러들이다 call in men one after another // ~ 물어보다 ask (them) one after another // 일을 ~ 처리하다 dispose of matters in due order / settle things one by one[one after another] // ~ 설명하겠습니다 I'll[Let me] explain it in order. // 우리는 문제를 ~ 해결했다 We solved the problems one by one. // 학생들이 ~ 들어왔다 The pupils came in one after another. // 그는 ~ 손님과 악수했다 He shook hands with each guest in turn.

차륜(車輪) a (wagon) wheel. ⇨ 수레바퀴(⇨수레).

차르랑 clinking; with a clink[tinkle]. **차르랑하다** clink; tinkle; make a tinkling sound.

차리다 1 [장만하여 갖추다] make; prepare; set up; get ready. ¶음식을 ~ serve (a person) with a meal / 식탁[밥상]을 ~ set the table (for dinner) / lay covers (for four guests) // 저녁상을 ~ get supper ready / 잔칫상을 ~ give[spread] a feast[banquet] / give[hold] a party / 살림을 ~ make a new home (at / in) // 점포를 ~ set up a store // 떠날 채비를 ~ make oneself ready for the start (on a trip) // 아침 식사는 내가 차리겠습니다 I will set the table for breakfast [prepare breakfast]. / 차린 것이 아무것도 없습니다 We have nothing special to offer you.

2 [옷 등을 갖추어 꾸미다] dress (oneself) up; be dressed up.

3 [겉으로 드러내다] keep; maintain; save; preserve; observe; pay attention (to). ¶체면을 ~ keep up appearances // 그는 체면을 차리기 위해 봉급을 많이 받고 있는 채했다 He pretended to be receiving a high salary in order to keep up appearances.

4 [스스로 깨치다] understand; catch up (the meaning). ¶…을 눈치 ~ get the wind of (it).

5 [정신을 가다듬어 되찾다] come to; collect (oneself); concentrate (one's mind).

6 [욕망을 채우려 하다] be avaricious / be covetous / be greedy / 제 욕심만 ~ be self-interested / put one's own interests above everything else.

차림새 [차린 그 모양] dress; attire; getup; guise; one's (personal) appearance. ¶행상인 ~의 남자 a man looking like a peddler // 예술가 ~의 남자 a man dressed like an artist // 단정한 ~로 decently dressed // 여자 ~로 in the (dis)guise of a woman / disguised in female attire // 나그네의 ~로 fitted out as a traveler / in a traveling outfit // ~가 말쑥하다 [야하다] be neatly[loudly] turned out / be neat[loud] in one's dress // ~가 간소하다 be simply attired // ~를 하다 dress shabbily / be shabbily dressed / be humbly clad // 그녀는 ~에 매우 신경을 쓴다 She is very careful about her appearance. // 이런 ~로는 남 앞에 못 나간다 I am not fit to be seen. / I am not presentable. // 그는 ~에 개의치 않는 사람이다 He is quite indifferent to [careless about] his personal appearance. //

~만 봐도 그녀의 성격을 알 수 있었다 You could judge her character through her outfit.

차림표(-表) a menu; a bill of fare.

차마 ¶~ …하지 못하다 do not have the heart (to punish him) / be loath (to leave / to part) / be reluctant [unwilling / averse] (to do) / cannot allow [bring] oneself (to leave) // ~ 눈 뜨고 볼 수 없는 참상이다 be too miserable [cruel] to look at // ~ 그대로 보아 넘길 수 없다 be unable to let (it) pass unnoticed / cannot remain indifferent // 나는 ~ 그렇게 할 수 없었다 I couldn't find it in my heart to do so. // 그를 ~ 바로 쳐다볼 수 없었다 I had to turn off my face from him. // 나는 그의 부탁을 ~ 거절할 수가 없었다 I could not find it in my heart to refuse his request.

차멀미(車-) car sickness. **차멀미하다** get [be] carsick. ¶나는 차멀미했다 I got carsick.

차명하다(借名-) assume (a person's) name; use (a person's) name; masquerade under (a person's) name; impersonate (another). ¶차명하여 in the name of / under the (assumed) name of.

차바퀴(車-) a wheel; a rundle. ¶~ 자국 a (wheel) track / a rut / the print of a wheel / ~에 깔리다 be run over by (a car) // ~에 기름을 치다 put oil on the wheels // ~가 빠졌다 The wheel has come off.

차반(茶盤) a tea tray [server / board].

차변(借邊) the debit [debtor] (약어 Dr, dr.); (차변란) the debit [debtor] side. ¶~과 대변 debtor and creditor // ~에 기입하다 debit (a sum) against [to] (a person) / enter (an item) to (a person's) debit [to the debit of (a person's) account].

●**차변 계정** [잔고] a debtor account [balance]. **차변 항목** a debit item.

차별(差別) (a) distinction; (a) discrimination; differentiation. ¶인종 ~ racial discrimination / a color bar [line] / (남아프리카의) apartheid // 인종 ~ 철폐 abolition of racial discrimination // ~적인 discriminative / discriminatory / preferential / differential // 상하의 ~ 없이 without distinction of rank or class // 남녀의 ~ 없이 irrespective of sex / men and women (all) like // 연령의 ~ 없이 irrespective [regardless] of age // ~을 두지 않고 indiscriminately / without distinction [discrimination] // 두 사람 사이에 ~을 두다 [두지 않다] discriminate [make no distinction] between two people // ~을 두지 않고 취급하겠습니다 I will treat you all alike [without partiality]. **차별하다** draw [establish / set up] a distinction (between); differentiate (one from another); distinguish (between); discriminate (against A / in favor of B). ¶여성을 ~ discriminate against women // 외국인을 ~ discriminate against foreigners // 사람에 따라 ~ discriminate against certain persons.

●**차별 관세** discriminating duties. **차별 대우** discriminative [discriminatory / discriminating / preferential] treatment; discrimination in treatment; inequality of treatment. ¶~를 받다 be treated discriminately / be discriminated against (by) // ~을 하다 give discriminative [preferential] treatment (to) / treat (people) with discrimination [differently] / discriminate against // 나는 심한 ~를 받았다 I was horribly discriminated against.

차부(車夫) a driver; a cabman; (짐수레의) a carter.

차분하다 calm; quiet; composed; tranquil; placid; serene; subdued; sedate; collected; self-possessed. ¶차분한 기분 a quiet mood // 차분한 빛깔 a sober [subdued] color // 아주 차분한 목소리로 in a skilled, severely controlled voice // 차분한 태도로 in a calm [graceful] manner // 비상 사태 속에서 그녀의 차분한 태도는 우리에게 용기를 주었다 Her composure in the midst of the emergency gave us courage. **차분히** calmly; quietly; composedly; serenely; with serenity [composure]. ¶~ 생각해 보다 think over (a matter) / ponder (over the plan) // ~ 공부하다 settle [set] down to one's studies // 마음을 ~ 가라앉히다 calm [compose] oneself / keep cool / gather one's wits // 그는 ~ 회장을 둘러보았다 He looked around the hall quite composedly [calmly]. // 아이들이 떠들어 ~ 책을 읽을 수가 없다 The children are so noisy that I cannot settle down to my reading. // 모든 가능성을 ~ 생각해 보십시오 Take your time and think over all the possibilities.

차비(車費) (철도 승차비) the railroad [railway] fare; (전차 등의) the (car) fare; (일반적으로) the transit fee; (운반료) freight; carriage; cartage. ¶~를 내다 pay the fare // ~를 할인하다 discount [reduce] the fare (for students) // 서울까지의 왕복 ~는 얼마입니까 What is the fare to Seoul and back?

차비(差備) preparation(s); arrangement. ⇨ 채비

차사(差使) [역] an emissary (with the police power).

차석(次席) the next seat [position]. ¶~이다 rank next to (the captain) // 그녀는 고교를 반에서 ~으로 졸업했다 She graduated from high school second in her class. // 그는 ~으로 입상했다 He finished in second place. / He was the runner-up.

●**차석자** (관리 등) an official next in rank; an associate; (수상자 등) the second winner. **차석 판사** an associate [a side] judge.

차선(次善) the second best.

●**차선책** the second [next] best policy. ¶~을 택하다 take the second best (for / to) // 최선의 계획이 안 되면 우리는 ~을 쓸 수밖에 없다 If we can't use the best plan, we'll have to settle for the second best.

차선(車線) a (traffic) lane. ¶4~의 고속도로 a four-lane speedway // ~을 지키다 [지키며 달리다] keep one's lane / stay in one lane // 서울-대전 간의 고속도로를 8~으로 확장하다 expand the Seoul-Daejeon Expressway into an eight-lane road.

●**차선 분리대** a divisional strip [island]. **차선폭**

차수(次數) [수] (the second) degree. ¶다항식의 ~ the degree of a polynomial.

차수(差數) difference (in number); balance; disparity.

차아(次兒) one's [the] second son.

차압(差押) [법] attachment; seizure. ⇨ 압류

차액(差額) the difference; (특히 수지의) the balance; (매매의) the margin. ¶큰 [작은] ~ a wide [narrow] margin // 두 가격의 ~ the difference between two prices // 5만 원의 ~ a

차양

difference of fifty thousand won // ~을 메우다 make up the difference // ~이 얼마인가 What is the balance[margin]? // 예금의 예입과 인출의 ~이 꼭 만 원이 되었다 The balance[difference between the debit and credit sides] of my account comes to exactly ten thousand won.

차양(遮陽) **1** (지붕의) a penthouse; a pent roof; (창·문의) an awning; a (sun / Venetian) blind. **2** a visor; an eyeshade. ⇨챙². ¶~이 넓은 모자 a broad-brimmed hat / ~이 달린 모자 a peaked[visored] cap.

차용(借用) borrowing; loan. **차용하다** (무료로) borrow; (유료로) rent. ¶돈을 차용하다 달라고 부탁하다 ask (a person) for a loan of money / apply to (a person) for an advance of money // 일금 10만 원을 정히 차용했습니다 I owe you[IOU] 100,000won.
● **차용금** borrowed money; a loan; a debt. **차용어** a borrowed word; a loanword; a loan. **차용인** a borrower; (돈의) a debtor. **차용 증서 / 차용증** a bond of debt[loan]; an IOU(▶ I owe you의 음(音)에서); a due bill; (속의) the three vowels. ¶150파운드의 ~를 쓰다 write out an IOU for 150 pounds.

차원(次元) **1** [수] a dimension. ¶2[3]~의 of two[three] dimension / two-[three-]dimensional // 제4~ 공간 four-dimensional space. **2** [입장·수준] a point of view; a level. ¶~이 낮은[높은] 이야기 a gutter-level[an elevated] conversation / a conversation on commonplace[lofty] topics // 그가 하는 일은 내가 하는 일과 ~이 다르다 His work belongs to a different sphere from mine. // 그들의 의견은 ~이 달라 일치하지 않는다 They look at the matter on different levels, so there is no way to bring their opinions into line.

차월(借越) a debt balance; (당좌 예금의) an overdraft; overdrawing. **차월하다** overdraw.

차위(次位) the second rank[place / position].

차이(差異) (a) difference; (a) divergence; disagreement; (a) distinction(구별); (a) discrepancy(불일치); (a) disparity(불균형); (a) dissimilarity(같지 않음); a gap. ¶연령[신분]의 ~ (a) discrepancy[disparity] in age[social standing] // 빈부의 ~ a gulf between the rich and the poor // 의견의 ~ a difference[divergence] of opinion[views] // 취미의 ~ (a) disparity of tastes (between A and B) // 능력의 ~ a discrepancy in ability // 현저한 ~ a striking[remarkable / sharp] contrast // 세 살 ~의 형[아우] a brother three years older[younger] than (one) // ~가 있다 there is a difference (between) / disagree (with) / differ[vary] (from) // 큰 ~가 있다 differ greatly (from) / there is a wide difference (between) / make a vast difference (to one) // 큰 ~가 없다 differ little (from) / make little difference // ~를 두다 make difference // [차별을 두다] discriminate / [등급을 두다] grade / graduate // 그들 사이에는 큰 능력의 ~가 있다 There is a great difference in ability between them. // 그와 나의 인생관에는 큰 ~가 있다 There is a great difference between his philosophy of life and mine. // 두 사람 사이의 연령의 ~는 크다 There is a great age gap[difference in ages] between the two. // 두 나라 사이에는 큰 의견의 ~가 있다 There is a great gulf between the two nations. // 두 세대 사이의 ~는 불가피하다 A gap between two generations is inevitable. // 회원 간에 많은 의견(의) ~가 있었다 There were many differences of opinion among the members. // 두 사람의 태도에는 현저한 ~가 있었다 There is a striking contrast between the attitudes of the two men. // 두 보고 사이에는 상당한 ~가 있다 There are considerable discrepancies between the two reports. // 지출과 수입 간에 큰 ~가 있다 There is a great discrepancy between the outlay and the income. // 두 사람 사이에는 의견의 ~가 있었다 There was a difference[(문어) divergence] of opinion[views] between the two. // 부부의 사회적 신분의 ~ 때문에 결혼은 실패했다 The disparity in the social standing of the couple ruined their marriage. // 그것은 엄청난 ~이다 [~가 별로 없다] It makes a great[little] difference. // 5분 ~로 그를 만나지 못했다 I missed him by five minutes. // 그 사람과는 두 살 ~입니다 He is two years older[younger] than I am. // 어느 길을 가나 별 ~가 없다 It makes very little difference which road we take. // 승급률은 능력에 따라 ~가 있다 Rates of salary increases vary depending on ability. // 이 반의 학생들은 성적의 ~가 크다 The grades of the students in this class vary widely. // 양자 사이에는 하늘과 땅의 ~가 있다 They are poles asunder. // 보는 것과 듣는 것과는 엄청난 ~가 있다 There is all the difference in the world between seeing and hearing. // 신제품의 개발에 있어서 양사 간에는 처음부터 우열의 ~가 났었다 As for the development of new products, there was a gap between the two firms from the beginning.

차이다 get kicked; rejected. ⇨채다³. ¶차이고 짓밟혀 죽다 be trodden down and trampled to death.

차익(差益) marginal profits; a margin. ¶환~ exchange gain[profit] // 매매 ~ trading profit.

차인꾼(差人-) an employee (of a merchant).

차일(遮日) a sunshade; an awning; a blind; a marquee; a tent. ¶~을 치다 shade[protect] a thing from the sun / fix a marquee / pitch a tent // ~을 내려 주시오 Please pull down the blind.

차일피일(此日彼日) ¶일을 ~ 미루다 put the work off from day to day. **차일피일하다** delay (a matter) from day to day; put off[leave over] (a matter) day by day; procrastinate. ¶차일피일하고 빚을 갚지 않다 defer payment on the debt time and again // 차일피일하다가 기회를 놓치다 procrastinate until an opportunity is lost // 차일피일하다가 오늘에 이르렀다 And it has thus been delayed until now.

차임 a chime.
● **차임벨** a chime bell.

차입(借入) borrowing; loaning. **차입하다** borrow; obtain (money) on loan. ¶은행에서 500만 원을 ~ borrow[get a loan of] five million won from a bank.
● **차입금** a loan (of money); borrowed money; a debt.

차입하다(差入-) send in (a thing) to a prisoner. ¶그녀는 복역 중인 아들에게 옷가지를 차입했다 She sent some clothes to her son in prison.
● **차입품** a thing sent in to a prisoner; outside supplies for a prisoner.

차자(次子) one's[the / a] second son.
차작(借作) [남의 손을 빌려 글[물건]을 만듦] vicarious writing[making]; ghostwriting; writing[making] for (another); [남의 손을 빌려 만든 작품] a vicarious work. **차작하다** write[compose / make] for (another); ghost-write; ghost.
● **차작자** a ghost(writer).
차장(次長) a vice-chief[-director]; a deputy chief; an assistant director (general). ¶**편집** ~ a senior[an associate] editor.
● **차장 검사** the assistant prosecutor general.
차장(車掌) (미국의 열차·버스 및 영국 버스의) a conductor; (영국 열차의) a guard. ¶**여**~ a woman[girl] conductor / a conductress.
차점(次點) the second highest mark[number of points]; the next[second] score; (선거) the second largest number (of votes). ¶~**이 되다** rank second / stand second on the list // 300표로 ~이 되다 come second, polling 300 votes // 그는 ~으로 낙선했다 He finished[came in] just behind the successful candidate(s). // 그는 선거에서 ~이었다 He was the runner-up in the election.
● **차점자** (선거에서) the candidate with the next highest number of votes; (경기 등에서) the runner-up (*pl.* runners-up); the second-place finisher.
차제(此際) ¶~에 now / on this occasion [opportunity] / under[in] these circumstances / ~에 깨끗이 거절하지 않으면 안 된다 You must give a flat refusal right now. // ~에 보고드리고 싶은 것은 다음과 같습니다 Let me take this opportunity to tell you[On this occasion I will tell you] this.
차조 [식] glutinous millet.
차좁쌀 polished[hulled] glutinous millet.
차종(車種) the type[model] of a car.
차주(車主) a car owner; the owner of a car [bus].
차주(借主) a borrower; a debtor; a hirer(임차인); a tenant(토지·가옥의); a renter(가옥의); a lessee(토지의).
차중(車中) ¶~**에서** in a train[car] // ~에서 도시락을 먹었다 I had lunch on the train[car].
차지[1] occupancy; occupation; possession. ¶(남의) ~**가 되다** (물건이) come[fall] into one's hands / pass into one's possession / (사람이) come into possession of (something). **차지하다** occupy; hold; have; possess; get; take(up); make (a thing) one's own; take possession of; (경기 등에서) gain; obtain; secure; score; win; (수량·비율을) account for; amount to. ¶높은 지위를 ~ secure[occupy] a high position // 수석을 ~ be[sit] at the top[head] of (one's class) / stand first in (one's class) // 승리를 ~ win a battle[victory] / win(out) (over) / gain [secure / clinch] a victory (over) / earn a win (over) // 절대다수를 ~ command an overwhelming[absolute] majority (in the House) // 장소를 너무 ~ (세간 등이) occupy [take up] much space[room] // 노벨상을 수상함으로써 그는 문학가로서의 명성을 차지하게 되었다 He received an Nobel prize and won literary fame. // 그 트럭이 도로 폭을 온통 차지했다 That truck took up the whole width of the road. // 그는 은행에서 중요한 자리를 차지하고 있다 He occupies[holds] an important position in the bank. // 그는 고교 3년 동안 수석을 차지했다 He was at the top of his class for three years in high school. // 누가 1위를 차지하고 있는가 Who stands [ranks] first? // 그의 당은 국회에서 절대다수를 차지하고 있다 His party commands[has] an absolute majority in the National Assembly. // 수출의 3할을 전기 제품이 차지하고 있다 Electric appliances form[make up] thirty percent of our exports. // 호텔들이 해변가의 아름다운 곳을 모조리 차지하고 있다 The hotels occupy[take up] all the beautiful site along the beach. // 그는 마침내 회장의 자리를 차지했다 He finally landed the presidency [the post of president]. // 그는 마침내 그녀의 마음을 차지했다 In the end he captured [won] her heart. // 그들은 그의 벌이의 일부를 차지했다 They took a percentage[a cut] of his earnings.
차지[2] 1 [호텔 등에서의 요금] charge. ¶**테이블** ~ a cover charge. 2 charging. ⇨**차징**
차지(借地) [땅을 빌림] lease of land; rented land; a leasehold. ¶나는 30년간의 ~ 계약으로 이 땅을 빌렸다 I took this land on a lease of thirty years[a 30-year lease].
● **차지권** a lease; a leasehold. **차지료** (a) (land) rent; (영) (a) ground rent. **차지인** a leaseholder; a tenant; [법] a lessee.
차지다 1 [쌀 등이 끈기가 많다] glutinous; sticky. ¶**차진 쌀**[밀] glutinous rice[wheat] // 이 쌀은 ~ The rice is rich in gluten. 2 [성질이 깐깐하다] tenacious; persistent; stick-to-itive. ¶**차진 사람** a man of tenacity // 그는 차지지가 못하다 He sticks to nothing. / He lacks tenacity of purpose.
차질(蹉跌) a failure; a frustration; a miscarriage; a fiasco (*pl.* ~(e)s); a setback; a deadlock; a snag. ¶계획에 ~**을 가져오다** (원인이) upset[frustrate] in one's plan / (사람이) be frustrated[baffled] in one's scheme // 사업에 ~**이 생겼다** The undertaking failed [fell through]. // 이 사건이 그의 생애에 ~을 초래했다 This incident wrecked his career.
차징 [축구·농구] charging.
차차(次次) 1 [조금씩] gradually; by degrees; bit by bit; little by little; step by step; by inches; [점점] increasingly; growingly; more and more(더하여); less and less(덜하여). ¶~ **더워지다**[추워지다] be getting warmer [colder] // ~ **좋아지다** show gradual improvement // ~ 일에 익숙해지다 become accustomed gradually[more and more] // ~ **어려워지다** become increasingly difficult // ~ 높은 지위로 올라가다 advance to a higher position step by step // 나는 건강이 ~ 나아지고 있다 I am getting better (day by day). // 기운이 빠졌다 ~ My courage oozed away. // 해가 ~ 길어진다 The days are getting longer. // 개울은 비 온 뒤에 ~ 맑아진다 A stream will work itself clear after rain.
2 [조만간] by and by; in (course of) time; in due time[course]; in process of time; with the lapse of time; as time goes[passes]. ¶~ 아시게 됩니다 You will come to understand it by and by. // 이 책은 어렵지만 ~ 쉬워진다 This book is difficult, but it will become easy in time. // 돈은 ~ 갚아도 됩니다 You may return the money later on at your convenience.
차차차 [음] a cha-cha(-cha). ¶~**를 추다** cha-

차창

cha / dance the cha-cha.

차창(車窓) a car[train] window. ¶~에 비치는 경치 the scenery seen from a car[train] window // ~ 밖을 내다보다 look out (of) a car window // ~의 풍경을 바라보며 즐겼다 I enjoyed looking at the scenery from the train window.

차체(車體) a car body; the body (of a car); the chassis (of a carriage); the frame(자전거의). ¶~가 대파됐다 Our car was badly damaged.
● **차체 검사** checking an automobile.

차축(車軸) a wheel axle; an axle.

차츰차츰 gradually; by degrees; step by step; little by little; inch by inch; by and by; more and more; slowly and[but] steadily. ¶~ 나아가다 advance gradually / inch[edge] one's way forward.

차치하다(且置-) let alone; set[put] aside [apart]. ¶농담은 차치하고 joking aside [apart] // 만사 차치하고 before everything [anything] else / first of all // 이 문제는 차치하고 apart from[setting aside] this question // 그것은 차치하고 이 문제에 대해 먼저 토의합시다 Let's leave that for the time being and discuss this matter first. // 그것은 차치하고 기록은 어느 분이 하시겠 됩니까 Well, that aside, who will take the minutes? // 옳고 그르고를 차치하더라도 그것은 엄연한 사실이다 It may be right or wrong, but it is a stern reality.

차트 a chart.

차편(車便) a (public) conveyance; (by way of) a vehicle. ¶~을 이용하다 avail oneself of a vehicle // ~으로 여행하다 travel by (a) vehicle // 거기 가려면 어떤 ~이 있습니까 What kind of conveyance is available to go there? / 그 곳까지는 버스 ~을 이용할 수 있다 A bus service is available as far as there.

차폐(遮蔽) cover; shelter; [군] defilade(축성의); [전] screening; shielding. ¶방사선 ~ radiation shielding. **차폐하다** shelter; (주로 위쪽에서 빛·열 등을) shade; (포격을) defilade. ¶전등을 ~ cover an electric lamp.
● **차폐물** a cover; a shelter; [군] a defilade; [전] a screening; a shielding.

차폭(車幅) the breadth of a car.

차표(車票) a (railroad / bus / streetcar) ticket; a passenger ticket; a coupon (ticket)(회수권). ¶당일 유효 ~ a day ticket / 3일간 유효 ~ a ticket available for 3 days / 왕복 ~ (영) a return ticket / (미) a round-trip ticket // 할인 ~ a cheap ticket / ~를 조사하다 examine tickets // ~를 적다[개찰하다] punch [clip] a ticket // ~를 보여 주세요 Ticket please. // 자, ~를 끊으십시오 All fares, please. // 이 ~는 2일간 유효함 This ticket is valid for two days. // 이 ~는 판매 당일만 유효함 This ticket is available[valid / good] on the day of issue only. // (역에서) ~를 팔기 시작한다 The ticket window is open.
● **차표 판매소** the ticket window[office]; (영) a booking office. **차표 판매원** (미) a ticket agent; a ticket girl; (영) a booking clerk.

차필하다(借筆-) have (a person) write for one.

차하지다(差下-) be inferior to; be worse than; be below; fall behind; be second to; yield; compare unfavorably with.

차형(次兄) one's second elder brother.

차호(次號) the next issue (of a magazine); the forthcoming issue.
● **차호 계속** To be continued (in the next issue). **차호 완결** To be concluded (in the forthcoming issue).

차환(借換) [먼저 것을 갚음] conversion; refunding. **차환하다** renew (a debt).
● **차환 공채** a converted loan. **차환 발행** a conversion issue.

차회(此回) this time; (on) this occasion.

차회(次回) next time; the following sequence; the next round(경기의).

차후(此後) after this; hence(forth); hereafter; in future; for the future; from this time on; from now[here] on. ¶~로는 이런 짓을 절대로 안 하겠습니다 I will never do anything like this in future. // ~로는 조심해야 해 Be more careful hereafter[after this]. / Take my warning for the future.

착 closely; without hesitation; loosely; imposingly. ⇨<척²

착각(錯覺) [사실과 다르게 지각함] an illusion; (청각·망각) a hallucination; [잘못 알거나 생각함] a wrong guess; misunderstanding; a mistake. ¶~에서 벗어나다[깨어나다] awake from an illusion / be disillusioned // ~을 일으키다 be hallucinated / have [be under] an illusion / be confused into thinking (that ...) // 눈의 ~으로 그것이 둥글게 보였다 It looked round because of an optical illusion. // 그는 순간적으로 외국에 와 있는 것 같은 ~에 빠졌다 He was momentarily under the illusion that he was in a foreign country.

착각하다 be hallucinated; be under an illusion; misunderstand; misjudge; (make a) mistake; guess wrong. ¶도둑으로 ~ mistake [take] (a person) for a robber // ~하고 있다 be mistaken / be under a misapprehension / be under an illusion (about / as to / that) // 나는 그를 그의 동생으로 착각했다 I mistook him for his brother. // 나는 네가 그곳에 가는 것으로 착각하고 있었다 I was under the false impression that it was you who were to go there.

착검(着劍) [구령] Fix bayonets! **착검하다** fix a bayonet; carry a sword; wear a sword. ¶착검하고 with a fixed bayonet / with bayonets fixed.

착공(着工) ¶새 교사는 다음 달 ~ 예정이다 The construction of the new school building will start next month. / We shall begin to build the new school next month. / The new school building will be started next month. **착공하다** start (construction) work.
● **착공식** a ground-breaking ceremony.

착란(錯亂) distraction; derangement; aberration; confusion. ¶정신 ~ dementia / distraction / mental derangement[aberration] / insanity. **착란하다** (서술적) go distracted; go[run] mad; aberrate; be (mentally) deranged. ➔ 정신을 착란시키다 (사물이) drive (a person) distracted / derange one's mind // 그는 정신이 착란되어 있다 He is mentally deranged.
● **착란 상태** a state of dementia.

착륙(着陸) (a) landing; alighting; touchdown; (로켓의) a blastdown. ¶계기[맹목] ~ blind landing // 비상 ~ a forced [an emergency] landing // 야간 ~ a night landing // 연(軟)

soft landing // 지상 유도 ~ the ground-controlled approach // 무~ 비행 a nonstop flight // 외바퀴 ~ landing on one wheel // ~ 태세를 취하다 (비행기 등이) stand by [take up position / prepare] for landing // 강제 ~을 하다 make a forced landing // 강제 ~을 시키다 force a plane down. **착륙하다** land; make a landing; alight; reach the ground; ground; touch [(미) set / put] down. ¶공항에 ~ land on an airport // 훌륭히 [용케] ~ make a good landing // 무사히 ~ make a safe landing // 빌딩 옥상에 헬리콥터가 착륙했다 The helicopter landed on the roof of the building.
● **착륙장** a landing field [ground]; a landing strip; an airstrip. **착륙 장치** landing gear; an undercarriage. ¶자동식 ~ automatic landing gear. **착륙 지점** a touchdown point. ¶헬리콥터 ~은 알려지지 않았다 It is not known where the helicopter landed.

착발(着發) **1** [발착] arrival(s) and departure(s). **착발하다** arrive and depart. **2** [격발] (firearm) percussion; detonation by impact. **착발하다** percuss; detonate by impact.
● **착발 신관** a percussion fuse. **착발탄** a percussion shell.

착복(着服) **1** [옷의] clothing. **착복하다** clothe [dress] oneself (in); put on clothes. **2** (재물의) embezzlement; misappropriation; appropriation; peculation. **착복하다** pocket; embezzle; misappropriate (to oneself); peculate; divert (public money) into one's own pocket. ¶그는 이익의 대반을 착복했다 He misappropriated [embezzled] most of the profit. // 그는 그 돈을 절반 이상 착복했다 More than half of the money stuck to his fingers.

착빙(着氷) [얼어붙음] an ice coating (on an airplane). ¶~이 추락 사고의 원인이었다 The crash was caused by a coat of ice on the plane. **착빙하다** ice forms on; (물체가) ice (up).

착상(着床) [생] nidation; implantation. **착상하다** nidate; become implanted (on the uterine wall).

착상(着想) (hitting on) an idea; a conception; a turn of thought. ¶훌륭한 [재치 있는] ~ a good [clever] idea // 기발한 [독창적인] ~ a novel [an original] idea // 좋은 ~ a happy thought [idea] // a good [capital / splendid] idea // 재미있는 ~ an interesting [a fascinating] idea // ~이 좋다 be cleverly conceived / be a clever conception [idea] // ~이 떠오르다 hit upon an idea // 멋진 ~이 떠올랐다 A capital idea flashed into his mind. // 그건 좋은 ~이다 That's a good idea. // 그의 참신하고도 대담한 ~에는 모두 놀랐다 Everybody was surprised by the novelty and boldness of his conception. **착상하다** conceive; think of (doing); hit upon (a plan); (사물이) cross [come into / enter] one's mind; come to mind.

착색(着色) coloration; (영) colouration; coloring; (영) colouring. **착색하다** color; paint; tint. ¶데생에 ~ put in colors to an outline picture.
● **착색유리** colored glass; stained glass. **착색제** a coloring agent. ¶인공 ~ 함유 (표시) Artificially colored.

착생(着生) [생] insertion.

착석(着席) taking a seat. ¶~순으로 in the order of seats. **착석하다** take one's seat [place]; take a chair; sit (down). ¶착석하고 있다 be seated / be in one's seat [place] // 일동은 착석했다 They all took their seats [seated themselves]. // 어서 착석해 주십시오 Please be seated. // 가족 모두가 식탁 앞에 착석했다 (미) All the family sat down at the table. / (영) All the family sat at table. // 속히 착석하시오 Take your seats [Be seated] quickly. ➔¶착석시키다 seat (a person) / cause (a person) to take a seat.

착선(着船) **1** [배의 도착] the arrival of a ship (in a harbor). **2** [도착한 배] a ship which has arrived.

착수(着水) (a) landing on the water; (우주선의) a splashdown. **착수하다** (비행기가) land [(문어) alight] on the water; (우주선이) splash down. ➔¶엔진 고장으로 조종사는 비행기를 호수 위에 착수시켰다 Engine trouble made the pilot ditch his plane in the lake.

착수(着手) start; commencement; outset. **착수하다** start; commence; begin; set about (business); get to (work); undertake; set one's hand to; enter upon (one's work); (새 사업에) embark on (an enterprise); launch (upon). ¶일을 ~ set [go] to work // 문제 해결에 ~ take steps toward solving [the solution of] a problem // 자동차 생산에 ~ launch upon the production of cars // 그는 마침내 일에 착수하기로 마음을 먹었다 He finally made up his minds to undertake the job. // 불가피한 사정으로 그 일을 착수할 수 없었다 Unavoidable circumstances prevented me from setting about the work. // 나는 지금 새로운 일에 착수했다 I am (working) on a new job now. // 지금 막 일에 착수했다 We've just begun our work [set to work / set about the work / started our work]. // 너무 바빠서 그 일에는 아직 착수하지 못하고 있다 We are so busy we have not got around to it yet. // 지금 곧 일에 착수하라 Get to work right this moment. // 그들은 새로운 사업에 착수했다 They started [launched] a new enterprise. // 일단 착수하기만 하면 간단히 될 일이다 It's not at all a difficult job once you get started.
● **착수금** a deposit; an earnest; [deposit [earnest] money; a retaining fee(변호사의). ¶~을 주다 make [leave] a deposit (of 300,000 won on a car) / place money on deposit.

착시(錯視) [심] an optical illusion.

착신(着信) the receipt (of a message / of a telegram); [우편의 도착] the arrival of the mail [post].
● **착신국** a receiving [the destination] post office.

착실하다(着實-) **1** [꾸준하고 성실하다] steady (and honest); steady-going; [안정되다] sound; stable; sober; [믿을 만하다] trustworthy; [충실하다] faithful. ¶착실한 남자 a steady (and honest) man // 착실한 방법 [투자] a sound method [investment] // 착실한 사업가 a solid [trustworthy] businessman // 착실한 사람 an industrious [a hardworking] man // 착실한 성격 a stable [steady] character // 그는 천재는 아니지만 착실한 형이다 He's not a genius, but he keeps at it. **착실히** steadily; soberly; faithfully. ¶~ 일을 하다 work like a bee [beaver] // 연구를 ~ 진행하다

착안 make (sure and) steady progress in one's studies // ~ 공부하다 study hard[steadily / untiringly] // ~ 돈을 모으다 save (money) steadily // 그는 더디지만 ~ 일한다 He is slow but steady. // 그는 목표를 향해 ~ 나아가고 있다 He is moving toward his goal steadily [step by step]. // 자 그러면 ~ 시작하자 All right now, settle down (and get) to work. // 그는 ~ 진전하고 있다 He is making steady progress. **2** [충분하다] enough; full; sufficient; good. **착실히** enough; sufficiently; fully. ¶집에서 2마일은 ~ 된다 It's a good two miles from home.

착안(着眼) ¶~이 좋다[나쁘다] be right [wrong] in one's way of looking at [one's view of] the matter // 날카로운 ~이다 That's an astute[interesting] observation. **착안하다** notice; perceive; aim at; pay[turn] one's attention to; have an eye to; fix one's eyes upon. ¶그는 아주 훌륭한 것에 착안했다 He directs his attention to the relevant points. // 좋은 일에 착안했는걸 You have surely directed your attention to the right thing.
● **착안점** the point aimed at; the point of one's observation; [견지] a point of view; one's viewpoint. ¶이곳이 문제의 ~이다 This is the aspect[point] of the question which we must consider. // 우리는 ~이 다르다 You and I view the matter from different angles [see the matter differently].

착암기(鑿巖機) [광] a rock drill; a jackhammer (손에 드는).

착염(錯鹽) [화] complex salt.

착오(錯誤) a mistake; an error; [불일치] (a) disagreement; [차이] a discrepancy. ¶시행 ~ trial and error // 시대 ~ anachronism // 어떤 ~로 by some mistake // ~가 생기다 go wrong / misfire // ~를 일으키다 make a mistake // 계획에 ~가 생겼다 Our plans miscarried [went wrong / went awry]. **착오하다** mistake; make [commit] a mistake; err.

착용하다(着用-) put on; wear; have (a coat) on. ¶모닝코트를 ~ wear a morning coat / have a morning coat on // 등교 시에는 제복을 착용할 것 The pupils must attend school in uniform. // 그는 제복을 착용하고 있다 He is in uniform.

착유(搾油) oil expression. **착유하다** press [express] oil (from); extract oil by pressing.
● **착유기** an oil press [mill].

착유(搾乳) milking. ¶1회분의 ~량 a milking. **착유하다** milk (a cow).
● **착유기** a milker; a milking machine.

착의하다(着衣-) get dressed; dress (oneself); get [put] on clothes.

착잡하다(錯雜-) complicated; intricate; knotty; (en)tangled; complex; involved. ¶착잡한 표정 an expression of mixed feelings // 그 여자의 표정은 착잡한 심정을 나타내고 있었다 Her face betrayed a mixture of emotions within. **착잡히** intricately; complicatedly; involvedly; knottily; complexly.

착지 1 [도착지] the place of arrival. 2 [점프 등의] (a) landing. ¶체조 선수는 멋진 ~를 보여 주었다 The gymnast made a superb landing. // 체조 선수는 완벽한 ~로 연기를 끝냈다 The gymnast finished his performance with a perfect landing. **착지하다** land.

착착 close(ly); tightly. ⇨척척1

착착(着着) steadily; step by step. ¶~ 진행되다 progress steadily / make steady progress [headway] // 그는 계획을 ~ 실행한다 He carries out his plans one by one. // 도로 공사를 ~ 진행했다 The construction of the road made steady progress. // 일은 ~ 진행 중이다 The work is well under way.

착취(搾取) 1 [짜냄] expression; extraction. **착취하다** squeeze; extract; press. 2 (고혈의) exploitation; sweating; extortion; squeezing. ¶중간 [자본가] ~ intermediary [capitalist] exploitation. **착취하다** exploit; sweat (one's employees); squeeze (money out of a person); extort. ¶노동자를 ~ exploit the workmen // 식민지를 ~ exploit a colony // 백성의 고혈을 ~ exploit [bleed] the people / grind the people down // 고용주가 고용인을 착취한다 The employer sweats his workers.
● **착취 계급** the exploiting class. ¶피 ~ the exploited classes.

착탄(着彈) impact (of a missile).
● **착탄 거리** the range of fire; gunshot (range). ¶~ 안 [밖]에 있다 be within [out of] gunshot // 이 대포의 ~는 4킬로미터이다 This cannon has a range of 4 kilometers. **착탄 지점** an impact area.

착하(着荷) an incoming delivery [shipment]; arrivals; receipts; goods received. **착하하다** arrive.
● **착하 인도 [지급]** delivery [payment] on arrival.

착하다 (아이가) good; nice; (마음씨가) good (-natured); kindhearted; [온순하다] meek; gentle; quiet; [순종하다] obedient; docile. ¶착한 아이 a good boy [girl] / a lamb of a boy // 착한 일 a good work [deed] / a virtuous act // 마음이 ~ be kindhearted / have one's heart in the right place // 착한 일을 하다 do something good / do (what is) good / practice virtue // 착하게 굴다 act in a virtuous [kindly] manner / be good [nice] to (a person) // 조금은 남을 위해 착한 일을 해라 Do something for the good of others. // 착한 일과 악한 일을 구별 못 하는 사람이 있다 There are people who do not know what is right and what is wrong [who cannot tell right from wrong]. // 착하지, 울지 마라 Don't cry, there's a good boy [girl]. // 착하기도 해라 What a good boy [girl]!

착함(着艦) (비행기의) deck-landing; [귀함] rejoining one's ship. **착함하다** land (on a carrier / on the deck of a ship). ¶비행기 한 대가 항공모함(의 갑판)에 착함했다 An airplane [영] aeroplane) landed on (the deck of) the aircraft carrier.

착항(着港) arrival (in port). **착항하다** make port [harbor]; arrive in port [harbor].

찬(讚) praise(s); a eulogy; a legend; a panegyric.

찬(饌) a (side) dish. ⇨반찬
● **찬 가게** a pickle shop; a grocer's (store).

찬가(讚歌) a paean; a poem [song] in praise (of); a hymn. ¶청춘 ~ a song in praise of youth // 크리스마스 ~ a Christmas carol.

찬간(饌間) a kitchen; a pantry where side dishes are prepared.

찬간자 a white-faced bluish horse.

찬거리(饌-) groceries; materials for making side dishes.

찬기(-氣) cold air [steam]; chilly atmosphere; cold draft. ¶~가 돌다 be chill with cold air / have a cold fit // ~를 느끼다 feel chilly / feel a chill // ~가 가시다 warm slightly // ~을 쏘이다 be exposed to cold air.

찬동(贊同) approval; endorsement; support; approbation. ¶남의 ~을 구하다 request approval[support] of a person / ask for a person's approval[support] // ~을 얻다 obtain (a person's) consent[approval] // 그녀의 계획은 많은 사람들의 ~을 얻었다 Her plan won the approval of many people. **찬동하다** approve of; support; give one's approval (to); endorse (a plan).

찬란하다(燦爛-) brilliant; bright; shining; radiant; glittering; lustrous; dazzling; resplendent. ¶찬란한 별 bright[glittering] stars // 찬란한 문화 the glorious civilization // 찬란한 보석 a brilliant[radiant] jewel // 찬란한 업적 a splendid accomplishment // 찬란한 장식 a glittering decoration // 광채가 ~ have bright[resplendent] colors / be lustrous. **찬란히** brilliantly; brightly; radiantly; resplendently; glitteringly; dazzlingly. ¶~ 빛나다 shine brightly // ~ 보석을 아로새긴 왕관 a brilliantly bejeweled crown.

찬모(饌母) a woman cook in charge of making side dishes.

찬물 cold water. ¶~ 한 컵 a glass of (cold) water // ~을 한 잔 들이켜다 drink a cup of cold water.
찬물을 끼얹다 discourage (a person from); throw a cold blanket (over); put a damper (on).

찬미(讚美) praise; glorification; laudation; extolment; admiration; adoration. **찬미하다** praise; admire; laud; glorify; extol; hymn; chant hymns of praise (to a person). ¶신을 ~ praise God / give praise[glory] to God // 인생을 ~ sing[chant] the praises of life // 극구 ~ extol[laud / praise] (a person) to the sky[skies].
● **찬미가** a hymn. ⇨ ☞찬송가(⇨찬송) **찬미자** an admirer; an adorer.

찬바람 coolness; cold-bloodedness. ¶애인 사이에 ~이 일기 시작했다 Their love has begun to cool.

찬반양론(贊反兩論) pros and cons; arguments for and against (a matter). ¶이 문제에 관해서는 ~이 활발하게 벌어졌다 There were many pros and cons presented concerning this question. / They argued at length for and against this question.

찬밥 1 [식은 밥] cold rice. 2 [하찮은 사물·사람] a trifling thing; a worthless fellow.

찬부(贊否) yes or no; approval or disapproval; for and against; ayes or noes; yeas or nays; pros and cons. ¶~를 묻다 put (a question / a matter) to a vote / submit (a measure) to a ballot / take a vote[ballot] (on a question) // ~를 결정짓다 (투표에서) vote on (a matter) // 그 문제의 ~을 논했다 We argued the pros and cons of the matter. // ~ 반반이다 The ayes and nays split evenly.
● **찬부 양론** pros and cons; arguments for and against. ¶그 의안에 대해서는 ~이 있다 They are arguing for and against the bill. **찬부 투표** ayes and noes; votes for and against.

찬비 a cold[chilly] rain.

찬사(讚辭) a eulogy; praise(s); a compliment;
laudatory remarks; a panegyric; an encomium (pl. ~s, -mia). ¶아낌없는 ~ (give) unstinted praise // ~를 드리다[보내다] eulogize / pay one's tribute of praise (to) / compliment (a person on his performance) // ~를 아끼지 않다 be unsparing of[in] one's praise // 그녀는 그의 업적에 대해 ~를 아끼지 않았다 She was unstinting in her praise of his work. / She lavished praise on his work. // 그들의 노고에 ~를 보내자 Let's congratulate them on their efforts.

찬성(贊成) approval; approbation; agreement; assent; suffrage; seconding(동의(動議)의); support; endorsement; favor. ¶~ 투표하다 vote for[in favor of] (a bill) / cast a favorable[an aye] vote for (a measure) // ~을 얻다 gain a person's approval / ~을 표명하다 express one's approval // ~을 구하다 ask (a person's) approval / beg (a person's) suffrage // ~ Yes. / Aye! // 불 ~ No. / Nay! // 10표, 반대 5표였다 The vote was 10 for and 5 against. // ~ 다수에 의해 가결합니다 (의장의 말) The ayes have it. **찬성하다** approve of (a plan); give one's approval to (a plan); agree (to a person's opinion / with a person); subscribe to (a person's view); fall in with (a person's view); assent to (a person's opinion); support (a bill); second (a motion); vote for (a measure); favor (a proposal); be in favor of (a reform); endorse [indorse] (a plan). ¶의안에 ~ support a bill / (투표로) vote for a bill // 동의에 ~ second a motion // 만장일치로 ~ be unanimous in (their) approval[consent] / consent unanimously // 제안에 찬성하는 분들은 손을 들어 주십시오 Those (who are) in favor (of the proposal), please raise your hands.
● **찬성론** a supporting argument. **찬성자** an approver; a supporter; (동의(動議)에 대한) a seconder; a standby. ¶~가 많다 The ayes have it.

찬송(讚頌) glorification (of God); praise (to God).
● **찬송가** a hymn; a psalm. ¶~를 부르다 sing a hymn.

찬스 a chance; an opportunity. ¶절호의 ~ a capital chance / a golden opportunity // ~를 놓치다 lose[pass up] a chance.
● **찬스 메이커**(*chance maker) a heads-up player.

찬양(讚揚) praise; admiration; laudation; applause; commendation. **찬양하다** praise; admire; laud; applaud; extol; commend; give [accord] high praise to. ¶찬양할 만한 admirable / laudable / praiseworthy // 신을 ~ praise[give glory to] God / sing[chant] the praises of Him / doxologize // 그녀의 아름다움을 ~ admire (a person) of her beauty // 극구 ~ extol[laud] (a person) to the skies[sky-high] / bestow unstinted praise (on) // …을 찬양하는 연설을 하다 give an address of homage to (Shakespeare) // 모든 사람이 그녀를 찬양하였다 She was the admiration of everyone.

찬연하다(燦然-) brilliant; radiant; resplendent. ¶찬연한 광채 brilliant light / radiant brightness // 찬연한 태양 the radiant sun. **찬연히** brilliantly; radiantly; resplendently. ¶~ 빛나다 shine brilliantly / glitter // 그의 무용

찬의 (武勇)은 역사에 ~ 빛나고 있다 His valor shines on in history. / His valor remains a brilliant spot in history.

찬의(贊意) approval. ¶~를 표하다 express [show / give / nod / voice] one's approval (to / toward) / give one's assent (to).

찬장(饌欌) a cupboard; a sideboard; a dresser.

찬조(贊助) support; backing; patronage; approval. ¶A 씨의 ~ 아래 under the support [auspices] of Mr. A / supported by Mr. A / ~를 얻다 obtain (a person's) patronage [support] / ~를 청하다 solicit (a person's) support. **찬조하다** support; back (up); patronize.
● **찬조금** a contribution. ¶~을 내다 contribute (10,000 won to the project) / make a contribution (to / for). **찬조 연설** a supporting speech; a campaign speech for a candidate. ¶~을 하다 speak for a candidate. **찬조자** a supporter; a patron. **찬조 출연** appearance as a guest (artist). ¶우리는 송 씨의 ~으로 극을 상연한다 We will present the play with Mr. Song as a guest star.

찬찬하다 1 [꼼꼼하다] attentive; staid; careful; prudent; cautious. ¶그녀는 성격이 아주 ~ She has a very steady character. **찬찬히** [침착하게] staidly; deliberately; calmly; quietly; [꼼꼼하게] carefully; cautiously; attentively. ¶~ 준비하다 make thoroughgoing preparations (for) // 무슨 일이나 ~ 하다 be deliberate [cautious] in doing anything // 그는 내 얼굴을 ~ 보았다 He looked hard [fixedly / steadily] at me. / He fixed his eyes on me. // ~ 이야기해 봐라 Compose yourself before you speak.
2 [느리다] slow; leisurely; deliberate (of movement). **찬찬히** slowly; leisurely; deliberately; (wait) with patience. ¶~ 하다 take one's time (in doing / over something) / go easy (with one's work) / take it easy.

찬탄(讚歎·贊嘆) praise; admiration. **찬탄하다** admire; extol(l); speak highly of; be filled with admiration (at). ¶크게 찬탄할 만하다 be worthy of the highest admiration / merit the highest praise // 찬탄하여 마지않을 be lost in admiration (for).

찬탈(簒奪) usurpation. ¶왕위 ~의 기도 a plot to usurp the throne. **찬탈하다** usurp. ¶왕위를 ~ usurp [seize] the throne.
● **찬탈자** a usurper.

찬합(饌盒) a nest of box; a tub (with a lid) for cooked rice. ¶~에 담다 pack (food) in a nest of boxes.

찰- [차진] glutinous; gluey; [지독한] excessive; extreme; deadly.

찰가난 extreme [dire / abject] poverty; utter destitution; penury; indigence; beggary.
● **찰가난뱅이** a needy [destitute] person; a pauper; (집합적) the destitute [indigent].

찰거머리 [동] a leech. ¶~ 같은 사람 a barnacle / a hanger-on / a leech // ~처럼 붙어 떨어 지지 않다 cling to (a person) like a leech / fasten on (a person) like a tick.

찰것 food made of glutinous grain.

찰과상(擦過傷) an abrasion; a chafe; a skin-deep wound; a scratch. ¶ 나는 팔에 ~을 입 었다 I got a scratch on my arm. / I scraped my arm. // 그는 보도에서 넘어져 양 무릎에 ~ 을 입었다 He skinned both knees when he fell on the sidewalk.

찰기(-氣) glutinousness; glutinosity; stickiness. ¶~가 있는 sticky / glutinous // ~가 생기기까지 가루를 반죽하다 knead the dough till it develops a sticky consistency // 수입 쌀 은 밥을 지었을 때 ~가 없다 Imported rice doesn't hold together very well when cooked.

찰깍 with a snap [click / crack]; snap; crack. ¶걸쇠를 ~ 채우다 snap the clasp.

찰깍거리다 [단단한 것이] click; clack; (시계가) ticktack; ticktock; tick; (타자기가) click, click, click ....

찰나(刹那) a moment; an instant; a trice. ¶~ 적 쾌락 passing [fleeting] pleasures / the pleasures of the moment // …하는 ~에 the moment [minute] ... / instantaneous [simultaneous] with ... // 문을 연 ~에 the instant [minute] I opened the door // 바로 그 ~에 at that very moment.
● **찰나주의** the principle of living only for the pleasure of the moment; impulsiveness; momentalism.

찰싹거리다 cling [stick] to; hang on to; keep clinging round (the limbs).

찰떡 a glutinous-rice cake.

찰랑거리다 1 [액체가] lap; splash. ¶해변에 찰 랑거리는 파도 waves lapping on the beach / 찰랑거리는 잔물결 laughing wavelets // 뱃전에 물결이 찰랑거렸다 The water lapped against the boat. // 독의 물이 찰랑거린다 The water in a jar is slopping from side to side. 2 clink; jingle; tinkle.

찰랑찰랑 1 [액체가 가득 괴어 있는 모양] to the brim; brimfully; to the full; overflowingly. ¶~ 부은 술잔 an overbrimming cup. **찰랑찰랑하다** brimful; overflowing. ¶물이 찰랑찰랑한 대야 a basin filled to the brim with water // 술잔에 술을 찰랑찰랑하게 따르다 fill a glass (up) to the brim with wine / pour a glass full of wine / brim a cup with wine // 물 이 찰랑찰랑하게 차 있다 be filled with water to the brim. 2 jingling; tinkling; clinking.

찰바닥 with a splash. ⇨ 찰바닥

찰밥 boiled glutinous rice.

찰벼 a glutinous rice plant.

찰상(擦傷) an abrasion; a chafe. ⇨ 찰과상

찰싹 with a splash; with a slap. ⇨ 철썩

찰쌈지 a tobacco pouch carried on one's side.

찰찰 overflowingly. ⇨ 철철

찰카닥 with a snap; with a click. **찰카닥하다** give a snap [click]; slap; slurp. ¶라이터를 찰 카닥하고 켜다 light a lighter with a click [snap] // 찰카닥하고 덱 속에 카세트를 넣다 snap a cassette into a deck // 찰카닥하고 셔터 가 내려졌다 The shutter clicked. // 뚜껑이 찰 카닥하고 닫혔다 The lid closed with a click.

찰칵 with a snap. ⇨ 찰카닥

찰흙 clay; slime; plastacine(학교에서 쓰는). ¶ ~질의 clayey (soil) / argillaceous (rocks) // ~으로 만들다 make (a model) of clay / model (an image) in clay.

참¹ [진실] truth; reality; verity; fact(사실). ¶…이 ~임을 증명하다 certify the truth of ....

참² 1 [정말로] really; truly; indeed; quite; very. ¶~ 재미있었다 I had such a good time, indeed. // ~ 난처하게 되었다 This is a nice kettle of fish. / It's really annoying. // ~ 좋은 집이구나 What a fine house! // ~ 안됐어 What a pity! // 오늘은 ~ 덥다 How hot it is today! // 그 여

자 ~ 미인인데 She is a real beauty.// 나는 ~ 운이 좋았다 I had capital luck.// ~ 아름답다 It is really beautiful.
2 [감탄사] well; oh; what; really; by the way. ¶~, 자네한테 물어볼 말이 있네 Well, now, I have something to ask you.// ~, 오늘이 월요일이지 Oh, it's Monday, isn't it?// ~ 별사람 다 보겠네 Really now, I have never seen such a dreadful person!// ~ 별소리 다 듣겠다 Just what do you mean talking to me that way?// ~ 한 씨를 알고 있나 By the way, do you (happen to) know Mr. Han?

참³ **1** [휴식] a (short) rest (from work); a recess; a (coffee) break; a respite (from work); a spell; [쉬는 시간에 먹는 식사] a snack taken during a recess. **2** [계제] the occasion; [찰나·순간] the instance; the moment; the time. ¶…하려는 ~에 just as [when] one is about to (do) / the moment one is going to (do) / on the point of (doing) // 너를 부르러 사람을 보내려던 ~이었다 I was just on the point of sending for you.

참- true; real; veritable; genuine. ¶~뜻 the true meaning [sense] // ~사람 a true [an honest] man // ~사랑 a true love.

참(站) [역참] a post; a station; a stage.

참가(參加) participation; joining; entry. ¶~를 신청하다 send an entry for (a game) / enter for (a contest). **참가하다** participate (in); take part (in); enter (a sporting event); join (in) (a party). ¶토론에 ~ join (in) [take part in] a discussion // 세미나에 ~ participate in a seminar // 하기 강습회에 ~ be enrolled in a class at the summer school / 참가하지 않다 keep aloof (from) / stand aside // 누구나 참가할 수 있다 be open to all competitors [comers / outsiders] / welcome volunteers // 나는 그 기획에 참가했다 I participated in the project.// 독일은 다시는 전쟁에 참가하지 않을 것이다 German will never participate in [enter] another war.
● **참가국** a participating nation. **참가자** a participator; a participant; (경기 등의) an entrant; an entry; (집합적) the list [field]. ¶지난주 파업의 ~는 5만 명이었다 There were fifty thousand people who took part in the strike last week.// 투표 의 ~의 수는 많았다 [적었다] There was a good [poor] turnout at the polls. **참가 팀** a participating team.

참개구리 [동] a leopard frog.

참게 [동] a king crab; a horse-shoe crab.

참견(參見) **1** [간섭] interference; meddling; [관여] participation. ¶쓸데없는 ~이다 This is [That's] none of your business.// 그는 언제나 쓸데없는 ~을 한다 He is always meddling (in other people's affairs). **참견하다** meddle [interfere / intermeddle] in (another's affair); intrude oneself (into another's affair); obtrude on [upon]; put [poke / thrust] one's nose into; put [thrust] one's oar in; poke into (관여하다) participate (in); take part (in); have [play] a part (in); mix up (in); have a share [hand] (in); be concerned (in). 참견하는 사람 a busybody / a meddlesome [an officious] person / (영국 구어) a nosy parker // 참견하는 intrusive / presumptuous / (구어) pushy / (문어) officious // 그가 참견하는 데 나는 어처구니가 없었다 I was dumbfounded by his intrusion [officious interference].// 젊은이들은 남이 자기들 일에 참견하는 것을 싫어한다 Young people don't want others to meddle in their affairs.// 그는 내 일에 언제나 참견하려 든다 He is always trying to meddle in my affairs.// 그는 무엇에든지 참견하는 자다 He pokes [thrusts / puts] his nose into everything.// 참견하지 마라 Mind your own business. / Don't butt in! / Hands off! / Don't poke your nose into others' affairs. / Don't dabble in other people's business. / Keep out of it! / It's none of your business. / Keep your fingers out of my business. / Don't interfere with my work! // 내가 무슨 일을 하든 참견하지 마라 Never mind what I do.// 나는 참견하지 않을 수가 없다 I cannot look on in silence.
2 a visit. ⇨참관

참고(參考) (a) reference; consultation. ¶~를 위해 for reference / for one's information // 책을 ~로 하다 refer to [consult] a book // ~가 되다 serve as a reference / furnish a person with information // 나는 송 씨의 주석을 ~로 했다 I referred to Mr. Song commentary.// 이 책은 크게 ~가 되었다 This book was very helpful.// 훗날의 ~를 위해 이 서류를 보관해 두었다 I kept these papers for future reference.// ~로 알고 싶은데 이 워드 프로세서의 값은 얼마죠 Just for my information could you tell me how much this word processor cost? **참고하다** refer to (a dictionary); consult (a book). ¶…을 참고하는 in the light of ... / with reference to ... // 문헌을 ~ refer to literature / consult a document // 여러 사람의 의견을 참고하여 계획을 세우다 consult (the views of) several people before setting the plan up // 참고하시라고 여기 지난 5년간의 통계를 준비해 두었습니다 Just for reference [your information], here are statistics for the past five years.
● **참고 문헌** a bibliography; literature cited. **참고서** a reference book; a book of reference. ¶영어 ~ a reference book for [a key to] the study of English // ~류 books for reference. **참고인** a reference; a witness; a person who has information about [can provide evidence in] a case. **참고 자료** reference data [materials].

참고둥 [동] a rock shell.

참관(參觀) a visit; inspection; (증인으로서의) witnessing. **참관하다** visit; inspect; (증인으로서) witness; be (a) witness to. ¶투표 [개표]를 ~ witness the voting [ballot counting] // 수업을 ~ visit [inspect] a class at work / go to see classwork // 참관할 수 있다 [없다] (사물이) be open [closed] to visitors // 나는 어제 딸의 수업을 참관했다 I visited my daughter's class (at work) yesterday. / I went to observe my daughter's class yesterday.
● **참관인** a visitor; (선거의) a witness. ¶개표 ~ a ballot-counting witness // 투표 ~ a voting witness / a referee of voting. **참관일** a visiting day.

참극(慘劇) a tragedy; a tragic event. ¶~의 현장 the scene of the tragedy // ~을 빚어내다 enact a tragedy // 여기서 ~이 벌어졌다 This was the scene of the tragedy.

참기름 sesame oil; gingili.

참깨 sesame; (알맹이) a sesame seed. ¶~를 빻다 grind sesame seeds.

참나리 [식] a tiger lily.

참나무 [식] a black oak.

참다

참다 1 [인내하다] be patient; have [take / keep / practice] patience; [견디다] endure; put up with; bear; stand(▶ 앞의 두 가지 말은 구어로 많이 씀, bear와 stand는 부정문에서 쓸 때가 많음); tolerate(▶ 남의 행동에 대하여 보통 부정문으로 씀). ¶참을 수 있는 bearable / tolerable / endurable / sufferable // 참을 수 없는 unbearable / intolerable / insufferable / insupportable / unendurable / beyond [past] endurance // 참을 수 없는 고통 unbearable [intolerable] pain // 잘 ~ bear and forbear // 치욕을 ~ bear up under one's shame // 마지막까지 ~ hold [hang] on till the end // 그는 참을 수 있는 충동에 휩쓸렸다 He was driven by an irresistible impulse. // 나는 그런 모욕을 참을 수 없다 I can't bear [endure] such an insult. // 돈이 그다지 없었으므로 점심은 국수 한 그릇으로 참았다 Since my money was almost gone I had to make do with a bowl of noodles for lunch. // 이번만은 참아 주겠다 I won't punish you for what you've done just this once. // 여기가 바로 네가 참고 견뎌야 할 고비다 This is where your patience [perseverance] is needed most. // 저런 사람에게는 참을 수 없습니다 I cannot endure [have no patience with] a man like that. // 그의 뻔뻔스러움은 참을 수가 없다 I can't tolerate [stand] his impudence. // 나는 끝내 참지 못했다 My patience was finally worn out. / I could not endure [stand / bear / put up with] it any longer. // 조금만 더 참는 게 좋겠어 You'd better be patient a little while longer. // 일 년만 더 참아야 한다 You've got to grin and bear it [You just have to hang on] for one more year. // 결혼 생활에는 참아야 할 일이 많다 There are many things to be endured [(一) put up with] in married life. // 꾸준한 참은 보람이 있어 그는 그 사업에 마침내 성공했다 His perseverance was rewarded [paid off] when the undertaking finally succeeded. // 아프겠지만 잠시 참아라 It must hurt, but just hang on for a minute. // 이 소음은 참을 수가 없다 I can't stand [bear] this noise. // 이 이상 참고 기다릴 수는 없다 It is beyond my endurance to wait a moment longer. // 오늘은 참지 못할 지경으로 덥다 It is unbearably hot today. / Today's heat is unbearable [intolerable]. // 참는 것도 한도가 지났다 I can't put up with it any longer. / My patience is exhausted. // 그녀는 그의 되는 대로 하는 방식에는 도저히 참을 수가 없었다 She had no tolerance whatever for [She simply could not tolerate] his slipshod ways. // 나는 이 고통을 더 이상 참을 수 없다 I can't bear this pain any longer.
2 [억제하다] control (oneself); restrain (oneself); stifle; repress; suppress; forbear; keep [hold] back; contain (one's passion); subdue [deny] oneself. ¶참을 수 없는 욕망 an uncontrollable desire // 하품을 ~ suppress [stifle] a yawn // 눈물을 ~ hold back one's tears // 노여움을 ~ repress one's anger // 그는 소변을 참고 있었다 He controlled [fought off] his need to urinate. // 나는 흐르는 눈물을 참을 수 없었다 I could not hold back my tears. // 너무나 우스워서 소녀들은 웃음을 참지 못했다 It was so funny that the girls couldn't help giggling. // 나는 웃음 [하품] 을 가까스로 참았다 I could hardly suppress [stifle] a smile [yawn]. // 그녀는 눈물이 나오

는 것을 간신히 참았다 She fought her tears back with difficulty.

참다랑어 a tuna (pl. ~, ~s); a tunny.
참담하다(慘澹-) pitiful; pitiable; piteous; wretched; dire; harrowing; grim; miserable; terrible; horrible; tragic; appalling; disastrous. ¶참담한 사고 a terrible accident // 참담한 광경 a horrible sight // 참담한 결과로 끝나다 end in tragedy // 참담한 지경에 처하다 be in extreme distress [dire want] / be in depth of misery // 참담한 비극이 계속되었다 There was one appalling tragedy after another.
참답다 true; real; genuine; honest; sincere; faithful; truthful; upright; right-minded. ¶참다운 친구 a true friend / a faithful friend // 참다운 영웅 a hero worthy of the name // 참다운 인간 an honest man / a genuine [sincere] person // 참다운 뜻으로 in the true [truest] sense of the word [term].
참대 [식] a common Korean bamboo.
참돔 [동] a red sea bream; a porgy.
참되다 true; real; genuine; honest; sincere; faithful; truthful; upright. ¶참되게 honestly / faithfully / sincerely / truthfully // 참된 우정 true friendship // 그것이야말로 참된 친절이다 That is true [real] kindness.
참뜻 [참된 뜻] the true meaning; [본디의 속뜻] one's real intention.
참례(參禮) attendance; presence. **참례하다** attend; be present (at); present oneself (at); sit (at). ¶장례식에 ~ attend a (person's) funeral // 집회는 회원 다수가 참례한 가운데 열렸다 The meeting was held with a large number of members attending.
참말 a true remark [story]; an authentic story; the truth; a (real) fact. ¶~의 true / real / actual // 을 하다 tell [speak] the truth // ~로 받아들이다 believe / take (it) seriously / accept (an account) as true // 남의 말을 ~로 믿다 take a person at his word // ~다 So it is. // ~일까 Can it be true? / I wonder if it is true. / (놀라서) ~입니까 Indeed? / Really? / Really and truly? / You don't say so! (설마) // 그 소문은 ~인가 Is there any truth in the rumor? // ~인지 아닌지 확실히 모르는 말은 하지 마라 Never say anything which you do not know to be true. // 누가 그런 말을 ~로 믿는담 Who would believe it? / Tell that to the (horse) marines [the Jews]. // 그의 말은 ~인 것 같다 He seems to be telling the truth. // ~이야, 믿어도 좋아 (You may) Depend upon it. / (You may) Take it from me [Take my word for it]. / Believe me. // 그는 대단한 부자다, ~이야 He is very rich, I can tell you.
참말로 [진실로] really; truly; in truth; actually; [진지하게] in (good / real) earnest; [전적으로] really; quite; indeed; very. ¶너 ~ 잘 왔다 It is a jolly good job that you came. / I declare, I'm very glad that you are here.
참먹 an ink stick of high quality.

참모(參謀) **1** [군의 고급 지휘관] a staff officer; (집합적) the staff. ¶일반 ~ the general staff // 그는 사령관의 ~로 일했다 He served on the staff of the commander-in-chief. **2** [상담역] an adviser; a counselor; (구어) a brain. ¶정 씨의 ~역 Mr. Jeong's brain trust / an adviser [a brain truster] to Mr. Jeong // …의 ~로 활동하다 act as adviser to ….

●**참모 본부** the General staff Office. **참모장** the chief of staff. **참모 총장**[차장] the Chief [vice-chief] of the General staff. **참모 회의** a council of war; a war council.

참모습 one's true face; one's true character [colors]. ¶~을 드러내다 throw off one's disguise / throw off the mask.

참배(參拜) worship. **참배하다** go and worship at (a shrine); pay reverence at (a tomb); enter (a temple) and pray before the altar; visit [pay a visit to] (a shrine).
●**참배자** a worshiper.

참벌[동] a honeybee. ⇨ 꿀벌

참변(慘變) a disastrous accident; a tragic incident; a disaster; a terrible disaster; a catastrophe; a tragedy. ¶~을 당하다 suffer a disastrous accident.

참빗 a fine-toothed bamboo comb (used for removing loose hairs or dandruff).

참사(參事) an adviser; a counselor; (영) a counsellor.
●**참사관** (대사관 등의) a councilor; (영) a councillor.

참사(慘死) a tragic [miserable / violent] death. **참사하다** meet with (a tragic) death; come to [meet with] a violent end. ¶그는 복병을 만나 참사했다 He was ambushed and met with a violent death.∥그는 게릴라의 손에 참사했다 He was cruelly murdered at the hands of the guerrillas.

참사(慘事) a tragic [terrible] incident; a disastrous accident. ¶탄광의 ~ a terrible accident in a coal mine∥여객기가 추락하여 대~가 되었다 The (air)plane crash was a tragic accident.∥운전기사의 사소한 부주의가 이 ~를 일으켰다 Just a moment's carelessness on the part of the driver caused this horrible [dreadful] accident.

참사람 an honest man; a good citizen; a respectable member of society; a new man(갱생한). ¶~이 되다 become a new man / turn over a new leaf / reform (oneself) / mend one's ways.

참살(斬殺) [목을 베어 죽임] decapitation; beheading. **참살하다** behead; decapitate; cut the head off (a person).

참살(慘殺) [참혹히 죽임] murder; slaughter; butchery; carnage; massacre. **참살하다** murder cruelly; butcher. →일가 7명이 참살되었다 All seven members of the family were brutally murdered.∥마을 사람들은 한 사람도 남김없이 참살되었다 The whole village was [All the villagers were] massacred in cold blood.
●**참살 사건** a murder case.

참상(慘狀) a disastrous scene; a wretched spectacle; a pitiable condition; a miserable state; a sad [tragic] state of things; misery. ¶기근의 ~ the misery of a famine∥~을 나타내다 present a terrible sight [spectacle] / be in a miserable [wretched] condition∥재해의 ~을 목격하다 witness the terrible sights of a disaster∥항공기 추락 현장은 처참한 ~이었다 The scene of the plane crash was a terrible sight [a horrible spectacle].

참새 a sparrow. ¶~처럼 재잘거리다 chatter like a sparrow∥~가 쩍쩍 울고 있다 Sparrows are chirping [twittering].
●**참새 떼** a flock of sparrows.

참석(參席) attendance; presence; appearance; participation. ¶…의 ~하에 in the presence of / attended by. **참석하다** attend; be in attendance (at); be present (at); [참가하다] participate in; take part in. ¶나도 옵서버로 회견에 참석했다 I was also present at the interview as an observer.∥시체 해부에 참석해 주십시오 Your presence is requested at the autopsy.∥친척들이 모두 결혼식에 참석했다 All the relatives attended the wedding.∥머리가 아파서 나는 회의에 참석하지 않았다 I excused myself from attending the meeting because I had a headache.∥각 도시의 대표자가 참석했다 All the cities were represented at the meeting.
●**참석자** [출석자] an attendant; (집합적) an attendance; [참가자] a participant.

참선(參禪) meditation in Zen Buddhism; [좌선의 수행] practices of [in] Zen meditation. **참선하다** practice Zen meditation at [in] a Buddhist temple.
●**참선자** a Zen devotee [votary].

참소(讒訴) a false charge; (a) slander; calumny; defamation. **참소하다** make a false charge (against); make a false representation (of); slander; calumniate; defame. ¶그는 친구를 참소했다 He brought [made] a false [fake] charge against his friend. (▶ bring은 법정에 제소했을 경우이고, 그 밖에는 make를 씀)
●**참소자** a slanderer; a calumniator.

참수(斬首) decapitation; beheading; decollation. **참수하다** behead; decapitate; cut the head off (a person). →살인범은 참수당했다 The murderer was beheaded.
●**참수대** a guillotine; a scaffold; the (executioner's) block.

참숯 hard charcoal.

참신하다(斬新-) new; novel; original; unconventional; up-to-date. ¶참신한 디자인 a novel design / an original design∥참신함이 결여되다 be lacking in freshness / lack freshness∥그의 처녀작은 문단에 참신한 바람을 불어넣었다 His first novel inspired [revitalized] the literary world. / His first novel was like a breath of fresh air to the literary world.∥그녀는 항상 참신한 아이디어를 내놓는다 She always has [come up with] original ideas.

참언(讒言) a false charge; (a) slander. ¶그는 ~의 화를 입었다 He fell victim to slander. **참언하다** slander; make a false charge (against); libel; calumniate; defame.

참여(參與) participation (in public affairs). **참여하다** participate [join] in; take part in; play one's part in; be a party to; have one's share in. ¶국정에 ~ take part in the conduct of state affairs∥입법에 ~ have a voice [say] in legislation∥경영에 참여할 권리가 있다 have a voice in the management (of)∥총선거는 국민이 직접 국정에 참여하는 유일한 기회다 The general election is the nation's sole chance to participate directly in government.
●**참여자** a participant.

참예(參詣) [신·부처에게 나아가 뵈는 것] a visit to a temple [shrine]; worship; a pilgrimage. **참예하다** visit [pay a visit to] (a temple); pay homage [one's respects] (to); worship before [at] (a temple); make a pilgrimage (to).

참예인 / 참예자 a visitor (to a temple); a worshipper; a pilgrim.

참외 [식] a melon.
● **참외밭** a melon field; a melon patch.

참으로 [정말로] really; truly; in truth; in fact; indeed; [매우] very; (very) much; quite; (감탄) how; what. ¶공주님은 ~ 아름다운 분이셨습니다 The princess was indeed very, very beautiful.∥슬픈 일이 아닐 수 없다 Oh my, how sad!∥~ 상심이 되시겠습니다 You must be deeply grieved.∥내 자식답다 That's my boy[girl]. / (미국 구어) Attaboy [Attagirl]!∥~ 신사다 How like a gentleman! ¶원통해 주셔서 ~ 고맙습니다 I thank you from the bottom of my heart for your kind help.

참을성(一性) patience; endurance; perseverance; forbearance; persistence; longsuffering; [관용] tolerance; sufferance; [자제] self-control; self-command. ¶~ 있는 patient / forbearing / persevering / enduring / long-suffering∥~ 있는 사람 a person of perseverance / a man of patience / a patient worker∥~ 없는 impatient / lacking perseverance∥그는 ~ 있게 기다렸다 He waited patiently.∥그는 ~이 없다 He can stick to nothing.∥그는 기회가 무르익기를 ~ 있게 기다렸다 He waited patiently for the opportunity to mature.

참의원(參議院) the Senate(미국의); the House of Councilors(일본의); the Upper House; the House of Lords(영국의).

참작(參酌) consideration; allowance(s); deliberation; reference. ¶아무런 ~도 없이 남에게 벌을 주다 show no leniency in punishing a person∥어떤 ~도 보일 필요가 없다 You need not show any mercy. **참작하다** consider; take (something) into consideration [account]; show consideration for; allow for; deliberate; refer to; consult. ¶평소의 좋은 자네 행위를 참작하여 in consideration of your usual conduct∥자네 부친의 낯을 참작하여 용서하고 보내 주겠다 I will let you off out of respect for your father.∥내 사람이 소중한 아들을 잃고 난 직후라는 것을 참작해 주지 않으면 안 됩니다 We must take into consideration [make allowance for] the fact that he has just lost a dear son.∥그가 젊다는 것을 우리는 참작하여 처리했다 We considered [made allowance(s) for] his youth.

참전(參戰) participation in a war; entry into a war. ¶러시아의 ~이 승패를 결정하게 되었다 Russia's entry into the war decided the outcome. **참전하다** enter a war; participate in the war; join a war. ¶그 나라는 미국 편에서 참전했다 That country entered the war on the American side.

참정(參政) participation in government. **참정하다** participate in government.
● **참정권** the right to vote; the franchise; suffrage; [보통 선거권] universal suffrage. ¶여성 ~ woman[women's] suffrage∥~을 부여하다 give the franchise[suffrage] (to)∥~을 획득하다 acquire the franchise∥~을 잃다 forfeit the franchise.

참조(參照) reference; consultation; comparison. ¶전후 ~ cross reference∥그는 그것을 ~로 내세웠다 He referred to it. / He mentioned it. / He cited it as an example. **참조하다** [참고로 보다] refer (to); [조사하다] consult; [비교하다] compare (with). ¶원문을 ~ refer to the original∥사전을 ~ consult [refer to] a dictionary∥25페이지의 예문 5를 참조할 것 See[Cf.] p. 25, ex. 5(▶ cf.는 비교 대조하라는 뜻).∥이 문제에 있어서 참조할 만한 것이 하나도 없다 There is nothing to refer to[go by] in this matter.

참주(僭主) a usurper (of the throne); a tyrant; a despot.

참참이 sometimes. ⇨ =이따금

참치 a tuna. ⇨ =참다랑어

참패(慘敗) a crushing[humiliating] defeat; a dismal failure. ¶그 정당은 지방 선거에서 ~를 당했다 That party suffered a crushing defeat in the local elections.∥우리는 ~를 당했다 (구어) We were beaten (all) hollow. **참패하다** suffer [sustain] a crushing[disastrous] defeat; be crushed; be beaten utterly [all hollow]. ¶우리는 그 시합에서 참패했다 We were completely defeated in the match.

참하다 1 [생김새가 곱다] nice; fair; charming; good-looking; handsome; pretty; comely; [말쑥하다] neat; clean; tidy; smart; (구어) natty. ¶참한 얼굴 a fair countenance[face] / nice features∥참한 아가씨 a pretty girl / a nice-[smart-]looking girl∥옷차림이 ~ be neatly[smartly] dressed / be dressed in style. 2 [성질이 얌전하다] quiet[calm] and gentle; mild; sedate; modest.

참하다(斬一) behead; decapitate; decollate; slay (with a sword). ¶저놈을 빨리 끌어내어다 참하여라 To death with this fellow!

참해(慘害) heavy[ruinous] damage; havoc; ravage. **참해하다** work havoc with (the crops); cause severe damage (to).

참형(斬刑) execution[death] by beheading; decapitation; beheading. ¶그들은 ~에 처해야 한다 They shall pay for it with their heads. **참형하다** punish by beheading; decapitate; behead.

참형(慘刑) a cruel punishment; a relentless [ruthless] penalty.

참호(塹壕) a trench; [대피호] a dugout. ¶~를 파다 dig trenches / dig in∥적은 견고한 ~에 들어박혔다 The enemy was[were] strongly entrenched.
● **참호 공사** trench work. **참호 생활** trench life. **참호전** trench warfare.

참혹하다(慘酷一) 1 [비참하다] miserable; wretched; tragic(al); sad; pitiable; sorrowful. ¶참혹한 광경 a pitiful sight∥참혹한 사건 a tragic accident / a tragedy / a disaster∥참혹한 생활 a life of misery / a wretched[miserable] life∥그 사고 현장은 정말 참혹한 광경이었다 The scene of the accident was simply horrible.∥실로 참혹한 광경이었다 It was a really pitiable sight to see. **참혹히** miserably; sadly; pityingly. ¶그는 ~ 죽었다 He met with a tragic end. / He died a miserable death.

2 [잔인하다] cruel; atrocious; brutal; merciless; ruthless; cold-hearted. ¶참혹한 짓을 하다 do a cruel thing / commit cruelties[atrocities]. **참혹히** cruelly; brutally; atrociously. ¶~ 대하다 be cruel to[hard on] (a person) / treat (a person) harshly[with brutality]∥~ 도 …하다 be cruel enough to (do) / have the cruelty to (do).

참화(慘禍) a terrible disaster; a crushing calamity; a tremendous catastrophe. ¶전쟁

창녀

의 ~ the ravages[horrors] of war // 전쟁의 ~를 입다 suffer the ravages of war.
참회(懺悔) [회오] penitence; repentance; contrition; [고백] (a) confession. ¶~의 눈물 penitential tears // ~를 듣다 hear a person's confession. **참회하다** repent (of one's sins); be penitent; [고백하다] confess; make a confession (of). ¶참회하는 생활 a penitential life / a penitent's life // 참회하러 가다 go to confession // 참회하여 죄를 용서받다 be confessed of a crime // 나는 신부에게 참회했다 I confessed my sins to the priest. // 참회하면 죄가 소멸된다 Repentance wipes out sin. → ¶참회시키다 draw a confession from (a person).
● **참회록** (저서명) Confessions. **참회자** a penitent; a repentant sinner; [고백하는 사람] a confessant.
찹쌀 glutinous rice; sticky rice. ¶~ 경단 rice-flour dumplings.
● **찹쌀떡** (a) glutinous rice cake. **찹쌀밥** boiled glutinous rice.
찹찹하다 1 (물건이) neatly piled[heaped] up; stacked in good order. 2 (마음이) calm and serene; self-possessed; composed.
찻간(車間) [차내] the inside of a car[train]; a compartment. ¶~에서 in[on] a train / in a car.
찻값(茶一) a tea[coffee] charge.
찻길(車一) 1 [기차·전차 등의 궤도] a (train) track; a railroad[(영) railway]. 2 [차도] a roadway; (미) a driveway.
찻삯(車一) the railroad fare; the (car) fare. ⇨ 차비(車費)
찻숟가락(茶一) a teaspoon. ¶두 ~의 설탕 two teaspoonfuls[teaspoonful] of sugar.
찻잎 tea leaves.
찻잔(茶盞) a tea-things; (한 벌) a tea set [service]; a teacup.
찻종(茶鍾) a teacup; a teabowl. ¶차를 ~에 따르다 pour tea into a cup.
찻집(茶一) a teahouse; a tearoom. ⇨ 다방
창¹ (구두의) sole leather; the sole of a shoe. ¶~ 속 an inner sole // ~ 안 a liner // ~을 갈다 put a new sole (on) / resole / (시커서) have one's shoes resoled (by) // ~이 나갔다 Shoe soles got[were] worn out.
창² [구멍] a hole made in paper[cloth] (a tear; a rent. ¶~이 나다 a hole is made (in cloth) / get a hole in (a thing).
창(窓) a window. ⇨ 창문 ¶~을 열다 open a window / raise[pull up] a window // ~을 닫다 shut[close / let down] a window // ~을 열면 잔디밭이다 The window looks out upon a lawn.
창(槍) a spear; a spike; a javelin(투창 경기의); a lance(기병 등의); (쌍날 칼을 꽂은) pike. ¶~ 자루 the handle of a spear[lance] // ~을 겨누다 lower[couch] a spear[lance] (for attack) // ~으로 찌르다 lance / spear / tilt (at a person) // ~을 쓰다 wield [brandish] a spear.
창가(窓一) [낱것의] ~ 좌석 a window seat // ~에 앉다 sit by[at] the window.
창가(娼家) a brothel; a house of ill fame; a bawdyhouse.
창가(唱歌) [노래] a song; vocal music. **창가하다** sing.
● **창가집** a collection of songs.
창간(創刊) the first publication[edition]; foundation (of a periodical). **창간하다** launch (a newspaper); found[start] (a periodical). ¶1965년 창간됐다 Founded[First published] in 1965. // 본지는 2000년에 창간했다 Our magazine was first issued [published] in 2000. // 신문을 창간할 계획이 있다 There are plans for starting a newspaper. // 그 잡지는 창간된 지 10년이 된다 The magazine has been in existence for ten years.
● **창간호** the first[inaugural] issue; the initial[inaugural] number. ¶~를 내다 issue (its) initial number.
창건(創建·刱建) foundation; establishment; organization; inauguration. **창건하다** found; establish; organize; start; inaugurate; create. → 그 회사는 창건된 지 오래되지 않다 It is not very long since the company was established.
창고(倉庫) a storehouse; a warehouse(▶ storehouse는 추상적인 뜻으로도 쓰임); (지하의) a cellar; (곡물의) a granary; (영) a depot; a godown(인도 등지의); a magazine(군수품의). ¶술 ~ a wine cellar // 쌀 ~ a rice granary / a storehouse for rice // 보세 ~ a bonded warehouse // 잉여 쌀은 ~에 저장되어 있다 The surplus rice is stored in warehouses. // 나는 이사할 때 가구를 ~에 맡겼다 I put my furniture in storage when I moved.
● **창고 계원** / **창고지기** a warehouse keeper. **창고료** warehouse[storage] charges. **창고업** warehousing. **창고업자** a warehouseman. **창고 증권** a warehouse bond.
창공(蒼空) a blue[an azure] sky; the blue heavens; the vault of heaven.
창구(窓口) a window; a wicket. ¶매표 ~ a ticket window // 은행 ~ a bank window // 출납 ~ a cashier's[teller's(은행의)] window [case] // ~ 담당자 a clerk at a window // ~에서 사무를 보다 attend at the window // ~의 서비스가 나쁘다[를 개선하다] give poor [better] service at the window // 3번 ~에서 좌석을 예약해 주십시오 Reserve [(영) Book] your seat at Window No. 3. // 윌리엄 씨가 이 교류 계획의 ~ 입니다 Mr. William is the man to contact about this exchange program.
● **창구 계원** a clerk at the window.
창궐(猖獗) rage; fury; rampancy; rifeness; virulence. **창궐하다** rage; be rife[virulent / rampant]. ¶유행성 감기가 창궐하고 있다 Influenza is raging (just now). // 질병이 그 지방에 창궐하고 있었다 The plague was rampant in the area.
창극(唱劇) a Korean classical opera.
창기(娼妓) a prostitute.
창기병(槍騎兵) a lancer.
창끝(槍一) a spearhead; the point of a spear. ¶나는 그에게 ~을 겨누었다 I pointed my spearhead at him.
창난젓 salt-pickled pollack guts.
창녀(娼女) a prostitute; a streetgirl; a trollop; a streetwalker; a woman of the street; a harlot; a whore. ¶~ 출신 an ex-prostitute // ~가 되다 enter into[practice] prostitution // ~로 팔리다 be sold for prostitution // ~와 놀다 consort with a whore / go to bed with a prostitute // 몸값을 물고 ~를 빼내다 ransom [buy out] a prostitute / take a woman out of a life of shame // ~ 생활을 하다 live on the street.

창달(暢達) fluency; liveliness; briskness; development; growth; promotion. ¶언론 ~에 공헌하다 contribute to the promotion of the freedom of speech. 창달하다 develop; promote.

창당(創黨) the formation of a political party. 창당하다 form[organize] a political party.
●창당 정신 the founding spirit of a party; the spirit underlying the formation of the party.

창대(槍-) a spear handle[shaft].

창던지기(槍-) 〔체〕 the javelin (throw). 창던지기하다 throw a javelin.
●창던지기 선수 a javelin thrower.

창도(唱導) advocacy. 창도하다 advocate; preach; advance[introduce] (a new doctrine). ¶평화주의를 ~ advocate pacifism / 자유를 ~ espouse the cause of liberty / preach[uphold] liberty // 신학설을 ~ advance[introduce] a new theory.
●창도자 an advocate (of democracy); a proponent; an exponent.

창립(創立) founding; establishment; organization. ¶~ 50주년을 축하하다 celebrate the 50th anniversary of the foundation (of a school) // 그 회사는 ~ 이래 발전을 계속해 왔다 The company has continued to prosper since its foundation. 창립하다 found; establish; organize; build; set up; start. →¶이 학교는 1900년에 창립되었다 This school was founded in 1900. // 하버드 대학은 1636년에 창립되었다 Harvard University saw the light of day in 1636. // 이 학교는 창립된 지 30년이 된다 This school has reached the 30th year of its existence. // 그 회사는 창립된 지 얼마 안 된다 It is not very long since the company was established.
●창립 기념일 the anniversary of the founding[establishment] (of a school). 창립자 the founder[foundress(여자)]; the organizer. ¶그 가 이 병원의 ~다 He is the founder of this hospital. 창립 총회 the inaugural[first general] meeting.

창문(窓門) a window; a sash window (내리닫이의); a casement (window)(좌우로 여닫는); (배의) a port(hole); (채광창) a sky light. ¶~을 열어 두다 leave a window open[up] // ~을 닫아 두다 keep a window shut[closed / down] // ~ 안을 들여다보다 look into[in through] a window // ~에서 목을 내밀다 stick one's head out of a window // ~으로 들어가다 get in by a window // ~에서 뛰어내리다 jump (down) from a window // 도둑은 ~으로 침입했다 The thief entered by the window.

창밖(窓-) ¶~을 내다보다 look out (of) a window // ~으로 몸을 내밀다 lean out of a window // ~의 경치가 좋다 The window commands a very fine view.

창백하다(蒼白-) (deathly / ashy) pale; pallid; white (as a sheet). ¶환자의 창백한 얼굴 the pallid[pale] face of a sick person // 얼굴이 ~ look pale // 그는 화가 나서 얼굴이 창백해졌다 He turned livid with anger. // 그는 순간적으로 얼굴이 창백해졌다 His face turned (deathly) pale in an instant. // 그는 그 소식을 듣고 창백해졌다 He went pale[turned white] at the news. // 그녀는 몹시 창백한 얼굴을 하고 있다 She looks ghastly[deathly] pale. / Her face is as white as a sheet. // 안색이 몹시 창백하구나 You are looking awfully washed out.

창부(倡夫) an actor.

창부(娼婦) a prostitute. ⇨창녀(娼女)

창살(窓-) (문의) a lattice; a latticework; a lattice strip; a frame; a grille; iron bars(감옥의). ¶~ 없는 감옥 a prison without bars.

창상(創傷) a gash; a wound[injury] (by an edged weapon); a cut.

창생(蒼生) (백성) the people; the populace; the masses.

창설(創設) establishment; founding; organization. 창설하다 found; establish.

창성(昌盛) prosperity; flourishing; thriving. 창성하다 prosper; thrive; flourish; be prosperous; do well.

창세(創世) the creation of the world. 창세하다 create the world.
●창세기 [성] (The Book of) Genesis(약어 Gen.). ¶~ 5장 27절 Genesis, chapter five, verse twenty-seven / Genesis 5:27(▶ five twenty-seven이라고 읽음).

창시(創始) origination; creation; establishment; foundation. 창시하다 originate; create; found; establish; initiate. ¶그건 K 씨가 창시한 것이다 It originated with[It was invented by] Mr. K.
●창시자 the originator; the founder; the initiator. ¶교파의 ~ the founder of a sect // 새로운 학설의 ~ the originator of a new theory.

창안(創案) an original idea[plan]. ¶이것은 한상수 씨의 ~입니다 This idea originated with Mr. Han Sangsu. 창안하다 originate; devise; invent. ¶이 기계는 A 박사가 창안한 것이다 This machine has originated from[is originally designed by] Dr. A.
●창안자 the originator; the inventor. ¶이 기계의 ~ the inventor of this machine.

창업(創業) (사업의) inauguration of an enterprise; 〔창립〕 foundation; establishment; the establishment[founding] of a business. ¶내년에 우리 회사는 ~ 50주년을 경축한다 Next year we are celebrating the (golden) jubilee of our company. 창업하다 (사업을) inaugurate[start] an enterprise; 〔창립하다〕 found; establish. ¶창업한 이래 since the foundation. →¶우리 회사는 1965년에 창업되었다 Our firm was founded[established] in 1965.
●창업비 initial expenses[expenditure]. 창업자 the founder.

창연(蒼鉛) 〔화〕 bismuth. ⇨비스무트

창연하다(蒼然-) 〔푸릇푸릇하다〕 dark blue; bluish; 〔어둑어둑하다〕 dim; gloomy; gray; shady; somber; (고색이) antiquated; patinated. ¶고색이 ~ be antique-[hoary-]looking / be hoary with antiquity / be timeworn.

창유리(窓琉璃) window glass; (끼우는) a (window) pane. ¶~를 깨(뜨리)다 break a window (pane) // ~를 끼우다 glaze a window.
●창유리 닦개 (자동차의) a windshield washer[cleaner].

창의(創意) an original idea[view]; originality. ¶그녀의 시는 ~성이 부족하다 Her poems lack originality.
●창의력 an initiative spirit; initiativeness. ¶~이 풍부한 사람 a man of ideas[ingenuity] / an original[an inventive / a creative] thinker / an imaginative person // ~을 짜낸 연출 imaginative staging // ~을 발휘하다 use

찾다

one's originality / exercise [exert] one's ingenuity

창의적(創意的) original; inventive; ingenious. ¶~인 기술 개발로 값싼 고급 상품을 개발하기 위해 노력하다 make efforts to develop cheap but quality commodities through creative development of technologies.

창자 [대장과 소장] intestines; [내장] entrails; (구어) guts; insides(▶ 위도 포함). ¶닭의 ~를 빼다 clean a chicken / take out the insides of a chicken.

창자가 끊어지다 ¶창자가 끊어지듯이 아프다 have a splitting stomachache // 창자가 끊어지는 것 같다 I am brokenhearted. // 그녀와 헤어져야 한다고 생각하니 창자가 끊어지는 듯하다 It was heartrending to think that I had to part from her.

창작(創作) [새로이 만들어 냄] creation; [작품] a creative work; [소설] a novel; [저작] production; [소설 쓰기] story [fiction] writing; a story; (집합적) fiction. ¶~적인 creative / original // ~에 종사하다 engage in writing a creative [an original] work / engage in the profession of letters // ~을 그만두다 quit writing [penning] novels. **창작하다** create; invent; [소설을 쓰다] write a novel [story].
● **창작가** a creator; an originator; an author; a writer; [소설가] a novelist; a creative [story / fiction] writer. **창작력** creative power [talent]; [독창력] originality. **창작 활동** creative activity.

창제(創製) (an) invention; creation; origination. **창제하다** (사람이) create; invent; (사물이) originate with one.

창조(創造) creation. ¶~의 재능 creative genius // 천지 ~ the Creation. **창조하다** create; make; call into being. ¶하느님께서 천지를 창조하셨다 God created heaven and earth.
● **창조력** creative power [faculty]; creativity; originality (독창성). **창조물** a creature; (집합적) creation. ¶모든 (피)~ all creation. **창조성** creativity. **창조자** a creator. **창조주** the Creator.

창조적(創造的) creative; [독창적] original. ¶~ 예술[예술가] a creative art [artist] // ~ 진화 creative evolution.

창창하다(蒼蒼-) 1 [매우 푸르다] deep blue [green]; azure. ¶창창한 바다 the blue sea / the deep // 창창한 하늘 a deep blue sky. 2 [멀다] far-off; remote; dim; uncertain; long; [끝없다] vast; boundless; (서술적) be far away. ¶창창한 장래 a bright [rosy / great] future // 앞길이 창창한 청년 a young man who has the world before him / one who is in the prime of youth // 갈 길이 아직 ~ still have along way to go [before one] // 앞길이 ~ be still young / have a long future before one / have a great [bright / rosy] future before one / have the whole world before one.

창천(蒼天) a blue [(문어) an azure] sky; the blue heavens.

창출(創出) creation. ¶새로운 문화의 ~ creation of a new culture. **창출하다** create. ¶새 유행을 ~ create a new fashion // 햄릿의 새로운 형을 ~ create a new Hamlet.

창칼 [작은 칼] a small knife; a pointed knife(공작용-); a penknife; [접을 수 있는 소형의] a pocketknife; [접을 수 있는 대형의] a jackknife.

창틀(窓-) a window frame; (바깥쪽의) a window sash.

창파(滄波) sea waves; billows; big rollers. ¶만경 ~ the billowy sea / the boundless expanse of sea / the endless waves.

창포(菖蒲) [식] a sweet flag; an iris (*pl.* ~es, irides); a sweet rush.

창피(猖披) shame; disgrace; ignominy; dishono(u)r. ¶큰 ~ an open [a public] disgrace / burning [crying] shame // ~를 주다 put [bring] (a person) to shame / shame [make (a person) blush [ashamed] / put (a person) out of countenance / humiliate (a person) / insult / shame [disgrace] (a person) publicly // 소년의 나쁜 행실 때문에 어머니가 ~를 당했다 The boy's bad behavior embarrassed his mother. // 그게 무슨 ~니 What a disgrace! / Shame on you! **창피하다** shameful; scandalous; disreputable; ignoble; ignominious; (서술적) be embarrassed [abashed]; be a shame; [초라하다] unsightly; shabby; miserable; unpresentable. ¶창피한 일 a shame / a disgrace // 창피한 짓 disgraceful behavior / shameful conduct // 창피한 꼴을 당하다 be put to shame / disgrace [humiliate] oneself / bring disgrace upon oneself / be put out of countenance / (크게) expose oneself to public disgrace / be disgraced [insulted] in public // 창피한 짓을 하다 behave disgracefully // 창피해서 머리를 숙이다 hang one's head for shame // 창피함을 무릅쓰고 돈을 알선해 달라다 swallow one's pride to ask (a person) to lend one money // …하는 것을 창피하게 여기다 think [feel] shame to (do) // …을 창피하게 여기지 않다 be lost [dead] to all sense of shame // 나는 너무 창피해서 아무 말도 못했다 I was too embarrassed to speak. // 그녀는 창피한 듯이 작은 목소리로 대답했다 She replied in an embarrassed whisper. // 술에 취하여 창피한 짓을 저질렀다 I behaved shamefully after I got drunk. // 여러 사람 앞에서 넘어져서 창피했다 I fell down right in front of everybody, I was so embarrassed. // 그는 회의에 늦어서 창피한 표정을 하고 방으로 들어왔다 He was late for the meeting and entered the room with a sheepish [an embarrassed] look on his face.

창해(滄海) a blue expanse of water; the vast blue sea; the ocean.
● **창해일속**(--粟) a drop in the bucket.

창호(窓戶) windows and doors; [건구] fittings; fixtures; (household) furnishings. **창호하다** paper a window frame; a doorframe.
● **창호지** window paper; sliding screen paper; paper for sliding doors. ¶~를 바르다 paste the paper on the window frame / paper a sliding door [screen].

창황하다(蒼黃-·倉皇-) hasty; flurried; hurried; precipitated; (서술적) be in haste; be in a great hurry; be in a rush; be in a flurry. **창황히** with precipitation; hastily; hurriedly; in great haste [big great hurry]; in a flurry; hurry-scurry. ¶~ 달아나다 run away helter-skelter / beat a hasty retreat.

찾다 1 (사람·물건 등을) search (for); be on the search (for); look for; look up; [수색하다] hunt(up); trace; [구하다·요구하다] seek (for / after); look out for; look for; hunt for;

찾아내다

be out after. ¶사람을 찾으러 가다 go looking [hunting] for a person∥책을 찾으려고 뛰어다니다 run around looking for a book∥전화번호를 ~ find out a person's telephone number∥연줄을 ~ hunt up connections∥일자리를 ~ look out for[hunt for] a job∥열쇠를 찾으려고 온 집 안을 뒤지다 search all over the house for a key∥행방불명의 친구를 찾아다니다 search for one's missing friend∥버섯을 찾아다니다 gather mushrooms∥잃어버린 시계를 찾았다 나는 온 집 안을 뒤졌다 I searched all over the house for the missing watch.∥무엇을 찾고 있니 What are you looking for?∥지도에서 ~ 보아라 Look up the place on a map.∥이 학교에서는 영어를 가르칠 교사를 찾고 있다 A teacher of English is wanted in[(미) at] this school./We are looking for someone to teach English at this school.∥나는 열쇠가 있을까 하고 내 주머니를 찾았다 I fished in my pocket for the key.∥그는 재미있는 잡지를 찾고 있다 He is hunting[searching / looking] for an interesting magazine.∥시계를 아직 못 찾았다 The watch is still missing.∥이 행사의 근원을 거슬러 찾아보면 고려 시대로 이르게 된다 We can trace this function back to the Goryeo period.∥친척들을 여기저기 찾아다녀서 그녀는 가문의 내력을 알아낼 수 있었다 By asking around among her relatives, she found out the family's background. **2** [발견하다] discover; detect; find (out); locate(장소를). ¶경찰은 마침내 그의 거처를 찾았다 The police finally found out where he was./The police finally tracked him down [located him].∥나는 옥스퍼드 사전에서 그 단어를 겨우 찾았다 I looked in the Oxford Dictionary and finally found[located] the word. **3** [되가지다] take[get / win] back; have (it) back; regain; retake; resume; recover; restore; reclaim; redeem; retrieve; draw out [from]; take out. ¶(은행에서) 예금을 ~ draw [withdraw] one's savings(from a bank)∥그 전 지위를 도로 ~ retrieve one's former position∥전당포에서 시계를 ~ redeem[recover / take out] a pawned watch / take[get] a watch out of pawn[pledge]∥(미국 속어) get a watch out of hock∥실지(失地)를 ~ recover[regain] lost territory∥그 슈트케이스를 찾아가는 사람이 없었다 No one claimed the suitcase./The suitcase was left unclaimed. **4** [방문하다] call (on a person / at a person's house); come[go round] to see; visit; pay[make] a visit to; pay one's respects to (a person); pay (a person) a call; look (a person) up; (미) visit with (a person). ¶우리는 경주의 절을 찾았다 We visited temples in Gyeongju.∥내가 서울에 있을 동안에 나를 찾아 주게 Call on me while I'm (still) in Seoul.∥요전에 나는 그들의 집을 찾았다 I called at their house the other day.∥오늘 아침에 그가 나를 찾아왔다 He came to see me this morning.∥그는 이따금 나한테 찾아온다 He calls at my house[calls on me / comes to see me] once in a while.∥회사로 그를 찾았다 I went to see him in[at] his office. **5** (사전 등을) consult[use / see / turn to / refer to] (a dictionary for the meaning of a word); (미) look up (a word in a dictionary); (영) look (a word) out (in a dictionary). ¶단어를 불한사전에서 ~ look a word up in a French-Korean dictionary∥사전[지도]을 ~ consult a dictionary[a map]∥그는 사전 찾는 법을 모른다 He does not know how to use a dictionary.

찾아내다 discover; detect; find(out); locate. ¶우리 마침내 용의자의 소재[거처]를 찾아냈다 We finally discovered the suspect's whereabouts. / We finally located the suspect.

채¹ [가늘고 긴 물건의 길이] the length (of a long and slender object). ¶수염의 ~가 길다 have[wear] a long beard.

채² (수레·가마의) poles attached to the sides [ends] of a carriage for carrying it; a shaft; a bearing pole. ¶가마 ~ a palanquin pole∥상여 ~ the pallbearers' poles on a funeral bier.

채³ **1** a whip. ⇨**채찍** ¶종아리 ~ a switch to use on the legs∥파리 ~ a fly swatter[flap]. **2** (악기의) a drumstick; a stick; a pick.

채⁴ [집을 셀 때의 단위]. ¶두 ~ two houses∥이 마을에는 20 ~ 안짝의 농가가 있다 This hamlet consists of less than twenty farmhouses.

채⁵ [잘게 썰기] shredding vegetables; cutting in thin strips; [썬 것] thin strips (of a vegetable); shredded vegetables; vegetable shreds. ¶무를 ~ 치다 cut a radish into fine strips.

채⁶ [그대로] just as it is[stands]; intact; with no change; in the original state of; […한 이후] since. ¶산 ~로 alive∥외투를 걸친 ~ with one's overcoat on∥불을 켠 ~로 자다 sleep with the electric light on∥미해결인 ~로 남아 있다 remain unsolved[unsettled]∥산 ~로 묻다 bury (a person) alive∥호랑이를 산 ~로 잡다 catch[capture] a tiger alive∥나무는 넘어진 ~로 있다 The tree lies as it fell.∥아기가 입을 벌린 ~ 잠자고 있다 The baby is sleeping with its mouth open.∥그는 내 책을 가져간 ~ 돌려주지 않았다 He took my book and never returned it[and that's the last I've seen it].∥신을 신은 ~ 방에 들어가서는 안 된다 You can't enter the room with your shoes on.∥나는 딴 일은 아무것도 하지 않은 ~ 바로 자 버렸다 I went right to bed without doing anything else.∥그는 의자에 앉은 ~ 우리를 맞았다 He greeted us from his chair (without getting up).∥누가 수돗물을 틀어 놓은 ~로 두었니 Who has left the water running?

채⁷ [아직] (not) yet; as yet; so far; before; [겨우] only. ¶날이 밝기도 전에 before light / 3분도 ~ 못 되어 in less than three minutes∥그의 말이 ~ 끝나기도 전에 before he could finish his sentence∥(일이) ~ 자리가 잡히지 않다 be not yet on the right track∥시간이 ~ 되지 않다 be not yet time∥열 달이 ~ 못 된다 It is not yet ten months.∥사과가 ~ 익지 않았다 Apples are not ripe yet.

-채 [집의 덩이] a section of a building; a wing. ¶본~ the main house[building / wing]∥딴~ a separate building∥사랑~ a detached building[the detached wing of a house] use for a reception room.

채(菜) vegetable salad.

채결(採決) [의안의 가부를 물어 정함] (a) decision; a vote; ballot taking; (미) a roll call; (영) a division. ¶~을 요구하다 call for a division (on a matter). **채결하다** vote (on); take a vote (on a question); take a ballot (for); put (a matter) to(the) vote; (미) take a roll call; (영) go into division. ¶가부(可否)를 ~ take the ayes and noes∥의제에 대하여 ~ take a vote on a subject / put an issue to the vote∥채결한 결과 본 법안에 대한 찬성은 30, 반대는 50이었다 The result of voting was 30 for and 50 against the bill.

채광(採光) lighting(arrangements). ¶~이 좋은[나쁜] 방 a well-[poorly-]lighted room∥~이 나쁘다 be ill lighted. **채광하다** light; let in light; admit light. ¶천창(天窓)에서 ~ let in light through a skylight.
● **채광창** an aperture for admitting light; a skylight; a loophole; [지붕 경사면에 낸 창] a dormer window; (갑판·선체 등의) a deadlight.

채광(採鑛) mining. **채광하다** mine; work (a mine); dig for (minerals).
● **채광권** mining rights.

채굴(採掘) mining; digging; exploitation; working. **채굴하다** dig out; mine (gold, coal, etc.); work [exploit] (a mine). ¶석탄을 ~ mine [extract / dig] coal∥금광을 ~ work [exploit] a gold mine.
● **채굴권** a mining[mineral] right; a mining concession. **채굴량** outturn; output. **채굴장** a stope.

채권(債券) (국공사채) a bond; (회사채 등) a debenture. ¶개발 ~ a development bond∥국고 ~ a treasury [(영) an exchequer] bond∥기명 ~ a registered bond∥무기명 ~ a bond to bearer∥무담보 ~ a plain bond∥보증 ~ a guaranteed bond∥유기명[무기명] ~ a redeemable[perpetual] bond∥장기[단기] ~ a long-[short-] term bond∥저축 ~ a savings debenture∥~의 상환 redemption of bonds[securities]∥연리 5푼의 ~을 발행하다 issue bonds bearing a yearly interest of five percent∥이 ~은 이율이 좋다 This bond yields a good return.
● **채권 소유자** a bondholder. **채권 입찰제** the bond bidding system; (아파트의) the bond-accompanied apartment bidding system.

채권(債權) credit; a claim; an obligatory. ¶~의 면제[변제] exemption from (liquidation of) claims∥~을 징수하다 obtain performance of an obligation∥나는 그에게 ~이 있다[없다] I have a claim [no claim] against him.
● **채권국** a creditor power[nation]. **채권 압류** garnishment. **채권 양도** cession[assignment] of an obligation. **채권자** a creditor; an obligee. ¶~들이 몰려들다 have one's door thronged[besieged] by creditors.

채근하다(採根一) [뿌리를 캐다] dig roots out; [근원을 캐다] trace (a thing) to its origin; [독촉하다] press (a person for a thing); urge (a person to do); demand; call upon (a person to do). ➔¶돈을 갚으라고 채근당하다 be pressed to pay.

채금(採金) mining gold; mining. **채금하다** mine[dig] gold.

채널 (텔레비전의) a channel. ¶입출력 ~ [컴] an input-output channel∥~ 7로 영화를 보다 watch a movie on Channel 7∥~을 돌리다 change channels∥~을 맞추다 pick up [select] a channel∥~ 쟁탈전을 벌이다 quarrel over what program to watch∥제9 ~에서는 무엇을 하나 What is on Channel 9?

채다¹ 1 [낚아채다] snatch (away) (from / off); catch away; take by force; tear (off / away) (a thing) from (a person); [덮치다] swoop off; [가로채다] seize (a thing) by force; steal. ¶남의 단골을 ~ intrigue with another's customer∥손에서 핸드백을 ~ snatch a handbag out of her hand∥(솔개 등이) 병아리를 채 가다 pounce away with a chicken∥그는 파도에 발이 채어 휩쓸렸다 He was carried [swept] off his feet by the wave(s).∥그녀는 화술에 능해 언제나 우리들의 화젯거리를 채 간다 She is such a great talker that she always monopolizes our conversation.
2 [혀 당기기] jerk; pull with a jerk. ¶낚싯대를 ~ jerk one's fishing rod out∥소매를 ~ jerk (a person) by the sleeve.

채다² (눈치·낌새를) sense; suspect; spot; smell out (the secret); get wind[scent] of; become aware (of / that). ¶좋아하지 않는 눈치를 ~ sense that people don't like one∥눈치 채지 못하도록 하다 avoid (another's) suspicion.

채다³ 1 [걷어채다] get kicked; get a kick; (돌부리에) stumble (over / upon / against). ¶당나귀에게 ~ get kicked by a donkey∥돌부리에 ~ trip on[against] a stone∥옆구리를 ~ get a kick[get kicked] on the side. 2 [딱지 맞다] be rejected[rebuffed]; be jilted; be kicked out; get the mitten. ¶여자에게 챈 남자 a rejected lover.

채다⁴ →채우다¹·²·³

채단(綵緞) silk stuffs; silks.

채도(彩度) chroma. ¶이 색은 ~가 낮다 This color has a low chroma.

채독(菜毒) [채소 등에 섞인 독기] food poisoning from vegetables; [중독증] a vegetable-borne disease. ¶~에 걸리다 get[suffer from] a vegetable-borne disease.

채록(採錄) recording in a book. **채록하다** select[extract] (a passage) and put (it) on record; record. ¶우리는 민화를 테이프에 채록했다 We recorded the folktales on tape. ➔¶채록되어 있다 (사서가) contain (a word) / (낱말 등이) be given[found] (in a dictionary).

채롱 [채그릇의 한 가지] a box-shaped wicker basket; a hamper.

채료(彩料) colo(u)ring materials; an artist's colo(u)rs; pigment; paint. ¶~를 칠하다 paint / color (a picture).
● **채료 그릇** a palette.

채마(菜麻) vegetables. ⇨²채소

채무(債務) a debt; an obligation; liabilities. ¶고정 ~ fixed liabilities[indebtedness]∥보증 ~ a suretyship obligation∥연대 ~ a joint obligation∥~가 있다 be liable for debts / owe / be [stand] in (a person's) debt∥~를 이행하다 perform one's obligation / meet [discharge] one's liabilities∥~를 청산하다 liquidate one's liabilities / clear up one's debts∥~를 면제하다 release a person from a debt∥나는 그에게 100만 원의 ~가 있다 I owe him one million won.∥나는 그에게 ~가 있다 I stand in his debt.
● **채무 불이행** default[nonfulfillment] of an obligation. **채무 상환** redemption of a debt. **채무 이행** fulfillment of an obligation. **채무자** a debtor, a loanee; [법] an obligor. ¶지불 능력이 없는 ~ an insolvent debtor.

채반(-盤) 1 [싸릿개비로 결어 만든 그릇] a

wicker tray. 2 [진미] delicacies (which a bride takes to her parents).

채발 long shapely feet; slender feet.

채벌(採伐) felling. ⇨¨벌채(伐採)

채비 preparation(s); arrangement; a getup; (an) outfit; equipment. ¶아무 ~도 없이 without any preparation // ~를 하다 fix oneself for going out // 길 떠날 ~를 하다 equip oneself[fit oneself out] for a trip / arrange[make preparations]for a journey // 여행 ~는 다 되었다 All arrangements have been made for our trip. // 갈 ~는 되었소 Are you ready to go? / 우리는 떠날 ~가 되어 있다 We are ready to start. // 그녀는 무도회에 갈 ~를 하고 나왔다 She came out dressed for the ball. **채비하다** prepare (oneself) (for); arrange (for); make preparations[arrangements] (for); get(oneself) ready (for / to do); equip oneself (for).

채산(採算) (commercial) profit. ¶독립 ~제 the self-supporting system // ~만 따지다 be given to calculation / be calculative // ~이 맞다[맞지 않다] be profitable[unprofitable] / be paying[not paying] // ~이 맞는 조건으로 거래하다 make transactions on a commercial basis // ~이 맞는 사업이다 This is a paying business. // 이 일은 ~이 맞지 않는다 This work doesn't pay. // 이 계획은 ~이 맞지 않는다 The project won't pay. / This is not a paying project. // 우리는 그것들을 ~을 무시하고 팔았다 We sold them without regard for profit. // 하려면 할 수는 있지만 ~이 맞지 않는다 Though possible, it is not commercially practicable.

● **채산 가격** a remunerative price. **채산성** payability.

채색(彩色) 1 [그림에 색을 칠하기] coloring; painting; coloration; a color scheme(배합). ¶그 방의 ~이 참신하다 The color scheme of the room is novel[original]. // ~하다 color; paint; variegate; decorate. ¶채색한 colored / painted // 지도에 ~ color a map. ➔¶항아리는 불에 굽기 전에 채색된다 The pots are colored before being fired. // 서쪽 하늘은 석양으로 아름답게 채색되어 있었다 The western sky was beautifully colored by the setting sun. 2 coloring materials. ⇨¨채색품(⇨채색).

● **채색감** coloring materials; colors; paint; pigment. **채색 인쇄** color[chromatic] printing. **채색화** a colored picture.

채석(採石) quarrying. **채석하다** quarry (marble).

● **채석공** a quarryman. **채석장** a quarry.

채소(菜蔬) vegetables; greens; greenstuff; greengrocery; garden products; (미) (garden) truck. ¶~를 가꾸다 grow[raise] vegetables / (미) grow garden truck(시장에 내려고).

● **채소 가게** (미) a vegetable store. **채소밭** a vegetable[kitchen] garden; (시장 판매용) (미) a truck farm[garden].

채송화(菜松花) [식] a sun plant; the rose moss; a garden portulaca.

채식(菜食) a vegetable diet. **채식하다** live on vegetables.

● **채식 동물** a herbivorous[grass-eating] animal. **채식주의** vegetarianism.

채신사납다 shameful; ignoble; indecent; disreputable; outrageous. ¶채신사납게 굴다 behave outrageously[indecentfly / unseemly] // 그런 짓을 해서야 채신사나워 쓰겠소 It will bring a scandal upon you if you behave like that. // 젊은이들 앞에서 이렇게 주책없이 이야기를 하다니 채신사납소 It is very unseemly to talk in this loose fashion before young men. // 나는 채신사납지 않을 정도로 가능한 한 빨리 퇴장했다 I took myself away from the ceremony as soon as I decently could.

채신없다 undignified; ungentlemanly; ungentlemanlike; unbecoming. ¶채신없는 짓 an undignified act[behavior] // 채신없는 사람 a person with no dignity // 남 앞에서 하품을 하면 ~ It's bad form[manners] to yawn in the presence of others.

채용(採用) 1 [채택] adoption; acceptance; introduction. **채용하다** adopt (a plan); accept (a proposal); introduce (a system); use (a textbook). ¶새 교수법을 ~ adopt a new method of teaching // 정부는 양로 연금 제도를 채용했다 The government introduced old age pensions.

2 [임용] appointment; [고용] engagement; employment. ¶임시 ~ appointment on trial / trial employment. **채용하다** employ; take (a person) into service. ¶임시로 채용한 점원 a clerk employed on a trial basis // 서기로 ~ employ (a person) as a clerk // 그녀를 비서로 ~ employ her as a secretary // 졸업생 4명을 ~ engage four graduates // 신입 사원을 ~ employ[take on] new personnel[(영) staff] // 임시로 ~ take (a person) on trial // 채용해 줄 것을 부탁하다 offer one's service(s) / apply for a position. ➔¶그는 운전기사로 채용되었다 He was employed[(문어) engaged] as a driver. // 나는 그 직장에 지원했으나 채용되지 않았다 I applied for the position, but I wasn't chosen[didn't get it].

● **채용 시험** an examination for service; an employment[a job] examination. **채용 조건** hiring requirements[specifications / qualifications]; conditions of employment. **채용 후보자** a prospective employee.

채우다[1] [자물쇠 등을 잠그다] fasten; lock; (형구를) shackle; fetter. ¶자물쇠를 ~ fasten a lock / lock(up) // 문을 ~ lock a door // 단추를 ~ fasten (a coat) with buttons / button up (one's coat) // 지퍼를 ~ zip (up) / run up a zipper // 호크를 ~ hook (up) (a dress) // 수갑을 ~ shackle (a person's) hands.

채우다[2] [차게 하다] cool; chill; (찬물에) put [keep] (something) in cold water; (얼음에) ice; keep (something) cool on ice; (냉장고에) refrigerate. ¶얼음에 채운 생선 iced fish / fish in ice // 맥주를 얼음에 ~ keep beer cool on ice // 우물에 수박을 채워 두고 있다 A watermelon is cooling down in the well.

채우다[3] 1 (수량을) make good; make up for; fill up. ¶부족을 ~ make good[make up (for)] a deficiency // 결원을 ~ fill a vacant place / fill up a vacancy // 100을 ~ make a round hundred / make (it) 100.

2 (기한을) complete (a period[term]); see it through. ¶임기를 ~ complete one's term of service // 계약 기간을 ~ fulfill the period [term] of a contract // 복역 기한을 채우고 출소하다 serve out one's time and be released from prison / be released on the expiration of the period of punishment.

3 [가득하게 하다] fill (up); (틀어넣어서)

pack(in); stuff. ¶술잔을 ~ fill a glass with wine / fill a wineglass // 통에 물을 ~ fill a tub with water / fill up a tub // 배를 ~ fill the stomach / eat one's fill // 사복을 ~ stuff one's own pocket // 보드상자에 책을 ~ pack a cardboard box with books // 욕조에 물을 채워 주게 Fill the bathtub. // 병에 기름을 채웠다 I filled the bottle with oil. // 이 이불에는 깃털이 채워져 있다 This quilt is stuffed [padded] with feathers. // 그는 자신의 지위를 이용하여 사복을 채웠다 He took advantage of his post and filled[lined] his own pocket [purse].
4 [만족시키다] satisfy; gratify; answer; meet; fulfill; fill. ¶욕망을 ~ gratify[satisfy] one's desire // 정욕을 ~ gratify one's lust // 수요를 ~ supply[meet] the demand // 조건을 ~ meet the conditions.

채유(採油) drilling for oil; oil extraction. **채유하다** drill for oil; extract oil (from olives).
● **채유권** an oil concession [right].

채자(採字) [인] type-picking. **채자하다** pick types.

채점(採點) marking; grading; scoring; (미) rating. ¶~이 박하다 [후하다] be bad[good] marker / be severe[liberal] in marking (examination papers) // 출석을 ~에 감안하다 consider attendances in awarding marks // 입시의 ~을 하다 mark entrance examination papers // 그는 ~이 엄격하다 He is a strict marker. **채점하다** give[award] marks; mark (examination papers); grade; (미) rate; score (a test). ¶백 점 만점으로 답안을 ~ mark examination papers on the basis of 100 // 답안을 채점하느라 바쁘다 be busy looking over the examination papers.
● **채점자** a marker; a grader; a scorer(경기의). **채점표** a list of marks.

채종(採種) seed-gathering. **채종하다** gather the seeds.
● **채종기** a seeder. **채종밭** a field for seed-raising.

채집(採集) collection; collecting; gathering. ¶곤충 ~ insect collecting / (구어) bugging / bug hunting // 곤충 ~망 an insect catcher // 식물[광물] ~ collection of plants[rocks] // 식물 ~ 상자 a vasculum (pl. vascula, ~s) // 약초 ~ a collection of herbs. **채집하다** collect; gather. ¶식물을 ~ collect plants / gather herbs // 나비를 ~ catch butterflies for specimens // 곤충을 채집하러 가다 go bugging[bug hunting / insect collecting].
● **채집가** a collector.

채쭉 a whip; (말의) a horsewhip. ¶말을 ~으로 때리다 whip [lash] a horse // ~을 휘두르다 wield a whip.
● **채쭉질** [매질] whipping; lashing; flogging. ¶~을 하다 [매질하다] whip / lash / [격려하다] lash / spur[urge] on.

채취(採取) picking; gathering. **채취하다** pick; gather; collect; harvest; fish (pearls); [추출하다] extract (alcohol / radium). ¶해초를 ~ gather seaweeds // 지문을 ~ take (a person's) fingerprints / fingerprint (a person) // 문의 손잡이에서 지문을 ~ lift fingerprints from a doorknob // 올리브에서 기름을 ~ extract oil from olives.
● **채취자** a picker; a gatherer; a collector.

채치다¹ 1 [채찍질하다] whip; lash; flog; flagel-

late. 2 [독촉하다] press; urge; dun. ¶빚을 갚으라고 ~ dun[press / push] (a person) for payment of a debt / urge (a person) to pay a debt.

채치다² snatch (away)(from / off); jerk. ⇨**채다**¹

채칼 a knife for shredding vegetables; a chef's knife.

채탄(採炭) coal mining. **채탄하다** mine[extract] coal.
● **채탄량** the output of coal. **채탄부** a pitman; a collier.

채택(採擇) [선택] choice; selection; option; [채용] acceptance; introduction; adoption (특히 의안 등의). ¶새 방법의 ~ the adoption[introduction] of a new method (of teaching). **채택하다** choose; select; accept (a proposal); adopt (a plan); use (a textbook). ¶결의안을 ~ adopt a resolution // 우리는 내년도용으로 새로운 교과서를 채택했다 For next year we chose[selected] a new textbook. // 이런 토픽도 가끔 채택해 주었으면 합니다 I wish you would take up[select] such topics sometime. // 그는 신문의 사설을 교재로 채택했다 He used newspaper editorials as teaching material. // 그는 남보다 앞서 새로운 아이디어를 채택했다 He was the first to adopt the new ideas. →¶그의 제안은 채택되었다 His plan was adopted. // 만장일치로 결의안이 채택되었다 The resolution was unanimously adopted. // 그들의 제안은 전혀 채택되지 않았다 Their proposal was given no consideration[was totally ignored / was not taken up at all].

채팅 (a) chat.

채플 a chapel.

채혈(採血) blood-gathering [-collecting]; drawing blood. ¶이동 ~차 a bloodmobile. **채혈하다** gather[collect] blood (from a donor); draw blood (from a vein).
● **채혈 기관** a blood-gathering agency.

채화(彩畵) a colored picture; a painting.

책(冊) a book; a volume; [작품] a work; [읽을거리] reading. ¶영어 ~ an English book // 과학 ~ a scientific book / a book on science // ~ 모양으로 [~이 되어] in book form // 한 권의 ~으로 되어 있다 be bound up in one volume // 한 권의 ~으로 엮다 collect (essays) into a single volume(쓴 것을 모아) / compile (data) into a book(편집하다) // ~으로 출판하다 publish in book form // ~을 쓰다 write a book // ~을 읽다 read a book // ~을 내다 publish[bring out] a book // 논문을 ~으로 내다 publish essays in book form // ~을 매다 bind a book // ~(장)을 넘기다 turn over the leaves of a book // ~을 읽어 주다 read to (a person) // ~을 읽다가 잠들다 read oneself to sleep // 단순히 ~에서 얻은 지식 mere book learning / knowledge gained only from books // 그 ~은 지금 떨어졌습니다 We haven't got any copies of the book on hand now. / The book is out of stock at present. // 그 ~은 대출 중이다 The book is out. // 이 ~은 잘 씌었다 This book is well written. // 형은 ~을 많이 가지고 있다 My brother has a large library. // 그녀는 ~을 많이 읽는다 She reads a lot. // 그는 ~을 많이 읽었다 He is well-read. // 그녀는 최근에 처음으로 ~을 냈다 She recently published her first book. // 그의 논문은 ~으로 출판되어 있다 His thesis has

been published in book form [as a book].
책(柵) **1** [울타리] a (picket) fence; a stockade; a paling; a railing; a palisade; a corral(가축 우리). ¶~을 두르다 set (up) [put up] a fence round / fence round [around / about] / enclose (a place) with a palisade. **2** (둑의) a stockade; a log dike [dyke].
책(責) **1** responsibility. ⇨⁼책임 **2** blame; charge. ⇨⁼책망
-책(責) a responsible person; a person in charge (of). ¶조직~ an organizer.
-책(策) a step; a measure; a plan; a scheme; a policy; a resource; a means; an expedient. ¶궁여지~ a shift / the last expedient // 대응~ a countermeasure // 해결~ a solution (to [of] a problem).
책갈피(册－) a space between the leaves (of a book). ¶~에 끼워 두다 keep (it) between the leaves of a book // ~에 돈을 넣어 두다 put money between the leaves of a book.
책권(册卷) a volume; a book. ¶그는 ~깨나 갖고 있다 He has a good many books.
책꽂이(册－) a bookstand; a bookrack; a bookshelf (*pl.* -shelves).
책동(策動) maneuvers; machination; scheming. ¶정치가들의 야비한 ~ the contemptible maneuvers of politicians. **책동하다** maneuver; machinate; scheme (for power). ¶뒤에서 ~ maneuver behind the scenes / pull the wires (from behind).
● **책동가** a schemer; a wirepuller; a maneuverer; a machinator.
책뚜껑(册－) a (book) cover.
책략(策略) a stratagem; a ruse; an artifice; a trick; tactics; strategy; maneuvers; a plan; a scheme; a policy; (미국 속어) a frame-up. ¶~을 쓰다 use [resort to] artifice / play a mean trick on (a person) // 온갖 ~을 다 쓰다 use every artifice / resort to every possible stratagem // ~을 써서 with stratagem [artifice] // 이 풍부하다 be resourceful / be full of resources // ~으로 적을 진지 안으로 꾀어 들이다 [진지 밖으로 꾀어내다] maneuver the enemy into [out of] position // 그들은 세력을 만회하려고 온갖 ~을 쓰고 있다 They are resorting to every stratagem to retrieve their power.
책력(册曆) an almanac; a book calendar.
책망(責望) blame; charge; (a) censure; (a)reproach; (a) rebuke; (a) reproof. ¶~을 듣다 be reproved [rebuked] / be called to task / receive a reproof (from) / catch [get] it (from) // 잘못에 대해 ~을 받다 take the blame for a mistake // 나는 약속을 어겼다고 ~을 들었다 I was reproached with having broken my promise. **책망하다** call (a person) to task [account]; blame; censure; charge; reproach; rebuke; reprove. ¶부주의를 ~ reproach (a person) for his carelessness // 남의 직무 태만을 ~ reproach [scold] a person for neglect of duty // 남의 약속 위반을 ~ call a person to account for breaking his promise // 배은망덕을 ~ rebuke (a person's) ingratitude // 자기 자신을 ~ blame oneself // 선생님은 학생들의 부주의를 책망했다 The teacher scolded the boys for being so careless. // 시장은 시(市) 공무원들의 불공직적인 업무를 책망했다 The mayor reproved the city officials for their irregularities. // 남을 책망하지 말고 자신을 책망하라 Find fault with yourself rather than with others.
책무(責務) [의무] duty; (an) obligation; [책임] responsibility. ¶국가에 대한 ~ one's duty to one's country // 자기의 ~를 다하다 discharge [fulfil(l)] one's obligations / do [perform] one's duty.
책받침(册－) a pad to rest writing paper on; a sheet of plastic [cardboard] placed under a sheet of paper when writing.
책방(册房) a bookseller's; a bookstore. ⇨⁼서점
책벌레(册－) [지나치게 공부하는 사람] a bookworm.
책보(册褓) [책보자기] a book wrapper; [책 보통이] a package of books.
책사(策士) a tactician; a schemer. ⇨⁼모사(謀士)
책상(册床) a desk; a (writing) table. ¶양소매 ~ a kneehole desk // 사무용 ~ an office desk // ~에 앉다 sit [be] at a desk // ~에 앉아서 졸다 doze at a desk // ~을 나란히 하여 함께 일하다 work side by side (with a person) // ~을 사이에 두고 앉다 sit across a table // 아들애는 ~에 앉아 있는 일이 좀처럼 없다 My son seldom sits at his desk. / My son doesn't study very much.
● **책상다리** [앉음새] sitting cross-legged. ¶~를 하다 sit cross-legged / sit down tailor-fashion / sit with one's legs crossed // 그는 ~를 하고 앉았다 He sat with his legs crossed.
책상물림 a naive academic. **책상보** a table cloth.
책임(責任) responsibility; liability(지불의); [책무] an obligation; duty. ¶무~ irresponsibility // 연대 [공동] ~ collective responsibility / joint liability // 유한 [무한] ~ limited [unlimited] liability // 전~ the whole responsibility // 무거운 ~ heavy responsibility // 의무 이행의 ~ responsibility for the fulfil(l)ment of obligations // 사고에 대한 ~ liability for an accident // 법률에 대한 ~ responsibility to the law // 일가족 부양의 ~ a family responsibility // 전쟁의 ~ war guilt / responsibility for war // ~ 있는 ~ 자리 a responsible post / a position of trust // ~ 있는 답변 a responsible answer // ~은 …에게 있다 the responsibility rests [lies] with … / the fault lies with … // ~이 있다 be responsible [answerable / accountable] (to a person for something) / be to blame (for) // …의 ~으로 돌리다 lay [place] the responsibility on … / charge (a thing) to (a person's) account // 자기의 ~하에 하다 act [do] on one's own responsibility // ~을 지다 bear [assume / take / shoulder] the responsibility (for / of) / hold oneself responsible (for) // ~을 느끼다 be sensible of one's responsibility (for) // ~을 느껴 사임하다 resign from a sense of responsibility // ~을 일체 지지 않다 disclaim all the responsibility (for) // ~을 다하다 fulfil(l) one's responsibility / discharge one's obligation(s) / do [perform] one's duty // ~을 해제하다 absolve [release] (a person) from his responsibility // ~을 묻다 call (a person) to account / take [call] (a person) to task (for) // ~을 회피하다 avoid [evade / shirk] one's responsibility (for) // ~을 지우다 place [put] the responsibility (for something) on (a person) / saddle (a person) with the responsibility (for) // ~을 전가하다 shift the

responsibility (for something) onto (a person) / pass the buck to (a person) // ~을 같이하다 share the responsibility (for something) with (a person) // ~의 소재를 밝히다 clarify where the responsibility lies / find out who is responsible (for) // 내 ~은 아니다 I'm not responsible [to blame] for it. // ~은 어디에[누구에게] 있는가 Where shall we place the responsibility for it? / Who is responsible for it? // 부모를 봉양하는 것은 너의 ~이다 It lies upon you to provide for your parents. // 자기 아이들을 기르는 것은 부모의 ~이다 It is the duty of parents to bring up their children. // 당신은 가족에 대하여 ~이 있다 You have obligations to your family. // 그는 모든 ~을 한 몸에 졌다 He took it upon himself to bear the whole burden. // 회사를 파산시킨 ~은 사장에게 있었다 The responsibility for the company's bankruptcy rested [lay] with the president. / The president was responsible for the company's bankruptcy. // 너는 ~을 회피하려 해서는 안 된다 You must not try to evade your responsibility. // 내 ~은 그것으로 끝난다 My responsibility ends with it. // ~의 태반은 은행 측에 있다 Much of the blame belongs with the bank. // 어떤 일을 하든 먼저 ~의 소재를 분명히 해야 한다 Whatever you do, you must first make it clear who is responsible. // 친구와 공동[연대] ~으로 이 공장을 경영하고 있다 My friend and I are jointly responsible for the management of this factory. // 화재의 ~을 지고 교장이 사임했다 Taking the blame for [Holding himself responsible for] the fire, the headmaster resigned. // 아들의 실패는 내게 ~이 있다 I am to blame [must answer] for my son's failure. // 나는 ~을 지고 문단속을 하겠습니다 I will see to it that the doors are locked. // 정보 통신부는 등기 우편 이외의 금전 분실에는 ~이 없다 The Ministry of Information and Communication is not liable for the loss of money unless it is registered.
● **책임감** a sense of responsibility. ¶~이 강하다 have a strong sense of responsibility // ~이 없다 lack all sense of responsibility. **책임자** a responsible person; a person in charge (of). ¶여기 ~는 누구냐 Who is in charge here? **책임 전가** imputation; (구어) buck-passing. **책임 회피** evasion [shirking] of responsibility. (구어) buck-passing.
책자(冊子) a book; a volume. ⇨책(冊)
책잡다(責-) find fault with (a person); call (a person) to account (for); take (a person) to task; blame [reproach] (for). ¶실언을 ~ take (a person) to task for a slip of the tongue // 직무 태만을 ~ denounce (a person) for his neglect of duty // 책잡을 데가 없다 have no fault to find with.
책잡히다(責-) be found fault with; be called to account [task]; be taken to task; be blamed [reproached]. ¶위약했다고 ~ be blamed for having broken one's promise // 직무 태만으로 ~ be accused of having neglected one's work // 회사의 돈을 썼다고 ~ be blamed for appropriating company money.
책장(冊張) a leaf of a book; the pages. ¶~을 넘기다 turn over the leaves of a book / turn [leaf] the pages of a book / leaf through a book / thumb the leaves of a book.
책장(冊欌) a bookshelf (*pl.* -shelves); a bookcase; a book chest.
책정(策定) appropriation; (가격 등의) fixing (prices). ¶봉급 ~ arrangement of a salary scale. **책정하다** appropriate; allot; earmark (for). ¶가격을 ~ fix a price // 학교 보조금으로 오백만 원을 ~ appropriate five million won for school aid // 연구비로서 얼마의 금액을 ~ earmark a sum of money for research work // 해마다 G.N.P.의 25%를 군비로 ~ earmark 25% of (its) G.N.P. each year for military preparedness // 나는 오천만 원을 집의 건축비로 책정했다 I set aside [earmarked / alloted] fifty million won for building a house.
책치레(冊-) make-up of a book. **책치레하다** make up a book.
책하다(責-) call (a person) to task; blame. ⇨책망하다(⇨책망)
챔피언 a champion; (속어) a champ. ¶레슬링 ~ a wrestling champion / a champion wrestler // 수영의 세계 ~ the swimming champion of the world // ~이 되다 win [gain] a championship // ~ 자리를 잃다 [유지하다] lose [retain] a championship.
● **챔피언십** (a) championship.
챙 1 a penthouse. ⇨차양1 **2** (모자 앞에 다는 조각) a visor; a peak; (운동모 등의) an eyeshade; an eye shield. ¶~이 넓은 모자 a broad-brimmed hat // ~이 달린 모자 a peaked [visored] cap.
챙기다 [정돈하다] put (things) in order; set (things) in (good) order; tidy up; [짐 꾸리다] pack; [모으다] gather all together; collect. ¶소지품을 ~ get one's things together / gather up one's belongings // 서류를 ~ get papers in order // 제 물건을 잘 ~ take good care of one's (own) things // 짐을 챙겨 들고 상경하다 come up to Seoul with one's things packed.
처(妻) a wife. ⇨아내 ¶내연의 ~ a common-law wife // 조강지~ one's wife married in poverty / one's old life partner // ~에게 쥐어지내는 남편 a henpecked husband // ~로 삼다 make (a woman) one's wife / take (a woman) to wife / have [get] (a woman) for one's wife // ~에게 쥐어지내다 be henpecked / be tied to one's wife's apron string // 그 녀석은 제 ~에게 쥐어지낸다 He is at the beck and call of his wife.
처(處) [정부 기구] an office.
-처(處) [곳] a place. ¶근무~ one's place of employment / one's office // 접수~ a reception desk [office] // 법제~ the Office of Legislation // 국가 보훈~ the ministry of Patriots and veterans Affairs.
처가(妻家) one's wife's home.
● **처가살이** living in one's wife's home. ¶~를 하다 live in one's wife's home.
처결(處決) settlement; disposal; disposition; decision. **처결하다** settle; dispose of; decide.
처남(妻男) one's wife's brother; one's brother-in-law.
처넣다 1 [무리하게 넣다] push [press / thrust / force / stuff / jam] in; crowd [jam / stuff] into; [마구 넣다] throw (a thing) into. ¶책을 상자에 ~ pack one's books into a box // 떡을 입에 ~ shovel down rice cake // 쓰레기통에 ~ throw (things) into a wastebasket //

처네 나는 불필요한 것은 다락방에 처넣기로 하고 있다 I usually throw unneeded things into the attic.// 나는 더러운 옷을 세탁기에 처넣었다 I threw[shoved] the dirty clothes in the washing machine. **2** [감금하다] lock (a person) up[in]; confine; imprison. ¶교도소에 ~ cast[throw] (a culprit) into prison// 어두운 방에 ~ confine [lock] (a person) in a dark room// 그 녀석을 교도소에 처넣겠다 I'm going to get him imprisoned.

처네 1 [덧이불] a coverlet; a counterpane; a quilt; a comforter. **2** [아이를 업는 포대기] a coverlet for carrying a baby on one's back.

처녀(處女) a virgin; a maiden; a maid. **숫**~ an immaculate virgin// ~의 virgin / maiden / ~다운 maidenlike / maidenly / virginal / ~답게 like a maiden / in a maidenlike manner// 꽃다운 ~ 시절에 in the flower of maidenhood / in virginal bloom// ~로 늙은 여자 women who have retained their virginity

처녀가 애를 낳아도 할 말이 있다(속담) Every evil-doer has his reasons.
●**처녀림** a primeval forest. ⇨=원시림(⇨=원시 (原始) **처녀막** [생] the maidenhead; the hymen. **처녀성** virginity; maidenhood; virgin hood. ¶~을 상실함 devirgination / defloration// ~을 잃어버리다[빼앗기다] lose[be deprived of] one's virginity / be deflowered// ~을 지키다 keep[retain] one's virginity. **처녀자리 / 처녀궁 / 처녀좌** [천] the Virgin; Virgo. **처녀작** a maiden work.

처단(處斷) [결단] judgment; decision; [처치] disposition; punishment. **처단하다** [결단하다] judge; decide; rule; [처치하다] punish; deal[do] with. ¶범법자를 엄히 ~ punish [deal with] an offender severely.

처대다 1 [불에 사르다] put[throw] (paper) into a fire; burn on a fire. **2** [자꾸 대 주다] keep supplying[providing] thoughtlessly.

처덕(妻德) **1** [아내의 덕행] the virtue(s) of one's wife. **2** [아내로 입는 덕] one's wife's assistance[help]. ¶~으로 by one's wife's help / thanks to one's wife// 그는 ~으로 성공했다 Thanks to his wife's help, he could succeed.

처덕거리다 1 [물건을 두드려 소리 내다] keep beating with a paddle; paddle; slap; flap; pound. ¶빨래를 ~ paddle the laundry. **2** [함부로 바르다] paste[affix / stick] haphazardly[at random]. ¶벽에 종이를 ~ paste papers all over a wall in a haphazard way// 얼굴에 분을 ~ paint one's face thick / powder one's face too thickly.

처덕처덕 [빨래를] paddling; beating; slapping; [바르는 모양] (paste) at random[haphazard]; thick(ly). ¶담에 전단을 ~ 붙이다 paste bills all over a wall// 분을 ~ 바르다 paint[plaster] (one's face) thickly. **처덕처덕 하다** keep beating with a paddle; paste haphazardly. ⇨처덕거리다

처뜨리다 (아래로) hang down; suspend; droop. ¶어깨를 ~ droop one's shoulders // 개가 귀를 처뜨렸다 A dog drooped his ears. // 긴 머리를 등 뒤로 ~ have one's long hair flowing down one's back.

처량하다(凄涼-) **1** [황량하다] desolate; dreary; bleak; deserted. **처량히** desolately; drearily; bleakly. **2** [구슬프다] sad; sorrowful; doleful; plaintive; melancholy. ¶처량한 이야기 a pathetic story// 처량한 느낌 a feeling of wretchedness// 처량한 심사 melancholy[pensive] mood// 처량한 노래 a plaintive song// 처량한 모습 a wretched[lonesome] look// 처량한 신세 a pitiable condition// 처량해지다 feel miserable [wretched] // 나는 몹시 처량한 느낌이 들었다 I felt awfully miserable[wretched].// 처량한 얼굴을 하지 마라 None of your wretched face! **처량히** sorrowfully; dolefully; plaintively. ¶~ 살다 live[lead] a dreary[wretched] life.

처럼 like; as; as ... as; (not) so ... as; as if [though]. ¶우후죽순~ (spring up) like mushrooms// 어느때~ as usual// 전~ as before / as in the past// 아무 일도 없었던 것 ~ as if nothing had happened// …~ 보이다 it seems[appears] that ... / look like ...// 친자 식~ 사랑하다 love (a child) like one's own // 한집안 식구~ 대하다 treat (a person) as one of the family// 눈~ 희다 be as white as snow// 대낮~ 밝다 be as bright as (noon) day// 남~ 행동하다 behave like a stranger// 그것은 돌~ 무겁다 It's as heavy as a stone. // 그는 자기 아버지~ 익살꾼이다 He is humorous like his father.// 그는 개를 아이~ 다룬다 He treats his dog like his child.// 그는 노인~ 천천히 말을 했다 He speaks slowly like an old man.// 그녀는 마누라~ 그를 돌봐 주고 있다 She looks after him like a wife.// 영어를 그 사람~ 잘하지는 못한다 I can't speak English so well as he.// 그 이야기는 정말[거짓말]~ 들렸다 The story sounds [doesn't sound] true.// 그는 마치 보고 온 것 ~ 이야기한다 He talks as if he had been there to see it himself.// 그녀는 마치 미친 사람~ 무언가를 외쳐 대고 있었다 She was screaming as if she had gone out of her mind.// 그것은 네가 생각하는 것~ 간단하지는 않다 It is not so simple as you think.

처리(處理) management; conduct; disposition; disposal; transaction; dealing; handling; settlement; (약품 등을 쓰는) treatment; (원료 등의) processing. ¶열 ~ heat treatment// 주방 찌꺼기[쓰레기]의 ~ garbage disposal// 하수 ~ sewage disposal// 나는 그 사건의 ~를 일임받았다 I was entrusted with the conduct of the affair.// 우리는 사고의 ~를 해야 한다 (마무리) We must tidy up the mess left after the accident. / (사후 조처) We must deal with the aftermath of the accident. **처리하다** manage (a matter); conduct (business); dispose of (a matter); deal with (an affair); take care of (a matter); transact; handle; settle (up) (a problem); (생산 원료 등을) process; (약품 등을 써서) treat. ¶폐기물을 ~ dispose of useless articles// 물질을 열[산]로 ~ treat a substance with heat [an acid] // 사무를 ~ conduct [transact] business// 일을 ~ manage[dispose of / deal with] a task// 어려운 문제를 ~ deal with [manage / cope with] a difficult problem// 대충 ~ break the neck[back] of (a task)// 자기 일을 잘 처리하고 있다 be in control[on top] of one's job// 그 문제는 간단히 처리할 수 있다 The question can't be settled easily. // 우선 이 문제부터 처리하자 Let's first settle [clear up] this question.// 마침내 쓰레기를 처리했다 The rubbish was at last disposed

처사

of. // 그녀는 일[사무]을 거침없이 아주 잘 처리한다 She manages [deals with / handles] business very efficiently. // 그는 밀려 있는 일을 솜씨 있게 처리하였다 He skillfully [smoothly] disposed of the accumulated work. // 아이는 이 일을 처리하지 못한다 A child can't handle this matter. // 고양이 새끼를 어떻게 처리해야 할지 모르겠다 I don't know what to do with the kittens. // 그는 그 문제를 능란하게 처리했다 He skillfully dealt with [disposed of] the problem. // 이 서류를 처리해 줘래 Will you take care of this paper? / (폐기) Will you dispose of this paper? // 사무를 좀 더 능률적으로 처리할 수 없소 Can't you handle [manage] the office work more efficiently? // 적당히 처리해 주게 I leave (the transaction of) the matter to your discretion. // 우선 이 일을 처리해야 한다 I must finish (off) this work first. // 그도 이 일을 사흘 동안에 처리할 수는 없을 것이다 Even he would not be able to finish this job in three days. // 이 문제는 내가 처리하기에는 너무 어렵다 This problem is too difficult for me to deal with. / This problem has got(ten) out of my control. // 그가 문제를 그럴싸하게 처리해 줄 것일세 He will deal with the matter as he thinks fit. / He will see to it that the matter is settled. // 조속한 시일 내에 처리해 주십시오 I want you to settle the matter as soon as possible. ➡ ¶ (사건이) 원만히 처리되다 be settled amicably / be brought to an amicable settlement // 그의 부상은 산업 재해 보험으로 처리되었다 He was allowed to claim workmen's compensation insurance for his injury. // 그 일은 서투르게 처리되었다 The affair was poorly managed. / He mishandled [made a mess of] the matter. // 그것은 사무적으로 처리되어야 한다 It should be handled [dealt with] in a businesslike manner. // 그 문제는 이미 처리되었다 That matter has already been settled.

처마 the eaves. ¶ ~의 홈통 an eaves gutter / an eave trough / ~에서 떨어지는 빗물 raindrops falling from the eaves // ~ 끝에 달린 고드름 icicles hanging from the eaves / ~에 풍경이 매달려 있다 A wind-bell is hanging from the eaves. // 비가 퍼붓고 있으니 이 집 ~ 밑에서 비를 피하자 It's really pouring. Let's take shelter under the eaves of this house.

처매다 〔감아 매다〕 bind up (a wound); bandage (a wound) up.

처먹다 〔몹시 세게 먹다〕 cram (food) into one's mouth; shove [shovel] down; eat greedily; devour. ¶떡을 ~ shovel down rice cake // 처먹어라 Dig [Tuck] in!

처박다 1 〔몹시 세게 박다〕 drive [strike] in(to); ram down (a stake); wedge in (쐐기 등을). ¶못을 ~ drive [hammer] a nail into (a wall). 2 〔처넣다〕 thrust [shove / tuck] in(to); stuff [cram / pack] into; ram in(to); (물속에) dive; dip. ¶서랍 속에 ~ shove [cram] (a thing) in a drawer / 트렁크에 옷을 ~ ram clothes into a trunk / 헛간에 ~ put (things) into a barn. 3 〔가두다〕 shut in [up]; lock in [up]; confine. ¶처박아 두다 keep (a person) penned (up) (in a place).

처박히다 be shut in [up]; be locked in [up]. ¶처박혀 있다 confine oneself to [in] (a room) / shut oneself up / be confined [closeted] in (one's room) / remain [keep] indoors // 하루 종일 방에 ~ keep (in) one's room all day long.

처방 〔處方〕 (a) prescription; a recipe. ¶ ~을 쓰다 write a prescription (for a disease) // ~대로 조제하다 prepare a medicine as prescribed [according to a prescription] // ~을 잘못하다 make out a wrong prescription (for) // 의사의 그에 대한 ~은 1주일간의 휴양이었다 The doctor prescribed a week's rest for him. / The doctor's prescription for him was a week's rest. // 그 의사는 나의 병에 대해서 ~을 써 주었다 The doctor prescribed medicine for my disease. / The doctor wrote out a prescription (of medicine) for my disease. // 그 약사는 의사의 ~대로 약을 조제했다 The pharmacist [druggist] filled the doctor's prescription. // 이 약은 의사의 ~ 없이는 조제하지 않음 This medicine is obtainable only on a physician's prescription.

●**처방전** a (medical) prescription. ¶ ~을 쓰다 write [make out] a prescription (for a disease) // ~에 따라서[대로] 조제해 받다 get [have] a prescription filled / receive a medicine according to a prescription.

처벌 〔處罰〕 〔벌하기〕 (a) punishment; 〔형벌〕 a penalty. ¶가벼운[무거운] ~ a light [heavy] penalty // ~을 면하다 escape the penalty (of) // 커닝에 대한 ~은 가혹하다 The penalty for cheating on [(영)] an examination is severe. // 그는 불법 주차로 ~을 받았다 He was penalized for illegal parking. // 그는 ~로서 벌금형을 선고받았다 He was punished with a fine. // 그는 유능한 변호사를 고용한 덕택에 ~을 면했다 Because he hired clever lawyers he managed to escape punishment [(구어) get off scot-free]. // 음주 운전에는 더 무거운 ~을 내려야 한다 The penalty for drunken driving should be much heavier. // 범인은 엄중한 ~을 받았다 The criminal was severely punished. // 그는 징계의 ~을 받았다 He was subjected to disciplinary punishment. // 관대한 ~을 바랍니다 I entreat you to be lenient. **처벌하다** punish (a person for a crime); inflict a penalty on (a person for an offense). ¶엄중히 ~ punish severely / inflict severe [heavy] punishment on. ➡그는 처벌되지 않고 석방되었다 He was set free unpunished.

처분 〔處分〕 〔처치〕 disposal; disposition; dealing; a measure; 〔형벌〕 punishment. ¶공매 ~ (disposition by) public sale / 매각 ~ disposition by sale / 부당 ~ an unwarrantable proceeding [measure] / 체납 ~ disposition for failure to pay (taxes) / 강제 execution by legal process // 행정 ~을 취하다 take an administrative measure // 포로는 적병의 ~에 달려 있었다 The captive was at the mercy of the enemy soldier. // 적당한 ~을 바랍니다 Deal with me as you think fit. **처분하다** dispose of; deal with; make a clearance of (unsold goods). ¶토지[재산]를 ~ dispose of one's land [property] // 위반자를 엄중히 [관대히] ~ deal with an offender severely [leniently] // 그 죄지은 학생을 어떻게 처분할까요 What shall we do with the guilty boy?

처사 〔處士〕 recluse; a retired scholar.

처사 〔處事〕 treatment; management (of an affair); dealing [handling] with (a matter);

처삼촌

처(處) conduct; disposal; [조치] a measure; a step. ¶적절한 ~ an appropriate[adequate] measure / a proper step // ~를 잘하다 take a proper step / deal with a matter properly // 그는 혹독한 ~를 받았다 He was subjected to cruel treatment. / He was cruelly treated. // 부인에 대한 그의 ~는 정말 이해할 수 없다 I simply can't understand the way he treats [his behavior toward] his wife. // 네 ~는 현명했다 You acted wisely. **처사하다** manage (a matter); deal[cope / do] with (an affair); dispose of (a matter).

처삼촌(妻三寸) one's wife's uncle; an uncle-in-law.

처서(處暑) [24절기의 하나] *cheoseo*; 'limit of heat' — a solar period (=about August 23rd).

처세(處世) conduct of life. ¶~에 능한 사람 a worldly-wise person // ~에 능하지 못하다 be lacking in worldly wisdom // 저 사람은 ~를 잘한다 That man knows how to get ahead [along] in the world. / He is worldly-wise. / He is good at making his way in life. // 그는 매우 위태로운 ~를 한다 He makes a living in a very risky way. // 정직함이 그의 ~ 방법이다 Honesty is the guiding principle of his life. **처세하다** get on[make one's way] in the world; get along with people.
● **처세술** a rule of life; the secret of success in life; the art of living[of managing in society]; how to get on in the world; social politics. ¶~이 서투르다 be lacking in worldly wisdom // 그는 ~에 아주 능하다 He is a man of the world. / He knows well how to get on in life. / He knows how to get along[ahead] in life. // 그는 ~을 터득하고 있다 He knows how to get[the secret of getting] along in life[this world]. **처세훈(-訓)** the (guiding) motto for one's life; rules of conduct in life; lessons of life.

처소(處所) [장소] a place; [거처] a living [dwelling] place; one's residence; one's abode; one's address(주소); [임시의] ~ one's temporary address[residence] // 그의 ~는 아직 모른다 His whereabouts is[are] still unknown.

처신(處身) behavior; deportment; demeanor; conduct. ¶남편과 사별한 뒤 나는 ~이 곤란하다 Having lost my husband, I don't know what to do with myself. **처신하다** behave [conduct / deport / comport / demean] oneself. ¶교묘히 ~ act[conduct oneself / maneuver / (영) manoeuvre] with great tact // 훌륭하게 [의젓하게] ~ behave fine[well / handsomely] // 그녀는 재치 있게 처신하여 큰 부자와 결혼했다 She played her cards cleverly and married a millionaire. // 그는 어떻게 처신해야 하는가를 안다 He knows how to conduct himself.

처연하다(凄然-) pathetic; sad; sorrowful.

처우(處遇) (a) treatment. ¶~를 개선하다 improve treatment / give better treatment to (workers). **처우하다** treat; deal[do] with. ¶나는 그를 어떻게 처우해야 할지 모르겠다 I don't know what to do with him[how to treat him].
● **처우 개선** better treatment.

처음 [시초] the beginning; the opening; the start; the outset; commencement; [최초] (the) first; the first time; [기원] the origin. ¶

~의 first / initial / incipient / lead-off(개시의) / original / early(초기의) // ~에는 at first / at the start // 맨 ~ the very first[beginning] / ~부터 끝까지 from the beginning to end / (책의) from cover to cover // ~으로 for the first time // ~의 계획 the original plan // ~[첫 / 처음으로 겪는] 경험 one's first experience // ~ 이틀 동안 the first two days // ~에는 학생이 10명이었다 There were ten students at the beginning[to start with]. // 그는 소심한[겁먹은] 태도였다 At first he seemed to be timid. // ~에 그것을 끓이고 다음에 양념을 한다 First boil it and then season it. // ~에[첫 번째로] 누가 왔는가 Who came first? // ~에 도착한 것은 톰이었다 Tom was the first to arrive. // ~으로 그를 만났을 때 나는 별로 강한 인상을 받지는 못했다 The first time I met him, he did not make much of an impression on me. // ~부터 시작하십시오 Start from[Begin at] the beginning. // 그런 것은 나는 ~부터 알고 있었다 I know that from the beginning[start]. // 나는 ~부터 그를 수상히 여겼다 I suspected him from the outset[the (very) beginning]. // 그 일이라면 ~부터 알고 있었다 I knew it all along. // ~에는 누구나 신중하다 Everyone is careful at first. // ~ 목표는 훨씬 높았다 The original goal was much higher than this. // ~이 잘못되었다 I got off on the wrong foot. / I made a false[wrong] start. // ~ 뵙겠습니다 How do you do? / I am glad[pleased] to meet you. // 우리는 맨 ~부터 다시 시작해야 한다 We must start again from scratch[from the very beginning]. / Back to the drawing board! // 그가 지각하기는 이번이 ~이 아니다 It is not the first time that he has come late. / It's nothing new for him to come late. // 서울은 ~이다 I am a stranger in Seoul. / I am unfamiliar with Seoul. // 내가 ~ 유럽에 갔을 때는 배 편이었다 When I first went to Europe, I went by ship. // 저 산에 ~ 절을 세운 사람은 저 스님이다 That priest was the first person to build a temple on the mountain. // 파리에 간 것은 그것이 ~이었다 That was my first visit to Paris. // 내가 그런 장관을 본 것은 ~이다 I have never seen such a spectacle before. // ~으로 배우는 사람은 천천히 활주하세요 We ask that beginners ski slowly. // 그것은 정말 ~ 겪는 경험이었다 It was an entirely new experience for me. // 나는 ~부터 실패했다 I made a mistake[(구어) I goofed] at the very beginning. / I got off on the wrong foot right at the start. // 녹화(錄畫)는 ~부터 본격적으로 행해졌다 The filming was done cold, without any rehearsal. // 뉴욕에 와서 ~ 이삼 년 동안은 자주 연극을 보러 다녔다 I often went to the theater during my first few years in New York.

처자(妻子) one's wife and children; one's family. ¶~를 부양하다 support[provide for] one's family // ~를 버리다 desert[discard] one's wife and children // ~를 돌보지 않다 have no regard for one's wife and children.

처자(處子) a virgin; a maiden. ⇨처녀

처절하다(悽絶-) extremely sad[melancholy / wretched / miserably]; heartbreaking; heartrending; [처참하다] ghastly; gruesome. ¶처절한 광경 a sorrowful[heartbreaking] sight / a gruesome scene // 처절한 싸움 a fierce battle.

처제(妻弟) one's wife's younger sister; one's sister-in-law.
처조모(妻祖母) one's wife's grandmother.
처조부(妻祖父) one's wife's grandfather.
처조카(妻-) one's wife's nephew[niece].
처지(處地) 1 〔형편〕 a situation; a condition; circumstances; one's lot; one's (financial) status; 〔입장〕 a standpoint; a position; one's standing; 〔신분〕 a station in life. ¶비참한 ~ a miserable [pathetic / wretched] situation / a hard plight / a fix∥곤란한 ~ a difficult[an awkward] situation / a delicate position / a dilemma∥어떤 ~에 있건 under [in] any circumstances / however circumstanced one may be / in any condition in life ∥어려운 ~에 있다 be in needy circumstances∥자기의 ~에 만족하다 be contented with one's lot∥같은 ~에 있다 be in the same circumstances∥괴로운 ~에 빠지다 be placed in a sad plight / fall into great straits / be put in a (nice) fix / get oneself into a nasty mess / (비참한) be driven into a piteous plight∥남의 딱한 ~에 동정하다 sympathize with a person's sad plight∥자기 ~를 모르다 do not know where one stands [is]∥남의 ~가 되어 보다 put[place] oneself in another's place[shoes]∥그는 몹시 어려운 ~에 빠져 사임하지 않을 수 없었다 Things came to such a pass[(구어) got into such a mess] that he had to resign.∥마침 내가 그 곳에 있었기 때문에 나는 그들을 돕지 않을 수 없는 ~에 있었다 I was obliged to help them just because I happened to be there.∥나는 어려운 ~에 빠졌다 I am in an awkward situation.∥(구어) I am in a nice [bad] fix.
2 〔사이〕 relations; terms. ¶우리는 서로 말을 놓고 지내는 ~다 We are on thee-and-thou terms with each other.
처지다 1 〔늘어지다〕 hang (down); droop; sag. ¶처진 어깨 drooping shoulders∥귀가 처진 개 a dog with button[drop] ears∥끝이 처진 콧수염 a handlebar mustache∥케이블이 처져 있다 The cable is slack[sagging].∥그녀의 뺨이 처지기 시작한다 Her cheeks are beginning to sag.∥그의 바지는 무릎이 처져 있다 There are bast at the knees of his trousers.∥열매가 많이 열려 가지가 처져 있다 The branches are drooping under the weight of the fruit.∥잎이 비를 맞아 처져 있다 The leaves are drooping in the rain.
2 〔뒤지다〕 fall[drop] behind; fall back; trail; be outstripped (by). ¶혼자만 뒤에 ~ fall [remain] behind all alone∥경주에서 ~ drop[fall] behind in a race∥행군하다가 ~ fall out while on the march.
처지르다 1 〔아궁이 등에 나무를 몰아 넣다〕 lay[put] plenty of (wood) (on the fire). ¶방에 불을 ~ make a huge fire. 2 put (paper) into a fire. ⇨처대다1
처참하다(悽慘-) ghastly; gruesome; lurid; grim; appalling; miserable; wretched. ¶처참한 생활 a wretched[miserable] life∥처참한 싸움 a bloody battle[fight] ∥공습 후의 처참한 광경 the desolate[dreary] scene (of a devastated area) after an air raid∥현장은 몹시 처참했다 The scene presented a ghastly sight. **처참히** ghastly; gruesomely; grimly.
처처(處處) several[various] places; this and that part; several parts. ¶~에(서) (here and) everywhere.

처첩(妻妾) one's wife and concubine.
처치(處置) 1 〔처분〕 disposal; disposition; management; (상처의) treatment; 〔조치〕 a measure; a step. ¶쓰레기 폐기 ~ the disposal of garbage∥피해자 구제를 위하여 긴급 ~를 취하다 take emergency measures for the relief of the victims∥그는 ~ 곤란한 놈이다 He is a tough[hard] customer (to deal with). **처치하다** 〔처리하다〕 dispose of; 〔대처하다〕 deal with; 〔대책을 세우다〕 take measures (to do). ¶잘못 ~ adopt the wrong measure∥부상자를 응급 ~ give first aid [first-aid treatment] to an injured person ∥상처를 빨리 처치해라 Treat the wound quickly.
2 〔제거〕 removal; clearance; elimination; liquidation. **처치하다** remove; get rid of; clear [take] away; do away with; eliminate; liquidate. ¶책상을 어디로 처치해야겠다 We have to move the table away somewhere.∥우리는 그를 처치하기로 했다 We marked him for death.
처하다(處-) 1 〔놓이다〕 be placed (in); be [get] faced with. ¶역경에 ~ be in adversity / be under unfavorable circumstances∥불리한 입장에 ~ be in a disadvantageous position∥위기에 ~ face[be confronted with] a crisis∥괴로운 지경에 처해 있다 be in great difficulty∥역경에 처하여 침착성을 잃지 마라 Don't lose your presence of mind in the face of difficulty.
2 〔처벌하다〕 sentence; condemn. ¶사형에 ~ sentence[condemn] (a person) to death / 5일간의 구류에 처해지다 be sentenced to five day's detention∥그는 사형에 처해졌다 He was condemned to death.∥그는 10년 징역에 처해졌다 He was sentenced to ten years in prison.∥그는 엄벌에 처해야 한다 He deserves severe punishment.
처형(妻兄) one's wife's elder sister; one's sister-in-law.
처형(處刑) 〔처벌〕 punishment; 〔사형 집행〕 execution. **처형하다** punish; (사형에) execute. ➔¶지도자는 처형되었다 The leader was liquidated[(미국 속어) rubbed out].∥그는 1789년에 파리에서 처형되었다 He was executed in Paris in 1789.
● **처형대**(교수·단두의) a scaffold; (교수의) a gallows. **처형장** an execution ground.
척¹ (false) show; make-believe. ⇨˝체²
척² 1 〔잘 붙는 모양〕 closely; tightly; hard; fast; clingingly. ¶~ 달라붙다 cling tight (to one's body)∥(풀이 손에) ~ 달라붙다 (paste) stick fast (to one's hand)∥젖은 옷이 몸에 ~ 들러붙다 wet clothes cling tight to one's body.
2 〔즉뜻〕 without hesitation[delay]; readily; 〔즉각〕 instantly; quickly; offhand; right away[off]. ¶~ 보고 at first sight / at the first glance∥~ 대답하다 answer (question) readily / give a ready answer∥돈을 ~ 내걸다 bet one's money without hesitation / be a ready bettor∥한 번 ~ 보고 그의 사기임을 알아보았다 One glance was enough to see through his fraud.∥딸이 말하자나 하는 것을 ~ 알아챘다 I sensed exactly[immediately] what my daughter was driving at.
3 〔늘어지는 모양〕 loosely; drooping (low); limply; flaccidly. ¶~ 늘어지다 hang limply / dangle.

4 〔의젓하게〕 imposingly; with dignity; 〔멋지게〕 smartly; becomingly; dashingly. ¶안경을 ~ 쓰다 look good in spectacles / put on one's glasses imposingly // 칼을 ~ 차다 wear a sword dashingly.

척³(공) a chuck; a vise.

척(尺) a *ja*; a foot. ⇨"자"2

척(隻) a vessel; a ship; a boat. ¶배 한 ~ [one] vessel[ship / boat] // 한 ~분의 뱃짐 a shipload // 거룻배 한 ~분의 석탄 a lighter-load of coal // 군함 한 ~을 출동시키다 dispatch a warship.

척결하다(剔抉−) 〔찾아내어 없애다〕 expose (a crime / fraud); lay bare (an evil design). ¶부정 사건을 ~ expose a scandal.

척골(脊骨) the backbone. ⇨"등골뼈(⇨등골)

척골(蹠骨) 〔생〕 a metatarsal (bone).

척도(尺度) 〔계량의 단위〕 a measure; 〔눈금〕 a scale; 〔기준〕 a standard; a criterion; a barometer. ¶문명의 ~ an index of civilization // …을 재는 ~가 되다 be a measure[a barometer / an index] of ... / be a yardstick for ... // 마일이나 야드는 길이의 ~이다 Miles and yards are measures of length. // 재산은 사람의 행복을 결정하는 ~가 아니다 You cannot measure a man's happiness by his wealth. / Wealth is no criterion of a man's happiness. / 너와 나는 인생을 보는 ~가 다르다 You view life with different standards from mine. / You look at life differently than I do. / 체중은 건강의 ~이다 Your weight is a barometer of your physical condition. // 출판물의 양은 문화의 ~로 일컬어진다 It is said that a culture can be measured by the volume of material published.

척력(斥力) 〔물〕 repulsion; repulsive force.

척박하다(瘠薄−) barren; sterile; infertile; meager; poor. ¶척박한 땅 barren[sterile / unproductive] soil[land] // 땅을 척박하게 하다 impoverish the soil.

척분(戚分) kinship; (ties of) relationship.

척살(刺殺) **1** 〔찔러 죽임〕 stabbing to death. **척살하다** stab (a person) to death. **2** tagging (a runner) out. ⇨"터치아웃(⇨터치)

척수(脊髓) 〔생〕 the spinal cord[marrow]; pith.

●**척수 신경** the spinal nerves. **척수액** the spinal fluid. **척수염** myelitis. **척수 주사** a spinal injection.

척식(拓殖) colonization; exploitation. **척식하다** 〔미개지를 개간하다〕 open up undeveloped land; 〔식민지를 건설하다〕 colonize; settle.

●**척식 은행** a colonial bank. **척식 회사** a colonization company.

척주(脊柱) 〔생〕 the backbone; the spine; the spinal column.

척지(尺地) 〔퍽 좁은 땅〕 a (single square) foot of land; a small strip of land; 〔썩 가까운 곳〕 a place a foot away[at a stone's throw].

척지다(隻−) 〔원한이 생기다〕 come to hate each other. ¶그 사람과 척진 일은 없다 I have no grudge against him.

척척 1 〔들러붙은 모양〕 close(ly); tightly; adhesively; fast. ¶~ 들러붙다 stick fast (to) / adhere (to) // 젖은 옷이 몸에 ~ 달라붙는다 Wet clothes cling fast to one's body.

2 〔서슴지 않고〕 without hesitation[delay]; readily; 〔얼른얼른〕 quickly; promptly; rapidly; speedily; with dispatch; briskly; right off; 〔수월하게〕 easily. ¶그는 오락에 돈을 ~ 쓴다 He lavishes money on amusement. // 그녀는 난문을 ~ 풀었다 She solved the difficult question easily[effortlessly / with hardly any effort]. // 일이 ~ 진행되었다 The work progressed rapidly. // 그는 ~ 결단을 내린다 He makes decisions quickly. / He is decisive. // 그는 질문에 ~ 대답하였다 He answered the question in a crisp manner.

3 〔차곡차곡〕 fold by fold; heap by heap (쌓다); tidily; neatly. ¶~ 쌓다 pile up in a heap // 이불을 ~ 개키다 fold up the bedding.

척척박사(−博士) a walking dictionary.

척척하다 wet; moist; damp(ish); clammy; 〔서술적〕 feel wet. ¶척척한 손 a moist[clammy] hands // 척척한 옷 wet clothes // 비에 젖어 척척해지다 get wet in the rain // 밤이슬을 맞아 ~ be wet from the rain // 밤이슬을 맞아 ~ be wet[damp] with night dew // 오줌을 싸서 옷이 척척해졌다 Clothes have been wet with urine // 마룻바닥이 ~ The floor is damp. **척척히** wetly; moistly; clammily.

척추(脊椎) 〔생〕 **1** the backbone; the spine; the spinal column. **2** the backbone. ⇨척주

●**척추동물** a vertebrate. ¶무~ an invertebrate. **척추 마취** spinal anesthesia; rachianesthesia.

척출(斥黜) 〔벼슬을 떼어서 내쫓음〕 ouster; ousting; expulsion; dismissal; discharge. **척출하다** dismiss[discharge] (a person) from office; oust[expel] (a person) from a position.

척탄(擲彈) a (hand) grenade.

●**척탄병** a grenade thrower.

척후(斥候) **1** 〔정탐〕 scouting; patrol duty(임무); reconnaissance. **2** a scout; a patrol. ⇨척후병(⇨척후)

●**척후대** a reconnoitering party. **척후병** a scout; a patrol; a reconnoitering soldier. ¶~을 내보내다 send out scouts. **척후전** skirmishes of scouts; a patrol encounter.

천 〔피륙〕 cloth; stuff; texture; (textile) fabrics; 〔재료로서의〕 material. ¶고급 ~ quality cloth // 조각 ~ a piece of cloth // 좋은 [나쁜] ~ good[bad] stuff // 결이 거친 [부드러운] ~ coarse[soft] cloth // ~의 견본 sample cloth // (미) a swatch // ~을 짜다 weave cloth // ~을 끊다 [사다] buy a piece of cloth // 이 ~은 질깁니다 This stuff wears well.

천(千) a[one] thousand. ¶~분의 1 a[one-]thousandth // 2~ 그루의 나무 two thousand trees // ~ 배(倍) a thousand times / 〔문어〕 a thousandfold // ~의 thousands of (students) // ~ 단위로 계산되다 be counted by the thousand // 몇 ~ 명이나 되는 사람이 죽었다 Thousands of people died.

천 리 길도 한 걸음부터(속담) A journey of a thousand miles starts with but a single step.

천거(薦擧) 〔추천〕 (a) recommendation. ¶…의 ~로 by[through] the recommendation of ... / on[at] the recommendation of ... // 그녀는 선생님의 ~로 비서 직을 구했다 She got a position as a secretary by[on] the recommendation of her teacher. // 아버지 친구의 덕분에 나는 취직이 되었다 Thanks to a recommendation[an introduction] from a friend of my father's, I was successful in getting a job. **천거하다** recommend; say[put in] a good word for. ➔¶그는 그 클럽의 회장

으로 천거되었다 He was nominated for the presidency of the club.

척격스럽다(賤格-) mean; base; vulgar; dirty; low-minded; (신분이) low; lowly; humble; ignoble.

천견(淺見) a shallow view; a superficial idea.
- **천견박식**(-薄識) little experience and small learning; superficial learning and a shallow view.

천계(天界) the celestial [heavenly] world; Heaven.

천계(天啓) a heavenly revelation; a sign from heaven.

천고(千古) [태고] remote antiquity; [영원] eternity; all ages. ¶~ 불멸의 everlasting / eternal / immortal // ~의 명언 an unchangeable maxim / an eternal truth.

천고마비(天高馬肥) ¶~의 가을에 in autumn, when the sky is high and clear, and horses grow fat and sturdy.

천골(賤骨) (a person with) a mean physiognomy.

천골(薦骨) the sacrum (*pl.* sacra). ¶~의 sacral.

천공(天空) the sky; the heavens; the air. ¶~을 날다 fly high in the air.

천공(穿孔) perforation; (편치로) punching; (송곳·드릴로) boring; drilling. **천공하다** drill; perforate; bore; punch.
- **천공기**(-機) a boring machine; a drill. ¶전기 ~ an electric drill. **천공 카드** a punch card.

천구(天球) the celestial sphere; the heavens; (문어) the vault (of Heaven).
- **천구도**(-圖) a celestial map. **천구의**(-儀) a celestial globe.

천국(天國) the kingdom of Heaven [God]; Heaven; Paradise; the blessed land. ¶~의 heavenly / celestial // 지상의 ~ an earthly [a terrestrial] paradise // ~에 가다 go to Heaven // 아버지는 ~에 가셨다 My father went to Heaven [died].

천군만마(千軍萬馬) thousands of troops and horses; large regiments of soldiers and war horses. ¶~의 맹장 a veteran of many battles.

천극(天極) [천] 1 the celestial poles. 2 the polar star. ⇨북극성(⇨북극)

천근(千斤) [아주 무거운 무게] great weight. ¶너의 한마디는 ~의 무게가 있다 What you say carries great weight with us.

천금(千金) [많은 돈] a lot of money; fortune; [귀중함] pricelessness. ¶일확~ making a big fortune with one swoop [at one stroke] // ~을 주고도 사지 못할 물건 an invaluable article // ~의 값어치가 있다 be priceless // 우리에게는 일각~이었다 We had a truly wonderful time (,which passed all too soon).

천기(天氣) the weather. ⇨일기(日氣)
- **천기도** a weather map [chart].

천기(天機) 1 [하늘의 기밀] the profound secret(s) of Nature [Heaven]; the hidden plans of Providence. 2 [큰 기밀] a profound [top] secret; a state secret(국가의). ¶~를 누설하지 마라 The secret should not be divulged. / It must be kept (a) secret.

천녀(天女) a celestial nymph; a heavenly maiden.

천년(千年) a thousand years; a millennium.
- **천년만년** myriad years. ⇨천만년(⇨천만)

천당(天堂) Heaven; the palace of Heaven; Paradise; the kingdom of Heaven. ¶~에 가다 go to glory [Heaven].

천대(賤待) (a) contemptuous [cold] treatment; inhospitable [cold] reception. **천대하다** treat (a person / a thing) contemptuously [with contempt]. →¶**천대받다** be treated contemptuously / get the cold shoulder // 천대받을 짓을 하다 incur the contempt of others // 가난하다고 그 소년은 천대받았다 The boy was looked down upon, because he was poor. / 그 소년은 의붓자식이라고 되게 천대받았다 Being a stepchild the boy suffered a real ill-treatment.

천더기(賤-) a despised person; a child of scorn. ¶~ 노릇을 하다 be treated as a child of scorn // 그는 동네의 ~다 He is the scorn of his neighbors.

천도(天桃) a mythical peach that is said to grow in Heaven.

천도(天道) 1 [천지의 도리] the ways of Heaven; the Heavenly way. ¶~가 무심하구나 Alas! God is indifferent. 2 [천] the orbits of heavenly bodies.

천도(遷都) the transfer [removal] of the capital (to). ¶~ 100년제(祭) the centenary of the transfer of the capital. **천도하다** transfer [remove] the capital (to); move [remove] the seat of government (to).

천도교(天道敎) [종] the *Cheondogyo*.

천동설(天動說) the Ptolemaic theory [system]; geocentricism.

천둥 [뇌명] thunder; a peal [roll] of thunder; [소리와 빛을 수반한 천둥] a thunderbolt(▶lightning은 번갯불). ¶~이 울리고 있다 It is thundering. / The thunder is rumbling. // 먼 곳에서 ~이 울렸다 Rolls of thunder were heard in the distance. // 지붕 위에서 ~이 우르릉거렸다 A clap [peal] of thunder broke above the house.
- **천둥소리** a peal [roar / roll] of thunder; cracks of thunder. ¶멀리서 ~가 났다 The thunder rolled [rumbled] in the distance.

천둥벌거숭이 [함부로 날뛰는 사람] a wild [reckless] fellow; an impetuous daredevil. ¶그는 ~라 아무것도 모르고 덤비기만 한다 He is a rank amateur but has to get mixed up in everything.

천랑성(天狼星) [천] the Dog Star; Sirius.

천량 [재물과 양식] money and food; supplies. ¶~이 다 떨어지다 have run through [out of] supplies.

천렵(川獵) river-fishing. **천렵하다** fish in a river [brook].

천륜(天倫) Natural Law; the natural relationships of man. ¶~에 벗어난 짓을 하다 transgress Natural Law // ~에 어그러지다 violate [transgress] moral laws.

천리(天理) natural laws; the laws of nature. ¶~를 거스르다 violate the laws of nature / go against natural laws.

천리마(千里馬) a fine [swift] horse.

천리안(千里眼) [투시력] clairvoyance; second sight; [통찰력] insight; penetration. ¶~을 가진 사람 a clairvoyant(남자) / a clairvoyante(여자) // 그는 ~이다 He is gifted with second sight. / He is clairvoyant.

천마(天馬) a flying horse; [그리스 신화] Pegasus; [명마] a fine steed.

천막(天幕) a tent; (배의) an awning; (집합적)

천만

천막 tentage. ¶피난용 ~ a shelter tent / 대형 ~ (hoist) a big top(서커스의) / (영) a marquee / 소형 ~ a shelter tent / (군인 속어) a dog tent // ~을 치다[접다] pitch[strike] a tent.
●**천막생활** camping; camping-out; camp life; (방랑의) a nomadic life. ¶~을 하다 camp out. **천막촌** a tent[camp] village.

천만(千萬) 〔1천만〕 ten million; 〔무수〕 a countless number; a myriad; 〔매우〕 exceedingly; extremely; very much. ¶몇 ~이나 는 tens of millions of // …은 유감~이다 It is really regrettable that …. / It is quite deplorable that …. / It is much to be regretted that ….
천만의 말씀 (당찮은) an inappropriate remark. ¶"훌륭한 정원이군요." "~입니다. 그저 넓기만 합니다." "This is quite a garden you have here." "Not really. It's big, but thats all."
●**천만고**(-古) remote[great] antiquity; most ancient times; 〔영원〕 eternity. **천만금** millions of money. **천만년** myriad years; a long long time. **천만다행** great good fortune [luck]; a stroke of good luck. ¶~으로 내 시도는 성공했다 I was fortunate enough to succeed in my attempt. // 다친 것이 그만하기 ~입니다 You were lucky not to have been hurt seriously (in the auto accident). // 거기서 그를 만난 것은 ~이었다 It was by a stroke of good luck[It was really providential] that I met him there. / I found him there by pure luck. **천만뜻밖** ¶~의 quite unexpected / least expected / unlooked-for / unforeseen / unanticipated / never dreamed of // ~의 일 the last thing one can think of / a (great) surprise / a bolt from the blue // ~에 quite unexpectedly / contrary to one's expectation / surprisingly enough / all of a sudden // 너를 여기서 만나다니 ~이다 It's quite a surprise to see you here. / You are the last man I expected to meet here. // 그가 성공하다니 ~이다 His success is really surprising. **천만번** times out of number; heaps [dozens] of times; (부사적) ever so many times; over and over again. ¶너 따위는 ~ 죽어 마땅하다 Thousands of death are too good for the likes of you. // 그 죄는 ~ 죽어 마땅하다 The crime definitely deserves certain death. / The guilt can only be atoned with death. **천만세**(-世) countless generation; all ages; eternity. ¶~에 걸쳐 for all ages to come / through all ages / forever. **천만장자** a billionaire; a multimillionaire.

천만부당하다(千萬不當-) utterly unjust. ⇨ 천부당만부당하다

천만에(千萬-) 1〔겸사〕 Don't mention it; Not at all; Never mind; 〔미〕 You're welcome. ¶"대단히 감사합니다." "~요." "Thank you very much." "You are welcome[No trouble at all / Don't mention it / My pleasure / It's a pleasure / It's my pleasure / The pleasure is [was] (all) mine / Think nothing of it]." // "노고에 감사드립니다." "원, ~요." "Thank you for your trouble." "Oh, no, not at all." 2〔부당〕 Oh, (dear) no!; Nothing of the kind[sort]!; Far from it!; Nothing could be farther from the truth!; What an absurd idea!; (미국 속어) Never happen! ¶그가 모르고 있었다고? ~ He didn't know? Of course he did!

천명(天命) 1〔하늘의 뜻〕 God's will; Heaven's decree; the appointment of heaven; 〔운명〕 fate; destiny; one's lot in life; karma. ¶~을 알다[~이라고 체념하다] submit to Heaven's will / take life philosophically / resign oneself to fate / 최근의 불행을 그는 ~으로 받아들였다 He accepted his recent misfortune as his destiny[fate]. // ~으로 단념하기는 아직 이르다 It is still too early to resign ourselves to fate[to call it fate and give up]. // 최선을 다하고 ~을 기다려야지요 We must do our best and leave the rest to Providence.
2〔타고난 수명〕 one's life; one's natural term of existence. ¶그는 ~이 다한 것을 알았다 He knew he had come to his journey's end [to the end of his life].

천명(闡明) clarification; elucidation. **천명하다** make clear; explain; give an explanation; elucidate; clarify; explicate. ¶교리를 ~ clarify[elucidate / give an explanation of] a doctrine // 중외에 ~ affirm before[declare to] the world.

천묘(遷墓) the removal[transfer / relocation] of a grave[tomb]. **천묘하다** remove[transfer / relocate] a grave[tomb] (to).

천문(天文) 1〔천체의 온갖 형상〕 astronomical phenomena. ¶~을 보다 make astronomical observations / study the stars / (점성술로) cast a horoscope. 2 astronomy. ⇨ 천문학(⇨ 천문)
●**천문 단위** an astronomical unit. **천문대** an astronomical observatory. **천문학** astronomy; uranology. ¶위치 ~ astrometry // 이론 〔실지 / 통계 / 항해 / 구면〕 ~ theoretical [practical / statistical / nautical / spherical] astronomy // ~상의 astronomical. **천문학자** an astronomer.

천문학적(天文學的) astronomical. ¶그 데이터는 ~ 숫자에 달했다 The data reached[ran into] astronomical figures.

천민(賤民) 〔집합적〕 lowly[humble] people; the lowly; the humble; low-class people.

천박하다(淺薄-) shallow; superficial; frivolous; flimsy; thoughtless. ¶천박한 사람 a shallow-minded person // 천박한 판단 a superficial judgment // 천박한 생각 a shallow idea // 천박한 행위 a thoughtless act // 그런 일을 저지르다니 내가 천박했다 It was superficial of me to have done a thing like that.

천방지축(天方地軸) 1〔덤벙댐〕 rashness; recklessness; harum-scarumness; foolhardiness; 〔덤벙대어〕 rashly; recklessly; harum-scarum; at a venture. ¶~ 덤비다[날뛰다] act rashly / rush recklessly / make a headlong [foolhardy] rush. 2〔허둥댐〕 hurry; flurry; 〔허둥대어〕 in a hurry[flurry]; hurry-scurry. ¶~ 달아나다 run away in a flurry.

천벌(天罰) Heaven's vengeance[judgment]; divine punishment[retribution]; the punishment of Heaven; the wrath of God; divine wrath. ¶~이 내리도록 빌다 imprecate [call down] the vengeance of Heaven upon (a person) // ~을 받다 incur the wrath of Heaven / bring down Heaven's vengeance on one's head / draw divine wrath on oneself / be punished by Heaven / be visited with Heaven's judgment // 그는 약자를 괴롭히다 ~을 받았다 He was punished by heaven for bullying the weak. / He incurred the wrath of Heaven by bullying the weak. // 나쁜 짓을 하면 ~을 받는다 An evil deed calls forth fearful retribution. // 이 ~을 받을 놈 Hang you! / Go to hell!

천변(川邊) the bank of a river. ⇨˝냇가

천변(天變) extraordinary phenomena in the heavens; a convulsion of nature.

● **천변지이**(-地異) an extraordinary natural occurrence; a natural disaster [calamity]; the disturbances of the elements; a convulsion of nature; a cataclysm. ¶작년은 ~가 계속하여 발생했다 Last year, natural disasters hit us one after another.

천복(天福) Heaven's blessing; benediction. ¶~을 빌다 ask a blessing (of Heaven) // ~을 받다 be blessed by Heaven.

천부(天賦) endowment; nature. ¶~의 natural / inherent / inborn / God-given / godsent // ~의 재주 a gift / a natural gift [talent] // 그의 작곡가로서의 ~의 재능은 만년에 가서 발휘되었다 His gift for composing music asserted itself only in his last years. // 그에게는 ~의 재능이 있다 He has God-given talent [a natural gift / an innate aptitude]. // 그녀는 ~의 시인이다 She is a born poet.

천부당만부당하다(千不當萬不當-) utterly [absolutely] unjust [unreasonable / unjustified]. ¶천부당만부당한 요구 an extravagant demand // 그 비난은 ~ The reproach is quite unjust. // 그들이 그렇게 하는 것은 ~ It isn't at all the thing for them to do so.

천분(天分) [타고난 재능] one's natural gifts [ability / talents]. ¶~이 있는 사람 a talented [gifted] man // ~**이 있다** be talented [gifted] / be endowed with talents (for) // ~**이 없다** be untalented / be endowed with no genius // ~**을 타고나다** be born with talents // 그에게는 음악가의 ~이 있다 He is talented [gifted] as a musician. // 그녀는 ~이 풍부한 시인이다 She is a highly gifted poet. / She has a great gift for poetry.

천사(天使) an angel; a herald of God; (집합적) hierarchy. ¶대~ an archangel // 수호~ a guardian angel / one's good genius // ~의 angelic / seraphic / cherubic // (와) 같은 angelic / seraphic / An angel of a (woman) // ~와 같은 소녀 an angel of a girl // ~와 같은 미소 an angelic smile // 백의의 ~ a white-robed angel / [종군 간호사] a war nurse // 아기는 ~처럼 그려져 있었다 The infant was painted like a cherub.

● **천사장** an archangel.

천사만고(千思萬考) [여러 가지로 생각함] deep meditation; careful [mature] consideration [deliberation]. **천사만고하다** meditate deeply; consider [deliberate] carefully.

천상(天上) [하늘 위] the heavens. ¶~에서부터 from above [heaven / on high] / [의외의 곳에서] (drop) out of the clouds // ~의 heavenly / celestial / ethereal.

● **천상천하 유아독존** I am my own Lord throughout heaven and earth.; Holy am I alone throughout heaven and earth.

천상(天象) an astronomical phenomenon; the aspect of the heavens.

천생(天生) **1** [타고난 본바탕] a product of nature [heaven]; nature. ¶~의 natural / born / designed by nature // 그는 ~의 시인이었다 He was born a poet.
2 [선천적으로] by nature; naturally; [두고두고] as [for] ever; [흡사하여] bearing as close resemblance; [부득불] unavoidably; inevitably; necessarily. ¶너는 ~ 사기꾼밖에 못해 먹겠군 A swindler is all [is the most] that you will ever be. // 이 아이는 ~ 제 아버지야 The boy is the very portrait [express image] of his father. / The boy is a chip of [off] the old block. // 그럴 수밖에 딴 도리가 없었다 There was no other alternative. / We had no choice left.

● **천생배필** a match made in heaven. **천생연분** predestined [Heaven-ordained] relation. ¶그 부부는 ~이다 They are a well matched couple. / They are made for man and wife.

천석꾼(千石-) a wealthy farmer (who can harvest 1,000 *seok* of rice).

천성(天性) (one's) nature; (one's) natural constitution; one's innate disposition [character / temperament]. ¶사람의 ~ the nature of human beings // ~의 [~적인] natural / constitutional / born / inborn / inherent // ~적으로 by nature / by birth / naturally // 그는 ~이 과묵하다 He is naturally reticent. / He is reticent by nature. // 습관은 제2의 ~이라 말한다 Habit is said to be second nature. // 낙천적인 것이 그의 ~이다 His optimism is inborn. / He is optimistic by nature. // 그는 ~적으로 명랑하다 He was born with a cheerful disposition. // 그의 ~인 의협심에서 그는 그녀를 도왔다 He helped the woman out of his natural [inborn / innate] sympathy for the weak and unfortunate.

천세(千歲) a thousand years; a millennium; perpetuity; eternity. ¶~ 불멸의 immortal // ~ 만세까지 forever / through all ages / in perpetuity // ~에 이름을 ~에 남기다 win (an) immortal fame / immortalize one's name.

천수(天水) rainwater.

● **천수답**(-畓) paddies dependent on rainwater.

천수(天壽) one's life. ⇨˝천명(天命)2

천수(天數) **1** one's life. ⇨˝천명(天命)1 **2** fate; destiny. ⇨˝천운1

천시(天時) **1** [하늘의 도움이 있는 시기] a heaven-appointed time; a time of providence [Heaven]. ¶~를 **기다리다** wait upon such times as Heaven should appoint // ~는 우리 편에 있다 The time is in our favor. **2** [때에 따른 자연현상] the times and seasons.

천시(賤視) contempt. ⇨˝멸시

천식(喘息) [의] (bronchial) asthma; (말의) broken wind. ¶~(성)의 asthmatic // 소아~ asthma in [of] childhood.

● **천식 환자** an asthmatic.

천신(天神) **1** [하늘에 있는 신령] the heavenly gods. **2** ➡ 천사

● **천신지기**(-地祇) the gods of heaven and earth.

천신(薦新) [민] **1** [새로 난 농산물을 신에게 올림] offering the first harvest of the season to gods. **천신하다** offer the first harvest [crop / fruits] of the season to gods. **2** [신을 위한 굿] a shamanist rite in spring [autumn]. **천신하다** have a spring [an autumn] shamanist rite.

천신만고(千辛萬苦) indescribable hardships; intense application. ¶~를 **겪다** experience [undergo / go through] all kinds of hardships / make intense application // 나는 다년간의 ~ 끝에 그 발명을 완성하였다 I consummated my invention after years of intense application.

천심(天心) **1** the will of Heaven. ⇨천의 **2** 〔하늘 복판〕 the zenith. ¶달이 ~에 걸렸다 The moon has reached its zenith. / The moon is hanging at the zenith.

천앙(天殃) Divine retribution.

천애(天涯) **1** 〔하늘 끝〕 the horizon; the skyline; the heavenly shores. **2** a far-off country; a remote region; a distant land. **3** 〔피붙이나 부모가 없음〕. ¶그녀는 ~의 고아가 되었다 She was left an orphan all alone in the world.

천야만야하다(千耶萬耶−) 〔높다〕 lofty; skyhigh; 〔깎아지르다〕 sheer; precipitous; 〔깊다〕 unfathomable. ¶천야만야한 계곡 an unfathomable ravine / an abyss.

천양(天壤) heaven and earth.
● **천양지차** a world of difference; extreme opposition; poles apart. ¶그들의 성격은 ~다 Their personalities are as different as day and night [poles apart]. // 이 대피아니스트와 젊은 제자 사이에는 연주에 있어 ~가 있다 The performance of this great pianist and that of his young pupil are as different as day and night.

천업(賤業) a mean [degrading] occupation; a dishonorable [shameful] calling [trade].

천역(賤役) a mean [dirty] job [service]; dishonorable [shameful] work [toil]; a discreditable role.

천연(天然) **1** 〔저절로 이루어진 상태〕 nature; spontaneity. ¶~의 〔인공을 가하지 않은〕 natural / unartificial / native(금속 등의) / spontaneous(자생의) / wild(야생의) / 〔타고난〕 natural / innate / inborn / inherent / congenital // ~의 아름다움 natural beauty / the beauty of nature // ~ 그대로의 바위 a rock in its natural form / a natural rock // 금은 ~으로 산출된다 Gold occurs in nature. / 그 돌은 ~적으로 그런 형태이다 The stone is so shaped by nature. **2** 〔비슷하게〕 just [exactly] (like another); as if. ¶그녀는 제 어머니다 She is the very [exact] image [likeness] of her mother.
● **천연가스** natural gas. ¶액화 ~ liquefied natural gas(약어 LNG). **천연기념물** a natural monument. ¶~로 지정하다 designate (a thing) as a precious natural product. **천연색** (a) natural color; 〔영〕 technicolor(상표명); cinecolor. **천연자원** natural resources. ¶~이 풍부하다 be rich in natural resources // ~을 개발[보호]하다 develop [conserve] natural resources.

천연덕스럽다(天然−) natural; looking like the truth; calm; just like (another). ⇨천연스럽다

천연두(天然痘) smallpox; variola. ¶~에 걸리다 suffer from [be attacked with] smallpox / have (the) smallpox / be taken ill of smallpox // 그녀의 얼굴에는 ~의 흔적이 있다 Her face is pitted with smallpox scars. // 나는 ~ 예방 주사를 맞았다 I had a smallpox vaccination [inoculation]. / I was vaccinated against smallpox.
● **천연두 자국** a pockmark; a pit. **천연두 환자** a case of smallpox; a smallpox patient.

천연스럽다(天然−) **1** 〔자연스럽다〕 natural; unartificial; 〔꾸민 테가 없다〕 unstudied; unaffected. ¶천연스러운 자세 a natural [an unaffected] posture // 천연스럽지 않은 unnatural / artificial / affected. **2** 〔그럴싸하다〕 looking like the truth; specious; plausible. ¶천연스럽게 plausibly / speciously / with seeming truth / as if it were true // 천연스럽게 거짓말을 하다 tell a clever lie / tell a lie that sounds like truth // 천연스럽게 말하다 talk with much show of truth // 천연스럽게 눈물을 흘리다 shed crocodile tears // 그는 천연스러운 표정으로 선생님 말씀에 귀를 기울이고 있었다 He listened to his teacher with a serious look.
3 〔태연하다〕 calm; cool; unmoved; unperturbed; 〔무관심하다〕 unconcerned; indifferent; nonchalant. ¶천연스럽게 calmly / coolly / in cool blood / as if nothing had happened / with an innocent look // 천연스러운 얼굴을 하고 있다 be innocent looking / look as if one would not harm a fly // 그는 천연스럽게 자리에 앉았다 He sat down as if nothing had been the matter with him [nothing had happened]. // 그는 중요한 서류를 잃어버렸는데도 아무 일 없다는 듯 ~ He lost some important papers, but he still looks (as cool) as if nothing had happened.
4 〔흡사하다〕 just [exactly] like (another); (서술적) be the exact image [likeness] (of); be (a person's) double.

천왕성(天王星) 〔천〕 Uranus.

천외(天外) **1** 〔하늘의 밖〕 beyond the heavens. **2** 〔아득히 먼 곳〕 farthest regions. **3** 〔상상을 초월하는 경지〕. ¶**기상-하다** be a most unexpected idea / be quite an original conception.

천우신조(天佑神助) God's [providential] help; special Providence; heavenly assistance; help from the gods; the grace of Heaven [God]. ¶~의 providential / miraculous // ~로[에 의하여] by the grace of Heaven / thanks to a benign disposition of fate // ~를 빌다 invoke the help of Heaven (for ...) / ~로 사지를 벗어났다 I returned from the jaws of death by the grace of Heaven. // 내가 다치지 않은 것은 ~였다 There was Providence in my getting off unhurt. // 네가 살아났 것은 정말 ~다 You must bless your stars that you have escaped! **천우신조하다** Heaven helps and God assists.

천운(天運) **1** 〔하늘의 운명〕 fate; destiny; the will of Heaven; Providence. **2** 〔다행한 운수〕 fortune; luck. ¶~으로 thanks to a benign dispensation of fate // ~에 맡기다 trust to chance [luck / Providence / Heaven] / leave (a matter) to chance [divine law] / leave one's fate to Heaven // 아직 ~이 다하지 않은 것 같다 It seems Fortune has not yet deserted me.

천은(天恩) **1** 〔하느님 은혜〕 the grace of God [Heaven]; divine grace [favor]; heavenly blessings. **2** 〔임금의 은혜〕 the benevolence [graciousness] of the King [Emperor].

천의(天意) the will of Heaven; the divine will; Providence; Heaven's decree [will]. ¶~에 따르다 obey [follow / bow to] the will of Heaven [Providence] // ~에 어긋나다 be against [be contrary to] the will of Heaven [the divine will].

천의무봉(天衣無縫) perfect beauty with no trace of artifice. ¶그의 글에는 ~의 아취가 있다 He writes flawlessly [exquisitely] without any trace of artifice.

천인(天人) **1** 〔하늘과 사람〕 God [heaven] and

man. ¶그는 ~공노할 죄를 지었다 He has sinned against God and man.
2 [천상과 인사] heavenly phenomena and human affairs.
3 [하늘에 사는 사람] an inhabitant of heaven; a heavenly being; a celestial; an angel.
4 [도사·선인] a supernatural being; a (Taoist) hermit with supernatural powers.
5 [뛰어난 사람] a superhuman person; a (man of) genius.
6 [매우 아름다운 여자] a woman of heavenly beauty.

천인(賤人) a lowly man; a person of humble [low] birth [origin].

천일(天日) **1** [해] the sun; sunshine; sunlight. **2** [하늘과 해] the sky and the sun. **3** [천도교의 창진 기념일] Heaven Day in the *Cheondogyo* (=5 April).
● **천일염** bay salt; sun-dried salt. **천일제염** the solar evaporation process.

천일 야화(千一夜話) [문] the Arabian Nights' Entertainments. ⇨ 아라비안나이트

천자(千字) the Thousand-Character Text. ⇨ 천자문(⊃천자)
● **천자문** the Thousand-Character Text [Classic]; a primer of Chinese characters.

천자(天子) a son of Heaven; an emperor.

천자만태(千姿萬態) an endless variety of forms; multifariousness. ¶~ 의 multifarious.

천자만홍(千紫萬紅) a dazzling variety of beautiful flowers. ¶정원에는 꽃들이 ~으로 피어 있다 The garden is a riot of colors with a variety of flowers in full glory.

천장(天障) the ceiling; the roof. ¶반자 ~ a boarded ceiling // ~ 밑의 전선 the electric wiring under the roof // ~ 이 높은 홀 a lofty hall // ~ 이 낮은 방 a low-ceilinged room // ~ 이 높다[낮다] be high-[low-]ceil(ing)ed / have a high[low] ceiling // ~ 에 매달려 있다 be hanging from the ceiling // ~ 을 대다 ceil (a room with cedar boards) / board a ceiling.
● **천장 선풍기** a ceiling fan.

천재(天才) (제주) (a) genius; a natural gift [endowment]; (사람) a (man of) genius; a prodigy; (구어) a wizard (at chemistry). ¶대[소] ~ a great[transcendent] genius // [뛰어난] ~ a great[transcendent] genius / 어학의 ~ (재능) a genius[an aptitude] for language / (사람) a linguistic genius / a born linguist // 그는 어학의 ~다 He has a gift for languages. / He is a genius at learning languages. // 그녀에게는 ~의 번뜩임이 있다 She has a streak[touch] of genius in her.
● **천재 교육** education of gifted children; genius education. **천재아** a gifted child; an infant[a child] prodigy; (미) a boy[girl] wonder; a budding genius.

천재(天災) a natural calamity [disaster]; [법] an act of God (불가항력). ¶~ 를 만나다[당하다] be visited by a natural calamity / meet with a natural disaster // ~ 라 어쩔 수가 없다 There is no help for it, for it is an act of God. / It is an act of God and beyond human control. // 이 지방은 갖가지 ~가 덮쳤다 This district is visited by various kinds of natural calamities [disasters]. // 검증 결과 이 사고는 ~ 었던 것으로 결론 났다 After the investigation, it was concluded that the accident was an act of God.
● **천재지변** a natural disaster [calamity]; the disturbances of the elements; a convulsion of nature; a cataclysm.

천재(千載) a thousand years. ⇨ 천세
● **천재일우**(ーー遇) [만나기 어려운 좋은 기회]. ¶~ 의 좋은 기회를 놓치다 throw away a golden[rare] opportunity / lose the chance of a lifetime.

천재적(天才的) talented; gifted. ¶그는 ~ 인 무용가이다 He is an extremely [exceptionally] talented dancer. // 그에게는 ~ 인 데가 있다 He shows flashes[sparks] of genius.

천적(天敵) [생] a natural enemy.

천정(天井) →천장(天障)

천정(天頂) [천] the zenith. ¶~ 에 at the zenith of the heavens.
● **천정 거리** the zenith distance [angle]. **천정의** a zenith telescope [tube].

천정부지(天井不知) skyrocketing. ¶~ 다 The sky's the limit. / No ceilings are foreseen. // 요즈음 물가는 ~ 다 Prices today are skyrocketing.

천제(天帝) God; Providence; the Creator; (the Lord of) Heaven.

천조(天助) Heaven's [providential] help; help from above [Heaven]; special Providence.

천주(天主) God; the Almighty. ⇨ 하느님
● **천주 삼위** the Trinity.

천주교(天主教) Catholicism. ⇨ 가톨릭

천지(天地) **1** [하늘과 땅] heaven and earth; the heavens and the earth; [우주] the universe; [자연] nature. ¶대[소] ~ a macrocosm [microcosm] // ~ 의 of heaven and earth / universal / mundane // ~ 가 무너져도 [뒤집혀도] though the heavens fall // ~ 에 맹세하다 swear by heaven and earth / call heaven to witness // ~ 를 진동시키다 (위업 등으로) shake the sphere [earth and sky / heaven and earth / the whole universe] / make the whole world wonder / (음향 등이) rend the air // 그 두 사람 사이에는 ~의 차가 있다 There is all the difference (in the world) between them. / They are poles asunder [worlds apart] in opinion. / They are as opposite as two poles. / There is a world of difference between the two. // ~ 를 뒤흔드는 함성이 일어났다 There arose a tumultuous shouting, seeming to rend the very sky.
2 [세상·세계] a land; a world; a realm; a sphere; a stage. ¶별 ~ a different world // 자유의 ~ a free land // 신 ~ a new world // 우리들의 ~ our own sphere.
3 [많음] (an) abundance; (a) plenty; (an) opulence; richness. ¶그곳은 거지 ~ 다 The place swarms with beggars. / The district is overflowing[crowded] with beggars. // 한강은 지금 서퍼 ~ 다 The Hangang(Han River) is a surfer's paradise now. / Along the Hangang(Han River), surfers are in their element now.
● **천지개벽** [창조] the Creation (of Heaven and Earth); the beginning of the world; [대변혁] a cataclysmic change; an upheaval; a revolution. ¶~ 이래 since the beginning [creation] of the world / since the world began / since the dawn of history // ~ 하다 create heaven and earth / undergo a cataclysmic change / revolutionize. **천지 만물** universal [all] nature; the universe; the creation; all creatures. **천지신명** the gods of

천지 heaven and earth. ¶~께 맹세코 그 일은 하지 않았습니다 I swear by heaven and earth [Upon my word] I did not do it. **천지 창조** the Creation. ¶~의 신 the Creator of the universe.

천지(天池) the crater lake on Baekdusan(Mt. Baekdu).

천직(天職) a mission; a vocation; a calling; one's divinely appointed work in life. ¶~을 다하다 fulfill one's mission∥그녀는 노인들을 돌보는 일을 ~으로 믿고 있었다 She believed that her true vocation was caring for old people. / She believed she had a calling to take care of old people.∥그는 의사로서의 ~을 완수했다 He fulfilled his mission as a physician.

천진난만하다(天眞爛漫-) naive; unaffected; artless; innocent; simple-hearted [-minded]. ¶천진난만한 미소 an innocent smile∥천진난만한 어린이 a simple and innocent child∥천진난만한 얼굴 an innocent face∥천진난만한 태도 an unaffected air / an unsophisticated attitude∥그녀는 그 이야기를 듣고 천진난만하게 기뻐했다 She was innocently pleased with the story.∥늙은 부인은 소녀처럼 천진난만했다 The old woman retained her childlike innocence.

천진무구하다(天眞無垢-) innocent; (문어) immaculate. ¶천진무구한 처녀 an immaculate virgin / an innocent girl.

천차만별(千差萬別) infinite variety. ¶~의 계급 infinite gradation of ranks∥~의 사람 all sorts of people / various kinds of people. **천차만별하다** multifarious; motley; of various kinds; an infinite variety of; in a thousand different ways. ¶사람의 성격은 ~ Each man has a character of his own.

천착(穿鑿) 1 [구멍을 뚫음] excavation. **천착하다** excavate. 2 [파고들어 연구함] inquiry; search; pursuit; exploration. **천착하다** dig [pry / delve] into; inquire into; search; seek [look] for; poke and pry; probe. ¶사건을 ~ pry [dig / poke one's nose] into an affair / be inquisitive about an incident∥기자는 그 스캔들을 끝까지 천착했다 The reporter probed until he got to the bottom of the scandal.

천창(天窓) a skylight; (갑판의) a companion; (현측·갑판의) a scuttle.

천천히 [느리게] slowly; without haste [hurry]; [한가롭게] leisurely; deliberately; in a leisurely manner [way]; at (one's) leisure. ¶더 ~ more slowly∥(일 등을) ~ 하다 take one's time (in doing)∥~ 이야기하다 speak slowly / speak leisurely∥~ 생각하다 take time [stop] to think∥~ 먹다 eat leisurely / take one's time with the meal∥~ 여행하다 make a leisurely trip / travel by easy stages∥~ 걷다 walk leisurely / walk at a leisurely pace∥~ 하세요 Take your time. / Take it easy. / Take plenty of time.∥뜨거운 물에 ~ 몸을 담그다 ease into a hot bath∥행렬은 ~ 나아갔다 The procession went forward very slowly.∥그는 ~ 차를 홀짝였다 He sipped tea in a leisurely manner.∥그 일은 뒤에 ~ 생각하자 I'll think it over at my leisure.∥~ 있다가 저녁이나 먹고 가게나 Stay long, won't you, and have supper with me. / Stay to supper, please.∥교통이 혼잡했기 때문에 ~ 운전하지 않으면 안 되었다 We had to slow to a crawl because of the heavy traffic.∥좀 더 ~ 말씀해 주십시오 Please speak more slowly.

천첩(賤妾) 1 [천한 출신의 첩] a concubine of low birth [origin]. 2 [부인이 자신을 낮춰 부르는 말] I.

천체(天體) a heavenly [celestial] body; a celestial sphere [object]; an orb. ¶~를 관측하다 observe (the) heavenly bodies / make an astronomical observation / survey the starry heavens.
● **천체 관측** an astronomical observation. **천체 망원경** an astronomical telescope. **천체 물리학** astronomical physics; astrophysics. **천체 사진** the photograph of a star [heavenly body]. **천체 운동** the movement of heavenly bodies. **천체학** uranography; uranology.

천추(千秋) [긴 세월] many years. ¶~의 한 a matter of great regret∥이름을 ~에 남기다 win (an) immortal fame / keep a corner in the Temple of Fame∥~은 ~의 한이다 It is a thousand pities that …
● **천추만세** myriad years. ➪ 천만년(➪ 천만)

천출(賤出) a child born of a concubine of low birth [origin].

천치(天癡·天痴) idiocy; an idiot. ➪ 백치

천칭(天秤) a balance. ➪ 천평칭
● **천칭자리** [천] the Balance; Libra.

천칭(賤稱) a derogatory term; a depreciatory term [word / name]. **천칭하다** call by a depreciatory term.

천태만상(千態萬象) all sorts of forms and figures; a great diversity in form and figure; multifarious states of things [affairs]; multifariousness.

천편일률(千篇一律) [한결같고 변화가 없음] monotony; humdrumness; lack of variety. ¶~의 인사장 stereotyped greeting cards.

천편일률적(千篇一律的) dull; monotonous; humdrum; stereotyped. ¶할머니가 하시는 말씀은 언제나 ~이다 The stories my grandmother tells me are always one and the same.∥그가 말하는 것은 늘 ~이다 He always harps on the same theme [topic].

천평칭(天平秤) a balance; a pair of scales. ¶비중 ~ a specific-gravity balance∥~에 달다 weigh (something) in the balance [on the scale].

천품(天稟) [타고난 기품] natural disposition; temperament; innateness. ¶훌륭한 ~을 타고나다 be born with an admirable disposition.

천하(天下) [일국] the whole country; the land; the realm; the State; the (whole) Empire; [세상] the public; the world; [세계] the world; the universe; [지배권] ruling power; [정권] administrative power; the reins of government. ¶~의 대사 a matter of grave concern to the state∥~의 대세 the general situation of the world / the trend of the international affairs∥~의 공흥 the greatest hero ever known∥~의 공론 public opinion∥~에 under the sun / under heaven / in the (whole) world / on earth∥~에 둘도 없는 [제일의] unique / peerless / matchless / unrivaled / inimitable∥~에 으뜸이다 beat [lead] the world∥~에 이름을 떨치다 make a noise [name] in the world / become world-famous∥~를 다스리다 rule over the whole country∥~를 호령하다 rule [reign over] the whole country / dictate to the whole country∥~를 얻다 conquer [rule

/ reign over] the whole country / [정권을 잡다] come to power / get into power / gain political power // ~를 **통일하다** unify a country / bring the whole country under one's rule [sway] / rule over the land / make oneself master of the realm // 그는 ~무적이다 He has no rival in the world [under the sun]. // 이것은 ~의 일대 사건이다 This is a very serious incident [matter] for the nation. // 민주당이 ~의 정권을 잡았다 The Democratic Party came to power. // 지금은 ~태평의 세상이다 Peace reigns over the land. / The world is at peace. // 그는 ~태평으로 자고 있다 He is sleeping as though he hadn't a care in the world. // 이런 훌륭한 경치는 ~에 둘도 없다 The place is unequaled [has no equal] in its scenic beauty. // ~없는 학자도 그것은 모른다 The best scholar does not know it.
● **천하 명창** one of the greatest [most excellent] singers in the world; a world-famous [-renowned] singer. **천하일색** the reigning beauty; a woman of matchless [unsurpassed] beauty; the fairest of the fair. **천하일품** a unique article; a nonesuch; the best specimen in existence. ¶~인 unique / peerless / unequaled / unparalleled // 이 포도주는 ~이다 This wine is unrivaled [beyond compare]. / This wine is superb [excellent]. // 그의 피아노 솜씨는 ~이다 His performance on the piano is unequaled. / No one can equal him in playing the piano. **천하장사** a man of unparalleled (physical) strength; the strongest man in the world; a man of Herculean strength; a Hercules; an Atlas. ¶그는 힘이 ~다 He is a Hercules [very powerful man]. / He is a pillar of strength. / He has the strength of a horse.

천하다(賤-) **1** [지체·지위가 낮다] humble; low; lowly; ignoble; obscure; low-lived; low-born. ¶천한 직업 a mean [humble] occupation // 천한 몸 a person of humble [low / ignoble] birth // 천한 신분 a lowly [humble] station in life / a low social position [standing / status] // 천하게 살다 live in a lowly way / live humbly // 그는 천한 집안 태생이다 He is of low [humble] birth.
2 [상스럽다] vulgar; base; mean; low; gross; rude; beastly. ¶천한 말씨 a vulgar (way of) expression / coarse language // 천한 티 a vulgar streak // 품성이 천한 사람 a man of mean [low] character / a low-minded person / a man of vulgar tastes // 행동이 ~ have vulgar manners // 그런 말투는 ~ It is bad manners to talk like that.
3 [흔하다] plenty; superfluous.

천하없어도(天下-) whatever may happen; by all means; under [in] any circumstances.

천학(淺學) superficial [shallow] learning [knowledge]. ¶~의 무리 an unlearned [unread] lot // ~이라 도움이 될 수 있을지 걱정입니다 With the little knowledge I have, I am afraid I cannot be of any service to you. // 비록 ~비재이나 최선을 다하겠습니다 Though I have little learning or ability, I will do my best. (▶ 이런 겸손한 표현은 영어에는 없음)

천행(天幸) the blessing [grace / help] of Heaven [God]; good fortune; a piece [stroke] of good luck [fortune]; a good-send. ¶~으로 by (a stroke of) good luck / as good luck would have it // ~으로 …하다 have the (good) fortune to (do) / be lucky enough to (do).

천형(天刑) Heaven's vengeance. ⇨ 천벌

천혜(天惠) Heaven's blessing; a gift of nature; natural advantage. ¶이 섬은 ~를 많이 입고 있다 This island is favored by nature. / This island is blessed with [rich in] natural resources.

천후(天候) (a) climate. ⇨ 기후(氣候)

철[1] [계절] a season; the time of the year. ¶사~ the four seasons / (부사적) (all) the year round / at all times of the year / throughout the year / in all seasons (of the year) // 제~ the right [best] season // 복숭아 ~ the peach season // 봄~ spring / springtime / spring tide // ~ 따라 피는 꽃 flowers of the season // 수확 ~ the harvest season / the season for harvesting // ~에 따르는 물건 things in season // ~ 늦은 사과 late apples / apples behind the season // ~ 따라 옷을 갈아입다 change one's clothes according to the season // ~ 아닌 장미꽃이 한 송이 피어 있다 There is a single rose blooming out of season. // 지금은 장사가 안 되는 ~이다 We're now in a dull season in trade. / Trade is now poor [inactive / quiet]. // 경치는 ~ 따라 바뀐다 The scenery varies from season to season.

철[2] [분별] discretion; judgment; prudence; wisdom; good sense. ¶~**이 없다** have no discretion [sense] // 그는 아직 ~이 덜 들었다 He is still immature in his way of thinking. / He has not yet arrived at the age of discretion. // 이젠 좀 ~이 나야지 You ought to know better now.

철(鐵) iron; steel(강철). ¶~의 ferrous / ferric // ~의 장막 the Iron Curtain // ~을 함유하는 containing iron / ferrous / ferriferous (rocks / soil).

-철(綴) a file. ¶서류~ a file of documents [papers] // 신문~ a newspaper file / a file of newspapers.

철각(鐵脚) iron legs. ¶~을 자랑하는 선수 a runner of iron legs.

철갑(鐵甲) [쇠로 만든 갑옷] iron armor; [칠갑] a coating; a crust.
● **철갑선** an ironclad (ship).

철강(鐵鋼) steel. ⇨ 강철(鋼鐵)

철거(撤去) [거두어 가지고 떠나감] removal; [부수어 치움] demolition; dismantlement. ¶무허가 판잣집의 ~ the removal of illegally built shacks // 빈민굴의 ~ the clearing of slums. **철거하다** remove; clear (away); (부수어서) demolish; pull [take] down; dismantle. ¶장애물을 ~ remove the obstacles / clear (the passage) of obstacles // 시설을 ~ dismantle [take away] facilities. ➔¶철거되다 be removed / be dismantled / be cleared away / be demolished / be pulled down / be taken down // 그 건물은 철거될 것이다 The building will be torn down [demolished] and cleared away.

철겹다 out of season; unseasonable; off-season. ¶철겹게 핀 꽃 a blossom out of season / a flower coming out unseasonably // 철겨운 날씨 unsettled [crazy] weather // 철겨운 옷 clothes worn beyond the season.

철골(徹骨) a skinny [bony / thin / meager /

철골 (鐵骨) a steel[an iron] frame; a steel skeleton. ¶~로 조립하다 build with an iron frame.
● 철골 공사 steel-frame work. 철골 구조 a cage; steel-frame structure; skeleton construction.

철공 (鐵工) an ironworker; an ironsmith.
● 철공소 an ironworks. ¶~ 주인 an ironmaster.

철관 (鐵管) an iron tube(가는); an iron pipe(큰). ¶~을 묻다 lay iron pipes // ~이 터졌다 An iron pipe burst.

철광 (鐵鑛) [철을 함유한 광석] iron ore; [철이 나는 광산] an iron mine.

철교 (鐵橋) [쇠다리] an iron bridge; (철도의) a railway bridge. ¶~을 놓다 construct[build] a railway bridge (over) // ~를 지나다 pass an iron bridge.

철군 (撤軍) withdrawal[removal] of troops; military withdrawal; evacuation. ¶~의 규모와 일정 the size and timetable of the pullout (of the troops) // ~을 요구하다 demand troop withdrawal(s) / demand evacuation // ~을 거부하다 refuse to withdraw the army / refuse evacuation. 철군하다 withdraw troops (from a place); evacuate (a place); pull troops out (of a place); pull out.

철권 (鐵拳) a (clenched) fist. ¶~을 먹이다 fist / strike (a person) with one's fist / use one's fist (on) // ~을 퍼붓다 rain blows upon (a person) // ~을 휘두르다 shake one's fist (at a person / in another's face) // 그들은 그를 향해 ~을 날렸다 They clenched fists showered upon him.

철궤 (鐵櫃) an iron box[chest]; [금고] a steel safe.

철그렁 with a clang. ⇨ˊ절그렁

철근 (鐵筋) [건] a[an iron] reinforcing rod [bar].
● 철근 콘크리트 ferro-concrete; reinforced concrete; (프) béton armée. ¶~ 건물 a ferro-concrete[concrete steel] building // ~로 되어 있다 be (built) of reinforced concrete.

철기 (鐵器) ironware; hardware; ironmongery.
● 철기 시대 the Iron Age.

철길 (鐵-) a railway; a railroad. ⇨ˮ철도

철꺽 with a snap. ⇨찰깍

철끈 (綴-) a binding string[strip].

철나다 know better; become possessed of discretion. ⇨철들다

철도 (鐵道) a railway; (미) a railroad; a railroad line. ¶경편 ~ a light railway // 고가 ~ an elevated[overhead] railroad // 고속 ~ a high-speed railroad // 관광 ~ a scenic railway // 광궤 ~ a broad-gauge[narrow-gauge] railroad // 교외 ~ a suburban railway // 국유 ~ a government[state] railway // 군용 ~ a military[strategic] railway // 단선[복선] ~ a single-track [double-track] railroad // 사설 ~ a private railroad // 전기 ~ an electric railway // 증기 ~ a steam railway // ~의 운행 operation of railways / (미) railroading // ~로 여행하다 travel by rail[train] // ~를 부설하다 construct[build / lay / make] a railway (line) // ~를 이용하다 avail oneself of the railway // ~가 통하다 have a railroad / a railroad runs // 서울에서 부산까지 ~가 통해 있다 A railroad [railway] runs from Seoul to Busan. / Seoul and Busan are linked by rail. // 이 도시에는 머지않아 ~가 통하게 된다 The city will soon be brought into railway communications.
● 철도망 a network[system] of railways; a railway network. 철도 사고 / 철도 참사 a railway accident[disaster]. 철도 선로 [철도의 궤도] a railway[railroad] track; a railway line; (집합적) trackage. 철도 여행 railway traveling; a railway journey; (미) railroading. 철도 운송 transportation by rail; railway transportation; (미) railroading. 철도 운임 / 철도 요금 (여객의) railway fare; (화물의) freight[goods] rates; freightage. 철도청 the National Railroad Administration. 철도편 transportation by rail. ¶~으로 per[by] rail / by train / by freight // ~으로 부치다 send (a thing) by rail. 철도 화물 railway goods; (미) freight.

철두철미 (徹頭徹尾) thoroughly; throughout; through and through; out-and-out; in every way; every inch; at all points; in every particular; to the core; from top to bottom; from beginning to end; from first to last; all the way. ¶그는 ~ 보수주의자이다 He is a conservative through and through. // 그는 ~ 신사였다 He was every inch a gentleman. / He was a gentleman in every way. 철두철미하다 thorough (going); exhaustive; complete; utter; out-and-out; all-out. ¶철두철미한 공산주의자 a dyed-in-the-wool communist / a communist to the core // 철두철미한 연구 a thorough[an exhaustive] study // 철두철미한 조사 a thoroughgoing investigation // 철두철미한 학자 a scholar to the core[bone] / a scholar through and through[to the last inch].

철들다 know better; become possessed of discretion; attain[reach] the age of discretion; cut one's wisdom teeth. ¶철들 나이 the age of discretion // 철들고 나서부터 from one's earliest recollection / ever since one could remember / for as long as one can remember // 그가 철들었을 무렵에 바로 그의 부모가 이혼했다 His parents got divorced just when he was getting old enough to remember things.

철딱서니 〈속〉 discretion; judgment. ⇨철²

철떡거리다 cling[stick] to. ⇨찰딱거리다

철렁거리다 a lap; clink ⇨찰랑거리다

철렁철렁 to the brim; jingling. ⇨찰랑찰랑

철로 (鐵路) a railway; a railroad. ⇨ˮ철도(鐵道)

철리 (哲理) the philosophy[philosophical principles / metaphysics] (of). ¶~를 탐구하다 study the philosophy of the matter // ~를 실천하다 carry one's philosophy into action.

철마 (鐵馬) a (railway) train; (구어) an iron horse.

철망 (鐵網) 1 (집합적) wire netting; a wire net; a (wire) gauze(그물코가 작은); (난롯가의) a fireguard. ¶창의 ~ a window screen // ~을 친 창 a wire-mesh window // ~을 치다 cover (a thing) with wire netting. 2 (barbed-)wire entanglements. ⇨철조망

철면 (凸面) a convex surface; a convexity.

철면피 (鐵面皮) a brazen-faced fellow; a brassy one; a man as bold as brass. 철면피

하다 brazen-faced; brazen; brassy; audacious; shameless; unblushing; barefaced; impudent; as bold as brass; cheeky; 《미국 속어》 fresh. ¶철면피하게 …하다 have the impudence[cheek / face / crust] to (do)/그는 정말이지 철면피한 녀석이다 What nerve he has got!

철모(鐵帽) a helmet; an iron hat. ¶~를 쓴 군인 a helmeted soldier∥~를 쓰다 wear a helmet.

철모르다 〔분별이 없다〕 lack judgment[discretion]; be imprudent[indiscreet / thoughtless / injudicious]; 〔천진하다〕 be simple-minded[innocent / untutored]. ¶철모르는 어린아이 a thoughtless[an innocent] child∥철모르고 날뛰다 do reckless things / behave recklessly∥어린애가 철모르고 한 짓이니 용서하십시오 Please forgive his behavior; he is only a child.

철문(鐵門) an iron door[gate].

철물(鐵物) metallic material; 〔쇠로 만든 기물〕 ironware; ironwork; hardware; a metal utensil; 《영》 ironmongery; 〔쇠장식〕 metal fittings.
●**철물상 / 철물 상인** an ironmonger; 《미》 a hardwareman; a hardware dealer. **철물점** 《미》 a hardware store[shop]; 《영》 an ironmongery; 《영》 an ironmonger's (shop).

철버덕 with a splash. ⇨철버덕

철벅거리다 〔물 등을〕 splatter; paddle; dabble; 〔물속에서〕 splash about in the water. ¶철벅거리며 내를 건너다 splash across a stream∥진창길을 철벅거리며 가다 go splashing in the mud∥물속에서 철벅거리며 놀다 disport oneself in the water∥우리는 철벅거리며 내를 건넜다 We splashed our way across the river.

철벅철벅 splashing(ly); dabbling; splash-splash; with splashing sounds. ¶~ 물을 튀기다 splash water about∥~ 물에 들어가다 〔내를 건너다〕 splash into the water[splash across a stream]. **철벅철벅하다** splatter; paddle. ⇨철벅거리다

철벽(鐵壁) an iron wall; 〔견고한 성벽〕 an impregnable fortress. ¶금성 ~ an impregnable fortress[castle]∥~같은 진을 치다 take up an impregnable position.

철병(撤兵) withdrawal of troops. ⇨철군

철봉(鐵棒) 1 〔쇠막대〕 an iron bar[rod]; an iron club(곤봉). 2 〔체조용의〕 a horizontal bar; gallows; (경기 종목의) the horizontal bar; gymnastics on the bar. ¶~을 하다 exercise on the horizontal bar.

철부지(-不知) 〔철없는 사람〕 an indiscreet[a thoughtless] person; a person who lacks good sense; 〔철없는 어린애〕 a mere child; just a child. ¶아직 ~이다 be just a child who does not know his mind as yet∥~ 노릇을 하다 act[behave] like a mere child / play a fool∥나는 ~가 아니다 I was not born yesterday.

철분(鐵分) iron (content). ¶~이 있는[을 함유한] containing iron / ferric / chalybeate (springs) / ferruginous∥~을 함유한 물 chalybeate water∥~이 많은[적은] rich [poor] in iron / high[low] in iron∥~이 많은 야채 vegetables which contain a lot of iron∥이 물은 ~이 많다 The water is strongly impregnated with iron.

철사(鐵絲) (a) wire; 《집합적》 wiring. ¶가시 ~ barbed wire∥~ 한 가닥 a (piece of) wire∥전기가 통하고 있는 ~ a live wire∥~의〔같은〕 wiry∥~로 묶다〔잇다〕 wire together.
●**철사 그물** a wire net.

철삭(鐵索) a cable; a wire rope.

철새 a migratory[passage] bird; a bird of passage; a transient(체류 기간이 짧은 사람); 〔집합적〕 migrants.

철석간장(鐵石肝腸) a hard heart; an iron [adamantine] will; a steadfast resolution. ¶~을 녹이다 disarm (a person's) hardheartedness / shake (a person's) steadfast resolution / make (a person's) firm purpose waver / captivate (a man)∥여자의 눈물에는 대장부의 ~도 다 녹는다 Man's hardheartedness is utterly disarmed by the tears of a woman.

철석같다(鐵石-) adamantine; firm as a rock. ¶철석같은 마음 an iron[adamantine] will / a steadfast resolution∥철석같은 언약 a solemn promise. **철석같이** ¶남을 ~ 믿다 pin one's faith[hope] upon another's sleeve.

철선(鐵船) an iron[a steel] vessel; an ironclad(철갑선).

철선(鐵線) (a) wire. ⇨철사

철수(撤收) withdrawal; removal; evacuation. ¶전면 ~ a total withdrawal∥군대의 즉시 ~ an immediate withdrawal of troops. **철수하다** withdraw (from); remove; evacuate (a place); draw off; pull out. ¶군대를 ~ pull the troops out of (Cambodia) / call (the armed forces) home(본국으로)∥지상군을 ~ withdraw one's ground forces (from)∥군대는 점령 지역에서 철수했다 The troops withdrew from the occupied area.

철시하다(撤市-) close the market; close up shops[stores]; suspend business. ¶철시한 상가 a closed shopping district[street] / a shopping street in suspension.

철심(鐵心) 1 〔철석같은 마음〕 an iron[adamantine] will; a steadfast resolution. 2 〔쇠로 박은 심〕 an iron core.

철썩 1 〔물소리〕 with a splash[splosh / swash]; with a dash. ¶물결이 바위에 ~ 부딪치는 소리 the swash of water against rocks∥파도가 바닷가에 ~ 부딪쳤다 The waves splashed on the beach. **철썩하다** splash; plash; swash. 2 〔때리는 소리〕 with a slap [pank / crack]. ¶따귀를 ~ 때리다 slap (a person) in[on] the face / slap (a person) on the cheek∥어린애의 볼기를 ~ 때리다 spank a child / paddle a child's bottom. **철썩하다** make a slapping[spanking / cracking] sound; slap.

철썩거리다 splash; swash; plash. ¶철썩거리는 파도 소리 the plash of the waves / the splosh of the surf∥물가에 철썩거리는 파도 waves dashing on the shore.

철썩철썩 〔파도 소리〕 splashing; dashing; with splashes[plashes]; 〔때리는 소리〕 with slaps[snaps / spanks]. ¶바닷물이 해안에서 ~ 파도치고 있다 The waves are lapping the beach.

철야(徹夜) an all-night vigil[sitting]. ¶~로 병구완하다 sit up with (an invalid) all night [all the night through]∥~로 회의하다 have an all-night conference∥~로 시험공부를 하다 sit up all night over one's textbooks for examination∥그들은 ~로 화투를 쳤다 They had an all-night hwatu session. **철야하다** sit

철없다 [stay / be] up all night; keep vigil. ¶섣달그믐에 ~ sit out New Year's Eve // 환자의 머리맡에서 ~ keep vigil at patient's bedside // 나는 간밤에 철야했다 I stayed up all night last night.
- ●**철야 운행** (버스 등의) all-night service. **철야 작업** all-night work. ¶~을 하다 work all night.

철없다 indiscreet; imprudent; thoughtless; reckless; rash; (서술적) have no sense [discretion]; lack judgment. ¶철없는 어린아이 a mere child / a greenhorn of a boy // 철없는 짓을 하다 commit a rash act / do something rash / act foolishly / behave like a mere child.

철옹(산)성 (鐵甕山城) an impregnable fortress. ¶~ 같다 [~이다] be impregnable / be very [ever so] strong / be hard of approach.

철완 (鐵腕) a cannonball [strong] arm. ¶저 투수는 철완을 휘둘러 제11회전을 끝까지 투구했다 That pitcher made it through eleven innings with his strong arm.
- ●**철완 투수** a pitcher with an iron arm; a strong-armed [an iron-armed] pitcher.

철인 (哲人) 〔현자〕 a wise man; a man of wisdom; a sage; 〔철학자〕 a philosopher.

철인 (鐵人) an iron man.

철자 (綴字) spelling; orthography. ¶정확한 ~ the exact spelling // ~가 잘못된 글자 a misspelt word // ~의 잘못 misspelling / cacography // ~를 잘못 쓰다 misspell // ~를 생략하지 않고 정식으로 쓰다 spell (out) (one's name) in full // "concerto"의 ~를 말해 보아라 Spell the word "concerto." // 이 단어의 ~를 알고 있는가 Do you know how to spell this word? / Do you know the spelling of this word? // 그 단어의 ~를 말해 주시오 Please tell me how to spell the word. **철자하다** spell. ¶"colonel"이라는 단어는 어떻게 철자하는가 How do you spell "colonel"? // 그녀의 이름은 그렇게 철자하지 않는다 That is not the way to spell her name.
- ●**철자법** the system of spelling; how to spell (a word).

철재 (鐵材) iron (material); an iron frame. ¶~를 써서 집을 짓다 build a house with iron frames.

철저하다 (徹底-) thorough(going); exhaustive; complete; perfect; utter; out-and-out; all-out; downright; drastic; radical. ¶철저한 변혁 a sweeping [drastic / radical] change // 철저한 악당 an unmitigated villain // 철저한 연구 a thorough [an exhaustive / an intensive] study // 철저한 공산주의자 a dyed-in-the-wool communist // 철저한 무신론자 a thoroughgoing atheist // 철저한 이기주의자 an out-and-out [a through-and-through / a dyed-in-the-wool] egoist // 철저한 낙관가 an incorrigible [incurable] optimist // 철저한 낙관주의 an incorrigible optimism // 철저한 조사가 필요하다 A thorough [thoroughgoing] investigation (of the matter) is needed. // 철저한 개혁이 요망된다 A drastic [An all-out] reform is called for. // 철저한 변혁은 시기상조이다 The time is not yet ripe for sweeping changes. // 문제의 철저한 연구가 시작되었다 An exhaustive [A comprehensive] study of the problem was begun. // 그는 무슨 일에나 ~ There is nothing half-and-half about him. / He is always thorough about anything. **철저히** thoroughly; thoroughgoingly; completely; thoroughly; downright; all out; through and through; (up) to the hilt. ¶~하다 do (anything) thoroughly / go all length // ~ 연구하다 exhaust (a subject) / probe (a matter) to the bottom / make exhaustive researches into (a subject) // ~ 조사하다 make a thorough [an exhaustive] investigation of (a matter) / search (a matter) to the bottom // 적을 ~ 쳐부수다 defeat the enemy decisively [thoroughly] / thrash the enemy // (사상 등을) ~ 주입시키다 dye in (the) grain [in the wool] // 이야기를 ~ 이해시키다 have oneself fully understood (by) // 글 뜻을 ~ 이해시키다 bring the meaning of a sentence home to (a person) // 공부를 하려면 ~ 해라 If you study at all, be sure to master your subject. // 그는 뭔가를 시작하면 ~ 한다 Whenever he starts something he goes all out [all the way]. / He always sees what he has started through to the end.

철제 (鐵製) ¶~의 (made of) iron / steel.
- ●**철제 기구** an iron tool; ironwork; ironware.

철제 (鐵劑) 〔의〕 iron; an iron preparation; a ferric medicine.

철조망 (鐵條網) (barbed-)wire entanglements; 〔군〕 a hedgehog. ¶~을 둘러친 빈 터 a field laid with barbed-wire entanglements // ~을 둘러치다 wire in (against) // ~을 치다 set [stretch / construct] wire entanglements // ~에 걸리다 get entangled in barbed wire // ~을 뚫다 break through wire entanglements.

철쭉 〔식〕 a royal azalea; a rhododendron.
- ●**철쭉꽃** a royal azalea blossom. **철쭉나무** 〔식〕 a royal azalea. ⇨=철쭉

철창 (鐵窓) 1 〔쇠 창살문〕 a steel-barred window. 2 〔교도소〕 prison bars; the bars; a prison. ¶~신세가 되다 be placed behind prison bars / be cast into prison / be imprisoned / be a prisoner // ~생활을 하다 pass (five years) in prison / pine behind (the) bars.

철책 (鐵柵) an iron railing [paling / fence]. ¶~을 두르다 put an iron fence around (something) // ~이 처져[둘러] 있다 be enclosed with an iron railing // ~으로 보호하다 protect (the lawn) by iron railings // ~을 쳐서 못 들어오게 하다 keep (people) away with an iron railing [fence].

철천지원 (徹天之冤) a lasting regret. ⇨=철천지한

철천지원수 (徹天之怨讐) a mortal foe; a sworn enemy.

철천지한 (徹天之恨) a lasting regret; a bitter [deep] grudge; deep-rooted enmity; an inveterate resentment. ¶~이 맺힌 원수 a bitter enemy // ~을 품다 bear [have / nurse] (a person) a deep(-rooted) grudge / cherish an implacable hostility (toward) // ~을 풀다 vent one's bitter spite / satisfy one's inveterate grudge // 우리는 그들에게 ~이 있다 We have deep-rooted rancor against them.

철철 overflowingly; brimmingly. ¶~ 넘치도록 to the brim / brimfully / to the full // (물 등이) ~ 넘치다 overflow (the bank) / run [flow] over (the brim) / brim over (with) // ~ 넘치도록 술을 따르다 fill a glass (up) to the brim with wine / brim a cup with wine.

철철이 each (and every) season; from season to season. ¶~ 피는 꽃들 flowers of each season // 경치는 ~ 달라진다 Scenery changes from season to season.

철칙 (鐵則) an ironbound [ironclad / inviolable] rule [regulation]; a hard and fast rule; an invariable principle. ¶「단결」이 우리의 ~이다 Unity is our ironclad motto. // 시험 문제는 아무도 실외로 가지고 나갈 수 없다는 것이 ~이다 It is a hard-fast rule that no one can take examination papers out of this room.

철커덕 with a snap. ⇨ 찰카닥

철탑 (鐵塔) a steel tower; (고압선용의) a pylon.

철통같다 (鐵桶-) be strong; be impregnable [impenetrable]; be airtight [watertight]; (경비가) be closely [rigorously] guarded; be on strict watch [guard]. ¶철통같은 방어진 an impenetrable defense cordon // 철통같은 방비 impregnable fortification // 철통같은 경계망 a strict police cordon // 철통같은 방위 태세를 유지하다 maintain an iron-tight defense posture // 수도 방위 태세는 ~ The defense system of the capital is just perfect. **철통같이** ¶~ 경계하다 be on strict watch / guard rigorously // ~ 에워싸다 surround (a place) like a ring of iron.

철퇴 (撤退) [철수] (a) withdrawal; (an) evacuation; a pullout; (후퇴) a retreat. ¶부분 ~ a partial pullout / a thinout // 전면 ~ the total withdrawal / a general pullout. **철퇴하다** withdraw [draw off] (troops); evacuate (a place); pull out (of a place). ¶군대는 어제 그 도시에서 철퇴했다 The soldiers withdrew from [pulled out of] the town yesterday. →¶병력을 진지에서 철퇴시키다 withdraw troops (from a position).
● **철퇴 명령** an evacuation order. ¶그 도시로부터의 ~을 받다 be ordered out of the city.

철퇴 (鐵槌) an iron hammer; an iron mace. **철퇴를 가하다[내리다]** give [deal] a hard [heavy / crushing] blow (to); (구어) crack down (on). ¶당국은 불법 도박에 철퇴를 가했다 The authorities dealt a hard blow to [cracked down on] illegal gambling.

철판 (凸版) [인] letterpress; relief [anastatic / surface] printing. ¶아연 ~ a zinc relief.
● **철판 인쇄** letterpress; anastatic [relief / surface] printing.

철판 (鐵板) an iron [a steel] plate [sheet]; sheet iron; a sheet of iron; (번철) a griddle; a hot plate. ¶고기를 ~에 굽다 grill meat on an iron plate // 쇠고기 ~구이를 내놓다 serve beef grilled on an iron plate / serve grilled strips of beef.
● **철판공** (-工) a plater.

철편 (鐵片) a piece [scrap] of iron. ¶얇은 ~ taggers.

철폐 (撤廢) abolition; removal. ¶쌀 통제 ~ the abolition of controls on rice. **철폐하다** abolish; remove; do away with; repeal (the excise tax); annul. ¶법률을 ~ rescind a law // …의 금지를 ~ lift the embargo [ban] on … // 제한을 ~ remove [take away] the restriction // 통제를 ~ take off controls / decontrol // 계급 차별을 ~ do away with [obliterate] class distinctions // 차별 대우를 ~ do away with [abolish] the discrimination // 이민 제한을 ~ let down the immigration barriers.

철필 (鐵筆) **1** a pen. ⇨ 펜 **2** [등사판용 필기도구] a steel pen; a stencil pen; an iron stylus; a metallic pencil. ¶~로 원지를 긁다 cut the stencil paper with a steel pen. **3** [새김날] a burin; a seal graver.

철하다 (綴-) bind (a book); file. ¶서류를 ~ file papers / place papers on file // 편지를 ~ file letters / put letters in a file // 신문을 ~ 두다 keep newspapers on [in a] file // 철해져 있다 be on file // 보고서에 참고 자료를 덧붙여서 ~ insert and fasten the reference data in a report.

철학 (哲學) philosophy. ¶경험 ~ empirical philosophy // 도덕 ~ moral philosophy // 동양 [서양] ~ Oriental (or Western) philosophy // 법 ~ philosophy of law // 분석 ~ analytic philosophy // 비판 (칸트의) critical philosophy // 사회 ~ social philosophy // 사변 [자연] ~ speculative [natural] philosophy // (칸트의) 선험적 ~ a priori philosophy (of Kant) // 실존 ~ existential philosophy / existentialism // 실증 ~ positive philosophy / positivism // 역사 ~ philosophy of history // 인생 ~ philosophy of life // 종교 ~ philosophy of religion // 그의 독특한 ~ a philosophy all his own // ~을 논하다 talk philosophy // ~을 공부하다 study philosophy // ~에 뜻을 두다 take up the study of philosophy // 그것이 내 ~이다 That is my way of thinking. // 그에게는 그 나름의 인생 ~이 있다 He has his own philosophy of life.
● **철학 개론** an introduction to [an outline of] philosophy. **철학 박사** (사람) a doctor of philosophy; (학위) Doctor of Philosophy(약어 Ph.D., D.Ph(il).). **철학자** a philosopher; a man of philosophy.

철학적 (哲學的) philosophical. ¶~ 사색 [사상] philosophical speculation [thought] // ~으로 philosophically // ~으로 생각하다 philosophize (about) // 인생을 ~으로 고찰하다 consider life from a philosophical point of view.

철혈 재상 (鐵血宰相) the Iron Chancellor.
철혈 정책 (鐵血政策) a blood-and-iron policy.
철형 (凸形) convexity. ¶~의 convex.

철회 (撤回) withdrawal; revocation; retractation; recantation; repeal; relinquishment; [법] ademption(유증(遺贈)의). **철회하다** withdraw (a bill); revoke (a license); recall (a decision); retract (a statement); relinquish [recede from] (one's demand); forgo (one's claim); repeal (a law); rescind (a contract); countermand (an order). ¶사표를 ~ withdraw one's resignation // 요구를 ~ withdraw [forgo] one's claims / relinquish [retract / recede from] one's demands // 앞서 한 말을 ~ withdraw [take back] one's words / back down on what one said // 제안을 ~ get the proposal abandoned / retract [withdraw] one's proposal // 약속 [전설 (前說)]을 ~ retract a promise [one's former statement]. →¶사표는 철회되었다 The resignation was withdrawn.

첨가 (添加) annexing; addition. ¶~ 기입하다 add (something) in writing. **첨가하다** annex (to); append (to); affix (to); add (to); attach (to). ¶됨으로 ~ throw in / fling in // 단맛을 ~ add sweetening // 편지에 추신(追伸)을 ~ add a postscript to a letter // 선물에 편지를 첨가해서 보내다 send a present along with a letter [note]. →¶이 식품에는 방부제가 첨가되어 있지 않다 This food has no pre-

첨단
servative additives [no added preservatives].
●**첨가물** an annex(e); an appendix; an addition; an additive. ¶식품 ~ an [a food] additive // 인공 ~ 미첨가 (식품의 라벨에) No Artificial Additives. **첨가어** an agglutinative language.
첨단(尖端) 1 [뾰족한 끝] a pointed end [head]; a (fine) point; a tip; a cusp(이·잎 등의). 2 [맨 앞장] the spearhead; the vanguard; a cutting edge. ¶유행의 ~ a ultra fashionable mode [style] // 유행의 ~을 걷다 set [lead] the fashion // 시대의 ~을 가다 be in the van of the era // 그녀는 유행의 ~을 걷는다 [유행을 만들어 낸다] She sets the fashion. / [유행을 좇는다] She follows the latest fashion.
●**첨단 기술** cutting-edge [leading-edge] technology; advanced technology and skills; (transfer of) updated [up-to-date] technology; high-technology. ¶~의 도입 new technical introduction // ~의 개발 the development of updated technology. **첨단 산업** a frontier industry; a high-technology industry.
첨벙 with a splash [plop]; splosh. ¶물속으로 ~ 떨어지다 fall plop into the water // 물속으로 ~ 뛰어들다 plunge [splash / jump] into the water.
첨병(尖兵) [경계·수색하는 병사] a point (of an advance guard); an advance guard point; [경계·수색하는 소부대] an advance detachment.
첨부(添附) appending; annexing. **첨부하다** attach (a thing to another); append; annex; be accompanied (by). ¶원서에 사진을 첨부해서 내다 submit an application (together) with [accompanied by] one's photograph // 성적 증명서를 첨부해서 원서를 제출했다 I submitted my school records with my application. // 최근의 사진을 신청서에 첨부할 것 A recent photograph should be attached to the application form.
●**첨부 사진** an accompanying photograph. **첨부 서류** appended [attached] papers; accompanying documents; an annex(e); [증거 서류] exhibits.
첨삭(添削) correction. ¶작문의 ~을 받다 have one's composition looked over and corrected (by) // ~을 부탁하다 submit (one's composition to a person) for correction / ask (a person) to look over (one's composition). **첨삭하다** correct; look over; touch up. ¶나는 영작문을 첨삭해 받았다 I had my English composition corrected.
첨예하다(尖銳-) [날카롭다] acute; sharp; [급진적이다] radical.
첨예화하다(尖銳化-) 1 [분쟁 등이] become [get] acute [tense]; be aggravated. ¶첨예화하는 분쟁 a sharpening conflict. 2 [사상 등이] be radicalized; become more radical (in one's ideas).
첨잔하다(添盞-) pour an additional wine into a cup.
첨지(籤紙) a paper bookmark.
첨첨(添添) heap upon heap; layer on layer; pile after pile. ¶돌 [벽돌]을 ~ 쌓다 heap up stones [bricks] / lay one stone [brick] upon another.
첨탑(尖塔) a pinnacle; a spire; a steeple.
첩(妾) a (kept) mistress; a concubine. ¶~을 두다 keep [set up] a mistress [concubine] // 남의 ~ 노릇을 하다 be [become] a person's concubine // ~의 소생이다 be born of a concubine.
첩(貼) a paper (of medicine); a chartula (pl. -lae) (가루약의); a dose (of) (복용량). ¶약 한 ~ a paper [wrapper] of medicine // 이 약은 식후에 한 ~씩 들도록 하시오 Take a dose of this medicine after each meal.
-첩(帖) an album; a (note) book. ¶견본~ a sample book // 사진~ a photograph [photo] album.
첩경(捷徑) 1 [지름길] a shortcut (to); [손쉬운 방법] a shorter way; a royal road. ¶성공의 ~ a short cut to success // 외국어를 배우는 ~ the shortest way to learn foreign languages // ~의 지식을 얻는 ~ a shortcut to knowledge // 학문에는 ~이 없다 There is no royal road to learning. 2 [흔히] most likely; in all probability; [쉽게] easily; readily. ¶친구에게 돈을 빌려 주면 ~ 돈도 잃고 친구도 잃기 쉽다 If you lend money to your friend, you are liable to lose money and your friend.
첩보(捷報) [싸움에 이긴 보고] news of a victory; the tidings of victory. ¶~를 올리다 report the victory (of / at) to the throne // 이윽고 ~가 들어왔다 It was not long before word came that they won the battle.
첩보(諜報) secret information; intelligence.
●**첩보 기관** an intelligence office [organization / agency]; a secret service. **첩보망** an intelligence [espionage] network; a spy net. **첩보원** an intelligence man; a secret agent. **첩보 활동** espionage activities.
첩부(貼付) [발라서 붙임] pasting. **첩부하다** paste [stick / put / affix / apply] on [up]. ¶편지에 우표를 ~ put a stamp on a letter / stamp a letter.
첩살림(妾-) living with a concubine. **첩살림 하다** live with a concubine; keep a second [separate] establishment.
첩실(妾室) a (kept) mistress. ⇨=첩(妾)
첩약(貼藥) a paper of medicine; a dose of medicine in a wrapper.
첩자(諜者) a spy; an (espionage) agent. ⇨=간첩 ¶~ 노릇을 하다 be engaged in espionage / act as spy // ~를 보내다 send (out) a spy (to) / send a spy (into).
첩첩산중(疊疊山中) ¶~에 in the heart of mountains rising one above another / deep in the mountains / far up (in) the mountain / in the recesses [depth] of a mountain // ~에 살다 live in the heart of the mountains.
첩첩수심(疊疊愁心) anxiety on anxiety; worry on top of worry. ¶~에 싸이다 have a lot of anxiety / have worries upon worries.
첩첩이(疊疊-) fold upon fold; layer upon layer; pile upon pile; heap (up) on heap. ¶~ 그를 둘러싼 기자들 the reporters crowding around him // 시체가 ~ 쌓이다 (장소가) be heaped with (the) dead // 구름이 ~ 쌓였다 Clouds hung in great bunches [heaps]. // 경찰이 그 집을 ~ 둘러싸고 있었다 The house was surrounded by droves of policemen.
첫 the first; new; maiden; starting; the beginning. ¶~째 the first // ~ 경험 one's first [new] experience // ~ 글자 the first letter (of a word) / (이름의) an initial (letter) // ~ 등장 one's debut / one's first appearance on

첫가을 the stage // ~아이 one's first(-born) child // ~ 공연(公演) the first performance (of a play) // ~차 the first bus [train] // ~ 출전 (make / set out upon) one's first campaign / a maiden battle // ~ 항해 a maiden voyage // ~ 무대 one's first appearance (on the stage) / one's debut.

첫가을 early autumn [(미) fall]; the beginning of autumn.

첫걸음 the first step (to); an initial step; a start; [초보·기본] the rudiments (of); the ABC (of); a beginners' course (in English). ¶성공의 ~ the first step to success // 영어 ~ elementary [beginner's] English / "First Steps in English" / a "Primer of English" // ~을 그르치다 make a false start / start in the wrong way // ~을 내딛다 take[mark] the first step / make[get] a start / set one's foot (on).

첫겨울 early winter; the beginning of winter.

첫고등 [맨 처음의 기회] the first opportunity [chance]; the very start.

첫국밥 [출산 후 처음 먹는 미역국과 밥] the first seaweed soup and rice taken after childbirth. ¶~을 먹다 take soup and rice for the first time after the delivery of a child.

첫기제(~忌祭) the first anniversary of (one's parent's) death after the three-year mourning period.

첫길 1 [초행길] an unaccustomed course [route]; one's first trip (to); a road one is on for the first time. ¶~이 되어 생소하다 I am not familiar with the road. 2 [신행길] (on) the way to one's wedding.

첫나들이 (갓난아이의) going out for the first time after one's birth; (신부의) the first outing of a bride marriage. **첫나들이하다** go out for the first time after one's birth; (신부가) make her first post-marriage outing; (비유) have something smeared on one's face.

첫날 the first day [night]; the opening day; (연극의) the première. ¶학년의 ~ the first day of school [of the school year] // 공연 ~ the first [opening] day [night] // ~ 공연을 놓치지 않는 사람 (연극의) a first-nighter // 회의의 ~ the opening session.

● **첫날밤** the bridal [first] night; the first night of a married couple.

첫낯 an unfamiliar face; a stranger; a first meeting.

첫눈¹ [일견] a first look [glance / glimpse / sight]. ¶그는 ~에 그 여자한테 반했다 He fell in love with her at first sight. / He had a crush on her at first sight. // 나는 ~에 그 집이 마음에 들었다 I took a fancy to the house at first sight.

첫눈² [초설] the first snow(fall) of the season. ¶어젯밤에 ~이 내렸다 It snowed last night for the first time this year.

첫더위 the first heat (of the season); the first spell of hot weather; the first hot spell [heat wave]. ¶~가 시작되었다 The first hot weather set in.

첫돌 (아기의) the first birthday of a baby; (행사의) the first anniversary [memorial day] (of). ¶창립 ~ 기념행사를 갖다 observe the first anniversary of the opening (of the firm).

첫딸 a female first-born; one's first(-born) daughter. ¶~을 낳다 give birth to a girl at one's first childbirth.

첫딸은 세간 밑천이다(속담) When the first child is a daughter, that is a great help around the house.

첫마디 an opening [initial] remark [word]; the first word. ¶~를 꺼내다 open one's word [case] / open the conversation / break the silence / break the ice(하기 어려운 말을) // ~를 어떻게 꺼내야 할지 모르다 do not know how to broach (a subject) // ~에 화를 내다 get angry at (a person's) first remark // ~부터 욕이었다 He abused me as soon as he opened his mouth. // 그는 ~가 나보고 왜 왔느냐는 것이었다 His first word to me was "Why did you come here?" // 나는 그의 ~가 어떻게 나올지 기다렸다 I waited for his opening words.

첫머리 the beginning; the outset; the opening; the head (of a column); the top; the first (part). ¶장(章) ~에 at the beginning of the chapter // 책을 ~부터 읽다 read a book from the beginning // 그의 이름이 명부 ~에 쓰여 있다 His name is marked at the top of a list. / His name heads a list. // 그의 연설은 ~가 재미있었다 The opening of his speech was interesting. // 그녀는 곡의 ~에서 조금 잘못 불렀다 She made a slight mistake at the beginning of the song. // 네 이름이 ~에 나와 있다 Your name heads [tops] the list.

첫물 1 (옷의) new clothes that have yet to be laundered; new clothes worn for the first time; first wear(ing). ¶~ 옷 clothes that have never been laundered // 옷이 ~에 못 쓰게 되다 one's clothes are worn out before they got laundered. 2 →만물

첫발 the first step (to / toward); an initial step; [발족] a start. ¶성공을 향한 ~을 내디디다 take the first step toward(s) success // 나는 ~을 그르쳤다 I got off to a bad start. / I started off on the wrong foot. // 그는 새 인생에 ~을 내디뎠을 뿐이다 He has just started on a new career. // 그들은 작년 5월 그 섬에 ~을 디뎠다 They first set foot on the island in May last year.

첫밥 the first feeding (of silkworms). ¶~을 주다 feed (silkworms) for the first time.

첫배 the firstborn (of animals). ⇨맏배

첫봄 early spring; the beginning of spring. ¶~에 in (the) early spring / early in spring.

첫사랑 one's first love; calf love(어릴 때의); (사람) one's first lover [sweetheart]; the first girl [boy] one fell in love with. ¶~에 빠지다 fall in love for the first time // ~에 실패하다 lose one's first love / be disappointed [betrayed] in one's first love // ~을 모르다 have never experienced calf love // 그녀는 내 ~의 여자였다 She was my [the object of my] first love. // 그의 ~은 기생이었다 His first love was a *gisaeng*.

첫새벽 early dawn [morning]. ¶~에 before dawn / in the early dawn [morning] // ~에 일어나다 get up early in the morning // ~이어서 아직 어두웠다 It was before dawn and the light was poor. // ~까지는 아직 시간이 있다 There is yet (some) time before daybreak.

첫서리 the first frost (of the season). ¶어젯밤에 ~가 내렸다 We had the first frost of the year last night.

첫선 [처음 등장] the first public appearance; [처음 공개] the first public exhibition

첫소리 [presentation]. ¶전국에 ~을 뵐 신형 텔레비전 a TV set of a new model that is put for the first time on the nation-wide sales network∥그가 젊은 외교관으로서 ~을 보인 것은 26세 때였다 He was twenty-six when he made his debut as a young diplomat.

첫소리 [언] an initial sound; an initial consonant (in a Korean orthographic syllable).

첫솜씨 a first try of one's skill; the first performance [execution]; a first doing [attempt]; a green hand. ¶~가 되어 잘 만들어질지 모르겠다 Since this is my first attempt, I don't know whether I can make it very well.

첫술 the first spoonful of food (one takes at a meal). ¶~을 뜨다 take one's first spoonful of food at a meal.
　첫술에 배부르랴(속담) You must not expect too much at your first attempt.

첫아들 a male first-born. ¶~을 낳다 give birth to a boy at one's first childbirth∥~을 보다 get a boy as one's first child.

첫여름 early summer; the beginning of summer. ¶~에 early in summer.

첫이레 the first week [the seventh day] after a childbirth.

첫인상(-印象) a first impression. ¶~이 좋다 make [have / give] a good [favorable] first impression (on / upon)∥좋지 않은 ~을 남기다 leave a bad [an unfavorable] first impression∥그의 ~은 좋지 않다 He impressed me unfavorably upon our first meeting.∥그의 ~은 좋지 않지만 아주 친절하다 He is repellent at first, but is really very kind.

첫잠 the first [early] stage of sleep; a sleep one has just fallen into; one's first sleep. ¶~에서 깨다 be aroused in one's first sleep / be awakened from one's first sleep∥애 우는 소리에 ~이 깨다 wake up at the cry of a baby soon after one has gone to sleep for the night.

첫정(-情) a first attachment [affection / love]. ¶서로 ~이 들다 fall in love each for the first time∥~을 못내 잊지 못하다 can't get over one's first attachment at all.

첫째 the first; number one; No. 1; the top [first] place; the foremost. ¶~의 first / primary / foremost / leading∥~로 first / firstly / in the first place / first of all / before everything / to begin with / at the outset∥~ 문제 the first [main] problem∥~ 날의 일정 the schedule for [on] the first day∥진보의 ~ 단계 the first [initial] stage of progress∥~로 오다 come first / be the first to come∥~가 되다 secure [take / win / get] (the) first place / stand [rank] first (in / among) / be at the top [head / best] (of) / head [top] the list (of) / finish [come in] first / come out first [top]∥(의) 목적은 …이다 The primary object is …∥~를 겨루다 compete for first place∥이 도시는 동해안에서 ~가는 큰 어항의 하나다 This town is one of the largest fishing ports on the east coast.∥하고 싶은 말이 세 가지 있다. ~ 너는 칠칠치 못해 I have three things to say to you. First [One is], you lack discipline.∥건강이 ~다 Health is the most important thing.∥이 기획의 ~ 목표는 무엇입니까 What is the primary [chief / principal] aim of this project?∥그 사람에게 돈을 요구해 보았자 소용없다. ~ 그 사람은 인색하니까 It's no good asking him for money. To begin with, he is so close-fisted.∥나는 보트를 사지 않기로 했다. ~ 너무 비싸고… I decided not to buy a cruiser, because in the first place it was too expensive, and ….∥나는 도덕 교육을 ~로 생각하고 있다 I consider moral education most important. / I attach the greatest importance to moral education.∥~도 공부, 둘째도 공부 study, study, nothing but study / study and more study.∥~ 시간이 없고 또 돈도 없다 For one thing there is no spare, and for another I don't have the money.∥우선 ~로 무엇을 해야 좋을까 What should we do first (of all)?

첫추위 the first cold weather (of the season); the first spell of cold weather. ¶~가 든다 The first cold weather sets in.

첫출발(-出發) a start; a beginning. ¶인생의 ~ one's (first) start in life∥인생의 ~을 하는 청년 a young man on the threshold of life∥~이 좋다[나쁘다] make a good[wrong] start∥이 차는 ~이 순조롭다 This car starts easily.∥그 말은 ~이 빨랐다[나빴다] The horse got off to a fast [bad] start.∥신제품의 ~은 그런대로 좋았다 The new product has gotten off to a pretty good start.

첫판 the first round [game / bout]; an initial round; the beginning. ¶~에 지다 get beaten in the first round [bout] (of).

첫해 the first year. ¶미국 간 ~ the first year one was in America.

첫해 권농(勸農) (속담) being clumsy because of inexperience; a greenhorn.

첫행보(-行步) 1 [처음 감] one's first visit [errand]. ¶~에 돈을 받아 오다 collect the money one's first trip (to get it). 2 [첫 행상] one's first venture at [trip of] peddling. ¶~에 상당한 이익을 보다 make a considerable profit on one's first peddling (trip).

첫혼인(-婚姻) one's first marriage. **첫혼인하다** marry for the first time.

청 [얇은 막] a membrane; a film; a pellicle. ¶갈대~ the white membrane inside a reed∥귀~ the drum membrane / the eardrum∥목~ the vocal cords [bands].

청(靑) [청색] a blue colo(u)r; green or blue; azure.

청(請) a request; a favo(u)r; one's wishes; [간청] an entreaty; a solicitation. ¶간절한 ~ an earnest request / an entreaty∥긴한 ~ an urgent [important] request∥…의 ~에 따라 at a person's request / in compliance [accordance] with a person's request∥친구의 모처럼의 ~으로 at the pressing request of a friend∥~을 넣다 make a request through (a person) / ask a favor (indirectly)∥~을 들어주다 comply with [accede to] (a person's) request / grant (a person's) request / do (a person) a favor / oblige (a person)∥~을 들어주지 않다 turn down [refuse / decline] (a person's) request / refuse (a person) a favor / turn a deaf ear to a request∥~이 있다 have a favor to ask of (a person) / wish to make (a person) a request / wish to ask a favor of (a person)∥~이 하나 있는데요 I have a favor to ask of you.∥무슨 ~인가요 What is your request? / What is that you would have me do?∥~을 하나 들어주시겠소 Would you do me a favor? // ~을 들어주지 You shall have your request.(▶불손스런 표현) / 당신 ~이야 안 들어줄 수 있나 How could I possibly refuse a request of yours? / I can refuse you nothing. // ~이라면 아니 갈 수도 없지 I may as well go if you wish me to. // 그는 나의 ~을 받아들여 그 계획을 단념했다 He gave up the project in compliance with my request. / He granted my request and gave up the project.

청(廳) the main hall. ⇨대청(大廳)

청각(聽覺) (the sense of) hearing; hearing sense; auditory[acoustic] sense; audition. ¶시~ 교육 audio-visual education // ~에 호소하는 효과 audio effects // ~에 호소하다 appeal to the ear // ~을 잃다 lose one's hearing // ~이 예민하다 have sensitive ears / have an acute[a keen] sense of hearing / be keen of hearing // 나이를 먹어 ~이 약해지기 시작했다 My hearing is beginning to fail with age. // 앞을 못 보는 사람들은 보통 ~이 좋은 법이다 People who cannot see usually have a fine sense of hearing.
●**청각 기관** a hearing[an auditory] organ. **청각 신경** the auditory[acoustic] nerve. ¶~을 곤두세우다 keep one's ears on the alert. **청각 장애인** a hearing challenged[handicapped / impaired] person(▶ handicapped 보다 impaired나 challenged가 완곡하고 부드러운 말임).

청강(聽講) attendance (at a lecture); auditing (a course). ¶~ 무료 [게시] Attendance[Admission] Free. // ~ 자유 (게시) Admission Is Open To All. // ~을 허락하다 grant (a person) admission. **청강하다** attend (a lecture); (미) listen to (a lecture); audit (a course at a university). ¶두세 개의 세미나를 ~ sit in on[(미) audit] a few seminars // 국제법을 ~ audit "International Law".
●**청강생** (미) an auditor(▶ 학점을 따지 않음); a special student(▶ 일부 수업의 학점을 땀); (영) an occasional[unregistered] student.

청개구리(靑-) 1 [동] a green frog; a tree frog; a hyla. 2 (만사에 엇나가고 엇먹는 짓을 하는 사람) a perverse[contrary] person; a cross-grained person.

청객(請客) (an) invitation; inviting guests. **청객하다** invite a guest.

청결하다(淸潔-) clean; neat; pure. ¶청결한 부엌 a clean kitchen / 청결한 몸 a clean body // 청결한 점에서는 이 호텔이 낫다 This hotel is superior in cleanliness. // 저 사람은 청결한 느낌을 준다 There's something untainted about him. / He gives one a feeling of purity. **청결히** cleanly; neatly; purely. ¶~ 닦다 wipe (a thing) clean // ~ 하다 clean (up) / make[keep] clean / cleanse / purify // ~해 두다 keep (a thing) clean // 몸을 ~ 해 두다 keep oneself (neat and) clean.

청계(淸溪) a clear[limpid / pellucid] stream[brook].

청과(靑果) fruits and (green) vegetables; green stuff; (미) (garden) truck.
●**청과 시장** a vegetable (and fruit)[a green-grocery] market; a fresh produce market. **청과점** a greengrocery; a vegetable stall; a fruit and vegetable shop; (영) a greengrocer's (shop).

청교도(淸敎徒) a Puritan. ¶~적인 puritanical / puritan.
●**청교도주의** Puritanism. **청교도 혁명** the Puritan Revolution.

청구(請求) [강한 요구] a demand; [요구] a request; [정당한 권리로서의 요구] a claim; asking; a call; an application. ¶손해[상환] ~ a claim for damages[reimbursement] // …의 ~에 따라 (응하여) in compliance[conformity] with (a person's) request / (의기하여) on the request of … // ~를 받아들이다 concede a demand / grant a request // ~를 거절하다 deny[reject / refuse / decline / turn down] a request // ~를 철회하다 withdraw one's claim / take back one's demand // 이 책의 ~는 내 앞으로 해 주시오 Charge this book to my account. **청구하다** ask[apply] for; request; demand; claim; call (up)on (a person to do); (대가 · 요금을) charge. ¶청구할 수 있는 claimable // 청구한 대로 as requested[demanded] // 지불을 ~ demand payment of a person // 견본 [원서 용지]을 ~ ask for a specimen[an application form] // 손해 배상을 ~ claim damages // 청구하는 대로 지불하겠습니다 I will play on demand. // 책의 목록은 청구하는 대로 보내 드립니다 Catalogs of our books will be sent on request. ➔전기료는 매달 내 구좌로 청구[지불]된다 The electric bill is charged directly to[paid from] my checking account every month.
●**청구권** (the right to make) a claim; claim rights. **청구서** a bill; a written claim; an account. ¶손해 배상 ~ a written claim for damages // 지불 ~ a bill (for payment) // ~를 내다 render[send in] an account / submit a bill (to) // ~를 쓰다 write[make] out a bill. **청구액** the amount asked[claimed]. **청구인 / 청구자** an applicant; a demandant; a claimant. ¶~ 없는 은행 예금 an unclaimed[a dormant] bank account.

청국장(淸麴醬) cheonggukjang; bean-paste soup prepared with ground fermented soybeans.

청기(靑旗) a blue flag.
청기와(靑-) a blue[green] tile.
청기와 장수(속담) one who makes a trade secret of his special process[technique].

청널(廳-) a floorboard. ⇨마루청(⑤)마루).

청년(靑年) a young man; a youth; (집합적) the younger [(문어) rising] generation; the youth; young people. ¶20세의 ~ a youth of twenty // 전도 유망한 ~ a promising youth // ~ 실업가 a young businessman // ~다운 웅지(雄志) youthful aspiration // 혈기 왕성한 ~ (집합적) young blood(s) / vigorous youth.
●**청년기**(-期) adolescence. **청년단** a young men's association; a young people's group. **청년 시대** youth; one's younger days[years]; one's salad days. **청년 운동** a youth movement. **청년회** a young men's association. ¶기독교 ~ a Young Men's Christian Association(약어 Y.M.C.A., YMCA) / 기독교 여자 ~ a Young Women's Christian Association(약어 Y.W.C.A., YWCA).

청담하다(淸淡-) 1 [마음이 깨끗하다] honest; upright; clean-handed; disinterested. 2 [맛 · 빛깔이 맑고 엷다] simple; plain; light; mild.
청대콩(靑-) beans not quite ripe.
청동(靑銅) bronze. ¶~의 bronze // ~색의 bronzy // ~의 상 a bronze statue / a statue in bronze.

●**청동기**(-器) bronze ware; a bronze tool. **청동기 시대** [고고] the Bronze Age. **청동 세공** bronze work; a bronze. **청동화**(-貨) a bronze coin.

청둥오리(동) a wild duck; a mallard (duck) (암수 또는 수컷); a greenhead(수컷).

청등(靑燈) a blue electric bulb.

●**청등홍가**(-紅街) the gay quarters; (미) a red-light district.

청딱따구리(靑-) [동] a gray-headed woodpecker; a black-naped green woodpecker.

청람(晴嵐) [아지랑이] shimmering of heated air; a thin haze in a fine day.

청량음료(淸凉飮料) a cooling [refreshing] beverage; (미) a soft [cold] drink; (영) a mineral (water); (속어) the dishwater.

청량제(-劑) a cooler; a refrigerant; a tonic; a restorative; (구어) a pick-me-up. ¶그 자그마한 여자애의 미소 짓는 모습은 한 모금의 ~였다 The sight of that little girl's smile gave me a real lift.

청량하다(淸凉-) clear and cool; cool and refreshing; crisp. ¶청량한 날씨 nice cool weather.

청력(聽力) (the power [sense] of) hearing; hearing ability; audition. ¶~이 좋다 have a keen sense of hearing / ~을 잃다 lose one's hearing / 나이 탓으로 ~이 쇠퇴했다 I lost my hearing with age. / My hearing got weaker with age. // 그는 ~이 약하다 He is hard of hearing.

●**청력 검사** a hearing test. **청력계** an audiometer; a sonometer.

청렴하다(淸廉-) clean-handed; upright; disinterested; incorruptible. ¶청렴한 사람 a man of integrity / a man of pure heart and clean hands / an upright man // 청렴하게 uprightly / incorruptibly.

청록색(靑綠色) a bluish green colo(u)r; bluish green; turquoise blue.

청룡(靑龍) a blue dragon.

●**청룡도**(-刀) an old Chinese broadsword; a falchion.

청루(靑樓) a brothel; a house of ill-fame [ill-repute]; a whorehouse. ¶~에 놀다 frequent brothels.

청류(淸流) a (clear) limpid stream.

청매(靑梅) a green [an unripe] plum.

청맹(과니)(靑盲-) [못 보는 눈] an eye that is blind though it looks perfect; [의] amaurosis; [못 보는 사람] an amaurotic [a batblind] person.

청명(淸明) [24절기의 하나] cheongmyeong; one of the 24 seasonal divisions (=about 5 April).

청명하다(淸明-) fine; clear; fair; bright. ¶청명한 날씨 fine [fair / bright] weather // 청명한 하늘 a clear [crystalline] sky / an azure sky // 지난주에는 청명한 날씨의 계속이었다 We enjoyed fine weather every day last week. / We had clear skies all last week. // 한국의 10월은 항상 청명한 날씨가 계속된다 October in Korea is always a month of beautiful weather.

청문(聽聞) audience; audition. **청문하다** listen (to); hear.

청문회 a (public) hearing.

청밀(淸蜜) honey; nectar. ⇨꿀

청바지(靑-) (blue) jeans. ¶~를 입은 in blue jeans / jeaned (teenager).

청백리(淸白吏) a clean-handed [an uncorrupted] government officer.

청백전(靑白戰) a contest [tourney] between two groups [between the blue and white camps].

청백하다(淸白-) clean(-handed); upright; irreproachable; uncorrupted; uncorruptible; innocent; spotless; stainless; pure. ¶청백한 사람 a man of integrity / a person with a clean record // 그는 너무 청백하여 꺼림한 일은 않는다 He has too much integrity to get involved in shady deals. **청백히** innocently; purely; honestly.

청부(請負) (a) contract (for work). ¶~로 by contract // ~를 맡다 (have a) contract (for the work) / receive a contract (for the work from a person) // ~를 주다 put out (the work) to contract / give out a contract (for the work) // 새 공사는 전부 ~를 준다 All the new work will be put out to contract.

●**청부 계약** a contract (with). **청부 공사** contract work; construction work done on contract. **청부 살인** murder by contract. **청부 살인자** a hired [professional] assassin [killer / murderer] / (속어) a hit man. **청부업자** a contractor. ¶건축 ~ a housebuilder / a building contractor // 토목 ~ an engineering contractor. **청부 입찰** a contract tender.

청빈하다(淸貧-) be poor but honest. ¶청빈한 생활을 하다 live [carry] a poor but honest life.

청사(靑史) history; annals. ¶이름을 ~에 남기다 leave one's name in history / 이름이 ~에 빛나다 be famous in history / one's name is immortalized in history.

청사(靑絲) blue thread. ⇨청실

청사(廳舍) a government office building.

청사등롱(靑紗燈籠) 1 a lantern covered with green silk in the middle and with red silk at both ends. 2 (벼슬아치의) a lantern covered with green silk carried by second and third grade officers.

청사진(靑寫眞) a blueprint. ¶새 빌딩의 ~을 만들다 make a blueprint for the new building // 선진 조국의 ~을 제시하다 present a blueprint for the advanced fatherland.

청사초롱(靑紗-) a lantern covered with green silk in the middle and with red silk at both ends; a lantern covered with green silk carried by second and third grade officers. ⇨청사등롱

청산(靑山) green mountains [hills]; blue mountains.

●**청산유수** eloquence; fluency. ¶~같이 with great fluency [volubility] / very fluently // 말이 ~다 be very eloquent / be a fluent speaker.

청산(靑酸) [화] hydrocyanic [prussic] acid; hydrogen cyanide.

●**청산가리** potassium cyanide. **청산 가스** hydrocyanic acid gas.

청산(淸算) 1 [채무·채권 관계를 매듭지음] settlement; clearance; squaring [settling / clearing up] accounts; clearing (off); (회사 등의) liquidation; winding up. **청산하다** liquidate; wind up; clear off [up]; settle. ¶어음을 ~ settle a bill // 셈을 ~ settle [square] accounts (with a person) // 부채를 청산하고 해산하다 (사람이) liquidate [wind up] (a

company) / (회사가) go into liquidation.// 그는 땅을 팔아 부채를 청산했다 He cleared off his debts by selling his land.// 회사가 잘되지 않아 청산할 수밖에 없었다 The company failed and had to go into liquidation. // 부채를 청산하니 남는 것이 없었다 Nothing was left when we had cleared off our debts. // 계산은 이달 말에 청산하기로 하자 Let's close[settle up] the accounts at the end of this month. 2 [죄·과거 등을 결말지어 없앰]. **청산하다** cleanse; become decent. ¶죄를 ~ atone for one's sin // 죽음으로써 죄를 ~ commit suicide in atonement for one's crime / atone [pay] for one's sin with one's life // 과거를 청산하고 다시 출발하자 Let's bury the past and start again. // 그녀는 애인과의 관계를 청산했다 She cleaned up accounts with her lover and left him.
● **청산 거래** [경] future transaction. **청산 계정** an open account. **청산액** an adjusted amount. **청산인** a liquidator; a balancer(청산서를 만드는).

청상과부(青孀寡婦) a young widow.

청색(青色) a blue colo(u)r; green or blue; azure. ¶짙은 ~ deep[dark] blue // 신호는 ~ 이다 The (traffic) light is green.

청서(淸書) copying fair. ⇨ ˙ 정서(淨書).

청소(淸掃) cleaning; sweeping(쓸기); dusting (먼지떨기); scrubbing(걸레질); (거리의) street cleaning; scavenge. ¶대~ (do) a general house cleaning // 도로 ~ street cleaning / scavengery / garbage disposal // 모든 방이 ~ 가 잘되어 있다 All the rooms are kept clean and tidy. **청소하다** clean; sweep; dust; scrub; scavenge(길을). ¶방을 ~ clean a room // 집 안을 ~ clean up a house / have [do] a house cleaning // 오물을 ~ collect [clear away] the night soil // 바닥을 걸레로 닦아 ~ wipe the floor // 방을 깨끗이 청소해 두어라 Give this room a good cleaning [sweeping].
● **청소기** a cleaner. ¶전기 ~ a vacuum cleaner // 그 방을 내가 지금 막 ~로 깨끗이 했다 I have just vacuum cleaned[vacuumed] that room. **청소 도구** dusting[scrubbing] things; cleaning equipment. **청소부** (-夫) a cleaner; a sweeper; (도로의) a street cleaner; a scavenger; (쓰레기의) a dustman; a garbageman. **청소차** a scavenger's[refuse] cart; a garbage wagon [truck].

청소년(青少年) young boys and girls; teenagers; adolescents; juveniles; the youth; the younger generation; young people.
● **청소년 범죄** juvenile delinquency[crimes]. ¶요즘 흉악한 ~가 급증하고 있다 The felonious juvenile crimes have been a sharp rise these days.

청송(青松) a green pine (tree).
청수(淸水) clear water.
청순하다(淸純-) pure (and innocent). ¶청순한 소녀 a pure girl / an innocent girl // 청순한 마음 a pure heart // 청순한 처녀 a chaste maiden // 그들의 사랑은 ~ Their love is pure.

청승 signs of a wretched fate. ¶~을 떨다 act like fortune's orphan / try to work on (another's) compassion.
● **청승꾸러기** a person with bad luck written on his face; a sad-looking person; (속어) a loser.

청승맞다 (서술적) be suggestive of ill luck; be doomed to misery; [애틋하다] miserable; wretched; poor; pitiful; ominously; sorrowful. ¶청승맞게 울다 wail ominously // 얘기하는 투가 ~ have a plaintive way of speaking.

청신경(聽神經) [생] the auditory[acoustic] nerve.
청신남(淸信男) a male Buddhist.
청신녀(淸信女) a female Buddhist.
청신하다(淸新-) new and fresh. ¶청신한 맛 freshness // 청신한 시풍(詩風) a new and fresh style in poetry // 청신한 맛이 없다 lack freshness / be stale // 그의 작품에는 청신한 맛이 하나도 없다 I can't find nothing new in his work.

청신호(青信號) 1 [진행을 나타내는 교통 신호] a green light; a green traffic signal; a go signal. ¶~가 켜져 있다 The light is on for "Go." // ~로 바뀌었을 때 횡단보도를 건너라 Cross at the crosswalk when the light is [turns] green. // ~가 나오면 가도 된다 You may go on the green light[when the light turns green]. 2 [시작의 순조로운 징조]. ¶개발 계획에 ~가 떨어졌다 A green light[The go-ahead] was given to the development project.

청실(青-) blue[green] thread[yarn].
청아하다(淸雅-) elegant; refined; clear; mellifluous. ¶청아한 목소리 a clear ringing voice.

청야(淸夜) a bright[clear] night.
청약(請約) subscription (for stocks). **청약하다** subscribe (for bonds / shares); send a subscription.
● **청약금** subscription money. **청약서** a written description; (미) (용지) a subscription blank[(영) form]. **청약자** a subscriber. ¶~에 불리한 보험 약관 the insurance terms disadvantageous to the subscribers.

청어(青魚) [동] a herring. ¶훈제 ~ a red herring / (배를 갈라 처리한) a kippered herring / a kipper / (통째 말린) a bloater.
● **청어 알** herring roe.

청옥(青玉) [광] sapphire.
청와대(青瓦臺) the Blue House; the (Korean) Presidential residence; the official residence of Korean President.
청요리(淸料理) Chinese dishes. ⇨ 중화요리
청우(晴雨) fair or rainy[foul] weather; sunshine and rain. ¶~에 관계없이 rain[wet] or shine / whether it may rain or not / in all weathers.
● **청우계** a barometer; a weatherglass; a rain glass.

청운(青雲) 1 [푸른 구름] blue clouds. 2 [높은 지위나 벼슬] high ranks. ¶~의 꿈을 지닌 청년들 ambitious young men / ~의 뜻을 품다 have lofty ambitions / (문어) aspire to greatness.

청원(請願) a petition; an appeal (to the authorities). ¶~을 들어주다 grant a petition. **청원하다** petition (the government for something); make a petition (to); present [submit] a petition (to); file[lodge] a petition (with the House of Representatives); hand[send] in a petition (to); apply (for). ¶감형을 ~ petition[send a petition to] (the authorities) for a commutation of a sentence // 나는 조세 문제를 청원했다 I peti-

청원하다

tioned [appealed to] the authorities for exemption from taxation.∥그 제도를 폐지해 달라고 정부에 청원했다 They petitioned the government for the abolition of the system [that the system be abolished].

● 청원 경찰관 a policeman specially detailed to protect (a person's) body. 청원서 a (written) petition [application]. 청원자 a petitioner; an applicant.

청원하다(請願-) ask for [seek / invoke] (a person's) assistance; seek (a person's) help; call in (a person's) aid; appeal [make an appeal] (to a person) for help.

청음(淸音) 1 [맑은 소리] a clear voice. 2 [언] a voiceless [an unvoiced] sound. ⇨ ˚안울림소리

청음기(聽音機) a sound locator [detector]; (수중의) a hydrophone.

청자(靑瓷·靑磁) *cheongja*; celadon porcelain; a type of Korean porcelain with a translucent, pale green glaze. ¶고려 ~ Goryeo celadon (porcelain)∥~ 꽃병 a vase of celadon porcelain.

● 청자색 celadon green.

청자(聽者) a listener.

청장(廳長) a director (of a government office).

청절(淸節) [정조] chastity; [절조] fidelity; faithfulness.

청정(淸淨) purity; cleanness; cleanliness. ¶~ 결백한 마음 a pure and undefiled heart∥ 순박한 처녀 a pure and innocent girl. 청정하다 pure; clean; stainless; undefiled; immaculate. ¶청정한 공기 pure, fresh air∥청정하게 하다 purify / cleanse. 청정히 purely; cleanly; immaculately; stainlessly.

● 청정 야채 clean vegetables. 청정 재배 parasite-free cultivation; sanitary [germ-free] culture; (수경법) hydroponics.

청조(靑鳥) 1 [동] a broad-billed roller. ⇨ 파랑새1 2 [반가운 사자·편지] a messenger (bearing good news).

청주(淸酒) *cheongju*; clear strained rice wine; refined rice wine. ¶특급 ~ special-grade rice wine.

청죽(靑竹) [푸른 대나무] a green bamboo; a newly cut bamboo(갓 벤); unseasoned bamboo(마르지 않은).

청중(聽衆) [집합적] an audience; an attendance; hearers; auditors. ¶많은 [적은] ~ a large [small] audience [attendance]∥약 5천 명의 ~ an audience of about 5,000∥~을 끌다 attract [draw] an audience∥~을 열광시키다 arouse [move] one's audience to enthusiasm∥~이 많았다 [적었다] There was a large [small] audience.∥그는 ~을 향해서 연설했다 He addressed the audience.

● 청중석 an auditorium; an audience seat.

청지기 a steward; a chamberlain; an attendant to a high official.

청직하다(淸直-) honest; upright; just; clean-handed. ¶청직한 사람 a man of integrity / an upright man.

청진(聽診) [의] auscultation; stethoscopy. 청진하다 auscultate; stethoscope; examine with a stethoscope.

● 청진기 a stethoscope. ¶~를 대다 apply a stethoscope (to)∥~로 진찰하다 stethoscope / examine with a stethoscope.

청참외(靑-) [식] a green melon.

청천(靑天) a blue [an azure] sky; the blue heavens.

● **청천벽력**(-霹靂) a bolt from [out of] the blue; a thunderbolt from a clear sky; a sudden and unexpected accident. ¶~같이 like a bolt from the blue / like a thunderbolt ∥그 소식은 그녀에게 ~이었다 The news struck her like a bolt from the blue.

청천(淸泉) a clear [crystal] spring.

청천(晴天) fine [fair] weather; a cloudless [clear / bright] sky.

청첩장(請牒狀) a letter of invitation; an invitation (card); (구어) an invite. ¶결혼 ~ a wedding invitation∥~을 내다 send [issue] an invitation (card) (to)∥~을 받다 have [receive] an invitation (from a person) / be invited.

청청하다(靑靑-) freshly [vividly] green; fresh and green; verdant. ¶청청한 대 bright green bamboos∥산들은 초목으로 ~ The hills are robed in green [covered with verdure].

청초(靑草) 1 [푸른 풀] green grass. 2 [풋담배] green tobacco.

청초하다(淸楚-) neat and clean; tidy; trim. ¶그녀는 검소하지만 청초한 옷차림을 하고 있었다 She is simply but neatly dressed. 청초히 neatly; tidily; smartly.

청춘(靑春) one's youth; the springtime [springtide] of life; the bloom [heyday] of youth. ¶꽃다운 ~ the bloom of (one's) youth∥~ 시절에 in one's youth / in one's youthful days [years] / in the flower [bloom] of (one's) youth∥~의 꿈과 야망 the dreams and ambitions of youth∥~의 피 young blood / the hot blood of youth∥~의 피가 불타다 burn with the fine of youth∥그는 ~의 정열을 일에 쏟아 부었다 He concentrated on his work with youthful enthusiasm.

● 청춘기(-期) adolescence; puberty. 청춘사업 love; amour. 청춘 시대 one's youth; one's youthful days [teens]; the morning [prime] of youth.

청출어람(靑出於藍) excelling [surpassing] one's master [teacher].

청취(聽取) listening; hearing; audition; [라디오] listening-in. 청취하다 [듣다] listen to; hear; (라디오를) listen (in) (to the radio). ¶라디오를 ~ listen to the radio∥증언을 ~ hear evidence∥무선 전신을 ~ pick up a wireless message∥위원회는 그에게서 사정을 청취했다 The committee heard what he had to say (for himself) [his explanation of the matter].

● 청취율 program (listener) ratings. 청취자 (라디오의) a (radio) listener. 청취 테스트 an audition. ¶~를 하다 audition (a person) / give an audition (to)∥~를 받다 audition.

청 코너(靑-) [권투] the challenger's corner.

청탁(淸濁) 1 [맑음과 흐림] purity and impurity. 2 [옳음과 그름] good and evil. ¶~을 가리다 discriminate good and bad∥~을 가리지 않다 be so broad-minded as to be tolerant of all sorts of men.

청탁(請託) [부탁] asking; begging; a request; a favor; [의뢰] trust; commission. ¶긴한 ~ an urgent [important] request∥~을 거절하다 reject [refuse] (a person's) request∥~을 받다 be asked [solicited] (to do)∥~이 하나 있습니다 I have a favor to ask of you.∥장관 은 어떤 업자로부터도 편의를 봐 달라는 ~을 받은 바 없다고 주장했다 The minister insisted that no manufacturer had ever solicited special favors from him. **청탁하다** request; ask (a person to do); beg; [의뢰하다] entrust (a person with a matter); commission (a person to do). ¶취직 자리를 ~ ask (a person) to get a job (for).

청태(青苔) 1 [푸른 이끼] moss [lichen]. ¶~가 낀 돌 stones covered with green moss. 2 [김] green laver.

청포(青布) bluish hemp cloth.

청포묵(青泡−) mung-bean jelly. ⇨녹두묵(⇨녹두).

청풍(清風) a cool [refreshing] breeze.
● **청풍명월** a cool breeze and a bright moon.

청하다(請−) 1 [부탁하다] ask; request; beg; call upon (a person) to (do); pray for; entreat; supplicate (him for pardon); apply; appeal; petition; sue for; solicit (for); plead for. ¶청컨대 (if you) please / I pray / I beg / I hope [wish] / It is to be hoped (that) // 청하지도 않았는데 unasked / without being asked // 도움을 ~ appeal (to a person) for aid / ask for (a person's) assistance / call for help // 면회를 ~ ask for [request / seek / solicit] an interview (with) // 연설을 해 달라고 ~ call on [upon] (a person) to make a speech // 출석해 주기를 ~ ask [request] (a person) to attend // 노래를 한 곡 ~ ask for a song from (a person) / call (up)on (a person) to sing // 그는 누구든 도움을 청하기만 하면 곧 도와준다 He is ever ready to help all who appeal to him for help.
2 [달라고 하다] beg; solicit. ¶무엇을 (달라고) ~ ask [beg / solicit] (a person) for something / apply (a person) for something.
3 [초대하다] invite; ask; engage; call in; send for. ¶청해서 at [by] (a person's) invitation // 청한 [불은] 손님 an invited [uninvited / uncalled-for] guest // 집으로 ~ ask (a person) to one's home // 의사를 ~ send for [call in] a doctor // 전문가를 ~ engage the service of an expert // 그것은 스스로 화를 청하는 것이다 With that he is inviting disaster of his own accord.
4 (잠을). ¶잠을 청해도 잠이 오지 않아서 unable to obtain the sleep for which one longs // 잠을 ~ try to sleep.

청허(聽許) permission; grant; sanction; approval. **청허하다** accept; assent to; approve; sanction; grant.

청혼(請婚) a proposal [an offer] of marriage (to); courtship; addresses. ¶~을 **승낙하다** accept (a person's) proposal of marriage / give one's hand (to) // ~을 **거절하다** decline (a person's) proposal of marriage. **청혼하다** propose (marriage) (to a girl); make an offer of marriage to (a girl); court; ask [sue] for (a lady's) hand; pay one's addresses to (a lady). ¶정 씨 집에 ~ propose to the Jeong family // 돈을 노리고 ~ seek (a woman's) hand in marriage for money // 그는 그녀에게 청혼했다 He proposed (marriage) to her. // 아직까지 그녀에게 청혼하는 사람이 없었다 No man has asked for her hand.
● **청혼자** a suitor (for a woman's hand).

청혼(請魂) [불] invocation of the spirit (of a dead person). **청혼하다** invoke [summon] the spirit.

청홍(색) (青紅色) blue and red.

체[1] [가루를 치거나 거르는 기구] a sieve; a sifter; a riddle(굵은); a grate(네모틀에 매운); a jig(선광용의); a griddle. ¶~로 **치다** sieve / sift / screen / weed out / put [pass / powder] (something) through a sieve [sifter] / sift (the flour from the bran).

체[2] [꾸민 태도] (false) show; make-believe; pretense; affectation; simulation; dissimulation; an air. ¶아는 ~ a knowing air [aspect]. **체하다** pretend; affect; feign; pose (as); put on a show of (doing); set up for (a gentleman); pose as (a rich man); sham; fake; make believe; make a pretense [feint / show] of (doing); make as if; assume [put on] an air of (a scholar); simulate; dissimulate. ¶잘난 체하는 말투 an affected way of speech // 못 들은 ~ pretend [make believe] not to hear (a person) // 아는 ~ pretend to know / assume an air of wisdom / set up for a wise man // 모르는 ~ pretend not to know / (문어) feign ignorance // 미친 ~ feign madness / pretend to be insane // 죽은 ~ feign [sham / simulate] death // 센 ~ pretend to be brave / bluff / put on a show of bravado // 끝까지 모르는 ~ wear an air of innocence throughout // 안에 [집에] 없는 ~ pretend not to be in [at home] / pretend to be out // 몸이 아픈 ~ pretend to be ill / feign illness // 나는 그 일을 모르는 체했다 I pretended not to know anything about it. / (문어) I assumed an air of [feigned] ignorance about it. // 거미는 위험할 때 흔히 죽은 체한다 A spider often plays dead when in danger. // 그는 예술가인 체하고 있다 He has the air of a true artist about him. // 그는 친절한 체하면서 반드시 무언가를 꾀하다 He's always scheming something under the pretense of kindness. // 그는 수염 같은 것을 길러서 음악가인 체하고 있었다 Wearing a mustache, he posed as a musician. // 그녀는 내 곁을 지나갈 때 모른 체했다 She cut me [ignored me / pretended not to know me] when she passed me. // 선생님이 누가 창문을 깨뜨렸냐고 물었을 때 최 군은 모른 체했다 When the teacher asked who had broken the window, Choe pretended ignorance [feigned innocence]. // 그녀는 정숙한 아내인 체했다 She acted the role of [pretended to be] a faithful wife. // 그는 점잖은 체하고 있다 He has the air of a gentleman [something of the gentleman in his manner]. // 그는 늘 잘난 체하고 있다 He always assumes [puts on] an air of importance. // 그는 예술가인 체한다 He poses as an artist. // 그는 다만 순진한 체할 뿐이다 He is only affecting innocence [acting innocent]. // 그는 어른인 체하지만 아직 어린애다 Precocious as he is, he is still (just) a child. // 그는 짐짓 대단한 사람인 체하며 엄숙하게 말문을 열었다 He began to talk solemnly, with an air of importance. // 그는 마약 밀수 경위를 알고 있는데도 모른 체했다 Even though he knew about how the drugs were being smuggled, he pretended not to know [feigned ignorance / (구어) played dumb]. // 그는 친구의 곤경을 모른 체했다 He kept his eyes shut [closed] to his friend's plight. / He turned a blind eye [deaf ear] to his friend's predicament. // 그는 사람들의 비난을 못 들은 체했다 He pretended not to hear other people's criticisms. // 그는 아는 체하며 나에게 대답했다 He answered me with a knowing look[in a knowing way / knowingly]. / When he replied he looked as if he knew more than I did. // 그녀는 귀부인인 체했다 She pretended to be[put on the airs of] a lady of rank. // 그는 (집에) 있으면서 일부러 없는 체했다 He pretended to be out. // 그는 그것을 전연 몰랐던 것처럼 놀란 체했다 He acted surprised just as if he knew nothing about it. // 그는 무엇이나 아는 체한다 He pretends to know everything about everything. // 그렇게 아는 체하면서 말하지 마라 Don't talk in such a knowing manner. / Don't speak so knowingly.

체³ 〔탄식할 때 내는 소리〕 tut!; shucks!; phew!; pshaw!; fie!; tsk!; hang it all!

체(體) 〔본보기·방식〕 a style; a form; a fashion. ¶~가 잡히다 take[get into] shape / take form // ~을 본받다 imitate a style.

체(滯) 〔한〕 indigestion; dyspepsia.

-체(體) 1 〔몸〕 the body; physique; build; frame; constitution. ¶건강~ a healthy body // 기업~ an enterprise. 2 〔수〕 a solid (body). ¶4면~ a tetrahedron // 8면~ an octahedron.

체감(遞減) successive diminution; decrease in order; gradual decrease. ¶수익 ~의 법칙 the law of diminishing returns / 효용 ~ diminishing returns[utility]. 체감하다 decrease in order; diminish successively.

● **체감 속도** (a) slowdown speed.

체감(體感) a feeling in the body; a bodily sensation.

● **체감 온도** sensible temperature.

체격(體格) a physique; (physical) constitution; frame; (physical) make; (a) (physical) build; physical features; structure of body; setup. ¶가냘픈 ~ a slight build / a delicate physique // 강철 같은 ~ an iron constitution // 탄탄한[짱짱한] ~ a compact[well-knit; well-set] frame // 탄탄하지 못한 ~ loose build // 중간 ~ medium build[stature] // 딱 벌어진 ~의 남자 a man with a strong [powerful] build / a burly, thickset man // 이 건장한 사람 a man of sturdy [stalwart] build // ~이 좋다 have a good constitution [fine physique] / be well-built[-constructed] // ~이 나쁘다 have a weak constitution / have a poor physique // 그와 나는 거의 비슷한 ~이다 He and I are pretty much of the same build. // 그는 ~이 날씬하다 He is slightly built. / He is slight of build.

체결(締結) conclusion. ¶평화 조약의 ~ the conclusion of a peace treaty. 체결하다 conclude; contract. ¶계약을 ~ agree on a contract / enter into an agreement // 차관을 ~ contract a loan // 10억 원의 차관 협정을 체결했다 A billion won loan agreement was concluded. // 우리는 100만 원에 매매 계약을 체결했다[타결지었다] We struck bargain[We came to terms] at a million won. // 우리나라는 미국과 강화 조약을 체결했다 Our country concluded a peace treaty with the United States.

체경(體鏡) a full-length[large] mirror; a large looking glass.

체계(體系) a system; an organization; a scheme. ¶철학 ~ a system of philosophy / a philosophical system // 자금 ~ a wage system // ~적(으로) systematic(ally) // ~가 선 논문 a well-organized treatise // ~적인 조사 systematic inquiry // 사상 ~를 세우다 formulate a system of thought // ~화하다 systematize // 완전한 ~를 이루고 있다 form a complete system // 그의 진술은 ~가 서 있지 않다 His presentation is unsystematic [lacks system].

체공(滯空) staying[remaining] the air. 체공하다 stay[remain] in the air.

● **체공 비행** an endurance flight. **체공 시간** duration of flight.

체구(體軀) the body; the frame; (a) (physical) build. ¶~가 당당한 사람 a man with a magnificent build / a magnificently built man // ~가 우람하다 have a magnificent physique / be huge of limb // ~가 건장하다 be of sturdy build.

체급(體級) 〔체〕 weight. ¶권투의 ~ boxing weight.

체기(滯氣) an indication[a symptom / a touch] of indigestion[dyspepsia]. ¶~가 있다 have a touch of indigestion / suffer from slight dyspepsia.

체납(滯納) nonpayment; arrearage; default (of payment); failure to pay; delinquency (in payment). ¶세금의 ~ nonpayment of taxes // 그는 세금 ~으로 압류를 당했다 He had his property attached[seized] because he had failed to pay his taxes. 체납하다 fail to pay; default; be remiss in one's payment; be delinquent in payment; be in arrear(s) with the payment; let (taxes) fall in arrears. ¶회비를 ~ let one's membership dues fall into arrears // 세금을 ~ fail to pay[default in paying] one's taxes // 나는 세금을 체납한 적이 없다 I had never had my taxes in arrears. → 세금이 체납되어 있다 I am behind[am in arrears] with my taxes. / My taxes are over due[in arrears].

● **체납금** arrears; arrearages. **체납액** an amount in arrears. **체납자** a defaulter; a delinquent; (세금의) a tax delinquent; a delinquent taxpayer. ¶~ 명부 a delinquent list. **체납 처분** disposition for failure to pay (taxes); coercive collection. ¶~에 의한 압류 attachment for default // ~을 하다 institute a process (against a person) for the recovery of taxes in arrears / make an attachment (on a person's property) for unpaid taxes.

체내(體內) the interior of the body. ¶~의 in the body[system] / intestine / internal // ~의 당분 body[tissue] sugar // ~에 에너지를 비축하다 save[store up] energy in the body.

● **체내 수정** 〔동〕 internal[entosomatic] fertilization.

체념(諦念) 〔희망을 버림〕 abandonment; renunciation; 〔운명이라고 생각하기〕 resignation; reconciliation. 체념하다 abandon; resign; reconcile. ¶실종[사망]한 것이라고 ~ give up (a person) for lost[dead] // (환자를) 살지 못할 것으로 ~ give over (a patient) for dead // 도리 없다고 ~ abide by[resign oneself to] the inevitable / submit to necessity // 그는 깨끗이 체념할 줄 모른다 He doesn't know when to give up. / He is a bad loser. // 그는 모든 것을 운명으로 체념했다 He accepted[resigned himself to] it as his fate. // 그는 대학에 갈 수 없는 것에 대해 좀체로 체념할 수 없었다 He couldn't reconcile himself to not going to college. // 사람이란 깨끗이 체념할 줄 알아야 한다 A person must know when to give up.∥나는 그것이 내 운명이라고 체념했다 I resigned myself to it as my lot.∥나는 제2지망을 택하기로 체념했다 I was reconciled to my second choice.∥그녀는 남편이 죽은 것으로 체념했다 She gave her husband up for dead.∥나는 영국으로 가려던 생각을 포기하고 체념했다 I gave up [abandoned] the idea of going to England.∥그는 사업에서의 손해에 대한 아쉬움을 체념하기가 어려웠다 He could not get over[accept] the loss in his business.

체능(體能) physical aptitude[ability].
● 체능 검사 a physical aptitude test.

체득(體得) 1 [체험] realization; experience. 체득하다 realize; learn (from experience). 2 [습득] comprehension; [숙달] mastery. 체득하다 comprehend; master. ¶사도(斯道)의 비법을 ～ master the mysteries of the art∥그는 스키 타는 요령을 드디어 체득했다 He finally mastered the art of skiing.

체력(體力) physical strength; stamina; the strength of one's body. ¶～의 양성 physical training / development of physical strength∥～을 기르다 build up one's physical strength / strengthen one's body∥～이 있다[없다] have[lack] physical strength∥～이 쇠약해졌다 I don't have as much stamina as I used to.∥원거리 수영은 현재의 네 ～으로는 무리다 A long-distance swim would be too much of a strain on you in your present physical condition.∥～에 있어서는 아무도 그를 따를 사람이 없다 No one can equal him in strength.
● 체력장(-章) the physical strength measurement.

체류(滯留) a stay; sojourn. ¶영국 ～ 중에 during my stay in English∥그는 유럽 ～ 중, 음악 콩쿠르에 입상했다 He won a prize in a musical contest during his stay in Europe. 체류하다 stay; make a (long) stay (at); remain; sojourn; stop(잠시 동안). ¶숙부 댁에 ～ stay with one's uncle[at one's uncle's]∥호텔에 ～ stay at hotel / stop in a hotel∥장기간 ～ make a long[an extended] stay [sojourn]∥그는 호텔에 장기 체류했다 He made a long stay at the hotel.∥나는 하와이에 1주일 동안 체류할 작정이다 I will stay in Hawaii for a week.
● 체류 기간 the length of one's visit[stay]. 체류자 a sojourner; a (hotel) guest; a visitor; a stayer. 체류지 a place of sojourn.

체머리 shaking one's head to and fro; a shaky head; spasmodic head-shaking. ¶～를 흔들다 shake one's head chronically / [싫증 나다] be sickened (of) / (구어) be sick and tired (of) / be fed up (with).

체면(體面) [면목] face; honor; [위신] dignity; prestige; [명성] reputation; a good name; [외관] appearances; decency. ¶～이 서는 face-saving (concession)∥～이 깎이는[손상되는] undignified / compromising / disgraceful∥～을 지키기 위한 방책 face-saving formulas∥～을 위하여 for appearance's sake / for form's[decency's] sake∥～을 무릅쓰고 without caring about decency∥～을 차리다 preserve[keep up / save] appearances∥～도 차리지 않고 알랑거리다 flirt openly[without any regard for decency]∥～에 관계되다 concern[touch] one's honor∥～을 중히 여기다 stress[be greatly concerned about] appearances∥～을 지키다 keep up appearances / save (one's) face∥～을 잃다 lose (one's) face∥～상 그들은 별거를 하지 않고 있다 They live together for the sake of appearances.∥그는 마누라 앞에서 짐짓 ～을 차렸다 He made it look right before his wife.∥그것은 내 ～에 관계된다 That would look bad. / That would hurt my reputation.∥지금은 ～을 걱정할 때가 아니다 This is no time for worrying about appearances. / We can't afford to worry about niceties now.∥우리 미혼모가 되어야 하니 ～이 서지 않게 되었다 We feel it's a disgrace[(문어) unseemly] that our daughter should be an unmarried mother.∥그녀의 음악 애호는 ～치레뿐이다 Her love of music is all show[just a pose].∥그는 (사나이로서의) ～을 잃었다 He lost face (as a man).∥그런 곳에 자주 드나들면 네 ～에 영향을 미칠 것이다 It would be beneath [It would reflect on] your dignity to frequent such a place.∥이것으로 그의 ～이 서게 될 것이다 This will be to his credit. / This will bring him credit.∥그의 ～을 생각해서 잠자코 있기로 하자 I will keep it (a) secret to save his face[honor].∥여자 친구 앞에서 ～을 잃다니 남자로서 참 무슨 꼴이냐 What a trial for a man to lose face[his dignity] in the presence of his girlfriend!∥그가 그렇게 한 것은 ～을 위해서이다 He did that (just) for appearances[to save face].∥그의 불찰로 나는 ～을 잃었다 I lost face because of his misconduct.∥～ 문제는 차치하고, 도의상으로도 용서할 수 없는 일이다 Apart from the question of honor, it is unpardonable from the moral point of view.∥그렇다면 내 ～은 어떻게 되나 How can I save my face[honor] then?

체모(體毛) hair.
체모(體貌) face; dignity. ⇒체면.
체벌(體罰) corporal[physical / bodily] punishment. ¶심한 ～을 가하다 inflict severe corporal punishment on (a person)∥～을 받다 suffer corporal punishment.

체불(滯拂) a delay in payment; delayed payment (of wages).
● 체불 임금 back pay[wages]; (pay) wages in arrears; wage arrears; delayed pay. ¶～의 청산을 요구하다 call for clearance of back wages.

체비지(替費地) a substitute lot; substitute land; an area of land secured by the authorities in recompense of development outlay.

체색(體色) (동물의) the color of the body.
체세포(體細胞) [생] a somatic [body].
체스 [서양 장기] chess. ¶～의 말 a chessman∥～를 하는 사람 a chess player∥～를 하다 play chess.
● 체스 판 a chessboard.

체신(遞信) transmission through stages; [통신] communications.

체액(體液) [생] body fluids; (중세의 생리학에서) a humor; (영) a humour. ¶사(四)～ the four cardinal humors.
● 체액 병리학 humoral pathology.

체언(體言) [언] indeclinable parts of speech in Korean grammar; the substantives.

체열(體熱) body heat; (동물의) animal heat. ¶～을 발산하다 give off body heat.

체온(體溫) (body) temperature; body heat. ¶～을 재다 take one's temperature∥～이 높다

체외 [낮다] have a high [low] temperature // 그의 ~이 내려갔다[올라갔다] His temperature fell [rose]. // 그의 ~은 정상이다 His temperature is normal.
- 체온계 a (clinical) thermometer. ¶항내(肛內) ~ a rectal thermometer.

체외(體外) ¶ ~로 배설되다 be discharged from one's body.
- 체외 수정 external fertilization.

체위(體位) 1 [체격] a physical standard; physical condition; physique. ¶평균 ~ the physical average (in the country) // 젊은이들의 ~가 현저히 향상되었다 The physique [physical build] of the younger generation has improved remarkably. 2 [자세] a posture; a position of the body.
- 체위 향상 [저하] improvement [deterioration] of physical condition.

체육(體育) physical training [culture]; the physical upbuilding (of a nation); (교과명) physical education; (체조) gymnastics; (운동) athletics.
- 체육관 a gymnasium (pl. ~s, -sia); (미국구어) a gym. 체육 대회 an athletic meeting. 체육 선생 a physical education teacher. 체육 특기자 an athletic meritocrat. 체육회 an athletic association [club]. ¶대한 ~ the Korea Amateur Athletic Association(약어 K.A.A.A.).

체인 a chain; (자동차의) a tire chain. ¶타이어 ~ a tire chain // 문 안쪽에 ~을 고정시키다 fasten a door from the inside with a chain // 대설 때문에 ~을 감지 않은 차는 고속도로 통행을 허용하지 않았다 Because of the heavy snowfall, no cars without (tire) chains [(영) (snow) chains] were allowed to enter the expressway.
- 체인 스토어 (미) a chain store; (영) a multiple shop [store].

체인지 [야구] a change.
- 체인지 오브 페이스 (야구에서) a change-up; a change of pace.

체재(滯在) a stay; sojourn. ⇨체류

체재(體裁) form; style; [겉보기] appearance; show; [만듦새] getup; format(책의). ¶논문의 ~ the form of the dissertation // 같은 ~의 uniform / of the same pattern // ~가 좋다 be of good style / be seemly [presentable] / look nice [presentable] // ~가 나쁘다 do not look nice / cut a sorry figure / be unsightly // ~를 갖추다 have proper form [style].

체적(體積) volume; cubic volume [content(s)]; cubage; [수] solid measure; [용적] capacity. ¶물체의 ~ the volume of a body // ~을 구하다 find the volume (of) / cube // 용기의 ~은 2세제곱미터이다 The volume of this container is two cubic meters.
- 체적계 a volumenometer; a stereometer. 체적 팽창 cubical expansion.

체절(體節) [동] an arthromere; a metamere; a somite; a segment. ¶~의 arthromeric / metameric / somitic / somital / segmental.
- 체절 기관 a segmental organ.

체제(體制) [조직 체계] a system; [구조] a structure; an order; a setup; organization; formation; (몸의) anatomy. ¶경제 ~ an economic structure // 구~ the old order [system / structure] // 전시 ~ a war footing // 정치 ~ a political system [dispensation] // 자본주의 ~ the capitalistic structure // 현 ~ the existing structure / the Establishment // 국내 ~를 강화하다 strengthen the internal structure of the nation // 그 나라는 전시 ~하에 있다 The country has been reorganized on a war footing.

체조(體操) gymnastics; physical [gymnastic] exercises; (미) gym work [exercises]; (영) jerks. ¶기계 ~ apparatus gymnastics // 라디오 ~ radio gymnastic exercises // 맨손 [도수] ~ gymnastic exercises without apparatus / (경기 종목) free standing exercises // 미용 ~ calisthenics / aesthetic gymnastics // 율동 ~ rhythmic gymnastics [calisthenics]. 체조하다 practice gymnastics; have gymnastic exercises.
- 체조 경기 gymnastics competition. 체조 기구 gymnastic appliances [apparatus / gear]. 체조 선수 a gymnast.

체중(體重) [몸무게] the weight (of one's body); one's body weight. ¶~의 증가 an increase in weight // ~의 감소 [저하] weight loss // ~의 조절 reduction of one's weight // ~을 재다 weigh oneself (on the scales) // ~을 외발에 싣다 put one's weight on one's left leg // ~을 감량하다 reduce [lessen] one's weight / (문어) reduce / get one's weight down // ~이 얼마예요 How much do you weight? / What is your weight? // 나는 ~이 45킬로그램입니다 I weigh 45 kilograms. / I am 45 kilograms in weight. / My weight is 45 kilograms. // 나는 ~이 3킬로그램 늘었다 [줄었다] I gained [lost] 3kilograms. // 그는 ~이 60킬로그램 나갔다 He tipped the scales at sixty kilograms.
- 체중계 the scales. ¶~에 오르다 step on the scales.

체증(滯症) [소화 불량 증세] indigestion; dyspepsia; [막히는 상태] a jam. ¶교통 ~ traffic congestion / a traffic snarl [back up] // ~이 생기다 impair [disturb] one's digestion // ~이 있다 suffer from indigestion.
- 체증 환자 a dyspeptic.

체증(遞增) gradual increase. 체증하다 increase gradually. ¶세율은 수입의 증가에 비례하여 체증한다 The tax rate rises in proportion to the increase in income.

체질 sieving; screening; sifting. 체질하다 sieve; screen (coal, sand, gravel, etc.); sift (out). ¶가루를 ~ sift flour / put flour through a sieve // 자갈을 ~ screen [riddle] gravel // 체질하여 좋은 것과 나쁜 것을 가르다 sift the good from the bad.

체질(體質) (physical) constitution; [소질] predisposition. ¶특이 ~ a diathesis (pl. -eses) // 병약한 ~ constitutional tendencies to disease // 폐병에 걸리기 쉬운 ~인 사람 a man constitutionally predisposed to consumption // ~이 약하다 be of weak constitution // 허약한 ~이다 have a sickly constitution [delicate frame] // 우리 경제의 ~을 개선하고 국제 경쟁력을 강화하다 improve the structure of our economy and raise our competitiveness in the world market // 그것은 나의 ~에 맞지 않다 That doesn't suit my constitution. / I haven't the constitution for that. / That doesn't agree with me.
- 체질 개선 improving one's physical constitution; (단체·기업 등의) radical reform; revamping; overhauling. ¶정계의 ~이 필요하다 An improvement in the way politics is

체취(體臭) 1 [몸의 냄새] body smell; evil smell of the body; the personal odor (of a beloved woman); [주로 겨드랑이 냄새] body odor(약어 B.O.). ¶~가 나다 give out[send forth] a body smell∥~가 깊이 배다 be powerfully impregnated with the personal odor∥~가 심하다 have strong body smell∥땀내 섞인 ~가 물씬 풍겨 왔다 The smell of a sweaty body greeted my nose. 2 [독특한 기분·버릇] something characteristic of the man; a special flavor[(영) flavour]. ¶그의 시에는 그 나름의 독특한 ~가 있다 His poems have his own flavor[characteristics].

체크 1 [검사·대조 표시] a check, **체크하다** check[tick] (off); mark. ¶지급 전표를 ~ check a payment slip∥정답을 체크하시오 Check the right answers.∥그는 사고 싶은 물건을 체크했다 He checked off the items he wanted to buy. 2 [바둑판무늬] a check; (영) a chequer. ¶~무늬 커튼 a check(er)ed [chequered] curtain.
● **체크아웃** (a) check-out. ¶~ 시간은 11시입니다 Check-out time is eleven.∥나는 9시에 호텔을 ~했다 I checked out of the hotel at nine. **체크인** (a) check-in. ¶호텔에 ~하다 check into[check in at] a hotel∥그녀는 프론트에서 손님의 ~을 담당하고 있다 She takes charge of check-ins at the front desk.

체통(體統) (an official's) decency; face; dignity prestige; honor; face. ¶~이 서는 face-saving (concession)∥~에 관한 문제 a matter of dignity / a question of 'face'∥~에 신경을 쓰다 be face-conscious / be too much concerned about one's official honor∥~을 세우다 save (one's) face[one's honor]∥~을 잃다 lose (one's) face / be put out of countenance∥~ 없이 굴다 act improperly[disrespectably]∥그는 대장부로서의 ~을 잃었다 He lost his dignity[honor] as a man.

체포(逮捕) (an) arrest; apprehension; (a) capture. **체포하다** arrest; (문어) apprehend; catch; seize (and hold); catch[take] hold (of); make an arrest. ¶범인을 ~ arrest a criminal∥당신을 체포합니다 I place you under arrest. →¶(아직) 체포되지 않고 있다 be (still) at large∥그 가족 중 한 사람이 범인으로 체포되었다 One member of the family was arrested for committing a crime.∥이탈자는 체포되었다 The deserters were captured[apprehended].∥그 살인범은 현장에서 체포되었다 The murderer was arrested[(문어) apprehended] on the spot.∥마약 밀수단은 아직 체포되지 않고 있다 The drug smugglers are still at large.∥여러 명의 학생이 불법 침입을 이유로 체포되었다 Several students were arrested for trespassing.
● **체포령** a mandate for an arrest; a warrant for the arrest. ¶…의 ~을 내리다 issue a warrant for the arrest of …. **체포 영장** an arrest warrant; a warrant for a person's arrest. ¶그에게 ~이 발부되었다 There is a warrant out for his arrest.

체표(體表) the surface of a body.

체하다(滯-) (음식이) sit[lie] heavy on one's stomach; remain undigested in the stomach; (사람이) have an attack of indigestion. ¶나는 체했다 The food is sitting heavy on my stomach. / I have indigestion.∥내가 먹은 생선이 체했을 것이다 The fish I ate must have disagreed with me.

체험(體驗) (an) experience. ¶귀중한[진귀한] ~ a valuable[an unusual] experience∥유아 ~ childhood experiences∥~으로 알다 learn by[from] experience∥~을 살리다 make effective use of one's experience. **체험하다** experience; undergo; go through. ¶직접 ~ gain one's experience at first hand∥큰 어려움을 ~ undergo[experience / go through] great hardships∥감옥 생활을 ~ experience prison life.
● **체험담** the story of one's experiences; talk of one's personal experiences. ¶유럽에서의 ~을 말씀해 주세요 Tell us about your experiences in Europe.

체현(體現) embodiment; personification; impersonation. **체현하다** embody; impersonate; personify; give a concrete form to.

체형(體刑) 1 [몸에 가하는 벌] corporal punishment. ¶~을 가하다 inflict physical [corporal / bodily] punishment (on). 2 [징역] penal servitude; imprisonment with hard labor[(영) labour]. ¶강도는 2년의 ~을 선고받았다 The robber was sentenced to two years at hard labor.

체형(體形) [몸의 생긴 모양] a form; a figure; a (bodily) shape.

체형(體型) [체격의 형] a body type. ¶표준 ~ standard proportions∥~에 맞추어 옷을 만들다 make clothes to measure.

체화(滯貨) [밀려 있는 화물] (an) accumulation of freight[goods]; [짐이 밀려 있음] freight congestion; [팔다 남은 상품] stock; a stockpile (of goods). **체화하다** accumulate; (화물이) be congested.

첼로 a cello (pl. ~s).
● **첼로 연주자** a cello player; a cellist.

쳄발로 a cembalo (pl. -li, ~s).

쳇다리 a fork-shaped sieve rails; a frame supporting a sieve (over a tub).

쳇바퀴 a sieve-frame; the frame of a sieve.

쳐내다 take[clear / sweep] away; clear off [out]; remove; clean up. ¶눈을 ~ clear away[off] snow / rake[shovel / sweep] away snow / clear (a yard) of snow / remove snow∥변소를 ~ dip out[up] night soil∥돼지우리를 ~ clean (up[out]) a pigsty [pigpen]∥우물을 ~ clean a well.

쳐다보다 look up (at); look upward; lift (up) [raise] one's eyes; cast up one's eyes (to). ¶천장을 ~ look up at the ceiling∥남의 얼굴을 ~ look up into a person's face∥흘깃 glance up (at)∥위를 쳐다보면 한이 없다 Don't compare yourself with those above you.

쳐들다 1 [올리다] lift (up); raise. ¶높이 ~ hold (a thing) aloft∥고개를 ~ raise one's head∥손을 번쩍 ~ raise[put up] one's hand high∥부끄러워 고개를 쳐들지 못하다 cannot hold up one's head for shame / cannot look (a person) in the face because of bad conscience∥뱀이 대가리를 쳐들었다 The snake raised its head. 2 mention; refer (to). ⇨초들다.

쳐들어가다 invade; drive[penetrate] deep into (enemy territory). ¶아군은 적의 본진으로 쳐들어갔다 Our troops made inroads into enemy territory. / Our troops carried the attack all the way to the enemy's headquar-

쳐들어오다 ters.∥그들은 외국의 영토에 쳐들어간 적이 없다 They have never invaded a foreign territory.
쳐들어오다 ¶강도가 그녀의 집에 쳐들어왔다 Burglars broke into her house.∥그는 내가 없는 사이에 내 방에 쳐들어왔다 He forced his way into my room in my absence.
쳐부수다 1 [때려 부수다] break (down). ¶폭도가 문을 쳐부수고 쏟아져 들어왔다 The mob broke down the door and came rushing in. 2 [격파하다] defeat; beat. ¶마침내 그들은 적을 쳐부수었다 They have defeated[beaten] the enemy at last.
쳐주다 [값을] appraise; value; evaluate; set [put] price (on); assess; estimate. ¶백만 원으로 ~ appraise [estimate] (the land) at one million won∥비싸게[싸게] ~ estimate (the cost) high[low] / rate (a thing) high [low]∥그 책을 5천 원 쳐줄 테니 나한테 파시오 Sell the book to me, I'll pay 5,000 won for it. 2 [간주하다] regard (as); consider; think of (as); deem; reckon; count (as / for); look on [upon] (as); take (for). ¶세상에서 쳐주지 않는 작가 an obscure[unacknowledged] writer ∥적임자로 ~ regard (a person) as fit [suitable] for the post∥이것은 그의 공로로 쳐주어야 한다 He must be given credit for this.
초 a candle; a taper(가는 것). ¶~의 심지 the wick (of a candle) / a candlewick∥~의 동강 a candle end∥~에 불을 붙이다 [당기다] burn[light] a candle∥~를 불어서 끄다 blow out a candle∥~의 심지를 자르다 snuff a candle∥~가 다 되어 간다 The candle is burning low.
초(草) 1 [초안] a rough copy; a draft. ¶법안의 ~ a draft of a bill∥~를 잡다 make a draft (of) / make a rough copy (of) / draft∥~를 잡지 않고 쓰다 write (an essay) offhand. 2 grass characters. ⇨ *초서 3 hay; dry grass. ⇨건초
초(醋) vinegar. ¶~에 절이다 pickle in vinegar ∥~를 치다 vinegar (something) / put vinegar in[on].
초(初) 1 [처음] the beginning; (the) first; the early part. ¶이달 ~ the beginning of this month∥학기 ~ the beginning of the (school) term∥5월 ~에 early in May∥작년 ~에 in the early months of last year∥20세기 ~에 in the early part[years] of the 20th century / early in the 20th century. 2 [야구] the first[upper] half; the top. ¶7회 ~를 끝냈으나 양 팀은 여전히 득점이 없었다 The top [The first half] of the seventh inning was over, and neither team had scored. / After seven and a half innings, still neither team had scored.
초(秒) a second (기호 ″). ¶천분의 1~ a millisecond∥백만분의 1~ a microsecond∥2분 40~ 걸렸다 It took two minutes and forty seconds.∥그는 백 미터를 10~ 5로 달렸다 He ran the 100-meter dash in 10.5 seconds. ∥1~에 10매 인쇄할 수 있는 기계를 샀다 We bought a machine which can print 10 pages per second.∥~를 다투는 문제다 [1~도 아깝다] There is no moment to lose.
초-(初) early. ¶~하루 the 1st of the month.
초-(超) super-; ultra-. ¶~강대국 a superpower∥~단파 ultrashort wave.

초가을(初-) early autumn[(미) fall]; the beginning of autumn[fall]. ¶~에 at the beginning of autumn / in early autumn.
초가(집)(草家-) a *choga*; (풀로 인) a thatched [thatch-covered] house; a hut roofed with thatch; (짚으로 인) a straw-thatched house[cottage]; a house thatched with straw.
● **초가삼간** a three-room thatched house; a small cottage. **초가지붕** a *chogajibung*; a thatch(ed) roof; a thatch; a straw-thatched roof.
초간(初刊) the first publication (of a book).
초간장(醋-醬) soysauce mixed with vinegar.
초개(草芥) bits of straw; [하찮은 것] a worthless thing; rubbish; dirt. ¶~ 같은 worthless / valueless / unworthy∥~ 같은 인생 a worthless life[existence] / a humble life∥목숨을 ~같이 여기다 think[make] nothing of one's life / hold one's life as nothing.
초겨울(初-) early winter; the beginning of winter. ¶~에 at the beginning of winter / in early winter.
초경(初更) the first watch of the night(=7-9 p.m.).
초경(初經) [생] menarche.
초계(哨戒) patrol; patrolling. ¶연안 ~ coastal patrol∥해상 ~ sea patrol. 초계하다 patrol. ¶초계하고 있다 be on patrol.
● **초계기**[선](哨戒機[船]) a patrol plane[line]. **초계 부대** a patrol force. **초계정** a patrol [picket / vedette] boat.
초고(草稿) a (rough) draft; a rough copy; notes; a manuscript(약어 MS., *pl.* MSS.). ¶강의의 ~ notes for a lecture∥연설의 ~ a draft of a speech∥~를 보면서 연설하다 speak from notes[a prepared text]∥~ 없이 강연하다 lecture without notes∥~를 작성하다 make (out) a draft (of) / draft (out) / prepare notes (for a lecture) / minute (a document)∥그의 시 가운데 몇몇은 아직 ~ 그대로 되어 있다 Some of his poems are still in manuscript (form).
초고속(도)(超高速度) (at) superhigh[ultrahigh] speed. ¶~의 super-speed (flight).
● **초고속도 촬영기** a superhigh-[a hyperhigh-/ an ultrahigh-]speed camera.
초고주파(超高周波) [통신] superhigh frequency(약어 S.H.F., SHF, s.h.f.); ultrahigh frequency(약어 U.H.F., UHF, u.h.f., uhf). ¶~의 ultrahigh-frequency.
초고추장(醋-醬) vinegared red pepper paste.
초과(超過) excess; [잉여] surplus; (an) extra. ¶수입[수출] ~ an excess of imports [exports] / unfavorable[favorable] balance of trade∥인원 ~ an excessive number of people∥사망에 대한 출산의 ~ an excess of births over deaths∥예산에 대한 10만 원의 ~ an excess of 100,000 won over the budget∥연령[체중] ~로 실격하다 be disqualified because of overage[overweight]. 초과하다 exceed; be in excess (of); be above[over / more than]. ¶규정 중량을 ~ exceed the fixed weight / overweigh∥정원을 ~ exceed the fixed number of people / exceed the number required∥그 차는 속도 제한을 시속 20킬로 초과했다 The car exceeded the speed limit by 20 kilometers per hour.∥이 소포는 규정된 무게를 30그램 초과하고 있다 This

package is 30g over the weight limit.// 지난달은 예산을 초과했다 We spent more than our budget last month.// 지출이 수입을 초과했다 My expenses exceeded my income.➔ 여비 예산에서 만 원이 초과되었다 The cost of the trip exceeded our budget by ten thousand won. / We ran ten thousand won over our budget.
● **초과 근무** overtime work[service]; extra duties. ¶~를 **하다** work overtime / do (two hours') overtime. **초과 시간** extra time; overtime. **초과 요금** excess fare(차의); excess baggage charge(수화물의). ¶한 시간당 500원의 ~을 받습니다 It's[We ask] 500won for each extra hour.

초교(初校) (교정의) the first proof (sheet). ¶~를 보다 read the first proof.

초구(初球) [야구] the first pitch[ball].

초극(超克) conquest. **초극하다** conquer; overcome[surmount / get over] (a difficulty); tide over (a crisis).

초근목피(草根木皮) [풀뿌리와 나무 껍질] the roots of herbs[plants] and the barks of trees; [악식] coarse and miserable food; [한약재] medicinal herbs. ¶~로 **연명하다** barely keep alive with the aid of herb roots and tree barks.

초급(初級) a primary[an elementary] grade; the first[beginner's] class (in English); the junior course (in French). ¶~용의 (books) for beginners.

초급(初給) an initial salary. ⇨ *초임급*(⇨*초임*)

초기(初期) 1 (한 시대의) the early days [years]; the beginning. ¶조선 ~에 in the early Joseon dynasty / 19세기 ~에 early in the nineteenth century. 2 (병 등의) the first [initial / incipient / early] stage. ¶~의 산업 (an) industry in its infancy // 문명의 ~ the early stage of civilization // 춘원의 ~ 작품 Chunwon's early works // (음모 등을) ~에 박살 내다 nip (a plot) in the bud // 그의 병은 폐결핵 ~이다 He is in the early stages of tuberculosis.// 암은 ~에 발견하는 것이 중요하다 It is important to detect cancer in its first stages.

초김치(醋) vinegared *gimchi*(kimchi).

초나흗날(初一) the 4th day of a month.

초년(初年) 1 [인생의 초기] one's youth; one's early years; one's younger days. ¶~에 when young / while in one's youth / in one's youth / at an early age // ~에 **등과하다** pass the state examination at an early age. 2 [첫해] the first year; [초기] the early years.
● **초년병** a new[raw] recruit. **초년생** a beginner; a novice; a greenhorn; a neophyte; a tyro.

초능력(超能力) preternatural[supernatural] power; [염력(念力)] telekinetic power; (mental) telepathy; [투시] clairvoyance; [미래 예지] prescience; [초감각적 지각] extrasensory perception(약어 ESP). ¶~으로 스푼을 구부리다 band a spoon with telekinetic power.

초단(初段) 1 [계단의 첫 단] the first step of a stair; the bottom step. 2 [바둑·유도 등의 첫 번째 단] the lowest grade of the senior class (in); the first grade. ¶**바둑** ~**자** a first-grade player of *baduk*(go) // 그는 태권도가 ~ 이다 He has reached the first grade in *taegwondo*.

초단파(超短波) ultrashort waves; very high frequency (약어 V.H.F., VHF, v.h.f., vhf); microwaves. ¶극~ ultra high frequency(약어 UHF) // 극~의 very-high-frequency.
● **초단파 방송** frequency modulation [FM] broadcasting; ultrashort wave broadcasting.

초닷샛날(初一) the 5th day of the month.

초당(草堂) a thatched cottage separated from the main building of a house.

초당파(超黨派) ¶~의 supra-partisan / non-partisan.
● **초당파 내각** a supra-partisan[coalition] cabinet. **초당파 외교** suprapartisan[nonpartisan / bipartisan] diplomacy.

초대(初代) [제1대] the first generation; (사람) the founder.
● **초대 대통령** the first President. **초대 왕** the first King[the founder] of a dynasty.

초대(招待) (an) invitation; (구어) (an) invite. ¶…의 ~로 at[on] the invitation of … // ~를 **받다** get[receive] an invitation / be invited (to dinner / by a person) / have an invitation (from a person) // ~를 **수락**[거절] **하다** accept[decline / turn down] an invitation // 나는 ~를 사절하는 편지를 냈다 I sent my regrets.// 선약이 있어서 ~에 응하지 못함을 미안하게 생각합니다 I regret that a previous engagement prevents me from accepting your kind invitation. **초대하다** invite; ask; extend an invitation (to a person). ¶만찬에 ~ invite[ask] (a person) to dinner / have (a person) in for dinner // 집으로 ~ ask (a person) to one's home / have (a person) over[in] // 초대해 주셔서 감사합니다 I thank you for your kind invitation.// 특별 세일에 초대합니다 You are cordially invited to a special sale. ➔ 홍 씨의 결혼식에 초대받아 갔다 I was a guest at the wedding of Mr. Hong.
● **초대권** a complimentary ticket(우대권); an invitation card[ticket]; a courtesy card(영화 등의). **초대석** a reserved seat for a guest. **초대장** a letter of invitation; an invitation (card); (구어) an invite. ¶~을 (보)내다 send [issue] an invitation (card) (to). **초대전** (그림 등의) (미) a preview; a private view.

초대면(初對面) the first meeting[interview] (with). ¶~인 사람 a stranger // 그들은 ~의 인사를 했다 They introduced themselves to each other.// 그것이 톰과는 ~이었습니다 That was the first time I met Tom. **초대면하다** meet (a person) for the first time.

초대작(超大作) a super-production; (영화의) a superfilm; a supra-feature film.

초대형(超大型) ¶~의 extra-large / (구어) outsize(d) // ~화하다 jumboize.
● **초대형 여객기** a superliner. **초대형 제트 여객기** a jumbo jet.

초도(初度) [첫 번] the first (time).
● **초도순시** one's first tour[round] of inspection.

초동(樵童) [땔나무를 하는 아이] a young woodcutter; a fuel-gathering boy.

초두(初頭) the beginning; the opening; the start; the outset; [애초] (the) first. ¶**회의** ~ the beginning of a meeting // 20세기 ~에 at the beginning of the twentieth century // (일이) ~부터 잘되어 가다 make a successful beginning / make a good start.

초들다 [말하다] mention; refer[allude] (to);

초등 make mention (of); [인용하다] cite (as an example); instance. ¶과거사를 ~ make reference to what had passed∥남의 약점을 ~ bring up (a person's) shortcomings∥잘못을 초들어 남을 면박하다 fling a fault in a person's teeth[face].

초등(初等) an elementary[a primary] grade; the lowest grade.
● **초등 교육** elementary school education. **초등학교** an elementary[a primary] school; a grade school. **초등학생** a primary[an elementary] schoolchild.

초라하다 (겉모양 등이) shabby; poor-[shabby-]looking; mean; miserable; wretched; seedy; scruffy; rusty; [미국 구어] tacky; [보잘것없다] humble; mean; poor. ¶초라한 집 a shabby[poor / wretched] house∥초라한 여인숙 a wretched[scruffy] inn∥초라한 오막살이 a humble cottage / a mean hut∥옷차림이 초라한 여자 a poorly dressed woman / a dowdy∥초라한 생활을 하다 be poorly[badly] off / live a miserable[wretched] life∥옷차림이 ~ be shabbily[poorly] dressed / be ill-clad / be down at heels[(the) heel] / be out at (the) heels∥초라해 보이다 cut a poor [sorry] figure∥그 옷을 입으니 좀 초라해 보인다 You look rather shabby in those clothes.

초래하다(招來-) bring about; give rise to; lead to; invite; incur; cause. ¶화를 ~ bring calamity upon oneself / court disaster∥집안에 불행을 ~ bring misfortune on one's family∥파멸을 ~ bring down ruin (on a person)∥죽음을 ~ court[occasion] death∥자기가 초래한 일이다 be of one's own making∥예기치 않은 사태를 초래하였다 It brought about an unexpected situation. / 사소한 실수가 중대한 결과를 초래했다 A little oversight led to[had / brought about] serious consequences.

초례(醮禮) a marriage[nuptial / matrimonial] ceremony; a wedding (ceremony); nuptials; hymeneal rite. ¶~를 지내다 hold[perform / celebrate / solemnize] a marriage[wedding].
● **초례청** a wedding hall.

초로(初老) middle age. ¶~의 middle-aged / elderly∥~의 남자 a man past middle age∥~에 접어들다 enter upon middle age.

초로(草路) a path[lane] across the grass.

초로(草露) dew on the grass. ¶인생은 ~와 같다 The world is but a fleeting shadow.
● **초로인생** a life as evanescent as the dew; an ephemeral[a transient] life.

초록(抄錄) [발췌된 것] an excerpt; an abstract; an extract; [적요] an epitome; a summary; a résumé. ¶시사 ~ a summary of current affairs. **초록하다** [발췌하다] abstract; excerpt; extract; [적요를 만들다] summarize; epitomize; write an epitome[a summary] (of).
● **초록자** [발췌자] an abstracter; an excerptor; [적요의 필자] an epitomist; a summarist.

초록(색)(草綠色) green. ¶밝은 ~ emerald (green)∥옅은 ~ light green∥~의 green; grassy-green / verdant∥~으로 물들다 be clad[robed] in verdure[green leafage]∥그 언덕은 진한 ~으로 뒤덮여 있다 The hill is covered with rich green.
초록은 동색(同色) (속담) One devil knows another.; Like knows like.; The wicked know the ways of their own kind.
● **초록빛** green. ⇨ 초록

초롱¹ a tin; [미] a can. ¶[석유 ~ an oilcan / (영) a kerosene tin∥석유 한 ~ a tin [can] of kerosene∥물 다섯 ~ five pails of water.

초롱² a (paper) lantern. ¶~을 밝히다[들다] light[carry] a lantern.
● **초롱꽃** [식] a bellflower; a Canterbury bell.

초롱초롱하다 (눈이) charmingly clear; limpid. ¶초롱초롱한 눈 limpid eyes.

초름하다 [적다] small; less; [불충분하다] insufficient; not enough; hardly ample; [미달하다] not up to the mark; less than due amount[quantity]; [모자라다] a bit short of. ¶그래도 아직 ~ It is not yet up to the mark.

초립(草笠) a straw hat.
● **초립둥이** a (married) youngster wearing a straw hat.

초막(草幕) [초가] a straw-thatched hut[cottage]; [중의 거소] a Buddhist monk's cell (near the temple).

초만원(超滿員) ¶~을 이룬 청중 an overflowing audience∥러시아워 동안은 통근 열차는 어느 것이나 ~이다 During rush hours, every commuter train is packed with people [packed to overflowing].∥연주회는 ~이었다 The concert drew a full house.

초면(初面) the first meeting (with). ¶~의 사람 a person met for the first time / a stranger∥그들은 서로 ~이었다 That was the first time they saw of each other.
● **초면 인사** greetings on the first meeting. ¶그들은 ~를 나누었다 They exchanged greetings as newly introduced person.

초목(草木) trees and plants; plant life; vegetation. ¶산천 ~ nature / natural scenery∥~이 우거진 산 a mountain with lush vegetation.

초문(初聞) a thing heard of for the first time. ¶그것은 금시 ~이다 That's news[a revelation] to me. / It's the first time I've heard that.

초미(지급)(焦眉之急) a crying[pressing] necessity; an urgent[a crying] need. ¶~의 urgent / pressing / exigent / impending∥~의 문제 an urgent[a burning] question / matter of urgent necessity.

초반(初盤) the opening part (of); an early stage. ¶그 조사는 아직도 ~이다 The investigation is still in its initial phase.

초밥(醋-) vinegared fish and rice.

초배(初褙) lining; underlining. **초배하다** line [underline] (a wall) with paper.
● **초배지** lining paper; a lining.

초벌(初-) [관형어적] first; preliminary.
● **초벌 그림** a rough sketch; a draft. ¶~을 그리다 make a rough sketch (of).

초범(初犯) (범죄) one's first offense[(영) offence]; (범인) a first offender.
● **초범자** a first offender.

초범하다(超凡-) extraordinary; uncommon; (서술적) be out of the common[ordinary]; be of an unusual order.

초병(哨兵) a sentry; a sentinel; a military guard. ¶~을 세우다 set up a sentry / picket (soldiers) / post[station] a guard∥~을 교대하다 relieve a sentry.

- **초병 근무** sentry[guard] duty.
초병(醋瓶) a vinegar bottle.
- **초병마개** 〔몹시 시큰둥한 체하는 사람〕 a person with repulsive and nauseous manners.
초보(初步) the first step (to / toward); the rudiments (of); the elements (of); the ABC (of); a beginners course (in French). ¶~의 〔적인〕 rudimentary / elementary // 화학의 ~ the rudiments of chemistry // 물리학의 ~적 지식 a rudimentary [an elementary] knowledge of physics // 독일어를 ~부터 배우다 learn German from the beginning // ~를 가르치다 initiate (a person) into (the elements of English grammar) / instruct (a person) in (the elements of English) / introduce (a person) into / give (a person) elementary lessons (in) / teach (a person) the rudiments (of) // ~를 배우다 receive first lessons (in French from a person) / take rudimentary lessons (in English) from (a person) / learn the rudiments (of Latin) from [under] (a person) / receive one's first (dancing) instruction // 나는 영어를 ~부터 다시 배우고 싶다 I want to study English from the ABC('s) [very beginning] again. // 그의 연구는 아직 ~ 단계에 있다 He is only at the ABC of his study. / He is still in an early stage of his study. / 나는 그에게서 독일어 ~를 배웠다 I first began to study German under his tutorship. / He was my first teacher of [in] German.
- **초보 운전자** a beginner's driver; a beginning driver. **초보자** a beginner; a novice. ¶이 책은 ~용이다 This book is for beginners. // 바둑에는 아직 ~이다 I'm a beginner at baduk. // ~ 환영 (게시) Welcome to beginners. **초보 지식** a rudimentary[an elementary] knowledge (of botany).
초복(初伏) the first 10-day period of the dog days (beginning around mid-July); the early dog days. ¶~이 들었다 The dog days began [set in].
초본(抄本) an extract; an abstract; an abridged transcript. ¶호적 ~ an abstract of one's family register.
초본(草本) 〔식〕 a herb; (집합적) herbage. ¶~의 herbal / herbaceous // 일년생 [이년생 / 다년생] ~ an annual [a biennial / a perennial] plant.
- **초본 식물** a herbaceous plant.
초봄(初-) early spring; the beginning of spring. ¶~에 at the beginning of spring / in early spring / early in spring.
초봉(初俸) an initial [a starting] salary [pay]; the hiring rate; (미국 속어) a starter. ¶~ 100만 원을 받다 start with a monthly salary of 1,000,000 won / get a starting salary of 1,000,000 won a month.
초부(樵夫) 〔나무하는 사내〕 a firewood cutter; a woodcutter; a woodman (pl. -men).
초빙(招聘) (an) invitation; a call; engagement(고용). ¶~으로 [~에 의하여] at [by] (a person's) invitation / ~에 응하다 accept the offer of a position / accept the call (to the chair of physics) // 나는 대학의 ~을 받아들이기로 결정했다 I decided to accept the invitation from the university. **초빙하다** invite (a lecturer); call in (a specialist); call on (a person to do); 〔고용하다〕 engage; enlist (a person's) service. ¶그들은 송 선생을 고문으로 초빙했다 They engaged Mr. Song as an adviser. →¶그는 팀의 감독으로 초빙되었다 He was invited to become the manager of the team. // 그는 미국 정부에 초빙되었다 He was offered a position [post] by [in] the United States government. (▶ in은 정부 내에)

초사흗날(初一) the third day of a month.
초산(初産) one's first childbirth [birth / confinement / delivery]. ¶그녀는 ~에 사내아이를 얻었다 Her first child was a boy. // ~은 순산[난산]이었다 Her first delivery was an easy [a difficult] one.
- **초산부** a woman expecting[bearing] her first baby; (출산 후의) a woman who has just had her first baby; a primipara (pl. -rae).
초산(硝酸) 〔화〕 nitric acid. ⇨=질산(窒酸)
초산(醋酸) 〔화〕 acetic acid. ⇨=아세트산
초상(初喪) (a period of) mourning. ¶~이 났다 A death occurs (in a person's family). // ~을 당하다 have a death in one's family // ~을 치르다 attend [see] to funeral ceremonies.
- **초상집** a house[family] in mourning; a bereaved family.
초상(肖像) a portrait; a likeness; 〔성상〕 an icon; an effigy; an image. ¶자기 ~을 그리게 하다 have one's portrait painted // 그녀는 앉아 ~을 그리게 하고 있다 She is sitting for her portrait.
- **초상권** the rights to one's portrait(s). **초상화** a portrait. ¶유화의 ~ a portrait in oils // ~를 그리다 take [paint] (a person's) portrait. **초상 화가** a portrait painter; a portraitist.
초생(初生) 〔처음 생겨남〕 (being) newborn.
- **초생아** a newborn child.
초서(草書) (글자) grass [cursive] characters; (서법) the grass [cursive] hand; cursive writing [calligraphy]; (서체) a very cursive style of writing Chinese characters; the grass style. ¶~로 쓰다 write in grass characters // ~를 잘 쓰다 be good at writing in grass characters.
- **초서체 활자** 〔인〕 secretary; a script.
초석(硝石) potassium nitrate. ⇨=질산칼륨(⇨질산)
초석(礁石) a submerged [sunken] rock; a reef.
초석(礎石) a foundation stone; a cornerstone; 〔토대〕 a foundation; a basis (pl. bases). ¶나라의 ~이라고 할 만한 인물 the pillar [mainstay] of the state // 민주 정치의 ~을 쌓다 lay the foundation (stone) of democracy // 그는 이 나라 민주 정치의 ~을 쌓았다 He laid the foundations [the cornerstone] of democracy in this country.
초선(初選) ¶~의 (당선) newly-elected.
- **초선 의원** a newly-elected member of the National Assembly.
초설(初雪) the first snow(fall) (of the season).
초성(初聲) 〔언〕 an initial sound. ⇨=첫소리
초소(哨所) a guard [sentry] post; (검문소의) a checkpoint. ¶감시 ~ an observation point.
초속(도)(初速度) initial velocity; (탄환의) muzzle velocity.
초속(도)(超速度) super-[ultra-] high speed; super velocity.

초속(도)(秒速度) the velocity[speed] per second. ¶~ 20미터로 at (a velocity[speed] of) 20 meters per[a] second∥~ 15미터의 바람이 불고 있다 The wind is blowing at a speed of 15 meters per[a] second.

초순(初旬) the first ten days (a month). ⇨˘상순(上旬)

초승 the first days[the beginning] of a month.
● 초승달 a new[young] moon; a crescent (moon); the sickle[horned] moon. ¶~ 모양의 crescent(-shaped)∥~이 하늘에 떠 있다 The young moon hangs in the sky.

초시계(秒時計) a microchronometer; a stopwatch.

초식(草食) ¶~의 plant-[grass-]eating / herbivorous / graminivorous. 초식하다 eat grass [vegetables]; live on grass[vegetables].
● 초식 동물 a plant-[grass-]eating animal; a grazer; a herbivorous animal; a herbivore (pl. -s, -ra).

초신성(超新星) [천] a supernova.

초심(初心) 1 [처음 마음] one's original intention. 2 a beginner. ⇨˘초심자(⇨초심) ¶~의 inexperienced / green (as grass).
● 초심자 a beginner; a novice; a greenhorn; a neophyte. ¶~용의 (books) for beginners.

초심(初審) a first-instance trial. ⇨˘제일심(⇨제일(第一))

초아흐렛날(初-) the ninth day (of a month).

초안(草案) a (rough) draft. ¶법안의 ~ a draft bill∥~을 기초(起草)하다 prepare[make out] a draft (for) / draft[draw up] (a bill)∥일정의 ~을 작성하다 draw up[prepare] a draft agenda∥그가 헌법 수정의 ~을 작성했다 He drafted the constitutional amendment.

초야(初夜) 1 the first watch of the night. ⇨˘초경(初更) 2 the bridal night. ⇨˘첫날밤(⇨첫날)

초야(草野) a remote village; an out-of-the-way hamlet[place]; the boondocks; the backwoods. ¶~에 묻혀 살다 live in rural retirement[seclusion] / lead a humble[a quiet country] life.

초여드렛날(初-) the eighth day (of a month).

초여름(初-) early summer; the beginning of summer. ¶~에 early in summer / at the beginning of summer.

초역(抄譯) an abridged[epitomized] translation; (a) translation of selected chapters [passages] (from Faust). 초역하다 make an abridged[a summarized] translation (of); translate selected chapters[passages] (from).

초연(初演) the first (public) performance [showing]; the premiere (performance) (of). 초연하다 give the first public performance (of); premiere (a play); perform (a play) first. →¶그 오페라는 1960년에 초연되었다 The opera was first staged in 1960.∥그 교향곡은 빈에서 초연되었다 The symphony was first performed in Vienna. / The first performance of the symphony was given in Vienna.

초연(硝煙) [화약의 연기] powder smoke. ¶~탄우(彈雨) 속에 amid the smoke of powder and hail of bullets / in the thick of the fight.

초연하다(超然-) transcendental; stand-offish. ¶…에 ~ stand[hold / keep] aloof from / rise[be] above (the world)∥돈 문제 [여론]에 ~ be above money matters[public opinion]∥속세에 ~ keep aloof from the crowd[masses] / rise above the world [vulgar herd]∥초연한 태도를 취하다 maintain[take] a stand of aloofness[detachment] / stand aloof∥초연하여 얼굴을 하고 있다 look droll, detached and unworldy∥그는 속세에 초연해 있다 He stands[holds himself / keeps himself] aloof from the world.∥그는 어딘지 초연한 데가 있다 He is somewhat aloof[detached] from the world. 초연히 aloof; detachedly; transcendently.

초열흘날(初-) the tenth day (of a month).

초엽(初葉) the early days[years]; the beginning; the initial phase. ¶20세기 ~에 in the early part of the 20th century.

초엽(蕉葉·草葉) [건] a bracket; a corbel(벽돌의); a console(처마 언저리 벽의).

초엿샛날(初-) the sixth day (of a month).

초옥(草屋) a thatched cottage.

초원(草原) a grassy [grass-covered] plain; grassland(s); a prairie(북미의); pampas(남미의); a steppe(러시아·중앙아시아의); a savanna(h) (미국 남부·서아프리카의). ¶~의 집 a home[house] on a prairie.

초월(超越) transcendence; transcendency. 초월하다 transcend; rise above; stand aloof from; be superior (to). ¶현세를 ~ rise above the world / stand aloof from the world ∥생사를 ~ disregard the peril of one's life∥이해를 ~ be disinterested∥그는 사욕을 초월해 있다 He is[has transcended] above self-interest.
● 초월수(-數) a transcendental (number). 초월 함수 a transcendental function.

초월적(超越的) transcendental. ¶~ 태도 a transcendental attitude.

초유(初有) ¶~의 first / initial / original / unprecedented / unexampled∥사상(史上) ~의 unprecedented[unparalleled] in history ∥우리나라 ~의 대지진 a record earthquake in (the history of) our country∥그것은 이 지방 ~의 일이다 That is an unheard-of event in this district.

초유(初乳) [의] (산부의) colostrum; foremilk; (암소의) beestings.

초음속(超音速) supersonic speed; hypersonic speed(음속의 약 5배 이상의 속도). ¶~의 supersonic.
● 초음속 비행 supersonic flight. 초음속 제트기 a supersonic jet plane.

초음파(超音波) [물] supersonic[ultrasonic] waves. ¶~의 supersonic / ultrasonic.
● 초음파 발생기 an ultrasonic generator.

초이렛날(初-) the seventh day (of a month).

초이튿날(初-) the second day (of a month). ¶9월 ~ the second of September / September 2(▶ (the) second라고 읽음).

초인(超人) a superman.
● 초인주의 superhumanism.

초인적(超人的) superhuman / preterhuman. ¶~으로 superhumanly∥~ 노력 superhuman efforts.

초인종(招人鐘) a (call) bell; a doorbell; a buzzer; a service bell(여관방의). ¶~을 울리다 ring a (door) bell / push a bell button∥[사람을 부르다] ring for (a servant)∥~을 누르다 push a doorbell / give a doorbell a push∥~이 울렸다 The doorbell rang.

초일(初日) the first[opening] day[night]; the premiere(연극의).

초읽기(秒-) countdown. ¶~를 하다 count down.

초임(初任) the first appointment.
- **초임급** an initial[a starting] salary[pay]. ¶나의 ~은 80만 원이었다 I started at a salary of 800,000 won. / My first salary was 800,000 won. **초임지** one's new post of duty.

초입(初入) 1 [길 등의 어귀] an entrance; an approach; a way in. ¶강[길] ~ an entry to a river[road] // 마을[터널] ~ an approach to a village[tunnel]. 2 [처음 들어감] the first entrance; entering for the first time.

초자연적(超自然的) supernatural; preternatural. ¶~ 존재 a supernatural being.

초자연주의(超自然主義) supernaturalism.

초장(初章) 1 (가곡의) the first part (of a song); (음악의) the first movement. 2 (시조의) the first of the three verses (of a *sijo*); (글의) the first chapter.

초장(初場) 1 (시장의) the opening[morning] market[session / sale]. ¶~부터 시세가 높았다 The market opened higher. 2 [일의 첫머리판] the outset; the start; the beginning. ¶~에는 at first / in the beginning // ~에는 실패했다 I failed (in it) at first.

초장(醋醬) soy sauce mixed with vinegar and pine-nut meal[parched sesame].

초장파(超長波) 〔통신〕 a very low frequency (약어 V.L.F., VLF, v.l.f., vlf).

초저녁(初-) 1 (the) early evening; the early hours of the evening[night]. ¶~에 early in the evening / in the early part[hours] of the evening // ~잠이 들다 fall asleep early in the night // 아직 ~이다 It's still early in the evening. / The night is still young. 2 the very first. ⇨애초

초전도(超傳導) 〔전〕 superconduction.
- **초전도성** superconductivity. **초전도체** a superconductor.

초점(焦點) a focus (*pl.* ~es, foci); a focal point. ¶고정 ~ [사진] a fixed focus // 자동 self-focus(s)ing // 허 ~ a virtual focus // 분쟁의 ~ the focus of trouble // ~이 맞다[맞지 않다] be in[out of] focus // ~을 맞추다 focus (one's glasses on an object) / adjust the focus (of a lens) // ~에 모이다 converge into a focus // 공격의 ~이 되다 bear the brunt of an attack // ~에 ~을 두다[…을 ~으로 하다] place the focus on (a question) / focus on (a matter) // 카메라의 ~을 맞추다 bring a camera into focus // 말의 ~을 흐리다 evade the point // 우리는 쌍안경의 ~을 새에 맞추었다 We focused our binoculars on the bird. // 그녀의 얼굴에 ~이 맞았다[맞지 않았다] Her face is in[out of] focus. // 네 사진은 모두 ~이 맞지 않는다 Your pictures are all out of focus. // 그 문제의 ~은 무엇인가 What is at the heart of the matter? // 그것이 바로 문제의 ~이다 That is the heart[the very point] of the matter. // 논의의 ~이 이 점에 압축되었다 The discussion (was) focused[centered] on this point.
- **초점 거리** the focal distance[length]. ¶~ 측정기 a focometer / a focimeter. **초점면** a focal plane. ¶~ 개폐 장치 a focal plane shutter.

초조하다(焦燥-) fretful; impatient; irritated; anxious; restless. ¶초조한 마음 an anxious [a nervous / a restless] state of mind // 초조한 기분으로 in an impatient mood // 초조한 빛[기색]이 보이다 seem impatient / look anxious[worried] // 초조해하다 fret / worry / be impatient / show impatience // 초조해지다 get impatient / (미) get jittery // 시험 결과를 몰라서 초조하다 be anxious to know the result of an examination // 그는 이번에도 또 실패했으므로 초조해하고 있다 He is fretting [in a fret] because he failed this time, too. // 일이 잘되어 가지 않아서 모두는 초조해하고 있다 They are all an edge[irritable] because their work is not going well. // 그렇게 초조해할 것 없다 You have nothing to fret about like that.

초주검(初-) ¶~이 되다 be more dead than alive / be all but dead / be half-dead / (남의 손에) be half-kill / (때려서) beat[flog] (a person) nearly to death // ~이 되게 얻어맞다 be thrashed[flogged] within an inch of one's life.

초지(初志) one's original intention[purpose / aim / object]. ¶~를 관철하다 accomplish [carry out] one's original intention / (굽히지 않다) abide by[stick to] one's original purpose // ~를 굽히다 give up one's original purpose // ~를 이루다 realize[fulfill] one's long-cherished desire // 그는 ~를 관철했다 He carried out his original purpose[intention].

초지(草地) 〔풀이 나 있는 땅〕 grassland; a grassy place; a green (field); 〔목초지〕 a pasture; a meadow.

초진(初診) the first medical examination. ¶~입니다 This is my first visit. / I am on my first visit.
- **초진 환자** a new patient[client]. ¶~는 보험 카드를 접수부에 제출해 주십시오 A new patient should present his health insurance card at the reception desk.

초집(抄集·抄輯) a collection of extracts [excerpts / abstracts]; a selection(선집). ¶법안 ~ extracts of bills / a copy of extracted bills. **초집하다** make a collection of extracts [excerpts / abstracts]; extract (from); excerpt (from).

초창기(草創期) the initial stage(s); the early period; the pioneer days. ¶~에 in the beginning / in the first stage / at the outset [inception] // 인류사의 ~ the early days of mankind / the most ancient days of human history // 사업의 ~ the beginning(s) of an enterprise // 문예 부흥의 ~ the dawning of the Renaissance // ~의 회사 운영 the management of a company in its early stage.

초청(招請) (an) invitation. ¶~에 의하여 at [by] (a person's) invitation // ~을 받아들이다[사절하다] accept[decline] an invitation // ~을 받지 않고 가다 go uninvited // ~을 받고 오다 come by invitation. **초청하다** invite [ask] (a person to a party) // ¶강사를 ~ invite[call in] a lecturer // 집에 남을 ~ ask a person to one's home // 각국 대표를 평화 회의에 ~ call the representatives[delegates] of each country to the Peace Conference.
- **초청객** an invited guest. **초청 경기** an invitation game. **초청장** a letter of invitation; an invitation (card). ¶~을 보내다 extend[issue / send] an invitation (to).

초출(抄出) extraction; excerption; selection.

초출

초출하다 extract (from); excerpt (from); select (from); make an extract (from).

초출(初出) the first appearance (of fruits).

초췌하다(憔悴・顦顇-) haggard; emaciated; gaunt; thin and worn; worn-out. ¶초췌한 얼굴 a haggard face / a worn-out look // 초췌한 모습 a haggard[worn] figure // 초췌해지다 get[become] haggard[gaunt / emaciated] (from) / be worn out // 근심[걱정]으로 초췌해지다 be careworn // 형편없이 초췌해지다 be worn to a shadow // 그는 오랫동안의 병으로 초췌하였다 He was emaciated[wasted] by his long illness.

초취(初娶) one's first wife.

초치(招致) summons; invitation. **초치하다** [불러들이다] summon; send for; [초대하다] call; [유치하다] attract (tourists). ¶회의에 대표를 ~ call in conference delegates (from) // 그들은 1988년의 올림픽을 서울에 초치하는 운동을 일으켰다 They launched a drive to bring the 1988 Olympic Games to Seoul.

초친놈(醋-) a worthless playboy; a rake of no promise; a hopeless roué.

초침(秒針) the second hand[the sweep-second] (of a watch).

초콜릿 chocolate; [코코아를 재료로 만든 과자] a chocolate; a stick[bar] of chocolate. ¶~색의 chocolate-colored.

초크 (a) chalk.

초탈(超脫) transcendency; transcendence; detachment. **초탈하다** transcend; stand aloof (from); rise above. ¶초탈한 태도 a disinterested attitude // 세속을 ~ rise above the world / stand aloof from the world / be in this world, but not of it // 그는 세속을 초탈한 사람이다 He cares little about worldly matters. / He is free from worldly cares.

초토(焦土) [불탄 흙] scorched earth; burnt ground; [불탄 자취] the ruins[site] of a fire; [불탄 재] burnt-out cinders and ashes. ¶~화하다 be burnt to the ground / be reduced to ashes // 아름다운 거리는 전쟁으로 ~화되었다 War turned the beautiful streets into ruins.

초특급(超特急) a superexpress (train).

초특작품(超特作品) a super production; (영화의) a superfilm.

초파리(醋-) [동] a drosophila (pl. -lae); a vinegar fly; a fruit fly.

초판(初-) the first round[period / bout / scene]; (승부의) the opening (of a game). ¶~에 in[at] the beginning / at the outset / in the early stage // ~부터 다시 하다 do all over again / begin afresh / make a new start // ~에 잘나가다 make a successful beginning / make a good start // 나는 ~에서 잠錯다 I began at the wrong end. / I made a false [wrong] start.

초판(初版) the first edition; the first impression; the original edition. ¶~을 3천 부 인쇄[발행]하다 print[issue / publish] the first edition of 3,000 copies (of a book) // ~은 1주일도 못 되어 매진되었다 The first edition was exhausted[sold out] in less than a week.

● **초판본** (집합적) the first edition; [낱권의] a copy of the first edition.

초필(抄筆) [가는 붓] a fine (writing) brush.

초하다(抄-) [추려 베끼다] make an extract (from); make an abstract (of); extract [excerpt / select / cull] (from). ¶편지의 한 귀절을 ~ transcribe a passage from the letter // 시편(詩篇) 중에서 ~ make a selection from the Psalms.

초하다(草-) [초안을 잡다] make a draft (of / on / from); draft out an address.

초하루(初-) the first day of a month. ⇨ 초하룻날(⇨초하루)

● **초하룻날** the first day of a month. ¶6월 ~ the 1st of June.

초학(初學) [처음 배움] learning first in one's life; the beginning of learning; [미숙한 학문] elementary learning. ¶아직 ~이라 그에 대해서는 아무것도 모릅니다 I am a mere beginner in such matters so I know nothing about it.

● **초학자** a beginner; a learner; a greenhorn; an abecedarian. ¶~용의 입문서 a manual [guidebook] for beginners.

초행(初行) going for the first time; one's first trip[journey]. ¶파리는 ~입니다 This is my first visit to Paris.

● **초행길** a road new to one; a road one has never been on before; one's first trip [journey].

초현대적(超現代的) ultramodern.

초현실주의(超現實主義) surrealism.

● **초현실주의자** a surrealist.

초호(礁湖) [환초로 둘러싸인 호수] a lagoon.

초혼(初昏) (the evening) dusk; twilight.

초혼(初婚) one's first marriage. ¶그 여자는 40세인데 ~이오 She is forty now and is marrying for the first time. // "그가 결혼한다고 하던데 ~입니까?" "아니오, 재혼입니다." "I hear he is going to get married. Is it his first marriage?" "No, it's his second marriage."

초혼(招魂) invocation of the spirits of the dead. **초혼하다** invoke the spirit of the deceased.

● **초혼제** a memorial service (for the war dead).

초회(初回) [첫 번] the first time.

● **초회 불입금** (월부의) the first installment; down payment. ¶~이 없는 월부 No money down.

촉(鏃) [뾰쪽한 끝] the point (of a pencil); the nib (of a pen); [화살촉] an arrowhead; the point of an arrow; a gad. ¶만년필 ~ the point of a fountain pen // 펜 ~ a penpoint / a nib.

촉(燭) candle power. ⇨ 촉광₁

촉각(觸角) (곤충의) a feeler; an antenna (pl. -nae); a tentacle; a horn (of a snail). ¶~을 내밀다 put out (its) feelers.

촉각을 곤두세우다 concentrate[focus] one's attention (on). ¶그는 촉각을 곤두세우고 사태의 진전을 지켜보았다 He was all attention to watch the development of the situation.

촉각(觸覺) the sense of touch; (a) tactile sensation. ¶~의 tactile / tactual.

● **촉각기** a tactile[touch] organ.

촉감(觸感) 1 [피부에 닿는 느낌] feel; touch. ¶~이 좋다 be pleasant[agreeable / smooth] to the touch[feel] / feel smooth / have a smooth feel // ~이 좋지 않다 be unpleasant to the touch // ~이 거칠다 [부드럽다] be rough[soft] to the touch / feel rough[soft] // 이 천은 ~이 부드럽다[거칠다] This cloth is soft[rough] to the touch. // 이것은 ~이 모피

같다 It feels like fur. // ~으로 이것이 무엇인지 알 수 있습니까 Can you tell what it is by the feel? 2 the sense of touch. ⇨ˉ촉각(觸覺)

촉광(燭光) 1 [광도의 단위] candle power(약어 c.p.). ¶60~의 전구 a 60 candle power bulb. 2 [촛불의 빛] candlelight.

촉구(促求) pressing; urging. **촉구하다** [재촉하다] press (a person for a thing); urge (a person to do); [요구하다] demand; call upon (a person to do). ¶주의를 ~ call [attract] (a person's) attention to (a matter) // 진지한 반성을 ~ demand (a person's) serious reflection // 대답을 ~ press (a person) for an answer // 사임을 ~ urge (a person) to resign / insist upon (a person's) resignation // 이 점에 대해서 너희들에게 주의를 촉구하고자 한다 I would like to draw [call] your attention to this point.

촉급하다(促急-) urgent; pressing; imminent. ¶촉급한 문제 a matter of great urgency // 촉급한 일로 on urgent business.

촉망(囑望) expectation; hope. ¶그는 주위 사람들의 ~을 받고 있다 He is the hope of those around him. **촉망하다** fasten [hang / pin / put] one's hopes on (a person); expect much of [from] (a person). ¶크게 ~ expect very much of [from] (a person) / entertain great expectations of (a person) // 온 가족이 그를 촉망하고 있었다 All his family pinned [fastened] their hopes on him. / He was the hope of the whole family. →¶앞날이 촉망되는 청년 a promising youth / a young man (full) of promise / a young man with a great [rosy] future // 장래가 촉망되는 화가 a promising artist // 당신은 장래가 촉망되는 아드님을 두셨습니다 You have a promising son. / You can expect much of your son. // 그는 장래가 촉망되고 있다 He is thought to be promising [have a brilliant future ahead of him]. // 그녀는 화가로서 장래가 촉망된다 She has a great future as a painter.

촉매(觸媒) [화] a catalyzer; a catalyst; a catalytic (agent).

● **촉매 반응** a catalytic reaction; catalysis.
촉매 작용 a catalytic action; (cause / bring about) catalysis.

촉모(觸毛) [동] a cirrus (*pl.* cirri); a tactile hair. ¶~가 있는 cirrate / cirrose.

촉박하다(促迫-) urgent; pressing; imminent. ¶시간이 ~ be pushed [pressed] for time // 약속 기일이 ~ The appointed day is now close [near] at hand.

촉발(觸發) 1 [접촉하여 폭발함] detonation by contact; contact detonation. **촉발하다** detonate [be detonated] by contact; be touched off. 2 [감정 등이 일어남] being excited [moved / stirred]. **촉발하다** be excited [moved / stirred].

● **촉발 장치** a contact-detonating device.

촉새 [동] a bunting.

촉성(促成) (식물 등의) forcing [hastening / accelerating] the growth of a plant. **촉성하다** stimulate [foster] the realization (of); promote the growth of.

● **촉성 재배** forcing culture. ¶~용 온실 a forcing house // ~용 식물 plants for forcing // ~를 한 야채 forced [hothouse] vegetables.

촉수(觸手) 1 [동] an antenna (*pl.* -ae); a feeler; a tentacle. 2 [사물에 손댐] touching.
촉수를 뻗치다 reach (for); try to get [obtain].

● **촉수 엄금** (게시) Hands off.
촉수(觸鬚) [동] (절지동물의) a palp; a palpus (*pl.* -pi); (물고기의) a barbel.

촉진(促進) promotion; acceleration; hastening; facilitation; furtherance. **촉진하다** promote (an undertaking); accelerate; expedite; facilitate; quicken; further; speed [step / gear] up (a job); give [lend] an impetus (to); give a boost (to). ¶식물의 성장을 ~ hasten [accelerate / force] the growth of a plant // 문명의 진보을 ~ expedite [facilitate / further / quicken / accelerate / speed up] the progress of civilization // 양국 간의 무역을 ~ give a boost to trade between the two countries // 식욕을 ~ quicken [sharpen / stimulate] the appetite // 정부는 농업의 기계화를 촉진했다 The government promoted the mechanization of farming. // 기술 개발은 자연 파괴를 촉진했다 The development of technology has quickened the destruction of nature. // 이 물질은 식물의 성장을 촉진한다 This substance stimulates [hastens / accelerates] plant growth.

촉진(觸診) [의] palpation; examination by touch [the hand]. **촉진하다** palpate; examine by touch [the hand].

촉촉하다 damp(ish); humid. ⇨축축하다

촉탁(囑託) [위촉] commission; entrusting; charge; part-time engagement; [위촉을 받은 사람] a part-time employee; a part-timer. ¶관청[은행]의 ~ a part-time employee of a government office [a bank] // 학교 ~의(醫) a part-time school doctor // 그는 정년퇴직 후에도 ~으로 남았다 He stayed on as a part-timer after he retired from regular employment. // 그는 ~이다 He's on part-time. **촉탁하다** entrust [charge] (a person) with (a job); commission (a person to do). ¶대학교수에게 외교 문제 연구를 ~ commission a university professor to study diplomatic problems // 우리는 그 회사에 자료 정리를 촉탁하고 있다 We entrust that company with the arrangement of our data.

● **촉탁 교원** a part-time teacher.

촌(村) [마을] a village; a hamlet(작은); a rural community; [시골] the country; a rural district; (미) the backcountry. ¶빈민~ a poor village // ~구석에서 살다 live in a secluded place.

촌(寸) 1 [친등(親等)의 단위] a degree. ¶삼~ an uncle // 사~ a cousin / a relative in the fourth degree // 사돈의 팔~ a cousin forty times removed. 2 a Korean inch. ⇨ˉ치¹

촌가(寸暇) a moment's leisure. ⇨촌극(寸隙)

촌가(村家) a village [country] house.

촌각(寸刻) a moment; a minute. ¶~은을 ~을 다투다 (병 등이) require [call for] prompt treatment / (문제 등이) need a speedy solution // ~을 …하다 lose no time in (doing) / (do) promptly [speedily] // 문제의 해결은 ~을 다툰다 Not a moment can be lost [we can't waste a moment] in finding a solution to the problem.

촌극(寸劇) a little dramatical performance; a short play; a sketch; a playlet; a skit.

촌극(寸隙) a moment's leisure; a spare moment. ¶~을 아껴 utilizing every odd moment // ~도 없다 have not a minute to call one's own // ~을 이용하다 make use

촌길 (村-) a village road[street]; a country path[road].

촌내 (寸內) 〔십촌 안의 친척〕 a relative within tenth degree; near relatives.

촌놈 (村-) a rustic; a rube; (조롱적) a boor; a (country) bumpkin; a churl; a yokel; a clod-hopper; (미) a backwoodsman; a hillbilly; (미국 속어) a hayseed. ¶그는 이를테면 서울 ∼이다 He is, so to speak, a Seoul rustic.// ∼ 수작 마라 Don't make you a boor!

촌뜨기 (村-) a rustic; a countryman; a bumpkin; a person from the country. ¶∼ 같은 여자 a boorish [countrified-looking] girl// ∼ 짓을 하다 commit untraveled man's blunders.

촌락 (村落) a village; a hamlet(작은).

촌로 (村老) a village senior [elder].

촌민 (村民) a villager; (집합적) countrypeople; countryfolk; villagers; village folk [people]; the inhabitants of a village.

촌보 (寸步) a few steps. ¶피로해서 ∼도 옮길 수 없었다 I was so fatigued that I was unable to take another step.

촌부 (村夫) a country[village] man.

촌부 (村婦) a country[village] woman.

촌사람 (村-) 〔시골에 사는 사람〕 a villager; a countryman; a rustic; (집합적) countryfolk.

촌색시 (村-) a country lass [girl].

촌수 (寸數) degrees; the degree of consanguinity [kinship / relationship (by blood)]. ¶혼인 금지의 ∼ (the) prohibited [forbidden] degrees (of marriage)// ∼가 가까운[먼] 사람 a person who is near [distant] relative.

촌스럽다 (村-) 〔촌티 나다〕 boorish; rustic; countrified(-looking); 〔세련되지 못하다〕 unfashionable (clothes); inelegant; unrefined; unpolished; uncouth; ungainly (figure). ¶촌스러운 사람 a lout / a rustic / a boor / a clod hopper / a bumpkin// 촌스럽게 차려입다 be unfashionably [uncouthly] dressed.

촌외 (寸外) 〔십촌이 넘는 먼 친척〕 a distant relative.

촌음 (寸陰) a moment; a minute; an instant; the slightest space of time. ¶∼을 아끼다 skimp on time / grudge even a minute / cannot spare a moment // ∼을 아껴 공부하다 use every available minute to study // ∼을 아껴 연구에 몰두하다 devote all one's time and energies to studies.

촌장 (村長) a village headman [chief].

촌지 (寸志) 〔작은 뜻을 나타낸 적은 선물〕 a little token of one's gratitude [appreciation]; a small present. ¶∼ 〔사례의 봉투에 쓰는 글〕 with compliments // 이것은 저의 (감사의) ∼입니다 This is only a small present [a small token of my gratitude]. // ∼로 받아 주십시오 Please accept this humble token of my gratitude. // 감사의 ∼로서 포도주 한 병을 보내 드립니다 I am sending you a bottle of wine as a small token of my gratitude.

촌철살인 (寸鐵殺人) ¶∼의 경구 a saw coming home to one's heart / a pithy epigram that stings [cuts / pierces] one to the quick // 그의 문장은 ∼의 감동을 준다 His writing is full of pithy sarcasms.

촌충 (寸蟲) ➡조충

촌탁 (忖度) 〔(마음을) 헤아림〕 guessing [surmising] (another's) mind [feeling]. **촌탁하다** guess [sense] (another's) feeling; conjecture; judge. ¶제 표준으로써 남의 마음을 ∼ judge others in terms of oneself / project (a person's) feelings / measure other's corn by one's own bushel.

촌티 (村-) rusticity; boorishness. ¶∼가 나다 be boorish / look rustic / be countrified (-looking) / have a rural appearance // 그 처녀는 아직 ∼를 벗지 못했다 The girl hasn't yet got the hayseed out of her hair.

촌평 (寸評) a brief review (of a play); a brief comment (on a political movement). **촌평하다** make a brief comment (on); comment briefly (upon).

촐랑거리다 1 〔까불다〕 act [be] frivolous [irresponsible / unserious / flippant]; behave carelessly [rashly]. ¶촐랑거리며 돌아다니다 gad [flit] about // 그녀는 촐랑거린다 [경박하다] She is imprudent [heedless / indiscreet]. 2 surge; roll. ➪촐렁거리다

촐랑이 a frivolous [careless] person.

촐싹거리다 1 〔경망스럽게 굴다〕 act frivolously [irresponsibly / unseriously / flippantly]. 2 〔부추기다〕 instigate; incite; stir up; urge; prod; needly; egg on. ¶촐싹거려 …하게 하다 set [needle] (a person) to do.

촐촐하다 hungry; feel a bit hungry. ➪출출하다

촘촘하다 (틈새 등이) close; thick; fine; dense. ¶나뭇결이 촘촘한 close-[fine-]grained // 촘촘한 박음새 close stitching / close stitches // ∼을 이 촘촘한 천 cloth of (a) close texture // 쳇불이 촘촘한 채 a sieve of fine mesh. **촘촘히** closely; thickly; finely. ¶모를 ∼ 심다 set young rice plants close together.

촛농 (-膿) guttered candle (wax); melted wax running down a candlestick. ¶책상 위에 ∼을 흘려 그 위에 초를 세우다 stick a candle in its own wax on the desk // ∼이 앉았다 The candle was guttered. // ∼이 흐른다 The candle gutters down. // ∼이 흐르고 있다 The candle is running.

촛대 (-臺) a candlestick; a candlestand; (벽에 붙인 것) a sconce; a flambeau (pl. ∼x, ∼s); a candle holder. ¶∼에 초를 꽂다 fix a candle in a candlestick.

촛불 candlelight. ¶∼을 켜다 light a candle // ∼을 (입으로) 불어서 끄다 blow out a candle // ∼에 글을 읽다 read by candlelight // ∼이 다 돼 간다 The candle is burning low.

총 (말갈기와 꼬리의 털) the hairs of a horse's mane [tail].

총 (銃) 〔총기〕 a gun; (집합적) firearms; arms; 〔소총〕 a musket; a rifle(강선총); (집합적) small arms. ¶따발∼ a Russian automatic rifle // 단발∼ a single-shot gun / a single-loader // 연발∼ a magazine rifle / a repeater // 6연발∼ a six-shooter // ∼을 맞다 be under fire / be shot // ∼을 쏘다 shoot [fire / (문어) discharge] a gun // 남에게 ∼을 겨누다 level a gun at a person // ∼을 메다 shoulder a gun // ∼을 들이대고 납치하다 kidnap (a person) at gunpoint // ∼을 바꿔 메다 change arms // ∼에 착검하다 fix a bayonet // 그는 나를 향해 ∼을 겨누었다 He leveled his rifle [pointed his gun] at me. // 세워∼ 〔구령〕

Order arms!// 걸어~ [구령] Pile arms!// 받들어~ [구령] Present arms!// ~이 불을 뿜었다 The gun spat fire.

총-(總) [통틀어] all; whole; entire; general; overall; gross; total; full. ¶~득점 the total score / the total points made // ~소득 the gross income // ~본부 general headquarters / the center // ~예산 the total budget / the general estimate // ~결산 a complete settlement of accounts // ~선거 a general election // ~대리점 a general agent / a sole agent.

총가(銃架) an arms rack; a rifle stand; a gun rest [mounting].

총각(總角) an unmarried man; a bachelor; a celibate; (미국 속어) a bach.
● **총각김치** chonggakgimchi; pickled young radishes. 총각 처녀 young people (of both sexes); unmarried (young) men and women.

총감(總監) an inspector general; a superintendent-general; a commissioner.

총감독(總監督) a general manager.

총검(銃劍) 1 [총과 검] rifles and swords. 2 a bayonet. ⇨ "대검 ¶~을 들이대고 at the point of a bayonet // ~으로 찌르다 bayonet (a person) / stab (a person) with a bayonet.
● **총검술** bayonet drill [exercise / practice].

총격(銃擊) (rifle) shooting; rifle fire. ¶~을 가하다 shoot (at) / fire (at) / direct fire (toward) // ~을 받다 be under fire / be shot (at) / draw shots. 총격하다 shoot a rifle (at a target); (숨은 곳에서) snipe (at); (기관총으로) machine-gun (a building); (저공에서) strafe.
● **총격전** an exchange of shots [fire]; a gun battle; a gunfight. ¶~을 벌이다 gunfight / fight a gun battle / exchange fire (with).

총결산(總決算) [총체적인 결산] the final settlement of all accounts; final balancing of books. ¶연말 ~ the year-end settlement of (the whole accounts). 총결산하다 make final settlement of (accounts); settle [balance] accounts. ¶연말에 수입 지출을 ~ balance the receipts and disbursements at the end of the year // 이제 10년간의 연구를 총결산할 때다 It is time to sum up the findings of my ten years of research.

총경(總警) a police superintendent; (영) a superintendent; (미) an inspector; a senior superintendent(약어 Sr. Supt.).

총계(總計) the total; the whole [total] amount [sum]; the sum [grand / full] total (소계에 대한); the aggregate. ¶내 여비는 ~ 5,000 달러 들었다 The trip cost me 5,000 dollars all told. // ~가 얼마나 됩니까 What does the total come to? / What is the sum? / What do you make the sum? / How much is it altogether? // 사상자는 ~ 200명에 달했다 The number of casualties reached 200. 총계하다 total; sum [add / count] up. ¶총계하여 in all / in total / in toto / all told / altogether / (미) in the aggregate // 손해를 ~ sum up the loss // 총계하여 약 100만 원이 된다 It makes a (grand) total of around a million won.

총공격(總攻擊) an all-out attack; a full-scale offensive. ¶우리는 적에 대해 ~을 개시했다 We launched an all-out attack on [against] the enemy. // 나는 모두에게서 ~을 받아 내 제안을 철회했다 I withdrew my proposal when everyone criticized it [when it was blasted by everyone]. 총공격하다 make [open / launch] an all-out attack (on / against); attack (the enemy) in full force. ¶전 전선에서 ~ launch on a general offensive along the entire front.

총괄(總括) [개괄] generalization; [요약] summarization; epitomization; recapitulation; summary. 총괄하다 generalize; summarize; sum up; epitomize. ¶총괄하면 generally speaking / to sum up / as a whole / to recapitulate // ~데이터를 ~ put together data // 모든 문제를 총괄하여 토의하다 discuss all the problems at one time.

총괄적(總括的) all-inclusive; all-embracing; overall; blanket; lump-sum; omnibus. ¶~으로 in the gross [mass / lump] / collectively / (프) en bloc [masse].

총구(銃口) the muzzle (of a gun / of a rifle). ¶~를 들이대고 (threat a person) at the point of a gun.

총급하다(悤急-) (서술적) be in a great hurry; be very urgent.

총기(銃器) [집합적] small arms; firearms.
● **총기실 / 총기고** a gun room; an armory.

총기(聰氣) [총명한 기운] brightness; intelligence; sagacity; spark of intelligence; [기억력] a good memory; retentiveness. ¶~가 있다 be bright [intelligent] // ~가 없다 be dull [unintelligent] // ~가 좋다 have a good [retentive] memory // 그의 얼굴에는 ~가 없다 There's no intelligence in his face.

총대(銃-) the barrel (of a gun); the gun barrel; (총) a gun [rifle]. ¶~를 메다 shoulder a rifle.

총대리점(總代理店) a general agency.

총독(總督) a governor-general (pl. governors-~); a viceroy. ¶캐나다 ~ the Governor-General of Canada.
● **총독부** the government-general; (영) the Vice-regal.

총동원(總動員) general [full] mobilization. 총동원하다 mobilize fully; make [effect] a general mobilization; mobilize all the resources (of). ¶온 가족이 총동원하여 with the combined [united] efforts of the whole family // 산업계를 ~ mobilize all (of) the industry // 전(全) 학교가 총동원하여 식목했다 All the teachers and students took part in planting trees. // 총동원해서 빨리 해치우자 Let us finish the work among us all. ➔ ¶기생을 총동원시키다 call in all the gisaeng.
● **총동원령** orders for the mobilization of the entire army; general mobilization orders.

총람(總覽) 1 [남김없이 봄] a comprehensive [general] survey; [개요·개략·개관] (문어) a conspectus. 2 [관계 사항을 종합한 책] a comprehensive bibliography (on a subject).

총람(總攬) superintendence; (general) control. 총람하다 superintend; oversee; preside over; control. ¶교육 인적 자원부는 국민의 교육을 총람한다 The Ministry of Education and Human Resources Development has control of [supervises] the education of the nation.

총량(總量) the total [aggregate] amount; the gross weight [volume] (▶ weight는 무게, volume은 부피). ¶~은 2톤이었다 The gross weight was two tons. // ~ 5세제곱미터까지는 그 상자 안에 들어갑니다 The box will hold a gross volume of five cubic meters.

총력(總力) all one's energy[strength]; the aggregate power. ¶~을 다하여 with concerted efforts / with all one's might (and main) / all-out // ~을 다하다 (기울이다 [direct] all one's energies (to) / (속어) go all-out // 우리는 ~을 다하여 싸웠다 We fought with all our might [strength / power].
● **총력 안보 (태세)** (strengthen) an all-out national security (posture); a total security (posture). **총력전** a total war; an all-out war.

총렵(銃獵) hunting; shooting. ⇨총사냥 ¶~ 금지기 the closed season.
● **총렵가** a hunter; a huntsman; a sportsman. **총렵기** the hunting[shooting] season; the open season.

총론(總論) general remarks; [대요(大要)] an outline (of); [서설(序說)] an introduction (to); a general summary; a survey (of). ¶~의 introductory // 민법 ~ an introduction to the study of civil law // ~에서 각론으로 들어가다 proceed from a summary to the details / proceed[descend] from the general to the particular.

총론(叢論) a collection of treatises[essays]. ¶문학 ~ a collection of essays on literature.

총리(總理) 1 [국무총리] the premier; the Prime; the prime minister; the Premier; Minister. 2 [총관리] general overseeing [control]; presiding over. **총리하다** preside over; oversee. ¶국무를 ~ preside over[run] affairs of state.
● **총리 공관** the premier's official residence. **총리실** the Office of Premier.

총림(叢林) a dense wood[grove]; [덤불숲] a bush; a thicket.

총망하다(悤忙-) very busy; hurried; rushed; flurried; (서술적) be in a hurry. **총망히** in a great hurry; hurriedly; in precipitation.

총면적(總面積) ¶이 홀의 ~은 500제곱미터이다 The total area[floor space] of this hall is five hundred square meters.

총명(聰明) [명민] brightness; intelligence; sagacity; wisdom; [기억력이 좋음] a good [retentive] memory. **총명하다** bright; intelligent; sagacious; wise; (기억력이) have a good[sharp / retentive] memory. ¶총명한 사람 a man of sagacity / an intelligent [a wise] person // 총명한 사람은 그런 일을 하지 않는다 No sagacious[sensible] man would do such a thing.

총목록(總目錄) the table of contents; a complete catalog(ue); a full list. ¶이것들은 ~에 기재되어 있다 These items are listed in the catalog.

총무(總務) (사무) general affairs[business]; (사람) a manager; a director; a leader; the director in charge of general affairs. ¶원내 ~ (미) a floor leader / (영) a whipper-in / a whip // 학생회 ~ a manager of the student's association.
● **총무과**[국(局)] the general affairs section [bureau]. **총무부** the general affairs department[division]. ¶~ 부장 the chief of the general affairs department.

총반격(總反擊) an all-out counterattack. **총반격하다** mount a general counteroffensive.

총받이(銃-) the firing[front / foremost] line; the forefront (of the battle).

총보(總譜) [음] a (full) score. ¶~에서 in (full) score.

총본산(總本山) [불] the head[mother] temple (of a Buddhist sect); the headquarters (of a sect).

총부리(銃-) the muzzle of a rifle. ¶~를 들이대고 (threat a person) at the point of a gun / (미) at gunpoint // ~를 들이대다 point [level / aim] a gun at (a person) / hold a gun (on the enemy).

총사냥(銃-) (미) hunting; (영) shooting; sporting. ¶~을 금하다 prohibit hunting. **총사냥하다** hunt with a gun; go shooting [hunting].

총사령관(總司令官) the supreme commander; the commander in chief(약어 C. in C., C in C). ¶연합군 ~ the Supreme Commander for the Allied Powers.

총사령부(總司令部) the General Headquarters(약어 GHQ). ¶유엔군 ~ United Nations Command(약어 UNC).

총사직(總辭職) general resignation; resignation in a body[(프) en masse / en bloc]. ¶내각 ~ the resignation of the Cabinet // ~을 요구하다 demand (that the Cabinet) resign en masse. **총사직하다** resign in a body[en masse]. ¶내각이 총사직했다 The Cabinet resigned en mass[in a body]. / The entire Cabinet resigned.

총살(銃殺) shooting (to death). **총살하다** shoot (a person) to death; kill (a person) by shooting. →그는 반역자로서 총살되었다 He was shot for treason.
● **총살형** execution by a firing squad(▶ by (a) firing squad는 몇 사람의 의한 것임). ¶~에 처하다 send a person before the firing squad / sentence a person to be shot // 전범은 ~으로 처형되었다 The war criminals were executed by a firing squad.

총상(銃傷) a bullet[gunshot] wound. ¶~을 입다 suffer gun shot (in one's right shoulder) // 그는 가슴을 관통한 ~으로 죽었다 He died on the spot of[from] a bullet which pierced his chest.

총상 꽃차례(總狀-次例) a raceme.

총색인(總索引) a general index (to an encyclopedia).

총생(叢生) growing in clusters; fasciculation. **총생하다** grow dense[in clusters]; be arranged in fascicles; form fascicles. ¶총생하는 [~의] arranged in fascicles / fasciculate / fascicular // 현장에는 키가 큰 풀이 총생하고 있었다 The site was overgrown[choked] with tall grass.
● **총생 식물** a social[gregarious] plant.

총서(叢書) (갖가지의) a collection of books; a library; [연속 출판물] a series (단수·복수 동형). ¶고전 문학 ~ a library of the classics // ~로 출판하다 publish in a series.

총선(總選) a general election. ⇨총선거

총선거(總選擧) a general election. ¶~에서 승리하다 win the general election // ~는 2개월 이내에 실시된다 A general election will take place within two months. **총선거하다** hold a general election; appeal[go] to the country.
● **총선거일** the general election day.

총성(銃聲) the report of a gun. ⇨총소리

총소리(銃-) the report of a gun[rifle]; a gun [rifle] report; a (gun) shot. ¶~가 들렸다 I heard a shot. / A shot was heard.

총수(總帥) [영도자] (supreme) leader; [총지휘관] a commander-in-chief (pl. commanders-in-chief); a commander. ¶K 재벌의 ～ the head of the K Group.

총수(總數) 〔전체의 수효〕 the total[aggregate] (number); the whole sum; 《부사적》 in all [total]; all told; altogether; in the aggregate. ¶～ 2백 a total of 200／～가 얼마나 되나 What does it amount to in all[in the aggregate]?／～는 2백이 된다 The total amounts to 200 (in all)./ The total number is 200./ They number 200 in all.／구경꾼의 ～가 4만 명이었다고 했다 The spectators were said to have totaled forty thousand.／불량품의 ～가 20개에 달했다 All told, there were as many as twenty articles of inferior make.／회원 는 2,500명이다 The total membership is 2,500.

총수입(總收入) the total[gross] income.

총신(銃身) the barrel (of a gun). ⇨총열

총신(寵臣) one's favorite retainer[subject]; a court favorite.

총아(寵兒) a favorite[pet] child; a darling; a pet;〔귀여운 아이〕a beloved child. ¶문단의 ～ the darling of the literary world／시대의 ～ lion of the day／그는 운명의 ～이다 He is a very fortunate[lucky] fellow./ Lady Luck always seems to smile on him.

총안(銃眼) a loophole (to shoot through); a crenel(le); an embrasure. ¶～이 있는 성벽 a crenellated wall.

총알(銃-) a ball; (피스톨·라이플 총의) a bullet; (장총의) a shell; a shot (산탄); a slug (납의); a staple (호치키스의). ¶～ 자국 a bullet hole／～이 나가지 않는 총 an unloaded gun／～이 뚫지 못하는 옷 a bulletproof jacket／～이 미치는[못 미치는] 곳에 within [out of] gunshot (of)／～로 꿰뚫다 send [fire] a bullet through (a person's brain)／ ～에 맞다 be hit by a bullet / get[receive] a bullet (in one's arm) / (영국 속어) catch a packet／～을 뽑(아내)다 extract the ball (from) / unload a gun／～을 쏘아 박다 (박아 넣다) pull a bullet in (a person's stomach)／ ～을 재다 load (a gun) (with shot) / charge (a gun)／～을 재어 발사 준비를 하다 load (a gun) ready for firing／적에게 ～을 퍼붓다 rain bullets on the enemy / subject the enemy to fire／～이 다하다 [～을 다 쏘다] fire away all one's shot／～이 무릎에 박히다 a bullet lodges[gets embedded] in one's knee ／～이 벽을 꿰뚫다 a bullet goes through [penetrates] a wall／～이 비 오듯 하다 bullets rain[shower like hail] / bullets come thick and fast／그 연발 권총은 ～이 장전돼 있다 The revolver is loaded.／그는 ～에 맞아 죽었다 He was shot dead./ The bullet hit and killed him./ He was killed by a bullet.

총애(寵愛) favor; good graces; love; patronage; affection. ¶왕비의 ～를 잃다 forfeit [lose] the queen's favor[affection]／그녀는 왕의 ～를 받았다 She was loved most tenderly by the king./ She was a favorite with the king. **총애하다** favor; bestow favor (up)on; make a favorite of; receive (a person) into one's favor; love (a person) tenderly; patronize. ¶총애하는 favorite / beloved / pet ／부모는 막내딸을 총애했다 The parents were partial to[felt special affection for] their youngest daughter.

총액(總額) the total sum[amount]; the sum total; the [a] total; 《문어》 the aggregate. ¶～ 5백만 원 ₩5,000,000 in total[in the aggregate]／수출 ～ the total exports／예산 ～ the total budget／～은 500달러가 된다 The total comes to 500 dollars./ It makes a total of 500 dollars.／피해 ～은 2억 원에 이른다 The total damages amount to two hundred million won.／차입금이 ～ 50만 원이 되어 버렸다 Our debts ran up to a total of five hundred thousand won./ We ran up a debt totaling five hundred thousand won.

총열(銃-) the barrel (of a gun); the gunbarrel.

총영사(總領事) a consul general (▶ 형용사가 뒤에 옴) (pl. consuls general, consul generals). ¶윤 싱가포르 ～ Consul-General Yun at Singapore.

●**총영사관** a consulate general. ¶뉴욕 한국 ～ the Korean Consulate General in New York.

총원(總員) 〔전체의 인원〕 the entire strength; the whole personnel; all members; total membership; all hands (배의); 《부사적》 in all; all told. ¶군대의 ～ the entire strength of an army／～ 30명 thirty persons in all [all told]／～ 5만 명의 조합 a union with a membership of fifty thousand／～ 갑판으로 All hands on deck!／～ 100명이 출석했다 There were a hundred persons present in all [all told].

총의(總意) the collective [general] will [opinion] (of); the consensus (of the people). ¶국민의 ～ the (collective) will of the people[the whole nation]／국민의 ～에 따라 in accordance with the general will[the consensus] of the people／그것은 의사의 ～에 따라 결정 되었다 It was determined by a consensus of medical opinion.

총잡이(銃-) 〔사격의 명수〕 a gunman; a (professional) killer; a gangster.

총장(總長) 1 (대학의) the president (of a university); a chancellor (영국 대학의); a prexy (미국 속어);〔사무총장〕 the secretary-general. ¶부～ a vice president／～에 취임하다 assume the presidency (of a university) / take[occupy] the presidential chair (of). 2 (군대의) the chief (of an army). ¶참모 ～ the Chief of the General Staff.

총재(總裁) a president; a governor; the presidency. ¶당 ～ the president of a party / a party chief／부～ a vice-president／한국은행 ～ the Governor of the Bank of Korea／명예 ～ an honorary president／그는 당의 ～ 후 보로 추천되었다 He was nominated for the presidency[《영》 leadership] of the party. / He was nominated as party president [chairman／《영》 leader] of the party.／그들 은 권 씨를 ～로 하여 당의 재건을 도모하고 있다 They are trying to rebuild their party under the chairmanship of Mr. Gwon.

총점(總點) one's total score; the total number of marks[points]; the aggregate of marks. ¶영어의 ～은 80점이었다 The total of marks in English was 80.／5과목의 시험에서 내 ～ 은 450점이었다 My total score for the five subjects was 450.

총좌(銃座) a gun support; an emplacement [position].

총지배인(總支配人) a general manager.

총지출(總支出) gross[total] expenditure. ¶～ 은 10만 원이었다 The total expenditure [《미》]

총지휘(總指揮) the supreme command. ¶공군의 ~자는 스미스 장군이었다 General Smith took supreme command of the air force. 총지휘하다 take the supreme command of (an army). ¶그날의 행사를 그가 총지휘했다 He took charge of the entire program for the day[entire day's program].∥그 전투는 스미스 장군이 총지휘했다 The fighting took place under the command of General Smith.
● **총지휘관** the (supreme) commander.

총질(銃−) shooting; firing. ¶~이 서투르다 be poor at shooting / be a bad[poor] shot. 총질하다 shoot[fire] (a gun); fire at (a person).

총채 a (horsehair) duster. ¶~로 털다 dust (the desk)∥나는 ~로 책의 먼지를 떨었다 I dusted the books.

총체(總體) the whole; all. ¶~적으로 on the whole / all things considered / in general∥우리 비용의 ~는 상당한 것이 될 것이다 Our total expenditure will be considerable.∥~적으로 말해, 젊은이들이 정치에 흥미를 잃었다 Generally speaking, young people have lost interest in politics.∥~적으로 그 계획은 성공이었다 By and large, the plan was successful.

총총걸음 (walking in) quick short steps; hurried walking. ¶~으로 at a quick[brisk] pace / with quick steps∥~을 치다 walk in quick short steps / hurry along∥~으로 걸어오다 come up (the pavement) with mincing steps.

총총하다 (별이) starlit; starry; starred; star-studded. ¶별이 총총한 밤 a bright starry night∥하늘에 별이 ~ The sky is studded [crowded / strewn] with stars.

총총하다(叢叢−) 〔나무 등이 무성하다〕 thick; dense; close. 총총히 thickly; densely; closely. ¶모를 ~ 심다 plant young rice plants close together∥산에 나무가 ~ 들어서다 a mountain is densely wooded∥그 정원에는 묘목이 ~ 심어져 있었다 Nursery-trees [Young trees] were planted close together in the garden.

총총하다(叢叢−) (사물이) dense; crowded; numerous. 총총히 densely; numerously; in large numbers.

총총(히)(悤悤−) in haste; hastily; in a hurry [rush]; hurriedly. ¶~ 떠나다 leave in haste ∥~ 집에 돌아가다 hurry[scurry] home∥~ 다녀가다 make a hasty visit∥~ 달아나다 run away helter-skelter / beat a hasty retreat∥그는 연회장을 ~ 돌아다니면서 모든 사람들의 뒤를 보살펴 주고 있었다 He rushed about[ran around] at the banquet seeing to everyone's needs. 총총하다 〔몹시 급하다〕 hasty; hurried; rushed.

총출동(總出動) general mobilization. ¶군대의 ~ the general mobilization of troops. 총출동하다 have a general mobilization; be all mobilized[called out]. ¶그의 가족이 총출동하여 나를 환영해 주었다 His whole family came out to welcome me.∥경찰관이 총출동하여 시체를 수색 중이다 The entire police force is out searching for the dead body.∥온 마을 사람이 총출동하여 지사를 맞이했다 All the villagers went out to greet the governor. ∥경관들이 총출동하여 경계를 했다 The police turned out in full force to prevent a breach of peace.

총칙(總則) general rules[provisions]. ¶민법 ~ general provisions of the civil code.

총칭(總稱) a general term; a generic name; an overall designation. 총칭하다 give a general name (to); name generically.

총칼(銃−) a gun and a sword; firearms. ¶~로 다스리다 rule over with guns and swords [by force].

총탄(銃彈) a ball; a bullet. ⇨ =총알

총톤수(總−數) gross tonnage. ¶~ 1만 톤의 배 a steamer of 10,000 tons gross.

총통(總統) 1〔총괄〕 presiding over. 2〔총괄하여 다스리는 관직〕 the President; the Generalissimo; (독) the Führer.

총퇴각(總退却) a general[full] retreat. ¶군대는 ~ 중이다 The army is in full retreat. 총퇴각하다 make a general retreat; retreat on all fronts.

총파업(總罷業) a general strike. ¶~으로 들어가다 go on a general strike / begin a general strike∥~ 중지의 지령이 내렸다 The general strike was called off.

총판(總販) an exclusive sale; sole agency [trade]. ¶~ 특약을 맺다 enter into a special contract for the sole agency∥~권을 주다 give the sole selling right[the franchise / an exclusive agency] (for). 총판하다 make an exclusive sale (of).

총평(總評) a general survey[review / critique]. ¶문단 ~ a sweeping criticism[a general review] of the literary world.

총포(銃砲) guns; firearms; 〔집합적〕 gunnery.
● **총포상** a gun store[〔영〕 shop]; a dealer in firearms. 총포 화약류 단속법 the Firearms & Explosive Control Law.

총할(總轄) superintendence. ⇨ =총람(總攬)

총화(銃火) rifle[musket] fire; gunfire. ¶~를 받다 come[be] under fire.

총화(總和) 〔전체를 합해 모은 수〕 the sum total. ¶전학급의 지출 ~를 내 주시오 Please add up the expenditure for all the classes.

총회(總會) a general meeting[assembly]; (본회의) a plenary session. ¶주주 ~ a general meeting of stockholder / [〔영〕 shareholders]∥임시 ~ an extraordinary general meeting∥유엔 ~ the United Nations General Assembly(약어 UNGA).
● **총회꾼** a rowdy who operates a protection racket in relation to company stockholders' meetings.

촬영(撮影) photographing; picture-taking; (영화) filming. ¶야간[고속도] ~ night[high-speed] photography∥야외 ~ (사진의) outdoor[nature] photography / (영화의) shooting on location∥실내 ~ indoor photographing∥재(再)~ a retake / rephotographing / reshooting∥적외선 ~ 장치 an infrared imaging system∥부감(俯瞰) ~ a crane[boom] shot∥~을 개시하다(영화의) start filming[shooting]. 촬영하다 (사진을) take a photograph[picture] (of); (영화를) make a film (of a wedding); film (a scene); shoot.
● **촬영 감독** a movie director. **촬영 금지** 〈게시〉 Taking Photographs (Is) Forbidden.; Cameras Are Forbidden.; No Pictures [Photography]. **촬영기** a moving-camera; a movie camera. **촬영 기사** a movie photogra-

pher; a cinematographer; a cameraman. **촬영 기술** camera technique; camera work; cinematography. **촬영 대본** a continuity. **촬영소** a cinema[film] studio; (미) a lot.

최-(最) the most; the extreme; ultra-. ¶~남단 the southernmost // ~첨단 the ultra-modern // ~우수 the very best.

최강(最強) the strongest. ¶~의 the strongest (team) / the most powerful (nation).

최고(最古) ¶~의 the oldest.

최고(最高) maximum; supremacy. ¶~의 highest / supreme / maximum / superlative // ~의 온도 the highest temperature // ~의 스태프 the best staff // ~의 솜씨 supreme skill // 벚꽃이라면 진해가 ~다 There is no place like Jinhae to see cherry blossoms. // 그는 그 팀에서의 ~ 선수이다 He is the star [the number one player] on the team. / He outshines all the other players on the team. // 누가 이 반의 ~의 학생인가 Who is the top student[pupil] in this class? // 따뜻하기로 말한다면 깃털 이불이 ~다 For warmth, nothing can beat[you can't beat] an eiderdown (quilt). // 따뜻하게 하고 집 안에 있는 것이 ~다 The best thing is to keep warm and stay indoors. // 신경통에는 온천이 ~다 Nothing is as good as (a both in) a hot spring for neuralgia. // 물가가 ~에 달했다 Prices have hit the ceiling.
● **최고 가격** the highest [top / maximum] price; [경] the ceiling price. **최고 기록** the highest record; a new [an all-time] high. ¶~을 내다 have the best record / set a new record // ~을 깨뜨리다 break[smash] the record. **최고봉** [가장 높은 봉우리] the highest peak (of the Alps); [비유] the highest authority; the acme. ¶문단의 ~ the most prominent figure in the world of letters // 현대 문학의 ~ the highest level of contemporary literature // 영시(英詩)의 ~ the high-water mark of English poetry // 화단(畫壇)의 ~ the greatest of all painters (in Korea) // 히말라야의 ~ the highest peak in the Himalayas // 당대 물리학계의 ~ the most prominent physicist of the day / the greatest authority the day / the greatest authority in physics at the present // 그림은 18세기 미술의 ~이다 This painting represents the peak [pinnacle] of eighteenth-century art. **최고 사령관** the supreme commander; the commander-in-chief. **최고 속도** (a) maximum [top] speed. **최고 수훈 선수** the most valuable player(약어 MVP). **최고점** the highest [top] point; (경기의) the highest score; (시험의) the highest mark. ¶그는 시험에서 ~을 땄다 He gained the highest marks in the examination. **최고 책임자 / 최고 수뇌자** (정부 등) the highest[chief] executive. **최고품** the best stuff; tops. **최고 품질** top[the best] quality. **최고 학부** the highest seat [institution] of learning. ¶~를 나오다 graduate [be graduated] from a university. **최고 회의** the supreme council; the top-level meeting; (옛 소련의) the supreme Soviet of the U.S.S.R.

최고(催告) (a) notification; [법] a peremptory notice; a call(불입의). **최고하다** notify; call on (a person) to (do).

최고급(最高級) the highest grade[class]. ¶~의 of the highest grade / top-level [-ranking] / first-rate / of the best[highest / finest]

quality / (구어) choicest // 우리 회사의 제품은 ~에 끼인다 Our products are numbered [classed] among the best.
● **최고급품** an article of the highest quality.
최고도(最高度) the highest degree; the maximum; the climax.
최고위(最高位) the highest rank; the top place. ¶~를 차지하다 hold (the) top place / rank first.
최고조(最高潮) (조수의) the high water-mark; [정점] the climax; the zenith; the acme. ¶~에 이르다[달하다] reach[hit] the climax // ~ 상태다 be in full swing / (사람이) be in top form / be at the tiptop of (one's profession) // 선거전은 ~에 달했다 The election campaign reached its climax. // 9회말 홈런에 관중의 열광은 ~에 달했다 The excitement of the spectators reached fever pitch when the batter hit a homer in the bottom half of the ninth inning.
최근(最近) (때의) the latest date; the nearest; the most recent; the latest; (거리의) the nearest[shortest]; [요즈음 들어] lately; in recent years. ¶~의 (시간) the latest / last / recent / up-to-date // ~ 5년간에 in the last five years // ~까지 until a recent date / up to recently // ~의 편지 a recent letter // ~에 결혼한 부부 a newly-married couple // ~에 일어난 사건들 recent events // ~에 지은 집 a house recently built // ~ 10년 동안에 in the last ten years // ~의 아이들 the children of today // 그는 ~에 결혼했다 He got married recently. // ~에 언제 그를 만났습니까 When did you see him last?
● **최근 소식** the latest news.
최근세(最近世) recent times; the modern period. ¶한국 ~사(史) (저서명) a History of Modern Korea.
최다(最多) the greatest[largest] in number [quantity]; being most numerous; the maximum. ¶~의 군중 the largest crowd [mob] // 홈런의 ~ 기록 the record for the most home runs.
최단(最短) the shortest; the nearest (distance). ¶~의 the shortest // ~ 코스를 가다 take the shortest course // 이 길은 로스앤젤레스로 가는 ~의 코스입니다 This is the shortest course[cut / route] to Los Angeles.
● **최단 거리** the shortest distance. ¶학교까지는 ~로 500미터이다 It is five hundred meters to school by the shortest route. **최단 시일** the shortest time.
최대(最大) the greatest; the biggest; the largest; the maximum. ¶~의 [가장 큰] the biggest / the largest / [최대한의] maximum // 세계 ~의 도시 the largest city in the world // 전후 ~의 철도 사고 the worst train accident since the war // ~의 업적 the crowning achievement // ~의 찬사 the highest possible compliment / the greatest possible praise // ~ 풍속 the maximum wind velocity // ~ 찬사를 보내다 pay one's highest tribute of admiration.
최대 다수의 최대 행복 the greatest happiness of the greatest number (of people); the greatest good for the greatest number.
● **최대 공약수** the greatest common divisor [denominator](약어 G.C.D.); the greatest common measure(약어 G.C.M.). ¶4, 20, 40의 ~는 4이다 The greatest common divisor

of 4, 20, and 40 is 4. // 반전론은 좌우 양파의 주장의 ~였다 The only common ground shared by the left and right wings was a belief in pacifism. / The only thing the left and right wings had in common was anti-war feeling. **최대량**[額] the largest [maximum] quantity [amount]. **최대치** ➡최댓값 (⇨최대) **최댓값** [수] the maximum (value).

최대한(도)(最大限度) the[a] maximum. ¶~의 능률 (put out / show) the maximum of efficiency // ~으로 to the highest degree / to the utmost // 재능을 ~으로 활용하다 make the utmost use of one's ability // ~의 노력을 하다 exert the greatest possible effort [maximum effort] // 능력을 ~으로 발휘하다 give full play to one's abilities / use one's abilities to the full // 이 학급의 정원은 ~ 40인이다 The class is limited to forty. // 우리는 재고품을 ~의 싼값으로 제공합니다 We'll offer the goods in stock at the lowest possible price. // ~으로 깎아 드리는 것입니다 I'll reduce the price of much as possible.

최루(催淚) causing[producing] tears. ¶~(성)의 lachrymal / lacrimal.
● **최루 가스** tear gas; lacrimatory gas. **최루탄** a tear bomb[shell]. ¶경찰은 데모하는 군중을 ~으로 저지했다 The city police stopped the crowd in demonstration by using teargas bomb.

최면(催眠) hypnosis; hypnogenesis; somnolency. ¶자기 ~ selfypnotism // ~의 hypnotic // ~에 걸린 사람 a hypnotic // ~에 걸려 있다 be in a hypnotic trance / be in a state of hypnosis.
● **최면 상태** a hypnotic state; hypnosis; hypnotism. ¶~에 빠지다 be hypnotized // ~에서 깨우다 bring (a person) out of a hypnotic trance / dehypnotize. **최면술** mesmerism; hypnotism. ¶~에 걸린 사람 a hypnotic / a person under hypnosis // ~의 hypnotic // ~을 걸다 mesmerize (a person) / hypnotize (a person) / exercise a mesmeric power (over) // ~에 걸리다 be mesmerized / be hypnotized // 연사의 웅변에 청중은 마치 ~에 걸린 듯했다 The speaker's eloquence hypnotized the audience. **최면술사** a hypnotist; a mesmerist. **최면 요법** a hypnotic cure; hypnotherapy. ¶~을 쓰다 use a hypnotic cure. **최면제** [의] sleeping drug. ⇨수면제(⇨수면(睡眠))

최북단(最北端) the northernmost. ¶~의 northernmost.

최상(最上) the best. ¶~의 the best / the finest / the highest / the nicest / supreme / superb / superlative / (미) topnotch // ~운 the best of luck // 의 행복 the supreme happiness // 그의 컨디션은 ~이었다 He was in the best of condition[the best possible condition]. // 그의 연주 가운데서 ~의 것은 쇼팽의 왈츠였다 The best part of his concert was the Chopin waltz. / The Chopin waltz was the high point of his recital.
● **최상권** supreme power; supremacy.

최상급(最上級) **1** [가장 높은 등급] the highest grade / (학교의) the top[graduating] class. **2** [언] the superlative (degree).

최선(最善) the best. ¶~의 노력 the utmost [best] efforts // ~을 다하다 do one's best [utmost] / do all one can // ~을 다하겠습니다 I will do[try] my best. // 그는 난민 구호에 ~의 노력을 기울이고 있다 He is doing his best [exerting every effort] to help the refugees.

최성기(最盛期) [전성기] the golden age [days]; the height of prosperity; (작물 등의) the peak of the season; (젊음·인기 등의) one's heyday. ¶문화의 ~에 이르다 reach the high watermark[zenith] of (its) culture // 자연주의는 그때가 ~였다 Naturalism was then in its heyday. / That was the golden age of naturalism. // 지금은 수박의 ~다 This is the season for watermelons. / Watermelons are at their best now.

최소(最小) (크기가) the smallest; (양·정도이) the minimum. ¶~의 the smallest / minimum / minimal // 위험을 ~화하다 reduce the danger to a minimum // ~의 노력으로 최대의 효과를 올리다 achieve a maximum of efficiency at a minimum of effort // 그는 ~의 비용으로 그것을 그럭저럭 해냈다 He managed to do it at the minimum of cost.
● **최소 공배수** [수] the least common multiple(약어 L.C.M.). **최소량** the minimum quantity. **최소치** ➡최솟값(⇨최소) **최솟값** [수] the minimum (value).

최소(最少) **1** [가장 적음] the least; the fewest; the minimum. ¶~의 the fewest / the least / the minimum / minimal // 나는 사내에서 ~의 보너스를 받았다 I received the smallest [lowest] bonus in the office. // 이달의 교통사고는 5년 동안에 ~다 The number of traffic accidents this month is the lowest in five years. **2** [가장 젊음] the youngest.

최소한(도)(最小限度) (명사) the[a] minimum; (부사) at a minimum; to say the least (of it); at (the) least. ¶~으로 at a minimum // 비용을 ~으로 줄이다 reduce the expenses to the minimum // 5년은 걸리다 take five years at least[at the minimum] // 청중 속의 여성은 ~ 20명은 될 것이다 There must be at least twenty women in the audience. // 그들의 노력으로 피해는 ~에 그쳤다 Their efforts held the damage to a minimum. // 이것이 우리가 생각할 수 있는 ~의 요구이다 This is the lowest conceivable demand we can make. // 그것은 ~으로 어림해도 500만 원은 들 것이다 It will cost five million won, ever estimating conservatively.

최신(最新) up-to-dateness. ¶~의 [가장 새로운] the newest / [최근의] the latest / up-to-date // ~ 뉴스 the latest news / red-hot news // ~ 머리형 the latest hairstyle // ~ 설비를 갖춘 병원 a hospital with the most up-to-date facilities.
● **최신식** the latest[newest] fashion[style]. ¶~ 백과사전 an up-to-date encyclopedia // ~ 호텔 a hotel with the latest improvements. **최신 유행** the latest fashion; the newest style. ¶~의 모자[양복] a new-look hat[suit] // ~의 구두를 신다 wear the latest thing in shoes // 모두 ~의 양장을 하고 있다 They are seen all dressed à la mode. **최신판** the latest edition. **최신형** a new[the latest] style [model / design].

최악(最惡) the worst. ¶~의 the worst // ~의 경우에는 When[If] (the) worst // ~의 시나리오 a worst-case scenario // ~의 경우에 대비하다 prepare for the worst // ~의 사태에 이르렀다 Things have reached the worst possible pass. // 우리는 ~의 경우를 예상해야만 한다 We must be prepared for the worst.

최우등(最優等) the top grade; the highest [greatest] distinction; top honors. ¶~의 most excellent / the best // ~으로 졸업하다 graduate (from a college) with the highest [greatest] distinction.
● **최우등생** the highest honorsman; the top student. **최우등품** the most excellent stuff; an article of superb quality; A-1 goods; a choice article.

최우수(最優秀) the very best; an A1; an ace. ¶~ 학생 the very best student.
● **최우수 선수** the most valuable player(약어 MVP).

최음제(催淫劑) an aphrodisiac (medicine); a lascivious drug.

최장(最長) the longest. ¶~의 (the) longest.
● **최장 거리** the longest [greatest] distance.

최저(最低) the lowest; the lowermost; the minimum. ¶~의 〔가장 낮은〕 the lowest / 〔최소한의〕 minimum // 경비를 ~한으로 줄이다 cut expenses to a minimum [to the bone] // 한 달에 ~5만 원의 경비가 들 것이다 It will cost at least [cost an absolute minimum of] fifty thousand won a month.
● **최저가** the lowest price. **최저 기록** the lowest record; 〔미국 구어〕 a new low. **최저 생활**[**생활비**] the minimum standard [cost] of living.

최적(最適) ¶~의 the most suitable (for) // 그 드레스는 파티에 ~이다 That is the most suitable [the perfect] dress for the party. // 그 역할에는 그가 ~이다 He is the very [just the right] man for the part. **최적하다** optimal; optimum.
● **최적 온도**[**밀도 / 속도**] the optimum temperature [density / speed]. **최적 조건** 〔생〕 the optimum.

최전방(最前方) the line of battle. ⇨ ̄**최전선**

최전선(最前線) the front line; the foremost front; the spearhead; the line of battle; (at) the forefront. ¶~의 병사들 soldiers at the front.

최종(最終) 〔맨 뒤〕 the last; 〔끝〕 the end. ¶~의 the last / the final / closing / ultimate // ~까지 to the last [end] // ~적으로 finally // ~수단 a trump card / one's last resort // 〔거래 소의〕 ~ **입회** the trading day's close // 내일 ~ 교섭을 하기로 되어 있다 We are going to make one last [final] attempt to negotiate (it) tomorrow. // 내가 ~ 수단을 쓰기에는 아직 시기상조다 It's too early to resort to my last trick [to play my trump card].
● **최종 결정** the final decision. **최종 목적** ultimate object. **최종 수요자 / 최종 소비자** an end user. **최종안** the final program [plan]. **최종회** (시합의) the last inning [round].

최첨단(最尖端) 1 〔맨 끝 부분〕 the end; the tip. 2 〔시대나 유행의 가장 선두〕 the forefront; (예술상의) the avant-garde. ¶~의 〔가장 진보한〕 the most advanced / [첨단 기술의] high-tech / [초근대적인] ultramodern / [전위적인] avant-garde // ~의 컴퓨터 기술 the most advanced computer technology.

최초(最初) the first; the outset; the beginning; the commencement. ¶~의 the first (doing) / initial (attempt) / opening (game) / 〔본래의〕 original (plan) / primary (object) / 〔가장 이른〕 the earliest (visitor) // ~의 경험 one's first [new] experience // ~에 first (of all) / in the first place / to begin [start] with // ~의 계획 the original plan // ~의 목적 one's primary object // ~의 3년간 the first three years // ~의 사건 the first happening // ~에는 그럴 계획이 아니었다 It wasn't my original plan to do so. // 그 회사의 금년 ~의 출판은 이 책이다 The publisher has begun the year with this book.

최하(最下) the lowest; the most inferior; the worst. ¶~의 ~ / the worst // 네 명의 소년들은 모두 수학을 못하는데 그 가운데서도 그가 ~였다 The four boys were all bad at mathematics, but he was the worst. // ~로 싸게 해서 얼마입니까 What is the very lowest price you will go down to? // 그것이 ~로 깎은 값입니다 That's the lowest (price) I can let it go for.
● **최하 가격** the lowest [minimum] price. **최하층** (사회의) the lowest stratum of society; the lowest class; (건물의) the lowermost story. **최하품** the worst stuff; an article of the lowest grade [quality].

최하급(最下級) the lowest grade [class]. ¶~의 of the lowest class / buck(군대 등에서의).

최하위(最下位) 〔가장 아래의 지위〕 the lowest rank; (경기 등에서의) last place (in the rankings). ¶~의 **장교** an officer of the lowest rank // ~의 팀 the tailender // ~**이다** rank lowest / be lowest in rank / (경기에서) be in the cellar // 반에서 ~이다 be at the bottom of the class // ~로 **떨어지다** fall into the cellar [into last place] // 우리 팀은 금년도에 ~이다 Our team is the tailender [(구어) in the cellar] this year.

최혜국(最惠國) a most favored nation.
● **최혜국 대우** most-favored-nation treatment. ¶~를 **받다** be treated as a most favored nation. **최혜국 조항 / 최혜국 약관** the most-favored-nation clause(약어 MFNC).

최후(最後) 1 〔맨 끝〕 the last; 〔결말〕 the end. ¶~의 the last / final / closing / ultimate // ~로 lastly / finally / in conclusion / in the end // ~까지 to the last end // ~의 희망 one's last hope // ~의 승리 the final [ultimate] victory // ~의 일격 the last [a final] blow // ~의 승리를 얻다 win in the long run / win an ultimate victory // 영화를 ~까지 보다 sit through the movie // ~까지 **저항하다** resist to the last (drop of one's blood) // ~의 5분이 중요하다 The last five minutes determines the issue. // 그 사람을 만난 것은 그것이 ~다 That was the last I saw of him. // ~에 누가 이길지는 두고 봐야겠다 It is yet to be seen who will win in the end.

2 〔죽음·임종〕 one's last moment; one's end; one's fate. ¶~의 말 one's dying words // (악운이 다하여) ~**가 오다** come to one's account day (having run out one's prosperous course of wickedness) // 그는 비참한 [장렬한] ~를 마쳤다 He met a tragic [heroic] end. / He died a tragic [heroic] death. // 나는 그의 ~를 지켜 볼 수 없었다 I was unable to be present at his deathbed.
● **최후 노력** a last-spurt effort. **최후 수단** (resort to) the last measure; one's [the] last resort; the ultimate [final] step. ¶그는 사흘 밤이나 잠을 못 자서 ~으로 수면제를 먹었다 After three sleepless nights, he took sleeping

pills as a last resort. 최후 순간 the last [critical] moment. 최후의 만찬 the Last Supper. 최후의 심판 the Last Judg(e)ment: the great[last] account; doom. 최후통첩 an ultimatum; a final note. ¶~을 보내다 send [deliver] an ultimatum // 그들은 그에게 ~을 내밀었다 They confronted him with an ultimatum.

추(錘) (낚싯줄의) a (fishing) sinker; a (fishing) weight; (저울의) a scale weight; (시계의) a pendulum; a bob; (먹줄의) a plummet.

추가(追加) (an) addition; an addendum (*pl.* -da); an appendix (*pl.* -dices, -ixes); [보충] a supplement. ¶~의 additional / supplementary. 추가하다 add[append] (something) to; supplement. ¶목걸이에 진주를 3개 ~ add three pearls to a necklace // 예산에 ~ supplement a budget // 우리는 맥주를 추가해서 주문했다 We ordered more beer.
● 추가 경정 예산(안) a revised supplementary budget (bill). 추가 비용 additional expenses. 추가 시험 a supplementary examination; a makeup (examination); (미) a condition(가진학 학생의). ¶~을 치르다 take a makeup / take a special test to make up for one's absence[failure] at the regular examination // 영어의 ~을 치르게 되다 be conditioned in English. 추가 신청 additional application. 추가 예산(안) an additional budget (bill). 추가 주문 an additional order.

추간(追刊) additional publication. 추간하다 publish in addition.

추격(追擊) (a) pursuit; (a) chase; a follow-up attack. ¶경찰의 맹~을 피하다 evade the hot pursuit of the police // 적은 우리를 맹렬히 ~ 중이다 The enemy is after us in hot pursuit. / (구어) The enemy is hot on our trail[tail]. 추격하다 pursue; chase; give chase to; run after. ¶적기를 ~ give chase to an enemy plane // 후퇴하는 적을 ~ pursue and attack [make further attacks on] a retreating enemy // 반란군을 맹~ pursue the rebels hotly[closely] / press hard on the rebel's heels.

추격(을) 붙이다 1 [전술을 연습시키다] hold [carry out] maneuvers; do military exercise; hold a sham battle[fight]. 2 [이간하여 싸우게 하다] make (persons) quarrel; set (persons) by the ears; alienate[estrange] (a person) from (another).
● 추격자 a pursuer; (복수의) a pursuing party; (미) a posse. ¶~를 따돌리다 give one's pursuer the slip / throw one's pursuer off the scent. 추격전 a battle fought in pursuit of an enemy.

추경(秋耕) autumn plowing. ⇨"가을갈이(⊙)가을)."

추경(秋景) autumn scene; autumnal scenery.

추계(秋季) autumn; (미) fall.
● 추계 운동회 an autumn sports[athletic] meet[meeting].

추계(推計) (an) estimation. 추계하다 estimate.
● 추계지(-紙) stochastic paper. 추계학 stochastics; the theory of statistical inference.

추고(追考) reminiscence; recollection; retrospection; looking back. 추고하다 look back upon[to] (the past); retrospect; reminisce.

추고 →퇴고(推敲)

추곡(秋穀) autumn grain.
● 추곡 수매 (가격) the government purchase (price) of rice.

추골(椎骨) [생] the backbone. ⇨"척추1."

추구(追求) pursuit; chase; search; following-up. ¶행복[명성]의 ~ the pursuit of happiness[fame]. 추구하다 pursue; seek after; chase; give chase to; follow after. ¶…을 추구하여 in quest[pursuit / search] of // 이상을 ~ pursue one's ideals/쾌락을 ~ pursue [seek] pleasure // 자본주의는 이윤을 추구한다 Capitalism seeks profit.

추구(追究) (an) investigation (of); a close inquiry (into). ¶진리의 ~ an inquiry into the truth // 진실의 본질에 대한 ~ an inquiry into the nature of truth. 추구하다 inquire into (a matter) closely; follow up an inquiry; investigate (a matter) thoroughly; probe (a matter) to the bottom.

추구(推究) inference. 추구하다 infer.

추궁(追窮) close inquiry; pressing hard; thorough investigation. ¶정치 헌금에 대한 ~ a searching investigation of political donations. 추궁하다 press hard; come down hard (on / upon). ¶책임을 ~ call (a person) to account / 그들은 도청(道政)의 부패를 추궁했다 They looked closely into corruption in prefectural politics. / 경찰관은 나의 음주 운전을 의심하여 추궁했다 Suspecting that I was driving under the influence of alcohol, the policeman grilled me. →¶나는 남에게 책임을 추궁당할 일을 한 적이 없다 I have never done anything to lay myself open to criticism. // 내 설명의 모순점을 추궁당하여 나는 답변의 말이 궁했다 I was at a loss what to say[answer] when they pointed out the inconsistencies in my explanation.

추근추근 tenaciously; persistently; pertinaciously; importunately. ¶~ 묻다 pester (a person) with questions // 여자를 ~ 쫓아다니다 keep after[pester] a girl / pursue a girl doggedly // 그렇게 ~ 캐묻지 마라 Don't be so inquisitive. 추근추근하다 persistent; tenacious; pertinacious; dogged; importunate; inquisitive. ¶추근추근한 요구 an importunate demand / 추근추근한 사람 a dogged person / a nuisance // 추근추근한 외판원 a high-pressure salesman. 추근추근히 doggedly; tenaciously; persistently; importunately; demandingly.

추급(追給) (a) supplementary payment. 추급하다 pay in addition.

추기(追記) an additional writing; a supplement; an addendum (*pl.* -da); a postscript(약어 PS, P.S.). ¶~에 이렇게 적혀 있다 The postscript goes[reads] like this. 추기하다 add a postscript (to); add (to); write (an addendum) later; supplement.

추기경(樞機卿) [가] a cardinal.

추기다 [꾀다] tempt; allure; seduce; entice; decoy; cajole; wheedle(달콤한 말로); [선동하다] incite; abet; instigate; stir up; (개 등을) set (a dog) on[at] (a person). ¶추겨서 싸우게 하다 egg (a person) on to fight // 노동자를 추겨서 파업을 시키다 instigate workers to go on strike.

추깃물 water from a rotting corpse; cadaveric fluid.

추남(醜男) a bad-looking[an ugly] man.

추납(追納) supplementary payment; a follow-

추납하다 up payment. 추납하다 pay in addition. ¶나는 세금을 2만 원이나 추납했다 I paid an extra [additional] twenty thousand won in taxes.

추녀 [건] an angle rafter. ¶~ 끝에 매달린 고드름 icicles hanging from the eaves.

추녀(醜女) an ugly [a bad-looking / (미) a plain-looking] woman; a hag.

추념(追念) commemoration; remembrance. **추념하다** cherish [honor] the memory of (a person).
●**추념사** a memorial address.

추다¹ [춤 동작을 벌이다] dance; step [foot] it. ¶왈츠를 ~ dance a waltz // 장단[피리]에 맞추어 춤을 ~ dance to music [the flute] // 남의 장단에 춤을 ~ dance to [after] a person's tune [pipe / piping] // 우리는 피아노 반주에 맞추어 춤을 추었다 We danced to the music of the piano.

추다² 1 [찾아 뒤지다] find out; recover; get back; rummage out; worm out of (비밀 등을). 2 →추리다 3 [채어 올리다] pull up; draw up; lift up. ¶멍석 한구석을 ~ pull up a corner of a mat // 그물을 ~ draw up a net / haul in a net.

추단(推斷) [미루어 판단함 또는 그 판단] (an) inference; (a) deduction; [처단] judgment; decision; punishment. ¶기지의 사실로부터의 정당한 ~ legitimate inference from known facts. **추단하다** infer [deduce / gather] (from evidence); [처단하다] render judgment on; mete out punishment for. →¶그의 말투로 보아 그가 이 조건에는 불복인 것으로 추단된다 I gather from his words that he is not satisfied with the terms.

추대하다(推戴-) have (a person) as head [president / director]; be under the (presidency of); have (a person) over (a society). ¶당회는 황태자를 총재로 추대하고 있다 Our society has the honor of having the Crown Prince as president. // 윤 씨를 회장에 추대하기로 했다 We selected Mr. Yun as president of the society.

추도(追悼) mourning. ¶~의 뜻을 표하다 do honor to (a person's) memory / pay a tribute to the memory of (a person). **추도하다** mourn (for the dead / over a person's death).
●**추도가** a dirge. **추도문 / 추도사** a memorial writing [address]. ¶고 M씨의 ~을 읽다 deliver a eulogy on [pay tribute to the memory of] the late Mr. M. **추도식 / 추도회** a ceremony held in memory of (a person). ¶우리는 고인의 ~을 가졌다 We held a memorial service for the departed [deceased].

추돌(追突) a rear-end collision; a bump. ¶~을 당하여 차가 대파되었다 Struck from behind, the car was damaged badly. **추돌하다** rear-end; collide [run into] (a car) from behind. ¶추돌하지 않도록 주의하시오 Drive (your car) carefully so as not to collide with another car from behind.

추락(墜落) a fall; an accidental fall; (a) precipitation; a crash; [구어] a cropper; (영국 속어) a mucker. ¶그는 비행기 ~으로 사망했다 He was killed in a plane crash. **추락하다** fall; drop; come to the ground; go over (an embankment); come a cropper; (구어) crash(항공기가). ¶거꾸로 ~ fall head over heels (from) / fall [go down / come down] headlong to the ground // 그는 낭떠러지에서 추락하여 죽었다 He fell off [from] a cliff and died. // 비행기가 산에 추락했다 A plane crashed into the mountain. // 그는 벼랑에서 곤두박질로 추락했다 He fell head over heels from the cliff. // 그는 배에서 바다로 추락했다 He fell overboard. // 그는 10미터쯤 추락했다 He had a drop of about ten meters.
●**추락사** death from a fall. **추락 사고** (비행기의) a plane crash.

추레하다 shabby; dirty; frowzy; slovenly; (영) scruffy. ¶그런 추레한 옷차림으로 남 앞에 나가서는 안 된다 Don't go out in public looking so shabby [scruffy].

추력(推力) (a) driving force; (프로펠러 등의) (a) thrust; (로켓 등의) propulsive force; propulsion. ¶35,000 파운드의 ~을 내다 produce [generate] 35,000 pounds of thrust.

추렴 [어떤 비용을 위해 얼마씩 내어 거둠] joint contribution; sharing the expenses; pooling; clubbing. ¶술~ a drinking party that goes Dutch / a Dutch drinking party // ~으로 at the joint expense of. **추렴하다** contribute jointly; contribute each his own share; pool (funds); club (the expenses). ¶그들은 그 비용을 추렴했다 They shared the expenses (among them). / Each paid his share of the expenses. / They all contributed some money to cover the expenses. // 그 형제는 저금을 추렴하여 자동차를 샀다 The brothers put their savings together [pooled their savings] to buy a car. // 그 소년들은 추렴해서 5천 원을 만들었다 The boys raised five thousand won among them.
●**추렴새** [추렴하는 금품] one's share (in the expenses); one's shot (at a tavern / at an inn); [추렴하는 일] joint contribution.

추록(追錄) [후기] a postscript; [보유] an addendum (pl. -da). **추록하다** add (notes to an article); write a postscript; write an addendum. ¶편집자는 그 작가의 일기에 연보를 추록했다 The editor appended a chronology to the writer's diary.

추론(推論) reasoning; ratiocination; (an) inference; induction(귀납); deduction(연역). ¶합리적인 ~을 내리다 make a reasonable inference [deduction]. **추론하다** reason; ratiocinate; infer (from); draw an inference (from); [귀납하다] induce; [연역하다] deduct. ¶버스 편이 아주 좋지 않으므로 그는 택시로 올 것이라고 나는 추론했다 Since bus service was very poor, I reasoned that he would probably come by taxi. // 이 자료에 입각해서 나는 다음과 같이 추론한다 From these data, I infer as follows [I draw the following conclusion]. →¶실패한 원인은 자금 부족에 있다고 추론되었다 It was concluded that the failure was caused by the lack of funds.

추리 the flank (of beef).

추리(推理) reasoning; ratiocination; (an) inference; (an) illation. ¶연역 [귀납] ~ deductive [inductive] inference // 직접 [간접] ~ immediate [mediate] inference // ~의 과정 a reasoning process // 너의 ~는 잘못되었다 Your reasoning [inference] isn't correct. **추리하다** [추론하다] infer (from); [논리적으로 생각하다] reason; [사실이나 가설로부터 사유하다] deduce (from). ¶하나하나 추리해 나가다 follow out a train of reasoning // 이러한 상황으로부터 사건의 전모를 추리해 보자

추리닝

Let's try to reconstruct a full picture of what happened, based on the evidence before us. ¶범인은 여자라고 추리되었다 It was deduced that the culprit was a woman.
● 추리력 one's reasoning; (문어) deductive powers. 추리 소설 a detective[mystery] story[novel]; (구어) a whodunit. 추리 소설가 a detective story writer; a mystery[crime] writer.

추리닝 training suit; sweat suit; jogging suit.
● 추리닝 바지 sweat pants. 추리닝 상의 sweat shirt.

추리다 〔선발하다〕 select (out of many); choose (from); pick out; single out; 〔선별하다〕 sort; assort. ¶여럿 중에서 ~ choose from among many // 짚을 ~ pick and trim straws (weeding out short ones) // 좋은 것을 ~ pick out the best ones // 지원자 5천 명 중에서 ~ single out of 5,000 applicants // 20명의 후보자 중에서 3명만 추려졌다 Only three were selected from among twenty candidates.

추맥(秋麥) autumn-sown barley; the late barley.

추명(醜名) an ill name; ill repute[fame]; infamy; notoriety; a scandal(추문). ¶~을 사다 earn[fall into] bad repute / become notorious (for) / raise[create / give rise to] a scandal.

추모하다(追慕-) cherish[respect] (a person's) memory; look back upon the memory of (a deceased person) with respect and affection. ¶선친을 ~ cherish[revere] the memory of one's late father // 그를 추모하는 사람들이 고향에 그의 기념비를 세웠다 His admirers set up a monument to his memory in his native place.

추문(醜聞) a scandal; ill fame. ¶끔찍한 ~ a frightful scandal // ~을 일으키다 create [cause / make up / give rise to] a scandal / 그에게는 ~이 그칠 새 없다 He is the object of continual[frequent] scandal. // 주간지가 그의 ~을 퍼뜨렸다 The weekly magazine published news of the scandal about him.
● 추문거리 a scandalous affair; a source of scandal; an object of public scandal.

추물(醜物) 〔물건〕 an ugly[a dirty] object [matter]; 〔사람〕 an ugly[a bad-looking / an unattractive] person; an indecent[a mean] person.

추밀원(樞密院) (영국의) the Privy Council.

추방(追放) **1** 〔쫓아냄〕 banishment; expulsion; (자국·고향으로부터) exile (from); 〔불법 입국자 등의 국외로의〕 deportation. ¶빈곤 ~ banishment of poverty // …의 ~을 선언하다 pronounce (a person's) exile // 악서 ~ 운동을 일으키다 start a campaign against harmful publications // ~을 당하다 get expelled[banished / exiled]. **추방하다** banish; expel; 〔불법 입국자 등을 쫓아내다〕 deport; 〔장소·지위 등에서 몰아내다〕 oust. ¶장교를 군에서 ~ cashier an officer from the army. →¶그는 국외로 추방되었다 He was banished[deported] from the country. // 그 아이는 학교에서 추방되었다 The child was expelled from school. // 그는 직장에서 추방되었다 He was ousted from office. // 그는 이단자로서 교회에서 추방되었다 He was excommunicated from the church as a heretic.
2 〔공직에서 몰아냄〕 a purge. ¶~을 해제하다 depurge / strike (a person's) name off the list of purgees / take (a person) off the line of purgees. **추방하다** purge. ¶공직에서 ~ remove[oust] (a person) from public office / purge (a person) from public life // 현직에서 ~ evict (a person) from his present post.
● 추방령 (불법 입국자 등의) a deportation order; (공직에서의) a purge directive. 추방자 an exile; (공직에서의) a purgee. ¶국외 ~ an exile / an expatriate.

추분(秋分) 〔24절기의 하나〕 *chubun*; the autumn(al) equinox.

추비(追肥) (an) additional manuring. ⇨ 덧거름

추사(秋思) autumnal sentiment[thought].

추산(推算) calculation; computation; reckoning. **추산하다** calculate; compute; reckon; 〔추정하다〕 estimate; put (at). ¶그는 내 집 수리비를 200만 원으로 추산했다 He estimated the cost of the repairs to my house at two million won. →¶이득은 2,000만 원으로 추산되었다 We estimated the profit at twenty million won.

추상(抽象) abstraction.
● 추상론 an abstract argument. 추상 명사 〔언〕 an abstract noun. 추상화(-化) abstraction. ¶~하다 abstract. 추상화(-畵) an abstract painting.

추상(秋霜) 〔가을의 찬 서리〕 autumn frost.

추상(追想) recollection; reminiscence. ⇨ 추억
● 추상록 reminiscences; memoirs; (a book of) recollections.

추상(推想) conjecture; surmise; supposition; presumption; inference; guess; imagination. ¶그것은 단순한 ~에 불과하다 It's a mere conjecture (and nothing more). / It is mere guesswork. **추상하다** conjecture; presume; suppose; surmise; infer (from); guess; imagine.

추상같다(秋霜-) severe; rigorous; rigid; stern merciless; relentless. ¶추상같은 명령 a stern order / 신 검사의 논고는 추상같았다 The final speech of prosecutor Sin was a scathing one.

추상적(抽象的) abstract. ¶사물을 ~으로 생각하다 consider things in the abstract [abstractly] // 그는 다만 ~으로 말했을 뿐이다 He was only talking in abstract[general] terms.

추색(秋色) 〔가을 경치〕 autumnal scenery; 〔단풍〕 autumnal tints[colo(u)rs]; 〔가을의 기색〕 signs of autumn. ¶~을 즐기다 enjoy autumnal tints // ~이 한창이다 The autumnal tints are in full glory. / The autumn colors are in flame. // ~이 깊어졌다 We are now in the midst of autumn.

추서(追敍) posthumous honors. **추서하다** confer posthumous honors on (a person); be promoted to (the third Court rank) posthumously.

추서다 〔몸이 회복되다〕 get well again; recover (from illness); be (about) oneself again; be restored to health. ¶그의 몸이 추서는 데 오래 걸렸다 He took a long time to come[get] round.

추석(秋夕) *chuseok*; the Korean (version of) Thanksgiving Day (celebrated on the 15th day of the eighth lunar month); Harvest Moon Day[Festival].

추세(趨勢) a tendency; a trend; a drift. ¶~효과 [경] a trend effect // 시대의 ~ the current of the times // 여론의 ~ the trend [set / tendency] of public opinion // 현대 철학의 ~ the trend[tendency] in modern philosophy // 일반적인 ~ a general tendency // 시대의 ~에 따르다 follow the trend of the times / swim with[go with] the current of the times • 시대의 ~에 거스르다 swim against the current of the times // 증가 ~에 있다 be on an increasing trend // 그것이 현대의 ~이다 That is the trend of the modern world[the times].

추소(追訴) a supplementary suit[indictment]. **추소하다** bring a supplementary suit [indictment] (against). ➡¶그는 절도죄에 상해죄가 더해져 추소되었다 He was indicted for[on charges of] assault and battery in addition to theft.

추속(醜俗) indecent[disgraceful / scandalous] customs; mean[base / foul] manners.

추수(秋收) harvesting; harvest. ¶~ 때 harvesttime / the time of harvest // 3백 석의 ~ a harvest[crop] of 300 *seok* of rice // ~가 많다 get[have] a good harvest[crop] / reap a rich harvest[crop] // 그들은 ~에 바빴다 They were busy harvesting[gathering in] the wheat. **추수하다** harvest; gather (in) a harvest; reap (a harvest); crop; take the crop up. ¶논에서 곡식을 ~ harvest the paddy fields.
● **추수 감사절** Thanksgiving Day. **추수기** harvesttime; harvest.

추스르다 1 [치켜 올리다] pick up and put in place. ¶업은 아이를 ~ jiggle a baby on one's back. 2 [수습하다] set (things) in order; manage; fix. ¶일을 ~ handle matters nicely / deal with an affair.

추시(追諡) a posthumous title. **추시하다** confer a posthumous title.

추시하다(趨時-) [시속(時俗)을 따르다] swim [go / float] with the stream[current]; follow the spirit of the times; keep abreast with[of] the times; keep pace[up] with the times.

추신(追伸·追申) a postscript(약어 P.S., PS, p.s.).

추심(推尋) (어음 등의) collection. ¶수표를 ~에 돌리다 put a check through for collection. **추심하다** collect.
● **추심금** money collected. **추심료** a collection charge. **추심 어음** a bill for collection; a collection bill. **추심 은행** the collection bank.

추썩거리다 (어깨 등을) shrug (one's shoulders) repeatedly; (옷을) keep rolling [pulling] up. ¶바지를 ~ keep pulling [hitching] up one's trousers // 그 노인은 여윈 어깨를 연방 추썩거렸다 The old man shrugged his thin shoulders repeatedly.

추악하다(醜惡-) [보기 흉하다] ugly; unsightly; misshapen; [비루하다] abominable; mean; base; foul; filthy; revolting; repulsive; scandalous. ¶추악한 노파 an ugly old woman / a hag // 추악한 광고 an unsightly advertisement // 추악한 이야기 a filthy[an indecent] talk // 추악한 행위 mean conduct / a scandalous[disgraceful] deed // 추악한 짓을 하다 behave unseemly / act dishonorably / (여자에게) take liberties with a woman / behave horribly toward a girl // 남이 없는 자리에서 욕을 하는 것은 ~ It's mean [cheap] to talk about a person behind his back.

추앙(推仰) reverence; veneration; adoration; respect; worship. ¶그는 세인의 ~을 받고 있다 He stands high in public esteem. / He enjoys the high esteem of the public. **추앙하다** revere; venerate; adore; respect; worship; look up to; hold (a person) in esteem [veneration]. ¶모두가 그를 지도자로 추앙하고 있었다 They all looked up to him as their leader. ➡¶추앙받다 be held in respect [esteem / veneration].

추야(秋夜) an autumn night. ¶~장 긴긴 밤에 in the long nights of autumn / in autumn when the nights are long.

추어(鰍魚·鯔魚) [동] a loach. ➪ ╒ 미꾸라지
● **추어탕** loach soup.

추어올리다 1 [끌어 올리다] pull up; lift (up); hoist. ¶바지를 ~ pull up one's trousers. 2 [정도 이상으로 칭찬하다] praise; applaud; compliment; speak well[highly] of (a person); (우쭐하도록) sing (a person's) praise; puff; (미) give (a person) a boost; flatter; say nice things (to). ¶부지런하다고 ~ praise (a person) for (his) diligence // 그렇게 추어올리지 말게 Spare my blushes. // 나는 그를 추어올려 승낙을 얻었다 I obtained his consent by flattery.

추어주다 praise; applaud. ➪ ╒ 추어올리다2 ¶조금만 추어주어도 우쭐대는 사람 a person easily elated[flattered] // 공부를 잘한다고 ~ praise (a student) for his good marks // 몹시 ~ praise (a person) sky-high / extoll[laud] (a person) to the skies / sing[chant] the praises of (a person) / speak very highly of (a person) // 어린이에게 행실이 착하다고 ~ compliment a child on his good behavior // 추어주어 싫어하는 사람은 없다 Nobody feels offended at compliments

추억(追憶) recollection; reminiscence; remembrance; retrospection; a retrospect; a memory. ¶옛날의 그리운 ~ a good old memory // 어린 시절의 ~에 잠기다 be lost in memories of one's childhood // ~에 잠기다 reminisce / indulge in reminiscence // 과거의 ~을 더듬다 recall[recollect / look back upon] the past // ~을 새롭게 하다 refresh one's memory // ~을 불러일으키다 (구어) ring a bell // 이 공원은 두 사람의 ~의 장소이다 This park has memories for us. // 그 사람은 내게 있어 이제 ~의 인물에 불과하다 He is only a memory to me now. // 이 여행은 즐거운 ~이 될 것이다 This trip will be something pleasant to look back on. **추억하다** recollect; reminisce; recall; look back upon [to] (the past); retrospect; review; go over (the past) in one's mind. ¶옛날을 추억하다 (사물이) make (a person) reminiscent of old times / remind (a person) of the old days / carry one's thoughts back to the past.
● **추억거리** a remembrancer; a reminder; a memento; a souvenir. **추억담** a reminiscence; a reminiscent talk; memoirs. ¶런던 유학 시절의 ~을 하다 tell a person of one's days as a student in London // 우리는 ~으로 이야기꽃을 피웠다 We got carried away reminiscing[talking about old times].

추완(追完) [법] subsequent completion.

추워지다 get[grow] cold; become chilly. ¶본

추워하다
격적으로 추워졌습니다 The cold weather has set in. / It's really gotten cold.

추워하다 feel (the) cold; feel chilly; complain of the cold. ¶추워하는 것 같다 appear uncomfortable with cold / look cold.

추월(追越) outrunning. **추월하다** (자동차 등이) pass (another motorcar) ahead; (배가) outsail; outsteam. ¶스포츠카가 우리 차를 추월했다 A sports car overtook ours.

●**추월 금지** (게시) (미) No passing; (영) No Overtaking; Overtaking Prohibited. **추월금지 구역** a no-passing zone.

추위 coldness; (the) cold. ¶**겨울 ~** the cold [rigors] of winter / **시베리아의 ~** the cold in Siberia / **심한 ~** the intense [bitter] cold / **살을 에는 듯한 ~** the biting [piercing / penetrating] cold / (속어) a bone chiller / **갑자기 닥치는 ~** a cold snap / **~를 몹시 타는 사람** a coldblooded person / a person exceedingly sensitive to cold / **이 ~에** in this cold season / **~가 뼈까지 스미다** be chilled to the marrow [bone] / feel very chilly [cold] / **~에 견디다** stand [bear] the cold / **~에 약하다** be oversensitive to cold / be easily affected by cold weather / **~에 떨다** shiver with cold / quiver from cold / **~에 지다** succumb to the cold / **~에 익숙해지다** inure oneself to cold / **~를 피하다** avoid [escape] the cold / **~를 면하다** [막다] keep off [out] the cold / **~를 느끼다** feel the cold / **~를 타다** be sensitive to cold / feel the cold readily / be easily chilled / have a cold constitution / **~로 몸이 얼다** be numb with cold / **~가 혹독하다** It is bitterly cold / **나는 ~ 속에 두 시간이나 거기에 서 있었다** I stood there for two hours in the cold. / **이 ~에 몸을 잘 보살피십시오** Please take care of yourself in this cold season. / **이 집 안에 있으면 ~를 잊게 된다** You'll never feel the cold in this house. / **금년의 ~는 유난하다** The cold of this winter is quite unprecedented. / **나는 유난히 ~를 탄다** I am unusually sensitive to cold.

추이(推移) [변화] a change; [이행] a transition; (a) shift; development. ¶**시대의 ~와 함께** [**~에 따라**] with the change of times / **사태의 ~를 지켜보다** watch the development of events / see how the wind blows / **우리는 사태의 ~를 방관하고 있을 수 없다** We can't just (sit back and) wait to see what happens. / **우리는 사태의 ~를 지켜볼 것이다** We'll watch how things will go. **추이하다** change; undergo a change; shift. ¶**끊임없이 추이하는** ever-changing [-shifting].

추인(追認) [사실을 인정함] ratification [confirmation] after the fact. **추인하다** confirm [ratify] after the fact. ¶**기정 사실을 추인하지 않을 수 없었다** We were obliged to accept it as an accomplished fact.

●**추인자** (법) a ratifier; a confirmor.

추잠(秋蠶) an autumn breed of silkworms.

추잡스럽다(醜雜-) dirty; disgusting. ⇨**추잡하다**

추잡하다(醜雜-) [더럽다] dirty; filthy; nasty; foul; [역겹다] disgusting; detestable; loathsome; repulsive; [음란하다] indecent; lascivious; scabrous; immoral; [상스럽다] low; vulgar. ¶**추잡한 말** a filthy [a foul / an obscene / an indecent / a dirty / an improper] talk / smut / coarse [ribald / gutter] language / vulgar expression / four-letter words / **추잡한 이야기** an off-color [a risqué] story / indecent topics / an obscene story / a dirty story / **추잡한 농담** a broad joke / (어) a water-closet joke / **추잡한 그림** an obscene [indecent] picture / (집합적) pornography / **추잡한 사람** a filthy [an indecent] person / a vulgar [mean] person / a nasty [an odious] fellow / **추잡한 소문** a scandal / **여자에게 추잡한 소리를 하다** say ugly [improper] things to a girl / make an obscene remark to a girl / **여자에게 추잡한 짓을 하다** take liberties with a woman / behave horribly toward a girl / **그것은 추잡한 광경이었다** It was a disgusting sight. / **그에 관한 추잡한 소문이 나돌고 있다** There is an off-color rumor about him.

추장(酋長) a chief; a head; a headman (pl. -men); a chieftain.

추저분하다(醜-) dirty; unclean; untidy; shabby; messy. ¶**추저분한 집** a squalid house.

추적(追跡) a chase; (a) pursuit; tracking; stalk. ¶**경찰은 유괴범의 ~ 중이다** The police are on the kidnapper's trail [in pursuit of the kidnapper]. / **우리는 적의 ~을 받으면서 도망쳤다** We ran off with the enemy following at our heels. **추적하다** chase; run after; pursue; track; stalk; make track for; give chase to. ¶**추적해 오다** come in pursuit / **우리는 살인범을 추적하여 붙잡았다** We tracked down the murderer (and captured him). / **경찰들은 즉시 범인을 추적했다** The policemen were immediately in pursuit [on the track] of the offender. →**추적시키다** send (a person) in pursuit of / put (a person) on the track of.

●**추적권** (외국 선박 등에 대해) the right of hot pursuit. **추적자**(-子) [화] a tracer. **추적자**(-者) a pursuer; a chaser. ¶**범인은 ~로부터 벗어났다** The criminal eluded the chase [pursuit]. / The culprit gave his pursuers the slip. **추적 조사** a follow-up survey.

추접스럽다(醜-) dirty; mean; base; low; sordid; squalid; abject. ¶**추접스러운 놈** a dirty guy / a low-down good-for-nothing / **추접스럽게 굴다** behave in a mean [low-down] fashion / **그런 추접스러운 짓은 안 한다** I am above such meanness.

추젓(秋-) tiny shrimps salted in autumn.

추정(推定) [어림] an estimate; (an) estimation; [추측·가정] an assumption; (a) presumption; (an) inference; (an) illation. ¶**당국의 ~에 의하면 인구 증가율은 약 10%이다** The authorities concerned estimate that the increase in population is about ten percent. / **그것은 단순한 ~에 불과하다** That's a mere assumption. / **피해자의 ~ 연령은 60세 전후였다** The age of the victim was estimated to be about sixty. / **그녀의 사망 ~ 시간은 오전 6시에서 7시 사이이다** The estimated time of her death was between six and seven in the morning. **추정하다** [어림하다] estimate; [짐작하다] presume; assume; infer. ¶**유죄로 ~ presume** (a person) to be guilty / **경찰은 내부인의 범행으로 추정하고 있다** The police assume [presume] that it was an inside job. →**¶손해는 500만 원으로 추정되었다** The loss was estimated at five million won.

●**추정 가격** the presumed value (of). **추정량** an estimated volume. **추정 범죄** constructive crime.

추종(追從) following; [모방] imitation. ¶남의 ~을 불허하다 be peerless / be without a peer / be inimitable / have no equal [second] / have no superior (in) / cannot be duplicated // 그 바이올린은 음색에 있어 타의 ~을 불허한다 That violin has no equal [is unrivaled] in timbre. **추종하다** follow; be servile to (public opinion); ko(w)tow (to) (비굴하게); [모방을] imitate. ¶남의 의견을 ~ follow the opinion(s) of other people // 스승의 작품을 ~ imitate [copy / follow] one's teacher [one's teacher's style] // 전후의 일본은 계속 미국을 추종해 왔다 Postwar Japan has consistently toed the U.S. line [followed in American footsteps]. // 일의 꼼꼼함에 있어서는 우리를 추종할 자가 없다 We are second to none [We have no rivals] in the care with which we do our work.

추증(追贈) posthumous conferment of honors. ¶정부는 고 W 씨에게 훈장의 ~을 결정했다 The government decided to award the late Mr. W. **추증하다** confer honors [court rank] posthumously.

추지다 [습기로 눅눅하다] moist; damp; wet. ¶추진 수건을 이마에 대다 apply a damp [moist] towel to one's forehead.

추진(推進) propulsion; drive. ¶분사 ~(식) 비행기 a jet-propelled plane. **추진하다** [앞으로 나아가게 하다] propel; drive [push / thrust] forward; [촉진하다] push forward; promote; further; step up. ¶계획을 ~ go ahead [move forward] with a plan // 당사는 이 계획을 추진하고 있다 Our company is promoting this project. // 이 계획을 추진해 주시오 Please go on [ahead] with this plan. / Please carry this program forward. // 새 공법은 공사를 추진하는 데 도움이 되었다 The new technique in engineering served to speed up the construction work. ➔¶우리는 이 일을 추진시켜야 한다 We should push forward with this work.

● **추진기** a propeller; a screw(배의). **추진력** a thrust; propulsive force; (a) driving [propelling] force; an impulse. ¶기계의 ~ the thrust of an engine // 그는 그 운동의 ~이 되었다 He was the driving force behind the campaign. **추진제** a propellant; a propellent.

추징(追徵) an additional collection; a supplementary collection. **추징하다** collect in addition; collect the balance (of a tax); make an additional collection of; (별로서) impose a penalty (of 10,000 won) on (a person). ➔¶나는 소득세를 10만 원 추징당했다 I was charged an additional hundred thousand won [had to pay a hundred thousand won more] for income tax.

● **추징금** money collected [paid] in addition. **추징세** a tax penalty; a penalty tax.

추천(推薦) recommendation. ¶…의 ~으로 by [through] the recommendation of … / on [at] the recommendation of … // 남에게 ~을 부탁하다 ask for another's recommendation // 교장의 ~으로 그를 채용했다 We hired him on the recommendation of the principal. // 이 영화는 교육 인적 자원부의 ~을 받았다 This movie [film] was given a commendation [was commended] by the Ministry of Education and Human Resources Development. **추천하다** recommend; propose; say [put in] a good word for (a person); [지명하다] nominate. ¶나는 그녀를 당신의 비서로 추천합니다 I recommend her to you for the job of secretary. // 한 선생을 회장 후보로 추천하고 싶다 I would like to nominate Mr. Han for the presidency. / I would like to propose Mr. Han as president. // 그 사람은 추천할 수 없다 I have not a good word to say for him. // 그분에게 잘 좀 추천해 주십시오 Please put in a good word for me with him.

● **추천인 / 추천자** a recommender; an introducer; a proposer; a sponsor; (신원 보증인) a reference. **추천 작가** a recommended writer. **추천장 / 추천서** a letter of recommendation; (신원 등의 소개서) a reference.

추첨(抽籤) (제비) a lot; (복권·복첨) a lottery; a raffle; [제비뽑기] the drawing of lots. ¶~으로 정하다 determine [decide] by lot // ~으로 순번을 결정하다 decide the order by lot [drawing lots] // ~에 당첨되다 draw a winning number / win a prize in a lottery // ~에 떨어지다 draw a losing number // 시합의 대전표는 ~으로 짜여졌다 The teams were paired [The pairings were determined] by lot. // 그는 ~에서 1등 상을 탔다 He won first prize in the lottery [raffle / drawing]. **추첨하다** draw lots; cast lots; hold a lottery.

● **추첨권** a lottery ticket. **추첨 번호** a lottery number. **추첨제** the lottery system. ¶~ 중학 입시 the lottery (and ward) system for middle school entrance.

추축(樞軸) (기계의) a pivot; an axle; an axis (pl. axes); [중추] a central point; the center (of power).

● **추축국** (제2차 대전 때의) the Axis powers.

추출(抽出) 1 [어떤 물질을 뽑아냄] abstraction; [화] extraction. **추출하다** abstract; extract; (증류하여) distill. ¶광석에서 불순물을 ~ abstract impurities from ore // 물질에서 진액을 ~ extract [distill] essence from a substance. 2 [뽑아냄] sampling.

● **추출물** an extract; an educt. **추출법** a sampling process. ¶여론 조사에는 임의 ~을 쓴다 We use random sampling for public opinion polls.

추측(推測) (a) conjecture; (a) surmise; (a) supposition; (a) presumption; (an) inference; speculation; a guess. ¶근거가 있는 [박약한] ~ a well-founded [an ill-founded] conjecture // ~대로 as conjectured [supposed] // 내 ~으로는 in my guess [estimation] // ~으로 대답하다 answer with a guess // 네 ~은 들어맞았다 You've guessed it. / You've guessed right. / Your guess hit the mark. // 내 ~이 틀렸다 I guessed wrong. / My guess was wrong. // ~에 의해 이 결론에 도달했다 I have come to this conclusion by inference. // 이것은 단지 ~에 불과하다 This is mere guesswork. / This is a mere conjecture. // ~만으로 결론을 맺어서는 안 된다 You must not form a conclusion merely by guessing. // 너는 사실에 입각하지 않고 ~으로 말하고 있어 What you say is based on supposition, not on fact. **추측하다** suppose; guess; (문어) infer; (문어) surmise; (문어) conjecture(▶ suppose는 사실일 것으로 생각하다, guess는 지레짐작으로 추측하다, infer는 무언가에 입각해서 추측하다, surmise는 단순히 상상을 근거로 하여 추측하다, conjecture는 확실한 정보 없이 추측하다); give a guess; form [make] a

추커들다 conjecture; gather (from); draw an inference (from). ¶한번 추측해 보다 venture a guess / hazard a conjecture // 도저히 추측할 수 없다 It is past conjecture. // 달리 추측할 길이 없다 I have no other conjecture to offer [make] on it. // 이들 자료에 의해서 그날 대지진이 있었음을 추측할 수 있을 것이다 It may be inferred from these data that there was a strong earthquake on that day. // 사투리로 보아 그가 프랑스 사람이라고 추측했다 I guessed [gathered / surmised] from his accent that he was a Frenchman. // 말씀하신 것으로 추측하건대 이 계획을 언짢게 생각하시는군요 I infer from what you say that you are dissatisfied with this plan.
● **추측 기사** a speculative article [news story].

추켜들다 raise; hold up; lift (up); heave. ¶돌을 ~ hold[lift] up a stone / 어린애를 ~ lift[pick up] a child.

추켜잡다 lift (up); hold up. ¶끌리지 않도록 치맛자락을 ~ hold up one's skirt to keep it from dragging[draggling].

추키다 〔치올리다〕 raise; lift (up); hold up; 〔채어 올리다〕 hitch [jerk / snatch] up. ¶바지를 ~ hitch up one's trousers.

추태(醜態) 〔행동〕 disgraceful behavior; shameful conduct; (외관) an unseemly sight; a sorry figure; (상태) a scandalous condition. ¶~를 부리다 act disgracefully / behave oneself in a shameful manner / make a show of oneself / cut a ridiculous [sorry] figure / 〔실수하다〕 come[fall] a cropper // ~를 연출하고 말았다 I'm afraid I disgraced myself[behaved abominably]. // 여러 사람 앞에서 그런 ~를 보이다니 How could you behave so shamefully in public?

추파(秋波) 1 [맑은 물결] autumn ripples. 2 〔아첨·은근한 눈짓〕 an ogle; an amorous[a coquettish] glance; an amatory look; (속어) the glad eye. ¶관리에게 ~를 던지다 (go out of one's way to) please[flatter] government officials // 그 여자는 청년에게 ~를 던지고 있다 The woman keeps making eyes [casting amorous glances] at the young man. / (구어) The woman is giving the young man the come-on.

추풍(秋風) an autumn(al) wind[breeze].
● **추풍낙엽** leaves blown off by the autumn wind. ¶~의 정객들 fallen politician like so many leaves blown off by the autumn wind.

추풍(醜風) indecent customs. ⇨ 추속(醜俗)

추하다(醜—) 1 〔아름답지 않다〕 ugly; bad [ugly-]looking; plain; ill-favored; unlovely; unattractive. ¶추한 여자 a plain[an ugly/(미)] a homely] woman.
2 〔망측하다〕 unseemly; unsightly; indecent; 〔수치스럽다〕 ignoble; ignominious; disgraceful; dishonorable; mean. ¶추한 싸움 a scandalous dispute // 추한 사람 a mean[vulgar] person / an indecent [odious] person / a dirty dog // 추한 짓 disgraceful [infamous / shameful / scandalous] conduct // 추한 관계를 갖다[맺다] have illicit[improper] connection (with) / have evil relations (with) // 추하게 굴다 behave unseemly[unbecomingly] / behave in a shameful[low-down] fashion / act dishonorably.

추한(醜漢) an ugly fellow[guy]; a mean fellow; a low-down type.

추행(醜行) disgraceful [infamous / shameful / scandalous] conduct; a misdeed; a scandal. ¶(여자에게) ~을 하다 commit obscene action upon (a woman) / make a sexual attack on (a girl) // ~을 들춰내다 bring a scandal to light / expose a scandal.

추호(秋毫) a bit; a whit; a hair; an atom. ¶~도 in the (very) least / (not) a jot [whit / bit] / (not) at all / (not) in the slightest degree / in no degree // 그들이 나에 대하여 온갖 말을 다했지만 나는 ~도 놀라지 않았다 Whatever they said about me, I was not surprised at all[I was not in the least surprised]. // 저는 그런 짓을 할 의도[생각]가 ~도 없었습니다 I had not the slightest[the least] intention of doing such a thing. // 제 진술에 거짓이란 ~도 없습니다 There is no falsehood whatever in my statement. // 저는 그것에 대해 ~도 개의하지[신경을 쓰지] 않습니다 I don't care a bit[a straw] about it. // 그에게 친절한 마음씨란 ~도 없다 He has not an atom[a trace] of kindness in him. // 그는 애정 같은 것은 ~도 없다 He had not a particle[an atom] of affection in him.

추후(追後) ¶~에 later (on) / afterward // ~ 통지가 있을 때까지 until further notice // ~에 알려 드리겠습니다 I'll let you know later. // 그것에 관해서는 ~에 논하기로 하자 We shall make mention of it further on. // 정확한 정보는 ~ 우송한다 More exact information follows by mail.

추흥(秋興) pleasures [delights] of autumn; autumn fun.

축[1] 〔무리〕 a group; a gang; a bunch (of people / things); a set; a party; a circle. ¶한 ~ (one and) the same gang // ~에 들다[끼이다] 〔어울리다〕 join (a party) / mix oneself (among) / (부류에) take one's place (in / among) / be reckoned [numbered] (among) // 선진국 ~에 끼이다 rank [be numbered] among the advanced nations // ~에도 못 들다 be insignificant / count for nothing [little] / be of no account / be beneath [not worth] one's notice / (속어) be off the map // 그따위 녀석과 같은 ~으로 치다니 말이 안 된다 I cannot stand being classed [lumped together] with that (sort of) fellow. // 그이도 똑똑한 ~에 든다 He is one of the clever ones. // 그 사람에 비하면 나 따위는 ~에도 못 듭니다 I am a mere nothing beside him. // 그래 뵈어도 그게 그중에서는 가장 나은 ~이라나 They may not look like much but they're the best of the lot, I guess. // 30명이 합격했는데 나도 그 ~에 꼈다 Thirty passed, including myself[myself included]. // 그래 가지고서는 영어를 하는 ~에 끼일 수가 없다 With that much knowledge, you can hardly be said to know English.

축[2] 〔처진 모양〕 drooping(ly); danglingly; limply. ¶~ 늘어진 귀 drooped [drooping / droopy] ears // 늘어지다 hang loose [limply] / dangle / (지쳐서) be dead tired / be dog-tired / be washed-out // 어깨가 ~ 늘어지다 one's shoulders droop / have drooping shoulders // 그의 머리칼은 이마에 ~ 처져 있었다 His hair hung loose over his brow. // 개의 혀가 ~ 늘어져 있었다 The dog's tongue was lolling out. // 그 아이는 뱃멀미로 ~ 늘어져 있었다 The child was limp[worn out] from being seasick.

축(祝) a form of invocation. ⇨축문(祝文)
축(逐) (바둑의) being cornered always by one move; a ladder.
축(軸) **1** [회전체의 중심] an axis (*pl.* axes); [수레바퀴의 중심] an axle; [기계의 회전축] a spindle; [선회지축] a pivot; [샤프트] a shaft; [시계의 용두 등의 중심] a stem. ¶**가로**[수평] ~ a horizontal [transverse] axis// **세로** ~ a vertical [longitudinal] axis// 차 앞바퀴[뒷바퀴]의 ~ the front [rear] axle of a car// **좌표** ~ a coordinate axis / an axis of coordinates// *x*~ the *x*-axis // **장**[단] ~ (타원형의) the major [minor] axis // 수레바퀴는 ~을 중심으로 하여 회전한다 Wheels turn on their axles. // 지구는 그 ~을 중심으로 24시간에 1회전한다 The earth turns on its axis once in 24 hours.
2 (지물의) a roll; a ream. ¶종이 두 ~ two rolls [reams] of paper.
축(縮) shortage; deficiency; want; lack; deficit.
축가(祝歌) a song of congratulation [celebration]; a festive song. ¶결혼 ~ a nuptial song.
축가다(縮—) decrease; become weaker. ⇨축나다
축객(逐客) turning a guest out; driving a guest away. ¶문전 ~을 당하다 be turned away at the door / be refused admittance. **축객하다** turn a guest out; drive a guest away.
축구(蹴球) [사커] soccer; (영) socker; association football; (집합적) football (▶ football 이라고 하면 미국에서는 주로 미식축구, 영국에서는 주로 럭비를 가리킴). ¶**미식**(美式) ~ American football // ~**를 하다** play soccer [football].
● **축구 경기 / 축구 시합** a soccer [football] game. **축구 선수** a soccer [football] player; a soccerite; a footballer; a gridder (미식축구의). **축구장** a soccer [football] field; (럭비의) a rugger field; (미식축구의) (미) a gridiron.
축나다(縮—) **1** (수량이) decrease; diminish; lessen; be deficient [lacking / missing]; become [fall / come] short (of); be found short (of); be reduced. ¶돈이 3천 원 축난다 There is a deficit [shortage] of 3,000 won. / 3,000 won is found missing. // 이 섬에 두 되가 축났다 The rice has dried out and comes to 2 *doe* short of a *seom*. **2** (몸이) become weaker; lose weight; fail in health; get run down. ¶공부를 너무하여 그는 몸이 좀 축났다 He lost some weight due to his hard study. // 슬픔과 근심은 고된 일보다 사람을 더 축나게 한다 Sorrow and anxiety wear(s) a man more than hard work.
축내다(縮—) **1** (수량이) cause a loss [deficit]; reduce a sum by (a certain amount); spend (part of a sum); take a bite of [so much out of] a sum; (공금 등을) defalcate; commit defalcation. ¶은행 돈을 약 백만 원 ~ appropriate about one million won of the bank's money for one's private use // 5천 원에서 천 원을 ~ reduce the 5,000 won by 1,000 / spend 1,000 of the 5,000 won / take 1,000 won from the 5,000 // 재산을 크게 ~ cause a serious gap in one's finances. **2** (몸을) reduce flesh [weight]; make weak; weaken.
축농증(蓄膿症) [의] ozena; empyema.
축다 become damp [moist / wet].
축대(築臺) an elevation; an embankment; a terrace. ¶~**를 쌓다** build a ground up high // ~**가 무너졌다** The stone and cement embankment collapsed.
축도(祝禱) (pronounce) a benediction. ⇨축복 기도(⇨축복) ¶~**를 하다** give the benediction / pronounce the benediction (upon the congregation).
축도(縮圖) [축소한 도면] a reduced (-size) drawing [copy]; a miniature (copy); [비유] an epitome; a microcosm. ¶사회의 ~ society in miniature // 세계의 ~ the world in epitome // 인생 [현대 생활]의 ~ an epitome of human [modern] life // 건물의 5분의 1의 ~를 작성하다 draw a building on a scale of 1/5 [one to five] // 그것은 바로 인생의 ~다 It's a veritable epitome of life.
● **축도기**(—器) a pantograph; an eidograph.
축문(祝文) a written prayer (offered at ancestor memorial service); a form of invocation. ¶~을 읽다 recite a written [ritual] prayer.
축배(祝杯) a toast; a celebratory drink. ¶~를 **들다** drink a toast (for / to) / drink [toast] (to) (a person's) health [success] / drink in celebration of (an event) // 서로 ~를 들다 toast each other // 신랑 신부를 위해 ~를 들다 toast the bride and bridegroom // 민 군의 도미(渡美)를 축하하여 ~를 들다 drink a toast for Min to celebrate his going to America // 그의 건강을 위해 ~를 들자 Let's toast [drink (a toast) to] his health.
축복(祝福) (a) blessing; (a) benediction. ¶분에 넘치는 ~이다 I cannot expect any greater blessing. / This is too good for me. // 하느님의 ~이 내리시기를 빕니다 God bless you! // 우리는 모두의 ~ 속에 결혼했다 We got married with everyone's blessings. **축복하다** bless; give (a person) one's blessing; give [pronounce] a benediction upon (a person). ¶전도를 ~ wish (a person) good luck [a happy future] // 당신의 장래를 축복합니다 I wish you the best of luck. ➔**축복받은 나라** a blessed [God-favored] country // **축복받다** be blessed / be given [receive] a benediction.
● **축복 기도** (pronounce) a benediction; a blessing.
축사(畜舍) (소의) a cattle shed [pen]; a barn; (돼지의) a pigsty [(미) a pigpen]; (특히 양·비둘기 등의) a cot [(영) a cote] (▶ a sheepcote, a dovecote처럼 합성어로 쓰임).
축사(祝辭) a congratulatory [complimentary] address [remark / speech]; a message of congratulations; greetings; felicitations. ¶~**를 낭독하다** read (aloud) a congratulatory address [message] // 결혼를 하다 offer congratulations [one's best wishes / (문어) felicitations] at a wedding // 여러분의 성공에 대해 먼저 ~를 드리고자 합니다 Let me first congratulate (all of) you on your success. // 내빈들의 ~가 한 시간 동안이나 이어졌다 The guests' congratulatory speeches [greetings] went on for a whole [all of an] hour. **축사하다** deliver a congratulatory [felicitatory] address (at a ceremony); offer [tender / extend] one's congratulations [felicitations] (to a person); congratulate (a person on his success).
축사(縮寫) making a reduced [an abridged] copy; a miniature [reduced] copy; a miniature reproduction. **축사하다** draw [copy] on

a smaller scale; make a reduced [an abridged] copy (of). ¶축사하여 in miniature // 신문을 5분의 1로 ~ copy a newspaper on a scale of one to five / 사진을 ~ reduce (the size of) a photograph // 실물의 5분의 1로 ~ reduce (a thing) to a scale of one fifth the natural size.
● 축사도 (-圖) a reduced drawing. 축사 사진 a small-size [reduced-size] photograph.

축산 (畜産) stock raising [farming]; stockbreeding; livestock raising; animal husbandry; livestock industry.
● 축산업 stockbreeding; stock raising; livestock raising [farming]; animal husbandry. 축산 자금 (government) loans for livestock industry. 축산학 (the study of) animal husbandry; zootechny.

축생 (畜生) 1 [짐승] animals; beasts. 2 [사람답지 못한 사람] a veritable beast; a brute (of a man).

축성 (祝聖) [가] consecration; sanctification. 축성하다 consecrate; sanctify.

축성 (築城) [성을 쌓음] construction of a castle; building a castle [wall]; [진지를 쌓음] fortification; establishment of a fortification. ¶야전 ~ [군] field fortification. 축성하다 build [construct] a castle [wall]; fortify.

축소 (縮小) (a) reduction; curtailment; retrenchment; abridg(e)ment; a cut; a scale-down; (속어) de-escalation. ¶군비 ~ (a) reduction of armaments / arms reduction / a cutback in military strength. 축소하다 reduce; curtail (expenses); retrench; abridge; cut [scale] down; shrink; dwindle; [단축하다] contract. ¶비용을 ~ curtail expenditure / cut down (on) expenses // 과(課)를 ~ reduce a section of an office in business and staff // 규모를 ~ reduce the plan (of) / downscale / 군비를 ~ reduce armaments // 사업을 ~ reduce [cut back] business / curtail the operation // 우리는 인원을 축소해야 한다 We have to cut back on personnel. / Staff cuts are necessary. →¶준비 기간이 1개월 축소되었다 The preparation period was shortened by a month.
● 축소판 a reduced- [smaller-] size edition. ⇨축쇄판(⇨축쇄)

축쇄 (縮刷) [인] printing in smaller type [reduced size]; reduced-size printing. 축쇄하다 print in smaller type [reduced size]; print a reduced-size edition (of).
● 축쇄판 a reduced- [smaller-] size edition; a tabloid [pocket] edition. ¶~의 사전 a pocket dictionary // ~으로 내다 publish [issue] in reduced size.

축수 (祝手) folding one's hands in prayer; invocation by prayer; wishing. 축수하다 pray with one's hands pressed together; pray with joined [folded] hands; invoke by prayer; wish. ¶병을 낫게 해 달라고 신에게 ~ implore God to heal one of a disease / pray to God for the recovery of one's health // 남의 건강[행운]을 ~ wish a person good health [luck].

축수 (祝壽) wishing (a person) a long life. 축수하다 wish (a person) a long life.

축승 (祝勝) celebration of a victory; rejoicing over a victory.

축어역 (逐語譯) literal translation. ⇨직역(直譯)

축연 (祝宴) a party held in celebration of (an event). ⇨축하연(⇨축하)

축우 (畜牛) a domestic cow[ox]; (집합적) cattle.

축원 (祝願) praying; a prayer; petition; supplication. 축원하다 pray (for); invoke; petition; supplicate; wish. ¶세계 평화를 ~ pray for the peace of the world // 신의 은총을 ~ pray to God for mercy // 아들의 성공을 ~ pray that one's son may succeed // 여행길이 무사하기를 ~ wish (a person) a good journey / 전승을 ~ pray for a victory in the war // 당신의 성공을 축원합니다 I wish you success. / May you succeed!
● 축원문 a written prayer.

축음기 (蓄音機) a gramophone; (미) a phonograph; a record player. ¶판이 자동적으로 바뀌는 ~ a phonograph with an automatic record changer // ~를 틀다 play [turn on] the gramophone // ~를 멈추다 [끄다] turn off a phonograph.

축의 (祝意) congratulations (on); one's good [best] wishes. ¶~를 표하여 in honor of (a person) / in celebration of (an event) / ~를 표하다 extend [offer] one's congratulations [felicitations] / express one's congratulations [good wishes] / congratulate [felicitate] (a person on his success) // 국기를 걸어 ~를 표하다 hoist the national flags to celebrate the day.

축이다 [축축하게 하다] wet; moisten; damp (-en). ¶밭과 목초지를 축이는 비 the rain that wets fields and pastures // 목[입술]을 ~ moisten one's throat [lips] // 수건을 ~ wet [damp] a towel / 수건을 축여서 이마에 대다 apply a damped [moist] towel to one's forehead // 몇몇 수로가 물을 공급하여 밭을 축이고 있다 The fields are watered by several canals. // 소년은 혀로 핥아 마른 입술을 축였다 The boy licked his dry lips to moisten them. // 여름에 갈증이 나는 목을 축이는 데에는 맥주가 제일이다 There is nothing like beer to quench one's thirst in summer. // 꺾은 꽃가지에 물을 축여 주지 않으면 시들어 버린다 Unless you do something to help a cut flower draw water, it will soon wither.

축일 (祝日) a festival (day); a festive [festal] day; a fête [feast] day; a gala day; a public [legal] holiday; a red-letter day (▶달력에 붉은 글씨로 표시한 일에 기인); a flag day. ¶개교 기념의 ~ a fête-day in commemoration of the founding of a school.

축재 (蓄財) (행위) accumulation of wealth [riches]; money-grubbing; (돈) a store of money; amassed [accumulated / piled-up] wealth; a hoard. ¶부정 ~ illegal profiteering / property amassed by illegal means // 그는 ~에 급급하고 있다 He is striving hard after wealth. / He is bent on moneymaking. 축재하다 accumulate [pile up / store up] wealth; gather wealth; amass [lay up / save up / make] money; hoard [save] up; amass wealth; accumulate property.
● 축재자 a moneymaker; a thrifty person. ¶부정 ~ an illicit fortune maker.

축적 (蓄積) storing up; accumulation; stockpiling. ¶달러의 ~ dollar deposits // 자본의 ~ accumulation of capital / capital accumulation // 장기간에 걸친 농약의 채내 ~ a long term accumulation of agricultural chemicals

inside the body. 축적하다 accumulate; amass; store[treasure] up; stockpile; hoard up. ¶부를 ~ accumulate wealth // 정력을 ~ store up energy // 재산을 ~ amass wealth / pile up a fortune. ➔¶축적된 지식 accumulated knowledge // 피로가 축적되었다 My fatigue accumulated.
● 축적물 accumulation.

축전(祝典) a celebration; a festival; festivities; a commemoration(기념제). ¶기념 ~ a commemoration festival // 25[50/60]주년 기념 ~ a silver[golden / diamond] jubilee(▶ 75주년을 diamond라고 하는 사람도 있음) // 50주년 기념 ~을 올리다 hold a celebration of the 50th anniversary (of) // 우리는 대학 창립 100주년을 ~을 거행했다 We held a ceremony to celebrate the centennial (of the foundation) of our university.

축전(祝電) a congratulatory telegram; a (telegraphic) message of congratulations; a telegram of good wishes. ¶~을 치다[보내다] send a congratulatory telegram (to) / telegraph[wire / cable] one's congratulations (to) / telegraph a congratulatory message (to) / send (a person) one's congratulations by wire // ~이 쇄도하다 wired congratulations pour in[come snowing in] // ~이 잇달아 날아들었다 Messages of congratulations came pouring in. // 나는 그에게 ~을 쳤다[보냈다] I sent him a congratulatory telegram [cable]. / I cabled my congratulations to him.

축전(蓄電) accumulation[storage] of electricity. 축전하다 store.
● 축전기(-器) a[an electric] condenser. ¶가변(可變) ~ a variable condensor // 고정 ~ a fixed condenser. 축전지 a storage battery [cell]; 《영》 an accumulator.

축제(祝祭) a festival; a fête; a gala. ¶~ 때에 on (the occasion of) a festival // ~ 기분이다 be in a festive mood // ~를 지내다 keep [observe / celebrate] a festival.
● 축제일 a national / public holiday; a fête day; a gala day; a festival (day).

축제(築堤) (em)banking; embankment. ¶강에 ~를 하다 embank[dike] a river. 축제하다 construct a riverbank; embank; dike.
● 축제 공사 embanking; embankment [(미)] levee] work(s).

축조(逐條) (부사적) article by article; item by item; point by point.
● 축조심의 an article-by-article[a clause-by-clause] discussion. ¶~를 하다 discuss (a thing) article by article / take the items up one by one.

축조(築造) building; construction. 축조하다 build; construct; erect. ¶철교를 ~ build [construct] a bridge // 기념비를 ~ erect a monument.
● 축조물 a building; a structure; an edifice.

축지다(縮-) 1 (명예 가치가) discredit oneself; fall into discredit; bring discredit on oneself. 2 become weaker. ⇨축나다2 ¶그는 앓아서 몸이 몹시 축졌다 He is terribly run down since his illness.

축지법(縮地法) a magic method of contracting space. ¶~을 쓰다 contract space by magic.

축척(縮尺) 1 [도면 상의 거리와 실제 거리와의 비] a reduced scale. ¶~ 5만분의 1의 지도 a map drawn on a scale of 1:50,000[one to fifty thousand] // ~ 7분의 1의 모형 a one-seventh model (of) // 미국 잠수함 「노틸러스」의 실제 크기 98미터에 대한 2미터 ~의 모형 a model of U.S. submarine Nautilus scaled down to 2 meters from a real-life 98. 2 (피륙의) (cloth) being short of the regular [standard] length.

축첩(蓄妾) keeping a concubine[mistress]; concubinage. ¶~ 공무원을 파면하다 fire a government official who has a concubine. 축첩하다 keep a mistress[concubine].

축축 [늘어진 모양] all drooping[dangling] low; all sagging low; dingle-dangle; all limply. ¶나뭇가지가 ~ 늘어져 있다 The branches are all drooping low. // 개들이 혀를 ~ 늘어뜨렸다 All the dogs lolled out their tongues.

축축하다 damp(ish); humid; moist; clammy; (서술적) feel damp; be slightly[moderately] wet. ¶축축한 날씨 damp weather // 축축한 시트 damp sheets // 축축한 세탁물 damp laundry[washing] // 축축한 공기 humid air // 축축한 바람 a damp[humid / moisture-laden] wind // 밤이슬을 맞아 ~ be wet [damp] with night dew // 축축하고 퀴퀴하다 be damp and musty // 축축해지다 become [get] damp[moist] / become[get] wet [moisten] // 등골에 땀이 ~ My back is damp [clammy] with sweat. // 옷이 ~ My clothes feel wet. // 땅이 비로 ~ The ground is wet from the rain. // 장마 때에는 모든 것이 ~ During the rainy season the dampness penetrates everything. 축축이 ¶~ 내리는 비 a soft[gentle] rain // 이슬에 ~ 젖은 풀 dewy grass / grass wet with dew // 이슬에 ~ 젖다 get moist[become wet] with dew / be bedewed // 내 셔츠는 땀으로 ~ 젖어 있다 My shirt is damp[wet] with perspiration.

축출(逐出) driving out; expulsion; dismissal; ejection; deportation; banishment. 축출하다 drive[turn / send / get / put] out; kick[run] (a person) out (of the house[company / army]); rout (a person) out (of home); (지위·직책 등에서) oust[expel / dislodge] (a person from a position); hoof out (아내를) divorce; (셋집·셋방 등에서) evict[eject] (a tenant from the house); put (a tenant) out; (문밖으로) turn (a person) out of doors; show (a person) the door. ¶당(黨)에서 ~ oust[expel] (a person) from the party // 사원을 회사에서 ~ fire an employee from the company // 선동자를 회장에서 축출했다 We drove out an agitator from the meeting. // 나는 그를 일자리[지위]에서 축출했다 I ousted him from his office[position]. ➔축출당하다 get driven[run / kicked] out / be expelled.

축포(祝砲) a cannon salute; a salute (of guns); (육군의) an artillery salute. ¶21발의 ~를 놓다 give[fire] a twenty-one gun salute / fire a feu de joie[salute] of 21 guns // 그를 맞이하여 10발의 ~가 발사되었다 A ten-gun salute was fired in his honor.

축하(祝賀) (일에 대한) a celebration; (사람에 대한) congratulations; felicitations; rejoicings; festivities; (congratulatory) greetings. ¶마을 사람들은 해마다 이날이면 ~ 행사를 한다 Every year the villagers observe a festival on this day. // 나는 자그마한 ~의 표시로 그에게 (접는) 부채를 선사했다 As a small token of my congratulations, I gave him a (folding) fan. **축하하다** (사람을) congratulate (a person on a thing); (일을) celebrate (an event); commemorate (a wedding); greet. ¶…을 축하하여 in celebration [commemoration] of … / for … / 생일을 축하하여 in celebration of a person's birthday // 결혼을 축하합니다 I congratulate you on your marriage. / I wish you every happiness. // 사진 콘테스트에서 1등 하신 것을 진심으로 축하합니다 I heartily congratulate you on winning first prize in the photo contest. / I offer [extend] my hearty congratulations on your winning first prize in the photo contest. // 부모님의 금혼식을 축하하는 만찬회를 열었다 We gave a dinner to celebrate our parents' golden wedding anniversary. // 새해를 축하합니다 (A) Happy New Year! / 생일을 축하합니다 Happy Birthday! / Congratulations on your birthday.

●**축하객** a congratulator; a well-wisher(결혼 등의). **축하 선물** a congratulatory gift. **축하연** (—宴) a party [banquet] held in celebration of (an event). ¶결혼의 ～ a wedding feast [reception] // ～을 베풀다 hold a feast in honor of (a person) / hold a banquet in celebration of (an event). **축하 인사** one's congratulations (on an event); a congratulatory address.

축합 (縮合) [화] condensation. **축합하다** condense.

●**축합물** a condensate; a condensation product.

축항 (築港) harbor [(영) harbour] construction [improvements]. **축항하다** construct [build / improve] a harbor.

춘경 (春耕) spring plowing. ⇨봄갈이

춘경 (春景) [봄 경치] spring scenery; a spring scene.

춘계 (春季) [관형어적] spring.

●**춘계 방학** the spring vacation.

춘곤 (春困) languor [lassitude] which affects people in spring; "spring fever".

춘광 (春光) **1** [봄볕] spring sunshine. **2** [봄철의 경치] spring scenery; the scenery in spring; the vernal beauty of nature.

춘궁 (春宮) [동궁] the Crown Prince.

춘궁 (春窮) the spring austerity; spring poverty; spring shortage of food.

●**춘궁기** the farm hardship period; the spring lean [food-short] season.

춘기 (春期) spring; springtime. ⇨"봄철

춘기 (春機) sexual desire.

춘난 (春暖) spring warmth; mild spring weather.

춘몽 (春夢) spring dreams; visionary fancies; a springtime fantasy. ¶일장～ a scene in one's springtime dreams.

춘부장 (春府丈) your hono(u)red father.

춘분 (春分) [24절기의 하나] *chunbun*; the vernal [spring] equinox.

춘사 (春思) **1** [봄의] feelings of springs; spring musings [sentiments]. **2** lust; sexual desire. ⇨"색욕(色慾)

춘사 (椿事) a disaster; a surprising [an unexpected] event; a disastrous accident; [비극] a tragedy. ¶일대(一大) ～ a great accident.

춘삼월 (春三月) March in [of] the lunar calendar. ¶～ 긴긴해에 in springtime when days are long.

●**춘삼월 호시절** (—好時節) the pleasant days of spring: the mild weather of spring.

춘색 (春色) spring scenery; a feel of spring. ⇨"봄빛 ¶～이 바야흐로 한창이다 The spring is now in full glory [is at its best]. / Spring is bu(r)sting out all over.

춘설 (春雪) spring snow. ⇨"봄눈

춘심 (春心) sexual desire. ⇨"춘정

춘약 (春藥) [성욕을 돋우는 약] an aphrodisiac (dose); a sexual stimulant.

춘잠 (春蠶) spring silkworms; a spring breed of silkworms. ¶～을 치다 raise silkworms in spring.

춘절 (春節) spring; springtime. ⇨"봄철

춘정 (春情) sexual [carnal] desire; sexual urge; lust; passion. ¶～을 돋우다 excite sexual desire / be suggestive / be provocative.

춘추 (春秋) [봄과 가을] spring and autumn; [세월] years and months; [연령] age. ¶～가 기울다 decline in age [one's years] // ～가 몇이십니까 What is your age, sir? / How old are you, sir? // 그 이후로 많은 ～가 흘렀다 Many years have passed since then.

●**춘추복** a suit for spring [autumn] wear; spring [autumn] clothes [wear]; a spring [an autumn] suit.

춘풍 (春風) a spring wind. ⇨"봄바람 ¶～에 돛단 듯하다 Everything goes all right [smoothly].

춘하추동 (春夏秋冬) [사계절] the four seasons; [일년 내내] all the year round; always.

춘화 (春花) spring flowers.

춘화 (도) (春畫圖) an obscene [licentious / dirty / filthy] picture; a pornography; an erotic picture.

춘흥 (春興) the charms [pleasures] of spring; the spring fever; the lure of spring. ¶～에 겨워하다 be overjoyed with the charms of spring.

출가 (出家) leaving home; [불문에 듦] entering the priesthood; becoming a (Buddhist) priest. **출가하다** leave home; renounce the world; enter the priesthood; take the tonsure; become a bonze; become a priest.

출가 (出嫁) a woman's being married (and leaving home). ¶～외인(外人)이다 A married daughter is no better than a stranger. **출가하다** be [get] married (to a person / into a family). ¶클가문(家門)에 ～ be married to one of the Mins // 좋은 곳에 ～ make a good marriage / marry well // 그녀는 이제 출가할 나이다 She is old enough to be [get] married. / She has reached the marriageable age. ➔¶딸을 출가시키다 marry one's daughter off / give one's daughter away in marriage.

출간 (出刊) publication. ⇨출판

출감 (出監) discharge from prison. ⇨출옥

출강 (出講) lecturing. ¶화요일은 나의 ～일입니다 I have classes on Tuesday. **출강하다** lecture; give lectures (at); teach (at); be a part-time teacher (at). ¶수요일이면 나는 이 대학에 출강합니다 I teach [give lectures] at this university on Wednesdays.

출격 (出擊) a sally; a sortie. ¶백 회 ～ 기록을 보유하다 have a record of 100 sorties. **출격하다** sally (forth); make a sortie [sally]. ¶우리는 포위하고 있는 적군을 향해 출격했다 We made a sally against the besieging forces.∥이 항공 부대는 자주 그 지역에 출격한다 This aviation corps often attack[carries out raids on] that region.

출결(出缺) attendance (and[or] absence). ¶~ 통계를 매기다 keep a record of 《students'》 attendance.

출고(出庫) delivery of goods from a warehouse[storehouse]. **출고하다** deliver 《goods》 from a warehouse; take 《goods》 out of a warehouse.
● **출고 가격** a factory[store] price. **출고 지시(서)** a delivery order.

출관(出棺) taking[carrying] a coffin out of the house. **출관하다** take[carry] a coffin out of the house.

출구(出口) 1 [나가는 어귀] a way out; an exit; an outlet; a gateway. ¶극장의 ~ the exit of a theater∥고속도로의 ~ a freeway[《영》 motorway] exit∥비상 ~ an emergency exit [door]∥화재 ~ a fire exit∥(지하철에서) 종로 방면 ~ the way out toward Jongno Street∥거리로 나가는 ~ a way out to the street / a street door∥~를 막다 block the exit[the way out]∥~는 이쪽입니다 This way out.∥~를 모르겠다 I can't find my way out.∥그는 둘러보며 ~를 찾았다 He looked around for a way out. 2 [상품을 항구 밖으로 수출함] sending[taking] out of a port; clearing a port. **출구하다** send[take] out of a port.
● **출구 조사** an exit poll.

출국(出國) departure from a country. ¶불법 ~ illegal departure. **출국하다** depart from [go out of] a country; leave a country.
● **출국 허가(서)** an exit[a departure] permit.

출근(出勤) (office) attendance; being on the job[on duty]; going to work. ¶~이 이르다 be early at office∥~이 늦다 be late for the office. **출근하다** attend one's office; go[come] to the office; go to work; show up at the office[for work]; go on duty; report for work [duty]. ¶회사에 ~ show up at one's desk in the (company) office∥아홉 시에 ~ go (down) to (the) office at nine o'clock∥출근해 있다 be at (one's) office / be present∥그가 오늘은 출근했다 He is at the office today.∥오늘은 오후에 출근한다 I am on the afternoon shift today.∥매일 버스로 출근한다 I take the bus daily to my work[office].∥8시 30분에 출근하시오 Come[Report] to the office at 8:30.∥총지배인은 아직 출근하지 않았습니다 The general manager is not in[here / at his desk / at the office] yet.∥그는 한 시간 늦게 출근했다 He reported to work an hour late.
● **출근부** an attendance book[record]; a time book. ¶~에 도장을 찍다 register[sign] one's name in the attendance book / punch the time clock. **출근 시간** the time one reports for work; the hour for going to work; the office-going hour. ¶~이 늦다 be late for the office.

출금(出金) [지출] payment; defrayal; (예금의) drawing; a withdrawal (of funds). **출금하다** [지출하다] defray; pay; (예금을) make a withdrawal.
● **출금 전표** a paying-out slip.

출납(出納) (금전) receipts and payments [disbursements / expenses]; revenue and expenditure; incomings and outgoings; depositing and drawing. ¶~을 맡아보다 have[be in] charge of accounts[revenue and expenditure] / hold the purse strings∥그는 회사의 ~ 담당이다 He is in charge of the accounts in the firm. / He is in charge of the firm's (books) accounts.∥이 창고는 물품 ~이 불편하다 This warehouse is hard to get things in and out of.∥예금의 ~에는 이 용지에 기입하여 사용하시오 We fill out these forms for deposits and withdrawals.∥나는 금전 ~의 계정 잔고가 맞는가를 검사했다 I checked to see whether the accounts balance or not. **출납하다** take in and pay out; receive and disburse; handle the cash accounts[transactions]. ¶현금을 ~ handle cash / be a cashier.
● **출납계** a cashier; (은행) a teller. **출납부** a cashbook; an account book.

출동(出動) dispatch; going[starting] out; moving (out); (군대의) marching; mobilization; (함대의) sailing. ¶군대[경찰]의 ~ the mobilization of troops[police]∥함대의 ~ the moving out of a fleet∥~을 명하다 order to move∥~ 준비를 하다 hold itself in readiness for action∥군대에 ~ 준비 명령이 내려졌다 The troops were alerted[put on alert]. **출동하다** go[set / start] out; go into action; move out[in]; start moving; (군대가) be called out; be mobilized; (함대가) sail; (소방대 등이) turn out. ¶폭동 진압을 위해 군대가 출동했다 The army was dispatched[went into action] to crush the riot. ➔**출동시키다** dispatch / send / move∥경찰을 출동시킬 정도의 일은 아니다 It's not serious enough to justify calling in the police.∥즉시 구조대를 출동시켜라 Get the rescue squad into action at once.
● **출동 명령** an order for moving[turning out]; marching orders(육군); sailing orders(해군). ¶(요격기의) 긴급 ~ a scramble order∥~을 내리다[받다] give[receive] marching[sailing] orders∥~을 받고 있다 (육군이) be under orders for the front / (해군이) be under orders to proceed (to).

출두(出頭) appearance; presence; attendance. ¶~를 요구하다 request the attendance[presence] of 《a person》 / ask 《a person's》 appearance∥자진 ~를 요구하다 ask 《a person's》 voluntary appearance. **출두하다** appear; attend; present oneself (at); be present (at); make one's[put in an] appearance; turn[show] up; report oneself (at); report personally[in person] (to a person / at an office). ¶법원에 ~ appear in court∥출두하라고 통고하다 serve notice to appear / summon to appear (in court)∥비자를 받으려면 본인이 영사관에 출두하여야 한다 You have to appear in person at the consulate to get a visa.∥경찰에 출두했다 I presented myself at the police station.∥내일 세무서에 출두한다 I will report to[at] the tax office tomorrow.
● **출두 명령** a summons; an order to appear. ¶법원 ~ (issue) a summons to appear in court.

출람(出藍) excelling one's master. ⇨청출어람

출렁거리다 (액체가) surge; roll; undulate; wave; slop[slosh] about[around] (in a bucket). ¶기슭에 출렁거리는 물결 little waves lapping (against) the shore∥출렁거리

는 가슴 a heaving bosom.// 물을 너무 마셔서 배가 출렁거린다 My stomach is all sloshy from drinking too much water.// 물이 독 안에서 출렁거린다 The water in a jar is slopping from side to side.

출력(出力) 1 [전] generating power; output (of power). ¶~ 3백 마력의 모터 a motor that develops [turns out / has a capacity of] 300 h.p.// ~ 25만 킬로와트의 발전소 a power plant that generates 250,000 kilowatts of electricity [with a 250,000 kw-capacity]// 이 크다 [작다] have a large [small] output// 이 원자력 발전소는 ~이 500만 킬로와트이다 This nuclear power plant has a generating capacity of five million kilowatts. / The output of this power station is five million kilowatts.// 100마력의 엔진을 갖추고 있다 It has a 100-horsepower engine. 2 [컴] output. **출력하다** output.
● **출력 장치** an output unit.

출렵하다(出獵-) go hunting [shooting]. ¶출렵해 있다 be out hunting [shooting].

출루하다(出壘-) [야구] go to (first) base. ¶출루해 있다 (주자가) be on (the second) base / (팀이) have (two) on (base)// 출루한 사람은 없다 There is no one on base.// 5회까지 출루한 사람이 한 사람도 없었다 No one got to first base during the first five innings.

출마(出馬) [말을 타고 나감] going out [forth] on horseback; [입후보] (미) candidacy; (영) candidature. ¶~를 **선언하다** declare one's candidacy (for). **출마하다** stand as a candidate for (an election); run for (the National Assembly). ¶총선거에 ~ run (as a candidate) at a general election // 국회의원에 ~ run for election to the National Assembly // 그는 대통령 선거에 출마한다 He is running for president [the presidency].

출몰하다(出沒-) appear and disappear; [자주 나타나다] make frequent appearance; frequent; haunt; infest. ¶산적이 출몰하는 고개 a (mountain) pass infested with bandits / a bandit-ridden pass// 산길에 도둑이 출몰했다 A mountain path was haunted by robbers.// 일당은 이 근방의 술집을 출몰한다 They frequent the bars in this neighborhood.// 이 고성에는 유령이 출몰한다고 한다 The ancient castle is said to be haunted by a ghost.// 이 근방에는 게릴라가 출몰한다 The area is infested with guerrillas.// 큰사슴 떼가 산기슭에 가끔 출몰한다 A herd of moose can often be seen at the foot of the mountain.// 적함이 자주 연안에 출몰했다 A hostile vessel has often been seen off the coast.// 호랑이가 그곳에 출몰했다 Tigers lurked there.

출발(出發) departure; starting. ¶~에 즈음하여 at [on] one's departure (to the front) // ~ 직전에 just before departure // 인생의 ~에 즈음하여 at the threshold of one's life // 잠시 ~을 미루겠다 We'll put off our departure temporarily.// 인생의 ~을 그르쳤다 I got off on the wrong foot in life.// 자네의 새 ~을 축하하네 I wish you the best of luck with your new life.// 나는 경주를 ~에서 끝일까지 보았다 I watched the race from start to finish.// 그가 인생의 ~을 잘하기를 바란다 I hope he will get off to a good start in life.// 505편의 ~은 두 시간 늦었다 The departure of Flight 505 was two hours behind schedule [delayed by two hours]. **출발하다** start (from); depart (from); leave (Seoul); set out (from); hop [take] off (비행기가). ¶그는 파리를 향해 인천을 출발했다 He left Incheon for Paris.// 비행기는 정각에 출발했다 The plane took off on schedule.// 행렬은 중앙 공원에서 출발했다 The procession started from Central Park.// 그가 맨 먼저 출발했다 He made a start.// 그 비행기는 예정 시간대로 출발했다 The plane took off on schedule.
● **출발선** a starting line. ¶선수들이 ~에 늘어섰다 The runners lined up at the starting line. **출발 시간** the starting [departure] time. ¶비행기 ~은 몇 시입니까 What time does the plane leave [take off]? **출발 신호** a starting [leaving] signal. ¶~를 **기다리다** wait for the starter's signal. **출발점** the starting [take-off] point; the point of departure; [육상 경기] the starting mark [line]. ¶(경기에서) ~에 **서다** toe the line [mark / scratch] // ~으로 돌아가 다시 하다 begin all over again / make a fresh start // 이번에 실패하면 우리는 ~으로 다시 돌아가게 된다 If we fail this time, we will be right back where we started.// 경기는 ~으로 되돌아갔다 The game is right back where it started.// 그는 급사로 ~으로 하여 마지막에는 사장이 되었다 He started out (his career) as an office boy and ended as (company) president.

출범(出帆) sailing; departure (of a ship). **출범하다** sail (out [forth]); set sail (from Busan); leave (Busan for America); clear (from Boston); put out to sea. ¶출범하는 배 an outgoing ship.
● **출범기**(-旗) the Blue Peter. **출범 시간** (ship's) sailing time. ¶~이 다가오고 있다 The time for sailing is drawing near. / We are going to sail [leave part] before long. **출범일** the sailing day.

출병(出兵) the dispatch of troops [an expeditionary force] (to). ¶소말리아 ~ the dispatch of troops to Somalia. **출병하다** dispatch [send] troops [an expeditionary force] (to). ¶해외로 ~ send troops overseas // 전선에 출병했다 Troops were sent [dispatched] to the front.

출비(出費) (an) expenditure; [드는 비용] expenses. ¶~를 바짝 줄이다 cut down (on) expenses // 내년에는 ~가 많아질 것 같다 Our expenses will mount next year.// 그 때문에 드는 ~가 그에게는 매우 벅찬 것이었다 It meant heavy expenditure for him. / It put a heavy financial burden on him.

출사(出師) the dispatch of troops (to). ⇨ **출병**

출사하다(出仕-) enter on an official career; go into government service.

출산(出産) delivery; (a) childbirth; (a) birth. ¶~는 3월 10일로 예정되어 있습니다 The baby is due [expected] on March 10.// 그녀는 ~으로 사망했다 She died in childbirth.// 100의 ~ 중 사산(死産)은 2의 비율이다 There are two stillbirths per hundred deliveries.// 그의 아내는 다음 주 ~ 예정이다 His wife is expecting her baby next week. **출산하다** give birth to (a child); be delivered of (a baby). ¶그녀는 여자 아기를 출산했다 She gave birth to [(문어) was delivered of] a baby girl.
● **출산율** a birthrate. **출산 휴가** (a) maternity leave.

출상(出喪) carrying the coffin out of the

house. 출상하다 carry the coffin out to the grave. ¶오전 9시에 출상할 예정으로 있다 The hearse is to leave home at 9 a.m.

출생(出生) (a) birth; coming into the world; origin(근본). ¶그의 ~의 비밀 the secret of his birth // 그들은 장남의 ~을 축하했다 They celebrated the birth of their first son. **출생하다** be born. ¶그들은 같은 날에 출생했다 They were born on the same day.
● **출생률** a birthrate. **출생 신고** a report [register] of a birth. ¶나는 아들의 ~를 했다 I have (just) registered the birth of my son. **출생 연월일** the date of one's birth. **출생지** one's birthplace; one's native place.

출석(出席) attendance; presence; appearance. ¶전원 ~ complete[perfect] attendance // ~을 요구하다 request[ask for] (a person's) attendance (at) // 먼저 ~을 부르겠습니다 I'll call the roll[take attendance] first(▶ call the roll은 명부에 의거하여). // 너희는 ~ 여부의 통지를 즉각 해야 한다 You should have let us know immediately whether you were coming or not. // 그는 ~이 고르지 않다[불규칙하다] He is irregular in his attendance. // 이달에는 자네 ~이 좋지 않았는걸 You've been very irregular in your attendance this month. **출석하다** attend; be present (at); present oneself (at). ¶출석하지 않다 do not[fail to] attend / absent oneself (from) // 부디 출석해 주십시오 We request the pleasure of your company. // 그 모임에 출석해 주도록 그들이 내게 요청을 했다 They have requested my presence at the meeting.
● **출석률** the percentage of attendance. ¶이 반의 ~은 매우 나쁘다 The attendance of this class is very bad. **출석부** a roll book. **출석자** a person present; an attendant (at); (집합적) attendance; those present. ¶~가 많았다[적었다] The meeting was well[poorly] attended. / There was a large[poor] turnout at the meeting.

출세(出世) success[advancement] in life; a successful career[life]; [영달] eminence; [승진] promotion. ¶~ 가도를 달리다 (steadily) move up the ladder under (a person) // ~가 빠르다 make a rapid rise / rise rapidly in the world // ~를 방해하다 stand in the way of (a person's) advancement. **출세하다** [입신하다] succeed in life; rise [go up] in the world; rise to a high position; [승진하다] win [get / obtain] promotion; be promoted (to); be advanced (to). ¶출세한 사람 a successful man / a success // 빨리 ~ mark a rapid rise in the world (승진이) win[get / obtain] rapid[quick] promotion // 갑자기 ~ suddenly rise to a higher position / rise suddenly in the world // 그는 끝내 출세하지 못했다 He never got ahead. // 그의 부모는 아들들이 출세한 것을 보고 기뻐했다 His parents were glad of their son's success[that their son had succeeded] in life. // 그는 급속도로 출세했다 He rose rapidly in the world. // 그는 국장으로 출세했다 / He was promoted to bureau chief. / He rose to the position of bureau chief. // 그가 고등학교 동창 중에서 가장 출세했다 He is the most successful person in my high-school class [of my high-school classmates]. // 그런 식으로는 출세할 수 없다 If he goes on at that rate he will never attain greatness. // 그는 출세할 기회를 놓치고 말았다 He missed a chance to get ahead in life.
● **출세 비결** secrets of social success[a successful life]. **출세욕** ambitions for success. **출세작**(작품) the work which (has) brought (a person) into prominence; one's maiden success-piece. ¶그 곡이 그의 ~이다 That work brought him recognition (as a composer).

출소(出所) [교도소에서 나옴] release from prison. **출소하다** be released [discharged] from prison / leave [come out of] prison. ¶그는 형기가 끝나 교도소에서 출소했다 He was released from [let out of] prison at the end of his term of imprisonment.
● **출소자** a released convict.

출소하다(出訴-) institute a lawsuit (against a person); bring [file] an action [a suit] (against a person); sue (a person for damage).

출수(出穗) [이삭이 팸] coming out in ears. **출수하다** be in (the) ear; come into ears; ear (up).
● **출수기** the earing season.

출신(出身) [신분] a graduate; affiliation; origin; birth. ¶군인 ~ a former military man // 부산 ~ a native of Busan // 대학 ~의 사람 a university graduate // 정당 ~의 장관 a minister affiliated with a political party / a party Minister // 도시[시골] ~이다 be town-[country-] bred // 그는 노동자 계급의 ~이다 He was born in a working-class family. // 나는 호남 ~입니다 I come [am] from the Honam District. // "부산 ~입니까?" "아닙니다, 마산입니다." "Do you come [Are you] from Busan?" "No, I'm from Masan." // 그는 귀족 ~이다 He comes of aristocratic stock. / He is descended from a noble [an aristocratic] family. // 그녀는 양갓집 ~이다 She is well-born. / She comes [is] from a good family. // 그는 제주도 ~이다 He comes from Jejudo. // 새 지사는 어느 당 ~인가 Which party is the new governor from?
● **출신교** the school from which one graduated (▶ graduated from은 (미)에서 어떤 학교에나 쓰이지만, (영)에서는 대학에만, 그 밖의 학교에 대해서는 the school one went to라고 함); (미) one's alma mater. **출신자** (학교의) a graduate; (남자) an alumnus (pl. -ni); (여자) an alumna (pl. -nae). **대학 ~** a university graduate. **출신지** where one was born [grew up]; one's native place; one's hometown.

출애굽기(出-記) [성] (The Book of) Exodus (약어 Exod.).

출어(出漁) going out fishing. ¶배는 그린랜드 앞바다에 ~ 중 나포되었다 The boat was seized while fishing off Greenland. **출어하다** sail [go] out fishing. ¶아프리카 동해안으로 ~ go to the east coast of Africa on a fishing expedition.
● **출어 구역** a fishing area. **출어기**[권] the fishing season [right].

출연(出捐) contribution; subscription; donation. **출연하다** contribute (money) to (a fund); donate.
● **출연금** a contribution; a donation. **출연자** a contributor; a donator.

출연(出演) appearance on the stage; performance. ¶스타 총~의 연극이었다 The play was performed with an all-star cast. **출연하**

출연 다 appear on the stage; play; perform; take part in (a concert); sing(노래하다). ¶춘향으로 ~ appear as[play the part of] Chun-hyang// 국립 극장에 ~ make one's appearance on the stage of the National Theater// 출연하여 주시기 바랍니다 Contributions are solicited.// 다가오는 청초 공연에 그는 출연하지 않는다 He will not appear in the coming New Year production.

● **출연 계약** a booking. ¶~이 없다 have no bookings// 그는 내년에 ~이 꽉 차 있다 He is fully booked for next year. **출연료** a performance fee; an actor's[a singer's] fee. **출연자** a performer; a player; an actor(남자); an actress(여자); a singer(가수); (퀴즈 프로 등의) a panelist; (집합적) the cast (of a drama). ¶주요한 ~ the leading actor[actress] / the main player.

출영(出迎) meeting; reception(영접). ¶~을 받다 be met[greeted] (at the airport)// 많은 친지의 ~를 받다 be met[received] by many friends[people] at (a place)// ~ 구중이 그 광장에 꽉 찼다 The stadium was bursting with the welcoming[cheering] crowd. **출영하다** receive; greet; meet; go[come] (out) to meet (a person) on arrival.

출옥(出獄) discharge[release] from prison. ¶가~ release on parole / provisional release. **출옥하다** be released[discharged] from prison; leave[come out of] prison. ¶만기 ~ be discharged upon expiration of one's term // 그는 15년 형기를 마치고 출옥했다 He was released after serving a sentence of 15 years' confinement. ➔¶출옥시키다 release / discharge / set (a prisoner) free[at liberty].

출원(出願) application; submitting. ¶특허 중 (게시) Patent applied for. / Patent Pending. **출원하다** make[file] an application; apply (for). ¶특허를 ~ apply (to the Patent Office) for a patent// 나는 이 약의 특허를 출원했다 I have applied[filed an application] for a patent on this medicine.

● **출원자** an applicant.

출입(出入) 1 [드나들기] coming in and out; entrance and exit. ¶청와대 ~ 기자 a newsman accredited to the Blue House// ~을 허락하다 give (a person) the run[entrée] of (a house) / allow (a person) access to (one's house)// 무단~을 금하다 warn (trespassers) off// 이 상자가 ~를 막고 있다 This box blocks the doorway.// 그의 우리 집 ~ 못하게 하겠다 I will forbid him to enter my house.// 공작은 이제 궁궐의 ~이 불가하게 되었다 The Duke was no longer received at court.// 그곳은 학생의 ~이 금지되어 있다 The place is off limits to the students.// 무단 ~을 금함 (게시) Unauthorized Entry (Is) Forbidden. **출입하다** go[come] in and out; enter and leave; (자주) frequent. ¶출입하는 배 incoming and outgoing vessels// 출입하는 상인 one's regular[usual] tradesman// 자유로이 출입할 수 있다 have[be allowed] free access to (a house)// 저 집은 많은 사람이 출입한다 The family has many visitors.// 나는 그의 집에 자유로이 출입한다 I have the run of his house. / I have free access to his house. / I can come and go freely at his house.

2 [외출]. **출입하다** go out for a short visit.

● **출입구** an entrance (and exit); a door (-way); a gate(way). **출입국** entry into, and departure from, the country. **출입국 관리** immigration control[management]. **출입 금지** (게시) Keep Out.; Keep Off.; Off Limits.; No Trespassing. ¶미성년자 ~ (게시) Minors Not Allowed. / No Minors (Allowed). **출입처** (신문 기자의) a beat.

출자(出資) (an) investment; financing. ¶공동 ~ a joint capital. **출자하다** invest[sink / lay out] money (in); finance (an enterprise); contribute money (to); make a contribution (of). ¶주식에 ~ invest one's money in stocks// 그는 광산에 출자했다 He invested (his money)[He made an investment] in a mine.// 세 개의 큰 회사가 이 사업에 출자하고 있다 Three major business concerns are backing this project financially.// 이 다섯 사람이 출자하여 그 회사를 만들었다 These five people provided the capital to establish the firm.

● **출자금** money invested; an investment. **출자액** the amount of investment[money invested]. **출자자** an investor; a financier.

출장(出張) (회사원의) a business trip; (공무원의) an official trip[tour]; a tour of duty. ¶~ 교수[지도]를 하다 give lessons at one's pupil's (home)// ~ 명령을 받다 be ordered (to go) to (Japan) on business// ~을 보내다 send[dispatch] (a person)on business to (Pusan)// 그는 ~ 중입니다 He is away on business. **출장하다** go (to Seoul) on business[on a business trip]; make an official trip (to).

● **출장비** traveling[(영) travelling] expenses; (수당) a travel allowance. **출장소** a branch[local] office; an agency.

출장(出場) 1 [어느 장소에 나감] appearance (in a place). **출장하다** appear (in a place). 2 participation (in). ⇨**출전**(出戰)2

출전(出典) the source; the authority. ¶~을 밝히다 indicate[name] the source (of) / give [cite] the authority (for)// 인용문은 ~을 명확히 밝힐 것 Be sure to give the source of each of your quotations.// 이 구절은 ~은 성경이다 This phrase is quoted from the Bible.// 이 논문은 ~의 기재가 불충분하다 This paper has insufficient documentation[is inadequately documented].

출전(出戰) 1 going to the front. ⇨=**출정**(出征) 2 (경기 등의) participation (in); an entry (for). ¶부정행위 때문에 그 야구 팀은 ~ 정지가 되었다 The baseball team was disqualified (from competition) for misconduct.// 그 경주에 20명 이상의 ~ 신청자가 있었다 There were over twenty entries for the race. **출전하다** take part (in); participate (in); enter (for an event). ¶경기에 ~ take part in a[an athletic] contest// 그는 100미터 경주에 출전했다 He took part[participated] in the hundred-meter dash.

● **출전 선수** a participating player[athlete]; an entrant; (집합적) the entry (of a race).

출정(出廷) appearance in court; a court appearance. ¶~ 명령을 받다 be ordered to (appear in) court. **출정하다** appear in court; attend court; be in court. ¶피고가 출정하지 않으면 in case of nonappearance of the defendant// 재판을 받기 위해 ~ be brought to court for trial// 9시에 출정할 것 You are to appear in court at nine.// 아직 그는 출정

하지 않고 있다 He is not yet in court.
출정(出征) going to the front; taking the field. **출정하다** go to war [the front]; take the field (against Rome); go on an expedition (against).
● **출정 군인** a soldier in active service at the front [going to the front].
출제(出題) setting a problem; making questions (for an examination). ¶한 선생의 ～는 예측하기 어렵다 Mr. Han's examination questions are hard to predict.// ～ 범위를 알려 주겠다 I'll tell you what the test will cover. **출제하다** set (a person) a problem (in mathematics); make questions (for an examination in English) out of (the textbook material); prepare an examination paper. ¶영어 시험 문제를 ～ make [prepare] questions for an English test.
● **출제자** a person who contributes questions for an examination; a person who prepares examination questions.
출중하다(出衆-) outstanding; conspicuous; prominent; preeminent. ¶출중한 인물 a distinguished figure// 출중한 작품 an excellent [outstanding] work// 출중한 재능 extraordinary [outstanding] talent// 출중한 재주가 있다 be of extraordinary talent// 그는 출중한 재주를 가지고 있었다 He was endowed with rare gifts.// 그는 무예가 ～ He is skilled beyond his fellows in every form of military exercise. **출중히** outstandingly; preeminently; by far (the best); far [out] and away; out of the common; extraordinarily. ¶～ 공부를 잘하다 be by far the best student.
출찰(出札) issue of a ticket.
● **출찰 계원** (미) a ticket agent [clerk]; (영) a booking clerk. **출찰구** a ticket [(영) booking] window [booth].
출처(出處) the origin; the source; provenance. ¶～가 분명한 authentic (news) / (information) (drawn / collected) from a sure [reliable] source// 뉴스의 ～ the source of (the) news// ～가 분명치 않다 be of doubtful origin [provenance / authenticity] / be from an unreliable source// ～를 밝히다 (정보 등의) disclose [indicate / name] the source (of) / locate (a report) / (인용문 등의) give chapter and verse// 믿을 만한 ～로부터의 정보에 의하면 전쟁은 종말에 가까워지고 있다 According to reports from reliable sources, the war is drawing to an end.// 소문의 ～를 찾아냈다 I have traced the source of the rumor.// 이 유행어의 ～는 알려져 있지 않다 The origin of this fad word is unknown.// 그 뉴스의 ～는 불명이다 [알 수 없다] That news item cannot be traced to a reliable source.// 이 구절의 ～는 셰익스피어이다 This phrase comes from Shakespeare.
출초(出超) an excess of exports. ⇨수출 초과 (⇩수출) ¶3억 원의 ～ an excess of exports amounting to three hundred million won.
출출하다 hungry; (서술적) feel a bit hungry; feel somewhat [rather] hungry [empty].
출타(出他) going out; an outing; leaving home. ¶～ 중에 in [during] one's absence / while one is away [absent] // ～ 중이라 죄송했습니다 I am very sorry I was not in (home / office) when you called on me.
출토품(出土品) a [an archaeological] find; an excavated [unearthed] article; an excavation.
출토하다(出土-) (물건이) be excavated [unearthed] (at a site / from the ruins of ...); (장소가) produce; yield. ➔¶이 항아리는 절의 경내에서 출토되었다 This pot was unearthed on the temple grounds.// 고분에서 여러 가지 도구가 출토되었다 The tumulus yielded various artifacts [(영) artefacts].
출판(出版) publication; publishing. ¶한정 ～ a limited edition// **예약** ～ publication by subscription// **자비** ～ publication on one's own account. **출판하다** publish; issue; bring [put] out (a book). ➔¶출판되다 be published / come out// 이 책은 지난달 막 출판되었다 The book came out [was published] only last month.// 이 책은 출판되었다 [출판되지 않았다] The book is in print [out of print].// 이 책은 10년 전에 출판되었다 This book was published ten years ago.
출판의 자유 freedom of the press.
● **출판계** the publishing world. **출판권** the right of publication; publication right. **출판 기념회** a party in celebration of the publication of a book. **출판물** a publication. ¶～을 **단속하다** exercise control over publications // ～**이 범람하다** have too many publications. **출판부** a publishing department. **출판사** a publishing company [house / firm]; a publisher; (미) a book concern. **출판업** the publishing business; publishing. **출판업자** a publisher.
출품(出品) exhibition; show; display. **출품하다** exhibit; show; display; put [place] on exhibition [show]. ¶전람회에 ～ send [submit] (one's painting) to an exhibition// 그는 사진 콘테스트에 3점을 출품했다 He entered three of his works in the photo contest.// 그녀는 전람회에 수채화를 출품했다 She sent her watercolor to the exhibition. ➔¶신형 자동차가 출품되어 있다 New model cars are on show [display].
● **출품 목록** a catalog of exhibits. **출품물** an exhibit; an article on show [exhibition]. **출품자** an exhibitor.
출하(出荷) forwarding; shipment; shipping; consignment. **출하하다** forward; ship; consign. ¶수원에서 서울로 포도를 ～ ship grapes from Suwon to Seoul// 화물을 ～ ship goods from (Seoul station).
● **출하자** a shipper; a forwarder. **출하지** the place of shipment.
출항(出港) departure from a port. ¶～**을 허가하다** give (a ship) clearance// ～**을 정지시키다** lay [put] an embargo on (a ship). **출항하다** leave port; set sail (from); clear a port. ¶몇 시에 배가 출항합니까 What time is the ship leaving port [setting sail / sailing / departing]?
● **출항 명령** an order for sailing. **출항 수속 / 출항 절차** clearance formalities. **출항 통지** [**허가장**] a clearance notice [permit / certificate].
출항(出航) sailing off; departure; (항공기의) a take off. **출항하다** start on a voyage; set sail (from). ¶그 배는 부산에서 뉴욕을 향해 출항했다 The ship left Busan for New York [for New York from Busan].
출현(出現) appearance; emergence; arrival; advent. ¶구세주의 ～ the advent of the Savior. **출현하다** appear; make one's appear-

ance; emerge; turn [show] up; come in. ¶국적 불명의 잠수함이 앞바다에 출현했다 A submarine of unknown nationality appeared [made an appearance] in the offing. ∥최초의 혁신당 내각이 출현했다 The first progressive cabinet came into existence. ∥핵무기가 출현하여 전쟁의 성격이 완전히 바뀌었다 Since the advent of nuclear weapons, the nature of war has changed drastically. (▶ advent는 보통 the advent of …의 형태로 쓰여, 중요한 사물·인물의 출현을 뜻함) ➔¶출현시키다 bring into existence.

출혈(出血) **1** [피가 남] bleeding; hemorrhage; loss of blood. ¶내[뇌] ~ internal [cerebral] hemorrhage ∥ 다량의 ~ profuse [copious] bleeding / excessive loss of blood ∥ ~이 심하다 bleed badly [copiously] ∥ ~ 과다로 죽다 die from excessive bleeding [loss of blood] ∥ ~을 멎게 하다 stop bleeding / stanch [arrest] the flow of blood ∥ 상처의 ~을 멈추게 하다 stanch one's wound ∥ ~ 과다로 그가 사망했다 He bled to death [died from loss of blood]. **출혈하다** bleed; lose blood.
2 [전쟁 등의 희생] casualties; sacrifices. ¶막대한 ~ many casualties ∥ 우리 편의 다소의 ~은 각오해야 한다 We must be prepared for some sacrifices on our side.
● **출혈 경쟁** (업계의) a cutthroat competition; a dumping war. **출혈 수출** below-cost export. **출혈 판매** a sacrifice [below-cost] sale.

출회(出廻) [물품이 시장에 나와 도는 것] movement (of commodities); flow (of goods); arrivals on the market; supply. ¶상품의 ~를 증가시키다 increase the flow of goods. **출회하다** arrive [appear] on the market; hit [come on to] the market; be moving; goods flow out to the market.
● **출회기** the crop-moving season; a season for movement (of crops).

춤¹ [무용] a dance; dancing; (속어) a step (무도); ¶양~ a western [an occidental] dance / ballroom dancing ∥ 어깨~ shoulder dancing ∥ 엉덩이~ hula(-hula) / a hula dance ∥ 추잡한 ~ an indecent [a vulgar] dance ∥ ~을 추다 dance / dance [perform] a dance / have a dance / tread a (dainty) measure ∥ / (구어) step it / foot [hoof] it / (속어) shake a leg ∥ ~을 잘 추다 dance well / be a good dancer ∥ …의 곡에 맞추어 ~을 추다 dance to the tone [melody] of … ∥ 음악에 맞추어 ~을 추다 dance to [after] music ∥ ~을 추러 가다 go dancing / go to a dance ∥ 남의 장단에 ~을 추다 dance to [after] another's tune [pipe / piping / whistle] / be made a puppet of another ∥ 탱고 ~을 출 줄 아세요 Can you do the tango?
● **춤 상대** [선생] one's dancing partner [master].

춤² [운두] the height of an upturned rim; [높이] height. ¶ ~이 높은 [낮은] 구두 a high-[low-]cut shoe.
춤³ inside the waist of one's trousers. ⇨ 허리
춤⁴ [한 손으로 쥘 만한 분량] a handful; a fistful. ¶모 한 ~ a handful of rice seedlings.
춤곡(-曲) [음] a dance music.
춥다 cold; chilly. ¶추운 지방 a cold area ∥ 추운 곳에 in the cold ∥ 추워서 떨다 shiver with cold / quiver from cold ∥ (사람이) 추워 보이다 appear uncomfortable with cold / look cold / be manifestly cold (in the thin coat) ∥ 혹독하게 ~ It's miserably cold. ∥ 밖은 살을 에는 듯이 추웠다 It was bitterly cold outdoors. ∥ 참으로 추운 겨울이었다 We had a very severe [very cold] winter. ∥ 오늘 아침은 몹시 추웠다 It was awfully cold this morning. / The temperature dipped very low this morning.

충(蟲) **1** an insect; a beetle. ⇨ 벌레 **2** a mawworm; an ascarid. ⇨ 회충
충격(衝撃) an impact; a shock; an impulse; percussion. ¶세상에 ~을 준 흉악한 범죄 an atrocious crime which shook the world ∥ 그에게는 ~이 너무 심했다 The shock was too much for him. / He took it harder than we expected. ∥ 나는 그 소식을 듣고 ~을 받았다 I was shocked by the news. ∥ 그의 죽음은 전 세계에 ~을 주었다 His death shocked the whole world. ∥ 나는 그 그림에서 강한 ~을 받았다 That painting had a great impact on me. ∥ 폭발의 ~으로 집이 흔들렸다 The house was shaken by the shock of the explosion. ∥ 아들의 죽음이 그에게 확실히 ~을 준 듯하다 The death of his son has definitely told on him. / The loss of his son seems to have hit him hard [really affected him].
● **충격 시험** an impact [a percussion] test. **충격 요법** shock therapy [treatment]. **충격파** a shock wave.
충격적(衝撃的) shocking. ¶ ~인 사건 a shock.
충견(忠犬) a faithful dog.
충고(忠告) [조언] (a piece of) advice (▶ 이 말은 복수가 되지 않음); counsel; [훈계] an admonition; [경고] a warning. ¶ ~에 따라 on (a person's) advice ∥ ~에 따르다 follow [act upon] (a person's) advice ∥ ~에 거역하다 [~를 저버리다] act against [disobey] (a person's) advice ∥ 남의 ~를 받아들이다 take [accept] a person's advice ∥ ~를 주다 give [offer / furnish / provide / tender] advice ∥ ~를 구하다 ask advice (of a person) / seek the advice (of a person) ∥ ~를 무시하다 disregard [give no heed to] (a person's) advice ∥ ~를 마음속에 새기다 grave (a person's) counsel on one's memory ∥ 그녀는 내 ~를 거역하고 [~에 따라] 나갔다 She went out against [on] my advice. ∥ 그는 어떠한 ~에도 귀머거리였다 He is deaf to all advice [warnings]. ∥ 오로지 네 장래를 생각해서 내가 네게 솔직한 ~를 하고자 한다 Precisely because I have your future at heart, I'd like to give you my frank advice. ∥ 그는 ~를 좋게 [나쁘게] 받아들였다 He took my advice in good [bad] part. **충고하다** advise; give (a person) advice [counsel]; counsel; [경고하다] give (a person) warning; caution; [훈계하다] admonish; remonstrate (with). ¶건강에 주의하라고 ~ advise (a person) to take (good) care of his health ∥ 동물 학대에 대해서 ~ remonstrate against cruelty to animals ∥ 그들은 그의 어리석은 행동에 대해서 충고했다 They remonstrated with him about [on] his foolish behavior. / They dissuaded him from his folly. ∥ 나는 그에게 담배를 피우지 말라고 충고했다 I advised him against [to stop] smoking. ∥ 한 가지 충고할 것이 있다 Let me give you a piece of advice.

●**충고자** an adviser; a counselor.
충군(忠君) loyalty [devotion] to one's sovereign [king]. **충군하다** be loyal (to one's king).
충나다(蟲-) [물건에 벌레가 생기다] get infested (with vermin).
충당(充當) appropriation; assignment; devotion. **충당하다** allot [assign] (some time for one's use / two hours to sleep); apply [devote] (a sum of money to amusement); appropriate (a sum for a purpose); earmark (a sum for house repair). ¶비용에 충당할 돈을 지급받다 be given the money to meet the expenses // 원고료를 빚 갚는 데 ~ apply copy money to the payment of debts // 임시 수입을 대금의 변제에 ~ allot the extra income to [for] the payment of a loan // 50만 달러를 새 교사의 건설비로 충당했다 Half a million dollars has been appropriated for the new school building. ➔¶그 수익은 빈민 구제 사업비에 충당될 것이다 The proceeds will go to the relief of the poor. ¶그 기금은 자선 사업에 충당되고 있다 The fund is appropriated for charitable purposes.
충돌(衝突) 1 [서로 맞부딪침] a collision; a clash; a bump; an impact; (구어) a pile-up(몇 대의 차이). ¶삼중 ~ a three-way collision (among) // 정면 ~ a frontal clash (between) / a head-on collision (with) // 자동차의 ~ a car crash // 연쇄 ~ a multicar collision / a pileup. **충돌하다** collide [come into collision] (with); run [smash / crash / bump] (against / into). ¶전봇대에 ~ run [smash] into a telegraph pole // 정면으로 ~ clash [collide] head-on (with) // 충돌하여 침몰하게 하다 run (a boat) down // 5,6대의 차가 연쇄 충돌했다 There was a pileup of five or six cars. / Five or six cars were involved in a pileup. // 나는 상점에서 튀어나온 사나이와 충돌했다 I collided with a man who dashed out of a shop.
2 [불일치·불화] a conflict; a clash; a collision; a discord; a feud; a quarrel. ¶군사적 ~ a military collision (between) // 무력 ~ an armed collision (with / between) // 감정의 ~ an emotional [a temperamental] clash (between / with) // 이해의 ~ a conflict [clash] of interests (between) // 의견의 ~ a collision of opinions / a collision of views // 부자 사이의 ~ a friction between father and son // 가격 문제를 둘러싸고 권 씨와 임 씨와의 의견 ~ 이 생겼다 Mr. Gwon and Mr. Im clashed on the question of price. // 학생과 경찰 사이에 유혈 ~ 이 있었다 A sanguinary collision took place between the students and the police. **충돌하다** (의견 등이) conflict [clash] (with); be in conflict (with); run counter (to); jar (with); [불화하다] fall out (with); quarrel (with). ¶...으로 남과 ~ clash [collide] with (a person) over ... // 충돌하지 않고 (잘)해 나가다 get on [along] well (with) // 충돌하기를 피하다 avoid [ward off] friction [a collision] (with) // 나는 그와 의견이 충돌했다 His opinion clashed [conflicted] with mine. / He and I disagreed entirely.
3 [전투] an encounter; (사소한) a skirmish; a brush. **충돌하다** encounter; have an encounter [a skirmish] (with).
충동(衝動) 1 [순간적 욕구] an impulse; an impetus; an urge; [심] a drive. ¶성적 ~ a sex urge [drive] // 육체적 ~ a body urge // 일시적 [순간적] ~ a sudden impulse / an impulse [a spur] of the moment // 순간적 ~ 으로 on the spur [impulse] of the moment // ~에 이끌리다 be urged (to do) by impulse / act on impulse / be swayed [carried away] by impulse // 일시적인 ~ 으로 돈을 훔치다 steal money on the impulse of the moment // ~을 억제하다 inhibit [resist] an impulse (to do) // ...하고 싶다는 ~ 을 느끼다 feel an impulse to (do) / have an urge to (do) // 나는 그 자리에서 도망치고 싶은 ~ 을 느꼈다 I felt an impulse [urge] to run away from the scene.
2 [교사·선동] instigation; abetment; incitement. ¶...의 ~ 으로 at the instigation of ... / abetted by ... // 교감의 ~ 으로 학생들은 교장 배척 운동을 시작했다 The students started a movement to expel the principal, egged on by the head instructor. **충동하다** instigate; abet; incite; stir up; egg [set] (a person) on (to do). ¶남을 충동하여 ...하게 하다 set [needle] a person to (do) // 둘이 싸우게 ~ egg two persons on to fight with each other / sick one person on [to] another // 이 사건은 누군가가 충동하고 있음에 틀림없다 Someone must be at the bottom of this affair.
●**충동구매** impulse buying. ¶옷가지의 ~를 하다 buy clothes on impulse.
충동적(衝動的) impulsive. ¶~으로 impulsively / on [from] impulse / on the spur of the moment / ~인 사람 an impulsive person / a man of impulse // ~으로 행동하다 act on impulse // 그는 ~으로 상점에서 물건을 훔쳤다 He stole goods in the store impulsively [on the spur of the moment].
충령탑(忠靈塔) a memorial to fallen heroes; a monument for the war dead.
충류(蟲類) insects and worms.
충만하다(充滿-) (서술적) be full (of vitality); be filled [pregnant / replete] (with); teem [swarm] (with); overflow (with); (연기 등이) permeate (the whole house). ¶사무실은 활기가 ~ The office is full of life. / The office is bustling with activity. // 종업원들 사이에는 불만이 충만해 있다 There is much dissatisfaction among the employees. **충만히** repletely; fully; abundantly.
충매(蟲媒) [식] entomophily; insect pollination.
●**충매화** an entomophilous flower.
충복(忠僕) a faithful [loyal / devoted / dutiful] servant; a man Friday.
충분조건(充分條件) a sufficient condition.
충분하다(充分-) enough; sufficient; full; plentiful; plenty of; good; goodly; [만족스럽다] satisfactory; [완전하다] perfect; thorough; generous (size / amount); adequate. ¶충분한 식사[음료] a good meal [drink] // 충분한 자산 ample means // 충분한 돈 enough money // 충분한 보수 satisfactory pay [remuneration] // 충분한 식량[필요품]의 공급 a sufficient [an ample / a bountiful] supply of food [necessaries] // 생활비에 충분한 연금 a sufficient pension for one's living expenses // 주전자의 물을 끓이는 데에 충분한 열 enough heat [heat sufficient] to boil the kettle // 충분한 이유 every [good] reason / adequate reason // 충분한 성적 satisfactory results // 충분한 조사[심리] a full [thorough] investigation [consideration] // 충분하다고 할

충성 수는 없으나 though not sufficiently complete [wholly satisfactory]//이 일을 위해서는 2주일이면 ~ Two weeks will be enough for this job.//이제 충분합니다. 그만두세요 Stop! That's enough.//변명은 그것으로 충분해 I think that's a good enough excuse.//그들은 충분한 식량을 갖고 떠났다 They started with an ample supply of provisions.//우리는 시간이 충분했다 We were in plenty of time. / We had ample time at our disposal.//그가 없어도 ~ We can do well without him.//지금 급료로 나는 충분하오 I'm (quite) content with my present salary. **충분히** (정도) enough; sufficiently; fairly; fully; thoroughly; in full; in its fullness; to the full; to perfection; perfectly; adequately; without restraint; (풍부하게) amply; copiously; plentifully; (만족하게) satisfactorily; to one's satisfaction; to one's heart's content. ¶~ 휴식한 뒤에 after a good rest//~을 알고서 with the full knowledge that (such is the case)//~ 생각한 끝에 after[upon] due consideration//~ 알고 있다 know well enough//~ 보답하다 reward abundantly [amply]//~ 설명하다 explain in full / explain at (full [great]) length//물을 ~ 주다 give a good watering//~ 먹다 eat one's fill / eat fully//자기가 가진 힘을 ~ 발휘하다 make the most of what one has//그 가치를 ~ 인정하다 come to a full appreciation of its value//볼 만한 가치가 있다 be well worth seeing//~ 즐기다 be sated with pleasure//고생은 넘칠 만큼 ~ 했다 I've had more than enough trouble.//수면을 ~ 취하지 않으면 안 된다 You must get plenty of sleep.//이제 ~ 먹었습니다 I've had plenty, thank you.//~ 생각한 뒤에 하여라 Think it over carefully first.//해 볼 가치는 ~ 있다 It's well worth trying.//집에서 2마일은 ~ 된다 It's a good two miles from home.//사정은 ~ 알고 있다 I'm fully aware of the situation.//~ 만족할 만한 결정은 아니었다 It was not a truly [an entirely] satisfactory solution.//식량은 ~ 준비되어 있었다 We had more than enough food.//~ 만족하시리라 믿습니다 I'm sure you will be fully [completely] satisfied.//보수는 ~ 받았습니다 I have been very well paid.//할 말은 ~ 했다 Enough has been said.//성사될 가망이 ~ 있다 There is every promise of success.//사정을 ~ 참작했으나 역시 그는 벌을 받아야 한다고 생각한다 After making all allowances, I think he ought to be punished [deserves punishment].

충성 (忠誠) loyalty; allegiance; fidelity. (▶ loyalty는 개인적인 감정, allegiance는 국민·단체의 의무감, fidelity는 약속·주의 등에 대한 충성의 뜻이 내포되어 있고, loyalty에 비해 애착심보다는 의무감을 강하게 암시함) ¶과잉 ~ excessive loyalty / an uncalled-for show of loyalty [fidelity] (to one's lord)//결혼의 서약에 대한 ~ conjugal fidelity / fidelity to one's wedding vows//…에 ~을 다하다 be loyal / render devoted service//조국에 ~을 맹세하다 pledge one's allegiance [loyalty] to one's country//국가에 ~을 다하다 give one's fealty to the nation / loyally serve one's country//그는 국왕에게 ~을 맹세했다 He swore allegiance to the king. **충성하다** show great integrity [sincerity] in one's service; render devoted service.

충성스럽다 (忠誠-) loyal; faithful; dutiful. ¶충성스러운 신하 a loyal retainer.

충수 (蟲垂) [생] the vermiform appendix [process].
●**충수염** (-炎) [의] appendicitis. 충수 절제 수술 appendectomy.

충신 (忠臣) a loyal [faithful] retainer [vassal]; a loyalist; a faithful subject. ¶~은 두 임금을 섬기지 않는다 A faithful retainer will not serve two master. / A loyal subject will not serve a second lord.//효자가 ~이 된다 A good son will make a good subject.

충실 (充實) [실질이 있음] substantiality; fullness; [충만·충족] repletion; replenishment; [완비] completeness; completion; perfection. ¶내용의 ~ meatness [substantiality] on contents//국력의 ~을 기하다 try to build up [consolidate] national power [strength].
충실하다 full; replete (with useful information); complete; rich; (실질·내용이) substantial (meal); solid (reading). ¶내용이 충실한 작품 a substantial [solid piece of] work//충실한 나날을 보내다 live a full life / live to the full//몸이 ~ be in perfect health / have a sound body//아이들은 모두 충실합니다 All our children are enjoying [are blessed with] excellent health.//책의 내용이 ~ The book is substantial [very rich / meaty] in content.
충실히 substantially; fully; repletely; perfectly. ¶~ 보낸 세월 wellfilled years//~ 하다 fill up / enrich / complete (armaments) / perfect (oneself in English)//일상생활을 ~ 하다 enrich one's life / fill one's days//규모를 확대하기보다 내용을 ~ 하는 것이 중요하다 It is more important to enrich the content than to enlarge the size.

충실하다 (忠實-) faithful; honest; devoted; true; trusty; sta(u)nch; loyal; [면밀하다] conscientious; scrupulous. ¶충실한 친구 a faithful [staunch] friend//충실한 하인 a faithful servant / a man Friday//아내에게 충실한 남편 a husband loyal to his wife//충실한 조사 a painstaking investigation//당시 풍속의 충실한 묘사 a detailed description of the customs of that time//그 번역은 원문에 ~ The translation closely follows the original.//그는 직무에 ~ He is faithful [dedicated] to his duties.//그는 자기 자신에 ~ He is true to himself. **충실히** faithfully; loyally; devotedly; truly; honestly; conscientiously. ¶원문을 ~ 번역하다 make one's translation faithful to the original//~ 근무[일]하다 serve [work] faithfully / be faithful in one's service / do one's work with sincerity / work like a horse//명령대로 ~ 수행하다 carry out one's order to the letter.

충심 (忠心) faithfulness; loyalty; allegiance; fidelity; sincerity.

충심 (衷心) [우러나는 참된 마음] one's innermost [inmost] heart; one's true heart. ¶~으로 wholeheartedly / from the bottom of one's heart / heartily / cordially / in one's heart of hearts / with one's whole heart / with all one's heart//~의 환영 a hearty welcome//~의 축사 heartfelt congratulations//~에서 우러나오는 소리 one's sincere remark//~으로 감사하다 thank (a person) from (the bottom of) one's heart//~으로 환영하다 welcome (a person) heartily [cordially] / give a hearty welcome//자당께서 별세하신 데

충양돌기(蟲樣突起) [생] the vermiform appendix. ⇨충수

충언(忠言) (good / honest) advice; honest words; counsel. ¶~은 귀에 거슬린다 Good advice is harsh to [grates on] the ear. / Honest advice jars on the ear. / Golden words offend the ears. **충언하다** give (a person) (good) advice [counsel]; advise; counsel.

충원(充員) supplement of the personnel; [군] the reserves; recruits; drafts. **충원하다** supplement the personnel; call up [recruit] personnel; recruit.
● **충원 계획** a levy plan.

충의(忠義) loyalty and uprightness [righteousness]; loyalty; fidelity; fealty. ¶~지사(之士)다 be loyal and righteous [good].

충이다 [곡식이 많이 들게 흔들다] shake (a rice bag) up and down or from side to side (to put [pack] rice to the full); joggle (rice in a bag).

충일(充溢) [가득 차서 넘침] overflow; affluence; exuberance; abundance; adequacy; sufficiency. **충일하다** overflow; be full (of energy); be overflowing (with water); be affluent [abundant] (in natural resources); be exuberant.

충적(沖積) [관형어적] alluvial.
● **충적기**[세] the alluvial epoch [period]. **충적토**[지] alluvial soil; alluvium. **충적 평야** an alluvial plain; a floodplain.

충전(充電) charge; charging; electrification. ¶재 ~ recharging // 전지 ~ battery charging / ~식의 면도기 a rechargeable shaver. **충전하다** (축전지에) charge (an accumulator) (with electricity); give a charge of electricity to (a storage battery); electrify.
● **충전기** a (battery) charger. **충전소** a charging station.

충전(充塡) filling up [in]; tamping; replenishment; plugging(충치 등의); inflation(가스의). **충전하다** fill up [in]; stop (up); replenish; plug; tamp; calk (with oakum)(배의 판자 틈을); inflate(가스를). ¶이에 금을 ~ fill a tooth with gold.
● **충전기** a plugger; a tamping tool; a filling machine. **충전제** (a) filler.

충절(忠節) loyalty; allegiance; fidelity; devotion. ¶~을 다하다 serve (one's lord) loyally [faithfully] / be devoted (to one's lord).

충정(衷情) one's inmost feelings; one's true [inmost] heart. ¶~을 호소하다 pour out one's heart (to a person) // ~을 털어놓다 [피력하다] open one's heart [mind] (to) / unbosom oneself (to).

충족(充足) filling up; sufficiency; adequacy; [만족] satisfaction; satisfactoriness. **충족하다** fill (up); fulfill; meet; answer; satisfy. ¶충족한 full / enough / sufficient / adequate / satisfactory // 그는 충족한 생활을 하고 있다 He lives in contentment. →**충족되지 않은 욕망** an unfulfilled desire // 조건 [수요]을 충족시키다 meet the requirements [demand] // 욕망을 충족시키다 satisfy one's desires.

충직하다(忠直-) faithful; sincere; honest; upright. ¶충직한 사람 an honest [a faithful] / a steady / a sterling man // 충직한 하인 a faithful [loyal] servant // 주인에게 충직한 체하다 affect [pretend] devotion to one's master. **충직히** faithfully / sincerely; honestly. ¶~일하다 be faithful to one's duty [in one's service].

충천하다(衝天-) rise high toward the sky; soar into the sky; go sky-high. ¶의기가 ~ one's spirit soars (to the skies) / be in high [towering / roaring / royal] spirits // 그는 노기가 ·충천했다 A wave of fierce wrath rolled up in him.

충충하다 [산뜻하지 못하고 흐림] depressingly dark [dusky]; drab; gloomy; dull; dingy; leaden; somber; opaque. ¶충충한 빛깔 a dark [subdued] color // 충충한 녹색 a subdued green (color).

충치(蟲齒) a carious [decayed / bad] tooth; (상태) dental caries. ¶~ 구멍 a cavity in a tooth // 치료 안한 ~ an untreated decayed tooth // ~를 치료하다 treat a cavity [decayed tooth] // ~를 예방하다 prevent tooth decay [cavities] // ~가 아프다 have a toothache / have an ache in one's carious [decayed] tooth // ~가 2개 있다 have two decayed teeth // ~를 뽑아 버리다 have a decayed tooth (pulled) out [extracted] // ~가 생기다 get a decayed tooth / have a tooth decay // ~에 봉을 박다 fill [stop] a decayed tooth.

충해(蟲害) damage from insects; insect damage; vermin damage; fly; a blight. ¶사과는 올해 ~를 입었다 The apple crop this year was damaged by insects.

충혈(充血) [의] congestion (of the brain); engorgement; injection; afflux (of blood to the head); hyper(a)emia. ¶뇌의 ~ the congestion of the brain // ~을 없애다 relieve (mucous membranes) of congestion / decongest. **충혈되다** be congested; congest; be engorged; (눈이) be bloodshot; become turgid with blood. ¶충혈된 눈 bloodshot [inflamed / injected] eyes.

충혼(忠魂) [충의의 정신] a loyal soul; a faithful spirit; [죽은 자의 넋] the departed spirit. ¶~을 위로하다 propitiate the departed spirit.
● **충혼비** a monument to the departed spirit.

충효(忠孝) loyalty (to one's master) and filial piety. ¶~를 다하다 do one's duty both to one's lord and to one's parents.

췌관(膵管) [생] a pancreatic duct.

췌액(膵液) pancreatic juice. ⇨이자액(⇨)이자(胰子))

췌언(贅言) [말] redundant [superfluous] words; (a) pleonasm; redundancy; tautology. ¶이 책의 진가에 대해서는 ~을 요하지 않는다 There is no need to dwell [reiterate] upon the value of this work.

췌장(膵臟) [생] the pancreas. ⇨이자(胰子)
● **췌장암** cancer of the pancreas. **췌장염** pancreatitis.

취객(醉客) a drunken man; a drunk; a drunkard.

취관(吹管) a blowpipe; a blast pipe.

취급(取扱) 1 (사람의) treatment; reception; dealing; usage; (고객의) service; business manners. ¶공평한 ~ a fair [square] deal / 개 같은 ~을 하다 use (a person) like a dog // 부하 ~을 하다 treat (a person) as an underling // 지독한 ~을 받다 be ill treated [used] / meet with harsh usage [treatment]

취기 /(구어) be given a raw deal // 정중한 ~을 받다 be treated[received] courteously[cordially] // 그 가게는 손님 ~이 나쁘다 Service in that store is bad[poor]. **취급하다** treat; deal with. ¶공평하게 ~ deal justly[fairly] with (a person) / give (a person) a square deal // 그는 나를 마치 어린애처럼 취급한다 He treats me as if I were a child.

2 (물건의) handling; manipulation; working; (사람의) treatment; handling; dealing; use. ¶~법 how to work[handle] // 난폭한 ~ rough handling. **취급하다** handle; manipulate; work[operate] (a machine); treat; deal with; manage. ¶사회 문제를 취급한 소설 a novel dealing with[treating of] social problems // 취급하기 편리하게 for convenience in handling // (기계 등이) 취급하기 쉽다[편리하다] be easy to work[manipulate / operate] / be convenient to handle[operate] // 잘못 취급하여 망가지다 be broken by ill usage // 이것은 정밀 기계이니까 조심해서 취급해야 한다 As this is a delicate[precision] machine, you must handle it with care.

3 (일의) transaction; conduct; management. ¶소화물 ~ parcels consignment // (문제의) 정당한 ~법 the proper method of approach // 사무 ~을 잘하다 be skillful in managing affairs. **취급하다** carry on; deal in; conduct; transact; manage. ¶사무를 ~ conduct [carry on] business / manage affairs // 외환을 ~ deal in foreign exchange // 전보를 ~ accept[take in] telegrams // 우리 가게에서는 주류는 취급하지 않습니다 We do not handle [sell] liquor. // 여기서는 외국 소포를 취급하지 않는다 Overseas parcels are not accepted here.

●**취급 설명서** an instruction manual. **취급소** an office; an agency. ¶수화물 ~ a luggage[(미) baggage] office // 화물 ~ (미) a freight agency / (영) a forwarding agency. **취급 주의** (게시) Handle with Care.; Fragile.

취기(臭氣) an offensive[odious] smell; a bad [foul / nasty / fetid / filthy] odor; a stench; a stink. ¶~가 있는 bad-smelling / malodorous / stinking // ~가 없는 inodorous / odorless // ~를 내다[뿜다] give[send] out an offensive smell / emit a foul[bad] odor // ~를 없애다 destroy the bad odor (of) / deodorize // ~가 코를 찌른다 It stinks (to heaven). / It is offensive to the nose. / It has an offensive smell.

취기(醉氣) drunkenness; (문어) intoxication; tipsiness; inebriation. ¶~를 이기지 못하다 be overcome by the effects of the liquor // ~가 돌다 grow[get / become] drunk[tipsy] / feel the effects of drink / feel the onset of inebriation / show signs of intoxication / the liquor begins to show its effect // ~가 깨다 [가시다] become sober / sober down[up] / recover from one's intoxication // 그는 ~가 머리에 올랐다 The drink went to his head. // 마침내 ~가 돌기 시작했다 The drinks finally hit him. / He finally began to feel the effects of what he had drunk. // 물을 좀 마시고 ~를 깨게 하세요 Drink some water and sober up. // 그는 ~가 심하여 자기의 아내마저 몰라보았다 He was so drunk that he did not even recognize his wife. // 계산서를 보자 ~가 단번에 가셨다 When I saw the bill, I sobered up in an instant.

취담(醉談) drunken burbling; drunken words. ¶취기가 돌면 ~이 나온다 When wine sinks, words swim. // ~이니 개의치 마시오 Don't mind his words — he's drunk. **취담하다** babble under the influence of alcohol.

취득(取得) (an) acquisition; [구입함] (a) purchase. **취득하다** acquire; gain; get; obtain; take possession of (the new property); purchase. ¶면허를 ~ acquire[get] a license // 소유권을 ~ acquire the ownership (of).

●**취득권** ownership. **취득세** an acquisition tax. ¶부동산 ~ (a) property acquisition tax / a real estate acquisition tax. **취득 시효** [법] acquisitive prescription. **취득자** an acquisitor.

취락(聚落) (생물의) a colony; (인간의) a colony; a community(공동 사회); a town(도시); a village(마을).

취로(就勞) [관형어적] working; job-producing. **취로하다** set to work; work; find work [employment].

●**취로 사업** a job-producing project.

취미(趣味) (an) interest; (a) liking; (a) taste; [도락] a hobby. ¶악~ vulgar[bad] taste / loud taste(복장 등의) // 고상한[저속한] ~ refined[vulgar / loud] taste // 다방면의 ~ varied[various / many-sided / versatile / wide] interests[tastes] // ~와 실용을 겸한 자기 porcelain of both beauty and utility // ~가 좋은 tasteful / elegant / refined // ~가 좋은 사람 a person of refined[well-cultivated] taste // ~가 없는 tasteless / dull / insipid / uninteresting // ~가 없는 사람 a man of few interests / a person who lacks taste // ~가 다양한 사람 a person with many interests [hobbies] // ~가 **좋다** (사람이) have (a) good [well-cultivated] taste (in clothes) / (사물이) be in good taste // 시에 ~가 없다 have no taste for poetry / have no interest in poetry // ~에 맞다 suit one's taste / be to one's liking // ~로 우표를 수집하다 collect stamps as a hobby // ~로 골동품을 만지다 dabble in curios as a hobby // …에 ~를 가지다 be interested (in) / take an interest (in) / have a taste (for) / have a fondness[liking] (for) // ~를 붙이다 acquire[attain / develop] a taste (for) // ~를 잃다 lose one's interest (in) / lose one's taste (for) // ~는 사람마다 다르다 Tastes differ. / Every man has his (own) taste. / Every man to his taste. / There is no accounting for tastes. / So many men, so many tastes. // 그는 다양한 ~를 가진 사람이다 He is a man of many accomplishments. // 재즈에는 ~가 없다 Jazz is not to my taste[liking]. // 가르치는 것이 ~입니다 I teach for pleasure. // 이것이라면 모든 사람의 ~에 맞을 것이다 This will please[suit] every taste[all tastes]. // 그는 일 이외에는 아무런 ~도 없다 He has[shows] no interest in anything outside his job. // 그것은 각자의 ~ 나름이겠지요 It is a matter of taste. / It is a matter of individual[personal] preference. // 그녀는 고상한 ~의 복장을 하고 있다 She is tastefully dressed. / She has excellent taste in clothing[dress]. // 편물은 ~와 실익을 겸비하고 있다 Knitting is my hobby as well as a source of income.

●**취미 생활** a dilettante('s) life.

취사(炊事) cooking; kitchen work. **취사하다** cook; do cooking.

● 취사 당번 the cook's duty; (병(兵)) a soldier on the cook's duty; (집합적) kitchen police. ¶그가 ~이었다 He was put on mess duty. // 메리가 ~이다 It's Mary's turn to cook. 취사도구 a kitchen utensil; (집합적) kitchenware. 취사장 a kitchen; (캠프·공사장 등의) a cookhouse; (배의) a galley. ¶(특히 아파트의) 간이 ~ (미) a kitchenet(te) // 공동 ~ a common[communal] kitchen.

취사선택 (取捨選擇) adoption or rejection; choice; option; selection. ¶~의 자유 freedom of choice // ~에 망설이다 be at a loss which to take[choose] (from among) // ~은 자유로이 하십시오 You are free to choose[make a choice]. 취사선택하다 adopt or reject (a thing); choose; select; make one's option[choice]. ¶잘못 ~ make the wrong choice / make a mistake in the choice (of) // 마음대로 취사선택하십시오 You may take it or leave it at your pleasure.
● 취사선택권 a right of selection; an option.

취생몽사 (醉生夢死) ¶그는 ~의 나날을 보내고 있었다 He lived an indolent life. / He dreamed[idled] his days away. 취생몽사하다 idle[slumber / sleep] one's life away; live idly[to no purpose].

취소 (取消) 〔삭제〕 cancellation; (약속·면허 등의) revocation; retraction; retractation; recantation; disaffirmation; 〔철회〕 withdrawal; (유증의) ademption; 〔폐지〕 abolition; (법률 등의) abrogation; cassation; repeal; (명령 등의) annulment; 〔해제〕 rescission; (신문의) retraction; correction. ¶면허(증)의 ~ revocation of a license // ~를 강요하다 compel recantation // …의 ~를 승낙시키다 obtain the annulment of ... // 나는 신문 기사의 ~를 요구했다 I demanded the withdrawal of the newspaper statement. // 그 계획[거래]은 ~다 The plan[deal] is off. 취소하다 cancel; strike[scratch] off[out]; nullify; void; revoke (a decision); rescind (a vote); 〔철회하다〕 withdraw; retract (one's statement); take back; (판결 등을) disaffirm; recall (a promise); repeal; revoke; (명령·주문 등을) cancel (out); annul; recall. ¶취소할 수 있는 retractable / recallable / revocable / 〔법〕 ambulatory (will) // 취소할 수 없는 irrevocable / beyond revoke[recall] / irreversible // 약혼을 ~ release (a person) from engagement / break[call] off one's engagement (to a girl) // 구독 신청을 ~ withdraw subscription // 면허를 ~ revoke a license // 영업 허가를 ~ cancel a business license // 약속을 ~ recall[declare off / retract / go back on] a promise / withdraw from an engagement / withdraw a promise / drop[depart from] one's promise // 예약을 ~ cancel a reservation // 먼저 한 말을 ~ take back what one has said / go back on[swallow / eat] one's word / retract one's former statements[one's speech] // 전부 ~ call[declare] the whole thing off // 취소합니다 I take it back. // 메리는 약혼을 취소했다 Mary broke off[ended] her engagement. (▶ break off는 갑자기 취소하다) // 그는 종전의 진술을 취소했다 He withdrew[retracted] his previous statement. →¶회의가 취소되었다 The meeting fell through[was called off]. // 야간 경기가 비 때문에 취소되었다 The night game was rained out.
● 취소권 〔법〕 right of rescission; the right to rescind. 취소 불능 신용장 an irrevocable letter of credit.

취안 (醉眼) drunken eyes. ¶~이 몽롱하여 with drunken eyes / sleepy from drink.

취안 (醉顔) a face flushed with liquor; a drunken look.

취약 (脆弱·貧弱) weakness; frailty; fragility brittleness; delicacy. 취약하다 weak; fragile; frail; delicate; tender; flimsy; brittle(부서지기 쉽다).
● 취약 지구[지점] 〔군〕 a vulnerable area [point].

취업 (就業) employment; entering a profession; working. ¶~ 중이다 be at work. 취업하다 enter a profession; be employed. ¶내년 봄부터 취업할 예정이다 plan to operate (the business) from next spring.
● 취업 규칙 the rules of employment; office [shop] regulations. 취업률 the percentage of employment. ¶금년도 대학 졸업자들의 ~이 좋다 The percentage of employment among the college graduates shows a favorable trend this year. 취업 시간[일수] working hours[days]; hours[days] worked. 취업 연령 working age. 취업 인구 the working population.

취역하다 (就役−) go into commission; be placed[put] in[into] commission; be commissioned. ¶그 화물선은 태평양 항로에 취역했다 The freighter has been placed on the Pacific line.

취음 (取音) transliteration. 취음하다 transliterate (Korean words) into[with] Chinese characters.

취임 (就任) assumption (of office); installation; inauguration. ¶대통령 ~일 the Inauguration Day. 취임하다 take[assume] office (as); take one's post (with a corporation); get into office (as); be inaugurated (as). ¶국무 위원에 ~ take office as State Minister // 대통령에 ~ be inaugurated[sworn in] as President // 나는 시장으로 취임했다 I assumed the office of[took office as] mayor.
● 취임사 an inaugural address[speech]. 취임식 an inaugural ceremony.

취입 (吹入) recording. 취입하다 record; blow in. ¶레코드를 ~ put (a song) on a record / have[get] (one's song) recorded // 그의 연설[노래]을 취입했다 His speech[song] was recorded on the phonograph[gramophone].

취재 (取材) collection of data[materials]; 〔신문〕 news gathering; coverage. ¶그는 ~를 위해 그 유족을 만나러 갔다 He went to interview the bereaved family. 취재하다 collect [gather / obtain] data[materials] (on / for); (신문 기자가) collect[gather] news materials (for / on); cover (a fire). ¶그 모임을 취재하기 위해 기자 한 사람이 파견되었다 A reporter was sent to cover the meeting. // 이 소설은 한국 전쟁에서 취재하였다 This novel took its story from the Korean War.
● 취재 기자 an assignment man; a beat reporter; (미국 속어) a legman. 취재원 (−源) a news source. 취재 활동 coverage activities; (미국 구어) legwork.

취조 (取調) investigation; inquisition; inquiry; examination; interrogation. ¶~는 매우 엄중했다 The investigation[examination] was exceedingly thorough. // 그는 경찰의 ~를 받았다 He was questioned by the police. // 피

의자는 엄한 ~를 받았다 The suspect was questioned relentlessly. **취조하다** investigate; inquire; examine. ¶엄중히 ~ conduct strict examination.

취주(吹奏) blowing; playing; a blow. **취주하다** blow[play] (the flute).

● **취주악** wind(-instrument) music. **취주 악기** a wind instrument. ⇨관악기(⇨관악) **취주악대** a brass band. **취주자** a player.

취중(醉中) ¶~에 in a drunken state // ~의 싸움 a drunken brawl // ~에 실수하다 make a drunken slip / make a mistake while in one's cups. **취중에 진담이 나온다**(속담) One often tells the truth when drunk.

● **취중 운전** drunken driving; driving (a car) while intoxicated[under the influence of liquor]; drink-and-driving (offense). ¶~을 하다 drive under the influence of alcohol.

취지(趣旨) 〔생각〕 an opinion; a view; 〔의미·요지〕 the meaning; the purport; the tenor; the effect; the point; the gist; 〔목적〕 an object; an aim; a purpose. ¶연설의 ~ the tenor[purport] of a speech // 본 회의 설립의 ~ the purpose for which this society was formed // 질문의 ~ the point[tenor] of one's question // 이 논문의 ~를 모르겠다 I don't understand the point of this thesis. // 그는 나의 신청을 받아들인다는 ~의 편지를 보내 왔다 He sent me a letter to the effect that he would accept my offer. // 그들이 교섭 재개에 응할 용의가 있다는 ~의 회답을 보내왔다 They answered to the effect that they were ready to reopen negotiations. // 사장의 ~을 받들어 세 사람을 골랐다 I selected three members at the command of the president. // 그것은 단체의 ~에 어긋난다 It runs counter to the aims of the organization. // 오늘 모임의 ~를 나는 전혀 알 수 없었다 I didn't quite understand what the meeting today was for[(구어) all about]. // 이 번역문은 원문의 ~을 충분히 전달하지 못하고 있다 This translation doesn't fully convey the meaning[tenor intent] of the original. // 전언(傳言)의 ~는 잘 알았습니다 I understand the gist of the message.

● **취지서** a prospectus. ¶~에 쓰여진 대로 as is mentioned in the prospectus / ~를 작성하다 draw up[write out] a prospectus.

취직(就職) finding employment; getting a job. ¶~을 신청하다 apply for a position // ~을 알선하다 help (a person) (to) find a job // ~을 부탁하다 ask (a person) for a job / 그의 ~을 도와주었다 I helped him get a job. // 출판사에 ~을 의뢰했다 I have applied for a job with a publishing firm. **취직하다** find employment [work]; secure[obtain / get] a position (in / with); get a job (with a firm); enter the service (of). ¶무역 회사에 ~ be employed in the trading company // 나는 은행에 취직했다 I have got(ten) [obtained] a job [post] in a bank. // 금년 졸업생들이 거의 다 취직하였다 The graduates of this year have almost been placed. ➔그는 제자를 회사에 취직시켰다 He placed his students in business firms.

● **취직난** the difficulty of finding employment; job shortage. ¶~을 완화하다 relieve the difficulty of finding employment // ~이 심각해졌다 The difficulty of finding employment has become acute[aggravated]. **취직 시험** an employment examination. **취직자리** employment; a position; a situation; a job; an opening; a place. ¶~를 찾다 seek employment / look[hunt] for a position // 서울에서는 ~를 찾을 수 없다 I can't find a job in Seoul.

취침(就寢) going to bed[sleep]. ¶~ 전에 before retiring / ~ 중에 while (one is) asleep // ~ 중 (게시) Don't disturb. **취침하다** go to bed; turn in; retire.

● **취침 시간** bedtime; time to go to bed. ¶아이들의 ~은 8시입니다 Our children's bedtime is eight o'clock. / Our children are sent to bed at eight. // 이제 ~이에요 It's time for [to go to] bed.

취태(醉態) drunkenness; intoxication; tipsiness. ¶~를 부리다 put on a drunken display / (미국 속어) hit the booze and become wild.

취하(取下) withdrawal; discontinuance. ¶소송의 ~ the discontinuance of an action. **취하하다** withdraw (a charge[suit] against a person / a petition). ¶신청을 ~ withdraw one's application // 소송을 ~ withdraw [call off / drop] a suit.

취하다(取−) 1 〔(방법 등을) 쓰거나 강구하다〕 adopt; take; assume. ¶강경한 태도를 ~ assume[take] a firm attitude // 방침을 ~ take[adopt] a course // 최후의[극단적인] 수단을 ~ resort to the last [an extreme] measure // 공세를 ~ assume[take] the offensive.

2 〔선택하다〕 prefer; choose; pick; take. ¶달리 취할 방도 the alternative // 많은 것 중에서 하나를 ~ choose[pick] one out of many // 죽음과 치욕 중에서 하나를 ~ choose between death and dishonor // 그 설(說)은 취할 것이 못 된다 The opinion is not worth serious consideration.

3 〔얻다〕 get; gain; take. ¶이(利)를 ~ derive benefit (from) / profit [benefit] by [from] (something) / 〔추구하다〕 seek personal gain [interests] / pursue [be bent upon] gain // 많은 이윤을 ~ gain a fair margin of profit.

4 (몸 자세를) assume a posture (of); pose; (…할 채비를) make ready (to do); be[stand] ready (for). ¶(총을) 쏠 자세를 ~ come to [hold the rifle at] the ready // 방어 자세를 ~ take[assume] a posture of defense // 포즈를 ~ pose (oneself) (as a model) / strike [get into] a pose / (사진을 찍기 위해) pose for one's picture / pose for a photography // 그는 덤벼들려고 자세를 취했다 He stood ready for a fight [to strike at me].

5 〔휴식·수면 등을〕 take; eat; have. ¶휴식을 ~ have[take] a rest // 충분한 수면을 ~ take [have] a good sleep.

6 〔꾸거나 빌리다〕 borrow; lend. ¶돈을 ~ borrow money // 돈을 취해 주다 lend money.

취하다(醉−) 1 (술에) get drunk [intoxicated / tipsy]; be overcome with liquor; be under the influence of drink; make [get] oneself drunk on liquor; get liquored up; (속어) hit the bottle; be tight. // 취하여 under the influence of liquor [drink] // 취하게 하다 make [get] a person drunk // 거나하게 ~ be a bit tipsy / be in a cheerful mood with drink / have [be] three [both] sheets in [to] wind('s eye) // 곤드레만드레 ~ drink oneself down / be drunk as a flesh [tailor / fiddler] / be

dead[blind / beastly] drunk / be under the table // 취해서 본성을 잃다 be dazed by liquor // 취해서 잠들다 drink oneself to sleep / go off into a vinous sleep // 그는 이미 꽤 취해 있다 He is already pretty high[mellow / drunk]. // 그는 너무 취한 것 같아 Looks like he's had one too many. / Looks like he's had all he can take. // 브랜디에 취해서 나의 머리는 이상한 환영을 쫓기 시작했다 Drunk on brandy, I began to pursue a mysterious fantasy in my mind. // 그는 곤드레만드레 취해서 돌아왔다 He came home dead drunk. // 그는 얼근히 취해 있다 He's a bit high. / He's feeling mellow. / He's tipsy. // 그는 취해서 말짱하다 He carries himself well even when he has been drinking. / He can hold his liquor [(영) drink]. // 아무래도 좀 취한 것 같군요 I'm a little tipsy[a bit high], I'm afraid. // 그는 취한 김에 옆에 앉아 있던 여자에게 키스를 하려고 했다 Emboldened by what he had drunk, he tried to kiss the girl sitting next to him.
2 〔도취하다〕 get intoxicated [fascinated / enraptured / spellbound / elated / exalted]; be in raptures. ¶승리감에 ~ be elated with victory // 행복에 ~ be in the raptures of happiness / be drunk with joy / beside oneself with happiness // 관객은 그 묘기에 취했다 The audience was spellbound by the fine performance. // 나는 음악에 취했다 I was intoxicated by[with] the music. // 그녀의 아름다운 목소리가 모든 청중을 취하게 했다 Her beautiful voice charmed[enchanted] the full house[the capacity audience].

취학(就學) entering school. **취학하다** enter [attend / go to] school. ➔¶어린이를 취학시키다 put[send] (a boy) to school.
● **취학률** the percentage of school attendance. ¶한국은 초등학교의 ~이 사실상 100퍼센트다 Elementary school attendance is virtually 100 percent in Korea. **취학 아동** school children. ¶미~ a preschooler. **취학 연령** the school age. ¶~이 되다 attain [reach] the school age.

취한(醉漢) a drunkard; a drunk; a drunken fellow; (속어) a lush.

취항(就航) putting out to sea; sailing; commission; service. **취항하다** go into commission; be placed[put] in commission; put out to sea; set sail; start on a voyage; enter service. ¶부산·제주 간을 취항하는 배 a boat plying between Busan and Jeju // 보잉 747이 서울·뉴욕 간에 취항했다 The Boeing 747 has been put into service [operation] between Seoul and New York. ➔¶취항시키다 place (a ship) in commission / commission (a vessel) in service.
● **취항선** vessels in commission.

취향(趣向) 〔기호〕 taste; liking; fondness; 〔경향〕 (follow she's artistic) bent; inclination. ¶~에 맞다 suit one's taste / please [suit / hit] one's fancy // 이 핸드백은 그녀의 ~에 맞을 것이다 This handbag will suit her taste [fancy]. / She will like this handbag. // 이 옷은 내 ~에 맞지 않는다 This dress is not to my taste. // 이번의 전시회는 아주 새로운 ~으로 해 볼 작정이다 I intend to try a completely new approach for the upcoming exhibition. // 그것은 개인 ~의 문제다 It's a matter of taste[individual preference].

취흥(醉興) exhilaration due to alcohol; a convivial mood. ¶~에 겨워 excited[elated] under the influence of drink / in drunken delight / heated by wine // ~이 일다 become cheerful in one's cups // ~을 돋우다 heighten [increase] the conviviality // ~에 겨워 춤을 추다 dance in drunken delight // 그 바람에 모처럼 올랐던 ~이 깨져 버렸다 That brought a chill to the merrymaking.

측(側) the side. ¶유엔 ~ the UN side // 회사 ~의 반론 a counterargument made by the management // 학생[노동자] ~의 요구 the demand on the part of students[workers] // 잘못은 우리 ~에 있다 The fault is on our side. // 우리 ~에서는 아무 반대도 없다 There is no objection on our part.

측간(廁間) a lavatory; a water closet. ⇨ **변소**

측근(側近) **1** 〔가까운 곁〕 the surroundings; around[nearby] a person. ¶~에 모시다 stand by (a person's) side / attend[wait] on // ~에 아무도 없다 have nobody around one / be unattended[unaccompanied] // 경찰은 수상 ~에서 수회 사건을 적발하였다 The police exposed[disclosed] a case of bribery among those [in circles] close to the premier. // 설마 내 ~에서 그런 일이 일어나리라고는 상상도 못했다 I never dreamed that such a thing would happen among those in my immediate circle.
2 those close to (the President). ⇨ **측근자**(⇨ 측근) // 총리 ~ 소식통에 의하면 according to sources close to the prime minister // ~과의 논하다 consult one's aides // 그는 왕의 ~으로서 다년간 일했다 He served as an attendant to the king for many years. // ~수상은 언제나 ~에 둘러싸여 있었다 The prime minister was always surrounded by members of his staff.
● **측근자** those close to (the President); one's close associates[staff members]; (미) an aide (to). **대통령 ~** a presidential aide.

측도(測度) measurement (of degree); gauging. **측도하다** measure; gauge.

측량(測量) **1** 〔길이 등의〕 measurement; measuring; (토지의) a survey; surveying. ¶고저 [수준] ~ leveling // 기선 ~ a base line measurement // 사진 [항공] ~ a photo[an aerial] survey // 삼각 ~ triangulation // 토지 ~ (의) land surveying. **측량하다** measure; take [make] a measurement (of); (토지를) survey; make a survey (of). // 산의 높이를 ~ measure the height of a mountain. **2** 〔헤아림〕 estimate; guess; conjecture. **측량하다** fathom; sound; plumb. ¶그의 의도를 측량하기 어렵다 I cannot fathom his intention.
● **측량기** a surveying instrument. **측량 기사** a (land) surveyor; a surveying engineer. **측량술** surveying (technique); measuration.

측면(側面) the side; the flank; a side[lateral] face. ¶~의 side / flank / lateral // 재정적인 ~에서 in the financial aspect // ~에서 보다 〔관찰하다〕 take a side view of (something) // 각재에는 상하의 면과 네 개의 ~이 있다 A block has a top, a bottom, and four sides. // 우리는 적 왼쪽의 ~을 공격했다 We attacked the enemy's left flank. // ~에서 원조하겠습니다 I'll give you indirect aid. / I'll help you from the sidelines. // 나는 그의 그런 ~을 미처 몰랐다 I hadn't noticed that side of his character before.

측면 공격 a flank attack; a flanking assault. ¶~을 하다 make[launch] a flank attack (against / on) / attack (the enemy) in the flank. **측면 방어** a flank defense. **측면 운동** a lateral movement.

측백나무(側柏-) [식] an Oriental[a Chinese] arborvitae; a thuja.

측벽(側壁) a side wall.

측사(側射) a flanking fire.

측선(側線) (철도의) a sidetrack; a siding; (어류의) a lateral line; (운동 경기의) a sideline; a touchline(축구의). ¶열차를 ~에 넣다 sidetrack a train // (열차가) ~에서 대기하고 있다 be (waiting) on a siding / 열차를 ~에 옮기다 shunt a train onto a siding.

측심(測深) (depth) sounding. **측심하다** measure the depth (of); fathom; sound.
● **측심기** a sounder; a depth finder; (상표명) a Fathometer. **측심연** a plumb (bob); a plummet; a sounding lead.

측우기(測雨器) a rain gauge; a pluviometer; a udometer; a hyetometer; an ombrometer.

측은지심(惻隱之心) compassion; pity; mercy; natural sympathy.

측은하다(惻隱-) pitiful; pitiable; piteous; poor. ¶측은한 마음이 들다 be overwhelmed [touched] with pity (for) / feel compassion [pity] for (a person) / take pity on (a person) / be touched with compassion / touch one's heart. **측은히** sympathetically, compassionately. ¶~ 여기다 sympathize / compassionate / commiserate / have compassion[pity] on / feel pity (for).

측점(測點) [측량의 기준이 되는 점] a surveying station; a measuring point.

측정(測定) measurement; survey(토지의); sounding(수심의); observation(관측). ¶**방사선 ~** radiation measurement. **측정하다** measure; survey; sound; gauge. ¶거리를 ~ find[measure] the distance (to) // 속력을 ~ determine the velocity (of) // 태양의 고도를 ~ take the height of the sun // 그 지역의 강우량을 ~ measure the rainfall in the region // 수온의 변화를 ~ measure the changes in water temperature // 체중을 ~ weigh oneself.
● **측정기** a measuring instrument. **측정법** a method[way] of measurement.

측지(測地) land surveying; a geodetic survey. **측지하다** survey (land); practice surveying.
● **측지학** geodesy.

측후(測候) a meteorological observation; meteorology. **측후하다** make a meteorological observation (of).
● **측후소** ➡ 기상대(⇨기상(氣象))

층(層) **1** (지층 등의) a stratum (*pl.* -ta); a layer; a seam; a bed(식탁 등의). ¶(석)탄~ a coal seam[bed] // 암석 ~ rock stratification // 화석의 ~ a layer of fossils // 중생대 ~ the Mesozonic stratum // 제3기 ~ the Tertiary formation // 대기(大氣)의 상~ the upper layers of the atmosphere // ~을 이루어 in layers.
2 [계층·단계] a class; a stratum. ¶근로자~ the working class // 지식 ~ the intellectual class / the intelligentsia / intellectuals // 고소득 ~ a high economic bracket // 독자~ a class of readers / a readership // 연령 ~ an age group[bracket] // 여러 ~의 사람들이 그의 팬이다 His fans include a wide variety of people.
3 (건물의) a story; (영) a storey; a floor. ¶1~ (미) the first floor[story] / (영) the ground floor // 2~ (미) the second floor [story] / (영) the first floor // 지하 ~ the basement // 지하 3~ the third basement (level) // 2~ 건물 a two-story [two-storied] house / (영) a two-storeyed house // 지상 15~ 지하 3~의 빌딩 a building with fifteen floors plus three basement levels // 각 ~ 정지의 엘리베이터 an elevator[(영) a lift] that stops at each floor // 3~ 집 a three-story [-storied] house // 이 빌딩은 몇 ~입니까 How many floors does this building have? // 그의 사무실은 몇 ~입니까 Which floor is his office on? // 내 방은 3~에 있다 My room is on the third[(영) second] floor.
4 [등급] a grade; a class. ¶배우에도 여러 ~이 있다 There are various grades of actors.

층계(層階) stairs; a staircase; a stairway; a flight (of stairs). ¶나선 ~ a spiral[corkscrew] staircase / a winding stair // 회전 ~ a winding stair // 위[아래]에서 at the head[bottom / foot] of the stairs // 마지막 ~ the top stairs // 가파른 ~ a steep staircase // 높은 ~ tall[long] stairs // ~를 올라가다 ascend[go up] the stairs / go upstairs // ~를 헛디디다 miss one's footing on the stairs // ~에서 떨어지다 fall downstairs // ~를 급히 오르다[내리다] hurry upstairs[downstairs] // ~에서 미끄러지다 slip on the stairs // ~에서 굴러 떨어지다 fall downstairs.
● **층계참** a landing (place); a (mean) landing.

층나다(層-) **1** (켜가) be in layers[strata]; be (formed) in seams; show[have] (a structure of) layers. **2** [차이 나다] be uneven; show disparity (in). ¶머리를 층나게 깎다 cut one's hair uneven // 연령이 층난다 There is disparity in age.

층널(層-) a layer board.

층루(層樓) a storied tower; a tower of several stories.

층류(層流) [물] laminar[streamline] flow.

층면(層面) [지] a stratification plane; (쌓인 물건의 겉면) the surface (of piled up things).

층상(層狀) ¶~의 stratiform / stratified / ~을 이루다 be stratified / have a stratified formation / be in layers[strata] // 화석이 ~을 이루고 있는 것이 발견되었다 We discovered layer upon layer of fossils.
● **층상운** a stratiform cloud.

층수(層數) the number of layers[strata]; the (total) number of floors[stories] (of a building).

층암절벽(層巖絕壁) a precipitous wall of stratified rock; a cliff; a precipice.

층애(層崖) [지] an escarpment; a stratified precipice[cliff].

층운(層雲) a stratus (*pl.* -ti).

층적운(層積雲) [기상] a stratocumulus; a roll cumulus.

층지다(層-) be in layers; be uneven. ⇨ =층나다 ¶머리를 층지게 깎다 cut one's hair uneven.

층층다리(層層-) steps; a stairway. ⇨ =층층대

층층대(層層臺) steps; a stairway; a terrace. ¶높은 ~ a long stairway / a high terrace // 가파른 ~ a steep stairway // ~를 올라가다[내려가다] ascend[descend] the steps.

층층시하(層層侍下) serving both parents and grandparents alive.

층층으로(層層-) layer upon layer. ⇨ 층층이 ¶~ 놓다 put [place] layer upon layer (of something).

층층이(層層-) layer upon layer; one story [(영) storey] after another; pile after pile; all layers; all stories. ¶~ 쌓다 pile (something) in layers // 벽돌을 ~ 쌓다 lay bricks course upon course.

층하(層下) ¶~를 두고 사람을 대하다 discriminate against a person. **층하하다** discriminate against (a person / a thing); treat (a person) with less respect [favor] than others. ¶사람을 ~ discriminate against a person / treat a person with disrespect [discrimination] // 사람을 층하하지 않다 treat every person just and fair / treat all alike.

치¹ (길이의 단위) a *chi*; a Korean inch(= 1.193 in.). ¶한 ~ 앞도 안 보이는 심한 눈보라 a blinding blizzard // 한 ~ 앞을 못 보다 be not farsighted / have no foresight // 캄캄하여 한 ~ 앞도 내다볼 수 없었다 It's pitch-dark and we cannot see an inch ahead of us.

치² 1 (사람) a fellow; a guy; a chap. ¶이 (그 / 저) ~ this [that] fellow [guy / chap] // 저~가 그렇게 말했다 That guy told me so. 2 (물건) an article; a thing; goods. ¶중간 ~ (크기) an article of in-between [medium] size. 3 (몫·분량) a share; a portion; a part. ¶사흘 ~의 약 medicine for three days // 이달 ~ 수업료 [분량 / 비용 / 회비 / 임대료 / 수입] the fee [amount / charge / dues / rent / income] for this month // 하루 ~ 식량 a day's ration.

치(値) (수) (numerical) value.

치(齒) a tooth.

치(를) **떨다** 1 (분해서 이를 떨다) grind [gnash] one's teeth. ¶분하여 ~ grind one's teeth with indignation. 2 (인색하다) stint; skimp; scrimp; pinch and scrape; be awfully stingy; be very sparing. ¶돈이라면 ~ be niggardly of money / be close with one's money / spend money sparingly // 그는 한 푼에도 치를 떤다 He has a fit every time he has to spend a penny. / He pinches a penny till it hurts.

치(가) 떨리다 1 (분하여 이가 떨리다) make one shudder; give one the shudders; be infuriated; be tense with indignation. ¶그 말을 들으니 치가 떨린다 His remark makes me mad. // 그 생각만 해도 치가 떨린다 The very thought of it gives me the shudders. 2 (지긋지긋하다) become (thoroughly / quite) disgusted (with); get sick (to death) (of).

치감다 wind [bind / coil] upward(ly) (around).

치강(齒腔) (생) the pulp cavity.

치경(齒莖) the gum(s). ⇨ 잇몸

●**치경음** (언) an alveolar (consonant).

치고 1 (예외 없이) when it comes to; as for; (…마다) every. ¶그것은 그렇다 ~ be that as it may / well, let me see // 사람 ~ 결점 없는 사람은 없다 No one is free from faults. / There is no one but has some faults. // 실력이 없는 사람~ 뽐내고 싶어 하지 않는 사람은 없다 It is always the people with the last ability who like to boast. // 돈 있는 사람~ 돈 아끼지 않는 사람 없다 Most of rich people are frugal of their money. // 비밀~ 탄로되지

않는 것이 없다 There is nothing so secret but it comes to light. // 노력 없이 얻을 수 있는 물건~ 가질 만한 값어치가 있는 것은 없다 Nothing is worth having that can be gained without labor. // 한국 사람~ 누가 통일을 반대하랴 What [Surely no] Korean will object to the unification of Korea!

2 (…을 감안하면) considering; seeing; (…자격으로는) as; for. ¶미국인~ 한국어를 잘하다 speak fluent Korean for an American.

치고는 when it comes to; considering. ⇨ 치고 ¶그 소년은 나이~ 키가 크다 The boy is tall for his age. // 7월~ 선선하다 It is cool for July. // 신인~ 꽤 잘했다 Seeing (Considering) that he is new to the job, he has done very well. // 그 애는 여자 아이~ 행동이 거칠다 For a girl, she behaves roughly.

치골(恥骨) (생) the pubis (*pl.* pubes); the pubic bone.

치골(齒骨) (의) (a) dentary bone; dentale.

치과(齒科) 1 (의) dental surgery; dentistry; dental service. 2 a dentist's (office); a dental clinic.

●**치과 기공(사)** a dental technician. **치과 대학** a dental college. **치과의 / 치과 의사** a dentist; a dental surgeon; (개업의(醫)) a dental practitioner. **치과 의원** a dentist's (office); a dental clinic.

치관(齒冠) the crown (of a tooth).

치국(治國) governing [ruling] a country [nation]; government; statecraft.

●**치국책** statecraft; statesmanship.

치근(齒根) the root of a tooth. ⇨ 이촉

치근거리다 annoy; tease. ⇨ 지근거리다₁

치근(덕)치근(덕) annoying; molesting. ⇨ 지근(덕)지근(덕)

치기(稚氣) childishness; puerility. ¶~ 넘친 childish / puerile // ~에서 벗어나다 get rid of childishness.

치다¹ 1 (파도가 일렁이다) wave; roll (in waves); undulate; (물결이 와서 부딪다) dash (against). ¶파도가 치는 대양 the billowy deep // 물결이 치는 소리 the sound [roar] of the waves // 물결이 치는 대로 (drift about) at the mercy of the waves // 바위에 파도가 ~ waves dash against a rock.

2 (눈보라·폭풍우가) rage; bluster. ¶들에는 눈보라가 치고 있었다 A blizzard was raging over the field.

3 (벼락 등이) strike; hit; thunder; lighten. ¶천둥이 친다 The thunder rolls. // 멀리서 천둥 치는 소리가 들렸다 Rolls of thunder were heard in the distance. // 때때로 번개가 쳤다 There were occasional flashes of lightning.

치다² 1 (때리다) strike; hit; beat; knock; give [deal] a blow; pommel; slap; slug; smack; thrash; smite; wallop; punch. ¶북을 ~ beat a drum // 어깨를 툭 ~ pat (a person) on the shoulder // 종아리를 ~ whip (a person) on the calves of the legs // 그 어머니는 개구쟁이 아들의 엉덩이를 쳤다 The mother spanked her naughty boy. // 그 아버지는 아이의 뺨을 쳤다 The father slapped the child on the face [the child's cheek]. // 그는 책상을 치면서 연설을 했다 He pounded on the desk during his speech. // 그는 주먹으로 테이블을 쾅 쳤다 He struck the table with his fist. // 그는 신문지를 접어서 파리를 쳤다 He swatted (at) the fly with a folded newspaper. (▶ at이 들어가면, 파리를 노려서 친 것이 됨) // 그는 공을 원

치다

쪽으로 빗나가게 쳤다(야구에서) He pulled the ball to left.∥그는 화를 내며 내 손에서 책을 쳐 떨어뜨렸다 He knocked the book from my hand in anger.
2 (운동에서 공을 때려 보내다) strike; hit. ¶공을 되받아 ~ strike back the ball / return the ball / (서로 계속적으로) rally / engage in a rally / 홈런을 ~ hit a home run / 배트로 공을 정통으로 ~ hit a ball squarely with a bat / 공을 상대방 코트에 쳐 넣다 smash a ball into one's opponent's court∥쳐 올리다 send (a thing) up∥그는 2사(二死) 만루에서 플라이를 쳐 올렸다 He hit a fly with two outs and the bases loaded.∥그는 맹렬한 라이너를 쳤다 He hit a sizzling liner.∥그는 초구를 정확히 쳤다 He hit the first pitch right on the nose.
3 [소리 내기 위해 때리다] beat (a drum); strike[toll / ring] (a bell); clang (a gong); clap (hands). ¶종을 ~ strike a bell / (올리다) ring a bell / (천천히 규칙적으로) toll a bell∥그녀는 손뼉을 치며 기뻐했다 She clapped her hands in delight.∥청중은 모두 손뼉을 쳤다 The audience clapped all together.
4 (손가락으로 악기를) play (on). ¶피아노를 ~ play (on) the piano.
5 (시계가) strike. ¶시계가 12시를 쳤다 The clock struck[sounded] twelve.∥지금 몇 시를 쳤지 What did it[the clock] strike?
6 (게임·운동을 하다) play (a game). ¶테니스[탁구]를 ~ play tennis[ping-pong] / 당구를 ~ play (at) billiards / have a game of billiards.
7 [못 등을 박다] drive[knock] in; hammer. ¶못을 ~ nail / drive a nail / hammer a nail into (wood).
8 [두들겨서 만들다]. ¶칼을 ~ temper[forge] a sword∥떡을 ~ pound steamed glutinous rice / make a rice cake.
9 [공격하다] attack; assault; assail; strike; [정벌하다] subjugate; conquer. ¶반역자를 ~ subjugate[crush] the rebels∥적의 후방을 ~ take[attack] the enemy in the rear.
10 [공박하다] attack; criticize; denounce; censure; impugn; speak[talk / write] against (a man); declaim against. ¶신문에서 남을 ~ write against a person / attack [pound] a person in the newspaper.
11 [자르다] cut. ¶나무의 가지를 ~ thin the branches (of a tree) / 정원수의 가지를 치게 했다 I had some branches trimmed off the trees in the garden.
12 [잘게 썰다] chop up. ¶채를 ~ cut (a carrot) into thin strips / cut into small [matchlike] pieces∥무채를 ~ cut a radish into fine strips.
13 [깎다] shave. ¶밤 보늬를 ~ shave the skin of a chestnut (with a knife).

치다³ 1 [설치하다] set; put up. ¶진(陣)을 ~ set up camp / take up a position∥강을 건너 밧줄을 ~ stretch a rope across a river∥두 기둥 사이에 [방을 가로질러] 밧줄을 ~ stretch a rope between two poles[across a room] / 창문에 커튼을 ~ hang a curtain over[at] a window∥이곳에 텐트를 치자 Let's pitch our tent here.∥경관은 줄을 치고 군중을 들이지 않았다 The policemen cordoned off the area and wouldn't let the crowd in.∥경찰이 비상선을 쳤다 The police posted a cordon.∥그들은 회장의 주위에 막을 쳤다 They put up curtains around the hall.
2 [엮다] weave. ¶돗자리[가마니]를 ~ weave a straw mat[bag] / 거미가 집을 쳤다 A spider has spun a web.
3 [감아서 매다] tie; do up. ¶각반을 ~ put on spats / do up puttees∥대님을 ~ tie one's trousers-cuffs[trousers around the ankles].

치다⁴ 1 [사육하다] raise (sheep / hogs / silkworms); rear (silkworms).
2 [새끼를 낳다] breed; procreate; propagate; bring forth the young; litter. ¶1년에 5, 6회 새끼를 ~ have five or six litters yearly.
3 [이자가 붙다] draw[bear / yield] interest. ¶이자가 새끼를 ~ bear double interest.
4 [꿀을 그러모으다] (bees) produce and store honey.
5 [내돋게 하다]. ¶가지를 ~ shoot out branches / ramify.

치다⁵ 1 (양념 등을) put (soy) into[in / on]. ¶양념을 ~ spice (a dish) / put a spice [spices] in∥생선에 소금을 ~ sprinkle salt on fish / 스테이크에 고깃국물을 약간 ~ dribble gravy onto the steak. **2** (기름을) apply (a lubricant). ¶기계에 기름을 ~ apply oil to a machine / grease a machine / lubricate a machine∥잔디 깎는 기계에 기름을 ~ oil a lawnmower. **3** [술을 따르다] pour; fill. ¶술을 ~ fill a glass with wine / serve wine.

치다⁶ 1 [계산에 넣다] count among; include. ¶그녀는 우리를 이제는 친구로 치지 않을 것이다 She will no longer count us among her friends.∥합격자는 나까지 쳐서 10명이었다 Ten applicants passed the examination, myself among the number.
2 [평가하다] price; value. ¶비싸게[싸게] ~ value at a high[low] rate / hold (anything) at a high[low] price / overestimate[underestimate]∥이것을 얼마로 치는가 How much would you put[estimate] this at?∥이것은 아무리 싸게 쳐도 1만 원은 나가는 물건이다 It is worth ten thousand won at the very least.
3 [가정하다] suppose; assume; presume; take it for granted that; postulate; presuppose. ¶…이라 치고 on the assumption that … / supposing[assuming] that … / suppose … / granted[granting] that …∥그들은 허가가 곧 나는 것으로 치고 있었다 They assumed[took it for granted] that permission would be given promptly.∥그것이 사실이라 치더라도, 역시 자네가 그르다 Granting that it is so, you are still (in the) wrong.
4 [간주하다] regard (as); consider; think of (as); look on[upon] (as); take (for). ¶남을 바보로 ~ consider a person (to be) a fool / look upon a person as a fool.

치다⁷ 1 [선·점 등으로 표하다]. ¶줄을 ~ draw a line / 방점을 ~ mark with a side dot [point]. **2** [발신하다]. ¶전보를 ~ send [dispatch] a telegram (to) / get[dash] off a telegram (to) / (구어) send a wire (to). **3** [점 패를 알아보다]. ¶점을 ~ practice divination / (남에게 부탁하여) have one's fortune told.

치다⁸ 1 [숙박시키다] lodge. ¶하숙을 ~ run [operate / keep] a lodging house. **2** [대하다] entertain. ¶손님을 ~ entertain guests. **3** (시험 등을) take; sit for; try. ¶시험을 [시행하다] conduct[hold / give / set] an

치다[9] 〔제거·청소하다〕 remove; take[clear / sweep] away; clear[take] out of the way; get rid of. ¶눈 치기 snow shoveling[(영) shovelling] // 눈 치는 넉가래 a snow shovel / (기계) a snowplow / (영) a snowplough // 우물을 ~ clean out a well / 강바닥을 ~ dredge a river / 도랑의 감탕을 ~ dredge mud from a ditch // 길의 눈을 ~ remove[clear] snow from a road // 우리는 집 주위의 도랑을 쳤다 We cleaned out the ditches around our house. // 나는 집 앞 보도의 눈을 쳤다 I shoveled the snow (away) from the pavement in front of our house.

치다[10] 〔체질을 하다〕 sift; sieve; put[pass / powder] (something) through a sieve [sifter]. ¶밀가루를 체에 ~ sift out flour.

치다[11] 1 〔소리를 지르다〕. ¶고함을 ~ shout / cry[call] out / storm // 호통을 ~ yell at / hurl words of thunder at / fulminate against / (미) bawl (a person) out. 2 〔동작·행위를 하다〕. ¶개구리헤엄을 ~ swim on one's chest // 물장구를 ~ paddle one's feet in the water.

치다[12] 〔차 등이 사람을〕 run over (a person); knock[run] (a person) down.

치다꺼리 1 〔일을 처리 냄〕 management; disposal; dealing (with); tidying (up); taking care of. ¶손님 ~ entertaining guests // 살림 ~ management of a household / housekeeping / taking care of the housework // 그 사건의 ~를 내가 맡았다 I was entrusted with the conduct[dealing] of the affairs. **치다꺼리하다** manage; dispose of; deal (with); take care of; look after; attend (to); tidy (up). ¶손님 ~ take care of[entertain / attend to] a guest // 살림 ~ manage a house. 2 〔바라지〕 help; aid; provision; supply(ing); taking care of; arranging; providing. ¶아들의 살림 ~ helping out one's son (with household necessities) // 친구의 장례 ~ providing [arranging] a funeral for a friend / taking care of the arrangements for a friend's funeral // 친구의 혼인 잔치 ~를 하다 take care of[arrange] the wedding banquet for a friend // 마침내 아이들 ~를 하지 않게 되었다 I was at last relieved of my children's care. **치다꺼리하다** help; aid; look after; take care of; provide; supply; arrange. ¶남의 일을 ~ help a person to do his work / assist a person.

치닫다 go[run] up; run uphill; run upstairs.

치대다 1 〔위쪽으로 대다〕 put[apply / place / stick / fix] on the upper side. ¶판자를 ~ fix a piece of board upward (of a wall). 2 〔문지르다〕 knead; rub. ¶반죽을 ~ knead dough // 빨래를 ~ rub laundry.

치도곤(治盜棍) a club (for the lash).
치도곤을 안기다 club[cudgel] (a criminal); 〔비유〕 teach (a person) a lesson; give (a person) a raw deal; give (a person) a hard time.

치독(治毒) treatment for poison; removal [neutralization] of poison; counteracting a poison; an antidote. **치독하다** treat for poison; remove[neutralize / counteract] poison.

치둔하다(癡鈍-) stupid; dumb; dull.

치뜨다 raise; lift (one's eyes). ¶눈을 ~ cast an upward glance / lift up one's eyes / turn up the eyes.

치란(治亂) 〔태평과 어지러움〕 peace reigns and[or] turbulent days; (평정) suppression of a rebellion. **치란하다** suppress a rebellion; put down a revolt.

치런치런 1 〔물이〕 full; overflowing. ¶우물에 물이 ~ 괴었다 The well is overflowing with water. 2 〔스칠락 말락 하는 모양〕 long; dragging; trailing. ¶치맛자락을 ~ 늘어뜨리고 걷다 walk dragging one's skirt along. **치런치런하다** long; dragging; (서술적) be trailing (down). ¶치런치런한 머리채 a long pigtail.

치렁거리다 1 〔부드럽게 움직이다〕 drag; trail; hang down; droop. ¶버들가지가 ~ willow branches droop low // 치맛자락이 ~ one's skirt drags // 긴 머리가 그녀의 등에서 치렁거리고 있다 Her long hair hangs loose(ly) down her back. 2 〔시일이 늦어지다〕 drag on; be prolonged[protracted].

치렁치렁 1 〔치렁거리는 모양〕 hanging (down); drooping; dragging. ¶허리까지 ~ 늘어진 땋은 머리 a pigtail that hangs down to one's waist // 치맛자락이 ~ 땅에 끌린다 My skirt drags. // 버들가지가 ~ 늘어졌다 Willow branches drooped. // 두꺼운 커튼이 창문에 ~ 늘어져 있다 Thick curtains hang loose at the window. **치렁치렁하다** drag; trail. ⇨ 치렁거리다 1 2 〔미적미적〕 prolonging; protracting; delaying; dragging (it) out. ¶몇 주일 동안 ~ 끈 다음에 after weeks' delay and postponement // 체류 일을 ~ 끌다 protract one's stay indefinitely. **치렁치렁하다** drag on. ⇨ 치렁거리다 2

치렁하다 dragging; trailing; drooping; droopy. ¶버들가지가 ~ Willow branches hang down droopily. // 치마가 ~ My skirt is long and trailing.

치레 embellishment; adornment; beautifying; prettifying; decorating. ¶겉~로만 for mere form's sake. **치레하다** embellish; adorn; decorate; deck[dress] up; smarten up; doll [pretty] up; beautify; pretty. ¶집을 ~ beautify a house / pretty a house up // 얼굴을 ~ pretty one's face up / work on[paint / apply makeup to] one's face // 몸을 ~ adorn oneself / dress up // 옷을 ~ dress[deck] up / be in gala dress / sport fancy attire / be in full feather.

치료(治療) (medical) treatment; remedy. ¶물리 ~ physical therapy // 심리 ~ a psychical cure // 자가 ~ doctoring oneself / home treatment / self-treatment // 전기 ~ electrotherapy // 외과 ~ surgical treatment // ~상의 효과 remedial[therapeutic / curative] value // 5일간의 ~를 요하는 화상 a burn requiring five days of treatment // ~중이다 be under (medical) treatment / be under the care of a doctor // 의사의 ~로 완쾌되다 recover under the treatment of a doctor // ~를 게을리 하다 neglect to have proper medical care // ~ 중에 절명하다 succumb under the treatment // ~의 효력도 없이 그는 사망했다 He died in spite of all the medical treatment he received. / He died, all medical treatment proving useless. // 나는 이를 ~ 중이다 I am undergoing dental treatment. // 그는 민 박사의 ~로 완쾌했다 He recovered

under the treatment of Dr. Min.∥어떤 ~도 그녀에겐 효과가 없었다 Her case resisted all treatment.∥그 ~는 효과가 좋았다 The treatment worked well. **치료하다** cure (a person of a disease); remedy; treat. ¶치료하기 어려운[치료할 수 없는] irremediable / incurable∥치료할 수 없는 병 an incurable disease / a disease beyond [insusceptible of] medical treatment / a trouble which resists all treatments∥병을 ~ cure a disease / have one's disease treated∥응급 ~ give first aid∥이 병은 빨리 치료하지 않으면 안 된다 This disease calls for[needs] prompt treatment. →¶치료받다 receive[obtain] treatment / be given treatment / take [undergo] medical [[외과] surgical] treatment / be placed under medical care∥암을 치료받는다 be treated for cancer∥아버지는 O 박사에게 치료받었다 My father was treated by Dr. O.∥나는 의무실에서 상처를 치료받었다 I had my injury treated[seen to] in the infirmary.
● **치료법** a curative means; (a method of) medical treatment; a remedy; a cure; therapeutic measures; therapeutics. ¶민간 a popular [folk] remedy∥암에 새로운 ~을 시도하다 try a new treatment[cure] for cancer ∥이 병에는 ~이 없다 There is no cure for the disease. / The disease is incurable. **치료비** a doctor's fee[bill]; a medical fee; smart money(배상 조의).

치루 [의] an anal fistula (pl. -las, -lae).
치르다 1 [지불하다] pay (off) (for); (구어) fork out. ¶물건 값을 ~ pay for (an article) ∥셈을 ~ pay[(미국 구어) foot] a bill / settle one's account∥계약금을 ~ advance money on a contract∥즉석에서[맞돈으로] ~ pay down∥계산을 치렀다 I have paid the bill[settled the accounts].∥이 차에 800 만 원을 치렀다 I paid 8,000,000 won for this car. / This car cost (me) 8,000,000 won.∥그는 나에게 만 원을 치러야 한다 He is liable to me for (the sum of) ten thousand won.
2 [겪다] undergo; go[pass] through; experience; (시험을) carry out. ¶시험을 ~ take an exam(ination) / undergo [go through] an examination∥홍역을 ~ have a hard time of it / have a bitter experience / be plagued [bored] to death by (a person)∥나는 의과 대학의 입학시험을 치렀다 I took[(영) sat for] the entrance examination of a medical school.∥그는 5년 형을 치렀다 He served a sentence of five years' imprisonment[five-year sentence].
3 [큰일을] carry out; go through; have; observe; put on (formalities). ¶손님을 ~ give [hold] a party / play host (to) / entertain∥제사를 ~ observe the formalities of ancestor worship∥결혼식을 ~ have a wedding ceremony.

치마 a skirt. ¶주름~ a pleated skirt∥~의 주름을 잡다[gather] on a skirt∥~를 **입다**[두르다] put on[wear] a skirt∥~를 벗다 remove[take off] one's skirt
● **치마폭** the width of joined parts in a skirt.
치맛바람 the swish of a skirt; the influence of woman's power; (학교에서의) the frequent appearance of mothers on campus (where their sons and daughters are attending school). ¶~이 무섭다 (a woman) be domi-neering [overbearing / swaggering]. **치맛자락** the edge [end / tail] of a skirt; the skirt; the trail; the train. ¶~을 걷어잡다 tuck up the skirt∥~을 끌며 걷다 walk trailing one's skirt behind∥신부의 ~을 들고 따라가다 carry the train of a bride.
치마분 (齒磨粉) tooth powder.
치매 (癡呆) [의] imbecility; dementia. ¶노인성 ~ senile dementia∥조발성(早發性)~ precocious dementia / schizophrenia.
● **치매증** [의] dementia.
치매기다 number in ascending order; start from the bottom in assigning numbers. ¶번지를 ~ number the houses in ascending order.
치명상 (致命傷) a mortal[fatal / deadly] wound; a fatal blow; a deathblow. ¶~을 주다 give (a person) a mortal wound / do (a person) a deadly injury∥~을 입다 be fatally[mortally] wounded / suffer[receive] a mortal wound / have a fatal wound inflicted on one∥그 부상이 ~이 되었다 The wound proved fatal.∥그는 그날의 전투에서 ~을 입었다 He was mortally wounded in the battle that day.∥그의 실책이 우리의 새 계획에 ~이 되었다 His blunder proved fatal to our new project.
치명적 (致命的) fatal; mortal; deadly; lethal; killing. ¶~인 병 a fatal disease∥~인 타격을 입다[받다] suffer[receive] a deathblow∥ ~인 타격을 주다 deal[strike] (a person) a fatal[mortal / deadly] blow∥정부로서는 그것이 ~인 타격이었다 It was a deathblow to the government.∥그는 ~인 손해를 입었다 He suffered fatal blow.
치명타 (致命打) [숨통을 끊는 타격] (deliver) a fatal [decisive] blow. ¶그는 검으로 그 남자의 목을 찔러 ~를 가했다 (문어) He delivered the coup de grâce by plunging his sword into the man's throat. / (구어) He finished the man off by thrusting his sword into his throat.∥그 비평가의 평은 그의 문필 생활에 ~를 가했다 The criticism proved to be the decisive[fatal] blow that put an end to his literary career.
치목 (稚木·穉木) [어린나무] a young plant [tree]; a sapling; a set.
치밀다 1 [복받치다] be filled[seized] (with); have a fit (of); surge; swell; well up. ¶분노가 ~ feel the surge of anger / have a fit of anger / get one's dander up / flare up∥욕심이 ~ be seized with greed∥치미는 정욕을 누르다 mortify [control] one's passions / regulate one's desires∥나는 메스꺼움이 치밀어 올랐다 I felt nauseated[sick at my stomach].∥그는 노여움이 치밀어 올랐다 Anger welled up in his heart.∥그는 증오심이 치밀어 올랐다 Hatred rose within him.∥그는 격렬한 증오심이 치밀자 몸을 떨었다 He trembled as a violent hatred welled up inside him.
2 (먹은 것이) heave; rise; come up. ¶먹은 것이 치밀었다 My food came back up.∥나는 (먹은 것이) 치밀어 올라 토할 것만 같았다 I was on the point of vomiting.
3 [위로 밀다] push[shove / force] up; thrust up; raise (up). ¶죽순이 흙을 치밀고 올라온다 Bamboo sprouts push up through the earth.
치밀하다 (緻密-) elaborate; close; minute; fine; nice; delicate. ¶너무 치밀한 overmin-

ute // 치밀한 관찰 (a) minute [exhaustive / close] observation // 치밀한 머리 an accurate [a precise] mind / a head for detail // 치밀한 계획 a very careful plan / a carefully drawn up plan / a minute [detailed] plan / an elaborate plan // 치밀한 생각 close [careful] thinking // 치밀한 세공 elaborate [delicate] workmanship // 치밀한 추리 a close reasoning // 치밀하지 못하다 be lacking in precision // 치밀한 주의를 요하다 require a close attention // 그의 문예 비평은 정말 ~ His criticism of literary works is precise. // 그의 일하는 솜씨는 아주 ~ His work is extremely detailed. // 그 조사는 치밀하지 않다 The investigation lacks accuracy. // 그는 관찰이 ~ He is a minute [nice] observer. // 치밀한 조사 결과 그것은 복제(複製)임이 드러났다 Under close examination it was found to be a reproduction. **치밀히** elaborately; closely; minutely; precisely. ¶결혼식의 만반의 준비는 아주 ~ 마련되었다 All the preparations for the wedding were made most carefully [with the utmost care].

치받다 butt up; push up counter (to); push up against. ¶남의 턱을 ~ give a person an uppercut on [to] the chin // 남을 머리로 ~ give a person a butt of head / butt a person (in the stomach) // 황소가 농사꾼을 치받아 죽였다 The bull gored the farmer to death.

치받이 1 [비탈] an upward [ascending] slope; an ascent; a climb; an upgrade; an uphill (road). ¶가파른[완만한] ~ a steep [gradual] ascent // ~ 길 an uphill road // 그 길은 언덕 쪽으로 가파른 ~ 길이 되어 있었다 The road made an abrupt rise in the direction of the hill. 2 [건] mud plastered on the ceiling. **치받이하다** plaster the ceiling.

치받치다 1 (버팀대로) support; (밀어 올려) push up. ¶토마토를 막대로 ~ support a tomato plant with a stick // 지붕을 ~ give support to a roof / hold up the roof // 포도 덩굴을 ~ stick a grapevine. 2 (연기·불길이) rise; soar; flare. ¶연기가 치받쳤다 Smoke rose. // 불길이 치받쳤다 A flame flared [blazed / flamed] up. 3 (감정이) surge; swell; well up. ¶분노가 ~ be seized with anger / flare up in anger / get one's dander up.

치부(恥部) 1 [생] the pubic region. ⇨음부(陰部) 2 [부끄러운 부분] a disgrace. ¶이 홍등가는 도시의 ~이다 This red-light district is a disgrace to the city. // 할렘 지구는 뉴욕의 ~이다 The city of New York ought to be ashamed to have such a place as Harlem.

치부(致富) acquisition of wealth; making money. **치부하다** make money; become rich; amass a fortune. ¶장사를 해서 크게 ~ make a great fortune by trade / do a good stroke of business // 주식으로 ~ profit handsomely from stock speculation / make a killing on the stock market.

치부(置簿) 1 [기입함] book-keeping; writing down. **치부하다** keep books; keep accounts; enter (an item) in a book; write down. ¶… 앞으로 ~ put [charge] (a sum) to (a person's) account // 취해 준 것을 ~ enter the loan // 모두 한데 치부해 주시오 Please put down all the items on the same bill. // 내 앞으로 치부해 두십시오 Charge the sum [Put it down] to my credit [account]. 2 [마음속에 새겨 둠]. **치부하다** keep [bear] in mind; make a mental note of; remember. 3 an account book. ⇨치부책(⇨치부)

●**치부책** an account book; a ledger.

치사(致死) being fatal [mortal / deadly]; killing. ¶~의 fatal / mortal / deadly / lethal // 과실 ~ (죄) accidental [unpremeditated] homicide / involuntary manslaughter / homicide [death] by misadventure // 상해 ~ a bodily injury resulting in death.

●**치사량** a fatal [lethal] dose. ¶~에는 이르지 않는 sublethal (dose of poison) // 그는 ~의 수면제를 먹었다 He took a lethal dose of sleeping pills. **치사율** lethality.

치사(致謝) appreciation; extending thanks; gratitude. **치사하다** extend thanks; appreciate; express one's gratitude [appreciation]. ¶ 남의 호의에 ~ thank a person for his kindness // 도와준 데 대해 ~ thank (a person) for his help.

치사스럽다(恥事-) shameful; dishonorable. ⇨치사하다 ¶치사스러운 꼴을 당하다 be put to shame / bring disgrace upon oneself / disgrace oneself / humiliate oneself // 치사스러운 줄을 모르다 know no shame / be shameless [brazen-faced] // 치사스러운 것을 무릅쓰고 그에게 돈을 빌려 달라고 했다 Pocketing my pride, I asked him for a loan.

치사하다(恥事-) shameful; dishonorable; disgraceful; ignoble; ignominious; mean; dirty. ¶내 몸에 손대지 말아요, 치사한 사람이군요 Keep your hand off me, you dirty creep! // 남의 논문을 표절하다니 정말 치사하군 What a disgrace [How shameful] to plagiarize somebody else's thesis! // 치사한 소리 같지만 그건 돈벌이가 안 된다 Though I am ashamed to say, it means [brings] no money.

치산(治山) [산소를 손질하여 다듬음] keeping ancestral graves in order; [산림을 잘 다스림] forestry conservancy [conservation / protection]; antiflood [flood control] afforestation; afforestation (as part of a disaster-control program). **치산하다** keep ancestral graves in good shape; take good care of the forests; protect the forests.

●**치산치수**(-治水) antiflood [flood control] afforestation; conservation of rivers and forests. ¶~ 사업 anti-erosion project.

치산(治産) (가사의) management of household affairs; (재산의) management of one's property [estate]. ¶금 ~ [법] incompetency / 금~자 a person adjudged incompetent / an interdict. **치산하다** manage household affairs; manage one's property.

치살리다 praise (a person) to the skies; plaster (a person) with praise; sing (a person's) praises; give (a person) a boost; speak highly of; flatter. ¶너무 치살리지 마라 Spare my blushes.

치석(齒石) tartar (on the teeth); dental calculus; odontolith. ¶~으로 더러워진 tartar-coated teeth // ~이 붙다 be coated with tartar // ~을 제거하다 remove [scrape] tartar from (a person's) teeth / scale (a person's) teeth // 그 사람의 이에 ~이 형성되었다 Tartar has formed on his teeth.

●**치석 제거** scaling (of the teeth).

치성(致誠) [정성을 다함] devotion; loyal [faithful] service; (신령·부처에게) sacrificial service (to spirits); a devout prayer. ¶~을

치세 1834

드리다 offer a sacrifice (to spirits) / offer a devout prayer // 그는 아들을 점지해 달라고 신령님께 ~을 드렸다 He prayed fervently to divine spirits for a son.

치세(治世) (제왕의) a reign; [통치] a rule; a regime; [태평 시대] peaceful times; peaceful ruling. ¶…의 ~에 in[under / during] the reign of … // 빅토리아 여왕 ~하에 under[in] the reign of Queen Victoria // 영국은 엘리자베스 여왕 ~에 해외로 대발전을 했다 England made a great overseas expansion in the reign of Queen Elizabeth. **치세하다** reign [rule] (over).

치솟다 1 [솟아오르다] rise (suddenly); soar; skyrocket; shoot up; zoom(비행기가). ¶불길이 ~ burst into flame / flame[blaze] up // 하늘 높이 ~ rise[soar] to the sky / shoot into the blue // 물가가 천정부지로 치솟고 있다 Prices are skyrocketing. // 불길이 치솟았다 Flames shoot up[rose higher]. 2 (감정 등이) be filled[seized] (with); have a fit (of).

치수(-數) the number of *chi*[inches]; measure; measurements; dimensions; size. ¶~대로 to measure / according to the measurements // ~에 맞추어 to measure / ~를 재다 measure the length / take (a person's) measure(ments) (for a new suit) / measure the size[dimension] (of) / measure (a person for clothes) / take the size (of) // 자로 ~를 재다 take the measurements of (a box) with a rule // ~가 모자라다 be short (of measure) / be wanting in length // ~가 틀리다 [잘못 재다] take a wrong measure / [잘못 만들다] make (a thing) to wrong measurements // 내 가슴둘레의 ~는 95센티이다 I measure ninety-five centimeters around my chest. // 나는 상자의 ~를 자로 쟀다 I measured the box with a ruler. // 종이의 ~는 세로 20센티, 가로 30센티였다 The paper was twenty by thirty centimeters (in size). // 나는 ~대로 책상을 만들었다 I made the desk (exactly) to specification[according to the specifications]. // 이 옷은 네 ~에 맞춰 만들었다 The clothes are made to your measure.

치수(治水) river[riparian] improvement; river training; flood control. ¶~는 정치의 가장 중요한 과제가 되어 왔다 Flood control has been a prime subject[duty] of government. **치수하다** regulate (rivers); improve water communications; control flood.

● **치수 공사** embankment[flood prevention / levee / river] works; water conservation works; river embanking; riparian work(s); flood control (work).

치아(齒牙) a tooth (*pl.* teeth). ⇨ 이¹ 1

치안(治安) (the) public peace (and order); security. ¶~을 유지하다 keep[maintain] public peace and order // ~을 어지럽히다 disturb public peace and order // 이 지역은 ~이 안전하다[나쁘다] This area is safe[not safe].

● **치안감** Senior Superintendent General(약어 Sr. Supt. Gen.). **치안 당국** law enforcement authorities. **치안 유지** maintenance of (the) public peace. ¶~법 [법] the Maintenance of the Public Order Act // ~상 for security reasons. **치안총감** Director General (of the National Police).

치약(齒藥) toothpaste; dental cream; (가루) tooth powder; (집합적) dentifrice. ¶~으로 칫솔질하다 brush one's teeth with toothpaste.

치어(稚魚) a fry; a fingerling; (집합적) fry; the young of fishes.

치어걸(ˣcheer girl) a cheerleader; a pompom girl.

치열(治熱) [한] controlling a fever. **치열하다** control[check] a fever.

치열(齒列) a row[set] of teeth. ¶~이 고르다 [고르지 않다] have a regular[an irregular] set of teeth // 당신은 ~이 가지런하군요[가지런하지 못하군요] Your teeth are well[poorly] aligned.

● **치열 교정** correction of irregularities of the teeth; straightening of irregular teeth; orthodontics(단수 취급); orthodontia.

치열하다(熾烈―) intense; keen; severe; fierce. ¶치열한 경쟁 (a) keen[hot / sharp / fierce / cutthroat] competition / hot[bitter] rivalry // 치열한 논쟁 a heated[fiery] discussion / a hot argument // 치열한 전투 a fierce battle[fight] // 그 법안은 치열한 논쟁 끝에 통과되었다 The bill was passed at the end of a bruising debate. **치열히** intensely; keenly; severely; fiercely. ¶~ 싸우다 fight hard[furiously] / have a fierce battle[engagement] / engage in hot[harsh] fighting.

치오르다 rise (up); go up. ¶동쪽 하늘로 치오르는 태양 the sun climbing the eastern sky // 끝이 치올라 간 콧수염 a mustache with the ends curled up // 하늘로 ~ soar[go up] in the air.

치올리다 lift up; push up. ¶공을 하늘로 ~ throw a ball up in the air // 그녀의 머리를 치올린 모습이 아주 멋지게 보였다 She looked very nice with her hair up.

치와와 (멕시코 원산의 작은 개) a Chihuahua.

치외 법권(治外法權) [법] extraterritoriality; extraterritorial rights[jurisdiction]; (외교관의) diplomatic immunity. ¶~상의 extraterritorial // ~을 철폐하다 abolish[relinquish] extraterritoriality // ~을 행사하다 exercise (one's) extraterritoriality.

치욕(恥辱) [불명예] (a) disgrace; dishonor [(영) dishonour]; [수치] shame; [모욕] an insult(▶ 남을 모욕하는 언동); humiliation(▶ 모욕을 당한 사람의 기분·상태); indignity; stigma. ¶심한 ~ a crying[burning] shame / a deep disgrace / a sore indignity // 국가의 ~ a disgrace to the nation / a national disgrace / a stain upon the national honor // ~을 당하다 be disgraced[dishonored / insulted] / be subject to humiliation // ~을 주다 disgrace / dishonor / insult / humiliate / bring shame on (a person) / make (a person) ashamed / put (a person) to shame / subject (a person) to humiliation // ~을 씻다 wipe away[off] a disgrace / clear one's reputation // ~을 초래하다[가져오다] bring shame[disgrace] upon one's head / suffer disgrace / disgrace oneself // 집안에 ~을 가져오다 bring disgrace[dishonor] upon (the name of) one's family // ~을 참다 bear disgrace / pocket[book] an insult / (영) eat humble pie / (미) eat crow / endure shame [an insult] // …을 ~으로 여기다 be ashamed of (a person / doing) / feel[think] it disgraceful (to do) / feel shame (to do) // 이로써 ~을 씻을 수가 있었다 This has taken away my reproach. // 그의 행위는 부모의 ~이 된다

His conduct reflects on his parents.∥그는 여러 사람 앞에서 ~을 당했다 He was humiliated[put to shame / disgraced / insulted] in public.

치우다 1 [없애다·옮기다] put[take] away; clear away[off]; work off; remove; get[put] out of the way; 〔챙기다〕keep; store; put [play] (a thing) away[up / by]; put away(옆으로 비켜 두다); put back(본디 있던 곳에); stow away; tuck away (in a box). ¶팔아 치울 물건 goods for clearance sale∥갈퀴로 잔디의 낙엽을 ~ rake fallen leaves from the lawn∥길에 있는 눈을 ~ shovel (away) the snow from a road∥식탁을 ~ clear the table∥장난감을 ~ put toys away∥테이블(의 접시들)을 ~ clear (the dishes from) the table∥쓰레기를 ~ dispose of junk∥걸리적거리는 것을 ~ remove an obstacle / do away with a nuisance∥길의 돌을 ~ remove stones from the road∥의자를 ~ put the chairs back in their places∥읽던 책을 ~ put aside the book one read∥잠동사니를 ~ shift rubbish out of the way∥차를 좀 치워 주시오. Move your car, please.∥이것을 좀 치워 다오 Get this out of the way.∥상자를 모두 치워 버렸다 I have removed all the boxes.∥깨진 꽃병은 벌써 치워 버렸다 The broken vase has already been cleared away[removed].∥일꾼들이 빈 깡통 더미를 치우고 있다 The workers are disposing of the piles of empty cans.∥그는 의자를 방 한구석에 치웠다 He moved the chairs to a corner of the room.∥다 들은 테이프를 치웠다 I put away the tapes I had finished listening to.∥어린애가 장난 못 하게 칼을 치워라 Put the knife away so that the child can't toy with it.
2 [정돈하다] put (things) in order; put[set] (a room) to rights; tidy (up); clean up; straighten up (a room); put[set] (a room) straight; fix up. ¶방을 ~ tidy up a room / put[set] a room to rights∥책상 위[서랍]를 ~ tidy up a desk[drawer]∥연회가 끝난 방을 ~ put a room in order after a party is over∥잠다하게 늘어놓은 방을 ~ tidy (up) a disordered[cluttered] room∥부엌을 ~ straighten (out) the kitchen∥하던 일을 ~ clean up unfinished work.
3 〔시집보내다〕give (one's daughter) in marriage; dispose of (one's daughter) (in marriage); get (one's daughter) off; marry off (one's daughter). ¶딸을 변호사에게 치웠다 I married (off) my daughter to a lawyer.
4 [기타] finish; put an end to; bring to an end[a close]; complete. ¶먹어 ~ eat up all / finish(off) / make short work (of)∥책 한 권을 읽어 ~ finish a book∥나는 저녁을 막 먹어 치웠다 I have just had my supper.

치우치다 1 [한쪽으로 쏠리다] lean (to / toward); incline (toward); slant (toward). ¶약간 동쪽으로 치우친 곳에 a little to the east (of)∥벽이 서쪽으로 치우쳤다 A wall slanted to the west.
2 [편파적이다] be biased[one-sided / prejudiced]; be lopsided[unbalanced]; 〔불공평하다〕be partial; have a partiality (for / to); 〔도를 넘기다〕go to excess. ¶치우치지 않는 〔공정한〕fair / unbiased / 〔편견이 없는〕unprejudiced∥치우친 생각 a biased[one-sided / lopsided / partial / distorted] view / a prejudice∥치우친 식사를 하지 않도록 하다

take a well-balanced diet∥감정에 ~ give way to[be carried away by] one's feelings∥학문에 ~ have a bent[partiality] for learning[study]∥막내아들을 치우치게 사랑하다 be partial toward the youngest son∥그의 의견은 치우쳐 있다 He is prejudiced. / His view is one-sided.∥부하를 다루는 데 치우쳐서는 안 된다 You must not be partial in dealing with your subordinates.

치유(治癒) healing; cure; recovery. **치유하다** 〔고치다〕cure; heal; 〔낫다〕heal; cure; recover; be cured. ¶치유할 수 있는[없는] curable[incurable]. ➔그의 손가락의 벤 상처는 2, 3일로 치유됐다 His cut finger healed in a few days.
● **치유기**(一期) convalescence. **치유력** healing power; curative properties.

치음(齒音) 〔언〕a dental sound. ⇨'잇소리

치이다[1] 1 [무거운 것에 부딪히거나 깔리다] get hit; be crushed[squeezed]; be pressed[held / caught] under. ¶손이 장도리에 ~ one's hand gets hit by a claw hammer∥무너지는 바위에 치여(서) 죽다 be crushed to death under the loosened rocks.
2 [차(車)에 깔리다] get[be] run over[knocked down] (by); be hit (by). ¶그는 차에 치였다 He was hit[knocked down] by a car.∥그 소녀는 덤프트럭에 치여 죽었다 The girl was run over and killed by a dump truck.
3 [덫에 걸리다] get trapped[entrapped]; be caught in a trap. ¶곰이 덫에 치였다 A bear was trapped.∥쥐가 덫에 치였다 A rat was caught in the trap[was trapped].

치이다[2] [피륙의 올이 한쪽으로 쏠리다] lose (its)weave; 〔솜 등이 뭉치다〕form into a lump; lump (up) to one side. ¶항라(亢羅)는 빨면 치인다 Silk gauze loses its weave when it is washed.

치이다[3] [가격이 얼마씩 들다] cost; amount to (so much); be calculated (at the rate of); take (cost of); be priced; be valued. ¶비싸게 ~ come[prove to be] expensive / run into (big) money∥싸게 ~ cost little / come cheap / be less expensive / be economical∥그것은 한 개에 300원씩 치였다 It cost me three hundred won a piece.∥가스를 쓰면 숯보다 싸게 치인다 Gas is less expensive than charcoal.

치인(癡人) [어리석고 못난 사람] a simpleton; an idiot; a dunce; a fool.

치자(治者) the ruler; the governor.

치자(梔子) a gardenia; a Cape jasmine.
● **치자나무** a Cape jasmine[jessamine]; a gardenia.

치장(治粧) 〔장식〕ornamentation; decoration; adornment; embellishment; 〔화장〕toilet; makeup; dressing. ¶몸 ~ personal adornment[ornament] / dressing up∥가게의 ~ shop decoration∥진열창 ~ window dressing. **치장하다** ornament; decorate (a room with flowers); adorn; deck[trick] out[up]; bedeck; embellish (a house); dress (a window); (옷 등으로) dress (oneself) up; 〔화장하다〕make[touch] up. ¶보석으로 아름답게 치장한 귀부인 a lady glittering[bedecked] with jewels∥몸을 ~ dress up[out] / deck up (with jewels) / adorn oneself (with jewels) / (구어) titivate∥얼굴을 ~ put on makeup / make up one's face∥집을 ~ dec-

치장 orate [pretty up] one's house // 말쑥하게 치장하고 나서다 go out all dolled up.

치장(治裝) [행장을 차림] preparations for a journey. **치장하다** make preparations [equip oneself / fit oneself out] for a journey; start packing one's bags for a journey; prepare for a trip [journey].

치적(治績) (the results of an) administration; administrative record(s) [achievements]. ¶…의 치적을 기념하여 비를 세우다 erect a monument in commemoration of (a person's) remarkable executive services.

치정(癡情) foolish passion; blind love; infatuation; [질투] jealousy. ¶~에 미쳐 있다 be consumed with a blind passion (for) // 그는 ~ 때문에 여자를 죽였다 He murdered a woman out of jealousy. // 그는 ~에 빠져 처자식을 버렸다 Infatuated with a woman, he abandoned his wife and children.
● **치정 관계** connection with a love affair; amorous relationship. **치정 살인** a sex [scandalous] murder (case).

치조(齒槽) [생] an alveolus (pl. -li); an alveole; the socket of a tooth. ¶~의 alveolar.

치졸하다(稚拙-·穉拙-) naïve; (awkwardly) artless. ¶치졸한 그림 a poorly-drawn [an awkwardly-done] picture / an amateurish [unpolished] painting.

치주염(齒周炎) paradentitis.

치중(置重) attachment of weight [importance] (to / on / upon). **치중하다** attach (great) weight to; stress; emphasize; lay stress [emphasis] on [upon]; attach importance to; set importance on; value; put [set] value on; set (great) store by. ¶지나치게 ~ give undue value to // 일보다는 노는 데 ~ place more importance on having fun than on working / attach greater importance to fun than to work.

치즈 cheese. ¶가루 ~ powdered cheese // 얇게 썬 [강판으로 간] ~ sliced [grated] cheese.

치질(痔疾) piles; haemorrhoids; (미) hemorrhoids. ¶수~ external hemorrhoids / blind piles // 암~ internal hemorrhoids // ~을 절제하다 remove hemorrhoids // 그는 ~이 있다 He is suffering from hemorrhoids.
● **치질 환자** a victim of [a sufferer from] piles.

치켜들다 [위로 올려 들다] raise; lift. ¶머리를 ~ raise one's head // 해바라기는 태양을 향하여 머리를 치켜들었다 The sunflower lifted its head to the sun.

치켜세우다 praise [extol] (a person) to the skies; pay (a person) a compliment; pass out compliments; be complimentary; say pretty [nice] things (to); flatter; (구어) soft-soap (a person into doing). ¶치켜세워 …시키다 flatter (a person) into doing // 치켜세워도 소용없다 Flattery won't work with me. / Flattery will get you nowhere. // 그는 영웅으로서 국민에게 치켜세워졌다 He was lionized as a hero by the people. // 그는 남이 자기를 치켜세우는 것을 좋아하지 않는다 He does not like to be fussed over.

치키다 raise; lift; heave; boost; pull [draw] up. ¶바지를 ~ pull up one's trousers // 눈썹을 ~ raise one's eyebrows // 머리를 치켜 깎다 trim (a person's hair) up / (여성의 머리를) shingle.

치킨 chicken.

치타 [동] a cheetah.

치통(齒痛) (a) toothache; odontalgia; dentalgia. ¶주사를 맞았더니 ~이 좀 가라앉았다 The injection eased the toothache a little.

치하(治下) under the rule [regime / reign]. ¶~의 government / regime] (of) // 나세르 ~의 이집트 Egypt under the Nasser regime // 나폴레옹 ~의 프랑스 France under (the reign [rule] of) Napoleon // ~에 있다 be ruled by.

치하(致賀) appreciation; compliment; congratulation(축하); praise(칭찬). **치하하다** appreciate; compliment; praise; admire; congratulate; felicitate. ¶…을 치하하기 위하여 in honor [celebration] of … // 종업원의 노고를 ~ do something to thank the employees for their services / appreciate the service of employees // 여왕은 그를 기사로 제수하여 공을 치하했다 The queen rewarded him by dubbing him a knight. // 사장은 그의 공로를 치하하여 금일봉을 주었다 The president gave him money in appreciation of his service.

치한(癡漢) 1 [호색한] (구어) a molester; (구어) a pervert; (속어) a wolf; a masher. ¶혼잡한 차 속의 ~ a molester of women on crowded trains / a man who molests women on crowded trains. 2 a simpleton; an idiot. ⇨치인

치환(置換) transposition; [수][화] substitution; replacement; displacement; metathesis. **치환하다** substitute; displace; replace; transpose; metathesize. ¶치환할 수 있는 [화] displaceable // A로 B를 ~ substitute A for B / replace B with [by] A.

칙령(勅令) a Royal [a King's] order. ⇨칙명

칙명(勅命) [임금의 명령] a Royal [a King's] order [command / commission / mandate]. ¶~을 내리다 issue [give] an Imperial order // 그는 ~에 따라 파리에 파견되었다 He was sent to Paris by Imperial order.

칙사(勅使) an Imperial envoy [messenger].

칙서(勅書) an official letter from the Emperor; an Imperial message.

칙임(勅任) Royal appointment.

칙칙폭폭 [증기 기관차의 소리] chug-chug [chuff-chuff]; puff-puff. ¶~ 증기 기관차는 비탈을 올라갔다 The steam locomotive huffed and puffed [chugged] up the hill.

칙칙하다 dark; somber; dull; drab. ¶칙칙한 청색 sordid blue // 칙칙해 보이다 look dark and dull (in the lamplight) // 그 커튼은 빛깔이 좀 ~ The curtain is a bit too gaudy [loud].

칙허(勅許) Imperial sanction. ¶~를 청하다 ask for [submit (a matter) for] Imperial sanction.

친-(親) 1 [직계의] true; real; by blood; german. ¶~사촌 a cousin-german // ~부모 one's real [blood] parents // ~형제 [자매] full [real / blood] brothers [sisters]. 2 [친밀한] favoring; pro-. ¶~한파의 pro-Korean // ~정부의 pro-government // ~영주의자 an Anglophile.

친가(親家) one's old [parents'] home.

친고(親告) [법] a (formal) complaint from the victim. **친고하다** make a criminal complaint.
● **친고죄** a crime requiring a (formal) complaint from the victim for prosecution.

친교(親交) (intimate) friendship; intimacy;

good fellowship; friendly [intimate] relations. ¶50년 동안의 ~ a friendship of fifty years [years' standing] // …과 ~가 있다 be on friendly [close / intimate] terms with … / enjoy the friendship of / enjoy a close intimacy with / be good friends with// ~를 굳히다 deepen [cement] a friendship // ~를 끊다 break a friendship (with) // ~를 도모하다 promote [develop] friendly [cordial] relations (with) // …과 ~를 지속하다 maintain friendly relations with … ¶그는 그 청년과 ~를 맺었다 He made friends [formed a friendship] with the young man. ¶나는 안 군과 30년 동안의 ~가 있다 I have enjoyed An's friendship [An and I have been friends] for thirty years.

친구(親舊) a friend; [동지] a companion; a mate; a fellow; a comrade; (구어) a pal; (구어) a chum; [교우] a circle; company. ¶학교 ~ a schoolmate // 한 방 ~ a roommate // ~의 친구 a friend of a friend / one's friend's friend // 장난 ~ one's companion in fun // 남자 ~ a boyfriend // 여자 ~ a girlfriend // 술 ~ a drinking companion [(구어) buddy] // 미덥지 못한 ~ a fair-weather friend // 오랜 ~ an old friend / a friend of long standing // 좋은 ~ a good friend // 참된 ~ a true [tried] friend // 친한 ~ an intimate [a close] friend / a chum / a crony // 불행을 함께 나누는 ~ a companion of one's misery // ~ 간의 다툼 a quarrel [fight] among friends // 좋은 [나쁜] ~와 사귀다 keep good [bad] company // 못된 ~와 어울리다 get [fall] into bad company // ~와 의절하다 part company (with) / break (friendship) (with) // ~가 되다 make friends [a friend] (with) / form [contact / strike up] a friendship (with) / (구어) pal up (with) // …과 ~가 되고 싶어 하다 seek the company [friendship] of / seek to form a friendship with // ~가 되어 주다 keep company (with them) // ~가 없다 have no friends / be friendless // 그는 ~ 간에 호평을 받고 있다 He is well thought of among [is well liked by] his companions. // 그는 ~ 간에 「울프」라는 별명으로 통하고 있다 He goes by the nickname "wolf" among his friends [in his circle]. // 그와는 10년간이나 ~ 사이이다 We have been companions [pals] for ten years. // 그는 당신과 ~가 되고 싶어 한다 He wants to be friends with you. // 좋은 ~와 사귀어라 Please seek out good company. / Choose your companions well. // 그는 참된 ~가 못 된다 He is not true to his friends. // 사람은 사귀는 ~를 보고 알 수 있다 You can judge a man by the company he keeps. // ~는 얻기보다 잃기가 쉽다 A friend is easier lost than found. // 어려울 때 도와주는 ~야말로 참다운 ~다 A friend in need is a friend indeed.

친권(親權) parental authority [prerogatives]. ¶~을 행사하다 exercise parental authority.
● **친권자** a person with parental authority [rights].

친근감(親近感) a feeling of intimacy [familiarity]; friendly feeling; affection; a sense of closeness. ¶~이 있는 [없는] friendly [unfriendly] / familiar [unfamiliar] / kind [unkind] / intimate [cold] // …에 대하여 ~을 품다 feel strong affinities with … / find in … something congenial to oneself // 나는 그에 대해 ~을 가진 적이 없다 I have never felt close to him. // 그에게는 어쩐지 ~이 안 든다 There is something unapproachable about him.

친근하다(親近-) intimate; friendly; close; familiar (with). ¶친근한 사이 intimate relationship / first-name basis // 친근한 사이다 be on good [friendly] terms (with) / be friends [(구어) chums] (with) / have a close [friendly] relation (with) // 매우 ~ be hand and [in] glove (with each other). **친근히** intimately; friendly; closely. ¶그는 ~ 내게 말을 걸어왔다 He spoke to me in a friendly way.

친남매(親男妹) one's full [whole / real / blood / own] brothers and sisters. ¶그들은 ~간이다 They are brother and sister of the full blood.

친누이(親-) one's real [own] (younger) sister; one's sister by blood.

친동생(親同生) one's true [real] (younger) brother [sister]; one's brother [sister] by blood (as opposed to stepbrother [stepsister]).

친딸(親-) one's own [real] daughter.

친모(親母) one's true [real] mother. ⇨=친어머니

친목(親睦) friendship; friendliness; intimacy; amity. ¶상호 간의 ~을 도모하다 promote mutual friendship. **친목하다** [친밀하다] intimate; affectionate; friendly; [화목하다] harmonious; happy; peaceful.
● **친목 단체** a friendly society. **친목회** an informal social gathering; (구어) a mixer; (구어) a (friendly) get-together (▶ 소수 인원의 격식 없는 모임); a reunion. ¶~를 열다 hold a social gathering [meeting].

친미(親美) ¶~의 pro-American / pro-United States.
● **친미 노선** [외교] the pro-American line [diplomacy].

친밀하다(親密-) intimate; friendly; familiar; close; (구어) chummy; thick. ¶친밀한 태도로 in a friendly [an affectionate] manner // …과 ~ […과 친밀한 사이다] be on intimate [friendly] terms (with) / be on terms of intimacy (with) / be in close connection (with) / be in intimate relations (with) // …과 친밀해지다 become intimate (with) / establish [form / effect] an intimacy (with) / make friends (with) // 그 일로 해서 그들은 서로가 더욱 친밀해졌다 It brought them all the closer to each other. // 우리는 아주 친밀한 사이는 아니다 We are not on the best of terms. **친밀히** intimately; closely.

친부(親父) one's true [real] father. ⇨=친아버지

친부모(親父母) one's real [blood] parents. ¶~처럼 돌보아 주다 look after (a person) with parental affection [tenderest care] / display a fatherly interest (in) / bring up (a child) with motherly care.

친분(親分) [지면] acquaintance; acquaintanceship; [가까운 관계] friendship; intimacy; familiarity. ¶~을 맺다 make (a person's) acquaintance / get [become] acquainted (with) / make (an) acquaintance (with) / form the acquaintance (of) / strike up an acquaintance (with) / be introduced (to) // ~이 있다 be acquainted [familiar] (with) // ~이 없다 have no acquaintance (with) / be

친사돈

not acquainted (with) / be not close [intimate] (with) // ~이 두터워지다 get more closely acquainted // 어떻게 해서든 그들과 ~을 유지하는 편이 좋다 You'd better keep up your acquaintance with them. // 그와는 ~이 두텁다 I am on familiar terms with him.

친사돈(親査頓) the parents of one's son-[daughter-]in-law.

친상(親喪) mourning for one's parent; bereavement of one's parent. ¶~을 당하다 lose one's parent / be bereaved of one's parent / have one's parent die.

친생자(親生子) [적출자] a legitimate[lawful] child; a child born in lawful wedlock.

친서(親書) a letter written in a person's own hand; an autograph letter. ¶국왕[대통령]의 ~ an autograph letter[a personal message] from the King[President] // ~를 휴대하다 carry a personal letter (from). **친서하다** write (a letter) in person.

친선(親善) friendship; amity; friendly relations[ties]; goodwill. ¶국제 ~ international goodwill[friendship] // 국제 ~에 기여하다 contribute to a better international friendship // 국제 ~을 도모하다 cultivate[promote] international friendship // 한미 ~을 증진[촉진]하다 promote friendly relations between Korea and the U.S.

● **친선 경기** a goodwill match. ¶국제 ~ an international goodwill match. **친선 방문** a (four-day) goodwill visit (to a country). **친선 사절** a goodwill envoy; (사절단) a goodwill mission. ¶~로 캐나다에 가다 go to[visit] Canada on a goodwill mission.

친손자(親孫子) a son of one's son; one's real [blood] grandson.

친솔(親率) the members of one's family; one's family.

친수성(親水性) [화] hydrophile property.

친숙하다(親熟-) intimate; close; familiar; well acquainted. ¶친숙한 사이 a friendly relationship / close acquaintanceship // 남과 친숙해지다 get to know a person // …과 친숙한 사이다 be well acquainted with (a person) // 그것은 우리의 귀에 친숙한 말이다 The word sounds familiar to us. **친숙히** intimately; closely; familiarly.

친아들(親-) one's true[real] son; one's son by blood (as opposed to stepson).

친아버지(親-) one's true[real] father; one's father by blood (as opposed to stepfather).

친애(親愛) affection; love; [친근] intimacy. **친애하다** love; feel affection for. ¶친애하는 …/beloved // 친애하는 벗 one's dear friend // 친애하는 여러분 (연설 등에서) Ladies and gentlemen! // 나는 그에게 친애하는 정을 느끼고 있다 I have deep affection for him.

친어머니(親-) one's true[real] mother; one's mother by blood (as opposed to stepmother). ¶~처럼 대하다 be[act as] a mother to (a child) / take a motherly interest in (a child).

친언니(親-) one's true[real] (elder) sister; one's sister by blood (as opposed to stepsister).

친우(親友) a good[close / bosom / great] friend; one's best friend; a buddy; an intimate (friend).

친위대(親衛隊) the Royal guards; the bodyguards (to the King).

친일(親日) ¶~의 pro-Japanese // ~적인 사람 a Japanophil(e) / a sympathizer for Japan.

● **친일파** a pro-Japanese group[faction]; Japanese sympathizers.

친자식(親子息) one's true[real / own] child; one's child by blood (as opposed to stepchild). ¶그 부인에게는 ~이 없었다 The woman had no children of her own.

친전(親展) Personal; Confidential; To be opened by addressee only(편지 봉투에 적는 말).

친절(親切) kindness; goodness; goodwill; a favor. ¶조그만 ~ a small kindness / a little act of kindness // ~을 가장하여 [명계로] under the mask[show / pretense] of friendship[kindness] // ~에 보답하다 repay (a person's) kindness // ~을 베풀다 be kind [good] to (a person) / show (a person) kindness / do (a person) a good turn / do well by (a person) / treat (a person) with kindness // ~을 다하다 show (a person) every kindness // ~을 이용하다 take (mean) advantage of (a person's) kindness / avail oneself of (a person's) kind offer / presume upon (a person's) kindness // ~에 감사합니다 Thank you for your kindness. // 너의 ~이 오히려 그를 망하게 했다 Your kindness proved his ruin. // 내가 베푼 ~이 헛되지는 않았다 My kindness was not wasted[thrown away] upon him. **친절하다** kind; kindly; good; obliging; accommodating; friendly. ¶친절한 행위 a kind act / an act of kindness // 친절한 사람 a kind person // 참으로 친절하기도 하시오 How kind [sweet] of you! (▶ sweet 는 여성 용어) // 그는 친절한 마음에서 그렇게 한 것이다 He did it out of kindness[goodwill]. // 우리는 친절한 대접을 받았다 We were treated cordially[with consideration]. // 각주 (脚註)는 친절하고 자상했다 The footnotes were exhaustive and painstaking. **친절히** kindly; obligingly; kindheartedly; with kindness. ¶~ …하다 be kind[good] enough to (do) / be so kind as to (do) / have the kindness to (do) // ~ 가르쳐 주셔서 고맙습니다 It was very kind of you to teach me. / Thank you very much for your kindness in teaching me. // 따님께서 ~ 역까지 마중 나와 주셨습니다 Your daughter was good enough [had the kindness] to meet me at the station. // 그는 나를 항상 ~ 대해 주었다 He always treated me kindly. / He was always kind to me.

친정(親政) direct government by the King. **친정하다** (the King) govern in person.

친정(親庭) [아내의 본집] a woman's native home; a woman's parents' home[house]; one's maiden home. ¶아내는 자식을 데리고 ~으로 갔다 My wife took our son and went back to her parents'.

친족(親族) a relative; a relation. ¶남계 [부계] ~ an agnate // 직계 [방계] ~ a lineal [collateral] relative [relation] / (관계) lineal [collateral] consanguinity // 여계 [모계] ~ a cognate.

● **친족 관계** kinship; relationship by blood and marriage. **친족법** the Domestic Relations Law.

친지(親知) an acquaintance; a friend. ¶~ 간 [관계] acquaintanceship / contacts // ~가 많다 have a wide acquaintance / have a large circle of acquaintances / (미) have many contacts // 그는 ~를 의지하여 서울로 갔다 He went to Seoul, looking to an acquaintance for help.

친척(親戚) a relative; a relation; (남자) a kinsman; (여자) a kinswoman; (집합적) kinfolk; (영) kinsfolk. ¶가까운[먼] ~ a near [distant] relative // 핏줄이 같은 ~ a blood relative // 일가 ~ one's kith and kin / all one's relatives / one's kindred / one's relatives in blood and law[by blood and marriage] // 그녀는 나의 먼 ~이다 She is a distant[remote] relative of mine. // 그는 내게는 ~이 되는 사람입니다 He is a relative [relation] of mine. // 그는 외가 쪽 ~입니다 He is related to me on my mother's side. // 멀리 있는 ~보다 가까운 이웃이 낫다 A good neighbor is better than a relative far away. // 너희 두 사람은 ~이니 Are you two related?
● **친척 관계** kinship; relationship.

친친 [감거나 동여매는 모양] round and round (about); coil upon coil; in circles. ¶구렁이가 (먹이를) ~ 감다 wrap coils around (a prey) / loop (a victim) in several coils / throw turns of (its) body around (a prey) // 범인은 포승으로 ~ 묶였다 The criminal was trussed up with a rope.

친칠라 [동] a chinchilla.

친탁하다(親─) take after[resemble] one's father's[paternal] side of the family.

친필(親筆) one's own handwriting; an autograph; [법] a holograph. ¶~ 편지 an autograph letter (of Keats) / a holograph letter // ~로 in one's own hand [handwriting] / autographically // 그 편지는 그의 ~입니다 The letter was written by himself.

친하다(親─) [가깝다] intimate; familiar; close; friendly; near. ¶친한 친구 a good [great / close] friend / a bosom[an intimate] friend / a familiar / (구어) a chum // …과 ~ be on good[friendly] terms (with) / be friends[(구어) chums] (with) / have a close [friendly] relation (with) / (구어) be chummy[in] (with) // …과 친해지다 make friends (with) / grow intimate (with) / become familiar[intimate] (with) / get to know (a person) better // 친해 보이다[친한 것 같다] seem to be on intimate terms (with) / seem to be great friends (with) // 그는 너에게 지나치게 친하게 군다 He's too friendly[familiar] with you. // 손님에게 도가 넘게 친하게 대해서는 안 된다 Your manner toward your customers shouldn't be too familiar. // 그가 자기 젊은 비서와 친해진 것은 언제인가 When did he become intimate with his young secretary? // 나는 그와 친하게 지내고 있습니다 I am on friendly terms with him. // 우리는 서로 친한 사이다 We are on familiar terms[at home] with each other. // 그는 송 씨와 친하게 되었다 He became closely to Mr. Song. / [아는 사이가 되다] He got acquainted with Mr. Song.

친할머니(親─) (의붓할머니에 대하여) one's true[real] grandmother; one's grandmother by blood; (외할머니에 대하여) a grandmother on one's father's side; a paternal grandmother.

친할아버지(親─) (의붓할아버지에 대하여) one's true[real] grandfather; one's grandfather by blood; (외할아버지에 대하여) a grandfather on one's father's side; a paternal grandfather.

친형(親兄) one's real elder brother.

친형제(親兄弟) one's full[real / own] brothers and sisters.

친화(親和) [우호] friendship; friendly relations; [화] an affinity; an appetency. **친화하다** make[be] friends[chums] (with); get on [along] (with); [화] develop[have] an [a natural] affinity (for).
● **친화력** [화] an affinity; an appetence; an appetency.

친히(親─) [몸소] personally; in person. ¶~ 보다 see with one's own eyes // ~ 지휘하다 take[assume] personal command (of) / be in personal command (of) // ~ 방문하다 pay a visit in person / make a personal call (on a person / at a person's house).

칠(七) seven.

칠(漆) 1 lacquer; lacquering. ⇨옻칠 2 [도료] paints; paint and varnish; daubs; varnishes; [마르기] coating; varnishing(니스의); painting(페인트의). ¶니스 ~ varnishing // 페인트 ~ painting // 회 ~ plastering / whitewash // 회를 한 벽 a white-plastered wall // 회색 ~을 한 벽 a gray-plastered wall // 마무리 ~을 하다 give a final[last] coat (of) paint (to) // 식탁에 바니시로 마무리 ~을 하다 finish a table with a coat of varnish // 이 책상은 니스 ~이 아직 마르지 않았다 This desk is freshly varnished. / This desk is still wet with varnish.
● **칠 조심** (게시) Wet Paint.

칠각형(七角形) a heptagon. ¶~의 heptangular / heptagonal.

칠거지악(七去之惡) the seven valid causes for divorce.

칠기(漆器) 1 lacquer(ed)[japan] ware; lacquer(work). 2 wooden lacquer[japan] ware. ⇨칠목기

칠뜨기(七─) 〈속〉 an infant born in the 7th month of pregnancy; a half-wit. ⇨칠삭둥이

칠면조(七面鳥) [동] a turkey. ¶수~ a male turkey / a gobbler / (영) a turkey cock // 암~ a turkey hen // ~ 같은 얼굴을 하다 turn red and white.

칠목기(漆木器) wooden lacquer[japan] ware.

칠보(七寶) [불] the seven treasures(▶ gold, silver, lapis, crystal, coral, agate, pearls를 말함).

칠삭둥이(七朔─) 1 [조산아] an infant born in the 7th month of pregnancy[born three months early]. 2 [바보] a half-wit; a lackbrain.

칠생(七生) [불] seven lives.

칠석(七夕) 1 [음력 7월 7일] chilseok; the seventh evening of the seventh month of the lunar calendar. 2 the seventh day of the seventh month of the lunar calendar. ⇨칠석날(☆칠석)
● **칠석날** chilseoknal; the seventh day of the seventh month of the lunar calendar.

칠성(七星) [천] the Big Dipper. ⇨북두칠성

칠성판(七星板) a mortuary plank (containing seven holes representing the Dipper). ¶~을 지다 [죽다] die / [사지에 들다] risk death / enter the jaws of death.

칠순(七旬) 1 [70일] seventy days. 2 [70세] seventy years of age.
● **칠순 노인** a septuagenarian; an old man

칠십 [woman] at the age of seventies.

칠십(七十) seventy; (수명을 말할 때의) three-score (years) and ten; the Biblical span; (로마 숫자) LXX. ¶제~ the seventieth // ~ 대 the seventies / the 70s / the 70's // ~ 대의 노인 a septuagenarian.

칠야(漆夜) a jet-black[pitch-dark] night.

칠언(七言) [문] a composition in classical Chinese verse which has seven characters [syllables] in a line.
● **칠언 절구** a quatrain with seven words to a[each] line.

칠오조(七五調) the seven-and-five-syllable meter. ¶~의 시 a poem[verse] in seven-and-five-syllable meter.

칠월(七月) July(약어 Jul.).

칠장이(漆-) (옻칠의) a lacquerer; (페인트칠의) a painter.

칠전팔기(七顚八起) indomitability; inflexibility. ¶~의 정신 an indomitable spirit / fortitude of mind. **칠전팔기하다** fall down seven times and[but] get up eight (times); never give in to adversity; stand firm in difficulties. ¶그는 칠전팔기했다 He kept (on) bouncing back after each failure. // 칠전팔기해라 If at first you don't succeed, try, try again.

칠정(七情) the seven feelings[emotions] (=joy, anger, sorrow, fear, love, hate, lust).

칠칠맞다 decent; brisk. ⇨ **칠칠하다** ¶칠칠맞지 못한 녀석 a slovenly guy.

칠칠찮다 slovenly (appearance, work, etc.); untidy[dowdy] (dress); sloppy[slipshod] (work); unkempt (hair); loose; messy; draggletailed. ¶칠칠찮은 사람 a slovenly person / (구어) a slob // 칠칠찮은 방법으로 in a sloppy way[manner] // 그는 칠칠찮은 사람이다 He is of a careless disposition. / He is sloppy by nature. // 너 칠칠찮게 보여. 정신 좀 차려 You look slovenly. Shake up! // 그는 무엇을 시켜도 ~ He does everything in a slovenly way[slipshod manner]. // 그는 만사에 ~ He is sloppy in everything.

칠칠하다 1 [몸가짐이 깨끗하다] decent; decorous; proper. **칠칠히** decently; decorously; properly. 2 [민첩하다] brisk; smart; nimble; sharp. ¶솜씨가 ~ have nimble hands // 그렇게 칠칠하지 못한 사람은 성공을 못 한다 Such sluggard will not succeed in anything. **칠칠히** briskly; smartly; sharply.

칠판(漆板) a blackboard(흑판). ¶~을 지우다 wipe[erase / clean (off)] the blackboard // ~에 분필로 글씨를 쓰다 write on the blackboard with chalk.
● **칠판지우개** an[a chalk] eraser; a wiper.

칠하다(漆-) (그림물감·페인트를) paint; (회반죽을) plaster; (니스를) varnish; (에나멜을) enamel; (옻을) lacquer; coat; (비누·페인트 등을) apply. ¶갓 칠한 freshly-painted // 갓 칠한 벤치 a freshly-painted bench // 갓 칠한 freshly-plastered wall // 처덕처덕 ~ daub (paint) all over (the wall) / bedaub // 벽을 하얗게 ~ paint a wall white / whitewash // 식탁에 니스를 두 번 ~ give a table two coats of varnish // 마루에 밀랍을 ~ wax the floor // 타월에 비누를 ~ apply soap to a towel // 나는 집에 페인트를 칠렸다 I had my house painted. // 게임에 진 사람의 얼굴에는 먹물을 칠한다 We smear the face of the person who loses the game with ink. // 아이가 그림에 물감을 칠하고 있다 The child is coloring a picture.

칠현금(七絃琴) a heptachord; a seven-stringed lute [harp].

칠흑(漆黑) pitch-black; coal-black; jet-black. ¶~ 같은 어둠 utter [total] darkness // ~ 같은 밤 a pitch-dark [jet-black] night // ~ 같은 머리 raven(-black) hair // ~**같이 어둡다** be too dark to see an inch before one / be pitch-dark / be as dark as pitch.

칡 [식] an arrowroot; a kudzu.

칡덩굴 the vines of arrowroots. ¶~에 엉키다 get entangled in arrowroot vines.

칡범 a striped tiger; a striped tigress(암컷).

칡소 a striped ox [cow].

침 spit; spittle; sputum (pl. -ta); saliva. ¶~을 뱉다 spit (on / at) / expectorate / salivate // ~을 튀기다 froth at the mouth // ~이 마르도록 칭찬하다 be very loud in another's praises / speak in the highest terms (of) // 남의 얼굴에 ~을 뱉다 spit in a person's face / spit at a person / (비유) humiliate / insult // 자기 얼굴에 ~을 뱉다 disgrace oneself // ~을 흘리다 (口) drool / (영) dribble // 그는 손에 ~칠을 하여 밧줄을 잡았다 He wet his hand with saliva[spit] and gripped the rope. // 그는 내 얼굴에 ~을 튀기면서 지껄여 댔다 He spluttered in my face as he spoke. // 사과를 보니 입에 ~이 고였다 My mouth watered at the sight of the apple. // 그의 얼굴에 ~이라도 뱉어 주고 싶었다 I would have spat on[at] him. // 그는 ~을 꿀꺽 삼켰다 He swallowed hard. // 갓난아이가 ~을 흘리고 있다 The baby is dribbling[slobbering] // 바닥에 ~을 뱉지 마시오 (게시) No spitting on the floor.

침을 삼키다 [흘리다] [탐내다] lust (for); gloat (on / over); be envious (of).

침(針) 1 a (sewing) needle. ⇨ 바늘1 2 [시곗바늘] the hands of a clock [watch]. 3 a thorn; a prickle. ⇨ **가시1**

침(鍼) [한방의 혈을 찌르는 바늘] a needle. ¶~을 놓다 acupuncture / apply [treat with] acupuncture // 환자에게 ~을 놓다 treat a patient with acupuncture // ~을 맞다 get acupunctured / be treated with acupuncture // 삔 발에다 ~을 놓다 acupuncture a sprained ankle.

침감(沈-) a persimmon sweetened in salt water.

침강(沈降) sedimentation; precipitation. ¶적혈구 ~ 시험 a blood sedimentation test. **침강하다** precipitate; subside; settle (down).
● **침강 속도** [의] (혈액의) sedimentation rate. ¶적혈구 ~ blood sedimentation rate.

침공(侵攻) (an) invasion; a raid; an attack; an inroad. **침공하다** invade; make an invasion (upon); raid (into); attack.
● **침공 작전** invasion operations.

침구(寢具) bedclothes; bedding. (▶ 두 낱말 모두 이불 덮는 것에 쓰는데, bedding일 때에는 밑에 까는 것에도 씀) ¶~를 개다[펴다] fold up [lay out] bedclothes [bedding] // ~를 치우다 put away the bedding.

침구(鍼灸) acupuncture and moxibustion.
● **침구술** (the art of) acupuncture and moxibustion.

침낭(寢囊) a sleeping bag.

침노하다(侵攎-) invade; raid; make an inroad upon (a country); encroach upon (the territory of). ¶변경을 ~ invade the frontier districts // 남의 권리를 ~ encroach upon another's rights // 이웃 나라를 ~ invade a neighboring country.

침담그다(沈－) cure[marinate] (persimmons) in salt water.

침대(寢臺) a bedstead; a bed; (기차·기선의) a (sleeping) berth. ¶(침대차의) 상단[하단] ~ an upper[a lower] berth // 접는 식 ~ a folding bed // ~을 예약하다 book[reserve] a berth // ~에서 나오다[~에 들다] get out of [go to] bed // ~에 누워 있다 be[lie] in bed // ~에서 벌떡 일어나다 jump out of bed // ~에서 일어나다 sit up in bed.
● **침대보 / 침대 커버** a bedspread; a bedcover. **침대차** a sleeping car[carriage]; (미) a sleeper.

침독(鍼毒) poisoning caused by improper practice of acupuncture.

침략(侵掠) [약탈함] pillage; plunder; spoilage; spoliation. **침략하다** plunder; pillage; despoil; loot. ¶사람의 재물을 ~ despoil (a person) of his goods.

침략(侵略) (an) aggression; (an) invasion; an inroad. ¶경제 ~ an economic invasion // 무력 ~ an armed aggression // 직접[간접] ~ a direct[an indirect] invasion // 바다[하늘]로부터의 ~ a seaborne[an airborne] invasion // ~적(인) aggressive. **침략하다** invade; raid; make a raid (on); make an inroad (into); conquer. ¶그 군대는 이웃 나라를 침략했다 The army invaded the neighboring country.
● **침략국** an aggressor nation; an aggressor. **침략군** an invading army. **침략자** an aggressor; an invader. **침략 전쟁** a war of aggression; an aggressive war. **침략주의** a policy of aggression; an aggressive policy. **침략 행위** an act of aggression. ¶이것은 명백히 경제적 ~이다 This is clearly an act of economic invasion.

침례(浸禮) [기] baptism by immersion; immersion.
● **침례교도** a Baptist. **침례교회** the Baptist Church.

침로(針路) a course. ¶~를 벗어나다 swerve from one's course / be driven[taken] off (one's) course (by a storm) // ~를 잡다 direct[set] one's course (toward / for) // ~를 제주도로 돌리다 head for Jejudo / direct one's course toward Jejudo // ~를 북동쪽으로 잡다 take a northeasterly course // ~를 벗어나지 않도록 배를 몰다 hold one's ship on course // ~를 바꾸다 turn[change / alter] (one's) course (toward) // ~를 잘못 잡은 것 같다 I'm afraid I've taken the wrong course.

침모(針母) a seamstress; a needlewoman. ¶난 ~ a daily[live-out] seamstress // 든 ~ a resident[live-in] seamstress.

침목(枕木) (영) a (railroad) tie; a crosstie; (영) a sleeper. ¶철도 ~ a sleeper / a railroad tie // ~을 갈다 renew the ties // ~을 괴다 support with a block.

침몰(沈沒) sinking (in water); submersion; foundering(침수에 의한). ¶배는 가까스로 ~을 면했다 The ship narrowly escaped sinking. **침몰하다** sink; go down; go to the bottom; be submerged; founder. ¶배는 천천히 침몰했다 The ship sank[went down / went under the water] slowly. // 유람선은 50명의 승객을 태운 채 침몰했다 The pleasure[excursion] boat sank[went down] with 50 passengers on board. // 배는 독도 앞바다에서 침몰했다 The ship sank[went down] off Dokdo. ➔¶침몰시키다 sink[submerge] (a vessel) / send (a ship) to the bottom // 구멍을 뚫어 침몰시키다 scuttle (a ship) // 2척의 배가 어뢰로 침몰되었다 Two vessels were sunk by torpedoes.
● **침몰선** a sunken[submerged] ship. ¶~을 인양하다 salve a sunken vessel.

침묵(沈默) silence; [무언] taciturnity; reticence. ¶깊은[무거운] ~ a deep[an oppressive] silence // ~을 지키다 keep silent / observe[keep / maintain / preserve] silence / remain silent[mute / dumb] / keep one's tongue quiet // ~을 깨다 break one's[the] silence // 그들 사이에 무거운 ~이 흘렀다 An oppressive silence continued between them. // 그는 ~을 깨뜨리고 이야기하기 시작했다 He broke his silence and began to talk. // 그 일에 대해서는 모두 굳게 ~을 지키고 있었다 All of them observed a strict silence concerning the matter. **침묵하다** hold one's tongue; become silent; fall into silence. ¶그는 그 사이 죽 침묵하고 있었다 He remained [kept] silent the whole time. // 침묵하고 간과할 일이 아니다 This is not a thing to be passed over in silence. ➔¶침묵시키다 silence / put[reduce] (a person) to silence / (의론으로) argue (a person) into silence // 그 대성일갈(大聲一喝)이 그를 침묵시켰다 The thundering cry made him hold his tongue [(구어) shut him up].

침방(寢房) a bedroom. ⇨ ➔ 침실

침범(侵犯) (영토의) (an) invasion; encroachment; intrusion; (권리의) violation; infringement. ¶국경 ~ a border[frontier] violation // 타국 영토 ~ the invasion of another country. **침범하다** invade; raid; make a raid upon; (권리 등을) violate; infringe on; (en)trench on; trespass on; encroach [intrude] on. ¶권한을 ~ infringe upon (a person's) authority // 사생활을 ~ violate [infringe upon] (a person's) privacy // 인권을 ~ violate personal rights // 국적 불명의 비행기가 한국의 영공을 침범했다 An airplane of unknown nationality violated Korean airspace.

침봉(針峯) (꽃꽂이의) a frog.
침상(針狀) ¶~의 needle-shaped / pointed.
침상(寢牀) a couch; a cot; a bed(stead).
침샘 a salivary gland.
침소(寢所) a sleeping place; a bedchamber; a bedroom.

침소봉대(針小棒大) exaggeration; overstatement; magnification. **침소봉대하다** exaggerate; magnify; overstate; aggrandize; overdo; overshoot oneself; make a mountain (out) of a molehill. ¶침소봉대하여 with exaggeration / exaggeratedly // 자기 고생을 침소봉대하여 말하다 exaggerate[overstate] one's troubles // 그는 언제나 침소봉대하여 말하는 버릇이 있다 He always makes a mountain out of a molehill.

침수(浸水) inundation; flood(ing); submersion. **침수하다** be flooded[inundated / submerged]; be under water; (배가) spring a leak; leak; make water. ➔¶(배가) 침수되다 be[become] waterlogged // 가옥이 마루 밑[위]까지 침수되었다 The house was flooded up to[above] the floorboards. // 그 배는 침수

침술

되기 시작하여 5분 만에 가라앉았다 The boat began to leak[be filled with water] and sank in five minutes.
● 침수 가옥 submerged house; houses under water. 침수 지역 a flooded[submerged] area.
침술(鍼術) acupuncture.
● 침술사 an acupuncturist.
침식(侵蝕) erosion; (특히 금속의) corrosion. ¶비[바람/물]에 의한 ~ rain[wind/water] erosion∥비바람의 ~ corrosion of the elements∥토양 ~ soil erosion∥풍우에 의한 토양의 ~이 심하다 The soil has been badly eroded by wind and rain.∥이 골짜기는 빙하의 ~으로 형성되었다 This valley was formed by glacial erosion. 침식하다 erode; corrode; eat away; (물이) wash out; (바다가 육지를) gain[encroach] on. ¶강이 바위를 침식해서 깊은 곳을 이루고 있다 The river has won deep channels through the soft rock. →¶금속은 산(酸)에 침식되기 쉽다 Metals are easily corroded by acids.
● 침식 작용 erosion; erosive action. ¶바닷물의 ~ the inroads of the sea.
침식(寢食) food and sleep; one's bodily comfort. ¶~을 잊고 without sparing oneself / heart and soul / devotedly∥~을 함께하다 share board and room (with) / live under the same roof (with)∥그녀는 ~을 잊고 자식을 간호했다 She was so busy nursing her child that she had no time to eat or sleep.∥나는 그와 2년간 ~을 함께했다 I lived under the same roof with him for two years.∥그는 ~을 잊고 연구에 몰두했다 He devoted himself to his research. / He was absorbed in his research.∥그는 ~을 잊고 회사의 원상 회복에 있는 힘을 다 쏟았다 He poured all his energy into putting[He almost forgot to eat or sleep in trying to put] the company back on its feet.
침실(寢室) a bedroom; a bedchamber; a sleeping room. ¶~ 겸 거실 a bed-sitting room.
침엽(針葉) [식] a needle (leaf); a needle-shaped leaf.
● 침엽수 [식] a needle-leaf[coniferous] tree; a conifer.
침울하다(沈鬱−) melancholy; dismal; gloomy; depressed; heavyhearted. ¶침울한 안색 a gloomy expression∥침울한 표정 a depressed[melancholy] look∥침울한 목소리로 in a gloomy voice∥침울해지다 mope / be depressed∥침울해 있다 be gloomy and depressed / be moping∥(구어) really down / in low spirits∥그것을 꼭 해야 한다고 생각하니 마음이 ~ It makes me feel heavyhearted[heavy at heart / despondent] to think I must do it.∥그녀는 침울해 보인다 She looks blue[depressed / melancholy].∥그는 아들의 거동 때문에 침울해 보인다 He looks gloomy[disheartened] because of his son's behavior.∥무엇 때문에 넌 침울한 얼굴이냐 What makes you pull a long face[look so glum]? / (속어) Why do you look so down in the dumps?∥어머님은 침울한 채 돌아오셨다 Mother looked depressed[dejected] when she came back. / Mother came back with a melancholy look.
침윤(浸潤) (액체의) permeation; infiltration; saturation. ¶폐 ~ infiltration of the lungs.

침윤하다 permeate (in/through); infiltrate [soak] (into).
침의(鍼醫) an acupuncturist.
침입(侵入) (타국에의) an invasion; (급습) an incursion; a raid(▶ invasion은 침입하여 거기에 머물러 있음. incursion, raid는 모두 습격한 다음 철수하는 것을 나타냄); (남의 집에 대한) an intrusion; (a) trespass(무단 침입).
¶가택 ~ (죄) housebreaking / (an action of) trespass∥구내[잔디밭] ~을 금함 Keep off the premises (the grass). 침입하다 (타국에) invade; make an invasion (upon); make a raid (on); raid (into); (남의 집에) break (into); (사유지 등에) trespass (on). ¶이웃 나라에 ~ invade a neighboring country∥남의 세력권을 ~ encroach on a person's territory∥이웃집 밭에 불법으로 ~ trespass on one's neighbor's fields∥강도단이 아침 일찍 은행에 침입했다 Early in the morning a group of burglars robbed[broke into / made a raid on] the bank.∥도둑은 창문으로 집 안에 침입했다 The robber broke into the house by [through] the window.∥몇 대의 전차가 갑자기 아군 진지에 침입했다 Some tanks suddenly carried out an invasion upon[made a raid on / raided into] our positions.∥그 비행기는 타국의 영공에 침입했다 The plane trespassed upon[violated] another country's airspace.
● 침입군 an invading army. 침입자 an invader; a trespasser; an intruder. ¶무단 ~는 고발함 Trespassers will be prosecuted.
침잠하다(沈潛−) 1 [물속에 가라앉다] sink [settle] (to the bottom). 2 [사색하거나 몰입하다] be lost[absorbed / engrossed] in thought. ¶그는 사색에 침잠해 있다 He is lost [engrossed / absorbed] in thought. →¶가슴 속 깊이 침잠된 슬픔 a sorrow deep (down) inside of him.
침쟁이(鍼−) an acupuncturist; an acupuncturator.
침전(沈澱) precipitation; deposition; sedimentation; settlement. 침전하다 settle (to the bottom); precipitate; be precipitated [deposited]. ¶고형물은 금방 침전한다 Solid matter soon settles.∥플라스크 안에 녹말이 침전했다 Starch settled[formed a deposit] in the flask. →¶밑바닥에 뭔가 침전되어 있다 Something is deposited at the bottom.
● 침전물 a deposit; a sediment; a precipitate; a lodgement; settlings; lees(찌꺼기). ¶때로 밑바닥에 흰 ~을 볼 수 있으나 해는 없습니다 (병 등의 주의 사항) White sediment [A white deposit] may form[be found] at the bottom, but it is harmless. 침전지(−池) a settling pond; a settling[depositing] basin [reservoir].
침주다(鍼−) [침을 놓다] acupuncture; apply [treat with] acupuncture.
침질(鍼−) acupuncture. 침질하다 perform acupuncture.
침착(沈着) composure; self-possession; presence of mind; calmness; coolness. ¶~을 잃다[유지하다] lose[keep] one's head[presence of mind] / (구어) blow[keep] one's cool∥~을 되찾다 recover[regain] one's presence of mind / (구어) pull oneself together∥우리는 옆집에 불이 났을 때 ~을 잃고 허둥댔다 We lost our presence of mind when the fire broke out next door. 침착하다

composed; self-possessed; calm; cool; collected; serene; (서술적) have presence of mind. ¶침착한 표정 a collected look∥침착한 사람 a self-possessed person / a calm (and collected) person∥침착한 성격 a staid character∥침착한 태도 (with) a calm attitude∥침착한 태도를 보이다 bear oneself with coolness / show presence of mind∥그는 침착한 태도를 잃지 않았다 He never lost his poise. / He remained unperturbed[calm].∥그는 위험에 직면해서도 침착했다 He remained calm and collected in (the) face of danger. **침착히** calmly; coolly; composedly; with composure; with presence of mind. ¶그는 ~ 행동했다 He acted with composure[self-possession].

●**침착성** composure; equanimity; self-possession; presence of mind; poise. ¶~을 잃지 않다 remain composed / be[remain] absolutely calm and self-possessed.

침체(沈滯) stagnation; inactivity; dullness; slackness. ¶~ 상태에 있다 be dull / be stagnant / be depressed∥시황은 다소 ~ 상태다 The market is rather depressed [inactive / stagnant].∥나는 마침내 오랜 ~ 에서 벗어날 수 있었다 I finally managed to get out of [(문어) emerge from] my long slump[depression].∥주가는 수요 부족으로 ~ 상태에 있다 Stock prices are held in check for lack of sufficient demand. **침체하다** stagnate; become sluggish[dull]. ¶침체해 있다 be stagnant[stagnating] / be dull[slack / inactive]. ➔¶침체된 시장 a dull[slack] market∥침체시키다 depress (trade) / cause the stagnation (of)∥선수들의 사기는 완전히 침체되었다 The members of the team were utterly depressed[dejected].∥주식 시장이 몹시 침체되어 있다 The stock market is extremely dull[stagnant / inactive].∥이 팀은 최하위에서 침체되어 있다 This team is floundering at the bottom of the league.

침침하다(沈沈-) **1** [어둡다] gloomy; somber; dim. ¶침침한 방 안 a dimly-lit[ill-lighted] room∥침침한 곳에서 in the gloom[semi-dark]∥침침한 등불 밑에서 독서하다 read in the dim[poor] light of a lamp. **2** (눈이) dim(med); dim-sighted; blurred; bleared; misty; purblind. ¶눈이 침침하다 have dim eyes[sight] / one's eyes glaze over∥눈물로 눈이 침침해지다 dim[be blurred] with tears∥나이를 먹으면 눈이 침침해진다 Our sight grows dim with age.∥눈이 침침해서 모든 것이 흐릿하다 Everything looks blurred to my dim eyes.

침탈(侵奪) [법] (부동산의) disseisin; disseizin. **침탈하다** disseise; disseize. ¶재산을 ~ dispossess (a person) of property.

침통(鍼筒) a case[box] for acupuncture needles.

침통하다(沈痛-) grave; serious; anguished; sorrow-stricken; sad; mournful. ¶침통한 얼굴로 with a sad look∥침통해하다 be distressed[anguished] (at) / grieve (at / over) / one's heart aches (at)∥그는 침통한 어조로 그 결과를 발표했다 He announced the result in a sad[grave / serious] tone.∥그는 침통한 모습으로 앉아 있었다 He looked sad[sorrowful / mournful / grave / serious].∥아버지를 잃은 그녀의 마음은 침통하였다 Her heart was heavy with sorrow because of the loss of her father.

침투(浸透) permeation; infiltration; penetration. ¶마르크스 사상의 ~ the infiltration of Marxist ideas∥공산주의의 ~ infiltration of communism (into)∥경제 ~ economic penetration. **침투하다** permeate; infiltrate; penetrate; spread itself (into / through). ¶정계에 ~ infiltrate (into) political circles∥용액이 천에 침투했다 The solution permeated the cloth.∥이곳에 묻힌 위험한 화학 약품이 흙에 침투하기 시작했다 The dangerous chemicals buried here have begun to seep into the soil.∥동양 철학이 미국 젊은이들의 마음에 침투하다 Eastern philosophy filtered into the hearts of young Americans.∥젊은이들에게 그 디자인이 침투하기 시작하고 있다 The design is beginning to spread[(구어) catch on] among young people.∥그들은 한국 제품이 그들 나라의 시장에 침투하는 것을 두려워한다 They fear Korean penetration of their markets.

●**침투 작전** infiltration operation.

침팬지 [동] a chimpanzee.

침하(沈下) subsidence; sinking; settlement. ¶지반 ~ ground sinkage[subsidence]. **침하하다** subside; sink; dip(지층이). ¶지반이 10 센티 침하했다 The ground has sunk ten centimeters.∥토대가 지진으로 침하했다 The foundation sank because of an earthquake.∥그 지역의 지반이 서서히 침하하고 있다 The land in the area is gradually sinking[subsiding].

침해(侵害) infringement; violation; encroachment; trespass; invasion; obstruction; disturbance. ¶저작권 ~ an infringement of copyright∥사생활의 ~ an invasion of a person's privacy∥인권의 ~는 헌법에 위배된다 The violation of human rights is against the Constitution. **침해하다** infringe (on); encroach[trespass / trench] (on); violate; disturb(권리를). ¶침해할 수 없는 inviolable ∥권한을 ~ impinge upon (a person's) authority∥그는 특허권을 침해했다 He infringed (on) the patent right.∥그는 나의 사유 재산을 침해했다 He trespassed on my private property. ➔¶사상 및 양심의 자유는 침해되어서는 안 된다 We must not encroach upon[infringe upon] freedom of thought and conscience.

●**침해자** a trespasser.

침흘리개 a slobberer; a slaverer; a driveler; a drooler.

칩 [물] a chip.

칩거(蟄居) keeping the house; seclusion. **칩거하다** keep the house; keep[stay] indoors; confine oneself in one's house; shut oneself up (in a room).

칩떠보다 [눈을 치뜨고 보다] cast an upward glance (at); lift (up) one's eyes; cast up one's eyes (to).

칫솔(齒-) a toothbrush. ¶~로 이를 닦다 brush one's teeth.

칭송(稱頌) praise; applause; admiration; eulogy; laudation. ¶그 고귀한 행동은 사람들로부터 ~을 받았다 This noble deed won him the admiration of the people. **칭송하다** admire; applaud; laud; extol; commend; praise. ¶고인의 덕을 ~ eulogize the virtue of the deceased∥극구 ~ be loud in (a person's) praises / extol[laud] (a person)

칭얼거리다 sky-high[to the skies] / speak in highest terms of (a person).

칭얼거리다 fret; be peevish[fussy]; whine; whimper; cry peevishly.

칭얼칭얼 fretfully; peevishly; whining; whimpering; fussing. ¶어린애가 ~ 울다 a baby cries peevishly. **칭얼칭얼하다** fret; be peevish[fussy]. ⇨ 칭얼거리다

칭찬(稱讚) praise; applause; admiration; commendation; laudation. ¶~의 말 a word of praise (for) / a eulogy // 이웃의 ~이 자자한 사람 the center of appreciation in the neighborhood // 그 작품은 많은 비평가의 ~을 받았다 The work won the praise of many critics. // 그녀는 그를 ~의 눈으로 바라보았다 She looked up at him with admiration. // 그 피아니스트가 독주를 끝내자 ~의 박수갈채를 보냈다 They applauded the pianist when he finished playing. // 그는 모두의 ~을 받고 우쭐해졌다 Applauded by all of them, he felt quite proud of himself. **칭찬하다** praise; commend; admire; extol; applaud; eulogize; compliment; laud; pay a tribute of praise to; speak well[highly] of (a person); speak in high terms of (a person). ¶칭찬할 만한 행위 an admirable[a praiseworthy] deed // 극구 ~ speak very highly of / cry[praise / talk] up / sing[chant] the praises of / extol[laud] (a person) sky-high[to the skies] / be loud in (a person's) praise // 사람들은 소년의 선행을 극구 칭찬했다 People praised [(문어) lauded] the boy to the skies for his good deed. // 사람들은 이구동성으로 그 친절한 의사를 칭찬했다 They chorused their heartfelt praise of the kindhearted doctor. // 모두가 그를 칭찬했다 Everybody praised him. / Everybody admired[expressed admiration for] him. // 그의 행위는 칭찬할 만하다 His conduct is worthy of praise[praiseworthy]. / His action is greatly to his credit. // 그는 그 학생의 정직성을 칭찬했다 He praised the pupil for his honesty. // 그녀의 헌신은 아무리 칭찬해도 모자라다 We cannot praise her selflessness too much. / We cannot overpraise her devotion to her work. // 평론가들은 이 신진 작가를 칭찬하고 있다 Critics speak highly of this new writer. // 그것은 별로 칭찬할 만한 것이 못 된다 There is nothing commendable about it. // 사람들은 그의 용기 있는 행동을 칭찬했다 People applauded his courageous conduct. / People were loud in praise of his brave deed. // 그는 그녀의 훌륭한 지성을 칭찬하고 인사말을 맺었다 He concluded his remarks with words of admiration for her dazzling intelligence. ➔¶그들의 노력은 칭찬 받을 만하다 Their effort is praiseworthy [laudable]. // 칭찬받고 화내는 사람은 없다 Nobody feels offended at compliments.

칭하다(稱一) **1** [부르다] call; name; term; designate. ¶A라고 칭하는 남자 a man who gives the name of A / (그 이름의) a man of [by] the name of A // …이라 칭해지고 있다 be said[reputed / cracked up] to be … // 진정한 교육자라고 칭할 만한 사람은 극히 드물다 There are very few, if any, who really deserve the name of educationist. // 이것을 「완전 고용」이라고 칭한다 To this is given the term of "full employment."
2 [사칭하다] pretend; feign; [주장하다] claim; [항변하다] plead. ¶렘브란트의 그림이라고 칭하는 것 what purports to be a Rembrandt // …이라 칭하여 on[under] the plea[pretext] of (illness) / under (the) pretense of / representing oneself as (a newspaper man) // 왕이라고 ~ assume the title of king // 친척이라고 ~ claim to be (a person's) relative.

칭호(稱號) [작위·관직명 등] a title; [명칭] a name; an appellation; a designation; [학위] a degree. ¶…에게 ~를 주다 give a person a title // 「위대한 화가」라는 명예 ~ the honorary title of "a great painter."

ㅋ

카 [맛·냄새 등이 맵거나 독할 때 내는 소리] Phew!; Wow!; Ouch!
카나리아 [동] a canary; a canary bird.
카나마이신 [항생 물질의 하나] kanamycin.
카네이션 [식] a carnation; a clove pink. ¶빨간 ~을 가슴에 달고 있다 wear a red carnation on one's breast.
카논 [음] a canon.
카누 a canoe. ¶~를 젓는 사람 a canoeist // ~를 타고 내려가다 canoe down (a river) // ~를 젓다 paddle a canoe.
● **카누 경주** a canoe race; a canoeing event.
카니발 a carnival.
카덴차 [음] a cadenza; cadence.
카드 1 (일반적인) a card; a slip (of paper)(종이쪽지). ¶백지 ~ a blank card // 수강 등록 ~ a course registration card // 자료를 ~에 적어 두다 put down the data on cards // 단어를 ~로 분류[정리]하다 classify[arrange] the words in order on cards // ~를 철하다 file cards // (물건 값을 지불하면서) ~ 받습니까 Do you accept credit cards? // 나는 그 신발을 비자 ~로 구입했다 I charged the shoes on Visa. 2 [트럼프의 패] a card.
● **카드놀이** card playing; a game of cards; a card game. ¶~를 하는 사람 a cardplayer // ~에서 이기다[지다] win[lose] at cards // ~를 하다 play cards / have[play] a game of cards // ~를 하고 있다 be at cards // ~를 잘하다 be good at cards / be a good card player. **카드 목록** a card catalog[file]. **카드 번호** [색인] a card number[index].
카드뮴 [화] cadmium(기호 Cd).
● **카드뮴 중독** cadmium poisoning.
카디건 a cardigan (sweater).
카라반 [대상(隊商)] a caravan. ¶~을 짜서 아프리카로 여행하다 caravan through Africa.
카랑카랑하다 1 (날씨가) clear and cold. 2 (목소리가) clear and high-pitched; shrill; piercing; penetrating.
카레 curry.
● **카레라이스** curry and rice.
카로틴 [화] carotin; carotene.
카르복시기 (-基) [화] a carboxyl group [radical].
카르스트 지형 (-地形) [지] karst.
카르텔 (㉭Kartell) a cartel. ¶불황 ~ a (business) recession cartel // 수출 ~ an export cartel // ~을 만들다 form[establish] a cartel.
카리스마 [종] (a) charisma (pl. -mata); (a) charism (pl. ~s). ¶~적 charismatic.
카리에스 [의] caries. ¶요추 ~ lumbar caries // 척추 ~ caries[tuberculous osteitis] of the vertebrae / spinal caries / Pott's disease.
카메라 a camera. ¶소형 ~ a miniature camera / a minicam(era) // 일안[이안] 리플렉스 ~ a single-lens[twin-lens] reflex camera // ~를 들이대고 with a camera at the ready // ~에 필름을 넣다 load a camera // 성을 ~로 찍다[~에 담다] take a picture [photograph] of a castle // ~로 찰칵 찍다 click a camera / snap a camera (at) // ~를 대다 [겨냥하다] aim one's camera / level the camera (at) // 그는 ~에 익숙해 있다[서툴다] He is camera-wise[camera-shy].
● **카메라맨** (주로 영화·TV의) a cameraman; (스틸 사진의) a photographer. ¶신문사의 ~ a press photographer. **카메라 앵글** a camera angle. ¶이 사진은 ~이 좋았다 This picture was taken from a good angle.
카멜레온 [동] a chameleon. ¶~ 같은 사람 [변덕스러운 사람] a chameleon / a fickle [an inconstant] person.
카무플라주 a camouflage. **카무플라주하다** camouflage (a war plant); [위장하다] disguise (one's real intention); dissemble. ¶카무플라주한 전차 a camouflaged tank // ~로 ~ veil[disguise] one's true intentions // 그는 자신의 무지를 허세로 카무플라주했다 He hid [concealed] his ignorance by bluffing.
카바레 a cabaret. ¶~의 댄서 a cabaret dancer.
카바이드 [화] carbide(▶ calcium carbide의 속칭).
카본 [탄소봉] a carbon (rod).
● **카본지** (-紙) carbon paper.
카뷰레터 [기화기] a carburet(t)or.
카빈총 (-銃) a carbine (rifle). ¶자동 ~ a machine carbine.
카세인 [화] casein.
카세트 a cassette.
● **카세트테이프** a cassette tape. **카세트테이프 리코더** a cassette tape recorder.
카센터 (˟car center) a car[auto] repair shop; a body shop; a garage.
카스텔라 (㉠castella) sponge cake.
카스트 [인도의 신분제] a caste.
카시오페이아자리 [천] Cassiopeia.
카약 a kayak.
카우보이 a cowboy; [미] a ranchman (pl. -men); (미국 구어) a cow-puncher; a cow-poke.
● **카우보이 모자** a cowboy hat.
카운슬러 a counselor; [영] a counsellor.
카운슬링 counseling; [영] counselling.
카운터 (은행·상점 등의) a (service) counter; a cash counter; a counting house[[미] room]; (출입구에 있는) a check-out counter; (호텔의) the (front) desk; the reception desk. ¶~에 앉다 sit at the counter // 귀중품을 ~에 맡기다 check one's valuables at the front desk // ~에 문의해 주십시오 Ask at the counter.
카운터블로 [권투] a counterblow.
카운트 a count; counting. ¶풀 ~ a full count // 저 투구는 노 ~가 되었다 That pitch didn't count. // 심판원은 ~를 시작했다 The referee began the count. // 투 스트라이크 스리 볼이다 The count is three balls and two strikes. // 그는 ~ 투에서 일어섰다 He got up at the count of two. **카운트하다** take the count; count (the score).
● **카운트다운** (로켓 발사 시 등의) a countdown. ¶로켓 발사 전의 ~이 시작되었다 The countdown for the rocket launch has begun.

카지노 a casino (pl. ~s).
카카오 [카카오나무·열매] a cacao (tree [bean]).
카키색 (-色) khaki. ¶그는 ~의 옷을 입고 있다 He is dressed in khaki.
카타르 [의] catarrh. ¶[비][장] ~ nasal[intestinal] catarrh // 위 ~ catarrh of the stomach // 대장 ~ catarrh of the large intestine.
카타르시스 [그] (a) catharsis.
카탈로그 [영] a catalogue. ¶가격이 적힌 ~ a priced catalog // 신제품을 ~에 올리다 put new products in a catalog // 냉장고 ~를 한 부 보내 주십시오 Please send me a copy of the catalog of refrigerators.
카테고리 [철] a category.
카톨릭 →가톨릭
카투사 KATUSA; Katusa(▶ Korean Augmentation Troops to the United States Army의 약어). ¶~는 미군과 합동 근무를 한다 Katusas are on a joint duty with U.S. soldiers.
카트리지 a cartridge.
카퍼레이드 (˘car parade) [환영·축하 차량 행렬] a motorcade. (▶ car parade는 차 전시를 위한 차량 행렬을 가리킴)
카페 a café; coffeehouse.
카페리 a car ferry.
카페인 caffeine. ¶탈~ 커피 caffeine-free coffee // ~을 제거하다 remove caffeine from (coffee) / decaffeinate.
카페테리아 a cafeteria; a self-service restaurant.
카펫 a carpet. ¶~을 깔다 spread a carpet / carpet (a room / a floor).
카폰 a car phone.
카풀 carpooling.
●**카풀제** a car pool.
카프리치오 [음] a capriccio.
카피 a copy. ¶이 편지의 ~를 한 장 만들어 주세요 Please make a copy of this letter.
●**카피라이터** a copywriter.
칵칵 with coughs (to clear one's throat); (토하려고) retching. **칵칵하다** keep coughing (to clear one's throat). ⇨칵칵거리다
칵칵거리다 keep coughing (to clear one's throat); (토하려고) keck; retch.
칵테일 [혼성주] a cocktail.
●**칵테일글라스** a cocktail glass. **칵테일파티** a cocktail party.
칸 1 [방을 세는 단위] a room; a chamber. ¶네 ~ 집 a four-room(ed) house. **2** [칸막이] a partition; a compartment. ¶방의 일부를 ~을 막다 partition off a part of a room. **3** [공백] (a) space; a blank (space). ¶알맞은 전치사를 써서 빈 ~을 채워라 Fill (in) the blanks with appropriate prepositions.
칸나 [식] a canna (flower).
칸델라¹ [광도의 단위] a candela(약어 cd).
칸델라² (@kandelaar) [석유등] a (kerosene) hand lantern.
칸막이 [막음] partitioning; screening off; [막는 것] a screen; a partition. ¶판자 ~ a wooden partition. **칸막이하다** partition; screen off; put up a (board) screen. ¶칸막이한 방 a partitioned room.
칸살 1 [면적] the size of a room(usually 7 or 9 feet square). ¶~ 넓은[좁은] 방 a large [small] room. **2** [거리] a space; an interval; distance.
칸초네 [음] a canzone (pl. -ni).

칸칸이 [방마다] (in) each [every] room; from room to room; room by room. ¶~ 사람이 들어 있다 Every room is occupied.
칸타빌레 [음] cantabile.
칸타타 [음] a cantata.
칼¹ **1** [나이프] a knife (pl. knives); (선원용) a jackknife; (부엌칼) a kitchen knife; (식탁용) a table knife; [단검·비수] a dagger; a dirk; a stiletto (pl. ~(e)s). ¶면도 ~ a razor // 조각 ~ a burin / an engraver // 주머니 ~ a pocket knife / a penknife // 과일 깎는 ~ a fruit knife // ~로 찌르다 stab (a person) with a dagger / plunge a dagger [knife] (into a person's breast) / knife (a person) // ~로 베다 cut with a knife // ~이 잘 든다[안 든다] The knife cuts well [won't cut].
2 [검] a sword; a saber(군도·지휘도). ¶~ 가는 사람 a sword-sharpener [-grinder] // ~을 차고 with a sword at the [one's] side // ~을 들이대고 (rob a person of his money) at the point of the sword // ~ 솜씨가 좋다 [어설프다] be a good [poor] swordsman // ~ 쓰는 법을 배우다 learn how to use a sword // ~을 차다 wear [carry] a sword (at one's side) // ~을 갈다 sharpen [burnish] a sword // ~을 뽑다 draw [unsheathe] a sword / whip out a sword (힘차게) // ~을 휘두르다 brandish [flourish] a sword // ~을 푹 찌르다 drive a sword home / run [thrust] a sword (through the body) // ~을 버리고 붓을 잡다 give up the sword for the pen // 내리치는 ~을 받아넘기다 parry [turn aside / ward off] a sword thrust.
칼(을) 맞다 suffer a sword-stroke. ¶칼을 맞아 죽다 be put to the sword / fall a victim to the sword of (an assassin) / die [beneath] the sword (of an enemy).
칼² [형틀] a cang(ue); a pillory. ¶~을 씌우다 put (a person) in the pillory / cangue.
칼(을) 쓰다 wear a cangue; be put in pillory; be pilloried. ¶칼을 쓴 죄인 a cangued criminal [convict].
칼국수 *kalguksu*; (hand-made) chopped noodles.
칼깃 a flight feather; a remex (pl. remiges); (집합적) the pinion.
칼끝 the point of a sword.
칼날 the edge [blade] of a sword [knife]. ¶~을 세우다 put an edge (on) / give an edge (to) / edge / sharpen (a knife) // ~이 무디다 The edge of a knife is dull [blunt].
칼데라 [지] a caldera.
칼등 the back of a sword [knife].
칼라 (깃) a (shirt) collar. ¶소프트[더블/케이프] ~ a soft [turn-down / cape] collar.
칼럼 a column.
칼럼니스트 a columnist.
칼로리 [물] a calorie [calory] (약어 Cal.). ¶킬로그램 ~ a kilogram calorie / a kilocalorie // ~가 높은 음식 calorific food // ~가 낮은 low-caloric (soda pop) // 하루 1,800~를 유지하다 maintain an average of 1,800 calories [maintain as much as a 1,800 caloric diet] per day // 이 식품은 ~가 높다 [낮다] This food is high [low] in calories. // 그들은 하루 3,000~의 식사를 한다 They consume 3,000 calories a day.
●**칼로리 섭취량** caloric [calorie] intake (of 1,800 units). **칼로리 함유량** caloric content. ¶~이 높은 식품 food with higher caloric

칼륨 content.
칼륨 [화] potassium; kalium(기호 K).
● **칼륨염** a potassic salt.
칼리 (@kali) **1** [화] potassium. ⇨ =칼륨 **2** a potassic salt. ⇨ =칼륨염(⇨칼륨)
칼리프 [이슬람 제국 주권자의 칭호] a caliph.
칼립소 [음] a calypso.
칼부림 wielding a sword[knife]; bloodshed.
칼부림하다 wield[brandish / flourish] a sword at (a person).
칼새 [동] a white-rumped swift.
칼슘 [화] calcium. ¶**염화**[산화]~ calcium chloride[oxide] // **인산**[황산 / 탄산]~ calcium phosphate[sulphate / carbonate] // ~분을 함유하다 contain calcium.
● **칼슘 비누** calcium soap.
칼자국 a sword cut.
칼자루 the hilt of a sword; the haft of a dagger; the handle of a knife.
칼자루(를) 잡다[쥐다] have the (final[last]) say. ¶칼자루를 쥔 사람은 그다 He is the one with the say.
칼잡이 1 a butcher. ⇨ =백정 **2** a swordsman. ⇨ =검객
칼질 cutting. **칼질하다** cut; do cutting.
칼집 (검의) a sheath; (주머니칼의) a case. ¶~에서 칼을 뽑다 draw one's sword // 칼을 ~에 넣다 sheathe one's sword.
칼춤 a sword dance. ¶~을 추다 perform a sword dance.
칼침 (-鍼) the thrust of a knife[dagger / sword]. ¶~을 놓다 give a thrust (at a person) with a knife[dagger / sword] // ~을 맞다 get stabbed / suffer a sword stroke.
칼칼하다 be thirsty. ⇨킬킬하다
캄보 [소규모의 재즈 악단] a combo.
캄브리아기 (-紀) [지] the Cambrian period [system]; the Cambrian.
캄캄하다 1 [어둡다] pitch-dark; (as) dark as pitch; (as) dark as midnight. ¶터널 속은 칠흑같이 캄캄했다 It was pitch-dark[as dark as pitch] in the tunnel. // 캄캄해서 아무것도 보이지 않았다 Nothing was to be seen in the utter[total] darkness.
2 [암담하다] dark; gloomy; dismal; somber. ¶앞길이 ~ I can't see ahead at all. / [희망이 없다] The future looks black [hopeless]. // 그 말을 들으니 눈앞이 캄캄해졌다 When I heard it, I was plunged into despair. // 우리의 앞날은 ~ Our prospects are black[gloomy]. / We have a dark future before us.
3 [모르다] (서술적) be ignorant (of); be not familiar[well acquainted] (with); be ill informed (of); be a stranger (to). ¶세상 일에 ~ know nothing about the world / know but little of the world / be ignorant of[inexperienced in] the ways of the world // 그는 법률에 대해서는 ~ His knowledge of law is very limited[poor].
캅셀 →캡슐
캉캉 [프랑스의 춤] (프) the cancan. ¶~을 추다 do the cancan.
캐내다 dig up; excavate. ⇨파내다
캐다 1 dig up; unearth; (식물을) gather; pick. ¶금을 ~ dig gold / 나물을 ~ dig up[gather] edible plants // 약초를 ~ pick[gather] medicinal herbs.
2 [알아내려고 따지다] examine closely; pry into (a person's secret); peck[pick] at (a person's faults). ¶캐기 좋아하는 inquisitive / prying / curious / nos(e)y // 비밀을 ~ pry into a secret / probe[trace] a secret / ferret [worm] out a secret / 신원을 ~ inquire [look] into (a person's) antecedents[birth and parentage] / look into (a person's) family background / check up (a person's) record // 사건의 근원을 ~ go to the root of a matter / probe a matter to the bottom // 꼬치꼬치 ~ split hairs(세밀히 구별하다) / scrutinize / rake / ransack / poke and pry / dig [pry / delve] into // 넌 참 캐기를 좋아하는구나 How inquisitive you are! / You always want to know too much. // 그들은 나의 과거를 캐기 시작했다 They began poking around into my past.

캐드 CAD(▶ computer-aided design의 약어).
캐디 a caddie; a caddy.
캐러멜 (a) caramel.
캐럴 a (Christmas) carol.
캐럿 [보석 무게의 단위] a carat; [금의 순도] (미) a karat; (영) a carat. ¶7~의 다이아몬드 a diamond of 7 carats / a 7-carat diamond / 14~의 금 fourteen-karat gold / 14k gold.
캐리커처 a caricature.
캐릭터 1 [성격] (a) character. **2** [소설·만화에 나오는 인물·동물] a character.
● **캐릭터 상품** products featuring popular comic characters.
캐묻다 question closely; press[drive] a question home; press (a person) for an answer; cross-question; cross-examine. ¶일의 진상을 ~ make sure of[(문어) ascertain] the truth of a matter // 우리는 돈의 출처에 대해서 그에게 꼬치꼬치 캐물었다 We questioned him in detail[closely] about the source of the money. // 그녀는 내 부모에 대해 꼬치꼬치 캐물었다 She kept asking all sorts of questions[She persistently questioned me in the most detailed way] about my parents.
캐비닛 a cabinet.
캐비지 [양배추] a cabbage.
캐스터 a caster; a newscaster; (미) an anchorman.
캐스터네츠 [음] castanets. ¶~를 치다 click castanets.
캐스트 [배역] the cast (of characters). ¶이 영화는 호화 ~다 This movie has a star-studded cast.
캐스팅 보트 (의장이 갖는) the casting vote; (소수파가 쥐는) the say. ¶의장은 ~를 행사했다 The chairman used his casting vote.
캐시미어 cashmere. ¶~ **코트** a cashmere coat.
캐시 카드 a cash card; a money card(▶ 은행에 따라 말하는 방법이 다름). ¶~로 돈을 인출하다 withdraw money with a cash card.
캐어묻다 question closely. ⇨캐묻다
캐주얼 [평상시 입는 옷·구두] casuals.
● **캐주얼슈즈** casual shoes. **캐주얼웨어** casual wear[clothes].
캐처 a catcher. ¶그는 자이언츠의 ~이다 He catches[is a catcher] for the Giants.
캐치볼 (*catch ball) playing catch. ¶~을 하다 play[have a] catch.
캐치프레이즈 a catch phrase.
캐치하다 catch. ¶극비 정보를 캐치했다 We got hold of[obtained] top secret information.

캐터필러 〔무한궤도〕 a caterpillar [tread / track]. ¶~ 트랙터 a caterpillar tractor.
캑 with a cough or sputter (to get something out of one's throat).
캑캑 with repeated coughs or splutters; hacking away. 캑캑하다 cough and cough. ⇨캑캑거리다
캑캑거리다 cough and cough.
캔디 (미) (a piece of) candy; (영) sweets.
캔버스 (미) canvas.
캔슬 (a) cancellation. 캔슬하다 cancel. ¶예약[계약]을 ~ cancel a reservation [contract].
캘리퍼스 〔측정 용구〕 (a pair of) cal(l)ipers. ¶내측[외측] ~ inside[outside] calipers.
캘린더 〔달력〕 a calendar. ¶벽걸이 ~ a wall calendar // 탁상 ~를 넘기다 turn over a page [leaf] of a desk calendar.
캠 CAM(▶ computer-aided manufacturing의 약어).
캠코더 a camcorder.
캠퍼 〔약〕 camphor.
캠퍼스 a campus. ¶~에(서) on campus(▶ 이 경우 관사를 붙이지 않음).
캠페인 a campaign. ¶우리는 새 상품 판매 촉진 ~을 벌이고 있다 We are conducting a sales campaign to promote our new product. // 공해 반대 ~을 전개할 계획이다 We intend to build up an antipollution movement[campaign] among the people.
캠프 a camp; (운동선수의) a training camp. ¶~를 거두다 break (up a) camp.
●캠프촌 a camping village. 캠프파이어 a campfire.
캠핑 camping. ¶~을 가다 go (out) camping / leave for camping (in). 캠핑하다 camp (out). ¶캠핑하는 사람 a camper // 숲으로 캠핑하러 가다 go camping in the woods // 호반에서 ~ camp (out) by a lake.
캡 1 〔모자〕 a cap. 2 〔만년필 등의 뚜껑〕 a cap.
캡션 〔삽화·사진의 설명문〕 a caption.
캡슐 (약·인공위성의) a capsule. ¶~에 싼 capsulated // 우주 ~ a space capsule.
캥거루 〔동〕 a kangaroo (pl. ~s, (집합적) -roo). ¶~ 새끼 a baby kangaroo / a joey.
캥캥 〔강아지·여우 등이 우는 소리〕 yap, yap, yap; yelp, yelp, yelp. ¶여우가 숲 속에서 ~ 울었다 A fox yelped in the forest. 캥캥하다 yap; yelp. ⇨캥캥거리다
캥캥거리다 yap; yelp; yip.
커녕 far from (doing); anything but at all; in no wise; instead of; [말할 것도 없고] not to mention; not to speak of; to say noting of. ¶실망하기는~ far from being disappointed // 즐겁기는~ none too pleasant // 그는 기뻐하기는 ~ 몹시 화를 냈다 Far from being pleased, he got very angry. // 그는 사과하기는~ 거꾸로 불평을 늘어놓았다 He didn't even try to apologize. On the contrary, he complained to us. // 아기는 뛰기는~ 아직 걷지도 못한다 The baby cannot walk yet, much less run. // 먹을 것은~ 물도 떨어졌다 It's not a question of food. We don't even have any water left. // 야조 관찰에는 개똥지빠귀는~ 참새 한 마리도 보지 못했다 I went bird watching, but I could not find even a sparrow, to say nothing of a thrush. // "그 말을 듣고 기뻤니?" "그렇기는~ 나는 정말로 실망했어." "Weren't you glad to hear that?" "Far from it! I was really disappointed." // 그는 영어는~ 우리말도 모른다 He doesn't know Korean, to say nothing of English.
커닝 (*cunning) cheating (on[(영) in] an examination); cribbing(▶ cunning은 「교활하다」의 뜻). 커닝하다 cheat; crib. ¶커닝하다가 들키다 be caught cribbing // 선생님은 학생이 커닝하는 것을 발견했다 The teacher caught a student cheating on[in] the examination.
●커닝 페이퍼 (*cunning paper) a crib (sheet); a cheat sheet.
커다랗다 huge; great; gargantuan; gigantic; monstrous; mammoth; colossal. ¶커다란 잘못 a gross[glaring] mistake / a grave[fatal] error // 커다란 몸집 a gigantic figure // 커다란 건물 a massive[colossal] building / a stupendous structure // 눈을 커다랗게 뜨고 with one's eyes wide open // 신문에 커다랗게 광고를 내다 place[put in] a large advertisement in a newspaper // 너처럼 커다란 사나이가 울다니 꼴사납다 It's shameful for a grown man like you to cry.
커다래지다 become[grow] larger[bigger]; wax large; increase in size; [성장하다] grow (up); become taller; [증대하다] swell; expand; be enlarged. ¶눈이 커다래져서 with one's eyes wide open / with saucer[bulging] eyes // 눈이 ~ open one's eyes wide // (놀라서) stare with[in] wonder / (미국 속어) be popeyed.
커리어 a career. ¶그는 이 분야에 30년의 ~가 있다 He has a career of thirty years in this field. // 이번 일에서 그의 법률가로서의 ~가 모든 것을 말해 주었다 His career in law meant[counted for] a great deal in this case.
커리큘럼 〔교육 과정〕 a curriculum (pl. -s).
커뮤니케이션 communication.
커미션 〔수수료·구전〕 a commission.
커버 〔덮개〕 a cover; a covering. ¶책 (book) jacket / a wrapper // 기저귀 ~ a diaper cover // ~를 씌우다 lay a cover / cover (a chair) / (책에) jacket // ~를 벗기다 take off the cover (from). 2 〔보충하기〕. 커버하다 cover (a loss); make up for (a loss); [원호하다] cover; back up. ¶3루를 ~ cover third base.
●커버걸 a cover girl.
커버링 covering.
커브 1 〔곡선〕 a curve; a curved line. ¶하강[상승] ~ a falling[rising] curve // 상승 ~를 그리는 암의 사망률 the up-curving cancer mortality. 2 〔도로·선로의 굽은 곳〕 a curve; a bend. ¶도로의 급 ~ a sharp turn[bend] in the road // ~를 돌다 round a curve // ~를 틀다 curve / turn sharply / make a sharp turn (at the intersection). 3 〔야구〕 a curve (ball). ¶인[아웃] ~ an incurve[outcurve] / a pitch that breaks toward[away from] a batter // ~를 던지다 throw a curve // 저 투수는 날카로운 ~가 장기이다 His best pitch is a sharp curve.
커서 〔컴〕 〔입력 위치 표시〕 a cursor.
커스터드 custard.
커지다 grow[become] larger[bigger]; wax large; increase in size; [성장하다] grow (up); become[grow] taller; [증대하다] swell; expand; be enlarged; be extended; [대성하다] attain greatness; [중대해지다] assume serious proportions[great dimensions];

grow serious. ¶부피가 ~ increase[grow] in volume∥담이 ~ become emboldened∥수요가 ~ the demand rises (for it) / be more in demand∥~ one's influence is extended∥문제가 커졌다 The problem has grown serious.∥인구가 는다고 해서 국력이 커지는 것은 아니다 A nation does not necessarily grow in power, if its population increases.

커터 [자르는 도구] a cutter.

커트 1 (머리·보석·구기 등의) a cut. ¶브릴리언트 ~의 다이아몬드 a brilliant-cut diamond. **커트하다** cut. ¶유리를 ~ cut glass∥볼을 ~ cut a ball∥머리를 짧게 커트했다 I had my hair cut short. 2 [필름을 잘라 냄] cutting; a cut. **커트하다** cut. ¶필름을 ~ cut a film / edit a film by omitting some parts.

커트라인 (*cut line) a cutoff point.

커튼 a curtain (at a window); (미) drapes(엷은 커튼 위에 치는 두꺼운). ¶두꺼운 천의 ~ a thick curtain / (~)에 a drape / ~을 치다 draw the curtains together / 창의 ~을 닫다 draw the curtains over[across] a window / 창문에 ~을 달다 hang curtains on a window / 방의 3분의 1을 ~으로 막다 curtain off one third of a room∥~을 열어 주세요 Please draw the curtains.∥~은 모두 닫혀 있었다 The curtains were pulled to[together].
●**커튼콜** a curtain call.

커틀릿 a cutlet.

커프스 [블라우스 등의 소맷부리] cuffs.
●**커프스단추** a cuff button; 《영》 a sleeve button; (사슬이 달린) a cuff link; 《영》 a sleeve link.

커플 a couple. ¶그들은 어울리는 ~이다 They are a well-matched couple.

커피 coffee. ¶~ 가는 기계 a coffee grinder∥진한[엷은] ~ strong[weak] coffee∥아이스 ~ iced coffee∥드립 ~ drip coffee∥밀크 ~ (프) a café au lait / ~를 타다 make coffee∥~를 한 잔 마시다 drink a cup of coffee / (속어) have a coffee∥~에 크림과 설탕을 타서 마시다 drink[have] coffee with cream and sugar∥~은 어떤 것을 좋아하십니까 How do you like your coffee?∥~는 블랙[진한 것]을 좋아합니다 I like my coffee black[strong].
●**커피숍** a coffee shop. **커피 여과기** a coffee filter. **커피 잔** a coffee cup. **커피점** [커피콩 등을 파는 상점] a coffee shop(▶ coffee shop은 《미》에서는 간단한 식사가 가능한 호텔 등의 식당을 말함); [찻집] a tearoom; 《영》 a tea shop. **커피포트** a coffeepot.

컨디션 condition. ¶몸의 ~ one's physical condition / ~이 좋다 be[feel] well / be in good condition / (운동선수가) be in fine [good] shape / ~이 나쁘다 be[feel] unwell / be out of condition[sorts / form] / be in bad shape / be[feel] under the weather∥경기에 대비하여 몸의 ~을 조절하다 get into [in] (good) shape for the match∥~을 유지하다 keep in training[form / trim] / ~을 되찾다 regain one's form / ~은 최상이다 be in the best condition[form] / be in top form∥오늘은 몸의 ~이 별로 좋지 않다 I'm not quite feeling myself today. / I am not up to the mark today. / I do not feel quite well today.(▶ "I am in bad condition."은 몸이 허약해져 있을 때 쓰는 말로, 감기 등으로 몸이 좋지 않을 때에는 쓰지 않는 말임).

컨베이어 a conveyer; a conveyor.
●**컨베이어 시스템** a conveyor system.

컨설턴트 a consultant. ¶경영 ~ a management consultant.

컨소시엄 [자본·기업 합작] a consortium (pl. -tia).

컨테이너 a container. ¶~용 크레인 (부두의) a container crane.
●**컨테이너선**(一船) a container ship. **컨테이너 차** (트럭) a container truck; (열차) a container train. ¶화물을 ~로 운반하다 carry goods in a container truck[train].

컨트롤 control. ¶~이 좋다[나쁘다] have a good[poor] control / ~이 잘 안 되다 [야구] lose control (of pitching).

컨트리클럽 a country club.

컬 a curl. **컬하다** [머리털을 지지다]. ¶머리털을 ~ curl one's hair.

컬러 1 [색] (a) color; (영) (a) colour. 2 [특색]. ¶로컬 ~가 짙은 제전 a festival rich in local color.
●**컬러 사진** a color picture[photo]. **컬러텔레비전** a color television.

컬렉션 a collection. ¶그의 우표 ~은 대단하다 He has an excellent [quite a] collection of stamps.

컬컬하다 (서술적) be[feel] thirsty[dry]; have a dry throat. ¶목이 컬컬한데 맥주 한 잔 했으면 좋겠다 I am thirsting for a glass of beer.

컬트 영화(—映畵) a cult movie.

컴맹(—盲) [상태] computer illiteracy; [사람] a computer illiterate.

컴백 a comeback. **컴백하다** come back (to one's former work); make one's comeback. ¶영화계에 ~ find one's way back into the screen / make one's comeback on the screen∥그 가수는 멋있게 컴백했다 The singer made[staged] a splendid comeback.

컴컴하다 1 pitch-dark; dark. ⇨깜깜하다 1·2 2 [음흉하다] blackhearted; evil-minded; wicked; treacherous; sly; dark; black. ¶속이 컴컴한 사람 a blackhearted[treacherous] person / an insidious man / a deep one / a snake.

컴파일러 [컴] a compiler.

컴퍼스 1 [걸음쇠] (a pair of) compasses; a compass. ¶~로 원을 그리시오 Draw a circle with a pair of compasses[a compass]. 2 [나침반] a mariner's compass. 3 a step; a stride. ⇨보폭 ¶~가 긴 사람 a long-legged person∥그는 ~가 길다[짧다] He walks with long[short] strides[steps].

컴퓨터 a computer. ¶~화하다 computerize∥데이터를 ~에 넣다 put data into a computer / computerize data / feed data into a computer∥~로 정보 검색을 하다 obtain data from a computer / use a computer to search for data.
●**컴퓨터 그래픽스** computer graphics(약어 CG). **컴퓨터 바이러스** computer virus. **컴퓨터 언어** computer language.

컵 1 [잔] a cup; a glass; a mug. (▶ 영어에서 glass는 cup이라고는 하지 않으나, 우리말에서는「글라스」를「컵」이라고 할 수 있음. 또한, 영어에서 mug는 cup의 한 종류이긴 하지만 cup과 구별되는 이름으로 쓰이는 경우가 많으나, 우리말에서는「머그잔」이라는 말이 최근 들어서야 드물게 쓰일 뿐, 대개는「컵」이라는 말이 사용됨) ¶한 ~ 가득한 물 a glass[a glassful] of water∥종이 ~ a paper cup∥우유 반 ~을 주십시오 May I have half a glass of milk?// 그는 ~으로 술을 꿀꺽꿀꺽 마셨다 He gulped (down) wine from a glass.//물을 한 ~ 주십시오 Let me have [Get me] a glass of water. **2** [우승배] a cup; a trophy. ¶데이비스 ~ the Davis Cup// 우승~을 타다 win the cup [trophy].

컷 1 [작은 삽화] a cut; an illustration. ¶~을 넣다 fill (the space) with a cut. **2** (영화·필름의) cutting; a cut. ¶원 ~ [영] one cut.

케도 KEDO(▶ Korean Peninsula Energy Development Organization의 약어).

케라틴 [화] ceratin; keratin.

케이블 a cable. ¶해저 ~ a submarine cable. ●케이블 부설 cable laying [placing]. 케이블 철도 a cable [funicular] railway [tramway]. 케이블카 a funicular railway coach. 케이블 티브이 cable television [TV].

케이스 1 [용기·그릇] a case. ¶담배 ~ a cigarette case// ~에 넣다 put a thing in a case. **2** [사례] a case. ¶모델 ~ a model [typical] case// ~ 바이 ~로 case by case / on a case-by-case basis// ~ 바이 ~로 결정하다 decide on a case-by-case basis// 이것은 특수한 ~이다 This is an unusual case[example].

케이에스 KS(▶ Korean Standards의 약어). ●케이에스 마크 a KS mark.

케이오 KO; K.O.; (미국 속어) a kayo(▶ knockout의 약어). ¶제11라운드에서 ~로 이기다 score an 11th round knockout victory// 그는 ~승을 했다 He KO'd his opponent.

케이크 (a) cake. ¶생일 ~ a birthday cake// ~를 자르다 knife a (wedding) cake.

케이프 a cape. ¶~를 걸치다 wear a cape.

케일 [양배추의 일종] kale; kail.

케첩 ketchup; catsup. ¶토마토~ tomato ketchup.

케케묵다 antiquated; old; timeworn; worm-eaten; [시대에 뒤지다] old-fashioned; outmoded; out of date; musty(곰팡내 나는); [진부하다] stale; trite; hack. ¶케케묵은 책 a musty[fusty] book// 케케묵은 말[격언] a hackneyed[stale / worn-out] saying / an old platitude / a copybook maxim// 케케묵은 이야기 an old story / fiddler's news// 케케묵은 농담 a stale[worn] joke / (구어) a chestnut// 귀가 따갑도록 들은 케케묵은 이야기 I'm sick and tired of hearing that hackneyed phrase.// 그는 또 케케묵은 이야기를 꺼내었다 He began to talk his tired old stories again.

케톤 [화] keton(e).

케페우스자리 [천] Cepheus.

켄타우루스자리 [천] the Centaur; Centaurus.

켄트지 (-紙) Kent paper.

켈트 인 (-人) (사람) a Celt; (민족) the Celts. ¶~의 Celtic.

켕기다 1 [팽팽해지다] be stretched tightly[to the full]; become tense[taut]; be strained. ¶힘줄이 ~ have a strain on the sinew / feel a sinew taut// 줄이 켕긴다 A rope is stretched taut.// 바지가 켕긴다 My trousers are tight.// 밧줄은 팽팽하게 켕겨 있었다 The rope was stretched taut[taut]. **2** [불안해지다] feel uneasy[ill at ease]; feel guilty[compunction]; be affected with guilt; be[feel] afraid (of). ¶네가 대답을 못하는 것은 켕기는 데가 있기 때문이다 You cannot answer me because you have a guilty conscience.// 나는 마음에 켕기는 것이 없다 / I have a clear [a clean / an easy] conscience. **3** [팽팽하게 하다] strain; stretch tightly; tighten; brace up; stiffen. ¶밧줄을 ~ tighten[strain] a rope / stretch a rope tight / haul a rope taut / pull all the slack out of a rope. **4** [서로 버티다] stand against[up to]; hold out against; face[confront] each other; be over against each other.

켜 a layer. ¶얇은 ~ a thin layer / a lamina (pl. -ae)// ~로 쌓다 heap[pile] up in several layers// ~를 이루다 form layers.

켜다 1 [불을 밝게 하다] burn; light (up) (a lamp); set (a lamp) alight; make (a light); turn[switch] on (an electric lamp). ¶촛불을 ~ light a candle / get a candle alight//가스불을 ~ turn on the gas//전등을 ~ turn[switch] on the electric light / light up (a house) with electricity//성냥을 ~ (불을 일으키기) light [strike / scrape] a match// 밤새도록 불을 켜 두다 keep a light burning [an electric light turned on] all night// 그녀의 방에 전등이 켜져 있다 The (electric) light is on in her room.// 이 성냥은 불이 켜지지 않는다 I can't get these matches to light. / These matches won't strike.// 이 라이터는 불이 켜지지 않는다 This lighter doesn't work.// 방에는 등불이 환하게 켜져 있었다 A lamp was burning brightly in the room.// 복도에는 희미하게 불이 켜져 있었다 The passage was dimly lit. **2** [톱으로 쪼개다] saw (wood). ¶가로 켜는 톱 a crosscut saw// 톱으로 ~ cut with a saw / saw// 나뭇결을 가로[세로] ~ saw crossways [lengthways] of the grain// (재목이) 잘 켜지다[켜지지 않다] saw easily[badly]. **3** [현악기를] play (the violin); scrape (on) (a fiddle); sweep (the strings). ¶곡을 바이올린으로 ~ fiddle a tune. **4** [한꺼번에 마시다] drink deeply[in large draughts]; quaff; take draughts (of); swill; guzzle (beer). ¶단숨에 ~ empty (the glass) at a draught / drain (the cup) at one gulp / quaff (the glass) to the dregs / drink (the cup) dry// 술 한 병을 다 ~ drink[drain] a bottle of wine to the dregs / crack a bottle of brandy. **5** [(기지개를) 하다] stretch (oneself); stretch one's body with raised hands. ¶하품과 기지개를 켜며 with a stretch and a yawn. **6** [실을 뽑다] spin off. ¶누에고치에서 실을 ~ reel silk off a cocoon. **7** [우레 등을 불어 소리를 내다] whistle (a birdcall); give a mating call; imitate an animal call. ¶우레를 ~ imitate a pheasant call.

켤레[1] [수] a conjugate. ¶~의 conjugate[1]. ●켤레 복소수 a conjugate complex number.

켤레[2] a pair. ¶한 ~의 양말 a pair of socks// 두 ~의 구두 two pairs of shoes.

코 1 (사람·동물의) a nose; (속어) a nozzle; (미국 속어) a snoot; (돼지 등의) a snout; (개·말 등의) a muzzle; (코끼리의) a trunk; a proboscis. ¶높은[낮은 / 잘생긴] ~ a high-bridged[flat / shapely] nose// 사자~ a snub[pug] nose// 매부리~ an aquiline nose// 들창~ a turned-up nose// ~가 납작한 flat-nosed// ~ 먹은 소리를 하다 speak through the nose / nasalize (words)// ~로 숨 쉬다 breathe through the nose// ~가 좋다 [냄새

를 잘 맡다) have a good[sharp/keen] nose / have a good scent∥~가 예민하다 have a sharp[keen] nose∥~를 후비다 pick one's nose∥~를 콩콩거리다 sniff/whimper/whine(개 등이)∥~를 쥐다 pinch one's nose[nostrils] / hold one's nose∥~를 닦다 wipe[clean] one's nose∥~를 찡그리다 wrinkle one's nose∥~를 맞대고 의논하다 lay heads together (over)∥(냄새가) ~를 찌르다 be offensive to the nose[smell] / stink∥나는 ~가 막혔다 My nose is stopped up[blocked]. **2**〔콧물〕 snivel; nasal mucus; (비어) snot. ¶~를 흘리는 아이 a child with a running [runny] nose∥~를 훌쩍이다 snuff/snivel∥종이로 ~를 닦다 wipe one's nose with paper∥~를 풀다 blow the[one's] nose∥그는 손수건으로 ~를 풀었다 He blew his nose into[with] his handkerchief.∥그는 감기로 ~를 흘리고 있다 He is sniveling[sniffling] with a cold. **3**〔물건의〕 the nose; the tip; the cap; the toe. ¶신~ the toe[cap/toecap] of a shoe∥버선 ~ the toe of a sock. **4**〔편물의〕 a stitch; a link; 〔그물의〕 a knot. ¶그물~ a net knot∥~를 성기게[촘촘하게] 뜨다 knit with large[small] stitches∥한 ~를 빠뜨리다 drop[let down] a stitch∥한 ~가 풀리면 전부 다 풀린다 If one stitches gives, the other will.

코가 납작해지다 be put to shame; feel depressed[dispirited].

코가 높다 be proud.

코(를) 골다 snore. ¶코 고는 소리 a snore∥코 고는 사람 a snorer∥드르렁드르렁 ~ snore loudly[terribly] / blow[snore] like a grampus∥코를 골기 시작하다 fall to snoring∥드러눕자 ~ plunge into a noisy sleep∥그의 코 고는 소리에 잠이 깼다 His snores woke me up.

코를 납작하게 만들다 humble (a person's) pride; snub (a person); put (a person's) nose out of joint; take (a person) down a peg[notch] or two; take the conceit out of (a person); knock (a person) down to size.

코를 떼다 get snubbed[humbled / spurned / rejected]; get put to shame. ¶돈 꾸어 달랬다가 ~ get turned down cold trying to borrow money∥월급을 올려 달랬다가 ~ have one's request for a raise flatly rejected.

코(가) 세다 〔고집이 세다〕 hard-nosed; stiff-necked; stubborn; headstrong; self-assertive. ¶저렇게 코가 센 친구는 처음 보겠다 His obstinacy really beats me.

코감기(-感氣) a cold in the head[nose]; coryza. ¶~에 걸려 있다 have a cold in the nose[head]∥~로 냄새를 못 맡는다 I cannot smell with a cold in the nose.

코걸이 1〔씨름〕 a nose-grip; a nostrilgrip. **2**〔코에 거는 물건〕 a nose pendant[ring].

코끝 the tip of a nose. ¶~에 종기가 생겼다 I have a boil[spot] on the tip of my nose.∥강도가 내 ~에 총을 들이댔다 The robber thrust a gun under my nose.

코끼리 an elephant. ¶~ 같은 elephantine / elephant-like∥수〔암〕 ~ a bull[cow] elephant∥새끼 ~ a calf[baby] elephant∥아프리카〔인도〕 ~ an African[Indian] elephant.

코납작이 1〔코가 납작한 사람〕 a flat-nosed person. **2**〔기가 꺾인 사람〕 a person who has been taken down a peg or two; a person frustrated by shame.

코냑 〔브랜디의 일종〕 (프) cognac.

코너 1〔모퉁이·구석〕 a corner; (백화점 등의) a special counter[section] (for children's wear). ¶선두 주자는 벌써 네 번째 ~를 돌았다 The first runner has already turned the fourth corner.∥투수는 플레이트의 ~로 스트라이크 볼을 던졌다 The pitcher threw [hurled] a strike across the corner of the plate.∥신사복 ~는 어디에 있습니까 Where is the men's wear department[counter for men's wear]? **2**〔궁지〕 a corner. ¶~로 몰아넣다 drive[put] (a person) into a corner.
●**코너킥**〔축구〕 a corner kick.

코넷〔음〕 a cornet; a cornet-à-pistons. ¶~ 연주자 a cornet(t)ist.

코담배 snuff. ¶한 줌의 ~ a pinch of snuff∥~를 맡다 take (a pinch of) snuff.

코대답(-對答) an indifferent[a nonchalant] answer. **코대답하다** answer indifferently [nonchalantly / with no great enthusiasm].

코데인〔화〕 codein(e).

코드¹〔음〕 a chord.

코드²〔암호〕 a code. ¶프레스 ~ the press code∥오산(誤算) 검출 ~ 〔컴〕 an error-detecting code∥자동 검사 ~ 〔컴〕 a self checking code.

코드³〔줄〕 a cord; 〔전깃줄〕 an electric cord; a flex.

코디네이터 a coordinator.

코딱지 dried mucus from the nose; nose dirt; nose wax; (dried) snot. ¶~를 후비다 pick one's nose∥~만 한 방 a very small room / a poky[tiny] little room∥~가 생겼다 Nose wax gathered.

코뚜레 a cow's[bull's] nose ring.

코란〔종〕 the Koran. ¶~의 Koranic.

코랄〔음〕 a choral(e). ¶바흐의 ~ a Bach chorale.

코러스〔음〕 a chorus.

코로나〔천〕 a corona (pl. ~s, -nae).
●**코로나그래프** a coronagraph. **코로나 방전** corona discharge.

코르덴 corduroy.
●**코르덴 바지** corduroy pants[trousers]; (a pair of) corduroys.

코르셋 a corset; corsets; (영) stays. ¶올인원 ~ an all-in-one corselet(te)∥~을 입다 wear a corset∥외과 의사는 변위 추간 연골의 치료에 ~을 입혀 주었다 The surgeon made me wear a corset for my slipped disk.

코르크 cork; a cork(마개). ¶~의〔식〕 suberic∥~ 같은 corky / 〔식〕 subereous / suberose∥~제(製) cork / 〔식〕 ~는 물에 뜬다 A cork floats in water.

코린트식(-式)〔건〕 the Corinthian order. ¶~의 Corinthianesque∥~의 성당 a Corinthian temple∥~의 원주 a Corinthian column.

코맹맹이 a person who twangs; a person who speaks through the nose.
●**코맹맹이 소리** a nasal voice; a twang. ¶~를 하다 twang / speak through the nose.

코머거리 a person with a stopped-up[congested] nose.

코메디 →코미디

코메콘 〔공산권 경제 상호 원조 회의〕 COMECON(▶ the Council for Mutual Economic Assistance의 약어).

코멘트 (a) comment (on). ¶~를 하다 make comment (on)∥노~ No comment.

코뮈니케 (프) a communiqué. ¶공동 ~ a joint communiqué // ~를 발표하다[읽다] issue[read] a communiqué.
코뮤니스트 a communist.
코뮤니즘 communism(▶ 종종 C-).
코미디 a comedy.
코미디언 a comedian.
코믹하다 comic(al); humorous; funny; jocular; jocose. ¶코믹한 표정 a comic look on one's face.
코민테른 the Comintern(▶ Communist International의 약어).
코민포름 the Cominform(▶ Communist Information Bureau의 약어).
코밑 ¶~에 under the nose.
● **코밑수염** a m(o)ustache. ¶~을 기르다 wear[cultivate / grow] a mustache.
코바늘 (편물의) a crochet hook[needle]. ¶~로 숄을 짜다 crochet a shawl.
코발트 [화] cobalt(기호 Co). ¶~빛의 cobaltic.
● **코발트블루 / 코발트청** cobalt blue; azure blue.
코방아 찧다 fall flat on one's face.
코브라 [동] a cobra. ¶킹 ~ a king cobra.
코빼기 a nose. ⇨코1 ¶나는 1년 이상 그의 ~도 보지 못했다 I've seen neither hide nor hair of him in over a year.
코뼈 [생] the nasal bone.
코뿔소 [동] a rhinoceros (pl. ~es, ~); a rhino (pl. ~s, ~).
코사인 [수] cosine(약어 cos).
코스 1 (경주·여행 등의) a course; (경기장 등의) a lane; a track; (경기의) a route; (골프의) a fairway; (일부) a lap; a leg. ¶제3 ~ Lane No. 3 // 남쪽[북쪽] ~ the southern[northern] route // 당일치기 ~ a one-day course of a trip // ~를 바꾸지 않다 hold[keep on] one's course // 같은 ~를 밟다 follow the same course // 전(全) ~를 완주(完走)하다 stay the course // 낮은 ~로 던지다 throw a low pitch // (로켓 등이) 제 ~에서 벗어나다[벗어나지 않다] be off[on] true course // 이 하이킹 ~에는 위험한 곳이 몇 군데 있다 There are several dangerous places along this hiking trail. // 이 골프 ~는 매우 넓다 This golf course is very large.
2 [학과 과정] a course of study. ¶박사 학위 ~ the doctor's course // 프랑스 어 ~를 택하다 take a course in French // 진학 ~를 택할까, 취직 ~를 택할까 망설이고 있다 I can't decide whether to choose the college course or the vocational course. // 나는 대학 진학 ~를 밟기로 했다 I decided to take the college preparatory course. // 그는 속성 ~로 영어 회화의 능력을 길렀다 He acquired (his) ability in English conversation through an intensive course.
3 (양식의). ¶풀 ~ a full-course meal.
코스닥 [벤처 기업을 위한 주식 장외 시장] KOSDAQ(▶ Korea Securities Dealers Automated Quotations의 약어).
코스모스 [식] a cosmos (pl. ~, ~es).
코스트 cost. ¶~를 낮추다 reduce[cut into] the cost // 생산 ~의 절감을 꾀하다 try to reduce the cost of production.
코시컨트 [수] a cosecant(약어 cosec).
코안경 (-眼鏡) (프) a pince-nez.
코알라 [동] a koala (bear).
코앞 ¶~에 straight before one / under one's (very) nose / before one's eyes // ~에 닥친 impending / imminent (danger) // ~에 닥치다 be near[close] at hand / be imminent / be just ahead // 단도를 ~에 들이대다 present a dagger under (a person's) nose // ~의 것을 못보다 fail to see what is right under one's nose.
코요테 a coyote.
코웃음 a sneer; sneering.
코웃음(을) 치다 sniff (at); sneer (at); laugh ironically.
코일 [전] a coil. ¶유도[감응] ~ an induction coil // 2차 ~ a secondary coil.
코즈머폴리터니즘 a cosmopolitanism.
코즈머폴리턴 a cosmopolitan; a cosmopolite.
코찡찡이 a habitual sniffer[sniffler].
코청 the nasal septum.
코치 (사람) (행위) coaching; training. ¶배팅 ~를 받다 be coached on batting // 그는 우리 야구 팀의 ~를 맡고 있다 He coaches our baseball team. **코치하다** coach (a team).
코침 (-鍼) tickling (a person's) nose.
코침(을) 주다 tickle (a person's) nose.
코카인 [화] cocain(e); (미국 속어) coke; (미국 속어) snow.
● **코카인 중독** cocainism; cocaine poisoning [addiction]. ¶~자 a cocainist / (미국 속어) a coke addict[fiend].
코카타르 [의] nasal catarrh.
코코넛 a coconut.
코코아 (가루·음료) cocoa. ¶~를 마시다 drink [have] cocoa // ~를 홀짝거리다 sip cocoa // 뜨거운 ~를 마시고 싶다 I want a cup of hot chocolate[(영) cocoa].
● **코코아 열매** a cocoa[cacao] bean; a cacao (pl. ~s).
코코야자 (-椰子) [식] a coconut palm[tree]; a coco.
코콤 COCOM(▶ Coordinating Committee for Export to Communist Area의 약어).
코크스 (a piece of) coke. ¶~용의 탄(炭) coking coal // ~를 연료로 하다 use coke for fuel.
코탄젠트 [수] a cotangent(약어 cot).
코털 the hairs in[of] the nostrils; a vibrissa (pl. -rissae). ¶~을 뽑다 pull out the hairs out of the nostrils.
코트¹ [외투] a coat; an overcoat. ¶~를 입다 [벗다] put on[take off] a coat // ~를 입고 있다 wear a coat.
코트² [경기장] a (tennis) court. ¶~를 만들다 lay out a court.
코팅 (천·렌즈 등의) (a) coating.
코펠 (⑤Kocher) a nested cooking set.
코피 blood from the nose; nosebleed(ing); nasal hemorrhage; [의] epistaxis. ¶그 아이는 ~를 흘리고 있다 The child's nose is bleeding. / The child has a nosebleed[bloody nose]. / The child is bleeding at the nose. // 나는 아침에 종종 ~를 쏟는다 I often have [get] a nosebleed in the morning.
코허리 the narrow part of the nose (at the base). ¶~가 시큰해지다 be almost moved to tears / be touched with compassion.
코흘리개 a snotty(-nosed) kid; a snotnose; a snivel(l)er.
콕¹ [공] a cock; (수도·가스의) a tap; (미) a faucet; a spigot; a valve. ¶비상 ~ an emergency handle // 수도의 ~을 열어 놓은 채로 두다 leave the water running // 밸브 ~ a

valve cock /~을 완전히 틀어 물이 나오게 하다 release the water on[at] full cock// 저 ~을 열어라[잠가라] Turn on[off] that cock [faucet / tap].

콕² 1 [찌르는 모양] stinging[piercing / thrusting / poking / pricking] hard[fast / sharply / abruptly]. ¶~ 쏘는 약 냄새 a sharp odor of medicine// ~ 찌르는 말 spicy[poignant] remarks// 바늘로 ~ 찌르다 prick with a needle// 팔꿈치로 ~ 찌르다 nudge (a person) with one's elbow// 아무의 옆구리를 ~ 찌르다 poke (a person) in the ribs// 코를 ~ 쏘다 assail one's nostrils// (나무) 가시에 발을 ~ 찔리다 run a splinter into one's foot// 벌이 ~ 쏘았다 A bee stung abruptly[sharply].// 고추가 ~ 쏜다 Red pepper stings[bites] the tongue[is stinging hot]. **2** [쪼는 모양] pecking; picking. ¶닭이 땅을 ~ 쫀다 A hen pecks at ground.

콕콕 1 [찌르는 모양] repeatedly stinging [piercing / thrusting / poking / pricking]. ¶~ 쏘는 통증 a smarting pain// ~ 쑤시다 sting / have a throbbing pain / (상처가) tingle [smart / throb] (with pain)// 맛이 ~ 쏘다 be pungent[piquant / cutting]// 바늘로 ~ 찌르다 keep pinpricking with a needle// 아무의 옆구리를 ~ 찌르다 poking (a person) in the ribs// 고추가 매워 ~ 쏜다 Red pepper keeps my tongue stinging. **2** [쪼는 모양] repeatedly pecking; picking. ¶닭이 병아리를 ~ 쫀다 A hen keeps pecking away at a chick.

콘 a[an ice-cream] cone.
콘덴서 [전] a condenser; a capacitor.
콘도(미니엄) a condominium (unit).
콘돔 a condom; (미국 구어) a rubber; a (contraceptive) sheath; (영국 속어) a French letter.
콘사이스 (*concise*) [소형 사전] pocket (-sized) dictionary. (▶ "concise"는 「간결한」의 뜻을 나타낼 뿐, 「사전」의 의미는 없음)
콘서트 a concert. ¶레코드 ~를 열다 give [hold] a record concert.
● **콘서트홀** a concert hall.
콘센트 (*concent*) [전] (미) an (electric) outlet; a wall socket; a plug receptacle [(영) socket]. ¶~에 플러그를 꽂다 insert a plug in a wall outlet / plug in.
콘셉트 a concept.
콘솔 [바닥 설치형의 대형 캐비닛] a consol.
콘체르토 [음] a (piano / violin) concerto (*pl.* ~s, -ti).
콘체른 (ⓖKonzern) a (business) concern; a combine; a pool.
콘크리트 concrete. ¶~의 concrete// 아직 굳지 않은 ~ fresh concrete// 철근 ~ steel-reinforced[armored] concrete// 현장 배합 cast-in-place concrete// ~를 바르다 concrete (the pavement) / cover[lay / treat] (something) with concrete.
● **콘크리트 건물** a concrete building. **콘크리트 믹서** a concrete mixer. **콘크리트 믹서차** a cement mixer on wheels. **콘크리트 블록** a concrete block. **콘크리트 포장** concrete pavement.
콘택트렌즈 a contact lens. ¶~를 끼다 wear contact lenses / have contact lenses stuck on to eyeballs.
콘테스트 a contest. ¶미인 ~ a beauty contest.

콘텐츠 [디지털 정보] contents.
콘트라베이스 [음] a contrabass; a bass; a double bass.
콘트라스트 a contrast. ¶~를 이루다 (be in) contrast with.
콘트랄토 [음] contralto.
콘플레이크 cornflakes.
콜걸 a call girl.
콜드 게임 [야구] a called game. ¶시합은 일몰로 ~이 되었다 The game was called when the sun set.
콜드크림 cold cream.
콜라 [콜라 음료] Coke; kola [cola].
콜라주 (a) collage.
콜레라 [의] cholera. ¶의사 ~ a suspected case of cholera// ~가 발생[만연 / 유행]하다 cholera breaks out[spreads / prevails]// ~에 걸리다 be infected with cholera.
● **콜레라균** a cholera germ[bacillus (*pl.* -cilli)]; a comma (bacillus). **콜레라 백신** cholera vaccine. **콜레라 예방 주사** (an) anti-cholera injection. ¶~를 하다[놓다] inoculate (a person) against cholera. **콜레라 환자** a cholera patient; a case of cholera.
콜레스테롤 [화] cholesterol. ¶나의 혈중 ~은 정상치보다 높다 I have more than the normal amount of blood cholesterol.
콜로라투라 [음] coloratura; coloarature.
● **콜로라투라 소프라노** coloratura soprano. ¶~ 가수 a coloratura (soprano).
콜로세움 [원형 경기장] the Colosseum.
콜로이드 [화] colloid. ¶~(성)의 colloidal.
● **콜로이드 용액** colloidal solution.
콜록거리다 keep coughing[hacking].
콜록콜록 coughing[hacking] away. ¶~ 기침을 하다 give[emit] a dry cough / have a hacking cough / keep coughing[hacking]// 그는 밤이 되면 ~ 기침이 나와 고통스러웠다 At night he was plagued by a persistent cough. / After dark he would start coughing [hacking] and couldn't stop. **콜록콜록하다** keep coughing. ⇨ᐸ**콜록거리다**
콜론¹ [경] a call loan.
콜론² [이중점] a colon.
콜리 [개의 한 품종] a collie.
콜머니 [경] call money; money on call.
콜 사인 [전파 호출 부호] a call sign[signal]; call letters.
콜콜 gurgling; snoring. ⇨ᐸ**쿨쿨**¹·²
콜타르 [화] coal tar. ¶~ 크레오소오트 [피치] coal tar creosote[pitch]// 판자에 ~를 칠하다 tar a board / cover a board with coal tar.
콜택시 a call taxi.
콜호스 a kolkhoz; a Russian farm; a collective farm.
콤마 1 [구두점] a comma. ¶두 단어 사이에 ~를 넣다 insert[put] a comma between two world. **2** →점(點)5
콤바인 [수확기] a combine (harvester).
콤비 1 a combination; a partner; [2인조] a pair; a duo. ¶…과 ~로 in combination with …// …과 ~가 되어(서) 하다 join force with … / tie up with …// 저 두 사람은 좋은 ~다 Those two are really a good[happy] pair.// ~로 합시다 Let's do it together (, you and me).// 두 사람은 ~로 짜서 일을 마쳤다 The two combined their efforts[got together] and finished the work.// 그는 B 씨와 ~다 His closest partner[associate] is Mr. B. **2** [상하가 다른 양복] the matching of the coat and

콤비나트 (@kombinat) an industrial complex; a complex. ¶석유 화학 ~ a petrochemical complex.

콤비네이션 [수] a combination.

콤팩트 [화장 도구] a compact. ¶~의 거울 a compact mirror.

콤플렉스 (have / develop) an inferiority complex. ¶~를 없애다 rid (a person) of his inferiority complex / dismiss a sense of inferiority (out of one's mind) // 나는 그에 대하여 ~를 갖고 있다 I feel inferior to him. / He gives me an inferiority complex.

콧구멍 a nostril; the naris (*pl.* nares). ¶~이 narial / narine // ~이 큰 wide-nostrilled // ~을 벌름거리다 flare one's noses.

콧기름 grease about the nostrils.

콧김 the breath from the nose. ¶~을 쐬다 be exposed to the breath from the nose of (a person).

콧날 the ridge[line] of the nose. ¶~이 오똑한 사람 a person with a shapely[well-formed] nose // ~이 서다 have a straight[high] nose // 그는 ~이 좀 비뚤어져 있다 His nose is a bit crooked.

콧노래 a hum; humming through the nose. ¶~를 부르다 hum / sing through the nose // ~를 부르며 일하다 do one's work humming a tune / hum songs at work // 그녀는 ~를 부르면서 저녁 식사를 만들었다 She was humming as she cooked dinner. // 그는 ~를 부르면서 일하고 있었다 He was humming over his work [while he worked].

콧대 the nose ridge[bridge].

콧대(가) 높다 be proud; be elated (over); be puffed up (with pride); have (unreasonably) high standards. ¶콧대가 높은 사람 a high-hatted man / a high hat / a stuck-up person.

콧대를 꺾다 put a person's nose out of joint; humble (a person's) pride; snub (a person); take (a person) down a peg; take the conceit out of (a person). ¶젠체하는 저 녀석의 콧대를 꺾어 주고 싶다 I'd like to outwit [outsmart] that complacent fellow. // 저 거만한 녀석의 콧대를 꺾을 방법이 없을까 Isn't there any way of taking that boastful fellow down a peg[notch]?

콧대(가) 세다 be self-assertive; be defiant [aggressive]; be imperious[haughty]. ¶콧대가 센 사람 a self-assertive fellow / a defiant [an aggressive] person // 그 사람은 한밑천 잡기자 요즘 콧대가 세어졌다 Having acquired a fortune he has grown quite arrogant lately.

콧등 the ridge of the nose.

콧마루 the ridge [the bridge] of the nose. ¶~가 높다 have a high-bridged nose.

콧물 snivel; snot; nose runnings[drippings]. ¶~을 닦다 wipe one's (running) nose // ~을 흘리다 snivel / drivel / run at the nose // ~을 훌쩍거리다 snivel / snuff // 그는 ~을 흘리고 있다 His nose is running. / He has a runny nose.

콧방귀 a pooh-pooh; a snort; pooh-poohing; snorting (at).

콧방귀를 뀌다 snort[sniff] at; turn up one's nose at; treat (a person) with contempt [disdain].

콧방울 the wings of the nose.

콧병 (-病) [코의 병] nose trouble[ailment]. ¶~을 앓다 have nose trouble.

콧소리 1 [언] a nasal sound. ⇨비음 2 [코 먹은 소리] a nasal voice[tone / accent]; a twang. ¶~로 말을 하다 speak through one's nose / nasalize the words / have a nasal tone[twang] // 그는 감기가 들어 심한 ~를 냈다 He had an awful nasal voice because of a cold. // 그는 영어를 말할 때 ~를 낸다 He speaks English with a (nasal) twang. / He speaks English through his nose. // 그 여자는 "아직 가지 마세요" 하고 ~로 애교를 부렸다 The woman said in her ingratiating nasal voice, "Oh, don't go yet."

콧수염 (-鬚髥) a moustache; (미) a mustache. ¶~이 많이[적게] 난 남자 a man with a heavy[thin] mustache // ~을 기르다 grow [cultivate] a mustache // 우리 할아버지는 ~을 기르고 계신다 My grandfather wears[has] a mustache.

콧숨 breathing through the nose; a snort. ¶~이 거칠다 breathe hard through the nose // 말이 거칠게 ~을 내보냈다 The horse snorted violently[gave a violent snort]. // 환자가 ~을 가쁘게 쉬고 있다 The patient is breathing hard through the nose.

콧잔등(이) the narrow part of the nose (at the base). ⇨코허리

콩¹ [집합적] the pulses; [잠두 등] a bean; [완두] a pea; [대두] a soybean; a soya bean. ¶풋 [검은] ~ a green[black] soybean // ~의 꼬투리 a (bean) pod // 꼬투리에서 깐 ~ shelled beans // 강낭~ a kidney bean / a French bean // 땅~ a peanut / 튀긴 ~ pop-bean / ~을 볶다 parch[roast] beans // ~을 심다 sow beans // ~을 물에 담가(서) 불려 두다 keep beans steeped[soaked] in water // ~을 재배하다 grow soybeans.

콩 심은 데 콩 나고 팥 심은 데 팥 난다 (속담) Don't expect the extraordinary.; Like father, like son.

콩으로 메주를 쑨다 해도 곧이듣지 않는다 (속담) Deliberately deny the truth of what was said.; Shut one's ears to a person.

콩 튀듯 팥 튀듯 하다 jump up with anger; be hopping mad. ¶성이 나서 ~ be[get] hopping mad / be carried away by anger / be wild with rage.

콩² with a thump. ⇨<쿵

콩가 [쿠바의 민속춤(곡)] a conga; [그 음악에 쓰는 드럼] a conga (drum).

콩가루 soybean flour.

콩고물 soybean flour.

콩국 soybean soup.

콩기름 soy(bean) oil; (soya) bean oil; peanut oil (땅콩 기름).

콩깍지 bean chaff; a bean hull[shuck]; peasecod (완두의). ¶~를 까다 pod[hull] beans / shell peas.

콩깻묵 (soy) bean cake; the remains of soybeans from which the oil has been extracted.

콩꼬투리 a bean pod; a pea pod.

콩나물 bean sprouts.
●**콩나물 교실** an overcrowded classroom. **콩나물국** bean-sprout soup. **콩나물밥** rice cooked with bean sprouts. **콩나물시루** a jar for growing sprouts. **콩나물~ 같다** be packed [jammed] like sardines / (미국 속어) be jammed up.

콩대 a beanstalk.

콩밥 bean-mixed rice.
콩밥(을) 먹다 serve a jail[prison] term; do [serve] time (at); "feed on bread and water". ¶콩밥을 먹은 일이 있다 I have been in prison.∥하마터면 콩밥을 먹을 뻔했다 I was nearly sent to prison.
콩밥(을) 먹이다 send (a person) in jail.
콩버무리 bean-mixed rice cake.
콩설기 layered bean-mixed rice cake.
콩소메 〔요리〕 (프) consommé; consomme; clear soup.
콩알 a grain of beans. ¶간이 ~만 해지다 be held[kept] in suspense / have one's heart in one's throat / be in great fear.
콩엿 wheat gluten mixed with popped beans.
콩자반 bean-boiled in soy sauce.
콩장 (-醬) parched, seasoned beans.
콩켸팥켸 a medley; a topsy-turvy; a pell-mell; a jumble; an utter confusion. ¶~가 되다 be at sixes and sevens / be mixed up (promiscuously) / be jumbled up∥~ 쌓아 놓다 pile (it) up pell-mell.
콩콩 with thumps. ⇨쿵쿵1
콩쿠르 〔경연〕 (프) a concours; a contest; a competition. ¶사진[영화] ~ a camera[movie] concours / a photo[movie] contest∥음악 ~ a musical contest∥그는 사진 ~에 참가했다 He participated[took part] in a photo contest.
콩테 (크레용의 하나) (프) a conté (crayon).
콩트 〔문〕 (프) a conte; a short-short; a short story.
콩팔칠팔 incoherently; ramblingly; pointlessly. ¶~ 지껄이다 say incoherent things / make a rambling[pointless] speech / talk wild. **콩팔칠팔하다** gibber; ramble; talk incoherently.
콩팥1 〔콩과 팥〕 soybeans and red beans.
콩팥2 〔생〕 a kidney. ⇨˝신장(腎臟)
콰르텟 〔음〕 a quartet(te).
콱 1 〔세게〕 strongly; hard; violently; pungently(냄새가); (밀거나 당길 때) with a jerk; 〔단단히〕 tightly; firmly; fast. ¶~ 밀다 push with a (sudden) jerk / push (a thing) with force∥(냄새가) ~ 코를 찌르다 assail one's nostrils∥칼로 ~ 찌르다 stab (a person) through / thrust a dagger home∥옆구리를 ~ 쥐어박다 keep poking (a person) in the ribs∥화살이 나무에 ~ 박혔다 Arrows are stuck fast in a tree.∥기둥에 머리를 ~ 부딪쳤다 I smacked[banged / bashed] my head against a pillar.∥턱을 한 대 ~ 얻어맞았다 I took a good wallop on the chin. / I got socked on the jaw.
2 〔막히는 모양〕 quite; strongly; stiflingly. ¶(구멍·관 등이) ~ 막히다 be stopped[plugged] up / be[get] blocked / get clogged / be choked∥대답이 ~ 막히다 be at a loss for an answer∥숨이 ~ 막히다 be chocked[suffocated] / be stifled∥코가 ~ 막혀 있다 My nose is stopped[stuffed] up.∥하수가 ~ 막혀 있다 The drain is completely bunged up.
콸콸 gushingly; in spouts; in profusion; in a steady stream. ¶~ 쏟아져 흐르다 flow out steadily / gush out (of)∥샘이 ~ 솟아 나오다 a spring bubbles[gushes / wells] up / a spring spouts forth∥세면대의 물이 배수구로 ~ 빨려 들어갔다 The water in the washbasin gurgled[was sucked] down the drain.

∥물이 병의 주둥이에서 ~ 흘러나왔다 The water gurgled out of the mouth of the bottle.
콸콸하다 spout; gush. ⇨콸콸거리다
콸콸거리다 spout; gush; gurgle; bubble. ¶콸콸거리는 소리 a gurgling sound.
쾅 (터질 때) with a boom[roar]; bang; (떨어질 때) with a bump[thud / thump]. ¶~ 하고 부딪치다 bump against (a wall) / bump into (a man)∥바위를 쇠망치로 ~ 쳐서 부수다 bang[chink] away at a rock with a hammer∥~ 떨어지다 fall heavily[with a thump]∥~ 소리가 나다 (go) bang / go off with a bang∥대포를 ~ 쏘다 boom a gun∥담벽에 ~ 하고 부딪히다 bang against a wall∥뒷차가 ~ 하고 내 차에 부딪쳤다 The car behind banged[crashed] into my car.∥마루에 ~ 하고 내려놓지 마시오 Don't bang it down on the floor.∥그는 문을 ~ 하고 닫았다 He shut the door with a bang.
쾅쾅거리다 (터질 때) keep booming[roaring]; (떨어질 때) keep bumping[thumping / thudding]; reverberate; resound. ¶복도를 쾅쾅거리며 달리다 run through a passage noisily∥뜰에 쾅 내려놓는 소리가 ~ bundles come bumping down into the yard∥마루를 쾅쾅거리며 걷다 stamp along the floor∥대포가 쾅쾅거린다 Guns are booming away.∥발을 쾅쾅거리지 마라 Keep your feet still.∥누군가가 문을 쾅쾅거리고 있다 Someone is knocking[rapping] at the door.
쾌 〔북어 스무 마리를 셀 때의 단위〕 a string (of 20 dried pollacks). ¶북어 두 ~ two strings of 20 dried pollacks.
쾌감 (快感) a pleasant[an agreeable] feeling[sensation]; a feeling of pleasure; (성교 시의) (an) orgasm. ¶~을 느끼다 feel pleasure / feel comfortable[agreeable / fine / nice / good]∥형언할 수 없는 ~을 느꼈다 I felt an indescribable pleasure.
쾌거 (快擧) an inspiring[a heroic] deed; a gallant act[step / enterprise / undertaking]; a glorious[gallant / heroic] venture; a splendid[heroic] achievement. ¶근래의 ~이다 be the most (heart-)stirring enterprise in these days∥그는 큼직한 타이틀 모두를 손에 넣는 ~를 성취했다 He accomplished the splendid feat of winning all the major titles.
쾌남아 (快男兒) a nice[fine / spirited / good] fellow; a jolly (good) fellow; (속어) a brick; (미) a regular guy[fellow]; (미) a nice guy.
쾌도 (快刀) a sharp knife[sword].
쾌락 (快樂) pleasure; enjoyment; delight; comfort. ¶인생의 ~ pleasures[joys] of life∥육체적[관능적] ~ the pleasures of senses / sensual[carnal] pleasures∥~에 빠지다 given[give oneself up] to pleasure / wallow[revel] in pleasure∥~을 추구하다 seek[pursue] pleasure / gather (life's) roses∥인생의 온갖 ~을 만끽하다 drain the cup of pleasure to the dregs∥온갖 인생의 ~을 버리다 cut off all comforts in life.
● **쾌락주의 / 쾌락설** 〔논〕 Epicureanism; hedonism. **쾌락주의자** a hedonist.
쾌락 (快諾) a ready[willing] consent; a ready assent. **쾌락하다** consent[agree / accept] readily; give a ready[hearty / prompt / willing] consent; accept (an offer) readily. ¶그는 나의 요청을 쾌락했다 He willingly[readily] consented to my request. / He consented to my request with a ready answer.

쾌변(快辯) eloquence; fluent speech. ¶~을 토하다 make an eloquent address[speech] / have a flow of words.

쾌보(快報) good[cheerful / encouraging / pleasant / welcome] news; glad tidings; a joyful report. ¶~를 전하다 convey the joyous news (to) // ~에 접하다 receive welcome news // ~로 전 시가(市街)는 들끓었다 The good news threw the whole city into a wild joy.

쾌사(快事) a pleasant thing[event / matter]; a joyful event; a delight; amenities (of life). ¶그것은 근래의 ~로 여겨졌다 It was really regarded as a most gratifying event. // 우리 학교 야구 팀의 우승은 근래의 ~였다 The victory of our school baseball team was one of the best things that has happened recently.

쾌속(快速) a high[great] speed. ¶~으로 달리다 run at a high speed / (속어) run at a rattling pace / advance[sail] at a great clip. 쾌속하다 very fast; swift; speedy.
● 쾌속 열차 a fast train; a rapid-transit train. 쾌속정 / 쾌속선 a speedboat; fast sailing ship[boat].

쾌승(快勝) a clear[joyful / signal / sweeping] victory; an easy victory (over). 쾌승하다 win a sweeping[a signal / an overwhelming] victory (over); win easily; come off with flying colors. ¶그는 테니스 시합에서 쾌승했다 He won a clear-cut victory[won easily] over his opponent in a tennis match.

쾌유(快癒) complete recovery. ⇨쾌차

쾌재(快哉) cry out "bravo" / yell[shout] for[with] delight[joy] / utter yells of delight / shout with exultation.

쾌적하다(快適-) agreeable; comfortable; delightful; pleasant; (속어) comfy; (속어) nice. ¶쾌적한 침대 a comfortable bed // 쾌적한 기차 a comfortable train ride // 소풍에 쾌적한 날씨 agreeable[lovely] weather for picnic // 쾌적한 항해 a pleasant voyage // 아담하고 쾌적한 집 a cozy little house // 새 자동차를 타는 기분은 몹시 ~ The new car rides very comfortably. // 이곳의 기후는 매우 쾌적합니다 The climate here is quite pleasant [agreeable].

쾌조(快調) a good[best / perfect / favo(u)rable] condition. ¶~이다 be in the best condition // ~를 보이다 go on smoothly / progress favorably // 컨디션은 아주 ~입니다 I am in excellent condition. // 만사는 ~로 진행되고 있다 Everything is going smoothly.

쾌주(快走) fine running; fast sailing. 쾌주하다 sail[run] fast[at an exhilarating speed]; run well; make a good run. ¶쾌주하는 요트 a racing sailboat // 주자는 쾌주하여 단숨에 3루에 나아갔다 The runner put on a burst of speed and made it all the way to third base. // 배는 순풍을 타고 쾌주했다 The boat scudded[ran] before the wind.

쾌차(快差) complete recovery; restoration to health. 쾌차하다 be completely cured; recover completely; regain one's health; be restored to health; be perfectly well again; be (quite) oneself again; come round completely. ¶병이 ~ get over an illness / recover from illness // 어머니는 ~쾌차하셨다 Mother is quite strong again.

쾌척(快擲) generously throwing[tossing out; making a generous contribution. 쾌척하다 generously throw out; make a generous contribution; contribute generously; give (a fund) willingly. ¶천만 원을 ~ generously give a donation of ten million won (to / toward).

쾌청(快晴-) (very) fine; nice and fine. ¶쾌청한 날 a clear day // 쾌청한 토요일 a beautiful Saturday // 개회식 날은 쾌청하여 날씨마저 알맞았다 The opening day was favored with very fine weather. // 전국적으로 쾌청한 날씨가 될 것이다 Fair skies will prevail over the peninsular.

쾌투(快投) pitch well. ¶그 투수는 멋지게 쾌투했다 He pitched very well. / The pitcher was in marvelous form.

쾌하다(快-) 1 [기쁘다] happy; delightful; delighted. 쾌히 delightfully; agreeably; pleasantly; cheerfully; comfortably; [기꺼이] gladly; readily; willingly; with pleasure; with readiness; with a good grace. ¶~ 승낙하다 readily[willingly] consent (to it) / give a ready consent (to) / readily accept (an invitation) // ~ 청을 들어주다 comply with another's request with a good grace // ~ 돈을 꾸어 주다 lend money with a good grace // ~ 떠맡다 be delighted to undertake (the work) / undertake (something) with pleasure // 남의 충고를 ~ 받아들이다 take another's advice in good part.
2 [병이 완전히 낫다] well again; recovered. ¶몸이 이제는 아주 ~ I am perfectly well again. 쾌히 completely; nicely. ¶병이 ~ 낫다 be completely recovered from illness.

쾌활하다(快活-) cheerful; cheery; merry; jolly; gay; lively; vivacious; sprightly; light-hearted; volatile; (구어) rattling. ¶쾌활한 성미 cheerful spirit // 쾌활한 사람 a jolly[lively] fellow // 그는 쾌활한 사람이다 He is a cheerful man. 쾌활히 cheerfully; lively; lightheartedly; with a light heart. ¶~ 웃다 laugh gaily[merrily] // ~ 대답하다 answer cheerfully // 그녀는 ~ 웃었다 She laughed merrily.

괴괴하다 ill-[foul-] smelling. ⇨퀴퀴하다

쿠데타 a coup d'état (pl. coups d'état, coup d'états); a coup. ¶군사[군부] ~ a military coup // 무혈 ~ a bloodless coup // ~를 일으키다 effect[carry out] a coup d'état / pull (off) a coup // 젊은 장교들이 ~를 기도했다 Young officers tried to carry out a coup d'état.

쿠리다 ill-[foul-] smelling; suspicious. ⇨구리다

쿠린내 a bad smell. ⇨구린내

쿠션 a cushion. ¶스리 ~ [당구] three-cushion billiards[carom] / three cushions // ~이 좋은 의자 a soft, comfortable chair // ~을 대다 cushion (a seat).

쿠키 (미) a cookie; a cooky; (영) a biscuit.

쿠페 (소형 자동차) (프) a coupé; a coupe; (미국 속어) a coop.

쿠폰 a coupon. ¶주문용 ~ an order coupon // 호텔 ~ a hotel coupon // ~으로 사다 purchase by means of coupon.

쿡 stinging hard; pecking. ⇨콕²

쿨롬 [전] a coulomb(약어 C).

쿨룩쿨룩 coughing away. ⇨콜록콜록

쿨쿨¹ (물이) gurgling. 쿨쿨하다¹ keep gurgling. ⇨쿨쿨거리다¹

쿨쿨² (잠을) snoring; z-z-z. ¶~ 코를 골다

쿨쿨거리다¹ keep gurgling; gurgle and gurgle.

쿨쿨거리다² keep snoring; snore and snore.

쿵 with a thump[plump / bump / thud / bang / clunk]. ¶~ 하고 넘어지다 fall down with a thud // ~ 하고 엉덩방아를 찧다 fall flat on one's behind[rear] // ~ 하고 마룻바닥에 떨어지다 come down bump on the floor // 나무가 ~ 하고 쓰러졌다 A tree fell with a thud [thump]. // 나는 바나나 껍질에 미끄러져서 ~ 하고 넘어졌다 I slipped on a banana peel and went down with a wham.

쿵쾅거리다 keep banging[roaring / pounding]; make din; raise [kick up] a racket; romp about. ¶쿵쾅거리며 걷다 stamp along (the floor) / walk along (the passageway) pit-a-pat [noisily] // 쿵쾅거리며 방을[에서] 나가다 stamp violently out of a room / stamp out of the room (in anger) // 아이들이 2층에서 쿵쾅거리며 뛰놀고 있다 The kids are romping[thudding] away upstairs. // 건축 현장에서 들려오는 저 쿵쾅거리는 소리가 신경에 거슬린다 All that pounding over at the construction site is getting on my nerves.

쿵쿵 1 [떨어지거나 넘어질 때 나는 소리] with thumps[plumps / bumps / thuds / bangs]. **쿵쿵하다** thump; plump; bump; thud; bang. **2** [북·대포 소리] bang, bang; boom, boom. ¶~ 울리는 대포 소리 the booming sound of cannon // 북을 ~ 울리다 rataplan / tom-tom / beat loudly. **쿵쿵하다** bang, bang; boom, boom. **3** [찧는 소리]. ¶방아를 ~ 찧다 pound (grain) heavily with a pestle.

쿵푸 (⑧功夫) kung fu.

쿼터¹ [4분의 1] a [one] quarter.

쿼터² [할당] quota; allotment. ¶수입 ~ an import quota // ~를 삭감하다 cut the quota.
●**쿼터제** the quota system.

쿼터백 [미식축구] (a) quarterback(약어 q.b.). ¶~을 맡아보다 quarterback (for a team).

퀀셋 a Quonset [영] Nissen] hut.

퀭하다 [눈이 들어가 정기가 없다] cavernous; sunken; deep-set; hollow. ¶퀭한 눈 sunken [cavernous / deep-set] eyes.

퀴놀린 [화] quinoline.

퀴륨 curium(기호 Cm).

퀴리 [방사능 단위] a curie(기호 Ci, c). ¶마이크로~ a microcurie.

퀴즈 a quiz; a quiz game. ¶~를 풀다 answer a quiz question.
●**퀴즈 프로** [라디오·TV] a quiz program [show]; a panel show. ¶~의 사회자 a quizmaster // 나는 텔레비전의 ~에 출연했다 I appeared on a TV quiz show.

퀴퀴하다 ill- [foul-] smelling; stinking; malodorous; offensive; 《구어》 smelly. ¶퀴퀴한 냄새 an offensive [a bad / a foul] smell // 생선이 썩어 ~ The fish is rotten and stinking.

퀼로트 [치마바지] (a pair of) culottes.

큐 1 [당구] a cue. ¶~를 잡다 play billiards (with). **2** [신호] a cue. ¶~를 보내다 cue / give a cue // 연출자는 배우에게 말을 시작하라고 ~를 보냈다 The director signaled the actor to begin to speak. / The director gave the actor his cue.

큐비즘 [미] cubism.

큐피드 [로마 신화] Cupid.

크기 (a) size; dimensions; magnitude; volume(용적); bulk(부피). ¶~는 in size / in dimensions / in area(면적) // ~에 따라서 according to size // 상당한 ~의 fairly large-sized / good-sized / of reasonable dimensions // 중간 정도~의 medium- [moderate-] sized // ~가 다르다[같다] differ[be equal] in size // 엽서 ~의 한 조각의 종이 a piece of paper of a postcard size // 달걀 ~의 혹 a lump as big as an egg // 대체로 같은 ~다 They are much of a size. // 이 사진은 실물 ~이다 This photograph is natural [actual] size. // 이 돌은 ~에 비해 무겁다 This stone is heavy for its size. // ~는 어느 정도로 할까요 What size shall I make it?

크나큰 huge; gigantic; giant; enormous; mammoth; mountainous; vast; tremendous. ¶~ 손실 a tremendous [an enormous] loss // ~ 은혜 a great favor [obligation] // ~ 잘못 a gross [glaring] mistake / a grave [fatal] error.

크낙새 [동] a Korean redheaded woodpecker.

크다¹ [자라다] grow (up); become taller; grow larger; increase in size; [증대하다] swell; expand; be enlarged; be extended; be expanded; [대성하다] attain greatness. ¶다 큰 아이 a grown-up child // 도시[시골]에서 큰 아이 a city [country] -bred child // 모유 [인공영양]로 큰 아이 a breast-bred [bottle-fed] child // 너는 커서 무엇이 될래 What are you going to do [be] when you grow up, dear? // 얘야 너 많이 컸구나 What a big boy you have grown up, dear! // 그는 시골에서 컸다 He grew up in the country. // 진달래가 많이 컸다 The azalea has grown a lot. // 요전에 보았을 때보다 키가 컸구나 You have grown since I saw you last.

크다² [형상이] big; large; [위대하다] great; grand; [강대하다] mighty; powerful; [막심하다] severe; heavy; [거대하다] gigantic; monstrous; mammoth; huge; colossal; enormous; [광대하다] vast; extensive; spacious; broad; of vast dimensions; (부피가) bulky; massive; voluminous(용적이); (마음이) generous; liberal; magnanimous. ¶큰 사람[읍] a big person [town] // 큰 건물 a large building // 큰 치수의 여성복 a large size [(미) queen-sized] dress(▶ (미) 남성용은 king-sized) // 매우 [터무니없이] 큰 방 a huge [an enormous] room // 100보다 큰 수 a number higher [larger / bigger] than one hundred // 큰 기대 high hopes / great expectations // 큰 소란 a big fuss // 큰 희망[슬픔] a great hope [sorrow] // 큰 규모가 큰 사업[project] a large-scale undertaking [project] // 큰 실패 a big [terrible] mistake // 목소리가 ~ have a loud voice // 큰 기대를 걸다 expect great things from (a person / a thing) // 마음이 ~ be broad-minded [big-hearted / generous / magnanimous] / have a big heart // 손이 ~ have an open hand / be liberal (of [with] one's money) / be generous (with one's money) // 야심이 ~ have a high ambition // 그렇게 큰 소리로 말하지 마라 Don't shout like that. // 텔레비전 소리가 너무 ~ The television is too loud [noisy]. (▶ noisy는 시끄러운의 뜻) // 우리는 큰 저항에 부딪혔다 We met strong [heavy / great] resistance. // 작물에 큰 피해를 가져왔다 It caused great [serious / severe] damage to the crops. / It did a lot of

크라운

[considerable] damage to the crops.∥나는 큰 빚을 지고 있다 I'm deeply in debt.∥상대방 팀에 크게 졌다 Our opponents beat us by a wide margin. / We were badly beaten by our opponents.∥그 뉴스는 크게 보도되었다 The story was given extensive coverage.∥이러한 스타일의 큰 장갑은 다 팔렸습니다 Large-sized gloves in this style are sold out.∥태풍에 의한 농작물의 피해는 매우 컸다 The crops suffered heavy damage from the typhoon.∥나는 그 일로 해서 크건 작건 불편을 겪었다 I was more or less inconvenienced by the affair.∥그것은 크게 도움이 된다 It helps me greatly. / It is a great help to me.∥그는 큰 문방구점을 가지고 있다 He has a large stationery shop.∥그것은 큰 성공[실패]이었다 It was a great success[a complete flop].∥큰 고기는 놓치고 송사리만 잡아두었다 Laws catch flies, but let hornets go free.

큰 방죽도 개미구멍으로 무너진다(속담) A little leak will sink a great ship.

크라운 [왕관 모양을 새긴 영국의 5실링짜리 은화] a crown.

크래커 [과자] a cracker; (영) a biscuit; [작은 폭죽] a cracker. ¶~를 아삭아삭 깨물다 crunch a cracker∥~를 울리다 set off a cracker.

크랭크 a crank. ¶~의 회전 속도 crank speed∥~를 돌리다 crank / turn a crank∥~ 인을 하다 [영] start filming∥~ 업을 하다 [영] finish filming.
● **크랭크축** a crankshaft.

크레디트 카드 a credit card. ¶~ 소지자에게 더 나은 서비스를 제공하다 provide better service to holders of credit cards.

크레센도 [음] crescendo(약어 cres., cresc.; 기호 <).

크레용 (a) crayon. ¶파란색[노란색] ~ a stick of blue[yellow] crayon / a blue[yellow] crayon∥~으로 그림을 그리다 draw a picture in crayon(s).

크레인 [공] a crane.

크레졸 cresol.
● **크레졸 비눗물** a saponated cresol solution. **크레졸수** cresol water.

크레파스 a pastel crayon(▶ crayon과 pastel을 합성한 말로, 일본에서 만들어진 조어임).

크렘린 the Kremlin.

크로마뇽인(―人) [고고] Cromagnon[Cro-Magnon] man.

크로스바 [체] a crossbar.

크로스워드퍼즐 a crossword puzzle. ¶~을 하다 do[work on] a crossword puzzle.

크로스컨트리 [체] a cross-country.

크로켓 [서양 요리의 하나] a croquette.

크로키 [미] (프) a croquis; a rapid sketch; a rough draft.

크롤 스트로크 [수영] the crawl stroke.

크롬 [화] chromium(기호 Cr); chrome.
● **크롬 도금** chromium plating.

크루즈 미사일 a cruise missile.

크리스마스 Christmas (약어 Xmas); Christmas day. ¶~다운[기분의] Christmasy / Christmassy∥~에 on Christmas Day∥~를 경축하다 keep[observe] Christmas∥~ 축하, 인사를 하다 extend[offer] Christmas greetings (to)∥~를 축하합니다 A merry Christmas (to you)! / I wish you a merry Christmas.
● **크리스마스 선물** a Christmas present [gift]; a Christmas box(아이에게 주는). **크리스마스실** a Christmas seal. **크리스마스이브** (on) Christmas Eve. **크리스마스카드** a Christmas card. ¶~를 받다 get a Christmas card (from)∥~를 보내다 send a Christmas card (to). **크리스마스 캐럴** a Christmas carol. **크리스마스트리** Christmas tree.

크리스천 a Christian.
● **크리스천 네임** a Christian name.

크리스털 crystal.
● **크리스털 유리** crystal glass. **크리스털 제품** a crystal.

크리스트교(―教) Christianity; the Christian religion[faith]. ¶~의 Christian∥~를 믿다 believe in Christianity / be a Christian∥~를 전도하다 propagate[spread] Christianity∥그는 ~로 개종했다 He was converted Christianity.
● **크리스트교도** a Christian.

크리켓 [체] cricket. ¶~을 하다 play cricket.

크림 1 [식용] cream. ¶~ 모양의 creamy / creamlike∥생~ fresh cream∥커피에 ~을 타다 add cream to coffee∥우유에서 ~을 뜨다 skim the cream from milk∥우유를 휘저어 ~을 만들다 churn cream. **2** (화장용) (skin) cream. ¶화장용 ~ cosmetic[facial / face] cream∥콜드 ~ cold cream∥배니싱 ~ vanishing cream∥셰이빙 ~ shaving cream∥~을 바르다 cream (one's face) / apply cream to (one's hands). **3** (an) ice cream. ⇨아이스크림
● **크림빵** a cream bun.

큰개자리 [천] the (Great) Dog; Canis Major.

큰골 [생] the cerebrum. ⇨대뇌

큰곰자리 [천] the Great Bear; the Big Dipper; Ursa Major.

큰기침 a big "ahem." ¶~으로 그 자리를 얼버무리려 하다 try to save the situation with a big "ahem." **큰기침하다** clear one's throat loudly (to draw a person's attention). ¶큰기침하고 방에 들어가다 go into the room with a big "ahem."

큰길 a main road[street]; a thoroughfare; a highway; a broad street. ¶~에서 on[(영) in] the main street.

큰달 [긴 달] a long month. ¶1월은 ~이다 January has thirty-one days.

큰댁(―宅) the house of one's eldest brother; the head family; the house of the legal wife. ⇨큰집

큰돈 a large[a big] sum (of money); a lot[a great deal] of money. ¶~을 벌다 make a lot of money∥~을 들이다 go to great expense / [투자하다] invest a large sum (in)∥~이 들다 cost a great deal of money[a fortune]∥내게는 그런 ~이 나올 데가 없다 I don't know where I can get such a large sum.∥그에게 ~이 굴러 들어왔다 He has come into a fortune.∥무슨 ~이라도 굴러 들어왔나 Has your ship come home?

큰딸 the eldest daughter. ⇨맏딸

큰마누라 one's wedded wife; a legal[lawful] wife.

큰마음 1 [대망] a great desire; (an) ambition; (an) aspiration; best wishes. ¶~을 품다 have[cherish / harbor] an ambition / be full of ambitions. **2** [후한 마음] a big[large] heart; a generous heart. ¶~ 먹고 자네에게 시계를 사 주겠네 I will buy you a watch generously.∥그는 웨이터에게 ~ 먹고 팁을 후하

게 주었다 He tipped the waiter generously. // 나는 ~ 먹고 모피로 된 코트를 샀다 I splurged on[treated myself to] a fur coat.

큰물 a heavy flood; an inundation; an overflow. ¶~이 지다[나다] have a flood / get flooded / be in flood / be inundated // ~에 집이 떠내려갔다 Houses were swept away by a flood. // 이렇게 비가 계속되다가는 ~ 지겠는걸 If it goes on raining, there will be a flood[it will cause a flood].

큰북 [음] a big drum; (오케스트라용의) a low [bass] drum.

큰불 [큰 화재] a big[great] fire; a destructive [disastrous] fire; a conflagration; a holocaust; [큰 짐승을 잡기 위해 쏘는 총알] a shot (for hunting big game). ¶~을 만나다 be visited by a disastrous fire // ~이 났다 A big fire broke out[took place]. / There was a big fire.

큰불(을) 놓다 [발포하다] fire a shot (at big game).

큰비 a heavy rain; a big[heavy / torrential] rainfall; (구어) a drencher. ¶~가 왔다 It rained heavily. / There was[We had] a downpour[heavy rainfall].

큰사람 [위대한 사람] a great[magnanimous] man; a man of virtue[high caliber]; a great [master] mind. ¶~이 되다 attain greatness.

큰사랑 (-舍廊) (웃어른이 거처하는) the living room of one's elders; the main guest room.

큰사위 the husband of one's firstborn [eldest] daughter. ⇨ 맏사위

큰살림 a luxurious household; high living. **큰살림하다** live high.

큰상 (-床) a formal table laden with food presented to the guest of honor.

큰상(을) 받다 be presented with a formal table.

큰소리 1 [야단치는 소리] a shout; a yell; a roar; a bawl; a brawl. ¶~로 꾸짖다 address vehemently / thunder out / vociferate / fulminate / give (a person) hell[what for] / haul (a person) over the coals // ~ 한 번 못 하다 be very submissive [docile] / never raise one's voice. 2 [호언] big[tall] talk; boasting; a bombast; a (loud) boast; boastful words; bragging; high-sounding words; magniloquence.

큰소리치다 talk tall[big]; [자랑하다] boast (of / that); brag; make wild[exaggerated] claims. ¶그 사나이는 자기가 세계적인 스키어라고 큰소리쳤다 The man bragged[boasted] that he was the world's top skier. // 그는 입으로는 큰소리쳐도 실은 대단찮다 It's all bark and no bite. // 큰소리치는 녀석치고서 겁쟁이 아닌 녀석이 없다 It's the ones who talk big who are really the cowards. // 그는 집 안에서만 큰소리치고 밖에서는 꼼짝도 못한다 He is bossy at home but timid elsewhere. / He is a lion at home and a mouse abroad. / He is a bully at home and a coward abroad.

큰손녀 (-孫女) one's firstborn granddaughter by one's eldest son. ⇨ 맏손녀

큰손자 (-孫子) one's firstborn grandson by one's eldest son. ⇨ 맏손자

큰아기 1 [다 큰 처녀] an adolescent girl; a grown-up girl; a girl in her late teens. 2 [맏딸] one's eldest[(미) oldest] daughter.

큰아들 the firstborn[eldest] son. ⇨ 맏아들

큰아버지 an(older) uncle; one's father's [dad's] older brother.

큰어머니 an(older) aunt; the wife of one's father's[dad's] older brother.

큰언니 one's eldest brother[sister].

큰오빠 one's eldest brother.

큰일 1 [큰 사업] a great undertaking; a big [great] enterprise[task]; a big business; a big plan. ¶~을 이룩하다 achieve[do] a great thing[work] // ~을 계획하다 plan a big enterprise // 그놈은 꼭 ~ 할 걸세 He is sure to do something big some day. // ~은 작은 일에서 비롯된다 Great things have small beginnings.
2 [중대한 일] a matter of grave concern [great consequence / great importance]; a serious[grave] affair; a great trouble; a disaster; no joke; an alarming accident. ¶~을 저지르다 cause[invite] a disaster / cause a serious trouble // ~을 저질렀군 Now you're done it! / See what you have done. // 자네 ~을 저질렀구먼 Now you're done it! / 너에게 무슨 일이 생기면 ~이다 What if anything should happen to you! // 그놈은 하도 게으름쟁이라서 ~이야 I don't know what to do with him. He is such a lazy fellow. // ~이다! 호랑이가 우리에서 도망쳤다 Good God! The tigers gotten out of its cage! // 그런 짓을 하면 ~이다 If you do something like that, it will have serious consequences. // 한 발짝만 잘못 디디면 ~이다 A single false step could prove fatal[disastrous]. // 들키면 나는 ~이다 If I am discovered, I am done for. // 기차를 놓치면 ~이니 곧 떠나세요 Leave at once. You simply mustn't miss the train
3 [예식·잔치] a great occasion; a big ceremony[banquet]; a wedding; a funeral. ¶~을 치르다 go through[carry out] a wedding [funeral] // ~이 닥쳐온다 A big occasion draws near.

큰일(이) 나다 assume alarming[menacing / serious] proportions; grow[get] serious; face a matter of grave[serious] concern; face disaster. ¶큰일 났다고 떠들다 cry alarm // 이거 큰일 났구나 Good Heavens! We really are in trouble! / We are in for it. / Here's a (nice[pretty]) go. / What a fine fix we're in! // 이대로 놔 두면 큰일 나겠다 If we leave it like this, it will grow[develop] into a serious matter. // 큰일 날 사람이로군 What a man! / (구어) He's a caution. // 큰일 날 뻔했다 That was close. / It was a close call.

큰절[1] [의식·웃어른에 가장 공손한 절] a deep bow. **큰절하다** make a deep bow; (초례청에서) make one's ceremonial deep bows. ¶차례가 끝나면 어린이들은 부모에게 큰절한다 After the ceremony, children make deep bows to their parents.

큰절[2] [큰 사찰] the main temple.

큰집 1 [만형의 집] the house of one's eldest brother. 2 [종가] the head[main] family; the head house; the main stock. 3 [적가(嫡家)] the house[home] of the legal wife.

큰창자 [생] the large intestine. ⇨ 대장(大腸)

큰처남 (-妻男) the eldest brother of one's wife; one's eldest brother-in-law.

큰코다치다 have a bitter experiences; have [get] the worst of it; have a hard[bad] time (of it) (with a person); pay dearly (for); (속어) get[catch / take] it in the neck. ¶그런 짓을 하다가는 큰코다칠걸 You will suffer if

큰할아버지 you do such a thing. / You shall smart for this.∥믿지 못할 사람을 믿었다가 큰코다쳤다 I made the bitter mistake of putting my faith in someone who could not be trusted.

큰할아버지 one's grandfather's eldest brother.

큰형(-兄) one's eldest brother. ⇨맏형

큰형수(-兄嫂) the wife of the eldest brother; one's eldest sister in-law.

클라리넷 [음] a clarinet. ¶~ 연주자 a clarinet(t)ist / a clarinet player∥~을 연주하다 play (on) the clarinet.

클라이맥스 a climax. ¶~에 달하다[이르다] reach[come to] the climax (of a story) / culminate (in) 이야기는 ~에 이르렀다 The story has reached[come to] its climax.∥음악회의 ~는 그녀의 바이얼린 독주였다 Her violin solo marked the climax of the concert.∥이 소설의 ~는 두 사람의 재회(再會) 장면이다 The climax in the novel is the scene in which the two meet again.

클래스메이트 a classmate.

클래식 classical music.

클랙슨 a klaxon; a horn; [자동차의 경적 소리] a honk; a beep. ¶~을 울리다 sound[toot] the klaxon[horn] / honk.

클러치 [공] a clutch. ¶노 ~의 자동차 a car with automatic transmission[automatic drive]∥(자동차의) ~를 연결하다 let in the clutch (of a car)∥~를 떼다 release the clutch∥~를 밟다 step on the clutch (pedal).

클럽 1 [동호회] a club. ¶테니스 ~ a tennis club∥사교 ~ a social club / (미)(남학생의) a fraternity / (미)(여학생의) a sorority∥~에 들다 join a club / become a member of a club∥~을 조직하다 organize a club. **2** [카드놀이의] clubs. ¶~의 잭 the jack of clubs. **3** [골프의 채] a club.
●클럽 활동 club[extracurricular] activities. ¶그녀는 ~에 열심이었다 She took an enthusiastic part in club activities. 클럽 회원 a member of a club; a clubman; a clubber.

클레이 사격(-射擊) clay pigeon shooting; trapshooting; skeet shooting.

클레임 [경] [손해 배상 청구] a claim. ¶~에 응하다 pay a claim (for damages)∥~을 붙이다 make[institute / bring forward / put in] a claim for compensation∥~을 제기하다 advance a claim / make a claim on (a company) / send in a claim (as per).

클렌징크림 [화장용 크림] cleansing cream.

클로로벤젠 [화] chlorobenzene.

클로로포름 [화] chloroform. ¶환자를 ~으로 마취했다 I chloroformed the patient.

클로로필 [식] chlorophyll.

클로르칼크(⒮Chlorkalk) [화] chloride of lime; bleaching powder.

클로버 [식] a clover. ⇨토끼풀¶네 잎 ~ a four-leaf(ed) clover∥세 잎 ~ a trefoil / a honeywort.

클로즈업 [영] [대상의 일부를 확대함] a close-up(약어 CU); a close shot; a close-up view (of the moon). **클로즈업하다** take[obtain] a close-up (of); bring into a close-up. ➔¶클로즈업되다 be brought into a close-up / [비유] be high lighted / be in the limelight / (신문 등에서) be played up (by the papers)∥새끼 고양이가 클로즈업되어 있다 The kitten is shown in (a) close-up.∥정세가 바뀌면서 그의 이름이 다시 클로즈업되기 시작했다 The new situation has brought him into the public eye again. / As the situation has changed, he is being given a great deal of attention again.

클리토리스 [생] the clitoris.

클릭 [컴] [마우스 누름] a click. **클릭하다** click (on).

클린업 트리오 [야구] a cleanup trio.

클린치 [권투] a clinch; clinching. **클린치하다** clinch. ¶클린치하고 있다 be in a clinch.

클린 히트 [야구] a clean hit[single]. ¶~를 치다 smash out a clean hit∥센터 쪽으로 ~를 날리다 smack the ball cleanly into center for a hit.

클립 1 [종이끼우개] a (paper) clip. ¶~으로 꽂다 fasten (papers) with a clip. **2** [머리말이용의] a curling pin; a curler. ¶그녀는 머리를 ~으로 감고 있었다 Her hair was in curlers.

큼직하다 quite[fairly] big[large]; good-sized; fair-sized; on the large side; (도량이) quite generous[liberal]. ¶큼직한 집 quite a big house∥큼직한 사람 quite a big person∥큼직한 글씨로 쓰다 write large∥신문에 큼직한 광고를 내다 place[put in] a large advertisement in a newspaper. **큼직이** big; large(ly); [대규모로] on a large[grand] scale; in a large[big] way; [도량이 크게] generously; liberally. ¶집을 ~ 짓다 build a house big∥(옷을) 좀 ~ 해 주세요 Cut the coat rather full[with some allowance].

킁킁 "Sniff, sniff!" ¶~ 냄새를 맡다 sniff (at) / give a sniff (at). **킁킁대다** whine; grunt. ⇨킁킁거리다

킁킁거리다 (개 등이) whine; (돼지 등이) grunt; (말 등이) snort; (사람이 경멸의 표시로) snort. ¶코를 ~ snuffle / sniffle∥그 아이는 코를 킁킁거리는 버릇이 있다 The child is in the habit of sniffling.

키¹ [신장] (one's) height; (one's) stature; inches. ¶~가 큰[작은] 사람 a man of great [small / low / short] stature / a tall[short] person∥보통 ~의 사람 a man of ordinary stature∥중~의 사람 a person of mean [medium / middle / middling] stature∥~가 크다 be tall (of stature) / be high[tall] in stature / be of great stature / have a good height∥~가 작다 be short (of stature) / be small[low / short] (in stature) / be of small stature∥~가 거의 같다 be nearly of the same height∥~가 자라다 grow tall[in height] / increase[grow] in stature∥~가 장대같이 크다 be as tall as a lamppost∥~를 재다 measure[take] (a person's) height∥~를 대보다 measure oneself with (another) / compare one's stature back to back with (another)∥~가 얼마예요 How tall are you? / What is your height?∥나는 ~가 165센티미터다 I am 165 centimeters tall[in height / in stature]. / I stand 5 feet 4 inches (tall / high).∥그는 ~가 크다[작다] He is tall [short].∥자네는 ~가 크다 You have grown.∥깊이가 ~를 넘는 곳에 가면 안 된다 Don't go beyond[get out of] your depth.∥누이동생은 나보다 ~가 크다 My younger sister is taller than I am.∥두 사람은 나란히 ~ 재보기를 했다 The two of us stood side by side [back to back] to see which was the taller [to compare heights] (▶ back to back은 등을 맞대고 서서의 뜻).

키 크고 속 없다(속담) be tall and lack insides.

키 크고 싱겁지 않은 사람 없다(속담) There are no tall people who knows how to behave properly.

키² [곡식을 까부르는 기구] a ki; a winnow; a winnowing basket; a winnowing fan; a winnower; a fan. ¶~로 **까부르다** winnow (grain / chaff) // ~로 까불러서 겨를 없애다 winnow the chaff away [out] (from the grain).

키³ [조종타] a rudder; [조종 장치] a helm; [타륜(舵輪)] a (steering) wheel. ¶~를 **잡다** steer / be at the helm // [조종하다] manage / control / handle / direct / lead // 그때 선장이 ~를 잡고 있었다 The captain was at the helm at the time.

키⁴ a key. ¶~를 **누르다** press down a key // 타자기의 ~를 두드리다 pound [strike / tap] the keys of a typewriter // 전신의 ~를 치다 operate a telegraph key.

키니네 [약] quinine.

키다리 a tall lank person; (영국 구어) a daddy longlegs; (미) a gangling fellow. ¶그는 전봇대 같은 ~다 He is as tall as a lamppost.

키보드 1 [컴퓨터·피아노 등의] a keyboard. 2 [호텔 등에서 열쇠를 걸어 두는 판] a keyboard.

키부츠 [이스라엘의 집단 농장] a kibbutz (pl. -zim).

키순(-順) the order of stature [height]. ¶~으로 in order of [according to] stature // ~으로 **서다** [늘어서다] stand [line up] in order of height // 소년들은 ~으로 늘어섰다 The boys lined up in order of height.

키스 a kiss (on the cheek); a smack(소리가 나는). ¶~를 **보내다** [던지다] send [blow / throw] a kiss (to) // ~를 **허락하다** give one's lips (to) // ~를 하며 이별의 ~를 하다 kiss (a person) good-by (to) / kiss (a person) good-by // …에게 몰래 ~를 하다 steal a kiss from (her) // 사랑의 ~를 하다 kiss (her) with love // 두 사람은 ~를 했다 Their lips met. // 그녀는 아기에게 안녕의 ~를 했다 She kissed the child good-bye [good-night]. **키스하다** kiss (a girl on the lips / a person's lips); give (a person) a kiss; give (a person) a smack(소리 내어). ¶아이에게 ~ give a kiss to a child // 성서에 키스하여 선서하다 kiss the Bible [the Book] // 키스하고 헤어지다 [자나] kiss (a person) good-bye [good night] // 키스하지 않고 헤어지다 part with dry lips.

키우다 1 [양육하다] bring up; rear; raise; foster; nurse; (동·식물을) breed; raise; rear. ¶어머니 손으로만 키운 (a child) brought up exclusively by his mother // 아이를 우유 [모유]로 ~ feed [raise] a child on the bottle [at the breast] // 아이를 훌륭히 ~ nurture a child the way a child should be brought up(바람직하게) / breed a child a good boy [girl] (가정교육이 좋게) // 손수 돌보아 ~ bring up (a child) under one's care // 금이야 옥이야 하고 키우다 be reared [brought up] with the utmost care and affection // 그녀는 세 아이를 훌륭히 She brought up [raised] three children. // 그들은 몇 천 마리나 되는 양을 키우고 있다 They keep thousands of sheep. // 그녀는 다섯 아이를 혼자서 키웠다 She brought up her five children all by herself. // 아이는 부모가 키우기에 달렸다 A child is what his parents make it.

2 [육성하다] promote; support; protect; (재질 등을) develop; cultivate; [훈련·교육하다] educate; train; bring up. ¶운동선수를 ~ develop an athlete // 법률가로 ~ bring up (a boy) to the legal profession // 외교관으로 ~ train (a person) for the diplomatic service // 담력을 ~ cultivate [foster / develop] courage // 국내 산업을 ~ promote domestic [home] industry // 인재를 ~ cultivate men of talent // 제자를 어엿한 장인으로 ~ train an apprentice until he becomes a full-fledged craftsman // 그가 그녀의 음악적인 재능을 키웠다 He fostered her musical talent. // 정부는 국내 산업을 키우는 조처를 취했다 The Government took measures to promote domestic industry.

3 [병·습관 등을 악화시키다] aggravate; make serious.

키 워드 a key word.
키위 [동] a kiwi; an apteryx.
키잡이 a helmsman; a steerman; (경주용 보트의) a coxswain; a cockswain; a cox.
키질하다 winnow. ¶쌀을 ~ winnow rice.
키퍼 a goalkeeper. ⇨`골키퍼
키펀처 a key puncher; a key-punch operator.
키펀치 [컴] a key punch.
키포인트 (*key point) [주안점] the main [essential] point; [요점] the point. ¶문제 해결의 ~ a key to solving a question // ~를 **파악하다** get [catch] the point [the main idea] of (a subject) // 이것이 ~다 This is the point.

킥 (축구·럭비 등에서) a kick. ¶코너 ~ a corner kick // 드롭 [플레이스] ~ a drop [place] kick // 페널티 ~ a penalty kick // ~으로 골을 넣다 kick a goal // 그는 ~이 강하다 He's got a strong kick. / He's a strong kicker. **킥하다** kick (the ball). ¶공을 ~ kick a ball.

킥복싱 kick boxing.
킥오프 [축구] a kickoff. **킥오프하다** kick off.
킥킥 tittering; chuckling. **킥킥하다** titter; chuckle. ⇨`킥킥거리다

킥킥거리다 titter; chuckle; laugh to oneself. ¶킥킥거리며 쳐다보다 look at (a person) with furtive laughter // 소녀들은 배를 쥐고 킥킥거리며 웃었다 The girls were doubled up with suppressed laughter. // 그녀는 킥킥거리며 웃었다 She broke into a giggle. // 어린 소녀가 킥킥거리면서 방을 빠져나갔다 The tittering little girl slipped out of the room.

킬로 a kilo.
● **킬로그램** a kilogram(me)(약어 kg). **킬로리터** a kiloliter(약어 kl). **킬로미터** a kilometer (약어 km). ¶시속 3백 ~ a velocity of 300 km [kilometers] an hour. **킬로볼트** a kilovolt(약어 kV). **킬로와트** a kilowatt(약어 kW). **킬로칼로리** a kilocalorie(약어 kcal). **킬로헤르츠** a kilohertz(약어 kHz).

킬킬거리다 giggle; titter; chuckle. ⇨`낄낄거리다
킷값 behavior appropriate to [benefitting] one's height [stature]. ¶~도 못 하다 be unworthy of one's stature.
킹사이즈 ¶~의 king-size(d).
킹킹거리다 (어린애가) fret; be peevish [fractious]; whine; blubber; (개가) whimper; whine.

E

타(他) **1** [다른 사람] another person; other people; (the) others. ¶~의 추종을 불허하는 peerless / matchless / unequaled / unrivaled / beyond[without] compare / without (an) equal∥그의 용감한 행위는 ~의 모범이 되었다. His brave deed served as a pattern for others. **2** [다른] another (person); other (people); alien; foreign; strange (land). ¶~계정으로 이월하다 transfer to other accounts.

타(打) [다스] a dozen. ¶반 ~ half a dozen∥10~ ten dozen / a small gross∥한 ~에 얼마로 팔다 sell by the dozen.

타가(他家) another family[house].

타개(打開) a break; a development; a new turn; a solution. ¶정국의 ~ a new turn of the political situation / introduction of a new situation in politics. **타개하다** break (through); effect a break[development]. ¶교착 상태를 ~ break[resolve] the deadlock / bring a deadlock to an end / save the situation∥난국을 ~ find a way out of the difficulties∥위기를 타개할 실마리를 찾았다 We have found an idea that may lead to a breakthrough in the crisis.

● **타개책** a way out; a remedy; a countermeasure; a plan for the way out. ¶~을 강구하지 않으면 안 된다 We must find some way out of the difficulty.

타격(打擊) **1** [때려치기] a blow; a hit; a knock; (구어) a clout; [기세를 꺾기] (구어) a crusher; (구어) a stinger; [충격] a shock; [손해] damage. ¶치명적인 ~ a fatal[mortal / smashing / crushing] blow∥~을 주다[가하다] strike a blow (at / against)∥심한[큰] ~을 받다 be hard hit (by) / receive[get] a severe blow∥(구어) take a terrific walloping / (속어) take a bad knock∥주가의 폭락으로 큰 ~을 받다 lose heavily by a slump in the stocks∥~을 피하다 fend off a blow∥~을 완화시키다 soften a blow∥그는 상대의 머리에 ~을 가했다 He hit[struck] his opponent (a blow) on the head.∥그의 실패가 그에게는 크나큰 ~이었다 The failure was a great blow[shock] to him.∥태풍으로 사과는 큰 ~을 입었다 The apples were heavily damaged by the typhoon. / The typhoon did serious damage to the apple crop.∥철도 파업은 서울의 중앙 시장에 큰 ~을 주었다 The railroad strike hit the Central Market in Seoul hard.∥근간의 실패가 그에게 큰 ~을 준 것 같다 His recent failure seems to have been a great shock to him.∥석유 위기의 결정적 ~을 받아 그의 회사는 도산했다 His company went down under the crushing blow of the oil crisis.∥그녀는 마음속에 심한 ~을 받았다 Her heart was broken. / It was a terrible [hard] blow to her.

2 [야구] batting; hitting; a clout. ¶~이 좋은 선수 a good[strong] hitter / a slugger(강타자)∥계속하여 무서운 ~을 보이다 swat streaks of long basers / swat a succession of hits / pound out hit after hit[a series of hits]∥그 팀은 ~이 좋다[신통찮다] The team is[isn't] hitting well. / The team is strong [weak] in hitting.∥멋진 ~이다 It's a clean hit. / The ball has been well kissed.

● **타격력** hitting[batting] power. **타격률** a batting average. ⇨ =타율(打率) **타격 상** the batting award. **타격수** the number of times at bat. ⇨ =타수(打數) **타격순** the batting order. ⇨ =타순 **타격왕** the batting champion; the leading[top] hitter (for this season). **타격전** a game with many hits; (미국 속어) a slugging match[contest]; (구어) a slugfest.

타견(他見) **1** [남이 보는 바] showing to others; exposure. **2** [남의 의견] another person's opinion[view]; others' ideas[views / suggestions]. ¶~을 들어 보다[구하다] ask [invite / seek / solicit] another's opinion [views].

타결(妥結) a compromise settlement; (협정) an agreement. ¶원만하게[성공적으로] 일의 ~을 짓다 settle a matter satisfactorily / bring a matter to a successful conclusion. **타결하다** come to terms[a settlement] (with); reach an agreement (with); make a compromise agreement (with). ➡¶교섭은 5시간 뒤에 드디어 타결되었다 They finally reached an agreement[came to terms] after five hours of negotiations.∥노조와 회사 간의 임금 인상 교섭은 15,000원에 타결되었다 The union and the management settled on a wage increase of fifteen thousand won.

● **타결점** a point of agreement.

타계(他界) **1** [다른 세계] another world; the other world. **2** [죽음] death; demise. **타계하다** depart this life; depart from life; join the majority; pass away; die. ¶그는 지난달 타계하였다 He died[passed away] last month.

타고나다 be born (with / into); be gifted [endowed] (with); be made for; be cut out for. ¶타고난 born / inborn / inbred / inherent / natural∥타고난 음악의 재능 a natural talent[gift] for music∥타고난 시인 a born poet∥장님으로 ~ be born blind / have been blind from birth∥좋은 팔자를 ~ be born under a lucky star∥비운을 ~ be born to sorrow∥그녀는 타고난 재능을 지니고 있다 She has natural talent.∥그의 고집은 타고난 것이다 He is stubborn by nature.∥나는 불운을 타고났다 I was born under an unlucky star. / I was destined to be miserable.∥그는 예술가로 타고났다 He is a born[natural] artist.∥타고난 현인은 없다 No man is born wise.

타고장(他−) an alien[a strange] place; another place.

타관(他官) another countryside. ⇨ =타향

타구(打球) [야구] batting; [친 공] a batted ball. ¶~는 쭉쭉 뻗어 나가 스탠드로 들어갔다 The ball flew deeper and deeper and landed in the stands.

타구(唾具) a spittoon; (미) a cuspidor.

타국(他國) [외국] a foreign country; [미지의 땅] a strange land. ¶~의 foreign / alien // ~ 땅에 묻히다 die in a strange [foreign] land / die far from home.
● **타국어** a foreign language; a strange tongue. **타국인** a foreigner. ⇨외국인(⇨외국)
타기(舵機) [해] steering gear; a helm.
타기하다(唾棄-) detest; hate; abominate; abhor; reject; have [hold] in detestation [abomination / abhorrence]. ¶타기할 detestable / disgusting / abhorrent / abominable / odious.
타깃 a target. ¶이 상품은 ~을 젊은 층에 맞추고 있다 These articles are aimed at the teenage market.
타 누르기 [씨름] holding [pressing] (a person) down with one's body.
타닌 [화] tannin.
● **타닌산** tannic acid; tannin.
타다¹ **1** (불에) burn; blaze; be in flames. ¶활활 타는 불길 roaring flame // 반쯤 탄 통나무[시체] a half-burned log [body] // 옷의 탄 자국 a burn on one's clothes // 타서 생긴 구멍 a hole made by burning / a burnt hole / a burn (from tobacco) // 잘 ~ be easy to burn / catch fire easily / be combustible / be inflammable // 잘 타지 않다 do not burn (easily) / be noncombustible / be noninflammable / burn ill [dull(y) / badly / poorly] // 불꽃을 내며 ~ burn with flame // 소리 없이 ~ burn quietly // 홀딱 다 버리다 be burnt out [up / down / away / off] / burn to nothing / go out / burn itself out / be destroyed [consumed] by fire / be reduced to ashes // 새까맣게 ~ be burnt black / be blackened with fire // 타기 시작하다 begin to burn / 불붙다 catch [take] fire / ignite // 옷이 타서 구멍이 나다 burn a hole in one's clothes // 그 화재로 많은 사람이 타 죽었다 Many persons were burnt to death in the fire. // 그 집이 타고 있다 The house is burning [is on fire]. // 그 집이 다 타 버렸다 The house burned down [was reduced to ashes]. // 이 장작은 잘 탄다 This wood burns well. // 목조 가옥은 타기 쉽다 Wooden houses burn [catch fire] easily. // 그 큰불로 수천 호의 가옥이 탔다 Thousands of houses were destroyed [burnt down / reduced to ashes] in the great fire.
2 [눋다] be [get] scorched [charred]; be parched; be singed. ¶탄 밥 scorched rice // 새까맣게 ~ be burnt [scorched] black // 밥이 탄다 The rice is scorched [get burned]. // 타지 않게 자꾸 저어라 Stir it constantly to prevent scorching [burning]. // 무슨 타는 냄새가 난다 I smell something burning [scorching].
3 [햇볕으로 변색되다] be sunburned [sunburnt]; be suntanned; be sunbaked; be browned (with the sun). ¶햇볕에 탄 얼굴 a sunburnt [suntanned / unbrowned] face // 바닷바람에 검붉게 탄 어부 a fisherman tanned leathery in the salt air // 햇볕에 타지 않도록 하다 keep (oneself) from getting sunburnt // 그는 살갗이 탔다 (알맞게) He got tanned [got a suntan]. / (염증이 나게) He got sunburned.
4 [바짝 마르다] dry up; be dried up; parch; be parched (up); dry as a brick; [목이 마르다] have a dry throat; be [feel] thirsty. ¶바짝 탄 논 a dried up [parched] rice paddy // 목이 ~ be parched with thirst.
5 (정열에) burn; glow; blaze; be aflame; be kindled; (속이) be anguished [agonized / anxious]. ¶애가 ~ be anxious [worried] / be agonized // 그의 연구에 대한 정열이 다 타 버렸다 He has exhausted his enthusiasm for the research.
6 (기타). ¶타는 듯한 주홍빛 blazing scarlet // 저녁놀이 붉게 타는 하늘 the sky aglow with the setting sun // 아지랑이가 아른거리며 타고 있다 The air is shimmering with heat. // 온 산이 단풍으로 타는 듯하다 The whole mountain is ablaze with autumn colors.
타다² **1** [탈것에] ride (a horse); take (a train); take [have] a ride in (a car); ride in (a cab); [오르다] get on [into] (a train); board (a bus); [배에 오르다] go [get] aboard [on board] (a ship); embark on [in] (a ship). ¶마차를 ~ ride in a cab // 자동차를 ~ ride in a motorcar // 자동차를 타고 가다 drive a motorcar / go by car // 기차를 ~ take a train / board a train [car] / ride in a train [car] // 기차를 타고 가다 travel [go] by rail [train] / go on [in] a train / take a train (to a place) // 자전거를 ~ ride a bicycle // 자전거를 타고 가다 go by [on a] bicycle // 말을 ~ ride [mount / get on] a horse / ride horseback // 말을 타고 가다 go [travel] on horseback / ride (to a place) // 소를 ~ seated on the back of a cow // 보트를 타러 가다 go boating / go for a row (in [on] a boat) // 부산에서 배를 ~ embark [take ship] at Busan / sail from Busan // 비행기를 타고 가다 fly (to Hawaii) / go [travel] (to San Francisco) by air [plane] // 엘리베이터를 타고 오르내리다 go up and down in an elevator // 갈아~ (차를) change (cars / into a car) / transfer to (another bus) / (배를) transship (from a steamer to another) // 2등을 타고 가다 go second-class // 열차를 잘못 ~ take the wrong train // 여러분 버스를 타 주십시오(승선하세요) All aboard! // 마지막 버스를 타려면 우리는 서둘러야 한다 We must hurry if we intend to catch the last bus. // 그 배[비행기]에는 망명 중인 국왕이 타고 있었다 There was an exiled King on board the ship [plane]. // 이 자동차는 6명이 탈 수 있다 This car can hold six people.
2 [올라가다] walk up; climb [go up] (a mountain / tree); ascend [make an ascent of] (a mountain). ¶문지방을 타고 넘다 cross [step across] the threshold // 밧줄을 ~ walk a rope [tightrope] / (재주로) dance [walk] on a tightrope / tightrope // 나는 능선을 타고 나아갔다 I went along the ridges. // 그는 배수관을 타고 내려왔다 He climbed down along a drainpipe. // 나는 사다리를 타고 담 위로 올라갔다 I climbed the fence by means of a ladder. // 물이 쇠사슬을 타고 똑똑 떨어졌다 The water trickled down a chain. // 땀이 그의 뺨을 타고 흘러내렸다 Sweat streamed down his cheeks. // 그 도둑은 지붕을 타고 도망쳤다 The thief fled from roof to roof. / The thief escaped over the rooftops.
3 [전파·바람 등을 이용하다] take; get (on). ¶전파를 ~ be broadcast (by radio) / be [go / get] the air (waves) / take the air // 종소리가 바람을 타고 들려왔다 The sound of a bell was carried to me on the wind. // 꽃가루는 바람을 타고 살포된다 Pollen is scattered by the

타다

wind.∥수상의 연설은 전파를 타고 전국에 전달되었다 The Prime Minister's address was broadcast throughout the country.∥그의 목소리는 마이크를 잘 탄다 His voice carries well over a mike.
4 [얼음 위를 닫다] skate (on the ice); do skating; glide (over the ice); slide[walk] (on the ice). ¶얼음을 잘 ~ be a good skater.
5 [기회·틈 등을 이용하다] seize (an opportunity); seize on the situation; (사물이) be opportune[timely]; be suited[pertinent] to the occasion; [인기를 누리다] catch popularity; catch on; take; hit (the public taste); [기회로 삼다] take (mean) advantage[avail oneself] of (someone's weakness). ¶혼란한 틈을 타서 in the confusion of the moment / taking advantage of the confusion∥틈을 ~ get time free / avail oneself of some free time / take the opportunity∥혼잡한 틈을 타 달아나다 take advantage of the confusion to run away∥그는 인기의 파도를 타고 있다 He is riding a wave of popularity.∥시류를 타지 않으면 그는 성공하지 못할 것이다 If he doesn't swim with the tide[current] he will not succeed.

타다³ [섞다] mix (with); admix; add (to); put (to/in). ¶물을 탄 브랜디 brandy and water∥물을 타지 않은 브랜디 brandy straight / pure undiluted brandy∥물을 ~ mix (alcohol) with water / dilute (a solution) with water / water down∥포도주에 물을 ~ dash wine with water / water wine∥술에 물을 ~ mix[temper / dilute] wine with water / put some water to wine∥음식에 독을 ~ poison (a person's) food∥물감을 ~ dissolve dye (in water)∥물에 소금을 ~ dissolve salt in water / salt the water∥위스키를 아무것도 타지 않고 마시다 take (a glass of) whisky neat[clear] / drink whisky straight∥위스키에 물을 탄 것을 한 잔 줘 Give me a whisky-and-water.∥홍차에 우유를 타시나요 Do you take milk in your tea?

타다⁴ [받다] get; have; receive; take; gain; obtain; be given; secure (the doctor's degree); win[carry off / bear away] (a prize); [수여되다] be awarded; (구어) cadge. ¶연금을 타는 사람 a recipient of a pension∥100만 원의 월급을 ~ draw[receive] a salary of 1,000,000 won / get 1,000,000 won a month∥어머니한테서 용돈을 ~ get pocket money from one's mother∥졸업장을 ~ receive a graduation certificate[diploma]∥노벨상을 ~ be awarded a Nobel prize∥우등상을 ~ get[win] a honor prize∥정부에서 보조금을 ~ get a subsidy from the government∥그는 몹시 탐내던 상을 탔다 He won the most coveted prize.

타다⁵ **1** [맷돌에 갈다] grind. ¶탄 보리 ground[cracked] barley∥맷돌에 콩을 ~ grind peas on a grindstone∥이 밀은 잘[곱게] 타진다 This wheat grinds well[fine]. **2** [두 쪽으로 가르다] split; divide; halve(반으로); part; crack. ¶박을 ~ halve a gourd∥가르마를 ~ part one's hair (down the middle).

타다⁶ **1** [잘 느끼다] be apt to feel; be sensitive to; be tender; be alive (to pain); [격하기 쉽다] be excitable. ¶부끄럼을 ~ be shy[bashful / coy / self-conscious]∥간지럼을 ~ be ticklish / be sensitive to tickling∥노염을 ~ be resentful[testy / touchy / irascible] / be liable to lose one's temper[get angry].
2 [영향을 받다] be susceptible[sensitive] to; be allergic to; suffer easily from; be affected. ¶여름을 ~ suffer from the summer heat∥추위를 ~ be sensitive to cold∥옻을 ~ be poisoned with lacquer / be allergic to lacquer∥가뭄을 ~ be easily damaged from want of rain∥흰옷은 더럼을 잘 탄다 White clothes pick up dirt easily.

타다⁷ [악기 등을 켜다] play (on); twang on (a banjo); strum on (a mandolin). ¶하프를 ~ play the harp∥슬픈 곡을 ~ play a sad tune∥그녀는 거문고 타는 솜씨가 훌륭하다 She has a good touch on the *geomungo*.

타다⁸ [솜을 퍼지게 하다] (cotton) out; willow[willy / whip] (cotton); (헌솜을) rewhip; whip[willow] willowed (old cotton). ¶탄 솜 rewhipped[renovated] old cotton.

타닥거리다 1 [살살 두드리다] thump; beat pat-pat. ¶바지의 먼지를 타닥거려 털다 beat the dust off one's trousers. **2** [맥없이 걷다] trudge along[one's (weary) way]; trudge on (the street); tread along[on]; plod on; jog[pad] along. ¶타닥거리며 totteringly / trudgingly / with tottering steps. **3** [겨우겨우 살아가다] barely manage to live along; rub along; make a bare[pick up a scanty] living; eke out a precarious living[existence].

타달거리다 walk wearily; jolt; clink dully. ⇨터덜거리다

타당성(妥當性) propriety; appropriateness; adequacy; soundness; pertinence; validity.

타당하다(妥當−) proper; appropriate; adequate; valid; sound; reasonable; fit; apposite; pertinent. ¶타당한 비판 (a) valid criticism / (an) apt criticism∥타당하지 않은 improper / inappropriate / inadequate / unfit / inapposite / impertinent∥타당하다고 인정하다 regard (it) as appropriate∥그 경우에 있어서는 타당한 조치였다 The measure was appropriate[proper] under the circumstances.∥그 사람을 위대한 소설가라고 하는 것은 타당하지 않다 It is not fitting[right] that he is[should be] ranked as a great novelist.∥나는 타당한 이유도 없이 해고되었다 They dismissed me without any good reason.∥그 조치가 타당한 것인지 의심스럽다 I doubt the propriety[suitability] of the measures.

타도(打倒) overthrow. ¶정부 ~ Down with the government! **타도하다** overthrow; throw out; defeat; knock down; topple (a person) from power. ¶독재 정권을 ~ overthrow a dictatorial government∥군국주의를 ~ wipe out militarism.

타도(他道) another province; other provinces.
타동사(他動詞) [언] a transitive verb.
타락(墮落) (도덕상의) depravity; (moral) corruption; degradation; debasement; fall; degeneration; decadence; delinquency; [종] apostasy. ¶정신의 ~ desolation of the spirit∥예술의 ~ decadence in art∥도덕의 ~ moral decay∥상류 사회의 ~ the decline of the upper classes∥요즘은 교내 폭력으로 학교가 ~ 상태가 되었다 Schools are falling apart[going downhill] as a result of classroom violence. **타락하다** degrade; degenerate (into); lapse (from / into); descend (to); fall into decadence; (문어) become depraved; backslide; go to the bad; be morally ruined;

타락 go wrong; fall (away); go astray; fall from grace(종교적으로). ¶타락한 여자 a fallen [dissolute] woman // 타락한 사회 a corrupt [degenerate / depraved] society // 거리의 여자로 ~ come down to streetwalking / sink to the level of a streetwalker // 나쁜 친구들과 사귄 것이 그가 타락한 원인이었다 Keeping bad company caused him to go astray [go to the bad]. // 술 때문에 그는 타락했다 Drink led to his ruin [downfall]. ➔¶저질 프로그램은 어린이들을 타락시킬 위험이 있다 Trashy programs may corrupt children.

타락줄 a hair-rope.

타래 a hank; a skein; a bunch; a round; a coil; a coiled bundle (of). ¶실 한 ~ a skein of thread // 새끼 두 ~ two bunches[coils] of rope // 한 ~의 머리 a lock[tuft / tress] of hair.

타래박 a long-handled well-dipper; a well bucket.

타래버선 children's quilted socks with decorations on them.

타래송곳 1 [나사 송곳] a gimlet; an auger. 2 [마개뽑이] a corkscrew.

타래타래 in coils[skeins]; in spirals; round and round. ¶새끼를 ~ 감다[사리다] oil the rope up. **타래타래하다** wound into coils [skeins] (서술적) in coils[spirals].

타력(他力) the power of another; help from without; outside help; [종] salvation from outside. ¶~에 의존하지 않도록 하다 try not to rely upon others.

타력(打力) hitting[batting] power. ¶~에서 우세하다 have better batters than / be superior to (the opposing team) in hitting power / outbat[outhit] (the other team).

타력(惰力) (an) inertia; (a) momentum (pl. -ta, -s); force of habit. ¶~으로 달리다[언덕을 내려가다] run[go downhill] on inertia; coast[downhill] // 일의 ~에 끌려 나는 쉽사리 멈출 수 없었다 I could not stop easily because of my momentum.

타령 [곡조의 한 가지] a kind of tune; [민요] a ballad.

타륜(舵輪) [해] a steering wheel; the wheel; a helm. ¶~을 잡다 be at the wheel.

타르 tar. ¶~를 칠한 지붕 a tarred roof // ~ 같은 냄새 a tarry odor // ~ (성분)이 적은 담배 a low-tar cigarette.

타르타르산(-酸) [화] tartaric acid.

타면(打綿) cotton beating. **타면하다** beat cotton out; whip[willow] cotton.
● **타면기** a willow(er). ⇨솜틀

타박 [나무라거나 판잔함] faultfinding; carping; caviling; criticism; censure; blame; condemnation; grumbling. ¶음식 ~ grumbling at[about / over] food. **타박하다** find fault with (a person); carp[cavil / pick] at (another's faults); blame; criticize; censure; condemn; reproach; grumble (at / about / over). ¶음식을 ~ grumble at[about / over] the food // 이러니저러니 ~ criticize (a person) for one thing or another // 그는 남을 타박하기를 좋아한다 He is ready to find faults with others. / He is too critical of others.
● **타박쟁이** a grumbler; a faultfinder; a momus.

타박상(打撲傷) a bruise; a contusion; a contused wound. ¶~을 입히다 bruise[contuse] (a person's arm) // 그는 어깨에 ~을 입었다 He was bruised[He got a bruise] on the shoulder.

타박타박 totteringly. ⇨<터벅터벅

타방(他方) 1 another side. ⇨타방면 2 another province. ⇨타지방

타방면(他方面) [다른 방면] another side [place / quarter]; a different direction; [다른 한편] the other side[hand].

타봉(打棒) batting. ¶~을 휘두르다[~이 부진하다] hit[bat] very well[badly] // 그 팀의 ~은 더한층 날카로웠다 The batting of the team was especially sharp.

타분한 stale; musty; moldy; ill-[foul-]smelling. ¶타분한 생각 a musty idea.

타블로이드 a tabloid. ¶~판 신문 a tabloid (newspaper) // 신문을 ~판으로 발행하다 publish a newspaper in tabloid (format / form).

타산(打算) calculation; self-interest; selfishness. **타산하다** calculate the loss and gain (of); consult one's own interests.

타산적(打算的) calculating; selfish; self-interested; self-centered; mercenary; mindful only of one's own interest. ¶~인 정치가 a calculating politician // ~인 결혼 marriage for mere lucre // ~인 사랑 interested [cupboard] love // ~인 생각에서 from a self-centered viewpoint / in a spirit of calculation / from[out of] self-interest / for mercenary [selfish] purposes / from selfish[interested] motives // ~으로 with a mercenary spirit / mercenarily / for gain[profit] // 그 사나이는 만사를 ~으로 처리한다 He does everything for his own profit. // 그는 ~인 녀석이다 He is a calculating[mercenary / self-seeking] fellow.

타산지석(他山之石) a lesson; an example (from which one can profit). ¶그의 실패를 ~으로 삼으시오 Let his failure be a lesson to you.

타살(他殺) murder; manslaughter; homicide. ¶~의 흔적이[혐의가] 있다 There is a suspicion of foul play. / The body bears marks of violence. // 아무래도 ~ 같다 There is every reason to believe that it is a murder. // 시체의 상태를 보고 경찰은 ~로 단정했다 From the condition of the body, the police concluded that it was (a case of) murder.
● **타살체** the body of a murder victim.

타살하다(打殺-) strike[knock / beat / club] (a dog) to death; strike (a cat) dead; kill by a blow.

타석(打席) [야구] [타수] (times) at bat(약어 ab.); [배터 박스] a batter's box. ¶규정 ~수 the required minimum number of times at bat (for qualifying to be included in the batting records) // 3번째 ~에서 when he was at bat[came to bat] the third time / in his third at bat // ~에 나가다 go to the plate // ~에 서다 take one's turn at the bat / be at bat / come up to bat // 그는 5~에 1안타였다 In five times at bat[trips to the plate] he had one hit.

타선(打線) [야구] the batting lineup[order]. ¶~이 작렬하다 make many hits / pump out hits // 상대 팀의 ~을 침묵시키다 keep the opposing team's bats silent // 상위 ~이 부진하다 The top of the batting order isn't hitting.

타선(唾腺) a salivary gland. ⇨타액선(⇨타액)

타성(他姓) another surname[family name]. ¶~을 쓰다 assume another surname / be adopted into another family.

타성(惰性) 1 [물] inertia. ⇨ˇ관성 ¶~으로 움직이다 be carried by inertia (자전거나 자동차가) coast / (비행기가) glide. 2 [습관] force of habit. ¶외출을 하면 ~에서 발이 그쪽으로 향한다 When I go out, my legs carry me there from sheer force of habit. / 그는 지금까지의 ~으로 그렇게 하고 있는 데 불과하다 He continues to do so simply from[by] force of habit. / It is only from habit that he is doing so now. // 그는 그저 ~으로 움직이고 있을 뿐이다 He is just coasting.

타수(打數) [야구] the number of times at bat.

타수(舵手) a helmsman; a steersman; (보트의) a coxswain; (구어) a cox.

타순(打順) [야구] the batting order. ¶~을 바꾸다 juggle the batting order // 코치는 9명 가운데 3명의 ~을 바꿨다 The coach shifted the batting position of three of the nine players. // 그는 ~ 2번을 친다 He bats second.

타악기(打樂器) [음] a percussion instrument.

타액(唾液) spit; spittle. ⇨ˇ침

●**타액 분비** salivation; flow of saliva. **타액선** a salivary gland. ⇨ˇ침샘

타오르다 blaze[light] up; burn[go] up (in a flame); burst into flame(s). ¶타오르는 정열 a burning passion // 확 ~ flare up (in flames) // 밤하늘에 불길이 타올랐다 Flames shot up into the dark night. / The fire flared [blazed] up in the dark sky. / 그 건물은 단숨에 타올랐다 The building instantly went up in a burst of flame. / The building burst into flames in an instant.

타워 a tower.

타원(楕圓) an ellipse; an oval. ¶~의 elliptic(al) / oval(-shaped) // ~으로 elliptically.

●**타원 운동** elliptic motion. **타원체** an oval figure; an ellipsoid. ¶~의 ellipsoidal / spheroidal // 회전 ~ an ellipsoid of revolution / a spheroid. **타원형** an oval. ¶~의 elliptical / oval.

타월 a towel. ¶목욕 ~ a bath towel // 세면 ~ a facecloth / (미) a washcloth / (영) a (face) flannel // ~로 몸[얼굴]을 닦았다 I dried myself[my face] with a towel.

타월을 던지다 [권투 경기 중 기권하다] throw in the towel.

●**타월걸이** a towel rack.

타율(他律) 1 [윤] heteronomy. ¶~적(으로) heteronomous(ly). 2 [다른 규율] another[a different] order[rule / discipline].

타율(打率) [야구] a batting average. ¶그는 이번 시즌 ~이 2할 7푼 5리이다 He has a .275 this season (▶ 275를 two seventy-five 라 읽음). // 이번 시즌의 그의 ~은 상당히 높다 His batting average is quite high this season. / He is hitting the ball pretty well this season.

타의(他意) [다른 생각] any other intention; [남의 뜻] another person's will. ¶~가 없음을 보여 줄 필요가 있었다 We had to show that we had no other intentions. // ~가 있어서 한 일은 아니다 I had no ulterior motive in doing so. // 그는 ~는 없었다 He didn't mean anything by it.

타이 1 a necktie. ⇨ˇ넥타이 2 a tie score. ⇨ˇ타이스코어(⇨타이) 3 [음] a tie. ¶~로 연결된 음표 tied notes.

●**타이기록** a tie record. ¶그는 400미터 자유형에서 세계 ~을 냈다 He tied the world record for[in] the 400-meter freestyle. **타이스코어** [동점] a tie score. ¶7회 말에 5대 5 ~가 되었다 The score was tied at 5-5 in the bottom of the seventh inning. // 게임은 4대 4 ~로 끝났다 The game ended in a 4-4 tie. **타이 핀** a tiepin; (영) a scarfpin; (미) a stickpin.

타이가 [상록 침엽수림대] a taiga.

타이곤 [동] a tigon.

타이르다 admonish (a person for his fault); give admonition to (a person); remonstrate (with a person on a fault); [충고하다] counsel[advise] (a person to do); warn (a person of danger); [설득하다] persuade (a person to do); [도리로써 깨닫게 하다] reason (with a person). ¶그릇된 짓을 하지 않도록 ~ admonish (a person) against doing wrong // 순한 말로 ~ speak (to a person) in a voice of sweet reason // 타일러 납득시키다 reason (a person) into compliance // 나는 다시는 같은 잘못을 저지르지 않도록 그를 타일렀다 I admonished him not to repeat the same mistake. // 내가 그를 타일렀지만 허사였다 My admonitions [remonstrances] fell flat upon him. // 나는 그를 타일러 가출하지 못하게 했다 I persuaded him not to run away from home. // [문어] I dissuaded him from running away from home. // 나는 그의 잘못을 간곡히 타일렀다 I tried hard to make him see that he was at fault. // 그는 아들에게 도리를 타일렀지만 허사였다 He tried in vain to reason with his son. // 그는 그 소년들을 타일러 순종케 했다 He persuaded the boys to obey him. // 의사는 임신부들에게 흡연은 태아에게 해롭다고 타일렀다 The doctor warned the expectant mothers of the harmful effects of smoking on their babies.

타이머 a timer. ¶~를 5시에 맞추어 놓다 set a timer for five o'clock.

타이밍 timing. ¶적절한[아쉬운] ~ good[bad] timing // 그가 하는 일은 언제나 ~이 나쁘다 [빗나간다] His timing is always bad[off]. // 정말 ~이 좋았다 It was quite timely[well timed]. / It came at just the right time.

타이어 a tire; (영) a tyre. ¶스페어 ~ a spare tire // 고무 ~ a rubber tire // 공기 ~ a pneumatic (tire) // 자동차 ~ an automobile tire // ~ 자국 a tire track // ~를 바꿔 끼우다 fix a new tire (to a wheel) // ~에 바람을 넣다 inflate[pump up] a tire // ~에 체인을 달다 put chains on a tire / [스키드 방지 처리를 하다] make a tire skidproof // ~가 펑크가 났다 I had a flat tire.

타이츠 tights. ¶~를 신은 소녀 a girl in tights.

타이트스커트 a tight skirt.

타이틀 1 [표제] a title. ¶책[영화]의 ~ the title of a book[movie]. 2 [선수권] a championship; a title.

●**타이틀 매치** a title match. ¶논~ a non-title match. **타이틀 뮤직** title music.

타이프(라이터) a typewriter. ¶국문 ~ a Korean typewriter // 영문 ~ an English-character typewriter // ~로 친 편지 a typed letter // ~를 치다 [찍다] typewrite / type / tap

[use / work] a typewriter // ~를 짤깍짤깍 치다 tap away at one's typewriter // 편지를 ~로 찍다 type a letter / write a letter on a typewriter // 카본지 4장 넣고 ~를 치다 type (it) with four carbons // ~로 서류를 만들다 type up a form // ~의 키를 두드리다 pound [strike] the keys of a typewriter // 원고를 [구술하는 것을] ~ 치다 type from a copy [from dictation] // ~를 연습하다 practice [(영) practise] typing // 1분 동안에 몇 자나 ~로 칠 수 있습니까 How many words can you type a minute? // 그는 ~로 작문을 하고 있다 He is writing his composition at typewriter.
● 타이프 용지 typewriter paper.

타이피스트 a typist. ¶영문 ~ an English typist / a typist of English // 국문 ~ an operator of the Korean-character typewriter / a typist in Korean.

타이핑 typing; typewriting. **타이핑하다** typewrite; type. ¶이것 좀 타이핑해 줄래요 Will you type this up, please?

타인(他人) 1 [다른 사람] another person; (the) others; other people. ¶~은 어떻든 as for myself / for my part / I don't know about others, but .... 2 [남] an unrelated person; a stranger. ¶~ 앞에서 in the presence of others / before strangers [other people] // ~ 취급을 하다 treat (a person) like a stranger / make a stranger of (a person) // ~처럼 굴다 behave like a stranger / be reserved / have a distant manner [air] // ~은 참견하지 마라 A third party should not thrust his nose in these matters. / It is none of your business.

타인(打印) punching.
● 타인기 a punch; a punching machine.

타일 a tile. ¶~을 깐 tiled (bathroom) // ~을 깔다 [붙이다] lay [set] tiles (on) / face [cover] with tiles / tile (a bathroom).
● 타일공(-工) a tiler; a tile-setter. 타일 공사 tiling; tiler's work.

타임 1 [시간] time. ¶경주[주자]의 ~을 재다 time a race [a runner] // 그 주자의 최고 ~은 10초 8이다 The sprinter's [runner's] best time is 10.8 seconds. 2 [시합 능의 일시 중지] a time-out; a time out. ¶심판이 ~을 선언했다 The official [referee] called a timeout.
● 타임리코더 a time clock [recorder]. 타임머신 a time machine. 타임스위치 a time switch; a timer. 타임아웃 a time-out; a time out. 타임 테이블 a timetable; [철도] a train schedule.

타입 [어떤 부류의 형] (a) type; (a) pattern; (a) stamp. ¶학구적 ~의 사람 a scholarly [an academic] type of man // 같은 ~의 사람 a person of the same type // 이 가게에는 여러 ~의 사람이 모여들고 있다 People of various types [Various types of people] frequent this shop. // 그녀는 내가 좋아하는 ~의 여성이다 She is my type. / She is the type [kind] of woman I like. // 나는 저런 ~의 사내가 싫다 I don't like men of that type. / I don't like that type of men.

타자(打者) [야구] a batter; a batsman; a hitter. ¶강~ a slugger / (영) a slogger // 1번 ~ a leadoff man / the first batter // 대~ a pinch hitter // 왼손 ~ a left-handed batter // 3할 ~ a three hundred hitter / a 0.300 hitter // 다음 ~ the next batter.

타자기(打字機) a typewriter.
타자수(打字手) a typist.
타작(打作) thresh; thrashing. **타작하다** thresh; thrash. ¶발로 밟아서 ~ treadthresh (rice).
● 타작마당 a threshing [thrashing] floor [ground].

타전(打電) sending a telegram; telegraphing. **타전하다** telegraph; wire (to); send a wire (to); send a telegram (to); communicate by wire; (해저 전선으로) cable; (무선으로) radio (to); send a radio (to); (영) wireless (to).

타점(他店) (영) another store; (영) another shop; another firm.

타점(打點) 1 [점을 찍음] marking with a dot [point]; dotting; pointing. **타점하다** mark with a dot [point]; dot; point; spot. 2 [마음속으로 정하여 둠]. **타점하다** single [pick] out (a house for hire); spot (a man); fix one's choice on (a person); select (a thing) as desirable; mark out [down] (a thing / a person) for (some purpose). 3 [야구] a run batted in(약어 RBI); a run. ¶~으로 연결된 싱글 히트 with a runscoring single // 그는 5~을 올렸다 He drove [knocked] in five runs.
● 타점 기록 the record for runs batted in. 타점왕 the RBI king. ¶그는 이번 시즌의 ~이 되었다 He won the RBI title [crown] this season.

타조(駝鳥) [동] an ostrich.
타종(他宗) another sect; other sects.
타종(打鐘) the ringing [tolling] of a bell. **타종하다** strike [toll / ring] a bell; sound [ring] a gong.

타지(他地) [다른 지방] an other province; a different part of the country; [외국 땅] a foreign country; an alien [a strange] land. ¶~ 사람 a stranger.
타지방(他地方) another province.
타진(打診) 1 [의] percussion; tapping. **타진하다** examine (a part of the body) by percussion; sound; tap. ¶의사가 내 가슴을 타진했다 The doctor sounded my chest. 2 [의향을 살핌] sounding; tapping. **타진하다** sound [feel] out (a person's feeling). ¶정세를 ~ float a trial balloon / throw out feelers // 여론의 추세를 ~ gauge the trend of public opinion / put up a ballon d'essai // 이 문제에 대한 그의 의향을 타진해 봅시다 Let's sound [feel] him out about the matter.
● 타진기 a plexor; a plessor. 타진음 a percussion sound. 타진판 a pleximeter.

타짜(꾼) a hoodwinker (in card game); a humbug; a swindler; a (card) sharper; (미국 속어) a gyp(per).

타처(他處) another place; a different part of the country; strange parts. ¶~에서 elsewhere / at [in] another [some other] place / somewhere else / in a strange quarter.

타파(打破) breaking; destruction; overthrow. ¶계급 ~ the abolition of class distinctions. **타파하다** break down; do away with (conventionalities); destroy; overthrow (bureaucracy). ¶구습[현상]을 ~ do away with the old practices [the existing state of things] / break down the old practices [the existing state of things] // 그들은 인습을 타파하기 위해 궐기했다 They rose (up) to break down [do away with / abolish] the old convention-

타합

alities.
타합(打合) a previous[preliminary] arrangement; preliminaries. **타합하다** make (previous) arrangements (as to time); arrange (a matter with a person, that …, etc.); prearrange. ¶그 일에 대해서는 그와 타합해 놓았다 I have made prior arrangements with him about that. ➔¶그 건에 관해서는 미리 타합되어 있다 Arrangements have been made on that matter.//내일 아침 8시에 서울역에 집합하기로 타합되어 있다 It has been arranged that we are to meet at Seoul Station at eight tomorrow morning.

타향(他鄕) another countryside; a place away from home; a foreign land; foreign parts. ¶~ 사람 a stranger / (미국 구어) an out-of-towner//~에서 away from home / in a strange land / ~에서 떠돌다 wander in a strange land / be an exile from home//~에서 죽다 die in a strange land / die far from home//10년이나 ~살이를 하다 be absent from home for 10 years//~의 하늘 밑에서 울다 be distressed under a foreign sky//~ 사람은 한눈에 알아볼 수 있다 We can distinguish strangers[people from other parts of the country] at a glance.

타협(妥協) (a) compromise; an agreement; an understanding; (미) (정당 간의) trade. ¶~의 여지가 없다 There is no room for compromise.//우리는 이 점 때문에 ~이 되지 않았다 We failed to reach[come to] a compromise on this point.//내가 상대방에게 10만 원을 지불하기로 하여 우리는 그 일에 ~을 지었다 We settled the matter by agreeing that I would pay the other party 100,000 won. / A compromise was reached to the effect that I would pay the other party 100,000 won. **타협하다** compromise (with); come to terms (with); make[effect] a compromise; reach [arrive at] a compromise; show a conciliatory tone; temporize (with); reach an agreement (with); meet (a person) halfway; split the difference. ¶우리는 이 조건으로 상대방과 타협했다 We came to terms[reached an agreement] with them on these conditions.//이제 이쯤에서 서로 타협합시다 Let's compromise (with each other) at this point.//우리 둘은 서로 타협하여 화해했다 We both made concessions and reconciled our differences[buried the hatchet].//그 문제는 그들과 타협하여 원만하게 타결하는 것이 어떻습니까 How about compromising with them to bring the matter to an amicable settlement?
● **타협안** a compromise; a compromise plan [proposal]. ¶~이 드디어 성립되었다 A compromise agreement was finally arrived at. **타협점을 모색하다** seek mutually-agreeable compromise terms//~을 발견하다 find out a meeting point[common grounds] / come to an agreement//우리는 마침내 ~을 찾았다 Finally we found a point of compromise.//양측의 회담은 마침내 ~을 찾지 못한 채 끝나 버렸다 The meeting between the two sides ended without their being able to find any common ground.

타협적(妥協的) compromising; concessive. ¶~인 태도 (assume) a compromising[concessive] attitude// 비~ unyielding / uncompromising / intransigent / hard-shell(ed) (미국 속어)//그 사람에 대해 ~인 태도를 취할 수가 없다 I cannot take a conciliatory attitude toward him.

탁 1 [부딪거나 터지는 소리] with a bump [clunk]; with a crack; with a pop[bang]. ¶ 고무풍선이 ~ 터지다 a balloon pop[bursts]//문을 ~ 닫다 slam[snap / bang] the door to[closed] / shut the door with a bang//(병 등이) ~ 터지다 break with a crack//책을 ~ 덮다 shut a book with a snap[clap]//무엇인가 ~ 소리가 들렸다 I heard a rap[tap].//나는 테이블 위에 글라스를 ~ 내려놓았다 I put the glass down on the table with a clink.// 그녀는 텔레비전의 채널을 ~ 돌렸다 She flicked the TV switch to another channel.// 문에 이마를 ~ 부딪혔다 I smacked[whacked / whammed] my fore head against the door. //~ 소리를 내고 타구가 우익 외야석으로 날아갔다 There was the crack of a bat and the ball flew into the right-field bleachers.
2 [손으로 치는 소리] with a slap[snap]; with a crack. ¶막대기로 머리를 ~ 치다 rap [whack / smack] a person on the head with a stick//무릎을 ~ 치다 slap one's knee (when one has an inspiration)//어깨를 ~ 치다 pat (a person) on the shoulder.
3 [끊어지거나 풀리는 소리] with a snap; snappingly; with force. ¶손가락 마디를 ~ 꺾다 crack[pop] one's knuckles//(감긴 것이) ~ 풀어지다 run down / come unwound / (맨 것이) come untied[off].
4 [트이어 시원한 모양] widely; extensively; vastly; (가슴속이) refreshingly. ¶~ 트인 뜰 an extensive[a spacious] garden//~ 트인 목장 a wide open meadow//~ 트인 전원 a wide spread of country//시야가 ~ 트이다 command extensive views//갑자기 눈앞이 ~ 트이다 a wide prospect bursts upon one's sight[view].
5 [숨 막히는 모양] stiflingly; chokingly. ¶숨이 ~ 막히는 더위였다 It was stifling hot.

탁견(卓見) [뛰어난 의견] a fine[capital] idea [suggestion]; distinguished[excellent] views; [뛰어난 통찰] lofty outlook; foresight; farsightedness; clear-sightedness; penetration. ¶~이 있는 clear-sighted / long-headed [-sighted] / farseeing//~이 있다 have a long head[view] / have a broad vision.

탁구(卓球) (정식으로) table tennis; ping-pong. ¶~를 치다 play ping-pong.
● **탁구공** a ping-pong ball. **탁구대** a ping-pong table.

탁론(卓論) a lofty[sound] argument; a clever view.

탁류(濁流) a turbid[muddy] stream; turbid [dark] waters (of a river). ¶~는 마을을 휩쓸었다 The muddy water rushed through the village.

탁마(琢磨) [옥석을 갊] polishing (a gem); [학문·덕행을 닦음] improvement; cultivation. **탁마하다** polish; improve (one's virtue); cultivate (one's mind). ¶절차탁마한 덕으로 by dint of hard work.

탁발(托鉢) [불] religious mendicancy (in Buddhism). **탁발하다** go about asking for alms. ¶승려는 이 집 저 집 탁발하며 다녔다 The priest went from house to house begging for alms.
● **탁발승** a mendicant priest; a friar.

탁본(拓本) a rubbed copy; a rubbing. ¶~을

뜨다 make a rubbing (of) / rub a copy (from a monument) // 그 비(碑)의 ~을 떴다 I made a rubbing of the monument. **탁본하다** take a rubbing (of).

탁상(卓上) ¶~의[에] on a table[desk] // ~용의 desk (dictionary).
● **탁상공론** a desk[mere] theory; an impracticable proposition. ¶~가 an armchair theorist. **탁상시계** a table clock.

탁선(託宣) an oracle; a divine revelation.

탁설(卓說) an excellent[a supreme] opinion [theory]; remarkable[excellent] views. ¶명론 ~ sound arguments and excellent views / a sound, well-argued thesis.

탁성(濁聲) a thick voice.

탁송(託送) consignment. ¶직접 ~ a direct consignment. **탁송하다** consign (goods to a forwarding agency); send (goods) on consignment; send along (with); send (a thing) by[through / under the care of] (a person); book (a parcel) for[to] (Busan); check (baggage).
● **탁송품** a consignment.

탁아소(託兒所) a day[public] nursery; (프) a crèche; (백화점 등의 일시적인) a nursery; [유치원에 들어가기 전의 보육원] a nursery school; a children's home; a baby farm. ¶아이를 ~에 맡기다 leave a child to the care of a day nursery.

탁월하다(卓越-) excellent; eminent; prominent; distinguished; superb. ¶탁월한 수완 superior ability // 탁월한 위인 a person of transcendent greatness // 탁월한 학자 a prominent scholar // 인물과 역량이 모두 ~ surpass others both in character and ability // 그는 웅변가로서[수학에서] ~ He was an outstanding orator[outstanding in mathematics].

탁음(濁音) a voiced sound. ⇨ 올림소리

탁자(卓子) a table. ¶둥근 ~ a round table // 4인용의 ~ a table for four // 를 끼고 마주 앉다 (두 사람이) sit across a table / (한 쪽이) sit across from (a person) at a table // ~에 둘러앉다 sit (a)round a table // ~에 놓다 put (a thing) on the table.

탁절하다(卓絶-) excellent; eminent; prominent.

탁주(濁酒) raw rice wine. ⇨ 막걸리

탁탁 1 [일을 결단성 있게 해치우는 모양] promptly; quickly; speedily; with (brisk) dispatch; in a businesslike way. ¶일을 ~ 해치우다 finish one's business with dispatch / do a thing quickly / be prompt in one's work / make short[quick] work of one's business.
2 [픽픽 쓰러지는 모양] (fall) in rapid [quick] succession; (come down) one after another. ¶적탄에 병사들이 ~ 쓰러졌다 The soldiers fell thick and fast under the enemy's fire.
3 [소리 나는 모양] with cracks; with pops; flapping; clattering; rattling. ¶날개를 ~ 치다 flap[flutter] (its) wings // 먼지를 ~ 털다 beat the dust off (one's trousers) // (총체로) dust bustlingly with a duster // 손뼉을 ~ 치다 clap one's hands // 장작이 ~ 소리를 내며 타다 wood burns crackling // 마른 가지를 ~ 꺾어서 불쏘시개로 만들었다 I made kindling by breaking [snapping] up dry branches.
4 [침을 세게 뱉는 모양] spitting hard or in rapid succession. ¶침을 ~ 뱉다 spit kerslop[ker-plunk]! / go spit-spit-spit.
5 [숨이 막히는 모양] stifling; short of [out of] breath; gasping. ¶숨이 ~ 막히는 방 a very stuffy[close] room // 숨이 ~ 막히다 be stifled / be gasping for breath / lose one's breath // 숨이 ~ 막히는 더위였다 It was stifling hot. // 동굴 안의 공기는 숨이 ~ 막혔다 The air in the cave was very close.

탁탁거리다 keep cracking[popping / snapping / banging]. ¶장작이 타느라고 탁탁거린다 Firewood crackles as it burns.

탁탁하다 1 [피륙이 촘촘하고 두껍다] closewoven; thick and strong. 2 [살림이 넉넉하다] abundant; plentiful. ¶살림이 ~ be well [comfortable] off.

탁하다(濁-) 1 [물 등이 흐리다] muddy; turbid; dull; thick; [불순하다] impure; [음성 등이 거칠다] thick. ¶탁한 공기 impure[foul / hazy / murky] air // 탁한 목소리 a thick voice // 탁한 물 muddy water // 마음이 탁한 사람 a person with dark designs / an inscrutable [untrustworthy] person // 탁해지다 become muddy[turbid / impure / thick] / muddy / become cloudy(술 등이) // 가스는 방 안 공기를 탁하게 한다 Gas spoils[poison] the air of a room. // 우물이 탁해졌다 The well has got muddy. 2 [안색이 훤하지 않다] dark; swarthy.

탄(炭) 1 coal. ⇨ 석탄 2 a briquet(te). ⇨ 연탄

탄갱(炭坑) [광] a coal mine; a coal pit. ¶~을 파다 work a coal mine.

탄고(炭庫) a coal cellar[bin / bunker].

탄광(炭鑛) [광] a coal mine; (영) a colliery.
● **탄광부** a coal(-mine) worker; a collier. **탄광업** the coal-mining industry. ¶~자 a coal-mine operator. **탄광 지대** a coal-mining region[area]; (영) the black country.

탄내(炭-) (char)coal fumes; [연탄가스] briquet gas. ¶~를 맡다 get poisoned by briquet gas.

탄대(彈帶) a bandolier[bandoleer]. ⇨ 탄피

탄도(彈道) a trajectory; a line of fire; the path of a projectile[missile]; a ballistic trajectory. ¶곡사 ~ a curved trajectory.
● **탄도 곡선** a ballistic curve. **탄도 비행** a trajectory[suborbital] flight. **탄도탄** a ballistic missile. ¶단거리 ~ a short range ballistic missile(약어 SRBM) // 대륙 간 ~ an intercontinental ballistic missile(약어 ICBM) // 중거리 ~ an intermediate range ballistic missile(약어 IRBM) // 준중거리 ~ a medium range ballistic missile(약어 MRBM). **탄도학** ballistics.

탄두(彈頭) a warhead; a head. ¶미사일 ~ a missile warhead // 핵 ~ a nuclear warhead // 수폭 ~ an H-bomb[a hydrogen] warhead // 원자 ~ an atomic warhead.

탄띠(彈-) a bandolier[bandoleer]; a cartridge [(군대 속어) an ammo] belt.

탄력(彈力) elasticity; resilience; elastic force; spring; bounce; give; rebound. ¶~ 있는 elastic / springy / buoyant / resilient // ~이 없는 inelastic / nonelastic // 공의 ~ the rebound[bounce] of a ball // ~이 좋은 공 a ball that bounces well // ~적인 flexible (attitude) // ~이 있다 be elastic [resilient / springy] // 그의 다리는 ~을 잃었다 His legs have lost their spring. / His step has lost its

bounce.// 나의 근육이 ~을 잃어 가고 있다 My muscles are losing their resilience.
● 탄력성 elasticity; resilience; flexibility; adaptability. ¶그는 ~이 있는 태도를 보였다 He showed flexibility in his attitude.

탄로(綻露) disclosure; revelation; exposure; divulgence; detection. ¶~가 나다 get found out [detected / divulged / exposed / disclosed] / be revealed [laid bare] / be brought [come] to light / come [be] out / transpire / 틀림없이 ~ 날 것이다 It is bound to come out.// 음모는 ~ 나고 말았다 The plot has been laid bare. // 그의 거짓말이 ~ 났다 He was caught in a lie. / His lie was discovered [exposed]. // 우리의 계책이 ~ 난 것 같다 Our trick seems to have been seen through [detected]. // 일이 ~가 나서 그는 도시에서 떠나야만 했다 What he had done came to light, and he had to leave town. // 일[비밀]이 ~ 났다 The secret is [got] out. / The cat is out (of the bag).

탄막(彈幕) a barrage; an artillery barrage. ¶엄호 ~ a covering barrage // ~을 치다 put up a barrage.
● 탄막 포화 covering fire; a curtain fire.

탄맥(炭脈) a coal seam [vein].

탄미(歎美) admiration; adoration; appreciation. 탄미하다 admire; be filled with admiration; appreciate; adore; praise; laud. ¶탄미할 만한 admirable // 그녀는 정원의 장미를 탄미하고 있었다 She was admiring the roses in the garden.

탄복하다(歎服-) admire; be struck [moved] with admiration; be deeply impressed (with / by); think well of. ¶탄복할 만한 admirable / praiseworthy / worthy of admiration // 탄복케 하다 excite [demand] (a person's) admiration / strike [fill] (a person) with admiration / impress // 그녀의 아름다움[재능]에 ~ be struck by her beauty [ability] // 그의 깊은 통찰력에 탄복했다 We admired [were impressed by] the depth of his insight.

탄산(炭酸) [화] carbonic acid. ¶~의 carbonic // ~을 없애다 decarbonize.
● 탄산가스 carbon dioxide. ⇨ 이산화탄소 탄산나트륨 / 탄산소다 sodium carbonate; carbonate of soda. 탄산석회 / 탄산칼슘 calcium carbonate. 탄산수 carbonated water; soda (water). 탄산수소나트륨 sodium bicarbonate. 탄산염 a carbonate. 탄산지(-紙) carbon paper. ¶~로 복사한 카피 a carbon copy // ~로 복사하다 take copies with carbon paper. 탄산천(-泉) a carburetted spring. 탄산칼륨 potassium carbonate; carbonate of potash; pearl ash(조제의).

탄생(誕生) (a) birth; nativity. ¶새로운 클럽의 ~ the birth of a new club // ~을 축하하다 celebrate (a person's) birth // 그들은 공공 도서관의 ~을 축하했다 They celebrated the establishment of their public library. 탄생하다 get [be] born; come into the world; first see the light of day. ¶민주주의가 탄생하였다 Democracy came into being [existence]. // 영어 잡지가 또 탄생했다 Another English magazine has appeared. // 그 나라에 자유가 새로이 탄생했다 Freedom had a new birth in the country.
● 탄생석 a birthstone. 탄생일 one's birthday. 탄생지 one's birthplace.

탄성(彈性) [물] elasticity. ¶~이 있는 elastic / springy / buoyant / resilient // ~이 없는 inelastic / nonelastic.
● 탄성 고무 elastic gum; gum elastic; (India) rubber. 탄성률 the modulus [coefficient] of elasticity. 탄성체 an elastic body.

탄성(歎聲·嘆聲) [한탄하는 소리] a sigh; a groan; [감탄의 소리] a sigh of admiration; an exclamation. ¶~을 발하다 heave a sigh / groan / admire with a deep sigh // 그는 ~을 올렸다 He uttered an admiring cry.

탄소(炭素) [화] carbon. ¶~질의 carbonaceous // 방사성 ~ radiocarbon / radioactive carbon // 방사성 ~에 의한 연대 측정 radiocarbon dating // 수소와 ~의 화합물 a compound of hydrogen and carbon // 일[이]산화 ~ carbon monoxide [dioxide] // ~를 함유하다 be carbonaceous // ~를 제거하다 decarbonize // ~와 화합시키다 carburet / carburize // ~화하다 carbonate.
● 탄소강 carbon steel. 탄소 동화 작용 carbon dioxide assimilation. 탄소봉 a carbon point. 탄소 화합물 carbon compounds.

탄수화물(炭水化物) [화] a carbohydrate; a saccharide. ¶~의 적은 식사 a low carbohydrate diet // ~의 섭취를 줄이다 cut down (on) one's intake of carbohydrates.

탄식(歎息·嘆息) [비탄] a sigh; lamentation; [한탄] deploring. ¶~으로 나날을 보내다 sigh away one's days. 탄식하다 sigh (over); heave [draw] a sigh; sigh for grief; lament; deplore. ¶정계의 부패를 ~ deplore the corruption of political circles // 자신의 불운을 ~ lament (over) one's misfortune // 그의 낙선 소식을 듣고 일동은 탄식했다 Everybody heaved a sigh at the news of his defeat in the election. // 그는 자신의 불운을 생각하고 탄식했다 He lamented [grieved over] his misfortune.

탄신(誕辰) a (royal) birthday; the king's birthday; the birthday of a sage [saint]. ¶제84회 ~ the 84th birthday.

탄알(彈-) a shot; a bullet. ¶~ 자국 a bullet hole // ~에 맞다 be hit by a bullet / get [receive] a bullet (in one's arm) / (영국 속어) catch a packet // ~에 맞아 죽다 be killed by a bullet / be shot dead // ~을 재다 load (a gun) (a shot) / charge (a gun) // ~을 뽑(아내)다 extract the ball (from) / unload a gun // ~을 쏘아 박다 pull a bullet in (a person's stomach) // ~이 넓적다리에 박히다 A bullet is lodged [embedded] in one's thigh. // ~이 비 오듯 하다 Bullets fall thick and fast.

탄압(彈壓) oppression; pressure; suppression (▶ oppression은 압제·학대, suppression은 진압이나 활동의 금지, pressure는 압박·강제의 뜻이 담겨 있음); coercion. ¶무력 ~ military pressure // ~을 가하다 bring pressure (to bear) upon / subject (a person) to pressure / bear hard on (a person) / clamp down on // ~을 받다 be suppressed / be subjected to pressure [suppression] // 그들은 노동자에게 ~을 가했다 They put pressure on the laborers. // 그 운동은 치안 방해로서 ~을 받았다 The movement was suppressed as a breach of the public peace. 탄압하다 suppress; oppress; repress; coerce; crush; clamp down (on); run rough shod over. ¶언론을 ~ shackle speech and writing / place a gag on the freedom of speech. →¶자유는 결

코 탄압되어서는 안 된다 Freedom should never be suppressed.
● **탄압 정책** an oppressive[a repressive] measure.

탄약(彈藥) ammunition; munition; 〔군대 속어〕 ammo. ¶~ 50발 fifty rounds of ammunition.
● **탄약고** a powder magazine[dump]; a shot locker. **탄약 상자** an ammunition box [chest]; a cartridge box; 〔군〕 a caisson. **탄약통** a cartridge; a cartouch(e).

탄우(彈雨) a shower[rain / hail] of bullets [shells]. ¶~ 속에서 under a rain of shells / amid a hail of bullets.

탄원(歎願) 〔간절히 바람〕 (an) entreaty; 〔문어〕 (a) supplication; 〔문서에 의한 청원〕 a petition; 〔지지 등을 호소함〕 an appeal; (a) solicitation; (a) suit. ¶~을 받아들이다 listen[lend an ear] to (a person's) entreaties / grant a petition[an entreaty] / ~을 받아들이지 않다 reject an entreaty / turn a deaf ear to (a person's) entreaties / turn down a petition∥그는 마을 사람들의 ~으로 석방되었다 He was released on the petition of the villagers.∥그는 나의 ~을 딱 잘라 거절했다 He turned down my entreaty[supplication]. **탄원하다** entreat; supplicate; implore; beseech; obtest; solicit (relief); sue (a person for something); petition (the government); appeal (to a person for something); make suit; beg. ¶정부에 구제를 ~ petition the government for relief∥국민은 그의 구명을 탄원했다 The people sent in a petition for his life.∥그들은 정부에 감세를 탄원했다 They petitioned the government for a tax cut.
● **탄원서** a (written) petition. ¶~를 내다 present[send in] a (written) petition to / file a petition with (the government)∥많은 사람들이 그 ~에 서명했다 Many people signed the petition. **탄원자** a supplicant; a petitioner.

탄저병(炭疽病) (가축·사람의) anthrax; 〔식〕 anthracnose.

탄전(炭田) 〔광〕 a coalfield.

탄젠트〔수〕 a tangent(약어 tan).

탄주(彈奏) 〔음〕 play; (a) performance. **탄주하다** play (on) (the piano); perform; pluck [touch] (the strings of). ¶하프를 ~ play the harp / perform on the harp.
● **탄주법** touch. **탄주자** a player; a performer.

탄지 burnt tobacco left over in a pipe.

탄진(炭塵) coal dust. ¶~에 의한 호흡기 질환 a respiratory disease caused by inhaling coal dust.

탄질(炭質) the quality of coal. ¶~이 좋다〔나쁘다〕 The coal is of good[poor] quality.

탄차(炭車) a coal waggon; 〔영〕 a coal truck.

탄착(彈着) hit; impact.
● **탄착 거리** 〔군〕 range; gunshot; the range of gun. ¶미사일의 ~는 2천 킬로미터이다 The missile has a range of 2,000 kilometers. **탄착점** the point of impact.

탄창(彈倉) 〔군〕 a magazine (of a machine gun).

탄층(炭層) 〔지〕 a coal seam; a coal bed. ¶~이 깊은 탄갱이 있는 탄전 a colliery with a thick [deep] bed.

탄탄대로(坦坦大路) a broad and level highway; a royal road.

탄탄하다 strong; sturdy; steady; healthy. ⇨ 튼튼하다

탄폐(炭肺) anthracosis; black lung; a respiratory trouble due to the inhalation of coal dust; a lung disease due to coal dust.

탄피(彈皮) an empty cartridge.

탄핵(彈劾) impeachment; denunciation; accusation; arraignment. ¶판사는 뇌물을 먹고 ~을 받았다 The judge was impeached for taking bribes. / The judge was accused of taking bribes. **탄핵하다** impeach (a person of[with] a crime); denounce; accuse (a person of misdemeanor); censure; arraign.
● **탄핵안** an impeachment motion[resolution]; a vote of censure. ¶정부 ~을 제출하다 introduce a motion of impeachment against the Government. **탄핵자** an impeacher; a denunciator. **탄핵 재판소** the Impeachment Court.

탄화(炭化) 〔화〕 carbonization; 〔탄소와의 화합〕 carburetting. **탄화하다** carbonize; char; carburet.
● **탄화규소** silundum. **탄화물** a carbide. **탄화수소** hydrocarbon; carburetted hydrogen. **탄화철** cementite. **탄화칼슘** calcium carbide; carbide of calcium; carbonized calcium.

탄환(彈丸) 〔집합적〕 a projectile; lead; (산탄) a shot; (작은) a bullet; (포탄) a ball; a cannon ball; a shell(파열탄); a shrapnel(유산탄). ¶~이 꿰뚫지 못하는 bulletproof / shellproof∥빗발치는 ~ a shower of lead / ~이 떨어지다 fire away all one's shots / 빗발치는 ~ 속을 나아가다 advance under a shower[hail / rain / storm] of bullets∥적에게 ~을 퍼붓다 rain [shower] shells upon the enemy / subject the enemy to fire.

탄흔(彈痕) a bullet mark[hole]; a shot hole. ¶온통 ~투성이의 벽 a bullet-pocked wall∥~이 남아 있는 창문 a bullet-holed window∥그 선체에는 ~이 많았다 The hull was riddled with shot[bullets].

탈 〔가면〕 a (face) mask; 〔위선〕 hypocrisy; false modesty. ¶위선의 ~을 쓴 사람 a hypocrite / a wolf in sheep's clothing[in a lamb's skin] /···의 ~을 쓰고 under the mask[cloak] of (friendship / charity) / in [under] the semblance of (a sage) / under the color of (religion)∥~을 쓰다 wear[put on] a mask / mask one's face / use a mask / cover one's face with a mask / (위선의) dissemble / play the hypocrite / simulate the modesty one does not feel∥~을 벗다 take [throw] off one's mask / unmask / show one's true colors(정체를 드러내다)∥···의 ~을 벗기다 unmask[take off the mask of] (a hypocrite) / debunk.

탈(頉) 1 〔사고〕 an accident; an incident; an untoward event; 〔장애〕 a hitch; a snag; a failure; a trouble; a mishap; 〔지장〕 a hindrance; an impediment; interruption. ¶별 ~이 없는 if nothing interferes∥~ 없이 without a hitch[trouble] / smoothly / well / 〔순조로이〕 all along / safely / in safety / safe and sound / 〔무사히〕 with a whole skin / 〔건강하게〕 in good health∥~ 없이 진행되다 go on without hitch[trouble] / keep going in good shape / go all right∥~ 없이 run smoothly∥~이 나지 않도록 조심해라 See to it that nothing goes wrong[there are no slipups].∥우리 계획에 ~이 생겼다 Something went wrong with our plans. / A hitch developed in our plans.// 역에 누이를 마중하러 갔는데 무슨 ~이 있었는지 나타나지 않았다 I went to the station to meet my sister, but by some mistake she did not appear.// 그가 경관을 때린 것이 ~이었다 The trouble was that he struck the policeman. / What made it so bad was that he hit the policeman./ 시계를 마루에 떨어뜨렸지만 아무 ~이 없었다 I dropped the watch on the floor, but it was all right.// 술 담배를 조금 하는 것쯤은 별 ~ 없을 테지 A little wine and tobacco will do you no harm.// 애 큰 ~이 났다 Good heavens, we're in real trouble!

2 [병] sickness; (영) illness; a disease; a trouble; a disorder. ¶배 ~ a stomach trouble // 몸에 ~이 나다 get ill[sick] / have (health) difficulties// 과식을 해서 ~이 나다 make oneself ill by overeating / overeat oneself ill// 과로하여 ~이 나다 work[fag] oneself ill// 무리를 한 것이 ~이 된 겁니다 This comes of the strain of work. / The strain has begun to tell on me.// 그는 ~ 없이 아주 잘 있다 He is in the best of health. / He is as fit as a fiddle.

3 [흠] a fault; a defect; a flaw; [평계] a plea; an excuse; a pretext; [트집] faultfinding. ¶~을 잡다 find fault with / pick flaws with / haggle (about) / cavil at / (시비를) accuse (a person) falsely / make a false charge (against) // 남의 ~을 찾다 examine (a person) closely for little defects / try to point out other's faults// 그 친구는 게으른 것이 ~이다 The bad thing about him is his laziness.

탈-(脫) ¶~공업화 the post-industrialization process.

탈각(脫却) a breakaway (from). ¶그들은 아직도 구습(舊習)에서 ~을 못 하고 있다 They cannot get rid of[free themselves from] the old custom yet. **탈각하다** get rid[clear] of; rid[extricate] oneself of; slough off; shake oneself free from; free oneself from; emerge from.

탈각(脫殼) [동] exuviation. **탈각하다** exuviate; cast off a shell[skin]; slough.

탈것 (육지의) a vehicle; (해상의) a vessel; (비행기) an airplane; [교통 기관] means of transportation; a (public) conveyance.

탈격(奪格) [언] the ablative case.

탈고(脫稿) completion of a manuscript. **탈고하다** finish writing; complete (a novel); (원고가) be completed. ¶그가 집필 중인 소설은 곧 탈고한다 The novel he is writing is near completion.// 마침내 100페이지의 논문을 탈고했다 I finally managed to complete my hundred-page thesis. → ¶그 저작은 이미 탈고되었다 The work is already complete in manuscript.

탈곡(脫穀) threshing (grain); thrashing. **탈곡하다** thresh[thrash] (wheat); do the threshing.

●**탈곡기** a threshing machine; a thresher.

탈구(脫臼) [의] dislocation; luxation. **탈구하다** get[be] dislocated; be luxated; slip[be put] out of joint. →¶그의 왼팔이 탈구되었다 He has dislocated his left arm. / His left arm is out of joint.

●**탈구 교정** extension.

탈놀음 a masque; a masque[mask] play.

탈당(脫黨) secession; withdrawal from [breaking with] a party; defection; (미) (party) bolting; (영) cave. **탈당하다** secede; withdraw[resign / defect / bolt] from a party; desert[leave / abandon] a party; break with a party. ¶그는 민주당을 탈당했다 He resigned his membership of the Democratic Party.

●**탈당 성명**(서) a (written) statement of one's secession from a party. **탈당자** a seceder; a renegade; (속어) a rat; [미] a bolter; a defector. ¶~가 속출했다 One member after another left the party.

탈락(脫落) **1** [누락] an omission; a lacuna (*pl.* ~s, -cunae); a hiatus (*pl.* ~ (es)). **탈락하다** be omitted; be left out; be excluded [eliminated]; be missing. ¶공천에서 ~ be left out the public nomination// 예선에서 ~ be eliminated (from the tournament) / be rejected in an elimination match / be disqualified (from) // 그들은 연속 두 게임에서 저서 탈락했다 They lost two games in succession and were eliminated. → ¶2, 3명의 이름이 명단에서 탈락되어 있다 A few names had been left off[omitted from] the list.

2 [이탈] defection; desertion(탈당 등); straggling. ¶(대학생의) 중도 ~ the expulsion before[prior to] graduation. **탈락하다** fall away (from); fall[drop] behind; drop out (of school). ¶레이스에서 탈락하는 사람이 많다 Many people have dropped out of the race.

탈락탈락 flop; swingingly. ⇨˘털럭털럭.

탈력(脫力) exhaustion; loss of strength.

탈모(脫毛) falling-out[-off] of hair; loss of hair; depilation; fallen hair. ¶~ 작용을 하는 depilatory // 이 로션은 ~를 방지한다 This lotion stops the hair from falling out. **탈모하다** (one's hair) fall out[off]; lose hair; bald; (새털이) molt.

●**탈모제** a depilatory (agent); a hair remover. **탈모증** [의] alopecia; depilatory disease. ¶원형 ~ alopecia areata.

탈모(脫帽) doffing one's hat[cap]; [구령] Hats off! **탈모하다** take[pull] off one's hat [cap]; doff the hat; raise[lift / remove] one's hat[cap]; uncover[bare] one's head. ¶남자들은 탈모하고 서 있었다 The men stood bareheaded[with their heads uncovered].

탈무드 [역] Talmud.

탈바가지 a mask (made from a calabash [gourd]).

탈바꿈 (a) transformation; (a) metamorphosis. **탈바꿈하다** change (the shape of); assume another[a different] shape; metamorphose; transform; transmute.

탈바닥 splashing; spattering. **탈바닥하다** keep splashing. ⇨˘탈바닥거리다.

탈바닥거리다 keep splashing[slopping / spattering]; splash about in (the water). ¶진창을 탈바닥거리며 걷다 go splashing in the mud.

탈법(脫法) (an) evasion of the law. **탈법하다** evade[dodge] the law.

●**탈법 행위** an evasion of the law; a slip from the grip of the law. ¶그건 분명히 ~가 된다 That constitutes a clear evasion of the law.

탈복하다(脫服-) go out of[leave off] mourning.

탈산(脫酸) [화] deoxidization; deoxidation. **탈산하다** deoxidize.

탈상(脫喪) expiration of the period of mourning; the end of mourning. **탈상하다** finish [come out of] mourning; leave off [get over] mourning. ¶내일로 탈상합니다 Tomorrow the mourning period will end.

탈색(脫色) decolo(u)ration; decolorization; discharge; bleaching. **탈색하다** decolo(u)r; decolorize; bleach; blanch; discharge.
● **탈색제** a decolorant; a decolorizer; (표백제) a bleach; a bleaching agent.

탈선(脫船) running away from a ship; desertion from a ship. **탈선하다** desert a ship; jump ship; run away from a ship.

탈선(脫線) 1 (열차 등의) derailment. **탈선하다** be [get] derailed; derail; run off the line [rails]; leave the rails; (영) leave [run off] the metals; (미) jump [leave] the track; (미) be ditched. ¶열차가 탈선했다 The train ran off the track. / The train (was) derailed. →¶ 탈선되어 있다 be off the track / be on the ties.
2 (행동 등의) deviation; aberration; departure; divergence; (이야기 등의) a ramble; (a) digression; an excursion; sidetracking. ¶~적인 연설 an irrelevant speech / a speech full of deviations [of rambling remarks] // ~직전의 학생들은 그 복장을 보면 알 수 있다 You can tell which students are on the brink of delinquency by their appearance. **탈선하다** (행동이) deviate [go away] from the right path; get on the loose; go astray [wild]; be erratic [eccentric]; (이야기 등이) digress [go adrift] (from the subject); make a digression; go off the rails; go [run] off the (main) track; get sidetracked; be off the subject; talk (away) [wander / stray] from the subject [point]; get off the point; go wild; wander (in one's talk). ¶이론이 ~ argue beside the point // 이야기가 탈선했다 The talk digressed from the subject. / The talk got sidetracked.
● **탈선 학생** an erratic student.

탈세(脫稅) evasion of taxes; tax evasion [dodging]. ¶~의 수단 a tax dodge // ~ 혐의로 수사하다 investigate (a person) on suspicion of tax evasion // ~를 묵인해 주고 돈을 받다 pocket money after conniving at the tax dodgings // 그 회사는 ~의 혐의가 있다 The firm has fallen under suspicion of tax-dodging. **탈세하다** evade [dodge] a tax; defraud the revenue (수입을 속여서).
● **탈세액** the amount of the tax evasion. **탈세자** a tax evader [dodger]; an evade of taxes.

탈속(脫俗) unworldliness; absence of vulgarity. **탈속하다** rise above the world; be superior to worldly aims. ¶탈속한 unworldly / unearthly / supermundane / saintly // 그는 탈속한 입장에서 생각한다 He sees things from an unworldly point of view. // 그는 출가 탈속하여 도를 닦은 사람이다 He has risen above [transcended] the world and cultivated his moral sense.

탈수(脫水) [수분 제거] dehydration; [가열 등에 의한 수분 제거] evaporation; [건조시킴] desiccation; (공학에서) dewatering. ¶~ 장치가 있는 전기세탁기 a washer-dryer. **탈수하다** dehydrate; dry; dewater; (원심력으로) spin-dry.
● **탈수기** a hydroextractor; a desiccator; a drying machine; a dehydrator; a dryer; a dewaterer; (세탁기의) a spin-drier. **탈수제** a dehydrator; a dehydrating [desiccating] agent; desiccant. **탈수증** dehydration.

탈수소(脫水素) [화] dehydrogenation.

탈습(脫濕) dehumidification. **탈습하다** dehumidify.
● **탈습기**(-器) a dehumidifier.

탈염(脫鹽) desalinization; [화] desalting. **탈염**

탈영(脫營) desertion from barracks; decampment. **탈영하다** desert from barracks; desert one's colors; break barracks; (미) go over the hill.
● **탈영병** a deserter; a runaway soldier.

탈옥(脫獄) prison breach; prison [jail] breaking; (미국 구어) jailbreak. ¶~을 기도하다 attempt an escape from jail / try to break prison. **탈옥하다** break (from a) prison; break jail; escape from prison. ¶지금까지 두 번 탈옥한 사람 a two-time escapee from prison // 한 죄수가 탈옥했다 A convict broke out of prison.
● **탈옥수** a prison-breaker; a jail-breaker; an escaped prisoner [convict].

탈의(脫衣) divestiture; divestment. **탈의하다** undress oneself; take off one's clothes.
● **탈의장 / 탈의실** a dressing [changing] room; (해수욕장 등의) a bathhouse; (체육관·학교 등의) a locker room.

탈자(脫字) an omitted word; an omission. ¶~가 많다 Many words are left out.

탈장(脫腸) [의] (a) hernia (pl. ~s, -niae); (a) rupture. ¶~이 되었다 I have a hernia. **탈장하다** rupture; herniate.
● **탈장대**(-帶) a truss.

탈저(脫疽) [의] gangrene; sphacelation; necrosis (pl. -ses). ¶~에 걸리다 sphacelate / be attacked by gangrene.

탈적하다(脫籍-) have one's name removed [deleted] from the (family, military, etc.) register; strike one's name off the register.

탈주(脫走) (an) escape; flight; abscondence; decampment; a break; a breakaway; (a) desertion. ¶자유에의 ~ a break for freedom // ~를 꾀하다 plan [attempt] an escape. **탈주하다** flee; escape; run away; (군인이) desert (from the army); (수병이) jump ship; (육군에서) (미국 구어) go over the hill; make off (with oneself); break loose [away]; bolt; (구어) give [take] leg bail(탈옥·탈영). ¶탈주한 죄수 an escaped convict // 집단으로 ~ stage a mass breakout (from a reformatory).
● **탈주병** a deserter; a fugitive [runaway] soldier. **탈주자** an absconder; a runaway; a refugee; an escapee; a bolter; a fugitive; a defector.

탈지(脫脂) removal of fat [grease]. **탈지하다** remove grease [fat] (from). ¶양모에서 ~ remove grease from wool.
● **탈지면** absorbent [sanitary] cotton; (미) cotton wool. **탈지유** (powdered) skim [nonfat] milk.

탈진(脫盡) total exhaustion. **탈진하다** be utterly exhausted [fatigued]; be tired to death; be worn [fagged] out.

탈출(脫出) (an) escape; extrication. **탈출하다** escape from (a prison); extricate oneself from (danger); get away (from a place); get out. ¶국외로 ~ escape to another country /

탈춤

flee one's country // 비행기에서 낙하산으로 ~ make a parachute jump[bail out] from a plane // 집단으로 ~ stage a mass breakout (from a reformatory) // 마침내 그는 곤경에서 탈출했다 At last he got himself out of[(문어) extricated himself from] the difficult situation. // 그 군인은 적의 수용소에서 탈출했다 The soldier escaped from the enemy's camp.

탈춤 a *talchum*; a mask(ed) dance.

탈취(脫臭) deodorization. **탈취하다** deodorize; remove[kill] the odor (of).
● **탈취제** deodorant; a deodorizer.

탈취(奪取) capture; seizure. **탈취하다** capture; carry; seize; snatch (from / out of / away). ¶왕위를 ~ usurp the throne // 요새를 ~ carry[take] a fortress // 그는 적의 군기를 탈취했다 He snatched away[grabbed] the enemy banner. ¶그는 회사를 탈취하려고 음모를 꾸미고 있었다 He was conspiring to take over the company. →¶수도가 적군에 탈취되었다 The capital was seized[captured] by the enemy.

탈탈 plodding; with dull clinks. ⇨탈털

탈퇴(脫退) (단체 등으로부터의) withdrawal (from); (교회·당파 등으로부터의) (문어) secession (from). ¶~서를 내다 submit a written notice-to-quit (to an association). **탈퇴하다** withdraw (from); leave; (문어) secede (from); break (away) from; bolt from; disconnect oneself from. ¶조합에서 ~ secede from the union // 몇몇 지부가 그 단체에서 탈퇴했다 Several branches withdrew from the organization. // 그는 그 운동에서 탈퇴했다 He has dropped out of the movement.

● **탈퇴자** a seceder; a bolter.

탈피(脫皮) **1** (곤충·뱀의) ecdysis (*pl*. -dyses); casting off. **탈피하다** cast (off) the skin; shed the skin; slough (off). ¶뱀이 탈피했다 The snake has cast off[has shed] its skin. // 누에는 탈피할 때마다 자란다 A silkworm grows every time it casts off the skin. **2** (비유) self-renewal. **탈피하다** ¶구태(舊態)에서 ~ break from the convention / outgrow one's former self / come out of oneself // 그는 부모에 대한 의타심에서 탈피했다 He outgrew his dependence on his parents.

탈항(脫肛) (의) (suffer from) prolapse of the anus.

탈환(奪還) recapture; recovery; retaking. ¶(죄수 등의) 불법 ~ rescue. **탈환하다** recapture; win back; regain; recover; retake. ¶적으로부터 진지를 ~ recapture a position from the enemy // 해외 시장을 ~ recapture the overseas market // 우승기를 ~ win back the pennant // 아군은 적군에 점령되었던 섬을 탈환했다 Our troops retook the island which had been captured by the enemy.

탈회(脫會) secession[withdrawal] (from a society); defection. ¶이 지역의 의사들은 의사회에 ~서를 냈다 The local medical association submitted a notice of secession to the Medical Society. **탈회하다** withdraw[secede / resign] from (an association); break away from[leave] (a society); drop out (of an organization); drop[give up] one's membership; cease to be a member (of). →¶탈회시키다 expel (a person) from (a club) / force (a person) to resign from (an association).

탐(貪) [탐욕] covetousness; avarice; greed; [욕심] desire; want; [탐닉] indulgence.

탐관(貪官) a greedy[grasping] official.
● **탐관오리** a corrupt official; a graft-happy official; a venal official.

탐광(探鑛) searching for coal beds[oil fields]; prospecting. **탐광하다** prospect (a region for gold).

탐구(探究) [조사] (an) investigation; (an) inquiry; [연구] research; (a) study. ¶과학적 ~ scientific inquiry[research / study] // 진리의 ~ the search for truth // 사고 원인의 ~ investigation of the cause of an accident. **탐구하다** investigate; inquire into; make researches in; explore. ¶진리를 ~ search for[(문어) seek after] truth // 중국인의 국민성을 ~ do research on the national traits of the Chinese.
● **탐구심** the spirit of inquiry. ¶선천적으로 ~이 강한 사람들이 있다 Some people are inquiring by nature. **탐구자** [조사하는 사람] an investigator; [연구하는 사람] a researcher.

탐나다(貪-) (사물이) be desirable; be appetizing; be tempting; be desirous [covetous] of; be envious of; desire; rust after[for]. ¶탐나는 여자 a desirable[lust-arousing] woman // 탐나는 음식 appetizing [mouth-watering] food // 탐나는 물건 a want / a thing desired / an object of desire // 돈이 탐나서 for love of money // 탐나는 듯이 wistfully / longingly // 돈이 ~ be covetous of money // 권력이 탐난다 I am covetous of power. / I lust for power. // 나는 그 자리가 몹시 탐났다 I wanted the post very badly. // 나는 명예 따위는 탐나지 않는다 I have no desire[don't care] for fame.

탐내다(貪-) desire; want; crave (for); hanker for[after]; covet; be greedy (after); be desirous (of acquiring / to acquire); be covetous (of). ¶명성을 ~ covet for[after] fame // 돈을 ~ be greedy for money / be money-mad // 음식을 ~ be ravenous (for food) // 남의 것을 ~ covet what belongs to others // 남의 아내를 ~ covet another's wife // 남의 재산을 ~ be covetous of another's property // 남의 것을 탐내서는 안 된다 You should not covet what[anything which] belongs to others. // 그는 재물을 탐내지 않는다 He has no desire for wealth. // 남의 것을 탐내지 마라 Don't covet what is not yours. // 돈은 누구든지 탐내는 법이다 Love of money is common to all.

탐닉(耽溺) [열중] indulgence; addiction; [주색에의 몰입] dissipation; debauchery. **탐닉하다** indulge in; be addicted to; be given (up) to; give oneself up to; abandon oneself to (the pursuit of pleasure); be dissipated; dissipate. ¶마약에 탐닉하고 있다 be addicted to[hooked on] drugs // 여색에 ~ be given (up) to debauchery // 그는 주색에 탐닉하고 있다 He was given to wine and women. / He indulged in sensual pleasures.

탐독(耽讀) indulgence in reading; avid reading. **탐독하다** read avidly[with avidity]; be absorbed[engrossed] in reading; steep oneself (in); pore over (a novel); be immersed in (a book); devour (novel after novel). ¶소설을 ~ pore over[be immersed in] novels // 이 연애 소설을 탐독했다 I couldn't put this love story down. // 그는 그

책을 탐독하고 있었다 He was poring over the book.

탐리(貪利) love of undue gain[profits]; greed of gain; profiteering. **탐리하다** covet[make] undue[unreasonable] profits; profiteer; be greedy[avaricious / covetous] of gain.

탐문(探問) indirect inquiry; roundabout investigation. **탐문하다** inquire about indirectly; sound (out) by indirect inquiry.

탐문(探聞) obtaining information (by inquiry). **탐문하다** obtain information (by inquiry); hear; get wind of(소문을); (형사 등이) snoop[beat the bushes] for information. ¶탐문한 정보 information (obtained by inquiry) / a tip (on) / a pickup / (구어) a wrinkle // 탐문한 바에 의하면 according to what I[we] have learned // 그 사나이에 대해서 탐문한 것이라도 있나 Have you heard anything about him?
● **탐문 수사** legwork. ¶경찰은 목격자를 찾기 위하여 널리 ~를 벌였다 The police did a lot of legwork in an effort to find an eyewitness. // 경찰은 단서를 찾기 위하여 인근에서 ~를 벌였다 The police questioned everyone in the neighborhood in their search for a lead.

탐미(耽美) love of beauty ¶~적인 (a)esthetic.
● **탐미주의** (a)estheticism. **탐미주의자** an (a)esthete.

탐방 (with a plop[splash]. ⇨탐병

탐방(探訪) (private) inquiry; an interview(기자 등의); investigation. ¶사회 ~ private inquiry into social life // 카메라 ~ a photographic interview. **탐방하다** inquire (into); make inquiry of; have an interview (with). ¶ 경주의 가을을 ~ enjoy the autumnal beauty of the Gyeongju // 기자는 슬럼가를 탐방했다 The reporter looked into[investigated] the conditions in the slums.
● **탐방기** a report of inquiries. **탐방 기자** a (newspaper) reporter; an interviewer; a legman; a leg writer.

탐사(探査) (an) inquiry; (an) investigation; probing. ¶심해(深海) ~용 선박 a vessel designed for deep sea probes. **탐사하다** make inquiries; investigate; inquire[look] into. ¶달 표면을 ~ probe the surface of the moon // 철저히 ~ make a thorough[rigid] inquiry // 석유를 ~ explore for oil // 고적을 ~ visit a place of historical interest // 내정(內情)을 ~ inquire into the real state.

탐색(探索) 1 [수색] search; hunt; quest. **탐색하다** search (for); look[quest] for; delve into; seek for; hunt up; probe. ¶범인의 자취를 ~ trace the movements[whereabouts] of the criminal // 단서를 따라 ~ follow up a clue // 철저히 ~ trace (rumors) to earth.
2 [조사] (a) probe; inquiry; investigation; research. **탐색하다** [손으로 더듬어서 찾아내다] grope for and find (a thing); [찾아 발견하다] hunt out; discover; [장소를 알아내다] locate; [상세히 조사하다] investigate. ¶광맥을 탐색하여 찾아내다 locate[discover] a vein of ore // 상대의 심중을 탐색하여 알아내다 come to understand a person's innermost feelings // 고대사(古代史)를 ~ inquire into ancient history // 사건의 원인을 ~ investigate the cause of[find out what caused] the incident // 나는 그의 경력을 탐색해 보겠다 I'll probe into his past. // 우리는 적의 움직임을 탐색할 필요가 있다 We need to spy on the enemy's movements. // 자넨 그의 의중을 탐색해 보았나 Have you sounded him out?
● **탐색자** an investigator. **탐색전** an engagement in reconnaissance; a reconnoitering skirmish.

탐스럽다 desirable; appetizing; coveted; attractive; tempting; charming. ¶탐스러운 여자 a desirable woman // 탐스러운 사과 an appetizing apple // 탐스러운 듯이 wistfully / longingly // 탐스러운 꽃 a very beautiful flower // 탐스러운 검은 머리 abundant dark hair // 그녀의 머리털은 탐스럽게 어깨에 내려와 있었다 Her hair hung in abundant masses over her shoulders.

탐식(貪食) voracity; edacity; gluttony. **탐식하다** eat voraciously[greedily]; eat avidly; devour; gormandize. ¶탐식하는 사람 a voracious person / a glutton / a gormandizer.

탐심(貪心) avarice; greed; cupidity.

탐욕(貪慾) avarice; rapacity; covetousness; cupidity. ¶~의 화신 (be) avarice itself / (be) the incarnation of avarice // 그는 ~으로 인해 남의 돈을 훔쳤다 His greed[avarice] drove him to steal another's money.
● **탐욕가** a shark; a vulture; a harpy; a greedy fellow.

탐욕스럽다(貪慾−) avaricious; rapacious; greedy; covetous; insatiable; insatiate. ¶명예에 대하여 ~ be greedy[hungry] for fame // 금전에 대하여 ~ be greedy about money // 권력에 대하여 ~ be greedy for power // 탐욕스러운[게걸스러운] 아이로구나 What a glutton you are! **탐욕스레** avariciously; rapaciously; greedily; covetously. ¶…을 ~ 바라보다 cast greedy eyes on.

탐재(貪財) 〔재물을 탐함〕 love of money; desire for wealth. **탐재하다** love money; desire wealth; covet (for) property.

탐정(探偵) (행위) detective work; covert investigation; espionage; espial; (사람) a detective; (미) an investigator; a spy; a plainclothesman(사복형사); (미) a sleuth. ¶군사 ~ a military spy // 비밀 ~ a secret agent / a secret(-service) detective // 사설 ~ a private detective / (속어) a private eye // 아마추어 ~ an amateur detective // ~에게 미행당하다 be shadowed by a detective // ~을 도중에 따돌리다 give a detective the slip on the way / shake off a detective // ~을 붙이다 set [put] a detective upon (a person). **탐정하다** spy (on a person / into a secret); trace (a crime); detect; do detective work.
● **탐정물** a detective[crime] story; (미국 속어) a whodunit(▶ Who done it?을 발음대로 표기한 것. 바른 용법은 Who did it?). **탐정 소설** a detective story[novel]; (집합적) detective fiction

탐조(探照) throwing a searchlight. **탐조하다** throw[beam] a searchlight (on).
● **탐조등** a searchlight. ¶~으로 비추다 turn [flash] a searchlight (on something) / sweep (the sea) with a searchlight // ~을 켜다 switch on a searchlight.

탐지(探知) ascertaining; detection; finding out by indirect inquiry. **탐지하다** detect; spy [search] out (a secret); trace[ferret / smell] out (a crime); get wind of (an affair); learn (a fact) by inquiry; monitor (radio communications). ¶비밀을 ~ smell out a secret // 음모를 ~ scent[trace] out a plot / smell out

탐측 treachery.// 그 해역에서 기뢰를 쉽게 탐지할 수 있었다 We succeeded in detecting the mines laid in that sea area.// 그들은 내 신원을 탐지한 것 같았다 They seem to have uncovered[discovered] my past history.// 나는 그 비밀을 탐지해 냈다 I have smelled[ferreted / nosed] out his secret.
● **탐지기** a detector; a locator. ¶전파 ~ a radar / a radar set // **방향** ~ a radar / a direction finder // **어군** ~ a fish finder [detector]. **탐지 기지** a detection station. **탐지 장치** detection equipment; a monitoring [detection] device; a detecting device.

탐측 (探測) sounding; probing.
● **탐측 기구** [기상] a pilot balloon. **탐측 로켓** a sounding rocket.

탐탁하다 desirable; satisfactory; pleasant; pleasing; agreeable; acceptable. ¶탐탁한 사람 a lik(e)able person // 탐탁하지 않은[못한] undesirable / unsatisfactory / disagreeable / unpleasant // 탐탁한 구혼자 an eligible suitor // 탐탁하지 않은 손님 an unlooked-for guest / an unwelcome visitor // 탐탁치 않은 평판 an unsavory reputation // 탐탁치 않은 인상을 주다 give (a person) an unfavorable impression // 별로 탐탁한 일은 못 돼 The work has no particular attraction for me.// 하나도 탐탁한 게 없다 None of them seem quite the thing.// 그와 동행하는 것은 별로 탐탁치 않다 I am rather unwilling to go with him.// 그런 사람은 별로 탐탁하게 여기지 않는다 I have no opinion of that sort of man.

탐폰 [의] a tampon.

탐하다 (貪-) covet (fame); be greedy (of / for); be covetous (of). ¶명리(名利)를 ~ covet [thirst after] fame and gain // 안일을 ~ live in idleness / pass one's days in indolence / idle away one's time // 폭리를 ~ eager to make an excessive[undue] profit / profiteer.

탐험 (探險) (an) exploration; (탐험 여행) an expedition. ¶남아프리카 ~ an expedition to [into] South Africa // 남극 ~ an Antarctic expedition // 심해(深海) ~ 은 매우 흥미롭다 The exploration of the ocean depth is very interesting.// 그는 북극 ~ 에 나섰다 He went on an expedition to the North Pole. **탐험하다** explore; make an exploration. ¶무인도를 ~ explore an uninhabited island // 미지의 나라를 ~ explore[make an exploration of] an unknown country
● **탐험가** an explorer; an expeditionary. **탐험대** an expeditionary[exploration] party. ¶남극[북극] ~ an Antarctic[Arctic] expedition // ~를 **조직[지휘] 하다** organize[lead / command] an expedition // ~를 **파견하다** dispatch an expeditionary[exploration] party.

탐혹 (耽惑) indulgence; addiction; infatuation. **탐혹하다** indulge in; be addicted[given] to; be infatuated with; immerse oneself in. ¶여자에게 ~ be infatuated with a woman.

탑 (塔) a tower; (성 등의 작은 탑) a turret; [불] a pagoda. ¶첨 ~ a steeple / a spire // **방첨** ~ an obelisk // **기념** ~ a monument // **석** ~ a stone monument // **교회의** ~ a church steeple[spire] // **텔레비전** ~ a television tower // **철** ~ (고압선용의) a pylon // ~**을 세우다** erect [build] a tower.

탑본 (揚本) a rubbed copy. ⇨=탁본

탑비 (塔碑) a tower and a monument (at a tomb).

탑승 (搭乘) boarding; riding (a ship / a plane). **탑승하다** get into; board; [비행기를 타다] get on (a plane); [함선에 오르다] embark on [go on board] a ship. ¶비행기에 ~ have a ride[go up] in an airplane / get into[get aboard] an airplane // 이륙 30분 전에 비행기에 탑승해 주십시오 Please (go on) board the plane half an hour before takeoff.
➔ ¶**탑승시키다** embark [enplane / entrain] (troops).
● **탑승권** a boarding card. **탑승자 / 탑승객** a passenger. ¶~ **명단** a (passenger) manifest.

탑재 (搭載) loading; embarkation; entrainment. **탑재하다** load; embark; entrain; take in. ¶탑재해 있다 be loaded (with goods) / have (a rocket guns) on board // 배에 화물을 ~ load a ship with goods / get[take] goods on board // 기차에 군수품을 ~ entrain military supplies // 많은 식량을 탑재하고 출범하다 sail (laden) with a large cargo of foodstuff // 그 군함은 12인치 포 10문을 탑재하고 있다 The warship carries[mounts] ten 12-inch guns.// 그 전투기는 미사일을 탑재하고 있다 The fighter is carrying a missile.// 다량의 무기를 탑재하고 출항했다 The ship set sail loaded with a large supply of arms.
● **탑재량** burden; (have) a carrying capacity (of 5,000 tons).

탓 [잘못] fault; blame; responsibility; [이유] reason; cause; ground(s); [결과] consequences; a result; [영향] influence; an effect. ¶… **—이다** be one's fault / be to blame / be due[attributable] to … / be caused by … // 내 ~ 으로 through my fault // 잘못을 남의 ~ 으로 돌리다 lay the fault at a person's door / put the blame on a person // 실패를 불운한 ~ 으로 돌리다 attribute [ascribe / impute] one's failure to bad luck / set one's failure down to bad luck // 그 사고는 그의 ~ 이 아니다 He not to be blamed[not responsible] for the accident.// 내가 기차를 놓친 것은 오래 끈 네 전화 ~ 이다 I missed my train because of your long telephone call.// 그의 친구들은 그 실패를 그의 ~ 으로 돌렸다 His friends put the blame for the failure on him.// 내 ~ 이 아니다 Don't blame me (for it) ! / It's not my fault.// 이것은 오랜 습관 ~ 이다 This comes from long habit.// 내 기분 ~ 인지 도무지 술 맛이 좋지 않다 Perhaps it's my imagination, but this wine isn't very good.// 날씨 ~ 인지 몸이 나른하다 I feel tired. Maybe it's the weather.// 다 내 ~ 입니다 I'm all my fault. **탓하다** put[lay] blame upon; lay the fault to; find fault (with); blame [reproach] (a person for something); impute; charge; accuse. ¶자신을 ~ reproach oneself (for) / 하늘을 ~ quarrel with Providence // 네가 잘못하고 왜 나를 탓하느냐 Why do you try to shift the blame on me when all the time you are to blame?// 나만 잘못한다고 탓하지 마시오 Don't lay the blame upon me alone. / Don't make me the scapegoat.// 네가 게을러서 낙제한들 누구를 탓하랴 If you fail because of your idleness, you will only have to reproach[thank] yourself for it.

탕 [총소리] bang; with a bang; [부딪는 소리] with a clang. ¶주먹으로 책상을 ~ 치다 bang one's fist on the table // 대포 소리가 ~ 하고 울렸다 The gun bang out.// 권총 소리가 ~ 하고 들렸다 I heard the bang[bam] of a pistol.∥그녀는 문을 ~ 하고 닫고 나갔다 She slammed the door[banged the door shut] and left.

탕(湯) **1** [욕조] a (hot) bath; [목욕탕] baths. ¶남[여]~ the men's[women's] section (of a bathhouse)∥~에 들어가다 have a dip in the bathtub∥~에 가다 go to a bathhouse. **2** [제사에 쓰이는 국] soup offered at ancestor memorial service.

-탕(湯) [국] soup; [달인 약] a (medical) decoction; an infusion. ¶살미~ beef and rice soup∥보신~ dog soup.

탕감(蕩減) writing-off; cancellation; remission. **탕감하다** write off (debt); cancel (out). ¶빚을 탕감해 주다 remit (a person's) debt / write off (a person's) debt∥내게 진 네 빚을 탕감해 주겠다 I'll write off your debt to me. ➔¶빚이 탕감되었다 I had my debts canceled [written off].

탕거리(湯−) soup makings; soup stock.

탕건(宕巾) *tanggeon*; a horsehair skullcap; a horsehair inner cap.

탕관(湯罐) a pipkin.

탕기(湯器) a soup bowl.

탕메(湯−) soup and rice offered at ancestral rites.

탕면(湯麵) noodles in soup.

탕솥(湯−) a soup kettle.

탕심(湯心) [방탕한 마음] propensity to dissipation; salacious thinking.

탕아(蕩兒) a debauchee; a libertine; a rake; a fast liver; a prodigal[profligate] son. ¶성경에 나오는 ~ 이야기는 잘 알려져 있다 Everybody knows the Biblical story of the prodigal son.

탕약(湯藥) a (medical) decoction; an infusion; herb tea.

탕자(蕩子) a debauchee; a libertine. ⇨ᐧ탕아

탕진하다(蕩盡−) squander; dissipate (a fortune); run[go] through (one's fortune); run [give] out of. ¶재산을 ~ squander[run through] one's fortune∥방탕한 생활로 가산을 ~ squander[dissipate / exhaust] one's fortune by fast living∥그는 부모의 유산을 탕진했다 He has squandered every penny of the legacy from his parents.∥그는 가산을 탕진해 버렸다 He has gone bankrupt.∥그는 경마로 재산을 탕진했다 He gambled away his entire fortune at the race.∥그는 나의 재산을 탕진했을 뿐만 아니라 내 모든 생활까지 파멸시켰다 He not only squandered my fortune but also destroyed my whole existence.

탕치(湯治) a hot-spring cure; treating an illness with hot baths. **탕치하다** cure (an illness) by hot baths; take a hot-spring cure; try the baths for medical purposes. ¶온천에 탕치하러 가다 go to a hot-spring resort to recover one's health / go to a spa for [and take] a hot-spring cure.

탕치다(湯−) **1** [재산을 다 날리다] squander [dissipate] one's fortune. ¶노름으로 ~ gamble away one's fortune. **2** [탕감하다] write off; cancel (out). ¶빚을 ~ write off a debt / remit (a person's) debt.

태¹ [새 쫓는 데에 쓰는 기구] a clap(ping) [cracking] whip.

태² [그릇의 깨진 금] a crack; a fissure.

태(胎) the placenta and the umbilical cord. ¶그는 ~를 길렀다 [어리석다] He is stupid [defective].

태(態) **1** shapeliness. ⇨ᐧ맵시¶귀여운 ~ a certain loveliness about one∥이 양복은 그가 입으면 ~가 난다 This suit looks good[nice] on him[when he wears it]. **2** [태도] an air. ¶갑부~를 내다 play the millionaire / display[show off] one's wealth∥형은 외출하면 형님~를 낸다 When we go out together, my brother puts on a patronizing air[(속어) likes to act patronizing]. **3** [언] voice. ¶능동 [수동]~ active[passive] voice.

태가다 crack; be cracked; have a crack. ¶태간 그릇 a cracked ware / a crackle.

태고(太古) ancient times; remote ages[antiquity]. ¶~의 ancient / primeval / primitive / 태곳적 사람들 ancient[primitive] peoples∥~에는 eons ago.

● **태고사** ancient history. **태고 시대** ancient times; antiquity.

태교(胎敎) prenatal care (of an unborn child); prenatal culture[education]; antenatal training. ¶아름다운 음악을 듣는 것은 ~에 좋다고 한다 Listening to good music is said to have a good effect on one's unborn baby.

태권도(跆拳道) *taegwondo*; *taekwondo*; the Korean art of emptyhanded self-defense. ¶세계 ~ 연맹 the World Taekwondo Federation(약어 WTF).

태그 매치 a tag-team (wrestling) match.

태극(太極) *taegeuk*; the Great Absolute (in Chinese philosophy); the entity of the cosmos. ¶~무늬가 있는 기와 a two-comma-patterned roofing tile.

● **태극기** *Taegeukgi*; the national flag of Korea; the *taegeuk* flag. **태극선**(−扇) a fan with a *taegeuk* design.

태기(胎氣) [임신을 한 기미] signs[indications] of pregnancy; a feeling that one is pregnant.

태깔(態−) **1** [모양과 빛깔] form and colo(u)r. **2** [교만한 태도] a haughty attitude.

태깔(이) 나다 look nice.

태깔스럽다(態−) haughty; proud; arrogant.

태껸 *taekkyeon*; the kicking and tripping art (as a sport).

태내(胎內) the interior of the womb. ¶~의[~에 있는] 아기 a child in the womb / an unborn child / a fetus∥~에서 죽다 die while in the (mother's) womb.

태도(態度) an attitude; [거동] bearing; demeanor; deportment; a manner; an air; (문어) a mien. ¶심적 ~ a mental attitude∥강경한 ~ a firm attitude (toward) / a strong stand (against the U.S.)∥친절한 ~ a friendly attitude∥태연한 ~로 nonchalantly / as if nothing had happened∥결연한 ~로 in a determined attitude / with a determined air∥위협적인 ~로 나오다 take[assume] a threatening attitude∥~를 **고치다** revise [modify] one's attitude / improve one's behavior / mend one's ways∥~를 **바꾸다** change[modify] one's attitude / alter one's stand / change one's tune∥~를 **정하다** determine one's attitude (toward a problem) / decide (on doing, on the words, etc.)∥~를 **밝히다** define[clarify] one's attitude / make one's attitude clear / stand up and be counted∥~를 밝히지[분명히 하지] 않다 do not commit oneself / be noncommittal [uncommitted] (on an issue)∥명백한 ~를 취하다 take a clear stand (on a problem)∥

태동 모호[애매]한 ~를 취하다 assume[maintain] an ambiguous[a dubious] attitude (toward a problem) / sit on the fence∥오만한 ~를 취하다 strike a haughty attitude∥쌀쌀한 ~를 보이다 behave oneself toward (another) like a stranger / wear a distant air∥~가 부드럽다[점잖다] move[bear oneself] / be of gentle manners∥말하는 ~가 조심스럽다 be modest in one's speech∥경찰관은 그 남자의 ~가 수상하다고 생각했다 The policeman thought the man's manner suspicious. ∥그들은 안절부절못하는 ~였다 They behaved very nervously. / They acted very nervous.∥그는 수업 ~가 나쁘다 [장난을 친다] He misbehaves in class. / [주의가 산만하다] He has a poor attitude in class.∥그는 그들에 대하여 반항적인[단호한] ~로 나왔다 He took a rebellious[firm] attitude toward(s) them.∥그 말을 듣자 그녀의 ~는 싹 변했다 She changed her attitude completely when she heard that.∥너의 ~가 확실치 않아 난처하다 Your indecision[ambivalent attitude] puts us in a difficult position.∥한국 정부는 미국 정부에 대하여 강경한 ~를 취했다 The Korean government adopted a firm stance toward(s) the United States.∥우리가 그에게 우호적인 ~를 취하면 그도 부드러워질 것이다 If we take a friendly attitude toward him, he will soften.∥그가 먼저 취하는 ~를 기다리며 지켜보자 Let's wait and see what line he takes[tack he takes / he does] first.∥그의 이야기하는 ~가 마음에 들지 않는다 I don't like his way of talking[the way he talks].∥그녀의 손님을 대하는 ~는 빈틈이 없다 Her manner of serving[waiting on] the customers is perfect.∥마치 대가나 된 듯한 ~를 보이고 있다 He has the bearing[air] of an important person.∥그는 늘 소극적인 ~로 말한다 He always speaks in defensive manner.∥그는 누구에게나 한결같은 ~로 대한다 He has an equable way of dealing with people.

태동(胎動) (태아의) quickening; fetal movement; the movements of the fetus; [비유] signs[indications] (of forthcoming activities); fomentation. ¶군국주의의 ~의 signs of the militarism∥혁명의 ~을 감지했다 There is a scent[whiff / feeling] of revolution in the air. **태동하다** quicken; [비유] show signs of (democratization).
● **태동기** the quickening period.

태두(泰斗) a great authority (on); a leading light; a luminary; a star. ¶지질학의 ~ a great authority on geology∥한국 의학계의 ~ a luminary in the medical profession of Korea.

태막(胎膜) a fetal[foetal] membrane; an embryonic membrane.

태만(怠慢) [게을리 함] negligence; neglect; dereliction; procrastination; [게으름] idleness; laziness. ¶정부의 ~ the supineness of the government∥직무 ~자 a defaulter / a delinquent∥그는 직무 ~으로 직장을 잃었다 He lost his job through[because of] negligence.∥자네는 직무 ~이야 You have been remiss (in your duties). / You have been negligent[have neglected your duties]. **태만하다** negligent; neglectful; derelict; delinquent; supine; idle; lazy. ¶태만한 사람 a quitter / a shirker / a sluggard / a lazybones. **태만히** negligently; delinquently; idly; lazily. ¶직무를 ~ 하다 shirk[neglect] one's duties.

태몽(胎夢) a dream of forthcoming conception.

태무하다(殆無—) (very) scarce; virtually nonexistent; very few[rare]; (there is) little; (서술적) be next to nothing. ¶내가 얻은 것이라곤 태무하였다 I scarcely gained anything.∥성공의 가망은 ~ There is not the remotest chance of success.∥큰 도시에서는 화재 없는 날이 ~ Hardly a day passes without a fire in a big city.

태반(太半) (양적으로) the greater[best / most] part; the great[large] portion; (수적으로) the great; majority; the bulk. ¶~은 mostly / for the most part / in large part / generally / nearly all∥일생의 ~ the greater[better] part of one's life∥주민의 ~은 강의 서쪽에 살고 있다 Most[The greater part] of the inhabitants live on the west side of the river.∥이곳 노동자의 ~은 지방 출신이다 The majority of the laborers here come from rural areas.∥일의 ~을 끝냈다 Our task is mostly finished.∥공사는 ~이 완성되었다 The work is very nearly completed.

태반(胎盤) [생] the placenta (pl. -tae, ~s). ¶~의 placental∥~이 있는[없는] placental [implacental].

태변(胎便) meconium. ⇨배내똥

태부족(太不足) a great want[shortage / lack / dearth]. **태부족하다** greatly wanted; (서술적) be in great shortage; be much lacking.

태산(泰山) [높고 큰 산] a great[big / high] mountain; [사물이 크고 많음] a heap; a pile; a huge amount; a mountain (of). ¶~처럼 확고부동하다 be firm[as steady] as a rock∥~같이 믿다 give the fullest confidence[credit / credence] to (a statement)∥할 일이 ~ 같다 have lots[a heap] of things to do / have so many things to do∥~처럼 쌓여 있다 be piled up mountain-high.
● **태산준령** high and steep mountains.

태상왕(太上王) an abdicated King; an ex-King.

태생(胎生) 1 [출생] birth; origin. ¶~이 좋은 wellborn / of noble [high / good] birth / gently born∥~이 천한 lowborn / of low [obscure / humble] origin∥외국 ~의 foreign-born∥시골 ~의 사람 a country-born person∥하와이 ~의 한국인 a Hawaiian-born Korean∥명문 ~이다 be highborn / be of noble birth / be born with a silver spoon in one's mouth∥어디 ~이십니까 Where do you come from? / Where are you from?∥그는 ~으로 따지자면 미국인이지만, 지금은 한국으로 귀화했다 He is an American by birth[was born an American], but he is now a naturalized Korean.

2 [동] viviparity. ¶~의 viviparous.
● **태생 동물** viviparous animals. **태생지** one's birthplace; one's place of birth; one's native place. **태생학** [의] embryology; ontogenesis.

태선(苔蘚) moss; lichen. ⇨이끼

태선(苔癬) [의] lichen. ¶~의 lichenous.

태세(態勢) [태도] an attitude; setup; a posture; [준비] preparedness; arrangements; [상태] a condition. ¶받아들일 ~ preparations to receive∥…할 ~에 있다 be[stand] ready[prepared / poised] (for / to do) / be in fit shape (to do) // 방어 ~에서 공격 ~로 전환하다 move away from a defensive posture and shift toward the offensive // 만반의 준비 ~로 있다 I am prepared for anything. // 적함의 공격을 요격할 ~가 되어 있다 We are ready [prepared] for an attack from the enemy warships. // 전쟁을 개시할 ~가 되어 있다 We are ready to go to war [open hostilities]. // 노조는 4월 15일에 파업을 ~를 갖추고 있다 The Labor Union is (all) ready to [is posed to] go on strike on April 15.

태수(太守) a governor-general (*pl.* governors-general, governor-generals); a viceroy; a governor; a prefect.

태아(胎兒) an unborn child [baby]; (임신 3개월까지의) an embryo (*pl.* ~s); (3개월 이후의) a fetus; a conceptus (*pl.* ~es, -ti). ¶~의 embryonic / fetal // ~의 순조로운 발육 the normal development of a fetus.

태양(太陽) **1** [해] the sun. ¶~의 solar / heliacal // ~의 빛 sunlight / sunshine / [태양 광선] the sun's rays / sunbeams // ~ 표면의 대폭발 a solar flare / a chromospheric eruption // ~의 햇무리 a halo round the sun // ~은 동쪽에서 뜬다 [서쪽으로 진다] The sun rises in the east [sets in the west]. **2** [남에게 희망을 주는 것]. ¶그녀는 난민들의 마음의 ~이었다 She was light and hope to the refugees.

● **태양계** the solar system. **태양년** a solar year. **태양등** a sun lamp; an artificial sunlight; a mercury(-vapor) lamp. **태양력** the solar calendar. **태양 숭배** heliolatry; sun worship. **태양시** solar time. **태양신** the sun god [goddess]; [그리스 신화] Helios. **태양 에너지** solar energy [power]. **태양열** solar heat; the heat of the sun's rays. ¶~ 온수기 a solar water heater // ~ 발전 solar power generation // ~ 냉난방 solar heating and cooling // 앞으로 대규모 발전에 이 이용될 것이다 In the future solar heat will be used to generate electric power on a large scale. **태양 전지** a solar battery [cell]. **태양 흑점** a sunspot; a solar spot.

태어나다 be born; come into being [existence / world]; see the light. ¶태어난 곳 one's birthplace // 태어난 나라 one's native country [land] // 태어날 아기 the coming [expected] child // 갓 태어난 아기 a newborn baby / a newborn // 태어날 때부터 from birth // 내가 태어난 뒤로 줄곧 ever since my birth [I was born] / in (all) my born days / in my life // 세상에 태어나서 처음으로 for the first time in one's life [since one was born] // 부자로 ~ be born rich [to wealth / with a silver spoon in one's mouth] // 운을 타고 ~ be born under a lucky star // 특별한 재능을 가지고 ~ be born with a rare gift of nature // 다시 ~ be born again / be [get] reborn // 새로 태어난 듯한 느낌이 들다 feel like a new man / feel as if one were reborn // 나는 1982년 11월 2일 서울에서 태어났다 I was born in Seoul on November 2, 1982. // 나는 가난한 집안에 태어났다 I was born poor [into a poor family]. // 그들에게 여자 아이가 태어났다 A girl baby was born to them. / They had a baby girl. // 그는 미국인 어머니에게서 태어났다 He was born of an American mother. // 다음 달 누이에게 아기가 태어날 예정이다 My sister is going to have a baby next month. // 우리 집에 갓 태어난 새끼 고양이 두 마리가 있다 I have two newborn kittens.

태업(怠業) a work stoppage; deliberate idleness; [스트라이크] a go-slow (strike); (미) a slowdown (strike); (영) a ca'canny. **태업하다** go on a slowdown strike; start a work slowdown.

태연자약하다(泰然自若-) perfectly calm; cool and collected; imperturbable; calm and self-possessed. ¶태연자약하게 calmly / with composure / quite unruffled / without turning a hair // 그는 태연자약하게 경찰관의 심문에 대답했다 He answered the policeman's questions with perfect serenity [great composure]. // 그는 태연자약했다 He kept his presence of mind. / He never lost his presence of mind [his composure].

태연하다(泰然-) calm; cool; composed; self-possessed; unruffled; imperturbable; unimpassioned; firm; immovable; unmoved. ¶그녀는 태연한 태도를 잃지 않았다 She remained calm [self-possessed]. / She kept her presence of mind. // 그는 그런 소동을 피우고 나서도 ~ He himself looks perfectly cool after having alarmed us like that. // 다음 날 그는 태연한 얼굴로 회사에 나왔다 The next day he came to the office as if nothing had happened. // 그녀는 그런 불행한 일을 겪고도 ~ Even after such an unhappy experience, she looks quite unconcerned. // 그는 성공하거나 실패하거나 언제나 ~ He is indifferent to success or failure. // 그 이야기를 듣고도 그는 태연했다 He was unmoved [unimpressed] by the story. // 톰은 자기가 거짓말을 하고 있다는 것이 탄로가 났어도 천연스럽게 태연했다 Tom was as cool as a cucumber when he was found to be telling a lie. **태연히** coolly; calmly; with composure; in a self-possessed manner. ¶그는 ~ 앉아 있었다 He was sitting calmly. / He was sitting with great composure. // 그는 ~ 거짓말을 한다 (구어) He makes no bones about lying. / He thinks nothing of telling lies.

태열(胎熱) [의] congenital fever.

태엽(胎葉) a spring; a windup spring. ¶~이 풀린 시계 a run-down clock // ~이 풀리다 run down / come unwound // ~을 감다 wind (the spring of) a wall clock // 장난감의 ~이 끊어졌다 This spring [clockwork] of the toy is broken.

● **태엽 장치** clockwork. ¶~가 된 장난감 a windup [spring-driven] toy // 이 인형은 ~로 움직인다 This doll moves if you wind it up.

태우다[1] **1** [불에 타게 하다] burn; put into the fire; set (the hay) on fire; have [get] (one's house) burnt down. ¶쓰레기를 ~ burn rubbish / make a bonfire of rubbish // 담배를 ~ smoke a cigarette // 화재로 전 재산을 ~ have all one's property burnt in the fire // 마른 풀을 불에 버리다 burn off dead grass // 레이저 광선으로 점을 태워 없애다 burn off a mole with laser beams // 태워서 재를 만들다 reduce to ashes // 태워 버리다 burn up [away] / destroy by fire / commit to the flames / incinerate / throw into the fire // 나는 옛날 편지를 전부 태워 버렸다 I burned up all the old letters. / I threw all the old letters into the fire. // 그들은 마을의 집들을 깡그리 태워 버렸다 They set fire to all the houses in the village and burned them

태우다

1 [그슬리다] burn; scorch; singe; char(새까맣게). ¶새까맣게 ~ burn a thing black [to a cinder] // 다리미질을 하다가 와이셔츠를 ~ scorch a shirt while ironing it // 나는 해변에서 살갗을 태우고 왔다 I got a suntan on the beach.

3 (시체를) cremate; burn (a corpse) to ashes. **4** (가슴·속을) burn (one's soul); agonize; worry. ¶속을 ~ be worried[anxious / agonized / anguished] / burn with anguish // 애를 ~ worry oneself // 남의 속을 ~ make (a person) worry / make (a person) awfully anxious.

태우다² [사람·물건을 싣다] carry; take in; take (a person) on board; place (a man) in a train; pick up; (선원을) ship (a new crew); (수용하다) accommodate. ¶군인들을 태운 열차 a train carrying soldiers / a train with soldiers in it // 승객 백 명을 태울 수 있는 여객기 an airliner that can accommodate 100 persons / an airliner with a hundred-passenger capacity // 배가 ~ take passengers on board(배가) / take in passengers(기차·버스가) // 도중에서 승객을 ~ pick up passengers // 말에 ~ put[set] (a person) on a horse / 어린아이를 목말 태우고 가다 ride[carry] a child on one's shoulders // 태워 주다 (탈것에) give (a person) a lift [ride] (in one's car) / give (a person) a passage (on one's boat) / (도와서) help (a person) into (a car) / put[place] (a child) on (a train) / 나는 그 어린애를 부축하여 스키 리프트에 태워 주었다 I helped the child (to) get on the ski lift. // 그는 자기 차에 나를 태워 주었다 He gave me a lift in his car. // 자네를 집까지 태워 주겠다 I will drive you home. // 그 비행기[배]는 수상과 그 일행을 태우고(탑승시키고) 있었다 The plane[ship] was carrying the Prime Minister and his party. / The plane[ship] had the Prime Minister and his suite on board. // 그의 어머니를 부산행 열차에 태워 주도록 나는 그에게 부탁을 받았다 I was asked to put his mother on the train bound for Busan.

태우다³ **1** [재산·월급 등을 타게 하다] divide (something among); portion out; apportion. ¶재산을 아들에게 ~ divide one's property among one's sons / settle one's property on one's sons. **2** [가르마를 갈라붙이게 하다] have (one's) hair parted. ¶가르마를 왼쪽으로 ~ have one's hair parted on the left-hand. **3** [노름이나 내기에서 돈을 지르다] place a bet (on); lay (a wager); bet; stake; wager.

태우다⁴ [연줄·그네를] put[let] in and out. ¶연줄을 ~ let the string of a kite in and out // 그네를 ~ [앉히어] put[set] (a child) on a swing / (타게 하다) let (a child) get on [have] a swing.

태위(胎位) [태아의 위치] presentation (of the fetus).

태음(太陰) the moon.
● **태음력** the lunar calendar. **태음시** the lunar time.

태자(太子) the Crown Prince. ⇨황태자

태장(笞杖) [볼기 치는 형구] a bamboo paddle (used for punishment); [매로 볼기를 침] beating (on the buttocks); flogging; flagellation.

태점(胎占) divination of the sex of an unborn child.

태조(太祖) a founder (of a dynasty); the first King (of the dynasty).

태중(胎中) ¶~ in pregnancy // ~에 during the period of pregnancy[maternity].

태질 **1** [타작] threshing (grain); flailing; beating hard. **태질하다** thresh; beat out (grain); beat hard. ¶벼를 ~ thrash[thresh] rice / beat the rice grains out. **2** [메어치기] throwing[casting] down. **태질하다** throw [cast / fling] down; get (a person) down.

태질치다 throw down. ⇨태질하다(⇨태질²) ¶사람을 ~ throw a person down // 짐을 땅에 ~ fling one's pack down on the ground.

태초(太初) the beginning of the world.

태클 [체] a tackle. **태클하다** tackle.

태평(太平·泰平) **1** [세상의 평안함] (perfect) peace; quiet; tranquility. ¶~을 구가하다 enjoy the blessing of peace / sing the praises of undisturbed peace. **태평하다** peaceful; quiet; tranquil. ¶태평한 세상 in time of peace / in the piping times[days] of peace // 천하가 ~ The world is at peace. / Peace reigns over the land. **태평히** peacefully; quietly; tranquilly.

2 [몸·마음의 평안함] easygoingness; optimism. ¶네가 어떻게 그렇게도 ~일 수 있는지 참 모르겠다 I wonder how you can take things[it] so easy. // 자넨 아주 천하~이로군 You look quite carefree. / You look free from all care. // 그것을 눈치 채지 못했다니 자넨 얼마나 천하~인 사람인가 How easygoing you are not to have noticed it! **태평하다** free and easy; carefree; easygoing; optimistic; devil-may-care; happy-go-lucky; insouciant. ¶태평한 사람 an easygoing person / a person who takes life[things] easy / a lighthearted person // 그런 무사태평한 사고방식으로는 이 세상을 살아 나가기가 어렵지 Such an easygoing[happy-go-lucky] way of thinking will be of no use in the real world. **태평히** optimistically; insouciantly. ¶~ 살다 lead an easy life // 이런 판국에 내가 ~ 있을 수 있겠는가 How can I take it easy[(속어) hang loose] in such circumstances?
● **태평가**(-歌) a song of peace. **태평성대** a peaceful reign; a reign of peace.

태평소(太平簫) [음] a conical oboe; a Korean clarinet.

태평스럽다(太平-) free and easy; carefree. ⇨태평하다(⇨태평) ¶자기는 항상 운이 좋다고 믿고 있는 그도 정말 태평스런 사람이다 How easygoing[optimistic] of him to believe fortune will always smile on him!

태평양(太平洋) the Pacific (Ocean). ¶북[남] ~ the North[South] Pacific // ~의 Pacific // 환~ 국가 the Pacific rim nations.
● **태평양 고기압** a Pacific high. **태평양 연안** the Pacific coast; (미국의) the west coast. **태평양 전쟁** the Pacific War. **태평양 횡단 비행**[항로] a transpacific flight [line].

태풍(颱風) a typhoon. ¶~이 북상했다 A typhoon came up north. // ~이 이 섬을 덮었다 The island was hit[struck] by a typhoon. // ~은 남방의 해상에서 발달하고 있다 A typhoon is brewing to the south. // ~이 발생하였다 A typhoon formed[was formed / was born / was spawned]. // ~이 제주도로 다가오고 있다 A typhoon is approaching Jejudo. // ~은 인천 쪽으로 서서히[빠른 속도로] 진행하고

고 있다 The typhoon is cruising in the direction of[racing toward] Incheon.// ~은 해상으로 물러갔다 The typhoon blew out to sea.// ~은 동해 상에서 소멸되었다 The typhoon dissipated on the East Sea.
  ●**태풍의 눈** the eye[center] of a typhoon; [크게 영향을 미치는 사람·물건] a person[thing] at the center[eye] of a storm.
태피스트리 a tapestry (*pl.* -tries).
태형(笞刑) (a) whipping; (영) (a) flogging; lashes.
태환(兌換) conversion. ¶마르크와 달러의 ~ conversion of marks into dollars. **태환하다** convert (to / into). ¶태환할 수 있는[없는] 지폐 convertible[non-convertible] paper money.
  ●**태환 은행** an issuing bank; a bank of issue; (영) a clearing bank. **태환 지폐** / **태환권** a convertible note.
태후(太后) the Empress Dowager. ⇨⁼황태후
택시 a taxi; a taxicab; a cab. ¶개인 ~ an owner-driven cab// 손님을 찾아 돌아다니는 ~ a cruising taxi// ~로 가다[~를 타다] go by[take a] taxi// ~를 **잡다** flag up[flag down] a taxi(▶ flag down은 달리고 있는 차를 신호하여 멈추게 함)// ~ 영업을 하다 operate a taxi service// 요금을 내고 ~에서 내리다 pay off a taxi// 큰맘 먹고 ~를 타다 treat oneself to a taxi// ~를 **대절하다** hire a taxi// (손을 들어) ~를 세우다 halt a taxi// ~를 부르다 (소리 질러) hail a taxi / (전화로) call a taxi.
  ●**택시 강도** taxi robbery; (범인) a taxi robber. **택시 운전사** a taxi driver; a cabdriver; a cabman; (구어) a cabby[cabbie]; (영) a taximan; (여자) a cabette. ¶개인 ~ an owner-driver cabby. **택시 정류장** (미) a taxi stand; (미) a cabstand; (미) a cab zone [line]; (영) a taxi rank.
택일(擇日) choice of an auspicious day. **택일하다** choose an auspicious day.
택일(擇一) alternative.
택지(宅地) a house site. ⇨⁼집터 ¶~를 조성하다 prepare housing sites / turn (the land) into housing lots.
  ●**택지 분양** sale of building lots. **택지 정리** laying out of a tract [of grounds].
택하다(擇~) [선택하다] prefer; choose; pick; take. ¶많은 중에서 하나를 ~ choose[pick] one out of many // 가장 좋아하는 것을 ~ take the one one likes best / take one's first choice// 이 밖에 택할 길은 없읍니다 There is no alternative.// 나 같으면 항복하느니 차라리 최후까지 싸우는 쪽을 택하겠소 I would prefer to fight to the end rather than to surrender. / I would rather fight to the end than surrender.// 나는 이 방법을 택하겠다 I'll adopt this method.// 어느 쪽을 택할까 망설이고 있다 I am at a loss which to choose.// 어느 것을 택하셨습니까 Which is your choice?
탤런트(*talent*) a TV actor[actress]; an actor [actress] in TV. ¶TV ~ a TV star[personality]// 신인 ~를 스카웃하다 scout for new talent.
탬버린 [음] a tambourine. ¶~을 흔들어[손으로 두드려] 울리다[소리 내다] play[sound] the tambourine by shaking it[striking it with one's hand].
탭 댄서 a tap dancer; (속어) a soft-shoe shuffler.
탭 댄스 a tap dance. ¶그들은 ~를 추고 있다 They are tap-dancing.
탯줄(胎~) the umbilical cord; the navel string[chord]; [생] the funiculus (*pl.* -li).
  탯줄 잡듯 하다 hold very tight[fast]; take fast hold of.
탱고 the tango. ¶~를 **추다** dance the tango.
탱자 [탱자나무의 열매] a fruit of the trifoliate orange.
  ●**탱자나무** [식] a trifoliate orange tree.
탱커 a tanker; an oiler; a crude carrier. ¶오일 ~ an oil tanker.
탱크 1 [용기] a tank. ¶가스[석유] ~ a gas[an oil] tank// ~에 가득 채우다 fill up the tank (of a car). 2 a tank. ⇨⁼전차(戰車)
  ●**탱크로리** (미) a tank truck; (영) a tank lorry.
탱탱 tautly; tightly. **탱탱하다** blown up to the tautness of surface; inflated; swollen up [out]; puffed up; distended; hard and taut [tense / tight]. ¶종기가 부어 ~ A boil is swollen up taut.// 뺀 발목은 탱탱하게 붓는다 A sprained ankle puffs up.
탱화(幀畵) [불] an altar portrait of Buddha.
터¹ [자리] a site (for a school); a (building) lot; land (for); a place; a plot. ¶집~ land for housing / a house[home / building] lot// 장 ~ a marketplace// 일~ [근무처] one's place of work / one's jobsite / one's post// 빈 ~ a vacant lot// 옛날의 ~ the site of an ancient temple// 공원으로서 좋은 ~ a good site for a park// ~를 **돋우다** build up[fill in / raise] the land (for)// ~를 **잡다** select[pick out / secure] a site[lot / land].
  2 [일이 벌어지는 장소] an arena; a theater. ¶싸움~ a field of battle / a battlefield// 빨래 ~ a wash place / a place for doing the laundry (at the streamside).
  3 [기초] the foundation; the ground; footing; foothold; groundwork; spadework. ¶~를 **다지다** consolidate[solidify] the foundation // ~를 **잡다** establish the foundation (of)// ~가 **잡히다** have a firm foothold / be well grounded.
  터(를) 닦다 prepare[level] the ground (for); clear the foundation (of).
터(가) 세다 (a site is) ill-omened; unlucky; ill-fated; jinxed; (서술적) have an unfortunate site.
터² 1 [예정] a plan; an expectation; hope; [의도] intention. ¶…할 ~이다 be going to (do) / plan to / expect to / be set to / be supposed to / be supposed to// 너는 어떻게 할 ~인가 What are you going to do? / What do you intend to do?// 이번에는 성공할 테다 I hope [expect] to succeed this time.// 서울엔 얼마나 있을 텐가 How long do you plan to remain in Seoul?
  2 [추측·짐작]. ¶오늘은 물결이 사나울 텐데 I fear the waves will be high today.// 그랬더라면 잘되었을 텐데 If he had done so, he might have succeeded.// 지금쯤 도착했을 ~인데 He ought to have arrived there by this time.// 그것은 잘될 테지 I trust it will work out well.// 그에게는 이미 알려졌을 테니까, 그것을 말할 필요는 없다 You don't need to tell him about it, since he is supposed to have already been informed.
터널 1 [굴] a (railway) tunnel; an excavation. ¶사직 ~ the Sajik Tunnel// 해저 ~ an

터놓다

undersea [an underwater / a submarine] tunnel // ~에서 나오다 come out of a tunnel // 산에 ~을 파 나가다 tunnel one's way into a mountain // 열차가 ~을 통과하였다 The train passed through a tunnel. 2 [야구] [두 다리 사이로 공을 놓침] failure to field a grounder. ¶1루수가 땅볼을 ~시켰다 The first baseman let the grounder go through his legs.
● **터널 공사** tunneling work; tunnel construction.

터놓다 1 [막힌 것을 치우다] lay [make] open; open (it) up; break; undam (a river, a reservoir, etc.). ¶터놓은 두 방 a double room knocked into one // 둑을 ~ break [burst] a dam (on a river) // 물꼬를 ~ open a sluice [floodgate].
2 [금했던 것을 풀다] remove (a prohibition); lift (a ban). ¶봉쇄를 ~ raise a blockade // 통제를 ~ remove control (on) / decontrol.
3 [마음을 트고 지내다] open one's heart; open up one's mind; be frank [candid / open] (with a person); be unreserved; throw [lay aside] reserve [formalities]; break down all reserve; throw [shake / cast] off all restraint; come out of one's shell; break the ice; hobnob (with a person). ¶흉금을 터놓고 이야기하다 talk in a familiar way / have a friendly talk [chat] (with) / have a heart-to-heart talk (with) / speak without restraint. // 그는 좀처럼 남에게 흉금을 터놓지 않는다 He would not come out of his shell. // 터놓고 이야기하자 Let's have a heart-to-heart talk. / Let's talk turkey. / Let's talk frankly. // 그와는 터놓고 의논할 수 있다 I can consult him without reserve. / I can ask his advice without any inhibitions.

터덜거리다 1 [걸음이] walk wearily; trudge; jog (on); plod; walk heavily (over / along); travel with labor. ¶지친 아이들은 터덜거리며 집에 돌아갔다 The tired boys jogged home. 2 (수레 소리가) jolt; rattle along (a stony road). 3 (질그릇 등이) clink dully.

터덜터덜 [걷는 모양] plodding; trudging. **터덜터덜하다** walk wearily. ⇨ 터덜거리다 1 2 [소리 나는 모양] rattling. **터덜터덜하다** jolt; clink dully. ⇨ 터덜거리다 2·3

터득(攄得) understanding; comprehension; grasp; apprehension; realization; mastery. **터득하다** understand; apprehend; comprehend; master; make out; grasp; have a grasp of …; realize; learn. ¶터득하기 쉬운 [어려운] easy [hard] to understand [learn] // 골프의 퍼팅 요령을 ~ get the hang [knack] of putting / 하는 방법을 완전히 ~ acquaint oneself thoroughly with the procedure // 프랑스 어를 ~ master French / acquire [get] a mastery of French language / perfect oneself in French // 나는 마침내 숨은 진리를 터득했다 At last I realized [(문어) perceived / the hidden truth. // 그는 도교의 심오한 뜻을 터득했다 He mastered the profound principles [secrets] of Taoism. // 그는 그 기술을 완전히 터득했다 He completely mastered [gained a complete mastery of] the art.

터뜨리다 1 [막힌 것 등을] break; burst; tear; have (something) break [burst / tear]. ¶종기를 ~ break one's boil / have one's boil break // 풍선을 ~ break [burst] a balloon // 벚나무가 꽃망울을 터뜨리기 시작했다 The cherry blossoms have begun to bloom [have begun to open / are coming into bloom].
2 (폭발물·감정을) explode; burst; detonate. ¶폭탄을 ~ explode a bomb // 다이너마이트를 ~ set [touch] off a dynamite // 웃음을 ~ explode with laughter / burst out laughing / burst [break out] into (fits of) laughter // 그 소식을 듣자 그녀는 울음을 터뜨렸다 She burst into tears [broke down crying] at the news. // 모든 사람이 격렬한 분노를 터뜨렸다 Everybody gave full vent to his anger.

터럭 hair. ¶~만큼도 (not) in the least / (not) a bit [whit / feather].

터무니없다 [근거 없다] unfounded; baseless; groundless; (서술적) have no foundation; [엉뚱하다·당치않다] extraordinary; wild; absurd; fabulous; preposterous; exorbitant; (미국 속어) darned; [말도 안 되다] unreasonable; [말의 조리가 서지 않다] incoherent; [무모하다] reckless; [도를 지나치다] excessive. ¶터무니없는 요구 a preposterous [an unconscionable] demand / an excessive [unreasonable / inordinate] demand // 터무니없는 값 an exorbitant [an outrageous / a ridiculous / an unreasonable / an incredible / a fancy / a fabulous] price // 터무니없는 거짓말 a damned [whopping] lie / a whacking big lie / a whopper // 터무니없는 말 a pure fabrication / an unfounded report / nonsense / rotten stuff / rubbish // 터무니없는 일 [것] a walloper // 터무니없는 논법 [논쟁] an illogical argument // 터무니없는 값을 매기다 set an unreasonable [exorbitant] price // 터무니없는 의심을 받다 be suspected when one is innocent / incur groundless suspicion / be falsely suspected (of theft) // 그것은 터무니없는 오해다 That is a gross misunderstanding. // 그런 터무니없는 말을 하지 마라 Don't say such ridiculous [absurd] things. // 그것은 터무니없는 거짓말이다 It's an outrageous lie. // 터무니없는 소리 By Jingo! / By Jove! / Confound it! / Stuff and nonsense! **터무니없이** absurdly; monstrously; enormously; exorbitantly; fabulously; unreasonably; unconscionably; impossibly; ridiculously; incredibly; uncommonly. ¶~ 싸게 at an absurdly low price / (buy an article) dirt cheap // ~ 앞뒤가 맞지 않는 문장 incoherent writing // 그는 말과 하는 짓이 모두 ~ 엉망이다 Both his words and his actions are utterly confused. // 그것에는 ~ 오랜 시간이 걸렸다 It took an incredibly long time. // 그것은 ~ 비싸다 It is a staggering [an exorbitant / a mind-boggling] price.

터미널 1 [종점] (미) a terminal; (영) a (bus) terminal; a (railway) terminus. 2 [공항의 사무 시설] a terminal. 3 [단자·컴퓨터의 단말 장치] a terminal.

터벅거리다 trudge (along / on); tread (along / on); plod (on); hobble (along / about); jog [pad] (along).

터벅터벅 totteringly; trudgingly. ¶~ 걷다 plod one's way / trudge along // 그는 비탈길을 걸어 올라갔다 He trudged wearily up the slope. **터벅터벅하다** trudge (along / on). ⇨ 터벅거리다

터번 a turban. ¶~을 감은 사람 a turbaned man // ~을 감다 wear (a) turban.

터부 a taboo; a tabu. ¶~시하다 taboo / put

the taboo on (something) / put (something) under taboo // 그 말은 그들 사이에서는 ~로 되어 있다 That word is taboo with them.

터부룩하다 tufty; fringy. ⇨ 더부룩하다1

터빈 a turbine (engine). ¶가스[수력 / 증기 / 공기] ~ a gas[a water / a steam / an air] turbine / 압력[충동 / 반동 / 충격] ~ a pressure[an impulse / a reaction / an action] turbine.

터수 1 〔처지〕 circumstances; one's lot; a station in life; a condition of life. ¶자기의 ~를 알다 know one's station in life[one's distance] // 나보다 그의 ~가 낫다 He is better off than I (am). / He has it better than I. 2 〔관계〕 relationship; friendship; terms; a footing. ¶…과는 서로 너너하는 ~다 be on thee-and-thou terms with ... // 그와는 아주 친한 ~다 I am on very close terms with him.

터울 an age span between siblings; the difference[disparity] of age between siblings. ¶~이 잦다 be frequent in having a baby // 나는 삼 형제 중의 가운데인데 형이나 동생이나 세 살 ~이었다 I was the middle child of the three, but there was a gap of three years on either side.

터전 a site; a lot; the grounds; a base. ¶필요한 개혁의 ~ the base of needed reforms // 그는 상인으로서 ~을 잡았다 He has established himself as a trader.

터주 the tutelary spirit of a house site; (라) a genius loci. ¶그는 창사 때부터 일하고 있으므로 다들 터줏대감으로 간주하고 있었다 He worked for this company from the very beginning, so everyone regarded him as the real boss.

터지다 1 〔파열되다〕 burst (open); break; split; splinter; (종기) burst; break; open; collapse. ¶터져 나갈 듯한 갈채 a storm[thunder / volley] of applause / an avalanche of cheers / (목재의) 말라 터진 데 [건] a check // 터진 손 chapped hands // 살쪄서 터질 듯한 bulging // …으로 터질 듯하다 be busting with ... / be filled to a breaking point with ... / be packed to a busting point with ... // 박수갈채가 ~ break into a loud applause // 둑이 터졌다 A dike collapsed [gave way]. // 입술이 터졌다 My lips cracked. // 타이어가 터졌다 The tire was punctured. / The tire had a blowout. // 그 연주회장은 열광적인 청중으로 터질 지경이었다 The concert hall was crowded[packed to overflowing] with an enthusiastic audience. // 목의 종기가 마침내 곪아 터졌다 The boil on my neck has burst[popped open] at last. // 배가 터질 것 같다 I am full. / My stomach's about to burst. // 풍선이 터졌다 The ballon burst. // 구경꾼들에게서 야유가 터져 나왔다 The spectators booed and jeered. // 나는 슬픔으로 가슴이 메어 터질 듯했다 My heart was breaking with grief. // 나는 분노로 가슴이 터질 것만 같았다 I felt as if I would burst with anger. // 이 양복은 솔기가 여기저기 터졌다 Seams have popped open[come apart / come undone] here and there in this suit. // 내 스웨터의 소매가 터졌다 The cuff of my sweater has unraveled[is unraveling / (영) has unravelled / (영) is unravelling]. // 벚나무의 꽃망울이 터지기 시작했다 The cherry blossoms have begun to bloom[open]. / The cherry trees have started blooming. // 어망은 정어리로 터질 것 같았다 The fishing net was bursting[crammed to the breaking point] with sardines. // 그 사내아이는 자주 소매나 옆구리가 터져서 집에 돌아온다 The boy often comes home with a sleeve torn loose or a side seam torn open.

2 〔폭발하다〕 explode; burst (out); go off; break out; blow up. ¶굉장한 소리를 내고 ~ blow up[go off] with a terrific explosion // 울화통을 ~ (사람이) fly into a passion / burst into a rage // 화약이 터졌다 Gunpowder exploded. // 평소의 울분이 터지고 말았다 Their smoldering resentment flared up. // 요란한 웃음소리가 갑자기 터져 나왔다 There was a sudden burst[roar] of laughter. // 그 계획에 대한 반대의 목소리가 터져 나왔다 There was an outcry against the plan.

3 〔발생하다〕 occur[happen] suddenly; break [burst] out; take place. ¶중대한 사건이 터졌다 A serious matter popped up. // 전쟁이 터졌다 A war broke[burst] out.

4 (샘·피 등이) spout (out); spurt (out / up); gush out. ¶코피가 ~ bleed at the nose / have a bloody nose.

5 〔얻어맞다〕 get a blow; be beaten; be struck on.

터치 a touch. ¶부드러운[멋있는] ~ with a delicate[an admirable] touch // 이 타자기의 키는 ~가 가볍다[무겁다] This typewriter has a light[heavy] touch. **터치하다** touch. ¶러너를 ~ touch the runner // 그 사건은 전혀 터치하지 않고 있다 I have nothing to do with the affair.

● **터치다운** 〔미식축구〕 touchdown. **터치라인** 〔럭비·축구〕 a touchline. **터치아웃** (*touch out) 〔야구〕 tagging (a runner) out. ¶3루에서 주자를 ~시키다 throw[put] a runner out at third // 러너는 1루 바로 앞에서 ~되었다 The runner was tagged out short of first base.

터프 가이 (구어) a tough guy [(영) egg].

턱[1] (입의 위아래) the jaws; 〔생〕 maxilla (*pl.* -lae); (아래턱의 바깥 부분) the chin; the chops; the mandible (포유동물·어류 등의, 특히 아래턱). ¶아래~ the lower jaw / the mandible / the chin // 위~ the upper jaw / the maxilla // 이중 ~ a double chin // 이중의 double-chinned // 긴 ~ lantern jaws // 긴 ~의 lantern-jawed // 외투 깃에 ~을 파묻고 (walk) with one's chin sunk into one's coat // ~이 빠지다 dislocate one's jaw // ~을 당기다[내밀다] draw in[stick out] one's chin // 너무 웃다가 ~이 빠지다 laugh one's jaw out of joint // ~을 치켜 올리다 turn up one's nose // 손으로 ~을 괴다 rest one's chin on[in] one's hand / cup one's chin in one's hands / prop one's head in one's hands / sit with one's head between one's two palms[hands] // ~을 당기고 가슴을 펴라 Chin down, chest out!

턱[2] (높은 데) a projection; an elevated place; a rise; a sill. ¶고개~ the top of a pass [slope] // 마루~ the top / the summit // 문~ a door[window] sill.

턱[3] (음식 대접) a treat; a feast; a banquet; an entertainment; (미국 속어) a set-up. ¶~을 내다 stand treat for (one's friend) / give (a person) a treat / treat (a person) to (something) / (구어) stand (a person) dinner.

턱⁴ **1** [까닭] reason; grounds. ¶그럴 ~이 있나 It cannot be so.∥내가 알 ~이 있나 How should I know that? **2** [그만한 정도] that extent. ¶아직 그 ~이다 That's all the further we've gotten. / It's still much the same.∥그의 병세는 그저 그 ~이다 He has not been making any perceptible recovery. / His condition shows little improvement.∥"경기가 어떤가?" "그저 그 ~이지." "How's business?" / "Oh, not too bad." / "Just so-so."

턱⁵ **1** [긴장이 풀리는 모양] at complete ease [rest]. ¶마음을 ~ 놓다 put one's mind at complete ease / feel greatly relieved / be [feel] quite at ease. **2** [반가워 손·어깨 등을 잡는 모양] affectionately. ¶손을 ~ 잡다 grasp (a person's) hand affectionately. **3** [자연스럽게 구는 모양] without hesitation; with a grand air; composedly. ¶손을 ~ 내밀다 ask for (something) with no hesitation.

턱걸이 **1** [체조] a chin-up; chinning exercises. ¶~를 10번 하다 do 10 chin-ups∥~를 몇 번이나 할 수 있나 How many times can you chin yourself (up)? **2** (씨름·싸움에서의) a chin hold [catch]. **턱걸이하다** topple with a chin hold [catch]. **3** [기식(寄食)] parasitism; dependence; sponging. **턱걸이하다** sponge [hang] on (one's relations); be parasitic on; be a dependent on (a person).

턱밑 [가까운 곳]. ¶~에 beneath one's chin / right under one's nose∥~에 두고 보지 못하다 can't see [fail to find] what is right under one's nose.

턱받이 a bib; a pinafore; (영) a feeder.
턱뼈 [생] a jawbone; a maxillary bone; the maxilla (pl. ~s, -lae).
턱살 the lower jaw; the chin.
턱수염(―鬚髯) a beard. ¶~을 기른 남자 a bearded man∥~을 기르다 grow [raise] [wear] a beard(▶ wear는 상태를, grow는 행위를 나타냄) / 긴 ~이 있다 have a long beard.
턱시도 a tuxedo (pl. ~es); a tuxedo jacket; (영) a dinner jacket [coat].
턱없다 **1** [근거·이유 없다] groundless; unfounded. ¶턱없는 소문 a groundless rumor / an unfounded gossip. **턱없이** unfoundedly; groundlessly; without reason. ¶~ 때리다 knock (a person) on no provocation∥~하다 abuse (a person) without rhyme [reason].
2 [지나치다] immoderate; exorbitant; extreme; excessive; (속어) tall; (미국 속어) darned; [당치 않다] extraordinary; unreasonable; absurd; wild; preposterous; (속어) blithering. ¶턱없는 값 an exorbitant [a fancy] price / 턱없는 계획 a wild [an absurd] project / a wildcat scheme / 턱없는 요구 an extravagant [unreasonable] demand / a wholly unacceptable demand / 턱없는 소리를 하다 say extraordinary [absurd] things / talk nonsense [wild]. **턱없이** excessively; immoderately; unreasonably; preposterously; absurdly. ¶~ 돈을 쓰다 fool one's money away / make extravagant expenditures∥~ 술을 먹다 drink immoderately∥~ 키가 크다 be extremely tall∥이 동네는 물가가 ~ 비싸다 Prices are unduly [unreasonably] high in this town.∥그건 ~ 싸다 That's ridiculously cheap.
3 [신분에 맞지 않다] (서술적) be not suitable to one's means; [능력 밖이다] (서술적) be beyond one's reach [power]. ¶턱없는 생각을 갖다 have ideas above one's station∥그런 사치는 나에겐 ~ Such a luxury is beyond my reach. **턱없이** beyond one's reach [power].

턱잎 [식] a stipule.
턱주가리 〈속〉 the lower jaw. ⇨아래턱(⇨아래).
턱지다 swell; form a rise; be hilly. ¶턱진 길 a hilly road.
턱짓 moving one's chin as a gesture; pointing with one's chin. ¶~으로 부리다 have (a person) at one's beck / order (a person) about∥그는 ~으로 사람을 부려 먹는다 He bosses people around. / He barks orders at people. **턱짓하다** make a gesture by moving one's chin; point with one's chin.
턱턱 promptly; (fall) in rapid succession; with cracks; spitting hard or in rapid succession; stifling. ⇨탁탁

턴 (수영 등의) a turn. ¶퀵 ~ a quick turn∥공중제비 ~ a somersault turn∥그는 ~을 잘한다 He makes a good turn. **턴하다** turn; make [execute] a turn; tip off the wall (풀에서). ¶50m 지점에서 ~ turn (around) at the 50-meter mark.

털 **1** (사람의) hair. ¶겨드랑이 ~ hair under the arm / armpit hair∥곱슬곱슬한 ~ curly [crisp] hair∥부드러운 ~ soft hair∥빳빳한 ~ coarse [bristly] hair∥센 ~ gray hair∥솜 ~ downy hair∥같은 hairy∥~이 있는 haired / hairy∥~이 없는 hairless / bald∥~이 많은 hairy / thick-haired∥~ 나는 약 a hair-grower [-restorer]∥~을 뽑다 pull out a hair / unhair∥~ 많은 사람 a hairy person∥~을 지지다 frizzle [friz] and curl hair / have one's hair frizzled and curled∥~이 성기다 be thinly-haired∥~이 빠지다 (사람이) lose one's hair / hair falls out [comes off]∥~이 성기어 [엉성해]지다 be losing one's hair∥~이 났다 Hair grew [appeared / came out].∥그녀는 머리에 ~이 길다 She has long hair.∥그의 가슴에 ~이 나기 시작했다 Hair has begun to grow on his chest.∥~이 몇 개 빠졌다 A few hairs fell out [came off].
2 (짐승의 털) fur; wool; [깃털] feathers. ¶새 ~ bird feathers / down (양털)∥~의 결 (동물의)the lie of fur∥~의 결이 고운 개 a dog with a fine coat of hair∥~ 많은 개 a shaggy dog∥~을 갈다 (깃털을) mo(u)lt / (짐승이) shed (its) hair [coats]∥~ 가는 시기 the molting season∥~ 뜯다 (닭의) pluck a chicken∥~도 안 뜯고 먹으려 하다 be hasty [impatient] / be out to get all (a person's) possessions.
3 [보풀] nap; shag; fuzz; fluff. ¶~이 일다 get [be] fuzzy [fluffy].
4 wool(l)en yarn. ⇨털실.
털가죽 a fur; a fell. ⇨모피
털갈이 (새의) mo(u)lting; (짐승의) coat-shedding; shedding hair. ¶~ 새 a molter. **털갈이하다** mo(u)lt; shed (its) hair [coats]. ¶닭이 털갈이한다 Hens are molting.∥동물은 봄이 되면 털갈이한다 Animals shed their coats in spring.
털구멍 pores (of the skin).
털끝 **1** [털의 끝] the end of a hair; an end of hair; the tips of hair; hair tips.
2 [조금] a bit; a jot; a whit; [아주 작은 일] a minor detail; (집합적) trivia; minute. ¶~만큼도 (not) in the least / (not) at all / (not)

a bit[whit] / (not) in the slightest degree / in no degree∥ ~만큼도 개의치 않다 don't care at all / don't care a straw / don't give a damn∥그에게는 친절함이 ~만큼도 없다 He doesn't have a scrap of human kindness in him.∥그에 대해서 ~만큼의 원한도 품고 있지 않다 I don't bear the slightest malice toward(s) him.∥그는 자기 아들을 ~만큼도 사랑하고 있지 않다 He does not love his son a bit. / He hasn't a particle of love for his son.∥그의 태도에는 ~만큼의 열의도 보이지 않았다 There was no trace[particle] of enthusiasm.∥~만큼도 의심할 여지가 없다 There isn't the faintest shadow of doubt about it.∥그것을 할 생각은 ~만큼도 없다 I haven't the slightest[smallest] intention of doing it.∥그에게는 양심이라고는 ~만큼도 없다 He has not an atom[ounce] of conscience in him.∥그의 말에는 진실이 ~만큼도 없다 There is not an ounce of truth in what he says.

털다 1 (먼지 등을) sweep[brush] off; shake down; (담뱃재를) knock off. ¶거미줄을 ~ sweep away[off] cobwebs/(발을 굴러서) 눈을 ~ stamp the snow from (one's boots)∥윗도리의 먼지를 옷솔로 털어 내다 brush one's jacket∥모자의 먼지를 ~ shake the dust from one's hat∥뿌리의 흙을 ~ shake the earth away from the roots∥옷에 묻은 눈을 ~ wipe the snow from one's clothes∥그는 책장의 먼지를 털어 냈다 He dusted the bookcase.∥그는 바지에 묻은 진흙을 털어 냈다 He beat the dirt[mud] from his trousers. 2 [가진 돈 등을 전부 써 버리다] empty. ¶돈 지갑[주머니]을 ~ empty one's purse (to the last penny) / clear one's purse out∥가진 돈을 몽땅 ~ give all the money one has in hand∥나는 가진 돈을 전부 털어서 시디를 샀다 I spent all my money on a CD.∥그는 지갑을 털어 복권을 샀다 He emptied his pockets to buy a lottery ticket.∥주머니를 털어 만 원을 주었다 I gave him ten thousand won, all that I happened to have with me. 3 (도둑 등이) rob (a person) of; strip (a person) of; steal (a thing from a person); pilfer[filch] (articles from a shop). ¶금고를 ~ rob a safe∥은행을 ~ (도둑이) break into [burglarize / (속어) burgle] a bank / (강도가) rob a bank∥소매치기가 주머니를 털었다 A pickpocket picked my pocket.∥그는 그 집을 털었다 He burglarized[robbed] the house.

털럭거리다 [늘어진 것이 흔들거리다] keep slapping; flap; flop. ¶신 뒤축이 떨어져 털럭거린다 The sole of my shoe gets loose and keeps slapping.∥열어 놓은 창문에서 커튼이 털럭거리고 있다 The curtains are flapping at the open window.

털럭털럭 flop; swingingly; with jolt; clatteringly. **털럭털럭하다** keep slapping. ⇨"털럭거리다

털리다¹ 1 (붙은 것·묻은 것이) get shaken [knocked / beaten] off; (먼지가) get dusted [brushed] off. ¶옷의 먼지가 잘 ~ Dust brushes off my clothes readily. / My clothes are easily dusted.∥담뱃재가 좀체 털리지 않는 파이프 The ashes just won't knock out of the pipe. 2 [모두 빼앗기다] get robbed (of). ¶금고를 ~ have one's safe robbed∥(소매치기한테) 주머니를 ~ have one's pocket picked / have (a thing) stolen∥소매치기에게 지갑을 털렸다 A pickpocket stole[(구어) lifted] my wallet.∥집을 비운 사이에 도둑에게 털렸다 We had our house robbed in our absence. / Our house was robbed while we were away.

털리다² [털게 하다] have (a person) shake [knock / beat / dust / brush] off.

털모자 (-帽子) a fur hat; a woolen cap(털실로 짠).

털목도리 a comforter(털실로 짠); a boa(모피로 만든); a woolen muffler.

털방석 (-方席) a fur cushion.

털버덕 splashing. ⇨"탈바닥

털벙 with a plop; with a splash.

털보 a hairy[shaggy] person.

털복숭아 a fuzzy[downy] peach.

털북숭이 a hairy person[thing]. ¶~의 hairy / shaggy (dog).

털붙이 1 a fur; a fell. ⇨"털가죽 2 [털로 된 물건] fur pieces; fur goods; [털옷] fur clothes.

털실 wool(l)en yarn; worsted (yarn); wool; knitting wool. ¶~로 짠 양말 woolen socks∥~로 스웨터를 짜다 knit wool into a sweater / knit a sweater out of wool∥그녀는 ~로 짠 옷을 입고 있다 She is dressed in woolens.

털썩 with a thud[plump / thump / bump / flump]; heavily. ¶그는 ~ 무릎을 꿇었다 He sagged[abruptly dropped] to his knees.∥그는 마루에 ~ 쓰러졌다 He fell to the floor with a thud. / He flopped down on the floor. (▶ flopped는 의도적으로 쓰러졌다는 뜻)∥(충돌의) 충격으로 선반에서 짐이 ~ 떨어졌다 A piece of baggage fell from the rack with a crash.∥노파는 의자에 ~ 주저앉았다 The old lady flopped down[sank heavily] into a chair.∥그녀는 ~ 엉덩방아를 찧었다 She fell flat on her behind.∥의자에 ~ 주저앉으면 못 써 Don't flop down into chairs.∥우편함에 연하장 뭉치가 ~ 떨어졌다 A whole bunch of New Year's cards were dropped in our mailbox.∥짐꾼은 짐을 땅바닥에 ~ 내려놓다 The porter dumped his load on the ground.∥무거운 쌀부대를 ~ 내려놓았다 I plunked the heavy rice bag down.∥노예는 땅바닥에 ~ 주저앉았다 The slave sat flat [flopped] on the ground. / The slave squatted down on the ground. **털썩하다** thud; flop; plump; bump. ¶어디선가 털썩하는 소리가 들렸다 There was a dull thud somewhere.

털썩거리다 keep plopping[thudding]; keep bobbing; jolting. ¶궁둥이를 ~ move one's bottom up and down∥털썩거리며 걷다 jolt [bob] along.

털어놓다 (마음속을) open one's heart; take (a person) into one's confidence; confide in (a person); disclose; reveal; lay bare; confess; tell[talk] frankly[without reserve]. ¶털어놓고 말하면 to be frank[candid] with you / frankly speaking∥자, 다 털어놔 봐 Come on, spit it out!∥그는 마음을 털어놓는 성미이고 솔직한 사람이다 He's open and straightforward and not at all stuffy[pretentious]. / He's really down-to-earth.∥마침내 그는 울적한 심정을 털어놓았다 Finally he gave vent to his pent-up feelings.∥(마음에 걸리는 일이 있으면) 남김없이 털어놓는 게 어때 How about making a clean breast of it?∥사실을 털어놓고 싶은 기분이 되었다 I felt inclined to tell the truth.∥이제 슬슬 본심을 털어놓는 게

털어먹다

어때 Isn't it about time you told me your real intentions?∥털어놓고 이야기하자 Let's have a heart-to-heart talk. / Let's have a frank talk. / Let's talk turkey.∥그녀는 아무에게도 말하지 않고 그에게만 자기 비밀을 털어놓았다 She confided her secret to no one but him.∥이 일에 대해 털어놓고 의견을 말해 주면 좋겠다 I would like you to give your opinion about this matter frankly. / Let me hear your frank opinion about this matter.∥털어놓고 말하는데 너는 사내에서 인기가 없어 To tell you the truth, you are not popular in the company.∥그는 아무것도 털어놓으려고 하지 않았다 He kept everything secret to himself.∥나는 네게 무슨 일이든 털어놓을 수 있다 I can keep nothing from you.

털어먹다 spend the last cent; run through; eat (a person / oneself) out of house and home; eat (a person / oneself) up. ¶재산을 ~ squander [go[run] through] one's fortune∥이러다간 집이건 땅이건 그는 다 털어먹을 게다 At this rate he will soon eat himself out of house and land.∥나는 한 푼 없이 다 털어먹었다 I have spent my last penny. / I am down to my last cent.∥그는 가진 재산을 톡톡 다 털어먹었다 He ran through his fortunes.

털옷 a fur[woolen] robe.
털외투(-外套) a fur coat; a fur-lined overcoat.
털장갑(-掌匣) fur[woolen] gloves.
털터리 a penniless person. ⇨빈털터리
털털¹ (걷는 모양) plodding; trudging(ly). **털털하다**¹ trudge. 2 (소리) with dull clinks; with clatter. ¶~ 소리가 나다 make a rattling sound.
털털거리다 1 (걸음을) plod along; trudge along. 2 (소리를) keep clinking dull; keep clattering [rattling]. ¶털털거리는 차 a rattling thing / a cheap motorcar / (미국 속어) a flivver / 마차의 털털거리는 소리 the rattling of a cart / 자동차가 털털거리며 지나간다 A motorcar rattles[rumbles] along the road.
털털이 1 [털털한 사람] an unassuming person; a free and easy person. 2 [탈것] a rattling thing; a rattletrap; (미) a (junk) flivver; (미) a jalopy.
털털하다² (사람이) unaffected; free and easy.
털토시 fur-lined wristlets; a muff. ¶~를 끼다 wear[put on] fur-lined wristlets.
텀벙 with a plop[splash]. ¶물에 ~ 떨어지다 drop into the water with a plop[dull splash] / fall plump into the water / flop into the water / 탕(湯)에 ~ 들어가다 plump into the bath / 물속에 ~ 뛰어들다 jump into the water with a splash / plop[splash] into the water∥~ 소리를 내다 make a splash∥그는 강물에 ~ 뛰어들었다 He plunged into the river with a plop. / He plunged plop into the river. **텀벙하다** splash; plop.
텀벙거리다 keep splashing[plopping]; splash about; dabble. ¶물속에서 ~ splash about in the water∥발을 물에 담그고 ~ dabble one's feet in the water.
텀블러 [큰 잔] a tumbler.
텀블링 [공중제비] tumbling.
텁석 with a snatch; with a snap; greedily. ¶~ 물다 snap[bite] at∥(물고기를) 미끼를 ~ 물다 snap at[rise to] the bait∥~ 받아먹다 snap (it) up∥~ 움켜잡다 snatch / grasp greedily∥저고리를 ~ 쥐다 grasp a fistful of (a person's) coat∥매가 획 덮쳐 먹이를 발톱으로 ~ 움켜잡았다 The hawk swooped down and clutched its prey with its claws.

텁석나룻 bushy whiskers; a thick and short heavy beard.
텁석부리 a man with bushy whiskers [beards]; a heavily bearded man.
텁석텁석 with snatches; with snaps; greedily. ¶~ 그러쥐다 keep snatching∥~ 받아먹다 keep snapping at (it).
텁수룩하다 thick; shaggy; bushy. ¶텁수룩한 머리 long unkempt hair / a mop of hair∥텁수룩한 얼굴 a hairy face / a face with a shaggy beard(▶ shaggy는 길고 거친 털이 어지럽게 난 상태)∥수염이 ~ have a thick [bushy] beard / be heavily bearded (apparently unshaved for weeks)∥구레나룻이 텁수룩하게 나다 have a shaggy growth of whiskers∥그의 팔은 온통 털이 ~ He has really hairy arms. / He's got hair all over his arms.
텁석이 a sloppy person.
텁텁하다 1 (입맛이) thick and tasteless; unpleasant-tasting; (서술적) have a muddy taste; be rough and unpleasant to the palate. ¶텁텁한 된장국 thick and tasteless bean-paste soup∥입이 ~ have a muddy [brown] taste in one's mouth. 2 (성미가) free and easy; broad-minded; careless. ¶성미가 텁텁해서 누구나 가리지 않고 잘 사귀다 be so broad-minded as to associate with men of all shades. 3 (눈이) dim; blear(y); blurred.
텃마당 the threshing ground of a community.
텃밭 a vegetable[kitchen] garden; a family garden.
텃새 [동] a resident (bird); a permanent resident.
텃세(-貰) (a) ground[land] rent; rent for a (house) site. ¶연(年) 30만 원의 ~로 토지를 빌려 주다 lend land at a rental of 300,000 won per year∥차지인(借地人)에게서 높은 ~를 징수하다 collect high land rent from tenants.
텃세(-勢) defending one's territory[turf / eminent domain]; pulling rank. **텃세하다** take advantage of being on one's own ground[in one's own sphere of influence] to act high-handedly; play cock-of-the-walk; lord it over a newcomer.
텅 ¶~ 빈 empty / vacant / bare / void / hollow / deserted∥(속이) ~ 빈 나무 a hollowed tree∥~ 빈 느낌 a sense of emptiness / hollowness∥~ 빈 방 an empty room∥지갑이 ~ 비었다 I have spent my last penny.∥열차는 ~ 비어 있었다 There were few passengers in the train. / We had the train almost to ourselves.∥우리가 헛간에 와 보니 그 안은 ~ 비어 있었다 Arriving at the shed, we found it completely empty.∥큰 불상(佛像)의 안쪽은 ~ 비어 있다 The inside of the Great Statue of Buddha is hollow.∥오두막은 반년이나 ~ 비어 있었다 The hut had been deserted for half a year.∥그는 머리가 ~ 비었다 He doesn't have any brains[(구어) anything up to].∥오늘은 지갑이 ~ 비었다 I am broke today.∥사무실은 ~ 비어 있었다 Nobody was in the office.
텅스텐 [화] tungsten; wolfram(기호 W). ¶~의

tungstic / tungstenic.
● **텅스텐 전구** a tungsten bulb[lamp].

텅텅 all hollow. ¶~ 비다 be quite empty // 방은 ~ 비어 있다 The room is all empty. // 쌀뒤주가 ~ 비어 있다 There isn't any rice left in the rice box. / The rice box is empty. // 여러 술집을 돌아다니고 있다가 우리는 주머니가 ~ 비어 버린 것을 알았다 We did the rounds of bars[went from one bar to another] until we found ourselves dead-broke[stone-broke].

테¹ 1 (둘러매는) a hoop. ¶~를 두르다 hoop / put a hoop (on) / bind with hoops // ~를 벗기다 unhoop / take the hoops off // ~가 느슨해졌다[벗겨졌다] A hoop got loose[came off]. // 통의 ~가 벗겨졌다 The hoop of the barrel came loose. // ~가 헐거워졌다 The hoop worked loose.
2 (안경 등의) a rim; a frame. ¶은~의 안경 silver-framed glasses // 검은 ~ 테의 a black rim[edge] // ~ 없는 안경 rimless glasses // 금-안경 gold-rimmed spectacles // 검은 ~ 안경 black-rimmed spectacles.
3 (모자 띠) a band; a stripe; (언저리) a brim; a rim. ¶금~ 두른 모자 a cap banded with gold stripes // ~가 넓은 모자 a broad-brimmed hat.
4 [테두리] a border; a rim. ¶장식 ~ an ornamental border[rim] // 검은 ~ a black frame / mourning borders // ~의 black-edged / black-bordered // 검은 ~의 광고 [사망 광고] an obituary (notice) / (신문 등의) the obituaries.

테² [실 묶음] a reel; a skein; a bunch. ¶실 한 ~ a skein of thread.

테너 [음] (음역) tenor; (사람) a tenor (singer). ¶~로 부르다 sing tenor.

테니스 (lawn) tennis. ¶단식[복식] ~ a tennis match[game] of singles[doubles] // 경식[연식] ~ hardball[softball] tennis // ~를 하다 play tennis.
● **테니스 라켓** a tennis racket. **테니스 선수** a tennis player; (미국 속어) a netter. **테니스장** / **테니스 코트** a tennis court. **테니스화**(-靴) tennis shoes; (미) sneaker.

테두리 1 [가장자리] the border; the edge; [테] the brim; the rim; the frame. ¶검은 ~ black borders[edges] / (부고 등의) mourning borders // ~를 두르다 put a border on / rim / border / margin / frame // 바깥 ~ an outer frame.
2 [비유] an outline; an overall picture; a rough sketch. ¶계획의 ~ an outline of a scheme.
3 [범위] a limit; a framework; the confines (of). ¶~ 밖에(서) outside[beyond] the limit (of) // ~ 안에(서) within the limit [framework] (of) // 사회적 관습의 ~ 안에 있다[밖으로 나가다] stay within[go beyond] the bounds of social custom // 법의 ~ 안에서 within the legal limit / without infringement of the law // ~를 넘어서다 exceed[go beyond] the limit // ~를 정하다 fix the limit / set limits[bounds] (to) / set framework (for) // 통제의 ~를 넓히다[좁히다] widen[narrow] the sphere of control // 합법의 ~을 벗어나다 pass[overstep] the bounds of legality / commit a trespass // 정부는 금년도 예산의 ~ 밖에서 재해 지역에 긴급 원조를 해 주기로 했다 The government decided to appropriate aid for the disaster area outside this year's budget.

테라마이신 [약] terramycin.
테라스 a terrace. ¶~에(서) on the terrace.
테러 terror; terrorism. ¶백색[적색] ~ a white [red] terror // 우익의 ~ right-wing terrorism // ~ 습격 a terroristic raid / a terror raid // ~에 희생되다 fall a victim to terrorism. **테러하다** terrorize.
테러단 a gang of terrorists; the terrorists.
테러리스트 a terrorist.
테러리즘 terrorism.
테레빈유(-油) turpentine (oil); gum spirits; oil of terebinth; spirits of turpentine. ¶~를 바르다 turpentine.
테르븀 [화] terbium(기호 Tb). ¶~의 terbic.
테리어 [동] a terrier. ¶스코치 ~ a Scottish [Scotch] terrier // 폭스 ~ a fox terrier.
테마 (⑤Thema) a theme; subject matter. ¶음악의 ~ the theme of a music // 연구 ~ a subject of study // 자연을 ~로 한 시 a poem with a nature theme // 연구의 ~를 잡다 select a subject of study // 삼각관계를 ~로 소설을 쓰다 write a novel with a love triangle as its theme // 논문 ~가 무엇이죠 What is the subject of your thesis? // 연설의 ~는 인권이었다 The speaker's theme was human rights.
● **테마 뮤직** theme music[song]; (방송 개시·종료의) a signature (tune).
테스터 a tester.
테스트 a test; testing; an examination; (구어) an exam; (미) a workout; a quiz; (배우·가수의) an audition; a tryout. ¶학력 ~ an achievement test // 성능 ~ a performance [an efficiency] test // 지능 ~ an intelligence test // 객관식 ~ an objective test // 실력 ~ an ability test // 체력 ~ a physical test // ~를 하다 give a test // ~를 받다 take a test / (가수 등이) get an audition // ~에 합격하다 pass a test // 오늘 수학 ~가 있었다 We had a test in mathematics today. // 기계는 지금 ~ 중이다 The machine is being tested. **테스트하다** test. ¶음성을 ~ test one's voice // 우리는 그 기기의 내구력을 실제로 테스트했다 We put the endurance of the appliance to an actual test. / We actually tested the endurance of the appliance.
테이블 a table; a desk. ¶사이드 ~ a side table // ~에 자리 잡고 앉다 sit down to[at] table // ~에 둘러앉다 sit around a table // ~을 사이에 두고 앉다 (두 사람이) sit across a table / (한 쪽이) sit across from (a person) at a table.
● **테이블 매너** table manners. **테이블보** a table cover; a tablecloth(식탁의); (미) a table spread.

테이프 1 (종이·헝겊·비닐 등의) (a) tape; (축하용) a paper streamer; a colo(u)red tape ribbon; (녹음테이프) a (sound recording) tape; (창 등에서 흩뿌리는 색 테이프) ticker-tape. ¶골인 지점의 ~ (육상 경기의) the finish tape // ~ 한 권 a reel[spool] of tape // 절연 ~ insulating tape // 스테레오 ~ a stereo tape // 스테레오 ~ 재생 장치 a stereophonic tape player // 접착~ adhesive tape // 자기(磁氣) ~ magnetic tape // 비디오 ~ (a) video tape // 셀로판~ cellophane tape / (상표명) (미) Scotch tape / (영) Sellotape // 고무 ~ an elastic (band) // ~에 녹음한 대화 taped

테제 dialog(ue) // ~를 끊다 (개통식 등에서) cut the ribbon[tape] (at a opening ceremony) // 100미터 경주에서 ~를 끊다 break[breast] the tape in the 100-meter dash // 그는 자기 아이들의 노래를 ~에 수록했다 He taped his children's songs. / He recorded his children's songs on tape. **2** [줄자] a tape (measure).
● **테이프 녹음** tape recording. **테이프리코더** a (magnetic) tape recorder. ¶~로 녹음하다 record on a tape recorder / ~를 작동시키다 set a tape recorder in operation.

테제(⑤ These) [철] a thesis (pl. theses).
테크노크라시 technocracy.
테크노크라트 a technocrat.
테크닉 (a) technique; (a) technic. ¶연주의 ~ a playing technique (on the piano) // ~이 뛰어나다 be superior in technique / show [display] an excellent technique.
텍사스 히트 (*Texas hit) [야구] a Texas leaguer; a blooper; a bloop hit.
텍스트 [원문·본문] a text. ¶~대로의 인용 a textual quotation.
텐트 a tent; (집합적) tentage. ¶큰 ~ (hoist) a big top(서커스의) / (영) a marquee(가든파티 등에 쓰이는) // 원형 ~ a bell tent / 소형 ~ a shelter tent / (군대 속의) a dog[pup] tent // ~의 줄을 매는 쐐기 a tent peg // ~를 치다 pitch[set up / put up] a tent // ~를 걷어치우다 strike[pull down] a tent.
텔레비전 [방송 프로그램] television; (구어) TV; (영국 구어) telly; (미국 속어) the boob tube(텔레비전을 바보 취급한 말투); (수상기) a television (set); a TV (set); (영국 구어) a telly; a teleset. ¶~의 televisioning / televisional // 29인치 ~ a TV set with a 29 in. wide screen // 컬러 ~ color television / (수상기) a color television (set) // 폐쇄 회로 ~ closed-circuit television // 흑백 ~ black-and-white television // ~으로 watch television[TV] / (영국 속어) on the telly // ~을 보다 watch television // ~을 켜다[끄다] turn on[off] television[a TV set] // ~에 나오다 make a television appearance / make an appearance on TV / appear [go] on television / get on television[TV] // ~에 출연하다 appear on a television show / do a television program // ~ 앞에서 떠날 줄 모르다 glue oneself to a television set / be planted in front of a TV set // ~으로 보다 teleview / see (a person) on television / watch (a soccer game) on TV // ~의 화상(畵像)을 보내다 radio TV pictures (to) // ~ 생방송에 나오다 go on live television // ~을 켜 놓은 채 두었다 I left the television on. // 나는 야구 시합을 ~으로 보았다 I watched [saw] the baseball game on TV. // 저 가수는 ~에 자주 나온다 That singer often appears on television.
● **텔레비전광**(一狂) a television fanatic; (미국 속어) a vidiot. **텔레비전 드라마** a teleplay; a television play. ¶연속 ~ a television serial drama / (미) a soap opera. **텔레비전 방송** a television[TV / video] broadcast; a telecast; a videocast. ¶컬러 ~ (프로) a color broadcast / (방송함) color broadcasting // ~을 하고 있는 축구 a televised [telecast] soccer // ~을 하다 telecast / televise / make a telecast. **텔레비전 수상기** a television (set); a TV set. **텔레비전 시청률** an audience rating. **텔레비전 시청자** a televiewer; a viewer; (집합적) the TV audience. **텔레비전 영화** a telefilm; a vidfilm; a movie produced for television. **텔레비전 프로** a television program; a TV show. ¶장시간 방송의 ~ a telethon / 어린이용 ~ a kid program on television / a kidvid.
텔레타이프 a teletype(writer); a teletype printing system; a teleprinter. ¶~로 보낸 통신 a teletype (message) // ~를 치다[~로 송신하다] teletype / send (a message) by teletype.
텔레파시 [정신 감응] telepathy. ¶~의 pathic // ~로 전하다 communicate by telepathy / telepath // ~를 행하다 telepathize.
텔렉스 (상표명) Telex(▶ teleprinter exchange의 약어); telex; (통신문) a telex. ¶공중 ~ 부스 a public Telex booth // 뉴스를 ~로 보내다 telex news.
템포 (a) tempo (pl. ~s, -pi); speed. ¶빠른[느린] ~로 at quick[slow] tempo / rapidly [slowly] // ~가 빠른[느린] 곡 a tune with a quick[slow] tempo // 한 ~ 느리다 be one beat behind[late] // 연극의 ~를 조금 더 빨리 하다 speed up the pace of the drama a little // ~에 맞추다 keep pace with the tempo (of modern life) // ~가 맞지 않다 be out of tempo // ~가 빠르다[느리다] be quick[slow] of moving / be fast-moving [slow-moving] / be quick[slow] in tempo // ~를 빨리 하다 quicken the tempo / pick up in tempo // 그가 하는 일은 다른 사람보다 한 ~ 느리다 He is always one step slower than[one step behind] others in doing things.
토 1 (한문 구절 끝에 붙이는) Hangeul letters suffixes added to aid the reading of Chinese texts. **2** [언] a postpositional word functioning as an auxiliary to a main word. ⇨토씨
토건업(土建業) civil engineering and construction industry; construction work; the construction industry.
● **토건업자** a civil engineering and building constructor.
토공(土工) **1** (작업) earthwork(s). **2** a plasterer. ⇨미장이
토관(土管) an earthen pipe[tube]; a clay pipe; a (drainage) tile(하수의). ¶~을 묻다 lay an earthen pipe.
토굴(土窟) a dugout. ⇨땅굴2 ¶~에서 사는 사람 a cave dweller.
토기(土器) an earthen(ware) vessel[utensil / pot]; (집합적) earthen ware; crockery.
● **토기장이** an earthenware maker; a potter.
토기점 an earthenware shop.
토끼 [집토끼] a (house) rabbit; [산토끼] a hare.
토끼 둘을 잡으려다가 하나도 못 잡는다(속담) If you run after two hares, you will catch neither.; Grasp all, lose all.
● **토끼 굴** a rabbit hole[burrow]. **토끼뜀** (a) leapfrog; leapfrogging. ¶~을 하다 leapfrog (over) / play leapfrog / hop forward in a squatting position (with one's hands behind one's back). **토끼잠** a light sleep. ¶~을 자다 have a poor sleep / sleep lightly[badly] / be wakeful. **토끼장** a rabbit hutch.
토끼풀 [식] a clover.
토너먼트 a tournament; a tourney. ¶골프 ~ a golf tournament // 테니스 ~에 출전하다 take part in a tennis tournament // ~에서 1위가 되다 take first place in a tournament // 테니스 ~에서 (끝까지) 이겨 남다 remain a

토닉 a tonic. ¶진~ a gin and tonic // 헤어 ~ hair tonic.

토닥거리다 keep patting[tapping / knocking / rapping / beating]. ¶남의 뺨을 ~ pat a person's cheek / pat a person on the cheek // 고기를 다지느라고 ~ be chopping meat on the kitchen board // 토닥거리며 아기를 잠재워라 Let a baby fall into sleep by patting.

토닥토닥 patting[rapping / knocking / beating] repeatedly. ¶그는 그녀의 어깨를 ~ 두드렸다 He patted her on the shoulder. **토닥토닥하다** keep patting. ⇨토닥거리다

토담(土-) an earthen wall; a mud[dirt] wall; an adobe wall.
● **토담집** a mud-wall hut; an adobe hut.

토대(土臺) **1** [토단] a terrace of earth.
2 (건축의) a foundation; a stereobate; a sill. ¶~로 쓴 돌 a cornerstone / a foundation stone // 건물의 ~를 놓다 lay the foundations of a building // ~를 굳히다 solidify the foundation // ~를 쌓다 build up the foundation / 이 집의 ~는 든든하다 This house is built on a firm foundation. / This house has a firm foundation.
3 [(사물의) 기초] a foundation; groundwork; a base; a basis (pl. bases); a cornerstone. ¶…을 ~로 한 based upon … // …을 ~로 하여 on the basis of … // ~가 되다 form the basis (of) // ~를 쌓다 pave the way for / prepare the ground (for) / lay the groundwork (for) // 실지 체험을 ~로 소설을 쓰다 write a novel based on one's actual experience // ~가 마련되었다 The groundwork was done. / The way was paved. / A cornerstone was laid. // 교육은 사람의 성격의 ~가 된다 Education lays the foundation of a man's character. // 이 결론은 내가 직접 관찰한 바를 ~로 하고 있다 This conclusion is based on my own personal observations. // 그는 조그만 자본을 ~로 장사를 시작했다 He started a business on small capital.

토라지다 **1** (성이 나서) pout; sulk; be(come) sulky[peevish]; go into the sulks; be in the sulks. ¶토라진 소리를 하다 say spiteful things // 그 아이는 토라져 있다 The child has the sulks. // 아내는 토라져서 잠자리에서 일어나지 않았다 My wife stayed in bed sulkily [out of spite]. // 저 아이는 야단맞으면 곧 토라진다 That child starts to sulk whenever he's scolded. **2** (음식이) lie heavy on one's stomach; (사람이) have heartburn; have a sour stomach.

토란(土卵) [식] a taro (pl. ~s).
● **토란국** soup with taro in it; taro soup.

토로(吐露) exposing[revealing] one's thoughts. **토로하다** lay bare (one's heart); express; utter; deliver; speak (one's mind); give mouth[vent] (to); disclose[reveal] (a secret to a person); voice; set forth. ¶의견을 ~ give[express / set forth] one's opinion / deliver oneself of an opinion // 진정을 ~ pour forth[lay open] one's heart // 심정을 ~ lay bare one's heart // 그는 그의 심정을 일기장에 토로했다 He expressed his true feelings in his diary. // He gave vent to his innermost feelings in his diary.

토록 [정도] as much as; to the extent of. ¶그~ 많은가 Is there that much? // 종일~ 노시오 Stay all day long.

토론(討論) (a) discussion; (a) debate (▶ discussion은 의견을 서로 주고받음, debate는 다른 의견을 맞부딪쳐 논의함); a talk. ¶자유[집단] ~ free[group] discussion // 대체~ (전반적인) general debate / (예비적) preliminary discussion / (안건의) first reading // 무익한 ~ a sterile discussion // ~의 광장 the forum of debate // ~의 명수 a good debater / a master of fence // 많은 ~ 끝에 after much discussion // ~에 참가하다 join the debate / take the floor // ~에 들어가다 enter upon[open] a debate / go into a discussion (on / concerning) // ~에 부치다 put (a question) to debate / bring (a question) up for debate // ~을 끝내다[종결짓다] close[wind up / closure] a discussion[debate] / apply the closure to the debate // ~ 종결의 동의를 제출하다 (의회에서) bring a motion for closure // 그 문제는 아직 ~ 중이다 The question is still under discussion[debate]. // 그 건에 대해서 ~이 벌어지고 있다 A discussion of the matter is underway. // 그들은 ~을 종결했다 They closed the discussion. **토론하다** debate (on); discuss (a subject with a person); dispute; have[hold] a debate; (미) talk up. ¶조합의 방침에 대해서 ~ argue about the union's policy // 평화에 관해 ~ debate on peace.
● **토론자** a debater; a discussant. **토론회** a debate; (공개 토론회) a panel discussion[an open forum]; (TV 토론회) a TV debate; a debating society; an oratorical contest.

토륨 [화] thorium(기호 Th).

토르소 [몸통만으로 된 소상] a torso (pl. ~(e)s, -si).

토리 [실 뭉치] a spool of thread.
● **토리실** thread in spools.

토마토 [식] a tomato (pl. ~es); a love apple.
● **토마토소스** tomato sauce. **토마토케첩** tomato ketchup[catchup / catsup].

토막 a piece; a block; a bit; a fragment; a strip; a scrap(끄트러기). ¶고기 한 ~ a slice of meat / (돼지·새끼 양의) a piece of pork [lamb] / a pork[lamb] chop / (쇠고기의) a chop of beef / a steak // 나무 한 ~ a piece [block] of wood // 역사의 한 ~ a page [scene] of history // 엿 한 ~ a piece[bar] of taffy // ~ 살인 사건 a mutilation murder case // ~ 시체 a mangled[dismembered] body // ~ 지식 fragmentary[scrappy] knowledge // ~으로 in pieces / in fragments // ~이 나다 be broken into pieces // ~을 내다[치다] cut[chop] into pieces / cut (a thing) in slices / cut[hack] to pieces / slice / fillet(생선 등을) // 생선을 셋으로 ~ 치다 cut a fish into symmetrical right and left halves with the insides and bones removed
● **토막극** a little dramatical performance; a short play; a skit.

토막(土幕) a dugout. ⇨움집
토막토막 (in)to pieces; piece by piece. ¶~ 자른 무 thick slices of radish // 생선을 ~ 자르다 chop fish into pieces // 나무를 ~ 베다 saw wood into pieces / (깍두기를 하려고) 무를 ~ 썰다 cut a radish into cubes.

토목(土木) (공사) engineering[public] works. ¶~ (사업)을 일으키다 undertake public works.
● **토목건축(업)** civil engineering and con-

토민(土民) natives; the aborigines. ⇨ 토착민(⇨토착)

토박이(土-) a native. ⇨ 본토박이(⇨본토)

토박하다(土薄-) (땅이) infertile; meager; sterile; barren; unproductive; sick. ¶토박한 땅 unproductive land // 이곳은 땅이 너무 토박해서 아무것도 안 된다 The soil here is poor. // 이 밭은 너무 토박해서 아무것도 안 된다 This field is too sterile to yield anything.

토방(土房) an earth-floored [a dirt-floored] room.

토벌(討伐) conquest; subjugation; suppression. **토벌하다** conquer; subjugate; suppress; put down; subdue. ¶게릴라를 ~ subdue the guerrillas // 반란군을 ~ suppress a rebellion.
● **토벌군 / 토벌대** a punitive force. ¶~을 보내다 send a punitive force [expedition] (against).

토벽(土壁) a mud-plastered wall. ⇨ 흙벽

토사(土沙) earth and sand. ¶선로가 ~로 덮였다 The railroad tracks were covered by earth and sand (from the landslide).
● **토사 붕괴** a washout; a landslide. ¶~로 학교가 흙더미에 묻혔다 The school collapsed and was buried under a landslide.

토사(吐瀉) vomiting and diarrh(o)ea. **토사하다** vomit; suffer from vomiting fits and diarrhea; vomit and run off at the bowels; throw up.
● **토사곽란**〔한〕 acute gastroenteritis; vomiting and diarrhea. **토사물** vomit and excreta; the matter vomited.

토산물(土産物) products of the district [place]; local produce; native produce.

토색(土色) (an) earthlike color. ⇨ 흙빛

토색(討索) 〔금품을 억지로 달라고 함〕 (an) extortion; exaction; blackmail(ing). **토색하다** extort (money from a person); blackmail (a person) for; practice extortion.

토석(土石) soil and stone.

토성(土星) 〔천〕 Saturn. ¶~의 고리 Saturn's rings; the belts of Saturn.

토성(土城) a wall of earth; a mud wall; mud fortifications.

토속(土俗) local customs; folkways. ¶~적인 folk (dances).
● **토속 신앙** (a) folk belief.

토슈즈 〔토 댄스용 신발〕 toeshoes.

토스 a toss. ¶어느 편이 먼저 공격하느냐를 ~로 정했다 We tossed up to decide [decided by a toss of a coin] which side should take the offensive first. // 저 배구 선수는 ~가 좋다 That volleyball player is good at setting the ball up. **토스하다** toss (a ball).

토스터 a toaster; an electric toaster. ¶자동 ~ a pop-up toaster // ~로 빵을 굽다 make toast [toast (a slice of) bread] in a toaster.

토스트 toast. ¶버터를 바른 [안 바른] ~ buttered [dry] toast // 프렌치 ~ French toast // ~ 한 장 a slice of toast // ~를 굽다 make toast / toast (~) // ~에 버터를 바르다 butter toast / spread toast with butter / spread butter on toast.

토시 wristlets (to protect against the cold).

토신(土神) 〔민〕 a deity of the soil.

토실토실 plump; chubby; fat. ¶~ 살이 찌다 be plump [chubby]. **토실토실하다** plump; chubby; rotund; tubby; fat. ¶토실토실한 볼 chubby cheeks // 토실토실한 아기 a chubby baby // 토실토실한 얼굴 a full face.

토씨 〔언〕 a postpositional word functioning as an auxiliary to a main word. ⇨ 조사(助詞)

토악(吐-) 1 〔구토〕 an attack [a fit] of vomiting. **토악질하다** vomit; fetch [bring / throw] up; spew out the vomit; 《영국 속어》 shoot the cat. ¶먹은 것을 ~ throw up what one has eaten. 2 〔부정 소득의 반환〕 coughing up [repaying / refunding / replacing] ill-gotten money. **토악질하다** cough up [repay / refund / replace] ill-gotten money; disgorge. ¶먹었던 돈을 ~ repay what one has embezzled.

토양(土壤) soil. ¶메마른 [비옥한] ~ poor [rich / good / fertile] soil // ~을 개량하다 improve the soil.
● **토양 오염** soil pollution. **토양학** pedology; soil science.

토어(土語) 1 〔토착민의 언어〕 the language [tongue] of the natives; 〔그 지역의 말〕 a local language. 2 an [a provincial] accent. ⇨ 사투리

토역(土役) earthwork(s). ⇨ 흙일
● **토역꾼** a navvy; a construction worker.

토옥(土屋) a mud-wall hut. ⇨ 토담집(⇨토담)

토요일(土曜日) Saturday(야어 Sat.). ¶~은 반공일이다 We have a half day off on Saturdays.

토욕질(土浴-) a dust bath; (a hen / horse) wallowing in mud [dirt]; dusting. **토욕질하다** have [take] a dust bath; wallow in mud [dirt].

토우(土雨) dust in the air. ⇨ 흙비

토의(討議) (a) discussion; (a) debate(▶ discussion은 여러 가지 견해를 내놓고 서로 이야기하는 일, debate는 다른 의견을 다투게 하는 일); (a) deliberation. ¶자유 ~ free discussion // ~에 들어가다 enter into a discussion / open a debate // ~를 마치다 close a discussion // ~에 부치다 submit (a subject) to debate / bring up (a matter) for discussion // 개혁안을 ~에 부치다 submit a reform bill for debate / bring up a reform bill for discussion // 문제를 ~ 대상으로 삼다 take up a matter for discussion // ~를 종결하다 close a discussion // ~ 중이다 be under discussion [debate] // 지금 열띤 ~가 진행 중에 있다 A heated debate [discussion] is now going on. **토의하다** discuss (politics / a social problem); hold a discussion (with another); deliberate upon [over] (a matter); debate on [about] (a question, a subject, a matter, a problem, etc.). ¶반의 학생은 그 문제에 대해 토의했다 The class discussed [debated] that problem.
● **토의 사항** items on the agenda. **토의안** a subject for debate [discussion].

토인(土人) a native; an aboriginal(원주민); aborigines(집단).

토장(土葬) burial; 《문어》 interment; inhumation. **토장하다** inter; inhume; bury in the ground. ¶아버지의 유해를 ~ bury one's father's remains / 《문어》 inter one's father's remains.

토제(土製) ¶~의 earthen // ~의 인형 a clay doll // ~의 그릇 an earthen vessel / (집합적) earthenware.

토제(吐劑) 〔약〕 an emetic (medicine); a vomitory.

토족(土族) (relatives of) native gentry.
토지(土地) 1 〔지면〕 land; a piece[tract] of land(한 구획의 땅); 〔소유지〕 lands; a lot [plot] (좁은); an estate; a landed property [estate]; real estate(넓은). ¶넓은 ~ broad acres / a large[big] tract of land // 작은 ~ a patch of land / a small piece of land // 백 제곱미터의 ~ 100 square meters of land // ~를 사다 buy (a piece of) land [a lot] // ~에 투자하다 invest in real estate // ~를 개척하다 clear[exploit] the land [ground] // ~를 매매하다 deal in real estate // ~를 빌리다 lease [rent] land [a lot] // ~를 갖고 있다 own [hold / have / possess] land // ~를 놀려 두다 keep land idle // ~를 임대해 주다 grant the lease of a piece of land // 그는 메마른 ~를 비옥하게 만들었다 He enriched the poor [barren] soil. // 그는 넓은 ~를 개발했다 He developed a large tract of land.
2 〔지질〕 soil; land. ¶기름진 ~ fertile land [soil] / rich land // 메마른 ~ poor [barren] soil / barren [sterile] land // ~를 **경작하다** cultivate [till] the soil [land] / (쟁기 등으로) plow the ground // ~를 기름지게 하다 enrich the soil
● **토지 개량** land improvement. ¶~을 하다 improve land. **토지 개혁** land reform. **토지 구획 정리** land (re)adjustment [reallocation / (re)plotting]. **토지 대장 / 토지 등기부** a land ledger [register]; a terrier; a cadastre. **토지 매매** dealings in real estate. **토지 소유권** landownership; 〔법〕 a (possessory) title to land. **토지 소유자** a landowner; a landholder; a landed proprietor; (집합적) the landed interest. **토지 수용** expropriation of land; eminent domain.
토질(土質) (the nature of) the soil; soil quality; the quality of the soil. ¶단단한 ~ hard soil // ~을 **검사하다** analyze [test] the soil // ~이 비옥[척박]하다 The soil is fertile (or rich) [poor].
토착(土着) 〔관형어적〕 native(-born); aboriginal; indigenous. ¶~의 인디언 a native-born Indian // 담배는 한국 ~의 식물이 아니다 Tobacco is not a plant indigenous to the soil of Korea.
● **토착민** natives; the aborigines; original settlers; autochthon(e)s. ¶흑인은 아메리카의 ~이 아니다 Negroes are not indigenous to America.
토치카 (러) tochka; a pillbox.
토코페롤 〔화〕 tocopherol.
토큰 〔대용 화폐〕 a token (coin).
토키 〔발성 영화〕 a talkie; a talking film [picture].
토탄(土炭) peat; turf. ¶~ 같은 peaty.
토템 a totem. ¶~의 totemic // ~ **연구가** a totemist.
● **토템 숭배** totemism.
토플 TOEFL(▶ Testing of English as a Foreign Language의 약어).
토픽 a topic; a subject. ¶오늘의 ~ current topics / the topics of the day.
토하다(吐-) 1 〔게우다·뱉다〕 vomit; spew; bring[fetch] up; throw [cast] up; (영국 구어) cat. ¶먹은 것을 ~ throw [bring] up what one has eaten // 피를 ~ spit [vomit / cough up] blood // 토하기 위해 목구멍에 손가락을 넣다 put one's fingers down his throat to make himself vomit // 토하게 하다 induce (a person) to vomit [throw up] // 그는 먹은 것을 전부 토해 냈다 He vomited [threw up] everything he had eaten. // 나는 자동차 안에서 토할 것만 같았다 While I was in the car, I began to feel like vomiting [to feel sick at my stomach]. // 나는 어제저녁에 먹은 것을 모두 토해 버렸다 I vomited [threw up] what I ate last night. // 나는 갑자기 토할 것처럼 메스꺼워졌다 I suddenly felt very sick at my stomach. // 환자는 먹는 족족 토해 버린다 The patient cannot keep food down. // 그는 방바닥에 토해 버렸다 He threw up on the floor. / He was sick on the floor.
2 (부정·이득을) 〔구어〕 disgorge. ¶횡령한 돈을 토해 내다 disgorge [fork over] the embezzled money // 그는 그 보상으로 1년 동안의 수입을 몽땅 토해 내지 않으면 안 되었다 He had to surrender [give up] all his earnings for the year to compensate for it.
3 〔내뿜다〕 emit; vomit; puff out; breathe out(숨을); belch forth; send forth [up] (연기 등을). ¶(화산이) 불과 연기를 ~ belch fire and smoke // 저 화산은 끊임없이 검은 연기를 토하고 있다 The volcano is constantly emitting clouds of black smoke.
4 〔씩씩하고 기백 있게 말하다〕. ¶기염을 ~ wag one's tongue [jaw] / give rein to one's tongue / argue furiously [vehemently] / talk big / (속어) spread oneself // 열변을 ~ speak with fervor [heat] / make an eloquent speech.
토혈(吐血) vomiting [spitting] of blood; hematemesis; hemorrhage of the stomach. **토혈하다** spit [vomit] blood.
토호(土豪) a landed proprietor; a wealthy local farmer; 〔호족〕 a powerful local family.
● **토호질** (practice) tyranny; oppression.
톡 1 〔튀어나는 모양〕 protruding; protuberant; bulging; 〔불거짐·비어짐〕 popping; bulging out (of a pocket). ¶눈알이 ~ 불거지다 have protruding [protuberant / bulging] eyes / be bug-eyed [lobster-eyed] / (미국 속어) be popeyed // 밤알이 송이에서 ~ 비어졌다 The chestnut popped out of its burr. // 접은 신문이 호주머니 밖으로 ~ 비어져 있다 A folded newspaper is sticking out of his pocket. // 토끼가 풀숲에서 ~ 튀어나왔다 Suddenly a rabbit jumped [sprang] out from the grass.
2 〔치는 모양·소리〕 with a pat [rap]. ¶어깨를 ~ 치다 tap (a person) on the shoulder // 공깃돌을 손가락으로 ~ 튀기다 fillip off a marble.
3 〔부러지거나 끊어지는 소리〕 with a snap; snappingly. ¶(실이) ~ 끊어지다 snap (off / short) // 바늘을 ~ 부러뜨리다 snap a needle // 잔가지를 ~ 꺾다 snap off a twig // 연필이 ~ 부러지다 a pencil snaps [breaks with a snap] // 그는 바이올린의 줄이 ~ 끊어지는 소리를 들었다 He heard a string snap in his violin.
4 〔쏘는 모양〕 sharply; prickingly; spicily. ¶~ 쏘는 말 spicy [poignant] remarks // 맛이 ~ 쏘다 taste hot / have a burning taste / be pungent / bite // ~ 쏘아붙이다 make cutting remark / give a sharp rejoinder / make a biting retort // 고추는 혀를 ~ 쏜다 Red pepper bites [burns] the tongue.
5 〔튀는 모양〕. ¶손톱으로 ~ 튀기다 fillip / flip // 벼룩이 ~ 튀었다 The flea hopped.
톡탁 tapping; rapping; beating; dabbing. **톡탁**

톡탁거리다
하다 trade blows.
톡탁거리다 1 ticktack; click, click, click …. ⇨ 똑딱거리다 2 [티격태격 싸우다] exchange blow after blow.
톡톡 1 [불거진 모양] protruding[bulging] in several places; [버어진 모양] popping out and popping out. ¶게 눈이 ~ 불거졌다 The crabs popped their eyes out. ∥보따리가 ~ 비어졌다 A bundle was bulging out here and there.
2 [부러지는 모양] with snaps; [별안간] suddenly; abruptly; (말을) sharply. ¶남의 말을 ~ 쏘아 주다 give a series of sharp rejoinders / make one biting retort after another∥연필심이 ~ 부러졌다 The lead of a pencil broke easily.
3 [치거나 부딪는 소리] with pats[raps / thuds / bumps]. ¶문을 ~ 두드리다 tap[rap] at[on] the door / knock on[at] the door / give a rat-tat∥(땀을 훔치려고) 손수건으로 이마를 ~ 치다 dab one's forehead with a handkerchief∥어깨를 ~ 치다 keep patting (a person) on the shoulder∥돌을 ~ 쪼아내다 chip away at a stone∥그는 손가락으로 테이블을 ~ 두드렸다 He beat a tattoo with his fingers on the table.
톡톡하다 1 [액체가 묽지 않다] thick; rich; heavy. **톡톡히** thickly; richly. ¶국을 ~ 끓이다 prepare soup thick.
2 [피륙이 도톰하다] thick; close; close-woven. ¶톡톡한 천 a fabric of a close[firm] texture. **톡톡히** closely; thickly. ¶배를 ~ 짜다 weave cloth thick.
3 [꾸중 등이 심하다] harsh; severe; smart. **톡톡히** harshly; severely; smartly. ¶~ 꾸짖다 scold[(미)] berate] (a person) scathingly / give (a person) a good scolding∥~ 책망듣다 get severely scolded / be given a good scolding / get a round rating∥홍수를 만나서 ~ 혼이 났다 I had a terrible experience on account of the flood.
4 [재산 등이 많다] (a great) many; much; plenty of. **톡톡히** quite a lot; much; loads of. ¶이문을 ~ 남기다 make a big profit∥~ 사례를 받다 be given a liberal[handsome] reward / be rewarded generously∥그는 그 거래로 ~ 재미를 보았다 He pocketed a nice sum over the transaction.
톤 a ton; [배·화물의 톤수] tonnage(▶영국에서는 a long ton(약 1016kg), 미국에서는 a short ton(약 907kg), 프랑스에서는 a metric ton (1000kg)을 씀). ¶배수 ~ a displacement ton∥용적 ~ a measurement[volume / freight] ton∥적재 ~ a shipping ton∥중량 ~ a deadweight ton(약어 DWT)∥총 ~ a gross ton∥6~ 덤프 트럭 a six-ton dump truck∥석탄 10~ ten tons of coal∥8,000~의 배 a ship of 8,000 tons∥5천 ~의 기선 a steamer of 5,000 tons (burden) / a 5,000-tonner∥이 배는 몇 ~입니까 What is the tonnage of this ship?
톤세(-稅) tonnage dues.
톤수(-數) tonnage. ¶등록 ~ registered tonnage∥배수(~순) ~ displacement (net) tonnage∥재화 중량 ~ deadweight capacity [tonnage]∥적재 ~ capacity tonnage∥총~ gross tonnage / the total tonnage ∥(한 company's fleet)∥이 배의 ~는 3천 톤이다 This steamer is 3,000 tons burden. / This ship displaces 3,000 tons(배수량).

톨 a nut(밤 등의); a grain (of rice). ¶밤 한 ~ a chestnut∥쌀 한 ~이라도 고맙게 여겨야 한다 You must be thankful for a grain of rice.
톨게이트 [통행료 받는 곳] a tollgate.
톨루엔 [화] toluene.
톱¹ [자르거나 켜는 연장] a saw; (한 사람이 켜는 것) a handsaw; a tenon saw; (두 사람이 켜는 것) a crosscut saw. ¶가두리 ~ an edger∥기계 ~ a sawing machine∥내릴 ~ a ripsaw∥둥근 ~ a circular saw / (미) a buzz saw(소형의 것)∥따 ~ a pit saw∥동가리 ~ a crosscut saw∥톱니가 양쪽에 달린 ~ a reversing saw∥~으로 판자를 켜다 saw a board∥~의 날을 세우다 set (the teeth of) a saw∥나뭇가지를 ~으로 잘라 내다 saw a branch off a tree.
톱² top. 1 [선두]. ¶원반던지기가 그 체육 대회의 ~을 장식했다 The discus throw was the first event at the athletic meet. 2 [일 등]. ¶~으로 시험에 합격하다 pass an examination first on the list∥존은 클래스에서 ~이다 John stands first in his class. / John is at the top[head] of his class. 3 [신문 등의 상단 오른쪽]. ¶일면 ~ 전단(全段)의 표제 a banner (headline) on the front page∥그 뉴스는 석간의 ~을 장식했다 The news was given top priority in the evening paper.
톱기사(-記事) a front-page[lead] story; a lead; the top[leading] article in a newspaper.
톱날 a saw blade; a saw tooth. ¶~을 세우다 set a saw.
톱뉴스 top news; big news; (미국 속어) the front-pager. ¶(잡지에 대한) ~ 기고가(寄稿家) a man who writes a story dealing with a major news item and sells it to a magazine publisher∥~로 다루다 take (an article) as top news∥어느 신문이나 그 사건을 ~로 다루었다 Every newspaper treated the affair as top news.
톱니 the tooth of a saw; a sawtooth (pl. -teeth). ¶~ 모양의 saw-toothed / lacerated / jagged / serrate(d)∥~ 세우는 기계 a saw sharpener / a sharpening machine∥~를 세우다 set (the teeth of) a saw.
● **톱니바퀴** a toothed wheel. ¶맞물림 ~ a cogwheel∥베벨[엇물림] ~ a bevel[skew] gear∥큰 ~ a gear wheel∥작은 ~ a pinion∥~의 이 a cog / a tooth∥~가 물리지 않았다 The gears didn't mesh.
톱밥 sawdust.
톱상어 [동] a saw shark.
톱질 sawing. **톱질하다** saw. ¶톱질하는 사람 a sawyer.
톱칼 a handsaw. ¶빵 베는 ~ the serrated blade of a bread knife.
톱톱하다 (국물이) thick; rich; heavy.
톳 a 100-sheet bundle (of laver).
통¹ 1 (배추 등의) a head (of cabbage); the body (of a gourd). ¶박 한 ~ a gourd∥배추 세 ~ three heads of cabbage∥배추 ~이 크다 The cabbage has a large head.
2 [사람됨] caliber; scale; [도량] magnanimity; generosity; [담] boldness. ¶~이 큰 generous / large-[broad-]minded / liberal / [대담한] bold / daring∥~이 큰 사람 a man who does things in a big way∥~이 작다 be a person of small caliber∥그는 ~이 큰 사람이다 He is a man of big caliber. / He is a person who think big.

3 [피륙의 세는 단위] a roll; a bolt. ¶광목 열 ~ ten rolls of calico.
4 (노름의) 10 or 20 points obtained from 3 cards.
5 [바지 지름] the inside diameter; [둘레] girth; [굵기] thickness; [넓이] width; breadth. ¶소매 ~ a sleeve opening∥허리 ~ one's girth.

통² 1 [정신차릴 수 없는 상황]. ¶~에 in the midst (of) / amid / amidst / in the bustle [confusion] (of) / during the confusion (over) / taking advantage of the confusion / in the influence (of)∥충돌하는 ~에 by the force of impact∥북새 ~에 in the confusion / during the commotion∥전쟁 ~에 사람이 많이 죽었다 Many lives were lost in the ravages of war.∥그는 과음하는 ~에 머리가 빠개질 것같이 아팠다 He had a racking headache, consequent on drinking too much.
2 [동아리] a gang; a group; a junto[junta]; cahoots. ¶한~이 되다 be in cahoots with / be in collusion[league] with.

통³ [전혀] quite; entirely; utterly; absolutely; completely; [조금도] (not) at all; (not) in the least; (not) a bit[straw / particle / fig]. ¶~ 모르겠다 cannot make head or tail of (something)∥헤엄을 ~ 못 치다 cannot swim a stroke / swim to the bottom[like a stone / like a tailor's goose]∥장사가 ~ 안 된다 Business is quite dull. / There is no business at all.∥그 물건은 ~ 안 팔린다 The goods do everything but sell.∥그는 그날 이후 ~ 오지 않는다 It was the last day he came here.∥그런 사람을 저는 ~ 모릅니다 I don't know any such man. / I know no such man.∥그것이 무엇인지 ~ 짐작할 수가 없다 I don't have the slightest idea what it is.∥그런 일에 그는 ~ 마음을 쓰지 않았다 He did not care a bit about it.∥당신의 제의는 ~ 말도 되지 않습니다 What you propose is entirely out of the question.

통(通) [편지 세는 말] a letter; a note; [문서를 세는 말] a document; a paper; [증서를 세는 말] a bond. ¶편지 한 ~ a letter / a note∥엽서 한 ~ a postcard∥호적 등본 두 ~ complete copies of one's family register∥서류 세 ~ three copies of a document∥(증서 등을) 한 ~ 써 주다 give a signed statement [pledge] (to) / give[let (a person) have] (it) in black and white / (차용증을) write an I.O.U.∥2 [3 / 4 / 5]~ 작성하다 make out (a document) in duplicate[triplicate / quadruplicate / quintuplicate]∥계약서는 두 ~ 작성되었다 They made two copies of the contract.∥후일을 위해 한 ~ 써 드리겠습니다 I will give you a written statement for future reference.∥나는 세 ~의 편지를 썼다 I wrote three letters.∥서약서를 2~ 제출했다 I submitted a written promise in duplicate[two copies of a written promise].

통(桶) [나무 그릇] a cask; a barrel; (큰) a hogshead; a butt; (작은) a keg; (물통 등) a pail; (wooden) bucket; a tub; a kit; (槽) a tank; a vessel; a trough; a cistern(수조). ¶물 두 ~ two bucketfuls[tubs] of water∥맥주 ~ a beer barrel∥~에 담은 맥주 barreled beer∥마개 a bung∥~의 귀때 a tap∥석유~ a kerosene can[tin] / an oil can∥작은 나무 ~ a keg∥~에 든 포도주 wine in[from] the wood∥~에 넣다 put (a thing) in a barrel / barrel∥~에서 술을 따르다 draw wine from a cask∥술을 ~에 담다 put wine in a cask

통(筒) [속이 빈 물건] a pipe; a tub; a case; a (gun) barrel; (기계의) a sleeve; (깡통의) a tin; (미) a can. ¶대~ bamboo.

통(統) [지] a series (단수·복수 동형). **2** [행정구역] a *tong*; the second-lowest city administrative unit.

-통(通) **1** [정통한 사람] an authority (on); an expert (in / at / on); [감정가] a connoisseur (of). ¶소식~ informed sources∥법률~ an authority on law / a legal expert∥재정~ an expert on financial affairs / a financial expert∥그는 상당한 경제~이다 He is very well informed[versed] in economics. / He's an expert on economics.∥그녀는 아랍~이다 She is an authority on Arabia. / She is well acquainted with Arabic affairs.∥그녀는 영화 ~이다 She is very knowledgeable[in (구어) in the know] about movies. **2** [거리] a street. ¶종로~ a Jongno street.

통가리(桶-) [곡식 더미] a heap of grain put in a straw rain-shelter.

통각(痛覺) [아픔을 느끼는 감각] a sense [sensation] of pain. ¶무(無)~의 analgesic.

통감하다(痛感-) feel strongly[deeply / acutely]; fully realize; take to heart. ¶어학의 필요성을 ~ feel strongly the necessity of the knowledge of foreign languages∥이 실패로 평소의 연습이 중요함을 통감했다 This failure brought home to me[made me realize keenly] how important daily practice was.∥그때 비로소 나는 어머니의 사랑을 통감했다 I had never felt mother's love so strongly.∥전쟁에 살아남은 자들은 생명의 존엄성을 통감했다 The survivors of the war were filled with an appreciation of the value of life.

통계(統計) statistics; figures; a numerical statement. ¶~의 statistical∥~적인 statistical (observation)∥~상으로는 statistically / in the statistics∥~에 의하면 according to statistics∥인구[범죄] ~ statistics of population[crimes]∥사망[출산] ~ statistics of mortality[birth]∥~를 잡다 collect[gather] statistics (of) / take[get] the statistics / prepare[compile] statistics of ...∥출생률의 ~를 내다 compile[gather] statistics on the birthrate∥이것은 신뢰할 만한 자료에 근거한 ~이다 These figures are compiled from reliable sources.
●**통계연감** a statistical yearbook. **통계 자료** statistical data. **통계 조사** (a) statistical research[investigation]; statistics and research. **통계청** the National Statistical Office. **통계표** a statistical table; returns. ¶사망~ mortality returns. **통계학** (the science of) statistics.

통고(通告) (a) notice; (a) notification; announcement; warning. ¶일방적인 ~ a one-sided[unilateral] notice∥최후 [final] notice / an ultimatum (pl. ~s, -ta)∥아무 ~도 없이 without any advance notice [warning]∥~를 보내다 issue a notification∥~ 없이 불참하다 absent (oneself) without notice∥퇴거 ~를 하다[받다] give[receive / be given] notice to quit a house∥경찰서 출두 ~를 받다 be served with a notice to appear at the police station∥그는 또 아무

통곡 ~없이 결석했다 He was absent again without notice.// 통행증이 없는 사람은 건물 안에 들어오는 것을 금한다는 내용의 ~가 있었다 An announcement was made to the effect that no one without a pass would be allowed to enter the building.// 하루 전 ~를 요한다 A day's notice is required. **통고하다** notify (a person of[that]); give (a person) notice (of / that ...); warn (a person[that]); [법] garnish. ¶사전에[나를 전에] ~ give (a person) previous[four day's] notice / 일을 그만두려 할 경우에는 1개월 전에 (고용주에게) 통고할 것 You should give a month's notice (to your employer). / You may quit the job on a month's notice.
● **통고서** a (written) notice; a notice in writing. **통고 처분** noticed disposition; disposition of notification.

통곡(痛哭·慟哭) lamentation; wailing. **통곡하다** [비탄하다] (문어) bemoan; lament (a person's death); [몹시 울다] weep bitterly (over the loss of a friend). ¶유족은 통곡했다 The bereaved family cried their hearts[eyes] out. / The bereaved family were overcome with tears. // 그는 아들의 시체를 끌어안고 통곡했다 Embracing his son's dead body, he wailed[wept bitterly].

통과(通過) passage; passing; a pass; transit; carriage(의안의). ¶~의 자유 freedom of transit // 법안의 ~를 지연시키다 stall a bill // 국내 ~를 허가[거절]하다 give[refuse] a passage through the country // 의안의 ~를 저지하다 block the passage of a bill. **통과하다** pass (through); go[get] through; be carried. ¶세관을 ~ go[pass] through the customs // 시험에 ~ pass an examination // 자동차는 터널 내부를 통과했다 The car passed through a tunnel. // 지금 부산 상공을 통과하고 있다 We are now flying[passing] over Busan. // 열차가 통과했다 A train passed by. // 차는 다리를 통과했다 The car crossed a bridge. // 이 의안은 만장일치로 국회를 통과했다 This bill passed[was carried in] the National Assembly by a unanimous vote. // 이 법안은 쉽게 통과했다 This bill had an easy passage. // 제1차 심사를 통과했다 I passed the first screening. // 그것은 세관을 통과했다 It passed customs. → ¶(세관에서) 화물을 통과시키다 pass goods // 의안을 통과시키다 carry[pass] a bill / rush[get] a bill through the House // 구멍에 밧줄을 통과시키다 pass rope through the hole // 모래는 물을 잘 통과시킨다 Sand easily lets water through. // 국회는 그 의안을 통과시켰다 The National Assembly passed the bill. // 그는 국회에서 그 의안을 우격다짐으로 통과시켰다 He rammed the bill through the National Assembly. // 동의는 15 대 3으로 통과되었다 The motion (was) carried by fifteen votes to three.
● **통과 화물** transit goods; (포장 표기) "Transit."

통관(通關) entry; clearance; customs clearance; clearance (of goods) through the customs. **통관하다** enter[clear] (a ship); clear[pass] the customs; clear[pass] (baggage) through the customs. ¶국외 정세를 ~ survey[take a general look at] foreign affairs.
● **통관세** a customs [clearance] fee. **통관 신고서** a bill of entry. **통관 절차** customs formalities [procedure]; clearance; customs entry. ¶~를 마치다 go through the customs formalities / clear[go through] customs / pass customs entry.

통괄(統括) generalization; summarization; recapitulation; synthesis. **통괄하다** summarize; generalize; synthesize; epitomize. ¶여러 가지 의견을 ~ put various opinions together to form a united view // 지방의 조직을 ~ unify the local organizations // 지금까지 수집한 정보를 통괄해 보자 Let's put together the information we have collected. → ¶마지막 에서 책의 내용 전체가 통괄되어 있다 The content of the entire book is summarized in the last chapter.

통권(通卷) the consecutive number of volumes. ¶제5권 제2호(~ 10호) Vol. 5 No. 2 (Serial Number 10) // 그의 전집은 ~ 50권이 되었다 His complete works came to fifty volumes. // 이 계간지의 37권 2호는 ~ 146호이다 Vol. 37, No. 2 of this quarterly is the 146th issue.

통근(通勤) attending office; going to work; commuting; commutation; (입주 근무의 상대어로) living out. **통근하다** attend[go to] (one's / the) office; (영) commute; live out; come[go] to work from outside. ¶매일 열차로 ~ take the train daily to and from one's office // 버스와 지하철로 통근하고 있다 I go to work by bus and subway. // 그는 상당히 먼 데서 통근하고 있다 He comes to work[comes to the office / commutes] from a great distance. // 회사는 수월하게 통근할 수 있는 거리에 있다 The company is within easy commuting distance.
● **통근 시간 / 통근 시각** time to attend office; rush hours. **통근 열차** a commuter [commuting] train; a train for commuters. **통근자** a commuter; (영) a daily-breader.

통금(通禁) suspension of traffic. ⇨ "통행금지 (⇨통행)
● **통금 시간** curfew hour. **통금 위반** a curfew violation. **통금 해제 구역** a curfew-lifted area.

통기(通氣) ventilation; airing. ⇨ "통풍(通風)
● **통기공**(-孔) a breathing hole; a vent (hole); a ventilator; (공) an air hole[vent]. **통기성** [화] (air-)permeability.

통김치 pickles made of whole cabbages.

통나무 a log. ¶~를 켜다 saw up a log.
● **통나무 다리** a log bridge; (미) a footlog. **통나무집** a log cabin[hut / house].

통념(通念) a common idea; a generally [commonly] accepted idea. ¶그것이 사회 ~ 이다 The idea is universally accepted. / That is the idea generally accepted[the received view]. // 지금의 사회 ~으로는 그건 통용되지 않는다 That will not be generally accepted by society today.

통달(通達) 1 [막힘이 없이 통함] mastery; conversance; thorough knowledge (of). **통달하다** be well[deeply] versed (in); be at home (in / on); have a thorough knowledge (of); be conversant (with). ¶영어에 ~ be proficient in English / have a good[thorough] knowledge of English // 사무에 ~ be well versed in business methods // 그는 고대사에 통달해 있다 He is well versed in[acquainted with] ancient history. / He is at home in

ancient history.// 맡은 일에 통달하기란 쉽지가 않다 It is not easy to be a master of one's work.
2 [위에서 아래로의 연락] (a) notification; a communication; [회람(장)] a circular. **통달하다** communicate; notify 《a person of a matter》.

통닭 a whole chicken; [닭요리] a chicken cooked whole.
● **통닭구이** a roast chicken; a chicken roasted whole.

통독하다(通讀-) read[go/get] through 《a book》; read 《a book》 from cover to cover; peruse 《a book》. ¶그 책을 통독하는 데 5일은 걸린다 It will take me five days to read through the book[read the book from cover to cover].

통람하다(通覽-) survey; look over; glance 《one's eyes》over; take a general view of; [통독하다] peruse; read[run] through. ¶보고서를 ~ look over[read through] a report.

통렬하다(痛烈-) severe; fierce; bitter; biting; sharp; scolding; scathing; cutting; incisive 《criticism》. ¶통렬한 일격 a knockdown [telling / terrible] blow // 내 소설은 통렬한 비판을 받았다 My novel was criticized severely. // 나는 그의 통렬한 비판에 주춤했다 I winced at his scathing comments. ¶그는 통렬한 풍자로 알려져 있다 He is known for his biting sarcasm. **통렬히** severely; sharply; bitterly; fiercely. ¶~ 비판하다 criticize bitterly [severely / cuttingly / scathingly].

통례(通例) common[usual] practice; a (common) usage; a[an established] custom. ¶~적으로 출제되는 문제 questions which are usually set in the examination // ~에 따르다 follow the usage[custom] // 우리 회사에서는 연 1회의 위로 여행을 하는 것이 ~로 되어 있다 It is our custom in this company to take a trip together for recreation once a year. // 이 지방에서는 이런 때 그렇게 하는 것이 ~로 되어 있다 In these parts it is customary to do so on such occasions.

통로(通路) a passage; a passageway; a way; a pathway; a path; a roadway; a road for passage; an avenue; an alley(좁은); a walkway(정원·공원 등의); the entrance(극장·교회 등의); a track(동물의). ¶~ 옆의 좌석 an aisle seat // ~를 내다 clear the passage[make way] 《for》// ~를 막다 block[stand in] the way 《of》// ~에 있다 lie[be] in one's way / be in the route 《of》// ~의 방해가 되다 be[stand / get] in 《a person's》way // 입구까지의 ~를 트다 clear a path to the entrance // 이것은 종업원 전용~이다 This passage is for the exclusive use of our employees. // (게시) Employees Only.

통론(通論) [개론] an outline (of sociology); [입문] an introduction (to economics). ¶문학 ~ an introduction to literature // 법학 ~ an outline of law.

통마늘 a whole bulb of garlic.

통명(通名) a given name; a popular[common]; an alias.

통모하다(通謀-) conspire with; work[act] in concert[collusion / league]. ¶통모하여 in conspiracy with / in collusion[league].

통문(通文) a circular (letter). ¶~을 돌리다 send (out)[issue / address] a circular (letter) / circularize.

통발 [식] a bladderwort.

통보(通報) a report; (공보) a bulletin; (내무 보도) 《give / get》 a tip. ¶기상 ~ a weather report. **통보하다** report; notify; inform. ¶경찰에 ~ notify the police (about a matter) // 누군가 경찰에 그것을 통보한 사람이 있다 Someone must have reported it to[informed /(구어) tipped off] the police.

통보(通寶) a coin; currency. ¶삼한(三韓)~ a coin of the Sam-Han period.

통보리 uncracked grains of barley.

통분(通分) [수] reduction (of fractions) to a common denominator. **통분하다** reduce (fractions) to a common denominator. ¶2/3에서 1/4을 통분해서 빼시오 Subtract one fourth from two thirds by reducing to a common denominator.

통분(痛憤·痛忿) great indignation. **통분하다** be greatly indignant. ¶나는 그들의 냉대에 통분했다 I strongly resented[was very indignant at] their cold treatment.

통사(通史) ¶경제학 ~ a (complete) history of economics.

통사정(通事情) **1** [사정을 잘 알아줌] having sympathetic understanding; having an understanding heart. **통사정하다** have sympathetic understanding; have an understanding heart; understand. **2** [사정함] an appeal; a complaint; unbosoming oneself 《to》; speaking one's mind letting 《a person》 know one's situation[mind]; a frank talk of one's difficulties》. **통사정하다** make an appeal 《to》; complain 《of》; unbosom oneself 《of》; divulge; get 《it》off one's chest; speak one's mind[tell frankly] 《about》. ¶곤란한 사정을 친구에게 ~ tell a friend quite frankly about one's difficulties.

통산(通算) summing up; [총액수] the aggregate; the sum total. ¶미결 40일 ~ 1년의 금고 one year's imprisonment with credit for forty days service as an unconvicted prisoner // 그는 ~ 성적 2위이다 He ranks second on the overall[all-time] list. // 그는 ~ 500개의 홈런을 날렸다 He has hit five hundred home runs in all[a career total of five hundred home runs]. **통산하다** sum[add] up; aggregate; total; [포함시키다] include. ¶통산하여 20년 이상의 for the total period of twenty years or more // 비용은 통산해서 500만 원이 되었다 The expenses amounted [added up] to five million won.

통상(通常) [평소] usually; [보통] normally; [일반적으로] generally; as a rule; commonly; under normal conditions.

통상(通商) commerce; trade; trade intercourse; commercial relations[intercourse]. ¶덴마크와 ~을 시작하다 open trade with Denmark / establish trade[commercial] relations[links] with Denmark // 전쟁으로 양국 간의 ~은 단절되었다 The war interrupted the flow of commerce between the two countries. **통상하다** trade (with a country).
● **통상 관계** trade relations. **통상 대표부** the Trade Representation. ¶미국 ~ the Office of the U.S. Trade Representative. **통상 무역** trade and commerce. **통상 사절단** a trade delegation. **통상 조약** a commercial treaty. ¶~을 맺다 conclude[sign] a commercial treaty.

통설(通說) [일반적인 학설] a common[popular] view [opinion]; a commonly-[popularly-]held opinion. ¶~에서는 기원전 2세기 후반에 실크 로드가 열리기 시작한 것으로 되어 있다 It is commonly accepted that people began to travel along the Silk Road in the latter half of the second century B.C.

통성명하다 (通姓名-) introduce (themselves) to each other; exchange (their) names. ¶우린 아직 통성명하지 않았죠 We haven't met yet, have we?

통속 〔단체〕 a gang; a cabal; 〔협잡꾼의〕 a decoy; 〔미〕 a shrill; 〔영〕 a bonnet; 〔경매 때의〕 a by-bidder; a puffer; 〔음모〕 a cabal; a secret intrigue [plot]; a secret agreement. ¶한~이 되다 conspire (with) / act [be] in collusion [concert / complicity] (with) / 〔미〕 go (into) cahoots (with) // 그놈의 ~을 누가 알 수 있나 Who can tell what secret agreement they've made? / I can't guess what secret game they have made.

통속 (通俗) 1 〔일반적인 풍속〕 a common [popular] custom. 2 〔관용어적〕 popular; common.
● **통속극** a play dealing with the domestic life of commoners. **통속 문학** [소설] popular literature [novels]. **통속 음악** popular music. **통속화** popularization. ¶~하다 popularize / 〔속악하다〕 vulgarize.

통속적 (通俗的) 〔대중적〕 popular; 〔평범한〕 common; 〔속악한〕 vulgar. ¶~인 과학 서적 a popular book of science // ~인 의견 [사고방식] common opinion [way of thinking], the opinion [way of thinking] of the main in the street // ~인 기사 an unscientific account // ~인 책 a book for the lay reader // ~으로 popularly / in a popular style // ~으로 말하면 to use plain language / in common parlance.

통솔 (統率) command; generalship; leadership. ¶…의 ~하에 있다 be under the command [leadership] of. **통솔하다** command; lead; direct; take the lead of. ¶일군 〔一軍〕을 ~ be at the head [in command] of an army // 해군을 ~ be at the head [in command] of the navy // 그는 부하를 훌륭히 통솔하고 있다 He leads his men well. / He exercises excellent leadership over his subordinates. ➔그 연대는 잘 통솔되어 있었다 The regiment was well officered.
● **통솔권** (the right of) command. **통솔력** leadership; ability to command. ¶그녀는 ~이 있다 She has good leadership ability. / She is an able leader. **통솔자** a leader; a commander. ¶~가 되다 take the lead of / stand at the head of.

통수 (統帥) the supreme [high] command. ¶육해공군의 ~자 the supreme commander of the army, navy and air force. **통수하다** command; have the supreme command (of). ¶삼군 [전군]을 ~ command all the armed forces.
● **통수권** the prerogative of supreme command.

통신 (通信) (a) communication; (편지 등에 의한) correspondence; (보도) news; (특전 (特電)) a dispatch; (정보) information; (국가적인 기밀 정보) intelligence. ¶**데이터 ~** data communication // 북경의 ~에 의하면 according to a dispatch [message / news] from Peking / a Peking dispatch says (that …) // ~을 계속하다 maintain a correspondence (with) / keep in touch [communication] (with) // ~을 개시하다 get into communication [correspondence] (with) / begin to communicate [correspond] (with) // 전쟁으로 본국과 이곳과의 ~은 일체 두절되었다 All communication between our country and this place has been interrupted [cut off] by the war. // 본국과 무선으로 ~을 계속했다 I kept in touch with home by wireless. // 폴란드발 ~은 전국적인 파업을 보도했다 A dispatch from Poland reported nationwide strikes. **통신하다** correspond (with a person); communicate (with a person); communicate a message (to a person); report (for a paper); keep up a correspondence (with a person).
● **통신 강좌** a correspondence course. ¶~로 공부하다 do a correspondence course (in accounting) // ~로 부기를 공부하고 있다 I am taking a correspondence course in bookkeeping. / I am taking courses in bookkeeping by correspondence. **통신 교육** education by correspondence; a correspondence course of (high school [college]) education. ¶~을 하다 teach by correspondence / ~을 받다 take [do] a correspondence course (in economics). **통신 기관** a means [a medium / an organ] of communication. **통신 대학** a home study college. **통신망** news-gathering facilities [organization]; a communications net. **통신문** correspondence; a communication; a written message. **통신병** (미) a signalman; a signal corpsman; (영) a telegraphist. **통신사** a news agency; a news [(미) wire] service. ¶연합 ~ the Associated press (약어 A.P.) / 타스 ~ Tass News Agency. **통신원** (신문사 등의) a correspondent; a reporter; (회사의 통신계원) a correspondence clerk. ¶특파 [종군] ~ a special [war] correspondent // 본사 뉴욕 ~으로부터의 전문에 의하면 our correspondent in New York cables (that …) // 신문의 ~으로 일하다 report [correspond] for a newspaper. **통신 위성** a communications satellite. **통신 판매** mail order; mail-order sale [selling]. ¶~ 회사로부터 차를 샀다 I bought tea from a mail-order house [firm]. // ~로 차를 팔고 있다 They sell tea to mail-order customers.

통어 (統御) (통치) rule; (제어) control; (관리) management. **통어하다** rule; govern; control; bring [hold] under one's control [girdle]; manage; (미) administrate. ¶통어하기 힘드는 unmanageable / uncontrollable / ungovernable / unruly // 부하를 ~ control one's subordinates / control the men under one // 잘 ~ control (one's subordinates) properly // 통어할 수 없게 되다 get beyond [out of] control / get out of hand.

통역 (通譯) (일) interpretation; (사람) an interpreter. ¶**동시 ~** simultaneous translation // 믿을 만한 ~ a reliable interpreter // ~ 없이 without an interpreter / without interpretation // B씨의 ~으로 이야기하다 speak through the interpreter, Mr. B // ~을 통해서 [두지 않고] 그와 이야기했다 I talked with him through [without] an interpreter. **통역하다** interpret; act as (an) interpreter.
● **통역관** an official interpreter; a secretary-interpreter.

통용 (通用) popular [common] use; circulation; currency. ¶지폐의 ~을 제한하다 restrict the currency of bank notes // ~ 기한 당일[1개월] 한 (표의 표기) Good [Available / Valid] for the day of issue[for a month] only. **통용하다** be in common use; pass (for); circulate; be[pass / go / run] current; (표 등이) be available; be good; (규칙 등이) hold good[true]. ¶국제간에 ~ have international currency // 통용하기 시작하다[통용하지 않게 되다] gain[lose] currency // 그 화폐는 어디서나 통용된다 That coin goes[can be used] everywhere. → ¶세상에 통용되다 pass current with the world // 일반적으로 통용되다 pass[go / run] current // 이 말은 지금은 통용되지 않는다 This word is not used[in common use] today. / This word is obsolete now. // 그의 이론은 오늘날에도 통용된다 His theory holds good[true] even today. // 영어는 세계 어느 곳에서나 통용된다 English is spoken all over the world. // 원화는 이 나라에서 통용됩니까 Can won be used in this country?

● **통용문**(-門) a side gate[door]; a service [back] entrance. **통용어** a current word [language]; a password; a word[language] in current use. **통용 화폐** currency; a current coin.

통운(通運) transportation; forwarding; express. **통운하다** transport; forward; ship.

● **통운 회사** a transport company; a forwarding agent[agency]; (미) an express agency[company].

통원(通院) ¶1개월의 ~을 요하는 부상 an injury requiring one month's treatment as an outpatient. **통원하다** go to hospital regularly; attend a hospital (as an outpatient); receive regular outpatient treatment; see a doctor regularly. ¶나는 벌써 3개월이나 통원하고 있다 I've been seeing a doctor regularly for three months now.

● **통원 치료** (require) a treatment as an outpatient. **통원 환자** an outpatient.

통으로 wholly; entirely.

통일(統一) unity; unification; consolidation; coordination; uniformity; coherence; oneness; (표준화) standardization; (통어) rule; sway; dominance; (집중) concentration. ¶남북~ unification of North and South (Korea) // 재~ reunification (of Germany) // 정신 ~ psychic[mental] concentration // 평화 ~적인 peaceful unification // 국가의 ~ the unification of the nation // ~적인 unific // ~이 되어 있다 be in union / be united / be unified // ~이 안 되어 있다 lack unity[coordination] / be without coordination / be incoherent // ~에의 길은 아직도 멀다 The unification is still a long way off. // 그러면 당내의 ~이 안 될 것이다 That would cause disunity among the party members. **통일하다** unify; consolidate; coordinate; [표준화하다] standardize; [통어하다] rule; bring under sway. ¶나라를 ~ unify a nation / bring a country under a single authority [one sway] // 가격을 ~ standardize the prices // 철자법을 ~ standardize spelling rule // 그는 중국 전토를 통일했다 He united the whole land of China under his sway. → ¶통일된 unified / uniform / systematic / homogeneous // 통일되지 않은 diverse / incoherent.

● **통일부** the Ministry of Unification. **통일성** unity. **통일 정부**[전선] a unified government [front]. **통일체** a unity; a whole.

통장(通帳) (은행의) a bankbook; a passbook; (외상 거래의) a chit-book. ¶예금 ~ a bankbook / a deposit passbook // 저금 ~ a savings passbook // ~에 **가입하다** enter (an item) in a bankbook // 잠시 ~을 주시겠습니까 May we keep your passbook[bankbook] for a while?

통장(統長) the head of a *tong*.

통절하다(痛切-) [절실하다] keen; poignant; acute; urgent. ¶통절한 회한[뉘우침] acute [keen / sharp] remorse. **통절히** keenly; poignantly; severely; acutely. ¶~을 느끼다 (사물이) be keenly felt (that ...) / (사람이) feel keenly[vividly] // 결함을 ~ 느끼다 feel the shortcomings severely / 스스로의 결점을 ~ 느끼다 feel one's shortcomings keenly // 필요성을 ~ 느끼다 keenly feel the necessity of [for] ... // 무언가 종교적 믿음이 필요하다는 것을 ~ 느꼈다 I felt keenly the need of religious faith.

통점(痛點) [의] a pain spot.

통정(通情) 1 having sympathetic understanding; an appeal. ⇒ 통사정 2 [마음을 주고받음] shared sympathy. 3 [세상 인정] the way of the world; the rules of affairs in the world. 4 [간통] adultery; illicit intercourse [intimacy].

통제(統制) control; regulation; regimentation. ¶물가 ~ price control // 식육의 ~ the control of meat / meat control // 정부의 ~ governmental control // 항공[언론]의 정부 ~ government regulation of the airlines[press] // ~가 없는[통제하지 않는] uncontrolled / noncontrolled // ~를 **강화하다** tighten [strengthen] the control (of / over) // 엄격한 ~를 하다 exercise strict[close] control (over) // ~를 **완화하다** alleviate[ease] the control // ~를 해제하다 [풀다] remove control (from / on) / lift control / decontrol // …에 대한 ~를 철폐하다 lift the control on ... // 그 나라는 군의 ~하에 있다 The country is under military control. // 금융에 대한 ~가 점점 더 엄격해지고 있다 Monetary controls are becoming more stringent[rigid]. // 전체 학생은 ~가 잘되어 있다 The student body is well under control. // 정부는 산업에 대한 ~를 완화할 방침이다 The Government intends to ease controls on industry. **통제하다** control; regulate; govern; regiment. ¶산업을 ~ regulate[regiment] industries.

● **통제 가격** controlled prices. **통제 경제** controlled economy. **통제 구역** a restricted area; a control zone. **통제 기관** a control organ[agency]; an organ for control.

통조림(桶-) (제조) packing; (미) canning; (영) tinning; (제품) (미) canned[(영) tinned] provisions[goods]. ¶고기 ~ canned [tinned] meat // 과일 ~ canned[tinned] fruit // 쇠고기 ~ canned[tinned] beef / bully (beef) // 연어[생선] ~ canned[tinned] salmon[fish] // ~을 따다 open a tin[can] / saw out the top of a can[tin].

통증(痛症) a pain; an ache; a pang(급작스런); pricking(따끔따끔한). ¶격렬한 ~ a severe[a sharp / a poignant / an acute] pain // 등[무릎]의 ~ a (sharp) pain in the back[knee] // 옆구리의 ~ a pain[stitch] in one's side // 쿡

통지

쿡 찌르는 듯한 ~ a sharp stab of pain // 상처의 ~ the smart of a wound // ~이 더하다 [줄어들다] the pain increases [abates] // ~이 멎다 the pain stops // ~이 심하다 feel a bad [severe] pain (in one's teeth) // ~을 느끼다 feel [have / suffer] a pain // ~을 누그러뜨리다 [가라앉히다] allay [alleviate / mitigate / ease / relieve] the pain / make the pain easier // ~을 멈추다 stop (the) pain // ~을 없애다 remove [banish / kill] (the) pain // ~을 참다 stand [bear / endure] the pain // 오른쪽 눈에 욱신거리는 ~이 있다 I feel a smarting pain in my right eye. // 나는 오른쪽 옆구리에 찌르는 듯한 ~을 느꼈다 I felt a sharp stab of pain in my right side. // 이 주사를 맞으면 ~은 가라앉습니다 This injection will stop [get rid of] the pain.

통지 (通知) [통고] (a) notice; (a) notification; [통보] (a) report; information; [통신] communication; (상업상의) an advice. ¶계약 만기 ~ a notice of expiration of contract // 어음 부도[집회] ~ a notice of dishonor [meeting] // 착하(着荷)[이전 / 해약] ~ a notice of arrival [removal / cancellation] // 송금 ~ a remittance advice // 회사로부터의 채용 ~ a notice of one's employment by a company / (영) a letter of appointment to the staff of a company // 추후 ~가 있을 때까지 till further notice [advice] / until one hears further from (a person) // ~를 받는 즉시 at a minute's notice / immediately on receipt of one's notice // …이라는 ~가 있었다 word has reached (this office) that … / word was received (at the headquarters) that … // …이라는 ~에 접하다 advice has been received to the effect that … // ~를 받다 be informed (of / that …) / have [receive] notice (of / that …) / be notified [advised] (of / that …) / receive advices // ~를 기다리다 await word // 그에게서 동창회의 ~를 받았다 I received notice of our class reunion from him. // 나는 건강 진단의 ~를 받았다 I have been notified [informed] about the physical examination. **통지하다** notify (a person that [of]); inform (a person that [of]); let (a person) know (that / of); communicate (news to / with a person); advise [apprise] (a person that [of]); (주로 해약·해고 등의) give (a person) notice (that / of). ¶미리 ~ give (a person) previous notice / send word beforehand // ~임을 통지해 드립니다 This is to give notice [notify / inform you] that …. // 도착하면 바로 통지해 주십시오 Please write to me immediately upon your arrival. // 초보 운전자의 강습에 나오시도록 통지합니다 We advise you that [This is to notify you to] attend the lecture for new drivers. // 자세한 것은 또 통지하겠습니다 I'll let you know more about it later. / I'll send you more detailed information about it later.

● **통지서** a (written) notice; a written message. ¶부도 ~ (어음의) a notice of dishonor [protest] // 출하(出荷) ~ a consignment note / a shipping advice / a bill of landing. **통지 예금** a deposit at call [notice]. **통지인** an informer. **통지표** a report card. ⇨생활 통지표(⇨생활)

통짜 the whole mass [lump] (of).

통짜다¹ [한동아리가 되기로 약속하다] pledge oneself to become a member of a gang [group / cabal]; form a gang [group]. ¶~과 통짜고 in collusion [league / conspiracy] with // 그녀는 정부와 통짜고 남편을 살해하려고 했다 She conspired with her lover to murder her husband.

통짜다² [각 부분을 하나가 되도록 맞추다] put [fit / piece] together; frame; assemble.

통째(로) whole; altogether; bodily; entirely; in (its) entirety. ¶~ 굽다 roast (a chicken) whole // ~ 먹다 eat (something) whole // ~ 삼키다 swallow up without chewing / swallow (a biscuit) whole // 고기 한 토막을 ~ 삼키다 swallow a piece of meat whole // 생선을 ~ 먹다 eat up a fish whole / eat a fish, bone and all // 그녀는 닭을 ~ 구웠다 She roasted a whole chicken. // 금고 속에 든 것들을 ~ 도둑맞았다 The contents of the safe were stolen in their entirety [en masse].

통찰 (洞察) discernment; penetration; insight. **통찰하다** discern; penetrate [see] into; see through; fathom (a person's heart).

● **통찰력** an insight; penetration; vision; discernment. ¶~이 있는 discerning / penetrative / penetrating / perceptive / perspicacious // ~이 있는 사람 a man of insight / a discerning person // ~이 빼어난 사람 a man of great insight // ~이 있다 have an insight into … // 예리한 ~이 있다 can see through a brick wall // 그는 인간성에 대한 ~이 없었다 He had no insight into human nature. // 그는 놀랄 만한 ~을 가지고 있다 He can see through a brick wall. // 그는 ~이 예리한 사람이다 He is a man of keen insight. // 그는 부하의 심리에 대한 ~이 없었다 He had no insight into the mentality of his subordinates.

통첩 (通牒) a note; a circular; instruction. ¶외교 ~ a diplomatic note // 최후 ~ an ultimatum (pl. ~s, -ta) // ~을 보내다 issue [send] a notification // 노조는 경영자측으로부터 최후~을 받았다 The labor [(영) trade(s)] union received an ultimatum from the management. **통첩하다** notify (a person of [that]); give notice (to); communicate.

통촉 (洞燭) (sympathetic) understanding; comprehension; judgment; discernment. **통촉하다** (design to) see; understand; comprehend; judge; discern; consider; realize.

통치 (統治) rule; reign; government; administration. ¶신탁 ~ trusteeship // 위임 ~ mandatory rule [administration] // 국가의 ~ the administration of the state // 국가 ~의 대권(大權) the rights of sovereignty of the state // …의 ~하에 있다 be under the rule [reign] of … // 여왕의 ~가 50년 계속되었다 The queen's reign lasted fifty years. // 그 나라는 프랑스 ~하에 있었다 The country was under French rule. **통치하다** rule over [govern] (a country / a people); hold sway over; administer; guide. ¶한 나라를 ~ rule (over) a country / reign over a country / govern [administer] a country.

● **통치권** (exercise one's) sovereign [supreme] power; sovereignty; majesty. ¶~을 행사하다 exercise the sovereign power. **통치 기관** government organs [machinery]. **통치자** the ruler; the sovereign. **통치 제도** a ruling system.

통치마 a pleatless [seamless] skirt.

통칙 (通則) general [common] principles;

통

general rules. ¶~으로서 as a general rule.
통칭(通稱) 〔공통으로 쓰이는 이름〕 a common designation[title]; 〔널리 통하여 불리는 이름〕 a popular[common] name; (an) alias. ¶~…으로 알려진 T 씨 Mr. T better known as ... // 조지, ~은 톰 George, commonly called Tom / George alias Tom // ~ X로 통하다 go by the name of X // 그 고개는 무악재라는 ~으로 통하고 있다 This pass is commonly known as[goes by the name of] Muakjae.
통쾌감(痛快感) smart[thrilling] feelings.
통쾌하다(痛快−) 〔유쾌하다〕 awfully pleasant; extremely delightful; piquant; 〔만족스럽다〕 affording intense satisfaction; very gratifying. ¶통쾌한 사나이 a man of spirits // 통쾌한 문제[연설] an incisive[a trenchant / a stunning] style[speech] // 가장 통쾌한 것은 …이었다 the thing that gave me the most kick[that was the most gratifying] was ... // 매우 ~[통쾌하게 여기다] be highly delighted // 야 통쾌하구나 How delightful and gratifying! / (미) How thrilling! // 지프로 산을 넘는 일은 참으로 통쾌했다 It was really thrilling to cross the mountains in a jeep. / (구어) I got a real kick out of crossing the mountains by jeep. // 우리의 상대 팀이 완패하는 것을 보고 정말 통쾌했다 It gave us real pleasure[great satisfaction] to see our rivals beaten thoroughly. **통쾌히** to one's great satisfaction; delightfully; pleasantly; thrilling; incisively; trenchantly. ¶그의 약점이 ~ 폭로되었다 His weakness has been mercilessly disclosed.
통타(痛打) a crushing[stinging / telling / punishing] blow; a shrewd knock; a crusher; a crasher; a stinger. ¶신인 투수는 ~를 얻어맞았다 The new pitcher was hit hard. **통타하다** give a crushing blow (to / on); 〔야구〕 send a crasher (to left field). ¶그는 풀카운트 후의 투구를 통타하여 20호 홈런을 날렸다 He socked a 3-2 pitch for his twentieth homer. ➔**통타당하다** get a crushing blow (from a person).
통탄(痛歎) deep lamentation; bitter grief; deep regret. **통탄하다** lament[regret] deeply; grieve bitterly; deplore. ¶통탄할 deplorable / lamentable / grievous / regrettable // 통탄할 대참사 a lamentable[deplorable] disaster // 아주 통탄할 일 a matter of great regret // …은 통탄할 일이다 It is deplorable[much to be regretted] that ... should ... . // 미성년자의 범죄가 증가하고 있는 것은 정말 통탄할 일이다 The increase in juvenile delinquency is quite deplorable.
통탕 beating; pounding. ⇨〈퉁탕
통통¹ 〔몸피가 굵은 모양〕. **통통하다**¹ round; plump; chubby; buxom; full. ¶통통한 아이 a chubby[plump] child // 통통한 젖가슴 a full breast // 얼굴이 통통한 여자 a chubby-faced woman // 볼이 통통한 어린애 a baby with chubby[plump] cheeks // 통통하게 살찐 여자 a plump[buxom] woman // 통통하게 찌다 become round / plump (up / out) // (얼굴) 모습이 ~ look chubby // 그녀의 몸매는 점점 통통해진다 Her form is rounding.
통통² 〔두드리는·구르는 소리〕 pounding; beating; stamping; tramping; resounding. **통통하다**² pound; beat. ⇨〈통통거리다 2 〔발동기 소리〕 chug-chug (of a motorboat).
통통거리다 pound; beat; stamp; tramp. ¶통로에서 통통거리는 발소리 the pound of feet in the passageway // 통통거리며 계단을 오르다 stamp upstairs // (발동선이) 통통거리며 지나가다 chug off [along] // (발로) 통통거리며 박자를 맞추다 (one's feet) tom-tom out a pattern of rhythm (one is whistling) // 어린애가 마루를 통통거리며 돌아다닌다 A child scampers around on the floor. // 계단을 통통거리며 올라오는 발소리가 들렸다 I heard the light footsteps of someone coming quickly up the stairs.
통통배 a motorboat; a motor-powered boat.
통틀다 lump[put] together; sum up; draw into one mass.
통틀어 〔모두 합하여〕 all put together; in total; (all) in all; (in) all told; in the gross [mass / lump]; in one lot; collectively; (프) en bloc[masse]. ¶~ 스물 twenty in all / twenty all told // ~ 3만 원 (물건 값이) 30,000 won for the whole lot[in all told] // ~ 말하면 taking all (things) together / to sum up // ~ 5만 원이 되다 total up to 50,000 won // ~ 얼마냐 What do you charge for them all? / How much (is it) all together? / How much does it make altogether?
통판(通販) mail order. ⇨〈통신 판매(⇨통신)
통폐(通弊) a common evil[abuse / weakness]. ¶이러한 일들은 현대 사회의 ~이다 These happenings are evils common to all the classes in this society. // 배타적인 것은 한국민의 ~이다 Exclusiveness is fault common among the Koreans. / Koreans are apt to be exclusive.
통폐합(統廢合) (conduct) the merger and abolition (of). ¶재정의 핍박으로 부과(部課)의 ~이 단행되었다 Because of the tight financial situation, some departments and sections were abolished and others were merged.
통풍(通風) ventilation; airing; draft; draught. ¶자연[인공] ~ a natural[an artificial] draft // ~이 잘되는 방 a well-ventilated room // ~이 좋은[나쁜] a well-[an ill-]ventilated room // ~이 잘되다[잘 안 되다] be well[ill] ventilated // 이 아파트는 ~이 좋다[나쁘다] This apartment house is well[poorly] ventilated. **통풍하다** let (fresh) air in; admit air; ventilate.
●**통풍관** an air pipe[line]; a vent pipe; a ventiduct. **통풍구** a ventilation opening; an air hole; an airway; a vent; a ventilator. **통풍기** a ventilator; an aerator. **통풍 장치** a ventilation arrangement[device / apparatus].
통풍(痛風) 〔의〕 gout; podagra. ¶~에 걸리다 be afflicted with gout.
통하다(通−) 1 (길·통로·교통 기관 등이) run; lead (to / into) (…에 이르다); open (into a room / upon a corridor[garden]); communicate (with); 〔개통하다〕 be opened (to [for] traffic); be connected (by a railway) (이어지다). ¶해안으로 통하는 길 a road leading [going] to the seashore // 안뜰로 통하는 대문 a large gate leading[giving] into the court // 서울에서 춘천으로 통하는 가도 a highway leading to Chuncheon from Seoul // 아침 5시부터 지하철이 통한다 The subway runs from 5 a.m. // 이 문은 뜰로 통한다 This door leads to the garden. // 이 길은 이웃 도시로 통한다 This road leads to the next town. // 얼마 안 있으면 우리 시에도 철도가 통한다 A railway

통하다

will soon be laid to our town. // 여기서 목포까지 철도가 통해 있다 A railway runs [extends] from here to Mokpo. // 이 마을에서 해안까지 철도가 통하고 있다 A railroad runs [There is railroad service] from this town to the seaside. // 이 방의 한쪽은 다른 방으로 통해 있다 One end of this room communicates with another room. // 지금은 그 지방에 철도가 통한다 A railroad is now open to that locality. / A railway service is now available in that district.

2 (공기가) vent (through a chimney); (be) ventilate(d); (빛·열 등이) pass [run / go] through; penetrate; permeate; (혈액 등이) (be) circulate(d); (파이프 등이) draw; drain. ¶공기가 (잘) 통하지 않는 방 an unaired room / an ill-ventilated room // 공기가 잘 ~ have a good ventilation [vent] // 빛이 ~ be penetrable to light // 피가 잘 ~[안 ~] have a good [poor] circulation of blood // 피를 잘 통하게 하다 improve [facilitate] the circulation of blood // 이 담뱃대는 연기가 잘 통한다 This pipe draws well. // 이 굴뚝[파이프]은 연기가 잘 통하지 않는다 This chimney [pipe] does not draw well. // 이 하수도는 물이 잘 통한다 The sewer runs [drains] well. // 유리 섬유는 열이 통하지 않는다 Glass fiber does not transmit heat.

3 (전류가) transmit; flow. ¶전기가 통하고 있는 전선 a live [an electrified] wire // 금속류는 전기가 통한다 Metals transmit electricity. // 이 철사는 전류가 통하고 있다 This wire is charged with electricity. / This is a live wire.

4 (전화가) (a call) be put [go / get] through; be on (the line); (the phone) be working; get connected (with). ¶전화가 통하지 않는다 The phone [wire] is dead. / The line is out. // B씨에게 전화를 걸었으나 통하지 않았다 I could not get Mr. B on the phone. / I couldn't get through to Mr. B. // 전화가 잘 통하지 않는다 My call won't go through. / I can't get through on the phone. // 통화 중이어서 전화가 통하지 않습니다 The line is busy [(문어) The number is engaged] and I can't reach [get] him.

5 [내용·사정 등에 정통하다] be well [deeply] versed (in); be an expert (in / on); be well up (in); be proficient (in); be at home (in / on); be a master (of); be well acquainted (with); be well informed (of); be conversant (with). ¶시사 문제에 통해 있다 be in touch with current problems // 영어에 통해 있다 be proficient in English / have a good [thorough] knowledge of English // 내막에 통해 있다 be well up on the inside story // 그는 현대 음악에 통해 있다 He is well informed about [well versed in] modern music. / He knows a lot about modern music.

6 (말·의사 등이) be understood; be comprehended; be spoken; make oneself understood; understand (each other); be congenial. ¶말이 통하는 사람 a man of sense / a sensible person / a nice [good] fellow // 일반적으로 통하는 말 a popular [common] word // 영어가 ~ be able to speak English / make oneself understood in English // 말이 서로 ~ [통하지 않다] be able [unable] to communicate with each other (in English) // 서로 기분이 ~ understand each other's sentiments // 마음과 마음이 ~ commune [hold communion] (with) // 자기의 의사를 (남에게) ~ let one's desire [intention] be known (to others) // 서로 잘 ~ be very responsive to each other // 그는 이야기가 통한다 He talks sense. / He is quick of understanding. // 멕시코에서는 무슨 말이 통하지 What language do they speak [is spoken] in Mexico? // 한국에서는 에스파냐 어가 통하지 않는다 Spanish isn't spoken in Korea. // 그에게는 농담이 통하지 않는다 He doesn't appreciate [understand] jokes. // 그 사람에게는 이치가 통하지 않는다 He is dead to reason. // 그와 나는 마음이 서로 통한다 He and I get along very well with each other. / He and I understand each other (very well). / He and I hit it off well. // 교육에 있어서는 교사와 학생의 마음이 서로 통하는 것이 가장 중요하다 The most important thing in education is that the teacher and the pupil come to understand [come in close touch with] each other. // 힌트를 주어도 그녀에게는 통하지 않았다 My hint was lost upon her. // 내 영어는 영국에서 통하지 않았다 People in Britain did not understand my English.

7 (글의 뜻이) make sense; be understandable. ¶뜻이 통하지 않는 문장 an incomprehensible sentence // 이 문장은 뜻이 통하지 않는다 This sentence doesn't make sense. // 고치니까 이제야 글의 뜻이 통하는군 Now your correction makes sense of the sentence.

8 (정 등을) become intimate (with); have relations (with); form a liaison (with); commit misconduct [adultery] (with); intrigue (with). ¶정을 ~ have an illicit intercourse (with) // 유부녀 [기혼녀]와 정을 ~ have an affair [relations] with a married woman // 그녀는 하인과 정을 통했다 She gave herself to his servant. // 그가 그녀와 정을 통한 지 2년이 된다 It has been two years since he became intimate with her.

9 [내통하다] communicate secretly [intrigue] (with the enemy); betray; be in touch with (the other party). ¶적과 ~ prostitute oneself to the enemy // 어떤 사람과 (비밀히) 통하고 있다 be in secret communication with somebody // 그는 라이벌 회사의 이사와 (비밀히) 통하고 있다 He is in secret touch with a director of a rival company.

10 [알려지다] pass (for / as); figure as; be known as. ¶…의 이름으로 ~ pass under the name of / go [be known] by the name of // 진짜로 ~ pass for [as] genuine // 대가(大家)로 ~ be reputed [acknowledged] as an authority // 그는 송이라는 이름으로 통하고 있다 He passed under [went by] the name of Song. / He was known as [by the name of] Song.

11 [허용되다] pass; get by; be admissible. ¶내 의견은 그들에게 통하지 않을 거다 My opinion will not go down with them. // 그런 핑계는 통하지 않는다 Such excuses will not do. // 그런 어리석은 짓이 통하다니 How can such an absurd thing be accepted [allowed]? // 그런 논리는 통하지 않는다 Such an argument will not do. // 법률은 몰랐다는 것으로 통하지 않는다 Ignorance of the law excuses no one. // 요즘 세상에 그런 생각은 통하지 않는다 Such ideas [views] are unacceptable today. // 저런 짓이 버젓이 통할 수 있다니 세상도 말세다 That such things can

pass unremarked [That a person can do such a thing with impunity] is a sign of the collapse of civilization.
12 [통용되다] be valid; hold [be / stand] good; be available (차표 등이); [유통되다] pass; circulate. ¶규칙이 통한다 A regulation holds good.∥이 돈은 어디서나 This money passes [can be used / goes] freely everywhere.∥이 표는 이 노선에서는 통하지 않는다 This ticket is not good [valid] on this line.∥그 증명서는 이제는 통하지 않는다 The certificate is no longer valid, now.
13 [거치다] pass [go] through; go by way of. ¶…을 통해서 through / through the medium of / via∥C 씨를 통해 through Mr. C / through Mr. C's good offices∥신문과 라디오를 통해서 via [through] the radio and newspapers∥중매인을 통해서 청혼하다 propose to (a girl) through a go-between∥시베리아를 통해서 가다 [오다] go [come] by way of [via] Siberia∥부인은 엷은 커튼을 통해 밖을 내다보고 있었다 The lady was looking out through the thin curtain.∥빛이 벽 틈을 통해 들어왔다 Light came in through a crack in the wall.∥부인을 통하여 그의 의향을 알아 볼 생각이다 I will sound him out through his wife.∥그는 신 씨를 통하여 회사에 취직이 되었다 He was employed by the company through the influence of Mr. Sin.∥그 정보는 프랑스 대사관을 통해 입수했다 We received the information through the French Embassy.∥그것에 대해서는 책을 통해 얻은 지식밖에 없다 I know about it only through books.∥My knowledge about it comes from books only.∥나는 친구를 통해 그녀에게 내 전갈을 보냈다 I sent a message to her via a friend.∥그것이 여론 조사를 통해서 본 젊은 사람들의 경향이다 That is the tendency among young people as seen through a public opinion poll.
14 [시간·공간에 걸치다]. ¶일생을 통하여 throughout [during] one's life / all one's life∥1년을 통하여 all the year around [round] / throughout the year∥전국을 통하여 throughout [all over] the country∥그 일은 내 일생을 통해 잊혀지지 않을 것이다 I will remember it all my life [as long as I live].∥도서 교환권 [상품권]은 전국을 통하여 사용할 수 있다 Book coupons are good all over [anywhere in] the country.
15 [관계가 있다] be concerned [connected] (with); have a relation [connection] (with). ¶피가 서로 ~ [일가 관계에 있다] be in kinship with / be a relative (of)∥문학과 음악은 서로 통한다 There is an interrelation between the literature and the music.

통학(通學) attending school. **통학하다** attend [go to] school [classes]. ¶도보로 ~ attend school on foot∥버스[열차]로 ~ go to school by bus [train]∥자기 집에서 ~ attend school from one's home.
●**통학 구역** a school district [zone]; (영) a school catchment area. **통학생** (기숙 제도 도 학교의) a day scholar [boy]; an extern. **통학차** (버스) a school bus; (열차 등) a student train; a student commuter train.

통한(痛恨) great sorrow; deep grievance [regret / mortification]; bitter remembrance; bitterness. ¶~의 눈물 tears of bitter grief. **통한하다** regret deeply; grieve bitterly. ¶…은 통한하기 그지없다 [짝이 없다] it is to be greatly regretted that ….

통할(統轄) (general) control; control and jurisdiction. **통할하다** control; exercise general control (over); supervise; be in charge of. ¶그가 전 기획을 통할하고 있다 He is in charge of [supervises] the whole undertaking.
●**통할 구역** the area under the direct control (of).

통합(統合) integration; unification; unity; combination; consolidation; synthesis. ¶야당 ~ unification of parties out of power∥국민 ~의 상징 the symbol of the unity of the people. **통합하다** integrate; combine; unify; unite; consolidate; put [bring] together; make into one. ¶그 지역에서는 초등학교를 하나로 통합할 계획을 갖고 있다 There is a plan to combine all the elementary schools in the area into one. ➔¶통합된 united / combined / integrated∥세 개의 고등 교육 기관이 통합되어 대학이 되었다 Three institutions of higher education were integrated [brought together] into one university.

통행(通行) passing; passage; transit; (street) traffic. ¶~을 **방해하다** obstruct the traffic / bar the way∥~을 **금하다** close (up) a road / seal a street to traffic / block a street∥좌측~ (게시) Keep to the left. / Walk on the left.∥**일방** ~ (게시) One way only. / One-way traffic.∥이 앞으로는 차량 ~이 금지되어 있다 Automobile traffic is prohibited beyond this point.∥여기는 일방 ~이다 This is a one-way street.∥이 나라에서 차량은 좌측~이다 Vehicles drive on the left in this country.∥주차 중인 차량이 보행자의 ~을 가로막고 있다 A parked car is blocking the path of pedestrians.∥이 길은 차량 ~이 많다 [적다] There is heavy [little] traffic on this road. **통행하다** pass (through); go [get] past; go through [along]. ¶통행할 수 있는 [없는] passable [impassable]∥거리를 ~ pass [go] along a street / walk down a street∥이 길은 통행할 수 없다 This road is impassable [closed to traffic].
●**통행권**(-券) a pass; a ticket; a pass token. **통행금지** suspension of traffic. ¶~ (게시) Road closed. / Closed to traffic.∥차량 ~ (게시) No thoroughfare for vehicles.∥야간 ~ (시간) the curfew (hour)∥야간 ~를 실시하다 impose a curfew∥이 도로는 수리 때문에 자주 일시 ~가 된다 This road is often closed temporarily for repairs. **통행료** a toll; passage money. ¶~ 징수소 a toll house / a toll station∥이 도로는 ~를 내야 한다 This is a toll road. **통행세** a traveling tax; transit duty; a toll. **통행인** a passerby (pl. passersby); a foot passenger; a pedestrian; a wayfarer; a passer. **통행증** a pass; (적국·피점령지 등의) a safe-conduct (pass); a safeguard.

통혼(通婚) **1** [혼인 의사를 표시함] making a proposal [an offer] of marriage. **통혼하다** make an offer of marriage (to a girl). **2** [혼인 관계를 맺음] entering into matrimony. **통혼하다** enter into matrimony.

통화(通貨) currency; current money [coins]; the medium of circulation; the circulating medium. ¶관리 ~ managed [controlled] currency∥금속[강제] ~ metallic [forced] currency∥준~ near money∥보조[자동] ~

통화 fractional [automatic] currency // 총~ 공급 중가율 the total money supply increase rate // ~ 가치의 절하 (currency) devaluation // ~로 천 원 1,000 won in currency // 그 나라의 ~로 지불하다 pay in (the) coin of the realm / pay the bill in the currency of the country. ●**통화량** the amount of currency in circulation. **통화 수축** deflation. ⇨"디플레이션 **통화 안정** the stabilization of currency. **통화 정책** a monetary policy. **통화 팽창** inflation (of currency). ⇨"인플레이션

통화(通話) a (telephone) call; a (telephone) message; telephone conversation; telephonic communication. ¶한 ~ one call / a conversation // 한 ~ 3분간 a call of three minutes // ~ 중이다 be talking over [be on] the telephone // 한 ~ 3분간의 요금은 70원입니다 The fee is seventy won for each conversation of three minutes. // 한 ~입니다 Your three minutes are up, sir. // 지금 몇 ~였습니까 How many minutes did we speak? // 전화는 지금 ~ 중입니다 (미) The telephone[line] is busy now. / (영) The telephone[line] is engaged now. // ~ 중 (전화) (미) Line's busy. / (영) Number's engaged. // 그분은 지금 ~ 중입니다 He is on another line. **통화하다** speak [talk] over [upon] the telephone.
●**통화량** telephone traffic. **통화료** the fee [charge] for a telephone call. ¶시외 ~ the fee for trunk call / the distance-call charge.

통회(痛悔) [가] contrition. **통회하다** be contrite.

퇴각(退却) 1 [후퇴] (a) retreat; (a) withdrawal; retirement; falling back; backdown. ¶총~ a full [general] retreat // ~ 중인 적군 retreating enemy troops // ~ 중이다 be in retreat / be on the run // ~ 나팔을 불다 sound the retreat [retire] // 예정된 ~을 하다 make a prearranged withdrawal [retreat] / retreat as prearranged // ~을 엄호하다 cover a retreating army / protect the retreat // 군대의 ~은 정연하게 이루어졌다 The army retreated in orderly fashion. **퇴각하다** retreat (from / to); beat [make] a retreat; withdraw; retire; fall back; give ground. ¶서둘러 beat a hasty retreat // 무사히 ~ make good one's retreat // 전 전선에서 ~ retreat along the whole line // 질서 있게 [무질서하게] ~ retreat in good order [in disorder].
2 [거절] rejection; refusal to accept. **퇴각하다** reject; refuse to accept.
●**퇴각군** an army in retreat; a retreating army. **퇴각로** a route of retreat; a withdrawal route. ¶~를 차단하다 cut off [intercept] a retreat. **퇴각 명령** an order to retreat; the retire.

퇴거(退去) [이전] leaving; quitting; removal; [명도·철수] evacuation; withdrawal; eviction; dispossession; [추방] deportation; [도망] an exodus (from a country) (다수의). ¶~를 명하다 order to leave (a place / a house) / order (a person) out of a place [to quit a place] // 세든 사람에게 ~를 요구하다 give a tenant a notice to quit [move]. **퇴거하다** leave; quit; depart; evacuate; withdraw [go away] (from a place); vacate (a house); remove; move out. ¶불법 입주자는 ~하라는 명령을 받았다 The illegal tenants [The squatters] were ordered to leave the building. // 그들은 대학 구내에서 퇴거하라는 명령을 받았다 They were ordered off the campus. ➔¶**퇴거시키다** cause (a person) to withdraw (from) // 수비대를 진지로부터 퇴거시키다 evacuate a garrison from a post.
●**퇴거 명령** an order for departure; a deportation order; an expulsion order; an eviction [evacuation] order. ¶~을 받다 be ordered to quit (a place) // 폭발 위험 때문에 주민들은 ~을 받았다 The residents were ordered to evacuate (the area) because of the danger of an explosion. **퇴거 신고** a removal report.

퇴고(推敲) polish; elaboration. ¶~의 여지가 있다 admit of further polish [elaboration] // ~에 ~를 거듭하다 work [do] (one's composition) over again and again / spend much time [be very scrupulous] in the choice of diction // 그는 그 논문의 ~를 거듭했다 He worked hard to polish his theses. **퇴고하다** polish; elaborate (on); improve. ¶퇴고한 글 an elaborate style // 그는 자기의 작품을 많은 시간을 들여서 퇴고했다 He spent a great deal of time improving [revising] his composition.

퇴골(腿骨) a leg bone. ⇨다리뼈(⇨다리)

퇴교(退校) leaving school (before graduation); expulsion from school. ⇨퇴학

퇴근(退勤) leaving one's office [work]. ¶~길에 on one's way back [home] from the office. **퇴근하다** leave the office; come [go] home from work; finish one's daily work and leave (the office). ¶공장에서는 몇 시에 퇴근하느냐 When is quitting time at your factory? // 그는 5시에 퇴근했다 He left the office at five.
●**퇴근 시간** the closing hour.

퇴기(退妓) a retired gisaeng; an ex-gisaeng.

퇴락(頹落) dilapidation; ruin. **퇴락하다** dilapidate; go [fall] to ruin; fall [go] into decay [dilapidate]; collapse. ¶퇴락한 가옥 a dilapidated house / a house in decay.

퇴로(退路) the path of retreat; the retreat; a withdrawal route. ¶~를 차단하다 [끊다] intercept [cut off] the [a person's] retreat / block the way of retreat / cut the line of retreat.

퇴물(退物) 1 [물려받은 물건] a hand-me-down(의류 등); articles handed down (from one's elder brother); [쓰던 물건] a used [secondhand] article. 2 [거절된 물건] a thing [an article] rejected [refused / declined] to accept; an article sent back. 3 [물러난 사람] a retired person (from one's occupation). ¶~ 배우 an ex-film star / a failed actor.

퇴박맞다(退一) [물리침을 받다] be rejected [repelled / rebuffed / refused]; get rejected; be sent back; be turned down; meet with a refusal [repulse]. ¶면허 신청이 ~ an application for a license is turned down // 선물을 주려다가 ~ get one's present rejected to accept // 면회 신청이 ~ one's request for an interview is refused.

퇴박하다(退一) [물리치다] refuse (a bribe / a gift); reject; repel; repulse; rebuff; turn down; decline (an invitation); (미) throw (a person) down; tell [beg] off.

퇴보(退步) retrogression; retrocession; a return; a step backward; a backward step; [퇴화] degeneration; deterioration. ¶문명의 ~ the retrogression of civilization / a backward step [movement] in civilization. **퇴**

하다 go [move / fall] backward; suffer a relapse; retrograde; retrocede; take a backward step; retrogress (to); degenerate; deteriorate. ¶퇴보한 국민 a degenerate people // 계산 능력은 나이와 함께 퇴보했다 My computation(al) ability has deteriorated [declined] with age.

퇴비(堆肥) compost. ⇨ ="두엄 ¶~ 더미 a compost pile [heap] / a manure heap // 땅에 ~를 주다 manure [compost] the land // ~를 만들다 compost (grass).

퇴사(退社) 1 [회사를 그만둠] retirement [withdrawal] from a company [firm]; [법] termination of membership. **퇴사하다** retire [withdraw] from a company; leave a company. ¶그는 일신상의 이유로 퇴사했다 He resigned for personal reasons. 2 leaving one's office. ⇨ "퇴근

퇴색(退色·褪色) fading (of color); discoloration. **퇴색하다** (색이) go [come] off; fade (away); (사물이) grow dull in color; lose color; discolor; be discolored. ¶퇴색하기 쉬운 색깔 a fugitive [fading] color // 퇴색하지 않는 푸른색 fadeproof blue // 퇴색하지 않도록 물들이다 dye in grain // 이 색은 빨아도 퇴색하지 않는다 This color will stand wash.

퇴석(堆石) 1 [쌓여진 돌] a pile of stones. 2 [지] a moraine. ¶측(側)[중(中) / 종(終)]~ a lateral [medial / terminal] moraine.

퇴속(頹俗) corrupt customs; degenerate morals; decadence.

퇴송하다(退送-) send back; reject; decline [refuse] to accept.

퇴역(退役) retirement (from service). **퇴역하다** retire (from service); leave office [the army]; go out of commission; be discharged from military service. ¶퇴역한 retired / out of commission // 아버지는 60세에 퇴역했다 My father retired from the service at the age of sixty. ➔ ¶퇴역시키다 decommission / put [place] (an officer) on the retired list / mothball (a ship) / place (a ship) out of commission.

● **퇴역 군인** an ex-service man; (미) a veteran. **퇴역 장교** a retired officer.

퇴영(退嬰) conservatism; retrogression. ¶~적 [보수적] conservative / [진취적 기상이 없는] unenterprising / retiring (disposition). **퇴영하다** retrograde; retrogress.

퇴원(退院) leaving (the) hospital; (감화원에서의) discharge from a reformatory. ¶~을 명하다 order (a patient) out of (the) hospital // ~을 허락받다 be given permission to leave (the) hospital / be allowed to go home // 그 환자는 내달 말까지 ~ 허가가 나오지 않을 것이다 The patient will not be discharged [released] from (the) hospital until the end of this month. (▶ 병원의 건물을 뜻하지 않는 경우, 영국에서는 hospital에 the를 붙이지 않음) **퇴원하다** leave (the) hospital; be discharged [released] from (the) hospital. ¶퇴원해도 좋다 [퇴원하기에는 빠르다] be [be not] well enough to leave (the) hospital // 그는 어제 퇴원했다 He left [got out of] (the) hospital yesterday.

● **퇴원 환자** a discharged patient.

퇴위(退位) (an) abdication. **퇴위하다** abdicate (the throne [crown]); step down from the throne (in favor of one's son). ¶황제는 퇴위했다 The emperor abdicated [gave up] the throne. ➔ ¶퇴위시키다 depose / dethrone (a king).

퇴임(退任) retirement (from one's office). **퇴임하다** (정년으로) retire (from); (임기 도중에) resign (from). ¶임기 만료로 퇴임한 이사 the director retiring from office on account of his term of office.

퇴장(退場) 1 (회의·식·경기장 등에서의) leaving. ¶선수는 ~ 명령을 받았다 The player was thrown out of the game. **퇴장하다** leave (the hall); go away. ¶전원 퇴장할 때까지 until everyone leaves.

2 (무대에서) exit(한 사람); exeunt(두 사람 이상의). ¶햄릿 ~ (극본의 지시) Exit Hamlet (▶ exit를 주어 앞에 놓아 3인칭 단수 현재에서도 s를 붙이지 않음. 주어가 복수인 경우는 exeunt로 됨). **퇴장하다** make one's exit; leave the scene. ¶주연 여배우는 얌전히 퇴장했다 The leading actress made a graceful exit.

3 (회의장에서) a walkout. ¶총~ a general walkout // ~을 명하다 order (a person) out of the room [hall] / order (a person) out / order (a person) to retire from the room. **퇴장하다** walk out of the chamber; walk out on the debate. ¶대표단은 퇴장하기로 결정했다 The delegation decided to walk out of the meeting. ➔ ¶퇴장당하다 be banished from / be ordered away from the hall // (재판의) 방청인을 퇴장시키다 send the gallery out of court.

퇴적(堆積) accumulation; a pile; a heap; [지] sedimentation. ¶하안(河岸) ~층 a river drift // 화물의 ~ accumulation of freight. **퇴적하다** pile [build] up; accumulate. ¶그들은 도로에 퇴적한 진흙더미를 치웠다 They cleared the streets of the (heaps of) mud. / They removed the mud which had accumulated on the roads. // 방대한 자료가 퇴적해 있었다 A huge amount of data had accumulated [had piled up]. / (구어) There were heaps of materials.

● **퇴적물** sediment; a deposit. **퇴적암** a sedimentary rock.

퇴정(退廷) leaving the court. ¶재판관은 그에게 ~을 명령했다 The judge ordered him to leave the courtroom. **퇴정하다** leave (the) court; withdraw from the court.

퇴조(退潮) 1 an ebb tide. ⇨ 썰물 2 [쇠퇴] the ebb [low] tide; the ebbing [falling] tide; low water; reflux. ¶사운(社運)은 ~의 조짐을 보이고 있다 The company's fortunes are beginning to ebb [are on the wane]. **퇴조하다** ebb. ¶경기는 퇴조하고 있다 Business is on the ebb.

● **퇴조기** a period of ebb.

퇴주(退酒) wine that has been used in a ritual libation.

● **퇴주잔** a cup containing used libation wine.

퇴직(退職) retirement (from office); resignation. **퇴직하다** retire [withdraw] from office [public service]; be relieved of office; go out of office; go on the retired list; retire from [leave] the service; resign an office. ¶그는 연금을 받고 퇴직했다 He retired on a pension. // 그는 일신상의 이유로 퇴직했다 He quit [resigned from] his job for personal reasons. // 그는 정년으로 퇴직했다 He had to quit his post on reaching (the) retirement

퇴진 age. →¶퇴직시키다 place (a person) on the retired list / retire (a person) // 연금을 주어 퇴직시키다 pension off (a person).

● **퇴직금** a retirement allowance; retirement pay[benefits]; (해고 수당) a discharge allowance. ¶일시 ~ lump sum retirement payment / a retirement lump sum grant. **퇴직 연령** retirement age. **퇴직자** a retired employee.

퇴진(退陣) decampment; [비유] retirement. ¶내각의 ~을 요구하다 ask the cabinet to resign en bloc // 그들은 수상의 ~을 요구했다 They demanded the resignation of the Prime Minister. **퇴진하다** decamp; withdraw; [비유] retire (from a position); step down; resign; exit; go out; disengage oneself (from). ¶아군은 부득이 퇴진했다 Our army had to retreat. // 그는 지금 제일선에서 퇴진하고 있다 He is now relieved of a responsible position. // 그는 곧 퇴진한다 He is on the way out.

퇴짜 [거절] rejection; refusal; a setdown; a turndown; a rebuff; a reject; [거절된 물건] a reject; a rejected article; a throw-out.

퇴짜(를) 놓다 refuse (to accept); reject; repel; repulse; snub; turn down; (구혼자에게) give (a suitor) the mitten; reject (a suitor). →¶조악품을 ~ reject[weed out] inferior articles // 그는 그녀를 매정스럽게 퇴짜 놓았다 He repelled her with his harshness.

퇴짜(를) 맞다 be rejected; be turned down; suffer[meet with] a rebuff[refusal / repulse]; get snubbed; (구혼자가) get the mitten; be kicked. ¶퇴짜 맞은 사내 a rejected lover[suitor] // 우리 제의는 퇴짜를 맞았다 Our offer was flatly rejected. // 그는 시험에서 퇴짜 맞았다 He was eliminated through an examination. // 그는 여자 친구로부터 퇴짜를 맞아 기가 죽어 있다 He is dejected because he was jilted[(구어) dumped / (구어) ditched] by his girlfriend.

퇴청하다(退廳-) leave the office.
퇴출하다(退出-) leave; withdraw.
퇴치(退治) 1 [정복] subjugation; subdual; conquest; suppression. **퇴치하다** subdue; subjugate; suppress. ¶괴물을 ~ slay[kill] a monster // 해적을 ~ clear the sea of pirates // 마귀를 퇴치하러 가다 go on an expedition against fiends.
2 [박멸] extirpation; eradication; elimination; extermination; control; destruction. **퇴치하다** wipe[stamp / root] out; clean up; extirpate; eradicate; eliminate; get rid of; destroy; control; fight; combat. ¶말라리아를 ~ eliminate[stamp out] malaria // 이를 ~ delouse // 그들은 쥐를 퇴치했다 They exterminated[got rid of] the rats. (▶ exterminate 는 모두 죽임, get rid of 는 그곳에서 없어지게 함)
3 [비유] crusade. ¶문맹 ~ a crusade against illiteracy. **퇴치하다** launch a campaign against. ¶질병과 가난을 뿌리째 ~ root[wipe] out disease and poverty. →¶빈곤은 퇴치되어야 한다 Poverty must go.

퇴침(退枕) a wooden pillow with drawers; a box pillow. ¶~을 베고 자다 sleep with one's head on a box pillow.

퇴폐(頹廢) (도덕·기풍 등의) corruption; degeneration; demoralization; decay; decline; deterioration; dry rot. **퇴폐하다** be corrupted; be demoralized; be degenerated; decay; fall into decay; decline. ¶퇴폐한 세상 the decadent world / the decadence[degeneration] of the age // 도의가 퇴폐하고 있다 Moral standards are collapsing. / Corruption[Degeneracy] is rampant.

● **퇴폐 문학** decadent literature. **퇴폐주의** decadence; decadentism. **퇴폐풍조** decadent (and degenerating) trend.

퇴폐적(頹廢的) decadent; declining; degeneration. ¶~인 영화 a decadent film.

퇴학(退學) 1 (학생 스스로의) leaving school (before graduation); (a) withdrawal. ¶개인 사고[권유]에 의한 ~ leaving school for personal reasons [at the request of the principal]. **퇴학하다** leave[give up] school [college]; withdraw from school[college]. ¶중도 ~ leave school halfway / leave (university) before graduation / drop out (of school) // 가정 형편으로 ~ leave school for family reasons [owing to family circumstances] // 낙제하여 ~ flunk out of (a university) // 그녀는 건강상의 이유로 퇴학했다 She left[quit] school for health reasons.
2 (학교 당국의 벌로서의) expulsion from school. **퇴학하다** dismiss[expel] (a student). →¶그는 퇴학당했다 He was expelled from school. / He was expelled[(영) sent down] from (the) university.

● **퇴학생** a dropout; an expelled student. ¶중도 ~ a school dropout.

퇴행(退行) 1 [역행] regression. 2 [기관 등의 퇴화] retrogression; (정신적인) regression. **퇴행하다** retrograde; regress.

퇴화(退化) [쇠퇴하여 축소됨] degeneration; [퇴행] retrogression; (기관·조직의) atrophy. ¶~적 degenerative / retrogressive. **퇴화하다** degenerate; degrade; retrograde; atrophy; become atrophied(기관 등이). ¶퇴화하여 잡초가 되다 degenerate into weeds // 그 기관은 사용하지 않아 퇴화했다 That organ has degenerated[atrophied] because of disuse. →¶퇴화시키다 degrade / degenerate // 교배에 의하여 퇴화시키다 breed (wild qualities) out of (dogs).

● **퇴화 기관** [생] a rudiment; a rudimentary organ. **퇴화 동물** a degenerate. **퇴화 작용** the process of degeneration.

툇마루(退-) a veranda(h); a narrow porch; a stoop. ¶~에서 햇볕을 쬐자 Let's bask in the sun on the porch[veranda(h)].

투(套) 1 [버릇] a manner; a way; a fashion; a habit. ¶말~ one's way[manner] of talking / the way one talks / a turn of words // 이런 ~로 in this way[manner] like this. 2 [법식] a form; a style. ¶편지 ~ the forms of letter writing // 옛 ~ an old style / a conventional form // K 씨 ~의 소설 a novel written in the style of Mr. K.

투견(鬪犬) [개싸움] a dogfight; [싸움용 개] a fighting dog. ¶~시키다 fight dogs.
투계(鬪鷄) 1 cockfighting. ⇨ 닭싸움 2 [싸움닭] a fighting cock; a game cock[fowl].
● **투계장** a cockpit.
투고(投稿) (a) contribution. ¶~ 환영 All contributions (are) welcome. / Open to all contributors. **투고하다** contribute ((an article) to a periodical); write (for a magazine). ¶나는 문예지에 매월 시조를 투고하고 있습니다 Every month I contribute a *sijo* to a literary magazine. // 이 소녀는 이 잡지에 자주 투고하

고 있다 This girl is a regular [frequent] contributor to this magazine.
- **투고란** a readers' [contributors'] column; a letter-to-the-editor column.

투과(透過) transmission; permeation. **투과하다** (빛 등이) penetrate; transmit; (액체 등이) permeate. ¶방사능은 철판도 투과한다 Radioactivity can even penetrate an iron plate.// 이 흙은 물이 투과하기 쉽다 Water easily passes through [permeates] this soil.
- **투과성** permeability. **투과율** transmissivity.

투광기(投光器) a floodlight.

투구 a helmet; a headpiece. ¶~를 쓰다 wear a helmet // ~를 벗다 take off one's helmet.

투구(投球) throwing a ball; a throw; a toss; [야구] pitching; a pitch; hurling; (공) a pitched ball. ¶왼손 ~ left-handed pitching // 멋진 ~ fine delivery / neat pitching //속임수 ~를 하다 try to fool the batter with a bad pitch // 저 소년은 ~를 잘한다 That boy pitches very well. / (폼이) That boy has a fine delivery. **투구하다** pitch; hurl; deliver; bowl; make a throw [toss] (to third). ¶계속 ~ continue to pitch // 그는 2일간 계속 투구했다 He took the mound for two days running. →¶감독은 투수에게 계속 투구시킬 작정이다 The manager's going to leave the pitcher in.
- **투구 동작** a windup. ¶투수는 ~에 들어갔다 The pitcher wound up to throw. / The pitcher went into his delivery.

투기(投棄) [내던져 버림] abandonment. **투기하다** abandon; give up; throw [cast] away.

투기(投機) (a) speculation; (구어) (a) spec; a venture; an adventure; an operation; gambling; chances; (증권) stockjobbery; stockjobbing. ¶돈벌이가 되는 ~ a profitable venture // 부동산 ~ speculation in real estate // 빚나간 ~ (구어) a bad spec //~로 떼돈을 벌다 make a killing in speculation // ~에 손을 대다 dabble [engage] in speculation / play the market / speculate //~로 빈털터리가 되다 beggar oneself by speculation / 위험한 ~를 하다 play a dangerous game / play for high stakes / speculate (on) //주식 ~를 하다 speculate in stocks //아버지는 ~에 손대어 큰 손해를 보았다 My father went in for [tried speculation] and lost heavily. / My father lost heavily through speculating. // 나는 증권 ~를 한번 해 보았다 I tried my hand at playing the stock market. / I ventured into a bit of speculation in stocks. //그는 ~에서 한몫 잡았다 He was lucky on the stock market. / He made a fortune through speculation. **투기하다** speculate in (stocks); deal in futures; engage in speculation; make a venture; gamble (in stocks).
- **투기꾼 / 투기업자** a (professional) speculator; a stockjobber. **투기사업** a speculative enterprise [business / venture]. **투기 시장** a speculative market. **투기심** a speculative spirit [disposition]; a gambling spirit; [기업심] enterprise. ¶~을 일으키다 be tempted to speculate. **투기열** a craze [mania] for speculation; speculative enthusiasm [craze].

투기(妬忌) unreasonable [burning / intense] jealousy.

투기(鬪技) a competition; a contest; a match. ¶~에 이기다[지다] win [lose] a game.

- **투기장** an arena; a ring.

투덕거리다 keep patting [tapping / knocking / rapping / beating].

투덕투덕하다 plump; plump-cheeked; fat and well-looking.

투덜거리다 [불평하다] complain; [혼잣말처럼 투런거리다] grumble; mutter; murmur(알아듣지 못할 만큼 작은 소리로); (미국 속어) gripe. ¶투덜거리는 사람 a grumbler // 그는 봉급이 적다고 투덜거렸다 He grumbled at his low salary. // 그는 마누라에게 음식을 가지고 투덜거렸다 He complained [grumbled] to his wife about the meals. // 집주인들은 집세를 올려야 한다고 투덜거리고 있다 The tenants are complaining obstinately against the raising of the rent. // 언제까지 투덜거리고만 있을 테냐 Haven't you done enough grumbling?// 그는 항상 무엇이가 투덜거리고 있다 He is always complaining [grumbling] about something. // 이제 와서 실수했다고 투덜거려 봐야 소용없다 It is no good lamenting [moaning about] my blunder now. / (구어) There's no use my crying over spilt milk. // 그는 비난하는 투로 나를 보고 무언가 투덜거렸다 He gave me a reproachful look and muttered something. // 투덜거리지 마라 Don't grumble! / (미) None of your gripes.

투망(投網) a cast(ing) net; a fishing net. ¶~을 던지다 cast a (fishing) net / throw a cast net. **투망하다** cast [throw] a net.

투매(投賣) (손해를 무릅쓰는) a sacrifice sale; [덤핑] dumping; (재고 일소의) a clearance sale. ¶출혈 ~ a distress [slaughter] sale. **투매하다** sell at a loss [sacrifice]; dump.
- **투매 상품** distress merchandise; goods sold at a sacrifice.

투명(透明) transparency; pellucidity; limpidness; clearness; clarity. ¶반~인 translucent / semitransparent / translucid. **투명하다** transparent; limpid; pellucid; lucid; diaphanous; clear (as crystal); crystalline. ¶투명한 유리 transparent glass // 투명한 물 clear water // 무색투명한 colorless and transparent // 불투명한 opaque // 투명해지다 become transparent / clarify.
- **투명도** (the degree of) transparency. ¶이 호수의 ~는 30미터이다 The water in this lake is transparent to a depth of thirty meters.

투묘(投錨) anchoring; anchorage. **투묘하다** anchor; cast anchor. ¶배는 서둘러 투묘했다 The boat was anchored hurriedly. // 배는 항구에 투묘해 있었다 The ship was [lay] at anchor in the harbor.

투미하다 [어리석고 둔하다] dull; sluggish; stupid; thickheaded; dull-witted. ¶투미한 남자 a boorish man / a boor / a blockhead / a dull [stupid] fellow // 이미 알고 있는 것을 묻다니 너도 참 투미하구나 It is very stupid of you to ask about something you already know.

투박스럽다 unshapely; unrefined. ⇨=**투박하다** ¶투박스러운 사내 a lout / a rustic / a churl / a boor / a backwoodsman / a bumpkin.

투박하다 (물건이) unshapely; shapeless; ill-formed; ill-shaped; unsightly; coarse; rough; gross; crude; (사람이) unrefined; rustic; boorish; uncouth; awkward; stiff; senseless. ¶투박한 손 rough hands / stubby hands // 투

투베르쿨린 [의] tuberculin.
● **투베르쿨린 검사** (take) a tuberculin test. ¶~ 결과 양성[음성]이었다 The tuberculin test turned out to be positive[negative]. **투베르쿨린 반응** a tuberculin reaction.

투병(鬪病) one's struggle against disease [illness]. **투병하다** struggle against disease.
● **투병 생활** one's life under medical treatment. ¶만 2년의 ~ 끝에 직장에 복귀했다 After two whole years of struggle against [fighting] my illness, I was able to return to work.

투사(投射) 1 [심] projection. **투사하다** project. 2 [물] incidence. ⇨[입사(入射)]
● **투사각** an angle of incidence. ⇨[입사각(⇨입사(入射)) **투사면** a plane of incidence. **투사물** a projectile.

투사(透寫) tracing. **투사하다** trace (out) (a writing / drawing). ¶형지[型紙][도면]를 ~ trace (out) a pattern [a drawing].
● **투사지** tracing paper.

투사(鬪士) a fighter; a combatant; a champion; (미국 속어) a bearcat. ¶독립~ a leader of national independence movement // 혁명 ~ a champion of revolution // 자유의 ~ a fighter for [champion of] freedom // 여성 해방의 ~ a champion of women's liberation // 여성 참정권 운동의 ~ a militant suffragette / 민주화 운동의 ~ a fighter for democratization.

투서(投書) a hate letter[mail]; (익명의) an anonymous notice [communication / letter]. **투서하다** write a hate letter to. ¶경찰에 투서하여 알리다 inform the police (of a crime) by sending an anonymous letter.
● **투서함** a complaints [suggestion] box.

투석(投石) stone-throwing [-hurling]. **투석하다** cast [throw / hurl] a stone [rock] (at); stone (at). ¶기동대에 투석했다 We threw [hurled] stones at the riot squad.
● **투석전** a fight with stone missiles.

투석(透析) [화] dialysis. ¶인공 ~ artificial dialysis. **투석하다** dialyze.
● **투석기** a dialyzer; (영) dialyser.

-투성이 [뒤덮여 있음] covered with ...; [묻거나 배어 있음] daubed [soiled / stained / smeared] with ...; [가득함] full of ...; filled with .... ¶피~의 bloodstained / bloody / gory // 기름~의 oil-stained / oily / grease-stained / greasy // 오식~의 책 a book full of misprints // 땀~다 be all of[in] a sweat // 기름~다 be stained [smeared] all over with grease [oil] // 이 작문은 잘못~다 This composition is full of mistakes. // 그는 온몸이 상처~였다 He was wounded all over. // 나는 빚~다 I am deep in debt. // 그의 입 언저리는 피~였다 His mouth was smeared with blood. // 그 소년은 진흙~가 되어 집으로 왔다 The boy came home covered with mud. // 거리는 쓰레기~였다 The street was littered with trash. // 나는 먼지[진흙]~가 되었다 I got covered with dust[mud] all over. // 그 여자의 이야기는 모두 거짓말~였다 Her whole story was a tissue of lies.

투수(投手) [야구] a pitcher; a hurler; (구어) a twirler; a moundsman; (미국 속어) a heaver. ¶선발[구원] ~ a starting [relief] pitcher // 주전 ~ an ace pitcher // 완투 ~ a pitcher who pitches a complete game // 승리 [패전] ~ a winning [losing] pitcher // 좌완 ~ a southpaw / a lefthand(ed) pitcher / a lefthander // 속구 ~ a speedball pitcher // ~를 바꾸다 [교체하다] change the pitcher // (난타하여) ~를 지치게 만들다 belabor the pitcher // 첫 시합의 ~는 손철수였다 Son Cheolsu pitched [took the mound] in the first game.
● **투수력** pitching strength (of a team). **투수전** pitchers' battle; a pitching duel. **투수진** the pitching staff; the hill staff. **투수판** a pitcher's plate [box]; the mound; (미국 속어) the rubber.

투숙객(投宿客) a guest (registered at hotel); a lodger.

투숙하다(投宿-) put up at (a hotel); lodge in (a hotel); check into (a hotel); register [be a guest] at (a hotel). ¶함께 ~ stay at the same hotel / lodge in the same inn (with another) / (한방의) share a room (with).

투시(透視) 1 [비치어 봄] seeing through. **투시하다** see through. 2 (X선의) fluoroscopy; roentgenoscopy; examination by fluoroscopy. **투시하다** examine by fluoroscopy; look at (a person's chest) through the fluoroscope. 3 [꿰뚫어 봄] clairvoyance; second sight. **투시하다** divine; see through. ¶저 점쟁이는 정말로 미래를 투시할 능력이 있는 모양이다 That fortuneteller is said to be a real clairvoyant.
● **투시도** a perspective drawing [view]; an opened-up view (of a factory) showing the interior. **투시 도법** [미] perspective (representation). **투시력** clairvoyant powers; clairvoyance.

투신(投身) 1 [몸을 던짐]. **투신하다** drown [die by drowning] oneself (in the water); throw oneself into the water [river]; commit suicide by drowning; precipitate oneself into the water; kill oneself by plunging (from); plunge to death. ¶투신한 시체를 건져 올리다 pull a body from a watery grave // 그는 근처의 강에 투신하였다 He drowned himself in a nearby river.
2 [종사]. **투신하다** go into; launch [plunge] into; enter upon; embark [launch out] on (an enterprise); start out to (do something); concern oneself in; be concerned in [with]; have a hand [finger] in. ¶실업계에 ~ go into [engage in] business / enter upon a business career // 영화계에 ~ go into the movies / find one's way into filmdom // 정계에 ~ enter upon a political career / go [launch] into politics / make one's debut on the political stage // 사회 개혁에 ~ start out to reform the society.
● **투신자살** a death leap (from); committing suicide by jumping (on the track) in front of a [an onrushing] train; suicide by drowning. ¶~을 하다 (물에) drown oneself (in a river) / commit suicide by drowning / (건물 등에서) leap [plunge] to one's death / kill oneself [commit suicide] by plunging (from) // 강에 ~을 하다 jump in the river to kill oneself // 그는 옥상에서 ~을 하였다 He committed suicide by jumping [leaping] from the roof of the building. / He jumped to his death from

a high building.

투실투실 plump. ⇨토실토실

투약(投藥) medication; (medical) prescription; dosage; exhibition; administration (of medicine). **투약하다** prescribe[administer / compound / give] a medicine[drug / dose]; medicate. ¶나는 환자에게 투약했다 I gave [administered] medicine to the patient.
● **투약구** a medicine window; a pharmacist office(약국).

투여(投與) [약을 줌] (a) dosage; medication. ¶이 약의 ~에는 주의를 요함 Administration of this medicine requires care. / This medicine must be administered carefully. // 비타민 C의 대량 ~가 이 병에는 효과가 있다 A high dosage of vitamin C is effective for this disease. **투여하다** give a medicine; medicate. ¶환자에게 약을 ~ give medication to a patient / [처방된] prescribe (a) medicine for a patient.

투영(投影) 1 [물체가 비치는 그림자] a cast shadow. **투영하다** reflect; cast a reflection; throw an image on. 2 [수] projection. **투영하다** project (an article).
● **투영도** [미] a projection (chart); a projected figure.

투옥(投獄) imprisonment; confinement; incarceration. ¶그는 ~을 모면하였다 He escaped imprisonment. **투옥하다** put a person in prison; cast[throw] a person into prison; imprison a person; (속어) run in; (속어) lag. →**투옥되다** be put in jail / be taken[sent] to jail / be flung into jail / be jailed / be put behind bars / be consigned to prison // 그는 억울한 죄로 투옥되었다 He was imprisoned[jailed / put in jail] on a false charge.

투우(鬪牛) (경기) a bullfight; bullfighting; (소) a fighting bull. **투우하다** have a bullfight; have bulls fight (each other); fight a bull.
● **투우사** a bullfighter; a matador; (말을 타고 하는) a toreador. **투우장** a bullring.

투원반(投圓盤) the discus throw. ⇨원반던지기(⊙원반)
● **투원반 선수** a discus thrower.

투입(投入) 1 [던져 넣음] throwing in; injection; (노력) (몸의) output. ¶우편물 ~구 a letter drop // (자동판매기 등의) 화폐 ~구 a slot. **투입하다** throw[cast] into; order (troops) in; commit to; [화] project (ion / on). ¶투표지를 투표함에 ~ deposit a ballot in the ballot box // 공격에 ~ throw (a battalion) into attack // 단계적으로 [서서히] ~ phase in (new machinery) for increased automation // 그 나라는 전쟁[전선]에 10만의 병력을 투입했다 The nation committed 100,000 men to that battle[the front]. 2 [경] [투자] investment; [기업이 매입하는 재화 또는 용역] input. **투입하다** invest [sink] (money) in (factory equipment). ¶공공 사업에 사재를 ~ expend private funds on a public enterprise // 회사는 많은 돈을 설비에 투입했다 The company invested[sank] a lot of money in plant and equipment. →¶터널 건설에 투입된 노력은 엄청나다 The work that has been put into[has gone into / building] the tunnel is immeasurable.
● **투입량** an input(자본재나 용역의). **투입 자본** an investment.

투자(投資) (an) investment. ¶거액 ~ a heavy investment // 공공 ~ public investment // 민간 ~ private investment // 사전 ~ preinvestment // 설비 ~ investment in plant and equipment / (plant and) equipment investment // 자본 ~ capital investment // 주식 ~ investment in stocks / stock speculation // 총 ~ gross investment // 해외 ~ overseas investment // 확실한[유리한] ~(물) a sound [good] investment // ~에서 얻은 이자 an interest from investments // 위험한 ~를 하다 make a risky investment. **투자하다** invest in; make an investment in; lay[put] out (one's money) in; (현지이 또는 회수 곤란한 사업에) sink (money / a capital) in. ¶토지에 ~ invest (one's money) in land / put one's money into land // 있는 돈을 가장 유리하게 ~ (이익을) 다시 그 사업에 ~ plow back (the profits) into enterprise // 나는 신규 사업에 거액을 투자했다 I invested heavily in the new project. // 가지고 있는 돈을 가장 유리하게 투자하려면 어떤 방법이 제일 좋을까요 What would be the best way to lay out my money to do the most work for me? // 아버지는 전 재산을 그 사업에 투자했다 My father invested [put] all his fortune in the project.
● **투자가** an investor. ¶기관[개인] ~ an institutional[individual] investor // 일반 ~ the investing public / general investors. **투자 신탁** (an) investment trust. ¶~에 돈을 맡기다 have one's money trusted with an investment company. **투자액** an amount invested. **투자 유인** an investment incentive. **투자 은행** an investment bank. **투자 자본** invested capital. **투자 회사** an investment company.

투쟁(鬪爭) [다툼·싸움] a fight; (문어) strife; a struggle (for a thing / with a person); (권리를 찾기 위한) a struggle; a fight. ¶계급 ~ class struggle[strife / war] // 권력 ~ power struggle / struggle for power // 무력 ~ a armed struggle // 임금 인상 ~ a fight for higher wages // 준법 ~ work-to-rule strike tactics / a slowdown strike // ~적인 combative // 주부들은 소비세 반대 ~에 나섰다 The housewives roses in opposition to the excise tax. **투쟁하다** fight; combat; struggle.
● **투쟁심** a combative spirit. **투쟁 의식** strife consciousness.

투전(鬪牋) [노름 제구] Korean playing cards; (놀이) a game of cards; (노름) gambling. ¶~ 한 벌 a pack[(미) deck] of cards. **투전하다** play cards; gamble.
● **투전꾼** a cardplayer; a gambler.

투정 complaining; grumbling; growling. ¶밥 ~ grumbling over one's food // 잠 ~ grouchiness in the morning // 아이들은 이가 날 때면 ~을 한다 Children are fretful when cutting their teeth. **투정하다** grumble (at / over); complain (about / of); growl. ¶돈 달라고 ~ importune (one's father) for money // 과자를 사 달라고 ~ clamor for candy // 투정하는 아이를 달래다 soothe a fretful child.

투지(鬪志) a combative[fighting] spirit; fight. ¶~가 없다 be gritless / have cold feet // ~를 보이다 show fight // ~를 잃다 lose fight // 나는 완전히 ~를 잃었다 I have lost all my fighting spirit. / There is no fight left in me. // 그 소식을 듣고 우리는 ~를 잃고 말았다 Hearing it, we lost our fighting spirit. / The news took the edge off our excitement about

투지만만하다 [enthusiasm for] the game. // 지금이야말로 ~를 보여 줄 때다 Now is the time for you to show fight.

투지만만하다(鬪志滿滿-) burn with combativeness; be highly combative; be full of fight; have plenty of fight (in one). ¶나는 ~ I have plenty of fight in me. / I am full of fight. // 그도 젊었을 때는 투지만만했다 He was much of a fighter in his younger day.

투창(投槍) [체] the javelin (throw). ⇨ "창던지기
● **투창 선수** a javelin thwrower. ⇨ 창던지기(⇨ 투창수)

투척(投擲) a throw; throwing. **투척하다** throw. ¶수류탄을 ~ throw a hand grenade.
● **투척 경기** the distance throw; a throwing event.

투철하다(透徹-) clear; limpid; lucid; pure; thorough; thoroughgoing. ¶투철한 민족주의자 a nationalist to the bone // 투철한 두뇌 clear brains / a clear head // 투철한 책임감을 지닌 사람 a person with a thoroughgoing sense of responsibility // 전문가 기질이 ~ act like a professional / be a thoroughgoing professional. **투철히** through and through; out and out; throughout; thoroughly; (up) to the hilt; to the core.

투포환(投砲丸) the shot put. ⇨ "포환던지기(⇨ 포환)

투표(投票) [표결] vote; suffrage; [투표하기] poll; ballot; voting; balloting. ¶결선 ~ a final[decisive] ballot / a show-down vote / a runoff ballot / 결정 ~ a casting vote / 국민 ~ a plebiscite / the referendum (pl. ~s, -da) // 기립 ~ a rising[standing] vote // 기명 ~ an open vote / a signed ballot // 단기(單記) [연기(連記)] ~ a vote with single [plural] entry / 대리 ~ voting by proxy // 무기명 [비밀] ~ a secret vote / an unsigned vote // 복식 [단식] ~ plural [single] vote // 부재자 ~ absentee voting // 부정 ~ an illegal [unjust] ballot // 불신임 ~ a vote of nonconfidence / a nonconfidence vote // 신임 ~ a vote of confidence // 일반 ~ a referendum / a popular vote // 지명 ~ a roll-call vote // 직접 ~ (put it to) a direct (popular) vote / (elected by) direct vote of the people // ~의 마감 closing of the poll [vote] // 무~로 without vote [voting] // ~의 재실시를 요구하다 demand a new ballot [a fresh vote] // ~에 부치다 put (the question / a bill) to the [a] vote / put (a proposition) on the ballot // ~에 이기다 beat (another) at the poll / outvote (another) / win a ballot // ~에서 지다 be outvoted // ~로써 결정하다 determine [decide / settle] by ballot [vote / poll] // ~로 선출하다 elect by vote / vote by ballot // ~를 실시하다 take [hold] a ballot / take a vote (for …) // …에 찬성 ~를 하다 vote for [in favor of] … / ballot for … // …에 반대 ~를 하다 vote against [in opposition to] … / ballot against … // 다수의 ~를 얻다 poll [get] a majority of votes // 다수 [최다수]의 ~를 얻어 당선되다 be returned by [receiving] a majority of votes [at the head of the poll] // …의 ~를 요청하다 invite votes for … // ~를 마치다 close polls // 가수의 인기 ~를 하다 take a vote on who is the most popular singer // 그 문제는 ~에 부쳐야 한다 The question should be put to a vote. // ~ 결과는 찬성 20 반대 10표였다 The vote stood at twenty ayes and ten noes. // ~ 결과 250 대 200으로 법안은 가결되었다 The bill carried 250 votes [by a vote of 250] to 200. // 누구를 리더로 할 것인가는 ~로 결정합시다 Let's decide by a vote [vote on] who should be the leader. // 그들은 그 동의에 찬성 [반대] ~를 했다 They voted for [against] the motion. // 새 법안은 ~에서 부결되었다 The new bill was voted down. // 새 교황은 세 번째 [3차] ~로 선출되었다 A new pope was elected on the third ballot. **투표하다** ballot (for); cast a ballot; (미) vote; (미) cast a vote (for); poll. ¶민주당에 ~ vote Democratic / B 씨에게 ~ give one's vote [vote for] Mr. B // 투표하러 가다 go to the poll(s) // 나는 L씨에게 투표했다 I gave my vote to Mr. L. // 내일 투표하러 가십니까 Are you going to the polls [to vote] tomorrow? // 나는 혁신 후보자에게 투표할 작정이다 I intend to vote [cast my ballot] for the reform candidate.
● **투표구** a polling district. **투표권** the (right to) vote; the right of voting [casting the ballot]; suffrage; a voice; the voting power. ¶~을 행사하다 exercise one's voting power // ~을 박탈하다 deprive (a person) of the right to vote // ~을 주다 qualify (a person) as voter // ~을 잃다 lose one's vote // 나는 위원회에서 ~을 갖고 있지 않다 I am not a voting member of the committee. **투표소 / 투표장** a polling place; (미) the polls. **투표수** the number of votes. ¶그의 득표는 총~의 1할에도 미치지 않았다 He polled less than a tenth of the (total) votes cast. **투표용지** a ballot (paper); a voting card; a ticket. **투표율** a turnout (of voters). ¶높은 [낮은] ~ heavy [light] vote // 지사 선거의 ~은 높았다 There was a heavy [light] turnout (at the polls) for the gubernatorial election. **투표일** a voting day. **투표자** a voter. **투표 참관인** a voting witness; a referee of voting. **투표함** a ballot (box). ¶투표가 끝나면 ~은 봉인된다 After voting is over, the ballot box is sealed.

투피스 a (business) suit; a two-piece (suit). ¶갈색 ~를 입은 부인 a woman in a brown suit.

투하(投下) 1 [아래로 떨어뜨림] throwing down; dropping; an airdrop (of supplies). **투하하다** throw down; drop; (비행기에서) airdrop. ¶폭탄을 ~ drop a bomb // 의료품을 ~ (air)drop medical supplies // 비행기가 수도에 폭탄을 투하했다 The airplanes dropped bombs on [bombed] the capital. 2 [투자] investment. **투하하다** invest (in). ¶신제품 개발에 막대한 자본을 ~ invest a large amount of capital in the development of a new product.
● **투하 자본** invested capital; an investment; [경] investment [venture] capital.

투하(投荷) (짐) jetsam; jettisoned cargo; (행위) jettison. **투하하다** jettison cargo; cast [throw] cargo overboard.

투항(投降) surrender. ¶적에게 ~을 다그치다 urge [call on] the enemy to surrender. **투항하다** surrender (to the enemy); lay down one's arms.
● **투항자** a surrenderer.

투해머(投-) hammer throwing. ⇨ "해머던지기(⇨ 해머)

투혼(鬪魂) fighting [combative] spirit.

툭 protruding; with a pat; with a snap;

톡 sharply. ⇨>톡

톡톡 protruding in several places; with snaps; with pats. ⇨>톡톡

톡톡하다 thick; close; harsh; (a great) many. ⇨>톡톡하다

톡하면 (too) often; on[at] the slightest provocation; ready to; always. ¶~ …하다 be apt [liable / prone] to (do) / be inclined [disposed] (to do) / it (too) often happens that … 싸우다 pick a fight at the slightest provocation. ∥~ 울다 will cry over nothing ∥ 그는 ~ 조그만 일로 화를 낸다 He is likely to fly off the handle at the slightest provocation. ∥ 그녀는 ~ 죽겠다고 한다 She constantly talks of dying. ∥ 그는 ~ 나의 욕을 한다 Whenever he opens his mouth, he must say something against me.

툰드라 the tundra.
● **툰드라 지대** the tundra area.

툴툴거리다 grumble (at / over / about); mutter (about); complain (of). ¶대우가 나쁘다고 ~ complain of ill treatment / (봉급의 경우) complain about one's salary / complain that one is not paid well ∥ 그는 아버지에게 컴퓨터를 사 주지 않는다고 툴툴거렸다 He grumbled at his father for not buying him a computer.

툼벙 with a plop[splash].

툼벙거리다 keep splashing[ploping]; splash about; dabble.

퉁 (소리) with a boom; booming; ringing hollow. ¶가야금 줄을 ~ 울리는 소리 the twang of a *gayageum* string / 북을 ~ 울리다 boom a drum / beat a drum / 대포를 ~ 쏘다 fire a gun with a boom / boom a gun.

퉁겨지다 1 [불쑥 나오다] get disclosed; come to light; come out; be revealed. ¶비밀이 퉁겨졌다 The secret is disclosed. 2 [어긋나서 틀어지다] come apart; get dislocated; be disjointed. ¶실밥이 퉁겨졌다 The seam came apart. ∥ 책상다리가 퉁겨졌다 The leg of a table got disjointed. ∥ 뼈마디가 퉁겨졌다 The joint became dislocated.

퉁기다 1 [버틴 것을] loosen (it); take (it) apart; get (it) out of place. ¶기둥 받침을 ~ slip a pillar stay. 2 [악기 등을] pluck the strings (of a musical instrument with one's fingers); play with one's fingers. ¶만돌린을 퉁기는 소리 the tinkle of a mandoline ∥ 기타 줄을 ~ pick[thrum (on)] a guitar ∥ 악기의 현을 ~ strum the strings of an instrument. 3 [뼈 등을] put (it) out of joint; dislocate (one's knee joint). ¶어깨의 관절을 ~ put one's shoulder out. 4 [기회 등을] let (a chance) slip[missed]; let go (a chance); miss (an opportunity). ¶좋은 자리를 ~ miss a good position.

퉁명스럽다 blunt; brusque; gruff; snappish; curt; unaffable. ¶퉁명스러운 사나이 a gruff [short-spoken] man ∥ 퉁명스러운 대답 a curt[blunt] answer ∥ 퉁명스럽게 bluntly / snappishly / brusquely / curtly ∥ 퉁명스럽게 답하다 answer bluntly / give[make] a curt [blunt] answer ∥ 퉁명스럽게 말대답하다 give a surly[tart] reply / reply brusquely[snappishly] ∥ 퉁명스럽게 말하다 talk bluntly[shortly] / speak stiffly [brusquely / bluntly / curtly] ∥ 그녀는 말투가 하도 퉁명스러워서 언제나 화를 내고 있는 것처럼 들린다 She has such a curt[brusque] way of speaking that she always sounds angry.

퉁방울 a brass bell.

퉁방울눈 protruding[protubarant / bulging] eyes; goggle[pop / lobster] eyes; (사람) a lobster-eyed person.

퉁방울이 a lobster-eyed[goggle-eyed / pop-eyed] person; a person with protruding eyes.

퉁소 a *tungso*; a six-holed bamboo flute. ¶~를 불다 play (on) a *tungso*.

퉁탕 [두드리거나 발로 구르는 소리] beating; pounding; striking; stamping; [총소리] banging repeatedly; bang.

퉁탕거리다 1 [두드리거나 발로 구르는 소리를 내다] beat; pound; beat loudly. ¶마룻바닥을 퉁탕거리며 걷다 stamp along the floor ∥ 복도를 퉁탕거리며 걷다 walk along the passageway pit-a-pat[noisily] / bounce along the passageway ∥ 어린아이가 퉁탕거리며 마루 위를 뛰어다닌다 A child is scampering around on the floor. 2 (총소리가) keep banging away.

퉁퉁 pounding; chug-chug (of a motorboat). ⇨>퉁퉁[1,2] ¶눈이 ~ 붓다 one's eyes are all swollen[puffed up].

퉤 spitting. ¶~~ spit-spit!

튀각 fried kelp[tangle]; flakes of fried tangle.

튀기 1 [수나귀와 암소 사이에서 난 새끼] a hybrid between a male donkey and a cow. 2 a child of mixed racial origins. ⇨>혼혈아(⇨ 혼혈) 3 [동식물의 잡종] a hybrid.

튀기다[1] 1 (손가락으로) fillip; flip; snap; (주판알을) move[work] counters; (용수철 등을) spring out. ¶손가락으로 ~ flip (a thing) away with one's finger / (현악기의) 줄을 ~ touch the strings ∥ 고무줄을 탁 ~ snap (a person) with a rubber band. 2 (물 등을) splash; (be) spatter; dabble; (침을) spit; sputter. ¶온 방에 물을 ~ splash water all about / 책장에 잉크를 ~ splash a page with ink / splash ink on a page / 흙탕물을 ~ splash mud about[over / on] / (사람에게) splash (a person) with mud ∥ 남의 얼굴에 침을 ~ spit[sputter] in one's face ∥ 흙탕물을 튀기며 걷다 drabble along ∥ 우리는 물을 튀기며 물속을 걸었다 We splashed through the water. ∥ 자동차가 흙탕물을 내게 튀겼다 A car splashed me with mud. / A car splashed mud on me. ∥ 에이프런에 물이 튀겼다 Water splashed on my apron. / My apron was splashed with water. ∥ 급류가 바위 위로 튀기며 흐르고 있었다 The rapid current was splashing over the rocks. ∥ 그는 침을 튀기며 이야기를 계속했다 He talked on, with his spittle flying. ∥ 자동차는 흙탕물을 사방에 튀기며 내뺐다 A car sped away splashing the muddy water about. 3 [달아나 놓치다] send (a thing) flying[off]; let (a captive) escape[loose]; let (a person) off; (놀라게 하여) start; rouse; scare away. ¶토끼를 굴에서 ~ start a hare from its burrow.

튀기다[2] (기름에) fry (in a hot pan); frizzle; (곡식을 불에) pop. ¶기름을 많이 붓고 튀긴 야채 deep-fried vegetables ∥ 기름에 ~ fry[frizzle] in oil ∥ 쌀을[옥수수를] ~ pop rice[corn] ∥ 닭을 기름에 ~ fry a chicken (in oil) ∥ 기름을 많이 붓고 ~ deep-fry / fry in deep oil ∥ 새우[생선]를 ~ (deep-)fry shrimps[a fish] ∥ 새우가 바삭바삭하게 튀겨졌다 The shrimps were fried crisp. ∥ 새우가 다 튀겨지면 곧 먹기로 하

튀김 자 Let's start eating as soon as the shrimps are ready[fried].

튀김 [기름에 튀긴 음식] fried food; a fried dish; a fry fritters. ¶굴~ fried oysters // 생선[야채] ~ deep-fried fish[vegetables] // ~ 기름 frying oil.

튀다 1 (탄력이 있는 물건이) bound; rebound; bounce; spring. ¶(공이) 잘 ~ bound well // 덫이 ~ a trap springs // 튀어 오르게 하다 bounce (a ball) // 이 공은 잘 튄다 This ball bounces well. // 공이 튀지 않게 되었다 The ball has lost its bounce. // 그는 튀어 오른 공을 잡았다 He caught the ball on the bound. // 공은 1루 베이스를 맞고 높이 튀었다 The ball hit first base and bounced[bounded] high into the air.
2 (불똥이) spark; sparkle; sputter; (장작 등이 타면서) snap; crack; crackle; (볶는 것이) burst[crack] open; pop open. ¶불꽃이 ~ sparks fly[shoot up] // 불 속의 밤이 튀었다 The chestnuts popped in the fire. // 숯불에서 불꽃이 튀었다 Sparks flew from the charcoal fire. // 팝콘이 열을 받아 튀기 시작했다 The popcorn began to pop as it was heated. // 장작이 불에 타면서 탁탁 튄다 The firewood crackles as it burns.
3 (물·침 등이) splash; spatter; sputter; get spattered; splashed. ¶흙탕물이 튄 바지 bespattered[splashed] trousers // 옷에 흙탕물이 ~ have one's clothes spattered with mud // 얼굴에 침이 ~ one's face is spattered with saliva // 물이 사방에 튀었다 The splashing water flew about. // Water splashed about. // 치마에 흙탕물이 튀었다 My skirt was splashed[spattered] with mud. // 튀김 요리를 하는 중에 기름이 튀었다 The fat spat while I was deep frying.
4 (달아나다) fly (away); run away; make off; take (to) flight. ¶도둑은 뒷문으로 튀었다 The burglar bolted through the back door.

튀밥 popped rice.

튀어나오다 1 (숨은 것·동물 등이) jump[leap / bounce] out; spring out; [뛰쳐나오다] rush[burst] out; (말 등이) rush. ¶침대에서 ~ spring[(영국 구어)] nip) out of bed // 방에서 ~ rush[run / dash / dart] out of the room // 우리 속에서 ~ break out of a cage / break loose // (짐승 등이) 숨은 곳에서 ~ break cover // 토끼가 굴에서 튀어나왔다 A rabbit sprang out of the burrow. // 낯선 사나이가 튀어나왔다 A strange man bolted out[came rushing out]. // 호랑이가 우리에서 튀어나왔다 A tiger broke out of its cage. // 말이 그의 입 밖으로 튀어나왔다 Words rose to[poured from] his lips. / He poured out words in a steady flow. // 뜻밖의 증언이 증인의 입으로부터 튀어나왔다 Unexpected testimony came[(문어) issued] from the witness's mouth.
2 (돌출하다) project; protrude; jut (out); shoot out. ¶담 밖으로 튀어나와 있는 소나무 a pine tree jutting beyond the walls // 광대뼈가 튀어나와 있는 얼굴 a face with prominent cheek bones // (길게) 바다로 튀어나와 있다 jut[push / run] out (a long way) into the sea // 입구의 일부가 보도에 튀어나와 있다 Part of the entrance projects[protrudes] over the sidewalk. // 그의 눈은 튀어나와 있다 His eyes are starting out of their sockets.

튜너 (라디오·텔레비전의) tuner.

튜브 a tube; (타이어 속의) an inner (air-)tube. ¶~에 든 치약 a tube of toothpaste // ~에 든 그림물감 tube colors / a tube paint // ~에서 그림물감을 짜내다 squeeze paint from a tube.

튤립 [식] a tulip.

트기 →튀기

트다¹ 1 [싹이 돋아나다] sprout; bud (out); shoot; spring up. ¶싹이 ~ put forth[shoot out] buds / bud / sprout // 나무의 싹이 텄다 The tree put forth buds. // 나무의 싹이 트기 시작했다 The trees have begun to bud[sprout].
2 [살갗이 벌어지다] chap; be[get] chapped; be cracked. ¶튼 손 a chapped[chappy] hand // 살갗이 잘 트는 사람 a person liable to have a chappy skin // 손이 ~ one's hands chap / (사람이) get chapped hands // 피부가 트는 것을 막다 keep the skin from chapping[becoming chapped] // 그 아이의 손은 추위로 터 있었다 The child's hands were chapped by the cold. // 입술이 텄다 My lips are chapped. // 내 피부는 잘 튼다 My skin chaps easily.
3 [동쪽이 훤해지다] break; dawn; turn gray. ¶동이 튼다 The day breaks. / The sky turns gray. // 먼동이 터 온다 The eastern sky is gradually turning gray. / The dawn breaks. // 먼동이 트면서 하늘이 밝아졌다 The sky began to lighten[grew gray] just before daybreak. / The sky grayed[lightened / (영) greyed] with the approach of dawn.

트다² 1 [막힌 것을 통하게 하다] break (it) open; sit (it) open; cut; open. ¶길을 ~ cut a path / build[open] a road // 황야에 길을 open up[cut] a road through a wilderness // 둑을 ~ break[burst] a dam // 막은 칸막이를 ~ take off a partition // 아귀를 ~ make an opening / put in a slit // 성공의 길을 ~ pave the way for success // 두 방을 터서 한 방으로 만들다 throw two rooms into one // 후진들을 위해 길을 터 주다 (retire from service to) give younger men a chance / open the way for the promotion of one's juniors // 우리는 두 개의 방을 터서 연회장으로 만들었다 We made a banquet[(영) banqueting] room by knocking down the wall[removing the sliding doors] between the two rooms. (▶ removing the sliding doors는 장지문을 떼어 내어)
2 [거래 관계를 맺다] open; begin; initiate. ¶거래를 ~ enter into a connection[business relation] (with) // 은행과 거래를 ~ open an account with[at] a bank // 외상을 ~ open a charge account.

트라이 [럭비] a try. ¶~를 올리다 score a try / make a successful try // ~로 득점하다 score on a try.

트라이애슬론 [철인 레이스] triathlon.
트라이앵글 [음] a triangle.
트래핑 [체] trapping.
트랙 a track. ¶~과 필드 track and field. ● **트랙 경기** track events[athletics]; running events. ¶~의 주자 a track runner.
트랙터 a tractor. ¶경작용 ~ a farm[an agricultural] tractor / an agrimotor // 대형 ~ a heavy-duty tractor // 무한궤도 ~ a caterpillar tractor.
트랜스 a (power) transformer. ¶~가 탔다 The transformer burned out.

트랜스젠더 [성 전환자] a transgender.
트랜지스터 [물] a transistor.
  ●**트랜지스터라디오** a transistor radio.
트랩 a movable flight of steps; (배의) a gangway (ladder); (미) an accommodation ladder; (비행기의) a (plane) ramp; landing steps. ¶~을 올라[내려]가다 go[step] up [down] the ladder[ramp].
트러블 a trouble; a scandal. ¶가정의 ~ a family trouble/~을 일으키다 make[stir up] trouble / cause trouble /…과의 사이에 ~을 일으키다 get into trouble with (the police).
트러스 [건] a truss.
  ●**트러스교** a truss bridge. ¶나무 ~ a wooden[timber] truss bridge.
트러스트 a trust. ¶~를 만들다[조직하다] organize a trust.
트럭 a (motor) truck; an autotruck; (영) a (motor-)lorry. ¶군용 ~ a camion // 소형 ~ a pickup / 자갈을 실은 대형 ~ a large truck loaded with gravel // 3대분의 화물 three truckloads of goods // ~으로 나르다 carry in a truck / haul by truck[(영) by lorry] / truck (goods) // ~으로 석탄을 나르다 carry coal on a truck // ~이 간선 도로는 항상 ~의 왕래가 많다 This highway is always busy with truck traffic.
트럼펫 [음] a trumpet.
  ●**트럼펫 주자** a trumpeter; a trumpet player.
트럼프 (*trump) (a game of) cards. (▶ trump 는 카드의 으뜸 패를 뜻함) ¶한 벌의 ~ a pack of cards / (미) a deck of cards // ~의 으뜸패 a trump (card) // ~를 하는 사람 a cardplayer // (점치기 위해) ~의 패를 늘어놓다 lay cards (on the table) // ~의 패를 떼다[도르다 / 섞다] cut[deal / shuffle] the cards // ~로 도박을 하다 gamble at cards // ~로 점을 치다 tell one's fortune from cards // ~를 하고 있다 be at cards // ~를 젖히다 turn over a card // ~에서 이기다[지다] win[lose] at cards.
트렁크 1 [여행용의 큰 가방] a (cabin) trunk; (드는) a portmanteau (*pl.* ~s, ~x); (미) a suitcase; a valise(여행용 손가방). ¶~에 가득 한 옷 a trunkful of dress. 2 [자동차 뒤에 짐 싣는 곳] the trunk (compartment); the luggage compartment; the boot.
트레머리 swept-back hair with a bun[knot / chignon] at the back of the head. ¶~를 한 다 dress[do (up)] one's hair in a "swept-back" style with a bun at the back of the head.
트레이너 a trainer.
트레이닝 training. ¶하드 ~ hard training // ~을 하고 있다 be in training (for the game) / ~을 받고 있다 be under training (for the coming season) // 이번 시합에 대비해서 ~에 들어가다 go into training for the coming match.
트레이드 [야구] trade; trading of players. **트레이드하다** trade (a player) for (another). ➔¶그 선수는 라이언즈에서 베어스로 트레이드 되었다 The player was traded from the Lions to the Bears.
트레이드마크 a trademark.
트레이싱 페이퍼 [투사지] tracing paper.
트레일러 a trailer.
트로이카 a troika. ¶(옛 소련 외교의) ~ 방식 the "troika" plan[principle].

트로트 a trot.
트로피 a trophy. ¶~를 타다 win a trophy.
트롤 a trawl. ¶오터 ~ an otter trawl // ~로 고기를 잡다 trawl.
  ●**트롤망**(一網) a trawl net; a trawl; a ground net. **트롤선** a trawlboat; a trawler. **트롤 어법** trawl fishery; trawling.
트롤리버스 a trolley bus(coach).
트롬본 [음] a trombone. ¶~을 불다 blow a [play the] trombone.
  ●**트롬본 주자** a trombonist.
트리밍 [사진] trimming. **트리밍하다** trim. ¶확대할 때에 트리밍해서 왼쪽 끝 사람은 빼 주세요. In enlarging, please trim the picture and leave out the person at extreme left in the negative.
트리오 a trio (*pl.* ~s). ¶보컬 ~ a vocal trio // ~로 노래하다 sing in a trio.
트리코마이신 [약] trichomycin.
트리플 triple.
트릭 a trick; a catch; a shenanigan. ¶영화의 ~ 제작 the fabrication of faked pictures // ~ 을 쓰다 resort to tricks // ~에 걸리다 be taken in / be tricked / be a victim of somebody's shenanigans // ~을 써서 …하게 하다 trick (a person) into doing // 그는 완전히 ~ 에 걸렸다 He was completely taken in.
트림 belching; a belch; eructation; (속어) burp. ¶~을 참다 stifle a belch // ~이 나왔다 I belched[(구어) burped]. **트림하다** belch; eruct; burp. ¶아기를 트림하게 하다 burp a baby.
트립신 [생] trypsin.
트립토판 [화] tryptophan(e).
트릿하다 1 [가슴이 거북하다] (서술적) feel stuffed up; have congestion in the chest. 2 [맺고 끊는 데가 없다] dull; slow; vague. ¶트 릿한 대답 a dubious[vague] reply // 트릿한 사람 an indecisive character / a wishy-washy sort of fellow // 트릿한 태도를 취하다 assume a lukewarm[an indecisive] attitude // 셈이 ~ be unpunctual in one's payment.
트위스트 the twist. ¶~를 추다 twist / dance [do] the twist / do the twisty steps.
트이다 1 (막혀 있던 것이) get cleared; be open(ed); be cut(길 등이); (운이) be in the ascendant. ¶시계가 트인 extensive views // 확 트인 길 a clear passage / a open road // 탁 트인 경치 an open view // 운이 ~ be in luck's way / one's fortune changes for the better / fortune turns in one's favor // 가슴속이 시원히 ~ feel refreshed[relieved] // 터널이 트였다 The tunnel was opened. // 길이 ~ A road was opened up. // 운이 트이기 시작했다 Fortune has begun to smile on me. / Luck is beginning to turn my way. // 운이 조금도 트이지 않는다 Luck is against me. / I'm having a run of bad luck. // 40세가 되었을 때 그의 운이 트였 다 A lucky turn in his fortunes came[His luck began to look up] when he was forty. // 숲을 빠져나오자 갑자기 눈앞이 탁 트였다 A wide prospect burst upon my view as I came out of the forest.
2 (마음 등이) be liberal[generous]; be open-minded[open-hearted]; be sensible; [물정에 밝아지다] come to know much of the world; get used to the ways of the world. ¶속이 트 인 사람 a man of the world / a person of a liberal turn of mind // 속이 ~ be liberal

[open-hearted] / have a liberal [generous] mind / have an understanding heart // 눈이 ~ come [be brought] to one's senses / awake from an illusion // 그는 속이 탁 트인 사람이다 He is a most open-hearted person.

트집 1 (탈) a fault; a blemish; (생트집) a false charge. ¶~이 나다 get cracked / have a split // 그것은 엉뚱한 ~이다 That's a preposterously unjust charge to make against me. 2 (틈새) a crack; a break; a fissure. ¶찻잔에 ~이 생겼다 The teacup cracked. / There is a crack in this teacup. // 그 때문에 두 사람의 우정에는 ~이 갔다 That has caused a crack in their (bond of) friendship.

트집(을) 잡다 find fault (with); pick holes [flaws] (in); make a false charge (against); cavil at; split hairs. ¶트집 잡기를 좋아하는 captious / faultfinding / caviling // 말에 ~ find fault with (a person's) remark // 물건에 ~ pick a hole in an article // 사소한 일에도 ~ trump up charges on the slightest pretext // 트집을 잡아 싸움을 걸다 pick a quarrel with (a person) // 그는 언제나 동료와 트집만 잡고 있다 He is always finding fault with his colleagues. // 그녀는 며느리가 하는 일에 대해 일일이 트집을 잡았다 She found fault with everything her daughter-in-law did. // 그는 내 말에 대해 일일이 트집을 잡는다 He finds fault with everything I say. / He takes me to task for everything I say. // 그는 내가 하는 일에 대해 일일이 트집을 잡는다 He picks holes in [finds fault with] everything I do. // 그들은 내가 일부러 그 화분을 깼다고 트집을 잡았다 They accused me unjustly [falsely] of having broken that pot on purpose. // 그는 사소한 일로 트집을 잡아 나를 구타했다 He picked a quarrel with me over a trifle and hit me. // 그는 내 작품이 독창성이 없다고 트집을 잡았다 He ran down my work, saying it lacked originality.

●**트집쟁이** a faultfinder; a nit-picker; a nag; a nagger.

특가(特價) a special [bargain] price; a specially reduced price. ¶정가의 6할이라는 ~로 at the special price of sixty percent of its original price // ~로 팔다 sell at a special [reduced / bargain] price / sell at sacrifice / (팔다 남은 책을) remainder // ~로 카메라를 팔다 sell cameras at bargain prices.

●**특가 판매** sale at a special price; a bargain sale. **특가품** an article offered at a special [bargain] price; a bargain; a bargain-priced article.

특공(特功) a great achievement; distinguished service; a special merit.

특공대(特攻隊) a "special attack" unit [corps]; a suicide unit; a commando unit; commandomen; (미) a Ranger. ¶인질들을 구출하기 위해 ~를 파견하다 send the commandos to rescue the hostages (held by pro-Palestinian highjackers).

특과(特科) a special course; an arm (of the army) other than infantry; a technical corps (pl. corps); a technical troop.

특권(特權) a privilege; a special [an exclusive] right; a prerogative; a charter; (법) special privilege. ¶여성의 ~ a woman's prerogative // 외교관의 ~ diplomatic privileges (and immunities) // 국회의 ~ the prerogatives of parliament // ~이 있는 [주어진] privileged // ~을 부여하다 privilege / grant [give] (a person) a privilege // ~을 가지다 [누리다] possess a special right / hold [enjoy] a privilege // ~을 전유(專有)하다 ~을 누리다 enjoy an exclusive prerogative of ... // ~을 행사하다 exercise a privilege // ~을 잃다 be deprived of a privilege // ~을 남용하다 abuse a privilege // 우리는 도서관을 이용할 수 있는 ~이 부여되었다 We were given the special right to use the library. // 젊은이만이 이런 종류의 도전적인 일을 해 볼 ~을 가지고 있다 Only young people are privileged to attempt this sort of challenging work.

●**특권 계급 / 특권층** the privileged class. ¶소수 ~ a privileged minority / the privileged few.

특근(特勤) [과외의 일] extra duty [assignment]; [시간 외 근무] overtime work. **특근하다** work overtime; work extra hours; do extra work.

●**특근 수당** overtime pay [allowance].

특급(特急) [특별 급행열차] a limited [special] express (train); a super-express; (속어) a cannonball. ¶부산행 ~ the limited express for Busan // ~을 타다 take [board] a limited express.

특급(特級) special grade.

특기(特技) one's special ability [talent / gift]; one's special skill; one's special art; speciality; one's special flair in (mathematics, music, etc.). ¶군사 ~ military occupational speciality(약어 MOS) // 이 화가의 ~는 정물이다 This artist's forte is still life. // 그의 ~는 물구나무를 서서 걷는 일이다 His speciality [special trick / special stunt] is to walk (standing) on his hands. // 남의 이름을 잘 외우는 것이 그녀의 ~이다 Remembering names is her strong point. / She has a special gift [talent] for remembering names. // 나는 각자가 ~를 살릴수 있도록 일을 그들에게 안배하려고 노력했다 I tried to assign them tasks in which they could make the most of their own special abilities.

특기(特記) special mention. ¶~ 사항 없음 No comments in particular. / Nothing (noteworthy) to report. **특기하다** mention specially; make special mention of; write in large characters. ¶특기할 만한 noteworthy / remarkable // 특기할 만한 일 what is specially noteworthy // 특기할 만하다 be worth [deserve] special mention // 이 사건은 특기할 만하다 This incident is worthy of special mention. // 오늘은 나의 생애에서 특기할 만한 날이다 Today is a very important [a red-letter] day in my life. // 그녀의 헌신적인 근무는 특기할 만하다 Her self-sacrificing service deserves special mention. / We must make special mention of her self-sacrificing service.

특대(特大) outsize. ¶~의 outsize(d) / extra large / king-size(d) // ~의 구두 king-size(d) [oversize(d)] shoes // ~의 스커트 a queen-size(d) skirt.

●**특대품** [경] an imperial. **특대호** a special enlarged issue [number]. ¶창간 10주년 ~ an enlarged special issue of the journal in commemoration of the tenth anniversary of its founding.

특대(特待) (a) special treatment; distinction. ¶~를 받다 be treated with distinction. **특대**

하다 treat (a person) with distinction; give a special treatment.

특등(特等) a special grade[class]; the top grade.
● **특등석** a special seat; a box[극장의]. **특등실** a special(-class) room; (기선의) a cabin deluxe. **특등품** an article of special quality; an A1 article; an extra-fine[superfine] article[brand].

특례(特例) **1** [특별한 예] a special case[example]; a particular instance[case]. ¶그의 경우는 ~이다 He is a special case. **2** [예외] an exception. ¶전시 ~ a wartime exception//~로서 as an exception//~에 의해서 in accordance with the exception provided for//~를 만들다 make an exception to the rule / [선례를 만들다] provide[create] a precedent//우리는 어떤 ~도 인정하지 않습니다 We make[grant] no exceptions.
● **특례법** [법] a special law. ⇨특별법(⇨특별)

특매(特賣) (a) special sale; sale at a special price; a bargain sale. **특매하다** sell at a special price; conduct a special sale; sell at specially reduced prices. ¶대할인 가격으로 ~ make a special offer at greatly reduced prices//저 가게는 이번 주에 의류를 특매한다 That store has a bargain sale on clothes this week.
● **특매장** a bargain counter; (지하층의) a bargain basement. **특매품** articles for special sale; articles sold at special prices; an article offered at a bargain (price). ¶~이므로 반환이나 교환을 사절합니다 No returns or exchanges on sale items.

특명(特命) [특별한 명령·임명] a special command[appointment / assignment]; [군] a mission. ¶~의 extraordinary//~을 띠고 on special mission//그는 ~을 띠고 한국을 방문했다 He visited Korea on a special mission. **특명하다** command[order / appoint] specially.
● **특명 전권 대사**[공사] an ambassador[a minister] extraordinary and plenipotentiary.

특무(特務) special duty[service].
● **특무 기관** (-機關) the Special Service Agency[Organization]; a secret (military) agency[service].

특배(特配) **1** [배급] special distribution; a special[an extra] ration. **특배하다** distribute specially[exceptionally]. **2** [배당] a special[a bonus] dividend.

특별(特別) [관형어적]. **특별하다** special; especial; express; [특수하다] particular; [고유하다] peculiar; [보통이 아니다] extraordinary; uncommon; (여분의) extra; (예외의) exceptional. ¶특별한 것 a special thing / a special / a specific//특별한 이유 a particular [special] reason//특별한 이유도 없이 without any particular reason//특별한 관계에 있는 사람들 those with whom we have a special connection//특별한 배려로 by special grace//특별한 취급을 하다 give (a person) special treatment//그는 보통 사람과는 다른 특별한 인물이다 He is a special [different from the run-of-the-mill].//그는 특별한 대접을 받았다 He was given special treatment.//나는 생일날에 유달리 특별한 일은 하지 않습니다 I do nothing special on my birthday.//이것은 특별한 주의를 필요로 한다 This needs (e)special attention(▶ 형용사인 especial은 문어적임).//신 씨는 그 여자와 특별한 관계에 있었다 Mr. Sin was on intimate terms[had a special relationship] with the woman.//그는 아무도 특별한 취급을 하지 않는다 He doesn't give anyone special treatment. / He does not make exceptions of anyone. **특별히** specially; especially; particularly; in particular. ¶~ 정한 경우를 제외하고(는) unless otherwise provided for//~ 주의하다 pay special attention (to) / exercise special care//이 옷은 ~ 맞춘 것이다 This suit was (specially) made to order.//그는 ~ 신용할 수 있는 인물이다 He is an especially reliable person.//그는 정치에 ~ 관심이 없는 것은 아니다 He is not particularly indifferent to politics.//지금으로서는 ~ 말씀드릴 것이 없습니다 I have nothing in particular to say at the moment.//그의 목소리는 ~ 크다 His voice is exceptionally loud.//올겨울은 ~ [유난히] 춥다 It is unusually cold this winter. ¶낯선 나라에서 보내는 최초의 1주일은 ~ 길게 느껴졌다 I felt my first week in the strange country extraordinarily long.
● **특별 규정** an express provision. **특별 기금** a special fund. **특별 메뉴** special. ¶오늘는 무엇입니까 What is special today?//오늘 ~가 있습니까 Is anything special today? **특별법** [법] a special law. **특별 사면** (an) amnesty; (a) mercy; a particular[special / free] pardon. **특별상** a special prize (for outstanding performance in watch-repairing). **특별석** a reserved[special] seat; a box. **특별 소비세** special excise tax. **특별 수당** a special[an extra] allowance. **특별시** a special municipality[city]. **특별 예산** a special[an extraordinary] budget. **특별 운임** a special fare. **특별 위원회** [정] a special[an ad hoc] committee. **특별 임무** a special mission. **특별 임용** special appointment. **특별호** a special[an extra] number[issue / edition]. ¶스미스 박사 추모 ~ a special number in memory of Dr. Smith(▶ 임시인 경우는 special 대신 extra를 씀). **특별 회계** special accounts.

특보(特報) a special report; special news; a (news) flash. ¶뉴스 ~ a news flash. **특보하다** flash; give a special report (on). ¶개표 결과를 ~ flash the ballot-counting results. → ¶내각 총사퇴의 뉴스가 특보되었다 There was a news flash announcing that the Cabinet had resigned.

특사(特使) a special envoy; a special[an express] messenger. ¶대통령 ~ a presidential envoy//~를 파견하다 dispatch a special envoy / send an express messenger//정부는 그를 ~로 미국에 파견했다 The Government dispatched[sent] him to the United States as its special envoy.

특사(特赦) (an) amnesty; (a) mercy. ⇨특별사면(⇨특별) ¶~로 출감하다 be released from prison on (special) amnesty//~를 받다 be accorded[granted] amnesty//~에서 빠지다 be excluded from the amnesty//새 정권에 의해서 정치범에 대한 ~가 있었다 The new regime granted a general amnesty to political offenders. **특사하다** grant an amnesty (to offenders); give amnesty (to); amnesty. ¶정치범을 ~ grant an[a special] amnesty to political prisoners.
● **특사령** an act of grace[amnesty]; a decree

특산물

of amnesty[oblivion].

특산물(特産物) a special[a specialty / an indigenous] product; a speciality. ¶인삼은 개성의 ~이다 Insam is a speciality[indigenous to the soil] of Gaeseong.∥전복은 이 지방의 ~이다 Abalones are a special product [speciality] of this district.

특산지(特産地) special production localities.

특상(特上) ¶~의 the finest[choicest] (Turkish tobacco).
● **특상품** choice goods.

특상(特賞) a special prize[reward]. ¶~은 한씨가 받았다 The special prize went to Mr. Han. / Mr. Han was awarded the special prize.

특색(特色) a specific character; a characteristic; a (specific) feature; a peculiarity; a distinction; (개성) an idiosyncrasy; an individuality; (특히 인격상의) a color; (personal) coloring. ¶한국 소설의 주요 ~ the chief distinction of Korean novel∥~ 있는 special / characteristic / peculiar / distinctive / distinguishing∥~ 없는 indistinctive / featureless / common∥…이 ~이다 be characterized by∥(어떤 일이) …의 ~을 나타내다[보이다] be characteristic of / characterize / feature / mark / stamp / be typical of∥~을 발휘하다 display one's characteristic [salient] feature∥~을 살리다 make the best of (its) characteristic traits∥그녀는 ~ 있는 작가다 There is something in the writer which distinguishes her from others.∥이 작품에는 시대의 ~이 잘 나타나 있다 This work clearly reveals the features characteristic of the period.∥강한 의지가 그녀의 ~이다 Strong-mindedness is her outstanding characteristic.∥전편에 넘치는 밝음이 그의 작품의 ~이다 His works are characterized [marked] throughout by a sunny outlook.∥목이 긴 것이 기린의 ~이다 The distinctive peculiarity[feature] of the giraffe is its long neck.

특선(特選) (a) special selection; (a) special approval; (a) recognition. ¶전람회에서 ~이 되다 be specially selected[win a special recognition] at an art exhibition. **특선하다** choose[select] specially.
● **특선품** a choice[deluxe] article.

특설(特設) 〔관형어적〕 specially installed [prepared]. **특설하다** set up[organize / establish / install] specially. ➔¶이 회의를 위해서 구내에 우체국이 특설되었다 A special post office was opened[set up] on the premises to serve this congress.
● **특설 링** a specially prepared ring. **특설 전화** a specially installed telephone.

특성(特性) a special[distinctive] quality; a specific[special / peculiar] character; a specificity; a characteristic; a peculiarity; a (peculiar) property; a feature; (개인의) a trait of character; a stamp; an idiosyncrasy; an individuality; 〔생〕 a diagnosis (pl. -noses); genius. ¶정신적 ~ a peculiarity of mind∥개인적[국민적]인 ~ individual[national] peculiarities∥소다의 ~ the properties of soda∥약의 ~ the peculiar properties of a drug∥~을 발휘하다 show a special quality∥(어떤 일이) …의 ~을 나타내다 characterize / mark / be characteristic of∥…의 ~을 갖다 possess the characteristics of∥~을 살리다 make the most of (its) characteristics∥사원 개개인의 ~을 살려서 일을 맡기다 assign each of the employees to a position where he can give full play to his natural abilities∥전성(展性)은 모든 금속의 ~이다 Malleability characterizes[is characteristic of] all metals.∥소다에는 기름을 녹이는 ~이 있다 The ability to dissolve grease is a special property of soda.∥이 민족은 참을성이 강한 것이 ~이다 Perseverance marks the nation[race]. / This nation[race] is characterized by perseverance.∥독일어는 긴 복합어를 만드는 ~이 있다 The formation of long compound words is a marked characteristic of the German language.∥비둘기는 귀소성이 강하다는 ~ 때문에 통신에 널리 이용되고 있다 Because of their characteristically homing instinct, pigeons are used extensively to carry messages.

특수(特殊) speciality; peculiarity; characteristic(s). **특수하다** special; specific; particular; peculiar; characteristic; distinct; distinguishing; unique(독특한). ¶특수한 목적 a particular object / a special purpose∥특수한 성질 one's own nature / (개성) an individuality / an idiosyncrasy∥특수한 예 a special example∥특수한 원인 a specific cause∥특수한 재능 an unusual talent∥특수한 방법으로 in a particular way∥이 장치는 특수한 목적으로 만든 것이다 This device was designed for a special purpose.
● **특수강**(-鋼) special steel. **특수 교육** education for the handicapped. **특수 부대** 〔군〕 special forces. **특수성** peculiarity; speciality; particularity; special characteristics. **특수 은행** a special[chartered] bank. **특수층 / 특수 계급** a privileged class. **특수학교** a school for handicapped children. **특수화** specialization; specification. ¶~하다 specialize / specify / differentiate. **특수 효과** 〔영〕 special effect(s). **특수 훈련** special training.

특수(特需) 〔특별한 수요〕 special procurements; emergency[special procurement] demands[orders] (due to the outbreak of war).

특실(特室) a special(-class) room; a cabin deluxe. ⇨특등실(⇨특등)

특약(特約) a special contract[agreement]. ¶…과 ~을 맺다 make a special arrangement with …∥…과 ~이 되어 있다 be under a special contract with / have a special agreement with …∥우리는 생산자와 ~을 맺고 있다 We have a special contract with the producers.∥A지(紙)는 AP 통신과 ~을 맺고 있다 The A newspaper has an A.P. franchise. **특약하다** make a special contract [agreement] (with).
● **특약점** a special agent. ¶우리는 그 회사의 ~을 맡았다 We became special[sole] agents for this firm.

특용(特用) (a) special use. **특용하다** use specially; use (a thing)[be used] for a special purpose.
● **특용 작물** a crop for a special use; a cash crop.

특위(特委) 〔정〕 a special committee. ⇨특별위원회(⇨특별)

특유(特有) peculiarity. ¶그 사람 ~의 필체 his special style of penmanship∥아프리카의 이 지방 ~의 습관 custom peculiar to this

part of Africa // 이것들은 한국 ~의 식물[동물]이다 These are plants[animals] indigenous to Korea. **특유하다** characteristic (of); peculiar[special] (to); unique; unusual; (all) its own. ¶특유한 맛 a peculiar flavor // 유머의 결여는 그 집안의 특유한 성격이다 A lack of a sense of humor is a marked characteristic of this family. // 개미는 특유의 통신 수단을 가지고 있다 Ants have a means of communication all their own. // 이 작곡가의 화음에는 뭔지 그 나름의 특유한 것이 있다 This composer has something peculiarly his own in the chords he uses.
● **특유성** a peculiarity; uniqueness.
특이성(特異性) peculiarity; particularity; singularity; uniqueness.
특이하다(特異-) singular; peculiar; unique. ¶특이한 복장 unusual clothes // 특이한 모양의 꽃 a flower of singular shape // 특이한 재능의 소유자 a person of unique talent // 이것은 특이한 예이다 This is a peculiar case. / This case is out of the ordinary. // 이것은 특이한 사건이다 This is an unprecedented case. // 그 가게는 장식이 특이하게 되어 있다 The store is decorated with original designs. / The shop has an unusual decor. // 그녀의 문장은 표현 형식이 아주 Her writing style is highly idiosyncratic [very eccentric / too individualistic].
특작(特作) a special production; [영] a special film; a feature (production). ¶초~ a super production / [영] a super picture.
특장(特長) a good[strong] point; a forte; a merit. ¶연료비가 적게 드는 것이 이 차종의 ~이다 The low cost of fuel is the strong point of this kind of automobile.
특전(特典) a special favor; a benefit; (개인적인) a privilege; [가] an indult. ¶본회 회원의 ~ advantages of membership in this society // 세금 면제의 ~ the privilege of exemption from taxation // ~을 주다 grant a special favor[a privilege] / privilege // ~을 입다 be granted a special favor // 그들에게는 공공 교통 기관의 운임 무료라는 ~이 부여되어 있다 They enjoy[are granted] the privilege [special favor] of traveling on public vehicles free of charge. // 이 제도는 고용자 측에 몇 가지 ~을 부여하고 있다 This system offers employees several benefits.
특전(特電) a special telegram; a telegraphic dispatch. ¶로이터 ~ Reuter's special (service) // ~을 띄우다 dispatch a telegram.
특전대(特戰隊) a ranger-commando force.
특정(特定) specification. ¶~의 specific // ~행위의 금지 prohibition of specific acts // ~의 남자 친구는 없습니다 I have no particular [special] boyfriend. **특정하다** specify. ¶이러저러한 것을 원한다고 특정하지 않았다 I did not specify what I wanted. // 현재 상태에서는 범인을 특정하기는 어렵다 It is difficult to determine the offender under these circumstances. // 산불의 발화 지점을 특정할 수가 없다 We cannot pinpoint where the forest fire started.
● **특정 계약** a specified contract. **특정물** a specific thing. **특정 요금** a specified [a special / an exceptional] fare[rate]. **특정 운임** special freight rates. **특정인** a specified person. **특정 지역** a specific region; (투기 억제의) the special (tax) zones.

특제(特製) special make[manufacture]. ¶당사 ~의 냄비를 싸게 제공합니다 We offer pans specially made by our company at reduced prices. // 기념식 후에 학생들에게 ~ 케이크가 배급되었다 After the celebration, the pupils received cakes specially prepared for the occasion. **특제하다** make[manufacture] specially.
● **특제품** [특별히 만든 것] a specially make article; specially manufactured goods; [특급품] an extra fine article.
특종(特種) **1** [특별한 종류] a special kind [type].
2 [특종 기사] exclusive news; an exclusive; a scoop; a news beat. ¶~을 캐내다 scoop / get a scoop / (구어) pull a (big) scoop // 이것은 멋진 ~이 되겠다 This will make a marvelous[terrific] scoop. // 이 신문에 연구 데이터 날조의 ~이 실려 있다 There is a scoop on the fabrication of research data in this paper. // 이번에는 우리 신문이 ~으로 다른 신문을 앞질렀다 This time our paper beat the other papers to the punch[scooped the other papers]. // 타임스는 그 수회 사건을 ~으로 다루어 또다시 타사를 앞질렀다 The Times again beat[scooped / got the scoop on] all the other newspapers with the story of the bribery scandal.
특진(特進) accelerated promotion; a special promotion of rank. ¶2계급 ~ a double promotion / promotion by two ranks / promotion skipping a grade.
특질(特質) a characteristic; a property; a special quality. ¶고딕 건축의 ~ the characteristics of Gothic architecture // 이 건축 재료는 불에 강하다는 ~을 갖고 있다 A special property of this building material is that it is fire-resistant.
특집(特輯) a special edition. ¶뉴스 ~ a special news program // 어느 신문이나 독직 사건을 ~으로 다루고 있다 There are special stories on the bribery case in every paper. / Every paper has given extra space to special stories on the bribery case. // 그 주간지는 금주에 총선거를 ~으로 다루었다 The weekly this week has put together a special issue on the general election.
● **특집 기사** a special feature article. ¶이달호의 ~ the special feature in the current issue. **특집호** a special number[issue]. ¶신년 ~ a January number (of a magazine) with new year features // 올림픽 ~ a special number on the Olympics.
특징(特徵) a (special / distinctive / distinguishing) feature[character]; a distinguishing[characteristic / distinctive] mark; (a) distinction; (인상 등의) identifying marks; a characteristic; a peculiarity; (개인의) a trait of character; individualities; an idiosyncrasy; a stamp; [생] a diagnostic character. (▶ feature는 주의를 끄는 두드러진 특색, 특히 얼굴 등 그 자체 내에서 눈에 띄는 부분, peculiarity는 다른 것과 달라 눈에 띄는 특색) ¶~ 있는 characteristic / peculiar / remarkable / striking // ~ 없는 얼굴 a face without (any) character[lacking in character] // 한국 지형의 두드러진 ~ the notable geographical features of Korea // 그의 음악의 ~적인 목가성 the idyllic quality peculiar to his music // 한국의 여름철 기후의 ~은 고온 다습한 것이다

The summer climate of Korea is characterized by high temperatures and high humidity. / High temperatures and high humidity are characteristic of summer in Korea. ∥ 맹크스 고양이는 꼬리가 없는 것이 ~이다 The lack of a tail is a peculiarity[distinctive characteristic] of the Manx cat. ∥ 장수는 그들의 가족성 ~이다 Longevity is a family trait with them. ∥ 그녀의 표정에는 두드러진 ~이 있다 There is something striking about her facial expressions. ∥ 그녀의 웃음에는 ~이 있다 She has a peculiar manner[way] of laughing. ∥ 그는 ~이 있는 인물이다 He is a character. ∥ 이 도시에는 ~이 없다 This town is lacking in character[has nothing distinctive about it]. ∥ 현대의 ~적인 경향은 과학에 대한 신앙이다 One of the characteristic trends of modern times is faith in science.

특징짓다 (特徵−) characterize; distinguish; mark; stamp; feature.

특채 (特採) special appointment[engagement/employment]. **특채하다** employ specially; take (a person) into service[a company] specially.

특청 (特請) (a) special request. ¶한 가지 ~이 있습니다 I would like to make a special request to you. **특청하다** request specially; make a special request (to a person).

특출하다 (特出−) outstanding; conspicuous; prominent; distinguished; striking; remarkable. ¶특출한 인물 a great[an outstanding] figure (in history) / (미) a standout ∥ 별로 특출한 게 없다 cut no striking figure (in one's class) ∥ 그는 특출하게 머리가 좋다 He is exceptionally[extraordinarily] bright. ∥ 그는 수학을 특출하게 잘한다 He is excellent [outstanding] in mathematics.

특칭 (特稱) special designation; a special name; [논] the particular. **특칭하다** give a special name (to); designate in particular.

특파 (特派) dispatch; sending off (a person) for a special purpose. **특파하다** dispatch [send] (specially); send off (a person) for a special purpose; send on a special mission; tell off. ¶정부는 유엔에 홍 씨를 특파했다 The government dispatched Mr. Hong to the United Nations as a special envoy.

● **특파 대사** a special ambassador. **특파원** [특별 임무를 위해 파견된 사람] a mission; a representative; a delegate; [신문·통신사의 파견 기자] a (special) correspondent. ¶AP (서울) ~ an AP correspondent (in Seoul) ∥ **이동 ~** a roving correspondent ∥ 본지의 런던 ~에 의하면 according to our London correspondent.

특필 (特筆) special mention. **특필하다** mention [write] specially; make special mention of; (신문 등이) make a feature of; feature; give (special) prominence to; lay special stress on. ¶대서 ~ write in golden[red / large] letters / single (something) out for special mention ∥ 이것은 특필할 만한 사건이다 This is an incident worthy of mention. ∥ 신문은 그 흉악 범죄를 특필했다 The newspaper featured that atrocious crime. ∥ 오늘은 나의 생애에서 특필할 만한 날이다 Today is a very important[a red-letter] day in my life.

특허 (特許) 1 [특별한 허가] a special permission; [면허] a license. **특허하다** license (a person to do); grant (a person) a special permission[license]. 2 (채굴·부설권 등의) a concession; a government privilege. 3 (정부에서 은행·회사 등에 주는) a charter. ¶버스 영업에 대한 ~ a franchise for a bus service. **특허하다** charter (a company to do). 4 (전매의) a patent (for / on). ¶~를 주다 give[grant] a patent ∥ ~를 **신청하다** apply for a patent ∥ 자동 제어 장치에 관한 ~를 따다 patent a device for automatic control / obtain[get / take out] a patent on an automatic control device ∥ ~를 가지고 있다[보유하다] hold a patent ∥ 신안 ~를 받다 take out a patent for[on] a new invention. 5 a patent right. ⇨ **특허권**(⇨**특허**)

● **특허권** a patent right; the right to a patent. ¶~을 가진 patent ∥ ~을 **갖다**[얻다] hold[obtain / secure] a patent right (for). **특허료** [특허 신청 수수료] a patent fee; [특허권 사용료] royalty. **특허법** the patent law. **특허 사무소** a patent attorney's office. **특허 사용료** (a) patent royalty. **특허 소유자** a patentee. **특허청** the Korean Industrial Property Office(약어 KIPO). **특허 출원** a patent application. ¶~ 중 (표시) Patent Pending. / Patent applied for. **특허품** a patented article; a patent.

특혜 (特惠) a special favor[benefit]; preference; preferentialism. ¶세제 ~ a tax favo(u)r / tax privileges ∥ ~의 preferential / privileged ∥ ~를 **주다** offer[afford] a preference ∥ ~를 **받다** receive a preference ∥ ~ 세율을 적용받다 receive a preference / enjoy a tariff preference (of 5%).

● **특혜 관세** a preferential duty[tariff].

특효 (特效) (a) special virtue[efficacy] (for). ¶~가 있다 be specially efficacious for (a disease) ∥ 알로에는 여러 가지 병에 ~가 있다 Aloe is very good[(문어) efficacious] for various diseases. ∥ 이 약은 다음 여러 병에 ~가 있다 This medicine is effective for the following diseases.

● **특효약** a specific remedy; a miracle [wonder] drug. ¶두통의 ~ a remedy that works wonders for headaches.

특히 (特−) specially; expressly; in special (measure); in specialty; [각별히] especially; in special; particularly; in particular; peculiarly; [무엇보다] above all; before everything else. ¶이 과자는 이 일 때문에 ~ 만들어진 것이다 This cake has been specially prepared for the occasion. ∥ 그의 공적에 대하여 ~ 언급되지 않으면 안 된다 Special mention should be made of his contribution. ∥ 오늘은 ~ 안개가 짙다 It is especially foggy today. ∥ ~ 재미있는 이야기는 없었다 No one said anything particularly interesting[of particular interest]. ∥ "이번 주말에는 어느 곳으로 가실 작정입니까?" "~ 어느 곳이라고 정한 곳은 없습니다." "Where are you planning to go this weekend?" "Nowhere in particular." ∥ 그녀의 얼굴은 아버지를 빼쏘았다. ~ 화가 나 있을 때는 그렇다 Her face is very much like her father's, particularly when she is cross. ∥ 이 기부금은 ~ 장애 아동의 교육에 사용된다 This donation is to be used exclusively for the education of handicapped children. ∥ 이 모임은 ~ 주부를 위해 계획된 것이다 This gathering was expressly planned for housewives. ∥ 이것은 ~ 중요한

다 This is particularly important.// 나는 꽃을 좋아하는데 ~ 흰 꽃을 좋아한다 I like flowers, expecially white ones.

튼실하다(-實-) [튼튼하고 실하다] (사물이) strong and firm; solid; substantial; (사람이) strong and healthy; sturdy; stout.

튼튼하다 [견고하다] strong; solid; stout; stanch; [골격·짜임새 등이 실하다] sturdy; stalwart; substantial; [견실하다] steady; secure; firm; stable; sound; [건강하다] healthy; sound; strong; well and strong; lusty; vigorous; robust. ¶튼튼한 창고 a strongly built warehouse// 튼튼한 철문 solid iron door// 튼튼한 오두막집 a sturdily-[stoutly-]built mountain cabin// 건물의 튼튼한 토대 the strong base[foundation] of a building// 튼튼한 체격 a well-built [strong] physique// 튼튼한 사람 a strong person / (체격이) a man of solid [sturdy] build [physique] / a powerfully-[strongly-]built man// 튼튼한 자본 a substantial capital// 튼튼해지다 become healthy / grow strong / gain[improve] in health / [회복되다] be all right again / be well again// 눈이 ~ have a good eyesight// 아들에게는 건전한 정신과 튼튼한 몸을 갖기를 바란다 I would like[wish] my son to be sound in mind and strong in body.// 나는 위장이 ~ I have a sound[good] digestive system.// 이 사다리는 튼튼한가요 Is this ladder secure? **튼튼히** strongly; solidly; firmly; stoutly; sturdily. ¶국방을 ~ 하다 strengthen the national defense// ~ 자라다 grow up in good[perfect] health// 몸을 ~ 하다 build[build up] one's health / fortify oneself (against cold) / strengthen one's body// 이 책상은 ~ 만들어져 있다 This desk is solidly built[made].// 우리는 통나무를 짜 올려 오두막집을 지었다 We built a cabin by placing one log firmly on top of another.

틀 1 [창문·액자 등의 테두리] a frame; framework; [필름을 감는] a reel. ¶사진~ the frame of a picture / a picture frame// 자수~ a tambour / an embroidery frame// 창~ a window frame / a sash(내리닫이 창문의)// ~에 끼운 그림 a framed picture// ~에 끼우다 frame (a picture) / set [put] (a picture) in (a) frame.
2 [주형(鑄型)] a mo(u)ld; a matrix; cast; [공] a die; (의치의) an impression; a mold; [모형] a model; a pattern. ¶~을 뜨다 make a model of / model (a tooth in wax)// ~에 부어 뜨다 cast in a mold.
3 [일정한 윤곽·형태] a (definite) shape [form]. ¶~을 잡다 get [lick] (a matter) into shape / give shape to (a matter)// ~이 잡히다 take[be in] shape / take a concrete [definite] form / materialize// ~이 잡히지 않다 remain[be] in a nebulous state.
4 [정해진 형식·격식] formality; a formula (pl. -lae, ~s); [관례] usage; conventionality; tradition; rule. ¶~에 박힌 grooved / conventional / stereotyped(상투적인) / hackneyed(진부한) / mannieristic / (일정한) fixed / regular / definite / too common / machine-made / ~에 박히지 않은 unconventional / offbeat / (자유로운) free and easy[open] // ~에 박힌 표현 a conventional [stereotyped] expression// ~에 박히다 squeeze (an individual) into a pattern / regiment / standardize// 모든 학생을 하나의 ~에 박히게 하려고 하다 try to mold all one's pupils to one and the same type// 나는 ~에 박히지 않은 그의 아이디어가 좋다 I like his unconventional ideas.// 그의 노래는 ~에 박힌 데가 없다 His singing is free of mannerisms.
5 [기계] a machine; a device. ¶형~ an instrument of torture / a frame for punishing (offenders)// 솜~ a cotton gin / a (saw) gin.
6 a (good) frame; a figure. ⇨틀거지
7 a sewing machine. ⇨재봉틀(⇨재봉)

틀거지 a (good) frame; a figure; dignity; an imposing manner[shape / appearance]. ¶~가 있다[없다] be dignified[lack dignity].

틀국수 machine-made noodles.

틀니 an artificial[a false] tooth; a denture. ¶~를 끼우다[빼다] put in[take out] one's false teeth// ~를 해 박다 have a false[an artificial] tooth put in.

틀다 1 [비틀다] twist; wrench; wring; screw; give (something) a twist. ¶부상자는 아픔으로 몸을 비비 틀었다 The injured man twisted (and turned) about in pain.
2 [돌리다] turn; wind; [기계 등을 작동시키다] set [put] (a machine) going. ¶시계태엽을 ~ wind (up) a clock / 축음을 ~ turn on a phonograph / put[play] a record on a phonograph// 가스를 ~ turn on gas// 문의 손잡이를 ~ turn a doorknob// 방향을 ~ shift (its) turn / turn (to)// 핸들을 오른쪽으로 ~ turn a handle to the right// 수도꼭지를 ~ turn the tap on// 누군가가 라디오를 틀어 놓은 채로 두었다 Someone has left the radio on.// 그는 어린이를 피하려고 핸들을 급히 틀었다 He turned the steering wheel sharply in an effort to miss the child.
3 [일 등을 방해하다] thwart; counteract (a plan); cross; work against. ¶일을 ~ thwart / counteract / cross (a person's) plan[design].
4 [솜을 타다] gin (out)[willow] (cotton). ¶솜을 ~ gin[willow] cotton / clean cotton by beating[whipping] with machinery.
5 [머리털을 뭉쳐 올려 붙이다] tie [do] up (one's hair). ¶머리를 틀어 올리다 do[put] one's hair up// 상투를 ~ do one's hair up into a topknot.

틀리다[1] 1 [비틀리다] get twisted[wrenched]; be distorted; grow warped. ¶넥타이가 ~ one's tie gets twisted. 2 [돌아가다] get turned[wound]; wind; turn. ¶나사가 틀렸다 A screw turned. 3 [솜이 틀어지다] get ginned[willowed]. ¶솜이 틀렸다 Cotton was ginned[willowed]. 4 [머리털이 틀어지다] be done up; tie. ¶상투가 잘 틀리지 않는다 The topknot won't tie properly.

틀리다[2] 1 [잘못되다] be mistaken (in); become [be] wrong[erroneous / incorrect]; be in error; be in the wrong; be at fault; [잘못하다] mistake; err; make [commit] a mistake[an error] (in); do wrong[amiss]. ¶계산이 ~ make an error in calculation / miscalculate // 판단이 ~ err in one's judgment / misjudge// 전혀 ~ be completely [absurdly] mistaken / be quite [dead] wrong / be far off base / (미국 속어) be all wet// 틀린 mistaken / wrong / erroneous / incorrect / errant / improper / false// 내 기억이 틀리지 않는다면 if I remember right[rightly / aright / correctly] / if my memory does not fail me// 틀린 것을 찾아내다 detect an error [a

틀림없다

mistake] // 틀리지 않도록 주의하다 guard against error / be cautious to prevent mistakes // 그것은 분명히 틀린다 It is glaringly erroneous. // 너의 추측은 전혀 틀린다 Your guess is quite wide of the mark. // 자네 생각[말]은 틀렸네 You are wrong. / You are in error. // 계산에는 틀린 데가 하나도 없었다 There were no mistakes[There was not a single error] in the calculation. // 색인 카드의 순서가 틀렸다 The index cards are arranged in the wrong order[all mixed up]. // 이 편지는 주소가 틀렸다 The address on this letter is wrong. // 그녀에 대한 자네 생각은 틀렸네 You are mistaken about her. // 네가 틀린 곳은 바로 거기다 That's where you are mistaken[wrong]. // 틀린 곳이 있으면 고쳐라 Correct errors, if any.
2 [나쁘다] be bad[evil / wrong / inferior]. ¶틀린 생각 an evil intention / a bad idea // 이 물건[달걀]은 틀렸다 These articles[eggs] are inferior[bad].
3 [끝장나다] be done for; be ruined[spoilt][이루지 못하다] end in catastrophe[failure]. ¶나는 이제 다 틀렸다 I am done for. / It's all up[over] with me. / I'm gone. / (구어) I'm a goner. // 일은 다 틀렸다 The game is up. / All is lost. // 그것 때문에 계획이 다 틀렸다 That upset all my plan.
4 [심사가 좋지 않다] become crooked[perverse / distorted]; be[get] warped. ¶너 왜 그렇게 심사가 틀려 있느냐 Why are you looking so crooked[distorted / cross]?
5 [사이가 나쁘다] fall out (with); be at odds (with); get estranged (from); get on bad terms (with). ¶서로 틀려 말을 하지 않다 have fallen out with each other and aren't on speaking terms.
6 →다르다

틀림없다 [잘못이 없다] correct; exact; (all) right; free from mistakes[errors]; [믿음성 있다] trustworthy; reliable; [확실하다] sure; certain; unfailing; infallible. ¶틀림없는 사람 a reliable person / a person of steady[firm / strong] character / a man of stability // 틀림없는 사실 a plain[an indisputable / a glaring] fact // …에 ~ must (be) / there is no[it is beyond] doubt that ... / it is certain that ... / I am sure (that) ... / certainly / surely // …이라고 해도 ~ It may safely be said that .... // "자네 틀림없나?" "틀림없고말고." "Are you quite sure?" "I am sure." / "As I'm alive." / "You bet!" / "Sure (things)!" / (미국 속어) "I can bet any money." // 저 사람은 변호사임에 ~ That man is no doubt a lawyer. / He must be a lawyer. // 상기와 같이 틀림없음 (서류 등에서) I hereby affirm the above statement to be true and correct (to the best of my knowledge). // 틀림없는 사실이다 It is an obvious fact. // 그의 집은 이 근처 어딘가에 있음이 ~ His house should be around here somewhere. // 그는 틀림없는 사람인가 Can he be trusted[relied upon]? // 그건 절대로 틀림없이 You may bet your boots on that. // 그의 판단에 맡겨 두면 틀림없을 터야 It may safely be left to his judgment. // 그는 시험에 합격했음에 ~ He must have passed the examination. // 그것은 틀림없는 그의 목소리였다 There was no doubt that it was his voice. **틀림없이** [정확히] correctly; rightly; errorlessly; [확실히] certainly;

surely; beyond [no / without] doubt; [분명히] evidently; [꼭·반드시] without fail. ¶~ …하다 do not fail[forget] to do / make it a rule to (do) / be in the habit of (doing) / ~ 그렇게 하겠다 I will go it, or I am a Dutchman. // 돈은 ~ 갚겠소 I will return the money to you without fail. // 이것은 ~ 그의 필적이다 This is undoubtedly his hand writing. // 그는 ~ 이길까요 Are you certain [sure] he will win? // 그것이면 ~ 합격될 게다 That is sure to[There's no doubt that it will] pass muster. // 내일 ~ 와 주십시오 Be sure [Don't fail] to come tomorrow. // 이것은 ~ 그의 모자다 It is most certainly his hat. // 내가 그것을 여기 ~ 두었다 I'm sure I put it here. // 그 사람이라면 ~ 믿을 수 있다 We can trust him all right. // 그는 ~ 성공한다 I am confident of his success. / He is sure to succeed. / I am sure he will succeed. // 우리 팀은 ~ 이긴다 You may depend upon it that [Depend upon it,] we will win. // 그런 말을 하면 그들은 ~ 너를 웃음거리로 만들 것이다 If you say such a thing, they'll be sure to make a laughingstock of you.

틀어넣다 cram; stuff; load; wad; squeeze (into); jam; (짐 등을) pack; (사람을) crowd (into). ¶음식을 배 속에 잔뜩 ~ stuff[load] one's stomach with food / stuff[gorge / prime] oneself with food / eat one's fill // 가방에 ~ pack (books) in a bag // 옷을 트렁크에 ~ ram[squeeze] clothes into a trunk.

틀어막다 1 (구멍 등) stop (up) (a hole); fill (up); stuff (up); plug (up). ¶구멍을 ~ stop [block] up a hole / fill [stop] a hole (with rags) // 솜으로 귀를 ~ stuff[fill / stop / wad] one's ears with cotton // 벌어진 틈을 ~ stop [fill] up a crevice with (something) / stuff (cotton) into a crevice / chink (up) // 그는 신문지로 쥐구멍을 틀어막았다 He stopped up a rathole with newspaper.
2 [억제·제지하다] stop; curb; check; put a stop to; put a stopper[gag] on. ¶입을 ~ forbid (a person) to mention (it) / stop (a person's) mouth / impose silence on (a person) / put a gag on (a person) / bind (a person) to secrecy / hush up (a matter) // 돈을 주어 입을 ~ buy (a person's) silence / put a gold muzzle (on newspapers).

틀어박다 1 cram; stuff. ⇨틀어넣다 2 [오래 넣어 두다] hoard; keep in dead storage; keep (a thing) idle (in stock).

틀어박히다 confine oneself to[in] (a room); stay in[indoors / at home]; closet oneself in (one's office); shut oneself up; be confined [closeted] in (one's room); keep (the house); remain[keep] indoors. ¶세상을 등지고 ~ retire from the public eye // 시골에 ~ retire into[to] the country // 그는 자기 방에 틀어박혔다 He shut himself up in[(문어) confined himself to] his room. // 그는 감기 때문에 집에 틀어박혀 있다 A cold confined him to his house. / He was kept at home by a cold. // 집에 틀어박혀 있지 말고 밖에 나가 아라 You shouldn't shut yourself up in the house — go outdoors. // 이 아이는 자기 세계 속에 틀어박혀서 마음을 터놓으려고 하지 않는다 This child has withdrawn into his shell and won't open his heart to anyone.

틀어지다 1 [빗나가다] turn aside[away]; swerve; deviate; (탄환 등이) miss (the

target); go wild [astray]. ¶(이야기가) 옆길로 ~ wander [digress] from the subject // 표적에서 ~ miss the target / go wide of the mark.
2 [불화하다] break (with); quarrel [fall out] (with); be alienated [estranged] (from); split (with); get into a dispute (with). ¶친구들과 몹시 틀어져 있다 be on very bad terms with one's friends // 서로 틀어져 말도 하지 않는다 have fallen out with each other and aren't on speaking terms // 그것 때문에 가족들 사이가 틀어졌다 That led to bad feelings between the members of the family. // 둘의 사이가 틀어졌다 The relationship between the two went sour.
3 [어그러지다] go wrong [amiss]; break down; fall through; fail. ¶다 ~ come to nothing [naught] / end in failure / end up in a failure [fiasco] / be unsuccessful // 악천후가 계획을 완전히 틀어놓게 했다 The bad weather upset [frustrated] our plans completely. // 교사의 몰이해한 태도가 그의 진로를 틀어지게 했다 The teacher's lack of understanding put him on the wrong in life. // 요즈음은 만사가 틀어지고 있소 Lately everything has gone wrong. // 건널목 사고로 철도의 운행 계획이 틀어졌다 The accident at the crossing has upset the railroad schedule. // 그의 목적이 틀어졌다 He missed [failed to hit] the mark. // 병 때문에 나의 계획은 틀어졌다 My plan fell apart because of my illness.
4 [꼬이다] get [be] twisted; be distorted; go [be] awry; kink. ¶넥타이가 틀어져 있다 have one's tie twisted.

틀지다 (서술적) be dignified; have dignity. ¶그는 틀지고 믿음직하다 He is dignified and reliable.

틀톱 a frame saw; a pit saw.

틈 1 [갈라진 자리] a crevice; a crack; a chink; a chasm; a fissure; a cleft; a gap; space; an interstice. ¶문~ an opening left by a door ajar / a chink in the door // 벽~ a crevice in the wall // ~을 막다 stop [fill] up (a crevice) with (something) / stuff (cotton) into a crevice / chink.
2 [공간·여지] room; space; a margin; a blank (여백). ¶그는 군중의 ~ 사이로 빠져나갔다 He made his way through the crowd. // 발을 디딜 ~이 없다 There is no room [place] to step [put one's foot down].
3 [불화] a discord; a difference; a breach (of friendship); a split; an estrangement. ¶두 사람 사이에 ~이 생겼다 The two became estranged. / Their relationship cooled. // 그것은 그들 사이의 ~을 잠시 메웠을 뿐이다 It only patched up their differences for the moment. // 양국 간에 깊은 ~이 생겼다 A gulp has formed [exists] between the two countries.
4 [기회] a chance; an opportunity. ¶~만 있으면 whenever one gets a chance / at all spare moments // ~을 노리다 watch for a chance // ~을 봐서 도망칠 작정이다 I am just waiting for a chance to escape.
5 [여가] time; leisure (hours); spare [leisure] time; time to spare; spare [odd] moments. ¶~만 있으면 at all spare moment // ~을 보아 at some convenient time // 그는 ~만 있으면 독서를 했다 He read whenever he could snatch a moment. / He spent every free moment (in) reading. // 독서하랴 가르치랴 조금도 ~이 없다 Between reading and teaching my time is fully taken up. // 오후엔 ~이 좀 있습니다 I have some leisure from my work in the afternoon.

틈나다 be free; be not busy; be at leisure. ¶틈나면 그것을 해 놓겠습니다 I will do it when I have time. // 틈나는 대로 저 노인을 찾아봐 주세요 Please go and see the old man when you can spare a moment.

틈내다 make time (to do); find time. ¶나는 온종일 틈낼 시간이 없다 My time is all taken up.

틈바구니 a crevice; room. ⇨ 틈1·2

틈새 a break; a rift; a gap; an opening; (문어) an aperture. ¶커튼의 ~에서 햇빛이 비쳤다 The sun shone in through an opening between the curtains. // 긴 산울타리에는 조그만 ~도 없었다 There was not even a small gap in the long stretch of hedge. // 구름의 ~에서 푸른 하늘이 보인다 Blue sky is visible through the breaks [rifts] in the clouds. // 울타리 ~로 고양이가 들락날락하고 있다 Cats go in and out through the opening in the fence. // 벽의 ~로부터 달빛이 새어 들어왔다 A streak of moonlight came into the room through a chink [crack] in the wall. // 바위 ~에 조그마한 도마뱀이 있었다 There was a tiny lizard in a crevice [crack] in the rock.

틈새기 [틈의 아주 좁은 부분] a narrow crack [opening / space]; a crevice; a cranny; a chink.

틈입 (闖入) intrusion; forced entry. **틈입하다** intrude [force / break] into; force one's way into; trespass on. ¶우익의 일단이 강연회장에 틈입해 왔다 A group of rightists broke into the lecture hall. // 댁까지 틈입해서 죄송합니다 I am very sorry to intrude on the privacy of your home.
● **틈입자** an intruder; a trespasser.

틈타다 [···을 이용하다] take (mean) advantage [avail oneself] of (someone's weakness); seize; take. ¶기회를 틈타서 도망치다 seize the moment [that opportunity] to run away // 그는 그녀의 약점을 틈타 그것을 이용했다 He took advantage of her vulnerable position. // 그의 선량한 성품을 틈타서 그들은 그것을 이용했다 They presumed on his good nature. // 그 사나이는 내 남편이 부재중임을 틈타 대담하게 뚜벅뚜벅 집 안으로 걸어 들어와 He picked a time when my husband was away and came boldly into our house.

틈틈이 1 [틈마다] at each gap; in every opening. **2** [여가마다] in one's spare time; [시간의 중간에] in the intervals (between). ¶수업 도중 ~ 학생과 만난다 I see students (in the intervals) between classes. // ~ 이 일을 해 두세요 Please get this work done in your spare time. // ~ 스웨터를 짜고 있다 I knit sweaters in my leisure hours [when I have time to spare]. // 그는 화가인데 ~ 시도 쓰고 있다 He is an artist, but he writes poetry as well when he has the time.

티[1] **1** (먼지) a mote; dust; a particle; a grit; (불순물) impurities; (이물질) a foreign element. ¶눈에 ~가 들어가다 have a mote in one's eye // 집 안에는 ~ 하나 없었다 There was not a speck of dust in the whole house.
2 [흠] a flaw; a speck; a spot; a blemish; a

stain; a blot; a blur; a defect. ¶옥에 ~ a fly in the ointment / a flaw in an otherwise perfect thing.
3 [기색·작태] an air; a look; a touch (of melancholy); a dash; a shade; a tinge; [태도] a manner; behavior; an attitude; bearing; [몸짓] gesture. ¶학자~를 부리지 않는 학자 an unpedantic scholar∥유식한 ~를 내며 with a knowing air∥…(한) ~가 있다 smack of (recklessness) / have a touch [dash] of ... / look like (an old man)∥~를 내다 act (like / as if) / behave[bear] oneself / assume[put on] the air (of a scholar)∥시골~가 나다 have a rural appearance / look rustic / be rustic-looking / (사람이) look like a countryman∥그는 되게 선배~를 낸다 He doesn't have to put on such a patronizing [superior] air (even) if he is my senior.∥그녀는 타격을 받은 ~가 전혀 없었다 Her manner showed no signs of shock.
티(를) 뜯다 [흠잡다] find fault (with); try to find a fault (in a person[thing]); cavil [carp] at (another's) faults; fault (a person [thing]); pick holes in (a person's) coat; (미국 구어) pick on (a person[thing]).
티(를) 보다 [흠을 살피다] see[look over] whether there is any flaw in (it).
티² [차] tea.
  ●**티 파티** [다과회] a tea party; tea; (구어) a tea fight. ¶~에 남을 초대하다 ask[invite] a person to tea.
티³ (골프의) a tee.
티격나다 break (with); quarrel[fall out] (with); be alienated[estranged] (from).
티격태격 wranglingly; bickeringly. ¶그들 형제는 언제나 ~ 다투기만 했다 There was always rancor[bad feeling / bad blood] between the brothers. / The brothers were hostile to[at odds with] each other. **티격태격하다** quarrel[dispute / wrangle] (with); bicker with each other.
티 그라운드 teeing ground.
티끌 1 [먼지] dust; a mote. ¶속세의 ~에 오염되다 be stained with the impurities of the world∥~을 털다 shake off the dust / dust (furniture) / brush (a hat)∥책상 위에는 ~ 하나 없었다 There wasn't a speck of dust on the desk. **2** [아주 작은[적은] 것] a tiny bit. ¶~만큼의 값어치도 없다 It is not worth a snap (of one's fingers). ¶그에게는 ~만큼의 양심도 없다 He has not an atom[ounce] of conscience in him.∥그 사람에 대해서는 ~만큼도 생각하지 않아요 I don't care a bit [at all] about him. / (속어) I don't give a damn about him.(▶ 남들 앞에서 자주 사용하지 않는 것이 바람직한 표현).
티끌 모아 태산 (속담) Many a little makes a mickle.; Little and often make a heap in time.; Many drops make a shower.
티눈 a corn. ¶~이 생긴 발가락 a toe with a callosity∥발바닥에 ~이 생겨 아프다 I have a corn on the sole of my foot and it hurts.
티브이 TV; television.
티샤쓰 a T-shirt. ⇨"티셔츠
티샷 a tee shot.
티셔츠 a T-shirt.
티스푼 a teaspoon.
티엔티 [폭약] TNT; trinitrotoluene; trinitrotoluol.
티오 [조직표] TO(▶ table of organization의 약어); [정원] authorized personnel.
티자 [T자형의 제도용 자] a T square.
티케이오 (권투에서) a TKO(▶ a technical knockout의 약어).
티켓 a ticket.
티크 (나무) a teak; (목재) teak(wood).
티타늄 [화] titanium(기호 Ti).
티타임 (오후의 차 마시는 시간) teatime; [오전·오후의 중간 휴식] (미) a coffee break; (영) a tea break.
티티새 [동] a dusky thrush.
티푸스 typhoid[enteric] fever; abdominal typhus(주로 장티푸스를 가리킴). ¶~(성)의 typhoid∥발진 ~ typhus (fever)∥파라 ~ paratyphoid fever.
틴에이저 a teenager(13세에서 19세까지); teener. ¶~ 소녀들의 우상 an idol among teenage girls∥내 딸애는 아직 ~입니다 My daughter is still in her teens.
팀 a team. ¶홈 ~ the home team∥~을 만들다 organize[get up] a team∥~의 일원이다 be a member of the team / be on the (baseball) team∥우리 학교 ~이 이겼다 Our school team won. ¶그는 우리 야구 ~에 들어 있다 He is in[on] our baseball team.
팀워크 teamwork; cooperation. ¶~가 좋다 [나쁘다] have fine[be poor in] teamwork∥~가 잘 짜여 있다 exhibit fine teamwork / work well together as a team.
팀파니 timpani (sing. -no) (복수형이지만 종종 단수 취급); a kettledrum.
  ●**팀파니 연주자** a timpanist.
팀플레이 team play.
팁 1 [행하·축의] a tip; a gratuity. ¶두둑한[약간의] ~ a large[small] tip∥~을 바라다 expect a tip∥~을 받다 receive[get] a tip∥웨이터에게 ~을 주다 tip a waiter∥후한 ~을 주다 give a generous tip∥~을 뿌리다 give tips all round∥~을 주어 …시키다 tip (a waitress) into (doing something)∥거스름돈은 자네 ~으로 받아 두게 Keep the change as a tip to you.∥그는 탁자에 몇 푼의 ~을 놓았다 He put a small tip on the table.∥~은 사양합니다 No tips accepted. / No tipping.∥보이에게 ~ 10,000원을 주었다 I tipped the waiter 10,000 won. / I gave the waiter 10,000 won tip. / I gave a tip of 10,000 won to the waiter.
2 [야구] a tip. ¶파울 ~ a foul tip.
팅크 (a) tincture. ¶요오드[캠퍼] ~ (tincture of) iodine[camphor].
팅팅 tautly; tightly. ⇨탱탱

ㅍ

파[1] [식] a Welsh[spring] onion; a green onion(양파); a shallot(골파).

파[2] [음] fa. ¶~ 을 F / f.

파[3] [골프] par. ¶그는 ~로 돌았다 He parred the course.∥그는 투 언더 ~로 돌았다 He went round (the course) in two under par.

파(派) **1** [패거리] a group; a coterie. ¶교장 ~ the supporters of the principal∥전전[전후]~ the prewar[postwar] generation∥지주~ the landed interests[group]∥친미~ a pro-American group∥소장(少壯)~ a young group∥관학(官學)~와 사학(私學)~의 다툼 a strife between the government and the private school factions∥나는 시장(市長)~가 아니다 I am not on the mayor's side.
2 [당파] a party; a faction. ¶민 씨 지지[반대]~ the pro-Min[anti-Min] faction∥주류~ the mainstreamers∥비주류~ the nonmainstreamers∥혁신~ the reformists∥강경~ the hardline faction∥온건~ the moderate faction / the moderates∥좌~ the left-wing faction / leftists∥우~ the right wing faction / rightists∥그 당은 두 ~로 갈라졌다 The party split into two factions.
3 [학파·유파] a school. ¶(문학·예술상의) 고전[낭만]~ the classical[romantic] school∥한 ~를 이루다 found a school of one's own.
4 [종파] a sect; a denomination; [족벌] a branch of a family[clan]. ¶감리교~ the Methodist communion∥장로교~ the Presbyterian denomination∥개신교의 여러 ~ Protestant denominations.

파(破) [물건의] damage; injury; breakage; breakdown; (사람의) a defect; a fault. ¶~가 나다 be damaged[destroyed / impaired / spoilt] / be broken (down)∥~가 난 물건 a defective[damaged / flawed] article∥그릇에 ~가 나다 a dish gets damaged.

파격(破格) an exception. **파격하다** make an exception.

파격적(破格的) exceptional; unprecedented; unconventional; special; abnormal. ¶~ 승진 an exceptional promotion∥~인 대우를 받다 enjoy exceptionally good treatment∥~인 값으로 봉사하다 sell (a thing) at an absurdly low price / offer (goods) at a great bargain∥~ 승진을 하다 obtain[get] an unprecedented[exceptional] promotion∥~으로 싼값에 팔다 sell at an absurdly low price∥하인으로서 그런 ~ 대우를 받은 사람은 없었다 No servant had ever been treated so well.

파견(派遣) dispatch; despatch. **파견하다** dispatch; despatch; send. ¶군대[함대]를 ~ dispatch an army[a fleet] (to)∥대사를 ~ accredit an ambassador (to)∥대표를 ~ delegate[send] a representative∥사절을 ~ dispatch[send] an envoy (to)∥정부는 사절을 국제 연합에 파견했다 The government dispatched[sent] an envoy to the U.N.

● **파견군** an expeditionary force[army]. **파견대** a contingent; a detachment.

파경(破鏡) [깨진 거울] a broken mirror; [이혼] (a) divorce; separation; [이지러진 달] a waned moon. ¶~에 이르다 be divorced.

파계(破戒) breaking[transgression of] a commandment; apostasy. **파계하다** violate [break] the Buddhist commandments; transgress; apostatize.

● **파계승** an apostate[a depraved] monk; a fallen[sinful] priest.

파고(波高) the height of a wave; wave height.

파고들다 [조사·검토하다] dig[delve / probe] into (a problem); investigate; make a thorough investigation; [침식·침투하다] eat into; gnaw (at one's heart); burn into (one's mind); cut into. ¶마음속에 ~ eat into one's heart∥상대방의 (선거) 기반에 ~ encroach upon the constituency of another candidate / bite[eat] into another candidate's constituency∥외국 시장에 ~ make an inroad into[up]on) a foreign market∥파고들며 연구하다 delve[dig] into (a matter) / make a thorough investigation of∥질투심이 어느덧 그녀의 가슴을 파고들었다 Jealousy wormed into her mind before she knew it.∥그는 사건의 진상을 파고들었다 He went to the root of the matter.

파곡(波谷) a trough[furrow] between waves.

파곳 [음] a fagotto (pl. -ti); a bassoon.

파괴(破壞) destruction; demolition; breakdown. **파괴하다** destroy; break; ruin; wreck; demolish; dilapidate(집 등을); work havoc (upon); make havoc (of / among); ravage. ¶한 마을을 완전히 ~ raze a village to the ground∥가정의 평화와 행복을 ~ destroy the peace and happiness of families. →¶파괴되다 be broken / be destroyed[demolished / smashed / razed / dilapidated] / collapse∥낡은 가옥이 파괴되고 아파트가 세워졌다 The old house was demolished[torn down] and an apartment house was built.∥그 두 사람 사이의 친밀한 관계가 파괴되었다 The friendly relationship between the two has been destroyed.∥그의 꿈은 완전히 파괴되었다 His dream was utterly shattered. / His hopes were completely ruined.∥태풍으로 많은 가옥이 파괴되었다 Many houses were demolished by the typhoon.

● **파괴력** destructive power. **파괴자** a destroyer; a disrupter; a devastator; a desolator.

파국(破局) [붕괴] a collapse; [비극적인 결말] a catastrophe. ¶~에 직면하다 be in the face of ruin∥~으로 몰고 가다 drive into catastrophe∥그 부부는 마침내 ~을 맞이했다 The couple were finally faced with ruin. / (이혼) They were finally divorced.∥그 독직 사건이 회사의 ~을 초래했다 The corruption case brought about the collapse of the company.

파국적(破局的) catastrophic.

파급(波及) spreading; extending; reaching. ¶그 새 약품 발표의 ~ 효과는 아주 컸다 The announcement of the new drug had far-

파기 reaching effects [considerable repercussions]. **파급하다** (…에 미치다) extend; spread; (영향을 끼치다) influence; affect. ¶이 사건은 정계에 파급하는 바가 컸다 This affair has greatly affected the political world. ➔¶파급되는 바가 큰 영향 a far-reaching influence [effect] // 전국에 파급되다 extend all over the country / raise [create] a nation-wide stir // 정계에 파급되다 affect the political world // 그 분쟁은 한국에까지 파급됐다 The dispute extended [spread] to Korea.

파기(破棄) (문서 등을 찢어 버림) destruction; (계약 등을 취소함) (an) annulment; (a) cancellation; (판결을 취소함) (a) reversal. ¶조약의 ~ the denunciation [abrogation] of a treaty // 외채(外債)의 ~ repudiation of foreign debts. **파기하다** destroy; (무효로 하다) annul (a decision); cancel (a contract); break (a promise); abrogate (a lease); scrap (a treaty). ¶원심 판결을 ~ quash the original judgment // 그는 자기 서약을 파기했다 He broke [went back on] his promise. // 나는 이 계약을 파기하기로 결정했다 I have decided to cancel this contract. // 대법원은 고등법원의 판결을 파기했다 The Supreme Court reversed [overturned] the high court's ruling. ➔¶상호 간 합의에 의해 계약이 파기되었다 The contract was annulled [canceled] by mutual agreement. // 원(原)판결이 파기되었다 The original verdict was reversed [overturned]. // 그 계획은 재정상 이유로 파기되었다 The project was abandoned [given up] for financial reasons.

파김치 *pagimchi*; pickled (Welsh) onion.

파김치(가) 되다 (몹시 지치다) be dead tired; be dog-tired; be worn [fagged] out; be totally [utterly] exhausted.

파내다 dig up [out]; unearth; (발굴하다) excavate; disinter. ¶땅속에서 ~ dig (something) from [out of] the ground // 석탄을 ~ dig coal (from a mine) // 나무뿌리를 ~ grub the roots of a tree // 시체를 ~ dig out [disinter / exhume] a corpse // 금을 ~ dig gold (from a mine) // 개가 흙 속에서 무엇인가를 파냈다 The dog has unearthed [dug up] something. // 그들은 많은 양의 도기를 파냈다 They excavated a great deal of pottery. // 그는 감자를 파내고 있었다 He was digging potatoes. // 이 산의 석탄은 이미 모두 파내어졌다 The coal of this mine has already been completely dug up.

파노라마 a panorama. ¶그것은 아주 ~ 같은 경치다 It is quite a panoramic view.

파니 idly; indolently; lazily. ¶~ 놀다 lead an idle life / be always idle.

파다 1 (땅·구멍을) dig; delve; bore (a hole); drive (a tunnel); (파서 뚫다) excavate (a canal); (후벼 내다) scoop out. ¶옷깃이 크게 파인 블라우스 a blouse with a low neckline / a low-cut blouse // 구멍을 ~ excavate [make] a hole (in) // 땅에 구멍이를 ~ dig a hole in the ground // 땅을 ~ delve [dig in] the ground / (동물이) burrow / (농사짓다) till the soil / do farm work // 우물을 ~ sink [dig] a well // 모래를 ~ dig up the sand // 참호를 ~ dig a trench // 삽으로 ~ dig with a shovel // 파 들어가다 dig (a hole) into (the earth) / dig one's way into // 파 내려가다 dig down // 송곳으로 판자에 구멍을 후벼 ~ bore a hole in a board // 그는 땅에 깊은 구멍을 팠다 He dug a deep hole in the ground. // 그들은 산을 파서 터널을 만들고 있다 They are digging [boring] a tunnel through the mountain.

2 (새기다) carve (in / on); engrave; chisel; cut. ¶명패에 이름을 ~ engrave a plate with a name / engrave a name on a plate // 도장을 ~ engrave a seal / (도장포에 의뢰하여) have one's seal cut [engraved].

3 (이치·문제 등을) make a search [inquiry] (for / into); delve [probe] into (a problem); dig (for / into). ¶깊은 학리(學理)를 ~ explore an abstruse theory // 진상을 ~ inquire into the true state of things / go (down) to [get at] the bottom of a matter // 문제를 깊이 ~ probe deeply into a matter / dig [get] to the bottom of a matter.

4 (공부를) study hard; work hard at (one's studies); (미) grind (away) (at); (구어) dig in [into] (one's subject); (속어) cram [bone] up (on). ¶공부만 파는 학생 (미국 속어) a dig / (미국 속어) a plugger / (미국 속어) a grinder // 영어를 들이 ~ study English in earnest / grind away at English.

파다하다(頗多─) abundant; numerous; large in number; quite frequent. ¶파다하게 일어나는 일 a matter of frequent occurrence // 그러한 예는 ~ We have a good many examples of the kind [sort]. / That sort of thing happens quite often. // 이것은 파다한 예 중의 하나에 지나지 않는다 This is only an instance among the many.

파다하다(播多─) widespread; (서술적) be widely known; be rife. ¶그 소문이 파다하게 퍼졌다 The rumor [report] went about [got abroad]. // 사장이 곧 사직하리라는 소문이 ~ The air is filled with rumors that the president of the company will soon resign his post. // 당지(當地)에서는 전쟁이 날 것이라는 소문이 ~ Rumors of war are rife in this part of the country.

파닥거리다 1 (새·깃털 등이) flutter; flap. ¶날개를 ~ flutter (its) wings // 파닥거리며 날아가다 fly with a flap of the wings / flop across the sky // 파닥거리며 땅에 떨어지다 (a wounded bird) flutter to the ground // 새 새끼는 파닥거렸지만 날지를 못했다 The fledgling's wings flopped again and again, but it could not get off the ground. // 새가 새장 안에서 파닥거렸다 The bird fluttered its wings in the cage.

2 (물고기가) leap; jump; flop; splash. ¶물고기가 둑 위에서 힘없이 파닥거렸다 The fish flopped helplessly on the bank. // 강물 속에서 파닥거리는 저 고기를 보아라 Look at that fish splashing about in the river.

파닥파닥 (새·돛 등이) flapping; fluttering; flip-flap; flip-flop; (물고기가) flopping; leaping; splashing. **파닥파닥하다** flutter; leap. ⇨ 파닥거리다

파도(波濤) waves; billows; surges; a beachcomber(밀려오는); a surf; a breaker(환). ¶큰 ~ a big [great] wave / a high sea / a billow / a mountain of a wave // ~ 모양의 wavelike // ~ 없는 calm / smooth // ~와 싸우다 buffet the waves // ~에 떠돌다 drift [float] on the waves // ~에 시달리다 be tossed about by the waves // ~에 휩쓸리다 be washed [carried] away by the waves // ~에 휘말리다 be swallowed up by the waves // ~처럼 밀려오다 surge [rush] upon // ~를 헤치다 plow the

waves / 그 배는 ~를 가르고 전진했다 The ship plowed[cut] its way through high seas. // 거친 ~가 일고 있었다 The waves were running high. // 거친 ~가 바위에 부서지고 있었다 Angry waves were breaking on the rocks. // 배는 거친 ~를 헤치고 나아갔다 The ship sailed on through the rough seas.
● **파도 소리** the sound[roar] of the waves.
파도타기 surfboard-riding; surfing. ¶~를 하다 surf / ride the surf (on a board) / ~를 하는 사람 a surfer / a surf rider.

파도치다 (波濤-) wave; surge; billow. ¶파도치는 대로 (drift about) at the mercy of the waves / 파도치는 바다 choppy sea / 파도치는 해변 the shore washed by the waves / 벼 이삭이 논에서 파도치고 있다 The ears of rice are waving in the field. // 그가 웃었을 때 그의 배는 파도치듯 흔들렸다 When he laughed, his belly heaved[wobbled]. // 내 가슴이 심하게 파도쳤다 My heart throbbed violently. / My heart beat fast.

파동 (波動) a wave[an undulatory] motion; undulation; fluctuation. ¶가격 ~ fluctuations in prices / 경제 ~ an economic crisis // 정치 ~ a political upheaval / 증권 ~ wild fluctuations of the stock market / a stock market crisis.
● **파동설** the wave[undulatory] theory (of light).

파두 (巴豆) [식] a croton (plant).
파라다이스 (a) paradise.
파라솔 [양산] a parasol. ¶비치 ~ a beach umbrella // ~을 받다 put up[hold] a parasol.
파라오 [고대 이집트 왕의 칭호] a Pharaoh.
파라티온 [화] parathion (insecticide).
● **파라티온 중독** parathion poisoning.
파라티푸스 [의] paratyphoid (fever).
● **파라티푸스균** a paratyphoid bacillus.
파라핀 [화] paraffin(e).
● **파라핀지** wax(ed) paper.
파란 (波瀾) 1 a wave; a billow. ⇨ 파랑(波浪)
2 [소동·분규] (a) disturbance; a commotion; troubles; a storm. ¶~이 많은 eventful // ~많은 의회 a stormy session of the Assembly / ~ 많은 인생 a varied[checkered / dramatic] life / a life full of ups and downs // ~만장의 생애 a checkered[an eventful] career // ~을 일으키다 create[cause] troubles / raise a disturbance (in a dead calm) // 그의 외도가 가족에게 ~을 일으켰다 His (love) affair caused all kinds of problems[trouble] in his family. // 수상의 조심성 없는 발언 때문에 정계에 ~이 일어났다 The prime minister's indiscreet utterance created a sensation[caused an uproar] in the political world. // 이번의 선거 운동에는 ~이 있을 것 같다 This election campaign is going to be a stormy one. // 그는 ~만장의 생애를 끝마쳤다 His stormy life came to an end. // 오늘의 씨름은 ~의 날이었다 It was a stormy day in ssireum today. / There was an upheaval in the ring today. // 앞으로 더욱 ~ 곡절이 있을 것이다 The situation will hence-forward grow more involved and troublesome.

파랄림픽 [국제 신체장애자 체육 대회] the Paralympics.
파랑 [청색인] blue; azure; [하늘색] skyblue; [녹색] green.
파랑 (波浪) a wave; a roller; [큰 파도] a billow; a surge.
● **파랑 주의보** a high sea warning.
파랑새 1 [동] a broad-billed roller. 2 [푸른 새] a bluebird (▶ 길조를 상징함).
파랗다 [청색인] blue; azure; [녹색인] green; [창백하다] pale; pallid (face). ¶파란 눈 blue eyes // 파란 풀 green grass / 파란 하늘 a blue sky // 파랗게 질린 얼굴 a pallid[wan / cadaverous] face / 파랗게 물들이다 dye (the cloth) blue / 파랗게 질리다 turn deadly pale / turn as white as a sheet (with fright).

파래 [식] green laver; (a) sea lettuce.
파래지다 (나뭇잎 등이) become[turn] blue [green]; (얼굴이) turn pale[pallid]; go green; lose color. ¶파래졌다 빨개졌다 하다 turn alternately pale and red / 나뭇잎이 파래졌다 Leaves of trees turned green. // 그의 얼굴이 파래졌다 His face turned pale.

파렴치 (破廉恥) shamelessness; infamy; ignominy; impudence; effrontery. **파렴치하다** shameless; infamous; ignominious; disgraceful; (사당적) be dead[lost] to (the sense of) shame; have the cheek of the devil. ¶파렴치한 거짓말쟁이 a shameless liar // 이 파렴치한 녀석 같으니 Shameless person, you! // 그는 파렴치한 사람이오 He has no[is lost to all] sense of shame.
● **파렴치한** (-漢) a shameless fellow.

파르르 seething; in a fit of anger; in a (sudden) burst of flame; trembling. ⇨ 바르르

파르스름하다 bluish; be tinged with blue; rather pale. ⇨ 푸르스름하다

파릇파릇 all spotted green. ⇨ 푸릇푸릇

파리 [동] a fly; a housefly. ¶~를 쫓다 fan [drive / scare] flies away / ~를 찰싹 치다 swat a fly // …에 ~가 꾀다 flies swarm (round / about) / (sugar) attract flies // ~가 과일에 쉬를 슬었다 A fly blowed fruit. // ~ 한 마리가 그 위에 앉아 있었다 A fly was sitting on it. // ~가 그것에 온통 꾀어 있었다 Flies were crawling all over it.

파리(를) 날리다 (one's business) be slack [dull]; fall off.
● **파리 목숨** transient[ephemeral] existence; mean[cheap] life. **파리약** fly poison; [액체] fly water. **파리채** a fly flap[swatter]; a flapper. ¶~로 파리를 잡다 flap[swat] a fly.

파리하다 [창백하다] pale; pallid; wan (look); [해쓱하다] emaciated; worn; gaunt. ¶파리한 얼굴 a thin[drawn] face / a pallid[haggard] face // 파리해지다 become thin / lose one's weight / lose flesh / fall off / 앓고 나서 파리해 보이다 look thin after an illness // 그녀는 오래 앓고 나서 얼굴이 파리해 보였다 Her face looked wan after her long illness.

파마 a permanent wave; (미) a permanent; (영국 구어) a perm. ¶미장원에 가서 ~를 하다 go to the beauty parlor for a perm(anent) [to have one's hair permed]. **파마하다** get a permanent; have one's hair permed. ¶그녀는 머리를 파마했다 She has a perm(anent).

파먹다 1 [먹어 들어가다] eat into[away / out]. ¶땅을 ~ live by farming // 벌레가 사과 흰개미가 집의 토대를 파먹어 버렸다 White ant ate away the foundation of the house. // 부패는 나라의 심장부를 파먹는다 Corruption eats at the heart of the country. 2 [도식하다] eat idle bread[the bread of idleness]; live [lead] an idle life; (재산 등을) eat away what

파면 one has. ¶하는 일 없이 재산을 다 ~ run through one's fortune in idleness.

파면 (罷免) dismissal; removal; discharge. **파면하다** dismiss; discharge; relieve (a person) of his post; remove (a person) from office; (미국 구어) fire. →¶파면되다 be fired [dismissed / discharged] / be relieved of one's post / 직무 태만으로 파면되다 lose one's position through neglect of duty // 그는 회사에서 파면되었다 He was dismissed from the company. // 그 검사는 부정행위 때문에 파면되었다 The prosecutor was discharged [dismissed] for doing something dishonest.

파멸 (破滅) ruin; destruction; wreck; collapse; downfall; fall. ¶~에 직면하고 있다 be on the brink of ruin // (일신의) ~을 초래하다 bring (down) ruin upon oneself / work one's own undoing // 그는 술로 몸의 ~을 자초했다 Alcohol was his ruin. / He ruined himself by drinking too much. // 그의 최초의 잘못이 그를 ~로 이끌었다 His first mistake led (him) to his ruin. / His first wrong step proved his undoing. // 그녀의 미모가 ~의 원인이었다 Her beauty was her ruin. // 그는 노름에 몰두해서 일신의 ~을 초래했다 His mania for gambling has brought about his ruin. **파멸하다** be ruined; be done for; go to ruin[the devil / dogs]; go under.

파문 (波紋) 1 [수면에 이는 잔물결] a ripple; a water ring; a (wave) ring on the water. ¶~을 이루다 ripple / make ripples // ~이 퍼지다 waves ripple out in all directions // ~을 그리다 ripple / start a water ring / purl / 수면에 ~이 퍼졌다 Ripples spread across the water.

2 [영향] a stir; a sensation; repercussions. ¶~을 일으키다 create a ripple[stir] / cause [make] trouble // 정계에 ~을 일으키다 [던지다] create a stir[cause repercussions] in the political world // 그 사건은 재계에 큰 ~을 던졌다 The incident created quite a stir [caused a great sensation] in financial circles. // 그 보도는 온 나라 안에 큰 ~을 일으켰다 The news created a stir in the country.

3 [물결무늬] a wave pattern.

파문 (破門) [종] excommunication; (사제간의) expulsion. **파문하다** excommunicate; (제자를) strike (a person) out of; expel. →¶파문당하다 be excommunicated / be expelled // 그는 가톨릭교회에서 파문되었다 He was excommunicated from the Catholic Church.

파묻다¹ 1 (땅속에) bury (in); entomb; [매장하다] inter; inhume. ¶얼굴을 두 손에 파묻고 with one's face buried in one's hands / 시체를 ~ bury a dead body / commit a body to the earth // 손수건에 얼굴을 파묻고 울다 weep in one's handkerchief // 가슴속 깊이 파묻어 두다 keep (a matter) all to oneself // 얼굴을 베개에 파묻고 울다 cry with one's face pressed into a pillow. 2 (일·사건을) bury in oblivion; smother [cover / hush] up. ¶사건을 쉬쉬 ~ hush[cover] up the scandal[matter].

파묻다² [꼬치꼬치 묻다] ask inquisitively [closely]; dig for information; quiz; grill. ¶그들은 나의 과거를 파묻기 시작했다 They began poking around into my past. // 그는 나에게 미주알고주알 파물었다 He questioned me to the minutest details. / He subjected me to searching inquiry.

파묻히다 be buried (in / under); (세상에) be buried in oblivion. ¶눈에 ~ be buried under[in] the snow / be snowed under // 시골에 ~ bury oneself[be buried] in the country // 세상에 파묻혀 살다 live in obscurity / live an obscure life // 일에 ~ be up to the neck in work // 파묻힌 재능을 발굴하다 unearth hidden talent // 우리는 눈(토사) 속에 파묻혀 있는 차를 겨우 찾아냈다 We had great difficulty finding the car which was buried in the snow[under the landslide]. // 오솔길은 낙엽 속에 파묻혀 있었다 The narrow path was covered with (a thick layer of) dead leaves. // 3개월 동안 마을은 눈 속에 파묻혀 있었다 For three months the village was snowed under. // 그는 시골에 파묻혀 버렸다 He buried himself[lived obscurely] in the country.

파발 (擺撥) a post station; a stage.
● **파발꾼** an express messenger; a courier.
파발마 a post horse. ¶~를 띄우다 dispatch a messenger on a post horse.

파밭 an onion patch.

파벌 (派閥) a clique; a faction; a coterie; a ring. ¶~을 짓다 form [join] cliques // ~을 없애다 eliminate the factionalism // 여러 ~로 갈라지다 split into petty factions // 그 당은 몇몇 ~로 갈라졌다 The party split into several factions. // 이 클럽 안에는 작은 ~이 많이 있었다 There were lots of little cliques in the club.
● **파벌 싸움** a factional[an interfactional] strife[dispute]; rivalry between factions. **파벌주의** factionalism.

파병 (派兵) the dispatch of troops. **파병하다** dispatch troops (to). ¶해외로 ~ send troops overseas.

파삭파삭하다 crisp; crumbly; friable; (과자 등이) short; (서술어) eat crisp[short]. ¶파삭파삭한 비스킷 a crisp biscuit // 파삭파삭한 흙 crumbly soil // (충분히 튀겨져서) 파삭파삭해지다 frizzle // 파삭파삭하게 구워지다 be burned to a crisp.

파산 (破産) insolvency; bankruptcy; (financial) failure; smash. ¶강제 [신청] ~ involuntary[voluntary] bankruptcy // 저 회사는 ~ 직전에 있다 That company is on the verge of failure[bankruptcy]. // 우리 재정은 ~ 직전에 있다 We are virtually bankrupt [(구어) broke]. **파산하다** become [go] bankrupt[insolvent]; go into bankruptcy; fail; be brought to ruin; come [go] to smash; (미국 구어) go under; (속어) go broke. ¶상점은 마침내 파산했다 That store has finally gone under. // 그 회사는 파산했다 The company went bankrupt. →¶그는 계획적으로 회사를 파산시켰다 He bankrupted his company deliberately.
● **파산 부도 세일** a bankrupcty sale. **파산 선고** an adjudication of bankruptcy. ¶~를 받다 be declared bankrupt // 법원은 그에게 ~를 했다 The court declared[(문어) adjudicated] him bankrupt[insolvent]. **파산자** a bankrupt; an insolvent. **파산 채권[채무]** claims[debts] provable in bankruptcy.

파상 (波狀) wave; undulation. ¶~의 wavy / wavelike / undulating // ~을 그리다 be wavy / rise and fall / undulate.

● **파상 공격** an attack in waves; a [an air] raid in waves; wave bombing. ¶~을 가하다 launch [make] a series of attacks 《on / upon》.

파상풍(破傷風) 〔의〕 tetanus; (턱뼈가 굳어지는) lockjaw; (말의) stag-evil. ¶~의 tetanic.

파생(派生) derivation. **파생하다** derive [be derived] 《from》; stem 《from》; originate 《in》. ¶뜻밖의 사태가 파생했다 An unexpected situation developed 《from it》.∥거기에서 중대한 사태가 파생했다 A serious situation developed as a result. →¶명사에서 파생된 형용사 an adjective derived from a noun.
● **파생어** a derivative.

파생적(派生的) derivative; secondary(이차적인). ¶~인 사건 a matter incidental to a main issue∥그것은 ~인 문제에 지나지 않는다 It's purely a secondary matter.

파선(波線) a wavy [an undulating] line; a wave.

파선(破船) 〔난파〕 shipwreck; 〔난파선〕 a wrecked ship; a wreck. **파선하다** be wrecked.

파손(破損) damage; injury; breakage; breakdown; dilapidation. ¶~이 크다〔작다〕 suffer a heavy [slight] damage∥~을 면하다 be intact∥태풍에 의한 가옥의 ~은 컸다 The typhoon did heavy damage to houses.∥수입된 도자기에 많은 ~이 있었다 There was a lot of breakage among the imported chinaware. / Many pieces of the imported chinaware were broken.∥그 배는 ~을 면했다 The boat remained intact. **파손하다** damage; break down. →¶파손되다 be broken (down) / be damaged [dilapidated / destroyed / impaired]∥파손되기 쉬운 easy to break / fragile / breakable∥파손되기가 쉬운 물건 a fragile item / something fragile∥파손된 오두막집 a tumble-down shack∥파손된 옛 성 a dilapidated old castle∥파손된 비행기는 2대뿐이었다 Only two planes were damaged.∥공장의 기계류는 모두 파손되어 있었다 All the machinery in the factory was out of order.∥이 종류의 그릇은 파손되기 쉽다 Vessels of this sort are fragile.
● **파손품** damaged goods.

파송(派送) dispatch; despatch. ⇨=파견

파쇄(破碎) crush(ing); smash(ing); cracking (to pieces); fragmentation. **파쇄하다** crush; smash; shatter; crack [break] to pieces; break up. ¶돌을 ~ crush stone (into pieces).
● **파쇄기** a disintegrator; a crusher.

파쇠(破-) scrap metal [iron]; iron scrap.

파쇼(ⓘFascio) (주의) fascism; (운동) the fascist movement.

파수(把守) 1 〔행위〕 watch; lookout; vigilance; surveillance; guard; vigil. ¶~를 보다 watch / keep (a) watch 《for / against》 / stand guard / be on the lookout [watch] ∥ 입구에다 ~를 세우다 place a watch [guard] at the door∥우리는 그의 집에 ~를 세웠다 We kept guard over his house. **2** a watchman. ⇨=파수꾼(⇨파수)
● **파수꾼** a watchman; a guard; a lookout; a keeper; a picket. ¶~을 두다 place a guard 《at》 / set [post] a lookout 《for》. **파수병**(-兵) a sentry; guard; a sentinel.

파스¹ 〔약〕 PAS(▶ para-aminosalicylic acid의 약어).

파스²(ⓢPasta) Ben-Gay(상표명); a muscle relaxant [relaxer]. ¶~를 붙여 보내세요 Try Ben-Gay, please.

파스칼 〔컴〕 PASCAL; Pascal.

파스텔 (a) pastel.
● **파스텔화** a pastel; a drawing in pastel.

파슬리 〔식〕 a parsley.

파시(波市) a seasonal fish market.

파시스트 〔파시즘 신봉자〕 a fascist; 〔파시스트 당원〕 a Fascist.

파시즘 fascism.

파악(把握) 〔바로 이해함〕 understanding; grasping (the situation, the meaning, etc.) ¶상세한 점의 충분한 ~ a good grasp of details. **파악하다** grasp; seize; understand; catch hold of. ¶요점을 ~ grasp the point∥그 사건의 진상을 ~ get at the truth of the matter∥상황을 ~ grasp the situation / take in the situation∥문장의 뜻을 ~ grasp the meaning of a sentence∥그는 사태를 잘 파악하지 못한 것 같다 It seems that he has but a poor [feeble] grip of the situation.∥그녀는 내가 한 말을 파악하지 못했다 She couldn't catch what I said.∥이 그림은 그 모델의 변별적 특징을 잘 파악하고 있다 This picture has captured the distinctive features of the model.∥그는 언뜻 보고 사태를 파악했다 He took in the situation at a glance.∥그는 산수의 요령을 잘 파악하고 있다 He has a good grasp of arithmetic.∥그는 일의 앞뒤를 빨리 파악하고 있다 He grasps things quickly.

파안대소하다(破顔大笑-) give [show] a broad smile; smile broadly; burst into laughter.

파약(破約) a breach of contract [promise]. **파약하다** break [infringe] an agreement [a contract]; break one's word [promise]. ¶이 협정은 1년간 파약할 수 없다 You cannot break off [cancel] this agreement for one year. →¶약혼자에게 파약당했다 I was jilted by my fiancée.

파업(罷業) a strike; (미) a walkout. ¶동정 ~ a sympathetic strike∥시한 ~ a strike for a limited number of hours∥총~ a general strike∥교육 법안에 반대하는 항의 ~ a protest strike against the education bill [measure] ∥~ 중이다 be on strike∥~에 들어가다 go on strike∥무기한 ~에 들어가다 go on strike indefinitely [for an indefinite period] ∥종업원들은 ~ 중이다 The employees are on strike.∥~이 진행되고 있다 A strike is going on.∥~ 중 (게시) On Strike. ∥~은 오전 5시에 해제되었다 The strike was called off at 5 in the morning.∥그들은 국회 의사당 앞에서 연좌 ~를 벌였다 They staged a sit-down strike in front of the National Assembly Building. **파업하다** strike; turn out; [미] walk out.
● **파업권** the right to strike. ¶~을 확립[행사]하다 establish [exercise] one's right to strike. **파업 기금 / 파업 자금** a strike fund. **파업자** a striker.

파열(破裂) (an) explosion; (a) bursting; (a) rupture; (an) eruption(화산의); 〔결】 (a) rupture. ¶보일러[수도관]의 ~ the bursting of a boiler [water pipe]∥심장 [혈관] 의 ~ the rupture of the heart [a blood vessel]∥타이어의 ~ the blowout [bursting] of a tire. **파열하다** explode; burst; erupt; blow [go] up. ¶폭탄이 파열했다 A bomb exploded [went off]. →¶추위로 수도관이 파열되었다 The water pipe

파운데이션 (화장품) foundation; (속옷) a foundation garment.

파운드 (화폐 단위) a pound(기호 £); (영국 화폐) a pound sterling; (영국 속어) a quid; (무게) a pound(기호 lb.) (*pl.* lbs.). ¶5~ 지폐 a five pound note∥~를 평가 절하 하다 devaluate the sterling∥그것은 10~의 무게가 나간다 It weighs 10 pounds[10 lbs].∥그 값은 3~ 6펜스입니다 It is[costs] 3.06[three pounds and six pence].∥그는 10~ 지폐로 지불했다 He paid with a ten-pound note.∥~의 가치가 올랐다[내렸다] The value of sterling has risen[fallen].∥몸무게가 몇 ~입니까 How many pounds do you weigh?
● **파운드 지역** the sterling area.

파울 [체] (a) foul play; a foul; [야구] a foul ball. ¶~의 foul / against the rules∥~을 하다 violate[act against] the rules / play foul / commit a foul∥~로 퇴장당하다 foul out of the game∥그는 곧 ~로 아웃이 되어 버렸다 He soon fouled out of the game.
● **파울 볼** [야구] a foul ball. ¶~을 치다 foul / hit a foul ball / foul the ball off.

파워 power. ¶우먼 ~ woman power∥~가 있는 엔진 a high-powered engine.
● **파워 핸들** (*power handle) a power steering wheel.

파이¹ (양과자) a pie; (미) a potpie(주로 고기의). ¶건포도 ~ a raisin pie∥과일 ~ a fruit pie∥민스 ~ a mince pie∥복숭아 ~ a peach pie∥소시지 ~ a sausage pie∥애플 ~ an apple pie∥크림 ~ a cream pie∥호박 ~ a pumpkin pie∥~의 껍질 (a) piecrust / the shell of a pie.

파이² [수] pi (*pl.* ~s); π.

파이다 be dug; be hollowed. ⇨패다⁴

파이트머니 fight money; a fighter's purse.

파이팅 (*fighting) [격려·응원의 구호] go; way to go; stick it out. ¶(한국) ~! Go[Way to go] (Korea)!

파이프 [관] a pipe; a tube. ¶비닐 ~ a vinyl pipe∥수도 ~ a water pipe∥~로 물을 끌다 draw[lead] water through a pipe. 2 [담뱃대] a (tobacco) pipe(대담배용의); a cigarette holder(궐련용). ¶~를 물고 a pipe in one's mouth / with a pipe between one's teeth∥~에 불을 붙이다 light a pipe∥~ 담배를 피우다 smoke a pipe∥~를 빨다 pull at a pipe∥~의 재를 떨다 tap one's pipe out / knock the ashes out of one's pipe∥~에 담배를 재다 fill one's pipe (with tobacco)∥~를 청소하다 clean a pipe∥~가 막혀 있다 The pipe is clogged.
● **파이프라인 / 파이프 배관** a pipeline. ¶두 나라 사이의 정보 교환을 위한 ~ a pipeline for (the) exchange of information between two countries∥가솔린은 ~으로 항구에서 수송된다 Gasoline [(영) Petrol] is transported from the port by a pipeline. **파이프 오르간** a pipe organ.

파인더 (망원경의) a finder; (카메라의) a viewfinder. ¶이 망원경의 ~를 들여다봐 Look through the finder of this telescope.

파인애플 a pineapple.

파인주스 pineapple juice.

파인 플레이 [체] a fine play. ¶~를 하다 make a fine play.

burst because of the cold.
● **파열음** an explosive sound; [언] a plosive consonant.

파일¹ (서류철) a file. ¶협회의 기록은 모두 ~이 되어 있다 All the transactions of the society are on file[filed].∥이건 ~을 해 두는 게 좋다 You had better keep this on file[in a file].
● **파일북** a file; a folder.

파일² 1 (기초 공사용 말뚝) a pile. ¶땅에 ~이 처박혔다 Piles were driven into the ground. 2 [방직] pile. ¶이 타월은 ~이 두꺼워 촉감이 좋다 The thick pile on this towel feels good.

파일(八日) [불] the anniversary of the birth of Buddha; Buddha's birthday (festival); the eighth of April of the lunar calendar.
● **파일등**(一燈) lanterns burned on Buddha's birthday.

파일럿 [항공기 조종사·도선사] a pilot.

파자마 (미) (a pair of) pajamas; (영) pyjamas(윗옷은 top, 바지를 bottoms라고 함). ¶타월 천의 ~ pajamas made of towel cloth∥~ 바람으로 in one's pajamas.

파장(波長) (a) wavelength. ¶고유 ~ a natural wavelength∥단[중 / 장] ~ a short[medium / long] wavelength∥KBS에 ~을 맞추다 tune in to KBS.
● **파장계** a cymometer; a wavemeter.

파장(罷場) (과거장의) the conclusion of state examinations; (시장의) close of a marketplace. **파장하다** bring (state examinations) to a close[an end]; close (a marketplace).
● **파장 떨이 세일** a closing out sale. **파장 시세** the closing quotation[price].

파쟁(派爭) a factional strife; an interfactional strife[dispute].

파종(播種) sowing; seeding. ⇨씨뿌리기 ¶늦~의 종자 late sown seeds∥~의 계절 the planting season. **파종하다** sow; sow seed; scatter (seed). ¶봄에 ~ sow seed in spring∥밭에 ~ scatter the fields with seed∥밭에 밀을 ~ sow a field with wheat.
● **파종기**(一期) the seedtime; the sowing season. **파종기**(一機) a seeder; a sowing[seeding] machine.

파죽지세(破竹之勢) irresistible force; crushing[overwhelming] power. ¶~로 with irresistible force / with progressive increase of force∥~로 나아가다 carry all[everything / the world] before one / sweep away everything in one's way∥그 유행은 현재 ~로 번지고 있다 The craze is carrying everything before it for the moment.∥그 군대는 ~로 진격했다 The troops swept away everything in their path.

파지(破紙) a defective[tattered] sheet of paper; remnants of paper; wastepaper.

파직(罷職) dismissal[removal] from office; discharge; deprivation of office. **파직하다** dismiss (a person) from office; discharge (a person) from (his) duties; remove (a person) from office; (미국 속어) fire.

파찰음(破擦音) [언] an affricate.

파천(播遷) royal flight from the palace; an evacuation of the capital. **파천하다** flee from the Royal Palace; evacuate the capital.

파천황(破天荒) unprecedentedness. ¶~의 record-breaking / unprecedented / unheard-of.

파초(芭蕉) [식] a banana plant; a plantain.

파출(派出) dispatch(ing); derivation. **파출하다** dispatch; send out; detach. →젊은 여성이 간호사로 파출되었다 A young woman was

●**파출부**(-婦) a day housekeeper; 〔영〕 a home help; a visiting housekeeper[maid]; 〔영〕 a charwoman. **파출소** a branch office; (경찰관의) a police box[stand]. ¶~에 신고하다 report to a policeman at the police stand / (습득물 등을) take[carry] (a thing) to a police box.

파충류(爬蟲類) the reptiles; creeping things. ¶~의 reptilian // ~를 먹고 사는 reptilivorous.

파치(破-) broken[damaged] articles; defective goods.

파킨슨병(-病) 〔의〕 Parkinson's disease; paralysis agitans.

파탄(破綻) 1 〔불성립〕 failure; a rupture(교섭의). 그 일에 ~을 가져왔다 The plan failed [went amiss]. // 그 계획에 ~이 생겼다 The plan failed[fell through]. // 마침내 그들의 가정생활은 ~으로 끝났다 Their family life ended in failure. **파탄하다** fail; come to a rupture. 2 〔은행·회사의 지급 정지〕 bankruptcy. ¶은행 ~ a bank failure. **파탄하다** become[go] bankrupt. 3 〔붕괴〕 breaking. ¶인격의 ~을 가져오다 break up one's personality / lead to the bankruptcy of one's character. **파탄하다** be ruined; break down.

파토스 pathos. ¶그의 작품에는 일말의 ~가 감돌고 있다 There is a touch of pathos in his works.

파트 1 〔일부〕 part. ¶이 소설은 여섯 ~로 갈라져 있다 This novel is divided into six parts. 2 〔음악·합창 등에서의 성부〕 a part. ¶당신은 어느 ~를 맡습니까 Which part do you sing [play]? 3 〔부서〕 a department. ¶수출 ~ the export department.

파트너 a partner. ¶댄스의 ~ a dancing partner // 댄스에서 나는 그녀를 ~로 택했다 I chose her as my partner for the dance.

파티 a party; a meeting; social gathering; 〔친목회〕 a social; (구어) a mixer. ¶댄스~ a dancing party / a dance (a dance party라고는 하지 않음) // 디너 ~ a dinner party // 티 ~ a tea party // 크리스마스 ~ a Christmas party // ~에 잘 나가는 사람 a partygoer // 남성[여성]만의 ~ a stag[hen] party // ~가 끝난 후 after the party is over / ~를 **열다** give [hold / have] a party // 신입생을 위한 환영 ~를 열다 have a party for freshman // 그의 환영 ~가 학생 회관에서 열렸다 A welcome party was held for him at the student hall. // 바야흐로 ~는 한창이다 The party is in full swing.

파파라치 paparazzi(▶ 단수형은 paparazzo).

파파야 〔식〕 a papaya.

파편(破片) a broken piece; a fragment; a scrap; 〔나무·돌 등의 조각〕 a chip; 〔나무·돌 등의 가시 모양의 조각〕 a splinter. ¶깨진 꽃병의 ~ fragments of a broken vase / broken pieces of a vase // 옛날 토기의 ~ shards of ancient earthenware // 폭탄의 ~ a splinter of a bomb // 유리의 ~ pieces[bits] of broken glass // 포탄 ~ shell fragments / shrapnel // 유리 ~이 내 손가락에 박혔다 A splinter of glass got stuck in my finger.

파피루스 〔식〕 a papyrus (*pl.* papyri); a paper reed[rush].

파하다(罷-) 〔끝나다〕 end; stop; discontinue; break off; bring to an end; be over[out]; give up; quit. ¶모임이 파할 무렵에 at the end [close] of the meeting // 회의를 ~ end a meeting / bring the meeting to a close // 일을 ~ stop work / leave off work // 공부를 중도에서 ~ give up studying halfway through / leave school in midterm // 혼담을 ~ break off marriage talks // 학교[회사]가 파하고 나서 만나자 Let's meet after school[office hours]. // 학교는 3시에 파한다 School is over at three. // 우리 회사는 6시에 파한다 Our office closes at six. // 연극은 10시에 파했다 The play finished at ten. / The show was over at ten. // 사건이 일어난 것은 마침 회사가 파할 무렵이었다 The accident happened just at closing time.

파행(爬行) creeping; crawling. **파행하다** creep; crawl.

●**파행 동물** a reptile.

파행(跛行) 〔절뚝거림〕 limping; 〔균형이 잡히지 않음〕 (an) imbalance. ¶~적 운영 the crippled operation of (of). **파행하다** limp.

●**파행 경기**(-景氣) spotty prosperity; an erratic economy. **파행 국회** (normalize) the crippled operation of the National Assembly; the limping[crippled] house operation.

파헤치다 (땅을) dig[turn] up (the soil); dig (the ground) over; tear up (a road); 〔비유〕 rake up (an old scandal); 〔깊이 생각·검토하다〕 investigate; delve[prove] into (a problem) ¶문제를 근본부터 ~ attack a problem at the grass-roots // 무덤을 ~ violate[open] a grave / break a grave open // 도로가 몇 군데 파헤쳐져 있다 The road is torn up at several places.

파혼(破婚) breaking off a marriage engagement; (a) breach of promise of marriage. **파혼하다** break the engagement; break (off) engagement (with). ¶나는 파혼했다 I cancel(l)ed[broke off] our engagement.

파훼(破毁) 1 〔파괴〕 destruction; demolition. **파훼하다** destroy; demolish; break. 2 〔법〕 ➡ 파기

팍 with a thrust; with a thud. ⇨ 퍽¹

팍삭 limply; (break) easily. ⇨ 퍽석

팍팍 thrusting repeatedly; with flop after flop. ⇨ 퍽퍽

판 〔벌어진 곳〕 a place; a spot; a site; a scene; 〔판국〕 (the) state of affairs; (the aspect [phase] of) the situation; circumstances; 〔때〕 the moment; 〔경우〕 the occasion; the case; 〔횟수〕 a game; a round; a bout; a match. ¶노름~ a gambling place // 씨름 한 ~ a round of *ssireum* // 이러한 ~에 at this juncture / in the present[critical] juncture of things // 위급한 ~에 in the moment of danger / at critical moment // 막~에 at the last moment // 바둑[장기]을 한 ~ 두다 play a game of *baduk*[*janggi*] // …할 ~이다 be going to / be about to do / be on the point of doing // 두 ~ 이기다[지다] win[lose] two games // 투전 한 ~ 벌여 볼까 How about a round of cards?

판(板) 1 a board. ⇨ 널빤지 2 〔축음기관·레코드판〕 a record; a disk[disc]. 3 a (printing) block. ⇨ 판(版)

판(版) 1 〔판목〕 a (printing) block; 〔도판〕 a plate; a cast. ¶~에 박은 듯한[박힌] stereotyped / cut-and-dried [-dry] / mannerisitic / conventional / formal // ~에 박은[박힌] 말 a set[conventional / hackneyed / stereotyped] phrase[expression] // ~에 박은 설날 선물 a

판 (版) **1** a valve. ⇨ 밸브 **2** [식] a (flower) petal. ⇨ 꽃잎 ¶ 4~화(花) a flower of four petals / a four-petal(l)ed flower. **3** [생] a valve. ⇨ 판막

-판 (判) [책·종이의 규격] size. ¶ 사륙~ duodecimo / crown octavo / 대(大)~의 종이 large-sized paper // 이절 [사절/팔절] ~ folio [quarto / octavo] / 국~ a small octavo // B4~ a legal size // A4~ a letter size // (사진의) 명함~ the size of a visiting card.

판가름 judging sides (which side is right and which side is wrong); a showdown; decision. ¶ ~이 나다 be decided / turn out [prove] to be ... / come to a conclusion. **판가름하다** judge (a competition, fight, etc.); decide; sit in judg(e)ment (on); (미국 속어) have a final showdown. ¶ 싸움을 ~ judge which of the two fighting parties is right and which is wrong // 나는 그를 판가름할 권리가 없다 I have no right to judge him. // 가부간 판가름해 주시오 Anyhow, judge between us.

판각 (板刻) engraving (on woodblocks); wood-cutting. **판각하다** engrave (designs, letters, etc.) on wood; make a print from a woodblock.
●**판각본** a woodblock-printed book; a xylographic book. **판각화** a woodcut; a woodblock print; xylograph.

판검사 (判檢事) judges and public prosecutors; judicial officers; (집합적) the bench.

판결 (判決) judg(e)ment; [법] a (judicial) decision; a decision of the court; a ruling; adjudication; finding; a sentence; a decree. ¶ 최종 ~ a final decree [decision] // ~의 번복 reversal of a decision // ~의 집행 execution of judgment // ~의 집행을 정지하다 suspend a judgment // ~을 내리다 give a decision (upon) / adjudicate (on a case) / rule (that ...) / find / judge // 사형 ~을 내리다 sentence (a person) to death // 남에게 [사건에 대해] ~을 내리다 pass sentence [judgment] upon a person [case] // ~을 유예 [연기] 하다 reserve [suspend] judgment // ~을 지지하다 sustain a decision // ~을 취소하다 set aside a decision // 사형 ~을 받다 receive a death sentence / get death // 유죄 [무죄] ~을 받다 receive a verdict [be given a decision] of guilty [not guilty] // 피고는 ~에 승복 [불복] 했다 The accused accepted [appealed] the court's decision. // 재판관은 피고에게 사형을 선고했다 The judge sentenced the defendant to death. // 그 사건에 대한 ~이 내일 내려진다 Judgment [A decision] will be given [passed] on the case tomorrow. // 그에게 유리 [불리] 한 ~이 나왔다 The judgment was [went] in his favor [against him]. // ~은 원고의 패소 [승소] 로 돌아갔다 The case was decided against [in favor of] the plaintiff. **판결하다** judge; decide (on a case); give (a) decision (on a case); pass judgment (on a vase); adjudicate [adjudge] (on an action); sentence (a person) to (death).
●**판결문** the decision. ¶ ~을 읽다 read the ruling / read out the decision. **판결 이유** reasons for decision [the judgment].

판공비 (辦公費) expediency fund; expense account (접대비); extra-expenses (예비비); confidential money [expenses] (기밀비).

판국 (-局) a situation; the position [state] of affairs; the state of things; the aspect of affairs. ¶ 험한 ~ a tricky [touchy / perilous] situation / 수습할 수 없는 ~ an uncontrollable situation // ~을 관망하다 watch the situation / watch how things develop / see how the wind blows / see which way the cat will jump // 새로운 ~으로 접어들다 take a new turn / take on a new aspect / enter upon a new phase // 일이 그 ~이라면 나도 잠자코 있을 수 없다 If it comes to that, I have something to say too.

판권 (版權) copyright; literary property. ¶ ~기한이 지난 out of copyright // ~을 침해 [양도] 하다 infringe on [transfer] a copyright // 1958년 맥밀런 사(社) ~ 획득 Copyright, 1958, by The Macmillan Company // 우리는 그 책의 ~을 갖고 있다 We hold [own] the copyright on the book. // 그들은 그의 화집의 ~을 취득했다 They copyrighted his collection of pictures. / They obtained [secured] the copyright for his collection of pictures. // 그의 저작에는 아직 ~이 살아 있다 His works are still copyright.
●**판권 소유** ownership of copyright; (출판물에 기재하는 문구) Copyrighted; All rights reserved. **판권 양도** transfer of copyright. **판권 침해** an infringement of copyright; a copyright infringement.

판금 (板金) a (metal) plate; sheet metal.
●**판금공** a sheet metal worker.

판나다 **1** [끝나다] get finished; come to an end [a close / a conclusion]; be over. ¶ 싸움은 판났다 A fight is over. / The winner is decided. // 그 사건은 아직 판나지 않았다 The matter has not been settled yet. / The matter still remains unsettled [is yet to be settled]. **2** [다하다] be all gone; run out; be exhausted. ¶ 떡이 판났다 The rice cake is all gone. // 양식이 판났다 Our provisions are running out. **3** [파멸하다] be ruined; go [fall] crash; go bankrupt. ¶ 회사가 판났다 The company is bankrupt. // 그 집안은 판났다 The family is ruined. // 그의 세도는 이제 판났다 His power is now in eclipse.

판다 (-) a panda; a bear cat; a cat bear.

판다르다 (서술적) be entirely different; be quite another thing; be poles apart. ¶ 사회학과 사회주의는 ~ Social science and socialism are two entirely different things.

판단 (判斷) [단정] (a) judg(e)ment; (an) adjudication; (a) decision; [결론] conclusion; [

산] estimation; [재량] discretion; [해석] (an) interpretation. ¶종합 ~ (a) synthetic judgment // (공정한) ~을 내리다 pass a (fair) judgment (on) // ~을 그르치다 misjudge / error in judgment // 경험으로 미루어 ~을 내리다 form conclusions from experiences // 그는 엄청난 ~의 실수를 저질렀다 He made a gross misjudgment. // 나의 ~으로는 틀림이 없다 There is no error in my judgment. // 당신의 ~에 맡기겠습니다 I will leave it to your judgment. // 나의 ~으로는 그는 아주 정직한 사람이다 I judge him to be a very honest man. **판단하다** judge; decide; [해석] interpret; [이해] understand; [예언] foretell; [꿈을] read; [점을] divine. ¶그의 말로 미루어 판단하건대… Judging from what he says … // 남을 겉보기로 판단해서는 안 된다 You should not judge a person by his appearance. // 보고로 판단하건대 그 피해가 상당히 큰 모양이다 Judging from the report, the damage seems to be considerable. // 어느 쪽이 좋은지 나는 판단할 수가 없다 I cannot tell which is better.

● **판단 기준** a yardstick for judgment; a standard of judgment. **판단력** judgment; discernment; sense. ¶~이 좋다 have good judgment // ~이 부족하다 be lacking[wanting] in judgment // ~을 잃다 lose one's judgment.

판도(版圖) [영토] a territory; dominion; [지배하는 영지] a domain. ¶~를 확장하다 expand one's territory [domain].

판독(判讀) decipherment(암호 등의); interpretation; making out; reading. **판독하다** decipher; make out; read; spell out. ¶고문서를 ~ decipher an old manuscript // 그 칼에 새긴 글은 좀처럼 판독하기 어렵다 The signature on the sword is hard for me to make out[decipher]. // 휘갈겨 쓴 글씨를 판독하는 데 애먹었다 I found it hard to read[make out] the scrawl.

판돈 stakes (in gambling). ¶~을 쓸다 sweep the board / take the pool // ~을 떼다 divide up the stakes [the money on the board].

판례(判例) [법] a (judicial) precedent; a (leading) case. ¶새로운 ~를 만들다 set [establish] a precedent // ~를 인용하다 cite [refer to] a precedent [case].

● **판례법** [법] case law; judicial precedents; judiciary law; judge-made law. **판례집** law reports.

판로(販路) a market (for goods); an outlet. ¶~가 있다 (상품이) be marketable[salable] / be in (good) demand / be in great request / be much in request // ~가 열리다 a market opens (for) // ~를 구축하다 build (up) a market (for) // ~를 잃다 lose one's market // 이 상품은 ~가 넓다[좁다] There is a good market[little demand] for these articles. // 그들은 그 기계의 ~를 확장[획득/개척]하는 데 성공했다 They succeeded in expanding the market[in securing a market / in opening up a market] for those machines. // 그들은 자기 회사 제품의 ~를 찾느라 애썼다 They had trouble finding outlets for their products. // 우리는 신제품의 ~를 찾고 있다 We are seeking a market for our new product. // 이 제품은 ~가 없다 There's no demand [outlet] for this product.

판막(瓣膜) [생] a valve. ¶심장의 ~ the valves of the heart.

● **판막염** valvulitis.

판매(販賣) (a) sale; selling; marketing. ¶위탁 ~ a consignment sale / a sale on consignment // 월부 ~ selling[a sale] (made) on the installment plan // 특가 ~ a bargain sale / sale at a special reduction // 자동 ~기 a vending machine / a slot machine // 신용 ~ a credit sale / a sale on credit // 할인 ~ a discount sale // 독점 ~ an exclusive sale // 그들은 자사의 상품 ~에 필사적이다 They are working frantically to sell[promote] their company's goods. **판매하다** sell; deal in; handle; dispose of; work off. ¶이 책은 예약 판매합니다 These books are sold by subscription (only). // 이 가게는 문방구를 판매하고 있다 This store deals in stationery. // 그 책은 전국의 어느 서점에서도 판매하고 있다 That book is available at every bookstore in the country. // 이런 종류의 카메라를 유럽에 판매하는 것은 어려운 일이다 It is difficult to find a market in Europe for this type of camera. ➔¶이 물건은 내일부터 판매됩니다 These articles will go on sale tomorrow.

● **판매 가격** a selling price. **판매고** sales volume. **판매 대리점** a distributor; an agency marketing; a sales agency. **판매망** a sales network. **판매부** a sales department. ¶~ 부장 a sales manager[chief] / a marketing executive / (신문·잡지의) a circulation manager. **판매 실적** sales performance. **판매업자** a distributor. **판매원** (미) a salesclerk; (영) a shop assistant; (미) a salesperson; a salesman(남자); a saleswoman(여자); a vendor(행상). **판매인** a seller; a merchandiser; a marketer; an agent. **판매점 / 판매소** (미) a store; (영) a shop. ¶총~ a selling agent. **판매 조합** a marketing cooperative; a marketing[selling] cooperative association; a sales guild. **판매 촉진** sales promotion. ¶~ 운동 a sales campaign // 신제품의 ~ 운동을 벌이다 conduct a sales campaign for a new product / (구어) plug a new product.

판명하다(判明-) make (a matter) clear [plain]; dig up; ascertain. ➔¶그의 소재는 아직 판명되지 않았다 His whereabouts is[are] still unknown. // 그가 무죄라는 것이 판명되었다 It has been proved that he is innocent. // 피해자의 신원이 최 씨로 판명되었다 The victim was found to be[was identified as] Mr. Choe. // 그의 말은 완전히 거짓임이 판명되었다 What he said proved[turned out] to be completely false. // 그의 범행 동기가 판명되었다 We found out[discovered] what his motive for the crime was. // 사건의 진상은 아직 판명되지 않았다 The truth about the case is still unknown.

판목(版木) a (printing) block. ¶~으로 인쇄된 그림 a picture printed from a wood block.

판무관(辦務官) a commissioner. ¶고등 ~ a high commissioner / (영) the High Commissioner.

판무식(判無識) illiteracy; illiterateness; ignorance. **판무식하다** 《서술적》 be utterly ignorant.

● **판무식쟁이** a densely illiterate person; an (utterly) unlettered person; an ignoramus.

판박이(版-) 1 [인쇄본] a printed book. 2 [아이들의 장난감용] a copy picture; (도자기·유리 등에 옮기는) a decalcomania; a decal. 3 [틀에 박힌 것] a fixed form; a stereotyped

판별

pattern. 4 [꼭 닮은 사람] the spitting image of (a person). ¶그녀는 엄마와 ~이다 She is the spitting image of her mother. / She is a carbon copy of her mother.

판별(判別) distinction; discrimination. **판별하다** distinguish (between A and B); tell (A) from (B); discriminate (between A and B / one from the other); make [notice] the difference (between); judge. ¶선악을 ~ tell right from wrong / know the difference between right and wrong // 양자는 판별할 수 없을 정도로 흡사했다 The two were so alike that they could not be distinguished from each other. // 화학 섬유와 양털을 판별할 수 있습니까 Can you distinguish [tell] synthetic fiber from wool?
● **판별력** discrimination; power of discernment; judgment. **판별식** [수] a discriminant.

판본(板本·版本) a woodblock-printed book. ⇨ 판각본(⇨판각)

판사(判事) a judge; a justice; (집합적) the judiciary; the bench. ¶수석[예심/배석] ~ presiding [a criminal court / an associate] judge // 대법원 ~ a Supreme Court judge // 부장 ~ a senior judge / a chief judge (of the district court) // K ~가 그 사건을 담당하고 있다 Judge K presides over [is in charge of] the case.
● **판사석** the bench; a judgment seat; a judge's bench. **판사 직** judgeship; the bench.

판서(判書) [역] a minister (in ancient times).

판서하다(板書—) write on the blackboard.

판설다 unfamiliar (with); inexperienced (in); unaccustomed (to); unused (to); new (to / at); not at home (in).

판세(—勢) [형세] the situation; the state of affairs [things]; the condition of affairs; the tide (of); (바둑 등의) the position; [전망] the prospects; the chances. ¶유리[불리]한 ~ a favorable [an unfavorable] turn of the situation // 지금의 ~로는 as the situation stands / as things are [stand] / according to the present situation / in view of the situation // ~가 일변하다 take a new turn / take on a new aspect / enter upon a new phase // ~를 관망하다 watch the situation [the development of affairs] / see how the land lies / see [watch] which way the cat jumps // ~는 어떠한가 What is the situation? / How lies the land? / (승부의) What are the chances? // ~가 불리[유리]해졌다 The tide turned against [to / in favor of] us.

판소리 pansori; a long epic song; a solo opera drama.

판수 1 [점쟁이 소경] a blind fortuneteller. 2 a blind person. ⇨소경1

판시(判示) judg(e)ment; (a) decision; a ruling. **판시하다** decide (on a case); give (a) decision (on a case); rule (that ... should ...).

판시세(—時勢) the market price; the current market quotations.

판연하다(判然—) distinct; evident; clear; express; explicit; plain; [명확하다] definite; [확실하다] certain. **판연히** clearly; distinctly; plainly; palpably; definitely; certainly.

판유리(板琉璃) flat glass; plate glass (두꺼운 것); sheet glass (얇은 것); (한 장) a glass plate; a pane.

판이하다(判異—) quite [widely / entirely] different (from); diametrically opposed (to);

(서술적) differ entirely [widely] (from); be a far cry (from); be poles apart [asunder] (in).

판자(板子) a board; a plank. ⇨ 널빤지
● **판자문** a wooden door. **판잣집** a board-framed house; a makeshift hut; a shack; a barrack; a shanty.

판재(板材) boards (for a coffin).

판정(判定) (a) judgment; (a) decision; (an) adjudication; finding; a verdict (매심원의). ¶심판의 ~ the umpire's decision // ~의 기준 a criterion for judging // ~으로 이기다 [판정 승하다] win a decision / win by points // ~으로 지다 [판정패하다] be defeated by a decision / lose on points // ~을 내리다 pass judgment (on) / give a decision (on) // …에게 이겼다는 ~을 내리다 decide [give a decision] in favor of ... / declare (a person) winner // 피고에 대하여 유리한[불리한] ~을 내리다 find for [against] the defendant // ~을 뒤엎다 reverse the (umpire's) decision // 우리 팀에게 승리 ~이 났다 Our team was declared [judged] the victor in the contest. // 심판의 ~에 승복했다 I accepted [abided by] the umpire's [referee's] decision. // 그 심판은 우리에게 불리한 ~을 내렸다 The referee decided against us. **판정하다** judge; decide; adjudicate (upon); adjudge; find. ¶잘못 ~ misjudge. ➔ ¶그 건축물은 표준에 합치된다고 판정되었다 The building was judged to be up to standard.
● **판정승** a decision. **~하다** win [score] a decision (over) / win by [on] points (over) / defeat [beat] (one's opponent) on points [by a decision] // 그는 심판 전원 일치의 ~을 거두었다 He won the match in a unanimous decision. **판정패** a loss on points. **~하다** be defeated [beaten] by a decision / lose [drop] a decision (to) / lose (a match) on points.

판지(板紙) board; pasteboard; cardboard; paperboard; carton. ¶~ 상자 a cardboard case / a pasteboard box / a carton.

판초 a pancho.

판촉(販促) sales promotion.

판치다 stand [be] unchallenged [unrivaled / without a rival]; reign supreme; lord it over; exercise great influence (over). ¶군인이 판치는 나라 a country ridden by soldiers // 당시 정계는 그가 판치고 있었다 At that time the whole political situation was entirely in his hands. / He reigned supreme in the political world then.

판타지 [음—] a fantasia; a fantasy.

판탈롱 [여성 바지] pantaloons.

판판이 every time; whenever; always; all the time [while]. ¶~ 실패하다 fail in every attempt [at every step] // ~ 지다 be defeated in every battle / lose every battle that one fights // ~ 놀다 [놀고먹다] eat idle bread / lead an idle life / be always playing [idle] // ~ 거짓말만 하다 lie all the time // 그녀는 ~ 굶고 있다 She goes hungry.

판판하다 even; level; flat; smooth; plane. ¶판판한 표면 a smooth [a plane / an even] surface // 판판한 땅 even [level / flat] ground.

판판히 evenly; smoothly. ¶땅을 ~ 하다 level [roll] the ground.

판하다 wide; vast; spacious; extensive; boundless. ¶판한 바다 a vast sea // 판한 들판 a wide plain. **판히** widely; vastly; spaciously;

판화(版畵) a print; a woodcut[block] print; [판화술] (pictorial) wood printing.
● **판화가** a woodblock artist.

판히(判-) clearly; distinctly. ⇨판연히(↔)판연하다) ¶~ 보이다 be seen clearly[distinctly] / be clearly seen∥~ 들여다보이다 be seen through clearly / be patently transparent∥그녀의 옷이 얇아서 속이 ~ 들여다보인다 Her skins can be seen through her thin dress.

팔 an arm. ¶오른[왼] ~ the right[left] arm∥근끌이 억센 ~ a brawny arm∥~이 없는 armless∥~에 완장을 두르고 with a band round one's arm∥~에 기장을 달고 with a badge on one's arm∥~이 부러지다[삐다] break[sprain] one's arm∥~에 의지하다 lean on (a person's) arm (for support)∥~에 의지하여 걷다 walk on (a person's) arm∥~로 들다 have (something) on one's arm∥~에 안다 hold[carry] (a thing / a person) in one's arms / embrace (a baby) / have (a baby) in one's arms∥~에 부상을 입다 be wounded in the arm∥~을 흔들다 swing one's arms∥~을 들다 raise one's arm∥(남이 잡도록) ~을 내밀다 lend[offer] one's arm∥(두) ~을 벌리다 spread out one's arms / open one's arms wide∥~을 끼다 lock arms with / link one's arms in[through] another's∥~을 끼고 걷다 walk[go] arm in arm with …∥~을 걷어붙이다[걷어올리다] bare one's arm / roll[turn / tuck] up the sleeves∥~을 펴다[뻗다] extend one's arm / reach[stretch] one's arm (toward) / reach (out)∥~을 굽히다 bend[hunch] one's arm∥~을 잡다 hold [take] (a person) by the arm / hold[take] (a person's)∥사내아이는 그쪽으로 ~을 뻗었다 The boy stretched[extended] his arm toward it.∥그는 나의 ~을 잡았다 He caught [seized / grabbed] me by the arm.∥그녀는 ~에 쇼핑백을 안고 있다 She has a shopping bag on her arm.∥그는 두 ~을 벌리고 앞길을 막아섰다 He stood blocking my way with both arms spread wide[outspread].∥우리는 두 ~을 벌리고 그녀를 맞이했다 We welcomed her with open arms.

팔이 들이굽지 내굽나(속담) Blood is thicker than water.

팔(八) eight. ¶~분의 1 one-eight.
● **팔각**(八角) eight angles.
● **팔각정** an octagonal pavilion. **팔각형** an octagon.

팔걸이 an armrest.
● **팔걸이의자** an armchair; an elbow chair.

팔괘(八卦) eight signs of divination.

팔꿈치 an elbow. ¶~ 관절 an elbow joint∥~가 닳아서 해어진 코트 an overcoat worn-out [threadbare] at the elbow(s)∥~로 치다 hit [poke / dig] one's elbow into (another's side) / jog / jostle / nudge(툭 치다)∥~로 밀어제치다 elbow (a person) aside∥~로 밀어제치고 지나가다 elbow one's way through (the crowd)∥~를 펴다 square one's elbows / spread[bend] out one's elbows∥…에 ~를 괴다 rest one's elbow(s) upon …∥내 코트 오른쪽 ~가 해졌다 My coat is worn out at the right elbow.∥~로 밀지 마시오 Don't elbow me.∥그녀는 그를 저지하려고 했지만 그는 그녀를 ~로 밀어냈다 She tried to stop him, but he elbowed her out of the way.∥나는 군중 속에 ~로 밀어제치고 나아갔다 I elbowed my way through the crowd.

팔다 1 [판매하다] sell; deal in (goods); offer (articles) for sale; put[place] (articles) on sale[on the market]; [(소지품 등을) 팔아 치우다] dispose of. ¶팔 수 있는 salable / marketable∥팔 수 없는 unsalable / unmarketable∥팔 것 an article for[on] sale / offerings∥팔 집 a house for[on] sale∥팔고 다니다 carry (fish) about for sale / hawk / peddle∥다 ~ sell off[out] / clear out∥팔아 치우다 dispose of / part with (a thing)∥비싸게 ~ sell dear / sell at a high[good] price∥싸게 ~ sell cheap / sell at a low[moderate] price / sell at a bargain∥이문을 (많이) 남기고 ~ sell at a profit / sell (a thing) with a good margin∥손해 보고 ~ sell at a loss[at a sacrifice] / sell under prime cost(밑지고)∥시세대로 ~ sell at the current market price∥정찰대로 ~ sell at the fixed price∥할인해서 ~ sell at a discount∥외상으로 ~ sell on credit[tick / trust] / give (a person) credit∥천 원에 ~ sell (a thing) for one thousand won∥한 개 1,000원에 ~ sell at 1,000 won apiece∥1다스에 얼마로 ~ sell by the dozen∥노예로 ~ sell (a person) for a slave∥점포를 ~ sell out one's shop∥몸을 ~ sell oneself for money / prostitute oneself∥미모를 ~ trade[capitalize] on one's beauty∥지조를 ~ sell[prostitute] one's honor [chastity] (for money)∥구형의 냉장고를 팔아 치우다 sell off[dispose of] all old model refrigerators∥낡은 가구를 팔아 치우다 dispose of old furniture∥집을 헐값으로 ~ sell one's house for a song∥장물을 외국에 팔아 치우다 sell (off) stolen articles in foreign countries∥오래 써서 낡은 자전거를 팔아 치웠다 I disposed of my old bicycle.∥그것은 신세계에서 팔고 있다 You can buy[get] it at Shinsegae.∥나는 넝마를 넝마장수에게 팔아넘겼다 I sold some rags to a junkman.∥저 가게에서는 과일을 싸게 팔고 있다 They sell fruit cheaply[at a low price] at that store.∥밑지고 팔아서는 장사가 안 된다 I can't do business if I have to sell at a loss.∥많이 남기고 팔고 있습니다 I am selling it at a nice profit.∥설탕은 1파운드 단위로 팔고 있다 Sugar is sold by the pound.∥중고차를 80만 원에 팔았다 I sold a used car for eight hundred thousand won.∥이것은 얼마에 팝니까 What[How much] are you asking for this?∥그것은 큰 백화점에 가면 판다 It is available[You can buy it. / It can be bought] at major department stores.∥그 농부는 야채를 팔고 다녔다 The farmer went about peddling vegetables.∥저 가게는 해산물의 신선함을 장점으로 내세워 팔고 있다 That store promotes[makes a selling point of] the freshness of its seafood.∥이 카메라를 팔아야겠는데 I would like to sell this camera.∥그는 내 카메라를 자기에게 팔았으면 좋겠다고 말했다 He asked me to sell him my camera.∥그는 가게를 팔려고 내놓았다 He put his shop up for sale.∥그 다방은 팔려고 나와 있다 The coffee shop is up for sale.∥그는 시세의 하락을 예상하고 팔기로 했다 (주식에서) He expected stocks[(영) share prices] to drop, so he decided to sell.∥가격을 인하한 상품은 하루에 다 팔아 치웠다 We sold everything that was marked down in one day.∥그는 집을 너무 서둘러 팔아서 큰 손해를 보았다 He

팔다리

suffered a heavy loss because he sold his house in too great a hurry [too hastily].
2 (노력 등을). do job work / do wage labor / work for wages // 날품을 ~ work by the day / work as a day laborer.
3 [배신·배반하다] betray; deceive; sell (out); delude; impose upon. ¶나라를 ~ sell[betray / turn traitor to] one's own country / become a quisling // 친구를 ~ betray a friend.
4 (이름 등을) take advantage of (one's name). ¶자선[우정]이라는 이름을 팔아서 under the guise [respectable] cloak] of charity[friendship] / 남[남의 이름]을 assume[use] (a person's) name / make a fraudulent use of (a person's) name // 자기 이름을 ~ [빌려 주다] lend one's name // 그런 일에 내 이름을 팔지 말아 주게 I don't want my name to be given[mentioned] in such a connection.
5 [곡식을 사다] buy[purchase] (grain, rice, etc.). ¶쌀을 ~ buy[purchase] rice / 양식을 ~ lay in provisions.
6 (한눈을) turn one's eyes away (from); avert one's eyes (from); look away (from); (정신을) distract[divert] one's attention (from). ¶책을 보지 않고 한눈을 ~ look away from one's book.

팔다리 the arms and legs; the limbs. ¶~가 없는 limbless // ~를 못 쓰다 lose the use of one's limbs.

팔도 (八道) the eight provinces of Korea.
● **팔도강산** the land of Korea; all Korea.

팔등신 (八等身) a well-proportioned figure. ¶~의 미인 a beautiful well-proportioned woman // 그녀는 ~이다 She has a well-proportioned figure.

팔딱거리다 **1** [맥박 치다] pulsate; palpitate; throb; beat. ¶맥이 팔딱거린다 The pulse pulsates[beats]. / 가슴이 팔딱거린다 My heart throbs[beats / palpitates]. **2** [가볍게 뛰다] hop; leap; jump; spring; bound.

팔딱팔딱 [맥박 치는 모양] pulsating; palpitating; throbbing; [뛰는 모양] hopping; leaping; jumping. **팔딱팔딱하다** pulsate; hop. ⇨ "팔딱거리다

팔뚝 the forearm.

팔라듐 [화] palladium (기호 Pd).

팔락팔락 fluttering(ly); flapping. ⇨ "펄럭펄럭

팔랑개비 **1** a pinwheel. ⇨ "바람개비(⇨바람') **2** [출랑거리는 사람] a frivolous[flippant / flighty] fellow.

팔랑거리다 flutter; flap; wave. ¶바람에 ~ flutter[flap / wave] in the wind // 나뭇잎이 바람에 팔랑거린다 The leaves flutter in the wind.

팔레트 [미] a palette.

팔리다 **1** (물건이) sell[be sold] (for 1,000 won); be in (great) demand[request]. ¶잘 팔리는 물건 a good[quick] seller / 잘 팔리지 않는 물건 a poor seller / unsalable goods / dead stock // 제일 잘 팔리는 책 the best[top] seller // 잘 팔리지 않는 책 a slow-selling book // 오랫동안 팔리지 않은 책 a shopworn [(영)shopsoiled] book // 우리 가게에서 가장 잘 팔리는 모델 our fast-selling model // 잘 sell well / be in good demand / have a good sale / command a large sale / enjoy a brisk [large] sale / (출판물이) have a large circulation // 잘 팔리지 않다 do not sell well / find no sale[market] / be in poor demand / have a poor sale // 금방 ~ sell right away / meet a ready sale / obtain an immediate sale // 날개 돋친 듯이 ~ sell like[wildfire / hot cakes] // 좋은 값으로 ~ fetch[bring / command] a good[an excellent] price // 갯값으로 ~ be sold for a song[an old song] // 제일 잘 ~ be the best[top] seller // 이 책은 잘 팔린다[팔리지 않는다] This book sells well [does not sell]. // 이번 겨울은 석유난로가 잘 팔린다[팔리지 않는다] Kerosene stoves are in great[poor] demand this winter. // 신제품이 잘 팔린다[팔리지 않는다] The new products are selling well[poorly]. / There is great[not much] demand for the new products. // 신형 자동차는 날개 돋친 듯이 팔리고 있다 The new model cars are selling like hotcakes. // 그것들은 더 비싼 값으로[1만 원에] 팔린다 They sell[are sold] for a higher price[for ten thousand won]. // 이 상품은 인기가 있어 하루에 100개는 쉽사리 팔린다 This product is so popular that we sell a hundred a day easily. // 이 물건은 장기간 팔리지 않고 우리 가게에 남아 있었다 This article lay unsold on our shelves for a long time.
2 (사람이) go into bondage[slavery]; (미혼녀가) get married; [고용되다] get[obtain] employment. ¶반대당으로 팔려 가다 sell out to the opposition party // 그 학교의 졸업생은 잘 팔린다 The graduates of that school are eagerly sought after. // 그녀는 팔리지 못했다 She has been left on the shelf. // 그녀는 티브이 사회자로서 한창 팔리고 있다 She is much in demand[much sought after] as a TV MC [master of ceremonies].
3 (이름·얼굴이) become well known; become popular; get around. ¶얼굴이 널리 팔리다 be widely known / be popular // 이 후보자는 대중에게 이름이 팔려 있지 않다 This candidate is not well enough known among the people. // 지금 가장 이름이 팔려 있는 가수는 누구냐 Who is the most popular singer today?
4 (눈이) gaze upon (something) in[with] rapture; look at something else; (정신이) be fascinated[captivated] (by); be absorbed [lost / engrossed / immersed] (in); be[get] carried away (by); lose oneself (in); go mad [crazy] (after / over). ¶…에 정신이 ~ absorbed (in reading) // 여자 배우에게 정신이 홀려 ~ run (mad) after[be infatuated with] an actress / be crazy about an actress // 낚시질에 정신이 팔려 있다 be given over to angling / be wild about fishing // 노는 것에 정신이 팔려 공부하는 것을 잊다 be too much absorbed in play to think of one's study // 그녀는 돈버는 일에만 정신이 팔려 있다 She is bent on moneymaking.

팔림새 sale; demand. ¶~가 나쁜[신통치 않은] 물건 a bad sell[seller] / a slow-selling article / ~가 좋은 물건 a good sell[seller] // ~가 좋다 be a good seller / be in great demand / have a large sale / sell[be selling] well // ~가 나쁘다 be a poor seller / be in poor demand / do not sell well // ~가 빠르다 [더디다] be quick-selling[slow-selling] // 이 상품은 ~가 좋다[나쁘다] The goods are much[little] in demand[do not sell] well. // 수입품의 ~가 좋아[나빠]졌다 Sales of imported goods improved[fell off].

팔만대장경 (八萬大藏經) the Tripitaka Ko-

팔매 throwing; slinging; hurling. ¶돌~ stone-throwing[-slinging]// ~를 **치다** throw / sling / hurl / fling (a stone at).
● **팔매질** throwing; slinging; hurling. ¶그는 ~을 잘한다 He throws well.// 그는 백 야드를 ~을 할 수 있다 He can throw a hundred yards.

팔면 (八面) **1** [여덟 개의 면] eight sides. ¶~의 [이 있는] having eight faces / octahedral. **2** [여러 방면] all sides.
● **팔면부지** an utter stranger. **팔면체** an octahedron (pl. -dra). ¶정~ a regular octahedron.

팔목 the wrist. ¶~이 가늘다 be slim-wristed // ~을 **잡다** take (a person) by the wrist / grasp[grab / grip] (a person) by the wrist.
● **팔목시계** →손목시계(⇨손목).

팔방 (八方) all directions; every side. ¶~에서 from all directions[sides / quarters] / from every side / from all around // ~으로 in all directions / in every direction[quarter] / on all sides[quarters] / all around // ~으로 **살피다** keep an eye on all quarters // 길은 여기서 ~으로 통한다 From here, roads run in all directions. // 그 소문은 ~으로 퍼졌다 The rumor spread far and wide. // 우리는 분실한 크레디트 카드를 ~으로 찾았다 We searched high and low for the missing credit card.
● **팔방미인** one who is affable to everybody; everybody's friend; a flunk(e)y. ¶그는 ~이다 He tries to please everybody. // 정부의 외교 정책은 ~가격이다 The government's diplomatic policy is to try to be every nation's friend.

팔베개 ¶~ **베고** with one's head (pillow) on one's arm / ~를 **하다** [베다] make a pillow of one's arm / pillow[rest] one's head on one's arm // ~를 하고 자다 sleep with one's head (pillowed) on one's arm / 그는 ~를 하고 잤다 He slept with his arm for a pillow. / He slept with his head on his arm(s).

팔분쉼표 (八分-標) [음] (미) an eighth rest; (영) a quaver rest.
팔분음표 (八分音標) [음] (영) a quaver; (미) an eighth note.
팔불출 (八不出) a good-for-nothing; a dull fellow.
팔삭둥이 (八朔-) **1** [조산아] an infant born in the 8th month of pregnancy. ¶그녀는 ~를 낳았다 She gave birth to a child two months premature. **2** [얼뜨기] a half-wit.
팔순 (八旬) eighty years; four score years. ¶~ 노인 an octogenarian.
팔심 the strength of one's arm. ¶~이 **세다** have strong arms.
팔십 (八十) eighty. ¶~ 대의 사람 an octogenarian.
● **팔십 노인** an 80-year-old man[woman]; an old man[woman] of eighty.
팔씨름 Indian[arm] wrestling. ¶~을 **하다** indian-wrestle (a person) / arm-wrestle with a person. **팔씨름하다** have a hand wrestling.
팔아먹다 1 [팔아 버리다] sell off[out]; dispose of (by sale). ¶헐값으로 ~ sell (an article) for a mere song // 가산을 다 ~ squander one's fortune. **2** [장사거리로 삼다] offer[put up] (something) for sale. ¶미모를 ~ trade[capitalize] on one's beauty // 명예를 ~ sell[prostitute] one's honor (for money) // 지식을 ~ peddle one's knowledge. **3** [곡식을 사 먹다] buy[purchase] grain.
팔오금 the bend[crook] of the arm.
팔월 (八月) August(약어 Aug.).
● **팔월 한가위** the 15th day of the eighth lunar month; the midautumn[harvest-moon] festival.
팔자 (八字) (a) destiny; fate; (a) lot; fortune; doom; one's star. ¶기구한 ~ 〈사나운 팔자〉 a hard[a hapless / an evil] fate / [기이한 팔자] a curious turn of fate // ~에 **맡기다** leave one's fate to Heaven / trust to Providence // ~로 알고 체념하다 [~소관으로 돌리다] resign oneself to one's fate[lot] / be reconciled to one's fate / accept (something) as fate // ~를 잘[잘못] 타고 나다 be born under a lucky [an unlucky] star // 불행을 ~로 돌리다 ascribe one's ill luck to fate // ~를 **한탄하다** bemoan[bewail] one's ill fate // ~를 **탓하다** grumble at[quarrel with] one's lot / 큰사람이 될 ~다 be destined to become a great man // 일찍 죽을 ~다 be fated to die young // 그녀는 젊어서 죽을 ~였다 It was fated that she should die young. / She was destined to die young. // 모두가 내 ~다 It is all due to the stars I was born under.
팔자(를) 고치다 [개가하다] marry again; remarry; [벼락출세하다] rise suddenly in the world; [벼락부자가 되다] gain quick riches; get[become] rich suddenly.
팔자(가) 늘어지다 be in easy circumstances; be comfortably off; be blessed with good fortune.
팔자(가) 사납다 be unlucky[unfortunate]; be out of luck; be ill-fated. ¶팔자가 사나운 사람 an unfortunate[ill-fated] person / a hapless person.
● **팔자땜** a compensation for one's doom [evil destiny]. ¶~을 **하다** suffer a minor misfortune in compensation for one's ill fate // ~으로 알고 체념하세 We will take it as the price for our escape from misfortune.
팔자걸음 (八字-) toeing out. ¶~으로 **걷다** toe out / walk with the toes turned out[outward].
팔죽지 the upper arm.
팔짓 arm gestures; the movements of the arms. **팔짓하다** make gestures with one's arms; move one's arms.
팔짝 suddenly; nimbly. ⇨<펄쩍
팔짝팔짝 jumping up and down. ⇨<펄쩍펄쩍
팔짱 folding one's arms.
팔짱(을) 끼다 fold one's arms (across one's chest[breast]); fold one's arms in front of one; lock one's arms across one's chest; (남과) lock arms with; link one's arm in [through] another's. ¶팔짱을 끼고 with folded arms / with one's arms folded [crossed] // …과 팔짱을 끼고 걷다 walk[go] arm in arm with … // 팔짱을 끼고 방관하다 look on with folded arms[with one's hands in one's pockets] / stand idle // 팔짱을 끼고 앉다 sit with one's arms folded (across one's chest / in front of one) // 나는 친구와 팔짱을 끼고 걸었다 I walked arm in arm with a friend. / My friend and I walked with our arms linked. // 그는 팔짱을 끼고 보고만 있었다 He looked on with folded arms. / He remained an indifferent spectator[onlooker]. // 그는 팔짱을 끼고 생각에 잠겼다 He

팔찌 folded his arms and fell into thought. // 그가 곤란에 처해 있는데 우리가 팔짱을 끼고 보고만 있을 수는 없다 We cannot just stand by with folded arms[sit idle by] when he is in trouble.

팔찌 1 [팔가락지] a bracelet; a bangle; a wristlet; an armlet. 2 [활 쏠 때에 매는 띠] a bracer. ¶~를 **끼다** wear a bracelet.

팔척장신(八尺長身) a very tall man.

팔촌(八寸) [삼종 형제되는 촌수] the eighth degree (of consanguinity); (사람) a third cousin; a first cousin twice removed. ¶사돈의 ~ a cousin 40 times removed / an unrelated person / a stranger.

팔팔 simmering; broiling; flapping. ⇨ 펄펄

팔팔하다 1 [성질이 괄괄하고 급하다] quick-[hot-]tempered; passionate; impatient. 2 [생기가 있다] sprightly; lively; snappy; spirited; animated; full of life. ¶**팔팔한 처녀** a young and lively girl // 그는 나이는 많으나 아직 ~ He may be old but he's still quite spry. // 보시는 대로 아직도 팔팔합니다 I am alive and kicking, as you can see.

팔푼이(八-) a fool; a simpleton; a dullard; a half-wit.

팜파스 [남미의 온대 초원] a pampas.

팜플렛 → 팸플릿

팝 pop (music).

팝송 a pop song.

팝콘 popcorn.

팡 with a bang; gaping. ⇨ 빵²

팡파르 [음] a fanfare; a flourish (of trumpets); a tucket. ¶~를 **울리다** sound a fanfare.

팡파짐하다 gently curved. ⇨ 펑퍼짐하다

팡팡 popping and popping; with a rush. ⇨ 펑펑

팥 an adzuki[adsuki] bean; a red bean.

팥고물 mashed adzuki bean; adzuki bean flour.

팥밥 cooked rice and red beans.

팥죽(-粥) rice and adzuki-bean porridge. ¶~**단** thick bean-meal soup (with sugar and rice cake).

패(牌) 1 [표로 쓰는 나뭇조각 등] a tag; a tab; a tablet; a plate; a tally. ¶**명~** a name plate // **문~** a doorplate // **상~** a medallion / a medal // **위~** a mortuary[memorial] tablet / (조상의) an ancestral tablet / a family memorial tablet // "**팔 것**"이라는 ~를 **붙이다** put up a "For Sale" sign (on one's truck). 2 (카드놀이·화투 등의) a (playing) card; a suit(같은 종류의). ¶**한 벌** ~ a pack[(미) deck] of cards // **손 안에 든** ~ the cards in one's hand // **바닥에 깐** ~ a lay card // ~**가 좋다**[**나쁘다**] have a good[bad] hand // ~**를 도르다** deal the cards // **그는 능숙한 솜씨로** ~**를 쳐서 돌렸다** He deftly shuffled and dealt the cards. // **자기의** ~**를 보이면 안 된다** Don't show your hand. 3 (마작의) a tile; a piece. 4 [무리] a party; a company; a group; a set; a circle; a gang; a clique. ¶**젊은** ~ young folks // **우리** ~ our group / our team // ~**를 짓다** form a party // **그런** ~**들과 사귀지 마라** Don't mix with such a set. // **저들** ~**에 들어가지 마라** Don't keep company with them. / Stay out of their circle.

패(를) 떼다 cut the cards.

패(霸) [바둑] eternal alternation. ¶~**를 쓰다**

make a no-man's point.

패가망신(敗家亡身) ruining both oneself and one's family; one's ruin. **패가망신하다** ruin oneself. ¶**그는 노름으로 패가망신했다** He gambled himself out of house and home.

패가하다(敗家-) ruin one's family; a family goes to ruin[is wrecked]; a family becomes [goes] bankrupt.

패각(貝殼) a shell. ⇨ 조가비 ¶~**상**(狀)**의** conchoidal / conchform / shell-shaped.

패거리(牌-) a party; a company. ⇨ 패(牌)4

패검(佩劍) [칼을 참] wearing[carrying] a sword; [차는 칼] side arms; a sword worn. **패검하다** wear[bear] a sword[saber] (at one's side).

패군(敗軍) a defeated army. ¶~**지장**(之將)**은 병법을 말하지 않는다** A defeated [vanquished] general should not talk of battles. / It is not for the vanquished to talk of war.

패권(霸權) supremacy; mastery; hegemony; domination; leadership; supreme power. ¶**미일**(美日)**의** ~ **다툼** contention for hegemonism by the United States and Japan // ~**을 쥐다** bear[hold] sway (over) / assume [have] the hegemony (of the land) / dominate / secure supreme power / hold supremacy // **해상의** ~**을 쥐다** dominate [rule] the seas / secure the mastery of the seas / be the mistress of the sea // ~**을 다투다** compete for dominance / (경기에서) fight [struggle / contend] for a championship // **세계 시장에서 상업상의** ~**을 다투다** struggle for commercial supremacy in the markets of the world // **영국은 에스파냐에게서** ~**을 빼앗았다** Britain wrested supremacy from Spain.

패기(霸氣) an ambitious spirit; ambition; aspiration. ¶~ **있는**[~**만만한** / ~**에 넘치는**] ambitious / aspiring / adventurous / gumptious // ~ **있는 사람** a man of spirit // ~ **없는** inert / spiritless / apathetic // ~ **없는 사람** a dull [an inert / an apathetic] person // **그는** ~**가 있다** He is full of go. / (미) He is full of pep. // **그는** ~**가 없다** He lacks spirit. / He has no gumption. // **그는** ~**가 있는 남자다** He is an ambitious[aspiring] man.

패널 [건] a panel.

패다¹ [이삭이 나오다] come out. ¶**이삭이** ~ come into ears / ear (up) // **이삭이 패어 있다** be in (the) ear // 2, 3**일만 있으면 벼가 모두 팰 것이다** The rice plants will all come into ears in a few days.

패다² [때리다] beat; strike; knock; hit; thrash; give [deal / deliver] (a person) a blow. ¶**늘씬하게** ~ give (a person) a sound thrashing / beat (a person) to a jelly [mummy] // **피가 들도록** ~ beat (a person) black and blue.

패다³ [쪼개다] break[strike] (wood) to pieces. ¶**장작을** ~ chop[split] (fire)wood.

패다⁴ [팜을 당하다] be[get] dug; be hollowed. ¶**옴폭 팬 볼** hollow[sunken] cheeks // **빗물로 팬 도랑** a channel hollowed out[worn] by the rainwater // **빗방울 때문에 땅이 팼다** The raindrops have hollowed out the ground. / The raindrops have worn holes in the ground[have worn away the soil]. // **비 때문에 땅이 패서 도랑이 생겼다** The rain has worn a channel in the ground.

패담(悖談) an unreasonable remark; indecent[improper] talk. 패담하다 say unreasonable thing; talk unreasonably; talk indecency.

패덕(悖德) immorality; demoralization; corruption; a lapse from virtue.
● 패덕자 / 패덕한 an immoral[a corrupt / a depraved] man; a scoundrel; a ruffian.

패도(霸道) ruling by force; military government[rule]; the rule of might.

패랭이 1 [역] a bamboo hat (worn by commoners). **2** [식] a pink. ⇨ 패랭이꽃(⇨ 패랭이)
● 패랭이꽃 [식] a pink; a China[a rainbow / an Indian] pink.

패러그래프 a paragraph.
패러다임 [틀·체계] a paradigm.
패러독스 [역설] a paradox.
패러디 (a) parody.
패류(貝類) shellfish.
패륜(悖倫) immorality. ¶∼의 immoral.
● 패륜아 an immoral person. 패륜 행위 immoral conduct.

패리티 [경] parity.
● 패리티 가격 a parity price.

패망(敗亡) (a) defeat; rout; ruin; wreck; collapse. 패망하다 be defeated; suffer[sustain] a defeat; be routed; be ruined; go[fall] crash; go to ruin. ¶그 나라는 사치로 패망했다 The country was ruined by rolling in luxurious habits[lavishing upon its pleasures].

패멸(敗滅) decay; ruin; a downfall; a fall; destruction. 패멸하다 fall[crumble] into decay; fall; be ruined; go to ruin; collapse; be destroyed.

패물(佩物) personal ornaments[outfittings / adornments]; accessories; trinkets.

패배(敗北) (a) defeat; a loss; a reverse; (a) discomfiture; a setback; (a) rout(패주). ∼를 맛보다 taste defeat / meet with defeat // ∼를 인정하다 acknowledge[admit] one's defeat / throw[chuck] up the sponge / throw in the sponge // 싸움은 반란군의 ∼로 끝났다 The battle resulted in the defeat of the rebel army. 패배하다 be defeated; be beaten; be worsted; have the worst; sustain [suffer] a defeat[reverse]; lose a battle[the day](싸움에서); lose a game(경기에서); be repulsed; be routed(패주하다). 완전히 ∼ be completely defeated // 총선거에서 ∼ lose[be defeated in] the general election // 한국 팀은 큰 차로 프랑스 팀에게 패배했다 The Korean team was beaten by[lost to] the French team by a lopsided score. ➔ ¶적을 패배시키다 defeat the enemy / put the enemy to rout.
● 패배자 a defeated person; a loser; a failure. 패배주의 defeatism. 패배주의자 a defeatist.

패병(敗兵) routed soldiers[troops]; a defeated army.

패보(敗報) the news[tidings] of defeat; a report of defeat.

패사(稗史) an unauthentic history; an unofficial history[chronicle].

패색(敗色) signs of defeat; unfavorable signs in battle. ¶∼이 짙다 Defeat seems certain.

패석(貝石) a fossil shell.
패설(悖說) an unreasonable remark. ⇨ 패담
패설(稗說) a folktale; a folk story; a legend; a fable; a romance.

패세(敗勢) the reverse tide of a war; signs of defeat; a losing situation; a backing[disadvantageous] situation. ¶우리는 ∼에 놓여 있다 The chance[odds] are against us.

패션 (a) fashion. ¶긴 듯한 옷이 올가을의 ∼입니다 Longer dresses are in fashion this autumn.
● 패션 디자이너 a fashion designer. 패션모델 a fashion model. 패션쇼 a fashion show.

패소(敗訴) losing a suit[case]; a lost case. ¶∼의 당사자 the party defeated // 그 소송은 원고의 ∼로 되었다 The case went[The verdict was] against the plaintiff. / The plaintiff lost the suit[case]. 패소하다 lose a suit[case]; fail in an action; be cast in a suit. ¶나는 손해 배상 소송에서 패소했다 I have lost my damage suit.

패스 1 [무료입장권·승차권] a pass; a free ticket[pass]; [정기권] (미) a commutation ticket; (영) a season ticket. ¶통근 ∼ a commutation ticket for workers // 지갑 ∼ a case for a commutation ticket // 철도의 ∼ a pass on the railroad.
2 [합격] passing. 패스하다 pass. ¶시험에 ∼ pass[succeed in] an examination[a test] // (물품의) 검사에 ∼ pass muster / stand the test.
3 [체] pass; passwork. 패스하다 pass (a ball to another). ¶공을 센터에 ∼ pass the ball to the center.
4 [카드놀이] (자기 차례를 거르고 다음 차례로 돌리는 일) pass. 패스하다 pass.

패스포트 a passport. ¶나는 ∼를 신청[갱신]했다 I have applied for a[renewed my] passport.

패싸움(牌─) a gang fight. 패싸움하다 have a gang fight; fight in groups.

패악하다(悖惡─) wicked; vicious; villainous; perverse.

패용(佩用) wearing (a decoration). 패용하다 wear (a decoration). ¶기장을 ∼ wear a badge[medal].

패운(敗運) a bad luck to lose; declining fortune; adverse fortune; one's waning star.

패이다 → 패다⁴

패인(敗因) a cause of defeat; a factor contributing to defeat. ¶그들의 ∼은 부실한 팀워크에 있었다 They were defeated on account of poor teamwork.

패자(敗者) the defeated (person); the vanquished; a loser. ¶∼ 쪽에서 서서 싸우다 fight for the underdog[on the losing side].
● 패자 부활전 a repechage. 패자전 a consolation match[game / race / round].

패자(霸者) **1** [무력에 의한 정복자] a supreme ruler. **2** [경기의 우승자] a champion; a winner; a titleholder.

패잔(敗殘) survival after defeat. ¶∼의 defeated / vanquished.
● 패잔병 remnants (of a defeated troop); stragglers; runaway troops. ¶적의 ∼ the (escaped) remnants of the enemy // ∼ 소탕작전 a mopping-up[clean-up] operation // 소탕 작전에서 5백 명의 ∼이 사살되거나 붙잡혔다 Five hundred stragglers were either killed or captured in the mopping-up operation.

패장(敗將) a defeated[vanquished] general.
패적(敗敵) a defeated[vanquished] enemy.
패전(敗戰) a lost battle; (a) defeat (in war); a failure in war; (a) reverse. 패전하다 lose a war[battle]; be defeated in a battle; lose the

패주 day.
● **패전국** a defeated [vanquished] nation [country]. **패전 투수** [야구] a losing pitcher.

패주(敗走) flight; rout; debacle. ¶~중이다 be on the run. **패주하다** be routed; be put to rout; take to flight; flee. ¶적은 무질서하게 패주했다 The enemy fled in disorderly retreat. →¶적을 패주시키다 put an enemy to rout / rout an enemy / set an enemy flying∥우리는 적을 패주시키는 데 성공했다 We succeeded in routing our enemy [putting our enemy to flight].

패총(貝塚) a shell heap. ⇨조개더미(⇨조개)

패킹 packing. **패킹하다** pack [stuff] up; fill (a crevice with cotton).

패턴 a pattern. ¶**테스트** ~ a test pattern∥사람의 성장 과정에는 여러 가지의 ~이 있다 There are many patterns in the process of man's growth.

패퇴(敗退) (a) defeat; (a) setback. **패퇴하다** [퇴각하다] retreat; [지다] be defeated; be beaten; lose a battle; (경기에서) lose a game; be out. ¶그는 첫 시합에서 패퇴했다 He was eliminated [defeated] in the first match [game].

패트롤카 a (police) patrol car.

패하다(敗-) 1 [싸움에 지다] be defeated; be beaten; lose (a game / a battle / the day); have the worst of it; suffer a defeat; come of a loser. ¶경기에 ~ lose a game [match / bout]∥전쟁에 ~ be defeated in a war / lose a war∥장기에 ~ be beaten in a game of *janggi*∥선거전에서 ~ suffer a defeat [be beaten] in an election campaign∥소송에 ~ lose a lawsuit∥1대 3으로 ~ be defeated [lose the game] by a score of 1 to 3∥시합에 패한 원인은 무엇인가 Why did you lose the game?
2 [살림이 거덜 나다] go [become] bankrupt; (미국 구어) go broke. ¶노름으로 집안이 ~ gamble oneself out of house and home.
3 [야위다] get [become] thin [haggard]; be worn out; waste away.

패혈증(敗血症) [의] blood [septic] poisoning; septicemia; (영) septicaemia; sepsis; sapremia. ¶~성 septicemic.

팩 with a thud; snap (off). ⇨픽2·4

팩시밀리 a facsimile (단수·복수 동형). ¶~로 in facsimile.

팬 [애호자] a fan; an enthusiast. ¶야구 ~ a baseball fan∥영화 ~ a movie fan∥A의 열렬한 ~ an enthusiastic [a fanatical] admirer of A∥~이 많은 여배우 an actress with a large number of admirers∥그는 씨름 [영화] ~이다 He is a *ssireum* [movie] fan.∥당신이 어느 투수의 ~입니까 Who is your favorite pitcher?∥이 지방에는 야구 ~이 많다 There are many baseball fans in this area.

팬더 →판다

팬레터 (write) a fan letter (to); (집합적) fan mail.

팬지 [식] a pansy; a heartsease; a heart's-ease. ¶야생 ~ a kiss-me-quick.

팬츠 1 (속옷) underpants; (영) pants; (남성용) (미) (under)shorts; (여성용) panties; (영국 구어) knickers. 2 (경기용의 반바지) shorts; (복싱 등의) trunks. ¶해수욕 ~ (bathing) trunks / swimming trunks / (미) swim trunks∥쇼트 ~ shorts∥핫 ~ hot pants.

팬케이크 a pancake; a griddlecake; a flapjack.

팬터마임 a (panto)mime; a dumb show. ¶~을 하다 (panto)mime (an act) / indicate by dumb show.

팬티 (a pair of) panties(여성용·아동용); (미) briefs; (주로 미) shorts(남성용); (영) pants. (▶ 한국어 "팬티"는 남성용·여성용·아동용 모두를 가리키나, 영어 "panties"는 남성용·아동용만을 가리키며, "briefs"는 남성용·여성용의 것을 가리킴) ¶삼각 ~ briefs / (상표명) jockey shorts(남성용)∥사각 ~ boxers / boxer shorts [briefs].
● **팬티스타킹** (*panty stocking) a panty hose; a pantihose.

팸플릿 a pamphlet; a brochure; a leaflet(한 장으로 된). ¶선전 ~ a propaganda pamphlet∥~을 찍어 내다 issue pamphlets / pamphleteer∥~으로 (되어) 나오다 be published in pamphlet form.

팻말(牌-) a notice [bulletin] board. ¶길가에는 통행금지의 ~이 서 있었다 At the side of the road stood a notice board saying "Closed to Traffic."

팽 round; around. ⇨'빙1·3

팽개치다 1 [내던지다] throw (away); cast (away); fling (at); hurl (at). ¶창밖으로 ~ throw (a thing) out of the window∥책을 책상 위에 ~ slam a book on the desk∥책가방을 바닥에 ~ throw [fling] one's satchel down on the floor∥그는 나에게 책을 팽개쳤다 He flung [hurled] a book at me.
2 [포기하다] give [throw] up; abandon; [내버려 두다] leave off; leave untouched; lay aside; neglect; desert. ¶공부 [직무]를 ~ neglect one's studies [duties]∥팽개쳐 둘 수 없다 cannot be left untouched / demand immediate attention∥시험이 끝나자마자 그는 공부를 팽개쳐 버렸다 As soon as the examination was over, he stopped studying.∥그는 일을 팽개치고 경마에 갔다 He ditched his work and went to the race.∥그런 문제를 그냥 팽개쳐 둘 수는 없다 The matter must not be left as it is. / The matter cannot wait any longer.

팽그르르 (turn / skate / glide) around smoothly. ⇨'뱅그르르

팽글팽글 round and round smoothly. ⇨'뱅글뱅글

팽나무 [식] a (Chinese) nettle tree; a (Chinese) hackberry. ¶~ 열매 a (Chinese) nettle-tree nut.

팽대(膨大) swelling; expansion; distension; [의] tumefaction. **팽대하다** swell; expand; distend.

팽만하다(膨滿-) be inflated. **팽만히** inflatedly.

팽배(澎湃) overflowing; surging; rampage; rage. **팽배하다** overflow; surge; rage; rise high. ¶팽배하는 민주 사상 the flood tide of democracy∥19세기 중엽에 팽배했던 혁명의 기운 the trend toward(s) revolution which surged forth in the mid-19th century.

팽압(膨壓) [식] turgor pressure.

팽이 a top. ¶~를 돌리다 spin a top∥~를 쳐서 돌리다 whip a top to make it spin∥~가 자리 잡았다 The top sleeps [is sleeping].∥어린이가 ~를 돌리고 있다 A child is spinning a top.∥~가 잘 돌고 있다 The top is spin-

ning smoothly [(문어) is sleeping].
- **팽이채** a whip for spinning a top. **팽이치기** top spinning.

팽창(膨脹) [부풀어 오르기] swelling; inflation; [확대] expansion; dilation; distension; [발전] growth; [증가] increase. ¶**통화 ~** inflation [expansion] of currency // **예산의 ~** an increase in the budget // **기체의 ~** expansion of gases // **도시의 ~** the growth of a city // **인구의 ~** the growth [increase] of population. **팽창하다** swell; expand; inflate; grow; increase; aggrandize. ¶**팽창한 예산** swollen estimates // **팽창한 배** a distended abdomen // **쇠는 열을 가하면 팽창한다** Iron expands when (it is) heated. / Heat expands iron. // **이 도시의 인구는 지금 2배로 팽창했다** The population of this city has now swollen twice as large as before. // **국고의 세출은 해마다 팽창한다** The State expenditure increases year by year.
- **팽창 계수 / 팽창률** the coefficient [rate] of expansion.

팽팽 round and round (quickly). ¶**~ 돌다** turn [go] round and round quickly [rapidly] / spin / twirl // **비행기가 ~ 돌면서 떨어졌다** The plane fell in a spin.

팽팽하다 1 [켕기어서] tight; taut; strained; tense; stretched to the full. ¶**팽팽해지다** tighten / become tight [taut]. **팽팽히** tightly; tautly; tensely. ¶**밧줄을 ~ 당기다** tighten [strain] a rope / stretch a rope tight // **너무 ~ 잡아당기면 끊어진다** If you strain it too hard, it will break.
2 (성질이) rigid; strict; stern; narrow-minded; illiberal; strait-laced; hide-bound. ¶**팽팽한 사람** a strict [narrow-minded] person. **팽팽히** rigidly; strictly; sternly; narrow-mindedly.
3 (세력이) close; equal; even; equally-matched [-balanced]; well-matched. ¶**팽팽한 경기** a close game / a well-matched game // **실력이 ~** be well matched [balanced] in strength [power]. **팽팽히** closely; equally; evenly. ¶**쌍방은 주장을 굽히지 않고 ~ 맞섰다** Both struck fast to their respective opinions.

퍼내다 bail [dip / ladle] out (water); scoop (water) out (of); pump out (a well)(펌프로). ¶**물을 펌프로 ~** pump water out // **배에서 물을 ~** bail water out of a boat / bail out a boat // **연못의 물을 남김없이 ~** drain a pond // **배에 괸 물을 ~** bail water from the bottom of a boat // **분뇨를 ~** pump up [out] night soil // **삽으로 모래를 ~** dip out sand with a shovel.

퍼덕거리다 flutter; leap. ⇨ 파닥거리다
퍼덕퍼덕 flapping; flopping. ⇨ 파닥파닥
퍼뜨리다 (종교·사상 등을) spread; disseminate; diffuse; circulate; propagate; make popular; popularize; (소문 등을) set (a rumor) afloat; start [circulate / spread] (a rumor); give (it) out that ...; make (a thing) public; make (a thing) known. ¶**유언비어를 ~** circulate [spread / set] a false rumor / put a rumor into currency // **공산 사상을 ~** propagate communism / spread Communist ideas // **그들은 근거도 없는 소문을 퍼뜨렸다** They spread [put about] a groundless rumor. // **그런 이상한 소문을 퍼뜨린 자는 누구냐** Who spread such a strange rumor? // **그는 온 동네에 그 소문을 퍼뜨리고 다녔다** He spread [circulated] the rumor throughout the village. // **누가 그 거짓 소문을 퍼뜨리기 시작했는가** Who started [circulated] the false rumor? // **그는 일부러 거짓 정보를 퍼뜨렸다** He deliberately [purposely] had false information [reports] circulated [spread].

퍼뜩 [별안간] suddenly; in a flash. ¶**~ 생각나다** it occurs to one (that) / flash across one's mind // **어떤 생각이 ~ 그의 머리에 떠올랐다** An idea struck [flashed into] his mind. // **그 소리에 ~ 제정신이 들었다** I was alarmed by the sound and gathered my wits about me. // **그 생각이 ~ 떠올랐다** The idea occurred to me in a flash. // **멋있는 생각이 ~ 떠올랐다** A wonderful idea flashed across [into] my mind. // **나는 창문을 잠그지 않고 나왔다는 생각이 ~ 들었다** It suddenly occurred to me that I had forgotten to lock the window before I left home.

퍼렇다 blue; green. ⇨ 파랗다
퍼레이드 a parade. ¶**~ 참가자** a parader // **~ 를 펼치다** hold a parade.

퍼먹다 [많이 먹다] bolt (one's dinner); shovel (food) into one's mouth. ¶**조반을 급히 ~** make [down] a hasty breakfast.

퍼붓다 1 (비난·욕설 등을) heap (shower / rain) (abuses) upon; (포화를) rain (fire) on; bring (the enemy) under (fire). ¶**악담[욕설]을 ~** curse and swear (at a person) // **입정 사납게 욕설을 ~** abuse (a person) in foul language // **질문을 ~** bombard (a person) with questions / rain questions on (a person) // **(야구에서) 맹타를 ~** shower hits (on the opposing team) // **그는 우리에게 욕을 마구 퍼부었다** He hurled a storm of curses at us. // **사람들은 그에게 비난을 [주먹 세례를] 퍼부었다** They showered abuse on him [showered him with blows]. // **그는 상대자에게 펀치를 퍼부었다** He showered punches on his opponent. // **그들은 적진에 포탄을 퍼부었다** They rained shells upon the enemy's camp. // **그 용의자에게 질문이 퍼부어졌다** The suspect was bombarded with questions. // **마을 사람들은 그에게 욕설을 퍼부었다** The villagers heaped insults and abuse upon him.
2 (비가) pour (down); pelt down; (눈이) fall thick and fast. ¶**(억수같이) 퍼붓는 비** pouring [heavy / pelting] rain // **퍼붓는 눈보라 속에** in a heavy snowstorm // **비가 (억수같이) 퍼붓는다** It is raining in torrents [(in) buckets]. / It's raining cats and dogs.

퍼석퍼석하다 crisp; crumbly. ⇨ 파삭파삭하다
퍼센트 percent; per cent(기호 %; 약어 p.c., per ct.); (a) percentage (of) (구어에서는 percent와 구별 없이 쓰이지만, 일반적으로는 수사 뒤에 percent를 쓰고, small, large, high 등의 수량 형용사 뒤에 percentage가 쓰임). ¶**백 ~ 의 성공** a one-hundred percent success // **우리는 연리 6 ~ 의 이자를 받고 있다** We get 6 percent interest per year. / It accumulates interest at six percent per year (percents로는 되지 않음). // **지진에 의한 사망자는 마을 전체 인구의 30 ~ 에 이르렀다** Thirty percent of all the villagers were [the whole population of the village was] killed in the earthquake.(▶「수사+percent of+명사」가 주어일 때, 동사의 수는 명사의 수에 일치시킨다) // **나의 예상은 적중률 99 ~ 다** My forecasts [guesses] are right 99 percent of

퍼센티지 the time.∥나는 100~ 자네의 의견에 찬성이다 I am one hundred percent in agreement with you.∥그들은 정찰의 20~ 할인으로 팔고 있다 They give a 20 percent discount [a reduction of 20 percent]. / They sell at a reduction of 20%. / They sell at 20% off (the regular price).∥높은[큰] ~를 차지하고 있다 It represents [accounts for] a high [large] percentage.

퍼센티지 (a) percentage. ¶~로 말하면 in terms of percentage∥상당히 큰 ~를 차지하다 take up [show] a considerably high percentage∥정확한 ~를 내다[파악하다] work out the exact percentage.

퍼스널 컴퓨터 a personal computer.

퍼스트레이디 〔대통령·원수의 부인〕 the First Lady.

퍼스트 베이스 first base.

퍼즐 a puzzle. ¶크로스워드~ a crossword puzzle∥~을 풀다 solve [work out] a puzzle.

퍼지다 1 〔넓어지다〕 spread out; widen; broaden; become wider [broader]. ¶딱 퍼진 앞가슴 a broad chest∥쫙 퍼진 나뭇가지 spreading branches∥자락이 퍼진 스커트 a flared skirt∥끝이 퍼져 있다 The tip spreading out.
2 〔유포 또는 보급되다〕 spread (abroad); be diffused; be propagated; pervaded (a city); be disseminated; be circulated; (소문 등이) get about [abroad / around]; go the rounds; get [take] air. ¶소문이 확 퍼졌다 The rumor spread like wildfire.∥소문이 학생들 간에 퍼졌다 The rumor got abroad among the students.∥불온한 공기가 온 마을에 퍼지기 시작했다 An air of unrest began to spread the through [pervade] the town.∥고기 굽는 냄새가 공중에 퍼져 다가왔다 The smell of roasted meat came drifting through the air.∥참석자 간에 우호적인 분위기가 퍼졌다 A friendly atmosphere prevailed among those present.∥큰 지진이 일어날 것이라는 뜬소문이 입에서 입을 통해 퍼졌다 The rumor that there would be a strong earthquake spread from mouth to mouth.∥그가 이혼했다는 소문이 퍼졌다 The rumor got abroad [around] that he had gotten a divorce.∥그가 인색하다는 소문이 퍼졌다 The rumor spread that he was stingy.∥소문이 읍내 전체에 퍼졌다 The rumor spread all over town.∥화재는 사방으로 퍼졌다 The fire spread in all directions.
3 〔만연하다〕 spread; prevail; be prevalent; be wide spread. ¶(병이) 퍼지기 시작하다 become prevalent / break out∥발진 티푸스가 퍼지는 것을 막다 prevent [check] the spread of typhus∥독감이 전국에 퍼졌다 Influenza has spread throughout the country.∥갖가지 전염병이 전국적으로 퍼지고 있었다 Various infectious disease were prevailing throughout the country.
4 〔유행하다〕 be in [come into] fashion [vogue]; become popular. ¶이 노래가 학생들 간에 널리 퍼져 있다 This song is much in vogue [very popular] with the students.
5 〔번식하다〕 breed; multiply; propagate; proliferate (동물이). ¶자손이 ~ have a flourishing progeny∥잡초는 급속히 퍼진다 The weeds propagate themselves rapidly.
6 〔불어서 커지다〕 swell up; (물을 먹어) become soaked; sodden; (밥이) be steamed (to a proper degree). ¶퍼진 콩 swollen [sodden] soybeans.

퍼트 (골프에서) a putt. ¶~의 연습을 하다 practice putting. 퍼트하다 putt.

퍼펙트게임 〔야구〕 a perfect game.

퍽¹ 1 〔찌르는 모양〕 with a thrust; (thrusting) hard. ¶칼로 ~ 찌르다 thrust with a knife. 2 〔쓰러지는 모양〕 with a thud; (collapsing) feebly; in a heap. ¶~ 쓰러지다 fall with a thud / fall plump (upon the ground) / fall down feebly∥그는 마루에 ~ 쓰러졌다 He fell flat on the floor.∥남편이 죽었다는 소식을 듣고 그녀는 ~ 쓰러져 울었다 She threw herself down in tears [broke down in tears] at the news of her husband's death.

퍽² 〔매우〕 very much; quite; terribly; awfully; (미국 속어) real; sure; (속어) right; damn (ed). ¶~ 많은 quite a number of (people) / a good many (books)∥~ 많은 수입 a handsome [good / tidy] income∥~ 잘생긴 quite good-looking∥~ 재미있는 be very interesting∥~ 춥다 be pretty cold∥~ 기뻐하다 be very glad / be much pleased∥영어를 ~ 잘하다 speak English fairly [tolerably] well∥~ 컸구나 What a big boy you've grown!∥~ 재미있었다 We had a mighty good time. / We were highly delighted.∥비가 ~ 많이 왔다 A fair amount [Quite a bit] of rain has fallen.∥환자가 ~ 좋아졌다 The patient is much better.

퍽³ (아이스하키의) a puck.

퍽석 1 〔맥없이 주저앉는 모양〕 limply; with a flump; heavily. ¶의자에 ~ 주저앉다 sink [flop down] into a chair / sit limply in a chair. 2 〔깨지는 모양〕 (break) easily; fragilely.

퍽퍽 1 〔내지르는 모양〕 thrusting repeatedly; with thrusts; (repeatedly thrusting) hard. ¶칼로 ~ 찌르다 thrust the knife in again and again. 2 〔쓰러지는 모양〕 with flop after flop; thudding and thudding. ¶병사들이 총에 맞아 ~ 쓰러졌다 The soldiers were (shot and) dropping one after another.

퍽퍽하다 (be) dry and crumbling; crisp; brittle.

펀둥거리다 lead an idle life; idle [dawdle] one's time away.

펀치 〔권투〕 a punch. ¶턱에 ~를 먹이다 punch (a person) on the jaw [chin] / land a punch on (a person's) jaw [chin]∥그는 강력한 ~의 소유자다 He has strong punches.∥그 녀석의 코에 ~를 먹여 주었다 I punched him on the nose.∥나는 턱에 ~를 맞았다 I took a punch on the chin.
●**펀치 카드** a punch [punched] card.

펀펀하다 even; level. ⇨ 판판하다

펀하다 wide; vast. ⇨ 판하다

펄 1 a tideland; a tidal flat. ⇨ 개펄 2 〔들판〕 a wide expanse of land; a vast plain; a prairie.

펄떡거리다 pulsate; hop. ⇨ 팔딱거리다

펄떡펄떡 pulsating; hopping. ⇨ 팔딱팔딱

펄럭이다 flutter; whip; wave; stream; float; fly. ¶바람에 펄럭이는 깃발 a streaming flag∥바람에 펄럭이는 머리 hair streaming in wind∥바람에 ~ flutter [wave / flap] in the wind [breeze]∥깃발이 바람에 펄럭이고 있다 The flag is fluttering in the wind.∥커튼이 바람에 펄럭였다 The wind flapped the curtain. / The curtain flapped in the wind.

펄럭펄럭 fluttering (ly); flapping; with a flutter. ¶바람에 ~ 나부끼다 flutter [flap] in

펄렁거리다 flutter; flap. ⇨ '팔랑거리다

펄썩 1 [먼지 등이 이는 모양] rising in a puff. ¶먼지가 ~ 일어났다 A cloud of dust rose. **2** [주저앉는 모양] plump; heavily; with a thud. ¶의자에 ~ 주저앉다 plump[flop] down into a chair / drop[sink] into a chair // 땅바닥에 ~ 주저앉다 plump (oneself) down on the ground / 소녀들은 방바닥 위에 ~ 주저앉아 있었다 The girls were sitting sprawled out on the floor.

펄쩍 1 [갑자기 여는 모양] suddenly; abruptly. **2** [갑자기 뛰는 모양] nimbly; lightly. ¶~ 뛰다 make a sudden leap / jump[start / leap / spring] to one's feet // ~ 뛰며 좋아하다 leap [dance] for joy (at).

펄쩍 뛰다 [억울하여 강력히 부인하다]. ¶그는 그녀를 만난 적이 없었다고 펄쩍 뛰었다 He denied that he had never met her.

펄쩍펄쩍 jumping[leaping / springing] up and down. ~ 뛰다 jump up and down // 성이 나서 ~ 뛰다 bounce with anger.

펄펄 1 [끓는 모양] simmering; seething; boiling. ¶물을 ~ 끓이다 keep water at a simmer // 물이 ~ 끓는다 Water is boiling hard. **2** [신열이나] feverish; (온돌방 등이) broiling; scorching. ¶그의 몸은 ~ 끓는다 He has a high fever. **3** [날리거나 나부끼는 모양] flapping; fluttering; (눈 등이) in flakes. ¶눈이 ~ 내린다 It snows in great flakes.

펄펄하다 quick-tempered; sprightly; lively. ⇨ 팔팔하다.

펄프 a pulp. ¶대용 ~ substitute for wood pulp // 인견[목재 / 제지] ~ rayon[wood / paper] pulp // ~ 로 만들다 reduce to pulp.
  ● **펄프 공장** a pulp mill. **펄프재**(-材) pulpwood.

펌블 [야구·미식축구] a fumble. **펌블하다** fumble (a grounder); boot (a ball); bobble; muff. ¶공을 ~ fumble a ball (▶야구에서는 동사형만이 쓰임).

펌프 a pump. ¶빨[밀] ~ a suction [force] pump // 소방 ~ a fire engine // 증기[압력] ~ a steam[pressure] pump // 배수[급수 / 양수] ~ a drainage[feeding / lift] pump // 수동(식) ~ a hand pump / (소방용의) a manual fire engine // 흡인식[회전식] ~ a suction[rotary] pump // 진공[배기] ~ a vacuum[exhaust] pump // 자전거의 ~ a bicycle pump // ~ 로 물을 퍼내다 pump the water out (of) // ~ 로 물을 퍼 올리다 pump up water (from) // ~ 질하다 work a pump.
  ● **펌프 우물** pump well.

펌프스 (a pair of) pumps(여성 구두의 일종). ¶슬링 ~ sling(-back) pumps / slings.

펑 with a bang; gaping. ⇨ '뻥²

펑크 1 (타이어의) a puncture; a blowout. ¶자동 ~ 방지 타이어 a self-sealing tire // ~ 가 나다 (타이어가) blow (out) / puncture / explode / go flat / (사람·차가) have a blowout / have[suffer] a flat tire / (구어) get a flat // ~ 를 때우다 (미) fix a flat / (영) mend a puncture // ~ 가 났다 (타이어가 주어일 때) The tire went flat. / The tire blew out. / (사람이 주어일 때) I've got a flat tire [blowout]. / (차가 주어일 때) My car's got a flat tire[blowout]. // 우리 회사 타이어는 쉽게 ~ 나지 않는다 Our tire do not puncture easily. **2** (양말·옷 등의) a puncture; a hole. ¶~ 가 나다 be punctured / get a hole (in one's sock) // (옷의) ~ 난 곳을 깁다 cover a hole // 양말이 ~ 나다 a sock is punctured / a sock gets a hole in it / (사람이) get a hole in one's sock // 네 양말이 ~ 나 있다 There is a hole in your sock. **3** [일이 틀어짐]. ¶~ 가 나다 be spoiled / end in a failure // ~ 를 내다 make a break (in the schedule) // 비 때문에 운동회가 ~ 나 버렸다 The rain has spoiled the field day. / Because of the rain our field day fell flat.

평퍼지다 (서술적) get well-developed[well-rounded].

평퍼짐하다 gently curved; broad and roundish. ¶평퍼짐한 엉덩이 well-rounded hips.

평평 1 [터지는 소리] popping and popping; [구멍 난 모양] with(several) holes (in a thing). **2** [세차게 쏟아지거나 솟는 모양] with a rush; violently; heavily; profusely; copiously. ¶~ 나오다 (water) gush out // 눈이 ~ 내린다 It snows heavily.

페넌트 (미) a pennant; (영) a championship flag.
  ● **페넌트 레이스** (야구에서) (미) a pennant race; (영) contention for a championship.

페널티 [체] a penalty. ¶그에게 ~ 가 과해졌다 He was (got) penalized. / He had a penalty imposed on him.
  ● **페널티 골** a penalty goal. **페널티 에어리어** a penalty area. **페널티 킥** a penalty kick.

페놀 [화] phenol.
  ● **페놀 수지** phenolic resins.

페놀프탈레인 [화] phenolphthalein.

페니 a penny(약어 p) (pl. pence(금액의), pennies(화폐의)). ¶반 ~ a halfpenny // 1~ 반 three halfpennies [halfpence].

페니실린 [약] penicillin. ¶10만 단위의 ~ 을 주사하다 give a person an injection of 100,000 units of penicillin.
  ● **페니실린 쇼크** a penicillin shock. **페니실린 연고** a penicillin ointment. **페니실린 주사** a penicillin shot [injection].

페달 a pedal; a treadle. ¶~ 을 밟다 work a pedal[treadle] / pedal (one's bicycle) // 나는 자전거의 ~ 을 밟으며 고개를 올라갔다 I pedaled my bicycle up the hill. // 나는 라우드[약음] 을 밟으며 피아노를 쳤다 I played the piano with the loud (or sustaining)[soft] pedal down.

페더급(-級) the featherweight.
  ● **페더급 선수** a featherweight (boxer).

페디큐어 (*pedicure) (발톱 물감) (미) (a) nail polish; (영) (a) nail varnish. (▶ pedicure는 발과 발톱을 다듬는 일을 가리킴)

페리보트 a ferry(boat).

페미니스트 [남녀 동등권론자·여권 신장론자] a feminist.

페미니즘 feminism.

페미돔 [여성용 콘돔] a Femidom.

페소 [통화 단위] a peso (pl. ~s).

페스트 [의] (the) pest; the black plague [death]; (the) plague; pestilence. ¶선(腺)~ (the) bubonic plague.
  ● **페스트균** a plague bacillus.

페스티벌 [축제] a festival.

페시미스트 [염세주의자] a pessimist.

페시미즘 pessimism.

페어플레이 fair play. ¶~ 를 하자 Let's play fair[cricket]. / Play the game!

페이 [봉급·임금] pay.
페이드아웃 [영화·TV] (a) fade-out.
페이드인 [영화·TV] (a) fade-in.
페이소스 [비애감] pathos. ¶~가 넘치는 이야기 a story full of pathos.
페이스 (a) pace. ¶자기 ~로 at one's own pace[speed] // ~를 지키다 proceed at one's own pace / keep within one's speed / do not overpace[outpace] oneself // 상대의 ~를 흐트러뜨리다 throw one's rival out of his stride / force the pace of one's rival / put (a person) out of his pace.
페이지 a page(약어 p.; pl. pp.); a leaf(▶ a page는 한 면, a leaf는 양면 즉 한 장을 말함). ¶반대 ~ the opposite page // 왼쪽 ~ the left-hand page / the verso (pl. ~s) // 오른쪽 ~ the right-hand page / the recto (pl. ~s) // (제)12~ page[p.] 12 // 500~의 책 a book of five hundred pages // ~ 위쪽[아래쪽]에 at the top[bottom] of a page // 5 내지 10~에 on pages[pp.] 5-10 // ~를 매기다 page (a book) / paginate (a book) / number the pages // 90~를 열다[펴다] open (the book) at[to] page 90 / find page 90 // ~를 넘기다 turn (over) the leaves[pages] of a book / thumb[leaf] through the pages // ~를 장식하다 adorn[decorate] the page (of history) // 그것은 10~에 있다 It is on page 10. // 15~을 펴십시오 Open your book(s) to[at] page 15. / 130~로 이어짐 Continued on page 130. / 12~로부터 이어짐 Continued from page 12.
페인트[1] [체] feint.
페인트[2] [도료] paint. ¶수성 ~ water paint / ~를 칠하다 paint // ~가 벗겨졌다 The paint came off. // ~ 주의 (게시) (미) Wet paint. / (영) Fresh paint. // ~가 벗겨져 있다 The paint is peeling[coming] off.
● **페인트칠** painting. ¶~이 벗겨지기 시작하다 The paint is beginning to come off[peel].
페치카 (@pechka) a Russian[Manchurian] stove.
페티시즘 [성적 상징물에 대한 집착증] fetishism.
페티코트 a petticoat; an under skirt.
페팅 [남녀의 관능적인 애무] petting. ¶소프트 ~ soft petting / necking // 헤비 ~ heavy petting.
페퍼민트 peppermint.
펜 a pen. ¶굵은[가는] ~ a broad[fine] pen // 펠트~ a felt-tipped pen // 볼 ~ a ball-point pen // 라이트 ~ (전산에서) a light pen // ~으로 쓰다 write with[in] pen and ink // "연필로 써도 됩니까?" "아니요, ~으로 쓰시오." "May I use a pencil?" "No, please use a pen." // ~을 놓으시오 Please put down your pen(s). // ~을 들고 쓰기 시작하시오 Pick up[Take up] your pen(s) and start writing.
펜은 검보다 강하다(속담) The pen is mightier than the sword.
펜글씨 pen writing.
펜대 a penholder.
펜더 [자동차의 흙받기] (미) a fender; (영) a mudguard.
펜스[1] [야구] a fence.
펜스[2] [영국의 화폐 단위] pence. ¶2~ (금액) twopence / (동화) a twopenny // 2~의 twopenny // 1~ 반 three half pence / three halfpennies(반 펜스화 3개) // 반 ~ a halfpenny // 4~짜리 우표 a fourpenny stamp.
펜싱 fencing; foils. ¶~ 교사 a fencing master // ~ 도장 a fencing school // ~ 시합 a fencing match / a match at foils // ~용의 칼 a fencing (foil) // ~ 연습을 하다 practice fencing.
● **펜싱 선수** a fencer; a foilsman.
펜촉(-鏃) a pen point; (영) a nib.
펜치 [철사를 끊거나 구부리는 도구] (a pair of) (cutting) pliers; pinc(h)ers.
펜클럽 the P.E.N. Club(▶ the International Association of Poets, Playwrights, Editors, Essayists, and Novelists의 약어).
펜타곤 [미국의 국방성] the Pentagon; the Department of Defense.
펜팔 a pen pal; a pen-friend.
펜화(-畵) a pen(-and-ink) picture[drawing]; a drawing in pen and ink.
펠리컨 [동] a pelican.
펠트 felt.
● **펠트 모자** a felt hat; (미) a soft hat.
펩신 [화] pepsin.
펩톤 [화] peptone. ¶~의 peptonic.
펭귄 [동] a penguin.
펴다 [말하다] publish; issue; bring out.
펴낸이 a publisher.
펴다 1 [펼치다] spread; lay (out); unfold (a newspaper); unroll (a scroll); open. ¶접부채를 ~ open[unfold] a fan // 책을 ~ open[unfold] the book // 우산[신문]을 ~ open[unfold] an umbrella[a newspaper] // 지도를 ~ spread a map // 담요를 ~ spread[lay out] a blanket / 자리를 펴 놓다 spread a mat // 이부자리를 펴 놓다 spread the bedclothes / make[prepare] a bed // 상품을 죽 펴 놓다 lay articles out for sale / display articles for sale // 빵에 버터를 넓게 퍼서 바르다 spread butter on a piece of bread // 새가 날개를 폈다 The bird spread its wings. // (책의) 25페이지를 펴시오 Open your book(s) at[Turn to] page 25.

2 [뻗다] stretch; outstretch; hold out; spread out. ¶팔을 ~ stretch[hold out] one's arm (to) / reach[put] out one's hand (to / for) / make a long arm (for) // 팔다리를 ~ stretch one's limbs / make oneself comfortable(편안히) // 가슴을 ~ stick out one's chest // 허리를 ~ stretch one's back / straighten oneself // (내로라하고) 가슴을 펴고 걷다 strut[walk] about with one's head in the air // 그는 의기 양양하게 가슴을 폈다 He puffed out his chest with pride.

3 [굽은 것을 곧게 하다] straighten; (말린 것을) uncoil; (금속판을) planish; roll; (구김살 등을) smooth out (creases); (다리미 등으로) iron out. ¶철사를 ~ stretch[uncoil] wire // 금을 두들겨 ~ beat out gold // 스커트의 구김살을 ~ smooth out the wrinkles in a skirt // 손수건의 주름을 ~ (다리미로) iron out the wrinkles in a handkerchief // 종이의 구김살을 ~ flatten[smooth out] crumpled paper.

4 [널리 실시하다·공포하다] promulgate (a law); issue; spread. ¶법률을 ~ put a law into force[effect] // 경찰은 수사망을 전국에 폈다 The police instituted a widespread search throughout the country.

5 [세력 등을 넓히다] extend[expand] (one's influence); establish (one's influence in a district).

6 [기세를 자유롭게 가지다] ease (one's mind); relieve; keep (one's spirits) up. ¶기를 못 ~ cower / shrink (with fear) / be timid / be in a funk.

펴이다 1 (형편이) become better; be changed for the better; improve; (일·어려움이) be smoothed (down / away); be reduced [eased]. ¶살림이 ~ become better off // 셈이 ~ become better off // 금년에는 형편이 펴이 시킬 빕니다 I hope you'll better it this year. **2** [펴지다] get unfolded [straightened / smoothed].

펴지다 1 [펼쳐지다] spread (out); overspread(온통); get unfolded [unrolled]. ¶책상 위에 지도가 펴져 있었다 A map lay spread out on the desk. **2** (구김살 등이) be straightened; be flattened; become smooth.

편 [떡] rice cake.

편(便) 1 (through) the agency of a person. ⇨ 인편(人便) ¶친구 ~에 보내다 [부치다] send (a thing) by (the hand of) a friend.
2 [우편] post; (미) mail. ¶항공 ~으로 부치다 send (a letter) by air mail / airmail (a letter) // 자세한 것은 다음 ~으로 알려 주겠다 I will inform you of the details by the next mail [post].
3 [교통] facilities; service. ¶교통 ~ communication [traffic] facilities / facilities for communication // 철도 ~으로 per [by] rail / by train // 배 ~으로 by ship [steamer / water / sea] // 교통 ~이 좋다 be convenient for transportation // 그 섬으로 가는 배 ~이 있습니까 Is there (a) steamer service to the island? // 항공 회사는 오늘의 제8~을 취소했다 The airline company has canceled the eighth flight today. // 당시 중국으로 건너가는 ~은 이것밖에는 없었다 In those days there was no way of getting to China except this. // 이 집은 버스 ~이 좋다 This house is conveniently near [is convenient to] the bus stop. // 그 도시로의 항공기 [열차] ~이 개설되어 있다 There is air [rail] service to that city. / Air [Rail] service is available to that city. // 이 지역 [부근]은 교통 ~이 나쁘다 Public transport is very poor in this area [neighborhood].
4 [쪽] a side; [방향] a direction; a way. ¶아버지 [어머니] ~의 (a relation) on the paternal [maternal] side / on the father's [mother's] side // 이 [저] ~에 this [that] way // 왼~에 on the left (-hand) side // 오른 ~으로 to the right // 아이들은 어머니 ~에 붙었다 The children took side with their mother.
5 [한 패] a party; a ring; a team (경기의); one's side. ¶우리 ~ our side [part] / we / a friend / our party [team] // 상대 ~ the other party / the opposite party / one's opponent party // 우리 ~과 적 (모두) friend and foe (alike) / both sides / allies and enemies // ~을 가르다 separate into groups [parties] / divide (the men) in two teams(두 패로) // ~을 갈라서 경기하다 play on opposite in a game // 제 ~으로 끌어들이다 win a person over to one's side // 나는 언제나 네 ~이다 I will always stand by you. // 당신은 어느 ~이냐 Which [Whose] ~ side are you on? // 학급의 농구 경기에서 황 군과 나는 각기 다른 ~이 되었다 In the class basketball game, Hwang and I were on different sides. // 나는 네 ~이다 I stand your friend.
6 [선택·경향]. ¶이렇게 하는 ~이 좋을 것이다 You'd better do it like this [(in) this way]. // 이것도 아직 큰 ~이다 Even this is a relatively large one. // 그와 가느니 집에 있는 ~이 낫다 I would rather [sooner] stay at home than go with him. // 그녀에게 그렇게 말하는 ~이 나을 뻔했다 You had better have told her so.

편(編) [편찬] compilation; editing. ¶윤 박사 ~ compiled [edited] by Dr. Yun. // G ~ 영한사전 The English-Korean dictionary compiled [edited] by G.

편(篇) 1 [권] a volume; a book. ¶상[중 / 하] ~ the first [second / third] volume / Book Ⅰ [Ⅱ / Ⅲ]. **2** [장·절] a chapter; a section; a part; (시 등의) a canto. ¶제1~ the first chapter / chapter Ⅰ / (시의) canto Ⅰ // 상 ~ the first volume / Volume Ⅰ / Book Ⅰ. **3** [시문·영화 등의 수효] a piece. ¶한 ~의 시 a poem // 한 ~의 수필 an essay // 다섯 ~ 5 pieces // 그녀의 편지는 그대로 한 ~의 시이다 Her letter is a piece of poetry in itself.

편각(偏角) [측량] declination; [수] amplitude; [항] variation.
● **편각계(-計)** a declinometer.

편견(偏見) a biased [distorted / prejudiced] view; prejudice; a bias. ¶인종적 ~ racial prejudice // ~이 있는 [없는] (un)prejudiced / (im-)partial // ~을 갖다 [품다] hold [harbor] a biased view (of) / have a prejudice [bias] against (a thing) // ~을 버리다 cast [put] away a prejudice // 당신은 그녀에게 ~을 가지고 있다 You are prejudiced [have a prejudice] against her. // 그렇게 생각하는 것은 나의 ~일까 Is it prejudice [bias] on my part to think that way? / Am I over sensitive to think that way? // 그것은 나의 ~ 때문일지 모른다 That may be due to my prejudice. / I may be biased [prejudiced / jaundiced]. // 그녀는 ~이 심하다 She has a strongly warped view. / She unnecessarily feels herself wronged. // 그것은 네가 부당하게 대우받고 있다는 네 ~에 지나지 않는다 You just imagine that you're being unfairly treated.

편곡(編曲) [음] (an) arrangement. ¶A씨 작곡 B씨 ~의 composed by Mr. A, arranged by Mr. B. **편곡하다** arrange. ¶곡을 오케스트라용으로 ~ orchestrate a piece / arrange a piece for orchestra // 이것은 바이올린용으로 편곡한 것이었다 This piece of music was arranged for the violin.
● **편곡자** an arranger; an adapter.

편광(偏光) polarized light; polarization (of light).
● **편광계** a polarimeter. **편광 현미경** a polarization microscope.

편년사(編年史) a chronicle; annals.
편년체(編年體) a chronological form [order]. ¶~로 in chronological order.

편달(鞭撻) 1 [격려] encouragement; urging; whipping. ¶여러분의 지도와 ~을 바랍니다 I will appreciate your further help and encouragement. **편달하다** encourage [urge / incite / goad] (a person to do); spur on (a person to industry); whip. ¶제가 성공한 것은 편달해 주신 덕택입니다 I owe my success to your encouragement. // 더욱 편달해 주시기 바랍니다 I must seek your further advice and encouragement. / I solicit your continued patronage [favors]. **2** [채찍질] lashing.
편달하다 lash.

편대(編隊) (a) formation. ¶비행 ~ flight formation // 폭격기의 대 ~ a large formation of bomber // 9대 ~로 in nine-plane formation

편도(片道) one way; each way. ¶요금은 ~ 5,000원입니다 The fare is 5,000won each way.// 부산까지 2등 ~ 한 장 주시오 (미) One second-class one-way ticket to Busan, please.// (영) Give me a second-class single to Busan.// ~입니까 왕복입니까 Do you want a one-way ticket or a round-trip?
● **편도 승차권** (미) a one-way ticket; (영) a single (ticket). **편도 요금** (미) a one-way fare; (영) a single fare.

편도(扁桃) [식] an almond (tree); [열매] an almond.

편도선(扁桃腺) [생] the tonsils; the amygdala (pl. -lae). ¶~의 tonsillar // 당신의 ~은 부어 있습니다 Your tonsils are swollen. / You have swollen tonsils.
● **편두선염** tonsillitis. ¶화농성 ~ septic tonsillitis.

편두통(偏頭痛) [의] (a) migraine; (a) megrim; a sick[migraine] headache. ¶~이 나다 have [suffer from] a migraine.

편들다(便-) take part[sides] (with); side (with); take (a person's) side[part]; be on (a person's) side; stand by (a person); back; support. ¶아들을 ~ side with one's son // 너는 어느 쪽에 편드니 Which side are you on?// 여론은 그에게 편들었다 Public opinion was in his favor.// 신은 정의의 편들어 주신다 God is on the side of justice.// 그는 항상 가난한 사람들을 편든다 He always takes sides with[takes up the cause of] the poor.

편람(便覽) a handbook; a manual; [안내서] a guide. ¶영어 ~ a handbook of English // 경제학 ~ a handbook of economics // 학생 ~ a handbook for students / (미) a college catalog(ue) / (영) a (university) prospectus.

편력(遍歷) 1 [널리 돌아다니기] travel; a pilgrimage. **편력하다** go on a pilgrimage; wander[travel] about[around]. ¶여러 나라 [국내 각지]를 ~ travel through many countries[provinces]. 2 [갖가지 경험을 하기]. ¶그의 인생 ~도 마지막에 가까웠다 He is nearing the end of his checkered life.// 그는 여성 ~에 종지부를 찍고 마침내 결혼했다 He finally got married after having been involved with many women.
● **편력자** a pilgrim; an itinerant.

편류(偏流) [항] (a) drift; (a) deflection; leeway.

편리(便利) convenience; expediency; serviceableness(쓸모 있음); handiness(간편); facilities(시설의). ¶남의 ~를 도모하다 consult [serve] the convenience of a person // 공공의 ~를 도모하다 promote the benefit of the public. **편리하다** convenient; expedient; handy; serviceable; useful. ¶편리한 기구 a convenient[serviceable / handy] utensil [tool] // 이 부엌에는 여러 가지 새로운 편리한 것이 갖추어져 있다 This kitchen has all the modern conveniences.// 지하철을 이용하면 편리합니다 It is convenient if you use the subway[(영) underground].// 이 호텔은 관광하기에 편리한 위치에 있다 This hotel is conveniently located for sightseeing.// 이 방은 도서관이 가까워서 ~ This room is conveniently near[is located conveniently close to] the library.// 그것 참 편리하군 (구어) That is very convenient for me.// 이 책은 참고하기에 ~ This book is convenient for reference.// 이 집은 교통이 편리한 역 가까이에 있다 This house is located conveniently near a station.

편린(片鱗) a part; a portion; something; a glimpse. ¶그 에세이로부터 그 당시 사람들의 생활의 ~을 엿볼 수 있다 You can get a glimpse of the way people lived then from the essay.// 그는 어릴 때 이미 그 비범한 재능의 ~을 보이고 있었다 As a young child, he had already given indications of his unusual talent.

편마암(片麻巖) [지] gneiss.

편면(片面) one side. ¶너는 사물의 ~밖에 보지 않는다 You look at only one side of things [the matter].

편모(偏母) one's widowed[lone] mother. ¶슬하에 있다 have mother only / live with one's widowed mother // ~ 슬하에서 자라다 grow up[be brought up] under widowmother's care.

편모(鞭毛) [생] a flagellum (pl. ~s, -la).
● **편모충** a flagellate. ¶~류 flagellates.

편무(片務) a unilateral duty[obligation / responsibility]. ¶~적 unilateral.
● **편무 계약** a unilateral contract[agreement].

편물(編物) [뜨개질] knitting; crochet(크로셰 뜨개질); [뜨개질한 것] knitted work; knitting; knit; [뜨개질한 옷] knitgoods; knitwear. **편물하다** knit; do knitting; crochet. ¶편물하는 사람 a knitter.
● **편물 기계** a knitting machine[frame]; a knitter.

편법(便法) an easier[a handy] method; a shortcut; a short way; an expedient; an expediency; convenient mode; an expedient means. ¶일시적인 ~ a temporary expedient // 무슨 ~을 강구해야겠다 We must devise [resort to] some expedient method.

편벽하다(偏僻-) eccentric; obstinate; bigoted; one-sided; prejudiced; bias(s)ed; partial.

편상화(編上靴) lace-ups; [장화] lace-up boots.

편서풍(偏西風) (the) westerlies; the prevailing westerlies(▶ 보통 복수형).

편성(編成) formation; organization; composition; a footing. ¶예산 ~ the compilation of a budget // 전시[평시] ~ a war[peace] footing [organization] // 프로그램 ~ program(m)ing // 그는 새 프로의 ~에 바쁘다 He is busy (with) arranging new programs.// 경기의 대전 ~은 추첨으로 결정한다 Who plays who(m)[The pairing] for the tournament will be decided by lot. **편성하다** form; organize; compose; compile; draw up; make up; frame; weave; [군] embody. ¶예산을 ~ draw [make] up a budget // 텔레비전 프로를 ~ plan a TV program // 신입생을 50명씩 여섯 반으로 편성했다 We organized the new pupils into six classes of fifty new pupils each. ➔ 이 열차는 10량으로 편성되어 있다 This train is ten cars long. / This train is composed[made up] of ten cars.// 위원회는 10명의 위원으로 편성되어 있다 The commit-

tee consists of [comprises] ten members.
● **편성국** (방송국의) the program(m)ing department.
편수 [공장의 우두머리] a master workman [artisan]; the chief workman; a boss handicraftsman; a foreman.
편수(編修) editing; compilation; redaction. **편수하다** edit; compile; prepare for the press.
● **편수관** an editorial officer; an (official) editor.
편술(編述) editing; compilation; writing. **편술하다** write (a book); edit; compile; redact.
편승하다(便乘-) 1 [교통편을 얻어 타다] (차에) get a lift (in a person's car); get (a free ride) along a road; make one's way (to a place) by thumbing rides; (미) hitchhike; (배에) take a ship; go on board (a ship). ¶운좋게 종로까지 친구가 차에 편승시켜 주었다 Fortunately a friend gave me a lift in his car as far as Jongno. 2 [기회를 틈타다] avail oneself of; take advantage of; (미국 구어) jump on [aboard] the bandwagon. ¶철도 운임의 인상에 편승하여 제조 업자는 물가를 올렸다 Manufacturers took advantage of the rise in railway fares to increase prices.
편식(偏食) an unbalanced[one-sided] diet. **편식하다** eat unbalanced meals; have an unbalanced diet. ¶편식하는 아이 a child who eats only what he likes // 아이들이 편식하지 않도록 길렀다 I brought my children up to eat everything they are served. // 건강한 사람은 편식하지 않는다 Healthy people eat balanced meals.
편싸움(便-) a gang fight. **편싸움하다** fight in groups; have a gang fight.
● **편싸움꾼** a gang fighter.
편안하다(便安-) [무사하다] safe; secure; [평온하다] peaceful; quiet; calm; tranquil; restful; [안락하다] comfortable; easy; easeful; carefree; [태평하다] lighthearted; easygoing; happy-go-lucky. ¶편안하고 한가롭게 있을 때가 아니다 This is no time to be idling[taking it easy]. // 그 그림을 보고 있으면 기분이 편안해진다 Looking at this painting sets my mind at ease. // 이 의자는 ~ This is a comfortable chair. // 이제 좀 편안해졌습니까 Do you feel better now? // 죽으면 편안해질 것이다 Death will release me from my pain. // 나는 대역을 마치고 나서 마음이 편안해졌다 I feel relieved, as I have accomplished this important duty. // 자기 아들이 전쟁에 나간 후부터 그녀는 한시도 마음이 편안하지 않았다 She had never felt easy[at ease] since her son went off to war. // 그는 편안한 생활을 하고 있다 He leads a carefree [comfortable] life. / He leads a life of ease.
편안히(便安-) safely; peacefully; quietly; calmly; comfortably; easily. ¶~ 앉으십시오 Please sit at ease[comfortably]. // 그는 고생도 모르고 ~ 자랐다 He had a protected childhood and grew up without experiencing life's hard knocks. // 범인은 붙잡히기까지 이웃 마을에서 뻔뻔스럽게도 ~ 살고 있었다 The criminal had been living a cozy[(영) cosy] life brazenly in the next town until he was arrested. // 아무것도 그의 마음을 ~ 할 수 없었다 Nothing could put[set] his mind at rest. // 그들은 연금으로 ~ 지내고 있다 They lead a comfortable life on a pension. // 그녀는 ~ 죽었다 She died[passed away] peacefully. // ~ 잠드소서 (묘비에서) Rest[May he rest] in peace.
편암(片巖) [광] schist. ¶~ (모양)의 schistose.
편애(偏愛) (a) partiality (for); a predilection (for); favoritism (to). ¶그는 ~를 한다 He shows partiality. **편애하다** be partial (to); show favoritism (to); be prejudiced in favor (of). ¶편애하여 상대를 망치다 give undue favor and spoil a person / run a person with kindness // 그는 학생을 편애하지 않는다 He treats all the pupils fairly. / He doesn't have any pets.
편육(片肉) slices of boiled beef.
편의(便宜) convenience; accommodation; facility; (교통 등의) facilities; [이익] advantage; benefit; [방편] expedience; expediency. ¶…의 ~를 도모하기 위하여 to meet[suit / serve] the convenience of ... // ~를 제공하다 offer[afford] convenience (to a person) / provide[afford] facility (for some purpose) / offer advantage (to) // 사용자의 ~를 위해 자세한 설명서가 붙어 있다 Detailed instructions are attached for the convenience of users. // 이 부근은 역이 가깝다는 ~가 있다 This neighborhood has the advantage of being near a station. // 조사의 ~를 위해 최선을 다하겠다 I'll do everything I can to facilitate the investigation. // ~상 그것을 셋으로 나누었다 I divided it into three categories for convenience sake[for the sake of convenience]. **편의하다** handy; convenient; expedient. ¶편의한 방법 an expediency / an expedient // 편의한 방법을 취하다 adopt [resort to] an expedient.
● **편의주의** opportunism; expediency; timeserving. **편의주의자** an opportunist. ¶그는 ~다 He is an opportunist[a timeserver].
편이하다(便易-) convenient; handy; easy; useful; serviceable.
편익(便益) [편리] convenience; facility; [이익] benefit; advantage; profit. **편익하다** beneficial; advantageous; helpful.
편입(編入) 1 [짜서 넣음] weaving (in). **편입하다** weave in. 2 [끼어 들어감] entry; admission; incorporation(합병); [군] enlistment; enrol(l)ment (in). **편입하다** (부류의) class (with / among); include (in); (예산에) insert; (학급에) admit[put] (into); enrol(l) (into); place (in a grade); (군대에) assign (to the infantry). ¶이것은 내년도의 예산에 편입된다 This amount can be carried over to next year's budget.
● **편입생** an enrol(l)ee; an enrolled student; a transfer student. **편입 시험** an entrance examination (for admission) for transfer students. ¶그는 ~을 보고 3학년에 들어왔다 After an examination he was admitted as a junior.
편자 [말굽의 쇳조각] a horseshoe. ¶말에 ~를 붙이다 shoe a horse.
편자(編者) an editor; a compiler.
편재(偏在) uneven[unfair] distribution; maldistribution. ¶부의 ~ the maldistribution of wealth. **편재하다** be unevenly distributed; be maldistributed. ¶출판사는 서울에 편재해 있다 There is an overconcentration of publishing companies in Seoul.
편재(遍在) omnipresence; ubiquity. **편재하다** omnipresent; ubiquitous.

편저(編著) compilation; redaction. ¶홍길동 ~ a book written and edited[compiled] by Hong Gildong. **편저하다** compile; redact.

편전(便殿) the king's private quarters[living room].

편제(編制) formation; organization; composition. ¶우리는 이미 전투 ~를 이루고 있었다 We were already in battle formation. **편제하다** form; organize; compose; make up; frame; [군] embody.
● **편제표** (군대의) a table of organization.

편주(片舟·扁舟) a little boat; a skiff. ¶일엽 ~ a little boat / a tiny leaf of a boat.

편중(偏重) preponderance. **편중하다** attach [give] too much importance (to); make too much of; lay disproportionate emphasis (on); overemphasize. ¶학교에서 입시 준비에 편중하는 것은 잘못이다 Placing too much emphasis[a disproportionate emphasis] on preparatory education at school is a mistake.

편지(便紙·片紙) a letter; a communication; a note; a missive; a line(단신); an epistle(서한); (집합적) mail. ¶감사 [사례] ~ a letter of thanks / an appreciative letter // 안부 ~ a letter inquiring after one's health // 연애 ~ a love letter / 인사 ~ a letter of greetings // ~를 쓰다 write a letter / (남에게) write (a person) a letter / write (to) (a person) // ~를 주고받다 correspond (with) / exchange letters (with) // ~로 신청하다 apply by letter // ~를 부치다 mail[(영) post] a letter // ~를 뜯다 open[unseal] a letter / cut a letter open // 3월 2일자로 보내 주신 ~ 고맙습니다 Thank you for your letter of[dated] March 2.(▶ March the second라고도 읽음) // 여동생으로부터 3주일 이상이나 ~가 오지 않았다 I have not heard from my sister for more than three weeks. // 그는 항상 ~ 회답을 즉시 해 준다 He always answers[replies to] my letters promptly. // 내가 그와 주고받은 ~는 거의 50통이나 된다 I have exchanged about fifty letters with him in all. // 그는 나에게 ~로 청혼했다 He proposed to me by letter. / He wrote and asked me to marry him. // 나한테 온 ~ 없습니까 Is there any mail for me? // 나는 1주일에 한 번 부모님께 ~를 쓴다 I write (a letter) to my parents once a week. // 이 ~ 좀 부쳐 주시겠습니까 Will you mail [(영) post] this letter for me? // 그는 ~를 자주 쓰는 사람이다 He is a good correspondent.
● **편지 봉투** an envelope; (미) an envelop. **편지지** letter[writing] paper; notepaper. ¶~ 다섯 장 five sheets of letter paper.

편집(偏執) bigotry; obstinacy; bias. **편집하다** be bigoted (to / in); stick to (one's prejudice); show bias.
● **편집광** (사람) a monomanic. **편집병** paranoia. ¶~ 환자 a paranoid.

편집(編輯) editing; compilation; redaction. **편집하다** edit (a magazine); compile (a dictionary); prepare for the press. ¶책을 [유명한 수필을 모아서] ~ edit a book [a collection of famous essays]. ➔ ¶이 책[테이프]는 아주 재치 있게 편집되어 있다 This book[tape] is ingeniously edited.
● **편집국** an editorial office. **편집부** an editorial department. **편집실** (신문사의) the desk; the editorial room. **편집자** an editor; [편집원] a member of the editorial staff; [필름 편집자] a (film) cutter. **편집장** the chief editor; (신문사의) the copy chief; (간행물의) the general editor. **편집 회의** (hold) an editorial meeting. **편집 후기** the editor's[editorial] comments.

편짜다(便-) form[make up] a party [team]; organize [get up] a team; team up; [편을 가르다] separate into groups. ¶…과 ~ take part with / partner (with) / pair (off) with / team up with / join forces with // 편짜서 놀이를 하다 play (on opposite) sides (in a game) // 넷이 편짰다 Four banded together to form a team[side].

편차(偏差) [물][공] (a) deflection; [수] (a) deviation; (측량의) (a) declination; [물] (a) variation; [공] windage; (항로의) (a) drift; driftage. 표준 ~ standard deviation // 자기 ~ magnetic declination.
● **편차계** a declinometer.

편찬(編纂) compilation; editing. **편찬하다** compile (a dictionary); edit (an anthology). ¶그 사전은 지금 편찬하는 중이다 The dictionary is in preparation[in course of compilation]. ➔ ¶이 책은 잘 편찬되어 있다 This book is excellently got up.
● **편찬자** a compiler; an editor.

편찮다(便-) **1** [편하지 않다] uncomfortable; uneasy. ¶옷이 꽉 끼어 ~ be uneasy [uncomfortable] in tight clothes. **2** [병으로 아프다] ill; sick; unwell; indisposed; ailing. ¶몸이 ~ be[feel] unwell[ill] / be [feel] out of sorts / be in a bad state of health / (구어) be under the weather // 배 속이 ~ have something wrong with one's inside / one's stomach is out of order // 어디 편찮으십니까 Is anything the matter[wrong] with you?

편충(鞭蟲) [동] a whipworm.

편취(騙取) a fraud; a swindle; an imposture; a cheat; (속어) a have. **편취하다** commit [practice] a fraud; swindle; defraud; cheat; deceive. ➔ ¶우리 집은 그 사람들에게 편취당하고 말았다 We were swindled out of our house by those people.

편친(偏親) one parent; an only parent; a single parent. ¶~의 아이 a fatherless[motherless] child.
● **편친시하** having only one parent to serve.

편파(偏頗) partiality; favoritism; (unfair) discrimination; [일방적임] one-sidedness; [불공평] unfairness; injustice. ¶저 심사원은 ~적이다 That judge is biased toward one side. // 심판은 ~적이어서는 안 된다 A referee should be impartial[not be partial]. // 그들은 ~적인 판정에 항의했다 They protested against the unfair[unjust] judgement. **편파하다** partial; one-sided; unfair; biased.

편편이(便便-) by each[every] messenger [mail].

편편하다(便便-) [아무 일 없이 편안하다] free from care; carefree; easy; comfortable. **편편히** comfortably; easily.

편평족(扁平足) [평평한 발] a flatfoot (pl. -feet); a splayfoot (pl. -feet). ¶~의 flatfooted.

편평하다(扁平-) flat; horizontal; even; level; [식] compressed. ¶편평한 길 a level road.

편하다(便-) **1** [안락하다] comfortable; easy; [걱정 없다] free from care; carefree; insouciant. ¶일하기에 편한 옷 an easy fit for work // 발이 편한 신발 comfortable shoes to wear / shoes easy to walk in∥속이 ~ feel comfortable in the stomach∥그와 함께 있으면 마음이 편하지 않다 I don't feel at ease [comfortable] in his presence.∥그는 있을 때가 없다 I never feel free from care. **편히** comfortably; easily; peacefully. ¶마음을 ~ 먹다 ease one's mind / take things[it] easy∥부모를 ~ 모시다 let one's parents lead a comfortable life∥여기에 계시는 동안 마음 ~ 지내시오 Make yourself at home [Take it easy] while you are here.

2 [편리하다] convenient; suited (for some purpose); handy; expedient. ¶쓰기가 ~ be convenient of use / be easy[handy] to use∥교통이 ~ have (good) facilities of communication∥자기 편할 대로 생각하다 indulge in wishful thinking∥자기 편할 대로 하다 consult[suit / follow] one's own convenience / suit oneself[one's convenience]. **편히** conveniently; suitably; handily; expediently.

3 [쉽다] easy; light; simple; soft. ¶편한 일 an easy task / a soft[cushy] job / light work [labor]∥그 일은 옆에서 보는 것처럼 그렇게 편한 일은 아니다 It is by no means so easy as it seems. **편히** easily; lightly; simply; softly.

4 [고통이 없다]. ¶편해지다 (고통이) be mitigated / be alleviated / (사람이) feel relief / get rid of (pain)∥이 약을 먹으면 편해진다 This medicine will bring[give] you relief[ease you of your pain].

편향(偏向) **1** (전자류 등의) deflection; (생물의 개체의 변이에 의한) deviation. **편향하다** deflect; deviate. **2** [치우친 경향] an inclination (to / toward); a tendency (to / toward). ¶그들은 분명히 좌익 ~이다 They obviously lean[They are obviously inclined] toward the left. / They are obviously leftists.∥최근 그는 보수주의적 ~을 보이기 시작했다 Recently he has begun to show an inclination[a tendency / leanings] toward conservatism. **편향하다** incline (toward); tend (toward / to). →¶편향된 교과서 a slanted [an ideologically biased] textbook.

편협하다(偏狹-·褊狹-) narrow-minded; illiberal; intolerant. ¶그는 그 문제에 대해서는 편협한 견해를 가지고 있다 He takes a jaundiced[prejudiced] view of the matter.

편형동물(扁形動物) a platyhelminth (*pl.* ~s, ~es); a flatworm.

펼치다 unfold (a package); lay out (one's clothes); unroll (a scroll); spread[open] a sail. ¶(새가) 날개를 ~ spread the wings∥책의 38페이지를 펼치시오 Open your book(s) to[at] page 38.∥활짝 트인 경치가 눈 아래에 펼쳐졌다 A broad view spread itself[opened out] below us.

폄하다(貶-) speak ill[evil] of; speak slightingly of; despise; depreciate (a person's abilities); disparage; run[cry / call] down; belittle.

평(坪) **1** [토지 면적] a *pyeong* (단수·복수 동형) (=3.954 sq. yds.); [체적] a *pyeong* (=7.9 cub. yds.). ¶이 뜰은 2백 ~이다 This garden covers (an area of) two hundred *pyeong*. **2** [유리·헝겊·벽의 한 자 평방] a *pyeong* (=0.11 sq. yds.). **3** [조각·동판의 한 치 평방] a *pyeong* (=1.4 sq. inches).

평(評) [비평] (a) criticism; a comment; a review; [평판] (a) reputation; (a) repute. ¶신문 기사에 대해 ~을 하다 comment on newspaper articles∥그는 동료 간에 ~이 좋다 He is popular among his colleagues.∥이 작품은 비평가들로부터 좋은 ~을 받지 못했다 This work was not well received by the critics. / This work did not get a favorable reception from the critics.∥그는 유능한 사업가라는 ~을 얻었다 He got the reputation of being an able businessman. / He earned[got /acquired] a reputation as an able businessman.

평가(平價) par; parity. ¶법정 ~ mint par / par of exchange∥실제[상업] ~ real[commercial] par of exchange∥~로 ~과 샀다 We bought it below[above] par.

●**평가 절상** revaluation; upward (re)valuation (of the won); upvaluation. ¶~을 하다 revaluate[revalue / upvalue] (the currency / the dollar). **평가 절하** devaluation. ¶~를 하다 devaluate[devalue] (the currency).

평가(評價) **1** [가격을 정함] (a) valuation; [견적] (an) estimation; [과세 등을 위한 사정] (an) assessment; [매기·과세 등을 위한] (an) appraisal. ¶재산의 ~ the assessment[[영] the rating] of one's property. **평가하다** value; estimate; appraise; assess. ¶토지를 높게 ~ set a high valuation on the land. →¶(과세를 위해) 5천만 원으로 평가된 집 a house assessed at fifty million won∥이익은 500만 원으로 평가되었다 The profit was estimated at five million won.

2 [사물의 가치를 정함] (문어) (an) evaluation; (a) valuation; (an) appraisal. ¶한국에 대한 공평한[정확한] ~ a fair[correct] evaluation of Korea∥성적의 5단계 ~ a rating of school children's performance on five levels∥정부에 대한 세간의 ~를 높이다 raise the public estimate[opinion] of the government∥세간의 ~가 높다 stand high in public estimation. **평가하다** evaluate; value; estimate. ¶업적을 ~ evaluate a person's achievements∥과대[과소]하게 ~ overestimate[underestimate]∥교사는 그녀의 재능을 정확하게 평가했다 The teacher estimated [sized up] her ability accurately.∥상사는 그의 능력을 높이[낮게] 평가했다 His boss had a high[low] opinion of his ability.∥외모로 사람을 평가해서는 안 된다 We should not judge (of) a man by his appearance.

●**평가익**[손] an appraisal profit[loss]; a paper profit[loss].

평각(平角) [수] a straight angle.

평결(評決) [법] a verdict; a decision; a deliverance. ¶원고에게 유리한 ~ a verdict for [favorable to] the plaintiff∥배심원은 유죄[무죄]의 ~을 내렸다 The jury returned [rendered / brought in] a verdict of guilty [innocent]. **평결하다** bring in[give / deliver / return] a verdict (of).

평교(平交) friends (of) about the same age; peer group friends; friends in the same age bracket.

●**평교간** friendly relationship between (one's) contemporaries.

평교사(平教師) a common teacher.

평균(平均) **1** [가지런하게 고름] an average. ¶1인 ~ per head / 조화 ~ the harmonic average∥10과 20의 ~은 15이다 The average of 10 and 20 is 15.∥나는 어린이들

평년 의 신장의 ~을 내 보았다 I calculated the average height of the children.// 기남이의 학업 성적은 ~ 이상, 민수는 ~ 이하, 신희는 ~ 에 이르고 있다 Ginam's work at school is above average, Minsu's is below average, and Sinhui's is about average.// 지난달의 강우량은 ~의 두 배였다[~보다 30퍼센트 불었다] Last month's rainfall was double the average [thirty percent over the [an] average].// 그들은 한 달에 ~ 12일밖에 일하지 않는다 They work only twelve days a month on the [an] average.// 한 사람당 3,000원이 된다 That comes to an average of thirty hundred won per person.// 내 수입은 월 ~ 100만 원이 된다 My income averages out at 1,000,000 won a month. **평균하다** average; take [strike] an average.// 나는 평균하여 하루에 2시간을 걷는다 I walk two hours a day on the average.// 그는 평균하면 한 달에 맥주를 약 10병 마신다 He averages about ten bottles of beer a month.

2 [균형] equilibrium; equipoise; balance. ¶한 발로 몸의 ~을 잡다 balance oneself on one leg.

3 [수] the mean. ¶산술[기하] ~ the arithmetical [geometric] mean // 연 ~ the yearly mean // 월 ~ the monthly mean.

● **평균값** the mean (value). ¶~의 정리 the mean value theorem. **평균 기온** the mean air [atmospheric] temperature. **평균대** (체조 용구) a balance beam; (체조 종목) the balance beam. ¶그녀는 ~ 체조에서 은메달을 땄다 She won the silver medal in the beam event. **평균 수명** the average life expectancy [span]. ¶여자의 ~은 남자보다 길다 On the average women live longer than men. **평균 연령** the average age (of children). **평균점** the average mark. ¶~ 70점 이상을 얻지 않으면 졸업할 수 없다 A student who fails to achieve an average (mark) of 70 cannot graduate.

평년(平年) **1** [윤년이 아닌 해] a common year; a year other than a leap year. **2** [보통의 해] an average [a normal] year. ¶~과 같은 기온 the temperature in an average year // 장마가 ~보다 길었다 The rainy season lasted longer than usual.

● **평년작** an average crop [harvest]. ¶쌀은 ~이 될 전망이다 The rice crop is expected to be about average.// 올해의 포도는 ~을 웃[밑]돌았다 This year's grape crop was better than [fell short of] the average.

평등(平等) [균등] equality; [공평] impartiality. ¶인권 ~ the equality of human rights // **기회** ~ equality of opportunity // **남녀** ~ equality of the sexes. **평등하다** equal; equable; even; impartial. ¶평등하게 [평등히] equally / evenly / [차별 없이] impartially // 남녀의 역할을 평등하게 하다 equalize male and female roles // 아이들에게 용돈을 평등하게 주었다 I gave an equal amount of pocket money to each child.// 그는 종업원을 평등하게 다루었다 He treated his employees impartially [without discrimination].// 우리는 모두 법 앞에서 ~ We are all equal before the law.// 사람은 모두 평등하게 태어났다 All men are created equal.

● **평등주의** equalitarianism; egalitarianism. **평등화** equalization; equaling out.

평론(評論) [논문 형식의 비평] criticism; [시평] a review; a comment. ¶문예 ~ literary criticism / [문예 시평] a (book) review / a (literary) review // **영화**[연극] ~ movie (or film) [play] reviews // 문학 작품의 ~을 하다 make critical remarks on [offer criticism of] a literary work. **평론하다** review; comment (on); criticize; make comments (on).

● **평론가** a critic; (신간 서적 등의) a reviewer; [시사 해설자] a commentator; 《영》 a publicist; [신문 등의 특별란 집필자] a columnist. ¶**미술**[음악 / 문예] ~ an art [a music / a literary] critic // **야구** ~ a baseball commentator // **영화**[연극] ~ a movie [play] critic.

평맥(平脈) the normal [regular] pulse.

평면(平面) a plane; a level. ¶~의 plane / level / flat // ~적인 관찰 (a) superficial observation // 접 ~ a tangent plane // 동일 ~상에 있다 be on the same level [plane] (with) / be in one plane / be flush (with).

● **평면각** a plane angle. **평면경** a plane mirror. **평면 기하학** plane geometry. **평면도** a ground [floor] plan.

평민(平民) a commoner; a plebeian; a man of the people; (집합적) the common people. ¶~적인 democratic // ~적인 사람 a democratic person // ~ 태생이다 be a commoner by birth.

평방(平方) **1** ➡ 제곱 **2** […을 길이로 하는 정사각형의 넓이] a square.

● **평방근** ➡ 제곱근(⇨제곱)

평범하다(平凡-) common; ordinary; commonplace; homely; humdrum; banal; trite; mediocre; [특색이 없다] featureless; tame; unremarkable; [평온무사하다] uneventful. ¶평범한 일 a commonplace / an everyday affair [occurrence] // 평범한 인간 a common [an ordinary] man / an everyday sort of man / a mediocrity // 평범한 얼굴 a featureless face / commonplace features (생김새) // 평범한 말 a trite [hackneyed] saying / a truism // 평범한 문장 an ordinary [indifferent] composition // 평범한 소설 a mediocre novel // 평범한 집 a commonplace [an ordinary] house // 그녀의 얼굴은 ~ Her face lacks distinction.// 그는 평범한 화가에 지나지 않는다 He is but the commonest kind of painter.// 그는 아주 평범한 사람이다 He is quite a mediocrity.// 그는 평범한 사람이 아니다 He is no ordinary person.// 그 이야기는 평범했다 The story fell flat.// 여자가 직업을 갖는다는 것도 평범한 일이 되었다 It is now quite a common(place) [an ordinary] thing for woman to have a job.// 나의 평범한 머리로는 이 문제를 못 풀 것 같다 With my second-rate mind, I cannot possibly solve this problem. **평범히** commonly; ordinarily; commonplacely; tamely; uneventfully. ¶~ 살다 live a humdrum life // 그날도 ~ 지나갔다 The day passed uneventfully.

평복(平服) an ordinary [everyday] dress [attire]; plain clothes; weekday clothes; undress (실내복); (군복에 대하여) civilian clothes; (군인 속어) mufti. ¶~을 입은 [~ 차림의] (dressed) in plain clothes / in everyday [ordinary] clothes [attire] // ~을 입은 신부와 수녀 Catholic priests and nuns in lay dress // ~ 차림으로 외출하다 go out casually dressed. **평복하다** wear plain clothes.

평분(平分) equal division. **평분하다** divide equally; divide into two equal parts.

평상(平牀・平床) a flat bench; a wooden bedstead.

평상(平常) ordinary times; time of peace. ⇨평상시(⇨평상)

● **평상복** an ordinary dress. ⇨평복 **평상시** [보통 때] ordinary[normal] times; [평화 시] time of peace; peace time. ¶~의 usual / ordinary / normal / common / everyday / [상습적인] customary / habitual // ~에 at ordinary[normal] times / [보통은] ordinarily / commonly / usually / [상습적으로] customarily / habitually // ~와는 달리 unusually / ~ 상태로 돌아가다 resume (its) normal conditions / ~로 복구되다 be restored to normal conditions // 철도는 5시간 후에 ~ 상태로 복구되었다 The railroad service was restored to normal five hours later. // 나는 오늘 아침 ~ 보다 일찍 일어났다 This morning I got up earlier than usual. // 근무는 ~대로 한다 Business will be carried as usual.

평생(平生) one's (whole) life; a lifetime. ¶~의 한(恨) a lifelong regret / ~의 친구 a lifelong friend // 연구에 ~을 바치다 devote one's lifetime to the study (of) // ~을 독신으로 지내다 remain single through life // ~을 편안하게 살다 live comfortably to the end of one's life // 이런 기회는 ~에 다시는 없다 Such a chance never comes twice in a lifetime. // 그는 그 일에 ~을 바쳤다 He devoted his (whole) life to the work. // 그녀는 ~ 독신으로 지냈다 She remained single all [throughout] her life. // 그는 ~에 소설을 20권 썼다 He wrote twenty novels in his lifetime. // 이것은 ~ 잊을 수 없는 경험이다 This is an experience I shall remember all my life [as long as I live]. // 그는 ~ 가난했다 He was poor through [to the end of] his life. // 내 ~에 이렇게 추운 겨울은 없었다 This is the coldest winter I have experienced in all my life. // 당신의 은혜는 ~ 잊지 않겠습니다 I shall [(미) will] never forget your kindness as long as I live.

● **평생 교육** lifelong education; continuing education. **평생소원** one's lifelong desire; a desire cherished for life.

평생토록(平生－) all one's life; as long as one lives; through life. ¶~ 변치 않는 우정 lifelong friendship.

평서문(平敍文) [언] a declarative sentence; an assertive sentence.

평소(平素) ordinary times. ⇨=평상시(⇨평상) ¶~처럼 [~대로 / ~와 같이] as usual // ~의 연습 everyday practice / **~대로 하다** do one's usual // ~의 소망이 이루어졌다 My longcherished desire [wish] was realized. // 그의 태도는 ~와 조금도 다르지 않았다 His attitude was no different from usual. // 그는 ~에 침착하다 He is usually [ordinarily] selfpossessed. // 그는 ~보다 창백해 보인다 He looked somewhat paler than usual. // 그는 ~와 전혀 달랐다 He was not at all his usual [normal] self. // ~ 건강에 조심해야 한다 You must always be careful of your health. // 나는 ~에 6시에 일어난다 I usually get up at six. // 오늘의 그는 ~와 다르다 He is not quite himself today. // 그는 ~ 과묵한 사람입니다 He is usually taciturn. // 그는 ~처럼 8시에 집을 나갔다 He left home at eight as usual. // 그는 ~대로 산책하러 나갔다 He went out for a walk as usual. // 그는 ~에 소식을 한다 Usually he doesn't eat much. // ~의 행동이 중요하다 Our everyday conduct is what counts [is important]. // 딸은 ~와 다른 점이 조금도 없었다 I noticed nothing unusual in my daughter's behavior. / I noticed nothing out of the ordinary about my daughter's behavior. // ~의 소원이 이루어져서 정원이 딸린 집을 갖게 되었다 Our long-cherished desire to own a house with a garden came true.

평수(坪數) 1 [평의 수] the number of *pyeong*; area. ¶~ 20평이다 cover 20 *pyeong*. 2 [평] floor space [area]; [넓이] space. ¶~가 꽤 많은 집 a spacious house.

평시(平時) ordinary times. ⇨=평상시(⇨평상)

평신도(平信徒) a lay believer; (남자) a layman; (여자) a laywoman; (집합적) the laity.

평안(平安) peace; calm(ness); quiet(ness); tranquility. **평안하다** peaceful; quiet; tranquil. ¶항해 중 평안하시기를 빕니다 I wish you a happy voyage. / Bon voyage! // 부모님은 평안하신가요 How are your parents — are they well? **평안히** in peace; peacefully.

평야(平野) a plain; plains; an open field. ¶호남~ the Honam plain(s) // 국토의 20%가 ~다 Twenty percent of the country is flat land.

평영(平泳) the breaststroke.

● **평영 선수** a breaststroker; a breaststroke swimmer.

평온(平溫) [평상시의 온도] a normal temperature; [평균 온도] an average [a mean] temperature.

평온(平穩) calmness; quiet(ness); quietude; tranquil(l)ity; serenity. ¶~무사한 peaceful / pacific / uneventful (life) // ~무사하게 살다 live in peace and quiet // 세상은 마침내 ~을 되찾았다 The world situation at last settled [calmed] down (again). / The world returned to normal at last. // ~무사함이 언제까지 계속될까 How long will the peace and quiet last? // 거리는 평소의 ~을 되찾았다 The street [block] regained its usual tranquil(l)ity. // 그날은 ~무사하게 지나갔다 The day passed uneventfully. **평온하다** calm; quiet; tranquil; serene; peaceful. ¶평온해지다 become quiet / quiet down // 그 소도시[읍]는 평온했다 The town was quiet. // 캠퍼스[교내]는 마침내 평온해졌다 The campus finally became peaceful [quieted down / (영) quietened down] again. // 그의 얼굴은 끝까지 평온했다 His face remained serene [tranquil] throughout. // 그는 마음이 평온한 것처럼 보이려고 애썼지만 얼굴은 점차 창백해졌다 He tried to look unperturbed, but his face gradually lost color.

평원(平原) a plain; (미) a prairie(대초원).

평의(評議) conference; consultation; discussion; deliberation. ¶문제를 ~에 부치다 submit a matter to discussion / have a conference on a matter. **평의하다** confer; consult (with a person); discuss (a matter); deliberate on (a matter); hold a conference [counsel]; counsel together; take counsel together. ¶오늘은 예산의 배분에 대해 평의한다 We will discuss [deliberate on] the allocation of the budget today.

● **평의원** a council(l)or; (재단의) a trustee.

평의회 a council; a conference; (대학 등의) a meeting of the board of trustees.

평이하다(平易-) easy; plain; simple. ¶평이한 문체 a simple [plain] style // 평이한 해설 a clear [lucid / plain] explanation // 평이한 영어로 in simple [easy / plain] English // 평이한 말로 하자면 to use simple [plain] language // 문제를 평이하게 설명하다 explain a question simply // 이것은 평이한 문장으로 쓰여 있다 This is written in a clear [simple / lucid] style.

평일(平日) 1 [일요일 이외의 날] a weekday; a workday; a business day. ¶~에는 on weekdays / on business days // ~에는 6시에 일어난다 On weekdays I get up at six. // ~은 5시까지 영업하고 있다 Weekdays [On weekdays] the store is open until 5:00. // 휴양지는 ~에는 한산하다 Holiday resorts are not crowded on weekdays. 2 ordinary times. ⇨ 평상시(⇔평상(平常))

평자(評者) a critic; a commentator; a reviewer(신간 서적 등의).

평작(平-) [보통 화살] a medium-size(d) arrow.

평전(評傳) a critical biography (of Milton).

평점(評點) [시험 점수] examination marks; [단계점] a grade; grading; [가치 평가의] evaluation marks. ¶최고의 ~을 받다 receive [get] the best mark [grade].

평정(平靜) [무사 평온] calm; serenity; tranquil(l)ity; [침착] equability; equanimity; sedateness. ¶마음의 ~ serenity [equability / peace] of mind / composure // 마음의 ~을 유지하다 remain calm [unperturbed] / keep composed / keep one's head [cool / presence of mind] // 마음의 ~을 잃다 lose one's composure [presence of mind / equilibrium] / be perturbed // 마음의 ~을 되찾다 recover composure / restore to tranquil(l)ity // ~을 가장하다 feign calmness. **평정하다** calm; serene; tranquil; sedate; equable. **평정히** serenely; calmly; tranquilly; sedately.

평정(平定) suppression; repression; subdual; subjugation(정복). **평정하다** suppress; repress; subdue; pacify; subjugate (the whole country). ¶반란을 ~ put down rebels // 천하를 ~ conquer [subjugate] the whole country / establish [restore] peace in the (whole) country.

평정(評定) rating; evaluation. ¶근무 ~ (teacher's) efficiency rating. **평정하다** rate; evaluate. ¶학생의 학력을 ~ rate a student's academic ability.

평준화(平準化) leveling (off); equalization; standardization. **평준화하다** level (the various classes); make equal; standardize (the mode of living).

평지 [식] a rape (plant). ⇨ 유채(油菜)
평지(平地) flatland; level land [ground]; a flat; a plain(평원); a flat country(지방). ¶~낙상하다 fall down and get hurt on the level ground / meet an accident / have an unforeseen disaster [calamity].
● **평지풍파** an unnecessary disturbance [trouble]. ¶~를 일으키다 create unnecessary trouble (intentionally) / raise troubles unnecessarily [where there is no cause] / flutter [cause flutter in] the dovecot(e)s / make waves.

평직(平織) plain weave [fabrics].

평탄하다(平坦-) 1 [지면이 평평하다] even; flat; plane; level (country / road). ¶평탄한 길 a level [flat] road // 도로를 평탄하게 하다 level a road. 2 [마음이 편하고 고요하다] calm; placid; peaceful; tranquil; even. 3 [일이 순조롭다] favorable; smooth; uneventful.

평토(平土) level(l)ing the ground after burying a body. **평토하다** level the ground after burying the body.
● **평토장**(-葬) burial without erecting a mound.

평판(平板) a flat board; a slat; [측량] a plane [plain] table.

평판(平版) a lithograph.
● **평판 인쇄** lithography; (미) lithoprinting. ¶~를 하다 lithograph / (미) lithoprint.

평판(評判) [비평하는 것] criticizing; [명성] fame; (a) reputation; (a) repute; [세평] the world's opinion; public estimation; popularity(인기); notoriety(악명); [소문] a report; a rumor; gossip. ¶대단한 ~ a sensation // ~이 난 reputed / famed / notorious // ~이 좋은 소설 (정평이 있는) a well-received novel / (대중적인) a popular novel // ~이 좋다 be well [highly] spoken of / have [enjoy] a good reputation [character / name] // ~이 나쁘다 be ill spoken of / have a bad reputation [character] / have an ill name / be unpopular // ~이 자자하다 be talked about / (come to)be much spoken [talked] of / become popular / win popularity // ~을 얻다 win reputation / become popular / win popularity // ~을 떨어뜨리다 [잃게 하다] lose one's good reputation / lose one's popularity // 새 시장은 항간의 ~이 좋다 The new mayor stands high in public estimation. / The new mayor is popular among the people. // 그 주간지는 영화배우의 스캔들 기사 때문에 ~이 나쁘다 The weekly is notorious for its scandalous stories about movie stars. // 그는 학자들 사이에 ~이 좋아 [나빠]졌다 He has risen [fallen] in the estimation of scholars.

평평하다(平平-) 1 [판판하다] flat; [평활하다] even; smooth; [수평이다] level; horizontal; [평면이다] plane. ¶평평한 땅 even [level / flat] ground // 평평한 면을 위쪽으로 돌리십시오 Turn it smooth side up. **평평히** flatwise; level; evenly; smoothly. ¶~ 하다 flatten / level (down [up / off]) / even / smooth / make even [smooth] / roll(금속 등을) // 길 [지면]을 ~ 하다 level a road [the ground] // 우리는 언덕을 ~ 깎았다 We leveled the hill. 2 [평범하다] common; ordinary; commonplace; featureless. **평평히** commonly; ordinarily; commonplacely.

평하다(評-) criticize; comment (on). ¶시사 문제를 ~ comment on the news of the day // 남을 사기꾼이라고 ~ speak of a person as an impostor // 타임지는 그의 저서를 좋게 평했다 The Times reviewed his book favorably.

평행(平行) [수] parallelism; parallel. ¶선로와 ~으로 뻗어 있는 길 a road running parallel to [with] the railway // …과 ~으로 선을 긋다 draw a line parallel to ... // A선과 B선은 ~이다 Lines A is parallel to [with] line B. / Lines A and B are parallel (to [with] each other). // 그 도로는 철도와 ~으로 뻗어 있다 The road runs parallel with the railroad. / The road parallels the railroad. **평행하다** parallel.

●**평행봉** parallel bars. ¶2단 ~ uneven bars. **평행 사변형** a parallelogram. **평행선** parallel lines; a line parallel to[with] another.

평형(平衡) equilibrium; balance; counterbalance; counterpoise; a state of perfect balance. ¶**안정**[**불안정**] **~** stable[unstable] equilibrium // **~을 유지시키다** balance / equilibrate / poise // **몸**[**마음**]**의 ~을 유지하다** keep[preserve] one's balance // **~을 잃다** lose the balance // **저울은 지금 ~을 유지하고 있지 않다** Now the scales are not in equilibrium. **평형하다** balanced; poised; (서술적) be in equilibrium.
●**평형감각** the sense of equilibrium. **평형 상태** (a state of) equilibrium.

평화(平和) peace; [화합] harmony. ¶**세계 ~** world peace / the peace of the world / universal peace // **마음의 ~** peace of mind / (one's) inward peace // **가정의 ~** the peace of the household[one's home] // **~의 길** an avenue of peace // **전쟁과 ~** war and peace // **~를 사랑**[**갈망**]**하다** love[covet] peace // **~를 유지하다** maintain[keep peace] // **~를 깨뜨리다** break[disturb] peace // **영원한 ~를 정착시키다** establish[secure] a lasting[permanent] peace // **~를 위태롭게 하다** endanger the peace (of Europe) // **~를 되찾다** restore peace // **~를 가져오다** bring (Palestine) to peace // **가정의 ~를 어지럽히다** disturb domestic harmony[peace] // **세계 ~가 회복되었다** Peace returned to the world. / World peace was restored. // **한국은 세계 각국과 ~를 유지하고 있다** Korea is at peace with all the world. // **국제 ~를 촉진함이 우리의 사명이다** Our mission is to promote peace among the nations.
●**평화 공세** a peace offensive. **평화 공존** peaceful coexistence. **평화 봉사단** (미국의) the Peace Corps. **평화 사절** a peace envoy. **평화 조약** a peace treaty. ⇨**강화 조약**(⇔**강화**(講和)) **평화주의** pacifism.

평화롭다(平和-) peaceful; pacific; amicable; tranquil; harmonious. ¶**평화로운 마음** a peaceful mind // **평화로운 방법** an amicable way // **평화롭게 살다** live in peace / lead a peaceful life / enjoy a life of peace // **그것은 평화로운 광경이었다** It was a peaceful scene. // **국내는 ~** The nation is at peace. // **문제는 평화롭게 해결되었다** The problem has been settled in an amicable way.

평활근(平滑筋) [생] a smooth muscle. ⇨**민무늬근**

평활하다(平滑-) smooth; level; flat; even. ¶**평활하게 하다** smooth / make smooth / (기름을 쳐서) lubricate.

평활하다(平闊-) level and spacious; flat and extensive[wide].

폐(肺) [생] the lungs. ¶**~가 나쁘다** have a weak chest // **~를 앓다** have lung trouble // **그는 오른쪽의 ~가 나쁘다** His right lung is affected.

폐(弊) 1 **an evil; an abuse**. ⇨**폐단**
2 [괴로움] (a) trouble; (a) worry; a bother (to a person); [귀찮은 일] (an) annoyance. ¶**~가 안 된다면** if it is not inconvenient to (you) // **~를 끼치다** trouble [bother / annoy] (a person) / give[cause] (a person) trouble / put (a person) to trouble [bother] / make oneself a nuisance (to a person) // **~가 많았습니다** I owe you very much. / I'm afraid I have caused you a great deal of trouble. // **조금도 ~가 되지 않습니다** It is no trouble at all. // **~를 끼쳐서 죄송합니다** I'm sorry to give you much trouble. / I'm sorry to trouble you. // **남에게 ~를 끼치지 않도록 해라** Try not to bother others. / You must not give others too much trouble.

폐가(弊家) my house[home].

폐가(廢家) 1 [버려두어 သ는 집] a deserted [dilapidated] house. ¶**~가 되다** fall into dilapidation[disrepair] / become dilapidated. 2 [상속자가 없는 집안] an extinct family; an abolished house. **폐가하다** (the family) become extinct.

폐간(廢刊) discontinuance (of publication); ceased publication. **폐간하다** cease to publish; discontinue issuing (a newspaper / a magazine). ➔¶**폐간된 잡지** a defunct magazine / a magazine now defunct // **폐간되다** be discontinued / go out of existence // **그 잡지는 폐간되었습니다** The magazine has ceased publication[to appear]. / The magazine has been discontinued. / That magazine is no longer being published.

폐결핵(肺結核) [의] phthisis; pulmonary tuberculosis; consumption; white plague. ¶**~을 앓다** suffer from tuberculosis of the lungs.
●**폐결핵 환자** a consumptive (patient).

폐경기(閉經期) the climacteric; the period of the menopause in women. ¶**~의 여자** a woman at the menopause.

폐관(閉管) [음] a closed pipe; a closed tube.

폐관(閉館) closing (its doors). ¶**~ 시각** the closing time[hour] (of a library) // **(도서관은) 저녁 5시 ~** Closed[The library will close] at 5 p.m. / The closing time (of the library) is 5 p.m. **폐관하다** close (its doors); be closed.

폐광(廢鑛) an abandoned[an unworked / a disused] mine; a dead pit [mine]. **폐광하다** abandon a mine; disuse a mine.

폐교(廢校) abolition [closing] of a school. **폐교하다** close[abolish] a school. ➔¶**폐교되다** be abolished[closed / discontinued] // **그 학교는 재정난으로 폐교되었다** The school was closed because of financial difficulties. // **그 학교는 3월 말에 폐교된다** The school will be closed[shut] down at the end of March.

폐기(廢棄) (제도・풍속의) disuse; abolition; abandonment; (법률 등의) abrogation; repeal; disaffirmation; defeasance; cassation; reverse(관결의); denunciation(조약의). **폐기하다** do away with; annul; disuse; abolish; abandon; renounce; discard(습관을); [법] abrogate; repeal; dissolve; denounce (조약을). ¶**구식 자동차를 ~** scrap [junk] an outdated car // **우리는 핵무기를 폐기해야 한다** We should do away with[renounce / give up] nuclear weapons. // **그런 제도는 즉시 폐기해 버려라** Abolish such a system at once. ➔¶**그 법령은 1954년에 폐기되었다** The law was repealed in 1954.
●**폐기물** waste (matter); wastes. ¶**미처리 ~** untreated waste (matter) // **방사성 ~** radioactive waste matter[products] / atomic waste // **산업 ~** industrial waste (products).

폐기종(肺氣腫) [의] emphysema of the lungs; pulmonary emphysema.

폐농(廢農) [농사의 포기] abandonment[giv-

폐단(弊端) an evil; an abuse; a vice; an obnoxious[evil] custom[practice]. ¶음주의 ~ the vice of intemperance // ~을 고치다 remedy[correct] an abuse // 거기에는 여러 가지 ~이 따른다 It is attended by many evils.

폐디스토마(肺-) [동] a pulmonary distoma; distoma pulmona.

폐렴(肺炎) [의] pneumonia; inflammation of the lungs. ¶급성 ~ acute pneumonia // 그는 감기가 악화하여 ~이 되었다 His cold turned [developed] into pneumonia.

폐롭다(弊-) 1 [귀찮다] troublesome; bothersome. 2 [성미가 까다롭다] particular; fussy; fastidious; crabbed (old age).

폐막(閉幕) the falling of the curtain; a curtainfall; a close; an end; the finish. ¶극장의 ~ 시간은 11시이다 The closing time for the theater is eleven. / The theater closes at eleven. **폐막하다** close[bring down] the curtain; close; end; finish; bring to an end. →¶연극은 9시에 폐막되었다 The curtain was dropped at nine. / The play ended at nine.

폐문(閉門) closing the gate. **폐문하다** close the gate; bar the gate. ¶몇 시에 폐문하죠 When will the gate be closed?

●**폐문 시간** the closing time; lockup.

폐물(廢物) a useless article[thing]; waste [discarded] material[products]; waste; junk; [부스러기·쓰레기] refuse; dregs; trash; garbage; rubbish; [낡은 것] an obsolete [outdated] thing; (구어) a has-been. ¶~이 되다 become useless / go[run] to waste // ~을 이용하다 utilize waste materials / recycle (a used bottle).

●**폐물 처리** waste disposal.

폐백(幣帛) 1 (신부의) bride's gifts to her parents-in-law. ¶~을 올리다 (a bride) make a deep bow and offer her gifts to her parents-in-law. 2 (신랑의) silks offered to the bride by the bridegroom. 3 (제자의) a present from a pupil on meeting his teacher for the first time.

폐병(肺病) [의] 1 [폐에 관한 질병] a lung [pulmonary] disease; a lung trouble [complaint]; a chest trouble[disease]. ¶그녀는 ~을 앓고 있다 She has lung[chest] trouble. 2 〈속〉 phthisis. ⇨폐결핵

폐부(肺腑) 1 [생] the lungs. ⇨폐(肺) 2 [마음속] the bottom[depths] of one's heart; one's inmost heart. ¶~에서 우러나오다 come from the heart.

폐부를 찌르다 give (a person) a home thrust; cut[sting] (a person) to the quick; go to (a person's) heart. ¶폐부를 찌르는 듯한 heart-breaking (news).

폐비(廢妃) [물러난 왕비] a deposed queen; a former queen; [왕비의 자리에서 물러나게 함] a deposal of a queen. **폐비하다** depose a queen; force a queen to abdicate.

폐사(弊社·敝社) our company[firm]; we.

폐사(廢寺) [폐지된 절] a ruined[dilapidated] temple.

폐색(閉塞) (a) blockade; blocking(-up); stoppage; [철도] a block; [의] imperforation; occlusion; obstruction. ¶장(腸) ~ [의] obstruction of the intestines / intestinal obstruction / ileus. **폐색하다** blockade; block (up); bottle up.

●**폐색 구간**[신호] [철도] a block section [signal].

폐선(廢船) a scrapped vessel; a vessel retired from service.

폐쇄(閉鎖) closing; closure; shutdown(일시적인); a lockout. ¶공장 ~ (미) a closedown / a lockout(노동 쟁의 때의) // ~적 사회 the closed society // (문 등이) 자동 ~의 self-closing // ~를 명하다 order (a school) closed // 그의 성격은 ~적이다 He is not at all open.

폐쇄하다 close (down / up); shut (down); lock (up); wind up; lock out. ¶그들은 극장을 폐쇄했다 They closed down the theaters. →¶수도원이라는 폐쇄된 사회 the narrow, closed world of a convent // 폐쇄되다 be closed down[up] / be shut (down) / be locked up // 그 광산은 불황으로 말미암아 폐쇄되었다 The mine was closed because of the business depression.

●**폐쇄기**(-機) breech mechanism. **폐쇄음**[언] a stop (sound); an implosive.

폐수(廢水) waste water. ¶공장 ~ factory wastes // 미처리(의) ~ untreated waste water // 공장 ~에 의한 환경오염 environmental pollution caused by effluent[liquid waste] from factories.

●**폐수 처리** waste-water treatment; liquid waste treatment. **폐수 처리 장치** a waste water disposal plant.

폐수종(肺水腫) [의] an edema of the lungs; a pulmonary edema (pl. -mas, -mata).

폐습(弊習) a bad habit; an evil practice; a corrupt[an evil] custom; an abuse; an evil; a vice; a detestable practice. ¶…의 ~에 물들다 be tainted with a bad habit of ... // ~을 타파하다[없애다] break down[do away with] evil customs // ~을 고치다 remedy[put a stop to] abuses.

폐암(肺癌) [의] cancer of the lungs; lung cancer; pulmonary carcinoma.

폐어(肺魚) [동] a lungfish; a dipnoan (fish).

폐어(廢語) a dead language. ⇨ˇ사어(死語)

폐업(廢業) discontinuance[abolishment] of business. **폐업하다** give up[discontinue / quit / close] one's business; shut up one's shop; close down one's store; (의사·변호사 등이) give up one's practice; (배우 등이) leave[retire from] the stage. ¶내 부친은 제과점을 폐업했다 My father closed down his bakery.

●**폐업 신고** a report of cessation of business[a business closing]. ¶~를 하다 report the cessation of business.

폐염 →폐렴(肺炎)

폐원(閉院) (의회의 마침) the closing[adjournment] of the National Assembly. **폐원하다** close[adjourn] (the session of) the National Assembly.

폐위(廢位) dethronement. **폐위하다** dethrone; depose (a sovereign); take the crown from (a king). →¶그 왕은 폐위되었다 The king was dethroned[deposed].

폐유(廢油) waste[rejected / defective] oil.

폐인(廢人) (불구에 의한) a person maimed [crippled] for life; a crippled[disabled] person; a cripple; (병에 의한) a confirmed invalid. ¶~이 되다 be crippled / be disabled // 그는 ~과 다름없다 He is practically[to all intents and purposes already] dead.

폐일언하다(蔽一言-) sum up (a story); boil down. ¶폐일언하고 in a word / in brief [short] / to be short / to sum up∥폐일언하고 네가 잘못했다 In short, you are to blame.

폐장(肺臟) [생] the lungs. ⇨⁼폐(肺)

폐장(閉場) the closing (of a place). ¶~ 후 [증권] after the close. **폐장하다** close; be closed.

폐적(廢嫡) disinheritance; [법] disherison. **폐적하다** disinherit; [법] disherison.

폐절(廢絶) extinction. **폐절하다** become extinct; be discontinued. ¶그 가계(家系)는 10대째에 폐절했다 The family died out ten generations later.
●**폐절가**(一家) an extinct family.

폐점(閉店) 1 [가게를 닫음]. ¶~ 후에 손님이 온 것 같다 There seems to have been a customer who came after closing time[after the store was closed]. **폐점하다** close (a) shop; close one's doors. ¶우리 가게는 6시에 폐점합니다 Our shop will be closed at six. 2 discontinuance of business. ⇨⁼폐업

폐점(弊店·敝店) our shop; we.

폐정(弊政) misgovernment; maladministration; misrule.

폐정하다(閉廷-) dismiss [adjourn] the court. ¶재판장은 판결을 내리고 폐정했다 The chief justice gave judgment and dismissed the court.∥5월 10일까지 폐정합니다 The court is adjourned till May 10.

폐지(廢止) abolition; disuse; discontinuance; (법률·제도 등의) abrogation; annulment; nullification. **폐지하다** abolish; discontinue; disuse; do away with; (법률 등을) abrogate; annul; quash; repeal; rescind; cancel. ¶노예 제도를 ~ abolish slavery. ➔**폐지되다** be abolished / go out of use [existence] / fall into disuse∥그 제도는 훨씬 이전에 폐지되었다 That system was abolished[discontinued] a long time ago.

폐진증(肺塵症) [의] pneumoconiosis. ⇨⁼진폐

폐질(廢疾) an incurable[a fatal] disease. ¶~이 되다 be disabled / be crippled for life.
●**폐질자** a disabled person; a cripple for life.

폐차(廢車) a disused car; a scrapped vehicle [car]; an out-of-service car; a junked car. ¶~ 처분 하다 scrap a car / put a car out of service.
●**폐차장** an auto junkyard.

폐포(肺胞) [생] an alveolus (*pl.* -li) (of the lung); pulmonary alveoli.

폐품(廢品) waste articles [materials]; [쓰레기] rubbish; (미) trash. ¶~을 회수[재생] 하다 collect [recycle] waste articles∥~이 되다 become useless / go [run] to waste / go to the scrap heap.
●**폐품 수집** collection [reclamation] of waste articles [materials]; recovery of scrap. **폐품 활용** the utilization of waste materials; wealth from waste.

폐하(陛下) (3인칭) His [Her] Majesty; (2인칭) Your Majesty. ¶황제 ~ H.M. [His Majesty] the Emperor∥황후 ~ H.M. [Her Majesty] the Empress∥황제 황후 양 ~ T.M. [Their Majesties] the Emperor and Empress∥엘리자베스 여왕 ~ Her Majesty Queen Elizabeth.

폐하다(廢-) 1 (제도 등을) abolish; abandon; discard. ¶노예 제도를 ~ abolish slavery. 2 (법률 등을) repeal; annul; abrogate(나중의 법률로써). 3 (어떤 지위에서) dethrone; depose; discrown. 4 (일·사용을) discontinue; quit; give up. ¶학업을 ~ give up one's studies / lay aside one's books∥허례허식을 ~ dispense [do away] with formalities.

폐합(廢合) abolition and amalgamation. **폐합하다** abolish and amalgamate; reorganize; consolidate.

폐해(弊害) an evil; an abuse; [악영향] an evil [a harmful] influence; a bad effect. ¶~를 끼치다[~가 있다] exert an evil influence upon (children) / have an injurious effect upon (society) / give [cause] trouble∥독재 정치의 ~를 바로잡다 remedy the abuses of autocratic government∥이 개혁에는 많은 ~가 따를 것이다 The proposed reform will be attended by many evils.

폐허(廢墟) (the) ruins; (the) remains(남아 있는 것). ¶옛 절의 ~ the ruins [remains] of an old temple∥~가 되다 be ruined / fall into ruins∥그 읍은 지금 ~가 되어 있다 The town is [lies] in ruins now.

폐활량(肺活量) lung [breathing] capacity; the capacity of the lungs.
●**폐활량계** a spirometer; a pulmometer. **폐활량 측정** pulmometry; spirometry.

폐회(閉會) the closing (of a meeting). ¶~가 되다 come to a close / be closed∥~를 선언하다 declare the meeting [sitting] closed∥국회는 지금 ~ 중이다 The National Assembly is not in session now. **폐회하다** close [adjourn] (a meeting)(▶ adjourn은 다음 회기까지).
●**폐회사** a closing address. ¶~를 하다 give a closing address. **폐회식** a closing ceremony.

폐회로(閉回路) [전] a closed circuit. ¶~로 방송하다 broadcast by closed circuit.
●**폐회로 텔레비전** closed-circuit television(약어 CCTV).

포(砲) a gun(총); a cannon (*pl.* ~s, (집합적) ~) (대포); an artillery piece; a fieldpiece(야포); (집합적) gunnery; ordnance; artillery. ¶~를 쏘다 fire a gun.

포(脯) dried slices of meat seasoned with spices. ¶육~ dried slices of beef∥~를 뜨다 slice meat (for the purpose of seasoning and drying it).

포가(砲架) a gun carriage; a naval gun mount(군함용). ¶~를 설치하다 set a gun carriage∥~에서 내리다 dismount (a gun).

포개다 [겹쳐 놓다] put [place] one upon [over] another; lay over; lay one on top of another [the other]; lap; overlap; [겹쳐 쌓다] pile up; heap up; stack; [접어 개다] lay in folds. ¶포개어(서) one over [upon] the other (2개를) / one over [upon] another (3개 이상을) / (겹쳐 쌓아) in piles / in layers∥책을 ~ pile books∥장작을 ~ stack firewood.

포개지다 lie one upon another; overlap; be laid over.

포격(砲擊) shelling; bombardment; cannonade; an artillery attack [strike]; artillery pounding; gunfire; gunshot. ¶~의 응수 an exchange of fire / an artillery duel∥~를 받다 be under fire / take fire∥적군을 향해 ~을 개시하다 open fire on the enemy. **포격하다** shell; fire on [at] (a ship, a fort, etc.); bombard; cannonade. ¶발견하는 대로 포격하라 Fire on sight.

포경(包莖) [의] phimosis (*pl.* -ses). ¶~의

포경 phimotic.
● 포경 수술 an operation for phimosis; phimosiectomy.

포경(捕鯨) whaling; whale hunting [fishing]. 포경하다 whale; catch [capture] whales.
● 포경 기지 a whaling station. 포경선 a whaler; a whale ship. 포경업 the whaling industry.

포고(布告) proclamation; declaration (of war); notification; ordinance. ¶~ 제1호 the initial proclamation // ~를 내다 issue a proclamation [declaration] / issue [publish] a decree // 선전 ~를 하다 declare [proclaim] war (on / against). 포고하다 proclaim; announce; declare; decree; notify. →¶그것은 1950년에 법령으로 포고되었다 It was declared by statute in 1950.
● 포고령 a decree; an edict. 포고문 a declaration; a decree.

포괄(包括) inclusion; comprehension. 포괄하다 include; comprehend; comprise; contain; embrace; cover; take in. ¶이 책은 광범한 문제를 포괄하고 있다 This book covers a wide field [range] of topics. →¶이 작품들은 모두 전위 예술에 포괄된다 These works (of art) all belong to [are all included in] the genre of avant-garde art.
● 포괄 범위 the coverage (of an agreement).

포괄적(包括的) inclusive; comprehensive; general. ¶~인 말 a comprehensive term // ~으로 정국을 보다 take an overall look at the political situation // 나는 먼저 그 건에 대해 ~인 견해를 말했다 I first presented an overview of the matter.

포교(布敎) propagation (of religion); missionary work; mission (work); propagandism. 포교하다 propagate (a religion); mission (a district, in an area, etc.); propagandize (a community, a country, etc.); proselytize (a person).
● 포교 사업 missionary work. 포교자 a propagator; a missionary (worker); an evangelist.

포구(浦口) an inlet; an estuary; (영) a creek.
포구(砲口) the muzzle of a gun. ⇨ 포문(砲門)
포구(捕球) [야구] a catch. ¶멋진 ~ a nice [good] catch. 포구하다 catch a (thrown) ball.

포근하다 1 [따뜻하다] comfortably warm; snug (and comfortable); [푹신하다] soft [downy] (and fluffy). ¶포근한 침대 a soft, comfortable bed // 포근한 이부자리 downy bedding // 어머니의 포근한 가슴 mother's warm breast // 아이들을 보면 마음이 포근해진다 The sight of the children warms my heart. 포근히 warmly; comfortably; snugly; softly. ¶어머니의 품에 ~ 안겨 있는 아이 an infant nestling in its mother's breast // 아이는 따뜻한 담요에 싸여 ~ 잠들어 있었다 The child was sleeping snugly in the warm blanket.
2 [겨울 날씨가] mild; soft; genial. ¶포근한 겨울 a soft [mild / green] winter // 올겨울은 예년에 비해 포근했다 We have had a milder winter than usual. 포근히 mildly; genially.

포기 a plant; a head (of cabbage); a root. ¶풀 한 ~ one plant // 배추 두 ~ two heads of cabbage // 국화의 ~를 나누다 separate the roots of a chrysanthemum // 배추 ~가 크다 The cabbage has a large head.

포기(抛棄) giving up; abandonment; resignation; renunciation; renouncement; surrender; waiver; [법] release; (요구의) relinquishment; disclaimer. ¶전쟁의 ~ renunciation of war. 포기하다 throw up (one's office); abandon [give up] (one's plan); forsake; renounce (war); resign (one's right); surrender; forfeit; [방치하다] lay aside; [법] release. ¶(학생이) 수업을 ~ boycott [(미) cut] a lecture // 권리를 ~ resign [forfeit] the right // 첫날부터 시험을 ~ throw [give] up the examination on the first day // 의사는 환자를 포기하였다 The doctor gave up on the patient. // 그가 두 번째 체포되자 그의 모친도 그를 포기하였다 After he was arrested for the second time, even his mother gave up on [washed her hands of] him. // 나는 죽어도 포기하지 않는다 I shall never give up as long as I live.

포대(布袋) a burlap [cloth] bag; a sack; a gunny sack.
포대(包袋) a (burlap) bag. ⇨ 부대(負袋)
포대(砲臺) a (gun) battery; (요새) a fort; a fortress; a casemate. ¶~를 구축하다 construct [erect] a battery / build a fort.

포대기 a wadded baby wrapper; a quilt for little children.

포도(葡萄) a grape. ¶건 ~ raisins // ~의 수확 a vintage // ~를 재배하다 raise [grow] grapes // 올해는 ~가 잘되었다 This has been an excellent [a vintage] year for grapes. / The grapes are [The grape crop is] doing very well this year.
● 포도나무 a grape (vine). 포도당 grape sugar; glucose; dextrose; D-glucose. 포도 덩굴 a grapevine. 포도밭 a vineyard; a grapery; a grape plantation. 포도송이 a bunch [cluster] of grapes. 포도주 (grape) wine; vinous liquor. ¶백~ white wine / Rhenish wine / hock / sherry // 적~ red [purple] wine / claret / Bordeaux // ~ 한 병 a bottle of wine. 포도즙 grape juice.

포도(鋪道) [포장된 도로] a paved road; [포장된 보도] (미) a sidewalk; (영) a pavement.

포도대장(捕盜大將) [역] a police chief (in ancient times).

포도청(捕盜廳) [역] the police bureau.

포동포동 ¶~ 살진 얼굴 a chubby [full] face. 포동포동하다 plump; fleshy; round; well-fleshed; chubby. ¶포동포동한 손발 plump arms and legs // 포동포동한 아기 [여자] a plump [buxom] baby [woman] // 포동포동하게 살이 쪄 있다 be plump / be chubby.

포로(捕虜) 1 (전쟁의) a prisoner (of war) (약어 P.O.W., POW) (pl. P.O.W.'s, POW's). a war prisoner; a captive. ¶~로 잡다 capture / take a person a prisoner // ~가 되다 be captured / be taken prisoner // ~를 수용하다 intern a prisoner. 2 [비유] a victim; a slave. ¶…의 ~가 되다 be a slave to / be enslaved / enslave oneself to // 여자의 ~가 되다 lose one's heart [be a slave] to a woman / be enamored of a woman.
● 포로 교환 an exchange of prisoners. 포로 송환 the repatriation of prisoners of war. 포로수용소 a depot for prisoners of war; a prison(er's) [POW] camp; a concentration camp.

포르노 pornography; (구어) porn(o). ¶~의 pornographic / (구어) porn(o).
● 포르노 숍 a porn(o) shop. 포르노 영화

pornographic film. **포르노 잡지** a pornographic magazine; a porno magazine.
포르르 1 [끓어오르는 모양] bubbling; seething; boiling. **포르르하다** bubble[boil] up; seethe. **2** [타는 모양] (burn) crisply. **포르르하다** burn up[be burned up] in no time. **3** [떠는 모양] trembling; quivering. **포르르하다** quiver; tremble. **4** [새 등이 갑자기 날아가는 모양]. (fly / whirr away) suddenly. **포르르하다** flush.
포르말린 [화] formalin. ¶그 표본은 ~에 담겨 보존되어 있다 The specimen is preserved in formalin.
● **포르말린 소독** formalin disinfection.
포르테 [음] forte(기호 *f*).
포르티시모 [음] fortissimo(기호 *ff*).
포름산 (一酸) a formic acid.
포마드 pomade; pomatum; hair grease. ¶머리에 ~를 바르다 pomade one's hair / apply pomade to one's hair.
포마이카 (상표명) Formica.
포만하다 (飽滿一) (서술적) be satiated[sated] (with). ¶나는 맛있는 음식을 포만하도록 먹었다 I ate my fill of delicious foods. / I'm satiated with delicacies.
포말 (泡沫) bubbles; a foam. ⇨¬물거품1
포목 (布木) linen and cotton (cloth); drapery; piece goods; (미) dry goods.
● **포목상** a draper; a linen-draper; (미) a dry-goods dealer. **포목점 / 포목전** a draper's shop; (미) a dry-goods store.
포문 (砲門) [포구(砲口)] the muzzle of a gun; (군함의 포안(砲眼)) a porthole; a gunport; (성벽의 포안) an embrasure; (화문(火門)의 뚜껑) the apron (of a gun).
포문을 열다 open fire; fire (the first gun). ¶논쟁의 ~ commence[start] a debate / broach a discussion.
포물선 (抛物線) [수] a parabola. ¶~을 그리다 describe a parabola // ~을 그리며 날다 pass (overhead) describing a parabola.
● **포물선 운동** a parabolic motion[movement].
포미 (砲尾) the gun breech; the breech (of a cannon).
포박 (捕縛) (an) arrest; apprehension; capture. **포박하다** arrest; apprehend; catch; seize; take; place under arrest; capture; (구어) nab.
포백 (布帛) linens and silks.
포병 (砲兵) (부대) artillery; (영) the Royal Artillery; (병사) an artilleryman; a gunner. ¶사단[군단] ~ division[corps] artillery.
● **포병 기지** an artillery base. **포병대** [단] an artillery unit[corps]. **포병전** an artillery duel [engagement]. **포병 학교** the Artillery School.
포복 (匍匐) creeping. ¶~ 전진을 하다 advance on all fours[on one's hands and knees] // 적의 참호에 ~으로 접근하다 approach to the enemy trench by crawling and creeping. **포복하다** creep; crawl; walk on one's hands and knees; go on all fours(손발로).
● **포복 식물** a creeper (plant); a vine.
포복절도하다 (抱腹絶倒一) hold[split] one's sides with laughter; laugh oneself into convulsions; be convulsed with laughter; double (up) with laughter; die with laughing. ¶그의 이야기가 우스워서 모두들 포복절도했다 His story was so funny that we were all in convulsions[we all laughed till our side began to ache]. // 원숭이의 웃기는 묘기에 관중은 포복절도했다 The spectators were all in fits of[thrown into convulsions of] laughter at the funny tricks of the monkey.
포볼 (*four ball) [야구] a base on balls; a pass; a walk. ¶~으로 1루에 나가다 walk / be walked / draw a walk ¶타자에게 ~을 허용하다 walk a batter / give a batter a walk.
포부 (抱負) [희망·대망] one's hopes; [문어] one's aspirations; [계획] a plan. ¶졸업 후의 ~를 말하다 tell what one plans to do after graduation // 그는 미래에 큰 ~를 지니고 있다 He has great hopes[ambitions] for his future. // 그들은 커다란 ~를 품고 있다 They aspire to great things. // 새 시장으로서의 ~를 말씀해 주십시오 Please tell us about your (ambitious) plans as (the) new mayor. // 그는 도무지 ~가 없어 보인다 He shows no desire to improve himself.
포상 (褒賞) a prize; a reward. ¶그는 ~을 받았다 He received[won] a prize. **포상하다** give a prize (to); praise and reward. ¶시장은 그를 포상했다 The mayor awarded him a prize. / The mayor gave him an award.
포석 (布石) **1** [바둑] the arrangement of stones at the beginning of a game of *baduk*(go). **포석하다** arrange[place] stones in strategic position. **2** [전략적 움직임] a strategic move; [준비] preparations. ¶그것은 다가오는 선거에 대한 ~이다 That is part of his strategy for the coming election. **포석하다** prepare; arrange; take precautions (against); pave the way for the future.
포석 (鋪石) a paving stone; a flagstone.
포섭 (包攝) **1** [받아들임] ¶~ 공작을 하다 contrive to win (a person) over. **포섭하다** win [gain] (a person) over to one's side; bring (a person) round. ¶뇌물로 남을 ~ fix[bring round] a person by bribery. **2** [논] connotation; subsumption. **포섭하다** connote; subsume.
포성 (砲聲) the sound of firing[gunfire]; the roaring [boom] of a gun[cannon] (먼 곳의). ¶~이 울려 퍼졌다 The roar[thunder] of artillery[guns] filled the air. // 멀리서 ~이 들렸다 We heard the distant boom of guns.
포수 (砲手) **1** [총을 가진 군사] an artilleryman; a gunner; an artillerist. **2** [사냥꾼] a hunter.
포수 (捕手) [야구] a catcher. ¶톰은 우리 팀의 ~이다 Tom is the catcher for[on] our team.
포술 (砲術) gunnery; artillery.
포스 아웃 [야구] a force-out. ¶3루 주자는 홈베이스에서 ~이 되었다 The third-base runner was forced out at home plate.
포스터 a poster; a placard; a bill; (그림이 있는) a pictorial poster; (글자만의) a plain poster. ¶광고 ~ an ad-poster // 연극[영화]의 ~ a theatrical[movie] poster // ~를 붙이다 [떼다] put up[tear off] a poster // ~로 선전하다 advertize with posters.
● **포스터물감 / 포스터컬러** (a) poster color [(영) colour / paint].
포스트 [지위] a post. ¶그는 중요한 ~에 임명되었다 He was appointed to an important post.
포승 (捕繩) a rope (for tying up criminals). ¶~을 지우다 bind up (a criminal) / fasten the waist (of a criminal suspect) with a cord /

포식 arrest (a wanted person) // ~에 묶이다 be arrested / be apprehended / be caught (by the police) // 순순히 ~을 받다 surrender tamely / suffer oneself to be bound [arrested] / be arrested without resistance.

포식 (捕食) predation; predatism. **포식하다** prey on (birds).
● **포식 동물** a predator; a predatory animal.

포식 (飽食) gluttony; 《문어》 satiation; engorgement. **포식하다** satiate oneself (with rich food); glut oneself (on); eat one's fill.

포신 (砲身) a gun barrel; the barrel of a gun.

포악 (暴惡) violence(난폭); tyranny(폭정); savagery(야만); atrocity(잔학). ¶~무도한 살인범 a ruthless [diabolical] murderer. **포악하다** atrocious; ruthless; outrageous; barbarous. ¶부상을 입은 호랑이 a furious wounded tiger // 포악한 군주[임금] a tyrannical ruler / a tyrant // 적군은 점령지에서 포악하게 굴었다 The enemy tyrannized the occupied area. // 약탈자는 온갖 포악한 짓을 다했다 The plunderers committed all sorts of atrocities.

포안 (砲眼) 〔군〕 an embrasure.

포연 (砲煙) the smoke of artillery. ¶~이 자욱한 사막 a desert shrouded in smoke from artillery fire // 그는 ~을 뚫고 돌아왔다 He came through (the worst of) the battle alive. / He made his way[came] safely through the thick of the battle.

포옹 (抱擁) an embrace; (특히 애정을 지닌, 열렬한) a hug. ¶그의 정열적인 ~으로 그녀는 숨도 쉴 수 없었다 His passionate embrace took her breath away. / He took her breath away with a passionate embrace. **포옹하다** embrace; hug; cuddle; hold (a person) to one's breast[in one's arms]; wrap one's arms about (a person). ¶두 손을 벌리고 ~ give (a person) a bear hug // 서로 ~ embrace[hug] each other // 그녀는 자기 아들을 포옹했다 She embraced[hugged] her son.

포용 (包容) tolerance; magnanimity. **포용하다** tolerate; accept with magnanimity. ¶사람을 포용하는 아량이 있다 have the capacity for tolerance.
● **포용력** tolerance; catholicity; broad-mindedness; magnanimity. ¶~ 있는 사람 an understanding[a magnanimous / a broad-minded] person // ~이 강하다 possess a capacious mind / be so broad-minded as to admit men of all shades.

포워드 a forward(약어 F.W.).

포위 (包圍) encirclement; envelopment; (a) siege; besiegement; investment; beleaguerment. ¶적의 ~를 돌파하다 break through the lines of the besieging enemy forces. **포위하다** 〔에워싸다〕 surround; encircle; hem [close] in; (군대 등이) invest; envelop; beleaguer; besiege; lay siege to (a fort); (경관이) throw a cordon round (a place). ¶경찰이 그 구역을 포위했다 The police threw a cordon around the block. → 우리는 적에게 완전히 포위되었다 The enemy closed in on us from all sides. / We were completely besieged [surrounded / hemmed in] by the enemy. // 그 성은 2개월 동안이나 적군에게 포위되어 있었다 The castle was besieged[laid siege to] by enemy forces for two months.
● **포위망** an encircling net; an iron ring. **포위 작전** an encircling[enveloping / outflanking] operation.

포유 (哺乳) lactation; suckling; nursing. **포유하다** suckle[nurse / give suck to] one's baby.
● **포유동물** a mammal. **포유류** the mammals.

포육 (脯肉) jerked meat; jerk; jerky; charqui; charque.

포의 (布衣) 1 〔벼슬 없는 선비〕 a scholar holding no office; a civilian; a commoner. 2 〔베로 만든 옷〕 hemp clothes.
● **포의한사** (一寒士) a poor scholar holding no office.

포인터 〔사냥개〕 a pointer.

포인트 1 〔득점〕 a point. ¶~를 따다[잃다] win [lose] a point // 매치 ~ a match point. **2** 〔요점〕 the point. ¶키~ the main[crucial] point / 〔단서〕 a key (to) // 세일즈 ~ a selling point. **3** 〔전철기〕 a switch; 〔영〕 points. ¶~를 바꾸다 switch a train from one track to another. **4** 〔활자의 크기 단위〕 point. ¶이 책은 8~ 활자로 찍다 We will set the book in 8-point type.

포자 (胞子) 〔생〕 a spore; a cyst. ¶무~ 생식 apospory.
● **포자낭** a sporocyst. **포자엽** a sporophyl(l).

포장 (包裝) packing; packaging(상품의 개장(装)); baling(곤포·꾸리미의); crating(운송용 상자·틀·바구니 등의). ¶~이 잘[단단하게] 되어 있다 be well [properly / securely] packed // ~이 나쁘게 [허술하게] 되어 있다 be badly [poorly / defectively] packed // ~을 풀다 unwrap (a package) / unpack (a box) // ~ 상자 무료 제공 〔게시〕 Case free. / Packaging free. / No charge for case. **포장하다** pack (up); 《미》 package; wrap (it) up. ¶종이로 ~ wrap (it) up in paper // 깨지는 물건을 꾸릴 때는 충분히 포장할 것 Use plenty of wrapping when you pack fragile articles.
● **포장물** a package. **포장비** a packing charge. **포장지** packing[brown / wrapping] paper.

포장 (布帳) a blackout curtain; a linen screen [awning]; (수레·자동차 등의) a hood; a (folding) top. ¶접고 걷는 ~이 달린 자동차 a convertible (car) // ~을 씌우다[걷다] pull up [put down] the top // ~을 걷고 운전을 하다 drive a car with the top down.
● **포장마차** 〔포장을 둘러친 마차〕 a covered wagon; a (horse and) buggy; 〔미국 역사〕 a prairie schooner [wagon]; (술·국수 등을 파는) a movable bar on a covered cart in which liquor and some simple side dishes are served; a covered cart bar.

포장 (褒章) 〔칭찬의 표징인 휘장〕 a medal (of merit).

포장 (鋪裝) pavement; paving. **포장하다** pave [surface] (a road with asphalt). →¶포장되어 있는[포장되어 있지 않은] 길 a paved[an unpaved] road.
● **포장 공사** paving[surfacing] work; pavement work(s). **포장도로** a paved road [street]; a pavement. ¶아스팔트 ~ an asphalt-paved[-surfaced] road / 《미》 a blacktop road.

포졸 (捕卒) 〔역〕 a constable; a policeman.

포좌 (砲座) 〔대포를 올려놓는 장치〕 a gun platform; a barbette; 〔포가(砲架)〕 the cage of a (field) gun.

포주 (抱主) a keeper of a brothel; a whore-

포즈 [자세] a pose. ¶~를 취하다 pose (oneself) (as a model) / strike [get into] a pose / take one's pose / posture / arrange oneself // ~를 바꾸다 [고치다] change one's pose / enter into a new pose // 사진을 찍기 위해 ~를 취하다 pose for a picture // 그 ~로 움직이지 마세요. Hold that pose!

포지션 a position. ¶스코어링 ~ scoring position // ~이 바뀌다 be changed in one's position // ~을 지키다 stand [guard] one's position // 전원이 각자의 ~에 붙었다 Everybody is (stationed) in his position.

포진(布陣) the lineup (of); lines. **포진하다** take up a position; (군대를) array one's force for battle. ¶그들은 공격하기 위해 당당히 포진했다 They formed a splendid [an impressive] battle array (for an attack).

포차(砲車) a gun carriage.

포착(捕捉) capture; apprehension; prehension. **포착하다** catch; seize; grasp; catch [take] hold of; (레이더가) pick up. ¶포착하기 어려운 elusive / evasive / intangible / slippery / [애매한] vague / hard to understand [catch] // 기회를 ~ seize (on) [embrace] an opportunity // 레이더가 태풍의 눈을 포착했다 The radar picked up the eye of the typhoon.

포충망(捕蟲網) an insect net; a butterfly net.

포츠담 선언(-宣言) the Potsdam Declaration [Conference].

포커 poker. ¶~를 하다 play poker.
● **포커페이스** a poker face. ¶~를 짓다 wear [assume] a poker face.

포켓 a pocket. ¶(속이) ~에 들어가는 pocket(-size(d)) / pocketable / vest-pocket (dictionary) // ~ 속을 뒤져 보다 search one's pocket / feel in one's pocket for (something) // ~에 넣다 pocket / put (a thing) in [into] a pocket / drop (a volume) into one's pocket // ~에 쑤셔 넣다 cram [stuff] one's pocket (with) // ~에 손을 넣다 reach in one's pocket // ~에서 꺼내다 take (a letter) out of one's pocket / draw (a newspaper) from one's pocket // ~을 달다 sew up a pocket (on a coat) // ~을 뒤지다 fish in one's pocket (for).
● **포켓북** a pocket(-sized) book. **포켓판** a pocket edition. ¶~ 사전 a pocket dictionary.

포크 (식사용) a fork. ¶한 벌의 나이프와 ~ a knife and fork // 디저트용 [샐러드용] ~ a dessert [salad] fork // 세[네] 날 ~ a three-pronged [four-pronged] fork // 식사용 [식탁용] ~ a dinner [table] fork.
● **포크 볼** [야구] a fork ball.

포크 댄스 a folk dance.

포크 송 a folk song.

포클레인 (*Poclain) a hydraulic shovel; a steam shovel.

포타슘 [화] potassium.

포탄(砲彈) a cannon ball; a shell; a shot. ¶우리는 적에게 ~을 퍼부었다 We rained artillery fire on the enemy. / We showered the enemy with shells.

포탈(逋脫) [과세를 피하여 면함] tax evasion; evasion of taxes. ¶세금 ~액 the amount of the tax evasion // 세금 ~자 a tax dodger [evader / cheat] / an evader of taxes. **포탈하다** evade [dodge] a tax; defraud the revenue.

포탑(砲塔) a gun turret; a cupola; (진지·군함 등의) a gunhouse.

포터 a (baggage) porter; (미) a redcap.

포터블 portable.
● **포터블 라디오** a portable radio.

포털 사이트 a portal (site).

포테이토칩 (미) potato chips; (영) (potato) crisps.

포트란 [컴퓨터의 실용 언어] FORTRAN (▶ formula translation의 약이).

포플러 [식] a poplar. ¶~ 가로수 거리 an avenue lined with poplar trees.

포플린 poplin.

포피(包皮) the foreskin; the prepuce.

포학하다(暴虐-) tyrannical; cruel; despotic; outrageous. ¶포학한 군주 a tyrant // 포학한 짓을 하다 commit [perpetrate] atrocities [outrages] // 온갖 포학한 짓을 다하다 perpetrate all possible atrocities / go through [run] the whole gamut of outrages.

포함(包含) inclusion; comprehension; implication (뜻을). ¶세금 ~ [경] duty paid // 운임 ~ [경] (미) freight prepaid / (영) carriage paid. **포함하다** include; comprise; comprehend; embrace; cover; contain; have (in); hold. ¶…을 포함하여 including / inclusive of …// …을 포함하지 않고 excluding / exclusive of …// 나는 세금을 포함해서 100만 원의 월급을 받고 있다 I receive a monthly salary of 1,000,000 won, taxes included [before taxes (are deducted)]. // 재료비를 포함한 가격입니다 The cost of material is included in the price. // 송료를 포함해서 얼마가 되겠습니까 How much will it be, shipping [freight charge] included? // 어린이들을 포함하여 300명이었다 There were 300 people, including children. // 송료를 포함해서 5,000원이었다 It cost 5,000 won, postage included. → ¶공장 견학을 스케줄에 포함시키다 work a factory tour into the schedule // 나를 그의 동류에 포함시키지 말게 Don't put me in the same category with him. // 이 속담에는 적어도 두 가지 뜻이 포함되어 있다 This proverb implies at least two things. / This proverb has at least two implications. // 그 일행에는 두 사람의 여성이 포함되어 있다 The group includes two women. / Two women are included in the party.
● **포함량** the (amount of) content. **포함률** the percentage of content.

포함(砲艦) a gunboat.

포핸드 [테니스·탁구] a forehand. ¶~로 타구하다 hit a ball with one's forehand.

포화(砲火) (a) gunfire; (a) shellfire; (an) artillery fire; (a) fire. ¶십자 ~ cross fire // 맹렬한 ~ a heavy fire / drumfire(연속적인) // ~를 퍼붓다 rain fire on (the enemy) / bring (the enemy) under fire // 서로 ~를 주고받다 exchange fire.

포화(飽和) [화] saturation. **포화하다** be [become] saturated (with). → ¶포화시키다 saturate [charge] (with).
● **포화 상태** saturation. ¶환자의 수용은 ~이다 There are no spare beds for new patients. / The ward is full. // 서울의 도로 교통은 ~이다 The streets of Seoul are completely choked [extremely congested]. // 이 물에 소금을 ~가 될 때까지 넣어라 Put salt in the water to saturation. **포화 용액** a saturated solution. **포화점** the saturation point; a saturated point. **포화 화합물** a saturated compound.

포환(砲丸) 1 [포탄] a cannonball. 2 [체] a shot.
● 포환던지기 the shot put. ¶~ 선수 a shot-putter // ~를 하다 put the shot.

포획(捕獲) capture; seizure. **포획하다** capture; seize; catch. ¶그들은 이번 겨울에 100 마리의 사슴을 포획했다 They caught as many as a hundred deer this winter.
● 포획고 / 포획량 a (good / poor) catch (of fish). 포획물 a prize; a booty. 포획자 a captor.

포효(咆哮) [사나운 짐승이 울부짖음] roaring; howling; [울음 소리] a roar; a howl; a bellow. **포효하다** roar; howl; bellow; yell. ¶포효하는 파도 소리를 듣다 hear the roar of the sea.

폭¹ [셈·정도]. ¶하루 만 원 ~으로 at the rate of 10,000 won a day // … ~ 이다 be equivalent to / be as good as // 시간당 3천 원 ~ 이다 be 3,000 won an hour // 1달러는 한국 돈으로 1,300원 ~ 이 된다 One dollar is equivalent to 1,300 won in Korean money.

폭² home; completely; fast; throughly; well; deep; (fall) with a heavy fall; sharply. ⇨폭

폭(幅) 1 width. ⇨"너비 ¶~이 넓은[좁은] 도로 a wide(or broad) [narrow] road // 길이 50cm. ~ 10cm의 천 a piece of cloth 50 centimeters long and 10 centimeters wide / a piece of cloth fifty centimeters in length and ten centimeters in breadth // 그것은 ~이 1미터이다 It is one meter wide[in width / in breadth]. // 무대가 ~은 넓지만 길이가 없다 The stage is wide but not deep enough[is wide enough / but lacks depth].
2 [도량·포용성] generosity; magnanimity; caliber; [범위] range; [규칙·제한 등의 여유] permitted freedom; latitude. ¶일의 ~을 넓히 다 broaden the scope of one's work.
3 (그림·병풍 등의) a scroll; a strip; a piece (of). ¶한 ~의 그림 a (picture) scroll // 두 병풍 a double-leaf [-folded] screen // 논에서 거니는 백로의 모습은 한 ~의 그림 같다 The white herons in the rice fields are very picturesque.

폭거(暴擧) [난폭한 행동] a rash [reckless] act; outrage; violence; [폭동] a riot; an insurrection; a disturbance; [무모한 기도] a reckless attempt; a leap in the dark. ¶~ 하다 act recklessly / resort to [use] violence // 를 경고하다 warn (a person) against recklessness // 대장은 젊은 대원들의 ~에 주의를 주었다 The captain warned the young soldiers not to be reckless.

폭격(爆擊) (aerial) bombing [bombardment]; a bombing attack [raid]. ¶무차별 ~ indiscriminate bombing // 융단 ~ carpet [pattern] bombing // 전략 ~ strategic bombing / 정밀 ~ precision bombing // 그 항구는 공중 과 육지의 양쪽에서 ~과 포격을 받았다 The port was bombarded from both land and air. **폭격하다** bomb; drop a bomb (on); make a bombing raid. ¶그들은 그 도시의 중심부를 폭격했다 They bombed the central part of the city. ➡¶폭격당한 지역 a bombed [bomb-blasted] area.
● 폭격기 a bombing plane; a bomber; (집합 적) bombing craft. ¶전투 ~ a fighter-bomber // 중[경] ~ a heavy [light] bomber. 폭격대 a bombing squad; an air strike force.

폭군(暴君) a tyrant; a despot (전제 군주). ¶~ 네로 Nero, the tyrant // ~을 타도하라 Down with the tyrant!

폭넓다(幅-) wide; broad; extensive. ¶폭넓은 지식 wide [extensive] knowledge // 그는 그 분야에서 폭넓은 활약을 하고 있다 He is very active in many areas in that field. / He is playing an active part over a wide area in his field. // 그는 폭넓은 지식을 지니고 있다 He has broad knowledge.

폭도(暴徒) rioters; a mob; mobsters; insurgents; mutineers (군대의). ¶~의 무리 a mob of rioters // ~에게 습격당하다 be mobbed // ~ 를 진압하다 put down [suppress / pacify] a mob // 경찰은 ~를 진압했다 The police got the mob [rioters] under control. // 시민들은 ~로 변하여 시청사를 습격했다 The townspeople turned into rioters and attacked the town hall.

폭동(暴動) a riot; a disturbance; rioting; an uprising; [병란] a mutiny; [반란] an insurrection; a rebellion. ¶무장 ~ an armed revolt // ~으로 뒤끓는 도시 a riot-torn town // ~을 일으키다 riot / raise [start / get up] a riot / start rioting / rise in riot [insurrection] / create a disturbance // ~을 진압하다 suppress [quell / put down] a riot / repress a disturbance // ~이 일어났다 A riot arose [broke out] // 학생들이 ~을 일으켰다 The students have started a riot [have rioted]. // ~은 진압되었다 The riot was suppressed [put down].
● 폭동자 a rioter; an insurgent; a rebel; a mutineer (군대의).

폭등(暴騰) a sudden rise; a sharp rise; (미) a boom; a (big) jump; skyrocketing. ¶원유 가격의 ~ a jump [steep rise] in crude oil prices. **폭등하다** (갑자기) rise suddenly; (미) boom; (엄청나게) jump; soar; shoot skyward; skyrocket. ¶폭등하는 물가 soaring prices / (미) boom prices // 천 원에서 2천 원 으로 ~ jump from 1,000 won to 2,000 won // 물가가 폭등했다 Prices have taken a jump. / There has been a sudden rise in prices. // 임대료가 폭등했다 Rents have risen remarkably. // 인플레로 물가가 폭등하고 있다 Prices are soaring owing to the inflation. // 땅값이 폭등하고 있다 Land prices are soaring [skyrocketing].

폭락(暴落) a slump; a (sharp) break; a crash; a smash; sagging; a heavy fall [decline]; a tremendous drop. ¶주식의 ~ a slump [crash] in stocks // 그는 주가의 ~으로 큰 손 해를 보았다 He suffered heavy losses in the stock market slump [crash]. // 주식 시장은 공전의 주가 ~을 기록했다 The stock market recorded an unprecedented slump. **폭락하다** (크게) decline heavily [sharply]; slump; (갑자기) fall suddenly; (미) toboggan (가치가); [증권] plunge; plummet; nosedive. ¶인기가 ~ have a sudden fall in one's popularity // 500 원 대로 ~ slump to the 500 won level // 주가 가 폭락했다 The stock market suffered a sharp decline. // 상품 값[물가]이 폭락하기 시 작했다 Prices are collapsing. // 생사 가격이 폭락했다 The price of raw silk slumped. // 철 강주(株)가 폭락했다 There was a sharp fall [sudden decline] in steel stocks. / Steel stocks plunged [went into a nosedive].

폭력(暴力) violence; (brute) force. ¶조직 ~ violence committed by a criminal organization // 집단 ~ mass violence / organized violence // ~으로 [~에 의해서] be force [violence] / [법] by force and arms // ~을 가하다 cause[employ] violence (to) / commit violence (toward) / commit an outrage (on) // ~을 행사하다[휘두르다] use[employ] violence[force] (on a person) / use one's fist / (미) employ strong-arm methods (upon) / strong-arm (another) // 이 난무하다 an act of violence prevails (on) // 그들은 마침내 ~을 휘둘렀다 They finally used[resorted to] violence. // 그는 아내에게 ~을 휘두른다 He does violence to his wife. / (때린다) He beats his wife. // 그는 우두머리의 자리를 ~으로 빼앗았다 He seized the position of boss by force [violence]. // ~은 사용하지 마라 Don't use [employ] violence[force]. // 그들은 목적을 달성하기 위해서는 ~도 불사한다 They are ready to use[employ / resort to] violence [force] in order to achieve their ends.

●폭력단 a band of thugs; a gangster organization given to using violence; a goon squad(노동 쟁의 등의); (단원) a gangster; a goon. ¶~ 일제 검거[소탕] a rounding-up of gangsters. 폭력배 hoodlums; hooligans; (street) gangsters; street toughs. ¶~의 단속을 강화하다 tighten control on hooligans. 폭력 범죄 a crime of violence. 폭력 행위 use [an act] of violence; gangsterism.

폭로(暴露) exposure; disclosure; divulgence; debunking. ¶독직 사건의 ~ the disclosure [exposure] of bribery. 폭로하다 disclose [reveal / divulge / air] (a secret); expose (another's crime); betray (another's plot); lay bare (an evil design); bring (a matter) to light; give away (another's secret). ¶폭로하겠다고 위협하여 under threat of exposure // 비밀을 ~ divulge (a person's) secret / reveal[expose] a secret // 사기꾼의 정체를 ~ expose an imposter // 회사의 실정을 ~ make a public disclosure of the real condition of a company // 주간지가 그녀의 재혼을 폭로했다 The weekly disclosed her remarriage. // 시키는 대로 하지 않으면 네가 한 일을 폭로할 테다 If you don't obey me, I'll let out what you've done. →¶폭로되다 be discovered / be revealed [disclosed / exposed] / come [be brought] to light // 그의 비밀이 폭로되었다 His secret was exposed[brought to light]. // 이 사건으로 그의 무능함이 폭로되었다 This incident revealed his incompetence. // 그는 과거의 비행이 폭로되지 않을까 하여 두려워하고 있다 He is afraid that his past misdeeds may be discovered.

●폭로 기사 a telltale story; a muckraking article. ¶그 주간지는 연예계의 ~로 독자를 끈다 That weakly magazine attracts readers with disclosures about the entertainment world. 폭로 전술 exposure tactics.

폭뢰(爆雷) a[an anti-submarine] depth bomb[charge].

폭리(暴利) excessive profits. ¶전쟁을 이용하여 ~를 취하는 자 a war profiteer // ~를 취하다 make undue[unreasonable] profits (on) / profiteer (in house rents) // 는 단속하다 control profiteering // 그들은 ~를 취했다 They made undue profits. // 그는 무기 밀수로 ~를 취했다 He made enormous profits by smuggling weapons. // 악덕업자들은 토지 매매로 ~를 취했다 Dishonest dealers made excessive[unwarranted] profits on the land sales.

●폭리배 a profiteer; a "robber."

폭민(暴民) a mob; rioters; insurgents; riotous people.

●폭민 정치 mob[mass] rule; mobocracy; ochlocracy.

폭발(暴發) explosion; blowing up. ¶인구 ~ a population explosion // 분노의 ~ explosion of anger. 폭발하다 explode; blow up; burst into. ¶분노가 ~ (사람이) fly into a passion / burst into a rage // 그는 마침내 분노가 폭발했다 In the end he flew into a rage. →¶분노를 폭발시키다 let loose one's indignation.

폭발(爆發) explosion; detonation; blast(ing); burst(ing); blowing up; eruption(화산의). ¶원자[핵] ~ atomic[nuclear] explosion // 가스의 ~ explosion of gas. 폭발하다 explode; burst (up); blow up; go up[off]; detonate; (화산이) erupt; burst into eruption. ¶굉장한 소리를 내면서 ~ blow up [go off] with a terrific explosion // 화약 공장이 엄청나게 폭발했다 The powder plant went up in a tremendous explosion. // 가스 탱크가 굉장한 소리를 내며 폭발했다 The gas tank blew up with a terrific blast[explosion]. →¶폭발시키다 explode / detonate / blow up / blast / burst // 다이너마이트를 폭발시키다 set[touch] off a dynamite.

●폭발 가스 explosive gas; (광산) firedamp. 폭발력 explosive power. 폭발물 an explosive (substance). ¶~ 위험 (게시) Danger-Explosives!

폭발적(暴發的) explosive; tremendous. ¶인기 tremendous popularity // 인구의 ~인 증가 a population explosion / an explosive increase of population // ~으로 explosively (accelerate).

폭사(爆死) death resulting from bombing. 폭사하다 be killed by a bomb; be bombed to death.

폭삭 1 [온통] entirely; wholly; completely; thoroughly. ¶지붕에 쌓인 눈의 무게로 곳간이 ~ 주저앉았다 The weight of the snow on the roof caused the shed to collapse. 2 [먼지가 갑자기 가볍게 일어남] puffing; in a cloud. ¶탄환이 떨어져 그의 주위에서 온통 흰 먼지가 ~ 일었다 Bullets puffed up the white dust all around him.

폭서(暴暑) intense[severe / torrid] heat.

폭설(暴雪) a tremendous[very heavy] snowfall[fall of snow]. ¶~ 지역 an area of high snowfall // 영동 지방에 ~이 내렸다 There was a very heavy snowfall in[A tremendous amount of snow fell on] the Yeongdong area.

폭소(爆笑) a[an uncontrolled] burst[roar] of laughter; an explosive laugh[laughter]; uproarious laughter. ¶~가 터졌다 There was a burst of laughter. // 그 순간 장내에 ~가 일었다 At that instant there arose a roar laughter in the hall. 폭소하다 roar with laughter; burst out laughing; burst into laughter. ¶청중은 그의 개그[익살]에 폭소했다 The audience burst out laughing[burst into laughter] at his gag.

폭스트롯 a fox trot.

폭식(暴食) voracious[excessive] eating; gorging; gluttony; voracity. 폭식하다 overeat (oneself); eat too much; eat to[in] excess;

폭신폭신
gorge.
● **폭식가** an excessive[a voracious] eater; a glutton.

폭신 softly; gently. ⇨ `폭신폭신`
폭신하다 soft; downy. ⇨ `폭신하다`
폭압(暴壓) oppression (by force); coercion; repression. **폭압하다** oppress; coerce; repress.
폭약(爆藥) an explosive (compound); detonator; blasting powder; Hercules powder(광산용). ¶**고성능** ~ a high explosive // ~을 장치하다 lay an explosive // ~에 점화하다 set off the blasting powder // 그들은 선로에 강력한 ~을 장치했다 They planted[laid] a powerful explosive on the tracks.
폭양(曝陽) the parching[scorching] heat (of the sun); the blazing sunlight; the burning sun.
폭언(暴言) violent[harsh / intemperate] language; abusive[bad] language; wild[strong] words. **폭언하다** abuse; use violent[strong] language; speak vehemently; utter wild words.
폭우(暴雨) a heavy rain[rainfall]; a torrential [hard] rain; a down pour; cataracts (a deluge] of rain. ¶~ 속에 in a pouring rain // ~로 피해를 입다 be damaged by a heavy rain.
폭음(暴飮) heavy[deep / excessive / immoderate] drinking; carousal; intemperance. ¶~ 폭식하다 eat and drink immoderately // 어젯 밤에는 ~을 했다 I had too much to drink last night. / I drank heavily[to excess] last night. // 그는 ~폭식으로 인해 건강을 해쳤다 He injured his health by eating and drinking immoderately[too much]. **폭음하다** drink hard[heavily / deep]; drink like a fish; drink too much[to excess]; booze. ¶그는 폭음한 탓으로 신장을 앓게 되었다 He suffers from kidney trouble on account of heavy drinking.
● **폭음가** a hard drinker; a soaker.

폭음(爆音) (비행기의) buzzing; burring; drumming; whizzing; a roar; (폭발의) an explosion; a detonation; a report; (내연 기관의) knocking. ¶제트기의 ~ the roar of a jet plane // ~을 내며 날다 fly with a whirr // ~이 1마일 떨어진 곳에서 들렸다 The explosion was heard a mile away. // 그 모터사이클은 ~을 내며 달려가 버렸다 The motorcycle roared away.
폭정(暴政) tyrannical government[rule]; oppressive sway; despotism; tyranny. ¶~을 펴다 tyrannize over a country // ~에 신음하다 [시달리다] groan under tyranny // 그 총독은 식민지에 ~을 폈다 The governor tyrannized the colony. // 그 국민은 ~에 신음하고 있었다 The people were groaning under the yoke of tyranny[despotism].
폭주(暴走) (자동차 등의) reckless driving; speeding; (가축 떼 등의) a stampede; [야구] a reckless run.
● **폭주족** (오토바이의) a motorcycle gang; a hell's angel; (차의) a gang of hot-rodders.
폭주(暴酒) heavy[excessive] drinking; toping(상습적). **폭주하다** drink heavily [excessively]; drink too much; overdrink; tope.
폭주(輻輳·輻湊) overcrowding; congestion (of goods[traffic]); influx[deluge / flood] (of people). ¶교통량의 ~ a traffic congestion [jam] // 화물[우편물의]의 ~ a congestion of goods[mail] // 주문의 ~ pressure of orders // ~를 완화하다 relieve the congestion (of goods). **폭주하다** congest; be congested (with); be (over) crowded (with). ¶편지가 폭주했다 Letters came in showers.
폭죽(爆竹) a (fire)cracker; a squib; a flip-flap; a petard. ¶~을 터뜨리다 set off firecrackers / fire squibs // 그들은 승리를 축하하려고 ~을 터뜨렸다 They set off[exploded] firecrackers to celebrate the victory.
폭탄(爆彈) a bomb; a bombshell. ¶고성능 ~ a TNT bomb / a high explosive bomb // 시한 ~ a time bomb // 원자[수소] ~ an atomic [a hydrogen] bomb // 초대형 ~ a superbomb / a blockbuster // 화염 ~ a liquid-flame bomb // ~을 투하하다 drop[deliver] a bomb (on a city) // ~을 던지다 throw[hurl] a bomb at (a train) // ~을 싣다 (비행기에) bomb up // 그는 열차에 ~을 던졌다 He threw a bomb at the train.
● **폭탄선언** a bombshell declaration[statement]. ¶~을 하다 drop[throw] a bombshell / make a bombshell announcement.
폭투(暴投) [야구] a wild throw; a wild pitch; wild pitching. ¶~로 2루에 진루하다 advance to second on wild throw. **폭투하다** pitch [throw] wild; throw a wild ball.
폭파(爆破) blasting; blowing up; explosion. **폭파하다** blast; blow up; explode. ¶철로를 ~ pound rail lines (with bombs) // 다이너마이트로 암석을 ~ dynamite a rock / blast a rock with dynamite // 우리는 배를 폭파했다 We blew up a ship.
폭포(수)(瀑布水) a waterfall; a falls; a cascade(작은); a cataract(큰). ¶나이아가라 ~ (the) Niagara Falls // ~처럼 쏟아지다 fall [come down] in cataracts[torrents] // ~가 되어 떨어지다 fall in a cascade[in torrents] / cascade down // ~를 이용하여 발전하다 harness a waterfall to generate electricity.
폭폭 piercing repeatedly; blunt(ly); freely; (boiling) completely; rotting rapidly; sinking deep(ly). ⇨ `푹푹`
폭풍(暴風) a storm; a windstorm; a wild [violent / stormy] wind; a high wind; a gale(강풍); a hurricane; a typhoon(태풍). ¶(월면의) ~의 바다 the Ocean of (Lunar) Storms // ~의 중심 a storm center / the eye of a storm // ~이 불고 있었다 It was blowing a gale. // ~이 지나갔다 The storm is over [gone]. / The storm has blown over. // ~이 불 것 같다 It looks like a storm. / A storm is rising. // ~이 사납게 불고 있다 A storm is raging. // 밤새도록 ~이 몰아쳤다 It blew a gale all (through the) night. // 스키어 일행은 ~ 속에 갇혔다 [휩싸였다] The skiing party was caught in the storm. / (움직일 수 없게 되었다) The skiing party was stranded by the storm.
폭풍 전의 고요 the lull[calm] before a storm.
● **폭풍 경보 / 폭풍 주의보** a storm warning. ¶~가 내렸다 A storm warning is out. **폭풍권** a storm zone[area]. **폭풍우** a rainstorm; a storm; a tempest.
폭풍(爆風) a bomb blast; a blast (from an explosion). ¶창문 유리가 ~에 날아갔다 The windowpanes were blown out by the blast.

폭한(暴寒) severe[intense sharp] cold; cold snap.

폭한(暴漢) a ruffian; a rowdy; a rough; a roughneck; a thug; (미국 속어) a goon; a tough; a bully.

폭행(暴行) **1** [난폭한 행동] (an act of) violence; riotous conduct; an outrage; an assault. ¶~을 가하다 do violence (to)∥폭도들은 그 사진 기자에게 ~을 가했다 The mob did violence to the cameraman. **폭행하다** behave violently; use violence; assault (criminally). **2** [강간] (a) violence; (a) rape; (a) violation. **폭행하다** violate; rape. ➔¶그녀는 폭행당했다 She was violated[raped / assaulted].

● **폭행자** an outrager; a rioter; an assaulter; a violator[rapist] (능욕자).

폰 [물] [음의 크기의 단위] a phon. ¶비행기의 폭음은 120~이다 An airplane engine registers 120 phons. ¶역전에서 자동차의 소음은 70~이다 The traffic noise in front of the station is 70 phons.

폰섹스 phone sex.

폰트 [글꼴] a font.

폰팅 (*phone ting) a telephone blind date.

폴더 a folder.

폴라로이드 카메라 (상표명) a Polaroid (Land) camera.

폴로 [체] polo. ¶~의 볼 a polo ball.

● **폴로셔츠** a polo shirt.

폴로늄 [화] polonium (기호 Po).

폴리에스테르 [화] polyester.

폴리에틸렌 [화] polyethylene.

폴짝 opening the door suddenly; lightly leaping. ⇨²**풀쩍**

폴카 [음] a polka. ¶~를 추다 dance the polka / polka.

폼 [모양·형태] form; carriage; way of holding oneself. ¶~이 좋다 have a nice form / have a smart carriage∥그는 투구의 ~이 좋다[나쁘다] His pitching form is[is not] good.

퐁당 plop; plump; with a plop[flop / splash]. ¶~ 빠지다 fall plop into (the water) / drop into (the water) with a plop∥물에 뛰어들다 jump into the water with a plop[splash] / plump[splash] into the water.

퐁당거리다 make a plopping sound; keep plopping[flopping / splashing]. ¶물속에서 ~ splash[spatter] about in the water.

퐁당퐁당 plop, plop; plopping; with plops [flops]. ¶~ 물에 떨어지다 fall plop-plop into the water. **퐁당퐁당하다** make a plopping sound. ⇨**퐁당거리다**

퐁퐁 1 [구멍이 터지는 소리] breaking open repeatedly. **2** [샘 솟는 소리] bubbling; gurgling.

표(表) **1** [일람표의] a table; a tabular statement[exhibit]; a schedule (예정표); a diagram; a chart (도표); a list (목록); [표의 형식] tabular form. ¶시간~ a timetable / (학교의) a schedule∥정가~ a price list∥통계~ the tabulation of statistics∥~에(서) 보인 바와 같이 as shown in the table[on the list]∥~에 실려 있다 be listed / be (placed) on the list∥~로 만들다 tabulate / tabularize / put into tabular form / make into a table / make a list[table] of / 자세한 것은 아래의 ~와 같음 Details are tabulated as under.∥레몬은 다음 ~의 세 번째에 있다 Lemons stand third on the following list.∥이 ~로 지난 10년간의 지가의 변동을 알 수 있다 This table shows the changes in land prices for the past ten years.∥회원의 이름이 이 ~에 실려 있다 The names of the members are listed here[are on this list].
2 [제왕께 올리는 글] a memorial to the Throne. ¶출사(出師)~를 올리다 memorialize the Emperor on an expedition / appeal to the Emperor for an expedition.
3 a proof (of); a token. ⇨²**표적**(表迹) ¶~가 나다 [두드러지다] be conspicuous[striking / evident / obvious] / stand out / [겉으로 드러나다] show signs / show[give] proof [evidence] (of) / be shown (clearly)∥~ 나게 markedly / conspicuously / notably / remarkably / strikingly∥~ 나게 예쁘다 be strikingly beautiful∥유난히 ~ 나다[~ 내는 짓을 하다] make oneself (too) conspicuous∥회색은 먼지가 묻어도 ~ 나지 않는다 Gray does not show the dust.

표(票) **1** [각종 딱지] a card; a label; a name card (이름표); a place card (좌석표); a tab; a tag (꼬리표); [(짐·신발 등의) 보관표] a receipt; a check; [번호표] a number check; [정가표·전당표 등] a ticket; a tally (꼬리표); (한 장씩 떼어 내는) a chit; a coupon. ¶~를 붙이다 paste a card[label] / label (a bottle) ∥~를 달다 label (a trunk) / put a tag (on an article) / ticket∥수화물에 짐~를 달다 attach a tag to (one's) baggage∥나는 소포에 꼬리~를 붙였다 I put a tag on the bundle. ∥트렁크에는 「취급 주의」라는 ~가 붙어 있었다 The trunk was labeled "Handle with care."
2 [차표·배표·입장권 등] a ticket; a coupon (ticket)(메어 쓰게 된). ¶**당일 유효**~ a day ticket / a ticket available on the day of issue only∥반~ a half ticket∥배~ a steamboat[boarding] ticket∥왕복~ (미) a round-trip ticket / (영) a return (ticket)∥편도~ (미) a one-way ticket / (영) a single ticket∥3일간 유효~ a ticket valid for three days∥서울까지의 직행~ a through ticket to Seoul ∥~ 받는 사람 a ticket[check] taker∥~ 파는 곳 a ticket office / (영) a booking office ∥~를 사다 get[buy / take] a ticket / book (for Seoul)∥기차~를 사다 buy a train ticket∥~를 찍다 punch[clip] a ticket∥~를 검사하다 examine a ticket∥부산까지의 2등 ~를 한 장 주시오 (Please give me) One second-class ticket to Busan.∥경주까지의 새마을 왕복 ~를 두 장 주시오 Give me two round-trip deluxe-class tickets to Gyeongju.
3 (선거의) a vote; a ballot. ¶**고정** votes[support] / loyal votes[support]∥**동정** ~ sympathy votes∥**부동**~ floating[shifting / drifting / uncommitted] votes∥**여성**[청년] ~ women's[young people's] votes∥**조직**~ organized votes∥1인 1~ one man one vote ∥깨끗한 한 ~ an honest[a fair / a clean / a conscientious] vote∥~를 얻다[모으다] win [get / draw / gather / round up] votes∥…한 ~를 던지다 cast a vote[ballot] (for)∥500~ 중 325~를 얻다 poll[win] 325 votes of 500 cast∥장 씨에게 ~를 던지다 vote for Mr. Jang∥그는 종교 단체의 고정~로 당선됐다 He is elected on loyal support from religious organization.∥그 안은 250대 350 ~로 가결되었다 The bill was passed by a vote of 250 to 350.∥이번 선거에서 그는 약 5만 ~를 얻었다 He received[got / polled]

about 50,000 votes in the election.∥그는 20 ~ 대 5∶로 위원장에 선출되었다 He was elected chairman of the committee by a vote of 20 to 5.∥보수계의 두 후보 간에 ~가 갈라졌다 The votes were split between the two conservative candidates.∥각 후보는 ~ 모으기에 안간힘을 쓰고 있다 Each candidate is frantically trying to secure votes.

표(標) **1** [부호] a mark; a sign; a note. ¶물음 ~ a note of interrogation∥「○」를 한 단어 a word marked (with a) "○"∥~를 **하다 mark** (a thing) / **put**[**place**] **a mark on** (a thing)∥단어에 별~를 하다 mark a word with an asterisk[a star] / put an asterisk by a word.
2 [징표] a symbol; an emblem.
3 [휘장] a badge; a mark. ¶회원~를 달고 있다 wear a membership badge.
4 [증거] a proof (of); evidence (of / for); a testimony (to). ¶차에는 격투의 ~가 있었다 There were evidences of struggle in the car.
5 [상표] a trademark; a brand. ¶비둘기~ 노트 a Pigeon brand notebook.

표결(表決) ballot taking; a vote; (미) a roll call; (영) a division. ¶~에 **들어가다 come to a vote**∥~을 **요구하다 call for a division** (an a measure)∥~ 결과 법안에 대한 찬성이 22표 반대가 14표였다 The result of voting was 22 in favor and 14 against the bill.∥그 안건에 대한 ~이 행해졌다 A vote[division] was taken on the matter. / They voted on the matter.∥자유당은 단독 ~을 감행하였다 The Liberal party took a vote in the absence of the other parties.∥그 법안은 ~에 부쳐졌다 The bill came[was put] to the vote. **표결하다 vote** (on); **take a vote** (on a question); **take a ballot** (for); (미) **take a roll call**; (영) **take a division**; **divide** (on). ¶동의를 ~ **make a decision**[**vote**] **on a motion**∥무기명 투표로 ~ vote by secret ballot∥기립에 의해 ~ vote by standing up / take a standing vote.

표결(票決) a vote; voting; a decision by vote. ¶아슬아슬한 (차이의) ~ (by) a close vote (of 100 to 98)∥~에 **부치다 put**[**submit**] (a bill) to a **vote**[**ballot**]. **표결하다 take a vote** (on); **vote** (on).

표고(버섯) [식] a shiitake (mushroom).

표구(表具) mounting. **표구하다 mount** (a picture); **put** (a picture) **in a mount**. ¶표구하도록 하다 have (a picture) mounted∥족자로 그림을 표구하게 했다 I had the picture mounted on a hanging scroll.
 ● **표구사** a paper hanger; a paperer; a mounter.

표기(表記) **1** [표면에 쓰기] inscription on the face. ¶~의 inscribed[mentioned] on the face[outside]∥~의 금액 the sum inscribed on the face∥~의 주소 the address mentioned[written] on the outside / the above address. **표기하다 inscribe**[**write**] **on the face**. ➔ **표기된 declared** / **insured**∥편지에 표기된 주소 the address written on the face of a letter. **2** [철자] spelling; transcription (다른 글에 의한). **표기하다 spell**; **transcribe**. ¶한글을 로마자로 ~ **romanize Korean**[**Hangeul**]∥단어의 발음을 발음 기호로 ~ **transcribe**[**show**] **the pronunciation of a word in phonetic symbols**.
 ● **표기 가격 declared**[**insured**] **value**. **표기법 notation**. ¶음성 ~ **phonetic notation**.

표기(標記) marking; a mark. **표기하다 mark**.

표독스럽다(慓毒−) ferocious; fierce. ⇨ **표독하다** ¶표독스러운 얼굴로 with a look of venom.

표독하다(慓毒−) ferocious; fierce; venomous; vicious; (구어) shrewd. ¶표독한 여자 a ferocious woman / a shrew / a she-devil∥표독하게 말하다 speak daggers to∥표독하게 노려보다 look daggers at.

표류(漂流) **1** [떠서 흘러감] drift; drifting. **표류하다 drift** (about / with the current / on the tide); **be adrift**. ¶물결치는 대로 ~ **be**[**drift**] **about**] **at the mercy of the waves**∥보트는 꼬박 주야를 표류했다 The boat had drifted about[was adrift] for one whole day and night. **2** [정처 없이 돌아다님]. **표류하다 wander aimlessly**; **tramp**; **rove**.
 ● **표류물 floatage**; **driftage**; **flotsam**(표류 화물); **a drifter**. **표류선 a drifting ship**; **a castaway** (**ship**); **a derelict**(난파선). **표류자 a person adrift on the sea**; **a castaway** (**on an island**); **a drifter**.

표리(表裏) **1** [속과 겉] inside and outside; obverse and reverse. **2** [양면] two sides (of a thing); [표면과 내심] appearance and mind [real intention]. ¶~가 있는[~부동(不同)한] **double-dealing** / **double-faced** / **double-hearted** / **treacherous** / **unfaithful** / **dishonest**∥~가 없는 **single-hearted** / **single-minded** / **faithful** / **honest**∥~ 없이 **single-heartedly** / **faithfully**∥~ 없이 주인을 섬기다 serve one's master faithfully[single-heartedly]∥그는 ~가 있는 사람이다 He is double-faced[two-faced / a double-dealer / a hypocrite]. / He wears a double face. / He plays a double game.
 ● **표리일체 inside and outside together**; **both sides** (**as one**). ¶~가 되어 일하다 **work in close cooperation** (**with**).

표리부동하다(表裏不同−) (be) treacherous; deceptive; double-faced. ¶표리부동한[표리가 있는] 사람 **a double-dealer** / **a double-faced person**∥그는 표리부동해서 우리의 신용을 잃었다 Because he was a double-dealer [Because of his double-dealing] he lost our trust.

표면(表面) [거죽] the surface; the face; the obverse; [외부] the exterior; the outside; [외양] (an) appearance; (a) show. ¶물의 ~ the surface of the water∥지구의 ~에 on the face[surface] of the earth∥~의 **external** / **outside** / **outward** / **superficial** / **surface** / **apparent** / **seeming** / **ostensible**∥~(상)의 이유 **an ostensible reason** / **a plausible excuse**∥~**상으로**[**적으로**] (**는**) **externally** / **outwardly** / **apparently** / **on the surface** (**of things**) / **ostensibly**∥~상으로 남을 판단하다 **judge a man by his outward**[**external**] **appearance**∥(사람이) ~에 **나서다 be**[**appear**] **in the limelight** / **show oneself in the public eye**∥~에 **나타나다 get shown on the face**[**surface**] / **appear**[**be**] **in the public eye** / **appear above**[**come to**] **the surface**∥그는 ~에 나서기를 좋아한다 He loves to be in the limelight.∥그는 ~에 나서기를 좋아하지 않는다 He likes to keep in the background.∥~상으로는 순해 보이지만 그에게는 아주 고집 센 데가 있다 He seems to be gentle, but there is a very stubborn side to him.∥그는 ~상으로는 친절한 듯한데 본심은 알 수 없다 He is seemingly very kind, but I don't know about his real feelings. // ~상으로는 아무 일 없는 것처럼 보인다 Outwardly [On the surface] there seems to be no trouble.

●**표면 장력** [물] surface tension. **표면화** ¶~하다 come [be brought] to the fore [front] / come out in the open / come up to the surface / come to a head / become an issue // ~시키다 bring (a matter) to the surface [fore / front] / make (a matter) public // 사건이 ~되었다 The affair was brought to public notice. // 내부의 불화가 마침내 ~되었다 Finally the internal strife came to the surface [fore]. // 일이 ~되기 전에 처리하고 싶다 I want to take care of the matter before it attracts public attention.

표면적(表面積) the surface [superficial] area.

표명(表明) expression; demonstration; manifestation. ¶입후보의 ~ the announcement of one's candidacy. **표명하다** [표시하다] state; express; make an expression (of); indicate; demonstrate; show; manifest. ¶사의 [감사의 뜻]를 ~ express [show] one's gratitude // 반대를 ~ express oneself against (a matter) / declare against (a plan) // 그는 유감의 뜻을 표명했다 He expressed his regret. // 그는 손을 저으며 불만의 뜻을 표명했다 He demonstrated his dissatisfaction by waving his hands. // 그는 그 계획에 반대를 표명했다 He declared [professed himself] against the project. / He professed opposition to the project.

표박(漂泊) 1 [정처 없이 떠돌아다님] wandering; roaming; vagabondage; tramp. **표박하다** wander about; tramp; vagabondize. 2 [표류] drifting. **표박하다** drift.

표방(標榜-) profess (oneself to be); adopt a platform [slogan / motto] (of); advocate [champion / espouse / sponsor] (the cause of democracy); stand for. ¶민주주의를 표방하는 교육 education which advocates the cause of democracy // 정의를 ~ be professedly for justice / champion the cause of justice / be clothed with righteousness // 인도주의를 ~ claim to stand for humanitarian principles / advocate the cause of humanitarianism // 그들은 정의를 표방하여 싸웠다 They fought for the cause [under the slogan] of justice.

표밭(票-) a favorable voting constituency (for the Liberal party); an area where a candidate has many supporters; a candidate's stronghold. ¶노조가 그의 ~이다 He has many supporters in the labor unions.

표백(表白) (an) expression; (a) manifestation; exhibition; [자백] (a) confession. **표백하다** express; manifest; [자백하다] confess.

표백(漂白) bleaching; decoloration; decolorization. **표백하다** bleach; decolor; decolorize. **표백한**[표백하지 않은] 무명 bleached [unbleached] cotton (cloth).
●**표백분** bleaching powder; chloride of lime. **표백제** a bleaching agent; a bleach; a decolorant; a decolorizer.

표범(豹-) [동] a leopard; a panther. ¶아메리카~ an American leopard / a jaguar // 암~ a leopardess / a pantheress.

표변(豹變) a sudden change; a change of front; a volte-face; an about-face. **표변하다** change suddenly; change front; make [perform] a volte-face; volte-face; [변절하다] turn one's coat. ¶당선되자 그는 표변하여 보수파로 전환했다 Once he was elected, he did an about-face [a political flip-flop] and became a conservative.

표본(標本) 1 [실물 견본] a specimen. ¶동물 [식물] ~ a zoological [botanical] specimen // 박제 ~ a stuffed [mounted] specimen (of a bird) // 알코올 보존 ~ a specimen preserved in alcohol. 2 [견본] a sample. ¶임의 [무작위] ~ 추출 [수] random sampling. 3 [전형] a type; an example. ¶그는 우등생의 ~이다 He is a typical honor student. / He is a typical example of an honor student. // 그 행위는 정직의 ~이다 That is a good example of an honest act.
●**표본실** a specimen room [gallery]; (식물의) a herbarium (pl. ~s, -ria). **표본 조사** a sample survey.

표상(表象) 1 [심] (a) representation; (a) presentation; [철] an idea. ¶부분 ~ a partial idea. 2 a symbol (of). ⇨상징 ¶자유의 ~ a symbol of liberty [freedom].
●**표상주의** symbolism. ⇨상징주의(↔)상징)

표석(標石) a stone marker. ⇨푯돌

표시(表示) 1 [나타냄] (an) indication; (an) expression; (a) manifestation; (a) demonstration. ¶의사 ~ expression of one's intention. **표시하다** indicate; show; manifest; express; give expression to. ¶의사를 ~ indicate one's intention / express one's will. ➔ ¶비상구는 녹색 문자로 표시되어 있다 The emergency [fire] exit is indicated [shown] in green letters. 2 [표적] a token; a mark; a sign; a manifestation. ¶감사의 ~로 as a token [in token] of one's gratitude [appreciation] / 사랑의 ~로 in sign of love // 데 마음의 ~입니다 It's a mere mark of kind regard.

표어(標語) a slogan; a motto (pl. ~(e)s); a catchword; a watchword; a rallying word. ¶적절한 ~ a fitting motto (for) // 「안전 제일」을 ~로 삼고 under the slogan "Safety First" // ~를 모집하다 offer a prize for the best motto // 그 정당은 「깨끗한 정치」라는 ~를 내걸고 결성되었다 The party was formed under the slogan [catchword / watchword] "Clean Politics."

표음(表音) (문자의) phonetic representation. **표음하다** represent [write] phonetically.
●**표음 문자** a phonogram. **표음주의** phoneticism.

표의(表意) (문자의) ideography. **표의하다** represent [write] the meanings; write in ideographs.
●**표의 문자** an ideogram; an ideograph; an ideographic character.

표장(標章) an ensign; an emblem; a badge; a mark.

표적(表迹) 1 [증표] a proof (of); evidence (of / for); a testimony (to). ¶~을 남기지 않다 leave no trace behind. 2 [마음의 표시물] a token; a mark; a sign; a manifestation. ¶감사의 ~으로 in token [as a token] of one's gratitude.

표적(標的) a target; a mark. ¶공격[비난]의 ~ an object [a target] of criticism // ~을 맞히다 [벗어나다 / 겨냥하다] hit [miss / aim at] the mark [target].
●**표적 사격** target shooting.

표절(剽竊) plagiarism; piracy; crib; abstrac-

표정 tion. **표정하다** pirate; plagiarize; crib; gut (a book); abstract. ¶남의 문장을 ~ plagiarize another person's writing.
- **표절물** a plagiarism; a crib. **표절자** a (literary) pirate; a plagiarist.

표정(表情) (a) (facial) expression; a look(얼굴·눈의). ¶불만스러운 ~ a discontented look / 근심스러운 ~ a look of anxiety[worry] // ~이 풍부한 expressive / full of expression // ~이 없는 expressionless / inexpressive / blank / wooden / flat // ~이 없는 얼굴 (무표정한) an expressionless face / (미국 속어) a dead pan / (속마음을 감춘) a poker face // ~이 굳어지다 harden one's face / freeze // ~을 살피다 read (a person's) face // 이상한 ~을 짓다 make a strong expression // 그녀는 슬픈 ~을 짓고 있다 She looks sad. // 화난 ~이 그의 얼굴에 떠올랐다 An angry look came over his face. // 곤혹스러운 ~이 그의 얼굴을 스쳤다 A puzzled expression[look] crossed[passed over] his face. // 섣달 그믐날의 전국 각지의 ~을 전해 드리겠습니다 We will report on how people in various parts of the country are spending New Year's Eve. // 그 뉴스를 둘러싼 각국의 ~은 가지각색이었다 The reactions of other nations to the news were varied. // 그는 미심쩍은 ~을 지었다 He put on a suspicious look[expression]. / He looked suspicious. // 그는 놀란 ~으로 일어섰다 He stood up with a look of surprise.

표제(標題·表題) (책 등의) a title; (장·절 등의) a heading; (사진 등의) a caption; (신문 기사 등의) a headline (over an article); a head(ing); (문장의) a superscription. ¶부(副) ~ a subtitle / a subhead(ing) // 2단 ~ a double head // 「한국의 전통」이라는 ~의 책 a book entitled [with the title (of)] Korean Traditions // 큰 ~ (신문의) a banner [big] headline / (교과서 등의) a major heading // 책의 ~ the title of a book // ~을 달다 give a title [headline] to / headline [head] (an article) / put a caption on (a cartoon) // 그는 그 논문에 「꿈」이라는 ~를 붙였다 He entitled his essay "Dreams." He gave the title "Dreams" to his essay. // 그는 「중세의 미술」이라는 ~로 연설했다 He spoke on the topic [subject] (of) "Medieval Art."
- **표제어** (사서 등의) a headword; an entry word; a vocabulary entry; (난외(欄外)의) a catchword; a guide[direction] word. **표제 음악** program music.

표주박(瓢-) a small gourd.

표준(標準) 1 [기준] a standard; (판단의) a criterion (*pl.* -ria); [수준] a level. ¶~의 standard / ~대로 in conformity to[in accordance with] the standard // ~을 정하다 fix [set up / establish] a standard / lay down a criterion / 일정한 ~에 달하다 reach [come up to / be up to] a fixed standard // ~ 이상 [이하]이다 be above[below] the standard / 최근에 수상자의 ~이 높아졌다[낮아졌다] The level of competition for the prize has recently risen [fallen]. / 이것은 고교생을 ~으로 해서 쓴 책이다 This book is written on[at] the high-school level.
2 [보통·평균] the average; norm. ¶~이 normal / average // 내 수입은 ~ 이상[이하]이다 My income is above [below] normal [the average].
- **표준 가격** the standard price. **표준 상태** [물] a normal state. **표준시** (the) standard time; Greenwich (Mean) Time(약어 G.M.T.). ¶만국[그리니치] ~ universal time / Greenwich Mean Time / **한국** ~ Korean Standard Time(약어 KST). **표준어 / 표준말** the standard language (of a nation / in a country); standard Korean[English]. **표준 편차 [수]** standard deviation. **표준형** a standard type. ¶~의 가구 standard furniture. **표준화** standardization.

표준적(標準的) normal; average. ¶~인 한국인 an average Korean // ~인 3세아 a normal child of three.

표지(表紙) a cover; binding(등부분도 포함한). ¶두꺼운 ~ a hard [stiff] cover // 종이 [가죽] ~ a paper [leather] binding // 겉[뒤] ~ a front [back] cover // 천 [가죽] ~의 책 a book bound in cloth [leather] // 종이 ~의 책 a paperback / a soft-cover / a softbound book / 딱딱한 ~의 책 a hardback / a hard-cover [hardbound / hardbacked] book // ~의 커버 a jacket / a dust jacket [wrapper] // ~를 붙이다 bind a book (in leather) // ~를 씌우다 cover a book (in paper) / put the covers on (a book).

표지(標識) a mark(ing); a sign; a signal; [항] a beacon; a guide. ¶경계 ~ a landmark / a boundary mark(er) // 공중 ~ (비행장의) a pylon // 도로 [교통] ~ a signpost / a guidepost // (집합적) signposting // 지상 [항로] ~ a ground [channel] mark // 항공 ~ an air [aerial] beacon // 해상 ~ a sea mark / a beacon // 「우회전 금지」의 ~가 있다 There's a "No Right Turn" sign. // 대문 앞의 큰 나무가 우리 집의 ~다 The big tree in front of the gate is a guide [landmark] to my house.
- **표지등(-燈)** a beacon light. **표지물** a signal.

표징(表徵) a sign; a mark; a symbol; an indication.

표착(漂着) drifting ashore. **표착하다** be cast [thrown] ashore; be washed ashore; drift [float] ashore; be driven (to). ¶어선이 해안에 표착했다 A fishing boat was washed up on the shore.

표찰(標札) a label; a bill; a tally(나무·쇠 등); a sticker(풀로 붙이는). ¶~을 붙이다 paste a bill.

표창(表彰) (official) commendation; honoring; awarding. **표창하다** commend (officially); honor [do honor to] (a person); give recognition (for); make public recognition (of a person's services). ¶숨은 선행을 ~ honor (a person) publicly for an unrecognized good deed // 정부는 녹화 운동에 전력한 임녹화 씨의 공적을 표창했다 The government made public recognition of the services rendered by Mr. Im Nokhwa in the tree planting campaign. → ¶표창받다 win official commendation / be cited (for) // 뛰어난 봉사로 표창받다 be given a citation for (one's[its]) excellent service (to) // 그는 진화에 협력하여 표창되었다 He was officially commended [He won official commendation] for helping the firemen fight a fire.
- **표창식** a commendation ceremony; a ceremony of awarding an honor. **표창장** a certificate [letter] of commendation; a citation; a testimonial.

표창(鏢槍) a dart; a dirk; a javelin.

표출(表出) expression. **표출하다** express. ¶감정을 ~ express one's feelings.
표층(表層) [표면의 층] the outer layer[stratum (*pl.* -ta)]. ¶지구의 ~ the crust of the earth.
표토(表土) topsoil; surface soil; regolith.
표표하다(表表-) conspicuous; distinguished; famous; renowned; noted. **표표히** conspicuously; famously; remarkably.
표피(表皮) 1 [생] the outer(most) layer of the skin; the scarfskin; the cuticle; the epidermis(최상층의). 2 [식] the epidermis; the exterior coating; the bark(수피).
● **표피 세포** an epidermal cell. **표피 조직** epidermal tissue.
표하다(表-) [나타내다] express (one's gratitude); show; manifest; demonstrate; pay (one's respects); offer (one's congratulations). ¶…에 경의[사의]를 표하여 in honor [appreciation] of …//그의 협력에 대한 사의를 표하여 in appreciation of his cooperation //경의를 ~ express[show] one's respect (to) / pay one's respects (to)//유감의 뜻을 ~ express one's regret (over a matter)//충심으로 …의 뜻을 표합니다 I wish to [beg to] inform you that ….//충심으로 조의를 표합니다 Allow me to express my sincere sympathy (on the death of …).
표하다(標-) mark (a thing); put[place] a mark on (a thing). ¶연필로 ~ mark in pencil//그 페이지를 접어서 ~ double over a leaf to mark the page//상자에 ~ mark a box//기억할 만한 구절에 ~ mark passages to be memorized.
표현(表現) (주로 말에 의한) (an) expression; (a) representation; (a) presentation; (a) manifestation. ¶~의 자유 freedom of expression//이솝 이야기의 그림에 의한 ~ a pictorial representation of Aesop's fables // ~적인 expressive / expressional / ~이 교묘한 well-turned (phrase) // 이 대목은 ~의 방법이 훌륭하다 This is well put. **표현하다** express; be expressive of; represent; manifest; give expression[words] to (thoughts). ¶표현할 수 없는 inexpressible / indescribable / beyond expression // 멋지게 ~ express happily [cleverly] // 감상을 글로 ~ write one's impressions / express one's feelings in writing // 자기의 생각을 ~ express one's opinion / express oneself // 내 기분을 반도 표현할 수 없다 I cannot tell half of what I feel. // 그 기분은 무어라 표현하기 어렵다 The feeling is indescribable. // 나는 감사의 마음을 어떻게 표현해야 할지 모르겠다 I don't know how to express my gratitude. // 그 광경은 말로 표현할 수 없는 것이었다 The sight was beyond words [description]. // 그 경치의 아름다움은 말로 표현할 수 없을 정도다 The beauty of the view is beyond words [expression]. // 이것은 어떻게 표현하면 좋을까 How should I word [phrase / express] it?//취지는 좋은데 표현하는 것이 서투르다 The idea is good, but it is poorly expressed [put / worded]. //그의 그림에는 자연을 사랑하는 마음이 잘 표현되어 있다 His love of nature is well expressed in his painting.
● **표현력** one's power of expression; ability to express oneself. **표현법** expression; how to express oneself. **표현주의** expressionism.
푯대(標-) a signpost; a mark(ing) post; a (signal) post; a pillar.
푯돌(標-) [길 표지] a stone marker; a marker stone; a landmark[boundary] stone; [이정표] a milestone. ¶~을 세우다 set up a landmark stone.
푯말(標-) a post; a signpost. ¶~을 세우다 set up a signpost (by the roadside).
푸 1 [내뿜는 소리] whew!; whoo!; with a light whistle. ¶포도 씨를 ~ 하고 내뱉다 spit out grape seeds. 2 [방귀 소리] foof.
푸가(⑩fuga) [음] a fugue. ¶~풍의 곡 a fugate.
푸근하다 comfortably warm; mild. ⇨ 포근하다
푸념 1 [불평] an idle[a doleful] complaint; a grumble; grumbling. ¶노인의 ~ an old man's repeated grumbling. **푸념하다** grumble (at); complain (of / about); make complaints (to a person about something); whine (about); dwell on grievances; (미국구어) gripe (at / about). ¶물가고를 ~ complain [grumble] about high prices // 불운을 ~ complain about one's bad luck / (문어) deplore one's misfortune(s) // 그는 술을 마시기만 하면 푸념하기 시작한다 Whenever he drinks, he starts griping.
2 [무당의 꾸짖음] the ravings of a shaman (transmitting the rage of a spirit while in a trance). **푸념하다** rave.
푸다 (물 등을) draw (from); (국자 등으로) scoop (up); dip (up); (펌프로) pump (up); (배에 있는 물을) bail out. ¶국을 ~ ladle [spoon up] soup // 우물물을 ~ draw water from a well // 분뇨를 ~ dip up night soil // 삽으로 ~ shovel / take up with a shovel // 국자로 양동이에 물을 퍼 담다 ladle water into a bucket with a dipper / 솥에서 밥을 ~ scoop rice out of a pot / 밥그릇에 밥을 ~ serve rice in a bowl / serve out rice / fill a bowl with rice (from the pot) // (못물을) 다 ~ drain (a pond) / dry / bail out (a pond) / scoop water out of (a pond) / 독에서 쌀을 ~ scoop rice out of a jar
푸닥거리 [무당의 굿] an exorcism. **푸닥거리하다** perform an exorcism.
푸대접(-待接) unkind[uncivil] treatment; a cold[frigid] reception; inhospitality. ¶~을 받다 receive unkind treatment / be treated inhospitably // 그는 ~을 받고 있다 He is treated coldly. / He is kept in a low position. // 그는 점원에게 ~을 받아 화가 나 있다 He is angry because he was not given polite service by the clerk. **푸대접하다** treat [receive] (a person) coldly [with coldness / unkindly / in a cold way]; receive (a person) with indifference; be inhospitable (to); give (a person) a cold [frosty] reception (to); give [show / turn] the cold shoulder (to). ¶은혜를 베푼 사람을 푸대접해서는 안 된다 You should never be inhospitable to anyone to whom you are indebted.
푸드덕 flapping; fluttering. ¶ ~ 날개를 치다 flap [flutter] (its) wings.
푸드덕거리다 flap; flutter.
푸들 [개의 한 품종] a poodle.
푸딩 (a) pudding.
푸르다 1 [청색이다] blue; azure; [초록이다] green. ¶푸른 하늘 an azure sky // 푸른 눈의 소녀 a blue-eyed girl // 천을 푸르게 물들였다 I dyed the cloth blue. // 푸른 야채를 더 먹어

푸르디푸르다 freshly[vividly] blue; fresh and green; (서술적) be blue as blue can be; be green as green can be; be ever so blue [green]. ¶푸르디푸른 하늘 a pure blue sky / a perfectly clean blue sky.

푸르르 bubbling; (burn) crisply; trembling; (fly / whirr away) suddenly. ⇨ 포르르

푸르스름하다 (빛깔이) bluish; greenish; (서술적) be tinged with blue[green]; have a bluish[greenish] tint; (얼굴이) rather pale [pallid]. ¶등불이 푸르스름한 불꽃을 내며 타고 있었다 The lamp was burning palely.

푸르죽죽하다 sordidly bluish[greenish].

푸른곰팡이 [식] green mold; a penicillium (pl. -lia).

푸릇푸릇 all spotted green[blue]; green [blue] here and there. ¶온몸이 ~ 멍 들다 turn black and blue all over∥나뭇잎이 ~ 돋아났다 The leaves came out on the trees all fresh and green.∥그녀의 얼굴은 ~ 멍이 들어 있다 Her face is bruised dark here and there. **푸릇푸릇하다** verdant; fresh and green; be green[blue] here and there; be all spotted green[blue]. ¶푸릇푸릇한 신록의 계절 the season of fresh verdure.

푸새¹ (풀을 먹임) starching. **푸새하다** starch (linen). ¶옷을 ~ starch clothes.

푸새² (풀) grasses; plants; pasturage.

푸석돌 a crumbly stone; a loose rock.

푸석이 1 [부스러지기 쉬운 물건] a crumbly thing; fragile stuff. 2 [무르게 생긴 사람] a fragile[frail] person.

푸석푸석 [부스러지기 쉬운 모양] all crisp [crumbly / rotting away]. ¶~ 부서지다 crumble / break into crumbs. **푸석푸석하다** crumbling; crumbly; loose (soil); friable; (과일 등이) dry and tasteless[insipid]; (감자 등이) dry and crumbling; not pasty; (치즈가) snappy. ¶(나무가) 푸석푸석해지다 become crumbly / undergo dry rot.

푸석하다 [부스러지기 쉽다] crisp; crumbly; friable.

푸성귀 greens; green vegetables; greenstuff. ¶~를 가꾸다 grow greens / raise vegetables∥~로 김치를 담그다 pickle greens.

푸싱 [체] pushing.

푸주한(-漢) a butcher; (미국 속어) a meatman.

푸줏간(-間) a butcher's (shop); (미) a meat store[shop].

푸지다 abundant; plentiful; ample; lavish; profuse; generous. ¶푸진 음식 abundant food / generous portion∥푸진 대접 liberal treatment∥푸지게 in (great) plenty[abundance] / abundantly / plentifully / (미) aplenty / amply / fully / lavishly / generously / liberally∥푸지게 먹다 eat plenty.

푸짐하다 plentiful; abundant; copious; generous. ¶푸짐한 성찬 an abundance of good cheer. **푸짐히** abundantly; plentifully; profusely; amply; fully.

푸푸 puffing; in puffs. ¶~ 불다 puff and blow.

푹 1 [찌르는 모양] home; hard; through. ¶~ 찌르다 stab through / plunge (a knife into a person's breast) / thrust (a dagger) home∥사나이는 날카로운 칼로 가슴이 ~ 찔렸다 The man was stabbed in the chest with a sharp knife.∥그녀의 말 한마디가 내 가슴을 ~ 찔렀다 Her remark to me really hit home.
2 [뒤집어쓰거나 싸는 모양] completely; entirely. ¶모자를 ~ 눌러쓰다 pull[flap] one's hat over one's eyes / wear one's hat pulled low over one's eyes∥눈이 온 땅을 ~ 덮었다 The snow covered the ground completely.∥그는 담요를 머리 위로 ~ 덮어썼다 He pulled the blankets (up) over his head.∥그녀는 자기 아기를 담요로 ~ 둘러쌌다 She wrapped her baby up in a blanket.
3 [잠자는 모양] fast; sound(ly). ¶~ 자다 sleep soundly / be sound asleep / sleep like a top[log].
4 [쉬는 모양] thoroughly; completely; quite. ¶~ 쉬다 rest up / rest completely / have a good slack.
5 [흠씬] thoroughly; well; through. ¶고기를 ~ 삶다 do meat thoroughly∥~ 젖다 be wet [soaked] through [to the skin]∥그는 온천에 몸을 ~ 담가 피로를 풀었다 The long soak in the hot spring soothed his tired body.
6 [빠지거나 팬 모양] deep; deeply. ¶~ 파다 dig deep(ly)∥진창에 ~ 빠지다 be caught [stuck] deep in the mud∥악의 구렁텅이에 ~ 빠지다 be up to one's neck in crime / be steeped in vice∥그는 고개를 ~ 숙였다 His head sank forward on his breast.∥그는 편안하고 조용한 생활에 ~ 잠겨 있었다 He enjoyed a life of peace and tranquillity to the full.∥그는 그녀에게 ~ 빠졌다 He fell head over heels in love with the woman. / He fell headlong for the woman.
7 [쓰러지는 모양] (fall) with a clash[thud]; plump; flop. ¶~ 쓰러지다 fall with a clash [thud] / fall flat[plump].
8 [갑자기 줄어든 모양] sharply. ¶~ 줄다 decrease [decline / fall off] sharply [remarkably]∥지붕이 눈의 무게로 ~ 꺼졌다 The roof suddenly caved in under the weight of the snow.
9 [고개를 깊이 숙이는 모양]. ¶고개를 ~ 숙이다 bow one's head far down / sink one's head on one's breast[chest].
10 [썩는 모양] rotting completely.

폭신폭신 softly; gently; lightly. **폭신폭신하다** soft; downy; cottony; flossy; fluffy; spongy. ¶폭신폭신한 이불 a soft and fluffy quilt∥폭신폭신한 소파 a soft, comfortable sofa∥폭신폭신하고 따뜻해 보이는 방석 a bulging and warm-looking cushion∥이 의자는 폭신폭신하고 기분이 좋다 This chair gives comfortably.

폭신하다 soft; downy; cottony; flossy; fluffy; spongy. ¶폭신한 깃털 이불 a fluffy down quilt∥폭신한 스웨터 a fluffy sweater∥폭신한 베개 a fluffy pillow∥폭신한 쿠션 a soft cushion.

폭폭 1 [찌르는 모양] piercing[pricking] repeatedly. ¶바늘로 ~ 찌르다 keep pricking with a needle∥그는 쌀 가마를 칼로 ~ 찔렀다 He thrust his knife into the rice bag repeatedly.
2 [사정없이] blunt(ly); sharp(ly).
3 [아낌없이] freely; liberally; lavishly. ¶돈을 ~ 쓰다 spend money freely / be lavish [liberal] of one's money.
4 [삶는 모양] (boiling) completely; thor-

풀다

5 [날씨가 무더운 모양]. ¶~ 찌는 sultry / muggy / (damp and) close // 날이 ~ 찐다 It is steaming hot[sultry].
6 [썩는 모양] rotting rapidly[completely]. ¶날이 더워 고기가 ~ 썩는다 Meat rots fast because of the hot weather.
7 [빠지는 모양] sinking deep(ly). ¶발이 눈에 ~ 빠졌다 My feet sank deep in the snow.

푹하다 [퍽 따뜻하다] unseasonably warm; mild; soft. ¶푹한 겨울 a soft[mild / green] winter.

푼 1 [화폐 단위] a pun; Korean penny(=1/10 don). ¶돈 한 ~(도) 없다 be penniless / have not a penny[brass farthing / red cent] in the world / (미) be utterly broke // ~의 값어치도 없다 be not worth a farthing // 한 ~ 주십시오 (거지의 말) Tip[Spare] us a copper. / Alms, please. // 한 ~도 못 깎아요 I won't take a cent less. / I wouldn't come down a cent.
2 [무게 단위] a pun; a Korean penny-weight (=0.01323 ounce, 0.375 gram).
3 [길이 단위] a pun (=1/10 chi, 0.119 inch).
4 [백분비] percentage; percent. ¶3할 5~ thirty-five percent / 35% // 8~ 이자 8% interest // 이 채권은 5~의 이자가 붙는다 This bond bears five-percent interest.

푼돈 [적은 돈] a little[small amount of] money; a small sum; [얼마 안 되는 돈] (save) a small fortune; a trifling amount (of money); small change; a (mere) pittance; small[loose] coins; loose money. ¶~을 모으다 save money little by little / save pocket money[a petty penny] // ~을 아끼다 be penny-wise // 그는 ~깨나 모았다 He has piled up a small fortune. / He has saved a nice bit of money.

푼수 1 [정도] degree; extent; [율] rate; [비] ratio. ¶…의 ~로 at a rate of … // 세 사람 ~를 일하다 do three men's work // 이 ~로 나간다면 (if things go on) at this rate. 2 [어리석은 사람] a fool; a foolish person; an idiot.

푼푼이 penny by penny. ¶~ 모은 돈 money saved penny by penny[little by little].

푼푼하다 1 [넉넉하다] ample; sufficient; abundant. ¶푼푼한 돈[음식] abundant money[food]. **푼푼히** amply; abundantly; sufficiently. ¶옷의 품을 ~ 하다 ease a coat under the arms. 2 [너그럽다] large-hearted; broad-minded; liberal; generous; openhanded. ¶푼푼한 태도 an air of magnanimity / free and open manners. **푼푼히** liberally; generously.

풀¹ [초본 식물] grass(▶ 풀의 종류를 말할 때는 가산(可算) 명사); [잡초] a weed(▶ 종종 복수형); [약초] an herb; [집합적] herbage. ¶~잎 a blade of grass // ~이 무성한 언덕 a grassy hill / 한 포기의 ~ one clump of grass // ~ 베는 사람 a mower / ~을 깎는 기구 a (lawn-)mower // ~이 무성한 벌판 a field overgrown with grass // ~을 베다 cut[mow] grass // 정원의 ~ a weed in a garden // ~이 무성하다 be overrun[overgrown / rank] with grass[weeds] // 잔디밭의 ~을 뽑다 weed the lawn // 정원은 ~로 온통 뒤덮여 있었다 The garden was overrun[overgrown] with weeds. // 소가 목장에서 ~을 뜯어 먹고 있다 The cattle are grazing[feeding on

grass] in the pasture.

풀² 1 [끈끈한 물질] paste(밀가루로 만든); starch(녹말로 만든); glue(아교풀); gum(고무풀); a size(피륙에 먹이는). ¶~이 잘 먹은 well-starched (cloth) / starchy (shirt) // ~과 가위로 하는 일 [누덕누덕 깁는 수공] mere patchwork / [주워 모아 독창성 없는 일] a scissors-and-paste job // ~이 너무 먹은 셔츠 a stiffly starched shirt // ~을 개다 temper starch with water // ~을 쑤다 make paste // 이 손수건은 ~이 잘 먹었다 This handkerchief is well starched. 2 [기운] spirit(s); heart; starch.

풀(을) 먹이다 starch (linen). ¶빳빳하게 풀을 먹인 옷 stiffly starched clothes // 이것에 풀을 먹여 주시오 I want this to be starched.

풀(이) 서다 become stiff with paste.

풀(이) 죽다 1 (옷 등이) lose (its) starch; get limp. ¶풀이 죽은 칼라 a limp collar. 2 (사람이) be disheartened; be down in[at] the mouth; be in the blues[dumps]; be cast down; be downcast; be downhearted; be crestfallen; be dejected; be dispirited; be out of spirits. ¶풀 죽은 얼굴을 하다 look blue [downcast] / be down (in the mouth) // 몹시 풀 죽어 있군그래! 어찌된 일이냐 You look awful(ly) blue! What's the matter (with you)? // 선생님께 꾸지람 들었다고 풀 죽지 마라 Don't be so dejected just because you were scolded by the teacher. // 그런 일을 갖고 풀 죽을 필요 없다 What is the use of losing heart over such an affair? // 그는 의기양양하여 담판하러 갔으나 풀 죽어 돌아왔다 He went in high spirits to negotiate, but came away disheartened[downcast]. // 위원회에서 계획을 거부당하여 그는 완전히 풀 죽었다 After the committee rejected his plan, he looked utterly crestfallen. // 그는 경마에서 많은 돈을 잃고 풀 죽어 있었다 Having lost a lot of money at the horse races, he was crestfallen[in a dejected state]. // 그는 풀 죽은 표정을 하고 있었다 He looked discouraged[(구어) let down]. // 뜻밖의 불행으로 그는 아주 풀이 죽었다 He was completely discouraged[disheartend] by the unexpected misfortune. // 너무 성적이 나빠서 나는 아주 풀이 죽었다 I did so badly that I felt just terrible. / I was down in the dumps because I did so badly. // 기대했던 돈이 들어오지 않아서 그는 풀 죽어 있다 He is dejected[downhearted / very depressed] because the money he was expecting did not come through. // 넌 왜 그렇게 풀 죽어 보이니 Why are you looking so dejected[depressed / dispirited / disheartened]? // 자기의 제안이 거절되자 그는 풀 죽어 돌아갔다 His offer having been refused, he went back dejectedly[crestfallen].

풀³ 1 [수영장] a swimming pool; (영) a swimming bath. ¶온수 ~ a warm pool. 2 [경] a pool. ¶이익을 ~제로 하다 pool (a group's) profits.

풀기(-氣) 1 [빳빳함] stiffness; starchiness. ¶~가 있다 be starchy[starched / stiffened] // ~가 없다 be not starched / be unstarched [unstiffened]. 2 [활기] stamina; pep; vim; energy; vigo(u)r; vitality.

풀다 1 [묶은 것 등을 끄르다] untie (a string); undo (a bundle); unbind (a bandage); loosen (one's hair); unloose; unpack (a

풀리다

package); unfasten (a rope); unravel (a thread); disentangle (a knot); fray(천 등을); unknit(편물을); untwist; untwine(꼰 것을). ¶밧줄을 ~ untie a rope // 꾸러미를 ~ undo a package // 구두끈을 ~ unlace one's shoes // 매듭을 ~ disentangle a knot // 여장을 ~ one's traveling clothes // 머리를 ~ let down one's hair // 복잡하게 얽힌 매듭을 ~ disentangle a complicated knot // 매듭이 진 실을 ~ disentangle a knotted thread // 편물을 ~ unravel one's knit // 헝클어진 털실을 풀었다 I untangled [disentangled] the yarn.
2 [문제 등을 해결하다] solve (a question); work out (a difficult problem); answer (a question); explain; clear up (the meaning). ¶방정식을 ~ solve [reduce] an equation // 고대의 수수께끼를 ~ solve [clear up] the mysteries of ancient times // 수학 문제를 ~ solve a problem in mathematics // 제곱[세제곱]을 ~ extract [find / take] the square [cubic] root (of) // 암호문을 ~ decipher / decode // 3차 방정식을 ~ solve a cubic equation // 서로 상의해서 문제를 ~ clear up [get at the nub of] a problem by talking about it // 그는 그들의 의혹을 풀어 주었다 He dispelled their doubts.
3 [해제하다] dissolve [cancel / rescind] (a contract); remove (a prohibition); lift (a ban); absolve (a person from an obligation); release; disengage. ¶포위[봉쇄]를 ~ raise a siege [blockade] // 자금 동결을 ~ thaw the frozen assets // 계엄령을 ~ lift martial law // 금지령을 ~ remove [lift] a ban // 요새의 포위를 ~ raise [lift] the siege of a fort.
4 [의심 등을 없애다] dispel (doubts); clear away [up]; remove (a misunderstanding). ¶기분을 ~ dispel [dissipate] the gloom / distract [divert] oneself // 의심을 ~ clear oneself of the charge (of theft) / dispel doubts // 원한을 ~ pay off old scores (with a person) // 오해를 ~ dispel a person's misunderstanding // 그의 노여움을 푸는 데 애먹었다 I had difficulty in appeasing his anger. // 나는 어떻게든 이 의심을 풀고 싶다 I want to clear myself of this suspicion somehow or other. // 나는 일요일에 낚시로 기분을 풀고 있습니다 I forget my troubles by going fishing on Sundays. // 이 오해를 어떻게 풀어야 할지 모르겠다 I don't know how to explain away [talk my way out of] this misunderstanding.
5 [감긴 실 등을 끄르다] draw [work] out.
6 [사람을 동원하다] call [send / draw] out (troops). ¶증원 부대를 ~ send out fresh troops / reinforce (the guards).
7 [액체에 다른 물질을 타다] dissolve; melt. ¶도료를 ~ dissolve a paint.
8 [피로 등을 사라지게 하다] relieve; banish. ¶피로를 ~ relieve one's fatigue / freshen up // 몸을 ~ [준비 운동을 하다] warm up / limber up // [해산하다] deliver a child / give birth to a child // 굳어진 목의 근육을 ~ get rid of the stiffness in one's neck / loosen up the stiff muscles around a person's neck / massage a person's neck and shoulders // 헤엄치기 전에 몸을 풀어라 Limber up before swimming.
9 [긴장을 없애다] relieve; relax; ease; unwind. ¶긴장을 ~ relieve the tension // 마음을 ~ ease oneself / ease one's mind // 빳빳한 어깨를 부드럽게 ~ ease [relieve] the stiffness in one's shoulders // 식후의 위스키 한 잔은 긴장을 풀어 준다 A drink of whisky after dinner relaxes me [(구어) helps me unwind].
10 [화 등을 가라앉히다] appease; calm; pacify. ¶화를 ~ quell [appease] one's anger // 갈증을 ~ quench thirst // 시장기를 ~ appease [alleviate] one's hunger // 한 조각의 빵은 내 굶주림을 풀어 주지 못했다 A (single) piece of bread was not enough to satisfy [appease] my hunger. // 나는 샘물로 갈증을 풀었다 I quenched my thirst with water from the spring. // 그녀는 어머니에게 화풀이를 하여 울분을 풀었다 She vented her anger on her mother.
11 [소원을 이루다] realize; satisfy; gratify. ¶소원을 ~ realize one's desire / gratify one's wishes / have one's wish fulfilled.
12 [콧물을 나오게 하다] blow (one's nose). ¶코를 세게 ~ blow one's nose hard // 손수건으로 코를 ~ put a handkerchief to one's nose.
13 [논으로 만들다] turn land into (a paddy); create (a paddy) out of land. ¶개펄에 논을 ~ turn shoreland into paddies.

풀리다 1 (맺힌 것이) get [come] loose; come untied [undone]; (얽힌 것이) become disentangled; (가장자리 등이) fray; be frayed; (구두끈이) become unlaced. ¶풀리지 않는 양말 (미) runproof [(영) ladderproof] stockings / (비유) 실마리가 ~ find a clue (to) // 얽힌 실뭉치가 풀리지 않는다 The ball of yarn just won't come untangled. / I can't get the ball of yarn untangled. // 내 구두끈이 풀렸다 My shoelace has come undone. // 매듭이 풀리려 한다 The knot is coming untied.
2 (화 등이) be allayed; (마음이) relent (toward a person). ¶그녀는 아직도 가슴속에 노여움이 풀리지 않고 있었다 Anger smoldered in her heart. // 그의 노여움이 풀렸다 His anger melted away. / His anger disappeared [vanished]. // 그들의 (나쁜) 사이는 아직도 풀리지 않았다 There still has been no thaw in the chilly relations between them.
3 (의혹 등이) be solved; be resolved; be dispelled; be removed; be cleared; be dissipated; disappear; vanish. ¶풀리지 않는 문제 an unsolved [insoluble] problem / 혐의가 ~ be cleared of a charge // 그의 오해가 아직도 풀리지 않았다 So far we have not been able to dispel [clear up] his misunderstanding. // 마침내 그 수수께끼가 풀렸다 I have finally solved the puzzle. // 그에 대한 의심은 아직도 풀리지 않고 있다 My suspicions about him have not yet cleared up [(문어) been dispelled]. // 그의 설명을 듣고 의혹이 풀렸다 His explanation has dispelled [resolved] my doubts. // 나는 혐의가 풀려 기쁘다 I am glad to be cleared of suspicion [the charge].
4 (수학 문제 등이) work out. ¶그 문제는 좀처럼 풀리지 않는다 The sum won't work out.
5 [해방되다] be (get) freed. ¶갇혔던 몸이 ~ be released (from prison).
6 [해제・제거되다] be removed; be lifted [raised]. ¶금지령이 풀렸다 The ban was removed [lifted]. // 포위가 풀렸다 The siege was raised [lifted]. // 독기운이 차츰 풀렸다 The poison worked [wore] off. // 수도의 계엄령은 아직 풀리지 않고 있다 The capital is still under martial law. / Martial law has not yet been lifted in the capital.

7 [용해되다] dissolve; become dissolved; melt; (언 것이) be thawed out; thaw. ¶물에 ~ (풀 수 있다) be soluble in water∥땅은 곧 풀릴 것이다 The ground will thaw soon.
8 (소원이) get realized; be fulfilled. ¶소원이 ~ have[get] one's desire fulfilled / have one's wish realized.
9 (긴장이) become[get] remiss; remit; relax; slack(en); flag. ¶그 한 마디로 그의 기분이 풀렸다 That one word made him feel relieved. ∥양자 간의 긴장된 감정이 차차 풀렸다 The emotional tension between the two parties has gradually relaxed.∥그녀의 말 한마디로 좌중의 긴장이 풀렸다 At her words, the tension in the room lifted[everyone relaxed].
10 (추위가) abate; moderate; go down. ¶추위가 한결 풀렸다 The cold has remarkably abated.
11 (피로가) be relieved (of); get over (from); recover (from). ¶피로가 ~ be relieved of one's fatigue / get over[recover] from one's fatigue∥더운 목욕을 하고 나니 뻣뻣한 어깨가 풀렸다 A hot bath relieved[eased] the stiffness in my shoulders.∥커피 한 잔에 피로가 풀렸다 A cup of coffee relieved my fatigue.
12 (눈이) become bleared; get[go] bleary. ¶눈이 풀렸다 My eyes got bleared. / I had bleary eyes.

풀무 (a pair of) bellows; a blower; a forge. ¶손 ~ a hand bellows∥~로 불을 피우다 use bellows on a fire and get it going.
●**풀무질** blowing with the bellows. ¶~을 하다 blow with a bellows / work[blow] a bellows.

풀밭 grassland; a grassy[weedy] place; a lawn(잔디밭); a green (field); [목초지] a meadow; a pasture. ¶~에서 놀다 play on the grass∥~에 누워 뒹굴다 lie down on the grass∥~에 누워 자다 sleep on a bed of grass.

풀백 [축구] a fullback(약어 f.b., fb).
풀베이스 (*full base) loaded bases.
풀빛 (dark) green.
풀뿌리 grass roots; the roots of grass.
풀 세트 [테니스] a full set. ¶시합이 ~가 되었다 The match went the full five sets.
풀숲 a bush; a thicket.
풀썩 **1** [먼지·연기 등이 별안간 일어나는 모양] rising lightly. ¶먼지가 ~ 났다 A great cloud of dust rose lightly.∥연기가 ~ 났다 A cloud of smoke rose suddenly.∥자동차가 지날 때 먼지가 ~ 났다 A motorcar raised a cloud of dust as it passed. **2** [주저앉는 모양] collapsing. ¶땅 위에 ~ 주저앉다 flop down on the ground∥집이 ~ 내려앉았다 A house collapsed completely.

풀어내다 **1** [줄 등을 끌러 내다] pay out (a line); (얽힌 것을) unravel (a thread); disentangle (a knot). ¶거미는 실을 풀어내어 거미집을 쳤다 The spider spun out its thread and made a wed. **2** [밝혀내다] clear up (the meaning); work out (a difficult problem); solve (a question). ¶수수께끼를 ~ solve [untangle] a mystery / solve[read / undo] a riddle / work[make] out a puzzle ∥방정식을 ~ solve[reduce] an equation.

풀어놓다 (여러 사람을) put; send; dispatch. ¶형세를 알아보려고 사람들을 ~ put[dispatch] men to feel the situation.

풀어지다 **1** get loose; be allayed; be solved; work out. ⇨**풀리다** **2** [국수·죽이 느슨히 풀리다] lose (its) glutinousness; become loose[unstuck].

풀오버 a pullover.
풀이 (an) explanation; elucidation; exposition; (an) interpretation. **풀이하다** interpret; construe; explain; elucidate; expound. ¶옳게 [잘못] ~ interpret rightly[falsely].
풀잎 a blade of grass; a grass leaf.
풀질 pasting; applying paste. **풀질하다** paste; apply paste (to).
풀쩍 [문을 갑자기 열거나 닫는 모양] [closing] the door suddenly; [뛰거나 나는 모양] lightly leaping[jumping]. **풀쩍하다** keep opening and closing (the door). ⇨**풀쩍거리다**
풀쩍거리다 keep opening and closing (the door); come in and go out all the time; keep coming in and going out; lightly leap [jump].
풀치다 release; free from (troublesome thoughts). ¶생각을 ~ put one's mind at ease.
풀칠(-漆) **1** pasting. ⇨**풀질** **2** [겨우 끼니를 이어 감] bare living[livelihood]. **풀칠하다** make one's living; keep the pot boiling; eke out a living. ¶겨우 입에 ~ eke out a scanty livelihood / live from hand to mouth∥입에 풀칠하기도 어렵다 have no means of livelihood / find it difficult to make a living.
풀 카운트 [야구] a full count. ¶투 스리로 ~가 되었다 There is a full count on the batter.
풀타임 full-time. ¶~의 교사 a full-time teacher∥~ 임금 full-time wages∥~으로 일하다 work full time.
풀풀 **1** [눈 등이 흩날리는 모양] in flakes. **2** [뛰거나 나는 모양] flying[running] swiftly [nimbly]. **3** [끓는 모양] boiling hard; seething. ¶물이 ~ 끓는다 Water is boiling up.
풀피리 a grass harp.
품¹ **1** [옷의 폭] width (of a coat). ¶앞[뒤] ~ the breast[shoulder] width∥~이 손 저고리 a too tightly cut coat. **2** [가슴] the bosom; the breast. ¶산[대자연]의 ~ the bosom of a mountain[of Nature]∥단도를 ~에 넣고 with a dagger in one's bosom∥어머니의 ~에 안긴 갓난아기 an infant nestling in its mother's breast∥상대[적]의 ~속으로 뛰어들다 get in close to one's adversary.
품² [수고·힘] trouble; labor; work. ¶하루 ~ a day's work[labor]∥~이 많이 드는 일 a troublesome[time-consuming] job∥열 사람 ~이 드는 일 work requiring ten hands to do∥~이 들다 require[cost] (much) labor / be troublesome∥~을 덜다 save (oneself) labor ∥그 일은 꽤 ~이 든다 The work requires much labor.
품(을) 갚다 work in return; do return service to (a person's) help.
품(을) 팔다 work for (daily) wages; do piecework [job work / odd jobs]; work as a day laborer; work by the day.
품³ [외양] (personal) appearance; [방식] a way; a fashion. ¶사람 생긴 ~ a person's (personal) appearance∥사람된 ~ (a) personal character / (a) personality∥날뛰는 ~ the way one gambols about / the wild [arrogant] way one behaves.

품(品) 1 quality. ⇨ 품질 2 [품계] (official) rank; order. ¶정[종]2~ the senior[junior] grade of the second (court) rank. 3 (a) grace. ⇨ 품격

-품(品) [물품] an article; a piece; an item. ¶국산~ home made[domestic] goods∥가공~ processed goods∥필수~ a necessary article.

품값 charge for labor. ⇨ 품삯
품갚음하다 do return service to (a person's) help; work in return.
품격(品格) (a) grace; dignity; character. ¶~이 있다 be elegant[refined / dignified].
품계(品階) a (court) rank; rank.
품귀(品貴) a scarcity[shortage / paucity] of goods[stock / supply]; an inadequate supply[an undersupply] of goods. ¶등유는 지금 ~ 상태가 되어 있다 The kerosene in stock is running short[low]. / Kerosene is in short supply.
품꾼 a piecework man. ⇨ 품팔이꾼
품다 1 [안다] hold[take] (a child) in one's arms; embrace; hug; [품속에 지니다] conceal. ¶악한은 단도를 품고 있었다 The villain carried a dagger concealed. / A dagger was found on the ruffian's person.
2 [마음에 지니다] harbor (suspicion); entertain; cherish; nourish; bear; hold; nurse [foster]; hoard; have. ¶반감을 ~ harbor [have] ill feelings / feed antipathy (toward(s))∥의심을 ~ harbor suspicions / have doubts∥원한을 ~ bear a grudge (against a person) / bear ill will (toward(s) a person)∥희망을 ~ cherish a hope (that)∥나는 그에게 살의를 품었다 I felt the urge to kill him.∥이 분쟁은 많은 문제를 품고 있다 This dispute involves many problems.∥그녀는 마음속에 그에 대한 원한을 품고 있었다 She held[harbored] a deep grudge against him.∥그는 그 방식에 의문을 품고 있었다 He had[entertained] doubts about that method. / He was skeptical about that method.
3 [알을] brood; sit (on eggs). ¶알을 품고 는 암탉 a sitting hen∥알을 품게 하다 set (a hen) on eggs∥암탉이 알을 품고 있다 The hen is sitting on (her) egg.
품등(品等) [등급] a grade; [품질] quality.
품명(品名) the name of an article.
품목(品目) [물품의 종류] an item; [목록] a list of articles. ¶~별로 by item∥수입 ~ (a list of) the items imported∥영업 ~ business items / items of business.
품사(品詞) [언] a part of speech. ¶8~ the eight parts of speech.
품삯 charge[pay / wages] for labor. ¶~을 치르다 pay (a person) for his trouble[labor] / pay (a person) by the piece∥~을 받다 receive one's wages[pay] for the labor∥~을 받고 일하다 work by the day / hire out.
품성(品性) character. ¶~의 도야 character building / cultivation of character∥~을 도야하다 build one's character∥그는 ~이 고결한[비열한] 남자이다 He is a man of noble [ignoble] character.
품성(稟性) [타고난 성질] nature; character.
품속 the bosom; the breast. ¶~에 안다 hold [take] (a child) in one's arms[breast]∥그는 ~에 한 푼도 없었다 He was utterly penniless.∥그는 사표를 ~에 지니고 출근했다 He went to the office with his resignation in his pocket.

품앗이 exchange of services; an exchange of labor. **품앗이하다** exchange services.
품위(品位) 1 [품격] dignity; (a) grace; nobility. ¶~ 있는 [위엄이 있는] dignified / [고상한] noble∥~가 없는 unrefined / coarse∥~를 떨어뜨리다 degrade[disgrace] oneself / lose one's dignity∥그런 일을 하면 당신의 ~를 떨어뜨립니다 Such an act would be beneath your dignity. / You will degrade yourself by such an act.∥노력은 사람의 ~를 높인다 Effort ennobles a man.∥그녀는 ~ 있는 사람이다 She has grace and dignity.
2 [광석 중의 금속의 비율] (a) grade; [금이나 다이아몬드의 성분 비율] a carat. ¶저~광 low-grade ore∥~ 18의 금반지는 순금 75퍼센트를 함유한다 An 18-karat gold ring is 75 percent pure gold.
3 [품계] a (court) rank. ¶~가 높은 사람 a person of high rank.
품의하다(稟議-) circulate the draft of a plan to obtain the sanction of (executives).
품절(品切) absence of stock. ¶~이 되다 run out of stock / be sold out∥일용품이 ~되지 않도록 하다 keep daily necessities in stock all the time∥흑설탕은 ~입니다 Brown sugar is out of stock. / We are out of brown sugar.∥~ 〈게시〉 All gone. / All sold. / Sold out.
품종(品種) [물품의 종류] a kind; [동물의] a breed; [동식물의 변종] a variety. ¶양의 ~을 개량하다 develop a better breed of sheep∥포도의 새 ~을 만들어 내다 produce a new variety of grapes.
● **품종 개량** (동물의) improvement of breed; cattle breeding; (식물의) improvement of plants; plant breeding. ¶토마토의 ~ improvement of a species of tomato.
품질(品質) quality. ¶~이 좋은 물건 a high-quality[superior / fine] article∥~이 떨어지는 상품 inferior goods∥…에 비하여 ~이 떨어지다 be inferior to (a thing) in quality∥이 비누는 ~이 좋다[나쁘다] This soap is of good[poor] quality.
● **품질 관리** quality control(약어 QC). **품질 보증** a guarantee of quality; 〈게시〉 Quality Guaranteed.
품팔이꾼 a piecework man; a pieceworker; a day laborer; a casual laborer; a charwoman(여자).
품팔이하다 work for (daily) wages; do piecework[job work]; do odd jobs; work as a day laborer; be hired[(미국 구어) hire out] by the day.
품평(品評) estimation; evaluation; judgment; criticism. **품평하다** estimate; evaluate; judge; criticize.
● **품평회** a (competitive) show[exhibition]; (미) a fair. ¶농수산물 ~ an agricultural fair∥~에 참가하다 enter a competition for the prize.
품하다(稟-) proffer (something) to a superior for approval; submit (a plan) to a superior; inquire of a senior (about something).
품행(品行) (moral) conduct; behavior; demeanor; deportment; moral character; morals. ¶~이 나쁜 남자[여자] a libertine[a wanton woman] / a man[woman] of loose morals∥그는 ~이 좋다[나쁘다] He behaves [conducts] himself well[badly].∥그는 ~이

단정하다 He is a man of good conduct. / His conduct is above reproach [perfect / exemplary]. // 그는 아들의 ~이 나빠서 걱정하고 있다 His son's loose morals worry him.

풋- [덜 익은] green; unripe; [새로 나온] new; fresh; [미숙한] green; novice; inexperienced.

풋감 a green [an unripe] persimmon.

풋거름 green manure.

풋것 [처음 것] the first product (of fruit, vegetables, etc.) of the season [year]; [덜 익은 농산물] unripe product (of grain, fruit, vegetables, etc.).

풋고추 an unripe hot pepper.

풋곡식(-穀食) unripe grain.

풋과실(-果實) green [unripe] fruit.

풋김치 gimchi (kimchi) prepared with young vegetables.

풋나기 → 풋내기

풋나물 (a dish of) young herbs.

풋내 smell of fresh young greens [herbs]. ¶~가 나다 smell of greens / [비유] be green [unfledged / callow] / smell of one's mother's milk / be inexperienced [unskilled].

풋내기 1 [미숙한 사람] a new [green / raw] hand; a beginner; a novice; (미) a tenderfoot; a neophyte; a freshman; (영) a fresher; (구어) a greenhorn; (직공 등) a new [green] hand; [신참자] a newcomer. ¶~ 변호사 a newly-qualified lawyer / a lawyer who has just begun to practice // ~ 기자 a novice [cub] reporter // ~ 시인 a poetaster // ~ 화가 a daubster // ~ 문필가 a hack writer / a scribbler // ~ 의사 a quack (doctor). 2 [경솔한 사람] a rash person; a hotspur.

풋담배 green tobacco.

풋바심 harvesting grain before it is ripe. 풋바심하다 harvest (rice) too early [before it is ripe / while it is unripe].

풋밤 a green [an unripe] chestnut.

풋벼 unripe rice.

●풋벼바심 harvesting unripe rice.

풋볼 [축구] association football; soccer; [럭비] rugby; (구어) rugger (▶ 정식으로는 rugby football). ¶아메리칸 ~ (American) football (▶ 미국에서는 단순히 football이라고 함) // ~ 경기 a football game [match] // ~ 선수 a football player / a footballer // ~을 하다 play football.

풋사랑 transient [fleeting] love; calf [puppy] love (소년 소녀의); fickle love (들뜬).

풋워크 [체] footwork. ¶~가 흐트러지다 lose one's footwork // 그는 ~가 좋다 He has good footwork.

풋콩 green [unripe] beans.

풍(風) 1 a boast; a brag. ⇨ 허풍 2 [풍병] palsy; paralysis.

-풍(風) [차림] a look; appearance; one's getup; [태도] bearing; mien; deportment; manner; [유파·식·형] a style; a fashion; a type; a mode; [풍습] manners (and customs); a custom; ways; [기질] disposition; turn of mind. ¶도회~ town [urbane] manners / urbanity // 프랑스~ a French style.

풍경(風景) 1 scenery; a view. ⇨ 경치 2 a landscape. ⇨ 풍경화(⇨ 풍경)

●풍경화 a landscape. ¶유화의 ~ a landscape in oil.

풍경(風磬) a wind-bell; a small hanging bell that tinkles in the wind.

풍광(風光) scenery; a view. ⇨ 경치 ¶부근의 ~을 해치다 spoil the natural beauty of an area.

풍구(風-) 1 [바람을 일으켜 쭉정이 등을 제거하는 농기구] a winnowing machine; a winnower. 2 (a pair of) bellows. ⇨ 풀무

풍금(風琴) [오르간] an organ; a harmonium; (손으로 돌리는) a hand organ.

풍기(風紀) discipline; (사회의) public morals; (남녀간의) (sexual) morality. ¶사회의 ~ public [social] morals // 학교의 ~ school discipline // ~를 문란케 하다 [유지하다] corrupt [maintain] public morals. // ~를 단속하다 enforce discipline (among) / watch over [control] public morals // ~가 문란하다 Morals are corrupt. // 그 같은 일은 사회 ~를 몹시 해치는 것이다 That would be a gross offense against public decency.

●풍기 문란 demoralization; the decay of public morality.

풍기다 1 (냄새를) perfume; scent; give out [off / forth] an odor [a scent] (of); (냄새가) smell (of); hang [float] in the air [in midair]; (좋은 냄새가) be fragrant; (악취가) stink; reek (of / with). ¶올리브 꽃향기가 풍기는 마을 a village fragrant with olive blossoms // 옆방에서 가스 냄새가 풍겨 왔다 I smelled gas coming from the next room. // 그는 술 냄새를 풍기며 내게로 왔다 He came at me reeking of liquor. // 하수도가 악취를 풍긴다 The ditch stinks (offensively).

2 (새를) start [flush (up) / rise] (a bird); (새가) flush; fly [start] out; take wing; rise in the air; begin (its) flight. ¶개들은 새를 풍기려고 내달렸다 The dogs ran ahead to rise the birds.

3 (곡식을) winnow (grain); fan. ¶왕겨와 티를 ~ winnow chaff and dirt away.

풍년(豊年) a year of abundance; a rich [bumper] year; (풍작) a bumper harvest [crop]. ¶올해는 ~이 들 것 같다 We probably have a good harvest this year. / A bumper crop is expected this year. // 금년은 귤의 ~이다 This is a bumper year for the orange crop [harvest].

풍덩 plop; plump. ⇨ 풍당

풍뎅이 [동] a gold beetle; (미) a goldbug; (영) a chafer.

풍랑(風浪) wind and waves; heavy seas. ¶~에 시달리다 be buffeted by [at the mercy of] the wind and waves // ~과 싸우다 battle with [struggle against] the wind and waves.

풍력(風力) the velocity [force] of the wind; wind velocity. ¶자동 ~ 기록계 an anemograph // ~이 강해졌다 The wind gained in force.

●풍력계 an anemometer.

풍로(風爐) a mov(e)able [portable] cooking stove. ¶전기 [석유 / 가스] ~ an electric [an oil / a gas] cooker.

풍류(風流) 1 [운치] elegance; taste; refinement. ¶~의 (우아한) elegant / [품위가 있는] tasteful / [세련된] refined // ~의 길 elegant accomplishments / refined pursuits // ~를 아는 사람 a man of refined tastes // ~가 있는 정원 an elegant [a tastefully laid out] garden // ~를 알다 have an eye for the picturesque / have a love of the poetical // 그는 ~를 이해하지 못한다 He cannot appreci-

풍만하다

ate the poetic. 2 [음악] music.
● 풍류가 / 풍류객 / 풍류인 a man of taste; a person of a romantic turn of mind.

풍만하다(豊滿-) 1 [물건이 넉넉하다] abundant; opulent. 2 [몸에 살이 탐스럽게 많다] plump; corpulent; voluptuous(▶「육감적인」이라는 느낌을 가짐); buxom; well-developed (breasts); stout (lady). ¶풍만한 가슴 well-rounded breasts // 풍만한 육체 a voluptuous figure // 그녀는 몸집이 ~ She is buxom. / She has an ample body.

풍매(風媒) [식] pollination by wind; anemophily. ¶~의 pollinated by wind / anemophilous.
● 풍매화 an anemophilous [a wind-pollinated] flower.

풍모(風貌) [용모] looks; [풍채] appearance. ¶~가 좋은 사람 a man of a fine appearance / a fine-looking man.

풍문(風聞) a report; a rumor; hearsay. ¶~에 듣다 hear from someone / know by [from] hearsay / (고) hear tell [say] (of / that ...) // ~을 퍼뜨리다 spread [start / circulate] a rumor / set a rumor afloat // …이라는 ~이다 rumor has it that ... / it is said [they say] (that) ... / there is a story going round that ... / there is a rumor (in the air) that ... // 세상의 ~ 따위엔 개의치 않는 것이 좋다 One shouldn't be concerned with hearsay. // 나는 그 소식을 ~으로 들었다 A little bird told me about it. // ~이 떠돌았다 A rumor got afloat [abroad].

풍물(風物) 1 scenery; a view. ⇨ˇ경치 ¶그는 전원의 ~을 사랑한다 He loves rural scenery. // 반딧불은 여름의 ~이다 Fireflies bring us the real feeling of summer. 2 [그 고장의 생활과 관계되는 것]. ¶독일의 ~ the scenery and customs [scenes and manners] of Germany / things German. 3 [농악에 쓰이는 악기] farmers' musical instruments.

풍미(風味) flavor; savor; taste; relish; tang(얼얼한); bouquet(술 등의). ¶고급 와인이 요리의 ~를 돋운다 Fine wine enhances the taste of a dish [brings out the best in food].

풍미하다(風靡-) overwhelm; dominate; predominate; sway; sweep; carry all (before one). ¶그는 일세를 풍미하였다 He was the most powerful [influential] politician of his day. // 그의 예술은 그 세기를 풍미했다 His art was a dominant influence during that century.

풍병(風病) [한] nervous diseases.

풍부하다(豊富-) abundant; plentiful; plenteous; rich; ample; abound in [with]; (서술적) be fertile in (schemes). ¶천연자원이 풍부한 나라 a country rich [abundant] in natural resources // 경험이 풍부한 사람 a man rich in experience // 풍부한 음색 a mellow tone [sound] // 상품의 풍부함 the great variety of articles for sale // 천연자원이 ~ be rich [(문어) abound] in natural resources // 경험이 ~ have a lot of experience / have a wealth of experience // 상상력이 ~ have a fertile [a lot of] imagination // 기지가 ~ be witty / have a wealth of wit // 그는 화제가 ~ He has a great [plentiful] stock of topics. // 그 상점은 재고가 ~ They have an abundant [(문어) a copious] supply of goods in stock at that store. **풍부히** plentifully; abundantly; richly; in abundance; in plenty. ¶지식을 ~ 하다 enrich one's knowledge // 내용을 ~ 하다 enrich the contents.

풍비박산하다(風飛雹散-) scatter [disperse / be scattered] (in all directions); [부서지다] break [be broken] to [into] fragments [splinters].

풍상(風霜) 1 [바람과 서리] wind and frost. 2 [세상의 고난] hardships; troubles; sufferings. ¶10년 ~ ten years' hardships // ~에 견디고 살다 endure the hardships of life.

풍선(風船) 1 [고무풍선] a (toy) balloon; a rubber balloon. ¶실을 맨 ~ a balloon on a string // ~을 불다 inflate a balloon // ~을 터뜨리다 break a balloon // ~이 터졌다 The balloon burst. 2 a balloon. ⇨ˇ기구(氣球) ¶광고 ~ an advertising [ad] balloon // ~을 띄우다 send up [fly] a balloon.
● 풍선껌 (a piece of) bubble gum. ¶~을 부풀리다 blow a bubble.

풍설(風雪) [바람과 눈] wind and snow; [눈보라] a snowstorm; [장기간의 맹렬한 눈보라] a blizzard. ¶배는 심한 ~ 속에 난항했다 The ship had a rough voyage in [fought against] the violent wind and snow. // 이 탑은 500년의 ~에 견뎌 왔다 This tower has weathered five hundred years.
● 풍설 주의보 a snowstorm warning.

풍설(風說) a report; a rumor. ⇨ˇ풍문

풍성하다(豊盛-) [넉넉하다] abundant; plentiful; ample; affluent; opulent; exuberant. ¶풍성한 수확 (추수) an abundant crop [harvest] (of rice). **풍성히** abundantly; plentifully; amply; affluently.

풍속(風俗) [풍습] manners and customs; [풍기] (public) morals. ¶고장의 ~ native [local] customs // ~을 문란케 하다 corrupt [degrade] public morals / vitiate public morals / encourage immorality / commit an indecent act // 남의 나라에 가면 그 나라 ~을 따라야 한다 When at [in] Rome, do as the Romans do.
● 풍속 사범 (행위) a violation of public morals; an indecent offence; (사람) violaters of public morals. **풍속화 / 풍속도** a genre picture [painting].

풍속(風速) wind velocity; the velocity of the wind. ¶순간 최대 ~이 초속 25미터에 달했다 The maximum instantaneous wind velocity reached 25 meters per second. / The wind blew at speeds of up to 25 meters per second. // 현재의 ~은 초속 30미터이다 The wind is blowing (at) [has attained a velocity of] 30 meters per second.
● 풍속계 an anemometer; a wind gauge.

풍수(風水) [민] 1 [음양오행설에 기초한 지술 (地術)] feng-shui; wind-and-water magic. 2 a geomancer. ⇨지관
● 풍수설 (the theory of) geomancy. **풍수지리설** [민] the theory of divination based on topography; Chinese geomantic principles.

풍수해(風水害) storm and flood damage. ¶논은 ~를 입었다 The rice fields were damaged by the storm and flooding.

풍습(風習) [풍속] manners and customs; [습관] a custom. ¶~의 customary // 사회[지방]의 ~ social [local] customs // 그 고장의 ~에 따라서 according to the custom of the place // ~에 따르다 observe [conform to] custom // 그녀는 찌쎄 집안의 ~을 따랐다 [따르지 못했다] She copied [could not adapt herself to]

the ways of the Choes.
풍식(風蝕) [바람에 의한 침식] wind erosion.
풍신(風神) 1 [바람을 주관하는 신] the god of wind. 2 (one's personal) appearance. ⇨ˇ풍채
풍악(風樂) (Korean) music. ¶~을 잡히다 have music performed[played] // ~이 울렸다 Music began.
풍압(風壓) wind pressure.
● **풍압계** a pressure-tube anemometer.
풍어(豊漁) a big[good] catch; a large haul. ¶~를 기원하다 pray for a good haul // 해변은 청어의 ~로 흥청거렸다 The shore was alive with people rejoicing over the large haul of herring. // 꽁치 ~였다 We got a big catch of mackerel pike.
풍요(豊饒) richness; abundance; fertility; productiveness; fruitfulness. **풍요하다** rich; affluent; fertile; productive; fruitful; abundant. ¶풍요한 땅 fertile[productive] land // 그들은 풍요한 사회에서 자랐다 They were brought up in an affluent society.
풍우(風雨) wind and rain; a rainstorm. ¶~ 대작하다 have a driving rainstorm.
풍운(風雲) 1 [바람과 구름] winds and clouds; elements. 2 [어지러운 형세] an unsettled situation. ¶~의 뜻을 품다 cherish an ambition / have an adventurous spirit // ~을 타다 take advantage of an unsettled situation (to do) // 유럽의 정세가 일대 ~을 안고 있다 A stormy outlook faces Europe.
● **풍운아** a lucky adventurer; a spirited fellow who seizes every opportunity and cuts a conspicuous figure.
풍월(風月) [청풍과 명월・아름다운 자연] the bright moon and cool breezes; beauties of nature; [시가(詩歌)] poetry. ¶~을 즐기다 enjoy the beauties of nature / take delight in communion // ~을 짓다 compose a poem / make verses // ~을 알다 know[understand] how to make verses // 그는 홀로 ~을 벗 삼아 살고 있다 He lives all alone, conversing only with nature[making nature his sole companion].
● **풍월객** a person who dabbles in poetry; a poet.
풍유(諷諭) a hint; insinuation; an indirect suggestion (of); [문] an allegory. **풍유하다** insinuate; suggest indirectly; allegorize; use allegory.
풍자(諷刺) a (stroke of) satire; a sarcasm; an innuendo (*pl.* ~(e)s); an irony; a squib; a skit. ¶사회 ~ a satire society. **풍자하다** satirize; innuendo; lampoon(신랄히); squib. ¶이 책은 (이 책이) 쓰여진 당시를 통렬히 풍자하고 있다 This book is a stinging satire on the times of its author.
● **풍자 문학** a satire; satirical literature. **풍자 소설** a satirical novel[story]. **풍자시** a satirical poem; a satire; a lampoon; a pasquinade. **풍자화**(-畫) [회화] a caricature; [풍자만화] a cartoon.
풍자적(諷刺的) satirical; sarcastic; ironical.
풍작(豊作) a good[an abundant] harvest [crop] (of rice); a bumper crop (of apples). ¶계속되는 ~ a succession crop[harvest] // 올해의 쌀농사는 잘 될 것 같다 The rice crop [harvest] looks good this year.
풍재(風災) wind damage. ⇨ˇ풍해(風害)
풍전등화(風前燈火) a light before the wind; a precarious situation to be in. ¶회사의 운명은 ~와 같다 The firm is in a precarious state. // 그의 목숨은 ~와 다름없다 His life hangs by a hair[a thread]. // 그 건물은 화재로 ~의 상태였다 The building was in imminent danger of fire.
풍조(風鳥) [동] a bird of paradise. ⇨ˇ극락조 (⇨극락)
풍조(風潮) 1 [해] the tide. 2 [세상이나 시대의 추세] a tendency; a trend; a drift; a genius; the tide[current / stream]. ¶세상의 ~에 따르다[거스르다] go with[swim against] the current[trend] of the times // 그는 돈이 만능이라는 ~를 개탄하고 있다 He deplores the public tendency to regard money as almighty.
풍족하다(豊足-) abundant; opulent; affluent; plentiful; rich; wealthy. ¶풍족한 군자금 abundant war fund / a well filled war chest. **풍족히** abundantly; opulently; affluently; plentifully; richly; wealthily. ¶큰 부자는 돈을 ~ 쓸 수 있다 A very rich man can be lavish with money. // 아버지는 용돈을 내게 ~ 주셨다 My father gave me a generous allowance.
풍진(風疹) [의] German measles; rubella. ¶~에 걸리다 contract German measles.
풍진(風塵) 1 [먼지] (wind-scattered) dust. 2 [세속 일] worldly[mundane] affairs; cares of life. ¶~을 피하다 stand aloof from worldly affairs.
● **풍진세계** this world of woe and tumult.
풍차(風車) a windmill.
풍채(風采) (one's personal) appearance; air; mien; getup; dash(씩씩한); presence. ¶~가 좋은 사람 a person of fine appearance [presence] / a person of good bearing // ~가 좋지 않은 사람 an insignificant-[undistinguished-]looking man / a man of no presence / a hog in armor // ~가 돋보이지 않는 사람 a person who doesn't look very impressive // ~가 좋다 be stately in mien / look stately / have a fine presence[appearance] // 그는 ~가 당당하다 He has fine[dignified] appearance. / He has a commanding presence.
풍치(風致) taste; [우아] elegance; (풍경의) scenic beauty. ¶~ 있는 경치 elegant / tasteful / charming // ~ 없는 경치 tame[dry and monotonous] scenery // ~를 해치다 spoil the beauty of a scene / disfigure a landscape (with advertisements) // 소나무가 경치에 ~를 더했다 Pine trees added to the beauty of the view.
● **풍치 지구** a scenic area; a landscape area; nature preservation area.
풍토(風土) natural features (of a region); climate. ¶~의 차이 climatic differences // 유럽의 ~에 익숙해지다 get acclimatized[(미) acclimated] in Europe / get used to the European climate.
● **풍토병** an endemic (disease); a local disease.
풍파(風波) 1 [바람과 물결] the wind and waves[sea]; (폭풍우) a storm; a tempest; (거친 파도) rough seas. ¶~를 만나다 be caught by a storm // 바다는 ~가 심하다 The wind and waves are high. / The sea is rough. // ~가 조용해졌다 The storm has[The wind and waves have] subsided. // 포경선은 ~를 무릅쓰고 출발했다 The whalers set sail in spite of the storm.

풍해

2 [인생의 고초] a storm. ¶인생의 ~ the storm [rough and tumble] of life // 그는 세상의 모진 ~를 이겨 내 온 사람이다 He has weathered the hard-ships of everyday life.
3 [불화] (a) discord; a quarrel; a trouble; disturbances; dissensions. ¶우리 집은 ~가 끊일 새가 없다 There is constant trouble in my family. // 그는 가는 곳마다 ~를 일으킨다 He causes trouble wherever he goes. // 우리 집에서는 ~가 인 적이 없다 There have not been any discord in my family. // 그 정책에 지금은 반대하지 마라. 지금은 ~를 일으킬 때가 아니다 Don't object to the policy now. This isn't the time to make waves.

풍해(風害) wind damage; damage from the wind; crop loss caused by the wind. ¶중부 지방은 ~가 격심했다 The storm did a great deal of damage in the central district.

풍해(風解) [화] efflorescence. **풍해하다** effloresce.

풍향(風向) the direction of the wind. ¶~이 좋다 The wind is favorable. // ~을 살펴 보자 Let's see which way the wind is blowing. // ~이 남쪽에서 서쪽으로 변했다 The wind has changed [shifted] from the south to the west.
● **풍향계** an anemoscope; a weathercock; a (weather) vane. ¶~는 바람 따라 돈다 The vane turns with the wind.

풍화(風化) 1 [지] weathering; aeration. **풍화하다** weather. ¶암석이 풍화해서 여러 가지 모양을 하고 있었다 The rocks had weathered [the elements had worn (down) the rocks] into various shapes. →¶풍화된 바위 a weathered rock. 2 [화] efflorescence. ⇨**풍해**(風解)
● **풍화 작용** weathering.

퓨리턴 [청교도] a Puritan.
퓨마 [동] a puma; a cougar.
퓨즈 a fuse. ¶안전 ~ a safety fuse // ~를 붙이다 fit a fuse (to) // ~를 교체하다 replace a fuse / replace a blown-out fuse with a new one // ~가 끊어졌다 The fuse has blown (out).

퓰리처상(—賞) a Pulitzer Prize (for poetry). ¶~ 수상자 a Pulitzer prizewinner.

프라이 [튀김] fry. ¶달걀 ~ fried eggs / (미) a sunny-side up // ~로 하다 fry.
● **프라이팬** a frying pan; (미) a frypan.

프라이드 pride. ¶~가 강하다 be (very) proud // 그는 자기가 하는 일에 ~를 가지고 있다 He is proud of [He takes pride in] his work.

프라이버시 privacy. ¶~의 침해 an intrusion [invasion] of privacy // 가정의 ~를 지키다 guard the privacy of one's home // 나는 아무에게도 ~를 침해당하고 싶지 않다 I don't want anyone to intrude (up)on [disturb] my privacy.

프라임 레이트 the prime rate. ¶~를 인하하다 lower [cut] the prime rate.

프락치 (@fraktsiya) a fraction.
● **프락치 활동** fraction activities.

프랑 [화폐 단위] a franc(약어 Fr, F). ¶프랑스 ~ a French franc(약어 Fr) / 스위스 ~ a swiss franc(약어 SFr) // ~화는 안정되어 있다 [하락했다] The franc is stable [has fallen].

프랑스 France; (공식명) the French Republic. ¶~의 French.
● **프랑스 어** French; the French language.

프래그머티즘 [철] pragmatism.

프러포즈 a proposal of marriage. ¶그녀는 최근 두 사람으로부터 ~를 받았다 She has recently had proposals (of marriage) from two men. **프러포즈하다** propose (to a girl). ¶나는 그녀에게 프러포즈하였다 I proposed to her [asked her to marry me].

프런트 [호텔 현관 접수계] (미) the front [reception] desk. ¶차봉수 씨, ~로 와 주시기 바랍니다 Mr. Cha Bongsu, please come to the (front) desk.

프런트 코트 a front court.
프레스 [압축 기계] a press.
프레스 센터 the press center.
프레올림픽 the Pre-Olympics; the Pre-Olympic Games.
프렌치드레싱 [요리] French dressing.

프로[1] 1 a professional (player). ⇨**프로페셔널** ¶~급의 (a player) on a professional level // ~로 전향하다 turn professional [pro] // ~의 세계에서 성공하다 make it among the pro / succeed as a professional // 그 권투 선수는 ~로 전향했다 The boxer has turned professional. 2 a proletarian. ⇨**프롤레타리아** 3 [퍼센트] percent.
● **프로 레슬링** pro(fessional) wrestling. **프로 야구** pro(fessional) baseball. ¶~ 선수 a professional baseball player // ~팀 a professional baseball team / a pro baseball team // ~ 올스타전 the game of the (1990) Korean Pro Baseball All-Star series. **프로 축구** a pro football.

프로[2] a program(me). ⇨**프로그램** ¶교양 ~ an educational program // 대북(對北) 방송 ~ a program beamed at North Korea / 라디오 [텔레비전] ~ a radio [T.V.] program // 연극 ~ a playbill / a theater program // 청취자 [시청자] 참가 ~ an audience-participation program [show] // 특별 ~ a feature [special] program // 다채로운 ~ a varied [diversified] program // ~ 중의 하나 an item [a number] on [in] the program // 그 ~는 몇 시부터입니까 What time does the program [show] come on? // 그 ~는 끝났다 The program was gone through. // 뉴스 해설이 ~에 삽입되었다 Commentary on the news was inserted in [worked into] the program. // 이것으로 오늘의 ~를 마칩니다 This concludes today's program [the program for today].
● **프로 편성** program(m)ing.

프로그래머 [컴] a (computer) programmer.
프로그래밍 [컴] program(m)ing.
프로그램 a program(me); (미국 구어) a card. ¶(운동회 등의) ~을 진행시키다 run off the events // ~을 짜다 arrange [prepare] a program / draw [get] up a program // 오늘은 ~이 다채롭다 We have a varied program today. // 그것을 ~에 싣자 Let us put it on the program. // 그녀의 노래가 ~의 맨 처음에 나와 있다 Her song is the first (item) on the program. // 만사는 ~대로 진행됐다 Everything went on as previously scheduled. // 그는 컴퓨터에 ~을 입력시켰다 He fed a program into the computer. // 그는 컴퓨터의 ~을 만들었다 He programmed a computer.

프로덕션 [영] a production; a (movie) studio.
프로듀서 (제작자) a producer; (연출가) a (program) director.
프로모터 a promoter.
프로세스 a process.

프로젝트 a project.
프로테스탄트 [기] a Protestant.
프로톤 [물][화] a proton.
프로파간다 propaganda; publicity.
프로판 가스 propane[liquefied petroleum] gas; LP gas; propane.
프로페셔널 a professional (player); (구어) a pro.
프로펠러 a propeller; (영) an airscrew; (항공속어) a prop. ¶~를 돌리다 spin the propeller // ~가 돌기 시작했다 The propeller began whirling.
프로포즈 →프리포즈
프로필 [옆모습] a profile; [인물 단평] a profile; a brief character sketch. ¶텔레비전에서 그 배우의 ~을 소개했다 There was a profile of that actor on television. / A profile of the actor was given on television.
프론트 (미) the front desk; (영) the reception (desk). ¶호텔 ~ 앞에서 만납시다 Let's see at the front desk of the hotel.
프롤레타리아 [무산자] a proletarian; [무산자계급] the proletariat.
● 프롤레타리아 문학[예술] proletarian literature[art]. 프롤레타리아 혁명[작가] a proletarian revolution[writer].
프롤로그 a prolog(ue) (to).
프롬프터 [연] a prompter.
프리랜서 a free lance; a free-lancer. ¶그녀는 ~로 일하기 위해 정규직을 버렸다 She gave up her regular job in order to free-lance.
프리마 돈나 a prima donna (*pl.* ~s, prime donne).
프리미엄 [할증금] a premium. ¶~이 붙다 command a premium // ~을 붙이다 put a premium (on) // 티켓에는 ~이 붙어 있다 A ticket commands a premium. / They are asking a premium for the ticket.
프리 배팅 (*free batting*) [야구] batting practice.
프리섹스 free sex[love].
프리 스로 [자유투] a free throw. ¶~를 넣다 [~로 득점하다] sink a free throw.
프리즘 [물] a prism. ¶직각 ~ a right-angled prism // ~의 prismatic.
프리지어 [식] a freesia.
프리 킥 [축구] a free kick.
프린터 [인쇄기·등사기] a printer.
프린트 a print; [인쇄물] a mimeographed copy[sheet]; (옷감의 무늬); (미) calico. ¶강의의 ~ a printed[mimeographed] synopsis of a lecture. 프린트하다 print; mimeograph. ¶우리는 전단을 프린트했다 We mimeographed the handbills. / We had the handbills mimeographed.
프림 (커피의) creamer.
프토마인 [화] ptomaine.
● 프토마인 중독 ptomaine poisoning.
플라멩코 flamenco. ¶~를 추다 dance the flamenco.
플라밍고 [동] a flamingo. (*pl.* ~(e)s).
플라스마 [물] plasma.
플라스크 a flask; a flasket(소형의).
플라스틱 (a) plastic; plastics.
● 플라스틱 제품 a plastic; plastic goods.
플라이 [야구] a fly (ball). [내야[외야] ~ an infield[outfield] fly // 희생 ~ a sacrifice fly // ~를 치다[쳐 올리다] fly (a ball) / pop (up / out) / hit a fly ball // ~를 잡다 catch a fly // 그는 좌익으로 ~를 쳤다 He flied out to left (field).
플라이급 (-級) [체] the flyweight. ¶세계 ~ 선수권 the world flyweight championship.
● 플라이급 선수 a flyweight.
플라잉 스타트 (*flying start*) [체] a premature start; a breakaway.
플라타너스 [식] a plane (tree); a platan(e); (미) a sycamore. ¶~ 길 an avenue lined with plane trees on both sides.
플라토닉 러브 [정신적인 사랑] platonic love.
플란넬 flannel. ¶면 ~ cotton flannel / flannelet(te).
플랑크톤 [생] plankton. ¶동물성 ~ zooplankton / animal plankton // 식물성 ~ phytoplankton / plant plankton // ~을 먹고 사는 물고기 a planktivorous[plankton-feeding] fish.
플래시 1 [사진] a flash; (a) flashlight. ¶~ 세례를 받다 be in a flood[flares] of flashlights // ~를 터뜨리다 light a flashbulb / snap a flashlight // 그는 ~ 세례를 받았다 He was the focus of a million flashing cameras. / He was bathed in the light from[in the glare of] camera flashes. 2 an electric torch. ⇨ 손전등
● 플래시 전구 a flashbulb; a flash lamp.
플래카드 a placard. ¶~를 들고 행진하다 march with placards lifted up // 우리는 ~를 들고 거리를 행진했다 We marched through the streets holding[carrying] placards. / We marched through the streets with placards raised.
플랜 [계획] a plan; a scheme. ¶~을 세우다 make[form / map out] a plan / form [contrive / lay down] a scheme.
플랜트 [설비 시스템] a plant.
● 플랜트 수출 export of (industrial) plants.
플랫 1 [음] a flat(기호 b). 2 [경기에서]. ¶10초 ~ flat at ten seconds / ten seconds flat // 100미터를 11초 ~으로 달리다 run a hundred-meter race[the hundred meters] in eleven seconds flat.
플랫폼 a platform (of a railway station). ¶2번선 ~ No.2 platform / platform No. 2 // 상행[하행] ~ an up[a down] platform // ~의 역명 표시판 a station name sign at a platform // ~에서 on the platform // ~을 떠나다 move [go] out of the platform // ~으로 들어가다 enter the platform // 상행[하행] ~에서 마중하다 meet (a person) on the up[down] platform.
플러그 [전] a plug. ¶단로(斷路) ~ a disconnecting plug // 연결 ~ an attaching plug // ~를 꽂다 plug in // ~를 소켓에 꽂다 put a plug in the socket // ~를 소켓에서 빼다 pull a plug out of the socket // 텔레비전의 ~를 전원에 꽂다 plug in a television (set).
플러그 인 [기능 확장용 소프트웨어] plug-in.
플러스 plus; [이익] a gain (to one's happiness); an advantage; an asset. ¶~ 요소 a plus factor // 조금이라도 ~가 된다면 if there is any gain // 4 ~ 8은 12 Four plus eight is [makes / equals] twelve. / Four plus eight are[make / equal] twelve. // 모두 해서 2,000원의 ~밖에 안 된다 All told, that means only a 2,000 won profit for me. // ~는커녕 도리어 손해가 되었다 Far from being a gain, it proved (to be) a loss. // 당신이 중국어를 할 수 있다는 것은 큰 ~가 된다 It's quite a plus [an asset / an advantage] that you can

speak Chinese. **플러스하다** 〔더하다〕 add to; 〔기여하다〕 contribute to; do (much) for. ¶500원을 더 플러스해 주겠다 I'll give you another 500 won. / I will add 500 won to it. ➔마이너스되는 점보다 플러스되는 점이 많다 The pluses outweigh the minuses.
● **플러스 기호** a plus (sign). **플러스마이너스** plus or minus. ¶그러면 ~ 제로다 〔이익이 없다〕 That means no gain[profit] for us. / 〔변함이 없다〕 That adds up to zero[nothing]. **플러스알파**(ˇplus alpha) plus something; plus extra; something extra. ¶보수는 90만원 ~가 될 것이다 Compensation will be 900,000 won plus a little more[plus something else].

플레어스커트 a flared[flaring] skirt.
플레이 a play. ¶**파인 ~** a fine play / 좋은 ~를 보이다 perform[do] a fine play // 그 팀은 거친 ~로 유명하다 The team is well-known for its rough play. // 그 시합에서 진기한 ~가 속출했다 In that game there was a crop of odd plays.
플레이보이 a womanizer; a lady-killer; a ladies' man; a Don Juan. (▶ playboy는 「바람둥이」의 뜻보다는 돈 많고 놀기 좋아하는 「한량」의 뜻이 강함)
플레이 볼 〔야구·테니스〕 play ball.
플레이어 〔선수·연주자〕 a player; 〔음반 연주기〕 a record player.
플레이오프 〔동점자의 결승 시합〕 a play-off. ¶~ 시합을 하다 have a play-off.
플레이트 〔물〕〔사진〕 a plate.
플로피 디스크 a floppy disk.
플롯 a plot. ¶소설의 ~ the plot of a story.
플루오르 〔화〕 fluorine.
● **플루오르화** (—化) 〔화〕 fluoridation.
플루토늄 〔화〕 plutonium(기호 Pu).
플루트 〔음〕 a flute. ¶~를 불다 play (on) the flute.
● **플루트 주자** a flutist; a flute player.
피¹ 1 〔혈액〕 blood. ¶**~바다** a pool[sea] of blood // ~의 순환 circulation of the blood / ~ 묻은 bloodstained / bloody // ~ 묻은 칼 a bloody[blood-stained] blade[sword] // ~와 땀의 결정 the fruit of[a thing won with] one's blood and sweat // ~에 주린 bloodthirsty / 코에서 ~가 나다 bleed at the nose // ~가 멎다 stop bleeding // ~가 묻다 become tainted with blood // ~를 토하다 smear with blood // ~를 흘리다 spill[shed / let] blood / ~를 토하다 spit (up) blood / eject blood / cough blood(기침하여) / vomit blood(위에서) // ~를 뽑다 draw blood / ~를 멎게 하다 stop the bleeding / check the flow of blood // ~를 뿜으며 쓰러지다 fall in a spray of blood // ~를 멎게 하려고 상처에 붕대를 감다 bandage a wound to stop the bleeding // ~가 흐른다 Blood flows[runs / courses]. // ~가 줄줄 흐른다 Blood streams[rains / trickles] down. // ~가 솟는다 Blood spurts[spouts / gushes out]. // 손수건은 ~가 묻어 있었다 The handkerchief was stained with blood. // 잇몸에서 ~가 나온다 The gums bleed. // 그의 입술에서 ~가 흐르고 있었다 His lip was bleeding. // 상처에서 ~가 흐르고 있었다 Blood was oozing from the wound. // 나는 아내에게 수혈하려고 ~를 150cc 뽑았다 I had 150cc of my blood taken as a transfusion for my wife.
2 〔혈연·겨레〕 blood; lineage; consanguinity. ¶~를 이어받다 descend (from) / be blood-related (to) // ~로 맺어져 있다 be related by blood (ties) (to) // 그녀에게는 시인의 ~가 흐르고 있다 A poet's blood runs in her veins. // 그에게는 동양인의 ~가 섞여 있었다 He had Oriental blood in his veins. // 그녀는 외국인의 ~를 이어받았다 She is of alien blood.
3 〔비유〕 ¶~를 끓게 하다 cause the blood to tingle / inflame the blood[ardor] (of) / stir (a person's) blood // 정의를 위해 ~를 흘리다 bleed for a righteous cause // 전쟁터는 ~바다를 이루었다 The battlefield was flooded with blood. // 그것을 보고 나는 ~가 얼어붙는 것 같았다 The sight made my blood curdle. // 나에게도 ~와 눈물이 있다 I am made of flesh and blood. / I am not a stock nor a stone. // 그는 아직 머리에 ~도 안 마른 녀석이다 He is wet behind the ears.
피는 물보다 진하다(속담) Blood is thicker than water.
피가 거꾸로 솟다 One's blood runs backward in one's veins.
피(가) 끓다 One's blood stirs[boils / tingles].
피도 눈물도 없다 be cold-blooded; be stony hearted; be stonehearted; be insusceptible to pity. ¶그는 피도 눈물도 없는 사람이다 He is cold-blooded[cruel].
피로 피를 씻다 have a quarrel with blood relations; Blood will have blood.
피를 나누다 be blood-related; be of the same blood; be consanguineous. ¶피를 나눈 형제 a blood brother / a brother by blood / a brother-german.
피를 말리다 curdle the blood.
피를 보다 result[end] in bloodshed. ¶그 사건은 끝내 피를 보게 됐다 The affair resulted in bloodshed.
피를 빨다 suck up blood; 〔착취하다〕 exploit.
피에 주리다 thirst for blood; be bloodthirsty.
피² 〔식〕 a Deccan grass; a barnyard grass [millet].
피³ 〔경멸·비웃음 소리〕 pooh!; pish!; pshaw! ¶~! 웃기지 마라 Pshaw! You're fooling me.
피검 (被檢) ¶~되다 be arrested (for violation of the election law).
● **피검자** the arrested; a person in custody.
피겨 (스케이팅) figure skating.
● **피겨 스케이팅 선수** a figurer; a figure skater.
피격 (被擊) ¶~되다 be attacked[assailed / assaulted] (by).
피고름 bloody pus.
피고용인 (被雇傭人) an employee; the employed(총칭).
피고(인) (被告人) (민사상의) a defendant; (형사상의) the accused; a prisoner at the bar.
● **피고(인)석** the dock; the bar. **피고(인) 측 변호인** the counsel for the defense[accused].
피곤 (疲困) fatigue; weariness; exhaustion; tiredness. **피곤하다** tired; weary; fatigued; exhausted. ¶오래 서 있으니 ~ be tired from standing // 아, ~ Oh, I'm tired. // 걸어 다녀서 피곤했다 I got tired walking round. // 그녀와 이야기하고 있으면 피곤해진다 Talking to her is tiring[tires me].
피골 (皮骨) skin and bones. ¶~이 상접[상련] 한 사람 an anatomy / a man of skin and bones // ~이 상접[상련] 하다 be reduced to a (mere) skeleton[bag of bones] / be all[just] skin and bones / be worn to a shadow.

피그미 a Pygmy; a Pigmy.
피난(避難) refuge; shelter; harborage; evacuation. **피난하다** seek safety in flight; take [seek] refuge (in a place / with a person); take [find] shelter (in); flee (to a place) for safety; evacuate(다른 지방으로). ¶사람들은 이웃 나라로 피난했다 People sought refuge in a neighboring country. / People fled to a neighboring country for safety. // 해일로 마을 사람들은 언덕 꼭대기로 피난했다 The villagers took refuge from the tidal wave on a hilltop. // 홍수 경보가 내렸으므로 마을 사람들은 각자의 집을 비우고 피난했다 A (general) flood warning was issued, and so the villagers evacuated their houses.
● **피난민** refugees; evacuees; displaced persons. **피난살이** refugee life. **피난처** a place of refuge [safety]; a shelter; a refuge; an asylum; a haven (of rest).

피날레 [음] a finale; [오페라] a grand finale.
피눈물 tears of blood [pain / great sorrow]; bitter tears. ¶~ 나게 번 돈 money raised by desperate means // ~을 흘리다 shed tears of blood [bitter tears] / weep tears of pain // ~나는 슬픔을 맛보다 (사람이) make one's heart bleed // 그는 ~ 나는 심정으로 처자와 이별했다 He bade farewell to his wife and children with a bleeding heart.

피닉스 [불사조] the ph(o)enix.
피다¹ **1** [꽃봉오리가 벌어지다] bloom; blossom; flower; open; come out; come [open] into flowers. ¶갓 핀 장미 a new-blown rose // 빨리 피는 early / precocious // 늦게 피는 꽃 a late flower // 제철이 아닌 때 핀 꽃 a flower which has bloomed out of season // 봄에 피는 화초 plants blooming [flowering] in spring // 활짝 burst into blossom // 한창 ~ be in all (its) glory // 복숭아꽃이 필 때에 in the peach blossom time // 피기 시작하다 begin to bloom / come into blossom [bloom] // 피어 있다 be in bloom [blossom] / be in flower / be out / be open // 꽃을 피게 하다 make flowers open [bloom] // 꽃이 피었다 The flowers opened [bloomed]. / The flowers are out. // 벚꽃이 피기 시작했다 The cherry blossoms are beginning to bloom. // 튤립은 봄에 핀다 Tulips bloom [are in bloom / are out] in (the) spring. (▶ blossom은 쓸 수 없음) // 이 꽃은 언제 핍니까 When does this flower come out? // 달리아가 멋지게 피어 있다 The dahlias are in magnificent bloom. // 사과나무가 꽃이 피기 시작했다 The apple trees are beginning to blossom. // (때 아닌) 철쭉꽃이 다시 피었다 The azaleas have bloomed twice. // 우리 집 벚나무가 제철이 아닌 2월에 꽃이 피었다 Our cherry tree bloomed unseasonably in February.
2 [불이 일어나 번지다] begin to burn; get lively; be kindled; be made; [연기가 일어나다] go up; rise; ascend; yield. ¶하늘로 피어오르는 연기 smoke rising into the air // 불이 피었다 The fire is made. // 석탄불이 피어 있다 The coal is living [burning]. // 불이 잘 피지 않는다 The fire is not made [started] well yet.
3 (얼굴 등이) bloom; (형편이) thrive; flourish; prosper; get on well. ¶활짝 피어 미인이 되다 bloom into a beautiful woman // 얼굴빛이 피었다 One's complexion bloomed. // 그도 이제는 아주 형편이 피었다 He is now in quite comfortable circumstances.
4 [곰팡이가 생기다] become [get] moldy [musty / fusty].
피다² → 피우다
피대(皮帶) a (leather) belt; (집합적) belting.
피동(被動) passivity; passiveness.
● **피동형** [언] the passive form.
피동사(被動詞) [언] a passive verb.
피동적(被動的) passive. ¶~으로 passively.
피둥피둥 1 (몸이). ~ 살찐 사람 a plump person / a fatty. **피둥피둥하다** fatty; fleshy; puffy; plump; (노인이) vigorous; hale and hearty; in green old age. ¶그는 여든이면서도 아직 ~ He wears his four score years lightly. **2** obstinately; stubbornly; headstrongly.
피땀 [무엇을 이루기 위한 노력과 정성] greasy sweat. ¶~ 흘려 번 돈 money raised by desperate means // ~ 흘리며 일하다 sweat blood / toil and moil // 이 돈은 ~이 어린 돈이다 The money was earned by hard work. / This money was earned with my blood, sweat, and tears.
피똥 bloody excrement [stool / feces].
피라미 [동] a minnow; a dace.
피라미드 a pyramid. ¶~형의 pyramidal / pyramidic(al) // ~식 조직 a pyramid organization // 이 건조물은 역~형이다 This building is an inverted pyramid.
피란(避亂) refuge; evacuation. ¶~을 가다 get away from war / take [seek] refuge (in a place) / flee (to a place) for safety / evacuate.
피랍(被拉) [납치됨] being kidnapped. **피랍되다** be taken away [captive / prisoner]; be kidnapped.
피력하다(披瀝-) express (one's opinion); give expression [vent] to (one's thoughts); make known; reveal. ¶흉중을 ~ unbosom oneself (to) / open [lay bare] one's heart (to) // 그는 흉중을 피력했다 He revealed what was on his mind. / He spoke his mind. / He expressed his true feelings.
피로(疲勞) fatigue; weariness; exhaustion. ¶정신적 [육체적] ~ mental [physical] fatigue [exhaustion] // 눈의 ~ eye strain // 여행의 ~ fatigue from a journey // ~를 모르는 tireless / inexhaustible // ~를 느끼다 feel fatigue [tired] // ~를 없애다 relieve [banish] one's fatigue / freshen up // 잠자서 ~를 없애다 sleep off one's fatigue // ~를 풀다 rest oneself / rest from one's fatigue // ~가 풀리다 be relieved of one's fatigue / get over [recover from] one's fatigue // 나는 ~가 풀렸다 [회복되었다] I have recovered from my fatigue. // 우리는 온천물에 목욕을 하여 여행의 ~를 풀었다 We had a bath at a hot spring to get over the fatigue of our journey. // 나는 잠을 자서 ~를 풀었다 I slept off my fatigue. // 목적지에 다다르자마자 나는 ~를 느꼈다 As soon as I arrived at my destination, I realized how tired I was. **피로하다** tired; weary; fatigued; exhausted. ¶녹초가 될 정도로 ~ be reduced to pulp / be dog-tired / be tired to death // 피로한 기색을 보이다 show signs of fatigue // 피로한 기색을 보이지 않다 show no trace of fatigue // 피로한 기색도 없이 tirelessly // 몹시 피로해 보이다 look very tired // **피로해지다** become fatigued / be tired / grow weary / become exhausted / be fagged / be knocked

피로연 a dinner for making an announcement. ¶결혼 ~ (give) a wedding reception[dinner] / (hold) an after-wedding celebration∥~을 베풀다 give a dinner in announcement of (one's marriage)∥그들은 그 호텔에서 결혼 ~을 열었다 They held the wedding reception at the hotel.

피뢰침(避雷針) a lightning rod[conductor].

피륙 piece goods; (미) dry goods; (영) drapery; textiles.
● **피륙 장수** a dealer in textile fabrics; (영) a draper.

피리 1 [국악기] a *piri*. 2 [리코더의 통속적인 말] a recorder.

피리어드 a period; a full stop. ¶~를 찍다 put a period (to).

피마자(蓖麻子) [식] a castor-oil plant; (씨) a castor bean.
● **피마자유** castor oil.

피막(皮膜) [의] a membrane; a film; a tapetum (*pl*. -ta).

피막(被膜) [의][동] a tunic; [의] a capsule.

피막이풀 [식] a marsh pennywort.

피망 [식] a green pepper; a pim(i)ento (*pl*. ~s).

피맺히다 extravasate; get bruised.

피멍 a bruise; a contusion.

피보험물(被保險物) an insured article[thing]; insured property.

피보험자(被保險者) a person insured; the insured; an insurant.

피보호자(被保護者) (프) a protégé(남자); a protégée(여자); a ward.

피복(被服) clothes; clothing. ⇨ 옷
● **피복비** clothing expenses.

피복(被覆) covering; coating. **피복하다** cover; coat.
● **피복선** a covered wire.

피부(皮膚) the skin. ¶~가 약하다[강하다 / 거칠다] have a delicate[strong / rough] skin ∥ ~가 희다 have a fair complexion ∥ ~로 느끼다 get the feel of (political sentiment) with the skin ∥ 그녀는 ~가 거칠다 She has rough [coarse] skin. / Her skin is chapped. ∥ 그녀의 ~는 부드럽다[매끈하다] She has soft [smooth] skin. ∥ 그녀는 ~가 희다 She has fair skin.
● **피부과** [피부에 관한 의학의 한 분과] dermatology; (병원의) the department of dermatology. **피부병** a skin[cutaneous] disease. **피부색** the color of the skin. ⇨ 살빛 **피부암** cutaneous cancer; cancer of the skin. **피부염** dermatitis.

피붙이 one's sons and daughters. ⇨ 혈육

피브리노겐 [화] fibrinogen.

피브린 [생] fibrin.

피비린내 bloodiness. ¶~ 나는 bloody / sanguinary ∥ ~ 나는 싸움 a bloody fight[battle] ∥ ~ 나는 광경 a bloody sight ∥ ~ 나는 사건 a sanguinary incident ∥ ~ 나는 싸움이 한 달이나 계속되었다 The bloody battle lasted a month.

피사리 weeding. **피사리하다** pick out[pluck] weeds; weed (a rice field).

피사체(被寫體) a subject (for photography); a thing pictured.

피살(被殺) being killed[murdered]. **피살되다** be killed[murdered]. ¶피살된 시체 the body of a murdered person / the body of the victim of a murder.
● **피살자** a murderee; the victim of a murderer.

피상(皮相) [외관] an outward look.

피상속인(被相續人) [법] an ancestor; a predecessor; an inheritee.

피상적(皮相的) superficial; shallow. ¶~인 견해를 지니다 take a superficial view (of) ∥ 그의 지식은 ~이다 His knowledge is superficial. ∥ 그것은 ~인 논의이다 That's a shallow [feeble] argument. ∥ 사태를 ~으로만 보지 마라 Don't look only at the surface of things.

피서(避暑) summering. **피서하다** summer (at / in); pass[spend] the summer (at / in). ¶피서하러 가다 go to a summer resort ∥ 해운대로 피서하러 가다 go to Haeundae for the summer[to avoid the heat of town] ∥ 올여름엔 제주도로 피서하러 갈 예정이다 We are planning to go to Jejudo to avoid the heat this summer.
● **피서객** a summer visitor[resident]. **피서지** a summer resort.

피선(被選) [선거에 뽑힘]. **피선되다** be elected. ¶의장으로 피선되었다 I was elected chairman. / I was elected to the chair.

피선거권(被選擧權) eligibility for election. ¶국회의원의 ~이 있다 be eligible for election to [be qualified to run for] an M.P.[a member of the National Assembly].

피선거인(被選擧人) an eligible person.

피스톤 [공] a piston.

피습(被襲) ¶~당하다[받다] be attacked / be assaulted / be set upon.

피승수(被乘數) [수] a multiplicand.

피시 PC (▶ personal computer의 약어).

피시에스 PCS(▶ Personal Communications Service의 약어).

피신(避身) escape; flight; refuge. **피신하다** escape; get off[away]; flee; take refuge (in); [숨다] conceal[hide] oneself. ¶저 오두막집에 피신하자 Let's take refuge in that hut. ∥ 나는 숙부 집에 피신했다 I sought refuge with my uncle.

피아(彼我) self and others; both sides; he and I; they and we; that and this; [상호] each other. ¶~의 [상호의] mutual.

피아노 1 [건반 악기의 하나] a piano (*pl*. ~s). ¶그랜드 ~ a (concert) grand piano ∥ 업라이트 ~ an upright piano ∥ 자동 ~ a player piano / Pianola(상표명) ∥ ~를 치다 play (on) the piano ∥ ~를 배우다 take piano lessons (from) ∥ ~를 가르치다 teach (a person) the piano ∥ ~를 연습하다 practice on the piano ∥ ~에 맞춰 노래하다 sing to the piano ∥ 그녀는 ~를 잘 친다[못 친다] She plays the piano well[badly]. / She is good[poor] at playing the piano. ∥ 그녀는 ~ 반주에 맞춰 노래했다 She sang to the piano. 2 [음] [여리게] piano(약어 p).
● **피아노 독주** a piano solo (by). **피아노 사중주** a piano quartet. **피아노 삼중주** a piano trio. **피아노 조율사** a piano tuner. **피아노 협주곡** a piano concerto.

피아니스트 a pianist.

피아르 P.R.(▶ public relations의 약어). ¶~가 잘돼 있다 be well publicized ∥ 당국은 새로운 세제(稅制)의 ~에 힘을 쏟고 있다 The au-

thorities are trying to get the public informed about the new tax system. **피아르하다** publicize; advertise.
● **피아르 영화** a P.R. film. **피아르 활동** public relations (activities); publicity activities. ¶그는 ~을 하고 있다 He does P.R. work.
피안(彼岸) 〔불〕〔범〕 paramita; entrance into Nirvana(열반).
피압박 민족(被壓迫民族) the oppressed [downtrodden] people[nation]. ¶~ **해방 (운동)** (the campaign for) liberation of the oppressed people[nation].
피어나다 1 〔불이 다시 일다〕 light[blaze] up (again); burn up; get lively. ¶숯불이 피어났다 The charcoal fire got lively again. 2 〔형편이 좋아지다〕 begin to prosper[flourish / thrive]. 3 〔의식이 차츰 깨어나다〕 come to (oneself); come to life again; revive (from a swoon). 4 〔꽃 등이 피게 되다〕 begin to bloom[come out]; come[burst] into flower; effloresce(문화 등이). ¶꽃이 ~ come into full bloom.
피에로 〔연〕 a pierrot; a (circus) clown.
피엑스 〔미 육군〕 a post exchange; a PX (*pl.* PXs).
피엘오 PLO(▶ the Palestine Liberation Organization의 약어).
피우다 1 〔꽃을 피게 하다〕 make (flowers) open[bloom].
2 〔불을 피게 하다〕 kindle; burn; make (up). ¶석탄불을 ~ burn coal // 난로를 ~ make a fire in the fireplace // 향을 ~ burn incense.
3 (담배를) smoke; puff. ¶담배를 ~ smoke a pipe[tobacco] / puff at one's pipe / smoke a cigar[cigarette] // 한 대 ~ have[take] a smoke (a pipe) // 담배를 피워도 괜찮겠습니까 Do you mind my smoking[if I smoke]? // 여기서 담배를 피우면 안 된다 You must not smoke here.
4 〔냄새를 퍼뜨리다〕 emit; give out[off]; send forth[out].
5 〔먼지를 일으키다〕 raise[make / kick up] (dust).
6 〔부리다〕 do; play; use; perform; display. ¶익살을 ~ play the fool / jest // 재주를 ~ play [do] tricks // 소란을 ~ make[create] a commotion // 난봉을 ~ indulge in follies.
피육(皮肉) skin and flesh.
피의자(被疑者) 〔법〕 a suspected person; a suspect; a person under suspicion. ¶강도 ~ a robber-suspect // 살인 사건의 ~ a suspect in a murder // a suspected murderer // ~의 사진 the photograph of a criminal suspect.
피임(被任) 〔임명됨〕 appointment to an office. **피임되다** be appointed; get[receive] an appointment.
● **피임자** an appointee; an appointed person.
피임(避妊) contraception; prevention of conception[maternity]; 〔산아 제한〕 birth control. **피임하다** prevent conception; practice birth control.
● **피임법** sterilization; a contraceptive measure[method]; a preventive method of conception. **피임 수술** a contraceptive operation; contraceptive treatment. **피임약** / **피임제** a contraceptive (pill); an anticonceptive. ¶경구 ~ an oral contraceptive / the pill.
피자 pizza; (a) pizza pie.

피자식물(被子植物) an angiosperm. ⇨ **속씨식물**
피장파장 evenness; equality; a tie. ¶~**이다** be quits (with a person) // 이제 ~이다 Now we are quits[all square / even].
피점령국(被占領國) an occupied country.
피제수(被除數) 〔수〕 a dividend.
피조물(被造物) a created thing; a creature; (집합적) creation.
피지(皮脂) sebum; sebaceous matter.
● **피지선**(一腺) a sebaceous gland.
피진(皮疹) 〔의〕 an efflorescence; a rash; an exanthema (*pl.* -mata).
피질(皮質) 〔의〕 the cortex; a cortical layer.
피차(彼此) 〔저것과 이것〕 that and this; 〔서로〕 each other; you[he] and I; they and we; both sides[parties]. ¶~ 사랑[미워]하다 love [hate] each other // ~의 구별을 할 수 없다 be unable to tell friend from foe // ~ 다툴 것이 없다 There's no need for quarrelling back and forth.
● **피차간** each other; between you and me; between both sides[parties]. ¶~의 약점을 알고 있다 We know each other's weak point. **피차일반** both the same; no difference between them[us / him and me]; equality between each other. ¶~이다 be mutually equal[the same] // 잘못하기는 ~이다 They are both to blame. // 가난하기는 ~이다 You are not rich, nor I either. / When it comes to being poor, we're in the same boat. // 날 보고 비겁하다니, ~ 아닌가 If I am a coward, you're another.
피처 〔야구〕 a (baseball) pitcher. ¶~를 맡아 하다 pitch / play as a pitcher // 프로 팀에서 ~를 보다 pitch on a pro team // ~ 앞 땅볼로 아웃이 되다 ground out to the pitcher // ~ 플레이로 아웃이 되다 line out to the pitcher.
피천 〔아주 적은 액수의 돈〕 the smallest sum (of money). ¶~ 한 닢 a coin of the smallest value / a farthing // ~ 닢도 쪼개 쓰는 녀석 a pinch-farthing / a skinflint // 나는 그에게 ~ 한 닢의 빚도 없다 I don't owe him a cent.
피천 한 닢 없다(속담) be penniless; have not a penny[brass farthing / red cent] in the word; have not a single stiver; (미) be utterly[stone] broke.
피치 1 〔일정 시간 내의 동작 속도〕 a pace. ¶급 ~로 at high[great] speed / 일의 ~를 올리다 [늦추다] speed up[slow / slacken] the pace of one's work // 조금 ~를 올려서 걷자 Let's walk a little faster[at a slightly faster pace].
2 〔노의 횟수〕 a stroke. ¶선원은 36의 ~를 냈다 The crew put in 36 strokes a minute.
3 〔투구〕 a pitch. ¶와일드 ~ a wild pitch / 나이스 ~ (지금 던진 한 구에 대하여) That was a nice pitch! / (시합을 통해서, 어느 회·장면을 통해서) Nice pitching!
4 〔음〕 a pitch. ¶~가 높은 목소리로 in a high-pitched voice.
5 〔석유 등의 증류 잔류물〕 pitch.
6 〔기어의 톱니와 톱니 사이의 거리〕 pitch.
피치카토 〔음〕 pizzicato. ¶~로 연주된 악곡[악절] a pizzicato (*pl.* -ti, ~s) // ~로 **연주하다** play (a passage) pizzicato.
피칭 1 〔야구〕 pitching. 2 〔배·비행기 등의 흔들림〕 pitching. ¶~ 연습을 하다 practice pitching.
● **피칭 머신** a pitching machine. ¶~으로 연

피켈 습하다 practice batting with a pitching machine.

피켈 [등산 용구의 하나] a pickel.

피켓 a picket. ¶~을 치다 keep a picket (at a factory) / picket (a place)//공장에 ~을 두다 picket a factory.

피크 [절정·정점] a peak. ¶그의 인기는 ~에 달했다 His popularity has reached its peak.

피크닉 a picnic. ¶~을 가다 go (out) on a picnic / go picnicking.

피클 [절인 서양식 음식] pickles.

피타고라스의 정리 (一定理) the Pythagorean theorem.

피투성이 ¶~의 bloodstained / bloodsoaked / gory / bloody//~가 되어 bathed with [in] blood//~가 되다 be smeared [covered] with blood / be bathed in blood / be spattered [covered] all over with blood / be bloodied// 그는 ~가 되어 누워 있었다 He was lying there covered with blood.//노인은 얼굴이 ~가 되어 땅에 쓰러져 있었다 The old man was lying on the ground, his face covered with blood.

피트 feet (sing. foot)(약어 ft.; 기호 ′). ¶길이 30~의 풀 a thirty-foot swimming pool//2~ 자 a two-foot rule//나는 키가 5~ 2인치 된다 I am five feet two inches [5′2″] tall.

피펫 [화] a pipet(te).

피폐 (疲弊) impoverishment; exhaustion. ¶재정의 ~ financial exhaustion//농촌의 ~ the impoverished conditions of rural communities. **피폐하다** become [be] impoverished [exhausted]. ¶전쟁으로 피폐한 나라 a country impoverished [exhausted] by war.

피폭 (被爆) ¶~되다 be bombed.
● **피폭자** an A-bomb [atomic bomb] victim.
피폭 지구 a bombed block [area].

피피엠 ppm; ppm.; p.p.m.; P.P.M.(▶ parts per million의 약어).

피하 (皮下) ¶~의 hypodermic / subcutaneous.
● **피하 주사** a hypodermic [subcutaneous] injection. ¶~를 놓다 inject (medicine) under the skin / inject hypodermically. **피하 지방** subcutaneous fat.

피하다 (避-) 1 [회피하다] avoid (the heat); escape; evade (punishment); elude (payment); dodge [duck] (a blow); [막다] avert (danger); (사람·요구 등을) put off; (비바람을) take [seek / find] shelter (from). ¶피할 곳 a shelter (from the enemy's fire) / a place of safety//피할 수 없는 unavoidable / unescapable / inevitable//전쟁의 포화를 피해 오는 사람들 refugees fleeing from the fires of war//위험을 ~ escape danger / get out of danger//오해를 ~ avoid misunderstanding//차를 얼른 ~ dodge a car//상대방의 질문을 ~ evade [parry] another's questions//난을 ~ find a refuge//자리를 leave [quit] one's seat / slip away (from)// 남의눈을 ~ avert people's eyes//타격을 ~ dodge [elude] a blow//그런 표현은 점잖지 않다고 일반적으로 피한다 People generally avoid using such expressions because they sound indecent.//이 판잣집으로는 도저히 비바람을 피할 수 없다 This rickety hut will not protect [shelter] us from the weather.//그는 상대방의 타격을 교묘하게 피했다 He skillfully dodged his opponent's blow.//그녀는 나의 질문에 대답하기를 피했다 She evaded my question.//쇼핑 손님들은 불타는 백화점에서 피했다 The shoppers fled the burning department store.//그는 이제 피할 수 없다고 체념 [단념]했다 He resigned himself to his fate.//저녁 식사를 끝낸 그는 시끄럽게 떠드는 아내를 피해 항상 서재에 틀어박히곤 했다 After supper he used to retreat from his yapping wife into his study. / After supper he used to go into his study to get away from his fussy [nagging] wife.//나는 간신히 재난을 피했다 I had a narrow escape.//우리는 위험을 피하려고 했다 We tried to avoid danger.//그들은 햇볕을 피하여 그늘에 앉았다 They sat in the shade to get away from [keep out of] the sun.//나는 몸을 날려 내게로 쓰러지는 나무를 피했다 I jumped out of the way just before the tree fell on me.//이것은 피할 수 없는 문제이다 This is a problem we have to face [we cannot avoid].//양측 의견의 충돌은 피할 수 없다 A clash of opinion between the two (parties) is inevitable.//여러 사람 앞에서의 비평은 피하는 편이 좋다 You had better withhold comment [not say anything] in public.//저 검사의 날카로운 심문에는 나는 피할 길이 없다 I cannot evade [sidestep] that prosecutor's penetrating questions.//자네 그 질문을 교묘히 피했군 You evaded [parried] the question very cleverly.//나무 밑에서 비를 피했다 I took shelter [sheltered myself] from the rain under a tree.

2 [멀리하다] keep away from (danger); stand [keep] clear of (politics); keep aloof from (bad company); shun (evil company). ¶암초를 ~ steer clear of the rocks [reef]//만나기 싫은 사람을 ~ give (a person) a wide berth//좋지 못한 친구는 피하는 편이 낫다 You had better avoid [keep away from] bad company.//그는 자기 부친을 피했다 He shunned [gave a wide berth to] his father.

3 (책임 을) shirk (responsibility); evade (an answer). ¶책임을 ~ shirk [evade / avoid] one's responsibility//사장은 명확한 발언을 피했다 The president did not commit himself to [didn't say] anything definite.

피한 (避寒) wintering; hibernation. **피한하다** winter (at / in); pass the winter (at / in); go to (a place) for the winter; hibernate (at / in). ¶제주도에서 ~ winter [pass the winter] at Jejudo.
● **피한지** a winter resort; winter quarters.

피해 (被害) (무생물의) damage; (주로 사람의) (an) injury; harm; casualties(사상). ¶태풍에 의한 ~ damage caused by a typhoon//~가 많다 [적다] suffer heavily [lightly] (from)//~를 입다 be damaged (by) / be injured / suffer damage (from a flood)//~를 주다 (농작물 등에) damage / do damage (to) / (주로 남에게) injure / do harm (to)//~를 모면하다 be intact / come out unhurt / (사람이) escape injury//그 사고로 지나가는 사람이 ~를 입었다 Some passersby were injured in the accident.//전원이 ~를 입지 않았다 No harm came to us. / All of us escaped injury.//화재를 만났지만 창고의 물건은 ~를 면했다 The goods in the storehouse remained intact [were undamaged] despite the fire.//우리 측엔 인명 ~가 없었다 We suffered no casualties. / There were no casualties on our side.//올겨울의 폭설로 중앙선 ~가 가장 컸다 The Jungang [Seoul-Gyeongju] Line of the

National Railways suffered most from the heavy snowfalls this winter.∥마을이 입은 홍수 ~는 막심했다〔가벼웠다〕The village suffered heavy〔only slight〕damage from the flood.∥그는 지난번 태풍으로 큰 ~를 입었다 He suffered a great deal of damage from the recent typhoon.∥이 고장은 대지진으로 ~를 입었다 This area was hit by a great earthquake.
●**피해망상** a delusion of persecution. **피해액** the amount of damage; (범위·정도) the extent of damage; the damage. **피해자** a victim; a sufferer; the injured person. ¶홍수 ~ the victims of the flood(▶ 집을 잃은 사람·사망자 등을 포함).

피험자(被驗者)(시험의) an examinee; a testee; (실험의) a subject. ¶새로운 치료법의 ~ (구어) a guinea pig for the testing of a new treatment.

피혁(皮革)〔짐승 가죽〕 hides (and skins); leather(무두질한). ¶인조〔합성〕 ~ artificial [synthetic] leather.
●**피혁공** a tanner. **피혁 공업** the leather industry. **피혁 제품** leather articles.

피후견인(被後見人) a ward.

픽¹ 1〔바람 빠지는 소리〕. ¶~ 하는 소리 a hiss / a hissing sound / a swish / a whoosh∥~ 하며 풍선의 바람이 빠졌다 The toy balloon got deflated with a whoosh. 2〔쓰러지는 모양〕with a thud; (collapsing) feebly; in a heap. 3〔웃는 모양〕grinningly; sneeringly. ¶~ 웃다 grin / sneer / let go a despising laugh∥그는 그를 보자 ~ 웃음을 터뜨렸다 The girls looked at him and burst into laughter[burst out laughing]. 4〔끊어지는 모양〕snap (off). ¶연줄이 ~ 끊어졌다 The string of the kite has broken[snapped].

픽² (악기의) a pick; a (bone) plectrum (pl. -tra, ~s).

픽션 (a) fiction.

픽업 1〔레코드플레이어의〕 a pickup. 2〔트럭의 일종〕a pickup (truck).

픽픽 〔쓰러지는 모양〕with flop after flop; thudding and thudding. ¶~ 쓰러지다 several fall down feebly / fall down feebly again and again∥병사들이 총에 맞아 ~ 쓰러졌다 The soldiers were (shot and) dropping one after another. 2.〔싱거운 웃음〕all smiling[laughing] aimlessly. ¶~ 웃다 several laugh listlessly / keep laughing listlessly / give listless smiles. 3〔바람이 힘없이 빠짐〕. ¶~ 바람이 빠지다 lose what little air they have.

핀 1〔고정 바늘〕a pin. ¶넥타이 ~ a tiepin∥안전 ~ a safety pin∥두 장의 천을 ~으로 고정하다 pin two pieces of cloth together∥사진을 벽에 ~으로 고정하다 pin up a picture on the wall. 2〔머리에 꽂는〕 a hairpin. ¶그녀는 머리에 ~을 꽂고 있다 She pins up her hair. 3〔골프의〕 a pin. ¶그는 홀에 ~을 꽂았다 He set the [put a] pin into the hole. 4〔볼링의〕 a pin. ¶그는 10개의 ~을 1회에 전부 넘어뜨렸다 He knocked down all ten pins with one bowl.

핀둥거리다 loaf one's time away. ⇨ 빈둥거리다

핀둥핀둥 idly; lazily. ⇨' 빈둥빈둥

핀셋(@pincette)(a pair of) tweezers; forceps(의료용). ¶~으로 집다 pick up with a pincette∥~으로 가시를 뽑다 pull out a thorn with tweezers.

핀잔 (a) scolding; (구어) a wipe; a snub; a rebuff. ¶~을 주다 〔호통을 치다〕 scold / rebuke severely / 〔거절하다〕 give a rebuff (to)∥~을 받다 〔꾸지람을 듣다〕 (구어) catch it / get scolded / get a scolding / 〔거절당하다〕 get a rebuff.

핀치 〔at / in / on / upon〕 a pinch; 〔야구〕 a clutch. ¶~에 빠지다〔~를 맞다〕find oneself in a fix[pinch]∥~을 벗어나다 tide over a crisis∥그는 ~에 강하다 He is tough when the going is rough[when it comes to a pinch].∥9회 초에서 우리는 ~에 몰렸다 In the top[first half] of the ninth inning, we got into a pinch.
●**핀치 러너** a pinch runner. ⇨'대주자 **핀치 히터** a pinch hitter; a substitute batter. ¶~가 되다 〔야구〕 be sent in as a pinch hitter∥그는 ~로 나가 홈런을 쳤다 He pinch-hit a homer.

핀트 〔초점〕 a focus; 〔요점〕 the point. ¶~가 맞다 be[get] in focus∥~가 안 맞다 be out of focus∥~를 맞추다 get (a thing) in focus / adjust[take] the focus / focus (one's camera)∥얼굴에 ~를 맞추다 focus on the face∥이 사진은 ~가 맞지 않았다 The picture is out of focus.∥피사체에 ~를 맞추었다 I focused my camera on the subject. / I brought my subject into focus.∥그의 이야기는 ~가 맞다[맞지 않다] What he says is to [off] the point.

필(匹)〔마소의 세는 단위〕 a head. ¶말 세 ~ three horses∥두 ~의 소 two head of cows.

필(疋)〔피륙을 세는 단위〕 a roll of cloth. ¶무명 세 ~ three rolls of cotton cloth∥~로 사다〔팔다〕 buy[sell] by the roll.

필(筆)(a lot of (land). ⇨'필지(筆地)

-필(畢)〔이미 마침〕. ¶지불~ (기재 사항) Paid ∥검사~ Examined∥영수~ Sold∥그것은 검사~이라고 표시되어 있었다 It was labeled "Examined."

필경(筆耕) copying; stencil-paper writing. **필경하다** copy; (등사하다) stencil.
●**필경료** a copying fee. **필경사** a copyist; a scribe; a stenciler(등사판의).

필경(畢竟) after all; in the end; finally; in the long run; in the final[last] analysis. ¶~는 오지 않을 것이다 He will not come after all.∥그는 돈을 낭비하여 ~에는 빈털터리가 되었다 He squandered his money until he became penniless.

필기(筆記)〔글씨를 씀〕 taking notes; 〔받아씀〕 notes. **필기하다** take a note[notes] of; write [note / put] down. ¶강연을 ~ write down a speech∥요점을 ~ jot down the main points∥그는 비서에게 편지를 구술하여 필기하게 했다 He dictated a letter to his secretary.
●**필기도구** writing utensils. **필기시험** a written examination. **필기장** a notebook.

필담(筆談) conversation by writing. **필담하다** communicate in[by means of] writing; talk by means of writing; carry on a talk by writing.

필답(筆答) a written answer[response]. **필답하다** answer in writing.
●**필답시험** a written examination. ⇨'필기시험(⇨필기)

필독(必讀) required reading.
●**필독서** a must book. ¶학생의 ~ a book which every student must read / a must

book for students // 이 책은 학생의 ~이다 This book is a must for students.

필두 (筆頭) 1 [붓 끝] the tip of a writing brush. 2 [연명의 첫째] the first on a list [in a roll]. ¶민순도 씨를 ~로 with Mr. Min Sundo at the head of the list // 클린턴 대통령을 ~로 from President Clinton down // 그는 우승 후보의 ~에 올라 있다 He heads the list of likely winners. 3 [우두머리] the head; senior.

필드 [체] the field.
● 필드 경기 a field event. 필드하키 field hockey.

필라멘트 [전] a filament.

필력 (筆力) the power [force] of a brush stroke [the pen]; [문장의 힘] the force of one's written style. ¶~이 있는 글 powerful writing.

필름 (a) film. ¶네거[포지] ~ (a) negative [positive] film // 컬러 [흑백] ~ (a) color [black-and-white] film // 한 통의 ~ a reel [spool] of film // ~에 담ും film (a scene) // ~을 감다 wind (a roll of) film // 카메라에 ~을 넣다 load a camera // ~을 현상하다 develop film // 이 ~ 한 통으로 사진 24장을 찍을 수 있다 This roll of film has twenty four exposures. // 그 영화는 5권에 담겨 있다 The movie is on five reels of film. // 사고의 장면을 ~에 담았다 I filmed the scene of the accident.

필마 (匹馬) [한 필의 말] one [a] horse.
● 필마단기 (一單騎) riding alone without servants [retinue].

필명 (筆名) 1 [글로써 떨치는 명성] a name [fame] as a calligrapher. ¶~이 높다 be a famous calligrapher [writer]. 2 [펜네임] a pen name. ¶…의 ~으로 under the pen name of … // 김소월이라는 ~으로 under the pen name [pseudonym] of Kim Sowol.

필묵 (筆墨) brush and Chinese ink; pen and ink; writing materials.

필법 (筆法) the technique of calligraphy; rules for wielding the brush; a style of brushmanship; penmanship. ¶힘찬 ~ a powerful stroke of the brush // ~을 터득하고 있다 know how to use a brush.

필봉 (筆鋒) [붓의 위세] the power of a piece of writing. ¶~이 날카로운 비평가 a critic who wields [writes with] a sharp pen // ~이 날카롭다 be forcible [sharp] in one's argument [style].

필부 (匹夫) [한 남자] a man; [태생이 천한 사내] a man of humble birth; [교양이 없는 사내] an uncultured man.
● 필부필부 (一匹婦) humble men and women; common people; Jack and Jill.

필부 (匹婦) [한 여자] a woman; an individual woman; [신분이 낮은 여자] a lowly woman; [평범한 여자] an ordinary woman.

필사 (必死) [반드시 죽음] inevitable death; [사력을 다함] desperation. ¶~의 frantic / desperate // ~의 공격 a desperate [frantic] attack // ~의 각오로 with a firm resolve to lay down one's life (for) / (fully) prepared for death.

필사 (筆寫) copying; transcription. 필사하다 copy; transcribe.

필사적 (必死的) desperate; frantic. ¶~으로 frantically / for one's (dear) life / desperately / in desperation / (속어) like hell // ~인 노력 desperate [frantic] efforts // ~으로 일하다 work away like one possessed / work for one's life // ~으로 도망치다 run dead away / run for dear life // ~으로 헤엄치다 swim for one's life // ~이 되다 become desperate / be driven to desperation / make desperate [frantic] efforts / turn to bay // 사람이 ~이 되면 무섭다 A desperate man will go to any length. // 그들은 ~으로 싸웠다 They fought in desperation [desperately]. // 그는 ~으로 허우적거렸다 He struggled for his life. // ~으로 임한다면 틀림없이 목적을 달성할 수 있다 If you are prepared to risk everything, you are sure to accomplish your purpose. // 그는 ~인 사랑을 하고 있다 He is desperately in love.

필산 (筆算) calculation with figures written down [arithmetic worked out] on paper. 필산하다 do the sums on a piece of paper.

필생 (畢生) one's life. ¶~의 사업 one's lifework // ~의 대작 one's masterpiece // ~의 노력 lifelong [lifetime] efforts // 이것이 나의 ~의 사업이다 This is my lifework.

필생 (筆生) a copyist; an amanuensis.

필설 (筆舌) brush and tongue; writing and speech. ¶~로 다할 수 없다 It is beyond all description. / It beggars description. // 그녀의 아름다움은 ~로 다할 수 없다 Her charm is beyond description. / Words cannot describe her allure.

필세 (筆勢) one's stroke of the brush [pen].

필수 (必須) ¶~의 indispensable / essential / requisite / mandatory / ~ 조항 a mandatory clause.
● 필수 과목 a required [compulsory] subject [course]. 필수 조건 an essential [an indispensable] condition. ¶전제가 되는 ~ a precondition // 병역을 마쳐야 함은 취직의 ~이다 The completion of military service is a prerequisite to employment. // 비자는 여러 나라에 있어서 아직 여행의 ~이다 A visa is still a prerequisite for travel in many countries.

필수품 (必需品) a necessary article; (집합적) necessities; necessaries; requisites. ¶생활 ~ the necessaries [necessities] of life / living necessaries // 여행 [등산] 용 ~ travelling [mountaineering] requisites.

필순 (筆順) the stroke order (of Chinese characters).

필승 (必勝) (a) certain [sure / unfailing] victory. ¶~의 신념 faith in certain victory // ~의 신념을 가지고 with every confidence of victory // ~을 기하다 be sure of victory (자신) / resolve to secure a victory at any cost (각오) // 나는 ~을 기하고 있다 I am sure of ultimate victory.

필시 (必是) certainly; surely; definitely; without doubt; I am sure. ¶그녀는 ~ 기뻐할 거야 She'll be very pleased, I'm sure.

필연 (必然) 1 inevitability; necessity. ¶논리적 [물리적] ~ logical [physical] necessity // ~의 결과로서 by a natural process (of cause and effect) / automatically // 사장이 부정을 저질렀으니 회사가 망하는 것도 ~이다 As a necessary consequence of the president's dishonesty, the company will go bankrupt. 2 [틀림없이 꼭] certainly; surely; definitely; without doubt; necessarily; inevitably.
● 필연성 inevitability; necessity.

필연적(必然的) inevitable; necessary.
필연코(必然-) certainly; surely. ⇨**필연2**
필요(必要) (a) necessity (for / of / to do); (a) need (of / for / to do); requirement. ¶~ 없는 unnecessary / needless∥즉각 행동할 ~ the need for[of] immediate action / the need to act immediately∥~에 따라서 as occasion demands / at need∥…을 ~로 하다 need / be[stand] in need of / require / want∥~할 ~가 있다 it is necessary (to do) / must (do) / have to (do)∥…할 ~가 없다 there is no necessity for (doing) / need not[don't have to] (do)∥(하여도) there is no use in (doing) / ~를 충족시키다 meet the requirements / serve the[one's] need∥그에게 알릴 ~가 있다 We must let him know.∥당신은 나갈 ~가 없습니다 You don't have[need] to go out.∥그에게 이야기할 ~가 있을까 Is there any need[Is it necessary] for me to tell him?∥어째서 그렇게 서둘 ~가 있나요 Why are you in such a hurry?∥~에 따라서 대책을 강구해 가면 될 것이다 It will be all right if we take action as the need arises[as the occasion demands / as necessity requires].∥지금 당장 대답할 ~는 없다 It is not necessary to answer at once. / You don't need[have] to answer at once.∥진찰의 결과, 그녀는 입원 치료의 ~가 있다고 결정되었다 As a result of the examination, it was concluded that she needed medical treatment[care] in a hospital.∥재고할 ~가 있다 We must think it over again. / We must reconsider (it). **필요하다** necessary; needful; needed; required; requisite; indispensable; essential. ¶필요하면 if necessary / in case of need[necessity] / if need be∥여행에 필요한 물품 articles necessary for travel∥필요한 물건 a necessity∥~(꼭) 필요해서 out of[from] (sheer) necessity [need]∥우표는 몇 장이 필요합니까 How many stamps do you want[need]?∥급히 유능한 비서가 ~ A competent secretary is needed immediately.∥돈 얼마가 필요합니까 How much do you need[want]?∥당신에게 필요한 것은 용기입니다 What you need is courage.∥그는 휴양이 ~ He needs (to) rest.∥이 일은 인내가 ~ Patience is required[necessary] for this job.∥예정을 변경한 것은 필요했기 때문이다 I changed the schedule because I had to.∥필요하면 자금을 빌려 드리겠소 I'll lend you money if you need some. **필요는 발명의 어머니**(속담) Necessity is the mother of invention.
●**필요성** necessity. **필요악** a necessary evil.
필요조건 a necessary condition; a requirement. ¶타자할 수 있는 능력이 ~의 하나이다 Ability to type is one of the requirements. **필요충분조건** a necessary and sufficient condition (for).
필자(筆者) the writer; the author. ¶이 글의 ~ (자신을 가리켜) the present writer / (통신원) this correspondent∥이 글의 ~는 여성이다 This was written by[from the pen of] a certain lady.
필적(匹敵) a rival; a match; an equal. **필적하다** equal; rival; be a match (for); be equal (to); compare (with); stand comparison (with). ¶필적할 만한 것이 없다 have no equal (in experience) / be unequaled[unrivaled] (in cooking)∥그에 필적할 사람은 없다 He has no equal[rival]. / He is peerless.

/ He is second to none.∥도저히 그에게는 필적할 수 없다 I am no match for him.∥나는 당신에 필적할 만하지 않소 I am no match for you.∥단단하기로는 다이아몬드에 필적하는 것이 없다 Nothing can compare with diamond in hardness.
필적(筆跡) **1** [글씨 형적] a specimen of handwriting; a calligraphic specimen; a holograph. ¶이것은 아버지의 ~입니다 This is my father's calligraphy. **2** [글 솜씨] one's handwriting; one's hand; one's style of handwriting. ¶남자[여자] ~ a masculine[feminine] hand∥뛰어난[서투른] ~ good[bad] handwriting / beautiful[messy] handwriting∥~을 흉내 내다 copy (a person's) hand / imitate (a person's) handwriting∥~을 감정하다 analyze handwriting∥유려한 ~으로 쓰여 있다 be written in a beautiful, flowing hand∥이것은 분명히 그의 ~이다 This is unquestionably his hand(writing).
●**필적 감정** (an) analysis of one's handwriting.
필주(筆誅) [죄 등을 글로 써서 꾸짖음]. ¶~을 가하다 denounce (a person) in writing∥수상은 실언으로 전 신문의 ~를 받았다 The Prime Minister was denounced[(문어) censured / (구어) lambasted] for his indiscreet remark in every newspaper.
필지(必至) inevitability; necessity. ¶~의 inevitable∥회사의 파산은 ~의 상황이다 The company is headed toward inevitable bankruptcy. **필지하다** follow as a necessary[an inevitable] consequence. ¶국회 해산은 ~ The dissolution of the National Assembly is unavoidable.
필지(必知) required knowledge.
●**필지 사항** matters everyone must[should] know; indispensable information.
필지(筆地) a lot[plot / piece] (of land).
필진(筆陣) [집필 진용] the writing[editorial] staff; (포진) a maneuver in paper warfare. ¶~을 펴다 set forth one's argument《for / against》.
필촉(筆觸) a touch of a brush.
필치(筆致) [필세의 운치] a stroke of the brush; a touch; [글 솜씨] style of writing. ¶입신(入神)의 ~ a master stroke∥가벼운[거친] ~ a light[rough] touch∥원숙한 ~ a mellowed style∥그의 ~는 멋있다 The strokes of his brush are fine.∥그의 ~는 경묘하고 원숙하다 His style is easy and well mellowed.∥그는 경묘한 ~로 쓴다 He writes with a light touch. / His style is light and carefree.
필터 [사진] a light filter; (렌즈의) a (color[(영) colour]) filter; (담배의) a filter tip. ¶적외선 ~ an infrared filter.
●**필터 담배** a filter-tip(ped) cigarette; a filter cigarette.
필통(筆筒) (꽂아 두는) a pencil vase; a pen[brush] stand; (넣고 다니는) a pencil case.
필하다(畢-) end; finish; complete; get[be] through. ¶검사를 ~ stand the test / come [measure] up to the standards(규격에 맞다) / be O.K.'d∥납세를 ~ pay one's taxes∥입항[출항] 수속을 ~ clear inward[outward]∥대학 과정을 ~ complete a[one's] university course.
필하모니(⑤Philharmonie) [음악 협회(주최의 콘서트)] a philharmonic; [교향악단] a

필화(筆禍) [글이 제재를 받음] a serious slip of the pen. ¶~를 초래하다[입다] be indicted for one's article (in a magazine) // 그는 잡지에 쓴 기사로 ~를 입었다 An article he wrote in a magazine got him into trouble [caused him a lot of trouble].

필히(必−) certainly; surely; necessarily; by all means; at any cost. ¶~ 하다 be sure [certain] to (do) / be bound to (do) / never fail to (do) // ~ 그 편지를 부칠 것 Be sure to mail the letter.

핌피 Pimfy(▶ Please in my front yard의 약어).

핍박(逼迫) pressure (for money); stringency (of the money market); tightness (of money). ¶재정의 ~ stiffened [tight] financial conditions. **핍박하다** be tight; get stringent. ¶금융 사정이 ~ 하다 Money is tight [scarce]. // 자금이 핍박해 있다 I am pressed for funds. // 정세가 핍박해지고 있다 The situation is growing strained [tense]. / A crisis is impending.

핏기(−氣) the color of the skin [face]; one's complexion. ¶~ 없는 얼굴 a pale face / a face as white as a sheet // ~가 없다 have a bad complexion / look pale [sallow / unwell] // ~가 가시다 become [turn] pale / 그녀는 몸이 아파서 얼굴에 ~가 없다 Her cheeks are pale with sickness. // 그녀의 얼굴에서 ~가 가셨다 The color drained from her face.

핏대 a vein; a blood vessel.

핏대(를) 올리다[세우다] get angry; boil [turn purple] with rage. ¶핏대를 올리고 다투다 have a hot dispute // 그는 핏대를 세우고 화를 냈다 He turned purple with rage.

핏덩어리 1 [피의 덩어리] a clot of blood; clotted blood; gore. 2 [갓난아이] a newborn baby.

핏덩이 a clot of blood; a newborn baby. ⇨ 핏덩어리

핏발 congestion; being bloodshot; a bloodshot condition. ¶~이 삭다 congestion [bloodshot condition] clears up // ~이 서다 become bloodshot / become turgid with blood // ~ 선 눈 bloodshot eyes.

핏빛 blood red. ¶~으로 물들다 be dyed in blood red.

핏자국 a bloodstain; a blood mark. ¶~이 있는 bloodstained.

핏줄 1 a blood vessel. ⇨ 혈관 ¶~이 불거진 손 a veinous [veiny] hand. 2 blood; lineage. ⇨ 혈통 ¶좋은 ~ a good strain [stock] // ~이 같다 be blood-related (to) / be of the same blood / be related by blood (to) // 그와 나는 ~이 같은 척분이다 He and I are blood relatives. / He is related to me (by blood). // ~은 속일 수 없다 Heredity will out. // 우리는 같은 성씨이지만 ~은 같지 않다 We have the same surname, but are not related (by blood). // 내 급한 성미는 아버지의 ~을 이은 것이다 I get my quick temper from my father.

핑 round; around. ⇨ 빙¹·³·⁴

핑계 an excuse; a pretext; a pretense; a plea. ¶그럴듯한 ~ a plausible excuse / a specious pretense // ~로 남을 따돌리다 put a person off with an excuse // 병을 ~ 삼아 사직하다 resign (from) one's post under the pretext of ill health // 그는 병을 ~ 삼아 일을 맡지 않았다 He turned down the job under the pretense of illness. // 그런 ~를 누가 믿겠나 Who could believe such an excuse? // 그의 약속이란 단지 ~일 뿐이다 His promises are a mere show [pretense / (영) pretence]. // 그녀는 일을 ~ 삼아 외출했다 She used an errand as a pretext [an excuse] for going out. // 그는 병을 ~ 삼아 출석하지 않았다 He excused himself from attending under [on] the pretext of ill health [that he was ill]. // 그는 언제나 이 ~ 저 ~로 우리 초대를 거절한다 He always finds some pretext or other for declining our invitations. **핑계하다** make a pretext [a pretense / an excuse] of; pretend (to be ill); use (something) as pretext.

핑계 없는 무덤이 없다(속담) A pretext is never wanting.

핑그르르 (turn / skate / glide) around smoothly. ⇨ 빙그르르

핑글핑글 round and round smoothly. ⇨ 빙글빙글

핑크 pink.
● 핑크 무드 an amorous mood.

핑퐁 ping-pong; table tennis. ¶~을 치다 play ping-pong.
● 핑퐁대 a ping-pong table.

핑핑 round and round (quickly). ⇨ 팽팽 ¶(눈이) ~ 돌다 feel dizzy [giddy] // 탄환이 ~ 귓전을 스쳐 갔다[공중을 날아갔다] The bullets whistled [whizzed] past my ears [through the air].

ㅎ

하[1] with a hot wet breath. ¶거울에 입김을 ~ 하고 내뿜다 breathe on a glass.

하[2] 〔놀람〕 ha!; huh!; O!; oh!; Oh my goodness!; Dear me!; 〔의문〕 eh?; what? ¶~, 돈을 잃어버렸다 Say you lost your money, eh?

하(下) **1** 〔하등〕 the low class [grade]; inferiority. ¶~의 inferior / low / mean // 그의 품성은 ~의 ~이다 He is of the meanest [lowest / 〔문어〕 basest] character. **2** 〔상하 2권의 하〕 the second volume; 〔상중하 3권의 하〕 the third [last] volume.

-하(下) 〔아래〕. ¶~에서 under / on // …의 지휘〔지도 / 감독〕~에 under the command [direction / supervision] of … / under ….

하감(下疳) 〔의〕 chancre; the initial lesion of syphilis. ¶연성〔경성〕 ~ soft [hard] chancre.

하감하다(下鑑-) read a letter from one's inferior [subordinate].

하강(下降) a descent; a fall; (경기 등의) a decline; a downturn. ¶~ 도중에 on the way down. **하강하다** descend; go [come] down. ¶기구(氣球)는 서서히 하강하고 있다 The balloon is gradually descending [coming down]. // 갓난아기의 사망률은 하강하고 있다 The infant mortality rate is declining [is on the decline]. // 그래프의 곡선은 여기서 갑자기 하강하기 시작한다 The curve in the graph begins to drop [fall] sharply at this point.
● **하강 곡선** a downward curve. ¶~을 그리다 be on a downhill run / be on the decline.

하객(賀客) a congratulator; a well-wisher.

하계(下界) 〔인간의 세계·이 세상〕 this world; the world here below; 〔지상〕 the earth. ¶~의 earthly / sublunary / mundane / temporal // ~에서 here below // 그는 우주선에서 ~를 내려다보았다 He looked down at the earth from a spaceship.

하계(夏季) summer; summer time. ⇨ 하기(夏期)

하고 〔및〕 and; 〔함께〕 with; along [together] with. ¶아버지~ 아들 father and son // 부모님~ 살다 live with one's parents.

하고많다 〔많고 많다〕 innumerable; countless; numberless; incalculable; (stars) without number; no end of. ¶그 전쟁으로 하고많은 인명과 재산이 희생되었다 The war cost heavily in human life and wealth.

하곡(夏穀) summer crops [harvests]; barley and wheat.
● **하곡 수매가** the government purchase price of barley.

하관(下官) a minor official [employee] (of the government); a subordinate (official); a minion.

하관(下顴) the lower part of the face; the jaws. ¶~이 빨다 have a pointed jaw / have drooping [sagging] jaws.

하관하다(下棺-) lower a coffin into the grave; deposit a coffin in the grave.

하교(下校) ¶~ 도중에 톰을 만났다 On my way home from school I met Tom. // ~ 시에 비가 오기 시작했다 Just when school was over, it started to rain. **하교하다** come [return] home from school.

하교(下敎) 〔교시〕 instructions; an order; directions; 〔전교〕 orders from the king; the king's command. ¶~를 바라다 ask for instructions (from). **하교하다** deign to direct [instruct]; direct; instruct; order; command; give directions [orders] (to).

하구(河口) the mouth of a river; a river-mouth; 〔조수의 간만이 있는 넓은 하구〕 an estuary. ¶이 강의 ~는 2킬로이다 This river is two kilometers wide at the mouth.

하권(下卷) the last volume; the third volume(상·중·하권에서); the second volume(상·하권에서).

하극상(下剋上) the lower dominating the upper; overpowering of seniors by juniors; a revolt against seniors; a mutiny. ¶~의 시대에는 그런 예가 헤아릴 수 없이 많다 Such examples abound during a period of social upheaval.

하급(下級) a lower class [grade]. ¶~의 low-class / lowe-grade / 〔연하의〕 junior.
● **하급 관리 / 하급 공무원** a lower-level [junior / petty] official; minor government official. **하급 관청** a subordinate agency. **하급 법원** a lower [a lesser / an inferior] court. **하급생** a lower-grade [-class] student [boy / girl]; an underclassman. **하급심**(-審) a trial by a lower court. **하급 장교** a junior officer; (집합적) officers at the junior level. **하급품** lower-grade goods.

하기(下記) the writing given below; the following; the undermentioned statements [paragraphs]. ¶~와 같이 as in the following / as follows / as undermentioned [under-written] / as given [listed] hereunder // ~의 the following / undermentioned / mentioned below // ~의 이유 때문에 For reasons given below, … // ~조건은 ~와 같습니다 The conditions are as follows. // ~의 학생은 내일 9시에 등교할 것 The students listed below are to come to school at nine tomorrow.
● **하기 사항** the following items.

하기(夏期) summer; summer time; the summer season; the summer period. ¶~의 (a)estival.
● **하기 강좌** (a) summer lecture course. **하기 방학** the summer vacation (from school). **하기 학교** a summer school. ⇨ 여름학교(⇨여름) **하기휴가** the summer vacation; 〔영〕 the summer holidays.

하기는 in fact; indeed. ¶~ …이지만, 그러나 (It is) true, but … // ~ 그래 It's a fact. / Yes, you are right. // 그는 힘이 세다. ~ 몸집도 크지만 He is strong, but then he is big, too. // 여자는 이 일을 할 수 없다. ~ 예외는 있지만 Women cannot do this job, though [of course] there are some exceptions.

하기식(下旗式) a flag-lowering ceremony; (군) a retreat.
● **하기식 나팔** a retreat.

하나 1 (숫자의) one; a unit. ¶그녀는 ~를 들으면 열을 안다 Drop a hint, and she will understand everything.
2 [한 개] one; a piece. ¶흔히 쓰이는 동사가 ~ 빠져 버렸다 One very common verb was left out.∥솔을 ~ 샀다 I bought a brush.∥이것들은 ~에 30원입니다 These are thirty won each[a piece].∥그는 방금 재미있는 정보를 ~ 들려주었다 He has just given me an interesting piece of information.(▶ an interesting information이라고는 하지 않음)∥그는 아이들에게 오렌지를 ~씩 나누어 주었다 He gave one orange to each child.∥그들은 순식간에 음식을 ~도 남기지 않고 먹어 치웠다 They ate up the food in no time.∥흉작의 원인 중의 ~는 불순한 기후 조건이다 The crop failure is due in part to the unusual weather conditions. / One of the causes of the crop failure is the unusual weather.
3 [유일] a single one; only one. ¶단 ~의 the only / the sole (survivor) / the one (and only) / solitary / single / unique / exclusive ∥ ~뿐인 친구 one's[the] one and only friend∥사과는 없습니다. 남은 것이 ~도 없습니다 We have no apples. There are none left.∥이 페이지에는 오식이 ~도 없다 There isn't a single misprint on this page.∥그것은 사장의 생각 ~로 결정된다 It depends ultimately on the president's decision.∥이것 ~밖에 없다 This is the only one.
4 [동일] the same. ¶~의 (one and) the same / identical∥우리의 생각은 ~다 Our ideas are the same.∥그들의 의견은 ~로 통일[조정]하는 것은 곤란하다 It is hard to put their views together into one unified opinion [reconcile their views].
5 [일체] one (body); one flesh. ¶~로 만들다 make into one / unite (into one) / unify / merge ∥ ~가 되다 become[get into] one / unite into one / be unified / be merged / come together∥세계는 ~다 The world is one.∥바다와 하늘이 수평선에서 ~로 되어 있다 The sea and the sky blend together at the horizon.∥전 국민이 ~가 되어 국난에 임했다 The whole nation rose as one man in the national crisis.
6 [조차] not even; not so much as. ¶그녀는 찌개 ~도 끓이지 못한다 She cannot even make a pot stew.∥그녀는 싫은 얼굴 ~ 하지 않고 부지런히 일했다 She worked hard with no sign of reluctance.∥그 일에 대해서는 ~도 아는 것이 없습니다 I know nothing about it.∥그에게 좋은 데가 ~도 없다 He has no special merit. / I can see nothing in him.∥나는 ~도 부끄러운 점이 없다 I have nothing to be ashamed of. / I am quite free from blame.
하나를 듣고 열을 알다 be quick to understand; be quick on the uptake.
하나만 알고 둘은 모르다 judge everything by one thing he knows.
하나부터 열까지 from beginning to end; in everything. ¶골프에 관한 일이라면 그는 ~ 알고 있다 He knows everything about golf.
하나님 God. ⇨하느님
하나하나 one after another; one by one; one at a time; piece by piece; [개별적으로] individually; separately; minutely; in all particulars; fully; in detail. ¶그것들을 ~ 수효를 헤아리려면 한이 없을 것이다 If you start counting them one by one, there will be no end to it.∥24권에 이르는 셰익스피어 전집이 ~ 출간됩니다 Shakespeare's Complete Works will come out in twenty-four volumes one after another.∥그는 자기 결점을 ~ 고쳐 갔다 He corrected his faults one by one.

하녀 (下女) a maid; a maidservant; a servant girl.

하느님 [가][기] God; the Almighty; the Lord; the Supreme Being; the Most High; a deity. ¶~의 가호 divine protection∥~의 말씀 the word of God / the word of the Spirit∥~의 은총 the blessing[grace] of God / divine blessing[grace]∥~을 믿다 believe in God∥~을 공경하다 revere God∥~을 찬양하다 glorify God∥~께 기도하다 pray to God∥~께 복을 빌다 pray to God for help[aid]∥~께 맹세코 그것은 진실이다 I swear to[by] God that it's true.∥무슨 일이 일어날지 ~만이 안다 God alone knows what will happen.∥~만이 알고 있다 God only knows.

하느작거리다 swing; sway. ⇨흐느적거리다

하늘 1 [천공] the sky; the blue; the heavens; (시어) the firmament; [창공] the skies; [공중] the air. ¶맑은[흐린] ~ a clear[cloudy] sky∥금방 비가 쏟아질 것 같은 ~ a threatening sky∥~로 치솟은 준봉 a rugged peak towering against the sky∥남쪽 ~에 빛나는 별 stars shining in the southern sky∥~에 닿을 것 같은 고층 건물 a sky-high building∥~을 날다 fly through the air∥~을 쳐다보다 look up at the sky[to Heaven] / raise one's face to[at] the sky[Heaven]∥연이 ~로 날아올랐다 The kite soared up into the sky.∥~ 높이 종달새가 지저귀고 있다 High up in the sky a lark is singing.∥시험에 합격하니 ~에 오른 것 같은 기분이었다 Having passed the examination, I was in (the) seventh heaven.∥그들은 ~을 찌르는 것 같은 기분으로 출발했다 They started out in the highest spirits.
2 [천국] heaven. ¶~에 계신 우리 아버지 (주기도문) Our Father which art[who is] in Heaven(▶ who is는 현대의 말투).
3 [하느님] God; Providence; Heaven. ¶~의 소리 a heavenly voice∥~의 도움 providential help∥그의 악독함은 ~이 알고 땅도 안다 Even though nobody seems to notice his evil acts, Heaven and earth know.∥그는 운을 ~에 맡겼다 He left it in the hands of Providence. / He entrusted it to Providence [chance].∥그는 이것도 ~의 뜻이라고 체념하였다 He resigned himself to it as God's will.∥~은 한 사람에게 두 가지 재능을 내리지 않는다 God does not give two gifts (to one person).

하늘 보고 침 뱉기(속담) What you are doing will backfire on you one of these days.
하늘은 스스로 돕는 자를 돕는다(속담) Heaven helps those who help themselves.
하늘이 무너져도 솟아날 구멍이 있다(속담) There is a way out of every situation, however bad.; Every cloud has its silver lining.; When one door closes, another one opens.

● **하늘나라** (the kingdom of) Heaven; Paradise; Elysium(천당). ¶그는 ~로 불리어 갔다 He was summoned to Heaven. / He was called to his heavenly home. **하늘색** sky blue; sky-blue color; azure.
하늘가재 [동] a stag beetle.

하늘거리다 idle one's time away; waver. ⇨하늘거리다
하늘소 [동] a long-horned beetle; a longicorn (beetle).
하늘하늘 idly; waveringly. ⇨ㅎ흐늘흐늘
하늘하늘하다 soft; pulpy. ⇨흐늘흐늘하다
하늬(바람) a west wind.
하다[1] **1** [행하다] do; perform; undertake; deliver (a speech); [해 보다] try; attempt; [실행하다] practice; put into practice; execute; set about; go in for. ¶하는 수 없이 unavoidably / inevitably / for want of any other alternative / for lack of anything better / [마지 못해서] reluctantly / unwillingly //…하려고 하여 in an effort [endeavor] to (do) / by way of (doing) // 하지 않으려고 ~ be reluctant [unwilling / disinclined / loath] to (do) / hate (doing / to do) / be backward in (doing) // 해야 할 일을 ~ do what is due to one / 하는 일 없이 idle away one's time / live an idle life [a life of ease] / eat the bread of idleness //…하게 되다 learn to (do) / come to (do) //…까지 하게 되다 go the length of (doing) // 해 버리다 get through (a task) / get (a thing) done / finish / make an end of (one's task) // 할 수 있는 데까지 해 보다 do one's best [utmost] / do all one can / 다시 한 번 해 보다 try again / make another attempt // 숙제를 해 주다 do a homework for (a boy) / help (a boy) with his homework / 심부름을 해 주다 run an errand (for a person) //…하기로 하고 있다 make it a rule to (do) / 할 생각이 있다 have a mind (to do) / be willing (to do) / feel like (doing) // 나는 하루분의 일을 했다 I've done a full day's work. / I've done a day's worth of work. // 그는 하는 일마다 잘되지 않았다 Nothing he did went right. // 거기까지 할 생각은 없다 I don't want to go that far [(영) to resort to such measures]. // 할 테면 해 보아라 Go ahead and do it! / Go ahead and try it, if you dare! // 어쩌자고 성급한 짓을 했는가 What a reckless thing you [he] did! / What a rash act! // 그렇게 해 주시면 고맙겠습니다 You will oblige me by doing so. // 그들은 그렇게밖에 할 수 없었다 There was nothing else they could do. / They had no other choice. // 왜 좀 더 여자답게 행동하지 못하니 Why don't you behave [act] a little more like a lady? // 제가 하겠습니다 I will do it. / 어떻게 할까요 What shall I [we] do (about it)? // 그녀는 어찌할 바를 모르고 우두커니 서 있었다 At a loss what to do, she stood there vacantly. // 「하면 된다」는 격언이 있다 As the saying goes, if you have a mind to do something, you can do it. // 나는 아들이 하는 대로 내버려 두겠다 I will let my son do as he likes. // 그는 하는 일도 없이 빈둥거리고 있다 He is idling his time away. / He lives an idle life. // 참 잘했다 Well done! // 한번 해 보시지요 Go on [ahead]! / (구어) Go to it! // 그것은 너무 어려워서 나는 할 수 없다 It is too difficult for me. // 나는 이런 일을 해 본 적이 없다 I am quite new [an utter stranger] to this kind of work.
2 (음식 등을) take; have; help oneself to; eat (먹다); drink (마시다), smoke (피우다). ¶나는 술도 담배도 하지 않소 I neither drink nor smoke. // (주문을 받을 때) 뭘로 하시겠습니까 Your order?
3 [부르다] call; name; style; term. ¶X라고 하는 사나이 (자칭하는) a man who gives the name of [calls himself] X / (그런 이름의) a man of [by] the name of X / a man named [called] X / a man, X by name // 나는 최민수라고 합니다 My name is Choe Minsu. (▶ 영어로는 성과 함께 이름도 말하는 것이 보통임) // 그 사람은 결코 학자라고 할 수는 없다 He has no claim to scholarship.
4 [사칭하다] pretend; feign; [주장하다] claim; [항변하다] plead. ¶친척이라고 ~ claim to be (a person's) relative // 왕이라고 ~ assume the title of king.
5 [소문에 듣다] they [people] say; it is said; I hear; I am told; I understand. ¶그렇다고 하더군 So I understand. / So I hear. // 그는 지금 앓고 있다고 한다 He is reported [said] to be ill. // 그는 내일 상경한다고 한다 He is expected in Seoul tomorrow.
6 [알다] know; [배우다] study; learn. ¶나는 일주일에 두 번 독일어 공부를 하고 있다 I take lessons in German twice a week. // 대학에서는 수학을 했소 (전공했다) I majored in mathematics at the university. / (연구했다) (미) I studied mathematics in college. / (영) I studied mathematics at university.
7 (직업·노릇을) act [officiate / serve] as; [종사하다] engage [be engaged] in; [경영하다] keep; run (a restaurant); work; operate. ¶아버님은 약국을 하고 있습니다 My father keeps [runs] a drugstore. / My father is a pharmacist [druggist]. // 그는 무슨 장사를 하는 사람이냐 What does he do? / What line of business is he in? / What is he engaged in? // 그는 변호사 [의사]를 하고 있다 He practices law [medicine]. // 나는 두 사람의 중매인 노릇을 했다 I acted as the go-between for the two. // 저는 전에 선생 노릇을 했습니다 I used to be a teacher.
8 [공연·연기하다] perform; act; play. ¶이 역은 누가 하지 Who will play this part?
9 (놀이·운동을) play (baseball); have (a game at billiards). ¶체스를 하자 Let's play chess.
10 [말하다] say; remark; talk; speak. ¶남들이야 뭐라고 하든 whatever others may say (about / of) // 지금 뭐라고 했니 What did you say just now? // 한마디 하게 해 주시오 Let me say one thing, if I may. / There is one thing I would like to say.
11 (값이) cost; be worth. ¶이 그림은 500만 원 한다 This picture is worth [will fetch] five million won. // 이 종류의 시계는 10만 원은 할 것이다 A watch of this kind will easily cost a hundred thousand won. // 그 양복은 얼마나 하던가요 How much did you pay for that dress?
12 [경험하다] experience; go through. ¶고생을 많이 ~ go through hardships and privations.
13 [착용하다] wear; have on; be dressed in. ¶형편없는 옷차림을 하고 있다 be shabbily [poorly] dressed / be ill-clad.
14 [정하다] fix; decide; make. ¶구류 기간은 2개월(이하)로 한다 The term of detention shall not exceed two months.
-하지 않도록 (so as) not to (do); so that ... may not (do); lest ... should; for fear (that). ¶지각~ 서두르자 Let's hurry so we won't be

late.∥그녀에게 말~ 해라 Take care to tell her.∥나는 시험에 낙제~ 열심히 공부한다 I work hard so as not to fail in the examination. / I work hard lest I should fail in the examination.

-하지 않을 수 없다 cannot help doing; cannot but do; (미) cannot help but do; be obliged [compelled] to (do). ¶사직하지 않을 수 없게 되다 be compelled to resign one's post∥이 사실을 개탄~ I cannot help deploring this fact.∥그녀는 진실을 말하지 않을 수 없었다 She could not help telling the truth.

할 말 1 [해야 할 말] one's say; what one has to say; [주장] one's claim. ¶~은 해야 한다 You should say what you have to say. ∥~이 있으면 하도록 내버려 두어라 If he has anything to say, let him speak out.∥너 ~이 있느냐 What have you to say?∥~ 있으면 해 봐라 Say your say. / Tell me what you have to say.∥별로 ~이 없다 I have no say in the matter.∥I have nothing special to say for myself.∥사람에게는 누구나 ~이 있다 Each has his own claims.∥양쪽 모두 ~이 많다 There is much to be said [Much can be said] on both sides. **2** [이의] an objection; [불평] a complaint; a grievance. ¶~이 있다 have an objection (to / against) / have something to complain of / be dissatisfied (with) / ~이 없다 have no objection (to / against) / have nothing to complain of / be satisfied (with) ∥너는 아무것도 ~이 없을 텐데 I don't think you have anything to complain of.∥이거라면 그도 ~이 없을 게다 This will satisfy him.∥너에게 ~이 많다 I have a bone to pick with you.

해야 하다 have to (do); must (do); should (do); ought to (do). ¶곧 출발을 해야 한다 I must set out at once.∥자기 일은 자기가 해야 한다 You ought to look after yourself.

하다² consider; think (of / about / over); make. ¶그는 서울에 가 볼까 했다 He took it into his head to go up to Seoul.∥그녀의 아버지는 그녀에게 화분의 나무에 물을 주게 하였다 Her father made her water the potted plants.∥그녀는 자기 아들에게 개집을 짓게 하였다 She got her son to build a doghouse. ∥그의 어머니는 그를 역으로 보내 그의 할아버지를 마중하게 하였다 His mother sent him [had him go] to the station to meet his grandfather.

하다³ [매우] really; quite; indeed; very. ¶아름답기도 ~ be really beautiful∥빠르기도 ~ be speedy indeed∥참 이상하기도 ~ How strange!∥정말 날씨가 좋기도 ~ How fine! / Fine day, isn't it?

하다못해 [심지어] so far as; to the extent of; even; [적어도] at (the) least; at the lowest; to say the least (of it); [별도리 없이] under the pressure of necessity; driven by necessity; [종국에는] in the end; finally. ¶~ …하다 be compelled [forced / obliged] to (do) / be [find oneself] under the necessity of (doing) / be driven by dire [sheer] necessity to (do) ∥그의 하인들까지도 주인을 멸시하였다 Even his servants despised him.∥~ 하루만이라도 더 계십시오 Stay just [at least] one day longer.∥그가 ~ 말이라도 그렇게 해 주었으면 좋았을걸 He might at least have told me so.∥~ 만 원이라도 주었으면 좋겠다 At least you can let me have 10,000 won.∥~ 나에게 이야기라도 했었더라면 좋았을걸 I wish you had told me about it, though.

하단(下段) a lower portion [division / paragraph].

하단(下端) the bottom tip [point / part] (of); the lower end (of).

하단하다(下壇-) leave [go down / descend from] the platform [rostrum / pulpit].

하달하다(下達-) notify (to an inferior); convey (to the people); pass down (word); (명령을) give [lay on] (a command); issue (orders). ¶상의(上意)를 ~ convey the will and ideas of a superior officer to subordinate officials / pass down word (that …)∥명령을 ~ issue an order [a command] / give orders.

하대(下待) **1** [낮게 대접함] inhospitable treatment; a disrespectable reception; inhospitality. **하대하다** treat [receive] (a person) inhospitably; be inhospitable (towards). **2** [상대에게 낮은말을 씀]. **하대하다** call (a person) by name without any honorific title; call (a person) by his last name only; do not mister (a person).

하도 too; too much; excessively; to excess; (미) overly; very much; ever so much [hard / fast …]. ¶~ 기뻐서 in the excess [fullness] of one's joy / through excess of joy / elated by joy / in one's joy / for joy∥~ 슬퍼서 in one's grief / in a passion of grief∥~ 보고 싶어서 in one's eagerness to see it∥~ 바빠서 잠도 제대로 잘 수 없다 be too busy to get enough sleep∥이 책은 ~ 어려워서 읽을 수가 없다 This book is too difficult for me to read.

하도급(下都給) subcontracting; a subcontract. ¶~ 주다 sublet / underlet.
●**하도급업자** a subcontractor; a subcontract firm(업체).

하도롱지(-紙) brown paper; sulfate paper; kraft paper.

하드 디스크 a hard disk.

하드 록 [음] hard rock.

하드보드 [건] hardboard.

하드보일드 hard-boiled. ¶~의 문체[추리 소설] a hard-boiled style [detective story].

하드웨어 [컴] hardware.

하등(下等) [하급] a low(er) class [grade]; [열등] inferiority; [조잡] coarseness; [천속(賤俗)] bad form; bad taste. ¶~의 low / lower (plant) / inferior / mean / coarse / vulgar / (구어) infamous / (속어) rotten.
●**하등 동물** the lower animals; animals of the lower orders; (무척추동물) invertebrates. **하등 식물** the lower plants; the plants of a lower order. **하등품** an inferior article; an article of inferior quality.

하등(何等) what; whatever; (not) any; no; (not) in any way. ¶~의 이유도 없이 without any reason / for nothing∥~의 위험도 없이 without the least danger∥~의 관계도 없다 have no relation [connection] whatever (with) / have nothing to do (with) / be not in any way related (with)∥~ 이상할 것 없다 There is nothing strange about it.∥~ 이상이 없다 Nothing is wrong [the matter]. / (미) Everything's O.K.

하락(下落) (가격의) a fall [drop / decline] (in price); depreciation; a slump(폭락); (품질의) deterioration; [증권] a sag; a downturn. ¶

가의 ~ a fall [decline] in the price of commodities // 쌀값의 ~ a fall in the price of rice // 급격한 ~ a sharp [precipitate] drop // ~을 예상하고 in anticipation of a decline [drop]. **하락하다** fall (off); decline; come [go] down; depreciate; sink; [(가치가) 떨어지다] deteriorate; degrade; [증권] sag; show a downward [declining] tendency. ¶물가가 하락했다 Prices have come down [fallen]. // 주가가 하락하고 있다 Stock prices are falling [declining]. // 그녀의 인기는 하락하고 있다 She is declining in popularity. / Her popularity is on the wane [decline]. ➔¶하락시키다 depreciate / lower / bring down (prices) / degrade(가치를 떨어뜨리다).
● **하락세** (show) a declining tendency; (take) a downward trend; a downtrend.
하략(下略) the rest [last part] omitted. **하략하다** omit the rest [the concluding part].
하렘 a harem.
하례(賀禮) [축하식] a congratulatory ceremony; a celebration; [축하] congratulation; felicitations; greetings. ¶신년 ~ the New Year's ceremony // ~를 **받다** accept (a person's) felicitation. **하례하다** hold [perform] a congratulatory ceremony; celebrate; congratulate [felicitate] (a person on [upon]); offer one's felicitations (on).
하루 1 [일수] a day. ¶~의 일 a day's work // ~ **종일** all day (long) // 온 ~ a whole day // ~ 건너서 every other [second] day // ~이 틀에 in a day or two // 2번 twice a day // ~도 빠짐없이[거르지 않고] hardly a day goes by but [that ... not] // 10년을 ~같이 for ten years as one day / for ten years without intermission // ~ 3,000원을 쓰다 spend 3,000 won a day // ~라도 빨리 하다 lose no time in doing (something) // ~를 헛되이 보내다 idle away a day // ~ 종일 기다리다 wait for (someone) all day long // ~ 세 끼 먹다 take three meals a day. // 그는 단 ~도 불평하지 않는 날이 없다 There's not a single day when he doesn't complain.
2 the first day of a month. ⇨초하룻날(⇨초하루).
3 [어느 날] one day. ¶~ **저녁** one evening // ~는 근교의 몇몇 절에 가 보았다 One day I visited some temples in the suburbs.
● **하루갈이** an area of land that takes a day's plowing. **하루거리** [의] malignant [falciparum / subtertian] malaria. ¶~에 걸리다 be taken with malignant [subtertian] malaria. **하루살이** [동] a mayfly; a dayfly; an ephemera (*pl*. ~s, -rae). ¶~ 같은 [덧없는] ephemeral / transitory / [짧은 목숨의] short-lived // 그 당시 나는 ~와 같이 근근이 생활하고 있었다 At the time I was living from hand to mouth [I was barely making ends meet]. // 그는 ~ 인생이다 He lives from day to day. **하루치** a day's portion; a ration (식량의). ¶~의 일 a day's work. **하룻날** the first day (of a month). **하룻밤** [한 밤] a night; one evening [night]; [온 밤] all night (long); all the night through; [어느 낮 밤] one night. ¶~ **사이에** in one night / overnight // ~의 숙박 a night's lodging / lodging for one night // ~을 **묵다** stay overnight / put up for the night // 우리는 들판에서 캠핑을 하며 ~을 지냈다 We spent the night camping in the field. // 나는 옛 친구와 이야기를 나누며 ~을

새웠다 I stayed up all night talking with an old friend of mine. // ~이 지나 깨어 보니 온 통 눈세계였다 I woke up to find the whole world covered with snow.
하루바삐 without a day's delay; as soon as possible; as soon as one can. ¶~ 회복되시기를 **빕니다** I pray for your earliest possible recovery. // 이 병은 ~ 치료해야만 한다 This illness calls for [requires] prompt treatment.
하루아침에 overnight; in a day; in a brief space of time. ¶~ 유명해지다 leap [flash / spring at a bound] into fame // 로마는 ~ 이루어진 것이 아니다 Rome was not built in a day.
하루하루 every day; daily; from day to day; day after [by] day. ¶~ **나아지다** get better day by day // 그는 해야 할 일을 ~ 늦추는 경향이 있다 He tends to put off what he has to do from day to day. / He tends to procrastinate. // 나는 ~를 뜻있게 보내고 싶다 I want to use each day meaningfully. // 그는 나무를 베어 ~의 양식을 벌고 있었다 He earned his daily bread by cutting wood. // 나는 겨우 ~의 생활비를 버는 것이 고작이다 I just manage to earn enough for my day-to-day [daily] needs.
하룻강아지 a (one-day-old) puppy [pup / whelp].
하룻강아지 범 무서운 줄 모른다(속담) Fools rush in where angels fear to tread.; Boldness is blind.
하류(下流) **1** [하천의] the lower reaches of a river [stream]. ¶배는 ~를 향해 나아가고 있었다 The boat was going downstream [down the river]. // 50미터 ~에 선착장이 있다 There is a landing place 50 meters down the river. // 이 ~에 작은 부락이 있다 [There is a hamlet downstream [downriver]. **2** [사회의 하층 계급] the lower classes.
● **하류 계급** the lower classes. **하류 사회** the lower classes; the lower order [strata] of society. **하류 생활** (a) low life.
하륙(下陸) unloading; discharge; landing; disembarkation. **하륙하다** land (cargo); discharge [unload] (a ship / cargo from a ship).
하르르 thin(ly); flimsily; sleazily. **하르르하다** thin; flimsy; sleazy. ¶하르르한 종이 flimsy paper.
하릅 a one-year-old (horse, ox, dog, etc.); a yearling.
하리놀다 [중상하다] slander; calumniate; malign; scandalize; defame.
하릴없다 1 [어찌할 수 없다] inevitable; unavoidable; inescapable; (서술적) cannot help (it); (it) cannot be helped; cannot choose but (do). ¶네게 비난을 받아도 ~ I know I deserve your reproaches. **하릴없이** unavoidably; inevitably; helplessly. ¶~ …하다 be compelled [obliged / forced] to (do) / be hard put to it to (do) // ~ 최후의 수단을 쓰다 be driven [impelled] to extreme measures. **2** [틀림없다] not a bit different (from); just like; absolutely identical (with). **하릴없이** correctly; precisely.
하마(河馬) [동] a hippopotamus (*pl*. ~es, -mi); (구어) a hippo (*pl*. ~s).
하마터면 almost; nearly; (속어) as near as a toucher. ¶나는 ~ 목숨을 잃을 뻔했다 I came within an inch of being killed. / I very

하마평 (下馬評) an outsider's irresponsible talk; gossip; an advance rumor. ¶내각 개편에 관하여 여러 가지 ~이 나돌고 있다 There are all sorts of rumors [things being whispered] about the Cabinet reshuffle.

하면 (夏眠) (a)estivation. **하면하다** (a)estivate.

하명 (下命) [명령] orders; a command. ¶그에게 곧 전선에 출동하라는 ~이 있었다 He was ordered [commanded] to depart for the front at once. ∥ 무엇이든 ~만 해 주십시오 I am always at your service. **하명하다** order; command.

하모니 harmony. ¶그 그룹은 ~가 결여되어 있다 There is no harmony within the group.

하모니카 [음] a harmonica; a mouth organ. ¶~로 징글벨을 불다 play "Jingle Bells" on a harmonica.

하묘 (下錨) anchoring; anchorage; dropping anchor. **하묘하다** anchor; cast [let fall] anchor; drop (its [her]) anchor; come to (an) anchor; let go the anchor.

하문 (下門) [생] the vulva. ⇨=음문

하문 (下問) ¶그 사건에 대해서 폐하의 ~이 있었다 There was an inquiry from the Emperor concerning that incident. **하문하다** ask [consult] one's subordinates. ¶불치(不恥)~ be not ashamed to seek counsel of an inferior.

하물 (荷物) a load; a burden. ⇨=짐1
● **하물 취급소** a baggage office [room].

하물며 (긍정) (how) much more; still more; (부정) much [still] less; to say nothing of. ¶나는 동요도 잘 못 부르는데 ~ 오페라는 더 말할 것도 없다 I cannot even sing children's songs well, to say nothing of [much less, let alone] opera. ∥ 이 일이 당신에게 어렵다면 ~ 내게는 더 말할 것도 없다 If this task is hard for you, think how much harder it must be [it must be still harder] for me! ∥ 제자의 작품이 저토록 훌륭한데, ~ 스승의 작품은 훨씬 훌륭했음에 틀림없다 If the disciple's work is so splendid, his teacher's (work) must have been much more so. ∥ 그녀는 말도 제대로 할 줄 모르는데, ~ 범절을 알 리가 없다 She does not even know how to speak properly, let alone how to behave.

하바네라 [음] (a) habanera.

하박 (下膊) the forearm.
● **하박골** forearm bones.

하반기 (下半期) the second [latter] half of the year; the half-year ending December 31.

하반신 (下半身) the lower half of one's body.

하복 (夏服) summer clothes; (제복) a summer uniform.

하복부 (下腹部) [생] the abdominal [hypogastric] region; the abdomen; the underbelly; the hypogastrium (pl. -tria).

하부 (下部) the lower part.
● **하부 구조** a substructure; the understructure (of). **하부 기관** subordinate agencies [offices]. **하부 조직** a substructure; a subordinate organization. ¶어느 도시에나 이 정당의 ~이 있다 This (political) party has an organization [a branch] in every town.

하분하분하다 soft and juicy.

하비다 1 [할퀴다] scratch; claw; maul(맹수가). 2 [헐뜯다] find fault (with); try to find a fault (in a person [thing]); pick flaws with.

하사 (下士) [군] (육군·공군·해병) a staff sergeant; (해군) a petty officer second class.

하사 (下賜) a royal [an imperial] grant [donation / gift]. **하사하다** give; grant; confer; bestow (a sword on a person). ¶군주가 하사한 땅 land bestowed [granted] by one's lord.
● **하사금** an Imperial [a Royal] donation. **하사품** an Imperial [a Royal] gift.

하사관 (下士官) ➡부사관

하산하다 (下山-) 1 [산에서 내려오다] climb [come] down a mountain. 2 [절을 떠나다] leave a temple.

하상 (河床) [하천의 바닥] a riverbed.

하선 (荷船) a small cargo vessel.

하선하다 (下船-) leave a steamer; go ashore; get off a ship; disembark.

하소 (煆燒) [화] calcination; calcining; roast. **하소하다** calcine; roast.

하소연 appealing; complaining; making a plea (to). ¶~을 들어주다 give (a person) a hearing. **하소연하다** make an appeal [a plea] (to); appeal (to); complain of (a grievance); whine (about). ¶서러운 사정을 ~ complain of one's sad plight / plead one's sad situation ∥ 억울함을 ~ complain of an injustice.

하수 (下水) foul water; sewage; sewerage. ¶~가 넘치고 있다 The sewage has overflowed [overflown].
● **하수구** a cesspipe; a sewer pipe; a drainpipe. **하수구** a ditch; a drain; a kennel; a sewer; a gutter. ¶~를 치다 clear (out) a ditch / clean a drain ∥ ~가 막혔다 The drain is obstructed. **하수도** sewerage; drainage; a sewer system. **하수 정화** sewage purification. **하수 처리장** a sewage disposal [treatment] plant.

하수¹ (下手) [낮은 솜씨] unskillfulness; awkwardness; [낮은 솜씨의 사람] a poor hand; (장기·바둑의) a lower grader; a low-grade player.

하수² (下手) 1 [살인] murder; killing. **하수하다** murder; kill; slay; put (a man) to death. 2 start. ⇨=착수(着手)
● **하수인** the perpetrator (of a crime); an offender; a culprit; a criminal(범인); [살인자] the murderer; the slayer. ¶폭행의 ~을 밝혀내다 trace the outrage home to its perpetrator.

하숙 (下宿) [숙박하기] boarding; lodging; board and lodging; (미) board and room. ¶~ 생활을 하다 live in lodgings [a lodging house] ∥ ~을 옮기다 change one's lodgings ∥ ~을 치다 run [operate / keep] a lodging house ∥ ~을 찾고 있다 be on a hunt for lodgings ∥ 나는 학교 근처에 ~을 잡았다 I have taken rooms near the school. **하숙하다** lodge [board / room] 《at a house / with a person》. ¶나는 양 씨 댁에 하숙하고 있다 I lodge at Mr. Yang's. / I have a room at Mr. Yang's.
● **하숙방** a room for boarding; a lodger's [boarder's] room. **하숙비** board charge; the

boarding expenses[charges]. ¶나의 ~는 식비까지 합해서 월 40만 원이다 I pay 400,000 won a month for room and board. **하숙생** a student boarder. **하숙집** (one's) lodgings; a boardinghouse.

하순(下旬) the last ten days[third] (of a month). ¶9월 ~에 toward the end of September / late in September // 10월 ~ 중에 during the last ten days of October.

하악(下顎) [생] the lower jaw. ⇨°아래턱(⇨아래)
● **하악골** the lower jawbone. ⇨°아래턱뼈(⇨아래)

하안(河岸) a riverside; a riverbank; a waterfront.

하야말갛다 whitish and thin. ⇨°허여멀겋다
하야말쑥하다 white and clean. ⇨°허여멀쑥하다

하야하다(下野―) go out of office; retire[go back] to private life; retire from public life; resign one's public[government] post; step down.

하양 white; whiteness.

하얗다 pure white; snow(y)-white; (as) white as snow; immaculately white. ¶하얀 시트 an immaculate sheet // 문을 하얗게 칠하다 paint a door white // 그녀의 머리가 ~ She has snow-white. // 일어나 보니 눈이 하얗게 쌓여 있었다 I awoke to find the ground covered over with white snow.

하얘지다 become pure white[snow(y)-white]; (머리가) turn gray[white]. ¶그녀의 머리가 하얘졌다 Her hair turned white[gray]. // 그의 얼굴이 하얘졌다 His face went pale[got white as a sheet]. // 그녀의 얼굴은 화장을 해서 하얘졌다 Her face has been whitened with makeup.

하여간(에)(何如間―) anyhow; anyway; at any rate; somehow or other.

하여금 […을 시키어]. ¶그로 ~ 다시 한번 해 보게 해라 Let him have another try! / Give him one more chance! / 내 아들로 ~ 역까지 모셔다 드리게 할까요 Shall I have my son accompany you to the station? // 그로 ~ 나에게 편지를 쓰도록 해라 Let[Make] him write a letter to me.

하여튼(何如―) anyway; anyhow. ⇨°아무튼 ¶그것은 ~ be that as it may / be the matter what it may // ~ 그렇게 하겠다 I will do so, anyway. // ~ 저녁 식사나 하자꾸나 At any rate, let's have supper. // ~ 점심때까지 기다려 보자 Well, at any rate, I will wait for him till noon. // ~ 그가 싫다 I don't like him anyway. // ~ 그에게 물어보자 Let's ask him anyway. // ~ 출발을 연기해야겠다 In any case[At all events], we have to postpone our departure. // ~ 사실이다 Believe it or not, it's a fact. // ~ 나는 끝까지 하렵니다 Anyhow, I'm going to stick it out. // ~ 도중에 계획을 변경할 수는 없다 In any case[At any rate], we can't change our plans halfway. // ~ 그가 적어도 회답만이라도 해야 했다 Be that as it may, he should at least have answered.

하역(荷役) loading and unloading (of vessels); shipping and discharging; stevedoring; cargo work. ¶석탄의 ~ coal-handling // 그들은 석탄의 ~ 작업을 완료했다 They finished the work of loading the coal. // 부두의 하역부들은 ~을 끝내고 휴식했다 After loading the ship[Having finished loading], the longshoremen took a break[stopped for a rest]. **하역하다** load and unload; ship and discharge.
● **하역부** a stevedore; (미) a longshoreman (pl. -men); a wharf[(영) dock] laborer. **하역장치** a cargo gear.

하염없다 1 [아무 생각이 없다] absentminded; vacant; blank; abstracted. ¶하염없는 이야기 hollow[empty] words / a meaningless talk. **하염없이** blankly; vacantly; absentmindedly; abstractedly; (헛되이) idly. ¶~ 생각에 잠기다 be in a brown study / be lost in reverie[in the clouds] / ~ 바라보다 look vacantly [blankly] (at) / stare into space // ~ 세월을 보내다 idle one's time away / loaf away one's time[days] // ~ 걸어가다 stroll absentmindedly. 2 [끝이 없다] endless; boundless; unlimited; infinite. **하염없이** endlessly; ceaselessly; unceasingly. ¶~ 눈물을 흘리다 give free vent to one's tears.

하염직하다 worth (doing); (서술적) be worthy of (praise). ¶그것은 하염직한 일이다 It is a job worth doing.

하오(下午) afternoon. ⇨°오후(午後)

하옥(下獄) imprisonment; confinement. **하옥하다** put (a person) in prison[in jail]; throw [cast] (a person) into prison; imprison; send (a criminal) to prison. ➔¶하옥되다 be put in jail / be sent to prison[jail].

하원(下院) the Lower House[Chamber]; (영국의) the House of Commons; (미국의) the House of Representatives; (프랑스의) the Chamber of Deputies.
● **하원 의원** a member of the House of Representatives; (영국의) a member of Parliament; an M.P.; (미국의) a Representative.

하위(下位) a low(er) rank; a subordinate position; a low(er) grade. ¶~에 있다 occupy [hold] a subordinate position (to) / be placed under (another) / be below (another) in rank / be inferior (to) // ~로 떨어지다 sink in the scale // 그는 부사장보다 ~에 있다 He is below the vice-president in rank.
● **하위 타자** [야구] a low-ranking batter.

하의(下衣) (a pair of) trousers; (미) pantaloons; pants.

하의(下意) 1 [아랫사람의 뜻] the will and ideas[the wishes] of the lower-grade personnel. 2 [민의] the will of the people; the popular opinion. ¶~를 **상달**(上達)**하다** convey the will of those who are governed to those who govern.

하이 다이빙 high diving; a high dive.

하이라이트 a highlight. ¶올림픽의 ~ the highlights of the Olympics // 우리 대학 제전의 ~는 셰익스피어 극이다 The highlights of our College Festival is a Shakespearean play.

하이볼 (미) a highball; (영) a whisky and soda.

하이에나 [동] a hyena.

하이재킹 [항공기의 탈취] hijacking (of an airplane); skyjacking.

하이칼라(°high collar) 1 [멋쟁이] a stylish man; a smart fellow; a man of fashion; a dandy; [멋있음] stylishness; smartness; chic. ¶~의 [맵시를 낸] foppish / dandyish / [멋있는] smart / chic / stylish / fashionable / of the latest fashion. 2 (헤어스타일의)

하이킹 one's hair in foreign style. ¶~ 머리를 하다 dress one's hair in foreign style.

하이킹 (a) hiking; a hike. **하이킹하다** go on a hike; go hiking; hike (to).

하이테크 high-tech; high technology.

하이틴(*high teen) one's late teens. ¶~의 소년 [소녀] a boy[girl] in his[her] late teens // 그녀는 ~이다 She is late in her teens.

하이파이 hi-fi; high fidelity. ¶~의 hi-fi / high-fidelity.

하이퍼링크 a hyperlink.

하이픈 a hyphen. ¶~을 넣다[~으로 잇다] hyphen / hyphenate // 이 단어에는 ~이 들어가야 한다 This word needs to be hyphenated.

하이힐 high-heeled shoes; (wear) high heels. ¶그녀는 ~을 신고 있다 She is wearing high heels[high-heeled shoes].

하인(下人) a servant; a domestic (servant). ¶~을 두다 keep a servant / have a servant in one's service.

하인(何人) [어떤 사람] everyone; every person; all. ¶~을 막론하고 whoever it may be / irrespective of age, sex and nationality / no matter who he may be // ~을 막론하고 들어서는 안 된다 You shouldn't let anybody in, whoever it may be.

하인방(下引枋) [건] a lower lintel; a skirting board beam.

하자(瑕疵) a flaw; a blemish; a blur; a defect. ¶~ 있는 권원(權原) a defective title // ~ 없는 flawless / immaculate / all-perfect.

하잘것없다 trifling; trivial; petty; insignificant; worthless; poor. ¶하잘것없는 선물 a trifling gift / 하잘것없는 일로 소란을 피우다 make a fuss about trifles / make much of a trifling matter // 하잘것없는 일로 다투었다 We quarreled[We had a quarrel] over a trifle.

하저(河底) a riverbed; the bed[bottom] of a river.

하전(荷電) [전] electric charge.
● **하전 입자** a charged particle.

하절(夏節) summertime. ⇨"여름철(⇨여름)

하정(賀正) New Year's congratulations[greetings]; [연하장의 문구] A Happy New Year!

하제(下劑) a purgative; a purge; [완하제] a laxative; a cathartic. ¶~를 쓰다 use[take] a purgative[laxative] / purge the bowels.

하종가(下終價) [증권] (hit) the daily permissible bottom.

하주(荷主) a shipper(적적인) a consignor(하송인); the owner of goods(소유주).

하중(荷重) load. ¶동(動)~ live[mobile / dynamic] load // 마력 ~ [항] weight per horsepower loading // 안전 ~ safe load // 유료 ~ pay load // 정(靜)~ dead load // 부동 ~ static load // 제한 ~ proof load.

하지(下肢) a leg. ⇨"다리'1

하지(夏至) [24절기의 하나] *haji*; the summer solstice.
● **하지선** the tropic of Cancer.

하지만 but; however; yet; nevertheless; still; though. ¶그날 아침은 비가 몹시 왔다. ~ 우리는 출발했다 It was raining hard that morning, but we set out all the same.

하지하(下之下) the lowest of its kind; the poorest[worst] of all.

하직(下直) leave-taking; leave; a farewell; good-by(e). ¶~ 인사를 하러 가다 go for a parting call / pay (a person) a farewell visit // ~을 고하다 bid (a person) adieu. **하직하다** take (one's) leave (of); say good-bye (to); bid farewell. ¶부모의 슬하를 ~ leave[bid farewell to] one's parental roof / live away from one's parents / 고향을 ~ leave one's hometown [native place] // 이 세상을 ~ leave this world / depart this life / die.

하차(下車) getting off[out]; alighting (from a train). ¶~ 시에는 발밑을 조심하십시오 Watch your step when you get off[leave] the train. **하차하다** get off (the train); get down (from a car); alight (from a train); get out (of a car). ¶나는 부산에서 하차한다 I shall break my journey[stop off / stop over] at Busan.

하찮다 [사소하다] trifling; trivial; petty; insignificant; [무가치하다] worthless; valueless; good-for-nothing; poor; trashy; [쓸모없다] useless. ¶하찮은 일 a matter of no importance[account] / a trifling thing / a trifle / a trivial affair[matter] // 하찮은 너석 a worthless fellow / a petty underling / (미) a nothing // 일상생활의 하찮은 근심 걱정 petty worries of everyday life // 하찮은 의견 an opinion of little significance[weight] // 하찮은 일을 걱정하다 worry about little things [trifles / trivial matters] // 하찮은 일로 언쟁을 하다 quarrel about[over] trifles[trivial matters] // 하찮게 여기다 make light[little] of / think little[nothing] of / belittle // 하찮은 일을 크게 떠벌리다 make much of a trifling matter / make a mountain of molehill / overdraw a matter // 그는 하찮은 일에도 툭하면 법석을 떤다 He tends to fret[fuss] over little things[trifles].

하천(河川) rivers; watercourses.
● **하천 공사** river conservation work. **하천 부지** the[dry] riverbed. **하천 오염** the river contamination. ¶공장 폐수에 의한 ~ industrial pollution of a river.

하청(下請) a subcontract. ¶~을 주다 sublet / subcontract // 저 회사는 수주한 일을 모두 ~ 주고 있다 That company farms[parcels] out all their orders to subcontractors.
● **하청 공사** subcontracted work. **하청 공장** a subcontract factory. **하청인** a subcontractor.

하체(下體) [아랫도리] the lower part of the body; the nether limbs; [음부] the pubic region; the pubes.

하층(下層) **1** [아래층] a lower layer[stratum]; an underlayer; a substratum (*pl.* -rata). **2** [아래의 계급] a lower social stratum. ¶~의 lower-class.
● **하층 계급** the lower classes. **하층민** the people of the lower classes; the great unwashed; common[vulgar] herd; the rabble. ¶최~ the dregs of society. **하층 사회** the lower strata of society. **하층 생활** (a) low life. **하층운** lower clouds.

하치(下-) low-grade goods; goods of inferior [poor] quality. ¶이 물건은 ~이다 This article is of inferior quality.

하치장(荷置場) a yard; a storage space; a depository; a repository. ¶노천의 석탄 ~ an open storage yard for coal.

하키 [체] hockey. ¶필드~ field hockey // 아이스~ ice hockey // ~를 하다 play hockey.
● **하키 선수** a hockey player. **하키 스틱** a hockey stick.

하퇴(下腿) the (lower) leg; [생] the crus (*pl.* crura).
● **하퇴골** the leg bones.
하트 [카드놀이의] a heart. ¶~의 퀸[에이스/잭] the queen[ace/knave] of hearts.
하편(下篇) the last volume.
하품 [하품하기] yawning; (한 번의) a yawn. ¶~을 크게 하다 yawn a big long yawn / give a big yawn // ~을 하면서 말하다 yawn out (something) // ~을 참다 suppress[stifle] a yawn / choke down a yawn / bite off a yawn // 손으로 ~을 가리다 hide a yawn behind one's hand // ~을 하며 기지개 켜다 stretch oneself with a yawn // 하품은 옮는다 Yawning is catching. // 그의 말을 들으면 ~이 난다 His speeches are boring. **하품하다** yawn; gape. ¶신문을 보며 ~ yawn over the papers.
하품(下品) **1** [낮은 품격] vulgarity; coarseness; grossness; indecency. **2** low-grade goods. ⇨⌜하치⌝
하프 [음] a harp. ¶~를 연주하다 play the harp.
하프백 [축구] a halfback; [럭비] a scrum half. ¶~을 맡다 play halfback.
하프시코드 [음] a harpsichord.
하프 타임 half time.
하필 of all things (in the world); of all occasions[places]; of all people[persons] (사람일 때). ¶~ 그날에 on that day of all days [all others] // ~ 왜 제가 가야만 합니까 Why should I go of all persons? // ~ 왜 그 사람에게 부탁했지 Why did you ask him, of all people? // ~ 오늘 교통사고를 당하다니 That I should have a traffic accident today, of all days! // 하고많은 여자 중에 ~ 그가 저런 여자와 결혼하다니 Of all the women in the world, I can not imagine why he had to marry her. // ~ 옛날의 스캔들을 지껄이다니 What sort of a man is he to talk about the old scandal, of all thing! / Of all thing, to talk about an old scandal!
하하¹ ha! ha! ⇨⌜허허¹⌝
하하² Oh; Alas!; Oops! ⇨⌜허허²⌝
하학(下學) [수업이 끝남] ending of the school day. ¶~ 후에 after school (is over). **하학하다** leave school; come home from school; school ends for the day; school gets[lets] out.
● **하학 시간** dismissal time. **하학종** the dismissal bell.
하한(下限) the lowest limit; the greatest lower bound; the inferior limit(날짜의).
● **하한선** the lowest limit; the minimum.
하항(河港) a river port.
하해(河海) rivers and seas. ¶~ 같은 은혜 a great debt of gratitude / unlimited grace.
하행(下行) going down (from Seoul). **하행하다** go down (from Seoul); go into the country.
● **하행선** a down line. **하행 열차** an outbound[a down] train.
하향(下向) **1** [아래로 향함] a downward look. **하향하다** (얼굴을) look down; lower one's gaze[eyes]; (방향이) point downward. **2** [증권] a downward tendency[trend]. **하향하다** begin to decline[fall]; show a downward tendency[trend].
● **하향세** a downward[declining] tendency; a downtrend. ¶주식 시장은 ~에 있다 Stock [(영)] Share] prices are declining[falling]. / The market has turned downward [weakened]. **하향 조정** a downward adjustment.
하향하다(下鄕-) go away from the capital; go to one's native place.
하현(下弦) the last phase[quarter] of the moon.
● **하현달** a waning[an old] moon.
하혈(下血) a bloody flux[discharge]; [의] melena; melaena. **하혈하다** discharge blood (from the bowels); flux.
하회(下回) **1** [다음 차례] next time; next chapter (of a novel). **2** [윗사람이 내리는 회답] a reply; an answer; a response. ¶~를 기다리다 await (a person's) reply.
하회하다(下廻-) be less[lower] than …; be [fall] below (the average). ¶(결과를) 예상을 ~ fall short of one's expectation(s) // 금년 수출액은 작년의 그것을 하회한다 This year's exports fall short of last year's.
학(鶴) [동] a red-crested white crane. ⇨⌜두루미⌝
학감(學監) a school superintendent[overseer]; a dean(대학의).
학계(學界) learned[academic] circles; the academic[learned / scientific] world. ¶~의 권위 an authority of the academic world / ~에 공헌하다 advance the cause of learning // ~에 큰 공로를 세우다 do much[render great services] for the cause of learning.
학과(學科) [과목] a school subject; a subject of study. ¶정규 ~ regular academic work // 그는 ~에는 뛰어났으나 실기에서 실패했다 He did well in academic subjects but failed the practicals.
● **학과목** subjects on a school curriculum. **학과 시간표** a teaching schedule; a schedule (of lesson hours). **학과 시험** examinations in academic subjects.
학과(學課) a course of study; a lesson; school [class] work. ¶~를 배우다 learn a lesson // ~를 복습하다 review one's lessons // 내일의 ~를 예습하다 prepare tomorrow's lessons.
학관(學館) an educational institution; an academy; an (educational) institute.
학교(學校) a school; a college(대학 정도의); an academy(중학교 이상 고등학교 정도의); (집합적) an educational establishment[institution]; an institution of learning. ¶~ 시절에 in one's school days // ~가 파하고 나서 after school (is over) // (아직) ~에 다닐 때 while a student at school / when (one was) at school / in one's school days // ~를 갓 나온 fresh from[just out of] school[college] / ~ 차를 없애다 diminish the scholastic disparity among schools // ~에 들어가다 enter a school / go to[into] school // 아이를 ~에 보내다[넣다] send[put] a boy to school // ~에 다니다[가다] attend[go to] school // (교사가) ~에서 가르치다 teach (a) school // ~에서 돌아오다 come home from school // ~에서 제적하다 dismiss[expel] (a student) (from school) / (이름을) remove (a student's) name from the school register // ~에서 쫓겨나다 be expelled from (the) school // ~를 쉬다 stay away from school / absent oneself[be absent] from school // ~를 때먹다 play truant (from school) / cut school // ~를 쉬게 하다 keep (a boy) out of school // ~를 조퇴

학구

하다 leave school early / leave the class before it is dismissed / come away before school is out // ~를 그만두다[중퇴하다] leave [stop / quit] school // ~를 ӹ게 하다 make (a boy) leave school // ~를 졸업하다 complete the school course / graduate from [at] a college // ~를 세우다[설립하다] establish [found] a school // ~는 8시 반에 시작된다 School begins at eight thirty. // ~는 몇 시에 파합니까 What time is School over? / ~는 6시에 파한다 School is over[ends] at six. / Classes are dismissed at six. // 너 어느 ~에 다니니 Where do you go to school? / What school do you study at? // 내일은 ~가 논다 I have no school tomorrow. // 그는 1년 전에 ~를 그만두었다 He left[quit] school a year ago.

● 학교 교육 school education; schooling. ¶ 정규 ~ regular[formal] schooling // 그의 아버지는 ~을 받지 못했다 His father had no schooling. 학교 급식 school feeding; school lunch. 학교 선생 a schoolteacher. ¶그녀는 ~을 하고 있다 She teaches (in a) school. / She is a schoolteacher. 학교 성적 one's school[academic] record[achievements]. ¶ ~이 좋다[나쁘다] do well[badly] at school / have a good[bad / poor] school record. 학교장(一長) the principal[headmaster] of a school.

학구(學究) 1 [학문 탐구] study; learning; (사람) an academical person; a scholar; a student. 2 [글방 선생] a village-school teacher.

학구(學區) a school district.
● 학구제 the school district system.

학구적(學究的) scholastic; academic. ¶~인 생활 an academic[scholastic] life // ~인 정신 a scholastic spirit // ~인 저작 a scholastic [an academic] work // ~인 생활을 하다 live a studious life.

학군(學群) a school group. ¶제8~ the eighth school group.
● 학군제 the school group system.

학급(學級) a class; (미) a grade; (영) a form. ¶~을 편제하다 organize a class // 두 ~으로 나누다 divide (pupils) into two classes // ~에서 몇 째나 하나 How do you stand in your class?
● 학급 담임 a homeroom teacher; the teacher in charge of a class. 학급 문고 classroom library.

학기(學期) a (school) term; (미) a session; (미) a semester (1년 2기의). ¶신~ a fresh [new] term[semester] // 제1[2] ~ the first [second] term // 이번 ~ this[the current] term // 이번 ~의 교과 과정 the curriculum for this term / the courses offered this term.
● 학기말 (at) the close[end] of a term. 학기말 시험 a term[terminal] examination. 학기초 (at) the beginning of a term.

학내(學內) school grounds; (미) the school yard; (미) a campus. ¶~의 intramural / within the campus / in the university // ~에 (서) in the school / within school bounds / in the school[college] grounds / (미) on the campus(대학의) // ~의 질서를 지키다 maintain order on the campus [school premises].

학년(學年) a school[an academical / a scholastic] year; a class; (미) a grade; (영) a form. ¶1~ (미) the first grade / (영) the first form (▶ 미국에서는 주나 학교에 따라 초·중·고의 학년 구분이 다르나, 대체로 6·3·3제이거나 6·2·4제 또는 8·4제이며, 우리나라와 달리 초등학교에서 고등학교까지의 학년을 연속하여 부르기 때문에 고등학교의 최종 학년은 12학년, 즉 the twelfth가 됨) // 1[2 / 3 / 4] ~생 a first-[second- / third- / fourth-]year student / (미) a first[second / third / fourth] grader / (미) (4년제 고등학교나 대학교일 때) a freshman[sophomore / junior / senior] // 3~ A반 3A class // 나는 오는 3월에 3~이 된다 I shall be in the third year[grade / form] next March. // "너는 몇 ~이냐?" "3~입니다." "What grade[year] are you in?" "I'm in the third grade[third-year class]." // 저는 대학교 3~입니다 (미) I am junior. / (영) I am in my third year at the university. // 내 막내 누이동생은 초등학교 1~이다 My youngest sister is in the first grade[is a first grader]. / (영) My youngest sister is in the first year at primary school. // 그는 중학교 2~(생)입니다 He is in the second year of junior high school. / (미) He is the eighth grade. // 그는 나보다 2~ 위[아래]이다 He is two years ahead of[behind] me at school. // 이 중학교는 ~당 200명씩이다 There are 200 pupils in each grade at this junior high school.
● 학년말 the end of a school year. 학년말 시험 an annual[a final] examination.

학당(學堂) an educational institution; [학교] a school.

학대(虐待) cruel treatment; ill-treatment; maltreatment; mistreatment; abuse; cruelty; wrong. ¶동물 ~ 방지 협회 the Society for the Prevention of Cruelties to Animals(약어 S.P.C.A.) // 정신적 ~ mental cruelty // ~에 못 견뎌 being unable to endure[bear] the severity of the treatment // ~를 감수하다 submit to ill-treatment / suffer [allow] oneself to be maltreated. 학대하다 treat (a person) with cruelty[badly / ill / cruelly]; use (a person) ill; be cruel to (a person / an animal); use (animals) cruelly; ill-treat; maltreat; mistreat; abuse. ¶약자를 ~ oppress[bully] the weak // 동물을 ~ be cruel to animals // 아내를 ~ treat one's wife cruelly / abuse one's wife // 너무 학대하지 말아 다오 Don't be so cruel to me. / Have mercy on me. ➔ ¶학대당하다[학대받다] suffer maltreatment / receive cruel [bad] treatment / be ill-treated / be maltreated / be subjected to harsh usage // 이 나라에서는 동물이 학대당하고[학대받고] 있다 Animals are treated cruelly in this country. / People are hard on animals[are cruel to animals] in this country.
● 학대 음란증 sadism. ¶피(被)~ masochism.

학덕(學德) learning and virtue. ¶~을 겸비하다 be eminent in both learning and virtue.

학도(學徒) a student; a scholar.
● 학도병 a student soldier.

학동(學童) a schoolboy; a schoolgirl; a school child; a pupil.

학력(學力) scholarship; scholastic ability; scholarly[scholastic] attainments. ¶~이 뛰어난 사람 a person of great scholastic ability / a person excellent in scholarship // 고교생의 ~ 저하 a decline in the scholastic ability of high school students // ~이 뛰어나다 be excellent in scholarship // ~이 있다[없다] be a good[poor] scholar / have[have no] scholarly competence // 대학 출신 이상의 ~이 있다 surpass college graduates in scholarly attainments // 그는 그 시험을 칠 만한 ~이 못 된다 His scholarship[attainment] is not yet equal to[He has not scholarship enough to take] the examination. // ~이 저하되고 있다 There is a lowering in scholarship. // 그는 고등학교 졸업 ~이 있다[없다 / 이상이 있다] He is equal to[falls below / surpasses] a high school graduate in scholastic achievement[ability].

● **학력고사** a scholastic ability[an achievement] test; an examination in academic subjects.

학력(學歷) a school career; an academic career[background]; (formal) schooling. ¶~을 불문하고 irrespective of the academic background // ~이 없는 사람 a person without any school education[any academic background] // 고졸 또는 동등 이상의 ~이 있는 자 those who possess attainments equal to or higher than those of upper secondary school graduates // ~이 거의 없다 have little formal[regular] schooling // 그는 별다른 ~도 없이 박사가 되었다 He has been made a Doctor, though he has pursued no regular studies.

학령(學齡) school age. ¶~ 미달의 아이 a preschool child / a child under school age // ~이 되다 reach[attain] school age // 저 아이는 ~이 되지 않다 below school age // 저 아이는 ~에 달했다[미달이다] That child has reached [is under] school age.

● **학령 아동** children of school age; school-aged children.

학리(學理) a theory; a scientific principle. ¶~적[~(상)의] theoretical // ~상(으로) theoretically / in theory // ~적인 연구 theoretical study (of).

학명(學名) a scientific name; a technical name; (식물의) a botanical name; (동물의) a zoological name. ¶~을 붙이다 give a scientific name (to).

학문(學問) [면학] (pursuit of) learning; (the prosecution of) studies; [학식] learning; scholarship; scholarly attainments; [지식] knowledge; [교육·교양] education; schooling; [학술] a science. ¶~적(으로) scientific(ally) // ~의 진보 the advancement of learning // ~이 있는 learned / erudite(깊은) / educated(교육을 받은) // ~이 없는 사람 a person without learning / an unlettered [uneducated] person // ~이 뛰어나다 stand high[be proficient] in one's studies // ~에 정진하다 devote oneself to one's studies // ~을 좋아하다 like[be fond of] learning // ~을 하다 pursue learning / prosecute[follow] one's studies // ~이 있다 have learning[education] / be learned[educated] // ~이 매우 깊다 be very learned / be a good scholar // ~이 넓고 깊다 possess learning both broad and deep // ~을 뽐내다 be proud of one's learning [scholarship] // ~을 과시하다 parade[display] one's learning // ~의 길을 걷다 tread the path of learning // (국가 등의) ~이 진보해 있다 be advanced in learning // 저 사람은 ~이 있다 He is a learned[(문어) an erudite] man. / He is a man of learning. // 형은 ~을 좋아한다 My brother likes studying. / My brother has an academic bent. // ~만으로는 훌륭한 사람이 될 수 없다 Scholarship alone does not make a person great.

● **학문의 자유** academic freedom.

학벌(學閥) an academic clique; academical cliquism[sectionalism / sectarianism]. ¶~의 폐단 the evils of an academic clique // ~을 형성하다 form an academic clique // ~을 타파하다 break down academic cliques.

학병(學兵) a student soldier. ⇨ **학도병**(⇨학도)

학보(學報) a gazette; a school bulletin.

학부(學府) an educational institution; a seat of learning; an academic center. ¶최고 ~ the highest seat[institution] of learning / the highest educational institution // 최고 ~에 가다 go to an institution of higher learning.

학부(學部) a faculty; a college; a school; a department. ¶교양 ~ the Faculty of Liberal Arts // 이공 ~ the college[institute] of science and engineering[technology].

학부모(學父母) parents of students.

● **학부모회** a parent's association.

학부형(學父兄) parents of students.

학비(學費) school(ing)[educational] expenses. ¶학생의 ~를 대 주다 pay a boy's educational expenses / supply a boy with his school[college] expenses // (일하면서) ~를 벌다 earn one's school expenses (by working) // ~에 곤란을 받다 be hard up for school expenses / be unable to pay one's own way through school // 그는 나에게 ~를 대 주겠다고 말했다 He offered to pay for[to finance] my education.

학사(學士) [학위] a bachelor; [대학 졸업자] a university[college] graduate. ¶문~ a Bachelor of Arts(약어 B.A.) // 이(理)~ a Bachelor of Science(약어 B.S.).

● **학사 학위** a bachelor's degree.

학사(學事) [교육 사무] school affairs; education(al) matters.

● **학사 보고** a report on education(al) matters.

학살(虐殺) slaughter; (대량의) a massacre; carnage; a holocaust; (인종·민족 등의) genocide. ¶집단 ~ mass slaughter // 대량 ~ a large-scale massacre / a holocaust. **학살하다** slaughter; massacre; slay. → ¶인디언이 대량 학살되었다 The Indians were massacred [slaughtered]. // 그는 학살되었다 He was cruelly murdered. / They butchered him (in cold blood). // 약 5백 명의 죄수가 하루 만에 학살당했다 About 500 prisoners were slaughtered in a day.

● **학살자** a slaughterer.

학생(學生) 1 a pupil; a student(▶ (미)에서는 중학·고교생에게도 쓰지만, (영)에서는 대학생에만 씀); (대학생) an undergraduate(▶ 대학원생에 대하여); (대학원생) a graduate student. ¶초등학교 ~ (남자) a schoolboy / (여자) a schoolgirl(▶ 중학생을 가리킬 때도 있음) / a schoolchild // 고등학교 ~ (미) a high school student // ~ 시절에 in one's school days // 여~ a female student / (남녀 공학 대학의) (미국 구어) a co-ed // 학교를 잘 빼먹는 ~ a student with a high truancy record // ~다운 태도 bearing like a student /

a manner proper[appropriate] to a student / behavior worthy of[befitting to] a student // 법률[화학] 전공의 ~ a law[chemistry] student / a student of law[chemistry] // 그는 서울 대학교 ~이다 He is a student at Seoul University.(▶ 특정한 대학의 학생임을 나타낼 때는 전치사 of를 사용하지 않고 at을 사용)// ~ 시절에 책을 많이 읽는 것은 중요한 일이다 It is important that you should read many books while you are at school.// 우리 학교의 ~ 수는 1,000명이다 Our college has an enrollment of one thousand students.// 전교 ~이 식에 참가하도록 되어 있다 The whole school is[All the school is / All the students are] to attend the ceremony.
2 (생전에 벼슬을 못한 사람을 가리켜) a deceased scholar who lacks official rank.
● **학생 군사 교육단** Reserve Officer's Training Corps(약어 ROTC). **학생복** [모] a school uniform[cap]. **학생 운동** a student movement. ¶그는 대학 시절에 ~에 가담했었다 He was a student political activist[took part in student political activities] when he was in college. **학생증** a student identification card. **학생회** a students' association; (미) a student council. ¶총~ the General Students Association. **학생 회관** a students' hall; a student union (building). **학생회 회장** the president of the student council.

학설(學說) a theory; a doctrine. ¶~을 세우다 advance[set up / formulate] a theory // 그는 새로운 ~을 발표했다 He published a new theory.// 그 사실은 지금까지의 ~을 뒤엎었다 That fact upset the accepted theory.

학수(鶴壽) a long life; longevity.

학수고대하다(鶴首苦待-) wait with impatience; (eagerly) look forward to (doing); wait with bated breath; wait with a craned [an outstretched] neck; long[pine] for. ¶그들은 좋은 소식을 학수고대하고 있었다 They were waiting impatiently for the good news.

학술(學術) 1 [학예] arts and sciences: ¶~상의 (과학적) scientific / [전문적] technical // ~ 진흥을 위해 필요한 조처를 취하다 adopt the necessary measures to promote scientific research. 2 [학문] learning; [전문 분야의 지식] scholarship; [개인의 연구] studies. ¶그녀는 ~ 연구를 위해 도미했다 She went to America to pursue her studies.
● **학술 강연** an academic lecture. **학술 논문** a treatise[an essay / a study] (on). **학술 서적** learned[scientific] books. **학술 용어** a technical term. **학술원** the Academy. ¶한국 ~ the National Academy of Sciences / the Korean Academy. **학술회의** a Science Council.

학습(學習) learning; study. **학습하다** learn; study. ¶나는 영어를 제1외국어로서 학습하고 있다 I'm studying English as a first foreign language.
● **학습서** a study book; a handbook for students. **학습자** a learner. **학습장** a workbook; a drill book; a notebook.

학승(學僧) [학문에 뛰어난 승려] a learned [(문어) an erudite] monk[priest]; [학문을 공부하고 있는 승려] a monk studying Buddhism.

학식(學識) scholarship; learning; scholarly attainments[acquisition]; knowledge. ¶심오한 ~ profound knowledge[learning] / erudition // ~과 경험이 많은 a man of learning and experience // ~이 있는[없는] learned[unlettered] // ~이 있는 사람 a man of learning / a learned man / [학자] a scholar // ~을 뽐내다 make a display of one's learning / be pedantic // 저 사람은 ~이 깊다 That man is very learned.

학업(學業) studies; classwork; schoolwork. ¶~에 힘쓰다 study hard // ~을 게을리 하다[마치다 / 계속하다] neglect[complete / continue] one's schoolwork[studies] // ~이 우수하다 do well at school // ~을 중단하다 give up one's studies / leave off one's scholastic studies // 나는 돈이 없어서 ~을 그만두지 않으면 안 되었다 I had to leave school due to lack of money.
● **학업 성적** school records; (대학 등의) scholarly attainments.

학예(學藝) 1 [학문과 예능] arts and sciences; the liberal arts. 2 [소양] cultural attainments.
● **학예회** (hold)literary exercises.

학용품(學用品) school things[supplies].

학우(學友) [동창생] a schoolmate; a schoolfellow; a fellow student; [동급생] a classmate.
● **학우회** (재학생의) a students' association; (졸업생의) an alumni[alumnae] association (▶ alumnae는 여성의); (영) an Old Boys' [Girls'] association.

학원(學院) an (educational) institute; an academy; a seminary(종교 단체가 운영하는); a (private) school. ¶입시 ~ a preparatory school (for examinees) // 자동차 ~ a drivers' school.

학원(學園) an educational institution; a school; a campus.
● **학원 분쟁** a campus dispute. **학원 자율화** campus liberalization; campus autonomy; autonomy of universities.

학위(學位) a[an academic] degree[title]. ¶명예 ~ an honorary degree // 박사 ~ a doctor's degree / a doctorate // ~를 갖다[취득하다 / 받다] have[take / receive] a degree (from a university) / ~를 수여하다 grant a degree (to a person) / confer a degree (on a person) / award (a person) a degree // ~를 가지고 있다 hold[bear / have] a degree // 명예 ~를 받다 receive[be granted] an honorary degree // 그는 경제학 박사 ~를 땄다[취득했다] He got[received] Ph. D in economics.
● **학위 논문** a thesis (pl. -ses); (석사의) a master's thesis; (박사의) a doctor's[doctoral] thesis; a dissertation. **학위 수여식** the (ceremony of) conferment of a degree; commencement.

학자(學者) a scholar; a learned man; a man of learning; an erudite; a savant; [학구] an academical person. ¶저명한 ~ an eminent [a distinguished / a noted] scholar (in astronomy) // ~다운 태도 a scholarly attitude / an attitude appropriate to a scholar // ~로서의 양심 one's scholarly conscience / ~인 체하다 be pedantic / assume the air of a scholar / set up for a scholar // 그는 법~이다 He is a scholar in law. // 그에게는 ~적인 데가 있다 He has something of the scholar in him.

학자금(學資金) school(ing) [educational] expenses.

학장(學長) a president; a dean; a chancellor; a rector(▶ 영국의 대학의 chancellor는 명예직으로 실권이 없으며, vice-chancellor가 사실상의 학장임. 미국에서는 규모가 매우 큰 대학의 학장을 가리키는 수가 있음).

학적(學籍) a school[college] register. ¶~에 올리다 put one's name on the school register / enroll [matriculate] a student on the school register(▶ matriculate는 격식을 차린 말)∥~에서 빼다 strike a student's name off the school register∥~에 올라 있는 학생 총수는 1만 명이다 The total registration of students is ten thousand.
●**학적부** [학적을 기록한 장부] a school [college] register.

학점(學點) [교] a unit; (미) a point; (미) a credit. ¶3~짜리 독어를 수강하다 take German for three credits∥~이 모자라다 do not have sufficient credits (to graduate)∥30~을 따다 take 30 units∥1주에 3시간씩, 30주의 강의로 3~을 주다 give three credits for [to] a lecture of three hours per week for a term of thirty weeks∥그는 졸업에 필요한 ~을 따지 못했다 He failed to earn enough credits to graduate.
●**학점 제도** the credit[unit] system.

학정(虐政) [폭정] tyranny; oppressive[tyrannical] government; [독재] despotism; autocracy. ¶~에 신음하다 groan under (ruthless) tyranny∥왕은 ~을 폈다 The king tyrannized the people.

학제(學制) an educational system; a school system. ¶~를 개편하다 reorganize the system of education.

학질(瘧疾) malaria; paludism; ague. ¶~에 걸리다 be infected with malaria∥~에 걸린 것처럼 벌벌 떨다 tremble as though one had the ague.
학질(을) 떼다 be cured of[recover from] malaria; [비유] have a hard time; be disgusted[bored] (with).
●**학질모기** an anopheles mosquito; a malaria mosquito.

학창(學窓) a school; an educational institution. ¶~을 떠나다 leave[graduate from] school.
●**학창 생활** school life. **학창 시절** one's school days.

학춤(鶴-) the Crane Dance.

학칙(學則) school[college / university] regulations. ¶~을 만들다 frame [lay down] school regulations∥~을 지키다 observe [stick by] school regulations / follow[obey] school regulations∥~을 어기다 break [violate / go against] school regulations∥그것은 ~에 위배된다 It's against the school regulations.

학파(學派) a school; a sect. ¶스토아 ~ the Stoic school / the Stoics∥에피쿠로스 ~ the school of Epicurus∥헤겔 ~의 철학 the Hegelian school of philosophy∥~를 이루다 found a school∥두 ~로 갈라지다 be divided into two different schools.

학풍(學風) 1 [학문상의 전통·경향] academic traditions[features]. ¶저 두 학자는 ~이 다르다 Those two scholars belong to different schools. 2 [교풍] school traditions. ¶하버드의 ~을 따르다 keep[follow] Harvard traditions.

학행(學行) [학문과 덕행] scholarship and virtue; [학문과 실행] learning and practice.

학형(學兄) my learned friend; [학우 간의 호칭] you; (편지에서) Mr. ....

학회(學會) a learned[scientific] society; an academic society; an institute; an academy. ¶한국 영어 영문 ~ the English Literary Society of Korea∥한글 ~ the Korean Language (Research) Society∥수학 ~의 회원 a member of the mathematical society∥한국 물리 ~에 출석하다 attend a meeting of the Physical Society of Korea.

한 1 [하나의] one; a (single). ¶분필 ~ 개 a piece of chalk∥연필 ~ 자루 a pencil∥맥주 ~ 병 a bottle of beer∥~ 해 a (one) year∥동전 ~ 푼 a single penny / (even) a penny∥~ 줌의 쌀 a handful of rice∥~ 줄기의 희망 a ray[gleam] of hope∥~ 줄기의 빛 a streak of light∥~ 줄기의 연기 a wisp of smoke∥~ 바퀴 돌다 take a turn / go round / make a tour (of) (담당 구역을) go one's rounds∥하루에 ~ 끼밖에 못 먹다 have only one meal a day∥~ 치의 땅도 양보하지 않다 cede not an inch of ground∥이 주변에는 나무 ~ 그루도 나 있지 않다 Not a tree is to be seen (growing) around here.∥~ 푼 줍쇼 (거지의 말) Tip[Spare] us a copper.
2 [대략] about; some; nearly. ¶~ 10마일[시간] about [some] ten miles[hours] / (미) around ten miles[hours]∥~ 2백 미터 갔을 무렵 when I had gone about two hundred meters∥~ 20명이 마침 거기에 있었다 Some [About] twenty people happened to be there.

한 푼 아끼다 백 냥 잃는다 (속담) Penny-wise and pound-foolish; Grasp all, lose all.

한 귀로 들어와 한 귀로 흘러 나가다 go in one ear and out the other.

한 손 놓다 [하던 일이 일단 끝나다] come[be brought] to an end for the time being; be completed. ¶일은 이것으로 한 손 놓았다 This has brought the job to a pause for the present.

한 치 앞을 못 보다 be not farsighted; have no foresight.

한- 1 [큰] large; big; great. ¶~길 a main [broad] street[road] / a high road∥~시름 a big worry / a great anxiety. **2** [한창] right [just] in the middle (of); midmost (of). ¶~낮 midday / high noon∥~겨울 midwinter. **3** [같은] the same; the selfsame(똑같은). ¶~집안 one's family / the same family∥~패 one of the (same) party∥~방을 쓰다 share the same room (with).

한(限) 1 [한계] a limit; limits; bounds; an end. ¶탐욕에는 ~이 없다 There are no bounds to avarice.∥그의 야망은 ~이 없다 His ambition is boundless.∥그가 결심하는 것을 기다린다면 ~이 없다 If you wait for him to make up his mind you'll have to wait forever.∥사고 싶은 물건을 들자면 ~이 없다 There is no limit to what I want to buy.
2 [범위 내] so far as; as far as; to the limit that ...; unless. ¶내가 알고 있는 ~은 as far as I know∥사정이 허락하는[나에 관한] ~ as far as circumstances permit [I am concerned]∥될 수 있는 ~ 일찍 와라 Come as soon as possible [you can].∥지장이 없는 ~ 출석하겠습니다 I will attend the meeting if nothing intervenes.∥내가 살아 있는 ~ 너를

한 부자유스럽게 하지는 않겠다 You shall want for nothing as long as I live.∥네가 빌지 않는 ~ 용서하지 않겠다 I shall not forgive you unless you apologize.∥우리는 일이 있는 ~ 집에 돌아갈 수 없다 We cannot go home till we have finished our work.∥내가 아는 ~ 좋은 학교다 So[As] far as I know this is a fine school.

한(恨) 〔원한〕 heartburnings; a bitter[an ill] feeling; a grudge; 〔spite〕; 〔증오〕 (a) hatred; hate; rancor; 〔한탄〕 regret; a regrettable [deplorable] matter; an unsatisfied desire. ¶천추의 ~ a lasting regret / a matter for great regret∥~ 많은 regrettable / deplorable / lamentable∥~이 골수에 사무치다 bear (him) a bitter grudge / be full of rancor (against)∥~을 품다 bear[cherish / nurse / owe] (a person) a grudge / have a grudge[rancor / spleen] against (a person) ∥~을 풀다 vent one's spite / satisfy[wreak / work off] one's grudge / be avenged / avenge oneself∥~ 많은 일생을 보내다 lead a life full of tears and regrets / lead a life of deep sorrows∥~이 많다[없다] have much [nothing] to regret∥젊어서 공부 못 한 것이 ~이 되다 regret that one could not study while young∥그는 나에게 ~을 품고 있는 것 같다 I feel he has[bears] a grudge against me.

한(韓) Korea. ⇨ 한국(韓國)

한가롭다(閑暇-) free; disengaged. ⇨ 한가하다

한가운데 the middle; the center; the heart. ¶방 ~에 in the middle[center] of the room∥~에서 둘로 가르다 break[cut] in two in the middle / cut into two exact halves∥머리를 ~에서 가르다 part one's hair in the middle ∥넓은 바다 ~를 떠돌다 drift in the middle [(문어) midst] of the ocean∥그 탑은 읍내 ~ 있다 The tower is in the center[heart] of town.∥화살이 과녁 ~를 맞혔다 The arrow hit the target right in the center.

한가위 hangawi; the Korean (version of) Thanksgiving Day (celebrated on the 15th day of the eighth lunar month). ⇨ 추석

한가을 〔한창 무르익은 가을철〕 the depth [dead] of autumn[(미) fall]; 〔추수기〕 the busy harvesting season; the busy harvest time.

한가지 〔똑같음〕 (one and) the same thing. ¶그것은 어느 쪽이나 ~다 It is all one to me. / It makes no difference. / It is quite the same thing.∥고개를 끄덕이는 것은 찬성하는 것이나 ~다 Nodding your head is equivalent to saying yes. / 10센트짜리 주화 10개는 1달러와 ~다 Ten dimes are equal to one dollar.

한가하다(閑暇-) free; disengaged; (서술적) be at leisure; have no work to do; have spare time[time to spare]; have leisure. ¶한가한 때 when one is free[at leisure] / in one's leisure hours / at one's leisure∥손님이 없이 ~ be without a client[(속어) john]∥내 일은 온종일 한가하니 나를 방문해 주세요 I'll be free all day tomorrow, so please come and see me.∥한가한 사람들은 나를 도와주세요 Those who are not busy[occupied], please lend me a hand.∥두 가지 일을 떠맡아 한가한 시간이 전혀 없다 With two jobs, I don't have a moment to spare[I have my hands full]. **한가히** in a leisurely way; with leisure. ¶~ 지내다 idle away one's time.

한갓 only; merely; simply; solely; alone; just. ¶~ …이라는 이유로 simply because … / for the sole reason that …∥나는 ~ 장사꾼에 지나지 않는다 I am a mere tradesman. / I am nothing but[no more than] a tradesman.∥그것은 ~ 핑계에 불과하다 That is simply an excuse, and nothing more.∥그것은 ~ 모방에 지나지 않는다 It is a mere imitation.

한갓지다 tranquil; quiet; restful; peaceful; leisurely. ¶한갓진 곳 a quiet [secluded] place / an out-of-the-way place∥한갓진 시골 생활 leisurely[quiet] country life.

한객(閑客) a man of leisure; a leisured man; an idler(놀고 있는 사람).

한거(閑居) 〔조용한 생활〕 a quiet life; 〔은퇴한 생활〕 a retired life; 〔한가한 생활〕 a life of leisure; an idle life. **한거하다** live in retirement; lead a quiet life.

한걱정 great cares[worries]; big troubles.

한걸음에 〔단숨에〕 at a breath; at[on] a stretch; in a single spell; 〔쉬지 않고〕 without rest[a break]. ¶~ 언덕을 달려 올라가다 go up a hill with one rush[at a dash].

한겨울 midwinter; the dead[depth] of winter.(▶ midwinter는 종종 동지의 무렵을 가리키며, the dead of winter는 the coldest season을 의미함) ¶~에 in midwinter / in the depths[dead] of winter.

한결 〔눈에 띄게〕 conspicuously; noticeably; markedly; remarkably; 〔한층 더〕 more; much[still] more. ¶~ 두드러지다 stand out conspicuously / cut a conspicuous[splendid / brilliant] figure∥언니보다는 그녀가 인물이 ~ 낫다 She is far[decidedly] more beautiful than her elder sister.∥조금이라도 있는 쪽이 전혀 없는 것보다는 ~ 낫다 Something is far better than nothing.

한결같다 〔변함없다〕 constant; unchanging; unvarying; 〔일관성이 있다〕 consistent; coherent. ¶한결같은 태도 a consistent attitude∥한결같은 속도로 at a steady pace∥아내에 대한 그의 사랑은 한결같았다 His affection[devotion] for his wife remained unabated. **한결같이** 〔변함없이〕 constantly; invariably; as ever; 〔시종일관〕 consistently; coherently; 〔모두〕 all alike; without a single exception; every one of them. ¶~ 사랑하다 love (a person) as ever∥그는 평생을 ~ 노동자의 편이었다 He remained a stalwart friend of working people all his life.∥최 씨의 딸들은 ~ 미인이다 Mr. Choe's daughters are all beautiful.

한계(限界) a limit; a boundary(▶ 둘 다 흔히 복수형으로); a margin.(▶ limit는 가장 널리 쓰이는 말, boundary는 주로 영토 등의 경계에 관해서, bounds는 행위 등에, limitations는 능력 등의 추상적인 사항에 관해서 쓰임, margin은 끝, 극한을 나타냄) ¶~를 설정하다 limit / set limits (to)∥~에 이르다 reach the (highest) limit∥나는 내 힘의 ~를 알고 있다 I know my limitations. / I know the limit(s) of my power[strength].∥그것은 인간의 지식의 ~를 넘어서고 있다 It exceeds the bounds of human knowledge.∥실크의 국내 수요는 ~에 이르렀다 The domestic demand for silk has gone as high as it can go[has peaked]. ∥나는 인내의 ~에 달했다 I have reached the limits of my patience. / I cannot stand it any more.∥그것은 지식의 ~를 넘고 있다 It lies beyond the boundaries of our knowledge.

● **한계 비용** marginal cost. **한계 상황** a critical situation. **한계 생산비** marginal cost of production. **한계선** a boundary line; [물] a limiting line. **한계점** the critical point; the uppermost limit; the superior limit; the maximum. ¶~에 도달하다 reach[be at] the top[uppermost limit] (of the pay list for one's rank). **한계 효용** [경] marginal[final] utility.

한고비 [위기] the crisis; the critical moment [point / stage]; the most serious moment; [절정] the peak; the climax; the pay-off. ¶~ 넘기다 pass the crisis[critical point] / pass out of[pass the peak of] danger / turn the corner[병세 등] / be over the hump // 이 일도 이제 ~ 넘겼다 The hardest part of this work is over. / We are over the hump with the job. / We have broken the neck of this work. // 병세도 이제 ~ 넘겼다 The worst symptoms are gone.

한구석 a corner; a nook. ¶~에 in a corner (of a room) / in a nook (of a town) // 어디та 사람 눈에 띄지 않는 ~에 in some odd corner // 그 광경이 지금도 마음 ~에 남아 있다 The scene still remains somewhere in the background of my mind.

한국(寒國) a cold country[region / climate].
한국(寒菊) [식] a winter chrysanthemum.
한국(韓國) Korea; (공식명) the Republic of Korea(약어 ROK). ¶~의 Korean // ~화하다 Koreanize // ~ 사정에 밝다 be well informed on Korean affairs // 그게 바로 ~적인 사고방식이다 That's a very Korean way of thinking [point of view].

● **한국 국민** the Korean (people). **한국 사람** a Korean. **한국 산업 규격** the Korean Industrial Standards(약어 KS). **한국어** Korean; the Korean language. **한국 요리** a Korean-style dish; Korean-style cuisine. **한국은행** the Bank of Korea. **한국은행 총재** the Governor of the Bank of Korea. **한국 전쟁** the Korean War. ⇨육이오 전쟁 **한국학** Korean studies; Koreanology. **한국화**(一畫) (화법) Korean painting; (그림) a picture painted in Korean style.

한군데 [일정한 장소] the same place[spot]. ¶그들은 토요일마다 늘 ~에서 만나곤 했다 They used to meet together at the same place on every Saturday.

한그루 [농] raising a single crop (of rice) a year; single-crop farming.

한극(寒極) the coldest place[spot] in the world.

한글 Hangeul; Hangul; the Korean alphabetic writing system.

● **한글날** Hangeul Proclamation Day. **한글 맞춤법** Hangeul orthography; the rules [system] of spelling of Hangeul.

한기(寒氣) **1** [추위] cold weather; cold; a chill. ¶~를 느끼다 feel[have] a chill // 오싹 ~를 느끼다 feel cold // ~에 몸이 떨리다 (feel a) shudder / shiver // 그 광경을 보기만 해도 오싹오싹 ~를 느낀다 The mere sight of it gives me cold shivers. // 요즈음 ~가 한층 더 해졌다 It has become colder these past few days. // 이 식물은 0도 이하의 ~를 쐬면 죽고 만다 If exposed to temperatures below the freezing point, this plant will die. **2** [오한] a chill; chilliness; rigor. ¶~가 나다 feel a chill / feel chilly / have a chill[a cold fit].

한길 a main[principal / broad] street[road]; a high road; a street; a (leading) thoroughfare; an arterial highway[road]. ¶~로 통하는 골목길 an access road // ~에서 in the open street // ~에 나앉다 become[be rendered] homeless / be thrown on the streets / be out in the cold.

한꺼번에 [동시에] at once; at a time; at the same time; simultaneously; [단숨에] at a stretch[sitting]; [모두] all together; [한목에] in the[a] lump; in the gross. ¶~ 두 가지 일에 집중할 수는 없다 You can't concentrate on two things at a time. // ~ 들어가려고 하지 말게 Don't try to get in all together. // 피로가 내게 ~ 몰려왔다 Suddenly[All at once] I was overwhelmed by fatigue. // 아이들이 ~ 내게 덤벼들었다 The children attacked me in a group[(구어) ganged up on me]. // 책이 너무 많아 ~ 나를 수 없다 There are too many books for me to carry all of them at once.

한껏 1 [힘껏] with all one's might; with might and main; to the best of one's ability. ¶~ 노력하다 do one's (level) best / make every effort / exert oneself as hard as possible / exert oneself to the utmost. **2** [한도껏] to the utmost limit; to the maximum. ¶끈을 ~ 잡아당기다 draw a string out to its (full) length. **3** [실컷] to one's heart's content; as much as one likes; to the full; to the fullest measure. ¶~ 울다 weep oneself out / weep one's fill / have a good cry / give free vent to one's tears // ~ 즐기다 enjoy oneself to one's heart's content // ~ 먹다 eat one's fill / eat fully.

한끝 1 [한쪽 끝] an edge; one end. ¶밧줄의 ~을 잡다 hold one end of a rope. **2** [맨 끝] the (tail) end; the tip; the extremity. ¶줄의 ~에 서다 stand at the end of a row.

한나절 half a day; (미) a half day. ¶어제는 낮잠으로 ~을 보냈다 I slept away half the day yesterday. // 그것을 끝내는 데 ~이 걸렸다 It took me half a day or so[nearly half a day] to finish it.

한낮 [정오] midday; high noon; [백주] broad daylight. ¶~에 [정오에] at midday[noon] / [백주에] in broad daylight // ~의 태양 the midday sun // 눈을 뜨니 ~이었다 It was full day[daylight] when I awoke.

한낱 mere; merely; only. ¶~ …에 지나지 않다 be nothing but ... / be no more than ... // 나는 ~ 엑스트라에 지나지 않았다 I was only one of the extras. // 그것은 ~ 구실에 불과하다 It is a mere excuse. / That is an excuse, and nothing more.

한눈 [한 번 보기] a look; a (single) glance; a glimpse. ¶~에 at a glance / at first glance // 가짜인지 어떤지 ~에 알 수 있다 One glance will be enough to tell it is an imitation or not. // 그는 그녀한테 ~에 반했다 He fell in love with her at first sight.

한눈팔다 look away[aside / off]; take one's eyes[see] off (one's book); look at something else. ¶내가 한눈파는 사이에 가방이 없어져 버렸다 My suitcase had disappeared while I was looking the other way. // 운전할 때는 한눈팔지 마라 Don't take your eyes off the road when you are driving.

한다하는 distinguished; eminent; celebrated;

한닥거리다 respectable. ¶~ 인물 a person of consequence / (a) somebody // ~ 집안 a decent family // 정계에서 ~ 사람 a celebrity in the political world.

한닥거리다 shake; move (to and fro).

한달음에 at a run; without a pause for breath; straight through. ¶~ 가서 가져오겠다 I will run for [and fetch] it.

한담(閑談) a chat; an idle talk; a rambling talk; a gossip. ¶~으로 시간을 보내다 chat the time away / pass one's time in a quiet talk // 노인들은 ~으로 소일하고 있다 The old people spend all their time in idle talk. 한담하다 chat (with); have a chat (with); have a gossip [rambling talk] (with); coze (with). ¶나는 옛 친구와 한담했다 I had a chat with an old friend.

한대(寒帶) the frigid [frozen] zones; the arctic regions. ¶남[북]~ the south [north] frigid zone / the antarctic [arctic] zone [region].
● **한대 기후** a polar climate. **한대 동물[식물]** a polar [an arctic] animal [plant]. **한대 지방** (in) the cold latitudes.

한댕거리다 dangle; swing; hang pendulous; sway (to and fro); oscillate.

한더위 fierce [violent] heat; the midsummer heat; the canicular heat. ¶그곳은 8월의 ~ 때에도 기온이 섭씨 25도를 넘는 일이 드물다 The temperature there seldom rises above 25℃ even in August, the climax of summer.

한데[1] the same place. ⇨ 한군데

한데[2] **1** [노천] the open (air); the outdoors. ¶~의 open-air / outdoor // ~서 하는 식사 a cookout // ~서 자다 sleep in the open (air) / sleep under the open sky. **2** [정해진 곳의 밖] the outside (of a fixed area); the wrong place. ¶물을 ~에 붓다 pour water outside a vessel.

한도(限度) a limit; limits; bounds; a ceiling. ¶신용 ~ a credit limit // 최소[최대] ~ the minimum [maximum] // ~ 내에서 within the limit(s) (of) // 시속 30마일을 ~로 하여 within the 30 mile-an-hour limit // 최소 ~의 비용으로 at a minimum of expense // ~를 넘다 exceed the limit // ~에 달하다 reach the limit // ~를 정하다 fix the limit(s) / set a limit [limits] / put a ceiling (on) // ~를 넘지 않도록 하다 keep within bounds [the limits] // 그의 체력에는 ~가 있었다 There was a limit to his physical strength. // 이 과의 정원은 55명을 ~로 한다 This section is limited to five employees. // 내가 원조할 수 있는 ~는 10만 원이다 I can't contribute any more than [I can give only up to] 100,000 won in aid. // 그것이 내가 양보할 수 있는 최대 ~이다 That is the (ut)most that I can concede. // 인내에도 ~가 있다 Human patience has its limits.

한 독(韓獨) Korea and Germany. ¶~의 Korean-German.

한돌림 (차례의) one [a] round; (둘레의) one circumference [girth]. ¶~ 돌릴 술이 없다 There is not enough wine to go round.

한동기(一同氣) a half [whole] brother [sister]; brother and sister of the full blood; a brother [sister-]german.
● **한동기간** full [whole] brotherhood [sisterhood].

한동안 (for) a fairly [(미국 구어) considerable] long time; (for) quite some time [while]; (for) a good while. ¶그 후 ~ for some time since // ~ 있다가 after a long stretch [period] of time // ~ 머무르다 (구어) stay quite a while // ~ 뵙지 못했습니다 I haven't seen you for a long time [for an age]. / It is a long time since I saw you last.

한두 one or two; a few. ¶~ 번 one or twice // ~ 번이 아니고 again and again / time [once] and again / more than once / several times // ~ 가지 일 a thing or two / one or two things.

한둘 one or two. ¶사과 ~ one or two apples / a few apples.

한드랑거리다 dangle; swing; sway (to and fro); oscillate. ¶(나뭇잎 등이) 바람에 ~ tremble [rustle] in the breeze / be swayed by the wind / sway to the wind.

한들거리다 sway; waver; shake; tremble; (매달린 것이) swing; oscillate; (불꽃이) flicker; flare. ¶나뭇가지가 바람에 한들거리고 있다 The branches are swaying in the wind. // 물에 비친 그림자가 한들거렸다 The reflection on the water flickered and danced.

한들한들 shaking; trembling; swaying. **한들한들하다** sway; waver. ⇨ 한들거리다

한때 1 [같은 때] one time; the same time. ¶(무엇을 하는) ~에는 한 가지 일만 하시오 Do one thing at a time.
2 [과거의 어느 때] at one time; once. ¶나는 ~ 직업을 바꿀 것을 심각하게 생각했었다 At one time I seriously thought of changing jobs. // 이 도시는 ~ 수출 산업의 중심지로 번창했었다 This town once enjoyed prosperity as the center of the export industry. // 그녀는 ~ 인기 있는 여배우였었다 She was once a popular actress.
3 [잠시] for a time; for a while; [지금 얼마 동안] for the time being. ¶~의 인기 ephemeral [short-lived] popularity // ~의 생각[변덕] a passing thought [fancy] // ~의 변명 a makeshift excuse // ~의 충동에 끌려 그녀는 많은 액수의 돈을 그 사나이에게 주었다 Carried away by the impulse of the moment, she gave him a large sum of money. // ~는 어떻게 될지를 몰라 근심스러웠다 At one point [For a while] I was really worried. // 남편과 사별한 다음 그녀는 ~ 어찌할 바를 몰라 멍해 있었다 After her husband's death she was quite unable to cope for some time.

한란(寒暖) heat and cold; [온도] temperature. ¶~의 차 difference in temperature.
● **한란계** a thermometer. ¶섭씨[화씨] ~ a Celsius (or Centigrade) [Fahrenheit] thermometer // 최고 최저 ~ a maximum-minimum registering thermometer // ~가 15도를 가리키고 있다 The thermometer reads [registers / stands at] 15 degrees.

한랭(寒冷) cold; coldness; chilliness. **한랭하다** cold; chilly.
● **한랭 전선** a cold front. ¶~이 남하했다 A cold front advanced south. // 오늘은 ~이 호남 지방을 통과하겠습니다 A cold front will pass over the Honam District today.

한량(閑良) 1 [무과에 급제하지 못한 호반] a man of the military class who has not passed the examination for an official post. **2** [하는 일 없이 돈 잘 쓰고 잘 노는 사람] an idle youth of the gentry; a libertine; a prodigal; (미국 구어) a playboy.

한량없다(限量─) unlimited; limitless; bound-

less; endless; infinite. ¶욕심에는 ~ Avarice knows no bounds.∥위를 보면 ~ Don't compare yourself with those above you.∥그의 말을 일일이 들어주었다가는 ~ If we grant every wish of his, there is no end of[to] it.
한량없이 unlimitedly; boundlessly; endlessly; infinitely. ¶그의 친절이 ~ 고마웠다 I was overwhelmed by[with] gratitude for his kindness.
한련 (旱蓮) [식] a nasturtium; a tropaeolum (*pl.* ~s, -la).
한류 (寒流) a cold current.
한림 (翰林) the Royal Academy; an academic society; an institute.
● **한림원** an academy; an institute.
한마디 a (single) word; one word. ¶~로 말하면 in a[one] word / in short∥~ ~ word for word∥말 ~ 없이 without (saying) a single world∥마지막으로 ~ just a word before I close (my speech)∥~ **하다** speak[say] a word (about) / pass a remark∥너에게 ~ 해 두고 싶다 I want to say something to you.∥나는 ~도 놓치지 않으려고 귀를 기울였다 I listened attentively so as not to miss a single word.∥사장의 말 ~에 모두 조용해졌다 A word from the president hushed them all.∥그것을 하기 전에 나한테 ~ 해 주었으면 좋았을 텐데 You might have let me know before you did it.∥제게는 ~도 변명의 여지가 없습니다 There's not a word I can say for myself. / I have no excuse.∥그녀는 내 부탁을 ~로 거절했다 She flatly refused my request. / She turned me down flat[point-blank / (구어) cold].
한마음 one mind; a whole mind. ¶~ 한뜻으로 with one accord∥~이 되어 일하다 act in concert (with) / work in close cooperation / cooperate in harmony∥그들은 ~ 한뜻이다 They have one mind[soul] between[among] them. / They think alike.
한목 in the[a] lump; in one sum; by the gross. ¶3개월분의 봉급을 ~ 받다 receive three months' pay in a lump∥물건을 ~ 보내다[나르다] send[carry] things together∥~ 돈을 ~ 치르다 pay in a lump sum[in one sum]∥그렇게 ~ 돈을 지출했다가는 생활에 지장이 있을 것이다 Such an expenditure in one lot will affect the safety of living.
한몫 a share; one's portion[lot / quota] (미국 구어) a cut; (속어) a whack. ¶~ **차지하다** take one's share / get in on (the profit)∥~ **주다** give a share (to).
  한몫 끼다 have a share (in); take one's share (in); share in (the profits); take part [participate] in. ¶나도 그 일에 한몫 낍시다 Let me in on the job, will you?∥나도 그 일에 한몫 끼워 주게 Will you let me join[take part] in the work?∥그 계획에 나도 한몫 끼겠소 I will join in[take part in] the project. ∥나도 그 계획에 한몫 끼워 주시오 Will you let me in on that plan? / Let me have a share in the project, won't you?
  한몫 잡다[보다] make a profit (from); make money. ¶그는 이 사업에서 단단히 한몫 보고 있다 He is making very good money out of this enterprise.
한문 (漢文) Chinese writing. ¶~으로 씌어 있는 책 a book written in classical Chinese∥~으로 시를 짓다 compose a poem in classical Chinese.

● **한문학** Chinese classics[classical literature]; (한문 연구) study of Chinese classics. **한문학자** a scholar of Chinese classics.
한물 (채소 등의) the season; the best time (for); the prime.
한물가다 be out of season; be past (its) season[best]; be over the hill. ¶수박이 한물갔다 Watermelons have passed its season. ∥딸기는 한물갔다 Strawberries are out of season. / Strawberries are past their best. ∥그 여자도 이제 한물갔다 She has seen her best days. / She is over the hill.
한물지다 be[come] in season; be at (its) best. ¶수박이 한물졌다 Watermelons are in (season). / This is the season for watermelons now. / We have plenty of watermelons now.
한미 (韓美) Korea and America. ¶~의 Korean-American.
● **한미 경제 협력 위원회** the Korea-U.S. Economic Cooperation Committee(약어 ECC). **한미 관계** the relations between the United States and Korea; Korean-American relations. **한미 상호 방위 협정** the ROK-U.S. Mutual Defense Agreement. **한미 안보 협의회** the Korea-U.S. Security Consultative Meeting. **한미 연합군** the ROK-U.S. Combined Forces. ¶~ **사령부** the ROK-U.S. Combined Forces Command(약어 CFC)∥~ **사령관** (General R.) commander-in-chief of the ROK-U.S. Combined Forces Command. **한미 원자력 협정** the ROK-U.S. Atomic Energy Agreement. **한미 환율** a won-dollar exchange rate.
한민족 (漢民族) the Han race. ⇨ ̄한족(漢族)
한민족 (韓民族) the Korean race.
한밑천 a sizable amount of capital. ¶~ **잡다** make[amass] a (sizable) fortune.
한바닥 the central part; the heart; the center. ¶시장 ~ (in) the center[heart] of a market (place).
한바탕 a round; a bout; a (short) spell; a scene; a fall(씨름). ¶~ 부는 바람 a gust [blast] of wind∥~ 울다 cry for a spell∥~ 시합하다 have a (hot) game[bout]∥~ 싸우다 have a passage of arms (with) / make a (hard) fight (with) / (활극을 벌이다) have a nice scene (with)∥~ 야단치다 give (a person) a good scolding∥~ 연설을 하다 make a harangue∥~ 일을 하다 take a turn of work∥소나기가 ~ 올 것 같다 The (look of the) sky threatens a shower∥우리는 그것 때문에 ~ 웃었다 We had a good laugh over it.
한반도 (韓半島) the Korean peninsula. ¶~에서의 평화와 안정의 유지 the maintenance of peace and stability on the Korean peninsula ∥~에서의 긴장을 완화하다 defuse tension on the Korean peninsula.
한발 ¶~ ~ step by step / (서서히) slow(ly) / gradually / by (slow) degrees∥~ 앞서다 be [stay] one jump ahead∥~ 늦어 기차를 놓치다 miss a train by a step∥~ 늦어 그를 만나지 못했다 I missed him by a second[little].
한발 (旱魃) a drought. ⇨ ̄가뭄
한밤중 (-中) midnight; the middle[dead] of the night. ¶~에 at midnight / at dead of night / in the dead[middle / depth] of the night / at the deepest hour of the night∥~까지 far into the night / until the middle of the night / into the small hours of the

morning // ~까지 자지 않고 일어나 있다 sit up till the small hours (of the night) // ~까지 일하다[공부하다] burn the midnight oil.

한방 (一房) [같은 방] a[one] room; the same room; [온 방] the whole room. ¶~을 쓰다 share a room (with) // ~에 거처하다 live in the same room with (a person) / share a room with // 나는 언니와 ~을 쓴다 I share a room with my sister. // 사람들이 ~ 가득했다 The room was packed[crammed] with people. // 우리는 세 사람이 ~을 썼다 The three of us occupied the same room[roomed together]. (▶ room together는 주로 기숙사 등에서)

한방 (韓方) Oriental (herb) medicine.
●**한방약** a[an] herb medicine. ⇨한약 **한방의**-(醫) a herbalist; a herb doctor.

한배 1 [동물의] a litter (a pigs); a brood (of chickens). ¶강아지의 ~ a litter of puppies // ~의 새끼 a litter (of) / a hatch // 암돝은 ~에 세 마리 내지 여섯 마리의 새끼를 낳는다 The female produces from three to six young ones at a litter. 2 ⟨속⟩ children born of the same mother. ⇨동복(同腹)

한번 (一番) once. ¶~ 보다 have[take] a look at (a picture) // ~ 해 보다 have a try[go] (at a thing) // 그것을 ~ 보세요. Have a look at it. // 그곳을 ~ 해 보고 싶다 I would like to have a try at it. // 그곳은 ~ 가 볼 만한 곳이 다 The place is worth a visit. // ~ 해 봅시다 Let's have a try. / I'll just try it.
한번 엎지른 물은 다시 주워 담지 못한다(속담) It is no use crying over spilt milk.

한복 (韓服) a *hanbok*; Korean clothes[costume / dress / attire]. ¶~을 입은 in Korean clothes[dress] // ~을 입고 있다 be in Korean clothes / wear[have on] Korean clothes // 그녀에게 ~을 입혀 주었다 I helped her on with her Korean clothes. // 그녀는 ~을 입으면 아름답다[~이 잘 어울린다] She looks beautiful in Korean clothes.

한복판 the middle; the center; the heart. ¶~의 middle / central // ~에 right[just] in the middle[midst / center] (of) / midmost (of) // 서울 ~에 right in the heart of Seoul // bang in the center of Seoul // 방 ~에 in the middle[center] of the room // 길 ~을 걷다 walk in[keep to] the middle of the road // 과녁의 ~을 맞히다 hit the target right[fairly] in the center // 바로 그의 이마 ~에 맞았다 It struck him full in the forehead. // 그는 길 ~에 쓰러졌다 He fell on the middle of the road.

한불 (韓佛) Korea and France. ¶~의 Korean-French.

한사리 the flood[spring] tide; the spring(s).

한사코 (限死-) to the death; at the risk of one's life; for[with] one's life; desperately; frantically; ⟨구어⟩ like hell. ¶~ 반대하다 be dead set against / persist in one's opposition // ~ 버티다 persist to the bitter end / hold on to it through thick and thin // ~ 거절하다 decline[refuse] positively.

한산하다 (閑散-) dull; inactive (market); slack; [한가하다] leisurely; quiet. ¶시장은 ~ The market is slack[inactive]. // 이 가게는 이 시간엔 ~ It is the slack hour now in this store. // 거리는 이맘때는 ~ The traffic is light about this time.

한살되다 1 [물건이] be incorporated; be united. 2 (남녀가) be united; become one flesh; become man and wife.

한색 (寒色) [미] a cold color.

한서 (寒暑) [추위와 더위] heat and cold; [겨울과 여름] winter and summer. ¶~의 차가 심한 나라 a country with extremes of temperature // 그 나라는 ~의 차가 심하다 The country is marked by a wide range of temperature between the hottest and coldest periods of the year.

한서 (漢書) 1 [중국의 서적] a Chinese book; [집합적] Chinese classics[literature]. 2 [한문으로 기록된 책] a book in Chinese.

한선 (汗腺) [생] a sweat[a sudoriferous] gland.

한세상 (一世上) 1 [평생] a lifetime; one's (whole) life. ¶~을 마치다 end one's life // ~을 편안히 지내다 live comfortably to the end of one's life // 사람의 ~은 잠시에 불과하다 Our life is but a span. // 울며 살아도 ~이요, 웃으며 살아도 ~이다 Life is life, whether spent in tears or laughter. 2 [한창때] one's bright[best] days; the heyday of one's life. ¶~ 만나다 have one's day.

한센병 (一病) [의] Hansen's disease.

한속 1 [한마음] one mind. ¶~이다 be of a [one] mind. 2 [같은 속셈] the same intention[design]. ¶~과 ~이 되어 in collusion [league / conspiracy] with ... / in secret understanding with ... // ~이 되다 act[be] in collusion (with) / (미) go (into) cahoots (with).

한솥밥 the same mess. ¶~을 먹다 break bread (with) / live under the same roof (with) / eat at the same mess / be a messmate (with) // 그와는 ~을 먹은 사이다 I have broken bread with him. / We have lived under the same roof. / I have shared food with him.

한술 a spoonful (of food); [적은 음식] a bite [morsel] (of food). ¶~ 뜨다 take a spoonful of food / have a bite[morsel] // 점심 ~ 들자 Let's take a spot of lunch.

한술 더 뜨다 be more serious[extreme]. ¶나도 술꾼이지만 그의 아버지는 한술 더 뜬다 He's quite a drinker, but his father is an even heavier drinker. // 머리 좋은 학생은 때로 시험 출제자보다 한술 더 뜨는 경우가 있다 Sometimes the bright student can outwit the examination maker.

한숨¹ [호흡] a breath; [휴식] a pause; a rest; a relief; [잠] a (wink of) sleep. ¶~에 at a breath[stroke] / (all) in a breath / at a stretch // ~ 돌리고 after a pause // ~ 돌릴 틈도 없다 I have no time to rest[take a rest]. // 이젠 ~ 돌리겠다 Now I feel relieved. // ~ 돌리고 나서 다시 일을 시작하자 Let's pick up the work again after taking a break. // 이것이 끝나면 ~ 돌리자 When we finish this, let's take a break[breather] // 나는 어젯밤에 ~도 못 잤다 I didn't sleep a wink last night. / I couldn't catch some Z's last night.

한숨² [탄식] a sigh; a heave[long] breath. ¶~을 짓다[쉬다] sigh / heave[draw] a sigh / draw a deep[long] breath // ~을 쉬면서 with a (deep) sigh / sighing(ly) // 안도의 ~을 쉬다

heave a sigh of relief // 그는 ~을 쉬었다 He sighed. / He heaved [drew] a sigh.

한시 (一時) **1** ~도 잊지 않다 do not forget (it) even for a moment / keep (something) in mind all the time // ~도 몸에서 떼지 않다 always carry (a thing) about [on] one / 당신을 ~도 잊지 않을 것입니다 I'll never forget you for a moment [an instant]. // ~의 여유도 없다 I have no time to spare. / I haven't got [don't have] a moment to spare. // 그는 ~도 쉬지 않았다 He hasn't rested for as much as a second. // 그녀는 어머니 일을 ~도 잊은 적이 없다 She never forgets her mother for even a moment.

한시 (漢詩) a Chinese poem; 《집합적》 Chinese poetry.

한시름 a (big) worry; an [a great] anxiety. ¶~놓다 have peace of mind [feel relieved] for a while / feel temporarily relieved // 모두들 ~ 놓았다 Everybody gave a sigh of relief. // 자네 말을 듣고 ~ 놓았네 What you told me made me feel relieved. // 아버지가 무사히 돌아오셔서 ~ 놓았다 As my father came back safely, I felt [was] quite relieved.

한시바삐 without a moment's delay; as soon as possible; in no time.

한식 (寒食) *hansik*; "Cold Food" day (which falls on the 105th day after the winter solstice or about early April).

한식 (韓式) Korean style.
● **한식집** a Korean-style house; a house built in Korean style.

한식 (韓食) Korean-style food; a Korean (-style) meal. ¶저녁 식사는 ~을 드시겠습니까, 양식을 드시겠습니까 Will you have Korean-style food or Western-style food for dinner?

한심하다 (寒心－) 〔가엾고 딱하다〕 pitiful; pitiable; wretched; miserable; sorry; 〔통탄스럽다〕 lamentable; deplorable; grievous; woeful. ¶한심한 인간 a wretch / a hopeless fellow // 한심한 일 a matter for regret // 한심한 처지 [지경] a sorry [piteous] plight // 내 신세가 한심하구나 Ah me! How miserable I am! // 참으로 한심한 세상이다 What a wretched [sorry] world we live in! // 사회 기강이 이토록 문란한 것은 한심한 노릇이다 It is deplorable that the public morals should be so corrupt. // 자기 중심적으로 생각하는 사람이 많아진다는 것은 한심한 노릇이다 The increase in the number of self-centered people is deplorable [regrettable].

한약 (韓藥) a [an] herb medicine.
● **한약국 / 한약방** a dispensary of herbal medicine; a herbal medicine shop.

한어 (漢語) a Chinese word; a Chinese expression.

한없다 (限－) 〔끝이 없다〕 unlimited; limitless; boundless; endless. ¶한없는 바다 the boundless sea / 한없는 생명 eternal life // 한없는 기쁨 limitless [boundless] joy // 욕심에는 ~ Avarice knows no bound. **한없이** unlimitedly; boundlessly; without limit [end]; endlessly; infinitely; 〔더없이〕 extremely. ¶~ 넓은 바다 a boundless sea // 아들을 ~ 사랑하다 love one's son ever so much // 논의는 ~ 계속되었다 There was no end to the argument.

한여름 1 〔한창 더위〕 midsummer; the middle of summer; high [full] summer. ¶~ 더위 the midsummer heat // ~의 midsummer // ~에 in midsummer / in [at] the height of summer // 산꼭대기는 ~에도 시원하다 It is cool at the top of a mountain at [in] the height of summer. **2** 〔여름 한철〕 the summer season; the whole summer; all the summer (long / through). ¶~을 지내다 pass [spend] the summer (at).

한역 (漢譯) (번역) translation into classical Chinese; (역문) the classical Chinese version [rendering]. **한역하다** translate [put / turn] into classical Chinese.

한역 (韓譯) (번역) translation into Korean; (역문) the Korean rendering [version]. **한역하다** translate [render / put] into Korean.

한열 (寒熱) heat and cold; chillness and fever.

한염 (旱炎) the burning heat in the drought.

한영 (韓英) Korea and Britain. ¶~의 Korean-English.
● **한영사전** a Korean-English dictionary.

한옆 the [one] side. ¶~에 on [to] one side / aside / by the side (of) // ~으로 밀다 push aside // ~으로 비키다 step [stand] aside / step [move] to one side // 길 ~에 남자가 서 있었다 A man was standing by the side of the road.

한옥 (韓屋) a *hanok*; a Korean-style house.

한외 현미경 (限外顯微鏡) an ultramicroscope.

한우 (韓牛) a Korean cow [bull].

한유 (閑遊) idling; loafing. **한유하다** idle; loaf; idle one's time away.

한은 (韓銀) the Bank of Korea. ⇨ 한국은행 (⇨ 한국 (韓國))

한의사 (韓醫師) a herbalist; a herb doctor.

한의학 (韓醫學) Oriental medicine.

한인 (閑人) a man of leisure; a leisured man; an idler.
● **한인물입** (一勿入) 《게시》 No admittance except on business.

한인 (韓人) a Korean; (프) a Coréen.

한인 (漢人) a Chinese.

한일 (韓日) Korea and Japan. ¶~의 Korean-Japanese.
● **한일 각료 회담** the Korea-Japan Ministerial Conference. **한일사전** a Korean-Japanese dictionary. **한일 회담** the Korea-Japan talks; the Korean-Japanese Conference.

한일자 (－－字) ¶~로 in a straight line / in a beeline // ~로 다문 입 firm-set lips // 입을 ~로 다물다 firmly close one's lips.

한입 a mouthful; a bite. ¶~에 at [in one] mouthful // 그는 그것을 ~에 먹었다 He ate it [gulped it down] in one mouthful.

한자 (漢字) a Chinese character [ideograph]. ¶상용 (常用) ~ the Chinese characters in common [daily] use // 중고교 한문 교육용 기초 ~ the basic Chinese characters to be taught at middle and high schools // ~로 쓰다 write in Chinese characters.
● **한자어** a word written in Chinese characters. **한자 철폐** abolition of Chinese characters.

한잔 (一盞) 〔한 차례 마시는 술〕 a drink (of liquor); (구어) a spot (of drink). ¶~ 들면서 이야기하다 talk over a drink [bottle] // ~ 들어가 열큰한 기분이다 be a little drunk / be tipsy / be (feeling) a little high // 그는 ~ 들어가면 말문이 열린다 Wine loosens his tongue.

한잔하다 have [take] a drink; take a drop; (속어) get a wet. ¶한잔하시겠소 Won't you

한잔 have a drink? / What do you say to a drink? ∥ 오늘 밤 한잔하세 Let's have a drink tonight. ∥ How about having a drink tonight? ∥ 가끔 한잔합니다 I enjoy a glass now and then. ∥ 그는 한잔하면 시비조가 된다 He gets quarrelsome in his cups.

한잔 걸치다 have[take] a drink. ⇨ ˝한잔하다 (⇨한잔)

한잠 1 [깊이 든 잠] (a) deep sleep [(문어) slumber]; [숙면] (a) sound sleep. ¶~ 푹 자다 have a sound[deep] sleep. **2** [잠시 자는 잠] a sleep; a snatch[wink] of sleep; a doze; a nap (졸기). → **자다** get a sleep / sleep [have] a wink / take a nap ∥ ~도 못 자다 can not get a wink of sleep / do not sleep a wink ∥ 그날 밤 나는 ~도 못 잤다 I did [could] not get a wink of sleep that night.

한재 (旱災) a drought disaster[calamity]; damage from a drought. ¶~를 입다 suffer from a drought.

● **한재 지구** a drought(-stricken) district [area].

한적하다 (閑寂-) quiet; tranquil; secluded. ¶ 한적한 곳 a quiet[secluded] place ∥ 한적한 주택가 a quiet residential quarter[area] ∥ 한적한 시골 생활 a quiet life in the country. **한적히** quietly; tranquilly.

한정 (限定) [제한] limitation; qualification; [의미를 좁히기] definition; [논] determination. **한정하다** [제한하다] limit; restrict; set limits to; qualify; [의미를 좁히다] define; [논] determine. ¶회원을 50명으로 ~ limit membership to 50 / 시일[날짜]을 ~ put [set] a time limit (to) / 행동 범위를 ~ limit the sphere of one's activities. → ¶한정된 limited / defined ∥ 한정된 지면(紙面)으로는 with limited space at one's disposal ∥ …으로 한정되다 be limited[restricted] to … ∥ 수가 한정되어 있다 be limited in number ∥ 면회 시간은 30분으로 한정되어 있다 Visits are [Visiting time is] limited to thirty minutes. ∥ 회원은 여자만으로 한정되어 있다 Membership is limited to women. ∥ 우리의 예산은 5만 원으로 한정되어 있다 Our budget is limited to five hundred thousand won.

● **한정 가격** the ceiling price. **한정 치산** quasi-incompetence. **한정 치산자** a quasi-incompetent (person).

한제 (寒劑) [물] a freezing mixture; a cryogen; a refrigerant.

한제 (韓製) Korean make[manufacture]. ¶~의 Korean-made / (articles) of Korean make [manufacture] / (국산의) homemade.

한족 (漢族) the Han race; the Chinese.

한족 (韓族) the Korean race. ⇨˝한민족(韓民族)

한종신 (限終身) all life long; for life; throughout one's life; till death; till the end of one's life.

한종일 (限終日) all day (long); all the day.

한줄기 [한바탕의 빗줄기] a spell (of shower). ¶소나기가 ~ 오다 have a (spell of) shower.

한중 (寒中) midwinter; the cold season; the depth of winter. ¶~에 during the cold season / in (the depth of) winter.

한중 (韓中) Korea and China. ¶~의 Korean-Chinese / Sino-Korean.

● **한중 무역** Korean-Chinese trade. **한중사전** Korean-Chinese dictionary.

한중간 (-中間) the middle. ⇨˝한가운데

한즉 if so; then; in that case. ¶ 인제 어떻게 하는 것이 좋을까 Then, what should we do now?

한증 (汗蒸) a sweating bath; a steam[vapor / Turkish] bath; a sudatorium (pl. -ria). **한증하다** take a sweating[steam] bath. ¶마치 한증한 것 같았다 I felt as if I were taking a steam bath.

● **한증막** a sweating bathroom. ¶~ 같다 be sweltering / be oppressively hot and humid.

한지 (寒地) a cold area.

한지 (韓紙) hanji; Korean paper.

한직 (閑職) an easy[a leisurely] post; a sinecure. ¶~에 있는 사람 a sinecurist / ~에 있다 occupy a post of leisure / retire from the forefront ∥ ~으로 좌천되다 be relegated to a less important post ∥ 회장이라는 자리는 일종의 ~이었다 The post of company president was a kind of sinecure for him. ∥ 그는 몸이 약해서 ~으로만 돌려졌다 He was given a leisurely job [An easy job was assigned to him] because of his poor health.

한집안 1 [한 가족] one's family[people]; (미) one's folks. ¶~ 식구 (the people in) one's family / one's folk ∥ ~ 식구처럼 대하다 treat (a person) as a member of one's family ∥ ~이나 다름없다 be in close relation with each other. **2** [친척] one's relatives; a clan; the same family[clan].

한쪽 [어느 하나의 방향] a quarter; [한편 쪽] one side; (길의) one way; (사람의) a party. ¶ ~ 끝 an edge / one end ∥ ~ 눈[손] an eye[a hand] ∥ 다른 ~ 눈[손] the other eye[hand] ∥ 길 ~에 나 있는 풀 grass growing along one side of a road / 계약의 ~ 당사자 a party to the contract / 다른 ~ the other side ∥ ~만의 이야기[주장]을 듣다 hear (only) [listen to] one side of the story ∥ ~에 치우치다 be one-sided ∥ ~으로 기울다 lean to one side ∥ ~ 귀가 안 들리다 be deaf in one ear ∥ 상자의 ~이 망가져 있다 One side of the box is broken. ∥ 그는 ~ 손이 부자유하다 He has lost the use of one hand. ∥ 그는 ~ 눈이 안 보인다 He is blind in one eye. ∥ 벽에 걸린 그림이 ~으로 기울어져 있다 The picture on the wall is tilted to one side.

한참 [한동안] (for) a good while; for a (long) time[while]. ¶~ 있다가 after a good while ∥ ~ 있다가 대답하다 answer after a spell ∥ (시간이) ~ 걸리다 take long / take a long time ∥ ~ 만일세 It is a long time since we met [I saw you last].

한창 [절정] the height; the climax; the summit; the peak; the zenith; (인생의) (in) prime; flower; bloom; (꽃의) (in) full bloom; [부사적] in the midst[middle / thick] of; at the height of. ¶~ 일할 나이의 젊은이들 youths of working age ∥ 폭풍우가 ~ 휘몰아칠 때 at the height of the storm ∥ ~ 전쟁 중에 in the midst of the war ∥ (낮의) ~ 더운 때에 in the heat of the day ∥ 더운 여름이 ~ 일 때에 in the height of summer ∥ ~ 젊었을 때에 in the prime of youth ∥ ~ 의 one's days ∥ ~이다 be in full swing / (꽃이) be in full bloom ∥ 사과가 지금 ~이다 Apples are in season. ∥ 지금은 진달래꽃이 ~이다 The azaleas are in full bloom [at their best] now. ∥ 지금은 스케이팅이 ~이다 Now is the best time for skating. / It is now the skating season. ∥ 지금이 ~ 추울 때이다 We are in the worst part of the cold season. ∥ 그는 ~ 일할 나이

이다 He is at the height of his powers.// 더위도 지금이 ~이다 This is the hottest time of the year.// 작업은 지금이 ~이다 The work is in full swing. / We are right in the middle of our work.// 그 당시는 이 도시에 재즈가 ~이었다 At that time jazz was in its heyday in this town.// 그 당시는 권씨 문중이 ~ 권력을 누리고 있을 때였다 At that time the Gwon clan was at the height of its power.// 지금 시합[회의／토론／일]이 ~ 진행 중이다 The game[conference／argument／work] is in full swing now.// 내가 도착해 보니 파티가 ~이었다 When I arrived, the party was in full swing.// 논쟁이 ~일 때 한 발의 총성이 울렸다 In the middle of the dispute, there was a shot fired[a shot was fired].// 전투가 ~ 치열한 속을 뚫고 그는 전령으로 왕복해야 했다 He had to carry messages back and forth through the thick of the fighting.// ~ 붐빌 때에 쇼핑 센터에서 불이 났다 There was a fire at the shopping center just when it was most crowded.

한창때 〔청춘〕 the prime[spring] of life; the bloom of youth; 〔좋은 때〕 one's palmy[best] days; heyday; 〔과일 등의〕 the season; the best time (for). ¶ ~의 여자 a woman in her bloom// 인생의 ~가 지난 사람 a man past his prime// ~가 지난[한물간] 프로 야구 선수 a pro baseball player who is past his peak [(구어) over the hill]// ~에 있다 be in the prime of life[manhood(남자) / womanhood(여자)]// ~를 **지나다** be past one's prime / go to seed// 그녀의 남편은 (일하기에) ~이다 Her husband is in his prime.// 그녀는 여자로서 ~이다 She is in the bloom of womanhood.// 그들은 ~이다 They are in their prime[at the height of their powers]. / They have come into their own.// 그때가 그의 ~었다 (사회적으로) Those were his best days. / (신체적으로) He was in his prime[at the height of his powers] then.

한천(旱天) dry weather; a (spell of) drought.

한천(寒天) **1** 〔우무〕 agar(-agar); Chinese isinglass[gelatin]. ¶ ~질[모양] gelatinous / jellylike. **2** 〔추운 철〕 a cold season.

한철 one season.

한촌(寒村) a poor[lonely／deserted] village; an out-of-the-way hamlet.

한추위 〔한 차례의 추위〕 a spell of cold weather; 〔큰 추위〕 (the) intense[severe／bitter] cold.

한층(一層) 〔한 단계 더〕 more; still[much] more; (all) the more. ¶ ~ 힘드는 일 (much) harder work// ~ 더 조심하다 take all the more care// ~ 더 노력하다 make greater efforts// ~ 더 외로운 생각이 든다 My sense of isolation became doubly acute.// 홀로 남게 되자 슬픔이 ~ 더했다 Left all alone, I felt all the more sad.// 상대가 챔피언이라고 생각하니 투지가 ~ 왕성해졌다 My opponent was the champion, and this made me all the more determined to win[want to beat him even more].

한칼 1 〔한 번 휘둘러서 베는 칼질〕 a single stroke of the sword. ¶ ~에 **베다** cut down with[at] one[single] stroke of the sword. **2** 〔고기의〕 a slice[piece] (of meat). // 고기 ~ 살 돈도 없다 cannot afford to buy a single slice of meat.

한탄(恨歎) deploring; lamentation; regret. 한

탄하다 deplore; lament; sigh; regret; grieve. ¶ 한탄할 lamentable／deplorable／regrettable// 한탄할 일이다 It is a lamentable fact that ... / It is to be regretted that ... // 일신의 불행을 ~ bewail one's misfortune// 자식이 없음을 ~ regret that one is childless// 정치의 부패를 ~ deplore the corruption of politics// 친구의 죽음을 ~ lament over[for] the death of one's friend// 한탄해 마지않는 바이다 It is really a matter for her regret.// 그녀는 자기 아이의 죽음을 한탄했다 She lamented [grieved] over her child's death. / She mourned for her dead child.// 내 불운을 한탄해 보았자 무슨 소용이냐 What is the use of bewailing your misfortune?

한턱 〔향응〕 an entertainment; a treat; 〔향응〕 a feast. **한턱하다** entertain; treat; stand treat for (one's friend); give (a person) a treat.
● **한턱거리** something happy to make a treat out of.

한턱내다 entertain; treat; stand treat for (one's friend); give (a person) a treat. ¶ 술을 ~ treat (a person) to a drink /（미국 구어）set (a person) up to a drink /（미국 구어）blow (another) to a drink// 돌려 가며 ~ treat friends by turns// 이번엔 내가 한턱낼 차례다 It is my treat now.

한턱먹다 be feasted[treated]; have a feast.

한테 to; for. ⇨ ˉ에게

한테로 to; toward. ⇨ ˉ에게로

한테서 from; of. ⇨ ˉ에게서

한통 fellow adherents. ⇨ ˉ한통속 ¶ ~이 되어 사람을 속이다 conspire together[with someone] to cheat a person.

한통속 fellow adherents[conspirators]; a party (to a plot); a ring; a gang. ¶ ~이 **되다** conspire (with) / act in collusion (with) / plot together /（미）go (in) cahoots (with) // ...과 ~이 되어서 in collusion with ... / in secret understanding with ... / hand in glove with ...// ~이 되어 남을 속이다 conspire together[with someone] to cheat a person// 그들은 모두 ~이다 They are all part of the same.// 시장과 경찰서장은 ~이라고 비난을 받았다 The mayor and the police chief were accused of being hand in glove.

한파(寒波) a cold wave[snap]. ¶ ~가 전국을 엄습했다 A cold wave swept[hit] (over) the country. / Freezing weather gripped[seized] (over) the country.// 근래에 보기 드문 ~가 한국을 덮쳤다 Korea was visited by the coldest weather in recent years.

한판 a[one] game; a round; a bout; a turn(레슬링 등의). ¶ 씨름을 ~ 벌이다 have a bout at *ssireum*// 바둑을 ~ 두다 have a game of *baduk*(go)// 바둑 ~ 어떻습니까 How about a game of *baduk*?// 그는 결정적 ~이 될 때에 정말로 잘한다 When it counts[comes to an important game], he plays really well.
● **한판 승부** a contest of single round.

한패(一牌) one of the (same) party; an accomplice(공범자); a confederate(일당); 〔한 동아리〕 a company; a party; a set; a gang(악당의). ¶ ~가 **되다** join (others in something) / participate[take part] in (something) / mix oneself (among)// 그도 ~임에 틀림없다 He must be one of the party.// 이 녀석도 그놈들과 ~다 This fellow is one of them, too.// 이 범죄에는 틀림없이 그의 ~가 있다 He must have had an accomplice in this crime.// 너도

한편 (一便) **1** [한쪽] one side; one way; [당사자의 한쪽] one side [party]; [자기 편] friend; an ally; one's side. ¶~에 치우치다 be one-sided // ~이 되다 (게임에서) partner; pair (off) (with) // ~으로는 … 다른 ~으로는 … on the one hand [side] ... on the other (hand [side]) // 나는 자네와 ~일세 I stand your friend. // 다음 게임에서는 나와 ~이 되지 않겠니 How about pairing with me in the next game? / Will you be my partner in the next game? // 그는 짐과 ~이 되어도 승산이 없다 Even he joins forces [pairs] with Jim, he has no chance of winning. // ~이 되어 최선을 다해 보자 Let's join forces and do our best together. // 그의 의견은 ~에 치우쳐 있다 His opinion is one-sided. // 이 경우에는 반드시 ~을 가해자, 다른 ~을 피해자라고 말할 수 없다 In this case we cannot necessarily say that one party is the assailant and the other the victim. // 정부는 ~으로는 재정 재건의, 다른 ~으로는 감세라는 어려운 과업에 직면하고 있다 The government is faced with the difficult task of financial rehabilitation on the one hand and reducing taxes on the other. **2** [⋯한 외에] in addition to; while; but (at the same time); [⋯하는 한편] besides; while; [한편으로는] somewhat; in a way; a bit; [이야기는 바뀌어] in the meantime; meanwhile; on the other hand. ¶그의 큰아들은 사교적이지만 ~ 동생은 내성적이다 His oldest son is sociable, while [whereas] his younger son is more introverted. // 그들은 친지끼리는 예의 바르지만 ~ 대중 속에서는 아주 무례하다 They are very polite among acquaintances, but, on the other hand, they are extremely rude in public. // 그는 농사를 짓는 ~ 직물도 겸하고 있다 Besides farming, he does some weaving. // 그는 장사를 하는 ~ 그림도 그린다 He runs a store, and paints pictures as a sideline [on the side].

한평생 (一平生) a lifetime; one's (whole) life. ¶연구에 ~을 바치다 devote one's lifetime to the study.

한평생 (限平生) all [throughout] one's life; for life; through life; to the end of one's life. ¶~ 잊지 못할 일 a memory for life // ~ 독신으로 지내다 remain single through life // ~ 편히 지내다 live comfortably to the end of one's life // 나는 그것이 ~ 잊혀지지 않을 것이다 It will never be forgotten. / I shall never forget it.

한풀 꺾이다 be discouraged [disheartened / downhearted]; be downcast [cast down / crestfallen]. ¶한 번쯤의 실패로 한풀 꺾일 사나이가 아니다 He is not a man to be daunted by a single failure. // 추위도 한풀 꺾인 듯하다 The cold seems to have decreased in severity. // 첫 번에 실패하자 그의 열의는 한풀 꺾였다 The initial failure daunted [chilled] his ardor.

한풀이하다 (恨-) vent one's spite; satisfy one's grudge; avenge [revenge] oneself; pay off old scores with.

한풍 (寒風) a cold [chilly / bleak] wind. ¶살에는 듯한 ~ a biting [piercing] wind.

한하다 (限-) limit (to); restrict (to); confine (something to). ¶성인에 한한 영화 an adult film / a movie for adult entertainment // 이번에 한하여 for this time only / for this once // 정당한 사유가 있는 경우에 한하여 provided that there is just reason for it // 1인 1매에 한함 (입장권에 적힌 글) Admit one. / Admission for one person only. // 학생에 한하여 입장 (게시) No admission except to students. // 일요일에 한해서 입장 무료다 Admission is free on Sundays only. // 입장자는 여성에 한합니다 Only women are admitted. / Admission to women only. // 정당한 이유가 있는 경우에 한하여 고려한다 We will take it into consideration provided there is just reason for it.

한학 (漢學) the study of the Chinese classics; [중국학] Sinology. ¶~의 대가 an authority on Chinese classics.
● **한학자** a scholar of the Chinese classics; [중국 학자] a Sinologist.

한한자전 (漢韓字典) a Chinese-Korean dictionary.

한해 (旱害) drought damage; damage from a drought. ¶~를 입다 suffer from a drought // 농작물은 극심한 ~를 입었다 The crops suffered serious damage from the drought.
● **한해 지구** a drought(-stricken) area.

한해 (寒害) damage caused by cold weather; cold-weather damage. ¶농작물을 ~로부터 지키다 protect crops from being damaged by cold weather // ~ 대책을 강구하다 study how to protect (farm crops) from // 올해는 ~를 입어 쌀이 흉작이다 Due to the cold weather, the rice crop has failed this year.

한해살이풀 [식] an annual plant.

한화 (韓貨) [한국의 돈] Korean money.

할 (割) ten percent. ¶연(年) 1~2푼 5리의 이자 an interest of 12.5 percent per annum / 정가의 8~로 팔다 sell at 80 percent of the price [at a discount of 20 percent] // 3~ 할인해서 팔다 sell at 30% discount // 그 가게는 시디를 정가의 8~로 팔고 있다 The shop sells CD at eighty percent [(영) per cent] of the usual price [at a discount of twenty percent]. // 일의 8~은 [거의 / 절반 이상이] 다 되었다 The work is eighty percent [almost / more than half] finished. // 학생의 몇 ~이나 결석을 했습니까 What percentage of children were absent?

할거하다 (割據-) hold each his own sphere of influence; hold one's own ground; defend one's own territory.

할깃거리다 keep sharply (at a person). ⇨<흘깃거리다

할당 (割當) assignment; allotment; allocation; apportionment; quota; [부과] assessment; [배급] rationing. **할당하다** assign(▶ assign은 보통 권위를 가지고 특정인에게 할당하다의 뜻); allot; allocate; apportion; [부과하다] assess. ¶각자에게 ~ allot a share to each // 숙소들 ~ [군] billet (soldiers on houses) // 방을 ~ assign rooms (to persons) // 역(役)을 ~ assign a role (to each actor) // 예산을 각 부에 ~ apportion the budget among the sections // 그는 재산을 5명의 자식에게 균등하게 할당했다 He divided his property equally among his five children. ➔역(役)을 할당받다 be cast for [in] a role // 교정 일이 나에게

할당되었다 The task of proofreading was assigned to me.∥그의 강연에는 30분이 할당되었다 He was given[allotted] thirty minutes for his lecture.
● 할당량 / 할당액 a quota; an allotment. 할당제 a quota system. ¶수출 ~ the export quota system.

할딱거리다 pant; gasp (for breath). ⇨헐떡거리다

할딱할딱 gasping and panting. ⇨헐떡헐떡

할렐루야 hallelujah; halleluiah.

할례(割禮) circumcision. ¶~를 하다 circumcise (a person).

할로겐(족 원소)(一族元素) [화] a halogen.
● 할로겐화물 a halide; a halogenide.

할망구 an old lady. ⇨²할머니2

할머니 1 [조모] a grandmother; [호칭] Grandmother[Grandma / Granny]. ¶~의[~ 같은] grandmotherly (love)∥그녀는 ~가 키운다 [양육하고 있다] She is being raised by her grandmother. / [애지중지하고 있다] Her grandmother dotes on her. / [응석받이이다] She is spoiled[pampered] by her grandmother. 2 [늙은 여자] an old lady[woman]; a granny. 3 (친척의) a related woman of one's grandmother's generation.

할멈 [노파] an old woman; a granny; [하녀] an old maid.

할미 1 [조모] a grandma. 2 [노파] an old woman; an aged woman.
● 할미꽃 [식] a pasqueflower; a windflower.

할미새 [동] a wagtail.

할복(割腹) disembowelment. 할복하다 disembowel oneself; commit disembowelment; rip oneself up.
● 할복자살 suicide by disembowelment.

할부(割賦) allotment; quota. ¶~(제)로 팔다 sell (motorcars) on the installment plan ∥ 텔레비전 대금을 ~로 내고 있다 We're paying for the television by monthly installment. 할부하다 put[set] quota (on / to).
● 할부 구매 installment purchase. 할부금 an allotment. 할부 상환 amortization. 할부 판매 selling on an installment basis.

할선(割線) [수] secant (line)(약어 sec.).

할아버지 1 [조부] a grandfather[(구어) a grandpa]; [호칭] Grandfather[Grand(d)ad / Grandpa]. ¶~ 대(代)부터 이 마을에서 살고 있다 We have lived in this town since my grandfather's time. 2 [노인] an old man. 3 (친척의) a related man of one's grandfather's generation.

할아범 [늙은 남자] an old[aged] man.

할애하다(割愛—) spare (something); [내어 주다] part with (something). ¶지면을 ~ allow space (for)∥그렇게 하잖은 것을 위해 우리 잡지에서 1페이지의 지면을 할애할 수는 없다 We cannot give a whole page of our magazine to such an insignificant matter as that.∥이 교과서에서는 새 헌법에 1개 장(章) 을 할애하고 있다 This textbook devotes one whole chapter to the new Constitution.

할양(割讓) cession (of territory). ¶영토의 ~ the cession of territory. 할양하다 cede (territory). ➔영토의 반을 이웃 나라에 할양당했다 They were forced to cede[surrender] half of their territory to a neighboring country.

할인(割引) 1 (a) discount; (a) reduction. ¶단체 ~ a group reduction / (여행 시의) a partytrip reduction∥동업자 (간) ~ (a) trade discount∥은행 ~ bank[banker's] discount∥재~ rediscount∥현찰 ~ (a) cash discount∥수표 ~ 중매인 a discount broker∥조조 ~ 영화 (see) a morning movie at reduced admission∥조금 ~이 되지 않습니까 [할인해 주지 않겠어요] Will you make it a little cheaper? / (구어) Can't you knock a little off the price? **할인하다** discount; cut off; reduce. ¶25퍼센트 ~ make a reduction in price of[reduce the price by] 25 percent / give a discount of 25 percent∥500원 할인해 드리겠습니다 I'll give you a discount of 500 won.∥대량이면 할인해 드립니다 We make a reduction on a quantity.∥단체에 대해서는 운임을 할인해 준다 A discount is allowed on party tickets.∥현금 지불이라면 10퍼센트 할인됩니다 You get a 10 percent discount[We take 10 percent off] if you pay (in) cash.∥책은 할인되지 않습니다 They sell books at fixed prices.
2 discounting a bill. ⇨ 어음 할인(⇨)어음)
● 할인 가격 a reduced price. 할인권 a discount ticket[coupon]. 할인 기간 the term of discount. 할인 어음 a discounted bill. 할인 요금 a discount charge[commission]. 할인율 a discount rate. 할인 판매 a discount sale.

할인(割印) a tally impression; affixing a seal over two edges. ¶~을 찍은 서류 documents with a tally impression∥~을 찍다 affix a seal over two edges[at the joining of two papers].

할증(割增) a premium; a bonus; an extra (charge / fare / dividend). ¶시간 외 ~ 임금 overtime pay∥노무 임금의 ~제 a premium plan[system] of paying for labor∥~부(附)로 판매하다 be selling at a premium∥채권이 ~부로 판매되고 있다 They are selling the bonds at a premium. **할증하다** give[pay] an extra[a premium].
● 할증금 a premium; a bonus (on a loan). ¶~부 채권 a premium bond / a premium-bearing debenture. 할증 요금 an extra fare [charge]; a surcharge.

할짝거리다 keep licking; keep lapping. ¶개가 우유를 할짝거리고 있다 The dog is lapping milk.

할퀴다 1 (손톱으로) scratch; claw. ¶할퀸 상처 a scratch / a nail mark∥손톱으로 얼굴을 ~ scratch (a person's) face with one's fingernails∥고양이가 그를 할퀴었다 A cat clawed him. 2 [휩쓸거나 스쳐 지나가다]. ¶그곳에는 전쟁이 할퀴고 간 자국이 아직도 남아 있다 There are still scars left by the war.

핥다 lick; lap; taste. ¶깨끗이 핥아 먹다 lick (the plate) clean∥입술에 묻은 잼을 핥아 먹다 lick the jam off one's lips∥고양이가 제 발을 핥고 있다 The cat is licking its paws.∥아기가 손가락을 핥고 있다 The baby is sucking her fingers.∥나는 프랑스 어를 수박 겉 핥기로 알고 있을 뿐이다 I have only a smattering of French.∥개는 접시를 깨끗이 핥아 비웠다 The dog licked the plate clean.∥고양이가 물을 핥아 먹고 있다 The cat is lapping up the water.∥그 아이는 막대 캔디를 핥아 먹고 있다 The child is sucking on a lollipop.

핥아먹다 [빼앗다] cheat (a person) of; swindle (a person) out of.

함(函) a box; a case; a chest. ¶사서 ~ a postoffice box (P.O.B.)∥우편 ~ a mailbox∥서류 ~ a filing cabinet.

함교(艦橋) the bridge (of a warship); the navigating platform. ¶전[후]~ the fore [after] bridge.
● **함교 갑판** the bridge deck.

함구(緘口) holding one's tongue; keeping one's mouth shut. ¶~불언하다 refuse to talk / shut one's mouth and remain silent // 그는 여전히 ~무언이었다 He kept silence[mum] as before. **함구하다** hold one's tongue; keep one's mouth shut; keep one's lips tight; keep silent.
● **함구령** a gag; a gag rule [law]. ¶~을 내리다 forbid mentioning (a matter) / gag [muzzle] 《the press》// 보도에 ~을 내리다 gag the press / put a gag on the press // 그 일에 대하여 공무원들에게 ~을 내린 것 같다 The government officials seem to have been ordered not to talk about the matter. // 그 문제에 대해서는 ~이 내려져 있다 Our lips are sealed concerning the matter.

함께 together (with); [다같이] one and all. ¶모두 ~ all together // 부부 ~ both husband and wife / 남과 ~ 일하다 [행동하다] work [act] in cooperation with a person // 배와 ~ 가라앉다 go down with the ship // ~ 서다 put together / mix up // 죽으려면 모두 ~ 죽어야 한다 If we must die, let us all die together. // 공장은 기계와 ~ 몽땅 폭파되었다 The factory was blown up machinery and all. // 나는 그와 ~ 저녁 식사를 했다 I had dinner with him. // 여러분 모두 ~ 와 주시기를 바랍니다 I hope you will all come together to see us. // 우리는 모두 ~ 선생님을 뵈러 갔다 We went to see the teacher all together. // 형과 ~ 집을 떠났다 I left home with my brother. // 책의 송료는 대금과 ~ 보내 주십시오. Please send (us) the postage as well as [with] the price of the books. // 텔레비전의 보급과 ~ 사투리의 표준화가 촉진되어 왔다 With the spread of television, the standardization of dialects has been accelerated. // 가족과 ~ 찾아뵙겠습니다 I'll come with my wife and children. / I'll bring my wife and children. // 남편과 ~ 뵈올 날을 고대하고 있습니다 Both my husband and I are looking forward to seeing you. // 선물과 ~ 꽃다발이 보내졌다 A bouquet was delivered together with the present. // 비와 ~ 거센 바람이 불었다 The rain was accompanied by a high wind. // 나는 땅과 ~ 집을 샀다 I bought the house and the lot [together with the land]. // 우리는 날마다 학교에 ~ 가곤 했다 We used to go to school together every morning. // ~ 가시지 않겠습니까 Won't you go with me? / ~ 놀이를 하지 않겠습니까 Won't you join us in the game? // 초인종과 전화가 ~ 울렸다 The doorbell and the telephone rang at the same time. // 그들은 눈이 맞아 ~ 도망갔다 They ran away [eloped] together. // 나는 누이 동생의 쇼핑에 ~ 따라갔다 I went shopping with my sister to keep her company.

함께하다 share (something) with; take part in. ⇨같이하다 ¶나는 내 상사와 저녁 식사를 함께했다 I had dinner with my boss. // 나는 의리상 그와 술자리를 함께했다 I kept him company for a drink out of a sense of duty. // 그의 집을 방문했더니 손님과 불고기를 먹던 중이어서 자리를 함께했다 When I went to see him, he was eating *bulgogi* with some guests, and so I joined them [I had some, too].

함닉하다(陷溺) 1 (물속으로) drown; sink. 2 (주색 등에의 구렁에) indulge (in); be addicted [given] (to); give oneself up (to); abandon oneself (to).

함대(艦隊) a fleet; (소함대) a squadron (flotilla). ¶연합 ~ a combined fleet // 무적 ~ (16세기 에스파냐의) the Invincible Armada // 주력 ~ the main fleet // 의용 ~ a volunteer fleet // 연습 ~ a training squadron // 분견[상비] ~ a detached [standing] squadron // ~를 파견하다 dispatch a squadron [fleet] (to) // 태평양에 ~를 배치하다 station a squadron in the Pacific.
● **함대 기지** a fleet base. **함대 사령관** the commander of a fleet.

함락(陷落) (땅의) depression; collapse; a cave-in; sinking; [낙성] fall; surrender. **함락하다** (땅의) fall in; subside; sink; cave in; collapse; (적진의) fall; surrender; be reduced. → ¶요새를 함락시키다 take a fortress // 드디어 성을 함락시켰다 Finally they took the fortress. // 적의 요새는 3개월간의 포위 끝에 함락됐다 The enemy fortress fell to us after three months' siege. / The enemy surrendered their fortress to us after a siege of three months.
● **함락 지진** a fallen [cave-in] earthquake.

함량(含量) content. ¶알코올 [비타민] ~ alcohol [vitamin] content // 높은 지방 ~ a high fat content // 주철(鑄鐵)은 탄소의 ~이 많다 Cast iron has a high carbon content.

함령(艦齡) the age [life] of a warship. ¶~초과의 overage (warship).

함몰(陷沒) depression; subsidence; a cave-in; sinking; [몰락] ruin. **함몰하다** sink; subside; be depressed; cave [fall] in; collapse.
● **함몰호**(~湖) a depression [cave-in] lake.

함묵(緘默) holding one's tongue. ⇨ㄱ함구

함미(艦尾) the stern (of a warship).

함박꽃 [식] a peony (flower).

함박눈 large [feathery] snowflakes; the fleeces of descending snow. ¶~이 내린다 The snow is coming down in large flakes.

함부로 1 [무분별하게] thoughtlessly; carelessly; roughly; rashly; recklessly; indiscriminately; at random. ¶~ 말하다 speak thoughtlessly / make unthinking remarks // ~ 믿다 believe too readily // 저 사람에게는 ~ 말을 해서는 안 된다 We must be careful [watch our words] in talking with him. // 그녀는 ~ 행동하는 사람이 아니다 She is not the sort of person to act rashly. // 그는 몽둥이를 ~ 휘둘렀다 He swung the stick about frantically. // 그는 입에서 나오는 대로 ~ 말한다 He makes irresponsible remarks at random [on the spur of the moment]. // 그는 ~ 입을 놀리지 않는다 He weighs [picks] his word.
2 [허가 없이] without permission; [이유 없이] without (good) reason. ¶남의 집 정원에 ~ 들어가서는 안 된다 You must not go into somebody else's garden without permission.
3 [지나치게] immoderately; excessively; inordinately; to [in] excess; absurdly; unduly; (불필요하게) unnecessary; needlessly. ¶종이를 ~ 쓰다 waste paper.

함빡 fully; thoroughly. ⇨<흠뻑

함상(艦上) ¶~의[에서] aboard / on board (a warship).

함석 zinc; tin; galvanized iron. ¶~을 입히다 zinc // ~으로 지붕을 이다 roof with galvanized iron sheets.
- **함석지붕** a zinc[tin] roof; galvanized sheet iron roofing. ¶~의 tin-roofed. **함석판** sheet zinc; galvanized iron sheet.

함선(艦船) warships and other ships; (해군) naval vessels; all vessels[ships]; (집합적) a fleet. ¶~ 5척이 피해를 입었다 Five vessels were damaged.

함성(喊聲) a great outcry; a war[battle] cry; shouting; a war whoop. ¶승리의 ~ a shout of victory[triumph] // ~을 올리다[지르다] raise[give] a war[battle] cry / raise a great war whoop / give a great outcry // ~이 크게 진동하였다 A tremendous hubbub was heard.

함소하다(含笑-) [웃음을 머금다] hold a laugh in one's mouth; have[wear] a smile about one's mouth.

함수(含水) [화] ¶~의 hydrous / hydrated.
- **함수량** water content.

함수(函數) [수] a (mathematical) function. ¶~의 functional // **미분**[로그 / 삼각] ~ a differential[a logarithmic / trigonometric] function.
- **함수 관계** functional relation. **함수론** the theory of functions. **함수 방정식** a functional equation.

함수(鹹水) [염수] salt water; brine; [해수] sea water. ¶~의 saline.
- **함수어** [동] a salt-water fish. **함수호** a salt [saline] lake; a lagoon.

함수(艦首) the bow (of a war vessel).
- **함수포** a bow chaser.

함수초(含羞草) [식] a mimosa. ⇨=미모사

함씨(咸氏) an hono(u)red nephew; your nephew.

함양(涵養) fostering; cultivation; culture. ¶도의심의 ~ cultivation of moral sensitivity. **함양하다** foster; cultivate; develop; build up. ¶덕성을 ~ cultivate moral character // 관용의 정신을 ~ cultivate the spirit of tolerance.

함유량(含有量) content (by amount). ¶알코올 ~이 많다 contain a high percentage of alcohol // 이 약은 모르핀 ~이 매우 적다 Only a small amount of morphine is contained in this medicine.

함유하다(含有-) contain; include; have (in); hold. ¶철분을 함유한 물 water containing iron / chalybeate water // 이 광석은 금을 다량으로 함유하고 있다 This ore contains a lot of gold. / This ore has a lot of gold in it.

함입(陷入) depression; subsidence. **함입하다** be depressed; subside; sink; cave[fall] in; collapse.

함자(銜字) an hono(u)red name; your[his / her] name. ¶선생님의 ~가 어떻게 되십니까 What is your name, sir?

함장(艦長) the captain (of a warship); (소형 함선의) the commander. ¶잠수함의 ~ the captain of a submarine // 기함(旗艦)의 ~ the flag captain.

함재(艦載) carrying aboard a warship; loading on a warship. **함재하다** carry[load] aboard a warship.
- **함재기** a ship(-based) airplane; (미) a deck plane; (집합적) carrier-borne aircraft.

함적(艦籍) the Navy list. ¶~에서 빼다 strike (a ship) off the Navy list.

함정(陷穽) a pitfall; a pit; a trap. ¶~ 수사 (a) decoy investigation / a sting operation // ~에 빠지다 fall into a pit / be caught in a trap / (문어) fall victim to a person's plot // ~을 만들다 set[lay] a trap // ~에 빠뜨리다 ensnare / entrap / catch (an animal) in a trap // 그가 만든 ~에 감쪽같이 빠졌다 I fell right into the trap that he had set for me. // 남을 ~에 빠뜨리려고 하면 자기가 먼저 빠진다 He who digs a pit for others falls in himself.

함정(艦艇) war[naval] vessels; warships.

함지 1 [나무 그릇] a large scooped wooden bowl. **2** (금을 잡는) a pan for gold panning.

함지(陷地) low[depressed] ground; a basin; a sunken place; a depression; a hollow.

함지박 a wooden bowl; a porringer; a scooped wooden dish.

함진아비(函-) a box bearer[carrier].

함축(성)(含蓄性) implication; significance; suggestiveness. ¶함축성 있는 significant / pregnant (sentence) / suggestive // 함축성이 풍부한 말 a word (which is) full of meaning [significance] / a word pregnant with meaning // 그녀의 말에는 특별한 함축성이 있었다 There was a special implication in her words. // 그들의 말과 그녀의 말 사이에는 약간 다른 함축성[뉘앙스]이 있었다 There is a slight difference in nuance between what they said and what she said. // 그에게는 이러한 ~ 있는 말이 통하지 않았다 These words with their hidden meaning were beyond him. / The implication of these words was lost on him. // 그가 한 말에는 함축성이 많다 His remark suggests[implies] a great deal. **함축하다** imply; signify; suggest.

함포(艦砲) a ship's gun; the guns of a warship.
- **함포 사격** the bombardment of land by warships; naval bombardment. ¶~을 하다 bombard (a city) from the sea / shell (a fort) by war vessels // 그 도시는 ~을 받았다 The city was bombarded from the sea.

함함하다 smooth; soft and glossy[lustrous] (hairs).

함흥차사(咸興差使) a lost[corbie] messenger; a messenger sent out on an errand who never returns. ¶그에게 편지를 냈지만 ~다 I wrote to him but got no answer[but I heard nothing in reply]. // 그는 한 번 가면 ~다 Once he goes, he's gone[not likely to return].

합(合) **1** [합계] the sum (total); the total (amount). ¶~을 구하다 do the sum (of) / find[figure] out the sum (of) // ~이 50이다 be 50 in total[in all]. // 5와 5의 ~은 10이다 The sum of five and five is ten. **2** [천] conjunction. ¶~과 충 conjunction and opposition. **3** [철] (a) synthesis (pl. -theses).

합(盒) a brass[brazen] bowl with a lid.

합각(合閣) gable; (건축) a principal rafter. ¶~의 건축 양식으로 된 집 a house with a rafter roof.
- **합각 지붕** a gable roof.

합격(合格) success in an examination; passing an examination. ¶~ 여부의 판정 a yes-no decision / a decision to pass or fail (a person) // 입사 지원자의 ~ 여부는 추후 통지함 The results of our examination of the applicants will be announced later. / You will be notified later of our decision on your

합계

application.∥~ 여부의 결정이 날 때까지는 바늘방석에 앉아 있는 기분이었다 I was on pins and needles until I found out whether I had passed or not. **합격하다** (수험자가) pass an examination[a test]; succeed in an examination; (기준·검사 등에) come up to the standard[mark]; stand the test; pass inspection; (역할 등에) be found eligible; [채용되다] be accepted. ¶가까스로 ~ barely pass (the entrance examination)∥전 과목에 ~ pass every subject∥합격한 것을 축하합니다 I congratulate you on your success in the examination.∥그는 대학 입학시험에 합격했다 He passed[succeeded in passing] the university entrance examination. →¶선생님은 선심을 써서 나를 합격시켜 주셨다 My teacher passed me out of the kindness of his heart.
● **합격률** the ratio of successful applicants. **합격자** a successful candidate[applicant]. **합격점** (상품) (get) a passing mark; standards marks; (사람) the qualifying marks[score]. **합격증** a certificate; (미) a credit(어떤 과목의). **합격 통지** a notice of success. **합격품** tested goods.

합계(合計) the sum total; the total (amount [sum]); an aggregate (of). ¶~ 10,000원 ₩10,000 in total∥~ 백 권의 책 a total of 100 books / 100 books all told∥~액 3,000원 3,000 won in total∥~를 내다 figure out a sum∥~ 5만 원이 들었다 It cost 50,000 won in all[altogether / all told].∥지출이 ~ 10만 원에 달했다 Our expenses reached a total of[amounted to / totaled] 100,000 won.∥~가 얼마나 되나 What does the total come to? **합계하다** add[sum] up; add together; total; count up. ¶합계하여 in total / in the aggregate / altogether / in all / all told.

합금(合金) an alloy; a compound metal. ¶구리 3에 은 1의 비율로 섞은 ~ an alloy of three parts of copper to one of silver. **합금하다** alloy (metals); make an alloy of (copper and zinc). ¶금과 구리를 ~ make an alloy of gold and copper / alloy gold with copper.
● **합금강**(-鋼) alloy(ed) steel.

합기도(合氣道) *hapgido*; an art of self-defense.

합당(合黨) the merger[fusion] political parties. **합당하다** merge the parties; the parties merge.

합당하다(合當-) fit; suitable; proper; befitting; adequate; appropriate; right. ¶그 경우에 합당한 조치 measures appropriate to the occasion∥합당한 가격으로 at a reasonable price∥합당하지 않다 be improper[unsuitable / inappropriate]∥이 정도가 합당한 가격이라고 생각한다 I suppose this is about the right price.∥그것은 남에게 부탁을 하기에 합당한 방법이 아니다 That is not a proper way of asking a favor of a person.∥조건이 합당하면 받아들이겠다 I will accept your offer on fair terms.

합동(合同) [합병] combination; union; amalgamation; incorporation; merger; fusion; coalition(정당 등의); [수] congruence. ¶~の joint / united / combined / (in)corporated∥~ 기업 ~ a trust / (미) a combine∥~으로 jointly / in union. **합동하다** combine; unite (in one body / with others); amalgamate (with); merge (in something greater); incorporate (in / with). ¶합동하여 일에 대처하다 make a joint effort / form a united front (against)∥야당이 합동해서 지사 선거에 임했다 The opposition parties united[combined forces] for the gubernatorial election.
● **합동결혼식** a joint wedding. **합동 군사 훈련** the joint military service. **합동 위령제** a joint service for the (war) dead. **합동 위원회** a joint committee (of both Houses). **합동 작전** concerted[united / combined] operations. **합동 정견 발표회** a joint election speech [campaign] rally. **합동 조사반** a joint investigation team.

합력(合力) (힘을 합침) collaboration; cooperation; a joint effort; [물] a resultant (force). **합력하다** unite one's strength; join forces (with); make united efforts; collaborate (with); cooperate (with). ¶합력하여 by united efforts / in cooperation (with).

합류(合流) **1** [강이 합침] confluence; conflux. **합류하다** join; flow[run] together. ¶이 강은 어디서 한강과 합류합니까 Where does this river join the Hangang(Han river)?∥세 강이 이 지점에서 합류한다 Three rivers meet one another at this point.
2 [합동] joining; linking; union. **합류하다** join; unite[link up] (with); be merged (into). ¶데모대와 ~ unite[merge] with the demonstrators∥모임에 ~ join a party [meeting]∥우리와 합류하지 않겠소 Won't you join us?∥나는 그들의 산행에 합류했다 I joined in on their mountaineering.∥건방지게 보이는 녀석이 우리 기자단에 합류했다 An impudent-looking fellow joined our press group.∥선발대는 본대와 합류했다 The advance troops joined the main force. →¶당신 모임에 나도 합류시켜 주시오 Please take me into your group[circle].
● **합류점** the junction[confluence] of two rivers; the meeting point (of two civilizations).

합리(合理) rationality; reasonableness.
● **합리론 / 합리주의** [철] rationalism. ¶~자 a rationalist. **합리성** rationality. **합리화** rationalization. ¶경영의 ~ the rationalization of management∥산업의 ~ industrial rationalization∥~ 하다 rationalize / make (it) more rational[reasonable]∥자기 행위를 ~하다 rationalize one's behavior∥그는 그렇게 생각함으로써 자기 행위를 ~했다 He rationalized his conduct by thinking so.

합리적(合理的) rational; reasonable; logical. ¶~으로 rationally / logically / in a rational manner∥그것은 ~인 생각이다 It is a rational[sensible / reasonable] idea.

합명(合名) merger; partnership. **합명하다** merge; form a partnership.
● **합명 회사** an unlimited partnership; a general partnership.

합목적성(合目的性) [철] finality; purposiveness.

합반(合班) a combined class. **합반하다** combine (two) classes.
● **합반 수업** combined classwork[teaching].

합방(合邦) [병합] annexation of a country; [통합] unification of (two) countries. ¶한일 ~ the Japanese annexation of Korea. **합방하다** annex a country; unite (two) countries. →¶합방되다 be annexed (to).

합법(合法) lawfulness; legality; legitimacy. ¶그 행위가 ~임은 논의할 여지가 없다 The legality of the act cannot be disputed.
- **합법성** lawfulness; constitutionality. **합법주의** legalism. **합법화** legalization. ¶비-outlawing // ~하다 legalize // 주류 판매를 ~하다 legalize the sale of alcoholic drinks.

합법적(合法的) 〔적법한〕 lawful; 〔법정의〕 legal; 〔법률상 적당한〕 legitimate. ¶~ 투쟁 a law-abiding struggle // ~ 수단으로 by lawful means // 비~ unlawfully / illegally / illicitly // ~ 거래 white market // ~ 암시장 grey market. // 거래는 ~으로 행해졌다 The transaction was conducted lawfully [legally / legitimately].

합병(合倂) union; (a) combination; 〔연립〕(a) coalition; (회사 등의) (a) merger; amalgamation; consolidation; fusion (정당 등의); affiliation (작은 회사 등의); 〔병합〕 annexation; incorporation (편입). ¶신설 ~ consolidation // 흡수 ~ merger // 두 정당의 ~ a fusion [merger] of two political parties // 읍과 마을의 ~ the merger of towns and villages. **합병하다** combine; unite; amalgamate; merge; affiliate; be incorporated with; annex (영토를). ¶갑과 을을 ~ combine [unite] one thing with another // 영토를 ~ annex a territory (into) // 단과 대학을 종합 대학교에 ~ affiliate a college with [to] a university // 세 회사가 합병하여 대회사가 되었다 The three companies have been merged [amalgamated / combined] into a big enterprise.
- **합병 절차〔조건〕** amalgamation procedure [conditions]. **합병증** 〔의〕 a complication. ¶~을 일으키다 develop a complication / a complication occurs [sets in] // 그는 감기에서 ~이 생겼다 His cold led to complications. // After catching a cold, he developed complications. // 아버지는 원래의 병은 나았으나 지금은 ~을 앓고 계신다 My father was cured of his original disease, but is suffering from a secondary illness.

합보시기(盒-) a bowl with a lid.
합본(合本) **1** 〔책의〕 copies (of) bound together in book form; bound volumes (of a magazine). ¶일 년분의 ~ a bound set of all the issues (of a magazine) for a (certain) year. **합본하다** bind (copies) together; combine in a single volume. **2** partnership. ⇨합자(合資)

합사(合絲) (a) braid; a plaited [braided] cord; twisted thread [yarn]; twine. **합사하다** twist threads; twine threads into a string.

합삭(合朔) the conjunction [conjuncture] of moon and sun.

합산(合算) adding up. **합산하다** add up; add [put] together; sum up; total. ¶비용을 ~ add up the expenses // 송료, 관세를 합산하면 약 15만 원이 된다 With the postage and customs charges included, the total cost adds [runs] up to about 150,000 won.
- **합산액** total (amount).

합석(合席) a shared table. **합석하다** sit with (a person); sit in company with (a person); share a table (with). ¶식당에서 다른 사람과 ~ share a table with another at a restaurant // 죄송합니다만 합석해도 될까요 Excuse me, but would you mind sharing your table?

합선(合線) 〔전〕 (a) short (circuit). **합선하다** make a short circuit; short-circuit. ¶전선이 합선하면 대개 퓨즈가 끊어진다 A short circuit usually blows a fuse.

합성(合成) 〔물〕 composition; 〔화〕 synthesis. ¶힘의 ~ composition of forces // ~의 compound / composite / 〔화〕 synthetic. **합성하다** compose; compound; 〔화〕 synthesize.
- **합성 고무〔연료 / 염료〕** synthetic rubber [fuel / dyestuff]. **합성물** a complex; a compound; a composite thing; a synthetic (product); a synthesized product. **합성 사진** a montage picture [photo]. **합성 섬유** synthetic [chemical] fiber. **합성 세제** a synthetic detergent. **합성수지** synthetic resins; plastics. **합성어** a compound (word). **합성 피혁** synthetic leather.

합세하다(合勢-) join forces; form an alliance. ¶운동에 ~ join in the movement // 마을 사람들이 합세하여 그 사람에게 달려들었다 The villagers all turned upon the man. // 그 사람들은 합세하여 그를 실컷 때려 주었다 The men joined in giving him a sound thrashing.

합수(合水) a confluence; joining [meeting] of two streams. **합수하다** flow together; join; meet. ¶세 강이 이 지점에서 합수한다 Three rivers meet one another at this point.

합숙(合宿) joint billet. **합숙하다** lodge [board] together; be billeted together [with]. ¶강화 ~ stay in a training camp.
- **합숙소** a boarding house; a dormitory; a training camp. **합숙 훈련**(운동의). **합숙 훈련** camp training. ¶~을 하다 live together in a training camp.

합승(合乘) riding together; sharing a vehicle. **합승하다** ride together; share the car (with). ¶택시에 ~ share a cab (with) // 오토바이를 ~ ride on a motorcycle together // 그와 택시를 합승했다 I shared a taxi with him. / He and I shared a taxi. // 그들은 ~ 합승하여 왔다 They came in the same car.
- **합승객** a fellow passenger. **합승 자동차** an omnibus; a (motor) bus; an autobus; a motor coach.

합심(合心) union; unity; concert. **합심하다** unite; be of one accord [mind]; be in union (with); cooperate in harmony. ¶합심하여 with one accord // 그들은 합심하여 일했다 They worked together in perfect accord. // 서로 합심해서 하자 Let's work in unison.

합의(合意) mutual agreement; mutual [common] consent; concurrence. ¶~하에 별거하다 live apart by mutual consent // 양측 사이에 …하는 ~가 이루어졌다 It was agreed between the two that .... // ~에 의해 그 모임 [회의]은 연기되었다 The meeting was postponed by mutual consent. // 우리는 ~하에 이혼했다 We got a divorce through [by] mutual agreement. // 건축 부지에 관해서 그와 ~에 도달했다 We came to an arrangement with him as to building site. // 어떻게든 원만한 ~에 이르게 되기를 간절히 바랍니다 I would be very happy if we could reach an amicable agreement. **합의하다** agree (on / about / to do). ¶지불 기일에 합의했다 We agreed on the date of payment.
- **합의서** a written agreement; the text of minute. **합의 이혼** a divorce by mutual agreement.

합의(合議) consultation; conference; counsel. ¶~를 거쳐 after consultation / by mutual consent // 서로 간의 ~가 이루어졌다 We

합일 arrived at [reached] a conclusion [an agreement].∥회의의 변경은 회원의 ~ 아래서만 이루어진다 The revision of the rules shall be made by the mutual consent of [after consultation with] the members. **합의하다** consult [counsel] together; confer (with); take [go into] counsel. ¶회(會)의 운영에 대해 ~ confer [consult / hold a conference] about the management of an association.
● **합의 사항** items of understanding. **합의 재판** collegial [collegiate] judgment. **합의제** a representative [council / parliamentary] system.

합일(合一) union; unity; oneness. **합일하다** unite; be united (with / in one body); be in accord (with).

합자(活字) (활자의) a ligature.

합자(合資) partnership; joint capital [stock]. **합자하다** enter [go] into partnership (with); join stocks.
● **합자 회사** a limited partnership. ¶A ~ A & Company, Ltd.

합작(合作) coauthorship; collaboration; a joint work [production]; (협력) cooperation; (공동 경영) joint management [undertaking]; a joint venture; (미) a pool. ¶국공(國共) ~ Kuomintang-communist cooperation∥한불 ~ 사업 a Franco-Korean joint enterprise. **합작하다** collaborate with a person (on a book); produce conjointly; write jointly; cooperate with a person (in a work). ¶그 영화는 한미가 합작한 작품이다 The movie is a joint production of Korean and American film companies.
● **합작자** a collaborator; a joint author. **합작 투자** joint venture. **합작 회사** a joint corporation.

합장하다(合掌-) join one's hands; put one's hands flat together; clasp one's hands (in veneration). ¶그들은 합장하고 인사했다 They greeted people by joining their palms together (as if in prayer).

합장하다(合葬-) bury [inter] together. ¶부인을 남편과 ~ bury the wife's body [remains] with her husband's.

합제(合劑) a medical mixture; a compound; (화) a flux.

합주(合奏) (a) concert; (an) ensemble. ¶2[3/4/5]부 ~ a duet [trio / quartet / quintet]. **합주하다** play in concert.
● **합주단** an ensemble.

합죽거리다 mumble toothlessly.

합죽선(合竹扇) (a folding) fan with ribs made of double strips of bamboo.

합죽이 a toothless person.

합죽하다 toothless and puckered.

합죽할미 a toothless old woman.

합중국(合衆國) a federal state; a federation. ¶아메리카 ~ the United States (of America) / (구어) the States.

합창(合唱) chorus; concerted singing; ensemble. ¶혼성 ~ a mixed chorus∥남[여]성 ~ a men's [women's] chorus∥2[3/4/5]부 ~ a duet [trio / quartet / quintet]. **합창하다** sing in chorus; sing together.
● **합창곡** a chorus; a choral; a part-song. ¶남[여 / 혼]성 ~ a chorus for men's [women's / mixed] voices. **합창대** a chorus; (교회의) a choir.

합체(合體) union; incorporation; combination; consolidation; amalgamation. **합체하다** unite; be united; incorporate; combine (into one); consolidate.

합치(合致) agreement; coincidence; concurrence. **합치하다** agree (with); accord (with); be in accord (with); concur (with); consist (with); conform (to); coincide (with). ¶…에 합치하여 in (strict) conformity with … ∥현실과 ~ correspond to reality∥사실과 ~ square with the facts∥주의와 ~ [합치하지 않다] be in [out of] accord with one's principles.

합치다(合-) 1 [하나로 만들다] put [bring] together; combine; unite; join together; [병합하다] amalgamate; merge; annex. ¶두 물줄기가 합치는 지점 the confluence of two streams / the point where two streams meet∥세 방을 합쳐서 하나로 만들다 throw three rooms into one∥본부[본대]에 ~ join the headquarters [main body]∥도중에서 일행과 ~ join [rejoin] a party on the way∥그 면적은 한국과 일본을 합친 정도이다 The area is about that of the Korea and the Japan put together.∥3개의 마을을 합쳐서 하나의 시로 만들었다 The three villages were merged into a city.∥이 길은 그곳에서 국도와 합쳐진다 This road joins the highway there.
2 [섞다] mix (up); compound; [모으다] combine; assort. ¶한데 합쳐서 팔다 [사다] sell [buy] in bulk∥크고 작은 것을 합쳐서 계란을 팔다 sell eggs of all sizes together.
3 [합산하다] sum up; add up; total; put together. ¶3과 5를 ~ add three to five∥합쳐서 15개 있다 There are fifteen all together [all told / in all].∥미국의 인구는 영국과 프랑스의 인구를 합친 것보다 더 많다 The population of the United States is larger than that of Britain and France combined.
4 [하나가 되다] be united; be made into one; be put [joined] together; merge; combine (with).

합판(合板) a veneer board; plywood. ¶프린트 ~ printed plywood.

합판(合版) joint publication. **합판하다** publish (a book) jointly.

합판(合辦) joint management [undertaking]; a joint venture; (미) a pool. ¶한미 ~ 회사 a Korean-American joint concern [company / corporation].

합판화(合瓣花) [식] a gamopetalous [compound] flower.

합하다(合-) 1 [하나로 만들다] put [bring] together; combine; unite; join together; [병합하다] amalgamate; merge; annex. ¶두 장의 종이를 ~ put two sheets of paper together∥두 회사를 하나로 ~ merge [amalgamate] two companies∥그들은 힘을 합해 공통의 이익을 지켰다 They joined forces [united their efforts] to defend their common interests.
2 [섞다] mix (up); compound; [모으다] combine; assort. ¶물과 술을 ~ mix liquor with water.
3 [합산하다] sum up; add up; total; put together. ¶합해서 in total / in the aggregate / altogether / in all / all told∥합해서 얼마입니까 How much does it come to [amount to / total]? / How much is it all together?∥숙박료는 세금과 봉사료를 합해서 1박에 5만 원이었다 The hotel charge was fifty thousand

won including tax and service [tax and service included].
4 [하나가 되다] be united; be made into one; be put [joined] together; merge; combine (with). ¶마음을 ~ be united / act in concert with.

합헌(合憲) constitutionality. ¶~의 constitutional.
● **합헌성** constitutionality.

합환주(合歡酒) (혼례 때의) nuptial cups (of wine) exchanged between the bride and bridegroom; the wedding toast; (동침 전의) a drink before making love. ¶~를 나누다 exchange nuptial cups.

핫- **1** [솜을 둔] wadded [padded] (garment). **2** [배우자가 있는] having one's spouse. ¶~아비 a married man // ~어미 a married woman.

핫길(下-) [하등의 품질] inferior quality; a low grade [class]; [하등의 물건] an article of inferior quality; low-grade goods.

핫뉴스 hot news(▶ 부정관사를 붙이지 않으며 단수 취급).

핫도그 a hot dog(▶ 영어 "hot dog"는 길쭉한 빵에 소시지를 끼운 음식만을 가리키나, 우리말 「핫도그」는 소시지에 막대기를 꽂고 기름에 튀긴 음식을 가리키기도 함).

핫라인 a hot line.
핫 머니 hot money.
핫바지 **1** [솜바지] (a pair of) padded trousers. **2** [촌뜨기] a countryman; (경멸) a bumpkin; a clodhopper.

핫옷 wadded [padded] clothes.
핫이불 padded bedclothes.
핫저고리 a wadded [padded] jacket.
핫케이크 a hot cake; a pancake.
핫팬츠 hot pants.

항(項) **1** [조항] a clause; a paragraph; (예산표 등의) an item. ¶이 ~은 계속 [다음 페이지에] to be continued / (이면에) over / more / P.T.O.(▶ Please turn over의 약어) // 제3조 제1~에 해당하다 come under Sub-Section 1, Section 3. **2** [수] a term. ¶2[3 / 다]~식 a binomial [trinomial / polynomial] expression.

-항(港) a port; a harbor. ¶부산~ Busan Harbor // 자유~ a free port.

항간(巷間) the world; the town; the street. ¶~의 소문 a current rumor / the talk of the town // ~에 [on] the streets / abroad // ~에 전해지고 있는 이야기 a topic widely talked about / the talk of the town // ~에 떠도는 말에 의하면 a rumor has it that ... / people say that ... / it is said [rumored] in the town that ... / according to the current version // (소문이) ~에 퍼지다 be rumored abroad / get abroad.

항거(抗拒) resistance. **항거하다** resist; defy; oppose; antagonize. ¶여론에 ~ defy public opinion // 독재 정치에 ~ resist [rise against] dictatorial government.
● **항거죄** an offense [(영) offence] of resisting lawful order.

항고(抗告) [법] a complaint; an appeal (from); a protest. ¶준~ a quasi-complaint // 즉시 ~ an immediate complaint. **항고하다** protest (a ministry directive); appeal (a court decision); lodge [enter] a protest [an appeal]. ¶그들은 이 재판에 대하여 즉시 항고했다 They appealed the sentence [decision] immediately.
● **항고심** hearing of a complaint. **항고인** a complainant.

항공(航空) aviation; flight; aerial navigation; air traffic [voyage]. ¶~의 aerial / aeronautic // 국제 [국내] ~ international [domestic] aviation service // 민간 ~ civil aviation // 국제 민간 ~ 기구 the International Civil Aviation Organization // 대한 ~사 the Korean Air.
● **항공 공학** aeronautical engineering. **항공 교통 관제** air traffic control(약어 A.T.C.). ¶~를 하다 control air traffic. **항공권** an airline ticket. **항공기** **1** a plane; (미) an airplane; (영) an aeroplane; (집합적) aircraft. ¶정기 ~ an airliner // 민간 ~ a civil passenger airliner. **항공대** a flying corps (단수·복수 동형); an air force. **항공로** an airline [air route]; an airway; an air lane; a skyway. ¶~를 열다 establish [open] an air route [line]. **항공모함** an aircraft carrier; (미국 속어) a flattop; a seaplane tender. **항공법** a civil aeronautics law. **항공병**(-病) aviation sickness. **항공사진** an aerial photograph. **항공 수송** air transportation; air service; an airlift. **항공 시설** air service; airline facilities. **항공 요금 / 항공 운임** an air fare. **항공 우주 공학** aerospace engineering. **항공 우주 산업** aerospace industry. **항공 우편** (집합적) airmail; air mail; (편지) an airmail [air-mail] letter. ¶그 녀에게 ~으로 편지를 보냈다 I sent a letter to her by airmail. / I airmailed [air-mailed] her a letter. **항공 지도** an aeronautical chart. **항공 표지** an air(way) beacon. **항공학** aeronautics. **항공 학교** an aviation school. **항공 협정** a civil aviation agreement. **항공 화물** an air cargo. **항공 회사** an airline; (영) an airway.

항구(港口) [자연적인 항만] a harbor; (영) a harbour; [주로 상업항] a port. ¶~에 들르다 call at a port // ~에 들르지 않다 make no port // ~를 떠나다 clear a port / leave (a) port / sail from a port // 배가 ~에 닿았다 A ship came into port. / A ship arrived in port [the harbor]. / 배가 ~에 정박하고 있다 A ship is at anchor in the harbor. / A ship is in port.
● **항구 도시** a port town. ¶~ 목포 the port town of Mokpo.

항구성(恒久性) permanency; imperishability (of the universe).

항구적(恒久的) permanent; everlasting. ¶~ 평화 permanent [lasting] peace // ~ 대책 permanent measures.

항구하다(恒久-) permanent; perpetual; lasting; eternal.

항균성(抗菌性) antibiosis. ¶~의 antibacterial / antimicrobial.
● **항균성 물질** antibiotics.

항내(港內) (the inside of) a harbor. ¶~에 within [in] the harbor / in port // 유람선은 ~를 일주했다 The excursion boat went around the port.
● **항내 설비** harbor [port] facilities.

항도(港都) a port town. ⇨항구 도시(⇨항구)

항독소(抗毒素) [의] an antitoxin(e); an antivenom. ¶~를 주사하다 inject an antitoxin (serum).

항등식(恒等式) [수] an identical equation; an identity.

항라(亢羅) (silk) gauze; gossamer; sheer silk.

항렬(行列) generations of the clan. ¶같은 ~

항로(航路) 〔정해진 경로〕 a route; 〔진로〕 a course; 〔정기 항(공)로〕 a line; 〔배 등의 편(便)〕 service. //배(비행기)의 ~ a steamship [an air] route // 원양 ~의 배 an ocean liner // 정기 ~ regular service // ~에 오르다 enter service // ~를 정하다 lay a course / shape one's course // ~를 바꾸다 change one's course // ~를 잘못 잡다 take a wrong course / mistake one's course // ~를 동쪽으로 잡다 steer east // 배를 유럽 ~에 취항시키다 put a ship on the European run[line] // 대한 항공은 곧 그 도시와 서울 사이에 새로운 ~를 개설한다 Korean Airlines is going to open [inaugurate] a new line between that city and Seoul.
● **항로 변경** a deviation (of route). **항로 부표** a fairway buoy. **항로 신호** a marine signal; plying signals. **항로 이탈** (항공기의) deviation from the (international) flight route. **항로 표지** a beacon.

항론(抗論) refutation; repudiation; contradiction. **항론하다** refute (an argument); repudiate (a charge); contradict.

항만(港灣) harbors; harbour(s) and bay(s).
● **항만 사업** harbor works. **항만 시설** harbor [port] facilities.

항명(抗命) disobedience. **항명하다** disobey (a person's) order.

항목(項目) 〔제목〕 a head(ing); 〔표나 계산서 등의 세목〕 an item; 〔조항〕 an article; a clause; a provision (in a will). ¶~으로 나누다 itemize // 내용을 ~별로 검토하다 examine the contents item by item // 나는 논문을 5개 ~으로 나누었다 I divided the thesis into five heads. // 파충류는 이 ~에 들어 있다 The reptiles are included [come / fall] under this heading. / The reptiles belong to this category.
● **항목화** itemization; specification.

항무(港務) harbor [port] service.

항문(肛門) 〔생〕 the anus; the back passage; the fundament.
● **항문 괄약근** the anal sphincter. **항문병** an anal disease.

항법(航法) navigation. ¶극지 ~ 〔항〕 polar navigation.
● **항법사** a navigator.

항변(抗辯) 〔항의〕 a protest; 〔반론〕 (a) refutation; (피고의) a plea. ¶각하 ~ a plea in abatement // 사실 부인의 ~ a plea of the general issue. **항변하다** protest; refute; (피고가) plead; defend oneself; make a plea. ¶상관에게 ~ remonstrate with one's superior.

항병(降兵) a surrendered soldier.

항복(降伏·降服) (a) surrender; submission(복종); capitulation(일정한 조건에 따른); 〔굴복〕 yielding. ¶조건부[무조건] ~ a conditional [an unconditional] surrender // ~을 권하다 invite (the enemy) to surrender / summon [urge] (the enemy) to surrender // 무조건 ~을 강요당했다 We were forced to surrender unconditionally. **항복하다** surrender (oneself) (to); capitulate (to the enemy); strike one's flag; lower the colors; lay down one's arms; 〔굴복하다〕 submit[yield / bow / give in] (to one's rival); throw up the sponge; throw [toss] in the towel. ¶…이라는 조건으로 ~ surrender[capitulate] on the condition that ... // 이젠 항복하면 어때 Why not admit that you're beaten? // 우리는 힘이 다하여 적군에 항복했다 Our strength exhausted, we surrendered to the enemy. // 적은 싸우지도 않고 항복했다 The enemy surrendered without fighting. // 어때, 항복하겠지 Well, do you give up? / Well, have you had enough?
➔ ¶항복시키다 make (the enemy) to surrender / bring (the enemy) under [to his knees].

항산성균(抗酸性菌) an acid-fast bacterium (pl. -ria).

항상(恒常) always; all the time. ⇨늘 ¶그는 ~ 바쁘다고 말하고 있다 He always says he is busy. // ~ 아껴 주셔서 감사합니다 Thank you very much for your constant patronage. // 그는 ~ 자식 자랑을 한다 He always boasts about his son.

항상성(恒常性) 〔생〕 homeostasis.

항생 물질(抗生物質) an antibiotic.

항설(巷說) a town talk; a talk of the town; a rumor; a hearsay; a street-corner gossip. ¶그의 의견은 ~에 지나지 않는다 His opinion has no more weight than hearsay. // ~에 의하면 그는 자살했다고 한다 Rumor has it [There is a rumor] that he killed himself.

항성(恒性) constancy; permanency. ¶~의 constant.

항성(恒星) 〔천〕 a fixed [permanent] star; a sun. ¶~의 sidereal.
● **항성년** a sidereal year. **항성일** a sidereal day.

항소(抗訴) 〔법〕 an appeal (to a higher court); an intermediate appeal. ¶~를 철회하다 withdraw an appeal // 그의 ~는 기각되었다 His appeal was dismissed. **항소하다** bring an intermediate appeal (in a court); appeal to a court of intermediate appeal; enter [lodge / file] an intermediate appeal. ¶그들은 대법원에 항소하기로 하였다 They decided to appeal to the Supreme Court. // 피고는 지방 법원의 판결에 대하여 항소했다 The defendant appealed (against) the decision of the district court.
● **항소권** the right of intermediate appeal. **항소 기각** dismissal of intermediate appeal. **항소 법원** a court of appeal(s); an appellate court. **항소심** a review by an appellate court on an appeal. **항소장** a petition of appeal.

항속(航續) (배의) cruising; (항공기의) flight.
● **항속 거리** (배의) a cruising range; (항공기의) a flying range. ¶이 기종은 ~가 길다 This type of aircraft has a long[considerable] range. **항속력** cruising[flying] capacity. ¶배의 ~이 떨어졌다 The cruising capacity of this ship has dropped considerably. **항속 시간** cruising[flying] time.

항시(恒時) always; all the time. ⇨늘

항심(恒心) constancy; steadiness; steadfastness.

항아리(缸-) a *hangari*; a pot; a jar(아가리가 넓은 것). ¶물~ a water jar[pot] // 도기 ~ an earthen pot.

항아리손님(缸-) 〔의〕 parotitis; mumps (단수 취급).

항암제(抗癌劑) an anticancer drug.

항언(抗言) a protest; a retort; (a) refutation; confutation; contradiction. **항언하다** protest;

make a protest; refute; confute.
항온 constant temperature.
● **항온 동물** a warm-blooded [homoiothermic] animal.
항외(港外) ¶~에 outside the port[harbor] // ~에 **정박하다** lie at anchor off the harbor // 배가 ~로 나가다 sail out of a harbor.
항용(恒用) **1** [보통임] ordinariness; a commonplace. **2** [늘] always; usually; all the times; constantly.
항원(抗原·抗元) [생] an antigen.
항의(抗議) a protest; protestation; a remonstrance(항의); an objection(반대); an exception(이의); a representation(진정); a complaint(불평); [법] a demur. ¶**엄중 ~** a strong protest // **정식 ~** [체] a protest // **집단 ~** a mass protest. **항의하다** protest [make a protest] (to a person against a measure); object (to); offer [raise] an objection (to); take an exception (to). ¶**항의할 일이 있으면 말하시오** Inform[Tell] us if you have any objections. // 야당은 정부의 원안에 당연히 항의했다 The opposition party naturally protested against the government's proposal. // 나는 불공평한 대우에 대해 항의했다 I protested against the unfair treatment I had received. // 공장의 소음에 대하여 인근 주민들은 항의했다 The people in the neighborhood filed a complaint about the noise from the factory. // 시장의 망언에 대해 시민들이 항의했다 The citizens protested to the mayor over his improper language.
● **항의문** a note of protest. **항의 성명** a statement of protest. **항의 집회** a protest rally; a rally (against).
항일(抗日) anti-Japanese; resistance to Japan.
● **항일 운동** an anti-Japanese movement; the resistance to Japan.
항쟁(抗爭) contention; resistance; (a) struggle. **항쟁하다** contend; struggle (with / against); resist; offer resistance.
항적(航跡) a (boat's) wake; a furrow; a track; [항] a flight path; a vaportrail. ¶**다른 배의 ~을 따라가다** follow up the wake of another vessel.
항전(抗戰) resistance. ¶**철저한 ~** do-or-die resistance // **대일**(對日) **~** resistance to Japan. **항전하다** offer [make] resistance (to / against); resist. ¶**그들은 집요하게 항전했다** They put up stubborn resistance.
항주력(航走力) cruising speed.
항진(亢進) rise; [의] exasperation; exacerbation; (인플레 등의) aggravation; advance. ¶**심계 ~** palpitation / heart acceleration / tachycardia // **혈압 ~** a rise in blood pressure. **항진하다** rise; exasperate; accelerate.
항진하다(航進-) sail; proceed; steam; fetch; gather; gain ground; be on a voyage. ¶**매시 10해리를 ~** steam ten miles an hour.
항체(抗體) [생] an antibody.
항풍(恒風) a constant wind; a trade wind.
항해(航海) a voyage; (sea) navigation; (a) sailing; a crossing; a passage (over the sea); a (sea) trip; (순항) a cruise; [해상 교통] sea traffic. ¶**연안 ~** coastwise sailings // **원양 ~** ocean navigation // **처녀 ~** a long cruise // a maiden voyage / (사람의) one's first voyage // 즐거운 **~** a happy and delightful sail [voyage] // ~ 길에 오르다 start [go]

on a voyage / (사람·배가) set sail / (배가) put out to sea // ~ **중이다** (사람이) be on a voyage / (배·사람이) be out at sea / (배가) be under canvas / be afloat // ~ **중 바다가 거칠어지다** have a stormy [rough] passage [crossing] // ~에 **견디다** [견디지 못하는] be seaworthy [unseaworthy] // ~에 **강한** [**약한**] be a good [bad] sailor(사람이) // ~를 **계속하다** (사람이) continue the voyage / (배가) keep the sea / hold on her course. **항해하다** sail; make a voyage (to); navigate; make a crossing (over the ocean); cruise(순항하다). ¶**넓은 바다를 ~ go** [sail] across a wide sea // **태평양을 ~** sail the Pacific // **무사히 ~** make a safe voyage / have a smooth passage [crossing] // 그 배는 3개월간 항해하고 있었다 That ship has been three months at sea.
● **항해권** the right of navigation. **항해도** a (navigator's) chart. **항해등** a navigation light. **항해사** a mate; a navigation officer. ¶**1등 ~** the chief mate / the first mate [officer] // **2**[**3**]**등 ~** the second [third] mate [officer]. **항해선** a service ship. **항해 속도** sea [service] speed. **항해술** (the art of) navigation; seamanship. **항해 일지** a (voyage) log; a logbook; a ship's journal [log]. ¶~**를 적다** keep a logbook // ~**에 기입하다** enter (events) in a logbook / log (the miles run). **항해자** a mariner; a seaman; a navigator.
항행(航行) navigation; sailing; passage. ¶**샌프란시스코를 향해 ~ 중에** enroute to San Francisco. **항행하다** navigate; sail; steam; cruise. ¶**강의 상**[하]**류로 ~** sail up [down] a river.
● **항행권** the right of navigation.
항혈청(抗血淸) [의] an antiserum (pl. ~s, -ra).
항히스타민제(抗-劑) [약] an antihistamine; an antihistaminic (medicine).

해[1] **1** [태양] the sun. ¶**~ 질 녘** sunset / (미) sundown / evening // **질 녘에** toward evening [nightfall] / at dusk [dark] // **~가 드는 곳에** in a sunny place / in the sun // **~가 들지 않는 곳에** in a sunless [shady] place / in the shade / out of the sun // **~가 지기 전에** before dark [sunset / the sun sets] // **~가 중천에 있을 때에** while it is light // **~가 중천에 있을 때에** under a high sun // **~를 향하여** heliotropically // **~를 등지고** with the sun to one's back / apheliotropically // **~를 피하여** keep off the sun / shield oneself from the sun // **~가 떴다** [**졌다**] The sun has risen [set]. // **~가 밝게 비치고 있다** The sun is shining brightly. // **~가 비치기 시작했다** [**구름에 가려졌다**] The sun has begun to shine [has gone behind the clouds]. // **우리는 ~가 지기 전에 목적지에 다다른다** We got to our destination before sunset [dark]. // **~가 중천에 떠 있다** The sun is high. // **~ 질 녘이 되면 아이들은 집으로 돌아간다** When it began to get dark, the children went home.
2 [낮] daytime. ¶**하루 ~를 보내다** pass [spend] a day // **~가 길어지고** [**짧아지고**] **있다** The days are getting longer [shorter] // **곧 ~가 질 것이다** It will get dark soon. // **그는 ~가 져서 집으로 돌아왔다** He returned home after dark.
해가 서쪽에서 뜨겠다 Did hell freeze over?; Are my eyes deceiving me? ¶**네가 나한테 술을 산다고? 해가 서쪽에서 떴나** Are you

해² [연] a year. ¶이~ this year // 다음다음 ~ the year after next // 새~에 at the beginning of the year // 그~ 안에 before the end of the year / within the year / ~마다 every year / year after [by] year / with every passing year / with each year that goes by / ~를 보내다 see out the old year and see in the new // ~를 넘기다 extend from this year to next [from one year to the next] / keep over the winter(식물 등이) // 그녀는 ~가 갈수록 아름다워진다 She has grown more beautiful with the years. // ~가 지남에 따라 그 소문은 사라졌다 As the years passed [went by], the rumor faded away. // 그~는 눈이 많이 왔다 There was a lot of snow that year.

해³ [소유물] a possession. ¶내 ~ mine // 이것은 뉘 ~냐 Whose is this?

해⁴ [웃는 모양] (smile) with one's mouth open.

해- [그해에 새로 난] (of the current year); this year; new; fresh.

해(害) [위해] injury; harm; mischief; hurt; [손상] damage; injury; detriment; [해독] evil; injury; an evil [baneful] influence; evil [harmful / injurious] effects. ¶~을 끼치다 harm / do harm (to) / (손상을) damage / do damage (to) / (나쁜 영향을) have a harmful influence (on) // ~를 입다 (손상을) suffer damage / (악영향을) suffer harmful [evil] effects (from) // 담배는 건강에 ~가 된다 Smoking is bad for [harmful to] the health. // 그 법률은 ~가 많고 이익은 적다 That law does more harm than good. // 그 책은 풍기상 ~가 된다 The book has a bad effect on public morals. // 아무 ~가 없는 약은 있을 수 없다 No medicine is entirely harmless [without harmful effects].

-해(海) ¶북~ the North Sea.

해갈하다(解渴-) (갈증을) appease [quench / slake / relieve] one's thirst; (가뭄을) wet dry weather; be relieved from drought; bring the end of drought; (금전 면에) be relieved from financial drought.

해감 silt; slime; ooze. ¶~내가 나다 smell of slime [ooze].

해거름 sunset; (미) sundown; dusk(황혼); twilight; gloaming. ¶~에 at sunset / at dusk [twilight] / (미) in the shank of evening.

해거리 every other [second] year; (in) alternate years.

해결(解決) (a) settlement; [문제 등을 해명하는 일] (a) solution; (a) resolution. ¶분쟁의 실마리 a key to the settlement of a dispute // 원만한 [평화적] ~ an amicable [a peaceful] solution // 그것은 아직 미~로 남아 있다 It remains unsolved [unsettled]. 해결하다 settle; solve; work out a solution (to); resolve. ¶해결할 수 없는 insoluble (problem / mystery) / unsolvable // 원만히 ~ arrange [settle] (an affair) amicably / iron out (a knotty problem) / bring to an amicable settlement // 교섭에 의해서 ~ negotiate a settlement (of a problem with a person). // 그가 두 집안의 분쟁을 해결하였다 He settled the trouble between the two families. // 이 일을 될 수 있는 대로 빨리 해결하고 싶다 I'd like to have this matter settled as soon as possible. // 돈으로 해결할 수 있다면 돈을 내겠다 If it can be settled [put right] with money, I will pay. / If money can solve [settle] the matter, I will pay. / If I can settle the matter with money, I will. // 화해로 해결할 수 없느냐 Can't you settle the matter out court? ➔¶일은 평화적으로 해결되었다 The matter was brought to a peaceful settlement. // 당신의 결단 덕택으로 만사가 해결되었다 Your decision has resolved [settled] the whole problem.

● 해결사 a trouble-solving broker. 해결책 a solution; a method of settlement. ¶문제의 ~ a solution to a problem.

해고(解雇) (a) dismissal (from); (일시적이) a layoff. ¶집단 ~ mass dismissal // 회사는 조합에 대해 70명의 ~를 통고했다 The company notified the labor union of the dismissal of seventy employees. 해고하다 discharge; dismiss; part with (a servant); put (a person) to the door; put [send / turn (out)] to grass; give (a person) a shake; (미국 속어) fire (out). ¶즉시 ~ send [turn / put] (a person) to right-about(s) // 일시적으로 ~ (미) lay off (workman) / pay off. ➔¶그녀는 회사에서 해고당했다 She was dismissed [[미국 구어] fired] by the company. / (영국 구어) She got the sack from the company. / (미) She got the pink slip. // 직장에서 해고당한 뒤 1년이 되었다 A year has already passed [gone by] since I was fired. // 의무 불이행 때문에 사관은 해고되었다 The officer was dismissed [cashiered] from the service for neglecting has duty. (▶ cashier 는 군대의 경우에만 씀) // 하인은 부정 때문에 해고되었다 The servant was discharged [[구어] fired / (구어) sacked] for being dishonest.

● 해고 수당 a dismissal [discharge] allowance. 해고장 a notice of discharge; a dismissal notice. 해고 통지 a dismissal [discharge] notice.

해골(骸骨) (사람·동물의) a skeleton; bones; (속어) an anatomy; (머리뼈) a skull; a cranium (pl. -nia). ¶~같은 사람 a walking [living] skeleton / a mere skeleton // ~같은 얼굴 skull-faced.

해괴망측하다(駭怪罔測-) be extremely strange [outrageous / scandalous / disgraceful].

해괴하다(駭怪-) strange; queer; odd; mysterious; weird; outrageous; extraordinary; scandalous; monstrous. ¶해괴한 소문 a wild rumor // 그 참 해괴한 말이로구나 That is an extraordinary thing to say! 해괴히 strangely; queerly; oddly; outrageously.

해구(海口) the entrance to an inlet.
해구(海溝) a [an ocean] deep; a (sea) trench.
해구(海狗) [동] a fur seal; a sea bear.
● 해구신(-腎) the penis of a sea bear (used as an aphrodisiac).
해구(海寇) pirates; sea robbers [marauders].
해국(海國) an island country. ⇨﹦섬나라
해군(海軍) the navy; the naval service; the naval forces. ¶~의 naval / navy // 그는 ~에 있다 He is in the navy.
● 해군기(-機) a navy plane. 해군기(-旗) the navy flag. 해군 기지 a naval base. 해군력 naval power [strength]; sea [marine] power. 해군복 a seaman's uniform. 해군 본부 the Navy Headquarters. 해군 사관 / 해군 장교 a naval officer. 해군 사관학교 the Naval

Academy; (영) the Royal Naval College. **해군 사관학교 생도** a naval cadet; a midshipman. **해군 참모 총장** the Chief of Naval Operations(약어 C.N.O.). **해군 함선** naval vessels.

해금(解禁) removal[lifting] of a ban[an embargo]; (사냥 등의) the opening (of the shooting[fishing] season). ¶보도 금지 기사의 ~ the lifting of the press ban. **해금하다** remove[take off / lift] an embargo (on [upon] the export of coal); lift[remove] a ban (on); cancel a ban (placed on). →¶은어 잡이는 내주에 해금된다 The sweetfish season opens next week.// 수뢰 사건의 기사가 해금되었다 The press ban on the scandal case has been lifted.

● **해금기** (수렵의) the open season (on partridges).

해금(奚琴) [음] haegeum; a Korean fiddle.
해기(海氣) sea air; a breeze from the sea; a sea breeze.

● **해기욕** sea-air bathing.

해껏 [해가 질 때까지] during all the daylight hours; till dark [sunset / the sun sets]; all day long. ¶~ 일하다 work till sunset[dark].
해끄무레하다 whitish. ⇨ 희끄무레하다
해낙낙하다 satisfied; contented; pleased.
해난(海難) a disaster at sea; a shipwreck; (shipping) casualty. ¶~을 당하다 meet with a disaster at sea / be in distress (at sea) / be shipwrecked// 그들은 태평양 상에서 ~을 당했다 They were shipwrecked[met with a disaster] in the Pacific Ocean.

● **해난 구조** salvage. **해난 구조선** a salvage boat [steamer]. **해난 구조원** a lifesaver; (집합적) the Life-saving Service. **해난 신호** an SOS; a distress signal. ¶~를 보내다 radio [flash] an SOS / flash a distress signal.

해납작하다 white and broad[flat]. ¶해납작한 얼굴 a white and flat face.

해내다 1 [이겨 내다] beat; defeat; vanquish; get[gain] the better of (a person). ¶레슬링에서 세 사람을 ~ overmatch three persons in wrestling// 그는 주인을 말로 해냈다 He argued his master down.
2 [치러 내다] carry through[out]; succeed (in doing); complete; finish; accomplish; achieve; fulfill. ¶맡은 일을 ~ perform the work assigned to one// 계획한 바를 ~ carry through an undertaking// 훌륭히 ~ make a success[fair job] of (it) // 이럭저럭 ~ manage to do (a thing) (somehow) // 어려운 역할을 그는 아주 잘 해냈다 He fulfilled[(영) fulfiled / carried out] his difficult role very well.// 그는 그 대사업을 멋지게 해냈다 He accomplished[carried off / (구어) pulled off] that great undertaking successfully.// 그 사람이라면 그 일을 능히 해낼 것이다 He should be able to manage that task quite easily.// 이 일을 해낼 것 같지가 않다 I am afraid I am not equal to this job.// 그는 그것을 단기간에 해내겠다고 말한다 He says he will manage it in a short time.// 그녀는 점포의 확장을 그럭저럭 해냈다 She managed to enlarge the store [expand the store's business] somehow or other. (▶ enlarge the store는 점포의 면적을 늘리는 일, expand the business는 영업 범위를 넓히는 일)// 그것은 너 혼자 해내라 See it through by yourself.// 아무도 그것을 그가 할 수 있다고 생각하지 않았지만 그는 해냈다 No one expected him to do it, but he pulled it off.

해넘이 sunset; (미) sundown. ¶~에 at sunset.
해녀(海女) a woman diver. ¶진주 캐는 ~ a woman pearl diver// 제주도는 ~로 유명하다 Jejudo is famous for woman divers.
해단(解團) disbanding. **해단하다** disband (an expeditionary party).

● **해단식** the ceremony of disbanding.

해달(海獺) [동] a sea otter.
해답(解答) a solution (to a problem); an answer (to a question). ¶시험 문제의 ~ answers to examination questions // 방정식 [미분 방정식]의 ~ the solution[answer] to an equation [a differential equation] // 문제의 ~을 겨우 알아냈다 I finally worked out [found the answer to] the problem.// 이 수학 문제의 올바른 ~은 무엇이냐 What is the correct answer to this mathematics problem?// ~이 좀처럼 나오지 않았다 I simply could not work out a solution.// 그것으로는 이 문제의 ~이 되지 않는다 That is no solution to this problem. **해답하다** solve (a problem); answer (a question). ¶옳게[잘못] ~ answer correctly[incorrectly].

해당(該當) (관형어적) concerned; appropriate. ¶~ 항목을 보다 turn to the appropriate heading. **해당하다** [(조항 등에) 들어맞다] come [fall] under; come [fall] within the purview of; be applicable to; [(⋯에) 상당하다] correspond to; deserve. ¶3개월분의 봉급에 해당하는 보너스 a bonus equivalent to three months' pay// 그것에 해당하는 예 a case in point// 각서에 ~ fall under the Memorandum// 제2조에 ~ conform to Article 2// 「짐」에 해당하는 독일어는 무엇인가 What is the German (word) for jip?// 이 어구에 해당하는 영어는 없다 There is no English equivalent for the phrase.// 이 경우는 제3조에 해당한다 Article 3 applies [is applicable] to this case.// 국무 장관은 우리 외교 통상부 장관에 해당한다 The Secretary of State is equivalent to [the counterpart of] our Secretary of Foreign Affairs and Trade. →¶ 그것은 계약의 제5조에 해당된다 It comes [falls] under Article 5 of the contract.// 면제품은 이 부류에 해당된다 Cotton products come under this category.// 해당되는 항에 ○표를 하시오 Circle each applicable item.// 오늘날의 성인식은 옛날의 관례(冠禮)에 해당된다 The present coming-of-age ceremony corresponds to the *Gwallye* of old times.

● **해당 사항** pertinent [relevant] data.

해당화(海棠花) [식] a sweet brier.
해도(海圖) a (marine) chart; a hydrographical chart. ¶~에 실려 있지 않은 uncharted / not marked on the chart// 이 근처에는 ~에 실려 있지 않은 섬이 있다 There are some uncharted islands in this area.
해독(害毒) evil; harm; mischief; virus; poison; an evil[a baneful] influence; taint; canker; blast; blight. ¶문명의 ~ the canker of civilization// ~을 끼치다 cause damage (to) / work great mischief// 사회에 ~을 끼치다 exert a baneful [harmful] influence on society / poison society / contaminate [corrupt] society// 저런 책은 사회에 ~을 끼친다 That sort of book exerts a harmful[an evil] influence on society. / That sort of book poisons society.

해독(解毒) [의] detoxification; detoxication. ¶~의 antidotal (virtue). **해독하다** counteract [neutralize] the poison; detoxify; detoxicate.
● **해독제** an antidote; a toxicide; a counter-poison. ¶~를 먹이다 administer an antidote (to).

해독(解讀) decipherment; decoding. ¶암호기 [장치] a decoder. **해독하다** decipher; decode; decrypt. ¶해독하기 어려운 indecipherable / 해독할 수 있는 decipherable / 암호를 ~ decipher a code / 부호를 ~ interpret the signs [marks] // 고대의 비문을 ~ decipher [make out] an ancient inscription.

해돋이 sunrise; (미) sunup. ¶~에 at sunrise // ~를 보다 see the sunrise (from the peak) // 한라산 정상에서 ~를 보다 see the sunrise from the top of Hallasan(Mt. Halla).

해동(解凍) thawing; a thaw. **해동하다** (it) thaw. ¶올해는 일찍 해동할 것이다 This year the thaw will set in earlier.

해동청(海東靑) [동] a hawk; a falcon. ⇨ 매³

해득(解得) understanding; apprehension; grasp; comprehension. ¶~이 빠르다 [느리다] be quick [show] of apprehension. **해득하다** understand; apprehend; comprehend; grasp. ¶해득하기 어려운 incomprehensible / hard to understand.

해뜨리다 wear; wear (it) out. ⇨ 해어뜨리다

해로(海路) a sea route; a seaway. ¶~로 해서 by sea // ~로 부산에 가다 go to Busan by sea [water] / take a sea route to Busan.

해로(偕老) living together to an old age; growing gray together. ¶백년 ~ (husband and wife) sharing the years happily together. **해로하다** live together to an old age; grow old [gray] together.

해롭다(害-) harmful; injurious; detrimental; bad. ¶건강에 ~ be bad for (the) [injurious to] health // 풍기 면에 ~ be detrimental [destructive] to public morals // 심신에 ~ be harmful to mind and body [body and soul] // 농작물에 ~ be bad for [harmful to] the crops // 눈에 ~ be bad for [injurious to] the eyes / impair one's eyesight // 술은 건강에 ~ Drinking is injurious to one's health. // 그것은 몸에 ~ It will be bad for [(문어) injurious to] your health. // 이 영화는 청소년에게 ~ This film poisons [is harmful to] young people. // 이 책은 아이들에게는 ~ This book poisons [harms] young minds. // 어두컴컴한 곳에서 책을 읽는 것은 눈에 매우 ~ Reading in dim light is very hard on the eyes. // 그와 교제해도 해로울 것은 없다 There's no harm in association with him. // 너에게 해롭게는 하지 않겠다 I will do nothing to your disadvantage [against your interests]. // 포르노 영화의 선정적인 포스터는 아이들에게는 ~ It is harmful [not good] for children to see provocative posters advertising pornographic films.

해롱거리다 frolic; act [play] the giddy goat; play pranks; joke; jest; sport; get funny with (a person).

해류(海流) an ocean current; a (marine) current. ¶~를 타다 ride an ocean current.
● **해류도**(-圖) a current chart.

해륙(海陸) land and sea. ¶~으로 by land and sea.
● **해륙풍** a land and sea breeze.

해리(海里) a nautical [sea] mile; a knot. ¶200~ 어업 수역 the 200-mile fishing zone.

해리(海狸) [동] a beaver; a castor.

해리(解離) [화] dissociation. **해리하다** dissociate.
● **해리열** heat of dissociation.

해마(海馬) 1 [동] a sea horse. 2 a walrus. ⇨ 바다코끼리(⇨ 바다)

해마다 every year; yearly; annually; from year to year; year by [after] year. ¶물가는 ~ 오른다 Prices go up every year. // 수입은 ~ 증가 하고 있다 Imports are increasing year by [after] year. // ~ 그녀는 여자다워진다 With each passing year she has become less (of) a girl and more (of) a woman.

해말갛다 fair; fair-complexioned. ⇨ 희멀겋다

해말쑥하다 fair and clean (face). ⇨ 희멀쑥하다

해맑다 white and clean.

해머 a hammer. ¶공기 ~ an air hammer / a pneumatic (power) hammer // 증기 ~ a steam hammer.
● **해머던지기** hammer throwing. ¶~ 선수 a hammer thrower.

해먹 a hammock; a hanging bed; a swinging couch; a cot(배 안의). ¶~에서 자다 slip in a hammock // ~을 치다 [걸다] sling [lash] a hammock / 나무와 나무 사이에 ~을 쳤다 I slung a hammock between the trees. // 그는 ~을 걷었다 He lashed his hammock.

해면(海面) the surface of the sea; (표준 해면) the sea level. ¶거울 같은 ~ a glassy sea // ~에 떠오르다 float up to the surface of the sea / surface // ~은 거울처럼 잔잔하다 The sea is as smooth as glass [a mirror].

해면(海綿) a sponge. ¶목욕용 ~ a bath sponge // ~ 모양의 spongy // ~으로 빨아들이 다 sponge up (spilled milk).
● **해면동물** a poriferan. **해면질** spongy matter; spongin. **해면체** a spongy body; [생] a cavernous body.

해면(解免) 1 [책임의 해제] release; absolution; discharge; acquittal; exoneration. **해면하다** release; free; absolve; exonerate (a person from an obligation); relieve; acquit (a person of his responsibility). 2 dismissal from office. ⇨ 면직

해명(解明) elucidation; explication; explanation. ¶~을 요구하다 demand [call for] an explanation (from). **해명하다** make clear; clarify; elucidate; throw [shed] light upon; explicate; explain. ¶객관적으로 ~ throw an objective light (on) // 그는 자기의 괴상한 행동에 대해서 해명하지 못했다 He was unable to give any reason [explanation] for his extraordinary conduct.
● **해명서** a letter of explanation; a written explanation.

해몽(解夢) the reading [interpretation] of a dream; dream reading. **해몽하다** interpret [read] a dream.
● **해몽가** a dream reader; an oneirocritic; an oneiroscopist.

해무(海霧) a sea fog; a fog on the sea. ¶~에 덮이다 be enveloped in a sea fog // ~가 걷혔다 The sea fog lifted [cleared (off) [up])].

해묵다 be carried [brought] over from the previous year. ¶해묵은 일 work brought over from the previous year // 해묵은 쌀 (전년도의 쌀) rice of the previous year's crop / (오래된 쌀) old rice / long-stored rice // 해묵은

골칫거리 an outstanding[a long-pending] trouble.
해묵히다 carry over to next year.
해물(海物) marine products. ⇨해산물
해바라기 [식] a (common) sunflower; a helianthus; (미) a combflower.
● **해바라기 기름** sunflower oil.
해박하다(該博─) extensive; profound; exhaustive. ¶해박한 지식 profound learning / an exhaustive[extensive] knowledge / erudition∥해박한 지식의 소유자 a man of wide knowledge / a man of erudition[great learning]∥해박한 지식을 가지고 있다 have[be possessed of] vast stock of knowledge.
해발(海拔) the height above (the) sea level; altitude. ¶그 산은 ～ 2,700미터이다 The mountain is 2,700 meters above sea level [the sea].
해방(解放) release; liberation; freedom (from care, fear, etc.); deliverance; disengagement; emancipation (of ego); disenthralment. ¶노예 ～ emancipation of slaves / manumission∥노예 ～ 령 the Emancipation Proclamation(미국 남북 전쟁 때의)∥8·15 ～ the 1945 Liberation (of Korea)∥빈곤으로부터의 ～ freedom from poverty∥아, 드디어 ～이다 At last I am free! **해방하다** release; liberate; disengage; disenthral(l); emancipate; enfranchise; free (a person) from (bondage, restraint, etc.); rescue (a prisoner, a slave, etc.); extricate; deliver. ¶여성을 부엌으로부터 ～ emancipate women from the drudgery of the kitchen. ➔¶공부로부터 해방되었다 I was freed from study.∥나는 아이들을 돌보는 일에서 마침내 해방되었다 At last I was freed [released] from having to care for my children.
● **해방감** a feeling of freedom. **해방 신학** liberation theology. **해방 운동** a liberation movement[campaign]. ¶여성 ～ a movement for the emancipation of women.
해법(解法) a solution; a key to solution; how to solve (a problem).
해변(海邊) the seashore; the seaside; the beach; the coast(해안). ¶～의 coastal / seaside∥～에(서) on the seashore / at the seaside∥～에 **살다** live by the sea∥～을 **산책하다** take a walk along the beach / ramble [stroll] about the beach∥～**으로 나가다** go [come] down to[out on] the beach.
● **해변 도시** a coast[seacoast] town; a town along the coast.
해병(海兵) a marine.
● **해병대** (미) the (U.S.) Marine Corps.
해보다 [맞겨루다] fight (against); contend [compete] with; stand[rise] against. ¶그놈과는 끝까지 해볼 테다 I will never yield to him until he says[cries] uncle.
해부(解剖) 1 (의학상의) dissection; anatomy; (검시의) a postmortem (examination); autopsy. ¶병리 ～ pathological anatomy∥생체 ～ vivisection∥시체 ～ a postmortem examination / autopsy / [의] necropsy.∥인체 ～ dissection of a human body∥～ 결과 타살임이 판명되었다 The postmortem examination showed that it was a case of murder. **해부하다** dissect; cut up; vivisect(생체를); anatomize(동물체를); (검시를 위해) hold a postmortem[an autopsy] (on); necropsy. 2 [분석] (an) analysis (pl. analyses). **해부하다** analyze. ¶그의 성격을 해부해 보자 Let's analyze his character.
● **해부대** [실] a dissecting table[room]. **해부도**(─刀) a dissecting knife; a scalpel. **해부도**(─圖) an anatomical[anatomy] chart. **해부용 시체** a subject for dissection. **해부학** anatomy. ¶동물 ～ animal anatomy / zootomy∥식물 ～ plant anatomy / phytotomy∥인체 ～ human anatomy / anthropotomy. **해부학자** an anatomist.
해빙(海氷) sea ice.
해빙(解氷) thawing (of ice); a thaw. ¶～과 더불어 밭에는 보리의 파란 싹이 보이기 시작한다 As it thaws, green barley appears in the fields. **해빙하다** (it) thaw; break (up). ¶압록강은 해빙했다 The Amnokkang[The Yalu] is now free from[of] ice.
● **해빙기** the thawing season.
해사(海事) maritime affairs[matters].
● **해사법** [법] the law of admiralty.
해산(解産) (a) childbirth; (a) delivery; parturition; confinement. ¶～의 고통을 겪다 go through labor / undergo the pangs of childbirth∥(산과가) ～**구완하다** attend a case of confinement / assist at a childbirth∥그녀의 ～이 가까워지고 있다 She is nearing her confinement.∥그녀의 ～ 예정일은 언제지요 When does she expect her baby? / When is her baby due? **해산하다** be delivered of a child; give birth to a baby. ¶쉽게[힘들게] ～ have an easy[a difficult] labor [delivery]∥남아를 ～ give birth to a boy / be delivered of a boy∥그녀는 어젯밤에 해산했다 She had a baby last night. / She was delivered of (a son) last night.∥그녀는 내달에 해산할 예정이다 She is expected to give birth to a child next month.
● **해산기** one's time; period of delivery.
해산(解散) 1 (모임의) breakup; breaking-up; dispersion. ¶～을 **명하다** order (a crowd) to disperse. **해산하다** break up; disperse. ¶집회를 ～ break up a meeting∥역에서 해산한다 We'll break up[disband] at the station.∥오늘 시위는 행렬이 공원에 이르면 바로 해산할 겁니다 Today's demonstration will break up as soon as the marchers reach the park. ➔¶군중을 해산시키다 disperse a crowd∥군인들을 해산시키다 dismiss soldiers∥경찰이 시위자들을 해산시켰다 The police dispersed the demonstrators.∥그 집회는 경찰에 의해 해산되었다 The meeting was broken up by the police.∥수위가 모여든 기자들을 해산시켰다 The guards dispersed[scattered] the assembled reporters.
2 (회사 등의) dissolution (of a company); disorganization; liquidation; disbandment. ¶강제 ～ compulsory winding-up∥임의 ～ voluntary winding-up∥～을 **명하다** order (an organization) to be disbanded∥그 정당은 ～ 명령을 받았다 That party was ordered to be dissolved.∥우리 회사는 이제 재조직을 위한 ～을 하기에 이르렀다 Our company has grown to the point that it is now being dissolved for purposes of reorganization. **해산하다** dissolve (partnership); disorganize; wind up; [해산되다] be dissolved; be disorganized; be liquidated; go into liquidation; be disbanded. ¶조직을 ～ dissolve an organization∥비틀스는 언제 해산했지 Do you remember when the Beatles broke up?∥재

해산물

정 문제를 해결하지 못해 그 클럽은 해산했다 Unable to solve its financial problems, the club disbanded.
3 (국회의) dissolution. **해산하다** dissolve (the National Assembly); [해산되다] be dissolved. ¶국회를 해산하겠다고 위협하다 threaten to dissolve the National Assembly ➔¶의원의 임기 종료 전에 국회는 해산되었다 The Assembly was dissolved before the term of the members was completed.
● **해산권** the right to dissolve (the National Assembly).

해산물(海産物) marine products; the yield of the sea. ¶~이 풍부하다 be rich in marine products.

해삼(海蔘) [동] a trepang; a sea slug[cucumber].

해상(海上) ¶~의 maritime / marine / on the sea // ~의 패자(霸者) the mistress of the sea(s) // ~에(서) at sea / on the sea / during the voyage(항해 중) // ~에 있다 [항해 중이다] be at sea // ~에서 폭풍을 만나다 be overtaken by a storm at sea.
● **해상공원** a marine park. ¶국립 ~ a national sea park. **해상권** the command of the sea. ⇨"제해권 ¶~을 장악하다 rule [command] the sea / have the command of the sea. **해상 무역** maritime[sea / floating] trade; overseas trade. **해상법** [법] the maritime[marine] law. **해상 보험** marine [maritime] insurance. ¶~에 들다 effect [take out] marine insurance / insure (the cargo) against sea perils. **해상 생활** a seafaring[sailor's] life; life afloat[at sea] / ocean life. ¶~을 하다 go to sea / follow the sea. **해상 운송** marine transport(ation); sea-lift.

해상(海床) the bed[bottom] of the sea; the sea[ocean] floor[bed].

해상(海象) a warlus. ⇨"바다코끼리(⇨바다)

해상력(解像力) [사진] resolving power; resolution. ¶~이 높은 렌즈 a high resolution lens.

해서(楷書) the printed style of writing; the print[square] hand; the square[standard] style of Chinese handwriting. ¶~로 쓰다 write in the printed style / write in the square[block] style.

해석(解析) analysis; analytic research. ¶~적인 analytic(al). **해석하다** analyze.
● **해석 기하학** analytic(al) geometry. **해석학** analysis; analytics.

해석(解釋) (an) interpretation; construction; [설명] (an) explanation; elucidation; exposition. ¶문법적 ~ a grammatical interpretation // 법의 ~ the construction[interpretation] of law // 헌법[고전]의 ~ the interpretation of the Constitution[classics] // 영어 ~력 ability of reading English / reading ability in English // 일방적인 ~ a one-sided interpretation // ~ (상)의 차이 a discrepancy in interpretation. **해석하다** interpret; construe; put [place] a construction on; [설명하다] explain; elucidate; expound; [이해하다] take; make out (the meaning). ¶선의[악의]로 ~ take (a person's words) in good[bad] part / interpret favorably[unfavorably] / put a good[bad] construction (upon) // 잘못 ~ misinterpret / misconstrue // 여러 가지로 ~ interpret variously // 뜻을 다르게 ~ take the meaning differently // 법을 엄밀히 ~ take a strict interpretation of a law // 나는 그의 행동을 선의[악의]로 해석했다 I took his behavior in good[bad] part. // 이 절을 해석하시오 Explain this passage. // 그는 상대방의 행동을 잘못 해석한 것 같다 He seems to have misinterpreted his rival's behavior. // 그는 그녀의 말을 익살스럽게 해석했다 He put a humorous construction on[gave a humorous interpretation to] her words. ➔¶그것은 여러 가지로 해석될 수 있다 It may be interpreted [taken] in various ways[variously]. // 수줍음이 거만으로 해석된 것 같다 Her shyness seems to have been interpreted as[misconstrued as / taken for] arrogance.

해설(解說) (an) explanation; (an) interpretation; a commentary; a comment; an expository comment; exposition. ¶뉴스 ~ a news commentary // 야구 방송의 ~ commentary during the broadcast of a baseball game // 저명한 평론가의 ~이 붙은 작품집 an anthology with the comments of a distinguished critic. **해설하다** explain; comment on (the news); interpret; expound. ¶과학 이론을 쉽게 ~ explain a scientific theory in plain terms // 그는 라디오에서 시사 문제를 해설하고 있다 He comments on current topics on the radio. // 이 책은 식물 재배법을 자세하게 해설하고 있다 This book gives us detailed instruction on how to grow plants.
● **해설자** a commentator(뉴스 등의); an expounder(서적 등의).

해성층(海成層) [지] the sea[marine] layer; marine deposits.

해소(解消) **1** [해결] solution; settlement. **해소하다** solve; settle. ¶난관을 ~ iron out the difficulties // (…의) 부족을 ~ supply[cover / fill up / remedy] the shortage (of) // 주택난을 ~ solve the housing problem // 이것은 스트레스를 해소하는 데에 도움이 된다 This is useful in getting rid of stress. / This will help you (to) cope with stress. ➔¶곤란은 곧 해소될 것이다 The difficulty will soon ravel out. // 정계의 불안은 해소되었다 The political unrest died down. // 그에 대한 의혹은 해소되었다 My suspicions about him have been dispelled.
2 [해체] (a) dissolution; disorganization; liquidation. ¶당(黨)의 발전적 ~ the developmental liquidation of a party / the dissolution of a party for the better // 발전적 ~를 하다 be dissolved to form a better organization. **해소하다** dissolve; disorganize; liquidate. ➔¶해소되다 be dissolved / be disorganized / be liquidated.

해손(海損) [보험] an average (loss); sea damage. ¶공동[단독] ~ a general[particular] average.
● **해손 계약** an average agreement. **해손 계약 증서** an average bond. **해손 조항** an average clause.

해송(海松) **1** [곰솔] a black pine. **2** [식] a Korean nut pine. ⇨잣나무

해수(咳嗽) a cough. ⇨"기침
● **해수약** a cough medicine. ⇨"기침약(⇨기침)

해수(海水) seawater. ⇨"바닷물(⇨바다) ¶~의 침입을 막다 hold back the seawater // ~에서 얻은 민물 desalinated seawater.
● **해수욕** sea bathing; a sea(water) bath. ¶~을 하다 bathe in the sea / swim in the sea

//해운대에서 ~을 하다 bathe on the beach of Haeundae // ~을 하러 가다 go for a swim in the sea / go sea-bathing / go bathing in the sea. **해수욕장** a bathing resort[place]; a (bathing) beach; a beach[seaside] resort.
해수(海獸) a marine[sea] animal.
해시계(-時計) a sundial; a dial.
해식(海蝕) erosion of the sea; coastal[beach] erosion.
해신(海神) the god of the sea; the sea god; [로마 신화] Neptune; [그리스 신화] Poseidon.
해심(害心) [해치려는 마음] malicious intent; an evil intention; malice; ill will; murderous intent(살의). ¶~을 품다 bear (a person) malice / mean mischief.
해심(海深) the depth of the sea. ¶~을 재다 plumb[sound] the sea / take soundings // ~은 30피트다 The water is 30 feet deep.
해쓱하다 pale; pallid; wan; waxy. ¶몹시 ~ be deathly[ashy] pale // 얼굴이 해쓱해지다 turn pale[white] // 해쓱해 보이다 look pale // 앓고 나서 그녀의 얼굴은 ~ Her complexion is pasty from an illness.
해악(害惡) evil; harm; mischief; [악영향] an evil influence[effect]. ¶전쟁, 역병(疫病), 그 밖의 ~ war, pestilence and other evils // 사회의 ~을 바로잡다 cure the ills of society.
해안(海岸) the seashore; the (sea) coast; the seaside; the seaboard; the waterfront; [해변] the beach; the strand. ¶~의 coastal / seaside // ~의 경치 a coastal landscape // ~의 호텔 a seaside hotel / a hotel by the sea // ~에(서) on the shore[beach] / by the sea / at the seaside // ~에서 일광욕을 하다 bask in the sun on the beach // (배에서 보아) ~쪽에 coastwards // ~을 끼고[따라] along the shore[beach] / coastwise // ~ 가까이 inshore // ~을 산책하다 take[have] a walk along the beach // ~을 따라 항해하다 sail coastwise[along the coast] // 그는 ~에 별장을 가지고 있다 He has a villa at the seaside.
●**해안 경비대** the coast guard. **해안 단구**[지] the sea[marine] terrace. **해안선** the shoreline; the coastline; [철도] a coast railway. **해안 지방** a seaside[coast] district; a coastal region. **해안 평야** a coastal plain.
해약(解約) cancellation[annulment] of a contract; [법] rescission. **해약하다** cancel[annul / rescind] a contract; call[break] off (one's engagement); surrender (an insurance policy); (구독을) discontinue. ¶은행의 계좌를 ~ close a bank account.
해양(海洋) the sea(s); the ocean. ¶~의 자유 the freedom of the seas.
●**해양 개발** ocean development. **해양 경찰청** the National Maritime Police Agency. **해양성 기후** oceanic[maritime] climate. **해양 소설** a sea story. **해양 수산부** the Ministry of Maritime Affair and Fisheries. **해양 오염** sea contamination; contamination of sea water. **해양 자원** resources of the sea; marine resources. **해양학** oceanography.
해어뜨리다 wear; wear (it) out[away / down]. ¶옷을 ~ wear out one's clothes (to rags) // 구두를 구멍이 나도록 ~ wear one's shoes (away) into holes.
해어지다 wear; wear[get worn] out[away / down]; get tattered; become tattery. ¶너덜너덜 ~ be reduced to[fall into] tatters / tatter / be worn to rags // 다 해어진 worn / wornout / ragged / tattered / tattery / frayed / threadbare // 다 해어진 옷 (well) worn-out clothes / threadbare[tattered] clothes // 사전이 너덜너덜 해어졌다 The dictionary has been worn to tatters. // 코트를 여러 해 입었더니 소매가 해어졌다 My coat is frayed in the edges of its sleeves with the use of years.
해역(海域) a sea area. ¶한국 ~ the area of sea around Korea.
해연(海淵) the lowest depth of an ocean; the deep; the abyss.
해연풍(海軟風) a sea breeze.
해열(解熱) removal[alleviation / subsiding] of fever. ¶이 약은 ~에 잘 듣는다 This will lower[bring down] your fever. **해열하다** alleviate fever; break a fever.
●**해열제** a medicine for fever; an antifebrile; an antipyretic; a febrifuge.
해오라기 [동] a night heron.
해오라기난초(-蘭草) [식] a fringed orchis [orchid].
해왕성(海王星) [천] Neptune.
해외(海外) foreign countries. ¶~의 oversea(s) / abroad / foreign // ~의 사정 foreign affairs // ~로부터 from over[beyond] the sea / from abroad // ~에서 돌아오다 return from abroad // ~로의 발송 an overseas shipment // ~로 가다[여행하다] go[travel] abroad // ~로 수출하다 export (goods) abroad // 군대를 ~에 파견하다 send an army overseas // ~에 이름을 떨치다 obtain an international reputation // 그의 작품은 ~에서 번역되고 있다 His works have been translated in foreign countries.
●**해외 공관** diplomatic establishments [offices] abroad; embassies and legations abroad. **해외 근무 (수당)** overseas service (allowance). **해외 무역** overseas[foreign] trade. **해외 방송** overseas broadcasting [radio service]; an overseas radio broadcast. ¶~으로 듣다 listen to (music) on an overseas radio broadcast. **해외 사절** an envoy sent abroad. **해외 시장** an oversea(s) [a foreign] market. ¶~ 조사 foreign market research. **해외여행** a foreign travel[trip]; a trip abroad. ¶~을 자유화하다 liberalize the overseas trips. **해외 유학** study(ing) abroad. ¶~ 알선 업체 the overseas study brokerage companies. **해외 이민 / 해외 이주** emigration. **해외 진출** overseas expansion; (기업의) overseas ventures. ¶한국 상품의 ~ appearance of Korean merchandize on foreign markets / export of Korean commodities. **해외 통신** news from abroad; transoceanic communication. **해외 특파원** overseas [foreign] correspondents.
해우(海牛) [동] a sea cow; a manatee; a dugong.
해운(海運) marine[sea / ocean] transport [transportation]; (merchant) shipping.
●**해운업** marine transportation business; maritime trade; the shipping industry [business / trade]. **해운업자** a shipping agent; (집합적) shipping interests.
해원(海員) a seaman; a mariner; a sailor; (미) a crewman; (집합적) a crew. ¶~이 되다 become a seaman / go to sea.
해이(解弛) relaxation; slackness. **해이하다** slacken up; relax; grow lax; become remiss.

¶해이한 규율 slack discipline // 기강이 ~ discipline slackens[grows lax] // 마음이 해이해지다 one's attention[mind] relaxes[becomes remiss].

해인초(海人草) [식] Corsican weed.

해일(海溢) flood[high] tide; a storm surge; a tidal[storm] wave; a tsunami. ¶~이 덮치다 be struck[hit] by a tidal wave // ~에 휩쓸리다 be washed away by a tidal wave // 남해안에 ~이 일어났다 A tidal wave struck[visited / swept along] the south coast.
● 해일 경보 a tidal wave warning.

해임(解任) release from office; dismissal; discharge. 해임하다 release (a person) from office; relieve (a person) of (his) post; dismiss. ¶지점장을 해임했다 They removed the branch manager from his post. →¶해임되다 be released from[relived of] one's office / be dismissed from service // 회계원이 공금 횡령으로 해임되었다 The accountant was discharged[dismissed] for embezzlement.
● 해임장 a letter of dismissal; (속어) walking paper.

해자(垓子) a moat; a fosse. ¶~로 둘러싸인 성 a castle surrounded by a moat // 성에 ~를 두르다 moat a castle // ~를 파다 dig a moat.

해장 drinking (in the morning) to relieve the hangover. 해장하다 have a morning drink (to relieve the hangover); take a hair of the dog.
● 해장국 haejangguk; broth[soup] to relieve the hangover. 해장술 a drink of wine (on) the morning after; a morning drink; (구어) a hair of the dog.

해장(海葬) a burial at sea[in the sea]. 해장하다 bury at sea; consign (a person's body) to a watery grave.

해저(海底) the bottom[bed] of the sea; the ocean floor[bed]; the seabed. ¶~의 seabed // ~에 가라앉다 sink[go down] to the bottom of the sea // ~의 물고기밥으로 되다 be swallowed by the sea / be buried in a watery grave.
● 해저 유전 a submarine oil field. 해저 전선 a submarine cable; the cable. ¶~을 부설하다 lay a submarine cable. 해저 터널 an undersea[a submarine] tunnel. 해저 화산 a submarine volcano.

해적(海賊) a pirate; a sea robber. ¶~의 piratical // ~이 출몰하는 바다 a sea infested with pirates / pirate-infested waters // ~질하다 commit piracy / pirate (a ship) / rob at sea.
● 해적기 a black flag; the Jolly Roger; the skull and crossbones. 해적선 a pirate ship; a sea rover. 해적판(-版) a pirated edition [version / reprint].

해전(海戰) a naval battle[engagement] (▶ battle은 특정한 장소에서의 전투. engagement 는 조우전); a sea fight[battle]. ¶트라팔가 ~ the Battle of the Trafalgar.

해제(解除) 1 [취소] cancellation; dissolution; removal (of a ban). ¶풍풍 경보 ~ lifting of a storm warning / "all clear" // (공습) 경보 ~ 의 신호를 하다 give an all clear. 해제하다 (계약 등을) cancel (a contract); call off (an alert); (금지를) lift (a ban); remove (control). ¶계약을 ~ cancel a contract // 통제를 ~ remove control (on) / decontrol // 계엄령을 ~ lift martial law. →¶금지가 해제되다 obtain the annulment of the ban // 홍수 경보가 해제되었다 The flood alert was canceled.
2 [해방] release; absolution; discharge. ¶무장 ~ disarmament / demilitarization. 해제하다 release; free; absolve (a person from an obligation); relieve[acquit] (a person of responsibility). →¶그들은 무장을 해제당했다 They were deprived of their weapons.

해제(解題) a bibliographical introduction (to); bibliographical notes (of). ¶고전의 ~ the bibliographical introduction of a classical work // 한서(漢書) ~ bibliographical notes of Chinese classics[literature]. 해제하다 make a bibliographical introduction (to); annotate bibliographically.

해조(害鳥) an injurious[a harmful] bird.

해조(海鳥) a sea bird; a seafowl.
● 해조분(-糞) guano (pl. ~s).

해조(海藻) seaweeds; marine algae[plants].

해죽 with an affable[a sweet] smile; smilingly. ¶~ 웃다 smile sweetly (at a person) / break into a smile.

해중(海中) the middle[bottom] of the sea. ¶~에 in the sea / undersea(s) / overboard // ~에 뛰어들다 dive into the sea.
● 해중 핵 실험 an undersea nuclear test.

해지(解止) [법] termination. ¶파산 절차의 ~ the termination of bankrupt procedure. 해지하다 abandon; terminate; close.

해지다 wear; wear out. ⇨=해어지다

해직(解職) release from office; dismissal; discharge. 해직하다 release (a person) from his office[position]; relieve (a person) of his post; dismiss; discharge; fire. →¶해직되다 be relieved of one's post / be released from one's office[position] / be dismissed[fired].
● 해직 수당 a discharge allowance. 해직 통고 (hand) a dismissal notice.

해체(解體) 1 [분해] taking to pieces; dismantling; dismantlement. ¶선박 ~업자 a ship breaker. 해체하다 disjoint; dismantle (a machine); take (a machine) to pieces; break up (a ship); pull down (a building). ¶비행기를 ~ dismantle an airplane // 전시장의 가설 건축물을 ~ take a pavilion to pieces // 집을 ~ take down a house // 공장을 ~ dismantle a factory // 폐차를 ~ scrap a used car.
2 [해산] (a) dissolution; disorganization; liquidation. 해체하다 dissolve; disorganize; disband; liquidate; break up. ¶비밀 결사[정당]를 ~ dissolve[break up] a secret organization[a political party] // 재벌을 ~ break up[liquidate] a big business.
3 dissection. ⇨해부1

해초(海草) seaweeds. ⇨=해조(海藻)

해충(害蟲) a noxious[harmful] insect; (집합적) vermin. ¶~의 피해 insect plague // ~을 구제하다 exterminate vermin.
● 해충 구제 extermination of harmful insects.

해치 a hatch. ¶~의 뚜껑 a hatch cover.

해치다(害-) injure; harm; hurt; impair; do (a person) harm; spoil; damage; do damage [mischief] (to); inflict injury (upon). ¶건강을 ~ injure[ruin] one's health // 감정을 ~ hurt[injure] (a person's) feeling / hurt [offend] (a person) // 미관을 ~ mar[injure] the beauty (of) // 그 소문은 그의 명성을 해쳤

다 The rumor adversely affected his reputation.∥간판은 도시의 미관을 해친다 Billboards mar[spoil / ruin] the city's beauty.∥과음은 건강을 해친다 Too much drinking is bad for your health.∥그녀의 감정을 해치지 않도록 조심해라 Be careful not to hurt her feelings.∥그는 과음하여 건강을 해쳤다 Excessive drinking ruined[(문어) impaired] his health.∥과로로 건강을 해쳤다 I ruined my health with overwork.∥그의 감정을 해치고 싶지 않다 I don't want to hurt his feelings[offend him].∥급속한 도시화가 이 지방의 미풍을 해치게 될 것이다 Rapid urbanization will prove destructive to the fine customs of this district.

해치우다 〔지우다〕 defeat; beat; 〔끝장내다〕 finish; accomplish; 〔죽이다〕 kill; do away with. ¶일을 ~ get through with one's work / get a job finished∥간단히 ~ defeat (an opponent) with one hand∥나는 숙제를 해치웠다 I have finished my homework. / I am through with my homework.∥이 일을 되도록 빨리 해치우자 Let's get through with this work as soon as we can.∥저런 놈이 상대라면 한 손으로도 해치우겠다 I can beat an opponent like that with one hand tied behind me.

해커 〔해킹하는 사람〕 a hacker.

해킹 〔남의 컴퓨터 시스템에 무단 침입 하는 일〕 hacking.

해탈(解脫) deliverance (of one's soul); emancipation; salvation; (범) vimukti. **해탈하다** be delivered from (sin, passions, attachments, etc.). ¶사바를 ~ be delivered from worldly existence / be cut loose from the ties of the earth.

해태 a *haetae*; a mythical unicorn-lion; an omniscient mythical beast.

해태(海苔) laver; sloke. ⇨ ᵂ김¹

해태(懈怠) laziness; indolence; idleness. **해태하다** lazy; indolent; idle.

해토(解土) thawing (of the ground); a thaw. **해토하다** (the ground) thaw.

해파리 〔동〕 a jellyfish; a sea jelly; a medusa (*pl.* -sae, ~s). ¶~의 medusan.

해판(解版) 〔인〕 distribution of type. **해판하다** distribute type.

● **해판공** a distributor.

해팥 the year's new crop of red beans; new red beans.

해표(海豹) 〔동〕 a seal. ⇨ᵂ바다표범(⇨ᵂ바다)

해풍(海風) a sea wind; a sea breeze.

해프닝(*happening*) an accident; an unexpected incident. ¶재미있는 ~을 만났다 I came across an amusing happening.

해피 엔드 a happy ending. ¶~로 끝나는 이야기 a story with a happy ending∥둘이 화해하여 ~로 끝났다 The two were reconciled and the matter ended happily.

해하다(害—) injure; harm. ⇨ᵂ해치다

해학(諧謔) a jest; a joke; humor; (a) pleasantry.

● **해학가**(—家) a humorist; a man of humor; a joker; a jester. **해학극** a farce; a burlesque; a comedy. **해학 소설** a humorous story.

해학적(諧謔的) humorous; witty. ¶~인 시 a humorous poem.

해해거리다 keep laughing playfully[in fun]; laugh frolicsomely[silly].

해협(海峽) 〔지〕 a strait(▶ 고유 명사에 붙일 때는 straits로 단수 취급); (strait보다 넓은 경우) a channel; narrows; (미) a sound. ¶대한 ~ the Straits of Korea∥지브롤터 ~ the strait(s) of Gibraltar∥도버 ~ the Straits of Dover∥~을 건너다 cross a strait[channel].

해화석(海花石) 〔동〕 star coral.

해후(邂逅) a chance[casual] meeting; encounter. **해후하다** meet by chance; happen [chance] to meet; come across (a person); encounter. ¶두 사람은 20년 만에 해후했다 Chance brought the two together after a separation of twenty years. / The two happened to meet after twenty years' interval.

핵(核) **1** (세포 등의) a nucleus (*pl.* nuclei); 〔과실의 심〕 a core; 〔과실의 씨〕 a kernel; a stone. ¶세포~ a cell nucleus∥원자~ an atomic nucleus / the nucleus of an atom∥~의 nuclear. **2** 〔사물의 가장 중요한 점〕 the nucleus; the core; the heart.

핵가족(核家族) a nuclear family.

핵과(核果) 〔식〕 a drupe; a stone fruit.

핵막(核膜) 〔생〕 the nuclear membrane.

핵무기(核武器) a nuclear weapon. ¶전략[전술] ~ a strategic[tactical] nuclear weapon∥~에 의한 파괴[보복] nuclear destruction [retaliation]∥~의 개발 nuclear-weapons development∥~의 확산을 방지하다 check the spread[dissemination] of nuclear weapons / prevent nuclear proliferation∥~를 배치하다 deploy nuclear weapons∥우리나라는 ~의 반입을 금지하고 있다 The bringing of nuclear weapons into our country is banned.

● **핵무기 보유국** a nuclear power[nation]. ¶비(非)~ a non-nuclear power.

핵 무장(核武裝) nuclear armament(s). ¶비~지역 nuclear-free zone∥비~화 denuclearization∥~을 금지하다 denuclearize (a country).

● **핵 무장국** a nuclear-armed country; a nuclear power. **핵 무장 철폐** nuclear disarmaments.

핵물리학(核物理學) nuclear physics.

핵반응(核反應) nuclear reaction.

핵분열(核分裂) 〔물〕 (nuclear) fission; 〔생〕 nuclear division. ¶~을 일으키다 cause nuclear fission.

● **핵분열 연쇄 반응** fission chain reaction.

핵붕괴(核崩壞) disintegration of a cell nucleus; karyoclasis.

핵산(核酸) 〔화〕 nucleic acid. ¶디옥시리보 ~ deoxyribonucleic acid(약어 DNA)∥리보 ~ ribonucleic acid(약어 RNA).

핵 실험(核實驗) a nuclear test[experiment]; nuclear testing. ¶고공(高空) ~ a high altitude nuclear test∥공중[대기권 내] ~ a nuclear test in the air[atmosphere] / an open-air[atmospheric] nuclear test∥지하 ~ underground nuclear testing / an underground nuclear test∥~을 재개하다 resume nuclear weapons tests.

● **핵 실험 금지** a ban on nuclear tests; a nuclear test ban. **핵 실험장** a nuclear testing ground.

핵심(核心) the (hard) core; a kernel; 〔요점〕 the point. ¶문제의 ~ the heart[kernel] of a problem∥문제의 ~을 파악하다 go[get] to the heart of a matter / tear the vitals out of a subject∥~을 찌르다 touch the core (of a subject) / come to the point∥토론에서 우리

는 그 문제의 ~에 도달했다 In our discussion, we got to the heart of the matter.//그 문제에 대해 아무도 깊이 ~을 찔러 의견을 말하는 사람이 없었다 No one really went deeply into the matter.//이사회가 이 조직의 ~으로 되어 있다 The board of directors is the linchpin of this organization.//그의 이야기는 ~을 찔렀다 His speech was to the point.//그의 이야기는 결국 ~을 찌르지는 못했다 His talk, after all, never came to the point.//그 문제 해결의 ~을 그는 알고 있다 He knows what lies at the heart of the matter. / He knows which button to push to solve the problem.//그의 견해는 문제의 ~을 바로 본 것이다 His opinions go straight to the heart of the matter.//이 시민 단체가 그 운동의 ~이 되어 있다 This citizen's group is at the core[forms the core] of the movement.

핵에너지(核-) nuclear energy.
핵연료(核燃料) nuclear fuel.
핵우산(核雨傘) the (U.S.) nuclear umbrella. ¶~의 보호하에 두다 put (a nation) under the protection of (American) nuclear umbrellas.
핵융합(核融合) [생] fusion of cell nuclei; karyogamy; [물] nuclear fusion.
핵자(核子) 1 the (hard) core. ⇨ °핵심 2 [물] a nucleon. ¶중(重)~ a hyperon.
핵전쟁(核戰爭) (a) nuclear[atomic] war [warfare]. ¶~의 위협 a nuclear threat//~의 위험을 줄이다 reduce the threat of a nuclear war.
핵탄두(核彈頭) a nuclear warhead.
핵폐기물(核廢棄物) nuclear waste.
핵폭발(核爆發) a nuclear explosion[blast].
핵폭탄(核爆彈) a nuclear bomb.
핸드백 a handbag; (정장할 때 드는 작은) an evening bag; (작고 납작한) (미) a pocketbook.
핸드볼 [송구] handball.
핸드북 a handbook (of practical English).
핸드폰(*hand phone) a cellular[mobile] phone; a cellphone.
핸들(*handle) (자동차의) a (steering) wheel; (자전거·오토바이의) handlebars. (▶ "handle"은 손잡이를 가리킬 뿐 자동차 조종 장치를 가리키지 않음) ¶오른[왼]쪽 ~의 자동차 a car with right-hand[left-hand] drive / a righthand[left-hand] drive car//~을 잡다 be[sit] at the wheel / take the wheel (of the car)//~을 우[좌]로 돌리다[꺾다] wheel right[left]//그는 ~을 잡으면 아주 다른 사람처럼 변해 버린다 He seems to become quite another man when he is at[behind] the wheel.//그 사람에게 ~을 잡게 해서는 안 된다 Don't let him drive.//그는 당황해서 ~을 오른쪽으로 꺾었다 He hurriedly cut the steering wheel to the right.//~을 놓쳤다 The steering wheel slipped through my hands. / I couldn't hold onto the steering wheel.
핸들링 [축구] handling.
핸디캡 a handicap. ¶~ 20의 골퍼 a 20 handicap player / a 20-handicapper//~을 주다 handicap (a person)//…에 ~ 3을 주다 give three points to …//신체적 ~을 극복하다 overcome a physical handicap//그는 3년간의 공백이라는 ~에도 불구하고 훌륭하게 무대에 컴백하였다 Though handicapped by a three-year absence from the stage, he made a splendid comeback.//그는 ~ 9의 골프 실력이다 He is a 9-handicap player. / His (golf) handicap is 9.//그에게 ~을 얼마 주면 될까 What handicap shall we give him?

핸섬하다 handsome; good-looking. ¶핸섬한 남자 a handsome[good-looking] man.
핼리 혜성(-彗星) [천] Halley's comet.
핼쑥하다 pale; pallid; wan; ashy; blanched; waxy; pasty. ¶핼쑥한 사람 a pale-faced / sickly person//핼쑥한 얼굴 a pallid[wan] face//핼쑥해지다 turn ghastly[deadly] pale//앓고 나서 ~ look thin after an illness.
햄[1] (식품) ham. ¶훈제 ~ smoked[cured] ham / gammon.
● **햄 샌드위치** ham sandwiches.
햄[2] (아마추어 무선사) a (radio) ham.
햄버거 a hamburger.
햄버그 스테이크 a Hamburg steak; a hamburger.
햄샐러드 ham and salad.
햄에그 ham and eggs.
햅쌀 new rice; the year's new crop of rice.
● **햅쌀밥** boiled new rice.
햇- new; (crop) of the year. ¶~감자 a new crop of potatoes.
햇것 the year's (new) crop; a new crop (of the year).
햇곡식(-穀食) a new crop of the year; the year's new grain.
햇무리 the halo of the sun; the ring[corona] around the sun.
햇물 1 the halo of the sun. ⇨ °햇무리 2 (샘물의) a spring which gushes out only after the rainy season.
햇발 sunbeams. ⇨ °햇살
햇병아리 1 [새로 깐 병아리] a chicken; a chick. 2 [풋내기] a fledg(e)ling; a greenhorn; a new[green] hand; a novice; a tender foot. ¶대학을 갓 나온 ~ a new-fledged university man.
● **햇병아리 기자** a cub reporter.
햇볕 the heat[warmth] of the sunbeams [sunlight]; the sun. ¶(살갗이) ~에 타다 get sunburned[sunburn(t)] / get a (sun) tan(▶ sunburn은 피부가 빨개져서 벗겨지기, suntan은 갈색이 되기)//~을 쬐다 bask in the sun //옷을 ~에 말리다 dry one's clothes in the sun//이 약은 ~에 두지 않도록 하십시오 Keep this medicine out of the sun.//이 셔츠는 ~에 말린 것 같다 This shirt smells of the sun.//교실에는 ~에 탄 얼굴을 한 소년들로 가득했다 The classroom was full of boys with tanned faces.//그녀의 피부는 ~에 잘 탄다 Her skin sunburns[gets sunburnt] easily.
햇빛 sunshine; sunlight; sunbeams. ¶강렬한 ~ glaring[hard] sunlight//~을 보지 못하다 keep indoors / (식물·장소 등이) be sunless / have no sunshine / [밖에 알려지지 않고 있다] remain obscure / (법안 등이) be shelved [tabled] //~을 보다 see the light of day / (계획 등이) be realized / materialize//그는 ~을 보지 못한 채 죽고 말았다 He died in obscurity.//그의 계획은 ~에 탄 얼굴을 한 소년들로 가득했다 His plan materialized[was realized] at last. //감세 법안은 끝내 ~을 보지 못했다 The tax reduction bill was shelved[pigeonholed].//그의 작품은 ~을 보지 못하고 묻혀 버렸다 His works never saw the light of day.//방은 ~이 나날이 더 잘 들고 있다 The room gets

햇살 sunbeams; beams [streaks] of sunlight; the rays of the sun; the sunlight. ¶부드러운 ~ soft sunlight / soft[gentle] rays of sun // 나무 사이로 비치는 ~ sunbeams shining through branches of trees // ~을 받다 bathe [bask] in the sun // ~이 퍼지고 있다 The sun is spreading its beams.

햇수(-數) the number of years. ¶-로 5년 five calendar years // 여기에 온 지 -로 4년이다 It is my fourth year here.

행(行) 〔줄〕 a line; a row. ¶시의 한 ~ a line of verse / a verse // 한 ~ 걸러 (write) on every other line / 밑에서 5~째 the fifth line from the bottom // ~을 바꾸다 begin a new line / start a new paragraph / write on another line // ~의 끝에 구두점을 찍다 put a period at the end of a sentence // 나는 한 ~ 걸러서 썼다 I wrote on every other line. // 학위 논문은 두 ~ 걸러서 타자하시오 Double-space your thesis. // 한 페이지에 몇 ~ 있습니까 How many lines are there to a page? / 위[아래]에서 7~째 미스프린트가 있다 There is a misprint on the seventh line from the top[bottom] of the page.

행(幸) (good) luck. ⇨다행 ¶~인지 불행인지 for good or for evil / luckily or unluckily / fortunately or unfortunately.

-행(行) ¶부산~ 특급 열차 a limited express train for Busan / 뉴욕~ 선박 a ship bound for [to] New York.

행각(行脚) 1 〔승려가 수행하기 위해 돌아다님〕 (go on) a pilgrimage. **행각하다** go on (a) pilgrimage. **행각하다** make a pilgrimage. 2 〔여러 곳을 돌아다님〕 (go on) a walking tour; traveling on foot. ¶사기 ~에 나서다 go on a fraud[pilferage] tour. **행각하다** travel on foot; make a walking tour.

● **행각승** an itinerant monk; a priest on a pilgrimage.

행간(行間) space between lines. ¶~을 띄지 않는 조판물 solid [close] matter // ~의 여백 interlinear space // ~을 띄다 leave space between lines / space out // 〔인〕 ~을 넓고 짜다 set solid / close up / get in // ~을 넓히다[좁히다] leave more[less] space between the lines // ~을 읽다 read between the lines. // 그의 수필의 ~에는 비애감이 있다 There is a sense of pathos between the lines of his essay. // 편지는 간결하였으나 ~에 애정이 넘쳐 있었다 The letter was brief, but was filled with unexpressed affection.

행객(行客) a travel(l)er; a wayfarer.

행군(行軍) a march; marching. ¶강행 ~ a forced march / 무장 ~ an armed march / 설중(雪中) ~ a march in[through] the snow // 철야 ~ an overnight march // ~ 중인 군대 an army on the march // 무리한 ~으로 사망자가 나왔다 Some men died during the hard march. **행군하다** march. ¶우리 부대는 하루 60킬로미터를 행군했다 Our unit marched sixty kilometers a day.

● **행군 대형** a march formation. **행군 속도** a rate of march.

행궁(行宮) a rural palace; the King's traveling lodge; a temporary Palace.

행글라이더 a hang glider.

행낭(行囊) 〔미〕 a mailbag; a mail pouch; 〔영〕 a postbag.

행동(行動) action; an act; conduct; behavior; 〔군〕 operations. ¶군사 ~ military movements / hostile operations // 단독 ~ separate action // 단체 ~ group behavior / collective action // 자유 ~ free [independent] action / (have / get) a free hand // 적대 ~ hostile operations // 직접 ~ direct action // ~의 자유를 속박하다 restrain (a person's) freedom of action / tie (a person's) hands // 이론을 ~으로 옮기다 put a theory into action // 자유~을 하다 act on one's own // ~을 같이하다 [협력하다] 〔문어〕 act in concert with (a person) / 〔운명을 같이하다〕〔문어〕 cast one's lot in with (a person) // 훌륭한 ~을 하다 do a good deed / behave [conduct / 〔문어〕 bear] oneself well // ~을 고치다 mend one's ways // 장한 ~을 하다 behave admirably / give a good account of oneself // 말만이 아니라 ~으로 보여 주게 Don't just say it. Do it. / I want to see you doing it, not just talking about it. / Stop paying lip service and do something. / Put your money where your mouth is. // 그는 기민하게 ~을 취했다 He took quick action. / He acted immediately. // 지금부터 2시간은 자유~의 시간이다 (소풍 등에서) You may do whatever [go wherever] you like for the next two hours. // 남들 앞에서는 ~에 조심해요 Be careful about your behavior in public. // 그가 그런 ~을 했다고는 믿을 수 없다 I can't believe he did such a thing. // 그의 ~은 훌륭했다 He conducted himself splendidly. // 말보다 ~이 더 잘 나타낸다 Actions speak louder than words. **행동하다** act; behave (oneself); conduct oneself; move. ¶단독으로 ~ act separately (from) / act independently (of) // 남자답게 [신사적으로] ~ behave [〔문어〕 bear oneself] like a man [gentleman]. // 스포츠맨답게 ~ act [behave oneself] in a sportsmanlike manner / act as a sportsman should // 경솔하게 ~ act [behave] rashly // 그는 현명하게 행동해서 아무 탈이 없었다 He acted so wisely that there was no trouble.

● **행동거지** behavior; deportment; manner; conduct. **행동 과학** behavioral sciences. **행동대** an action corps [group]. **행동력** acting power. **행동반경** 〔군〕 a radius of action [operation]; a cruising [an action] radius. ¶(비행기가) 750마일의 ~을 가지다 have a radial range of 750 miles // 그는 ~이 넓다 He has a wide range of activities. / He is active in many fields. **행동주의** 〔심〕 behaviorism. **행동 통일** action in concert (with); united action. ¶~을 하다 act in concert (with) // ~을 무너뜨리다 break the concerted steps (of the strikers) // 파업자들끼리 ~이 안 되고 있다 There is lack of unity among the strikers.

행락(行樂) (휴일 등의) holiday-making; (작은 단체 여행) an excursion; (피크닉) a picnic; (나들이·산책) an outing. **행락하다** have a good time; enjoy oneself; have an outing.

● **행락객** 〔미〕 a weekender; vacationer; people enjoying their leisure [a day off]; 〔영〕 a holiday-maker; a hiker. **행락지** a pleasure [holiday / picnic] resort; a holiday haunt.

행랑(行廊) 〔하인들의 방〕 the servants' quarters (on both sides of the gate).

● **행랑것** a servant; a menial. **행랑살이** the life of a servant; servantship. **행랑아범** 〔어멈〕 a man [woman] servant.

행려(行旅) (행위) travel; (사람) a traveler.
- **행려병자** a person fallen sick on the road; an ill wayfarer; a charity patient.

행렬(行列) 1 (쇼핑이나 극장의) a queue; [행진] a procession; a parade. ¶**가장~** a masquerade parade // **연등[깃발]~** a lantern [flag] parade // **~의 선두[후미]** the head [tail] of a procession [queue] // **자동차의~** an array of cars // **~을 지어** in procession / in a line / in a queue // **~을 지어 나가다** march in procession / parade // **~에 끼어들다** go in a queue / join a (waiting) line // **~이 시가를 누비고 있다** Processions parade the streets. // **그녀는 ~의 앞장을 섰다** She headed the procession. 2 [수] a matrix (*pl.* -trices, ~es).
- **행렬식** a determinant.

행로(行路) 1 [길] one's course. 2 [세상살이] one's path [course] in life; one's career. ¶**인생~** the path [course] of life / life's journey // **인생 ~를 벗어나다** stumble on life's path // **인생 ~에는 어려움이 많다** The path of human life is thorny. / Life is full of rubs and worries.

행방(行方) one's whereabouts (단수 취급); one's traces. ¶**~이 묘연한** missing / lost // **오랫동안 ~을 몰랐던** long-lost (sister) // **~을 감추다** cover one's traces / conceal oneself [one's whereabouts] / run away // **~을 찾다** trace / search [hunt / look] for (a person) // **~을 알아내다** locate (a person) / discover the trace of (a missing man) / find out one's whereabouts / track down (a criminal) // **그녀의 ~이 알려져 있지 않다** Her whereabouts are unknown. / We don't know where she is. // **경찰은 마침내 그의 ~을 찾아냈다** The police have finally tracked him down. // **경찰은 범인의 ~을 쫓고 있다** The police are after [looking for] the criminal. // **그는 돈을 받은 즉시 ~을 감추었다** He disappeared the instant he received the money. // **내 부친은 1년 전부터 ~을 모르게 되었다** My father disappeared a year ago. // **찾아보았지만 그녀의 ~은 묘연했다** We failed to find any trace of her.
- **행방불명** ¶**~의** missing / lost // **~이 되다** be [get] lost / be heard of no more / be spirited off [away] // **그 아이는 마치 귀신에게 잡혀간 듯이 ~이 되었다** It was as if the child had been spirited off [away]. / The child seemed to have vanished into thin air. // **배가 가라앉았을 때 선장 한 사람만 ~이 되었다** The captain alone was lost when the boat sank. **행방불명자** a missing person; (집합적) the missing; the lost. ¶**사망자 5명, ~ 12명이다** Five have been found dead, and twelve are still missing.

행보(行步) walking; going on foot. **행보하다** walk; go on foot.

행복(幸福) happiness; welfare; bliss. ¶**인생의 ~** human happiness / happiness of life // **최대 다수의 최대 ~** the greatest happiness of the greatest number // **~의 절정** the seventh heaven // **~의 추구** pursuit [quest] of happiness // **~을 빌다** pray for a person's happiness / wish (a person) every happiness // **~을 누리다** enjoy happiness // **~을 빕니다** I wish you every happiness! // **~의 길은 여러 가지 있다** There are different ways to happiness. // **진심으로 귀댁의 ~을 기원합니다** Please accept my best wishes for your happiness. / May happiness live with you. **행복하다** happy; blessed; blissful. ¶**행복하게** happily / in happiness // **행복하게 살다** live [lead] a happy life / live happily // **나는 더할 나위 없이 ~** I'm as happy as a king [lark]. / I'm as happy as happy can be. // **두 사람의 생활은 행복한 일만 있었던 것은 아니었다** It wasn't all just roses with them.
- **행복감** [심] euphoria; the sense of well-being.

행불행(幸不幸) happiness or misery; weal or woe; good or ill fortune; good and evil. ¶**인생의 ~** the lights and shadows of life // **사람에 따라서 ~이 있다** Some are born lucky and others not.

행사(行使) use; exercise. **행사하다** use; employ; exercise (one's rights). ¶**무력을 ~** appeal [resort] to arms // **(경찰 등이) 실력을 ~** resort to forced measures / use [employ] force // **투표권을 ~** exercise the privilege of voting // **특권을 ~** exercise [employ] a [one's] privilege // **그는 직권을 행사했다** He exercised his authority. // **그들은 마침내 무력을 행사했다[실력 행사로 나왔다]** They finally resorted to arms [force].

행사(行事) an event; function. ¶**경축 ~** festivities // **경축 ~의 하나로서** as one item of the celebration program // **국제적 ~** an international event / **연중~** an annual function / a regular annual event / (집합적) the year's regular functions // **봄의 주요 ~** the main [chief] events of spring // **궁중의 ~** court functions // **1학기 ~ 예정표** the schedule for the first semester // **성년이 됨을 축하하는 갖가지의 ~** all kinds of ceremonies and festivities to celebrate the coming of age of young people // **신임 대사 환영의 ~를 베풀다** hold a reception for the new ambassador.

행상(行商) 1 peddling. ⇨*도붓장사(⇨도부). ¶**(지방으로) ~을 나가다** go on a peddling tour / 마을에서 마을로 건어물 ~을 하다 peddle dried fish from town to town // **~사절** (게시) No solicitors allowed! / No hawkers! 2 a peddler. ⇨*도붓장수(⇨도부).

행색(行色) 1 [태도] demeanor; a manner; an attitude. 2 [차림새] one's appearance in traveling outfit; one's appearance [look]. ¶**중의 ~을 한** (a person) attired as a priest // **~이 초라하다** be shabbily [poorly] equipped for travel / look shabby / be down at heels [(the) heel].

행서(行書) [한자 서체의 하나] a semi-cursive style of writing (Chinese characters).

행선지(行先地) [목적지] one's destination; the end of one's journey; (행방) one's whereabouts; (간 장소) the place where one has gone. ¶**배의 ~는 호놀룰루입니다** The boat is bound for Honolulu. / The destination of the boat is Honolulu. // **열차의 ~ 표시가 잘못되어 있었다** The sign on the train showed the wrong destination. // **그의 ~를 가르쳐 주십시오** Please tell us where he is [has gone]. / Let us know his whereabouts. // **아버지는 ~를 말하지 않고 아침에 나갔다** My father went out in the morning without telling us where he was going. // **이 열차의 ~는 어디죠** What is the destination of this train? / Where does this train go (to)? // **그는 ~를 밝히지 않고 나갔다** He went out without telling me where he was going.// 그의 ~는 분명치 않다 I am not sure where he has gone [of his whereabouts].

행성(行星) [천] a planet. ¶소~ a planetoid / a minor [small] planet // ~의 planetary.
● **행성 운동** planetary motion.

행세(行世) **1** [처세] conduct of life; [처세하는 태도] one's bearing [behavior / manners]. ¶~를 잘못하다 misconduct [misbehave] oneself. 행세를 하다 conduct [go] through life [the world]; behave [conduct] oneself. **2** [격에 맞지 않는 처신을 함] show; pretense; affectation. 행세하다 pass oneself off (as); pretend; affect; set up for; assume an air of (a scholar). ¶교수로 ~ set up for a professor / 백만장자로 ~ pose as a millionaire / 주인으로 ~ assume [put on] a proprietary air // 중으로 ~ assume the air of a priest.

행세(行勢) [세도를 부림]. 행세하다 wield [exercise / exert] power [authority] 《over》; hold sway. ¶행세하는 집안 a distinguished [an influential] family.

행수(行數) the number of lines; lineage.

행습(行習) a habit; a practice. ¶~이 사납다 have a bad habit of. 행습하다 make it a habit to; cultivate a habit.

행실(行實) conduct; behavior; deportment; demeanor. ¶좋은 [훌륭한] ~ good [honorable] conduct // 나쁜 [못된] ~ misconduct / misbehavior // ~이 좋다 be well-behaved [-conducted] / show good deportment [conduct] // ~이 나쁘다 misbehave / live fast and loose / lead a dissipated life // ~을 조심하다 be careful [prudent / discreet] in one's conduct // ~을 고치다 reform oneself [one's conduct] / (a)mend one's ways [conduct] / turn over a new leaf // ~이 나빠서 해고당하다 get the sack for one's misconduct // 그의 ~은 비난할 점이 없다 His morals are above reproach.

행여(나)(幸-) possibly; by (some) chance; by any chance [possibility]. ¶행여나 하고 on the chance 《of finding you》 / [요행을 바라고] on the off-chance // ~올까 하여 너를 기다렸다 I have waited in case you might drop by. // 행여나 했던 일이 사실로 판명되었다 A possibility has become an actuality. / My hope has come true.

행운(幸運) (a stroke of) good fortune; (good) luck; (미) a lucky [good] break. ¶~의 fortunate / lucky / happy // ~의 여신 the Goddess of Fortune // ~의 연속 repeated strokes of luck // ~의 편지 a chain letter // ~의 사나이 a very lucky man // ~의 날 a lucky [(문어) an auspicious] day // ~을 빌다 wish (a person) good luck [break] // ~을 타고나다 be born under a lucky star // ~을 얻다 have (a piece of) good luck / get a lucky [good] break // 우연히 그것을 들은 것이 ~이었다 It was a piece [a stroke] of luck that I happened to hear about it. // ~을 빕니다 Good luck (to you)! / I wish you good luck. // 내게 ~을 빌어 줘 Wish me luck. // 내게는 불원간에 ~이 돌아오겠지 Fortune will begin to smile on me [roll my way] in time. // ~의 여신은 용기 있는 자를 좋아한다 Fortune favors the brave.
● **행운아** a child of fortune; a Fortune's favorite [pet / minion]; a lucky person [fellow].

행원(行員) a bank clerk. ⇨은행원(⇨은행(銀行))

행위(行爲) [행동] an act; (an) action; (의도적인) a deed (▶ an act와 an action은 거의 같은 뜻이며, 개개의 행위를 가리키지만, an act of kindness처럼 한편으로만 쓰는 경우가 있음. 불가산 명사인 action은 계속적인 행위를 집합적으로 가리킴); [품행] conduct; behavior; (영) behaviour (▶ conduct는 도덕적으로 판단한 행위, behavior는 남에 대한 몸가짐); [소행] a work; (one's) doings. ¶도덕(적) ~ a moral act // 법률 ~ a juristic act / a legal action // 부정 ~ irregularities / irregular practices // 불법 ~ an illegal [unlawful] act / a wrong // 상 ~ a commercial transaction // 영웅적 ~ a heroic deed // 자선 ~ an act of charity / 정당한 ~ a justifiable [legitimate] act // 용감한 ~ a brave act // 친절한 ~ an act of kindness // 나쁜 ~ bad conduct.
● **행위 능력** (legal) capacity. **행위자** a doer; a performer (of a deed); [법] an actual offender; a transactor (상행위의).

행인(行人) a passerby (pl. passersby); a foot passenger; [나그네] a wayfarer. ¶저녁이 되자 ~의 발길이 끊어졌다 Toward evening the street was deserted.

행인(杏仁) [살구 씨 알맹이] an apricot stone [kernel].

행자(行者) [불] an ascetic; an ascetic devotee; (회교·바라문교 등의) a fakir.

행장(行狀) **1** (죽은 이의) records of a deceased person's life; records of one's doings during one's lifetime; a necrology; a history of the deceased. **2** (수감자의) (a record of) one's behavio(u)r; the conduct mark.

행장(行裝) a traveling [traveler's] outfit [suit / kit]; a traveler's equipment. ¶~을 차리다 [갖추다] make preparations [prepare / equip oneself] for a journey // ~을 풀다 take off one's traveling attire / [숙박하다] stop at an inn / (미) check in at a hotel.

행적(行跡·行績·行蹟) one's (lifetime) achievements [doings / work]; one's record of performances.

행전(行纏) leggings; uppers; gaiters; puttees. ¶~을 치다 put on leggings.

행정(行政) administration. ¶~적(인) [~상의] executive / administrative // ~ 수완이 있다 have administrative ability [talent].
● **행정 각 부** administrative branches. **행정 감독** [관리] administrative control [management]. **행정 개혁** a reform of the administrative structure; an administrative reform. ¶~ 위원회 the Administration Reform Commission. **행정관** an executive [administrative] official; an administrator; 《집합적》 the executive. **행정 관청** a government [an administrative] office. **행정권** administrative [executive] power [authority]. **행정 기관** an administrative organ [body / machinery]; an executive agency. **행정 명령** an administrative [executive] order. **행정법** [법] the administrative law. **행정부** the Executive; the Administration. **행정 소송** administrative litigation. **행정 자치부** the Ministry of Government Administration and Home Affairs. **행정 재판(소)** (a court of) administrative litigation. **행정 처분** an administrative measure [disposition]. **행정학** public administration.

행정(行程) **1** [거리] (a) distance; a journey; (행군의) a march; [일정] an itinerary. ¶하루의 ~ a day's journey∥나는 10일간의 ~을 마치고 무사히 돌아왔다 I returned safe after a journey of ten days.∥서울에서 (기차로 / 자동차로) 하루의 ~이다 It is a day's journey (train ride / car ride) from Seoul. **2** [공] a stroke; a throw (of a switch); a travel; an excursion. ¶공(空)~ a noncutting stroke∥내향(內向)~ an instroke∥상[하]~ an up[down] stroke∥외향 ~ an outstroke∥4~의 four-stroke (engine).

행주 (식기를 훔치는 헝겊) (미) a dishtowel; (영) a teatowel; (식탁 등을 훔치는 헝겊) a dishcloth.
● **행주치마** an apron.

행중(行中) a party; a company. ¶~에 끼다 join a party.

행진(行進) marching; a march; a parade. ¶고적대의 ~ the parade of a drum and fife corps∥결혼 ~ a wedding march∥죽음의 ~ a death's march∥~ 중이다 be on the march / be marching. **행진하다** march; proceed; parade. ¶거리를 ~ march along [down] the streets∥속보로 ~ march in quick time∥군대가 거리를 행진했다 The soldiers marched down the street.∥모델들은 무대 위를 행진했다 Models paraded on the stage.∥학생들의 가장행렬이 교정을 누비며 행진했다 The costumed students marched in procession around the school grounds.∥그들은 중심가[번화가]를 행진했다 They marched along the main street.
● **행진가** a marching song. **행진곡** a march. ¶군대 ~ a military march∥장송 ~ a funeral march.

행차(行次) the going[coming] (of an august personage); a visit (of a high personage) to a place. ¶그것은 ~ 뒤에 나팔 부는 격이다 That is the case of coming a day after the fair. **행차하다** go (out); come; visit. ¶임금님이 그 의식에 행차하셨다 His Majesty the King honored the ceremony with his presence.

행패(行悖) misconduct; misbehavior; violence. ¶술에 취하여 ~를 부리다 be drunk and disorderly∥(남에게) ~를 부리면서 위협하다 threaten (a person) with violence∥침략군은 마음대로 ~를 부렸다 The invading troops displayed the most unbridled license. **행패하다** misconduct[misbehave] oneself; behave rudely; do[resort to] violence.

행하(行下) **1** (하인에게 주는) a gift to one's servant on a joyous occasion[in consideration of his service]. **2** [놀음차] a tip; a gratuity; a consideration; (영) a perquisite. ¶~를 주다 give (a person) a tip[gratuity] / consider[remember] (a comedian).

행하다(行一) **1** [행위하다] do; act; [처신하다] behave (oneself); conduct oneself.
2 [실행하다] do; practice (asceticism); carry out (a plan); commit; [수행하다] perform; discharge (one's duty). ¶선을 ~ do good / practice virtue∥악을 ~ do wrong[evil] / commit vice∥나는 그의 지시대로 행했다 I did as he told me.∥우리는 올바르게 행할 뿐이다 We can only do what is right. / (문어) We can only conduct ourselves according to our conscience.∥말하기는 쉽고 행하기는 어렵다 Easier said than done.∥왜 그런 일이 행해지고 있는가 Why are such things being done?∥그 풍습은 이 나라에서 지금도 행해지고 있다 The custom is still observed in this country.
3 [실시하다] conduct (education); exercise (control); (법률 등을) put in force; enforce; give effect to; [행사하다] exercise (authority). ¶그것은 그의 동의하에 행해진 것이다 It was done with his consent.∥자세한 조사가 주민들 사이에 행해졌다 A detailed survey was conducted[carried out] among the residents.∥공연 예행 연습이 행해졌다 They had a rehearsal.∥그의 집에 대한 가택 수색이 행해졌다 He had his house searched.∥그의 연설은 프랑스 어로 행해졌다 He made his speech in French.∥여기서 결정적인 대전투가 행해졌다 The decisive battle was fought here.
4 [거행하다] hold (a funeral); give (an examination); observe (a festival). ¶기적을 ~ perform miracles.

행형(行刑) the execution of a sentence; (재산형의) the execution of a pecuniary punishment; (사형의) execution. **행형하다** execute a sentence[a pecuniary punishment].

행화(杏花) an apricot blossom.

향(向) [집 등의 앉음새] an exposure; an aspect; a prospect. ¶남~집 a house facing (the) south / a house with a southern aspect[exposure]∥서~이다 (집이) look to[toward] the west / look west / have a western exposure / (창문이) open to the west.

향(香) (an) incense; (a) perfume ¶~을 피우다 burn incense / incense (an image) / cense (the room).

향가(鄕歌) a *hyangga*; old Korean folk songs [ballads]; Korea's native songs.

향갑(香匣) an incense case.

향교(鄕校) a *hyanggyo*; a local school annexed to the confucian shrine.

향군(鄕軍) **1** the homeland reserve forces. ⇨향토 예비군(⇨)향토 **2** an ex-soldier. ⇨재향군인

향긋하다 somewhat fragrant[aromatic]; (서술적) have a faint sweet smell[odor / scent].

향기(香氣) [좋은 냄새] (a) fragrance; a scent; (a) perfume; (커피·스튜 등 주로 요리에 대한) (an) aroma; (브랜디 등의) bouquet. ¶~가 좋은 비누 scented[good-smelling] soap∥예술의 ~ 높은 작품 a work rich in artistic flavor∥그녀의 방에서 장미꽃 ~가 풍기고 있었다 Her room was perfumed with the sweet smell of rose. / Her room was fragrant with roses.∥월계수는 강한 ~를 풍긴다 A daphne gives off a strong fragrance[smell].∥나는 커피 ~를 맡았다 I breathed[inhaled] the aroma of the coffee.∥이 꽃은 ~가 좋다 This flower smells sweet.∥그윽한 장미꽃 ~에 나 자신을 잊었다 The fragrant[sweet-smelling] roses made me forget myself. / The fragrance of the roses made me forget myself.

향기롭다(香氣-) fragrant; aromatic; balmy; sweet-smelling; sweet; odoriferous. ¶매화의 향기로운 냄새 the fragrance[sweet smell] of plum blossoms∥이 나무를 때면 향기로운 냄새가 난다 This wood gives off a fragrant smell as it burns.

향꽂이(香-) an incense holder[burner].

향나무(香-) [식] a juniper.

향낭(香囊) an incense pouch[bag]; a sachet.

향내(香-) (a) fragrance; a scent. ⇨향기

향년(享年) one's age at death. ¶~ 83세 He died at (the age of) 83. / Died at 83.(▶ 약력 등에 간단히 쓰는 경우)

향도(嚮導) (일) guidance; conduct; leading; (사람) a leader; a guide; [군] a fugleman; a pivot. **향도하다** guide; conduct; lead.

향락(享樂) enjoyment. ¶~적 pleasure-seeking / pleasure-loving / hedonistic. **향락하다** enjoy. ¶인생을 ~ enjoy life.
● **향락 업소** a pleasure-seeking business establishment. **향락주의** epicureanism(▶ 지적·미적 쾌락을 추구함); hedonism(▶ 쾌락이 인생에서 최선의 것이라 생각함. 종종 비판적으로 쓰임). ¶~의 epicurean. **향락주의자** an epicurean; a hedonist.

향로(香爐) an incense burner.
● **향로석** the stone before a tomb that the incense burner is put on.

향료(香料) 1 (식품의) (a) spice. ¶박하 ~ peppermint (flavoring) // ~를 **넣다** season with spice. 2 (화장품의) perfume.

향리(鄕里) one's home town[native village].

향미(香味) a flavor.
● **향미료** spices; seasoning.

향방(向方) a direction; bearings; a course [line] (진행하는); a destination(목적지); an aspect(집 등의). ¶~을 **모르다** do not know the direction[which way is up] / lose one's way[bearings] / cannot find one's way.

향배(向背) for or against; pro or con; [태도] one's attitude. ¶~를 **정하다** decide one's attitude[whether to obey or not] // 이것은 그의 ~에 달려 있다 It depends on his attitude.

향불(香-) an incense fire; (a) burning incense. ¶~을 **피우다** burn[offer] incense.

향사(向斜) [지] a syncline; a synclinal (fold).

향상(向上) elevation; rise; [개선] improvement; betterment; uplift; [진보] (self-)advancement; progress. ¶질의 ~을 촉진하다 press for improvement in the quality (of) // (국민) 생활수준의 ~을 볼 수 있었다 There was a rise in the standard of living. // 여성의 지위 ~을 위하여 노력했다 We made efforts to raise[elevate] the status of women. // 젊은 이들의 체격 ~이 현저하다 The improvement of the young people is remarkable. // 그녀는 영어에 현저한 ~을 이룩했다 She has made remarkable[marked] progress in English. **향상하다** rise; be elevated; become higher; improve; advance; progress; make (good) progress. ¶향상하려고 노력하다 struggle for betterment // 2학년 학생들은 영어 실력이 향상하였다 The second-year students have made progress in English. → 사회 복지를 향상시키다 improve the social welfare system // 학문이 향상되다 improve [advance] in one's studies // 2학기에 너의 성적은 상당히 향상되었다 Your grades have [Your school record has] improved considerably in the second term. // 전후에 민주주의는 노동자 계층의 사회적 지위를 향상시켰다 Democracy helped (to) raise the social status[position] of the working class after the war.

향속(鄕俗) rustic[rural] (manners and) customs.

향수(享受) enjoyment. **향수하다** enjoy; have.

향수(享壽) 〔오래 사는 복〕. **향수하다** live long; enjoy longevity; live to a great [ripe old] age. ¶백 세까지 ~ live to be a hundred.

향수(香水) perfume(▶ 종류를 말할 때만 a perfume; perfumes); (a) scent; cologne.(▶ perfume이 여성들이 사용하는 짙은 향수를 가리키는 데 반해, cologne은 주로 남성들이 바르는 연한 향수를 가리킴) ¶~를 바른[넣은] perfumed / scented // 그녀는 ~를 바르고 있다 (상태) wear scent // 그녀는 ~를 바르고 있다 She is wearing perfume. // 손수건에 ~를 뿌렸다 I perfumed[sprayed perfume on] my handkerchief. // 너는 ~를 사용하기에는 너무 어리다 You are too young to use perfume.
● **향수병** a perfume bottle. **향수 비누** perfumed[scented] soap.

향수(鄕愁) homesickness; nostalgia. ¶~를 **느끼다** be[feel] homesick (for) / feel nostalgia (for) // 많은 도시인들은 전원생활에 ~를 느끼고 있다 Many city people feel nostalgic toward(s) rural life. // 저 가락은 ~를 자아내게 한다 That tune makes me homesick. // 저무는 저녁 풍경에 문득 ~를 느꼈다 The evening scene stirred a vague nostalgia in me.

향습성(向濕性) [식] positive hydrotropism.

향신료(香辛料) spice.

향악(鄕樂) the indigenous[native] Korean music.

향연(香煙) 1 [향 연기] the smoke of incense. 2 [향기로운 담배] fragrant tobacco.

향연(饗宴) a feast; (공식의) a banquet. ¶~을 **베풀다** hold a banquet.

향유(享有) enjoyment; possession. **향유하다** enjoy; possess oneself[be possessed] of. ¶모든 사람은 기본적 인권을 향유한다 Everyone has certain fundamental human rights as his birthright. // 그 나라는 부존자원을 향유하고 있다 The country is blessed with natural resources.

향유(香油) 1 perfumed oil; balm. ¶머리에 ~를 바르다 put perfumed oil on one's hair // 유해에 ~를 발랐다 The body of the deceased was embalmed[perfumed]. 2 sesame oil. ⇨ 참기름

향유고래(香油-) [동] a sperm whale.

향응(響應) 1 [메아리] resonance; consonance; response; respondence; an echo (pl. ~s); reverberation. **향응하다** resonate; be resonant (with); respond (to); echo. 2 [호응] acting in concert. **향응하다** act in concert[unison] (with); follow suit; chime in (with).

향응(饗應) an entertainment; a treat; [연회] a banquet; a dinner; a feast. ¶~을 **베풀다** entertain (a person at dinner) // 나는 ~을 받았다 I was treated to food and drink. / I was wined and dined. **향응하다** entertain (a person at dinner); regale (a person with wine); treat (a person) to a dinner; give a (dinner) party.

향일성(向日性) [식] heliotropism.
● **향일성 식물** a heliotropic plant.

향점(向點) [천] an apex (pl. ~es, apices). ¶태양 ~ the solar apex.

향정신성 의약품(向精神性醫藥品) a psychotropic (medicine).

향지성(向地性) [식] positive geotropism.

향초(香草) 1 [향기 나는 풀] fragrant [aromatic] grass[plants]; herbs. 2 [향기로운 담배] fragrant tobacco.

향촉(香燭) incense and candles (used in

향촌(鄕村) [시골] the country.
향취(香臭) (a) fragrance; a scent. ⇨ 향기
향토(鄕土) [고향·향리] one's native district; one's hometown; [출생지] one's birthplace. ¶~의 home∥이 대음악가는 우리 ~의 자랑이다 This great musician is the pride of our hometown.
● **향토 무용**[민요] a folk dance[song]. **향토 문학** folk literature. **향토색** local colo(u)r. ¶짙은 축제를 보여 드리겠소 I'll show you a festival full of local color. **향토애** love for one's home district. **향토 예비군** the homeland[local] reserve forces. **향토 예술** provincial art. **향토 음악** folk[local] music.

향하다(向-) **1** [대하다] face; look[direct] (to); front (on); turn (on / upon / toward). ¶얼굴을 위로 향하게 하고 with one's face upward∥정면을 ~ face (the) front∥위를 look up[upward] / turn up / turn one's face upward∥이쪽[저쪽]을 ~ look this[that] way∥벽 쪽을 향해서 서다 stand facing to a wall / stand with one's face turned toward a wall∥남쪽을 향해 향해하다 head south / sail south[toward the south]∥적을 향하여 진격하다 advance on the enemy∥두 사람은 서로 마주 향해 앉았다 The two sat facing each other[face to face].∥강도는 경관을 향해 발포했다 The robber fired at the policeman.∥그는 결승선을 향하여 달렸다 He ran toward(s) the finish line.∥그는 본루를 향하여 질주했다 He dashed madly for home base.
2 [가다] proceed (to); repair (to); go (to / toward); start (for); leave (for); make (for); head (toward); take one's way (toward). ¶서울로 ~ leave for Seoul∥제주도로 ~ head for Jejudo∥전ցtower로 ~ go to the front∥그녀는 부산을 향하여 출발했다 She set out for Busan.∥그들은 런던에서 뉴욕으로 향하고 있었다 They were on their way[en route] from London to New York.∥태풍은 북쪽으로[동해안으로] 향하고 있다 The typhoon is heading north[for the East coast].
3 [면하다] face (on); front (on); look (out) (on). ¶내 방은 뜰을 향해 있다 My room looks out into[opens into / opens out on] the garden.
4 [지향하다] be inclined[disposed] (to / toward); tend (to); lean[trend] (toward). ¶임향한 일편단심 one's sincere heart[sincerity] toward one's (liege) lord∥민심이 향하는 바를 살피다 see[watch] the trend of popular feelings∥사태는 악화 쪽으로 향하기 시작했다 The situation has begun to take a turn for the worse.

향학열(向學熱) an ardent love of learning; enthusiasm for learning. ¶~에 불타는 사람 an ardent lover of learning∥~에 불타다 burn with the desire for learning / aspire after further knowledge / be ardent[very eager] to seek knowledge.
향합(香盒) an incense box[jar].
향화(香火) **1** an incense fire. ⇨ 향불 **2** (a) sacrifice. ⇨ 제사(祭祀)
향후(向後) after this; from now on; hereafter; henceforth; henceforward. ¶~ 거짓말을 절대로 하지 않겠습니다 I will never tell a lie after this.∥~ 당신과 함께 일하고 싶습니다 I want to work with you from now on.

허 ha!; huh! ⇨ 하² ¶~, 또 당했군 Gosh, I've lost again.∥~, 우산 갖고 온다는 걸 깜빡 잊었네 Goodness (gracious), I have forgotten to bring an umbrella with me!
허(虛) a blind spot[point]. ⇨ 허점 ¶~를 찌르다 catch (a person) off guard / take advantage of (a person) at an unguarded moment∥그녀는 그의 ~를 찔렀다 She caught him unprepared.∥아군은 적의 ~를 찔렀다 Our army took the enemy unawares. / Our army made a surprise attack on the enemy.
허가(許可) **1** [허락] permission; leave(▶leave는 직장을 떠나거나 결혼하는 등의 허가에 쓰이는 경우가 많음). ¶상륙 ~ shore leave∥~를 바라다 ask a person's permission (to do)∥~를 얻다 be permitted / get a permit / obtain permission∥~ 없이 이 방은 사용할 수 없다 No one is to use this room without permission[leave].∥~ 없이 우산을 빌려 가서 죄송합니다 Excuse me for borrowing your umbrella without asking your permission.∥나는 외출 ~를 받았다 I got leave[permission] to go out.∥~가 났다 Permission was given[granted]. **허가하다** permit; give leave; (입학·입장을) admit. ¶누가 그런 일을 하라고 허가했지 Who gave you permission to do such a thing? ➔나는 연세 대학에 입학이 허가되었다 I have been admitted to Yonsei University.∥면허증이 없으면 자동차 운전은 허가되지 않는다 Nobody is permitted to drive a car without a (driver's) license.
2 [승인] (an) approval; sanction; (미국 구어) an O.K.[OK / okay] (pl. O.K.'s). ¶~가 났다 At long last the approval came through. **허가하다** sanction; approve (of); give one's approval (to). ¶정부는 2개 대학의 신설을 허가하였다 The Government has sanctioned the establishment of two new universities.
3 [면허] license; [인가] authorization; (미국구어) go-ahead. ¶~가 나다 be licensed / get a license / be authorized∥~를 받고 영업하다 do business under license. **허가하다** [면허하다] license; grant[give] a license; (인가하다) authorize; give the go-ahead. ➔우리는 독자적 결정을 내리도록 허가받고 있다 We are authorized to make our own decisions.∥이 음식점은 주류 판매를 허가받고 있다 This restaurant is licensed to sell liquor.∥그는 음식점 영업을 허가받았다 He got a license to run a restaurant.
● **허가제** a license system. **허가증** a permit; (법적인) a license; (영) a licence. ¶건축 ~ a construction permit∥취업 ~ a work permit.
허겁지겁 helter-skelter; hurry-scurry. ⇨ 허둥지둥
허공(虛空) the (empty) air; (empty) space; the (empty) sky; the void. ¶~에 in the air [sky]∥~을 잡다 grasp[clutch] at the air∥~을 가르며 날다 flash across the sky / fly through the air∥그의 주먹이 ~을 쳤다 He beat the air with his fist.∥그녀는 아까부터 ~을 뚫어지게 보고 있다 She has been staring into space[thin air] for some time.∥그는 ~을 잡듯이 팔을 뻗었다 He stretched out his arm as if he were grasping at thin air.
허구(虛構) (a) fiction; a fabrication; a lie; a

허구하다(許久-) very long; longtime; eternal. ¶허구한 세월 a long (period[space] of) time / a long stretch of time // 허구한 나날 day after[by] day / day in (and) day out.
falsehood; (a) concoction; (an) invention; a figment; a fake. ¶~의 false / fictitious / made-up // 순전한 ~ a pure fabrication / a perfect fake // 그 뉴스는 완전한 ~였다 The news was a complete invention.

허근(虛根) [수] an imaginary root.

허기(虛飢) hunger; hungriness. ¶~를 달래다 appease[alleviate / allay] one's hunger (with a slice of apple) // ~를 채우다 satisfy one's appetite (with some food) / gratify one's hunger (on) // ~를 느끼다 feel hungry [empty] / (농조) feel a vacuum in the lower regions.
● **허기증** hungry feeling; a sense of hunger. ¶~이 나다 be[feel / go] hungry / have a wolf in one's stomach.

허기지다(虛飢-) 1 [배고프다] go hungry; famish; be famished; be exhausted with hunger. ¶허기져서 쓰러질 것 같다 be faint from hunger. 2 [욕망이 생기다] be hungry [avid] for[after]; hunger[starve / hanker / thirst] for[after].

허깨비 [환영] a phantom; a phantasm; an apparition; an eidolon (pl. ~s, -la); [유령] a ghost; a specter; a bogle; a spook. ¶~을 보다 see (something) in a vision // ~에 홀리다 be lured by an illusion / be under an illusion.

허니문 a honeymoon.

허다하다(許多-) (많다) many; numerous; innumerable; abundant; plentiful; (흔하다) (very) common; commonplace; ordinary; (서술적) be met with everywhere. ¶허다한 일 a common[familiar] affair / not an uncommon case / a matter of common occurrence // 이 문제에 관한 서적은 ~ Books written on this subject are legion. // 그러한 일은 ~ Such things are by no means rare[uncommon].

허덕거리다 1 [숨이 차다] pant; gasp (for breath); puff (and blow); breathe hard [heavily]. ¶허덕거리며 말하다 gasp[puff / pant] out. 2 [애쓰다] struggle (hard) (for bare existence); fight hard (with poverty / against difficulties); toil and moil; have [fight] a hard fight[tough struggle] (with). ¶생활에 ~ live with one's nose at the grindstone / be in needy circumstances / find it hard to make a living // 너무 일이 바빠서 허덕거리고 있습니다 I'm so busy with my work that I can barely keep my head above water.

허덕이다 1 pant; gasp (for breath). ⇨ 허덕거리다1 ¶그는 물에 빠져 허덕이다가 가까스로 구조되었다 He was rescued just when he was on the point of drowning. 2 struggle (hard) (for bare existence). ⇨ 허덕거리다2 ¶국민은 근근이 생계를 이어가는 데 몹시 허덕이고 있다 The people are struggling[barely able] to make ends meet[keep body and soul together]. // 빚을 갚아야 하기 때문에 우리 집 식구는 생활에 허덕이고 있다 Loan payments are making it hard for my family to keep its head above water (financially).

허두(虛頭) the beginning; the opening (of a speech); the head (of a column); the opening paragraph.
허두를 떼다 open words; begin to say.

허둥거리다 fluster oneself; be all in a flurry [fluster / hurry-scurry]; be confused; be upset; be thrown into confusion. ¶사람들은 허둥거리지 않았다 The people remained calm[kept their head / kept their presence of mind]. // 그의 갑작스러운 죽음은 유족들을 허둥거리게 했다 His sudden death left his family in a state of turmoil.

허둥지둥 helter-skelter; hurry-scurry; hurriedly; in a great hurry; in hot[great] haste; in confusion. ¶불이야 하는 소리에 그는 ~ 달려갔다 Hearing somebody shout "Fire", he rushed up at breakneck speed. // 그들은 ~ 도망갔다 They fled helter-skelter[in a great hurry]. / 그는 ~ 방에서 나갔다 He hurried [walked hastily] out of the room. / He rushed hurry-scurry[helter-skelter] out of the room.

허드레 odds and ends; things of little value that can be used for sundry purposes.
● **허드레꾼** an odd(-job) man; an odd-jobber; a handy man; (미) a scrubman. **허드렛물** water for sundry uses. **허드렛일** odd jobs; chores; underwork; subordinate work(공사장 등의); kitchen work(부엌의).

허들 (경기) the hurdles; (장애물) a hurdle. ¶100미터 ~ (경기) the 100-meter hurdles. // ~을 넘다 [~에 걸려 넘어지다] clear (or leap) [stumble / trip] a hurdle.
● **허들 선수** a hurdler.

허락(許諾) (승낙) consent; assent; approval; sanction; (미국 구어) an O.K. [OK / okay]; (허가) permission; leave. ¶…의 ~을 받고 with (a person's) permission[leave / consent / authority] // ~을 받다[얻다] get [obtain / have / secure] permission[leave] (to do) / win[obtain] (a person's) consent [assent]. // 그는 부모의 ~을 받지 않고 그 집을 팔아 버렸다 He (has) sold the house without (obtaining) his parents' consent [permission]. // 그녀는 아버지에게 결혼 ~을 청했다 She asked her father's consent to her marriage. // 너는 누구의 ~을 받고 이 방에 들어왔느냐 Who gave you permission to (said you could) come into this room? // 너는 다리를 골절했으니 체육 면제의 ~을 받을 것이다 You will be excused from physical education class because of your broken leg. **허락하다** (승낙하다) consent (to); assent (to); grant; (찬성하다) approve (of); give one's approval (to); (허가하다) permit; (입학 등을) admit; (경제 사정 등이) can afford; (마음 등을) trust [confide in] (a person); (몸을) surrender (one's chastity to a man); give oneself (to a man). ¶시간[사정]이 허락하는 한 so far as time permits[circumstances permit] // 지면이 허락하는 한 to the limit of space / within the limits of the space allowed // 즉석에서 [선뜻] ~ give a ready consent (to) // 두말 않고 ~ accept (a proposal) without question // 결혼을 ~ give (a person) permission to marry / consent to (a person's) marriage // 남자에게 몸을 ~ surrender one's chastity to a man / give oneself to a man's embrace // 제의를 ~ assent [consent] to a proposal // 교칙 (校則)은 장발을 허락하지 않는다 School regulations do not permit long hair. ➔그는 이 학교에 입학이 허락되었다 He was admitted to this school.

허랑방탕하다(虛浪放蕩-) loose; licentious;

허례 unbridled; dissolute; profligate; dissipated. ¶허랑방탕한 자식 a profligate[wastrel] son / 허랑방탕한 사람 〔깡패〕 a scoundrel / 〔방탕자〕 a profligate / a rake / 〔낭비하는 사람〕 a wastrel // 그는 허랑방탕한 생활을 하다가 끝내 아버지한테 쫓겨났다 He led such a dissipated life that he was finally disinherited.

허례(虛禮) dead forms; empty[useless] formalities. ¶~에 빠지다 lapse into an empty formality // ~를 없애다 dispense[do away] with empty forms[formalities].
● **허례허식** empty formalities and vanity [ostentation].

허름하다 1 (낡아서) shabby; humble; worn-out; used; old. ¶허름한 옷 old[shabby] clothes / worn-out[used / secondhand] clothing. 2 (싸다) cheap(-looking); cheapish; mean. ¶허름한 물건 a cheap[low-priced] article.

허리 1 (몸의) the waist; the small of the back; the loin; the hip; the haunch(짐승의); the pelvic region. ¶~가 가는 여자 아이 a slender-waisted girl // ~까지 덮는 스웨터 a hip-length sweater // ~를 굽히다 stoop (down) // ~를 펴다 stretch [straighten] oneself[one's back] // ~가 길다 be long-waisted // ~가 굵다 have a big trunk[waist] // 깊이가 ~까지 닿다[차다] be waist-deep / be up to one's waist // ~가 날씬하다 have a slender[slim] waist // ~가 절구통 같다 have no waist // ~를 삐다 have one's waist dislocated // ~가 휘도록 일하다 break one's back // 그녀는 ~가 잘록하다 She has a wasp waist // 그는 아프다 I have pain in the waist. // 그는 일어서서 ~를 폈다 He stood up and stretched[straightened] (himself). // 그는 늙어서 ~가 굽어 있다 He is bent with age. / He stoops from age. // 그는 ~에 권총을 차고 있다 He wears a revolver on his belt.
2 (옷의) the waist; the hip; the yoke(스커트의). ¶치마~를 달다 attach the waist part of a skirt.
● **허리곤** a (leather) belt. ⇨ ⁼허리끼 **허리둘레** one's waist measurement; one's girth. ¶~ 24인치 a waist measure of 24 inches // ~를 재다 take waist measurement / measure (round) one's waist. **허리뼈** the hipbone; the hucklebone. **허리春** inside the waist of one's trousers. ¶~에 감추다 slip (something) in the waist of one's trousers // 치맛자락을 ~에 걷어 올리다 tuck up one's skirt at the waist. **허리통** one's girth. ¶~이 굵어지다 grow fat round the middle // ~이 절구통이다 have no waist. **허릿매** the shape of one's waist; the waistline ¶~가 날씬한 여자 a woman with shapely[well-formed / attractive] waist / a woman with a wasp waist.

허리띠 a (leather) belt; a waistband; a waist sash; a girdle; (집합적) belting. ¶~를 매다 tie a belt[sash / girdle] // ~를 조르다[느슨하게 하다] tighten[loosen] one's belt.
허리띠를 졸라매다 tighten (up) one's belt [gird (up) one's loins / pull up the trousers / gird oneself up] 《for an effort》; buckle down to (one's task).

허리케인 a hurricane. ¶~이 해안을 덮쳤다 A hurricane hit the coast.

허망하다(虛妄-) false; untrue; nonsensical; groundless; fabulous.

허명(虛名) a false reputation; an empty name. ¶~을 찾는 사람 a publicity seeker // ~을 찾다 court publicity // ~을 얻다 win a reputation that outruns one's ability.

허무(虛無) nothingness; nihility; futility. ¶~적인 nihilistic. **허무하다** nonexistent; null; futile; vain. ¶인생은 허무한 것이다 Life is but an empty dream. / All is vanity in life.
● **허무감** a sense of futility. **허무주의** nihilism. **허무주의자** a nihilist.

허무맹랑하다(虛無孟浪-) fabulous; groundless; absurd; extraordinary; wild. ¶허무맹랑한 소문 a groundless rumor / an unfounded gossip // 허무맹랑한 소리를 하다 say extraordinary[absurd] things / talk wild.

허물¹ 1 (살갗의) the outer(most) layer of the skin; the cuticle; the epidermis ¶햇볕에 타서 어깨의 ~이 벗어졌다 The skin of my shoulders peeled off from too much exposure to the sun. 2 (매미·뱀 등의) a cast-off skin (of a cicada); an ecdysis (pl. -ses); a slough.
허물(을) 벗다¹ (뱀 등이) cast (off) the skin; shed the skin; slough (off); exuviate. ¶뱀이 허물을 벗었다 The snake sloughed its skin [cast (aside) its slough].

허물² 〔실수〕 a fault; an error; a misstep; 〔잘못〕 a slip; a mistake; an error; 〔흠〕 a defect (in one's personality); a flaw; a blot; a blemish. ¶~을 인정하다 admit[acknowledge / recognize / own up to] one's fault / admit that one is in error // ~을 용서하다 forgive (a person) (for) his fault / excuse (a person) for his fault // ~을 뉘우치다 repent one's fault // ~을 눈감아 주다 overlook[pass over / wink at] (a person's) fault // ~을 들추어내다 find out another's faults / find fault with (a person) // ~을 남에게 씌우다 lay a fault to a person's charge[at a person's door] / lay one's fault on (a person).

허물(을) 벗다² 〔누명을 씻다〕 remove the stigma[disgrace] that has (been) attached to one's name; clear[purge] oneself of a false charge; wipe out the disgrace.

허물다 pull[tear] down; break up[down]; demolish; destroy. ¶그들은 새 집을 지으려고 고옥을 허물었다 They pulled[tore] down the old house to build a new one.

허물어지다 crumble (to the ground); fall (down); come down; collapse; break (down); give way; be destroyed. ¶허물어진 집들 houses collapsed / fallen houses // 허물어져 가는 crumbling (wall) / ruinous (hut) // 지진으로 집 2백 채가 허물어졌다 Two hundred houses were destroyed by the earthquake. // 벽이 허물어지기 시작했다 The wall has begun to crumble.

허물없다 unreserved; unconstrained; unceremonious; free; open(-minded); candid; frank; familiar; genial. ¶허물없는 태도로 in a friendly[candid] way // 허물없는 친구 a candid friend / a friend on frank terms // 그들은 곧 허물없는 사이가 되었다 They soon threw off[laid aside] their reserve. / They soon opened[warmed] up to each other. // 거기서는[그와는] 허물없이 굴 수 있다 I feel at ease[home] there[with him]. **허물없이** unreservedly; candidly; frankly; without constraint. ¶그는 결코 우리를 ~ 대하려고 하지 않았다 He would not open his heart to us. // 그녀에게는 ~ 말할 수 있다 I can talk to her quite easily[comfortably]. // 그녀는 누

구하고도 ~ 말을 건넨다 She will start a friendly conversation with just about anyone.

허밍 [음] humming.

허방 [움푹 팬 땅] a hollow; a cavity; a pit. ¶~을 디디다 step in a hollow / make a false step // ~에 빠지다 fall in(to) a pit.

허방(을) 짚다 [잘못 짚다] miscalculate; misjudge; make a miscalculation; shoot at the wrong mark. ¶나는 완전히 허방 짚었다 My calculations went all wrong. / My guess was wide of the mark.

허방다리 a pitfall. ⇨ ＝함정(陷穽)

허벅다리 the (upper) thigh. ¶~를 내놓다[드러내다] expose[bare] one's thighs.

허벅살 the flesh of the thigh(사람의); round(소의); ham(돼지의); dark meat(새의).

허벅지 the inside[inner part] of a thigh; the inguinal region.

허벅허벅하다 soft and somewhat dry.

허보(虛報) a false report; false news. ¶그 뉴스는 ~였다 The news has proved false.

허비(虛費) a wasteful use; waste (of); wastage; wastefulness. ¶시간의 ~ waste[a wasteful use / dissipation] of time. **허비하다** use[spend] wastefully; waste; use to no purpose; throw[chuck / fritter] away. ¶부질없은 일에 돈과 시간을 ~ waste one's time and money on worthless things // 이 문제를 더 이야기해 봐야 시간만 허비할 뿐이다 It is a mere waste of time to discuss this further.

허사(虛事) a useless thing; a vain effort[attempt]. ¶~가 되다 fall through / go up in smoke // 계획이 ~가 되어 버렸다 The plan fell through[came to nothing]. // 그의 실책으로 그 계획은 죄다 ~가 되어 버렸다 His blunder upset the whole scheme. // 우리의 모든 노력이 ~가 되어 버렸다 All our efforts were wasted[came to nothing]. / All the work we did went down the drain.

허사(虛辭) 1 [언] an expletive. 2 a lie; a falsehood. ⇨ ＝허언

허상(虛像) 1 [물] a virtual image. 2 [참모습과는 다르게 만들어진 모습] a false image; (a) pretense. ¶그들의 번영은 ~에 불과했다 Theirs was only a false prosperity.

허섭스레기 rubbish; trash; odds and ends; odd ends; lumber.

허세(虛勢) (a) bluff; a false show of power [courage]. ¶~를 부리는 사람 a bluff / a bluffer // ~를 부리다[짓다] put on a bold front // 취중에 ~를 부리다 become bold under the influence of alcoholic drink / become pot-valiant // 그는 그녀에게 ~를 부려 대단한 사람이라고 생각하게 했다 He bluffed her into believing[He pulled the wool over her eyes and convinced her] that he was really somebody. // 소년들은 ~를 부리며 유령의 집으로 향해 갔다 The boys headed for the haunted house with bravado.

허송(虛送) passing time idly. **허송하다** idle one's time[hours / life] away; pass one's time idly[in idleness]. ¶학생 시절에 병으로 2년간 허송했다 I lost[wasted] two years while I was in school because of illness.

●**허송세월** passing time idly. ⇨ ＝허송 ¶그는 ~을 보내고 있다 He is idling his time away. / He is leading an idle life.

허수(虛數) [수] an imaginary number.

허수아비 1 a scarecrow. ¶~를 세우다 set [put] up a scarecrow. 2 [비유] a (mere) figurehead; a dummy; a puppet. ¶~을 ~로 만들다 make a puppet of (a person). ¶저 사람은 ~다 He's absolutely useless. // ~처럼 서 있지만 말고 이것을 들고 있으면 어때 Why don't you hold this instead of just standing there like a dummy? // 그는 ~에 지나지 않는다 He is no more than a puppet.

허술하다 1 [초라하다] shabby; poor-looking; plain; humble; miserable. ¶허술하게 만들어진 가구 shabby furniture / poorly made furniture // 나는 허술한 집에 살고 있다 I live in a humble[shabby] house. **허술히** shabbily; plainly; humbly; miserably.
2 [부주의하다] careless; negligent; inattentive; rude; rough; loose. ¶허술한 방비 a loose defense / 허술한 틈을 노리다 watch for an unguarded moment / try to catch (a person) off his guard // 국무총리 공관의 경호가 허술했었다 The prime minister's official residence was scantily guarded. // 그 조사는 너무 ~ The investigation is too slipshod [sloppy]. **허술히** carelessly; negligently; rudely; loosely.

허스키하다 husky. ¶허스키한 목소리 a husky [harsh / throaty] voice.

허식(虛飾) [과시] ostentation; display; [허세 부림] affectation. ¶~이 없는 unaffected / plain // ~ 없이 without affectation // ~으로 가득 찬 삶 a life full of show and display // ~을 싫어하다 detest[hate] ostentation // ~을 좋아하다 love[be fond of] ostentation. **허식하다** show off; make a show; affect; cut a dash.

허실(虛實) truth and falsehood; weakness and firmness. ¶~을 밝히다 ascertain the truth of a matter / find out whether it is true (or not) // 적의 ~을 알아내다 discover the strong and weak points of the enemy.

허심(虛心) disinterestedness; freedom from prejudice.

허심탄회하다(虛心坦懷－) open-minded [-hearted]; candid; frank; free and easy. ¶허심탄회하게 [솔직히] frankly / [거리낌 없이] candidly / [마음을 터놓고] with an open heart // 우리는 허심탄회하게 이야기를 나누었다 We had a heart-to-heart talk. // 허심탄회하게 충고하여 주십시오 Please give me your candid advice.

허심하다(許心－) [마음을 허락하다] trust [confide in] (a person); admit[take] (a person) into confidence; allow oneself (to); make confident of (a person); [마음을 놓다] relax one's caution against (a person).

허약자(虛弱者) a weakly[an infirm] person.

허약하다(虛弱－) weak; weakly; infirm; delicate; feeble; frail; sickly(병약하다). ¶허약한 남자 a man in poor health // 그는 몸이 ~ He is in poor health. / He has a weak[delicate] constitution.

허언(虛言) a lie; a falsehood; an untruth. **허언하다** tell a lie[falsehood]; lie.

허여멀겋다 (액체 등이) whitish and thin; washy (milk); (피부 등이) nice and fair; (서술적) have a fair complexion.

허여멀쑥하다 white and clean.

허영(虛榮) vanity; vainglory. ¶여자의 ~ feminine vanity // ~에 찬 여자 a woman full of vanity / a vain woman // ~에 차다 be full of vanity / be vainglorious.

허영다

- **허영심** vanity. ¶~이 강한 vain / full of vanity / vainglorious // ~에 들떠서 driven by vanity / out of vanity // ~을 만족시키다[버리다] satisfy[give up] one's vanity // ~을 부채질하다[자극하다] inflate[excite / stimulate / appeal to] one's vanity // 여자는 대개 ~이 강하다 Women are generally vain creatures.

허옇다 pure white. ⇨ 하얗다

허예지다 become pure white. ⇨ 하얘지다

허욕(虛慾) a vain[wild] desire; avarice; greed(iness). ¶~이 많은 사람 an avaricious[a grasping] person // ~이 많다 be blind with avarice / be avaricious.

허용(許容) 〔용인〕 permission; allowance; approval; sanction; admission; tolerance. ¶(약의) **최대 ~량** the maximum permissible dose (of). **허용하다** permit; approve; allow; admit; tolerate. ¶체납을 허용하지 않다 admit of no default of payment. ➔ ¶이것은 관례로 허용되어 있다 This is sanctioned by usage. // 그 정도밖에 허용되지 않는다 That is about as much as can be permitted.
- **허용 범위** a permitted limit. ¶방사능 오염은 ~를 넘었다 Radioactive contamination has exceeded the permitted limits. **허용 오차** an allowable[a permissible] error. **허용 한계 / 허용 한도** a tolerance limit. ¶방사능의 ~ the maximum permissible exposure to radiation.

허우대 a robust physique; a fine appearance; a good constitution. ¶~가 좋다 be of sturdy build.

허우적거리다 struggle; flounder; paw the air. ¶물에서 헤어나려고 ~ paw the air to get out of the water.

허우적허우적 struggling; floundering; pawing the air. ¶~ 걷다 walk swinging one's arms. **허우적허우적하다** struggle; flounder. ⇨ 허우적거리다

허울 outward appearance[features / show]; exterior. ¶~뿐인 자유 the shadow of freedom // ~뿐이다 be not so good as it looks / be deceptive.

허울 좋은 도둑놈(속담) a wolf in a lamb's skin.

허울 좋은 하눌타리(속담) a person[a thing] only superficially attractive.

허울 좋다 look nice; be seemly; make a good figure[appearance]. ¶허울 좋은 nice-looking / fair-seeming / [그럴듯한] plausible / fair-spoken // 허울 좋은 친구 a seeming friend // 허울 좋았지 (속은) 별것 아니었다 It was not so good as it looked. // 집이 허울은 좋지만 안은 보잘것없다 The house looks nice from the outside but the inside is nothing much to look at.

허위(虛僞) (a) falsehood; falsity; an untruth; a lie; 〔논〕 fallacy. ¶~의 false / sham / untrue / fictitious / mendacious // ~ 기재를 하다 make a false description // 그의 진술은 ~였다 His statement proved false[untrue].
- **허위 보고** a false[mendacious] report. **허위 신고** a false return. **허위 진단서** a false diagnosis; (the issuance of) a wrongful medical examination[checkup] certificate. **허위 진술** 〔법〕 misrepresentation; a false representation. ¶~을 **하다** make a false statement (of) / misrepresent / (증인이) give false evidence / commit perjury.

허위대 →허우대

허장성세(虛張聲勢) bluster; bluff; bravado; swashbuckling. **허장성세하다** bluster; bluff; swashbuckle; pretend to power and influence.

허적거리다 ransack; rummage (in); scatter; disperse. ¶서랍 속을 ~ ransack[rummage in] a drawer (for) // 서류를 ~ rummage among papers // 닭들이 낟알을 찾느라 짚단을 허적거리고 있었다 Hens were scattering the bunch of straw for grains of rice.

허전하다 〔서술적〕 feel empty; feel something lacking; miss something. ¶호주머니가 ~ have a light[lean / slender] purse / have empty pockets // 그녀가 가고 나니 허전하였다 Her going away left sensible void. // 이 방은 가구가 없어서 ~ This room looks bare[empty] without furniture. // 이 그림은 어딘가 ~ Something is lacking[wanting] in this picture. // 나뭇잎이 없으면 뜰은 ~ The garden looks bare without any leaves on the trees.

허점(虛點) a blind spot[point]; an unguarded point. ¶현행법의 ~ loopholes in the existing law // 법의 ~을 찾다[노리다] find a loophole in the law // ~을 노리다 watch for an unguarded moment // ~을 보이다 lay oneself open to attack // ~을 찌르다 touch (a person) on the most vulnerable point // 너의 작전 계획에는 어딘가 ~이 있다 There is something missing in your plan of operations.

허정거리다 〔비틀비틀하다〕 walk with a tottering[an unsteady] gait; be unsteady on one's feet.

허족(虛足) 〔생〕 a pseudopodium. ⇨ 위족

허청대고 rashly; recklessly; blindly; thoughtlessly; at random. ¶무슨 일을 ~ 하다 do (something) on the spur of the moment[at random] // ~ 돈을 쓰다 spend money recklessly // ~ 남을 찾아가다 go to visit a person without making sure whether he will be home / give a person a reckless visit.

허초점(虛焦點) 〔물〕 a virtual focus.

허출하다 hungry; 〔서술적〕 feel hungry; get hungry. ¶배가 허출한데 먹을 것 좀 주시오 I'm hungry. Give me something to eat.

허탈(虛脫) 〔의〕 (physical) collapse; prostration. **허탈하다** collapsed; prostrated.
- **허탈감** despondency. **허탈 상태** 〔무기력〕 a state of lethargy; 〔멍한 상태〕 absentmindedness. ¶~에 있다 be in a state of lethargy / be utterly absentminded / look absent / be in a state of utter bewilderment // ~에 빠지다 fall into a state of lethargy.

허탕 vain[fruitless] effort; vain attempt; lost labor. ¶모든 노력이 ~이 되었다 All our efforts were in vain. // 범인 수색은 ~으로 끝났다 The search for the culprit ended in failure.

허탕(을) 치다 prove fruitless[abortive / all in vain]; come to nothing; labor in vain; make vain efforts. ¶만나러 갔다 ~ go on an empty errand / go in vain / make a fruitless call // 나는 낚시질하러 갔다 세찬 파도 때문에 허탕 치고 돌아왔다 I went fishing, but came home empty-handed[without a catch] because of the rough sea.

허투루 〔경솔하게〕 carelessly; heedlessly; lightly; 〔아무렇게나〕 negligently; in a slovenly way; roughly. ¶~ 볼 수 없는 사나이

crafty[tricky] fellow / a sly dog∥~ 보다 make[think] light of / make little account of / slight[neglect] (a person)∥~ 말하다 talk without thinking / make irresponsible remarks∥~ 다루다 handle (a thing) roughly [carelessly]∥일을 ~ 하다 do a slapdash job / work in a perfunctory manner.∥저 사람은 ~ 볼 수 없는 친구다 He is not a man to be trifled with. / He is a man deserving [worthy] of due consideration.∥그는 말을 ~ 하는 사람이 아니다 He weighs his words carefully.

허튼계집 a loose woman; a woman of easy virtue[loose morals]; a slut; a slattern.

허튼모 rice seedlings planted in random fashion (not in even rows).

허튼소리 a random remark; absurd remarks; a silly talk; nonsense; [잠소리] idle gossip; an empty prattle. ¶~를 하다 say silly things / talk nonsense∥~ 좀 작작 해라 Away with you lies!

허튼수작(—酬酌) (말) silly talk; idle talk; nonsense; (짓) a foolish act. ¶~하지 마라 Don't make yourself ridiculous. / Shame on you!

허파 [생] the lungs. ⇨폐(肺)

허파에 바람 들다 be easily tempted to laugh; laugh over nothing; be giggly.

허풍(虛風) a boast; a brag; tall[big] talk; a gasconade; a fanfaronade; (미국 속어) hot air. ¶그가 하는 말은 모두 ~이다 Everything he says is exaggerated.∥그건 ~이다 That's just hot air.

허풍(을) 치다 boast; brag; talk big[tall]; tell a tall tale; (구어) talk through one's hat; (미국 속어) blow hot air; blow hard; draw a long blow; (미국 속어) blow[toot] one's own trumpet. ¶그는 성공했다고 허풍을 쳤다 He boasted of[about] his success. / He bragged that he had succeeded.∥여느 때처럼 그는 아들의 성공에 대해 허풍을 치고 있었다 As usual he was bragging about his son's success.∥허풍을 쳐도 분수가 있지 There is a limit to bragging!

● **허풍선이** a boaster; a braggart; a windbag; (속어) a big talker; a gasbag; (미국 속어) a blowhard.

허하다(虛—) 1 [속이 비다] hollow; empty; void; vacant. ¶허한 느낌 a hollow feeling (inside of one). 2 [허약하다] weak(ly); infirm; delicate; feeble; frail. ¶몸이 ~ have a weak[delicate] constitution / be in delicate health∥기가 ~ lack vitality[spirit].

허하다(許—) [허락하다] permit; give (a person) permission[leave]; allow; (원하는 바를) grant; admit; approve; (경제력이) can afford.

허한(虛汗) (a) cold sweat[perspiration].

허허¹ (웃는 소리) ha-ha. ¶~ 웃으면서 (answer) with a (high) laugh∥~ 웃다 laugh aloud.

허허² [놀람 등의 탄식 소리] Oh; Well; Why; Good gracious!; Heavens!; Dear me!; [슬픔을 나타내는 소리] Alas!; [일이 틀어졌을 때 내는 소리] Oops!; Damn it! ¶~ 이거 망쳐 놨는걸 Oh, I have made a mess of it!∥~ 또 졌는걸 Gosh, I've lost again.

허허바다 a boundless (expanse of the) ocean; a waste of waters.

허허벌판 a vast stretch of land; a wild plain; a desert land(황야).

허혼하다(許婚—) give (a person) permission to marry; permit (a person) to marry (to); consent to (a person's) marriage.

허황되다(虛荒—) unreliable; absurd. ⇨허황하다 ¶허황된 생각 a fantastic idea[notion] / a wild idea∥허황된 계획 a wild[an unwise] project / a wildcat scheme / a wild-goose chase∥허황된 이야기 an incredible story / an absurd story / a cloud of words / sheer [clotted] nonsense∥허황된 소리를 하다 say absurd things / talk something incredible [fantastic / absurd / nonsensical] / talk wild.

허황하다(虛荒—) unreliable; untrustworthy; absurd; nonsensical; fantastic(al); wild (rumor); groundless.

헌 old; used; secondhand; worn-out; shabby.

헌거롭다(軒擧—) (서술적) (의기가) be in high spirits; be high-spirited; be elated; be in exaltation; (풍채가) have a fine presence [appearance]; look stately.

헌것 worn-out[used] things; a secondhand thing[article].

헌계집 a woman[girl] who has lost her virginity; a deflowered girl; a woman once married.

헌금(獻金) a gift of money; a contribution; a donation; a subscription; (교회 등에서의) a collection; an offering. ¶정치 ~ contribution of political funds∥~을 모으다 collect contributions / make[take up] a collection. **헌금하다** contribute; donate; subscribe to (a fund). ¶나는 교회에 만 원을 헌금했다 I made a contribution of[donated] ten thousand won to the church.

● **헌금함** a collection[contribution] box; (교회의) an offertory box.

헌납(獻納) [금품을 바침] presentation; offering; contribution; donation. **헌납하다** present (an airplane to the army); offer; contribute; donate.

● **헌납자** a contributor; a donor. **헌납품** an offering; a present.

헌당(獻堂) the dedication of a church; consecration. **헌당하다** consecrate a church.

헌데 [부스럼] a sore; a boil; an abscess. ¶~가 나다 have a boil∥발에 ~가 생겼다 I have got a boil on my foot. / A boil has formed on my foot.

헌등(獻燈) a votive lantern.

헌배하다(獻杯—) offer (a person) a cup of wine.

헌법(憲法) the constitution; the constitutional law. ¶성문[불문] ~ a written[an unwritten] constitution∥~상 constitutionally∥~(상)의 constitutional∥~상의 권리 one's constitutional rights∥~ 제1조 Article 1 of the Constitution∥민주주의에 입각한 ~ a constitution based on democracy / a democratic nation's constitution∥~의 규정에 위반하여 contrary to the constitutional provision∥~의 개정을 제안하다 initiate a constitutional amendment∥~을 제정하다 establish[frame] the constitution∥~을 시행하다 enforce the constitution∥~을 기초하다 draft a constitution∥~을 옹호하다 safeguard [defend / support] the constitution.

● **헌법 개정** an amendment to the constitution; a constitutional reform[change]. **헌법**

기관 a constitutional institution. **헌법 위반** a breach[violation] of the constitution. **헌법 재판소** the constitutional court. **헌법 정신** the spirit of the constitution; constitutional principles. **헌법 제도** a constitutional regime. **헌법 제정** enactment of constitution.

헌병(憲兵) 〔육군〕 a military policeman(약어 an MP); 〔집합적〕 the military police(약어 MP); 〔해군〕 a shore patrol(man)(약어 an SP); 〔집합적〕 the shore patrol(약어 SP).

헌사(獻辭·獻詞) (a) dedication; a dedicatory letter.

헌상(獻上) 〔봉정〕 presentation. **헌상하다** present (a thing to a person / a person with a thing); make (a person) a present of (a thing).
● **헌상품** an offering; a present.

헌수(獻壽) offering (a person) a cup of wine for his longevity. **헌수하다** offer (a person) a cup of wine for his longevity.

헌시(獻詩) a dedicated poem. **헌시하다** present[dedicate] a poem (to).

헌신(獻身) self-sacrifice; devotion; dedication. **헌신하다** devote oneself (to); dedicate oneself (to); sacrifice oneself (to). ¶사업[정치]에 ~ dedicate one's time[one's life / oneself] to business[politics] // 그녀는 가난한 자와 병든 자를 돕는 데 헌신하였다 She devoted herself to helping the poor and the sick. // 그는 일생을 인도에서 전도하는 데 바쳤다 He devoted his life to missionary work in India. // 그녀는 한평생 사회사업에 헌신했다 She devoted herself to social work all her life. / She devoted her whole life to social work. // 그는 나라의 통일을 위해 헌신했다 He devoted himself[was devoted] to the unification of his country.

헌신적(獻身的) self-sacrificing; devoted. ¶어머니의 자식에 대한 ~인 애정 the devotion of a mother for[to] her child // ~으로 devotedly / with (selfless) devotion // ~으로 일하다 work faithfully / work in dead earnest // ~으로 일에 종사하다 devote oneself to one's work // 병난 아이를 ~으로 간호하다 nurse one's sick child with devotion.

헌신짝 worn-out shoes. ¶~**같이 버리다** throw (a thing) away like an old shoe / cast (a thing) away like dirt / reject (a thing) as worthless // 지위를 ~같이 버리다 throw up one's office just as one would throw away an old hat[without any regrets] // 그는 나를 버리듯 했다 He deserted[abandoned] me as though I were a worn-out rag[an old glove].

헌장(憲章) a constitution; a charter. ¶국민 교육 ~ The Charter of National Education // 국제 연합[유엔] ~ the United Nations Charter // 대 ~ 〔영국 역사〕 the Magna Charta[Carta] / the Great charter // 대서양 ~ the Atlantic Charter // 어린이 ~ the Children's Charter.

헌정(憲政) 〔입헌 정치〕 constitutional government; constitutionalism. ¶~의 위기 a constitutional crisis // ~을 펴다 adopt constitutional government // ~의 실효를 거두다 act up to the principles of constitutional government / realize constitutional government.

헌정(獻呈) presentation; dedication. **헌정하다** present (a copy) to (a person); dedicate; offer.
● **헌정본** a presentation[complimentary] copy.

헌책(-冊) a secondhand[used] book; 〔고본〕 an old book. ¶~으로 사다 buy a book at second hand.
● **헌책방** a secondhand bookstore.

헌칠하다 tall and handsome; slender as a lily(특히 여자가).

헌팅캡 a hunting cap(경마 기수용); a sports cap(일반적인 것).

헌혈(獻血) blood donation; donating blood. ¶집단 ~ group blood donation. **헌혈하다** donate[give] (one's) blood.
● **헌혈 운동** a blood (donation) drive[campaign]. **헌혈자** a blood donor.

헌화(獻花) 〔꽃을 바침〕 wreath-laying; a floral tribute. ¶영전에는 많은 ~가 바쳐졌다 Many flowers were offered to the spirit of the deceased. **헌화하다** lay wreaths[flowers] (at). ¶무명용사의 무덤에 ~ lay flowers[a wreath] on the tomb of the unknown soldier.
● **헌화식** a wreath-laying ceremony.

헐값(歇-) a giveaway[wretched] price. ¶~의 dirt-[dog-]cheap / cheap as dirt // ~으로 사다 buy (a thing) cheap as dirt / get (an article) for a mere song // ~으로 팔다 sell (something) for its scrap value / sell (an article) dirt-cheap // 그는 ~으로 우표 컬렉션을 팔아 버렸다 He sold his stamp collection dirt cheap[for a song]. // 그 자전거는 ~으로도 팔리지 않을 게다 That bicycle won't fetch much, if anything.

헐겁다 loose(-fitting); baggy; too large. ¶헐거운 웃옷 a loose coat // 무릎이 헐거운 바지 trousers baggy at the knees // 이 카디건은 내게 너무 ~ This cardigan is too big for me.

헐다¹ 〔부스럼 등이〕 form[develop] a boil; break out in sores; be inflamed. ¶무릎이 헐었다 I have got a boil on my knee. // 다친 데가 헐었다 The wound was inflamed.

헐다² 〔낡아지다〕 become[get] old; wear[be worn] out; (옷 등이) become shabby. ¶헐어빠진 블라우스 a tired-looking blouse // 헐어서 누더기가 되다 be worn to rags.

헐다³ 1 〔허물다〕 break[pull / take / tear] down (a house); demolish; destroy. ¶돌담을 ~ demolish a stone wall // 그 극장을 헐어서 회사의 건물 부지로 만들었다 The theater was torn down[demolished] to make room for an office building. 2 〔돈을 쓰다〕 break; change. ¶만 원짜리를 ~ break[change] a 10,000 won note (into small money).

헐다⁴ 〔헐뜯다〕 speak ill of; slander; defame. ¶뒷전에서 남을 헐어 말하다 speak ill of (a person) behind his back / backbite (a person).

헐떡거리다 pant; gasp (for breath); puff (and blow); breathe hard[heavily / with difficulty]; be out[short] of breath; be panting[gasping] for breath. ¶헐떡거리며 gasping(ly) / panting(ly) / between gasps / out of breath // 헐떡거리면서 말하다 gasp[puff / pant] out // 그는 숨을 헐떡거리며 5층까지 올라갔다 He climbed panting up to the fifth floor. // 그는 헐떡거리며 비탈을 올라갔다 He climbed the slope panting[breathing hard]. // 나는 헐떡거리며 정상을 향했다 Gasping for breath, I set out for the peak. // 우리는 헐떡거리며 학교로 달려갔다 We ran to school, panting.

헐떡헐떡 gasping and panting; puffing and blowing. **헐떡헐떡하다** pant; gasp (for breath). ⇨ =헐떡거리다

헐뜯다 revile; slander; speak ill of (a person); disparage; speak against (a person); paint (a person) black; (구어) run down. ¶뒷전에서 남을 헐뜯는 사람 a backbiter // 뒷전에서 남을 ~ backbite (a person) / speak ill of (a person) behind his back // 남의 성공을 ~ belittle [disparage / run down] other people's success // 비평가들은 그의 작품을 헐뜯었다 The critics disparaged [condemned / (문어) denigrated] his work. // 그는 내가 하는 일은 뭐든지 헐뜯는다 He runs down everything I do.

헐렁거리다 1 [헐거워서 흔들리다] be loose; fit [work] loose. ¶신이 ~ one's shoes fit loose. 2 [행동을 조심하지 않다] act [behave] carelessly [recklessly / imprudently].

헐렁이 a careless person; a harum-scarum; a scatterbrain.

헐렁하다 loose(-fitting); baggy. ¶헐렁한 티셔츠 a baggy T-shirt.

헐렁헐렁하다 1 [헐겁다] loose(-bodied) (coat); too large; baggy. ¶헐렁헐렁한 옷 baggy clothes // 헐렁헐렁한 바지 baggy [loose] trousers // 헐렁헐렁한 신 loose (-fitting) shoes // 이 스커트는 ~ This skirt is too big for me. 2 [행동이 들뜨다] all unstable; terribly unstable. ¶그는 ~ He is very unstable [pretty shaky].

헐레벌떡 [헐떡거리며] puffing and blowing; gasping and panting; out of breath; [황급히] hurry-scurry; helter-skelter. ¶~ 달려가다 run along panting and puffing // 계단을 ~ 내려가다 tumble [hurry] down the stairs. **헐레벌떡하다** puff and pant; gasp for breath; be out of breath.

헐레이션 [사진] halation. ¶태양광의 반사로 이 사진에 ~이 생겼다 There is a halation in this picture from reflected sunlight.

헐리다 be pulled [torn] down; be demolished [destroyed]. ¶헐리고 있는 건물 a building under demolition // 그 집은 헐렸다 The house was removed [cleared / pulled down].

헐벗다 1 [사람이 누더기를 입다] (서술적) be in rags. ¶헐벗은 아이들 poorly [shabbily] clothed children. 2 [나무가 없다] bare; bald. ¶헐벗은 산 a bare [bald] mountain.

헐하다 (歇-) 1 [값싸다] cheap; inexpensive; moderate [reasonable] in price. ¶헐한 물건 low-priced goods / a (good) bargain // 헐하게 cheap / at a bargain. 2 [쉽다] easy; simple; light. ¶헐한 일 an easy [a light] task / a soft job / 헐한 상대 a poor [weak] rival. 3 [가볍다] light; lenient. ¶헐한 벌 a mild [lenient / light] punishment.

험객 (險客) 1 [성질이 험악한 사람] a person of (a) rough disposition; a man of violent temper. 2 a foul-mouthed person. ⇨ 험구가 (⇨험구)

험구 (險口) an evil [a malicious / a wicked] tongue; abuse; (사람) a foul-mouthed person; a slanderer; a knocker; a carper. **험구하다** wag one's slanderous tongue (at); slander; speak ill of; abuse; curse.
●**험구가** a foul-mouthed person; a slanderer; a carper.

험난하다 (險難-) difficult; hard; arduous; tough; steep; precipitous. ¶험난한 길 a thorny path / the way of the Cross // (등산의) 험난한 코스 a dangerous trail [course] // 전도가 ~ There is rocky going ahead.

험담 (險談) abuse; (a) slander; calumny; [뒷전에서 하는 말] backbiting; malicious gossip; scandal. ¶~을 잘하는 사람 a scandalmonger / a backbiter. **험담하다** speak ill of (a person); talk scandal about; slander; abuse; calumniate; (뒷전에서) backbite. ¶그들은 남 험담하기를 좋아한다 They love gossip [to gossip].

험로 (險路) a rough [rugged] road; a breakneck road; a hard [steep] pass. ¶다음 마을까지는 정글을 뚫고 가는 ~였다 It was rough walking [a hard journey] through the jungle to the next village. // 그들은 ~로 이름난 길에 다다랐다 They came to a path noted for its ruggedness.

험산 (險山) a steep [precipitous] mountain.

험상궂다 (險狀-) terrible; horrible; threatening; ugly-looking.

험상스럽다 (險狀-) terrible; horrible. ⇨ =험상 궂다 ¶험상스런 얼굴을 하고 있다 have a forbidding countenance.

험악하다 (險惡-) dangerous; perilous; (날씨 등이) threatening (sky); stormy; (사태가) serious; critical; grave. ¶험악한 날씨 stormy [threatening / rough] weather // 험악한 형세 a critical [tense] situation // 험악한 얼굴 a threatening [menacing] look / an angry look // 험악한 얼굴로 보다 look darkly [sternly] at (a person) / survey (a person) with a stern look // 날씨가 ~ It is threatening weather. // 사태가 험악해졌다 The affair took on a bad [an ugly] look. // 회의의 분위기는 점점 험악해졌다 The mood of the conference gradually grew uglier. / Trouble seemed to be looming ahead at the conference.

험준하다 (險峻-) steep; precipitous; rugged; sheer. ¶험준한 산길 a steep [rugged] trail // 험준한 산맥 a rugged mountain range // 그 산은 험준하게 보였다 The mountain looked quite forbidding.

험하다 (險-) 1 steep; precipitous. ⇨ =험준하다 2 dangerous; perilous. ⇨ =험악하다 3 [거칠다] rough; rude; harsh. ¶험한 운동 [장난] a rough sport [play] // 험하게 다루다 handle roughly [in a rough manner] // 넌 참 양말을 험하게 신는구나 You're terribly hard on stockings.

헙수룩하다 1 (머리털이) unkempt; untrimmed; shaggy; bushy. ¶헙수룩한 머리 a mop of hair // 머리를 ~ have long unkempt hair. **헙수룩히** unkemptly; shaggily; bushily. 2 (옷차림이) shabby; poor-looking; seedy. ¶헙수룩한 옷차림을 하고 있다 be shabbily [poorly] dressed. **헙수룩히** shabbily; seedily.

헛간 (-間) a shed; a (storage) barn.

헛걸음하다 go on a bootless [fool's] errand; make a visit (on a person) in vain; make a fruitless call (on a person); make a trip for nothing. ¶그가 집에 없을지 모르지만, 헛걸음을 셈 치고 가 보는 것도 좋겠지 He may not be at home, but you might go just on chance.

헛것 useless work; a wasted effort. ⇨ =헛일

헛구역 (-口逆) [의] vomiturition. ¶~질하다 try to vomit in vain.

헛기침 clearing one's throat; a hem. **헛기침하다** clear one's throat; hem.

헛김 leakage air[steam]; an air leak.

헛김나다 get an air leak; [맥빠지다] be disappointed; be dispirited.

헛노릇 a fruitless[useless / vain] effort; waste labor. **헛노릇하다** make vain efforts; waste[lose] one's labor.

헛다리 짚다 bark up the wrong tree; guess wrong; make a wrong guess; misjudge; shoot at the wrong mark.

헛돈 money thrown away; wasted money. ¶~을 쓰다 waste[throw away] one's money (on).

헛돌다 skid; race; (기계 등이) run idle; idle.

헛되다 1 [보람이 뜻이 없다] vain; fruitless; ineffective; unavailing; futile; useless; (서술적) be in vain; be no good; come to nothing; prove fruitless. ¶헛된 노력 a vain[fruitless / useless] effort / 헛된 세상 the futile world // 헛된 죽음 useless death // 헛된 시도 a vain attempt // 헛된 꿈 an empty dream // 헛된 희망을 품다 have a vain hope / hope against hope (that ...) // 헛되지 않다 be worthwhile (to do) / be worth (doing) // 내 노력은 헛되지 않았다 I have not labored in vain. // 그녀의 노력은 헛되었다 Her efforts proved ineffective. // 그는 그것을 되찾으려고 했지만 헛된 일이었다 He tried in vain to get it back. // 여기서 단념하면 지금까지의 노력이 헛되고 만다 If you give up now, all your previous efforts will be[have been] in vain [come to nothing]. **헛되이** [무익하게] in vain; vainly; uselessly; to no purpose; [보람 없이] fruitlessly; futilely; to no avail; [목적도 없이] aimlessly; [한가롭게] idly. ¶~ 세월을 보내다 pass one's time idly / live in idleness / idle one's time away // ~ 일생을 보내다 loaf through life // ~ 돈을 쓰다 spend money uselessly / waste (one's) money // ~ 죽다 die a useless death / die to no purpose[in vain] 2 [허황하다] wild; groundless; false; untrue. ¶헛된 소문 a groundless[wild] rumor / a canard.

헛듣다 [잘못 듣다] hear (it / him) wrong [amiss]; mishear; misunderstand (what was said); [예사로 들어 넘기다] listen to (a person) in an absent sort of way; pay little [no] attention to (a person's talk). ¶헛들은 것이 아닌가 하고 다시 들어 보았다 I listened again, to make sure I had heard aright. // 그건 자네가 내 말을 헛들은 것이겠지 You must have misheard me. / You haven't heard me aright[rightly / correctly].

헛디디다 miss one's foot[step]; lose one's footing; make a false step; slide down (a cliff). ¶층계를 ~ miss one's footing on the stairs // 벼랑을 헛디디어 바다 속으로 떨어지다 step over the cliff into the sea // 발을 헛디딨다 My foot slipped. // 그는 계단을 헛디디어 떨어졌다 He missed[lost] his footing on the stairs and fell.

헛맹세 a false[an empty / an idle] pledge [vow]. **헛맹세하다** make a false[an empty] vow (that / to do).

헛물관 (-管) [식] a tracheid.

헛물켜다 exert oneself to no purpose; make vain efforts; catch at shadow.

헛발 1 [잘못 디딘 발]. ¶~ 디디다 take[make] a false step / tread on air. 2 [생] a pseudopodium. ⇨헛족

헛방 (-放) 1 [빗맞은 총질] a miss shot; a mis-hit; a wrong hit. 2 [실탄을 재지 않은 총탄] a blank shot[cartridge]. 3 [헛된 말] empty talk; (속어) gas; (속어) hot air.

헛방 (-房) a lumber room; a storeroom.

헛방귀 a gentle fart.

헛방놓다 (-放-) [빗맞히다] miss one's shot [the mark]; fail to hit; [공포를 쏘다] fire blank cartridges[shots]; [빈말하다] (미국 구어) talk through one's hat; (미국 속어) shoot the bull.

헛배 부르다 have gas in the stomach; be troubled with flatulence[tympanites]; feel flatulent; have a false sense of satiety.

헛보다 [잘못 보다] miss (seeing); mistake; [못 보고 넘어가다] fail to see[notice]; [허께 비로 보다] see (something) in a vision.

헛보이다 get improperly seen; be misviewed; get[be] mistaken.

헛소리 1 [혼미 중에 하는 소리] talking in delirium; delirious utterances. ¶고열로 ~를 하다 be in a delirious fever // 그녀는 고열로 ~를 하고 있었다 She talked wildly[She was delirious] because of a high fever. **헛소리하다** talk in delirium; utter ravings. 2 [허튼 말] a falsehood; a lie; idle words; an empty talk; nonsense. **헛소리하다** talk nonsense.

헛소문 (-所聞) a groundless[false] rumor; a canard. ¶~을 퍼뜨리다 set a false rumor afloat.

헛손질 a mishit. **헛손질하다** hit space; beat the air[wind].

헛수 (-手) (바둑·장기의) an ineffective [a wrong] move. ¶~를 두다 make an ineffective[a wrong] move.

헛수고 fruitless[useless / vain] efforts; waste of labor; lost labor. ¶~로 돌아가다 prove fruitless / end in a (mere) waste of labor // 난 ~만 했다 I had all my trouble for nothing. / I gained nothing for all my trouble[efforts]. // 그것은 ~였다 It proved fruitless. // 너는 애쓴 보람도 없이 ~만 할 것이다 You'll get nothing for your trouble. // 나는 결국 ~를 하고 말았다 All my efforts turned out to have been wasted[in vain]. // 그를 찾아갔지만 부재 중이어서 ~만 했다 He was out when I went to see him so it was a waste of effort [energy]. **헛수고하다** make vain efforts; work[labor] in vain; exert oneself to no purpose; lose one's labor. ¶공연히 헛수고하지 말게 Don't look for a needle in a haystack.

헛심 wasteful strength; a useless effort. ¶~을 쓰다 strain oneself in vain.

헛웃음 a feigned[an affected] laugh[smile]; a smirk; a (conscious) simper. ¶~을 치다 affect[feign] a laugh / put on a feigned smile / simper.

헛일 useless work; a wasted effort; waste of labor; lost labor. ¶~이다 be (of) no use / be of no avail / be useless / be in vain / be no good // 저 아이에게는 아무리 말해도 ~이다 No matter how many times you tell that child, it's useless[it will have no effect]. **헛일하다** do useless work; labor in vain; make vain efforts; lose one's labor; labor for nothing.

헛잠 [자는 체하는 잠] sham[feigned / pretended] sleep; a simulation of sleep; [선잠]

a nap; a catnap. ¶~을 자다 sham[feign] sleep / pretend to be asleep / play possum / (선잠을) take[have] a nap.

헛잡다 fail to catch[grasp]; miss catching; miss one's hold; let slip. ¶공을 ~ miss a ball / fail to catch a ball / fumble (a grounder)// 찻잔을 헛잡아 떨어뜨리다 let a cup slip and drop.

헛총(-銃) a blank cartridge; a blank shot.
헛총을 놓다 fire blank cartridges[shots]. ¶3발을 ~ fire three blank shots.
● **헛총질** blank firing.

헛코골다 pretend to snore; feign sleep by snoring.

헛헛증(-症) hungriness; chronic hunger. ¶~이 있다 suffer from limosis.

헛헛하다 (서술적) be[feel] hungry.

헝겊 a piece of cloth; a patch; rags.
● **헝겊 조각** a small piece of cloth; a scrap of cloth. ¶~을 기워서 이불을 만들었다 I made a patchwork quilt with odds and ends of cloth.

헝클다 tangle; entangle; ravel; dishevel. ¶머리를 ~ dishevel one's hair // 실을 ~ tangle thread.

헝클어지다 tangle; get[become] tangled; be entangled; be in a tangle. ¶헝클어진 머리 tangled[matted] hair / disheveled[unkempt] hair // 헝클어진 실을 풀다 unravel [unloose] tangled thread // 그녀는 헝클어진 머리를 하고 문 앞에 나타났다 She came to the door with disheveled hair.

헤 ¶입을 ~ 벌리고 with one's mouth wide open / agape // 입을 ~ 벌리다 open one's mouth wide / gape // 입을 ~ 벌리고 쳐다보다 stare with open mouth (at) / gape (at).

헤게모니 hegemony. ¶~ 싸움 strife over hegemony / ~를 잡다 hold hegemony.

헤근거리다 become[get] loose; shake; be shaky[rickety / unstable].

헤근헤근 in a tottering[shaking] manner; unstably. ¶사개가 ~ 놀다 dovetails wobble.
헤근헤근하다 become loose. ⇨ 헤근거리다

헤다 wash out; rinse. ⇨ 행구다

헤드라이트 a headlight. ¶~를 켠 headlighted (car) / ~를 켜다[끄다] turn on[off] the headlight.

헤드라인 a headline.

헤드폰 a headphone.

헤딩 [축구] heading. ¶~으로 슛을 성공시키다 head the ball into the opponent's net. **헤딩하다** head (the ball).

헤뜨러지다 be[get] scattered (about); be dispersed; disperse; be littered (up). ¶사방으로 ~ disperse in all directions.

헤뜨리다 scatter; strew; disperse; put in disorder; clutter. ¶방 안에 종이쪽지를 ~ litter a room with scraps of paper // 닭이 모이를 헤뜨렸다 Chickens scattered their feed.

헤로인 [약] heroin.
● **헤로인 중독** heroinism. ¶그는 ~에 걸려 있다 He is addicted to heroin.

헤르니아 [의] hernia. (*pl.* ~s, -niae).

헤르츠 a hertz(약어 Hz).

헤르쿨레스자리 [천] Hercules.

헤매다 1 [돌아다니다] wander[roam / knock] about; hover (about / in); stray about(길을 잃고). ¶여기저기를 ~ wander from place to place // 들판을 ~ wander over[roam about] the field // 거리를 ~ wander about in the street // 생사지경을 ~ hover[linger] between life and death // 숲 속을 정처 없이 ~ stray aimlessly through the wood // 길을 잃고 숲 속 깊이 ~ miss one's way and wonder deep into the forest // 그는 여기저기를 여러 해 동안 헤맨 끝에 여기에 정착했다 He finally settled down here after years of roaming (about). // 어머니는 5일 동안이나 생사의 갈림길을 헤매고 계신다 My mother has been in critical condition[hovering between life land death] for five days.
2 [어찌할 바를 모르다] be puzzled[perplexed] (what to do); be at a loss (what to do); be quite embarrassed.

헤모글로빈 [생] hemoglobin.

헤무르다 (사물이) soft; flabby; flaccid; (사람이) weak; feeble; weak-kneed. ¶헤무른 사람 a weak[feeble] person / a weak-spirited [weak-hearted / fainthearted] person.

헤묽다 watery; (wishy-)washy; sloppy; thin (porridge).

헤벌어지다 open[be opened] wide; (서술적) be agape (with joy) (입이).

헤벌쭉하다 wide open; agape(입이).

헤브라이즘 Hebraism.

헤비급(-級) (권투 등의) the heavyweight division[class].
● **헤비급 선수** a heavyweight.

헤비메탈 [음] heavy metal.

헤비스모커 a heavy smoker.

헤살 hindrance; interference; disturbance. ¶~을 놓다[부리다] thwart / hinder / interfere with (a person) / disturb / throw an obstacle in (another's) path / put[thrust] a spoke in (another's) wheel // 계획에 ~을 놓다 thwart (a person's) plan // 남의 출세에 ~을 놓다 stand in the way of another's promotion[advancement] // 재수 없게 ~이 끼었는걸 What a provoking interference!
● **헤살꾼** a slanderer; an obstructionist.

헤식다 [무르다] brittle; soft; weak; infirm; feeble; flabby; fragile; crumbly; unenergetic; sluggish ¶헤식은 쌀 soft rice / 헤식은 사람 a person of weak constitution / a person who lacks vitality.

헤실바실 1 [모르는 사이에] inadvertently running out of; frittering away. ¶~ 없어지다 run out[be used up] before one is aware of it // 돈을 ~ 다 써 버리다 fritter away all the money one has. 2 [일하는 것이 흐지부지하여] indifferently; halfheartedly. ¶~ 일하다 scamp[fudge] one's work.

헤아리다 1 [신중히 생각하다] consider (a matter); think over (a matter); ponder on (a problem); deliberate. ¶(앞뒤를) 잘 헤아린 뒤에 after due[careful] consideration / 일을 잘 헤아려서 하다 undertake a plan with due consideration // 앞날을 헤아리지 않으면 머지 않아 우환이 따르기 마련이다 Lack of consideration for the distant future is sure to be followed by trouble in the near future.
2 [추측하다] guess; conjecture; see through; fathom; sound; plumb. ¶헤아릴 수 없는 깊이 unfathomable[immeasurable] depth // 남의 마음을 ~ fathom (a person's) heart / enter into another's feeling / (동정하다) sympathize with (a person) / (의도를) 알아차리다 read (a person's) mind // 복잡한 사정을 ~ understand the complicated circumstances // 남의 기분을 ~ understand a person's

feelings.∥그의 참뜻은 헤아리기 어렵다 I find it difficult to surmise what he really means. ∥그는 남의 마음을 통찰하여 잘 헤아린다 He is a good mind reader. / He is good at guessing what other people are thinking.∥그의 말투로 헤아려 보면 그는 명문대가 출신인 것 같다 Judging from the way he talks, I gather [presume] (that) he is from a distinguished family.∥그의 안색에서 헤아려 보건대 그가 실패한 모양이다 From the way he looks, I would say [it would appear] that he failed.∥심상치 않은 낌새를 헤아려(알아채고) 그는 잠자리에서 벌떡 일어났다 Sensing that something was wrong, he leaped out of bed.∥저는 충심으로 댁의 심중을 헤아릴 수 있습니다 I sympathize with you very much. / I feel for you very deeply.∥그녀의 심중을 헤아리면 그냥 잠자코 있을 수는 없다 Knowing how she feels, I cannot possibly stand idly by.∥그녀의 고충은 헤아리고도 남음이 있다 I can just imagine how hurt she must be.∥사람의 마음에는 헤아릴 수 없는 무엇이 있다 There is something inscrutable [unfathomable] in men's hearts.∥그는 화학의 발전에 헤아릴 수 없이 많은 기여를 했다 He contributed immensely to the development of chemistry.∥그의 진정한 의도를 헤아릴 수 없다 I cannot make out his true intentions.
3 [수량을 세다] count; calculate; estimate; amount to; come up to. ¶헤아릴 수 없는 incomputable / incalculable / immeasurable / inestimable ¶수(數)를 ~ count [estimate] the number∥얼마나 많은 사람이 그 약의 혜택을 입고 있는지 헤아릴 수 없다 Innumerable people have benefited from that medicine.∥그에게는 헤아릴 수 없을 만큼 많은 신세를 졌다 The debt of gratitude I owe him is beyond measure.∥그러한 예는 헤아릴 수 없이 많다 There are countless [numerous] instances like that.

헤어나다 escape from (danger); get out of (a predicament); extricate oneself from (difficulties); free oneself from (a bondage); find one's way out of (a fix). ¶위기에서 ~ get through [tide over] a crisis∥난관 [어려움]에서 ~ get out of trouble / find one's way out of difficulty [a scrape] / tide over a difficulty∥슬럼프에서 ~ pull oneself out of the slump∥파돈 한 닢 없지만 무슨 헤어날 방도가 있겠지 I'm stone-broke, but I think I can get by somehow.

헤어네트 a hairnet.

헤어드라이어 a hair dryer. ¶~로 머리를 말리다 dry one's hair with a dryer.

헤어브러시 a hairbrush. ¶~로 머리를 빗다 brush one's hair.

헤어스타일 a hairstyle; (여성의) a hairdo. ¶~을 바꾸다 change one's hairdo [hairstyle / haircut] (▶ haircut는 머리의 커트 방법을 바꾸는 일)∥어떤 ~로 하겠습니까 How do you want to have your hair done?

헤어스프레이 hair spray. ¶~를 뿌리다 spray one's hair.

헤어지다 1 [이별하다] part (from / with); separate; be separated (from); be parted (from); [이혼하다] divorce oneself (from). ¶아내와 ~ divorce one's wife∥헤어질 때에 on [at] parting / when [as] one parts from (a friend)∥서로 헤어져 살다 live separately / live apart from each other∥둘은 서로 싸우고 헤어졌다 They quarreled with each other [had a falling out] and split up.∥나는 그 사람과 역에서 헤어졌다 I parted from him at the station. / I said good-bye to him at the station.∥그는 헤어질 때 그녀의 손을 꼭 잡았다 He grasped her hands at parting.∥그와 헤어진 지 꽤 오래 된다 It's such a long time since I saw him last.
2 [흩어지다] break up; disperse; be scattered. ¶삼삼오오 헤어져서 가다 disperse by twos and threes∥졸업생들은 각처로 헤어졌다 The graduates were scattered in all directions.∥동기생들은 뿔뿔이 헤어져 있다 The graduates in my class are now scattered all over [far and wide].

헤어 토닉 hair tonic. ¶~을 바르다 apply hair tonic to one's hair.

헤어핀 a hairpin; (미) a bobby pin.

헤엄 swimming; a swim; a swimming stroke. ¶개 ~ the dog paddle∥~ 잘 치는 사람 a good swimmer∥~을 잘 치다 swim well / be a good swimmer / be good at swimming∥~을 잘 못 치다 be a poor swimmer∥풀에서 ~을 치다 take a swim in a pool. **헤엄하다** swim; have a swim.

헤엄치다 swim; have a swim. ¶어린이를 풀에서 헤엄치게 하다 let the children swim in the pool∥물가로 헤엄쳐 가다 swim to shore [ashore]∥강을 헤엄쳐 건너다 swim across a river.∥흐름을 거슬러 헤엄쳐 올라가다 swim against the current∥시류를 타고[거슬러] ~ swim with [against] the current.∥나는 전혀 헤엄칠 줄 모른다 I cannot swim a stroke.∥헤엄치지 마시오 (게시) No swimming.∥헤엄치는 법을 좀 가르쳐 다오 Teach [Show] me how to swim.

헤적이다 (찾으려고) ransack; rummage (in); [파헤치다] stir [dig] up (the mud); [흩뜨리다] scatter (about); disperse. ¶서류를 ~ rummage among papers∥공을 찾느라 수풀을 ~ rummage the thicket to search a ball.

헤죽거리다 swing one's arms as one goes [walks].

헤죽헤죽 walking briskly swinging one's arms. **헤죽헤죽하다** swing one's arms as one goes. ⇨**헤죽거리다**

헤집다 dig up [over]; turn up; tear up. ¶닭들이 벌레를 찾아 흙을 헤집고 있다 Hens are scratching the ground for worms.

헤치다 1 [파헤치다] dig up; turn up. ¶무덤을 ~ open [violate] a grave / dig [lay] a grave open∥흙을 ~ dig up earth∥나는 쓰레기를 헤치고 잃어버린 물건을 찾아냈다 I searched through the debris and found what I had lost.
2 [흩어 버리다] scatter; disperse; break up. ¶모인 사람을 ~ disperse a crowd.
3 [좌우로 물리치다] push aside; make one's way (through); plow [edge / push / work / elbow] one's way (through). ¶인파를 헤치고 나아가다 push [elbow / thrust] one's way through the crowd∥배가 물결을 헤치고 나아갔다 The boat plowed through the waves.∥잉어가 물을 헤치고 뛰어올랐다 A carp broke the water.∥나는 극도의 가난을 헤쳐 나갔다 I clawed my way up from extreme poverty.∥그는 인파를 헤치고 나아갔다 He wriggled [worked] his way through the crowd.

헤프다 1 (물건이) not durable; soon used up; (서술적) do not stand long use [give a long service]; do not last long; go fast. ¶요새 돈이 ~ Money doesn't go far these days.∥이 비누는 ~ This soap doesn't last long. **2** (씀씀이가) uneconomical; wasteful; prodigal; unthrifty. ¶돈을 헤프게 쓰다 be too free with one's money / be wasteful of money / be careless with money. **헤피** uneconomically; unthriftily; wastefully. ¶돈을 ~ 쓰다 spend money wastefully. **3** (몸가짐이) loose; dissolute; dissipated. ¶몸가짐이 헤픈 여자 a loose [fast] woman. **4** (말이) talkative; voluble; glib-tongued. ¶그는 말이 ~ He speaks too much.

헥타르 a hectare(기호 ha).
헥토그램 a hectogram.
헥토리터 a hectoliter.
헥토미터 a hectometer.
헥토파스칼 a hectopascal.
헬기(-機) a helicopter. ⇨=헬리콥터
헬레니즘 Hellenism. ¶~ (양식)의 Hellenistic∥~풍으로 하다 [되다] Hellenize.
헬륨 [화] helium(기호 He).
헬리콥터 a helicopter; (속어) a copter; (미국속어) a chopper; an egg beater. ¶~로 가다 helicopter (off) (to) ∥ ~로 운반되다 be transported by helicopter / be helicoptered (to)∥그는 ~를 타고 현장으로 날아갔다 He flew to the scene by[in a] helicopter. / He helicoptered to the scene.
헬리포트 a heliport. ¶우리는 옥상의 ~에 내렸다 We landed at the heliport on the roof.
헬멧 a helmet; (오토바이 타는 사람의) a crash helmet; (공장에서 쓰는) a hard hat.
헬스클럽 a health club.
헷갈리다 [갈피를 못 잡다] be hardly distinguishable (from); hardly tell[discriminate] (A from B); [머리가 혼란하다] be thrown into confusion; be confused[perplexed]. ¶머리가 헷갈린다 I'm getting confused. / (미국속어) My head is buzzy.∥어느 게 어느 건지 헷갈린다 I can't tell which is which.∥A와 B는 다른 것이니까 헷갈리지 말아야 한다 A is one thing, B is another. You must discriminate between them.
헹가래 tossing (a person); hoisting (a person) shoulder-high. ¶~를 치다 hoist (a person) shoulder-high / toss∥그들은 감독을 ~ 쳤다 They tossed the manager shoulder-high into the air.
헹구다 wash out; rinse; give (a thing) a rinse [swill]. ¶빨래를 ~ rinse laundry in clean water after washing ∥ 맑은 물로 ~ rinse a thing (in clear water)∥접시를 뜨거운 물에 ~ rinse a plate in hot water∥머리를 감으면 잘 헹구어라 Give your hair a good rinse after washing it. / Rinse all the soap out of your hair after you wash it.∥차 껍질이 남지 않도록 찻주전자를 헹구어라 Rinse all the tea leaves out of the teapot.∥잘 헹구지 않으면 세탁물에서 비누 냄새가 난다 If you don't rinse (out) the wash well, it will smell of soap.
혀 1 (사람의) a tongue; (동물의) a lingua. ¶~를 깨물다 bite one's tongue∥~가 까칠까칠하다 My tongue is rough[furry].∥~가 아리다 My tongue is tingling[burning].∥~를 내미십시오 Stick out your tongue. **2**⇒서¹

혀(가) 꼬부라지다 be tongue-tied; have an impediment in one's speech. ¶혀가 꼬부라져 아무 말도 할 수 없었다 I was tongue-tied.

혀를 굴리다 1 [무심코 말을 하다] make a slip of the tongue(실언하다); blurt out(비밀 등을). **2** [「ㄹ」소리를 내다] trill (the "r").
혀를 내두르다 ¶그의 노래에는 동급생들도 혀를 내둘렀다 His classmates were filled with admiration for his singing.∥그의 먹성이 좋은 것에 그녀는 혀를 내둘렀다 She was astounded at his appetite.
혀를 내밀다 [비웃다] laugh at. ¶그녀는 그의 등 뒤에서 혀를 내밀었다 She laughed at him [made a fool of him] behind his back.
혀를 놀리다 make a slip of the tongue; blurt out.
혀를 차다 click[clack] one's tongue; tut; be wonder-struck. ¶혀를 차는 소리 a tongue-clicking sound / a click[clack] of the tongue / (못마땅하여) Tut, tut∥그는 마음에 들지 않아 혀를 찼다 He clucked his tongue in disapproval.∥그는 그 제의에 혀를 찼다 He tutted the proposal(▶ 불찬성을 나타냄).
혀꼬부랑이 an inarticulate person; a person with a speech impediment.
혀끝 (혀의 끝) the tip of the tongue.
혀끝에서 뱅뱅 돌다 [어떤 말이 생각날 듯 말 듯하다] be on[at] the tip of one's tongue. ¶그의 이름이 ~ His name is on the tip of my tongue.
혀끝에 오르내리다 be talked about by people; be on the tongues of people.
혀뿌리 [생] the root of the tongue; the lingual radix.
혀옆소리 [언] a lateral (sound).
혀짤배기 a lisper; a tongue-tied person. ¶~의 lisping (child) / tongue-tied∥~ 어린이 a lisping child∥~소리를 하다 lisp (out) / speak with a lisp∥그녀는 ~소리를 한다 She speaks with a lisp. / She lisps.
혁대(革帶) a leather belt.
● **혁대 고리** a buckle; a clasp; a clamp.
혁명(革命) a revolution; [특히 무력에 의한 정부 전복] a coup d'état (pl. coups d'état). ¶무력 ~ an armed revolution∥무혈 ~ a bloodless revolution∥**사회** ~ a social revolution∥**산업** ~ an industrial revolution / [역] the Industrial Revolution∥**평화** ~ a pacific revolution∥**폭력** ~ a revolution by force[violence]∥**프랑스** ~ the French Revolution∥~**적(인)** revolutionary (ideas)∥**명예** ~ (영국의) the Glorious Revolution∥~을 일으키다 start[bring about] a revolution∥~이 일어났다 A revolution broke out.∥그 발명은 근대 사회에 일대 ~을 가져왔다 The invention caused[brought about] a tremendous revolution in modern society. / The invention revolutionized modern society. **혁명하다** revolutionize.
● **혁명가** a revolutionist; a revolutionary. **혁명군** a revolutionary army.
혁신(革新) [사회적·정치적 개혁] (a) reform; [쇄신] (an) innovation. ¶**기술** ~ technical innovation∥**자기** ~ **운동** the self-reform drive∥~**적(인)** innovative / [진보적] progressive∥~**적인 사상** a progressive[an innovative] idea∥**정치의 대** ~**을 행하다** make [(문어) effect] great reforms in politics∥**전술에 일대** ~**을 가져오다** bring about a revolution in the art of war. **혁신하다** reform; make a reform (in); renovate; innovate. ¶낡은 제도를 ~ reform an old system∥회사는 많은 기술을 혁신했다 The company has put

through many technical improvements.
● 혁신 세력 the progressive force; the progressive political group. 혁신 정당 a progressive party; a reformist (political) party. 혁신주의 progressivism. 혁신파 a reformist group. ¶그는 ~이다 He is a reformer. / He has progressive ideas.

혁혁하다 (赫赫-) splendid (reputation); brilliant (victory); glorious (exploit); distinguished (service). ¶혁혁한 승리를 거두다 win a glorious [brilliant] victory // 혁혁한 전과를 거두다 achieve brilliant war results. **혁혁히** splendidly; brilliantly; gloriously; distinguishedly.

현 (弦) **1** a bowstring. ⇨ "활시위 **2** [수] a chord(호의); a subtense(사선); a hypotenuse(직각 삼각형의 빗변). **3** [천] (달의) a quarter.

현 (絃) [현악기에서 소리 내는 줄] a string; a chord. ¶4~의 악기 a four-stringed instrument // 바이올린의 ~을 매다 string a violin (a bow) // 가야금의 ~을 죄다 tighten a string of a *gayageum* // ~을 퉁기다 strum the strings.

현 (舷) the sides of a boat. ⇨ "뱃전"

현 (現) [현재의] current; present; [현직의] incumbent. ¶~ 시점에서는 at present / at this point in time // ~ 시대 the present age // ~ 정부 the present [existing] Government // ~ 주민 present inhabitants [residents] // ~ 시장 the incumbent mayor.

현가 (現價) the current price.

현격하다 (懸隔-) far [wide] apart (from); widely different (from). ¶현격한 차이 a great disparity // 차이 a wide difference [gap] // 그의 영어 실력은 다른 학생에 비해 현격하게 뛰어났다 His ability in English is far better than [far superior to] that of the other students. / Of all the students, he is by far [far and away] the best in English. / (구어) He is way ahead of the other students in English. // 둘 사이에는 현격한 차이가 있다 There is a marked difference between the two. // 빈부의 차가 현격하지 않다 The gulf between rich and poor is not very wide.

현관 (玄關) [입구] the entrance; the porch (way); the (front) door. ¶~으로 들어가다 enter at the front door // 자동차를 ~에 대다 drive a motorcar up to the door // ~으로 들어와 주십시오 Please go [come] in by the front door.

현교 (懸橋) a suspension bridge. ⇨ "현수교(⇨ 현수)

현군 (賢君) a wise lord [king].

현금 (現今) the present time [day]; these days; now; nowadays. ¶~의 present(-day) / current / of today // ~에는 now / at the present time / today / nowadays / (in) these days // ~의 세계 정세 the current [present] world situation.

현금 (現金) cash; cold [hard] cash (▶ 수표나 카드 결제가 아닌 현금); [현재 있는 금전] actual [ready] money; [정금(正金)] specie; [맞돈] prompt [spot] cash; ready funds. ¶~이 필요 없는 cashless // 100만 원을 ~으로 지불하다 pay one million won in (hand) cash // ~이 부족하다 be [run] short of cash // ~이 없다 be out of cash // ~으로 치르다 pay in cash / present ready money / (미) pay down // ~으로 거래하다 deal in cash / conduct business on a cash / conduct business on a cash basis // ~으로 사다 [팔다] buy [sell] (a thing) for cash // 나는 반은 ~, 반은 월부로 지불했다 I paid half down, and the balance in monthly installments. // ~만 받음 Cash Only. // ~으로 1만 파운드 준비해 주게 Have 10,000 pounds ready in cash. // 지불은 ~입니까 Are you paying in cash? // 그것이라면 수중에 있는 ~으로 살 수 있다 I can buy that with the cash I have in hand. // 우리는 ~이 바닥났다 We are out of cash. // 이 수표를 ~으로 바꾸고 싶습니다 I'd like to have this check cashed. / I'd like to cash this check. // ~을 가지고 다닐 필요가 없는 시대가 한국에도 왔다 The time has come in Korea, too, when we don't have to carry cash with us any more.

● 현금 거래 a cash transaction; cash business. 현금 보유고 cash in [(미) on] hand. 현금 인출기 / 현금 자동 지급기 an automatic teller machine(약어 ATM); a cash dispenser. 현금 카드 a cash card. 현금화 encashment. ¶~하다 (수표 등을) encash / cash (in) (a check) / convert (a bond) (into cash) / (증권을) realize / liquidate (one's securities) // ~할 수 있는 liquid / (미) quick.

현기증 (眩氣症) giddiness; dizziness; [의] (a) vertigo (*pl.* ~s). ¶산후(産後) ~ puerperal vertigo // ~이 날 것 같은 절벽 a giddy precipice // ~이 나는 높이에서 at a giddy [dizzy(ing)] height (from the ground) // ~이 나다 grow [be] dizzy [giddy] // 때때로 ~이 나다 have frequent dizzy spells / be subject to attacks of vertigo // 일어설 때 ~이 나다 feel [get] dizzy [giddy] on standing up // 나는 병이 나기 전에 자주 ~이 일어나곤 했었다 I had frequent spells of dizziness [giddiness] before I became ill. // 숙취 때문인지 나는 ~이 난다 [머리가 빙빙 돈다] My head is swimming; I think I've got a hangover. // 그는 ~을 느껴 웅크렸다 He felt dizzy and squatted down. // 강한 햇살에 나는 ~이 났다 I was dazzled by the bright light.

현대 (現代) the present age [day / generation]; modern times; today. ¶~의 present-day / contemporary / present / current / of our time / modern / of the day // ~에 있어서 in our time // ~의 중요한 과제 important issues of the day // ~의 생활 the jostling life of today // ~의 한국 modern [contemporary] Korea / (the) present-day Korea / Korea (of) today.

● 현대극 a modern play; a drama of present-day life. 현대 문학 contemporary [current] literature. 현대 사상 modern ideas [thought]; modernism. 현대어 a living [modern] language. 현대 영어 present-day [up-to-date] English. 현대인 a modern; (집합적) the moderns. 현대 작가 modern [contemporary] writers. 현대주의 modernism. 현대풍 the present [latest / up-to-date] fashion; the modern style [fashion]; modernism. ¶~으로 in the modern style / up-to-date // ~으로 in the present fashion [style] / fashionably. 현대화 modernization; updating. ¶~하다 modernize / update / [현대풍으로 되다] be modernized // 완전히 ~하다 be completely modernized.

현대적 (現代的) modern(-type); modernistic

현상

up-to-date; up-to-the-minute. ¶~ 건물 a building in modern style // ~으로 in a modern style / along[on] modern lines // 아버지는 나이에 어울리지 않게 아주 ~인 분입니다 My father is quite modern[(구어) with it] for a man his age.

현란하다(絢爛-) gorgeous; brilliant; dazzling; (문체 등이) flowery; ornate; florid; gaudy. ¶현란한 문체 a flowery[richly ornate] style // 현란한 채색 rich[brilliant] coloring[(영) colouring] // 현란하여 눈이 부신 광경 a spectacle[sight]of dazzling gorgeousness // 그 현란함에는 눈이 부실 지경이었다 We were all dazzled by its brilliance. // 왕비는 현란한 의상을 입고 있었다 The queen was gorgeously[dazzlingly] dressed.

현명하다(賢明-) wise; clever; intelligent; (미) smart(▶ wise는 현명한, clever는 재치 있는, 때로는 교활하다는 뜻도 있음. intelligent, smart는 높은 지능을 가진. 단, intelligent는 고도의 지성이라는 느낌을 주는 데 비해, smart는 구어적); (분별 있다) judicious; sensible; prudent; discreet; well-advised. ¶현명한 방책 a wise policy // 현명한 사람 a wise man / an intelligent person / a man of intelligence // 현명한 조치를 취하다 adopt a wise policy // 현명하지 못한 ill-considered / injudicious / inadvisable / ill-advised / unwise // 현명하게 처신하다 act wisely [sensibly] // 그 방법은 현명한 방법이라고는 할 수 없다 That's not a wise[clever] way of doing it. // 그것을 알아차렸다니 정말 현명하구나 How clever of you to notice that! // 그는 현명하게 처신하여 많은 동지를 만들었다 He maneuvered cleverly and won many people over to his side. // 왕복 차표를 사 둔 것은 현명했어 It was wise of you to have gotten a round-trip[(영) return] ticket. // 당장 사과하는 것이 현명하다고 생각해 I think it's advisable[it would be wise] for you to apologize to him at once. // 선생에게 상의한 것은 현명한 일이었다 It was wise of him to consult his teacher. // 그것은 현명한 해결 방법이 아니다 That's no way to solve the problem. / That's not a sensible way to solve the problem. // 그렇게 하는 것이 과연 현명할까 몰라 I can't help wondering if we are wise to do so.

현모(賢母) a wise mother.
●**현모양처** a wise mother and good wife. ¶~가 되다 make a good wife.

현몽하다(現夢-) appear in one's dream; appear[come] to one in a dream.

현묘하다(玄妙-) abstruse; occult; recondite; mysterious; miraculous; [포착하기 힘들다] subtle (meaning).

현무암(玄武巖) [지] basalt; whinstone. ¶~의 basaltic.

현물(現物) [실물] the (actual) thing[article]; [거래에서 즉시 매매할 수 있는 물품] spot goods; spots. ¶~을 보지 않고 ~로 지불하다 pay (taxes) in kind // ~을 보지 않고 결정할 수 없습니다 I cannot decide unless I see the goods[actual article]. // 대금은 ~과 교환으로 지불하겠습니다 I will pay for it on delivery. // 나는 빚을 ~로 갚았다 I paid my debt in kind.
●**현물 가격** spot prices. **현물 거래** spot trading; spot transaction(물산の). **현물 인도** delivery of my goods. **현물 출자** investment in kind.

현미(玄米) unpolished[uncleaned / unmilled] rice; (구어) brown rice.
●**현미기**(-機) a (rice) huller; a husker. **현미빵** bread made of wheat flour mixed with whole rice flour.

현미경(顯微鏡) a microscope. ¶고배율 ~ a powerful[huge-power(ed)] microscope // 복합 ~ a compound microscope // 쌍안 ~ a binocular microscope // ~전자 an electron microscope // ~적(인) microscopic (exactness) // ~적 유기체 a microscopic organism // ~적으로 microscopically // ~으로 보다 look at a thing through a microscope / see a thing under a microscope // ~의 초점을 맞추다 focus a microscope (on / upon) // ~으로 조사하다 examine (a thing) with a[the] microscope / inspect (a thing) microscopically // 천 배의 ~으로 조사하다 examine a thing under a microscope with a magnification of 1,000.
●**현미경 분석** microscopic analysis. **현미경 사진** a microphotograph; a photomicrograph; microphotography; photomicrography.

현부(賢婦) a wise[sagacious] woman.

현부인(賢夫人) a wise wife; [남의 부인] your wife.

현사(賢士) a wise man[scholar]; a sage.

현상(現狀) the present state[situation]; the present[existing] condition[state of things]; the existing state[circumstances]; the status quo. ¶~으로는 under (the) existing circumstances / under (the) present conditions / as matters stand // ~ 그대로 in status quo / as (it) is // ~에 만족하다 be content with things as they are // ~을 유지하다 maintain the status quo // 경제의 ~에서 볼 때 감세는 무리이다 With economic conditions as they are now, it will be difficult to reduce taxes.
●**현상 유지** maintenance of the status quo. **현상 타파** destruction of the status quo.

현상(現象) a phenomenon (pl. -na); an appearance (in the sky); [사건] a happening; [국면] a phase. ¶자연[사회] ~ a natural[social] phenomenon // 물리 ~ a physical phenomenon // 언어 ~ phenomena of language // 사회 발달에 있어서의 일시적 ~ a passing phase in the development of society // 단순한 ~에 사로잡히지 않고 사물의 본질을 살피다 look into the true nature of a thing instead of looking merely at its surface // 이상한 ~이 일어났다 A strange phenomenon occurred[was observed]. // 그것은 사춘기의 일시적인 ~이다 That is a passing phase of adolescence. // 이번 사건은 황금만능의 세태가 낳은 ~이다 This incident reflects an aspect [is characteristic] of the present world where money is everything.
●**현상학** phenomenology.

현상(現像) [사진] developing; development. **현상하다** develop (a negative / (a) film). ¶필름을 현상하여 인화하다 develop (and print) a film. → ¶너무[덜] 현상된 필름 overdeveloped [underdeveloped] film.
●**현상실 / 현상소** a processing laboratory. **현상액** a developing solution; a developer. **현상지**(-紙) developing-out paper(약어 D.O.P.).

현상(懸賞) 〔상품·상금 등을 걸기〕 a prize contest [competition]; offer of a prize [reward]. ¶소설의 ~ 모집 a prize novel competition.
● **현상 광고** an advertisement for a prize contest; a prize ad. **현상금** prize money; a reward; a prize (on his head). ¶~이 붙은 with a prize offered // ~을 걸다 offer a prize [reward] (for) / (범인 등에) set[put] a price on (an offender's head) // ~을 타다 win [carry off] a prize (in a contest) // 지명 수배자에게 1만 달러의 ~이 걸려 있다 A reward of 10,000 dollars is being offered for the wanted man. // 잃어버린 아이에 대한 정보 제공자에게 500만 원의 ~을 드립니다 A reward of five hundred thousand won is offered for information about the lost child. **현상 논문** a prize essay. **현상 소설** a prize novel. ¶~ 응모 작품은 20편이나 되었다 There were as many as twenty entries for the (prize) novel contest.

현세(現世) **1** 〔지금 세상〕 this (present) world; the transient life; 〔불〕 the land of the living; this life. ¶~의 worldly / earthly / temporal / 〔속세의〕 secular // ~의 쾌락 temporal [worldly] pleasures // ~와 내세 this world and the next. **2** the alluvial period. ⇨="충적세(㊂충적)
● **현세주의** secularism.

현세(現勢) 〔현재의 정세〕 the present state (of affairs); the current [existing] situation [circumstances]; 〔현재의 세력〕 the present strength (of a party).

현손(玄孫) a great-great-grandson.

현수(懸垂) **1** 〔아래로 늘어짐〕 hanging; suspending. **2** 〔현수 운동〕 〔철봉의〕 chinning exercises.
● **현수교** 〔매달아 놓은 다리〕 a suspension bridge. **현수막** (극장의) a drop curtain; (거리·건물의) a banner; (방 등의) a hanging screen; a curtain; 〔플래카드〕 a placard. **환영 ~** welcoming banners // ~을 내걸다 put up a placard // 옥상에 대출 ~이 걸려 있다 There was a banner hanging from the roof advertising a big sale.

현숙하다(賢淑-) wise and virtuous.

현시(現時) the present time; today; now. ¶~와 같은 (때에) in times like the present.

현시(顯示) (a) revelation; (a) manifestation (of God's power); 〔가〕 exposure. ¶**성체 ~** the exposure of the Host // 그는 자기 ~욕이 강하다 He likes to make himself conspicuous. **현시하다** show; unfold; be revealed; uncover; unveil; open out.

현신(賢臣) a wise retainer [vassal].

현신하다(現身-) present oneself before a superior; put in one's appearance; appear.

현실(現實) actuality; the actual; the realities of life; a hard fact(공론(空論)에 대하여). ¶~의[로] actual(ly) / real(ly) // ~의 문제로서 as a matter of fact // 가혹한 ~ grim[hard / harsh] realities // 답답한 ~ heavy actualities // ~에 눈뜨다 awake to realities // ~로 되다 become reality // ~의 냉혹함을 직시하다 face up to the cold, hard facts of the situation // ~에 입각하여 계획을 세우다 plan practically [on a realistic basis] // 그 해결책은 ~에 맞지 않는다 The solution is inconsistent with reality. // 그의 생각은 ~과 동떨어져 있다 His ideas are out of touch with reality. // 계획을 세울 때는 ~에 입각해야 한다 You must have your feet on the ground when you make plans.
● **현실감** the sense for the real. **현실 도피** escape from reality. **현실성** actuality; reality. **현실주의** actualism; realism. **현실주의자** an actualist; a realist. **현실화** actualization; realization; materialization. ¶~하다 actualize / realize / materialize / (물가 등을) readjust (prices) to a realistic level // 그는 계획을 ~했다 He carried out[realized] his plan.

현실적(現實的) realistic; materialistic. ¶~인 사람 a realistic person // 네 생각은 ~이 아니다 Your ideas are not realistic. // 너는 더 ~이어야 한다 You've got to get your feet on the ground[to be more realistic / to settle down].

현악(絃樂·弦樂) string music.
● **현악기** a stringed (musical) instrument; a string instrument; 〔집합적〕 the strings. **현악 사중주(단)** a string quartet(te). **현악 삼중주(단)** a string trio.

현안(懸案) a pending[an outstanding] problem[question]. ¶노사간의 ~ a problem pending between management and labor // 한미 간의 ~ 경제 문제 the economic problems pending between Korea and America // 그 법안은 심의되지 않은 채 ~으로 남아 있다 The bill hasn't (even) been discussed and is still in limbo. // 쇠고기 관세 인하 문제는 아직 ~으로 남아 있다 The issue of reducing import taxes on beef is still up in the air [has been pushed onto a back burner]. (▶ be pushed onto a back burner는 관심이 없어 뒤로 미루어지는 것을 말함)

현양하다(顯揚-) exalt; extol.

현업(現業) work in the field; a work-site operation.
● **현업원** a field [an outdoor] worker; 〔집합적〕 the outdoor staff. ¶비 ~ a desk [clerical] worker / 〔집합적〕 the clerical staff.

현역(現役) (군무의) active service[duty]; (휴직에 대하여) service on full pay; commission(군함의). ¶~ 정치가 an active politician / a politician who is currently in office // ~ 투수 a pitcher on the active list // ~에서 퇴역하다 retire from active service // ~에 복귀시키다 demothball(군함을) // ~에 머무르다 stay in uniform // 아버지는 아직 ~으로 일하고 있다 My father is still working regularly.
● **현역 군인** a soldier in active service; a serviceman on active duty; a soldier with the colors. **현역 선수** a player on the playing list. **현역 장교** an officer in active service [on the active list]; 〔집합적〕 the effectives. **현역함** a commissioned vessel; a vessel in commission [service].

현연하다(顯然-) 〔명백하다〕 evident; obvious; clear; manifest; palpable. **현연히** distinctly; visibly; clearly; plainly.

현우(賢友) a wise friend.

현우(賢愚) 〔현명함과 어리석음〕 wisdom and folly; 〔현자와 우자〕 the wise and the foolish.

현월(弦月) a new moon. ⇨초승달(㊂초승)

현위(顯位) a high rank; a higher position.

현인(賢人) a wise man; a sage; a man of high intelligence; a Nestor. ¶~도 바보에게서 조언을 받는 일이 있다 A fool may give a wise man counsel.

현임(現任) the present office [post].

●현임자 the present holder of the office.
현자(賢者) a wise man. ⇨ =현인
현장(現場) (사건의) (the actual) spot; the scene (of action); (작업의) the scene of labor; a job site; (건축의) a building site; a construction field. ¶사고[범죄]의 ~ the scene of the accident[crime] // ~의 재현 reconstruction of the scene // 건설[공사] ~ a building[construction] site // 조난 ~ the scene of a disaster // ~에 있었던 사람들 those who happened to be there / those present // ~에서 on the spot[ground / scene] / then and there // ~에 닿다[있다] arrive[be] on the scene // ~에서 체포되다 be arrested on the spot[then and there] // ~에서 죽다 be killed on the spot // ~에서 들키다 be caught red-handed[in the act] // ~을 목격하다 be an eyewitness of the disaster [accident] // ~에 있는 사람들의 의견을 존중하다 respect the opinion of those who are doing the actual work // 우리는 즉각 ~으로 달려갔다 We ran to the spot immediately. // 그는 절도 ~에서 붙잡혔다 He was caught in the act of stealing. // 경관은 범인을 ~에서 체포했다 The police caught the criminal red-handed. // 우연히 나는 ~에 있었다 I just happened to be there (at the time).
●현장 감독 a field overseer; an on-the-job superintendent. ¶~을 하다 supervise the work of construction in the field. 현장 검증 an inspection of the scene (of a murder); an on-the-spot inspection[investigation]. 현장 근무 field service. 현장 부재 증명 [법] an alibi. 현장 조사 an on-the-spot survey; a field investigation. 현장 중계 a live relay broadcast. 현장 취재 on-the-spot coverage.
현재(現在) 1 [지금 이 시간] now; the present (time); [이 시점에] now; at present. ¶~ present / existing / current (prices) // ~까지 up to now / up[down] to date // ~는 [바로 지금] at present / now / at the present time / [지금 당장] for the time being // ~의 상황 present[existing] circumstances // ~ 대학 재학 중인 자 those presently at college // ~ 진행 중인 on-going (summit conference) // ~의 남편[주소] one's present husband [address] // ~ 그대로 놔두다 leave (a matter) as it is // 그는 ~의 지위에 만족하지 않고 있다 He is not content with his present post. // 그는 해고당하여 ~ 실업 중이다 He was fired and is now[presently / currently] out of work. // ~대로 두면 큰일 난다 If you leave it as it is, the results will be grave indeed. // ~까지 그와 같은 유적이 13군데 발견되었다 To date[Up to now], thirteen such sites have been discovered.
2 (문법에서) the present tense. ¶그 동사는 ~다 The verb is in the present (tense).
●현재 분사 a present participle. 현재 완료 (시제) the present perfect (tense). 현재 진행형 the present progressive.
현저하다(顯著-) conspicuous; remarkable; striking(▶ conspicuous는 눈에 잘 띄는, remarkable은 보통의 것과 주목받는, striking은 다른 것과의 차이가 인상적인 등이 함축되어 있음); notable; noticeable; marked; distinguished; salient; eminent; prominent; outstanding; [명백하than] obvious (fact). ¶현저한 진보 remarkable[marked] progress // 현저한 유사점 a striking resemblance / marked similarities // 현저한 차이 a sharp [striking] difference (in) // 앞뒤의 두 사건에는 현저한 차이가 있다 The former case is the direct opposite of the latter. // 그 병의 현저한 징후가 나타났다 The patient has begun to exhibit obvious symptoms of the disease. // 그는 그림 그리기에서 현저한 향상을 이룩했다 He has made remarkable progress in painting. // 이 석불의 영검은 현저하다고 한다 It is said that the power of this stone image of the Buddha is miraculous. // 그 약의 효험은 현저하여 열이 곧 내렸다 Obviously the medicine worked, for my fever went down at once. / The medicine had a miraculous effect. It reduced my fever immediately. 현저히 conspicuously; remarkably; strikingly; markedly; noticeably. ¶매상고가 ~ 감소했다 There has been a sharp[marked] decrease in our sales. // 그는 가수로서 명성이 ~[눈에 띄게] 상승하고 있다 His reputation as a singer has been rising remarkably.
현제(舷梯) an accommodation[a gangway] ladder.
현존(現存) ¶~의 [지금도 살아 있는] living / [지금도 있는] (now) existent. 현존하다 exist; be in existence; be extant; subsist. ¶현존하는 건물 the existing[present] building // 그 사건의 당사자로서 현존하는 인물은 이제 아무도 없다 No one involved in the incident is alive[living] today. // 신라 시대의 그림으로 현존하는 것은 드물다 There are few pictures of the Silla Dynasty still extant. (▶ extant는 서화·골동품에 대해서 씀)
●현존 작가 living writers.
현주소(現住所) one's present address[domicile / abode / residence].
현지(現地) the spot; the field; the actual place; the (actual) locale. ¶~의 on-the-spot // ~에서 촬영한 photographed on the actual location.
●현지 기관 a field organization. 현지 로케이션 [영] an on-the-spot location. 현지 르포 / 현지 보고 a spot[an on-the-spot / an on-scene] report; a report from the spot; (프) reportage. 현지 방송 an on-the-spot broadcast. 현지 생산 local production (국산 T.V. 등의). 현지 시간 local time. ¶~으로 오후 3시 (한국 시간으로 일요일 오전 4시) at 3 p.m. local time (04:00 KST Sunday). 현지 시찰 여행 a field trip; a fact-finding tour. 현지인 (-人) the natives. 현지 조달 self-subsistence[-sufficiency] on the spot. 현지 조사 an on-the-spot[a field] survey[investigation / inquiry]; investigation on the scene; an on-site study. ¶~를 하다 study (the question) on the spot[scene] / conduct a spot investigation. 현지 특파원 / 현지 파견원 a correspondent on the scene.
현직(現職) the present post[office]; the office now held. ¶~의 incumbent / on the active list / in active service // ~의 국회의원 an incumbent National Assembly member // ~에 있는 사람 an incumbent // ~에 머물다 remain in one's present post / stay on the job // ~이라는 유리한 이점을 안고 존슨 시장이 압승했다 Having the advantage of being the incumbent, Mayor Johnson won (reelection) by a wide margin.
●현직 경찰관 a policeman on the active list [in active service]. 현직 대통령 the incum-

bent President.

현직(現職) a high office; an eminent post. ¶~에 있는 사람 dignitaries / men of high office.

현찰(現札) [현재 가지고 있는] (hard) cash; actual [ready] money; [현금이 되는 지폐] a (bank) note; (속어) bread; dough. ¶~로 50만 원 five hundred thousand won in notes // ~로 **지불하다** pay in cash / present ready money.

현창(舷窓) [해] a porthole; a port.

현처(賢妻) an intelligent wife; a good housewife.

현철하다(賢哲―) wise; intelligent.

현충일(顯忠日) the Memorial Day.

현충탑(顯忠塔) a memorial monument.

현측(舷側) the sides of a boat. ⇨뱃전

현탁액(懸濁液) [화] suspension. ⇨서스펜션

현판(懸板) a tablet; a hanging board (with a picture or some calligraphy on it); a framed picture(그림으로 된).

현품(現品) the (actual) thing; the actual article[goods]; [경] spots; spot commodities [goods]; merchandise on spot. ¶~을 조사해보다 check up on the number of articles // ~은 견본과 달랐다 The actual article was different from the sample. // ~을 보지 않고는 뭐라 말할 수 없다 I cannot say either way before I inspect the article.

현하(現下) the present time. ¶~의 present / existing / of the hour [day] / at the present moment // ~의 급박한 pending / imminent / pressing / urgent // ~의 문제 the question of the hour / a current question[topic] // ~의 국제 정세 the existing state of international affairs // ~의 주택 사정 the present housing situation.

현학(衒學) pedantry; display[parading] of one's (book-)learning. ¶~적(인) pedantic.

● **현학자** a pedant; a gerund-grinder.

현행 ¶~의 present / existing / current (▶ present는 현재 행해지고 있다는 뜻에서 그 시간이 강조되며, existing, current는 현재 통용되고 있다는 데서 그 존재가 문제가 된다는 뜻이 담김) / (법률·규정 등이) in operation // ~대로 same as at present // ~의 교통 법규로는 under the present[current / existing] traffic regulations // ~의 조약 the treaty now in force // 수도 요금은 당분간 ~대로 둘 것 같다 The water rate is likely to be left as it is for some time. // ~ 임금률(率)은 너무 낮다 The ruling rates of wages are too low.

● **현행 교과서** the textbooks now in use. **현행 맞춤법** the current spelling system. **현행범** [법] (행위) a flagrant delict[offense]; a crime committed in the presence of a policeman; (사람) a criminal taken in an act of crime; a flagrant delictor[offender]. ¶~으로 **잡히다** be caught[taken] in the (very) act / be caught red-handed / be apprehended while committing a crime // 그는 폭행의 ~으로 체포되었다 He was caught in the act of assault. / He was caught red-handed (flagrante delicto) committing assault. **현행법** the existing[operative] law; the law (actually) in force. ¶~에 의하면 according to the law now in force // ~의 적용을 받다 be subject to the existing laws.

현현(顯現) a manifestation; an expression; evidence. **현현하다** manifest; express; evidence. ¶인간애가 이 의사의 모습으로 현현하다고 할 수도 있다 One might say that human love has manifested itself in the form of this doctor.

현혹(眩惑) dazzlement; bewilderment; a daze. **현혹하다** [당혹하게 하다] perplex; [혼란시키다] confuse; [판단을 그르치게 하다] delude; [유혹하다] seduce; tempt; make dizzy[giddy]; mystify[bewilder] (a person). ¶인심을 ~ confuse the mind of the people // 그 사나이는 달콤한 말로 여인을 현혹했다 He seduced the woman with honeyed words. → ¶현혹시키는 듯한 dazzling / blinding // 현혹되다 be dazzled [by] / be bewildered / be mystified // 나는 그 편지에 현혹되었다 I was deluded by the letter. / The letter misled me. // 나는 그녀의 요염한 자태에 현혹되었다 I was blinded by her enticing beauty. // 그에게 현혹되어 그의 정체를 알아내지 못했다 Taken in by his appearance, I failed to see him for what he was.

현화식물(顯花植物) [식]a phanerogam.

현황(現況) the present condition[state] (of). ¶회사의 자산 ~ the existing[present] state of a company's assets.

혈(穴) 1 [민] (bury one's father's body in) a propitious spot. 2 [한] [침 놓는 자리] a spot on the body important for acupuncture.

혈거(穴居) cave dwelling. ¶~의 cave-dwelling. **혈거하다** live [(문어) dwell] in a cave.

● **혈거 생활** cave dwelling. **혈거인** a cave dweller; a caveman.

혈관(血管) a blood vessel. ¶동맥, 정맥, 모세관은 ~이다 Arteries, veins, and capillaries are blood vessels.

● **혈관 경련** an angiospasm; a vascular spasm. **혈관 경화** hardening[sclerosis] of the blood vessels. **혈관 압축** thlipsis. **혈관 파열** the rupture[bursting] of a blood vessel.

혈괴(血塊) [한] gore; clot of blood.

혈구(血球) a blood corpuscle. ¶백[적]~ a white [red] corpuscle.

혈기(血氣) 1 [생명력] vigor[(영) vigour]. ¶~있는 젊은이 a vigorous[high-spirited] youth. 2 [왕성한 의기] hot blood. ¶~ 왕성한 사람 a hot-blooded man // ~가 넘치는 행동 an impetuous act // ~가 **왕성하다** be full of youthful vigor / be in the prime of health / be in one's hot[raw / vigorous] youth // 젊은 ~로 나는 바보 같은 짓을 했다 I did something stupid on account of youthful zeal.

혈농(血膿) bloody pus [matter].

혈뇨(血尿) [의] bloody urine; h(a)ematuria.

혈담(血痰) blood(y) phlegm. ¶~을 **뱉다** cough up bloody phlegm.

혈당(血糖) blood sugar. ¶~ 검사를 받다 receive a blood sugar test.

● **혈당치** the blood sugar level.

혈로(血路) [어려운 고비의 길] a hard way [means] of escape. ¶~를 **찾다**[**뚫다**] seek [find] a way out // 적 속에서 ~를 열다 cut one's way through the enemy.

혈루(血淚) tears of blood. ⇨피눈물

혈맥(血脈) 1 [혈관] a blood vessel. 2 blood; lineage. ⇨혈통

● **혈맥상통** blood relationship [bond].

혈맹(血盟) [피로써 굳게 맹세함] a blood pledge; a blood alliance.

혈반(血斑) a blood spot.

혈변(血便) bloody excrement. ⇨⁼피똥
혈병(血餠) [생] a clot of blood; a blood clot.
혈색(血色) one's complexion; color. ¶~이 좋은[나쁜] 남자 a ruddy[pallid] man∥~이 좋다[나쁘다] have a healthy[bad] complexion / look healthy[pale]∥~이 좋아[나빠]지다 gain[lose] color∥~을 되찾다 regain color∥그는 ~이 좋다[나쁘다] He looks healthy[pale]. / He has a healthy[sickly] complexion.
● **혈색소** [생] hemoglobin. ⇨⁼헤모글로빈
혈서(血書) a writing in blood. ¶~로 쓴 탄원서 a petition written in blood∥~를 쓰다 write in blood.
혈석(血石) [광] bloodstone.
혈세(血稅) a tax paid by the sweat of one's brow. ¶국민의 ~ taxes squeezed[extorted] from the common people.
혈소판(血小板) [의] a thrombocyte; a blood platelet; a plaque.
혈속(血屬) blood relatives[relation].
혈손(血係) [혈통을 이어 가는 자손] descendants related by blood; one's direct descendants.
혈안(血眼) a bloodshot eye. ¶그들은 딸의 입학시험 때문에 ~이 되어 있다 They can't think of anything but their daughter's entrance examination.∥그들은 도둑맞은 보석을 ~이 되어 찾았다 They searched desperately[made a mad search / made a frenzied search] for the stolen jewels.
혈압(血壓) blood pressure. ¶고~ high blood pressure / hypertension∥저~ low blood pressure / hypotension∥나는 ~이 높다[낮다] I have high[low] blood pressure.∥그는 ~이 정상이다 His blood pressure is normal. / He has normal blood pressure.∥몹시 흥분해서 ~이 10이 올라갔다 I was so excited that my blood pressure rose[went up] by ten.∥그의 ~은 아래가 85이고 위가 130이었다 His blood pressure was 130 over 85.∥나는 ~을 쟀다 I had my blood pressure taken.∥이 약을 먹으면 ~이 내려갑니다 This medicine will lower your blood pressure.
● **혈압 강하제** a hypotensive. **혈압계** a sphygmomanometer; a tonometer. **혈압 측정** sphygmomanometry.
혈액(血液) blood. ⇨⁼피¹
● **혈액 검사** a blood test. ¶~를 받다 have one's blood examined. **혈액 순환** the circulation of the blood. ¶~을 원활하게 하다 promote blood circulation. **혈액은행** a blood bank. **혈액 투석** hemodialysis. **혈액형** a blood type; the type of one's blood. ¶내 ~은 B형이다 I have type B blood.∥나와 그의 ~은 맞지 않는다 My blood has an incompatible reaction to his.
혈연(血緣) a blood relative.
● **혈연관계** (blood) relationship. ¶그와는 ~이다 I am related to him by blood. **혈연 사회** blood society.
혈온(血溫) [의] blood heat; the temperature of blood.
혈우병(血友病) [의] h(a)emophilia. ¶~의[~에 걸려 있는] h(a)emophilic.
● **혈우병 환자** a hemophiliac.
혈육(血肉) [자식] one's sons and daughters; [피붙이] one's own flesh and blood. ¶~의 형제 a brother of the same flesh and blood.
혈장(血漿) [생] blood plasma. ¶건조 ~ dried plasma∥인공 ~ a plasma substitute / dextran.
혈전(血栓) (a) thrombus (pl. -bi).
● **혈전증** (a) thrombosis. ¶뇌~ cerebral thrombosis.
혈전(血戰) a bloody battle; a desperate fight. **혈전하다** fight a bloody battle; fight desperately.
● **혈전지** a scene of desperate fighting.
혈족(血族) blood relatives; relative by blood.
● **혈족 관계** blood relationship.
혈청(血淸) [의] (a) (blood) serum (pl. ~s, -ra). ¶예방 ~ a preventive serum.
● **혈청 검사** (conduct) serum test. **혈청 반응** (a) serum reaction; (a) seroreaction. **혈청 요법** / **혈청 치료** serum treatment[therapy]; serotherapy. **혈청 주사** a serum injection.
혈통(血統) blood; [문어] lineage; pedigree; family line; descent. ¶~이 좋은 집안 a family of good lineage∥아버지[어머니] 쪽의 ~ the paternal[maternal] line / blood relationship on one's father's[mother's] side∥~이 좋다[나쁘다] come of a good[bad] stock / be of a good[bad] strain∥~을 조사하다 inquire into (a person's) lineage / trace back (a person's) family line∥~을 캐다 trace (a person's) descent (to)∥~이 끊어졌다 The line has died out.∥~은 속이지 못한다 Blood will tell. / Heredity will out.∥그는 무사 가문의 ~이다 He is descended from a brave warriors family.∥그는 예술가의 ~이다 The blood of artists runs in his veins.
혈투(血鬪) a bloody fight; a desperate struggle[fight]. **혈투하다** fight a bloody fight.
혈한(血汗) greasy sweat. ⇨⁼피땀
혈행(血行) blood circulation; the circulation of the blood. ¶~을 좋게 하다 improve the circulation of the blood∥~이 좋다[나쁘다] have normal[poor / bad] blood circulation.
● **혈행 장애** interruption in blood circulation.
혈혈단신(孑孑單身) being without a single human tie; being all alone; having no kith or kin. ¶나는 ~이다 I stand all alone in the world.
혈흔(血痕) a bloodstain. ¶~이 묻은 손수건 a bloodstained handkerchief∥그의 바지에 ~이 묻어 있었다 There were bloodstains on his trousers.
● **혈흔 검사** the examination of bloodstains.
혐기(嫌忌) dislike; aversion; abhorrence. **혐기하다** dislike; abhor; hold (a person) in abhorrence.
혐오(嫌惡) hatred; dislike; disgust; aversion; abhorrence. ¶자기 ~ self-hatred∥나는 독선적인 남편에게 심한 ~를 느꼈다 I felt a strong hatred[loathing] for my self-complacent husband. **혐오하다** hate; loathe; detest. ¶그의 얼굴에 혐오하는 빛이 보였다 I observed signs of repugnance on his face.
혐오스럽다(嫌惡—) hateful; disgusting; detestable. ¶정치가의 독직만큼 혐오스러운 것도 없다 Nothing makes one's gorge rises like corruption in politicians.
혐의(嫌疑) 1 [꺼리고 싫어함] dislike; aversion. **혐의하다** dislike; feel an aversion to.
2 [의심] suspicion; charge; accusation. ¶그는 살인의 ~를 받고 있다 He is suspected of murder.∥그는 절도 ~로 체포되었다 He was arrested on (the) suspicion of theft.∥그는

협객 살인의 ~를 썼었다 He cleared himself of the charge of murder.// 그는 뇌물을 받은 ~를 벗어나기가 어렵다 He is open to the charge of taking bribes.// 그를 둘러싼 ~가 좀처럼 풀릴 것 같지 않다 The suspicions surrounding him seem unlikely to be dispelled easily.// 경찰은 타살의 ~가 있다고 말하고 있다 The police suspect murder[it to be a case of murder].// 나는 어떻게든 ~를 씻지 않으면 안 된다 I must clear myself of suspicion[the charge] no matter what. / I must prove my innocence[exonerate myself] at any cost.// 아무래도 그에게 ~가 있는 것 같다 I suspect that he is the guilty one[the one who did it]. / He looks suspicious to me.// 그에게 ~가 있는지 없는지는 아직 확실하지 않다 It is not yet certain whether he is guilty or not. **혐의하다** suspect.
● **혐의자** a suspect; a person under suspicion.

협객(俠客) a man of chivalrous spirit. ¶그에게는 다소 ~ 기질이 있다 He has a touch of chivalry in him.

협곡(峽谷) 〔험하고 좁은 골짜기〕 a gorge; 〔급류의 침식으로 생긴 좁고 깊은 골짜기〕 a ravine; (대협곡) a canyon; (스코틀랜드 등의) a glen.

협공(挾攻) an attack on both flanks; a pincer attack[movement]; double envelopment. ¶도둑은 두 경비원에게 ~을 당하였다 The thief found himself[caught] between two guards. **협공하다** catch (the enemy) in a crossfire; attack (the enemy) from both sides; launch [make] a pincer attack against (the enemy). ¶우리는 적을 협공하였다 We attacked the enemy on[from] both sides[flanks].
● **협공 작전** a pincer movement; a pincer operation; pincer tactics.

협궤(狹軌) a narrow gauge.
● **협궤 철도** a narrow-gauge railway.

협기(俠氣) a chivalrous spirit; chivalry. ¶~가 있는 chivalrous // ~를 부리다 perform an act of chivalry / show one's manly spirit // 그는 ~를 부려 그 여자를 보호했다 He gallantly [chivalrously] protected the woman.

협동(協同) cooperation; collaboration; union; combination. ¶~의 communal / joint / concerted / united // ~으로 in partnership (with) / jointly / communally. **협동하다** cooperate (with); collaborate (in); work together; act in concert[union] (with); join forces[hands] (with); team up (with).
● **협동 기업** a joint enterprise[undertaking / venture]. **협동 정신** a spirit of cooperation; a cooperative spirit. **협동조합** a cooperative (association)(약어 co-op, coop). ¶소비자[농업] ~ a consumers'[farmers'] cooperative // ~에 가입하다 join a coop.

협력(協力) cooperation; collaboration; working together. ¶경제 ~ economic cooperation // 기술 ~ technical cooperation // 상호 ~ mutual cooperation // 긴밀한 ~ close cooperation / intimate collaboration // …의 ~을 얻다 obtain cooperation from ... / win [secure] the cooperation of ... / get (a person) into line // ~을 구하다 ask[appeal to] (a person) for help[assistance] // 시 당국은 도의 ~으로 전염병 유행을 간신히 예방했다 The municipal authorities, in cooperation with[assisted by] the prefecture, managed to control the epidemic. **협력하다** cooperate (with); work[pull] together; collaborate (with); unite one's efforts (with); make united[concerted] efforts; join forces [hands] (with); team up (with); (미국 구어) play ball (with). ¶**협력하여** in cooperation (with) // 교통안전에 협력해 주세요 Please cooperate in promoting traffic safety. // 그들에게 협력하시오 Team up[Work together] with them. // 협력하여 해치우자 Let's unite our efforts and see it through. // 그는 사장 축출 계획에 협력했다 He took part[had a hand] in the plot to oust the president from his post. // 네가 이 일에 협력해 주면 좋겠다 I'd like you to be my partner in this project. // 헬리콥터와 배는 협력해서 조난선을 구조했다 The helicopter and the ship worked in concert to help the wrecked ship.
● **협력자** a collaborator; a supporter.

협로(夾路) a bypath; a byroad; a side path.
협로(峽路) a mountain path; a defile.
협로(狹路) a (narrow) path. ⇨ **소로**(小路)
협만(峽灣) a fjord[fiord].
협문(夾門) a side door[gate]; a paneled door.
협박(脅迫) a threat; a menace; intimidation. ¶~에 의한 자백 confession under threat [duress] // ~의 눈초리 a menacing[threatening] look // 그는 ~을 받고 회사 기밀을 훔쳤다 He was intimidated[blackmailed] into stealing the company's secrets. // 그들의 ~이 두려워 지역 주민은 아무 말도 하려 들지 않았다 Their intimidation was so fierce that the neighbors shut their mouths and remained silent. **협박하다** threaten; intimidate; menace; blackmail; blackjack; (미국 구어) bulldoze. ¶죽이겠다고 ~ threaten (a person) with death // 협박하여 …하게 하다 intimate[force] (a person) into (doing / confession) // 그들은 100만 원을 내놓지 않으면 죽이겠다고 협박했다 They threatened to kill him unless he paid one million won. // 백화점 경비원은 물건을 훔친 주부를 협박했다 The security guard blackmailed a housewife who had stolen things from the department store.
● **협박자** a blackmailer. **협박장** a threatening letter. **협박 전화** a threatening[menacing] telephone call. **협박죄** a crime of intimidation[blackmail].

협살(挾殺) 〔야구〕 a rundown (play). **협살하다** run down[touch out] (a runner). ➔ 주자는 3루와 본루 사이에서 협살되었다 The runner was tagged out in a rundown between third base and home.

협상(協商) 〔교섭〕 negotiation(s); bargaining; (a) conversation; 〔외교〕 (프) an entente; an understanding; an agreement. ¶3국 ~ the Triple Entente // 비밀 ~ a closed-door negotiation // 평화 ~ peace negotiations // 캐나다와 ~을 맺다 conclude an agreement with Canada // ~을 재개하다 put negotiations back on track / get negotiations going again // ~은 교착 상태에 빠졌다 The negotiations reached a deadlock. **협상하다** negotiate (with a person a matter / for a purpose); bargain (with); confer (with).
● **협상국** a party to an entente; an entente.

협소하다(狹小−) 〔폭이 좁다〕 narrow; 〔한정되다〕 limited; 〔면적이 작다〕 small. ¶협소한 땅 a small plot[piece] of land // 한국은 국토가

~ Korea is limited in area [space].

협실(夾室) a small room attached to the main one. ⇨ 곁방1

협심(協心) unison; concert; cooperation. **협심하다** unite; be of one accord [mind]; be in union (with).

협심증(狹心症) [의] stricture of the heart; angina pectoris [cordis]; heart attack. ¶~으로 죽다 die of [from] heart attack.

협약(協約) an agreement; a convention; a pact; [협상] an entente; an understanding. ¶노동 ~ a labor agreement // 단체 ~ a collective [(영) trade] agreement // 신사 ~ a gentleman's [gentlemen's] agreement // 구두에 의한 ~ a verbal agreement. **협약하다** conclude [enter into] an agreement (with).

협업(協業) cooperation; cooperative work. **협업하다** cooperate; work together; work in cooperation.

협의(協議) a conference; (a) consultation; (a) deliberation. (▶ conference는 문제에 관하여 의견을 교환하는 일, consultation은 전문가 등의 의견을 청하는 일, deliberation은 정식의 심의·토의) ¶문제에 대하여 ~를 계속하다 hold deliberations on a question / ~ 후 결정하다 decide after due consultation [upon deliberation] // 사장은 중역과 ~ 중입니다 The president is in conference with the directors. **협의하다** talk (a matter over with a person); discuss (a matter with a person); consult [confer] (with a person about a matter). ¶그들은 경기 전에 작전을 협의하였다 They discussed tactics before the game. // 나는 그녀와 여행 일정을 협의했다 I discussed [made] traveling arrangements with her. // 협의한 대로 일이 진행되었다 Things proceeded according to the arrangements [as arranged]. / Everything went as planned. // 위원회 전원과 협의하였습니까 Did you ask the opinion of all the members of the committee?
● **협의 사항** a subject [topic] of discussion. **협의 이혼** a divorce by consent. ¶그는 아내와 ~ 했다 He divorced his wife by agreement. **협의회** a conference; a meeting.

협의(狹義) a narrow sense. ¶~의 교육 education in a narrow sense // ~로 해석하다 take (a word) in a narrow sense.

협잡(狹雜) trickery; (a) fraud; a swindle; (an) imposture; (구어) a take-in; (a) humbug; a hoax; (미국 속어) monkey business. ¶~의 tricky / fake / sham / bogus / false // ~에 걸리다 be imposed upon / be cheated / be taken in / become a victim of a deception // 이건 순전한 ~이다 This is all humbug. / It's all a trick [(미국 속어) do]. **협잡하다** cheat; deceive; swindle; take [let] (a person) in; play off a fraud (upon); play a trick (upon); (승부에서) play a foul game; play foul.
● **협잡꾼 / 협잡배** an impostor; a crook; a fraud; a trickster; a cheat.

협장(脇杖) a crutch. ⇨ 목발

협정(協定) an agreement; a convention; a pact; a concordat. ¶국제 ~ an international agreement / an accord // 관세 ~ a customs agreement // 신사 ~ a gentlemen's agreement // 운임 (군사) ~ a freight [military] convention // 정전 ~ cease-fire [an armistice] agreement / a truce accord // 통상 ~ a trade agreement / an agreement on commerce // 평화 ~ a peace accord // 행정 ~ an administrative agreement // ~에 의해서 by agreement / under an agreement made (with) // ~을 맺다 make [enter into] an agreement (with) // 미국과의 ~을 파기하다 break an agreement with the United States // ~에 조인하다 sign an agreement // ~이 성립되었다 They came to [arrived at] an agreement. **협정하다** agree upon (the price); arrange (with); make arrangements (with). ¶가격을 ~ make an agreement with (a person) on prices // 그들은 협정하고 성명을 발표했다 They issued a statement by agreement [arrangement].
● **협정서** a protocol. **협정안** a draft agreement. **협정 임금** wages agreed upon; agreed wages.

협조(協助) help; aid; assistance; support(후원); cooperation(협력). ¶상호 ~ mutual help [aid] / cooperation / helping one another // 양 씨의 ~로 by the help [the kind assistance] of Mr. Yang / through Mr. Yang's aid // ~를 바라다 ask for help / turn [look] to (another) for assistance // 너의 ~가 필요하다 I stand in need of your assistance. / I need your assistance. **협조하다** help (a person in his work); aid [assist] (in a person's work); render [give] (a person) aid [assistance] (in doing). ¶서로 협조하며 살아가다 live together interdependently.
● **협조자** a helper; an assistant; a supporter.

협조(協調) cooperation; harmony(조화); conciliation(타협). ¶노사 ~ cooperation between capital and labor. **협조하다** cooperate; act in concert [union / alignment] (with).
● **협조심** a spirit of cooperation.

협조적(協調的) cooperative; conciliatory; harmonious. ¶~ 정신으로 in a spirit of cooperation / cooperatively.

협주곡(協奏曲) a concerto (pl. ~s, -ti). ¶바이올린 [피아노] ~ a violin [piano] concerto // 합주 ~ a concerto grosso.

협죽도(夾竹桃) [식] a sweet-scented oleander; a rosebay.

협착증(狹窄症) [의] (a) stricture. ¶식도 ~ stricture of the esophagus // 요도 [직장] ~ stricture of the urethra [rectum].

협착하다(狹窄─) narrow; (서술적) be strangulated.

협찬(協贊) support; cooperation. ¶그 회사의 ~으로 under the sponsorship of the company // 우리의 자선 바자에 신문사의 ~을 얻었다 Our charity bazaar got the support of a newspaper. **협찬하다** approve of (a plan); give one's approval (to); support; aid; assist; help; cooperate (with). ¶문화 단체가 주최하는 연주회를 ~ support a musical concert sponsored by a cultural society.

협하다(狹─) [지대가 좁다] small; narrow; [마음이 좁다] narrow-minded; small-minded.

협화(協和) [서로 화합함] harmony; concord; concert. **협화하다** be in harmony [concord] (with); act in concert (with); get along [on] well (with).
● **협화음** [음] a consonance. ⇨ 어울림음

협회(協會) a society; an association. ¶동물 애호 ~ the Society for the Prevention of Cruelty to Animal // 농구 ~ the Basketball

혀바늘 a rash[an eruption] on the tongue. ¶~이 돋다 have eruption on one's tongue // ~이 돋았다 My tongue broke out in a rash. / My tongue became inflamed.

혀바닥 1 [혀의 윗면] the flat of the tongue. 2 〈속〉 a tongue.

혀소리 [언] a lingual (sound).

형(兄) 1 [손위 동기] one's older [elder] brother; one's big brother (▶ 종종 어린이가 말하는 경우). ¶큰~ one's oldest [eldest] brother ((미)에서는 older, oldest를 쓰는 경향이 강함) // 이복~ one's [an] older half brother // 나는 ~과 함께 살고 있다 I live with my brother. (▶ 영어에서는 특별한 경우를 제외하고는 남자 형제에 대해 손위·손아래를 구별하지 않고 그냥 brother라고 함. 그것을 굳이 구별할 때에는 「형」은 older brother, 「동생」은 younger brother라고 함. 한편, brother는 우리말 「형」과는 달리 호칭어로는 쓰이지 않으며, 형을 부를 때에는 그의 이름을 사용함) 2 [친구간의 높임말] Mr. ...; [당신] you. ¶최~ Mr. Choe // ~ (씨) Hey, pal! / Young man!

형(刑) a penalty; a sentence. ¶재산~ a pecuniary punishment // 종신~ a life sentence / imprisonment for life // 무거운[가벼운] ~ a heavy [light] punishment // 엄한~ (a) severe punishment // ~을 면하다 escape punishment // ~을 받다 receive a punishment // ~을 면제해 주다 let (a person) off a penalty / indemnify // ~을 집행[유예]하다 carry out [suspend] a sentence // ~을 가하다 inflict [impose] a punishment [penalty] (on) // ~을 언도하다 give [pass / pronounce] a sentence (on a person) // ~을 치르다 serve one's term of imprisonment / (속어) do a term of punishment // 그는 중~에 처해졌다 He was given a severe punishment. // 그는 절도죄로 2년 ~을 복역하고 있다 He is serving a two year sentence for theft. // 재판관은 피고에게 금고 6월의 ~을 선고했다 The judge sentenced the accused to six months in prison. / The judge passed [pronounced] a sentence of six months' imprisonment on the accused.

● **형 집행 정지** the stay of execution of the sentence.

형(形) 1 [형상] (a) shape; [형식] (a) form. ¶V자~의 V-shaped // ~이 망가지다 get out of shape / lose shape. 2 [만듦새] (a) cut; (a) make; [크기] (a) size. ¶포켓~의 사전 a dictionary of pocket size / a pocket-size(d) dictionary.

형(型) 1 [양식] (a) style; (a) type; a pattern; a make; [형식] form; mode; [종류] kind; stamp. ¶84년~ 캐딜락 a 1984 model Cadillac // 최신~ 비행기 the latest model of an airplane // B~의 혈액 blood type B // 신~의 전기스탠드 a desk lamp of a new design // 그는 돈키호테~의 남자이다 He is a Don Quixote [a quixotic man]. // 저런 ~의 사람과는 마음이 맞지 않는다 I cannot get along with men of that type [stripe]. // 그녀들은 같은 ~의 드레스를 입고 있었다 They were wearing dresses of the same style. 2 a block. ⇨ 꼴 3 a mo(u)ld; a matrix. ⇨ 거푸집1

형강(形鋼) section [shape] steel.

형광(螢光) 1 [물] fluorescence. ¶~을 발하다 fluoresce. 2 the glow of a firefly. ⇨ 반딧불

● **형광 도료** fluorescent [luminous] paint. **형광등** a fluorescent light [lamp]. **형광 물질** / **형광 재료** a fluorescent material. **형광판** a fluorescent plate.

형구(刑具) an implement of punishment.

형국(形局) 1 [형세] the situation; the state of things [affairs]. 2 [관상·풍수지리의 겉모양] an aspect; a phase; a facet; a facies (단수·복수 동형).

형극(荊棘) brambles; thorns. ¶~의 길 (가시밭길) a thorny path / a brambly way / (수난의 길) the way of the Cross.

형기(刑期) a prison term; a term of imprisonment [penal servitude]. ¶~를 치르다 serve one's term of imprisonment / serve a prison term / do a jail term / (구어) do [serve] time (at) // ~를 마치다 complete [serve out] one's sentence // 그는 3년 ~를 마치고 출소했다 He was released from prison at the end of his three-year (prison) term.

형기(衡器) a balance; scales.

형률(刑律) criminal law. ⇨ 형법

형명(刑名) the denominations [designations] of penalties.

형무소(刑務所) ➡ 교도소

형벌(刑罰) a penalty; [선고된 형] s sentence; [죄] (a) punishment.

형법(刑法) [법] (집합적) criminal [penal] law; (협의의) the Criminal Law Act; [형법전] the Criminal [Penal] code. ¶국제 ~ the international criminal law // ~상의 criminal / penal // ~상의 죄인 a penal offender // ~에 따라 처벌하다 deal with (a person) according to the provisions of the criminal code.

● **형법 위반** a penal offense. **형법학** criminal jurisprudence.

형부(兄夫) one's [a girl's] elder sister's husband; one's brother-in-law.

형사(刑事) 1 [형법의 사건] a criminal [penal] case. ¶그 사건에서 ~상의 문제가 제기되었다 Some were prosecuted under the criminal law with the affair. 2 [경찰] a (police) detective; (영) an operative; (미국 속어) a gumshoe; (수사계의) an investigator. ¶사복~ a plainclothes man // 살인 사건을 담당하고 있는 ~ a detective on the murder case.

● **형사과** the detective division. **형사 기동대** a police task force squad. **형사범** a criminal offense. **형사 사건** a criminal case. **형사 소송** a criminal action [suit]. ¶~을 상대로 ~을 제기하다 proceed against (a person) criminally. **형사 소송법** the Criminal Procedure Code. **형사 재판**(刑事裁判) a criminal trial. **형사 책임** criminal liability. ¶어린이라서 ~은 없다 As he is a child, he is not criminally liable for what he did. **형사 처분** (suffer) a criminal punishment.

형상(形狀) (a) shape. ⇨ 형상(形象)

형상(形象) (a) shape; (a) form. (▶ 추상적인 경우는 관사 없음)

● **형상화** ~하다 give shape [form] to.

형색(形色) 1 [형상과 빛깔] form [shape] and color. 2 [용색] features; looks; appearance.

형석(螢石) [광] fluorite; fluorspar; (영) fluor.

형설(螢雪) diligent study. ¶~의 공을 쌓다 prosecute one's studies for years / apply oneself closely to one's studies / burn the midnight oil.

● **형설지공** the fruits of diligent study.

형성(形成) formation; (천체의) evolution. ¶인격 ~ character building [formation]. **형성**

다 form; build (up); mold. ¶인격을 ~ shape [mold] one's character. ➔¶그 시대에 이 화산이 형성된 것으로 추정된다 It is assumed that this volcano was formed in that period. // 그의 인격은 아직 형성되지 않았다 His character is not yet fully developed.
● **형성기** the formative period (of a nation); the formative years (of an individual). ¶인격 ~ the formative period (in the life of a man). **형성층** [식] the formative layer; a cambium (*pl.* ~s, -bia).

형세 (形勢) [정세] the situation; the state of affairs[things]; the condition of affairs; the tide (of war); how the land lies; the trend [run] of events; [전망] the prospects; the chances. ¶세계의 ~ the world situation / the position[state] of world affairs // 현재의 ~로는 as matters stand / as things are [stand] // 지금 당장의 ~로는 큰 변화는 없을 것 같다 Judging by[from] the present situation[state of affairs], there will not be a great change. // ~는 우리에게 유리[불리]하다 The situation is in our favor[against us]. // 당분간 ~를 살펴보고 태도를 결정하자 Let's determine our attitude after watching for a while to see how the situation develops. // ~는 날로 악화되어 간다 Things are going from bad to worse every day. // 두 나라 사이의 ~는 매우 험악해졌다 The relation between the two countries is taking a critical turn. // 그들의 ~는 불리[유리]했다 The tide of the war was going against them[in their favor]. / (경기 등에서) Chances[The odds] were against them[were in their favor]. // 우리의 ~가 불리해지자 그는 우리를 배반했다 When the situation[outlook] worsened[became unfavorable], he betrayed us. // ~가 일변하였다 The tide of events turned. / The tide has turned. / The tables are turned (on Korea).

형수 (兄嫂) an elder brother's wife; a sister-in-law.

형식 (形式) (a) form; (a) formality; [철] a mode; form. ¶~상 in form / for form's sake // ~(상)의 formal / [철] modal // 희곡 ~으로 in the form of a drama // 어떤 ~으로든 in any form // ~에 치중하다 attach importance to form // ~에 구애되다 stick to forms / adhere to formality // ~에 빠지다 degenerate into formalism // 그의 보고서는 ~에만 치우쳐 내용이 없었다 He stuck so closely to form that his report had no content. / His report was all form and no substance. // 지시문은 질의응답의 ~으로 적혀 있다 The instructions are written in a question-and-answer form. // 그 축제는 전래의 ~으로 진행되었다 The festival proceeded according to the time-honored [traditional] pattern.
● **형식론** formalism. ¶~의 formalistic. **형식미** the beauty of form. **형식주의** [예] formalism; (관청의) red-tapism; officialism. **형식주의자** a formalist.

형식적 (形式的) formal; perfunctory (inspection). ¶~으로 formally / perfunctorily / for form's sake // ~의 의례 formality (at a wedding[funeral]) // 그에게서는 ~인 전근 인사장이 한 통 날아왔을 뿐이었다 All he sent me was a perfunctory form letter notifying me of his transfer. // ~입니다만 일단 여기에 사인해 주십시오 It's only a formality, but please sign here. // ~인 면접은 있었지만 그의 채용은 이미 정해져 있었다 It had already been decided to hire him although there was an interview for formality's[form's] sake.

형안 (炯眼) a sharp[keen / quick] eye; a penetrating eye; a keen insight.

형언 (形言) description; expression. **형언하다** describe; express (by words); give expression[words] to. ¶형언할 수 없는 indefinable / inexpressible[indescribable] (beauty) / surpassing[beyond] description / too (beautiful) for words // 형언할 수 없는 아름다움 indescribable beauty / exquisite beauty // 저녁노을의 아름다움은 형언할 수 없는 것이었다 The beauty of the evening glow was beyond description. // 나는 낯선 사람의 친절에 형언할 수 없는 감격을 맛보았다 I felt an inexpressible sense of gratitude at[I was in describably moved by] the stranger's kindness. // 그 참상은 도저히 형언할 수 없는 것이었다 The terrible scene was beyond description. / The horror of the scene defied description.

형용 (形容) [생긴 모양] figure; shape; [서술] qualification; modification; description; [비유] a simile; a metaphor; figure of speech. **형용하다** [수식하다] qualify; modify; [비유적으로 말하다] express figuratively[metaphorically]. ¶그녀의 아름다움은 말로 형용할 수 없다 Words cannot describe her beauty. // 형용사는 명사를 형용한다 Adjectives modify [qualify] nouns. // 이 아름다움은 형용할 수가 없다 This beauty beggars all description.
● **형용사** [언] an adjective.

형이상학 (形而上學) metaphysics; metaphysical philosophy.

형이하학 (形而下學) a concrete[physical] science.

형장 (刑場) a place of execution; an execution ground.
형장의 이슬로 사라지다 die on the scaffold; be executed.

형적 (形迹) [흔적] traces; vestiges; marks; [증거] indications; sign; evidence(s). ¶~을 나타내다 give[bear / show] evidence(s) (of) // ~을 남기지 않다 leave no trace behind // ~을 없애다 cover (up) one's traces / destroy all evidence // 그 ~은 찾아볼 수가 없다 I can find no trace of it. // 도둑이 뒷문으로 들어온 ~이 있다 There are evidences of the thief having entered the house by the back door.

형정 (刑政) penal[criminal] administration.

형제 (兄弟) a sibling; brothers; [동포] brethren. ¶사촌 ~ cousins // 의 ~ plighted brothers // 이복[배다른] ~ a half brother / a brother of the half blood // 이부 ~ half brothers / uterine brothers / brothers on the mother's[maternal] side // 친 ~ a full[whole] brother[sister] // 의리의 ~ a sworn brother // ~가 몇이나 됩니까 How many brothers do you have? // ~도 이해가 갈리면 남이다 Even brothers forget their bonds when there is a conflict of interest. // 내가 어렸을 때는 ~가 곧잘 다투었다 I often quarreled with my brother[brothers] when I was young.
● **형제간** brotherhood; brotherly ties; fraternity. **형제애** fraternal love; brotherly affection. **형제자매** brothers and sisters; brethren(동포).

형지 (型紙) a (paper) pattern (for a dress); a dress pattern (for a suit).

형질(形質) 1 [형태와 성질] form and nature [quality]. 2 [생] a character. ¶유전[획득] ~ an inherited [acquired] character.
● 형질 세포 a plasma cell.

형체(形體) (a) form; (a) shape; (an) appearance; a figure(모습); bodily appearance; the body(몸). ¶사람의 ~를 한 괴물 a monster in human shape // ~를 알아볼 수 없게 become [out of] recognition // ~를 갖추다 be given a form / be embodied // ~를 이루다 take [get into] shape.

형태(形態) 1 [사물의 생김새] (a) form; (a) shape. ¶정치의 한 ~ a form of government // …의 ~를 취하다 assume the form of … / ~를 바꾸다 transform / transfigure // 얼음·눈·수증기는 모두 물의 다른 ~다 Ice, snow and steam are different forms of water. 2 [심] configuration; (독) a Gestalt (pl. ~en).
● 형태론 [언] morphology; morphemics; accidence. 형태소 [언] a morpheme. ¶~의 morphemic. 형태학 morphology. ¶사회 ~ social morphology // ~상(으로) morphological.

형통하다(亨通—) go well [fine / smoothly / all right]; progress favorably. ¶만사형통하였다 Everything [All] went well [favorably] with them. / Everything turned out as they (had) wished.

형틀(刑—) (죄인을 신문할 때 앉히던) a chair in which a criminal is fastened to be interrogated; [고문대] a rack.

형편(形便) 1 [상태] a state; (a) condition; a situation; the state of things [affairs]; an aspect; [사정] circumstances; reasons. ¶가정 ~ one's family circumstances [reasons] // 국내 ~ domestic situation [reasons] / domestic [internal] affairs // 일이 되어 가는 ~ the course [run / development] of events [affairs] / the turn of events // ~상 in view of circumstances // ~상 하는 수 없이 [부득이] from the force [by force] of circumstances // ~의 여하를 불문하고 in any circumstances / regardless of circumstances // ~이 허락하면 if circumstances permit [favor] // ~이 이러하므로 [이런 ~이므로] such being the case / in [under] these [such] circumstances // ~에 의하여 owing to circumstances / in view of [to meet] changed circumstances / for certain reasons / for reasons of one's own // (그때의) ~에 따라서(는) according to circumstances / according to the development of the situation / according as things go // 가정 ~으로 on account of family affairs / for family reasons // 경제적 ~으로 owing [due] to economic circumstances // 여러 가지 ~으로 for many reasons combined // 피치 못할 [부득이한] ~으로 for some unavoidable reasons / under [owing to] unavoidable circumstances // 지금 ~으로는 under the present circumstances / in the present state of things [affairs] / as the matters [things] stand now / for the time being / as of now // 나는 ~상 갈 수 없다 Circumstances do not permit [admit] (of) my going. // 지금 ~으로는 걱정할 것이 없다 As things stand now, there's nothing to worry about. // 그의 가정 ~은 지금은 어떻습니까 What is the state of affairs in his family? // 지금 ~으로 보아서는 그는 2, 3일 끌 것 같다 Judging from his present condition, I think he will linger on for two or three days. // 그는 여행할 ~이 못 된다 He is in no condition to travel. // ~에 따라서는 일정이 변경될 수도 있다 The schedule may be altered according to circumstances. // 지금 ~으로는 회의가 길어질 것 같다 As matters stand now [Judging from the present state of things], the meeting will be prolonged.
2 [살림 형세] living conditions; one's circumstances; (a). living. ¶~이 넉넉하다 [좋다] be well [comfortably] off / be in easy circumstances / be well-to-do // ~이 어렵다 [옹색하다] be badly [poorly] off / be in needy [narrow / bad] circumstances / find it hard to make a living // ~이 말이 아니다 live a wretched [dog's] life / lead a miserable existence / eat the bread of affliction // 그녀는 전보다 ~이 더 어려워졌다 She is worse off than before. // 그는 나보다 ~이 낫다 He is better off than I (am).
3 [편의] convenience; [계제] time; an occasion; [기회] an opportunity; a chance. ¶~상 for convenience' sake / to suit one's convenience // ~에 따라 according to convenience // …의 ~으로 on [for] the convenience of … // ~이 좋은 convenient / suitable / suited (for some purpose) / opportune / expedient // ~이 나쁜 inconvenient / unsuitable / inopportune / untoward // ~이 좋을 때에 at one's convenience / at a propitious moment / in one's own good time // ~이 되면 if (it is) convenient (to you) / if it suits your convenience // ~이 닿으시는 대로 (빨리) at your earliest convenience / at the earliest practicable time // 남의 ~을 들어 보다 consult the convenience of others // 오늘은 내 ~이 좋지 않다 It is not convenient [is in convenient] for me today. // 그러니 ~이 좋으시다면 6시에 만납시다 So, if you are agreeable [it is agreeable to you / it is all right with you], we will meet at 6 o'clock. // 언제든 ~이 좋으실 때 만나러 오십시오 Come and see me whenever you like [it suits you]. // 그는 언제나 자기 ~ 좋은 대로 일을 처리한다[정한다] He always makes arrangements to suit his own convenience.

형편없다(形便—) (지독하다) terrible; dreadful; frightful; awful; wretched; (터무니없다) exorbitant; unreasonable; absurd; nonsensical. ¶형편없는 놈 an impossible fellow // 그의 문법은 ~ His grammar is simple terrible. // 이 작품은 ~ This work is no good at all. // 네 태도는 영 ~ Your attitude is simply awful. **형편없이** [몹시] terribly; dreadfully; frightfully; awfully; extremely; (터무니없이) unreasonably; absurdly; exorbitantly. ¶~ 고생하다 suffer terribly [a great deal] (from) / go through many hardships // ~ 비싸다 be fearfully [absurdly / exorbitantly] high (in price) // ~ 지다 be soundly defeated / be beaten all hollow / suffer a crushing [an ignorable] defeat // ~ 취하다 be heavily [hopelessly / dead] drunk / drink oneself dead drunk // 그 집은 손질을 안 해서 ~ 되어 있었다 The house was in very bad repair [in a dilapidated condition].

형평(衡平) balance; equilibrium; equipoise.
● 형평 원칙 the principle of equity. ¶~을 무시하다 [~에 어긋나다] ignore [be against] the principle of equity.

형해(形骸) 〔골격〕 a framework; a skeletal structure; a skeleton. ¶그 성은 ~만이 남아 있을 뿐이다 The castle remains only in ruins.∥인제 그 절은 ~조차도 남아 있지 않다 Nothing remains of the temple now.

형형색색(形形色色) every kind and description. ⇨ 가지각색 ¶~의 물건 articles of every sort and kind / a great variety of things / sundry articles / all sorts of things∥~의 자전거 bicycles of every description∥~으로 variously / diversely / severally / in many[various / different] ways / manifoldly.

형형하다(炯炯-) 〔빛나다〕 glaring; glittering; 〔눈빛이〕 piercing; penetrating. ¶안광(眼光)이 형형한 sharp-[eagle-]eyed∥(a man) with penetrating eyes∥형형한 눈빛의 병사 a warrior with piercing[sharp] eyes.

혜서(惠書) your (kind) letter.

혜성(彗星) 〔천〕 a comet. ¶인공 ~ an artificial [a man-made] comet∥핼리 ~ Halley's comet∥정계의 ~ a dark horse in politics∥~의 cometic / cometary∥~의 꼬리[광망] the tail[trail] of a comet∥~같이 나타나다 be brought into sudden prominence / make a meteoric rise from obscurity.

혜시(惠示) your kind instruction[information]. **혜시하다** kindly show[instruct / inform].

혜안(慧眼) 〔총명한 눈〕 a quick[sharp / keen] eye; a piercing[penetrating] eye; a keen insight. ¶~의 quick-sighted / sharp-[keen- / clear-]sighted / keen-[sharp-]eyed.

혜존(惠存) 〔증정본에〕 "With compliments (of the author)"; (사진 등에) "To[Presented to] Mr. ..., with best wishes from ..."

혜찰(惠札) your (kind) letter. ⇨ 혜서

혜택(惠澤) (a) benefit; (a) boon; (a) benefaction; (a) favor; grace. ¶~을 입다[받다] owe (something to a person) / be indebted (to a person for something) / benefit[profit] (by something)∥~을 주다 bestow a favor (on)∥문명의 ~을 받다 share in the benefits of civilization / be benefited by civilization∥미국은 천연자원의 ~을 많이 받고 있다 America is blessed with abundant natural resources.∥이 발명은 인류에게 커다란 ~이다 This invention is a great boon to mankind.

혜한(惠翰) your (kind) letter. ⇨ 혜서

호 a whiff[puff]. ¶촛불을 ~ 하고 끄다 whiff out a candlelight[candle]∥등불을 ~ 하고 불어서 끄다 blow out a lamp with a puff.

호(戶) a house; a door; a family. ¶30~ 되는 작은 마을 a hamlet of thirty houses[families].

호(弧) an arc. ¶백구(白球)가 푸른 하늘에 ~를 그리며 날았다 The white ball described an arc as it flew through the blue sky.

호(湖) a lake. ⇨ 호수(湖水)

호(號) **1** 〔번호〕 a number; an issue(잡지·신문의). ¶제1~ number one(약어 No. 1,) / the first number[issue]∥다음 ~ the next number [issue]∥15~실 Room No. 15∥타임스 5월 ~ the May number[issue] of the "Times" / the "Times" for May∥낡은 ~ a back number∥50~의 풍경화 a landscape about 32 (inches) by 46 inches∥도화동 3번지의 2~ 3-2, Dohwa-dong∥이하 다음 ~에 계속 To be continued.∥다음 ~로 완결 To be concluded (in the next number). **2** 〔장신구의 크기〕 size; 〔실의 굵기〕 count. ¶2~ 더 큰 모자 a hat two sizes larger∥12~의 방적사 12-count cotton. **3** 〔항목〕 an item; a head. ¶제5조 제3항 제2~에 해당하다 come under Paragraph 2, Subsection 3, Section 5. **4** 〔본명·자(字) 이외에 쓰는 이름〕 a pen name; a pseudonym. ¶~가 춘원인 작가 a writer with the pen name of Chunwon∥완당이라는 ~로 알려지다 be well known under the nom de plume of Wandang.

호(壕) a trench. ⇨ 참호

호-(好) good; favorable. ¶~기회 a fine opportunity∥~적수 a good rival[match]∥~재[증권] an encouraging factor / good news.

-호(號) (비행기·배 등의) "the ...". ¶기선 부산~ the S.S. Busan (Ho)∥(넬슨의 기함) 빅토리~ the Victory.

호가(呼價) 〔경〕 a nominal price[quotation]; 〔부르는 값〕 the price asked; the asking price; 〔제공가〕 the price offered; an offer; 〔경매의〕 a bidding; a bid. ¶매입[판매] ~ a nominal quotation for buying[selling]∥물건을 ~대로 사다 buy goods at the price named. **호가하다** ask[bid / offer] a price (for). ➔ 20원 비싸게 호가되다 be quoted twenty won higher.

호가호위(狐假虎威) acting arrogantly through borrowed authority; as an ass in a lion's skin. **호가호위하다** act arrogantly through borrowed authority.

호각(互角) 〔역량이 비슷함〕 equality; evenness; par; a good match. ¶~의 equal / even / equally-matched [-balanced] / well-[evenly-]matched∥~의 경기[접전] a close game / a well-matched game / an equal contest[fight] / an even match / (미) a nip and tuck game∥…과 ~이다 be equal with ...∥~을 이루다 get even (with) / draw level (with)∥~의 형세이다 be well matched [balanced] in strength[power]∥~의 경기를 하다 play an even game.

호각(號角) (a signal) whistle. ¶~을 불다 blow a whistle∥교통순경이 ~을 불어 나를 불러 세웠다 A traffic cop blew his whistle to signal me to stop.

호감(好感) (a) good feeling; (a) good will; (a) goodwill; 〔좋은 인상〕 a favorable [good] impression. ¶~이 가는 amiable / affable / attractive / pleasing∥~이 안 가는 unaffable / unattractive / repulsive∥~이 가는 얼굴 a likable look / a pleasant face∥~을 주다 impress (a person) favorably / give [make] a favorable impression (on [upon] a person)∥~을 가지다 be favorably disposed[inclined] toward (a person) / feel friendly toward (a person) / have a friendly feeling toward (a person)∥남의 ~을 사다 win[find] a person's favor [good will] / be in a person's favor∥그는 사장의 ~을 사고[사지 못하고] 있다 He is in[out of] favor with his boss.∥그녀는 어딘지 모르게 ~이 가는 데가 있다 She has something attractive about her.∥그것은 당국의 ~을 사지 못하고 있다 It is viewed unfavorably by the authorities.

호강 comfort; luxury; sumptuousness. **호강하다** live in luxury [comfort / clover]; live in easy circumstances; be comfortably off; live in the lap of luxury. ¶호강하고 자라다 be

호강스럽다 bred [brought up] in (the lap of) luxury / grow up in well-off circumstances.
호강스럽다 (easy and) comfortable; luxurious. ¶호강스러운 살림 a luxurious life / a life of luxury / comfortable [high] living.
호객(呼客) touting. **호객하다** tout; solicit patronage.
● **호객꾼** a tout(er); (미) a (hotel) runner; (구경거리의) (속어) a barker; (미국 속어) a spieler; (매춘의) a pander; a pimp.
호걸(豪傑) a hero; a great man; an extraordinary man.
● **호걸풍** a heroic [gallant] air.
호걸스럽다(豪傑−) heroic; gallant. ¶호걸스럽게 웃다 laugh broadly.
호격(呼格) [언] the vocative case.
호경기(好景氣) (a wave of) prosperity; a prosperous condition; a brisk market; good times; [벼락 경기] a boom. ¶전시의 ~ a war boom // ~의 prosperous / lively / good / brisk / active (market) / booming (town) // ~의 물결을 타다 take advantage of a boom // 최근 시장은 ~이다 The market has been active [brisk / lively] recently. // 1980년대는 ~였다 There was a (business) boom [Business was good] in the 1980's. // ~를 보이고 있다 Business is looking up.
호곡(號哭) wailing; (wild) lamentation; load weeping. **호곡하다** wail; weep aloud; bewail; weep [cry] bitterly; lament aloud.
호광(弧光) [물] an (electric) arc.
● **호광등** an arc lamp. ⇨ 아크등 **호광로**(−爐) an arc furnace.
호구(戶口) houses and inhabitants; population.
● **호구 조사** census taking; a census. ¶~를 하다 take a census.
호구(虎口) 1 [위태로운 처지나 형편] the jaws of death; danger. ¶~를 벗어나다 escape from the tiger's jaws / escape from the jaws of death / get out of danger // ~에 들어가다 put one's head into the lion's mouth / go into the jaws of death. 2 [바둑] a cross surrounded by three white [black] stones.
호구지책(糊口之策) a means of livelihood [living]; a way to make both ends meet; a living. ¶~이 막히다 have no means of livelihood / find it difficult to make a living // ~을 얻다 make [get] a living / gain a livelihood // 당장의 ~으로 슈퍼마켓에서 일했다 I worked in a supermarket as a stopgap measure [to make ends meet for the moment]. // 그녀는 임시직의 수입으로 ~를 세우고 있다 She is living from hand to mouth [(영) She is living a bare existence] on the income she gets from a part-time job. // 그녀의 변변치 못한 벌이가 가족의 ~이었다 The family lived on her scanty earnings.
호국(護國) defense of the fatherland. ¶~의 꽃으로 산화하다 die fighting gloriously for the country / die a heroic death in action. **호국하다** defend the fatherland.
호기(好期) a good time [occasion]; a good [favorable] season.
호기(好機) a good [golden / favorable] opportunity; a favorable [good] chance; a good time [occasion]; a most appropriate moment. ¶~를 잡다 [포착하다] seize [take] an opportunity / take time by the forelock / take the tide as it offers // ~를 놓치다 miss [lose / let slip] a golden opportunity / miss [lose / let go] a chance // ~를 기다리다 wait and see / gain time / (가만히) lie low // ~를 이용하다 improve one's opportunity / avail oneself of a good opportunity // 이런 ~는 두 번 다시 오지 않을 것이다 Such a chance will never come [offer itself].

호기(豪氣) 1 [씩씩하고 장한 기상] a heroic temper; a sturdy spirit; a stout heart. ¶~를 부리다 make a show of one's sturdy spirit / display one's gallantry. 2 [뽐냄] pride; haughtiness; arrogance; pomposity. ¶~를 부리다 bear oneself haughtily / hold one's head high / mount [ride] the high horse / wear a high hat.
호기롭다(豪氣−) 1 [호걸스럽다] heroic; intrepid; gallant; plucky; daring; stout-hearted. 2 [의기양양하다] proud; haughty; (속어) high-hat(ted).
호기성(好氣性) aerotropism. ¶~의 aerotropic / aerobic.
● **호기성 세균** aerobic bacteria (sing. -rium).
호기심(好奇心) curiosity; inquisitiveness. ¶~이 강한 curious / full of curiosity / inquisitive // ~이 강한 사람들 curious [curiosity-seeking] people / curiosity seekers / the curious // ~에 끌려서 [~에서] prompted [impelled] by curiosity / from [out of] curiosity // ~이 생기다 become [feel] curious // ~에 끌리다 be impelled [prompted] by curiosity / be seized with curiosity // ~을 일으키다 (자신의) become [feel] curious / (남·사물이) stimulate [excite / arouse] (a person's) curiosity / intrigue (a person) // ~을 만족시키다 gratify [satisfy] one's curiosity // 아이들은 ~이 강하다 Children are curious [full of curiosity]. // 그 사람의 과거에 대해 ~을 갖고 있다 [알고 싶다] I am curious to know his past. / I am curious about his past (history). // 그 이야기는 ~을 일으켰다 The story excited [aroused / whetted] my curiosity. // ~에 이끌려 방 안을 들여다보았다 I peeped into the room out of curiosity. // 그는 ~에서 그 이상한 과일을 한입 깨물어 보았다 Out of curiosity [Just to satisfy his curiosity], he took a bite of the strange fruit.
호남(湖南) (지방) the Honam district [area]; the Jeolla-do provinces.
● **호남 고속도로** the Honam [Daejeon-Suncheon] expressway. **호남선** the Honam [Daejeon-Mokpo] Line.
호남아(好男兒) [미남자] a handsome man; a good-[fine-]looking man; an Adonis; [멋진 사내] a fine fellow; a nice fellow [chip]; (미) a regular guy.
호다 sew (seams) with large stitches.
호담하다(豪膽−) stouthearted; bold (hearted); dauntless; (서술적) be stout of heart.
호두(胡桃) → 호두
호도(糊塗) temporizing; a makeshift. ¶일시적인 ~책 (미) a stopgap measure // 그것은 시간을 얻기 위한 ~책에 불과하다 That's a mere shift to gain time. **호도하다** patch up; shuffle; gloss over; varnish. ¶일시적으로 ~ temporize / patch up (things) for the moment / make (a) shift (with) / gloss over (a mistake) // 그는 결코 사실을 호도할 사람이 아니다 He is the last man to gloss over the matter.

호다 severe; harsh; terrible; pitiless; merciless; cruel. ¶호된 더위[추위] intense heat [cold] // 호된 공격 a severe attack // 호된 비평 merciless criticism // 호된 타격을 가하다 strike hard at (the enemy) // 호되게 야단치다 scold (a person) scathingly [unsparingly] / give (a person) a good [sharp] scolding // 호되게 얻어맞다 suffer a heavy blow / be hard hit // 나는 선생님에게 호되게 꾸지람을 들었다 I got a good scolding [telling-off] from my teacher. // 그 작품은 신문에서 호되게 비평을 받았다 The work was criticized [attacked] severely in the newspaper. // 나중에 호되게 야단을 맞을 거야 You are going to get a good scolding later.

호두 [식] a walnut. ¶~ 까는 기구 (a pair of) nutcrackers // ~를 까다 crack a walnut.
● 호두까기 인형 [음] the Nutcracker Suite.
호두나무 a walnut (tree).

호드기 a reed pipe [flute].

호드득거리다 1 [튀는 소리가 나다] crackle; crepitate; decrepitate; snap; pop (옥수수 등이). ¶불이 호드득거리며 타다 burn crackling / burn with a crackling sound / crackle // 콩을 볶으면 호드득거린다 Beans crackle when parched. // 숯이 불붙으면서 호드득거렸다 The charcoal crackled catching fire. 2 [방정 떨다] act frivolously [rashly].

호드득호드득 [튀는 소리] crackling; crepitating; decrepitating; snapping; popping; (방정맞게) rashly; imprudently; frivolously. 호드득호드득하다 crackle; act frivolously. ⇨호드득거리다

호들갑 떨다 [과장해서 말하다] exaggerate; say extravagantly; make too much of (a matter); [야단스럽게 말하다] say [speak] in a histrionic manner. ¶그까짓 생채기로 뭘 그렇게 호들갑 떠냐 What a fuss about such a scratch!

호들갑스럽다 [경망스럽다] flippant; frivolous; [흥감스럽다] exaggerated; bombastic; grandiloquent; hyperbolical; [야단스럽다] histrionic. ¶호들갑스럽게 웃다 laugh in a flippant [frivolous] manner // 하찮은 일로 호들갑스럽게 떠들어 대다 make much ado [a great fuss] about nothing.

호떡 (胡-) a Chinese pancake stuffed with sugar [bean jam].

호락호락 easily; readily; without ado. ¶~ 속아 넘어가다 be deceived easily / be easily taken in [duped] // 네가 생각하는 것처럼 ~ 넘어갈 내가 아니다 I am not such an easy prey [mark] as you'd take me for. // 나는 ~ 넘어가지 않는다 I won't let [allow] myself to be taken in. // 절대로 그것을 ~ 넘겨 줄 수는 없다 I'll be hanged if I let him take it without a (good) fight. 호락호락하다 ready; easily manageable; tractable. ¶호락호락하지 않다 be very hard to manage [deal with].

호랑나비 (虎狼-) [동] a swallowtail (butterfly).

호랑이 (虎狼-) 1 [범] a tiger; a tigress (암컷). ¶~가 으르렁거렸다 A tiger growled [roared]. 2 [사납고 무서운 사람] a cruel [merciless] person; inhumanly sharp person. ¶~ 영감 a snarling old man // ~ 상사 a tough sergeant // ~ 형사 a crack detective // ~ 검사 a relentless prosecutor.
호랑이 굴에 가야 호랑이 새끼를 잡는다 (속담) Nothing venture, nothing have [win].;
Nought venture, nought have.
호랑이 담배 먹을 적 (속담) in ancient [old] time [days]; a long time ago.
호랑이도 제 말 하면 온다 (속담) Talk of the devil, and he is sure to appear.; Talk of angels, and you will hear their wings.

호령 (號令) a (word of) command; an order. ¶ ~에 따라 [~이 떨어지자] at the word of command // ~을 내리다 give a (word of) command / (큰 소리로) shout a command (to). 호령하다 command; order; give an order [a command]; dictate (명령하다). ¶천하를 ~ dictate to the Empire / hold sway over the whole country.

호로자식 (-子息) →후레자식

호롱 a small kerosene lamp (without a chimney).

호루라기 a whistle.

호르르 1 [불타는 모양] rapidly; lightly. ¶~ 타 오르다 (strips of paper) burn [go] up lightly in a flame. 2 [나는 모양] flapping; fluttering. ¶~ 날아가 버리다 fly away with a flap of the wings. 3 [호각 소리] whistling; piping. ¶~ 불다 whistle / pipe // 호각 소리가 ~ 났다 The warbling [trilling] of a whistle was heard.

호르몬 [생] hormone. ¶남[여]성 ~ male [female] (sex) hormone // ~의 hormonal / hormonic.
● 호르몬 결핍증 anhormonia; hormone deficiency. 호르몬제 a hormone drug [preparation].

호른 [음] a horn. ¶~을 불다 play [sound / toot] a horn.

호리다 1 [넋을 잃게 하다] bewitch; enchant; fascinate; captivate. 2 [유혹하다] seduce; allure; entice. ¶여자를 잘 호리는 남자 a woman-killer / a Don Juan // 남자를 잘 호리는 여자 a vamp / (속어) a man-killer.

호리 (-瓶) a gourd (bottle); a calabash. ¶~ 모양의 gourd-shaped.
● 호리병박 [식] a bottle gourd. ¶~ 모양의 gourd-shaped.

호리호리하다 slim; slender; thin; lean; lanky; (구어) weedy. ¶호리호리한 소녀 a slim girl // 호리호리한 몸매 a thin [slender] figure / slender build // 호리호리한 소년 a lanky [gangling] boy // 호리호리하게 자라다 grow tall and thin [slender] // 소년은 호리호리하고 키가 크다 The boy is lanky [tall and slender].

호마이카 →포마이카

호명 (呼名) calling (a person) by name; roll call. ¶~에 대답하다 answer to one's name. 호명하다 call (a person) by name; make a roll call; call the roll. ¶학생을 하나하나 ~ call over the names of the pupils one after another // 선생님은 학생들을 호명하였다 The teacher called out the students' names.
● 호명자 a caller.

호모 (경멸적 속어) a homo; a gay.
호모 사피엔스 [고고] Homo sapiens.

호미 a hoe with a short handle. ¶~로 감자를 캐다 dig out [up] potatoes with a hoe.
호미로 막을 것을 가래로 막는다 (속담) A stitch in time saves nine.; Prevention is better than cure.
● 호미자락 the lower part of a hoe blade. ¶비가 ~만큼 오다 have a rain that soaks the soil an inch deep.

호밀(胡-) [식] rye.
호박 a pumpkin; a squash(호리병박 모양의). ¶ 같은 얼굴 a pumpkin-like[an ugly] face / 굴러 들어온 ~ It is a piece of good luck[a godsend / a windfall].// 그들에게 경고해 주었지만 ~에 침묵기었다 My warning fell flat[was lost / had no effect] on them.
● 호박고지 dried slices of young pumpkin. 호박씨 a pumpkin seed. 호박죽 winter squash porridge.
호박(琥珀) [광] amber; succinite; glessite. ¶인조 ~ artificial amber / amberoid // ~의 suc-cinic.
● 호박산 succinic acid. 호박색 amber (color); lime.
호반(湖畔) the shores of a lake; a lakeside; a lakefront. ¶ ~의 lakeside / by[on] the lake// ~의 호텔 a hotel by the lake / a lakeside hotel.
● 호반새 [동] a Korean ruddy kingfisher. 호반 시인 (one of) the Lake poets.
호방하다(豪放-) manly and large-minded [broad-minded / open-hearted].
호배추(胡-) [식] a Chinese cabbage; a pe-tsai.
호별(戶別) each house. ¶ ~로 from house to house / from door to door.
● 호별 방문 a house-to-house[door-to-door] visit; (선거에서) a house-to-house canvass. ¶ ~을 하다 make[pay] house-to-house calls [visits] / visit from door to door / (선거에서) make a house-to-house canvass / canvass door to door // 그는 ~하여 백과사전을 팔고 있다 He is a door-to-door encyclopedia salesman. / He goes from house to house selling encyclopedias. 호별 조사 a house-to-house investigation; a door-to-door inspec-tion.
호봉(號俸) a pay step; a salary class. ¶ 5~ a fifth-class salary // 그는 ~ 조정 외에는 공무원들의 봉급이 동결될 것이라고 언급했다 He noted that the wages of government officials would be frozen except in the case of promo-tion in the salary step.
호부(好否) good and[or] bad; likes and[or] dislikes. ¶ ~ 간에 whether it is good or not [proper or not] / whether one likes it or not.
호불호(好不好) good and[or] bad. ⇨호부
호사(豪奢) extravagance; luxury; sumptuous-ness; magnificence. 호사하다 repose in the lap of luxury; roll in luxury.
● 호사바치 a dandy; a gallant; a fop; a coxcomb; (미) a dude; a beau (pl. beaux, ~s).
호사가(好事家) a dilettante (pl. ~s, -ti); a busybody; a curiosity seeker; a curious person; a person of fantastic taste(s).
호사다마(好事多魔) Lights are usually fol-lowed by shadows; There's many a slip between the cup and the lip.
호사스럽다(豪奢-) luxurious; extravagant; sumptuous; magnificent; grand. ¶호사스러운 만찬 a grand dinner[feast] // 호사스럽게 꾸민 집 a sumptuously furnished house // 호사스러운 생활을 하다 live in great splendor [grand style] / live in extravagance[luxury] / live like a lord[prince] // 호사스러운 여행을 하다 travel like a lord[prince] / travel in an expensive way[in great style] / (미) go on a junket(공비로).

호상(好喪) a propitious mourning (of a per-son dying old and rich).
호상(湖上) ¶ ~에서 [의] on[in] the lake// ~의 일몰 [보트 놀이] sunset[boating] on the lake.
● 호상 가옥 a lake dwelling. 호상 생활자 a lake dweller.
호상(豪商) a wealthy merchant[business-man]; a merchant prince; a business mag-nate; (미국 속어) a baron.
호상(護喪) (행위) taking charge of a funeral ceremony; (사람) the master[a man in charge] of a funeral ceremony. 호상하다 take charge of a funeral ceremony.
● 호상소 the office in charge of a funeral ceremony.
호색(好色) sensuality; amorousness; lewd-ness; lechery; lasciviousness; lust; eroti-cism. ¶ ~의 sensual / amorous / lewd / las-civious / lustful / lecherous / erotic / inde-cent / (미국 속어) horny.
● 호색가 / 호색꾼 a lewd[lustful] man; a lecher; a goat; a satyr; a sensualist; a person devoted to sex life; a Don Juan.
호선(互先) an unhandicapped match of baduk. ⇨맞바둑
호선(互選) co-optation; mutual election. 호선하다 co-opt; elect by mutual vote; elect from among (themselves). → 사무장은 당원 중에서 호선되었다 The secretary-general was elected from among the members of the party.
호선(弧線) an arc.
호세아서(-書) [성] (The Book of) Hosea(약어 Hos.).
호소(呼訴) (불평 등의) a complaint; (법 등에의) an appeal; a petition. ¶무언의 ~ a mute appeal // ~력이 약하다 be of little appeal to people). 호소하다 (불평을) complain of; (정의·힘·무기 등에) appeal to (a sense of justice); appeal[resort] to (arms); have recourse to (violence); appeal (to the eye, to the pictori-al instinct, etc.). ¶고통을 ~ complain of a pain / 이성 [정의감]에 ~ appeal to one's reason[sense of justice] // 법에 ~ appeal to the law / bring an action[a suit] (against a person) // 완력에 ~ resort[go] to force [violence] / use force / have recourse to vio-lence // 국민에게 ~ appeal to the people [nation] // 자비심에 ~ throw oneself (a person's) charity / appeal to (a person) for mercy // 온 천하에 ~ appeal to the world // 환자는 고통을 호소했다 The patient com-plained of pain. // 그 연설은 국민에게 호소하는 힘이 없다 The speech does not have the power to appeal to the people. // 나는 법에 호소할 준비가 되어 있다 I am ready to go to law. // 소녀는 호소하듯이 말없이 나를 보았다 The girl looked at me in mute appeal. // 우리는 법에 호소하는 수밖에 없다 We have no choice but to fall back on the law[to take legal action].
호소(湖沼) lakes and marshes. ¶ ~의 lacus-trine.
호송(護送) escort; convoy. ¶ ...의 ~하에 under escort of ... // 군대의 ~을 받다 be sent under convoy of troops. 호송하다 escort; convoy; send (a person) under due escort; (죄수를) send[transport] (a person) under guard[under police escort] (to a prison). ¶

수송선을 ~ convoy transports // 국왕의 배는 5척의 구축함이 호송했다 The king's ship had an escort of five destroyers. ➔ ¶5억 원의 지폐는 경찰의 순찰차로 은행까지 호송되었다 The 500,000,000 won banknotes were sent to the bank guarded by a police patrol car.
● **호송차** a convoy. **호송차** (죄수의) a prison (motor-)van; a patrol wagon; a paddy wagon.

호수 (戶數) the number of houses[families]. ¶~가 100쯤 되는 마을 a village of about 100 houses.

호수 (湖水) a lake. ¶산정 ~ Lake Sanjeong // ~에 사는[나는] [생] lacustrine // ~가 많은 laky // ~의 lacustrine (dwellings) // 호숫가에 on the shore of a lake // 호숫가에 있는 다방 a lakeside[lakefront] teahouse / a teahouse on the lake // 호숫가에 있는 별장 a lakeside vacation cottage / a villa on[by] the lake.

호수 (號數) number; a register[serial] number. ¶집 ~ the number of a house // ~를 거듭하다 go through[run into] several editions // ~마다 연재하다 publish (a novel) serially.

호스 a hose; a hosepipe. ¶고무 ~ a rubber hose // 소방 ~ a fire hose // ~로 물을 뿌리다 hose water (over / on) / water (the garden) with a hose // 그들은 불타고 있는 집으로 ~를 돌렸다 They trained hoses on the burning house.

호스텔 a hostel. ¶유스 ~ a youth hostel.
호스티스 a hostess; a barmaid(여급).
호스피스 a hospice.

호시절 (好時節) a good season (for). ¶…의 ~이다 It is a good time for …. / We are in the best season for ….

호시탐탐 (虎視眈眈) with vigilant hostility; gloatingly. ¶그는 ~ 공격의 기회를 노렸다 He watched thirstily for a chance to attack. **호시탐탐하다** glare at with fierceness; be vigilantly hostile; keep a vigilant eye (on a person); watch for an opportunity [a chance] (to prey upon one's opponent).

호신 (護身) self-protection; self-defense. ¶~용의[으로] for self-protection / for use in self-defense // ~용 칼 a sword for self-protection [for one's own protection]. **호신하다** protect oneself; defend oneself.
● **호신술** the art of self-defense.

호심 (湖心) the heart[center] of a lake.
호안 (護岸) shore[bank] protection.
● **호안 공사** shore[bank] protection works; embankment; riparian works.

호언 (好言) kind words; nice words.
호언 (豪言) big[tall] talk; boasting; a bombast; high-flown words. ¶~을 하다 talk big / boast / talk boastfully[bombastically] / brag / swagger / vaunt // ~이라고 ~을 하다 boast that … / say boastfully that ….
● **호언장담** big talk; boasting.

호연 (好演) good acting; an excellent performance (of a play). ¶~을 하다 put up a good show.

호연지기 (浩然之氣) ¶~를 기르다 revive one's exhausted[spent] energy / refresh[recreate] oneself (with) / enliven one's spirits.

호열자 (虎列刺) 〈음역〉 cholera. ⇨콜레라
호외 (戶外) the open air; the open. ¶~ 의 out-of-door / open-air.

호외 (號外) an extra (edition) (of a newspaper); a special. ¶~를 발행하다 publish [issue] an extra // ~로 보도하다 announce (an event) in an extra // "~요! ~!" 하며 외치다 shout "Extra, Extra!"

호우 (豪雨) a heavy rain[rainfall]; a torrential [hard] rain; a downpour; cataracts [a deluge] of rain. ¶집중 ~ a localized torrential downpour // 그 지역에 ~가 내렸다 A heavy rain visited the area. / There was a heavy rainfall in the area.
● **호우 주의보** a torrential[heavy] rain warning.

호위 (護衛) a guard; an escort; a bodyguard; (집합적) guard; bodyguard; escort; convoy. ¶…의 ~ 아래[~를 받고] under the escort of …. **호위하다** guard; escort; (군함·군대가) convoy (a ship / supplies). ➔ ¶경관에 호위되어 under police escort // 이들 유조선은 군함에 호위되어 인도양을 건넜다 These tankers were escorted[convoyed] by warships across the Indian Ocean.
● **호위병** a guard; a military escort. **호위함** a naval escort; a convoy; an escort (warship).

호응 (呼應) 1 [기맥 상통] acting in concert. **호응하다** act in concert[unison] (with); be in sympathy (with); respond to (a request). ¶호응하여 in concert[cooperation] (with) / in response (to) / in collusion (with)(공모) // 바다와 육지에서 서로 호응하여 적을 공격하였다 Land and sea forces attacked the enemy in concert. 2 [언] concord; agreement. ¶시제의 ~ sequence of tenses. **호응하다** agree.

호의 (好意) good will; goodwill; good wishes; friendliness; kindness; favor; courtesy. ¶M 씨의 ~ kindness of Mr. M // ~로[~에서] out of courtesy / through kindness / out of good will // …의 ~로 through the kindness of … / by the courtesy of … // ~으로 ~에 보답하다 return (a person's) favor by … // ~를 가지다 feel[entertain] good will (toward) / be friendly[warm] (to) / regard (a person) kindly / have a liking (for) // …에게 ~를 보이다 show a friendly feeling for … / show a feeling of amity toward … // ~를 저버리다 [무시하다] fail to return[respond to] (a person's) kindness / reject (a person's) kind intentions / decline (a person's) kind offer // 남의 ~를 받아들이다 accept another's favor with pleasure // ~에 감사드립니다 Many thanks for your kindness. // ~로 한 것이 오히려 그에게 폐가 되었다 What I meant for her good proved harmful to her. // 모처럼의 ~가 악의로 받아들여졌다 My good intentions were taken amiss. // 친구의 ~로 이 일자리를 얻었다 I got this job through the kindness[good offices] of my friend. // 극장에 초대하겠다는 그녀의 ~를 저버려서는 안 된다 You had better not turn down her kind invitation to the theater.

호의 (好誼) good[warm] friendship; good terms; intimacy.

호의적 (好意的) friendly; amicable; kind; kindly. ¶~인 충고 well-meant advice // ~인 회답 a favorable answer[reply] // ~으로 in a friendly way / out of good will / with good intentions / with a good will // 아무리 ~으로 보아도 even when considered in a most favorable light / to say the most of it / at best // ~인 눈으로 보다 see (a thing) with a favorable eye / view (a thing) in a favorable light // 우리는 ~인 답변을 얻어 내지 못했다

호의호식 We didn't get a favorable answer.∥아무리 ~으로 보아도 그는 수재는 아니다 Even viewed in the most favorable light, he can't be called brilliant. / No matter how partial to him you may be, you can't call him brilliant.

호의호식(好衣好食) dressing well and faring richly; high living; comfort; luxury. **호의호식하다** dress well and fare richly; live high [well / in clover].

호인(好人) a good-natured person; a good [nice] fellow; a nice chap; (미) a regular guy.

호인(胡人) 1 (만주 사람) a Manchurian. 2 a barbarian. ⇨⁼야만인(⇨)야만).

호재(好材) good material; excellent data; [증권] favorable [strong] indications; bullish factors; favorable news.

호적(戶籍) (등록) census registration; [호적부] a census [family] register. ¶~에 올리다 [~에서 빼다] have (a person's) name entered in [deleted from] the family register ∥~ 조사를 하다 (개인이) inquire into a person's family register / (호적리가) take the census∥~의 정정을 신청하다 apply for the rectification of one's family register.
●**호적계**(원) a registrar. **호적부** a family register. **호적 초본**[등본] an extract [a copy] of one's family register.

호적(胡笛) →태평소

호적(號笛) a hooter; a horn; a siren; a klaxon. ¶~을 울리다 hoot / whistle.

호적수(好敵手) a good match [rival]; a worthy opponent; a lively competitor; a foeman worthy of one's steel. ¶~를 만나다 meet one's match∥~가 나타났다 A noticeable rival came up (in our line of business).∥그는 나의 테니스의 ~다 He is a good match for me at tennis.∥두 팀은 서로 ~이다 The two teams are well matched.

호적하다(好適-) suitable; good; best; fitted; ideal. ¶~에 ~ be suitable [suited] for ... / be right fit for ....

호전(好轉) a favorable turn [move]; a turn [change] for the better; improvement; a rally; pickup. ¶식량 사정의 ~ improvement in the food situation. **호전하다** take a favorable turn; change [take a turn] for the better; improve. ➜¶그의 병세가 호전되었다 He has rallied. / He has gotten better. / He is feeling better. / His illness took a turn for the better.∥경기가 호전되었다 Business has improved.∥환자의 상태가 호전되었다 The patient's condition has taken a turn [changed] for the better.∥주식 시장은 호전될 것이다 The stock market will pick up.

호전성(好戰性) bellicosity.

호전적(好戰的) jingoistic; bellicose; warlike; pro-war. ¶~ 민족 a warlike race∥~인 언사를 쓰다 employ warlike language∥~인 국민이라는 딱지가 붙다 be branded as a warlike nation [people].

호접(胡蝶) [동] a butterfly. ⇨나비².

호젓하다 still; quiet; hushed; deserted; lonely; solitary; desolate. ¶호젓한 곳 an out-of-the-way place∥호젓한 거리 a deserted street∥호젓한 산길 a lonely [lonesome] mountain path∥산속의 호젓한 마을 a lonely [isolated] village in the mountains∥그 작은 집은 숲 속에 호젓하게 서 있었다 The little house stood quietly and alone among the trees.

호정(糊精) [화] dextrin(e).

호조(好調) favorableness; satisfactoriness; a favorable tone [tendency / trend]; [증권] improvement. ¶~다 good / favorable / satisfactory / improved / promising∥~다 (선수 등이) be in good condition [shape] / be in (good) form / (몸의 컨디션이) be in the pink (of health)∥~로 진행되다 go off well [smoothly] / progress favorably [satisfactorily]∥~차츰 ~를 보이다 take a favorable turn / turn for the better / show a favorable tendency.

호족(豪族) a powerful family [clan].

호주(戶主) the head of a family [household]; the master of a house; a householder. ¶~와의 관계 one's relation to the head of the family.
●**호주권** the headship of a family; the leadership of a household. **호주 상속** succession to (the headship of) a house. **호주 상속인** an heir(ess).

호주머니(胡-) [주머니] a pocket; (속어) a kick. ¶뚜껑 ~ a flap pocket∥바지 ~ a trouser(s) pocket∥바지 뒤 ~ a hip [back] pocket∥스커트 ~ a placket∥안 ~ an inside pocket∥옆 ~ a side pocket∥조끼 ~ a vest pocket∥~ 속의 작은 ~ a small change pocket∥~가 없는 pocketless∥~에 들어가는 pocket(-size(d)) / pocketable (radio) / vestpocket (dictionary)∥~에 손을 찔러 넣고 with one's hands (buried) in the pockets∥~에 넣다 pocket / put (a thing) in [into] one's pocket∥~에 손을 넣다 reach in one's pocket∥~에 손을 넣어 더듬다 feel [fumble / dip] in one's pocket (for)∥~를 뒤지다 fish in one's pocket (for) / search one's pocket∥~에서 꺼내다 take (a letter) out of one's pocket / draw (a newspaper) from one's pocket∥~가 두둑하다 have a long [heavy / plump / well-filled] purse / have a fat pocketbook [purse] / be flush of money∥~가 비다 have a light [a lean / a slender / an empty] purse∥~에 한 푼도 없다 be penniless / have no money with one∥제 ~를 채우다 [살찌우다] fill one's own pockets / fatten one's purse∥남의 ~를 생각하다 be mindful of another's pocketbook∥~를 톡톡 털다 empty one's purse to the last penny [cent] / clear one's purse out∥~를 잔뜩 채우다 cram [stuff] one's pocket (with)∥~ 속에 있는 것을 전부 내놓아라 Turn out your pocket.∥~에 무엇을 넣고 다니니 What are you carrying in your pockets?∥이 라디오는 ~에 쏙 들어간다 You can carry this radio in your pocket.∥그 남자는 한 손을 ~에 넣고 서 있었다 The man was standing with his hand in his pocket.∥전철 안에서 ~에 든 것을 소매치기당했다 I had my pocket picked in a train.∥모자라는 내 ~에서 냈다 I made up the deficit of my pocket.
●**호주머니 사정** one's financial condition. ⇨주머니 사정(⇨주머니).

호출(呼出) [불러냄] a call; calling out; [소환] a summons; citing; a subpoena(법원의). ¶자동 ~ an automatic calling∥장거리 전화(의) ~ a trunk [long-distance] call(경찰 등의). ~에 응하다 [응하지 않다] answer [ignore] a summons∥월요일에 경찰서에 오라는 ~을 받았다 I got a summons to be at the police

station on Monday. **호출하다** call (a person) out; (전화로) ring (a person) up on the phone; (법정으로) summon; cite; subpoena. ¶원고[피고]를 ~ cite the plaintiff[defendant] (before the judge). →¶법정으로 호출당하다 be summoned to the court∥사장에게 호출당하다 be called before the president∥그는 법원에 호출당했다 He was summoned to appear in court.
● **호출 부호** (무선 전신국의) a call sign; call letters. **호출장** (a writ of) summons (*pl.* ~es); a subpoena. ¶~을 송달하다 serve a summons[subpoena] on (a person).
호치키스 a stapler; a stapling machine; (상표명) a Hotchkiss (paper fastener). ¶~로 철한 서류 stapled papers∥이 서류를 ~로 철해 주시오 Please staple these papers together.
호칭(呼稱) a name; a title; a designation; an appellation. **호칭하다** call; name; designate.
호콩(胡-) [식] a peanut. ⇨땅콩
호쾌하다(豪快-) exciting; stirring; animating; heroic (attempt). ¶호쾌한 인물 a large-hearted man.
호크(㏌haak) [갈고리 단추] a hook; a snap hook; a hook and eye. ¶~로 채우다 hook (up) (a dress)∥~를 벗기다 unhook / undo a hook and eye∥등을 ~로 채우는 블라우스 a blouse that hooks in the back∥그는 칼라의 ~를 끌렀다 He unhooked his collar.
호탕하다(豪宕-) magnanimous; large-minded. ¶호탕한 웃음 a broad[a hearty / an open] laugh.
호텔 a hotel. ¶~의 로비 hotel lobby∥~에 lounge in a hotel∥~ 생활을 하는 사람 a hotel resident∥~의 경영자[지배인] a hotel-keeper / a hotelier∥~의 종업원 a hotel employee / [사무원] a hotel clerk / [접객원] a room clerk∥~ 생활을 하다 make one's home in a hotel∥~에 묵다 put up at a hotel / (미) register[check in] at a hotel∥~에 묵고 있다 stay at a hotel∥~을 경영하다 keep[run] a hotel∥~ 예약을 해 놓았습니다 I've arranged your hotel accommodation. ∥나는 저 ~에 방을 하나 예약했다 I made a reservation for a room in that hotel. / I reserved a room at that hotel.
● **호텔 시설** hotel facilities. **호텔업자** hotelman.
호통 hurling words of thunder; a yell. **호통(을) 치다** hurl words of thunder (at); storm[nag / thunder / roar / snarl / snap] (at a person); give (a person) a good scolding[blowing-up]. ¶벽력같이 ~ shout in a voice of thunder.
호투(好投) [야구] good[fine / nice] pitching. ¶~를 계속하다 keep up the good pitching. **호투하다** pitch well[a good pitch]. ¶그는 시종 호투했다 He pitched well throughout the game.
호평(好評) (a) favorable criticism; a favorable comment [reception / notice / opinion]; public favor. ¶~의 of good repute / well-reputed∥~이다 be popular[be highly[favorably] spoken of/enjoy[win / gain] popularity∥학생들 사이에 ~이다 be popular with[among] (college) students∥~을 받다 be favorably commented upon / meet with public approval / gain public favor / be given a favorable reception∥신문의 ~을 받다 be favorably noticed by the press / have a good press∥그의 소설은 ~을 받았다 His novel was favorably[well] received. / His novel received favorable reviews.∥그의 강연은 학생들 사이에 ~이었다 His lectures were popular with[among] the students. **호평하다** criticize favorably; give a favorable reception to; receive well[favorably].
호피(虎皮) a tiger skin.
호학(好學) love of learning; intellectual appetite[thirst]. **호학하다** love[be fond of] learning.
호한(好漢) a nice[jolly] fellow; (미국 속어) a regular guy; (속어) a brick.
호항(湖港) a lake harbor.
호헌(護憲) [헌법을 옹호함] protection[safe-guarding] of the constitution.
● **호헌 운동** a Constitution protection movement; a movement for the defense of the Constitution.
호형(弧形) an arc (form / shape).
호형호제(呼兄呼弟) close[intimate] friendship. **호형호제하다** call each other brother; be intimate with each other.
호혜(互惠) reciprocity; mutual benefits.
● **호혜 조약** a reciprocal treaty. **호혜주의** a principle of reciprocity.
호호[1](呼-) [입김 뿜는 소리] blowing and blowing; in puffs[whiffs]. ¶추위서 손을 ~ 불다 warm one's hands with one's breath / breathe upon one's hands to keep them warm. **호호하다** whiff; puff (at).
호호[2] [웃음소리] ha-ha; haw-haw.
호호백발(皓皓白髮) hoar(y) hair; snowy[snow-white] hair; a white-headed[-haired] old man(사람).
호화(豪華) [관형어적]. **호화하다** splendid; gorgeous. ⇨호화롭다
● **호화 주택** a palatial mansion. **호화판** an edition deluxe; a deluxe edition. ¶이건 ~이군 This is really wonderful. / This is quite a thing.
호화롭다(豪華-) splendid; gorgeous; most luxurious; deluxe (car); (a hotel) de luxe. ¶호화로운 식사 a sumptuous meal / a luxurious table∥호화로운 생활을 하다 live in luxury / live in grand style∥호화로운 여행을 하다 travel like a prince∥나는 오늘 호화로운 식사를 했다 I had a sumptuous meal today. **호화로이** splendidly; gorgeously; luxuriously.
호화스럽다(豪華-) splendid; gorgeous. ⇨호화롭다
호화찬란하다(豪華燦爛-) gorgeous; brilliant; gaudy; dazzling; pompous; sumptuous. ¶호화찬란하게 치장하다 be gorgeously dressed.
호환(互換) an interchange. ¶~이 가능한 compatible / interchangeable. **호환하다** interchange.
● **호환성** compatibility; interchangeability. **호환성 컴퓨터** a compatible computer.
호환(虎患) a disaster caused by a tiger; the ravages of tigers.
호황(好況) a prosperous condition; prosperity; a boom; a brisk market. ¶~의 prosperous / favorable / brisk (market) / thriving[flourishing] (business)∥~이다 be prosperous / be in a prosperous condition / (미) boom / (물건이) be in good demand∥~을 보이다 show signs of prosperity / present a favorable aspect∥한국의 자동차 공업은 ~이

호흡

다 The Korean car industry is flourishing [thriving / booming]. (▶ flourishing은 최전성기에 있음, thriving은 유리한 조건하에서 번영함, booming은 일시적 경기로 들끓음) // 그의 장사는 ~을 누리고 있다 He is doing a flourishing business. / His business is flourishing. // 출판업은 ~으로 접어들고 있다 The publishing business has taken a turn for the better [is looking up]. // 최근의 ~ 덕분에 실업자가 급격히 줄었다 Thanks to the healthy economy, the number of the unemployed has dropped sharply in recent years. // 금년은 여름이 더워 맥주홀이 대~이다 It's so hot this summer that the beer halls are having a great year [doing a great business]. // 새 정거장이 생겨서 근방 가게들이 ~을 보이고 있다 With the construction of a new station, the nearby stores are doing a lively [brisk] business.

● 호황 국면(-局面) a booming stage. ¶~에 접어들다 enter a booming stage.

호흡(呼吸) 1 a breath; breathing; respiration. ¶심~ deep breathing // 복식 ~ abdominal breathing // 인공~ artificial breathing [respiration] // 정상 ~[의] eupn(o)ea // ~이 곤란하다 have difficulty in breathing / breathe with difficulty / breathe hard / labor for breath // ~이 급박하다 be pressed for breath / be hard of breathing // ~이 끊기다 expire / cease to breathe / breathe one's last // ~을 세다 count the respirations // 그는 ~이 빠르다 He breathes fast. / His breath [respiration] is rapid. // ~은 정상입니다 Respiration is normal. 호흡하다 breathe; respire.

2 (일을 함께할 때의 장단) tone; time. ¶~이 맞다 be in rhythm / tune (with) / be in harmony (with) / hit it off together // 남과 ~을 맞추다 attune oneself (to) / make oneself agreeable to another / keep tune (with) / (구어) keep in with another // 저 두 배우는 서로 ~이 완벽하게 맞는다 The two actors balance each other perfectly. / The two actors agree in tone. / Those two actors work with each other in perfect harmony. // 두 사람은 서로 ~이 잘 맞았다 The two of them hit it off very well together.

● 호흡 곤란 difficulty in breathing; difficult breathing; laboring breath. 호흡기 the respiratory organs. 호흡 기능 respiratory function. 호흡 정지[의] apn(o)ea.

혹¹ 1 (피부의) a wen; a lump; a bump; a swelling; a protuberance; (낙타의) a hump. ¶얼굴 왼쪽에 ~이 있다 have a wen on the left side of one's face // 목에 ~이 생기다 have a growth on one's neck // ~을 떼다 cut away a wen // 나는 머리를 얻어맞아 ~이 생겼다 I developed a bump [lump] on my head where I was hit. 2 (식물의 줄기·뿌리 등의) a knot (on a tree); a knob; a gnarl; a node. ¶~투성이의 knotty / knurly / knurled / gnarled.

혹 떼러 갔다 혹 붙여 온다 (속담) Many go out for wool and come home shorn.

혹² 1 (마시는 소리·모양) with a gulf [breath]. ¶한숨에 ~ 들이마시다 drink (it) down in one gulf. 2 (입김 부는 소리·모양) with a puff [whiff / blow]. ¶촛불을 ~ 불어 끄다 blow [puff] out a candle.

혹(或) possibly; if. ⇨ 혹시

혹간(或間) occasionally; at times. ⇨ 간혹

혹독하다(酷毒-) [모질다] severe; hard; harsh; cruel; unfeeling; [엄하다] strict; stringent; rigorous; exacting. ¶혹독한 벌 a cruel [severe] punishment // 혹독한 비평 harsh [bitter] criticism // 혹독한 추위 intense cold // 혹독한 처사 cruel act / severe practices. 혹독히 cruelly; severely; harshly; with severity [cruelty]. ¶~ 다루다 treat (a person) harshly [cruelly / hardly] / deal harshly (with) / handle cruelly.

혹부리 a person who has a wen [growth] (on his face). ¶~ 영감님 이야기 the story of an old man who got his wen snatched off by demons.

혹사(酷使) driving hard; abuse; ill-usage; exploitation. ¶육체[두뇌]의 ~ an immoderate use of one's physical [mental] powers / abuse of one's body [brain] // (물건이) ~에 견디다 withstand rough use. 혹사하다 work [drive] (a person) hard; keep [hold / put] (a person's) nose [face] to the grindstone; sweat (one's employees). ¶혹사하는 사람 a hard master [mistress] // 몸을 ~ overwork [overdrive] oneself / work too hard // 가정부를 ~ drive one's housemaid too hard // 불충분한 임금으로 일꾼을 ~ underpay and sweat one's workers // 그는 부하를 혹사하고 있다 He overworks his men. // 주인이 그들을 혹사했다 The boss drove them hard. / Their boss worked them very hard. → ¶혹사당하는 노동자 downtrodden workers // 죽도록 혹사당하다 be worked [squeezed] to death (by one's master) // 그는 사용주에게 값싼 임금으로 혹사당했다 He was underpaid and overworked by his employer.

혹서(酷暑) the intense [severe / scorching / fierce / violent / torrid] heat of summer. ¶~의 계절 the hot season / the hottest weather // ~에 견디다 stand the heat of summer // 그는 도시의 ~를 피해서 온양으로 갔다 He went to Onyang to escape the intense heat of the city. // ~에 건강 조심하십시오 Please take good care of yourself in this terrible heat.

혹설(或說) one opinion; a certain view [argument].

혹성(惑星) a planet. ⇨ 행성

혹세무민하다(惑世誣民-) delude the world and deceive the people.

혹시(或是) 1 [어쩌면] possibly; by some possibility; maybe; by (some) chance. ¶~ 집에 계신가 하고 on the chance that I may find you at home // ~ 그럴지도 모른다 It may be so. // ~ 그를 만날 수 있을까 해서 그의 사무실을 찾아갔다 I called at his office on the (off-)chance that I might be able to see him. // ~ 내가 못 가면 혼자 가 주십시오 Please go alone, if by any chance I cannot go. // ~ 런던에서 그를 만나면 안부나 전해 주시오 If you happen to see him in London, give my best regards. // ~ 자네가 그를 만나게 되면, 내가 만나고 싶어 한다고 전해 주게 If by (any) chance you should see him, tell him I want to see him.

2 [행여나] [걱정하여] lest ... should ...; for fear of ... [that ... may ...]. ¶~ ...하지나 않을까 하여 for fear of ... [that ... may ...] // 그것을 보시지 않으셨습니까 I was wondering if you might have seen it. / Did you happen

to see it?// 그가 집에 있으리라고는 생각하지 않았지만 ~나 하고 전화를 걸어 보았다 I did not expect him to be home, but I called just in case.// ~나 하고 생각한 것이 사실이 되었다 A possibility has become an actuality. / What I feared has come to pass.// ~ 남이 보지 않을까 하고 그는 나무 뒤에 숨어 있었다 He hid (himself) behind a tree for fear that he should be seen[(문어) lest he should be seen].

혹심하다(酷甚−) severe; hard; harsh; rigorous; intense; extreme; violent. ¶혹심한 벌 a cruel[severe] punishment//혹심한 더위 severe[intense] heat//혹심한 피해를 입다 suffer heavy losses.

혹여(或如) possibly; if. ⇨°혹시

혹은(或−) or; either ... or. ⇨°또는

혹자(或者) 1 [어떤 사람] some; someone; somebody; a certain[some] person; a Mr. So-and-so. ¶~는 이렇게 ~는 저렇게 말한다 Some say one thing and others another. 2 possibly; if. ⇨°혹시

혹평(酷評) (a) severe[harsh / bitter / sharp / scathing / slashing] criticism; a cruel remark; strictures; hypercriticism. ¶(저서가) ~을 받다 be subjected to severe criticism / be condemned//그럴 만하게 deserve critical censure//그의 소설은 ~을 받았다 His novel was severely criticized. / His novel was subjected to severe[harsh] criticism. **혹평하다** criticize sharply[bitterly / severely]; pass[offer] harsh[incisive] criticism (on); speak bitterly[badly] of (a person); say harsh things about (an opposition party); hypercriticize; (미) pound[score / beat] (a person) like anything. ¶그는 그 연극을 혹평했다 He panned[ran down] the play.
● **혹평가** a bitter[sharp / severe] critic; a hypercritic.

혹하다(惑−) 1 [유혹되다] be tempted; be seduced; [홀딱 빠지다] be infatuated with (a woman); be captivated[fascinated] by (a woman's beauty); fall a victim to (a woman's charms); lose one's head over (a woman); give oneself up (to). ¶물욕에 ~ be blinded by love of gain//여색에 ~ be smitten with[by] a woman's charms / be addicted to lust(정욕에)//돈에 혹하여 나쁜 짓을 하다 commit a crime for money. 2 [미혹되다] be deluded; be misled; be led into error; be trapped. ¶무당의 말에 ~ be deluded by a shaman's predictions.

혹한(酷寒) severe[bitter / intense] cold; a hard[severe] winter. ¶어느 ~의 겨울 밤 a bitterly cold winter night//~에 견디다 endure[stand] the intense cold.

혹형(酷刑) a severe[cruel] punishment [penalty]. ¶~을 과하다 inflict a severe punishment (to). **혹형하다** punish severely; inflict a severe punishment (on).

혼(魂) a soul; a spirit; a ghost; one's spirit(s) (기력). ¶~을 부르다 call back the spirit of the dead//~이 떠났다 The spirit departed the body.//죽음은 ~과 육체를 떼어놓는다 Death separates the soul from the body.

혼가(婚家) a house with a wedding occurring. ⇨°혼인집(⇨°혼인)

혼기(婚期) the marriageable age; nubility. ¶~가 된 처녀 a marriageable girl//~가 되다 be[become] of marriageable age//~를 놓치다 lose[miss] a chance of marriage//~가 지나다 be past the marriageable age / become an old maid//그녀는 ~가 되었다[지났다] She is of[is past] marriageable age. / She is at a[is past] marriageable age.//그녀는 ~를 놓쳤다 She has lost all chance of getting married.

혼나다(魂−) [놀라다] get frightened out of one's wits; be startled; [무서워하다] be scared[horrified]; [호된 경험을 겪다] have bitter experiences; have[get] the worst of it; have a hard[bad / (구어) rough / tough] time (of it) (with a person); pay dearly (for); have hard luck; suffer severely (from); [꾸지람 듣다] catch it hot; burn one's fingers. ¶나는 혼났다 I had a horrible experience.//혼났겠군요 You've had a terrible experience, haven't you?//너 이런 짓을 했으니 혼나야 하겠다 You will have to pay for this.//댁의 개가 짖어서 혼났습니다 Your dog gave me a bad time.//나중에 혼나 봐라 You shall smart for this.//I'll show you a thing or two.//그 때문에 혼났다 I paid dearly for it. / It cost me dear.

혼내다(魂−) [맛을 보이다] treat (a person) cruelly[badly]; give (a person) a hard [rough] time; do[serve] (a person) a bad [an ill] turn; give (a person) a raw deal; give it to (a person) (pretty) stiff; teach (a person) a lesson; put it across (a person); (구어) tell off (a person); [놀래 주다] frightened (a person) out of his wits; startle; horrify; scare. ¶내가 그를 한번 혼내 주어야 하겠다 I'll give him a hard time.//저 녀석을 혼내 주겠다 I'll let him have it. / I'll teach him a lesson he'll never forget.//댁의 말씀을 까따끔하게 혼내 주겠다 I'll teach him what's what. / I'll tell him a thing or two.//선생님은 소년을 따끔하게 혼내 주었다 The teacher taught the boy a good lesson.//따끔하게 혼내 줄 테다 I'll teach you a lesson you won't soon forget!//나는 그 말썽꾸러기 소년을 혼내 주었다 I gave it to the naughty boy. / I let the naughty boy have it. 나중에 혼내 줄 테다 You'll catch it afterwards. / Just wait! I'll teach you to do that!

혼담(婚談) an offer of marriage. ¶깨진 ~ unrealized marriage//~에 응하다 accept an offer of marriage//~이 있다 have[hear of] an offer[a proposal] of marriage//~이 쏟아져 들어오다 be flooded with offers of marriage//~이 깨지다 (a proposed match) be broken off//~을 꺼내다 bring word of a prospective marriage partner//~을 성사시키다 arrange[make up] a marriage//~을 거절하다 refuse[decline] an offer of marriage//~을 깨뜨리다 break up a proposed marriage//~이 성사되었다 The match has been made [arranged].//그녀에게 ~이 들어왔다 She has received an offer of marriage.//그 ~은 깨지고 말았다 The proposed match was broken off. / The suggestion of marriage between them did not realized.

혼돈(混沌·渾沌) chaos; nebulosity; confusion. ¶~ 상태에 있다 be in a chaotic state / be in (a state of) chaos[confusion]// ~ 상태에 빠지다 be reduced to a chaotic state / be thrown into confusion[disorder]//그 나라의 정국은 ~ 상태에 있다 The political situation of the country is chaotic. **혼돈하다** chaotic;

혼동 nebulous; confused; disorderly.

혼동(混同) confusion; mixing. 혼동하다 confuse [confound / mix up] (one thing with another); mistake (one) for (the other). ¶공과 사를 ~ mix up public and private matters / 자유와 방종을 ~ confuse liberty with license / take license for liberty / 목적과 수단을 ~ confuse [confound] the means with the end / confuse means and ends // (남의) 이름을 ~ confuse [mix up] names // 그는 언제나 공사를 혼동한다 He always confuses official and private matters. / He can't keep official and private matters straight. // 내 의견을 그의 의견과 혼동하지 않기를 바란다 I hope you won't mistake my opinion for his. / I wish you wouldn't confuse my opinion with his. // 공과 사를 혼동하고 있는 사람이 많다 There are a lot of people who do not draw a clear line between public and private matters.

혼란(混亂) confusion; disorder; disorganization; disarrangement; chaos; pell-mell; mixup; a jumble; a pretty [nice / fine] kettle of fish. ¶정치적 ~ political chaos / 경제의 ~ economic dislocation / 내부의 ~ internal disorder / 재정의 ~ financial derangement // 정신[사상]의 ~ a confusion of mind [thought / ideas] / 화재 현장의 ~ utter confusion at the scene of a fire / the confusion of a fire // ~을 틈타 taking advantage of the confusion // 큰 ~에 빠져 in great [utter] confusion [disorder] / utterly disorganized // ~ 상태에 있다 be in a state of disorder / 극심한 ~ 상태에 있다 be in utter confusion // ~에 빠지다 fall into disorder [confusion] / ~을 틈타 부정 이득을 얻다 fish in troubled waters // ~을 야기하다 [가져오다] lead to [occasion / give rise to] confusion // 사회적 ~을 조성하다 foment social order // 온 시가 ~에 빠져 있다 The whole city is plunged in confusion. / The whole city is turned upside down [in utter confusion / panic-stricken]. // 전 도시가 대~에 빠졌다 The entire city fell [was thrown] into great confusion [disorder]. / 회의는 대~에 빠졌다 The meeting fell into great confusion. / The meeting lapsed into pandemonium. // 잇따른 전쟁으로 나라는 큰 ~에 빠졌다 The successive wars threw the country into chaos [a chaotic state]. / 그의 거절로 회의는 일대 ~에 빠졌다 His refusal threw the meeting into great confusion. // 적이 쳐들어온다는 소식에 시민들은 큰 ~에 빠졌다 The news of the enemy's invasion threw the citizens into utter confusion. / 그녀는 화재 현장의 ~으로 크게 다쳤다 She was seriously injured in the confusion of the fire. 혼란하다 confused; disordered; disorderly; chaotic; (서술적) be in confusion; be in a tangle; be at sixes and sevens; be mixed up. ¶혼란해지다 be [get / become] confused [disordered] / be thrown into confusion [disorder] // 나는 머릿속이 너무 혼란해서 아무 말도 할 수 없었다 I was too confused [mixed up] to say anything. → ¶정세를 혼란시키다 confuse the situation / introduce confusion into the situation / 거래를 혼란시키다 dislocate business relations / 수상의 급작스런 죽음은 형세를 혼란시켰다 The sudden death of the premier confused the situation.

혼령(魂靈) the spirit (of the dead); (a person's) departed soul; the soul.

혼례(婚禮) a marriage [wedding / nuptial] ceremony; a wedding; nuptials. ¶~의 축하 선물 a wedding [marriage] present [gift] // ~를 치르다 [올리다] solemnize a marriage / celebrate a wedding // ~에 초대받다 be invited to a wedding // ~에 참석하다 attend [be present at] a wedding.

혼문(混文) [언] a mixed sentence; a compound-complex sentence.

혼미(昏迷) stupefaction; (bewildering) confusion; [의] stupor. ¶~ 상태에(서) in a fuddled state // ~ 상태에 빠지다 be thrown into confusion / 정국은 ~ 상태에 있었다 The political situation was in (a) turmoil. 혼미하다 stupefied; confused. ¶혼미한 정신 a confused mind / 혼미해지다 lose one's consciousness // 그는 의식이 혼미해졌다 He lost consciousness [became unconscious]. // 정국은 갈수록 더 혼미해졌다 The political situation has become more and more chaotic [confused].

혼방(混紡) mixed [blended] spinning. ¶~의 mixed (spun) (fabric) / 나일론 20% ~의 면 직물 cotton cloth with a 20% nylon mix.
● 혼방사 (一絲) mixed yarn.

혼백(魂帛) a temporary spirit tablet.
● 혼백상자 a spirit box.

혼백(魂魄) a soul; a spirit; a ghost. ⇨넋 ¶~이 이승을 떠돌고 있다 The spirit is haunting the old scenes. / One's spirit lingers around where one died.

혼비백산하다(魂飛魄散一) be frightened out of one's wits; be terrified out of one's senses. ¶혼비백산하여 with one's heart in one's mouth.

혼사(婚事) a matrimonial [marital / nuptial] matter; (a) marriage.

혼색(混色) [색을 섞기] mixing colors; [섞은 색] a compound [mixed] color. 혼색하다 mix colors.

혼서(婚書) a matrimonial epistle sent to the bride's family from the bridegroom's.

혼선(混線) 1 (전신·전화국의) cross; [전] contact; entanglement of wires. ¶~이 되고 있다 (전화기) The wires [lines] are mixed. / The lines are crossed. / (라디오가) The radio signals are jammed up. // ~으로 그와 통화하지 못했다 The wires are crossed and I can't get him. 혼선하다 get entangled; be mixed up; be crossed. 2 [혼란] confusion. 혼선하다 confuse. → ¶회의에서는 이야기가 혼선된 것 같다 They seemed to be talking at cross-purposes at the conference.

혼성(混成) mixture; composition; [영] mixing; [언] blending; contamination; hybridization; hybridism. 혼성하다 mix; mingle; compound.
● 혼성곡 [음] a medley. 혼성물 a mixture; a compound; a medley. 혼성팀 a combined team.

혼성(混聲) [음] (a work for) mixed voices.
● 혼성 (4부) 합창 a mixed chorus (in four parts).

혼수(昏睡) 1 [정신 없이 깊이 잠듦] a deep sleep. 2 [의식을 잃음] a coma; a trance; stupor; sinking; lethargic sleep. ¶~상태에 빠지다 fall [slip] into a comatose state [condition] / lapse into a coma // ~상태에 있

다 be in a (state of) coma // 최면술로 ~상태가 되다 be put into a trance by mesmerism.
혼수(婚需) (물건) necessary articles for marriage; (비용) marriage expenses.
혼식(混食) mixed [compound] food. **혼식하다** eat mixed food.
혼신(渾身) the whole body. ¶~의 힘을 다하여 with all one's might [strength] / with might and main // ~의 힘을 내다 put forth every ounce of one's energies / 그는 ~의 힘을 다해 돌을 던졌다 He threw the stone with all his might. // 그의 ~의 연기가 호평을 얻었다 The performance, into which he threw himself completely, was highly praised [was well received].
혼약(婚約) an engagement. ⇨약혼
혼연(渾然) wholly; in perfect harmony. ¶~일체가 되다 be united [jointed] together / from [constitute] a perfect [complete / harmonious] whole // 그 절과 배경의 산맥이 ~일체를 이루고 있었다 The temple and the range of hills in the background were in complete harmony.
혼외정사(婚外情事) extramarital intercourse.
혼욕(混浴) mixed [promiscuous] bathing. **혼욕하다** bathe promiscuously. ¶산의 온천에서는 남녀가 혼욕하였다 Men and women were bathing together at the hot spring in the mountain.
혼용하다(混用-) mix; mingle; use (one thing) together with (another). ¶한글과 한자를 ~ mingle Hangeul with Chinese characters.
혼음(混淫) group sex.
혼인(婚姻) marriage. ¶~을 빙자한 간음 행위 the behavior of inducing women into sexual relations under the pretext of marriage // ~을 취소하다 annul one's marriage // ~을 무효화하다 dissolve one's marriage // 목사가 두 사람의 ~을 주관했다 The minister married them. **혼인하다** marry; be [get] married (to); be united (with); enter into matrimony; [법] intermarry (with).
● **혼인 신고** registration of one's marriage. ¶~를 하다 register one's marriage. **혼인집** a house [family] with a wedding occurring.
혼일(混一) unification; consolidation; amalgamation. **혼일하다** unify; consolidate; amalgamate.
혼입(混入) [섞어 넣음] mixing; mixture; admixture; blending. **혼입하다** [섞다] mix (A with B / A and B); mingle (A and B); add (A to B); [섞이다] get mixed (with). ¶포도주에 독을 ~ mix poison in wine / add poison to wine. ➡¶설탕에 소금이 혼입되었다 Some salt got mixed (in) with the sugar.
혼자 [한 사람] one person; [홀몸] a single person; alone(단독으로); by oneself; for oneself(독력으로). ¶이익을 ~ 차지하다 monopolize the profit // ~서 고민하다 suffer by oneself // ~ 있기를 좋아하다 love solitude // ~ 여행하다 travel alone / ~ 있을 때는 무엇을 하나 What do you do when you are alone? / 그녀는 어둠 속에서 ~ 남아 있었다 She was left alone in the dark. // ~서 생각해 보아라 Think [Figure it out] for yourself. // 그 여자는 ~다 She is single. / She is unmarried. // 그는 그 일을 ~ 맡았다 He undertook the task alone [single-handed / by himself]. // 내 생질 아이가 ~ 걸을 수 있게 되었다 My sister's child can now walk by herself. // 밤에 ~ 나가는 것은 위험하다 It's dangerous to go out alone after dark. // 그녀는 ~서 다섯 아이를 키웠다 She brought up her five children alone. // 이것은 ~만 알고 계십시오 Please keep this to yourself.
혼작(混作) growing mixed crops; mixed cultivation; crop-mixing. **혼작하다** grow [cultivate] as mixed crops.
혼잡(混雜) [혼란] confusion; disorder; [붐빔] crowdedness; congestion; a jam; a bustle. ¶유흥가의 ~ the din and bustle of the amusement district / 도시 생활의 ~ the din and bustle of city life // ~ 통에 in the confusion // 교통의 ~을 완화하다 ease traffic congestion [jam] // 거리가 자동차와 보행자들로 ~의 극에 달해 있다 The streets are congested with cars and pedestrians. // 번화한 명동 거리의 ~ 속에서 그를 놓쳐 버렸다 I lost sight of him in the crowd on a busy Myeongdong street. // 재고품떨이 판매장은 대~이었다 There was a terrible crush at the clearance scale. **혼잡하다** confused; disordered; crowded; congested; bustling; (미국 속어) jammed. ¶불난 곳의 혼잡한 틈을 타서 in the confusion of the fire / 혼잡한 섣달의 거리 the crowded streets of December / 저녁때의 혼잡한 시간에 in the evening rush hour / 세모의 거리는 쇼핑 손님으로 ~ At the end of the year, streets are crowded with shoppers. // 그 휴양지는 휴가를 즐기려는 사람들로 혼잡했다 The tourist spot was overrun with throngs of holiday makers. / Crowds of vacationers thronged the tourist spot. // 도로는 여러 가지 차들로 혼잡했다 The road was jammed with various kinds of vehicles.
혼잣말 talking to oneself; a soliloquy; a monologue. ¶~처럼 말하다 say half to oneself // 노파는 노상 중얼중얼 ~을 하고 있다 The old woman is always muttering to herself. **혼잣말하다** say [speak / talk] to oneself; soliloquize; think aloud.
혼잣손 single-handedness; a single hand. ¶~으로 by one's own effort // ~으로 일하다 work single-handed / do (a thing) single-handed.
혼전(婚前) ¶~의 premarital // ~에 before marriage.
● **혼전 관계** premarital sex; sex before marriage.
혼전(混戰) 1 [난전] a confused [mixed / free] fight; a melee. ¶양 팀의 럭비 선수는 흥분해서 종반에는 ~이 되었다 Both rugger teams were excited and the game ended in a confused fight [melee / free-for-all] (▶ free-for-all은 난투의 뜻). **혼전하다** fight in confusion. 2 [결과를 알 수 없는 상태] ¶9월이 되어도 A 리그의 ~이 계속되었다 Even as late as September, there were still many teams in contention for the A League pennant. // 이 선거구는 ~ 상태의 A이다 It is impossible to tell who win the election in this district.
혼절(昏絕) fainting; a swoon. **혼절하다** faint; swoon; fall into a swoon.
혼쭐나다(魂-) 1 be startled; be scared. ⇨혼나다 ¶추락하는가 생각되어 나는 혼쭐났다 I was scared (half) death when I thought we were going to crash. 2 (황홀감으로) be transported [entranced]; fascinated.
혼처(婚處) a marriageable family or person. ¶

혼탁하다 마땅한 ~를 구하다 look around for some suitable candidates for (bride).

혼탁하다(混濁-) 1 [흐리다] (강 등이) turbid; muddy; (액체가) cloudy; (공기가) foul; (말소리가) thick. ¶흙먼지로 혼탁해진 공기 air thick with dust // 물이 혼탁하게 하다 muddle (water) // 혼탁해지다 become turbid [muddy]. 2 [세상이 어지럽다]. ¶혼탁한 세상 the corrupt world.

혼합(混合) mixing; mixture; admixture. **혼합하다** mix [blend / mingle] (A with B); compound; intermix. ¶혼합하기 쉬운 mixable / easy to mix // 혼합하기 어려운 unmixable // 모래와 자갈을 ~ mix sand with pebbles // 위스키를 ~ blend whisk(e)y. ➔ ¶혼합된 mixed / compound / blended(▶ mingle은 혼합된 후에도 혼합된 것을 식별할 수 있는 경우, blend는 식별할 수는 없지만 각 성분의 특질이 어느 정도 남도록 혼합하는 경우) // 물과 기름은 혼합되지 않는다 Oil and water do not mix. / Oil does not mingle with water.

● **혼합 경기** a medley race. **혼합물** a mixture; a blend; a medley; a compound; an amalgam; alloy; an admixture. **혼합주**(-酒) blended liquor; mixed spirits; a mixed drink; a cocktail.

혼혈(混血) mixed blood [breed]; racial mixture. ¶~의 (of) mixed blood [breed] / half-blood(ed) / half-breed.

● **혼혈아** a child of mixed racial origins; a half-blood; (흑인과 백인의) a mulatto; (유럽과 아시아의) a Eurasian; (미국인과 아시아 인의) an Amerasian. ¶미국인과 한국인의 ~ a person of mixed American and Korean parentage [extraction].

홀[1] a hall. ¶댄스~ a dance [dancing] hall // 콘서트~ a concert hall.

홀[2] [골프] a hole. ¶공을 ~에 넣다 hole a ball.

홀- [짝 없음] single. ¶~몸 a single man [woman] // ~아비 a widower.

홀가분하다 light; free and easy; light-hearted (마음이). ¶홀가분한 복장 casual clothes // 홀가분한 마음으로 with a light heart / lightheartedly // 홀가분해지다 (마음이) be lightened in heart / (무거운 책임 등이 없어지다) get [be] rid of one's encumbrances // 시험이 끝나 마음이 홀가분했다 I felt a load off my mind when the examination was over. **홀가분히** lightly; lightheartedly. ¶~ 이야기할 수 있는 친구 a friend who is easy to talk to // ~ 혼자 살다 enjoy a carefree life alone / enjoy the carefree life of a single person // 좀 더 ~ 생각하는 편이 좋다 Don't think [take it] so seriously. / Try to take things in a lighter vein [in a more free-and-easy way].

홀대(忽待) inhospitable [unkind] treatment; neglecting; slighting. **홀대하다** treat (a person) unkindly [inhospitably]; neglect [slight] (a person). ¶손님을 ~ treat a guest unkindly / neglect a guest.

홀딩 [체] holding. ¶~을 범하다 be penalized for holding.

홀딱 1 [반한 모양] deeply; dead; madly. ¶~ 반하다 be deeply [dead / madly] in love (with) / lose one's heart (to) // 그는 그녀에게 ~ 반했다 He is madly in love with her. / He is head over heels in love with her. // 나는 그 여배우에게 ~ 반해 있었다 I was head over heels in love [(구어) was really smitten] with the actress.
2 [여지없이] fairly; nicely; completely; thoroughly. ¶~ 속아 넘어가는 be nicely [fairly] taken in / 돈을 ~ 날리다 become (quite) penniless.
3 [벗는 모양] (removing it) completely; entirely; quickly. ¶옷을 ~ 벗다 strip oneself of all one's clothes / strip oneself bare [stark-naked] // (머리가) ~ 벗어져 있다 be bald as an egg.
4 [뒤집히는 모양] (turning a thing) inside out. ¶바람에 ~ 뒤집힌 우산 an umbrella blown inside [wrong side] out by the wind.

홀랑 1 [벗는 모양] (removing it) completely; entirely; quickly. 2 [뒤집히는 모양] (turning a thing) inside out. 3 [헐겁게] loosely; easily. ¶~ 들어가다 slip into place / slip in loosely.

홀로 alone; by oneself; single; single-handed(ly). ¶~ 살다 live alone / remain single // ~ 싸우다 fight alone [single-handed] // ~ 외출하다 go out by oneself.

홀로되다 become a widow [a widower].

홀리다 1 (귀신 등에) be possessed (by / with); be obsessed (by); be bewitched (by). ¶홀린 사람처럼 like one possessed // 무엇에 홀린 듯이 as if possessed by some devil or other // 여우 [귀신]에게 ~ be possessed by a fox [devil]. 2 (이성에게) get infatuated [captivated / bewitched]. ¶여자에게 ~ get infatuated with a woman / be gone on a woman. 3 (현혹되다) get tempted; be deluded [tricked / deceived / seduced]. ¶돈에 홀려 나쁜 짓을 하다 be tempted by money to do wrong.

홀몸 [단신] a single person; [독신] an unmarried person; (남자) a bachelor; (여자) a spinster. ¶평생을 ~으로 지내다 remain single all one's life.

홀뮴 [화] holmium (기호 Ho).

홀소리 [언] a vowel (sound). ⇨모음

홀수(-數) an odd [uneven] number.

홀스타인종(-種) [동] a Holstein (cow).

홀시(忽視) contempt; neglect; negligence. **홀시하다** despise; make light of; slight; treat snubly; snub; ignore; neglect.

홀씨 [생] a spore. ⇨포자

홀아비 a widower. ¶~로 살다 live in widowerhood // 그는 20년 동안이나 ~로 지내고 있다 He has remained a widower for twenty years.

● **홀아비살림** the life of a widower; a single life; a bachelor life. ¶~을 꾸려 나가다 maintain a widower's [bachelor's] home.

홀앗이살림 [가족이 단출한 살림] a household with few encumbrances; a small family.

홀어미 a widow.

홀연(히)(忽然-) suddenly; all of a sudden; all at once; unexpectedly; in an instant. ¶~ 사라지다 vanish as if by magic // ~ 왔다 ~ 사라지다 disappear as suddenly as one appears // 그는 ~ 안개 속으로 사라졌다 He faded in a flash into fog. // 그는 ~ 나타났다 가 또 ~ 떠났다 He disappeared as suddenly as he had appeared.

홀인원 (make) a hole in one.

홀짝 lightly; at a gulp; sniffling. ⇨홀쩍 1·2·3

홀짝거리다 sip (up); snivel. ⇨홀쩍거리다

홀쭉하다 →홀쭉하다

홀쭉이 a lanky person.
홀쭉하다 1 [가늘고 길다] lank; lanky; spindly; slender; spindling; [야위다] lean. ¶홀쭉한 사내 a lanky man // 홀쭉한 처녀 a slim girl // 볼이 ~ have hollow cheeks / have a pinched look // 허리가 ~ have a slim waist // 홀쭉해지다 grow [become] thin / lose flesh // 근심으로 홀쭉해지다 become thin from worries // 그녀는 몸매가 ~ She is of slender [delicate] build. // 앓고 나더니 홀쭉해졌다 Your illness has left you very thin. 2 [뾰족하다] pointed; tapering. ¶꼬리가 ~ have a pointed tail // 한쪽 끝이 ~ One end tapers.
홀치다 tie[knot] (a thing) firmly.
홀태 1 (생선) a slim fish without spawn[roe]. 2 (물건) a slim thing.
● **홀태바지** slender-legged trousers. **홀태버선** a tight sock.
홀하다 (忽-) 1 [경솔·소홀하다] careless; inconsiderate; negligent; hasty; rash; thoughtless. ¶대접이 ~ be careless [inhospitable] in treating (a person) // 행동이 ~ act[behave] rashly. 2 [대수롭지 않다] worthless; insignificant; (서술적) be of little importance; be of no account [value].
홈¹ a groove; a furrow; (세로 난) a flute; (쇠시리의) a quirk. ¶LP음반의 좁은 ~ a microgroove (on a record) / 창틀에 ~을 내다 [파다] groove [cut a groove in] a window frame.
홈² [야구] the home base [plate]; an asylum.
● **홈 플레이트** a home plate.
홈그라운드 home (ground). ¶~에서 경기를 하다 play at home (ground) / play as host [franchise team].
홈드라마 (*home drama) a family drama.
홈런 [야구] a home run; a homer; a round-tripper; a circuit clout; a four bagger. ¶만루 ~ a grand-slam homer // ~을 치다 hit [clout / slam] a home run (over the left field fence).
● **홈런왕** a home-run king [leader].
홈룸 [교] a homeroom; (시간) homeroom; one's homeroom period. ¶~ 위원 a member of the homeroom committee // ~의 선생 a homeroom teacher.
홈뱅킹 [인터넷 은행 업무 서비스] home banking.
홈 베이스 a home base.
홈 쇼핑 [안방 구매] home shopping.
홈스트레치 [체] (미) the homestretch. ¶~에 들어오다 get on the homestretch // ~에 들어서서 스퍼트하다 put on a spurt in the homestretch.
홈인하다 (*home in-) [야구] get [reach / go] home; cross the (home) plate; score. ¶3명의 주자가 잇따라 홈인했다 Three runners scored [crossed home plate / made it home] one after another. ➔¶그는 2루타를 쳐서 주자를 홈인시켰다 He drove in a runner with a two-base hit.
홈질 broad-stitching. **홈질하다** broadstitch.
홈통 (-桶) 1 (물을 이끄는) a bamboo water pipe (in a garden); a drainspout (세로의); an eaves trough (가로의); a gutter; a spout; an aqueduct; a conduit. ¶대나무 ~ an aqueduct of bamboo pipes // 빗물받이 ~ a gutter at the eaves / an eave(s) trough // 집에 ~을 달다 gutter a house. 2 (창틀·장지 등의) a groove on a window frame [doorstill].

홈 페이지 a home page. ¶~를 만들다 create a home page.
홉¹ [용량의 단위] a hop(=1/10 doe, 3.558 sq. ft.)
홉² [식] a hop; (암꽃) hops(▶ 보통 복수형). ¶~으로 쓴맛을 내다 hop.
홉뜨다 turn up the whites of one's eyes.
홋홋하다 unencumbered; carefree; (서술적) have few encumbrances. ¶홋홋한 살림 a (carefree) household with few encumbrances. **홋홋이** without encumbrances; with few dependents. ¶그 부부는 딸린 식구 없이 둘이서 ~ 산다 The couple leads a carefree life with no one else to worry about.
홍당무 (紅唐-) [무의 하나] a red radish; [당근] a carrot. ¶~ 같다 be as red as a lobster / be all of a glow // 얼굴이 ~가 되다 turn [become] red [crimson] / turn as red as a turkey cock [beet] / go [turn] red in the face / blush scarlet [to the roots of one's hair] / flush deeply.
홍도 (紅桃) (나무) a red-blossoming peach tree; (꽃) red blossoms of a peach tree.
홍두깨 1 (다듬이질의) a wooden fulling roller. ¶그것은 아닌 밤중에 ~ 격이었다 It burst upon us like a thunderclap. 2 [농] a ba(u)lk. 3 (소의 홍두깨살) fore rump (of beef).
● **홍두깨질** fulling cloth on a wooden roller.
홍등가 (紅燈街) the gay quarters; a red-light district.
홍루 (紅淚) 1 [미인의 눈물] tears of a fair. 2 [피눈물] tears of blood.
홍반 (紅斑) red spots; [의] erythema.
홍백전 (紅白戰) a contest between two groups.
홍보 (弘報) public information; public relations (▶ 단수 취급)(약어 P.R.); publicity. **홍보하다** publicize.
● **홍보과** (-課) the Public Information Section. **홍보지** (-誌) a public relations magazine. **홍보 책자** a publicity booklet [pamphlet]. **홍보 활동** a campaign of publicity (for a new camera); information work; publicity activities. ¶해외 ~ the (government's) overseas publicity activities // ~을 더욱 강화하다 further [strengthen / step up] publicity activities (on).
홍보석 (紅寶石) [광] a ruby. ⇨홍옥1
홍살문 (紅-門) a *hongsalmun*; a red gate with spiked top.
홍삼 (紅蔘) *insam*(ginseng) steamed red.
홍색 (紅色) [붉은색] red; a red colo(u)r. ¶~을 띤 reddish / pinkish // 암~ dark red // 심~ crimson.
홍소 (哄笑) loud laughter; a roar of laughter; a guffaw. ¶~를 터뜨리다 roar with laughter / burst into laughter. **홍소하다** laugh loudly; roar with laughter; guffaw.
홍수 (洪水) 1 [큰물] a heavy flood; a deluge. ¶대~ a deluge // 노아의 ~ Noah's flood / the Noachian deluge / the Deluge // ~와 가뭄이 없는 비옥한 땅 fertile land free of flood and drought // ~가 나다 have a flood / get flooded / be flooded [under water] / be inundated // ~로 유실되다 [떠내려가다] be carried [washed] away by a flood // ~ 피해를 입다 (사람이) suffer from a flood / (집·논 밭이) be flooded. ¶이 일대는 종종 ~가 난다 This area often suffers from floods [flooding]. / This area is often flooded. // 강물이 불어나서

유역은 ~가 났다 The water rose in the river and the surrounding fields were inundated. // 하류 일대의 ~가 났다 The lower reaches of the river were flooded. **2** [쇄도] a deluge; a flood; a rush. ¶편지의 ~ a deluge[flood] of letters // 자동차의 ~ a torrent of automobiles // 책의 ~ 속에서 좋은 책을 고르기란 무척 어렵다 Amidst the flood [torrent] of books being published, it is not easy to select really good ones.
● **홍수 경보[예보]** a flood warning[forecast]. **홍수 조절** flood control.
홍순(紅脣) **1** [여자의 붉은 입술] cherry[red] lips. **2** [막 피어나는 꽃송이] a half-open flower.
홍시(紅柿) a ripe and soft persimmon; a mellow persimmon.
홍실(紅－) (a) red thread.
홍안(紅顔) a ruddy[rosy] face; peachy[pink] cheeks. ¶~의 rosy-cheeked / ruddy-faced // ~의 미소년 a handsome rosy-cheeked youth / a fair youth / an Adonis.
홍어(洪魚·鱝魚) [동] a skate; a thornback.
홍역(紅疫) the measles; rubeola. ¶~을 하다 catch[get / have] the measles. **홍역(을) 치르다** have bitter experiences; have a hard time (of it).
홍염(紅焰) **1** [붉은 불꽃] red blazes[flares] of flame. **2** [천] a solar prominence[protuberance].
홍엽(紅葉) (단풍이 든) red leaves; autumn colo(u)rs[tints]; (단풍나무의) red maple foliage.
홍예(虹霓·虹蜺) **1 a** rainbow. ⇨무지개 **2** the arch of a gate. ⇨홍예문⊙홍예).
홍예(를) 틀다 span with an arch; arch (a gate).
● **홍예 다리** an arch(ed) bridge. **홍예문** the arch of a gate; an arched gate.
홍옥(紅玉) [광] a ruby. **2** [사과 품종의 하나] a Jonathan (apple).
홍익인간(弘益人間) devotion to the welfare of mankind. ¶~의 이념 the humanitarian ideal.
홍일점(紅一點) the only member of the fair sex (among); the only woman in the company. ¶그녀는 ~이었다 She was the only woman (that was) present among male members.
홍적세(洪積世) [지] the Pleistocene; the diluvial epoch.
홍조(紅潮) **1** [붉어진 얼굴] flushing; a glow. ¶~를 띠다 flush / (부끄러움 등으로) blush. **2** [붉은 해조] the seascape aglow with the rising sun. **3** menstruation. ⇨월경(月經)
홍차(紅茶) black tea; (a cup of) tea.
홍채(虹彩) [생] the iris.
● **홍채염** [의] iritis.
홍 코너(紅－) [권투] the champion's[defender's] corner.
홍학(紅鶴) [동] a flamingo (pl. ~(e)s).
홍합(紅蛤) [동] a hard-shelled mussel.
홍해(紅海) the Red Sea.
홑 [겹이 아님] one layer. ¶~이다 be one-layered.
홑－ [한 겹·외톨] single; onefold.
홑겹 a layer; a single layer.
홑꽃 [식] a single[single-petaled / monopetalous] flower.
● **홑꽃잎** a single petal.

홑눈 [동] a stemma (pl. -mata, ~s); an ocellus (pl. -lli). ¶~의 ocellar.
홑몸 1 [단신] a single person; a person without encumbrances. ¶~으로 여행하다 travel alone // ~으로 적진에 뛰어들다 penetrate the enemy position single-handed. **2** [임신하지 않은 몸] a woman who is not pregnant. ¶~이 아니다 be with child / be having a baby.
홑바지 unlined trousers; (Korean women's) undergarment.
홑벌 1 [한 겹의 물건] a one-layered[onefold] thing. ¶~ 바지 unlined trousers. **2** →단벌
홑소리 [언] a single sound; a monosyllabic sound.
홑실 (a) single-ply[-strand] thread.
홑열매 a simple fruit.
홑옷 unlined clothes; a thin linen clothing without lining.
홑원소 물질(－元素物質) [화] a simple substance.
홑이불 a single-layer quilt; a (bed) sheet.
홑잎 1 [한 잎사귀로 된 잎] a simple leaf. **2** a single petal. ⇨꽃잎⊙홑꽃)
홑치마 1 (한 겹의) an unlined skirt. **2** [맨몸에 입은] a skirt worn without an underskirt.
화 1 (性) pent-up resentment; anger; ire; wrath. ¶~가 나는 annoying / provoking / offensive / invidious / infernal // ~를 잘 내는 hot-[quick- / short-] tempered / irritable // ~를 잘 내는 사람 a person with an explosive temper / a hot-[short-]tempered person / a touchy person // 걸핏하면 ~를 내다 easily take offense // ~를 내다 lose one's temper / fly into a rage / (구어) fly off the handle // 속았다고 생각하니 ~가 났다 I am infuriated to think that I was cheated. // ~를 참을 수 없을 I could not control my temper. // 그는 ~가 나서 탁자를 뒤집었다 He turned over the table in a fit of anger. // 아버지는 노년에 들어서 ~를 잘 내게 되었다 My father has become quick-tempered[touchy] in his old age. // 그런 말을 들으니 ~가 난다 I'm outraged by your remarks. / Your remarks are outrageous. // 당신이 ~를 내는 것도 당연합니다 There is every reason for you to be angry. // ~가 나서 죽겠다 How vexatious! // 나는 ~가 나서 견딜 수 없었다 I was exceedingly angry. / I was beside myself with anger. // 그는 사소한 일로 ~를 낸다 He gets angry[(구어) flies off the handle] over little things. // 나는 그가 ~를 내는 것을 본 적이 없다 I have never known him to lose his temper. // (▶영)에서는 부정사 to가 없이도 무방함)// 그는 또 ~를 냈다 He lost his temper again. **2** (오행의) "Fire" — one of the five primary elements(=Metal, Wood, Water, Fire and Earth).
3 Tuesday. ⇨화요일
4 the heat of a fire. ⇨화기(火氣)
화(禍) (serious) trouble; (an) evil; a curse; [불행] (a) misfortune; [재앙] (a) disaster; a calamity; woe. ¶~를 당하다 meet with a calamity / [살해되다] be killed // ~를 부르다 invite[court] a disaster // ~를 자초하다 bring a calamity upon oneself // ~를 모면하다 escape a disaster // 그의 부주의가 ~를 초래했다 His carelessness brought about the disaster.
－화(化) -ization. ¶합리~ rationalization // 기

계~ mechanization // 대중~ popularization.
-화(畵) a picture; a drawing; a painting. ¶서양~ a Western painting // 인물~ a figure painting.
화가(畵架) [미] an easel.
화가(畵家) a painter; an artist. ¶동양[서양]~ a Eastern-style[Western-style] painter / a painter in the Eastern[Western] style // 일요~ a Sunday[an amateur] painter // 인물[풍경]~ a portrait[landscape] painter.
화간(和姦) fornication. 화간하다 fornicate (with).
화강석(花崗石) [광] granite. ⇨"화강암
화강암(花崗巖) [광] granite. ~이 granitic.
화객선(貨客船) a cargo-passenger ship; a ship carrying both cargo and passengers.
화공(火攻) a fire attack; an attack by fire. 화공하다 attack with fire. ¶적은 성을 화공했다 The enemy attacked the castle and set it on fire. / The enemy tried to take the castle by setting it on fire.
화공(畵工) a painter.
화공(靴工) a shoemaker.
화관(花冠) 1 [식] the corolla of a flower. ⇨"꽃부리 2 [장식의 관] a coronet; an ornamental crown. 3 [여자의 관] a woman's ceremonial coronet.
화광(火光) light from fire. ⇨"불빛
화교(華僑) a Chinese residing abroad; (집합적) overseas Chinese.
화구(火口) 1 (아궁이의) a fire hole. 2 [불을 내뿜는 아가리] a burner; a muzzle; a nozzle. 3 a crater.
●화구호(－湖) a crater lake.
화근(禍根) the root of evil; a source of calamity. ¶~을 없애다 cut off the evil at its root / eliminate[lay the axe to] the root of evil // ~이 되다 form a source of calamity / be the ruin (of) // ~을 뿌리 뽑다 eradicate the root of the evil // 그의 악정은 뒤에 ~을 남겼다 His misrule[misgovernment] was the cause of later trouble. // 그녀는 미모가 ~이 되었다 Her personal beauty was her ruin. // ~의 뿌리 깊다 The cause of the trouble is deep-rooted[lies deep-seated].
화급(火急) urgency; exigency; emergency. ¶이 계획의 중단 여부를 결정짓는 것은 ~을 요하는 문제이다 We must decide immediately whether to give up this plan or not. 화급하다 urgent; pressing; demanding; exigent; immediate; (서술적) be an emergency. ¶화급한 경우에는 in case of emergency / in an emergency // 그는 화급한 용무로 외출 중이다 He is out on urgent[pressing] business. // 화급한 경우에는 벨을 울려 주십시오 Ring the bell in an[in case of] emergency.
화기(火氣) 1 [답답증] a stifling sensation in the chest. 2 [노여움] anger; ire. 3 [불기운] the heat of a fire. ¶스토브의 ~ heat given off from a stove // ~ 주의 (게시) Watch out for fire hazards. // ~가 있는 데서 사용하지 마시오 (게시) Do not use near fire or flame.
●화기 엄금 (게시) No Fire.; Caution: [가연성 물질을 있는] Inflammable.
화기(火器) firearms. ¶공용 ~ a crew-served weapon // 경[중 / 소]~ light[heavy / small] firearms // 자동 ~ automatic firearms.
화기(和氣) 1 [화창한 일기] mild[genial / agreeable] weather. 2 [온화한 기색] geniality; peacefulness; harmoniousness.
화기(花期) the flowering season.
화기애애하다(和氣靄靄－) harmonious; peaceful; happy (home). ¶화기애애한 가정 a happy[harmonious] family // 화기애애한 모임 a congenial gathering // 화기애애하게 full of harmony / harmoniously / peacefully // 그의 집은 화기애애한 집안이다 Peace and harmony reign over his household.
화끈 with a sudden flush[glow]; with a sudden flash of heat; with a burning sensation. ¶(얼굴이) ~ 달다 flush up (hotly) / blush / feel (with shame). 화끈하다 hot; burning; flushing; glowing.
화끈거리다 feel hot[warm]; burn; flush; glow. ¶부끄러워서 얼굴이 ~ burn with shame // 귀가 화끈거린다 Running makes me hot. // 추워서 볼이 화끈거린다 The cold air makes the cheeks glow.
화끈화끈 burning; flushing; glowing. 화끈화끈하다 feel hot. ⇨"화끈거리다
화나다(火－) be angered[vexed / irritated / enraged / offended / provoked]; be riled (at); feel irritated[injured]; be[feel] sore (at / about). ¶화난 김에 in a fit of anger [temper / rage / the spleen] / in the heat of passion / in a moment[tumult] of anger // 그는 나를 화나게 하는 짓만 한다 He always rubs me (up) the wrong way. // 네 말이 그를 화나게 했다 Your remarks have exasperated him. / Your remarks have made him angry. // 내가 늦게 왔기 때문에 그녀는 화났다 She went into a huff because I arrived late. // 아버지가 편찮으시니 화나시게 해서는 안 된다 We mustn't upset father, because he's ill[sick]. // 그녀의 우유부단한 태도가 그를 화나게 한 것 같다 Her indecisive attitude seems to have enraged him.
화내다(火－) get angry (about a thing / with [at] a person); (구어) get mad (at a person / about a thing); give vent to one's anger; blow one's top. ¶그것은 화낼 만한 일이 못 된다 It's not worth getting angry about. // 그는 어떤 일에도 화내지 않는다 His temper is equal to any trial. // 그녀의 편지를 보고 그는 화냈다 He got angry at her letter. / Her letter made him angry. // 그는 곧잘 화낸다 He gets angry easily. / He loses his temper easily. // 무엇 때문에 그가 나한테 화내는지 모르겠다 I don't understand why he got angry with me. / I don't understand what I did to offend him[hurt his feelings].
화냥년 an adulteress; an adulterous[unfaithful] wife; a woman of easy[loose] morals; a slattern; a slut; a whore.
화냥질 adultery (of a married woman). ⇨"서방질(⇨서방(書房))
화농(化膿) suppuration; maturation; maturity; purulence. ¶~성의 suppurative / suppurating / festering // ~성 염증 purulent inflammation. 화농하다 suppurate; maturate; mature; fester; (종기가) come[draw / grow / gather] to a head.
●화농균 suppurative germs; pyogenic bacteria.
화닥닥 suddenly; hastily. ⇨"후닥닥
화단(花壇) a flower bed; a flower garden; a parterre. ¶~에 튤립을 심었다 I planted tulips in the flower bed.
화단(畵壇) painting[artistic] circles.
화답(和答) a response. 화답하다 respond (in

화대(花代) 1 [놀음차] a gratuity [tip] given to entertainers at a party. 2 [해웃값] a charge for *gisaeng*'s service.

화덕(火-) [화로] a (charcoal) brazier; [솥 거는] a (cooking) stove; a kitchen[cooking] range; an oven.

화독(火毒) inflammation caused by a burn.
● 화독내 the smell of burnt food; scorching smell of food.

화두(話頭) a topic[subject](of conversation). ¶~를 돌리다 change to subject[topic of conversation] / shift the conversation.

화드득 1 [묽은 똥이 갑자기 나오는 소리] with a slush[slosh]. 2 [총포 등이 터지는 소리] with a crackling[bursting] sound. 3 [경망한 모양] foolishly; giddily.

화드득거리다 slush repeatedly; bang[crackle/whizz] repeatedly.

화들짝 with surprise; with a start.

화딱지(火-) 〈속〉 pent-up resentment; anger. ⇨화(火)1

화락하다(和樂-) harmonious; peaceful; happy; (서술적) be full of harmony; be at peace with each other; dwell in unity [harmony]. ¶그의 집은 정말 ~ Peace and harmony reign over his household.

화랑(花郞) a *hwarang*; an elite youth corps of Silla.
● 화랑도(-道) *hwarangdo*; the code of Silla chivalry.

화랑(畫廊) an art gallery; a picture gallery.

화려하다(華麗-) splendid; magnificent; gorgeous; ornate; gallant; gaudy; flowery; brilliant; gay; showy. ¶화려한 무도회 a magnificent [gorgeous] ball // 화려한 문체 a gaudy style // 화려한 업적 a splendid achievement // 화려한 도시 파리 the gay city of Paris / gay Paris // 화려하게 등장하다 make a spectacular debut // 화려한 것을 좋아하다 be fond of show[display] // 화려한 옷을 입다 be flashily [loudly] dressed // 눈이 부시도록 ~ dazzle one with brilliance [splendor] // 너무 ~ be too gaudy[gay] (for a person) // 이 옷은 내게는 지나치게 ~ This dress is too colorful [loud] for me. // 회장은 화려하게 장식되어 있었다 The hall was gaudily decorated. // 외국에서 온 방문객들은 그 극장의 화려함에 놀랐다 The visitors from abroad were amazed at the splendor of the theater.

화력(火力) 1 [불의 힘] heat; heating power. ¶~이 세다[약하다] have a high[low] caloric value // ~에 견디다 resist the action of fire // 이 가스버너는 ~이 세다 This gas burner has strong heating power. 2 [화기의 위력] fire power.
● 화력 발전소 a thermoelectric [steam] power plant[station]. 화력 지원 fire support.

화로(火爐) a (charcoal) brazier; a fire pot [box]. ¶~에 손을 쬐다 warm one's hands over a brazier // ~를 쬐어 몸을 녹이다 warm oneself at a brazier.
● 화롯가 the fireside.

화룡점정(畫龍點睛) the finishing strokes [touches] (that set off the whole work to advantage).

화류계(花柳界) the gay quarters[world]; the frivolous community; (미) a red-light district. ¶~에 몸을 던지다 become a prostitute / sell oneself into prostitution.

화륜선(火輪船) a steamship.

화면(畫面) 1 (그림의) a picture. 2 [영화·TV] a screen; a scene on the screen. ¶~의 뒤틀림 picture distortion // 이 텔레비전의 ~은 20인치다 This TV set has a 20-inch screen. // ~에 비치고 있는 것이 무엇이죠 What's that on the screen now? // ~이 어둡다 The screen [picture] is dark. // ~이 바뀌었다 The scene shifted[changed].
● 화면 구성 the composition of a picture.

화목(火木) firewood. ⇨"땔나무

화목(和睦) harmony; concord; peace. 화목하다 harmonious; peaceful; (서술적) be in harmony[concord]; be at peace with each other. ¶화목하게 harmoniously / in harmony [peace] / happily / affectionately // 부부 사이가 ~ They are happily married. // 두 집안은 매우 화목한 사이였다 The two families were on very friendly terms. // 리셉션은 화목한 분위기 속에 개최되었다 The reception was held in a congenial[harmonious] atmosphere.

화무십일홍(花無十日紅) Pride will have a fall.; Every flood[tide] hath its ebb.

화문석(花紋席) a *hwamunseok*; a figured [fancy] mat; a flowered mat.

화물(貨物) (미) freight; (영) goods; [선하(船荷)] cargo; [상품] commodities. ¶선적 ~ ship freight[cargo] // 일반 선적 ~ general cargo // 중량 ~ hard goods // 표류 ~ [해상 보험] flotsam // 철도 ~ rail freight // 항공 ~ air freight [cargo] // 저 배는 ~을 운송합다 That ship carries freight. // 그 ~은 항공 ~로 발송되었다 The goods were sent by air cargo [freight].
● 화물 보관증 a warrant; (창고의) a warehouse receipt [(영) certificate]. 화물선 a cargo boat [steamer / liner(정기선)]; a transport(수송선); a tramp(부정기선); an ocean tramp(원양 부정기선); (미) a freighter. 화물 수송 (미) freightage; freight traffic; (영) (육상) the carriage of goods; (수상) freightage. 화물 열차 (미) a freight train; (영) a goods train; (무개의) a waggon. 화물 운임 (영) goods rates; (미) freight (rates); freightage. 화물 자동차 (미) a truck; (영) a (motor) lorry. 화물 취급소 (미) a freight [(영) goods] office. 화물칸 (열차의) a goods car; (항공기의) a cargo compartment.

화방(畫房) a studio. ⇨"화실

화방수(-水) a whirl (current); a whirlpool; an eddy.

화백(畫伯) a painter. ⇨"화가(畫家)

화법(話法) [언] narration; speech. ¶직접[간접] ~ the direct[indirect] speech.

화법(畫法) the art of drawing; drawing technique. ¶산수 ~ landscape painting // ~에 맞다[맞지 않다] be in[out of] drawing.

화병(火病) a disease caused by pent-up rage.

화병(花瓶) a flower vase. ⇨"꽃병

화보(畫報) a pictorial; a graphic; an illustrated magazine; (보도를 겸한) pictorial [illustrated] news; a picture report. ¶시사 ~ news in pictures / a pictorial record [survey] of current events.

화보(畫譜) a picture book[album].

화복(禍福) fortune and misfortune; good and evil. ¶인생의 ~ the vicissitudes [ups and downs] of life.

화부(火夫) (기선의) a fireman; (보일러·기관차의) a stoker; (화장터의) a cremator; a burner

at a crematory.
화분(花盆) a flowerpot. ¶~에 심은 장미 a potted rose / a rose planted in a pot.
화분(花粉) [식] pollen; another-dust; farina.
화사첨족(畫蛇添足) [사족] superfluity; redundancy; padding.
화사하다(華奢-) gorgeous; splendid; brilliant; pompous; gaudy; luxurious; sumptuous. ¶그녀가 나타나자 그 파티의 분위기가 화사해졌다 Her appearance created a cheerful atmosphere [an air of resplendence] at the party. // 잘 차려입은 젊은 여성들로 회장은 한층 화사하였다 The well-dressed young women lent festivity [gaiety] to the hall.
화산(火山) a volcano (pl. ~(e)s). ¶활[휴/사]~ an active[a dormant / an extinct] volcano // 해저 ~ a submarine volcano // ~의 폭발 a volcanic eruption // ~이 폭발했다 A volcano erupted. // ~이 활동하고 있다 The volcano is now active.
●**화산대** a volcanic zone[belt]. **화산 분출물** ejecta. **화산섬/화산도** a volcanic island. **화산암** an effusive rock. **화산 열도** a chain of volcanic islands. **화산 작용** volcanism; volcanic action. **화산재** volcanic ash(es); puzzolana. ¶~가 쏟아졌다 Volcanic ash fell from the sky. **화산 지대** a volcanism; volcanic region [zone]. **화산 활동** volcanic activity.
화살 an arrow; a shaft; a clothyard shaft(긴); a bolt(굵은); a dart(던지는). ¶빗발치듯 하는 ~ a shower [volley / barrage] of arrows // 처럼 날다 shoot like an arrow / fly with lightning speed // ~에 깃을 달다 fledge [fletch / feather] (at arrow) // ~을 시위에 메기다 fix [notch / fit] an arrow to the string // ~을 쏘다 shoot [send / discharge / let fly / let off] an arrow (at) // 그는 멧돼지에게 ~을 쏘았다 He shot an arrow at a boar. // ~은 과녁을 맞혔다 [놓쳤다] The arrow hit [missed] the target. // 세월은 ~처럼 빠르다 Time flies like an arrow.
●**화살대** an arrow shaft. **화살촉** an arrowhead; a barb of an arrow. **화살표** an arrow. ¶지도에 그려진 ~대로 가면 회의장에 닿을 수 있습니다 Follow the arrows on the map, and you will come to the meeting place.
화상(火傷) a burn(불에 덴); a scald(뜨거운 물에 덴). ¶제1[2/3/4]도 ~ a first-[second-/third-/fourth-]degree burn // ~을 입다 get [be] burnt / have [suffer] a burn / burn oneself / be [get] scorched(부지깽이 등으로) / get [be] scalded(뜨거운 물로) / scald oneself // 손에 ~을 입다 get burnt in the hand / burn one's hand // ~을 입히다 produce [cause] a burn // 크게 ~을 입다 be badly burned // 그녀는 뜨거운 프라이팬에 손이 닿아 ~을 입었다 She burned [burnt] her hand on a hot frying pan. // 그는 온몸에 ~을 입었다 He suffered burns all over his body.
화상(和尙) a Buddhist priest (in charge of a temple); a bonze.
화상(華商) a Chinese merchant (residing abroad).
화상(畵像) 1 [초상] a portrait; one's likeness. ¶~을 그리다 paint a person's portrait. 2 [TV] picture; screen. ¶~이 비틀어졌다 The picture is distorted.
●**화상 면적** a picture area.
화색(和色) (온화한) a serene [peaceful] countenance; a gentle look; (밝은) a healthy [bright] complexion.
화생방전(化生放戰) chemical, biological and radiological warfare; CBR warfare.
화서(花序) [식] an inflorescence. ⇨꽃차례
화석(火石) (a) flint. ⇨부싯돌
화석(化石) (작용) petrifaction; fossilization; (돌) a fossil. ¶~(질)의 fossilized / fossil // ~화하다 fossilize // 동물[식물]의 ~ a fossilized animal[plant] // 조개의 ~ a fossil seashell // 그는 ~ 같은 인물이다 He is an old fossil [a remnant from the Stone Age].
●**화석 인류** fossil men. **화석층** a fossil bed; fossilferous stratum (pl. -ta).
화선지(畵宣紙) Chinese drawing paper.
화성(火星) [천] Mars. ¶~의 Martian // ~ 중심의 areocentric.
●**화성인** a Martian. **화성학** areology.
화성(和聲) [음] harmony; concord; consonance. ¶~의 harmonic.
●**화성법** the law of harmony. **화성학** harmonics; the science of harmony.
화성(畵聖) a master painter; a great artist.
화성암(火成巖) igneous [eruptive] rocks. ¶심성 ~ Plutonic rocks.
화수분 an inexhaustible supply [treasury]; a golconda; a widow's cruse.
화술(話術) the art of narration; the storyteller's art; narrative skill. ¶~에 능한 사람 a master storyteller / a master of narrative / a man of great narrative power / a brilliant conversationalist // ~의 대가 황 씨 Mr. Hwang, a well-known narrator.
화승(火繩) a fuse (cord); a match.
●**화승총** a matchlock; a harquebus; a firelock; a hackbut.
화식(火食) cooked food; eating of cooked food. **화식하다** eat (fish) cooked; eat cooked food.
화식(和食) [일본식 음식] Japanese-style food; a Japanese (-style) meal; [일본 요리] Japanese dish [cuisine / cooking]. ¶~과 양식, 어느 쪽을 좋아하십니까 Which do you like, Japanese-style food or Western-style food?
화신(化身) (an) incarnation; (an) embodiment (of courage); (a) manifestation. ¶악마의 ~ a devil incarnate // 신의 ~ God incarnate / a manifestation of a God // 그녀는 미덕의 ~이다 She is the incarnation of virtue. / She is virtue itself.
화신(花信) tidings of flowers [blossoms]; information about flowers for viewing; news of the (cherry) trees coming in bloom.
화실(畵室) a studio; an atelier.
화씨(華氏) Fahrenheit(약어 Fahr., F.). ¶~(영하) 5도 ~ (minus) 5 degrees Fahrenheit // (-)5°F // 섭씨 100도는 ~로 212도이다 A hundred degrees centigrade is 212° on the Fahrenheit scale.(▶ 문장 첫머리에 숫자가 올 때는 아라비아 숫자를 쓰지 않음. 따라서 여기서는 100℃ is ...라 하지 않음)
●**화씨온도계** a Fahrenheit thermometer.
화약(火藥) gunpowder; powder. ¶무연[백색] ~ smokeless [white] gunpowder // ~을 폭발시키다 blow up [explode] explosives [gunpowder] // ~이 폭발했다 The gunpowder exploded.
화약을 지고 불로 들어간다(속담) invite danger; be a case of insect flying into a

화염

flame to death.
- **화약고** a powder magazine; an explosive warehouse; a powder house. **화약류** explosives. **화약 제조소** a powder plant. **화약통** a powderflask.

화염(火焰) a flame; a blaze. ¶집은 ~에 휩싸였다 The house was enveloped [wrapped] in flames. // ~은 하늘이라도 태울 듯 치솟았다 The flames rose so high that they seemed to scorch the heavens.
- **화염병** a Molotov cocktail; (영) a petrol bomb; an (incendiary) bottle grenade; a fire bottle [bomb].

화요일(火曜日) Tuesday(약어 Tues., Tue.).

화용월태(花容月態) a fair face and graceful carriage.

화원(花園) 1 [꽃동산] a flower garden. 2 a flower shop. ⇨꽃집

화음(和音) [음] a chord; an accord. ¶변화 ~ an altered chord // 주[부] ~ a tonic [secondary] chord // ~의 chordal.

화의(和議) 1 [화해 협상] negotiations for peace; [화해] reconciliation. ¶~를 맺다 make peace / conclude peace (with the enemy) // ~를 제의하다 make overtures for [for] peace / extend [hold out] the olive branch // ~를 청하다 sue for peace. **화의하다** negotiate for peace; make overtures for [for] peace. 2 [법] composition.
- **화의법** [법] the Composition Act. **화의 신청** application [petition] for composition. **화의 절차** composition proceedings(상법의); procedures of composition(화의의).

화이트칼라 an office worker; a white-collar worker. ¶~의 white-collar.

화이트 하우스 [백악관] the White House.

화인(火印) 1 [낙인] a brand (mark). 2 [되] a stamped grain measure.

화인(火因) the origin [cause] of a fire. ¶~ 불명의 화재 a fire of unknown origin // ~을 조사하다 inquire into the cause of the fire.

화인(禍因) the cause [root] of evil; the cause of trouble. ¶~을 남기다 sow the seeds of evil.

화장(火葬) cremation. ¶전기 ~ electric cremation. **화장하다** cremate (the remains); burn (the body) to ashes. ➔¶유해는 화장되었다 The body was cremated.
- **화장터** a crematorium (pl. ~s, -ria); a crematory.

화장(化粧) (a) makeup; (a) toilet; dressing. ¶밑~ a powder base / a foundation // 짙은[엷은] ~ heavy [light] makeup // 엷게 ~을 한 얼굴 a lightly made-up [powdered] face // ~을 하지 않은 얼굴 an unpainted face // 엷게 ~을 하다 put on a little makeup / powder one's face lightly // 짙은 ~을 하고 있다 wear heavy makeup / be heavily made up // ~을 지우다 remove one's makeup // ~을 고치다 adjust [fix] one's makeup // 나는 ~을 한 적이 없다 I have never worn makeup. // 그녀는 ~을 하지 않는 편이 예쁘다 She looks prettier without makeup. // 그녀는 오늘은 ~을 하지 않아서 더 늙어 보였다 She looked older today because she had on [wore] no makeup. // 그녀는 지금 ~ 중이다 She is touching up [redoing] her makeup. / She is putting on her makeup. **화장하다** make up (one's face); put on makeup; make one's toilet; paint [powder / embellish] one's face.

¶그녀는 화장실에서 화장하고 있다 She's in the ladies' room doing her face. // 그녀는 화장하는 데 1시간이나 걸린다 It takes her an hour to put on her face. // 그녀는 자기 나이보다 젊게 보이도록 화장한다 She makes up her face to look younger than she really is.
- **화장대** a dressing table; (미) a dresser; (미) a vanity. **화장 도구** a toilet set; toilet articles. **화장비누** toilet soap. **화장수** face [toilet] lotion; (beauty) wash. **화장실** (가정 등의) a bathroom; (영) a toilet; (극장·백화점 등의) (미) a restroom; (영) a toilet; (빌딩·공장 등의) a washroom; (학교·병원·비행기 등의) a lavatory; (남성용의) men's room; (여성용의) ladies' room; a powder room; (속어) the john. ¶~에 가다 (미) go to the bathroom / (영) go to the toilet // ~은 어디입니까 (개인의 집에서) Where can I wash my hands? / (미) Where is the bathroom?(▶ 이 경우 toilet이라든가 water closet이라고는 보통 말하지 않음) / (호텔·백화점·극장 등에서) Where is the restroom [the ladies' room / the gentlemen's room]? // ~에 가고 싶어요 Nature is calling me. / (소아어) I have to go potty. **화장지** (a roll of) toilet paper [tissue]; bathroom tissue. **화장품** cosmetics; toilet articles; makeup; a beauty product. ¶남성용 ~ men's toiletries.

화재(火災) a fire; a conflagration(큰); a blaze(작은). ¶원인 불명의 ~ a fire of unknown origin // 석유난로가 쓰러져 일어난 ~ a fire caused by the overturning of a kerosene stove // ~의 발생 장소 the origin of a fire // ~를 진압하다 put out a fire // ~를 만나다 be caught in a fire // ~를 일으키다 [내다] start [cause] a fire // ~로 타 버리다 be burnt in a fire / be destroyed by fire // ~로 집을 잃다 be burnt out (of house and home) / become [be rendered] homeless by fire // ~를 조심하다 be careful with fire / take precautions against fire // 어제 이 마을에는 대~가 있었다 Yesterday there was a big fire in this town. // 그 ~는 부엌에서 시작되었다 The fire started [broke out / originated] in the kitchen. // 백화점에 ~가 났다 The department store was on fire. // 건물은 ~로 완전히 타 버렸다 The building was completely destroyed by fire. / The building was burned down [reduced to ashes] in a fire. // 이 집은 ~로도 타지 않는다 This house is fireproof. // ~는 누전으로 일어났다 A leakage of electricity caused [occasioned] the fire. // 어디에 ~가 났느냐 Where is the fire?
- **화재경보** a fire alarm. **화재경보기** a fire alarm. ¶~를 울리다 sound a fire alarm. **화재경보 장치** fire-warning facilities. **화재 보험** fire insurance. ¶(집을) ~에 들다 insure (a house) against fire / get (one's house) insured against fire. **화재 현장** (rush to) the scene of a fire.

화재(畫才) artistic talent [skill]. ¶그는 ~가 있다 He is gifted with artistic talent. / He has the makings of an artist.

화재(畫材) [그림의 소재] subject matter for a painting.

화적(火賊) (a gang of) burglars. ⇨불한당1

화전(火田) a slash-and-burn field. ¶~에 메밀을 심었다 They planted buckwheat after they burned off the fields.
- **화전민** slash-and-burn farmers; fire field

farmers; brand-tillers.
화전(花煎) a flower-shaped (rice) cake.
화제(畫題) [그림의 제명] the title (of a painting).
화제(話題) a topic[subject] (of conversation). ¶일상 ~ a subject of everyday conversation∥오늘의 ~ current topics / the topics of the day∥항간의 화젯거리 be the talk of the town∥~가 풍부하다 have a large[an ample] stock of topics∥~가 떨어지다 find one's topics of conversation exhausted / have nothing more to talk about∥~에 오르다 become the topic[subject] of a talk[conversation] / come up in conversation / be talked about∥~가 궁하다 can think of nothing to talk about∥~를 일으키다 be much talked about / make a stir∥~를 바꿉시다 Let us change the subject.
화조(花鳥) 1 [꽃과 새] flowers and birds. ¶~풍월을 벗 삼아 생애를 보내다 spend one's life in communion with nature. 2 [꽃을 찾아 다니는 새] birds that visit flowers. 3 [꽃과 새의 그림이나 조각] a painting[sculpture] of flowers and birds.
화조월석(花朝月夕) flowery mornings and moonlit nights; the most beautiful time of the year.
화주(火酒) spirits; hard liquor; hard drink.
화주(花柱) [식] a style. ⇨=암술대⇨암술.
화주(貨主) (짐의 소유주) a consignor; a shipper; the owner of goods. ¶손해는 ~ 부담으로 화물을 보내다 consign goods at the owner's risk.
화중지병(畵中之餠) something unavailable[of no practical use]; a prize beyond one's reach.
화증(火症) anger; (a) passion; ire; a quick [hot / short] temper. ¶~이 나다 get angry [mad] / lose one's temper / get out of temper / get[fly / burst] into a temper[passion / rage].
화집(畫集) a picture album. ⇨=화첩1
화차(火車) 1 (화공용의) a fire-attack(ing) car; (지옥의) a fiery car. 2 [우리나라의 옛 전차] an ancient tank. 3 a steam locomotive. ⇨=기차1
화차(貨車) 1 a truck. ⇨=화물 자동차(⇨화물) 2 [짐차] a freight[(영) goods] train; (차량) a freight car; (영) a goods wagon. ¶무개 ~ an open[a flat] wagon / a (goods) truck / (영) a flat car∥~로 (미) by freight / (영) by goods.
화창하다(和暢−) balmy; bright; sunny. ¶화창한 봄날 a clear and mild[lovely] spring day.
화채(花菜) honeyed juice with fruits as a punch.
화첩(畫帖) 1 [화집] a picture album[book]; a book of paintings. 2 [사생첩] a sketchbook; [떼어 쓰는 도화지첩] a drawing pad.
화초(花草) a flowering plant; a flower. ¶~를 가꾸다 cultivate[grow] flowering plants∥그는 정원에 ~를 많이 심고 있다 He grows many flowers in his garden.
●**화초밭** a flower garden. **화초 재배** floriculture; cultivation of flowers; flower gardening.
화촉(華燭) 1 [혼례] a wedding; a marriage ceremony. 2 [그림용] candle for painting; (색이 든) a colored candle.
화촉을 밝히다 celebrate a wedding; solem-

nize a marriage.
화친(和親) friendship; friendly relations; amity; harmony. **화친하다** contract[form] a friendship (with); come into friendly [intimate] relations (with).
●**화친 조약** a peace treaty; a treaty of peace and amity.
화톳불 a bonfire. ¶~을 놓다[피우다] make a bonfire.
화통(火筒) a smokestack; a funnel(기관차·기
화투(花鬪) 1 [딱지] *hwatu*; Korean playing cards; "flower cards". 2 [놀이] *hwatu*; Korean cards. **화투하다** play "flower cards"; play Korean "*hwatu*" cards.
●**화투 놀이** playing "flower cards"; gambling at cards; card playing.
화판(花瓣) [식] a (flower) petal. ⇨=꽃잎.
화판(畫板) [도화지를 고정시키는 받침] a drawing[drafting] board; [유화를 그리는 판] a painting[drawing] board.
화평(和平) peace. ¶~을 제의하다 make a peace offer. **화평하다** peaceful; placid; harmonious.
화폐(貨幣) (통화) money; currency; (경화) a coin; (집합적) coinage. ¶대용 ~ token money[coin]∥법정 ~ legal tender∥보조 ~ a subsidiary coin∥본위[표준] ~ a standard coin∥위조 ~ counterfeit money / an imitation coin∥100원 ~ a 100-won coin∥~의 표면[이면] the head[tail] of a coin∥~의 대내[대외]적 가치 domestic [foreign] value of money∥~의 구매력 purchasing power of money∥~를 주조[위조]하다 mint[forge] coins∥~를 발행하다 issue coins.
●**화폐 가치** monetary[currency] value; the value of money[currency]. ¶인플레로 ~가 떨어졌다 The value of money has declined because of inflation. **화폐 개혁** currency [monetary] reform; [평가 절하] devaluation. **화폐 경제** a monetary economy. **화폐 단위** a monetary unit. **화폐 본위** a monetary standard. **화폐 제도** the monetary[currency] system.
화포(火砲) a gun; (집합적) artillery.
화포(畫布) canvas. ⇨=캔버스
화포(畫幅) a drawing paper; a canvas.
화풀이(火−) venting of one's anger. ¶그것으로 ~가 된다면 얼마든지 나를 때려라 Beat me as much as you like, if it makes you feel better[give you any satisfaction].∥그에게 ~를 해야겠다 I will get even with him. **화풀이하다** give vent to one's anger[indignation]; satisfy one's resentment[grudge]; vent[work off] one's anger[fury / rancor / indignation] (on a person); (구어) let off the steam. ¶아버지는 언제나 우리들에게 화풀이한다 My father always vents[takes out] his anger on us.∥아무리 화가 나더라도 나에게 화풀이하지는 마라 Don't take it out on me just because you're angry.
화품(畫品) a style of painting[drawing].
화피(花被) [식] the perianth. ⇨=꽃덮이.
화필(畫筆) a paintbrush; a painter's [an artist's] brush.
화하다(化−) [변화하다] change[turn] (into / to); convert (into / to); [변형하다] transform (into / to); be transformed; […으로 되다] be turned; be reduced (to). ¶돌로 ~ change[turn] into (a) stone / petrify∥타서

화학(化學) chemistry. ¶농예 ～ agricultural chemistry // 물리 ～ physical chemistry // 분석 ～ analytical chemistry // 응용 ～ applied chemistry // 열 ～ thermal chemistry // 이론 ～ theoretical chemistry // 유기[무기] ～ organic [inorganic] chemistry.
- 화학 결합 chemical combination; a chemical bond. 화학 공업 chemical industry. 화학 기호 the symbol of element. ⇨ 원소 기호(元素) 화학 무기 chemical weapons [arms]. 화학 반응 a chemical reaction. 화학 비료 chemical fertilizer. 화학 섬유 a synthetic [chemical] fiber. 화학식 a chemical formula. ¶물의 ～은 H_2O 다 The (chemical) formula for water is H_2O. 화학 약품 chemicals. 화학 요법[의] chemotherapy. ¶～제(劑) a chemotherapeutic agent / a chemotherapeutant. 화학자 a chemist. 화학 작용 chemical action. ¶～을 일으키지 않는 inert / neutral. 화학전 chemical warfare. 화학제품 chemical goods [products]; chemicals. 화학조미료 a chemical seasoning.

화학적(化學的) chemical. ¶～으로 chemically.

화합(化合) [화] chemical combination. 화합하다 combine (with). ¶수소는 산소와 화합하여 물이 된다 Hydrogen combines with oxygen to form water. // 질소는 수소와 화합하여 암모니아가 된다 Nitrogen combines with hydrogen to form ammonia.
- 화합물 a (chemical) compound.

화합(和合) harmony; concord; union; unity. ¶부부의 ～ conjugal harmony // 일가의 ～ a harmonious family life // 국민의 ～과 단결 national reconciliation and unity. 화합하다 harmonize (with); be harmonious [harmonized]; agree (with each other); be in accord (with). ¶화합하여 살다 live in perfect harmony // 부부는 서로 화합해야 한다 Man and wife should live together in unity.

화해(和解) amicable [friendly / peaceful] settlement; reconcilement; reconciliation; accommodation; (타협·사화) composition; compromise. ¶A와 B와의 ～ a reconciliation between A and B // ～에 의해 사건은 해결되었다 A friendly settlement closed the incident. 화해하다 make up (with); make peace (with); come to terms (with); reconcile oneself (with); be [become] reconciled (with); accommodate [compromise] (with); (사건이) be settled amicably; come to an amicable settlement. ¶화해할 수 있는[없는] reconcilable [irreconcilable] // 나는 그들과는 이미 화해했다 I have already made (it) up [made my peace] with them. // 소녀들은 바로 화해했다 The girls were soon friends again.
→ ¶화해시키다 conciliate / reconcile (persons to) / make peace (between) / mediate a settlement (between) // 저 두 사람을 화해시키기는 어려울 것이다 It will be hard to reconcile [make peace between] the two.

화형(火刑) (burning at) the stake; (fire and) faggot; burning to death. ¶～에 처해지다[～을 당하다] be burnt at the stake / be condemned at [to] the stake / be burned alive // 그 죄인은 ～에 처해졌다 The criminal was burned at the stake. // 그녀는 마녀로서 ～에 처해졌다 She was burned at the stake as a witch.

화환(花環) a wreath; a garland; a lei (목에 거는). ¶～ 3개 three wreaths of flowers // ～을 바치다 place [lay] a wreath (at the tomb / before a monument) / place a floral tribute (on the grave of) // ～을 만들다 make [wreathe] a garland.

화훼(花卉) a flowering plant.
- 화훼 원예 / 화훼 재배 floriculture; cultivation of flowers. 화훼 원예가 / 화훼 재배가 a floriculturist.

확[1] [절구] a mortar; [절구의 움푹 팬 부분] the hollow of a mortar. ¶이 절구는 ～이 깊다 This mortar has a deep hollow.

확[2] (갑자기) suddenly; [잽싸게] in a flash; alertly; (힘차게) with a jerk. ¶～ 당기다[밀다] pull [push] with a (sudden) jerk // ～ 덮치다 (짐승·새가) spring [leap / jump] upon [at] (사람이) ～ 덤비다 throw[hurl] oneself upon / be down on [upon] // ～ 열다 fling [throw] (a window) open // (불길이) ～ 타오르다 burst into flame(s) / flare [flame] up // 촛불을 ～ 불어 끄다 blow out a candle (light) // 종이에 불이 ～ 당겼다 Paper catched (on) fire. // 개가 ～ 달려들었다 Suddenly, a dog sprang at me. // 바람이 ～ 불었다 There was a gust of wind. // 소문이 ～ 퍼졌다 The rumor has spread in a flash. / The rumor spread like wildfire. // 불이 ～ 타올랐다 The fire flared up. // 불길이 ～ 솟아올랐다 The flames shot up high. // 근처가 ～ 밝아졌다 It suddenly became bright. // 그녀는 그를 보자 얼굴이 ～ 붉혔다 She blushed at the sight of him. // 촛불이 꺼지기 전에 ～ 타올랐다 The candle flared up a little before it went out. // 벚꽃은 일시에 ～ 피었다가 곧 진다 Cherry blossoms come out all at once and are soon gone.

확고하다(確固−) firm; definite; resolute; fixed; determined. ¶확고한 신념 a firm faith // 확고한 결심 a firm [fixed] resolution // 확고한 의지 an iron [adamant] will // 확고한 정책 a rock-ribbed policy // 확고한 태도 a determined [a resolute] attitude // 확고한 지위 a secure position // 확고한 증거 a positive proof // 확고한 기초[기반] 위에 on a firm foundation [basis] // 확고한 증거를 찾아내다 find positive [irrefutable / indisputable] evidence // 그것은 확고한 사실이다 It is an undeniable [established / indisputable] fact. // 그녀의 결의는 ～ Her resolution is firm [unshakable]. // 확고한 증거가 있다 There is irrefutable [positive / indisputable] evidence. // 그녀는 남편이 성공할 것이라는 확고한 신념을 갖고 있었다 She had a firm [an unshakable] faith that her husband would succeed.

확고히 firmly; resolutely; determinedly; unswervingly. ¶국가의 기초를 ～ 하다 place the country on a firm [solid] basis.

확답(確答) a definite answer [reply]; a determinate reply; a categorical answer. ¶～을 주지 않다 give no definite answer / be noncommittal // ～을 얻다 secure [gain] a definite answer // ～을 피하다 evade a definite answer // ～을 재촉하다 press (a person) for a definite answer / insist on a definite answer from (a person) // 장관은 ～을 피했다 The minister evaded committing himself in his answer. 확답하다 answer [reply] definitely; give a definite answer [reply].

확대(擴大) extension; augmentation; magnification; magnifying. ¶(전쟁의) 단계적 ~ escalation (of war) // 전화(戰火)의 ~ the spread of war(-fire) // 대미 무역의 ~ expansion of trade with the U.S. // 법을 자기에 유리하게 ~ 해석하다 stretch the law in one's favor. **확대하다** magnify; scale up; [퍼지다] spread; expand; (사건 등이) assume serious proportions. ¶사진을 ~ enlarge a photograph // …의 크기로 ~ magnify to the size of … // 사진을 실물 크기로 ~ make a life-size enlargement of a photograph // 양국 간의 경제 분야의 협력을 ~ expand bilateral partnership in the areas of economy // 이 사진을 명함판 크기로 확대해 주시오 Please make a carte de visite size enlargement of this photograph. ➜¶두 배로 확대된 사진 a twice enlarged photo // 이 현미경으로 보면 박테리아가 천 배로 확대된다 This microscope magnifies a bacteria one thousand times. // 전쟁은 반도 전역에 확대되었다 The war has spread throughout the peninsula. // 핵 군비는 더욱 확대될 모양이다 Nuclear armament is likely to escalate.
● **확대경** a magnifying glass [lens]; a magnifier; (현미경의) an amplifier. **확대율** magnifying power; [사진] an enlargement ratio; the scale of enlargement. **확대 재생산** expanded (re)production; reproduction on an enlarged scale.

확론(確論) an infallible argument; an incontrovertible [indisputable] opinion; a solid argument; sound reasoning; an established theory.

확률(確率) probability. ¶…할 ~이 크다 There is every probability that [of] … // 저 팀이 이길 ~은 4분의 1이다 The probability of the team winning [that the team will win] is one in four.

확립(確立) establishment; settlement. ¶세계 평화의 ~ the establishment of world peace. **확립하다** establish (a theory); build up; fix; settle. ¶명성[신용]을 ~ establish one's reputation [credit] // 방침을 ~ fix [decide on] a policy // 여성의 지위를 ~ establish women's status. ➜¶**확립된** established (fame) / settled (habit).

확보(確保) security; insurance; guarantee. **확보하다** secure (a seat / success); make sure of (a copy of a book); make good (one's position); ensure [insure] (one's life); assure (one's comfort); guarantee; maintain (place and order). ¶식량을 ~ secure foodstuffs // 교두보를 ~ secure [establish] a bridgehead // 좌석을 ~ secure a seat // 극동의 영원한 평화를 ~ ensure the lasting peace of the Far East // 역사에 불후의 위치를 ~ vindicate oneself a permanent place in history // 수송력을 ~ secure transportation facilities / secure transport capacity // 좌석을 두 개 확보해 주십시오 Please secure [save] two seats for me. (▶ 연극·경기 안내나 여행사 안내 등에서 예약할 때는 secure라고 하지만, 학생끼리 자리를 잡아 주기를 바랄 때는 save라고 말할 때는 save) ➜¶확실하게 일을 하면 살기에 어렵지 않은 수입이 확보될 것이다 Honest work will ensure you enough to live on.

확산(擴散) spread(ing); dissemination; proliferation; [물][화] diffusion (of light, gas, etc.). ¶핵 ~ spread of nuclear arms / nuclear proliferation // 핵 ~ 금지 조약[협정] a nuclear (weapons) nonproliferation [antiproliferation] treaty [agreement] // 빛의 ~ the diffusion of light // 핵무기의 ~을 막다 check the spread of nuclear weapons / prevent nuclear proliferation // 핵무기의 ~에 반대하는 결의 a resolution to oppose the spread of nuclear weapons.

확성기(擴聲器) a (loud) speaker; a megaphone; a speech amplifier; a speaking trumpet. ¶~로 (speak) through a megaphone / on [over] a loudspeaker // ~를 단 헬리콥터 a loudspeaker helicopter // ~를 단 트럭 a sound [loudspeaker] truck // ~로 말하다 speak over [through] a loudspeaker.

확신(確信) a conviction; a firm [confident] belief; assurance; confidence (자신). ¶~을 갖다 have confidence (that) / feel sure (of / that) // ~을 얻다 gain confidence // ~을 주다 carry conviction (to / with) // 성공할 ~이 없다 be not confident of success // 이 일은 ~을 갖고 말씀드릴 수 있습니다 This much I can say with confidence [certainty]. // ~은 없습니다 I am not certain. // 그가 훌륭한 사람이라는 ~을 굳혔다 My conviction that he is an admirable man was confirmed. **확신하다** believe firmly; be [feel] confident (of / that); feel certain (of / that); have a firm belief (that). ¶…임을 완전히 확신하고 in the full assurance that … // 나는 그의 결백함을 확신하고 있다 I am convinced of [believe firmly in] his innocence. / I am convinced that he is innocent. // 너는 성공을 확신하고 있니 Are you sure of success? / Are you sure (that) you will succeed? // 그는 시험에 합격되리라고 확신하고 있었다 He hadn't a doubt in the world [was absolutely sure] that he would pass the examination. ➜¶**확신시키다** convince.

확실성(確實性) certainty; reliability.
확실하다(確實-) [틀림없다] certain; sure (method); secure; positive; [믿을 만하다] reliable (news); trustworthy (person); [확정되다] definite. ¶확실한 근거 solid [sure] grounds (for belief) // 확실한 증거 positive [indisputable] proof [evidence] // 확실한 투자 [사업] a sound investment [business] // 확실한 담보 a good security // 확실한 대답 a definite answer // 확실한 방법 a sure [safe / valid] method // 확실한 사실 an established [a certain] fact // 확실한 정보 accurate information // 확실한 증인 [보증인] a reliable witness [guarantor / surety] // 확실한 약속 a positive promise // 확실한 저축법 a sure [dependable] way of saving money // 그 병에 대한 확실한 치료법 a sure cure for the disease // 확실한 소식통에서 듣다 hear from a reliable source // ~이 확실하다고 생각하다 be confident [sure] of (success) // 확실한 것은 말할 수 없다 I cannot say for certain. // 그가 내일 돌아올 것은 ~ There is no doubt that he will come back tomorrow. / He is sure [certain] to come back tomorrow. // 이 학설은 확실한 근거에 기초를 두고 있다 This theory is based on solid ground. // 그가 이른 시간의 열차에 탄 것은 ~ It is certain that he took the earlier train. // 이 문제가 시험에 나올 것은 ~ This question is on the test. // 이 정보는 확실한 소식통에서 나온 것이다 This information came [is] from a

reliable source.// 그가 범인이라는 확실한 증거는 없다 There is no positive proof that he committed the crime.// 그의 당선은 ~ He is safe to get in.// 그의 신원은 ~ He has good references.// 그의 실력을 생각하면 성공은 ~ Judging from his ability, he is sure to succeed.// 그가 승진하게 될지 어떨지 아직은 확실치 않다 It's not certain yet whether he'll get a promotion or not./ It's up in the air whether he'll get a promotion or not. 확실히 certainly; surely; for certain; to be sure; positively; definitely; no doubt; doubtless; beyond doubt; decidedly. ¶내가 ~ 아는 바로는 to my certain knowledge // ~ 하다 ensure / make sure (of) // ~ 그렇다[보증한다] I assure you it is so. // ~ 별난 여자다 She is a funny girl, and that's the truth. // ~ 그는 오게 되어 있다 He is bound to come. // ~ 차후 사태가 어떻게 될지 ~ 모른다 I don't know for certain how things will turn out. // ~ 은 모르지만 그 두 회사가 합병할 것이라는 소문으로 I don't know for certain that it's true, but it is said that the two companies are going to merge.

확약(確約) a strict[definite] promise. ¶~은 할 수 없다 I cannot make a definite promise. // 그의 ~을 받을 때까지 기다려라 Wait till you get a definite promise from him. **확약하다** promise positively; make a definite promise; give one's word (to); commit oneself (to). ¶확약하셨지요 You gave me your word, didn't you?

확언(確言) a positive[definite] statement; assertion; affirmation. **확언하다** state[say] positively[definitely]; assert; affirm; commit oneself; lay down. ¶그 점은 확언하기 어렵다 I am not positive about the point.// 나는 그녀가 거기 있었다고 확언할 수 없다 I cannot affirm that she was there.// 그는 그것이 사실이라고 확언했다 He said definitely[declared / asserted] that it was true./ 그 진술이 사실임을 확언할 수 있습니까 Can you affirm [vouch for] the truth of the statement? / Can you say for certain[(구어) sure] that it's true?// 그는 그 건에 대해 확언하기를 회피했다 He avoided making any definite comment[statement] on the matter.

확연하다(確然−) definite; positive; sure; certain. **확연히** definitely; positively; surely; certainly.

확인(確認) confirmation; affirmation; certification; validation. **확인하다** confirm; affirm; certify; validate; identify; ascertain; make sure (of / that). ¶시체를 ~ identify a corpse // 정체를 ~ discern (a person's) true character // 사실 여부를 ~ ascertain whether[if] it is true // 사실을 ~ make certain of the truth of the matter // 필요한 물건은 모두 샀는지 확인하세요 Make sure (that) you've bought everything necessary.// 그는 수험생 한 사람 한 사람을 확인했다 He checked the identity of the examinees one by one. // 진부를 확인해 봐야지 I'll see if it is true or not. // 그 이야기는 확인해 볼 필요가 있다 The story requires confirmation. // 손님이 도착했는지 확인하기 위해 집에 전화를 걸었다 I telephoned home to make sure[(문어) ascertain] that the guest had arrived. // 그 남자의 신원을 확인할 만한 것은 아무것도 없었다 There was nothing to identify the man. ➔ ¶ 확인되지 않은 unconfirmed / naked (confession) / 그것은 사실이라는 것이 확인되었다 The truth of it was confirmed. // 이 보도는 아직 확인되어 있지 않다 This report is not yet [has yet to be] confirmed.

● **확인서** a (written) confirmation; a confirmation document.

확장(擴張) extension (of one's premises); expansion (of trade); enlargement; aggrandizement; increment; dilation. ¶군비 ~ the expansion of armaments // 영토 ~ territorial expansion // (영토) ~ 정책 a policy of expansion // 도로 ~ 계획 a street-widening project // 기업이 ~ 일로에 있다 The enterprise is still expanding[growing]. **확장하다** extend (one's domains); expand (business); enlarge; aggrandize; increase; dilate. ¶가로 [거리]를 ~ widen a street // 교사(校舍) [가게]를 ~ enlarge[expand] the school-building [shop] // 병원을 ~ expand[enlarge] a hospital // 사업[업무]을 ~ expand[extend] business / branch out one's business // 사업을 해외로 ~ extend[expand] one's business abroad // 판로를 ~ extend the market (for) // 그는 유럽으로 사업을 확장하려 하고 있다 He intends to expand his business to Europe.

● **확장 공사** extension work.

확전(擴戰) escalation (of the war).

확정(確定) decision; settlement. ¶취해야 할 조처는 아직 ~을 못 보았다 The step to be taken is not yet decided upon. **확정하다** decide upon (a matter); settle; fix; confirm. ¶우리는 날짜를 아직 확정하지 않았다 We haven't fixed[settled on] a date yet. ➔ ¶확정된 사실 an established fact // 확정되다 be decided (upon) / be settled / become definite [certain] / be fixed (upon) // 이것은 확정된 사실이다 This is an established fact. // 그것은 아직 확정되지 않았다 The matter is not yet definitely settled. // 그의 도착은 6월 10일로 확정되었다 June 10 was set[fixed] as the date of his arrival. // 올해의 쌀값이 확정되었다 The price of rice for this year has been fixed. // 그의 유죄[무죄]가 확정되었다 His guilt[innocence] was established. // 재판은 피고의 승소[패소]로 확정되었다 The case has been decided in favor of[against] the defendant. // 그의 해외 파견이 확정되었다 It is decided that he shall be sent abroad.

● **확정 금액** a definite amount. **확정 신고** (소득세의) a final (income tax) return[declaration]. ¶소득세 ~(서) a final income tax return (for the year) // ~ 하다 turn in a final return (of one's income tax). **확정안** a final draft. **확정 일자** a fixed date; an inconvertible date. **확정 판결** [법] an irrevocable judgment; a final and conclusive judgment.

확정적(確定的) definite. ¶~으로 definitely / conclusively // 그가 승진할 것이 거의 ~이다 It is almost definite[certain] that he will be promoted.

확증(確證) corroboration; confirmation; [증거] (a) corroborative[decisive / clear / convincing / positive] proof; conclusive evidence. ¶~을 수반하지 않는 uncorroborated (confession) // …의 ~을 쥐다[잡다] secure [obtain] positive evidence of … // 그의 유죄의 ~을 잡다 secure[obtain] conclusive evidence of his guilt // 그가 그것을 했다는 ~은

없다 There is no positive proof that he did it.∥그의 이론의 정당함은 실험에 의해 ~을 얻었다 The validity of his theory was confirmed experimentally. **확증하다** prove [show] positively; corroborate; confirm; verify; give positive proof of; be corroborative of.

확충(擴充) (an) expansion; (an) amplification; [물] generalization; [논] distribution; [논][문] amplification. ¶생산력 ~ the expansion of productive capacity. **확충하다** expand (productivity); amplify. ¶교육 시설을 ~ expand[enlarge] educational facilities.

확확 1 [바람·연기 등이] with great puffs; with [in] gusts. ¶바람이 ~ 불다 have gust after gust of wind∥연기를 ~ 내뿜다 send out puffs of smoke. 2 [불길이] briskly; in flareups[blazes]; with flame after flame; broilingly; scorchingly. ¶[불이] ~ 타오르다 burn hot[briskly / furiously]∥(뺨이나 얼굴이) ~ 달아오르다 flush up (hotly) / blush / feel (one's face) burning (with shame). 3 [힘차게 풀리는 모양] off the reel; in rapid succession.

환¹ [줄] a fine file; a wooden stick covered with shark skin.

환² [마구 그린 그림] a poor drawing; a wretched painting; a daub. ¶~을 치다 draw [paint] poorly / daub.

환(丸) a (medicinal) pill. ⇨"환약 ¶청심~ pills that clear one's chest∥~을 짓다 make a pill / pill.

환(換) a money order; exchange; [경] transfer. ¶내국~ domestic exchange∥소액~ a postal note∥송금~ remittance by draft∥외국~ foreign exchange∥우편~ a postal money order∥달러~ dollar exchange∥전신~ a telegraphic transfer∥~의 자유화 liberalization of exchange∥~으로 송금하다 remit [send] (10,000 won) by money order∥~을 쳐넣하다 draw a money order (on a person for 10,000 won)∥~을 현금으로 바꾸다 have a money order cashed.

환가(換價) conversion (into money); realization. **환가하다** convert into money; cash; sell; realize. ¶재산을 ~ realize property.

환각(幻覺) a hallucination; an illusion. ¶~에 의해 보이는 상 a hallucinatory image∥~을 일으키다 hallucinate / have hallucinations∥취한 사람은 가끔 ~을 경험한다 Drunken men are sometimes subject to hallucinations.

● **환각제** a hallucinogenic drug; a hallucinogen.

환갑(還甲) the 60th anniversary of one's birth; one's 60th birthday. ¶그는 올해 ~을 맞이했다 He reached the age of sixty this year.∥그는 ~으로 생각되지 않을 만큼 젊게 보인다 He looks too young to be sixty.

● **환갑잔치** (give) a banquet on one's 60th birthday.

환 거래(換去來) exchange transactions.

환경(環境) environment; surroundings; circumstances. ¶가정~ (bad) home environment∥사회~ social environment∥생활~ one's living environment∥자연~ natural environment∥~의 변화 a change in one's circumstances∥~의 영향 the influence of environment∥건전한 ~ healthy surroundings∥한국의 지리적 ~ the geographic setting of Korea∥~이 나쁜 장소 a place with bad surroundings∥좋은 ~에서 자란 아이 a child raised in a good neighborhood∥(근처) ~이 좋다[나쁘다] be in a decent[an undesirable] neighborhood∥~에 영향받다 be influenced by one's environment∥~에 순응하다 adapt oneself to circumstances∥비위생적인 ~에서 작업하다 toil under unfavorable hygienic surroundings∥~을 극복하다 master one's circumstances∥어떠한 ~의 변화에도 순응하다 adjust to any change in one's environment[situation]∥어린이 교육에는 ~이 매우 중요하다 Environment is the first consideration in the education of children.∥그것은 ~ 탓이다 The surroundings are to blame for it.∥사람은 ~의 지배를 받는다 Man is a creature of circumstances.∥그들은 아무 불편 없는 ~에서 자라났다 They were brought up in comfortable[easy] circumstances.∥그는 ~에 순응하는 것이 더디다 He is slow in adapting himself to his surroundings[environment].∥사람은 유전과 ~에 의해 좌우된다 Man is conditioned by heredity and environment.

● **환경 공학** [파피] environmental engineering[disruption]. **환경 보존법** the Environmental Preservation Law. **환경 보호** the protection of environment. **환경부** the Ministry of Environment. **환경오염** environmental pollution[contamination]. **환경 요인** a habitat factor. **환경 호르몬** [내분비계 장애 물질] an endocrine disruptor.

환관(宦官) a eunuch; a gelding.

환국(還國) returning home from abroad. ⇨"귀국(歸國).

환궁(還宮) return(ing) to the Royal Palace. **환궁하다** return to the Royal Palace.

환금(換金) 1 [물건을 팔아서 현금으로 바꾸기] realization; conversion (of goods) into money. **환금하다** realize (one's securities / property); convert[turn] (goods) into money; [수표 등을 현금화하다] cash (a check); have[get] (a check) cashed. 2 [환전] exchange (of money); money exchanging. **환금하다** exchange. ¶100만 원을 달러로 ~ exchange 1,000,000 won into dollars.

● **환금 작물** a cash crop.

환급(還給) (a) refundment; (a) refund; (a) repayment; (a) reimbursement(상환·보상). **환급하다** refund; repay; reimburse.

환기(喚起) [불러일으킴] awakening; evocation. **환기하다** awaken (one's sympathy); call forth (great emotions); rouse (romantic images); arouse (public attention); excite (attention / curiosity); evoke. ¶여론을 ~ [환기시키다] rouse[stir up / excite] public opinion∥주의를 ~[환기시키다] call (a person's) attention (to a fact). ➔¶그는 새로운 사태에 대하여 그들의 주의를 환기시켰다 He called their attention to the new situation.∥각자에게 책임감을 환기시키고 싶다 I would like to awaken each of you to a sense of responsibility.∥이 문제는 사람들에게 주의를 환기시킬 필요가 있다 We have to call the attention of the people to this problem.

환기(換氣) ventilation; a change of air. ¶~가 잘되다[안 되다] be well[badly / ill] ventilated∥~를 위해 창문을 열다 open the windows to let fresh air in∥이 창고는 ~가 잘된다 [안 된다] This storehouse is well[poorly]

환난

환난 ventilated. **환기하다** ventilate; air. ¶방을 ~ air (out) [ventilate / let fresh air into] a room.
● **환기구** a ventilating opening. **환기 장치** a ventilator; ventilating facilities [equipment / arrangement]; a ventilating device. ¶완전한 ~가 돼 있다 have the most thorough ventilation. **환기창** a vent; a window for ventilation. **환기통** a ventilator; a ventilation funnel.

환난(患難) afflictions; hardships; difficulties; evil; trouble; distress.

환담(歡談) a pleasant chat [talk]; a confabulation. **환담하다** have a pleasant chat [talk] (with); confabulate (with).

환대(歡待) a hospitable [warm / cordial / hearty] reception; hospitality; hospitable treatment; welcome. ¶~를 받다 be warmly received / be accorded a warm welcome / be received cordially / meet with a cordial reception / receive hospitable treatment. **환대하다** give (a person) a warm reception; entertain warmly; receive warmly [cordially]; treat hospitably; make (a person) welcome. ¶손님을 ~ receive [entertain] a guest hospitably [cordially] / give a warm [cordial] reception [welcome] to a guest.

환도(環刀) [군복에 차던 군도] a military sword; a saber.

환도(還都) the return of the Government (to); returning of an evacuated government; returning to the capital. **환도하다** (an evacuated government) return; return to the capital.

환등(幻燈) [필름에 의한] a filmslide; a color slide(컬러의); [옛날의] a magic lantern.
● **환등기** a slide projector; a stereopticon; a magic lantern apparatus.

환락(歡樂) pleasure(s); merriment; mirth; merrymaking; gaieties. ¶인생의 ~을 쫓는 [추구하는] 사람 a pleasure-seeker // ~을 쫓다 [추구하다] pursue [seek] pleasure / gather (life's) roses / lead a gay life / a merrymaker // ~에 빠지다 indulge in [give oneself up to] pleasure / ~의 꿈에서 깨어나다 awoke [sober down] from a dream of pleasure. **환락하다** enjoy oneself; have fun.
● **환락가**(-街) an amusement center [quarter]; gay quarters; a pleasure haunt; (미) a red-light district.

환류(還流) a return current; a back flow [current]; [기상] convection, [화] reflux.

환매(換買) barter; bartering truck. **환매하다** barter; (미) trade; truck.

환매(還買) [경] redemption; repurchase; [증권] covering. **환매하다** buy back; repurchase; redeem; cover short.
● **환매권** the right of repurchase; the redemptive right. **환매인** a redeemer.

환멸(幻滅) disillusion; disillusionment. ¶~의 비애 a sad disillusionment / anguish [sorrow] of disillusionment // ~적인 illusion-dispelling // ~을 느끼다 be greatly disillusioned [disenchanted] / feel the bitterness of disillusion // 그의 실체를 발견하고 나는 ~을 느꼈다 I was disillusioned when I discovered his true character.

환물(換物) conversion of money into goods. **환물하다** convert money into goods.

환부(患部) [상처 난 자리] the affected [diseased] part; the seat (of a disease). ¶~를 차게 [따뜻하게] 하다 cool (down) [warm (up)] the affected part // ~를 절개하다 cut out the affected part // ~에 약을 바르다 apply medicine to the affected part.

환부(還付) [도로 돌려줌] return; restoration; restitution; retrocession. **환부하다** return; give back; restore; retrocede; refund (a tax).

환불(還拂) (a) refundment; (a) refund; (a) drawback; (a) repayment. **환불하다** pay back; repay; refund; reimburse; rebate. ¶관세를 ~ draw back the duties paid // 대금을 ~ return the price paid. ➔소득세의 일부가 환불되었다 Part of my income tax has been refunded [rebated]. // 해약 시에는 신청금을 환불받을 수 있습니다 The application fee will be refunded if the contract is canceled.
● **환불금** a refund; a repayment.

환산(換算) conversion; change. **환산하다** convert (won into dollars); change (into). ¶미터로 환산하여 calculated in terms of meters // 달러를 파운드로 ~ convert [change] dollars into pounds // 에이커를 제곱킬로미터로 ~ turn acres into square kilometers // 한국 화폐로 환산하면 약 3천 원이 된다 The sum will come to about 3,000 won in Korean currency. // 현재의 돈으로 환산하면 5백만 원에 상당한다 It is equivalent to five million won in to day's Korean currency. // 마일로 환산하여 어느 정도의 거리입니까 How far is it in miles?
● **환산율** the exchange rate. **환산표** a conversion [an exchange] table.

환상(幻想) a fantasy; an illusion; a vision; a (day)dream; a reverie; a phantasm. ¶즐거운 ~ a sweet illusion // 산산조각이 된 ~ a shattered illusion // ~에서 깨어나다 wake from one's reverie // 그의 가족을 만나면서 그에 대한 ~은 사라졌다 Meeting his family shattered all my illusions about him. // 장래에 대한 달콤한 ~은 사라졌다 My sweet dreams [visions] of the future vanished.
● **환상가** a fantast; an illusionist; a dreamer. **환상곡** a fantasy; a fantasia.

환상(幻像) [심] an illusion.

환상(環狀) annulation; a ring shape. ¶~의 ring-shaped / annular / loop / circular.
● **환상 도로** a loop [ring] road; a loop [belt] highway; a beltline avenue(도시의).

환상적(幻想的) visionary; dreamy. ¶이 그림은 ~인 분위기를 자아내고 있다 There is an air of fantasy about this picture.

환생(還生) 1 [되살아남] revival; resuscitation; renascence. **환생하다** revive; be resuscitated; be restored to life. 2 [다시 태어남] rebirth; regeneration. **환생하다** be born again; be [get] reborn. ¶나는 환생한다면 남자가 되고 싶다 If I were reborn [born again], I would like to be a man (next time).

환성(歡聲) a shout of joy [jubilation]; a hurrah; a cheer. ¶와 ~을 올리며 with vociferous cheers // ~을 올리다 shout for joy / give [raise] a cheer / raise [set up] a shout (of joy) // 갑자기 ~이 터져 나왔다 Suddenly a great cheer arose.

환속(還俗) [불] retiring from the Buddhist priesthood; returning to the laity. **환속하다** retire from the Buddhist priesthood; return to the laity.

환송(還送) sending back [home]; repatriation. ¶~ 바람 Please for ward.// (열차의) ~ (게시) To Car Barn. 환송하다 send back; send home(본국으로); repatriate. ¶빈 차를 ~ deadhead an empty train[car] //그가 이사한 곳으로 편지[소포]를 환송했다 I forwarded the letter[parcel] to his new address. / I sent the letter[parcel] on his new address.

환송(歡送) sending off; a send-off. 환송하다 give (a person) a hearty[good] send-off; farewell. ¶그들 모두가 그를 환송했다 They all gave him a hearty[cordial] send-off.
● 환송식 a farewell[send-off] ceremony. 환송회 a send-off[farewell] party. ¶선수단의 ~를 열다 hold a send-off party for the delegation of athletes.

환수(還收) redemption. 환수하다 redeem.
● 환수권 the right of redemption.

환승(換乘) a transfer. 환승하다 transfer.
● 환승객 a transfer passenger. 환승역 a transfer station.

환시(幻視) a visual hallucination.

환시세(換時勢) the (foreign) exchange rate. ⇨ =환율

환시장(換市場) an exchange market.

환심(歡心) good graces; favor.
환심(을) 사다 curry favor with (a person); win (a person's) favor; ingratiate oneself with (a person); insinuate[ingratiate] oneself into (a person's) favor. ¶여자의 ~ 사다 win a girl's heart //그녀의 환심을 사려고 하다 woo a woman // 그는 상사의 환심을 사려고 하고 있다 He is trying to gain the favor of his superiors. // 그는 toadying to his superiors. //그는 여자의 환심을 사는 방법을 알고 있다 He knows how to get into a woman's good grace.

환약(丸藥) a (medicinal) pill; a globule; (큰) a bolus; (작은) a pellet; a pil(l)ule. ¶~을 만들다 make a pill / pill.

환어음(換-) a bill of exchange(약어 B.E., B/E, b.e.); a draft; a draught. ¶기명식 [무기명식] ~ a special bill [a bill to bearer] // 내국 ~ (미) a domestic bill / (영) an inland bill // 단기[장기] ~ a short-[long-]dated bill [paper] // 무담보 ~ a clean bill // 부도 ~ a dishonored draft // 일람불 ~ a bill at sight / a sight bill // 정기불 ~ a time bill [draft] // 아메리카 은행 앞으로 발행한 ~ a draft on Bank of America // 10파운드의 ~을 발행하다 draw a bill of exchange (on a person) for 10 pounds.

환언하다(換言-) say[put] in other words. ¶ 환언하면 in other words / that is (to say) / namely.

환영(幻影) a vision; a phantom; a phantasm; [심] an illusion. ¶~을 쫓다 be lured by an illusion / be under an illusion // ~을 보다 see a vision.

환영(歡迎) (a) welcome; an ovation; (a) reception. ¶대~ a hearty[cordial] welcome // 성대한 ~ (미) red carpet (welcomes) // ~ 준비를 갖추다 kill the fatted calf // ~의 뜻을 표하다 say welcome (a person) / bid (a person) welcome // ~의 말을 하다 say a few words of welcome (to) // 그는 성대한 ~을 받았다 He was received [welcomed] well. //나는 도처에서 따뜻한 ~을 받았다 I was warmly welcomed everywhere. //그의 새 작품은 비평가들의 ~을 받았다 His new work was favorably received by the critics. // 투고(投稿) ~ Contributions from readers are cordially invited. 환영하다 welcome; bid (a person) welcome; give a welcome to (a person); receive warmly[favorably]; (구어) give (a person) the glad hand. ¶따뜻이[성대히] ~ give a warm[hearty / cordial] welcome / receive (a person) with open arms / roll out a red carpet for (a person) // 대대적으로 ~ stage a festive welcome (for) // 박수로 ~ give an ovation (with clapping of hands) // 언제든지 환영합니다 You shall always be welcome. // 여러분을 충심으로 환영합니다 I want to express my hearty welcome to you. / I am happy to have you here. // 일할 마음이 있는 사람이면 누구나 환영합니다 Anyone (who is) eager to work is [will be] welcome. → ¶환영받지 못하는 손님 an unwelcome guest // 환영받다 be received favorably / be warmly[cordially] received / have a warm reception / be welcomed // 환영받지 못하다 be not welcomed / be given a cold shoulder // 성대하게 환영받다 be warmly [enthusiastically] received[welcomed] / receive a rousing welcome.
● 환영 만찬회 a reception dinner. 환영사 (give) an address of welcome (in honor of); a welcoming speech. 환영회 a welcome meeting[party]; a reception (dinner). ¶~를 개최하다 give[hold] a reception (dinner) (in honor of) // 미스터 송의 ~를 열다 give [hold] a reception to welcome [in honor of] Mr. Song.

환우기(換羽期) the molting season.

환원(還元) 1 [복귀] restoration. 환원하다 restore (to its original state). → ¶환원되다 be restored to (the former condition). 2 [화] reduction; [분해] resolution; (산화물의) deoxidization. 환원하다 reduce (to); deoxidize; (금속 등을) revive. ¶환원되다 be reduced (to) // (원래의 상태로) 환원시키다 [화] revivify // 화합물은 그 원소로 환원된다 The compound resolves itself into its elements.
● 환원 작용 a reducing process. 환원제 a reducing[deoxidating] agent; a reducer; a reductant.

환유법(換喩法) [문] metonymy.

환율(換率) the exchange rate; the rate of exchange. ¶대미 ~ the (exchange) rate on America / the U.S. dollar rate // ~이 높다[낮다] The exchange rate rules high[low]. // 오늘 ~이 얼마죠 What's the exchange rate today? // 1달러 ~은 1달러에 1,348원입니다 Today's exchange rate is 1,348 won per 1US dollar.
● 환율 변경 exchange (rate) fluctuations. 환율 인상 a raise in exchange rates.

환자(患者) a patient; a sufferer (from a cold); a case (of cholera)(▶ 통원 치료를 받는 사람은 patient, 병에 걸린 사람은 case, sufferer를 씀); a victim (of a disease); a subject (of operation). ¶내과[외과] ~ a medical [surgical] subject // 동상 ~ a frostbite victim // 무료 ~ a charity-patient / a free patient // 수술 ~ a subject to be operated on / a surgical patient / a surgery case // 외래 ~ an outpatient / a day patient // 입원 ~ an inpatient // 인플루엔자 ~ a flu victim // 소화불량 ~ sufferers of indigestion // 3명의 맹장

환장하다

염 ~ three cases of appendicitis // 회복할 가망이 있는[없는] ~ a good[bad] subject // ~가 많은 의사 a doctor with[who has] a large practice // ~를 진찰하다 see[examine] a patient // ~는 경과가 좋다 The patient is progressing favorably. // 이 ~는 아무래도 어렵다[절망적이다] This is a difficult[hopeless] case. // 금년에 콜레라 ~가 많이 발생했다 There have been many cases of cholera this year.
● **환자 명부** a sick list; a list of patients.

환장하다(換腸一) become [go] mad[crazy/insane]; go off[out of] one's mind[head]; lose one's mind [wits/reason]. ¶그는 완전히 환장했다 He's gone stone crazy. // 그것만으로도 환장할 지경이야 It's enough to drive me mad[crazy].

환쟁이 a dauber; a wretched painter.

환전(換錢) exchange (of money); money changing. **환전하다** exchange (dollar into won / American money into Korean); change (a 1,000-won note). ¶공항에서 한국 돈을 달러로 환전하였다 I changed some Korean money into U.S. dollars at the airport.
● **환전상** (사람) a money changer; (가게) an exchange house. **환전 수수료** a commission [fee] for exchanging money; an exchange commission.

환절(環節) [동] a segment; an annulated segment

환절기(換節期) a change [turning-point] of season. ¶~가 되면 뼈마디가 아프다 At the turning of seasons the pain comes back to my joints and bones.

환 조작(換造作) exchange operation.

환지(換地) replotting; land substitution; (토지) a substitute lot; the land substituted for.
● **환지 지정**(처분) the designation[disposal] of replotting.

환차손(換差損) a loss from exchange rate fluctuation.

환차익(換差益) a profit from exchange rate fluctuation.

환청(幻聽) an auditory hallucination. ¶~이 들리다 hear things / suffer from auditory hallucinations.

환초(環礁) an atoll; a (ring-shaped) coral island. ¶비키니 ~ the Bikini atoll.

환치다 daub; draw[paint] poorly[unskillfully].

환태평양(環太平洋) the Pacific rim.
● **환태평양 지진대** The Pacific rim earthquake zone.

환 투기(換投企) exchange speculation.

환풍기(換風機) a ventilation[ventilating] fan; an extractor fan.

환하다 1 [밝다] bright; light ¶달빛이 환한 밤 a bright moonlight night // 대낮같이 ~ be as bright as day // 환해지다 lighten / grow[get] light / light up // 환하게 하다 brighten / lighten / light up / make brighter // 바깥은 아직도 (폐) ~ It is still light (enough) outside. // 이 방은 ~ This room is well lighted. // 환한 동안에 일을 끝마치자 Let's finish our work while it is still light. // 하늘이 점점 환해지기 시작했다 The sky is starting to get[grow] light. / Day is breaking. **환히** bright; brightly. ¶한낮의 태양이 ~ 빛나고 있었다 The midday sun was shining bright(ly).

2 [탁 트이다] open; clear; unobstructed. **환히** ¶~ 보이다 get an unobstructed view / be fully exposed to view / be in plain sight // 숲을 나오자 눈앞에 들판이 ~ 펼쳐져 있었다 When we emerged from the forest, an open plain spread out before us.

3 [명백하다] clear (distinction); plain (truth); evident (proof); obvious; patent; explicit. ¶환한 사실 a plain truth / an obvious fact. **환히** clear; clearly; obviously; plainly. ¶~ 밝히다 make clear / clear up / clarify / manifest / define // 나는 그것을 ~ 알고 있다 I know it like a look[know it like the back of my hand / know every detail of it].

4 [정통하다] (서술적) be familiar (with); be versed (in); be learned[well up] (in); be conversant (with); be posted up (in). ¶사무에 ~ be well versed in business methods / 서양 풍습에 ~ be familiar with Western customs // 법률에 ~ be learned in the law // 그는 중국 고전에 ~ He has a profound knowledge of Chinese classics. // 그는 이 근처 지리에 ~ He knows his way around here. / He knows the geography of this area very well.

5 [얼굴이 잘생기다] fine-looking; handsome; big and open; bright; radiant; beaming. ¶환한 얼굴 a handsome face / a big open face / a bright[radiant] face // 환한 미소 a beaming [radiant] smile. **환히** brightly; handsomely. ¶그녀는 ~ 웃었다 She laughed and smiled happily. / Her face broke into a happy grim.

환향(還鄕) return(ing) home; return to one's native place[birthplace]; homecoming. ¶금의 ~ returning home loaded with honors / returning (to one's old) home in glory. **환향하다** go[come] home; return (to one's old) home; return to one's hometown.

환형(環形) a ring shape. ¶~의 looped / ring-shaped.
● **환형동물** an annelid; a round[segmented] worm. ¶~의 annelid(an).

환호(歡呼) a cheer; an ovation; an acclamation; a hurrah. ¶속에서 amid (hearty) cheers // …에게 ~를 보내다 give (a person) hearty cheers[an ovation] // ~ 속에 전송하다 send off (a person) with a roar of applause. **환호하다** cheer; give cheers; shout for joy; acclaim; jubilate. ¶우승자가 단에 오르자 전원이 일제히 환호하였다 When the champion stepped onto the platform, everybody cheered in unison.
● **환호성** a shout of joy; a cheer. ¶~을 올리다 give a shout of joy / shout for joy / send up rousing cheers.

환후(患候) sickness; a disease. ⇨¹병(病)1 ¶부친의 ~가 어떠하신지 How is your sick father?

환희(歡喜) (great) joy; delight; gladness; glee; jubilation.

활 1 [무기] a bow; (궁술) archery. ¶~의 명수 an expert archer / a master of archery / ~을 쏘다 shoot an arrow // ~을 힘껏 당기다 draw a bow to the full // ~을 당기다 draw[bend] a bow / ~에 화살을 재다 fix[put] an arrow to a bow // ~에 시위를 매우다 string a bow / fit a bowstring to a bow // ~쏘기를 배우다 practice archery / 가지를 ~ 모양으로 굽히다 bend a branch into an arch // 그는 몸을 ~ 모양으로 뒤로 제꼈다 He leaned[arched (his

body)] backwards.
2 (무명솜을 타는) a bow for fluffing out cotton into wadding. ¶~로 솜을 타다 fluff out cotton into wadding with a bow.
3 (현악기의) a bow. ¶~을 쓰다 manage the bow (in playing a violin) / bow.

활강(滑降) [스키] (a) descent. ¶직~ a schuss // 사~ a traverse. **활강하다** glide down.
● **활강 경기** a downhill (race).

활개 1 [사람의 두 팔] one's arms; one's limbs. ¶네 ~ one's arms and legs // ~를 치며 swinging one's arms / [비유] with nothing to fear / triumphantly / with impunity / ~를 치며 걷다 walk swinging one's arms // 네 ~를 치다 swing one's arms and legs / walk with a swaggering gait / strut. **2** [새의 두 날개] the wings of a bird. ¶~를 치다 flap [clap / beat] the wings / flutter.
● **활갯짓** swinging one's arms in walking; strutting; swaggering. ¶~을 하다 swing one's arms / swagger / strut / ~하며 거리를 걷다 strut down a street.

활공(滑空) [항] gliding; a glide; volplane. **활공하다** glide; volplane.
● **활공 거리** a gliding distance. **활공기** [항] a glider. ⇨글라이더

활극(活劇) **1** [격투가 많은 영화] an action film[picture]; an action drama(연극). ¶서부~ a horse opera / a western (film) / a cowboy picture / an oater. **2** [난투] a riotous scene. ¶국회에서 ~이 벌어졌다 There was a fight on the floor of the National Assembly.

활기(活氣) vigor; spirit; energy; liveliness; animation; briskness; activity. ¶~ 있는 대화 a spirited[an animated] conversation / a lively talk // ~가 있는 사람 a lively[vivacious] person // ~가 넘치는 청년 a youth full of vigor[life] // ~를 띠다 become active [enlivened / animated] / be animated / be exhilarated / grow lively / show activity / (시장·경기 등이) become brisk / pick[look] up // ~를 띠게 하다 give life to / animate / lend animation to / activate / enliven / invigorate / inspirit / (미국 속어) pep[jazz] up // ~를 되찾다 be recovering / come to life again // 그의 말은 좌중에 ~를 불어넣었다 His words enlivened[put life into] the whole group. // His words brought the whole group to life. // 새벽과 함께 시장은 ~를 띠기 시작했다 The marketplace started to hum[hop] at dawn. // 이 마을은 ~가 없어 보인다 This town looks inactive[dead / lifeless]. // 토론은 처음부터 끝까지 ~가 없었다 The discussion was dull from beginning to end. // 새 쇼핑 센터는 ~를 띠고 있다 [번창하고 있다] The new shopping center is humming with business [very busy]. // 그녀[그녀의 존재]는 파티에 ~를 더했다 She[Her presence] added to the gaiety of the party. // 사건 발생 소식을 듣고 신문 기자들은 ~를 띠었다 Word of the event woke up the newspaper reporters[brought the newspaper office to life].

활꼴 [수] a segment; a crescent.

활달하다(豁達-) generous; magnanimous; liberal; broad-minded; openhearted.

활대 a (sail) yard; a sail boom.

활동(活動) [활약] activity; action; operations; [노력] strenuous exertion; energy; service; [기능] function; working (of the bodily organs). ¶정치 ~ political activity // 연구 ~ learned activity // 다방면의 ~ one's multifarious[innumerable] activities // ~을 시작[개시]하다 go into action / come into play / cut loose / (사람이) get off the ground / (미국 구어) get going / (조직·단체가) come into operation / become operative // (화산이) burst into activity / (군대가) begin operations // ~중이다 be in action / be at work(일하고 있다) / (화산이) be in activity // ~을 무디게 하다 hamper one's activity // 학생들은 과외 ~에 흥미를 갖고 있다 Students are interested in extracurricular activities. // 경찰은 ~ 태세를 취하고 있었다 The police were on the alert.

활동하다 [활약하다] be active; lead an active life; play[take] an active part (in); (구어) be on the go; [운동하다] canvass; campaign; [기능을 하다] function; work. ¶ 정계에서 ~ be active[take an active part] in politics // 화산이 활동하기 시작했다 The volcano has become active. // 그는 20년간 화단의 일선에서 활동하고 있다 He has been active in the front rank of painters for twenty years. // 그는 아직도 활동할 수 있는 힘이 있다 He is still full of energy. // 쌓인 토사를 치우려고 불도저가 활동하기 시작했다 Bulldozers went into operation to remove the piled-up earth and sand. // 그들은 평화를 위해 활동하고 있다 They are working hard for peace.
● **활동가** an active person; (정치적인) an activist. ¶정치 ~ a political activist // 종교 ~ a religious hustler. **활동 무대** one's field [stage] of action[activity]. **활동 범위** [활동 분야] one's scope[sphere] of activity[action]. ¶~가 넓다 [좁다] He has a wide[limited] sphere of activity. **활동사진** motion pictures.

활동적(活動的) active; energetic; dynamic. ¶ ~인 정력가 a man of kinetic energy[force].

활등 the back of a bow.

활딱 1 [벗어진 모양] swept clear[bright]. ¶머리가 ~ 벗어지다 get all bald and shiny on top / get bald as an egg[a billiard ball] // 옷을 ~ 벗기다 strip (a person) of all (his) clothes / strip (a person) (down) naked. **2** [끓어 넘는 모양] overflowing suddenly; boiling over.

활량 1 [활을 쏘는 사람] an archer; (시어) a bowyer. **2** a man of the military class who has not passed the examination for an official post; an idle youth of the gentry. ⇨ =한량(閑良)

활력(活力) vitality; energy; vital power[force / energies]. ¶~이 넘치는 사람 an energetic person // ~이 있는 vital / animated / in blood // 그는 늘 ~이 넘쳐 있다 He is always full of vitality[vigor / energy]. / He is energetic [lively / vigorous].
● **활력소** a tonic; a vitamin.

활로(活路) a means of escape; a way out (of the difficulty). ¶…을 구하는 유일한 ~ the only alternative to relieve … // 가까스로 궁지에서 ~를 찾았다 At last I found a way out of the difficult situation. // 우리는 (어려움에서 탈출할) ~를 찾아야만 한다 We have to find a way out of[means of escape from] the difficulty.

활물(活物) a living being[creature].
● **활물 기생** [생] parasitism on a living thing.

활발하다(活潑−) lively; sprightly; active; brisk; full of life; (구어) corky; jazzy. ¶활발한 동작 brisk[lively] movements∥활발한 걸음걸이[어조] a brisk way of walking [speaking]∥(거래가) 활발한 시장 a brisk [lively / booming] market∥저 아이는 퍽 ~ That child is full of energy. / That child is alert and active. **활발히** actively; lively; briskly; sprightly; with animation; with animation; like a brick. ¶~ 행동하다 move about briskly[energetically]∥뛰놀다 skip about actively[briskly]∥그 문제에 관하여 우리는 ~ 토론했다 We had a lively[heated] discussion about the problem.

활보하다(闊步) stride; strut; swagger (about); walk with a swaggering gait. ¶거리를 ~ strut along a street.

활빈당(活貧黨) chivalrous robbers; benevolent picaroons; (a band of) Robin Hoods.

활석(滑石) [광] talc; talcum ¶~질[성]의 talcky∥~ (모양)의 talcoid.
● **활석분** talcum (powder).

활성(活性) [화] activity. ¶~의 active / activated∥비~의 inert.
● **활성 비타민제** an activated vitamin preparation. **활성 산소** [수소] active oxygen [hydrogen]. **활성탄** active[activated] carbon. **활성화** activation. ¶~하다 activate (carbon).

활수(滑手) generosity; liberality. **활수하다** liberal; generous; lavish. ¶형은 금전에는 ~ My brother is generous[free] with his money.

활시위 a bowstring. ¶~를 메우다 string a bow∥~가 끊어졌다 The bowstring snapped.

활액(滑液) [생] synovia.
● **활액낭** a bursa (pl. ~s, -sae).

활약(活躍) activity; action. ¶그녀의 ~상 her activity∥이 분야에서는 여성의 ~이 두드러진다 A number of women have cut conspicuous figures in this field. **활약하다** be active (in); take[play] an active part (in); participate actively (in). ¶대~ have a lively time of it∥그는 정계에서 활약하고 있다 He is active[plays an active part] in the political world.

활어 live fish; live shellfish(갑각류).
● **활어조** a fish preserve; (얕은 어울의) a crawl; (어선의) a live well.

활엽수(闊葉樹) a broadleaf[broadleaved] tree.

활용(活用) 1 [응용] practical use; application. **활용하다** make use (of); put[turn] (knowledge) to practical use; apply; utilize. ¶새로운 방법을 산업에 ~ apply a new process in industry∥이곳에서는 영어를 활용할 수 없다 I cannot put my knowledge of English to practical use here.∥외국어를 배우는 데는 사전을 크게 활용하여야 한다 We have to make good use of dictionaries in studying foreign languages.∥기회를 가능한 한 활용하도록 힘쓰시오 Try to make the most of an opportunity.∥물은 여러 가지 용도에 활용할 수 있다 Water is utilized for various purposes.∥우리는 여가 시간을 더욱 활용해야 한다 We should make better use of our leisure time.∥나는 새로운 것을 사기 전에 갖고 있는 것을 활용하려고 한다 I try to utilize what I have before buying something new.

2 conjugation; inflection; (영) inflexion; declension. ¶동사 "go"의 ~을 들어 보이소 Conjugate[Give the conjugation of] the verb "go". **활용하다** conjugate; inflect; decline.
● **활용어** a conjugated word. **활용형** a conjugated form.

활인화(活人畫) a living picture; a tableau vivant.

활자(活字) (a) printing type; (집합적) type. ¶1호[9포인트] ~ No. 1[9-point] type∥고딕 [이탤릭]체 ~ Gothic[italic] type∥굵은 ~ bold[heavy] type∥~의 오식 a misprint / a typographical error∥~를 줍다 pick type∥~를 조판하다 compose[set up] type∥~로 식자(植字)하다 set in type∥~가 촘촘하다 The type is close-set.∥이 논문은 곧 ~화될 것이다 This article will soon appear in print[be printed].
● **활자 주조** type-founding; type-casting. **활자체** print. ¶~로 쓰다 write in block letters.

활주(滑走) gliding; a glide; (빙상의) sliding; (비행기의) a ground run. ¶공중 ~ gliding∥지상 ~ (비행기의) taxiing / taxying∥보조 ~ a minor runaway∥이륙 ~ a taking-off run∥착륙 ~ a landing run. **활주하다** (비행기가 활주로 등을) taxi; glide; run; (얼음 위 등을) slide. ¶비행기는 착륙하여 한동안 활주하다가 멈춰 섰다 The plane touched down, ran for a while (on the ground) and stopped.
● **활주로** a runway; a landing strip; (임시의) an airstrip. ¶비행기는 ~를 달렸다 The plane taxied down the runway.

활집 a bow-case.

활짝 1 (탁 트인 모양) widely; exceedingly (wide); broad; open; extensively. ¶~ 열어 둔 창문 a wide-open window∥바람이 잘 들어오라고 방문을 ~ 열어 두었다 The room was completely opened up so that there would be good ventilation. 2 (웃음·꽃 등이) brightly; radiantly; happily. ¶~ 편 장미 a full-[broad-]blown rose / a rose in full bloom∥~ 웃다 beam (upon[at] a person) / smile radiantly / beam[be radiant] with joy∥(꽃이) ~ 피다 bloom in all their glory. 3 (날씨가 개거나 환히 밝은 모양) clearly; brightly. ¶~ 갠 하늘 a bright, blue sky∥~ 개었다 It has cleared up.

활차(滑車) a pulley. ⇨도르래

활착(活着) rootage; rooting. **활착하다** take [strike] root.

활촉(−鏃) an arrowhead. ⇨화살촉(⇨화살)

활터 (야외의) an archery ground[range]; (실내의) an archery[a shooting] gallery[parlor].

활판(活版) letterpress (printing). ¶원고를 ~으로 짜다 set a manuscript in type.
● **활판소** a printing house; (미) a print shop. **활판 인쇄** letterpress printing; (인쇄물) printed matter. ¶그는 자작시를 ~ 했다 He had his poems printed.

활화산(活火山) an active volcano.
● **활화산대** an active volcano belt.

활활 1 (불타는 모양) in (fierce / great / tall) flames; in a blaze; (all) ablaze. ¶난로의 불이 ~ 타오르고 있었다 A fire was blazing [burning brightly] in the fireplace.∥그는 어린애를 구하기 위해 ~ 타오르고 있는 집 안으로 뛰어들었다 He dashed into the blazing house to save the child. 2 (부채질하는 모양) (fan oneself / use a fan) slowly and vigorously. 3 (새가 나는 모양) with great flaps of

the wings. ¶~ 날아가다 fly with a steady flap of the wings. 4 [옷 벗는 모양] (taking off) briskly. ¶옷을 ~ 벗다 slip [whip / hurry] off one's clothes.
활황(活況) activity; briskness; prosperity. ¶~을 띠다[보이다] show (signs of) activity / present animated [brisk / lively] appearance / become active // 매매는 ~이다 The market is lively [active].
홧김에(火-) under the influence of anger; in a fit of anger [rage / temper / the spleen]; in the heat of passion; out [in a fit] of pique. ¶~ 술을 마시다 drink liquor in anger // 그는 ~ 동생에게 책을 내던졌다 He threw a book at his brother in a fit of anger [rage / temper].
홧술(火-) liquor drunk in anger. ¶~을 마시다 drown one's anger [cares] in drink / drink out of anger [pique].
홧홧 hot(ly); fierily; feverishly. ¶얼굴이 ~ 달아오른다 flush up (hotly) / blush / feel one's face burning (with shame) // 몸이 ~ 달다 feverish. 홧홧하다 (feel) hot; warm; fiery; feverish; (서술적) burn; flush. ¶술을 마셔서 얼굴이 ~ I feel my face burning from the drink. / My cheeks are flushed with wine.
황(黃) 1 [황색] yellow. 2 [화] sulfur; sulphur(기호 S).
황갈색(黃褐色) light brown; yellowish brown; claybank; tan; (be of a) tawny color. ¶~의 yellowish brown / fulvous / tawny.
황감하다(惶感-) exceedingly thankful; deeply [reverently] grateful. ¶재정적으로 도와주신다면 황감하겠습니다 Financial help would be very welcome.
황계(黃鷄) a yellow hen [cock].
황고집(黃固執) obstinacy; stubbornness; bullheadedness; (사람) a bullheaded [pieheaded] person.
황공하다(惶恐-) fearful; awed; awe-struck [-stricken]; frightened; afraid; overwhelmed with awe. ¶황공하게도 graciously / condescendingly // 황공하오신 말씀입니다만 it may be said with due reverence that ... / with due respect I may say ... // 황공하오나 제가 저지른 행위에 대해 해명하고자 합니다 With all due respect, I would like to be allowed to explain my conduct. ¶황공하게도 폐하께서 내 작품에 대해 칭찬해 주셨다 His Majesty the Emperor very graciously praised my work.
황구(黃狗) a yellow dog.
황국(黃菊) [식] a yellow chrysanthemum.
황금(黃金) 1 gold. ⇨[금]金)1 2 [화폐] money. 3 [금빛] gold. ¶논에 보이는 것은 온통 ~물결뿐이다 As far as one can see the rice fields are waving their golden ears. 4 [가치가 큰 것]. ¶저 투수는 ~의 팔을 가졌다고 한다 That pitcher is said to have a golden arm.
● 황금률 the golden rule. 황금만능주의 the almighty dollar principle; mammonism. 황금분할 [수] the golden section. 황금빛 a gold(en) color. 황금시대 the golden age; (라틴 문학의) the Golden Age.
황급하다(遑急-) urgent; pressing; hurried. 황급히 in great haste; hastily; in a great [violent / deuced / mortal] hurry. ¶~ 달아나다 run away in a flurry / beat a hasty retreat // ~ 귀가하다 hurry home.
황기(黃芪·黃耆) [식] a hedysarum.

황녀(皇女) an Imperial [a Royal] princess. ¶조선 왕조의 마지막 ~ the last Royal princess of [in] the Joseon Dynasty.
황달(黃疸) [의] (yellow) jaundice; the yellows; icterus. 신생아 ~ jaundice of the newborn / (영) yellow gum.
● 황달 환자 an icteric(al).
황당무계하다(荒唐無稽-) absurd; nonsensical; fantastic(al); wild (rumor); fabulous; preposterous. ¶황당무계한 이야기 an absurd [a cock-and-bull] story // 그 계획은 ~ The plan is quite absurd.
황당하다(荒唐-) absurd; preposterous; wild.
황도(黃桃) a yellow peach.
황도(黃道) [천] the ecliptic; the girdle.
● 황도대 the zodiac.
황동(黃銅) brass. ⇨놋쇠
황량하다(荒凉-) desolate; bleak; deserted (village). ¶우리들 앞에는 황량한 벌판이 펼쳐져 있다 There spread a desolate plain before us. // 창문을 통해 추운 겨울의 황량한 풍경을 바라보았다 I saw a bleak scene of a cold winter day through the window.
황록색(黃綠色) yellowish green; pea green. ¶~의 yellow-green.
황린(黃燐) white phosphorus. ⇨흰인
황마(黃麻) [식] a jute.
황망하다(慌忙-) hurried; bustling; restless; flurried; confused. 황망히 hurriedly; flurriedly; in a hurry [flurry]; confusedly. ¶나는 ~ 떠나는 바람에 열쇠를 잊었다 I left in such a haste [flurry] that I forgot my keys.
황무지(荒蕪地) waste [wild / barren / bad] land; a barren tract; a wilderness; a waste. ¶~를 개간하다 reclaim [break up] wild land / clear waste land // 그 토지의 대부분은 아직도 ~이다 The greater part of the land still lies waste.
황밤(黃-) a dried chestnut which is hulled.
황비(皇妃) an empress.
황사(黃沙) yellow sand.
● 황사 현상 sandy dust phenomena; yellow dust cloud that often blows over Korea.
황산(黃酸) [화] sulfuric [(영) sulphuric] acid; vitriol. ¶농(濃)~ concentrated sulfuric acid // ~의 vitriolic // ~으로 태우다 vitriolize // ~을 끼얹다 [뿌리다] throw vitriol (at / on / over) / throw acid (at / on).
● 황산구리 copper sulfate [(영) sulphate]. 황산암모늄 ammonium sulfate [(영) sulphate]. 황산염 a sulfate; salt of sulfuric acid; vitriol. 황산 제일[제이]철 ferrous [ferric] sulfate.
황새 [동] stork. ¶뱁새가 ~를 따라가려 하다 try to do what is beyond one's capacity.
● 황새걸음 the gait of a stork; a long [great / swinging] stride; long [big] steps. ¶~으로 걷다 walk with long [big / large / great] steps [strides].
황색(黃色) yellow.
● 황색 신문 a yellow journal [paper / rag / sheet]; (집합적) the yellow press. 황색 인종 the yellow race. ⇨황인종
황소 a bull. ¶~같이 일하다 work like blazes [a horse / a tiger].
황소 뒷걸음치다가 쥐 잡는다(속담) The net of the sleeper catches fish.
● 황소걸음 (황소의) the gait of a bull; (느린) a snail's pace; a slow step; (착실한) a steady pace [step]. ¶~을 치다 walk slowly

황손(皇孫) an Imperial grandchild.
황송하다(惶悚−) fearful; awed. ⇨"황공하다
황실(皇室) the Imperial Household[Family].
황야(荒野) a wilderness; the wilds; a waste; wasteland; a desert land. ¶~를 헤매다 wander[roam] in the wilderness.
황어(黃魚) [동] a dace (*pl.* ~(s)); a chub (*pl.* ~(s)).
황열(병)(黃熱病) [의] yellow fever[jack].
황엽(黃葉) yellow leaves. ¶~이 되다 turn yellow.
황옥(黃玉) [광] (a) topaz.
황인종(黃人種) the yellow race; the yellow-skinned races; the Asiatics.
황자(皇子) an Imperial prince; a prince of the blood.
황적색(黃赤色) yellowish[poppy] red.
황제(皇帝) an emperor. ¶~ Imperial // 신성로마 ~ the Roman Emperor // 독일[오스트리아] ~ (옛날의) the Kaiser // 러시아 ~ (제정시대의) the Czar // 나폴레옹 ~ the Emperor Napoleon // ~의 자리에 오르다[~의 자리에서 물러나다] accede to[abdicate from] the (Imperial) throne.
● **황제 폐하** His Majesty the Emperor.
황조(皇祖) 1 [황제의 조상] Imperial ancestors. 2 [죽은 자기 할아버지] one's own revered dead grandfather.
황조롱이(黃−) [동] a kestrel; a Eurasian kestrel.
황족(皇族) the Imperial[Royal] family; royalty; a member of the Imperial family. ¶~의 Imperial / Royal / of Royal blood.
황지(荒地) waste land; barren land; desert [desolate] land; a waste; a desolation; a wilderness; wild(s).
황차(況且) (how) much more. ⇨"하물며
황채(黃菜) a dish of sliced ripe cucumber.
황천(荒天) stormy weather. ¶~의 항해 a rough voyage // 그들은 ~의 날씨에 출항했다 They set sail in the stormy[rough] weather.
황천(黃泉) the other world. ⇨"저승
● **황천객** a dead person. ¶~이 되다 go down to the shades / go on a journey whence no traveller returns / join the majority / depart (from) this life / pass away / die // 다음 날 그는 ~이 되었다 The next day he died[passed away]. **황천길** the way to Hades.
황철석(黃鐵石) [광] (iron) pyrites; (통속적으로) fool's gold.
황체(黃體) [생] (난소의) a corpus luteum (*pl.* corpora lutea).
● **황체 호르몬** progesterone; progestin; luteohormone; progestational hormone.
황촌(荒村) a deserted[desolate] village; a ghost town.
황태손(皇太孫) the eldest grandson of an Emperor.
황태자(皇太子) the Crown Prince; the Prince Imperial; the Heir Apparent (to the Throne). ¶영국 ~ the Prince of Wales // ~을 책봉하다 proclaim the Heir Apparent to the Throne.
● **황태자비** the Crown Princess; the wife [consort] of a prince.
황태후(皇太后) the Empress Dowager; the Queen Mother.
황토(黃土) [지] (yellow) ocher; loess; yellow soil; Chinese yellow.
● **황토색** ocher. ¶~의 ocherous.
황통(皇統) the Imperial line. ¶~을 잇다 accede to the Throne.
황폐(荒廢) desolation; (재해·전쟁 등에 의한) devastation; (토지·건물 등의) dilapidation; waste; ruin; abandonment. ¶삼림 ~ forest denudation. **황폐하다** be devastated; go to ruin; be laid waste; (건물이) go[fall] into decay; run waste. ¶황폐한 절 a ruined[run-down] temple // 황폐해진 오두막집 a run-down[tumbledown] hut // 황폐한 땅 desolate[desert] land // 전쟁으로 황폐해진 지역 war-devastated areas // **황폐해지다** (건물 등이 무너져 가다) be dilapidated / (집 등이 황폐해지다) go to ruin[rack and ruin] / (토지가) lie waste // 황폐하게 하다 devastate / lay waste / rage / ruin // 사람이 살지 않는 집은 황폐해져 있다 The deserted house was dilapidated. // 밭이 황폐해져 있다 The field lies waste[neglected]. // 온 마을이 황폐해졌다 The whole village fell into ruin[was devastated].
황해(黃海) the Yellow Sea.
황혼(黃昏) dusk; (evening) twilight; crepuscule. ¶~에 in the dusk of the evening / in the twilight / at dusk[twilight] // 인생의 ~기에 in the twilight years of one's life // ~이 깃들다 dusk falls // 이제 인생의 ~이다 I have reached the twilight years of my life[my twilight years].
황홀하다(恍惚−·慌惚−) 1 [무아경이다] charmed; enchanted. ¶황홀하여 in ecstasies [an ecstasy] / in raptures / in a trance / with rapture / (listen) spellbound // 황홀할 정도로 우아한 fascinatingly elegant // 황홀해져서 in an ecstasy / in raptures // 황홀한 사랑의 속삭임 the enchanting murmurs of love // **황홀해지다** be in raptures[ecstasies] (over) / be enraptured[entranced / charmed / enchanted / spellbound] (by / with / at / over) / be carried away (by) / fall into a trance // 황홀하게 하다 charm / enrapture / enchant / fascinate / spellbind // 나는 황홀한 마음으로 음악에 귀를 기울였다 I was filled with rapture listening to the music. // 너무나 아름다운 풍경에 나는 황홀했다 I was enchanted[enraptured] by the extremely beautiful scenery. // 그는 기쁜 소식을 듣고 구름 위에 뜬 것처럼 황홀했다 He felt as if he was walking[treading] on air at the good news. // 상을 탄 이야기를 그는 황홀한 기분이 되어 우리에게 말해 주었다 He told us ecstatically how he had won the prize. // 그는 새 캐딜락을 보고 황홀해졌다 He was thrown into ecstasies at the sight of his new Cadillac. // 그녀는 남을 황홀하게 할 만큼 아름다웠다 She was enchantingly beautiful. // 그녀는 황홀하게 음악에 도취되었다 She was absorbed in the music.
2 [몽롱하다] dim; vague; faint.
3 [눈부시다] gorgeous; showy; brilliant.
황화(黃化) [화] sulfuration; sulphuration; sulfurization. **황화하다** sulfurize; (영) sulphurise; sulfurate; sulphurate.
● **황화물** a sulfide. **황화수소** sulfuret(t)ed hydrogen.
황후(皇后) an empress; a queen; (여왕과 구별하여) an empress consort.
● **황후 폐하** Her (Imperial) Majesty[H.(I.)M.]

홰¹ 1 [새장의 나무 막대] a perch; a roost. ¶~에 오르다 (a hen) go to roost// 새가 ~에 앉아 있다 A bird is on the perch. 2 [새벽에 닭이 우는 번수]. 닭이 두 ~ 울었다 The cock crowed twice.

홰² [횃불의] a torch.

홰치다 flap[beat] the wings; flutter. ¶닭이 홰친다 A hen flaps its wings.

홱 1 [갑자기] suddenly; [잽싸게] quickly; with dispatch; nimbly. ¶~ 돌아보다 turn right round // ~ 지나가다 pass quickly / flit (across the sky) // 몸을 ~ 비키다 dodge oneself / dodge (a blow) nimbly // 창밖으로 얼굴을 ~ 내밀다 pop one's head out of the window // 문이 ~ 열렸다 The door swung [sprang / flew] open. // 바람이 ~ 불었다 There was a gust of wind. // 차는 왼쪽으로 ~ 돌았다 The car swerved [suddenly swung] to the left.
2 [힘차게] vigorously; with a jerk; with a shove; with a whack[swish]. ¶~ 당기다[밀다] pull[push] with a (sudden) jerk / give (it) a vigorous[quick] pull[push] // ~ 던지다 throw[fling / hurl] (a thing) at (a person) // (문 등을) ~ 열다 fling[throw] (a window) open // ~ 뿌리치다 jerk (one's arm) loose / shake oneself loose[free] from (a person's grasp) // ~ 뿌리치고 도망치다 tear oneself away from (another's grasp) // 어머니는 아이의 손을 ~ 잡아당겼다 The mother jerked her child by the hand.

횃대 a clothes rack; a clotheshorse; a rack for hanging clothes.

횃불 a (pine) torch; a flambeau (pl. ~x, ~s); a torchlight; a link. ¶~로 길을 밝히다 light one's way with a torch // ~을 켜다 kindle a torch // ~을 들다 carry a torch in one's hand.
● 횃불 행렬 a torchlight procession [parade].

행댕그렁하다 hollow; empty; deserted; look bare[empty / hollow]. ¶행댕그렁한 방 an empty room // ~ 가구가 없어서 방이 ~ The room looks bare without furniture. // 손님이 다 가서 방이 ~ The room feels empty now that all the guests have left.

행하다 1 [잘 알다] (서술적) be familiar (with); be well acquainted (with); be well [deeply] versed in; be well posted (in); be at home (in). ¶길을 행하게 알다 know the road well // 그는 그 내부 사정을 행하게 알고 있다 He is well informed of the inside facts. // 그는 이 부근 지리에 ~ He knows every inch of this neighborhood. 2 hollow; empty. ⇨행댕그렁하다

회(蛔) [동] a mawworm. ⇨회충

회(灰) 1 lime. ⇨석회 2 calcium oxide. ⇨산화칼슘(⇨산화(酸化))

회(回) [돌림 횟수] a time; (경기의) a round; a game; [야구] (미) an inning; (연재물의) an instalment. ¶1 ~ once / one time // 3 ~ three times // 7 ~ 초[말] the first[second] half of the seventh inning (권투 등의) 10 ~ 전 a bout[fight] of ten rounds // (토너먼트의) 2 ~ 전 the second round // (경기가) ~를 거듭함에 따라 as the game advances[progresses] // 9 ~ 초[말] 수비를 하다 take the field in the top[bottom] of the ninth inning // ~를 채우다 play the full game / finish the round // 2 ~

초반에 3점을 얻었다 (야구에서) They scored three runs in the top half of the second inning. // 2 ~ 전에서 이겼다 He won the second round. // 구경꾼들은 경기가 ~를 거듭함에 따라 흥분해 갔다 The spectators got excited as the game advanced [progressed].

회(會) 1 [모임] a meeting; an assembly; a gathering; a party; (미) a get-together; a conference. ¶~에 참석하다 attend [be present at] a meeting // ~에 참석치 않다 fail to attend [be absent from] a party // ~를 개최하다 hold [have / give] a party / hold a meeting. 2 [조직] a society; an association(협회); a club(클럽). ¶문학 ~ a literary society [club] // 금주 ~ a teetotal party [society] // ~를 조직하다 form[organize] a society // ~에 가입하다 join a society / associate oneself with a society.

회(膾) (생선회) slices of raw fish; sliced raw fish; (육회) minced raw beef. ¶다랑어 ~ slices of raw tuna / sliced raw tuna // 생선 ~ 를 치다 slice raw fish / prepare sliced raw fish.

회갑(回甲) the 60th anniversary of one's birth. ⇨환갑
● 회갑연(一宴) (give) a banquet on one's 60th birthday. ⇨환갑잔치(⇨환갑)

회개(悔改) repentance; penitence. 회개하다 repent (of one's sins); renounce one's former sins; be[become] penitent; reform oneself; turn over a new leaf. ¶잘못[비행]을 ~ acknowledge one's mistakes [misdeeds] and reform // 회개하면 죄도 사하여진다 Repentance wipes out sin. // 회개하라, 천국이 가까웠느니라 [성] Repent: for the kingdom of heaven is at hand.

회견(會見) an interview; an audience. ¶공식[비공식] ~ a formal[an informal] interview // 기자 ~ a press conference // 단독 ~ a single interview / an exclusive interview (with) // ~을 청하다 ask for an interview (with) // ~을 허락하다 grant[give] an interview (to a journalist) // 수상과의 ~을 신청하다 ask for[seek] an interview with the prime minister. 회견하다 have an interview (with); interview; meet [(미) meet with] (a person); have a talk with; give an interview to (the pressmen). ¶그에게 생각이 있다면 기꺼이 회견하겠다 I would be pleased to meet him if he wishes it. // 기자가 수상과 회견했다 A reporter interviewed the prime minister.
● 회견기 / 회견담 an interview. 회견자 an interviewer.

회계(會計) 1 [금전의 출납에 관한 일] accounts. ¶일반 ~ a general account // 특별 ~ special accounts // 그는 가 상점에서 ~를 담당하고 있다 He is in charge of the accounts at the store. 2 [계산] an account; [지불] a payment. ¶~를 마치다 pay the bill. 3 [금전 출납 담당자] an accountant; a treasurer.
● 회계 감사 audit; auditing. 회계사 a treasurer; an accountant; (공인 회계사) (미) a certified public accountant (약어 C.P.A.); (영) a chartered accountant. 회계 연도 a fiscal [(영) financial] year. ¶2002 ~ the 2002 fiscal year / the fiscal year 2002. 회계장부 an account book; a ledger. 회계학 accounting.

회고(回顧) recollection; retrospect; retrospection; review. **회고하다** recollect; retrospect; look back (upon / over / at); recall; review (one's past life); pass (one's life) in review. ¶지난날을 회고하면 on looking back upon [into] the past // 과거를 ~ look back upon one's old days // 1993년을 ~ review 1993 in retrospect.
- **회고록** reminiscences; memoirs.

회고(懷古) yearning for the old days; retrospection; reminiscence. ¶~의 정 sweet memories of the past / nostalgia // ~에 잠기다 think fondly of the past. **회고하다** recollect[look back upon] the past; recall the old days to one's mind.
- **회고담** reminiscences; recollections.

회관(會館) a hall; an assembly hall; a clubhouse. ¶기독교 청년 ~ the Young Men's Christian Association [Y.M.C.A.] Hall // 학생 ~ the students' hall.

회교(回敎) Islam. ⇨ =이슬람교
- **회교국** a Mohammedan country. **회교도** a Mohammedan; a Muslim [Moslem] (*pl.* ~(s)).

회군(回軍) withdrawl of troops. **회군하다** withdraw troops (from a place).

회귀(回歸) [한 바퀴 돌고 제자리로 돌아옴] (a) revolution; (a) recurrence. ¶~적 recurring / [주기적] periodic. **회귀하다** revolve; recur; come round again.
- **회귀년** a tropical year. **회귀선** the tropics. ¶남[북] ~ the tropic of Capricorn [Cancer].

회규(會規) the regulations of a society. ⇨ =회칙

회기(回忌) an anniversary of (a person's) death. ¶7~ the seventh anniversary of (a person's) death.

회기(會期) [회의하는 시기] a session; [국회의 개회에서 폐회까지의 기간] a sitting; a period. ¶국회의 ~ 중에 during the session of the National Assembly // 국회는 지금 ~ 중이다 The National Assembly is in session [is sitting] now. // 의회는 ~를 10일 연장했다 The parliament extended its session for ten days.
- **회기 연장** a prolongation [an extension] of the (present) session.

회담(會談) a conversation; a talk; a parley; a conference(정식의). ¶일련의 ~ a series of talks // 본~ full-dress [main] talks // 비공식 ~ an informal get-together // 3국 ~ a tripartite conference // 실무 ~ the workinglevel talks // 여야 (중진) ~ bipartisan conference (of key leaders) // 예비 ~ preliminary talks // 정상 ~ a summit(-level) meeting // 평화 ~ peace talks // 한일 ~ the ROK-Japan talks // ~은 제네바에서 열렸다 The summit conference was held in Geneva. **회담하다** talk together; have a talk (with); (정식으로) have a conference (with); confer (with). ¶장시간 ~ have a long talk (with a person) // 한미 양국은 3월에 회담하기로 했다 The Korean-American talks are to take place in March. // 장관은 그 일에 대해 그들과 회담했다 The minister conferred [had a talk] with them about [on] the matter.

회답(回答) a reply; an answer; a response. ¶…의 ~으로서 in reply [answer] to … // 기본급 인상 요구에 대한 ~ a reply to a demand for an increase in base pay // 아무런 ~도 없다 hear nothing in reply // ~을 받다 hear (from a person) in reply / get an answer (from) // 편지의 ~을 내다 answer [reply to] a letter // 편지 [전보]로 ~을 하다 reply by letter [wire] // ~은 문서로 하여 주십시오 You are requested to reply in writing. // 수상은 조속한 ~에 쫓기고 있다 The Prime Minister is being pressed for [under pressure to give] an immediate answer. // 앙케트에 ~을 보내 온 사람은 극소수였다 Very few people filled out the questionnaire. // ~을 하지 않은 편지가 아직도 한 통 있다 I still have one letter to answer. / One letter is still unanswered. // ~을 기다리고 있겠습니다 (편지 문투) I am looking forward to hearing from you. **회답하다** reply (to); answer; give [send] a reply [an answer]. ¶구두로 ~ give one's answer verbally [orally / by word of mouth] // 편지 [전보]로 곧 회답하십시오 Please reply by letter [wire] immediately. / Please write [wire] back once.
- **회답자** (앙케트 등의) a respondent; (퀴즈 프로 등의) a contestant; a panelist.

회당(會堂) 1 [교회] a church; a chapel. 2 a hall. ⇨ =회관 ¶청중이 ~에 꽉 차 있었다 The hall was crowded with audience.

회동(會同) an assembly; a meeting; a gathering. **회동하다** meet (together); assemble; gather (together); have an assembly.

회두리 the end; the finish; the last turn [round].
- **회두리판** the last round; the finals.

회람(回覽) circulation. ¶~을 돌리다 send out a circular (letter). **회람하다** circulate; read and pass on. ¶이 통지를 회람하여 주시오 Please read this notice and pass it on.

회랑(回廊) a corridor; a gallery; an ambulatory. ¶공중 ~ an air corridor (to Berlin).

회로(回路) 1 an electric circuit. ⇨ 전기 회로 (⇨전기(電氣)) ¶병렬 [직렬] ~ a parallel [series] circuit // 진공관 ~ a vacuum tube circuit // 집적 ~ an integrated circuit (약어 I.C.) // 전기 ~ an electric circuit // ~를 열다 [닫다] open [close] a circuit. 2 [돌아오는 길] the return way.
- **회로 차단기** a circuit breaker.

회류(會流) confluence; conflux. **회류하다** join; flow together; merge (into).

회반죽(灰―) mortar; plaster; stucco. ¶~을 바르다 plaster / stucco.

회백색(灰白色) ash color; light gray. ¶~의 ash / ash-colored [(영) -coloured] / light gray [(영) grey].

회백질(灰白質) [생] gray matter.

회벽(灰壁) a (lime-)plastered wall.

회보(回報) 1 [대답으로 하는 보고] a reply; an answer. **회보하다** send an answer; give a reply. 2 [돌아와서 아룀] bring back a report. **회보하다** report to (a person on one's work); report one's mission (to).

회보(會報) a bulletin; a report; the transactions(학회의). ¶동창회 ~ an alumni [alumnae] bulletin. (▶ alumnae는 여자 학교의)

회복(回復·恢復) 1 [본디 상태로 돌이킴] recovery; restoration; retrieval; rehabilitation; (시세의) recovery; reaction; [법] recovery. ¶경기의 ~ a return to prosperity // 기적적인 ~ a miraculous recovery // 날씨의 ~ improvement of the weather. **회복하다** get back; recover (strength); regain (one's reputa-

tion); restore (peace); rehabilitate (one's character); retrieve (one's honor / position); get over (a loss); repair (one's exhausted energies); make good; (실지 등을) (속이) win back; [법] (소송에 의해) replevy; be restored to (one's honor). ¶원 상태로 ~ return to the original condition∥평상으로 ~ return[go back] to normal∥사회 질서를 ~ restore public order∥명예를 ~ restore one's good name∥나라의 경제를 ~ reconstruct[restore stability to] the country's economy∥실지(失地)를 ~ recover lost territory. ➔¶날씨가 회복됐다 The weather has improved.∥경기가 회복되었다 The market has revived.∥(주식) 시세가 봄가지는 회복될 전망이다 The (stock) market will improve [pick up / rally] by spring.
2 [건강을 되찾음] recovery; recuperation. ¶건강을 ~ the return[restoration] of health ∥~ 중의 환자 a convalescent (patient)∥~이 **빠르다** recover (more) speedily∥~이 **늦다** be slow in recovery / make a slow recovery. **회복하다** recover (from illness); get well again; recuperate; be restored to health; recruit[regain] (one's health); get round. ¶회복할 가망이 없는 환자 a hopeless case∥건강을 ~ regain one's health∥그는 원기를 회복했다 He recovered his spirits.∥그는 결국 의식을 회복하지 못했다 He died without regaining consciousness. ➔¶그는 급속히 회복되고 있다 He is quickly recovering from his illness[getting better].∥부친의 병은 곧 회복될 것이오 Your father's illness will soon take a turn for the better.
● **회복기** convalescence; a convalescent stage. ¶~의 환자 a convalescent[recovering] patient / a convalescent∥~의 경제 reflationary[reflating / recovering / resurgent] economy∥~에 **있다** be in the convalescent stage / be convalescent. **회복실** (병원의) a convalescent ward.

회부(回附) transmission; [법] return; committal reference. ¶위원회 ~ devolution. **회부하다** transmit (to); refer (to); send (over) (to); forward (to); pass on (to); commit (to); [법] remit (to). ¶의안을 위원회에 ~ refer[relegate] a bill to a committee∥제안을 회의에 ~ submit a proposal to a meeting / put a proposal before a meeting∥사건을 재판에 ~ take a matter to court∥의안을 국회에 ~ refer[submit] a bill to the parliament. ➔¶그 사건은 하급 법원에 회부되었다 The case was remitted to a lower court.

회비(會費) a fee(일시적인); a membership fee(회원의); (영) a subscription(▶ 회보 등을 예약하고 불입하는). ¶클럽의 ~ club dues∥파티의 ~ one person's share of the cost of a party∥PTA의 ~ 를 모으다 collect PTA dues ∥~를 **납부하다** pay one's membership fee [dues]∥~를 **징수하다** collect dues∥연액 5,000원의 ~를 치르다 pay dues[a membership fee] of five thousand won a year∥그는 ~를 체납하고 있다 He is in arrears with his membership fee.

회사(會社) a company(약어 Co.); (미) a corporation; a firm; a concern(상사). ¶모[자] ~ a parent[subsidiary] company∥주식 ~ a corporation / a joint-stock company∥상사 ~ a trading company [corporation]∥보험 ~ an insurance company∥유한 ~ a corporation(약어 Inc.) / (영) a limited liability company(약어 Co., Ltd.)(▶회사명에는 생략하여 (미) Inc. (영) Co., Ltd.를 붙임)∥유령 ~ a bogus company∥합자 ~ a limited partnership∥합명 ~ an ordinary partnership∥동족 ~ a family partnership∥자매 ~ an affiliated company / an affiliate∥~에 **무하다** work for a company∥~에 **가다** go to work[the office](▶ the office는 사무직)∥~에 **들어가다** enter a company's service∥~를 **설립하다**[해산하다] establish[dissolve] a company∥~를 **만들다** organize[establish] a company∥~를 **합병하다** merge companies.
● **회사원** a clerk of a company; a company employe(e); an office worker[man]; a whitecollar worker.

회상(回想) recollection; [과거의 추억] reminiscence; retrospection; reflection. ¶~에 **빠지다** indulge in reminiscences. **회상하다** recollect; recall; call to mind; retrospect; remember; reflect on. ¶회상하건대 in retrospect∥과거를 ~ look back on the past / recall old times∥1970년대를 ~ recollect [look back upon] the 1970's.
● **회상록** reminiscences; memoirs. ¶그는 제 2차 대전 ~을 출판했다 He published his memoirs of World War Ⅱ.

회색(灰色) ash color; gray[(영) grey] (color). ¶~의 ash-colored / ashy / gray / (영) grey.
● **회색분자** a wobbler.

회생(回生) revival. ➪=**소생**(蘇生).

회석(會席) [모인 장소] a meeting place [room]; [모임] a meeting.

회선(回船) [돌아오는 배] a return boat; [배를 돌림] turning a boat around. **회선하다** turn a boat around; a boat turns around.

회전(回旋·廻旋) [그 자체가 회전함] rotation; [축을 중심으로 돌림] revolution. **회전하다** rotate; revolve.
● **회선곡** [음] a rondo. **회선교**(-橋) a swing bridge. ¶~선개교 **회선 운동** a rotary motion.

회선(回線) [전] a circuit. ¶전화 ~ a telephone circuit∥~ 고장으로 통화를 할 수 없었다 The lines were cut[out of order], so we couldn't get through to each other.∥전화 ~이 모두 통화 중이다 All the lines are busy [(영) engaged].

회송(回送) sending back. ➪=**환송**(還送).

회수(回收) (a) withdrawal; (a) collection; recovery; call-back(판 물건의); drawing in(은행권 등의). ¶자본의 ~ the revulsion of capital∥폐품 ~ collection of waste materials / the recovery of disused things∥그 돈은 ~ **불능이다** The money is uncollectible. / It is a bad debt.∥~ 불능의 대출금이 많아져서 그는 금전적 곤경에 빠져 있었다 He was in tight financial straits because he was struck with a lot of bad debts.∥제조 회사는 결함품의 ~를 시작했다 The manufacturer began to recall the defective goods. **회수하다** withdraw (coins / books) from circulation; collect; draw back; call in; retire; reclaim (disused things). ¶대출금을 ~ withdraw [draw in] loans / collect[call in] debts∥외상값을 ~ collect bills∥폐품[빈 병]을 ~ collect waste articles[empty bottles]∥외상 매출금을 ~ collect bills∥잡지를 ~ withdraw magazines from circulation∥파손된 헌 지폐를 ~ retrieve soiled old bills from circulation.

회수권(回數券) a coupon ticket. ¶50회의 ~ a ticket of 50 coupons.
회식(會食) dining together; mess(군인의). ¶~중이다 be at mess. 회식하다 dine together; dine (with); take a meal together; (군인 등이) have a mess (with); mess (with).
회신(回信) a reply. ⇨반신(返信)
● 회신료 postage for a reply; return postage. ¶~로 190원짜리 우표를 동봉하다 enclose a 190 won stamp for return postage[for a reply].
회심(回心) [마음을 고침] a change of heart; [종] conversion. 회심하다 be[get] converted.
회심(會心) congeniality; complacency. ¶~의 미소를 짓다[띠다] have[smile] a smile of satisfaction / smile complacently / have a self-satisfied smile.
● 회심작 a work after one's (own) heart. ¶이것은 나의 ~입니다 This is a work after my (own) heart.
회양목(-楊木) [식] a box tree; [재목] box; boxwood.
● 회양목과(-科) Buxaceae(학명).
회오(悔悟) repentance (for one's sins); remorse; penitence; contrition. ¶~의 눈물을 흘리다 shed tears of repentance[remorse] / shed penitent tears // ~의 빛을 보이다 show repentance // 피고는 ~의 정을 보이지 않았다 The accused did not show any sign of remorse. 회오하다 repent (of); be sorry (for); feel remorse (for); regret; become penitent. ¶깊이 ~ be smitten with remorse.
회오리바람 a whirlwind; an eddywind; a vertiginous wind; a cyclone; a (whirling) tornado (pl. ~(e)s); (미) a twister.
회원(會員) a member (of a society / an association); (집합적) a membership. ¶보통[특별/명예] ~ an ordinary[a special / an honorary] member // 정~ a regular member / a member in full and regular standing // 종신 ~ a life member // 준~ an associate member // 찬조[유지(維持)]~ a patronage[supporting] member // ~의 자격(qualifications for) membership // ~의 특전 privileges of membership // ~이 아닌 사람 nonmembers // ~의 자격을 잃다[다시 얻다] lose [regain] one's membership // ~으로서의 자격이 있다 be eligible for membership / be entitled to the membership (of) // ~이 되다 become a member / enroll oneself as a member / join (a society) // ~이 되어 있다 hold membership (in the club) / keep one's name on the list of membership[on the books] / be on the books // ~이 많다[적다] have a large[small] membership // ~을 모집하다 invite[seek] a membership // 널리 ~을 모집하다 seek a wide membership among the nation // ~을 제한하다 limit the membership (to 500) // ~을 사퇴하다 retire from membership (of an academy) // 정식 ~ 자격을 얻다 gain full membership // 나는 클럽의 ~이 되었다 I was admitted to the club. // 그는 의사회 ~의 한 사람이다 He is one of the members of the medical association. // 그는 테니스 클럽의 ~이 되었다 He joined[became a member of] the tennis club. // 이 클럽에는 2천 명의 ~이 있다 This club has two thousand members. / There are two thousand people in this club.
● 회원국 a member nation. 회원 명부 a

membership list[directory] (▶ directory는 주소가 기재된 것). ¶~에 올리다 enroll (a person) on the list of membership. 회원제 the membership system. ¶이 골프장은 ~로 되어 있다 This golf links is not open to non-members. 회원증 a membership card.
회유(回遊·洄游) migration. 회유하다 migrate.
● 회유어(~魚) a migratory[wandering] fish.
회유(回遊) [유람] an excursion; a circular trip[tour]. 회유하다 make an excursion[a circular tour].
● 회유선(~船) an excursion boat.
회유(懷柔) conciliation; pacification; appeasement; [매수] winning over. 회유하다 conciliate; pacify; appease; placate; bring (a person) round; [매수하다] buy[win] (a person) over; draw[bring] over (a person) to one's side. ¶그를 어떻게든 회유해서 우리 편으로 할 수 있었다 We managed to win him over to our side.
● 회유책 a conciliatory[pacification] measure[policy]; an appeasement policy. ¶~을 쓰다 take a conciliatory[pacification] measure[policy] / resort to an appeasement policy.
회음(會陰) [생] the perineum.
● 회음부 the perineal region.
회의(會議) a conference; a meeting; a council; a talk; a convention(대회); a congress(대표자 회의); a sitting(회기 중인); a session. ¶각무 ~ a Cabinet council[conference] // 국제 ~ an international conference // 긴급 ~ (hold / convoke) an urgent conference[meeting] // 당무 ~ an executive committee[meeting] // 본 ~ a plenary session // 비밀 ~ a closed[secret] meeting / a secret[closed-door] session / a secret conference[sitting] / a conclave // 평화[군축] ~ a peace[disarmament] conference // 원탁 ~ a round-table conference // ~에 참석하다 attend a conference / meet in conference [convention] // ~에 소집되다 be summoned to council // ~에 참가하다 join[take part in / participate in] a conference // 문제를 ~에 부치다 refer[submit / send] (a matter) to conference / lay[bring] (a question) before the council // ~를 개최하다 hold[call] a council[conference / session] / sit in [go into] conference // ~를 소집하다 call[assemble] a conference[a council] / convene [convoke] a convention // ~를 하고 있다 be in conference (with) // 교장은 지금 ~ 중이다 The principal is in conference now. // 오늘은 ~가 없다 There is no session today. // ~ 중 (게시) Now in session. // 그 문제에 대해서 지금 ~ 중입니다 They are sitting on the question. 회의하다 meet; confer (with); sit (in conference); hold a meeting[conference].
● 회의록 the minutes; proceedings. 회의소 a meeting hall; an assembly hall. 회의실 a council[board / conference] room; an assembly room. 회의장 a conference hall; a council house.
회의(懷疑) doubt; skepticism; incredulity; unbelief. 회의하다 doubt; be skeptical (of).
● 회의론 / 회의주의 (the principle of) skepticism. 회의론자 a skeptic; a Pyrrhonian; a Pyrrhonist.
회의적(懷疑的) skeptic(al); incredulous. ¶~으로 보다 take a skeptical[dim] view (of) //

그들은 상관의 생각에 ~이었다 They were skeptical about their boss's principles.
회자정리(會者定離) We never meet without parting.; Those who meet must part.
회자하다(膾炙-) be in everyone's mouth; be on everybody's lips; become a household word; be well known. ¶인구에 회자된 말 a common saying / a household word∥그 언은 인구에 회자되어 있다 The maxim is well-known to everybody[is a household phrase].
회장(回裝) 1 (여자 저고리의) colorful strips of cloth for trimmings (on a woman's coat). 2 (병풍 등의) edging《of a screen[scroll / map]》.
회장(回腸) 〖생〗 the ileum. ¶~의 ileac.
●**회장염** ileitis.
회장(會長) the president (of a society); the chairman (of a committee); a grand (of a club); 〖이사회〗 ~ (회사의) the chairman of the board of directors∥~이 되다 be elected chairman[president] / become chairman∥그 협회는 최 박사를 ~으로 모시고 있다 The society is under the presidency of Dr. Choe.
●**회장 직** presidency; chairmanship.
회장(會場) the place of meeting. ¶~에 넘치는 청중 an overflowing audience∥산업 박람회의 ~ 예정지 the planned site of the industrial Exhibition∥~은 어딥니까 Where is the meeting (going) to be held?∥~은 신라 호텔로 정했습니다 We have chosen the Silla Hotel as the place of meeting.∥여기가 박람회의 ~이 될 곳이다 This is to be the site for the exhibition.
회장(會葬) attendance at a funeral. **회장하다** attend a funeral.
●**회장자** attendants at a funeral. ¶그 장례식에는 ~가 많았다 The funeral was largely attended.
회전(回電) a reply telegram. ⇨¯답전(答電)
회전(回轉·廻轉) (a) revolution; (a) rotation; (a) gyration(선회). ¶매분 200 ~ 200 revolutions per minute(약어 200 r.p.m.)∥시계 방향과 반대 방향으로의 ~ counterclockwise rotation∥자금 ~을 촉진하다 quicken the turnover[circulation] of the fund∥그는 머리(의) ~이 빠르다 He is bright[smart]. / He has a quick mind. / (구어) He's quick on the uptake.∥그는 머리(의) ~이 더디다 His mind works slowly. / He doesn't have a very quick mind. / He has a dull mind. / He's slow to catch on.∥이 상품은 ~이 빠를 것 같다 We can expect a quick turnover from[on] these goods. **회전하다** revolve; rotate; gyrate; turn[spin] round; go[move] round; run(기계가). ¶180도 ~ rotate in a 180-degree arc∥1~ make one revolution (round) / make a turn / swing[come] full circle / go a full cycle / (공중제비로) somersault / turn a somersault / (위를 아래로) turn upside down / turn bottom over top / turn over∥바퀴가 회전한다 The wheels go[turn] round.∥바퀴가 축을 중심으로 하여 회전한다 A wheel turns [works] on its axle[axis].∥지구는 태양 주위를 회전한다 The earth revolves[travels / goes / moves] round the sun.∥이 선풍기는 1초에 몇 번 회전하지요 How many revolutions a second does this fan make? ➔¶회전시키다 turn (a thing) round / turn (a wheel) / [돌리다] give a turn (to) / roll 프로펠러를 회전시키다 swing the propeller∥공을 회전시키다〖야구〗give a ball a spin [spinning motion] / put spin on a ball∥자본을 회전시키다 circulate[rotate] capital.
●**회전 경기** 〖스키〗 special slalom. **회전등** a rotary lamp. **회전목마** a merry-go-round; a giddy-go-round; a whirligig; (미) a car(r)ousel; (영) a roundabout. ¶~를 타다 ride a carousel pony. **회전 무대** a turning [revolving / rotating / rotative] stage. **회전문** a revolving door. **회전의자** a swivel[pivot / revolving] chair. **회전 자금** a revolving fund. **회전축** the axis of rotation[gyration]; a pivot; a shaft.
회절(回折) 〖물〗 diffraction.
●**회절격자** 〖물〗 a diffraction grating. **회절파** a diffracted wave. **회절 현상** 〖물〗 a diffraction phenomenon.
회중(會衆) an attendance; an audience; attendants; (교회의) a congregation. ¶~에게 인사하다 address the meeting[an audience] ∥~은 다수[소수]였다 There was a large [small] attendance at the meeting.
회중(懷中) 1 the bosom. ⇨¯품속 2 one's inmost feelings. ⇨마음속(㊀마음)
●**회중시계** a pocket watch. **회중전등** an electric torch. **회중품 / 회중물** a pocketbook; a purse; a wallet(큰 것).
회지(會誌) a bulletin; the transactions(학회의). ¶동창회 ~ an alumni bulletin / an alumnae bulletin (여학교의).
회진(回診) a (doctor's) round of visits. ¶이제 곧 ~ 시간입니다 (환자를 향해서) The doctor will soon come in to see you. **회진하다** make a round of visits (to one's patients); go the round of (one's patients); visit one's patients; make sick calls; go round the beds.
회집(會集) (a) gathering; (a) meeting; (an) assemblage; (a) congregation. **회집하다** 〖모이다〗 gather; collect; assemble; meet; congregate; get together; [모으다] gather (together); collect; assemble.
회초리 a switch; a whip; a cane; a pointer(교사용). ¶버들 ~ a willow switch∥~로 때리다 switch (a boy) (with a cane) / cane / lash [flog / whip / swish] (a boy) (with a switch) ∥~를 맞다 be whipped / be caned[lashed] / get the cane.
회춘(回春) 〖도로 젊어짐〗 rejuvenation; restoration of youth. **회춘하다** grow[get] younger; be[become] rejuvenated; undergo rejuvenation; be restored to youth; become [grow] young again. ➔¶회춘시키다 rejuvenate / rejuvenize.
●**회춘제**(-劑) a rejuvenator; an erogenous drug.
회충(蛔蟲) 〖동〗 a mawworm; an intestinal worm; a roundworm; [의] an ascarid [ascaris] (pl. ascarid(e)s). ¶~이 생기다 get (intestinal) worms∥그는 ~이 있는 것 같다 He seems to have roundworms.
●**회충약** a medicine for expelling mawworms; a vermifuge; an anthelmint(h)ic (drug).
회칙(會則) the regulations[rules / (미) bylaws] of a society; the articles of an association; the constitution of a club. ¶그것은 ~에 반한다 That is against the regulations of our society.

회포(懷抱) one's inmost[intimate] thoughts; one's heart[mind]. ¶~를 풀다 unburden [unbosom] oneself (to a person).

회피(回避) evasion; avoidance; shirking; elusion; [법] refrainment. 회피하다 evade; avoid; shirk; dodge; shun; sidestep; elude (payment); get around (the difficulty). ¶책임을 ~ evade[shirk] one's responsibility / flee from responsibility // 언급을 ~ evade [decline] to comment (on) // 교전을 ~ disengage action // 동맹 파업을 ~ head off a strike // 일을 ~ shirk one's job.
● 회피책 / 회피 전술 dodging[evasive] tactics.

회한(悔恨) remorse; (a) regret; (a) repentance; contrition; compunction. ¶뼈저린 ~ poignant regret // ~의 contrite // ~의 눈물 tears of remorse.

회합(會合) a meeting; an assembly; a gathering; a party; (미국 구어) a get-together. ¶서울에서의 at a meeting in Seoul // ~ 날짜를 정하다 fix the day for meeting / make an appointment. 회합하다 meet; gather; assemble; get together. ¶우리는 월 1회 회합한다 We assemble[meet together] once a month.
● 회합 장소 a place of meeting.

회항(回航) 1 [항로] navigation; cruise; sailing about. 회항하다 sail round; double (a cape). 2 [특정항으로 배를 돌림]. 회항하다 bring [take] a ship (to Incheon). ➔ ¶부산항으로 회항시켰다 We brought[took] the ship into Busan Harbor. 3 [귀항] a homeward [return] voyage. 회항하다 make a homeward voyage; sail home.

회혼(回婚) the sixtieth anniversary of one's wedding; a diamond wedding. ¶~례를 올리다 celebrate one's diamond wedding (anniversary) / have one's diamond jubilee.

회화(會話) (a) conversation; a talk. ¶영어 ~ English conversation // 영어 ~를 잘하다 speak English well / be a good speaker of English / speak fluent English. 회화하다 talk [speak] (with); have a conversation[talk] (with); converse (with). ¶영어로 ~ converse in English (with) // 저 영국인과 몇 번 회화한 적이 있다 I have had several conversations with that Englishman.
● 회화 독본 a conversational reader. 회화책 a conversational book. 회화체 colloquialism; colloquial style. ¶~ 영어 colloquial English // ~로 쓴 책 a book written in colloquial [conversational] style.

회화(繪畵) pictures; paintings; drawings.
● 회화 전람회 an exhibition of pictures; an art[a painting] exhibition; a picture show.

회회교(回回敎) Islam. ⇨ ˭이슬람교

획 with a swerve; whizzing; with full force. ⇨ˌ휙

획(畫) (글자의) a stroke. ¶5~의 글자 a character of five strokes / a 5-stroke character // ~을 긋다 make a stroke // ~을 내리긋다 make a vertical[downward] stroke / stroke downwards // ~을 가로 긋다 make a horizontal[side] stroke.

획기적(劃期的) epoch-making; epochal. ¶~ 기록 an epoch-making record // 미술사상 ~ 작품 a landmark in the history of art.
● 획기적 사건[발견] an epoch-making event [discovery].

획득(獲得) acquisition; acquirement; possession; gain; taking. ¶부의 ~ the acquisition of wealth // 지식의 ~ the acquirement of knowledge. 획득하다 gain; acquire; obtain; secure; get; win; take (the first prize). ¶권리를 ~ acquire[secure] rights // 정권을 ~ come to power // 직책[직위]을 ~ obtain an appointment[a position] // 시민권을 ~ acquire citizenship // 면허를 ~ obtain a license // 그들은 자유를 획득하려고 싸우고 있다 They are fighting for liberty.
● 획득물 an acquisition; gainings. 획득 형질 [생] an acquired character.

획수(畫數) the number of strokes (in a Chinese character); the stroke count.

획순(畫順) the order of making strokes (in writing a Chinese character). ¶~을 틀리다 make strokes in a wrong order.

획일적(劃一的) [한결같은] uniform; standardized; [한결같음] uniformity. ¶~인 교육 uniform education // 경영자는 종업원을 ~으로 다루려고 했다 The manager tried to deal with all the employees in the same way.

획일주의(劃一主義) (the principle of) standardization.

획정(劃定) demarcation; delimitation. 획정하다 demarcate; delimit; mark out. ¶경계를 ~ delimit[demarcate] the boundary[frontier] line / mark off[draw up] the boundaries[a boundary].

획책(劃策) [일을 꾀함] planning; scheming; maneuvering; [계획] a plan; a project; a scheme. 획책하다 plan; project; scheme; form a plan; map out a plan; lay [concoct] a scheme; [책동하다] maneuver; use artifice; (미) frame (up); plot; conspire. ¶반란을 ~ conspire to rise in revolt // 그들은 사장을 축출하려고 획책하고 있다 They are scheming [planning / working] to oust the president from his post. // 배후에서 획책하는 자가 있다 Someone is maneuvering behind the scenes.

휙휙 1 [연달아 돌아가는 모양] round and round; whirling; speedily; fast. ¶~ 돌다 turn[go] round and round / spin / twirl / whirl. 2 [바람이 잇달아 세게 부는 모양] whistling; with a whistle[whiz(z)]. ¶바람이 하루 종일 ~ 불었다 The wind whistled all day long.

횟가루(灰-) calcium oxide. ⇨ ˭산화칼슘(⇨)산화(酸化))

횟감(膾-) raw fish (for preparing a sliced raw-fish dish).

횟돌(灰-) limestone. ⇨ ˭석회암(⇨)석회)

횟배(蛔-) stomach trouble caused by worms. ⇨ˌ거위배(⇨)거위)

횟수(回數) the number of times; frequency. ¶~를 거듭하다 repeat (so many times) // 그는 열 몇 번이나 ~를 거듭했다 He repeated it more than ten times. // 그가 상을 받은 ~는 열 번도 넘는다 He has been awarded prizes more than ten times. // ~를 거듭할수록 나는 그것에 익숙해졌다 In the process of repeating it, I got used to it.

횟집(膾-) a restaurant specializing in sliced raw fish.

횡(橫) width; across. ⇨ ˭가로

횡격막(橫隔膜) [생] the diaphragm; the midriff. ¶~의 phrenic.

횡단(橫斷) crossing; crosscutting; intersection; traversing. ¶대륙 ~ 철도 a transcontinental railway // 태평양 ~ 비행 a transpacific flight / a flight across the Pacific. **횡단하다** cross; traverse; sail[go / travel / swim / make a journey] across; run[lie] across [through]; intersect; cut transversely. ¶도로를 ~ cross a road / walk[go] across a street // 비행기[배]로 태평양을 ~ fly[sail] across the Pacific / make a flight[sail / cruise] across the Pacific / make a transpacific flight[sail / cruise] // 교통 법규를 무시하고 도로를 ~ jaywalk // 사막을 ~ cross[traverse] a desert.

● **횡단로** a crosscut (road); a shortcut; a (park) transverse. **횡단면** a cross[transverse] section; a transection. **횡단보도** a pedestrian crossing; (영) a zebra crossing; a crosswalk (for pedestrians).

횡대(橫隊) a rank; a line; a line abreast. ¶~로 in line // 2열 ~로 in a double line // ~로 되다 form in line / be drawn up in[into] line // 2열 ~로 되다 [정렬하다] form[be drawn up in] a double line // ~로 서 [구령] Line up facing the front!

● **횡대 비행** flying in line abreast. **횡대 행진** a march in a line.

횡듣다(橫-) [잘못 듣다] hear (it / him) wrong[amiss]; mishear; [오해하다] misunderstand (what was said).

횡렬(橫列) a rank; a line. ¶~을 짓다 stand in a row.

횡령(橫領) (a) usurpation; (a) seizure; dispossession; assumption; (an) embezzlement; misappropriation; [법] conversion(동산의). ¶공금의 ~ embezzlement[misappropriation] of public money[funds]. **횡령하다** usurp; seize upon; jump (a claim); embezzle; dispossess (a person of his property); assume; misappropriate unlawfully; misappropriate; help oneself to (the money); grab; [법] convert(동산을). ¶재산을 ~ seize upon (a person's) property / dispossess (a person) of his property // 은행[남]의 돈을 ~ embezzle money from a bank[person] // 공금을 일부 ~ embezzle part of official money.

횡문근(橫紋筋) [생] a striated [striped] muscle.

횡보다(橫-) [잘못 보다] see (a thing) wrongly; misjudge; make a wrong estimation[estimate] (of); misread[mistake] (a signal).

횡보하다(橫步-) walk sideways; sidle (through the door); edge along.

횡사(橫死) a violent[an unnatural / an untimely] death; death by violence; an accidental death; a suspicious death; a tragic death(참사). **횡사하다** die[meet] a violent [a tragic / an unnatural / an accidental] death; die by violence.

횡서(橫書) horizontal writing. ⇨가로쓰기
횡선(橫線) a horizontal line; a cross line; [수] an abscissa. ¶~을 긋다 cross.

● **횡선 수표** a crossed check[(영) cheque].

횡설수설(橫說竪說) incoherent talks; disjointed remarks; jargon; gibberish; jabberwock(y); nonsense. **횡설수설하다** talk incoherently; make disjointed remarks; talk jargon[nonsense]; jargon; gibber; jabber. ¶횡설수설하는 대답 an incoherent reply // 년 횡설수설해서 무슨 소린지 모르겠다 You speak a perfect jargon. / You talk in a perfect gibberish. // 그의 진술은 점점 횡설수설해졌다 His statement became more and more incoherent[confused].

횡액(橫厄) an unforeseen[unexpected] accident; a sudden accident; [재난] an unforeseen calamity[disaster]; [불행] (a) misfortune; a mishap. ¶~을 만나다 suffer an unexpected misfortune / have an accident / meet with (a) misfortune[calamity].

횡재(橫財) a windfall; a godsend; an acquisition; a find; [크게 한 몫보기] a killing; a cleanup; a bonanza(투기 등에서). ¶이건 ~다 It is an unexpected piece of windfall[good luck]. // 골동품 가게에서 뜻밖의 ~를 했다 I made a great find at an antique shop. **횡재하다** fall in with a piece of (good) luck; make a rare find; realize a windfall profit (of); receive one's share of the windfall; make a killing[cleanup]; strike a bonanza.

횡축(橫軸) ➡가로축(⇨가로)
횡파(橫波) [물] a transverse wave.
횡포(橫暴) oppression(압제); violence(폭력); tyranny(포학); high-handedness(위압). ¶군부(軍部)의 ~ the despotism of the militarists. **횡포하다** arbitrary; tyrannical; despotic; high-handed; overbearing; oppressive; violent; unreasonable. ¶횡포한 말단 관리 high-handed[overbearing] petty officials.

횡행하다(橫行-) [제멋대로 날뛰다] be[run] rampant; prevail; overrun; thrive; be prevalent. ¶해적이 횡행하는 바다 a pirate-ridden sea / a sea infested with pirates // 경찰조차도 불량배들이 횡행하는 데는 애를 먹고 있다 Even the police are having difficulty dealing with the rampage of delinquent groups. // 여기서는 증수회가 횡행하고 있다 Here bribery is rampant. // 관리들 사이에 독직이 횡행하고 있다 Bribery is rampant among the officials.

효(孝) filial piety [devotion]; filial duty; obedience to parents. ¶부모에게 ~를 다하다 tend one's parents with filial piety / be dutiful to one's parents // ~는 백행(百行)의 근본이다 Filial devotion is the basis of human conduct. / Filial piety is the source of all virtues.

효과(效果) (an) effect; effectiveness; avail; (the) good (of something); efficacy(약 등의); efficiency(능률); [결과] a result; fruit. ¶광고 ~ effectiveness of advertising // 무대 ~ stage effect / scenic effects // 선전 ~ propaganda effect // 음향 ~ (produce) sound effects // (예술등의) 전체적 ~ the general effect / (프) the tout ensemble // 열이 금속에 미치는 ~ the effect of heat upon metals // ~ 가 있는 effective / effectual / fruitful / efficient / successful / efficacious(약품 등이) // ~가 없는 ineffectual / inefficient / fruitless / resultless / vain / unavailing / to no purpose / of no avail[use] / yielding no results // ~를 거두기 위해서는 to be effective / in order to reap the fruits / (일 등이) to produce satisfactory results // ~가 있다 be effective / be effectual / take effect / have an effects (on) / do (a person) good / prove fruitful[successful] / bear fruit / be efficacious(약 등이) // ~가 없다 be ineffectual / be ineffectual / be fruitless / be (of) no good / (약 등이) be inefficacious / have [produce] no effect (on) // ~가 별로 없다 have little effect (on) / be of little avail / serve little // ~ 가 빠르다 be quick in (its) effect // …하는 ~

가 있다 have the effect of ...ing // 충분한 ~를 거두다 bear (its) full fruit // 극적 ~를 높이다 heighten the dramatic effect // 소기의 ~를 거두다 obtain the desired result / produce the intended effect // ~를 노리다 calculate upon an effect // ~를 내다 have an effect (on) // ~는 만점이다 It has gone quite for. // 해 질 녘의 멋진 구름의 ~는 묘사하기 어렵다 It is very hard to describe the wonderful cloud effects at sunset. // 여러 가지로 해 보았지만 그다지 ~가 없었다 Repeated attempts have been made without any noticeable result. // 그들에게는 아무리 주의를 주어도 ~가 없다 No matter how I warn them, it has no effect [does no good]. // 어머니의 꾸짖도 그 아이에게는 별로 ~가 없는 것 같았다 His mother's scolding seemed to have little effect on the child.

효과적(效果的) [효과 있는] effective; effectual; successful; efficacious(약 등이); [효과가 있음] effectiveness; effectuality; effectualness; efficaciousness. ¶비-인 ineffective / ineffectual // ~으로 effectively / with effect / ~인 교수법 efficient methods of teaching / 질병에 대한 ~인 치료법 an efficacious cure for a disease.

효녀(孝女) a filial [dutiful] daughter.

효능(效能) effect; efficacy; virtue; properties (of a medicine); benefit; good; use. ¶약의 ~ the virtue [effect] of (a) medicine / the efficacy of a remedy / the good that a medicine does // 온천의 ~ the medical benefits of hot springs (in the cure of a disease) // ~이 있다 [없다] be efficacious [inefficacious] / prove effective [ineffective] / be good [no good] (for) // (약의) ~이 나타나다 take effect / prove efficacious // ~이 있다 work wonders (on a headache) / do (a person) a lot of good // 그것은 어떤 ~이 있느냐 What is the good of it? / 이 약은 무엇에 ~이 있습니까 What is this medicine good for? // 이 약은 심장병에 ~이 있었다 This medicine has proved efficacious against heart disease. // 이 온천은 류머티즘에 ~이 있다 This hot spring is good for [has medicinal benefits in the treatment of] rheumatism. // 이 약은 나에게는 대단한 ~이 있었다 This medicine benefited me a great deal. // 그 약은 나에게는 조금도 ~이 없었다 The medicine had no effect on me.

효도(孝道) filial piety [devotion]; filial duty; obedience to parents. **효도하다** be dutiful [obedient / devoted] to one's parents; be a good son [daughter]; practice filial piety toward one's parents; discharge one's filial duties. ¶효도하고 싶을 때는 이미 부모는 안 계신다 By the time you are inclined to treat them properly, your parents are already gone. / When one would be filial, one's parents are gone.

효력(效力) 1 (약 등의) (an) effect. ¶파리 구제 (驅除)에 ~이 있는 약 chemicals good for eliminating flies // 약의 ~ the effectiveness of a medicine // ~이 있다 have an effect / work / (문어) be efficacious // 이 세제는 별로 ~이 없다 This detergent has little effect. // 그 약은 그의 두통에 아무런 ~이 없었다 This medicine did not relieve [help] his headache. // 그의 연설은 군중을 진정시키는 데 큰 ~이 있었다 His speech was very effective in calming the crowd. / His speech had a great pacifying effect on the crowd.
2 [법률의 작용] effect; [유효성] validity. ¶~이 있다 be valid / be in force // ~을 잃다 lose effect / become invalid // 그 계약의 ~이 발생하는 것은 1년 뒤부터이다 The contract will come into force after one year.

효모(균)(酵母菌) a yeast fungus (pl. ~es, -gi).

효부(孝婦) a dutiful [an obedient] daughter-in-law.

효성(孝誠) filial piety [devotion / affection]. ¶~스러운 아들 a dutiful [an obedient] son / an affectionate and dutiful son // ~이 지극하다 be devoted to one's parents // 그녀는 어머니에게 ~스럽다 She shows great devotion [behaves filially] to her mother. / She is faithful to her mother.

효성(曉星) 1 the morning star. ⇨ 샛별1 2 [희귀한 것] a rarity.

효소(酵素) [화] ferment; enzym(e); [의] zyme. ¶소화 ~ digestive enzyme.
● **효소학** enzymology.

효수하다(梟首-) gibbet [expose] a head.

효순하다(孝順-) affectionate and dutiful; filial obedient to one's parents.

효시(嚆矢) [맨 처음] the beginning; the first; the first person (to do); the pioneer (in). ¶···한 것은 그를 ~로 한다 He was the first (man) to (do). // 이것이 ···의 ~였다 This was the first instance of ....

효심(孝心) filial affection; filial piety. ¶~이 지극한 사람 a very dutiful person.

효용(效用) 1 [용도] use; [유용성] usefulness; utility. ¶비 ~ [경] disutility // 자연 [잉여] ~ [경] gratuitous [surplus] utility // 한계 ~ marginal utility // ~이 있다[없다] be of use [no use] // 그 이외에는 ~이 없다 That is the only use for it. 2 (an) effect. ⇨ 효험
● **효용 가치** effective value; utility value. **효용 체감의 법칙** [경] the law of diminishing utility [returns].

효율(效率) the utility factor; [물] efficiency; (엔진의) duty. ¶열~ thermal efficiency // 높은 ~ a high degree of efficiency // 비~적인 일 inefficient work // ~을 높이다 promote efficiency // 3안타로 5점이면 ~적인 공격이다 It's really an efficient offense when you get five runs on just three hits.
● **효율 곡선** an efficiency curve.

효자(孝子) a dutiful [filial] child [son]; a good [devoted] son.

효행(孝行) filial conduct; a filial deed.
● **효행상** a prize for filial conduct.

효험(效驗) (an) effect; (문어) efficacy; virtue; benefit. ¶~이 없다 be inefficacious / be ineffective / do (a person) no good / have no effect // ~이 없어지다 lose (its) effect // 이것은 기침에 ~이 있는 약이다 This is a good remedy for coughs. // 노인에게 주술적인 말은 ~이 있었다 The incantation worked wonders on the old man. / The magic spell had an immediate effect on the old man. // 이 약은 어디에 ~이 있느냐 What is this medicine good for?

후 with a whiff. ⇨ 호

후(後) 1 [사후]. ¶그 ~ after that (▶ 과거형을 씀) / [그 이래] since then (▶ 현재 완료형을 씀) / thereafter / afterward // 그 ~에 그는 어

떻게 하였습니까 What did he do after that? // 나는 그 ~로 여기에 살아왔다 I have lived here since then. // 그 ~로 죽 그를 본 사람은 아무도 없다 Nobody has seen him ever since. // 그는 물을 마신 ~에 말을 하기 시작했다 He drank some water, and then began to speak. // 그 며칠 만에 그는 위독하게 되었다 A few days later his condition became critical. // 그 ~ 며칠 동안 나는 두통이 났다 I had a headache for several days afterwards. **2** [앞날] future. ¶2주일 ~에 two weeks hence[from now] // ~의 future / coming // 그 일은 ~로 미룹시다 We will put it off till some other time. // 천 년 ~의 세계는 어찌 될 것인가 What will become of the world a thousand years hence[from now]?
후각(嗅覺) the sense of smell; the smell; the olfactory sense. ¶예민한[둔한] ~ a keen [poor] sense of smell // 개는 ~이 예민하다 The dog has a keen nose[sense of smell].
● **후각 신경** the olfactory nerve.
후견(後見) [보좌] guardianship; wardship; tutelage; tutorage; [원조] assistance. ¶숙부의 ~으로 under the guardianship of my uncle // ~을 받고 있다 be in[under] ward / be (placed) under the guardianship (for) / look after (children) / have the wardship of (a person).
● **후견인** [법] a guardian; a tutor; a curator; a committee; (연기자의) a prompter; (권투 선수의) a (personal) manager. ¶피 ~ a ward / 유언으로 ~을 지정하다 designate a guardian by will // 나는 조카의 ~이 되었다 I assumed responsibility for my nephew's upbringing. / I became my nephew's guardian.
후계(後繼) succession. **후계하다** succeed (a person / to another's office).
● **후계자** [대를 이을 사람] an heir(남자); an heiress(여자); an inheritor; (학문·예능 등의) a successor. ¶아들이 회장의 ~가 되었다 He succeeded his father as chairman of the board. // 누가 당신의 ~가 됩니까 Who will succeed to your post? / Who will take over your position[take over from you]? // 수제자인 그가 그 파를 영도하는 ~가 되었다 As the foremost disciple, he became heir to the leadership of that school.
후고(後顧) **1** [과거를 돌아봄] looking back. **후고하다** review; retrospect; look back upon. **2** [미래의 근심] anxiety[solicitude] about one's future. ¶~의 염려를 없애다 free (a person) from family cares[from anxiety about one's home] / free (a person) from solicitude[anxiety] about the future. // 그는 ~의 염려가 끊이지 않는다 He is always anxious about future affairs[his family and affairs after his death]. **후고하다** worry over the future; worry about one's family left behind.
후골(喉骨) the Adam's apple.
후광(後光) a glory; an aureole[aureola]; a gloria; [광륜] a halo (*pl.* ~(e)s); a nimbus (*pl.* -bi, ~es); (태양의) a corona. ¶성자의 머리에 ~이 비치고 있다 The saint has a halo around his head. / A halo is visible around the saint's head.
후군(後軍) [군] the rear guard.
후굴(後屈) [의] retroflexion. ¶자궁~ retroflexion of the uterus.
후궁(後宮) **1** [뒤쪽에 있는 궁전] a king's harem; a seraglio (*pl.* ~s). **2** [왕의 첩] a royal concubine.
후기(後記) a postscript(약어 P.S., p.s.). ¶편집 ~ the editor's postscript.
후기(後期) [뒤의 기간] the latter period; the latter[second] half year; (미) the second semester. ¶18세기 ~에 in the later[latter part of the] eighteenth century // ~에 latterly.
● **후기 대학** universities[colleges] in the second (screening) group. **후기 인상파** [미] (사람) the post-impressionists; (주의) post-impressionism.
후년(後年) [다음 해의 다음 해] the year after next; [후세] later years. ¶내 ~ three years from now // ~에 in future years / in years to come / (나중에) later / afterward(s) // 그는 ~에 후회할 것이다 He will regret it afterward [later in life].
후뇌(後腦) [생] the hindbrain; the afterbrain.
후닥닥 1 [갑자기] suddenly; abruptly; all at once; [열째게] quickly; nimbly; alertly; (as) quick as thought. ¶~ 뛰어가다 break into a run // 방에서 ~ 뛰어나가다 rush[bounce] suddenly out of the room // 옷을 ~ 벗다 whip off one's coat // 침대에서 ~ 뛰어 일어나다 jump[start] out of bed. **2** [서둘러] hastily; hurriedly; in a hurry; in haste; in a flurry. ¶계단을 ~ 오르다[내리다] hurry upstairs[downstairs] // 밥을 ~ 먹다 take a hasty[hurried] meal / rush through one's meal / snatch a hurried meal.
후닥닥거리다 1 [열째게 행동하다] act quickly; keep quick action; be in a flurry. ¶후닥닥거리며 도망치다 run away in a flurry / bundle off[away] / beat a hasty retreat. **2** [급히 서두르다] be hurried; be in a hurry; be in hot haste; be hasty. ¶일을 빨리 끝내려고 ~ rush to get a job done in a hurry.
후대(後代) the next [coming / oncoming] generation; [후세] after[coming] age. ¶창립자의 정신을 ~에 전하다 hand down the founder's spirit to future generations[posterity] // 그의 이름은 ~에까지 남을 것이다 His name will go down in history.
후대(厚待) a warm[cordial / hearty] reception; kind[hospitable] treatment; hospitality. ¶~를 받다 be kindly treated / be received warmly[cordially] / be accorded a cordial reception // 체재 시의 ~에 대하여 깊이 감사드립니다 Many thanks for the hospitality you showed me during my stay. **후대하다** give a warm[cordial] reception (to a person); receive (a person) warmly.
후덕하다(厚德−) virtuous; of high virtue.
후두(後頭) the back (part) of the head; [생] the occiput (*pl.* ~s, -pita).
● **후두골** the occipital (bone). **후두부** [생] the back part of the head; the occipital region. **후두엽** the occipital lobe.
후두(喉頭) the larynx (*pl.* ~es, larynges). ¶~의 laryngeal.
● **후두개** the epiglottis. **후두암** cancer of the larynx. **후두염** laryngitis.
후두두 in large drops; scatteringly; sprinklingly; with a clatter[patter]; pattering. ¶비가 ~ 내리기 시작했다 The rain has begun to sprinkle. / The rain has begun to fall in large drops.
후드 [두건] a hood. ¶~가 달린 오버 an over-

후들거리다 coat with a hood.∥~를 쓴 남자 a man with his head hooded∥~를 쓰다 put on a hood.

후들거리다 tremble; quiver; quake; shake; shiver. ¶무릎이 후들거렸다 My knees shook [were about to give away]. / I felt wobbly about the knees.

후들후들 tremblingly; shiveringly. ¶~ 떨다 tremble all over[like an aspen leaf] / shiver like a jelly / (구어) be all of[in] a tremble∥추워서 ~ 떨다 shiver with[from] (the) cold / quiver from (the) cold∥다리가 ~ 떨렸다 My legs trembled. **후들후들하다** tremble; quiver.

후딱 quickly; rapidly; nimbly; agilely; alertly; (as) quick as thought. ¶~ 해치우다 finish (one's work) quickly / dispatch (one's work) / make short work of (a thing / a person)∥~ 일어서다 rise quickly[nimbly] from one's seat / spring[jump / get up] to one's feet∥~ 다녀오다 do an errand in no time at all.

후딱후딱 all quickly[rapidly / with dispatch / with alacrity]. ¶일을 ~ 해치우다 finish up one's work briskly.

후락(朽落) [썩음] deterioration; decay; [퇴색] fading. **후락하다** [썩다] deteriorate; decay; molder (away). [퇴색하다] fade; lose color.

후레아들 an ill-bred fellow. ⇨후레자식

후레자식(-子息) an ill-bred[ill-mannered] fellow; a boor; a clown.

후려치다 give (a person) a sound thrashing [good licking]; hit (a person) hard; (속어) tan (a person's) hide (good). ¶상대의 칼끝을 ~ knock away one's opponent's sword∥갑자기 그가 지팡이로 내 다리를 후려쳤다 Suddenly he swept my feet out from under me with a stick.

후련하다 (feel) relieved; (feel one's mind) unburdened. ¶후련해지다 feel heartily gratified[satisfied]∥할 말을 다 하고 나니 가슴속이 후련했다 After I had said my say I felt my mind unburdened[as if a burden had been lifted off my mind]. / Now (that) I have had my say, I feel the easier for it.∥그가 단념했다는 말을 듣고 나는 속이 후련해졌다 I was delighted to learn that he'd given up.

후렴(後斂) (노래의) a burden; a refrain.

후루루 [호각 소리] whistling. **후루루하다** whistle; pipe.

후루룩 1 [나는 소리] flap-flap; with a flutter. 2 [들이마시는 소리] slurping; sipping. ¶뜨거운 죽을 ~ 마시다 sip (rice) gruel boiled hot. **후루룩하다** (날짐승이 날개를) flap[flutter] (its wings). [들이마시다] sip[slurp] (gruel).

후륜(後輪) a rear wheel.

후리다 1 [몰다] hunt up[out]; round up; (그물로) net (fish / birds); catch (fish) in a net. ¶산돼지를 ~ hunt down[out] wild boars. 2 [모난 곳을] round[rub] off (the angles[corners / edges]); soften down (the edges). 3 [채다] snatch (away) (from / off); wrest (from); catch away; take by force. ¶손에서 핸드백을 ~ snatch a handbag from [out of] (a woman's) hand. 4 [유혹하다] seduce; wheedle; cajole; deceive; coax; [매혹하다] captivate; charm; fascinate; bewitch. ¶남자를 ~ captivate a man with wiles∥여자를 ~ seduce a woman.

후리질 fishing with a net; seining. **후리질하다** fish with seine; seine.

후리후리하다 tall and slender[lanky / lean]; gangling. ¶키가 후리후리한 미인 a beautiful girl, slender as a lily.

후림 [유혹] (an) allurement; (an) enticement; seduction; a beguiling trick; a lure. ¶~에 넘어가다 yield[succumb] to seduction / be nicely taken in / fall an easy victim to (another's) trick.

후릿그물 a seine; a dragnet; a seine[towing] net; a flue. ¶~을 당기다 drag a seine∥~로 물고기를 잡다 fish with a seine / seine.

후면(後面) [뒷쪽] the backside; [뒷면] the reverse (side); the wrong[back / other] side. ~ 동전의 ~ the tail[reverse] of a coin.

후무리다 filch; make free with (money); (미국 속어) sneak; pocket; make (something) one's own surreptitiously. ¶그는 거스름돈을 후무렸다 He pilfered[pocketed] the change. ∥그는 누군가가 빠뜨리고 간 담뱃갑을 무무렸다 He filched a packet of cigarettes somebody had left behind.

후문(後門) a back[rear] gate; a postern (gate); a back door.

후문(後聞) lingering rumors; anecdotes [stories / rumors] that are spread after the event.

후물거리다 mumble.

후물림(後-) (a thing) handed down (from one's elder brother); a hand-me-down.

후미 an inlet; a bay; (영) a creek; (작은 후미) a cove. ¶육지로 깊이 들어간 ~ an arm of the sea running deep into the land / a fiord [fjord]∥그곳은 ~를 이루고 있다 The place forms an inlet.

후미(後尾) the rear; the tail; the stern(선미); (행렬 등의) the tail end. ¶~ 경호 the rear guard∥~의 back / (선미의) aft∥행렬의 ~에 붙다 be at the end of a procession / bring up the rear.

후미지다 1 [물굽이가] deeply indented; penetrated (far into the land); deep (into the land). ¶해안의 후미진 곳 a recess in the shoreline∥깊이 후미진 만 a landlocked bay. 2 [깊숙하다] sequestered; secluded; retired; unfrequented; lonely. ¶후미진 곳 a recess / a nook / a quiet, secluded place / an out-of-the-way place∥후미진 산속 the recess of a mountain / a mountain recess.

후박(厚薄) [두께의] (relative) thickness [thinness]; [정도 등의] (relative) generosity [partiality]. ¶~ 없이 impartially / without partiality[prejudice].

후박하다(厚朴-) generous; warmhearted; liberal. ¶인심이 ~ be liberal / have an open hand / be generous.

후반(後半) the latter half; the second half. ¶19세기 ~에 in the latter half of the 19th century / late in the 19th century.
●**후반기** the second half of the year[term].
후반전 the second half of the game.

후발(後發) ¶~ 그룹이 2주일 후에 도착했다 The group that started later arrived in two weeks.∥그 회사는 ~ 메이커지만 기술은 앞선다 That manufacturer got into the business late, but is technically advanced.
●**후발대** a backup group[party].

후방(後方) [뒷쪽; 군] the home[civilian] front; rear service. ¶~에 in[at] the rear / at the back / behind∥~의 rear / back / backward∥~에서 적을 공격하다 en-

gage [attack] the enemy in the rear [from behind] ∥ ~을 교란시키다 harass the rear (guards) ∥ ~을 지키다 back up the fighting forces.
● **후방 근무** rear service (at the base); duties in the rear [behind the (battle) line / on the home front(본국의)]. **후방 부대** troops in the rear.

후배(後輩) 〔경험·나이가 뒤진 사람〕 younger men; the younger generation; (one's) junior(▶ junior는 단순히 연하의 사람이나 하급자를 뜻할 뿐, 우리말의 「후배」가 가지는 서열 의식을 전혀 나타내고 있지 않음. 영어에는 「후배」에 꼭 들어맞는 말이 없음). ¶**학교** ~ one's junior in school ∥ 대학에서 나는 그보다 2년 ~였다 He was my senior by two years at the university. ∥ 최상급 학생들은 ~들에게 으스댔다 The upperclassmen lorded it over the underclassmen [younger students].

후배주(後配株) 〔증권〕 a deferred stock [share].

후배지(後背地) a hinterland.

후보(後報) a later report [dispatch]; further information; later [further] news. ¶~를 기다리고 있다 The report remains to be confirmed. / We are in expectation of further details.

후보(候補) 〔입후보함〕 (미) candidacy; (영) candidature; a candidate(사람); (운동 팀의) substitution. ¶(비)공인 ~ an (un)official candidate ∥ 당선 [낙선] ~ a successful [defeated] candidate ∥ 만년 ~ a permanent candidate ∥ 차기 시장 ~ a candidate in the next mayoral election ∥ 입상 ~의 작품 works under consideration for awards [being considered for prize] ∥ 위원장의 ~를 사퇴한다 withdraw [stand down] as a candidate for the chairmanship ∥ ~로 나서다 (미) run for / (영) stand for ∥ 그는 학장 후계자로서 첫째 ~다 He is the most likely candidate to succeed the president of the university. ∥ 다음 대통령 선거에서는 누가 ~로 나설까요 Who will run for the presidency in the next election?
● **후보생** a cadet. ¶사관 ~ a cadet (officer) / a military cadet(육군) / a naval cadet(해군) / an aviation cadet(공군). **후보 선수** a reserve; a substitute (player). **후보자** a candidate (for the election); an applicant (for a position). ¶공천 ~ a recognized [an official / an authorized] candidate ∥ **대통령** ~ a candidate for president / a presidential candidate ∥ **신랑**[신부] ~ a prospective groom [bride] ∥ 유력한 ~ a strong candidate ∥ (정당이) 두 사람의 ~를 내세우다 put up two candidates ∥ ~를 지지 [후원]하다 support [back up / boost] a candidate ∥ ~의 난립을 막다 check random candidacy ∥ 총선거에서 10명의 ~가 나섰다 Ten candidates ran [stood] in the general election(▶ run은 (미), stand는 (영)).
후보지 a site proposed (for); a most suitable place (for). ¶어린이 공원의 ~ the place [site] proposed for the children's park.

후부(後部) the hind [back] part; the rear (end) (of a train); (배의) the stern; the quarter. ¶~에 at the rear ∥ 버스의 ~ the rear of a bus.

후분(後分) one's luck [fortune] in the latter part on one's life. ¶~이 좋다 be lucky late in life / be fortunate in one's latter [later] days.

후불(後拂) 〔뒤에 치름〕 deferred payment; future [after] payment.

후비다 dig up; grub; (귀·코 등을) pick. ¶귀를 ~ clean [pick] one's ears ∥ 콧구멍을 ~ pick one's nose ∥ 담뱃대를 ~ poke a pipe.

후비적거리다 keep scooping [scraping] out; keep gouging; (코 등을) keep picking. ¶코를 ~ keep picking one's nose.

후사(後事) 〔장래 일〕 future affairs; 〔사후의 일〕 affairs after one's death. ¶~를 맡기다 [부탁하다] entrust (another) with future affairs / ask (another) to look after one's affairs while one is away / give (another) the charge of the affairs after one's death ∥ 그는 죽기 전에 ~를 동생에게 부탁했다 Before he died, he asked his brother to look after his family and affairs after his death.

후사(後嗣) a successor (to); an inheritor; an heir(남자); an heiress(여자). ¶그에게는 ~가 없다 He has no heir to succeed him. ∥ 그 집은 ~가 끊어졌다 The family became extinct. / The family line broke.

후사(厚謝) 〔감사〕 hearty [sincere / warm] thanks; deep [heartfelt] gratitude; 〔사례〕 a handsome [liberal] recompense [reward]. **후사하다** recompense handsomely; thank heartily; reward warmly.

후산(後産) delivery of the afterbirth. **후산하다** bear the afterbirth [secundines].

후살이(後一) remarriage [a second marriage] (of a woman).

후생(厚生) **1** 〔국민 생활의 향상〕 the welfare [well-being] of people; public [social] welfare. **2** 〔건강의 증진〕 (promotion of) health.
● **후생 사업** public welfare work. **후생 시설** welfare facilities.

후생(後生) **1** 〔후진〕 juniors; younger fellows; young scholars [students]. **2** a descendant. ⇨ "후예 **3** 〔불〕 the life to come. ⇨ "내생

후세(後世) **1** 〔후대〕 after [coming / future] ages; posterity; future generations. ¶~의 귀감 a model for coming generations ∥ ~에 전해지다 go down [be handed down] to posterity (as a traitor) ∥ 그는 ~에 이름을 남길 것이다 He will be remembered forever. / His name will live in history. ∥ 그 이야기는 ~에까지 전해졌다 The story was handed down [transmitted] to posterity. ∥ 그의 공적은 ~에까지 기억될 것이다 His distinguished achievements will be remembered for years [in the ages] to come. **2** a better world. ⇨ "내세

후속(後續) succession. ¶~의 following / succeeding ∥ ~ 차에 주의 Be careful of the cars behind you. ∥ 선 채로 꼼짝 못하는 열차로부터 1마일 떨어진 곳에서 ~ 열차가 달려오고 있었다 The next train had closed in to only a mile from the one that had come to a standstill. **후속하다** succeed; follow.
● **후속 부대** rear guard; a rear party (육군); reinforcements. **후속 조치** (take) follow-up measures.

후손(後孫) a descendant; a scion(명문의); 〔집합적〕 posterity; progeny. ¶왕족의 ~ a scion of a royal stock ∥ …의 ~이다 be a descendant of … / come [be descended] from (the Yang family) ∥ ~이 없다 have no descendant(s) ∥ ~에게 전하다 hand down (a thing) to one's offspring.

후송(後送) evacuation; sending back (to the rear). 후송하다 send back (to the rear). ➔중상병은 후송되었다 Seriously wounded soldiers were sent back to the rear.
● 후송 병원 an evacuation hospital. 후송환자 an evacuated casualty.
후수(後手) [바둑·장기에서 뒤에 둠] playing as second mover (at a game of *baduk*(go)).
후술하다(後述−) say[mention / describe / touch upon] later. ¶상세한 것은 후술하는 부분을 참조하시오 Refer to the following section[See below] for further details.// 이 문제에 대해서는 후술하기로 한다 I will discuss[touch upon] this issue later.
후식(後食) (a) dessert. ⇨"디저트
후신(後身) 1 [다시 태어난 몸] a reincarnation. ¶나는 무엇의 ∼일까 I wonder what I am the reincarnation of. 2 [이전의 형태에서 변화한 것] a transformation. ¶이 대학은 옛날 전문학교의 ∼이다 This college used to be a vocational school.
후신경(嗅神經) an olfactory nerve.
후실(後室) a second wife. ⇨¹후처
● 후실 자식 a child born of the second wife.
후안무치하다(厚顔無恥−) shameless; unabashed; unblushing; barefaced; impudent; audacious. ¶후안무치한 사람 a brazen and unscrupulous fellow / one who is lost to shame / a shameless fellow.
후열(後列) the rear (rank / row); the back row. ¶그는 ∼ 오른쪽에서 다섯 번째입니다 He is the fifth person from the right in the back row.
후예(後裔) a descendant; a scion; offspring (*pl.* ∼(s)). ¶그는 귀족의 ∼다 He is descended from a noble family.// 그는 윤씨 가문의 직계 ∼다 He was directly descended[was in direct descent] from the Yun clan.
후원(後園) a back[rear] garden; (미) a backyard; a rear yard.
후원(後援) support; backing; patronage; assistance; (구어) boosting; help; aid; favor. ¶…의 ∼ 아래 with the support[help] of ... / supported[aided] by ... / under the auspices[aegis] of ... // ∼이 끊어져서 for lack of further reinforcements// 국민의 ∼을 얻다 have the people behind one's back. 후원하다 support; give[lend] support (to); be[stand] behind (a movement); give backing (to); back up; patronize; help (a person); aid; stand by (a person); sponsor. ¶많은 친구가 그를 후원했다 Many (of his) friends backed him (up)[gave him support].// 도지사가 그를 후원하고 있다 The prefectural governor is behind[supporting] him.// 그는 그 계획을 열렬히 후원하고 있다 He is backing up the project enthusiastically.
● 후원자 a backer; a supporter; a patron(▶ 특히 예술가 등의 재정적 후원자); a sponsor; (경기의) an enthusiast. ¶돈 많은 ∼ a rich patron / a patron with an ample person // 그녀의 뒤에는 K라는 ∼가 있다 She has a supporter in the person of Mr. K. 후원회 a supporters' association; an association of supporters (for). ¶K 씨의 ∼을 조직하다 form [organize] a society for the support of Mr. K.
후위(後衛) the rear guard; (운동 경기에서의) a back (player). ¶∼를 보다 play the back.
후유 with a sigh; whew! ¶그는 긴 한숨을 ∼ 내쉬었다 He gave a deep sigh (of relief).// 이제 살았다 Hallelujah! We are safe at last.
후유증(後遺症) 1 [의] a sequela (*pl.* ∼s); an aftereffect (of a disease / of an injury). ¶방사능의 ∼ the aftereffects[delayed effects] of radiation. 2 [비유] aftermath. ¶학원 분쟁의 ∼ the aftermath of[unpleasant consequences of / (구어) fallout from] a campus dispute[riot].
후은(厚恩) great favor[kindness]; great obligations; indebtedness. ¶∼을 입다 receive [meet with] great kindness / owe (a person) great obligations / lie under deep obligations (to) / be deeply[much] indebted (to).
후의(厚意) kind intentions; kindness; favor; good wishes[offices]; goodwill. ¶…의 ∼로 through the courtesy[good offices / kindness] of ... // ∼를 거절하다 reject (a person's) kind intentions / decline (a person's) kind offer // ∼에 감사드립니다 Thank you very much (for your kindness).// 그의 ∼를 기꺼이 받기로 작정했다 (문어) I decided to avail myself of his kindness. / (구어) I decided to take him up on his offer.
후의(厚誼) kindness; favor; patronage; [우정] warm[fast / close] friendship. ¶∼에 보답하다 repay (a person) for his kindness / do something for (a person's) favor // 끊임없는 ∼에 감사드립니다 Thank you (very much) for your continued favor[patronage / custom].
후인(後人) (집합적) posterity; future generations.
후일(後日) the future; a later day. ⇨"뒷날 ¶∼에 in (the) future / later on / some (other) day / some day or other // ∼로 미루다 postpone till a later date // ∼을 도모하다 provide for the future // 새 사실이 ∼ 밝혀졌다 New facts came to light later.// 그것은 ∼에 화를 남기는 일이 된다 That will lead to trouble later on[be the root of future trouble / be laying up trouble for the future].// ∼에 다시 이야기합시다 Let's have a talk another day.
● 후일담 a sequel (to a story); an aftermath. ¶사건의 ∼ a sequence[sequel] to the event.
후임(後任) [뒤에 맡은 임무] the duty left over by one's predecessor; [후임자] a successor (to a post); an incomer; a replacement. ¶…의 ∼으로 in succession to / to succeed (a person) / as (a) successor to / in place of / 남의 ∼이 되다 succeed another[to another's post] / succeed a person at a post[in a position] / sit in another's place / replace a person / take another's place // ∼으로 뽑히다 [지명되다] be elected[designated] to a vacancy // 그의 ∼은 손 씨이다 Mr. Son will succeed[replace] him in his post. Mr. Son will fill[succeed to] his place[post].// 호텔의 지배인으로 적격인 ∼을 찾지 못했다 We haven't found a suitable person to take over the management of the hotel.// 그는 최 씨를 황 씨의 ∼으로 했다 He put Mr. Choe in Mr. Hwang's place.// 그는 한 씨의 퇴진을 획책하고 자기가 그 ∼이 되었다 He engineered Mr. Han's downfall and then took over his position.
● 후임자 a successor.
후자(後者) the latter. ¶∼의 경우에는 in the latter case // 전자와 ∼ the former and the

latter // 전자는 …, ~는 … the one [former] … while the other [latter] … // 전자가 ~보다 낫다 The former is better than the latter. // ~의 경우, 사태는 우리에게 상당히 불리해질 것이다 In the latter case, things will become pretty unfavorable for us. // 캐나다와 미국은 북미 대륙에 있으며, 전자는 ~의 북쪽에 있다 Canada and the United States are in North America; the former lies north of the latter.

후작(侯爵) a marquis; a marquess.
● 후작 부인 a marchioness.

후장(後場) [증권] the afternoon session [market / sale].

후조(候鳥) a migratory bird. ⇨ 철새

후줄근하다 (wet and) limp; flaccid; a little soggy. ¶후줄근하다 become limp / droop / flap // 후줄근한 옷차림을 하고 있다 be sloppily dressed.

후진(後陣) [예비대] reserves; reserve troops [forces]; troops held in reserve; [후위] a rear guard.

후진(後進) 1 [후배] a junior; a younger man [fellow]; [집합적] the rising [younger] generation. ¶~의 길을 막다 block [check] the promotion of one's juniors // ~을 가르다 train the younger [next] generation // ~을 돌보다 look after [be helpful to] one's juniors // ~에게 길을 터 주다 give younger men a chance / create vacancies for others pushing up // ~을 위한 길을 열어 주기 (in order) to facilitate the promotion of younger men / to open the way for one's juniors // ~을 위해 용퇴하다 resign in favor of one's juniors / resign to open the way for the promotion of one's juniors // 그는 ~에게 길을 열어 주기 위해 용퇴했다 He resigned to make way for younger men.
2 [미발달] underdevelopment; backwardness; lagging (behind). ¶문화적 ~ cultural backwardness / a cultural lag(지체).
3 [후퇴] backing; backward motion; retreat; [해] sternway. ¶전속 ~ [구령] Back full! 후진하다 back (away from); retrocede; (배가) go [move] astern; make sternway. // 차가 후진했다 The car backed up. // 배가 후진했다 The ship moved astern.
● 후진국 a backward country [nation]; a less developed country; an underdeveloped country. 후진성 backwardness(민족 등의). ¶~을 탈피하다 emerge from backwardness.

후처(後妻) a second wife. ¶~를 얻다 [맞다] marry a second wife // ~로 맞아들이다 take (a woman) for [as] a second wife.

후천성(後天性) ¶~의 postnatal / acquired.
● 후천성 면역 결핍증 [의] acquired immune deficiency syndrome(약어 AIDS).

후천적(後天的) a posteriori; acquired (immunity); learned (behavior pattern). ¶~으로 a posteriori // 성격은 ~으로 형성된다 You can form your own personal character in the course of your lifetime.

후추 pepper; black pepper. ¶~를 치다 sprinkle pepper on / pepper (a dish).
● 후춧가루 ground pepper.

후취(後娶) a second marriage. ⇨ 재취

후치사(後置詞) [언] a postposition.

후탈(後頉) 1 later complications of a disease.
2 after-trouble. ⇨ 뒷탈

후텁지근하다 sultry; sticky; stuffy. ¶오늘 밤은 몹시 ~ It is very sultry [hot and humid] tonight.

후퇴(後退) 1 [뒤로 물러남] backdown; (a) retreat; retrocession; regress; regression; retrogression; withdrawal; retirement; falling back; backdown. ¶경기의 ~ (a) recession // 작전상 [전략적] ~ a strategic retreat // ~ 중이다 be in retreat / be on the run. 후퇴하다 retreat; go [fall] back; back (away); retrocede; recede; retrograde; backtrack; (배가) drop [move / go] astern. ¶서둘러 ~ beat a hasty retreat // 질서 정연하게 [무질서하게] ~ retreat in good order [in disorder]. 2 [건] setback.
● 후퇴 명령 an order [a signal] to retreat.

후편(後便) 1 the backside. ⇨ 뒤쪽 2 [나중 인편] a later messenger; [나중 차편] (on) a later train.

후편(後篇) [후반] the latter part (of a book); the concluding part; [속편] a sequel (to); (전편에 대해) the second volume.

후하다(厚一) 1 (인심 · 인정이) kind (hearted-); tender (hearted); warm (hearted); hearty; cordial; hospitable; friendly; (보수 · 대우 등이) generous; lenient; liberal; magnanimous; handsome; openhanded. ¶후한 보수 a generous [rich] reward [recompense] // 마음이 후한 사람 a kindhearted [tenderhearted / softhearted] person / a kindly soul // 후한 대접 warm [cordial / hospitable] treatment [reception] / warm hospitality // 후한 선물 a handsome present // 돈에 ~ be liberal of [generous with] one's money // 점수가 ~ be liberal [generous] in marking (examination) papers / be an easy grader // 후하게 사례하다 reward (a person) handsomely // 분량을 후하게 주다 give a good measure.
2 thick. ⇨ 두껍다

후학(後學) 1 [후진 학자] a junior scholar. 2 [후일의 참고] future information [reference]. ¶~을 위하여 for one's future information [edification] / for one's future benefit / for future use [reference] // ~을 위하여 저의 어디가 나빴는지 가르쳐 주십시오 Just for future reference, I'd like to know what I've done wrong.

후항(後項) 1 [뒤에 적힌 조항] the succeeding clause; the latter item. 2 [수] the consequent; the latter term.

후환(後患) future troubles. ¶~이 두려워 for fear of future troubles // ~을 없애다 get rid of [remove] the source of all possible troubles // ~이 두려워서 아무도 피해를 신고하지 않는다 No one reports the damage for fear of the consequences [of reprisals]. // 그를 없애지 않으면 ~이 될 것이다 If you do not remove him, it will go ill with you.

후회(後悔) (a) repentance; (a) regret; penitence; remorse; contrition; compunction. 후회하다 repent (of); regret; be sorry (for); be penitent [repentant] (for); feel regret (for); feel remorse (for). ¶후회하여 with regret / with penitence // 게을렀던 것을 ~ repent (of) one's idleness // 과거의 잘못을 ~ regret one's past mistakes // 쓰라려게 ~ regret [repent] bitterly // 나중에 후회하지 않도록 지금 조심해야 한다 You'd better be careful now so that you won't [don't] have to be sorry later. // 그런 짓을 하면 나중에 후회한다 You will regret it later if you do such a thing. // 나중에 후회하지 않도록 최선을 다해

라 Do your best so that you won't regret it afterwards. // 이렇게 낡은 집을 산 일을 후회한다 I regret buying such an old house as this. // 후회해 봤자 이젠 너무 늦다 It is too late now for regrets. // 교사가 된 것을 후회한 적은 없다 I have never regretted being a teacher. // 후회했어도 소용없었다 I repented too late. / It was too late for me to be sorry.

후후 blowing and blowing. ⇨ 호호¹
후후년(後後年) the year after next. ⇨ 내후년
훅¹ (권투) a hook. ¶상대의 턱에 레프트 ~을 먹이다 deliver[let go] a left hook to the opponent's jaw.
훅² 1 [들이마시는 소리] with a sip[slurp]; at a gulp[draft / draught]. ¶국을 ~ 들이마시다 slurp up[gulp down] soup. 2 [부는 소리] with a whiff[puff]. ¶촛불을 ~ 불어 끄다 whiff[puff] out a candlelight[candle] / 성냥불을 ~ 불어 끄다 blow out a burning match // 그녀는 담배 연기를 ~ 하고 내뿜었다 She blew[puffed] out a cloud of cigarette smoke. // 그는 촛불을 ~ 불어 껐다 He blew out the candle in one long breath.
훈계(訓戒) (an) admonition; exhortation; a lecture; [타이러 주의시킴] caution; warning. ¶감독 불충분으로 ~ 처분을 받다 be given warning for careless supervision // 여러 차례의 ~에도 불구하고 그는 학교에 지각하는 일이 많았다 Though he had been admonished over and over again[In spite of repeated admonitions], he was often late for school.
훈계하다 admonish[exhort] (a person to do something); caution[warn] (a person against errors). ¶선생님은 학생들에게 위험한 놀이를 즉각 중지하도록 훈계했다 The teacher warned[told] the pupils to stop their dangerous game immediately.
  ●**훈계 방면** release with a warning. ⇨ 훈방
훈공(動功) distinguished[conspicuous] services; meritorious deeds; merits; exploits (of war). ¶혁혁한 ~ brilliant exploits // ~을 세우다 render distinguished services (to the state) / distinguish oneself (in) / serve with distinction / win honorable distinctions // 그는 훌륭한 ~을 세우되고 개선했다 He returned in triumph after his brilliant exploits[with many brilliant exploits to his credit]. // ~에 의해 훈장이 수여되었다 He was decorated in recognition of his distinguished services.
훈기(薰氣) 1 [훈훈한 기운] warm air; heat. ¶몸의 ~ body heat / human warmth // ~ 있는 방 a warm room // 난로는 ~라고 없었다 The fireplace gave out no heat. 2 influence. ⇨ 훈김²
훈김(薰-) 1 [훈기] warm fumes[vapor / steam]. 2 [세력] influence; power; strength; clout. ¶아버지 ~으로 출세하다 rise in the world through one's father's influence.
훈도(薰陶) [훈련] discipline; training; [교육] education; instruction; tuition. ¶선생님의 적절한 ~를 받아서 under a teacher's wise guidance // 장 선생님의 ~를 받았다 I studied under Mr. Jang. **훈도하다** discipline; train; instruct; educate.
훈독(訓讀) the Korean translation of a Chinese character. **훈독하다** read Chinese characters in their Korean translation.
훈등(勳等) the order of merit.
훈련(訓練) training; (a) drill; practice; exercise; (a) discipline; schooling. ¶자기 ~ self-discipline // 맹 ~ hard training // 제식(制式) ~ close-order drill // 화재 대피 [소방] ~ a fire drill // 직업 ~ professional[job] training // ~ 부족의 ill-trained // 배팅의 특별 ~을 받다 be given special training[instruction] in batting // ~을 받다 be trained[disciplined] (in) / train (for) / undergo training[discipline] / get training // ~ 중이다 be under [in] training // 그녀는 간호사가 되는 ~을 받았다 She was trained[received training] as a nurse. // 테이프 청취로 프랑스 어 듣기 ~을 하시오 Improve your aural comprehension of French by listening to tapes. **훈련하다** train; drill; exercise; discipline; school. ¶군대를 ~ drill troops // 무엇인가에 숙달되려면 매일 훈련할 필요가 있다 It requires daily practice to make progress in something. →¶ 잘 훈련된 well-trained[-disciplined] // 잘 훈련된 개 a well-trained dog.
  ●**훈련 교관** [군] a drillmaster. **훈련 교본** a drill book[manual] (for the infantry); a training manual. **훈련소** a training school [station / institute / center]. ¶육군 신병 ~ an army recruit[recruits] training center / an army training camp for recruits. **훈련장** a training ground[field].
훈령(訓令) instructions; an (official) order; a directive. ¶~을 내리다 give[issue] instructions[an order] // 본국 정부에 ~을 요청하다 ask for instructions from the home Government. **훈령하다** instruct; give[issue] instructions.
  ●**훈령 전보** telegraphic instructions. **훈령집** a directory.
훈민정음(訓民正音) [한글] Hunminjeongeum; the Korean script.
훈방(訓放) release with a warning. **훈방하다** dismiss (a person) with a caution. ¶경찰은 그를 훈방했다 The police dismissed him with a caution.
훈사(訓辭) an admonitory[exhortative] address (to students, to one's subordinates, etc.). ¶졸업식에서의 총장의 ~ the principal's address on a commencement day // ~를 하다 address[speak to] students.
훈수(訓手) (장기·바둑의) help from an outsider; a hint; a tip. ¶~ 없다 No help from the outsiders! **훈수하다** help from the side (with); give a hint[tip] (on). ¶장기 ~ help (a person) with a move in *janggi*(chess).
  ●**훈수꾼** kibitzer.
훈시(訓示) [훈계] instruction; admonition; exhortation; counsel; lecture; [훈사(訓辭)] an admonitory speech[address]; (an address of) instructions; (공무상의) official instructions; a directive. ¶교장 선생님은 학생들에게 ~를 하셨다 The principal gave the students instructions (in his address). **훈시하다** instruct; admonish; exhort; counsel; give (a person) counsel; give an address of instructions; make an admonitory speech; give[issue] official instructions; give a directive.
훈육(訓育) (moral) education; educative instruction; discipline. ¶~상의 disciplinary / educational. **훈육하다** instruct; train; discipline.
  ●**훈육 주임** a teacher in charge of moral training.
훈장(訓長) a (village) schoolmaster; a

teacher; an instructor.
훈장(勳章) a decoration; an order(▶ decoration은 훈장 그 자체를 가리키고, order는 훈장의 명칭 앞에 붙여 써서 수장자(受章者)의 한 사람이 되었다는 뜻을 내포함); a medal. ¶국민 ~ the Order of National Service Merit∥~을 달다[차다] wear a decoration∥~을 타다 be decorated / have an order conferred upon (one)∥장군은 병사의 가슴에 ~을 달아 주었다 The general pinned a decoration on the breast of the soldier.∥그는 공훈을 세우고 ~을 받았다 He was awarded[decorated with] a medal for distinguished service.
훈제(燻製) smoking. ¶~의 smoked / smoke-dried / bloated. **훈제하다** smoke; bloat; kipper; dry (fish) in the smoke.
● **훈제소 / 훈제실** a smokehouse. **훈제 연어** smoked salmon. **훈제품** smoked fish [meat].
훈 족(一族) the Huns; the Hun tribes.
훈증(燻蒸) fumigation. **훈증하다** fumigate; smoke. ¶황으로 ~ sulfur / sulfurize / fumigate (a room) with sulfur / smoke out (a sickroom).
● **훈증제** a fumigant.
훈풍(薫風) a light, balmy breeze; a summer breeze; a zephyr. ¶~이 부는 5월 May, with its fresh breezes.
훈화(訓話) (give) a moral discourse; an admonitory lecture. ¶지금부터 교장 선생님의 ~가 있겠습니다 The principal is going to speak to you.
훈훈하다(薫薫−) comfortably warm; nice and warm. ¶훈훈한 방 a nice and warm room∥훈훈한 감정 a tender feeling / (a) tender affection∥마음이 훈훈해지는 이야기 a heart-warming story∥그의 말을 듣고 있으면 마음이 훈훈해진다 Every time I listen to him, my heart is warmed[I feel a warm glow in my heart].∥그의 친절한 말에 마음이 훈훈해졌다 My heart was warmed[touched] by his kind words.
훌닦다 [몹시 나무라다] nag[snarl] (an); abuse[criticize / attack] (a person) severely; scold[reprimand / berate] vehemently; take[call / bring] (a person) to task. ¶훌닦아 세우다 give (a person) snuff.
훌떡 fairly; (removing it) completely; (turning a thing) inside out. ⇨²훌떡².³.⁴
훌떡훌떡 loosely; slipperily. ¶신이 ~ 벗어진다 My shoes keep slipping all the time. **훌떡하다** be apt to slip out; (one's shoes) slip all the time.
훌라 댄스 hula(-hula). ¶~를 추다 dance the hula.
훌라후프 a hula hoop; hula-hooping.
훌렁 (removing it) completely; (turning a thing) inside out; loosely. ⇨²훌랑
훌렁하다 loose; baggy; too large; loose-fitting [-bodied]. ¶훌렁한 바지 loose(-fitting) trousers.
훌륭하다 1 [멋지다] fine; handsome; nice; excellent; superb; splendid; brilliant; magnificent; grand. ¶훌륭한 선물 a wonderful present∥훌륭한 솜씨의 도기 pottery of excellent workmanship∥훌륭한 식사 an excellent dinner[meal]∥훌륭한 조처 a superb [an excellent] way of handling a matter∥훌륭한 복장을 한 여인 a well-dressed woman∥훌륭한 저택 a magnificent[fine] mansion∥그는 훌륭한 승리를 거두었다 He won a splendid victory.∥그는 훌륭한 선물을 내게 주었다 He gave me a wonderful present.∥맛이 훌륭합니다 It's delicious[very good]. **훌륭히** fine(ly); nicely; superbly; handsomely.
2 [(태도 등이) 당당하다] stately; imposing; commanding. ¶훌륭한 풍채 commanding presence / imposing appearance. **훌륭히** imposingly; stately; commandingly.
3 [존경할 만하다] honorable; respectable; [가치 있다] worthy; [떳떳하다] decent; presentable. ¶훌륭한 뜻 an honorable intention∥훌륭한 목적[업적] a worthy end[achievement]∥훌륭한 목표 a worthy objective∥훌륭한 일생을 보내다 lead a worthy[reputable] life∥그가 매우 훌륭한 사람이라고 생각하고 있다 I have a high opinion of him.∥그는 훌륭한 사람이다 He is a respectable person.∥모든 것이 훌륭했다 Everything was just perfect. **훌륭히** respectably; decently.
4 [칭찬할 만하다] admirable; praiseworthy; creditable; commendable. ¶훌륭한 글씨 admirable writing∥훌륭한 행위 a commendable[meritorious] act∥훌륭한 마음[태도] an admirable spirit[attitude]∥그의 용기는 ~ His courage is admirable.∥솜씨가 훌륭하십니다 Your performance does you credit. **훌륭히** admirably; creditably; commendably. ¶~ 해내다 carry something through admirably.
5 [고상하다] noble; lofty; high. ¶훌륭한 정신 a noble spirit∥훌륭한 인격자 a person of noble character. **훌륭히** nobly; loftily.
6 [위대하다] great; prominent; eminent. ¶훌륭한 학자 a great scholar∥훌륭한 예술가 a great[master] artist∥그는 훌륭한 학문적 업적을 남겼다 He left behind him outstanding academic achievements.∥그는 웅변가로서 ~ He is an excellent orator.∥그는 학력에서는 다른 사람들보다 ~ He excels[surpasses / is superior to] the others in scholastic ability[academically].∥수학에서는 그보다 훌륭한 사람은 없었다 He had no superior[rival / match] in mathematics. / He was unsurpassed in mathematics.∥그는 학자로서 훌륭했다 He was a great scholar.∥훌륭했어 Well done! / You've done it now.∥그것이 그의 훌륭한 점이다 That's where he is so great. **훌륭히** greatly; prominently; eminently.
7 [공명정대하다] fair; square; honest. ¶훌륭한 경기 fair play∥훌륭한 조치 a square deal. **훌륭히** fairly; honestly; squarely.
8 [충분하다] sufficient; good; [그럴 만하다] justifiable; warrantable; worthy. ¶훌륭한 이유 a good reason∥훌륭한 증거 sufficient evidence∥이 집은 내가 살기에 ~ This house is good enough for me to live in. **훌륭히** sufficiently; justifiably; warrantably.
훌리건 [극렬 스포츠 팬] a hooligan.
훌부시다 1 [깨끗이 씻다] rinse out; wash clean; wash off[out] well. ¶병을 ~ rinse out a bottle. 2 [죄다 먹다] eat up; eat (anything) clean; clean (the board).
훌쩍 1 [가볍게 날거나 뛰는 모양] lightly; [단번에 뛰는 모양] with[at] a jump[bound]; [재빨리 움직이는 모양] nimbly; quickly. ¶~ 말에 올라타다[말에서 내리다] spring on[off] the horse / swing into[from] the saddle∥담을 ~ 뛰어넘다 jump clean over the fence / fly over the fence at a bound∥그는 울타리를 ~ 뛰어넘었다 He hopped[jumped lightly]

훌쩍거리다

over the fence. ¶그는 ~ 말에 올라탔다 He lightly sprang onto[jumped on] the horse. **2** [단숨에 들이마시는 모양] at a gulp[draft / draught]; gulping; slurping; sipping; supping. ¶국을 ~ 들이마시다 drink[empty] (a bowl of) soup at a draft[one gulp] / gulp down soup.
3 [코를] sniffling; snivel(l)ing. ¶코를 ~ 들이마시다 sniffle / snivel.
4 [떠나가는 모양] aimlessly; without any definite purpose. ¶~ 나가다 go out with no definite purpose[destination] in mind // 집을 ~ 떠나다 leave one's house[home] aimlessly // 그는 자주 ~ 여행을 떠난다 He often goes on trips without any fixed itinerary. / 그는 이따금 ~ 찾아오곤 했다 Once in a while he used to pay us a casual call. / He used to drop in (on us) occasionally.

훌쩍거리다 1 [액체를 들이마시다] sip[sup / suck] (up); slurp (up); gulp down; [콧물을 들이마시다] sniffle; snivel. ¶국수를 훌쩍거리며 먹다 slurp up noodles // 그는 생각에 잠겨서 술을 훌쩍거리고 있었다 He was sipping liquor pensively. // 그는 감기에 걸려서 코를 훌쩍거리고 있다 He is sniffing[snivel(l)ing] with a cold. // 어린이들은 우유를 훌쩍거리며 마시고 있다 The children were slurping their milk. // 어린이는 코를 훌쩍거리고 있었다 The child kept sniffling.
2 [울다] snivel; sob; blubber; whine. ¶그 아이는 훌쩍거리며 집으로 돌아갔다 The child went home sobbing[in tears]. // 그는 훌쩍거리며 사과했다 He sobbed out an apology.

훌쩍훌쩍 1 (액체를) sipping repeatedly; with slurp after slurp; sucking away; [콧물을] sniffling; sniveling. ¶~ 마시다 drink (wine) by sips[in little sips] / drink in small gulps / sip (at) (wine) / drink thimblefuls of liquor. **훌쩍훌쩍하다** sip (up); sniffle. ⇨ 훌쩍거리다 **2** [우는 모양] weeping and sniffling away. ¶무엇 때문에 ~ 울고 있니 What are you sniveling about? **훌쩍훌쩍하다** snivel. ⇨ 훌쩍훌쩍₂

훌쭉하다 lank; lean; pointed. ⇨ 홀쭉하다 ¶밑이 훌쭉한 유리컵 a glass which is slender at the bottom // 볼이 ~ have hollow cheeks // 훌쭉해지다 lose much flesh / grow very thin.

훌훌 1 [나는 모양] fluttering(ly); lightly. ¶~ 날아가다 (a bird) fly away[off] / wing off / flutter away.
2 [뛰는 모양] with an easy jump; with leaps and bounds; nimbly. ¶재를 ~ 넘어가다 (dear) leap and bound over a pass[hill] // 개울을 ~ 뛰어넘다 skip[jump] across a stream with ease.
3 [던지는 모양·뿌리는 모양]. ¶짐짝을 ~ 내던지다 hurl[fling / toss] baggages lightly[with ease] // 씨앗을 ~ 뿌리다 scatter seeds.
4 [옷의 먼지 등을 터는 모양]. ¶옷의 먼지를 ~ 털다 dust one's clothes bustlingly / shake dust off one's clothes.
5 [옷 등을 벗어부치는 모양]. ¶옷을 ~ 벗다 throw[fling / shuffle / shuck] off one's clothes / slip one's clothes off.
6 [들이마시는 모양] with slurps. ¶죽을 ~ 마시다 slurp one's porridge
7 [불타는 모양] in flames; briskly. ¶~ 타다 blaze / flare.

훑다 1 (벼 등이) hackle; thrash; strip. ¶벼를 ~ hackle[thrash / thresh] rice // 뽕잎을 ~ strip off the leaves of a mulberry twig // 손으로 잡아 ~ draw[squeeze] (a thing) through one's hand // 훑어 내리다 hackle down // 그가 밀 이삭을 훑으면 밀알이 아래로 떨어졌다 As he stripped off the ears of wheat[stripped the wheat with his hands], the grains fell to the ground. **2** [제거하는] remove; scrub (off / away / out). ¶나뭇가지의 껍질을 ~ scrub away the bark of a twig // 생선 속을 ~ remove the guts from a fish / gut a fish. **3** look (a person) up and down; look over (the page). ⇨ 훑어보다

훑어보다 1 (위아래를) look (a person) up and down; stare[look hard] at (a person); survey[search / study] (a person's face); scrutinize[peruse] (a person's face). ¶남의 위아래를 ~ stare a person up and down / survey a person from head to foot // 남의 얼굴을 훑어보는 것은 실례다 It is rude[bad form] to look[stare] a person up and down. // 그가 내 얼굴을 자꾸 훑어봐서 무안했다 I was embarrassed because he kept surveying [searching / studying] my face. // 그는 나를 자세히 (위아래로) 훑어봤다 He measured me with his eyes. / He surveyed me from top to bottom. / He devoured me with his eyes.
2 [죽 살피다] look[go] over[through] (the page); pass an eye over (the manuscript); scan (a newspaper). ¶대강 ~ run one's eyes through (a book) / glance[run] (one's eyes) over (the papers) / skim over [through] (a letter) / dip into (a book) / give a hurried glance (to) // 책을 죽 ~ look through a book // 청구서[편지]를 죽 ~ look over a bill[letter] // 서류를 대충[쫙] ~ run one's eyes through[over] the papers // 그들은 시체를 찾기 위해 강바닥을 훑어보았다 They dragged the river bottom[the bottom of the river] for the dead body. // 그는 그녀를 죽 훑어보았다 His eyes swept over the woman. // 그는 신문을 죽 훑어보았다 He scanned[ran his eyes over] the newspaper.

훑이다 1 (벼 등이) be hackled[thrashed / threshed / stripped]. ¶잘 훑이지 않을 때는 hard to hackle[thrash / strip]. **2** [제거되다] be[get] removed; get scrubbed (off / away / out). **3** [빠지다·줄다] shrink; contract; get thin. ¶설사로 몸이 ~ get thin after a siege of watery diarrh(o)ea.

훔쳐보다 steal a glance[look] (at); look [glance] furtively (at). ¶슬쩍 ~ steal a glance at // 그는 옆 사람의 답안을 훔쳐봤다 He stole a glance[looked furtively] at the answer sheet of the student sitting next to him.

훔치다 1 [도둑질하다] steal (a thing from a person); pilfer[filch / purloin] (articles from a shop); make free with (another's possessions); (구어) lift; (속어) sneak; (속어) hook; (미국 속어) swipe. ¶훔친 물건 stolen goods // 남의 돈을 ~ pocket another person's money // 가게의 매상금을 ~ steal [filch] the store's receipts // 그는 메리의 지갑을 훔쳤다 He stole Mary's billfold. / He robbed Mary of her billfold. // 그는 동료의 돈을 훔쳤다 He stole some money from a fellow worker.
2 [닦다] wipe (off / out / up); swab; mop (up); [걸레질하다] scrub (a floor). ¶행주로 ~ dry (a dish) with a cloth // 걸레로 훔쳐 내

다 wipe up with a floorcloth // 먼지를 훔쳐 내다 wipe off the dust // 엎질러진 차를 ~ wipe up spilled[spilt] tea. **3** [도루하다] steal a base.

훔치적거리다 search[fumble] leisurely. ¶주머니를 ~ search[fumble around in] ones pocket leisurely.

훔켜잡다 grasp; clasp. ⇨'움켜잡다

훗날(後-) the future; a later day. ⇨='뒷날 ¶ ~에 in (the) future / later (on) / some (other) day // 그 화근을 남기지 leave evils to spring up in the future / sow seed of trouble for the future // 자세한 것은 ~ 말씀드리겠습니다 (언젠가) I will go into detail some other day. // ~ 회사로 찾아뵙겠습니다 (근일 중) I will call at your office one of these days. // 그는 ~을 기약하고 묵묵히 일하고 있다 (장래) He works on in silence, hoping for something better in the future.

훗배앓이(後-) complications following childbirth; afterpains.

훗일(後-) the aftermath of an event; future affairs. ⇨='뒷일

훗훗하다 uncomfortably warm; very warm [hot]; rather close.

훤칠하다 strapping; tall; (서술적) be high in stature; have a full well-developed figure. ¶훤칠한 여자 a strapping girl.

훤하다 1 [흐릿하게 밝다] dimly white; light; gray; dimly-lit. ¶훤한 하늘 a light sky // a dawning sky // 훤해지다 lighten / grow[get] light / turn gray / light up // 지금은 훤한 대낮이오 It is broad daylight now. // 동녘 하늘이 훤하며 밝아 오고 있다 The sky is growing light in the east. **2** open; clear (distinction); be familiar (with); fine-looking. ⇨='환하다·3·4·5

훨씬 fair; by far; a great deal; a lot; out[far] and away; by long[all] odds; by a long way; much (bigger, broader, etc.). ¶~ 좋은 물건 a much[far] better article // ~ 이전에 a long time[while] ago / long ago // 그보다 ~ 전에 long[a long time] before that // ~ 뒤에 와서 long afterward(s) // 무엇보다도 ~ 뛰어나다 be far and away[by far] the best of all. // 그녀는 생각보다는 ~ 미인이었다 She was a far more beautiful woman than I had expected. / She was even more beautiful than I had been led to expect. // 네가 그녀보다 ~ 아름답다 You are far more beautiful than she (is). // 어머님은 ~ 좋아지시고 있다 Mother is getting much better. // 이 책은 (다른 것보다) ~ 재미있다 This is by far the most interesting book (of them all). // 저는 아버지보다 솜씨가 ~ 못합니다 I am far behind my father in skill. // 지난번 보았을 때보다 ~ 자랐구나 You've really grown since I last saw you. // ~ 좋아졌다 It got markedly better. / It improved remarkably. // 음악의 재능에 있어서는 그녀는 우리보다 ~ 두드러져 있다 She is far above us in musical talent. // 이것이 ~ 길다 This is much longer (than that). // 둘 중에서 이것이 ~ 낫다 This is by far[far and away] the better of the two. (▶ far and away 가 뜻이 강함) // 너는 빨강을 입으면 ~ 돋보인다 You look much[even] better in red. // 그는 나보다 ~ 영리하다 He is a lot[a great deal / far] cleverer than I.

훨훨 in a blaze; (fan oneself) slowly and vigorously; with great flaps of the wings; (taking off) briskly. ⇨>활활

훼방(毁謗) **1** [방해] interruption; interference; intrusion; prevention; disturbance; trouble. **훼방하다** interfere with (a person); thwart; hinder; disturb; stand in (another's) way; put a spoke in (another's) wheel. **2** [비방] (a) slander; calumny; vilification; reprobation; defamation; (an) aspersion. **훼방하다** slander; calumniate; malign; reprobate; defame; asperse; speak ill of; fling mud at (a person).

훼방(을) 놓다[치다] interrupt; slander. ⇨="훼방하다(⇨훼방) ¶남의 계획을 ~ thwart a person's plan[design].

훼손(毁損) damage; (명예의) defamation of character. ¶명예 ~ a libel / defamation (of character) / a slander. **훼손하다** damage; injure; impair; spoil; compromise. ¶명예를 ~ defame / injure to a person's reputation. ➔¶그녀는 마약 사건에 연루되어 명성을 훼손시켰다 The narcotic case in which she was involved damaged her reputation.

휑댕그렁하다 hollow; empty; deserted; look bare[empty / hollow]. ¶집 안이 휑댕그렁했다 The house seemed deserted.

휑하다 1 [잘 알다] (서술적) be familiar (with); be well acquainted (with); be well [deeply] versed (in); be well posted (in); be at home (in). ¶이곳 지리에 ~ know the lay of the land around here // 문학에 ~ be well versed in literature. **2** hollow; empty. ⇨="휑댕그렁하다

휘 1 [바람 소리] whistling; with a puff[whiff]. ¶바람이 ~ 불었다 The wind was whistling [hissing / piping]. / There was a gust of wind. **2** [숨소리] with a puff[sigh]. ¶숨을 ~ 내쉬다 let out a long breath / puff away / 한숨을 쉬다 give a heavy sigh. **3** [둘러보는 모양] sweepingly. ¶좌중을 ~ 둘러보다 make a survey of the company.

휘(諱) [돌아간 높은 어른의 이름] a posthumous designation[name / title].

휘갈기다 (매 등을) give[whip / lash] (a person) a sound thrashing[good licking]; trail one's whip; hit hard; (글씨를) write hurriedly [hastily]; scribble; scrawl. ¶휘갈긴 편지 a scribbled note // 회초리로 등을 ~ lash (a person) on the back // 그는 종이에 주소를 휘갈겼다 He dashed off[hurriedly wrote] his address on a sheet of paper.

휘감기다 1 [감기어 붙다] twine[coil / wind] itself round; coil around; twist about; get wound[twisted] round. ¶담쟁이에 휘감긴 나무 a tree entwined with ivy // 울타리에 나팔꽃이 휘감기게 하다 entwine a morning glory around a fence // 덩굴이 나무에 휘감겨 있다 A vine is twisted[twined] around[about] the tree. **2** [달라붙다] cling[stick] to; hang on to; [얽히다] be caught in. ¶(기계의) 피대에 ~ be caught by[entangled in] the belt // 치맛자락이 발에 휘감겨서 걷기가 힘들다 I have trouble in walking with my skirt clinging to my legs.

휘감다 twine round; coil round; wind round [around]; entwine; tie[fasten] round. ¶뱀이 (친친) ~ wrap coils around (a prey) // 밧줄을 ~ wind a rope round (a thing) // 부러진 다리에 붕대를 ~ swathe broken limb in bandages // 뱀이 나뭇가지를 휘감았다 The snake wound itself around the stick. // 담쟁이덩굴이

휘갑치다

나무를 휘감고 있다 A vine has twined [coiled itself] around the tree. / The tree is entwined with a vine.∥굴욕감이 마음을 휘감고 떠나지 않았다 I could not drive away the feeling of humiliation from my mind.

휘갑치다 1 [가장자리를 꿰매다] hem (up); stoat; overcast; whipstitch. ¶손수건의 가장자리를 ~ hem a handkerchief. 2 [일을 잘 마무르다] wind up (one's work); settle (a matter); bring (a matter) to a settlement [finish]; round (a thing) off [out]. ¶집안 일을 ~ clear up one's household affairs. 3 [말막음하다] make it doubly sure so as not to raise any objection (to).

휘날리다 [나부끼다] wave; flutter; flap; fly; float; stream; (이름을) make (one's name) resound. ¶바람에 휘날리는 기 a streaming flag∥바람에 ~ flutter [wave / flag] in the wind∥명성을 천하에 ~ make a noise in the world / win [enjoy] a worldwide reputation.

휘늘어지다 hang (down); dangle; droop; trail. ¶땅에 닿을 듯 말 듯 휘늘어진 버들가지 drooping willow branches that almost sweep the ground∥그녀의 머리는 허리까지 휘늘어져 있다 Her hair hangs (down) to her waist.

휘다 1 [구부러지다] bend; curve; become bent [curved]; warp; [뒤틀리다] crook; buckle (up); [낭창낭창하다] be pliant [pliable]; be flexible [supple]; yield (압력에); (손가락·몸이) bend back (ward); lean backward (몸이). ¶잘 휘는 가지 a supple branch∥열을 받아 휜 판자 a board warped by heat∥가지가 휘도록 열매가 달린 나무 a tree overburdened [overbowed] with fruit∥열 때문에 재목이 휘었다 The heat has warped the timber.∥소년이 오르자 가지가 휘었다 The branch bent when the boy climbed on it.
2 [구부리다] bend; warp; curve; crook. ¶철사를 ~ curve a wire.
3 [휘어잡다] bend (a person) to one's will; force (a person) to give in; control (a person).

휘도(輝度) [물] brightness.

휘돌다 go [turn] round; circle (around); gyrate; whirl; wheel. ¶(배가) 갑(岬)을 double [(go) round] a cape∥연못을 한 바퀴 ~ go round a pond.

휘돌리다 turn; revolve (a wheel); spin; wheel; whirl; rotate.

휘두르다 1 [돌리다] brandish; flourish; wield; wave (about); throw about; swing (around); sway. ¶팔을 ~ throw one's arms about∥칼[창]을 ~ brandish [wield] a sword [spear]∥단도[곤봉]를 ~ brandish a dagger [club]∥채찍을 힘차게 ~ swish a whip∥권력을 ~ exercise [wield] one's power∥붓을 ~ drive a quill [pen]∥주먹을 휘둘러 위협하다 shake one's fist (at a person / in a person's face)∥그는 도끼를 휘둘렀다 He swung an ax around.∥그는 단도를 휘두르며 그녀에게 달려들었다 Brandishing a dagger, he dashed her.∥그는 정계에서 대단한 권력을 휘둘렀다 He wielded [exercised] enormous power in the political world.
2 [얼을 빼다] bewilder; upset; baffle; take (a person) aback.
3 [제 뜻대로 하다] turn [twist] (a person) round one's (little) finger; have (a person) at one's beck and call. ¶남에게 휘둘리다 be turned [twisted] around a person's (little)

finger / be at the mercy of a person∥아내에게 휘둘려 지내다 be tied to one's wife's apron strings∥나는 그녀에게 휘둘렸다 She twisted me around her little finger. / She did what she liked with me.∥그는 자기 마누라에게 휘둘리고 있다 He lets his wife lead him around by the nose.∥그는 아내를 휘두른다 He keeps his wife under his thumb.

휘둥그렇다 wide-eyed; pop-eyed; moon-eyed. ¶눈을 휘둥그렇게 뜨고 보다 stare wide-[bug-]eyed at (a person).

휘둥그레지다 open (one's eyes) wide; (미국속어) be pop-eyed. ¶눈이 휘둥그레져서 with wide eyes / with one's eyes wide open (in astonishment)∥놀라서 눈이 ~ stare [open one's eyes wide] with [in] wonder / be pop-eyed with alarm∥그들은 놀라서 눈이 휘둥그레졌다 Their eyes were popping with amazement.∥앵무새가 노래하기 시작하자 아이들은 눈이 휘둥그레졌다 When the parrot began to sing, the children stared at it in round-eyed wonder.

휘두루 [닥치는 대로] for general [all] purposes; for various uses. ¶~ 쓰이다 be used for general purposes / have various [wide] uses / be of wide [extensive] use.

휘뚝거리다 1 [흔들리다] shake; be shaken; be unsteady; be shaky; [비틀거리다] totter; wobble. ¶뾰족구두를 신고 ~ totter along on highheels∥책상이 휘뚝거려 글씨 쓰기가 어렵다 The table shakes so much that I cannot write. 2 [위태하여 마음을 놓을 수 없다] worry (oneself) (with); fidget (about); jitter (about); feel nervous [uneasy].

휘뚝휘뚝 in a tottering [shaking] manner; unsteadily. ¶~ 두서너 발 떼다 make a few tottering steps. ⇨ 휘뚝하다 shake; worry (oneself) (with). ⇨ **휘뚝거리다**

휘말다 1 [마구 휘감다] wind [twine / coil] (something) round carelessly. 2 [적셔서 더럽히다] make (one's clothes) wet and dirty; soil; stain. ¶바지를 휘말아 놓았다 I have got my pants all dirty.

휘말리다 1 [말리다] be rolled [wrapped] (up) in. 2 [휩쓸리다] be involved (in); be embroiled (on); (파도 등에) be engulfed; be swallowed up; be dragged in. ¶음모에 ~ be entangled in a plot / 전쟁에 휘말려 들다 be involved in a war / be drawn [dragged] into a war∥권력 싸움에 휘말려 들다 be caught up in a power struggle∥그 다섯 사람은 탁류에 휘말려 행방불명이 되었다 [실종되었다] The five men were swallowed up by the muddy stream and disappeared.

휘몰다 1 [말·차 등을 급히 몰다] hurry (up); hasten; drive fast; urge [spur] (a horse) on; whip up (a horse). ¶마차를 ~ hurry up [on] a carriage∥말을 ~ gallop a horse∥차를 ~ drive fast [hurry / hasten] (to a place) in a car∥차를 휘몰아 현장으로 달려가다 rush [hasten] to the scene in a car. 2 [가축·사냥감 등을 마구 몰다] drive; round up; chase (a fox); run (a hare) (down). ¶소 떼를 휘몰아 놓다 drive in cattle∥양을 목장으로 ~ drive sheep to a meadow.

휘몰아치다 (바람이) blow violently [boisterously]; blow hard (and strong); bluster; rage; rave; roar; (눈이) fall in whirls; fall thick and fast. ¶휘몰아지는 눈 a swirling snow / whirls of snow / a blizzard∥휘몰아

는 바람 a raging[roaring] wind // 폭풍우가 휘몰아치고 있다 A storm is raging.
휘묻이 layering; layerage. **휘묻이하다** lay (one's layer) (a tree).
휘발(揮發) volatilization. **휘발하다** volatilize. ¶휘발하기 쉬운 volatile.
● **휘발성** volatility. ¶~ 바니시 spirit varnish // ~ 용제(溶劑) a volatile solvent. **휘발유** gasoline. ⇨ 가솔린
휘선(揮線) [물] a bright line.
● **휘선 스펙트럼** bright-line spectrum.
휘슬 a whistle. ¶~을 불다 blow a whistle.
휘어들다 get[be] forced[squeeze / pushed] in; (사람이) come[work] (to); give in (to).
휘어잡다 1 [구부려 거머잡다] hold (a thing) bent[doubled up] in one's hand; grasp; take [catch / grab / clutch] hold of. ¶버들가지를 ~ hold willow branches in one's hand // 머리채를 휘어잡고 끌다 drag (a woman about the floor) by the hair.
2 [손아귀에 넣고 부리다] gain[win] (a person) over (to one's side); have (a person) under one's control; bend (a person) to one's will. ¶돈의 힘으로 ~ win (a person) over by money // 여자를 ~ control a woman at will // 부하를 ~ win over the hearts of men under one // 부인이 그를 휘어잡고 있다 His wife has him firmly under control. // 그는 부하를 완전히 휘어잡았다 He kept his men under tight control.
휘어지다 bend; be bent; be crooked; be pliant; be supple. ¶철사가 휘어졌다 A wire got bent[bents]. // 열로 판자가 휘어져 버렸다 The board (became) warped in the heat.
휘영청 (shine) bright(ly). ¶달이 ~ 밝다 The moon beams down.
휘우뚱 off balance. ¶~ 넘어지다 be (thrown) off one's balance. **휘우뚱하다** lose (one's) balance; be off one's balance.
휘장(揮帳) a curtain; a screen; hangings; (집합적) bunting.
휘장(徽章) a badge(모표·회원 표지 등); an emblem(표상); an insignia(소매·깃의); an ensign(군인). ¶~을 달다 [달고 있다] put on[bear / wear] a badge.
휘적거리다 swing (one's arms); sway (one's hand) to and fro. ¶팔을 휘적거리며 걷다 swing one's arms as one goes[walks].
휘적휘적 swinging (one's arms). ¶~ 걷다 swagger. **휘적휘적하다** swing (one's arms). ⇨ 휘적거리다
휘젓다 1 [뒤섞다] stir (up) (coffee); give (the porridge) a stir; beat up (cream); churn (milk). ¶스푼[숟가락]으로 ~ stir (one's tea / coffee) with a spoon // 커피에 설탕을 넣어 ~ stir sugar into one's coffee // 계란을 휘저어 거품이 일게 하다 whip[beat] an egg // 그는 스푼으로 커피를 휘저었다 He stirred his coffee with a spoon.
2 [흔들다] swing (one's arms). ¶팔을 휘저으며 걷다 swing one's arms as one goes [walks].
3 [어지럽게 하다] disturb; disarrange; upset; confuse; ruffle; ransack (a drawer); rummage [rout / root] (in a drawer). ¶마음의 평화를 ~ disturb the peace of mind // 그는 교실을 온통 휘저어 놓았다 He threw the whole class into disorder.
휘지다 be exhausted[worn out].
휘청거리다 1 [낭창거리다] be pliant[pliable / flexible / supple]. ¶버들가지는 잘 휘청거린다 Willow twigs are pliable. 2 [힘이 없어 흔들리다] be unsteady; reel; be shaky (on one's legs); be groggy(권투에서). ¶휘청거리는 unsteady / shambling / reeling / groggy / dotty / tottery // 세게 얻어맞고 ~ reel under a heavy blow // 휘청거리며 걷다 walk unsteadily [with unsteady steps] / shamble along // 병을 앓고 난 뒤에 다리가 좀 휘청거렸다 After my illness my legs were shaky[weak].
휘청휘청 [휘어져 흔들리는 모양] yielding; flexibly; pliantly; [가누지 못하는 모양] unsteadily; shakily; groggily; with an unsteady [ungainly] gait. ¶~ 걷다 shamble along / walk unsteadily / go with an unsteady gait. **휘청휘청하다** yield; be unsteady. ⇨ 휘청거리다
휘추리 a slender twig[sprig].
휘파람 a whistle. ¶~을 불다 whistle / give a whistle / whistle on one's fingers(손가락을 넣어서) // …을 ~ 으로 부르다 whistle for (a taxi) // ~ 을 불어 알리다 whistle by way of signal // ~ 을 불어 개를 부르다 whistle for a dog // 소년은 ~ 을 길게 불었다 The boy gave a long whistle. // 그는 그 멜로디를 ~ 으로 불었다 He whistled the tune. // 그녀가 수영복 차림으로 나타나자, 그는 희롱하는 ~ 을 불었다 He gave a wolf whistle when she appeared in a bathing suit.
휘하(麾下) troops under one's command; one's men. ¶~ 의 under one's command / under the banner (of) // ~ 에 모이다 rally round (a person) / join[follow] the banner (of) / enlist[gather together] under the banner (of).
휘호(揮毫) (글씨) (hand)writing; (그림) painting; drawing. **휘호하다** (글씨를) write; (그림을) draw; paint.
휘황찬란하다(輝煌燦爛-) brilliant; bright; radiant; dazzling; glittering; resplendent. ¶휘황찬란한 보석 a brilliant[radiant] jewel // 휘황찬란하게 조명된 무대 a highlighted stage // 휘황찬란한 전등 아래 under bright electric lights // 거리는 네온사인으로 휘황찬란했다 The street was blazing with (varicolored) neon signs. // 실내는 전등으로 휘황찬란했다 The room was brilliantly lighted with electricity. / The room was brightly lit by electric lamps.
휘황하다(輝煌-) brilliant; bright. ⇨ 휘황찬란하다
휘휘 round and round (about); in circles. ¶~ 감아 wind (a rope) round (a thing) // 곤봉을 ~ 내두르다 brandish a club // 단장을 ~ 휘두르다 brandish[flourish] a cane.
획 1 [빨리 돌아가는 모양] with a swerve; with a jerk; with a whirl; [갑자기] suddenly; abruptly; with a jerk; [재빨리] quickly. ¶~ 뒤돌아보다 turn right round / look round // ~ 열리다 fling [throw] open // ~ 둘러보다 see with a sweep of the eye // ~ 지나가다 pass quickly / flit (across the sky) // ~ 돌다 (방향을 바꾸어) turn round [around] / wheel about / whirl [spin] around // 그 사내아이는 ~ 둘러보고는 도망쳤다 The boy took one look around and took to his heels.
2 [바람 등이 세게] whizzing; whistling; with a whistle[whiz(z)]. ¶총알이 머리 위를 ~ 지나갔다 A bullet whistled[whizzed] past me.

휠체어

3 [힘껏] with full force; with all one's strength. ¶창을 ~ 던지다 hurl[dart] a spear∥그는 트럭에서 짐을 ~ 던졌다 He chucked the load off the truck.
휠체어 a wheelchair.
휩싸다 1 [감아 싸다] wrap (in); lap (in); tuck up (in). ¶홑이불로 어깨를 ~ tuck the bedcovers about one's shoulders / tuck the bedcovers in round one's shoulders∥망토로 몸을 ~ wrap oneself up in a cloak∥담요로 몸을 ~ envelop[roll] oneself in a blanket[rug]∥갓난아기를 포대기로 ~ wrap a baby in a baby blanket. 2 [온통 뒤덮다] cover (with); veil (in); shroud (in); mantle (in).
휩싸이다 1 [감겨 싸이다] be wrapped up (in); be bundled[swaddled] (in). ¶담요에 ~ be wrapped[tucked] up in a blanket. 2 [덮어 가려지다] be covered (with); be veiled [enveloped / shrouded] (in). ¶구름에 휩싸인 산꼭대기 mountaintops enveloped in clouds ∥안개에 ~ be enveloped[wrapped] in mist ∥불길에 ~ be enveloped in flames∥비밀에 ~ be shrouded[veiled] in mystery / be wrapped in a shroud of mystery.
휩쓸다 1 [일소하다] sweep away[off]; clear (away / off); clean out[away]; make a clean sweep (of); (병·재해 등이) sweep (over / through); [풍미하다] overwhelm; sway. ¶경기를 ~ sweep[win] all the games[matches / bouts] / win a sweeping victory∥판돈을 ~ sweep away[rake up] the money on the gambling table / sweep the board[deck]∥전 유럽을 ~ sweep over the whole Europe∥우리는 출전 팀을 모두 휩쓸었다 We beat all the other teams. / We won a sweeping victory over the other teams.∥우리는 적을 휩쓸었다 (구어) We licked all our opponents.
2 [설치다] overrun; rampage; rave[rage / ramp] about. ¶부랑배가 시내를 ~ Hoodlums tore the town up.
휩쓸리다 1 [모조리] be swept away[off]; [말려 들다] be involved[entangled] in; be drawn into. ¶인파에 ~ be swept along in the crowd / be caught up into the crowd∥물결에 ~ be swept away by the waves / be swallowed up by the waves∥권력 싸움의 와중에 ~ be caught up in a power struggle∥음모에 ~ be entangled[implicated] in a plot∥작은 보트가 파도에 휩쓸렸다 A small boat was swept off by the waves.∥나는 인파에 휩쓸려 들어갔다 I was drawn into the throng of people.∥그들은 전쟁에 휩쓸려 들어갔다 They were embroiled in the war.∥불어난 강물 때문에 다리가 휩쓸려 내려갔다 Bridges were washed[swept] away by the swollen river.
2 (설치는 힘에) be overrun; suffer a rampage.
휴가(休暇) a holiday; a vacation; time off; [말미] a leave of absence; (a) furlough. ¶여름 ~ the summer vacation[holidays]∥생리 ~ a special holiday for woman workers∥유급 ~ a paid holiday∥크리스마스 ~ the Christmas holidays∥특별 ~ a special leave∥짧은 ~ a short leave (from service)∥~ 중(에) during the vacation∥~ 때에 in vacation time∥~의 기한을 넘기다 outstay one's leave (of absence)∥~로 여행 중이다 be away on vacation / be vacationing (in the country)∥~로 바닷가에 가 있다 be vacationing[(미) holidaying] at the seaside∥~를 얻다 take a vacation / get[obtain / secure] a leave of absence / have a furlough / (미) take one's day off / (영) take a holiday∥~를 주다 grant (a person) a leave of absence[furlough]∥사흘 ~을 얻다 take [have] three days off∥~를 얻어 고향에 가 있다 be home on leave[furlough] / be home on vacation[for the vacation]∥~를 보내다 spend one's holiday[leave] (in the country) / vacation[(영) holiday] (in Korea)∥~를 마치고 돌아오다 come back from holiday∥산에서 1주간의 ~를 보내다 spend a one-week vacation in the mountains∥내일부터 ~다 Our vacation begins tomorrow.∥그는 지금 ~로 집에 있다 He is home on vacation [leave].∥나는 2주일의 ~를 얻었다 I took two weeks off.∥오늘은 ~를 얻었다 I took a day off today.∥그는 2개월의 ~를 얻었다 He got[was granted] two month's leave.∥1주일간 ~를 주셨으면 합니다 Would you please give me a week off?∥그들은 ~가 되어 모두 집에 돌아갔다 They are home on their vacation.∥그는 ~를 얻어 산으로 갔다 He took a vacation in the mountains.∥그녀는 ~로 어디가 가고 없었다 I found her away on vacation.∥~ 중에는 즐겁게 보냈다 I have had a pleasant holiday.∥~ 때 어디에 가십니까 Where are you going for the holiday(s)?

● **휴가원** a leave application. ¶~을 내다 send[hand] in one's leave application / apply for leave of absence.

휴간(休刊) suspension[discontinuation] of publication. ¶연중 무~이다 be issued all the year round / be issued daily throughout the year∥이 잡지는 ~ 중이다 This magazine has suspended publication. **휴간하다** suspend[discontinue] publication; stop issuing (a newspaper). ¶본지는 내일 휴간합니다 There will be no issue of this paper tomorrow.∥다음 주 호(號)는 휴간합니다 No issue next week. / Next week's issue will not appear.

● **휴간일** (신문의) a "no-issue" day; a newspaper holiday.

휴강(休講) no lecture (for the day). ¶L 교수 금일 ~ (게시) No class-Professor L. **휴강하다** give no lecture (for the day); absent oneself from school. ¶L 교수가 금일 휴강했다 Professor L was absent today.∥교수가 아파 3주간 휴강하게 되었다 There were no lectures[classes] for three weeks because the professor was sick.∥태풍 때문에 오늘은 전면 휴강하게 되었다 Because of the typhoon all the classes were canceled today.

휴게(休憩) (a) rest; a recess; a break; time-off; a time-out; [막간] (미) an intermission; (영) an interval. **휴게하다** rest; take a rest [recess]; take one's time off; take[have] a break.

● **휴게소** a resting place; a rest area. **휴게실** a resting[retiring] room; (호텔 등의) a lounge room; a lobby.

휴경지(休耕地) [농] land in fallow. ⇨**휴한지**
휴관(休館) closure (of a museum). ¶~이 되다 be closed (for the day)∥금일 ~ (게시) Closed today. **휴관하다** close (a museum). ¶미술관은 월요일에 휴관한다 The art museum is closed on Mondays.
휴교(休校) closure of a school. ¶오늘은 ~다

The school is closed [There are no classes] today. 휴교하다 close (a school) temporarily; be closed. ¶학교는 1개월간 휴교한다 School is closed for a month (beginning on March 15).

휴대(携帶) carrying. ¶총포의 ~는 금지되어 있다 The carrying of guns is prohibited. 휴대하다 carry; bring [take] (a lunch) with one; have (a thing) with one; equip oneself with (a camera); (미국 구어) pack (a gun). ¶무기를 ~ carry [be armed with] a weapon // 여행에 안내서를 ~ provide oneself with a guidebook to one's trip // 그는 큰 가방을 휴대하고 있었다 He was carrying a big bag. // 그는 큰돈을 휴대하고 있었다 He had a lot of money with him. // 그는 중요한 서류를 휴대하고 있었다 He was carrying important papers with him. // 이 사전은 휴대하기 편리하다 This dictionary is handy to carry. // 나는 지금 여권을 휴대하고 있지는 않습니다 I don't have my passport with [on] me. // 나는 마침 가위를 휴대하고 있었다 I happened to have scissors with me. // 현금을 휴대하는 것은 위험하다 It is dangerous to carry cash about with you [to carry cash on your person]. // 그 도둑은 흉기를 휴대하고 있지 않았다 The robber had [combat] no weapon with him.

● 휴대용 [관형어적] portable; hand; pocket; handy. ¶~ 녹음기 a portable recording machine // ~ 라디오 a portable radio // ~ 무선 전화기 a portable radiophone / (구어) a walkie-talkie // ~ 스테레오 카세트테이프 플레이어 a portable stereo cassette tape player // ~ 연료 pocket fuel / canned [(영) tinned] fuel / (군) fuel ration. 휴대 전화 / 휴대폰 a cellular [mobile] phone; a cellphone. 휴대품 one's personal effects [belongings]; hand luggage [(미) baggage]; (구어) one's things.

휴머니스트 [인문주의자] a humanist; [인도주의자] a humanitarian.

휴머니즘 [인문주의] humanism; [인도주의] humanitarianism.

휴머니티 humanity.

휴면(休眠) dormancy. ¶~ 중인 dormant; resting.
● 휴면기 a period of dormancy; a resting stage; diapause.

휴식(休息) (a) rest; repose; relaxation; a respite; (미) a breather. ¶중간 ~ an intermission / an interval / a recess // 10분간의 ~ a ten minutes' [ten-minute] break // 점심을 위한 1시간의 ~ an hour's recess for lunch // (회의 등이) ~에 들어가다 adjourn / (미) recess // 정오에 한 시간의 ~이 있다 We have an hour's recess at noon. 휴식하다 rest (oneself); take rest [respite / breather]; repose; relax. ¶잠시 ~ rest awhile [for a moment] / take a blow [short rest] // 충분히 ~ rest quite a long while / take a long [good] rest // 잠간 휴식합시다 Let's take a short break. / Let's have a short rest. / Let's take [have] a tea [coffee] break. // 충분히 휴식하셨습니까 Did you have a good rest? ➔ 휴식시키다 give (a person) a rest / rest.
● 휴식 시간 time to rest; a recess; a breathing time [spell]. ¶10분간의 ~ a 10 minute [ten minutes'] recess. 휴식처 a resting place; a place for refreshment.

휴양(休養) (a) rest; (미) a layoff; repose; relaxation; recreation; recuperation (병후의).
휴양하다 rest; take a rest; repose; relax; (병후에) recuperate; recruit (oneself). ¶(병으로) 1년간 ~ have a year's holiday to recruit [recuperate] (at) // 자네는 휴양하는 것이 좋겠다 You'd better have a rest.
● 휴양 시설 recreation facilities. 휴양지 a recreation center; a rest area; one's vacation spot.

휴업(休業) (점포 등의) suspension of business [operations]; closure; (회사·공장의) a shutdown. ¶~ 중인 공장 an idle factory // 금일 ~ (게시) Closed today. // 학교 [은행 / 관청]는 당일 ~ 이다 School [Banks / Government offices] are closed for the day. // 흡사 개점 ~ 상태다 The door is opened, but practically no business is done with. 휴업하다 (사람이) take a holiday; take a day off; (점포 등이) be closed (to business); suspend business (operations). ¶저 공장은 원료 부족으로 아직껏 휴업하고 있다 The factory still remains idle owing to want of raw materials. // 내일은 휴업합니다 This store will be closed tomorrow. // 당분간 휴업합니다 (게시) Closed for the present.
● 휴업일 a holiday; the day a shop is closed; a day off. ¶금일은 ~입니다 There is no business today.

휴일(休日) a holiday; a rest day; (비번 날) a day off; an off day. ¶법정 ~ a legal holiday // 은행 (영) a bank holiday // 임시 ~ a special holiday // 이틀 계속되는 ~ (have) two consecutive holidays / (have) two holidays in succession // ~ 기분으로 in a holiday mood [spirit / vein / atmosphere] // (밖에서) ~을 즐기는 사람 a holidaymaker / a holidayer // 매주 1회 ~을 주다 give a day off every week // ~을 이용하여 여행하다 go vacationing / go away for a holiday // 해안에서 ~을 보내다 spend a holiday at the seaside / spend a seaside holiday // 내일은 ~이다 We have a holiday tomorrow. / Tomorrow is a holiday. // 학교는 내일 ~ We have no school tomorrow. // 매주 수요일은 정기 ~입니다 We close the shop every Wednesday. // ~이라 그는 외출 중이다 He is out for a holiday. / It's a holiday and he has gone out. // 한 달에 ~이 다섯 번 있다 I have a day off five times [five days off] a month. // 그 가게는 일요일은 ~이다 The shop doesn't open on Sunday.
● 휴일 근무 holiday work. 휴일 여행 a holiday trip; (미) a vacation trip; (주말의) a weekend trip.

휴전(休電) suspension of power supply.
● 휴전일 a no-power day; (게시) No power supply day.

휴전(休戰) suspension [cessation] of hostilities; an armistice; a truce; a cease-fire. ¶전면적 [무장] ~ a general [an armed] truce // 중립국 ~ 감시단 the Neutral Nations Supervisory Commission for Armistice // ~ 상태를 유지하다 maintain a cease-fire // ~을 요구하다 ask for [call for] a truce [cease-fire] // 전 전선에 걸쳐 ~이 명령되었다 A cease-fire has been ordered on all fronts. // 2건의 ~ 위반이 있었다 There were two cases of truce violation. / Two incidents marred the cease-fire. 휴전하다 suspend [call off] hostilities; cease firing; conclude an armistice

휴정
(with); make a truce (with).
● **휴전선** a cease-fire[an armistice] line. **휴전 협정** a cease-fire agreement; the Armistice Agreement. **¶중대한 ~ 위반** a serious violation of the Armistice Agreement // **~을 체결하다** reach[arrive at / come to] a cease-fire agreement (with). **휴전 회담** a truce conference; truce[cease-fire] talks. **¶~을 개최하다** hold a truce conference / talk cease-fire (with).

휴정(休廷) recess[adjournment] of court. **¶토요일은 ~입니다** No court will be held on Saturday. **휴정하다** hold no court; adjourn the court (until). **¶5월 20일까지[1주일간] 휴정합니다** The court will adjourn[The court will be adjourned / The court will not sit] until May 20th[for a week].
● **휴정일** a non-judicial day; (라) a dies non (juridicus) (*pl.* dies nons, dies non juridici).

휴지(休止) a pause; a standstill; cessation; suspension; stoppage; discontinuance; (미국구어) a letup. **¶~ (악보 등의 지시)** (라) tacet! **/그 두 단어 사이에 보통 조금 ~를 둔다** We usually make a slight pause between those two words. // **교전국의 해외 무역은 거의 ~ 상태가 되었다** The seaborne trade of the belligerents has practically come to a standstill. **휴지하다** [중지하다] cease; pause; stop; suspend; discontinue; [멈추다] come to a standstill.

휴지(休紙) 1 [못 쓰는 종이] wastepaper; a scrap of paper; paper scraps. **¶~를 줍다** pick up wastepaper // **약속을 ~화하다** break one's word[promise] / go back on one's word[pledge] // **~가 되다[~화되다]** become wastepaper / be invalidated / become null (and void) // **그 서류[계약서]는 이제는 ~나 다름없다** The document[contract] is now no better than wastepaper[is a mere scrap of paper now]. **¶~를 함부로 버리지 말 것** Don't be a litterbug.
2 [뒤지] toilet[lavatory] paper[tissue]; a toilet roll(두루말이); [코 푸는 종이] paper for wiping the nose; a paper handkerchief. **¶~로 코를 풀다** blow one's nose on tissue paper.
● **휴지통** (미) a wastebasket; (영) a wastepaper basket.

휴직(休職) temporary retirement from office; (미) a layoff(단기의). **휴직하다** retire temporarily from office; [명을 받고] be put [placed] on the half-pay list(군인이); be laid off; be suspended from duty[office].

휴진(休診) suspension of medical examination. **¶금일 ~ (게시)** Office is closed today. / No consultations[appointments] today. / No office Hours Today. **휴진하다** accept[see] no patients[close the office] (for the day).

휴학(休學) a leave of absence from school; temporary absence from school. **¶동맹 ~** a strike of students / a school[college] strike // **3개월의 ~계를 내다** send in a notice of absence for three months // **그는 1년간의 ~계를 제출했다** He ask for a year's leave of absence from school. **휴학하다** withdraw [absent oneself] from school temporarily[for a time]. **¶오랫동안 휴학하고 있다** be long absent from school // **그는 병으로 6개월 동안 휴학하고 있다** He has been absent from school for six months because of illness. // **나는 군대에 가기 위해 휴학하였다** I took a leave of absence from university to join the army. / I took time off from university because of military service.
● **휴학생** a student who stays out of school temporarily.

휴한지(休閑地) 1 [농] land in fallow; fallow land; a fallow (ground). **¶~를 이용하다** make use of idle land. 2 vacant land. ⇨ **공지**(空地)

휴항(休航) suspension of a steamboat service. **휴항하다** suspend (its) steamboat service; (배가) be laid up.

휴화산(休火山) a dormant[a quiescent / an inactive] volcano. **¶그것은 ~이다** The volcano lies dormant[asleep].

휴회(休會) adjournment; a recess. **¶~ 직후의 국회** the post-recess National Assembly // **~ 중이다** be in recess / be out of session // **~를 선언하다** call[declare] a recess // **그 위원회는 ~ 중이다** That committee is in recess[is out of session]. // **국회는 연말연시의 자연 ~로 들어갔다** The National Assembly has entered its regular year-end recess. **휴회하다** adjourn (for a vacation); rise; take a recess; go into recess; recess. ➔**¶휴회되다** be adjourned / adjourn / go into recess // **회의는 다음 달까지 휴회되었다** The meeting was adjourned till next month.

흉 1 [흉터] a scar. **¶~이 있는 얼굴** a scarred face / a face with a scar / a face marked with wounds // **이마에 ~이 있다** have a scar on the forehead / one's forehead bears a scar // **~이 없어졌다. / The scar left no trace.** 2 [흠] a fault; a defect; a flaw; a blemish; a drawback. **¶~ 없는 사람은 없다** No one is free from faults. / There is no man but has some faults. / Nobody is perfect.

흉가(凶家) a house of ill[evil] omen; an ominous house; a haunted house.

흉계(凶計) a wicked[sinister] design; an evil scheme; a plot; a trick. **¶~를 꾸미다** devise wicked designs / hatch a plot / concoct tricks // **~에 빠지다** fall a victim to (another's) scheme.

흉골(胸骨) [생] the sternum (*pl.* ~s, -na); the breastbone. **¶~의** sternal.

흉곽(胸廓) the chest; the thorax (*pl.* ~es, races). **¶~의** thoracic / thoracal // **~이 넓다** [좁다] have a broad[narrow] chest.

흉금(胸襟) the bosom; the heart; the inner mind.
흉금을 털어놓다 unbosom oneself (to); open [lay bare] one's heart (to); take (a person) into one's confide (in); disclose one's innermost intention (to). **¶흉금을 털어놓고 이야기하다** talk without reserve / have a heart-to-heart talk (with) / have a frank chat (with) // **흉금을 털어놓고 이야기를 나누자** Let's have a heart-to-heart talk.

흉기(凶器) a murder[death / lethal / mortal / deadly / dangerous] weapon. **¶~를 지닌 강도** an armed rubber[burglar] // **~고 무장하고** armed with a deadly weapon // **자동차는 이따금 달리는 ~로 불린다** Cars are sometimes called deadly weapons on wheels.

흉내 (an) imitation; mimicry; apery; impersonation; (구어) a takeoff. **¶~를 내다** imitate / copy / ape / follow (another's example)

/ mimic / (구어) take off / (구어) do a take-off (of) / follow suit / take a leaf out of (a person's) book // 남의 목소리를 ~ 내다 mimic [feign] a person's voice / imitate [take off] the voice [tone] of a person // 그의 말씨를 ~ 내다 mimic a person's way of talking // 남의 걸음걸이를 ~를 내다 mimic a person's manner of walking / mimic the way a person walks // ~를 잘 낸다 be clever at mimicking (various sounds) // 앵무새는 사람의 말을 ~ 낸다 Parrots imitate human speech. // 그는 남의 ~를 잘 낸다 He is a clever mimic. / He is clever at imitating others [mimicking people]. / 그 배우는 여자를 잘 낸다 The actor plays the part of woman [imitates the movements of a woman] very well. // 그는 동물의 울음소리를 ~를 잘 낸다 He is good at mimicking [imitating] the cries [calls] of animals. / He mimics the cries of animals very well. // 그는 자기 아버지의 목소리를 ~ 냈다 He imitated his father's voice. // 그는 집오리의 울음소리를 ~ 내어 모두를 웃겼다 He made them by mimicking a duck's quack.
●**흉내쟁이** an imitator; a mimic; (구어) a copycat.
흉년(凶年) a bad year; a lean year; a year of bad [poor] harvest; a year of famine. ¶~이 들다 have a bad (rice) crop [harvest] / have a short crop [yield] (of rice) / be a bad year (for the rice crop).
흉년에 윤달(속담) Ill comes often on the back of worse.
흉노(匈奴) [역] the Huns.
흉몽(凶夢) an ominous dream; a dream of ill omen; an evil [ill-boding] dream; a nightmare. ¶~을 꾸다 dream an ominous dream / have (a) nightmare // ~에서 깨다 start from a nightmare.
흉문(凶聞) [부고] news of (a person's) death; [나쁜 소식] bad [dire / ill] news.
흉물(凶物) an evil [a treacherous] person; a deep one; a snake.
흉물스럽다(凶物-) be tricky; be sly; be wily; be crafty.
흉배(胸背) 1 [가슴과 등] breast and back. 2 [옛 관복의 표장] embroidered insignia on the breast and the back of an official robe.
흉벽(胸壁) 1 [흉곽의 외벽] walls of the chest. 2 [군] a breastwork. ⇨ 흉장
흉변(凶變) a calamity; a disaster; a tragic accident; (an) assassination(암살); murder(살인). ¶~을 당하다 meet with [suffer] a calamity [disaster] / get [be] assassinated [murdered]
흉보(凶報) [불길한 기별] bad [dire / ill] news; evil tidings; [부고] news of (a person's) death. ¶~를 전하다 break sad news (to his family).
흉보다 find fault with; pick out (another's) defects; speak ill of; run [cry / play] down; abuse; disparage; censure; criticize. ¶안 듣는 데서 흉보는 사람 a backbiter // 안 듣는 데서 ~ backbite (a person) / speak ill of (a person) behind his back [in his absence].
흉복(胸腹) [가슴과 배] chest and abdomen; breast and belly; [가슴의 복부] the phrenic area (between chest and abdomen).
흉부(胸部) [가슴] the chest; [생] the thorax (*pl.* ~es, thoraces); [동] the corselet. ¶~의 [생] thoracic // ~에 통증을 느끼다 feel a pain in the chest // (총알로) ~에 관통상을 입다 be shot through the breast.
●**흉부외과** chest [thoracic] surgery. **흉부 질환** a chest disease [complaint]; a trouble in the chest.
흉사(凶事) [불길한 일] an event of ill omen; [흉악한 일] an unfortunate incident; a tragic accident; a calamity; a disaster; a misfortune; [죽음] death. ¶잇달아 ~가 일어났다 One misfortune followed another. / Accidents occurred in quick succession.
흉상(凶相) [좋지 못한 생김] an evil physiognomy; [흉한 외모] (an) ugly [unsightly / unseemly] appearance; an evil countenance [face].
흉상(胸像) a bust.
흉식 호흡(胸式呼吸) thoracic respiration.
흉악범(凶惡犯) a brutal criminal; a vicious criminal.
흉악 범죄(凶惡犯罪) an atrocious crime; (문어) a heinous crime.
흉악하다(凶惡-) bad; wicked; heinous; villainous; atrocious; brutal; crude; ugly; unseemly. ¶가장 흉악한 범죄 a crime of the blackest dye.
흉어(凶漁) (have) a poor catch [haul]. ¶올해는 ~의 해였다 We have had a poor catch this year.
흉업다(凶-) ugly; unsightly; unseemly; indecent; awful; terrible. ¶보기에 ~ be (too) ugly [offensive] to look at // 색깔이 ~ The color is dreadful.
흉위(胸圍) the girth of one's chest; (여성의) one's bust measurement. ¶~를 재다 measure a person's chest / take a person's chest [bust] measurement // 그녀의 ~는 90 센티미터 된다 She measures 90 centimeters around the chest. / Her bust measurement is 90 centimeters.
흉일(凶日) an unlucky [evil] day; a black (-letter) day; an ill-starred day.
흉작(凶作) a bad [poor] harvest [crop]; a scanty harvest; a failure of crops. ¶~의 해 a lean year // 쌀농사의 ~ failure of the rice crop // 서리가 늦게 내렸기 때문에 사과가 ~이다 Owing to a late frost the apple crop turned out badly. // 금년은 쌀이 ~이다 The rice crop has turned out a failure this year. / The rice crop has failed this year. / We have had a short crop of rice this year. / This has been a bad year for the rice crop.
흉잡다 find fault with; pick [point] out (another's) defects; pick a hole in (another's) coat [character]; disparage.
흉잡히다 be found fault with; be spoken ill of; be picked on; be disparaged [criticized].
흉장(胸牆) [군] a breastwork; a parapet.
흉적(凶賊·兇賊) a thug; a brutal robber.
흉조(凶兆) an ill omen; an evil sign. ¶~다 bode ill [evil] (to / for).
흉중(胸中) [가슴속] one's bosom [mind / heart / feelings / thoughts / intentions]. ¶~에 간직하다 keep a matter to oneself / bury a matter deep in one's heart // ~을 털어놓다 bare one's innermost feelings // 남의 ~을 살피다 share a person's feelings / sympathize with a person // ~에 떠오르다 (사물이) enter [come across] one's mind / spring to mind / occur to one / (사람이) think of / hit upon (a plan) // 우리는 밤새 ~을 털어놓고 이야기

흉증 를 하였다 We had a heart-to-heart talk that lasted all through the night.

흉증(凶證) **1** an ill omen. ⇨ ⁼흉조 **2** [음흉함] slyness; craftiness; snakiness; insidiousness. ¶~을 부리다 use subtle tricks[treacherous measures] / act in a sly[snaky / treacherous] way.

흉추(胸椎) [생] a thoracic vertebra; (집합적) the thoracic vertebrae.

흉측하다(凶測-) (성질이) atrocious; heinous; brutal; (용모가) very ugly[crude]; bad-[ugly-]looking. ¶뱀은 움직이는 꼴이 흉측해서 싫습니다 I don't like snakes because the way they move is revolting.

흉탄(凶彈) a bullet shot by an assassin. ¶대통령은 ~에 쓰러졌다 The president was assassinated. / (문어) The president was felled by an assassin's bullet.

흉터 a scar; a seam (of an old wound); a mark. ¶팔의 덴 자리에 ~가 생겼다 The burn on my arm has left a scar.

흉통(胸痛) a pain in the chest; a chest pain; pleurodynia. ¶~을 느끼다 have a pain in one's chest.

흉포하다(凶暴-) atrocious; ferocious; brutal; outrageous. ¶지금 군중은 흉포해지고 있다 Now the crowd is turning savage.

흉하다(凶-) **1** [못생기다] ugly; bad-[ugly-]looking; plain; [보기 언짢다] unseemly; unsightly; ungainly; ugly. ¶다리에 보기 흉한 자국이 생겼다 An ugly scar remained[was left] on my leg. ¶그녀는 보기 흉하게 변해 버린 남편의 시신을 보자 통곡하였다 She burst into tears at the sight of her husband, dead and badly disfigured. // 그는 배가 나와 보기 ~ He looks awful with that potbelly. // 그 간판은 보기 흉하니 떼 버리시오 Please remove the signboard. It's unsightly.
2 [불길하다] ill; ill-omened; unlucky; inauspicious; sinister. ¶흉한 꿈 an unlucky dream // 흉한 예감 an ominous presentiment.
3 [마음씨 등이 나쁘다] wicked; vicious; villainous; bad. ¶흉한 놈 a wicked man / a villain / a godless person // 흉한 짓 a wicked [bad] act.

흉한(凶漢) [몹쓸 짓을 한 사람] a villain; a rioter; an assailant; a ruffian; an assassin (암살자). ¶~의 손에 쓰러지다 fall a victim to an assassin / be killed by an assassin / be murdered.

흉행(凶行) [폭행] (an act of) violence; (an) outrage; (an) atrocity; [살해] murder; [암살] (an) assassination. ¶여자가 남자에게 돌아가기를 거절하자 그 남자는 끔찍한 ~을 저질렀다 He committed the horrible deed[atrocious crime / murder] after the woman refused to come back to him. **흉행하다** do violence to (a person); commit an atrocity.

흉허물 a fault; a defect; a flaw.

흉허물(이) 없다 be on thee-and-thou terms with; be intimate enough to make no bones about each other's faults; be on intimate [friendly] terms (with); be frank [candid / open] with (a person). ¶흉허물 없는 친구 a friend with whom one need not stand on ceremony / a friend on frank terms / a good chum // 흉허물 없이 이야기하다 talk in a familiar way / speak without restraint // 흉허물 없이 지내다 associate on friendly [cor-dial] terms (with).

흉험하다(凶險-) cunning; insidious; crafty; tricky; sly; wily; dark.

흉흉하다(洶洶-) **1** (물결이) (the waves are) high; (the sea is) rough[furious / running high]. **2** (인심이) panic-stricken; filled with alarm; (서술적) be in great alarm[fear]. ¶그 소문으로 인심이 흉흉해졌다 The rumor aroused much fear in people's minds.

흐느끼다 sob; blubber; (아이 등이) whimper; whine. ¶흐느껴 우는 것 같은 바이올린 소리 the plaintive sound [the lament] of a violin // 흐느끼며 말하다 speak between sobs / blubber [sob] out (an apology) // 아이는 흐느끼다 잠들어 버렸다 The child sobbed itself to sleep. // 그 여자는 매우 비통하게 흐느꼈다 The woman sobbed bitterly [sobbed her heart out]. // 그 소녀는 흐느끼면서 경관에게 어떻게 되어 부모와 떨어지게 되었는가를 말했다 The child sobbed out to the policeman the story of how she had gotten separated from her parents.

흐느적거리다 swing; sway; shake; waver; flutter; (불꽃 등이) flicker; flare. ¶(나뭇잎 등이) 바람에 ~ be swayed by the wind / sway (about) to the wind / tremble [flutter] in the breeze.

흐늘거리다 1 [놀고 지내다] idle [dawdle / fiddle / snooze] one's time away; lead an idle life; loaf away one's time [days]. **2** [흔들거리다] waver; wave; swing [sway] (gently); flutter; play loosely.

흐늘쩍거리다 move around slowly [sluggishly / tardily / idly]; loiter along. ¶흐늘쩍거리며 걷다 walk slowly / loiter [poke] along / crawl.

흐늘흐늘 1 [빈둥빈둥] idly; lazily; at leisure. **흐늘흐늘하다** idle one's time away. ⇨ ⁼흐늘거리다 **2** [흔들흔들] waveringly; shaking; shakily. **흐늘흐늘하다** waver; wave. ⇨ ⁼흐늘거리다2

흐늘흐늘하다 soft; pulpy; limp; flabby. ¶흐늘흐늘해지다 be reduced to pulp [mash] // 흐늘흐늘하게 삶다 boil to pulp.

흐드러지다 1 [썩 탐스럽다] charming; fascinating; attractive; alluring; (구어) fetching. ¶꽃들이 흐드러지게 피었다 Flowers came out splendidly [gorgeously]. // 꽃들이 흐드러지게 피어 있다 Flowers are in full glory. **2** [흐뭇하다] gratifying; satisfying; pleasing. **3** [넉넉하다] plentiful; abundant; copious.

흐려지다 1 (하늘이) become cloudy [overcast]; be clouded [dull]; cloud up. ¶하루 종일 날씨가 흐려져 있었다 It was cloudy all day. // 갑자기 하늘이 흐려졌다 Suddenly the sky became overcast. // 하늘이 흐려져 있다 The sky is overcast.
2 [선명하지 않게 되다] become dim; dim; be clouded; fog up; be obscured; be blurred; become foggy (사진이); become turbid [muddy / impure / thick]. ¶김으로 거울이 흐려졌다 The mirror was clouded (up / over) with steam. // 나의 눈은 눈물로 흐려졌다 My eyes were dim with tears. // 안경이 흐려졌다 My glasses have fogged up. // 이 안경은 고온 다습에도 흐려지지 않는다 These glasses are not misted by high temperature or humidity. // 굴뚝 연기로 건물의 윤곽이 흐려지고 있다 The outline of the building is blurred by the smoke [emitted] from the chimney. // 진흙으

로 물이 흐려졌다 The water has become clouded with mud.
3 [걱정스러운 빛이 있다] be gloomy. ¶심노(心勞) 때문에 그의 마음은 흐려졌다 All his troubles have cast a cloud (of gloom) over his heart.

흐르다 **1** [유동하다] stream; flow; run; course; trickle(졸졸); ooze(스머 나오다); drain(배수되다); (양초의 촛물이) run; gutter. ¶그 강은 시내를 흐르고 있다 The river flows through the city. // 바위 위로 물이 가늘게 흐르고 있었다 Water was trickling down over the rocks. // 피가 그의 코에서 흐르고 있었다 He was bleeding at the nose. / Blood was trickling[gushing] from his nose.(▶ trickling은 소량을, gushing은 다량을 나타냄) // 구름이 달리듯[천천히] 하늘을 가로질러 흐르고 있다 Clouds are racing[drifting] across the sky. // 한강은 서해로 흘러 들어간다 The Hangang(Han River) flows[empties] into the Western Sea. // 시원한 공기가 창문으로 흘러 들어왔다 Fresh air streamed in through the window. // 나는 흐르는 물로 손발을 씻었다 I washed my hands and feet in running water. // 빗물은 배수관을 통해서 흐른다 The rainwater is carried off by[runs off through] drainpipes.
2 [떠다니다] float; drift; [유랑하다] drift; wander; knock about. ¶흘러 흘러 한국에 오다 drift to Korea // 나무토막이 강물 위로 흘러 내려왔다 A piece of wood came floating [drifting] down the river.
3 [쏟아지다] fall; spill; get[be] spilt; [넘치다] overflow; run[flow] over (the brim). ¶애교가 넘쳐 ~ be overflowing[beaming] with smiles // 책상에 잉크가 흘렀다 Ink has been spilt on the desk.
4 [윤기·광택이 나다]. ¶그의 얼굴에 기름이 흐른 Grease exudes on[oozes out of] his face. / His face is sleek[slick].
5 [쏠리다] lapse[fall] (into); run[incline / be inclined] (to); lean[tend / trend] (toward). ¶극단으로 ~ go to extremes[excess] / rush into extremes / go too far // 그들은 사치[난잡]에 흐르기 쉽다 They tend to be extravagant[rude].
6 (세월이) pass (by / away); elapse; go[roll / flow] by[on]. ¶그때부터 10년이 흘렀다 Ten years have passed[(문어) elapsed] since then.
7 [비유]. ¶초현실주의가 그의 전 작품에 흐르고 있다 Surrealism underlies all his works.

흐름 [흐르는 것] flowing; (물줄기 등의) a flow; a stream; a current; (페인트 등의) run; running; (시대 조류의) the current[tendency / trend] of the times. ¶물[공기]의 ~ the flow of water[air] // 시간의 ~ the passage of time // ~을 따라[거슬러] 헤엄치다 swim with [against] the current // ~을 올라[내려]가다 go up[down] stream // 시대[역사]의 ~에 역행하려고 하다 try to go against the current of the times[the flow of history] // 사람들의 ~에 따라 나는 밀려갔다 I was pushed along by the stream of people. // 시간의 ~은 참 빠르기도 하다 How (fast) time flies! // 세월의 ~에 따라 그 사건은 잊혀졌다 With the lapse of time[the passage of years] the event was forgotten.

흐리다[1] **1** [혼탁하게 하다] make (water) muddy[turbid / (미) roily]; roil; (미국 구어) rile; make foul[impure]; contaminate. **2** [명예를 더럽히다] tarnish; sully; defile; blemish; stain; spot. ¶이름[명예]을 ~ tarnish[stain] one's name[honor]. **3** [걱정스런 표정을 짓다] take on a anxious look; [언짢은 기색을 나타내다] make a sour face. **4** [애매하게 하다] make vague[obscure / indistinct / ambiguous / hazy]. ¶대답을 ~ equivocate in replying / give a vague[a non-committal / an evasive] answer // 그는 말꼬리를 흐리는 버릇이 있다 He has a way of slurring his word endings.

흐리다[2] **1** [불분명하다] not clear; unclear; vague; dim; obscure; hazy; misty; foggy; [애매하다] ambiguous; equivocal; evasive. ¶의식이 ~ have a dim consciousness // 기억이 ~ have a vague memory // 셈이 ~ be loose in settlement of accounts / be unpunctual [irregular] in one's payment // 태도가 ~ take an uncertain attitude (toward).
2 [희미하다] dim; clouded; foggy; obscure; blurred; smoked. ¶김이 창유리[전등]를 흐리게 했다 The steam fogged up the windows [dimmed the light].
3 [탁하다] muddy; turbid; thick (puddles); cloudy (wine); (목소리가) thick; hoarse; [혼탁하다] foul; impure. ¶흐린 물 muddy water // 흐린 데 없는 마음[양심] a clean [clear] conscience / a serene mind // 강물이 ~ The river runs thick. // 공장의 매연이 하늘을 흐리게 하고 있다 The smoke from the factory is clouding up the sky.
4 (날씨가) cloudy; clouded; overcast; murky. ¶흐린 하늘 a cloudy sky // 흐린 뒤 맑음 cloudy, clear(ing) later // 날씨가 ~ The weather is unsettled.
5 (시력이) dull; dim; blurred; bleary; bleared; dimmed; purblind. ¶눈이 ~ have bleared [dim] eyes // 청력이 ~ be hard[dull] of hearing.

흐리멍덩하다 **1** [분명치 않다] vague; dim; faint; obscure; indistinct; indeterminate; indecisive; indefinite; muddled; [애매하다] ambiguous; equivocal; evasive; dubious; noncommittal. ¶흐리멍덩한 눈 clouded [lackluster / fishy] eyes / glazed[glassy / remote] eyes // 흐리멍덩한 대답 (give) a vague[noncommittal / Delphic] answer / (give) an equivocal[indecisive] answer // 흐리멍덩한 셈 muddled accounts / 흐리멍덩한 태도 an uncertain[a noncommittal] attitude / an ambiguous[a dubious] attitude // 내 머리가 ~ My head doesn't feel clear. / My head feels fuzzy. **2** (귀가) dull; dim.

흐리터분하다 **1** [사물이 똑똑하지 않다] vague; dim; faint; obscure; indistinct; cloudy; hazy; misty; foggy. **2** [사람이 느슨하다] dull; sluggish; slovenly; loose; slack; [분명치 않다] shady; underhand. ¶그 자식은 흐리터분한 녀석이다 He's a slippery[tricky] one. // 자네 이야기는 ~ Your story has no point[makes no sense].

흐릿하다 **1** (날이) rather cloudy[overcast]. ¶흐릿한 날씨 rather cloudy[gray] weather.
2 [불분명하다] rather vague[dim / obscure / indistinct / hazy / ambiguous]; [뿌옇다] rather dim[clouded / blurred / smoked]; [둔탁하다] rather muddy[turbid / thick]. ¶달이 흐릿하게 보인다 The moon looks blurred. // 안개로 먼 산이 흐릿하게 보였다 Our view of

흐무러지다
the distant mountains was blurred by the mist.∥그때의 기억은 완전히 흐릿해졌다 My memory of the occasion has grown quite dim[hazy].∥카메라를 움직이지 않게 잠시 잡지 않아서 사진의 얼굴이 ~ The face in the picture is blurred because I didn't hold the camera steadily enough. **3** (눈이) rather dim[dull / blurred / bleary]; (청력이) rather hard[dull] of hearing. ¶나이를 먹으면 눈이 흐릿해진다 Our sight grows dim with age.∥나는 근시이기 때문에 먼 데 있는 것은 흐릿하게 보인다 As I am nearsighted, things in the distance look blurred.

흐무러지다 1 (익어서) overripe[overmature]; (물에 불어서) soaked[sodden]; soft[pulpy / limp / mushy]. **2** (뭉그러지다) crumble (into decay); mo(u)lder; collapse; give way; come [fall] down.

흐물흐물하다 overripe; (too) soft; pulpy; pulpous; limp; flaccid; mushy. ¶흐물흐물해지다 be reduced to pulp / become pulpy [mushy / flabby / limp]∥뭉클하고 무언가 흐물흐물한 것을 밟았다 I felt something squash under my feet. / I stepped upon something squashy.

흐뭇하다 [만족하다] gratifying; satisfying; satisfactory; gratified; [유쾌하다] pleasing; pleasant; [기쁘다] joyful; joyous; delightful; happy. ¶마음이 흐뭇해지는 편지 a heartwarming letter∥그것은 젊은 아버지가 태어난 자기 자식을 바라보고 있는 흐뭇한 정경이었다 It was the heartwarming scene of a young father looking at his newborn baby.

흐벅지다 plump; soft; full; round; fleshy; well-fleshed. ¶흐벅진 가슴 an ample [a well-rounded] bosom / a rich breast.

흐지부지 (answer) vaguely; halfheartedly; hazily. ¶일을 ~ 내버려 두다 leave things up in the air[unfinished / hanging]∥~ 대답하다 answer vaguely[halfheartedly]∥그는 ~ 일할 사람이 아니다 He is not a man for halfway measures. / He does not do things by halves.∥그 운동은 이윽고 ~ 끝이 나 버렸다 The movement petered out before long. ∥그 소문은 ~ 사라졌다 The rumor died out. **흐지부지한** vague; halfhearted; obscure; haze. ¶흐지부지한 태도 a lackadaisical[lukewarm] attitude. →**흐지부지되다** be dropped become hazy / end in smoke / come to nothing∥그의 계획은 결국 흐지부지되어 버렸다 His plan fizzled out in the end.∥한 달이 지나자 그 살인 사건도 흐지부지되었다 After one month, the murder case was forgotten.

흐트러뜨리다 1 (여기저기) scatter (about); strew; (군중 등을) disperse; break up. ¶물건들을 흐트러뜨려 놓다 leave things scattered[lying] about. **2** (머리칼 등을) dishevel (one's hair); rumple up (one's hair); (구어) muss (up) (one's hair). ¶머리를 흐트러뜨리고 with disheveled[unkempt] hair / with one's hair in disorder. **3** (정신을) distract. ¶정신을 ~ distract[divert] one's attention.

흐트러지다 1 [흩어지다] disperse; scatter; be scattered (about). ¶비행기는 산산이 흐트러져 바다에 처박혔다 The airplane plunged into the sea in pieces.∥카드의 순서가 흐트러져 있다 [제멋대로 되어 있다] The cards are out of order. / [잘못되어 있다] The cards are in the wrong order.∥실내는 조금도 흐트러진 데가 없었다 [잘 정돈되어 있었다] In the room everything looked in good order. / [어지른 흔적이 없었다] The room did not seem to have been disturbed at all. **2** (머리칼 등이) be disheveled; (구어) be mussed (up); be in disarray. ¶흐트러진 머리 [옷차림] disheveled[rumpled] hair [clothing]. **3** (정신이) be distracted. **4** (기타). ¶자세가 흐트러져 있다 I have bad posture.∥줄이 흐트러졌다 The line[(영) queue] got out of order[got confused].∥열은 맨 끝까지 조금도 흐트러지지 않고 있었다 The line was in perfect order to the last man.

흑 [흐느끼는 소리] with a sob; [목멘 소리] with a catch in one's voice.

흑(黑) **1** [흑색] a black color; black. **2** a black *baduk* stone. ⇨흑지

흑갈색(黑褐色) blackish brown.

흑단(黑檀) [식] an ebony.

흑두루미(黑-) [동] a hooded crane.

흑막(黑幕) [검은 장막] a black curtain. **2** [밀계(密計)] an ulterior design; something fishy; [내막] the inside (fact); concealed [undisclosed] circumstances; a behind-the-scenes story. ¶~을 폭로하다 expose a secret (of)∥거기에는 틀림없이 무슨 ~이 있을 거다 There must be something behind the scenes.

● **흑막 외교** secret[behind-the-scenes] diplomacy; diplomacy curtained off from the public.

흑반(黑斑) a black spot[patch / speckle]; melasma.

흑발(黑髮) black hair. ¶윤이 나는 ~ raven (-black) hair[locks].

흑백(黑白) **1** [흑과 백] black and white. **2** [선악] good and bad[evil]; [옳고 그름] right and wrong; [유죄와 무죄] guilt and innocence. ¶~을 밝히다 find out[make clear] which is right∥이 경우에는 우리는 ~을 가릴 수가 없다 In this case we cannot tell good from evil[right from wrong]. / In this case we cannot discriminate between good and bad.∥법정에서 ~을 가리기로 하자 Let's argue the rights and wrongs of the case in court.∥그것은 ~을 분간하기 어려운 사례이다 That is a borderline case.

● **흑백 논리** an all-or-nothing logic [attitude]. ¶그는 매사를 ~로 보는 경향이 있다 He tends to see everything in black and white. **흑백 사진** a black-and-white photograph; a photograph in black-and-white. **흑백 영화** a black-and-white picture; a monochrome film.

흑빵(黑-) (호밀로 만든) black bread; rye bread; (밀기울을 넣은) brown bread; whole wheat bread; (흑갈색의 달콤한) sweet brown bread.

흑사병(黑死病) [의] (the) pest; the black plague. ⇨페스트

흑사탕(黑沙糖) brown sugar. ⇨흑설탕

흑색(黑色) a black color; black.

● **흑색선전** a malicious[false] propaganda; a covert propaganda. **흑색 인종** the black race. ⇨흑인종(⇨흑인)

흑설탕(黑雪糖) brown sugar; unrefined [partially refined] sugar.

흑수병(黑穗病) smut; dustbrand. ⇨**깜부깃병**(⇨**깜부기**) ¶~**에 걸리다** smut / become smutted / become affected by smut.

흑수정(黑水晶) [광] smoky quartz.

흑심(黑心) a black heart; an evil[a wicked] heart; an evil[a dark] design. ¶~**을 품다** harbor an evil heart / cherish a dark design.

흑연(黑鉛) [광] black lead; graphite; plumbago.
● **흑연석** a graphite deposit.

흑운(黑雲) dark[black] clouds; [해] (태풍의 전조인) a brewing. ¶~**이 바다를 뒤덮었다** Dark[Black] clouds hung over the sea.

흑운모(黑雲母) [광] biotite.

흑인(黑人) a black; a Negro (*pl.* ~es); (미) an African American(▶ Negro에는 경멸적인 뜻이 담겨 있다 하여 black이라는 중립적인 말이 사용되어 왔으나, 최근에는 좀 더 완곡한 African American의 사용이 늘고 있음); (인종) the blacks. ¶~**에 대한 차별 대우** discrimination against blacks // ~**과 백인의 대립** the antagonism between blacks and whites.
● **흑인 분리 정책** the segregation policy. **흑인 영가** a black[Negro] spiritual. **흑인 음악** Negro music. **흑인종** the colored[black / Negro / African] race.

흑자(黑字) 1 [먹으로 쓴 글자] letters written in black ink; black characters[figures]. 2 (경제의) the black; a black-ink balance[figure]; (무역상의) a surplus. ¶**우리 회사는 ~다[~가 되었다]** Our company is in[got into] the black.
● **흑자 예산** a black-ink budget. **흑자 재정** balanced budget financing.

흑점(黑點) 1 [검은 점] a black spot. 2 a sunspot. ⇨**태양 흑점**(⇨**태양**(太陽))
● **흑점 주기** (태양의) a sunspot cycle.

흑지 a black *baduk*(go) stone.

흑책질하다 interfere with (a person) by sharp practices; thwart[frustrate] by shrewd tricks.

흑탄(黑炭) bituminous coal. ⇨**역청탄**(⇨**역청**)

흑토(黑土) [검은 빛깔의 흙] black soil [earth]; [기름진 땅] fertile soil.

흑판(黑板) a blackboard. ⇨**칠판**

흑해(黑海) the Black Sea; the Euxine Sea.

흑흑 1 [흐느껴 우는 소리] sobbing; with sobs. ¶~ **흐느끼다** sob / weep convulsively. **흑흑하다** [give a sob; whimper(어린아이가). 2 [찬 기운이 몸에 닿았을 때 내는 소리]. **흑흑하다** feel a cold thrill[shiver] through one; feel a chill creep over one.

흔덕거리다 shake. ⇨**한닥거리다**

흔드렁거리다 dangle; swing. ⇨**한드랑거리다**

흔들거리다 sway; waver. ⇨**한들거리다**

흔들다 1 [잇달아 움직이게 하다] wave (a flag, one's hand, etc.); shake (a stick, a bell, a coat, etc.); swing (a pendulum, a door, a hammock, etc.); give a (hard / good) shake (to); rock; wag. ¶**병[몸]을 ~** shake a bottle [oneself] // **주사위를 ~** shake and throw [cast] dice // **고개를 옆으로 ~** shake one's head // **고개를 세로로 ~** nod one's head // [비유] **nod one's agreement**[assent] // **팔[배트]을 ~** swing one's arms[a bat] // **흔들이를 ~** swing a pendulum // **손을 ~** wave one's hand // **잘 흔들어 드십시오**[사용하십시오] Shake well before drinking[use]. // **개가 꼬리를 흔들었다** The dog wagged its tail. // **그녀는 안녕이라고 손을 흔들었다** She waved me good-bye. // **경찰이 손을 흔들어 인파를 앞으로 나아가게 했다** A policeman waved the crowd on. // **그녀는 아들을 흔들어 깨웠다** She shook her son out of his sleep. / She woke her son up by shaking him. // **그는 어깨를 흔들며 웃었다** His shoulders shook with laughter. // **나는 아기를 흔들어 재웠다** I rocked the baby to sleep. // **나는 그네를 타고 있는 아이를 흔들어 주었다** I pushed the child in the swing[gave the child a swing]. // **어린이는 발을 흔들고 있었다** The child was swinging his legs. // **그는 느린 음악에 맞추어 몸을 흔들었다** He swayed to the slow music.
2 [감동·동요시키다] stir up; agitate; instigate; disturb; upset; move. ¶**민심을 ~** inflame[stir up] the popular passion // **결심을 ~** shake one's resolution.

흔들리다 1 (물체가) shake; quake; sway; wave; tremble(떨리다); vibrate(진동하다); (매동이) pitch(세로); roll(가로); rock(전후로); (상하로) toss; heave; bob; (매단 것이) swing; (차등이) joggle; (불빛이) flicker; quiver. ¶**바람에 흔들리는 갈대** reeds swaying in the wind // **열차가 지나갈 때마다 집이 흔들린다** The house shakes each time a train passes (by). // **바닷말이 해저에서 흔들리고 있는 것이 보인다** I can see sea weed swaying at the bottom of the sea. // **배가 몹시 옆으로[앞뒤로 / 전후 좌우로] 흔들렸다** The ship rolled [pitched / rocked] badly. // **우리는 택시를 타고 비포장도로를 달려 좌우로 흔들리던 끝에 그곳에 도착했다** We arrived there after being rocked from side to side[jolted] in a taxi on the unpaved road. // **작은 배는 파도에 흔들리고 있었다** A small boat was pitching[tossing] on the waves. // **카메라가 흔들렸다** The camera moved slightly. // **그때 나는 건물이 흔들리는 것을 느꼈다** At that time I felt the building shake. // **촛불이 흔들리다가 마침내 꺼졌다** The candle flickered and soon went out. // **화면이 흔들리고 있다** The picture is flickering up and down[back and forth] on the screen. // **미터의 바늘이 흔들렸다** The pointer on the meter shook. // **나는 발밑이 너무 흔들려서 서 있을 수가 없었다** I couldn't stay on my feet because the ground was rolling so violently. // **대지가 흔들리기 시작했다** The earth began to quake.
2 [동요하다] be shaken; be unsteady [shaky]; reel; vacillate; waver. ¶**흔들리는 세계 경제** the unstable world economy // **생각이 ~ have no fixed idea** // **마음이 ~** be changeable / be irresolute[indecisive] // **결단을 강요당하여 그의 마음은 흔들렸다** Pressed for a decision, he wavered. // **그 소식을 듣고 그의 결심은 흔들렸다** His resolution was shaken by the news. / His determination wavered at the news. // **과잉 생산으로 그 회사의 재정 상태는 흔들리기 시작했다** Overproduction has put the company in a shaky financial state. // **그들의 탈퇴로 조직이 흔들렸다** Their quitting shook the organization to its foundations. // **제의를 수락하느냐 거절하느냐로 그의 마음은 흔들리고 있었다** He wavered between accepting and rejecting the offer. // **그의 신념은 조금도 흔들리지 않았다** He remained firm in his faith. // **아침에 흔들리기 쉬운 것은 허영심이 강한 사람이다** Vain people are susceptible to flattery.

흔들의자(-椅子) a rocking chair; a rocker.
흔들흔들 swingingly; waveringly; swayingly; flickeringly. **흔들흔들하다** swing; rock; sway. ¶흔들흔들하는 테이블 a rickety [shaky] table // 이가 한 개 흔들흔들한다 I have a loose tooth. // 이가 흔들흔들하여 빠질 것 같다 This tooth is too loose it's about to come out.
흔연하다(欣然-) joyful; joyous; cheerful; delightful. **흔연히** joyfully; gladly; with a joyous smile; (기꺼이) willingly; readily; with a good grace. ¶~ 승낙하다 cheerfully accept / accept (an invitation) with pleasure [delight / alacrity / enthusiasm] // 부탁을 ～ 들어주다 comply with another's request with a good grace.
흔적(痕跡) (형적) traces; marks; vestiges; (말자취) tracks; evidences; signs. ¶고대 도시의 ～ vestiges of an ancient city // ～도 없이 사라지다 disappear without a trace / cover one's tracks / (문어) abscond // ～을 남기다 leave a trace // ～을 없애다 remove all traces (of) // …(의) ～이 있다 bear the marks of … / ～을 감추다 cover up one's traces // 많은 사람들이 지나간 ～이 있었다 There were tracks indicating that a large number of people had passed. // 금고의 자물쇠가 열린 ～은 없다 The safe shows no sign of having been unlocked. // 그에게는 지난날의 학식의 ～이 남아 있지 않다 There is not a trace left in him of his great learning. // 고향의 집은 ～도 남아 있지 않았다 Not a trace remained of the house where I had lived as a child. // 집 안에 사람이 살고 있는 ～은 없었다 We could not find any evidence that people were living in the house.
● **흔적 기관** a vestigial organ.
흔전만전 in (great) plenty [abundance]; abundantly; plentifully; amply. ¶돈을 ～ 쓰다 lavish [waste / squander] money / make the money fly. **흔전만전하다** abundant; plentiful; rich; ample; profuse; lavish.
흔쾌하다(欣快-) pleasant; happy; joyful; delightful. ¶이 성공은 나에게는 가장 흔쾌한 일이다 This success gives me the greatest happiness. **흔쾌히** (즐거이) gladly; happily; agreeably; (기꺼이) willingly; with pleasure. ¶～ 승낙하다 consent willingly.
흔하다 1 (많다) abundant; plentiful; rich; ample. ¶생선이 흔한 고장 a district rich [abundant] in marine products. **흔히** abundantly; plentifully.
2 (아무 데나 있다) common; commonplace; ordinary; familiar; common (or) garden; stock. ¶흔해 빠진 이야기 an old story / a twice-told tale / 흔해 빠진 일 a commonplace event / an everyday affair // 흔치 않은 미인 a rare beauty / a woman of rare [extraordinary] beauty // 지극히 흔한 수영복 a very commonplace [ordinary] bathing suit // 그런 여자는 흔해 빠졌다 She is the sort of woman whom you met by the dozen. // 그러한 예는 아주 흔합니다 Such cases are quite common. // 이런 귀한 물건을 만나기는 흔치 않읍니다 It is not every day that you come by such a find. **흔히** commonly; ordinarily; usually; generally; in general; often; (통속적으로) popularly; vulgarly. ¶～ 있는 실수 a common error // ～ 보는 굽 높은 구두 the kind of high-heeled shoe that everyone is wearing // 그런 것들은 아주 ～ 있다 Such things are not at all rare. // 이런 종류의 꽃은 어디에나 ～ 있다 This kind of flower grows [can be found] everywhere. // 10대의 소년에게 ～ 있는 일이지만, 그들은 오토바이에 열중하고 있다 As is often the case with teenagers, they are crazy about motorcycles. // 사고는 비 오는 날에 ～ 있다 Accidents tend to [frequently] happen on wet days. // ～ 말하듯이 피는 물보다 진하다 As is commonly said [To use a common expression], blood is thicker than water.
흘겨보다 squint [leer] (at); leer one's eyes (at); give a sharp sidelong glance (at).
흘금거리다 keep looking sideways; keep leering [ogling / eyeing].
흘금흘금 looking sideways over and over again; leering and leering. ¶～ 보다 keep eyeing. **흘금흘금하다** keep looking sideways. ⇨ 흘금거리다
흘긋 1 (얼씬 보이는 모양). ¶그가 차를 몰고 가는 것이 ～ 보였다 I caught [got] a glimpse of him as he drove past. 2 (재빨리 흘겨보는 모양) with a sidelong glance. ¶～ 보다 (곁눈질로) look askance [sideways] (at a person) / (잠깐) glance (at) / take a glance (a thing) // 그녀의 얼굴을 ～ 보다 steal a covert glance at her face.
흘기다 look disapprovingly out of the corner of one's eyes (at); cast a reproachful [disapproving] glance (at); scowl (at). ¶그는 번쩍이는 두 눈을 흘겨 만장의 청중을 노려보았다 He glared at the whole audience with his eyes glittering.
흘깃 with a glance. ¶～ 보다 cast a glance at (a person).
흘깃거리다 keep sharply [angrily] (at a person); keep glaring [scowling].
흘끔거리다 keep looking sideways. ⇨ 흘금거리다
흘끗 with a sidelong glance. ⇨ 흘긋
흘끗거리다 keep sharply [angrily] (at a person); keep glaring [scowling].
흘끗흘끗 scowling and scowling; glaring and glaring. **흘끗흘끗하다** keep sharply (at a person). ⇨ 흘끗거리다
흘러가다 flow; run; float [drift] along; fly (시간이). ¶덧없이 흘러가는 청춘 시대 the flying years of youth // (강이) 바로 ～ find its way to the sea // 세월은 흘러간다 Time flies. // 20년이란 세월이 흘러갔다 Twenty years have run their course. // 흘러가는 청춘이 아깝다 I regret the way my youth is flying away from me.
흘러나오다 (유출하다) flow out; run out; effuse; stream [pour] out; gush forth (뿜는다); ooze out (고름 등이). ¶졸졸 ～ drain through // 상처에서 피가 흘러나왔다 The blood flowed out from the wound. // 꼭지에서 물이 흘러나오고 있다 Water is running from the tap. // 고름이 흘러 나온다 The pus ran out. // 눈물이 그녀의 눈에서 흘러나왔다 Tears flowed [streamed] from her eyes. // 과장된 말이 그의 입에서 마구 흘러나왔다 Exaggerated words gushed from his lips.
흘러내리다 1 (떨어지다) fall; drop; run [stream / pour] down. ¶눈물이 그녀의 볼을 줄줄 흘러내렸다 Tears ran [streamed / coursed / rolled / trickled] down her cheeks. 2 (미끄러지다) slip [slide / glide] down; work down. ¶흘러내리는 바지를 치켜 올리다 pull

흠나다

[hitch] up one's trousers // 내 양말이 흘러내린다 My socks are sliding down.

흘리다 1 (액체를) let (water) flow[run out]; [쏟다] shed; spill; slop; pour over; [뚝뚝 떨어지게 하다] drop; let drop; drip; dribble. ¶눈물[피]을 ~ shed[drop] tears[blood] // 땀을 ~ perspire / sweat // 콧물을 ~ snivel / drivel / run at the nose // 국물을 ~ spill soup // 코피를 ~ bleed at the nose / have a bloody nose / one's nose bleeds // 나라를 위해 피를 ~ shed one's blood for one's country // 그는 이마에 땀을 흘리고 있었다 His forehead was dripping with sweat. // 그는 코피를 흘렸다 He had a nosebleed. // 그 아이는 콧물을 흘리고 있었다 The child's nose was running. // 그녀는 회한의 눈물을 흘렸다 She shed tears of remorse. // 그 전쟁에서 영국은 많은 피를 흘렸다 The war cost much British blood. // 그들은 피를 흘리지 않고 폭도를 진압했다 They suppressed the rioters without bloodshed. // 그는 물을 한 방울도 흘리지 않고 물동이를 날랐다 He carried the bucket without spilling a drop of water.
2 [잃어버리다] drop; lose. ¶지갑을 ~ lose one's purse / 돈을 ~ drop money.
3 [귀담아 듣지 않다] take no notice (of); pay no attention (to); give no heed (to); be deaf to (a person's remonstrances); let (an insult) go by. ¶농담으로 ~ take (it) as a joke // 그는 그녀의 말을 한쪽 귀로 듣고 한쪽 귀로 흘려버렸다 He let her words go in one ear and out the other. / He took no heed of what she said.
4 (글씨를) write in the grass hand[style]; [급히 쓰다] write hurriedly; scribble; scrawl(난폭하게).
5 [조금씩 나누어 주다] dribble out; give by[in] driblets.

흘림 grass characters. ⇨초서(草書)

흘수(吃水) draft; draught; sea gauge. ¶만재(滿載) ~ load draft / full (load) draft // 가 깊은[얕은] 배 a ship of deep[light] draft // (배가) ~ 18피트다 be of 18-feet draft / draw 18 feet (of water) // 를 재다 take the draft (of a ship) // 가 깊다[얕다] have a deep [light] draft // 이 배는 ~가 16피트이다 This ship draws sixteen feet (of water).
● **흘수선**(-線) the waterline; the draft (line). ¶만재 ~ the load (water) line.

흙 [토양] earth; soil; [진흙] mud; [찰흙] clay; [지면] the ground. ¶~으로 만든 earthen / clay // 내 눈에 ~이 들어가기 전에는 so long as I live[am alive] // ~을 파다 dig up earth / till the soil / do farming // ~을 덮다 heap up earth / cover with earth / earth up / mould up (potatoes) // ~으로 돌아가다 return[fall back] to dust / turn to clay / die // 이국땅의 ~이 되다 die in a strange [foreign] land // …의 ~을 밟다 set[plant] foot on (foreign) soil / tread (British) soil // 사람은 한 줌의 ~에 지나지 않는 Man is but a lump of clay. // ~으로 돌아가라 Back to the land!

흙감태기 a person[thing] covered all over with mud. ¶~가 되다 become muddy / muddy.

흙구덩이 a hole[cavity] in the ground; a pit.

흙내 (an) earthy smell. ¶~가 나는 감자 potatoes smelling of earth // ~를 맡다 take a smell at[have a smell of] earth / (초목이) take[strike] root.

흙담 →토담
흙더미 a heap[mound] of earth.
흙덩이 a lump of earth; a clod (of earth).
흙먼지 dust; a cloud of dust; a dust storm. ¶앞사람들이 일으킨 ~ dust stirred up by those in front // ~를 일으키다[날리다] raise [kick up] a cloud of dust // 트럭이 지나가면서 부연 ~를 날린다[일으킨다] Trucks raise thick clouds of dust as they pass.

흙받기 1 (자전거·자동차의) a mudguard; a splashboard; a fender; (마차의) a dashboard.
2 (미장이의) a mortarboard; a hawk.

흙벽(-壁) a mud-plastered wall; a clay wall.

흙비 dust in the air; a dust storm; a sandstorm(사막의).

흙빛 (an) earthlike color; the color of earth. ¶얼굴이 ~이 되다 turn ghastly[ashy] pale [pale as ashes] / turn ashen.

흙손 a (plasterer's) trowel; a float(끝칠용용).
● **흙손질** trowelling; plastering with a trowel. ¶~을 하다 trowel / plaster with a trowel / level with a float.

흙일 earthwork(s); mud work; [미장이 일] plaster work; plastering. **흙일하다** do earthwork; do mud work; plaster (a wall).
● **흙일꾼** a navvy. ⇨토역꾼(⇨토역(土役))

흙장난 playing with earth. **흙장난하다** play with earth.

흙칠하다 soil[smear / daub] with mud; be [soiled] with mud. ¶얼굴에 ~ smear one's face with mud / (비유) fling mud at / asperse (a person's character).

흙탕 muddy water. ⇨흙탕물(⇨흙탕)
● **흙탕길** a muddy road. **흙탕물** muddy water. ¶~에 빠지다 slip into a muddy pool (on the road) // ~을 튀기다 splash [spatter] (a person) with muddy water // ~을 뒤집어 쓰다 be spattered with muddy water.

흙투성이 being covered all over with mud [dirt]. ¶~가 되다 be covered all over with mud[dirt] / become[get] muddy / muddy // 그의 손은 ~었다 His hands were covered with mud.

흠 [비웃는 소리] pooh!; pish!; pshaw!; humph!; huh! ¶~ 웃다 laugh[smile] scornfully (at) / jeer (at).

흠(欠) 1 (물건의) a crack; a flaw; a disfigurement; a scratch; a speck; (과일의) a bruise. ¶찻잔의 가장자리에 난 ~ a nick in the lip [rim] of a teacup // ~이 있는 flawed / cracked / disfigured / bruised // ~이 없는 flawless / perfect // ~이 생기다 flaw / crack (금) / (과일이) bruise (easily) // (찻잔 등이) ~이 있다 have a flaw[crack] // 이 꽃병에는 ~이 있다 This vase is cracked. / There is a crack in the vase. // 이것은 ~이 있으니 싸게 드리지요 As these are defective goods I will part with them dirt cheap.
2 [결점] a fault; a defect; a flaw; a blemish; a mar; a stain; a blur. ¶그의 경력에 있어서의 ~ a blemish on his record // 말 많은 것이 그녀의 가장 큰 ~이다 Her great fault is talking too much. // ~ 없는 사람은 없다 Nobody is perfect. // 누구나 ~은 있다 Everyone has his foibles. // ~을 말하자면 그녀는 피부가 조금 검다 If she has any defect, it is that her complexion is a little too dark. // 그에게는 ~이 없다 He is free from faults.

흠나다(欠—) get marred. ⇨흠지다

흠내다 (欠-) (물건에) flaw; mar; crack; scratch; make a flaw[crack / scratch].

흠모 (欽慕) admiration; adoration; reverence; high regard. ¶그는 여전히 동향인의 ~를 받고 있다 He is still the idol of his countrymen. **흠모하다** admire; adore; esteem; idolize; entertain a high regard (for); make an idol of (a person).

흠뻑 fully; thoroughly; to the full; sufficiently; [마음이] to one's heart's content; to one's satisfaction. ¶~ 젖은 옷 dripping-wet clothes // 피에 ~ 젖은 셔츠 a blood-soaked shirt // ~ 젖다 be drenched[soaked / doused / wet] to the skin / get wet through[all over] / (옷이) get dripping[soaking] wet // 수건을 물에 ~ 적시다 soak a towel in water // 땀을 ~ 흘리다 be all of a sweat / get sweat all over / perspire profusely // 비가 ~ 오다 have sufficient rain // ~ 취하다 be dead [blind / beastly] drunk // 그 환자는 땀에 ~ 젖어 있었다 The sick man was wringing [soaking] wet with sweat. // 옷이 ~ 젖었다 My clothes are dripping[wringing / sopping] wet. // 그의 셔츠는 땀에 ~ 젖어 있었다 His shirt was soaked with sweat. // 네 코트가 ~ 젖었구나 Your coat is dripping[sopping] wet. // ~ 젖은 그 옷을 빨리 벗어라 Take off those dripping-wet clothes right away. // 그는 소나기를 만나서 온몸이 ~ 젖었다 He was caught in a shower and got wet[drenched] to the skin. // 나는 땀을 ~ 흘렸다 I was all in a sweat. / I perspired profusely. // 신문지가 비에 ~ 젖었다 The newspaper was soaked [dripping wet] with rain. // 그는 한 시간을 비를 맞고 걷더니 ~ 젖었다 He was dripping wet[soaked to the skin] after having walked in the rain for an hour. // 어머나 ~ 젖으셨군요 Why, you look like a drowned rat!

흠씬 enough; sufficiently; thoroughly; to the full; to the fullest measure. ¶~ 두들겨 주다 beat (a person) soundly / give (a person) a sound thrashing // 고기를 ~ 삶다 do meat well.

흠잡다 (欠-) find fault with; cavil[carp] at; pick holes in; (미국 구어) pick on (a person[thing]). ¶흠잡을 데가 없다 be above reproach / be faultless[unimpeachable] / leave nothing to be desired / be perfect [ideal] // 그의 솜씨는 흠잡을 데가 없다 His technique leaves nothing to be desired. / His technique is perfect[above criticism]. // 그의 경력에는 흠잡을 데가 없다 He has an impeccable record. / His record is unblemished. // He has a spotless[stainless] career. // 그는 흠잡을 데 없는 사람이다 I can find no fault in him.

흠정 (欽定) ¶~의 compiled by Royal order / laid down by Royal edict / authorized. **흠정하다** order[edict / authorize] (to compile).
●**흠정 헌법** a constitution granted by the King.

흠지다 (欠-) (물건에) get marred[cracked / scratched]; get[have] a flaw[crack / scratch / speck].

흠집 (欠-) (신체의) a scar; (물건의) a crack; a flaw; a scratch; a fault. ¶~ 있는 손 a scarred hand // 그림에 ~을 내다 damage a picture // 이 사과는 ~이 나 있다 This apple is bruised[has a bruise].

흠칫 cringing. **흠칫하다** shrink (back) (at / from); hold[fall] back (from); flinch (from); cringe in surprise[fright].

흡기 (吸氣) [들이마시기] inhalation of air [breath]; inspiration; (공기) air breathed in. **흡기하다** inhale; breathe in.

흡반 (吸盤) [동] a sucker. ⇨빨판

흡사 (恰似) just as; as if; as though; as it were. ¶~ 죽은 것 같다 look as if dead / be more dead than alive // ~ 미친 사람 같다 look as if one were mad // 그것은 ~ 그림 같았다 It was just like a picture.

흡사하다 (恰似-) be strikingly similar (to); resemble closely; bear a close resemblance [a strong likeness] (to); be the very picture of (one's father); be as like as two peas [eggs]; be exactly alike; be an exact counterpart (of); be a copy[replica] (of). ¶이 꽃병은 내 것과 ~ This vase is very similar to mine. / This vase looks almost exactly like mine. // 그는 아버지와 용모가 ~ He looks like his father very much. / He is the perfect image[very picture] of his father. // 그들의 성격은 ~ They are much alike in character. // 두 사람은 서로 ~ There is a close[great] resemblance between the two. **흡사히** similarly; exactly alike.

흡수 (吸水) [빨아올리기] suction of water; [빨아들이기] water absorption. **흡수하다** [빨아올리다] draw water by sucking[suction]; suck water; [빨아들이다] absorb water (from).
●**흡수관** a siphon; a suction pipe.

흡수 (吸收) absorption; [흡인] imbibition; suction; (열의) decalescence; (빛의) extinction; [동화] assimilation. ¶영양의 ~ absorption of nourishment // 우리나라는 서구 문화의 ~에 바빴다 Korea was busy (in) assimilating Western civilization. // 이 효소는 단백질의 소화 ~를 촉진한다 This enzyme aids the digestion and absorption of protein. // 그들은 새로운 지식의 ~에 몰두하였습니다 They were enthusiastic about absorbing new knowledge. / (구어) They soaked up new knowledge like crazy. **흡수하다** absorb; suck[take] in; imbibe; [동화하다] assimilate. ¶공기에서 수분을 ~ absorb moisture from the air // 실업자를 ~ absorb the unemployed into work // 해면은 물을 흡수한다 A sponge absorbs water. // 이 천은 땀을 잘 흡수한다 This material absorbs perspiration well. ➔ ¶혈액 내에 흡수되다 be absorbed into the blood // 피부를 통하여 체내에 흡수되다 be absorbed into the system through the skin // 소기업은 대기업에 흡수되었다 The small companies were absorbed by bigger ones.
●**흡수관** an absorption tube. **흡수력** absorbing[absorptive] power; absorbency; absorptivity. **흡수성** absorptive property; absorptiveness. ¶~의 absorbent / absorptive. **흡수제** an absorbent.

흡습성 (吸濕性) hygroscopic property; hygroscopicity. ¶~의 hygroscopic // 이 강하다 be highly [very] hygroscopic.

흡연 (吸煙) smoking (tobacco). ¶~으로 건강을 해치다 smoke oneself ill[sick] // 여기서는 ~이 금지되어 있다 No smoking is allowed here. / Smoking is prohibited here. // 과도한 ~은 성대를 해치기 쉽다 Much smoking tends to injure the voice. **흡연하다** smoke

(tobacco / a cigarette / a pipe); have a smoke.
● 흡연 금지 (게시) No smoking. 흡연실 a smoking[(영) smoke] room; (배의) a smoking saloon. 흡연자 / 흡연가 a smoker.
흡열(吸熱) heat absorption.
● 흡열 반응 [화] (an) endothermic [endoergic] reaction.
흡인(吸引) absorption; suction; imbibition; aspiration. 흡인하다 absorb; suck (in / up); imbibe; draw in (by suction).
● 흡인력 sucking force.
흡입(吸入) inhalation; indraft; imbibition; suction. 흡입하다 inhale; breathe[draw] in; suck (in); imbibe.
● 흡입기 an inhaler; an inhalator; an inspirator. ¶산소 ~ an oxygen haler // (환자에게) ~를 쓰다 treat (a patient) with an inspirator / give (a person) inhalation treatment / spray (a patient's) sore throat. 흡입 밸브 a sucking[suction] valve.
흡족하다(洽足-) 1 (아주 넉넉하다) sufficient; ample; enough; full. 흡족히 enough; sufficiently; fully; to the full; amply; in plenty. ¶~ 보답하다 reward amply[abundantly] paid // 물을 ~ 주다 give a good watering. 2 (만족하다) satisfactory; gratifying. 흡족히 satisfactorily; to one's satisfaction; to one's heart's content. ¶~ 여기다 be contented (with) / find (something) more than satisfactory.
흡착(吸着) [물][화] adsorption. 흡착하다 adsorb.
● 흡착제 an adsorbent.
흡혈(吸血) bloodsucking. 흡혈하다 suck blood.
● 흡혈귀 a vampire; a bloodsucker.
흥[1] [부사]. ¶코를 ~ 하고 풀다 blow one's nose with a hissing sound // (아이에게) ~ 해 Blow, honey!
흥[2] [감탄사] hm(m); hum(ph); hem; h'm. ¶~ 하고 코웃음 치다 turn up one's nose at (a person) // ~, 나를 놀리는군 Pshaw! You're fooling me!
흥(興) interest; fun; amusement; merriment; mirth; pleasure. ¶~이 나면 when fancy leads one // ~에 겨워(서) in the excess of mirth / driven by one's enthusiasm // ~을 깨뜨리는 사람 a killjoy / a spoilsport / a wet blanket // ~이 나다 become interested (in) / warm up (to one's work) / get excited [merry] (over / by) // ~이 깨지다 find one's fun spoiled (by) / one's enthusiasm is dampened (by) // ~이 나게 하다 amuse / interest / arouse (a person's) interest // ~에 겨워하다 be overwhelmed with mirth[fun] // ~을 돋우다 add to the fun (of) / heighten the interest (of) // ~을 깨뜨리다 spoil the fun (of) / cast a chill (upon / over) / dampen [chill] (a person's) enthusiasm (for) / wet-blanket (a person's) zeal (for) // 좌중의 ~이 깨지지 않도록 하다 keep the ball rolling / keep up the ball // 그는 늘 좌중의 ~을 깨뜨린다 He is an awful wet blanket. // 그녀의 아름다운 목소리가 파티의 ~을 돋우었다 Her sweet voice added to the fun of the party. // 그가 있으면 ~이 깨진다 He spoils our fun. // (구어) He is a killjoy[wet blanket]. // 그의 말이 모임의 ~을 깨 버렸다 His words cast a chill over the company. // 그녀가 나타나자 즐거운 파티의 ~이 깨졌다 Her appearance took all the fun out [spoiled the merry atmosphere] of the party.
흥건하다 1 (물 등이) brimful; full to the brim. ¶웅덩이에 물이 흥건하게 괴었다 A puddle is full of rainwater. 흥건히 brimfully. 2 (국물 등이) juicy; watery; (서술적) (have) much juice in it. ¶김칫국이 ~ The *gimchi*(kimchi) is much juicy. 흥건히 juicily; waterly
흥겹다(興-) delightful; merry; pleasant; joyous; cheerful; exciting; gay; full of fun. ¶ 흥겨운 하루 a day full of fun / an exciting day // 흥겨운 기분 a festive mood // 흥겨운 가락 a gay tune of (the guitar) // 흥겹게 gaily / merrily / joyously / pleasantly // 흥겨운 나머지 in the excess of mirth // 한창 흥겨운 판에 in the midst of one's merriment // 흥겨워하다 be amused (at) / enjoy oneself (over something / by doing) / have a good time of it // 흥겹게 놀다 make merry / have fun (at) / frolic.
흥기(興起) rise; ascendency. 흥기하다 rise; be in the ascendant.
흥망(興亡) rise and fall; ups and downs; vicissitudes; existence(존망); destinies (운명). ¶일국의 ~ the rise and fall of a nation / the destinies of a nation // 민족의 ~ the varied fortunes of races // 국가의 ~에 관한 중대 문제 a great question affecting the destinies of the nation // 우리나라의 ~이 이 싸움에 달려 있다 The fate of our country hinges on this battle. // 나는 ~을 걸고 이 사업을 해 보겠다 I will try my luck with this business.
● 흥망성쇠 rise and[or] fall together with prosperity and[or] decay. ¶인생의 ~ the vicissitudes[ups and downs] of life // 로마의 ~ the rise and fall of Rome.
흥미(興味) (an) interest; zest. ¶비상한 ~ great[keen] interest // ~ 있는 interesting (book) / attractive (show) / amusing (story) / exciting (game) // 다소 ~ 있는 이야기 a subject of some interest // ~ 없는 uninteresting / of no interest / wanting in interest / dull / stale / humdrum / insipid // 여러 가지 일에 ~를 갖고 있는 사람 a man of many interests / a person with multiple interests // 매우 ~를 끄는 뉴스 a most intriguing piece of news // ~를 가지고 with interest / with zest // 별로 ~가 없이 of little interest // ~를 가지다 take[feel] (an) interest (in) / be interested (in) // 문학에 지대한 ~를 가지다 take a great[warm] interest in literature // ~를 느끼다 (사람이) take [show] / evince] (an) interest (in) / find pleasure (in movies) / (사물이) appeal to (one's curiosity) // ~를 일으키다 interest / arouse[awake(n)] / stimulate / excite] (a person's) interest (in) // ~를 붙이게 하다 foster (a person's) interest (in) // ~를 잃다 lose (an) interest (in) // 많은 사람의 ~를 끌다 attract the interest of many people // 그는 스포츠에 ~가 있다[없다] He is[is not] interested in sports. / He takes an[no] interest in sports. // 그는 여러 가지 일에 ~를 가진 사람이다 He is a man of many[varied] interests. // 이런 것은 나에게는 ~가 없다 Such things have no interest for me. // 그녀는 점점 ~를 느끼게 되었다 She found her interest rising.
흥미진진하다(興味津津-) very[intensely]

흥미 interesting; of great [absorbing] interest; full of interest; absorbing (book). ¶흥미진진한 화제 topic of great interest (to one) / 이 책은 ~ This book is of absorbing interest. ∥ 이 영화는 흥미진진하였다 I've got a lot of fun out of [from] the picture. / The picture thrilled [excited] me a great deal. ∥ 그가 어떻게 나올지 흥미진진했다 It'll be very interesting [of great interest] to see how he reacts. ∥ 그는 흥미진진하다는 듯이 내 이야기를 듣고 있었다 He listened to me [my story] with great interest.

흥분(興奮) excitement; excitation; agitation; stimulation. ¶신경성 ~ [생] erethism. ∥ ~을 잘하는 excitable / (be) easily excited [agitated] ∥ ~을 느끼다 get [grow] excited (at) / feel excitement (at) ∥ ~을 가라앉히다 allay [calm down] one's excitement / cool down (a person's) hot temper ∥ 우리는 좀처럼 ~이 가라앉지 않았다 It took us a long time to calm down after the excitement. **흥분하다** be excited; be aroused (to activity); be [get] stimulated (into action); be highly strung; be wrought [worked] up (over); work oneself up (into a passion); get warm [hot]; (미) get a kick [thrill] (from). ¶흥분하여 in excitement / excitedly / in an excited state of mind / (영국 구어) in a flap ∥ 흥분하기 쉬운 excitable / hotheaded ∥ 흥분하지 않고 있다 keep calm ∥ 흥분해 있다 be excited (at / over) / be wild (over victory) ∥ 굉장히 흥분해 있다 be bubbling over with excitement ∥ 그 사건으로 흥분해 있다 be in a state of excitement about the affair ∥ 그는 쉽게 흥분한다 He is excitable. / He is easily excited [agitated]. ∥ 그는 무슨 일로 저렇게 흥분하고 있는가 What is he so excited [worked up] about? ∥ 흥분하지 마라 Don't be upset. / Calm down. / Take it easy. ∥ 그의 신경은 흥분해 있다 He is in a highly wrought-up [nervous] state. ∥ 그의 발언으로 그들은 흥분했다 They were stirred [were roused] by his speech. / They grew excited at his words. ∥ 그는 흥분해서 총을 쏘았다 He fired the gun in hot blood. ∥ 그는 하찮은 농담에도 잘 흥분하는 성미다 He gets easily excited at even the pettiest joke. ∥ 경마를 앞두고 말이 흥분해 있다 The horse is nervous before the race. ∥ 그는 흥분하기도 잘하고 가라앉기도 잘한다 He gets excited easily but soon cools down. / He blows hot and cold. / He doesn't stick with anything long. ∥ 그는 지금 너무 흥분해 있고 있으니까 그냥 내버려 두어라 Leave him alone, for he is too excited now. **→흥분시키다** stir (up) (a person's) feelings / work (a person) up / make (a person) hot / excite (a person) / stimulate (a person's) curiosity ∥ 환자의 기분을 흥분시켜서는 안 된다 Don't excite the patient.
● **흥분 상태** an excited condition [state]. **흥분제** a stimulant; an excitant; an exciter; an invigorator; (속어) a reviver; a pep pill. ¶~를 먹이다 [먹이다] take [administer] a stimulant.

흥성(興盛) prosperity. **흥성하다** grow in prosperity; become prosperous; prosper; thrive.

흥신소(興信所) an inquiry office [agency]; a detective agency; a credit bureau (상업 관계의).

흥얼거리다 hum (a tune); sing to oneself; croon (a song). ¶그녀는 작은 목소리로 민요의 마디마디를 흥얼거리고 있었다 She was singing snatches of a folk song softly to herself.

흥얼흥얼 humming; crooning. ¶~ 혼자 노래하다 hum [croon] to oneself.

흥정 [매매] buying and selling; purchase and sale; [거래] dealings; transactions; business; a bargain; [매매를 위한 값 등의 의논] bargaining; chaffering; haggling; [교섭] negotiation. ¶정치적 ~ (oppose to any sort of) political compromise ∥ 숯자리에서의 ~ a Dutch [wet] bargain ∥ 수지맞는 [수지맞지 않는] ~ a good [poor] bargain ∥ ~의 솜씨가 폐 있다 be a pretty keen hand at bargaining / ~이 없다 make few sales / do little business ∥ ~을 붙이다 act as broker / help strike a bargain / ~이 끝났습니다 The bargain has been concluded [closed]. ∥ 그는 사업상의 ~에는 거의 백지다 He knows little of the tricks of business. **흥정하다** buy and sell; make a deal (with); do business (with); (값을) bargain (with a person) over [about]; haggle (dicker) (with a person). ¶물건값을 놓고 ~ bargain [haggle] over the prices of an article with (a person) ∥ 가게 주인과 값을 ~ bargain with the storekeeper [shopkeeper] over the price.

흥정은 붙이고 싸움은 말리랬다(속담) One should help bargaining and stop quarrels.
● **흥정꾼** buyers and [or] sellers; a dealer; a trader; a broker.

흥진비래(興盡悲來) After fun comes sorrow.; After joy come tears.

흥청거리다 [마음껏 놀다] indulge in merrymaking; make merry; be on the spree; [거드럭거리다] be highly elated; exult; crow; be puffed up; swagger. ¶부어라 마셔라 하며 ~ go [be] on the spree / revel it / (구어) have a high time ∥ 흥청거리며 살다 live in a racket of enjoyment / live in luxury [great style] ∥ 그들은 만사를 잊고 흥청거렸다 They forgot themselves and went on the spree.

흥청망청 1 [즐기는 모양] merrily; gaily. ¶~놀기 a (hilarious) merrymaking / a spree / a racket / high jinks ∥ ~ 떠들며 놀다 indulge in a rowdy spree [boisterous merrymaking] / have high jinks / go on the spree. 2 [낭비하는 모양] in profusion. ¶돈을 ~ 쓰다 spend money most lavishly [in profusion].

흥취(興趣) interest; gusto; taste. ¶매우 ~가 있다 be of absorbing interest ∥ 아무런 ~도 없다 have no attractive features.

흥타령 a folksong with a "hum" at the end of each line.

흥패(興敗) rise and fall [decline]; fate; destiny. ¶제국의 ~가 이 일전에 달려 있다 The fate [future] of the Empire rests on this battle.

흥하다(興—) (나라 등이) rise; [번영·번창하다] thrive; flourish; prosper; boom; roar. ¶흥하는 집안 a thriving family ∥ 흥하든 망하든 whether one succeeds or fails / sink or swim / hit or miss / win or lose ∥ 장사가 흥한다 Business booms [flourishes / prospers]. ∥ 나라가 흥한다 A country rises. ∥ 흥하든 망하든 해 보겠다 I will try, sink or swim [kill or cure]. / I will make a spoon or spoil a horn.

흥행(興行) (사업) public entertainment; the amusement [entertainment] industry; show

business; (연예) (a) performance; (an) exhibition; a run; a show. ¶단기〔短期〕 ~ a short[long] run // 순회 ~ a roadshow. 흥행하다 give a performance; produce (a play); show; exhibit; run (a show). ¶연극을 ~ give[present] a play // 지방에서 흥행하고 있다〔미〕 be on the road. → ¶이 극은 6개월간이나 계속 흥행되었다 This play had a run of six months.
● 흥행권 the right of performance[production]; (연극의) a dramatic[stage / (미)play] right. 흥행물 a (public) performance; a show; a production; an exhibition. 흥행사 a showman; show projector. 흥행장 a show place.

흥흥 Hum hum!; Hmph hmph!

흩날리다 blow off[away]; be blown off; go to the winds; fly about[off]; scatter; flutter. ¶바람에 흩날리는 만 원짜리 지폐 ten-thousand-won bills scattered and blown about in the wind // 바람에 ~ be blown off by the wind // (꽃잎 등이) 바람에 흩날리며 떨어지다 fall fluttering in the wind // 꽃잎이 바람에 흩날리고 있었다 Flower petals were whirling[swirling / dancing] about in the wind. // 전단이 바람에 흩날렸다 The leaflets danced and whirled in the wind.

흩다 scatter; disperse. ⇨ 흩뜨리다

흩뜨리다 (꽃 등을) scatter; strew; (군중 등을) disperse; (구름 등을) dissipate; (머리를) dishevel. ¶머리를 흩뜨리고 with disheveled[disordered] hair // 자세를 ~ assume an easy posture // 종이 조각을 ~ scatter bits of waste paper // 주의력을 ~ distract[divert] one's attention // 물건들을 흩트려 놓다 leave things scattered[lying] about // 신문을 흩트려 놓은 채로 두다 leave pages of paper lying about // 군인은 자세를 흩뜨리지 않고 서 있었다 The soldier stood erect[straight].

흩뿌리다 scatter; strew; sprinkle. ¶씨를 ~ scatter seeds // 길에 물을 ~ sprinkle water on a road / sprinkle a street with water.

흩어지다 〔분산하다〕 disperse; scatter; be scattered (about); 〔어질러지다〕 be littered (up) (with); be in disorder. ¶흩어져 있는 것 scatterings / things lying scattered (on the ground) // (산산이) [사방에] ~ disperse in all directions / be scattered about // 흩어진 마음을 가라앉히다 collect[gather] one's scattered wits / compose oneself // 빈 깡통이 여기저기 흩어져 있었다 Empty cans[(영) tins] were scattered all over the place. / The place was littered[strewed] with empty cans. // 회원들이 이제는 각지로 흩어지고 말았다 The members are now scattered all over the country. // 군중은 경관이 오자 사방으로 흩어 졌다 The crowd dispersed[scattered] when the police arrived. // 동백꽃이 땅바닥에 흩어져 있었다 The camellias lay scattered on the ground. // 길에 종잇조각이 흩어져 있었다 The road is littered with paper. // 장난감이 여기저기 흩어져 있었다 Toys lay scattered about. // 길에는 전단이 어지럽게 흩어져 있었다 The street was littered with handbills. // 책상 위에는 원고지가 어지러이 흩어져 있었다 Sheets of manuscript paper were scattered about on the desk. // 동전이 길에 떨어져 사방으로 흩어졌다 Coins fell and scattered (in all direction) on the road. // 그는 드문드문 흩어져 있는 관중에게 열심히 이야기했다 He spoke eagerly [earnestly] to the sparsely scattered audience.

희가극(喜歌劇) a comic opera; an opera bouffe[comique].

희곡(戱曲) a drama; a play. ¶~적[의] dramatic / dramatical // ~을 쓰다 write a drama.
● 희곡 작가 a dramatist; a playwright; (미국 속어) a playwriter. 희곡집 a collection of plays.

희구(希求) desire; aspiration. **희구하다** desire (to do); aspire (to / after); seek; demand; call for; ask for. ¶명성을 희구하지 않다 have no aspiration for[after] fame.

희귀종(稀貴種) a rare variety; a rarity.

희귀하다(稀貴-) rare; infrequent. ¶희귀한 물건 a rarity / a curiosity / a black swan / a white crow // 희귀한 책〔병〕 a rare book[disease] // 희귀한 현상 a singular phenomenon // 희귀한 사건 a rare[an uncommon] occurrence[event].

희극(喜劇) a comedy; a farce (소극(笑劇)); (미) a funny show. ¶막간 ~ an interlude // 가벼운 ~ a light comedy / ~적(인) comic(al) / farcical // ~을 벌이다 play a comedy / 〔비유〕 play the fool / create a comic scene // 한바탕 ~이 벌어졌다 A comic scene was enacted.
● 희극 배우 a comic actor[actress(여자)]; a comedian(남자); a comedienne(여자); (구어) a comic. 희극 작가 a comic writer.

희끄무레하다 whitish; dimly white. ¶희끄무레한 얼굴 a clean and whitish face // 먼동이 희끄무레하게 트이기 시작한다 Day is beginning to break[dawn].

희꾼거리다 (어질증이 나서 어뜩어뜩해지다) get very dizzy[giddy].

희끗희끗 (흰 빛깔이) spotted[speckled] with white; grizzled; grizzly. **희끗희끗하다** grizzled; (옷감 등이) pepper-and-salt. ¶희끗희끗한 수염 a grizzled beard // 머리가 희끗희끗한 노신사 an old gentleman with a sprinkling of gray hairs // 머리가 희끗희끗한 사람 a grizzle-haired person // 머리가 ~ have grizzled [gray] hair // 그는 머리가 희끗희끗해지기 시작했다 His hair is beginning to frost a little.

회나리 wet[green] firewood.

희년(稀年) seventy years of age.

희다 1 (빛깔이) white; (피부가) fair; (머리칼이) gray; hoary. ¶흰 얼굴 a fair[white] face // 흰 머리 gray hair // 눈같이 흰 snow-white / white as snow // 살빛이 ~ have a fair complexion / be light-skinned // 흰 이를 드러내고 웃다 grin / be on the grin // 희게 하다 whiten / blanch(탈색하다) // 희게 칠하다 paint white / (회반죽으로) whitewash // 희게 되다 (회어지다) become white / (머리칼이) turn gray [white] // 흰 눈이 펄펄 내리기 시작했다 White flakes[snow] started to fall. 2 generous without competence. ⇨ 희떫다1

희대(稀代) uncommonness; rarity. ¶~의 uncommon / rare / peerless / unique / unheard-of // ~의 영웅 a unique[peerless] hero.

희디희다 [몹시 희다] very white; pure white; snow(y)-white; (as) white as snow; immaculately white.

희떫다 1 [실속은 없어도 마음이 넓다] generous [lavish / liberal] without competence; (허영적) showy; vain; vainglorious. 2 [배때 벗다] conceited; snobbish; (구어) uppish.

희뜩거리다 get very dizzy[giddy]; (one's

희뜩희뜩하다 head) swim.

희뜩희뜩하다 1 (현기증으로) very dizzy; get very giddy. 2 (흰 빛깔이) dotted [flecked] with white; (머리털에) grizzled; grizzly. ¶희뜩희뜩한 머리칼 grizzled [grizzly / frosty] hair∥머리가 희뜩희뜩한 노신사 an old gentleman with a sprinkling of grey hairs.

희락(喜樂) joy; gladness; happiness; ecstasy.

희로(喜怒) joy and anger; (감정) emotion;
● **희로애락** joy, anger, sorrow, and pleasure [happiness]; joy and anger; (감정) emotion; feelings. ¶~을 얼굴에 나타내지 않다 do not betray one's feelings [emotions].

희롱(戱弄) banter; raillery; rally; jeer; badinage; chaff; jest; (속어) a rag. ¶그녀는 그를 ~ 상대로 골랐다 She chose him as a partner to flirt with. **희롱하다** banter; chaff; tease (a person with his cowardice, a person with jest, etc.); poke fun (at); make a mock of; ridicule. ¶남을 ~ tease a person in jest / (미국 구어) josh a person∥그는 젊은 여자들을 희롱하기 좋아한다 He enjoys bantering with young women.

희롱거리다 frolic; act [play] the giddy goat. ➪해롱거리다

희맑다 white and clean. ➪해맑다

희망(希望) [바람] (a) hope; [소망] a wish; (강한 소망) a desire; an aspiration; [기대] prospect; expectation; [요구] a request; a demand. ¶절실한 [간절한] ~ an ardent desire / an earnest wish / one's dearest ambition∥일루의 ~ a ray [flash / gleam] of hope∥마지막 ~ one's last hope / the last ray of hope∥헛된 ~ an empty hope∥~이 있는 hopeful / promising∥~이 없는 hopeless / desperate / despairing∥최 씨의 ~에 따라 at Mr. Choe's wish [request] / in accordance with Mr. Choe's wishes∥~과는 반대로 against (contrary to) one's wishes∥…을 ~을 가지고 in hopes of … / in the hope that … / with the hope [desire] of …∥…의 ~이 있다 [없다] there is a [no] hope of … / see a [no] hope (for improvement)∥~에 (가득) 차 있다 be hopeful / be full of hope∥~이 이루어지다 have one's wishes fulfilled∥~을 가지다 [지니다・품다] hope / cherish a desire / cherish [entertain / nourish / foster] a hope (that …)∥…에 ~을 걸다 anchor one's hope (in / on) / attach one's hope (to) / pin [set / lay / fasten / hang] one's hope on (scientific projects)∥~을 이루다[달성하다] realize [gratify / get] one's wishes / attain one's desires∥~을 잃다 lose one's hope / one's hope goes down / be disappointed (in / of) / despair of (something)∥~을 버리다 despair (of) / relinquish [give up] (all) hope (of) / surrender [abandon] one's hopes∥~을 버리지 않다 hold on [cling] to one's hope∥모든 ~이 무너졌다 [깨졌다 / 사라졌다] My hopes have been all dashed to the ground [crushed to pieces]. / All my hopes were shattered. / It's all up with me.∥그녀는 마지막 ~을 그에게 걸고 달라붙었다 She clung to him as her last hope.∥그녀는 앞날의 ~을 잃었다 She can see no hope for the future.∥나는 배우가 되는 ~을 포기했다 I gave up all hope of [gave up on] becoming an actor.∥그가 돌아올 것을 기대해도 소용없는데도 나는 ~을 버리지 못하고 있다 I am hoping against hope that he will come back.∥그에게 너무 ~을 걸지 마라 Do not expect too much of him.∥나의 마지막 ~도 사라졌다 My only [last] hope was gone.∥그들은 거기에서 희미한 ~의 빛을 보았다 They found a faint gleam [glimmer] of hope in it. **희망하다** hope (for); be hopeful of; wish; aspire to [after]; expect; be anxious for (peace). ¶그녀는 희망한 대로 옥스퍼드 대학에 들어갔다 She got into Oxford University, just as she had hoped.∥어떤 직장을 희망하십니까 What kind of job are you looking for?
● **희망자** a person who wishes [desires] (something / to do); [지원자] an applicant; a candidate. ¶입회 ~ an applicant for membership.

희멀겋다 fair; fair-[light-]complexioned.

희멀쑥하다 fair and clean (face).

희미하다(稀微−) [미약하다] dim; faint; vague; indistinct; misty; hazy. ¶희미한 소리 a faint sound∥희미한 기억 a faint [dim] memory∥희미한 불빛의 방 a poorly lighted room / a dimly-lit room∥희미하게 밝은 dim / half-lighted∥등불을 희미하게 하다 dim the light∥내게는 희미한 희망조차 없다 I have not the faintest [slightest] hope.∥소리는 점점 멀어지고 희미해졌다 The sound grew fainter and fainter in the distance.∥섬이 희미하게 보인다 I can see an island dimly.∥나는 그 일을 희미하게 기억하고 있다 I have a dim [vague] memory of it.∥희미해서 잘 보이지 않는다 There isn't enough light to see well.∥I cannot see well in this dim light.∥동녘 하늘이 희미하게 밝아 왔다 The eastern sky grew faintly light.∥당시의 일은 그저 희미하게 기억날 뿐이다 I remember those days only vaguely. / I have only a faint memory of those days.

희박하다(稀薄−) [엷다] thin; weak; [묽다] dilute(d) (solution); (공기・가스 등이) rare; rarefied; [성기다] sparse. ¶염분이 희박한 액체 a dilute salt solution∥인구가 희박한 지역 a thinly populated area∥희박하게 하다 weaken / thin / (액체를) dilute / (기체를) rarefy∥그들은 위기 [정치] 의식이 ~ They lack a sense of crisis [political awareness].∥높은 산꼭대기에는 산소가 ~ Oxygen is thin at the top of a high mountain.

희번덕거리다 keep goggling [bulging / popping] one's eyes (from excitement, anger, etc.). ¶그는 놀라서 눈을 희번덕거렸다 He goggled in astonishment.

희번드르하다 1 (얼굴이) fair and bright [radiant / sleek] (complexion); (거죽이) showy; gaudy; ostentatious. ¶희번드르하게 옷만 잘 입었지 보잘것없는 사람이다 He wears showy clothes but there is not much of a person beneath them. 2 (말 등이) specious; glittering; fair-seeming. ¶거짓말을 희번드르하게 하다 tell a lie that sounds like the truth / lie like the truth.

희번지르하다 fair and sleek [well-looking] (face).

희보(喜報) good [auspicious / glad] news; joyful [glad] tidings.

희불그레하다 pale [light] red.

희붐하다 half-light; faintly light; dimly white; gray. ¶동쪽 하늘이 희붐하게 밝아 오고 있다 The sky is growing light in the east. / The eastern sky is brightening.

희비(喜悲) joy and sorrow. ¶나는 ~가 엇갈렸다 I have mixed feelings[emotions] about it. / Joy and grief[Sorrow and pleasure] alternated in my heart.
● **희비쌍곡선** a mingled feeling of joy and sorrow.

희비극(喜悲劇) a tragicomedy. ¶~의 tragicomic(al).

희사(喜捨) charity; almsgiving; alms; oblation; (a) donation; (a) contribution; (a) subscription. ¶~하다 beg for donations[offerings] / ask for alms[contribution] / make a collection (for)//응분의 ~를 하다 contribute one's mite[due share]//~를 받다 receive alms[donations]. **희사하다** give alms; give in charity; donate. ¶그는 복지 사업에 재산을 희사하였다 He made donations to charity[welfare work].
● **희사금** a gift of money; money given in charity[for charitable purposes]; alms; donations.

희색(喜色) a joyful look; a glad countenance. ¶그는 ~이 만면했다 He was beaming with joy. / He was all smiles.

희생(犧牲) a sacrifice; (자기희생) self-sacrifice; self-immolation; (남을 대신하는) a scapegoat. ¶~적 self-sacrificing//많은 ~을 치르고 at a considerable sacrifice / at heavy cost (in blood and treasure)//어떠한 ~을 치르더라도 at all costs / at any cost[price / sacrifice]//어떤 ~을 치르더라도 그 문서를 입수하고 싶다 I want that document no matter what the cost[at any cost]. **희생하다** sacrifice; victimize; make a sacrifice[scapegoat / victim] of (a person). ¶~을 희생하여 at the sacrifice of ... / at the cost[price / expense] of ...//자기 자신을 ~ sacrifice oneself / make a martyr of oneself//공익을 위해 사익을 ~ sacrifice one's personal interest to public good/그는 자유를 위해 한 몸을 희생했다 He died a martyr to the cause of liberty. →¶아버지는 화재로 희생되셨다 My father was a victim of the fire.//많은 시민이 전쟁에 희생되었다 A great many civilian lives were sacrificed during the war. / 나는 가족을 희생시키면서까지 출세하고 싶지는 않다 I do not intend to go so far as to sacrifice my family to[advance] my career. / I do not want to succeed in life at the expense of my family.
● **희생물** a scapegoat; a victim; a sacrifice. ¶홍 씨는 그들의 ~이 되었다 Mr. Hong was made their scapegoat.//그녀는 쉽게 그자의 ~이 되어 버렸다 She fell an easy prey[victim] to that man. **희생 번트** 〔야구〕 a sacrifice bunt. ¶그는 ~로 주자를 2루로 나아가게 했다 He bunted the runner to second base. / He advanced the runner to second base with a sacrifice bunt. **희생자** a victim (of a fire); a prey. ¶탄광 화재로 많은 ~가 생겼다 The fire in the coal mine took a heavy toll of lives.//댐은 30명의 귀중한 ~를 내고 완성됐다 The dam was completed at the cost of thirty lives. **희생정신** a spirit of (self-)sacrifice. **희생타** 〔야구〕 a sacrifice (hit); sacrifice batting. **희생 플라이** 〔야구〕 (hit) a sacrifice fly.

희서(稀書) a rare book.

희석(稀釋) dilution; attenuation. **희석하다** dilute; attenuate. ¶희석한 커피〔차〕 weakened coffee[tea] / 우유를 물로 ~ water milk down / thin milk with water//액체를 물로 ~ dilute a liquid with water.
● **희석액** a diluted[weak] solution. **희석제** a diluent.

희세(稀世) 〔진기함〕 uncommonness; rarity. ¶~의 uncommon / rare / extraordinary / unique / unheard-of / peerless / matchless//~의 영웅 a hero of extraordinary caliber / a hero for the century / ~의 악한 a notorious villain.

희소(稀少) scarcity; rarity. ¶~의 rare. **희소하다** scarce; rare.
● **희소가치** scarcity[rarity] value. **희소성** scarcity.

희소식(喜消息) good[favorable / happy / glad] news; joyful[glad] tidings. ¶~을 전하다 convey[bring] good news / give glad tidings//~이야 This is good news for you. / Here's a (pleasant) surprise for you.

희수(稀壽) 〔일흔 살〕 seventy years of age; one's seventieth birthday.

희수(喜壽) (reach) one's 77th birthday. ¶~ 축하 77th birthday celebration.

희열(喜悅) joy; gladness. ⇨＂희락

희원(希願) (a) hope; a wish. ⇨＂희망

희유기체(稀有氣體) 〔화〕 rare[noble / inert] gases.

희유원소(稀有元素) a rare element.

희읍스름하다 whitish; (서술적) be not quite white; be not white[clean] enough.

희토류 원소(稀土類元素) a rare-earth element.

희한하다(稀罕－) rare; uncommon; unusual; phenomenal; singular; extraordinary; curious(진기하다); novel(신기하다). ¶희한한 물건 a rare article / a rarity / a curiosity//희한한 일 a rare[an uncommon] occurrence / a rarity/그 사람이 화를 내다니 희한한 일이구나 It is unusual for him to get angry.

희화(戲畫) a caricature; (정치·사회 문제 등의) a cartoon. ¶그는 당시의 풍조를 ~화해서 그렸다 He depicted contemporary trends in cartoons. / He caricatured the trends of the day.

희희낙락하다(喜喜樂樂－) be (very) joyful [glad / delightful / gleeful / happy / pleasant]; rejoice[be rejoiced] (at / over); delight [take delight] (in). ¶희희낙락하여 merrily / joyfully / cheerfully.

흰개미 〔동〕 a white ant; a termite.

흰곰 〔동〕 a white[polar] bear.

흰나비 〔동〕 **1** a white (butterfly). **2** a cabbage butterfly. ⇨＂배추흰나비

흰둥이 (병적인) an albino (pl. ~s); 〔백인〕 a white man; (속어) a white.

흰떡 rice cake.

흰머리 white hair. ⇨＂백발 ¶~가 섞인 머리 hair streaked with gray / grizzled hair//~의 남자 a gray-haired[white-haired / silver-haired] man//~를 뽑아내다 pull out a white hair//~가 섞이다 (머리가) show white streaks / become grizzled//~를 검게 물들이다 dye one's (gray) hair black/갑자기 ~가 많아지고 있다 My hair is rapidly turning [going] gray. / My hair is graying rapidly.

흰무리 steamed rice cake in simple shape [without layers].

흰밥 plain white rice (cooked with nothing mixed in).

흰소리 a vain [an empty] boast; a big [a tall / an inflated] talk; a brag; (구어) a fish [tall] story; (속어) gas. ¶~ 작작해 There is a limit to bragging! **흰소리하다** talk big [tall]; brag; blow; draw [shoot] a long bow; (구어) talk through one's hat.
● **흰소리꾼** a vain [an empty] boaster; a braggart; (미국 속어) a blowhard.
흰쌀 polished rice. ⇨ °백미(白米)
흰인(-燐) white [yellow] phosphorus.
흰자(위) **1** (계란의) the white (of an egg); the albumen; glair. **2** (눈의) the whites of one's eyes. ¶~를 굴리다 show the whites of one's eyes.
흰죽(-粥) rice gruel. ¶~을 끓이다 boil rice into gruel.
히드라 [동] a hydra (*pl.* ~s, -drae).
히로뽕 methamphetamine(▶ 히로뽕은 상표명).
히브리서(-書) [성] the Epistle of St. Paul (the Apostle) to the Hebrews; Hebrews(약어 Heb.).
히스타민 [화] histamine. ¶항~제 an antihistamine.
히스테리 [의] hysteria; [발작] hysterics; (미국 구어) conniption; (미) PMS(▶ premenstrual syndrome의 약어); (영) PMT(▶ premenstrual tension의 약어)(생리 전의). ¶~의 hysterical // ~를 일으키다 go into hysterics / become hysterical // 그 화제가 나오면 그녀는 ~를 일으킨다 Whenever that topic comes up, she makes a scene.
히스테릭하다 hysteric(al). ¶히스테릭해지다 become hysterical // 그녀는 히스테릭하게 웃어 댔다 She burst into hysterical laughter.
히스패닉 [라틴 아메리카 출신의 미국 거주자] a Hispanic.
히아신스 [식] a hyacinth.
히어로 a hero. ¶이야기의 ~ the hero of a story // 오늘 [그날] 의 ~는 홍길동 투수였다 The pitcher, Hong Gildong, was today's hero [the hero of the day].
히어링(*hearing) [외국어 듣기] listening.
● **히어링 연습 / 히어링 훈련** a drill in listening. **히어링 테스트** listening [comprehension] test.(▶ hearing test는 청력 검사의 뜻임)
히죽 with an affable [a sweet] smile; smilingly. ¶~ 웃다 smile sweetly (at a person) / break into a smile.
히죽거리다 give one sweet smile after another.
히죽이 with a sweet [happy / contented / peaceful] smile; smilingly; beamingly. ¶~ 웃다 smile sweetly / beam with a smile / smile a sweet smile // 그는 좋아서 ~ 웃었다 He grinned with delight. // 그 아이는 하얀 이를 드러내며 ~ 웃었다 The boy flashed his white teeth in a quick grin.
히죽히죽 grinningly; with a broad grin. ¶~ 웃다 grin (broadly) (at). **히죽히죽하다** give one sweet smile after another. ⇨ °히죽거리다
히치하이크 a hitchhike; hitchhiking. ¶그들은 ~로 (대륙을 횡단하여) 뉴욕에 갔다 They hitchhiked to New York (across the continent). **히치하이크하다** hitchhike (one's way) (to).
히터 a heater. ¶전기 ~ an electric heater // ~를 켜다 [끄다] turn on [off] a heater.
히트 1 [야구] a (safe) hit; a single (hit). ¶클린 ~ a clean hit // 텍사스 ~ (속어) a blooper / a Texas leaguer // ~를 치다 (make a) hit // ~ 세 개로 2점 올리다 score two runs on three hits // 노~ 노런을 기록하다 pitch a no-hit, no-run game // (피처가) ~를 허용하지 않다 pitch [hurl] a no-hitter // 그가 ~를 쳤다 He got a (base) hit. **히트하다** hit; make a hit. **2** [대성공] a hit; a great (box-office) success. ¶~ 레코드 a recording hit // 기록을 깨는 대 ~였다 It was a record-breaking hit. // 그의 유행가가 대~를 쳤다 He made a great hit with his popular song. // His song was a great hit [success]. **히트하다** win a success; be a hit. ¶히트한 연극 a hit play.
● **히트송** a hit song. **히트 앤드 런** hit-and-run (play).
히프 one's hips. ¶~가 큰 large-hipped // ~ 길이의 코트 a hip-length coat.
히피 a hippie; a flower child; (집합적) hippies.
● **히피촌** a hippie commune.
히히 he-he!; hee-hee!
히히거리다 keep laughing playfully. ⇨ °해해거리다
힌두교(-敎) Hinduism; Hindooism.
● **힌두교도** a Hindu.
힌트 a hint; a tip-off. ¶~를 주다 give [drop / let fall] a hint // ~를 얻다 get [receive] a hint (from) / take (the) hint (from the scene) / pick up an idea // ~를 주겠다 I will give you a hint. // 그는 파도 소리에서 ~를 얻어 이 소나타를 만들었다 He got the hint for this sonata from the sound of waves.
힐 (wear) high-heeled shoes. ¶하이 [로] ~ high- [low-] heeled shoes.
힐끗 1 [얼씬 보이는 모양]. ¶~ 보이다 get [catch] a glimpse of. **2** [재빨리 흘겨보는 모양] with a sidelong glance. ¶그는 무관심한 태도로 이쪽을 보았다 He glanced this way casually [out of the corner of his eye].
힐난(詰難) blame; censure; reproach. **힐난하다** blame; censure; reproach; call (a person) to task.
힐문(詰問) cross-examination; close questioning; cross-questioning; a rigid [searching] inquiry; a demand (for an explanation); grilling. **힐문하다** cross-question; cross-examine; examine [question] closely; press (a person) hard with questions; inquire searchingly; put (a person) through severe examination; demand (an explanation); grill; call (a person) to account. ¶ ~의 실패를 ~ needle (a person) over the failure of ...
힐책(詰責) rebuke; reprimand; reproof; reproach; censure. **힐책하다** rebuke; reprimand; reprove; reproach; censure; call (a person) to task [account]. ¶약속 불이행을 ~ reproach (a person) for breaking his promise // 태만을 ~ rebuke (a person) for his neglect of duty. → ¶그는 감독 불충분으로 힐책당했다 He was reprimanded for insufficient control.
힘 1 [체력] (physical) strength; energy; force; might; power. ¶~만으로 by sheer strength // 근육의 ~ muscular strength // ~이 붙다 gain [gather] strength // ~이 장사다 have Herculean strength // ~을 겨루다 measure one's strength (with) / have a strength contest // ~이 세지다 [없어지다] gain [lose] strength // ~이 없다 be spiritless / lack

backbone // ~을 **내다** put forth[out] one's strength // ~을 **회복하다** regain[renew] strength // 그들은 온 ~을 다하여 싸웠다 They fought with all their strength. / They mustered (up)[summoned] all their strength to fight. // 그가 결승점에 도달했을 때는 온 ~이 빠져 있었다 He had exhausted his strength when he reached the goal. // 그는 야구에 온 ~을 쏟았다 He concentrated all his strength[energy] on baseball. // 그 일에는 큰 ~이 든다 The task requires plenty of energy. / It takes a lot of drive to do the job.

2 [물리적인 힘] force; power; energy. ¶열의 ~ energy of heat / caloric force // 자연의 ~ natural forces // 증기[전기]의 ~ steam[electric] power // ~이 좋은 엔진 a high-powered engine // 자석의 ~ the virtue of the magnet // 이 기계는 물의 ~으로 움직인다 This machine is driven by hydraulic power. // 보트는 바람의 ~으로 밀려갔다 The boat was swept away by the wind.

3 [작용] agency; action. ¶눈에 보이지 않는 ~ an invisible agency // 하느님의 ~ agency of Providence / divine agency.

4 [권세·위력] power; force; authority; sway; influence; weight. ¶전통의 ~ the weight of tradition // 여론의 ~ the force of public opinion // 경찰의 ~ the power[authority] of the police // 정부의 ~으로 through the influence[power] of the government // ~ 있는 사람 an influential person / a person who carries some weight // ~의 정치 power politics / rule by might // 부모의 ~으로 through the influence of one's parents // 그는 순전히 돈의 ~으로 정계에 진출했다 He got into politics by the sheer force of money. // 그는 부모의 ~으로 지금의 지위를 얻었다 He got his present position through the influence of his parents. // 그는 백부의 ~으로 그 회사에 들어갔다 He entered the company through his uncle's influence. // ~에는 ~으로 대항할 수밖에 없다 We must meet force with force.

5 [기운·용기] vigor; (미) nerve; heart; courage; (미국 속어) pep; ginger. ¶~을 북돋우다 invigorate / give vigor (to) / [격려하다] cheer up / encourage // ~을 잃다 lose courage[heart] / get dejected[dispirited / disheartened] // ~내 Cheer up! / Be of good cheer! / Snap out of it! / Perk up! // 한 잔의 차로 내게 새 ~이 났다 A cup of tea gave me fresh strength.

6 [강세] force; stress; emphasis. ¶~ 있는 문장 powerful sentences // ~ 있는 어조 a heavy accent // 그의 글에는 ~이 있다 He has a powerful pen. // 이 번역으로는 원문의 ~이 완전히 사라진다 The force of the original is entirely lost in this translation.

7 [노력] efforts; labor; exertions; endeavors. ¶~을 합쳐서 in cooperation (with) / by united effort // 자신의 ~으로 by one's own efforts // ~ 안 들이고 돈 벌기 making money without effort // ~을 합치다 cooperate / unite [join] efforts // 그들은 모든 ~을 다하여 시의 발전을 도왔다 They made[exerted] every possible effort to help the city develop. // 육해군이 ~을 합하여 적을 물리쳤다 The army and navy united to defeat the enemy. // 우리 모두가 ~을 합하지 않으면 이 사업은 성공할 가망이 없다 If we don't all pull together, the project has no chance of success.

8 [효력·효과] efficacy; effectiveness; effect. ¶약의 ~ the efficacy[virtue] of medicine [drug].

9 [조력] assistance; aid; help; support; good offices; service. ¶…의 ~으로 by[with] the aid of … / through (a person's) aid // ~이 되어 주다 help / assist / give assistance to / lend (a person) a helping hand // ~을 빌리다 get (a person's) help / enlist the help [aid] (of) // 언제건 ~이 되어 드리겠습니다 You will always find a friend in me. // ~이 되어 주는 것은 자네뿐일세 You are the only friend I can turn to for help. // 서로서로 ~이 됩시다 Let us help each other.

10 [능력] ability; power; faculty; capability; capacity; [재산] means. ¶듣는 ~ the faculty of hearing // ~이 자라는 데까지 as far [much] as one can / to best of one's ability [power] // ~을 **발휘하다** display one's ability // ~이 자라는 데까지 노력하다 strive with all one's might work as hard as one can / (구어) give it all[everything] one's got // 그에게는 남을 통솔하는 뛰어난 ~이 있다 He has fine leadership abilities[capabilities]. // 셰익스피어를 번역할 만한 ~은 내게 없다 I am not competent to translate Shakespeare. // 그와 씨름하기엔 ~에 부친다 I am not strong enough to wrestle with him. // 그 일은 내 ~에 부치는 일이다 The job is beyond my ability. // 이것을 들어 올리는 것은 내 ~에 부친다 It is impossible for me[I don't have the strength] to lift this.

11 [공헌] contribution; service. ¶…함에 있어서 ~이 크다 contribute greatly to … / make [do] much for … / be instrumental in (doing) // 새 학교를 설립하는 데에는 그의 ~이 컸다 He has contributed much in establishing the new school.

힘을 기르다 cultivate the faculty (of).

힘을 얻다 be encouraged (by); be cheered up (by). ¶그의 말에 나는 힘을 얻었다 I was encouraged by his words.

힘겨룸 a contest of strength. **힘겨룸하다** have a strength contest; have a trial of strength. ¶힘겨룸해 보자 Let's see who is the stronger, you or I.

힘겹다 (서술적) be not strong enough (to do); be beyond one's ability[power / reach]; be too much for one (to manage). ¶힘겨운 여행 a hard journey // 힘겨운 일 a laborous [heavy] task // 요즈음은 계단 오르기도 힘겹소 Lately I have had trouble going up the stairs. // 이 더위에 고개를 오른다는 것은 힘겨운 일이다 It is tiring to walk uphill in this hot weather. // 그는 힘겨운 듯이 걷고 있었다 He was walking with heavy steps[wearily]. // 그 사람과 교섭한다는 것은 힘겨운 일이다 It is a burdensome[an onerous] chore to negotiate with him.

힘껏 with all one's strength[might]; with might and main; to the best of one's ability [power]. ¶~ 하다 do one's best[utmost] / do everything in one's power[as one can] // ~ 당기다 pull with all one's force[strength] / pull with might and main // ~ 싸우다 fight for all one is worth // ~ 일하다 work with all one's strength / work at[up to] capacity // 활을 ~ 잡아당기다 draw a bow to the full // 발을 ~ 내디디다 plant one's feet firmly // 그는

힘들다

밧줄을 ~ 끌어당겼다 He pulled the rope with all his strength [with all his might / with all the strength he could muster]. // 나는 ~ 일했다 I worked with all my might. // 그들은 20년 만에 다시 만나 ~ 껴안았다 The two gave each other a good firm [hearty] hug when they met again after twenty years. // 그는 몸을 돌려 공을 ~ 쳤다 He swung at the ball with all the strength he possessed. // 나는 문을 ~ 밀었다 I pushed on the door with all my might. // ~ 해 보겠습니다 I will do my best. / (구어) I'll give it all I've got.

힘들다 1 [벅차다] laborious [arduous / strenuous / toilsome / troublesome / tough / painful]. ¶힘드는 일 a heavy [hard / laborious / toilsome / painful] task / a tough job // 힘들지 않는 일 a light [an easy] task / a soft job // 그 일은 무척 힘들었다 It cost me a great deal of trouble. / I went to considerable trouble in doing it.
2 [어렵다] hard [difficult / hard going / tough sledding]. ¶힘든 문제 a difficult problem // 더워서 일하기가 ~ be so hot that it is hard to work // 몸을 굽히기가 ~ have trouble in bending oneself // 일자리를 구하기가 ~ have difficulty in finding a job // 마침내 가장 힘드는 고비는 넘어섰다 At last we have broken the back of the work. // 그 일을 하는 데는 별로 힘들지 않았다 I had little difficulty [trouble] (in) doing the work.

힘들이다 1 (체력·노력을) put in one's strength [labo(u)r / efforts]; make efforts; exert oneself; endeavo(u)r. ¶일에 ~ throw oneself into one's work // 힘들여 운반하다 carry the load laboriously // 힘들인 보람이 있었다 My efforts were rewarded.
2 [애쓰다] take pains; take trouble; make (strenuous) efforts; labor. ¶힘들여서 laboriously / with (much) trouble / with (great) efforts // 일껏 힘들였는데도 after much trouble / after all one's efforts // 조금도 힘들이지 않고 without taking the least pains / without any effort / easily // 힘들여 번 돈 hard-earned money // 어려운 문제를 힘들이지 않고 풀다 solve a difficult problem with ease [with hardly any effort] // 그렇게 힘들이지 말고 쉽게 해라 Don't try so hard — take easy. // 힘들일 만한 가치가 없다 It is not worth the trouble.

힘살 muscle. ⇨근육

힘세다 strong; powerful; mighty. ¶힘세어 보이는 strong-looking // 힘센 자가 이긴다 The battle is to the strong. // 그는 굉장히 ~ He is of Herculean strength. / He is as strong as a horse.

힘쓰다 1 [노력하다] exert oneself; make efforts; endeavor; strive; try hard; labor (to do / for / after). ¶힘써 공부하다 study hard // 학업에 ~ attend to one's studies with diligence // 목적을 달성하려고 ~ strive after [for] one's object // 문제를 해결하려고 ~ set oneself to solve a problem // 출세하려고 ~ do one's best to succeed in life // 어학 연구에 특히 ~ lay special emphasis (up)on the study of languages // 힘쓴 보람도 없이 실패했다 In spite of my efforts, I failed. // 그는 파티에 출석할 때마다 새 친구를 사귀기에 힘썼다 Whenever he went to a party, he made an efforts [took every opportunity] to make new friends.
2 take pains. ⇨힘들이다2
3 [돕다] do (a person) a service; help; aid; extend help (to); lend a helping hand (to); (영향을) use one's influence (for a person). ¶남의 취직을 위해 ~ help (a person) find employment / assist (a person) to a position // 그는 나를 위해 여러 가지로 힘써 주었다 He has done lots of good turns for me. / He did me many good offices.

힘없다 [기력이 없다] weak; feeble; powerless; [능력이 부족하다] incapable; incompetent. ¶힘없는 목소리로 in a weak voice. **힘없이** feebly; droopingly; dejectedly. ¶~ 대답하다 give a feeble answer / answer feebly [dejectedly] // ~ 고개를 수그리다 hung down one's head much discouraged.

힘입다 owe; be indebted to (a person) for (something); be in (another's) debt. ¶아버지의 교육에 힘입어 성공하다 owe one's success to one's father's education // 그는 부친에게 힘입은 바 크다 He owes much to his father. / He is much indebted to his father.

힘자랑 boast of one's strength. **힘자랑하다** boast [be proud] of one's strength.

힘주다 1 (육체적으로) strain (at stool) (화장실에서); bear down (분만 때에). 2 [강조하다] emphasize; put stress (on). ¶힘주어 emphatically / with emphasis // 힘주어 말하다 emphasize [lay stress on] one's words / speak with emphasis.

힘줄 1 [근육의 희고 질긴 물질] a muscle; a tendon; a sinew. ¶~투성이의 sinewy // ~이 굵은 팔 a sinewy arm // ~이 당기다 have a strain in a muscle. 2 [혈맥·혈관] a vein. 3 [섬유질] a fiber; (영) fibre; a string. ¶~이 많은 stringy / fibrous // ~이 많은 고기 tough meat / stringy meat.

힘줌말 an intensive [emphatic] word.

힘차다 [활력이 넘치다] powerful; forceful; forcible; vigorous; energetic; full of strength. ¶힘찬 문체 a vigorous style // 힘찬 문장 a crisp [vigorous] style // 힘찬 연설 a powerful speech // 힘차게 powerfully / energetically / vigorously // 그는 힘차게 노를 젓기 시작했다 He started to row with vigor [with all his might / energetically].

힙합 hip-hop; hip hop.

힝 [코 푸는 소리] with a hissing sound; [비웃는 소리] pshaw! ¶코를 ~ 풀다 blow one's nose with a hissing sound.

힝힝 clearing one's nose repeatedly.

부 록

잘못 쓰기 쉬운 한국식 영어 ● 2120~2121
세계 주요 지명 ● 2122~2135
세계 주요 인명 ● 2136~2149
국어의 로마자 표기법 ● 2150~2152

잘못 쓰기 쉬운 한국식 영어

우리말 외래어 가운데에는 영어를 어원으로 하고 있음에도 불구하고 정작 그 본산지에서는 쓰이지 않는 말이 적지 않다. 이런 말들은 영어 회화나 작문에 그대로 쓰임으로써 잘못된 영어 표현을 만들어 내곤 한다. 이러한 잘못을 효과적으로 예방하기 위해, 한국식 영어에 토대를 둔 외래어를 한자리에 모아 보았다. [* 한국식 영어 앞에 ・ → 바른 영어 앞에]

개런티 연예인의 출연료. *guarantee → performance [appearance] fee.
겟투 야구에서, 병살. *get two → twin killing; double play.
골든아워 황금 시간대. *golden hour → prime time.
골 세리모니 골을 넣고 취하는 축하 제스처. *goal ceremony → goal celebration.
골인 구기에서, 골을 넣는 일. *goal in → scoring a goal.
그룹사운드 음악 연주 그룹. *group sound → musical band.
껌 *gum → chewing gum.
나이스 샷 골프에서, 훌륭한 샷. *nice shot → fine [good] shot.
내레이터모델 안내 도우미. *narrator model → pitch girl.
넥타이핀 *necktie pin → tiepin; tie clasp [clip]; (미) stickpin.
노트 공책. *note → notebook.
다운 권투에서, 쓰러지는 일. *down → knockdown.
댄스파티 *dance party → dance; dancing party; ball(화려한 고급 무도회); (미) prom (미국 고등학교 등의 파티).
더치페이 비용을 각자 부담하는 것. *Dutch pay → Dutch treat.
데드 볼 야구에서, 사구(死球). *dead ball → pitch which hits the batter; hit by a pitched ball.
데커레이션 케이크 *decoration cake → fancy cake.
드라이버 나사돌리개. *driver → screwdriver.
러닝머신 달리기 운동 기구. *running machine → treadmill.
러닝셔츠 *running shirt → (속옷) (미) undershirt; (영) vest; (운동용) athletic shirt.
러닝 호머 야구에서, 펜스를 넘지 않은 홈런. *running homer → inside-the-park homer.
레지 다방 여종업원. *register → tearoom waitress.
로스 타임 축구 등에서, 허비된 만큼 연장되는 경기 시간. *loss time → added time; injury time; lost time.
리모컨 원격 조정기. → remote (control).
리베이트 뇌물. *rebate → kickback; bribe.
리시버 귀에 꽂고 듣는 장치. *receiver → earphones.
리어카 손수레. *rear car → handcart; pushcart.
리포트 학교에 내는 소논문. *report → paper; essay.

마니아 광적으로 즐기는 사람. *mania → maniac; fan; buff.
마마보이 어머니에게 너무 의지하는 남자. *mama boy → mama's boy.
마카로니웨스턴 이탈리아 서부극. *macaroni western → spaghetti western; Italian western.
매니큐어 손톱 물감. *manicure → (미) nail polish; (영) nail varnish.
매스컴 언론 매체. → mass media.
매직펜 유성 잉크 필기구. *magic pen → marker (pen).
맨션 고급 아파트. *mansion → apartment [(영) flat] (of a better class).
무스탕 가공한 양모피. *mustang → sheepskin coat; lambskin coat.
미스 실수. → mistake.
미싱 재봉틀. → sewing machine.
미팅 모르는 남녀간의 만남. *meeting → blind date.
믹서 과일 가는 기계. *mixer → blender.
백넘버 선수의 등번호. *back number → uniform number.
백네트 야구에서, 뒤 그물. *back net → backstop.
백댄서 가수 뒤에서 춤추는 사람. *back dancer → background dancer.
백미러 자동차 뒷거울. *back mirror → rear view mirror.
볼펜 필기구의 하나. *ball pen → ballpoint (pen).
블루스 남녀가 안고 느리게 추는 춤. *blues → slow dance.
비닐하우스 채소 재배 온상. *vinyl house → plastic greenhouse.
비치파라솔 대형 파라솔. *beach parasol → beach umbrella.
사이다 청량 음료수. *cider → (미) soda (pop); (영) aerated water. ★cider의 본뜻은 미국에서는 '사과즙', 영국에서는 '사과주'임.
사인 유명인의 친필 서명. *sign → autograph.
사인펜 필기구의 하나. *sign pen → felt-tip (pen).
샐러리맨 봉급생활자. *salary man → office worker; salaried worker [man].
샤프펜슬 필기구의 하나. *sharp pencil → mechanical [automatic/(영) propelling] pencil.
서클 동아리. *circle → club.
선팅 창 유리에 색 필름을 붙이는 일. → (window) tinting.
스킨십 피부 접촉. *skinship → close physical contact.

잘못 쓰기 쉬운 한국식 영어

스탠드 전기 스탠드. *stand → desk[table] lamp.
스티커 교통 위반 딱지. *sticker → ticket.
시에프 모델 광고 모델. *CF model → commercial actor[actress]; ad actor[actress].
시엠 방송용 광고. *CM → commercial.
아이쇼핑 눈으로만 구경하는 일. *eye shopping → window shopping.
아이스케이크 막대 얼음과자. *ice cake → (미) popsicle.
아파트 1 개별 가구의 아파트. → (미) apartment; condominium; (영) flat. 2 건물 전체. → (미) apartment house[building]; condominium; (영) block of flats.
애프터서비스 사후 봉사. *after service → after-sale(s) service; warranty; (repair) service.
에어컨 냉방 장치. → air conditioner.
엠티 수련회. *MT → membership training.
오버 외투. *over → overcoat.
오버헤드 킥 축구에서, 머리 너머로 공을 차는 일. *overhead kick → bicycle kick.
오토바이 원동기 달린 이륜차. *auto bicycle → motorcycle.
오픈 게임 권투에서, 주 경기에 앞서 열리는 경기. *open game → open event[tournament].
오픈카 지붕 없는 자동차. *open car → convertible.
올드미스 노처녀. *old miss → old maid; spinster; (영) tabby.
와이셔츠 양복 안에 입는 셔츠. *white shirts → shirt; dress shirt.
워커 군화. *walker → combat[army] boots.
원룸 아파트 방 하나로 이뤄진 아파트. *one-room apartment → (미) studio apartment; (영) studio flat.
원샷 건배. *one shot → bottoms up.
윈도 브러시 자동차 유리 닦개. *window brush → wiper; (미) windshield wiper; (영) windscreen wiper.
인프라 기반 시설. → infrastructure.
점퍼 지퍼로 여미는 상의. *jumper → (zip-up) jacket. ★jumper는 (영)에서는 스웨터를, (미)에서는 점퍼스커트를 가리킴.
찬스 메이커 득점의 계기를 만드는 선수. *chance maker → heads-up player.
추리닝 운동 연습복. *training → training suit; sweat suit; jogging suit.
치어걸 여자 응원단원. *cheer girl → cheerleader; pom-pom girl.
카센터 자동차 정비소. *car center → car[auto] repair shop; body shop; garage.
카퍼레이드 차를 타고 벌이는 시가행진. *car parade → motorcade.
캐치볼 야구에서, 공을 주고받는 연습. *catch ball → playing catch.
커닝 시험에서, 부정행위. *cunning → cheating (on [(영) in] an examination); cribbing
커닝 페이퍼 커닝을 위한 쪽지. *cunning paper → crib(sheet); cheat sheet.
커트라인 합격선. *cut line → cutoff point.
콘사이스 소형 사전. *concise → pocket(-sized) dictionary.
콘센트 플러그 꽂는 장치. *concent → (미) (electric) outlet; wall socket; plug receptacle [(영) socket].
콤플렉스 열등감. *complex → inferiority complex.
키포인트 주안점. *key point → main[essential] point.
탤런트 텔레비전 연기자. *talent → TV actor[actress]; actor[actress] in TV.
터치아웃 야구에서, 주자를 아웃시키는 일. *touch out → tagging (a runner) out.
텍사스 히트 야구에서, 안타의 하나. *Texas hit → Texas leaguer; blooper; bloop hit.
트럼프 서양 놀이딱지 또는, 그 놀이. *trump → (game of) cards.
파이팅 잘 싸워라! 힘내라! *fighting → go; way to go; stick it out.
팬티 남자 팬티. *panties → [삼각 팬티] briefs; (상품명) jockey shorts; [사각 팬티] boxers; boxer shorts. ★한국어 '팬티'는 남성용·여성용을 다 포함하나, 영어 'panties'는 여성용을 가리킴. briefs는 남성용·여성용 모두를 가리킴.
팬티스타킹 허리까지 오는 스타킹. *panty stocking → panty hose; pantihose.
페디큐어 발톱 물감. *pedicure → (미) nail polish; (영) nail varnish.
포볼 야구에서, 사구(四球). *four ball → base on balls; pass; walk.
포클레인 굴삭기. *Poclain → hydraulic shovel; steam shovel.
폰팅 전화 데이트. *phone ting → telephone blind date.
풀 베이스 만루. *full base → loaded bases.
프리 배팅 자유 타격 연습. *free batting → batting practice.
플라잉 스타트 반칙 스타트. *flying start → premature start; breakaway.
플러스알파 더 보탬. *plus alpha → plus something; plus extra; something extra.
하이틴 10대 후반. *high teen → one's late teens.
해프닝 우발적 사건. *happening → accident; unexpected incident.
핸드폰 휴대 전화. *hand phone → cellular[mobile] phone; cellphone.
핸들 운전 장치. *handle → [자동차] (steering) wheel; [자전거·오토바이] handlebars.
홈드라마 가정극. *home drama → family drama.
히어링 외국어 듣기. *hearing → listening.

세계 주요 지명

가

가나 (국명) (the Republic of) Ghana
가나자와(金澤) (일본) (도시) Kanazawa
가론 강 (프랑스) the Garonne (River)
가봉 (국명) Gabon; (공식명) the Gabonese Republic
가오슝(高雄) (대만) (도시) Kaohsiung; Gaoxiong
가이아나 (국명) Guyana; (공식명) the Cooperative Republic of Guyana
가자 (중동 지중해 연안) (도시) Gaza
간다라 (아프가니스탄) (지역) Gandhara
간쑤 성(甘肅省) (중국) Gansu
갈라파고스 제도 (태평양 동부) the Galapagos (Islands)
감비아 (국명) (the Republic of) the Gambia
갠지스 강 (인도) the Ganges (River)
게티즈버그 (미국) (도시) Gettysburg
고드윈오스턴 산 (Mount) Godwin Austen ⇨케이투 봉
고리키 (러시아) (도시) Gorki; Gorky ('니주니노브고로드'의 구칭)
고베(神戶) (일본) (도시) Kobe
고비 사막 (몽골) the Gobi (Desert)
고아 주 (인도) Goa
골란 고원 (시리아) the Golan Heights
과달라하라 (멕시코) (도시) Guadalajara
과달루페 섬 (서인도 제도) Guadalupe
과달카날 섬 (태평양 서부) Guadalcanal
과테말라 (국명) (the Republic of) Guatemala
괌 섬 (태평양 서부) Guam
광둥 성(廣東省) (중국) Guangdong
광시좡 족(廣西壯族) 자치구 (중국) Guangxi Zhuang; (공식명) the Guangxi Zhuang Autonomous Region
광저우(廣州) (중국) (도시) Guangzhou
교토(京都) (일본) (도시) Kyoto
구마모토(熊本) (일본) (도시) Kumamoto
구이저우 성(貴州省) (중국) Guizhou
구자라트 (인도) (지역) Gujarat
규슈(九州) (일본) (섬) Kyushu
그단스크 (폴란드) (도시) Gdańsk
그라나다 (에스파냐) (도시) Granada
그랜드 캐니언 (미국) (협곡) the Grand Canyon
그레나다 (국명) Grenada
그레이트베어 호 (캐나다) Great Bear Lake
그레이트베이슨 (미국) (분지) the Great Basin
그레이트브리튼 (영국) (섬) Great Britain
그레이트샌디 사막 (오스트레일리아) the Great Sandy Desert
그레이트솔트 호 (미국) the Great Salt Lake
그레이트슬레이브 호 (캐나다) Great Slave Lake
그루지야 (국명) (the Republic of) Georgia
그르노블 (프랑스) (도시) Grenoble
그리니치 (영국) (도시) Greenwich
그리스 (국명) Greece; (공식명) the Hellenic Republic
그린란드 (북극) (섬) Greenland
그린즈버러 (미국) (도시) Greensboro
글로스터 (영국) (도시) Gloucester
기니 (국명) (the Republic of) Guinea
기니비사우 (국명) (the Republic of) Guinea-Bissau
기아나 (남아메리카) (지역) Guiana
기타큐슈(北九州) (일본) (도시) Kitakyushu

나

나가사키(長崎) (일본) (도시) Nagasaki
나고야(名古屋) (일본) (도시) Nagoya
나그푸르 (인도) (도시) Nagpur
나라(奈良) (일본) (도시) Nara
나리타(成田) (일본) (도시) Narita
나미비아 (국명) (the Republic of) Namibia
나소 (바하마) (수도) Nassau
나우루 (국명) (the Republic of) Nauru
나이로비 (케냐) (수도) Nairobi
나이아가라 폭포 (미국) Niagara Falls
나이지리아 (국명) Nigeria; (공식명) the Federal Republic of Nigeria
나일 강 (아프리카 북동부) the Nile (River)
나탈 (브라질) (도시) Natal
나폴리 (이탈리아) (도시) Naples
나훗카 (러시아) (도시) Nakhodka
난징(南京) (중국) (도시) Nanjing (구칭: Nanking)
남극해 (남극) the Antarctic Ocean
남아프리카 공화국 (국명) (the Republic of) South Africa
남중국해 (중국 남동 해역) the South China Sea
낭시 (프랑스) (도시) Nancy
낭트 (프랑스) (도시) Nantes
내몽골 (중국) (지역) Inner Mongolia; Nei Mongol; (공식명: 네이멍구 자치구) the Inner Mongolia Autonomous Region
내슈빌데이비드슨 (미국) (도시) Nashville-Davidson
네그루 강 (브라질 북부) the Rio Negro
네덜란드 (국명) the Netherlands, Holland; (공식명) the Kingdom of the Netherlands
네바다 주 (미국) Nevada (약어 Nev., NV)
네브래스카 주 (미국) Nebraska (약어 Nebr., Neb., NE)
네스 호 (영국) Loch Ness
네팔 (국명) Nepal; (공식명) the Kingdom of Nepal
노르망디 (프랑스) (지역) Normandy
노르웨이 (국명) Norway; (공식명) the Kingdom of Norway
노바스코샤 주 (캐나다) Nova Scotia
노보시비르스크 (러시아) (도시) Novosibirsk
노보쿠즈네츠크 (러시아) (도시) Novokuznetsk
노샘프턴 (영국) (도시) Northampton
노섬벌랜드 주 (영국) Northumberland
노스다코타 주 (미국) North Dakota (약어 N.Dak., N.D., ND)
노스요크셔 주 (영국) North Yorkshire
노스캐롤라이나 주 (미국) North Carolina (약어 N.C., NC)
노팅엄 (영국) (도시) Nottingham
노퍽 (미국) (도시) Norfolk
노퍽 주 (영국) Norfolk
녹스빌 (미국) (도시) Knoxville
놈 (미국) (도시) Nome
누벨칼레도니 섬 (남태평양 서부) Nouvelle Calédonie
누비아 사막 (수단) the Nubian Desert

세계 주요 지명

누악쇼트 (모리타니) [수도] Nouakchott
누쿠알로파 (통가) [수도] Nukuálofa
뉘른베르크 (독일) [도시] Nürnberg
뉴기니 (태평양 남서부) [섬] New Guinea
뉴델리 (인도) [수도] New Delhi
뉴멕시코 주 (미국) New Mexico (약어 N.Mex., N.M., NM)
뉴브런즈윅 주 (캐나다) New Brunswick
뉴사우스웨일스 주 (오스트레일리아) New South Wales
뉴올리언스 (미국) [도시] New Orleans
뉴욕 (미국) [도시] New York (City)
뉴욕 주 (미국) New York (State) [약어 N.Y., NY]
뉴잉글랜드 (미국) [지역] New England
뉴저지 주 (미국) New Jersey (약어 N.J., NJ)
뉴질랜드 [국명] New Zealand
뉴칼레도니아 섬 New Caledonia ('누벨칼레도니 섬'의 영어명)
뉴캐슬 (오스트레일리아) [도시] Newcastle
뉴캐슬어폰타인 (영국) [도시] Newcastle upon Tyne
뉴펀들랜드 주 (캐나다) Newfoundland
뉴포트 (미국) [도시] Newport
뉴햄프셔 주 (미국) New Hampshire (약어 N.H., NH)
뉴헤브리디스 제도 (태평양 남서부) New Hebrides Is.
뉴헤이번 (미국) [도시] New Haven
니가타(新潟) (일본) [도시] Niigata
니스 (프랑스) [도시] Nice
니아메 (니제르) [수도] Niamey
니아사 호 Lake Nyasa ⇨말라위 호
니주니노브고로드 (러시아) [도시] Nizhni Novgorod
니카라과 [국명] (the Republic of) Nicaragua
니코시아 (키프로스) [수도] Nicosia
님 (프랑스) [도시] Nîmes
닝샤후이 족(寧夏回族) 자치구 (중국) Ningxia Hui; [공식명] the Ningxia Hui Autonomous Region

다

낭 (베트남) [도시] Danang; Da Nang
다뉴브 강 (유럽) the Danube (River)
다롄(大連) (중국) [도시] Dalian; Talien
다르다넬스 해협 (터키) the Dardanelles
다르에스살람 (탄자니아) [수도] Dar es Salaam
다르질링 (인도) [도시] Darjeeling
다름슈타트 (독일) [도시] Darmstadt
다마스쿠스 (시리아) [수도] Damascus
다바(大巴) 산맥 (중국) the Daba [Tapa] Mountains
다바오 (필리핀) [도시] Davao
다볘(大別) 산맥 (중국) the Dabie [Tapieh] Mountains
다운 주 (영국) Down
다울라기리 산 (네팔) (Mount) Dhaulagiri
다윈 (오스트레일리아) [도시] Darwin
다카 (방글라데시) [수도] Dacca
다카르 (세네갈) [수도] Dakar
다카마쓰(高松) (일본) [도시] Takamatsu
다호메이 [국명] Dahomey ('베냉'의 구칭)
단둥(丹東) (중국) [도시] Dandong; Tantung
단치히 Danzig ('그단스크'의 독일어명)
달링 강 (오스트레일리아) the Darling (River)
담맘 (사우디아라비아) [도시] Dammam
대마도(對馬島) ⇨쓰시마 섬
대만(臺灣) ❶ [국명] Taiwan ❷ [섬] Taiwan
대서양 the Atlantic (Ocean)
대(大)순다 열도 (인도네시아) the Greater Sunda Islands; the Greater Sundas
대싱안링(大興安嶺) 산맥 (중국) the Greater [Great] Xing'anling Mountains
댈러스 (미국) [도시] Dallas
더럼 (영국) [도시] Durham
더반 (남아프리카 공화국) [도시] Durban
더블린 (아일랜드) [수도] Dublin
더비 (영국) [도시] Derby
더비셔 주 (영국) Derbyshire
던디 (영국) [도시] Dundee
덜루스 (미국) [도시] Duluth
데번 주 (영국) Devon
데이턴 (미국) [도시] Dayton
데칸 고원 (인도) the Deccan Plateau
덴마크 [국명] Denmark; [공식명] the Kingdom of Denmark
덴버 (미국) [도시] Denver
델라웨어 주 (미국) Delaware (약어 Del., DE)
델리 (인도) [도시] Delhi
델프트 (네덜란드) [도시] Delft
도네츠 강 (우크라이나) the Donets (River)
도르트문트 (독일) [도시] Dortmund
도미니카 공화국 [국명] the Dominican Republic
도버 해협 (영국·프랑스 사이) the Strait(s) of Dover
도빌 (프랑스) [도시] Deauville
도싯 주 (영국) Dorset
도체스터 (영국) [도시] Dorchester
도쿄(東京) (일본) [수도] Tokyo
도하 (카타르) [수도] Doha
독일 [국명] Deutschland; Germany; [공식명] the Federal Republic of Germany
돈 강 (러시아) the Don (River)
동중국해 (중국 동부 해역) the East China Sea
됭케르크 (프랑스) [도시] Dunkerque; Dunkirk
두바이 (아랍 에미리트) [토후국] Dubai
두샨베 (타지키스탄) [수도] Dushanbe
둥팅(洞庭) 호 (중국) Lake Dongting [Tungting]
뒤셀도르프 (독일) [도시] Düsseldorf
뒤스부르크 (독일) [도시] Duisburg
드네프르 강 (벨로루시·우크라이나) the Dnieper (River)
드레스덴 (독일) [도시] Dresden
드레이크 해협 (남아메리카·남극 사이) the Drake Passage
디모인 (미국) [도시] Des Moines
디엔비엔푸 (베트남) [도시] Dienbienphu; Dien Bien Phu
디종 (프랑스) [도시] Dijon
디트로이트 (미국) [도시] Detroit

라

라고스 (나이지리아) [도시] Lagos
라만차 (에스파냐) [지역] La Mancha
라바울 (파푸아 뉴기니) [도시] Rabaul
라바트 (모로코) [수도] Rabat
라벤나 (이탈리아) [도시] Ravenna
라스팔마스 (에스파냐) [도시] Las Palmas
라싸(拉薩) (중국) [도시] Lhasa
라오스 [국명] Laos; [공식명] the Lao People's Democratic Republic
라왈핀디 (파키스탄) [도시] Rawalpindi
라이덴 (네덜란드) [도시] Leiden
라이베리아 [국명] (the Republic of) Liberia
라이프치히 (독일) [도시] Leipzig
라인 강 (독일) the Rhine (River)
라자스탄 주 (인도) Rajasthan

세계 주요 지명

라트비아 〔국명〕 (the Republic of) Latvia
라파스 〔볼리비아〕 〔수도〕 La Paz
라플라타 강 〔아르헨티나〕 the Rio de La Plata
라플란드 〔스칸디나비아 반도〕 〔지역〕 Lapland
라호르 〔파키스탄〕 〔도시〕 Lahore
랑군 〔미얀마〕 〔수도〕 Rangoon ('양곤'의 구칭)
래브라도 〔캐나다〕 〔지역〕 Labrador
래브라도 반도 〔캐나다〕 the Labrador Peninsula
랭스 〔프랑스〕 〔도시〕 Reims; Rheims
랭커셔 주 〔영국〕 Lancashire
랴오닝 성(遼寧省) 〔중국〕 Liaoning
랴오둥(遼東) 반도 〔중국〕 the Liaodong (구칭: Liaotung) Peninsula
랴오허(遼河) 강 〔중국〕 the Liao (River)
러시아 〔국명〕 Russia; 〔공식명〕 Russian Federation
런던 〔영국〕 〔수도〕 London
레나 강 〔러시아〕 the Lena (River)
레닌그라드 〔러시아〕 〔도시〕 Leningrad ('상트페테르부르크'의 구칭)
레드 강 〔미국〕 the Red River
레만 호 〔스위스〕 Lake Leman
레바논 〔국명〕 (the Republic of) Lebanon
레소토 〔국명〕 Lesotho; 〔공식명〕 the Kingdom of Lesotho
레오폴드빌 〔콩고 민주 공화국〕 〔수도〕 Léopoldville ('킨샤사'의 구칭)
레이캬비크 〔아이슬란드〕 〔수도〕 Reykjavik
레이테 섬 〔필리핀〕 Leyte
렉싱턴 〔미국〕 〔도시〕 Lexington
렌 〔프랑스〕 〔도시〕 Rennes
로건 산 〔캐나다〕 (Mount) Logan
로드아일랜드 주 〔미국〕 Rhode Island (약어 R.I., RI)
로디지아 〔국명〕 Rhodesia ('짐바브웨'의 구칭)
로렌 〔프랑스〕 〔지역〕 Lorraine
로마 〔이탈리아〕 〔수도〕 Rome
로메 〔토고〕 〔수도〕 Lomé
로사리오 〔아르헨티나〕 〔도시〕 Rosario
로스앤젤레스 〔미국〕 〔도시〕 Los Angeles
로스토프나도누 〔러시아〕 〔도시〕 Rostov-na-Donu
로스 해 〔남극〕 the Ross Sea
로잔 〔스위스〕 〔도시〕 Lausanne
로조 〔도미니카〕 〔수도〕 Roseau
로지 〔폴란드〕 〔도시〕 Łódź ('우치'의 구칭)
로체스터 〔미국〕 〔도시〕 Rochester
로카르노 〔스위스〕 〔도시〕 Locarno
로키 산맥 〔북아메리카〕 the Rocky Mountains; the Rockies
로테르담 〔네덜란드〕 〔도시〕 Rotterdam
론 강 〔프랑스〕 the Rhône (River)
롬바르디아 주 〔이탈리아〕 Lombardy
롱비치 〔미국〕 〔도시〕 Long Beach
롱아일랜드 섬 〔미국〕 Long Island
루르 〔독일〕 〔지역〕 the Ruhr
루르드 〔프랑스〕 〔도시〕 Lourdes
루마니아 〔국명〕 Romania; Rumania
루붐바시 〔자이르〕 〔도시〕 Lubumbashi
루사카 〔잠비아〕 〔수도〕 Lusaka
루손 섬 〔필리핀〕 Luzon
루아르 강 〔프랑스〕 the Loire (River)
루안다 〔앙골라〕 〔수도〕 Luanda
루이빌 〔미국〕 〔도시〕 Louisville
루이지애나 주 〔미국〕 Louisiana (약어 La., LA)
룩셈부르크 ❶ 〔국명〕 Luxembourg; Luxemburg; 〔공식명〕 the Grand Duchy of Luxembourg ❷ 〔❶의 수도〕 Luxembourg

룩소르 〔이집트〕 〔도시〕 Luxor
룽먼(龍門) 〔중국〕 〔유적지〕 Longmen; Lungmen
뤄양(洛陽) 〔중국〕 〔도시〕 Luoyang (구칭: Loyang)
뤼베크 〔독일〕 〔도시〕 Lübeck
뤼순(旅順) 〔중국〕 〔도시〕 Lüshun
류블랴나 〔슬로베니아〕 〔수도〕 Ljubljana
류큐(琉球) 제도 〔일본〕 Ryukyu Islands
르망 〔프랑스〕 〔도시〕 Le Mans
르아브르 〔프랑스〕 〔도시〕 Le Havre
르완다 〔국명〕 (the Republic of) Rwanda
리가 〔라트비아〕 〔수도〕 Riga
리마 〔페루〕 〔수도〕 Lima
리모주 〔프랑스〕 〔도시〕 Limoges
리버풀 〔영국〕 〔도시〕 Liverpool
리보프 〔우크라이나〕 〔도시〕 L'vov
리브르빌 〔가봉〕 〔수도〕 Libreville
리비아 〔국명〕 Libya; 〔공식명〕 the Socialist People's Libyan Arab Jamahiriya
리비에라 〔프랑스·이탈리아〕 〔지역〕 the Riviera
리스본 〔포르투갈〕 〔수도〕 Lisbon
리야드 〔사우디아라비아〕 〔수도〕 Riyadh
리옹 〔프랑스〕 〔도시〕 Lyons
리우그란데 강 〔미국·멕시코 국경〕 the Rio Grande
리우데자네이루 〔브라질〕 〔도시〕 Rio de Janeiro
리치먼드 〔미국〕 〔도시〕 Richmond
리투아니아 〔국명〕 (the Republic of) Lithuania
리히텐슈타인 〔국명〕 Liechtenstein; 〔공식명〕 the Principality of Liechtenstein
린츠 〔오스트리아〕 〔도시〕 Linz
릴 〔프랑스〕 〔도시〕 Lille
릴롱궤 〔말라위〕 〔수도〕 Lilongwe
링컨셔 주 〔영국〕 Lincolnshire

마

마그달레나 강 〔콜롬비아〕 the Magdalena
마그데부르크 〔독일〕 〔도시〕 Magdeburg
마나과 〔니카라과〕 〔수도〕 Managua
마나마 〔바레인〕 〔수도〕 Manama
마나슬루 산 〔네팔〕 (Mount) Manaslu
마누카우 〔뉴질랜드〕 〔도시〕 Manukau
마닐라 〔필리핀〕 〔수도〕 Manila
마다가스카르 〔국명〕 Madagascar; 〔공식명〕 the Democratic Republic of Madagascar
마드라스 〔인도〕 〔도시〕 Madras
마드리드 〔에스파냐〕 〔수도〕 Madrid
마라카이보 〔베네수엘라〕 〔도시〕 Maracaibo
마라케시 〔모로코〕 〔도시〕 Marrakesh; Marrakech
마르마라 해 〔터키〕 the Sea of Marmara
마르세유 〔프랑스〕 〔도시〕 Marseilles
마르티니크 〔서인도 제도〕 〔섬〕 Martinique
마리아나 제도 〔태평양 서부〕 the Mariana Islands; the Marianas
마리아나 해구 〔태평양 서부〕 the Mariana Trench
마세루 〔레소토〕 〔수도〕 Maseru
마셜 제도 〔국명〕 (the Republic of) the Marshall Islands
마쓰야마(松山) 〔일본〕 〔도시〕 Matsuyama
마요르카 섬 〔에스파냐〕 Majorca
마이센 〔독일〕 〔도시〕 Meissen
마이애미 〔미국〕 〔도시〕 Miami
마인츠 〔독일〕 〔도시〕 Mainz
마젤란 해협 〔칠레·아르헨티나〕 the Strait of Magellan
마쭈(馬祖) 섬 〔중국〕 (중국 남동 근해) Matsu; Mazu
마추픽추 〔페루〕 〔유적지〕 Machu Picchu
마카오 Macao ⇨아오먼

마케도니아 〔국명〕 Macedonia
마터호른 (스위스) 〔산〕 the Matterhorn
마투그로수 (브라질) 〔고원〕 the Mato Grosso
마푸토 (모잠비크) 〔수도〕 Maputo
만달레이 (미얀마) 〔도시〕 Mandalay
만하임 (독일) 〔도시〕 Mannheim
말라가 (에스파냐) 〔도시〕 Málaga
말라보 (적도 기니) 〔수도〕 Malabo
말라위 〔국명〕 (the Republic of) Malawi
말라위 호 (아프리카 남동부) Lake Malawi
말라카 (말레이시아) 〔도시〕 Malacca ('멜라카'의 구칭)
말라카 해협 (말레이 반도·수마트라 섬 사이) the Strait(s) of Malacca
말레 (몰디브) 〔수도〕 Malé
말레이 (동남아시아) 〔제도〕 the Malay Archipelago
말레이 반도 (동남아시아) the Malay Peninsula; Malaya.
말레이시아 〔국명〕 Malaysia
말리 〔국명〕 (the Republic of) Mali
말뫼 (스웨덴) 〔도시〕 Malmö
매니토바 주 (캐나다) Manitoba
매사추세츠 주 (미국) Massachusetts (약어 Mass., MA)
매켄지 강 (캐나다) the Mackenzie River
매킨리 산 (미국) (Mount) McKinley
맨체스터 (영국, 미국) 〔도시〕 Manchester
맨해튼 (미국·뉴욕) Manhattan
머리 강 (오스트레일리아) the Murray River
메남 강 the Menam (River) ⇨차오프라야 강
메데인 (콜롬비아) 〔도시〕 Medellin
메디나 (사우디아라비아) 〔도시〕 Medina
메리다 (에스파냐, 멕시코, 베네수엘라) 〔도시〕 Mérida
메릴랜드 주 (미국) Maryland (약어 Md., MD)
메사비 산맥 (미국) the Mesabi Range
메소포타미아 (서남아시아) 〔지역〕 Mesopotamia
메시나 (이탈리아) 〔도시〕 Messina
메시나 해협 (이탈리아) the Strait of Messina
메인 주 (미국) Maine (약어 Me., ME)
메카 (사우디아라비아) 〔도시〕 Mecca
메콩 강 (인도차이나 반도) the Mekong (River)
멕시칼리 (멕시코) 〔도시〕 Mexicali
멕시코 〔국명〕 Mexico; 〔공식명〕 the United States of Mexico
멕시코 만 (북아메리카) the Gulf of Mexico
멕시코시티 (멕시코) 〔수도〕 Mexico City
멘도사 (아르헨티나) 〔도시〕 Mendoza
멜라네시아 (태평양 서부) 〔지역〕 Melanesia
멜라카 (말레이시아) 〔도시〕 Melaka
멜버른 (오스트레일리아) 〔도시〕 Melbourne
멤피스 (이집트, 미국) 〔도시〕 Memphis
모가디슈 (소말리아) 〔수도〕 Mogadishu
모나코 〔국명〕 Monaco
모데나 (이탈리아) 〔도시〕 Modena
모로니 (코모로) 〔수도〕 Moroni
모로코 〔국명〕 Morocco; 〔공식명〕 the Kingdom of Morocco
모리셔스 〔국명〕 Mauritius
모리타니 〔국명〕 Mauritania; 〔공식명〕 the Islamic Republic of Mauritania
모스크바 (러시아) 〔수도〕 Moscow
모잠비크 〔국명〕 (the Republic of) Mozambique
모잠비크 해협 (아프리카 대륙·마다가스카르 섬 사이) the Mozambique Channel
모젤 강 (프랑스·독일) the Moselle (River)
모카 (예멘) 〔도시〕 Mocha
모하비 사막 (미국) the Mojave [Mohave] (Desert)
모헨조다로 (파키스탄) 〔유적지〕 Mohenjo Daro
몬로비아 (라이베리아) 〔수도〕 Monrovia
몬태나 주 (미국) Montana (약어 Mont., MT)
몬터레이 (멕시코) 〔도시〕 Monterrey
몬테로사 산 (스위스·이탈리아) Monte Rosa
몬테비데오 (우루과이) 〔수도〕 Montevideo
몬테카를로 (모나코) 〔도시〕 Monte Carlo
몬트리올 (캐나다) 〔도시〕 Montreal
몰도바 〔국명〕 (the Republic of) Moldova
몰디브 〔국명〕 (the Republic of) Maldives
몰루카 제도 (인도네시아) the Moluccas; the Spice Islands
몰타 〔국명〕 (the Republic of) Malta
몸바사 (케냐) 〔도시〕 Mombasa
몽고(蒙古) ⇨몽골
몽고메리 (미국) 〔도시〕 Montgomery
몽골 〔국명〕 Mongolia; 〔공식명〕 the Mongolian People's Republic
몽마르트르 (프랑스·파리) 〔지구〕 Montmartre
몽블랑 산 (프랑스·이탈리아) (Mont) Blanc
몽파르나스 (프랑스·파리) 〔지구〕 Montparnasse
몽펠리에 (프랑스) 〔도시〕 Montpellier
뫼즈 강 (프랑스·벨기에·네덜란드) the Meuse (River)
무르만스크 (러시아) 〔도시〕 Murmansk
무스카트 (오만) 〔수도〕 Muscat
물탄 (파키스탄) 〔도시〕 Multan
뮌헨 (독일) 〔도시〕 Munich
미국 〔국명〕 the United States; the U.S.; the U.S.A.; America; 〔공식명〕 the United States of America
미네소타 주 (미국) Minesota (약어 Minn., MN)
미니애폴리스 (미국) 〔도시〕 Minneapolis
미드웨이 섬 (태평양 중부) Midway; the Midway Islands
미드 호 (미국) Lake Mead
미들랜드 (영국) 〔지역〕 the Midlands
미들즈브러 (영국) 〔도시〕 Middlesbrough
미시간 주 (미국) Michigan (약어 Mich., MI)
미시간 호 (미국) Lake Michigan
미시시피 강 (미국) the Mississippi (River)
미시시피 주 (미국) Mississippi (약어 Miss., MS)
미야자키(宮崎) (일본) 〔도시〕 Miyazaki
미얀마 〔국명〕 Myanmar; 〔공식명〕 the Union of Myanmar
미주리 강 (미국) the Missouri (River)
미주리 주 (미국) Missouri (약어 Mo., MO)
미케네 (그리스) 〔유적지〕 Mycenae
미크로네시아 ❶〔국명〕 Micronesia; 〔공식명〕 the Federated States of Micronesia ❷〔지역〕 Micronesia
민다나오 섬 (필리핀) Mindanao
민스크 (벨로루시) 〔수도〕 Minsk
밀라노 (이탈리아) 〔도시〕 Milan
밀로스 (그리스) 〔섬〕 Milos; Melos
밀워키 (미국) 〔도시〕 Milwaukee

바
바그다드 (이라크) 〔수도〕 Baghdad
바기오 (필리핀) 〔도시〕 Baguio
바누아투 〔국명〕 (the Republic of) Vanuatu
바덴바덴 (독일) 〔도시〕 Baden-Baden
바라나시 (인도) 〔도시〕 Varanasi
바랑키야 (콜롬비아) 〔도시〕 Barranquilla
바레인 〔국명〕 Bahrain; 〔공식명〕 the State of

세계 주요 지명

Bahrain
바르샤바 (폴란드) [수도] Warsaw
바르셀로나 (에스파냐) [도시] Barcelona
바마코 (말리) [수도] Bamako
바바리아 (독일) [지역] Bavaria
바베이도스 [국명] Barbados
바스라 (이라크) [도시] Basra
바스크 (에스파냐) [지방] the Basque Provinces
바오터우(包頭) (중국) [도시] Baotou [Paotow]
바이로이트 (독일) [도시] Bayreuth
바이아블랑카 (아르헨티나) [도시] Bahia Blanca
바이칼 호 (러시아) Lake Baikal
바젤 (스위스) [도시] Basel
바쿠 (아제르바이잔) [수도] Baku
바타비아 (인도네시아) [수도] Batavia ('자카르타'의 구칭)
바탄 반도 (필리핀) the Bataan Peninsula
바티칸 시국(市國) (유럽) Vatican City; [공식명] the Vatican City State
바하마 [국명] the Bahamas; [공식명] the Commonwealth of the Bahamas
반다르세리베가완 (브루나이) [수도] Bandar Seri Begawan
반둥 (인도네시아) [도시] Bandung
반줄 (감비아) [수도] Banjul
발 강 (남아프리카 공화국) the Vaal (River)
발레아레스 제도 (에스파냐) the Balearic Islands
발레타 (몰타) [수도] Valletta; Valetta
발렌시아 (에스파냐) [지역·도시] Valencia
발리 섬 (인도네시아) Bali
발칸 반도 (동유럽) the Balkan Peninsula; the Balkans
발트 해 (북유럽) the Baltic (Sea)
방갈로르 (인도) [도시] Bangalore
방글라데시 [국명] Bangladesh; [공식명] the People's Republic of Bangladesh
방기 (중앙아프리카 공화국) [수도] Bangui
방콕 (타이) [수도] Bangkok
백(白)나일 (수단) [강] the White Nile
백(白)러시아 [국명] White Russia ('벨로루시'의 구칭)
백해(白海) (러시아) the White Sea
밴쿠버 (캐나다) [도시] Vancouver
뱌트카 (러시아) [도시] Vyatka
버마 [국명] Burma ('미얀마'의 구칭)
버몬트 주 (미국) Vermont (약어 Vt., VT)
버뮤다 제도 (북대서양 서부) Bermuda; the Bermudas
버밍엄 (영국) [도시] Birmingham
버밍햄 (미국) [도시] Birmingham
버지니아 주 (미국) Virginia (약어 Va., VA)
버진 제도 (서인도 제도) the Virgin Islands
버크셔 주 (영국) Berkshire
버클리 (미국) [도시] Berkeley
버킹엄셔 주 (영국) Buckinghamshire
버펄로 (미국) [도시] Buffalo
베냉 [국명] (the Republic of) Benin
베네룩스 (유럽) [지역] Benelux
베네수엘라 [국명] (the Republic of) Venezuela
베네치아 (이탈리아) [도시] Venezia
베니스 Venice ('베네치아'의 영어명)
베드퍼드셔 주 (영국) Bedfordshire
베들레헴 (요르단 강 서안 지구) [도시] Bethlehem
베라크루스 (멕시코) [도시] Veracruz
베로나 (이탈리아) [도시] Verona
베르가모 (이탈리아) [도시] Bergamo
베르겐 (노르웨이) [도시] Bergen
베르됭 (프랑스) [도시] Verdun
베르사유 (프랑스) [도시] Versailles
베른 (스위스) [수도] Bern
베를린 (독일) [수도] Berlin
베링 해 (태평양 북부) the Bering Sea
베수비오 산 (이탈리아) (Mount) Vesuvius
베오그라드 (유고슬라비아) [수도] Beograd; Belgrade
베이루트 (레바논) [수도] Beirut
베이징(北京) (중국) [수도] Beijing (구칭: Peking)
베트남 [국명] Viet Nam; [공식명] the Socialist Republic of Viet Nam
벨기에 [국명] Belgium; [공식명] the Kingdom of Belgium
벨라우 Belau ⇨팔라우
벨로루시 [국명] (the Republic of) Belarus
벨로리존테 (브라질) [도시] Belo Horizonte
벨리즈 [국명] Belize
벨모판 (벨리즈) [수도] Belmopan
벨파스트 (영국) [도시] Belfast
벳푸(別府) (일본) [도시] Beppu
벵가지 (리비아) [도시] Benghazi
벵골 만 (인도·미얀마 사이) the Bay of Bengal
보고타 (콜롬비아) [수도] Bogota
보더스 주 (영국) Borders
보덴 호 (독일·오스트리아·스위스 국경) Boden See
보르네오 섬 (동남아시아) Borneo
보르도 (프랑스) [도시] Bordeaux
보스니아 헤르체고비나 [국명] (the Republic of) Bosnia-Herzegovina
보스턴 (미국) [도시] Boston
보스포루스 해협 (터키) the Bosporus
보츠와나 [국명] (the Republic of) Botswana
보터니 만 (오스트레일리아) Botany Bay
보트니아 만 (스웨덴·핀란드 사이) the Gulf of Bothnia
보팔 (인도) [도시] Bhopal
보하이(渤海) 만 (중국) Bo Hai; Po Hai
보헤미아 (체코) [지역] Bohemia
본 (독일) [도시] Bonn
볼가 강 (러시아) the Volga (River)
볼고그라드 (러시아) [도시] Volgograd
볼로냐 (이탈리아) [도시] Bologna
볼리비아 [국명] (the Republic of) Bolivia
볼티모어 (미국) [도시] Baltimore
봄베이 (인도) [도시] Bombay
부건빌 섬 (파푸아 뉴기니) Bougainville
부다페스트 (헝가리) [수도] Budapest
부룬디 [국명] (the Republic of) Burundi
부르고뉴 (프랑스) [지역] Burgundy; Bourgogne
부르키나파소 [국명] Burkina Faso
부에노스아이레스 (아르헨티나) [수도] Buenos Aires
부줌부라 (브룬디) [수도] Bujumbura
부쿠레슈티 (루마니아) [수도] Bucharest
부탄 [국명] Bhutan
북극해 (북극) the Arctic Ocean
북아일랜드 (영국) [지역] Northern Irland
북한 [국명] North Korea; [공식명] the Democratic People's Republic of Korea
북해 (북유럽) the North Sea
불가리아 [국명] (the Republic of) Bulgaria
불로뉴 (프랑스) [도시] Boulogne
불로뉴의 숲 (프랑스) the Bois de Boulogne
브라자빌 (콩고) [수도] Brazzaville
브라질 [국명] Brazil; [공식명] the Federative Republic of Brazil

브라질리아 (브라질) [수도] Brasília
브라티슬라바 (슬로바키아) [수도] Bratislava
브레머하펜 (독일) [도시] Bremerhaven
브레멘 (독일) [도시] Bremen
브레스트 (프랑스) [도시] Brest
브롱크스 (미국·뉴욕) [지구] the Bronx
브루게 (벨기에) [도시] Bruges
브루나이 [국명] Brunei; [공식명] Negara Brunei Darussalam
브루클린 (미국·뉴욕) [지구] Brooklyn
브뤼셀 (벨기에) [수도] Brussels
브르타뉴 (프랑스) [지역] Brittany; Bretagne
브리스틀 (영국) [도시] Bristol
브리즈번 (오스트레일리아) [도시] Brisbane
브리지타운 (바베이도스) [수도] Bridgetown
브리티시컬럼비아 주 (캐나다) British Columbia
브장송 (프랑스) [도시] Besançon
블라디보스토크 (러시아) [도시] Vladivostok
블루마운틴 산맥 (자메이카) the Blue Mountains
블룸폰테인 (남아프리카 공화국) [도시] Bloemfontein
비벌리힐스 (미국) [도시] Beverly Hills
비사우 (기니비사우) [수도] Bissau
비슈케크 (키르기스스탄) [수도] Bishkek
비스마르크 제도 (파푸아 뉴기니) the Bismarck Archipelago
비스케이 만 (프랑스·스페인 사이) the Bay of Biscay
비시 (프랑스) [도시] Vichy
비엔나 Vienna ('빈'의 영어명)
비엔티안 (라오스) [수도] Vientiane
비키니 환초 (마셜 제도) Bikini Atoll
비하르 주 (인도) Bihar
빅토리아 (세이셸) [수도] Victoria
빅토리아 (캐나다) [도시] Victoria
빅토리아 주 (오스트레일리아) Victoria
빅토리아 폭포 (잠비아·짐바브웨 국경) Victoria Falls
빅토리아 호 (탄자니아·우간다) Lake Victoria
빈 (오스트리아) [수도] Vienna
빈트후크 (나미비아) [수도] Windhoek
빌뉴스 (리투아니아) [도시] Vilnius
빌바오 (에스파냐) [도시] Bilbao

사나 (예멘) [수도] San'a; Sanaa
사라고사 (에스파냐) [도시] Zaragoza
사라예보 (보스니아 헤르체고비나) [수도] Sarajevo
사라와크 (말레이시아) [도시] Sarawak
사르데냐 (이탈리아) [섬] Sardinia
사마르칸트 (우즈베키스탄) [도시] Samarkand
사모아 제도 (남태평양) Samoa; the Samoa Islands
사세보(佐世保) (일본) [도시] Sasebo
사오싱(紹興) (중국) [도시] Shaoxing; Shaohsing
사우디아라비아 [국명] Saudi Arabia; [공식명] the Kingdom of Saudi Arabia
사우샘프턴 (영국) [도시] Southampton
사우스글러모건 주 (영국) South Glamorgan
사우스다코타 주 (미국) South Dakota 《약어 S.Dak., S.D., SD》
사우스요크셔 주 (영국) South Yorkshire
사우스캐롤라이나 주 (미국) South Carolina 《약어 S.C., SC》
사이공 (베트남) [도시] Saigon ('호치민'의 구칭)
사이판 섬 (마리아나 제도) Saipan
사하라 사막 (아프리카 대륙 북부) the Sahara (Desert)
사할린 (러시아) [섬] Sakhalin

사해(死海) (요르단·이스라엘) the Dead Sea
산다칸 (말레이시아) [도시] Sandakan
산둥(山東) 반도 (중국) the Shandong[Shantung] Peninsula
산둥 성(山東省) (중국) Shandong (구칭: Shantung)
산레모 (이탈리아) [도시] San Remo
산루이스포토시 (멕시코) [주] San Luis Potosi
산마리노 ❶ [국명] (the Republic of) San Marino ❷ [❶의 수도] San Marino
산살바도르 (엘살바도르) [수도] San Salvador
산세바스티안 (에스파냐) [도시] San Sebastián
산시 성(山西省) (중국) Shanxi (구칭: Shansi)
산시 성(陝西省) (중국) Shanxi; Shaanxi
산안토니오 (아르헨티나) [곶] Cape San Antonio
산타크루스 (카나리아 제도) [도시] Santa Cruz
산타페 (미국, 아르헨티나) [도시] Santa Fe
산토도밍고 (도미니카 공화국) [수도] Santo Domingo
산투스 (브라질) [도시] Santos
산티아고 (칠레) [수도] Santiago
산호세 (코스타리카) [수도] San José
산호해(珊瑚海) (오스트레일리아) the Coral Sea
살레르노 (이탈리아) [도시] Salerno
삿포로(札幌) (일본) [도시] Sapporo
상아 해안 Ivory Coast
상투메 (상투메 프린시페) [수도] São Tomé
상투메 프린시페 [국명] São Tomé and Principe; [공식명] the Democratic Republic of São Tomé and Principe
상트페테르부르크 (러시아) [도시] Saint Petersburg
상파울루 (브라질) [도시] São Paulo
상하이(上海) (중국) [도시] Shanghai
새크라멘토 (미국) [도시] Sacramento
새크라멘토 강 (미국) the Sacramento (River)
샌디에이고 (미국) [도시] San Diego
샌안토니오 (미국) [도시] San Antonio
샌프란시스코 (미국) [도시] San Francisco
샌프란시스코 만 (미국) San Francisco Bay
샤르트르 (프랑스) [도시] Chartres
샤먼(廈門) (중국) [도시] Xiamen
샤이엔 (미국) [도시] Cheyenne
샬럿 (미국) [도시] Charlotte
샹젤리제 (프랑스·파리) [지구] Champs-Élysées
샹파뉴 (프랑스) [지역] Champagne
서리 주 (영국) Surrey
서머싯 주 (영국) Somerset
서배너 (미국) [도시] Savannah
서(西)사모아 [국명] Western Samoa
서스캐처원 주 (캐나다) Saskatchewan
서식스 (영국) [지역] Sussex
서인도 제도 (중앙아메리카) the West Indies
서퍽 주 (영국) Suffolk
선양(瀋陽) (중국) [도시] Shenyang
선전(深圳) (중국) [경제 특별구] Shenzhen
세네갈 [국명] (the Republic of) Senegal
세미팔라틴스크 (러시아) [도시] Semipalatinsk
세바스토폴 (러시아) [도시] Sevastopol'
세부 섬 (필리핀) Cebu
세비야 (에스파냐) [도시] Sevilla
세이셸 [국명] (the Republic of) Seychelles
세인트로렌스 강 (캐나다) the Saint Lawrence River
세인트로렌스 수로 (캐나다) the Saint Lawrence Seaway
세인트루시아 [국명] Saint Lucia
세인트루이스 (미국) [도시] Saint Louis
세인트빈센트 그레나딘 [국명] Saint Vincent and the Grenadines

세계 주요 지명

세인트조지스 (그레나다) [수도] Saint George's
세인트존스 ❶ (앤티가 바부다) [수도] Saint John(')s ❷ (캐나다) [도시] Saint John's
세인트크리스토퍼 네비스 [국명] Saint Christopher and Nevis
세인트헬레나 섬 (대서양 남부) Saint Helena
세인트헬렌스 산 (미국) Mount Saint Helens
센 강 (프랑스) the (River) Seine
센트럴 주 (영국) Central
셀레베스 섬 (인도네시아) Celebes ('술라웨시 섬'의 구칭)
셰르부르 (프랑스) [도시] Cherbourg
셰틀랜드 제도 (영국) the Shetland Islands; the Shetlands
셰필드 (영국) [도시] Sheffield
셴양(咸陽) (중국) [도시] Xianyang; Hsienyang
소말리아 [국명] Somalia; [공식명] the Somali Democratic Republic
소시에테 제도 (프랑스령 폴리네시아) the Society Islands
소싱안링(小興安嶺) 산맥 (중국) the Lesser[Little] Xing'anling Mountains; the Xiaoxing'anling
소피아 (불가리아) [수도] Sofia
소호 (영국 런던·미국 뉴욕) [지구] Soho
손 강 (프랑스) the Saône (River)
솔로몬 [국명] the Solomons
솔즈베리 (짐바브웨) Salisbury ('하라레'의 구칭)
솔트레이크 시티 (미국) [도시] Salt Lake City
송네 협만 (노르웨이 서안 남부) the Sogne Fjord
수단 [국명] (the Republic of) the Sudan
수라바야 (인도네시아) [도시] Surabaya
수리남 [국명] (the Republic of) Suriname
수마트라 섬 (인도네시아) Sumatra
수바 (피지) [수도] Suva
수에즈 (이집트) [도시] Suez
수에즈 운하 (이집트) the Suez Canal
술라웨시 섬 (인도네시아) Sulawesi
쉬저우(徐州) (중국) [도시] Xuzhou (구칭: Sŭchow)
슈투트가르트 (독일) [도시] Stuttgart
슈프레 강 (독일) the Spree (River)
슈피리어 호 (미국·캐나다) Lake Superior
슐레지엔 (폴란드) [지역] Schlesien
스리나가르 (인도) [도시] Srinagar
스리랑카 [국명] Sri Lanka; [공식명] the Democratic Socialist Republic of Sri Lanka
스리자야와르데네푸라 (스리랑카) [수도] Sri Jayawardenepura
스미르나 (터키) [도시] Smyrna ('이즈미르'의 구칭)
스발바르 제도 (북극해) Svalbard
스와니 강 (미국) the Suwannee (River)
스와질란드 [국명] Swaziland; [공식명] the Kingdom of Swaziland
스와트 (파키스탄) [지역] Swat
스완지 (영국) [도시] Swansea
스웨덴 [국명] Sweden; [공식명] the Kingdom of Sweden
스위스 [국명] Switzerland; [공식명] the Swiss Confederation
스자좡(石家莊) (중국) [도시] Shijiazhuang
스칸디나비아 (북유럽) [지역] Scandinavia
스칸디나비아 반도 (북유럽) the Scandinavian Peninsula
스코틀랜드 (영국) [지방] Scotland
스코페 (마케도니아) [수도] Skopje
스탈린그라드 (러시아) [도시] Stalingrad ('볼고그라드'의 구칭)
스태퍼드셔 주 (영국) Staffordshire
스톡홀름 (스웨덴) [수도] Stockholm
스트라스부르 (프랑스) [도시] Strasbourg
스페인 Spain ⇨에스파냐
스프링필드 (미국) [도시] Springfield
슬로바키아 [국명] Slovakia; [공식명] the Slovak Republic
슬로베니아 [국명] (the Republic of) Slovenia
시나이 반도 (이집트) the Sinai (Peninsula)
시닝(西寧) (중국) [도시] Xining; Hsining
시드니 (오스트레일리아) [도시] Sydney
시러큐스 (미국) [도시] Syracuse
시리아 [국명] Syria; [공식명] the Syrian Arab Republic
시모노세키(下關) (일본) [도시] Shimonoseki
시베리아 (러시아) [지역] Siberia
시안(西安) (중국) [도시] Xian (구칭: Sian)
시암 [국명] Siam ('타이'의 구칭)
시애틀 (미국) [도시] Seattle
시에나 (이탈리아) [도시] Siena
시에라네바다 산맥 (미국, 에스파냐) the Sierra Nevada (Mountains); (▶미국 명칭에 한함) the Sierras
시에라리온 [국명] (the Republic of) Sierra Leone
시에라마드레 산맥 (멕시코) the Sierra Madre (Mountains); the Sierra Madres
시우다드트루히요 (도미니카 공화국) [수도] Ciudad Trujillo ('산토도밍고'의 구칭)
시장(西江) 강 (중국) the West River; the Xi[Hsi] (River)
시즈오카(靜岡) (일본) [도시] Shizuoka
시짱(西藏) 자치구 (중국) Xizang; [공식명] the Xizang Autonomous Region
시칠리아 (이탈리아) [섬] Sicily
시카고 (미국) [도시] Chicago
시코쿠(四國) (일본) [섬] Shikoku
시킴 주 (인도) Sikkim
신시내티 (미국) [도시] Cincinnati
신장웨이우얼(新疆維吾爾) 자치구 (중국) Xinjiang (구칭: Sinkiang); [공식명] the Xinjiang Uygur Autonomous Region
실레지아 Silesia ('슐레지엔'의 영어명)
실론 [국명] Ceylon ('스리랑카'의 구칭)
싱가포르 ❶ [국명] (the Republic of) Singapore ❷ [❶의 수도] Singapore
쑤저우(蘇州) (중국) [도시] Suzhou (구칭: Soochow)
쑹화(松花) 강 (중국) the Songhua[Sunghua] (River)
쓰시마(對馬) 섬 (일본) Tsushima
쓰촨(四川) 분지 (중국) the Sichuan Basin; the Red Basin of Sichuan
쓰촨 성(四川省) (중국) Sichuan (구칭: Szechwan)

아

아그라 (인도) [도시] Agra
아나폴리스 (미국) [도시] Annapolis
아덴 (예멘) [도시] Aden
아드리아 해 (지중해) the Adriatic (Sea)
아디스아바바 (에티오피아) [수도] Addis Ababa
아라비아 (서남아시아) [지역] Arabia
아라비아 반도 (서남아시아) the Arabian Peninsula
아라비아 해 (인도양) the Arabian Sea
아랄 해 (중앙아시아) the Aral Sea
아랍 에미리트 [국명] Arab Emirates; [공식명] the United Arab Emirates
아르노 강 (이탈리아) the Arno (River)

세계 주요 지명

아르메니아 [국명] (the Republic of) Armenia
아르항겔스크 (러시아) [도시] Arkhangelsk; Archangel
아르헨티나 [국명] Argentina; [공식명] the Argentine Republic
아마다바드 (인도) [도시] Ahmadabad
아마존 강 (남아메리카) the Amazon (River)
아메리카 ❶ [아메리카 대륙] America; [북미·중미·남미] the Americas ❷ America ⇨미국
아메리카령(領) 버진 제도 (서인도 제도) the Virgin Islands of the United States
아모이 Amoy ⇨샤먼
아무르 강 (중국·러시아 국경) the Amur (River)
아바나 (쿠바) [수도] Havana
아바단 (이란) [도시] Abadan
아부다비 (아랍 에미리트) [토후국 또는 수도] Abu Dhabi
아비뇽 (프랑스) [도시] Avignon
아비장 (코트디부아르) [수도] Abidjan
아삼 주 (인도) Assam
아순시온 (파라과이) [수도] Asunción
아스타나 (카자흐스탄) [수도] Astana
아오먼(澳門) (중국) [식민지] Aomen
아오모리(青森) (일본) [도시] Aomori
아우슈비츠 (폴란드) [도시] Auschwitz
아우크스부르크 (독일) [도시] Augsburg
아이다호 주 (미국) Idaho (약어 Id., Ida., ID)
아이보리코스트 Ivory Coast ('코트디부아르'의 영어명)
아이슬란드 [국명] (the Republic of) Iceland
아이오와 주 (미국) Iowa (약어 Ia., Io., IA)
아이티 [국명] (the Republic of) Haiti
아일랜드 [국명] Ireland
아제르바이잔 [국명] (the Republic of) Azerbaijan.
아조레스 제도 (대서양 북부) the Azores
아조프 해 (우크라이나) the Sea of Azov
아카바 만 (사우디아라비아·시나이 반도 사이) the Gulf of Aqaba
아카풀코 (멕시코) [도시] Acapulco
아칸소 주 (미국) Arkansas (약어 Ark., AR)
아콩카과 산 (아르헨티나) (Mount) Aconcagua
아크라 (가나) [수도] Accra
아테네 (그리스) [수도] Athens
아틀라스 산맥 (아프리카 북부) the Atlas (Mountains)
아페니노 산맥 (이탈리아) the Apennines
아프가니스탄 [국명] (the Republic of) Afghanistan
아피아 (서사모아) [수도] Apia
안나푸르나 (네팔) [연봉(連峯)] Annapurna; the Annapurna Massif
안달루시아 (에스파냐) [지역] Andalusia
안데스 산맥 (남아메리카) the Andes
안도라 [국명] Andorra
안도라라베야 (안도라) [수도] Andorra la Vella
안산(鞍山) (중국) [도시] Anshan
안타나나리보 (마다가스카르) [수도] Antananarivo
안트베르펜 (벨기에) [도시] Antwerpen
안후이 성(安徽省) (중국) Anhui (구칭: Anhwei)
알래스카 만 (미국) the Gulf of Alaska
알래스카 산맥 (미국) the Alaska Range
알래스카 주 (미국) Alaska (약어 Alas., AK)
알렉산드로프스크사할린스키 (러시아) [도시] Aleksandrovsk-Sakhalinski
알렉산드리아 (이집트, 미국) [도시] Alexandria
알류샨 열도 (미국) the Aleutian Islands; the Aleutians
알링턴 (미국) [도시] Arlington
알마티 (카자흐스탄) [도시] Almaty
알마아타 (카자흐스탄) [도시] Alma-Ata ('알마티'의 구칭)
알바니아 [국명] (the Republic of) Ablania
알자스 (프랑스) [지역] Alsace
알제 (알제리) [수도] Algiers
알제리 [국명] Algeria; [공식명] the Democratic and People's Republic of Algeria
알타이 산맥 (중앙아시아) the Altai Mountains
알프스 산맥 (유럽 중남부) the Alps
암만 (요르단) [수도] Amman
암스테르담 (네덜란드) [수도] Amsterdam
앙골라 [국명] Angola; [공식명] the People's Republic of Angola
앙카라 (터키) [수도] Ankara
앙코르 (캄보디아) [유적지] Angkor
애들레이드 (오스트레일리아) [도시] Adelaide
애리조나 주 (미국) Arizona (약어 Ariz., Az)
애버딘 (영국) [도시] Aberdeen
애틀랜타 (미국) [도시] Atlanta
애팔래치아 산맥 (미국) the Appalachian Mountains; the Appalachians
앤트림 주 (영국) Antrim
앤트워프 Antwerp ('안트베르펜'의 영어명)
앤티가 바부다 [국명] Antigua and Barbuda
앤티가 섬 (앤티가 바부다) Antigua
앨라배마 주 (미국) Alabama (약어 Ala., AL)
앨리스스프링스 (오스트레일리아) [도시] Alice Springs
앨버타 주 (캐나다) Alberta
앵커리지 (미국) [도시] Anchorage
야무수크로 (코트디부아르) [수도] Yamoussoukro
야운데 (카메룬) [수도] Yaoundé
야쿠츠크 (러시아) [도시] Yakutsk
얍 섬 (캐롤라인 제도) Yap
야하타(八幡) (일본) [지구] Yahata
얀마이엔 섬 (노르웨이 서해) Jan Mayen
얄타 (우크라이나) Yalta
양곤 (미얀마) [수도] Yangon
양쯔(揚子) 강 (중국) the Yangzi (구칭: Yangtze) (River)
어메이(峨眉) 산 (중국) (Mount) Emei[O-mei]
얼스터 (영국) [지역] Ulster
에게 해 (지중해) the Aegean (Sea)
에드먼턴 (캐나다) [도시] Edmonton
에든버러 (영국) [도시] Edinburgh
에리트레아 [국명] Eritrea
에베레스트 산 (네팔) (Mount) Everest
에센 (독일) [도시] Essen
에스토니아 [국명] (the Republic of) Estonia
에스파냐 [국명] España
에식스 (영국) Essex
에어 호 (오스트레일리아) Lake Eyre
에이레 [국명] Eire ('아일랜드'의 구칭)
에이번 주 (영국) Avon
에이설 호 (네덜란드) the IJsselmeer; the Ijsselmeer; Lake IJssel
에콰도르 [국명] (the Republic of) Ecuador
에티오피아 [국명] Ethiopia; [공식명] the People's Democratic Republic of Ethiopia
엘바 섬 (지중해) Elba
엘베 강 (독일) the Elbe (River)
엘살바도르 [국명] (the Republic of) El Salvador
엘파소 (미국) [도시] El Paso
영국 [국명] the United Kingdom; the U.K.; [공식명] the United Kingdom of Great Britain and Northern Ireland

세계 주요 지명

영국령 버진 제도 (서인도 제도) the British Virgin Islands
영국 제도 (영국) the British Isles
영국 해협 (영국·프랑스 사이) the English Channel; the Channel
영스타운 (미국) [도시] Youngstown
예나 (독일) [도시] Jena
예니세이 강 (러시아) the Yenisei[Enisei] (River)
예레반 (아르메니아) [수도] Yerevan
예루살렘 (이스라엘) [수도] Jerusalem
예멘 [국명] (the Republic of) Yemen
옌안(延安) (중국) [도시] Yanan
옌하이저우(沿海州) (러시아) [지역] the Maritime Territory; Primorski Krai; Primorye
옐로스톤 공원 (미국) Yellowstone (National Park)
오거스타 (미국) [도시] Augusta
오데사 (우크라이나) [도시] Odessa
오를레앙 (프랑스) [도시] Orléans
오리건 주 (미국) Oregon (약어 Oreg., Ore., OR)
오리노코 강 (베네수엘라) the Orinoco (River)
오리사 주 (인도) Orissa
오리사바 산 (멕시코) (Mount) Orizaba
오마하 (미국) [도시] Omaha
오만 [국명] Oman; [공식명] the Sultanate of Oman
오브 강 (러시아) the Ob' (River)
오사카(大阪) (일본) [도시] Osaka
오스트레일리아 [국명] Australia
오스트리아 [국명] (the Republic of) Austria
오스틴 (미국) [도시] Austin
오슬로 (노르웨이) [수도] Oslo
오아후 섬 (미국) Oahu
오이타(大分) (일본) [도시] Oita
오카야마(岡山) (일본) [도시] Okayama
오크니 제도 (영국) the Orkney Islands; the Orkneys
오크니 주 (영국) Orkney
오클라호마시티 (미국) [도시] Oklahoma City
오클라호마 주 (미국) Oklahoma (약어 Okla., OK)
오클랜드 ❶ (뉴질랜드) [도시] Auckland ❷ (미국) [도시] Oakland
오키나와(沖繩) (일본) [현] Okinawa
오타와 (캐나다) [수도] Ottawa
오트볼타 [국명] Upper Volta ('부르키나파소'의 구칭)
오하이오 강 (미국) the Ohio River
오하이오 주 (미국) Ohio (약어 O., OH)
오호츠크 해 (러시아·일본) the Sea of Okhotsk
옥스퍼드 (영국) [도시] Oxford
옥스퍼드셔 주 (영국) Oxfordshire
온두라스 [국명] (the Republic of) Honduras
온타리오 주 (캐나다) Ontario
온타리오 호 (캐나다·미국) Lake Ontario
올랜도 (미국) [도시] Orlando
올림피아 (미국, 그리스) [도시] Olympia
올림픽 반도 (미국) the Olympic Peninsula
올버니 (미국, 오스트레일리아) [도시] Albany
옴스크 (러시아) [도시] Omsk
와가두구 (부르키나파소) [수도] Ouagadougou
와이오밍 주 (미국) Wyoming (약어 Wyo., Wy., WY)
와이키키 (미국·호놀룰루) [해변] Waikiki (Beach)
와이트 섬 (영국) the Isle of Wight
요르단 [국명] Jordan; [공식명] the Hashemite Kingdom of Jordan
요르단 강 (서남아시아) the Jordan (River)
요세미티 (미국) [국립공원] Yosemite National Park
요코스카(橫須賀) (일본) [도시] Yokosuka

요코하마(橫濱) (일본) [도시] Yokohama
요크 (영국) [도시] York
요크셔 주 (영국) Yorkshire
요하네스버그 (남아프리카 공화국) [도시] Johannesburg
우간다 [국명] (the Republic of) Uganda
우랄 강 (러시아·카자흐스탄) the Ural (River)
우랄 산맥 (러시아·카자흐스탄) the Ural Mountains; the Urals
우루과이 [국명] Uruguay; [공식명] the Oriental Republic of Uruguay
우루무치(烏魯木齊) (중국) [도시] Ürümqi
우수리 강 (러시아) the Ussuri (River)
우스터 (영국) [도시] Worcester
우시(無錫) (중국) [도시] Wuxi; Wuhsi
우즈베키스탄 [국명] (the Republic of) Uzbekistan
우창(武昌) (중국) [도시] Wuchang
우치 (폴란드) [도시] Łódź
우크라이나 [국명] (the) Ukraine; [공식명] the Ukrainian Republic
우한(武漢) (중국) [도시] Wuhan
우후(蕪湖) (중국) [도시] Wuhu
울란바토르 (몽골) [수도] Ulan Bator
웁살라 (스웨덴) [도시] Uppsala
워릭셔 주 (영국) Warwickshire
워싱턴 (미국) [수도] Washington, D.C.)
워싱턴 주 (미국) the Washington (State) (약어 Wash., WA)
워털루 (벨기에) [전적지] Waterloo
웨스턴오스트레일리아 주 (오스트레일리아) Western Australia
웨스트글러모건 주 (영국) West Glamorgan
웨스트미들랜드 주 (영국) West Midlands
웨스트민스터 (영국·런던) [지구] Westminster
웨스트버지니아 주 (미국) West Virginia (약어 W.Va., WV)
웨스트서식스 주 (영국) West Sussex
웨스트요크셔 주 (영국) West Yorkshire
웨이수이(渭水) 강 (중국) the Wei (River)
웨이크 섬 (태평양 중서부) Wake Islands
웨일스 (영국) [지역] Wales
웰링턴 (뉴질랜드) [수도] Wellington
위니펙 (캐나다) [도시] Winnipeg
위스콘신 주 (미국) Wisconsin (약어 Wis., Wisc., WI)
위에 (베트남) [도시] Hue
위치토 (미국) [도시] Wichita
위트레흐트 (네덜란드) [도시] Utrecht
윈강(雲崗) (중국) [유적지] Yungang; Yünkang
윈난 섬(雲南島) (중국) Yunnan
윈저 (영국) [도시] Windsor
윈체스터 (영국) [도시] Winchester
윌밍턴 (미국) [도시] Wilmington
윌트셔 주 (영국) Wiltshire
윔블던 (영국) [지구] Wimbledon
유고슬라비아 [국명] Yugoslavia; Jugoslavia; [공식명] the Socialist Federal Republic of Yugoslavia
유주노사할린스크 (러시아) [도시] Yuzhno Sakhalinsk
유카탄 반도 (멕시코) the Yucatán Peninsula
유콘 강 (캐나다·미국) the Yukon (River)
유타 주 (미국) Utah (약어 Ut., UT)
유틀란트 반도 (덴마크) Jutland
유프라테스 강 (이라크) the Euphrates (River)
융프라우 산 (스위스) the Jungfrau
은자메나 (차드) [수도] N'Djamena
음바바네 (스와질란드) [수도] Mbabane

세계 주요 지명

이라와디 강 (미얀마) the Irrawaddy (River)
이라크 [국명] (the Republic of) Iraq
이란 [국명] Iran; [공식명] the Islamic Republic of Iran
이르쿠츠크 (러시아) [도시] Irkutsk
이리 호 (미국·캐나다) Lake Erie
이베리아 반도 (유럽) the Iberian Peninsula
이스라엘 [국명] Israel; [공식명] the State of Israel
이스마일리아 (이집트) [도시] Ismailia
이스탄불 (터키) [도시] Istanbul
이스터 섬 (태평양 남동부) Easter Island
이스트서식스 주 (영국) East Sussex
이스파한 (이란) [도시] Isfahan; Esfahan
이슬라마바드 (파키스탄) [수도] Islamabad
이오니아 (지중해) [지역] Ionia
이오니아 제도 (지중해) the Ionian Islands
이오니아 해 (이탈리아·그리스 사이) the Ionian Sea
이즈미르 (터키) [도시] Izmir
이집트 [국명] Egypt; [공식명] the Arab Republic of Egypt
이탈리아 [국명] (the Republic of) Italy
인더스 강 (파키스탄) the Indus (River)
인도 [국명] India
인도네시아 [국명] (the Republic of) Indonesia
인도양 the Indian (Ocean)
인도차이나 반도 (동남아시아) Indochina
인디애나 주 (미국) Indiana (약어 Ind., IN)
인디애나폴리스 (미국) [도시] Indianapolis
인스브루크 (오스트리아) [도시] Innsbruck
일리노이 주 (미국) Illinois (약어 Ill., IL)
일본 [국명] Japan
임팔 (인도) [도시] Imphal
잉글랜드 (영국) [지역] England

자

자그레브 (크로아티아) [수도] Zagreb
자르 Saar ⇨자를란트 주
자르 강 (독일·프랑스) the Saar (River)
자르브뤼켄 (독일) [도시] Saarbrücken
자를란트 주 (독일) Saarland; (the) Saar
자메이카 [국명] Jamaica
자바 섬 (인도네시아) Java
자이르 [국명] Zaire ('콩고 민주 공화국'의 구칭)
자이푸르 (인도) [도시] Jaipur
자카르타 (인도네시아) [수도] Jakarta
잔지바르 (탄자니아) [섬] (the Island of) Zanzibar
잘츠부르크 (오스트리아) [도시] Salzburg
잠베지 강 (모잠비크) the Zambezi (River)
잠비아 [국명] (the Republic of) Zambia
장시 성(江西省) (중국) Jiangxi (구칭: Kiangsi)
장쑤 성(江蘇省) (중국) Jiangsu (구칭: Kiangsu)
잭슨빌 (미국) [도시] Jacksonville
저장 성(浙江省) (중국) Zhejiang
적도(赤道) 기니 [국명] (the Republic of) Equatorial Guinea
전장(鎭江) (중국) [도시] Zhenjiang; Chenchiang
정저우(鄭州) (중국) [도시] Zhengzhou
제네바 (스위스) [도시] Geneva
제노바 (이탈리아) [도시] Genoa
제다 (사우디아라비아) [도시] Jedda; Jidda
제임스타운 (미국) [도시] Jamestown
조지아 주 (미국) Georgia (약어 Ga., GA)
조지타운 ❶ (가이아나) [수도] Georgetown ❷ (말레이시아) [도시] George Town
조호르바루 (말레이시아) [도시] Johore Bahru
존스턴 섬 (태평양 북부) Johnston Island

주네브 Genève ('제네바'의 프랑스 어명)
주노 (미국) [도시] Juneau
주룽(九龍) (중국) [도시] Kowloon; Jiulong
주장(九江) (중국) [도시] Jiujiang; Chiuchiang
주장(珠江) 강 (중국) the Zhu[Chu] (River)
중국 [국명] China; [공식명: 중화 인민 공화국] the People's Republic of China
중앙아프리카 공화국 [국명] the Central African Republic
중화민국 [국명] (the Republic of) China ('대만'의 구칭)
쥐라 산맥 (프랑스) the Jura Mountains; the Juras
지난(濟南) (중국) [도시] Jinan (구칭: Chinan)
지룽(基隆) (대만) [도시] Keelung; Jilong
지린 성(吉林省) (중국) Jilin (구칭: Kirin)
지바(千葉) (일본) [도시] Chiba
지부티 ❶ [국명] (the Republic of) Djibouti ❷ [❶의 수도] Djibouti
지브롤터 (이베리아 반도 남단) [식민지] Gibraltar
지브롤터 해협 (이베리아 반도 남단) the Strait(s) of Gibraltar
지중해 (유럽·아프리카 사이) the Mediterranean (Sea)
진먼(金門) 섬 (중국 남동부 근해) Quemoy; Jinmen
진주만(眞珠灣) (미국·하와이) Pearl Harbor
짐바브웨 [국명] (the Republic of) Zimbabwe

차

차드 [국명] (the Republic of) Chad
차드 호 (아프리카 중부) Lake Chad
차오프라야 강 (타이) Chao Phraya (River)
찰스턴 (미국) [도시] Charleston
창바이(長白) 산맥 (한반도·중국 국경) the Changbai[Changpai] Mountains
창사(長沙) (중국) [도시] Changsha
창춘(長春) (중국) [도시] Changchun
채널 제도 (영국 해협) the Channel Islands
청두(成都) (중국) [도시] Chengdu; Ch'engtu
체르마트 (스위스) [휴양지] Zermat
체셔 주 (영국) Cheshire
체스터필드 제도 (영국) the Chesterfield Islands
체코 [국명] Czech; [공식명] the Czech Republic (▶ 1993년 체코와 슬로바키아로 분리됨)
첼랴빈스크 (러시아) [도시] Chelyabinsk
추코트 반도 (러시아) the Chukotski [Chukot] Peninsula
추코트 산맥 (러시아) the Chukot Range
충칭(重慶) (중국) [도시] Chongqing (구칭: Chungking)
취리히 (스위스) [도시] Zürich
치앙마이 (타이) [도시] Chiang Mai; Chiengmai
치와와 (멕시코) [도시] Chihuahua
치체스터 (영국) [도시] Chichester
치치하얼(齊齊哈爾) (중국) [도시] Qiqihar; Chichihar (구칭: Tsitsihar)
치타 (러시아) [도시] Chita
치타공 (방글라데시) [도시] Chittagong
칠레 [국명] (the Republic of) Chile
칭다오(靑島) (중국) [도시] Qingdao (구칭: Tsingtao)
칭하이 성(靑海省) (중국) Qinghai
칭하이 (靑海) 호 (중국) Qinghai; Chinghai; Koko Nor

카

카나리아 제도 (대서양) the Canary Islands; the

세계 주요 지명

Canaries
카디건 (영국) [도시] Cardigan
카디건 만 (영국) Cardigan Bay
카디스 (에스파냐) [도시] Cadiz
카디프 (영국) [도시] Cardiff
카라치 (파키스탄) [도시] Karachi
카라카스 (베네수엘라) [수도] Caracas
카라코람 산맥 (파키스탄·인도·중국) the Karakoram Range; the Karakorams
카르타헤나 (콜롬비아, 에스파냐) [도시] Cartagena
카르파티아 산맥 (동유럽) the Carpathian Mountains; the Carpathians
카리브 해 (대서양 중서부) the Caribbean (Sea)
카메룬 [국명] (the Republic of) Cameroon
카보베르데 [국명] (the Republic of) Cape[Cabo] Verde
카불 (아프가니스탄) [수도] Kabul
카사블랑카 (모로코) [도시] Casablanca
카슈미르 주 (인도·파키스탄) Kashmir
카스피 해 (서아시아) the Caspian (Sea)
카슨시티 (미국) [도시] Carson City
카옌 (프랑스령 기아나) [도시] Cayenne
카이로 (이집트) [수도] Cairo
카이펑(開封) (중국) [도시] Kaifeng
카자흐스탄 [국명] (the Republic of) Kazakhstan
카타르 [국명] Qatar; [공식명] the State of Qatar
카탈루냐 (에스파냐) [지역] Catalonia
카트만두 (네팔) [수도] Katmandu; Kathmandu
카펀테리아 만 (오스트레일리아) the Gulf of Carpentaria
카프카스 산맥 (서아시아) the Caucasus (Mountains)
칸 (프랑스) [도시] Cannes
칸다하르 (아프가니스탄) [도시] Kandahar
칸첸중가 산 (네팔) (Mount) Kanchenjunga
칸푸르 (인도) [도시] Kanpur
칼라하리 사막 (아라비아 남부) the Kalahari (Desert)
칼레 (프랑스) [도시] Calais
캄보디아 [국명] Cambodia
캄차카 반도 (러시아) Kamchatka
캄팔라 (우간다) [수도] Kampala
캄페체 (멕시코) [도시] Campeche
캄페체 만 (멕시코) the Bay of Campeche
캄푸치아 Kampuchea ⇨캄보디아
캄피나스 (브라질) [도시] Campinas
캐나다 [국명] Canada
캐롤라인 제도 (태평양 중서부) the Caroline Islands; the Carolines
캐스케이드 산맥 (미국) the Cascade Range; the Cascades
캐스트리스 (세인트루시아) [수도] Castries
캐츠킬 산맥 (미국) the Catskill Mountains; the Catskills
캔버라 (오스트레일리아) [수도] Canberra
캔자스시티 (미국) [도시] Kansas City
캔자스 주 (미국) Kansas (약어 Kans., Kan., KS)
캔터베리 (영국) [도시] Canterbury
캘거리 (캐나다) [도시] Calgary
캘리컷 (인도) [도시] Calicut ('코지코드'의 구칭)
캘리포니아 만 (멕시코) the Gulf of California
캘리포니아 반도 (멕시코) Baja California; Lower California
캘리포니아 주 (미국) California (약어 Cal., Calif., Ca)
캘커타 (인도) [도시] Calcutta
컴벌랜드 강 (미국) the Cumberland (River)
컴브리아 주 (영국) Cumbria
케냐 [국명] (the Republic of) Kenya
케손시티 (필리핀) [도시] Quezon City
케이투(K2) 봉 (인도) (Mount) K2
케이프커내버럴 (미국) [곶] Cape Canaveral
케이프케네디 (미국) [곶] Cape Kennedy ('케이프커내버럴'의 구칭)
케이프타운 (남아프리카 공화국) [도시] Cape Town
케임브리지 (영국, 미국) [도시] Cambridge
케임브리지셔 주 (영국) Cambridgeshire
켄징턴 (영국·런던) [지구] Kensington
켄터키 주 (미국) Kentucky (약어 Ky., Ken., KY)
켄트 주 (영국) Kent
코나크리 (기니) [수도] Conakry; Konakry
코냐크 (프랑스) [도시] Cognac
코네티컷 주 (미국) Connecticut (약어 Conn., Ct., CT)
코드 곶 (미국) Cape Cod
코르도바 (에스파냐, 아르헨티나, 콜롬비아, 멕시코) [도시] Córdoba
코르시카 섬 (프랑스) Corsica
코모로 [국명] (the) Comoros; [공식명] the Federal Islamic Republic of the Comoros
코모로 제도 (마다가스카르 섬·아프리카 대륙 사이) the Comoro Islands; the Comoros
코모 호 (이탈리아) Lake Como
코벤트리 (영국) [도시] Coventry
코스타리카 [국명] (the Republic of) Costa Rica
코지코드 (인도) [도시] Kozhikode
코카서스 산맥 the Caucasus (Mountains) ('카프카스 산맥'의 영어명)
코코스 제도 (인도양 동부) the Cocos Islands
코크 (아일랜드) [도시] Cork
코타키나발루 (말레이시아) Kota Kinabalu
코트다쥐르 (프랑스) [해안] the Côte d'Azur
코트디부아르 [국명] (the Republic of) Côte d'Ivoire
코파카바나 (브라질) [해안] Copacabana
코펜하겐 (덴마크) [수도] Copenhagen
콘스탄티노플 (터키) [도시] Constantinople ('이스탄불'의 구칭)
콘월 주 (영국) Cornwall
콜럼버스 (미국) [도시] Columbus
콜로라도 강 (미국) the Colorado (River)
콜로라도 주 (미국) Colorado (약어 Col., Colo., CO)
콜롬보 (스리랑카) [도시] Colombo
콜롬비아 [국명] (the Republic of) Colombia
콩고 [국명] the Congo; [공식명] the People's Republic of the Congo
콩고 강 (아프리카 서부) the Congo (River)
콩고 민주 공화국 [국명] Democratic Republic of the Congo
콩코드 (미국) [도시] Concord
콸라룸푸르 (말레이시아) [수도] Kuala Lumpur
쾰른 (독일) [도시] Cologne
쿠릴 열도 (태평양 북부) the Kuril(e) Islands; the Kuril(e)s
쿠바 [국명] (the Republic of) Cuba
쿠스코 (페루) [도시] Cuzco
쿠웨이트 ❶ [국명] Kuwait; [공식명] the State of Kuwait ❷ [❶의 수도] Kuwait; Al Kuwait
쿡 산 (뉴질랜드) Mount Cook
쿡 제도 (뉴질랜드) the Cook Islands; the Southern Cook Islands
쿡 해협 (뉴질랜드) the Cook Strait
쿤룬(崑崙) 산맥 (중국) the Kunlun Mountains
쿤밍(昆明) (중국) [도시] Kunming
퀘벡 주 (캐나다) Quebec

퀸스타운 (뉴질랜드) [도시] Queenstown
퀸즐랜드 주 (오스트레일리아) Queensland
크노소스 (그리스) [유적지] Knossos
크라스노야르스크 (러시아) [도시] Krasnoyarsk
크라이스트처치 (뉴질랜드) [도시] Christchurch
크레타 섬 (그리스) [도시] Crete
크로아티아 [국명] (the Republic of) Croatia
크리스마스 섬 (태평양 중부) Christmas Islands
크림 반도 (우크라이나) Crimea; the Crimean Peninsula
클라이드 만 (영국) the Firth of Clyde
클레르몽페랑 (프랑스) [도시] Clermont-Ferrand
클론다이크 (캐나다) [지역] the Klondike
키갈리 (르완다) [수도] Kigali
키로프 (러시아) [도시] Kirov ('뱌트카'의 구칭)
키르기스스탄 [국명] (the Republic of) Kyrgyzstan
키리바시 [국명] (the Republic of) Kiribati
키시네프 (몰도바) [수도] Kishinev
키예프 (우크라이나) [수도] Kiev
키토 (에콰도르) [수도] Quito
키프로스 [국명] (the Republic of) Cyprus
킨샤사 (콩고 민주 공화국) [수도] Kinshasa
킬 (독일) [도시] Kiel
킬라우에아 산 (하와이) (Mount) Kilauea
킬리만자로 산 (탄자니아) (Mount) Kilimanjaro
킬 운하 (독일) the Kiel Canal
킹스타운 (세인트빈센트 그래나딘) [수도] Kingstown
킹스턴 (자메이카) [수도] Kingston

타

타나나리보 Tananarivo ⇒안타나나리보
타라와 (키리바시) [수도] Tarawa
타란토 (이탈리아) [도시] Taranto
타란토 만 (이탈리아) the Gulf of Taranto
타림 분지 (중국) the Tarim Basin
타밀나두 주 (인도) Tamil Nadu
타슈켄트 (우즈베키스탄) [수도] Tashkent
타이 [국명] Thailand; [공식명] the Kingdom of Thailand
타이난 (대만) [도시] Tainan
타이 만 (동남아시아) the Gulf of Thailand; the Gulf of Siam
타이베이(臺北) (대만) [도시] Taipei; Taibei
타이산(泰山) 산 (중국) Tai Shan; T'ai Shan
타이완(臺灣) Taiwan ⇒대만❷
타이완(臺灣) 해협 the Taiwan Strait ⇒대만 해협
타이중(臺中) (대만) [도시] Taichung; Taizhong
타이후(太湖) 호 (중국) Tai Hu; T'ai Hu
타인 위어 주 (영국) Tyne and Wear
타지키스탄 [국명] (the Republic of) Tajikistan
타클라마칸 사막 (중국) the Takla Makan [Taklimakan] Desert
타호 호 (미국) Lake Tahoe
타히티 섬 (프랑스령 폴리네시아) Tahiti
탄자니아 (탄자니아) Tanzania; [공식명] the United Republic of Tanzania
탈린 (에스토니아) [수도] Tallinn; Tallin
탕가니카 (아프리카 동부) [지역] Tanganyika
탕가니카 호 (아프리카 동부) Lake Tanganyika
탕구(塘沽) (중국) [도시] Tanggu; Tangku
탕헤르 (모로코) [도시] Tangier; Tangiers
태즈메이니아 (오스트레일리아) [섬] Tasmania
태평양 the Pacific (Ocean)
탬파 (미국) [도시] Tampa
터코마 (미국) [도시] Tacoma

터크스케이커스 제도 (서인도 제도) the Turks and Caicos Islands
터키 [국명] (the Republic of) Turkey
털리도 (미국) [도시] Toledo
테구시갈파 (온두라스) [수도] Tegucigalpa
테네리페 섬 (카나리아 제도) Tenerife
테네시 주 (미국) Tennessee (약어 Tenn., TN)
테이사이드 주 (영국) Tayside
테헤란 (이란) [수도] Tehran; Teheran
텍사스 주 (미국) Texas (약어 Tex., TX)
텔아비브 Tel Aviv ⇒텔아비브야파
텔아비브야파 (이스라엘) [도시] Tel Aviv-Jaffa
템스 강 (영국) the Thames
톈산(天山) 산맥 (중앙아시아) the Tian Shan; T'ien Shan
톈진(天津) (중국) [도시] Tianjin (구칭: T'ientsin)
톈타이(天台) 산 (중국) (Mount) Tiantai; T'ient'ai
토고 [국명] (the Republic of) Togo
토론토 (캐나다) [도시] Toronto
토리노 (이탈리아) [도시] Turin
토바고 섬 (트리니다드 토바고) Tobago
토켈라우 제도 (태평양 남부) the Tokelau Islands
토피카 (미국) [도시] Topeka
톰스크 (러시아) [도시] Tomsk
통가 [국명] Tonga; [공식명] the Kingdom of Tonga
통킹 만 (베트남·중국 근해) Tongking [Tonkin] Bay
투루판(吐魯番) (중국) [지역] Turfan; Turupan
투르 (프랑스) [도시] Tours
투르케스탄 (러시아) [지역] Turkestan
투르크메니스탄 [국명] Turkmenistan
투발루 [국명] Tuvalu
투아모투 제도 (프랑스령 폴리네시아) the Tuamotu Archipelago; the Tuamotus
툴레 (그린란드) [도시] Thule
툴롱 (프랑스) [도시] Toulon
툴루즈 (프랑스) [도시] Toulouse
튀니스 (튀니지) [수도] Tunis
튀니지 [국명] (the Republic of) Tunisia
튀링겐 주 (독일) Thuringia; Thüringen
트란스발 주 (남아프리카 공화국) the Transvaal
트란실바니아 산맥 (루마니아) the Transylvanian Alps
트란실바니아 주 (루마니아) Transylvania
트렌턴 (미국) [도시] Trenton
트론헤임 (노르웨이) [도시] Trondheim
트루크 제도 (미크로네시아 연방) the Truk Islands
트리니다드 섬 (트리니다드 토바고) Trinidad
트리니다드 토바고 [국명] (the Republic of) Trinidad and Tobago
트리에스테 (이탈리아) [도시] Trieste
트리폴리 ❶ (리비아) [수도] Tripoli ❷ (레바논) [도시] Tripoli
트빌리시 (그루지야) [수도] Tbilisi; Tiflis
티그리스 강 (소아시아·메소포타미아) the Tigris (River)
티라나 (알바니아) [수도] Tiranë; Tirana
티롤 주 (오스트리아) the Tyrol; the Tirol
티모르 섬 (인도네시아) Timor
티모르 해 (티모르 섬·오스트레일리아 사이) the Timor Sea
티미쇼아라 (루마니아) [도시] Timisoara
티베트(西藏) (중국) [지역] Tibet
티토그라드 (몬테네그로) [수도] Titograd ('포드고리차'의 구칭)
티티카카 호 (페루·볼리비아) Lake Titicaca
티후아나 (멕시코) [도시] Tijuana

팀푸 (부탄) [수도] Thimphu

파나마 ❶ [국명] (the Republic of) Panama ❷ ❶의 수도) Panama (City)
파나마 운하 (남아메리카) the Panama Canal
파나마 지협 (남아메리카) the Isthmus of Panama
파라과이 [국명] (the Republic of) Paraguay
파라마리보 (수리남) [수도] Paramaribo
파르마 (이탈리아) [도시] Parma
파리 (프랑스) [수도] Paris
파미르 고원 (중앙아시아) the Pamirs
파이크스 피크 (미국) [산] Pikes Peak
파키스탄 [국명] Pakistan; [공식명] the Islamic Republic of Pakistan
파타고니아 (아르헨티나) [지역] Patagonia
파푸아 뉴기니 [국명] Papua New Guinea
팔라우 [국명] Palau
팔레스타인 (요르단 강 유역) [지역] Palestine
팔리키르 (미크로네시아 연방) [수도] Palikir
팔마 (에스파냐) [도시] Palma
팜파스 (아르헨티나) [평원] the Pampas
패서디나 (미국) [도시] Pasadena
퍼스 (오스트레일리아) [도시] Perth
펀자브 주 (인도 북서부) Punjab
펑후(澎湖) 제도 (대만 해협) the P'enghu [Penghu] Islands; the Pescardores Islands
페나인 산맥 (영국) the Pennines; the Penine Chain
페낭 Penang ⇨조지타운❷
페라라 (이탈리아) [도시] Ferrara
페로스 제도 (태평양 북부) the Faeroes; the Faeroe Islands
페루 [국명] (the Republic of) Peru
페르시아 (남아시아) Persia
페르시아 만 (아라비아 반도·이란 사이) the Persian Gulf
페샤와르 (파키스탄) [도시] Peshawar
페스 (모로코) [도시] Fez; Fes
페어뱅크스 (미국) [도시] Fairbanks
펜실베이니아 주 (미국) Pennsylvania (약어 Pa., Penn., Penna., PA)
펠로폰네소스 반도 (그리스) the Peloponnese; the Peloponnesus; the Peloponnesos
포 강 (이탈리아) the Po (River)
포드고리차 (몬테네그로) [수도] Podgorica
포르토노보 (베냉) [수도] Porto Novo
포르토프랭스 (아이티) [수도] Port-au-Prince
포르투갈 [국명] (the Ripublic of) Portugal
포메라니아 Pomerania ⇨포모제
포모제 (폴란드) [지역] Pomorze
포스 만 (영국) the Firth of Forth
포이스 주 (영국) Powys
포츠담 (독일) [도시] Potsdam
포츠머스 (미국, 영국) [도시] Portsmouth
포클랜드 제도 (대서양 서남부) the Falkland Islands; the Falklands
포토맥 강 (미국) the Potomac River
포트루이스 (모리셔스) [수도] Port Louis
포트모르즈비 (파푸아 뉴기니) [수도] Port Moresby
포트빌라 (바누아투) [수도] Port Vila; Vila
포트사이드 (이집트) [도시] Port Said
포트오브스페인 (트리니다드 토바고) [수도] Port of Spain; Port-of-Spain
포트워스 (미국) [도시] Fort Worth
포틀랜드 (미국) [도시] Portland
포포카테페틀 산 (멕시코) (Mount) Popocatepetl

폴란드 [국명] (the Republic of) Poland
폴리네시아 (태평양) [지역] Polynesia
폼페이 (이탈리아) [유적지] Pompei
퐁텐블로 (프랑스) [도시] Fontainebleau
푸나 (인도) [도시] Poona
푸나푸티 (투발루) [수도] Funafuti
푸순(撫順) (중국) [도시] Fushun
푸아티에 (프랑스) [도시] Poitiers
푸에고 섬 (아르헨티나·칠레) Tierra del Fuego
푸에르토리코 섬 (서인도 제도) Puerto Rico
푸저우(福州) (중국) [도시] Fuzhou (구칭: Foochow)
푸젠 성(福建省) (중국) Fujian (구칭: Fukien)
퓨젓 사운드 (미국) [만(灣)] Puget Sound
프놈펜 (캄보디아) [수도] Phnom Penh
프라이부르크 (독일) [도시] Freiburg
프라이아 (카보베르데) [수도] Praia
프라하 (체코) [수도] Prague
프랑스 [국명] France; [공식명] the French Republic
프랑크푸르트 Frankfurt ⇨프랑크푸르트암마인
프랑크푸르트암마인 (독일) [도시] Frankfurt am Main
프레즈노 (미국) [도시] Fresno
프로방스 (프랑스) [지역] Provence
프로비던스 (미국) [도시] Providence
프룬제 (키르기스스탄) [수도] Frunze ('비슈케크'의 구칭)
프리지아 제도 (북해) the Frisian Islands; the Frisians
프리타운 (시에라리온) [수도] Freetown
프리토리아 (남아프리카 공화국) [수도] Pretoria
프린스에드워드아일랜드 주 (캐나다) Prince Edward Island
플랑드르 (프랑스·벨기에) [지역] Flanders
플로렌스 Florence ('피렌체'의 영어명)
플로리다 주 (미국) Florida (약어 Fla., FL)
플리머스 (영국) [도시] Plymouth
피닉스 (미국) [도시] Phoenix
피레네 산맥 (프랑스·에스파냐 국경) the Pyrénées
피레에프스 (그리스) [도시] Pireefs; Piraeus
피렌체 (이탈리아) [도시] Firenze
피사 (이탈리아) [도시] Pisa
피지 [국명] (the Republic of) Fiji
피지 제도 (태평양 중남부) the Fiji Islands
피츠버그 (미국) [도시] Pittsburgh
핀란드 [국명] (the Republic of) Finland
핀란드 만 (북유럽) the Gulf of Finland
필라델피아 (미국) [도시] Philadelphia
필리핀 [국명] (the Republic of) the Philippines
핏케언 섬 (남태평양) Pitcairn Island

하노버 (독일) [도시] Hannover
하노이 (베트남) [수도] Hanoi
하라레 (짐바브웨) [수도] Harare
하르툼 (수단) [수도] Khartoum; Khartum
하리코프 (우크라이나) [도시] Kwarkov
하얼빈(哈爾濱) (중국) [도시] Harbin; Haerbin; Haerhpin
하와이 (미국) [섬] Hawaii
하와이 제도 (미국) the Hawaiian Islands
하와이 주 (미국) Hawaii (약어 Haw., HI)
하이난(海南) 섬 (중국) Hainan
하이난 성(海南省) (중국) Hainan
하이데라바드 (인도) [도시] Hyderabad

세계 주요 지명

하이델베르크 (독일) [도시] Heidelberg
하이파 (이스라엘) [도시] Haifa
하이퐁 (베트남) [도시] Haiphong
하일랜드 주 (영국) Highland
하코다테(函館) (일본) [도시] Hakodate
하트퍼드 (미국) [도시] Hartford
하트퍼드셔 주 (영국) Hertfordshire
한커우(漢口) (중국) [도시] Hankou (구칭: Hankow)
할레 (독일) [도시] Halle
할리우드 (미국·로스앤젤레스) [지구] Hollywood
함부르크 (독일) [도시] Hamburg
항저우(杭州) (중국) [도시] Hangzhou (구칭: Hanchow)
해로 (영국) [도시] Harrow
해리스버그 (미국) [도시] Harrisburg
해밀턴 (캐나다, 뉴질랜드) [도시] Hamilton
핼리팩스 (캐나다, 영국) [도시] Halifax
햄프셔 주 (영국) Hampshire
허난 성(河南省) (중국) Henan (구칭: Honan)
허드슨 강 (미국) the Hudson (River)
허드슨 만 (캐나다) Hudson Bay
허베이 성(河北省) (중국) Hebei (구칭: Hopeh)
허페이(合肥) (중국) [도시] Hefei (구칭: Hofei)
헐 (영국) [도시] Hull [공식명: 킹스턴 어펀 헐] Kingston upon Hull
험버사이드 주 (영국) Humberside
헝가리 [국명] (the Republic of) Hungary
헤라트 (아프가니스탄) [도시] Herat
헤리퍼드 우스터 주 (영국) Hereford and Worcester
헤브리디스 제도 (영국) the Hebrides
헤센 주 (독일) Hessen
헤이그 (네덜란드) [도시] the Hague
헤이룽(黑龍) 강 the Heilongjiang (구칭: Heilungkiang) ⇨아무르 강

헬싱키 (핀란드) [수도] Helsinki
호놀룰루 (하와이) [도시] Honolulu
호니아라 (솔로몬) [수도] Honiara
호르무즈 해협 (이란·아라비아 반도 사이) the Strait of Hormuz
호바트 (오스트레일리아) [도시] Hobart
호치민 (베트남) [도시] Ho Chi Minh City
혼슈(本州) (일본) [섬] Honshu
홀름스크 (러시아) [도시] Kholmsk
홋카이도(北海道) (일본) [섬] Hokkaido
홍콩(香港) (중국 남부) [도시] Hong Kong
홍해(紅海) (아프리카·아라비아 반도 사이) the Red Sea
화이난(淮南) (중국) [도시] Huainan
화이허(淮河) 강 (중국) the Huai (River)
황금 해안 Gold Coast
황해(黃海) (중국·한반도 사이) the Yellow Sea
황허(黃河) 강 (중국) the Yellow River; the Huang He
후난 성(湖南省) (중국) Hunan
후베이 성(湖北省) (중국) Hubei (구칭: Hupeh)
후지(富士) 산 (일본) Mt. Fuji
후쿠오카(福岡) (일본) [도시] Fukuoka
후허하오터(呼和浩特) (중국) [도시] Huhehot; Huhhot
휴런 호 (미국·캐나다) Lake Huron
휴스턴 (미국) [도시] Houston
흑해(黑海) (유럽·아시아 사이) the Black Sea
희망봉(喜望峯) (아프리카 최남단) the Cape of Good Hope
히로시마(廣島) (일본) [도시] Hiroshima
히말라야 산맥 (남아시아) the Himalayas
히스파니올라 섬 (서인도 제도) Hispaniola
힌두쿠시 산맥 (아프가니스탄) the Hindu Kush

세계 주요 인명

부록

가

가린 Gagarin, Yuri(1934-68) (소련) 우주 비행사
가드너 Gardner, Erle Stanley(1889-1970) (미국) 변호사, 작가
가리발디 Garibaldi, Giuseppe(1807-82) (이탈리아) 군인
가마 Gama, Vasco da(1460-1524) (포르투갈) 항해가
가우디 Gaudi y Cornet, Antonio(1852-1926) (에스파냐) 건축가, 디자이너
가우스 Gauss, Karl Friedrich(1777-1855) (독일) 수학자
가이거 Geiger, Hans(1882-1945) (독일) 물리학자
가필드 Garfield, Jame Abram(1831-81) (미국) 20대 대통령
간디 ❶ Gandhi, Mahatma(1869-1948) (인도) 사상가, 독립 운동가 ❷ Gandhi, Indira(1917-84) (인도) 수상 ❸ Gandhi, Rajiv(1944-91) (인도) 수상
갈릴레이 Galilei, Galileo(1564-1642) (이탈리아) 천문[물리]학자
강희제(康熙帝) K'ang-hsi-ti(1654-1722) (중국) 청나라 4대 황제
갤럽 Gallup, George(1901-84) (미국) 여론 조사 창시자
갤브레이스 Galbraith, John Kenneth(1908-) (미국) 경제학자
건서 Gunther, John(1901-70) (미국) 언론인
게바라 Guevara, Che(1928-67) (아르헨티나 태생의 쿠바) 혁명가
게오르게 George, Stefan Anton(1868-1933) (독일) 시인
게오르규 Gheorghiu, Constantin Virgil(1916-92) (루마니아) 작가
게이뤼삭 Gay-Lussac, Joseph Louis(1778-1850) (프랑스) 물리[화학]학자
게이블 Gable, William Clark(1901-60) (미국) 영화 배우
게이츠 Gates, William H.(1955-) (미국) 마이크로소프트사 설립자
게인즈버러 Gainsborough, Thomas(1727-88) (영국) 화가
고갱 Gauguin, Eugène Henri Paul(1848-1903) (프랑스) 화가
고골리 Gogol, Nikolai Vasilievich(1809-52) (러시아) 작가
고든 Gordon, Charles George(1833-85) (영국) 군인
고르바초프 Gorbachev, Mikhail S.(1931-) (러시아) 정치가
고리키 Gorki[Gorky], Maksim(1868-1936) (러시아) 작가
고야 Goya y Lucientes, Francisco José de(1746-1828) (에스파냐) 화가
고티에 Gautier, Théophile(1811-72) (프랑스) 시인, 작가
고흐 Gogh, Vincent van(1853-90) (네덜란드) 화가
골드스미스 Goldsmith, Oliver(1730-74) (아일랜드 태생의 영국) 시인, 작가
골드윈 Goldwyn, Samuel(1879-1974) (폴란드 태생의 미국) 영화 제작자
골딩 Golding, William Gerald(1911-93) (영국) 작가
골즈워디 Galsworthy, John(1867-1933) (영국) 작가
공자(孔子) K'ung Fu-tzǔ (Confucius)(551-479 B.C.) (중국) 유교 철학자
공쿠르 Goncourt, Edmond Louis Antoine Huot de(1822-96) (프랑스) 작가
괴링 Göring, Hermann Wilhelm(1893-1946) (독일) 군인, 나치스 지도자
괴벨스 Goebbels, Paul Joseph(1897-1945) (독일) 정치가, 나치스 지도자
괴테 Goethe, Johann Wolfgang von(1749-1832) (독일) 작가
구노 Gounod, Charles François(1818-93) (프랑스) 작곡가
구텐베르크 Gutenberg, Johannes(1398?-1468?) (독일) 발명가
굴원(屈原) Chüyüan(343?-277? B.C.) (중국) 문인
궈모뤄(郭沫若) Guo Moruo(1892-1978) (중국) 정치가, 부수상
그라스 Grass, Günter(1927-) (독일) 작가
그라쿠스 Gracchus, Tiberius Sempronius(163-133 B.C.) (고대 로마) 호민관
그랜트 Grant, Ulysses Simpson(1822-85) (미국) 군인, 18대 대통령
그레셤 Gresham, Sir Thomas(1519-79) (영국) 금융가
그레이 Gray, Thomas(1716-71) (영국) 시인
그레코 Greco, El(1541-1614) (그리스 태생의 에스파냐) 화가
그로미코 Gromyco, Andrey(1909-89) (소련) 정치가
그로티우스 Grotius, Hugo(1583-1645) (네덜란드) 국제법의 창시자
그리그 Grieg, Edvard(1843-1907) (노르웨이) 작곡가
그린 Green, Thomas Hill(1836-82) (영국) 철학자
그린 Greene, Graham(1904-91) (영국) 작가
그림 Grimm, Jacob(1785-1863) (독일) 민속학자
글래드스턴 Gladstone, William Ewart(1809-98) (영국) 정치가, 수상
글루크 Gluck, Christoph Willibald von(1714-87) (독일) 작곡가
기번 Gibbon, Edward(1737-94) (영국) 역사가
기싱 Gissing, George Robert(1857-1903) (영국) 작가
기조 Guizot, François Pierre Guillaume(1787-1874) (프랑스) 정치가, 역사가
긴즈버그 Ginsberg, Allen(1926-97) (미국) 시인

나

나보코프 Nabokov, Vladimir(1899-1977) (소련 태생의 미국) 작가
나세르 Nasser, Gamal Abdul(1918-70) (이집트) 대통령
나이팅게일 Nightingale, Florence(1820-1910) (영국) 간호사
나폴레옹 1세 Napoleon I, Bonaparte(1769-1821) (프랑스) 군인, 황제
난센 Nansen, Fridtjof(1861-1930) (노르웨이) 탐험가
네로 Nero, Claudius(37-68) (고대 로마) 황제
네루 Nehru, Jawaharlal(1889-1964) (인도) 수상
네루다 Neruda, Pablo(1904-73) (칠레) 시인
네윈 Ne Win(1910-) (미얀마) 군인, 대통령
네이더 Nader, Ralph(1934-) (미국) 시민 운동가
넬슨 Nelson, Viscount Horatio(1758-1805) (영국) 군인
노발리스 Novalis(1772-1801) (독일) 시인

세계 주요 인명

노벨 Nobel, Alfred Bernhard(1833-96) (스웨덴) 발명가, 사업가, 노벨상 창시자
노스트라다무스 Nostradamus(1503-66) (프랑스) 예언자
노자(老子) Lao-tzu(?-?) (중국) 춘추 시대 사상가
누레예프 Nureyev, Rudolf(1938-93) (소련 태생의 영국) 무용가
뉴먼 Newman, Cardinal John Henry(1801-90) (영국) 신학자, 설교가
뉴턴 Newton, Sir Isaac(1642-1727) (영국) 수학자, 물리학자, 철학자
니진스키 Nijinsky, Waslaw[Vaslaw](1890-1950) (소련) 무용가
니체 Nietzsche, Friedrich Wilhelm(1844-1900) (독일) 철학자
닉슨 Nixon, Richard Milhous(1913-94) (미국) 37대 대통령
닌 Nin, Anaïs(1903-77) (미국) 작가
닐센 Nielsen, Carl(1865-1931) (덴마크) 작곡가

다비드 David, Jacque Louis(1748-1825) (프랑스) 화가
다얀 Dayan, Moshe(1915-81) (이스라엘) 군사 지도자
다윈 Darwin, Charles Robert(1809-82) (영국) 생물학자
단눈치오 D'Annunzio, Gabriele(1863-1938) (이탈리아) 작가
단테 Dante, Alighieri(1265-1321) (이탈리아) 시인
달라디에 Daladier, Edouard(1884-1970) (프랑스) 정치가, 수상
달라이 라마 14세 Dalai Lama XIV(1935-) (티베트) 티베트 불교 교주
달랑베르 d'Alembert, Jean le Rond(1717-83) (프랑스) 사상가
달리 Dali, Salvador(1904-89) (에스파냐) 화가
당통 Danton, Georges Jacques(1759-94) (프랑스) 혁명 정치가
대처 Thatcher, Margaret(1925-) (영국) 정치가, 총리
더스패서스 Dos Passos, John(1896-1970) (미국) 작가
던 Donne, John(1572-1631) (영국) 종교가, 시인
덜레스 Dulles, John Foster(1888-1959) (미국) 정치가
덩샤오핑(鄧小平) Deng Xiaoping(1904-97) (중국) 정치가
덩컨 Duncan, Isadora(1878-1927) (미국) 무용가
데라메어 de la Mare, Walter John(1873-1956) (영국) 문학가
데모스테네스 Demosthenes(384-322? B.C.) (고대 그리스) 정치가
데모크리토스 Democritus(460?-370? B.C.) (고대 그리스) 철학자
데시카 De Sica, Vittorio(1901-74) (이탈리아) 영화 감독
데아미치스 de Amicis, Edmondo(1846-1908) (이탈리아) 작가
데카르트 Descartes, René(1596-1650) (프랑스) 철학자, 수학자
도나텔로 Donatello(1386-1466) (이탈리아) 조각가
도데 Daudet, Alphonse(1840-97) (프랑스) 작가
도미에 Daumier Honoré(1808-79) (프랑스) 화가
도스토예프스키 Dostoevski, Fyodor Mikhailovich(1821-81) (러시아) 작가
도일 Doyle, Sir Arthur Conan(1859-1930) (영국) 추리 작가

두보(杜甫) Tu Fu (712-770) (중국) 시인
둡체크 Dubček, Alexander(1921-92) (체코슬로바키아) 정치가
뒤낭 Dunant, Jean Henri(1828-1910) (스위스) 사회사업가
뒤러 Dürer, Albrecht(1471-1528) (독일) 화가
뒤르켕 Durkheim, Émile(1858-1917) (프랑스) 사회학자
뒤마 ❶ Dumas, Alexandre(大 뒤마)(1802-70) (프랑스) 소설가·극작가 ❷ Dumas, Alexandre(小 뒤마)(1824-95) (프랑스) 작가
뒤비비에 Duvivier, Julien(1896-1967) (프랑스) 영화감독
뒤피 Dufy, Raoul(1877-1953) (프랑스) 화가
듀이 Dewey, John(1859-1952) (미국) 교육학자, 철학자
드가 Degas, Edgar(1834-1917) (프랑스) 화가
드골 De Gaulle, Charles André J.M.(1890-1970) (프랑스) 장군, 수상
드라이든 Dryden, John(1631-1700) (영국) 문학가
드라이저 Dreiser, Theodore Herman Albert(1871-1945) (미국) 작가
드랭 Derain, André(1880-1954) (프랑스) 화가
드레퓌스 Dreyfus, Alfred(1859-1935) (프랑스) 군인
드보르자크 Dvořák, Antonin(1841-1904) (체코슬로바키아) 작곡가
드뷔시 Debussy, Achille Claude(1862-1918) (프랑스) 작곡가
들라크루아 Delacroix, Ferdinand Victor Eugène(1798-1863) (프랑스) 화가
디드로 Diderot, Denis(1713-84) (프랑스) 사상가, 백과사전 편집자
디미트로프 Dimitrov, Georgi Mikhailovich(1882-1949) (불가리아) 정치가, 수상
디오게네스 Diogenes(412?-323 B.C.) (고대 그리스) 철학자
디오르 Dior, Christian(1905-57) (프랑스) 디자이너
디젤 Diesel, Rudolf(1858-1913) (독일) 발명가
디즈니 Disney, Walt(1901-66) (미국) 애니메이션 작가
디즈레일리 Disraeli, Benjamin(1804-81) (영국) 수상
디킨스 Dickens, Charles John Huffam(1812-70) (영국) 작가
디킨슨 Dickinson, Emily(1830-86) (미국) 시인
디포 Defoe, Daniel(1660-1731) (영국) 작가
딜타이 Dilthey, Wilhelm(1833-1911) (독일) 철학자

라겔뢰프 Lagerlöf, Selma Ottiliana Lovisa(1858-1940) (스웨덴) 작가
라그랑주 Lagrange, Joseph Louis(1736-1813) (이탈리아 태생의 프랑스) 수학·천문학자
라다크리슈난 Radhakrishnan, Sarvepalli(1888-1975) (인도) 철학자
라디게 Radiguet, Raymond(1903-23) (프랑스) 작가
라로슈푸코 La Rochefoucauld, François, Duc de (1613-80) (프랑스) 작가
라루스 Larousse, Pierre Athanase(1817-75) (프랑스) 사전 편찬자
라마르크 Lamarck, Jean Baptiste Pierre Antoine de Monet de(1744-1829) (프랑스) 생물학자
라마르틴 Lamartine, Alphonse Marie Louis de (1790-1869) (프랑스) 시인·정치가
라모 Rameau, Jean Philippe(1683-1764) (프랑스) 작곡가
라벨 Ravel, Maurice(1875-1937) (프랑스) 작곡가

세계 주요 인명

라부아지에 Lavoisier, Antoine Laurent(1743-94) (프랑스) 화학자

라브뤼예르 La Bruyère, Jean de(1645-96) (프랑스) 모럴리스트

라블레 Rabelais, François(1483?-1553?) (프랑스) 작가

라스무센 Rasmussen, Knun Johan Victor(1879-1933) (덴마크) 민속학자·탐험가

라스푸틴 Rasputin, Grigori Efimovich(1872-1916) (러시아) 승려

라신 Racine, Jean Baptiste(1639-99) (프랑스) 극작가

라오서(老舍) Lao She(1899-1966) (중국) 작가

라이샤워 Reischauer, Edwin Oldfather(1910-90) (미국) 역사가

라이트 ❶ Wright, Wilbur(1867-1912) (미국) 발명가 ❷ Wright, Orville(1871-1948) (미국) 발명가

라이프니츠 Leibniz, Gottfried Wilhelm(1646-1716) (독일) 철학자, 수학자

라파엘로 Raphaello(1483-1520) (이탈리아) 화가

라파에트 Lafayette, Marquis de(1757-1834) (프랑스) 군인·혁명가

라퐁텐 La Fontaine, Jean de(1621-95) (프랑스) 우화 작가

라플라스 Laplace, Pierre Simon(1749-1827) (프랑스) 천문학자, 수학자

라흐마니노프 Rachmaninoff, Sergei Vassilievich(1873-1943) (소련) 작곡가

랄로 Lalo, Edouard(1823-92) (프랑스) 작곡가

랑케 Ranke, Leopold von(1795-1886) (독일) 역사가

래스키 Laski, Harold Joseph(1893-1950) (영국) 정치학자

래티모어 Lattimore, Owen(1900-89) (미국) 동양학자

램 Lamb, Charles(1775-1834) (영국) 수필가

랭보 Rimbaud, Arthur(1854-91) (프랑스) 시인

량치차오(梁啓超) Liang Ch'i-ch'ao(1873-1929) (중국) 사상가, 정치가

러더퍼드 Rutherford, Ernst(1871-1937) (뉴질랜드 태생의 영국) 물리학자

러셀 Russell, Bertrand, 3rd Earl(1872-1970) (영국) 철학자, 평화 운동가

러스크 Rusk, Dean(1909-94) (미국) 정치가

러스킨 Ruskin, John(1819-1900) (영국) 비평가

런던 London, Jack(1876-1916) (미국) 작가

레닌 Lenin, Nikolai(1870-1924) (소련) 혁명가, 정치가

레르몬토프 Lermontov, Mikhail Yurievich(1814-41) (러시아) 문학가

레마르크 Remarque, Erich Maria(1898-1970) (독일) 작가

레비스트로스 Lévi-Strauss, Claude Gustave(1908-91) (벨기에 태생의 프랑스) 문화 인류학자

레셉스 Lesseps, Ferdinand de(1805-94) (프랑스) 수에즈 운하 건설자

레스피기 Respighi, Ottorino(1879-1936) (이탈리아) 작곡가

레싱 Lessing, Gotthold Ephraim(1729-81) (독일) 극작가

레오나르도 다빈치 Leonardo[Lionardo] da Vinci(1452-1519) (이탈리아) 화가, 조각가

레이건 Reagan, Ronald(1911-) (미국) 40대 대통령

레제 Léger, Fernand(1881-1955) (프랑스) 화가

렘브란트 Rembrandt(1606-69) (네덜란드) 화가

로댕 Rodin, François Auguste René(1840-1917) (프랑스) 조각가

로랑생 Laurencin, Marie(1885-1956) (프랑스) 화가

로렌스 ❶ Lawrence, David Herbert(1885-1930) (영국) 작가 ❷ Lawrence, T.E.(1888-1935) (영국) 군인, 작가

로렌츠 Lorenz, Konrad(1903-89) (오스트리아) 비교행동학자

로르샤흐 Rorschach, Hermann(1884-1922) (스위스) 정신 의학자

로맹 Romains, Jules(1885-1972) (프랑스) 작가

로멜 Rommel, Erwin(1891-1944) (독일) 군인

로베스피에르 Robespierre, Maximilien François Marie Isidore(1758-94) (프랑스) 혁명가, 정치가

로브그리예 Robbe-Grillet, Alain(1922-) (프랑스) 작가

로세티 ❶ Rossetti, Dante Gabriel(1828-82) (영국) 시인, 화가 ❷ Rossetti, Christina Georgina(1830-94) (영국) 시인

로스차일드 Rothschild, Nathan Meyer(1777-1836) (독일·영국) 은행가

로스탕 Rostand, Edmond(1868-1918) (프랑스) 극작가, 시인

로스트로포비치 Rostropovich, Mstislav L.(1927-) (러시아) 첼리스트, 지휘자

로시니 Rossini, Gioacchino Antonio(1792-1868) (이탈리아) 작곡가

로웰 Lowell, James Russell(1819-91) (미국) 시인, 비평가

로이드조지 Lloyd George, David, 1st Earl of Dufor(1863-1945) (영국) 수상

로이터 Reuter, Baron Paul Julius von(1816-99) (독일 태생의 영국) 통신사 창설자

로저스 Rodgers, Richard(1902-79) (미국) 작곡가

로크 Locke, John(1632-1704) (영국) 철학자

로트레크 Lautrec, Henri de Toulouse(1864-1901) (프랑스) 화가

로티 Loti, Pierre(1850-1923) (프랑스) 군인, 작가

록펠러 Rockefeller, John Davison(1839-1937) (미국) 실업가

롤랑 Rolland, Romain(1866-1944) (프랑스) 작가

롤리 Raleigh, Sir Walter(1554?-1618) (영국) 탐험가

롱사르 Ronsard, Pierre de(1524-85) (프랑스) 시인

롱펠로 Longfellow, Henry Wadsworth(1807-82) (미국) 시인

뢴트겐 Roentgen, Wilhelm Konrad(1845-1923) (독일) 물리학자

루벤스 Rubens, Peter Paul(1577-1640) (플랑드르) 화가

루빈스타인 Rubinstein, Artur(1887-1982) (폴란드 태생의 미국) 피아니스트, 작곡가

루소 ❶ Rousseau, Jean Jacques(1712-78) (프랑스) 사상가 ❷ Rousseau, Henri(1844-1910) (프랑스) 화가

루쉰(魯迅) Lu Xun(1881-1936) (중국) 문학가

루스벨트 ❶ Roosevelt, Franklin Delano(1882-1945) (미국) 32대 대통령 ❷ Roosevelt Theodore(1858-1919) (미국) 26대 대통령

루오 Rouault, Georges(1871-1958) (프랑스) 화가

루이스 Lewis, Harry Sinclair(1885-1951) (미국) 작가

루이 14세 Louis XIV(1638-1715) (프랑스) 황제

루이 필리프 Louis Philippe(1773-1850) (프랑스) 국왕

루터 Luther, Martin(1483-1546) (독일) 종교 개혁가

룩셈부르크 Luxemburg, Rosa(1870-1919) (폴란드 태생의 독일) 독일 공산당 지도자

뤼드베리 Rydberg, Johannes Robert(1854-1919) (스웨덴) 물리학자

류사오치(劉少奇) Liu Shao-ch'i(1898-1973) (중국) 정치가, 부주석

르나르 Renard, Jules(1864-1910) (프랑스) 작가
르낭 Renan, Joseph Ernest(1823-92) (프랑스) 역사가, 비평가
르누아르 Renoir, Pierre Auguste(1841-1919) (프랑스) 화가
르동 Redon, Odilon(1840-1916) (프랑스) 화가
르코르뷔지에 Le Corbusier(1887-1965) (스위스 태생의 프랑스) 건축가
리 Lee, Robert Edward(1807-70) (미국) 장군
리베라 Ribera, José de (Jusepe de Ribera)(1591-1652) (에스파냐) 화가, 판화가
리비히 Liebig, Justus von(1803-73) (독일) 화학자
리빙스턴 Livingstone, David(1813-73) (영국) 탐험가
리센코 Lysenko, Trofim Denisovich(1898-1976) (소련) 생물학자
리셴녠(李先念) Li Hsien-nien(1908-92) (중국) 국가주석
리슐리외 Richelieu, Armand Jean du Plessis, Duke of(1585-1642) (프랑스) 추기경, 정치가
리스먼 Riesman, David(1909-) (미국) 사회학자
리스트 Liszt, Franz von(1811-86) (헝가리) 작곡가
리처드슨 Richardson, Samuel(1689-1761) (영국) 작가
리카도 Ricardo, David(1772-1823) (영국) 경제학자
리케르트 Rickert, Heinrich(1863-1936) (독일) 철학자
리콴유(李光耀) Lee Kuan Yew(1923-) (싱가포르) 총리
리턴 Lytton, Victor Alexander George Robert, 2nd Earl of(1876-1947) (영국) 문학가, 정치가
리프먼 Lippmann, Walter(1889-1974) (미국) 언론인
리프크네히트 Liebknecht, Karl(1871-1919) (독일) 독일 공산당 지도자
린네 Linnaeus, Carolus(=Karl von Linné)(1707-78) (스웨덴) 생물학자
린드버그 Lindbergh, Charles Augustus(1902-74) (미국) 비행가
린뱌오(林彪) Lin Biao(1907-71) (중국) 군인, 정치가
린위탕(林語堂) Lin Yut'ang(1895-1976) (중국) 문학가
릴케 Rilke, Rainer Maria(1875-1926) (독일) 시인
림스키코르사코프 Rimski-Korsakov, Nikolai Andreevich(1844-1908) (러시아) 작곡가
립턴 Lipton, Sir Thomas Johnstone(1850-1931) (영국) 실업가
링컨 Lincoln, Abraham(1809-65) (미국) 16대 대통령

마네 Manet, Edouard(1832-83) (프랑스) 화가
마니 Manes; Mani(216?-276?) (페르시아) 마니교 창시자
마르셀 Marcel, Gabriel(1889-1973) (프랑스) 철학자, 극작가
마르코니 Marconi, Guglielmo(1874-1937) (이탈리아) 물리학자
마르코스 Marcos, Ferdinand E.(1917-89) (필리핀) 대통령
마르코 폴로 Marco Polo ⇨폴로
마르크스 Marx, Karl Heinrich(1818-83) (독일) 경제학자, 사회주의 제창자
마르탱뒤가르 Martin du Gard, Roger(1881-1958) (프랑스) 작가
마리보 Marivaux, Pierre Carlet de Chamblain de(1688-1763) (프랑스) 극작가
마리아 테레지아 Maria Theresia(1717-80) (오스트리아) 대공, 헝가리·보헤미아 여왕

마리 앙투아네트 Marie Antoinette(1755-93) (프랑스) 루이 16세 왕비
마셜 Marshall, George Catlett(1880-1959) (미국) 군인, 외교관
마야코프스키 Mayakovski, Vladimir(1893-1930) (소련) 시인, 극작가
마오쩌둥(毛澤東) Mao Tse-tung(1893-1976) (중국) 혁명가, 당 주석
마욜 Maillol, Aristide(1861-1944) (프랑스) 조각가
마운트배튼 Mountbatten of Burma, Earl (Louis Mountbatten)(1900-79) (영국) 해군 대장, 인도 총독
마이어 Mayer, Julius Robert von(1814-1978) (독일) 물리학자
마젤란 Magellan, Ferdinand(1480?-1521) (포르투갈) 항해가
마키아벨리 Machiavelli, Niccolò di Bernardo dei(1469-1527) (이탈리아) 사상가
마타 하리 Mata Hari(1876-1917) (독일) 독일 여간첩
마테를링크 Maeterlinck, Maurice(1862-1949) (벨기에) 문학가
마테오 리치 Matteo Ricci(1552-1610) (이탈리아) 이탈리아의 예수회 소속 중국 파견 선교사
마티스 Matisse, Henri(1869-1954) (프랑스) 화가
마호메트 Mahomet [Mohammed] (570?-632) (아랍) 이슬람교 창시자
마흐 Mach, Ernst(1838-1916) (오스트리아) 물리학자, 철학자
막사이사이 Magsaysay, Ramón(1907-57) (필리핀) 대통령
만 Mann, Thomas(1875-1955) (독일) 작가
만델라 Mandela, Winnie(1936-) (남아프리카 공화국) 대통령, 흑인 인권 운동가
말라르메 Mallarmé, Stéphane(1842-98) (프랑스) 시인
말로 Malraux, André(1901-76) (프랑스) 작가, 정치가
말리노프스키 Malinowski, Bronislaw Kasper(1884-1942) (폴란드 태생의 영국) 문화 인류학자
매디슨 Madison, James(1751-1836) (미국) 4대 대통령
매컬러스 McCullers, Carson(1917-67) (미국) 작가
매쿨리 Macaulay, Thomas Babington(1800-59) (영국) 역사가, 정치가
매킨리 McKinley, William(1843-1901) (미국) 25대 대통령
맥나마라 McNamara, Robert S.(1916-) (미국) 정치가
맥도널드 MacDonald, James Ramsay(1866-1937) (영국) 정치가, 수상
맥루언 McLuhan, Marshall(1911-80) (캐나다) 사회과학자
맥밀런 MacMillan, M. Harold(1894-1986) (영국) 정치가, 수상
맥스웰 Maxwell, James Clerk(1831-79) (영국) 물리학자
맥아더 MacArthur, Douglas(1880-1964) (미국) 군인
맨스필드 Mansfield, Katherine(1888-1923) (영국) 작가
맬서스 Malthus, Thomas Robert(1766-1834) (영국) 경제학자
맬컴 엑스 Malcolm X(1925-65) (미국) 흑인 운동가
맹자(孟子) Meng-tzu (Mencius)(372-289 B.C.) (중국) 사상가
머독 Murdoch, Iris(1919-99) (영국) 작가
먼로 ❶ Monroe, James(1758-1831) (미국) 5대 대통령 ❷ Monroe, Marilyn(1926-62) (미국) 여배우
메닝거 Menninger, Karl Augustus(1893-1990) (미

국) 정신 분석의
메디치 Medici, Cosimo de(1389-1464) (이탈리아) 정치가, 미술·문학 애호가
메리메 Mérimée, Prosper(1803-70) (프랑스) 작가
메시에 Messier, Charles(1730-1817) (프랑스) 천문학자
메이어 Meir, Golda(1898-1978) (이스라엘) 총리
메이저 Major, John(1943-) (영국) 정치가, 총리
메일러 Mailer, Norman(1923-) (미국) 작가
메치니코프 Metchnikoff, Élie(1845-1916) (러시아 태생의 프랑스) 생물학자
메테르니히 Metternich Klemens Wenzel Lothar(1773-1859) (오스트리아) 정치가
멘델 Mendel, Gregor Johann(1822-84) (오스트리아) 유전학자
멘델레예프 Mendeleev, Dmitri, Ivanovich(1834-1907) (러시아) 화학자
멘델스존 Mendelssohn, Felix(1809-47) (독일) 작곡가
멜빌 Melville, Herman(1819-91) (미국) 작가
모건 Morgan, Thomas Hunt(1866-1945) (미국) 유전학자
모네 Monet, Claude(1840-1926) (프랑스) 화가
모딜리아니 Modigliani, Amedeo(1884-1920) (이탈리아) 화가
모라비아 Moravia, Alberto(1907-90) (이탈리아) 작가
모루아 Maurois, André(1885-1967) (프랑스) 비평가, 작가
모리아크 Mauriac, François(1885-1970) (프랑스) 작가
모스 Morse, Samuel Finley Breese(1791-1872) (미국) 발명가
모어 More, Thomas(1477-1535) (영국) 사상가
모즐리 Moseley, Harry(1887-1915) (영국) 물리학자
모차르트 Mozart, Wolfgang Amadeus(1756- 91) (오스트리아) 작곡가
모파상 Maupassant, Henri René Albert Guy de (1850-93) (프랑스) 작가
몬드리안 Mondrian, Piet(1872-1944) (네덜란드) 화가
몰로토프 Molotov, Vyacheslav, Mikhailovich(1890-1986) (소련) 정치가
몰리에르 Molière(1622-73) (프랑스) 극작가
몰트케 Moltke, Helmuth,Graf von(1800-91) (프로이센) 군인
몸 Maugham, William Somerset(1874-1965) (영국) 작가
몽고메리 Montgomery, Bernard L.(1887-1976) (영국) 군인
몽골피에 Montgolfier Joseph Michel(1740-1810) (프랑스) 발명가
몽테뉴 Montaigne, Michel Eyquem, Seigneur de(1533-92) (프랑스) 사상가
몽테스키외 Montesquieu, Charles Louis de Secondat(1689-1755) (프랑스) 사상가
무리요 Murillo, Bartolomé Estéban(1618-82) (에스파냐) 화가
무바라크 Mubarak, (Muhammad) Hosni(1928-) (이집트) 대통령
무소르크스키 Moussorgsky, Modest Petrovich (1839-81) (러시아) 작곡가
무솔리니 Mussolini, Benito(1883-1945) (이탈리아) 파시스트당 총재
무어 Moore, Henry(1898-1986) (영국) 조각가
무제(武帝) Wu-ti(156-87 B.C.) 전한(前漢) 7대 황제
묵자(墨子) Mo-tzu(480-390 B.C.) (중국) 사상가

뭉크 Munch, Edvard(1863-1944) (노르웨이) 화가, 판화가
뮈르달 Myrdal, Karl Gunnar(1898-1987) (스웨덴) 정치가
뮈세 Musset, Louis Charles Alfred de(1810-57) (프랑스) 시인
미드 Mead, Margaret(1901-78) (미국) 문화 인류학자
미라보 Mirabeau, Honoré Gabriel Victor Riqueti(1749-91) (프랑스) 정치가
미로 Miró, Joan(1893-1983) (에스파냐) 화가, 조각가
미슐레 Michelet, Jules(1798-1874) (프랑스) 사학자
미첼 Mitchell, Margaret(1900-49) (미국) 작가
미치너 Michener, James(1907-97) (미국) 작가
미켈란젤로 Michelangelo(1475-1564) (이탈리아) 화가, 조각가
미테랑 Mitterand, François Maurice M.(1916-96) (프랑스) 정치가, 대통령
밀 Mill, John Stuart(1806-73) (영국) 철학자
밀러 ❶ Miller, Arthur(1915-) (미국) 극작가 ❷ Miller, Henry(1891-1980) (미국) 작가
밀레 Millet, Jean François(1814-75) (프랑스) 화가
밀른 Milne, A.A.(1882-1956) (영국) 시인, 작가
밀턴 Milton, John(1608-74) (영국) 시인

바

바그너 Wagner, Wilhelm Richard(1813-83) (독일) 작곡가
바르뷰스 Barbusse, Henri(1873-1935) (프랑스) 작가
바르토크 Bartók, Béla(1881-1945) (헝가리) 작곡가
바르트 Barth, Karl(1886-1968) (스위스) 신학자
바버 Barber, Samuel(1910-81) (미국) 작곡가
바서만 Wassermann, August von(1866-1925) (독일) 세균학자
바슐라르 Bachelard, Gaston(1884-1962) (프랑스) 철학자
바이런 Byron, George Gordon, Lord(1788-1824) (영국) 시인
바쿠닌 Bakunin, Mikhail(1814-76) (러시아) 무정부주의 혁명가
바흐 Bach, Johann Sebastian(1685-1750) (독일) 작곡가
반다이크 Van Dyck[Vandyke], Sir Anthony(1599-1641) (플랑드르) 화가
발레리 Valéry, Paul Ambroise(1871-1945) (프랑스) 시인
발작 Balzac, Honoré de(1799-1850) (프랑스) 작가
발트하임 Waldheim, Kurt(1918-) (오스트리아) 유엔 사무총장, 정치가
백낙천(白樂天) Po Chü-i(772-846) (중국) 시인
버거 Burger, Warren E.(1907-95) (미국) 법률가
버니언 Bunyan, John(1628-88) (영국) 작가
버드 Byrd, Richard E.(1888-1957) (미국) 탐험가
버질 Virgil ("베르길리우스"의 영어명)
버틀러 Butler, Samuel(1835-1902) (영국) 작가
벅 Buck, Pearl Sydenstricker(1892-1973) (미국) 작가
번스 Burns, Robert(1759-96) (영국) 시인
번스타인 Bernstein, Leonard(1918-90) (미국) 작곡가, 지휘자
번치 Bunche, Ralph J.(1904-71) (미국) 외교관
베긴 Begin, Menahem(1913-92) (이스라엘) 총리
베넷 Bennet, Enoch Arnold(1867-1931) (영국) 작가
베니딕트 Benedict, Ruth Fulton(1887-1948) (미국) 문화 인류학자
베르그송 Bergson, Henri(1859-1914) (프랑스) 철학자

세계 주요 인명

베르길리우스 Vergilius, Maro, Publius (70-19 B.C.) (고대 로마) 시인
베르디 Verdi, Giuseppe(1813-1901) (이탈리아) 작곡가
베른 Verne, Jules(1828-1905) (프랑스) 작가
베를렌 Verlaine, Paul(1844-96) (프랑스) 시인
베를리오즈 Berlioz, Louis Hector(1803-69) (프랑스) 작곡가
베리야 Beria, Lavrenti(1899-1953) (소련) 비밀 경찰 장관
베버 ❶ Weber, Karl Maria von(1786-1826) (프랑스) 작곡가 ❷ Weber, Max(1864-1920) (독일) 사회 과학자
베스푸치 Vespucci, Amerigo(1454-1512) (이탈리아) 항해자
베이컨 Bacon, Francis(1561-1626) (영국) 철학자
베케트 Beckett, Samuel(1906-89) (아일랜드 태생의 프랑스) 극작가
베토벤 Beethoven, Ludwig van(1770-1827) (독일) 작곡가
벤구리온 Ben-Gurion, David(1886-1973) (폴란드 태생의 이스라엘) 정치가, 수상
벤담 Bentham, Jeremy(1748-1832) (영국) 철학자, 법학자
벤츠 Benz, Karl(1844-1929) (독일) 발명가
벨 Bell, Alexander Graham(1847-1922) (미국) 발명가
벨라스케스 Velázquez, Diego Rodriguez de Silva y(1599-1660) (에스파냐) 화가
벨로 Bellow, Saul(1915-) (미국) 작가
벨리니 Bellini, Vincenzo(1801-35) (이탈리아) 오페라 작곡가
보나르 Bonnard, Pierre(1867-1947) (프랑스) 화가
보나파르트 Bonaparte, Napoléon ⇨나폴레옹 1세
보두앵 Baudouin(1930-93) (벨기에) 국왕
보들레르 Baudelaire, Pierre Charles(1821-67) (프랑스) 시인
보로딘 Borodin, Aleksandr Porfirievich(1833-87) (러시아) 작곡가
보르헤스 Borges, Jorge Luis(1899-1986) (아르헨티나) 작가
보마르셰 Beaumarchais, Pierre-Augustin Caron de(1732-99) (프랑스) 극작가
보부아르 Beauvoir, Simone de(1908-86) (프랑스) 작가, 비평가
보스 Bose, Subhas Chandra(1897-1945) (인도) 물리학자, 식물학자
보어 Bohr, Niels(1885-1962) (덴마크) 물리학자
보일 Boyle, Robert(1627-91) (영국) 물리학자, 화학자
보즈웰 Boswell, James(1740-95) (영국) 전기 작가
보카치오 Boccaccio, Giovanni(1313-75) (이탈리아) 시인
보티첼리 Botticelli, Sandro(1445?-1510) (이탈리아) 화가
본회퍼 Bonhoeffer, Dietrich(1906-45) (독일) 신학자
볼드윈 Baldwin, James(1924-87) (미국) 작가
볼테르 Voltaire(1694-1778) (프랑스) 사상가
뵐 Böll, Heinrich Theodor(1917-85) (독일) 작가
부르크하르트 Burckhardt, Jakob(1818-97) (스위스) 역사가
부세 Busse, Karl(1872-1918) (독일) 시인
부시 ❶ Bush, George(1924-) (미국) 41대 대통령 ❷ Bush, George W.(1946-) (미국) 43대 대통령
부알로 Boileau-Despréaux, Nicolas(1636-1711) (프랑스) 비평가, 시인
부하린 Bukharin, Nikolai(1888-1938) (소련) 볼셰비키 이론 지도자

분젠 Bunsen, Robert Wilhelm(1811-99) (독일) 화학자
분트 Wundt, Wilhelm(1832-1920) (독일) 생리학자, 심리학자
불가닌 Bulganin, Nikolai Aleksandrovich(1895-1975) (소련) 정치가, 수상
브라우닝 ❶ Browning, Robert(1812-89) (영국) 시인 ❷ Browning, Elizabeth Barrett(1806-61) (영국) 시인
브라운 ❶ Braun, Karl Ferdinand(1850-1918) (독일) 물리학자 ❷ Braun, Wernher von(1912-77) (독일 태생의 미국) 항공학자
브라크 Braque, Georges(1882-1963) (프랑스) 화가
브란트 Brandt, Willy(1913-92) (독일) 서독 총리
브람스 Brahms, Johannes(1833-97) (독일) 작곡가
브레주네프 Brezhnev, Leonid I.(1906-82) (소련) 공산당 서기장
브레히트 Brecht, Bertolt(1898-1956) (독일) 극작가
브렌타노 ❶ Brentano, Franz(1838-1917) (독일) 철학자 ❷ Brentano, Ludwig Joseph(1844-1931) (독일) 경제학자
브론테 ❶ Brontë, Charlotte(1816-55) (영국) 작가 ❷ Brontë, Emily Jane(1818-48) (영국) 작가
브뢰겔 Brueghel, Jan(1568-1625) (네덜란드) 화가
브루크너 Bruckner, Anton(1824-96) (오스트리아) 작곡가
브루투스 Brutus, Marcus Junius(85-42 B.C.) (고대 로마) 정치가
브르통 Breton, André(1896-1966) (프랑스) 시인, 사상가
블레이크 Blake, William(1757-1827) (영국) 화가
블로흐 Bloch, Ernest(1880-1959) (스위스 태생의 미국) 작곡가
블룸필드 Bloomfield, Leonard(1887-1949) (미국) 언어학자
비발디 Vivaldi, Antonio(1678-1741) (이탈리아) 작곡가
비스마르크 Bismarck, Otto Eduard Leopold von(1815-98) (독일) 정치가
비스콘티 Visconti, Luchino(1906-76) (이탈리아) 영화감독, 연출가
비용 Villon, François(1431-?) (프랑스) 시인
비제 Bizet, Georges(1838-75) (프랑스) 작곡가
비첨 Beecham, Sir Thomas(1879-1961) (영국) 지휘자
비트겐슈타인 Wittgenstein, Ludwig(1889-1951) (오스트리아 태생의 영국) 철학자
빅토리아 Victoria, Queen(1819-1901) (영국) 여왕
빌 게이츠 Bill Gates ⇨게이츠
빌드라크 Vildrac, Charles(1882-1971) (프랑스) 시인, 극작가

사

사강 Sagan, Françoise(1935-) (프랑스) 작가
사다트 Sadat, Anwar(1918-81) (이집트) 정치가, 대통령
사드 Sade, Donatien Alphonse Francois de (Marquis de Sade)(1740-1814) (프랑스) 작가, 사디즘의 창시자
사로얀 Saroyan, William(1908-81) (미국) 작가
사로트 Sarraute, Nathalie(1902-99) (프랑스) 작가
사르트르 Sartre, Jean-Paul(1905-80) (프랑스) 철학자, 작가
사마천(司馬遷) Ssu-ma Ch'ien(145?-86? B.C.) (중국) 전한 시대의 역사가
사비에르 Xavier, St. Francis (에스파냐 명 Francisco

세계 주요 인명

Javier)(1506-52) (에스파냐) 선교사
사포 Sappho (612? B.C.-?) (고대 그리스) 시인
사하로프 Sakharov, Andrei D.(1921-89) (소련) 물리학자
산타야나 Santayana, George(1863-1952) (에스파냐 태생의 미국) 철학자, 시인
상고르 Senghor, Léopold Sédar(1906-2001) (세네갈) 시인, 대통령
상드 Sand, George(1804-76) (프랑스) 작가
새뮤얼슨 Samuelson, Paul(1915-) (미국) 경제학자
새커리 Thackeray, William Makepeace(1811-63) (영국) 작가
샌드버그 Sandburg, Carl August(1878-1967) (미국) 시인, 작가
샐린저 Salinger, J.D.(1919-) (미국) 작가
생로랑 Saint-Laurent, Yves(1936-) (프랑스) 디자이너
생상스 Saint-Saëns, Charles Camille(1835-1921) (프랑스) 작곡가
생시몽 Saint-Simon, Claude Henri de Rouvroy, Comte de(1760-1825) (프랑스) 철학자
생어 Sanger, Margaret(1883-1966) (미국) 여권 운동가
생텍쥐페리 Saint-Exupéry, Antoine de(1900-44) (프랑스) 작가, 비행가
생트뵈브 Sainte-Beuve, Charles Augustin de (1804-69) (프랑스) 문학가, 비평가
샤갈 Chagall, Marc(1887-1985) (러시아 태생의 프랑스) 화가
샤넬 Chanel, Coco(1884-1971) (프랑스) 디자이너
샤를마뉴 Charlemagne (=Charles the Great) (742?-814) (서로마 제국) 황제
샤스트리 Shastri, Shri L.B.(1904-66) (인도) 정치가, 수상
샤토브리앙 Chateaubriand, François René, Vicomte de(1768-1848) (프랑스) 정치가, 문학가
샬리아핀 Chaliapin, Fyodor Ivanovich(1873-1938) (소련) 오페라 가수
샹폴리옹 Champollion, Jean François(1790-1832) (프랑스) 이집트 학자
서순 Sasoon, Siegfried(1886-1967) (영국) 시인
서 태후(西太后) Hsi-tai-hou(1835-1908) (중국) 청조 황후
석가모니 Sākyamuni; Gautama Buddha(563?-483? B.C.) (인도) 불교 창시자
세고비아 Segovia, Andrés(1893-1987) (에스파냐) 기타리스트
세네카 Seneca, Lucius Annaeus (4? B.C.-65 A.D.) (에스파냐 태생의 고대 로마) 정치가, 철학자
세르반테스 사아베드라 Cervantes Saavedra, Miguel de(1547-1616) (에스파냐) 작가
세잔 Cézanne, Paul(1839-1906) (프랑스) 화가
셀 Szell, George(1897-1970) (헝가리 태생의 미국) 지휘자
셰리든 Sheridan, Richard Brinsley(1751-1816) (아일랜드 태생의 영국) 극작가, 정치가
셰바르드나제 Shevardnadze, Eduard(1928-) (러시아) 정치가, 외무 장관
셰익스피어 Shakespeare, William(1564-1616) (영국) 극작가
셸리 Shelley, Percy Bysshe(1792-1822) (영국) 시인
셸링 Schelling, Friedrich Wilhelm Joseph von (1775-1854) (독일) 철학자
소로 Thoreau, Henry David(1817-62) (미국) 사상가
소쉬르 Saussure, Ferdinand de(1857-1913) (스위스) 언어학자
소크라테스 Socrates(470?-399 B.C.) (고대 그리스) 철학자
소포클레스 Sophocles(496?-406 B.C.) (고대 그리스) 시인
손다이크 Thorndike, Edward Lee(1874-1949) (미국) 교육 심리학자
손자(孫子) Sung-tzu(?-?) (중국) 춘추 시대 병법가
솔로몬 Solomon(971?-932? B.C.) (고대 이스라엘) 왕
솔제니친 Solzhenitsyn, Aleksandr I(1918-) (러시아) 작가
쇤베르크 Schönberg, Arnold(1874-1951) (오스트리아 태생의 미국) 작곡가
쇼 Shaw, George Bernard(1856-1950) (영국) 극작가
쇼스타코비치 Shostakovich, Dmitri(1906-75) (소련) 작곡가, 피아니스트
쇼팽 Chopin, Frédéric François(1810-49) (폴란드) 작곡가
쇼펜하우어 Schopenhauer, Arthur(1788-1860) (독일) 철학자
숄로호프 Sholokhov, Mikhail Alexandrovich(1905-84) (소련) 작가
수카르노 Sukarno, Achmed(1901-70) (인도네시아) 대통령
수하르토 Suharto(1921-) (인도네시아) 정치가, 대통령
슈니출러 Schnitzler, Arthur(1862-1931) (오스트리아) 작가
슈뢰딩거 Shrödinger, Erwin(1887-1961) (오스트리아) 물리학자
슈만 Schumann, Robert(1810-56) (독일) 작곡가
슈미트 Schmidt, Helmut(1918-) (독일) 정치가, 서독 총리
슈바이처 Schweitzer, Albert(1875-1965) (독일) 의사, 신학자, 철학자
슈베르트 Schubert, Franz Peter(1797-1828) (오스트리아) 작곡가
슈토름 Storm, Theodor(1817-88) (독일) 작가
슈트라우스 ❶ Strauss, Johann(父 1804-49; 子 1825-99) (오스트리아) 작곡가 ❷ Strauss, Richard(1864-1949) (독일) 작곡가
슈펭글러 Spengler, Oswald(1880-1936) (독일) 철학자
슐라이어마허 Schleiermacher, Friedrich Ernst Daniel(1768-1834) (독일) 신학자, 철학자
슐레겔 ❶ Schlegel, August Wilhelm von(1767-1845) (독일) 시인, 비평가 ❷ Schlegel, Friendrich von(1772-1829) (독일) 시인, 비평가
슐리만 Schliemann, Heinrich(1822-90) (독일) 고고학자
슐츠 Schulz, Charles(1924-) (미국) 만화가
슘페터 Schumpeter, Joseph(1883-1950) (미국) 경제학자
스노 Snow, Edgar Parks(1905-72) (미국) 언론인
스메타나 Smetana, Bedrich(1824-84) (체코) 작곡가
스미스 Smith, Adam(1723-90) (영국) 경제학자
스베덴보리 Swedenborg, Emanuel(1688-1772) (스웨덴) 철학자, 신비주의자
스위프트 Swift, Jonathan(1667-1745) (영국) 작가
스윈번 Swinburne, Algernon Charles(1837-1909) (영국) 시인, 비평가
스콧 ❶ Scott, Sir Walter(1771-1832) (영국) 작가 ❷ Scott, Robert Falcon(1868-1912) (영국) 탐험가
스크랴빈 Skryabin, Aleksandr Nikolaevich(1872-1915) (소련) 작곡가, 피아니스트
스타니슬라프스키 Stanislavsky, Konstantin(1863-1938) (러시아) 연출가
스타인 Stein, Gertrude(1874-1946) (미국) 시인, 작가, 극작가

스타인벡 Steinbeck, John Ernst(1902-68) (미국) 작가
스탈 Staël, Madame de(1766-1817) (프랑스) 문학가
스탈린 Stalin, Joseph V.(1879-1953) (소련) 정치가
스탕달 Stendhal(1783-1842) (프랑스) 작가
스탠리 Stanley, Sir Henry Morton(1841-1904) (영국) 탐험가
스턴 Sterne, Laurence(1713-68) (영국) 작가
스토 Stowe, Harriet Elizabeth Beecher(1811-96) (미국) 작가
스토코프스키 Stokowski, Leopold(1882-1977) (영국 태생의 미국) 지휘자
스트라빈스키 Stravinski, Igor Fedorovich(1882-1971) (러시아 태생의 미국) 작곡가
스트레이치 Strachey, Lytton(1880-1932) (영국) 전기 작가, 비평가
스트린드베리 Strindberg, August(1849-1912) (스웨덴) 문학가
스티븐스 Stevens, Wallace(1879-1955) (미국) 시인
스티븐슨 ❶ Stevenson, Adlai E.(1900-65) (미국) 정치가 ❷ Stevenson, Robert Louis Balfour(1850-94) (영국) 작가
스펜더 Spender, Stephen(1909-95) (영국) 시인, 비평가
스펜서 ❶ Spenser, Edmund(1552?-99) (영국) 시인 ❷ Spenser, Herbert(1820-1903) (영국) 철학자
스폭 Spock, Benjamin(1903-98) (미국) 소아과 의사, 교육자
스피노자 Spinoza, Baruch[Benedict de](1632-77) (네덜란드) 철학자, 신학자
스필버그 Spielberg, Steven(1947-) (미국) 영화감독
시라크 Chirac, Jacques(1932-) (프랑스) 정치가, 총리
시먼스 Symons, Arthur(1865-1945) (영국) 시인, 비평가
시몽 Simon, Claude(1913-) (프랑스) 작가
시벨리우스 Sibelius, Jean(1865-1957) (핀란드) 작곡가
시아누크 Sihanouk, Prince Norodom(1922-) (캄보디아) 정치가
시엔키에비치 Sienkiewicz, Henryk(1846-1916) (폴란드) 작가
시케이로스 Siqueiros, David Alfredo(1896-1974) (멕시코) 화가
시턴 Seton, Ernest Thompson(1860-1946) (영국 태생의 미국)「동물기」작가
실러 Schiller, Johann Christoph Friedrich von(1759-1805) (독일) 시인, 극작가
심농 Simenon, Georges(1903-89) (프랑스) 추리 작가
싱 Synge, John Millington(1871-1909) (아일랜드) 극작가, 시인
싱어 Singer, Issac Bashvish(1904-91) (미국) 작가
싱클레어 Sinclair, Upton Beall(1878-1968) (미국) 작가, 비평가
쑨원(孫文) Sun Yat-sen(1866-1925) (중국) 혁명 지도자, 중화민국 건립자
쑹메이링(宋美齡) Song Meiling(1897-) (중국) 장제스의 부인
쑹칭링(宋慶齡) Song Quingling(1892-1981) (중국) 쑨원의 부인, 중공 국가 부주석

아

아그리콜라 Agricola, Gnaeus Julius(40-93) (고대 로마) 장군
아그리파 Agrippa, Marcus Vipsanius (63?-12 B.C.) (고대 로마) 장군, 정치가
아나크레온 Anacreon (582?-485 B.C.) (고대 그리스) 시인
아낙사고라스 Anaxagoras (500?-428? B.C.) (고대 그리스) 철학자
아낙시만드로스 Anaximandros (610-546? B.C.) (고대 그리스) 철학자
아널드 Arnold, Matthew(1822-88) (영국) 시인, 비평가
아누이 Anouilh, Jean(1910-87) (프랑스) 극작가
아데나워 Adenauer, Konrad(1876-1967) (독일) 정치가, 수상
아라공 Aragon, Louis(1897-1982) (프랑스) 문학가
아라파트 Arafat, Yasir(1929-) (팔레스타인) PLO 의장
아롱 Aron, Raymond(1905-83) (프랑스) 사회 과학자
아르키메데스 Archimedes(287?-212 B.C.) (고대 그리스) 수학자, 물리학자
아리스토텔레스 Anaximandros(384-322 B.C.) (고대 그리스) 철학자
아리스토파네스 Aristophanes(450?-386? B.C.) (고대 그리스) 극작가
아리오스토 Ariosto, Lodovico[Ludovico] (1474-1533) (이탈리아) 시인
아문센 Amundsen, Roald(1872-1928) (노르웨이) 탐험가
아미엘 Amiel, Henri Frédéric(1821-81) (스위스) 철학자
아벨라르 Abélard, Pierre (Peter Abelard)(1079-1142) (프랑스) 신학자, 철학자
아보가드로 Avogadro, Count Amadeo(1776-1856) (이탈리아) 화학자, 물리학자
아소카 Asoka(263-226 B.C.) (고대 인도) 불교를 진흥시킨 왕
아스투리아스 Asturias, Miguel Angel(1899-1974) (과테말라) 작가
아우구스투스 Augustus (=Gaius Julius Caesar Octavianus) (63 B.C.-14 A.D.) (고대 로마) 황제
아우구스티누스 (Saint) Augustine(354-430) (고대 로마) 교부, 철학자
아웅산 Aung San(1915?-47) (미얀마) 독립 운동 지도자
아웅산수지 Aung San Suu Kyi(1945-) (미얀마) 민주화 운동 지도자
아유브 칸 Ayub Khan, Mohammad(1907-74) (파키스탄) 군인, 대통령
아이스킬로스 Aeschylus(525-456 B.C.) (고대 그리스) 비극 작가
아이젠하워 Eisenhower, Dwight David(1890-1969) (미국) 군인, 34대 대통령
아인슈타인 Einstein, Albert(1879-1955) (독일 태생의 미국) 이론 물리학자
아퀴나스 (Saint) Thomas Aquinas(1125?-74) (이탈리아) 신학자, 철학자
아크라이트 Arkwright, Richard(1732-92) (영국) 발명가
아키노 Aquino, Corazon(1933-) (필리핀) 대통령
아타튀르크 Atatürk, Mustafa Kemal ⇨케말 파샤
아폴리네르 Apollinaire, Guillaume(1880-1918) (프랑스) 시인
안녹산(安祿山) An Lu-shan(703?-757) (중국) 당나라 무장
안데르센 Andersen, Hans Christian(1805-75) (덴마크) 동화 작가
안드레예프 Andreyev, Leonid(1871-1919) (러시아) 작가
안드레오티 Andreotti, Giulio(1919-) (이탈리아) 정

세계 주요 인명

치가, 총리

안셀무스 Anselmus, Saint(1033-1109) (이탈리아 태생의 영국) 신학자

안젤리코 Angelico, Fra(1387-1455) (이탈리아) 종교화가

안토니오니 Antonioni, Michelangelo(1912-) (이탈리아) 영화감독

안토니우스 Antonius, Marcus (=Mark Antony)(82-30 B.C.) (고대 로마) 군인, 정치가

알랭 Alain, Emile Auguste Chartier(1868-1951) (프랑스) 에세이스트, 철학자

알렉산더 대왕 Alexander the Great(356-323 B.C.) (마케도니아) 대제국 창건자

알리 Ali, Muhammad (1942-) (미국) 프로 권투 선수

암스트롱 Armstrong, Sir William George(1810-1900) (영국) 기계 기술자

앙페르 Ampère, André Marie(1775-1836) (프랑스) 물리학자

애그뉴 Agnew, Spiro Theodore(1918-96) (미국) 정치가, 부통령

애덤스 ❶ Adams, Samuel(1722-1803) (미국) 독립 전쟁 지도자 ❷ Adams, John(1735-1826) (미국) 2대 대통령

애딩턴 Addington, Henry(1757-1844) (영국) 정치가

애치슨 Acheson, Dean G.(1893-1971) (미국) 정치가, 국무 장관

애틀리 Attlee, Clement R.(1883-1967) (정치가, 수상

앤더슨 ❶ Anderson, Sherwood(1876-1941) (미국) 작가 ❷ Anderson, Marian(1902-93) (미국) 오페라 가수

앨프레드 대왕 Alfred the Great(849-899) (영국) 웨섹스 왕

앵그르 Ingres, Jean Auguste Dominique(1780-1867) (프랑스) 화가

야마니 Yamani, Ahmed Zaki(1930-) (사우디아라비아) 석유·광물 장관

야스퍼스 Jaspers, Karl(1883-1969) (독일) 철학자

양귀비(楊貴妃) Yang Kouei-fei(719-756) (중국) 당나라 현종의 비

양제(煬帝) Yang-ti(569-618) (중국) 수(隋)나라 2대 황제

어빙 Irving, Washington(1783-1859) (미국) 작가, 역사가

업다이크 Updike, John(1932-) (미국) 작가

에디슨 Edison, Thomas Alva(1847-1931) (미국) 발명가

에라스무스 Erasmus, Desiderius(1469-1536) (네덜란드) 인문학자, 신학자

에렌부르크 Erenburg, Ilya Grigorievich(1891-1967) (소련) 작가

에르하르트 Erhard, Ludwig(1897-1977) (독일) 정치가, 서독 수상

에른스트 Ernst, Max(1891-1976) (독일) 화가·조각가

에를리히 Ehrlich, Paul(1854-1915) (독일) 세균학자, 화학자

에머슨 Emerson, Ralph Waldo(1803-82) (미국) 사상가, 시인

에우리피데스 Euripides(484?-406? B.C.) (고대 그리스) 시인

에이크 ❶ Eyck, Hubert van(1370?-1436) (네덜란드) 화가 ❷ Eyck, Jan von(1395?-1441) (네덜란드) 화가

에커만 Eckermann, Johann Peter(1792-1854) (독일) 작가

에코 Eco, Umberto(1932-) (이탈리아) 작가, 기호학자

에크하르트 Eckhart[Eckehart] Johannes(1260?-1327?) (독일) 신학자

에펠 Eiffel, Alexandre Gustav(1832-1923) (프랑스) 건축 기술자

에피쿠로스 Epicurus(341-270 B.C.) (고대 그리스) 철학자

에픽테토스 Epiktétos(55?-135?) (고대 로마) 철학자

엔데 Ende, Michael(1929-) (독일) 작가

엘로이즈 Héloise(1101?-64) (프랑스) 수녀원장

엘리엇 ❶ Eliot, George(1819-80) (영국) 작가 ❷ Eliot, Thomas Stearns(1888-1965) (미국 태생의 영국) 시인

엘리자베스 2세 Elizabeth Ⅱ(1926-) (영국) 여왕

엠페도클레스 Empedocles(490?-430? B.C.) (고대 그리스) 철학자, 정치가

엥겔 Engel, Christian Lorenz Ernst(1821-96) (독일) 통계학자, 경제학자

엥겔스 Engels, Friedrich(1820-95) (독일) 사회주의자, 경제학자

예수 Jesus (Christ)(4? B.C.-30? A.D.) 크리스트교 창시자

예스페르센 Jespersen, Jean Otto Harry(1860-1943) (덴마크) 영어학자

예이츠 Yeats, William Butler(1865-1939) (아일랜드) 시인

예젠잉(葉劍英) Yeh Chien-ying(1897-1986) (중국) 국가 부주석

예프투셴코 Evtushenko, Evgeny A.(1933-) (러시아) 시인

옐친 Yeltsin, Boris Nicolayevich(1931-) (러시아) 대통령

오닐 O'Neill, Eugene Gladstone(1888-1953) (미국) 극작가

오든 Auden, Wystan Hugh(1907-73) (영국 태생의 미국) 시인

오로스코 Orozco Jóse Clemente(1883-1949) (멕시코) 화가

오르먼디 Ormandy, Eugene(1899-1985) (헝가리 태생의 미국) 지휘자

오르테가이가세트 Ortega y Gasset, José(1883-1955) (에스파냐) 철학자

오리올 Auriol, Vincent(1884-1966) (프랑스) 정치가, 대통령

오스틴 Austen, Jane(1775-1817) (영국) 작가

오언 Owen, Robert(1771-1858) (영국) 공상적 사회주의자

오웰 Orwell, George(1903-50) (영국) 작가

오즈번 Osborne, John James(1929-) (영국) 극작가

오코너 ❶ O'Connor, Frank(1903-66) (아일랜드) 작가 ❷ O'Connor, Flannery(1925-64) (미국) 작가

오토 대제 Otto the Great(912-973) (신성 로마 제국) 황제

오파린 Oparin, Aleksandr Ivanovich(1894-1980) (소련) 생화학자

오펜바흐 Offenbach, Jacques(1819-80) (독일 태생의 프랑스) 작곡가

오펜하이머 Oppenheimer, Julius Robert(1904-67) (미국) 이론 물리학자

오 헨리 O. Henry(1862-1910) (미국) 작가

옥타비아누스 Octavianus ('아우구스투스'의 본명)

올리비에 Olivier, Sir Laurence, Baron(1907-89) (영국) 배우, 연출가

올컷 Alcott, Louisa May(1832-88) (미국) 작가

옴 Ohm, Georg Simon(1789-1854) (독일) 물리학자

와일더 Wilder, Thornton Niven(1897-1975) (미국) 극작가

와일드 Wilde, Oscar(1854-1900) (영국) 작가

와트 Watt, James(1736-1819) (영국) 기계 기술자, 발명가
왕안석(王安石) Wang Anshih(1021-86) (중국) 정치가, 문인
왕희지(王羲之) Wang Hsichih(307-365) (중국) 서예가
요한 바오로 2세 Johannes Paulus II(1920-) 264대 교황
우탄트 U Thant(1909-74) (미얀마) 정치가, 유엔 사무총장
울브리히트 Ulbricht, Walter(1893-1973) (독일) 동독 국가 평의회 의장
울워스 Woolworth, Frank Winfield(1852-1919) (미국) 실업가
울프 ❶ Woolf, Adelina Virginia(1882-1941) (영국) 작가 ❷ Wolfe, Thomas Clayton(1900-38) (미국) 작가
워 Waugh, Evelyn Arthur St. John(1903-66) (영국) 작가
워런 Warren, Robert Penn(1905-89) (미국) 작가
워싱턴 Washington, George(1732-99) (미국) 초대 대통령
워즈워스 Wordsworth, William(1770-1850) (영국) 시인
월폴 Walpole, Horace(1717-97) (영국) 저술가
웰링턴 Wellington, Arthur Wellesley, 1st Duke of(1769-1852) (영국) 군인, 수상
웰스 Wells, Herbert George(1866-1946) (영국) 작가
웹스터 Webster, Noah(1758-1843) (미국) 사전 편찬자
위고 Hugo, Victor Marie(1802-85) (프랑스) 작가
위안스카이(袁世凱) Yüan Shih-kai(1859-1916) (중국) 군벌, 중화민국 초대 총통
위클리프 Wycliffe [Wyclif], John(1330?-84) (영국) 종교 개혁가, 성경 번역가
위트릴로 Utrillo, Maurice(1883-1955) (프랑스) 화가
윌리엄스 Williams, Tennessee(1911-83) (미국) 극작가
윌슨 ❶ Wilson, (Thomas) Woodrow(1856-1924) (미국) 28대 대통령 ❷ Wilson, J. Harold(1916-) (영국) 노동당 당수, 총리
유클리드 Euclid(330-275 B.C.) (고대 그리스) 기하학자
율리아나 Juliana, Louise Emma Marie Wilhelmina(1909-80) (네덜란드) 여왕
융 Jung, Carl(1875-1961) (스위스) 심리학자
이든 Eden, Robert Anthony, Earl(1897-1977) (영국) 정치가, 수상
이백(李白) Li Po(701-762) (중국) 시인
이솝 Aesop(620?-560? B.C.) (고대 그리스) 우화 작가
이스트먼 Eastman, George(1854-1932) (미국) 발명가
이오네스코 Ionesco, Eugène(1912-94) (프랑스) 극작가
이홍장(李鴻章) Li Hung-chang(1823-1901) (중국) 청말 정치가
임칙서(林則徐) Lin Tse-hsü(1785-1850) (중국) 정치가
입센 Ibsen, Henrik(1828-1906) (노르웨이) 극작가

자

자라투스트라 Zarathustra(628?-551? B.C.) (고대 페르시아) 종교가
자멘호프 Zamenhof, Lazarus Ludwig(1859-1917) (폴란드) 언어학자
자오쯔양(趙紫陽) Chao Tzu-yang(1919-) (중국) 정치가
잔 다르크 Joan of Arc(1412-31) (프랑스) 구국 순교자
장자(莊子) Chuang-tzu(365?-270? B.C.) (중국) 전국 시대 사상가
장제스(蔣介石) Chiang Chieh-shih; Chiang Kai-shek(1887-1975) (중국) 중화민국 초대 총통
장징궈(蔣經國) Chiang Ching-kuo(1910-88) (중국) 중화민국 총통
장칭(江青) Ching Ching(1913-91) (중국) 마오쩌둥의 부인
잭슨 Jackson, Andrew(1767-1845) (미국) 7대 대통령
저우언라이(周恩來) Chou En-lai(1898-1976) (중국) 정치가
제너 Jenner, Edward(1749-1823) (영국) 의학자
제임스 ❶ James, William(1842-1910) (미국) 철학자 ❷ James, Henry(1843-1916) (미국) 작가
제퍼슨 Jefferson, Thomas(1743-1826) (미국) 3대 대통령
조로아스터 Zoroaster ('자라투스트라'의 영어명)
조머펠트 Sommerfeld, Arnold(1868-1951) (독일) 이론 물리학자
조이스 Joyce, James(1882-1941) (아일랜드) 작가
조토 디본도네 Giotto di Bondone(1266?-1337) (이탈리아) 화가, 건축가
존슨 ❶ Johnson, Samuel(1709-84) (영국) 시인, 비평가 ❷ Jonson, Ben(1572-1637) (영국) 시인, 극작가
졸라 Zola, Emile(1840-1902) (프랑스) 작가
졸리오퀴리 Joliot-Curie, Frédéric(1900-58) (프랑스) 물리학자
주공(周公) Chou-kung(?-?) (중국) 주대(周代) 정치가
주다노프 Zhdanov, Andrei Aleksandrovichu(1896-1948) (소련) 정치가, 공산당 지도자
주원장(朱元璋) Chu Yüan-chang(1328-98) (중국) 명나라 초대 황제
주자(朱子) Chu-tzu(1130-1200) (중국) 사상가
주코프 Zhukov, Georgi Konstantinovich(1896-1974) (소련) 장군, 국방상
주페 Suppé, Franz von(1819-95) (오스트리아) 작곡가
증국번(曾國藩) Tseng Kuo-fan(1811-72) (중국) 청말 정치가
지드 Gide, André(1869-1951) (프랑스) 작가
지멘스 Siemens, Ernst Werner von(1816-92) (독일) 기술자, 발명가
지브란 Gibran, Kahlil(1883-1931) (레바논 태생의 미국) 문학가
지스카르 데스탱 Giscard d'Estaing, Valéry(1926-) (프랑스) 정치가, 대통령
짐발리스트 Zimbalist, Efrem(1889-1985) (미국) 바이올리니스트, 작곡가

차

차가타이 Chagatai(?-1242) 차가타이 한국의 시조
차우셰스쿠 Ceauşescu, Nicolae(1918-89) (루마니아) 대통령
차이코프스키 Tschaikovsky, Pëtr Ilich [Peter Ilych] (1840-93) (러시아) 작곡가
채프먼 Chapman, George(1559?-1634) (영국) 극작가, 시인
채플린 Chaplin, Charles Spencer(1889-1977) (영국) 영화배우, 감독
처칠 Churchill, Sir Winston Leonard Spencer (1874-1965) (영국) 정치가, 수상
천두슈(陳獨秀) Ch'en Tu-hsiu(1880-1942) (중국)

세계 주요 인명

사상가
체르넨코 Chernenko, Konstantin Ustinovich(1911-85) (소련) 정치가
체르니 Czerny, Karl(1791-1857) (오스트리아) 피아니스트, 작곡가
체스터턴 Chesterton, Gilbert Keith(1874-1936) (영국) 문필가
체임벌린 ❶ Chamberlain, Joseph(1863-1937) (영국) 실업가, 정치가 ❷ Chamberlain, Neville(1869-1940) (영국) 정치가, 수상
체펠린 Zeppelin, Ferdinand von(1838-1917) (독일) 발명가
체호프 Chekhov, Anton Pavlovich(1860-1904) (러시아) 작가
초서 Chaucer, Geoffrey(1342?-1400) (영국) 작가, 시인
촘스키 Chomsky, Noam(1928-) (미국) 언어학자
츠바이크 Zweig, Stefan(1881-1942) (오스트리아 태생의 독일) 작가
츠빙글리 Zwingli, Ulrich(1484-1531) (스위스) 종교 개혁가
측천무후(則天武后) Tse-tien Wu-hou(624?-705) (중국) 당나라 고종 황후
칭기즈 칸(成吉思汗) Genghis[Ching(h)iz] Khan (1167?-1227) (중국) 몽골 제국 태조

카네기 Carnegie, Andrew(1835-1919) (영국 태생의 미국) 실업가
카네티 Canetti, Elias(1905-94) (불가리아 태생의 영국) 문인, 사상가
카다르 Kádár, Janos(1912-89) (헝가리) 정치가, 수상
카다피 Qaddafi, Muammaral(1942-) (리비아) 정치가
카라얀 Karajan, Herbert von(1908-89) (오스트리아) 지휘자
카로사 Carossa, Hans(1878-1956) (이탈리아 태생의 독일) 작가, 시인
카루소 Caruso, Enrico(1873-1921) (이탈리아) 오페라 가수
카르댕 Cardin, Pierre(1922-) (프랑스) 의상 디자이너
카를로스 Carlos, Juan(1938-) (에스파냐) 국왕
카메하메하 1세 (King) Kamehameha Ⅰ(1758?-1819) 하와이 원주민 왕
카뮈 Camus, Albert(1913-60) (프랑스) 작가
카사노바 Casanova, Giovanni Giacomo(1725-98) (이탈리아) (엽색으로 유명한) 작가
카스트로 Castro, Ruz Fidel(1927-) (쿠바) 혁명가, 정치가
카우츠키 Kautsky, Karl Johann(1854-1938) (독일) 사회주의자, 저술가
카이사르 Caesar, Julius(100-44 B.C.) (고대 로마) 군인, 정치가
카잔 Kazan, Elia(1909-) (터키 태생의 미국) 영화 감독, 작가
카터 Carter, James Earl, Jr.(1924-) (미국) 39대 대통령
카토 Cato, Marcus Porcius (234-149 B.C.) (고대 로마) 장군, 정치가
카트라이트 Cartwright, Edmund(1743-1823) (영국) 발명가
카프카 Kafka, Franz(1883-1924) (체코슬로바키아 태생의 독일) 작가
칸 Kahn, Herman(1922-83) (미국) 미래학자
칸딘스키 Kandinski, Vasili(1866-1944) (러시아) 화가

칸트 Kant, Immanuel(1724-1804) (독일) 철학자
칼라스 Callas, Maria(1923-77) (그리스계 미국) 성악가
칼라일 Carlyle, Thomas(1795-1881) (영국) 평론가, 역사가
칼뱅 Calvin, John(1509-64) (프랑스) 신학자, 종교 개혁가
캉유웨이(康有爲) K'ang Yu-wei(1858-1927) (중국) 정치가, 학자
캐더 Cather, Willa Sibert(1873-1947) (미국) 작가
캑스턴 Caxton, William(1422?-91) (영국) 활판 인쇄가
캘러헌 Callaghan, James(1912-) (영국) 총리
캠벨 Campbell, Thomas(1777-1844) (영국) 시인
커포티 Capote, Truman(1924-84) (미국) 작가
컨스터블 Constable, John(1776-1837) (영국) 화가
케네 Quesnay, François(1694-1774) (프랑스) 경제학자
케네디 Kennedy, John Fitzgerald(1917-63) (미국) 35대 대통령
케렌스키 Kerensky, Aleksandr(1881-1970) (소련) 정치가
케말 파샤 Kemal Pasha(1881-1938) (터키) 군인, 대통령
케스틀러 Koestler, Arthur(1905-83) (영국) 작가
케인스 Keynes, John Maynard(1883-1946) (영국) 경제학자
케플러 Kepler, Johannes(1571-1630) (독일) 천문학자
켈러 ❶ Keller, Gottfried(1819-90) (스위스) 작가 ❷ Keller, Helen Adams(1880-1968) (미국) 사회 교육가
켈로그 Kellogg, Frank Billings(1856-1937) (미국) 정치가
코다이 Kodály, Zoltán(1882-1967) (헝가리) 작곡가
코로 Corot, Jean Baptiste Camille(1796-1875) (프랑스) 화가
코르네유 Corneille, Pierre(1606-84) (프랑스) 극작가
코르테스 Cortez[Cortés], Hernando(1485-1547) (에스파냐) (남미 정복) 군인
코시긴 Kosygin, Aleksei Nikolaevich(1904-80) (소련) 수상
코엔 Cohen, Hermann(1842-1918) (독일) 철학자
코페르니쿠스 Copernicus, Nicolaus(1473-1543) (폴란드) 천문학자
코흐 Koch, Robert(1843-1910) (독일) 의사, 세균학자
콕토 Cocteau, Jean(1889-1963) (프랑스) 시인, 극작가
콘래드 Conrad, Joseph(1857-1924) (폴란드 태생의 영국) 작가
콘스탄티누스 대제 Constantine the Great(280?-337 B.C.) (고대 로마) 황제
콜드웰 Caldwell, Erskin(1903-87) (미국) 작가
콜럼버스 Columbus, Christopher(1451-1506) (이탈리아) 항해가
콜레트 Colette(1873-1954) (프랑스) 작가
콜리지 Coleridge, Samuel Taylor(1772-1834) (영국) 문학가
콜베르 Colbert, Jean-Baptiste(1619-83) (프랑스) 정치가
콩도르세 Condorcet, Marquis de(1743-94) (프랑스) 사회 철학자, 정치가
콩트 Comte, Auguste(1798-1857) (프랑스) 철학자
쾨헬 Köchel, Ludwig von(1800-77) (오스트리아) 식물·광물학자
쿠르베 Courbet, Gustave(1819-77) (프랑스) 화가
쿠베르탱 Coubertin, Pierre, Baron de(1863-1937)

세계 주요 인명

(프랑스) 근대 올림픽 창시자
쿠퍼 Cooper, James Fenimore(1789-1851) (미국) 작가
쿡 Cook, James (=Captain Cook)(1728-79) (영국) 항해가
쿨롱 Coulomb, Charles Augustin de(1736-1806) (프랑스) 물리학자
쿨리지 Coolidge, Calvin(1872-1933) (미국) 30대 대통령
퀴리 ❶ Curie, Marie Sklowdowska(1867-1934) (폴란드 태생의 프랑스) 물리학자, 화학자 ❷ Curie, Pierre(1859-1906) (프랑스) 물리학자
크라이슬러 ❶ Kreisler, Fritz(1875-1962) (오스트리아 태생의 미국) 바이올리니스트 ❷ Chrysler, Walter Percy(1875-1940) (미국) 자동차 사업가
크로체 Croce, Benedetto(1866-1952) (이탈리아) 역사가, 철학자
크로포트킨 Kropotkin, Pëter Alseevich(1842-1921) (러시아) 무정부주의자
크롬웰 Cromwell, Oliver(1599-1658) (영국) 군인, 정치가
크루프 Krupp, Alfred(1812-87) (독일) 제강업자
크리스티 Christie, Agatha Miller(1891-1976) (영국) 추리 작가
크릭 Crick, Francis Harry Compton(1916-) (영국) 생물학자
크세노폰 Xenophon(431?-350? B.C.) (고대 그리스) 역사가, 철학자
클라우제비츠 Clausewitz, Karl von(1780-1831) (독일) 군사 이론가
클라이스트 Kleist, Heinrich von(1777-1811) (독일) 극작가
클레 Klee, Paul(1879-1940) (스위스 태생의 독일) 화가
클레르 Clair, René(1898-1981) (프랑스) 영화감독
클레망소 Clemenceau, Georges Eugène Benjamin(1841-1929) (프랑스) 정치가, 수상
클레오파트라 Cleopatra(69-30 B.C.) (고대 이집트) 여왕
클로델 Claudel, Paul Louis Charles Marie(1868-1955) (프랑스) 시인, 외교관
클린턴 Clinton, Bill(1946-) (미국) 42대 대통령
키르케고르 Kierkegaard, Sören Aabye(1813-55) (덴마크) 철학자
키신저 Kissinger, Henry Alfred(1923-) (미국) 정치학자, 국무 장관
키츠 Keats, John(1795-1821) (영국) 시인
키케로 Cicero, Marcus Tullius(106-43 B.C.) (고대 로마) 정치가, 웅변가
키플링 Kipling, Joseph Rudyard(1865-1936) (영국) 작가
킨제이 Kinsey, Alfred(1894-1956) (미국) 동물학자, 사회학자
킹 King, Martin Luther. Jr.(1929-68) (미국) 종교인, 민권 운동가

타

타고르 Tagore, Sir Rabindranath(1861-1941) (인도) 시인
타소 Tasso, Torquato(1544-95) (이탈리아) 시인
타키투스 Tacitus, Publius Cornelius(56?-120?) (고대 로마) 역사가, 정치가
탈레스 Thales(636?-546? B.C.) (고대 그리스) 철학자, 천문학자
터너 Turner, Joseph Mallord William(1775-1851) (영국) 화가
테니슨 Tennyson, Alfred, 1st Baron(1809-92) (영국) 시인
테레사 Mother Teresa(1910-97) (알바니아 태생의 인도 거주) 수녀
텐 Taine, Hippolyte Adolphe(1828-93) (프랑스) 비평가, 철학자
토마스 아 켐피스 Thomas à Kempis(1380?-1471) (독일) 신비 사상가
토마스 아퀴나스 Thomas Aquinas ⇨아퀴나스
토스카니니 Toscanini, Arturo(1867-1957) (이탈리아) 지휘자
토인비 Toynbee, Arnold Joseph(1889-1975) (영국) 역사가
톨스토이 Tolstoi[Tolstoy], Count Lev[Leo] Nikolaevich(1828-1910) (러시아) 작가
톰슨 ❶ Thompson, Benjamin(1753-1814) (미국) 물리학자 ❷ Franciss(1859-1907) (영국) 시인 ❸ (Sir) George Paget(1892-1975) (영국) 물리학자 ❹ Thomson, (Sir) Joseph John(1856-1940) (영국) 물리학자
투르게네프 Turgen(y)ev, Ivan Sergeevich(1818-83) (러시아) 작가
투키디데스 Thucydides(460?-400? B.C.) (고대 그리스) 역사가
트로츠키 Trotski[Trotsky], Leon(1879-1940) (러시아) 혁명가, 공산당 지도자
트루먼 Truman, Harry S.(1884-1972) (미국) 33대 대통령
트뤼도 Trudeau, Pierre E.(1919-2000) (캐나다) 총리
트웨인 Twain, Mark(1835-1910) (미국) 작가
티치아노 Tiziano, Vecellio(1490?-1576) (이탈리아) 화가
티토 Tito, Josip Broz[Brozovich] (1892-1980) (유고슬라비아) 대통령
틴들 Tyndale[Tindal, Tindale], William(1494?-1536) (영국) 종교 개혁가
틴토레토 Tintoretto(1518?-94) (이탈리아) 화가

파

파가니니 Paganini, Niccolò(1782-1840) (이탈리아) 작곡가
파데레프스키 Paderewski, Ignace Jan(1860-1941) (폴란드) 피아니스트, 정치가
파렌하이트 Fahrenheit, Gabriel Daniel(1686-1736) (독일) 물리학자
파머 Palmer, Arnold(1929-) (미국) 골퍼
파바로티 Pavarotti, Luciano(1935-) (이탈리아) 성악가
파브르 Fabre, Jean Henri(1823-1915) (프랑스) 곤충학자
파블로바 Pavlova, Anna(1881-1931) (러시아) 발레리나
파블로프 Pavlov, Ivan Petrovich(1849-1936) (러시아) 생리학자
파스칼 Pascal, Blaise(1623-62) (프랑스) 철학자
파스테르나크 Pasternak, Boris Leonidovich(1890-1960) (소련) 시인, 작가
파스퇴르 Pasteur, Louis(1822-95) (프랑스) 세균학자
파운드 Pound, Ezra Loomis(1885-1972) (미국) 시인
파킨슨 Parkinson, C. Northcote(1909-93) (영국) 경제학자
팔레비 Pahlevi[Pahlavi], Mohammed Reza Shah(1919-80) (이란) 국왕
패러데이 Faraday, Michael(1791-1867) (영국) 물리·화학자
퍼싱 Pershing, John Joseph(1860-1948) (미국) 군인

세계 주요 인명

페로 Perrault, Charles(1628-1703) (프랑스) 비평가, 시인
페론 Perón, Juan D.(1895-1974) (아르헨티나) 군인, 대통령
페르미 Fermi, Enrico(1901-54) (이탈리아 태생의 미국) 원자 물리학자
페리 Perry, Matthew Calbraith(1794-1858) (미국) 해군 제독
페리클레스 Pericles(495?-429 B.C.) (고대 그리스) 장군, 정치가
페스탈로치 Pestalozzi, Johann Heinrich(1746-1827) (스위스) 교육 개혁가
페이터 Pater, Walter Horatio(1839-94) (영국) 비평가, 수필가
페인 Pain, Thomas(1737-1809) (영국 태생의 미국) 정치 평론가
페탱 Pétain, Henri Philippe(1856-1951) (프랑스) 2차 대전 시 비시(Vichy) 정권의 원수
페트라르카 Petrarca, Francesco(1304-74) (이탈리아) 시인, 인문주의자
펜 Penn, William(1644-1718) (영국) 아메리카 식민지 개척자
펠레 Pelé, Edson Arantes do Narcimento(1940-) (브라질) 축구 선수
펠리니 Fellini, Federico(1920-93) (이탈리아) 영화감독
포 Poe, Edgar Allan(1809-49) (미국) 시인, 작가
포드 ❶ Ford, Henry(1863-1947) (미국) 실업가 ❷ Ford, John(1895-1973) (미국) 영화감독 ❸ Ford, Gerald R.(1913-) (미국) 38대 대통령
포스터 Foster, Stephen Collins(1826-64) (미국) 민요 작사·작곡가
포이어바흐 Feuerbach, Ludwig Andreas(1804-72) (독일) 철학자
포크너 Faulkner, William(1897-1962) (미국) 작가
포터 Porter, Katherine Anne(1890-1980) (미국) 작가
포프 Pope, Alexander(1688-1744) (영국) 시인
폰테인 Fonteyn, Margot(1919-91) (영국) 발레리나
폴로 Polo, Marco(1254-1324) (이탈리아) 여행가
퐁파두르 Pompadour, Jeanne Antoinette Poisson, Marquise de(1721-64) (프랑스) 루이 15세의 연인
퐁피두 Pompidou, Georges(1911-74) (프랑스) 대통령
표트르 대제 Pyotr the Great(1672-1725) (러시아) 황제
푸리에 Fourier, Jean Baptiste Joseph(1768-1830) (프랑스) 수학자
푸슈킨 Pushkin, Aleksandr Sergeevich(1799-1837) (러시아) 시인, 작가
푸앵카레 Poincaré, Henri(1854-1912) (프랑스) 수학자
푸이(溥儀) P'u-i(1906-67) (중국) 청나라 마지막 황제, 만주국 황제
푸치니 Puccini, Giacomo(1858-1924) (이탈리아) 오페라 작곡가
푸코 Foucaut, Michel(1926-84) (프랑스) 철학자
풀브라이트 Fulbright, Jay William(1905-95) (미국) 정치가
풀턴 Fulton, Robert(1765-1815) (미국) 발명가
풀리처 Pulitzer, Joseph(1847-1911) (헝가리 태생의 미국) 언론인
프라 안젤리코 Fra Angelico(1400?-55) (이탈리아) 화가
프란체스코 Francis (of Assisi)(1182-1226) (이탈리아) 프란체스코 수도회 창시자
프랑스 France, Anatole(1844-1924) (프랑스) 작가, 비평가
프랑코 Franco Bahamonde, Francisco(1892-1975) (에스파냐) 군인, 총통
프랭클린 Franklin, Benjamin(1706-90) (미국) 정치가, 과학자, 저술가
프레보데그질 Prévost d'Exiles, François (=Abbé Prévost)(1697-1763) (프랑스) 작가
프레슬리 Presley, Elvis Aron (1935-77) (미국) 가수, 배우
프레이저 Fraser, John Malcolm(1930-) (오스트레일리아) 정치가, 총리
프로스트 Frost, Robert(1874-1963) (미국) 시인
프로이트 Freud, Sigmund(1856-1939) (오스트리아) 의사, 정신 분석학자
프로코피예프 Prokofiev, Sergei Sergeevich(1891-1953) (소련) 작곡가
프로타고라스 Protagoras(485?-410? B.C.) (고대 그리스) 철학자
프롬 Fromm, Erich(1900-80) (독일) 심리학자
프뢰벨 Froebel, Friedrich(1782-1852) (독일) 교육자
프루스트 Proust, Marcel(1871-1922) (프랑스) 작가
프리드먼 Friedman, Milton(1912-) (미국) 경제학자
프리스틀리 Priestley, Joseph(1733-1804) (영국) 종교인, 화학자
프톨레마이오스 Ptolemaios, Klaudios(127?-151?) (고대 그리스) 수학자
플라톤 Plato(428?-347? B.C.) (고대 그리스) 철학자
플랑크 Planck, Max(1858-1947) (독일) 물리학자
플레밍 ❶ Fleming, John Ambrose(1849-1945) (영국) 전기 공학자 ❷ Fleming, Alexander(1881-1955) (영국) 의학자, 세균학자
플로베르 Flaubert, Gustave(1821-80) (프랑스) 작가
플로티노스 Plotinus(205?-270) (이집트 태생의 고대 로마) 철학자
플루타르코스 Plutarchos(46?-120?) (고대 그리스) 도덕 철학자
플루타르크 Plutarch ('플루타르코스'의 영어명)
피란델로 Pirandello, Luigi(1867-1936) (이탈리아) 시인, 작가
피사로 Pizarro, Francisco(1475?-1541) (에스파냐) 잉카 제국 정복자
피아제 Piaget, Jean(1896-1980) (스위스) 아동 심리학자
피아프 Piaf, Edith(1915-63) (프랑스) 가수
피어슨 Pearson, Lester B.(1897-1972) (캐나다) 정치가, 수상
피츠제럴드 Fitzgerald, F. Scott(1896-1940) (미국) 작가
피카르 ❶ Piccard, Auguste(1884-1962) (스위스 태생의 벨기에) 물리학자 ❷ Piccard, Jean Félix (1884-1963) (미국) 화학자, 항공학자
피카소 Picasso, Pablo(1881-1973) (에스파냐) 화가
피타고라스 Pythagoras(580?-500? B.C.) (고대 그리스) 수학자, 철학자
피트 ❶ Pitt, (大) William, 1st Earl of Chatham(1708-78) (영국) 정치가, 수상 ❷ Pitt, (小) William(1759-1806) (영국) 정치가, 수상
피히테 Fichte, Johann Gottlieb(1762-1814) (독일) 철학자
필딩 Fielding, Henry(1707-54) (영국) 수필가, 작가

하

하디 Hardy, Thomas(1840-1928) (영국) 작가, 시인
하딩 Harding, Warren Gamaliel(1865-1923) (미국) 29대 대통령
하르트만 Hartmann, Karl Robert Eduard von

(1842-1906) (독일) 철학자
하비 Harvey, William(1578-1657) (영국) 생리학자, 의사
하웁트만 Hauptmann, Gerhart(1862-1946) (독일) 시인, 작가
하워드 Howard, Roy Wilson(1883-1964) (미국) 신문 경영자
하이네 Heine, Heinrich(1797-1856) (독일) 시인
하이데거 Heidegger, Johann Heinrich(1633-98) (스위스) 철학자
하이든 Haydn, Franz Joseph(1732-1809) (오스트리아) 작곡가
하이젠베르크 Heisenverg, Werner Karl(1901-76) (독일) 물리학자
하인켈 Heinkel, Ernst(1888-1958) (독일) 항공기 제작자
하일레 셀라시에 Haile Selassie(1892-1975) (에티오피아) 황제
한니발 Hannibal(247-183? B.C.) (카르타고) 장군
한비자(韓非子) Han Fei-tzu(280?-233 B.C.) (중국) 사상가
한센 Hansen, Armauer Gerhard Henrik(1841-1912) (노르웨이) 의학자
함마르셸드 Hammarskjöld, Dag(1905-61) (스웨덴) 유엔 사무총장
함무라비 Hammurabi(?-1750 B.C.) (바빌로니아) 법전 제작자, 국왕
함순 Hamsun, Knut(1859-1952) (노르웨이) 작가
핼리 Halley, Edmund(1656-1742) (영국) 천문학자
허드슨 ❶ Hudson, Henry(1550?-1611) (영국) 항해가 ❷ Hudson, W(illiam) H(enry)(1841-1922) (아르헨티나 태생의 영국) 작가
허스트 Hearst, William Randolph(1863-1951) (미국) 신문 경영자
헉슬리 ❶ Huxley, Thomas Henry(1825-95) (영국) 생물학자 ❷ Huxley, Aldous Leonard(1894-1963) (영국) 작가 ❸ Huxley, Julian Sorrell(1887-1975) (영국) 생물학자
헤겔 Hegel, Georg Friedrich Wilhelm(1770-1831) (독일) 철학자
헤라클레이토스 Herakleitos(540?-480? B.C.) (고대 그리스) 철학자
헤로도토스 Herodotus(484?-430? B.C.) (고대 그리스) 역사가
헤밍웨이 Hemingway, Ernest(1899-1961) (미국) 작가
헤벨 Hebbel, Christian Friedrich(1813-63) (독일) 시인, 극작가
헤세 Hesse, Hermann(1877-1962) (독일) 시인, 작가
헤시오도스 Hesiod(800? B.C.) (고대 그리스) 시인
헤위에르달 Heyerdahl, Thor(1914-) (노르웨이) 인류학자
헤이스팅스 Hastings, Warren(1732-1818) (영국) 정치가, 인도 총독
헤일리 Haley, Alex(1921-) (미국) 작가
헨델 Handel, George Frederick(1685-1759) (독일 태생의 영국) 작곡가
헨리 Henry, Patrick(1736-99) (미국) 정치가, 웅변가
헬름홀츠 Helmholtz, Hermann Ludwig Ferdinand von(1821-94) (독일) 생리학자, 물리학자
호가스 Hogarth, William(1697-1764) (영국) 풍속화가
호로비츠 Horowitz, Vladimir(1904-89) (소련 태생의 미국) 피아니스트
호메로스 Homer(?-?) (고대 그리스) 서사시인

호메이니 Khomeini, Ayatolla Ruhollah(1900-89) (이란) 이슬람교 지도자
호손 Hawthorne, Nathaniel(1804-64) (미국) 작가
호이징가 Huizinga, Jhon(1878-1945) (네덜란드) 역사가
호치민(胡志明) Ho Chi Minh(1890-1969) (베트남) 월맹 대통령
호킹 Hawking, Stephen William(1942-) (영국) 우주 물리학자
호프만 Hoffman, Ernst Theodor Amadeus Wilhelm(1776-1822) (독일) 작가, 화가, 음악가
호프만슈탈 Hofmannsthal, Hugo von(1874-1929) (오스트리아) 시인, 극작가
홀바인 Holbein, Hans(1497?-1543) (독일) 화가
홉스 Hobbes, Thomas(1588-1679) (영국) 철학자
홉킨스 Hopkins, Frederick Gowland(1861-1947) (영국) 생화학자
홍수전(洪秀全) Hung Hsiu-chüan(1814-64) (중국) 청말 태평천국 창시자
화이트 White, Patrick(1912-90) (오스트레일리아) 작가
화이트헤드 Whitehead, Alfred North(1861-1947) (영국) 수학자, 철학자
후버 Hoover, Herbert Clark(1874-1964) (미국) 31대 대통령
후설 Husserl, Edmund(1859-1938) (독일) 철학자
후세인 ❶ Hussein Ⅰ, Amir Abdullah(1935-99) (요르단) 국왕 ❷ Hussein, Saddam(1937-) (이라크) 대통령
후스(胡適) Hu Shih(1891-1962) (중국) 문학가, 사상가
후야오방(胡耀邦) Hu Yao-bang(1915-88) (중국) 정치가
훔볼트 ❶ Humboldt, Alexander Freiherr von (1769-1859) (독일) 자연과학자 ❷ Humboldt, Karl Wilhelm, Freiherr von(1767-1835) (독일) 언어학자
휘트먼 Whitman, Walt(1819-92) (미국) 시인
휴스 ❶ Hughes, Langston(1902-67) (미국) 시인 ❷ Hughes, Thomas(1822-96) (영국) 작가
흄 Hulme, Thomas Ernest(1883-1917) (영국) 철학자, 문예 비평가
흐루시초프 Khrushchev, Nikita(1894-1971) (소련) 정치가, 수상
히메네스 Jiménez, Juan Ramón(1881-1958) (에스파냐) 시인
히스 Heath, Edward R.G.(1916-) (영국) 정치가, 총리
히치콕 Hitchcock, Alfred(1899-1980) (영국 태생의 미국) 영화감독
히틀러 Hitler, Adolf(1889-1945) (오스트리아 태생의 독일) 나치 지도자, 제3제국 총통
히포크라테스 Hippocrates (460?-377? B.C.) (고대 그리스) 의학자
힉스 Hicks, John Richard(1904-89) (영국) 경제학자
힌덴부르크 Hindenburg, Paul von(1847-1934) (독일) 육군 원수, 바이마르 공화국 대통령
힐러리 Hillary[Hilary], Sir Edmund Percival (1919-) (뉴질랜드) 등산가, 탐험가
힐턴 ❶ Hilton, Conrad(1887-1979) (미국) 호텔 사업가 ❷ Hilton, James(1900-54) (영국 태생의 미국) 작가
힐티 Hilty, Carl(1833-1909) (스위스) 사상가
힘러 Himmler, Heinrich(1900-45) (독일) 나치 지도자, 군인

국어의 로마자 표기법

2000. 7. 7. 고시

제 1 장 표기의 기본 원칙

제 1 항 국어의 로마자 표기는 국어의 표준 발음법에 따라 적는 것을 원칙으로 한다.
제 2 항 로마자 이외의 부호는 되도록 사용하지 않는다.

제 2 장 표기 일람

제 1 항 모음은 다음 각 호와 같이 적는다.

1. 단모음

ㅏ	ㅓ	ㅗ	ㅜ	ㅡ	ㅣ	ㅐ	ㅔ	ㅚ	ㅟ
a	eo	o	u	eu	i	ae	e	oe	wi

2. 이중 모음

ㅑ	ㅕ	ㅛ	ㅠ	ㅒ	ㅖ	ㅘ	ㅙ	ㅝ	ㅞ	ㅢ
ya	yeo	yo	yu	yae	ye	wa	wae	wo	we	ui

[붙임 1] 'ㅢ'는 'ㅣ'로 소리 나더라도 ui로 적는다.

　〈보기〉 광희문　Gwanghuimun

[붙임 2] 장모음의 표기는 따로 하지 않는다.

제 2 항 자음은 다음 각 호와 같이 적는다.

1. 파열음

ㄱ	ㄲ	ㅋ	ㄷ	ㄸ	ㅌ	ㅂ	ㅃ	ㅍ
g, k	kk	k	d, t	tt	t	b, p	pp	p

2. 파찰음

ㅈ	ㅉ	ㅊ
j	jj	ch

3. 마찰음

ㅅ	ㅆ	ㅎ
s	ss	h

4. 비음

ㄴ	ㅁ	ㅇ
n	m	ng

5. 유음

ㄹ
r, l

[붙임 1] 'ㄱ, ㄷ, ㅂ'은 모음 앞에서는 'g, d, b'로, 자음 앞이나 어말에서는 'k, t, p'로 적는다. ([ ] 안의 발음에 따라 표기함.)

　〈보기〉 구미　　　　Gumi　　　　　영동　　　Yeongdong
　　　　 백암　　　　Baegam　　　　옥천　　　Okcheon
　　　　 합덕　　　　Hapdeok　　　　호법　　　Hobeop
　　　　 월곶[월곧]　 Wolgot　　　　 벚꽃[벋꼳] beotkkot
　　　　 한밭[한받]　 Hanbat

[붙임 2] 'ㄹ'은 모음 앞에서는 'r'로, 자음 앞이나 어말에서는 'l'로 적는다. 단 'ㄹㄹ'은 'll'로 적는다.

　〈보기〉 구리　　　　Guri　　　　　설악　　　Seorak

| 칠곡 | Chilgok | 임실 | Imsil |
| 울릉 | Ulleung | 대관령[대괄령] | Daegwallyeong |

제 3 장 표기상의 유의점

제 1 항 음운 변화가 일어날 때에는 변화의 결과에 따라 다음 각호와 같이 적는다.

1. 자음 사이에서 동화 작용이 일어나는 경우

   〈보기〉 백마[뱅마] Baengma   신문로[신문노] Sinmunno
         종로[종노] Jongno   왕십리[왕십니] Wangsimni
         별내[별래] Byeollae   신라[실라]   Silla

2. 'ㄴ, ㄹ'이 덧나는 경우

   〈보기〉 학여울[항녀울] Hangnyeoul   알약[알략] allyak

3. 구개음화가 되는 경우

   〈보기〉 해돋이[해도지] haedoji   같이[가치] gachi
         맞히다[마치다] machida

4. 'ㄱ, ㄷ, ㅂ, ㅈ'이 'ㅎ'과 합하여 거센소리로 소리 나는 경우

   〈보기〉 좋고[조코] joko   놓다[노타] nota
         잡혀[자펴] japyeo   낳지[나치] nachi

   다만, 체언에서 'ㄱ, ㄷ, ㅂ' 뒤에 'ㅎ'이 따를 때에는 'ㅎ'을 밝혀 적는다.

   〈보기〉 묵호 Mukho   집현전 Jiphyeonjeon

   〔붙임〕 된소리되기는 표기에 반영하지 않는다.

   〈보기〉 압구정 Apgujeong   낙동강 Nakdonggang
         죽변   Jukbyeon   낙성대 Nakseongdae
         합정   Hapjeong   팔당   paldang
         샛별   saetbyeol   울산   ulsan

제 2 항 발음상 혼동의 우려가 있을 때에는 음절 사이에 붙임표(-)를 쓸 수 있다.

   〈보기〉 중앙 Jung-ang   반구대 Ban-gudae
         세운 Se-un   해운대 Hae-undae

제 3 항 고유 명사는 첫 글자를 대문자로 적는다.

   〈보기〉 부산 Busan   세종 Sejong

제 4 항 인명은 성과 이름의 순서로 띄어 쓴다. 이름은 붙여 쓰는 것을 원칙으로 하되 음절 사이에 붙임표(-)를 쓰는 것을 허용한다. (( ) 안의 표기를 허용함.)

   〈보기〉 민용하 Min Yongha(Min Yong-ha)
         송나리 Song Nari(Song Na-ri)

   (1) 이름에서 일어나는 음운 변화는 표기에 반영하지 않는다.

   〈보기〉 한복남 Han Boknam(Han Bok-nam)
         홍빛나 Hong Bitna(Hong Bit-na)

   (2) 성의 표기는 따로 정한다.

제 5 항 '도, 시, 군, 구, 읍, 면, 리, 동'의 행정 구역 단위와 '가'는 각각 'do, si, gun, gu, eup, myeon, ri, dong, ga'로 적고, 그 앞에는 붙임표(-)를 넣는다. 붙임표(-) 앞뒤에서 일어나는 음운 변화는 표기에 반영하지 않는다.

〈보기〉 충청북도	Chungcheongbuk-do		
제주도	Jeju-do	의정부시	Uijeongbu-si
양주군	Yangju-gun	도봉구	Dobong-gu
신창읍	Sinchang-eup	삼죽면	Samjuk-myeon
인왕리	Inwang-ri	당산동	Dangsan-dong
봉천 1동	Bongcheon 1(il)-dong		
종로 2가	Jongno 2(i)-ga		
퇴계로 3가	Toegyero 3(sam)-ga		

〔붙임〕'시, 군, 읍'의 행정 구역 단위는 생략할 수 있다.

〈보기〉 청주시	Cheongju	함평군	Hampyeong
순창읍	Sunchang		

제 6 항 자연 지물명, 문화재명, 인공 축조물명은 붙임표(-) 없이 붙여 쓴다.

〈보기〉 남산	Namsan	속리산	Songnisan
금강	Geumgang	독도	Dokdo
경복궁	Gyeongbokgung	무량수전	Muryangsujeon
연화교	Yeonhwagyo	극락전	Geungnakjeon
안압지	Anapji	남한산성	Namhansanseong
화랑대	Hwarangdae	불국사	Bulguksa
현충사	Hyeonchungsa	독립문	Dongnimmun
오죽헌	Ojukheon	촉석루	Chokseongnu
종묘	Jongmyo	다보탑	Dabotap

제 7 항 인명, 회사명, 단체명 등은 그동안 써 온 표기를 쓸 수 있다.

제 8 항 학술 연구 논문 등 특수 분야에서 한글 복원을 전제로 표기할 경우에는 한글 표기를 대상으로 적는다. 이때 글자 대응은 제2장을 따르되 'ㄱ, ㄷ, ㅂ, ㄹ'은 'g, d, b, l'로만 적는다. 음가 없는 'ㅇ'은 붙임표(-)로 표기하되 어두에서는 생략하는 것을 원칙으로 한다. 기타 분절의 필요가 있을 때에도 붙임표(-)를 쓴다.

〈보기〉 집	jib	짚	jip
밖	bakk	값	gabs
붓꽃	buskkoch	먹는	meogneun
독립	doglib	문리	munli
물엿	mul-yeos	굳이	gud-i
좋다	johda	가곡	gagog
조랑말	jolangmal	없었습니다	eobs-eoss-seubnida

―― 부 칙 ――

1. (시행일) 이 규정은 고시한 날부터 시행한다.
2. (표지판 등에 대한 경과 조치) 이 표기법 시행 당시 종전의 표기법에 의하여 설치된 표지판(도로, 광고물, 문화재 등의 안내판)은 2005. 12. 31.까지 이 표기법을 따라야 한다.
3. (출판물 등에 대한 경과 조치) 이 표기법 시행 당시 종전의 표기법에 의하여 발간된 교과서 등 출판물은 2002. 2. 28.까지 이 표기법을 따라야 한다.